PRESENTED TO

BY

Compliments

of the School of Graduate and Continuing Studies

*Your word is a lamp to my feet
and a light for my path.*

PSALM 119:105

Old Testament Chronology

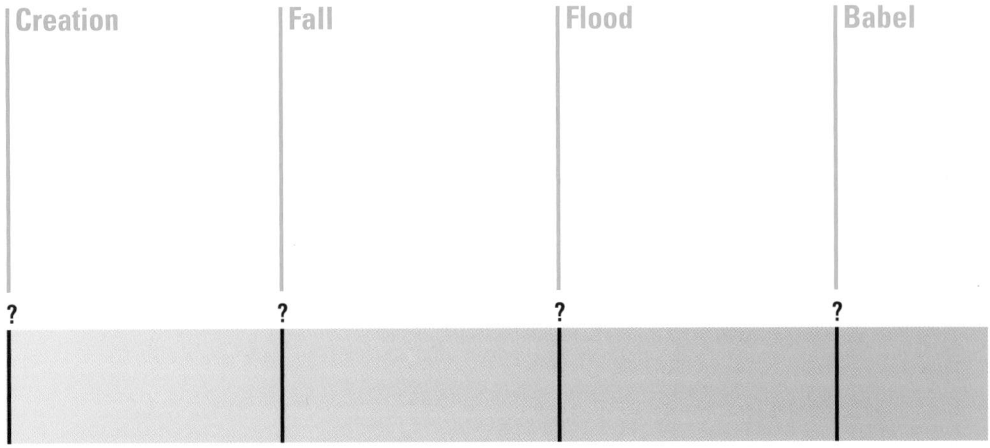

Creation

Fall

Flood

Babel

?

?

?

?

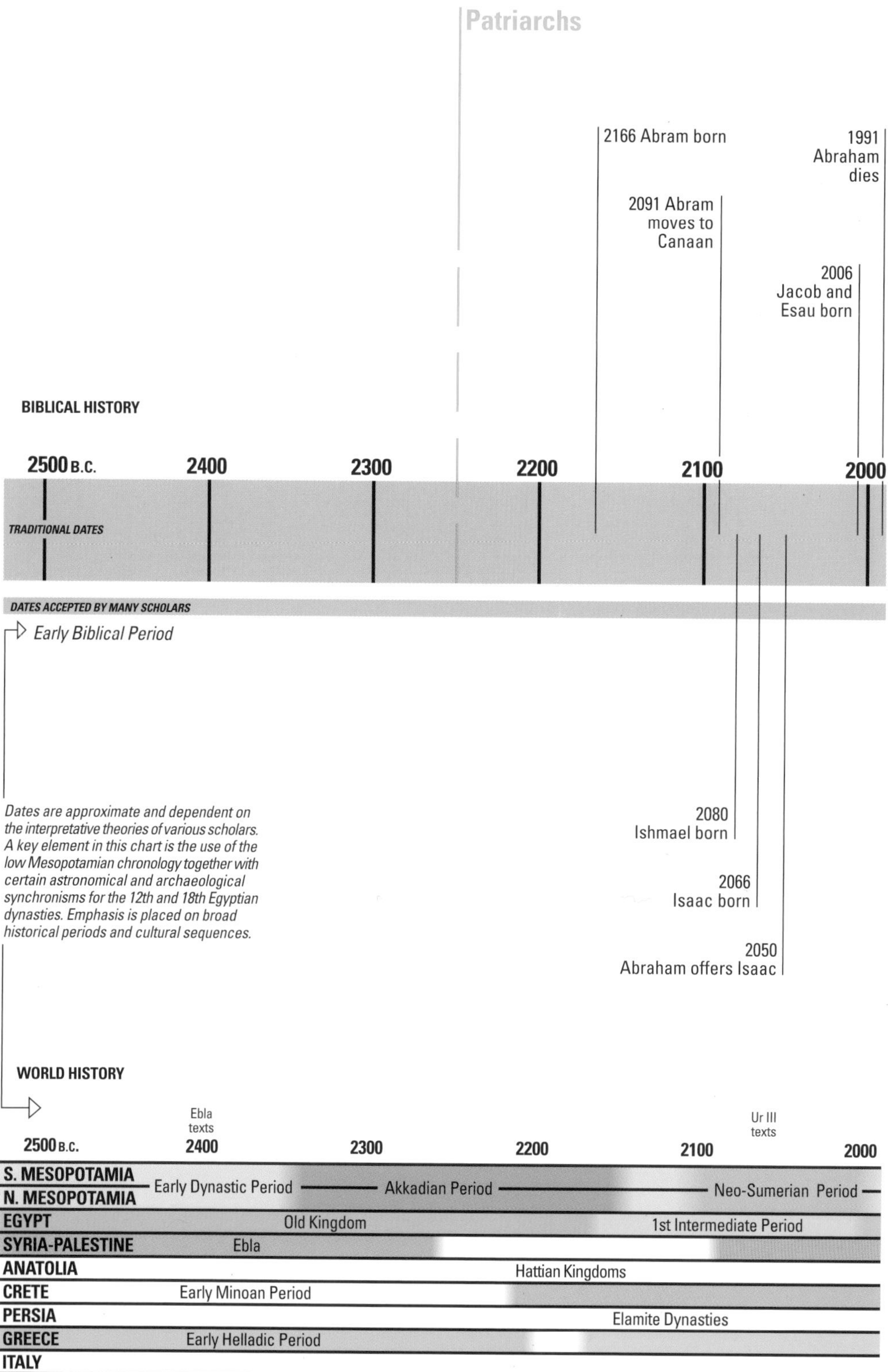
Patriarchs
2166 Abram born
1991 Abraham dies
2091 Abram moves to Canaan
2006 Jacob and Esau born
BIBLICAL HISTORY
2500 B.C.
2400
2300
2200
2100
2000
TRADITIONAL DATES
DATES ACCEPTED BY MANY SCHOLARS
Early Biblical Period
Dates are approximate and dependent on the interpretative theories of various scholars. A key element in this chart is the use of the low Mesopotamian chronology together with certain astronomical and archaeological synchronisms for the 12th and 18th Egyptian dynasties. Emphasis is placed on broad historical periods and cultural sequences.
2080 Ishmael born
2066 Isaac born
2050 Abraham offers Isaac
WORLD HISTORY
Ebla texts
Ur III texts
2500 B.C.
2400
2300
2200
2100
2000
S. MESOPOTAMIA
N. MESOPOTAMIA
Early Dynastic Period
Akkadian Period
Neo-Sumerian Period
EGYPT
Old Kingdom
1st Intermediate Period
SYRIA-PALESTINE
Ebla
ANATOLIA
Hattian Kingdoms
CRETE
Early Minoan Period
PERSIA
Elamite Dynasties
GREECE
Early Helladic Period
ITALY
©1985 The Zondervan Corporation

Old Testament Chronology

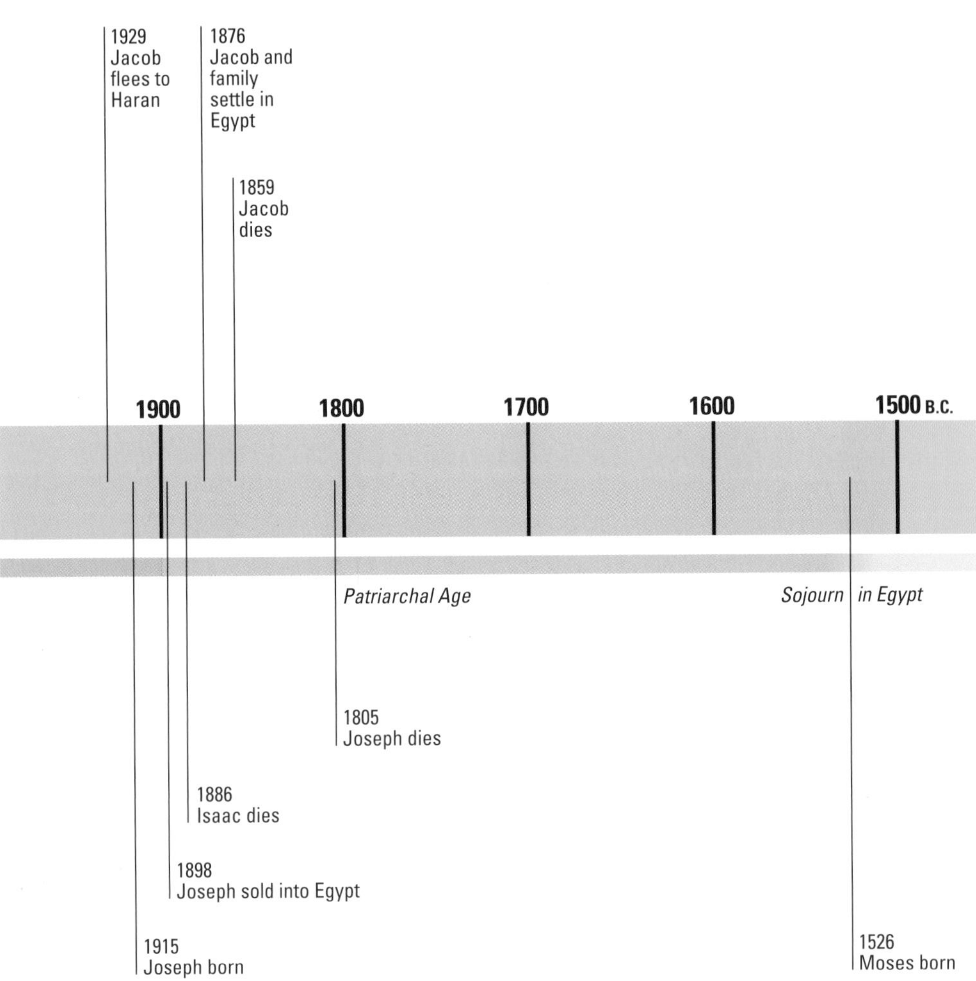

Cappadocian texts
Mari texts
Hammurapi texts
1900
1800
1700
1600
1500 B.C.
Isin-Larsa Period
Old Babylonian Period
Middle Kingdom
2nd Intermediate (Hyksos) Period
New Kingdom
Amorite Period
Hyksos Period
Late Canaanite Period
Hittite Old Kingdom
Middle Minoan Period
Middle Helladic Period

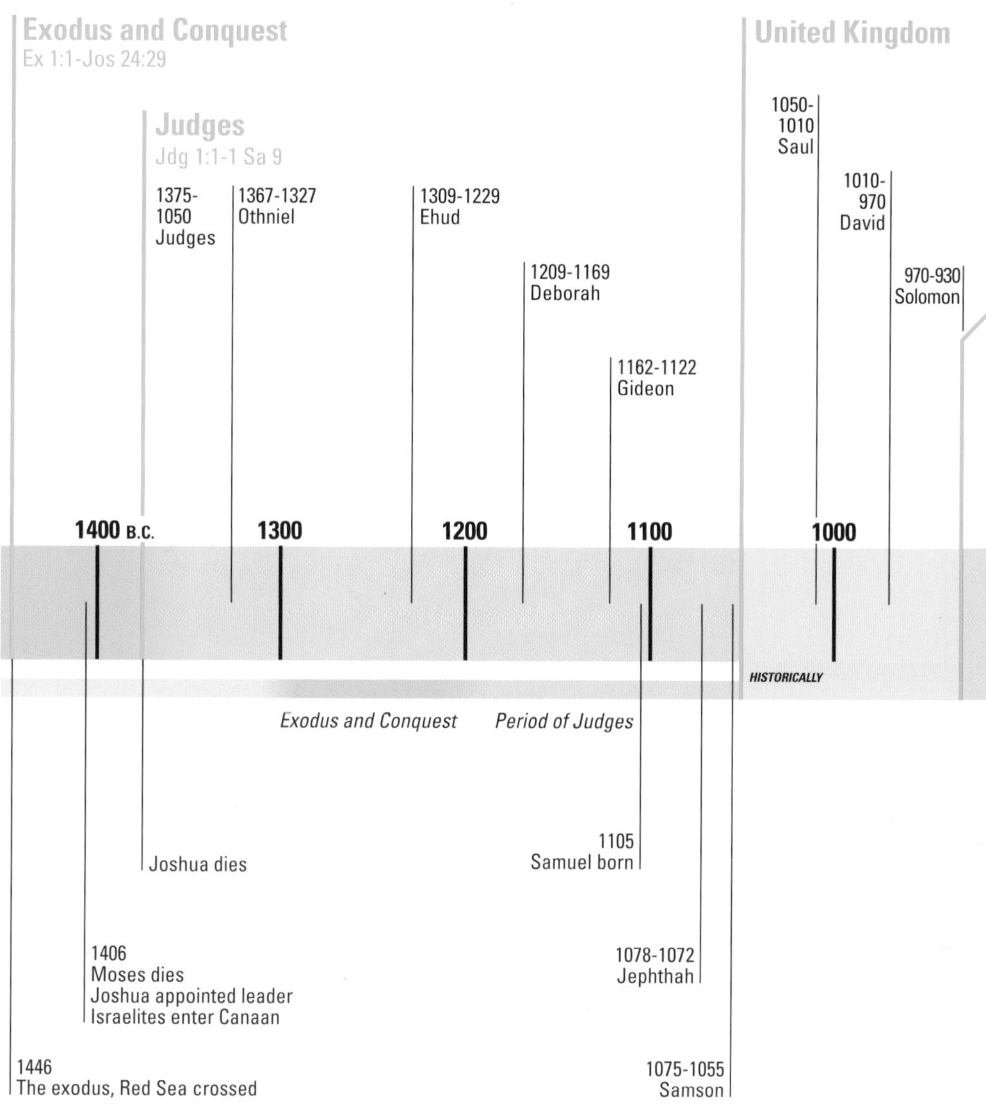

Nuzi texts · Ugaritic texts · Amarna texts · Merneptah inscription · Medinet Habu inscriptions · Shishak inscription

	1400 B.C.	1300	1200	1100	1000
S. MESOPOTAMIA	Kassite Period				
N. MESOPOTAMIA	←Mitannian Kingdom		Middle Assyrian Period		
EGYPT	New Kingdom				
SYRIA-PALESTINE	Late Canaanite Period		Sea Peoples		Phoenician,
ANATOLIA	Hittite Empire		Phrygian Period		
CRETE	Late Minoan Period				Dorian States
PERSIA					
GREECE	Late Helladic (Mycenean) Period				Dorian States
ITALY					

Old Testament Chronology

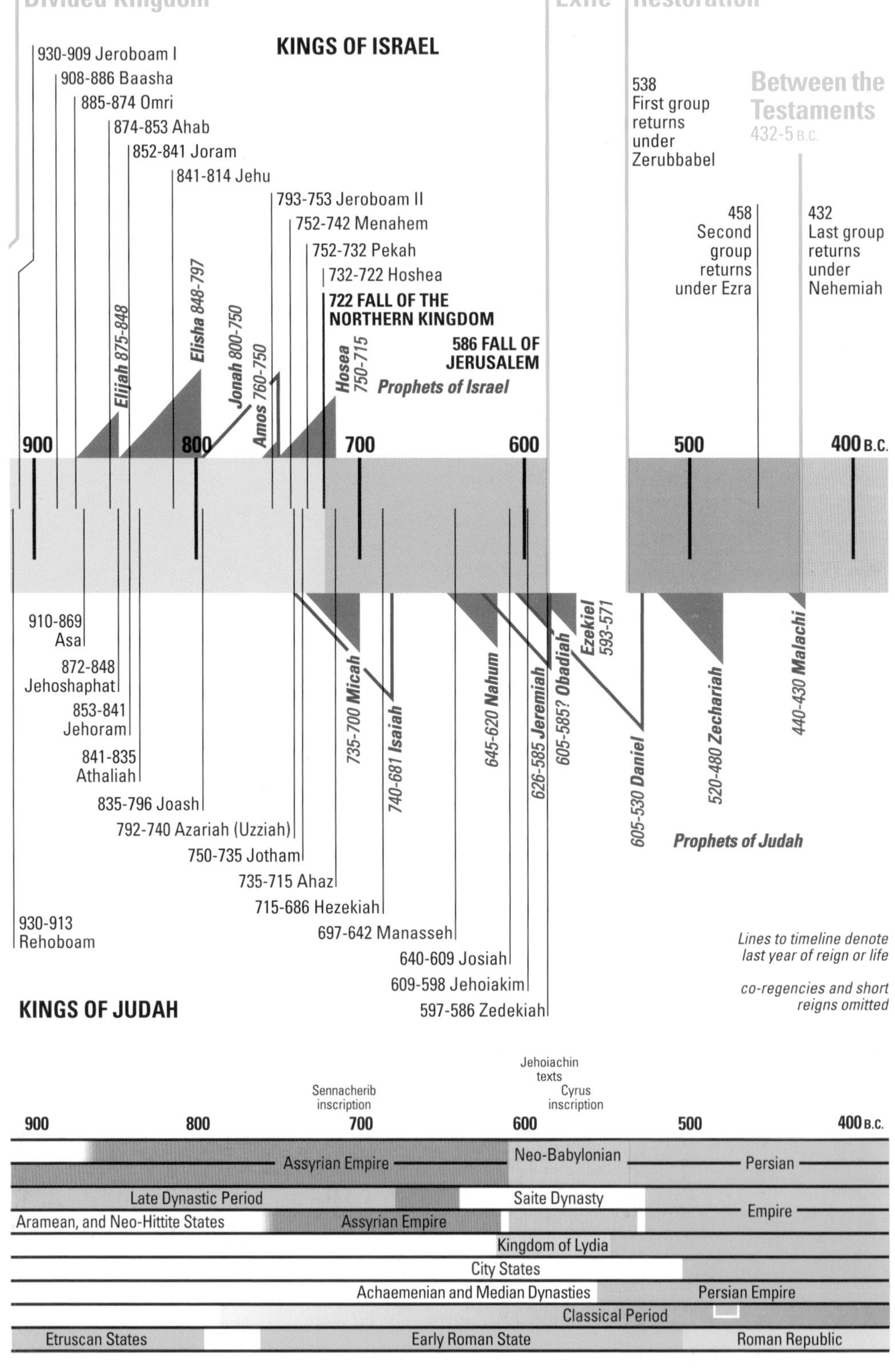

Divided Kingdom
Exile
Restoration
KINGS OF ISRAEL
930-909 Jeroboam I
908-886 Baasha
885-874 Omri
874-853 Ahab
852-841 Joram
841-814 Jehu
793-753 Jeroboam II
752-742 Menahem
752-732 Pekah
732-722 Hoshea
722 FALL OF THE NORTHERN KINGDOM
586 FALL OF JERUSALEM
Prophets of Israel
Elijah 875-848
Elisha 848-797
Jonah 800-750
Amos 760-750
Hosea 750-715
538 First group returns under Zerubbabel
Between the Testaments 432-5 B.C.
458 Second group returns under Ezra
432 Last group returns under Nehemiah
900
800
700
600
500
400 B.C.
910-869 Asa
872-848 Jehoshaphat
853-841 Jehoram
841-835 Athaliah
835-796 Joash
792-740 Azariah (Uzziah)
750-735 Jotham
735-715 Ahaz
715-686 Hezekiah
697-642 Manasseh
640-609 Josiah
609-598 Jehoiakim
597-586 Zedekiah
930-913 Rehoboam
KINGS OF JUDAH
735-700 Micah
740-681 Isaiah
645-620 Nahum
626-585 Jeremiah
605-585? Obadiah
Ezekiel 593-571
605-530 Daniel
520-480 Zechariah
440-430 Malachi
Prophets of Judah
Lines to timeline denote last year of reign or life
co-regencies and short reigns omitted
Sennacherib inscription
Jehoiachin texts
Cyrus inscription
900
800
700
600
500
400 B.C.
Assyrian Empire
Neo-Babylonian
Persian
Late Dynastic Period
Saite Dynasty
Empire
Aramean, and Neo-Hittite States
Assyrian Empire
Kingdom of Lydia
City States
Achaemenian and Median Dynasties
Persian Empire
Classical Period
Etruscan States
Early Roman State
Roman Republic

New Testament Chronology

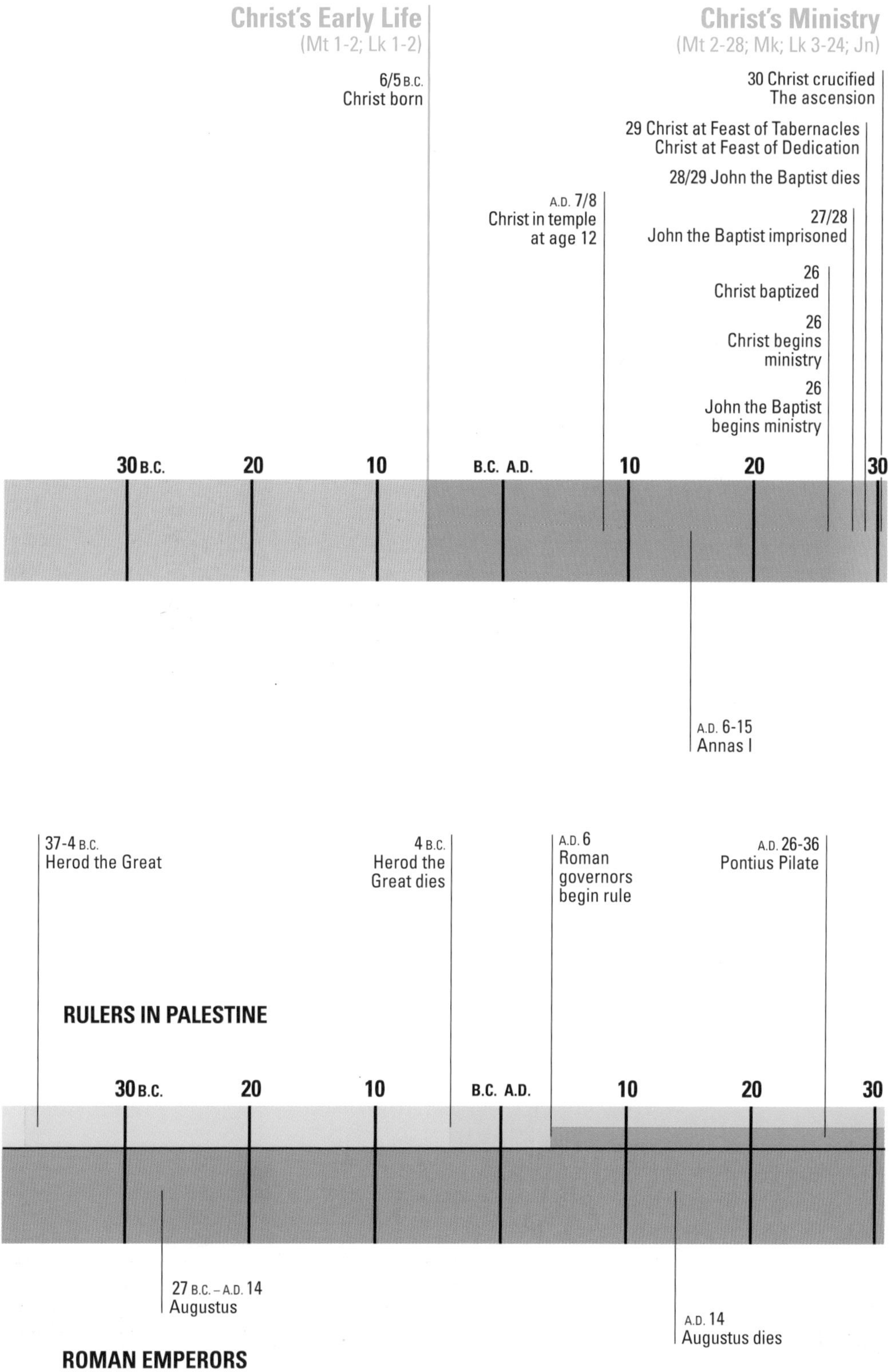

Christ's Early Life
(Mt 1-2; Lk 1-2)
Christ's Ministry
(Mt 2-28; Mk; Lk 3-24; Jn)
6/5 B.C.
Christ born
30 Christ crucified
The ascension
29 Christ at Feast of Tabernacles
Christ at Feast of Dedication
28/29 John the Baptist dies
A.D. 7/8
Christ in temple
at age 12
27/28
John the Baptist imprisoned
26
Christ baptized
26
Christ begins
ministry
26
John the Baptist
begins ministry
30 B.C.
20
10
B.C. A.D.
10
20
30
A.D. 6-15
Annas I
37-4 B.C.
Herod the Great
4 B.C.
Herod the
Great dies
A.D. 6
Roman
governors
begin rule
A.D. 26-36
Pontius Pilate
RULERS IN PALESTINE
30 B.C.
20
10
B.C. A.D.
10
20
30
27 B.C. – A.D. 14
Augustus
A.D. 14
Augustus dies
ROMAN EMPERORS

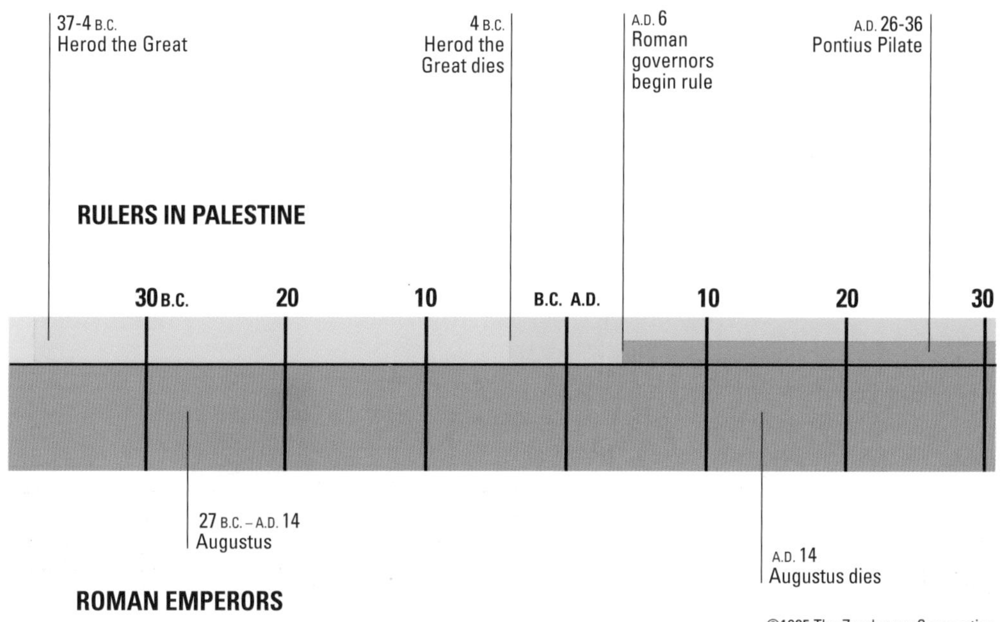

New Testament Chronology

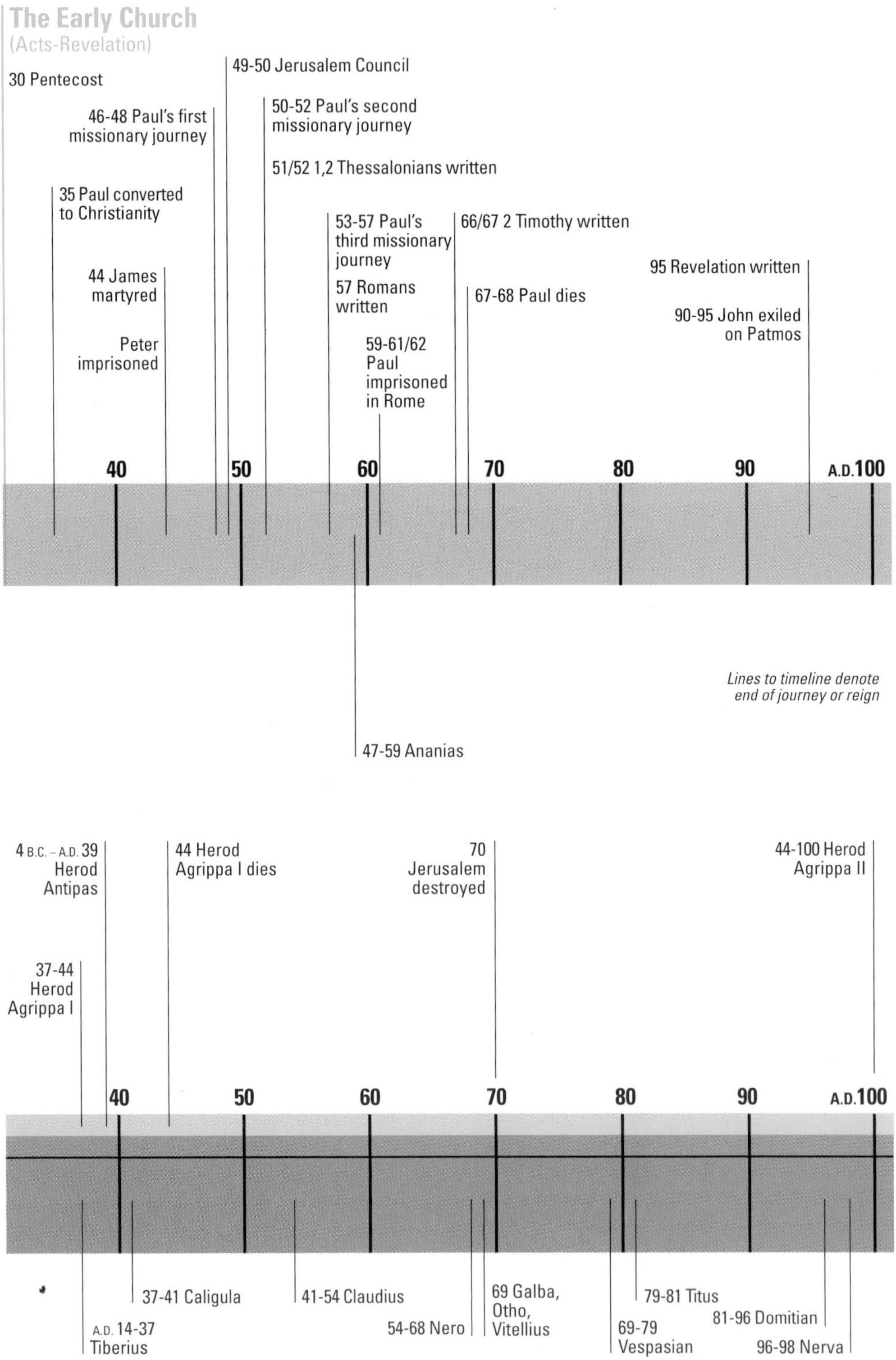

The Early Church
(Acts-Revelation)

30 Pentecost

35 Paul converted to Christianity

44 James martyred

Peter imprisoned

46-48 Paul's first missionary journey

49-50 Jerusalem Council

50-52 Paul's second missionary journey

51/52 1,2 Thessalonians written

53-57 Paul's third missionary journey

57 Romans written

59-61/62 Paul imprisoned in Rome

66/67 2 Timothy written

67-68 Paul dies

90-95 John exiled on Patmos

95 Revelation written

40 50 60 70 80 90 A.D.100

47-59 Ananias

Lines to timeline denote end of journey or reign

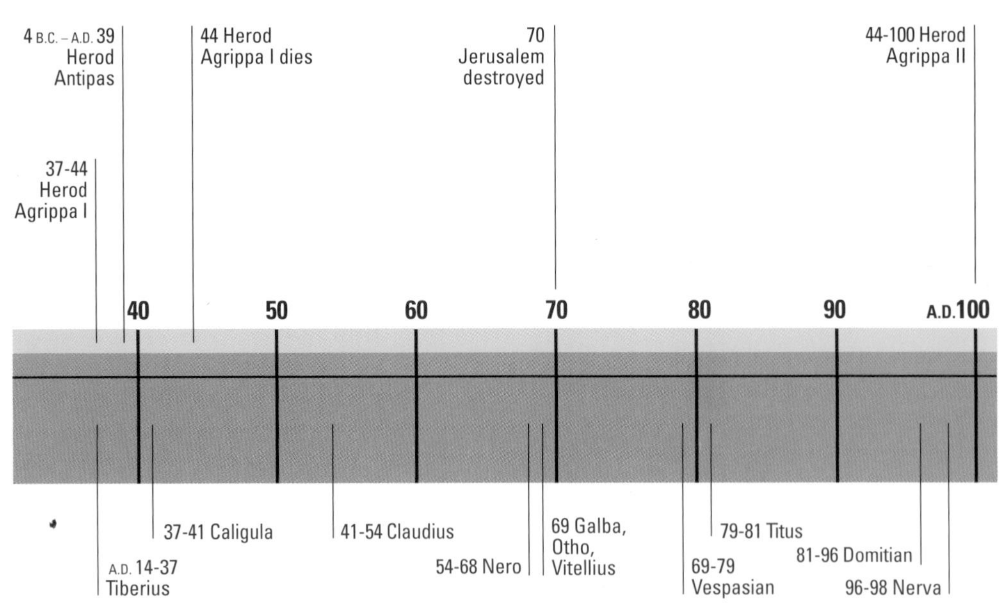

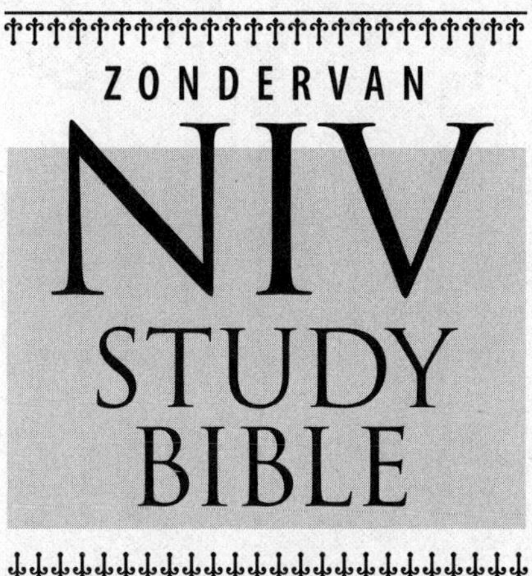
ZONDERVAN
NIV
STUDY
BIBLE

NEW INTERNATIONAL VERSION

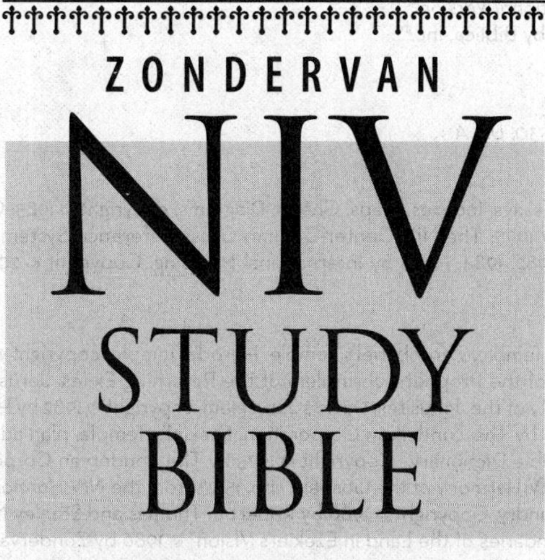

2008 UPDATE

EDITORS, 2008

General Editor
Kenneth L. Barker

Associate Editors
John H. Stek
Mark L. Strauss
Ronald F. Youngblood

ORIGINAL EDITORS, 1985

General Editor
Kenneth L. Barker

Associate Editors
Donald W. Burdick
John H. Stek
Walter W. Wessel
Ronald F. Youngblood

REVISION EDITORS, 2002

General Editor
Kenneth L. Barker

Associate Editors
John H. Stek
Walter W. Wessel
Ronald F. Youngblood

ZONDERVAN®

Zondervan NIV Study Bible
Copyright © 1985, 1995, 2002, 2008 by Zondervan

The Holy Bible, *New International Version®*
Copyright © 1973, 1978, 1984 by Biblica, Inc.™
All rights reserved

Published by Zondervan
Grand Rapids, Michigan 49530, U.S.A.

www.zondervan.com

Library of Congress Control Number 2008920783

Printed in the United States of America

10 11 12 13 14 15 16 17 18 /DCI/ 25 24 23 22 21 20 19 18 17 16 15 14 13 12 11 10 9 8 7 6 5

Tributes

Tribute to Edwin H. Palmer

Edwin Palmer, who had served so capably as Executive Secretary of the NIV Committee on Bible Translation and as coordinator of all translation work on the NIV, was appointed General Editor of the *NIV Study Bible* by Zondervan in 1979. On September 16, 1980, he departed this life to "be with Christ, which is better by far" (Philippians 1:23). Before his death, however, he had laid most of the plans for the *NIV Study Bible*, had recruited the majority of the contributors, and had done some editorial work on the first manuscripts submitted. We gratefully acknowledge his significant contribution to the earliest stages of this product.

Tribute to Donald W. Burdick

Donald Burdick was one of the original Associate Editors of the 1985 edition of the *NIV Study Bible*, with special responsibility for the New Testament. He departed this life on January 4, 1996, to be "at home with the Lord" (2 Corinthians 5:8)—before work commenced in 1997 on the fully revised edition of 2002. We gratefully acknowledge his outstanding work on the original *NIV Study Bible*.

Tribute to Walter W. Wessel

Walter Wessel was also one of the Associate Editors of the original *NIV Study Bible* (1985) as well as of the 2002 fully revised edition, with special responsibility for the New Testament. Althoug he was physically unable to be present at our work session iMarch of 2002, his handwritten proposals were available to uThen he went home to be with his Lord on April 21, 2002. Weankfully acknowledge his substantial contributions to the *NIStudy Bible* (fully revised). "Blessed are the dead who die in theord ... they will rest from their labor, for their deeds will follohem" (Revelation 14:13).

Quick Start Guide

Congratulations on your purchase of the *Zondervan NIV Study Bible*. You have in your hands a comprehensive, multiuse tool that has been designed specifically to enhance your understanding of and appreciation for God's Word.

About the *Zondervan NIV Study Bible*

The team of evangelical scholars who wrote and edited the notes for the *Zondervan NIV Study Bible* also served on the translation team for the New International Version translation itself. Since its release in 1985, the editors of the *Zondervan NIV Study Bible* have diligently worked to revise the notes to provide readers with the most up-to-date, relevant study notes available in the market today. Find out more about the New International Version translation itself by reading the NIV Preface on page xi.

What Is a Study Bible?

A study Bible contains the full text of the Bible, along with a library of study features to help the reader more completely grasp and understand what the text is saying. These notes introduce and explain a wide variety of background information to the Biblical text, providing deeper insights for individuals who are ready to devote themselves to serious study of the text.

What Help Do These Study Features Offer Me?

For a full discussion of each of these features — and others — see the Introduction on page xiv.

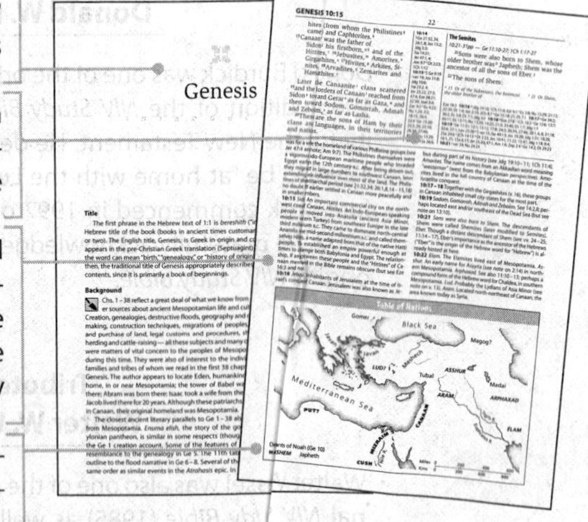

- Book Introductions answer the Who? What? Where? Why? and When? questions readers have about the Bible's 66 books.
- Center-column Cross References aid in deeper study of themes or concepts by leading readers to related passages on the same or similar themes.
- Over 20,000 Study Notes have been placed close to the text that they amplify and explain. These have been designed to provide background and context to the Scripture text, and will also answer questions that may arise as one reads through the Bible.
- In-text Maps, Charts, Diagrams and Illustrations summarize and explain important information and ideas from Scripture.
- The Topical Index has more than 700 entries that will help readers to study subjects of particular interest, allowing them to create their own study paths.
- Color Maps at the back of the Bible help readers to visualize the geographical context of what they're studying. The maps are supplemented by a complete map index.
- The NIV Concordance is a tool designed to help readers who remember a key word or phrase in a passage to locate the verses they're looking for. Words and names are listed alphabetically, along with their more significant verse references.

Why not go ahead and spend a few minutes trying out each of these features? If you're like most readers, certain helps will catch your interest and will eventually become trusted sources as you spend time with your Bible. May God bless you as you study and come to understand the timeless truths of the Bible as priceless treasures for today.

Table of Contents

Tributes, v

Quick Start Guide, vi

Contents: Maps, ix

Contents: Charts, x

Preface to the New International Version, xi

Introduction to the *NIV Study Bible*, xiv

Acknowledgments, xviii

Contributors, xix

Abbreviations, xx

Transliterations, xxi

Ancient Texts Relating to the Old Testament, xxii

THE OLD TESTAMENT

Introduction to Genesis, 1
Genesis 6
Introduction to Exodus, 85
Exodus 90
Introduction to Leviticus, 146
Leviticus 149
Introduction to Numbers, 186
Numbers 190
Introduction to Deuteronomy, 241
Deuteronomy 244
The Conquest and the Ethical Question of War, 286
Introduction to Joshua, 287
Joshua 291
Introduction to Judges, 325
Judges 330
Introduction to Ruth, 364
Ruth 367
Introduction to 1 Samuel, 373
1 Samuel 378
Introduction to 2 Samuel, 424
2 Samuel 426
Introduction to 1 Kings, 466
1 Kings 473
Introduction to 2 Kings, 526
2 Kings 528
Introduction to 1 Chronicles, 579
1 Chronicles 585
Introduction to 2 Chronicles, 624
2 Chronicles 626
Introduction to Ezra, 669
Ezra 672
Introduction to Nehemiah, 691
Nehemiah 693
Introduction to Esther, 715
Esther 717
Wisdom Literature, 727
Introduction to Job, 728
Job 734
Introduction to Psalms, 778
Psalms 790
Introduction to Proverbs, 952
Proverbs 958
Introduction to Ecclesiastes, 1003
Ecclesiastes 1007
Introduction to Song of Songs, 1018
Song of Songs 1021
Introduction to Isaiah, 1029
Isaiah 1034
Introduction to Jeremiah, 1128
Jeremiah 1133
Introduction to Lamentations, 1224
Lamentations 1227
Introduction to Ezekiel, 1237
Ezekiel 1243
Introduction to Daniel, 1311
Daniel 1313
The Book of the Twelve, or the Minor Prophets, 1333
Introduction to Hosea, 1334
Hosea 1337
Introduction to Joel, 1352
Joel 1354
Introduction to Amos, 1360
Amos 1363
Introduction to Obadiah, 1376
Obadiah 1378
Introduction to Jonah, 1380
Jonah 1383
Introduction to Micah, 1387
Micah 1390
Introduction to Nahum, 1398
Nahum 1400
Introduction to Habakkuk, 1404
Habakkuk 1406
Introduction to Zephaniah, 1411
Zephaniah 1413
Introduction to Haggai, 1418
Haggai 1421
Introduction to Zechariah, 1424
Zechariah 1428
Introduction to Malachi, 1443
Malachi 1446
The Time Between the Testaments, 1451

THE NEW TESTAMENT

The Synoptic Gospels, 1457

Introduction to Matthew, 1459

Matthew 1462

Introduction to Mark, 1518

Mark 1521

Introduction to Luke, 1559

Luke 1563

Introduction to John, 1618

John 1621

A Harmony of the Gospels, 1668

Introduction to Acts, 1674

Acts 1678

Introduction to Romans, 1736

Romans 1739

Introduction to 1 Corinthians, 1765

1 Corinthians 1769

Introduction to 2 Corinthians, 1794

2 Corinthians 1797

Introduction to Galatians, 1811

Galatians 1813

Introduction to Ephesians, 1822

Ephesians 1825

Introduction to Philippians, 1835

Philippians 1838

Introduction to Colossians, 1845

Colossians 1848

Introduction to 1 Thessalonians, 1854

1 Thessalonians . . . 1856

Introduction to 2 Thessalonians, 1862

2 Thessalonians . . 1864

The Pastoral Letters, 1867

Introduction to 1 Timothy, 1868

1 Timothy 1870

Introduction to 2 Timothy, 1878

2 Timothy 1880

Introduction to Titus, 1885

Titus 1887

Introduction to Philemon, 1890

Philemon 1891

Introduction to Hebrews, 1892

Hebrews 1895

The General Letters, 1914

Introduction to James, 1915

James 1917

Introduction to 1 Peter, 1923

1 Peter 1926

Introduction to 2 Peter, 1934

2 Peter 1937

Introduction to 1 John, 1942

1 John 1945

Introduction to 2 John, 1951

2 John 1952

Introduction to 3 John, 1953

3 John 1954

Introduction to Jude, 1955

Jude 1958

Introduction to Revelation, 1961

Revelation 1965

STUDY HELPS

Table of Weights and Measures, 1993

Index to Topics, 1994

Index to Notes, 2148

Index to Maps, 2188

Concordance, 2192

Index to Color Maps, 2337

MAPS

BOOK	Map Title	
Genesis	Table of Nations	22
	Jacob's Journeys	56
Exodus	The Exodus	108
Numbers	Cities of Refuge	239
Joshua	Conquest of Canaan: Entry	308
	Initial Conquests and the Submission of the Gibeonites	309
	Conquest of Canaan: Southern Campaign	310
	Conquest of Canaan: Northern Campaign	311
Judges	Five Cities of the Philistines	331
	Gideon's Battles	342
Ruth	The Book of Ruth	367
1 Samuel	David the Fugitive	409
	Exploits of David	418
2 Samuel	The City of the Jebusites/David's Jerusalem	432
	David's Conquests	444
1 Kings	Solomon's Jerusalem	477
	The Divided Kingdom	497
	Lives of Elijah and Elisha	518
2 Kings	Assyrian Campaigns against Israel and Judah	552
	Exile of the Northern Kingdom	558
	Nebuchadnezzar's Campaigns against Judah	572
	Exile of the Southern Kingdom	576
Ezra	Return From Exile	672
Nehemiah	Jerusalem of the Returning Exiles	695
Ezekiel	Boundaries of the Land in Ezekiel's Vision	1308
Daniel	The Neo-Babylonian Empire	1318
Hosea	Jerusalem During the Time of the Prophets	1333
Jonah	The Book of Jonah	1384
Matthew	Journey to Bethlehem, Flight to Egypt and Return to Nazareth	1467
	Jesus' Baptism and Temptation	1468
Mark	Jerusalem During the Ministry of Jesus	1527
	The Decapolis and the Lands beyond the Jordan	1530
	The Territories of Tyre and Sidon	1537
	Passion Week	1552
Luke	The Holy Land Under Herod the Great	1570
John	Jesus in Judea and Samaria	1629
	Jesus in Galilee	1635
Acts	Countries of People Mentioned at Pentecost	1680
	Philip's and Peter's Missionary Journeys	1692
	Roman Damascus	1695
	The Spread of the Gospel	1702
	Paul's First Missionary Journey	1704
	Paul's Second Missionary Journey	1711
	Paul's Third Missionary Journey	1718
	Paul's Journey to Rome	1731
Romans	Rome in the Time of Paul	1735
1 Corinthians	Corinth in the Time of Paul	1766
Ephesians	Ephesus in the Time of Paul	1823
Philippians	Philippi in the Time of Paul	1836
1 Timothy	Paul's Fourth Missionary Journey	1872
Revelation	The Seven Churches of Revelation	1967

CHARTS

BOOK	Chart Title	Page
	Old and New Testament Chronology	
	Ancient Texts Relating to the Old Testament	xxii
Genesis	Major Covenants in the Old Testament	19
	Integrated Chronology of the Patriarchs	26
	The Tribes of Israel	82
Exodus	Hebrew Calendar and Selected Events	104
	The Tabernacle	126
	Tabernacle Furnishings	127
Leviticus	Old Testament Sacrifices	153
	Old Testament Feasts and Other Sacred Days	178
Numbers	Encampment of the Tribes of Israel / Marching Order	193
Deuteronomy	Major Social Concerns in the Covenant	268
Joshua	Distances in Miles Between Old Testament Cities	313
1 Samuel	David's Family Tree	402
1 Kings	Chronology of Foreign Kings	472
	Solomon's Temple	484
	Temple Furnishings	487
	Rulers of the Divided Kingdom of Israel and Judah	504
	Ancient Near Eastern Deities	512
Ezra	Chronology: Ezra–Nehemiah	675
	Zerubbabel's Temple	677
Esther	Chiastic Structure of Reversals in Esther	724
Psalms	Significant Arrangement of the Psalter	786
	Types of Hebrew Parallelism	792
Proverbs	The Wise Man According to Proverbs: An Outline	957
	Character Traits in Proverbs	978
Ezekiel	Dates in Ezekiel	1239
	Ezekiel's Temple	1297
Daniel	Visions in Daniel	1323
	Ptolemies and Seleucids	1330
Malachi	From Malachi to Christ	1450
Matthew	Dating the Synoptic Gospels	1457
	House of Herod	1465
	Herod's Temple	1470
	Jewish Sects	1502
	The Life of Christ	1508
Luke	Capernaum Synagogue	1572
	Parables of Jesus	1598
	Resurrection Appearances	1615
John	Miracles of Jesus	1625
Acts	Major Archaeological Finds Relating to the New Testament	1667
	Timeline of Paul's Life	1696
Galatians	The Fruit of the Spirit	1819
1 Timothy	Qualifications for Elders/Overseers and Deacons	1874
Hebrews	The "Greater-Thans" in Hebrews	1897

Preface to the New International Version

THE NEW INTERNATIONAL VERSION is a completely new translation of the Holy Bible made by over a hundred scholars working directly from the best available Hebrew, Aramaic and Greek texts. It had its beginning in 1965 when, after several years of exploratory study by committees from the Christian Reformed Church and the National Association of Evangelicals, a group of scholars met at Palos Heights, Illinois, and concurred in the need for a new translation of the Bible in contemporary English. This group, though not made up of official church representatives, was transdenominational. Its conclusion was endorsed by a large number of leaders from many denominations who met in Chicago in 1966.

Responsibility for the new version was delegated by the Palos Heights group to a self-governing body of fifteen, the Committee on Bible Translation, composed for the most part of biblical scholars from colleges, universities and seminaries. In 1967 the New York Bible Society (now the International Bible Society) generously undertook the financial sponsorship of the project — a sponsorship that made it possible to enlist the help of many distinguished scholars. The fact that participants from the United States, Great Britain, Canada, Australia and New Zealand worked together gave the project its international scope. That they were from many denominations — including Anglican, Assemblies of God, Baptist, Brethren, Christian Reformed, Church of Christ, Evangelical Free, Lutheran, Mennonite, Methodist, Nazarene, Presbyterian, Wesleyan and other churches — helped to safeguard the translation from sectarian bias.

How it was made helps to give the New International Version its distinctiveness. The translation of each book was assigned to a team of scholars. Next, one of the Intermediate Editorial Committees revised the initial translation, with constant reference to the Hebrew, Aramaic or Greek. Their work then went to one of the General Editorial Committees, which checked it in detail and made another thorough revision. This revision in turn was carefully reviewed by the Committee on Bible Translation, which made further changes and then released the final version for publication. In this way the entire Bible underwent three revisions, during each of which the translation was examined for its faithfulness to the original languages and for its English style.

All this involved many thousands of hours of research and discussion regarding the meaning of the texts and the precise way of putting them into English. It may well be that no other translation has been made by a more thorough process of review and revision from committee to committee than this one.

From the beginning of the project, the Committee on Bible Translation held to certain goals for the New International Version: that it would be an accurate translation and one that would have clarity and literary quality and so prove suitable for public and private reading, teaching, preaching, memorizing and liturgical use. The Committee also sought to preserve some measure of continuity with the long tradition of translating the Scriptures into English.

In working toward these goals, the translators were united in their commitment to the authority and infallibility of the Bible as God's Word in written form. They believe that it contains the divine answer to the deepest needs of humanity, that it sheds unique light on our path in a dark world, and that it sets forth the way to our eternal well-being.

The first concern of the translators has been the accuracy of the translation and its fidelity to the thought of the biblical writers. They have weighed the significance of the lexical and grammatical details of the Hebrew, Aramaic and Greek texts. At the same time, they have striven for more than a word-for-word translation. Because thought patterns and syntax differ from language to language, faithful communication of the meaning of the writers of the Bible demands frequent modifications in sentence structure and constant regard for the contextual meanings of words.

A sensitive feeling for style does not always accompany scholarship. Accordingly the Committee on Bible Translation submitted the developing version to a number of stylistic consultants. Two of them read every book of both Old and New Testaments twice—once before and once after the last major revision—and made invaluable suggestions. Samples of the translation were tested for clarity and ease of reading by various kinds of people—young and old, highly educated and less well educated, ministers and laymen.

Concern for clear and natural English—that the New International Version should be idiomatic but not idiosyncratic, contemporary but not dated—motivated the translators and consultants. At the same time, they tried to reflect the differing styles of the biblical writers. In view of the international use of English, the translators sought to avoid obvious Americanisms on the one hand and obvious Anglicisms on the other. A British edition reflects the comparatively few differences of significant idiom and of spelling.

As for the traditional pronouns "thou," "thee" and "thine" in reference to the Deity, the translators judged that to use these archaisms (along with the old verb forms such as "doest," "wouldest" and "hadst") would violate accuracy in translation. Neither Hebrew, Aramaic nor Greek uses special pronouns for the persons of the Godhead. A present-day translation is not enhanced by forms that in the time of the King James Version were used in everyday speech, whether referring to God or man.

For the Old Testament the standard Hebrew text, the Masoretic Text as published in the latest editions of *Biblia Hebraica,* was used throughout. The Dead Sea Scrolls contain material bearing on an earlier stage of the Hebrew text. They were consulted, as were the Samaritan Pentateuch and the ancient scribal traditions relating to textual changes. Sometimes a variant Hebrew reading in the margin of the Masoretic Text was followed instead of the text itself. Such instances, being variants within the Masoretic tradition, are not specified by footnotes. In rare cases, words in the consonantal text were divided differently from the way they appear in the Masoretic Text. Footnotes indicate this. The translators also consulted the more important early versions—the Septuagint; Aquila, Symmachus and Theodotion; the Vulgate; the Syriac Peshitta; the Targums; and for the Psalms the *Juxta Hebraica* of Jerome. Readings from these versions were occasionally followed where the Masoretic Text seemed doubtful and where accepted principles of textual criticism showed that one or more of these textual witnesses appeared to provide the correct reading. Such instances are footnoted. Sometimes vowel letters and vowel signs did not, in the judgment of the translators, represent the correct vowels for the original consonantal text. Accordingly some words were read with a different set of vowels. These instances are usually not indicated by footnotes.

The Greek text used in translating the New Testament was an eclectic one. No other piece of ancient literature has such an abundance of manuscript witnesses as does the New Testament. Where existing manuscripts differ, the translators made their choice of readings according to accepted principles of New Testament textual criticism. Footnotes call attention to places where there was uncertainty about what the original text was. The best current printed texts of the Greek New Testament were used.

There is a sense in which the work of translation is never wholly finished. This applies to all great literature and uniquely so to the Bible. In 1973 the New Testament in the New International Version was published. Since then, suggestions for corrections and revisions have been received from various sources. The Committee on Bible Translation carefully considered the suggestions and adopted a number of them. These were incorporated in the first printing of the entire Bible in 1978. Additional revisions were made by the Committee on Bible Translation in 1983 and appear in printings after that date.

As in other ancient documents, the precise meaning of the biblical texts is sometimes uncertain. This is more often the case with the Hebrew and Aramaic texts than with the Greek text. Although archaeological and linguistic discoveries in this century aid in understanding difficult passages, some uncertainties remain. The more significant of these have been called to the reader's attention in the footnotes.

In regard to the divine name *YHWH,* commonly referred to as the *Tetragrammaton,* the translators adopted the device used in most English versions of rendering that name as "LORD" in capital letters to distinguish it from *Adonai,* another Hebrew word rendered "Lord," for which small letters are used. Wherever the two names stand together in the Old Testament as a compound name of God, they are rendered "Sovereign LORD."

Because for most readers today the phrases "the LORD of hosts" and "God of hosts" have little meaning, this version renders them "the LORD Almighty" and "God Almighty." These renderings convey the sense of the Hebrew, namely, "he who is sovereign over all the 'hosts' (powers) in heaven and on earth, especially over the 'hosts' (armies) of Israel." For readers unacquainted with Hebrew this does not make clear the distinction between *Sabaoth* ("hosts" or "Almighty") and *Shaddai* (which can also be translated "Almighty"), but the latter occurs infrequently and is always footnoted. When *Adonai* and *YHWH Sabaoth* occur together, they are rendered "the Lord, the LORD Almighty."

As for other proper nouns, the familiar spellings of the King James Version are generally retained. Names traditionally spelled with "ch," except where it is final, are usually spelled in this translation with "k" or "c," since the biblical languages do not have the sound that "ch" frequently indicates in English — for example, in *chant*. For well-known names such as Zechariah, however, the traditional spelling has been retained. Variation in the spelling of names in the original languages has usually not been indicated. Where a person or place has two or more different names in the Hebrew, Aramaic or Greek texts, the more familiar one has generally been used, with footnotes where needed.

To achieve clarity the translators sometimes supplied words not in the original texts but required by the context. If there was uncertainty about such material, it is enclosed in brackets. Also for the sake of clarity or style, nouns, including some proper nouns, are sometimes substituted for pronouns, and vice versa. And though the Hebrew writers often shifted back and forth between first, second and third personal pronouns without change of antecedent, this translation often makes them uniform, in accordance with English style and without the use of footnotes.

Poetical passages are printed as poetry, that is, with indentation of lines and with separate stanzas. These are generally designed to reflect the structure of Hebrew poetry. This poetry is normally characterized by parallelism in balanced lines. Most of the poetry in the Bible is in the Old Testament, and scholars differ regarding the scansion of Hebrew lines. The translators determined the stanza divisions for the most part by analysis of the subject matter. The stanzas therefore serve as poetic paragraphs.

As an aid to the reader, italicized sectional headings are inserted in most of the books. They are not to be regarded as part of the NIV text, are not for oral reading, and are not intended to dictate the interpretation of the sections they head.

The footnotes in this version are of several kinds, most of which need no explanation. Those giving alternative translations begin with "Or" and generally introduce the alternative with the last word preceding it in the text, except when it is a single-word alternative; in poetry quoted in a footnote a slant mark indicates a line division. Footnotes introduced by "Or" do not have uniform significance. In some cases two possible translations were considered to have about equal validity. In other cases, though the translators were convinced that the translation in the text was correct, they judged that another interpretation was possible and of sufficient importance to be represented in a footnote.

In the New Testament, footnotes that refer to uncertainty regarding the original text are introduced by "Some manuscripts" or similar expressions. In the Old Testament, evidence for the reading chosen is given first and evidence for the alternative is added after a semicolon (for example: Septuagint; Hebrew *father*). In such notes the term "Hebrew" refers to the Masoretic Text.

It should be noted that minerals, flora and fauna, architectural details, articles of clothing and jewelry, musical instruments and other articles cannot always be identified with precision. Also measures of capacity in the biblical period are particularly uncertain (see the table of weights and measures following the text).

Like all translations of the Bible, made as they are by imperfect man, this one undoubtedly falls short of its goals. Yet we are grateful to God for the extent to which he has enabled us to realize these goals and for the strength he has given us and our colleagues to complete our task. We offer this version of the Bible to him in whose name and for whose glory it has been made. We pray that it will lead many into a better understanding of the Holy Scriptures and a fuller knowledge of Jesus Christ the incarnate Word, of whom the Scriptures so faithfully testify.

The Committee on Bible Translation
June 1978
(Revised August 1983)

Names of the translators and editors may be secured
from the International Bible Society,
translation sponsors of the New International Version,
1820 Jet Stream Drive, Colorado Springs, Colorado 80921–3696 U.S.A.

Introduction to the *NIV Study Bible*

About the *NIV Study Bible*

The New International Version of the Bible (NIV) is unsurpassed in accuracy, clarity and literary grace. The commitments that led to the completion of this version later guided several of its translators to spearhead publication of the *NIV Study Bible*. Their purpose was unchanged: to communicate the word of God to the hearts of people.

Like the NIV itself, the *NIV Study Bible* is the work of a transdenominational team of Biblical scholars. All confess the authority of the Bible as God's infallible word to humanity. They have sought to clarify understanding of, develop appreciation for, and provide insight into that word.

But why a study Bible when the NIV text itself is so clearly written? Surely there is no substitute for the reading of the text itself; nothing people write *about* God's word can be on a level with the word itself. Further, it is the Holy Spirit alone — not fallible human beings — who can open the human mind to the divine message.

However, the Spirit also uses people to explain God's word to others. It was the Spirit who led Philip to the Ethiopian eunuch's chariot, where he asked, "Do you understand what you are reading?" (Ac 8:30). "How can I," the Ethiopian replied, "unless someone explains it to me?" Philip then showed him how an Old Testament passage in Isaiah related to the good news of Jesus.

This interrelationship of the Scriptures — so essential to understanding the complete Biblical message — is a major theme of the notes in the *NIV Study Bible*.

Doctrinally, the *NIV Study Bible* reflects traditional evangelical theology. Where editors were aware of significant differences of opinion on key passages or doctrines, they tried to follow an evenhanded approach by indicating those differences (e.g., see note on Rev 20:2). In finding solutions to problems mentioned in the book introductions, they went only as far as evidence (Biblical and non-Biblical) could carry them.

The result is a study Bible that can be used profitably by all Christians who want to be serious Bible students.

Features of the *NIV Study Bible*

The *NIV Study Bible* features the text of the New International Version, study notes keyed to and listed with Bible verses, introductions and outlines to books of the Bible, text notes, a cross-reference system (100,000 entries), parallel passages, a concordance (over 35,000 references), charts, maps, essays and comprehensive indexes.

The text of the NIV, which is divided into paragraphs as well as verses, is organized into sections with headings.

Study Notes

The outstanding feature of this study Bible is that it contains over 20,000 study notes located on the same pages as the verses and passages they explain.

The study notes provide new information to supplement that found in the NIV text notes. Among other things, they

1. explain important words and concepts (see note on Lev 11:44 about "holiness");
2. interpret difficult verses (see notes on Mal 1:3 and Lk 14:26 for the concept of "hating" your parents);

3. draw parallels between specific people and events (see note on Ex 32:30 for the parallels between Moses and Christ as mediators);
4. describe historical and textual contexts of passages (see note on 1Co 8:1 for the practice of eating meat sacrificed to idols); and
5. demonstrate how one passage sheds light on another (see note on Ps 26:8 for how the presence of God's glory marked his presence in the tabernacle, in the temple, and finally in Jesus Christ himself).

Some elements of style should be noted:

1. Study notes on a *passage* precede notes on individual verses within that passage.
2. When a book of the Bible is referred to within a note on that book, the book name is not repeated. For example, a reference to 2 Timothy 2:18 within the notes on 2 Timothy is written 2:18, not 2Ti 2:18.
3. In lists of references within a note, references from the book under discussion are placed first. The rest appear in Biblical order.
4. Certain kinds of material have been made more accessible through the use of the following symbols:

 The seedling calls attention to Scripture references containing study notes that have practical principles for personal application.

 The trowel points out references containing study notes that provide light from archaeology. Since there is more personal application material in the study notes than archaeological information, we have also indicated where archaeological data can be found in certain book introductions, maps and charts.

 The character symbol occurs in front of Scripture references containing study notes that provide descriptions and/or characterizations of persons or people groups. This symbol also sometimes appears in book introductions and essays.

Introductions to Books of the Bible

Each introduction to each book of the Bible is different. Introductions vary in length and reflect both the nature of the material itself and the strengths and interests of contributing editors.

An introduction frequently reports on a book's title, author, and date of writing. It details the book's background and purpose, explores themes and theological significance, and points out special problems and distinctive literary features. Where appropriate, such as in Paul's letters to the churches, it describes the original recipients of a book and the city in which they lived.

The "Quick Look" boxes in the book introductions contain incomplete information and are not intended to be adequate summaries of the introductions. They are only intended as graphic elements to stop the reader's eye and pique their interest. We strongly encourage readers to carefully read the full introductions for a better understanding of each Bible book.

A complete outline of the book's content is provided in each introduction (except for the introduction to Psalms). For Genesis, two outlines — a literary and a thematic — are given. Pairs of books that were originally one literary work, such as 1 and 2 Samuel, 1 and 2 Kings, and 1 and 2 Chronicles, are outlined together.

Text Notes

NIV text notes are indicated by raised, bold-faced letters following the words or phrases they explain. They examine such things as alternative translations, meanings of Hebrew and Greek terms, Old Testament quotations and variant readings in ancient Biblical manuscripts. There are also some explanatory notes. Text notes appear at the bottom of the right-hand column, preceded by their bold letters and verse numbers.

Cross-Reference System

The cross-reference system can be used to explore concepts, as well as specific words. For example, one can either study "angels as protectors" (see Mt 18:10) or focus on the word "angel" (see Jn 20:12).

The NIV cross-reference system resembles a series of interlocking chains with many links. The head, or organizing, link in each concept chain is indicated by the letter "S" (short for "See"). The appearance of a head link in a list of references usually signals another list of references that will cover a slightly different aspect of the concept or word being studied. The various chains in the cross-reference system — which is virtually inexhaustible — continually intersect and diverge.

Cross references are indicated by raised light-italic letters. When a single word is addressed by both text notes and cross references, the bold NIV text-note letter comes first. The cross references normally appear in the center column and, when necessary, continue at the bottom of the right-hand column after the NIV text notes.

The four lists of references are in Biblical order with one exception: If reference is made to a verse within the same chapter, that verse (indicated by "ver") is listed first. If an Old Testament verse is quoted in the New Testament, the New Testament reference is marked with an asterisk (*).

Genesis 1:1 provides a good example of the resources of the cross-reference system.

The four lists of references all relate to creation, but each takes a different perspective. Note *a* takes up the time of creation: "in the beginning." Note *b* lists three other occurrences of the word "created" in Genesis 1 – 2. Note *c* focuses on "the heavens" as God's creation. Because note *d* is attached to the end of the verse as well as to the word "earth," it deals with the word "earth," with the phrase "the heavens and the earth" and with creation itself (the whole verse).

The Beginning

1 In the beginning[a] God created[b]
the heavens[c] and the earth.[d] 2 Now
the earth was[a] formless[e] and empty,[f] darkness was over the surface of
the deep,[g] and the Spirit of God[h] was
hovering[i] over the waters.
3 And God said,[j] "Let there be light," and
there was light.[k] 4 God saw that the
light was good,[l] and he separated the
light from the darkness.[m] 5 God called[n]
the light "day," and the darkness he
called "night."[o] And there was evening, and there was morning[p] — the
first day.

1:1 [a] Ps 102:25; Pr 8:23; Isa 40:21; 41:4, 26; Jn 1:1-2 [b] ver 21, 27; Ge 2:3 [c] ver 6; Ne 9:6; Job 9:8; 37:18; Ps 96:5; 104:2; 115:15; 121:2; 136:5; Isa 40:22; 42:5; 51:13; Jer 10:12; 51:15 [d] Ge 14:19; 2Ki 19:15; Ne 9:6; Job 38:4; Ps 90:2; 136:6; 146:6; Isa 37:16; 40:28; 42:5; 44:24; 45:12, 18; Jer 27:5; 32:17; Ac 14:15; 17:24; Eph 3:9; Col 1:16; Heb 3:4; 11:3;

Parallel Passages

When two or more passages of Scripture are nearly identical or deal with the same event, this "parallel" is noted at the sectional headings for those passages. Such passages are especially common in Matthew, Mark, Luke and John; and in Samuel, Kings and Chronicles.

Identical or nearly identical passages are noted with *"pp."* Similar passages — those not dealing with the same event — are noted with *"Ref."*

To conserve space and avoid repetition, when a parallel passage is noted at a sectional heading, no further parallels are listed in the cross-reference system.

Concordance

The concordance is the largest ever bound with an English Bible. It was compiled and edited by John R. Kohlenberger III and Edward W. Goodrick. By looking up key words, you can find verses for which you remember a word or two but not their location. For example, to find the verse that states that the word of God is "sharper than any double-edged sword," you could look in the concordance under either "sharper," "double-edged," or "sword."

Maps

The *NIV Study Bible* includes 65 maps: 14 full-color and 51 black-and-white. The 14 full-color maps at the end of this Bible cover c. 2000 years of history.

Strategically placed throughout the text are 51 black-and-white maps. The Contents: Maps page contains a complete list of the topics covered.

The cities of Jerusalem, Damascus, Rome, Corinth, Ephesus and Philippi have been reconstructed as they might have been in ancient times. These re-creations allow Bible students to visualize David's city and, in the New Testament, the places through which Paul traveled on his missionary journeys.

Charts

Complementing the study notes are 44 charts, diagrams and drawings. Two full-color time lines, located in the front of this Bible, pinpoint significant dates in the Old and New Testaments. Other charts, carefully placed within the text, give detailed information about ancient, non-Biblical texts; about Old Testament covenants, sacrifices, and feast days; about Jewish sects; and about major archaeological finds relating to the Old and New Testaments.

Essays

Five brief essays provide additional information on specific sections of the Bible: Wisdom Literature, the Minor Prophets, the Synoptic Gospels, the Pastoral Letters, and the General Letters.

A sixth essay confronts the ethical question of war, and a seventh details the history, literature and social developments of the 400 years between the Old and New Testaments.

Subject, Notes and Map Indexes

The subject index contains references to key Biblical information and important topics. The notes index pinpoints other references to persons, places, events and topics mentioned in the *NIV Study Bible* notes.

Two map indexes help in locating place-names on a map.

Harmony of the Gospels

As an additional study tool for the Gospels and the life of Christ, this study Bible contains a portion of the *NIV Harmony of the Gospels* by Robert L. Thomas and Stanley N. Gundry.

The Divine Name Yahweh

The editors have sometimes elected to use the divine name Yahweh (rendered "the LORD" in the NIV) in the book introductions, study notes and essays instead of "the Lord" (or even "the LORD"). For the significance of this name see notes on Ge 2:4; Ex 3:14 – 15; 6:6; Dt 28:58.

Acknowledgments

1985 Edition

My greatest debt of gratitude is owed to God for giving me the privilege of serving as General Editor of the *NIV Study Bible*. Special thanks go to the four Associate Editors: Donald W. Burdick, John H. Stek, Walter W. Wessel, and Ronald F. Youngblood. Without their help, it would have been impossible to complete this project in approximately seven years.

In addition, grateful acknowledgment is given to all those listed on the Contributors page. Obviously the editors and contributors have profited immensely from the labors of others. We feel deeply indebted to all the commentaries and other sources we have used in our work.

I should also thank the following individuals for rendering help in various ways (though I fear that I have inadvertently omitted a few names): Caroline Blauwkamp, David R. Douglass, Stanley N. Gundry, N. David Hill, Betty Hockenberry, Charles E. Hummel, Alan F. Johnson, Janet Johnston, Donald H. Madvig, Frances Steenwyk, and Edward Viening.

Nehemiah 8:7–8, 12 says:

> *The Levites ... instructed the people in the Law while the people were standing there. They read from the Book of the Law of God, making it clear and giving the meaning so that the people could understand what was being read ... Then all the people went away ... to celebrate with great joy, because they now understood the words that had been made known to them.*

My associates and I will feel amply rewarded if those who use this study Bible have an experience similar to that of God's people in the time of Ezra and Nehemiah.

Kenneth L. Barker, General Editor

1995 Edition

Since 1995 marked the 10th Anniversary of the *NIV Study Bible*, the publisher and I decided to give it a new look. We added some features, corrected a few mistakes, and made certain kinds of material more accessible through the use of symbols in the study notes. Special thanks go to Walter Wessel for his significant contribution to the study notes in the Gospel of Matthew, and to Michael Vander Klipp and other Zondervan editors for their help.

Kenneth L. Barker, General Editor

2002 Edition

In the fully revised edition of the *NIV Study Bible*, the Associate Editors and I have added hundreds of new study notes, improved the book introductions (e.g., by paying greater attention to rhetorical, structural and other literary features) and enhanced other helps.

Special thanks go to Andrew J. Bandstra for providing additional study notes on the book of Revelation. We are also humbly grateful to God for the manner in which he has used this study Bible to bring edification and spiritual enrichment to literally millions of readers and users. It is my prayer that this will continue to be true of the fully revised edition of the *NIV Study Bible*.

Kenneth L. Barker, General Editor

2008 Edition

In this 2008 update of the *NIV Study Bible*, the Associate Editors and I have added some new study notes and charts, corrected a few mistakes, and brought greater continuity to certain kinds of material (e.g., there is now more consistency in the outlining of a few books and in the development of themes). We give a hearty welcome and special thanks to Mark Strauss as a new Associate Editor, with primary responsibility for the New Testament. "The unfolding of your words gives light" (Ps 119:130).

Kenneth L. Barker, General Editor

Contributors

General Editor: Kenneth L. Barker
Associate Editors: John H. Stek
Mark L. Strauss
Ronald F. Youngblood

1985 Edition

General Editor: Kenneth L. Barker
Associate Editors: Donald W. Burdick
John H. Stek
Walter W. Wessel
Ronald F. Youngblood

2002 Edition (Fully Revised)

General Editor: Kenneth L. Barker
Associate Editors: John H. Stek
Walter W. Wessel
Ronald F. Youngblood

The individuals named below contributed and/or reviewed material for the *NIV Study Bible*. However, since the General Editor and the Associate Editors extensively edited the notes on most books, they alone are responsible for their final form and content.

The chief contributors of original material to the *NIV Study Bible* are listed first. Where the Associate Editors and General Editor contributed an unusually large number of notes on certain books, their names are also listed.

Genesis	Ronald Youngblood
Exodus	Ronald Youngblood; Walter C. Kaiser, Jr.
Leviticus	R. Laird Harris; Ronald Youngblood
Numbers	Ronald B. Allen; Kenneth L. Barker
Deuteronomy	Earl S. Kalland; Kenneth L. Barker
Joshua	Arthur Lewis
Judges	John J. Davis; Herbert Wolf; John H. Stek
Ruth	Marvin R. Wilson; John H. Stek
1,2 Samuel	J. Robert Vannoy
1,2 Kings	J. Robert Vannoy
1,2 Chronicles	Raymond Dillard
Ezra	Edwin Yamauchi; Ronald Youngblood
Nehemiah	Edwin Yamauchi; Ronald Youngblood
Esther	Raymond Dillard; Edwin Yamauchi
Job	Elmer B. Smick; Ronald Youngblood
Psalms	John H. Stek
Proverbs	Herbert Wolf
Ecclesiastes	Derek Kidner; John H. Stek
Song of Songs	John H. Stek
Isaiah	Herbert Wolf; John H. Stek
Jeremiah	Ronald Youngblood
Lamentations	Ronald Youngblood; John H. Stek
Ezekiel	Mark Hillmer; John H. Stek
Daniel	Gleason L. Archer, Jr.; Ronald Youngblood
Hosea	Jack P. Lewis
Joel	Jack P. Lewis
Amos	Alan R. Millard; John H. Stek
Obadiah	John M. Zinkand
Jonah	Marvin R. Wilson; John H. Stek
Micah	Kenneth L. Barker; Thomas E. McComiskey; Allan A. MacRae
Nahum	G. Herbert Livingston; Kenneth L. Barker
Habakkuk	Roland K. Harrison; William C. Williams
Zephaniah	Roland K. Harrison
Haggai	Herbert Wolf
Zechariah	Kenneth L. Barker; Larry L. Walker
Malachi	Herbert Wolf; John H. Stek
Matthew	Walter W. Wessel; Ralph Earle
Mark	Walter W. Wessel; William L. Lane
Luke	Lewis Foster
John	Leon Morris
Acts	Lewis Foster
Romans	Walter W. Wessel
1 Corinthians	W. Harold Mare
2 Corinthians	Philip E. Hughes
Galatians	Robert Mounce
Ephesians	Walter L. Liefeld
Philippians	Richard B. Gaffin, Jr.
Colossians	Gerald F. Hawthorne; Wilber B. Wallis
1,2 Thessalonians	Leon Morris
1,2 Timothy	Walter W. Wessel; George W. Knight, III
Titus	D. Edmond Hiebert
Philemon	John Werner
Hebrews	Philip E. Hughes; Donald W. Burdick
James	Donald W. Burdick
1,2 Peter	Donald W. Burdick; John H. Skilton
1,2,3 John	Donald W. Burdick
Jude	Donald W. Burdick; John H. Skilton
Revelation	Robert Mounce; Andrew J. Bandstra
"The Time Between the Testaments" (essay)	David O'Brien

Abbreviations

GENERAL

c.	*about, approximately*
cf.	*compare, confer*
ch., chs.	*chapter, chapters*
e.g.	*for example*
etc.	*and so on*
i.e.	*that is*
KJV	*King James (Authorized) Version*
lit.	*literally, literal*
NT	*New Testament*
OT	*Old Testament*
p., pp.	*page, pages*
v., vv.,	*verse, verses (in the chapter being commented on)*

Standard abbreviations of month names are also sometimes used, as well as a few other common abbreviations.

BOOKS OF THE BIBLE

The Old Testament

Genesis	Ge
Exodus	Ex
Leviticus	Lev
Numbers	Nu
Deuteronomy	Dt
Joshua	Jos
Judges	Jdg
Ruth	Ru
1 Samuel	1Sa
2 Samuel	2Sa
1 Kings	1Ki
2 Kings	2Ki
1 Chronicles	1Ch
2 Chronicles	2Ch
Ezra	Ezr
Nehemiah	Ne
Esther	Est
Job	Job
Psalms	Ps
Proverbs	Pr
Ecclesiastes	Ecc
Song of Songs	SS
Isaiah	Isa
Jeremiah	Jer
Lamentations	La
Ezekiel	Eze
Daniel	Da
Hosea	Hos
Joel	Joel
Amos	Am
Obadiah	Ob
Jonah	Jnh
Micah	Mic
Nahum	Na
Habakkuk	Hab
Zephaniah	Zep
Haggai	Hag
Zechariah	Zec
Malachi	Mal

The New Testament

Matthew	Mt
Mark	Mk
Luke	Lk
John	Jn
Acts	Ac
Romans	Ro
1 Corinthians	1Co
2 Corinthians	2Co
Galatians	Gal
Ephesians	Eph
Philippians	Php
Colossians	Col
1 Thessalonians	1Th
2 Thessalonians	2Th
1 Timothy	1Ti
2 Timothy	2Ti
Titus	Tit
Philemon	Phm
Hebrews	Heb
James	Jas
1 Peter	1Pe
2 Peter	2Pe
1 John	1Jn
2 John	2Jn
3 John	3Jn
Jude	Jude
Revelation	Rev

Transliterations

A simplified system has been used for transliterating words from ancient Biblical languages into English. The only transliterations calling for comment are these:

Transliteration	Pronunciation
ʾ	Glottal stop
ḥ	Similar to the "ch" in the German word *Buch*
ṭ	Similar to the "t" in the verb "tear"
ʿ	Similar to the glottal stop
ṣ	Similar to the "ts" in "hits"
ś	Similar to the "s" in "sing"

Ancient Texts Relating to the Old Testament

Major representative examples of ancient Near Eastern non-Biblical documents that provide parallels to or shed light on various OT passages.

AMARNA LETTERS **Canaanite Akkadian** *14th century B.C.*	Hundreds of letters, written primarily by Canaanite scribes, illuminate social, political and religious relationships between Canaan and Egypt during the reigns of Amunhotep III and Akhenaten.
AMENEMOPE'S WISDOM **Egyptian** *Early 1st millennium B.C.*	Thirty chapters of wisdom instruction are similar to Pr 22:17–24:22 and provide the closest external parallels to OT wisdom literature.
ATRAHASIS EPIC **Akkadian** *Early 2nd millennium B.C.*	A cosmological epic depicts creation and early human history, including the flood (cf. Ge 1–9).
BABYLONIAN THEODICY **Akkadian** *Early 1st millennium B.C.*	A sufferer and his friend dialogue with each other (cf. Job).
CYRUS CYLINDER **Akkadian** *6th century B.C.*	King Cyrus of Persia records the conquest of Babylon (cf. Da 5:30; 6:28) and boasts of his generous policies toward his new subjects and their gods.
DEAD SEA SCROLLS **Hebrew, Aramaic, Greek** *3rd century B.C. to 1st century A.D.*	Several hundred scrolls and fragments include the oldest copies of OT books and passages.
EBLA TABLETS **Sumerian, Eblaite** *Mid-3rd millennium B.C.*	Thousands of commercial, legal, literary and epistolary texts describe the cultural vitality and political power of a pre-patriarchal civilization in northern Syria.
ELEPHANTINE PAPYRI **Aramaic** *Late 5th century B.C.*	Contracts and letters document life among Jews who fled to southern Egypt after Jerusalem was destroyed in 586 B.C.
ENUMA ELISH **Akkadian** *2nd millennium B.C.*	Marduk, the Babylonian god of cosmic order, is elevated to the supreme position in the pantheon. The 7-tablet epic contains an account of creation (cf. Ge 1–2).
GEZER CALENDAR **Hebrew** *10th century B.C.*	A schoolboy from west-central Israel describes the seasons, crops and farming activity of the agricultural year.
GILGAMESH EPIC **Akkadian** *Early 2nd millennium B.C.*	Gilgamesh, ruler of Uruk, experiences numerous adventures, including a meeting with Utnapishtim, the only survivor of a great deluge (cf. Ge 6–9).
HAMMURAPI'S CODE **Akkadian** *18th century B.C.*	Together with similar law codes that preceded and followed it, the Code of Hammurapi exhibits close parallels to numerous passages in the Mosaic legislation of the OT.
HYMN TO THE ATEN **Egyptian** *14th century B.C.*	The poem praises the beneficence and universality of the sun in language somewhat similar to that used in Ps 104.
ISHTAR'S DESCENT **Akkadian** *1st millennium B.C.*	The goddess Ishtar temporarily descends to the nether world, which is pictured in terms reminiscent of OT descriptions of Sheol.
JEHOIACHIN'S RATION DOCKETS **Akkadian** *Early 6th century B.C.*	Brief texts from the reign of Nebuchadnezzar II refer to rations allotted to Judah's exiled king Jehoiachin and his sons (cf. 2Ki 25:27–30).
KING LISTS **Sumerian** *Early 2nd millennium B.C.*	The reigns of Sumerian kings before the flood are described as lasting for thousands of years, reminding us of the longevity of the preflood patriarchs in Ge 5.
LACHISH LETTERS **Hebrew** *Early 6th century B.C.*	Inscriptions on pottery fragments vividly portray the desperate days preceding the Babylonian siege of Jerusalem in 588–586 B.C. (cf. Jer 34:7).
LAMENTATION OVER THE DESTRUCTION OF UR **Sumerian** *Early 2nd millennium B.C.*	The poem mourns the destruction of the city of Ur at the hands of the Elamites (cf. the OT book of Lamentations).
LUDLUL BEL NEMEQI **Akkadian** *Late 2nd millennium B.C.*	A suffering Babylonian nobleman describes his distress in terms faintly reminiscent of the experiences of Job.

Ancient Texts Relating to the Old Testament—*continued*	
MARI TABLETS **Akkadian** *18th century* B.C.	Letters and administrative texts provide detailed information regarding customs, language and personal names that reflect the culture of the OT patriarchs.
MERNEPTAH STELE **Egyptian** *13th century* B.C.	Pharaoh Merneptah figuratively describes his victory over various peoples in western Asia, including "Israel."
MESHA STELE (MOABITE STONE) **Moabite** *9th century* B.C.	Mesha, king of Moab (see 2Ki 3:4 and note on 1:1), rebels against a successor of Israel's king Omri.
MURASHU TABLETS **Akkadian** *5th century* B.C.	Commercial documents describe financial transactions engaged in by Murashu and Sons, a Babylonian firm that did business with Jews and other exiles.
MURSILIS'S TREATY WITH DUPPI-TESSUB **Hittite** *Mid-2nd millennium* B.C.	King Mursilis imposes a suzerainty treaty on King Duppi-Tessub. The literary outline of this and other Hittite treaties is strikingly paralleled in OT covenants established by God with his people.
NABONIDUS CHRONICLE **Akkadian** *Mid-6th century* B.C.	The account describes the absence of King Nabonidus from Babylon. His son Belshazzar is therefore the regent in charge of the kingdom (cf. Da 5:29–30).
NEBUCHADNEZZAR CHRONICLE **Akkadian** *Early 6th century* B.C.	A chronicle from the reign of Nebuchadnezzar II includes the Babylonian account of the siege of Jerusalem in 597 B.C. (see 2Ki 24:10–17).
NUZI TABLETS **Akkadian** *Mid-2nd millennium* B.C.	Adoption, birthright-sale and other legal documents graphically illustrate OT patriarchal customs current centuries earlier.
PESSIMISTIC DIALOGUE **Akkadian** *Early 1st millennium* B.C.	A master and his servant discuss the pros and cons of various activities (cf. Ecc 1–2).
RAS SHAMRA TABLETS **Ugaritic** *15th–14th centuries* B.C.	Canaanite deities and rulers experience adventures in epics that enrich our understanding of Canaanite mythology and religion and of OT poetry.
SARGON LEGEND **Akkadian** *1st millennium* B.C.	Sargon I (the Great), ruler of Akkad in the late 3rd millennium B.C., claims to have been rescued as an infant from a reed basket found floating in a river (cf. Ex 2).
SARGON'S DISPLAY INSCRIPTION **Akkadian** *8th century* B.C.	Sargon II takes credit for the conquest of Samaria in 722/721 B.C. and states that he captured and exiled 27,290 Israelites.
SENNACHERIB'S PRISM **Akkadian** *Early 7th century* B.C.	Sennacherib vividly describes his siege of Jerusalem in 701 B.C., making Hezekiah a prisoner in his own royal city (but cf. 2Ki 19:35–37).
SEVEN LEAN YEARS TRADITION **Egyptian** *2nd century* B.C.	Egypt experiences 7 years of low Niles and famine, which, by a contractual agreement between Pharaoh Djoser (28th century B.C.) and a god, will be followed by prosperity (cf. Ge 41).
SHALMANESER'S BLACK OBELISK **Akkadian** *9th century* B.C.	Israel's king Jehu presents tribute to Assyria's king Shalmaneser III. Additional Assyrian and Babylonian texts refer to other kings of Israel and Judah.
SHISHAK'S GEOGRAPHICAL LIST **Egyptian** *10th century* B.C.	Pharaoh Shishak lists the cities that he captured or made tributary during his campaign in Judah and Israel (cf. 1Ki 14:25–26 and note on 14:25).
SILOAM INSCRIPTION **Hebrew** *Late 8th century* B.C.	A Judahite workman describes the construction of an underground conduit to guarantee Jerusalem's water supply during Hezekiah's reign (cf. 2Ki 20:20; 2Ch 32:30).
SINUHE'S STORY **Egyptian** *20th–19th centuries* B.C.	An Egyptian offcial of the 12th dynasty goes into voluntary exile in Aram (Syria) and Canaan during the OT patriarchal period.
TALE OF TWO BROTHERS **Egyptian** *13th century* B.C.	A young man rejects the amorous advances of his older brother's wife (cf. Ge 39).
WENAMUN'S JOURNEY **Egyptian** *11th century* B.C.	An offcial of the Temple of Amun at Thebes in Egypt is sent to Byblos in Canaan to buy lumber for the ceremonial barge of his god.

The Old Testament

Genesis

INTRODUCTION

Title

The first phrase in the Hebrew text of 1:1 is *bereshith* ("in [the] beginning"), which is also the Hebrew title of the book (books in ancient times customarily were named after their first word or two). The English title, Genesis, is Greek in origin and comes from the word *geneseos,* which appears in the pre-Christian Greek translation (Septuagint) of 2:4; 5:1. Depending on its context, the word can mean "birth," "genealogy," or "history of origin." In both its Hebrew and Greek forms, then, the traditional title of Genesis appropriately describes its contents, since it is primarily a book of beginnings.

A Quick Look

Author:
Moses

Audience:
God's chosen people, the Israelites

Date:
Between 1446 and 1406 B.C.

Theme:
Genesis is a book of beginnings that introduces central themes of the Bible, such as creation and redemption.

Background

Chs. 1 – 38 reflect a great deal of what we know from other sources about ancient Mesopotamian life and culture. Creation, genealogies, destructive floods, geography and mapmaking, construction techniques, migrations of peoples, sale and purchase of land, legal customs and procedures, sheepherding and cattle-raising — all these subjects and many others were matters of vital concern to the peoples of Mesopotamia during this time. They were also of interest to the individuals, families and tribes of whom we read in the first 38 chapters of Genesis. The author appears to locate Eden, humankind's first home, in or near Mesopotamia; the tower of Babel was built there; Abram was born there; Isaac took a wife from there; and Jacob lived there for 20 years. Although these patriarchs settled in Canaan, their original homeland was Mesopotamia.

The closest ancient literary parallels to Ge 1 – 38 also come from Mesopotamia. *Enuma elish,* the story of the god Marduk's rise to supremacy in the Babylonian pantheon, is similar in some respects (though thoroughly mythical and polytheistic) to the Ge 1 creation account. Some of the features of certain king lists from Sumer bear striking resemblance to the genealogy in Ge 5. The 11th tablet of the *Gilgamesh* epic is quite similar in outline to the flood narrative in Ge 6 – 8. Several of the major events of Ge 1 – 8 are narrated in the same order as similar events in the *Atrahasis* epic.

In fact, the latter features the same basic motif of creation-alienation-flood as the Biblical account. Clay tablets found in 1974 at the ancient (c. 2500 – 2300 B.C.) site of Ebla (modern Tell Mardikh) in northern Syria may also contain some intriguing parallels (see chart, p. xxii).

Two other important sets of documents demonstrate the reflection of Mesopotamia in the first 38 chapters of Genesis. From the Mari letters (see chart, p. xxiii), dating from the patriarchal period, we learn that the names of the patriarchs (including especially Abram, Jacob and Job) were typical of that time. The letters also clearly illustrate the freedom of travel that was possible between various parts of the Amorite world in which the patriarchs lived. The Nuzi tablets (see chart, p. xxiii), though a few centuries later than the patriarchal period, shed light on patriarchal customs, which tended to survive virtually intact for many centuries. The inheritance right of an adopted household member or slave (see 15:1 – 4), the obligation of a barren wife to furnish her husband with sons through a servant girl (see 16:2 – 4), strictures against expelling such a servant girl and her son (see 21:10 – 11), the authority of oral statements in ancient Near Eastern law, such as the deathbed bequest (see 27:1 – 4,22 – 23,33) — these and other legal customs, social contracts and provisions are graphically illustrated in Mesopotamian documents.

As Ge 1 – 38 is Mesopotamian in character and background, so chs. 39 – 50 reflect Egyptian influence — though in not quite so direct a way. Examples of such influence are: Egyptian grape cultivation (40:9 – 11), the riverside scene (ch. 41), Egypt as Canaan's breadbasket (ch. 42), Canaan as the source of numerous products for Egyptian consumption (ch. 43), Egyptian religious and social customs (the end of chs. 43; 46), Egyptian administrative procedures (ch. 47), Egyptian funerary practices (ch. 50) and several Egyptian words and names used throughout these chapters. The closest specific literary parallel from Egypt is the *Tale of Two Brothers,* which bears some resemblance to the story of Joseph and Potiphar's wife (ch. 39). Egyptian autobiographical narratives (such as the *Story of Sinuhe* and the *Report of Wenamun*) and certain historical legends offer more general literary parallels.

Author and Date of Writing

Historically, Jews and Christians alike have held that Moses was the author/compiler of the first five books of the OT. These books, known also as the Pentateuch (meaning "five-volumed book"), were referred to in Jewish tradition as the five fifths of the law (of Moses). The Bible itself suggests Mosaic authorship of Genesis, since Ac 15:1 refers to circumcision as "the custom taught by Moses," an allusion to Ge 17. However, a certain amount of later editorial updating does appear to be indicated (see, e.g., notes on 14:14; 36:31; 47:11).

The historical period during which Moses lived seems to be fixed with a fair degree of accuracy by 1 Kings. We are told that "the fourth year of Solomon's reign over Israel" was the same as "the four hundred and eightieth year after the Israelites had come out of Egypt" (1Ki 6:1). Since the former was c. 966 B.C., the latter — and thus the date of the exodus — was c. 1446 (assuming that the 480 in 1Ki 6:1 is to be taken literally; see Introduction to Judges: Background). The 40-year period of Israel's wanderings in the desert, which lasted from c. 1446 to c. 1406, would have been the most likely time for Moses to write the bulk of what is today known as the Pentateuch.

During the last three centuries many interpreters have claimed to find in the Pentateuch four underlying sources. The presumed documents, allegedly dating from the tenth to the fifth centuries B.C., are called J (for Jahweh/Yahweh, the personal OT name for God), E (for Elohim, a generic name for God), D (for Deuteronomic) and P (for Priestly). Each of these documents is claimed to have its own characteristics and its own theology, which often contradicts that of the other documents. The Pentateuch is thus depicted as a patchwork of stories, poems and laws. However, this view is not supported by conclusive evidence, and intensive archaeological and literary research has tended to undercut many of the arguments used to challenge Mosaic authorship.

Theological Theme and Message

Genesis speaks of beginnings — of the heavens and the earth, of light and darkness, of seas and skies, of land and vegetation, of sun and moon and stars, of sea and air and land animals, of human beings (made in God's own image, the climax of his creative activity), of marriage and family, of society and civilization, of sin and redemption. The list could go on and on. A key word in Genesis is "account," which also serves to divide the book into its ten major parts (see Literary Features and Literary Outline) and which includes such concepts as birth, genealogy and history.

The book of Genesis is foundational to the understanding of the rest of the Bible. Its message is rich and complex, and listing its main elements gives a succinct outline of the Biblical message as a whole. It is supremely a book that speaks about relationships, highlighting those between God and his creation, between God and humankind, and between human beings. It is thoroughly monotheistic, taking for granted that there is only one God worthy of the name and opposing the ideas that there are many gods (polytheism), that there is no god at all (atheism) and that everything is divine (pantheism). It clearly teaches that the one true God is sovereign over all that exists (i.e., his entire creation), and that he often exercises his unlimited freedom to overturn human customs, traditions and plans. It introduces us to the way in which God initiates and makes covenants with his chosen people, pledging his love and faithfulness to them and calling them to promise theirs to him. It establishes sacrifice as the substitution of life for life (ch. 22). It gives us the first hint of God's provision for redemption from the forces of evil (compare 3:15 with Ro 16:17–20) and contains the oldest and most profound statement concerning the significance of faith (15:6; see note there). More than half of Heb 11—a NT list of the faithful—refers to characters in Genesis.

Literary Features

The message of a book is often enhanced by its literary structure and characteristics. Genesis is divided into ten main sections, each beginning with the word "account" (see 2:4; 5:1; 6:9; 10:1; 11:10; 11:27; 25:12; 25:19; 36:1—repeated for emphasis at 36:9—and 37:2). The first five sections can be grouped together and, along with the introduction to the book as a whole (1:1—2:3), can be appropriately called "primeval history" (1:1—11:26). This introduction to the main story sketches the period from Adam to Abraham and tells about the ways of God with the human race as a whole. The last five sections constitute a much longer (but equally unified) account, and relate the story of God's dealings with the ancestors of his chosen people Israel (Abraham, Isaac, Jacob and Joseph and their families)—a section often called "patriarchal history" (11:27—50:26). This section is in turn composed of three narrative cycles (Abraham-Isaac, 11:27—25:11; Isaac-Jacob, 25:19—35:29; 37:1; Jacob-Joseph, 37:2—50:26), interspersed by the genealogies of Ishmael (25:12–18) and Esau (ch. 36).

Genesis is supremely a book that speaks about relationships, highlighting those between God and his creation, between God and humankind, and between human beings.

The narrative frequently concentrates on the life of a later son in preference to the firstborn: Seth over Cain, Shem over Japheth (but see NIV text note on 10:21), Isaac over Ishmael, Jacob over Esau, Judah and Joseph over their brothers, and Ephraim over Manasseh. Such emphasis on divinely chosen men and their families is perhaps the most obvious literary and theological characteristic of the book of Genesis as a whole. It strikingly underscores the fact that the people of God are not the product of natural human developments, but are the result of God's sovereign and gracious intrusion in human history. He brings out of the fallen human race a new humanity consecrated to himself, called and destined to be the people of his kingdom and the channel of his blessing to the whole earth.

Numbers with symbolic significance figure prominently in Genesis. The number ten, in addition to being the number of sections into which Genesis is divided, is also the number of names appearing in the genealogies of chs. 5 and 11 (see note on 5:5). The number seven also occurs frequently. The Hebrew text of 1:1 consists of exactly seven words and that of 1:2 of exactly 14 (twice seven). There are seven days of creation, seven names in the genealogy of ch. 4 (see note on 4:17–18; see also 4:15,24; 5:31), various sevens in the flood story, 70 descendants of Noah's sons (ch. 10), a sevenfold promise to Abram (12:2–3), seven years of abundance and then seven of famine in Egypt (ch. 41), and 70 descendants of Jacob (ch. 46). Other significant numbers, such as 12 and 40, are used with similar frequency.

The book of Genesis is basically prose narrative, punctuated here and there by brief poems (the longest is the so-called Blessing of Jacob in 49:2 – 27). Much of the prose has a lyrical quality and uses the full range of figures of speech and other devices that characterize the world's finest epic literature. Vertical and horizontal parallelism between the two sets of three days in the creation account (see note on 1:11); the ebb and flow of sin and judgment in ch. 3 (the serpent and woman and man sin successively; then God questions them in reverse order; then he judges them in the original order); the powerful monotony of "and then he died" at the end of paragraphs in ch. 5; the climactic hinge effect of the phrase "But God remembered Noah" (8:1) at the midpoint of the flood story; the hourglass structure of the account of the tower of Babel in 11:1 – 9 (narrative in vv. 1 – 2,8 – 9; discourse in vv. 3 – 4,6 – 7; v. 5 acting as transition); the macabre pun in 40:19 (see 40:13); the alternation between brief accounts about firstborn sons and lengthy accounts about younger sons — these and numerous other literary devices add interest to the narrative and provide interpretive signals to which the reader should pay close attention.

It is no coincidence that many of the subjects and themes of the first three chapters of Genesis are reflected in the last three chapters of Revelation. We can only marvel at the superintending influence of the Lord himself, who assures us that "all Scripture is God-breathed" (2Ti 3:16) and that its authors "spoke from God as they were carried along by the Holy Spirit" (2Pe 1:21).

Outlines

Literary Outline:

- I. Introduction (1:1 — 2:3)
- II. Body (2:4 — 50:26)
  - A. "The account of the heavens and the earth" (2:4 — 4:26)
  - B. "The written account of Adam's line" (5:1 — 6:8)
  - C. "The account of Noah" (6:9 — 9:29)
  - D. "The account of Shem, Ham and Japheth" (10:1 — 11:9)
  - E. "The account of Shem" (11:10 – 26)
  - F. "The account of Terah" (11:27 — 25:11)
  - G. "The account of Abraham's son Ishmael" (25:12 – 18)
  - H. "The account of Abraham's son Isaac" (25:19 — 35:29)
  - I. "The account of Esau" (36:1 — 37:1)
  - J. "The account of Jacob" (37:2 — 50:26)

Thematic Outline:

- I. Creation (1:1 — 2:3)
- II. Primeval History (2:4 — 11:26)
  - A. Adam and Eve in Eden (2:4 – 25)
  - B. The Fall and Its Consequences (ch. 3)
  - C. Sin's Progression (4:1 – 16)
  - D. The Genealogy of Cain (4:17 – 26)
  - E. The Genealogy of Seth (ch. 5)
  - F. God's Response to Human Depravity (6:1 – 8)
  - G. The Great Flood (6:9 — 9:29)
    - 1. Preparing for the flood (6:9 — 7:10)
    - 2. Judgment and redemption (7:11 — 8:19)
      - a. The rising of the waters (7:11 – 24)
      - b. The receding of the waters (8:1 – 19)
    - 3. The flood's aftermath (8:20 — 9:29)
      - a. A new promise (8:20 – 22)
      - b. Renewed benediction and new ordinances (9:1 – 7)

c. A new relationship (9:8 – 17)
d. A new temptation (9:18 – 23)
e. A final word (9:24 – 29)
H. The Spread of the Nations (10:1 — 11:26)
1. The diffusion of nations (ch. 10)
2. The confusion of languages (11:1 – 9)
3. The first Semitic genealogy (11:10 – 26)
III. Patriarchal History (11:27 — 50:26)
A. The Life of Abraham (11:27 — 25:11)
1. Abraham's background (11:27 – 32)
2. Abraham's call and response (chs. 12 – 14)
3. Abraham's faith and God's covenant (chs. 15 – 22)
4. Abraham's final acts (23:1 — 25:11)
B. The Descendants of Ishmael (25:12 – 18)
C. The Life of Jacob (25:19 — 35:29)
1. Jacob at home (25:19 — 27:46)
2. Jacob abroad (chs. 28 – 30)
3. Jacob at home again (chs. 31 – 35)
D. The Descendants of Esau (36:1 — 37:1)
E. The Life of Joseph (37:2 — 50:26)
1. Joseph's career (37:2 — 41:57)
2. Jacob's migration (chs. 42 – 47)
3. Jacob's final days (48:1 — 50:14)
4. Joseph's final days (50:15 – 26)

The Beginning

1 In the beginning[a] God created[b]
the heavens[c] and the earth.[d] 2Now
the earth was[a] formless[e] and empty,[f] darkness was over the surface of
the deep,[g] and the Spirit of God[h] was
hovering[i] over the waters.

3And God said,[j] "Let there be light," and
there was light.[k] 4God saw that the
light was good,[l] and he separated the
light from the darkness.[m] 5God called[n]
the light "day," and the darkness he
called "night."[o] And there was evening, and there was morning[p]—the
first day.

6And God said,[q] "Let there be an expanse[r]
between the waters[s] to separate water
from water." 7So God made the expanse and separated the water under
the expanse from the water above it.[t]
And it was so.[u] 8God called[v] the expanse "sky."[w] And there was evening,
and there was morning[x]—the second
day.

9And God said, "Let the water under the
sky be gathered to one place,[y] and let
dry ground[z] appear." And it was so.[a]
10God called[b] the dry ground "land,"
and the gathered waters[c] he called

1:1 [a]Ps 102:25; Pr 8:23; Isa 40:21; 41:4,26; Jn 1:1-2 [b]ver 21,27; Ge 2:3 [c]ver 6; Ne 9:6; Job 9:8; 37:18; Ps 96:5; 104:2; 115:15; 121:2; 136:5; Isa 40:22; 42:5; 51:13; Jer 10:12; 51:15 [d]Ge 14:19; 2Ki 19:15; Ne 9:6; Job 38:4; Ps 90:2; 136:6; 146:6; Isa 37:16; 40:28; 42:5; 44:24; 45:12,18; Jer 27:5; 32:17; Ac 14:15; 17:24; Eph 3:9; Col 1:16; Heb 3:4; 11:3; Rev 4:11; 10:6 **1:2** [e]Isa 23:1; 24:10; 27:10; 32:14; 34:11 [f]Isa 45:18; Jer 4:23 [g]Ge 8:2; Job 7:12; 26:8; 38:9; Ps 36:6; 42:7; 104:6; 107:24; Pr 30:4 [h]Ge 2:7; Job 33:4; Ps 104:30; Isa 32:15 [i]Dt 32:11; Isa 31:5 **1:3** [j]ver 6; Ps 33:6,9; 148:5; Heb 11:3 [k]2Co 4:6*; 1Jn 1:5-7 **1:4** [l]ver 10,12,18,21,25,31; Ps 104:31; 119:68; Jer 31:35 [m]ver 14; Ex 10:21-23; Job 26:10; 38:19; Ps 18:28; 104:20; 105:28; Isa 42:16; 45:7 **1:5** [n]ver 8,10; Ge 2:19,23 [o]Ps 74:16 [p]ver 8,13,19,23,31 **1:6** [q]S ver 3 [r]S ver 1; Isa 44:24; 2Pe 3:5 [s]ver 9; Ps 24:2; 136:6 **1:7** [t]Ge 7:11; Job 26:10; 38:8-11,16; Ps 68:33; 148:4; Pr 8:28 [u]ver 9,11,15,24 **1:8** [v]S ver 5 [w]Job 9:8; 37:18; Ps 19:1; 104:2; Isa 40:22; 44:24; 45:12; Jer 10:12; Zec 12:1 [x]S ver 5 **1:9** [y]Job 38:8-11; Ps 33:7; 104:6-9; Pr 8:29; Jer 5:22; 2Pe 3:5 [z]Ps 95:5; Jnh 1:9; Hag 2:6 [a]S ver 7 **1:10** [b]S ver 5 [c]Ps 33:7

[a] 2 Or possibly *became*

1:1—2:3 In the ancient Near East, most of the peoples had myths relating how the world came to be. Prevalent in those myths were accounts of how one of the gods triumphed over a fierce and powerful beast that represented disorder, then fashioned the ordered world that people knew, and finally was proclaimed by the other gods to be the divine "king" over the world he had created—a position ever subject to the challenge of the forces of disorder.

Over against all those pagan myths, the author of Genesis taught a radically new doctrine of creation: The one and only true God did not have to overcome a mighty cosmic champion of chaos but simply by a series of his royal creation decrees called into being the ordered world, the visible kingdom that those decrees continue to uphold and govern. The author teaches this doctrine of creation in the form of a narrative that recounts the story of God's creative acts. The author narrates those acts from the perspective of one who was an eyewitness to events in God's royal council chamber, where he issues his creative decrees. For a similar narrative perspective see Job 1:6–12; 2:1–6. (For the different narrative perspective of what follows see note on 2:4—4:26.)

1:1 A summary statement introducing the six days of creative activity (see note on 2:1). The truth of this majestic verse was joyfully affirmed by poet (Ps 102:25) and prophet (Isa 40:21). *In the beginning God.* The Bible always assumes, and never argues, God's existence. Although everything else had a beginning, God has always been (Ps 90:2). *In the beginning.* Jn 1:1–10, which stresses the work of Christ in creation, opens with the same phrase. *God created.* "God" renders the common Hebrew noun *Elohim.* It is plural but the verb is singular, a normal usage in the OT when reference is to the one true God. This use of the plural expresses intensification rather than number and has been called the plural of majesty, or of potentiality. In the OT the Hebrew verb for "create" is used only of divine, never of human, activity. *the heavens and the earth.* "All things" (Isa 44:24). That God created everything is also taught in Ecc 11:5; Jer 10:16; Jn 1:3; Col 1:16; Heb 1:2. The positive, life-oriented teaching of v. 1 is beautifully summarized in Isa 45:18.

1:2 *earth.* The focus of this account. *formless and empty.* The phrase, which appears elsewhere only in Jer 4:23, gives structure to the rest of the chapter (see note on v. 11). God's "separating" and "gathering" on days 1–3 gave form, and his "making" and "filling" on days 4–6 removed the emptiness. *darkness ... the waters.* Completes the picture of a world awaiting God's light-giving, order-making and life-creating word. *and.* Or "but." The awesome (and, for ancient people, fearful) picture of the original state of the visible creation is relieved by the majestic announcement that the mighty Spirit of God hovers over creation. The announcement anticipates God's creative words that follow. *Spirit of God.* He was active in creation, and his creative power continues today (see Job 33:4; Ps 104:30). *hovering over.* Like an eagle that hovers over its young when they are learning to fly (see Dt 32:11; cf. Isa 31:5).

1:3 *God said.* Merely by issuing his royal decree, God brought all things into being (Ps 33:6,9; 148:5; Heb 11:3). *Let there be light.* God's first creative word called forth light in the midst of the primeval darkness. Light is necessary for making God's creative works visible and life possible. In the OT it is also symbolic of life and blessing (see 2Sa 22:29; Job 3:20; 30:26; 33:30; Ps 49:19; 56:13; 97:11; 112:4; Isa 53:11; 58:8,10; 59:9; 60:1,3). Paul uses this word to illustrate God's re-creating work in sin-darkened hearts (2Co 4:6).

1:4 Everything God created is good (see vv. 10,12,18,21,25); in fact, the conclusion declares it to be "very good" (v. 31). The creation, as fashioned and ordered by God, had no lingering traces of disorder and no dark and threatening forces arrayed against God or people. Even darkness and the deep were given benevolent functions in a world fashioned to bless and sustain life (see Ps 104:19–26; 127:2—see also NIV text note there).

1:5 *called.* See vv. 8,10. In the ancient Near East, for a king to name people or things was an act of claiming dominion over them (see 17:5,15; 41:45; 2Ki 23:34; 24:17; Da 1:7). In this creation account, God named the great cosmic realities of day, night, sky, land and seas. He left to human beings the naming of the creatures they were given dominion over (see vv. 26,28; see also 2:19 and note). *first day.* Some say that the creation days were 24-hour days, others that they were indefinite periods.

1:6 *expanse.* The atmosphere, or "sky" (v. 8), as seen from the earth. "Hard as a mirror" (Job 37:18) and "like a canopy" (Isa 40:22) are among the many pictorial phrases used to describe it.

1:7 *And it was so.* The only possible outcome, whether stated (vv. 9,11,15,24,30) or implied, to God's "Let there be" (see Ps 33:6,9 and note on 33:6).

1:9 *one place.* A picturesque way of referring to the "seas" (v. 10) that surround the dry land on all sides and into which the waters of the lakes and rivers flow. The earth was "formed out of water" (2Pe 3:5) and "founded ... upon the seas" (Ps 24:2), and the waters are not to cross the boundaries set for them (Ps 104:7–9; Jer 5:22).

1:10 *land.* Elsewhere usually rendered "earth" (as in vv. 15,17,20,22,26,28–30). In the Bible "earth" refers not to a

"seas."[d] And God saw that it was
good.[e]
11 Then God said, "Let the land produce vegetation:[f] seed-bearing plants
and trees on the land that bear fruit
with seed in it, according to their various kinds.[g]" And it was so.[h] 12 The
land produced vegetation: plants
bearing seed according to their kinds[i]
and trees bearing fruit with seed in
it according to their kinds. And God
saw that it was good.[j] 13 And there
was evening, and there was morning[k]—the third day.
14 And God said, "Let there be lights[l] in the
expanse of the sky to separate the day
from the night,[m] and let them serve
as signs[n] to mark seasons[o] and days
and years,[p] 15 and let them be lights
in the expanse of the sky to give light
on the earth." And it was so.[q] 16 God
made two great lights—the greater light[r] to govern[s] the day and the
lesser light to govern[t] the night.[u] He
also made the stars.[v] 17 God set them
in the expanse of the sky to give light
on the earth, 18 to govern the day and
the night,[w] and to separate light from
darkness. And God saw that it was
good.[x] 19 And there was evening, and
there was morning[y]—the fourth day.
20 And God said, "Let the water teem with
living creatures,[z] and let birds fly

1:10 [d]Job 38:8; Ps 90:2; 95:5 [e]S ver 4 1:11 [f]Ps 65:9-13; 104:14 [g]ver 12, 21,24,25; Ge 2:5; 6:20; 7:14; Lev 11:14,19,22; Dt 14:13,18; 1Co 15:38 [h]S ver 7 1:12 [i]S ver 11 [j]S ver 4 1:13 [k]S ver 5 1:14 [l]Ps 74:16; 136:7 [m]S ver 4 [n]Jer 10:2 [o]Ps 104:19 [p]Ge 8:22; Jer 31:35-36; 33:20,25 1:15 [q]S ver 7 1:16 [r]Dt 17:3; Job 31:26; Jer 43:13; Eze 8:16 [s]Ps 136:8 [t]Ps 136:9 [u]Job 38:33; Ps 74:16; 104:19; Jer 31:35; Jas 1:17 [v]Dt 4:19; Job 9:9; 38:7,31-32; Ps 8:3; 33:6; Ecc 12:2; Isa 40:26; Jer 8:2; Am 5:8 1:18 [w]Jer 33:20,25 [x]S ver 4 1:19 [y]S ver 5 1:20 [z]Ps 146:6 [a]Ge 2:19 1:21 [b]S ver 1

above the earth across the expanse of
the sky."[a] 21 So God created[b] the great
creatures of the sea[c] and every living
and moving thing with which the water teems,[d] according to their kinds,
and every winged bird according to
its kind.[e] And God saw that it was
good.[f] 22 God blessed them and said,
"Be fruitful and increase in number
and fill the water in the seas, and
let the birds increase on the earth."[g]
23 And there was evening, and there
was morning[h]—the fifth day.
24 And God said, "Let the land produce
living creatures[i] according to their
kinds:[j] livestock, creatures that move
along the ground, and wild animals,
each according to its kind." And it
was so.[k] 25 God made the wild animals[l] according to their kinds, the
livestock according to their kinds,
and all the creatures that move along
the ground according to their kinds.[m]
And God saw that it was good.[n]
26 Then God said, "Let us[o] make
man[p] in our image,[q] in our likeness,[r]
and let them rule[s] over the fish of
the sea and the birds of the air,[t] over

[c]Job 3:8; 7:12; Ps 74:13; 148:7; Isa 27:1; Eze 32:2 [d]Ps 104:25-26 [e]S ver 11 [f]S ver 4 1:22 [g]ver 28; Ge 8:17; 9:1,7,19; 47:27; Lev 26:9; Eze 36:11 1:23 [h]S ver 5 1:24 [i]Ge 2:19 [j]S ver 11 [k]S ver 7 1:25 [l]Ge 7:21-22; Jer 27:5 [m]S ver 11 [n]S ver 4 1:26 [o]Ge 3:5,22; 11:7; Ps 100:3; Isa 6:8 [p]Isa 45:18 [q]ver 27; Ge 5:3; 9:6; Ps 8:5; 82:6; 89:6; 1Co 11:7; 2Co 4:4; Col 1:15; 3:10; Jas 3:9 [r]Ac 17:28-29 [s]Ge 9:2; Ps 8:6-8 [t]Ps 8:8

planet in our solar system but to the land realm that is humankind's native habitat—in distinction from the "heavens" above and the "seas" below (see Ex 20:4).

1:11 *God said.* This phrase is used twice on the third day (vv. 9,11) and three times (vv. 24,26,29) on the sixth day. These two days are climactic, as the following structure of ch. 1 reveals (see note on v. 2 regarding "formless and empty").

Days of forming	*Days of filling*
1. "light" (v. 3)	4. "lights" (v. 14)
2. "water under the expanse ... water above it" (v. 7)	5. "every living and moving thing with which the water teems ... every winged bird" (v. 21)
3a. "dry ground" (v. 9)	$6a_1$. "livestock, creatures that move along the ground, and wild animals" (v. 24) $6a_2$. "man" (v. 26)
3b. "vegetation" (v. 11)	6b. "every green plant for food" (v. 30)

Both the horizontal and vertical relationships between the days demonstrate the literary structure of the chapter and stress the orderliness and symmetry of God's creative activity. *kinds.* See vv. 12,21,24–25. Both creation and reproduction are orderly.

1:14 *serve as signs.* In the ways mentioned here, not in any astrological or other such sense (see Ps 104:19; 136:7–9).

1:16 *two great lights.* The words "sun" and "moon" seem to be avoided deliberately here, since both were used as proper names for the pagan deities associated with these heavenly bodies. They are light-givers to be appreciated, not powers to be feared, because the one true God made them (see Isa 40:26). Since the emphasis is on the greater light and lesser light, the stars seem to be mentioned almost as an afterthought. But Ps 136:9 indicates that the stars help the moon "govern the night." *govern.* The great Creator-King assigns subordinate regulating roles to certain of his creatures (see vv. 26,28).

1:17–18 The three main functions of the heavenly bodies.

1:21 *creatures of the sea.* The Hebrew root underlying this phrase was used in Canaanite mythology to refer to a dreaded sea monster, which OT poets and prophets often employed as a metaphor for a powerful hostile force or empire (see Job 7:12; Ps 74:13; Isa 27:1; 51:9; Jer 51:34; Eze 29:3; 32:2 and notes; cf. notes on Job 3:8; 9:13; Ps 32:6; 87:4; 89:10). In Genesis, however, "the great creatures of the sea" are portrayed not as enemies to be feared but as part of God's good creation to be appreciated (cf. Ps 104:26 and note).

1:22 *Be fruitful and increase in number.* God's benediction on living things that inhabit the water and that fly in the air. By his blessing they flourish and fill both realms with life (see note on v. 28). God's rule over his created realm promotes and blesses life.

1:26 *us ... our ... our.* God speaks as the Creator-King, announcing his crowning work to the members of his heavenly court (see 3:22; 11:7; Isa 6:8; see also 1Ki 22:19–23; Job 15:8; Jer 23:18). *man.* Hebrew *'adam.* This noun (like the earlier Canaanite *'adam*) is a generic term, which, depending on context, is used to refer to a single human being or to a collectivity of human beings (whether males or females or both; see v. 27) or to humankind as a collective whole. It has no plural form. *image ... likeness.* No distinction

the livestock, over all the earth,[a] and
over all the creatures that move along
the ground."

27So God created[u] man[v] in his own
image,[w]
in the image of God[x] he created him;
male and female[y] he created them.[z]

28God blessed them and said to
them,[a] "Be fruitful and increase in
number;[b] fill the earth[c] and subdue it.
Rule over[d] the fish of the sea and the
birds of the air and over every living
creature that moves on the ground.[e]"
29Then God said, "I give you every seed-bearing plant on the face of
the whole earth and every tree that
has fruit with seed in it. They will be
yours for food.[f] 30And to all the beasts
of the earth and all the birds of the
air and all the creatures that move on
the ground—everything that has the
breath of life[g] in it—I give every green
plant for food.[h]" And it was so.
31God saw all that he had made,[i]
and it was very good.[j] And there was

1:27 [u]S ver 1 [v]Ge 2:7; Ps 103:14; 119:73 [w]S ver 26 [x]Ge 5:1 [y]Ge 5:2; Mt 19:4*; Mk 10:6*; Gal 3:28 [z]Dt 4:32 **1:28** [a]Ge 33:5; Jos 24:3; Ps 113:9; 127:3,5 [b]S Ge 17:6 [c]S ver 22; Ge 6:1; Ac 17:26 [d]ver 26; Ps 115:16 [e]Ps 8:6-8 **1:29** [f]Ge 9:3; Dt 12:15; Ps 104:14; 1Ti 4:3 **1:30** [g]Ge 2:7; 7:22 [h]Job 38:41; Ps 78:25; 104:14,27; 111:5; 136:25; 145:15; 147:9 **1:31** [i]Ps 104:24; 136:5; Pr 3:19; Jer 10:12 [j]S ver 4; 1Ti 4:4

[k]S ver 5 **2:1** [l]Dt 4:19; 17:3; 2Ki 17:16; 21:3; Ps 104:2; Isa 44:24; 45:12;

evening, and there was morning[k]—
the sixth day.

2 Thus the heavens and the earth
were completed in all their vast array.[l]

2By the seventh day[m] God had finished
the work he had been doing; so on
the seventh day he rested[b] from all
his work.[n] 3And God blessed the seventh day and made it holy,[o] because
on it he rested[p] from all the work of
creating[q] that he had done.

Adam and Eve

4This is the account[r] of the heavens and the earth when they were created.[s]

When the LORD God made the earth
and the heavens— 5and no shrub of the

[a] *26* Hebrew; Syriac *all the wild animals*
[b] *2* Or *ceased*; also in verse 3

48:13; 51:13 **2:2** [m]Dt 5:14 [n]ver 2-3; Ex 20:11; 31:17; 34:21; Jn 5:17; Heb 4:4* **2:3** [o]Ex 16:23; 20:10; 23:12; 31:15; 35:2; Lev 23:3; Ne 9:14; Isa 58:13; Jer 17:22 [p]Ps 95:11; Heb 4:1-11 [q]S Ge 1:1 **2:4** [r]Ge 5:1; 6:9; 10:1; 11:10,27; 25:12,19; 36:1,9; 37:2 [s]Ge 1:1; Job 38:8-11

should be made between "image" and "likeness," which are synonyms in both the OT (5:1; 9:6) and the NT (1Co 11:7; Col 3:10; Jas 3:9). Since human beings are made in God's image, they are all worthy of honor and respect; they are neither to be murdered (9:6) nor cursed (Jas 3:9). "Image" includes such characteristics as "righteousness and holiness" (Eph 4:24) and "knowledge" (Col 3:10). Believers are to be "conformed to the likeness" of Christ (Ro 8:29) and will someday be "like him" (1Jn 3:2). *and let them rule.* Probably to be understood in the sense "so that they may rule." Within the realm of his visible creation God places a creature capable of acting as his agent in relationship to other creatures (1) to represent God's claim to kingship over his creation and (2) to bring its full potential to realization to the praise of the Creator's glory. (In the ancient Near East, kings marked their conquest of lands by setting up images of themselves in the conquered territories as a sign of their authority and ruling presence. An especially noteworthy example is the life-size statue of the ninth-century B.C. Hadad-Yith'i, ruler of Gozan, found at Tell Fekheriyeh in northeastern Syria in 1979. An Aramaic inscription on the statue identifies it as the "image" and "likeness" of the ruler, using the Aramaic cognates of the Hebrew words.) For a celebration of humanity's exalted role (under God) in the creation see Ps 8:5–8 and notes. For the ultimate embodiment of humanity's dominion over the creation see Heb 2:5–9 and notes. *rule.* Humans are the climax of God's creative activity, and God has crowned them "with glory and honor" and made them rulers over the rest of his creation (Ps 8:5–8). Since they were created in the image of the divine King, delegated sovereignty (kingship) was bestowed on them.

1:27 This highly significant verse is the first occurrence of poetry in the OT (which is about 40 percent poetry). *created.* The word is used here three times to describe the central divine act of the sixth day (see note on v. 1). *male and female.* Alike they bear the image of God, and together they share in the divine benediction that follows.

1:28 *God blessed them ... fill ... subdue ... Rule.* Humankind goes forth from the hands of the Creator under his divine benediction—flourishing, filling the earth with their kind, and exercising dominion over the other earthly creatures (see v. 26; 2:15; Ps 8:6–8 and notes). Human culture, accordingly, is not anti-God (though fallen human beings often have turned their efforts into proud rebellion against God). Rather, it is the activity of those who bear the image of their Creator and share, as God's servants, in his kingly rule. As God's representatives in the creaturely realm, they are stewards of God's creatures. They are not to exploit, waste or despoil them, but to care for them and to use them in the service of God and humankind.

1:29–30 People and animals seem to be portrayed as originally vegetarian (see 9:3 and note).

1:31 *very good.* See note on v. 4. *the sixth day.* Perhaps to stress the finality and importance of this day, in the Hebrew text the definite article is first used here in regard to the creation days. Another possibility is that the purpose for the lack of the article with days 1–5 is to signal an order that is more literary/logical than strictly chronological (see note on v. 11).

2:1 A summary statement concluding the six days of creative activity (see note on 1:1).

2:2 *finished ... rested.* God rested on the seventh day, not because he was weary, but because nothing formless or empty remained (see NIV text note). His creative work was completed—and it was totally effective, absolutely perfect, "very good" (1:31). It did not have to be repeated, repaired or revised, and the Creator rested to commemorate it.

2:3 *God blessed the seventh day and made it holy ... rested.* Although the word "Sabbath" is not used here, the Hebrew verb translated "rested" (v. 2) is the origin of the noun "Sabbath." Ex 20:11 quotes the first half of v. 3, but substitutes "Sabbath" for "seventh," clearly equating the two. The first record of obligatory Sabbath observance is of Israel on her way from Egypt to Sinai (see Ex 16:5,23 and notes), but according to Ne 9:13–14 the Sabbath was not an official covenant obligation until the giving of the law at Mount Sinai. *holy.* See notes on Ex 3:5; Lev 11:44; Ro 1:7; 1Co 1:2.

2:4—4:26 The beginning of human history, in distinction from the account of creation in 1:1—2:3 (see note there).

2:4 *account.* The Hebrew word for "account" occurs ten times in Genesis—at the beginning of each main section (see Introduction: Literary Features). *the heavens and the earth.* See note on 1:1. The phrase "the account of the heavens and the earth" introduces the story of what happened

field had yet appeared on the earth[a] and
no plant of the field had yet sprung up,[t]
for the LORD God had not sent rain on the
earth[a u] and there was no man to work
the ground, 6but streams[b] came up from
the earth and watered the whole surface
of the ground — 7the LORD God formed[v]
the man[c w] from the dust[x] of the ground[y]
and breathed into his nostrils the breath[z]
of life,[a] and the man became a living being.[b]
8Now the LORD God had planted a garden in the east, in Eden;[c] and there he put
the man he had formed. 9And the LORD
God made all kinds of trees grow out of
the ground — trees[d] that were pleasing to
the eye and good for food. In the middle
of the garden were the tree of life[e] and the
tree of the knowledge of good and evil.[f]
10A river[g] watering the garden flowed
from Eden;[h] from there it was separated
into four headwaters. 11The name of the
first is the Pishon; it winds through the entire land of Havilah,[i] where there is gold.
12(The gold of that land is good; aromatic resin[d j] and onyx are also there.) 13The
name of the second river is the Gihon; it
winds through the entire land of Cush.[e]
14The name of the third river is the Tigris;[k]
it runs along the east side of Asshur. And
the fourth river is the Euphrates.[l]
15The LORD God took the man and put
him in the Garden of Eden[m] to work it and
take care of it. 16And the LORD God commanded the man, "You are free to eat from
any tree in the garden;[n] 17but you must not
eat from the tree of the knowledge of good
and evil,[o] for when you eat of it you will
surely die."[p]
18The LORD God said, "It is not good for
the man to be alone. I will make a helper
suitable for him."[q]
19Now the LORD God had formed out of
the ground all the beasts of the field[r] and
all the birds of the air.[s] He brought them to
the man to see what he would name them;
and whatever the man called[t] each living
creature,[u] that was its name. 20So the man

2:5 [t]Ge 1:11 [u]Job 38:28; Ps 65:9-10; Jer 10:13 **2:7** [v]Isa 29:16; 43:1,21; 44:2 [w]S Ge 1:27 [x]Ge 3:19; 18:27; Job 4:19; 10:9; 17:16; 34:15; Ps 90:3; Ecc 3:20; 12:7 [y]Ge 3:23; 4:2; Ps 103:14; Jer 18:6; 1Co 15:47 [z]S Ge 1:2; Job 27:3; Isa 2:22 [a]S Ge 1:30; Isa 42:5; Ac 17:25 [b]Job 12:10; 32:8; 33:4; 34:14; Ps 104:29; Isa 57:16; Eze 37:5; 1Co 15:45* **2:8** [c]ver 10,15; Ge 3:23,24; 4:16; 13:10; Isa 51:3; Eze 28:13; 31:9,16; 36:35; Joel 2:3 **2:9** [d]Eze 31:8 [e]Ge 3:22,24; Pr 3:18; 11:30; S Rev 2:7 [f]Eze 47:12 **2:10** [g]Nu 24:6; Ps 46:4; Eze 47:5 [h]S ver 8 **2:11** [i]Ge 10:7; 25:18

[a] *5* Or *land*; also in verse 6 [b] *6* Or *mist*
[c] *7* The Hebrew for *man (adam)* sounds like and may be related to the Hebrew for *ground (adamah)*; it is also the name *Adam* (see Gen. 2:20). [d] *12* Or *good; pearls*
[e] *13* Possibly southeast Mesopotamia

2:12 [j]Nu 11:7 **2:14** [k]Ge 41:1; Da 10:4 [l]Ge 15:18; 31:21; Ex 23:31; Nu 22:5; Dt 1:7; 11:24; Jos 1:4; 2Sa 8:3; 1Ki 4:21; 2Ki 23:29; 24:7; 1Ch 5:9; 18:3; 2Ch 35:20; Jer 13:4; 46:2; 51:63; S Rev 9:14 **2:15** [m]S ver 8 **2:16** [n]Ge 3:1-2 **2:17** [o]Ge 3:11,17 [p]Ge 3:1,3; 5:5; 9:29; Dt 30:15,19; Jer 42:16; Eze 3:18; S Ro 5:12; S 6:23 **2:18** [q]Pr 31:11; 1Co 11:9; 1Ti 2:13 **2:19** [r]Ps 8:7 [s]S Ge 1:20 [t]S Ge 1:5 [u]Ge 1:24

to God's creation. The blight of sin and rebellion brought a threefold curse that darkens the story of Adam and Eve in God's good and beautiful garden: (1) on Satan (3:14); (2) on the ground, because of Adam's sin (3:17); and (3) on Cain (4:11). *LORD God.* "LORD" (Hebrew *YHWH,* "Yahweh") is the personal and covenant name of God (see note on Ex 3:15), emphasizing his role as Israel's Redeemer and covenant Lord (see note on Ex 6:6), while "God" (Hebrew *Elohim*) is a general term. Both names occur thousands of times in the OT, and often, as here, they appear together — clearly indicating that they refer to the one and only God.

2:7 *formed.* The Hebrew for this verb commonly referred to the work of a potter (see Isa 45:9; Jer 18:6), who fashions vessels from clay (see Job 33:6). "Make" (1:26), "create" (1:27) and "form" are used to describe God's creation of both people and animals (v. 19; 1:21,25). *breath of life.* Humans and animals alike have the breath of life in them (see 1:30; Job 33:4). *the man became a living being.* The Hebrew phrase here translated "living being" is translated "living creatures" in 1:20,24. The words of 2:7 therefore imply that people, at least physically, have affinity with the animals. The great difference is that people are made "in the image of God" (1:27) and have an absolutely unique relation both to God as his servants and to the other creatures as God's stewards over them (Ps 8:5 – 8).

2:8 *in the east.* From the standpoint of the author of Genesis. The garden was thought of as being near where the Tigris and Euphrates rivers (see v. 14) meet, in what is today southern Iraq. *Eden.* A name synonymous with "paradise" and related to either (1) a Hebrew word meaning "bliss" or "delight" or (2) a Mesopotamian word meaning "a plain." Perhaps the author subtly suggests both.

2:9 *tree of life.* Signifying and giving life, without death, to those who eat its fruit (see 3:22; Rev 2:7; 22:2,14). *tree of the knowledge of good and evil.* Signifying and giving knowledge of good and evil, leading ultimately to death, to those who eat its fruit (v. 17; 3:3). "Knowledge of good and evil" refers to moral knowledge or ethical discernment (see Dt 1:39; Isa 7:15 – 16). Adam and Eve possessed both life and moral discernment as they came from the hand of God. Their access to the fruit of the tree of life showed that God's will and intention for them was life. Ancient pagans believed that the gods intended for human beings always to be mortal. In eating the fruit of the tree of the knowledge of good and evil, Adam and Eve sought a creaturely source of discernment in order to be morally independent of God.

2:11 *Pishon.* Location unknown. The Hebrew word may be a common noun meaning "gusher." *Havilah.* Location unknown; perhaps mentioned again in 10:29. It is probably to be distinguished from the Havilah of 10:7 (see note there), which was in Arabia.

2:13 *Gihon.* Location unknown. The Hebrew word may be a common noun meaning "spurter." Both the Pishon and the Gihon may have been streams in Lower Mesopotamia near the Persian Gulf. The names were those current when Genesis was written.

2:14 *Asshur.* An ancient capital city of Assyria ("Assyria" and "Asshur" are related words). *Euphrates.* Often called in Hebrew simply "the River" because of its size and importance (see note on 15:18).

2:15 *work … take care.* See notes on 1:26,28. The man is now charged to govern the earth responsibly under God's sovereignty.

2:16 *any tree.* Including the tree of life (v. 9).

2:17 *surely die.* Despite the serpent's denial (3:4), disobeying God ultimately results in death.

2:18 – 25 The only full account of the creation of woman in ancient Near Eastern literature.

2:18 *not good … to be alone.* Without female companionship and a partner in reproduction, the man could not fully realize his humanity.

2:19 *name them.* His first act of dominion over the creatures around him (see note on 1:5).

gave names to all the livestock, the birds
of the air and all the beasts of the field.
But for Adam[a] no suitable helper[v] was
found. 21So the LORD God caused the man
to fall into a deep sleep;[w] and while he
was sleeping, he took one of the man's
ribs[b] and closed up the place with flesh.
22Then the LORD God made a woman from
the rib[c][x] he had taken out of the man, and
he brought her to the man.

23The man said,

"This is now bone of my bones
and flesh of my flesh;[y]
she shall be called[z] 'woman,[d]'
for she was taken out of man.[a]"

24For this reason a man will leave his father and mother and be united[b] to his
wife, and they will become one flesh.[c]
25The man and his wife were both naked,[d] and they felt no shame.

The Fall of Man

3 Now the serpent[e] was more crafty than
any of the wild animals the LORD God
had made. He said to the woman, "Did
God really say, 'You must not eat from any
tree in the garden'?[f]"
2The woman said to the serpent, "We
may eat fruit from the trees in the garden,[g]
3but God did say, 'You must not eat fruit
from the tree that is in the middle of the
garden, and you must not touch it, or you
will die.'"[h]
4"You will not surely die," the serpent
said to the woman.[i] 5"For God knows
that when you eat of it your eyes will be
opened, and you will be like God,[j] knowing good and evil."
6When the woman saw that the fruit of
the tree was good for food and pleasing
to the eye, and also desirable[k] for gaining
wisdom, she took some and ate it. She
also gave some to her husband,[l] who was
with her, and he ate it.[m] 7Then the eyes
of both of them were opened, and they
realized they were naked;[n] so they sewed
fig leaves together and made coverings for
themselves.[o]
8Then the man and his wife heard the
sound of the LORD God as he was walking[p] in the garden in the cool of the day,
and they hid[q] from the LORD God among
the trees of the garden. 9But the LORD God
called to the man, "Where are you?"[r]
10He answered, "I heard you in the garden, and I was afraid[s] because I was naked;[t] so I hid."
11And he said, "Who told you that you
were naked?[u] Have you eaten from the tree
that I commanded you not to eat from?[v]"
12The man said, "The woman you put
here with me[w]—she gave me some fruit
from the tree, and I ate it."

2:20 [v]Ge 3:20; 4:1 **2:21** [w]Ge 15:12; 1Sa 26:12; Job 33:15 **2:22** [x]1Co 11:8, 9, 12; 1Ti 2:13 **2:23** [y]Ge 29:14; Eph 5:28-30 [z]S Ge 1:5 [a]1Co 11:8 **2:24** [b]Mal 2:15 [c]Mt 19:5*; Mk 10:7-8*; 1Co 6:16*; Eph 5:31* **2:25** [d]Ge 3:7, 10-11; Isa 47:3; La 1:8 **3:1** [e]Job 1:7; 2:2; 2Co 11:3; Rev 12:9; 20:2 [f]S Ge 2:17 **3:2** [g]Ge 2:16 **3:3** [h]S Ge 2:17 **3:4** [i]S Jn 8:44; 2Co 11:3 **3:5** [j]S Ge 1:26; 14:18, 19; Ps 7:8; Isa 14:14; Eze 28:2 **3:6** [k]Jas 1:14-15; 1Jn 2:16 [l]Nu 30:7-8; Jer 44:15, 19, 24 [m]2Co 11:3; 1Ti 2:14 **3:7** [n]Ge 2:25 [o]ver 21 **3:8** [p]Lev 26:12; Dt 23:14 [q]Job 13:16; 23:7; 31:33; 34:22, 23; Ps 5:5; 139:7-12; Isa 29:15; Jer 16:17; 23:24; 49:10; Rev 6:15-16 **3:9** [r]Ge 4:9; 16:8; 18:9; 1Ki 19:9, 13 **3:10** [s]Ex 19:16; 20:18; Dt 5:5; 1Sa 12:18 [t]Ge 2:25 **3:11** [u]Ge 2:25 [v]S Ge 2:17 **3:12** [w]Ge 2:22

[a] *20* Or *the man* [b] *21* Or *took part of the man's side* [c] *22* Or *part* [d] *23* The Hebrew for *woman* sounds like the Hebrew for *man*

2:24 *leave his father and mother.* Instead of remaining under the protective custody of his parents a man leaves them and, with his wife, establishes a new family unit. *united ... one flesh.* The divine intention for husband and wife was monogamy. Together they were to form as inseparable a union as that between parent and child. As parents and their children are the same "flesh and blood" (see 29:14 and note), so husband and wife should be bound together as "one flesh" as long as they live—of which sexual union is an expression (cf. 1Co 6:16 and note).

2:25 *naked ... no shame.* Freedom from shame, signifying moral innocence, would soon be lost as a result of sin (see 3:7).

3:1–24 The disobedience of Adam and Eve, and God's response that affects the whole course of human history (cf. Ro 5:12–21 and notes).

3:1 *serpent.* The great deceiver clothed himself as a serpent, one of God's good creatures. He insinuated a falsehood and portrayed rebellion as clever, but essentially innocent, self-interest. Therefore "the devil, or Satan," is later referred to as "that ancient serpent" (Rev 12:9; 20:2). *crafty.* The Hebrew words for "crafty" and "naked" are almost identical. Though naked, the man and his wife felt no shame (2:25). The craftiness of the serpent led them to sin, and they then became ashamed of their nakedness (see v. 7). *Did God really say ...?* The question and the response changed the course of human history. By causing the woman to doubt God's word, Satan brought evil into the world. Here the deceiver undertook to alienate people from God. Elsewhere he acts as an accuser (see NIV text note on Job 1:6), to alienate God from people (see Job 1–2; Zec 3:1 and note).

3:3 *and you must not touch it.* The woman adds to God's word (2:17), distorting his directive and demonstrating that the serpent's subtle challenge was working its poison.

3:4 *You will not surely die.* The blatant denial of a specific divine pronouncement (see 2:17 and note).

3:5 *God knows.* Satan accuses God of having unworthy motives. In Job 1:9–11 (see note on 1:9); 2:4–5 he accuses righteous Job of the same. *your eyes will be opened, and you will be like God.* The statement is only half true. Their eyes were opened, to be sure (see v. 7), but the result was quite different from what the serpent had promised. *knowing good and evil.* See note on 2:9.

3:6 *good for food ... pleasing to the eye ... desirable for gaining wisdom.* Three aspects of temptation. Cf. Lk 4:3,5,9; 1Jn 2:16.

3:7 *they realized they were naked.* No longer innocent like children, they had a new awareness of themselves and of each other in their nakedness, which now produced in them a sense of shame. *they ... made coverings.* Their own feeble and futile attempt to hide their shame, which only God could cover (see note on v. 21).

3:8 *garden.* Once a place of joy and of fellowship with God, it became a place of fear and of hiding from God.

3:9 *Where are you?* A rhetorical question (see 4:9).

3:12 *The woman you put here ... gave me.* The man blames God and the woman—anyone but himself—for his sin.

13Then the LORD God said to the woman,
"What is this you have done?"
The woman said, "The serpent deceived
me,[x] and I ate."
14So the LORD God said to the serpent,
"Because you have done this,

"Cursed[y] are you above all the
livestock
and all the wild animals!
You will crawl on your belly
and you will eat dust[z]
all the days of your life.
15And I will put enmity
between you and the woman,
and between your offspring[a][a] and
hers;[b]
he will crush[b] your head,[c]
and you will strike his heel."

16To the woman he said,

"I will greatly increase your pains in
childbearing;
with pain you will give birth to
children.[d]
Your desire will be for your husband,
and he will rule over you.[e]"

17To Adam he said, "Because you listened to your wife and ate from the tree
about which I commanded you, 'You must
not eat of it,'[f]

"Cursed[g] is the ground[h] because of you;
through painful toil[i] you will eat of it
all the days of your life.[j]
18It will produce thorns and thistles[k] for
you,
and you will eat the plants of the
field.[l]
19By the sweat of your brow[m]
you will eat your food[n]
until you return to the ground,
since from it you were taken;
for dust you are
and to dust you will return."[o]

20Adam[c] named his wife Eve,[d][p] because
she would become the mother of all the
living.
21The LORD God made garments of skin
for Adam and his wife and clothed them.[q]
22And the LORD God said, "The man has
now become like one of us,[r] knowing good
and evil. He must not be allowed to reach
out his hand and take also from the tree
of life[s] and eat, and live forever." 23So the
LORD God banished him from the Garden
of Eden[t] to work the ground[u] from which
he had been taken. 24After he drove the
man out, he placed on the east side[e] of the
Garden of Eden[v] cherubim[w] and a flaming
sword[x] flashing back and forth to guard
the way to the tree of life.[y]

[a] 15 Or *seed* [b] 15 Or *strike* [c] 20 Or *The man*
[d] 20 *Eve* probably means *living.* [e] 24 Or *placed in front*

3:13 [x]Ro 7:11; 2Co 11:3; 1Ti 2:14 **3:14** [y]Dt 28:15-20 [z]Ps 72:9; Isa 49:23; 65:25; Mic 7:17 **3:15** [a]Jn 8:44; Ac 13:10; 1Jn 3:8 [b]Ge 16:11; Jdg 13:5; Isa 7:14; 8:3; 9:6; Mt 1:23; Lk 1:31; Gal 4:4; Rev 12:17 [c]Ro 16:20; Heb 2:14 **3:16** [d]Ps 48:5-6; Isa 13:8; 21:3; 26:17; Jer 4:31; 6:24; Mic 4:9; 1Ti 2:15 [e]1Co 11:3; Eph 5:22 **3:17** [f]S Ge 2:17 [g]Ge 5:29; Nu 35:33; Ps 106:39; Isa 24:5; Jer 3:1; Ro 8:20-22 [h]Ge 6:13; 8:21; Isa 54:9 [i]Ge 29:32; 31:42; Ex 3:7; Ps 66:11; 127:2; Ecc 1:13 [j]Ge 47:9; Job 5:7; 7:1; 14:1; Ecc 2:23; Jer 20:18 **3:18** [k]Job 31:40; Isa 5:6; Heb 6:8 [l]Ps 104:14 **3:19** [m]Ps 104:23 [n]Ge 14:18; Dt 8:3, 9; 23:4; Ru 1:6; 2:14; 2Th 3:10 [o]S Ge 2:7; S Job 7:21; S Ps 146:4; 1Co 15:47; Heb 9:27 **3:20** [p]S Ge 2:20; 2Co 11:3; 1Ti 2:13 **3:21** [q]S ver 7 **3:22** [r]S Ge 1:26 [s]S Ge 2:9; S Rev 2:7 **3:23** [t]S Ge 2:8 [u]S Ge 2:7 **3:24** [v]S Ge 2:8 [w]Ex 25:18-22; 1Sa 4:4; 2Sa 6:2; 22:11; 1Ki 6:27; 8:6; 2Ki 19:15; 2Ch 5:8; Ps 18:10; 80:1; 99:1; Isa 37:16; Eze 10:1; 28:16 [x]Job 40:19; Ps 104:4; Isa 27:1 [y]S Ge 2:9

3:13 *The serpent deceived me.* The woman blames the serpent rather than herself.

3:14 *Cursed.* The serpent, the woman and the man were all judged, but only the serpent and the ground were cursed—the latter because of Adam (v. 17). *dust.* The symbol of death itself (v. 19) would be the serpent's food.

3:15 *he will crush your head, and you will strike his heel.* The antagonism between people and snakes is used to symbolize the outcome of the titanic struggle between God and the evil one, a struggle played out in the hearts and history of humankind. The offspring of the woman would eventually crush the serpent's head, a promise fulfilled in Christ's victory over Satan—a victory in which all believers will share (see Ro 16:20 and note).

3:16 *pains in childbearing.* Her judgment fell on what was most uniquely hers as a woman and as a "suitable helper" (2:20) for her husband. Similarly, the man's "painful toil" (v. 17) was a judgment on him as worker of the soil. Some believe that the Hebrew root underlying "pains," "pain" and "painful toil" should perhaps be understood here in the sense of burdensome labor (see Pr 5:10, "toil"; 14:23, "hard work"). *give birth to children.* As a sign of grace in the midst of judgment, the original benediction (see 1:28 and note) is not withdrawn. *desire … rule.* Her sexual attraction to the man, and his headship over her, will become intimate aspects of her life in which she experiences trouble and anguish rather than unalloyed joy and blessing.

3:17–19 *you will eat.* Though he would have to work hard and long (judgment), the man would be able to produce food that would sustain life (grace).

3:18 Cultivating the ground and sowing the seed of desired crops create a situation in which certain native plants become weeds—of which "thorns and thistles" are the most troublesome.

3:19 *return to the ground … to dust you will return.* Adam's labor would not be able to stave off death. The origin of his body (see 2:7) and the source of his food (see v. 17) became a symbol of his eventual death.

3:20 *named his wife.* Not an act of claiming dominion over her (see notes on 1:5; 2:19) but of memorializing her significance for him and the human race. *Eve.* See NIV text note.

3:21 *clothed them.* God graciously provided Adam and Eve with more effective clothing (cf. v. 7) to cover their shame (cf. v. 10).

3:22 *us.* See note on 1:26. *knowing good and evil.* In a terribly perverted way, Satan's prediction (v. 5) came true. *live forever.* Sin, which always results in death (Ps 37:1–2; Pr 11:19; Eze 33:8–9; Ro 6:23; Jas 1:14–15), cuts the sinner off from God's gift of eternal life.

3:23 *banished him from the Garden … to work the ground.* Before Adam sinned, he had worked in a beautiful and fruitful garden (2:15). Now he would have to till undeveloped land and struggle with the curse of thorns and thistles (v. 18).

3:24 *cherubim.* Probably similar to the statues of winged figures that stood guard at the entrances to palaces and temples in ancient Mesopotamia (see note on Ex 25:18). *to guard.* The sword of God's judgment stood between fallen humanity and God's garden. The reason is given in v. 22. Only through God's redemption in Christ do people have access again to the tree of life (see Rev 2:7; 22:2, 14,19).

Cain and Abel

4 Adam[a] lay with his wife[z] Eve,[a] and
she became pregnant and gave birth
to Cain.[b b] She said, "With the help of the
LORD I have brought forth[c] a man." 2Later
she gave birth to his brother Abel.[c]
Now Abel kept flocks, and Cain worked
the soil.[d] 3In the course of time Cain
brought some of the fruits of the soil as an
offering[e] to the LORD.[f] 4But Abel brought
fat portions[g] from some of the firstborn of
his flock.[h] The LORD looked with favor on
Abel and his offering,[i] 5but on Cain and
his offering he did not look with favor.
So Cain was very angry, and his face was
downcast.

6Then the LORD said to Cain, "Why are
you angry?[j] Why is your face downcast?
7If you do what is right, will you not be accepted? But if you do not do what is right,
sin is crouching at your door;[k] it desires to
have you, but you must master it.[l]"

8Now Cain said to his brother Abel,
"Let's go out to the field."[d] And while
they were in the field, Cain attacked his
brother Abel and killed him.[m]

9Then the LORD said to Cain, "Where is
your brother Abel?"[n]

"I don't know,[o]" he replied. "Am I my
brother's keeper?"

10The LORD said, "What have you done?
Listen! Your brother's blood cries out to
me from the ground.[p] 11Now you are under a curse[q] and driven from the ground,
which opened its mouth to receive your
brother's blood from your hand. 12When
you work the ground, it will no longer
yield its crops for you.[r] You will be a restless wanderer[s] on the earth.[t]"

13Cain said to the LORD, "My punishment is more than I can bear. 14Today you
are driving me from the land, and I will
be hidden from your presence;[u] I will be a
restless wanderer on the earth,[v] and whoever finds me will kill me."[w]

15But the LORD said to him, "Not so[e];
if anyone kills Cain[x], he will suffer ven-

4:1 [z]ver 17,25 [a]S Ge 2:20 [b]Heb 11:4; 1Jn 3:12; Jude 1:11 **4:2** [c]Mt 23:35; Lk 11:51; Heb 11:4; 12:24 [d]S Ge 2:7 **4:3** [e]Lev 2:1-2; Isa 43:23; Jer 41:5 [f]Nu 18:12 **4:4** [g]Lev 3:16; 2Ch 29:35 [h]Ex 13:2,12; Dt 15:19 [i]Heb 11:4 **4:6** [j]Jnh 4:4 **4:7** [k]Ge 44:16; Nu 32:23; Isa 59:12 [l]Job 11:15; 22:27; Ps 27:3; 46:2; S Ro 6:16 **4:8** [m]Mt 23:35; Lk 11:51; 1Jn 3:12; Jude 1:11 **4:9** [n]S Ge 3:9 [o]S Jn 8:44 **4:10** [p]Ge 9:5; 37:20,26; Ex 21:12; Nu 35:33; Dt 21:7,9; 2Sa 4:11; Job 16:18; 24:2; 31:38; Ps 9:12; 106:38; Heb 12:24; Rev 6:9-10 **4:11** [q]Dt 11:28; 2Ki 2:24 **4:12** [r]Dt 28:15-24 [s]Ps 37:25; 59:15; 109:10 [t]ver 14 **4:14** [u]2Ki 17:18; Ps 51:11; 139:7-12; Jer 7:15; 52:3 [v]ver 12; Dt 28:64-67 [w]Ge 9:6; Ex 21:12,14; Lev 24:17; Nu 35:19,21,27,33; 1Ki 2:32; 2Ki 11:16 **4:15** [x]Eze 9:4,6

[a] *1* Or *The man* [b] *1* *Cain* sounds like the Hebrew for *brought forth* or *acquired.* [c] *1* Or *have acquired* [d] *8* Samaritan Pentateuch, Septuagint, Vulgate and Syriac; Masoretic Text does not have *"Let's go out to the field."* [e] *15* Septuagint, Vulgate and Syriac; Hebrew *Very well*

4:1–26 How human sin progressed from murder of a brother in the second generation to arrogant assertion of independence from God and claim of total self-sufficiency in the seventh generation.

4:1 *With the help of the LORD.* Eve acknowledged that God is the ultimate source of life (see Ac 17:25).

4:2 *Abel.* The name means "breath" or "temporary" or "meaningless" (the translation of the same basic Hebrew word that is in Ecc 1:2 [see note there]; 12:8) and hints at the shortness of Abel's life.

4:3–4 *Cain brought some of the fruits ... But Abel brought fat portions from some of the firstborn of his flock.* The contrast is not between an offering of plant life and an offering of animal life, but between a careless, thoughtless offering and a choice, generous offering (cf. Lev 3:16 and note). Motivation and heart attitude are all-important, and God looked with favor on Abel and his offering because of Abel's faith (Heb 11:4). *firstborn.* Indicative of the recognition that all the productivity of the flock is from the Lord and all of it belongs to him.

4:5 *angry.* God did not look with favor on Cain and his offering, and Cain (whose motivation and attitude were bad from the outset) reacted predictably.

4:7 *sin is crouching at your door.* The Hebrew word for "crouching" is the same as an ancient Babylonian word referring to an evil demon crouching at the door of a building to threaten the people inside. Sin may thus be pictured here as just such a demon, waiting to pounce on Cain. He may already have been plotting his brother's murder. *it desires to have you.* In Hebrew, the same expression as that for "Your desire will be for [your husband]" in 3:16 (see also SS 7:10).

4:8 *attacked his brother ... and killed him.* The first murder was especially monstrous because it was committed with deliberate deceit ("Let's go out to the field"), against a brother (see vv. 9–11; 1Jn 3:12) and against a good man (Mt 23:35; Heb 11:4)—a striking illustration of the awful consequences of the fall.

4:9 *Where ...?* A rhetorical question (see 3:9). *I don't know.* An outright lie. *Am I my brother's keeper?* Demonstrating callous indifference—all too common through the whole course of human history.

4:10 *Your brother's blood cries out.* "Righteous Abel" (Mt 23:35), in one sense a "prophet" (Lk 11:50–51), "still speaks, even though he is dead" (Heb 11:4), for his spilled blood continues to cry out to God against all those who do violence to others. But the blood of Christ "speaks a better word" (Heb 12:24).

4:11 *curse.* The ground had been cursed because of human sin (3:17), and now Cain himself is cursed. Formerly he had worked the ground, and it had produced life for him (vv. 2–3). Now the ground, soaked with his brother's blood, would no longer yield its produce for him (v. 12).

4:12 *wanderer.* Estranged from other people and finding even the ground inhospitable, he became a wanderer in the land of wandering (see NIV text note on v. 16).

4:13 *My punishment is more than I can bear.* Confronted with his crime and its resulting curse, Cain responded not with remorse but with self-pity. His sin was virtually uninterrupted: impiety (v. 3), anger (v. 5), jealousy, deception and murder (v. 8), falsehood (v. 9) and self-seeking (v. 13). The final result was alienation from God himself (vv. 14,16).

4:14–15 *whoever ... anyone ... no one.* These words seem to imply the presence of substantial numbers of people outside Cain's immediate family, but perhaps they only anticipate the future rapid growth of the race. Alternatively, Cain's reference to himself was inclusive of his whole family line, which stood under judgment with him (as did the family line of Adam). Note that Cain built a city (v. 17) and that his descendant Lamech boasted of avenging (defending) himself (vv. 23–24).

4:15 *mark.* A warning sign to protect him from an avenger. For the time being, the life of the murderer is spared (but see 6:7; 9:6). For a possible parallel see Eze 9:4.

4:16 *Nod.* Location unknown. See NIV text note.

geance[y] seven times over.[z]" Then the LORD
put a mark on Cain so that no one who
found him would kill him. 16So Cain went
out from the LORD's presence[a] and lived in
the land of Nod,[a] east of Eden.[b]
17Cain lay with his wife,[c] and she became pregnant and gave birth to Enoch.
Cain was then building a city,[d] and he
named it after his son[e] Enoch. 18To Enoch
was born Irad, and Irad was the father of
Mehujael, and Mehujael was the father of
Methushael, and Methushael was the father of Lamech.
19Lamech married[f] two women,[g] one
named Adah and the other Zillah. 20Adah
gave birth to Jabal; he was the father of
those who live in tents and raise livestock. 21His brother's name was Jubal; he
was the father of all who play the harp[h]
and flute.[i] 22Zillah also had a son, Tubal-
Cain, who forged[j] all kinds of tools out of[b]
bronze and iron. Tubal-Cain's sister was
Naamah.
23Lamech said to his wives,

"Adah and Zillah, listen to me;
 wives of Lamech, hear my words.
I have killed[c][k] a man for wounding
 me,
 a young man for injuring me.
24If Cain is avenged[l] seven times,[m]
 then Lamech seventy-seven times.[n]"

4:15 [y]Ex 21:20 [z]ver 24; Lev 26:21; Ps 79:12 **4:16** [a]Jude 1:11 [b]S Ge 2:8 **4:17** [c]S ver 1 [d]Ps 55:9 [e]Ps 49:11 **4:19** [f]Ge 6:2 [g]Ge 29:28; Dt 21:15; Ru 4:11; 1Sa 1:2 **4:21** [h]Ge 31:27; Ex 15:20; 1Sa 16:16; 1Ch 25:3; Ps 33:2; 43:4; Isa 16:11; Da 3:5 [i]Job 21:12; 30:31; Ps 150:4 **4:22** [j]Ex 35:35; 1Sa 13:19; 2Ki 24:14 **4:23** [k]Ge 9:5-6; Ex 20:13; 21:12; 23:7; Lev 19:18; 24:17; Dt 27:24; 32:35 **4:24** [l]Dt 32:35; 2Ki 9:7; Ps 18:47; 94:1; Isa 35:4; Jer 51:56; Na 1:2 [m]S ver 15 [n]Mt 18:22

4:25 [o]ver 1 [p]Ge 5:3; 1Ch 1:1 [q]ver 8 **4:26** [r]Ge 5:6; 1Ch 1:1; Lk 3:38 [s]Ge 12:8; 13:4; 21:33; 22:9;

25Adam lay with his wife[o] again, and she
gave birth to a son and named him Seth,[d][p]
saying, "God has granted me another child
in place of Abel, since Cain killed him."[q]
26Seth also had a son, and he named him
Enosh.[r]
At that time men began to call on[e] the
name of the LORD.[s]

From Adam to Noah

5 This is the written account[t] of Adam's
line.[u]

When God created man, he made him
in the likeness of God.[v] 2He created them[w]
male and female[x] and blessed them. And
when they were created, he called them
"man.[f]"
3When Adam had lived 130 years, he
had a son in his own likeness, in his own
image;[y] and he named him Seth.[z] 4After
Seth was born, Adam lived 800 years and
had other sons and daughters. 5Altogether,
Adam lived 930 years, and then he died.[a]

[a] 16 *Nod* means *wandering* (see verses 12 and 14). [b] 22 Or *who instructed all who work in* [c] 23 Or *I will kill* [d] 25 *Seth* probably means *granted.* [e] 26 Or *to proclaim* [f] 2 Hebrew *adam*

26:25; 33:20; 35:1; Ex 17:15; 1Ki 18:24; Ps 116:17; Joel 2:32; Zep 3:9; S Ac 2:21 **5:1** [t]S Ge 2:4 [u]1Ch 1:1 [v]S Ge 1:27; Col 3:10 **5:2** [w]Ge 1:28 [x]S Ge 1:27; Mt 19:4; Mk 10:6; Gal 3:28 **5:3** [y]S Ge 1:26; 1Co 15:49 [z]S Ge 4:25; Lk 3:38 **5:5** [a]S Ge 2:17; Heb 9:27

4:17–18 *Cain ... Enoch ... Irad ... Mehujael ... Methushael ... Lamech.* Together with that of Adam, these names add up to a total of seven, a number often signifying completeness (see v. 15). Each of the six names listed here is paralleled by a similar or identical name in the genealogy of Seth in ch. 5 as follows: Kenan (5:12), Enoch (5:21), Jared (5:18), Mahalalel (5:15), Methuselah (5:25), Lamech (5:28). The similarity between the two sets of names is striking and may suggest the selective nature of such genealogies (see note on 5:5). For an example of such selectivity elsewhere see Ezr 7:3, where comparison with 1Ch 6:7–10 indicates that six names were omitted between Azariah and Meraioth. See also Introduction to 1 Chronicles: Genealogies and note on Mt 1:17.

4:17 *city.* The Hebrew for this word can refer to any permanent settlement, however small. Cain tried to redeem himself from his wandering and vulnerable state by the activity of his own hands—in the land of wandering he builds a city.

4:19 *married two women.* Polygamy entered history. Haughty Lamech, the seventh from Adam in the line of Cain, perhaps sought to attain the benefits of God's primeval blessing (see 1:28 and note) by his own device—multiplying his wives. Monogamy, however, was the original divine intention (see 2:23–24 and note on 2:24).

4:20–22 *Jabal ... Jubal ... Tubal-Cain.* Lamech's three sons had similar names, each derived from a Hebrew verb meaning "to bring, carry, lead," and emphasizing activity. Tubal-Cain's name was especially appropriate, since "Cain" means "metalsmith."

4:22 *tools.* For agriculture and construction; perhaps also for war (see 1Sa 13:19–21).

4:23 *killed a man for wounding me.* Violent and wanton destruction of human life by one who proclaimed his complete independence from God by taking vengeance with his own hands (see Dt 32:35 and note). Lamech proudly claimed to be master of his own destiny, thinking that he and his sons, by their own achievements, would redeem themselves from the curse on the line of Cain. This titanic claim climaxes the catalog of sins that began with Cain's unworthy offering and the murder of his brother.

4:24 *seventy-seven times.* Lamech's arrogant announcement of personal revenge found its counterpoint in Jesus' response to Peter's question about forgiveness in Mt 18:21–22 (see note on 18:22).

4:25 *again ... another child.* Abel was dead, and Cain was alienated; so Adam and Eve were granted a third son to carry on the family line.

4:26 *Enosh.* The name, like "Adam" (see NIV text note on 2:7), means "man" or "humankind." *began to call on the name of the LORD.* Lamech's proud self-reliance, so characteristic of the line of Cain, is contrasted with dependence on God found in the line of Seth.

5:1 *account.* See note on 2:4. *likeness.* See note on 1:26.

5:2 *male and female.* See note on 1:27. *blessed them.* See 1:28 and note. *called them.* See note on 1:5.

5:3 *his own likeness ... his own image.* See note on 1:26. As God created sinless Adam in his own perfect image, so now sinful Adam has a son in his own imperfect image.

5:5 *930 years.* See notes on v. 27; 6:3. Whether the large numbers describing human longevity in the early chapters of Genesis are literal or have a conventional literary function—or both—is uncertain. Some believe that several of the numbers have symbolic significance, such as Enoch's 365 (v. 23) years (365 being the number of days in a year, thus a full life) and Lamech's 777 (v. 31) years (777 being an expansion and multiple of seven, the number of completeness; cf. the "seventy-seven times" of the other Lamech in 4:24). The fact that there are exactly ten names in the Ge 5 list (as in the genealogy of 11:10–26) makes it likely that it includes gaps (see note on 4:17–18), the lengths of which may be

6When Seth had lived 105 years, he became the father[a] of Enosh.[b] 7And after he
became the father of Enosh, Seth lived 807
years and had other sons and daughters.
8Altogether, Seth lived 912 years, and then
he died.
9When Enosh had lived 90 years, he became the father of Kenan.[c] 10And after he
became the father of Kenan, Enosh lived
815 years and had other sons and daughters. 11Altogether, Enosh lived 905 years,
and then he died.
12When Kenan had lived 70 years, he
became the father of Mahalalel.[d] 13And
after he became the father of Mahalalel,
Kenan lived 840 years and had other sons
and daughters. 14Altogether, Kenan lived
910 years, and then he died.
15When Mahalalel had lived 65 years, he
became the father of Jared.[e] 16And after
he became the father of Jared, Mahalalel
lived 830 years and had other sons and
daughters. 17Altogether, Mahalalel lived
895 years, and then he died.
18When Jared had lived 162 years, he
became the father of Enoch.[f] 19And after
he became the father of Enoch, Jared lived
800 years and had other sons and daughters. 20Altogether, Jared lived 962 years,
and then he died.
21When Enoch had lived 65 years, he
became the father of Methuselah.[g] 22And
after he became the father of Methuselah,
Enoch walked with God[h] 300 years and
had other sons and daughters. 23Altogeth-
er, Enoch lived 365 years. 24Enoch walked
with God;[i] then he was no more, because
God took him away.[j]
25When Methuselah had lived 187 years,
he became the father of Lamech.[k] 26And
after he became the father of Lamech,
Methuselah lived 782 years and had other
sons and daughters. 27Altogether, Methuselah lived 969 years, and then he died.
28When Lamech had lived 182 years, he
had a son. 29He named him Noah[b][l] and
said, "He will comfort us in the labor and
painful toil of our hands caused by the
ground the LORD has cursed.[m]" 30After Noah
was born, Lamech lived 595 years and had
other sons and daughters. 31Altogether, Lamech lived 777 years, and then he died.
32After Noah was 500 years old,[n] he became the father of Shem,[o] Ham and Japheth.[p]

The Flood

6 When men began to increase in number on the earth[q] and daughters were
born to them, 2the sons of God[r] saw that
the daughters of men[s] were beautiful,[t] and
they married[u] any of them they chose.
3Then the LORD said, "My Spirit[v] will not
contend with[c] man forever,[w] for he is mortal[d];[x] his days will be a hundred and twenty years."

5:6 [b] S Ge 4:26; Lk 3:38 **5:9** [c] 1Ch 1:2; Lk 3:37 **5:12** [d] 1Ch 1:2; Lk 3:37 **5:15** [e] 1Ch 1:2; Lk 3:37 **5:18** [f] 1Ch 1:3; Lk 3:37; Jude 1:14 **5:21** [g] 1Ch 1:3; Lk 3:37 **5:22** [h] ver 24; Ge 6:9; 17:1; 24:40; 48:15; 2Ki 20:3; Ps 116:9; Mic 6:8; Mal 2:6 **5:24** [i] S ver 22 [j] 2Ki 2:1,11; Ps 49:15; 73:24; 89:48; Heb 11:5 **5:25** [k] 1Ch 1:3; Lk 3:36 **5:29** [l] 1Ch 1:3; Lk 3:36 [m] S Ge 3:17; Ro 8:20 **5:32** [n] Ge 7:6,11; 8:13 [o] Lk 3:36 [p] Ge 6:10; 9:18; 10:1; 1Ch 1:4; Isa 65:20 **6:1** [q] S Ge 1:28 **6:2** [r] Job 1:6 *fn*; 2:1 *fn* [s] ver 4 [t] Dt 21:11 [u] S Ge 4:19 **6:3** [v] Job 34:14; Gal 5:16-17 [w] Isa 57:16; 1Pe 3:20 [x] Job 10:9; Ps 78:39; 103:14; Isa 40:6

[a] 6 *Father* may mean *ancestor*; also in verses 7-26.
[b] 29 *Noah* sounds like the Hebrew for *comfort.*
[c] 3 Or *My spirit will not remain in*
[d] 3 Or *corrupt*

summarized in the large numbers. Other ancient genealogies outside the Bible exhibit similarly large figures. For example, three kings in a Sumerian list (which also contains exactly ten names) are said to have reigned 72,000 years each — obviously exaggerated time spans. *and then he died.* Repeated as a sad refrain throughout the chapter, the only exception being Enoch (see note on v. 24). The phrase is a stark reminder of God's judgment on sin resulting from Adam's fall.

5:22,24 *walked with God.* The phrase replaces the word "lived" in the other paragraphs of the chapter and reminds us that there is a difference between walking with God and merely living.

5:24 *then he was no more, because God took him away.* The phrase replaces "and then he died" in the other paragraphs of the chapter. Like Elijah, who was "taken" (2Ki 2:10) to heaven, Enoch was taken away (cf. Ps 49:15; 73:24) to the presence of God without experiencing death (Heb 11:5). Lamech, the seventh from Adam in the genealogy of Cain, was evil personified. But "Enoch, the seventh from Adam" (Jude 14) in the genealogy of Seth, "was commended as one who pleased God" (Heb 11:5).

5:27 *969 years.* Only Noah and his family survived the flood. If the figures concerning life spans are literal, Methuselah died in the year of the flood (the figures in vv. 25,28 and 7:6 add up to exactly 969).

6:1 – 8 How the early history of humankind led to such pervasive corruption that God was moved to bring a radical judgment on his creation.

6:1 *increase in number.* See note on 1:22.

6:2 *sons of God saw ... daughters of men ... and they married any.* See v. 4. The phrase "sons of God" here has been interpreted to refer either to angels or to human beings. In such places as Job 1:6; 2:1 it refers to angels, and perhaps also in Ps 29:1 (where it is translated "mighty ones"). Some interpreters also appeal to Jude 6 – 7 (as well as to Jewish literature) in referring the phrase here to angels.

Others, however, maintain that intermarriage and cohabitation between angels and human beings, though commonly mentioned in ancient mythologies, are surely excluded by the very nature of the created order (ch. 1; Mk 12:25). Elsewhere, expressions equivalent to "sons of God" often refer to human beings, though in contexts quite different from the present one (see Dt 14:1; 32:5; Ps 73:15; Isa 43:6; Hos 1:10; 11:1; Lk 3:38; 1Jn 3:1 – 2,10). "Sons of God" (vv. 2,4) possibly refers to godly men, and "daughters of men" to sinful women (significantly, they are not called "daughters of God"), probably from the wicked line of Cain. If so, the context suggests that vv. 1 – 2 describe the intermarriage of the Sethites ("sons of God") of ch. 5 with the Cainites ("daughters of men") of ch. 4, indicating a breakdown in the separation of the two groups.

Another plausible suggestion is that the "sons of God" refers to royal figures (kings were closely associated with gods in the ancient Near East) who proudly perpetuated and aggravated the corrupt lifestyle of Lamech son of Cain (virtually a royal figure) and established for themselves royal harems.

6:3 Two key phrases in the Hebrew of this verse are obscure: the one rendered "contend with" (see NIV text note) and the one rendered "for he is mortal." The verse seems to announce that the period of grace between God's declaration of judgment and its arrival would be 120 years (cf. 1Pe 3:20). But if the NIV text note reading is accepted, the verse announces

4The Nephilim[y] were on the earth in
those days — and also afterward — when
the sons of God went to the daughters
of men[z] and had children by them. They
were the heroes of old, men of renown.[a]
5The LORD saw how great man's wickedness on the earth had become,[b] and
that every inclination of the thoughts of
his heart was only evil all the time.[c] 6The
LORD was grieved[d] that he had made man
on the earth, and his heart was filled with
pain. 7So the LORD said, "I will wipe mankind, whom I have created, from the face
of the earth[e] — men and animals, and
creatures that move along the ground,
and birds of the air — for I am grieved that
I have made them.[f]" 8But Noah[g] found favor in the eyes of the LORD.[h]

9This is the account[i] of Noah.

Noah was a righteous man, blameless[j]
among the people of his time,[k] and he
walked with God.[l] 10Noah had three sons:
Shem,[m] Ham and Japheth.[n]
11Now the earth was corrupt[o] in God's
sight and was full of violence.[p] 12God
saw how corrupt[q] the earth had become,
for all the people on earth had corrupted their ways.[r] 13So God said to Noah, "I
am going to put an end to all people, for
the earth is filled with violence because of
them. I am surely going to destroy[s] both
them and the earth.[t] 14So make yourself
an ark of cypress[a] wood;[u] make rooms in
it and coat it with pitch[v] inside and out.
15This is how you are to build it: The ark
is to be 450 feet long, 75 feet wide and 45
feet high.[b] 16Make a roof for it and finish[c] the ark to within 18 inches[d] of the
top. Put a door in the side of the ark and
make lower, middle and upper decks. 17I
am going to bring floodwaters[w] on the
earth to destroy all life under the heavens, every creature that has the breath of
life in it. Everything on earth will perish.[x]
18But I will establish my covenant with

6:4 [y]Nu 13:33 [z]ver 2 [a]Ge 11:4 **6:5** [b]Ge 38:7; Job 34:26; Jer 1:16; 44:5; Eze 3:19 [c]Ge 8:21; Ps 14:1-3 **6:6** [d]Ex 32:14; 1Sa 15:11,35; 2Sa 24:16; 1Ch 21:15; Isa 63:10; Jer 18:7-10; Eph 4:30 **6:7** [e]Eze 33:28; Zep 1:2,18 [f]ver 17; Ge 7:4,21; Dt 28:63; 29:20 **6:8** [g]Eze 14:14 [h]Ge 19:19; 39:4; Ex 33:12,13,17; 34:9; Nu 11:15; Ru 2:2; Lk 1:30; Ac 7:46 **6:9** [i]S Ge 2:4 [j]Ge 17:1; Dt 18:13; 2Sa 22:24; Job 1:1; 4:6; 9:21; 12:4; 31:6; Ps 15:2; 18:23; 19:13; 37:37; Pr 2:7 [k]Ge 7:1; Ps 37:39; Jer 15:1; Eze 14:14,20; Da 10:11; S Lk 1:6; Heb 11:7; 2Pe 2:5 [l]S Ge 5:22 **6:10** [m]Lk 3:36 [n]S Ge 5:32 **6:11** [o]Dt 31:29; Jdg 2:19 [p]Ps 7:9; 73:6; Eze 7:23; 8:17; 28:16; Mal 2:16 **6:12** [q]Ex 32:7; Dt 4:16; 9:12,24 [r]Ps 14:1-3 **6:13** [s]Dt 28:63; 2Ki 8:19; Ezr 9:14; Jer 44:11 [t]ver 17; Ge 7:4,21-23; Job 34:15; Isa 5:6; 24:1-3; Jer 44:27; Eze 7:2-3 **6:14** [u]Heb 11:7; 1Pe 3:20 [v]Ex 2:3 **6:17** [w]Ps 29:10 [x]S ver 7,S 13; 2Pe 2:5

[a] *14* The meaning of the Hebrew for this word is uncertain. [b] *15* Hebrew *300 cubits long, 50 cubits wide and 30 cubits high* (about 140 meters long, 23 meters wide and 13.5 meters high) [c] *16* Or *Make an opening for light by finishing* [d] *16* Hebrew *a cubit* (about 0.5 meter)

that the human life span would henceforth be limited to 120 years (but see 11:10–26).

6:4 *Nephilim.* People of great size and strength (see Nu 13:31–33). The Hebrew word means "fallen ones." They were viewed by people as "the heroes of old, men of renown," but in God's eyes they were sinners ("fallen ones") ripe for judgment.

6:5 One of the Bible's most vivid descriptions of total depravity. And because human nature remained unchanged, things were no better after the flood (8:21).

6:6 *The LORD was grieved ... his heart was filled with pain.* Human sin is God's sorrow (see Eph 4:30 and note).

6:7 *I will wipe mankind ... from the face of the earth.* The period of grace (see v. 3 and note) was coming to an end. *animals ... creatures ... birds.* Though morally innocent, the animal world, as creatures under the corrupted rule of human beings, shared in their judgment (cf. 1Sa 15:3 and NIV text note).

6:8–9 *found favor ... righteous ... blameless ... walked with God.* See note on 5:22. Noah's godly life was a powerful contrast to the wicked lives of his contemporaries (see v. 5 and note; see also v. 12). This description of Noah does not imply sinless perfection.

6:9—9:29 In many legends circulating among the peoples of the ancient Near East, one of the major gods brought a devastating flood on the earth because he was disturbed by the noisy hubbub raised by humans (see Introduction: Background). The author of Genesis also tells of a devastating flood that destroyed all humankind except a single family. In his account, the Creator (who alone is God) was deeply grieved by the moral evil embraced and practiced by the creatures he had created in his own image and to whom he had committed the care of his creation. In his eyes they had so corrupted life in his good creation that only a radical cleansing judgment could check the rampant evil and bring humanity to account.

In his telling of the story to ancient Israel, the author of Genesis attacks the pervasive pagan notions about the gods and about humanity, as expressed in their stories of a mighty all-destroying flood. He casts this storied flood in a radically different theological light. In the deluge (i.e., in destructive floods and other "natural" disasters) humanity had (and has) to do with the righteous Creator. For just cause, and after long forbearance, he judged (and judges) the creature created in his image and called to be his image-bearer in the creation. God's judgment on human sin represented by the flood speaks of his radical "No" to humanity's corruption of its way in the world. But that "No" is not his final word (see 8:1 and note), and humanity is not at the mercy of a deity who at a whim might totally undo the creation order on which life depends. The God of the deluge has given another word, symbolized by the rainbow — a reassuring word about his enduring commitment to his creation. (See 9:8–17 and notes.)

6:9 *account.* See note on 2:4. *righteous.* See note on Ps 1:5.

6:14 *ark.* The Hebrew for this word is used elsewhere only in reference to the basket that saved the baby Moses (see Ex 2:3,5 and note on 2:3). *coat it with pitch.* Moses' mother made his basket watertight in the same way (see Ex 2:3).

6:16 *roof.* Perhaps overhanging, to keep the rain from coming in. *within 18 inches of the top.* Noah's ark probably had a series of small windows (see 8:6) encircling the entire vessel 18 inches from the top to admit light and air.

6:17 *floodwaters on the earth to destroy all life under the heavens.* Some believe that the deluge was worldwide, partly because of the apparently universal terms of the text — both here and elsewhere (vv. 7,12–13; 7:4,19,21–23; 8:21; 9:11,15; cf. 2Pe 3:6 and note). Others argue that nothing in the narrative of chs. 6–9 prevents the flood from being understood as regional — destroying everything on land that lay in its wake, but of relatively limited scope and universal only from the standpoint of Moses' geographic knowledge. "All life under the heavens" may mean all life within the range of Noah's perception. (See the universal language used to describe the drought and famine in the time of Joseph — 41:54,57; see also note on 41:57.)

6:18 *covenant.* See note on 9:9. Noah would not be given the particulars of God's covenant with him

you,[y] and you will enter the ark[z]—you
and your sons and your wife and your
sons' wives with you. 19You are to bring
into the ark two of all living creatures,
male and female, to keep them alive with
you.[a] 20Two[b] of every kind of bird, of every kind of animal and of every kind[c] of
creature that moves along the ground will
come to you to be kept alive.[d] 21You are to
take every kind of food that is to be eat-
en and store it away as food for you and
for them."
22Noah did everything just as God commanded him.[e]

7 The LORD then said to Noah, "Go into
the ark, you and your whole family,[f]
because I have found you righteous[g] in
this generation. 2Take with you seven[a] of
every kind of clean[h] animal, a male and
its mate, and two of every kind of unclean
animal, a male and its mate, 3and also sev-
en of every kind of bird, male and female,
to keep their various kinds alive[i] throughout the earth. 4Seven days from now I will
send rain[j] on the earth[k] for forty days[l] and
forty nights,[m] and I will wipe from the face
of the earth every living creature I have
made.[n]"
5And Noah did all that the LORD commanded him.[o]
6Noah was six hundred years old[p] when
the floodwaters came on the earth. 7And
Noah and his sons and his wife and his
sons' wives entered the ark[q] to escape the
waters of the flood. 8Pairs of clean and
unclean[r] animals, of birds and of all creatures that move along the ground, 9male
and female, came to Noah and entered the
ark, as God had commanded Noah.[s] 10And
after the seven days[t] the floodwaters came
on the earth.
11In the six hundredth year of Noah's
life,[u] on the seventeenth day of the second
month[v]—on that day all the springs of
the great deep[w] burst forth, and the floodgates of the heavens[x] were opened. 12And
rain fell on the earth forty days and forty
nights.[y]
13On that very day Noah and his sons,[z]
Shem, Ham and Japheth, together with his
wife and the wives of his three sons, entered the ark.[a] 14They had with them every
wild animal according to its kind, all livestock according to their kinds, every creature that moves along the ground according to its kind and every bird according to
its kind,[b] everything with wings. 15Pairs of
all creatures that have the breath of life in
them came to Noah and entered the ark.[c]
16The animals going in were male and
female of every living thing, as God had
commanded Noah.[d] Then the LORD shut
him in.
17For forty days[e] the flood kept coming
on the earth, and as the waters increased
they lifted the ark high above the earth.
18The waters rose and increased greatly
on the earth, and the ark floated on the
surface of the water. 19They rose greatly
on the earth, and all the high mountains
under the entire heavens were covered.[f]

6:18 [y]Ge 9:9-16; 17:7; 19:12; Ex 6:4; 34:10,27; Dt 29:13,14-15; Ps 25:10; 74:20; 106:45; Isa 55:3; Jer 32:40; Eze 16:60; Hag 2:5; 1Pe 3:20 [z]Ge 7:1,7,13 **6:19** [a]Ge 7:15 **6:20** [b]Ge 7:15 [c]S Ge 1:11 [d]Ge 7:3 **6:22** [e]Ge 7:5, 9,16; Ex 7:6; 39:43; 40:16, 19,21,23,25, 27,29,32 **7:1** [f]S Ge 6:18; Mt 24:38; Lk 17:26-27; Heb 11:7; 1Pe 3:20; 2Pe 2:5 [g]Ge 6:9; Eze 14:14 **7:2** [h]ver 8; Ge 8:20; Lev 10:10; 11:1-47; Dt 14:3-20; Eze 44:23; Hag 2:12; Ac 10:14-15 **7:3** [i]Ge 6:20 **7:4** [j]Ge 8:2 [k]1Ki 13:34; Jer 28:16 [l]Nu 13:25; Dt 9:9; 1Sa 17:16; 1Ki 19:8 [m]ver 12,17; Ex 24:18; 32:1; 34:28; Dt 9:9,11,18,25; 10:10; Job 37:6,13; Mt 4:2 [n]S Ge 6:7,13 **7:5** [o]S Ge 6:22 **7:6** [p]S Ge 5:32 **7:7** [q]S Ge 6:18 **7:8** [r]S ver 2 **7:9** [s]S Ge 6:22

[a] 2 Or *seven pairs*; also in verse 3

7:10 [t]S ver 4 **7:11** [u]S Ge 5:32 [v]Ge 8:4,14 [w]S Ge 1:7; Job 28:11; Ps 36:6; 42:7; Pr 8:24; Isa 51:10; Eze 26:19 [x]Ge 8:2; 2Ki 7:2; Ps 78:23; Isa 24:18; Mal 3:10 **7:12** [y]S ver 4; S 1Sa 12:17; S Job 28:26 **7:13** [z]Ge 8:16; 1Pe 3:20; 2Pe 2:5 [a]S Ge 6:18 **7:14** [b]S Ge 1:11 **7:15** [c]ver 8-9; Ge 6:19 **7:16** [d]S Ge 6:22 **7:17** [e]S ver 4 **7:19** [f]Ps 104:6

until after the floodwaters had dried up (see 9:8–17). *enter the ark.* The story of Noah's deliverance from the flood foreshadows God's full redemption of his people (see Heb 11:7; 2Pe 2:5) and is viewed by Peter as in some sense symbolic of Christian baptism (see 1Pe 3:20–21 and note on 3:21). *your sons and your wife and your sons' wives with you.* God extends his loving concern to the whole family of righteous Noah—a consistent pattern in God's dealings with his people, underscoring the moral and responsible relationship of parents to their children (see 17:7–27; 18:19; Dt 30:19; Ps 78:1–7; 102:28; 103:17–18; 112:1–2; Ac 2:38–39; 16:31; 1Co 7:14).

6:19 *two of all living creatures ... to keep them alive.* Most animals were doomed to die in the flood (see note on v. 7), but at least one pair of each kind was preserved to restock the earth after the waters subsided.

6:20 *kind.* See note on 1:11.

6:22 *did everything just as God commanded.* The account stresses Noah's obedience (see 7:5,9,16).

7:1 *Go into the ark.* The beginning of God's final word to Noah before the flood. God's first word to Noah after the flood begins similarly: "Come out of the ark" (8:16). *righteous.* See note on 6:8–9. Later, Noah was known as a "preacher of righteousness" (2Pe 2:5; see note there) who warned his contemporaries of coming judgment and testified to the vitality of his own faith (see Heb 11:7 and note).

7:2 *seven of every kind of clean animal ... two of every kind of unclean animal.* The "unclean" animals would only have to reproduce themselves after the flood, but the "clean" animals would be needed also for the burnt offerings that Noah would sacrifice (see 8:20) and for food (see 9:3 and note). For the distinction between "clean" and "unclean" animals and birds see Lev 11 and notes, especially the note on v. 2. How early this distinction came into use is unknown.

7:4 *forty days and forty nights.* A length of time often characterizing a critical period in redemptive history (see vv. 12,17; Dt 9:11; Mt 4:1–11 and notes on 4:1 and 4:2).

7:7 *entered the ark to escape the waters.* Noah and his family were saved, but life as usual continued for everyone else until it was too late (see Mt 24:37–39).

7:13 *Noah and his sons ... together with his wife and the wives of his three sons.* "Only a few people, eight in all" (1Pe 3:20; see 2Pe 2:5), survived the flood.

7:14 *every wild animal ... all livestock ... every creature that moves along the ground ... every bird.* Four of the five categories of animate life mentioned in 1:21–25. The fifth category—sea creatures—could remain alive outside the ark.

7:16 *God had commanded Noah ... the LORD shut him in.* "God" gave the command, but in his role as redeeming "LORD" (see notes on 2:4; Ex 6:6) he closed the door of the ark behind Noah and his family. Neither divine name is mentioned in the rest of ch. 7, as the full fury of the flood was unleashed on sinful humankind.

20The waters rose and covered the mountains to a depth of more than twenty
feet.[a,b] [g] 21Every living thing that moved
on the earth perished—birds, livestock,
wild animals, all the creatures that swarm
over the earth, and all mankind.[h] 22Every-
thing on dry land that had the breath of
life[i] in its nostrils died. 23Every living thing
on the face of the earth was wiped out;
men and animals and the creatures that
move along the ground and the birds of
the air were wiped from the earth.[j] Only
Noah was left, and those with him in the
ark.[k]
24The waters flooded the earth for a
hundred and fifty days.[l]

8 But God remembered[m] Noah and all
the wild animals and the livestock that
were with him in the ark, and he sent a
wind over the earth,[n] and the waters receded. 2Now the springs of the deep and
the floodgates of the heavens[o] had been
closed, and the rain[p] had stopped falling
from the sky. 3The water receded steadily
from the earth. At the end of the hundred
and fifty days[q] the water had gone down,
4and on the seventeenth day of the seventh
month[r] the ark came to rest on the mountains[s] of Ararat.[t] 5The waters continued to
recede until the tenth month, and on the
first day of the tenth month the tops of the
mountains became visible.
6After forty days[u] Noah opened the
window he had made in the ark 7and sent
out a raven,[v] and it kept flying back and
forth until the water had dried up from the
earth.[w] 8Then he sent out a dove[x] to see if
the water had receded from the surface of
the ground. 9But the dove could find no
place to set its feet because there was water over all the surface of the earth; so it returned to Noah in the ark. He reached out
his hand and took the dove and brought it
back to himself in the ark. 10He waited sev-
en more days and again sent out the dove
from the ark. 11When the dove returned to
him in the evening, there in its beak was
a freshly plucked olive leaf! Then Noah
knew that the water had receded from the
earth.[y] 12He waited seven more days and
sent the dove out again, but this time it
did not return to him.
13By the first day of the first month of
Noah's six hundred and first year,[z] the
water had dried up from the earth. Noah
then removed the covering from the ark
and saw that the surface of the ground
was dry. 14By the twenty-seventh day of
the second month[a] the earth was completely dry.
15Then God said to Noah, 16"Come out of
the ark, you and your wife and your sons
and their wives.[b] 17Bring out every kind
of living creature that is with you—the
birds, the animals, and all the creatures
that move along the ground—so they can
multiply on the earth and be fruitful and
increase in number upon it."[c]
18So Noah came out, together with his
sons and his wife and his sons' wives.[d]
19All the animals and all the creatures
that move along the ground and all the
birds—everything that moves on the
earth—came out of the ark, one kind after another.
20Then Noah built an altar to the LORD[e]
and, taking some of all the clean animals
and clean[f] birds, he sacrificed burnt offerings[g] on it. 21The LORD smelled the pleasing

[a] 20 Hebrew *fifteen cubits* (about 6.9 meters)
[b] 20 Or *rose more than twenty feet, and the mountains were covered*

7:20 [g] Ge 8:4-5; 2Pe 3:6 **7:21** [h] S Ge 6:7, 13; 2Pe 3:6 **7:22** [i] S Ge 1:30 **7:23** [j] Job 14:19; 21:18; 22:11,16; Ps 90:5; Isa 28:2; Mt 24:39; Lk 17:27; 1Pe 3:20; 2Pe 2:5 [k] Heb 11:7 **7:24** [l] Ge 8:3; Job 12:15 **8:1** [m] Ge 9:15; 19:29; 21:1; 30:22; Ex 2:24; Nu 10:9; Ru 4:13; 1Sa 1:11,19; 2Ki 20:3; 1Ch 16:15; Ne 1:8; 5:19; 13:14,22,31; Job 14:13; Ps 105:42; 106:4; Lk 1:54,72 [n] Ex 14:21; Jos 2:10; 3:16; Job 12:15; Ps 66:6; Isa 11:15; 44:27; Na 1:4 **8:2** [o] S Ge 7:11 [p] S Ge 7:4 **8:3** [q] S Ge 7:24 **8:4** [r] S Ge 7:11 [s] Ge 7:20 [t] 2Ki 19:37; Jer 51:27 **8:6** [u] Ge 7:12 **8:7** [v] Lev 11:15; Dt 14:14; 1Ki 17:4,6; Job 38:41; Ps 147:9; Pr 30:17; Isa 34:11; Lk 12:24 [w] ver 11 **8:8** [x] Job 30:31; Ps 55:6; 74:19; SS 2:12,14; Isa 38:14; 59:11; 60:8; Jer 48:28; Eze 7:16; Hos 7:11; 11:11; Na 2:7; Mt 3:16; 10:16; Jn 1:32 **8:11** [y] ver 7 **8:13** [z] S Ge 5:32 **8:14** [a] S Ge 7:11 **8:16** [b] S Ge 7:13 **8:17** [c] S Ge 1:22 **8:18** [d] 1Pe 3:20; 2Pe 2:5 **8:20** [e] Ge 12:7-8; 13:18; 22:9; 26:25; 33:20; 35:7; Ex 17:15; 24:4 [f] S Ge 7:8 [g] Ge 22:2,13; Ex 10:25; 20:24; 40:29; Lev 1:3; 4:29; 6:8-13; Nu 6:11; Jdg 6:26; 11:31; 1Sa 20:29; Job 1:5; 42:8

7:20 *covered the mountains to a depth of more than twenty feet.* The ark was 45 feet high (6:15), so the water was deep enough to keep it from running aground.

7:22 *breath of life.* God's gift at creation (see 1:30; 2:7 and note) was taken away because of sin.

8:1 *But.* So far the flood narrative has been an account of judgment; from this point on it is a story of deliverance and restoration. *God remembered Noah.* Though he had not been mentioned since 7:16 or heard from for 150 days (see 7:24), God had not forgotten Noah and his family. To "remember" in the Bible is often not merely to recall people to mind but to express concern for them, to act with loving care for them (see Ps 8:4 and note). When God remembers his children, he does so "with favor" (Ne 5:19; 13:31). *wind.* The Hebrew word translated "Spirit" in 1:2 is here rendered "wind," and introduces a series of parallels between the events of chs. 8–9 and those of ch. 1 in their literary order: Compare 8:2 with 1:7; 8:5 with 1:9; 8:7 with 1:20; 8:17 with 1:25; 9:1 with 1:28a; 9:2 with 1:28b; 9:3 with 1:30. Ch. 1 describes the original beginning, while chs. 8–9 describe a new beginning after the flood.

8:4 *mountains.* The word is plural and refers to a range of mountains. *Ararat.* The name is related to Assyrian Urartu, which became an extensive mountainous kingdom (see Jer 51:27; see also Isa 37:38), including much of the territory north of Mesopotamia and east of modern Turkey.

8:6 *window.* See note on 6:16.

8:11 *dove returned … in its beak was a freshly plucked olive leaf.* Olives do not grow at high elevations, and the fresh leaf was a sign to Noah that the water had receded from the earth. The modern symbol of peace represented by a dove carrying an olive branch in its beak has its origin in this story.

8:13 *first day of the first month of Noah's six hundred and first year.* The date formula signals humankind's new beginning after the flood.

8:14 *twenty-seventh day of the second month.* More than a year after the flood began (see 7:11).

8:16 *Come out of the ark.* See note on 7:1.

8:17 *multiply … be fruitful … increase in number.* See 1:22 and note. The animals and birds could now repopulate their former habitats.

8:20 *burnt offerings.* See Lev 1:3 and note.

8:21 *smelled the pleasing aroma.* A figurative way of saying that the Lord took delight in Noah's offering (cf. Eph

aroma[h] and said in his heart: "Never again
will I curse the ground[i] because of man,
even though[a] every inclination of his heart
is evil from childhood.[j] And never again
will I destroy[k] all living creatures,[l] as I
have done.

22 "As long as the earth endures,
seedtime and harvest,[m]
cold and heat,
summer and winter,[n]
day and night
will never cease."[o]

God's Covenant With Noah

9 Then God blessed Noah and his sons,
saying to them, "Be fruitful and increase in number and fill the earth.[p] 2The
fear and dread of you will fall upon all
the beasts of the earth and all the birds
of the air, upon every creature that moves
along the ground, and upon all the fish of
the sea; they are given into your hands.[q]
3Everything that lives and moves will be
food for you.[r] Just as I gave you the green
plants, I now give you everything.[s]
4"But you must not eat meat that has
its lifeblood still in it.[t] 5And for your lifeblood I will surely demand an accounting.[u] I will demand an accounting from
every animal.[v] And from each man, too, I
will demand an accounting for the life of
his fellow man.[w]

6 "Whoever sheds the blood of man,
by man shall his blood be shed;[x]
for in the image of God[y]
has God made man.

7As for you, be fruitful and increase in
number; multiply on the earth and increase upon it."[z]
8Then God said to Noah and to his sons
with him: 9"I now establish my covenant
with you[a] and with your descendants after you 10and with every living creature
that was with you—the birds, the livestock and all the wild animals, all those
that came out of the ark with you—every
living creature on earth. 11I establish my
covenant[b] with you:[c] Never again will all

[a] *21* Or *man, for*

8:21 [h] Ex 29:18, 25; Lev 1:9, 13; 2:9; 4:31; Nu 15:3, 7; 2Co 2:15 [i] S Ge 3:17 [j] Ge 6:5; Ps 51:5; Jer 17:9; Mt 15:19; Ro 1:21 [k] Jer 44:11 [l] Ge 9:11, 15; Isa 54:9 **8:22** [m] Jos 3:15; Ps 67:6; Jer 5:24 [n] Ps 74:17; Zec 14:8 [o] S Ge 1:14 **9:1** [p] S Ge 1:22 **9:2** [q] S Ge 1:26 **9:3** [r] S Ge 1:29 [s] S Ac 10:15; Col 2:16 **9:4** [t] Lev 3:17; 7:26; 17:10-14; 19:26; Dt 12:16, 23-25; 15:23; 1Sa 14:33; Eze 33:25; Ac 15:20, 29 **9:5** [u] Ge 42:22; 50:15; 1Ki 2:32; 2Ch 24:22; Ps 9:12 [v] Ex 21:28-32 [w] Ge 4:10 **9:6** [x] S Ge 4:14; S Jdg 9:24; S Mt 26:52 [y] S Ge 1:26 **9:7** [z] S Ge 1:22 **9:9** [a] ver 11; S Ge 6:18 **9:11** [b] ver 16; Isa 24:5; 33:8; Hos 6:7 [c] S ver 9

5:2; Php 4:18). *curse the ground.* Although the Hebrew here has a different word for "curse," the reference appears to be to the curse of 3:17. It may be that the Lord here pledged never to add curse upon curse as he had in regard to Cain (4:12). *even though every inclination of his heart is evil.* For almost identical phraseology see 6:5 and note. Because of humanity's extreme wickedness, God had destroyed them (6:7) by means of a flood (6:17; see note there). Although righteous Noah and his family had been saved, he and his offspring were descendants of Adam and carried in their hearts the inheritance of sin. God graciously promises never again to deal with sin by sending such a devastating deluge (see 9:11,15 and note on 9:11). Human history is held open for God's dealing with sin in a new and redemptive way—the way that was prepared for by God's action at Babel (see notes on 11:6,8) and that begins to unfold with the call of Abram (see notes on 11:27—25:11 and 12:1). *from childhood.* The phrase replaces "all the time" in 6:5 and emphasizes the truth that sin infects a person's life from conception and birth (see Ps 51:5; 58:3 and notes; cf. Eph 2:3).

8:22 Times and seasons, created by God in the beginning (see 1:14 and note), will never cease till the end of history.

9:1–7 At this new beginning, God renewed his original benediction (1:28) and his provision for humanity's food (cf. v. 3; 1:29–30). But because sin had brought violence into the world and because God now appointed meat as a part of the human diet (v. 3), further divine provisions and stipulations are added (vv. 4–6). Yet God's benediction dominates and encloses the whole (see v. 7).

9:2 *given into your hands.* God reaffirmed that human beings would rule over all creation, including the animals (see note on 1:26).

9:3 *Everything that lives and moves will be food.* Meat would now supplement the human diet.

9:4 *you must not eat meat that has its lifeblood.* Lev 17:14 stresses the intimate relationship between blood and life by twice declaring that "the life of every creature is its blood." Life is the precious and mysterious gift of God, and people are not to seek to preserve it or increase the life-force within them by eating "life" that is "in the blood" (Lev 17:11; see note there)—as many pagan peoples throughout history have thought they could do.

9:5 *for your lifeblood ... I will demand an accounting from every animal.* God himself is the great defender of human life (see 4:9–12 and note on 4:10), which is precious to him because people were created in his image (v. 6) and because they are the earthly representatives and focal point of God's kingdom. In the theocracy (kingdom of God) established at Sinai, a domestic animal that had taken human life was to be stoned to death (see Ex 21:28–32 and note on 21:28).

9:6 *Whoever sheds the blood of man, by man shall his blood be shed.* In the later theocracy, those guilty of premeditated murder were to be executed (see Ex 21:12–14; Nu 35:16–32; see also Ro 13:3–4; 1Pe 2:13–14). *for in the image of God has God made man.* See 1:26 and note. In killing a human being, a murderer demonstrates contempt for God (see also Pr 14:31; 17:5; Jas 3:9 and notes).

9:8–17 God's first and most basic covenant with his creatures (see chart, p. 19). It concerns the creation order itself and has its "sign" embedded in that creation order. Since divine judgment had seemed to undo the creation completely, sinful humanity needed God's covenanted assurance that his acts of judgment in history will not destroy the created order. This is the only divine covenant in which God pledges *not* to do something.

9:9 *I now establish my covenant.* God sovereignly promised in this covenant to Noah, to Noah's descendants and to all other living things (as a kind of gracious reward to righteous Noah, the new father of the human race—see 6:18) never again to destroy the earth and its inhabitants until his purposes for his creation are fully realized ("as long as the earth endures," 8:22). For similar commitments by God see his covenants with Abram (15:18–20), Phinehas (Nu 25:10–13) and David (2Sa 7). See chart, p. 19.

9:11 *Never again will all life be cut off by the waters of a flood.* A summary of the provisions of the Lord's covenant with Noah—an eternal covenant, as seen in such words and phrases as "never again" (see also v. 15), "for all generations to come" (v. 12) and "everlasting" (v. 16).

Major Covenants in the Old Testament

COVENANTS	REFERENCE	TYPE	PARTICIPANT	DESCRIPTION
NOAHIC	Ge 9:8-17	Royal Grant	Made with "righteous" (6:9) Noah (and his descendants and every living thing on earth—all life that is subject to human jurisdiction	An unconditional divine promise never to destroy all earthly life with some natural catastrophe, the covenant "sign" being the rainbow in the storm cloud
ABRAHAMIC A	Ge 15:9-21	Royal (land) Grant	Made with "righteous" (his faith was "credited . . . to him as righteousness," v. 6) Abram (and his descendants, v. 16)	An unconditional divine promise to fulfill the grant of the land; a self-maledictory oath symbolically enacted it (v. 17; see note there)
ABRAHAMIC B	Ge 17	Suzerain-vassal	Made with Abraham as patriarchal head of his household	A conditional divine pledge to be Abraham's God and the God of his descendants (cf. "As for me," v. 4; "As for you," v. 9); the condition: total consecration to the Lord as symbolized by circumcision
SINAITIC	Ex 19–24	Suzerain-vassal	Made with Israel as the descendants of Abraham, Isaac and Jacob and as the people the Lord has redeemed from bondage to an earthly power	A conditional divine pledge to be Israel's God (as her Protector and the Guarantor of her blessed destiny); the condition: Israel's total consecration to the Lord as his people (his kingdom) who live by his rule and serve his purposes in history
PHINEHAS	Nu 25:10-13	Royal Grant	Made with the zealous priest Phinehas	An unconditional divine promise to maintain the family of Phinehas in a "lasting priesthood" (implicitly a pledge to Israel to provide her forever with a faithful priesthood)
DAVIDIC	2Sa 7:5-16	Royal Grant	Made with faithful King David after his devotion to God as Israel's king and the Lord's anointed vassal had come to special expression (v. 2)	An unconditional divine promise to establish and maintain the Davidic dynasty on the throne of Israel (implicitly a pledge to Israel) to provide her forever with a godly king like David and through that dynasty to do for her what he had done through David—bring her into rest in the promised land (1Ki 4:20-21; 5:3-4)
NEW	Jer 31:31-34	Royal Grant	Promised to rebellious Israel as she is about to be expelled from the promised land in actualization of the most severe covenant curse (Lev 26:27-39; Dt 28:36-37, 45-68)	An unconditional divine promise to unfaithful Israel to forgive her sins and establish his relationship with her on a new basis by writing his law "on their hearts"—a covenant of pure grace

Major Types of Royal Covenants/Treaties in the Ancient Near East

ROYAL GRANT (UNCONDITIONAL)	PARITY	SUZERAIN-VASSAL (CONDITIONAL)
A king's grant (of land or some other benefit) to a loyal servant for faithful or exceptional service. The grant was normally perpetual and unconditional, but the servant's heirs benefited from it only as they continued their father's loyalty and service. (Cf. 1Sa 8:14; 22:7; 27:6; Est 8:1.)	A covenant between equals, binding them to mutual friendship or at least to mutual respect for each other's spheres and interests. Participants called each other "brothers." (Cf. Ge 21:27; 26:31; 31:44-54; 1Ki 5:12; 15:19; 20:32-34; Am 1:9.)	A covenant regulating the relationship between a great king and one of his subject kings. The great king claimed absolute right of sovereignty, demanded total loyalty and service (the vassal must "love" his suzerain) and pledged protection of the subject's realm and dynasty, conditional on the vassal's faithfulness and loyalty to him. The vassal pledged absolute loyalty to his suzerain—whatever service his suzerain demanded—and exclusive reliance on the suzerain's protection. Participants called each other "lord" and "servant" or "father" and "son." (Cf. Jos 9:6,8; Eze 17:13-18; Hos 12:1.)

Commitments made in these covenants were accompanied by self-maledictory oaths (made orally, ceremonially or both). The gods were called upon to witness the covenants and implement the curses of the oaths if the covenants were violated.

life be cut off by the waters of a flood;
never again will there be a flood to destroy
the earth.[d]"
12And God said, "This is the sign of the
covenant[e] I am making between me and
you and every living creature with you, a
covenant for all generations to come:[f] 13I
have set my rainbow[g] in the clouds, and it
will be the sign of the covenant between me
and the earth. 14Whenever I bring clouds
over the earth and the rainbow[h] appears in
the clouds, 15I will remember my covenant[i]
between me and you and all living creatures of every kind. Never again will the
waters become a flood to destroy all life.[j]
16Whenever the rainbow[k] appears in the
clouds, I will see it and remember the everlasting covenant[l] between God and all living creatures of every kind on the earth."
17So God said to Noah, "This is the sign
of the covenant[m] I have established between me and all life on the earth."

The Sons of Noah

18The sons of Noah who came out of the
ark were Shem, Ham and Japheth.[n] (Ham
was the father of Canaan.)[o] 19These were
the three sons of Noah,[p] and from them
came the people who were scattered over
the earth.[q]
20Noah, a man of the soil, proceeded[a] to
plant a vineyard. 21When he drank some
of its wine,[r] he became drunk and lay uncovered inside his tent. 22Ham, the father
of Canaan, saw his father's nakedness[s]
and told his two brothers outside. 23But
Shem and Japheth took a garment and laid
it across their shoulders; then they walked
in backward and covered their father's nakedness. Their faces were turned the other
way so that they would not see their father's nakedness.
24When Noah awoke from his wine and
found out what his youngest son had done
to him, 25he said,

"Cursed[t] be Canaan![u]
The lowest of slaves
will he be to his brothers.[v]"

26He also said,

"Blessed be the LORD, the God of
Shem![w]
May Canaan be the slave[x] of Shem.[b]
27May God extend the territory of
Japheth[c];[y]
may Japheth live in the tents of
Shem,[z]
and may Canaan be his[d] slave."

[a] 20 Or *soil, was the first* [b] 26 Or *be his slave*
[c] 27 *Japheth* sounds like the Hebrew for *extend.*
[d] 27 Or *their*

9:11 [d]S Ge 8:21 **9:12** [e]ver 17; Ge 17:11 [f]Ge 17:12; Ex 12:14; Lev 3:17; 6:18; 17:7; Nu 10:8 **9:13** [g]ver 14; Eze 1:28; Rev 4:3; 10:1 **9:14** [h]S ver 13 **9:15** [i]S Ge 8:1; Ex 2:24; 6:5; 34:10; Lev 26:42,45; Dt 7:9; Ps 89:34; 103:18; 105:8; 106:45; Eze 16:60 [j]S Ge 8:21 **9:16** [k]ver 13 [l]S ver 11; Ge 17:7,13,19; 2Sa 7:13; 23:5; Ps 105:9-10; Isa 9:7; 54:10; 55:3; 59:21; 61:8; Jer 31:31-34; 32:40; 33:21; Eze 16:60; 37:26; S Heb 13:20 **9:17** [m]S ver 12 **9:18** [n]S Ge 5:32; Lk 3:36 [o]ver 25-27; Ge 10:6,15 **9:19** [p]Ge 5:32 [q]S Ge 1:22; 10:32; 11:4,8,9 **9:21** [r]Ge 19:35 **9:22** [s]Hab 2:15 **9:25** [t]Ge 27:12 [u]ver 18; Ex 20:5; Ps 79:8; Isa 14:21; Jer 31:29; 32:18 [v]Ge 25:23; 27:29,37,40; 37:10; 49:8; Nu 24:18; Jos 9:23 **9:26** [w]Ge 14:20; Ex 18:10; Ps 7:17 [x]1Ki 9:21 **9:27** [y]Ge 10:2-5 [z]Eph 2:13-14; 3:6

9:12 *sign.* A covenant sign was a visible seal and reminder of covenant commitments. Circumcision would become the sign of the covenant with Abraham (see 17:11 and note), and the Sabbath would be the sign of the covenant with Israel at Sinai (see Ex 31:16 – 17 and note).

9:13 *rainbow.* Rain and the rainbow doubtless existed long before the time of Noah's flood, but after the flood the rainbow took on new meaning as the sign of the Noahic covenant. The Hebrew word is lit. "bow," as in 27:3; 48:22. The rainbow probably represents the bow with which God shoots the arrows of his lightning bolts toward the earth (see Ps 18:14; 77:17; 144:6; Hab 3:9,11 and note on 3:9; for other references to God wielding a bow see Ps 7:12; 21:12; Lam 2:4; Zec 9:13; for references to God's arrows see also Dt 32:23,42; Job 6:4; 34:6; Ps 38:2; 64:7; Lam 3:12 – 13; Eze 5:16). But after a rainstorm God's bow is aimed at himself (for weapons being turned back on those wielding them see Ps 37:15; 64:3 – 4,7 – 8; Jer 21:4). For that reason, God appointed the rainbow to be the sign of his self-maledictory covenant oath (see 15:17 and note); whenever he sees it, he is reminded of his oath-bound pledge (v. 16).

9:19 *who were scattered.* The clause anticipates the list of nations in ch. 10 (see note on 11:8).

9:20 *man of the soil.* Like his father Lamech (see 5:29).

9:21 *When he drank some of its wine, he became drunk.* The first person to make wine drank to excess (cf. Pr 20:1 and note). *uncovered inside his tent.* Excessive use of wine led, among other things, to immodest behavior (see 19:30 – 35).

9:22 *father of Canaan.* Mentioned here because Ham, in acting as he did, showed himself to be the true father of Canaan (i.e., of the Canaanites; see note on 15:16). *told his two brothers.* He broadcast, rather than covered, his father's immodesty.

9:23 *faces were turned … so that they would not see.* They wanted to avoid further disgrace to their father.

9:24 *from his wine.* From the drunkenness caused by the wine.

9:25 *Cursed be Canaan!* Some maintain that Ham's son (see vv. 18,22) was to be punished because of his father's sin (see Ex 20:5 and note), but Ex 20 restricts such punishment to "those who hate me." This account of Noah's cursing and blessing of his sons is addressed to Israel. Most likely it is for this reason that Canaan is here singled out from Ham's descendants as the object of Noah's curse. Israel would experience firsthand the depth of Canaanite sin (see Lev 18:2 – 3,6 – 30) and the harshness of God's judgment on it. In that judgment Noah's curse came to be fulfilled in the experience of this segment of Ham's descendants. But Ham's offspring, as listed in 10:6 – 13, included many of Israel's other long-term enemies (Egypt, Philistia, Assyria, Babylonia) who also experienced severe divine judgments because of their hostility to Israel and Israel's God. *lowest of slaves.* Joshua's subjection of the Gibeonites (Jos 9:27) is one of the fulfillments (see also Jos 16:10; Jdg 1:28,30,33,35; 1Ki 9:20 – 21). Noah's curse cannot be used to justify the enslavement of blacks, since most of Ham's descendants are known to be Caucasian, as the Canaanites certainly were (as shown by ancient paintings of the Canaanites discovered in Egypt).

9:26 *Blessed be the LORD.* The Lord (instead of Shem) is blessed (praised) because he is the source of Shem's blessing. He is also the "God of Shem" (and his descendants, the Semites — which included the Israelites) in a special sense.

9:27 *live in the tents of Shem.* Share in the blessings bestowed on Shem.

28 After the flood Noah lived 350 years.
29 Altogether, Noah lived 950 years, and
then he died.[a]

The Table of Nations

10 This is the account[b] of Shem, Ham
and Japheth,[c] Noah's sons,[d] who
themselves had sons after the flood.

The Japhethites

10:2-5pp — 1Ch 1:5-7

2 The sons[a] of Japheth:
Gomer,[e] Magog,[f] Madai, Javan,[g]
Tubal,[h] Meshech[i] and Tiras.
3 The sons of Gomer:
Ashkenaz,[j] Riphath and Togarmah.[k]
4 The sons of Javan:
Elishah,[l] Tarshish,[m] the Kittim[n] and
the Rodanim.[b] 5 (From these the
maritime peoples spread out into
their territories by their clans within their nations, each with its own
language.)[o]

The Hamites

10:6-20pp — 1Ch 1:8-16

6 The sons of Ham:
Cush,[p] Mizraim,[c] Put[q] and Canaan.[r]
7 The sons of Cush:
Seba,[s] Havilah,[t] Sabtah, Raamah[u]
and Sabteca.
The sons of Raamah:
Sheba[v] and Dedan.[w]

8 Cush was the father[d] of Nimrod,[x] who
grew to be a mighty warrior on the earth.
9 He was a mighty[y] hunter[z] before the
LORD; that is why it is said, "Like Nimrod, a mighty hunter before the LORD."
10 The first centers of his kingdom were
Babylon,[a] Erech,[b] Akkad and Calneh,[c] in[e]
Shinar.[f][d] 11 From that land he went to Assyria,[e] where he built Nineveh,[f] Rehoboth
Ir,[g] Calah 12 and Resen, which is between
Nineveh and Calah; that is the great city.

13 Mizraim was the father of
the Ludites, Anamites, Lehabites,
Naphtuhites, 14 Pathrusites, Caslu-

[a] 2 *Sons* may mean *descendants* or *successors* or *nations*; also in verses 3, 4, 6, 7, 20-23, 29 and 31. [b] 4 Some manuscripts of the Masoretic Text and Samaritan Pentateuch (see also Septuagint and 1 Chron. 1:7); most manuscripts of the Masoretic Text *Dodanim* [c] 6 That is, Egypt; also in verse 13 [d] 8 *Father* may mean *ancestor* or *predecessor* or *founder*; also in verses 13, 15, 24 and 26. [e] 10 Or *Erech and Akkad—all of them in* [f] 10 That is, Babylonia [g] 11 Or *Nineveh with its city squares*

9:29 [a] S Ge 2:17 **10:1** [b] Ge 2:4 [c] S Ge 5:32 [d] ver 32; 1Ch 1:4 **10:2** [e] Eze 38:6 [f] Eze 38:2; 39:6; Rev 20:8 [g] Eze 27:19 [h] Isa 66:19; Eze 27:13; 32:26 [i] Eze 39:1 **10:3** [j] Jer 51:27 [k] Eze 27:14; 38:6 **10:4** [l] Eze 27:7 [m] Ps 48:7; 72:10; Isa 2:16; 23:1,6,10,14; 60:9; 66:19; Jer 10:9; Eze 27:12,25; 38:13; Jnh 1:3 [n] Nu 24:24; Isa 23:12; Jer 2:10; Eze 27:6; Da 11:30 **10:5** [o] Ge 9:27 **10:6** [p] 2Ki 19:9; 2Ch 12:3; 16:8; Isa 11:11; 18:1; 20:3; 43:3; Jer 46:9; Eze 30:4,9; 38:5; Na 3:9; Zep 2:12; 3:10 [q] Eze 27:10; 38:5 [r] S Ge 9:18 **10:7** [s] Isa 43:3 [t] S Ge 2:11 [u] Eze 27:22 [v] Ge 25:3; 1Ki 10:1; 2Ch 9:1; Job 1:15; 6:19; 16:11; Ps 72:10,15; Isa 60:6; Jer 6:20; Eze 27:22; 38:13; Joel 3:8 [w] 1Ch 1:32; Isa 21:13; Jer 25:23-24; 49:8; Eze 27:15,20; 38:13 **10:8** [x] Mic 5:6 **10:9** [y] 2Ch 14:9; 16:8; Isa 18:2 [z] Ge 25:27; 27:3 **10:10** [a] Ge 11:9; 2Ch 36:17; Isa 13:1; 47:1; Jer 21:2; 25:12; 50:1 [b] Ezr 4:9 [c] Isa 10:9; Am 6:2 [d] Ge 11:2; 14:1; Zec 5:11 **10:11** [e] Ps 83:8; Mic 5:6 [f] 2Ki 19:36; Isa 37:37; Jnh 1:2; 3:2,3; 4:11; Na 1:1; Zep 2:13

9:29 *and then he died.* See note on 5:5. As the tenth and last member of the genealogy of Seth (5:3–32), Noah had an obituary that ends like those of his worthy ancestors.

10:1 *account.* See note on 2:4. The links affirmed here may not all be based on strictly physical descent, but may include geographical, historical and linguistic associations (see note on v. 5 and NIV text notes on vv. 2,8; 11:10). See also Introduction to 1 Chronicles: Genealogies.

10:2 *sons.* See NIV text note. *Japheth.* As the least involved in the Biblical narrative and perhaps also as the oldest of Noah's sons (see v. 21 and NIV text note), his descendants or successors are listed first. The genealogy of Shem, the chosen line, appears last in the chapter (see vv. 21–31; see also 11:10–26). The 14 nations that came from Japheth plus the 30 from Ham and the 26 from Shem add up to 70 (the multiple of 10 and 7, both numbers signifying completeness; see note on 5:5), perhaps in anticipation of the 70 members of Jacob's family who went down to Egypt (see 46:27 and note; Ex 1:5; see also Dt 32:8 and note). The Japhethites lived generally north and west of Canaan in Eurasia. *Gomer.* The people of Gomer (the later Cimmerians) and related nations (see v. 3) lived near the Black Sea (see map, p. 22). *Magog.* Possibly the father of a Scythian people who inhabited the Caucasus and adjacent regions southeast of the Black Sea. *Madai.* The later Medes. *Javan.* Ionia (southern Greece) and perhaps western Asia Minor. *Tubal, Meshech.* Not related to Tobolsk and Moscow in modern Russia. Together with Magog they are mentioned in later Assyrian inscriptions. See also Eze 38:2 and note. Probably Tubal was in Pontus, and Meshech was in the Moschian Mountains. Their movement was from eastern Asia Minor north to the Black Sea. *Tiras.* Possibly the Thrace of later times.

10:3 *Ashkenaz.* The later Scythians. All three names in this verse refer to peoples located in the upper Euphrates region.

10:4 *Elishah.* Either Alashia (an ancient name for Cyprus) or a reference to Sicily and southern Italy. *Tarshish.* Probably southern Spain. *Kittim.* A people living on Cyprus. *Rodanim.* A people whose name is perhaps reflected in Rhodes (a Greek isle).

10:5 See vv. 20,31. *territories ... clans ... nations ... language.* Geographic, ethnic, political and linguistic terms, respectively. These several criteria were used to differentiate the various groups of people.

10:6 *Ham.* The Hamites named here were located in southwestern Asia and northeast Africa. *Cush.* The upper Nile region, south of Egypt. *Mizraim.* Means "two Egypts," a reference to Upper (southern) and Lower (northern) Egypt. *Put.* Probably Libya (see note on v. 13). *Canaan.* The name possibly means "land of purple" (as does Phoenicia, the Greek name for the same general region). Canaan was a major producer and exporter of purple dye, highly prized by royalty. The territory was much later called Palestine after the Philistines (see v. 14).

10:7 *sons of Cush.* The seven Cushite nations here mentioned were all in Arabia. Sheba and Dedan (or their namesakes) reappear as two of Abraham's grandsons (see 25:3). Together with Raamah they are mentioned in Eze 27:20–22.

10:8 *Cush.* Probably not the same as in v. 6. Located in Mesopotamia, the name may be related to that of the later Kassites. *Nimrod.* Possibly the Hebrew name of Sargon I, an early ruler of Akkad (see v. 10).

10:10 *Erech.* The Hebrew name for Uruk (modern Warka), one of the important cities in ancient Mesopotamia (see map No. 1 at the end of this study Bible).

10:12 *great city.* Possibly a reference to Calah (or even Resen), but most likely to Nineveh (see Jnh 1:2; 3:2; 4:11), either alone or including the surrounding urban areas.

10:13 *Ludites.* Perhaps the Lydians in Asia Minor (see note on v. 22). *Anamites.* Located in north Africa, west of Egypt, near Cyrene. *Lehabites.* Perhaps the Libyan desert tribes (see note on v. 6). *Naphtuhites.* People of Lower Egypt.

10:14 *Pathrusites.* The inhabitants of Upper Egypt (see note on v. 6). *Captorites.* Crete, known as Captor in ancient times,

hites (from whom the Philistines[g]
came) and Caphtorites.[h]
15 Canaan[i] was the father of
Sidon[j] his firstborn,[a k] and of the
Hittites,[l] 16 Jebusites,[m] Amorites,[n]
Girgashites,[o] 17 Hivites,[p] Arkites, Si-
nites, 18 Arvadites,[q] Zemarites and
Hamathites.[r]

Later the Canaanite[s] clans scattered
19 and the borders of Canaan[t] reached from
Sidon[u] toward Gerar[v] as far as Gaza,[w] and
then toward Sodom, Gomorrah, Admah
and Zeboiim,[x] as far as Lasha.
20 These are the sons of Ham by their
clans and languages, in their territories
and nations.

10:14 [g] Ge 21:32,34; 26:1,8; Jos 13:2; Jdg 3:3; Isa 14:31; Jer 47:1,4; Am 9:7 [h] Dt 2:23; 1Ch 1:12 **10:15** [i] S Ge 9:18 [j] ver 19; Jos 11:8; Jdg 10:6; Isa 23:2,4; Jer 25:22; 27:3; 47:4; Eze 28:21; 32:30; Joel 3:4; Zec 9:2 [k] Ex 4:22; Nu 1:20; 3:2; 18:15; 26:5; 33:4 [l] Ge 15:20; 23:3,20; 25:10; 26:34; 27:46; 49:32; Nu 13:29; Jos 1:4; 1Sa 26:6; Eze 16:3 **10:16** [m] Jdg 19:10; 1Ch 11:4; Ezr 9:1 [n] Ex 3:8; Nu 13:29; 21:13; 32:39; Dt 1:4; Jos 2:10; 2Ch 8:7 [o] Ge 15:18-21; Dt 7:1 **10:17** [p] Ge 34:2; 36:2; Ex 3:8; Dt 7:1; Jdg 3:3 **10:18** [q] Eze 27:8 [r] 1Ch 18:3 [s] Ge 12:6; 13:7; 50:11; Ex 13:11; Nu 13:29; 14:25; 21:3; 33:40; Dt 1:7; Jdg 1:1 **10:19** [t] Ge 11:31; 12:1; 13:12; 17:8; 24:3; 26:34; 27:46; 28:1,6,8; 31:18; 35:6; 37:1; Lev 25:38 [u] S ver 15; Ge 49:13; Jos 19:28; Jdg 1:31; 18:28; 2Sa 24:6 [v] 2Ch 14:13 [w] Dt 2:23; Jos 10:41; 11:22; 15:47; Jdg 1:18; 6:4; 16:1,21; 1Sa 6:17; Jer 25:20; 47:1; Am 1:6; Zep 2:4 [x] Ge 14:2; Dt 29:23 **10:21** [y] ver 24; Nu 24:24

The Semites

10:21-31pp — Ge 11:10-27; 1Ch 1:17-27

21 Sons were also born to Shem, whose
older brother was[b] Japheth; Shem was the
ancestor of all the sons of Eber.[y]
22 The sons of Shem:

[a] 15 Or *of the Sidonians, the foremost* [b] 21 Or *Shem, the older brother of*

was for a while the homeland of various Philistine groups (see Jer 47:4 and note; Am 9:7). The Philistines themselves were a vigorous Indo-European maritime people who invaded Egypt early in the 12th century B.C. After being driven out, they migrated in large numbers to southwest Canaan, later extending their influence over most of the land. The Philistines of the patriarchal period (see 21:32,34; 26:1,8,14–15,18) no doubt had earlier settled in Canaan more peacefully and in smaller numbers.

10:15 *Sidon.* An important commercial city on the northwest coast of Canaan. *Hittites.* An Indo-European-speaking people who moved into Anatolia (ancient Asia Minor, modern western Turkey) from southeast Europe in the late third millennium B.C. They came to dominate north-central Anatolia in the mid-second millennium B.C. and called themselves Hittites, a name adapted from that of the native Hatti people. They established an empire powerful enough at times to challenge both Babylonia and Egypt. The relationship, if any, between these people and the "Hittites" of Canaan mentioned in the Bible remains obscure (but see Eze 16:3 and note).

10:16 *Jebusites.* Inhabitants of Jerusalem at the time of Israel's conquest of Canaan. Jerusalem was also known as Jebus during part of its history (see Jdg 19:10–11; 1Ch 11:4). *Amorites.* The name comes from an Akkadian word meaning "westerner" (west from the Babylonian perspective). Amorites lived in the hill country of Canaan at the time of the Israelite conquest.

10:17–18 Together with the Girgashites (v. 16), these groups in Canaan inhabited small city-states for the most part.

10:19 *Sodom, Gomorrah, Admah and Zeboiim.* See 14:2,8; perhaps located east and/or southeast of the Dead Sea (but see note on 13:10).

10:21 *Sons were also born to Shem.* The descendants of Shem were called Shemites (later modified to Semites). *Eber.* Though a distant descendant of Shem (see vv. 24–25; 11:14–17), Eber's importance as the ancestor of the Hebrews ("Eber" is the origin of the Hebrew word for "Hebrew") is already hinted at here.

10:22 *Elam.* The Elamites lived east of Mesopotamia. *Asshur.* An early name for Assyria (see note on 2:14) in northern Mesopotamia. *Arphaxad.* See also 11:10–13; perhaps a compound form of the Hebrew word for Chaldea, in southern Mesopotamia. *Lud.* Probably the Lydians of Asia Minor (see note on v. 13). *Aram.* Located north-northeast of Canaan, the area known today as Syria.

Table of Nations

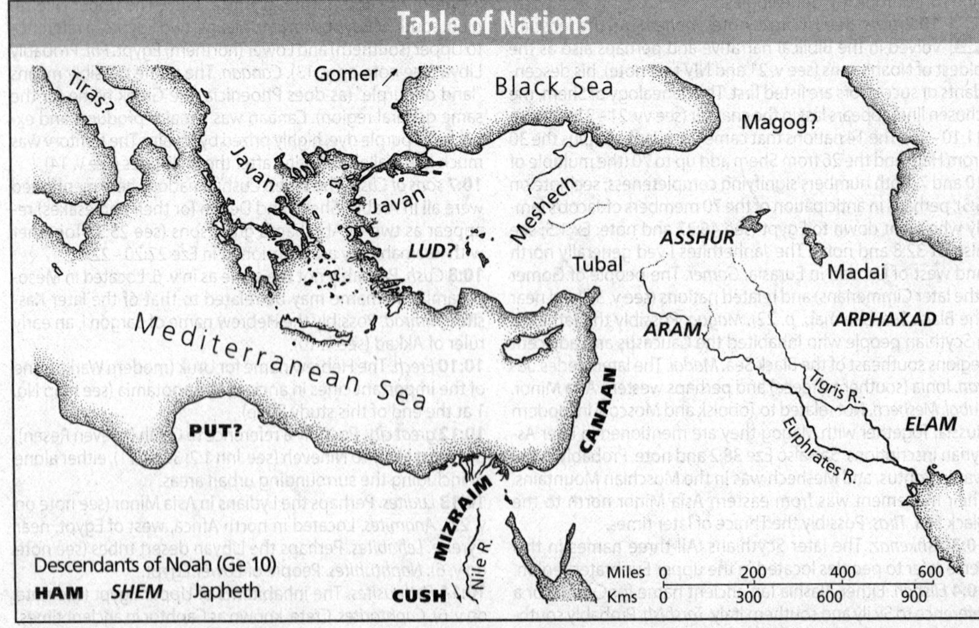

Elam,[z] Asshur,[a] Arphaxad,[b] Lud
and Aram.[c]
23 The sons of Aram:
Uz,[d] Hul, Gether and Meshech.[a]
24 Arphaxad was the father of[b] Shelah,
and Shelah the father of Eber.[e]
25 Two sons were born to Eber:
One was named Peleg,[c] because in
his time the earth was divided; his
brother was named Joktan.
26 Joktan was the father of
Almodad, Sheleph, Hazarmaveth,
Jerah, 27 Hadoram, Uzal,[f] Diklah,
28 Obal, Abimael, Sheba,[g] 29 Ophir,[h]
Havilah and Jobab. All these were
sons of Joktan.

30 The region where they lived stretched
from Mesha toward Sephar, in the eastern
hill country.
31 These are the sons of Shem by their
clans and languages, in their territories
and nations.

32 These are the clans of Noah's sons,[i]
according to their lines of descent, within their nations. From these the nations
spread out over the earth[j] after the flood.

The Tower of Babel

11 Now the whole world had one language[k] and a common speech. 2 As
men moved eastward,[d] they found a plain
in Shinar[e][l] and settled there.
3 They said to each other, "Come, let's
make bricks[m] and bake them thoroughly." They used brick instead of stone,[n] and
tar[o] for mortar. 4 Then they said, "Come,
let us build ourselves a city, with a tower
that reaches to the heavens,[p] so that we
may make a name[q] for ourselves and not
be scattered[r] over the face of the whole
earth."[s]
5 But the LORD came down[t] to see the city
and the tower that the men were building.
6 The LORD said, "If as one people speaking
the same language[u] they have begun to do
this, then nothing they plan to do will be
impossible for them. 7 Come, let us[v] go
down[w] and confuse their language so they
will not understand each other."[x]
8 So the LORD scattered them from there
over all the earth,[y] and they stopped building the city. 9 That is why it was called

[a] *23* See Septuagint and 1 Chron. 1:17; Hebrew *Mash.* [b] *24* Hebrew; Septuagint *father of Cainan, and Cainan was the father of* [c] *25* *Peleg* means *division.* [d] *2* Or *from the east*; or *in the east* [e] *2* That is, Babylonia

10:22 [z] Ge 14:1; Isa 11:11; 21:2; Jer 25:25; 49:34; Eze 32:24; Da 8:2 [a] Nu 24:22,24; Eze 27:23 [b] Lk 3:36 [c] Jdg 3:10; 1Ki 11:25; 19:15; 20:34; 22:31; 2Ki 5:1; 8:7 **10:23** [d] Ge 22:21; Job 1:1; Jer 25:20; La 4:21 **10:24** [e] S ver 21; Lk 3:35 **10:27** [f] Eze 27:19 **10:28** [g] 1Ki 10:1; Job 6:19; Ps 72:10,15; Isa 60:6; Eze 27:22 **10:29** [h] 1Ki 9:28; 10:11; 1Ch 29:4; Job 22:24; 28:16; Ps 45:9; Isa 13:12 **10:32** [i] S ver 1 [j] S Ge 9:19 **11:1** [k] ver 6 **11:2** [l] S Ge 10:10 **11:3** [m] Ex 1:14; 5:7; Jer 43:9 [n] Isa 9:10; Am 5:11 [o] Ge 14:10 **11:4** [p] Dt 1:28; 6:10; 9:1; Job 20:6; Jer 51:53 [q] Ge 6:4 [r] Dt 30:3; 1Ki 22:17; Est 3:8; Ps 44:11; Jer 31:10; 40:15; Eze 6:8; Joel 3:2 [s] S Ge 9:19; Dt 4:27 **11:5** [t] ver 7; Ge 18:21; Ex 3:8; 19:11,18,20; Ps 18:9; 144:5 **11:6** [u] S ver 1 **11:7** [v] S Ge 1:26 [w] S ver 5 [x] Ge 42:23; Dt 28:49; Isa 28:11; 33:19; Jer 5:15; 1Co 14:2,11 **11:8** [y] S Ge 9:19; Dt 32:8; S Lk 1:51

10:24 *Shelah.* See 11:12–15.
10:25 *Peleg.* See NIV text note and 11:16–19. *earth was divided.* Perhaps resulting from the dispersion of peoples described in 11:1–9.
10:26 *Joktan.* The predecessor of numerous south Arabian kingdoms.
10:28 *Sheba.* In southwest Arabia (roughly the area of Yemen). A later queen of Sheba made a memorable visit to King Solomon in the tenth century B.C. (see 1Ki 10:1–13).
10:29 *Ophir.* The source of much of King Solomon's gold (see 1Ki 9:28; 10:11). Its location seems to have been south of Canaan, perhaps somewhere in Africa or south Arabia (but see note on 1Ki 9:28).
11:1–9 This section provides the main reason for the scattering of the peoples listed in ch. 10. The narrative is a beautiful example of inverted or hourglass structure (see Introduction: Literary Features). The author of Genesis uses the story of the flood and the story of Babel to characterize the ways of humankind and God's responses through acts of judgment in order to thwart humanity's proud efforts to rule over the creation, not as God's faithful representatives but as rebels. With this characterization of human history outside God's saving work, the author sets the stage for God's call of Abram out of the post-Babel world to begin his redemptive work that would unfold in Israel's history.
11:1 *whole world.* The survivors of the flood and their descendants (see vv. 4,8–9).
11:3 *brick instead of stone, and tar for mortar.* Stone and mortar were used as building materials in Canaan. Stone was scarce in Mesopotamia, however, so mud brick and tar were used (as indicated also by archaeological excavations).
11:4 *us … ourselves … we … ourselves.* The people's plans were egotistical and proud. *tower.* The typical Mesopotamian temple-tower, known as a ziggurat, was square at the base and had sloping, stepped sides that led upward to a small shrine at the top. *reaches to the heavens.* A similar ziggurat may be described in 28:12. Other Mesopotamian ziggurats were given names demonstrating that they, too, were meant to serve as staircases from earth to heaven: "The House of the Link between Heaven and Earth" (at Larsa), "The House of the Seven Guides of Heaven and Earth" (at Borsippa), "The House of the Foundation-Platform of Heaven and Earth" (at Babylon), "The House of the Mountain of the Universe" (at Asshur). *name.* In the OT, "name" also refers to reputation, fame or renown. (The Nephilim were "men of renown [lit. 'name']," 6:4.) At Babel (see note on v. 9) the rebellious human race undertook a united and godless effort to establish for themselves, by a titanic enterprise, a world renown by which they would dominate God's creation (cf. 10:8–12; 2Sa 18:18). *scattered.* See note on v. 8.
11:6 *If … then.* If the whole human race remained united in the proud attempt to take its destiny into its own hands and, by its self-centered efforts, to seize the reins of history, there would be no limit to its unrestrained rebellion against God. A godless human kingdom would displace and exclude the kingdom of God. Cf. Cain's attempt to overcome his condition as one alienated from God, from a land and from other people by building for himself a city (see 4:17 and note).
11:7 *let us.* See notes on 1:1,26. God's "Come, let us" from heaven counters proud people's "Come, let us" (v. 4) from earth. *not understand each other.* Without a common language, joint effort became impossible (see v. 8).
11:8 *scattered.* See v. 4; 9:1,19. God dispersed the people because of their rebellious pride. Even the greatest of human powers cannot defy God and long survive.
11:9 *Babel.* See NIV text note and 10:10. The word is of Akkadian origin and means "gateway to a god" (Jacob's stairway was similarly called "gate of heaven"; see 28:17). *confused.* The Hebrew word used here (*balal*) sounds like "Babel," the

Babel[a][z]—because there the LORD confused the language[a] of the whole world.[b]
From there the LORD scattered[c] them over
the face of the whole earth.

From Shem to Abram

11:10-27pp — Ge 10:21-31; 1Ch 1:17-27

10 This is the account[d] of Shem.

Two years after the flood, when Shem
was 100 years old, he became the father[b]
of Arphaxad.[e] 11 And after he became the
father of Arphaxad, Shem lived 500 years
and had other sons and daughters.

12 When Arphaxad had lived 35 years, he
became the father of Shelah.[f] 13 And after
he became the father of Shelah, Arphaxad
lived 403 years and had other sons and
daughters.[c]

14 When Shelah had lived 30 years, he
became the father of Eber.[g] 15 And after he
became the father of Eber, Shelah lived
403 years and had other sons and daughters.

16 When Eber had lived 34 years, he became the father of Peleg.[h] 17 And after he
became the father of Peleg, Eber lived 430
years and had other sons and daughters.

18 When Peleg had lived 30 years, he
became the father of Reu.[i] 19 And after he
became the father of Reu, Peleg lived 209
years and had other sons and daughters.

20 When Reu had lived 32 years, he became the father of Serug.[j] 21 And after he
became the father of Serug, Reu lived 207
years and had other sons and daughters.

22 When Serug had lived 30 years, he became the father of Nahor.[k] 23 And after he
became the father of Nahor, Serug lived 200
years and had other sons and daughters.

24 When Nahor had lived 29 years, he became the father of Terah.[l] 25 And after he
became the father of Terah, Nahor lived 119
years and had other sons and daughters.

26 After Terah had lived 70 years, he became the father of Abram,[m] Nahor[n] and
Haran.[o]

27 This is the account[p] of Terah.

Terah became the father of Abram, Nahor[q] and Haran. And Haran became the
father of Lot.[r] 28 While his father Terah was
still alive, Haran died in Ur of the Chaldeans,[s] in the land of his birth. 29 Abram
and Nahor[t] both married. The name of
Abram's wife was Sarai,[u] and the name
of Nahor's wife was Milcah;[v] she was the
daughter of Haran, the father of both Milcah and Iscah. 30 Now Sarai was barren;
she had no children.[w]

31 Terah took his son Abram, his grandson Lot[x] son of Haran, and his daughter-
in-law[y] Sarai, the wife of his son Abram,
and together they set out from Ur of the
Chaldeans[z] to go to Canaan.[a] But when
they came to Haran,[b] they settled there.

[a] 9 That is, Babylon; *Babel* sounds like the Hebrew for *confused*. [b] 10 *Father* may mean *ancestor*; also in verses 11-25. [c] *12,13* Hebrew; Septuagint (see also Luke 3:35, 36 and note at Gen. 10:24) *35 years, he became the father of Cainan.* [13] *And after he became the father of Cainan, Arphaxad lived 430 years and had other sons and daughters, and then he died. When Cainan had lived 130 years, he became the father of Shelah. And after he became the father of Shelah, Cainan lived 330 years and had other sons and daughters*

11:9 [z] S Ge 10:10 [a] Ps 55:9 [b] Ac 2:5-11 [c] Isa 2:10,21; 13:14; 24:1 **11:10** [d] S Ge 2:4 [e] Lk 3:36 **11:12** [f] Lk 3:35 **11:14** [g] Lk 3:35 **11:16** [h] Lk 3:35 **11:18** [i] Lk 3:35 **11:20** [j] Lk 3:35 **11:22** [k] Lk 3:34 **11:24** [l] Lk 3:34 **11:26** [m] Lk 3:34 [n] Jos 24:2 [o] 2Ki 19:12; Isa 37:12; Eze 27:23 **11:27** [p] S Ge 2:4 [q] ver 29; Ge 31:53 [r] ver 31; Ge 12:4; 13:1,5,8,12; 14:12; 19:1; Lk 17:28; 2Pe 2:7 **11:28** [s] ver 31; Ge 15:7; Ne 9:7; Job 1:17; 16:11; Eze 23:23; Ac 7:4 **11:29** [t] S ver 27,31; Ge 22:20,23; 24:10,15,24; 29:5 [u] Ge 12:5,11; 16:1; 17:15 [v] Ge 22:20 **11:30** [w] Ge 16:1; 18:11; 25:21; 29:31; 30:1,22; Jdg 13:2; 1Sa 1:5; Ps 113:9; Lk 1:7,36 **11:31** [x] S ver 27 [y] Ge 38:11; Lev 18:15; 20:12; Ru 1:6,22; 2:20; 4:15; 1Sa 4:19; 1Ch 2:4; Eze 22:11; Mic 7:6 [z] S ver 28 [a] S Ge 10:19 [b] S ver 29; Ge 12:4; 27:43; 28:5,10; 29:4; 2Ki 19:12; Eze 27:23

Hebrew word for Babylon and the origin of the English word "babel."

11:10–26 A ten-name genealogy, like that of Seth (see 5:3–31; see also note on 5:5). Unlike the Sethite genealogy, however, the genealogy of Shem does not give total figures for the ages of the men at death and does not end each paragraph with "and then he died." It covers the centuries between Shem and Abram as briefly as possible.

11:10 *account.* See note on 2:4.

11:24 *Nahor ... became the father of Terah.* In c. 2296 B.C.

11:26 *Terah ... became the father of Abram, Nahor and Haran.* As in the case of Shem, Ham and Japheth, the names of the three sons may not be in chronological order by age (see 9:24; see also 10:21 and NIV text note). Haran died while his father was still alive (see v. 28). *became the father of Abram.* In c. 2166 B.C.

11:27—25:11 With God's calling of Abram out of the post-Babel peoples, the story of God's ways with humankind shifts focus from universal history to the history of God's relationship with a particular person and people. Here begins the history of his saving work in which human sin is not only judged (the flood) or restrained (Babel) but forgiven (through atonement) and overcome (through the purifying of human hearts). Throughout the rest of Scripture the unfolding of this history remains the golden thread and central theme. Its final outcome is made sure through Jesus Christ, "the son of Abraham" (Lk 3:33; see also Mt 1:1–17 and note on 1:1; Gal 3:16)—which is the core message of the NT.

The account of the God-Abram relationship found here foreshadows in many ways the God-Israel relationship, and the trials and triumphs of Abram's faith model the life of faith for his descendants.

11:27 *account.* See note on 2:4.

11:28 *Ur of the Chaldeans.* Possibly in northern Mesopotamia, but more likely the site on the Euphrates in southern Iraq excavated by Leonard Woolley between 1922 and 1934. Ruins and artifacts from Ur reveal a civilization and culture that reached high levels before Abram's time. King Ur-Nammu, who may have been Abram's contemporary, is famous for his law code. *Chaldeans.* See notes on Ezr 5:12; Job 1:17.

11:30 *Sarai was barren.* The sterility of Abram's wife (see 15:2–4 and notes; 17:17) emphasized the fact that God's people would not come by natural generation from the post-Babel peoples. God was bringing a new humanity into being, of whom Abram was father (17:5), just as Adam and Noah were fathers of the fallen human race.

11:31 *they came to Haran.* In Hebrew the name of the town is spelled differently from that of Abram's brother (v. 26). The moon-god was worshiped at both Ur and Haran, and since Terah was an idolater (see Jos 24:2 and note) he probably felt at home in either place. Haran was a flourishing caravan city in the 19th century B.C. In the 18th century it was ruled by Amorites (see note on 10:16).

32 Terah[c] lived 205 years, and he died in
Haran.

The Call of Abram

12 The LORD had said to Abram, "Leave
your country, your people and your
father's household[d] and go to the land[e] I
will show you.[f]

2 "I will make you into a great nation[g]
    and I will bless you;[h]
I will make your name great,
    and you will be a blessing.[i]
3 I will bless those who bless you,
    and whoever curses you I will curse;[j]
and all peoples on earth
    will be blessed through you.[k]"

4 So Abram left, as the LORD had told
him; and Lot[l] went with him. Abram was
seventy-five years old[m] when he set out
from Haran.[n] 5 He took his wife Sarai,[o] his
nephew Lot, all the possessions they had
accumulated[p] and the people[q] they had
acquired in Haran, and they set out for the
land of Canaan,[r] and they arrived there.
6 Abram traveled through the land[s] as
far as the site of the great tree of Moreh[t]
at Shechem.[u] At that time the Canaanites[v]
were in the land. 7 The LORD appeared to
Abram[w] and said, "To your offspring[a] I will
give this land.[x]"[y] So he built an altar there
to the LORD,[z] who had appeared to him.
8 From there he went on toward the hills

[a] 7 Or *seed*

11:32 [c] Jos 24:2 **12:1** [d] Ge 20:13; 24:4, 27, 40 [e] S Ge 10:19 [f] Ge 15:7; 26:2; Jos 24:3; Ac 7:3*; Heb 11:8 **12:2** [g] Ge 13:16; 15:5; 17:2, 4; 18:18; 22:17; 26:4; 28:3, 14; 32:12; 35:11; 41:49; 46:3; 47:27; 48:4, 16, 19; Ex 1:7; 5:5; 32:13; Dt 1:10; 10:22; 13:17; 26:5; Jos 11:4; 24:3; 2Sa 17:11; 1Ki 3:8; 4:20; 1Ch 27:23; 2Ch 1:9; Ne 9:23; Ps 107:38; Isa 6:13; 10:22; 48:19; 51:2; 54:3; 60:22; Jer 33:22; Mic 4:7 [h] Ge 24:1, 35; 25:11; 26:3; 28:4; Ex 20:24; Nu 22:12; 23:8, 20; 24:9; Ps 67:6; 115:12; Isa 44:3; 61:9; 65:23; Mal 3:12 [i] Ge 22:18; Isa 19:24; Jer 4:2; Hag 2:19; Zec 8:13 **12:3** [j] Ge 27:29; Ex 23:22; Nu 24:9; Dt 30:7 [k] Ge 15:5; 18:18; 22:18; 26:4; 28:4, 14; Dt 9:5; Ps 72:17; Isa 19:25; Ac 3:25; Gal 3:8* **12:4** [l] S Ge 11:27 [m] Ge 16:3, 16; 17:1, 17, 24; 21:5 [n] S Ge 11:31 **12:5** [o] S Ge 11:29 [p] ver 16; Ge 13:2, 6; 31:18; 46:6 [q] Ge 14:14; 15:3; 17:23; Ecc 2:7 [r] Ge 11:31; 16:3; Heb 11:8 **12:6** [s] Heb 11:9 [t] Ge 35:4; Dt 11:30; Jos 24:26; Jdg 7:1; 9:6 [u] Ge 33:18; 37:12; Jos 17:7; 20:7; 24:1; Jdg 8:31; 21:19; 1Ki 12:1; Ps 60:6; 108:7 [v] S Ge 10:18 **12:7** [w] Ge 17:1; 18:1; 26:2; 35:1; Ex 6:3; Ac 7:2 [x] Ex 3:8; Nu 10:29; Dt 30:5; Heb 11:8 [y] Ge 13:15, 17; 15:18; 17:8; 23:18; 24:7; 26:3-4; 28:13; 35:12; 48:4; 50:24; Ex 6:4, 8; 13:5, 11; 32:13; 33:1; Nu 11:12; Dt 1:8; 2:31; 9:5; 11:9; 34:4; 2Ki 25:21; 1Ch 16:16; 2Ch 20:7; Ps 105:9-11; Jer 25:5; Eze 47:14; Ac 7:5; Ro 4:13; Gal 3:16* [z] S Ge 8:20; 13:4

12:1 *had said.* God had spoken to Abram "while he was still in Mesopotamia, before he lived in Haran" (Ac 7:2; see note there). *Leave ... show you.* Abram must leave the settled world of the post-Babel nations and begin a pilgrimage with God to a better world of God's making (see 24:7; see also 11:1 – 9; Heb 11:10 and notes).

Here begins the story of how "the LORD [Yahweh] ... the God of Abraham, Isaac and Jacob" (Ex 3:16), "the God of Israel" (Ex 5:1), created for himself a people who acknowledged him as the only true God and who had as their homeland a place in the world that would be called "the LORD's [Yahweh's] land" (Jos 22:9) and even "the place ... you [Yahweh] made for your dwelling, the sanctuary ... your hands established" (Ex 15:17). In the ancient world of the OT, all the various gods that were worshiped and relied on were gods of a particular place and/or a particular people (a family, tribe, or nation — the choice of the gods to be venerated by the social unit resting in the hands of the communal leader[s]). The most effective way for the true God to break into such a religious world and gain world recognition was to establish a relationship with a patriarchal head of household and call him away from his idolatrous clan and from the place(s) with which its gods were linked and to establish that patriarch's household as the beginnings of a people who acknowledged only him as their God, and then locate them in a place/land that he claimed as his own. That is the program that Yahweh initiated with his summons to Abram to leave family and homeland and begin a prilgrimage led by Yahweh that would bring the nations to acknowledge that the God of Abraham, the God of Israel, is the only true God. The rest of Yahweh's dealings with the patriarchs and with Israel is the central focus of the OT Scriptures, which relate how that pilgrimage moved ever forward toward the fulfillment of Yahweh's purposes.

12:2 – 3 God's promise to Abram has a sevenfold structure: (1) "I will make you into a great nation," (2) "I will bless you," (3) "I will make your name great," (4) "you will be a blessing," or possibly "you will be seen as blessed," (5) "I will bless those who bless you," (6) "whoever curses you I will curse," and (7) "all peoples on earth will be blessed through you," or possibly "all peoples on earth will use your name in blessings" — as in 48:20. God's original blessing on the whole human race (1:28) would be especially fulfilled in the lives of Abram and his offspring. In various ways and degrees, these promises were reaffirmed to Abram (v. 7; 15:5 – 21; 17:4 – 8; 18:18 – 19; 22:17 – 18), to Isaac (26:2 – 4), to Jacob (28:13 – 15; 35:11 – 12; 46:3) and to Moses (Ex 3:6 – 8; 6:2 – 8). The seventh promise is quoted in Ac 3:25 with reference to Peter's Jewish listeners (Ac 3:12) — Abram's physical descendants — and in Gal 3:8 with reference to Paul's Gentile listeners — Abram's spiritual descendants.

12:3 *whoever curses you.* The ancient Near Eastern peoples thought that by pronouncing curses on someone they could bring down the power of the gods (or other mysterious powers) on that person (cf. 1Sa 17:43). They had a large conventional stock of such curses, preserved in many sources, such as the Egyptian Execration Texts, the Hittite suzerainty-vassal treaties, *kudurrus* (stone boundary markers [see note on Dt 19:14]), the Code of Hammurapi (Epilogue), etc. For examples see notes on Dt 9:14; Jer 15:3; see also note on Ge 27:33; cf. note on Ezr 6:11.

12:4 *Abram left, as the LORD had told him.* See Heb 11:8 and note. Prompt obedience grounded in faith characterized this patriarch throughout his life (see 17:23; 21:14; 22:3 and notes) — which served as a model for all of Abram's descendants. *Lot went with him.* See 13:1,5 and note on 13:5 – 18. Lot chose to go with his uncle Abram, seeking a better future. *seventy-five years old.* Although advanced in age at the time of his call, Abram would live for another full century (see 25:7 and note; see also note on 5:5).

12:5 *people they had acquired.* Wealthy people in that ancient world always had servants in their employ. Some were slaves, others were servants by choice; all were considered to be members of the "household" in which they served (see 14:14; 15:3; 17:12 – 13; 24:2).

12:6 *site of the great tree.* Perhaps the same tree referred to in 35:4 (see note there; see also Jdg 9:6,37). *Moreh.* The name means "teacher." It suggests that the Canaanites sought directions from their gods by this tree. *Shechem.* An important city in central Canaan, founded in the patriarchal period.

12:7 *The LORD appeared.* The Lord at times "appeared" in some way to the patriarchs and others, but not in all his glory (see Ex 33:18 – 20; Jn 1:18 and notes). *altar.* The first of several Abram built (see v. 8; 13:18; 22:9). He acknowledged that the land of Canaan belonged to the Lord in a special way (see Ex 20:24; Jos 22:19 and note).

12:8 *Bethel.* Just north of Jerusalem (see map, p. 497), it was an important town in the religious history of God's ancient people (see, e.g., 28:10 – 22; 35:1 – 15 and notes; 1Ki 12:26 – 29 and note on 12:29).

east of Bethel[a] and pitched his tent,[b] with
Bethel on the west and Ai[c] on the east.
There he built an altar to the LORD and
called on the name of the LORD.[d] 9Then
Abram set out and continued toward the
Negev.[e]

Abram in Egypt

12:10-20Ref — Ge 20:1-18; 26:1-11

10Now there was a famine in the land,[f]
and Abram went down to Egypt to live
there for a while because the famine was
severe.[g] 11As he was about to enter Egypt,
he said to his wife Sarai,[h] "I know what
a beautiful woman[i] you are. 12When the
Egyptians see you, they will say, 'This is
his wife.' Then they will kill me but will let
you live. 13Say you are my sister,[j] so that I

12:8 [a] Ge 13:3; 28:11, 19; 35:1, 8, 15; Jos 7:2; 8:9; 1Sa 7:16; 1Ki 12:29; Hos 12:4; Am 3:14; 4:4 [b] Ge 26:25; 33:19; Heb 11:9 [c] Jos 7:2; 12:9; Ezr 2:28; Ne 7:32; Jer 49:3 [d] S Ge 4:26; S 8:20 **12:9** [e] Ge 13:1, 3; 20:1; 24:62; Nu 13:17; 33:40; Dt 34:3; Jos 10:40 **12:10** [f] Ge 41:27, 57; 42:5; 43:1; 47:4, 13; Ru 1:1; 2Sa 21:1; 2Ki 8:1; Ps 105:19 [g] Ge 41:30, 54, 56; 47:20; Ps 105:16 **12:11** [h] S Ge 11:29 [i] ver 14; Ge 24:16; 26:7; 29:17; 39:6 **12:13** [j] Ge 20:2; 26:7

12:9 *Negev.* The dry wasteland stretching southward from Beersheba (see map No. 2 at the end of this study Bible). This Hebrew word is translated "south" in 13:14.

12:10 *went down to Egypt ... because the famine was severe.* Egypt's food supply was usually plentiful because the Nile's water supply was normally dependable. Abram's experience in this episode foreshadows Israel's later experience in Egypt, as the author of Genesis, writing after the exodus, was very much aware. The parallels are striking: a famine in the land (here; 47:4); affliction at the hands of the Egyptians (vv. 12 – 15; Ex 1:11 – 14); God's plagues on the Egyptians (v. 17; Ex 8 – 11); the Egyptians sending the people away as a result (vv. 19 – 20; Ex 12:31 – 32); the Egyptians letting them take with them all their possessions (v. 20; Ex 12:32); the people obtaining wealth from the Egyptians (v. 16; Ex 12:36); return to Canaan by stages through the desert (13:1 – 3; Exodus; Numbers; Deuteronomy; Joshua); arrival back in Canaan, where they worship the Lord (13:4; Jos 5:10; 8:30 – 35; 24:1 – 27). Abram was truly the "father" of Israel.

12:11 *As he was about to enter Egypt.* Having left the promised land to find food in a time of famine (see Ru 1:1), but doing so without God's guidance or consent

Integrated Chronology of the Patriarchs

ABRAHAM	Birth of ISAAC*	Birth of Esau and JACOB*	Birth of JOSEPH
AGE 75 To Canaan*			
100	(Birth of ISAAC*)		
140	AGE 40 Isaac's marriage*		
160	60	(Birth of Esau and JACOB*)	
175 Abraham's death*	75	AGE 15	
	100	40 Esau's marriage*	
	137	77 Jacob to Paddan Aram	
	151	91	(Birth of JOSEPH)
	157	97 Jacob's return to Canaan	AGE 6
	168	108	17 Joseph to Egypt*
	180 Isaac's death*	120	29
		121	30 Joseph enters Pharaoh's service*
		130 Jacob to Egypt*	39
		147 Jacob's death*	56
			110 Joseph's death*

Note: The ages marked with (*) are expressly given.

will be treated well for your sake and my
life will be spared because of you."
14When Abram came to Egypt, the Egyptians saw that she was a very beautiful
woman.[k] 15And when Pharaoh's officials
saw her, they praised her to Pharaoh, and
she was taken into his palace. 16He treated
Abram well for her sake, and Abram acquired sheep and cattle, male and female
donkeys, menservants and maidservants,
and camels.[l]
17But the LORD inflicted[m] serious diseases on Pharaoh and his household[n] because
of Abram's wife Sarai. 18So Pharaoh summoned Abram. "What have you done to
me?"[o] he said. "Why didn't you tell me
she was your wife?[p] 19Why did you say,
'She is my sister,'[q] so that I took her to
be my wife? Now then, here is your wife.
Take her and go!" 20Then Pharaoh gave orders about Abram to his men, and they
sent him on his way, with his wife and
everything he had.

Abram and Lot Separate

13 So Abram went up from Egypt[r] to the
Negev,[s] with his wife and everything
he had, and Lot[t] went with him. 2Abram
had become very wealthy[u] in livestock[v]
and in silver and gold.
3From the Negev[w] he went from place to
place until he came to Bethel,[x] to the place
between Bethel and Ai[y] where his tent had
been earlier 4and where he had first built
an altar.[z] There Abram called on the name
of the LORD.[a]
5Now Lot,[b] who was moving about
with Abram, also had flocks and herds
and tents. 6But the land could not support
them while they stayed together, for their
possessions were so great that they were
not able to stay together.[c] 7And quarreling[d]
arose between Abram's herdsmen and the
herdsmen of Lot. The Canaanites[e] and
Perizzites[f] were also living in the land[g] at
that time.
8So Abram said to Lot,[h] "Let's not have
any quarreling between you and me,[i] or
between your herdsmen and mine, for we
are brothers.[j] 9Is not the whole land before you? Let's part company. If you go to
the left, I'll go to the right; if you go to the
right, I'll go to the left."[k]
10Lot looked up and saw that the whole
plain[l] of the Jordan[m] was well watered, like
the garden of the LORD,[n] like the land of
Egypt,[o] toward Zoar.[p] (This was before the
LORD destroyed Sodom[q] and Gomorrah.)[r]
11So Lot chose for himself the whole plain
of the Jordan and set out toward the east.
The two men parted company: 12Abram
lived in the land of Canaan,[s] while Lot[t]
lived among the cities of the plain[u] and

12:14 [k]S ver 11 **12:16** [l]S ver 5; Ge 24:35; 26:14; 30:43; 32:5; 34:23; 47:17; Job 1:3; 31:25 **12:17** [m]2Ki 15:5; Job 30:11; Isa 53:4, 10 [n]1Ch 16:21; Ps 105:14 **12:18** [o]Ge 20:9; 26:10; 29:25; 31:26; 44:15 [p]Isa 43:27; 51:2; Eze 16:3 **12:19** [q]Ge 20:5; 26:9 **13:1** [r]Ge 45:25 [s]S Ge 12:9 [t]S Ge 11:27 **13:2** [u]S Ge 12:5; 26:13; Pr 10:22 [v]Ge 32:15; Job 1:3; 42:12 **13:3** [w]S Ge 12:9 [x]S Ge 12:8 [y]Jos 7:2 **13:4** [z]S Ge 12:7 [a]S Ge 4:26 **13:5** [b]S Ge 11:27 **13:6** [c]S Ge 12:5; 33:9; 36:7 **13:7** [d]Ge 26:20, 21; Nu 20:3 [e]S Ge 10:18 [f]Ge 15:20; 34:30; Ex 3:8; Jdg 1:4 [g]Ge 12:6; 34:30 **13:8** [h]S Ge 11:27 [i]Pr 15:18; 20:3 [j]Ge 19:9; Ex 2:14; Nu 16:13; Ps 133:1 **13:9** [k]Ge 20:15; 34:10; 47:6; Jer 40:4 **13:10** [l]1Ki 7:46; 2Ch 4:17 [m]Nu 13:29; 33:48 [n]Ge 2:8-10; Isa 51:3; Eze 31:8-9 [o]Ge 46:7 [p]Ge 14:2; 19:22, 30; Dt 34:3; Isa 15:5; Jer 48:34 [q]Dt 29:23; Job 39:6; Ps 107:34; Jer 4:26 [r]Ge 14:8; 19:17-29 **13:12** [s]S Ge 10:19 [t]S Ge 11:27 [u]S ver 10; Ge 19:17, 25, 29

(see 46:3–4; 2Ki 8:1), Abram showed that he needed to learn that the God who had called him and made promises to him could and would protect him and Sarai (see v. 3) even outside the promised land (see also ch. 20). Abram's attempt to secure his own safety matches Sarai's attempt to overcome her own barrenness (see ch. 16). *beautiful.* See v. 14. She was 65 at the time (see v. 4; 17:17). The Genesis Apocryphon (one of the Dead Sea Scrolls) praises Sarai's beauty.

12:13 *Say you are my sister.* If the pharaoh were to add Sarai to his harem while knowing that she was Abram's wife, he would have to kill Abram first.

12:15 *Pharaoh.* See note on Ex 1:11.

12:16 Livestock was an important measure of wealth in ancient times (see 13:2). *menservants and maidservants.* See note on v. 5. *camels.* Although camels were not widely used until much later (see, e.g., Jdg 6:5), archaeology has confirmed their occasional domestication as early as the patriarchal period.

12:19 *Why did you say, 'She is my sister' . . . ?* Egyptian ethics emphasized the importance of absolute truthfulness, and Abram was put in the uncomfortable position of being exposed as a liar.

12:20 *Pharaoh gave orders.* See Ex 12:31–32.

13:1,3 *Negev.* See note on 12:9.

13:2 *had become very wealthy.* Abram left Egypt with greater wealth than he had before—even as Israel would later leave Egypt laden with wealth from the Egyptians (Ex 3:22; 12:36).

13:4 *Abram called on the name of the LORD.* As he had done earlier at the same place (12:8).

13:5–18 Lot's separation from Abram and his choice of what appeared to him to be the most promising portion of the land alienated him from participating in the blessings promised to Abram. Rather, he became involved in the history of Sodom and Gomorrah (see 14:12–16; 19:1–38), whereas Abram received assurances that his descendants would multiply and would inherit the whole land (vv. 15–17).

13:6 *land could not support them.* Livestock made up the greater part of their possessions, and the region around Bethel and Ai did not have enough water or pasture for such large flocks and herds (see v. 10; 26:17–22,32; 36:7).

13:7 *Perizzites.* Their identity remains obscure, but reference may be to rural inhabitants in contrast to city dwellers.

13:8 *brothers.* Relatives (as often in the Bible).

13:9 *left . . . right.* Abram, always generous, gave his young nephew the opportunity to choose the land he wanted. He himself would not obtain wealth except by the Lord's blessing (see 14:22–24).

13:10 *plain.* The Hebrew for this word picturesquely describes this area as oval in shape. The precise location of the "plain" and its "cities" (v. 12) is still disputed. One plausible proposal locates them just southeast of the Dead Sea; another proposal locates them just northeast of the Dead Sea. *like the land of Egypt.* Because of its abundant and dependable water supply (see note on 12:10), Egypt came close to matching Eden's ideal conditions (see 2:10). *the LORD destroyed Sodom and Gomorrah.* See especially 18:16—19:29. The names of Sodom and Gomorrah became proverbial for vile wickedness and for divine judgment on sin (see note on Eze 16:47).

13:12 *Lot . . . pitched his tents near Sodom.* Since the people of Sodom were known to be wicked (see v. 13), Lot was flirting with temptation by choosing to live near them. Contrast the actions of Abram (v. 18).

pitched his tents near Sodom.[v] 13Now the
men of Sodom[w] were wicked and were
sinning greatly against the LORD.[x]
14The LORD said to Abram after Lot had
parted from him, "Lift up your eyes from
where you are and look north and south,
east and west.[y] 15All the land that you see
I will give to you and your offspring[a] forever.[z] 16I will make your offspring like the
dust of the earth, so that if anyone could
count the dust, then your offspring could
be counted.[a] 17Go, walk through the length
and breadth of the land,[b] for I am giving
it to you."[c]
18So Abram moved his tents and went to
live near the great trees of Mamre[d] at Hebron,[e] where he built an altar to the LORD.[f]

Abram Rescues Lot

14 At this time Amraphel king of Shinar,[b][g] Arioch king of Ellasar, Kedorlaomer[h] king of Elam[i] and Tidal king of Goiim
2went to war against Bera king of Sodom,
Birsha king of Gomorrah, Shinab king of
Admah, Shemeber king of Zeboiim,[j] and
the king of Bela (that is, Zoar).[k] 3All these
latter kings joined forces in the Valley of
Siddim[l] (the Salt Sea[c][m]). 4For twelve years
they had been subject to Kedorlaomer,[n] but
in the thirteenth year they rebelled.
5In the fourteenth year, Kedorlaomer[o]
and the kings allied with him went out
and defeated the Rephaites[p] in Ashteroth
Karnaim, the Zuzites in Ham, the Emites[q]
in Shaveh Kiriathaim 6and the Horites[r] in
the hill country of Seir,[s] as far as El Paran[t]
near the desert. 7Then they turned back
and went to En Mishpat (that is, Kadesh),[u]
and they conquered the whole territory of
the Amalekites,[v] as well as the Amorites[w]
who were living in Hazazon Tamar.[x]
8Then the king of Sodom, the king of
Gomorrah,[y] the king of Admah, the king
of Zeboiim[z] and the king of Bela (that is,
Zoar)[a] marched out and drew up their battle lines in the Valley of Siddim[b] 9against
Kedorlaomer[c] king of Elam,[d] Tidal king of
Goiim, Amraphel king of Shinar and Arioch king of Ellasar—four kings against
five. 10Now the Valley of Siddim[e] was full
of tar[f] pits, and when the kings of Sodom
and Gomorrah[g] fled, some of the men fell
into them and the rest fled to the hills.[h]
11The four kings seized all the goods[i] of
Sodom and Gomorrah and all their food;
then they went away. 12They also carried
off Abram's nephew Lot[j] and his possessions, since he was living in Sodom.
13One who had escaped came and reported this to Abram the Hebrew.[k] Now Abram

[a] *15* Or *seed*; also in verse 16 [b] *1* That is, Babylonia; also in verse 9 [c] *3* That is, the Dead Sea

13:12 [v]Ge 14:12 **13:13** [w]Ge 19:4; Isa 1:10; 3:9 [x]Ge 18:20; 19:5; 20:6; 39:9; Nu 32:23; 1Sa 12:23; 2Sa 12:13; Ps 51:4; Eze 16:49-50; 2Pe 2:8 **13:14** [y]Ge 28:14; 32:12; 48:16; Dt 3:27; 13:17; Isa 54:3 **13:15** [z]S Ge 12:7; Gal 3:16* **13:16** [a]S Ge 12:2; 16:10; 17:20; 21:13, 18; 25:16; Nu 23:10 **13:17** [b]ver 15; Nu 13:17-25 [c]S Ge 12:7; 15:7 **13:18** [d]Ge 14:13, 24; 18:1; 23:17, 19; 25:9; 49:30; 50:13 [e]Ge 23:2; 35:27; 37:14; Nu 13:22; Jos 10:3, 36; Jdg 1:10; 1Sa 30:31; 2Sa 2:1, 3, 11; 1Ch 11:1 [f]S Ge 8:20 **14:1** [g]S Ge 10:10 [h]ver 4, 9, 17 [i]S Ge 10:22 **14:2** [j]S Ge 10:19 [k]S Ge 13:10 **14:3** [l]ver 8, 10 [m]Nu 34:3, 12; Dt 3:17; Jos 3:16; 12:3; 15:2, 5; 18:19 **14:4** [n]S ver 1 **14:5** [o]S ver 1 [p]Ge 15:20; Dt 2:11, 20; 3:11, 13; Jos 12:4; 13:12; 17:15; 1Ch 20:4 [q]Dt 2:10 **14:6** [r]Ge 36:20; Dt 2:12, 22 [s]Ge 32:3; 33:14, 16; 36:8; Dt 1:2; 2:1, 5, 22; Jos 11:17; 24:4; 1Ch 4:42; Isa 34:5; Eze 25:8; 35:2; Am 1:6 [t]Ge 21:21; Nu 10:12; 12:16; 13:3, 26; Hab 3:3 **14:7** [u]Ge 16:14; 20:1; Nu 13:26; 20:1; 32:8; Dt 1:2; Jos 10:41; Jdg 11:16; Ps 29:8 [v]Ex 17:8; Nu 13:29; 14:25; 24:20; Dt 25:17; Jdg 3:13; 6:3; 10:12; 12:15; 1Sa 14:48; 15:2; 28:18; 2Sa 1:1; 1Ch 4:43; Ps 83:7 [w]Nu 13:29; Dt 1:4; Jos 2:10; 13:4 [x]2Ch 20:2; Eze 48:28 **14:8** [y]S Ge 13:10 [z]Dt 29:23; Hos 11:8 [a]S Ge 13:10 [b]S ver 3 **14:9** [c]S ver 1 [d]S Ge 10:22 **14:10** [e]S ver 3 [f]Ge 11:3 [g]ver 17, 21 [h]Ge 19:17, 30; Jos 2:16; Ps 11:1 **14:11** [i]ver 16, 21 **14:12** [j]S Ge 11:27 **14:13** [k]Ge 37:28; 39:14, 17; 40:15; 41:12; 43:32; Ex 3:18; 1Sa 4:6; 14:11

13:14 *Lift up your eyes . . . and look.* See Dt 34:1–4. Lot and Abram are a study in contrasts. The former looked selfishly and coveted (v. 10); the latter looked as God commanded and was blessed.

13:16 *like the dust of the earth.* A simile (one commonly used in the ancient Near East) for the large number of Abram's offspring (see 28:14; 2Ch 1:9 and note; see also Nu 23:10). Similar phrases are: "as numerous as the stars in the sky" and "as the sand on the seashore" (22:17).

13:17 *walk through the length . . . of the land.* Either to inspect it or to claim the right to live in it while looking forward to the promised ownership (cf. Dt 32:48–49).

13:18 *great trees.* See note on 12:6. *Mamre.* A town named after one of Abram's allies (see 14:13). *Hebron.* Kiriath Arba (see note on 23:2). *altar.* See note on 12:7.

14:1–24 Abram's act of faith successfully challenged the foreign kings who were seeking to bring the promised land under their sphere of rule and enabled him to rescue his nephew Lot. It also won for him and his God recognition among kings that they were a force to be reckoned with (see 12:2: "I will make your name great") and provided him with an opportunity to bear witness to his God.

14:1 *Amraphel king of Shinar.* Not the great Babylonian king Hammurapi, as once thought. *Elam.* See note on 10:22. *Goiim.* The Hebrew word means "Gentile nations" and may be a common noun here (as in Isa 9:1).

14:3 *Salt Sea.* The Dead Sea, whose water contains an approximately five times greater concentration of chloride and bromide salts than the water in the world's oceans, making it the densest large body of water on earth.

14:5 *Rephaites.* People of large stature (see Dt 3:11).

14:6 *Horites.* Formerly thought to be cave dwellers (the Hebrew word *hor* means "cave"), they are now commonly identified with the Hurrians, a non-Semitic people widely dispersed throughout the ancient Near East.

14:7 *En Mishpat.* Another name for Kadesh, it means "spring of judgment/justice." It is called Meribah Kadesh, "quarreling/litigation at Kadesh," in Dt 32:51 (see Nu 27:14). *Kadesh.* Located in the southwest Negev (see note on 12:9), it was later called Kadesh Barnea (see Nu 32:8). *territory of the Amalekites.* Reference is to a region later occupied by a semi-nomadic tribal people descended from Esau (36:12,16; 1Ch 1:36). Usually associated with the Negev (Nu 13:29) or the Sinai peninsula (Ex 17:8–9), they at times wandered from this territory (see Nu 14:25,43,45; Jdg 5:14 and note), often allying themselves with other peoples hostile to Israel (Nu 14:43,45; Jdg 3:13; 5:14; 6:3,33). *Amorites.* See note on 10:16. *Hazazon Tamar.* See note on Eze 47:18.

14:10 *tar pits.* Lumps of asphalt are often seen even today floating in the southern end of the Dead Sea. *hills.* The Dead Sea, the lowest body of water on earth (about 1,300 feet below sea level), is flanked by hills on both sides.

14:12 *Lot . . . was living in Sodom.* He moved into the town and was living among its wicked people (see 2Pe 2:8). Though Lot was "righteous," he was now in danger of imitating the "filthy lives of lawless men" (2Pe 2:7; see note there).

14:13 *Hebrew.* Abram, the father of the Hebrew people, is the first Biblical character to be called a Hebrew (see "Eber" in note on 10:21). Usually an ethnic term in the Bible, it was normally used by non-Israelites in a dis-

was living near the great trees of Mamre[l]
the Amorite, a brother[a] of Eshcol[m] and
Aner, all of whom were allied with Abram.
14When Abram heard that his relative[n] had
been taken captive, he called out the 318
trained[o] men born in his household[p] and
went in pursuit as far as Dan.[q] 15During
the night Abram divided his men[r] to attack
them and he routed them, pursuing them
as far as Hobah, north of Damascus.[s] 16He
recovered[t] all the goods[u] and brought back
his relative Lot and his possessions, together with the women and the other people.

17After Abram returned from defeating
Kedorlaomer[v] and the kings allied with
him, the king of Sodom[w] came out to meet
him in the Valley of Shaveh (that is, the
King's Valley).[x]

18Then Melchizedek[y] king of Salem[b][z]
brought out bread[a] and wine.[b] He was
priest of God Most High,[c] 19and he blessed
Abram,[d] saying,

> "Blessed be Abram by God Most High,[e]
> Creator[c] of heaven and earth.[f]
> 20And blessed be[d] God Most High,[g]
> who delivered your enemies into
> your hand."

Then Abram gave him a tenth of everything.[h]

21The king of Sodom[i] said to Abram,
"Give me the people and keep the goods[j]
for yourself."

22But Abram said to the king of Sodom,[k]
"I have raised my hand[l] to the LORD, God
Most High,[m] Creator of heaven and earth,[n]
and have taken an oath 23that I will accept nothing belonging to you,[o] not even a
thread or the thong of a sandal, so that you
will never be able to say, 'I made Abram
rich.' 24I will accept nothing but what my
men have eaten and the share that belongs
to the men who went with me—to Aner,
Eshcol and Mamre.[p] Let them have their
share."

God's Covenant With Abram

15 After this, the word of the LORD came
to Abram[q] in a vision:[r]

> "Do not be afraid,[s] Abram.
> I am your shield,[e][t]
> your very great reward.[f][u]"

2But Abram said, "O Sovereign LORD,[v]
what can you give me since I remain

[a] 13 Or *a relative*; or *an ally* [b] 18 That is, Jerusalem [c] 19 Or *Possessor*; also in verse 22 [d] 20 Or *And praise be to* [e] 1 Or *sovereign* [f] 1 Or *shield; / your reward will be very great*

14:13 [l] ver 24; S Ge 13:18 [m] Nu 13:23; 32:9; Dt 1:24 **14:14** [n] ver 12 [o] Dt 4:9; Pr 22:6 [p] S Ge 12:5 [q] Dt 34:1; Jdg 18:29; 1Ki 15:20 **14:15** [r] Jdg 7:16 [s] Ge 15:2; 2Sa 8:5; 1Ki 20:34; 2Ki 16:9; Isa 7:8; 8:4; 10:9; 17:1; Jer 49:23, 27; Eze 27:18; Am 1:3-5 **14:16** [t] 1Sa 30:8, 18 [u] S ver 11 **14:17** [v] S ver 1 [w] S ver 10 [x] 2Sa 18:18 **14:18** [y] Ps 110:4; Heb 5:6; 7:17, 21 [z] Ps 76:2; Heb 7:2 [a] S Ge 3:19 [b] Jdg 9:13; 19:19; Est 1:10; Ps 104:15; Pr 31:6; Ecc 10:19; SS 1:2 [c] ver 22; Ps 7:8, 17; Da 7:27 **14:19** [d] Heb 7:6 [e] ver 18 [f] ver 22; S Ge 1:1; 24:3; Jos 2:11; Ps 148:5; Mt 11:25 **14:20** [g] S Ge 9:26; S 24:27 [h] Ge 28:22; Dt 14:22; 26:12; Lk 18:12; Heb 7:4 **14:21** [i] S ver 10 [j] S ver 11 **14:22** [k] S ver 10 [l] Ex 6:8; Nu 14:30; Dt 32:40; Ne 9:15; Eze 20:5; Da 12:7; Rev 10:5-6 [m] S ver 18 [n] S ver 19 **14:23** [o] 1Sa 15:3, 19; 2Ki 5:16; Est 8:11; 9:10, 15 **14:24** [p] S Ge 13:18 **15:1** [q] 1Sa 15:10; 2Sa 7:4; 1Ki 6:11; 12:22; Jer 1:13; Eze 3:16; Da 10:1 [r] Ge 46:2; Nu 12:6; 24:4; Ru 1:20; Job 33:15 [s] Ge 21:17; 26:24; 46:3; Ex 14:13; 20:20; 2Ki 6:16; 2Ch 20:15, 17; Ps 27:1; Isa 7:4; 41:10, 13-14; 43:1, 5; Jer 1:8; Hag 2:5 [t] Dt 33:29; 2Sa 22:3, 31; Ps 3:3; 5:12; 18:2; 28:7; 33:20; 84:11; 119:114; 144:2; Pr 2:7; 30:5 [u] Ps 18:20; 37:25; 58:11; Isa 3:10 **15:2** [v] ver 8; Isa 49:22; Jer 44:26; Eze 5:11; 16:48

---

paraging sense (see, e.g., 39:17). Outside the Bible, people known as the Habiru/Apiru (a word probably related to the word "Hebrew") are referred to as a propertyless, dependent, immigrant (foreign) social class rather than as a specific ethnic group. Negative descriptions of them are given in the Amarna letters (clay tablets found in Egypt; see chart, p. xxii). *Mamre.* A town was named after him (see 13:18 and note).

14:14 *318 trained men born in his household.* A clear indication of Abram's great wealth. The Hebrew for "trained men" is found only here in the Bible. A related word used elsewhere in very ancient texts means "armed retainers." *Dan.* This well-known city in the north was not given the name "Dan" until the days of the judges (see Jdg 18:29). It was formerly called Laish or Leshem (see note on Jdg 18:7). Thus the designation here is most likely a later editorial updating.

14:17 *King's Valley.* Near Jerusalem (see 2Sa 18:18).

14:18 *Melchizedek king of Salem … priest.* See Heb 7:1. In ancient times, particularly in non-Israelite circles, kingly and priestly duties were often performed by the same individual. "Melchizedek" means "My king is righteous" or "king of righteousness" (Heb 7:2). "Salem" is a shortened form of "Jerusalem" (Ps 76:2) and is related to the Hebrew word for "peace" (Heb 7:2; see Jos 10:1 and note). *bread and wine.* An ordinary meal (see Jdg 19:19), in no way related to the NT ordinance of communion. Melchizedek's interest in Abram's military success was most likely political, and his entertainment of victorious Abram with refreshment and a priestly benediction constituted a recognition that Abram was a man to be reckoned with in kingly affairs.

14:19 *God Most High, Creator of heaven and earth.* The titles "most high," "lord of heaven" and "creator of earth" were frequently applied to the chief Canaanite deity in ancient times. But Abram, by identifying Melchizedek's "God Most High" with "the LORD" (see v. 22), bore testimony to the one true God.

14:20 *Abram gave him a tenth of everything.* A tenth was a king's share (see 1Sa 8:15,17 and note on 8:15). By offering Melchizedek a tenth, Abram responded to Melchizedek's action by showing that he in turn acknowledged his kingship in Salem. At the same time, having recognized Melchizedek's blessing as a benediction from the Lord, Abram's tithe to Melchizedek constituted a declaration that he would be indebted to no king but the Lord (see v. 23 and note). Melchizedek is later spoken of as a type or prefiguration of Jesus, our "great high priest" (Heb 4:14), whose priesthood is therefore "in the order of Melchizedek, not in the order of Aaron" (Heb 7:11; see note there; see also Ps 110:4 and note).

14:22 *I have raised my hand.* A standard oath-taking practice in ancient times (see Dt 32:40; Rev 10:5–6).

14:23 *I will accept nothing belonging to you.* Cf. 2Ki 5:16 and note. Abram refused to let himself become obligated to anyone but the Lord. If he had done so, this Canaanite king might later have claimed the right of kingship over Abram.

15:1–21 Here for the first time the Lord introduces a covenant into his relationship with Abram. In response to Abram's faltering faith, he graciously reinforces his promise (cf. 12:2–3) with a covenant oath.

15:1 *I am your shield.* Whether "shield" or "sovereign" is meant (see NIV text note), the reference is to the Lord as Abram's King. As elsewhere, "shield" stands for king (e.g., Dt 33:29; 2Sa 22:3; Ps 7:10; 84:9). *your very great reward.* Though Abram was quite rich (13:2; 14:23), God himself was Abram's greatest treasure (cf. Dt 10:9).

15:2 *Eliezer of Damascus.* A servant probably acquired by Abram on his journey southward from Haran (see 12:5). He may also be the unnamed "chief servant" of 24:2 (see note there).

childless[w] and the one who will inherit[a]
my estate is Eliezer of Damascus?[x]" 3And
Abram said, "You have given me no children; so a servant[y] in my household[z] will
be my heir."
4Then the word of the LORD came to
him: "This man will not be your heir, but
a son coming from your own body will
be your heir.[a]" 5He took him outside and
said, "Look up at the heavens and count
the stars[b]—if indeed you can count them."
Then he said to him, "So shall your offspring be."[c]
6Abram believed the LORD, and he credited it to him as righteousness.[d]
7He also said to him, "I am the LORD,
who brought you out[e] of Ur of the Chaldeans[f] to give you this land to take possession of it."[g]
8But Abram said, "O Sovereign LORD,[h]
how can I know[i] that I will gain possession of it?"[j]
9So the LORD said to him, "Bring me a
heifer,[k] a goat and a ram, each three years
old,[l] along with a dove and a young pigeon.[m]"
10Abram brought all these to him, cut
them in two and arranged the halves opposite each other;[n] the birds, however, he
did not cut in half.[o] 11Then birds of prey
came down on the carcasses,[p] but Abram
drove them away.
12As the sun was setting, Abram fell into
a deep sleep,[q] and a thick and dreadful
darkness came over him. 13Then the LORD
said to him, "Know for certain that your
descendants will be strangers in a country
not their own, and they will be enslaved[r]
and mistreated four hundred years.[s] 14But I
will punish the nation they serve as slaves,
and afterward they will come out[t] with
great possessions.[u] 15You, however, will
go to your fathers[v] in peace and be buried
at a good old age.[w] 16In the fourth generation[x] your descendants will come back
here,[y] for the sin of the Amorites[z] has not
yet reached its full measure."
17When the sun had set and darkness
had fallen, a smoking firepot with a blazing torch[a] appeared and passed between
the pieces.[b] 18On that day the LORD made
a covenant with Abram[c] and said, "To
your descendants I give this land,[d] from
the river[b] of Egypt[e] to the great river, the

[a] *2* The meaning of the Hebrew for this phrase is uncertain. [b] *18* Or *Wadi*

15:2 [w] Ac 7:5 [x] S Ge 14:15 **15:3** [y] Ge 24:2, 34 [z] S Ge 12:5 **15:4** [a] Gal 4:28 **15:5** [b] Job 11:8; 35:5; Ps 8:3; 147:4; Jer 33:22 [c] S Ge 12:2; S Jer 30:19; Ro 4:18*; Heb 11:12 **15:6** [d] Ps 106:31; Ro 4:3*, 20-24*; Gal 3:6*; Jas 2:23* **15:7** [e] Ge 12:1; Ex 20:2; Ac 7:3; Heb 11:8 [f] S Ge 11:28; Ac 7:4 [g] S Ge 13:17; 17:8; 28:4; 35:12; 48:4; Ex 6:8; Dt 9:5 **15:8** [h] S ver 2 [i] Lk 1:18 [j] Dt 12:20; 19:8 **15:9** [k] Nu 19:2; Dt 21:3; Hos 4:16; Am 4:1 [l] 1Sa 1:24 [m] Lev 1:14; 5:7, 11; 12:8 **15:10** [n] ver 17; Jer 34:18 [o] Lev 1:17; 5:8 **15:11** [p] Dt 28:26; Jer 7:33 **15:12** [q] S Ge 2:21 **15:13** [r] Ex 1:11; 3:7; 5:6, 10-14, 18; 6:5; Dt 5:15; Job 3:18 [s] ver 16; Ex 12:40; Nu 20:15; Ac 7:6, 17; Gal 3:17 **15:14** [t] Ge 50:24; Ex 3:8; 6:6-8; 12:25; Nu 10:29; Jos 1:2; Ac 7:7* [u] Ex 12:32-38 **15:15** [v] Ge 47:30; 49:29; Dt 31:16; 2Sa 7:12; 1Ki 1:21; Ps 49:19 [w] Ge 25:8; 35:29; Ex 23:26; Dt 34:7; Jos 14:11; Jdg 8:32; 1Ch 29:28; Job 5:26; 21:23; 42:17; Ps 91:16; Pr 3:16; 9:11; Isa 65:20 **15:16** [x] S ver 13; Ex 12:40 [y] Ge 28:15; 46:4; 48:21; 50:24; Ex 3:8, 17 [z] Lev 18:28; Jos 13:4; Jdg 10:11; 1Ki 21:26; 2Ki 16:3; 21:11; Eze 16:3 **15:17** [a] Jdg 7:16, 20; 15:4, 5 [b] S ver 10 **15:18** [c] Ge 17:2, 4, 7; Ex 6:4; 34:10, 27; 1Ch 16:16; Ps 105:9 [d] S Ge 12:7 [e] Nu 34:5; Jos 15:4, 47; 1Ki 8:65; 2Ki 24:7; 2Ch 7:8; Isa 27:12; Jer 37:5; 46:2; La 4:17; Eze 30:22; 47:19

15:3–4 Ancient documents uncovered at Nuzi (see chart, p. xxiii) near Kirkuk on a branch of the Tigris River, as well as at other places, demonstrate that a childless man could adopt one of his own male servants to be heir and guardian of his estate. Abram apparently contemplated doing this with Eliezer, or perhaps had already done so.

15:5 *count the stars — if indeed you can.* See 22:17. More than 8,000 stars are clearly visible to the naked eye in the darkness of a Near Eastern night. *So shall your offspring be.* The promise was initially fulfilled in Egypt (see Ex 1; see also Dt 1:10; Heb 11:12). Ultimately, all who belong to Christ are Abram's offspring (see Gal 3:29 and note).

15:6 Abram is the "father of all who believe" (Ro 4:11; see note there), and this verse is the first explicit reference to faith in God's promises (see Ro 4:3 and note). It also teaches that God graciously responds to faith by crediting righteousness to one who believes (see Heb 11:7 and note).

15:7 *I am the LORD, who brought you out.* Ancient royal covenants often began with (1) the self-identification of the king and (2) a brief historical prologue, as here (see Ex 20:2 and note).

15:8 *how can I know . . . ?* Cf. Lk 1:18 and note. Abram believed God's promise of a son, but he asked for a guarantee of the promise of the land.

15:9–21 This expression of God's covenant with Abram was cast in the form of ancient Near Eastern royal land-grant treaties and contained a perpetual and unconditional divine promise to fulfill the grant of land to Abram and his descendants (see 1Ch 16:14–18; Ps 105:8–11 and note on 105:8; see also chart, p. 19).

15:10 *birds . . . he did not cut in half.* Perhaps because they were so small (see Lev 1:17).

15:13 *country not their own.* Egypt (see 46:3–4). *four hundred years.* A round number. According to Ex 12:40 (see note there) Israel spent 430 years in Egypt.

15:15 The fulfillment is recorded in 25:8.

15:16 *In the fourth generation.* That is, after 400 years (see v. 13). A "generation" was the age of a man when his firstborn son (from a legal standpoint) was born — in Abram's case, 100 years (see 21:5). *sin of the Amorites has not yet reached its full measure.* Just how sinful many Canaanite practices were is now known from archaeological artifacts and from their own epic literature, discovered at Ras Shamra (ancient Ugarit) on the north Syrian coast beginning in 1929 (see chart, p. xxiii). Their "worship" was polytheistic and included idolatry, religious prostitution, divination (cf. Dt 18:9–12) and at times even child sacrifice. God was patient in judgment, even with the wicked Canaanites.

15:17 *smoking firepot with a blazing torch.* Symbolizing the presence of God (see Ex 3:2 and note; 14:24; 19:18; 1Ki 18:38; Ac 2:3 and note). *passed between the pieces.* Of the slaughtered animals (v. 10). In ancient times the parties sometimes solemnized a covenant by walking between the pieces of slaughtered animals (see Jer 34:18–19 and note on 34:18). The practice signified a self-maledictory oath: "May it be so done to me if I do not keep my oath and pledge." Having credited Abram's faith as righteousness, God now graciously ministered to his need for assurance concerning the land. He granted Abram a promissory covenant, as he had to Noah (see 9:9 and note; see also chart, p. 19).

15:18 *made a covenant.* Lit. "cut a covenant," referring to the slaughtering of the animals (the same Hebrew verb is translated "made" and "cut" in Jer 34:18). *I give this land.* The Lord initially fulfilled this covenant through Joshua (see Jos 1:2–9; 21:43–45 and note; see also 1Ki 4:20–21). *river of Egypt.* Prob-

Euphrates[f]— 19 the land of the Kenites,[g]
Kenizzites, Kadmonites, 20 Hittites,[h] Periz-
zites,[i] Rephaites,[j] 21 Amorites, Canaanites,
Girgashites and Jebusites."[k]

Hagar and Ishmael

16 Now Sarai,[l] Abram's wife, had borne
him no children.[m] But she had an
Egyptian maidservant[n] named Hagar;[o] 2 so
she said to Abram, "The LORD has kept me
from having children.[p] Go, sleep with my
maidservant; perhaps I can build a family
through her."[q]

Abram agreed to what Sarai said. 3 So
after Abram had been living in Canaan[r]
ten years,[s] Sarai his wife took her Egyptian maidservant Hagar and gave her to
her husband to be his wife. 4 He slept with
Hagar,[t] and she conceived.

When she knew she was pregnant, she
began to despise her mistress.[u] 5 Then Sarai said to Abram, "You are responsible for
the wrong I am suffering. I put my servant
in your arms, and now that she knows
she is pregnant, she despises me. May the
LORD judge between you and me."[v]

6 "Your servant is in your hands,[w]"
Abram said. "Do with her whatever you
think best." Then Sarai mistreated[x] Hagar;
so she fled from her.

7 The angel of the LORD[y] found Hagar
near a spring[z] in the desert; it was the
spring that is beside the road to Shur.[a]
8 And he said, "Hagar,[b] servant of Sarai,
where have you come from, and where are
you going?"[c]

"I'm running away from my mistress Sarai," she answered.

9 Then the angel of the LORD told her,
"Go back to your mistress and submit to
her." 10 The angel added, "I will so increase
your descendants that they will be too numerous to count."[d]

11 The angel of the LORD[e] also said to
her:

"You are now with child
and you will have a son.[f]
You shall name him[g] Ishmael,[a][h]
for the LORD has heard of your
misery.[i]
12 He will be a wild donkey[j] of a man;
his hand will be against everyone
and everyone's hand against him,
and he will live in hostility
toward[b] all his brothers.[k]"

13 She gave this name to the LORD who
spoke to her: "You are the God who sees
me,[l]" for she said, "I have now seen[c] the

15:18 [f]S Ge 2:14 **15:19** [g]Nu 24:21; Jdg 1:16; 4:11, 17; 5:24; 1Sa 15:6; 27:10; 30:29; 1Ch 2:55 **15:20** [h]S Ge 10:15; S Dt 7:1 [i]S Ge 13:7 [j]S Ge 14:5 **15:21** [k]S Ge 10:16; Jos 3:10; 24:11; Ne 9:8 **16:1** [l]S Ge 11:29 [m]S Ge 11:30; Lk 1:7, 36; Gal 4:24-25 [n]Ge 21:9; 24:61; 29:24, 29; 31:33; 46:18 [o]ver 3-4, 8, 15; Ge 21:14; 25:12 **16:2** [p]Ge 29:31; 30:2 [q]Ge 19:32; 30:3-4, 9-10 **16:3** [r]S Ge 12:5 [s]S Ge 12:4 **16:4** [t]S ver 1 [u]Ge 30:1; 1Sa 1:6 **16:5** [v]Ge 31:53; Ex 5:21; Jdg 11:27; 1Sa 24:12, 15; 26:10, 23; Ps 50:6; 75:7 **16:6** [w]Jos 9:25 [x]Ge 31:50 **16:7** [y]ver 11; Ge 21:17; 22:11, 15; 24:7, 40; 31:11; 48:16; Ex 3:2; 14:19; 23:20, 23; 32:34; 33:2; Nu 22:22; Jdg 2:1; 6:11; 13:3; 2Sa 24:16; 1Ki 19:5; 2Ki 1:3; 19:35; Ps 34:7; Zec 1:11; S Ac 5:19 [z]ver 14; Ge 21:19 [a]Ge 20:1; 25:18; Ex 15:22; 1Sa 15:7; 27:8 **16:8** [b]S ver 1 [c]S Ge 3:9 **16:10** [d]S Ge 13:16 **16:11** [e]S ver 7; S Ac 5:19 [f]S Ge 3:15 [g]Ge 12:2-3; 18:19; Ne 9:7; Isa 44:1; Am 3:2; Mt 1:21; Lk 1:13, 31 [h]Ge 17:19; 21:3; 37:25, 28; 39:1; Jdg 8:24 [i]Ge 29:32; 31:42; Ex 2:24; 3:7, 9; 4:31; Nu 20:16; Dt 26:7; 1Sa 9:16 **16:12** [j]Job 6:5; 11:12; 24:5; 39:5; Ps 104:11; Jer 2:24; Hos 8:9 [k]Ge 25:18 **16:13** [l]Ps 139:1-12

[a] 11 *Ishmael* means *God hears.* [b] 12 Or *live to the east / of* [c] 13 Or *seen the back of*

ably the modern Wadi el-Arish in northeastern Sinai (see map, p. 1308). *Euphrates.* The longest river in western Asia (about 1,700 miles; see note on 2:14). It marked the boundary between Israel and Israel's historic enemies (Assyria and Babylonia) to the east and northeast (cf. Isa 8:5–8).

15:19–21 A similar list associated with Canaan is found in 10:15–18 (see notes there). Here ten peoples are listed, the number ten signifying completeness. For other lists of the inhabitants of Canaan see Ex 3:8,17; 13:5; 23:23; 33:2; 34:11; Nu 13:29; Dt 7:1; 20:17; Jos 3:10; 9:1; 11:3; 12:8; 24:11; Jdg 3:5; 1Ch 1:13–14; 2Ch 8:7; Ezr 9:1; Ne 9:8.

16:1–15 A failure in faith leads to a brazen attempt to provide by human means what the Lord is accused of withholding. Sarai at the beginning (v. 2) and Abram at the end ("Ishmael"; see v. 15 and NIV text note on v. 11) express their mutual impatience with the Lord's failure as yet to overcome Sarai's barrenness.

16:1 *no children.* See note on 11:30. *Egyptian.* Perhaps Hagar was acquired while Abram and Sarai were in Egypt (see 12:10–20).

16:2 *The LORD has kept me from having children.* Some time had passed since the revelation of 15:4 (see 16:3), and Sarai impatiently implied that God was not keeping his promise. *Go, sleep with my maidservant.* An ancient custom, illustrated in Old Assyrian marriage contracts, the Code of Hammurapi and the Nuzi tablets (see note on 15:3–4), to ensure the birth of a male heir.

16:3 *ten years.* Abram was now 85 years old (see 12:4; 16:16).

16:4 *despise her mistress.* Peninnah acted similarly toward Hannah (see 1Sa 1:6).

16:5 *May the LORD judge between you and me.* An expression of hostility or suspicion (see 31:53; see also 31:49 and note).

16:7 *The angel of the LORD.* Since the angel of the Lord speaks for God in the first person (v. 10) and Hagar is said to name "the LORD who spoke to her: 'You are the God who sees me'" (v. 13), the angel appears to be both distinguished from the Lord (in that he is called "messenger"—the Hebrew for "angel" means "messenger") and identified with him (see also 48:16 and note). Similar distinction and identification can be found in 19:1,21; 31:11,13; Ex 3:2,4; Jdg 2:1–5; 6:11–12,14; 13:3, 6,8–11,13,15–17,20–23; Zec 3:1–6; 12:8. Traditional Christian interpretation has held that this "angel" was a preincarnate manifestation of Christ as God's Messenger-Servant. It may be, however, that, as the Lord's personal messenger who represented him and bore his credentials, the angel could speak on behalf of (and so be identified with) the One who sent him (see especially 19:21; cf. 18:2,22; 19:2). Whether this "angel" was the second person of the Trinity remains therefore uncertain (cf. Lk 2:9 and note). *Shur.* Located just east of Lower Egypt (see 25:18; 1Sa 15:7).

16:8 *I'm running away from my mistress.* Not yet knowing exactly where she was going, Hagar answered only the first of the angel's questions.

16:10 A promise reaffirmed in 17:20 and fulfilled in 25:13–16.

16:11 *Ishmael.* See NIV text note and 17:20.

16:12 *wild donkey.* Probably the onager, which roamed the dry steppes of the Near East. Ishmael would roam the desert like a wild donkey (see Job 24:5; Hos 8:9). *hostility.* The hostility between Sarai and Hagar (see vv. 4–6) was passed on to their descendants (see 25:18).

16:13 *I have now seen the One who sees me.* See NIV text note and cf. Ex 33:23. To see God's face was believed to bring death (see 32:30; Ex 33:20).

One who sees me."[m] 14That is why the
well[n] was called Beer Lahai Roi[a];[o] it is still
there, between Kadesh[p] and Bered.
15So Hagar[q] bore Abram a son,[r] and
Abram gave the name Ishmael[s] to the son
she had borne. 16Abram was eighty-six
years old[t] when Hagar bore him Ishmael.

The Covenant of Circumcision

17 When Abram was ninety-nine years
old,[u] the LORD appeared to him[v] and
said, "I am God Almighty[b];[w] walk before
me and be blameless.[x] 2I will confirm my
covenant between me and you[y] and will
greatly increase your numbers."[z]
3Abram fell facedown,[a] and God said
to him, 4"As for me, this is my covenant
with you:[b] You will be the father of many
nations.[c] 5No longer will you be called
Abram[c]; your name will be Abraham,[d d]
for I have made you a father of many nations.[e] 6I will make you very fruitful;[f] I will
make nations of you, and kings will come
from you.[g] 7I will establish my covenant[h i]
as an everlasting covenant[j k] between me
and you and your descendants after you
for the generations to come, to be your
God[l] and the God of your descendants
after you.[m] 8The whole land of Canaan,[n]
where you are now an alien,[o] I will give
as an everlasting possession to you and
your descendants after you;[p] and I will be
their God.[q]"
9Then God said to Abraham, "As for
you, you must keep my covenant,[r] you and
your descendants after you for the generations to come.[s] 10This is my covenant

16:13 [m] Ge 32:30; 33:10; Ex 24:10; 33:20,23; Nu 12:8; Jdg 6:22; 13:22; Isa 6:5 **16:14** [n] S ver 7 [o] Ge 24:62; 25:11 [p] S Ge 14:7 **16:15** [q] S ver 1 [r] Ge 21:9; Gal 4:22 [s] Ge 17:18; 25:12; 28:9 **16:16** [t] S Ge 12:4 **17:1** [u] S Ge 12:4 [v] S Ge 12:7 [w] Ge 28:3; 35:11; 43:14; 48:3; 49:25; Ex 6:3; Ru 1:20; Job 5:17; 6:4,14; 22:21; 33:19; 36:16; Isa 13:6; Joel 1:15; Mic 6:9 [x] S Ge 5:22; 20:5; Dt 18:13; 1Ki 3:6; 9:4; Job 1:1; Ps 15:2; 18:23; 78:72; 101:2 **17:2** [y] S Ge 15:18; S 22:16-18 [z] S Ge 12:2

[a] 14 *Beer Lahai Roi* means *well of the Living One who sees me.* [b] 1 Hebrew *El-Shaddai* [c] 5 *Abram* means *exalted father.* [d] 5 *Abraham* means *father of many.*

17:3 [a] ver 17; Ge 18:2; 19:1; 33:3; Ex 18:7; Nu 14:5; Jos 5:14; 7:6; Jdg 13:20; Eze 1:28; 3:23 **17:4** [b] S Ge 15:18 [c] ver 16; S Ge 12:2; 25:23 **17:5** [d] ver 15; Ge 32:28; 35:10; 37:3,13; 43:6; 46:2; 1Ki 18:31; 2Ki 17:34; 1Ch 1:34; Ne 9:7; Isa 48:1; S Jn 1:42 [e] Ro 4:17* **17:6** [f] Ge 1:28; 22:17; 26:22; 28:3; 35:11; 41:52; 47:27; 48:4; 49:22; Lev 26:9; Dt 7:13 [g] ver 16,19; Ge 18:10; 21:1; 36:31; Isa 51:2; Mt 1:6 **17:7** [h] S Ge 15:18; Lev 26:9,15 [i] S Ge 6:18 [j] S Heb 13:20 [k] S Ge 9:16 [l] Ex 6:7; 20:2; 29:45,46; Lev 11:44-45; 18:2; 22:33; 25:38; 26:12,45; Nu 15:41; Dt 4:20; 7:6,21; 29:13; 2Sa 7:24; Jer 14:9; Rev 21:7 [m] Ro 9:8; Gal 3:16 **17:8** [n] S Ge 10:19 [o] Ge 23:4; 28:4; 35:27; 37:1; Ex 6:4; 1Ch 29:15 [p] S Ge 12:7; S 15:7 [q] S ver 7; Jer 31:1 **17:9** [r] Ge 22:18; Ex 19:5; Dt 5:2 [s] Ge 18:19

16:14 *Beer Lahai Roi.* See NIV text note. Another possible translation that fits the context equally well is: "well of the one who sees me and who lives," i.e., Hagar. *Kadesh.* See note on 14:7.

17:1–27 God's covenant with Abram renewed and expanded (see chart, p. 19). After Abram's and Sarai's attempt to obtain the promised offspring by using the womb of Sarai's servant, God appears to Abram to reaffirm his promises. But he also makes it clear that, if Abram is to receive God's covenanted benefits, he must live out "the obedience that comes from faith" (Ro 1:5; see also ch. 22). To that end he calls on Abram to make with him a covenanted commitment of loyal obedience.

17:1 *ninety-nine years old.* Thirteen years had passed since Ishmael's birth (see 16:16; 17:24–25). *appeared.* See note on 12:7. *I am.* See note on 15:7. *God Almighty.* The Hebrew (*El-Shaddai*) perhaps means "God, the Mountain One," either highlighting the invincible power of God or referring to the mountains as God's symbolic home (see Ps 121:1). It was the special name by which God revealed himself to the patriarchs (see Ex 6:3 and note). *Shaddai* occurs 31 times in the book of Job and 17 times in the rest of the Bible. *walk before me and be blameless.* Perhaps equivalent to "walk with me and be blameless" (see notes on 5:22; 6:8–9).

17:2 *my covenant.* See 15:4–5. The covenant is God's; he calls it "my covenant" nine times in vv. 2–21, and he initiates (see 15:18), confirms (v. 2) and establishes (v. 7) it. *increase your numbers.* The language echoes 1:28 (Adam) and 9:7 (Noah), suggesting that God's original purpose for humankind, threatened by the sins of the race, will be achieved through Abraham and his descendants (see also Ex 1:7 and note). See 13:16 and note. Earlier God had covenanted to keep his promise concerning the land (ch. 15); here he broadens his covenant to include the promised offspring.

17:5 *Abram ... Abraham.* See NIV text notes. The first name means "Exalted Father," probably in reference to God (i.e., "[God is] Exalted Father"); the second means "father of many," in reference to Abraham. *your name will be.* By giving Abram a new name (see Ne 9:7) God marked him in a special way as his servant (see notes on 1:5; 2:19).

17:6 *nations ... kings.* This promise also came to Sarah (v. 16) and was renewed to Jacob (35:11; see 48:19). It referred to the proliferation of Abraham's offspring, who, like the descendants of Noah (see ch. 10), would someday become many nations and spread over the earth. Ultimately it finds fulfillment in such passages as Ro 4:16–18; 15:8–12; Gal 3:29; Rev 7:9; 21:24.

17:7 *everlasting.* God's commitment to his covenant was forever (see vv. 13,19), but descendants of Abraham could break it (see v. 14; cf. Isa 24:5 and note; Jer 31:32). *to be your God.* The heart of God's covenant promise, repeated over and over in the OT (see, e.g., v. 8; Jer 24:7 and note; 31:33; Eze 34:30–31; Hos 2:23; Zec 8:8 and note). This is God's pledge to be the protector of his people and the One who provides for their well-being and guarantees their future blessing (see 15:1).

17:8 *land.* See 12:7; 15:18; Ac 7:5. *everlasting possession.* The land, though an everlasting possession given by God, could be temporarily lost because of disobedience (see Dt 28:62–63; 30:1–10).

17:9 *As for you.* Balances the "As for me" of v. 4 (cf. also vv. 15,20). Having reviewed his covenanted commitment to Abraham (see 15:8–21), and having broadened it to include the promise of offspring, God now called upon Abraham to make a covenanted commitment to him—to "walk before me and be blameless" (v. 1). *keep my covenant.* Participation in the blessings of the Abrahamic covenant was conditioned on obedience (see 18:19; 22:18; 26:4–5).

17:10 *circumcised.* Circumcision was God's appointed "sign of the covenant" (v. 11), which signified Abraham's covenanted commitment to the Lord—that the Lord alone would be his God, whom he would trust and serve. It symbolized a self-maledictory oath: "If I am not loyal in faith and obedience to the Lord, may the sword of the Lord cut off me and my offspring [see v. 14] as I have cut off my foreskin" (analogous to the oath to which God had submitted himself; see note on 15:17). Thus Abraham was to place himself under the rule of the Lord as his King, consecrating himself, his offspring and all he possessed to the service of the Lord. For circumcision as signifying consecration to the Lord see Dt 10:16; 30:6; Jer 4:4 and note; 9:25–26; Eze 44:7 and note; 44:9; cf. Ro 2:29 and note. Other nations also practiced circumcision (see Jer 9:25–26; Eze 28:10 and note; 32:18–19), but not for the covenant reasons that Israel did.

with you and your descendants after you,
the covenant you are to keep: Every male
among you shall be circumcised.[t] 11You
are to undergo circumcision,[u] and it will
be the sign of the covenant[v] between me
and you. 12For the generations to come[w]
every male among you who is eight days
old must be circumcised,[x] including those
born in your household or bought with
money from a foreigner — those who are
not your offspring. 13Whether born in your
household or bought with your money,
they must be circumcised.[y] My covenant
in your flesh is to be an everlasting covenant.[z] 14Any uncircumcised male, who
has not been circumcised[a] in the flesh,
will be cut off from his people;[b] he has
broken my covenant.[c]"

15God also said to Abraham, "As for Sarai[d] your wife, you are no longer to call
her Sarai; her name will be Sarah.[e] 16I will
bless her and will surely give you a son by
her.[f] I will bless her so that she will be the
mother of nations;[g] kings of peoples will
come from her."

17Abraham fell facedown;[h] he laughed[i]
and said to himself, "Will a son be born
to a man a hundred years old?[j] Will Sarah
bear a child at the age of ninety?"[k] 18And
Abraham said to God, "If only Ishmael[l]
might live under your blessing!"[m]

19Then God said, "Yes, but your wife
Sarah will bear you a son,[n] and you will
call him Isaac.[a][o] I will establish my covenant with him[p] as an everlasting covenant[q] for his descendants after him.
20And as for Ishmael, I have heard you:
I will surely bless him; I will make him
fruitful and will greatly increase his numbers.[r] He will be the father of twelve rulers,[s] and I will make him into a great nation.[t] 21But my covenant[u] I will establish
with Isaac, whom Sarah will bear to you[v]
by this time next year."[w] 22When he had
finished speaking with Abraham, God
went up from him.[x]

23On that very day Abraham took his
son Ishmael and all those born in his
household[y] or bought with his money,
every male in his household, and circumcised them, as God told him.[z] 24Abraham
was ninety-nine years old[a] when he was
circumcised,[b] 25and his son Ishmael[c] was
thirteen; 26Abraham and his son Ishmael
were both circumcised on that same day.
27And every male in Abraham's household[d], including those born in his household or bought from a foreigner, was circumcised with him.

The Three Visitors

18 The LORD appeared to Abraham[e]
near the great trees of Mamre[f] while
he was sitting at the entrance to his tent[g]
in the heat of the day. 2Abraham looked
up[h] and saw three men[i] standing nearby.

[a] 19 *Isaac* means *he laughs.*

17:10 [t]ver 23; Ge 21:4; Lev 12:3; Jos 5:2,5,7; Jn 7:22; Ac 7:8; Ro 4:11 **17:11** [u]Ex 12:48; Dt 10:16 [v]S Ge 9:12; Ro 4:11 **17:12** [w]S Ge 9:12 [x]Ge 21:4; Lev 12:3; Jos 5:2; S Lk 1:59 **17:13** [y]Ex 12:44,48 [z]S Ge 9:16 **17:14** [a]ver 23 [b]Ex 4:24-26; 12:15,19; 30:33; Lev 7:20,25; 17:4; 18:29; 19:8; 20:17; Nu 9:13; 15:30; 19:13; Dt 17:12; Jos 5:2-8; Job 38:15; Ps 37:28 [c]Eze 44:7 **17:15** [d]S Ge 11:29 [e]S ver 5 **17:16** [f]S ver 6; S Isa 29:22 [g]S ver 4; Ge 24:60; Gal 4:31 **17:17** [h]S ver 3 [i]Ge 18:12; 21:6 [j]S Ge 12:4 [k]Ge 18:11,13; 21:7; 24:1,36; Jer 20:15; Lk 1:18; Ro 4:19; Gal 4:23; Heb 11:11 **17:18** [l]S Ge 16:15 [m]Ge 21:11 **17:19** [n]S ver 6,21; Ge 18:14; 21:2; 1Sa 1:20 [o]S Ge 16:11; Mt 1:21; Lk 1:13,31 [p]Ge 26:3; 50:24; Ex 13:11; Dt 1:8 [q]S Ge 9:16; S Gal 3:16 **17:20** [r]S Ge 13:16 [s]Ge 25:12-16 [t]Ge 25:18; 48:19 **17:21** [u]Ex 34:10 [v]S ver 19 [w]Ge 18:10, 14 **17:22** [x]Ge 18:33; 35:13; Nu 12:9 **17:23** [y]S Ge 12:5 [z]S ver 10, S 14 **17:24** [a]S Ge 12:4 [b]Ro 4:11 **17:25** [c]Ge 16:16 **17:27** [d]Ge 14:14 **18:1** [e]S Ge 12:7; Ac 7:2 [f]S Ge 13:18 [g]Ge 19:1; 23:10,18; 34:20,24; Ru 4:1; Ps 69:12; Heb 11:9 **18:2** [h]Ge 24:63 [i]ver 16,22; Ge 19:1,10; 32:24; Jos 5:13; Jdg 13:6-11; Hos 12:3-4; Heb 13:2

17:11 *sign of the covenant.* See notes on 9:12; 15:17. As the covenant sign, circumcision also (see note on v. 10) marked Abraham as the one to whom God had made covenant commitment (15:7 – 21) in response to Abraham's faith, which he "credited ... to him as righteousness" (15:6). Paul comments on this aspect of the covenant sign in Ro 4:11 (see note there).

17:12 *eight days old.* See 21:4 and Ac 7:8 (Isaac); Lk 1:59 (John the Baptist); 2:21 (Jesus); Php 3:5 (Paul). Abraham was 99 years old when the newly initiated rite of circumcision was performed on him (see v. 24). Many Arabs who consider themselves descendants of Ishmael are circumcised at the age of 13 (see v. 25) even today.

17:14 *cut off from his people.* Removed from the covenant people by divine judgment (see note on v. 10).

17:15 *Sarai ... Sarah.* Both names evidently mean "princess." The renaming stressed that she was to be the mother of nations and kings (see v. 16) and thus to serve the Lord's purpose (see note on v. 5).

17:16 *son.* Fulfilled in Isaac (see 21:2 – 3).

17:17 *laughed.* In temporary disbelief (see 18:12; cf. Ro 4:19 – 21 and note on 4:19). The verb is a pun on the name "Isaac," which means "he laughs" (see NIV text notes on v. 19 and 21:3; see also 18:12 – 15; 21:6).

17:20 *numbers.* See note on 13:16. *father of twelve rulers.* Fulfilled in 25:16.

17:21 Paul cites the choice of Isaac (and not Ishmael) as one proof of God's sovereign right to choose to save by grace alone (see Ro 9:6 – 13). *by this time next year.* See 21:2.

17:22 *God went up from him.* A solemn conclusion to the conversation.

17:23 *On that very day.* Abraham was characterized by prompt obedience (see note on 12:4).

18:1 – 33 God appears to Abraham with two representatives (identified as "angels" in 19:1) of his heavenly council (see 1Ki 22:19 – 22 and note on 22:19; Jer 23:18,22 and note on 23:18). He comes to announce to Abraham what he is about to do (see note on v. 17).

18:1 *appeared.* See note on 12:7. *great trees.* See note on 12:6. *Mamre.* See note on 13:18. *heat of the day.* Early afternoon.

18:2 *three men.* Two of the "men" were angels (see 19:1; see also note on 16:7). The third was the Lord himself (see vv. 1,13,17,20,26,33; see especially v. 22). *hurried.* The story in vv. 2 – 8 illustrates Near Eastern hospitality in several ways: (1) Abraham gave prompt attention to the needs of his guests (vv. 2,6 – 7). (2) He bowed low to the ground (v. 2). (3) He politely addressed one of his guests as "my lord" and called himself "your servant" (vv. 3,5), a common way of speaking when addressing a superior (see, e.g., 19:2,18 – 19). (4) He acted as if it would be a favor to him if they allowed him to serve them (vv. 3 – 5). (5) He asked that water be brought to wash their feet (see v. 4), an act of courtesy to refresh a traveler in a hot, dusty climate (see 19:2; 24:32; 43:24). (6) He prepared a lavish meal for them (vv. 5 – 8; a similar lavish offering was presented to a divine messenger in Jdg 6:18 – 19; 13:15 – 16). (7). He stood nearby (v. 8), assuming the posture of a servant (see v. 22), to meet their every wish. Heb 13:2 (see note there) is probably a reference to vv. 2 – 8 and 19:1 – 3.

When he saw them, he hurried from the entrance of his tent to meet them and bowed low to the ground.[j]

3 He said, "If I have found favor in your eyes,[k] my lord,[a] do not pass your servant[l] by. 4 Let a little water be brought, and then you may all wash your feet[m] and rest under this tree. 5 Let me get you something to eat,[n] so you can be refreshed and then go on your way—now that you have come to your servant."

"Very well," they answered, "do as you say."

6 So Abraham hurried into the tent to Sarah. "Quick," he said, "get three seahs[b] of fine flour and knead it and bake some bread."[o]

7 Then he ran to the herd and selected a choice, tender calf[p] and gave it to a servant, who hurried to prepare it. 8 He then brought some curds[q] and milk[r] and the calf that had been prepared, and set these before them.[s] While they ate, he stood near them under a tree.

9 "Where is your wife Sarah?"[t] they asked him.

"There, in the tent,[u]" he said.

10 Then the LORD[c] said, "I will surely return to you about this time next year,[v] and Sarah your wife will have a son."[w]

Now Sarah was listening at the entrance to the tent, which was behind him. 11 Abraham and Sarah were already old and well advanced in years,[x] and Sarah was past the age of childbearing.[y] 12 So Sarah laughed[z] to herself as she thought, "After I am worn out and my master[d][a] is old, will I now have this pleasure?"

13 Then the LORD said to Abraham, "Why did Sarah laugh and say, 'Will I really have a child, now that I am old?'[b] 14 Is anything too hard for the LORD?[c] I will return to you at the appointed time next year[d] and Sarah will have a son."[e]

15 Sarah was afraid, so she lied and said, "I did not laugh."

But he said, "Yes, you did laugh."

Abraham Pleads for Sodom

16 When the men[f] got up to leave, they looked down toward Sodom, and Abraham walked along with them to see them on their way. 17 Then the LORD said, "Shall I hide from Abraham[g] what I am about to do?[h] 18 Abraham will surely become a great and powerful nation,[i] and all nations on earth will be blessed through him. 19 For I have chosen him[j], so that he will direct his children[k] and his household after him to keep the way of the LORD[l] by doing what is right and just,[m] so that the LORD will bring about for Abraham what he has promised him."[n]

20 Then the LORD said, "The outcry against Sodom[o] and Gomorrah is so great[p] and their sin so grievous[q] 21 that I will go down[r] and see if what they have done is as bad as the outcry that has reached me. If not, I will know."

22 The men[s] turned away and went toward Sodom,[t] but Abraham remained standing before the LORD.[e][u] 23 Then Abraham approached him and said: "Will you sweep away the righteous with the wicked?[v] 24 What if there are fifty righteous peo-

[a] 3 Or *O Lord* [b] 6 That is, probably about 20 quarts (about 19 liters) [c] 10 Hebrew *Then he* [d] 12 Or *husband* [e] 22 Masoretic Text; an ancient Hebrew scribal tradition *but the LORD remained standing before Abraham*

18:2 [j] S Ge 17:3; S 43:28 **18:3** [k] Ge 19:19; 39:4; Ru 2:2, 10, 13; 1Sa 1:18; Est 2:15 [l] Ge 32:4, 18, 20; 33:5 **18:4** [m] Ge 19:2; 24:32; 43:24; Jdg 19:21; 2Sa 11:8; S Lk 7:44 **18:5** [n] Jdg 13:15; 19:5 **18:6** [o] Ge 19:3; 2Sa 13:8 **18:7** [p] 1Sa 28:24; Lk 15:23 **18:8** [q] Isa 7:15, 22 [r] Jdg 4:19; 5:25 [s] Jdg 6:19 **18:9** [t] S Ge 3:9 [u] Ge 24:67; Heb 11:9 **18:10** [v] S Ge 17:21; 21:2; 2Ki 4:16 [w] S Ge 17:6; Ro 9:9* **18:11** [x] S Ge 17:17; Lk 1:18 [y] S Ge 11:30; Ro 4:19; Heb 11:11-12 **18:12** [z] S Ge 17:17 [a] 1Pe 3:6 **18:13** [b] S Ge 17:17 **18:14** [c] Job 42:2; Isa 40:29; 50:2; 51:9; Jer 32:17, 27; S Mt 19:26; Ro 4:21 [d] S ver 10 [e] S Ge 17:19; Ro 9:9*; Gal 4:23 **18:16** [f] S ver 2 **18:17** [g] Am 3:7 [h] Ge 19:24; Job 1:16; Ps 107:34 **18:18** [i] S Ge 12:2; Gal 3:8* **18:19** [j] Ge 17:9 [k] Dt 4:9-10; 6:7 [l] Jos 24:15; Eph 6:4 [m] Ge 22:12, 18; 26:5; 2Sa 8:15; Ps 17:2; 99:4; Jer 23:5 [n] S Ge 16:11; S Isa 14:1 **18:20** [o] Isa 1:10; Jer 23:14; Eze 16:46 [p] Ge 19:13 [q] S Ge 13:13 **18:21** [r] S Ge 11:5 **18:22** [s] S ver 2 [t] Ge 19:1 [u] ver 1; Ge 19:27 **18:23** [v] Ex 23:7; Lev 4:3, 22, 27; Nu 16:22; Dt 27:25; 2Sa 24:17; Ps 11:4-7; 94:21; Eze 18:4; 2Pe 2:9

18:6 *bread.* A plural word referring to round, thin loaves.

18:10 See 17:21. Paul quotes this promise of Isaac's birth (see v. 14) in Ro 9:9 and relates it to Abraham's spiritual offspring (see Ro 9:7–8 and note on 9:8).

18:12 *laughed.* In disbelief, as also Abraham had at first (see note on 17:17). For Sarah's later laugh of joy and faith see 21:6–7.

18:14 *Is anything too hard for the LORD?* The answer is no, for Sarah as well as for her descendants Mary and Elizabeth (see Lk 1:34–37). Nothing within God's will, including creation (see Jer 32:17 and note) and redemption (see Mk 10:26–27 and note on 10:27), is impossible for him.

18:16 *Sodom.* See notes on 10:19; 13:10; Eze 16:47.

18:17 Abraham was God's friend (see v. 19; 2Ch 20:7; Isa 41:8; Jas 2:23). And because he was now God's covenant friend (see Job 29:4 and note), God convened his heavenly council (see note on 1:26) at Abraham's tent. There he announced his purpose for Abraham (v. 10) and for the wicked of the plain (vv. 20–21)—redemption and judgment. He thus even gave Abraham opportunity to speak in his court and to intercede for the righteous in Sodom and Gomorrah. Accordingly, Abraham was later called a prophet (see 20:7 and note). Here, in Abraham, is exemplified the great privilege of God's covenant people throughout the ages: God has revealed his purposes to them and allows their voice to be heard (in intercession) in the court of heaven itself.

18:18 *great and powerful nation ... blessed through him.* See note on 12:2–3.

18:19 *what is right and just.* See note on Ps 119:121.

18:20 *outcry.* A cry of righteous indignation (cf. the blood of Abel, 4:10 [see note there]) that became one of the reasons for the destruction of the cities (see 19:13). *Gomorrah.* See notes on 10:19; 13:10.

18:21 *I will go down.* The result would be judgment (as in 11:5–9), but God also comes down to redeem (as in Ex 3:8). *see.* Not a denial of God's infinite knowledge but a figurative way of stating that he as "Judge" (v. 25) does not act on the basis of mere complaints.

18:22 *Abraham remained standing before the LORD.* The text and NIV text note both illustrate the mutual accessibility that existed between God and his servant.

18:23 The second time Abraham intervened for his relatives and for Sodom (see 14:14–16).

ple in the city? Will you really sweep it
away and not spare[a] the place for the sake
of the fifty righteous people in it?[w] 25 Far
be it from you to do such a thing[x]—to kill
the righteous with the wicked, treating the
righteous[y] and the wicked alike.[z] Far be it
from you! Will not the Judge[b][a] of all the
earth do right?"[b]
26 The LORD said, "If I find fifty righteous
people in the city of Sodom, I will spare
the whole place for their sake.[c]"
27 Then Abraham spoke up again: "Now
that I have been so bold as to speak to
the Lord, though I am nothing but dust
and ashes,[d] 28 what if the number of the
righteous is five less than fifty? Will you
destroy the whole city because of five people?"
"If I find forty-five there," he said, "I
will not destroy it."
29 Once again he spoke to him, "What if
only forty are found there?"
He said, "For the sake of forty, I will
not do it."
30 Then he said, "May the Lord not be
angry,[e] but let me speak. What if only thirty can be found there?"
He answered, "I will not do it if I find
thirty there."
31 Abraham said, "Now that I have been
so bold as to speak to the Lord, what if
only twenty can be found there?"
He said, "For the sake of twenty, I will
not destroy it."
32 Then he said, "May the Lord not be
angry, but let me speak just once more.[f]
What if only ten can be found there?"
He answered, "For the sake of ten,[g] I
will not destroy it."
33 When the LORD had finished speaking[h]
with Abraham, he left,[i] and Abraham returned home.[j]

18:24 [w]ver 26; Jer 5:1 **18:25** [x]Ge 44:7,17; Dt 32:4; Job 8:3-7; 34:10 [y]Isa 5:20; Am 5:15; Mal 2:17; 3:18 [z]Dt 1:16-17 [a]Jdg 11:27; Job 9:15; Ps 7:11; 94:2; Heb 12:23 [b]Ge 20:4; Dt 32:4; 2Ch 19:7; Ezr 9:15; Ne 9:33; Job 8:3,20; 34:10; 36:23; Ps 58:11; 75:7; 94:2; 119:137; Isa 3:10-11; Eze 18:25; Da 4:37; 9:14; Mal 2:17; Ro 3:6 **18:26** [c]S ver 24 **18:27** [d]S Ge 2:7; S Job 2:8 **18:30** [e]ver 32; Ge 44:18; Ex 32:22 **18:32** [f]S ver 30; Jdg 6:39 [g]Jer 5:1 **18:33** [h]Ex 31:18 [i]S Ge 17:22 [j]Ge 31:55

19:1 [k]S Ge 18:2; Heb 13:2 [l]Ge 18:22 [m]S Ge 11:27 [n]S Ge 18:1 [o]S Ge 17:3; 48:12; Ru 2:10; 1Sa 25:23; 2Sa 14:33; 2Ki 2:15 **19:2** [p]S Ge 18:4; Lk 7:44 [q]Jdg 19:15,20 **19:3** [r]Ge 33:11 [s]Job 31:32 [t]Ex 12:39 [u]S Ge 18:6 **19:4** [v]S Ge 13:13 **19:5** [w]S Ge 13:13; Lev 18:22;

Sodom and Gomorrah Destroyed

19 The two angels[k] arrived at Sodom[l]
in the evening, and Lot[m] was sitting
in the gateway of the city.[n] When he saw
them, he got up to meet them and bowed
down with his face to the ground.[o] 2 "My
lords," he said, "please turn aside to your
servant's house. You can wash your feet[p]
and spend the night and then go on your
way early in the morning."
"No," they answered, "we will spend
the night in the square."[q]
3 But he insisted[r] so strongly that they
did go with him and entered his house.[s]
He prepared a meal for them, baking bread
without yeast,[t] and they ate.[u] 4 Before they
had gone to bed, all the men from every
part of the city of Sodom[v]—both young
and old—surrounded the house. 5 They
called to Lot, "Where are the men who
came to you tonight? Bring them out to us
so that we can have sex with them."[w]
6 Lot went outside to meet them[x] and
shut the door behind him 7 and said, "No,
my friends. Don't do this wicked thing.
8 Look, I have two daughters who have
never slept with a man. Let me bring them
out to you, and you can do what you like
with them. But don't do anything to these
men, for they have come under the protection of my roof."[y]
9 "Get out of our way," they replied.
And they said, "This fellow came here as
an alien,[z] and now he wants to play the
judge![a] We'll treat you worse than them."
They kept bringing pressure on Lot and
moved forward to break down the door.

[a] *24* Or *forgive*; also in verse 26 [b] *25* Or *Ruler*

Dt 23:18; Jdg 19:22; Ro 1:24-27 **19:6** [x]Jdg 19:23 **19:8** [y]Jdg 19:24; 2Pe 2:7-8 **19:9** [z]Ge 23:4 [a]S Ge 13:8; Ac 7:27

18:25 *Judge of all the earth.* Abraham based his plea on the justice and authority (see NIV text note) of God, confident that God would do what was right (see Dt 32:4 and note).

18:27 *Lord.* Abraham used the title "Lord" (Adonai), not the covenantal name "LORD" (Yahweh), throughout his prayer. He was appealing to God as "Judge of all the earth." *dust and ashes.* In contrast to God's exalted position, Abraham described himself as insignificant (see Job 30:19 and note; 42:6).

18:32 *just once more.* Abraham's questioning in vv. 23–32 did not arise from a spirit of haggling but of compassion for his relatives and of wanting to know God's ways. *ten.* Perhaps Abraham stopped at ten because he had been counting while praying: Lot, his wife, possibly two sons (see 19:12), at least two married daughters and their husbands (see 19:14 and NIV text note), and two unmarried daughters (see 19:8).

18:33 *home.* To Mamre (see v. 1). The next morning Abraham went back to see what God had done (see 19:27–28).

19:1–3 See note on 18:2.

19:1 *two angels.* See notes on 16:7; 18:2. *Lot was sitting in the gateway of the city.* Lot had probably become a member of Sodom's ruling council, since a city gateway served as the administrative and judicial center where legal matters were discussed and prosecuted (see Ru 4:1–12 and note on 4:1).

19:2 *square.* An open space near the main city gateway (see 2Ch 32:6) where public gatherings were held. Important cities like Jerusalem could have two or more squares (see Ne 8:16).

19:3 *bread without yeast.* A flat bread that could be baked quickly (see 18:6; Ex 12:8,39).

19:4–9 See Jdg 19:22–25.

19:5 *have sex with them.* Homosexual practice was open and common among the men of Sodom (see Jude 7 and note). The English word "sodomy" alludes to the perversions of the ancient city.

19:8 *under the protection of my roof.* Ancient hospitality obliged a host to protect his guests in every situation and in every possible way.

19:9 *This fellow came here as an alien, and now he wants to play the judge.* Centuries later, Moses was also considered an outsider and was accused of setting himself up as a judge (see Ex 2:14; Ac 7:27).

10 But the men[b] inside reached out and
pulled Lot back into the house and shut
the door. 11 Then they struck the men who
were at the door of the house, young and
old, with blindness[c] so that they could not
find the door.
12 The two men said to Lot, "Do you
have anyone else here — sons-in-law, sons
or daughters, or anyone else in the city
who belongs to you?[d] Get them out of
here, 13 because we[e] are going to destroy
this place. The outcry to the LORD against
its people is so great[f] that he has sent us
to destroy it."[g]
14 So Lot went out and spoke to his sons-
in-law, who were pledged to marry[a] his
daughters. He said, "Hurry and get out
of this place, because the LORD is about
to destroy the city![h]" But his sons-in-law
thought he was joking.[i]
15 With the coming of dawn, the angels
urged Lot, saying, "Hurry! Take your wife
and your two daughters who are here, or
you will be swept away[j] when the city is
punished.[k]"
16 When he hesitated, the men grasped
his hand and the hands of his wife and
of his two daughters[l] and led them safely
out of the city, for the LORD was merciful
to them.[m] 17 As soon as they had brought
them out, one of them said, "Flee for your
lives![n] Don't look back,[o] and don't stop
anywhere in the plain![p] Flee to the mountains[q] or you will be swept away!"
18 But Lot said to them, "No, my lords,[b]
please! 19 Your[c] servant has found favor in
your[c] eyes,[r] and you[c] have shown great
kindness[s] to me in sparing my life. But I
can't flee to the mountains;[t] this disaster
will overtake me, and I'll die. 20 Look, here
is a town near enough to run to, and it is
small. Let me flee to it — it is very small,
isn't it? Then my life will be spared."
21 He said to him, "Very well, I will grant
this request[u] too; I will not overthrow the
town you speak of. 22 But flee there quickly, because I cannot do anything until
you reach it." (That is why the town was
called Zoar.[d][v])

23 By the time Lot reached Zoar,[w] the sun
had risen over the land. 24 Then the LORD
rained down burning sulfur[x] on Sodom
and Gomorrah[y] — from the LORD out of the
heavens.[z] 25 Thus he overthrew those cities[a]
and the entire plain,[b] including all those
living in the cities — and also the vegetation in the land.[c] 26 But Lot's wife looked
back,[d] and she became a pillar of salt.[e]
27 Early the next morning Abraham got
up and returned to the place where he had
stood before the LORD.[f] 28 He looked down
toward Sodom and Gomorrah, toward all
the land of the plain, and he saw dense
smoke rising from the land, like smoke
from a furnace.[g]
29 So when God destroyed the cities of
the plain,[h] he remembered[i] Abraham, and
he brought Lot out of the catastrophe[j] that
overthrew the cities where Lot had lived.[k]

Lot and His Daughters

30 Lot and his two daughters left Zoar[l]
and settled in the mountains,[m] for he was
afraid to stay in Zoar. He and his two
daughters lived in a cave. 31 One day the
older daughter said to the younger, "Our
father is old, and there is no man around
here to lie with us, as is the custom all over
the earth. 32 Let's get our father to drink
wine and then lie with him and preserve
our family line[n] through our father."[o]
33 That night they got their father to drink
wine, and the older daughter went in and
lay with him. He was not aware of it when
she lay down or when she got up.[p]
34 The next day the older daughter said
to the younger, "Last night I lay with my
father. Let's get him to drink wine again
tonight, and you go in and lie with him so
we can preserve our family line through

[a] *14* Or *were married to* [b] *18* Or *No, Lord*; or *No, my lord* [c] *19* The Hebrew is singular. [d] *22* *Zoar* means *small.*

19:10 [b]S Ge 18:2 **19:11** [c]Dt 28:28-29; 2Ki 6:18; Ac 13:11 **19:12** [d]S Ge 6:18 **19:13** [e]Ex 12:29; 2Sa 24:16; 2Ki 19:35; 1Ch 21:12; 2Ch 32:21 [f]Ge 18:20 [g]1Ch 21:15; Ps 78:49; Jer 21:12; 25:18; 44:22; 51:45 **19:14** [h]Nu 16:21; Rev 18:4 [i]Ex 9:21; 1Ki 13:18; Jer 5:12; 43:2; Lk 17:28 **19:15** [j]Nu 16:26; Job 21:18; Ps 58:9; 73:19; 90:5 [k]Rev 18:4 **19:16** [l]2Pe 2:7 [m]Ex 34:6; Ps 33:18-19 **19:17** [n]1Ki 19:3; Jer 48:6 [o]ver 26 [p]S Ge 13:12 [q]S ver 19; S Ge 14:10; Mt 24:16 **19:19** [r]S Ge 6:8; S 18:3 [s]Ge 24:12; 39:21; 40:14; 47:29; Ru 1:8; 2:20; 3:10 [t]S ver 17,30 **19:21** [u]1Sa 25:35; 2Sa 14:8; Job 42:9 **19:22** [v]S Ge 13:10 **19:23** [w]S Ge 13:10 **19:24** [x]Job 18:15; Ps 11:6; Isa 30:33; 34:9; Eze 38:22 [y]Dt 29:23; Isa 1:9; 13:19; Jer 49:18; 50:40; Am 4:11 [z]S Ge 18:17; S Lev 10:2; S Mt 10:15; Lk 17:29 **19:25** [a]S ver 24; Eze 26:16; Zep 3:8; Hag 2:22 [b]S Ge 13:12 [c]Ps 107:34; Isa 1:10; Jer 20:16; 23:14; La 4:6; Eze 16:48 **19:26** [d]S ver 17 [e]Lk 17:32 **19:27** [f]Ge 18:22 **19:28** [g]Ge 15:17; Ex 19:18; Rev 9:2; 18:9 **19:29** [h]S Ge 13:12 [i]S Ge 8:1 [j]2Pe 2:7 [k]Ge 14:12; Eze 14:16 **19:30** [l]ver 22; S Ge 13:10 [m]S ver 19; S Ge 14:10 **19:32** [n]S Ge 16:2 [o]ver 34,36; Ge 38:18 **19:33** [p]ver 35

19:13 *we are going to destroy this place.* Sodom's wickedness had made it ripe for destruction (see Isa 3:9; Jer 23:14; La 4:6; Zep 2:8 – 9 and note on 2:9; 2Pe 2:6; Jude 7 and note).

19:14 *his sons-in-law thought he was joking.* Lot apparently had lost his power of moral persuasion even among his family members.

19:16 *hesitated.* Perhaps because of reluctance to leave his material possessions. *his hand and the hands of his wife and of his two daughters.* The ten righteous people required to save Sodom (see 18:32 and note) had now been reduced to four. *the LORD was merciful to them.* Deliverance is due to divine mercy, not to human righteousness (cf. Tit 3:5 and note).

19:24 *rained down burning sulfur.* Perhaps from a violent earthquake spewing up asphalt, such as is still found in this region (cf. Isa 34:9 and note).

19:26 *Lot's wife looked back, and she became a pillar of salt.* Her disobedient hesitation (see v. 17) became proverbial in later generations (see Lk 17:32). Even today, grotesque salt formations along the shores of the Dead Sea are reminders of her folly.

19:29 *God … remembered Abraham.* See note on 8:1. *he brought Lot out of the catastrophe.* Lot's deliverance was the main concern of Abraham's prayer (18:23 – 32), which God now answered.

19:33 *they got their father to drink wine, and the older daughter went in and lay with him.* Though Lot's role was mainly passive, he bore the basic responsibility for what happened here and reaped the harvest of his move toward Sodom (see 13:10 – 12 and notes).

our father."[q] 35So they got their father to
drink wine[r] that night also, and the younger daughter went and lay with him. Again
he was not aware of it when she lay down
or when she got up.[s]
36So both of Lot's daughters became
pregnant by their father.[t] 37The older
daughter had a son, and she named him
Moab[a];[u] he is the father of the Moabites[v]
of today. 38The younger daughter also had
a son, and she named him Ben-Ammi[b]; he
is the father of the Ammonites[w] of today.

Abraham and Abimelech

20:1-18Ref — Ge 12:10-20; 26:1-11

20 Now Abraham moved on from there[x]
into the region of the Negev[y] and
lived between Kadesh[z] and Shur.[a] For
a while[b] he stayed in Gerar,[c] 2and there
Abraham said of his wife Sarah, "She is
my sister.[d]" Then Abimelech[e] king of Gerar sent for Sarah and took her.[f]
3But God came to Abimelech[g] in a
dream[h] one night and said to him, "You
are as good as dead[i] because of the woman you have taken; she is a married woman."[j]
4Now Abimelech had not gone near
her, so he said, "Lord, will you destroy an
innocent nation?[k] 5Did he not say to me,
'She is my sister,[l]' and didn't she also say,
'He is my brother'? I have done this with a
clear conscience[m] and clean hands.[n]"
6Then God said to him in the dream,
"Yes, I know you did this with a clear conscience, and so I have kept[o] you from sinning against me.[p] That is why I did not
let you touch her. 7Now return the man's
wife, for he is a prophet,[q] and he will pray
for you[r] and you will live. But if you do
not return her, you may be sure that you
and all yours will die."[s]
8Early the next morning Abimelech
summoned all his officials, and when he
told them all that had happened, they
were very much afraid. 9Then Abimelech
called Abraham in and said, "What have
you done to us? How have I wronged you
that you have brought such great guilt
upon me and my kingdom? You have done
things to me that should not be done.[t]"
10And Abimelech asked Abraham, "What
was your reason for doing this?"
11Abraham replied, "I said to myself,
'There is surely no fear of God[u] in this
place, and they will kill me because of
my wife.'[v] 12Besides, she really is my sister,[w] the daughter of my father though not
of my mother; and she became my wife.
13And when God had me wander[x] from my
father's household,[y] I said to her, 'This is
how you can show your love to me: Everywhere we go, say of me, "He is my
brother." ' "
14Then Abimelech[z] brought sheep and
cattle and male and female slaves and
gave them to Abraham,[a] and he returned
Sarah his wife to him. 15And Abimelech
said, "My land is before you; live wherever you like."[b]
16To Sarah he said, "I am giving your
brother a thousand shekels[c] of silver. This
is to cover the offense against you before
all who are with you; you are completely
vindicated."
17Then Abraham prayed to God,[c] and
God healed Abimelech, his wife and his
slave girls so they could have children
again, 18for the LORD had closed up every

19:34 [q] S ver 32 **19:35** [r] Ge 9:21 [s] ver 33 **19:36** [t] S ver 32 **19:37** [u] Ge 36:35; Ex 15:15; Nu 25:1; Isa 15:1; 25:10; Jer 25:21; 48:1; Eze 25:8; Zep 2:9 [v] Nu 22:4; 24:17; Dt 2:9; Jdg 3:28; Ru 1:4,22; 1Sa 14:47; 22:3-4; 2Sa 8:2; 2Ki 1:1; 3:4; Ezr 9:1; Ps 108:9; Jer 48:1 **19:38** [w] Nu 21:24; Dt 2:19; 23:3; Jos 12:2; Jdg 3:13; 10:6,7; 1Sa 11:1-11; 14:47; 1Ch 19:1; 2Ch 20:23; 26:8; 27:5; Ne 2:19; 4:3; Jer 25:21; 40:14; 49:1; Eze 21:28; 25:2; Am 1:13 **20:1** [x] Ge 18:1 [y] S Ge 12:9 [z] S Ge 14:7 [a] S Ge 16:7 [b] Ge 26:3 [c] Ge 26:1,6,17 **20:2** [d] ver 12; S Ge 12:13 [e] ver 14; Ge 21:22; 26:1 [f] S Ge 12:15 **20:3** [g] Nu 22:9, 20 [h] Ge 28:12; 31:10,24; 37:5,9; 40:5; 41:1; Nu 12:6; Dt 13:1; Job 33:15; Da 2:1; 4:5 [i] Ex 10:7; 12:33; Ps 105:38 [j] ver 7; Ge 26:11; 1Ch 16:21; Ps 105:14 **20:4** [k] S Ge 18:25 **20:5** [l] S Ge 12:19 [m] S Ge 17:1 [n] Ps 7:8; 25:21; 26:6; 41:12 **20:6** [o] 1Sa 25:26, 34 [p] S Ge 13:13; Ps 41:4; 51:4

[a] *37 Moab* sounds like the Hebrew for *from father.*
[b] *38 Ben-Ammi* means *son of my people.*
[c] *16* That is, about 25 pounds (about 11.5 kilograms)

20:7 [q] Dt 18:18; 34:10; 2Ki 3:11; 5:3; 1Ch 16:22; Ps 105:15 [r] ver 17; Ex 8:8; Nu 11:2; 12:13; 1Sa 7:5; 1Ki 13:6; Job 42:8; Jer 18:20; 37:3; 42:2 [s] S ver 3; S Ps 9:5 **20:9** [t] S Ge 12:18; 34:7 **20:11** [u] Ge 42:18; Ne 5:15; Job 31:23; Ps 36:1; Pr 16:6 [v] S Ge 12:12; 31:31 **20:12** [w] S Ge 12:13 **20:13** [x] Dt 26:5; 1Ch 16:20; Isa 30:28; 63:17 [y] S Ge 12:1 **20:14** [z] S ver 2 [a] Ge 12:16 **20:15** [b] Ge 13:9; S 45:18 **20:17** [c] S ver 7; Job 42:9

19:36 – 38 The sons born to Lot's daughters were the ancestors of the Moabites and Ammonites (see Dt 2:9,19), two nations that were to become bitter enemies of Abraham's descendants (see, e.g., 1Sa 14:47; 2Ch 20:1 and note on 20:1 – 30).

20:1 – 18 See 12:10 – 20 and notes.

20:1 *Negev.* See note on 12:9. *between Kadesh and Shur.* See notes on 14:7; 16:7. *Gerar.* Located at the edge of Philistine territory, about halfway between Gaza near the Mediterranean coast and Beersheba in the northern Negev.

20:2 *Abimelech.* Probably the father or grandfather of the later king who bore the same name (see 26:1).

20:3 *dream.* Once again God intervened to spare the mother of the promised offspring. Dreams were a frequent mode of revelation in the OT (see 28:12; 31:10 – 11; 37:5 – 9; 40:5; 41:1; Nu 12:6; Jdg 7:13 – 14 and note; 1Ki 3:5 and note; Da 2:3; 4:5; 7:1).

20:7 *prophet.* See notes on 18:17; Zec 1:1. Abraham was the first man to bear this title (see Ps 105:15).

20:9 *brought such great guilt upon me and my kingdom.* Or "caused me and my kingdom to commit such a great sin." The "great sin" is adultery (see vv. 2 – 3,6; the same meaning for this expression is attested also in Egyptian and Canaanite texts). Everywhere else the Hebrew expression occurs in the OT it refers to idolatry (Ex 32:21,30 – 31; 2Ki 17:21), which is spiritual adultery (see Hos 1:2 and note). Adultery and idolatry are supreme forms of covenant infidelity (see note on Ex 34:15).

20:11 *fear of God.* A conventional phrase equivalent to "true religion." "Fear" in this phrase has the sense of reverential trust in God and commitment to his revealed will (word); see Ps 15:4; 34:8 – 14; Pr 1:7 and notes.

20:12 *she really is my sister, the daughter of my father though not of my mother.* Abraham's half-truth was a sinful deception, not a legitimate explanation.

20:14 – 16 Abimelech's generosity was a strong contrast to Abraham's fearfulness and deception.

20:16 *shekels.* Though not in the Hebrew, the word is correctly supplied here as the most common unit of weight in ancient times. Originally the shekel was only a weight, not a coin, since coinage was not invented till the seventh century B.C.

womb in Abimelech's household because of Abraham's wife Sarah.[d]

The Birth of Isaac

21 Now the LORD was gracious to Sarah[e] as he had said, and the LORD did for Sarah what he had promised.[f] 2Sarah became pregnant and bore a son[g] to Abraham in his old age,[h] at the very time God had promised him.[i] 3Abraham gave the name Isaac[a][j] to the son Sarah bore him. 4When his son Isaac was eight days old, Abraham circumcised him,[k] as God commanded him. 5Abraham was a hundred years old[l] when his son Isaac was born to him.

6Sarah said, "God has brought me laughter,[m] and everyone who hears about this will laugh with me." 7And she added, "Who would have said to Abraham that Sarah would nurse children? Yet I have borne him a son in his old age."[n]

Hagar and Ishmael Sent Away

8The child grew and was weaned,[o] and on the day Isaac was weaned Abraham held a great feast. 9But Sarah saw that the son whom Hagar the Egyptian had borne to Abraham[p] was mocking,[q] 10and she said to Abraham, "Get rid of that slave woman[r] and her son, for that slave woman's son will never share in the inheritance with my son Isaac."[s]

11The matter distressed Abraham greatly because it concerned his son.[t] 12But God said to him, "Do not be so distressed about the boy and your maidservant. Listen to whatever Sarah tells you, because it is through Isaac that your offspring[b] will be reckoned.[u] 13I will make the son of the maidservant into a nation[v] also, because he is your offspring."

20:18 [d]Ge 12:17 **21:1** [e]1Sa 2:21 [f]S Ge 8:1; S 17:16,21; 18:14; Gal 4:23; Heb 11:11 **21:2** [g]S Ge 17:19; S 30:6 [h]Gal 4:22; Heb 11:11 [i]S Ge 18:10 **21:3** [j]S Ge 16:11; S 17:19; Jos 24:3 **21:4** [k]Ge 17:10, 12; Ac 7:8 **21:5** [l]S Ge 12:4; Heb 6:15 **21:6** [m]Ge 17:17; Job 8:21; Ps 126:2; Isa 12:6; 35:2; 44:23; 52:9; 54:1 **21:7** [n]S Ge 17:17 **21:8** [o]1Sa 1:23 **21:9** [p]S Ge 16:15 [q]Ge 39:14; Gal 4:29 **21:10** [r]Ge 39:17 [s]Ge 25:6; Gal 4:30* **21:11** [t]Ge 17:18 **21:12** [u]Mt 1:2; Ro 9:7*; Heb 11:18* **21:13** [v]ver 18; S Ge 13:16 **21:14** [w]S Ge 16:1 [x]ver 31,32; Ge 22:19; 26:33; 28:10; 46:1,5; Jos 15:28; 19:2; Jdg 20:1; 1Sa 3:20; 1Ch 4:28; Ne 11:27 **21:16** [y]Jer 6:26; Am 8:10; Zec 12:10 **21:17** [z]Ex 3:7; Nu 20:16; Dt 26:7; Ps 6:8 [a]S Ge 16:7 [b]Ge 22:11,15 [c]S Ge 15:1 **21:18** [d]ver 13; S Ge 17:20 **21:19** [e]Nu 22:31 [f]S Ge 16:7 **21:20** [g]Ge 26:3,24; 28:15; 39:2,21,23; Lk 1:66 **21:21** [h]S Ge 14:6 [i]Ge 24:4,38; 28:2; 34:4,8; Jdg 14:2 **21:22** [j]S Ge 20:2 [k]ver 32; Ge 26:26 [l]ver 23; Ge 26:28; 28:15; 31:3,5,42; 39:2,3; 1Sa 3:19; 16:18; 2Ch 1:1; Ps 46:7; Isa 7:14; 8:8,10; 41:10; 43:5 **21:23** [m]ver 31; Ge 25:33; 26:31; 31:53; Jos 2:12; 1Ki 2:8

14Early the next morning Abraham took some food and a skin of water and gave them to Hagar.[w] He set them on her shoulders and then sent her off with the boy. She went on her way and wandered in the desert of Beersheba.[x]

15When the water in the skin was gone, she put the boy under one of the bushes. 16Then she went off and sat down nearby, about a bowshot away, for she thought, "I cannot watch the boy die." And as she sat there nearby, she[c] began to sob.[y]

17God heard the boy crying,[z] and the angel of God[a] called to Hagar from heaven[b] and said to her, "What is the matter, Hagar? Do not be afraid;[c] God has heard the boy crying as he lies there. 18Lift the boy up and take him by the hand, for I will make him into a great nation."[d]

19Then God opened her eyes[e] and she saw a well of water.[f] So she went and filled the skin with water and gave the boy a drink.

20God was with the boy[g] as he grew up. He lived in the desert and became an archer. 21While he was living in the Desert of Paran,[h] his mother got a wife for him[i] from Egypt.

The Treaty at Beersheba

22At that time Abimelech[j] and Phicol the commander of his forces[k] said to Abraham, "God is with you in everything you do.[l] 23Now swear[m] to me here before God

[a] *3 Isaac* means *he laughs.* [b] *12* Or *seed*
[c] *16* Hebrew; Septuagint *the child*

21:1 See 17:16. *did for Sarah what he had promised.* See Gal 4:22–23,28 and notes. The promised son through whom God will continue the covenant line (17:21) is born at last.

21:2–3 *Sarah ... bore a son to Abraham ... Isaac.* In c. 2066 B.C.

21:2 *very time God had promised.* See 17:21.

21:3 *Isaac.* See note on 17:17.

21:4 See notes on 17:10,12.

21:5 In fulfillment of the promise made to him (see 17:16), Abraham miraculously became a father at the age of 100 years (see 17:17 and chart, p. 26).

21:6 *laughter ... laugh.* See 18:12 and note on 17:17.

21:8 *weaned.* At age two or three, as was customary in the ancient Near East.

21:9 *the son whom Hagar the Egyptian had borne.* Ishmael, who was in his late teens at this time (see 16:15–16). *mocking.* Or "at play." In either case, Sarah saw Ishmael as a potential threat to Isaac's inheritance (v. 10).

21:10 *Get rid of that slave woman and her son.* See Gal 4:21–31 and notes. Driving them out would have had the effect of disinheriting Ishmael.

21:11 *The matter distressed Abraham.* Both love and legal custom played a part in Abraham's anguish. He knew that the customs of his day, illustrated later in the Nuzi tablets (see chart, p. xxiii), prohibited the arbitrary expulsion of a female servant's son (whose legal status was relatively weak in any case).

21:12 *Listen to whatever Sarah tells you.* God overruled in this matter (as he had done earlier; see 15:4), promising Abraham that both Isaac and Ishmael would have numerous descendants. *it is through Isaac that your offspring will be reckoned.* See 17:19; 22:18; see also Ro 9:6–8 and Heb 11:17–19 for broader spiritual applications of this statement.

21:14 *Early the next morning.* Though Abraham would now be separated from Ishmael for the first time, he responded to God's command with prompt obedience (see note on 12:4). *Beersheba.* See note on v. 31.

21:15 *one of the bushes.* See note on v. 33.

21:17 *God heard ... God has heard.* A pun on the name "Ishmael" (see NIV text note on 16:11; see also 17:20).

21:21 *Desert of Paran.* Located in north central Sinai. *his mother got a wife for him from Egypt.* Parents often arranged their children's marriages (see ch. 24).

21:22 *Abimelech.* See 20:2 and note. *Phicol.* Either a family name or an official title, since it reappears over 60 years later (25:26) in a similar context (26:26).

21:23 *swear to me ... before God ... Show to me ... kindness.*

that you will not deal falsely with me or
my children or my descendants.[n] Show
to me and the country where you are living as an alien the same kindness I have
shown to you."[o]
24Abraham said, "I swear it."
25Then Abraham complained to Abimelech about a well of water that Abimelech's servants had seized.[p] 26But Abimelech said, "I don't know who has done
this. You did not tell me, and I heard about
it only today."
27So Abraham brought sheep and cattle
and gave them to Abimelech, and the two
men made a treaty.[q] 28Abraham set apart
seven ewe lambs from the flock, 29and
Abimelech asked Abraham, "What is the
meaning of these seven ewe lambs you
have set apart by themselves?"
30He replied, "Accept these seven lambs
from my hand as a witness[r] that I dug this
well.[s]"
31So that place was called Beersheba,[a][t]
because the two men swore an oath[u]
there.

32After the treaty[v] had been made at Beersheba,[w] Abimelech and Phicol the commander of his forces[x] returned to the land
of the Philistines.[y] 33Abraham planted a
tamarisk tree[z] in Beersheba, and there he
called upon the name of the LORD,[a] the
Eternal God.[b] 34And Abraham stayed in the
land of the Philistines[c] for a long time.

Abraham Tested

22 Some time later God tested[d] Abraham. He said to him, "Abraham!"
"Here I am,"[e] he replied.
2Then God said, "Take your son[f], your
only son, Isaac, whom you love, and go to
the region of Moriah.[g] Sacrifice him there
as a burnt offering[h] on one of the mountains I will tell you about.[i]"

[a] 31 *Beersheba* can mean *well of seven* or *well of the oath.*

21:23 [n] 1Sa 24:21 [o] S ver 22; Jos 2:12 **21:25** [p] Ge 26:15, 18, 20-22 **21:27** [q] ver 31, 32; Ge 26:28, 31; 31:44, 53 **21:30** [r] Ge 31:44, 47, 48, 50, 52; Jos 22:27, 28, 34; 24:27; Isa 19:20; Mal 2:14 [s] ver 25; Ge 26:25, 32 **21:31** [t] S ver 14 [u] S ver 23, S 27 **21:32** [v] S ver 27 [w] S ver 14 [x] S ver 22 [y] S Ge 10:14 **21:33** [z] 1Sa 22:6; 31:13 [a] S Ge 4:26 [b] Ex 15:18; Dt 32:40; 33:27; Job 36:26; Ps 10:16; 45:6; 90:2; 93:2; 102:24; 103:19; 146:10; Isa 40:28; Jer 10:10; Hab 1:12; 3:6; Heb 13:8 **21:34** [c] S Ge 10:14 **22:1** [d] Ex 15:25; 16:4; 20:20; Dt 8:2, 16; 13:3; Jdg 2:22; 3:1; 2Ch 32:31; Ps 66:10; Heb 11:17; Jas 1:12-13 [e] ver 11; Ge 31:11; 46:2; 1Sa 3:4, 6, 8; Isa 6:8 **22:2** [f] ver 12, 16; Jn 3:16; Heb 11:17; 1Jn 4:9 [g] 2Ch 3:1 [h] S Ge 8:20 [i] ver 9

Phrases commonly used when making covenants or treaties (see vv. 27,32). "Kindness" as used here refers to acts of friendship (cf. v. 27; 20:14; Ps 6:4 and note). Such covenants always involved oaths.

21:27 *sheep and cattle.* Probably to be used in the treaty ceremony (see 15:10).

21:30 *as a witness.* "Witnesses" to covenant/treaty-making (or other events of continuing significance) served as disinterested (third-party) testimonies to the event they "witnessed" (see 31:44,48,52; Dt 4:26; 30:19 and note; 31:19,26; 32:1; Jos 22:27–28; 24:27; 1Sa 6:18) and could be appealed to (see Ps 50:1; Isa 1:2; Mic 6:1–2 and notes).

21:31 *Beersheba, because the two men swore an oath there.* See NIV text note. For a similar pun on the name see 26:33. Beersheba, an important town in the northern Negev, marked the southernmost boundary of the Israelite monarchy in later times (see, e.g., 1Sa 3:20 and note; 2Sa 17:11). An ancient well there is still pointed out as "Abraham's well" (see v. 25), but its authenticity is not certain. *because.* Or "when."

21:32 *Philistines.* See note on 10:14.

21:33 *tamarisk.* A shrub or small tree that thrives in arid regions. Its leafy branches provide welcome shade, and it is probably the unidentified bush under which Hagar put Ishmael in v. 15. *Eternal God.* Hebrew *El Olam,* a phrase unique to this passage. It is one of a series of names that include *El,* "God," as an element (see 14:19; 17:1 and notes; 33:20 and NIV text note; 35:7 and NIV text note).

22:1–19 The climax to the account of God's dealings with Abraham. Here we are told of God's supreme test of Abraham's faith and of his final confirmation of his covenanted promises—once again confirmed by an oath (vv. 15–18). After this, there follows only the account of how Abraham put his affairs in order with a view to the future: providing a place of burial for Sarah and himself in the promised land (ch. 23), obtaining a suitable wife for Isaac (ch. 24), and seeing to the distribution of his inheritance among his offspring (25:1–6).

This climax in many ways echoes the beginning (12:1–7), and with it frames the main body of the Abraham story. Note the striking parallels: (1) "Leave your country, your people and your father's household" (12:1); "Take your son, your only son, Isaac, whom you love … Sacrifice him …" (v. 2); (2) "go to the land I will show you" (12:1); "go to the region of Moriah … (to) one of the mountains I will tell you about" (v. 2); (3) having completed his "going" to the appointed land, Abram built an altar by "the great tree of Moreh" to God who had appeared to him (12:6–7); having completed his "offering" of Isaac, Abraham sacrificed on the altar he had built in "the region of Moriah" to God who had appeared to him (v. 13); (4) before Abram left his father's household God made promises to him (12:2–3); after Abraham showed his readiness to sacrifice his son Isaac, God confirmed those promises with an oath (vv. 15–18). In both events, Abraham let go of everything else and ventured his whole future on the trustworthiness of God's promises to him—the fundamental character of faith.

22:1 *Some time later.* Isaac had grown into adolescence or young manhood, as implied also by 21:34 ("a long time"). *tested.* Not "tempted," for God does not tempt (see Jas 1:13 and note). Satan tempts us (see 1Co 7:5) in order to make us fall; God tests us in order to confirm our faith (Ex 20:20) or prove our commitment (Dt 8:2). See note on Mt 4:1. *Here I am.* Abraham answered with the response of a servant, as did Moses and Samuel when God called them by name (see Ex 3:4; 1Sa 3:4,6,8).

22:2 *your son, your only son, Isaac, whom you love.* In the Hebrew text "Isaac" follows the clause "whom you love," in order to heighten the effect: "your son, your only son, whom you love—Isaac." Isaac was the "only son" of the promise (21:12). *region of Moriah.* The author of Chronicles identifies the area as the temple mount in Jerusalem (see 2Ch 3:1 and note). Today "Mount Moriah" is occupied by the Dome of the Rock, an impressive Muslim structure erected in A.D. 691. A large outcropping of rock inside the building is still pointed to as the traditional site of the intended sacrifice of Isaac. *Sacrifice him.* Abraham had committed himself by covenant to be obedient to the Lord and had consecrated his son Isaac to the Lord by circumcision. The Lord put his servant's faith and loyalty to the supreme test, thereby instructing Abraham, Isaac and their descendants as to the kind of total consecration the Lord's covenant requires. The test also foreshadowed the perfect consecration in sacrifice that another offspring of Abraham would undergo (see note on v. 16) in order to wholly consecrate Abraham and his spiritual descendants to God and to fulfill the covenant promises.

3Early the next morning[j] Abraham got
up and saddled his donkey. He took with
him two of his servants and his son Isaac.
When he had cut enough wood for the
burnt offering, he set out for the place
God had told him about. **4**On the third day
Abraham looked up and saw the place
in the distance. **5**He said to his servants,
"Stay here with the donkey while I and the
boy go over there. We will worship and
then we will come back to you.[k]"
6Abraham took the wood for the burnt
offering and placed it on his son Isaac,[l]
and he himself carried the fire and the
knife.[m] As the two of them went on together, **7**Isaac spoke up and said to his father
Abraham, "Father?"
"Yes, my son?" Abraham replied.
"The fire and wood are here," Isaac
said, "but where is the lamb[n] for the burnt
offering?"
8Abraham answered, "God himself will
provide[o] the lamb[p] for the burnt offering,
my son." And the two of them went on
together.
9When they reached the place God had
told him about,[q] Abraham built an altar[r] there and arranged the wood[s] on it.
He bound his son Isaac and laid him on
the altar,[t] on top of the wood. **10**Then he
reached out his hand and took the knife[u]
to slay his son.[v] **11**But the angel of the
LORD[w] called out to him from heaven,[x]
"Abraham! Abraham!"[y]
"Here I am,"[z] he replied.
12"Do not lay a hand on the boy," he
said. "Do not do anything to him. Now
I know that you fear God,[a] because you
have not withheld from me your son, your
only son.[b]"
13Abraham looked up and there in a
thicket he saw a ram[a] caught by its horns.[c]
He went over and took the ram and sacrificed it as a burnt offering instead of his
son.[d] **14**So Abraham called[e] that place The
LORD[f] Will Provide. And to this day it is
said, "On the mountain of the LORD it will
be provided.[g]"
15The angel of the LORD[h] called to Abraham from heaven[i] a second time **16**and
said, "I swear by myself,[j] declares the
LORD, that because you have done this
and have not withheld your son, your
only son,[k] **17**I will surely bless you[l] and
make your descendants[m] as numerous as
the stars in the sky[n] and as the sand on
the seashore.[o] Your descendants will take
possession of the cities of their enemies,[p]
18and through your offspring[b] all nations
on earth will be blessed,[q] because you
have obeyed me."[r]
19Then Abraham returned to his servants, and they set off together for Beersheba.[s] And Abraham stayed in Beersheba.

[a] *13* Many manuscripts of the Masoretic Text, Samaritan Pentateuch, Septuagint and Syriac; most manuscripts of the Masoretic Text *a ram behind ⌞him⌟* [b] *18* Or *seed*

22:3 [j]Jos 8:10 **22:5** [k]Ex 24:14 **22:6** [l]Jn 19:17 [m]ver 10; Jdg 19:29 **22:7** [n]Ex 29:38-42; Lev 1:10; Rev 13:8 **22:8** [o]ver 14 [p]ver 13; S Jn 1:29 **22:9** [q]ver 2 [r]S Ge 4:26; S 8:20 [s]Lev 1:7; 1Ki 18:33 [t]Heb 11:17-19; Jas 2:21 **22:10** [u]S ver 6 [v]ver 3; S Ge 18:19 **22:11** [w]S Ge 16:7 [x]S Ge 21:17 [y]Ge 46:2 [z]S ver 1 **22:12** [a]S Ge 18:19; 42:18; Ex 18:21; 1Sa 15:22; Job 1:1; 37:24; Pr 8:13; Jas 2:21-22 [b]S ver 2; Jn 3:16; 1Jn 4:9 **22:13** [c]S ver 8 [d]S Ge 8:20; Ro 8:32 **22:14** [e]Ex 17:15; Jdg 6:24 [f]Isa 30:29 [g]ver 8 **22:15** [h]S Ge 16:7 [i]S Ge 21:17 **22:16** [j]Ex 13:11; 32:13; 33:1; Isa 45:23; 62:8; Jer 22:5; 44:26; 49:13; 51:14; Am 6:8; Lk 1:73; Heb 6:13 [k]S ver 2 **22:17** [l]S Ge 12:2 [m]Heb 6:14* [n]S Ge 15:5; Ex 32:13; Dt 7:7; 28:62 [o]S Ge 12:2; S 26:24; Hos 1:10; Ro 9:27; Heb 11:12 [p]Ge 24:60; Est 9:2 **22:18** [q]S Ge 12:2,3; Ac 3:25*; Gal 3:8* [r]S ver 10; Ge 17:2,9; Ps 105:9 **22:19** [s]Ge 21:14; 26:23; 28:10

22:3 *Early the next morning.* Prompt obedience, even under such trying circumstances, characterized Abraham's response to God (see note on 12:4).

22:4 *third day.* Parts of three days were likely required for the journey from Beersheba (v. 19) to "the region of Moriah" (Jerusalem; see v. 2 and note), a distance of about 48 miles. On the other hand, a "journey of three days" may have been a conventional expression for a short trip rather than a journey of exactly three days (see 30:36; Ex 3:18; 5:3; 8:27; 15:22; Nu 10:33; 33:8; Jos 9:16; Jnh 1:17 and note; 3:3 and note).

22:5 *boy.* See v. 12; see also note on v. 1. The Hebrew for this word has a wide range of meaning, from an infant (see Ex 2:6) to a young man of military age (see 1Ch 12:28). *we will come back to you.* Abraham, the man of faith and "the father of all who believe" (Ro 4:11), "reasoned that God could raise the dead" (Heb 11:19) if that were necessary to fulfill his promise.

22:8 *God himself will provide the lamb.* The immediate fulfillment of Abraham's trusting response was the ram (see v. 13 and note), but its ultimate fulfillment is the Lamb of God (see Jn 1:29,36 and note on 1:29; see also 1Co 5:7 and note).

22:9 *laid him on the altar, on top of the wood.* Isaac is here a type (prefiguration) of Christ (see note on v. 16).

22:11 *angel of the LORD.* See note on 16:7. The "angel of the LORD" who had seen to the safety of Abraham's son Ishmael and had spoken of Ishmael's future (16:7–12; 21:17–18) now intervenes to save Abraham's son Isaac and afterward speaks of Isaac's future (vv. 17–18). *Abraham! Abraham!* The repetition of the name indicates urgency (see 46:2; Ex 3:4; 1Sa 3:10; Ac 9:4). *Here I am.* See note on v. 1.

22:12 *fear God.* See note on 20:11. *you have not withheld from me your son, your only son.* See v. 16 and note. Abraham's "faith was made complete by what he did" (Jas 2:21–22).

22:13 *instead of.* Substitutionary sacrifice of one life for another is here mentioned for the first time. As the ram died in Isaac's place, so also Jesus gave his life as a ransom "for" (lit. "instead of") many (see Mk 10:45 and note).

22:14 *The LORD Will Provide.* Thus Abraham memorializes the remarkable way in which God fulfilled his expectation (v. 8). The Hebrew for "will provide" is lit. "will see (to it)"; God's "seeing to it" spared Isaac just as God's "seeing" had spared Ishmael (in Hagar's womb; see 16:13–14 and notes; cf. 21:15–21). *mountain of the LORD.* During the Israelite monarchy the phrase referred to the temple mount in Jerusalem (see Ps 2:6 and note; Isa 2:3; 30:29; Zec 8:3).

22:16 *I swear by myself.* There is no greater name in which the Lord can take an oath (see Heb 6:13 and note). *you … have not withheld your son, your only son.* Abraham's devotion is paralleled by God's love to us in Christ as reflected in Jn 3:16 and Ro 8:32, which may allude to this verse.

22:17 *descendants as numerous as the stars in the sky.* See 13:16; 15:5 and notes. *sand on the seashore.* Fulfilled, at least in part, during Solomon's reign (see 1Ki 4:20 and note). *cities.* Lit. "gates." Taking possession of the gate of a city was tantamount to occupying the city itself (see 24:60).

22:18 *all nations on earth will be blessed.* See note on 12:2–3. *because you have obeyed me.* See note on 17:9.

Nahor's Sons

20 Some time later Abraham was told,
"Milcah is also a mother; she has borne
sons to your brother Nahor:[t] 21 Uz[u] the
firstborn, Buz[v] his brother, Kemuel (the
father of Aram), 22 Kesed, Hazo, Pildash,
Jidlaph and Bethuel.[w]" 23 Bethuel became
the father of Rebekah.[x] Milcah bore these
eight sons to Abraham's brother Nahor.[y]
24 His concubine,[z] whose name was Reu-
mah, also had sons: Tebah, Gaham, Ta-
hash and Maacah.

The Death of Sarah

23 Sarah lived to be a hundred and
twenty-seven years old. 2 She died at
Kiriath Arba[a] (that is, Hebron)[b] in the land
of Canaan, and Abraham went to mourn
for Sarah and to weep over her.[c]
3 Then Abraham rose from beside his
dead wife and spoke to the Hittites.[a][d]
He said, 4 "I am an alien and a stranger[e]
among you. Sell me some property for a
burial site here so I can bury my dead.[f]"
5 The Hittites replied to Abraham, 6 "Sir,
listen to us. You are a mighty prince[g]
among us. Bury your dead in the choicest
of our tombs. None of us will refuse you
his tomb for burying your dead."
7 Then Abraham rose and bowed down
before the people of the land, the Hittites.
8 He said to them, "If you are willing to
let me bury my dead, then listen to me
and intercede with Ephron son of Zohar[h]
on my behalf 9 so he will sell me the cave
of Machpelah,[i] which belongs to him and
is at the end of his field. Ask him to sell
it to me for the full price as a burial site
among you."
10 Ephron the Hittite was sitting among
his people and he replied to Abraham in
the hearing of all the Hittites[j] who had
come to the gate[k] of his city. 11 "No, my
lord," he said. "Listen to me; I give[b][l] you
the field, and I give[b] you the cave that is
in it. I give[b] it to you in the presence of my
people. Bury your dead."
12 Again Abraham bowed down before
the people of the land 13 and he said to
Ephron in their hearing, "Listen to me, if
you will. I will pay the price of the field.
Accept it from me so I can bury my dead
there."
14 Ephron answered Abraham, 15 "Listen
to me, my lord; the land is worth four hundred shekels[c] of silver,[m] but what is that
between me and you? Bury your dead."
16 Abraham agreed to Ephron's terms
and weighed out for him the price he had
named in the hearing of the Hittites: four
hundred shekels of silver,[n] according to the
weight current among the merchants.[o]
17 So Ephron's field in Machpelah[p] near
Mamre[q]—both the field and the cave in it,
and all the trees within the borders of the
field—was deeded 18 to Abraham as his
property[r] in the presence of all the Hittites[s]

[a] *3* Or *the sons of Heth*; also in verses 5, 7, 10, 16, 18 and 20 [b] *11* Or *sell* [c] *15* That is, about 10 pounds (about 4.5 kilograms)

22:20 [t] S Ge 11:29 **22:21** [u] S Ge 10:23 [v] Job 32:2; Jer 25:23 **22:22** [w] Ge 24:15, 47; 25:20 **22:23** [x] Ge 24:15 [y] S Ge 11:29 **22:24** [z] Ge 25:6; 35:22; 36:12; Jdg 8:31; 2Sa 3:7; 1Ki 2:22; 11:3; 1Ch 1:32; SS 6:8 **23:2** [a] Jos 14:15; 15:13; 20:7; 21:11 [b] ver 19; S Ge 13:18 [c] Ge 24:67 **23:3** [d] S Ge 10:15 **23:4** [e] S Ge 17:8; 19:9; Ex 2:22; Lev 25:23; Ps 39:12; 105:12; 119:19; Heb 11:9, 13 [f] Ge 49:30; Ac 7:16 **23:6** [g] Ge 14:14-16; 24:35 **23:8** [h] Ge 25:9 **23:9** [i] ver 17, 19; Ge 25:9; 47:30; 49:30; 50:13 **23:10** [j] ver 18 [k] S Ge 18:1; Dt 22:15; 25:7; Jos 20:4; Ru 4:11; 2Sa 15:2; 2Ki 15:35; Ps 127:5; Pr 31:23; Jer 26:10; 36:10 **23:11** [l] 2Sa 24:23 **23:15** [m] Eze 45:12 **23:16** [n] 2Sa 24:24; Jer 32:9; Zec 11:12 [o] 2Sa 14:26 **23:17** [p] S ver 9 [q] S Ge 13:18 **23:18** [r] S Ge 12:7 [s] ver 10

22:23–24 Abraham's brother Nahor became the father of eight sons by his wife and four by his concubine (see note on 25:6). They would later become the ancestors of 12 Aramean (see v. 21) tribes, just as Abraham's son Ishmael would become the ancestor of 12 tribes (see 25:16 and note) and Abraham's grandson Jacob would become the ancestor of the 12 tribes of Israel (49:28).

23:1–20 How Abraham provided a burial place for Sarah and himself in Canaan, thus in faith laying claim to Canaan as his homeland in accordance with God's promise.

23:2 *Kiriath Arba.* Means "the town of Arba" (Arba was the most prominent member of a tribe living in the Hebron area [see Jos 14:15 and note]). It can also mean "the town of four," referring to the place where Anak (see Jos 15:13–14; 21:11) and his three sons lived (see Jdg 1:10,20). *went.* Either from Beersheba to Hebron or into where Sarah's body was lying.

23:3 *Hittites.* See note on 10:15. They were apparently in control of the Hebron area at this time.

23:4 *an alien and a stranger.* The phrase was used often by the patriarchs and their descendants in reference to themselves (see 1Ch 29:15; Ps 39:12 and note; see also Heb 11:13 and note). On this earth Abraham "lived in tents" (Heb 11:9), the most temporary of dwellings. But he looked forward to the more permanent home promised him, which the author of Hebrews calls "the city with foundations, whose architect and builder is God" (Heb 11:10; see note there).

23:6 *You are a mighty prince.* Probably intended as flattery.

23:9 *cave of Machpelah.* The tombs of several patriarchs and their wives—Abraham and Sarah, Isaac and Rebekah, Jacob and Leah (see v. 19 and note; 25:8–10; 49:30–31; 50:12–13)—are, according to tradition, located in a large cave deep beneath the Mosque of Abraham, a Muslim shrine in Hebron. *end of his field.* Apparently Abraham wanted to buy only a small part of the field (namely, the part where the cave was located), but Ephron insisted that he purchase the entire field (see note on v. 15).

23:10 *in the hearing of all the Hittites who had come to the gate.* The main gateway of a city was usually the place where legal matters were transacted and attested (see v. 18; see also note on 19:1).

23:11 *my lord.* Perhaps intended to flatter Abraham (see v. 15). *give.* See NIV text note.

23:15 *four hundred shekels of silver, but what is that between me and you?* See note on 20:16. Despite Ephron's pretense of generosity, 400 shekels of silver was an exorbitant price for a field (see, e.g., Jer 32:9 and note). Ephron was taking advantage of Abraham during a time of grief and bereavement. He knew that Abraham had to deal quickly in order to have a place to bury Sarah, so he insisted that Abraham buy the entire lot (see note on v. 9).

23:16 *weight current among the merchants.* Subject to more variation and therefore greater dishonesty than the later royal standard (see 2Sa 14:26 and note), which was carefully regulated and more precise.

23:17 *the field and the cave in it, and all the trees.* Ephron had held out for the sale of the entire field and its contents (see notes on vv. 9,15).

who had come to the gate[t] of the city. 19Af-
terward Abraham buried his wife Sarah in
the cave in the field of Machpelah[u] near
Mamre (which is at Hebron[v]) in the land
of Canaan.[w] 20So the field and the cave in
it were deeded[x] to Abraham by the Hittites
as a burial site.[y]

Isaac and Rebekah

24 Abraham was now old and well advanced in years,[z] and the LORD had
blessed[a] him in every way.[b] 2He said to the
chief[a] servant[c] in his household, the one in
charge of all that he had,[d] "Put your hand
under my thigh.[e] 3I want you to swear[f] by
the LORD, the God of heaven[g] and the God
of earth,[h] that you will not get a wife for
my son[i] from the daughters of the Canaanites,[j] among whom I am living,[k] 4but will
go to my country and my own relatives[l]
and get a wife for my son Isaac.[m]"
5The servant asked him, "What if the
woman is unwilling to come back with me
to this land?[n] Shall I then take your son
back to the country you came from?[o]"
6"Make sure that you do not take my
son back there,"[p] Abraham said. 7"The
LORD, the God of heaven,[q] who brought
me out of my father's household and my
native land[r] and who spoke to me and
promised me on oath, saying, 'To your
offspring[b][s] I will give this land'[t]—he will
send his angel before you[u] so that you can
get a wife for my son from there. 8If the
woman is unwilling to come back with
you, then you will be released from this
oath[v] of mine. Only do not take my son
back there."[w] 9So the servant put his hand
under the thigh[x] of his master[y] Abraham
and swore an oath to him concerning this
matter.
10Then the servant took ten of his master's camels[z] and left, taking with him all
kinds of good things[a] from his master. He
set out for Aram Naharaim[c][b] and made his
way to the town of Nahor.[c] 11He had the
camels kneel down near the well[d] outside
the town; it was toward evening, the time
the women go out to draw water.[e]
12Then he prayed, "O LORD, God of my
master Abraham,[f] give me success[g] today, and show kindness[h] to my master
Abraham. 13See, I am standing beside this
spring, and the daughters of the townspeo-
ple are coming out to draw water.[i] 14May
it be that when I say to a girl, 'Please let
down your jar that I may have a drink,'
and she says, 'Drink,[j] and I'll water your
camels too'[k]—let her be the one you have
chosen for your servant Isaac.[l] By this I
will know[m] that you have shown kindness
to my master."
15Before he had finished praying,[n] Rebekah[o] came out with her jar on her shoulder. She was the daughter of Bethuel[p] son
of Milcah,[q] who was the wife of Abraham's brother Nahor.[r] 16The girl was very
beautiful,[s] a virgin;[t] no man had ever lain
with her. She went down to the spring,
filled her jar and came up again.
17The servant hurried to meet her and
said, "Please give me a little water from
your jar."[u]
18"Drink,[v] my lord," she said, and quickly lowered the jar to her hands and gave
him a drink.

[a] 2 Or *oldest* [b] 7 Or *seed* [c] 10 That is, Northwest Mesopotamia

23:18 [t]S Ge 18:1 **23:19** [u]S ver 9 [v]S Ge 13:18; Jos 14:13; 1Ch 29:27 [w]Ge 49:31 **23:20** [x]Jer 32:10 [y]S Ge 10:15; 35:29; 47:30; 49:30; 50:5, 13 **24:1** [z]S Ge 17:17; Jos 23:1 [a]Ge 12:2; Gal 3:9 [b]ver 35 **24:2** [c]S Ge 15:3 [d]Ge 39:4-6 [e]ver 9; Ge 47:29 **24:3** [f]Ge 47:31; 50:25 [g]ver 7 [h]S Ge 14:19; S Nu 20:14 [i]Dt 7:3; 2Co 6:14-17 [j]S Ge 10:15-19 [k]ver 37 **24:4** [l]S Ge 12:1; Jdg 14:3 [m]S ver 29; S Ge 21:21 **24:5** [n]ver 39 [o]Heb 11:15 **24:6** [p]ver 8 **24:7** [q]ver 3 [r]Ge 12:1 [s]Ro 4:13; Gal 3:16* [t]S Ge 12:7 [u]S Ge 16:7 **24:8** [v]ver 41; Jos 2:12, 17, 20; 9:20 [w]S ver 6 **24:9** [x]S ver 2 [y]Ge 32:4; 33:8 **24:10** [z]ver 19; 1Ki 10:2; 1Ch 12:40; Isa 30:6 [a]ver 22, 30, 47, 53; Ge 43:11; 45:23 [b]Nu 23:7; Dt 23:4; Jdg 3:8 [c]S Ge 11:29 **24:11** [d]Ex 2:15 [e]ver 13; Ge 29:2, 9-10; Ex 2:16; 1Sa 9:11; Jn 4:7

24:12 [f]ver 27, 42, 48; Ge 26:24; 28:13; 31:42, 53; 32:9; 43:23; 46:3; Ex 3:6, 15, 16; 4:5; 1Ki 18:36; Ps 75:9; 94:7 [g]ver 21, 40, 51, 56; Ge 27:20; Ne 1:11 [h]S Ge 19:19; Jos 2:12; Job 10:12 **24:13** [i]S ver 11, 43; Ge 29:8 **24:14** [j]ver 18, 46 [k]ver 19 [l]ver 44 [m]Jos 2:12; Jdg 6:17, 37; 1Sa 14:10; 1Ki 13:3; Ps 86:17; Isa 38:7; Jer 44:29 **24:15** [n]ver 45 [o]S Ge 22:23 [p]S Ge 22:22 [q]S Ge 11:29 [r]S Ge 11:29 **24:16** [s]S Ge 12:11 [t]Dt 22:15-21 **24:17** [u]ver 45; 1Ki 17:10; Jn 4:7 **24:18** [v]S ver 14

23:19 *buried his wife ... in the land of Canaan.* In that culture, people had a strong desire to be buried "with their fathers" (see note on 25:8) in their native land. By purchasing a burial place in Canaan, Abraham indicated his unswerving commitment to the Lord's promise. Canaan was his new homeland.

24:1–67 Abraham obtains a suitable wife for Isaac, relying on God who has made a covenant with him to provide an appropriate mother for his descendants who would inherit the land (see vv. 6–7).

24:2 *chief servant in his household.* Probably Eliezer of Damascus (see note on 15:2). *Put your hand under my thigh.* Near the organ of procreation, probably because this oath was related to Abraham's last will and testament and called for faithful implementation on the part of his son. Isaac must accept Abraham's and God's choice (see also 47:29 and note).

24:3 *the LORD, the God of heaven and the God of earth.* See v. 7; see also note on 1:1. For a similar majestic title used by Abraham in an oath see 14:22.

24:4 *my country.* Mesopotamia (see note on v. 10). *get a wife for my son.* See note on 21:21.

24:7 *To your offspring I will give this land.* Repeats the promise of 12:7. *his angel.* See note on 16:7.

24:10 *camels.* See note on 12:16. *Aram Naharaim.* See NIV text note; the name means "Aram of the two rivers"—the Euphrates and the Tigris. Aram (see note on Dt 26:5) Naharaim was the northern part of the area called later by the Greeks "Mesopotamia," meaning "between the rivers." *town of Nahor.* Nahor is the same name as that of Abraham's brother (see v. 15; 11:26). The town is mentioned in clay tablets excavated by the French beginning in 1933 at the ancient city of Mari on the Euphrates (see chart, p. xxiii). Nahor was located in the Haran (see note on 11:31) district and was ruled by an Amorite prince in the 18th century B.C.

24:11 *toward evening, the time the women go out to draw water.* After the midday heat had cooled.

24:14 *By this I will know.* Like his master Abraham, the servant asked God for a sign to validate his errand (see note on 15:8). *kindness.* See v. 27; probably a reference to God's covenant with Abraham, which had promised numerous descendants through Isaac (see 17:19; 21:12).

24:15 *Before he had finished praying.* God had already begun to answer. *Rebekah ... was the daughter of Bethuel son of ... the wife of Abraham's brother.* Isaac would thus be marrying his father's grandniece (see v. 48).

19 After she had given him a drink, she
said, "I'll draw water for your camels[w]
too,[x] until they have finished drinking."
20 So she quickly emptied her jar into the
trough, ran back to the well to draw more
water, and drew enough for all his camels.[y] 21 Without saying a word, the man
watched her closely to learn whether or
not the LORD had made his journey successful.[z]
22 When the camels had finished drinking, the man took out a gold nose ring[a]
weighing a beka[a] and two gold bracelets[b]
weighing ten shekels.[b] 23 Then he asked,
"Whose daughter are you?[c] Please tell me,
is there room in your father's house for us
to spend the night?[d]"
24 She answered him, "I am the daughter
of Bethuel, the son that Milcah bore to Nahor.[e]" 25 And she added, "We have plenty
of straw and fodder,[f] as well as room for
you to spend the night."
26 Then the man bowed down and worshiped the LORD,[g] 27 saying, "Praise be to
the LORD,[h] the God of my master Abraham,[i] who has not abandoned his kindness and faithfulness[j] to my master. As for
me, the LORD has led me on the journey[k] to
the house of my master's relatives."[l]
28 The girl ran and told her mother's
household about these things.[m] 29 Now Rebekah had a brother named Laban,[n] and
he hurried out to the man at the spring.
30 As soon as he had seen the nose ring,
and the bracelets on his sister's arms,[o]
and had heard Rebekah tell what the man
said to her, he went out to the man and
found him standing by the camels near the
spring. 31 "Come, you who are blessed by
the LORD,"[p] he said. "Why are you standing out here? I have prepared the house
and a place for the camels."
32 So the man went to the house, and the
camels were unloaded. Straw and fodder[q]
were brought for the camels, and water
for him and his men to wash their feet.[r]
33 Then food was set before him, but he
said, "I will not eat until I have told you
what I have to say."
"Then tell us," ⌞Laban⌟ said.
34 So he said, "I am Abraham's servant.[s]
35 The LORD has blessed[t] my master abundantly,[u] and he has become wealthy.[v] He
has given him sheep and cattle, silver and
gold, menservants and maidservants, and
camels and donkeys.[w] 36 My master's wife
Sarah has borne him a son in her[c] old
age,[x] and he has given him everything he
owns.[y] 37 And my master made me swear

24:19 [w]S ver 10 [x]ver 14 **24:20** [y]ver 46 **24:21** [z]S ver 12 **24:22** [a]ver 47; Ge 41:42; Isa 3:21; Eze 16:11-12 [b]S ver 10 **24:23** [c]ver 47 [d]Jdg 19:15; 20:4 **24:24** [e]ver 29, 47; S Ge 11:29 **24:25** [f]ver 32; Jdg 19:19 **24:26** [g]ver 48, 52; Ex 4:31; 12:27; 1Ch 29:20; 2Ch 20:18 **24:27** [h]Ge 14:20; Ex 18:10; Ru 4:14; 1Sa 25:32; 2Sa 18:28; 1Ki 1:48; 8:56; Ps 28:6; 41:13; 68:19; 106:48; Lk 1:68 [i]S ver 12 [j]ver 49; Ge 32:10; 47:29; Jos 2:14; Ps 98:3 [k]ver 21 [l]S ver 12, 48; S Ge 12:1 **24:28** [m]Ge 29:12 **24:29** [n]ver 4; Ge 25:20; 27:43; 28:2, 5; 29:5, 12, 13 **24:30** [o]S ver 10; Eze 23:42 **24:31** [p]Ge 26:29; Ps 115:15 **24:32** [q]S ver 25 [r]S Ge 18:4 **24:34** [s]S Ge 15:3 **24:35** [t]S Ge 12:2 [u]ver 1 [v]S Ge 23:6 [w]S Ge 12:16 **24:36** [x]S Ge 17:17 [y]Ge 25:5; 26:14 **24:37** [z]Ge 50:5, 25 [a]ver 3 **24:38** [b]S Ge 21:21 **24:39** [c]S ver 5 **24:40** [d]S Ge 5:22 [e]S Ge 16:7 [f]S ver 12 [g]S Ge 12:1 **24:41** [h]S ver 8 **24:42** [i]S ver 12 **24:43** [j]S ver 13 [k]Pr 30:19; Isa 7:14 [l]S ver 14 **24:44** [m]ver 14 **24:45** [n]1Sa 1:13 [o]ver 15 [p]S ver 17; Jn 4:7 **24:46** [q]ver 18-19 [r]ver 20 **24:47** [s]ver 23 [t]S Ge 22:22

an oath,[z] and said, 'You must not get a
wife for my son from the daughters of the
Canaanites, in whose land I live,[a] 38 but go
to my father's family and to my own clan,
and get a wife for my son.'[b]
39 "Then I asked my master, 'What if the
woman will not come back with me?'[c]
40 "He replied, 'The LORD, before whom
I have walked,[d] will send his angel with
you[e] and make your journey a success,[f]
so that you can get a wife for my son from
my own clan and from my father's family.[g] 41 Then, when you go to my clan, you
will be released from my oath even if they
refuse to give her to you—you will be released from my oath.'[h]
42 "When I came to the spring today, I
said, 'O LORD, God of my master Abraham,
if you will, please grant success[i] to the
journey on which I have come. 43 See, I am
standing beside this spring;[j] if a maiden[k]
comes out to draw water and I say to her,
"Please let me drink a little water from
your jar,"[l] 44 and if she says to me, "Drink,
and I'll draw water for your camels too,"
let her be the one the LORD has chosen for
my master's son.'[m]
45 "Before I finished praying in my
heart,[n] Rebekah came out, with her jar
on her shoulder.[o] She went down to the
spring and drew water, and I said to her,
'Please give me a drink.'[p]
46 "She quickly lowered her jar from her
shoulder and said, 'Drink, and I'll water
your camels too.'[q] So I drank, and she watered the camels also.[r]
47 "I asked her, 'Whose daughter are
you?'[s]
"She said, 'The daughter of Bethuel[t] son
of Nahor, whom Milcah bore to him.'[u]
"Then I put the ring in her nose[v] and
the bracelets on her arms,[w] 48 and I bowed
down and worshiped the LORD.[x] I praised
the LORD, the God of my master Abraham,[y]
who had led me on the right road to get
the granddaughter of my master's brother
for his son.[z] 49 Now if you will show kindness and faithfulness[a] to my master, tell
me; and if not, tell me, so I may know
which way to turn."
50 Laban and Bethuel[b] answered, "This is
from the LORD;[c] we can say nothing to you
one way or the other.[d] 51 Here is Rebekah;

[a] *22* That is, about 1/5 ounce (about 5.5 grams)
[b] *22* That is, about 4 ounces (about 110 grams)
[c] *36* Or *his*

[u]S ver 24 [v]S ver 22 [w]S ver 10; Isa 3:19; Eze 16:11-12 **24:48** [x]S ver 26 [y]S ver 12 [z]S ver 27 **24:49** [a]S ver 27 **24:50** [b]Ge 22:22 [c]Ps 118:23 [d]Ge 31:7, 24, 29, 42; 48:16

24:22 *beka.* Half a shekel (see Ex 38:26); see note on 20:16.
24:32–33 See note on 18:2.
24:34–49 The servant explained his mission to Rebekah's family. His speech, which summarizes the narrative of the earlier part of the chapter, is an excellent example of the ancient storyteller's art, which was designed to fix the details of a story in the hearer's memory.
24:40 *before whom I have walked.* See notes on 5:22; 6:8–9; 17:1.

take her and go, and let her become the wife of your master's son, as the LORD has directed.[e]"

52When Abraham's servant heard what they said, he bowed down to the ground before the LORD.[f] 53Then the servant brought out gold and silver jewelry and articles of clothing[g] and gave them to Rebekah; he also gave costly gifts[h] to her brother and to her mother. 54Then he and the men who were with him ate and drank and spent the night there.

When they got up the next morning, he said, "Send me on my way[i] to my master."

55But her brother and her mother replied, "Let the girl remain with us ten days or so;[j] then you[a] may go."

56But he said to them, "Do not detain me, now that the LORD has granted success[k] to my journey. Send me on my way[l] so I may go to my master."

57Then they said, "Let's call the girl and ask her about it."[m] 58So they called Rebekah and asked her, "Will you go with this man?"

"I will go,"[n] she said.

59So they sent their sister Rebekah on her way,[o] along with her nurse[p] and Abraham's servant and his men. 60And they blessed[q] Rebekah and said to her,

"Our sister, may you increase
to thousands upon thousands;[r]
may your offspring possess
the gates of their enemies."[s]

61Then Rebekah and her maids[t] got ready and mounted their camels and went back with the man. So the servant took Rebekah and left.

62Now Isaac had come from Beer Lahai Roi,[u] for he was living in the Negev.[v] 63He went out to the field one evening to meditate,[b][w] and as he looked up,[x] he saw camels approaching. 64Rebekah also looked up and saw Isaac. She got down from her camel[y] 65and asked the servant, "Who is that man in the field coming to meet us?"

"He is my master," the servant answered. So she took her veil[z] and covered herself.

66Then the servant told Isaac all he had done. 67Isaac brought her into the tent[a] of his mother Sarah,[b] and he married Rebekah.[c] So she became his wife, and he loved her;[d] and Isaac was comforted after his mother's death.[e]

24:51 [e]S ver 12 **24:52** [f]S ver 26 **24:53** [g]Ge 45:22; Ex 3:22; 12:35; 2Ki 5:5 [h]S ver 10,22 **24:54** [i]ver 56,59; Ge 30:25 **24:55** [j]Jdg 19:4 **24:56** [k]S ver 12 [l]S ver 54 **24:57** [m]Jdg 19:3 **24:58** [n]Ru 1:16 **24:59** [o]S ver 54 [p]Ge 35:8 **24:60** [q]Ge 27:4,19; 28:1; 31:55; 48:9,15,20; Jos 22:6 [r]S Ge 17:16 [s]Ge 22:17; Ps 127:5; Pr 27:11 **24:61** [t]S Ge 16:1; 30:3; 46:25 **24:62** [u]S Ge 16:14 [v]S Ge 12:9 **24:63** [w]Jos 1:8; Ps 1:2; 77:12; 119:15,27,48, 97,148; 143:5; 145:5 [x]Ge 18:2 **24:64** [y]Ge 31:17,34; 1Sa 30:17 **24:65** [z]Ge 38:14; SS 1:7; 4:1,3; 6:7; Isa 47:2 **24:67** [a]Ge 31:33 [b]S Ge 18:9 [c]Ge 25:20; 49:31 [d]Ge 29:18,20; 34:3; Jdg 16:4 [e]Ge 23:1-2 **25:2** [f]Jer 25:25 [g]Ge 36:35; 37:28,36; Ex 2:15; Nu 22:4; 25:6,18; 31:2; Jos 13:21; Jdg 6:1,3; 7:1; 8:1,22,24; 9:17; 1Ki 11:18; Ps 83:9; Isa 9:4; 10:26; 60:6; Hab 3:7 [h]Job 2:11; 8:1 **25:3** [i]S Ge 10:7 [j]S Ge 10:7

The Death of Abraham

25:1-4pp — 1Ch 1:32-33

25 Abraham took[c] another wife, whose name was Keturah. 2She bore him Zimran,[f] Jokshan, Medan, Midian,[g] Ishbak and Shuah.[h] 3Jokshan was the father of Sheba[i] and Dedan;[j] the descendants of Dedan were the Asshurites, the Letushites and the Leummites. 4The sons of Midian were Ephah,[k] Epher, Hanoch, Abida and Eldaah. All these were descendants of Keturah.

5Abraham left everything he owned to Isaac.[l] 6But while he was still living, he gave gifts to the sons of his concubines[m] and sent them away from his son Isaac[n] to the land of the east.[o]

7Altogether, Abraham lived a hundred and seventy-five years.[p] 8Then Abraham breathed his last and died at a good old age,[q] an old man and full of years; and he was gathered to his people.[r] 9His sons Isaac and Ishmael buried him[s] in the cave of Machpelah[t] near Mamre,[u] in the field of Ephron[v] son of Zohar the Hittite,[w] 10the field Abraham had bought from the Hittites.[d][x] There Abraham was buried with his wife Sarah. 11After Abraham's death, God blessed his son Isaac,[y] who then lived near Beer Lahai Roi.[z]

[a] 55 Or *she* [b] 63 The meaning of the Hebrew for this word is uncertain. [c] 1 Or *had taken* [d] 10 Or *the sons of Heth*

25:4 [k]Isa 60:6 **25:5** [l]S Ge 24:36 **25:6** [m]S Ge 22:24 [n]S Ge 21:10,14 [o]Ge 29:1; Jdg 6:3,33; 1Ki 4:30; Job 1:3; Eze 25:4 **25:7** [p]ver 26; Ge 12:4; 35:28; 47:9,28; 50:22,26; Job 42:16 **25:8** [q]S Ge 15:15 [r]ver 17; Ge 35:29; 49:29,33; Nu 20:24; 31:2; Dt 31:14; 32:50; 34:5 **25:9** [s]Ge 35:29; 47:30; 49:31 [t]S Ge 23:9 [u]S Ge 13:18 [v]Ge 23:8 [w]Ge 49:29; 50:13 **25:10** [x]S Ge 10:15 **25:11** [y]S Ge 12:2 [z]S Ge 16:14

24:53 The rich gifts bestowed on Rebekah and her family indicated the wealth of the household into which she was being asked to marry—far from her loved ones and homeland.
24:60 See 22:17 and note.
24:62 *Beer Lahai Roi.* See note on 16:14. *Negev.* See note on 12:9.
24:65 *she took her veil and covered herself.* Apparently a sign that she was unmarried (cf. 38:14,19).
24:67 *tent.* Often used as a bridal chamber (see Ps 19:4–5).
25:1–6 Abraham's final disposition of his estate.
25:1 *took.* Or "had taken" (see NIV text note), since Abraham would have been 140 years old at this time if the order is chronological. *wife.* Elsewhere called Abraham's "concubine" (1Ch 1:32).
25:2 *She bore him.* The listing of Keturah's offspring shows that Abraham indeed became "the father of many nations" (17:4–6; see note on 17:6).
25:5 *left everything he owned to Isaac.* Isaac was the "only son" (22:2; see note there) of Abraham's wife Sarah, so he was the legal heir to Abraham's estate (cf. 21:10 and note).
25:6 *concubines.* Secondary wives, a common cultural phenomenon in the ancient Near East. Polygamy was practiced even by godly men in ancient times, though it was not the original divine intention (see note on 4:19).
25:7 *a hundred and seventy-five years.* Abraham thus lived for a full 100 years in the promised land (see 12:4 and note).
25:8 *died at a good old age.* As God had promised (see 15:15). *old man and full of years.* A phrase used also of the patriarch Job (see Job 42:17). *was gathered to his people.* Joined his ancestors and/or deceased relatives in death (see 2Ki 22:20; 2Ch 34:28).
25:9 *Isaac and Ishmael.* Isaac, as the heir of covenant and estate (see note on v. 5), is listed first.
25:11 *Beer Lahai Roi.* See note on 16:14.

Ishmael's Sons

25:12-16pp — 1Ch 1:29-31

12This is the account[a] of Abraham's son
Ishmael, whom Sarah's maidservant, Hagar[b] the Egyptian, bore to Abraham.[c]

13These are the names of the sons of
Ishmael, listed in the order of their birth:
Nebaioth[d] the firstborn of Ishmael, Kedar,[e] Adbeel, Mibsam, 14Mishma, Dumah,[f]
Massa, 15Hadad, Tema,[g] Jetur,[h] Naphish
and Kedemah. 16These were the sons of
Ishmael, and these are the names of the
twelve tribal rulers[i] according to their settlements and camps.[j] 17Altogether, Ishmael lived a hundred and thirty-seven years.
He breathed his last and died, and he was
gathered to his people.[k] 18His descendants[l]
settled in the area from Havilah to Shur,[m]
near the border of Egypt, as you go toward
Asshur. And they lived in hostility toward[a]
all their brothers.[n]

Jacob and Esau

19This is the account[o] of Abraham's son
Isaac.

Abraham became the father of Isaac,
20and Isaac was forty years old[p] when he
married Rebekah[q] daughter of Bethuel[r] the
Aramean from Paddan Aram[b][s] and sister
of Laban[t] the Aramean.[u]

21Isaac prayed to the LORD on behalf of
his wife, because she was barren.[v] The
LORD answered his prayer,[w] and his wife
Rebekah became pregnant. 22The babies
jostled each other within her, and she
said, "Why is this happening to me?" So
she went to inquire of the LORD.[x]

23The LORD said to her,

"Two nations[y] are in your womb,
and two peoples from within you
will be separated;
one people will be stronger than the
other,
and the older will serve the
younger.[z]"

24When the time came for her to give
birth,[a] there were twin boys in her womb.[b]
25The first to come out was red,[c] and his
whole body was like a hairy garment;[d] so
they named him Esau.[c][e] 26After this, his
brother came out,[f] with his hand grasping
Esau's heel;[g] so he was named Jacob.[d][h]
Isaac was sixty years old[i] when Rebekah
gave birth to them.

27The boys grew up, and Esau became
a skillful hunter,[j] a man of the open country,[k] while Jacob was a quiet man, staying
among the tents. 28Isaac, who had a taste
for wild game,[l] loved Esau, but Rebekah
loved Jacob.[m]

29Once when Jacob was cooking some
stew,[n] Esau came in from the open country,[o]
famished. 30He said to Jacob, "Quick, let me
have some of that red stew![p] I'm famished!"
(That is why he was also called Edom.[e])[q]

[a] 18 Or *lived to the east of* [b] 20 That is, Northwest Mesopotamia [c] 25 *Esau* may mean *hairy*; he was also called Edom, which means *red.* [d] 26 *Jacob* means *he grasps the heel* (figuratively, *he deceives*). [e] 30 *Edom* means *red.*

25:12 [a]S Ge 2:4 [b]S Ge 16:1 [c]S Ge 17:20; 21:18 **25:13** [d]Ge 28:9; 36:3 [e]Ps 120:5; SS 1:5; Isa 21:16; 42:11; 60:7; Jer 2:10; 49:28; Eze 27:21 **25:14** [f]Jos 15:52; Isa 21:11; Ob 1:1 **25:15** [g]Job 6:19; Isa 21:14; Jer 25:23 [h]1Ch 5:19 **25:16** [i]Ge 17:20 [j]S Ge 13:16; Ps 83:6 **25:17** [k]S ver 8 **25:18** [l]S Ge 17:20; 21:18 [m]S Ge 16:7 [n]Ge 16:12 **25:19** [o]S Ge 2:4 **25:20** [p]ver 26; Ge 26:34; 35:28 [q]S Ge 24:67 [r]S Ge 22:22 [s]Ge 28:2,5,6; 30:20; 31:18; 33:18; 35:9,26; 46:15; 48:7 [t]S Ge 24:29 [u]Ge 31:20,24; Dt 26:5 **25:21** [v]S Ge 11:30 [w]Ge 30:17,22; 1Sa 1:17,23; 1Ch 5:20; 2Ch 33:13; Ezr 8:23; Ps 127:3 **25:22** [x]Ex 18:15; 28:30; 33:7; Lev 24:12; Nu 9:6-8; 27:5,21; Dt 17:9; Jdg 18:5; 1Sa 9:9; 10:22; 14:36; 22:10; 1Ki 22:8; 2Ki 3:11; 22:13; Isa 30:2; Jer 21:2; 37:7,17; Eze 14:7; 20:1,3 **25:23** [y]S Ge 17:4 [z]S Ge 9:25; 48:14,19; Ro 9:11-12* **25:24** [a]Lk 1:57; 2:6 [b]Ge 38:27 **25:25** [c]1Sa 16:12 [d]Ge 27:11 [e]Ge 27:1,15 **25:26** [f]Ge 38:29 [g]Hos 12:3 [h]Ge 27:36; 32:27; Dt 23:7; Jos 24:4; Ob 1:10,12 [i]S ver 7,S 20 **25:27** [j]S Ge 10:9 [k]ver 29; Ge 27:3,5 **25:28** [l]Ge 27:; 3,4,9,14,; 19 [m]Ge 27:6; 37:3 **25:29** [n]2Ki 4:38-40 [o]S ver 27 **25:30** [p]ver 34 [q]Ge 32:3; 36:1,8,8-9,19; Nu 20:14; Dt 23:7; Ps 137:7; Jer 25:21; 40:11; 49:7

25:12–18 A brief account of Ishmael's family line, showing the fulfillment of the promises made to Hagar (16:10) and Abraham (17:20) concerning their son but also noting the fulfillment of his predicted alienation from the descendants of Abraham and Sarah (see 16:12 and note).

25:12 *account.* See note on 2:4.

25:13 *names of the sons of Ishmael.* Many are Arab names, giving credence to the Arab tradition that Ishmael is their ancestor.

25:16 *twelve tribal rulers.* Twelve major tribes descended from Abraham's son Ishmael (as predicted in 17:20)—as was also true of Abraham's brother Nahor (see note on 22:23–24).

25:18 *in hostility toward.* See note on 16:12; or possibly "to the east of" (see NIV text notes here and on 16:12; see also 25:6).

25:19—35:29 The author now takes up the story of Jacob, which he continues until the death of Isaac. Isaac is the link between Abraham and Jacob, and his story is interwoven with theirs.

25:19 *account.* See note on 2:4.

25:20 *Paddan Aram.* See NIV text note; means "plain of Aram," another name for Aram Naharaim (see note on 24:10).

25:21 *because she was barren.* As Sarah had been (see 11:30 and note). Rebekah was barren for 20 years (vv. 20,26). Isaac's offspring, like Abraham's, were a special gift in fulfillment of God's covenant promises.

25:22 *jostled each other.* The struggle between Jacob and Esau began in the womb (see also v. 26 and note). *went.* Perhaps to a nearby place where it was thought that God was especially near.

25:23 *the older will serve the younger.* The ancient law of primogeniture (cf. Dt 21:15–17 and notes) provided that, under ordinary circumstances, the younger of two sons would be subservient to the older. God's election of the younger son highlights the fact that God's people are the product not of natural or worldly development but of his sovereign intervention in human affairs (see note on 11:30). Part of this verse is quoted in Ro 9:10–12 (see notes on 9:11–12) as an example of God's sovereign right to do "whatever pleases him" (Ps 115:3; see note there)—not in an arbitrary way (see Ro 9:14), but according to his own perfect will.

25:24–26 For another unusual birth of twin boys see 38:27–30.

25:25 *red.* A pun on Edom, one of Esau's other names (see v. 30 and NIV text note).

25:26 *his hand grasping Esau's heel.* Hostility between the Israelites (Jacob's descendants) and Edomites (Esau's descendants) became the rule rather than the exception (see, e.g., Nu 20:14–21; Ob 9–10; see also Introduction to Obadiah: Unity and Theme). *Jacob.* See NIV text note. The name became proverbial for the unsavory quality of deceptiveness (see NIV text note on Jer 9:4).

31 Jacob replied, "First sell me your birthright.[r]"
32 "Look, I am about to die," Esau said.
"What good is the birthright to me?"
33 But Jacob said, "Swear[s] to me first."
So he swore an oath to him, selling his
birthright[t] to Jacob.
34 Then Jacob gave Esau some bread and
some lentil stew.[u] He ate and drank, and
then got up and left.
So Esau despised his birthright.

Isaac and Abimelech

26:1-11Ref — Ge 12:10-20; 20:1-18

26 Now there was a famine in the
land[v]—besides the earlier famine of Abraham's time—and Isaac went
to Abimelech king of the Philistines[w] in
Gerar.[x] 2 The LORD appeared[y] to Isaac and
said, "Do not go down to Egypt;[z] live in
the land where I tell you to live.[a] 3 Stay in
this land for a while,[b] and I will be with
you[c] and will bless you.[d] For to you and
your descendants I will give all these
lands[e] and will confirm the oath I swore
to your father Abraham.[f] 4 I will make your
descendants[g] as numerous as the stars in
the sky[h] and will give them all these lands,[i]
and through your offspring[a] all nations on
earth will be blessed,[j] 5 because Abraham
obeyed me[k] and kept my requirements, my
commands, my decrees[l] and my laws.[m]"
6 So Isaac stayed in Gerar.[n]
7 When the men of that place asked him
about his wife, he said, "She is my sister,[o]"
because he was afraid to say, "She is my
wife." He thought, "The men of this place
might kill me on account of Rebekah, because she is beautiful."
8 When Isaac had been there a long time,
Abimelech king of the Philistines[p] looked
down from a window and saw Isaac caressing his wife Rebekah. 9 So Abimelech
summoned Isaac and said, "She is really
your wife! Why did you say, 'She is my
sister'?[q]"
Isaac answered him, "Because I thought
I might lose my life on account of her."
10 Then Abimelech said, "What is this
you have done to us?[r] One of the men
might well have slept with your wife, and
you would have brought guilt upon us."
11 So Abimelech gave orders to all the
people: "Anyone who molests[s] this man
or his wife shall surely be put to death."[t]
12 Isaac planted crops in that land and
the same year reaped a hundredfold,[u] because the LORD blessed him.[v] 13 The man
became rich, and his wealth continued
to grow until he became very wealthy.[w]
14 He had so many flocks and herds and
servants[x] that the Philistines envied him.[y]
15 So all the wells[z] that his father's servants
had dug in the time of his father Abraham, the Philistines stopped up,[a] filling
them with earth.
16 Then Abimelech said to Isaac, "Move
away from us;[b] you have become too powerful for us.[c]"
17 So Isaac moved away from there and
encamped in the Valley of Gerar[d] and settled there. 18 Isaac reopened the wells[e]

[a] 4 Or *seed*

25:31 [r] Dt 21:16-17; 1Ch 5:1-2 **25:33** [s] S Ge 21:23; S 47:31 [t] Ge 27:36; Heb 12:16 **25:34** [u] ver 30 **26:1** [v] S Ge 12:10; S Dt 32:24 [w] S Ge 10:14; Jdg 10:6 [x] S Ge 20:1 **26:2** [y] S Ge 12:7 [z] Ge 46:3 [a] S Ge 12:1 **26:3** [b] Ge 20:1 [c] S Ge 21:20; 27:45; 31:3, 5; 32:9; 35:3; 48:21; Ex 3:12; 33:14-16; Nu 23:21; Dt 31:23; Jos 1:5; Isa 43:2; Jer 1:8, 19; Hag 1:13 [d] ver 12; S Ge 12:2 [e] S Ge 12:7; Ac 7:5 [f] S Ge 17:19 **26:4** [g] ver 24; Ge 48:4 [h] S Ge 12:2; S Nu 10:36 [i] S Ge 12:7 [j] S Ge 12:3; Ac 3:25*; Gal 3:8 **26:5** [k] S Ge 18:19 [l] Ps 119:80, 112; Eze 18:21 [m] Lev 18:4, 5, 26; 19:19, 37; 20:8, 22; 25:18; 26:3; Nu 15:40; Dt 4:40; 6:2; 11:1; 1Ki 2:3 **26:6** [n] S Ge 20:1 **26:7** [o] S Ge 12:13 **26:8** [p] S Ge 10:14 **26:9** [q] S Ge 12:19

26:10 [r] S Ge 12:18 **26:11** [s] 1Sa 24:6; 26:9; Ps 105:15 [t] S Ge 20:3 **26:12** [u] Mt 13:8 [v] S ver 3 **26:13** [w] S Ge 13:2; S Dt 8:18 **26:14** [x] S Ge 12:16; S 24:36; 32:23 [y] Ge 37:11 **26:15** [z] S Ge 21:30 [a] S Ge 21:25 **26:16** [b] ver 27; Jdg 11:7 [c] Ex 1:9; Ps 105:24-25 **26:17** [d] S Ge 20:1 **26:18** [e] S Ge 21:30

25:31 *sell me your birthright.* In ancient times the birthright included the inheritance rights of the firstborn (see Heb 12:16 and note). Jacob was ever the schemer, seeking by any means to gain advantage over others. But it was by God's appointment and care, not Jacob's wits, that he came into the blessing.

25:33 *Swear to me first.* A verbal oath was all that was required to make the transaction legal and forever binding.

25:34 *lentil.* A small pea-like annual plant, the pods of which turn reddish-brown when boiled. It grows well even in bad soil and has provided an important source of nourishment in the Near East since ancient times (see 2Sa 17:28; 23:11; Eze 4:9 and note). *Esau despised his birthright.* In so doing, he proved himself to be "godless" (Heb 12:16; see note there), since at the heart of the birthright were the covenant promises that Isaac had inherited from Abraham.

26:1 – 33 The events of some of these verses (e.g., vv. 1 – 11) occurred before the birth of Esau and Jacob. Verses 1 – 11 are placed here to highlight the fact that the birthright and blessing Jacob struggled to obtain from his father (see 25:22,31 – 33; 27:5 – 29) involved the covenant inheritance of Abraham that Isaac had received.

26:1 *earlier famine of Abraham's time.* See 12:10 and note. *Abimelech.* Probably the son or grandson of the earlier king who bore the same name (see 20:2). *Philistines.* See note on 10:14. *Gerar.* See note on 20:1.

26:2 *appeared.* See note on 12:7.

26:3 *I will be with you.* God's promise to be a sustainer and protector of his people is repeated often (see, e.g., v. 24; 28:15 and note; 31:3; Jos 1:5 and note; Isa 41:10; Jer 1:8,19 and note on 1:8; Mt 28:20 and note; Ac 18:10; 2Co 13:14 and note; see also Ge 17:7 and note). *the oath I swore to your father Abraham.* See 22:16 – 18.

26:4 *descendants as numerous as the stars in the sky.* See 13:16; 15:5 and notes. *through your offspring all nations on earth will be blessed.* See note on 12:2 – 3.

26:5 *because Abraham obeyed me.* See note on 17:9. *requirements ... commands ... decrees ... laws.* Legal language describing various aspects of the divine regulations that God's people were expected to keep (see Lev 26:14 – 16,46; Dt 11:1). Addressing Israel after the covenant at Sinai, the author of Genesis used language that strictly applied only to that covenant. But he emphasized to Israel that their father Abraham had been obedient to God's will in his time and that they must follow his example if they were to receive the covenant promises.

26:7 *because she is beautiful.* See 12:11,14 and note on 12:11.

26:8 *caressing.* The word in Hebrew (a form of the verb translated "laugh" in 17:17; 18:12 – 13,15; 21:6 and "mock" in 21:9) is yet another pun on Isaac's name.

26:12 *reaped a hundredfold.* Indicative of the fertility of the promised land.

26:16 *you have become too powerful for us.* An indication that the covenant promises were being fulfilled.

that had been dug in the time of his father Abraham, which the Philistines had stopped up after Abraham died, and he gave them the same names his father had given them.

[19]Isaac's servants dug in the valley and discovered a well of fresh water there. [20]But the herdsmen of Gerar quarreled[f] with Isaac's herdsmen and said, "The water is ours!"[g] So he named the well Esek,[a] because they disputed with him. [21]Then they dug another well, but they quarreled[h] over that one also; so he named it Sitnah.[b] [22]He moved on from there and dug another well, and no one quarreled over it. He named it Rehoboth,[c][i] saying, "Now the LORD has given us room[j] and we will flourish[k] in the land."

[23]From there he went up to Beersheba.[l] [24]That night the LORD appeared to him and said, "I am the God of your father Abraham.[m] Do not be afraid,[n] for I am with you;[o] I will bless you and will increase the number of your descendants[p] for the sake of my servant Abraham."[q]

[25]Isaac built an altar[r] there and called on the name of the LORD.[s] There he pitched his tent, and there his servants dug a well.[t]

[26]Meanwhile, Abimelech had come to him from Gerar, with Ahuzzath his personal adviser and Phicol the commander of his forces.[u] [27]Isaac asked them, "Why have you come to me, since you were hostile to me and sent me away?[v]"

[28]They answered, "We saw clearly that the LORD was with you;[w] so we said, 'There ought to be a sworn agreement between us'—between us and you. Let us make a treaty[x] with you [29]that you will do us no harm,[y] just as we did not molest you but always treated you well and sent you away in peace. And now you are blessed by the LORD."[z]

[30]Isaac then made a feast[a] for them, and they ate and drank. [31]Early the next morning the men swore an oath[b] to each other. Then Isaac sent them on their way, and they left him in peace.

[32]That day Isaac's servants came and told him about the well[c] they had dug. They said, "We've found water!" [33]He called it Shibah,[d] and to this day the name of the town has been Beersheba.[e][d]

[34]When Esau was forty years old,[e] he married Judith daughter of Beeri the Hittite, and also Basemath daughter of Elon the Hittite.[f] [35]They were a source of grief to Isaac and Rebekah.[g]

Jacob Gets Isaac's Blessing

27 When Isaac was old and his eyes were so weak that he could no longer see,[h] he called for Esau his older son[i] and said to him, "My son."

"Here I am," he answered.

[2]Isaac said, "I am now an old man and don't know the day of my death.[j] [3]Now then, get your weapons—your quiver and bow—and go out to the open country[k] to hunt some wild game for me. [4]Prepare me the kind of tasty food I like[l] and bring it to me to eat, so that I may give you my blessing[m] before I die."[n]

[5]Now Rebekah was listening as Isaac spoke to his son Esau. When Esau left for the open country[o] to hunt game and bring it back, [6]Rebekah said to her son Jacob,[p]

[a] 20 *Esek* means *dispute.* [b] 21 *Sitnah* means *opposition.* [c] 22 *Rehoboth* means *room.* [d] 33 *Shibah* can mean *oath* or *seven.* [e] 33 *Beersheba* can mean *well of the oath* or *well of seven.*

26:20 [f] S Ge 13:7 [g] Ge 21:25 **26:21** [h] S Ge 13:7 **26:22** [i] Ge 36:37 [j] Ps 18:19; Isa 33:20; 54:2; Am 9:11 [k] S Ge 17:6 **26:23** [l] S Ge 22:19 **26:24** [m] S Ge 24:12 [n] S Ge 15:1; S Jos 8:1 [o] S Ge 21:20 [p] S ver 4 [q] ver 4; Ge 17:7; S 22:17; 28:14; 30:27; 39:5; Dt 13:17 **26:25** [r] S Ge 8:20 [s] S Ge 4:26; S Ac 2:21 [t] S Ge 21:30 **26:26** [u] S Ge 21:22 **26:27** [v] S ver 16 **26:28** [w] S Ge 21:22 [x] S Ge 21:27; Jos 9:6 **26:29** [y] Ge 31:29,52 [z] S Ge 24:31 **26:30** [a] Ge 31:54; Ex 18:12; 24:11; 1Sa 20:27 **26:31** [b] S Ge 21:23,27 **26:32** [c] S Ge 21:30 **26:33** [d] S Ge 21:14 **26:34** [e] S Ge 25:20 [f] S Ge 10:15; 28:9; 36:2; Jos 3:10; 1Sa 26:6; 1Ki 10:29 **26:35** [g] Ge 27:46; 28:8; Job 7:16 **27:1** [h] Ge 48:10; Dt 34:7; 1Sa 3:2 [i] S Ge 25:25 **27:2** [j] Ge 47:29; 1Ki 2:1

27:3 [k] S Ge 25:27 **27:4** [l] S Ge 25:28 [m] ver 10,25,31; S Ge 24:60; 49:28; Dt 33:1; Heb 11:20 [n] ver 7 **27:5** [o] S Ge 25:27 **27:6** [p] S Ge 25:28

Already in the days of the patriarchs, the presence of God's people in the land was seen as a threat by the peoples of the world. As the world's people pursued their own godless living, God's people aroused their hostility. A similar complaint was voiced by an Egyptian pharaoh hundreds of years later (Ex 1:9).

26:20 *The water is ours!* In those arid regions, disputes over water rights and pasturelands were common (see 13:6 and note; 21:25; 36:7).

26:25 *built an altar.* See note on 12:7. *called on the name of the LORD.* See 4:26 and note.

26:26 *Phicol.* See note on 21:22.

26:30 *made a feast.* Covenants were often concluded with a shared meal, signifying the bond of friendship (see 31:54; Ex 24:11 and notes).

26:33 *name of the town has been Beersheba.* See note on 21:31.

26:34 *When Esau was forty years old, he married.* As had his father Isaac (see 25:20). Forty years was roughly equivalent to a generation in later times (see Nu 32:13). *Judith ... Basemath.* In addition to these two wives, Esau also married Mahalath, "sister of Nebaioth and daughter of Ishmael" (28:9). The Esau genealogy of ch. 36 also mentions three wives, but they are identified as "Adah daughter of Elon the Hittite," "Oholibamah daughter of Anah ... the Hivite" and "Basemath daughter of Ishmael and sister of Nebaioth" (36:2-3). Possibly the lists have suffered in transmission, or perhaps alternative names or nicknames are used. It may also be that Esau married more than three wives.

26:35 *They were a source of grief.* Isaac and Rebekah were determined not to allow Jacob to make the same mistake of marrying Hittite or Canaanite women (see 27:46—28:2).

27:1-40 How Rebekah and Jacob manipulated Isaac's last will and testament.

27:1 *eyes were so weak that he could no longer see.* In ancient times, blindness and near blindness were common among elderly people (see 48:10; 1Sa 4:15). *Here I am.* See note on 22:1.

27:4 *the kind of tasty food I like.* Rebekah and Jacob took advantage of Isaac's love for a certain kind of food (see vv. 9,14). *give you my blessing before I die.* Oral statements, including deathbed bequests (see 49:28-33), had legal force in ancient Near Eastern law. *blessing.* See note on v. 36.

27:5 *listening.* Eavesdropping.

27:6 *Rebekah.* Throughout the Jacob story the author develops a wordplay on "birthright" (*bekorah*)

"Look, I overheard your father say to your
brother Esau, 7'Bring me some game and
prepare me some tasty food to eat, so that
I may give you my blessing in the presence
of the LORD before I die.'[q] 8Now, my son,
listen carefully and do what I tell you:[r] 9Go
out to the flock and bring me two choice
young goats,[s] so I can prepare some tasty
food for your father, just the way he likes
it.[t] 10Then take it to your father to eat, so
that he may give you his blessing[u] before
he dies."

11Jacob said to Rebekah his mother, "But
my brother Esau is a hairy man,[v] and I'm a
man with smooth skin. 12What if my father
touches me?[w] I would appear to be trick-
ing him and would bring down a curse[x] on
myself rather than a blessing."

13His mother said to him, "My son, let
the curse fall on me.[y] Just do what I say;[z]
go and get them for me."

14So he went and got them and brought
them to his mother, and she prepared
some tasty food, just the way his father
liked it.[a] 15Then Rebekah took the best
clothes[b] of Esau her older son,[c] which she
had in the house, and put them on her
younger son Jacob. 16She also covered his
hands and the smooth part of his neck
with the goatskins.[d] 17Then she handed to
her son Jacob the tasty food and the bread
she had made.

18He went to his father and said, "My
father."

"Yes, my son," he answered. "Who
is it?"[e]

19Jacob said to his father, "I am Esau
your firstborn.[f] I have done as you told me.
Please sit up and eat some of my game[g] so
that you may give me your blessing."[h]

20Isaac asked his son, "How did you
find it so quickly, my son?"

"The LORD your God gave me success,[i]"
he replied.

21Then Isaac said to Jacob, "Come near
so I can touch you,[j] my son, to know
whether you really are my son Esau or
not."

22Jacob went close to his father Isaac,[k]
who touched[l] him and said, "The voice
is the voice of Jacob, but the hands are
the hands of Esau." 23He did not recognize him, for his hands were hairy like
those of his brother Esau;[m] so he blessed
him. 24"Are you really my son Esau?" he
asked.

"I am," he replied.

25Then he said, "My son, bring me some
of your game to eat, so that I may give you
my blessing."[n]

Jacob brought it to him and he ate;
and he brought some wine and he drank.
26Then his father Isaac said to him, "Come
here, my son, and kiss me."

27So he went to him and kissed[o] him[p].
When Isaac caught the smell of his
clothes,[q] he blessed him and said,

"Ah, the smell of my son
 is like the smell of a field
 that the LORD has blessed.[r]
28May God give you of heaven's dew[s]
 and of earth's richness[t]—
 an abundance of grain[u] and new
 wine.[v]
29May nations serve you
 and peoples bow down to you.[w]
Be lord over your brothers,
 and may the sons of your mother
 bow down to you.[x]
May those who curse you be cursed
 and those who bless you be
 blessed.[y]"

30After Isaac finished blessing him and
Jacob had scarcely left his father's presence, his brother Esau came in from hunting. 31He too prepared some tasty food and
brought it to his father. Then he said to
him, "My father, sit up and eat some of
my game, so that you may give me your
blessing."[z]

32His father Isaac asked him, "Who are
you?"[a]

"I am your son," he answered, "your
firstborn, Esau.[b]"

33Isaac trembled violently and said,
"Who was it, then, that hunted game and
brought it to me?[c] I ate it just before you
came and I blessed him—and indeed he
will be blessed![d]"

34When Esau heard his father's words,
he burst out with a loud and bitter cry[e]

27:7 [q]ver 4 **27:8** [r]ver 13, 43 **27:9** [s]1Sa 16:20 [t]S Ge 25:28 **27:10** [u]S ver 4 **27:11** [v]Ge 25:25 **27:12** [w]ver 22 [x]S Ge 9:25 **27:13** [y]Mt 27:25 [z]S ver 8 **27:14** [a]S Ge 25:28 **27:15** [b]ver 27; SS 4:11 [c]S Ge 25:25 **27:16** [d]ver 22-23 **27:18** [e]ver 32 **27:19** [f]ver 32 [g]S Ge 25:28 [h]S ver 4 **27:20** [i]S Ge 24:12 **27:21** [j]ver 12 **27:22** [k]Ge 45:4 [l]ver 12 **27:23** [m]ver 16 **27:25** [n]S ver 4 **27:27** [o]Ge 31:28, 55; 33:4; 48:10; Ex 4:27; 18:7; Ru 1:9; 1Sa 20:41; 2Sa 14:33; 19:39 [p]Heb 11:20 [q]S ver 15 [r]Ps 65:9-13 **27:28** [s]Dt 33:13; 2Sa 1:21; Job 18:16; 29:19; Pr 3:20; Isa 26:19; Hos 14:5; Hag 1:10; Zec 8:12 [t]ver 39; Ge 49:25; Lev 26:20; Dt 33:13 [u]Ps 65:9; 72:16 [v]ver 37; Nu 18:12; Dt 7:13; 33:28; 2Ki 18:32; Ps 4:7; Isa 36:17; Jer 31:12; 40:10 **27:29** [w]2Sa 8:14; Ps 68:31; 72:11; Isa 19:21, 23; 27:13; 45:14, 23; 49:7, 23; 60:12, 14; 66:23; Jer 12:17; Da 2:44; Zec 14:17-18 [x]S Ge 9:25; S 25:23; S 37:7 [y]ver 33; Ge 12:3 **27:31** [z]S ver 4 **27:32** [a]ver 18 [b]ver 19 **27:33** [c]ver 35 [d]S ver 29 **27:34** [e]Heb 12:17

and "blessing" (*berakah*), both of which Jacob seeks to obtain; and Rebekah (*ribqah*) does her best to further the cause of her favorite son. *said to her son Jacob.* The parental favoritism mentioned in 25:28 is about to bear its poisonous fruit.

27:8 *my son, … do what I tell you.* Rebekah proves to be just as deceitful as Jacob, whose very name signifies deceit (see NIV text notes on v. 36; 25:26).

27:20 *your God.* Consistent with Jacob's language elsewhere (31:5,42; 32:9). Not until his safe return from Haran did he speak of the Lord as his own God (cf. 28:20–21 and note on 28:21; 33:18–20 and note on 33:20).

27:24 *Are you really my son Esau?* To the very end of the charade, Isaac remained suspicious.

27:29 *Be lord over your brothers.* Isaac was unwittingly blessing Jacob and thus fulfilling God's promise to Rebekah in 25:23 (see note there). *curse … be cursed … bless … be blessed.* Cf. 12:2–3 and notes.

27:33 *indeed he will be blessed.* The ancient world believed that blessings and curses had a kind of magical power to accomplish what they pronounced (see note on 12:3). But Isaac, as heir and steward of God's covenant blessing, acknowledged that he had solemnly transmitted that heritage to Jacob by way of a legally binding bequest (see note on v. 4).

27:34 *loud and bitter cry.* Esau's tears "could bring about no change of mind" (Heb 12:17; see note there).

and said to his father, "Bless[f] me — me
too, my father!"
35But he said, "Your brother came deceitfully[g] and took your blessing."[h]
36Esau said, "Isn't he rightly named
Jacob[a]?[i] He has deceived[j] me these two
times: He took my birthright,[k] and now
he's taken my blessing!"[l] Then he asked,
"Haven't you reserved any blessing
for me?"
37Isaac answered Esau, "I have made
him lord over you and have made all his
relatives his servants, and I have sustained
him with grain and new wine.[m] So what
can I possibly do for you, my son?"
38Esau said to his father, "Do you have
only one blessing, my father? Bless me
too, my father!" Then Esau wept aloud.[n]
39His father Isaac answered him,[o]

"Your dwelling will be
 away from the earth's richness,
 away from the dew[p] of heaven
 above.[q]
40You will live by the sword
 and you will serve[r] your brother.[s]
But when you grow restless,
 you will throw his yoke
 from off your neck.[t]"

Jacob Flees to Laban

41Esau held a grudge[u] against Jacob[v] because of the blessing his father had giv-
en him. He said to himself, "The days of
mourning[w] for my father are near; then I
will kill[x] my brother Jacob."[y]
42When Rebekah was told what her older son Esau[z] had said, she sent for her
younger son Jacob and said to him, "Your
brother Esau is consoling himself with the
thought of killing you.[a] 43Now then, my
son, do what I say:[b] Flee at once to my
brother Laban[c] in Haran.[d] 44Stay with him
for a while[e] until your brother's fury sub-
sides. 45When your brother is no longer
angry with you and forgets what you did
to him,[f] I'll send word for you to come
back from there.[g] Why should I lose both
of you in one day?"
46Then Rebekah said to Isaac, "I'm dis-
gusted with living because of these Hittite[h]
women. If Jacob takes a wife from among
the women of this land,[i] from Hittite wom-
en like these, my life will not be worth
living."[j]

28 So Isaac called for Jacob and
blessed[b][k] him and commanded him:
"Do not marry a Canaanite woman.[l] 2Go
at once to Paddan Aram,[c][m] to the house
of your mother's father Bethuel.[n] Take a
wife for yourself there, from among the
daughters of Laban, your mother's brother.[o] 3May God Almighty[d][p] bless[q] you and
make you fruitful[r] and increase your numbers[s] until you become a community of
peoples. 4May he give you and your descendants the blessing given to Abraham,[t]
so that you may take possession of the
land[u] where you now live as an alien,[v] the
land God gave to Abraham." 5Then Isaac
sent Jacob on his way,[w] and he went to
Paddan Aram,[x] to Laban son of Bethuel
the Aramean,[y] the brother of Rebekah,[z]
who was the mother of Jacob and Esau.
6Now Esau learned that Isaac had
blessed Jacob and had sent him to Paddan Aram to take a wife from there, and
that when he blessed him he commanded him, "Do not marry a Canaanite woman,"[a] 7and that Jacob had obeyed his father and mother and had gone to Paddan
Aram. 8Esau then realized how displeasing
the Canaanite women[b] were to his father
Isaac;[c] 9so he went to Ishmael[d] and married Mahalath, the sister of Nebaioth[e] and

a 36 *Jacob* means *he grasps the heel* (figuratively, *he deceives*). *b* 1 Or *greeted* *c* 2 That is, Northwest Mesopotamia; also in verses 5, 6 and 7 *d* 3 Hebrew *El-Shaddai*

27:34 [f]Ex 12:32 **27:35** [g]Jer 9:4; 12:6 [h]ver 19,45 **27:36** [i]S Ge 25:26 [j]Ge 29:25; 31:20,26; 34:13; 1Sa 28:12 [k]S Ge 25:33 [l]Heb 12:16-17 **27:37** [m]S ver 28; Dt 16:13; Ezr 6:9; Isa 16:10; Jer 40:12 **27:38** [n]Ge 29:11; Nu 14:1; Jdg 2:4; 21:2; Ru 1:9; 1Sa 11:4; 30:4; Heb 12:17 **27:39** [o]Heb 11:20 [p]ver 28 [q]Ge 36:6 **27:40** [r]2Sa 8:14 [s]S Ge 9:25 [t]2Ki 8:20-22 **27:41** [u]Ge 37:4; 49:23; 50:15; 1Sa 17:28 [v]Ge 31:17; 32:11; Hos 10:14 [w]Ge 50:4,10; Nu 20:29 [x]ver 42 [y]Ob 1:10 **27:42** [z]Ge 32:3,11; 33:4 [a]ver 41 **27:43** [b]S ver 8 [c]S Ge 24:29 [d]S Ge 11:31 **27:44** [e]Ge 31:38,41 **27:45** [f]S ver 35 [g]S Ge 26:3 **27:46** [h]S Ge 10:15 [i]S Ge 10:15-19 [j]S Ge 26:35; S Job 7:7 **28:1** [k]S Ge 24:60 [l]Ge 24:3 **28:2** [m]S Ge 25:20 [n]S Ge 25:20 [o]S Ge 21:21; S 24:29 **28:3** [p]S Ge 17:1 [q]Ge 48:16; Nu 6:24; Ru 2:4; Ps 129:8; 134:3; Jer 31:23 [r]S Ge 17:6 [s]S Ge 12:2

28:4 [t]S Ge 12:2,3 [u]S Ge 15:7 [v]S Ge 17:8 **28:5** [w]S Ge 11:31 [x]Hos 12:12 [y]S Ge 25:20 [z]S Ge 24:29 **28:6** [a]S ver 1 **28:8** [b]S Ge 10:15-19 [c]S Ge 26:35 **28:9** [d]S Ge 16:15 [e]S Ge 25:13

27:36 *Isn't he rightly named Jacob?* See NIV text notes here and on 25:26. *He took my birthright, and now he's taken my blessing!* The Hebrew for "birthright" is *bekorah,* and for "blessing" it is *berakah* (see note on v. 6). Though Esau tried to separate birthright from blessing, the former led inevitably to the latter, since both involved the inheritance of the firstborn (see Heb 12:16 – 17 and notes).

27:39 *away from the earth's richness, away from the dew of heaven.* Cf. v. 28. Isaac's secondary blessing of Esau could be only a parody of his primary blessing of Jacob.

27:40 See 25:22 – 23,26 and notes.

27:41 – 45 Esau's fierce hostility toward Jacob and its consequences. This account of Esau's "grudge" and the later account of the brothers' reconciliation (33:1 – 17) frame the story of Jacob's flight from Canaan to Paddan Aram, where he finds his wives, fathers many children and obtains great wealth before returning to the promised land. This chain of events parallels Joseph's experiences as seen in his words to his brothers in 50:20 (see note there).

27:43 *do what I say.* Bad advice earlier (see vv. 8,13 and note on v. 8), but sensible counsel this time.

27:44 *for a while.* Twenty years, as it turned out (see 31:38,41).

27:45 *both of you.* Jacob and Esau. If he had carried out his intent (v. 41), Esau would have to pay for his deed with his life (see 9:6 and note; see also Ex 21:12; Lev 24:17; Nu 35:19,21,27,33 and note on 35:33; 2Sa 14:6 – 7).

27:46 See note on 26:35.

28:2 *Paddan Aram.* See note on 25:20. *Take a wife for yourself there.* See 24:3 – 4.

28:3 *God Almighty.* See note on 17:1.

28:4 *the blessing given to Abraham.* See 12:2 – 3 and note. For Paul's application of this phrase to Christian believers see Gal 3:14.

28:5 See map and accompanying text, p. 56.

28:9 *in addition to the wives he already had.* See 26:34 and note.

daughter of Ishmael son of Abraham, in
addition to the wives he already had.[f]

Jacob's Dream at Bethel

10 Jacob left Beersheba[g] and set out for
Haran.[h] 11 When he reached a certain place,[i]
he stopped for the night because the sun
had set. Taking one of the stones there,
he put it under his head[j] and lay down
to sleep. 12 He had a dream[k] in which he
saw a stairway[a] resting on the earth, with
its top reaching to heaven, and the angels
of God were ascending and descending on
it.[l] 13 There above it[b] stood the LORD,[m] and
he said: "I am the LORD, the God of your
father Abraham and the God of Isaac.[n] I
will give you and your descendants the
land[o] on which you are lying.[p] 14 Your descendants will be like the dust of the earth,
and you[q] will spread out to the west and to
the east, to the north and to the south.[r] All
peoples on earth will be blessed through
you and your offspring.[s] 15 I am with you[t]
and will watch over you[u][v] wherever you
go,[w] and I will bring you back to this land.[x]
I will not leave you[y] until I have done what
I have promised you.[z]"[a]
16 When Jacob awoke from his sleep,[b] he
thought, "Surely the LORD is in this place,
and I was not aware of it." 17 He was afraid
and said, "How awesome is this place![c]
This is none other than the house of God;[d]
this is the gate of heaven."
18 Early the next morning Jacob took
the stone he had placed under his head[e]
and set it up as a pillar[f] and poured oil on
top of it.[g] 19 He called that place Bethel,[c][h]
though the city used to be called Luz.[i]
20 Then Jacob made a vow,[j] saying, "If
God will be with me and will watch over
me[k] on this journey I am taking and will
give me food to eat and clothes to wear[l]
21 so that I return safely[m] to my father's
house,[n] then the LORD[d] will be my God[o]
22 and[e] this stone that I have set up as a
pillar[p] will be God's house,[q] and of all that
you give me I will give you a tenth.[r]"

Jacob Arrives in Paddan Aram

29 Then Jacob continued on his journey
and came to the land of the eastern
peoples.[s] 2 There he saw a well in the field,
with three flocks of sheep lying near it because the flocks were watered from that
well.[t] The stone[u] over the mouth of the
well was large. 3 When all the flocks were
gathered there, the shepherds would roll
the stone[v] away from the well's mouth and
water the sheep.[w] Then they would return
the stone to its place over the mouth of
the well.
4 Jacob asked the shepherds, "My brothers, where are you from?"[x]
"We're from Haran,[y]" they replied.
5 He said to them, "Do you know Laban,
Nahor's grandson?"[z]
"Yes, we know him," they answered.
6 Then Jacob asked them, "Is he well?"
"Yes, he is," they said, "and here comes
his daughter Rachel[a] with the sheep.[b]"

28:9 [f] S Ge 26:34 **28:10** [g] S Ge 21:14 [h] S Ge 11:31 **28:11** [i] S Ge 12:8 [j] ver 18 **28:12** [k] S Ge 20:3; 37:19 [l] Jn 1:51 **28:13** [m] S Ge 12:7; 35:7, 9; 48:3 [n] S Ge 24:12; 48:16; 49:25; 50:17 [o] S Ge 12:7 [p] Ge 46:4; 48:21 **28:14** [q] Ge 26:4 [r] S Ge 12:2; S 13:14; S 26:24 [s] S Ge 12:3; Ac 3:25; Gal 3:8 **28:15** [t] S Ge 21:20 [u] Ps 121:5, 7-8 [v] ver 20 [w] ver 22; Ge 35:3 [x] ver 21; S Ge 15:16; 30:25; 31:30 [y] Dt 31:6, 8; Jos 1:5; Ne 4:14; Ps 9:10 [z] Lev 26:42 [a] Ps 105:10 **28:16** [b] 1Ki 3:15; Jer 31:26 **28:17** [c] Ex 3:5; 19:21; Jos 5:15; Ps 68:24, 35 [d] ver 22; Ge 32:2; 1Ch 22:1; 2Ch 3:1 **28:18** [e] ver 11 [f] ver 22; Ge 31:13, 45, 51; 35:14; Ex 24:4; Jos 24:26, 27; Isa 19:19 [g] Lev 8:11; Jos 4:9 **28:19** [h] S Ge 12:8 [i] Ge 35:6; 48:3; Jos 16:2; 18:13; Jdg 1:23, 26 **28:20** [j] Ge 31:13; Lev 7:16; 22:18; 23:38; 27:2, 9; Nu 6:2; 15:3; Dt 12:6; Jdg 11:30; 1Sa 1:21; 2Sa 15:8 [k] S ver 15 [l] 1Ti 6:8 **28:21** [m] Jdg 11:31 [n] S ver 15 [o] Ex 15:2; Dt 26:17; Jos 24:18; Ps 48:14; 118:28 **28:22** [p] S ver 18; 1Sa 7:12 [q] S ver 17 [r] S Ge 14:20; S Nu 18:21; Lk 18:12 **29:1** [s] S Ge 25:6 **29:2** [t] S Ge 24:11 [u] ver 3, 8, 10 **29:3** [v] S ver 2 [w] ver 8 **29:4** [x] Ge 42:7; Jdg 19:17 [y] S Ge 11:31 **29:5** [z] S Ge 11:29 **29:6** [a] Ge 30:22-24; 35:16; 46:19, 22 [b] Ex 2:16

[a] *12* Or *ladder* [b] *13* Or *There beside him* [c] *19* *Bethel* means *house of God.* [d] *20,21* Or *Since God . . . father's house, the LORD* [e] *21,22* Or *house, and the LORD will be my God, [22]then*

28:10–22 God's reassuring appearance to Jacob as he is about to leave the promised land. This event and God's appearance to him at the Jabbok River upon his return (32:22–32) form a frame around Jacob's stay in Paddan Aram, to which he went empty but from which he returned full.

28:11 *one of the stones . . . under his head.* In ancient times headrests (e.g., in Egypt) were often quite hard, sometimes being made of metal. People were used to sleeping on the ground.

28:12 *stairway.* Not a ladder with rungs, it was more likely a stairway such as mounted the sloping side of a ziggurat (see note on 11:4). *angels of God were ascending and descending on it.* A sign that the Lord offered to be Jacob's God. Jesus told a disciple that he would "see heaven open, and the angels of God ascending and descending on the Son of Man" (Jn 1:51; see note there). Jesus himself is the bridge between heaven and earth (see Jn 14:6 and note), the only "mediator between God and men" (1Ti 2:5; see note there).

28:13 *above it stood the LORD.* Mesopotamian ziggurats were topped with a small shrine where worshipers prayed to their gods.

28:14 *like the dust of the earth.* See note on 13:16. *All peoples on earth will be blessed through you.* Repeats the blessing of 12:3 (see note on 12:2–3).

28:15 *I am with you.* See note on 26:3. *I will not leave you.* Unlike the gods of pagan religions, in which the gods were merely local deities who were expected to give protection only within their own territories, the one true God assured Jacob that he would always be with him wherever he went (see Dt 31:6 and note).

28:17 *house of God . . . gate of heaven.* Phrases that related Jacob's stairway to the Mesopotamian ziggurats (see notes on 11:4,9).

28:18 *pillar.* A memorial of worship or of communion between people and God, common in ancient times. *poured oil on top of it.* To consecrate it (see Ex 30:25–29).

28:21 *return safely.* Partially fulfilled in 33:18 (see note there). *the LORD will be my God.* For the first time Jacob considered (conditionally: "If . . .," v. 20) acknowledging the God of Abraham and Isaac (see v. 13; 27:20) as his own. His full acknowledgment came only after his safe return from Haran (see 33:20 and note).

28:22 *this stone . . . will be God's house.* In the sense that it would memorialize Jacob's meeting with God at Bethel (see NIV text note on v. 19). *of all that you give me I will give you a tenth.* A way of acknowledging the Lord as his God and King (see note on 14:20).

29:5 *Laban, Nahor's grandson.* See 24:15,29. The Hebrew word here for "grandson" is lit. "son," which can refer to any male descendant (see NIV text note on 10:2).

[7]"Look," he said, "the sun is still high;
it is not time for the flocks to be gathered.
Water the sheep and take them back to
pasture."
[8]"We can't," they replied, "until all the
flocks are gathered and the stone[c] has
been rolled away from the mouth of the
well. Then we will water[d] the sheep."
[9]While he was still talking with them,
Rachel came with her father's sheep,[e]
for she was a shepherdess. [10]When Jacob
saw Rachel[f] daughter of Laban, his mother's brother, and Laban's sheep, he went
over and rolled the stone[g] away from the
mouth of the well and watered[h] his uncle's sheep.[i] [11]Then Jacob kissed[j] Rachel
and began to weep aloud.[k] [12]He had told
Rachel that he was a relative[l] of her father
and a son of Rebekah.[m] So she ran and
told her father.[n]
[13]As soon as Laban[o] heard the news
about Jacob, his sister's son, he hurried
to meet him. He embraced him[p] and
kissed him and brought him to his home,
and there Jacob told him all these things.
[14]Then Laban said to him, "You are my
own flesh and blood."[q]

Jacob Marries Leah and Rachel

After Jacob had stayed with him for a
whole month, [15]Laban said to him, "Just
because you are a relative[r] of mine, should
you work for me for nothing? Tell me what
your wages[s] should be."
[16]Now Laban had two daughters; the
name of the older was Leah,[t] and the
name of the younger was Rachel.[u] [17]Leah
had weak[a] eyes, but Rachel[v] was lovely
in form, and beautiful.[w] [18]Jacob was in
love with Rachel[x] and said, "I'll work for
you seven years in return for your younger
daughter Rachel."[y]
[19]Laban said, "It's better that I give her
to you than to some other man. Stay here
with me." [20]So Jacob served seven years
to get Rachel,[z] but they seemed like only
a few days to him because of his love for
her.[a]
[21]Then Jacob said to Laban, "Give me
my wife. My time is completed, and I want
to lie with her.[b]"
[22]So Laban brought together all the people of the place and gave a feast.[c] [23]But
when evening came, he took his daughter
Leah[d] and gave her to Jacob, and Jacob
lay with her. [24]And Laban gave his servant
girl Zilpah[e] to his daughter as her maidservant.[f]
[25]When morning came, there was Leah!
So Jacob said to Laban, "What is this you
have done to me?[g] I served you for Rachel,
didn't I? Why have you deceived me?[h]"
[26]Laban replied, "It is not our custom
here to give the younger daughter in marriage before the older one.[i] [27]Finish this
daughter's bridal week;[j] then we will give
you the younger one also, in return for another seven years of work.[k]"
[28]And Jacob did so. He finished the
week with Leah, and then Laban gave
him his daughter Rachel to be his wife.[l]
[29]Laban gave his servant girl Bilhah[m] to
his daughter Rachel as her maidservant.[n]
[30]Jacob lay with Rachel also, and he loved
Rachel more than Leah.[o] And he worked
for Laban another seven years.[p]

Jacob's Children

[31]When the LORD saw that Leah was
not loved,[q] he opened her womb,[r] but Rachel was barren. [32]Leah became pregnant
and gave birth to a son.[s] She named him

[a] *17* Or *delicate*

29:8 [c]S ver 2 [d]S Ge 24:13 **29:9** [e]Ex 2:16 **29:10** [f]ver 16 [g]S ver 2 [h]S Ge 24:11 [i]ver 3; Ex 2:17 **29:11** [j]ver 13 [k]Ge 33:4; 42:24; 43:30; 45:2, 14-15; 46:29; 50:1, 17; Ru 1:9 **29:12** [l]ver 15 [m]S Ge 24:29 [n]Ge 24:28 **29:13** [o]S Ge 24:29 [p]Ge 33:4; 45:14-15, 14; 48:10; Ex 4:27; 18:7; Lk 15:20 **29:14** [q]Ge 2:23; 37:27; Jdg 9:2; 2Sa 5:1; 19:12-13; 20:1; Ne 5:5; Isa 58:7 **29:15** [r]ver 12 [s]Ge 30:28, 32; 31:7, 41 **29:16** [t]ver 17, 23, 28, 30; Ge 30:9; 35:23; 47:30; 49:31; Ru 4:11 [u]ver 9-10 **29:17** [v]S ver 16 [w]S Ge 12:11 **29:18** [x]S Ge 24:67 [y]ver 20, 27, 30; Ge 30:26; Hos 12:12 **29:20** [z]S ver 18; Ge 31:15 [a]SS 8:7; Hos 12:12 **29:21** [b]Jdg 15:1 **29:22** [c]Jdg 14:10; Isa 25:6; Jn 2:1-2 **29:23** [d]S ver 16 **29:24** [e]Ge 30:9 [f]S Ge 16:1 **29:25** [g]S Ge 12:18 [h]S Ge 27:36 **29:26** [i]Jdg 15:2; 1Sa 14:49; 18:17, 20; 2Sa 6:23 **29:27** [j]Jdg 14:12 [k]S ver 18; Ge 31:41 **29:28** [l]S ver 16; S Ge 4:19 **29:29** [m]Ge 30:3; 35:22; 49:4; Dt 22:30; 1Ch 5:1 [n]S Ge 16:1 **29:30** [o]S ver 16 [p]S ver 20 **29:31** [q]ver 33; Dt 21:15-17 [r]S Ge 11:30; S 16:2; Ru 4:13; 1Sa 1:19; Ps 127:3 **29:32** [s]Ge 30:23; Ru 4:13; 1Sa 1:20

29:9 *shepherdess.* The task of caring for sheep and goats in the Middle East was shared by men and women.
29:10 *rolled the stone away.* A feat of unusual strength for one man, because the stone was large (see v. 2).
29:11 *weep aloud.* For joy.
29:13 *kissed him.* A common sign of affection among relatives, also between men (see 33:4; Ex 4:27; see also notes on Ro 16:16; 1Co 16:20).
29:14 *flesh and blood.* The English equivalent of a Hebrew phrase that means lit. "bone and flesh" and that stresses blood kinship (see, e.g., 2:23).
29:15 Laban's question and the author's observation in 30:43 (see note there) frame the account of Jacob's receiving the fulfillment of Isaac's blessing. See also God's blessing on Jacob (28:14).
29:16 *Leah … Rachel.* The names mean "cow" and "ewe" respectively, appropriate in a herdsman's family.
29:21 *my wife.* If Jacob had said "Rachel," Laban would have had no excuse for giving him Leah.
29:22 *feast.* A wedding feast was usually seven days long (see vv. 27–28; Jdg 14:10,12 and note on 14:10).
29:23 *when evening came … Jacob lay with her.* The darkness, or perhaps a veil (see 24:65), may have concealed Leah's identity.
29:24 See v. 29; a wedding custom documented in Old Babylonian marriage contracts.
29:25 *you deceived me.* Jacob, the deceiver in name (see NIV text notes on 25:26; 27:36) as well as in behavior (see 27:36), had himself been deceived. The one who had tried everything to obtain the benefits of the firstborn had now, against his will, received the firstborn (vv. 16,26).
29:28 *then Laban gave him his daughter Rachel.* Before Jacob worked another seven years (see v. 30).
29:31–35 Leah, though unloved, nevertheless became the mother of Jacob's first four sons, including Levi (ancestor of the Aaronic priestly line) and Judah (ancestor of David and his royal line, and ultimately of Jesus).
29:32 *named him Reuben … because the LORD has seen my misery.* See NIV text note. Ishmael had received his name in similar circumstances (see 16:11 and NIV text note).

Reuben,[a,t] for she said, "It is because the LORD has seen my misery.[u] Surely my husband will love me now."

33 She conceived again, and when she gave birth to a son she said, "Because the LORD heard that I am not loved,[v] he gave me this one too." So she named him Simeon.[b,w]

34 Again she conceived, and when she gave birth to a son she said, "Now at last my husband will become attached to me,[x] because I have borne him three sons." So he was named Levi.[c,y]

35 She conceived again, and when she gave birth to a son she said, "This time I will praise the LORD." So she named him Judah.[d,z] Then she stopped having children.[a]

30 When Rachel saw that she was not bearing Jacob any children,[b] she became jealous of her sister.[c] So she said to Jacob, "Give me children, or I'll die!"

2 Jacob became angry with her and said, "Am I in the place of God,[d] who has kept you from having children?"[e]

3 Then she said, "Here is Bilhah,[f] my maidservant.[g] Sleep with her so that she can bear children for me and that through her I too can build a family."[h]

4 So she gave him her servant Bilhah as a wife.[i] Jacob slept with her,[j] 5 and she became pregnant and bore him a son. 6 Then Rachel said, "God has vindicated me;[k] he has listened to my plea and given me a son."[l] Because of this she named him Dan.[e,m]

7 Rachel's servant Bilhah[n] conceived again and bore Jacob a second son. 8 Then Rachel said, "I have had a great struggle with my sister, and I have won."[o] So she named him Naphtali.[f,p]

9 When Leah[q] saw that she had stopped having children,[r] she took her maidservant Zilpah[s] and gave her to Jacob as a wife.[t] 10 Leah's servant Zilpah[u] bore Jacob a son. 11 Then Leah said, "What good fortune!"[g] So she named him Gad.[h,v]

12 Leah's servant Zilpah bore Jacob a second son. 13 Then Leah said, "How happy I am! The women will call me[w] happy."[x] So she named him Asher.[i,y]

14 During wheat harvest,[z] Reuben went out into the fields and found some mandrake plants,[a] which he brought to his mother Leah. Rachel said to Leah, "Please give me some of your son's mandrakes."

15 But she said to her, "Wasn't it enough[b] that you took away my husband? Will you take my son's mandrakes too?"

"Very well," Rachel said, "he can sleep with you tonight in return for your son's mandrakes."[c]

16 So when Jacob came in from the fields that evening, Leah went out to meet him. "You must sleep with me," she said. "I have hired you with my son's mandrakes."[d] So he slept with her that night.

17 God listened to Leah,[e] and she became pregnant and bore Jacob a fifth son. 18 Then Leah said, "God has rewarded me for giving my maidservant to my husband."[f] So she named him Issachar.[j,g]

19 Leah conceived again and bore Jacob a sixth son. 20 Then Leah said, "God has presented me with a precious gift. This time my husband will treat me with honor,[h] because I have borne him six sons." So she named him Zebulun.[k,i]

21 Some time later she gave birth to a daughter and named her Dinah.[j]

22 Then God remembered Rachel;[k] he

[a] *32 Reuben* sounds like the Hebrew for *he has seen my misery*; the name means *see, a son.* [b] *33 Simeon* probably means *one who hears.* [c] *34 Levi* sounds like and may be derived from the Hebrew for *attached.* [d] *35 Judah* sounds like and may be derived from the Hebrew for *praise.* [e] *6 Dan* here means *he has vindicated.* [f] *8 Naphtali* means *my struggle.* [g] *11* Or *"A troop is coming!"* [h] *11 Gad* can mean *good fortune* or *a troop.* [i] *13 Asher* means *happy.* [j] *18 Issachar* sounds like the Hebrew for *reward.* [k] *20 Zebulun* probably means *honor.*

29:32 [t] Ge 37:21; 46:8; 48:5,14; 49:3; Ex 6:14; Nu 1:5,20; 26:5; Dt 33:6; Jos 4:12; 1Ch 5:1,3 [u] S Ge 16:11 **29:33** [v] S ver 31 [w] Ge 34:25; 46:10; 48:5; 49:5; Ex 6:15; Nu 1:6,22; 34:20; 1Ch 4:24; Eze 48:24 **29:34** [x] Ge 30:20; 1Sa 1:2-4 [y] Ge 34:25; 46:11; 49:5-7; Ex 2:1; 6:16,19; Nu 1:47; 3:17-20; 26:57; Dt 33:8; 1Ch 6:1,16; 23:6-24,13-14 **29:35** [z] Ge 35:23; 37:26; 38:1; 43:8; 44:14,18; 46:12; 49:8; 1Ch 2:3; 4:1; Isa 48:1; Mt 1:2-3 [a] Ge 30:9 **30:1** [b] S Ge 11:30; Isa 49:21; 54:1 [c] S Ge 16:4; Lev 18:18 **30:2** [d] Ge 50:19; Dt 32:35; 2Ki 5:7 [e] S Ge 16:2 **30:3** [f] ver 7; S Ge 29:29 [g] S Ge 24:61 [h] Ge 16:2 **30:4** [i] ver 9,18 [j] Ge 16:3-4 **30:6** [k] Ps 35:24; 43:1 [l] ver 23; Ge 21:2; Ru 4:13; 1Sa 1:20 [m] Ge 46:23; 49:16-17; Nu 26:42-43; Jos 19:40-48; Jdg 1:34; 13:2; 18:2; Jer 4:15; 8:16; Eze 48:1 **30:7** [n] S ver 3 **30:8** [o] Ge 32:28; Hos 12:3-4 [p] Ge 35:25; 46:24; 49:21; Nu 1:42; 26:48; Dt 33:23; Jdg 4:6; 5:18; 1Ch 7:13 **30:9** [q] S Ge 29:16 [r] Ge 29:35 [s] Ge 29:24 [t] S ver 4 **30:10** [u] Ge 46:18

30:11 [v] Ge 35:26; 46:16; 49:19; Ex 1:4; Nu 1:24; 26:18; Jos 4:12; 1Ch 5:11; 12:8; Jer 49:1 **30:13** [w] Ps 127:3 [x] Ru 4:14; Ps 127:4-5; Lk 1:48 [y] Ge 35:26; 46:17; 49:20; Nu 1:40; 26:47; Dt 33:24; Jos 19:24-31; 1Ch 7:30-31 **30:14** [z] Ex 34:22; Jdg 15:1; Ru 2:23; 1Sa 6:13; 12:17 [a] ver 15,16; SS 7:13 **30:15** [b] Nu 16:9,13; Isa 7:13; Eze 34:18 [c] Ge 38:16; Eze 16:33; Hos 9:1 **30:16** [d] S ver 14 **30:17** [e] S Ge 25:21 **30:18** [f] S ver 4 [g] Ge 46:13; 49:14; Nu 1:8,28,29; 26:25; Dt 27:12; 33:18; Jos 17:10; 19:17; 21:6,28; Jdg 5:15; 10:1; 1Ch 7:1 **30:20** [h] S Ge 29:34; 1Pe 3:7 [i] Ge 35:23; 46:14; 49:13; Nu 1:30; 26:27; 34:25; Dt 33:18; Jdg 5:18 **30:21** [j] Ge 34:1; 46:15 **30:22** [k] S Ge 8:1

30:1 *she became jealous of her sister.* As Jacob was of his older brother. *Give me children, or I'll die!* Tragically prophetic words (see 35:16–19).

30:2 *Am I in the place of God . . . ?* Jacob was forever trying to secure the blessing by his own efforts. Here he has to acknowledge that the blessing of offspring could come only from God (see 31:7–13 for the blessing of flocks). Joseph later echoed these words (see 50:19).

30:3 *Sleep with her.* See v. 9; see also 16:2 and note. *for me.* Lit. "on my knees," apparently an expression symbolic of adoption (see 48:10–16 and note on 48:10) and meaning "as though my own" (see 50:23 and note and NIV text note).

30:4 *as a wife.* As a concubine (see 35:22).

30:5–12 Jacob's fifth, sixth, seventh and eighth sons were born to him through his concubines.

30:14 *give me some of your son's mandrakes.* The mandrake has fleshy, forked roots that resemble the lower part of a human body and were therefore superstitiously thought to induce pregnancy when eaten (see SS 7:13 and note). Rachel, like Jacob (vv. 37–43), tried to obtain what she wanted by magical means.

30:16 *hired.* The Hebrew for this word is a pun on the name Issachar (see NIV text note on v. 18).

30:17–20 Jacob's ninth and tenth sons were born through Leah, who was thus the mother of half of Jacob's 12 sons (see note on 29:31–35).

30:20 *presented . . . gift.* The Hebrew terms for these words are puns on the name Zebulun (see NIV text note).

30:21 *Dinah.* See ch. 34.

30:22 *God remembered Rachel.* See note on 8:1.

listened to her[l] and opened her womb.[m] 23She became pregnant and gave birth to a son[n] and said, "God has taken away my disgrace."[o] 24She named him Joseph,[a p] and said, "May the LORD add to me another son."[q]

Jacob's Flocks Increase

25After Rachel gave birth to Joseph, Jacob said to Laban, "Send me on my way[r] so I can go back to my own homeland.[s] 26Give me my wives and children, for whom I have served you,[t] and I will be on my way. You know how much work I've done for you."

27But Laban said to him, "If I have found favor in your eyes,[u] please stay. I have learned by divination[v] that[b] the LORD has blessed me because of you."[w] 28He added, "Name your wages,[x] and I will pay them."

29Jacob said to him, "You know how I have worked for you[y] and how your livestock has fared under my care.[z] 30The little you had before I came has increased greatly, and the LORD has blessed you wherever I have been.[a] But now, when may I do something for my own household?[b]"

31"What shall I give you?" he asked.

"Don't give me anything," Jacob replied. "But if you will do this one thing for me, I will go on tending your flocks and watching over them: 32Let me go through all your flocks today and remove from them every speckled or spotted sheep, every dark-colored lamb and every spotted or speckled goat.[c] They will be my wages.[d] 33And my honesty will testify for me in the future, whenever you check on the wages you have paid me. Any goat in my possession that is not speckled or spotted, or any lamb that is not dark-colored,[e] will be considered stolen.[f]"

34"Agreed," said Laban. "Let it be as you have said." 35That same day he removed all the male goats that were streaked or spotted, and all the speckled or spotted female goats (all that had white on them) and all the dark-colored lambs,[g] and he placed them in the care of his sons.[h] 36Then he put a three-day journey[i] between himself and Jacob, while Jacob continued to tend the rest of Laban's flocks.

37Jacob, however, took fresh-cut branches from poplar, almond[j] and plane trees[k] and made white stripes on them by peeling the bark and exposing the white inner wood of the branches.[l] 38Then he placed the peeled branches[m] in all the watering troughs,[n] so that they would be directly in front of the flocks when they came to drink. When the flocks were in heat[o] and came to drink, 39they mated in front of the branches.[p] And they bore young that were streaked or speckled or spotted.[q] 40Jacob set apart the young of the flock by themselves, but made the rest face the streaked and dark-colored animals[r] that belonged to Laban. Thus he made separate flocks for himself and did not put them with Laban's animals. 41Whenever the stronger females were in heat,[s] Jacob would place the branches in the troughs in front of the animals so they would mate near the branches,[t] 42but if the animals were weak, he would not place them there. So the weak animals went to Laban and the strong ones to Jacob.[u] 43In this way the man grew exceedingly prosperous and came to own large flocks, and maidservants and menservants, and camels and donkeys.[v]

[a] 24 *Joseph* means *may he add.* [b] 27 Or possibly *have become rich and*

30:22 [l] S Ge 25:21 [m] S Ge 11:30 **30:23** [n] S ver 6; S Ge 29:32 [o] Isa 4:1; 25:8; 45:17; 54:4; Lk 1:25 **30:24** [p] S Ge 29:6; 32:22; 33:2,7; 35:24; 37:2; 39:1; 49:22-26; Dt 33:13 [q] Ge 35:17; 1Sa 4:20 **30:25** [r] S Ge 24:54 [s] S Ge 28:15 **30:26** [t] S Ge 29:18 **30:27** [u] Ge 33:10; 50:4; Est 2:15 [v] Ge 44:5,15; Lev 19:26; Nu 22:7; 23:23; 24:1; Jos 13:22; 2Ki 17:17; Jer 27:9 [w] ver 30; S Ge 26:24; 31:38; Dt 28:11; 2Sa 6:11 **30:28** [x] S Ge 29:15 **30:29** [y] Ge 31:6 [z] Ge 31:38-40 **30:30** [a] S ver 27 [b] 1Ti 5:8 **30:32** [c] ver 33,35,39, 40; Ge 31:8,12 [d] S Ge 29:15 **30:33** [e] S ver 32 [f] Ge 31:39 **30:35** [g] S ver 32 [h] Ge 31:1 **30:36** [i] Ge 31:22; Ex 3:18; 5:3; 8:27 **30:37** [j] Jer 1:11 [k] Eze 31:8 [l] ver 38,41 **30:38** [m] S ver 37 [n] Ex 2:16 [o] ver 41; Jer 2:24 **30:39** [p] ver 41 [q] S ver 32 **30:40** [r] S ver 32 **30:41** [s] S ver 38 [t] S ver 37 **30:42** [u] Ge 31:1,9,16,43 **30:43** [v] S Ge 12:16

30:23 *disgrace.* Barrenness was considered to be shameful, a mark of divine disfavor (see 16:2 and note; 30:2).

30:24 *May the LORD add to me another son.* The fulfillment of Rachel's wish would bring about her death (see v. 1 and note; 35:16–19).

30:26 *I will be on my way.* Jacob had fulfilled his commitments. With his accounts squared with Laban, he asked permission to leave, taking only his family with him. Later, he will take with him also much of Laban's wealth (see 30:43—31:1)—just as Israel later left Egypt with much of Egypt's wealth (see Ex 12:35–36).

30:27 *divination.* The attempt to discover hidden knowledge through mechanical means (see 44:5), the interpretation of omens (see Eze 21:21 and note) or the aid of supernatural powers (see Ac 16:16 and note). It was strictly forbidden to Israel (see Lev 19:26; Dt 18:10,14 and note on 18:9) because it reflected a pagan concept of the world controlled by evil forces, and therefore obviously not under the sovereign rule of the Lord. *the LORD has blessed me because of you.* As God had promised Jacob at Bethel (28:14) and in accordance with the promise made to Abraham (see 12:2–3 and note; 22:18; see also 39:5,23 and note on 39:5; 41:41–57).

30:32 Most commonly the sheep were all white and the goats all black. So Jacob chose to identify as his wages the sheep with dark markings and the goats with white markings—on the face of it a very modest request.

30:35 *he removed.* Secretly and without telling Jacob.

30:36 *the rest of Laban's flocks.* Now made up of only pure-white sheep and all-black goats.

30:37 *poplar ... white.* The Hebrew terms for these words are puns on the name Laban. As Jacob had gotten the best of Esau (whose other name, Edom, means "red"; see note on 25:25) by means of red stew (25:30), so he now tries to get the best of Laban (whose name means "white") by means of white branches. In effect, Jacob was using Laban's own tactic (deception) against him.

30:39 The scheme worked—but only because of God's intervention (see Jacob's own admission in 31:9), not because of Jacob's superstition.

30:43 *the man grew exceedingly prosperous.* Over a period of six years (see 31:41). While in Haran Jacob obtained both family and wealth. His wealth came at the expense of people in Northwest Mesopotamia, just as Abram's (see 12:16 and note) and later Israel's (Ex 12:36) was obtained at the expense of the Egyptians (see also Isa 60:5–17 and note on 60:5; 61:6).

Jacob Flees From Laban

31 Jacob heard that Laban's sons[w] were saying, "Jacob has taken everything our father owned and has gained all this wealth from what belonged to our father."[x] 2And Jacob noticed that Laban's attitude toward him was not what it had been.[y]

3Then the LORD said to Jacob, "Go back[z] to the land of your fathers and to your relatives, and I will be with you."[a]

4So Jacob sent word to Rachel and Leah to come out to the fields where his flocks were. 5He said to them, "I see that your father's[b] attitude toward me is not what it was before,[c] but the God of my father has been with me.[d] 6You know that I've worked for your father with all my strength,[e] 7yet your father has cheated[f] me by changing my wages[g] ten times.[h] However, God has not allowed him to harm me.[i] 8If he said, 'The speckled ones will be your wages,' then all the flocks gave birth to speckled young; and if he said, 'The streaked ones will be your wages,'[j] then all the flocks bore streaked young. 9So God has taken away your father's livestock[k] and has given them to me.[l]

10"In breeding season I once had a dream[m] in which I looked up and saw that the male goats mating with the flock were streaked, speckled or spotted. 11The angel of God[n] said to me in the dream,[o] 'Jacob.' I answered, 'Here I am.'[p] 12And he said, 'Look up and see that all the male goats mating with the flock are streaked, speckled or spotted,[q] for I have seen all that Laban has been doing to you.[r] 13I am the God of Bethel,[s] where you anointed a pillar[t] and where you made a vow[u] to me. Now leave this land at once and go back to your native land.[v]'"

14Then Rachel and Leah replied, "Do we still have any share[w] in the inheritance of our father's estate? 15Does he not regard us as foreigners?[x] Not only has he sold us, but he has used up what was paid for us.[y] 16Surely all the wealth that God took away from our father belongs to us and our children.[z] So do whatever God has told you."

17Then Jacob put his children and his wives[a] on camels,[b] 18and he drove all his livestock ahead of him, along with all the goods he had accumulated[c] in Paddan Aram,[a][d] to go to his father Isaac[e] in the land of Canaan.[f]

19When Laban had gone to shear his sheep,[g] Rachel stole her father's household gods.[h] 20Moreover, Jacob deceived[i] Laban the Aramean[j] by not telling him he was running away.[k] 21So he fled[l] with all he had, and crossing the River,[b][m] he headed for the hill country of Gilead.[n]

Laban Pursues Jacob

22On the third day[o] Laban was told that Jacob had fled.[p] 23Taking his relatives[q] with him[r], he pursued Jacob for seven days and caught up with him in the hill

31:1 [w]Ge 30:35 [x]S Ge 30:42 **31:2** [y]ver 5 **31:3** [z]ver 13; Ge 32:9; Dt 30:3; Isa 10:21; 35:10; Jer 30:3; 42:12 [a]S Ge 21:22; S 26:3 **31:5** [b]ver 29,42,53; Ge 43:23; Da 2:23 [c]ver 2 [d]S Ge 21:22; S 26:3 **31:6** [e]Ge 30:29 **31:7** [f]Lev 6:2; Am 8:5 [g]S Ge 29:15 [h]ver 41; Nu 14:22; Job 19:3 [i]ver 52; S Ge 24:50 **31:8** [j]S Ge 30:32 **31:9** [k]Job 39:2; Eze 31:6 [l]S Ge 30:42 **31:10** [m]S Ge 20:3 **31:11** [n]S Ge 16:7 [o]S Ge 20:3 [p]S Ge 22:1; S Ex 3:4 **31:12** [q]S Ge 30:32 [r]Ex 3:7 **31:13** [s]Ge 28:10-22 [t]S Ge 28:18 [u]S Ge 28:20 [v]S ver 3 **31:14** [w]2Sa 20:1; 1Ki 12:16 **31:15** [x]Dt 15:3; 23:20; Ru 2:10; 2Sa 15:19; 1Ki 8:41; Ob 1:11 [y]S Ge 29:20 **31:16** [z]S Ge 30:42

[a] *18* That is, Northwest Mesopotamia [b] *21* That is, the Euphrates

31:17 [a]S Ge 27:41 [b]S Ge 24:63-64 **31:18** [c]S Ge 12:5 [d]S Ge 25:20 [e]Ge 35:27 [f]S Ge 10:19 **31:19** [g]Ge 38:12,13; 1Sa 25:2,4,7; 2Sa 13:23 [h]ver 30,32,34-35; Ge 35:2; Jos 24:14; Jdg 17:5; 18:14,17,24,30; 1Sa 7:3; 19:13; 2Ki 23:24; Hos 3:4 **31:20** [i]S Ge 27:36 [j]S Ge 25:20 [k]ver 27 **31:21** [l]ver 22; Ex 2:15; 14:5; 1Ki 18:46; 19:3; Jer 26:21 [m]S Ge 2:14 [n]ver 23,25; Ge 37:25; Nu 26:30; 32:1; Dt 3:10; Jos 12:2; Jer 22:6 **31:22** [o]S Ge 30:36 [p]S ver 21 **31:23** [q]ver 37 [r]Ex 14:9

31:1–55 Jacob's flight from Laban has a number of parallels with Israel's later flight from Egypt: (1) God's blessing of Jacob aroused the hostility of Laban and his sons, just as God's blessing of Israel aroused the hostility of Egypt's pharaoh; (2) Jacob took with him the wealth he had obtained at Laban's expense, just as Israel took with them the wealth they had obtained at the expense of the Egyptians; (3) in his flight Jacob crossed the great Euphrates River, just as Israel in their flight crossed the Red Sea; (4) Laban went in force to pursue Jacob, just as Egypt's pharaoh pursued Israel in force; (5) God intervened to secure Jacob against Laban's designs to keep Jacob's household under his control, just as God intervened to secure Israel against the pharaoh's design to keep the Israelites under his control.

31:1 *has taken everything.* Since Laban's sons had been caring for flocks containing the spotted and speckled animals that Laban had sorted out, Jacob could potentially lay claim to a large proportion of the flocks under their care.

31:3 *Go back to the land of your fathers.* Every sign Jacob was getting—from his wives (see vv. 14–16), from Laban (see v. 2), from Laban's sons (see v. 1) and now from God himself—told him that it was time to return to Canaan. *I will be with you.* See note on 26:3.

31:4 *Rachel and Leah.* At long last (see v. 14) Rachel, the younger, has been given precedence over Leah—but she will soon become a deceiver like her husband Jacob (see vv. 31,35).

31:7 *ten times.* See v. 41. "Ten" here probably signifies completeness. In effect, Jacob accused Laban of cheating him at every turn.

31:9 See note on 30:39.

31:11 *angel of God.* See note on 16:7. *Here I am.* See note on 22:1.

31:13 *Bethel, where you anointed a pillar.* See note on 28:18.

31:15 *what was paid for us.* Jacob had come empty-handed to Paddan Aram and had offered his labors instead of wealth for his wives (cf. 24:10). So what had been "paid" for them was the fruit of Jacob's labors for their father (30:27,30).

31:18 *Paddan Aram.* See note on 25:20; see also map on p. 56.

31:19 *household gods.* Small portable idols, which Rachel probably stole because she thought they would bring her protection and blessing. Or perhaps she wanted to have something tangible to worship on the long journey ahead, a practice referred to much later in the writings of Josephus, a first-century Jewish historian. In any case, Rachel was not yet free of her pagan background (see 35:2; Jos 24:2,14,23 and notes).

31:21 *So he fled.* As he had fled earlier from Esau (27:42–43). Jacob's devious dealings produced only hostility from which he had to flee. *Gilead.* An area of exceptionally good grazing land southeast of the Sea of Galilee (see Nu 32:1 and note; see also map on p. 56).

country of Gilead.[s] 24Then God came to Laban the Aramean[t] in a dream at night and said to him,[u] "Be careful not to say anything to Jacob, either good or bad."[v]

25Jacob had pitched his tent in the hill country of Gilead[w] when Laban overtook him, and Laban and his relatives camped there too. 26Then Laban said to Jacob, "What have you done?[x] You've deceived me,[y] and you've carried off my daughters like captives in war.[z] 27Why did you run off secretly and deceive me? Why didn't you tell me,[a] so I could send you away with joy and singing to the music of tambourines[b] and harps?[c] 28You didn't even let me kiss my grandchildren and my daughters good-by.[d] You have done a foolish thing. 29I have the power to harm you;[e] but last night the God of your father[f] said to me, 'Be careful not to say anything to Jacob, either good or bad.'[g] 30Now you have gone off because you longed to return to your father's house.[h] But why did you steal[i] my gods?[j]"

31Jacob answered Laban, "I was afraid, because I thought you would take your daughters away from me by force.[k] 32But if you find anyone who has your gods, he shall not live.[l] In the presence of our relatives, see for yourself whether there is anything of yours here with me; and if so, take it." Now Jacob did not know that Rachel had stolen the gods.[m]

33So Laban went into Jacob's tent and into Leah's tent[n] and into the tent of the two maidservants,[o] but he found nothing.[p] After he came out of Leah's tent, he entered Rachel's tent. 34Now Rachel had taken the household gods[q] and put them inside her camel's saddle[r] and was sitting on them. Laban searched[s] through everything in the tent but found nothing.

35Rachel said to her father, "Don't be angry, my lord, that I cannot stand up in your presence;[t] I'm having my period.[u]" So he searched but could not find the household gods.[v]

36Jacob was angry and took Laban to task. "What is my crime?" he asked Laban. "What sin have I committed[w] that you hunt me down?[x] 37Now that you have searched through all my goods, what have you found that belongs to your household?[y] Put it here in front of your relatives[z] and mine, and let them judge between the two of us.[a]

38"I have been with you for twenty years now.[b] Your sheep and goats have not miscarried,[c] nor have I eaten rams from your flocks. 39I did not bring you animals torn by wild beasts; I bore the loss myself. And you demanded payment from me for whatever was stolen[d] by day or night.[e] 40This was my situation: The heat consumed me in the daytime and the cold at night, and sleep fled from my eyes.[f] 41It was like this for the twenty years[g] I was in your household. I worked for you fourteen years for your two daughters[h] and six years for your flocks,[i] and you changed my wages[j] ten times.[k] 42If the God of my father,[l] the God of Abraham[m] and the Fear of Isaac,[n] had not been with me,[o] you would surely have sent me away empty-handed. But God has seen my hardship and the toil of my hands,[p] and last night he rebuked you.[q]"

43Laban answered Jacob, "The women are my daughters, the children are my children, and the flocks are my flocks.[r] All you see is mine. Yet what can I do today about these daughters of mine, or about the children they have borne? 44Come now, let's make a covenant,[s] you and I, and let it serve as a witness between us."[t]

45So Jacob took a stone and set it up as a pillar.[u] 46He said to his relatives, "Gather some stones." So they took stones and piled them in a heap,[v] and they ate there by the heap. 47Laban called it Jegar Sahadutha,[a] and Jacob called it Galeed.[b] [w]

48Laban said, "This heap[x] is a witness between you and me today."[y] That is why it was called Galeed. 49It was also

[a] 47 The Aramaic *Jegar Sahadutha* means *witness heap.*
[b] 47 The Hebrew *Galeed* means *witness heap.*

31:23 [s]S ver 21 **31:24** [t]S Ge 25:20 [u]S Ge 20:3 [v]S Ge 24:50 **31:25** [w]S ver 21 **31:26** [x]S Ge 12:18 [y]S Ge 27:36 [z]Ge 34:29; 1Sa 30:2-3 **31:27** [a]ver 20 [b]Ex 15:20; Jdg 11:34; 1Sa 10:5; 2Sa 6:5; Ps 68:25; Isa 24:8; Jer 31:4 [c]S Ge 4:21 **31:28** [d]ver 55; S Ge 27:27; Ru 1:14; Ac 20:37 **31:29** [e]S ver 7; S Ge 26:29 [f]S ver 5 [g]S Ge 24:50 **31:30** [h]S Ge 28:15; Job 29:2 [i]Ge 44:8 [j]S ver 19 **31:31** [k]S Ge 20:11 **31:32** [l]Ge 44:9 [m]S ver 19 **31:33** [n]Ge 24:67 [o]S Ge 16:1 [p]ver 37 **31:34** [q]S ver 19 [r]S Ge 24:63-64 [s]ver 37; Ge 44:12 **31:35** [t]Ex 20:12; Lev 19:3,32; Dt 21:18; 27:16; Jer 35:18 [u]Lev 15:19-23 [v]ver 19 **31:36** [w]1Sa 19:5; 20:32 [x]1Sa 23:23; 24:11 **31:37** [y]ver 33 [z]ver 23 [a]Dt 1:16; 16:18 **31:38** [b]S Ge 27:44 [c]S Ge 30:27 **31:39** [d]Ge 30:33 [e]Ex 22:13 **31:40** [f]Ps 132:4; 2Co 11:27 **31:41** [g]S Ge 27:44 [h]Ge 29:30 [i]S Ge 30:32 [j]S Ge 29:15 [k]S ver 7 **31:42** [l]S ver 5; S Ex 3:15 [m]S Ge 24:12 [n]ver 53; Ge 46:1 [o]S Ge 21:22; Ps 124:1-2 [p]S Ge 3:17 [q]S Ge 24:50 **31:43** [r]Ge 30:32,42 **31:44** [s]S Ge 21:27 [t]S Ge 21:30 **31:45** [u]S Ge 28:18 **31:46** [v]ver 48,51,52 **31:47** [w]S Ge 21:30 **31:48** [x]S ver 46 [y]S Ge 21:30; Jer 29:23; 42:5

31:24 *not to say anything ... good or bad.* Do not enter into a dispute with him; or do not press any claim against him (see also v. 29; cf. 24:50).

31:26 *deceived.* Jacob's character, reflected in his name (see NIV text notes on 25:26; 27:36), is emphasized in the narrative again and again.

31:27 *harps.* Much smaller, and with fewer strings (usually 6 to 12), than their modern counterparts.

31:32 *if you find anyone who has your gods, he shall not live.* Cf. 44:7–12 and note on 44:9. Though he made the offer in all innocence, Jacob almost lost his beloved Rachel. He had now been deceived even by his wife.

31:34 *inside her camel's saddle ... sitting on them.* Indicating the small size and powerlessness of the household gods.

31:35 *I'm having my period.* In later times, anything a menstruating woman sat on was considered ritually unclean (Lev 15:20).

31:39 *I bore the loss.* Ancient laws (as in Ex 22:13) held that a shepherd did not have to compensate for losses to wild animals.

31:42 *Fear.* Here a surrogate for God. Or perhaps the Hebrew for this word means "Kinsman," stressing the intimacy of God's relationship to the patriarch.

31:44 See vv. 48,52; see also 21:30 and note.

31:46 *ate.* See note on 26:30.

31:48 For the naming of an altar under similar circumstances see Jos 22:10–12,34.

31:49 *May ... other.* The so-called Mizpah benediction, which in context is in fact a denunciation or curse.

called Mizpah,[a][z] because he said, "May
the LORD keep watch between you and
me when we are away from each other.
50If you mistreat[a] my daughters or if you
take any wives besides my daughters,
even though no one is with us, remember that God is a witness[b] between you
and me."[c]
51Laban also said to Jacob, "Here is this
heap,[d] and here is this pillar[e] I have set
up between you and me. 52This heap is a
witness, and this pillar is a witness,[f] that
I will not go past this heap to your side to
harm you and that you will not go past
this heap[g] and pillar to my side to harm
me.[h] 53May the God of Abraham[i] and the
God of Nahor,[j] the God of their father,
judge between us."[k]
So Jacob took an oath[l] in the name of
the Fear of his father Isaac.[m] 54He offered
a sacrifice[n] there in the hill country and
invited his relatives to a meal.[o] After they
had eaten, they spent the night there.
55Early the next morning Laban kissed
his grandchildren and his daughters[p] and
blessed[q] them. Then he left and returned
home.[r]

31:49 [z]Jos 11:3; Jdg 10:17; 11:29
31:50 [a]Ge 16:6 [b]Dt 31:19; Jos 24:27; Jdg 11:10; 1Sa 12:5; 20:14,23,42; Job 16:19; Jer 29:23; 42:5; Mic 1:2 [c]S Ge 21:30; S Dt 4:26; S Jer 7:11
31:51 [d]S ver 46 [e]S Ge 28:18
31:52 [f]S Ge 21:30 [g]S ver 46 [h]S ver 7; S Ge 26:29
31:53 [i]S Ge 24:12

[a] *49 Mizpah* means *watchtower.*

[j]S Ge 11:27 [k]S Ge 16:5 [l]S Ge 21:23,27 [m]S ver 42 **31:54** [n]Ge 46:1; Ex 24:5; Lev 3:1 [o]S Ge 26:30 **31:55** [p]S ver 28; Ru 1:9 [q]S Ge 24:60; S Ex 39:43 [r]Ge 18:33

31:51 *heap ... pillar ... between you and me.* Boundary markers between Laban's territory and Jacob's territory. Galeed, Jacob's name for the heap, is a pun on Gilead (see v. 47 and NIV text note).
31:53 *God of their father.* Or possibly "gods of their father [i.e., Terah]," reflecting Laban's polytheistic background (see Jos 24:2). *Fear of his father Isaac.* See note on v. 42. Jacob had met the "God of Isaac" (28:13) at Bethel 20 years earlier.
31:54 *sacrifice ... meal.* Two important aspects of the covenant-making (see v. 44) process (see Ex 24:5–8,11 and note on 24:11). *relatives.* Those with whom he had now entered into a covenant. The common meal indicated mutual acceptance (see note on 26:30).
31:55 *blessed.* Or "said farewell to" (see NIV text note on 47:10; see also 31:28).

Jacob's Journeys

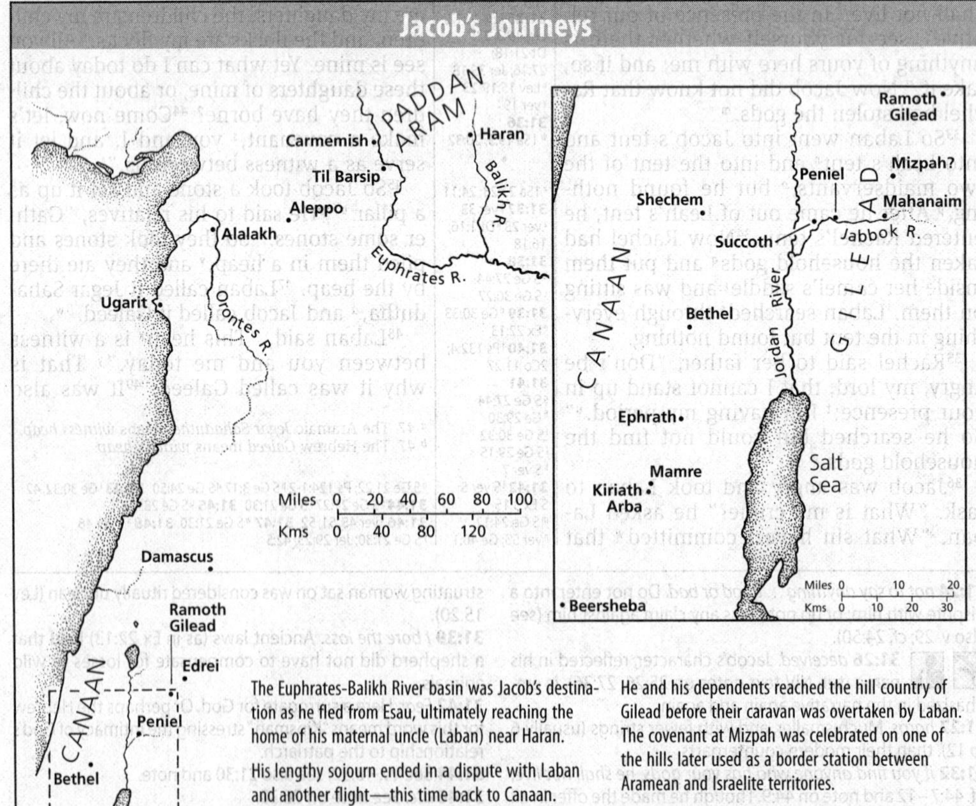

The Euphrates-Balikh River basin was Jacob's destination as he fled from Esau, ultimately reaching the home of his maternal uncle (Laban) near Haran.

His lengthy sojourn ended in a dispute with Laban and another flight—this time back to Canaan. His route likely took him toward Aleppo, then to Damascus and Edrei before reaching Peniel on the Jabbok River.

He and his dependents reached the hill country of Gilead before their caravan was overtaken by Laban. The covenant at Mizpah was celebrated on one of the hills later used as a border station between Aramean and Israelite territories.

Jacob tarried at Succoth, entered Canaan and proceeded to Shechem, where he erected an altar to the Lord.

Jacob Prepares to Meet Esau

32 Jacob also went on his way, and the
angels of God[s] met him. 2When Jacob saw them, he said, "This is the camp
of God!"[t] So he named that place Mahanaim.[a u]
3Jacob sent messengers[v] ahead of him
to his brother Esau[w] in the land of Seir,[x]
the country of Edom.[y] 4He instructed
them: "This is what you are to say to my
master[z] Esau: 'Your servant[a] Jacob says, I
have been staying with Laban[b] and have
remained there till now. 5I have cattle and
donkeys, sheep and goats, menservants
and maidservants.[c] Now I am sending this
message to my lord,[d] that I may find favor
in your eyes.[e] ' "
6When the messengers returned to Jacob, they said, "We went to your brother
Esau, and now he is coming to meet you,
and four hundred men are with him."[f]
7In great fear[g] and distress[h] Jacob divided the people who were with him into
two groups,[b i] and the flocks and herds
and camels as well. 8He thought, "If Esau
comes and attacks one group,[c] the group[c]
that is left may escape."
9Then Jacob prayed, "O God of my father Abraham,[j] God of my father Isaac,[k]
O LORD, who said to me, 'Go back to
your country and your relatives, and I
will make you prosper,'[l] 10I am unworthy
of all the kindness and faithfulness[m] you
have shown your servant. I had only my
staff[n] when I crossed this Jordan, but now
I have become two groups.[o] 11Save me, I
pray, from the hand of my brother Esau,
for I am afraid[p] he will come and attack
me,[q] and also the mothers with their children.[r] 12But you have said, 'I will surely
make you prosper and will make your descendants like the sand[s] of the sea, which
cannot be counted.[t] ' "

32:1 [s]S Ge 16:11; 2Ki 6:16-17; 1Ch 21:15; Ps 34:7; 35:5; 91:11; Da 6:22 **32:2** [t]S Ge 28:17 [u]Jos 13:26, 30; 21:38; 2Sa 2:8, 29; 17:24; 19:32; 1Ki 2:8; 4:14; 1Ch 6:80 **32:3** [v]Nu 21:21; Jdg 11:17 [w]S Ge 27:41-42 [x]S Ge 14:6; S Nu 24:18 [y]S Ge 25:30; S 36:16 **32:4** [z]S Ge 24:9 [a]S Ge 18:3 [b]Ge 31:41 **32:5** [c]S Ge 12:16 [d]S Ge 24:9 [e]Ge 33:8, 10, 15; 34:11; 47:25, 29; 50:4; Ru 2:13 **32:6** [f]Ge 33:1 **32:7** [g]ver 11 [h]Ge 35:3; Ps 4:1; 77:2; 107:6 [i]ver 10; Ge 33:1 **32:9** [j]S Ge 24:12 [k]S Ge 28:13 [l]S Ge 26:3; 31:13 **32:10** [m]S Ge 24:27 [n]Ge 38:18; 47:31; Nu 17:2 [o]S ver 7 **32:11** [p]S ver 7 [q]Ge 43:18; Ps 59:2 [r]S Ge 27:41 **32:12** [s]S Ge 22:17; 1Ki 4:20, 29 [t]S Ge 12:2; S 13:14; Hos 1:10; Ro 9:27 **32:13** [u]ver 13-15, 18, 20, 21; Ge 33:10; 43:11, 15, 25, 26; 1Sa 16:20; Pr 18:16; 21:14 **32:14** [v]Nu 7:88 **32:15** [w]S Ge 13:2;

13He spent the night there, and from
what he had with him he selected a gift[u]
for his brother Esau: 14two hundred female
goats and twenty male goats, two hundred ewes and twenty rams,[v] 15thirty female camels with their young, forty cows
and ten bulls, and twenty female donkeys
and ten male donkeys.[w] 16He put them in
the care of his servants, each herd by itself, and said to his servants, "Go ahead
of me, and keep some space between the
herds."[x]
17He instructed the one in the lead:
"When my brother Esau meets you and
asks, 'To whom do you belong, and where
are you going, and who owns all these animals in front of you?' 18then you are to
say, 'They belong to your servant[y] Jacob.
They are a gift[z] sent to my lord Esau, and
he is coming behind us.' "
19He also instructed the second, the
third and all the others who followed the
herds: "You are to say the same thing to
Esau when you meet him. 20And be sure
to say, 'Your servant[a] Jacob is coming
behind us.' " For he thought, "I will pac-
ify him with these gifts[b] I am sending on
ahead;[c] later, when I see him, perhaps he
will receive me."[d] 21So Jacob's gifts[e] went
on ahead of him, but he himself spent the
night in the camp.

Jacob Wrestles With God

22That night Jacob got up and took his
two wives, his two maidservants and his
eleven sons[f] and crossed the ford of the
Jabbok.[g] 23After he had sent them across

[a] 2 *Mahanaim* means *two camps.* [b] 7 Or *camps*; also in verse 10 [c] 8 Or *camp*

42:26; 45:23 **32:16** [x]Ge 33:8 **32:18** [y]S Ge 18:3 [z]S ver 13 **32:20** [a]S Ge 18:3 [b]S ver 13; 1Sa 9:7; 2Ki 8:8; Jer 40:5 [c]1Sa 25:19 [d]Ge 33:10; Ex 28:38; Lev 1:4; Mal 1:8 **32:21** [e]S ver 13 **32:22** [f]S Ge 30:24 [g]Nu 21:24; Dt 2:37; 3:16; Jos 12:2

32:1–32 Jacob's peaceful meeting with once hostile Esau and his safe arrival in the promised land.

32:1 *angels of God met him.* Jacob had just left the region of the hostile Laban and is about to enter the region of the hostile Esau. He was met by the angels of God, whom he had seen at Bethel when he was fleeing from Esau to go to Laban (see 28:12 and note). Thus God was with Jacob, as he had promised (see 28:15 and note; 31:3; see also note on 26:3).

32:2 *Mahanaim.* Located in Gilead (see note on 31:21) east of the Jordan and north of the Jabbok (see note on v. 22). Two camps (see NIV text note) had just met in hostility and separated in peace. Two camps were again about to meet (in hostility, Jacob thought) and separate in peace. But Jacob called this crucial place "two camps" after seeing the angelic encampment, suggesting that he saw God's encampment as a divine assurance. God's host had come to escort him safely to Canaan (see 33:12,15). Yet he also feared meeting with Esau, so he divided his household into two camps (see vv. 7,10 and NIV text note on v. 7), still trying to protect himself by his own devices.

32:3 *Seir . . . Edom.* Far to the south of Jacob's ultimate destination, but he assumed that Esau would come seeking revenge as soon as he heard that Jacob was on his way back.

32:4 *Your servant.* A phrase suggesting both courtesy and humility.

32:6 *four hundred.* A round number for a sizable unit of fighting men (see 1Sa 22:2; 25:13; 30:10). While Jacob lived the peaceful life of a shepherd, Esau lived "by the sword," as Isaac had foretold (27:40).

32:9 *Jacob prayed.* His first recorded prayer since leaving Bethel.

32:11 *mothers with their children.* Jacob knew that if Esau still had revenge in his heart, Jacob's wives and children would suffer with him.

32:12 *your descendants like the sand of the sea.* A reference to God's promise in 28:14 (see 22:17 and note).

32:13 *gift.* Probably a wordplay: Out of his "two camps" (Hebrew *maḥanayim,* v. 2; see vv. 7–8,10) Jacob selects a "gift" (*minḥah*) for his brother.

32:22 *Jabbok.* Today called the Wadi Zerqa, flowing westward into the Jordan about 20 miles north of the Dead Sea (see map, p. 56).

the stream, he sent over all his possessions.[h] 24 So Jacob was left alone,[i] and
a man[j] wrestled with him till daybreak.
25 When the man saw that he could not
overpower him, he touched the socket of
Jacob's hip[k] so that his hip was wrenched
as he wrestled with the man. 26 Then the
man said, "Let me go, for it is daybreak."
But Jacob replied, "I will not let you go
unless you bless me."[l]
27 The man asked him, "What is your
name?"
"Jacob,"[m] he answered.
28 Then the man said, "Your name[n] will
no longer be Jacob, but Israel,[a][o] because
you have struggled with God and with
men and have overcome."[p]
29 Jacob said, "Please tell me your
name."[q]
But he replied, "Why do you ask my
name?"[r] Then he blessed[s] him there.
30 So Jacob called the place Peniel,[b] saying, "It is because I saw God face to face,[t]
and yet my life was spared."
31 The sun rose above him as he passed
Peniel,[c][u] and he was limping because of
his hip. 32 Therefore to this day the Israelites do not eat the tendon attached to the
socket of the hip,[v] because the socket of
Jacob's hip was touched near the tendon.

Jacob Meets Esau

33 Jacob looked up and there was Esau,
coming with his four hundred men;[w]
so he divided the children among Leah,
Rachel and the two maidservants.[x] 2 He put
the maidservants and their children[y] in
front, Leah and her children next, and Rachel and Joseph[z] in the rear. 3 He himself
went on ahead and bowed down to the
ground[a] seven times[b] as he approached
his brother.
4 But Esau[c] ran to meet Jacob and embraced him; he threw his arms around his
neck and kissed him.[d] And they wept.[e]
5 Then Esau looked up and saw the women
and children. "Who are these with you?"
he asked.
Jacob answered, "They are the children
God has graciously given your servant.[f]"
6 Then the maidservants and their children[g] approached and bowed down.[h]
7 Next, Leah and her children[i] came and
bowed down.[j] Last of all came Joseph and
Rachel,[k] and they too bowed down.
8 Esau asked, "What do you mean by all
these droves I met?"[l]
"To find favor in your eyes, my lord,"[m]
he said.
9 But Esau said, "I already have plenty,[n]
my brother. Keep what you have for yourself."
10 "No, please!" said Jacob. "If I have
found favor in your eyes,[o] accept this gift[p]
from me. For to see your face is like seeing the face of God,[q] now that you have
received me favorably.[r] 11 Please accept the

[a] 28 *Israel* means *he struggles with God.* [b] 30 *Peniel* means *face of God.* [c] 31 Hebrew *Penuel,* a variant of *Peniel*

32:23 [h]S Ge 26:14 **32:24** [i]Da 10:8 [j]S Ge 18:2 **32:25** [k]ver 32 **32:26** [l]Hos 12:4 **32:27** [m]S Ge 25:26 **32:28** [n]Isa 1:26; 56:5; 60:14; 62:2,4,12; 65:15 [o]S Ge 17:5 [p]S Ge 30:8 **32:29** [q]Ex 3:13; 6:3; Jdg 13:17 [r]Jdg 13:18 [s]Ge 25:11; 35:9; 48:3 **32:30** [t]S Ge 16:13; 1Co 13:12 **32:31** [u]Jdg 8:9 **32:32** [v]ver 25 **33:1** [w]S Ge 32:6 [x]S Ge 32:7 **33:2** [y]ver 6 [z]S Ge 30:24 **33:3** [a]ver 6,7; S Ge 17:3; 37:7-10; 42:6; 43:26; 44:14; 48:12; 1Sa 20:41 [b]2Ki 5:10,14 **33:4** [c]S Ge 27:41-42 [d]S Ge 29:11; Lk 15:20 [e]S Ge 27:27 **33:5** [f]S Ge 18:3; Ge 48:9; Ps 127:3; Isa 8:18 **33:6** [g]ver 2 [h]S ver 3 **33:7** [i]ver 2 [j]S ver 3 [k]S Ge 30:24 **33:8** [l]Ge 32:14-16 [m]S Ge 24:9; S 32:5

33:9 [n]ver 11; S Ge 13:6 **33:10** [o]S Ge 30:27; S 32:5 [p]S Ge 32:13 [q]S Ge 16:13 [r]S Ge 32:20

32:24 *left alone.* As he had been at Bethel (see 28:10–22 and note). *a man.* God himself (as Jacob eventually realized; see v. 30) in the form of an angel (see Hos 12:3–4 and note on Ge 16:7). *wrestled.* God wrestled (*ye'abeq*) with Jacob (*ya'aqob*) by the Jabbok (*yabboq*)—the author delighted in wordplay. Jacob had struggled all his life to prevail, first with Esau, then with Laban. Now, as he was about to reenter Canaan, he was shown that it was with God that he must "wrestle"—not with Esau or any other human being.

32:25 *could not overpower him ... touched the socket.* God came to him in such a form that Jacob could wrestle with him successfully, yet he showed Jacob that he could disable him at will.

32:26 *I will not let you go.* Jacob's persistence was soon rewarded (v. 29). *unless you bless me.* Jacob finally acknowledged that the blessing must come from God.

32:28 *Your name will no longer be Jacob.* Now that Jacob had acknowledged God as the source of blessing and was about to reenter the promised land, the Lord acknowledged Jacob as his servant by changing his name (see 17:5 and note). *Israel.* See NIV text note. Here in Jacob/Israel, the nation of Israel got its name and characterization: the people who struggle with God (memorialized in the name Israel) and with human beings (memorialized in the name Jacob) and overcome. God later confirmed Jacob's new name (35:10).

32:29 *Why do you ask my name?* Such a request of God is both unworthy and impossible to fulfill (see Jdg 13:17–18).

32:30 *I saw God face to face.* See note on 16:13; see also Jdg 6:22–23; 13:22. Only God's "back" (see Ex 33:23) or "feet" (see Ex 24:10 and note) or "form" (see Nu 12:8), in a symbolic sense, may be seen with impunity. *yet my life was spared.* If Jacob's life was spared in his encounter with God, his prayer for his life to be spared in his encounter with Esau (v. 11) will surely be granted.

32:31 *The sun rose above him.* A new day dawns in Jacob's life (see Ps 5:3 and note).

32:32 *do not eat the tendon.* Probably the sciatic muscle. Mentioned nowhere else in the Bible, this dietary prohibition is found in the later writings of Judaism. Jacob retained in his body, and Israel retained in her dietary practice, a perpetual reminder of this fateful encounter with God.

33:2 *Rachel and Joseph in the rear.* Jacob wanted to keep his favorite wife and child farthest away from potential harm.

33:3 *bowed down to the ground seven times.* A sign of total submission, documented also in texts found at Tell el-Amarna in Egypt and dating to the 14th century B.C. (see chart, p. xxii).

33:4 All Jacob's fears proved unfounded. God had been at work and had so blessed Esau (v. 9) that he no longer held a grudge against Jacob.

33:9 *I already have plenty.* Esau had obtained his "plenty" while residing in "the land of Seir" (32:3; cf. 33:16) south of the promised land, just as Jacob had obtained his bounties in Paddan Aram north of the promised land. *my brother.* Esau's response was in contrast to Jacob's cautious and fearful "my lord" (v. 8).

33:11 *present.* The Hebrew for "present" is the same as that used for "blessing" in 27:35. The author of Genesis

present[s] that was brought to you, for God
has been gracious to me[t] and I have all I
need."[u] And because Jacob insisted,[v] Esau
accepted it.
12 Then Esau said, "Let us be on our
way; I'll accompany you."
13 But Jacob said to him, "My lord[w]
knows that the children are tender and
that I must care for the ewes and cows
that are nursing their young.[x] If they are
driven hard just one day, all the animals
will die. 14 So let my lord go on ahead of
his servant, while I move along slowly at
the pace of the droves[y] before me and that
of the children, until I come to my lord
in Seir.[z]"
15 Esau said, "Then let me leave some of
my men with you."
"But why do that?" Jacob asked. "Just
let me find favor in the eyes of my lord."[a]
16 So that day Esau started on his way
back to Seir.[b] 17 Jacob, however, went to
Succoth,[c] where he built a place for himself and made shelters for his livestock.
That is why the place is called Succoth.[a]
18 After Jacob came from Paddan Aram,[b][d]
he arrived safely at the[c] city of Shechem[e]
in Canaan and camped within sight of the
city. 19 For a hundred pieces of silver,[d] he
bought from the sons of Hamor,[f] the father
of Shechem,[g] the plot of ground[h] where he
pitched his tent.[i] 20 There he set up an altar[j] and called it El Elohe Israel.[e]

Dinah and the Shechemites

34 Now Dinah,[k] the daughter Leah had
borne to Jacob, went out to visit the
women of the land. 2 When Shechem[l] son
of Hamor[m] the Hivite,[n] the ruler of that
area, saw her, he took her and violated her.[o] 3 His heart was drawn to Dinah[p]
daughter of Jacob,[q] and he loved[r] the girl
and spoke tenderly[s] to her. 4 And Shechem
said to his father Hamor, "Get me this girl
as my wife."[t]
5 When Jacob heard that his daughter
Dinah had been defiled,[u] his sons were in
the fields with his livestock; so he kept
quiet about it until they came home.
6 Then Shechem's father Hamor went
out to talk with Jacob.[v] 7 Now Jacob's
sons had come in from the fields as soon
as they heard what had happened. They
were filled with grief[w] and fury,[x] because
Shechem had done a disgraceful thing in[f]
Israel[y] by lying with Jacob's daughter—a
thing that should not be done.[z]
8 But Hamor said to them, "My son Shechem has his heart set on your daughter.
Please give her to him as his wife.[a] 9 Intermarry with us; give us your daughters and
take our daughters for yourselves.[b] 10 You
can settle among us;[c] the land is open to
you.[d] Live in it, trade[g] in it,[e] and acquire
property in it.[f]"
11 Then Shechem said to Dinah's father
and brothers, "Let me find favor in your
eyes,[g] and I will give you whatever you
ask. 12 Make the price for the bride[h] and
the gift I am to bring as great as you like,
and I'll pay whatever you ask me. Only
give me the girl as my wife."
13 Because their sister Dinah had been

33:11 [s] 1Sa 25:27; 30:26 [t] Ge 30:43 [u] S ver 9 [v] Ge 19:3 **33:13** [w] ver 8 [x] Isa 40:11; Jer 31:8 **33:14** [y] Ex 12:38 [z] S Ge 14:6 **33:15** [a] S Ge 32:5 **33:16** [b] S Ge 14:6 **33:17** [c] Jos 13:27; Jdg 8:5, 6, 8, 14-16; 1Ki 7:46; 2Ch 4:17; Ps 60:6; 108:7 **33:18** [d] S Ge 25:20 [e] S Ge 12:6 **33:19** [f] Ge 34:2; Jdg 9:28; Ac 7:16 [g] Ge 34:2; Jos 24:32 [h] Ge 34:10, 16, 21; 47:27; Jn 4:5 [i] S Ge 12:8 **33:20** [j] S Ge 4:26; S 8:20 **34:1** [k] S Ge 30:21 **34:2** [l] S Ge 33:19 [m] S Ge 33:19 [n] S Ge 10:17 [o] Dt 21:14; 2Sa 13:14 **34:3** [p] ver 26 [q] ver 19 [r] S Ge 24:67 [s] Ge 50:21; Isa 14:1; 40:2 **34:4** [t] S Ge 21:21 **34:5** [u] ver 2, 13, 27; Ge 35:22; 49:4; Dt 27:20; 33:6; 1Ch 5:1 **34:6** [v] Jdg 14:2-5 **34:7** [w] 1Co 5:2 [x] Ge 39:19; 49:6-7; 2Sa 12:5; 13:21; Est 7:7; Pr 6:34 [y] Dt 22:21; Jdg 19:23; 20:6; 2Sa 13:12; Jer 29:23 [z] S Ge 20:9 **34:8** [a] S Ge 21:21; Dt 21:11 **34:9** [b] ver 16, 21; Dt 7:3; Jos 23:12 **34:10** [c] ver 23; Ge 46:34; 47:6, 27 [d] S Ge 13:9 [e] Ge 42:34 [f] S Ge 33:19 **34:11** [g] S Ge 32:5 **34:12** [h] Ex 22:16; Dt 22:29; 1Sa 18:25

[a] *17 Succoth* means *shelters.* [b] *18* That is, Northwest Mesopotamia [c] *18* Or *arrived at Shalem, a* [d] *19* Hebrew *hundred kesitahs*; a kesitah was a unit of money of unknown weight and value. [e] *20 El Elohe Israel* can mean *God, the God of Israel* or *mighty is the God of Israel.* [f] *7* Or *against* [g] *10* Or *move about freely*; also in verse 21

was conscious of the irony that Jacob now acknowledged that the blessing he had struggled for was from God. In his last attempt to express reconciliation with Esau, Jacob in a sense gave back the "blessing" he had stolen from his brother, doing so from the blessings the Lord had given him.

33:12 *I'll accompany you.* Resulting in another "two camps" (see 32:2 and note). Esau's proposal suggests that he had come with his 400 men to escort Jacob's vulnerable company safely home (see v. 15). Jacob declines the offer because he trusts the protection of God more than he trusts Esau and his men.

33:14 *until I come to my lord in Seir.* But Jacob, still the deceiver, had no intention of following Esau all the way to Seir.

33:18 *Paddan Aram.* See note on 25:20. *arrived safely.* The answer to Jacob's prayer 20 years earlier (see 28:21). *Shechem.* See note on 12:6. Jacob followed in the footsteps of Abraham (see 12:6). Jacob dug a well there (see Jn 4:5–6) that can still be seen today (see note on Jn 4:11).

33:19 *pieces of silver.* See NIV text note. The Hebrew word translated by this phrase is found only three times and always in patriarchal contexts (see Jos 24:32; Job 42:11 and note).

33:20 *set up an altar.* See note on 12:7. *called it El Elohe Israel.* See NIV text note. Jacob formally acknowledged the God of his fathers as his God also (see 28:21 and note). But he lingered at Shechem and did not return to Bethel (see 35:1), and that meant trouble (see ch. 34).

34:1–31 Jacob is now confronted in the promised land with the danger of being absorbed by the native Canaanites (vv. 9,16) and then with the threat of their hostility after his sons' vengeful acts (v. 30). These were dangers Israel constantly faced from the peoples around them—either absorption or hostility, both of which are perpetual threats to God's people. The name of God ends ch. 33 and begins ch. 35, but it is completely absent from this sordid chapter (see note on 7:16).

34:2 *Shechem.* See 33:19. He was probably named after the city.

34:4 *Get me this girl as my wife.* See note on 21:21.

34:7 *Israel.* The clan of Israel. *a thing that should not be done.* Cf. Tamar's plea to Amnon in a similar situation (2Sa 13:12).

34:9 *Intermarry with us.* The Canaanites wanted to benefit from the blessings Jacob had received from the Lord (both his offspring and his possessions—vv. 21–23).

34:12 *price for the bride.* For a specific example of this marriage custom see 24:53 and note.

34:13 *Jacob's sons replied deceitfully.* Like father, like son (see 27:24; see also note on 25:26).

defiled,[i] Jacob's sons replied deceitfully[j]
as they spoke to Shechem and his father
Hamor. 14They said to them, "We can't
do such a thing; we can't give our sister
to a man who is not circumcised.[k] That
would be a disgrace to us. 15We will give
our consent to you on one condition[l] only:
that you become like us by circumcising
all your males.[m] 16Then we will give you
our daughters and take your daughters for
ourselves.[n] We'll settle among you and become one people with you.[o] 17But if you
will not agree to be circumcised, we'll take
our sister[a] and go."

18Their proposal seemed good to Hamor
and his son Shechem. 19The young man,
who was the most honored[p] of all his father's household, lost no time in doing
what they said, because he was delighted
with Jacob's daughter.[q] 20So Hamor and
his son Shechem went to the gate of their
city[r] to speak to their fellow townsmen.
21"These men are friendly toward us,"
they said. "Let them live in our land and
trade in it;[s] the land has plenty of room
for them. We can marry their daughters
and they can marry ours.[t] 22But the men
will consent to live with us as one people only on the condition that our males
be circumcised,[u] as they themselves are.
23Won't their livestock, their property and
all their other animals become ours?[v] So
let us give our consent to them, and they
will settle among us.[w]"

24All the men who went out of the city
gate[x] agreed with Hamor and his son Shechem, and every male in the city was circumcised.

25Three days later, while all of them
were still in pain,[y] two of Jacob's sons,
Simeon[z] and Levi,[a] Dinah's brothers, took
their swords[b] and attacked the unsuspecting city,[c] killing every male.[d] 26They
put Hamor and his son Shechem to the
sword[e] and took Dinah[f] from Shechem's
house and left. 27The sons of Jacob came
upon the dead bodies and looted the city[g]
where[b] their sister had been defiled.[h]
28They seized their flocks and herds and
donkeys[i] and everything else of theirs in
the city and out in the fields.[j] 29They carried off all their wealth and all their wom-
en and children,[k] taking as plunder[l] everything in the houses.[m]

30Then Jacob said to Simeon and Levi,
"You have brought trouble[n] on me by making me a stench[o] to the Canaanites and
Perizzites, the people living in this land.[p]
We are few in number,[q] and if they join
forces against me and attack me, I and my
household will be destroyed."

31But they replied, "Should he have
treated our sister like a prostitute?[r]"

Jacob Returns to Bethel

35 Then God said to Jacob, "Go up to
Bethel[s] and settle there, and build an
altar[t] there to God,[u] who appeared to you[v]
when you were fleeing from your brother
Esau."[w]

2So Jacob said to his household[x] and
to all who were with him, "Get rid of the
foreign gods[y] you have with you, and purify yourselves and change your clothes.[z]
3Then come, let us go up to Bethel, where
I will build an altar to God,[a] who answered
me in the day of my distress[b] and who has
been with me wherever I have gone.[c]" 4So
they gave Jacob all the foreign gods they
had and the rings in their ears,[d] and Jacob
buried them under the oak[e] at Shechem.[f]
5Then they set out, and the terror of God[g]
fell upon the towns all around them so
that no one pursued them.[h]

6Jacob and all the people with him came
to Luz[i] (that is, Bethel) in the land of Canaan.[j] 7There he built an altar,[k] and he
called the place El Bethel,[c][l] because it was

[a] 17 Hebrew *daughter* [b] 27 Or *because* [c] 7 *El Bethel* means *God of Bethel.*

34:13 [i]S ver 5 [j]S Ge 27:36 **34:14** [k]Ge 17:14; Jdg 14:3; 1Sa 31:4; Isa 52:1 **34:15** [l]1Sa 11:2 [m]ver 22; Ex 12:48 **34:16** [n]S ver 9 [o]S Ge 33:19 **34:19** [p]Ge 49:3; 1Ch 11:21 [q]ver 3 **34:20** [r]S Ge 18:1 **34:21** [s]S Ge 33:19 [t]S ver 9 **34:22** [u]S ver 15 **34:23** [v]ver 28; S Ge 12:16 [w]S ver 10 **34:24** [x]S Ge 18:1 **34:25** [y]Jos 5:8 [z]S Ge 29:33 [a]S Ge 29:34 [b]Ge 49:5; Mal 2:16 [c]Jdg 18:7, 10, 27; Eze 38:11 [d]Ge 49:7 **34:26** [e]S ver 7; Ge 48:22 [f]ver 3 **34:27** [g]2Ki 21:14 [h]S ver 5 **34:28** [i]Ge 43:18 [j]S ver 23 **34:29** [k]S Ge 31:26 [l]Nu 14:3; 31:9, 53; Dt 2:35; Jos 7:21 [m]2Ki 8:12; Isa 13:16; La 5:11; Am 1:13; Zec 14:2 **34:30** [n]Ge 43:6; Ex 5:23; Nu 11:11 [o]Ex 5:21; 6:9; 1Sa 13:4; 27:12; 2Sa 10:6; 1Ch 19:6 [p]S Ge 13:7 [q]Ge 35:26; 46:27; Ex 1:5; Dt 10:22; 26:5; 1Ch 16:19; Ps 105:12 **34:31** [r]ver 2 **35:1** [s]S Ge 12:8 [t]S Ge 4:26; 8:20 [u]ver 3 [v]S Ge 12:7 [w]ver 7; Ge 27:43 **35:2** [x]Ge 18:19; Jos 24:15 [y]S Ge 31:19; S Jos 24:14 [z]Ex 19:10, 14; Nu 8:7, 21; 19:19 **35:3** [a]ver 1 [b]S Ge 32:7; S Jdg 2:15 [c]S Ge 26:3 **35:4** [d]S Ge 24:22; Ex 32:3; 35:22; Jdg 8:24; Pr 25:12 [e]ver 8 [f]S Ge 12:6 **35:5** [g]Ex 15:16; 23:27; Dt 2:25; Jos 2:9; 1Sa 7:10; 13:7; 14:15; 2Ch 14:14; 17:10; 20:29; Ps 9:20; Isa 19:17; Zec 14:13 [h]Ps 105:14 **35:6** [i]S Ge 28:19 [j]S Ge 10:19 **35:7** [k]S Ge 8:20 [l]Ge 28:19

34:15 Using a sacred ceremony for a sinful purpose (see vv. 24–25).

34:20 *gate of their city.* See notes on 19:1; 23:10.

34:23 The greed of the men of Shechem led to their destruction.

34:24 The Canaanites were even willing to submit to Israel's covenant rite (without any submission to Jacob's God) in order to attain their purposes.

34:25 *Simeon and Levi.* Because they slaughtered the men of Shechem, their own descendants would be scattered far and wide (see note on 49:7). *Dinah's brothers.* All three were children of Leah (29:33–34; 30:21). *killing every male.* Shechem's crime, serious as it was, hardly warranted such brutal and extensive retaliation (see vv. 27–29). Jacob's sons ran ahead of God's judgment on the Canaanites (see 15:16 and note).

34:30 *Perizzites.* See note on 13:7.

35:1–15 Whereas Abram's arrival at Shechem marked the end of his journey to Canaan—it was there that God promised to give the land to his offspring (12:6–7)—the final stage of Jacob's journey back was from Shechem to Bethel, where Jacob's pilgrimage with God had begun (28:10–22).

35:1 *God … appeared to you when you were fleeing.* See v. 7; 28:13.

35:2 *foreign gods you have with you.* See note on 31:19 (see also Jos 24:23).

35:3 *God … who has been with me.* See 26:3; 28:15 and notes.

35:4 *rings.* Worn as amulets or charms; a pagan religious custom (cf. Hos 2:13). *oak at Shechem.* Obviously a well-known tree, perhaps the "great tree" mentioned in 12:6 (see Jos 24:26).

35:5 *terror of God.* God protected his servant.

35:7 *built an altar.* See note on 12:7.

there that God revealed himself to him[m]
when he was fleeing from his brother.[n]
8Now Deborah, Rebekah's nurse,[o] died
and was buried under the oak[p] below
Bethel.[q] So it was named Allon Bacuth.[a]
9After Jacob returned from Paddan
Aram,[b][r] God appeared to him again and
blessed him.[s] 10God said to him, "Your
name is Jacob,[c] but you will no longer be
called Jacob; your name will be Israel.[d]"[t]
So he named him Israel.
11And God said to him, "I am God Almighty[e];[u] be fruitful and increase in
number.[v] A nation[w] and a community of
nations will come from you, and kings
will come from your body.[x] 12The land I
gave to Abraham and Isaac I also give to
you, and I will give this land to your descendants after you.[y]"[z] 13Then God went
up from him[a] at the place where he had
talked with him.
14Jacob set up a stone pillar[b] at the place
where God had talked with him, and he
poured out a drink offering[c] on it; he also
poured oil on it.[d] 15Jacob called the place
where God had talked with him Bethel.[f][e]

The Deaths of Rachel and Isaac

35:23-26pp — 1Ch 2:1-2

16Then they moved on from Bethel.
While they were still some distance from
Ephrath,[f] Rachel[g] began to give birth and
had great difficulty. 17And as she was having great difficulty in childbirth, the midwife[h] said to her, "Don't be afraid, for you
have another son."[i] 18As she breathed her
last—for she was dying—she named her
son Ben-Oni.[g][j] But his father named him
Benjamin.[h][k]
19So Rachel died and was buried on the
way to Ephrath[l] (that is, Bethlehem[m]).
20Over her tomb Jacob set up a pillar, and to
this day[n] that pillar marks Rachel's tomb.[o]
21Israel moved on again and pitched his
tent beyond Migdal Eder.[p] 22While Israel
was living in that region, Reuben went in
and slept with his father's concubine[q] Bilhah,[r] and Israel heard of it.

Jacob had twelve sons:
23The sons of Leah:[s]
Reuben the firstborn[t] of Jacob,
Simeon, Levi, Judah,[u] Issachar and
Zebulun.[v]
24The sons of Rachel:
Joseph[w] and Benjamin.[x]
25The sons of Rachel's maidservant Bilhah:[y]
Dan and Naphtali.[z]
26The sons of Leah's maidservant Zilpah:[a]
Gad[b] and Asher.[c]
These were the sons of Jacob,[d] who
were born to him in Paddan Aram.[e]

[a] 8 *Allon Bacuth* means *oak of weeping.* [b] 9 That is, Northwest Mesopotamia; also in verse 26 [c] 10 *Jacob* means *he grasps the heel* (figuratively, *he deceives*). [d] 10 *Israel* means *he struggles with God.* [e] 11 Hebrew *El-Shaddai* [f] 15 *Bethel* means *house of God.* [g] 18 *Ben-Oni* means *son of my trouble.* [h] 18 *Benjamin* means *son of my right hand.*

35:7 [m]S Ge 28:13 [n]S ver 1 **35:8** [o]Ge 24:59 [p]ver 4 [q]S Ge 12:8; 1Sa 10:3 **35:9** [r]S Ge 25:20 [s]S Ge 28:13; S 32:29 **35:10** [t]S Ge 17:5 **35:11** [u]S Ge 17:1 [v]S Ge 12:2 [w]S Ge 12:2 [x]S Ge 17:6 **35:12** [y]S Ge 28:13 [z]S Ge 12:7; S 15:7 **35:13** [a]S Ge 17:22 **35:14** [b]S Ge 28:22 [c]Ex 29:40; Lev 23:13; Nu 6:15, 17; 15:5; 28:7, 14; 2Sa 23:16; 2Ch 29:35 [d]S Ge 28:18 **35:15** [e]S Ge 12:8 **35:16** [f]ver 19; Ge 48:7; Ru 1:2; 4:11; 1Sa 17:12; Mic 5:2 [g]S Ge 29:6 **35:17** [h]Ge 38:28; Ex 1:15 [i]S Ge 30:24 **35:18** [j]1Sa 4:21; 14:3 [k]ver 24; Ge 42:4; 43:16, 29; 45:12, 14; 49:27; Nu 1:36; Dt 33:12 **35:19** [l]S ver 16 [m]Ge 48:7; Jos 19:15; Jdg 12:8; 17:7; 19:1, 18; Ru 1:1, 19; 1Sa 17:12; Mic 5:2 **35:20** [n]Jos 4:9; 7:26; 8:28; 10:27; 1Sa 6:18 [o]1Sa 10:2 **35:21** [p]Jos 15:21 **35:22** [q]S Ge 22:24 [r]S Ge 29:29; S 34:5; S Lev 18:8 **35:23** [s]S Ge 29:16 [t]Ge 43:33; 46:8 [u]S Ge 29:35 [v]S Ge 30:20 **35:24** [w]S Ge 30:24 [x]S ver 18 **35:25** [y]Ge 37:2 [z]S Ge 30:8 **35:26** [a]Ge 37:2 [b]S Ge 30:11 [c]S Ge 30:13 [d]S Ge 34:30; 46:8; Ex 1:1-4 [e]S Ge 25:20

35:8 *Deborah, Rebekah's nurse, died.* After long years of faithful service (see 24:59). *the oak.* Again probably a well-known tree (see note on v. 4), perhaps the "great tree" mentioned in 1Sa 10:3 (see note there). *below.* Either "lower than" or "to the south of."

35:9 *Jacob returned.* See map, p. 56. *Paddan Aram.* See note on 25:20.

35:10 *Jacob ... Israel.* The previous assignment of an additional name (see 32:28 and note) is here confirmed. For similar examples compare 21:31 with 26:33, and 28:19 with 35:15.

35:11–12 This event climaxes the Isaac-Jacob cycle (see Introduction: Literary Features). Now that Jacob was at last back at Bethel, where God had begun his direct relationship with him, God confirmed to this chosen son of Isaac the covenant promises made to Abraham (17:1–8; see 28:3). His words echo his original benediction pronounced on humankind in the beginning (1:28) and renewed after the flood (9:1,7). God's blessing on the human race would be fulfilled in and through Jacob and his offspring. See also 47:27; Ex 1:7 and note.

35:11 God identifies himself to Jacob here as "God Almighty" (El-Shaddai). At Bethel he had identified himself as "the God of your father Abraham and the God of Isaac" (28:13), but that was also as El-Shaddai (see 17:1 and note; see also 28:3; 48:3; Ex 6:3).

35:13 See note on 17:22.

35:14 See 28:18 and note. *drink offering.* A liquid poured out as a sacrifice to a deity.

35:15 See 28:19; see also note on v. 10 above.

35:16–29 The conclusion to the main story of Jacob's life.

35:16 *Ephrath.* The older name for Bethlehem (see v. 19) in Judah of the area in which Bethlehem was located (see Ru 1:2; Mic 5:2 and notes).

35:17 *another son.* An echo of Rachel's own plea at the time of Joseph's birth (see 30:24).

35:18 *Benjamin.* See NIV text note. The name can also mean "son of the south"—in distinction from the other sons, who were born in the north. One set of Hebrew terms for indicating direction was based on facing east, so south was on the right.

35:19 *Rachel died.* In childbirth (see note on 30:1). *Ephrath ... Bethlehem.* See note on v. 16.

35:20 *Rachel's tomb.* See 1Sa 10:2. The traditional, though not authentic, site is near Bethlehem.

35:21 *Migdal Eder.* Means "tower of the flock," doubtless referring to a watchtower built to discourage thieves from stealing sheep and other animals (see, e.g., 2Ch 26:10). The same Hebrew phrase is used figuratively in Mic 4:8, where "flock" refers to the people of Judah (see Mic 4:6–7).

35:22 Reuben's act was an arrogant and premature claim to the rights of the firstborn (see 2Sa 3:7; 12:8; 16:21; 1Ki 2:22 and notes). For this he would lose his legal status as firstborn (see 49:3–4; 1Ch 5:1 and note on 5:1–10; see also note on 37:21).

35:26 *sons of Jacob ... born to him in Paddan Aram.* Obviously a summary statement since Benjamin was born in Canaan (see vv. 16–18).

27 Jacob came home to his father Isaac[f]
in Mamre,[g] near Kiriath Arba[h] (that is,
Hebron),[i] where Abraham and Isaac had
stayed.[j] 28 Isaac lived a hundred and eighty
years.[k] 29 Then he breathed his last and
died and was gathered to his people,[l] old
and full of years.[m] And his sons Esau and
Jacob buried him.[n]

Esau's Descendants

36:10-14pp — 1Ch 1:35-37
36:20-28pp — 1Ch 1:38-42

36 This is the account[o] of Esau (that is,
Edom).[p]
2 Esau took his wives from the
women of Canaan:[q] Adah daughter
of Elon the Hittite,[r] and Oholibamah[s]
daughter of Anah[t] and granddaughter
of Zibeon the Hivite[u]— 3 also Basemath[v] daughter of Ishmael and sister
of Nebaioth.[w]
4 Adah bore Eliphaz to Esau, Basemath bore Reuel,[x] 5 and Oholibamah
bore Jeush, Jalam and Korah.[y] These
were the sons of Esau, who were born
to him in Canaan.
6 Esau took his wives and sons and
daughters and all the members of his
household, as well as his livestock
and all his other animals and all the
goods he had acquired in Canaan,[z]
and moved to a land some distance
from his brother Jacob.[a] 7 Their possessions were too great for them to
remain together; the land where they
were staying could not support them
both because of their livestock.[b] 8 So
Esau[c] (that is, Edom)[d] settled in the
hill country of Seir.[e]
9 This is the account[f] of Esau the father of the Edomites[g] in the hill country
of Seir.
10 These are the names of Esau's sons:
Eliphaz, the son of Esau's wife Adah,
and Reuel, the son of Esau's wife
Basemath.[h]

35:27 [f]Ge 31:18 [g]S Ge 13:18 [h]Ge 23:2; Jos 15:54; Jdg 1:10; Ne 11:25 [i]S Ge 13:18 [j]S Ge 17:8
35:28 [k]S Ge 25:7,20
35:29 [l]S Ge 25:8 [m]S Ge 15:15 [n]S Ge 23:20; S 25:9
36:1 [o]S Ge 2:4 [p]S Ge 25:30
36:2 [q]Ge 28:8-9 [r]Ge 26:34 [s]ver 14,18 [t]ver 25; 1Ch 1:40 [u]ver 24; S Ge 10:17; 1Ch 1:40
36:3 [v]ver 4,10,13,17 [w]S Ge 25:13
36:4 [x]S ver 3; 1Ch 1:35
36:5 [y]ver 14,18; 1Ch 1:35
36:6 [z]Ge 12:5 [a]Ge 27:39
36:7 [b]S Ge 13:6
36:8 [c]Dt 2:4 [d]S Ge 25:30 [e]S Ge 14:6
36:9 [f]S Ge 2:4 [g]ver 1,43
36:10 [h]S ver 3
36:11 [i]ver 15-16; 1Ch 1:45; Job 2:11; 4:1 [j]Jer 49:7,20; Eze 25:13; Am 1:12; Ob 1:9; Hab 3:3 [k]ver 15
36:12 [l]S Ge 22:24 [m]Ex 17:8,16; Nu 24:20; Dt 25:17,19; 1Sa 15:2; 27:8 [n]ver 16
36:13 [o]S ver 3
36:14 [p]S ver 2 [q]S ver 5
36:15 [r]ver 19,40; Ex 15:15 [s]Job 2:11; Jer 49:7; Eze 25:13; Am 1:12; Hab 3:3 [t]S ver 11
36:16 [u]S ver 11

11 The sons of Eliphaz:[i]
Teman,[j] Omar, Zepho, Gatam and
Kenaz.[k]
12 Esau's son Eliphaz also had a concubine[l] named Timna, who bore
him Amalek.[m] These were grandsons of Esau's wife Adah.[n]
13 The sons of Reuel:
Nahath, Zerah, Shammah and
Mizzah. These were grandsons of
Esau's wife Basemath.[o]
14 The sons of Esau's wife Oholibamah[p]
daughter of Anah and granddaughter
of Zibeon, whom she bore to Esau:
Jeush, Jalam and Korah.[q]
15 These were the chiefs[r] among Esau's
descendants:
The sons of Eliphaz the firstborn of
Esau:
Chiefs Teman,[s] Omar, Zepho, Kenaz,[t] 16 Korah,[a] Gatam and Amalek.
These were the chiefs descended
from Eliphaz[u] in Edom;[v] they were
grandsons of Adah.[w]
17 The sons of Esau's son Reuel:[x]
Chiefs Nahath, Zerah, Shammah
and Mizzah. These were the chiefs
descended from Reuel in Edom;
they were grandsons of Esau's wife
Basemath.[y]
18 The sons of Esau's wife Oholibamah:[z]
Chiefs Jeush, Jalam and Korah.[a]
These were the chiefs descended from Esau's wife Oholibamah
daughter of Anah.
19 These were the sons of Esau[b] (that is,
Edom),[c] and these were their chiefs.[d]
20 These were the sons of Seir the Horite,[e] who were living in the region:
Lotan, Shobal, Zibeon, Anah,[f]

[a] 16 Masoretic Text; Samaritan Pentateuch (see also Gen. 36:11 and 1 Chron. 1:36) does not have *Korah*.

[v]Ge 32:3; Ex 15:15; Nu 20:14; 33:37 [w]ver 12 **36:17** [x]1Ch 1:37 [y]S ver 3 **36:18** [z]S ver 2 [a]S ver 5 **36:19** [b]1Ch 1:35 [c]S Ge 25:30 [d]S ver 15 **36:20** [e]S Ge 14:6 [f]ver 29

35:27 *Mamre, near Kiriath Arba (that is, Hebron).* See notes on 13:18; 23:2.
35:29 See note on 25:8. *buried him.* In the family tomb, the cave of Machpelah (49:30 – 31).
36:1 – 43 A concise account of Esau's descendants, who also belonged to the "many nations" promised to Abraham and Sarah (17:5 – 6,16), before the more full-blown account of Jacob's descendants (see notes on 37:2—50:26 and 37:2). Cf. the account of Ishmael's offspring in 25:12 – 18 (see note there).
36:1 *account.* See note on 2:4. Though repeated in v. 9, the word does not mark the start of a new main section there since the information in vv. 9 – 43 is merely an expansion of that in vv. 1 – 8. *Esau (that is, Edom).* See 25:30 and NIV text note there. Reddish rock formations, primarily sandstone, are conspicuous in the territory of the Edomites, located south and southeast of the Dead Sea.
36:2 – 3 See note on 26:34.
36:7 See 13:6; 26:20 and notes.
36:8 *Seir.* Another name for Edom. The word itself is related to the Hebrew word meaning "hair," a possible meaning also for the name "Esau" (see NIV text note on 25:25). Esau's clan must have driven away the original Horite (see v. 20) inhabitants of Seir (see 14:6 and note). The descendants of Seir are listed in vv. 20 – 28.
36:10 – 14 The same list of Esau's descendants (see 1Ch 1:35 – 37) is repeated in vv. 15 – 19 as a list of tribal chieftains.
36:11 *Eliphaz: Teman.* One of Job's friends was named Eliphaz the Temanite (see Job 2:11 and note), and Job himself was from the land of Uz (see Job 1:1 and note). Thus Job probably lived in Edom (see vv. 28,34).
36:12 *Amalek.* See note on 14:7.
36:20 – 28 See note on v. 8. The same list of Seir's descen-

21 Dishon, Ezer and Dishan. These
sons of Seir in Edom were Horite
chiefs.[g]
22 The sons of Lotan:
Hori and Homam.[a] Timna was Lotan's sister.
23 The sons of Shobal:
Alvan, Manahath, Ebal, Shepho
and Onam.
24 The sons of Zibeon:[h]
Aiah and Anah. This is the Anah
who discovered the hot springs[b][i] in
the desert while he was grazing the
donkeys[j] of his father Zibeon.
25 The children of Anah:[k]
Dishon and Oholibamah[l] daughter
of Anah.
26 The sons of Dishon[c]:
Hemdan, Eshban, Ithran and Keran.
27 The sons of Ezer:
Bilhan, Zaavan and Akan.
28 The sons of Dishan:
Uz and Aran.
29 These were the Horite chiefs:
Lotan, Shobal, Zibeon, Anah,[m]
30 Dishon, Ezer and Dishan. These
were the Horite chiefs,[n] according
to their divisions, in the land of
Seir.

The Rulers of Edom

36:31-43pp — 1Ch 1:43-54

31 These were the kings who reigned in
Edom before any Israelite king[o] reigned[d]:
32 Bela son of Beor became king of
Edom. His city was named Dinhabah.
33 When Bela died, Jobab son of Zerah
from Bozrah[p] succeeded him as
king.
34 When Jobab died, Husham from the
land of the Temanites[q] succeeded
him as king.
35 When Husham died, Hadad son of
Bedad, who defeated Midian[r] in the
country of Moab,[s] succeeded him
as king. His city was named Avith.
36 When Hadad died, Samlah from Masrekah succeeded him as king.
37 When Samlah died, Shaul from Rehoboth[t] on the river[e] succeeded him
as king.
38 When Shaul died, Baal-Hanan son of
Acbor succeeded him as king.
39 When Baal-Hanan son of Acbor died,
Hadad[f] succeeded him as king. His
city was named Pau, and his wife's
name was Mehetabel daughter of
Matred, the daughter of Me-Zahab.

40 These were the chiefs[u] descended
from Esau, by name, according to their
clans and regions:
Timna, Alvah, Jetheth, 41 Oholibamah, Elah, Pinon, 42 Kenaz, Teman,
Mibzar, 43 Magdiel and Iram. These
were the chiefs of Edom, according
to their settlements in the land they
occupied.

This was Esau the father of the Edomites.[v]

Joseph's Dreams

37 Jacob lived in the land where his
father had stayed,[w] the land of Canaan.[x]

2 This is the account[y] of Jacob.

Joseph,[z] a young man of seventeen,[a]
was tending the flocks[b] with his brothers,

36:21 [g] ver 30 **36:24** [h] S ver 2 [i] Jos 15:19 [j] Job 1:14 **36:25** [k] S ver 2 [l] S ver 2 **36:29** [m] ver 20 **36:30** [n] ver 21 **36:31** [o] S Ge 17:6 **36:33** [p] Isa 34:6; 63:1; Jer 49:13,22 **36:34** [q] Jer 49:7; Eze 25:13; Ob 1:9 **36:35** [r] S Ge 25:2 [s] S Ge 19:37; Nu 21:11; 22:1; Dt 1:5; Jdg 3:30; Ru 1:1,6 **36:37** [t] Ge 26:22 **36:40** [u] S ver 15 **36:43** [v] S ver 9 **37:1** [w] S Ge 17:8 [x] S Ge 10:19 **37:2** [y] S Ge 2:4 [z] S Ge 30:24 [a] Ge 41:46; 2Sa 5:4 [b] Ge 46:32; 1Sa 16:11; 17:15; Ps 78:71; Am 7:15

[a] 22 Hebrew *Hemam,* a variant of *Homam* (see 1 Chron. 1:39) [b] 24 Vulgate; Syriac *discovered water;* the meaning of the Hebrew for this word is uncertain. [c] 26 Hebrew *Dishan,* a variant of *Dishon* [d] 31 Or *before an Israelite king reigned over them* [e] 37 Possibly the Euphrates [f] 39 Many manuscripts of the Masoretic Text, Samaritan Pentateuch and Syriac (see also 1 Chron. 1:50); most manuscripts of the Masoretic Text *Hadar*

dants (see 1Ch 1:38–42) is repeated in abbreviated form in vv. 29–30 as a list of tribal chieftains.
36:30 *divisions.* Tribal divisions (cf. Jos 11:23).
36:31 *before any Israelite king reigned.* Appears to presuppose the Israelite monarchy and thus to be a later editorial updating (see note on 14:14).
36:43 *This … Edomites.* A summary statement for the whole chapter (just as v. 1 is a title for the whole chapter).
37:1 *Canaan.* See note on 10:6. Jacob made the promised land his homeland and was later buried there (see 49:29–30 and note on 49:29; 50:13). His son Joseph also insisted on being buried in Canaan, which he recognized as the land the Lord had promised to Israel (see 50:24–25 and notes).
37:2—50:26 The Jacob-Joseph cycle (see Introduction: Literary Features). It focuses mainly on Jacob's sons and how they embodied for both good and ill the family line of Abraham, Isaac and Jacob, which God had chosen to be the channel of his saving acts in history.
37:2 *account.* See note on 2:4. The word here introduces the tenth and final main section of Genesis. *Joseph.* The author immediately introduces Joseph, on whom the last cycle of the patriarchal narrative centers. In his generation he, more than any other, represented Israel—as a people who struggled with both God and human beings and overcame (see 32:28 and note) and as a source of blessing to the nations (see 12:2–3 and note). It is, moreover, through the life of Joseph that the covenant family in Canaan becomes an emerging nation in Egypt, thus setting the stage for the exodus. The story of God's dealings with the patriarchs foreshadows the subsequent Biblical account of God's purpose with Israel. It begins with the election and calling out of Abram from the post-Babel nations and ends with Israel in Egypt (in the person of Joseph) preserving the life of the nations (see 41:57; 50:20 and notes). So God would deliver Israel out of the nations (the exodus), eventually to send them on a mission of life to the nations (cf. Mt 28:18–20; Ac 1:8). *bad report about them.* Doubtless about all his brothers (as the later context indicates), not just the sons of his father's concubines.

the sons of Bilhah[c] and the sons of Zilpah,[d] his father's wives, and he brought
their father a bad report[e] about them.
3Now Israel[f] loved Joseph more than
any of his other sons,[g] because he had
been born to him in his old age;[h] and he
made a richly ornamented[a] robe[i] for him.[j]
4When his brothers saw that their father
loved him more than any of them, they
hated him[k] and could not speak a kind
word to him.
5Joseph had a dream,[l] and when he told
it to his brothers,[m] they hated him all the
more.[n] 6He said to them, "Listen to this
dream I had: 7We were binding sheaves[o]
of grain out in the field when suddenly my
sheaf rose and stood upright, while your
sheaves gathered around mine and bowed
down to it."[p]
8His brothers said to him, "Do you intend to reign over us? Will you actually rule us?"[q] And they hated him all the
more[r] because of his dream and what he
had said.
9Then he had another dream,[s] and he
told it to his brothers. "Listen," he said, "I
had another dream, and this time the sun
and moon and eleven stars[t] were bowing
down to me."[u]
10When he told his father as well as his
brothers,[v] his father rebuked[w] him and
said, "What is this dream you had? Will
your mother and I and your brothers actually come and bow down to the ground
before you?"[x] 11His brothers were jealous
of him,[y] but his father kept the matter in
mind.[z]

Joseph Sold by His Brothers

12Now his brothers had gone to graze
their father's flocks near Shechem,[a] 13and
Israel[b] said to Joseph, "As you know, your
brothers are grazing the flocks near Shechem.[c] Come, I am going to send you to
them."
"Very well," he replied.
14So he said to him, "Go and see if all
is well with your brothers[d] and with the
flocks, and bring word back to me." Then
he sent him off from the Valley of Hebron.[e]
When Joseph arrived at Shechem, 15a
man found him wandering around in the
fields and asked him, "What are you looking for?"
16He replied, "I'm looking for my brothers. Can you tell me where they are grazing their flocks?"
17"They have moved on from here," the
man answered. "I heard them say, 'Let's
go to Dothan.[f]' "
So Joseph went after his brothers and
found them near Dothan. 18But they saw
him in the distance, and before he reached
them, they plotted to kill him.[g]
19"Here comes that dreamer![h]" they said
to each other. 20"Come now, let's kill him
and throw him into one of these cisterns[i]
and say that a ferocious animal[j] devoured
him.[k] Then we'll see what comes of his
dreams."[l]
21When Reuben[m] heard this, he tried to
rescue him from their hands. "Let's not
take his life," he said.[n] 22"Don't shed any
blood. Throw him into this cistern[o] here in
the desert, but don't lay a hand on him."
Reuben said this to rescue him from them
and take him back to his father.[p]
23So when Joseph came to his brothers,
they stripped him of his robe—the richly ornamented robe[q] he was wearing—
24and they took him and threw him into
the cistern.[r] Now the cistern was empty;
there was no water in it.

[a] *3* The meaning of the Hebrew for *richly ornamented* is uncertain; also in verses 23 and 32.

37:2 [c]Ge 35:25 [d]Ge 35:26 [e]1Sa 2:24 **37:3** [f]S Ge 17:5 [g]S Ge 25:28 [h]Ge 43:27; 44:20 [i]ver 23, 31, 32; 2Sa 13:18-19 [j]Ge 43:34; 45:22; 1Sa 1:4-5; Est 2:9 **37:4** [k]S ver 24; S Ge 27:41; Ac 7:9 **37:5** [l]S Ge 20:3; S 28:12 [m]ver 10 [n]ver 8 **37:7** [o]Ru 2:7, 15 [p]ver 9, 10; Ge 27:29; 42:6, 9; 43:26, 28; 44:14; 50:18; 2Sa 1:2; 9:6 **37:8** [q]Ge 41:44; 42:10; 44:16, 18; 48:22; 49:26; Dt 33:16 [r]ver 5 **37:9** [s]S ver 7; Ge 28:12 [t]Rev 12:1 [u]Dt 4:19; 17:3 **37:10** [v]ver 5 [w]Ru 2:16; Ps 9:5; 68:30; 106:9; 119:21; Isa 17:13; 54:9; Zec 3:2 [x]S ver 7; S Ge 9:25; S 33:3 **37:11** [y]Ge 26:14; Ac 7:9 [z]Lk 2:19, 51 **37:12** [a]S Ge 12:6 **37:13** [b]S Ge 17:5 [c]Ge 33:19 **37:14** [d]1Sa 17:18 [e]S Ge 13:18 **37:17** [f]2Ki 6:13 **37:18** [g]1Sa 19:1; 2Ch 24:21; Ps 31:13, 20; 37:12, 32; S Mt 12:14; Mk 14:1; Ac 23:12 **37:19** [h]S Ge 28:12 **37:20** [i]ver 22; Jer 38:6, 9 [j]ver 33; Lev 26:6, 22; Dt 32:24; 2Ki 17:25; Eze 34:25 [k]ver 31-33; S Ge 4:10 [l]Ge 50:20 **37:21** [m]S Ge 29:32 [n]Ge 42:22 **37:22** [o]S ver 20 [p]ver 29-30 **37:23** [q]ver 3 **37:24** [r]S ver 4; Ge 49:23; Jer 38:6; 41:7; Eze 22:27

37:3 *richly ornamented robe.* A mark of Jacob's favoritism, "the kind of garment the virgin daughters of the king wore" (2Sa 13:18).
37:5 *dream.* See note on 20:3.
37:7 *bowed down.* Joseph's dream would later come true (see 42:6; 43:26; 44:14 and notes).
37:8 *Will you actually rule us?* Joseph would later become the "prince among his brothers" (Dt 33:16) and receive "the rights of the firstborn" (1Ch 5:2), at least the double portion of the inheritance (see notes on 25:5; Dt 21:17), since his father adopted his two sons (see 48:5 and note).
37:10 *your mother.* Jacob possibly refers to Leah, since Rachel has already died (see 35:19). *bow down … before you.* An echo of Isaac's blessing of Jacob (see 27:29 and note).
37:11 *kept the matter in mind.* A hint that Jacob later recalled Joseph's dreams when events brought about their fulfillment. Cf. Mary's equally sensitive response to events during Jesus' boyhood days (Lk 2:19,51).
37:12 *Shechem.* See 12:6; 33:18 and notes.
37:17 *Dothan.* Located about 13 miles north of Shechem, Dothan was already an ancient city by this time.
37:19 *dreamer.* The Hebrew for this word means "master of dreams" or "dream expert" and is here used with obvious sarcasm.
37:21 *Reuben … tried to rescue him.* As Jacob's firstborn, he felt responsible for Joseph. He would later remind his brothers of this day (42:22). Initially Reuben's attempts to influence events seemed successful (30:14–17). But after his arrogant incest with Bilhah (see 35:22 and note) his efforts were always ineffective (see 42:37–38)—demonstrating his loss of the status of firstborn (see 49:3–4). Effective leadership passed to Judah (see vv. 26–27; 43:3–5,8–10 and note on 43:3; 44:14–34; 46:28; 49:8–12 and note on 49:8).
37:23–24 Similarly (see note on v. 21), in Egypt Joseph (though innocent of any wrongdoing) would be stripped of his position of privilege and thrown into prison—also as a result of domestic intrigue (ch. 39). His cloak also would be torn from him and shown to Potiphar, but he would be rescued (41:14).

25 As they sat down to eat their meal,
they looked up and saw a caravan of Ishmaelites[s] coming from Gilead.[t] Their camels were loaded with spices, balm[u] and
myrrh,[v] and they were on their way to
take them down to Egypt.[w]
26 Judah[x] said to his brothers, "What will
we gain if we kill our brother and cover
up his blood?[y] 27 Come, let's sell him to the
Ishmaelites and not lay our hands on him;
after all, he is our brother,[z] our own flesh
and blood.[a]" His brothers agreed.
28 So when the Midianite[b] merchants
came by, his brothers pulled Joseph up out
of the cistern[c] and sold[d] him for twenty
shekels[a] of silver[e] to the Ishmaelites,[f] who
took him to Egypt.[g]
29 When Reuben returned to the cistern
and saw that Joseph was not there, he tore
his clothes.[h] 30 He went back to his brothers and said, "The boy isn't there! Where
can I turn now?"[i]
31 Then they got Joseph's robe,[j] slaughtered a goat and dipped the robe in the
blood.[k] 32 They took the ornamented robe[l]
back to their father and said, "We found
this. Examine it to see whether it is your
son's robe."
33 He recognized it and said, "It is my
son's robe! Some ferocious animal[m] has
devoured him. Joseph has surely been
torn to pieces."[n]
34 Then Jacob tore his clothes,[o] put on
sackcloth[p] and mourned for his son many
days.[q] 35 All his sons and daughters came
to comfort him,[r] but he refused to be comforted.[s] "No," he said, "in mourning will I
go down to the grave[b][t] to my son.[u]" So his
father wept for him.
36 Meanwhile, the Midianites[c][v] sold Joseph[w] in Egypt to Potiphar, one of Pharaoh's officials, the captain of the guard.[x]

37:25 [s]S Ge 16:11 [t]S Ge 31:21; S SS 4:1 [u]Jer 8:22; 22:6; 46:11 [v]Ge 43:11; Ex 30:23; Ps 45:8; Pr 7:17; SS 1:13; Mt 2:11 [w]ver 28; Ge 39:1; Ps 105:17 **37:26** [x]S Ge 29:35 [y]S Ge 4:10 **37:27** [z]Ge 42:21 [a]S Ge 29:14 **37:28** [b]S Ge 25:2 [c]Jer 38:13 [d]Ex 21:16 [e]Lev 27:5; Mt 26:15 [f]S Ge 16:11 [g]ver 36; Ge 39:1; 45:4-5; Ps 105:17; Jer 12:6; Ac 7:9 **37:29** [h]ver 34; Ge 44:13; Nu 14:6; Jos 7:6; 2Sa 1:11; 2Ki 2:12; 5:7; 11:14; 22:11; Job 1:20; 2:12; Isa 36:22; 37:1; Jer 36:24; 41:5; Joel 2:13 **37:30** [i]ver 22 **37:31** [j]S ver 3 [k]Rev 19:13 **37:32** [l]S ver 3 **37:33** [m]S ver 20 [n]Ge 42:13, 38; 44:20, 28 **37:34** [o]S ver 29

Judah and Tamar

38 At that time, Judah[y] left his brothers
and went down to stay with a man of
Adullam[z] named Hirah.[a] 2 There Judah met
the daughter of a Canaanite man named
Shua.[b] He married her and lay with her;
3 she became pregnant and gave birth to a
son, who was named Er.[c] 4 She conceived
again and gave birth to a son and named
him Onan.[d] 5 She gave birth to still another son and named him Shelah.[e] It was at
Kezib that she gave birth to him.

[a] *28* That is, about 8 ounces (about 0.2 kilogram)
[b] *35* Hebrew *Sheol* [c] *36* Samaritan Pentateuch, Septuagint, Vulgate and Syriac (see also verse 28); Masoretic Text *Medanites*

[p]2Sa 3:31; 1Ki 20:31; 21:27; 2Ki 6:30; 19:1, 2; Job 16:15; Ps 69:11; Isa 3:24; 15:3; 22:12; 32:11; 37:1; Jer 48:37; 49:3; Joel 1:13 [q]Ge 50:3, 10, 11; Nu 20:29; Dt 34:8 **37:35** [r]Job 2:11; 15:11; 16:5; 42:11 [s]2Sa 12:17; Ps 77:2; Jer 31:15 [t]Ge 42:38; 44:22, 29, 31 [u]2Sa 12:23 **37:36** [v]S Ge 25:2 [w]S ver 28 [x]Ge 39:1; 40:3; 41:10, 12; 1Sa 22:14 **38:1** [y]S Ge 29:35 [z]Jos 12:15; 15:35; 1Sa 22:1; 2Sa 23:13; 2Ch 11:7 [a]ver 12, 20 **38:2** [b]ver 12; 1Ch 2:3 **38:3** [c]ver 6; Ge 46:12; Nu 26:19 **38:4** [d]ver 8, 9; Ge 46:12; Nu 26:19 **38:5** [e]Nu 26:20

37:25 *Ishmaelites.* Also called Midianites (v. 28; see Jdg 8:22, 24,26 and note on 8:24) and Medanites (see NIV text note on v. 36). These various tribal groups were interrelated, since Midian and Medan, like Ishmael, were also sons of Abraham (25:2). *Gilead.* See note on 31:21. *balm.* An oil or gum, with healing properties (see Jer 51:8), exuded by the fruit or stems of one or more kinds of small trees. The balm of Gilead was especially effective (see Jer 8:22 and note; 46:11). *myrrh.* Probably to be identified with labdanum, an aromatic gum (see Ps 45:8; Pr 7:17; SS 3:6; 5:13) exuded from the leaves of the cistus rose. Its oil was used in beauty treatments (see Est 2:12), and it was sometimes mixed with wine and drunk to relieve pain (see Mk 15:23 and note). As a gift fit for a king, myrrh was brought to Jesus after his birth (Mt 2:11) and applied to his body after his death (Jn 19:39–40).

37:28 *twenty shekels of silver.* In later times, this amount was the value of a male of Joseph's age who had been dedicated to the Lord (see Lev 27:5).

37:31–33 Again a slaughtered goat figures prominently in an act of deception (see 27:5–13).

37:34 *tore his clothes, put on sackcloth.* Tearing one's clothes (see v. 29) and wearing coarse and uncomfortable sackcloth instead of ordinary clothes were both signs of mourning (see note on Rev 11:3).

37:35 *daughters.* The term can include daughters-in-law (e.g., a daughter-in-law of Jacob is mentioned in 38:2). *grave.* According to some, the Hebrew word *Sheol* (see NIV text note) can also refer in a more general way to the realm of the dead, the netherworld, where, it was thought, departed spirits live (see note on Dt 32:22).

37:36 *sold.* "As a slave" (Ps 105:17). The peoples of the Arabian Desert were long involved in international slave trade (cf. Am 1:6,9 and note on 1:6). *guard.* The Hebrew for this word can mean "executioners" (the captain of whom was in charge of the royal prisoners; see 40:4), or it can mean "butchers" (the captain of whom was the chief cook in the royal court; cf. 1Sa 9:23–24).

38:1–30 The unsavory events of this chapter illustrate the danger that Israel as God's separated people faced if they remained among the Canaanites (see 15:16 and note). In Egypt the Israelites were kept separate because the Egyptians despised them (see 43:32 and note; 46:34). While there, God's people were able to develop into a nation without losing their identity. Judah's actions contrasted with those of Joseph (ch. 39)—demonstrating the moral superiority of Joseph, to whom leadership in Israel fell in his generation (see 37:5–9 and note on 37:8). Since Judah was with his brothers when they sold Joseph to the slave traders and was with them again when they went down to Egypt to buy food, the author seems to locate the events of this chapter within a period of approximately 21 years (see chart, p. 26). Or we may suppose that Judah returned to Canaan from time to time to look after his affairs there.

38:1 *left his brothers.* Joseph was separated from his brothers by force, but Judah voluntarily separated himself to seek his fortune among the Canaanites. *Adullam.* A town southwest of Jerusalem (see 2Ch 11:5,7).

38:3–4 *Er ... Onan.* The names also appear as designations of tribes in Mesopotamian documents of this time.

38:5 *Kezib.* Probably the same as Aczib (Jos 15:44), three miles west of Adullam. The "men of Cozeba" (another form of the same word) were descendants of Shelah son of Judah (see 1Ch 4:21–22). The Hebrew root of the name means "deception" (see Mic 1:14 and note), a theme running throughout the story of Jacob and his sons.

6Judah got a wife for Er, his firstborn, and her name was Tamar.[f] 7But Er, Judah's firstborn, was wicked in the LORD's sight;[g] so the LORD put him to death.[h]

8Then Judah said to Onan, "Lie with your brother's wife and fulfill your duty to her as a brother-in-law to produce offspring for your brother."[i] 9But Onan knew that the offspring would not be his; so whenever he lay with his brother's wife, he spilled his semen on the ground to keep from producing offspring for his brother. 10What he did was wicked in the LORD's sight; so he put him to death also.[j]

11Judah then said to his daughter-in-law[k] Tamar,[l] "Live as a widow in your father's house[m] until my son Shelah[n] grows up."[o] For he thought, "He may die too, just like his brothers." So Tamar went to live in her father's house.

12After a long time Judah's wife, the daughter of Shua,[p] died. When Judah had recovered from his grief, he went up to Timnah,[q] to the men who were shearing his sheep,[r] and his friend Hirah the Adullamite[s] went with him.

13When Tamar[t] was told, "Your father-in-law is on his way to Timnah to shear his sheep,"[u] 14she took off her widow's clothes,[v] covered herself with a veil[w] to disguise herself, and then sat down[x] at the entrance to Enaim, which is on the road to Timnah.[y] For she saw that, though Shelah[z] had now grown up, she had not been given to him as his wife.

15When Judah saw her, he thought she was a prostitute,[a] for she had covered her face. 16Not realizing[b] that she was his daughter-in-law,[c] he went over to her by the roadside and said, "Come now, let me sleep with you."[d]

"And what will you give me to sleep with you?"[e] she asked.

17"I'll send you a young goat[f] from my flock," he said.

"Will you give me something as a pledge[g] until you send it?" she asked.

18He said, "What pledge should I give you?"

"Your seal[h] and its cord, and the staff[i] in your hand," she answered. So he gave them to her and slept with her, and she became pregnant by him.[j] 19After she left, she took off her veil and put on her widow's clothes[k] again.

20Meanwhile Judah sent the young goat by his friend the Adullamite[l] in order to get his pledge[m] back from the woman, but he did not find her. 21He asked the men who lived there, "Where is the shrine prostitute[n] who was beside the road at Enaim?"

"There hasn't been any shrine prostitute here," they said.

22So he went back to Judah and said, "I didn't find her. Besides, the men who lived there said, 'There hasn't been any shrine prostitute here.'"

23Then Judah said, "Let her keep what she has,[o] or we will become a laughingstock.[p] After all, I did send her this young goat, but you didn't find her."

24About three months later Judah was told, "Your daughter-in-law Tamar is guilty of prostitution, and as a result she is now pregnant."

Judah said, "Bring her out and have her burned to death!"[q]

25As she was being brought out, she sent a message to her father-in-law. "I am pregnant by the man who owns these," she said. And she added, "See if you recognize whose seal and cord and staff these are."[r]

26Judah recognized them and said, "She is more righteous than I,[s] since I wouldn't give her to my son Shelah.[t]" And he did not sleep with her again.

27When the time came for her to give

38:6 [f]ver 11,13 **38:7** [g]S Ge 6:5 [h]ver 10; Ge 46:12; Lev 10:1-2; 1Ch 2:3 **38:8** [i]Dt 25:5-6; Ru 4:5; Mt 22:24-28 **38:10** [j]S ver 7; Dt 25:7-10 **38:11** [k]S Ge 11:31 [l]S ver 6 [m]Ru 1:8 [n]ver 14,26 [o]Ru 1:13 **38:12** [p]S ver 2 [q]ver 14; Jos 15:10,57; 19:43; Jdg 14:1,2; 2Ch 28:18 [r]S Ge 31:19 [s]S ver 1 **38:13** [t]S ver 6 [u]S Ge 31:19 **38:14** [v]ver 19 [w]S Ge 24:65 [x]Jer 3:2 [y]S ver 12 [z]S ver 11 **38:15** [a]Jdg 11:1; 16:1 **38:16** [b]Ge 42:23 [c]Lev 18:15; 20:12; Ru 1:6 [d]Ge 39:7,12; 2Sa 13:11 [e]S Ge 30:15 **38:17** [f]Jdg 15:1 [g]ver 20 **38:18** [h]ver 25; 1Ki 21:8; Est 3:12; 8:8; SS 8:6; Isa 49:16; Jer 22:24; Hag 2:23; 2Co 1:22; Eph 1:13 [i]S Ge 32:10; S Ex 4:2 [j]S Ge 19:32 **38:19** [k]ver 14 **38:20** [l]S ver 1 [m]ver 17 **38:21** [n]S Ge 19:5; Lev 19:29; Dt 22:21; 23:17; 2Ki 23:7; Hos 4:14 **38:23** [o]ver 18 [p]Ex 32:25; Job 12:4; Jer 20:7; La 3:14 **38:24** [q]Lev 20:10,14; 21:9; Dt 22:21,22; Jos 7:25; Jdg 15:6; 1Sa 31:12; Job 31:11,28; Eze 16:38 **38:25** [r]S ver 18 **38:26** [s]1Sa 24:17 [t]S ver 11

38:6 *Judah got a wife for Er.* See note on 21:21.
38:8 A concise description of the custom known as "levirate marriage" (Latin *levir* means "brother-in-law"). Details of the practice are given in Dt 25:5–6 (see note there), where it is laid down as a legal obligation within Israel (cf. Mt 22:24 and note). The custom is illustrated in Ru 4:5 (see note there), though there it is extended to the nearest living relative ("kinsman-redeemer," Ru 3:12; see note there and on 2:20), since neither Boaz nor the nearer kinsman was a brother-in-law.
38:9 *knew that the offspring would not be his.* Similarly, Ruth's nearest kinsman was fearful that if he married Ruth he would endanger his own estate (see Ru 4:5–6 and note on 4:6). *spilled his semen on the ground.* A means of birth control sometimes called "onanism" (after Onan).
38:10 *What he did.* His refusal to perform his levirate duty.
38:11 *he thought, "He may die too, just like his brothers."* Thus Judah had no intention of giving Shelah to Tamar (see v. 14).
38:12 *Timnah.* Exact location unknown, but somewhere in the hill country of Judah (see Jos 15:48,57).
38:14 *sat down ... the road.* Prostitutes (see v. 15) customarily stationed themselves by the roadside (Jer 3:2; see note there). *Enaim.* Means "two springs"; probably the same as Enam in the western foothills of Judah (see Jos 15:33–34 and note on 15:33).
38:18 *seal and its cord.* Probably a small cylinder seal of the type used to sign clay documents by rolling them over the clay. The owner wore it around his neck on a cord threaded through a hole drilled lengthwise through it.
38:21 *shrine prostitute.* The Hebrew here differs from that used for "prostitute" in v. 15. Judah's friend perhaps deliberately used the more acceptable term, since ritual prostitutes enjoyed a higher social status in Canaan than did ordinary prostitutes (see note on 20:9).
38:24 *have her burned to death.* In later times, burning was the legal penalty for prostitution (see Lev 21:9).
38:27–30 For a similarly unusual birth of twin boys see 25:24–26.

birth, there were twin boys in her womb.[u]
28As she was giving birth, one of them
put out his hand; so the midwife[v] took
a scarlet thread and tied it on his wrist[w]
and said, "This one came out first." 29But
when he drew back his hand, his brother
came out,[x] and she said, "So this is how
you have broken out!" And he was named
Perez.[a][y] 30Then his brother, who had the
scarlet thread on his wrist,[z] came out and
he was given the name Zerah.[b][a]

Joseph and Potiphar's Wife

39 Now Joseph[b] had been taken down
to Egypt. Potiphar, an Egyptian who
was one of Pharaoh's officials, the captain
of the guard,[c] bought him from the Ishmaelites who had taken him there.[d]
2The LORD was with Joseph[e] and he
prospered, and he lived in the house of his
Egyptian master. 3When his master saw
that the LORD was with him[f] and that the
LORD gave him success in everything he
did,[g] 4Joseph found favor in his eyes[h] and
became his attendant. Potiphar put him in
charge of his household,[i] and he entrusted
to his care everything he owned.[j] 5From
the time he put him in charge of his household and of all that he owned, the LORD
blessed the household[k] of the Egyptian because of Joseph.[l] The blessing of the LORD
was on everything Potiphar had, both in
the house and in the field.[m] 6So he left in
Joseph's care everything he had;[n] with Joseph in charge, he did not concern himself
with anything except the food he ate.
Now Joseph was well-built and handsome,[o] 7and after a while his master's wife
took notice of Joseph and said, "Come to
bed with me!"[p]
8But he refused.[q] "With me in charge,"
he told her, "my master does not concern
himself with anything in the house; everything he owns he has entrusted to my
care.[r] 9No one is greater in this house than
I am.[s] My master has withheld nothing
from me except you, because you are his
wife. How then could I do such a wicked
thing and sin against God?"[t] 10And though
she spoke to Joseph day after day, he refused[u] to go to bed with her or even be
with her.
11One day he went into the house to attend to his duties,[v] and none of the household servants[w] was inside. 12She caught
him by his cloak[x] and said, "Come to bed
with me!"[y] But he left his cloak in her
hand and ran out of the house.[z]
13When she saw that he had left his
cloak in her hand and had run out of the
house, 14she called her household servants.[a] "Look," she said to them, "this
Hebrew[b] has been brought to us to make
sport of us![c] He came in here to sleep with
me, but I screamed.[d] 15When he heard me
scream for help, he left his cloak beside
me and ran out of the house."[e]
16She kept his cloak beside her until
his master came home. 17Then she told
him this story:[f] "That Hebrew[g] slave[h] you

[a] 29 *Perez* means *breaking out.* [b] 30 *Zerah* can mean *scarlet* or *brightness.*

38:27 [u]Ge 25:24 **38:28** [v]S Ge 35:17 [w]ver 30 **38:29** [x]Ge 25:26 [y]Ge 46:12; Nu 26:20,21; Ru 4:12,18; 2Sa 5:20; 6:8; 1Ch 2:4; 9:4; Isa 28:21; Mt 1:3 **38:30** [z]ver 28 [a]Ge 46:12; 1Ch 2:4; Ne 11:24 **39:1** [b]S Ge 30:24 [c]S Ge 37:36 [d]S Ge 37:25 **39:2** [e]S Ge 21:20,22; Jos 1:5; 6:27; Jdg 1:19; 1Sa 18:14; Ac 7:9 **39:3** [f]S Ge 21:22 [g]ver 23; 1Sa 18:14; 2Ki 18:7; 2Ch 20:20; Ps 1:3; 128:2; Isa 33:6 **39:4** [h]S Ge 6:8; S 18:3 [i]Ge 47:6; 1Ki 11:28; Pr 22:29 [j]ver 8,22; Ge 40:4; 42:37 **39:5** [k]2Sa 6:11 [l]S Ge 26:24 [m]Dt 28:3; Ps 128:4 **39:6** [n]Ge 24:2 [o]S Ge 12:11; Ex 2:2; 1Sa 9:2; 16:12; 17:42; Est 2:7; Da 1:4 **39:7** [p]S Ge 38:16; Pr 7:15-18 **39:8** [q]Pr 6:23-24 [r]S ver 4 **39:9** [s]Ge 41:33,40 [t]S Ge 13:13; S Nu 22:34 **39:10** [u]Est 3:4 **39:11** [v]Ex 18:20; Dt 1:18 [w]ver 14 **39:12** [x]2Sa 13:11; Pr 7:13 [y]S Ge 38:16 [z]ver 15; Pr 5:8; 2Ti 2:22 **39:14** [a]ver 11 [b]S Ge 14:13 [c]S Ge 21:9 [d]Dt 22:24,27 **39:15** [e]S ver 12 **39:17** [f]Ex 20:16; 23:1,7; Dt 5:20; Ps 101:5 [g]S Ge 14:13 [h]Ge 21:10

38:29 *Perez.* Became the head of the leading clan in Judah and the ancestor of David (see Ru 4:18–22 and note) and ultimately of Christ (see Mt 1:1–6).

39:1–23 A continuation of the Joseph story (see 37:36)—the first stage in the movement of Israel from Canaan to Egypt.

39:1 *taken down to Egypt.* Joseph's experiences in Egypt, as well as those of his youth in Canaan (see note on 37:23–24), are similar to Israel's national experiences in Egypt. Initially, because of God's blessing, Joseph attains a position of honor (in Potiphar's house); he is then unjustly thrown into prison, his only crime being his attractiveness and moral integrity; and finally he is raised up among the Egyptians as the one who, because God is with him, holds their lives in his hands. Similarly Israel was first received with honor in Egypt (because of Joseph); then it was subjected to cruel bondage, its only crime being God's evident blessings upon it; and finally God raised Israel up in the eyes of the Egyptians (through the ministry of Moses) as they came fearfully to recognize that these people and their God did indeed hold their lives in their hands. The author of Genesis knew the events of the exodus and shows how the history of God and the patriarchs moved forward to and foreshadowed that event (see also 15:13–16; 48:21–22; 50:24–25). *Ishmaelites.* See note on 37:25.

39:2–6 See vv. 20–23. Though Joseph's situation changed drastically, God's relationship to him remained the same.

39:2 *The LORD was with Joseph.* See note on 26:3. This fact, mentioned several times here (vv. 3,21,23), is stressed also by Stephen (Ac 7:9–10).

39:5 *the LORD blessed the household of the Egyptian because of Joseph.* As God had blessed Laban because of Jacob (see 30:27 and note). The offspring of Abraham continue to be a blessing to the nations (see 12:2–3 and note).

39:6 *left in Joseph's care everything he had.* As Laban had entrusted his flocks to Jacob's care (30:31–34). Joseph had full responsibility for the welfare of Potiphar's house, as later he would have full responsibility in prison (vv. 22–23) and later still in all Egypt (41:41). Always this Israelite came to hold the welfare of his "world" in his hands—but always by the blessing and overruling of God, never by his own wits, as his father Jacob had so long attempted. In the role that he played in Israel's history and in the manner in which he lived it, Joseph was a true representative of Israel.

39:7 *took notice of.* Looked with desire at. The phrase is used in the same sense in Akkadian in Section 25 of the Code of Hammurapi (see chart, p. xxii).

39:9 *sin against God.* All sin is against God, first and foremost (see Ps 51:4 and note).

39:10 *though she spoke to Joseph day after day, he refused.* The ancient Egyptian "Tale of Two Brothers" tells a similar story (see chart, p. xxiii). Samson twice succumbed under similar pressure (Jdg 14:17; 16:16–17).

39:14 *this Hebrew.* See v. 17; see also note on 14:13.

brought us came to me to make sport of
me. 18But as soon as I screamed for help,
he left his cloak beside me and ran out of
the house."
19When his master heard the story his
wife told him, saying, "This is how your
slave treated me," he burned with anger.[i]
20Joseph's master took him and put him in
prison,[j] the place where the king's prisoners were confined.
But while Joseph was there in the prison, 21the LORD was with him;[k] he showed
him kindness[l] and granted him favor in the
eyes of the prison warden.[m] 22So the warden put Joseph in charge of all those held
in the prison, and he was made responsible for all that was done there.[n] 23The warden paid no attention to anything under
Joseph's[o] care, because the LORD was with
Joseph and gave him success in whatever
he did.[p]

The Cupbearer and the Baker

40 Some time later, the cupbearer[q] and
the baker[r] of the king of Egypt offended their master, the king of Egypt. 2Phar-
aoh was angry[s] with his two officials,[t] the
chief cupbearer and the chief baker, 3and
put them in custody in the house of the
captain of the guard,[u] in the same prison
where Joseph was confined. 4The captain
of the guard[v] assigned them to Joseph,[w]
and he attended them.
After they had been in custody[x] for some
time, 5each of the two men — the cupbearer and the baker of the king of Egypt, who
were being held in prison — had a dream[y]
the same night, and each dream had a
meaning of its own.[z]
6When Joseph came to them the next
morning, he saw that they were dejected.
7So he asked Pharaoh's officials who were
in custody[a] with him in his master's house,
"Why are your faces so sad today?"[b]
8"We both had dreams," they answered,
"but there is no one to interpret them."[c]
Then Joseph said to them, "Do not interpretations belong to God?[d] Tell me your
dreams."
9So the chief cupbearer[e] told Joseph his
dream. He said to him, "In my dream I
saw a vine in front of me, 10and on the
vine were three branches. As soon as it
budded, it blossomed,[f] and its clusters ripened into grapes. 11Pharaoh's cup was in
my hand, and I took the grapes, squeezed
them into Pharaoh's cup and put the cup
in his hand."
12"This is what it means,[g]" Joseph said
to him. "The three branches are three
days.[h] 13Within three days[i] Pharaoh will
lift up your head[j] and restore you to your
position, and you will put Pharaoh's cup in
his hand, just as you used to do when you
were his cupbearer.[k] 14But when all goes
well with you, remember me[l] and show
me kindness;[m] mention me to Pharaoh[n]
and get me out of this prison. 15For I was
forcibly carried off from the land of the Hebrews,[o] and even here I have done nothing
to deserve being put in a dungeon."[p]
16When the chief baker[q] saw that Joseph had given a favorable interpretation,[r]
he said to Joseph, "I too had a dream: On
my head were three baskets[s] of bread.[a]
17In the top basket were all kinds of baked
goods for Pharaoh, but the birds were eating them out of the basket on my head."
18"This is what it means," Joseph said.
"The three baskets are three days.[t] 19With-
in three days[u] Pharaoh will lift off your
head[v] and hang you on a tree.[b][w] And the
birds will eat away your flesh."[x]

[a] 16 Or *three wicker baskets* [b] 19 Or *and impale you on a pole*

39:19 [i]S Ge 34:7; S Est 1:12 **39:20** [j]Ge 40:3; 41:10; Ps 105:18 **39:21** [k]S Ge 21:20 [l]S Ge 19:19 [m]Ex 3:21; 11:3; 12:36; Est 2:9; Ps 106:46; Pr 16:7; Da 1:9 **39:22** [n]S ver 4 **39:23** [o]S Ge 21:20; S Nu 14:43 [p]S ver 3 **40:1** [q]ver 9,13,21; Ne 1:11 [r]ver 16,20 **40:2** [s]Pr 16:14,15; 19:12 [t]Ge 41:10; Est 2:21 **40:3** [u]S Ge 37:36; S 39:20 **40:4** [v]S Ge 37:36 [w]S Ge 39:4 [x]ver 7; Ge 42:17 **40:5** [y]S Ge 20:3 [z]Ge 41:11 **40:7** [a]S ver 4 [b]Ne 2:2 **40:8** [c]Ge 41:8,15 [d]Ge 41:16,25, 28,32; Dt 29:29; Da 2:22,28,47 **40:9** [e]S ver 1 **40:10** [f]Isa 27:6; 35:1-2; Hos 14:7 **40:12** [g]ver 16; Ge 41:12,15,25; Da 2:36; 4:19 [h]ver 18 **40:13** [i]ver 19,20; Jos 1:11; 3:2; Ezr 8:32; Ne 2:11 [j]ver 19 [k]S ver 1 **40:14** [l]1Sa 25:31; Lk 23:42 [m]S Ge 19:19; 1Sa 20:14,42; 2Sa 9:1; 1Ki 2:7 [n]ver 23; Ge 41:9; Ecc 9:15 **40:15** [o]S Ge 14:13 [p]Ge 39:20; Job 13:27 **40:16** [q]S ver 1 [r]S ver 12 [s]Am 8:1-2 **40:18** [t]ver 12 **40:19** [u]ver 13 [v]S ver 13 [w]ver 22; Dt 21:22-23; Est 2:23; 7:10 [x]Dt 28:26; 1Sa 17:44; 2Sa 21:10; 1Ki 14:11; 16:4; 21:24; Eze 39:4

39:20 – 23 See note on vv. 2 – 6.

39:20 *place where the king's prisoners were confined.* Though understandably angry (see v. 19), Potiphar put Joseph in the "house of the captain of the guard" (40:3) — certainly not the worst prison available.

40:1 – 23 God gives Joseph the interpretation of two dreams, which prepares the way for Joseph to be used by God to interpret the pharaoh's two dreams (ch. 41), leading to the subsequent fulfillment (chs. 42 – 46) of Joseph's two dreams (37:5 – 11).

40:2 *Pharaoh.* See note on Ex 1:11. *chief cupbearer.* Would be the divinely appointed agent for introducing Joseph to the pharaoh (see 41:9 – 14).

40:5 *each dream had a meaning.* Throughout the ancient Near East it was believed that dreams sometimes contained disclosures about the future that a proper interpretation would bring to light (see note on 20:3). God was beginning to prepare the way for Joseph's rise in Egypt.

40:8 *interpretations belong to God.* Only God, who knows the future, can properly interpret dreams (see 41:16,25,28; Da 2:28). *Tell me.* Joseph presents himself as God's agent through whom God will make known the revelation contained in their dreams — Israel is God's prophetic people through whom God's revelation comes to the nations (see 18:17 and note; 41:16,28,32).

40:13 *lift up your head and restore you to your position.* See Ps 3:3; 27:6. For this meaning of the idiom "lift up one's head" see 2Ki 25:27 and Jer 52:31, where the Hebrew for "released" in the context of freeing a prisoner means lit. "lifted up the head of."

40:14 *when all goes well with you, remember me.* Unfortunately, the cupbearer "forgot him" (v. 23) until two full years later (see 41:1,9 – 13).

40:15 *dungeon.* Probably hyperbole to reflect Joseph's despair (see note on 39:20). Since the same Hebrew word refers to a cistern in 37:24, the author of Genesis has established a link with Joseph's earlier experience at the hands of his brothers.

40:19 *lift off your head.* A grisly pun based on the same idiom used in v. 13 (see note there).

20Now the third day[y] was Pharaoh's birthday,[z] and he gave a feast for all his officials.[a] He lifted up the heads of the chief cupbearer and the chief baker[b] in the presence of his officials: 21He restored the chief cupbearer[c] to his position,[d] so that he once again put the cup into Pharaoh's hand,[e] 22but he hanged[a] the chief baker,[f] just as Joseph had said to them in his interpretation.[g]

23The chief cupbearer, however, did not remember Joseph; he forgot him.[h]

Pharaoh's Dreams

41 When two full years had passed, Pharaoh had a dream:[i] He was standing by the Nile,[j] 2when out of the river there came up seven cows, sleek and fat,[k] and they grazed among the reeds.[l] 3After them, seven other cows, ugly and gaunt, came up out of the Nile and stood beside those on the riverbank. 4And the cows that were ugly and gaunt ate up the seven sleek, fat cows. Then Pharaoh woke up.[m]

5He fell asleep again and had a second dream: Seven heads of grain,[n] healthy and good, were growing on a single stalk. 6After them, seven other heads of grain sprouted—thin and scorched by the east wind.[o] 7The thin heads of grain swallowed up the seven healthy, full heads. Then Pharaoh woke up;[p] it had been a dream.

8In the morning his mind was troubled,[q] so he sent for all the magicians[r] and wise men of Egypt. Pharaoh told them his dreams, but no one could interpret them for him.[s]

9Then the chief cupbearer said to Pharaoh, "Today I am reminded of my shortcomings.[t] 10Pharaoh was once angry with his servants,[u] and he imprisoned me and the chief baker in the house of the captain of the guard.[v] 11Each of us had a dream the same night, and each dream had a meaning of its own.[w] 12Now a young Hebrew[x] was there with us, a servant of the captain of the guard.[y] We told him our dreams, and he interpreted them for us, giving each man the interpretation of his dream.[z] 13And things turned out exactly as he interpreted them to us: I was restored to my position, and the other man was hanged.[a][a]"

14So Pharaoh sent for Joseph, and he was quickly brought from the dungeon.[b] When he had shaved[c] and changed his clothes,[d] he came before Pharaoh.

15Pharaoh said to Joseph, "I had a dream, and no one can interpret it.[e] But I have heard it said of you that when you hear a dream you can interpret it."[f]

16"I cannot do it," Joseph replied to Pharaoh, "but God will give Pharaoh the answer he desires."[g]

17Then Pharaoh said to Joseph, "In my dream I was standing on the bank of the Nile,[h] 18when out of the river there came up seven cows, fat and sleek, and they grazed among the reeds.[i] 19After them, seven other cows came up—scrawny and very ugly and lean. I had never seen such ugly cows in all the land of Egypt. 20The lean, ugly cows ate up the seven fat cows that came up first. 21But even after they ate them, no one could tell that they had done so; they looked just as ugly as before. Then I woke up.

22"In my dreams I also saw seven heads of grain, full and good, growing on a single stalk. 23After them, seven other heads sprouted—withered and thin and scorched by the east wind. 24The thin heads of grain swallowed up the seven good heads. I told this to the magicians, but none could explain it to me.[j]"

25Then Joseph said to Pharaoh, "The dreams of Pharaoh are one and the same.[k] God has revealed to Pharaoh what he is about to do.[l] 26The seven good cows[m] are seven years, and the seven good heads of grain are seven years; it is one and the same dream. 27The seven lean, ugly cows that came up afterward are seven years, and so are the seven worthless heads of grain scorched by the east wind: They are seven years of famine.[n]

28"It is just as I said to Pharaoh: God has shown Pharaoh what he is about to do.[o] 29Seven years of great abundance[p] are coming throughout the land of Egypt, 30but seven years of famine[q] will follow

[a] 22,13 Or *impaled*

40:20 [y]S ver 13 [z]Mt 14:6-10 [a]Est 2:18; Mk 6:21 [b]S ver 1 **40:21** [c]S ver 1 [d]2Ki 25:27; Jer 52:31 [e]ver 13 **40:22** [f]S ver 19 [g]Ge 41:13; Ps 105:19 **40:23** [h]S ver 14; S Ecc 1:11 **41:1** [i]S Ge 20:3 [j]ver 17; S Ge 2:14; Ex 1:22; 2:5; 7:15 **41:2** [k]ver 26; Jer 5:28 [l]ver 18; Ex 2:3; Job 40:21; Isa 19:6 **41:4** [m]ver 7 **41:5** [n]Jos 13:3; 2Ki 4:42; 1Ch 13:5; Isa 23:3; Jer 2:18 **41:6** [o]Ex 10:13; 14:21; Job 6:26; 11:2; 15:2; Ps 11:6; 48:7; Isa 11:15; 27:8; Jer 4:11; 18:17; Eze 19:12; 27:26; Hos 12:1; 13:15; Jnh 4:8 **41:7** [p]ver 4 **41:8** [q]Job 7:14; Da 2:1,3; 4:5,19 [r]Ex 7:11,22; Da 1:20; 2:2,27; 4:7; 5:7 [s]ver 24; S Ge 40:8; Da 4:18 **41:9** [t]S Ge 40:14 **41:10** [u]S Ge 40:2 [v]S Ge 37:36; S 39:20 **41:11** [w]Ge 40:5 **41:12** [x]S Ge 14:13; 39:17 [y]S Ge 37:36; 40:4 [z]S Ge 40:12 **41:13** [a]S Ge 40:22 **41:14** [b]Ps 105:20 [c]Isa 18:2,7 [d]S Ge 35:2; 45:22; Ru 3:3; 2Sa 12:20 **41:15** [e]S Ge 40:8 [f]S Ge 40:12; Da 4:18; 5:16 **41:16** [g]S Ge 40:8 **41:17** [h]S ver 1 **41:18** [i]S ver 2 **41:24** [j]S ver 8 **41:25** [k]S Ge 40:12 [l]S Ge 40:8; Isa 46:11; Da 2:45 **41:26** [m]S ver 2 **41:27** [n]S Ge 12:10 **41:28** [o]S Ge 40:8 **41:29** [p]ver 47 **41:30** [q]ver 54; Ge 45:6,11; 47:13; Ps 105:16

41:2 *out of the river there came up seven cows.* Cattle often submerged themselves up to their necks in the Nile to escape sun and insects.

41:6 *scorched by the east wind.* The Palestinian sirocco (in Egypt the khamsin), which blows in from the desert (see Hos 13:15) in late spring and early fall, often withers vegetation (see Isa 40:7; Eze 17:10 and note).

41:8 *his mind was troubled.* See 40:6–7. *magicians.* Probably priests who claimed to possess occult knowledge. *no one could interpret them.* See Da 2:10–11 and note on 2:10.

41:13 *things turned out exactly as he interpreted them.* Because his words were from the Lord (see Ps 105:19).

41:14 *Pharaoh sent for Joseph.* Effecting his permanent release from prison (see Ps 105:20). *shaved.* Egyptians were normally smooth-shaven, while Israelites and Canaanites wore beards (see 2Sa 10:4; Jer 41:5 and notes).

41:16 *I cannot do it … but God will give Pharaoh the answer.* See 40:8 and note; Da 2:27–28,30; cf. 2Co 3:5.

41:27 *seven years of famine.* See Ac 7:11. Long famines were rare in Egypt because of the regularity of the annual overflow of the Nile, but not uncommon elsewhere (see 2Ki 8:1 and note; see also chart, p. xxiii ["Seven Lean Years Tradition"]).

them. Then all the abundance in Egypt will be forgotten, and the famine will ravage the land.[r] 31 The abundance in the land will not be remembered, because the famine that follows it will be so severe. 32 The reason the dream was given to Pharaoh in two forms is that the matter has been firmly decided[s] by God, and God will do it soon.[t]

33 "And now let Pharaoh look for a discerning and wise man[u] and put him in charge of the land of Egypt.[v] 34 Let Pharaoh appoint commissioners[w] over the land to take a fifth[x] of the harvest of Egypt during the seven years of abundance.[y] 35 They should collect all the food of these good years that are coming and store up the grain under the authority of Pharaoh, to be kept in the cities for food.[z] 36 This food should be held in reserve for the country, to be used during the seven years of famine that will come upon Egypt,[a] so that the country may not be ruined by the famine."

37 The plan seemed good to Pharaoh and to all his officials.[b] 38 So Pharaoh asked them, "Can we find anyone like this man, one in whom is the spirit of God[a]?"[c]

39 Then Pharaoh said to Joseph, "Since God has made all this known to you,[d] there is no one so discerning and wise as you.[e] 40 You shall be in charge of my palace,[f] and all my people are to submit to your orders.[g] Only with respect to the throne will I be greater than you.[h]"

Joseph in Charge of Egypt

41 So Pharaoh said to Joseph, "I hereby put you in charge of the whole land of Egypt."[i] 42 Then Pharaoh took his signet ring[j] from his finger and put it on Joseph's finger. He dressed him in robes[k] of fine linen[l] and put a gold chain around his neck.[m] 43 He had him ride in a chariot[n] as his second-in-command,[b][o] and men shouted before him, "Make way[c]!"[p] Thus he put him in charge of the whole land of Egypt.[q]

44 Then Pharaoh said to Joseph, "I am Pharaoh, but without your word no one will lift hand or foot in all Egypt."[r] 45 Pharaoh gave Joseph[s] the name Zaphenath-Paneah and gave him Asenath daughter of Potiphera, priest[t] of On,[d][u] to be his wife.[v] And Joseph went throughout the land of Egypt.

46 Joseph was thirty years old[w] when he entered the service[x] of Pharaoh king of Egypt. And Joseph went out from Pharaoh's presence and traveled throughout Egypt. 47 During the seven years of abundance[y] the land produced plentifully. 48 Joseph collected all the food produced in those seven years of abundance in Egypt and stored it in the cities.[z] In each city he put the food grown in the fields surrounding it. 49 Joseph stored up huge quantities of grain, like the sand of the sea;[a] it was so much that he stopped keeping records because it was beyond measure.

50 Before the years of famine came, two sons were born to Joseph by Asenath daughter of Potiphera, priest of On.[b] 51 Joseph named his firstborn[c] Manasseh[e][d] and said, "It is because God has made me forget all my trouble and all my father's household." 52 The second son he named Ephraim[f][e] and said, "It is because God has made me fruitful[f] in the land of my suffering."

41:30 [r] ver 56; S Ge 12:10 **41:32** [s] Da 2:5 [t] S Ge 40:8 **41:33** [u] ver 39 [v] S Ge 39:9 **41:34** [w] Est 2:3 [x] Ge 47:24,26; 1Sa 8:15 [y] ver 48; Ge 47:14 **41:35** [z] ver 48 **41:36** [a] ver 56; Ge 42:6; 47:14 **41:37** [b] Ge 45:16; Est 2:4; Isa 19:11 **41:38** [c] Nu 27:18; Dt 34:9; Da 2:11; 4:8-9,18; 5:11,14 **41:39** [d] Da 2:11; 5:11 [e] ver 33 **41:40** [f] 1Ki 4:6; 2Ki 15:5; Isa 22:15; 36:3 [g] S Ge 39:9; Ps 105:21-22; Ac 7:10 [h] Est 10:3 **41:41** [i] ver 43,55; Ge 42:6; 45:8,13,26; Est 8:2; Jer 40:7; Da 6:3 **41:42** [j] S Ge 24:22; Est 3:10; 8:2,8 [k] 1Sa 17:38; 18:4; 1Ki 19:19; Est 6:8,11; Da 5:29; Zec 3:4 [l] Ex 25:4; Est 8:15; Da 5:29 [m] Ps 73:6; SS 4:9; Isa 3:18; Eze 16:11; Da 5:7,16,29 **41:43** [n] Ge 46:29; 50:9; Isa 2:7; 22:18 [o] Est 10:3 [p] Est 6:9 [q] S ver 41 **41:44** [r] S Ge 37:8; Est 10:2; Ps 105:22 **41:45** [s] Est 2:7 [t] Ex 2:16 [u] Eze 30:17 [v] ver 50; Ge 46:20,27

[a] 38 Or *of the gods* [b] 43 Or *in the chariot of his second-in-command*; or *in his second chariot* [c] 43 Or *Bow down* [d] 45 That is, Heliopolis; also in verse 50 [e] 51 *Manasseh* sounds like and may be derived from the Hebrew for *forget.* [f] 52 *Ephraim* sounds like the Hebrew for *twice fruitful.*

41:46 [w] S Ge 37:2 [x] 1Sa 8:11; 16:21; Pr 22:29; Da 1:19 **41:47** [y] ver 29 **41:48** [z] S ver 34 **41:49** [a] S Ge 12:2 **41:50** [b] S ver 45 **41:51** [c] Ge 48:14,18,20; 49:3 [d] Ge 46:20; 48:1; 50:23; Nu 1:34; Dt 33:17; Jos 4:12; 17:1; 1Ch 7:14 **41:52** [e] Ge 46:20; 48:1,5; 50:23; Nu 1:32; 26:28; Dt 33:17; Jos 14:4; Jdg 5:14; 1Ch 7:20; 2Ch 30:1; Ps 60:7; Jer 7:15; Ob 1:19 [f] S Ge 17:6

41:32 Repetition of a divine revelation was often used for emphasis (see 37:5–9; Am 7:1–6,7–9; 8:1–3).

41:38 *spirit of God.* See NIV text note. The word "spirit" should probably not be capitalized in such passages, since reference to the Holy Spirit would be out of character in statements by pagan rulers.

41:40 *You shall be in charge.* The pharaoh took Joseph's advice (see v. 33) and decided that Joseph himself should be "ruler over Egypt" (Ac 7:10; see also Ps 105:21). *all my people are to submit to your orders.* More lit. "at your command all my people are to kiss (you)"—i.e., kiss your hands or feet in an act of homage and submission (see Ps 2:12 and note).

41:42 Three symbols of transfer and/or sharing of royal authority, referred to also in Est 3:10 (signet ring); Est 6:11 (robe); and Da 5:7,16,29 (gold chain).

41:43 *second-in-command.* The position was probably that of vizier, the highest executive office below that of the king himself.

41:45 *gave Joseph the name Zaphenath-Paneah.* As a part of assigning Joseph an official position within his royal administration (see note on 1:5). The pharaoh presumed to use this marvelously endowed servant of the Lord for his own royal purposes—as a later pharaoh would attempt to use divinely blessed Israel for the enrichment of Egypt (Ex 1). He did not recognize that Joseph served a Higher Power, whose kingdom and redemptive purposes are being advanced. (The meaning of Joseph's Egyptian name is uncertain.) *Asenath.* The name is Egyptian and probably means "She belongs to (the goddess) Neith." *Potiphera.* Not the same person as "Potiphar" (37:36; 39:1); the name (also Egyptian) means "he whom (the sun-god) Ra has given." *On.* Located ten miles northeast of modern Cairo, it was called Heliopolis ("city of the sun") by the Greeks and was an important center for the worship of Ra, who had a temple there. Potiphera therefore bore an appropriate name.

41:46 *thirty years old.* In just 13 years (see 37:2), Joseph had become second-in-command (v. 43) in Egypt.

41:49 *like the sand of the sea.* A simile also for the large number of offspring promised to Abraham and Jacob (see 22:17; 32:12).

41:52 *Ephraim.* The wordplay on the name (see NIV text note) reflects the fact that God gave Joseph "two" (see v. 50) sons.

53The seven years of abundance in Egypt
came to an end, 54and the seven years of
famine[g] began,[h] just as Joseph had said.
There was famine in all the other lands,
but in the whole land of Egypt there was
food. 55When all Egypt began to feel the
famine,[i] the people cried to Pharaoh for
food. Then Pharaoh told all the Egyptians, "Go to Joseph and do what he tells
you."[j]
56When the famine had spread over the
whole country, Joseph opened the storehouses and sold grain to the Egyptians,[k]
for the famine[l] was severe throughout
Egypt.[m] 57And all the countries came to
Egypt to buy grain from Joseph,[n] because
the famine was severe in all the world.[o]

Joseph's Brothers Go to Egypt

42 When Jacob learned that there was
grain in Egypt,[p] he said to his sons,
"Why do you just keep looking at each
other?" 2He continued, "I have heard that
there is grain in Egypt. Go down there and
buy some for us,[q] so that we may live and
not die."[r]
3Then ten of Joseph's brothers went
down to buy grain[s] from Egypt. 4But Jacob
did not send Benjamin,[t] Joseph's brother, with the others, because he was afraid
that harm might come to him.[u] 5So Israel's
sons were among those who went to buy
grain,[v] for the famine was in the land of
Canaan[w] also.[x]
6Now Joseph was the governor of the
land,[y] the one who sold grain to all its
people.[z] So when Joseph's brothers arrived, they bowed down to him with their
faces to the ground.[a] 7As soon as Joseph
saw his brothers, he recognized them, but
he pretended to be a stranger and spoke
harshly to them.[b] "Where do you come
from?"[c] he asked.
"From the land of Canaan," they replied, "to buy food."
8Although Joseph recognized his brothers, they did not recognize him.[d] 9Then
he remembered his dreams[e] about them
and said to them, "You are spies![f] You
have come to see where our land is unprotected."[g]
10"No, my lord,[h]" they answered. "Your
servants have come to buy food.[i] 11We are
all the sons of one man. Your servants[j] are
honest men,[k] not spies.[l]"
12"No!" he said to them. "You have come
to see where our land is unprotected."[m]
13But they replied, "Your servants[n] were
twelve brothers, the sons of one man, who
lives in the land of Canaan.[o] The youngest is now with our father, and one is no
more."[p]
14Joseph said to them, "It is just as I told
you: You are spies![q] 15And this is how you
will be tested: As surely as Pharaoh lives,[r]
you will not leave this place unless your
youngest brother comes here.[s] 16Send one
of your number to get your brother;[t] the
rest of you will be kept in prison,[u] so that
your words may be tested to see if you are
telling the truth.[v] If you are not, then as
surely as Pharaoh lives, you are spies![w]"
17And he put them all in custody[x] for three
days.
18On the third day, Joseph said to them,
"Do this and you will live, for I fear God:[y]
19If you are honest men,[z] let one of your
brothers stay here in prison,[a] while the
rest of you go and take grain back for your
starving households.[b] 20But you must bring
your youngest brother to me,[c] so that your
words may be verified and that you may
not die." This they proceeded to do.

41:54 [g]S Ge 12:10 [h]Ac 7:11 **41:55** [i]Dt 32:24; 2Ch 20:9; Isa 51:19; Jer 5:12; 27:8; 42:16; 44:27 [j]S ver 41; Jn 2:5 **41:56** [k]S ver 36 [l]S Ge 12:10 [m]S ver 30 **41:57** [n]Ge 42:5; 47:15 [o]S Ge 12:10 **42:1** [p]Ac 7:12 **42:2** [q]Ge 43:2,4; 44:25 [r]ver 19,33; Ge 43:8; 47:19; Ps 33:18-19 **42:3** [s]ver 10; Ge 43:20 **42:4** [t]S Ge 35:18 [u]ver 38 **42:5** [v]S Ge 41:57 [w]ver 13,29; Ge 31:18; 45:17 [x]S Ge 12:10; S Dt 32:24; Ac 7:11 **42:6** [y]S Ge 41:41; S Ne 5:14 [z]S Ge 41:36 [a]S Ge 33:3 **42:7** [b]ver 30 [c]S Ge 29:4 **42:8** [d]Ge 37:2 **42:9** [e]S Ge 37:7 [f]ver 14,16,30; Dt 1:22; Jos 2:1; 6:22 [g]ver 12 **42:10** [h]S Ge 37:8 [i]S ver 3 **42:11** [j]ver 13; Ge 44:7,9,16,19, 21,31; 46:34; 47:3 [k]ver 15,16,19, 20,34 [l]ver 31 **42:12** [m]ver 9 **42:13** [n]S ver 11 [o]S ver 5; Ge 46:31; 47:1 [p]ver 24,32,36; S Ge 37:30,33; 43:7,29,33; 44:8; Jer 31:15 **42:14** [q]S ver 9 **42:15** [r]1Sa 17:55 [s]S ver 11; Ge 43:3,5,7; 44:21,23 **42:16** [t]ver 15 [u]ver 19 [v]S ver 11 [w]S ver 9 **42:17** [x]S Ge 40:4 **42:18** [y]S Ge 20:11; S 22:12; Lev 19:14; 25:43; 2Sa 23:3 **42:19** [z]S ver 11 [a]ver 16 [b]S ver 2 **42:20** [c]S ver 15

41:57 *all the world.* The known world from the writer's perspective (the Middle East). This description of the famine in the time of Joseph echoes the author's description of the flood in the time of Noah. God saved only Noah and his family from the flood, so that Noah became the new (after Adam) father of the race. With the call of Abram out of the post-flood and post-Babel nations, God once more singled out one man, now to be the father of his special people. God promised that, through this man and his descendants, "all peoples on earth will be blessed" (12:3; see note on 12:2–3). The author highlights the fact that in this new crisis hope rested with one of these descendants.

42:1—45:28 The reunion and reconciliation of Jacob's sons—but now in Egypt.

42:2–3 Stephen refers to this incident (Ac 7:12).

42:4 *did not send Benjamin, Joseph's brother.* Their mother Rachel had died (35:19), and Jacob thought Joseph also was dead (37:33). Jacob did not want to lose Benjamin, the remaining son of his beloved Rachel.

42:5 *famine was in the land of Canaan also.* As in the time of Abram (see 12:10 and note).

42:6 *they bowed down to him.* In fulfillment of Joseph's dreams (see 37:7,9 and note on 37:7; see also note on 40:1–23).

42:8 *Joseph recognized his brothers.* Although 21 years had passed since he had last seen them (see 37:2; 41:46,53–54), they had been adults at the time and their appearance had not changed much. *they did not recognize him.* Joseph, 17 years old at the time of his enslavement (37:2), was now an adult in an unexpected position of authority, wearing Egyptian clothes and speaking to his brothers through an interpreter (see v. 23). He was, moreover, shaven in the Egyptian manner (see note on 41:14).

42:9,14,16 *You are spies!* See note on Jos 2:1–24.

42:10 *my lord ... Your servants.* Unwittingly, Joseph's brothers again fulfilled his dreams and their own scornful fears (see 37:8 and note).

42:15 *As surely as Pharaoh lives.* The most solemn oaths were pronounced in the name of the reigning monarch (as here) or of the speaker's deities (see Ps 16:4 and note [see also note on 16:2–4]; Am 8:14 and note) or of the Lord himself (see Jdg 8:19; 1Sa 14:39,45 and note; 19:6; cf. Dt 6:13 and note).

21They said to one another, "Surely we
are being punished because of our brother.[d] We saw how distressed he was when
he pleaded with us for his life, but we
would not listen; that's why this distress[e]
has come upon us."
22Reuben replied, "Didn't I tell you not
to sin against the boy?[f] But you wouldn't
listen! Now we must give an accounting[g]
for his blood."[h] 23They did not realize[i] that
Joseph could understand them,[j] since he
was using an interpreter.
24He turned away from them and began
to weep,[k] but then turned back and spoke
to them again. He had Simeon taken from
them and bound before their eyes.[l]
25Joseph gave orders to fill their bags
with grain,[m] to put each man's silver back
in his sack,[n] and to give them provisions[o]
for their journey.[p] After this was done for
them, 26they loaded their grain on their
donkeys[q] and left.
27At the place where they stopped for
the night one of them opened his sack to
get feed for his donkey,[r] and he saw his
silver in the mouth of his sack.[s] 28"My
silver has been returned," he said to his
brothers. "Here it is in my sack."
Their hearts sank[t] and they turned to
each other trembling[u] and said, "What is
this that God has done to us?"[v]
29When they came to their father Jacob
in the land of Canaan,[w] they told him all
that had happened to them.[x] They said,
30"The man who is lord over the land
spoke harshly to us[y] and treated us as
though we were spying on the land.[z] 31But
we said to him, 'We are honest men; we
are not spies.[a] 32We were twelve brothers,
sons of one father. One is no more, and
the youngest is now with our father in Canaan.'[b]
33"Then the man who is lord over the
land said to us, 'This is how I will know
whether you are honest men: Leave one
of your brothers here with me, and take
food for your starving households and go.[c]
34But bring your youngest brother to me
so I will know that you are not spies but
honest men.[d] Then I will give your brother back to you,[e] and you can trade[a] in the
land.[f]' "
35As they were emptying their sacks,
there in each man's sack was his pouch

42:21 [d]Ge 37:26-28 [e]Ge 45:5
42:22 [f]Ge 37:21-22 [g]S Ge 9:5 [h]Ge 45:24
42:23 [i]Ge 38:16 [j]S Ge 11:7
42:24 [k]S Ge 29:11 [l]S ver 13; Ge 43:14,23
42:25 [m]Ge 43:2 [n]ver 27,35; Ge 43:12,18,21; 44:1,8 [o]Jer 40:5 [p]Ge 45:21,23
42:26 [q]S Ge 32:15; 44:13; 45:17; 1Sa 25:18; Isa 30:6
42:27 [r]Jdg 19:19; Job 39:9; Isa 1:3 [s]S ver 25
42:28 [t]Jos 2:11; 5:1; 7:5 [u]Mk 5:33 [v]Ge 43:23
42:29 [w]S ver 5 [x]Ge 44:24
42:30 [y]ver 7 [z]S ver 9
42:31 [a]ver 11
42:32 [b]S ver 13
42:33 [c]S ver 2
42:34 [d]S ver 11 [e]S ver 24 [f]Ge 34:10
42:35 [g]S ver 25 [h]Ge 43:18
42:36 [i]S ver 13 [j]S ver 24 [k]Job 3:25; Pr 10:24; Ro 8:31
42:37 [l]S Ge 39:4 [m]Ge 43:9; 44:32
42:38 [n]Ge 37:33 [o]ver 4 [p]S Ge 37:35 [q]Ge 44:29,34; 48:7
43:1 [r]S Ge 12:10
43:2 [s]Ge 42:25 [t]S Ge 42:2
43:3 [u]ver 8; Ge 44:14,18; 46:28 [v]S Ge 42:15
43:4 [w]S Ge 42:2
43:5 [x]S Ge 42:15; 44:26; 2Sa 3:13
43:6 [y]ver 8,11; S Ge 17:5 [z]S Ge 34:30
43:7 [a]ver 27; Ge 45:3 [b]S Ge 42:13; 44:19 [c]S Ge 42:15
43:8 [d]S ver 3; S Ge 29:35

of silver![g] When they and their father
saw the money pouches, they were frightened.[h] 36Their father Jacob said to them,
"You have deprived me of my children. Joseph is no more and Simeon is no more,[i]
and now you want to take Benjamin.[j] Everything is against me![k]"
37Then Reuben said to his father, "You
may put both of my sons to death if I do
not bring him back to you. Entrust him to
my care,[l] and I will bring him back."[m]
38But Jacob said, "My son will not go
down there with you; his brother is dead[n]
and he is the only one left. If harm comes
to him[o] on the journey you are taking,
you will bring my gray head down to the
grave[b][p] in sorrow.[q]"

The Second Journey to Egypt

43 Now the famine was still severe in
the land.[r] 2So when they had eaten
all the grain they had brought from Egypt,[s]
their father said to them, "Go back and
buy us a little more food."[t]
3But Judah[u] said to him, "The man
warned us solemnly, 'You will not see
my face again unless your brother is with
you.'[v] 4If you will send our brother along
with us, we will go down and buy food
for you.[w] 5But if you will not send him, we
will not go down, because the man said to
us, 'You will not see my face again unless
your brother is with you.[x]' "
6Israel[y] asked, "Why did you bring this
trouble[z] on me by telling the man you had
another brother?"
7They replied, "The man questioned us
closely about ourselves and our family. 'Is
your father still living?'[a] he asked us. 'Do
you have another brother?'[b] We simply
answered his questions. How were we to
know he would say, 'Bring your brother
down here'?"[c]
8Then Judah[d] said to Israel[e] his father,
"Send the boy along with me and we will
go at once, so that we and you and our
children may live and not die.[f] 9I myself
will guarantee his safety; you can hold me
personally responsible for him.[g] If I do not
bring him back to you and set him here

[a] *34* Or *move about freely* [b] *38* Hebrew *Sheol*

[e]S ver 6 [f]S Ge 42:2; Ps 33:18-19 **43:9** [g]1Sa 23:20

42:21 *how distressed he was … distress has come upon us.* The brothers realized they were beginning to reap what they had sown (see Gal 6:7 and note).

42:22 See 37:21–22 and note on 37:21.

42:24 *He had Simeon taken.* Jacob's second son (see 29:32–33) is imprisoned instead of the firstborn Reuben, perhaps because the latter had saved Joseph's life years earlier (37:21–22).

42:37 *both of my sons.* Reuben's generous offer as security for Benjamin's safety (see note on 37:21).

42:38 *grave.* See note on 37:35.

43:3 *Judah said.* From this point on, Judah became the spokesman for his brothers (see vv. 8–10; 44:14–34; 46:28). His tribe would become preeminent among the 12 (see 49:8–10 and notes), and he would be an ancestor of Jesus (see Mt 1:2–3,16–17; Lk 3:23,33).

43:9 Judah offered himself as security for Benjamin's safety — an even more generous gesture than that of Reuben (see 42:37 and note).

before you, I will bear the blame[h] before
you all my life.[i] 10As it is, if we had not delayed,[j] we could have gone and returned
twice."
11Then their father Israel[k] said to them,
"If it must be, then do this: Put some of the
best products[l] of the land in your bags and
take them down to the man as a gift[m]—a
little balm[n] and a little honey, some spices[o] and myrrh,[p] some pistachio nuts and
almonds. 12Take double the amount[q] of
silver with you, for you must return the
silver that was put back into the mouths
of your sacks.[r] Perhaps it was a mistake.
13Take your brother also and go back to the
man at once.[s] 14And may God Almighty[a][t]
grant you mercy[u] before the man so that
he will let your other brother and Benjamin come back with you.[v] As for me, if I
am bereaved, I am bereaved."[w]
15So the men took the gifts and double
the amount of silver,[x] and Benjamin also.
They hurried[y] down to Egypt and presented themselves[z] to Joseph. 16When Joseph
saw Benjamin[a] with them, he said to the
steward of his house,[b] "Take these men to
my house, slaughter an animal and prepare
dinner;[c] they are to eat with me at noon."
17The man did as Joseph told him and
took the men to Joseph's house.[d] 18Now
the men were frightened[e] when they were
taken to his house.[f] They thought, "We
were brought here because of the silver
that was put back into our sacks[g] the first
time. He wants to attack us[h] and overpower us and seize us as slaves[i] and take our
donkeys.[j]"
19So they went up to Joseph's steward[k]
and spoke to him at the entrance to the
house. 20"Please, sir," they said, "we came
down here the first time to buy food.[l] 21But
at the place where we stopped for the night
we opened our sacks and each of us found
his silver—the exact weight—in the mouth
of his sack. So we have brought it back
with us.[m] 22We have also brought additional silver with us to buy food. We don't
know who put our silver in our sacks."

43:9 [h]Ge 44:10, 17 [i]S Ge 42:37; Phm 1:18-19 **43:10** [j]Ge 45:9 **43:11** [k]S ver 6 [l]S Ge 24:10 [m]S Ge 32:13 [n]S Ge 37:25; Eze 27:17 [o]Ex 30:23; 1Ki 10:2; Eze 27:22 [p]S Ge 37:25 **43:12** [q]ver 15; Ex 22:4, 7; Pr 6:31 [r]S Ge 42:25 **43:13** [s]ver 3 **43:14** [t]S Ge 17:1 [u]Dt 13:17; Ps 25:6 [v]S Ge 42:24 [w]2Sa 18:33; Est 4:16 **43:15** [x]ver 12 [y]Ge 45:9, 13 [z]Ge 47:2, 7; Mt 2:11 **43:16** [a]S Ge 35:18 [b]ver 17, 24, 26; Ge 44:1, 4, 12; 2Sa 19:17; Isa 22:15 [c]ver 31; Lk 15:23 **43:17** [d]S ver 16 **43:18** [e]Ge 42:35 [f]Ge 44:14 [g]S Ge 42:25 [h]S Ge 32:11 [i]Ge 44:9, 16, 33; 50:18 [j]Ge 34:28 **43:19** [k]ver 16 **43:20** [l]S Ge 42:3 **43:21** [m]S ver 15; S Ge 42:25

43:23 [n]S Ge 24:12; S 31:5; Ex 3:6 [o]Ge 42:28 [p]S Ge 42:24 **43:24** [q]S ver 16 [r]S Ge 18:4 **43:25** [s]S Ge 32:13 [t]ver 16 **43:26** [u]S ver 16 [v]S Ge 32:13; Mt 2:11 [w]S Ge 33:3 **43:27** [x]S Ge 37:3 [y]S ver 7 **43:28** [z]Ge 44:24, 27, 30 [a]Ge 18:2; Ex 18:7 [b]S Ge 37:7

23"It's all right," he said. "Don't be
afraid. Your God, the God of your father,[n]
has given you treasure in your sacks;[o] I received your silver." Then he brought Simeon out to them.[p]
24The steward took the men into Joseph's house,[q] gave them water to wash
their feet[r] and provided fodder for their
donkeys. 25They prepared their gifts[s] for
Joseph's arrival at noon,[t] because they
had heard that they were to eat there.
26When Joseph came home,[u] they presented to him the gifts[v] they had brought
into the house, and they bowed down before him to the ground.[w] 27He asked them
how they were, and then he said, "How is
your aged father[x] you told me about? Is he
still living?"[y]
28They replied, "Your servant our father[z]
is still alive and well." And they bowed
low[a] to pay him honor.[b]
29As he looked about and saw his brother Benjamin, his own mother's son,[c] he
asked, "Is this your youngest brother,
the one you told me about?"[d] And he
said, "God be gracious to you,[e] my son."
30Deeply moved[f] at the sight of his brother,
Joseph hurried out and looked for a place
to weep. He went into his private room
and wept[g] there.
31After he had washed his face, he came
out and, controlling himself,[h] said, "Serve
the food."[i]
32They served him by himself, the
brothers by themselves, and the Egyptians
who ate with him by themselves, because
Egyptians could not eat with Hebrews,[j] for
that is detestable to Egyptians.[k] 33The men
had been seated before him in the order of
their ages, from the firstborn[l] to the youngest;[m] and they looked at each other in astonishment. 34When portions were served
to them from Joseph's table, Benjamin's

[a] 14 Hebrew *El-Shaddai*

43:29 [c]S Ge 35:18 [d]S Ge 42:13 [e]Nu 6:25; Ps 67:1; 119:58; Isa 30:18-19; 33:2 **43:30** [f]Jn 11:33, 38 [g]S Ge 29:11 **43:31** [h]Ge 45:1; Isa 30:18; 42:14; 63:15; 64:12 [i]S ver 16 **43:32** [j]S Ge 14:13; Gal 2:12 [k]Ge 46:34; Ex 8:26 **43:33** [l]S Ge 35:23 [m]S Ge 42:13; 44:12

43:11 *take them ... as a gift.* A customary practice when approaching one's superior, whether political (see 1Sa 16:20), military (see 1Sa 17:18) or religious (see 2Ki 5:15). *balm ... myrrh.* See 37:25 and note. *honey.* Either that produced by bees, or an inferior substitute made by boiling grape or date juice down to a thick syrup. *pistachio nuts.* Mentioned only here in the Bible; the fruit of a small, broad-crowned tree that is native to Asia Minor, Aram (Syria) and Canaan but not to Egypt.

43:14 *God Almighty.* See notes on 17:1; 35:1. *if I am bereaved, I am bereaved.* Cf. Esther's similar phrase of resignation in Est 4:16.

43:21 The brothers' statement to Joseph's steward compressed the details (see 42:27,35).

43:23 *Your God ... has given you treasure.* The steward spoke better than he knew.

43:24 See note on 18:2.

43:26 *bowed down.* Additional fulfillment of Joseph's dreams (see 37:7,9 and note on 37:7; see also 42:6 and note; 43:28).

43:29 *Benjamin, his own mother's son.* Joseph's special relationship to Benjamin is clear. *God be gracious to you.* Later blessings and benedictions would echo these words (see Nu 6:25; Ps 67:1).

43:30 *Joseph ... wept.* Both emotional and sensitive, he wept often (see 42:24; 45:2,14–15; 46:29).

43:32 *Egyptians could not eat with Hebrews.* The taboo was probably based on ritual or religious reasons (see Ex 8:26), unlike the Egyptian refusal to associate with shepherds (see 46:34), which was probably based on social custom.

43:34 *Benjamin's portion was five times as much.* Again reflecting his special status with Joseph (see note on v. 29; see also 45:22).

portion was five times as much as anyone else's.[n] So they feasted[o] and drank freely with him.

A Silver Cup in a Sack

44 Now Joseph gave these instructions to the steward of his house:[p] "Fill the men's sacks with as much food as they can carry, and put each man's silver in the mouth of his sack.[q] 2Then put my cup,[r] the silver one,[s] in the mouth of the youngest one's sack, along with the silver for his grain." And he did as Joseph said.

3As morning dawned, the men were sent on their way with their donkeys.[t] 4They had not gone far from the city when Joseph said to his steward,[u] "Go after those men at once, and when you catch up with them, say to them, 'Why have you repaid good with evil?[v] 5Isn't this the cup[w] my master drinks from and also uses for divination?[x] This is a wicked thing you have done.' "

6When he caught up with them, he repeated these words to them. 7But they said to him, "Why does my lord say such things? Far be it from your servants[y] to do anything like that![z] 8We even brought back to you from the land of Canaan[a] the silver[b] we found inside the mouths of our sacks.[c] So why would we steal[d] silver or gold from your master's house? 9If any of your servants[e] is found to have it, he will die;[f] and the rest of us will become my lord's slaves.[g]"

10"Very well, then," he said, "let it be as you say. Whoever is found to have it[h] will become my slave;[i] the rest of you will be free from blame."[j]

11Each of them quickly lowered his sack to the ground and opened it. 12Then the steward[k] proceeded to search,[l] beginning with the oldest and ending with the youngest.[m] And the cup was found in Benjamin's sack.[n] 13At this, they tore their clothes.[o] Then they all loaded their donkeys[p] and returned to the city.

14Joseph was still in the house[q] when Judah[r] and his brothers came in, and they threw themselves to the ground before him.[s] 15Joseph said to them, "What is this you have done?[t] Don't you know that a man like me can find things out by divination?[u]"

16"What can we say to my lord?[v]" Judah[w] replied. "What can we say? How can we prove our innocence?[x] God has uncovered your servants'[y] guilt. We are now my lord's slaves[z]—we ourselves and the one who was found to have the cup.[a]"

17But Joseph said, "Far be it from me to do such a thing![b] Only the man who was found to have the cup will become my slave.[c] The rest of you, go back to your father in peace."[d]

18Then Judah[e] went up to him and said: "Please, my lord,[f] let your servant speak a word to my lord. Do not be angry[g] with your servant, though you are equal to Pharaoh himself. 19My lord asked his servants,[h] 'Do you have a father or a brother?'[i] 20And we answered, 'We have an aged father, and there is a young son born to him in his old age.[j] His brother is dead,[k] and he is the only one of his mother's sons left, and his father loves him.'[l]

21"Then you said to your servants,[m] 'Bring him down to me so I can see him for myself.'[n] 22And we said to my lord,[o] 'The boy cannot leave his father; if he leaves him, his father will die.'[p] 23But you told your servants, 'Unless your youngest brother comes down with you, you will not see my face again.'[q] 24When we went back to your servant my father,[r] we told him what my lord[s] had said.[t]

25"Then our father said, 'Go back and buy a little more food.'[u] 26But we said, 'We cannot go down. Only if our youngest brother is with us will we go. We cannot see the man's face unless our youngest brother is with us.'[v]

27"Your servant my father[w] said to us, 'You know that my wife bore me two sons.[x] 28One of them went away from me, and I said, "He has surely been torn to pieces."[y] And I have not seen him since.[z] 29If you take this one from me too and harm comes to him, you will bring my gray head down to the grave[a a] in misery.'[b]

30"So now, if the boy is not with us when

[a] 29 Hebrew *Sheol*; also in verse 31

43:34 [n]S Ge 37:3; S 2Ki 25:30 [o]Lk 15:23 **44:1** [p]S Ge 43:16 [q]S Ge 42:25 **44:2** [r]ver 5, 10, 12, 16 [s]ver 8 **44:3** [t]Jdg 19:9 **44:4** [u]S Ge 43:16 [v]Ps 35:12; 38:20; 109:5; Pr 17:13; Jer 18:20 **44:5** [w]S ver 2 [x]S Ge 30:27; Dt 18:10-14 **44:7** [y]S Ge 42:11 [z]S Ge 18:25 **44:8** [a]S Ge 42:13 [b]ver 2 [c]S Ge 42:25; S 43:15 [d]Ge 31:30 **44:9** [e]S Ge 42:11 [f]Ge 31:32 [g]S ver 10; S Ge 43:18 **44:10** [h]S ver 2 [i]ver 9, 17, 33 [j]S Ge 43:9 **44:12** [k]S Ge 43:16 [l]S Ge 31:34 [m]S Ge 43:33 [n]ver 2 **44:13** [o]S Ge 37:29 [p]S Ge 42:26 **44:14** [q]Ge 43:18 [r]ver 16; S Ge 29:35; S 43:3 [s]S Ge 33:3 **44:15** [t]S Ge 12:18 [u]S Ge 30:27

44:16 [v]ver 22, 24; S Ge 37:8 [w]S ver 14 [x]Ps 26:6; 73:13 [y]S Ge 42:11 [z]S Ge 43:18 [a]S ver 2 **44:17** [b]S Ge 18:25 [c]S ver 10 [d]S Ge 43:9 **44:18** [e]S Ge 29:35 [f]S ver 16 [g]S Ge 18:30 **44:19** [h]S Ge 42:11 [i]S Ge 43:7 **44:20** [j]S Ge 37:3 [k]S Ge 37:33 [l]S Ge 42:13 **44:21** [m]S Ge 42:11 [n]S Ge 42:15 **44:22** [o]S ver 16 [p]S Ge 37:35

44:23 [q]S Ge 42:15; S 43:5 **44:24** [r]S Ge 43:28 [s]S ver 16 [t]Ge 42:29 **44:25** [u]S Ge 42:2 **44:26** [v]S Ge 43:5 **44:27** [w]S Ge 43:28 [x]Ge 46:19 **44:28** [y]S Ge 37:33 [z]Ge 45:26, 28; 46:30; 48:11 **44:29** [a]S Ge 37:35 [b]S Ge 42:38

44:4 *city.* Identity unknown, though Memphis (about 13 miles south of modern Cairo) and Zoan (in the eastern delta region) have been suggested.
44:5 *divination.* See v. 15; see also note on 30:27.
44:9 *If any of your servants is found to have it, he will die.* Years earlier, Jacob had given Laban a similar rash response (see 31:32 and note).
44:10 The steward softened the penalty contained in the brothers' proposal.
44:12 *beginning with the oldest and ending with the youngest.* For a similar building up of suspense see 31:33.
44:13 *tore their clothes.* A sign of distress and grief (see 37:29 and note on 37:34).
44:14 *threw themselves to the ground before him.* Further fulfillment of Joseph's dreams in 37:7,9 (see 42:6; 43:26,28).
44:16 *God has uncovered your servants' guilt.* Like Joseph's steward (see note on 43:23), Judah spoke better than he knew. Or perhaps he refers both to the present event and to the guilt of their sin against Joseph (see 42:21 and note).
44:18 *Judah … said.* See note on 43:3. *lord … servant.* See note on 42:10. *you are equal to Pharaoh.* Words more flattering than true (see 41:40,43 and notes).
44:29,31 *grave.* See note on 37:35.
44:30 *whose life is closely bound up with the boy's life.* The Hebrew underlying this clause is later used of Jonathan's becoming "one in spirit with David" (1Sa 18:1).

I go back to your servant my father[c] and
if my father, whose life is closely bound
up with the boy's life,[d] 31 sees that the boy
isn't there, he will die.[e] Your servants[f] will
bring the gray head of our father down to
the grave[g] in sorrow. 32 Your servant guaranteed the boy's safety to my father. I said,
'If I do not bring him back to you, I will
bear the blame before you, my father, all
my life!'[h]

33 "Now then, please let your servant remain here as my lord's slave[i] in place of
the boy,[j] and let the boy return with his
brothers. 34 How can I go back to my father
if the boy is not with me? No! Do not let
me see the misery[k] that would come upon
my father."[l]

Joseph Makes Himself Known

45 Then Joseph could no longer control
himself[m] before all his attendants,
and he cried out, "Have everyone leave
my presence!"[n] So there was no one with
Joseph when he made himself known to
his brothers. 2 And he wept[o] so loudly that
the Egyptians heard him, and Pharaoh's
household heard about it.[p]

3 Joseph said to his brothers, "I am Joseph! Is my father still living?"[q] But his
brothers were not able to answer him,[r] because they were terrified at his presence.[s]

4 Then Joseph said to his brothers,
"Come close to me."[t] When they had done
so, he said, "I am your brother Joseph,
the one you sold into Egypt![u] 5 And now,
do not be distressed[v] and do not be angry
with yourselves for selling me here,[w] because it was to save lives that God sent me
ahead of you.[x] 6 For two years now there
has been famine[y] in the land, and for the
next five years there will not be plowing
and reaping. 7 But God sent me ahead of
you to preserve for you a remnant[z] on
earth and to save your lives by a great deliverance.[a a]

8 "So then, it was not you who sent me
here, but God.[b] He made me father[c] to
Pharaoh, lord of his entire household and
ruler of all Egypt.[d] 9 Now hurry[e] back to
my father and say to him, 'This is what
your son Joseph says: God has made me
lord of all Egypt. Come down to me; don't
delay.[f] 10 You shall live in the region of Goshen[g] and be near me—you, your children and grandchildren, your flocks and
herds, and all you have.[h] 11 I will provide
for you there,[i] because five years of famine[j] are still to come. Otherwise you and
your household and all who belong to you
will become destitute.'[k]

12 "You can see for yourselves, and so
can my brother Benjamin,[l] that it is really I
who am speaking to you.[m] 13 Tell my father
about all the honor accorded me in Egypt[n]
and about everything you have seen. And
bring my father down here quickly.[o]"

14 Then he threw his arms around his
brother Benjamin and wept, and Benjamin[p] embraced him,[q] weeping. 15 And
he kissed[r] all his brothers and wept over
them.[s] Afterward his brothers talked with
him.[t]

16 When the news reached Pharaoh's palace that Joseph's brothers had
come,[u] Pharaoh and all his officials[v] were
pleased.[w] 17 Pharaoh said to Joseph, "Tell
your brothers, 'Do this: Load your animals[x] and return to the land of Canaan,[y]
18 and bring your father and your families
back to me. I will give you the best of the
land of Egypt[z] and you can enjoy the fat
of the land.'[a]

19 "You are also directed to tell them, 'Do
this: Take some carts[b] from Egypt for your
children and your wives, and get your father and come. 20 Never mind about your

[a] 7 Or *save you as a great band of survivors*

44:30 [c] S Ge 43:28 [d] 1Sa 18:1; 2Sa 1:26 **44:31** [e] S ver 22 [f] S Ge 42:11 [g] S Ge 37:35 **44:32** [h] S Ge 42:37 **44:33** [i] S ver 10; S Ge 43:18 [j] Jn 15:13 **44:34** [k] S Ge 42:38 [l] Est 8:6 **45:1** [m] S Ge 43:31 [n] 2Sa 13:9 **45:2** [o] S Ge 29:11 [p] ver 16; Ac 7:13 **45:3** [q] S Ge 43:7 [r] ver 15 [s] Ge 44:20; Job 21:6; 23:15; Mt 17:6; Mk 6:49-50 **45:4** [t] Ge 27:21-22 [u] Ge 37:28 **45:5** [v] Ge 42:21 [w] Ge 42:22 [x] ver 7-8; Ge 50:20; Job 10:12; Ps 105:17 **45:6** [y] S Ge 41:30 **45:7** [z] 2Ki 19:4,30,31; Ezr 9:8,13; Isa 1:9; 10:20,21; 11:11,16; 46:3; Jer 6:9; 42:2; 50:20; Mic 4:7; 5:7; Zep 2:7 [a] S ver 5; Ge 49:18; Ex 15:2; 1Sa 14:45; 2Ki 13:5; Est 4:14; Isa 25:9; Mic 7:7 **45:8** [b] ver 5 [c] Jdg 17:10; 2Ki 6:21; 13:14 [d] S Ge 41:41 **45:9** [e] S Ge 43:15 [f] Ge 43:10; Ac 7:14 **45:10** [g] Ge 46:28,34; 47:1,11,27; 50:8; Ex 8:22; 9:26; 10:24 [h] Ge 46:6-7 **45:11** [i] Ge 47:12; 50:21 [j] S Ge 41:30 [k] Ps 102:17 **45:12** [l] S Ge 35:18 [m] Mk 6:50 **45:13** [n] S Ge 41:41 [o] S Ge 43:15; Ac 7:14 **45:14** [p] S Ge 35:18 [q] S Ge 29:13 **45:15** [r] S Ge 29:11; Lk 15:20 [s] S Ge 29:11,13; S 46:4 [t] ver 3 **45:16** [u] S ver 2; Ac 7:13 [v] Ge 50:7 [w] S Ge 41:37 **45:17** [x] S Ge 42:26 [y] S Ge 42:5 **45:18** [z] ver 20; Ge 20:15; 46:34; 47:6,11,27; Jer 40:4 [a] Ezr 9:12; Ps 37:19; Isa 1:19 **45:19** [b] ver 21,27; Ge 46:5; Nu 7:3-8

44:33 *in place of the boy.* Judah's willingness to be a substitute for Benjamin helped make amends for his role in selling Joseph (see 37:26–27).
44:34 *Do not let me see the misery.* Judah remembers an earlier scene (37:34–35).
45:2 *wept.* See vv. 14–15; see also 43:30 and note.
45:3 *brothers … were terrified.* Either because they thought they were seeing a ghost or because they were afraid of what Joseph would do to them.
45:4 *I am your brother Joseph.* See v. 3; Ac 7:13. This time Joseph emphasized his relationship to them. *you sold.* See note on 37:28.
45:5 *God sent me.* See vv. 7–9; Ac 7:9; cf. 50:20 and note. God had a purpose to work through the brothers' jealous and cruel act (see Ac 2:23; 4:28 and notes).
45:6 Joseph was now 39 years old (see 41:46,53).
45:7 *remnant.* Although none had been lost, they had escaped a great threat to them all; so Joseph called them a remnant in the confidence that they would live to produce a great people.
45:8 *father.* A title of honor given to viziers (see note on 41:43) and other high officials (in the Apocrypha see 1 Maccabees 11:32).
45:9 *hurry back … don't delay.* Joseph is anxious to see Jacob as soon as possible (see v. 13).
45:10 *Goshen.* A region in the eastern part of the Nile delta, it was very fertile (see v. 18) and remains so today.
45:12 *I … am speaking.* Not through an interpreter as before (see 42:23).
45:14 *wept.* See 43:30 and note.
45:15 *his brothers talked with him.* In intimate fellowship and friendship, rather than hostility or fear, for the first time in over 20 years (see 37:2 and note on 45:6).
45:18 *you can enjoy the fat of the land.* An echo of Isaac's blessing on Jacob (see 27:28).

belongings,[c] because the best of all Egypt[d]
will be yours.' "
21 So the sons of Israel did this. Joseph
gave them carts,[e] as Pharaoh had commanded, and he also gave them provisions for their journey.[f] 22 To each of them
he gave new clothing,[g] but to Benjamin
he gave three hundred shekels[a] of silver
and five sets of clothes.[h] 23 And this is what
he sent to his father: ten donkeys[i] loaded
with the best things[j] of Egypt, and ten female donkeys loaded with grain and bread
and other provisions for his journey.[k]
24 Then he sent his brothers away, and as
they were leaving he said to them, "Don't
quarrel on the way!"[l]
25 So they went up out of Egypt[m] and
came to their father Jacob in the land of
Canaan.[n] 26 They told him, "Joseph is still
alive! In fact, he is ruler of all Egypt."[o]
Jacob was stunned; he did not believe
them.[p] 27 But when they told him everything Joseph had said to them, and when
he saw the carts[q] Joseph had sent to carry him back, the spirit of their father Jacob revived. 28 And Israel said, "I'm convinced![r] My son Joseph is still alive. I will
go and see him before I die."[s]

Jacob Goes to Egypt

46 So Israel[t] set out with all that was
his, and when he reached Beershe-
ba,[u] he offered sacrifices[v] to the God of his
father Isaac.[w]
2 And God spoke to Israel[x] in a vision at
night[y] and said, "Jacob! Jacob!"
"Here I am,"[z] he replied.
3 "I am God, the God of your father,"[a]
he said. "Do not be afraid[b] to go down
to Egypt,[c] for I will make you into a great
nation[d] there.[e] 4 I will go down to Egypt
with you, and I will surely bring you back
again.[f] And Joseph's own hand will close
your eyes.[g]"
5 Then Jacob left Beersheba,[h] and Israel's[i] sons took their father Jacob and their
children and their wives in the carts[j] that
Pharaoh had sent to transport him. 6 They
also took with them their livestock and
the possessions[k] they had acquired[l] in Canaan, and Jacob and all his offspring went
to Egypt.[m] 7 He took with him to Egypt[n] his
sons and grandsons and his daughters and
granddaughters—all his offspring.[o]
8 These are the names of the sons of Israel[p] (Jacob and his descendants) who went
to Egypt:

Reuben the firstborn[q] of Jacob.
9 The sons of Reuben:[r]
Hanoch, Pallu,[s] Hezron and Carmi.[t]
10 The sons of Simeon:[u]
Jemuel,[v] Jamin, Ohad, Jakin, Zohar[w] and Shaul the son of a Canaanite woman.
11 The sons of Levi:[x]
Gershon,[y] Kohath[z] and Merari.[a]
12 The sons of Judah:[b]
Er,[c] Onan,[d] Shelah, Perez[e] and Zerah[f] (but Er and Onan had died in
the land of Canaan).[g]
The sons of Perez:[h]
Hezron and Hamul.[i]
13 The sons of Issachar:[j]
Tola, Puah,[b][k] Jashub[c][l] and Shimron.
14 The sons of Zebulun:[m]
Sered, Elon and Jahleel.
15 These were the sons Leah bore to Jacob in Paddan Aram,[d][n] besides his daughter Dinah.[o] These sons and daughters of
his were thirty-three in all.

45:20 [c]Ge 46:6, 32 [d]S ver 18 **45:21** [e]S ver 19 [f]S Ge 42:25 **45:22** [g]S Ge 24:53 [h]S Ge 37:3; S 41:14; Jdg 14:12,13; 2Ki 5:22 **45:23** [i]S Ge 42:26 [j]S Ge 24:10 [k]S Ge 42:25 **45:24** [l]Ge 42:21-22 **45:25** [m]Ge 13:1 [n]Ge 42:29 **45:26** [o]S Ge 41:41 [p]S Ge 44:28; 1Ki 10:7 **45:27** [q]S ver 19 **45:28** [r]Lk 16:31 [s]S Ge 44:28 **46:1** [t]ver 5 [u]S Ge 21:14 [v]S Ge 31:54 [w]S Ge 31:42 **46:2** [x]S Ge 17:5 [y]S Ge 15:1 [z]S Ge 22:1 **46:3** [a]S Ge 28:13 [b]S Ge 15:1 [c]Ge 26:2 [d]S Ge 12:2 [e]Ex 1:7 **46:4** [f]S Ge 15:16; S 28:13 [g]ver 29; Ge 45:14-15; 50:1 **46:5** [h]S Ge 21:14 [i]ver 1 [j]S Ge 45:19 **46:6** [k]S Ge 45:20 [l]S Ge 12:5 [m]Nu 20:15; Dt 26:5; Jos 24:4; Ps 105:23; Isa 52:4; Ac 7:15 **46:7** [n]Ge 13:10 [o]ver 6; Ge 45:10 **46:8** [p]S Ge 35:26; Ex 1:1; Nu 26:4 [q]S Ge 29:32 **46:9** [r]Ex 6:14; Nu 1:20; 26:7; 1Ch 5:3 [s]Nu 26:5; 1Ch 5:3 [t]Nu 26:6 **46:10** [u]S Ge 29:33; Nu 26:14 [v]Ex 6:15; Nu 26:12 [w]Nu 26:13 **46:11** [x]S Ge 29:34; S Nu 3:17 [y]Ex 6:16; Nu 3:21; 4:38 [z]Ex 6:16; Nu 3:27; 1Ch 23:12 [a]Ex 6:19; Nu 3:20, 33; 4:29; 26:57; 1Ch 6:19 **46:12** [b]S Ge 29:35 [c]S Ge 38:3 [d]S Ge 38:4 [e]S Ge 38:29 [f]S Ge 38:30 [g]S Ge 38:7; Nu 26:19 [h]1Ch 2:5; Mt 1:3 [i]Nu 26:21 **46:13** [j]S Ge 30:18 [k]Nu 26:23; Jdg 10:1; 1Ch 7:1 [l]Nu 26:24 **46:14** [m]S Ge 30:20 **46:15** [n]S Ge 25:20; 29:31-35 [o]S Ge 30:21

[a] *22* That is, about 7 1/2 pounds (about 3.5 kilograms) [b] *13* Samaritan Pentateuch and Syriac (see also 1 Chron. 7:1); Masoretic Text *Puvah* [c] *13* Samaritan Pentateuch and some Septuagint manuscripts (see also Num. 26:24 and 1 Chron. 7:1); Masoretic Text *Iob* [d] *15* That is, Northwest Mesopotamia

45:22 *to Benjamin he gave … five sets of clothes.* See note on 43:34. *shekels.* See note on 20:16.

45:24 *Don't quarrel.* Joseph wanted nothing to delay their return (see note on v. 9), and he wanted them to avoid mutual accusation and recrimination concerning the past.

46:1—47:12 Israel's (Jacob's) move to and settlement in Egypt (see 15:13 and note).

46:1 *set out.* Probably from the family estate at Hebron (see 35:27 and note). *when he reached Beersheba, he offered sacrifices.* Abraham and Isaac had also worshiped the Lord there (see 21:33; 26:23–25).

46:2 *God spoke to Israel in a vision at night.* See 26:24. *Jacob! Jacob!* See note on 22:11. *Here I am.* See note on 22:1.

46:3–4 As Israel and his family were about to leave Canaan, God reaffirmed his covenant promises as he had done for Jacob at Bethel when Jacob was fleeing Canaan to escape Esau's wrath (see 28:13–15 and notes).

46:3 *I am … the God of your father … Do not be afraid.* A verbatim repetition of God's statement to Isaac in 26:24. *I will make you into a great nation.* The Lord reaffirmed one aspect of his promise to Abraham (see 12:2). *there.* See Ex 1:7.

46:4 *I will go down to Egypt with you.* God would be with Jacob as he went south to Egypt just as he was with him when he went north to Haran, and would again bring him back as he had done before (see 28:15 and note; see also 15:16 and note; 48:21). *will close your eyes.* A reference to Jacob's death (49:33—50:1).

46:8 *These are the names of the sons of Israel … who went to Egypt.* Repeated verbatim in Ex 1:1 (see note there), where it introduces the background for the story of the exodus (predicted here in v. 4).

46:15 *Paddan Aram.* See note on 25:20. *thirty-three in all.* There are 34 names in vv. 8–15. To bring the number to 33 the name Ohad in v. 10 should probably be removed, since it does not appear in the parallel lists in Nu 26:12–13; 1Ch

16The sons of Gad:[p]
Zephon,[a][q] Haggi, Shuni, Ezbon,
Eri, Arodi and Areli.
17The sons of Asher:[r]
Imnah, Ishvah, Ishvi and Beriah.
Their sister was Serah.
The sons of Beriah:
Heber and Malkiel.
18These were the children born to Jacob
by Zilpah,[s] whom Laban had given to his
daughter Leah[t]—sixteen in all.

19The sons of Jacob's wife Rachel:[u]
Joseph and Benjamin.[v] 20In Egypt,
Manasseh[w] and Ephraim[x] were
born to Joseph[y] by Asenath daughter of Potiphera, priest of On.[b][z]
21The sons of Benjamin:[a]
Bela, Beker, Ashbel, Gera, Naaman,
Ehi, Rosh, Muppim, Huppim and
Ard.[b]
22These were the sons of Rachel[c] who
were born to Jacob—fourteen in all.

23The son of Dan:[d]
Hushim.[e]
24The sons of Naphtali:[f]
Jahziel, Guni, Jezer and Shillem.
25These were the sons born to Jacob by
Bilhah,[g] whom Laban had given to his
daughter Rachel[h]—seven in all.

26All those who went to Egypt with Jacob—those who were his direct descendants, not counting his sons' wives—numbered sixty-six persons.[i] 27With the two
sons[c] who had been born to Joseph in
Egypt,[j] the members of Jacob's family,
which went to Egypt, were seventy[d] in
all.[k]

28Now Jacob sent Judah[l] ahead of him to
Joseph to get directions to Goshen.[m] When
they arrived in the region of Goshen, 29Jo-
seph had his chariot[n] made ready and
went to Goshen to meet his father Israel.[o]
As soon as Joseph appeared before him,
he threw his arms around his father[e] and
wept[p] for a long time.[q]
30Israel[r] said to Joseph, "Now I am ready
to die, since I have seen for myself that
you are still alive."[s]
31Then Joseph said to his brothers and
to his father's household, "I will go up
and speak to Pharaoh and will say to him,
'My brothers and my father's household,
who were living in the land of Canaan,[t]
have come to me.[u] 32The men are shepherds;[v] they tend livestock,[w] and they
have brought along their flocks and herds
and everything they own.'[x] 33When Pharaoh calls you in and asks, 'What is your
occupation?'[y] 34you should answer, 'Your
servants[z] have tended livestock from our
boyhood on, just as our fathers did.'[a] Then
you will be allowed to settle[b] in the region
of Goshen,[c] for all shepherds are detestable to the Egyptians.[d]"

47 Joseph went and told Pharaoh, "My
father and brothers, with their flocks
and herds and everything they own, have
come from the land of Canaan[e] and are
now in Goshen."[f] 2He chose five of his
brothers and presented them[g] before Pharaoh.
3Pharaoh asked the brothers, "What is
your occupation?"[h]
"Your servants[i] are shepherds,[j]" they
replied to Pharaoh, "just as our fathers
were." 4They also said to him, "We have
come to live here awhile,[k] because the famine is severe in Canaan[l] and your servants'
flocks have no pasture.[m] So now, please let
your servants settle in Goshen."[n]
5Pharaoh said to Joseph, "Your father
and your brothers have come to you, 6and
the land of Egypt is before you; settle[o]
your father and your brothers in the best
part of the land.[p] Let them live in Goshen.
And if you know of any among them with
special ability,[q] put them in charge of my
own livestock.[r]"
7Then Joseph brought his father Jacob
in and presented him[s] before Pharaoh.
After Jacob blessed[f] Pharaoh,[t] 8Pharaoh
asked him, "How old are you?"
9And Jacob said to Pharaoh, "The years
of my pilgrimage are a hundred and thirty.[u] My years have been few and difficult,[v]
and they do not equal the years of the

[a] *16* Samaritan Pentateuch and Septuagint (see also Num. 26:15); Masoretic Text *Ziphion* [b] *20* That is, Heliopolis [c] *27* Hebrew; Septuagint *the nine children* [d] *27* Hebrew (see also Exodus 1:5 and footnote); Septuagint (see also Acts 7:14) *seventy-five* [e] *29* Hebrew *around him* [f] *7* Or *greeted*

46:16 [p]S Ge 30:11; S Nu 1:25 [q]Nu 26:15 **46:17** [r]S Ge 30:13 **46:18** [s]Ge 30:10 [t]S Ge 16:1 **46:19** [u]S Ge 29:6 [v]Ge 44:27 **46:20** [w]S Ge 41:51 [x]S Ge 41:52 [y]Nu 26:28-37 [z]S Ge 41:45 **46:21** [a]Nu 26:38-41; 1Ch 7:6-12; 8:1 [b]Nu 26:40; 1Ch 8:3 **46:22** [c]S Ge 29:6 **46:23** [d]S Ge 30:6 [e]Nu 26:42 **46:24** [f]S Ge 30:8 **46:25** [g]Ge 30:8 [h]S Ge 24:61 **46:26** [i]ver 5-7; Ex 1:5; Dt 10:22 **46:27** [j]S Ge 41:45 [k]S Ge 34:30; Ac 7:14 **46:28** [l]S Ge 43:3 [m]S Ge 45:10 **46:29** [n]S Ge 41:43 [o]ver 1,30; S Ge 32:28; 47:29,31 [p]S Ge 29:11 [q]S ver 4; Lk 15:20 **46:30** [r]S ver 29 [s]S Ge 44:28 **46:31** [t]S Ge 42:13 [u]S Ge 45:10 **46:32** [v]Ge 47:3 [w]S Ge 37:2 [x]S Ge 45:20 **46:33** [y]Ge 47:3 **46:34** [z]S Ge 42:11 [a]Ge 47:3 [b]S Ge 34:10 [c]S Ge 45:10 [d]S Ge 43:32 **47:1** [e]S Ge 42:13 [f]S Ge 46:31 **47:2** [g]S Ge 43:15 **47:3** [h]Ge 46:33 [i]S Ge 42:11 [j]Ge 46:32 **47:4** [k]Ru 1:1 [l]S Ge 12:10 [m]1Ki 18:5; Jer 14:5-6; Joel 1:18 [n]Ge 46:34 **47:6** [o]S Ge 34:10 [p]S Ge 13:9; S 45:18 [q]Ex 18:21,25; Dt 1:13,15; 2Ch 19:5; Ps 15:2 [r]S Ge 39:4 **47:7** [s]S Ge 43:15 [t]ver 10; 2Sa 14:22; 19:39; 1Ki 8:66 **47:9** [u]S Ge 25:7 [v]S Ge 3:17; Ps 39:4; 89:47

4:24. The Hebrew form of "Ohad" looks very much like that of the nearby "Zohar" (see Ex 6:15), and a later scribe probably added Ohad to the text accidentally.
46:20 See note on 41:45.
46:26 *All those who went to Egypt with Jacob … numbered sixty-six persons.* The total of 33 (see v. 15 and note), 16 (v. 18), 14 (v. 22) and 7 (v. 25) is 70 (v. 27). To arrive at 66 we must subtract Er and Onan, who "had died in the land of Canaan" (v. 12), and Manasseh and Ephraim (v. 20), who "had been born … in Egypt" (v. 27).
46:27 *seventy.* See NIV text note; see also Dt 10:22. Seventy is the ideal and complete number (see Introduction: Literary Features; see also notes on 5:5; 10:2) of Jacob's descendants who would have been in Egypt if Er and Onan had not died earlier (see 38:7–10). For the number 75 in Ac 7:14 see note there.
46:28 *Jacob sent Judah ahead.* See note on 43:3.
46:29 *wept.* See 43:30 and note.
46:34 *shepherds are detestable to the Egyptians.* See note on 43:32.
47:9 *pilgrimage.* Jacob referred to the itinerant nature of patriarchal life in general and of his own in particular

pilgrimage of my fathers.[w]" 10Then Jacob blessed[a] Pharaoh[x] and went out from his presence.

11So Joseph settled his father and his brothers in Egypt and gave them property in the best part of the land,[y] the district of Rameses,[z] as Pharaoh directed. 12Joseph also provided his father and his brothers and all his father's household with food, according to the number of their children.[a]

Joseph and the Famine

13There was no food, however, in the whole region because the famine was severe; both Egypt and Canaan wasted away because of the famine.[b] 14Joseph collected all the money that was to be found in Egypt and Canaan in payment for the grain they were buying,[c] and he brought it to Pharaoh's palace.[d] 15When the money of the people of Egypt and Canaan was gone,[e] all Egypt came to Joseph[f] and said, "Give us food. Why should we die before your eyes?[g] Our money is used up."

16"Then bring your livestock,[h]" said Joseph. "I will sell you food in exchange for your livestock, since your money is gone.[i]" 17So they brought their livestock to Joseph, and he gave them food in exchange for their horses,[j] their sheep and goats, their cattle and donkeys.[k] And he brought them through that year with food in exchange for all their livestock.

18When that year was over, they came to him the following year and said, "We cannot hide from our lord the fact that since our money is gone[l] and our livestock belongs to you,[m] there is nothing left for our lord except our bodies and our land. 19Why should we perish before your eyes[n]—we and our land as well? Buy us and our land in exchange for food,[o] and we with our land will be in bondage to Pharaoh.[p] Give us seed so that we may live and not die,[q] and that the land may not become desolate."

20So Joseph bought all the land in Egypt for Pharaoh. The Egyptians, one and all, sold their fields, because the famine was too severe[r] for them. The land became Pharaoh's, 21and Joseph reduced the people to servitude,[b][s] from one end of Egypt to the other. 22However, he did not buy the land of the priests,[t] because they received a regular allotment from Pharaoh and had food enough from the allotment[u] Pharaoh gave them. That is why they did not sell their land.

23Joseph said to the people, "Now that I have bought you and your land today for Pharaoh, here is seed[v] for you so you can plant the ground.[w] 24But when the crop comes in, give a fifth[x] of it to Pharaoh. The other four-fifths you may keep as seed for the fields and as food for yourselves and your households and your children."

25"You have saved our lives," they said. "May we find favor in the eyes of our lord;[y] we will be in bondage to Pharaoh."[z]

26So Joseph established it as a law concerning land in Egypt—still in force today—that a fifth[a] of the produce belongs to Pharaoh. It was only the land of the priests that did not become Pharaoh's.[b]

27Now the Israelites settled in Egypt in the region of Goshen.[c] They acquired property there[d] and were fruitful and increased greatly in number.[e]

28Jacob lived in Egypt[f] seventeen years, and the years of his life were a hundred and forty-seven.[g] 29When the time drew near for Israel[h] to die,[i] he called for his son Joseph and said to him, "If I have found favor in your eyes,[j] put your hand under my thigh[k] and promise that you will show me kindness[l] and faithfulness.[m] Do not bury me in Egypt, 30but when I rest with my fathers,[n] carry me out of Egypt and bury me where they are buried."[o]

"I will do as you say," he said.

31"Swear to me,"[p] he said. Then Joseph swore to him,[q] and Israel[r] worshiped as he leaned on the top of his staff.[c][s]

47:9 [w] Job 8:9; Ps 39:12 **47:10** [x] S ver 7 **47:11** [y] S Ge 45:10,18 [z] Ex 1:11; 12:37; Nu 33:3,5 **47:12** [a] S Ge 45:11 **47:13** [b] S Ge 12:10; S 41:30 **47:14** [c] S Ge 41:36 [d] S Ge 41:34; Ex 7:23; 8:24; Jer 43:9 **47:15** [e] ver 16,18 [f] S Ge 41:57 [g] ver 19; Ex 16:3 **47:16** [h] ver 18,19 [i] ver 15 **47:17** [j] Ex 14:9 [k] S Ge 12:16 **47:18** [l] S ver 15 [m] S ver 16 **47:19** [n] S ver 15 [o] S ver 16 [p] ver 21,25 [q] S Ge 42:2 **47:20** [r] S Ge 12:10 **47:21** [s] S ver 19 **47:22** [t] ver 26 [u] Dt 14:28-29 **47:23** [v] Isa 55:10; 61:11 [w] Ne 5:3 **47:24** [x] S Ge 41:34 **47:25** [y] S Ge 32:5 [z] S ver 19 **47:26** [a] S Ge 41:34 [b] ver 22 **47:27** [c] S Ge 45:10,18 [d] S Ge 33:19 [e] S Ge 1:22; S 12:2; S 17:6 **47:28** [f] Ps 105:23 [g] S Ge 25:7 **47:29** [h] S Ge 46:29 [i] S Ge 27:2 [j] S Ge 32:5 [k] S Ge 24:2 [l] S Ge 19:19 [m] S Ge 24:27; Jdg 1:24; 2Sa 2:6 **47:30** [n] S Ge 15:15 [o] S Ge 23:20; S 25:9; S 29:16; 50:25; Ex 13:19; Jos 24:32; Ac 7:15-16 **47:31** [p] Ge 21:23; Jos 2:20; Jdg 15:12; 1Sa 24:21; 30:15 [q] S Ge 24:3 [r] S Ge 46:29 [s] S Ge 32:10; Heb 11:21 *fn* 1Ki 1:47

[a] *10* Or *said farewell to* [b] *21* Samaritan Pentateuch and Septuagint (see also Vulgate); Masoretic Text *and he moved the people into the cities* [c] *31* Or *Israel bowed down at the head of his bed*

as he hopefully awaited the fulfillment of the promise of a land (see also Dt 26:5 and note). *they do not equal the years of ... my fathers.* Abraham lived to the age of 175 (25:7), Isaac to 180 (35:28).

47:11 *best part of the land.* See note on 45:10. *district of Rameses.* The city of Rameses is mentioned in Ex 1:11; 12:37; Nu 33:3,5. The name doubtless refers to the great Egyptian pharaoh Rameses II, who reigned centuries later (the designation here involves an editorial updating). In addition to being known as Goshen (see v. 27), the "district of Rameses" was called the "region of Zoan" in Ps 78:12,43 (see note on Ge 44:4).

47:13 *famine was severe.* After the people used up all their money to buy grain (see vv. 14–15), they traded their livestock (vv. 16–17), then their land (v. 20), then themselves (v. 21).

47:21 The NIV text note reading would mean that the Egyptians were to move temporarily into the cities until seed could be distributed to them for planting (see v. 23).

47:26 *a fifth of the produce belongs to Pharaoh.* The same was true "during the seven years of abundance" (41:34)—but now all the land on which the produce grew belonged to the pharaoh as well.

47:27 *Israelites ... were fruitful and increased greatly in number.* See 35:11–12; 46:3 and notes.

47:29 *put your hand under my thigh.* See 24:2 and note. In both cases, ties of family kinship are being stressed.

47:30 *rest with my fathers.* See note on 25:8. *bury me where they are buried.* In the cave of Machpelah (see 50:12–13).

47:31 *worshiped as he leaned on the top of his staff.* Quoted

Manasseh and Ephraim

48 Some time later Joseph was told,
"Your father is ill." So he took his
two sons Manasseh and Ephraim[t] along
with him. 2When Jacob was told, "Your
son Joseph has come to you," Israel[u] rallied his strength and sat up on the bed.
3Jacob said to Joseph, "God Almighty[a][v]
appeared to me at Luz[w] in the land of Canaan, and there he blessed me[x] 4and said
to me, 'I am going to make you fruitful
and will increase your numbers.[y] I will
make you a community of peoples, and I
will give this land[z] as an everlasting possession to your descendants after you.'[a]
5"Now then, your two sons born to you
in Egypt[b] before I came to you here will be
reckoned as mine; Ephraim and Manasseh
will be mine,[c] just as Reuben[d] and Simeon[e] are mine. 6Any children born to you
after them will be yours; in the territory
they inherit they will be reckoned under
the names of their brothers. 7As I was returning from Paddan,[b][f] to my sorrow[g] Rachel died in the land of Canaan while we
were still on the way, a little distance from
Ephrath. So I buried her there beside the
road to Ephrath" (that is, Bethlehem).[h]
8When Israel[i] saw the sons of Joseph,[j]
he asked, "Who are these?"
9"They are the sons God has given me
here,"[k] Joseph said to his father.
Then Israel said, "Bring them to me so I
may bless[l] them."
10Now Israel's eyes were failing because
of old age, and he could hardly see.[m] So
Joseph brought his sons close to him, and
his father kissed them[n] and embraced
them.[o]
11Israel[p] said to Joseph, "I never expected to see your face again,[q] and now
God has allowed me to see your children
too."[r]
12Then Joseph removed them from Israel's knees[s] and bowed down with his face
to the ground.[t] 13And Joseph took both
of them, Ephraim on his right toward Israel's left hand and Manasseh on his left
toward Israel's right hand,[u] and brought
them close to him. 14But Israel[v] reached
out his right hand and put it on Ephraim's
head,[w] though he was the younger,[x] and
crossing his arms, he put his left hand on
Manasseh's head, even though Manasseh
was the firstborn.[y]
15Then he blessed[z] Joseph and said,

"May the God before whom my fathers
Abraham and Isaac walked,[a]
the God who has been my shepherd[b]
all my life to this day,
16the Angel[c] who has delivered me from
all harm[d]
—may he bless[e] these boys.[f]
May they be called by my name
and the names of my fathers
Abraham and Isaac,[g]
and may they increase greatly
upon the earth."[h]

[a] 3 Hebrew *El-Shaddai* [b] 7 That is, Northwest Mesopotamia

48:1 [t]S Ge 41:52; Heb 11:21 **48:2** [u]ver 8,9,11,14, 20 **48:3** [v]S Ge 17:1 [w]S Ge 28:19 [x]S Ge 28:13; S 32:29 **48:4** [y]S Ge 12:2; S 17:6 [z]S Ge 12:7; S 28:13 [a]S Ge 15:7 **48:5** [b]S Ge 41:50-52 [c]1Ch 5:1 [d]S Ge 29:32 [e]S Ge 29:33 **48:7** [f]S Ge 25:20 [g]S Ge 42:38 [h]Ge 35:19; Ru 1:2; 1Sa 16:4 **48:8** [i]S ver 2 [j]ver 10 **48:9** [k]S Ge 33:5 [l]S Ge 24:60 **48:10** [m]S Ge 27:1 [n]S Ge 27:27 [o]S Ge 29:13 **48:11** [p]S ver 2 [q]S Ge 44:28 [r]Ge 50:23; Job 42:16; Ps 103:17; 128:6 **48:12** [s]Ge 50:23; Job 3:12 [t]S Ge 19:1; S 33:3; 37:10 **48:13** [u]Ps 16:8; 73:23; 110:1; Mt 25:33 **48:14** [v]S ver 2 [w]ver 17,18 [x]S Ge 25:23 [y]S Ge 29:32; S 41:51 **48:15** [z]S Ge 24:60 [a]S Ge 5:22 [b]Ge 49:24; 2Sa 5:2; Ps 23:1; 80:1; Isa 40:11; Jer 23:4 **48:16** [c]S Ge 16:7 [d]S Ge 24:50; 2Sa 4:9; Ps 71:4; Jer 15:21; Da 3:17 [e]S Ge 28:3 [f]1Ch 5:1; Eze 47:13; Heb 11:21 [g]S Ge 28:13 [h]S Ge 12:2; S 13:14

in Heb 11:21. Compare 48:2 with the NIV text note reading here.

48:1–22 How Joseph, beloved Rachel's older son, received the inheritance of the firstborn among his brothers.

48:3 *God Almighty.* See notes on 17:1; 35:11. *Luz.* The older name for Bethel (see 28:19).

48:5 *your two sons … will be reckoned as mine.* Jacob adopts them as his own. *Ephraim and Manasseh.* See v. 1 for the expected order, since Manasseh was Joseph's firstborn (see 41:51). Jacob mentions Ephraim first because he intends to give him the primary blessing and thus "put Ephraim ahead of Manasseh" (v. 20; see note there). *mine, just as Reuben and Simeon are mine.* Joseph's first two sons would enjoy equal status with Jacob's first two sons (35:23) and in fact would eventually supersede them. Because of an earlier sinful act (see 35:22 and note), Reuben would lose his birthright to Jacob's favorite son, Joseph (see 49:3–4; 1Ch 5:2 and note on 5:1–10), and thus to Joseph's sons (see 1Ch 5:1).

48:6 *children born to you after them will be yours.* They would take the place of Ephraim and Manasseh, whom Jacob had adopted. *in the territory they inherit they will be reckoned under the names of their brothers.* They would perpetuate the names of Ephraim and Manasseh for purposes of inheritance (for a similar provision see 38:8; Dt 25:5–7 and notes). Joseph's territory would thus be divided between Ephraim and Manasseh, but Levi (Jacob's third son; see 35:23) would receive "no share of the land" (Jos 14:4). The total number of tribal allotments would therefore remain the same.

48:7 *Paddan.* That is, Paddan Aram (see note on 25:20). *Rachel died.* See 35:16–19. Adopted by Joseph's father, Ephraim and Manasseh in effect took the place of other sons whom Joseph's mother, Rachel, might have borne if she had not died. *Ephrath.* See note on 35:16.

48:8 *Israel … asked, "Who are these?"* Either because he had never met them or because, being old, he could not see them clearly.

48:10 *because of old age … he could hardly see.* See note on 27:1. *kissed them and embraced them.* While they were on Jacob's knees (see v. 12), probably symbolizing adoption (see note on 30:3).

48:13–20 See note on Ac 6:6.

48:13 *Manasseh … toward Israel's right hand.* Joseph wanted Jacob to bless Manasseh, Joseph's firstborn, by placing his right hand on Manasseh's head.

48:15 *blessed.* As his father Isaac had blessed him (27:27–29). *Joseph.* Used here collectively for Ephraim and Manasseh (see NIV text note on v. 21). *before whom … Abraham and Isaac walked.* See notes on 5:22; 17:1. *shepherd.* Widely used in the ancient Near East as a metaphor for the king. It highlighted his care for his people. Here and in 49:24 it is used of God (see Ps 23:1 and note).

48:16 *Angel.* See note on 16:7. The angel—God himself—had earlier blessed Jacob (see 32:29; see also note on 32:24).

17 When Joseph saw his father placing
his right hand[i] on Ephraim's head[j] he was
displeased; so he took hold of his father's
hand to move it from Ephraim's head to
Manasseh's head. 18 Joseph said to him,
"No, my father, this one is the firstborn;
put your right hand on his head."[k]
19 But his father refused and said, "I
know, my son, I know. He too will become
a people, and he too will become great.[l]
Nevertheless, his younger brother will be
greater than he,[m] and his descendants will
become a group of nations.[n]" 20 He blessed[o]
them that day[p] and said,

"In your[a] name will Israel[q] pronounce
this blessing:[r]
'May God make you like Ephraim[s]
and Manasseh.[t]'"

So he put Ephraim ahead of Manasseh.
21 Then Israel said to Joseph, "I am
about to die, but God will be with you[b][u]
and take you[b] back to the land of your[b]
fathers.[v] 22 And to you, as one who is over
your brothers,[w] I give the ridge of land[c][x]
I took from the Amorites with my sword[y]
and my bow."

Jacob Blesses His Sons

49:1-28Ref — Dt 33:1-29

49 Then Jacob called for his sons and
said: "Gather around so I can tell you
what will happen to you in days to come.[z]

2 "Assemble[a] and listen, sons of Jacob;
listen to your father Israel.[b]

3 "Reuben, you are my firstborn,[c]
my might, the first sign of my
strength,[d]
excelling in honor,[e] excelling in
power.
4 Turbulent as the waters,[f] you will no
longer excel,
for you went up onto your father's
bed,
onto my couch and defiled it.[g]

5 "Simeon[h] and Levi[i] are brothers—
their swords[d] are weapons of
violence.[j]
6 Let me not enter their council,
let me not join their assembly,[k]
for they have killed men in their anger[l]
and hamstrung[m] oxen as they
pleased.
7 Cursed be their anger, so fierce,
and their fury,[n] so cruel![o]
I will scatter them in Jacob
and disperse them in Israel.[p]

8 "Judah,[e][q] your brothers will praise
you;
your hand will be on the neck[r] of
your enemies;
your father's sons will bow down to
you.[s]
9 You are a lion's[t] cub,[u] O Judah;[v]
you return from the prey,[w] my son.
Like a lion he crouches and lies down,
like a lioness—who dares to rouse
him?

48:17 [i]ver 13 [j]S ver 14 **48:18** [k]S ver 14 **48:19** [l]Ge 17:20 [m]S Ge 25:23 [n]S Ge 12:2 **48:20** [o]S Ge 24:60 [p]Heb 11:21 [q]S ver 2 [r]Lev 9:22; Nu 6:23; Dt 10:8; 21:5 [s]Nu 2:18; Jer 31:9 [t]S Ge 41:51; Nu 2:20; 10:23; Ru 4:11 **48:21** [u]S Ge 26:3 [v]S Ge 15:16; S 28:13; Dt 30:3; Ps 126:1; Jer 29:14; Eze 34:13 **48:22** [w]Ge 37:8 [x]Jos 24:32; Jn 4:5 [y]S Ge 34:26 **49:1** [z]Nu 24:14; Dt 31:29; Jer 23:20; Da 2:28,45 **49:2** [a]Jos 24:1 [b]ver 16,28; Ps 34:11 **49:3** [c]S Ge 29:32; S 41:51 [d]Dt 21:17; Ps 78:51; 105:36 [e]S Ge 34:19 **49:4** [f]Isa 57:20; Jer 49:23 [g]S Ge 29:29; S 34:5 **49:5** [h]S Ge 29:33 [i]Ge 29:34 [j]S Ge 34:25; S Pr 4:17 **49:6** [k]Ps 1:1; Pr 1:15; Eph 5:11 [l]S Ge 34:26 [m]Jos 11:6,9; 2Sa 8:4; 1Ch 18:4 **49:7** [n]Ge 34:7 [o]Ge 34:25 [p]Jos 19:1,9; 21:1-42 **49:8** [q]S Ge 29:35 [r]Dt 28:48 [s]S Ge 9:25; 1Ch 5:2 **49:9** [t]Nu 24:9; Ps 7:2; 10:9; Eze 19:5; Mic 5:8 [u]Eze 19:2 [v]Rev 5:5 [w]ver 27; Nu 23:24; Job 38:39; Ps 17:12; 22:13; 104:21

[a] *20* The Hebrew is singular. [b] *21* The Hebrew is plural. [c] *22* Or *And to you I give one portion more than to your brothers—the portion* [d] *5* The meaning of the Hebrew for this word is uncertain. [e] *8* *Judah* sounds like and may be derived from the Hebrew for *praise.*

48:19 *his younger brother will be greater than he.* See note on 25:23. During the divided monarchy (930–722 B.C.), Ephraim's descendants were the most powerful tribe in the north. "Ephraim" was often used to refer to the northern kingdom as a whole (see, e.g., Isa 7:2,5,8–9; Hos 9:13; 12:1,8).

48:20 *he put Ephraim ahead of Manasseh.* Jacob, the younger son who struggled with Esau for the birthright and blessing and who preferred the younger sister (Rachel) above the older (Leah), now advanced Joseph's younger son ahead of the older.

48:21 *Joseph.* See note on v. 15. *I am about to die.* Years later, Joseph spoke these words to his brothers (50:24).

48:22 *ridge of land.* The Hebrew for this phrase is identical with the place-name Shechem, where Joseph was later buried in a plot of ground inherited by his descendants (see Jos 24:32 and note; see also 33:19; Jn 4:5 and note). *I took from the Amorites.* Possibly referring to the event of 34:25–29.

49:2–27 Often called the "Blessing of Jacob," this is the longest poem in Genesis. Its various blessings were intended not only for Jacob's 12 sons but also for the tribes that descended from them (see v. 28). For other poetic blessings in Genesis see 9:26–27; 14:19–20; 27:27–29; 27:39–40; 48:15–16; 48:20.

49:4 *Turbulent.* Reuben's descendants were characterized by indecision (see Jdg 5:15–16). *you will no longer excel, for you went up onto your father's bed.* See 35:22 and note; see also notes on 37:21; 48:5.

49:5 *Simeon and Levi are brothers.* They shared the traits of violence, anger and cruelty (see vv. 6–7; see also note on 34:25).

49:7 *I will scatter them.* Fulfilled when Simeon's descendants were absorbed into the territory of Judah (see Jos 19:1,9 and note on 19:1) and when Levi's descendants were dispersed throughout the land, living in 48 towns and the surrounding pasturelands (see note on 48:6; see also Nu 35:2,7; Jos 14:4; 21:41).

49:8 Cf. 27:29,40; 37:7,9. *Judah, your brothers ... will bow down to you.* See note on 43:3. As those who would become the leading tribes of southern and northern Israel respectively, Judah and Joseph were given the longest (vv. 8–12 and vv. 22–26) of Jacob's blessings. Judah was the fourth of Leah's sons and also the fourth son born to Jacob (29:35), but Reuben, Simeon and Levi had forfeited their right of leadership. So Jacob assigns leadership to Judah (a son of Leah) but a double portion to Joseph (a son of Rachel). See also 1Ch 5:2.

49:9 *You are a lion's cub.* A symbol of sovereignty, strength and courage. Judah (or Israel) is often pictured as a lion in later times (see Eze 19:2; Mic 5:8 and notes; and especially Nu 24:9). Judah's greatest descendant, Jesus Christ (see note on 43:3), is himself called "the Lion of the tribe of Judah" (Rev 5:5; see note there).

10"The scepter will not depart from Judah,[x]
nor the ruler's staff from between
his feet,
until he comes to whom it belongs[a][y]
and the obedience of the nations is
his.[z]
11He will tether his donkey[a] to a vine,
his colt to the choicest branch;[b]
he will wash his garments in wine,
his robes in the blood of grapes.[c]
12His eyes will be darker than wine,
his teeth whiter than milk.[b][d]

13"Zebulun[e] will live by the seashore
and become a haven for ships;
his border will extend toward
Sidon.[f]

14"Issachar[g] is a rawboned[c] donkey
lying down between two
saddlebags.[d][h]
15When he sees how good is his resting
place
and how pleasant is his land,[i]
he will bend his shoulder to the
burden[j]
and submit to forced labor.[k]

16"Dan[e][l] will provide justice for his
people
as one of the tribes of Israel.[m]
17Dan[n] will be a serpent by the roadside,
a viper along the path,[o]
that bites the horse's heels[p]
so that its rider tumbles backward.

18"I look for your deliverance,[q] O LORD.[r]

19"Gad[f][s] will be attacked by a band of
raiders,
but he will attack them at their
heels.[t]

49:10 [x]Nu 24:17,19; Jdg 1:1-2; 20:18; 1Ch 5:2; 28:4; Ps 60:7; 108:8 [y]Eze 21:27 [z]Ps 2:9; 72:8-11; 98:3; 110:2; Isa 2:4; 26:18; 42:1,4; 45:22; 48:20; 49:6; 51:5 **49:11** [a]Jdg 5:10; 10:4; Zec 9:9 [b]Dt 8:8; 2Ki 18:32 [c]Dt 32:14; Isa 63:2 **49:12** [d]SS 5:12 **49:13** [e]S Ge 30:20 [f]S Ge 10:19 **49:14** [g]S Ge 30:18 [h]Jdg 5:16; Ps 68:13 **49:15** [i]Jos 19:17-23 [j]Eze 29:18 [k]1Ki 4:6; 5:13; 9:21; Isa 14:2; 31:8 **49:16** [l]Ge 30:6 [m]S ver 2 **49:17** [n]Jdg 18:27 [o]Jer 8:17; Am 9:3 [p]ver 19 **49:18** [q]S Ge 45:7; Ps 40:1-3 [r]Ps 119:166,174 **49:19** [s]S Ge 30:11 [t]ver 17 **49:20** [u]S Ge 30:13 [v]Isa 25:6 [w]Job 29:6 **49:21** [x]S Ge 30:8 [y]Job 39:1 **49:22** [z]Ge 30:24 [a]S Ge 17:6; Ps 128:3; Eze 19:10 [b]Ps 80:10 **49:23** [c]1Ch 10:3 [d]S Ge 27:41; S 37:24 **49:24** [e]Job 29:20 [f]Ps 18:34; Isa 63:12 [g]Ps 132:2,5; Isa 1:24; 10:34; 49:26; 60:16 [h]S Ge 48:15 [i]Dt 32:4,15,18,31; 1Sa 2:2; 2Sa 22:32; Ps 18:2,31; 19:14; 78:35; 89:26; 144:1; Isa 17:10; 26:4; 30:29; 44:8; Hab 1:12 **49:25** [j]S Ge 28:13 [k]Ex 18:4; Ps 27:9 [l]S Ge 17:1 [m]S Ge 27:28 [n]Isa 66:11 [o]Dt 7:13; 28:4; Ps 107:38; Pr 10:22

20"Asher's[u] food will be rich;[v]
he will provide delicacies fit for a
king.[w]

21"Naphtali[x] is a doe set free
that bears beautiful fawns.[g][y]

22"Joseph[z] is a fruitful vine,[a]
a fruitful vine near a spring,
whose branches[b] climb over a wall.[h]
23With bitterness archers attacked
him;[c]
they shot at him with hostility.[d]
24But his bow remained steady,[e]
his strong arms[f] stayed[i] limber,
because of the hand of the Mighty One
of Jacob,[g]
because of the Shepherd,[h] the Rock
of Israel,[i]
25because of your father's God,[j] who
helps[k] you,
because of the Almighty,[j][l] who
blesses you
with blessings of the heavens above,
blessings of the deep that lies
below,[m]
blessings of the breast[n] and womb.[o]

[a] 10 Or *until Shiloh comes*; or *until he comes to whom tribute belongs* [b] 12 Or *will be dull from wine, / his teeth white from milk* [c] 14 Or *strong* [d] 14 Or *campfires* [e] 16 *Dan* here means *he provides justice.* [f] 19 *Gad* can mean *attack* and *band of raiders.* [g] 21 Or *free; / he utters beautiful words* [h] 22 Or *Joseph is a wild colt, / a wild colt near a spring, / a wild donkey on a terraced hill* [i] 23,24 Or *archers will attack . . . will shoot . . . will remain . . . will stay* [j] 25 Hebrew *Shaddai*

49:10 Though difficult to translate (see NIV text note), the verse has been traditionally understood as Messianic. It was initially fulfilled in David, and ultimately in Christ. *scepter.* See Nu 24:17 and note. *until he comes to whom it belongs.* Repeated almost verbatim in Eze 21:27 (see note there) in a section where Zedekiah, the last king of Judah, is told to "remove the crown" (Eze 21:26) from his head because dominion over Jerusalem will ultimately be given to the one "to whom it rightfully belongs."
49:11 Judah's descendants would someday enjoy a settled and prosperous life.
49:13 Though landlocked by the tribes of Asher and Manasseh, the descendants of Zebulun were close enough to the Mediterranean (within ten miles) to "feast on the abundance of the seas" (Dt 33:19).
49:17 *Dan will be a serpent.* The treachery of a group of Danites in later times is described in Jdg 18:27. *bites the horse's heels.* Samson, from the tribe of Dan, would single-handedly hold the Philistines at bay (Jdg 14–16).
49:18 Jacob pauses midway through his series of blessings to utter a brief prayer for God's help.
49:19 *Gad will be attacked.* Located east of the Jordan (see Jos 13:24–27), the descendants of Gad were vulnerable to raids by the Moabites to the south, as the Mesha (see 2Ki 3:4) Stele (a Moabite inscription dating from the late ninth century B.C.) illustrates (see chart, p. xxiii).
49:20 *Asher's food will be rich.* Fertile farmlands near the Mediterranean (see Jos 19:24–30) would ensure the prosperity of Asher's descendants.
49:21 *Naphtali is a doe set free.* Perhaps a reference to an independent spirit fostered in the descendants of Naphtali by their somewhat isolated location in the hill country north of the Sea of Galilee (see Jos 19:32–38 and note on 19:32).
49:22 *fruitful . . . fruitful.* A pun on the name Ephraim (see NIV text note on 41:52), who Jacob predicted would be greater than Joseph's firstborn son Manasseh (see 48:19–20 and notes). *branches climb over a wall.* Ephraim's descendants tended to expand their territory (see Jos 17:14–18).
49:24 *his bow remained steady.* The warlike Ephraimites (see Jdg 8:1 and note; 12:1) would often prove victorious in battle (see Jos 17:18). *Mighty One of Jacob.* Stresses the activity of God in saving and redeeming his people (see Isa 49:26). *Shepherd.* See note on 48:15. *Rock of Israel.* Israel's sure defense (see Dt 32:4,15,18,30–31)—a figure often used also in Psalms (see note on Ps 18:2) and Isaiah.
49:25 *Almighty.* See note on 17:1. *blessings of the heavens . . . of the deep.* The fertility of the soil watered by rains from above and springs and streams from below. *breast and womb.* The fertility of people and animals. For the later prosperity of Ephraim's descendants see Hos 12:8 and note.

[26]Your father's blessings are greater
than the blessings of the ancient
mountains,
than[a] the bounty of the age-old
hills.[p]
Let all these rest on the head of
Joseph,[q]
on the brow of the prince among[b]
his brothers.[r]

[27]"Benjamin[s] is a ravenous wolf;[t]
in the morning he devours the
prey,[u]
in the evening he divides the
plunder."[v]

[28]All these are the twelve tribes of Israel,[w] and this is what their father said to
them when he blessed them, giving each
the blessing[x] appropriate to him.

The Death of Jacob

[29]Then he gave them these instructions:[y] "I am about to be gathered to my
people.[z] Bury me with my fathers[a] in the
cave in the field of Ephron the Hittite,[b]
[30]the cave in the field of Machpelah,[c]
near Mamre[d] in Canaan, which Abraham
bought as a burial place[e] from Ephron the
Hittite, along with the field.[f] [31]There Abraham[g] and his wife Sarah[h] were buried,
there Isaac and his wife Rebekah[i] were
buried, and there I buried Leah.[j] [32]The
field and the cave in it were bought from
the Hittites.[c][k]"

[33]When Jacob had finished giving instructions to his sons, he drew his feet up
into the bed, breathed his last and was
gathered to his people.[l]

50 Joseph threw himself upon his father and wept over him and kissed
him.[m] [2]Then Joseph directed the physicians in his service to embalm his father Israel. So the physicians embalmed
him,[n] [3]taking a full forty days, for that
was the time required for embalming.
And the Egyptians mourned for him seventy days.[o]

[a] 26 Or *of my progenitors, / as great as* [b] 26 Or *the one separated from* [c] 32 Or *the sons of Heth*

49:26 [p] Hab 3:6 [q] 1Ch 5:1; Eze 47:13 [r] S Ge 37:8 **49:27** [s] Ge 35:18; Jdg 20:12-13 [t] Hab 1:8; Zep 3:3 [u] S ver 9 [v] Nu 31:11; Dt 2:35; Jos 7:21; 8:2; 22:8; Jdg 8:24 **49:28** [w] S ver 2 [x] S Ge 27:4 **49:29** [y] Ge 50:16 [z] S Ge 25:8 [a] S Ge 15:15; 50:25; 2Sa 2:32; 19:37 [b] S Ge 25:9 **49:30** [c] S Ge 23:9 [d] S Ge 13:18 [e] S Ge 23:4 [f] S Ge 23:20 **49:31** [g] Ge 25:9 [h] Ge 23:19 [i] S Ge 24:67 [j] S Ge 23:20; S 29:16 **49:32** [k] S Ge 10:15 **49:33** [l] S Ge 25:8; Ac 7:15

50:1 [m] S Ge 29:11; S 46:4 **50:2** [n] ver 26; 2Ch 16:14; Mt 26:12; Mk 16:1; Jn 19:39-40 **50:3** [o] S Ge 37:34; S Dt 1:3

49:26 *Joseph ... prince among his brothers.* See notes on v. 8; 48:19. Ephraim would gain supremacy, especially over the northern tribes (see Isa 7:1 – 2; Hos 13:1 and notes; see also Jos 16:9).

49:27 *Benjamin is a ravenous wolf.* See the exploits of Ehud (Jdg 3:12 – 30) and Saul and Jonathan (1Sa 11 – 15). See Jdg 19 – 21 for examples of the savagery that characterized one group of Benjamin's descendants.

49:28 *twelve tribes of Israel.* See note on vv. 2 – 27.

49:29 *Bury me with my fathers.* See note on 25:8. Jacob does not forget that the land of his ancestors is his God-appointed homeland (see note on 23:19).

49:33 *was gathered to his people.* See note on 25:8.

50:1 *wept.* See note on 43:30.

50:2 *physicians embalmed him.* Professional embalmers could have been hired for the purpose, but Joseph perhaps wanted to avoid involvement with the pagan religious ceremonies accompanying their services.

50:3 *forty days ... seventy days.* The two periods probably overlapped.

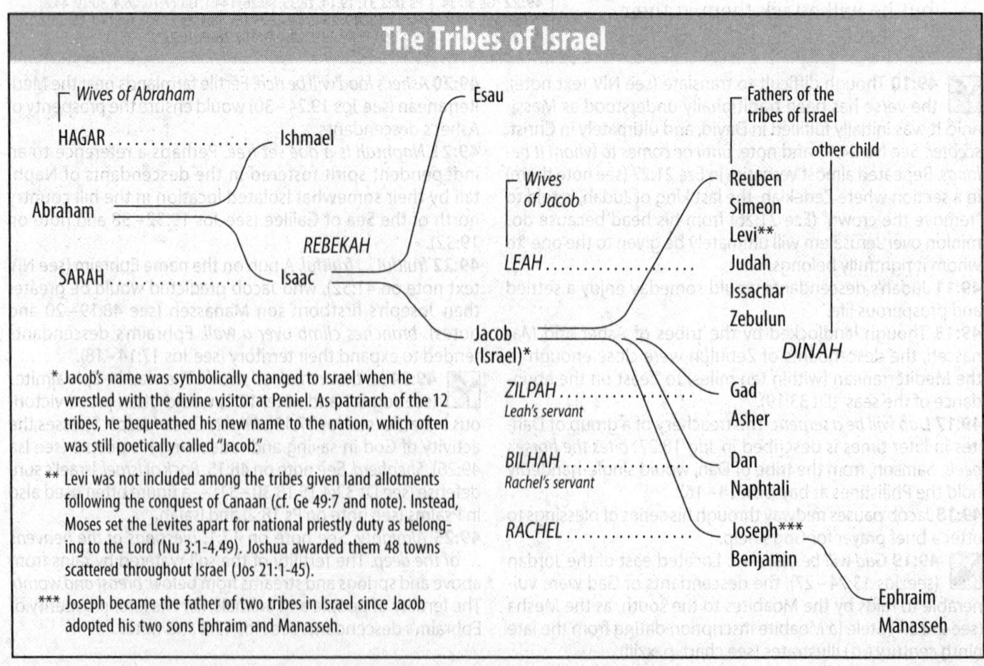
The Tribes of Israel
Wives of Abraham
HAGAR
Ishmael
Abraham
SARAH
Isaac
REBEKAH
Esau
Jacob (Israel)*
Wives of Jacob
LEAH
ZILPAH
Leah's servant
BILHAH
Rachel's servant
RACHEL
Fathers of the tribes of Israel
other child
Reuben
Simeon
Levi**
Judah
Issachar
Zebulun
DINAH
Gad
Asher
Dan
Naphtali
Joseph***
Benjamin
Ephraim
Manasseh
* Jacob's name was symbolically changed to Israel when he wrestled with the divine visitor at Peniel. As patriarch of the 12 tribes, he bequeathed his new name to the nation, which often was still poetically called "Jacob."
** Levi was not included among the tribes given land allotments following the conquest of Canaan (cf. Ge 49:7 and note). Instead, Moses set the Levites apart for national priestly duty as belonging to the Lord (Nu 3:1-4,49). Joshua awarded them 48 towns scattered throughout Israel (Jos 21:1-45).
*** Joseph became the father of two tribes in Israel since Jacob adopted his two sons Ephraim and Manasseh.

4 When the days of mourning[p] had
passed, Joseph said to Pharaoh's court,[q]
"If I have found favor in your eyes,[r] speak
to Pharaoh for me. Tell him, 5 'My father
made me swear an oath[s] and said, "I am
about to die;[t] bury me in the tomb I dug
for myself[u] in the land of Canaan."[v] Now
let me go up and bury my father;[w] then I
will return.'"

6 Pharaoh said, "Go up and bury your
father, as he made you swear to do."

7 So Joseph went up to bury his father.
All Pharaoh's officials[x] accompanied
him—the dignitaries of his court[y] and
all the dignitaries of Egypt— 8 besides all
the members of Joseph's household and
his brothers and those belonging to his
father's household.[z] Only their children
and their flocks and herds were left in
Goshen.[a] 9 Chariots[b] and horsemen[a] also
went up with him. It was a very large
company.

10 When they reached the threshing
floor[c] of Atad, near the Jordan, they lamented loudly and bitterly;[d] and there
Joseph observed a seven-day period[e] of
mourning[f] for his father.[g] 11 When the Canaanites[h] who lived there saw the mourning at the threshing floor of Atad, they
said, "The Egyptians are holding a solemn
ceremony of mourning."[i] That is why that
place near the Jordan is called Abel Mizraim.[b]

12 So Jacob's sons did as he had commanded them:[j] 13 They carried him to the
land of Canaan and buried him in the cave
in the field of Machpelah,[k] near Mamre,[l]
which Abraham had bought as a burial
place from Ephron the Hittite,[m] along with
the field.[n] 14 After burying his father, Joseph returned to Egypt, together with his
brothers and all the others who had gone
with him to bury his father.[o]

50:4 [p]S Ge 27:41 [q]ver 7 [r]S Ge 30:27; S 32:5 **50:5** [s]S Ge 24:37 [t]ver 24 [u]2Sa 18:18; 2Ch 16:14; Isa 22:16; Mt 27:60 [v]Ge 47:31 [w]Mt 8:21 **50:7** [x]Ge 45:16 [y]ver 4 **50:8** [z]ver 14 [a]S Ge 45:10 **50:9** [b]S Ge 41:43 **50:10** [c]Nu 15:20; Ru 3:2; 2Sa 24:18; 1Ki 22:10 [d]2Sa 1:17; 3:33; 2Ch 35:25; Eze 32:16; Ac 8:2 [e]1Sa 31:13; Job 2:13; Eze 3:15 [f]S Ge 27:41; S Lev 10:6 [g]S Ge 37:34 **50:11** [h]S Ge 10:18 [i]S Ge 37:34 **50:12** [j]Ge 49:29 **50:13** [k]S Ge 23:9 [l]S Ge 13:18 [m]S Ge 25:9 [n]S Ge 23:20 **50:14** [o]ver 8

50:15 [p]S Ge 27:41 [q]ver 17; S Ge 9:5; 37:28; Zep 3:11; 1Pe 3:9 **50:16** [r]Ge 49:29 **50:17** [s]S Mt 6:14 [t]S ver 15 [u]S Ge 28:13 [v]S Ge 29:11 **50:18** [w]S Ge 37:7 [x]S Ge 43:18 **50:19** [y]S Ge 30:2; S Ex 32:34; Ro 12:19; Heb 10:30

Joseph Reassures His Brothers

15 When Joseph's brothers saw that
their father was dead, they said, "What
if Joseph holds a grudge[p] against us and
pays us back for all the wrongs we did
to him?"[q] 16 So they sent word to Joseph,
saying, "Your father left these instructions[r]
before he died: 17 'This is what you are to
say to Joseph: I ask you to forgive your
brothers the sins[s] and the wrongs they
committed in treating you so badly.'[t] Now
please forgive the sins of the servants of
the God of your father.[u]" When their message came to him, Joseph wept.[v]

18 His brothers then came and threw
themselves down before him.[w] "We are
your slaves,"[x] they said.

19 But Joseph said to them, "Don't be
afraid. Am I in the place of God?[y] 20 You intended to harm me,[z] but God intended[a] it
for good[b] to accomplish what is now being
done, the saving of many lives.[c] 21 So then,
don't be afraid. I will provide for you and
your children.[d]" And he reassured them
and spoke kindly[e] to them.

The Death of Joseph

22 Joseph stayed in Egypt, along with all
his father's family. He lived a hundred and
ten years[f] 23 and saw the third generation[g]
of Ephraim's[h] children.[i] Also the children
of Makir[j] son of Manasseh[k] were placed at
birth on Joseph's knees.[c][l]

24 Then Joseph said to his brothers, "I am
about to die.[m] But God will surely come to
your aid[n] and take you up out of this land

[a] 9 Or *charioteers* [b] 11 *Abel Mizraim* means *mourning of the Egyptians.* [c] 23 That is, were counted as his

50:20 [z]Ge 37:20 [a]Isa 10:7; Mic 4:11-12 [b]Ro 8:28 [c]S Ge 45:5; Est 4:14 **50:21** [d]S Ge 45:11 [e]S Ge 34:3; Eph 4:32 **50:22** [f]S Ge 25:7; Jos 24:29 **50:23** [g]Job 42:16 [h]S Ge 41:52 [i]S Ge 48:11 [j]Nu 26:29; 27:1; 32:39,40; 36:1; Dt 3:15; Jos 13:31; 17:1; Jdg 5:14 [k]S Ge 41:51 [l]S Ge 48:12 **50:24** [m]ver 5 [n]Ru 1:6; Ps 35:2; 106:4; Isa 38:14

50:5 *My father made me swear an oath.* See 47:29–31. *dug.* Or "bought," as the Hebrew for this verb is translated in Hos 3:2 (see also Dt 2:6). *go up.* To Hebron, which has a higher elevation than Goshen.

50:10 *threshing floor.* Grain was threshed on a flat circular area, either of rock or of pounded earth. Threshing floors were located on an elevated open place exposed to the wind, usually at the edge of town or near the main gate (see 1Ki 22:10). See note on Ru 1:22.

50:15 *holds a grudge … and pays us back.* Similarly, Esau had once planned to kill Jacob as soon as Isaac died (see 27:41–45 and note).

50:17 *Joseph wept.* See note on 43:30. Joseph may have been saddened by the thought that his brothers might be falsely implicating their father in their story. Or he may have regretted his failure to reassure them sooner that he had already forgiven them.

50:18 *threw themselves down.* A final fulfillment of Joseph's earlier dreams (see note on 37:7; see also 37:9). *We are your slaves.* They had earlier expressed a similar willingness, but under quite different circumstances (see 44:9,33).

50:19 *Am I in the place of God?* See note on 30:2.

50:20 *God intended it for good.* Their act, out of personal animosity toward a brother, had been used by God to save life—the life of the Israelites, the Egyptians and all the nations that came to Egypt to buy food in the face of a famine that threatened the known world. At the same time, God showed by these events that his purpose for the nations is life and that this purpose would be effected through the descendants of Abraham.

50:23 *saw the third generation.* Cf. Job's experience (Job 42:16). *Makir.* Manasseh's firstborn son and the ancestor of the powerful Gileadites (Jos 17:1). The name of Makir later became almost interchangeable with that of Manasseh himself (see Jdg 5:14 and note). *placed at birth on Joseph's knees.* Joseph probably adopted Makir's children (see note on 30:3).

50:24 *brothers.* Perhaps used here in a broader sense than siblings. *I am about to die.* See note on 48:21. *God will … take you up out of this land.* Joseph did not forget God's promises (cf. 15:16; 46:4; 48:21) concerning "the exodus" (Heb 11:22).

to the land[o] he promised on oath to Abraham,[p] Isaac[q] and Jacob."[r] 25 And Joseph
made the sons of Israel swear an oath[s]
and said, "God will surely come to your
aid, and then you must carry my bones[t]
up from this place."[u]
26 So Joseph died[v] at the age of a hundred and ten.[w] And after they embalmed
him,[x] he was placed in a coffin in Egypt.

50:24 [o]S Ge 15:14 [p]S Ge 13:17 [q]S Ge 17:19 [r]S Ge 12:7; S 15:16 **50:25** [s]S Ge 24:37 [t]S Ge 49:29 [u]S Ge 47:29-30; Heb 11:22 **50:26** [v]Ex 1:6 [w]S Ge 25:7 [x]S ver 2

50:25 See 47:29 – 31 for a similar request by Jacob. *carry my bones up from this place.* Centuries later Moses did so to fulfill his ancestor's oath (see Ex 13:19). Joseph's bones were eventually "buried at Shechem in the tract of land that Jacob bought ... from the sons of Hamor" (Jos 24:32; see note there; see also Ge 33:19).

50:26 *Joseph died at the age of a hundred and ten.* See v. 22. Ancient Egyptian records indicate that 110 years was considered to be the ideal life span; to the Egyptians this would have signified divine blessing upon Joseph.

Exodus

I N T R O D U C T I O N

Title

"Exodus" is a Latin word derived from Greek *Exodos,* the name given to the book by those who translated the OT into Greek in the last centuries before Christ (the Septuagint). The word means "exit," "departure" (see Lk 9:31 and note; Heb 11:22). The name was retained by the Latin Vulgate, by the Jewish author Philo (a contemporary of Christ) and by the Syriac version. In Hebrew the book is named after its first two words, *we'elleh shemoth* ("These are the names of"). The same phrase occurs in Ge 46:8, where it likewise introduces a list of the names of those Israelites "who went to Egypt with Jacob" (1:1). Thus Exodus was not intended to exist separately, but was thought of as a continuation of the narrative that began in Genesis and continued on through Leviticus, Numbers and Deuteronomy. The first five books of the Bible are together known as the Pentateuch (see Introduction to Genesis: Author and Date of Writing).

> **A Quick Look**
>
> **Author:**
> Moses
>
> **Audience:**
> God's chosen people, the Israelites
>
> **Date:**
> Between 1446 and 1406 B.C.
>
> **Theme:**
> God reveals himself to his people and delivers the Israelites from slavery in Egypt to establish a covenant with them in the desert.

Author and Date of Writing

Several statements in Exodus indicate that Moses wrote certain sections of the book (see 17:14; 24:4; 34:27). In addition, Jos 8:31 refers to the command of Ex 20:25 as having been "written in the Book of the Law of Moses." The NT also claims Mosaic authorship for various passages in Exodus (see, e.g., Mk 7:10; 12:26 and NIV text notes; see also Lk 2:22–23). Taken together, these references strongly suggest that Moses was largely responsible for writing the book of Exodus — a traditional view not convincingly challenged by the commonly held notion that the Pentateuch as a whole contains four underlying sources (see Introduction to Genesis: Author and Date of Writing).

Chronology

According to 1Ki 6:1 (see note there), the exodus took place 480 years before "the fourth year of Solomon's reign over Israel." Since that year was c. 966 B.C., it has been traditionally held that the exodus occurred c. 1446. The "three hundred years" of Jdg 11:26 fits comfortably within this time span (see Introduction to Judges: Background). In addition, although Egyptian chronology relating to the 18th dynasty remains somewhat uncertain, some recent research tends to support the traditional view that two of this dynasty's pharaohs, Thutmose III and his son Amunhotep II, were the pharaohs of the oppression and the exodus respectively (see notes on 2:15,23; 3:10).

On the other hand, the appearance of the name Rameses in 1:11 has led many to the conclusion that the 19th-dynasty pharaoh Seti I and his son Rameses II were the pharaohs of the oppression and the exodus respectively. Furthermore, archaeological evidence of the destruction of numerous Canaanite cities in the 13th century B.C. has been interpreted as proof that Joshua's troops invaded the promised land in that century. These and similar lines of argument lead to a date for the exodus of c. 1290 B.C. (see Introduction to Joshua: Historical Setting).

The identity of the cities' attackers, however, cannot be positively ascertained. The raids may have been initiated by later Israelite armies, or by Philistines or other outsiders. In addition, the archaeological evidence itself has become increasingly ambiguous, and recent evaluations have tended to redate some of it to the 18th dynasty. Also, the name Rameses in 1:11 could very well be the result of an editorial updating by someone who lived centuries after Moses — a procedure that probably accounts for the appearance of the same word in Ge 47:11 (see note there).

In short, there are no compelling reasons to modify in any substantial way the traditional 1446 B.C. date for the exodus of the Israelites from Egyptian bondage.

The Route of the Exodus

At least three routes of escape from Pithom and Rameses (1:11) have been proposed: (1) a northern route through the land of the Philistines (but see 13:17 and note); (2) a middle route leading eastward across Sinai to Beersheba; and (3) a southern route along the west coast of Sinai to the southeastern extremities of the peninsula. The southern route seems most likely, since several of the sites in Israel's desert itinerary have been tentatively identified along it (see map No. 3 at the end of this study Bible). The exact place where Israel crossed the "Red Sea" is uncertain, however (see notes on 13:18; 14:2).

Themes and Theology

Exodus lays a foundational theology in which God reveals his name, his attributes, his redemption, his law and how he is to be worshiped. It also reports the appointment and work of Moses as the mediator of the Sinaitic covenant, describes the beginnings of the priesthood in Israel, defines the role of the prophet and relates how the ancient covenant relationship between God and his people (see note on Ge 17:2) came under a new administration (the covenant given at Mount Sinai).

Profound insights into the nature of God are found in chs. 3; 6; 33 – 34. The focus of these texts is on the fact and importance of his presence with his people (as signified by his name Yahweh — see notes on 3:14 – 15 — and by his glory among them). But emphasis is also placed on his attributes of justice, truthfulness, mercy, faithfulness and holiness. Thus to know God's "name" is to know him and to know his character (see 3:13 – 15; 6:3 and note).

What the Lord had promised centuries earlier to Abraham, Isaac and Jacob he now begins to bring to fruition as Israel is freed from Egyptian bondage and sets out for the land of promise.

God is also the Lord of history. Neither the affliction of Israel nor the plagues in Egypt were outside his control. The pharaoh, the Egyptians and all Israel saw the power of God. There was no one like him, "majestic in holiness, awesome in glory, working wonders" (15:11; see note there).

It is reassuring to know that God remembers and is concerned about his people (see 2:24 – 25). What the Lord had promised centuries earlier to Abraham, Isaac and Jacob he now begins to bring to fruition as Israel is freed from Egyptian bondage and sets out for the land of promise. The covenant at Sinai is but another step in God's fulfillment of his promise to the patriarchs (3:15 – 17; 6:2 – 8; 19:3 – 8).

The Biblical message of salvation is likewise powerfully set forth in this book. The verb "redeem" is used, e.g., in 6:6; 15:13 (see notes there). But the heart of redemption theology is best seen in the Passover narrative of ch. 12, the sealing of the covenant in ch. 24, and the account of God's gracious renewal of that covenant after Israel's blatant unfaithfulness to it in their worship of the golden calf (see 34:1 – 14 and notes). The apostle Paul viewed the death of the Passover lamb as fulfilled in Christ (see 1Co 5:7 and note). Indeed, John the Baptist called Jesus the "Lamb of God, who takes away the sin of the world" (Jn 1:29; see note there).

The foundation of Biblical ethics and morality is laid out first in the gracious character of God as revealed in the exodus itself and then in the Ten Commandments (20:1 – 17) and the ordinances of the Book of the Covenant (20:22 — 23:33), which taught Israel how to apply in a practical way the principles of the commandments.

The book concludes with an extended account of the building of the tabernacle. Though costly in time, effort and monetary value, the tabernacle, in meaning and function, points to the grace of God, who overcomes the alienation between himself and his (sinful) people. By means of the tabernacle, the omnipotent, unchanging and transcendent God of the universe came to "dwell" or "tabernacle" with his people, thereby revealing his gracious nearness as well (cf. Jn 1:14 and note). God is not only mighty in Israel's behalf; he is also present in the nation's midst.

However, these theological elements do not merely sit side by side in the Exodus narrative. They receive their fullest and richest significance from the fact that they are embedded in the account of God's raising up his servant Moses (1) to liberate his people from Egyptian bondage, (2) to inaugurate his earthly kingdom among them by bringing them into a special national covenant with him, and (3) to erect within Israel God's royal tent. And this account of redemption from bondage leading to consecration in covenant and the pitching of God's royal tent in the earth, all through the ministry of a chosen mediator, discloses God's purpose in history — the purpose he would fulfill through Israel, and ultimately through Jesus Christ the supreme Mediator (see 1Ti 2:5 and note).

Outline

- I. Prologue (chs. 1 – 2)
  - A. Israel Blessed and Oppressed (ch. 1)
  - B. A Deliverer Prepared (ch. 2)
    1. Infant Moses spared (2:1 – 10)
    2. Mature Moses' escape from Egypt (2:11 – 25)
- II. God's Deliverance of Israel (chs. 3 – 18)
  - A. The Deliverer Called (ch. 3)
  - B. The Deliverer's Objections and Disqualifications Overcome (ch. 4)
  - C. Unsuccessful Attempts to Deliver (5:1 — 6:12)
    1. Oppression made more harsh (5:1 – 21)
    2. Promise of deliverance renewed (5:22 — 6:12)
  - D. The Deliverers Identified (6:13 – 27)
  - E. Judgment of Plagues on Egypt (6:28 — 11:10)
    1. Deliverer's commission renewed (6:28 — 7:7)
    2. Presenting the signs of divine authority (7:8 – 13)
    3. First plague: water turned to blood (7:14 – 24)
    4. Second plague: frogs (7:25 — 8:15)
    5. Third plague: gnats (8:16 – 19)
    6. Fourth plague: flies (8:20 – 32)
    7. Fifth plague: against livestock (9:1 – 7)
    8. Sixth plague: boils (9:8 – 12)
    9. Seventh plague: hail (9:13 – 35)
    10. Eighth plague: locusts (10:1 – 20)
    11. Ninth plague: darkness (10:21 – 29)
    12. Tenth plague announced: death of the firstborn (ch. 11)

- F. The Passover (12:1–28)
- G. The Exodus from Egypt (12:29–51)
- H. The Consecration of the Firstborn (13:1–16)
- I. Crossing the "Red Sea" (13:17—15:21)
  1. Deliverance at the "Red Sea" (13:17—14:31)
  2. Song at the sea (15:1–21)
- J. Journey to Sinai (15:22—18:27)
  1. The waters of Marah (15:22–27)
  2. The manna and the quail (ch. 16)
  3. The waters of Meribah (17:1–7)
  4. The war with Amalek (17:8–16)
  5. Basic administrative structure (ch. 18)

III. Covenant at Sinai (chs. 19–24)
- A. The Covenant Proposed (ch. 19)
- B. The Decalogue (20:1–17)
- C. The Reaction of the People to God's Fiery Presence (20:18–21)
- D. The Book of the Covenant (20:22—23:33)
  1. Prologue (20:22–26)
  2. Laws on slaves (21:1–11)
  3. Laws on homicide (21:12–17)
  4. Laws on bodily injuries (21:18–32)
  5. Laws on property damage (21:33—22:15)
  6. Laws on society (22:16–31)
  7. Laws on justice and neighborliness (23:1–9)
  8. Laws on sacred seasons (23:10–19)
  9. Epilogue (23:20–33)
- E. Ratification of the Covenant (ch. 24)

IV. God's Royal Tent in Israel (chs. 25–40)
- A. Instructions concerning the Royal Tent (chs. 25–31)
  1. Collection of the materials (25:1–9)
  2. Furnishings of the tent (25:10–40)
     a. Ark and atonement cover (25:10–22)
     b. Table of the bread of the Presence (25:23–30)
     c. Gold lampstand (25:31–40)
  3. The tent and its courtyard (26:1—27:19)
     a. Curtains and frames (ch. 26)
     b. Altar of burnt offering (27:1–8)
     c. Courtyard (27:9–19)
  4. The tent's personnel (27:20—29:46)
     a. Priesthood (27:20—28:5)
     b. Garments of the priests (28:6–43)
     c. Ordination of the priests (ch. 29)
  5. Remaining provisions concerning the tent (ch. 30)
     a. Altar of incense (30:1–10)
     b. Census tax (30:11–16)
     c. Bronze basin (30:17–21)
     d. Anointing oil and incense (30:22–38)
  6. Appointment of Bezalel and his craftsmen (31:1–11)
  7. Observance of Sabbath rest (31:12–18)
- B. Rebellion Threatens Withdrawal of God (chs. 32–34)
  1. The golden calf (32:1–29)
  2. Moses' mediation (32:30–35)

3. Threatened separation and Moses' prayer (ch. 33)
4. Renewal of the covenant (ch. 34)

C. God's Royal Tent Set Up (chs. 35 – 40)

1. Summons to build (35:1 – 19)
2. Voluntary gifts (35:20 – 29)
3. Bezalel and his craftsmen (35:30 — 36:7)
4. Progress of the work (36:8 — 39:31)
5. Moses' blessing (39:32 – 43)
6. Erection of God's royal tent (40:1 – 33)
7. Dedication of God's royal tent (40:34 – 38)

The Israelites Oppressed

1 These are the names of the sons of Israel[a] who went to Egypt with Jacob, each
with his family: 2Reuben, Simeon, Levi
and Judah; 3Issachar, Zebulun and Benjamin; 4Dan and Naphtali; Gad and Asher.[b]
5The descendants of Jacob numbered seventy[a] in all;[c] Joseph was already in Egypt.
6Now Joseph and all his brothers and
all that generation died,[d] 7but the Israelites were fruitful and multiplied greatly
and became exceedingly numerous,[e] so
that the land was filled with them.
8Then a new king, who did not know
about Joseph, came to power in Egypt.[f]
9"Look," he said to his people, "the Israelites have become much too numerous[g]
for us.[h] 10Come, we must deal shrewdly[i]
with them or they will become even more
numerous and, if war breaks out, will join
our enemies, fight against us and leave the
country."[j]
11So they put slave masters[k] over them
to oppress them with forced labor,[l] and
they built Pithom and Rameses[m] as store
cities[n] for Pharaoh. 12But the more they
were oppressed, the more they multiplied and spread; so the Egyptians came
to dread the Israelites 13and worked them
ruthlessly.[o] 14They made their lives bitter
with hard labor[p] in brick[q] and mortar and
with all kinds of work in the fields; in all
their hard labor the Egyptians used them
ruthlessly.[r]
15The king of Egypt said to the Hebrew
midwives,[s] whose names were Shiphrah
and Puah, 16"When you help the Hebrew
women in childbirth and observe them on
the delivery stool, if it is a boy, kill him;
but if it is a girl, let her live."[t] 17The midwives, however, feared[u] God and did not
do what the king of Egypt had told them
to do;[v] they let the boys live. 18Then the
king of Egypt summoned the midwives
and asked them, "Why have you done
this? Why have you let the boys live?"
19The midwives answered Pharaoh,
"Hebrew women are not like Egyptian
women; they are vigorous and give birth
before the midwives arrive."[w]
20So God was kind to the midwives[x] and
the people increased and became even
more numerous. 21And because the midwives feared[y] God, he gave them families[z]
of their own.
22Then Pharaoh gave this order to all
his people: "Every boy that is born[b] you
must throw into the Nile,[a] but let every
girl live."[b]

[a] *5* Masoretic Text (see also Gen. 46:27); Dead Sea Scrolls and Septuagint (see also Acts 7:14 and note at Gen. 46:27) *seventy-five* [b] *22* Masoretic Text; Samaritan Pentateuch, Septuagint and Targums *born to the Hebrews*

1:1 [a] S Ge 46:8 **1:4** [b] Ge 35:22-26; Nu 1:20-43 **1:5** [c] S Ge 46:26 **1:6** [d] Ge 50:26; Ac 7:15 **1:7** [e] ver 9; S Ge 12:2; Dt 7:13; Eze 16:7 **1:8** [f] Jer 43:11; 46:2 **1:9** [g] S ver 7 [h] S Ge 26:16 **1:10** [i] Ge 15:13; Ex 3:7; 18:11; Ps 64:2; 71:10; 83:3; Isa 53:3 [j] Ps 105:24-25; Ac 7:17-19 **1:11** [k] Ex 3:7; 5:10, 13, 14 [l] S Ge 15:13; Ex 2:11; 5:4; 6:6-7; Jos 9:27; 1Ki 9:21; 1Ch 22:2; Isa 60:10 [m] S Ge 47:11 [n] 1Ki 9:19; 2Ch 8:4 **1:13** [o] ver 14; Ge 15:13-14; Ex 5:21; 16:3; Lev 25:43, 46, 53; Dt 4:20; 26:6; 1Ki 8:51; Ps 129:1; Isa 30:6; 48:10; Jer 11:4 **1:14** [p] Dt 26:6; Ezr 9:9; Isa 14:3 [q] S Ge 11:3 [r] Ex 2:23; 3:9; Nu 20:15; 1Sa 10:18; 2Ki 13:4; Ps 66:11; 81:6; Ac 7:19

1:15 [s] S Ge 35:17 **1:16** [t] ver 22 **1:17** [u] ver 21; Pr 16:6 [v] 1Sa 22:17; Da 3:16-18; Ac 4:18-20; 5:29 **1:19** [w] Lev 19:11; Jos 2:4-6; 1Sa 19:14; 2Sa 17:20 **1:20** [x] Pr 11:18; 22:8; Ecc 8:12; Isa 3:10; Heb 6:10 **1:21** [y] S ver 17 [z] 1Sa 2:35; 2Sa 7:11, 27-29; 1Ki 11:38; 14:10 **1:22** [a] S Ge 41:1 [b] ver 16; Ac 7:19

1:1 — 2:25 This first section of Exodus forms a prologue to the book. It describes how God blesses the Israelites to the point where they become a threat to the Egyptians. Oppression follows, but God raises up a deliverer in the person of Moses. Thus the stage is set for the conflict with the pharaoh and for Israel's redemption from Egypt.

1:1 – 5 These verses clearly indicate that Exodus was written as a continuation of Genesis.

1:1 *These are the names of.* The same expression appears in Ge 46:8 (see note there) at the head of a list of Jacob's descendants. *Israel ... Jacob.* Jacob had earlier been given the additional name Israel (see Ge 32:28; 35:10 and notes). *went to Egypt.* The Israelites lived in Egypt 430 years (see 12:40 and note).

1:2 – 4 The sons of Leah (Reuben through Zebulun) and Rachel (Benjamin; Joseph is not mentioned because the list includes only those "who went to Egypt with Jacob," v. 1) are listed in the order of their seniority and before the sons of Rachel's and Leah's female servants: Bilhah had Dan and Naphtali, Zilpah had Gad and Asher (see Ge 35:23 – 26).

1:5 *seventy.* See note on Ge 46:27.

1:6 – 7 From the death of Joseph to the rise of a "new king" (v. 8) was more than 200 years.

1:7 The language of this verse echoes that of God's benediction on humankind at the time of their creation (see Ge 1:28 and note). This benediction is renewed in the new beginning after the flood (see Ge 9:1 and note on 9:1 – 7) and subsequently becomes a centerpiece in the blessings promised and covenanted to Abraham (see Ge 17:2,6; 22:17 and notes), Isaac (Ge 26:4) and Jacob (Ge 28:14; 35:11; 48:4). God's good intentions for humans when he created them was beginning to be realized in a special way in Israel's history — not in the history of Egypt or of any other world power in which dreams of another, though perhaps lesser, Babel were still cherished. See also notes on 39:32; Nu 1:46. *land.* Goshen (see note on Ge 45:10).

1:8 See Ac 7:18. *new king.* Probably Ahmose, the founder of the 18th dynasty, who expelled the Hyksos (foreign — predominantly Semitic — rulers of Egypt). *did not know about Joseph.* That is, did not know about the great blessing Joseph had been to Egypt many years before.

1:11 *slave masters.* The same official Egyptian designation appears on a wall painting in the Theban tomb of Rekhmire during the reign of the 18th-dynasty pharaoh Thutmose III (see Introduction: Chronology). *oppress them with forced labor.* See Ge 15:13. *Rameses.* See note on Ge 47:11. *Pharaoh.* The word, which is Egyptian in origin and means "great house," is a royal title rather than a personal name.

1:14 *made their lives bitter.* A fact commemorated in the Passover meal, which was eaten "with bitter herbs" (12:8; see note there). *all kinds of work in the fields.* Including pumping the waters of the Nile into the fields to irrigate them (see Dt 11:10 and note).

1:15 *Hebrew.* See note on Ge 14:13. *Shiphrah and Puah.* Semitic, not Egyptian, names. Since the Israelites were so numerous, there were probably other midwives under Shiphrah and Puah.

1:16 *delivery stool.* The Hebrew term means lit. "two stones"; a woman sat on them while giving birth. *if it is a boy, kill him.* Boy babies are potential warriors and fathers.

1:17 See Ac 5:29 for a parallel in the early church (see also Ro 13:3 and note). *feared God.* See note on Ge 20:11.

1:22 *all his people.* Failing to accomplish his purposes through the midwives, the pharaoh mobilized all the Egyptians to deal with the Israelite threat.

The Birth of Moses

2 Now a man of the house of Levi[c] married a Levite woman,[d] 2and she became
pregnant and gave birth to a son. When
she saw that he was a fine[e] child, she hid
him for three months.[f] 3But when she
could hide him no longer, she got a papyrus[g] basket for him and coated it with
tar and pitch.[h] Then she placed the child
in it and put it among the reeds[i] along
the bank of the Nile. 4His sister[j] stood at
a distance to see what would happen to
him.
5Then Pharaoh's daughter went down
to the Nile to bathe, and her attendants
were walking along the river bank.[k] She
saw the basket among the reeds and sent
her slave girl to get it. 6She opened it and
saw the baby. He was crying, and she felt
sorry for him. "This is one of the Hebrew
babies," she said.
7Then his sister asked Pharaoh's daughter, "Shall I go and get one of the Hebrew
women to nurse the baby for you?"
8"Yes, go," she answered. And the girl
went and got the baby's mother. 9Phar-
aoh's daughter said to her, "Take this baby
and nurse him for me, and I will pay you."
So the woman took the baby and nursed
him. 10When the child grew older, she took
him to Pharaoh's daughter and he became
her son. She named[l] him Moses,[a] saying,
"I drew[m] him out of the water."

2:1 [c]S Ge 29:34 [d]ver 2; Ex 6:20; Nu 26:59
2:2 [e]S Ge 39:6 [f]Heb 11:23
2:3 [g]Isa 18:2 [h]Ge 6:14 [i]S Ge 41:2; S Job 8:11; Ac 7:21
2:4 [j]Ex 15:20
2:5 [k]Ex 7:15; 8:20
2:10 [l]1Sa 1:20 [m]2Sa 22:17

Moses Flees to Midian

11One day, after Moses had grown up, he
went out to where his own people[n] were
and watched them at their hard labor.[o] He
saw an Egyptian beating a Hebrew, one
of his own people. 12Glancing this way
and that and seeing no one, he killed the
Egyptian and hid him in the sand. 13The
next day he went out and saw two Hebrews fighting. He asked the one in the
wrong, "Why are you hitting your fellow
Hebrew?"[p]
14The man said, "Who made you ruler and judge over us?[q] Are you thinking
of killing me as you killed the Egyptian?"
Then Moses was afraid and thought,
"What I did must have become known."
15When Pharaoh heard of this, he tried
to kill[r] Moses, but Moses fled[s] from Pharaoh and went to live in Midian,[t] where he
sat down by a well. 16Now a priest of Midian[u] had seven daughters, and they came
to draw water[v] and fill the troughs[w] to water their father's flock. 17Some shepherds
came along and drove them away, but Moses got up and came to their rescue[x] and
watered their flock.[y]
18When the girls returned to Reuel[z] their
father, he asked them, "Why have you returned so early today?"
19They answered, "An Egyptian rescued

2:11 [n]Ac 7:23; Heb 11:24-26 [o]S Ex 1:11
2:13 [p]Ac 7:26
2:14 [q]S Ge 13:8; Ac 7:27*
2:15 [r]Ex 4:19 [s]S Ge 31:21 [t]Heb 11:27
2:16 [u]Ex 3:1; 18:1 [v]S Ge 24:11 [w]S Ge 30:38
2:17 [x]1Sa 30:8; Ps 31:2 [y]S Ge 29:10
2:18 [z]Ex 3:1; 4:18; 18:1,5,12; Nu 10:29

[a] 10 *Moses* sounds like the Hebrew for *draw out.*

2:1–10 The nativity of Moses. He was born a child of the oppression, was saved by means of an "ark" from the watery death decreed by the pharaoh, and was allowed to grow to maturity in the pharaoh's court. Thus Moses' early life paralleled in fundamental ways the life of Israel in Egypt, even as it contained also foreshadowings of things to come (see note on v. 2).

2:1 *a man ... a Levite woman.* Perhaps Amram and Jochebed (but see note on 6:20).

2:2 *a fine child.* Moses was "no ordinary child" (Ac 7:20; Heb 11:23), "fair in the sight of God" (see NIV text note on Ac 7:20). The account of Moses' remarkable deliverance in infancy foreshadows the deliverance from Egypt that God would later effect through him.

2:3 *papyrus basket.* Each of the two Hebrew words lying behind this phrase is of Egyptian origin. The word for "basket" is used only here and of Noah's ark (see note on Ge 6:14). Moses' basket was a miniature version of the large, seaworthy "papyrus boats" mentioned in Isa 18:2. *reeds.* The Hebrew word (*suph*) is of Egyptian derivation and occurs also (see also Ro 3:3 and note) in the name "Red Sea" (see NIV text note on 10:19).

2:4 *His sister.* Miriam (see 15:20–21 and notes).

2:5 *Pharaoh's daughter.* Perhaps the famous 18th-dynasty princess who later became Queen Hatshepsut. Throughout this early part of Exodus, all the pharaoh's efforts to suppress Israel were thwarted by women: the midwives (1:17), the Israelite mothers (1:19), Moses' mother and sister (vv. 3–4,7–9), the pharaoh's daughter (here). The pharaoh's impotence to destroy the people of God is thus ironically exposed.

2:6 *baby ... crying.* The only place in the Bible that tells of an infant crying.

2:10 *he became her son.* Thus "Moses was educated in all the wisdom of the Egyptians" (Ac 7:22; see note there). The narrator here was not interested in describing what this involved. Instead, he cited in the following verses (11–12,13,16–17) three incidents that illustrated Moses' character as a champion of justice. *Moses.* The name, of Egyptian origin, means "is born" and forms the second element in such pharaonic names as Ahmose (see note on 1:8), Thutmose (see note on v. 15) and Rameses (see note on 1:11). *drew him out.* A Hebrew wordplay on the name Moses (see NIV text note), emphasizing his providential rescue from the Nile. Thus Moses' name may also have served as a reminder of the great act of deliverance God worked through him at the "Red Sea" (see 13:17—14:31).

2:11–15 See Ac 7:23–29; Heb 11:24–27 and notes.

2:11 *Moses had grown up.* He was now 40 years old (see Ac 7:23).

2:14 *Who made you ruler and judge ...?* Unwittingly, the speaker made a prediction that would be fulfilled 40 years later (see Ac 7:27,30,35). The Hebrew word for "judge" could also refer to a deliverer, as in the book of Judges (see Ac 7:35); it was often a synonym for "ruler" in the OT (see Ge 18:25 and note) as well as in ancient Canaanite usage. *Moses was afraid.* See note on Heb 11:27.

2:15 *Pharaoh.* Probably Thutmose III (see Introduction: Chronology). *Midian.* Named after one of Abraham's younger sons (see Ge 25:2; see also note on Ge 37:25). Midian flanked the eastern arm of the Red Sea (Gulf of Aqaba) on both sides (see map, p. 108). Dry and desolate, it formed a stark contrast to Moses' former home in the royal court. He lived in Midian 40 years (see Ac 7:29–30).

2:16 *priest of Midian.* Reuel (see v. 18), which means "friend of God." His other name, Jethro (see 3:1), may be a title meaning "his excellency."

us from the shepherds. He even drew water for us and watered the flock.”
20“And where is he?” he asked his
daughters. “Why did you leave him? Invite
him to have something to eat.”[a]
21Moses agreed to stay with the man,
who gave his daughter Zipporah[b] to Moses in marriage. 22Zipporah gave birth to
a son, and Moses named him Gershom,[a][c]
saying, “I have become an alien[d] in a foreign land.”
23During that long period,[e] the king of
Egypt died.[f] The Israelites groaned in their
slavery[g] and cried out, and their cry[h] for
help because of their slavery went up to
God. 24God heard their groaning and he
remembered[i] his covenant[j] with Abraham, with Isaac and with Jacob. 25So
God looked on the Israelites and was concerned[k] about them.

Moses and the Burning Bush

3 Now Moses was tending the flock of
Jethro[l] his father-in-law, the priest of
Midian,[m] and he led the flock to the far
side of the desert and came to Horeb,[n]
the mountain[o] of God. 2There the angel
of the LORD[p] appeared to him in flames
of fire[q] from within a bush.[r] Moses saw
that though the bush was on fire it did
not burn up. 3So Moses thought, “I will go
over and see this strange sight—why the
bush does not burn up.”
4When the LORD saw that he had gone
over to look, God called[s] to him from within the bush,[t] “Moses! Moses!”
And Moses said, “Here I am.”[u]
5“Do not come any closer,”[v] God said.
“Take off your sandals, for the place where
you are standing is holy ground.”[w] 6Then
he said, “I am the God of your father, the
God of Abraham, the God of Isaac and the
God of Jacob.”[x] At this, Moses hid[y] his face,
because he was afraid to look at God.[z]
7The LORD said, “I have indeed seen[a]
the misery[b] of my people in Egypt. I have
heard them crying out because of their
slave drivers, and I am concerned[c] about
their suffering.[d] 8So I have come down[e] to
rescue them from the hand of the Egyptians and to bring them up out of that land
into a good and spacious land,[f] a land
flowing with milk and honey[g]—the home
of the Canaanites, Hittites, Amorites, Perizzites, Hivites[h] and Jebusites.[i] 9And now
the cry of the Israelites has reached me,
and I have seen the way the Egyptians are
oppressing[j] them. 10So now, go. I am sending[k] you to Pharaoh to bring my people
the Israelites out of Egypt.”[l]

2:20 [a]Ge 18:2-5 **2:21** [b]Ex 4:25; 18:2; Nu 12:1 **2:22** [c]Jdg 18:30 [d]S Ge 23:4; Heb 11:13 **2:23** [e]Ac 7:30 [f]Ex 4:19 [g]S Ex 1:14 [h]ver 24; Ex 3:7,9; 6:5; Nu 20:15-16; Dt 26:7; Jdg 2:18; 1Sa 12:8; Ps 5:2; 18:6; 39:12; 81:7; 102:1; Jas 5:4 **2:24** [i]S Ge 8:1 [j]S Ge 9:15; 15:15; 17:4; 22:16-18; 26:3; 28:13-15; Ex 32:13; 2Ki 13:23; Ps 105:10,42; Jer 14:21 **2:25** [k]Ex 3:7; 4:31; Lk 1:25 **3:1** [l]S Ex 2:18; Jdg 1:16 [m]S Ex 2:16 [n]ver 12; Ex 17:6; 19:1-11,5; 33:6; Dt 1:2,6; 4:10; 5:2; 29:1; 1Ki 19:8; Mal 4:4 [o]Ex 4:27; 18:5; 24:13; Dt 4:11,15 **3:2** [p]S Ge 16:7; S Ex 12:23; S Ac 5:19 [q]Ex 19:18; 1Ki 19:12 [r]ver 4; Ex 2:2-6; Dt 33:16; Mk 12:26; Lk 20:37; Ac 7:30 **3:4** [s]Ex 19:3; Lev 1:1 [t]Ex 4:5 [u]Ge 31:11; 1Sa 3:4; Isa 6:8

[a] *22 Gershom* sounds like the Hebrew for *an alien there.*

3:5 [v]Jer 30:21 [w]S Ge 28:17; Ac 7:33* **3:6** [x]S Ge 24:12; S Ex 4:5; Mt 22:32*; Mk 12:26*; Lk 20:37*; Ac 3:13; 7:32* [y]1Ki 19:13 [z]Ex 24:11; 33:20; Jdg 13:22; Job 13:11; 23:16; 30:15; Isa 6:5 **3:7** [a]1Sa 9:16 [b]ver 16; S Ge 16:11; 1Sa 1:11; Ne 9:9; Ps 106:44 [c]S Ex 2:25; Ac 7:34* [d]S Ex 1:10 **3:8** [e]S Ge 11:5; Ac 7:34* [f]S Ge 12:7; S 15:14 [g]ver 17; Ex 13:5; 33:3; Lev 20:24; Nu 13:27; Dt 1:25; 6:3; 8:7-9; 11:9; 26:9; 27:3; Jos 5:6; Jer 11:5; 32:22; Eze 20:6 [h]Jos 11:3; Jdg 3:3; 2Sa 24:7 [i]S Ge 15:18-21; Ezr 9:1 **3:9** [j]S Ex 1:14; S Nu 10:9 **3:10** [k]Ex 4:12; Jos 24:5; 1Sa 12:8; Ps 105:26; Ac 7:34* [l]Ex 6:13,26; 12:41,51; 20:2; Dt 4:20; 1Sa 12:6; 1Ki 8:16; Mic 6:4

2:23–25 These verses turn the reader's attention back to Israel's miserable plight in Egypt. They show that God truly cares for his people and has not forgotten his covenant promises made to their ancestors. This sets the stage for God's active intervention to bring about Israel's deliverance. Four expressions refer to Israel's suffering: "groaned," "cried out," "cry for help" (v. 23), "groaning" (v. 24); and four verbs describe God's response: "heard," "remembered" (v. 24), "looked on," "was concerned about" (v. 25).

2:23 *During that long period.* Thutmose III (see note on v. 15) enjoyed a long reign.

2:24 *covenant with Abraham.* See Ge 15:17–18; 17:7 and notes. *with Isaac.* See Ge 17:19; 26:24. *with Jacob.* See Ge 35:11–12.

3:1—18:27 The second main section of the book. It describes the deliverance of Israel from Egypt and includes the call of Moses, the plagues, the Passover, the exodus from Egypt, the crossing of the Red Sea and the journey to Sinai.

3:1 Like David (2Sa 7:8), Moses was called from tending the flock to be the shepherd of God's people. *Jethro.* See note on 2:16. *Horeb.* Means "desert," "desolation"; either (1) another name for Mount Sinai or (2) another high mountain in the same vicinity in the southeast region of the Sinai peninsula. Tradition identifies Mount Horeb with Ras es-Safsaf ("willow peak"), 6,500 feet high, and Mount Sinai with Jebel Musa ("mountain of Moses"), 7,400 feet high, but both identifications are uncertain.

3:2 *angel of the LORD.* Used interchangeably with "the LORD" and "God" in v. 4 (see note on Ge 16:7). *appeared to him in flames of fire.* God's revelation of himself and his will was often accompanied by fire (see 13:21 and note; 19:18; Ge 15:17 and note).

3:4 Every true prophet was called by God (see, e.g., 1Sa 3:4; Isa 6:8; Jer 1:4–5 and note on 1:5; Eze 2:1–8; Hos 1:2; Am 7:15; Jnh 1:1–2; see also note on 7:1–2). *Moses! Moses!... Here I am.* See notes on Ge 22:1,11.

3:5 *Take off your sandals.* A sign of respect and humility in the ancient Near East (see Jos 5:15). This practice is still followed by Muslims before entering a mosque. *holy.* The ground was not holy by nature but was made so by the divine presence (see, e.g., Ge 2:3). Holiness involves being consecrated to the Lord's service and thus being separated from the commonplace (see note on Lev 11:44).

3:6 See 2:24 and note. *afraid to look at God.* See notes on Ge 16:13; 32:30. Later, as the Lord's servant, Moses would meet with God on Mount Sinai (19:3) and even ask to see God's glory (see 33:18 and note).

3:8 *I have come down to rescue.* God may also come down to judge (see Ge 11:5–9; 18:21 and note). *land flowing with milk and honey.* The traditional and proverbial description of the hill country of Canaan—in its original pastoral state (see note on Isa 7:15). *honey.* The Hebrew for "honey" refers to both bees' honey and the sweet, syrupy juice of dates. *Canaanites ... Jebusites.* See notes on Ge 10:6,15–16; 13:7. The list of the Canaanite nations ranges from two names (see Ge 13:7) to five (see Nu 13:29) to six (as here; see also Jdg 3:5) to ten (see Ge 15:19–21 and note) to twelve (see Ge 10:15–18). The classic description includes seven names (see, e.g., Dt 7:1), seven being the number of completeness (see note on Ge 4:17–18).

3:10 *Pharaoh.* Probably Amunhotep II (see Introduction: Chronology).

11But Moses said to God, "Who am I,[m]
that I should go to Pharaoh and bring the
Israelites out of Egypt?"
12And God said, "I will be with you.[n]
And this will be the sign[o] to you that it
is I who have sent you: When you have
brought the people out of Egypt, you[a] will
worship God on this mountain.[p]"
13Moses said to God, "Suppose I go to
the Israelites and say to them, 'The God of
your fathers has sent me to you,' and they
ask me, 'What is his name?'[q] Then what
shall I tell them?"
14God said to Moses, "I AM WHO I AM.[b]
This is what you are to say to the Israelites: 'I AM[r] has sent me to you.'"
15God also said to Moses, "Say to the
Israelites, 'The LORD,[c] the God of your fathers[s]—the God of Abraham, the God of
Isaac and the God of Jacob[t]—has sent
me to you.' This is my name[u] forever, the
name by which I am to be remembered
from generation to generation.[v]
16"Go, assemble the elders[w] of Israel and
say to them, 'The LORD, the God of your
fathers—the God of Abraham, Isaac and
Jacob[x]—appeared to me and said: I have
watched over you and have seen[y] what
has been done to you in Egypt. 17And I
have promised to bring you up out of your
misery in Egypt[z] into the land of the Canaanites, Hittites, Amorites, Perizzites, Hivites and Jebusites—a land flowing with
milk and honey.'[a]
18"The elders of Israel will listen[b] to you.
Then you and the elders are to go to the
king of Egypt and say to him, 'The LORD,
the God of the Hebrews,[c] has met[d] with
us. Let us take a three-day journey[e] into
the desert to offer sacrifices[f] to the LORD
our God.' 19But I know that the king of
Egypt will not let you go unless a mighty
hand[g] compels him. 20So I will stretch out
my hand[h] and strike the Egyptians with
all the wonders[i] that I will perform among
them. After that, he will let you go.[j]
21"And I will make the Egyptians favorably disposed[k] toward this people, so
that when you leave you will not go empty-handed.[l] 22Every woman is to ask her
neighbor and any woman living in her
house for articles of silver[m] and gold[n] and
for clothing, which you will put on your
sons and daughters. And so you will plunder[o] the Egyptians."[p]

Signs for Moses

4 Moses answered, "What if they do not
believe me or listen[q] to me and say,
'The LORD did not appear to you'?"
2Then the LORD said to him, "What is
that in your hand?"
"A staff,"[r] he replied.

[a] *12* The Hebrew is plural. [b] *14* Or *I WILL BE WHAT I WILL BE* [c] *15* The Hebrew for *LORD* sounds like and may be derived from the Hebrew for *I AM* in verse 14.

3:11 [m]Ex 4:10; 6:12,30; Jdg 6:15; 1Sa 9:21; 15:17; 18:18; 2Sa 7:18; 2Ch 2:6; Isa 6:5; Jer 1:6 **3:12** [n]S Ge 26:3; S Ex 14:22; Ro 8:31 [o]Nu 26:10; Jos 2:12; Jdg 6:17; Ps 86:17; Isa 7:14; 8:18; 20:3; Jer 44:29 [p]S ver 1; Ac 7:7 **3:13** [q]S Ge 32:29 **3:14** [r]Ex 6:2-3; Jn 8:58; Heb 13:8; Rev 1:8; 4:8 **3:15** [s]Ge 31:42; Da 2:23 [t]S Ge 24:12 [u]Ex 6:3,7; 15:3; 23:21; 34:5-7; Lev 24:11; Dt 28:58; Ps 30:4; 83:18; 96:2; 97:12; 135:13; 145:21; Isa 42:8; Jer 16:21; 33:2; Hos 12:5 [v]Ps 45:17; 72:17; 102:12 **3:16** [w]Ex 4:29; 17:5; Lev 4:15; Nu 11:16; 16:25; Dt 5:23; 19:12; Jdg 8:14; Ru 4:2; Pr 31:23; Eze 8:11 [x]S Ge 24:12 [y]Ex 4:31; 2Ki 19:16; 2Ch 6:20; Ps 33:18; 66:7 **3:17** [z]S Ge 15:16; 46:4; Ex 6:6 [a]S ver 8 **3:18** [b]Ex 4:1,8,31; 6:12,30 [c]S Ge 14:13 [d]Nu 23:4,16 [e]S Ge 30:36 [f]Ex 4:23; 5:1,3; 6:11; 7:16; 8:20,27; 9:13; 10:9,26 **3:19** [g]Ex 4:21; 6:6; 7:3; 10:1; 11:9; Dt 4:34; 2Ch 6:32 **3:20** [h]Ex 6:1,6; 7:4-5; 9:15; 13:3,9,14,16; 15:6,12; Dt 4:34,37; 5:15; 7:8; 26:8; 2Ki 17:36; 2Ch 6:32; Ps 118:15-16; 136:12; Isa 41:10; 63:12; Jer 21:5; 51:25; Da 9:15 [i]Ex 4:21; 7:3; 11:9,10; 15:11; 34:10; Nu 14:11; Dt 3:24; 4:34; 6:22; Ne 9:10; Ps 71:19; 72:18; 77:14; 78:43; 86:10; 105:27; 106:22; 135:9; 136:4; Jer 32:20; Mic 7:15; Ac 7:36 [j]Ex 11:1; 12:31-33 **3:21** [k]S Ge 39:21 [l]Ex 11:2; 2Ch 30:9; Ne 1:11; Ps 105:37; 106:46; Jer 42:12 **3:22** [m]Job 27:16-17 [n]Ex 11:2; 12:35; Ezr 1:4,6; 7:16; Ps 105:37 [o]S Ge 15:14; Eze 39:10 [p]Eze 29:10 **4:1** [q]S Ex 3:18 **4:2** [r]ver 17,20; Ge 38:18; Ex 7:19; 8:5,16; 14:16,21; 17:5-6,9; Nu 17:2; 20:8; Jos 8:18; Jdg 6:21; 1Sa 14:27; 2Ki 4:29

3:11 Moses' first expression of reluctance (see v. 13; 4:1,10,13 and notes).
3:12 *I will be with you.* See note on Ge 26:3. The Hebrew word translated "I will be" is the same as the one translated "I AM" in v. 14 (see note there). *sign.* A visible guarantee that what God had promised he would surely fulfill (see notes on 4:8; Ge 15:8).
3:13 Moses' second expression of reluctance. *What is his name?* God had not yet identified himself to Moses by name (see v. 6; cf. Ge 17:1 and note).
3:14 *I AM WHO I AM.* The name by which God wished to be known and worshiped in Israel—the name that expressed his character as the dependable and faithful God who desires the full trust of his people (see v. 12, where "I will be" is completed by "with you"; see also 34:5–7 and notes). *I AM.* The shortened form of the name is perhaps found also in Ps 50:21 (see NIV text note there). Jesus applied the phrase to himself; in so doing he claimed to be God and risked being stoned for blasphemy (see Jn 8:58–59 and notes).
3:15 *The LORD.* The Hebrew for this name is *Yahweh* (often incorrectly spelled "Jehovah"; see note on Dt 28:58). It means "He is" or "He will be" and is the third-person form of the verb translated "I will be" in v. 12 and "I AM" in v. 14. When God speaks of himself he says, "I AM," and when we speak of him we say, "He is."
3:16 *elders.* The Hebrew for this word means lit. "bearded ones," perhaps reflecting the age, wisdom, experience and influence necessary for a man expected to function as an elder. As heads of local families and tribes, "elders" had a recognized position also among the Babylonians, Hittites, Egyptians (see Ge 50:7), Moabites and Midianites (see Nu 22:7). Their duties included judicial arbitration and sentencing (see Dt 22:13–19) as well as military leadership (see Jos 8:10) and counsel (see 1Sa 4:3).
3:18 *Hebrews.* See note on Ge 14:13. *three-day journey.* See note on Ge 22:4. *desert.* God had met with Moses there (see vv. 1–2) and would meet with him there again (see v. 12). *to offer sacrifices.* Entries in extant logs of Egyptian supervisors show that such a request was not exceptional.
3:20 *wonders.* A prediction of the plagues that God would send against Egypt (see 7:14—12:30).
3:21–22 See 11:2–3; 12:35–36.
3:21 *when you leave you will not go empty-handed.* God had promised Abraham that after Israel had served for 400 years they would "come out with great possessions" (Ge 15:14; see Ps 105:37). Israel itself was to live by the same principle of providing gifts to a released slave (see Dt 15:12–15).
3:22 *plunder the Egyptians.* As if they had conquered them in battle.
4:1–17 Moses has already voiced two reasons for his reluctance to obey God's call to rescue Israel from Egyptian bondage (see notes on 3:11,13). Here he states three more (vv. 1,10,13; see notes there). The Lord answers all three. Moses is now ready to return from Midian to Egypt (see vv. 18–31).
4:1 Moses' third expression of reluctance (in spite of God's assurance in 3:18).
4:2 *staff.* Probably a shepherd's crook.

3The LORD said, "Throw it on the
ground."
Moses threw it on the ground and it became a snake,[s] and he ran from it. 4Then
the LORD said to him, "Reach out your
hand and take it by the tail." So Moses
reached out and took hold of the snake
and it turned back into a staff in his hand.
5"This," said the LORD, "is so that they
may believe[t] that the LORD, the God of
their fathers—the God of Abraham, the
God of Isaac and the God of Jacob—has
appeared to you."
6Then the LORD said, "Put your hand inside your cloak." So Moses put his hand
into his cloak, and when he took it out, it
was leprous,[a] like snow.[u]
7"Now put it back into your cloak," he
said. So Moses put his hand back into his
cloak, and when he took it out, it was restored,[v] like the rest of his flesh.
8Then the LORD said, "If they do not
believe[w] you or pay attention to the first
miraculous sign,[x] they may believe the
second. 9But if they do not believe these
two signs or listen to you, take some water from the Nile and pour it on the dry
ground. The water you take from the river
will become blood[y] on the ground."
10Moses said to the LORD, "O Lord, I have
never been eloquent, neither in the past
nor since you have spoken to your servant. I am slow of speech and tongue."[z]
11The LORD said to him, "Who gave
man his mouth? Who makes him deaf or
mute?[a] Who gives him sight or makes him
blind?[b] Is it not I, the LORD? 12Now go;[c]
I will help you speak and will teach you
what to say."[d]
13But Moses said, "O Lord, please send
someone else to do it."[e]
14Then the LORD's anger burned[f] against
Moses and he said, "What about your
brother, Aaron the Levite? I know he can
speak well. He is already on his way to
meet[g] you, and his heart will be glad when
he sees you. 15You shall speak to him and
put words in his mouth;[h] I will help both
of you speak and will teach you what to
do. 16He will speak to the people for you,
and it will be as if he were your mouth[i]
and as if you were God to him.[j] 17But take
this staff[k] in your hand[l] so you can perform miraculous signs[m] with it."

Moses Returns to Egypt

18Then Moses went back to Jethro his
father-in-law and said to him, "Let me go
back to my own people in Egypt to see if
any of them are still alive."
Jethro said, "Go, and I wish you well."
19Now the LORD had said to Moses in
Midian, "Go back to Egypt, for all the
men who wanted to kill[n] you are dead.[o]"
20So Moses took his wife and sons,[p] put
them on a donkey and started back to
Egypt. And he took the staff[q] of God in
his hand.
21The LORD said to Moses, "When you
return to Egypt, see that you perform before Pharaoh all the wonders[r] I have given
you the power to do. But I will harden his
heart[s] so that he will not let the people
go.[t] 22Then say to Pharaoh, 'This is what
the LORD says: Israel is my firstborn son,[u]
23and I told you, "Let my son go,[v] so he
may worship[w] me." But you refused to let
him go; so I will kill your firstborn son.'"[x]
24At a lodging place on the way, the

[a] 6 The Hebrew word was used for various diseases affecting the skin—not necessarily leprosy.

4:3 [s]Ex 7:8-12, 15 **4:5** [t]ver 31; S Ex 3:6; 14:31; 19:9 **4:6** [u]Lev 13:2, 11; Nu 12:10; Dt 24:9; 2Ki 5:1, 27; 2Ch 26:21 **4:7** [v]2Ki 5:14; Mt 8:3; Lk 17:12-14 **4:8** [w]S Ex 3:18 [x]ver 30; Jdg 6:17; 1Ki 13:3; Isa 7:14; Jer 44:29 **4:9** [y]Ex 7:17-21 **4:10** [z]S Ex 3:11 **4:11** [a]Lk 1:20, 64 [b]Ps 94:9; 146:8; Mt 11:5; Jn 10:21 **4:12** [c]S Ex 3:10 [d]ver 15-16; Nu 23:5; Dt 18:15, 18; Isa 50:4; 51:16; Jer 1:9; Mt 10:19-20; Mk 13:11; S Lk 12:12 **4:13** [e]Jnh 1:1-3 **4:14** [f]Nu 11:1, 10, 33; 12:9; 16:15; 22:22; 24:10; 32:13; Dt 7:25; Jos 7:1; Job 17:8 [g]ver 27; 1Sa 10:2-5 **4:15** [h]ver 30; Nu 23:5, 12, 16; Dt 18:18; Jos 1:8; Isa 51:16; 59:21; Jer 1:9; 31:33 **4:16** [i]Ex 7:1-2; Jer 15:19; 36:6 [j]Nu 33:1; Ps 77:20; 105:26; Mic 6:4 **4:17** [k]S ver 2 [l]ver 20; Ex 17:9 [m]Ex 7:9-21; 8:5, 16; 9:22; 10:12-15, 21-23; 14:15-18, 26; Nu 14:11; Dt 4:34; Ps 74:9; 78:43; 105:27 **4:19** [n]Ex 2:15 [o]Ex 2:23; Mt 2:20 **4:20** [p]Ex 2:22; 18:3; Ac 7:29 [q]S ver 2 **4:21** [r]S Ex 3:19, 20 [s]Ex 7:3, 13; 8:15; 9:12, 35; 10:1, 20, 27; 11:10; 14:4, 8; Dt 2:30; Jos 11:20; 1Sa 6:6; Ps 105:25; Isa 6:10; 63:17; Jn 12:40; Ro 9:18 [t]Ex 8:32; 9:17 **4:22** [u]S Ge 10:15; Dt 32:6; Isa 9:6; 63:16; 64:8; Jer 3:19; 31:9; Hos 11:1; Mal 2:10; Ro 9:4; 2Co 6:18 **4:23** [v]Ex 5:1; 7:16 [w]S Ex 3:18 [x]Ge 49:3; Ex 11:5; 12:12, 29; Nu 8:17; 33:4; Ps 78:51; 105:36; 135:8; 136:10

4:3 *snake.* See 7:9–10 and note. Throughout much of Egypt's history the pharaoh wore a cobra made of metal on the front of his headdress as a symbol of his sovereignty.

4:8 *miraculous sign.* A supernatural event or phenomenon designed to demonstrate authority, provide assurance (see Jos 2:12–13), bear testimony (see Isa 19:19–20), give warning (see Nu 17:10) or encourage faith. See note on 3:12.

4:10 Moses' fourth expression of reluctance. *I am slow of speech and tongue.* Not in the sense of a speech impediment (see Ac 7:22). He complained, instead, of not being eloquent or quick-witted enough to respond to the pharaoh (see 6:12). Cf. the description of Paul in 2Co 10:10 (see note there).

4:13 Moses' fifth and final expression of reluctance (see note on 3:11).

4:14 *the LORD's anger burned against Moses.* Although the Lord is "slow to anger" (34:6), he does not withhold his anger or punishment from his disobedient children forever (see 34:7). *Levite.* Later, Aaron and his sons were chosen by the Lord to serve as Israel's priests down through the generations (see 28:1; 29:4–9).

4:15–16 See note on 7:1–2.

4:19 *all the men ... are dead.* Including Thutmose III (see 2:15,23 and notes; see also Introduction: Chronology).

4:20 *sons.* Gershom (see 2:22) and Eliezer. The latter, though unmentioned by name until 18:4, had already been born.

4:21 *wonders.* See note on 3:20. *I will harden his heart.* Nine times in Exodus the hardening of the pharaoh's heart is ascribed to God (here; 7:3; 9:12; 10:1,20,27; 11:10; 14:4,8; see Jos 11:20; Ro 9:17–18 and notes); another nine times the pharaoh is said to have hardened his own heart (7:13–14,22; 8:15,19,32; 9:7,34–35). The pharaoh alone was the agent of the hardening in each of the first five plagues. Not until the sixth plague did God confirm the pharaoh's willful action (see 9:12), as he had twice told Moses he would do (here; 9:12; see similarly Ro 1:24,26,28 and note).

4:22 *firstborn son.* A figure of speech indicating Israel's special relationship with God (see Jer 31:9; Hos 11:1 and note).

4:23 *kill your firstborn son.* Anticipates the tenth plague (see 11:5 and note; 12:12).

4:24 *lodging place.* Perhaps near water, where travelers could spend the night. *the LORD ... was about to kill him.* Evidently

LORD met ⌞Moses⌟[a] and was about to kill[y] him. 25But Zipporah[z] took a flint knife, cut off her son's foreskin[a] and touched ⌞Moses'⌟ feet with it.[b] "Surely you are a bridegroom of blood to me," she said. 26So the LORD let him alone. (At that time she said "bridegroom of blood," referring to circumcision.)

27The LORD said to Aaron, "Go into the desert to meet Moses." So he met Moses at the mountain[b] of God and kissed[c] him. 28Then Moses told Aaron everything the LORD had sent him to say, and also about all the miraculous signs he had commanded him to perform.

29Moses and Aaron brought together all the elders[d] of the Israelites, 30and Aaron told them everything the LORD had said to Moses. He also performed the signs[e] before the people, 31and they believed.[f] And when they heard that the LORD was concerned[g] about them and had seen their misery,[h] they bowed down and worshiped.[i]

Bricks Without Straw

5 Afterward Moses and Aaron went to Pharaoh and said, "This is what the LORD, the God of Israel, says: 'Let my people go,[j] so that they may hold a festival[k] to me in the desert.' "

2Pharaoh said, "Who is the LORD,[l] that I should obey him and let Israel go? I do not know the LORD and I will not let Israel go."[m]

3Then they said, "The God of the Hebrews has met with us. Now let us take a three-day journey[n] into the desert to offer sacrifices to the LORD our God, or he may strike us with plagues[o] or with the sword."

4But the king of Egypt said, "Moses and Aaron, why are you taking the people away from their labor?[p] Get back to your work!" 5Then Pharaoh said, "Look, the people of the land are now numerous,[q] and you are stopping them from working."

6That same day Pharaoh gave this order to the slave drivers[r] and foremen in charge of the people: 7"You are no longer to supply the people with straw for making bricks;[s] let them go and gather their own straw. 8But require them to make the same number of bricks as before; don't reduce the quota.[t] They are lazy;[u] that is why they are crying out, 'Let us go and sacrifice to our God.'[v] 9Make the work harder for the men so that they keep working and pay no attention to lies."

10Then the slave drivers[w] and the foremen went out and said to the people, "This is what Pharaoh says: 'I will not give you any more straw. 11Go and get your own straw wherever you can find it, but your work will not be reduced[x] at all.' " 12So the people scattered all over Egypt to gather stubble to use for straw. 13The slave drivers kept pressing them, saying, "Complete the work required of you for each day, just as when you had straw." 14The Israelite foremen appointed by Pharaoh's slave drivers were beaten[y] and were asked, "Why didn't you meet your quota of bricks yesterday or today, as before?"

15Then the Israelite foremen went and appealed to Pharaoh: "Why have you treated your servants this way? 16Your servants are given no straw, yet we are told, 'Make bricks!' Your servants are being beaten, but the fault is with your own people."

17Pharaoh said, "Lazy, that's what you are—lazy![z] That is why you keep saying, 'Let us go and sacrifice to the LORD.' 18Now get to work.[a] You will not be given any straw, yet you must produce your full quota of bricks."

19The Israelite foremen realized they were in trouble when they were told, "You are not to reduce the number of bricks required of you for each day." 20When

4:24 [y]Nu 22:22 **4:25** [z]S Ex 2:21 [a]Ge 17:14; Jos 5:2,3 **4:27** [b]S Ex 3:1 [c]S Ge 27:27; S 29:13 **4:29** [d]S Ex 3:16 **4:30** [e]S ver 8 **4:31** [f]S Ex 3:18 [g]S Ex 2:25 [h]S Ge 16:11 [i]S Ge 24:26 **5:1** [j]S Ex 4:23 [k]S Ex 3:18 **5:2** [l]Jdg 2:10; Job 21:15; Mal 3:14 [m]Ex 3:19 **5:3** [n]S Ge 30:36 [o]Lev 26:25; Nu 14:12; Dt 28:21; 2Sa 24:13 **5:4** [p]S Ex 1:11; 6:6-7 **5:5** [q]S Ge 12:2 **5:6** [r]S Ge 15:13 **5:7** [s]S Ge 11:3 **5:8** [t]ver 14,18 [u]ver 17 [v]Ex 10:11 **5:10** [w]ver 13; Ex 1:11 **5:11** [x]ver 19 **5:14** [y]ver 16; Isa 10:24 **5:17** [z]ver 8 **5:18** [a]S Ge 15:13

[a] 24 Or ⌞*Moses' son*⌟; Hebrew *him* [b] 25 Or *and drew near* ⌞*Moses'*⌟ *feet*

because Moses had failed to circumcise his son (see Ge 17:9–14 and note on 17:10).

4:25 *Zipporah ... cut off her son's foreskin.* Sensing that divine displeasure had threatened Moses' life, she quickly performed the circumcision on their young son. *flint knife.* Continued to be used for circumcision long after metal was introduced, probably because flint knives were sharper than the metal instruments available and thus more efficient for the surgical procedure (see Jos 5:2 and note). *feet.* Probably a euphemism for "genitals," as in Dt 28:57 ("womb," lit. "feet").

4:26 *bridegroom of blood.* Circumcision may have been repulsive to Zipporah—though it was practiced for various reasons among many peoples of the ancient Near East.

4:27 *kissed.* See note on Ge 29:13.

4:30 *Aaron told them everything the LORD had said to Moses.* See note on 7:1–2.

5:1 *Pharaoh.* See note on 3:10.

5:3 See 3:18 and note. The reason for sacrificing where the Egyptians could not see them is given in 8:26 (see note on Ge 43:32).

5:6 *slave drivers.* Probably the same as the Egyptian "slave masters" in 1:11 (see note there). *foremen.* Israelite supervisors whose method of appointment and whose functions are indicated in vv. 14–16.

5:7 *straw.* Chopped and mixed with the clay as binder to make the bricks stronger. Canaanite Amarna letter 148.30–34 probably refers to the use of straw in making clay bricks.

5:9 *lies.* See 4:29–31. The pharaoh labels all hopes of a quick release for Israel as presumptuous and false.

5:10 *This is what Pharaoh says.* In opposition to "This is what the LORD says" (4:22; 5:1). The pharaoh is now set on a collision course with the God of Israel.

5:15 *Israelite foremen ... appealed to Pharaoh.* During certain periods of Egyptian history slaves were permitted to appeal directly to the pharaoh, bypassing the ordinary chain of command. Egyptian records show that sometimes they were heard, but more often they were not.

they left Pharaoh, they found Moses and
Aaron waiting to meet them, 21and they
said, "May the LORD look upon you and
judge[b] you! You have made us a stench[c]
to Pharaoh and his officials and have put a
sword[d] in their hand to kill us."[e]

God Promises Deliverance

22Moses returned to the LORD and said,
"O Lord, why have you brought trouble
upon this people?[f] Is this why you sent
me? 23Ever since I went to Pharaoh to
speak in your name, he has brought trouble upon this people, and you have not
rescued[g] your people at all."

6 Then the LORD said to Moses, "Now
you will see what I will do to Pharaoh:
Because of my mighty hand[h] he will let
them go;[i] because of my mighty hand he
will drive them out of his country."[j]
2God also said to Moses, "I am the
LORD.[k] 3I appeared to Abraham, to Isaac
and to Jacob as God Almighty,[a][l] but by
my name[m] the LORD[b][n] I did not make myself known to them.[c] 4I also established
my covenant[o] with them to give them
the land[p] of Canaan, where they lived as
aliens.[q] 5Moreover, I have heard the groaning[r] of the Israelites, whom the Egyptians
are enslaving, and I have remembered my
covenant.[s]
6"Therefore, say to the Israelites: 'I am
the LORD, and I will bring you out from under the yoke of the Egyptians.[t] I will free
you from being slaves to them, and I will
redeem[u] you with an outstretched arm[v]
and with mighty acts of judgment.[w] 7I will
take you as my own people, and I will be
your God.[x] Then you will know[y] that I
am the LORD your God, who brought you
out from under the yoke of the Egyptians.
8And I will bring you to the land[z] I swore[a]
with uplifted hand[b] to give to Abraham, to
Isaac and to Jacob.[c] I will give it to you as
a possession. I am the LORD.'"[d]
9Moses reported this to the Israelites,
but they did not listen to him because of
their discouragement and cruel bondage.[e]
10Then the LORD said to Moses, 11"Go,
tell[f] Pharaoh king of Egypt to let the Israelites go out of his country."[g]
12But Moses said to the LORD, "If the Israelites will not listen[h] to me, why would
Pharaoh listen to me, since I speak with
faltering lips[d]?"[i]

Family Record of Moses and Aaron

13Now the LORD spoke to Moses and
Aaron about the Israelites and Pharaoh
king of Egypt, and he commanded them
to bring the Israelites out of Egypt.[j]
14These were the heads of their families[e]:[k]
The sons of Reuben[l] the firstborn
son of Israel were Hanoch and Pallu,
Hezron and Carmi. These were the
clans of Reuben.
15The sons of Simeon[m] were Jemuel, Jamin, Ohad, Jakin, Zohar and
Shaul the son of a Canaanite woman.
These were the clans of Simeon.
16These were the names of the sons
of Levi[n] according to their records:

[a] 3 Hebrew *El-Shaddai* [b] 3 See note at Exodus 3:15. [c] 3 Or *Almighty, and by my name the LORD did I not let myself be known to them?* [d] 12 Hebrew *I am uncircumcised of lips*; also in verse 30 [e] 14 The Hebrew for *families* here and in verse 25 refers to units larger than clans.

5:21 [b]S Ge 16:5 [c]S Ge 34:30 [d]Ex 16:3; Nu 14:3; 20:3 [e]S Ex 1:13; S 14:11 **5:22** [f]Nu 11:11; Dt 1:12; Jos 7:7 **5:23** [g]Jer 4:10; 20:7; Eze 14:9 **6:1** [h]S Ex 3:20; S Dt 5:15 [i]S Ex 3:20 [j]Ex 11:1; 12:31,33,39 **6:2** [k]ver 6,7,8, 29; Ex 3:14,15; 7:5,17; 8:22; 10:2; 12:12; 14:4,18; 16:12; Lev 11:44; 18:21; 20:7; Isa 25:3; 41:20; 43:11; 49:23; 60:16; Eze 13:9; 25:17; 36:38; 37:6,13; Joel 2:27 **6:3** [l]S Ge 17:1 [m]S Ex 3:15; 2Sa 7:26; Ps 48:10; 61:5; 68:4; 83:18; 99:3; Isa 52:6 [n]Ex 3:14; Jn 8:58 **6:4** [o]S Ge 6:18; S 15:18 [p]S Ge 12:7; Ac 7:5; Ro 4:13; Gal 3:16; Heb 11:8-10 [q]S Ge 17:8 **6:5** [r]S Ex 2:23; Ac 7:34 [s]S Ge 9:15 **6:6** [t]ver 7; Ex 3:8; 12:17,51; 16:1,6; 18:1; 19:1; 20:2; 29:46; Lev 22:33; 26:13; Dt 6:12; Ps 81:10; 136:11; Jer 2:6; Hos 13:4; Am 2:10; Mic 6:4 [u]Ex 15:13; Dt 7:8; 9:26; 1Ch 17:21; Job 19:25; Ps 19:14; 34:22; 74:2; 77:15; 107:2; Isa 29:22; 35:9; 43:1; 44:23; 48:20; Jer 15:21; 31:11; 50:34 [v]S Ex 3:19,20; S Jer 32:21; Ac 13:17 [w]Ex 3:20; Ps 9:16; 105:27 **6:7** [x]S Ge 17:7; S Ex 34:9; Eze 11:19-20; Ro 9:4 [y]S ver 2; 1Ki 20:13,28; Isa 43:10; 48:7; Eze 39:6; Joel 3:17 **6:8** [z]S Ge 12:7; Ex 3:8 [a]Jer 11:5; Eze 20:6 [b]S Ge 14:22; Rev 10:5-6 [c]Ps 136:21-22 [d]Lev 18:21 **6:9** [e]S Ge 34:30; Ex 2:23 **6:11** [f]ver 29 [g]S Ex 3:18 **6:12** [h]S Ex 3:18 [i]Ex 4:10 **6:13** [j]S Ex 3:10 **6:14** [k]Ex 13:3; Nu 1:1; 26:4 [l]S Ge 29:32 **6:15** [m]S Ge 29:33 **6:16** [n]S Ge 29:34

5:21 *May the LORD look upon you and judge you!* See Ge 16:5; 31:49 and notes. *stench.* See note on 1Sa 13:4.

6:1 *hand.* Often used figuratively in the Bible for power.

6:2 *I am the LORD.* Appears four times in this passage: (1) to introduce the message; (2) to confirm God's promise of redemption (v. 6) based on the evidence of vv. 2–5; (3) to underscore God's intention to adopt Israel (v. 7); (4) to confirm his promise of the land and to conclude the message (v. 8).

6:3 *God Almighty.* See note on Ge 17:1. *by my name the LORD I did not make myself known to them.* See notes on 3:14–15. This does not necessarily mean that the patriarchs were totally ignorant of the name Yahweh ("the LORD"), but it indicates that they did not understand its full implications as the name of the One who would redeem his people (see notes on v. 6; Ge 2:4). That fact could be comprehended only by the Israelites who were to experience the exodus, and by their descendants. *make myself known.* This experiential sense of the verb "to know" is intended also in its repeated use throughout the account of the plagues (see v. 7; 7:17; 8:10,22; 9:14,29; 10:2; 11:7) and in connection with the exodus itself (see 14:4,18 and note on 14:4; 16:6,8,12; 18:11).

6:5 *remembered.* See note on Ge 8:1.

6:6 *I will bring you out … will free you … will redeem you.* The verbs stress the true significance of the name Yahweh—"the LORD"—who is the Redeemer of his people (see note on v. 3). *outstretched arm.* Used figuratively of God's display of his power in the redemption of his people (see Dt 4:34; 5:15; see also Isa 51:9–11 and note on 51:9). *mighty acts of judgment.* See 7:4. The Lord's acts include redemption (for Israel) and judgment (against Egypt).

6:7–8 *brought you out from … will bring you to.* Redemption means not only release from slavery and suffering but also deliverance to freedom and joy.

6:7 *I will take you as my own people, and I will be your God.* Words that anticipate the covenant at Mount Sinai (see 19:5–6; see also Jer 7:23; 31:33; Zec 8:8 and notes).

6:8 See Ge 22:15–17. *swore with uplifted hand.* See note on Ge 14:22.

6:12 *I speak with faltering lips.* See note on 4:10.

6:13 *Moses and Aaron.* The genealogy contained in vv. 14–25 gives details concerning the background of Moses and Aaron. Only the first three of Jacob's 12 sons (Reuben, Simeon and Levi) are listed since Moses and Aaron were from the third tribe.

6:16 *Merari.* The name is of Egyptian origin, as are those of

Gershon,[o] Kohath and Merari.[p] Levi
lived 137 years.
17The sons of Gershon, by clans,
were Libni and Shimei.[q]
18The sons of Kohath[r] were Amram, Izhar, Hebron and Uzziel.[s] Kohath lived 133 years.
19The sons of Merari were Mahli
and Mushi.[t]

These were the clans of Levi according to their records.
20Amram[u] married his father's sister Jochebed, who bore him Aaron
and Moses.[v] Amram lived 137 years.
21The sons of Izhar[w] were Korah,
Nepheg and Zicri.
22The sons of Uzziel were Mishael,
Elzaphan[x] and Sithri.
23Aaron married Elisheba, daughter of Amminadab[y] and sister of Nahshon,[z] and she bore him Nadab and
Abihu,[a] Eleazar[b] and Ithamar.[c]
24The sons of Korah[d] were Assir, Elkanah and Abiasaph. These were the
Korahite clans.
25Eleazar son of Aaron married one
of the daughters of Putiel, and she
bore him Phinehas.[e]

These were the heads of the Levite
families, clan by clan.

26It was this same Aaron and Moses to
whom the LORD said, "Bring the Israelites
out of Egypt[f] by their divisions."[g] 27They
were the ones who spoke to Pharaoh[h] king
of Egypt about bringing the Israelites out of
Egypt. It was the same Moses and Aaron.[i]

Aaron to Speak for Moses

28Now when the LORD spoke to Moses in
Egypt, 29he said to him, "I am the LORD.[j]
Tell Pharaoh king of Egypt everything I tell
you."

30But Moses said to the LORD, "Since
I speak with faltering lips,[k] why would
Pharaoh listen to me?"

7 Then the LORD said to Moses, "See,
I have made you like God[l] to Pharaoh, and your brother Aaron will be your
prophet.[m] 2You are to say everything I
command you, and your brother Aaron is to tell Pharaoh to let the Israelites
go out of his country. 3But I will harden
Pharaoh's heart,[n] and though I multiply
my miraculous signs and wonders[o] in
Egypt, 4he will not listen[p] to you. Then
I will lay my hand on Egypt and with
mighty acts of judgment[q] I will bring out
my divisions,[r] my people the Israelites.
5And the Egyptians will know that I am
the LORD[s] when I stretch out my hand[t]
against Egypt and bring the Israelites out
of it."
6Moses and Aaron did just as the LORD
commanded[u] them. 7Moses was eighty
years old[v] and Aaron eighty-three when
they spoke to Pharaoh.

Aaron's Staff Becomes a Snake

8The LORD said to Moses and Aaron,
9"When Pharaoh says to you, 'Perform a
miracle,'[w] then say to Aaron, 'Take your
staff and throw it down before Pharaoh,'
and it will become a snake."[x]
10So Moses and Aaron went to Pharaoh
and did just as the LORD commanded. Aaron threw his staff down in front of Pharaoh
and his officials, and it became a snake.
11Pharaoh then summoned wise men and
sorcerers,[y] and the Egyptian magicians[z]
also did the same things by their secret

6:16 [o]S Ge 46:11 [p]Nu 3:17; Jos 21:7; 1Ch 6:1,16 **6:17** [q]Nu 3:18; 1Ch 6:17 **6:18** [r]Nu 3:27; 1Ch 23:12 [s]Nu 3:19; 1Ch 6:2,18 **6:19** [t]Nu 3:20,33; 1Ch 6:19; 23:21 **6:20** [u]1Ch 23:13 [v]Ex 2:1-2; Nu 26:59 **6:21** [w]1Ch 6:38 **6:22** [x]Lev 10:4; Nu 3:30; 1Ch 15:8; 2Ch 29:13 **6:23** [y]Ru 4:19,20; 1Ch 2:10 [z]Nu 1:7; 2:3; Mt 1:4 [a]Ex 24:1; 28:1; Lev 10:1 [b]Lev 10:6; Nu 3:2,32; 16:37,39; Dt 10:6; Jos 14:1 [c]Ex 28:1; Lev 10:12,16; Nu 3:2; 4:28; 26:60; 1Ch 6:3; 24:1 **6:24** [d]ver 21; Nu 16:1; 1Ch 6:22,37 **6:25** [e]Nu 25:7,11; 31:6; Jos 24:33; Ps 106:30 **6:26** [f]S Ex 3:10 [g]Ex 7:4; 12:17,41,51 **6:27** [h]Ex 5:1 [i]Nu 3:1; Ps 77:20 **6:29** [j]S ver 2 **6:30** [k]S Ex 3:11 **7:1** [l]S Ex 4:16 [m]Ex 4:15; Ac 14:12 **7:3** [n]S Ex 4:21; Ro 9:18 [o]S Ex 3:20; S 10:1; Ac 7:36 **7:4** [p]ver 13,16,22; Ex 8:15,19; 9:12; 11:9 [q]S Ex 3:20; Ac 7:36 [r]S Ex 6:26 **7:5** [s]S Ex 6:2 [t]Ex 3:20; Ps 138:7; Eze 6:14; 25:13 **7:6** [u]ver 2,10,20; Ge 6:22 **7:7** [v]Dt 31:2; 34:7; Ac 7:23,30 **7:9** [w]Dt 6:22; 2Ki 19:29; Ps 78:43; 86:17; 105:27; 135:9; Isa 7:11; 37:30; 38:7-8; 55:13; S Jn 2:11 [x]Ex 4:2-5 **7:11** [y]Ex 22:18; Dt 18:10; 1Sa 6:2; 2Ki 21:6; Isa 2:6; 47:12; Jer 27:9; Mal 3:5 [z]S Ge 41:8; 2Ti 3:8

Putiel and Phinehas (see v. 25) and of Moses himself (see note on 2:10). *Levi lived 137 years.* See vv. 18,20. In the OT, attention is usually called to a person's life span only when it exceeds 100 years.

6:20 *Amram ... Aaron and Moses.* There is some reason to believe that Amram and Jochebed were not the immediate parents but the ancestors of Aaron and Moses. Kohath, Amram's father (see v. 18), was born before Jacob's (Israel's) descent into Egypt (see Ge 46:11), where the Israelites then stayed 430 years (see 12:40–41). Since Moses was 80 years old at the time of the exodus (see 7:7), he must have been born at least 350 years after Kohath, who consequently could not have been Moses' grandfather (see v. 18). Therefore Amram must not have been Moses' father, and the Hebrew verb for "bore" must have the same meaning it sometimes has in Ge 10 (see NIV text note on Ge 10:8, where it is translated "was the father of"). *Jochebed.* The name appears to mean "The LORD is glory." If so, it shows that the name Yahweh (here abbreviated as *Jo-*) was known before Moses was born (see note on v. 3). *Aaron and Moses.* Aaron, as the firstborn (see 7:7), is listed first in the official genealogy.

6:26 *divisions.* The Hebrew word may imply that Israel is to serve as the Lord's army (also in 7:4; 12:17,41,51).

6:30 *faltering lips.* See v. 12 and note on 4:10.

7:1–2 As God transmits his word through his prophets to his people, so Moses will transmit God's message through Aaron to the pharaoh. The prophet's task was to speak God's word on God's behalf. He was God's "mouth" (4:15–16).

7:3 *harden.* See note on 4:21. *miraculous signs.* See notes on 3:12; 4:8.

7:4 *mighty acts of judgment.* See note on 6:6.

7:7 *Moses was eighty years old.* See notes on 2:11,15.

7:9–10 *snake.* The Hebrew for this word is different from that used in 4:3 (see Ps 74:13, "monster," and note on 74:13–14). A related word (also translated "monster") is used in Eze 29:3 as a designation for Egypt and her king (see note on 4:3).

7:11 *wise men and ... magicians.* See note on Ge 41:8. According to tradition, two of the magicians who opposed Moses were named Jannes and Jambres (see 2Ti 3:8 and note; the first is also mentioned in the pre-Christian Dead Sea Scrolls). *the Egyptian magicians also did the same things by their secret arts.* Either through sleight of hand or by means of demonic power.

arts:[a] 12Each one threw down his staff
and it became a snake. But Aaron's staff
swallowed up their staffs. 13Yet Pharaoh's
heart[b] became hard and he would not listen[c] to them, just as the LORD had said.

The Plague of Blood

14Then the LORD said to Moses, "Pharaoh's heart is unyielding;[d] he refuses to
let the people go. 15Go to Pharaoh in the
morning as he goes out to the water.[e]
Wait on the bank of the Nile[f] to meet him,
and take in your hand the staff that was
changed into a snake. 16Then say to him,
'The LORD, the God of the Hebrews, has
sent me to say to you: Let my people go,
so that they may worship[g] me in the desert. But until now you have not listened.[h]
17This is what the LORD says: By this you
will know that I am the LORD:[i] With the
staff that is in my hand I will strike the
water of the Nile, and it will be changed
into blood.[j] 18The fish in the Nile will die,
and the river will stink;[k] the Egyptians will
not be able to drink its water.' "[l]

19The LORD said to Moses, "Tell Aaron,
'Take your staff[m] and stretch out your hand[n]
over the waters of Egypt—over the streams
and canals, over the ponds and all the res-
ervoirs'—and they will turn to blood.
Blood will be everywhere in Egypt, even in
the wooden buckets and stone jars."

20Moses and Aaron did just as the LORD
had commanded.[o] He raised his staff in the
presence of Pharaoh and his officials and
struck the water of the Nile,[p] and all the
water was changed into blood.[q] 21The fish
in the Nile died, and the river smelled so
bad that the Egyptians could not drink its
water. Blood was everywhere in Egypt.

22But the Egyptian magicians[r] did the
same things by their secret arts,[s] and
Pharaoh's heart[t] became hard; he would
not listen to Moses and Aaron, just as the
LORD had said. 23Instead, he turned and
went into his palace, and did not take even
this to heart. 24And all the Egyptians dug
along the Nile to get drinking water[u], because they could not drink the water of
the river.

The Plague of Frogs

25Seven days passed after the LORD struck
8 the Nile. 1Then the LORD said to Moses,
"Go to Pharaoh and say to him, 'This is
what the LORD says: Let my people go, so
that they may worship[v] me. 2If you refuse
to let them go, I will plague your whole
country with frogs.[w] 3The Nile will teem
with frogs. They will come up into your
palace and your bedroom and onto your
bed, into the houses of your officials and
on your people,[x] and into your ovens and
kneading troughs.[y] 4The frogs will go up
on you and your people and all your officials.' "

5Then the LORD said to Moses, "Tell Aaron, 'Stretch out your hand with your staff[z]
over the streams and canals and ponds,
and make frogs[a] come up on the land of
Egypt.' "

6So Aaron stretched out his hand over
the waters of Egypt, and the frogs[b] came
up and covered the land. 7But the magicians did the same things by their secret
arts;[c] they also made frogs come up on the
land of Egypt.

8Pharaoh summoned Moses and Aaron
and said, "Pray[d] to the LORD to take the
frogs away from me and my people, and I
will let your people go to offer sacrifices[e]
to the LORD."

7:11 [a] ver 22; Ex 8:7,18; S Mt 24:24 **7:13** [b] S Ex 4:21 [c] S ver 4 **7:14** [d] ver 22; Ex 8:15,32; 9:7; 10:1,20,27 **7:15** [e] Ex 8:20 [f] S Ge 41:1 **7:16** [g] S Ex 3:18 [h] S ver 4 **7:17** [i] S Ex 6:2; 14:25 [j] ver 19-21; Ex 4:9; Rev 11:6; 16:4 **7:18** [k] Isa 19:6 [l] ver 21,24; Ps 78:44 **7:19** [m] S Ex 4:2 [n] Ex 14:21; 2Ki 5:11 **7:20** [o] S ver 6 [p] Ex 17:5 [q] Ps 78:44; 105:29; 114:3; Hab 3:8 **7:22** [r] S Ge 41:8 [s] S ver 11; S Mt 24:24 [t] ver 13, S 14; Ex 8:19; Ps 105:28 **7:24** [u] S ver 18 **8:1** [v] Ex 3:12,18; 4:23; 5:1; 9:1 **8:2** [w] Ps 78:45; 105:30; Rev 16:13 **8:3** [x] Ex 10:6 [y] Ex 12:34 **8:5** [z] S Ex 4:2; 7:9-20; 9:23; 10:13,21-22; 14:27 [a] S Ex 4:17 **8:6** [b] Ps 78:45; 105:30 **8:7** [c] S Ex 7:11; S Mt 24:24 **8:8** [d] ver 28; Ex 9:28; 10:17; Nu 21:7; 1Sa 12:19; 1Ki 13:6; Jer 42:2; Ac 8:24 [e] ver 25; Ex 10:8,24; 12:31

7:12 *Aaron's staff swallowed up their staffs.* Demonstrating God's mastery over the pharaoh and the gods of Egypt.

7:13 *heart became hard.* A hardened heart refers to a stubborn refusal to take God and his word seriously (see also note on 4:21).

7:14—10:29 The first nine plagues can be divided into three groups of three plagues each (7:14—8:19; 8:20—9:12; 9:13—10:29) with the first plague in each group (the first, the fourth and the seventh) introduced by a warning delivered to the pharaoh in the morning as he went out to the Nile (see v. 15; 8:20 and note; 9:13).

7:17 *my.* Moses'. *the water of the Nile . . . will be changed into blood.* See Ps 78:44; 105:29. Some interpreters believe that the first nine plagues may have been a series of unprecedented intensifications of events that were part of the Egyptian experience, events that in their more usual form did not have anything like the catastrophic effects of the disasters God brought on Egypt in order to deliver the Israelites from Egyptian imperial bondage. If that was the case, the first plague may have resulted from an unparalleled quantity of red sediment being washed down from Ethiopia during the annual flooding of the Nile in late summer and early fall, causing the water of Egypt's lifeline to become as red as blood (see v. 24 and note; cf. the incident in 2Ki 3:22–23).

7:19 *your staff.* Aaron was acting on Moses' behalf (see v. 17). *in the wooden buckets and stone jars.* Lit. "in/on the wooden things and in/on the stone things." Some think that, since the Egyptians believed that their gods inhabited idols and images made of wood, clay and stone (see Dt 29:16–17), the plague may have been intended as a rebuke to their religion (see 9:3; 12:12 and notes).

7:20 *Nile.* Egypt's dependence on the life-sustaining waters of the Nile led to its deification as the god Hapi, for whom hymns of adoration were composed. See note on v. 19.

7:24 *dug along the Nile to get drinking water.* Filtered through sandy soil near the river bank, the polluted water would become safe for drinking.

7:25 *Seven days passed.* The plagues did not follow each other in rapid succession.

8:2 *I will plague your whole country with frogs.* The frog (or toad) was deified in the goddess Heqt, who assisted women in childbirth.

8:3 *come up.* The frogs abandoned the Nile and swarmed over the land, perhaps because an unusually high concentration of bacteria-laden algae had by now proved fatal to most of the fish, thus polluting the river.

9Moses said to Pharaoh, "I leave to you
the honor of setting the time[f] for me to
pray for you and your officials and your
people that you and your houses may be
rid of the frogs, except for those that remain in the Nile."
10"Tomorrow," Pharaoh said.
Moses replied, "It will be as you say, so
that you may know there is no one like
the LORD our God.[g] 11The frogs will leave
you and your houses, your officials and
your people; they will remain only in the
Nile."
12After Moses and Aaron left Pharaoh,
Moses cried out to the LORD about the
frogs he had brought on Pharaoh. 13And
the LORD did what Moses asked.[h] The
frogs died in the houses, in the courtyards
and in the fields. 14They were piled into
heaps, and the land reeked of them. 15But
when Pharaoh saw that there was relief,[i]
he hardened his heart[j] and would not listen to Moses and Aaron, just as the LORD
had said.

The Plague of Gnats

16Then the LORD said to Moses, "Tell Aaron, 'Stretch out your staff[k] and strike the
dust of the ground,' and throughout the
land of Egypt the dust will become gnats."
17They did this, and when Aaron stretched
out his hand with the staff and struck the
dust of the ground, gnats[l] came upon men
and animals. All the dust throughout the
land of Egypt became gnats. 18But when
the magicians[m] tried to produce gnats by
their secret arts,[n] they could not. And the
gnats were on men and animals.
19The magicians said to Pharaoh, "This
is the finger[o] of God." But Pharaoh's heart[p]
was hard and he would not listen,[q] just as
the LORD had said.

The Plague of Flies

20Then the LORD said to Moses, "Get up
early in the morning[r] and confront Pharaoh as he goes to the water and say to
him, 'This is what the LORD says: Let my
people go, so that they may worship[s] me.
21If you do not let my people go, I will send
swarms of flies on you and your officials,
on your people and into your houses. The
houses of the Egyptians will be full of flies,
and even the ground where they are.
22" 'But on that day I will deal differently
with the land of Goshen,[t] where my people live;[u] no swarms of flies will be there,
so that you will know[v] that I, the LORD, am
in this land. 23I will make a distinction[a] between my people and your people.[w] This
miraculous sign will occur tomorrow.' "
24And the LORD did this. Dense swarms
of flies poured into Pharaoh's palace
and into the houses of his officials, and
throughout Egypt the land was ruined by
the flies.[x]
25Then Pharaoh summoned[y] Moses and
Aaron and said, "Go, sacrifice to your God
here in the land."
26But Moses said, "That would not be
right. The sacrifices we offer the LORD our
God would be detestable to the Egyptians.[z]
And if we offer sacrifices that are detestable in their eyes, will they not stone us?
27We must take a three-day journey[a] into
the desert to offer sacrifices[b] to the LORD
our God, as he commands us."
28Pharaoh said, "I will let you go to offer sacrifices to the LORD your God in the
desert, but you must not go very far. Now
pray[c] for me."
29Moses answered, "As soon as I leave
you, I will pray to the LORD, and tomorrow the flies will leave Pharaoh and his
officials and his people. Only be sure that
Pharaoh does not act deceitfully[d] again by
not letting the people go to offer sacrifices
to the LORD."
30Then Moses left Pharaoh and prayed to
the LORD,[e] 31and the LORD did what Moses
asked: The flies left Pharaoh and his officials and his people; not a fly remained.
32But this time also Pharaoh hardened his
heart[f] and would not let the people go.

8:9 [f] Ex 9:5 **8:10** [g] Ex 9:14; 15:11; Dt 3:24; 4:35; 33:26; 2Sa 7:22; 1Ki 8:23; 1Ch 17:20; 2Ch 6:14; Ps 71:19; 86:8; 89:6; 113:5; Isa 40:18; 42:8; 46:9; Jer 10:6; 49:19; Mic 7:18 **8:13** [h] Jas 5:16-18 **8:15** [i] Ecc 8:11 [j] S Ex 7:14 **8:16** [k] S Ex 4:2 **8:17** [l] Ps 105:31 **8:18** [m] Ex 9:11; Da 5:8 [n] S Ex 7:11 **8:19** [o] Ex 7:5; 10:7; 12:33; 31:18; 1Sa 6:9; Ne 9:6; Ps 8:3; 33:6; Lk 11:20 [p] S Ex 7:22 [q] S Ex 7:4 **8:20** [r] Ex 7:15; 9:13

[s] S Ex 3:18 **8:22** [t] S Ge 45:10 [u] Ex 9:4,6,26; 10:23; 11:7; 12:13; 19:5; Dt 4:20; 7:6; 14:2; 26:18; 1Ki 8:36; Job 36:11; Ps 33:12; 135:4; Mal 3:17 [v] Ex 7:5; 9:29 **8:23** [w] Ex 9:4,6; 10:23; 11:7; 12:13,23,27 **8:24** [x] Ps 78:45; 105:31 **8:25** [y] ver 8; Ex 9:27; 10:16; 12:31 **8:26** [z] S Ge 43:32 **8:27** [a] S Ge 30:36 [b] S Ex 3:18 **8:28** [c] S ver 8; S Jer 37:3; Ac 8:24 **8:29** [d] ver 15; Ex 9:30; 10:11; Isa 26:10 **8:30** [e] ver 12; Ex 9:33; 10:18 **8:32** [f] S Ex 7:14

[a] *23* Septuagint and Vulgate; Hebrew *will put a deliverance*

8:13 *the LORD did what Moses asked.* For similar occurrences see v. 31; 1Sa 12:18; 1Ki 18:42–45; Am 7:1–6. *The frogs died.* Probably because they had been infected by bacteria in the Nile algae (see note on v. 3).
8:15 *hardened his heart.* See note on 7:13.
8:16 *dust will become gnats.* The word "dust" is perhaps a reference to the enormous number (see, e.g., Ge 13:16 and note) of the gnats, bred in the flooded fields of Egypt in late autumn.
8:19 *finger of God.* A concise and colorful figure of speech referring to God's miraculous power (see 31:18; Ps 8:3). Jesus drove out demons "by the finger of God" (Lk 11:20). Cf. the similar use of the phrase "hand of the LORD" in 9:3, "work of his hands" in Ps 19:1 and "arm of the LORD" in Isa 51:9 (see note there).
8:20 *as he goes to the water.* As he goes to the Nile River. Perhaps the pharaoh went there (1) to worship at a shrine or (2) to bathe, as the princess had done in 2:5 (see also 7:15).
8:21 *I will send swarms of flies.* They probably would have multiplied rapidly as the receding Nile left breeding places in its wake. Full-grown, such flies infest houses and stables and bite people and animals.
8:22 *I will deal differently.* See 33:16. God makes a "distinction" (v. 23) between Moses' people and the pharaoh's people in this plague as well as in the fifth (see 9:4,6), the seventh (see 9:26), the ninth (see 10:23) and the tenth (see 11:7)—and probably also the sixth and eighth (see 9:11; 10:6)—demonstrating that the Lord can preserve his own people while judging Egypt. *Goshen.* See Ge 45:10 and note.
8:23 *miraculous sign.* See 4:8 and note.
8:26 *detestable to the Egyptians.* See Ge 46:34; see also Ge 43:32 and note.
8:31 *the LORD did what Moses asked.* See note on v. 13.

The Plague on Livestock

9 Then the LORD said to Moses, "Go to
Pharaoh and say to him, 'This is what
the LORD, the God of the Hebrews, says:
"Let my people go, so that they may worship[g] me." 2If you refuse to let them go
and continue to hold them back, 3the
hand[h] of the LORD will bring a terrible
plague[i] on your livestock in the field—on
your horses and donkeys and camels and
on your cattle and sheep and goats. 4But
the LORD will make a distinction between
the livestock of Israel and that of Egypt,[j]
so that no animal belonging to the Israelites will die.'"

5The LORD set a time and said, "Tomorrow the LORD will do this in the land."
6And the next day the LORD did it: All
the livestock[k] of the Egyptians died,[l] but
not one animal belonging to the Israelites
died. 7Pharaoh sent men to investigate and
found that not even one of the animals of
the Israelites had died. Yet his heart[m] was
unyielding and he would not let the people go.[n]

The Plague of Boils

8Then the LORD said to Moses and Aaron, "Take handfuls of soot from a furnace
and have Moses toss it into the air in the
presence of Pharaoh. 9It will become fine
dust over the whole land of Egypt, and
festering boils[o] will break out on men and
animals throughout the land."

10So they took soot from a furnace and
stood before Pharaoh. Moses tossed it into
the air, and festering boils broke out on
men and animals. 11The magicians[p] could
not stand before Moses because of the
boils that were on them and on all the
Egyptians. 12But the LORD hardened Pharaoh's heart[q] and he would not listen[r] to
Moses and Aaron, just as the LORD had
said to Moses.

The Plague of Hail

13Then the LORD said to Moses, "Get up
early in the morning, confront Pharaoh
and say to him, 'This is what the LORD,
the God of the Hebrews, says: Let my people go, so that they may worship[s] me, 14or
this time I will send the full force of my
plagues against you and against your officials and your people, so you may know[t]
that there is no one like[u] me in all the
earth. 15For by now I could have stretched
out my hand and struck you and your people[v] with a plague that would have wiped
you off the earth. 16But I have raised you
up[a] for this very purpose,[w] that I might
show you my power[x] and that my name
might be proclaimed in all the earth. 17You
still set yourself against my people and
will not let them go. 18Therefore, at this
time tomorrow I will send the worst hailstorm[y] that has ever fallen on Egypt, from
the day it was founded till now.[z] 19Give an
order now to bring your livestock and everything you have in the field to a place of
shelter, because the hail will fall on every
man and animal that has not been brought
in and is still out in the field, and they
will die.'"

20Those officials of Pharaoh who feared[a]
the word of the LORD hurried to bring their
slaves and their livestock inside. 21But
those who ignored[b] the word of the LORD
left their slaves and livestock in the field.

22Then the LORD said to Moses, "Stretch
out your hand toward the sky so that hail
will fall all over Egypt—on men and animals and on everything growing in the
fields of Egypt." 23When Moses stretched

9:1 [g]S Ex 8:1 **9:3** [h]Ex 7:4; 1Sa 5:6; Job 13:21; Ps 32:4; 39:10; Ac 13:11 [i]Lev 26:25; Ps 78:50; Am 4:10 **9:4** [j]ver 26; S Ex 8:23 **9:6** [k]ver 19-21; Ex 11:5; 12:29 [l]Ps 78:48-50 **9:7** [m]S Ex 7:22 [n]Ex 7:14; 8:32 **9:9** [o]Lev 13:18, 19; Dt 28:27, 35; 2Ki 20:7; Job 2:7; Isa 38:21; Rev 16:2 **9:11** [p]S Ex 8:18 **9:12** [q]S Ex 4:21 [r]S Ex 7:4 **9:13** [s]S Ex 3:18 **9:14** [t]S Ex 8:10 [u]Ex 15:11; 1Sa 2:2; 2Sa 7:22; 1Ki 8:23; 1Ch 17:20; Ps 35:10; 71:19; 86:8; 89:6; Isa 46:9; Jer 10:6; Mic 7:18 **9:15** [v]Ex 3:20 **9:16** [w]Pr 16:4 [x]Ex 14:4, 17, 31; Ps 20:6; 25:11; 68:28; 71:18; 106:8; 109:21; Ro 9:17* **9:18** [y]ver 23; Jos 10:11; Ps 78:47-48; 105:32; 148:8; Isa 30:30; Eze 38:22; Hag 2:17 [z]ver 24; Ex 10:6 **9:20** [a]Pr 13:13 **9:21** [b]S Ge 19:14; Eze 33:4-5

[a] 16 Or *have spared you*

9:3 *hand of the LORD.* See note on 8:19. *terrible plague on your livestock.* The flies of the fourth plague (see note on 8:21) possibly carried the bacteria (see note on 8:13) that would now infect the animals, which had been brought into the fields again as the floodwaters subsided. The Egyptians worshiped many animals and animal-headed deities, including the bull-gods Apis and Mnevis, the cow-god Hathor and the ram-god Khnum. Thus Egyptian religion is again rebuked and ridiculed (see note on 7:19). *camels.* See note on Ge 12:16.
9:4 *distinction.* See note on 8:22.
9:5 *Tomorrow.* To give those Egyptians who had come to fear the God of Israel time to bring their livestock in from the fields and out of danger (see also v. 20)—mercy in the midst of judgment.
9:6 *All the livestock of the Egyptians died.* That is, all that were left out in the fields. Protected livestock remained alive (see vv. 19–21).
9:8 *Take ... soot ... toss it into the air.* Perhaps symbolizing either the widespread extent of the plague of boils or their black coloration. *furnace.* Possibly a kiln for firing bricks, the symbol of Israel's bondage (see 1:14; 5:7–19). The same word is used in Ge 19:28 as a simile for the destruction of Sodom and Gomorrah.
9:9 *boils.* Possibly skin anthrax (a variety of the plague that struck the livestock in vv. 1–7), a black, burning abscess that develops into a pustule. *men and animals.* The plague on the livestock now extended to other animals as well as to the people of Egypt.
9:11 *magicians could not stand.* The "boils of Egypt" (Dt 28:27) seriously affected the knees and legs (see Dt 28:35).
9:12 *the LORD hardened Pharaoh's heart.* See note on 4:21.
9:16 Paul quotes this verse as an outstanding illustration of the sovereignty of God (see Ro 9:17).
9:18 *I will send ... hailstorm.* The flooding of the Nile (the possible occasion of the first six plagues) came to an end late in the fall. The hailstorm is thus in the proper chronological position, taking place in January or February when the flax and barley were in flower but the wheat and spelt had not yet germinated (see vv. 31–32).
9:19–21 See note on v. 6.
9:19 An example of God's compassion. Even in judgment he allows for the protection of both human beings and animals (see also note on Jnh 4:11).

out his staff toward the sky, the LORD sent
thunder[c] and hail,[d] and lightning flashed
down to the ground. So the LORD rained
hail on the land of Egypt; 24hail fell and
lightning flashed back and forth. It was
the worst storm in all the land of Egypt
since it had become a nation.[e] 25Through-
out Egypt hail struck everything in the
fields—both men and animals; it beat
down everything growing in the fields and
stripped every tree.[f] 26The only place it did
not hail was the land of Goshen,[g] where
the Israelites were.[h]
27Then Pharaoh summoned Moses and
Aaron. "This time I have sinned,"[i] he said
to them. "The LORD is in the right,[j] and I
and my people are in the wrong. 28Pray[k] to
the LORD, for we have had enough thunder
and hail. I will let you go;[l] you don't have
to stay any longer."
29Moses replied, "When I have gone out
of the city, I will spread out my hands[m] in
prayer to the LORD. The thunder will stop
and there will be no more hail, so you may
know that the earth[n] is the LORD's. 30But I
know that you and your officials still do
not fear[o] the LORD God."
31(The flax and barley[p] were destroyed,
since the barley had headed and the flax
was in bloom. 32The wheat and spelt,[q]
however, were not destroyed, because
they ripen later.)
33Then Moses left Pharaoh and went out
of the city. He spread out his hands toward
the LORD; the thunder and hail stopped,
and the rain no longer poured down on
the land. 34When Pharaoh saw that the
rain and hail and thunder had stopped,
he sinned again: He and his officials hardened their hearts. 35So Pharaoh's heart[r]
was hard and he would not let the Israelites go, just as the LORD had said through
Moses.

The Plague of Locusts

10 Then the LORD said to Moses, "Go
to Pharaoh, for I have hardened
his heart[s] and the hearts of his officials
so that I may perform these mi
signs[t] of mine among them 2that yo
tell your children[u] and grandchildren
I dealt harshly[v] with the Egyptians a
how I performed my signs among them,
and that you may know that I am the
LORD."[w]
3So Moses and Aaron went to Pharaoh
and said to him, "This is what the LORD,
the God of the Hebrews, says: 'How long
will you refuse to humble[x] yourself before
me? Let my people go, so that they may
worship me. 4If you refuse[y] to let them
go, I will bring locusts[z] into your country tomorrow. 5They will cover the face
of the ground so that it cannot be seen.
They will devour what little you have left[a]
after the hail, including every tree that
is growing in your fields.[b] 6They will fill
your houses[c] and those of all your officials and all the Egyptians—something
neither your fathers nor your forefathers
have ever seen from the day they settled
in this land till now.' "[d] Then Moses turned
and left Pharaoh.
7Pharaoh's officials said to him, "How
long will this man be a snare[e] to us? Let
the people go, so that they may worship
the LORD their God. Do you not yet realize
that Egypt is ruined?"[f]
8Then Moses and Aaron were brought
back to Pharaoh. "Go, worship[g] the LORD
your God," he said. "But just who will be
going?"
9Moses answered, "We will go with our
young and old, with our sons and daughters, and with our flocks and herds, because we are to celebrate a festival[h] to the
LORD."
10Pharaoh said, "The LORD be with
you—if I let you go, along with your
women and children! Clearly you are bent
on evil.[a] 11No! Have only the men go; and

9:23 [c]Ex 20:18; 1Sa 7:10; 12:17; Ps 18:13; 29:3; 68:33; 77:17; 104:7 [d]S ver 18; Rev 8:7; 16:21 **9:24** [e]S ver 18 **9:25** [f]Ps 105:32-33; Eze 13:13 **9:26** [g]S ver 4; Isa 32:18-20 [h]Ex 10:23; 11:7; 12:13; Am 4:7 **9:27** [i]ver 34; Ex 10:16; Nu 14:40; Dt 1:41; Jos 7:11; Jdg 10:10; 1Sa 15:24; 24:17; 26:21 [j]Ps 11:7; 116:5; 119:137; 129:4; 145:17; Jer 12:1; La 1:18 **9:28** [k]Ex 8:8; Ac 8:24 [l]S Ex 8:8 **9:29** [m]ver 33; 1Ki 8:22,38; Job 11:13; Ps 77:2; 88:9; 143:6; Isa 1:15 [n]Ex 19:5; Job 41:11; Ps 24:1; 50:12; 1Co 10:26 **9:30** [o]S Ex 8:29 **9:31** [p]Dt 8:8; Ru 1:22; 2:23; 2Sa 14:30; 17:28; Isa 28:25; Eze 4:9; Joel 1:11 **9:32** [q]Isa 28:25 **9:35** [r]S Ex 4:21 **10:1** [s]S Ex 4:21 [t]S Ex 3:19; S 7:3; Jos 24:17; Ne 9:10; Ps 74:9; 105:26-36 **10:2** [u]Ex 12:26-27; 13:8,14; Dt 4:9; 6:20; 32:7; Jos 4:6; Ps 44:1; 71:18; 78:4,5; Joel 1:3 [v]1Sa 6:6 [w]S Ex 6:2 **10:3** [x]1Ki 21:29; 2Ki 22:19; 2Ch 7:14; 12:7; 33:23; 34:27; Job 42:6; Isa 58:3; Da 5:22; Jas 4:10; 1Pe 5:6 **10:4** [y]Ex 8:2; 9:2 [z]Dt 28:38; Ps 105:34; Pr 30:27; Joel 1:4; Rev 9:3

[a] 10 Or *Be careful, trouble is in store for you!*

10:5 [a]Ex 9:32; Joel 1:4 [b]ver 15 **10:6** [c]Joel 2:9 [d]S Ex 9:18 **10:7** [e]Ex 23:33; 34:12; Dt 7:16; 12:30; 20:18; Jos 23:13; Jdg 2:3; 8:27; 16:5; 1Sa 18:21; Ps 106:36; Ecc 7:26 [f]S Ge 20:3; S Ex 8:19 **10:8** [g]S Ex 8:8 **10:9** [h]S Ex 3:18

9:27 *This time I have sinned.* For the first time the pharaoh acknowledges his sin and perceives its devastating results.

9:29 *spread out my hands.* See 1Ki 8:22,38,54; 2Ch 6:12–13,29; Ezr 9:5; Ps 44:20; 88:9; 143:6; Isa 1:15; 1Ti 2:8. Statues of men praying with hands upraised have been found by archaeologists at several ancient sites in the Middle East.

9:30 *LORD God.* See note on Ge 2:4.

9:31–32 See note on v. 18.

9:32 *spelt.* Grains of spelt, a member of the grass family allied to wheat, have been found in ancient Egyptian tombs. Although inferior to wheat, it grows well in poorer and drier soil.

10:2 *tell your children.* The memory of God's redemptive acts is to be kept alive by reciting them to our descendants (see 12:26–27; 13:8,14–15; Dt 4:9; Ps 77:11–20; 78:4–6,43–53; 105:26–38 and note on 105:28–36; 106:7–12; 114:1–3; 135:8–9; 136:10–15).

10:4 *I will bring locusts.* In March or April the prevailing east winds (see v. 13) would sometimes bring in hordes of migratory locusts. Fifty million of them could occupy a square kilometer and devour as much as 100,000 tons of vegetation in a single night. Such locust plagues were greatly feared in ancient times and became a powerful symbol of divine judgment (see Joel 1:4–7; 2:1–11; Am 7:1–3).

10:7 *How long . . . ?* The pharaoh's officials ironically echo the phrase used by Moses in v. 3. *Egypt is ruined.* Human rebellion and disobedience always bring death and destruction in their wake.

10:10 *The LORD be with you.* This may be irony (see NIV text note on "Clearly you are bent on evil").

10:11 *Have only the men go.* From the pharaoh's standpoint, (1) the women and children should remain behind as hostages, and (2) it was typically only the men who participated fully in worship.

since that's what you
or." Then Moses and
ut of Pharaoh's pres-

d to Moses, "Stretch
Egypt so that locusts
land and devour ev-
...ything growing in the fields, everything
left by the hail."
[13]So Moses stretched out his staff[j] over
Egypt, and the LORD made an east wind
blow across the land all that day and
all that night. By morning the wind had
brought the locusts;[k] [14]they invaded all
Egypt and settled down in every area of
the country in great numbers. Never before had there been such a plague of locusts,[l] nor will there ever be again. [15]They
covered all the ground until it was black.
They devoured[m] all that was left after the
hail—everything growing in the fields and
the fruit on the trees. Nothing green remained on tree or plant in all the land of
Egypt.
[16]Pharaoh quickly summoned[n] Moses and Aaron and said, "I have sinned[o]
against the LORD your God and against
you. [17]Now forgive[p] my sin once more and
pray[q] to the LORD your God to take this
deadly plague away from me."
[18]Moses then left Pharaoh and prayed
to the LORD.[r] [19]And the LORD changed the
wind to a very strong west wind, which
caught up the locusts and carried them
into the Red Sea.[a] Not a locust was left
anywhere in Egypt. [20]But the LORD hardened Pharaoh's heart,[s] and he would not
let the Israelites go.

The Plague of Darkness

[21]Then the LORD said to Moses, "Stretch
out your hand toward the sky so that darkness[t] will spread over Egypt—darkness
that can be felt." [22]So Moses stretched out
his hand toward the sky, and total darkness[u] covered all Egypt for three days.
[23]No one could see anyone else or leave
his place for three days. Yet all the Israelites had light in the places where they
lived.[v]
[24]Then Pharaoh summoned Moses and
said, "Go,[w] worship the LORD. Even your
women and children[x] may go with you;
only leave your flocks and herds behind."[y]
[25]But Moses said, "You must allow us to
have sacrifices and burnt offerings[z] to present to the LORD our God. [26]Our livestock
too must go with us; not a hoof is to be
left behind. We have to use some of them
in worshiping the LORD our God, and until
we get there we will not know what we
are to use to worship the LORD."
[27]But the LORD hardened Pharaoh's
heart,[a] and he was not willing to let them
go. [28]Pharaoh said to Moses, "Get out of
my sight! Make sure you do not appear
before me again! The day you see my face
you will die."
[29]"Just as you say," Moses replied, "I
will never appear[b] before you again."

The Plague on the Firstborn

11 Now the LORD had said to Moses, "I
will bring one more plague on Pharaoh and on Egypt. After that, he will let
you go[c] from here, and when he does, he
will drive you out completely.[d] [2]Tell the
people that men and women alike are to
ask their neighbors for articles of silver
and gold."[e] [3](The LORD made the Egyptians favorably disposed[f] toward the people, and Moses himself was highly regarded[g] in Egypt by Pharaoh's officials and by
the people.)
[4]So Moses said, "This is what the LORD
says: 'About midnight[h] I will go throughout Egypt.[i] [5]Every firstborn[j] son in Egypt
will die, from the firstborn son of Pharaoh,
who sits on the throne, to the firstborn son
of the slave girl, who is at her hand mill,[k]
and all the firstborn of the cattle as well.
[6]There will be loud wailing[l] throughout
Egypt—worse than there has ever been
or ever will be again. [7]But among the Israelites not a dog will bark at any man
or animal.' Then you will know that the
LORD makes a distinction[m] between Egypt

10:12 [i] Ex 7:19
10:13 [j] ver 21-22; Ex 4:17; 8:5,17; 9:23; 14:15-16,26-27; 17:5; Nu 20:8 [k] ver 4; 1Ki 8:37; Ps 78:46; 105:34; Am 4:9; Na 3:16
10:14 [l] Dt 28:38; Ps 78:46; Isa 33:4; Joel 1:4; 2:1-11,25; Am 4:9
10:15 [m] Dt 28:38; Ps 105:34-35; Joel 1:4; Am 7:2; Mal 3:11
10:16 [n] S Ex 8:25 [o] S Ex 9:27
10:17 [p] 1Sa 15:25 [q] S Ex 8:8
10:18 [r] S Ex 8:30
10:20 [s] S Ex 4:21
10:21 [t] Dt 28:29
10:22 [u] Ps 105:28; Isa 13:10; 45:7; 50:3; Rev 16:10
10:23 [v] S Ex 8:22; Am 4:7
10:24 [w] S Ex 8:8 [x] ver 8-10 [y] S Ge 45:10
10:25 [z] S Ge 8:20; S Ex 18:12
10:27 [a] S Ex 4:21
10:29 [b] Ex 11:8; Heb 11:27
11:1 [c] S Ex 3:20 [d] S Ex 6:1
11:2 [e] S Ex 3:21,22
11:3 [f] S Ge 39:21 [g] Dt 34:11; 2Sa 7:9; 8:13; 22:44; 23:1; Est 9:4; Ps 89:27
11:4 [h] Ex 12:29; Job 34:20 [i] Ex 12:23; Ps 81:5
11:5 [j] S Ex 4:23 [k] Isa 47:2
11:6 [l] Ex 12:30; Pr 21:13; Am 5:17
11:7 [m] S Ex 8:22

[a] *19* Hebrew *Yam Suph*; that is, Sea of Reeds

10:13 *east wind.* See note on v. 4.
10:19 *the LORD changed the wind.* He used the forces of his own creation to carry out his historical purpose and sovereign will (see v. 4; 14:21; Ps 104:4 and notes; cf. Mk 4:35–41 and notes). *Red Sea.* See NIV text note.
10:21 *darkness will spread over Egypt.* Like the third and sixth plagues, this ninth plague was unannounced to the pharaoh. It was possibly caused by the arrival of an unusually severe khamsin, the blinding sandstorm that blows in from the desert each year in the early spring. The darkness was an insult to the sun-god Ra (or Re), one of the chief deities of Egypt.
10:28 The pharaoh declares that he will never again grant Moses an audience. *The day you see my face.* During a plague of darkness, these words are somewhat ironic.
11:1 *and when he does.* The Hebrew for this phrase can also be read "as one sends away [a bride]"—i.e., laden with gifts (see Ge 24:53 and note).
11:2–3 See 3:21–22; 12:35–36.
11:4 *Moses said.* Continuing the speech of 10:29.
11:5 *Every firstborn son in Egypt will die.* See Ps 78:51; 105:36; 135:8; 136:10. This is the ultimate disaster, since all the plans and dreams of a father were bound up in his firstborn son, who received a double share of the family estate when the father died (see Dt 21:17 and note). Moreover, judgment on the firstborn represented judgment on the entire community. *slave girl, who is at her hand mill.* The lowliest of occupations (see Isa 47:2 and note).
11:7 *distinction.* See note on 8:22.

and Israel. 8All these officials of yours will
come to me, bowing down before me and
saying, 'Go,[n] you and all the people who
follow you!' After that I will leave."[o] Then
Moses, hot with anger, left Pharaoh.
9The LORD had said to Moses, "Pharaoh
will refuse to listen[p] to you—so that my
wonders[q] may be multiplied in Egypt."
10Moses and Aaron performed all these
wonders before Pharaoh, but the LORD
hardened Pharaoh's heart,[r] and he would
not let the Israelites go out of his country.

The Passover

12:14-20pp — Lev 23:4-8; Nu 28:16-25; Dt 16:1-8

12 The LORD said to Moses and Aaron
in Egypt, 2"This month is to be for
you the first month,[s] the first month of
your year. 3Tell the whole community of
Israel that on the tenth day of this month
each man is to take a lamb[a][t] for his family, one for each household.[u] 4If any household is too small for a whole lamb, they
must share one with their nearest neighbor, having taken into account the number
of people there are. You are to determine
the amount of lamb needed in accordance
with what each person will eat. 5The animals you choose must be year-old males
without defect,[v] and you may take them
from the sheep or the goats. 6Take care
of them until the fourteenth day of the
month,[w] when all the people of the community of Israel must slaughter them at
twilight.[x] 7Then they are to take some of
the blood[y] and put it on the sides and tops
of the doorframes of the houses where
they eat the lambs. 8That same night[z] they
are to eat the meat roasted[a] over the fire,
along with bitter herbs,[b] and bread made
without yeast.[c] 9Do not eat the meat raw
or cooked in water, but roast it over the
fire—head, legs and inner parts.[d] 10Do
not leave any of it till morning;[e] if some is
left till morning, you must burn it. 11This
is how you are to eat it: with your cloak
tucked into your belt, your sandals on
your feet and your staff in your hand. Eat
it in haste;[f] it is the LORD's Passover.[g]
12"On that same night I will pass
through[h] Egypt and strike down[i] every
firstborn[j]—both men and animals—and
I will bring judgment on all the gods[k] of
Egypt. I am the LORD.[l] 13The blood will be
a sign for you on the houses where you
are; and when I see the blood, I will pass
over[m] you. No destructive plague will
touch you when I strike Egypt.[n]
14"This is a day you are to commemorate;[o] for the generations to come you shall
celebrate it as a festival to the LORD—a lasting ordinance.[p] 15For seven days you are to

[a] 3 The Hebrew word can mean *lamb* or *kid*; also in verse 4.

11:8 [n]Ex 12:31-33 [o]Heb 11:27 **11:9** [p]S Ex 7:4 [q]S Ex 3:20 **11:10** [r]S Ex 4:21; Ro 2:5 **12:2** [s]ver 18; Ex 13:4; 23:15; 34:18; 40:2; Dt 16:1 **12:3** [t]Mk 14:12; 1Co 5:7 [u]ver 21 **12:5** [v]Ex 29:1; Lev 1:3; 3:1; 4:3; 22:18-21; 23:12; Nu 6:14; 15:8; 28:3; Dt 15:21; 17:1; Heb 9:14; 1Pe 1:19 **12:6** [w]ver 19; Lev 23:5; Nu 9:1-3,5,11; Jos 5:10; 2Ch 30:2 [x]Ex 16:12; Dt 16:4,6 **12:7** [y]ver 13,23; Eze 9:6 **12:8** [z]ver 10; Ex 16:19; 23:18; 34:25; Lev 7:15; Nu 9:12 [a]Dt 16:7; 2Ch 35:13 [b]Nu 9:11 [c]ver 19-20; Ex 13:3; Dt 16:3-4; 1Co 5:8 **12:9** [d]Ex 29:13,17,22; Lev 3:3 **12:10** [e]S ver 8; Ex 13:7; 29:34; Lev 22:30; Dt 16:4 **12:11** [f]ver 33; Dt 16:3; Isa 48:20; 52:12 [g]ver 13,21,27,43; Lev 23:5; Nu 9:2,4; 28:16; Dt 16:1; Jos 5:10; 2Ki 23:21,23; 2Ch 30:1; Ezr 6:19; Isa 31:5; Eze 45:21 **12:12** [h]Am 5:17 [i]Isa 10:33; 31:8; 37:36 [j]ver 29; S Ex 4:23; 13:15 [k]Ex 15:11; 18:11; Nu 33:4; 2Ch 2:5; Ps 95:3; 97:9; 135:5; Isa 19:1; Jer 43:12; 44:8 [l]S Ex 6:2 **12:13** [m]S ver 11,23; Heb 11:28 [n]S Ex 8:23 **12:14** [o]Ex 13:9; 23:14; 32:5 [p]ver 17,24; Ex 13:5,10; 27:21; Lev 3:17; 10:9; 16:29; 17:7; 23:14; 24:3; Nu 18:23

11:8 *Moses, hot with anger.* Moses' announcement of the death of the pharaoh's firstborn son is the Lord's response to the death threat to his servant Moses (10:28).

12:2 *This month is ... the first month.* The inauguration of the religious calendar in Israel (see chart, p. 104). In the ancient Near East, new year festivals normally coincided with the new season of life in nature. The designation of this month as Israel's religious New Year reminded Israel that its life as the people of God was grounded in God's redemptive act in the exodus. The Canaanite name for this month was Abib (see 13:4; 23:15; 34:18; Dt 16:1), which means "young head of grain." Later the Babylonian name Nisan was used (see Ne 2:1; Est 3:7). Israel's agricultural calendar began in the fall (see note on 23:16), and during the monarchy it dominated the nation's civil calendar. Both calendars (civil and religious) existed side by side until after the exile. Judaism today uses only the calendar that begins in the fall.

12:3 *community of Israel.* The Israelites gathered in assembly.

12:5 *animals ... without defect.* See Lev 22:18–25. Similarly, Jesus was like "a lamb without blemish or defect" (1Pe 1:19; see note there).

12:6 *at twilight.* Lit. "between the two evenings," an idiom meaning either (1) between the decline of the sun and sunset, or (2) between sunset and nightfall—which has given rise to disputes about when the Sabbath and other holy days begin.

12:7 *blood.* Symbolizes a sacrifice offered as a substitute, one life laid down for another (see Ge 9:4–6; 22:13; Lev 17:11 and notes). Thus Israel escapes the judgment about to fall on Egypt only through the mediation of a sacrifice (see Heb 9:22; 1Jn 1:7).

12:8 *bitter herbs.* Endive, chicory and other bitter-tasting plants are indigenous to Egypt. Eating them would recall the bitter years of servitude there (see 1:14 and note). *bread made without yeast.* Reflecting the haste with which the people left Egypt (see vv. 11,39; Dt 16:3; see also note on Ge 19:3).

12:9 *roast it ... head, legs and inner parts.* The method wandering shepherds used to cook meat.

12:11 *Passover.* Explained in vv. 13,23,27 to mean that the Lord would "pass over" and not destroy the occupants of houses that were under the sign of the blood.

12:12 *judgment on all the gods of Egypt.* See note on 15:11. Some had already been judged (see notes on 7:19; 8:2; 9:3; 10:21), and now all would be: (1) They would be shown to be powerless to deliver from the impending slaughter, and (2) many animals sacred to the gods would be killed.

12:13 *sign.* Just as the plagues were miraculous signs of judgment (see note on 7:17) on the pharaoh and his people (see 4:8 and note; 8:23), so the Lord's "passing over" the Israelites who placed themselves under the sign of blood from the Passover lamb was a pledge of God's mercy.

12:14 *celebrate it as ... a lasting ordinance.* Frequent references to Passover observance occur in the rest of Scripture (see Nu 9:1–5; Jos 5:10 and note; 2Ki 23:21–23; 2Ch 30:1–27; 35:1–19; Ezr 6:19–22; Lk 2:41–43 and note on 2:41; Jn 2:13,23 and note on 2:13; 6:4; 11:55—12:1). The ordinance is still kept by practicing Jews today.

12:15 *remove the yeast from your houses.* Yeast later was often used as a symbol of sin, such as "hypocrisy" (Lk 12:1; cf. Mk 8:15 and note) or "malice and wickedness" (1Co 5:8; see note there). Before celebrating Passover, observant Jews

Hebrew Calendar and Selected Events

NUMBER OF MONTH		HEBREW NAME	MODERN EQUIVALENT	BIBLICAL REFERENCES	AGRICULTURE	FEASTS**
1 Sacred sequence begins	7	**Abib; Nisan**	March–April	Ex 12:2; 13:4; 23:15; 34:18; Dt 16:1; Ne 2:1; Est 3:7	Spring (later) rains; barley and flax harvest begins	Passover; Unleavened Bread; Firstfruits
2	8	**Ziv (Iyyar)***	April–May	1Ki 6:1,37	Barley harvest; dry season begins	
3	9	**Sivan**	May–June	Est 8:9	Wheat harvest	Pentecost (Weeks)
4	10	**(Tammuz)***	June–July		Tending vines	
5	11	**(Ab)***	July–August		Ripening of grapes, figs and olives	
6	12	**Elul**	August–September	Ne 6:15	Processing grapes, figs and olives	
7	1 Civil sequence	**Ethanim (Tishri)***	September–October	1Ki 8:2	Autumn (early) rains begin; plowing	Trumpets; Day of Atonement; Tabernacles (Booths)
8	2	**Bul (Marcheshvan)***	October–November	1Ki 6:38	Sowing of wheat and barley	
9	3	**Kislev**	November–December	Ne 1:1; Zec 7:1	Winter rains begin (snow in some areas)	Hanukkah ("Dedication")
10	4	**Tebeth**	December–January	Est 2:16		
11	5	**Shebat**	January–February	Zec 1:7		
12	6	**Adar**	February–March	Ezr 6:15; Est 3:7,13; 8:12; 9:1,15,17,19,21	Almond trees bloom; citrus fruit harvest	Purim
		(Adar Sheni)* — Second Adar	This intercalary month was added about every three years so the lunar calendar would correspond to the solar year.			

*Names of months in parentheses are not in the Bible. **For more information on the feasts see chart, pp. 178–179.

eat bread made without yeast.[q] On the first
day remove the yeast from your houses, for
whoever eats anything with yeast in it from
the first day through the seventh must be
cut off[r] from Israel. 16On the first day hold
a sacred assembly, and another one on the
seventh day. Do no work[s] at all on these
days, except to prepare food for everyone
to eat—that is all you may do.
17“Celebrate the Feast of Unleavened
Bread,[t] because it was on this very day
that I brought your divisions out of Egypt.[u]
Celebrate this day as a lasting ordinance
for the generations to come.[v] 18In the first
month[w] you are to eat bread made without
yeast, from the evening of the fourteenth
day until the evening of the twenty-first
day. 19For seven days no yeast is to be
found in your houses. And whoever eats
anything with yeast in it must be cut off[x]
from the community of Israel, whether he
is an alien[y] or native-born. 20Eat nothing
made with yeast. Wherever you live,[z] you
must eat unleavened bread.”[a]
21Then Moses summoned all the elders
of Israel and said to them, “Go at once
and select the animals for your families
and slaughter the Passover[b] lamb. 22Take
a bunch of hyssop,[c] dip it into the blood
in the basin and put some of the blood[d]
on the top and on both sides of the doorframe. Not one of you shall go out the
door of his house until morning. 23When
the LORD goes through the land to strike[e]
down the Egyptians, he will see the blood[f]
on the top and sides of the doorframe and
will pass over[g] that doorway, and he will
not permit the destroyer[h] to enter your
houses and strike you down.
24“Obey these instructions as a lasting
ordinance[i] for you and your descendants.
25When you enter the land[j] that the LORD
will give you as he promised, observe this
ceremony. 26And when your children[k] ask
you, ‘What does this ceremony mean to
you?’ 27then tell them, ‘It is the Passover[l]
sacrifice to the LORD, who passed over
the houses of the Israelites in Egypt and
spared our homes when he struck down
the Egyptians.’ ”[m] Then the people bowed
down and worshiped.[n] 28The Israelites did
just what the LORD commanded[o] Moses
and Aaron.
29At midnight[p] the LORD[q] struck down
all the firstborn[r] in Egypt, from the firstborn of Pharaoh, who sat on the throne,
to the firstborn of the prisoner, who was
in the dungeon, and the firstborn of all the
livestock[s] as well. 30Pharaoh and all his officials and all the Egyptians got up during
the night, and there was loud wailing[t] in
Egypt, for there was not a house without
someone dead.

The Exodus

31During the night Pharaoh summoned
Moses and Aaron and said, “Up! Leave my
people, you and the Israelites! Go, worship[u] the LORD as you have requested.
32Take your flocks and herds,[v] as you have
said, and go. And also bless[w] me.”
33The Egyptians urged the people to
hurry[x] and leave[y] the country. “For otherwise,” they said, “we will all die!”[z] 34So
the people took their dough before the
yeast was added, and carried it on their
shoulders in kneading troughs[a] wrapped
in clothing. 35The Israelites did as Moses
instructed and asked the Egyptians for articles of silver and gold[b] and for clothing.[c]
36The LORD had made the Egyptians favorably disposed[d] toward the people, and
they gave them what they asked for; so
they plundered[e] the Egyptians.
37The Israelites journeyed from Rameses[f]

12:15 [q] Ex 13:6-7; 23:15; 34:18; Lev 23:6; Nu 28:17; Dt 16:3; 1Co 5:7 [r] S Ge 17:14 **12:16** [s] Nu 29:35 **12:17** [t] Ex 23:15; 34:18; Dt 16:16; 2Ch 8:13; 30:21; Ezr 6:22; Mt 26:17; Lk 22:1; Ac 12:3 [u] ver 41; S Ex 6:6,26; 13:3; Lev 19:36 [v] Lev 3:17 **12:18** [w] S ver 2 **12:19** [x] S Ge 17:14 [y] Nu 9:14; 15:14; 35:15; Dt 1:16; Jos 8:33 **12:20** [z] Lev 3:17; Nu 35:29; Eze 6:6 [a] Ex 13:6 **12:21** [b] S ver 11; Mk 14:12-16 **12:22** [c] Lev 14:4,6; Nu 19:18; Ps 51:7 [d] Heb 11:28 **12:23** [e] Isa 19:22 [f] S ver 7; Rev 7:3 [g] S ver 13 [h] S Ge 16:7; Isa 37:36; Jer 6:26; 48:8; 1Co 10:10; Heb 11:28 **12:24** [i] S ver 14 **12:25** [j] S Ge 15:14; Ex 3:17 **12:26** [k] Ex 10:2 **12:27** [l] S ver 11 [m] S Ex 8:23 [n] S Ge 24:26 **12:28** [o] ver 50 **12:29** [p] S Ex 11:4 [q] S Ge 19:13 [r] S Ex 4:23 [s] S Ex 9:6 **12:30** [t] S Ex 11:6 **12:31** [u] S Ex 8:8 **12:32** [v] Ex 10:9,26 [w] Ge 27:34 **12:33** [x] S ver 11 [y] S Ex 6:1; 1Sa 6:6 [z] S Ge 20:3; S Ex 8:19 **12:34** [a] Ex 8:3 **12:35** [b] S Ex 3:22 [c] S Ge 24:53 **12:36** [d] S Ge 39:21 [e] S Ex 3:22 **12:37** [f] S Ge 47:11

today conduct a systematic (often symbolic) search of their houses to remove every crumb of leavened bread that might be there (see v. 19). *cut off from Israel.* Removed from the covenant people by execution (see, e.g., 31:14; Lev 20:2–3) or banishment. See also Ge 17:14 and note.

12:17 *Feast of Unleavened Bread.* Began with the Passover meal and continued for seven days (see vv. 18–19; see also Mk 14:12 and note). *divisions.* See note on 6:26.

12:21 *Passover lamb.* Jesus is "our Passover lamb" (1Co 5:7; see note there), sacrificed "once for all" (Heb 9:12; see note there) for us.

12:22 *hyssop.* Here probably refers to an aromatic plant (*Origanum maru*) of the mint family with a straight stalk (see Jn 19:29) and white flowers. The hairy surface of its leaves and branches held liquids well and made it suitable as a sprinkling device for use in purification rituals (see Lev 14:4,6,49,51–52; Nu 19:6,18; Heb 9:19; see also Ps 51:7). *dip it into the blood.* Today at Passover meals a sprig of parsley or other plant is dipped in salt water to symbolize the lowly diet and tears of the Israelites during their time of slavery.

12:23 *pass over.* See note on v. 11. *the destroyer.* In Ps 78:49 the agent of God's wrath against the Egyptians is described as "a band of destroying angels." God often used angels to bring destructive plagues (see 2Sa 24:15–16 and note on 24:16; 2Ki 19:35; see also 1Co 10:10 and note).

12:26 *your children ask you, 'What does this ceremony mean to you?'* See 13:14. The Passover was to be observed as a memorial feast commemorating Israel's redemption and appropriating it anew. As observed today, it includes the asking of similar questions by the youngest child present.

12:27 *Passover sacrifice.* See note on v. 21. *passed over.* See note on v. 11.

12:29 *prisoner, who was in the dungeon.* The lowliest of situations (see note on 11:5; Jdg 16:21 and note).

12:31 *Pharaoh summoned Moses.* Though he had sworn never again to grant Moses an audience (see 10:28 and note), the pharaoh now humbles himself by summoning Moses and Aaron into his presence.

12:35–36 See 3:21–22; 11:2–3.

12:36 *plundered the Egyptians.* See note on 3:22.

12:37 *journeyed from Rameses.* See 1:11; see also note on Ge 47:11. The Israelite departure took place "the day after

to Succoth.[g] There were about six hundred
thousand men[h] on foot, besides women
and children. 38 Many other people[i] went
up with them, as well as large droves of
livestock, both flocks and herds. 39 With
the dough they had brought from Egypt,
they baked cakes of unleavened bread.
The dough was without yeast because they
had been driven out[j] of Egypt and did not
have time to prepare food for themselves.
40 Now the length of time the Israelite
people lived in Egypt[a] was 430 years.[k]
41 At the end of the 430 years, to the very
day, all the LORD's divisions[l] left Egypt.[m]
42 Because the LORD kept vigil that night to
bring them out of Egypt, on this night all
the Israelites are to keep vigil to honor the
LORD for the generations to come.[n]

Passover Restrictions

43 The LORD said to Moses and Aaron,
"These are the regulations for the Passover:[o]

"No foreigner[p] is to eat of it. 44 Any slave
you have bought may eat of it after you
have circumcised[q] him, 45 but a temporary
resident and a hired worker[r] may not eat
of it.

46 "It must be eaten inside one house;
take none of the meat outside the house.
Do not break any of the bones.[s] 47 The
whole community of Israel must celebrate it.

48 "An alien living among you who wants
to celebrate the LORD's Passover must have
all the males in his household circumcised;
then he may take part like one born in the
land.[t] No uncircumcised[u] male may eat of
it. 49 The same law applies to the native-
born and to the alien[v] living among you."

50 All the Israelites did just what the LORD
had commanded[w] Moses and Aaron. 51 And
on that very day the LORD brought the Israelites out of Egypt[x] by their divisions.[y]

12:37 [g]Ex 13:20; Nu 33:3-5 [h]Ge 12:2; Ex 38:26; Nu 1:46; 2:32; 11:13,21; 26:51 **12:38** [i]Nu 11:4; Jos 8:35 **12:39** [j]Ex 3:20; 11:1 **12:40** [k]Ge 15:13; Ac 7:6; Gal 3:17 **12:41** [l]S Ex 6:26 [m]S Ex 3:10 **12:42** [n]Ex 13:10; Lev 3:17; Nu 9:3; Dt 16:1,6 **12:43** [o]S ver 11 [p]ver 48; Nu 9:14; 15:14; 2Ch 6:32-33; Isa 14:1; 56:3,6; 60:10 **12:44** [q]S Ge 17:12-13 **12:45** [r]Lev 22:10 **12:46** [s]Nu 9:12; Ps 22:14; 34:20; 51:8; Pr 17:22; Jn 19:36* **12:48** [t]ver 49; Lev 19:18,34; 24:22; Nu 9:14; 10:32 [u]Eze 44:7 **12:49** [v]Lev 24:22; Nu 15:15-16,29; Dt 1:16 **12:50** [w]ver 28 **12:51** [x]S Ex 3:10; S 6:6 [y]S Ex 6:26

13:2 [z]ver 12,13,15; Ex 22:29; 34:20; Lev 27:26; Nu 3:13; 8:17; 18:15; Dt 15:19; Ne 10:36; Lk 2:23* **13:3** [a]ver 14; Ex 7:4; Lev 26:13; Nu 1:1; 9:1; 22:5; 26:4; Dt 4:45; 5:6; Ps 81:10; 114:1 [b]S Ex 3:20 [c]S Ex 12:8 **13:4** [d]S Ex 12:2 **13:5** [e]ver 11 [f]S Ex 3:8 [g]S Ex 3:8

Consecration of the Firstborn

13 The LORD said to Moses, 2 "Consecrate to me every firstborn male.[z]
The first offspring of every womb among
the Israelites belongs to me, whether man
or animal."

3 Then Moses said to the people, "Commemorate this day, the day you came out
of Egypt,[a] out of the land of slavery, because the LORD brought you out of it with
a mighty hand.[b] Eat nothing containing
yeast.[c] 4 Today, in the month of Abib,[d] you
are leaving. 5 When the LORD brings you
into the land of the Canaanites,[e] Hittites,
Amorites, Hivites and Jebusites[f]—the
land he swore to your forefathers to give
you, a land flowing with milk and honey[g]—you are to observe this ceremony[h]
in this month: 6 For seven days eat bread
made without yeast and on the seventh
day hold a festival[i] to the LORD. 7 Eat unleavened bread during those seven days;
nothing with yeast in it is to be seen
among you, nor shall any yeast be seen
anywhere within your borders. 8 On that
day tell your son,[j] 'I do this because of
what the LORD did for me when I came out
of Egypt.' 9 This observance will be for you
like a sign on your hand[k] and a reminder
on your forehead[l] that the law of the LORD
is to be on your lips. For the LORD brought
you out of Egypt with his mighty hand.[m]
10 You must keep this ordinance[n] at the appointed time[o] year after year.

11 "After the LORD brings you into the
land of the Canaanites[p] and gives it to
you, as he promised on oath[q] to you and
your forefathers,[r] 12 you are to give over to

[a] *40* Masoretic Text; Samaritan Pentateuch and Septuagint *Egypt and Canaan*

[h]Ex 12:25-26 **13:6** [i]S Ex 12:15-20 **13:8** [j]S Ex 10:2; Ps 78:5-6 **13:9** [k]Isa 44:5 [l]ver 16; Dt 6:8; 11:18; Pr 3:3; Mt 23:5 [m]S Ex 3:20 **13:10** [n]S Ex 12:14 [o]Ps 75:2; 102:13 **13:11** [p]S ver 5 [q]S Ge 22:16; Dt 1:8 [r]S Ge 12:7; S 17:19; Ps 105:42-45

the Passover" (Nu 33:3). *Ramses ... Succoth.* See map, p. 108. *about six hundred thousand men.* A round number for 603,550 (38:26; see Introduction to Numbers: Special Problem; see also Nu 1:46 and note).

12:38 *Many other people.* Possibly including such Egyptians as those mentioned in 9:20.

12:40 *length of time ... in Egypt was 430 years.* About 1876–1446 B.C., but see NIV text note.

12:41 *430 years, to the very day.* See notes on Ge 15:13; Ac 7:6.

12:44 See Ge 17:12–13 and note on 17:10.

12:46 *Do not break any of the bones.* See Nu 9:12 and note; Ps 34:20; possibly the passage quoted in Jn 19:36 in reference to Jesus (see NIV text note on Jn 19:36; see also notes on Ps 34:20; Jn 19:36).

12:48 *No uncircumcised male may eat of it.* Only those consecrated to the Lord in covenant commitment could partake of Passover; only for them could it have its full meaning (see Ge 17:9–14). Concerning participants in the Lord's Supper see 1Co 11:28 and note.

13:2 *Consecrate to me every firstborn male.* God had adopted Israel as his firstborn (see 4:22 and note) and had delivered every firstborn among the Israelites, whether human or animal, from the tenth plague (see 12:12–13). All the firstborn in Israel were therefore his. Jesus, Mary's firstborn son (see Lk 2:7), was presented to the Lord in accordance with this law (see Lk 2:22–23 and note on 2:22).

13:5 See note on 3:8.

13:9 *like a sign on your hand and a reminder on your forehead.* A figure of speech (see v. 16; Dt 6:8–9 and note; 11:18; see also Pr 3:3; 6:21; 7:3; SS 8:6). A literal reading of this verse has led to the practice of writing the texts of vv. 1–10, vv. 11–16, Dt 6:4–9 and Dt 11:13–21 on separate strips of parchment and placing them in two small leather boxes, which the observant Jew straps on his forehead and left arm before his morning prayers. The boxes are called "phylacteries" (Mt 23:5; see note there). This practice seems to have originated after the exile to Babylon.

the LORD the first offspring of every womb.
All the firstborn males of your livestock
belong to the LORD.[s] 13Redeem with a lamb
every firstborn donkey,[t] but if you do not
redeem it, break its neck.[u] Redeem[v] every
firstborn among your sons.[w]
14“In days to come, when your son[x] asks
you, ‘What does this mean?’ say to him,
‘With a mighty hand the LORD brought us
out of Egypt, out of the land of slavery.[y]
15When Pharaoh stubbornly refused to let
us go, the LORD killed every firstborn in
Egypt, both man and animal. This is why
I sacrifice to the LORD the first male offspring of every womb and redeem each of
my firstborn sons.’[z] 16And it will be like a
sign on your hand and a symbol on your
forehead[a] that the LORD brought us out of
Egypt with his mighty hand.”

Crossing the Sea

17When Pharaoh let the people go, God
did not lead them on the road through the
Philistine country, though that was shorter. For God said, “If they face war, they
might change their minds and return to
Egypt.”[b] 18So God led[c] the people around
by the desert road toward the Red Sea.[a]
The Israelites went up out of Egypt armed
for battle.[d]
19Moses took the bones of Joseph[e] with
him because Joseph had made the sons of
Israel swear an oath. He had said, “God
will surely come to your aid, and then you
must carry my bones up with you from
this place.”[b f]
20After leaving Succoth[g] they camped at
Etham on the edge of the desert.[h] 21By day
the LORD went ahead[i] of them in a pillar of
cloud[j] to guide them on their way and by
night in a pillar of fire to give them light,
so that they could travel by day or night.
22Neither the pillar of cloud by day nor the
pillar of fire by night left[k] its place in front
of the people.

14 Then the LORD said to Moses, 2“Tell
the Israelites to turn back and encamp near Pi Hahiroth, between Migdol[l]
and the sea. They are to encamp by the
sea, directly opposite Baal Zephon.[m] 3Phar-
aoh will think, ‘The Israelites are wandering around the land in confusion, hemmed
in by the desert.’ 4And I will harden Pharaoh’s heart,[n] and he will pursue them.[o]
But I will gain glory[p] for myself through
Pharaoh and all his army, and the Egyptians will know that I am the LORD.”[q] So
the Israelites did this.
5When the king of Egypt was told that
the people had fled,[r] Pharaoh and his officials changed their minds[s] about them
and said, “What have we done? We have
let the Israelites go and have lost their services!” 6So he had his chariot made ready
and took his army with him. 7He took six
hundred of the best chariots,[t] along with
all the other chariots of Egypt, with officers over all of them. 8The LORD hardened
the heart[u] of Pharaoh king of Egypt, so
that he pursued the Israelites, who were
marching out boldly.[v] 9The Egyptians—all
Pharaoh’s horses[w] and chariots, horsemen[c] and troops[x]—pursued the Israelites and overtook[y] them as they camped
by the sea near Pi Hahiroth, opposite Baal
Zephon.[z]

[a] *18* Hebrew *Yam Suph*; that is, Sea of Reeds
[b] *19* See Gen. 50:25. [c] *9* Or *charioteers*; also in verses 17, 18, 23, 26 and 28

13:12 [s]S Ge 4:4; Lev 27:26; Nu 3:13; 18:15,17; Lk 2:23* **13:13** [t]ver 15; Lev 27:11 [u]Ex 34:20; Isa 66:3 [v]Nu 3:46-47 [w]Nu 18:15 **13:14** [x]S Ex 10:2 [y]Ex 20:2; Dt 7:8; 28:68 **13:15** [z]S ver 2 **13:16** [a]S ver 9 **13:17** [b]Ex 14:11; Nu 14:1-4; Dt 17:16; Hos 11:5 **13:18** [c]Ex 15:22; Ps 136:16; Eze 20:10 [d]Jos 1:14; 4:13 **13:19** [e]Jos 24:32; Ac 7:16; Heb 11:22 [f]S Ge 47:29-30 **13:20** [g]S Ex 12:37 [h]Nu 33:6 **13:21** [i]Ex 32:1; 33:14; Dt 2:7; 31:8; Jdg 4:14; 5:4; Ps 68:7; 77:20; Jer 2:2; Hab 3:13 [j]Ex 14:19,24; 24:16; 33:9-10; 34:5; 40:38; Nu 9:16; 12:5; 14:14; Dt 1:33; Ne 9:12,19; Ps 78:14; 99:7; 105:39; Isa 4:5; 1Co 10:1 **13:22** [k]Ne 9:19 **14:2** [l]Nu 33:7; Jer 44:1; Eze 29:10 [m]ver 9 **14:4** [n]S Ex 4:21 [o]ver 8,17,23; Ps 71:11 [p]S Ex 9:16; Ro 9:17,22-23 [q]S Ex 6:2; Eze 32:15 **14:5** [r]S Ge 31:21 [s]Ps 105:25 **14:7** [t]Ex 15:4 **14:8** [u]S Ex 11:10 [v]Nu 33:3; Ac 13:17 **14:9** [w]Ge 47:17 [x]ver 6-7,25; Jos 24:6; Isa 43:17 [y]Ex 15:9 [z]ver 2

13:13 *Redeem.* See 6:6 and note. The verb means “obtain release, often (as here) by means of payment.” *donkey.* An “unclean” domestic animal (see Lev 11) that was not to be offered as a sacrifice to God (see also 34:20). *every firstborn among your sons.* Humans were to be consecrated to the Lord by their life, not by their death (see Ge 22:12; Nu 3:39–51; cf. Ro 12:1 and note).
13:14 See note on 12:26.
13:16 See note on v. 9.
13:17 *road through the Philistine country.* Although the most direct route from Goshen to Canaan, it was heavily guarded by a string of Egyptian fortresses.
13:18 *desert road.* Leading south along the west coast of the Sinai peninsula. *Red Sea.* See NIV text note. Various locations of the crossing have been proposed along the line of the modern Suez Canal and including the northern end of the Gulf of Suez (see map No. 3 at the end of this study Bible; but see also note on 14:2). *armed for battle.* Probably only with spears, bows and slings.
13:19 See notes on Ge 50:24–25.
13:21 *pillar of cloud . . . pillar of fire.* The visible symbol of God’s presence among his people (see 14:24; see also note on 3:2). The Lord often spoke to them from the pillar (see Nu 12:5–6; Dt 31:15–16; Ps 99:6–7).
14:2 *turn back.* Northward, in the general direction from which they had come. *Pi Hahiroth.* Located “east of Baal Zephon” (Nu 33:7). *Migdol.* The name means “watchtower.” *sea.* The sea that the NIV, in accordance with established tradition, calls the Red Sea—in Hebrew *Yam Suph*, i.e., Sea of Reeds (see 13:18 and NIV text note). Reference can hardly be to the northern end of the Gulf of Suez since reeds do not grow in salt water. Moreover, an Egyptian papyrus document seems to locate Baal Zephon in the vicinity of Tahpanhes (see note on Jer 2:16), a site near Lake Menzaleh about 20 miles east of Rameses. The crossing of the “Red Sea” thus probably occurred at the southern end of Lake Menzaleh (see map, p. 108; but see note on 13:18). *Baal Zephon.* Means “Baal of the north” or “Baal of North (Mountain)”—also the name of a Canaanite god.
14:4 *harden.* See v. 8 and note on 4:21. *know that I am the LORD.* See notes on 6:3; Eze 6:7.
14:7 *chariots.* Introduced into Egypt from Canaan, they brought about a revolutionary change in the art of warfare. Where the terrain was open and relatively flat, as much of Egypt was, they were especially effective. *officers.* The Hebrew for the singular of this word means “third man,” perhaps referring to his place in a chariot crew.
14:8 *hardened.* See v. 4 and note.

The Exodus

The exodus and conquest narratives form the classic historical and spiritual drama of OT times. Subsequent ages looked back to this period as one of obedient and victorious living under divine guidance. Close examination of the environment and circumstances also reveals the strenuous exertions, human sin and bloody conflicts of the era.

Marah—Oasis
Rameses—City or settlement
Trade routes
Probable Israelite route

Miles 0 20 40 60 80 100
Kms 0 50 100 150

Sea of Kinnereth
Jordan R.
CANAAN
AMMON
Rabbah
Jericho
Heshbon
Mt. Nebo
Ashdod
Lake Menzaleh
Way of the Land of the Philistines
PHILISTIA
Gaza
Lachish
Hebron
Salt Sea
Beersheba
Rameses
DESERT OF SHUR
AMALEKITES
DESERT OF ZIN
GOSHEN
Way to Shur
Punon
Pithom
Succoth
Kadesh Barnea
EDOM
SHASU NOMADS
Wadi of Egypt
On
Exact crossing place through the Biblical "Yam Suph" is unknown.
Trade route
DESERT OF PARAN
Way of the Land of the Red Sea
Memphis
EGYPT
SINAI
Ezion Geber
Marah
Elim
MIDIAN
DESERT OF SIN
Nile R.
Gulf of Suez
Dophkah
Hazeroth
Rephidim
Mt. Sinai
DESERT OF SINAI
Gulf of Aqaba
Red Sea

The Israelite tribes fled past the Egyptian system of border posts, through the Red Sea and into the desert, where they avoided the main military and trade routes leading across northern Sinai. The less frequently traveled "Way of the Sea" led to the remote turquoise and copper mining region northwest of Mt. Sinai.

It was necessary for Moses to take refuge in Midian where the Egyptian authorities could not reach him. The decades spent on "the far side of the desert" were an important formative part of his life.

In historical terms, the exodus from Egypt was ignored by Egyptian scribes and recorders. No definitive monuments mention the event itself, but a stele of Pharaoh Merneptah (c. 1205 B.C.) claims that a people called Israel were encountered by Egyptian troops somewhere in northern Canaan.

Finding precise geographical and chronological details of the period is problematic, but new information has emerged from vast amounts of fragmentary archaeological and inscriptional evidence. Hittite cuneiform documents parallel the ancient covenant formula governing Israel's "national contract" with God at Mount Sinai.

The Late Bronze Age (c. 1550–1200 B.C.) was a time of major social migrations. Egyptian control over the Semites in the eastern Nile delta was harsh, with a system of brickmaking quotas imposed on the labor force, often the landless, low-class "Apiru." Numerous Canaanite towns were violently destroyed. New populations, including the "Sea Peoples," made their presence felt in Anatolia, Egypt, Canaan, Transjordan, and elsewhere in the eastern Mediterranean.

Correspondence from Canaanite town rulers to the Egyptian court (the Amarna letters; see chart, p. xxii) in the time of Akhenaten (c. 1375 B.C.) reveals a weak structure of alliances, with an intermittent Egyptian military presence and an ominous fear of people called "Apiru" (= "Habiru").

10As Pharaoh approached, the Israelites
looked up, and there were the Egyptians,
marching after them. They were terrified
and cried[a] out to the LORD. 11They said
to Moses, "Was it because there were no
graves in Egypt that you brought us to the
desert to die?[b] What have you done to us
by bringing us out of Egypt? 12Didn't we
say to you in Egypt, 'Leave us alone; let us
serve the Egyptians'? It would have been
better for us to serve the Egyptians than to
die in the desert!"[c]

13Moses answered the people, "Do not
be afraid.[d] Stand firm and you will see[e]
the deliverance the LORD will bring you today. The Egyptians you see today you will
never see[f] again. 14The LORD will fight[g] for
you; you need only to be still."[h]

15Then the LORD said to Moses, "Why
are you crying out to me?[i] Tell the Israelites to move on. 16Raise your staff[j] and
stretch out your hand over the sea to divide the water[k] so that the Israelites can
go through the sea on dry ground. 17I will
harden the hearts[l] of the Egyptians so that
they will go in after them.[m] And I will gain
glory through Pharaoh and all his army,
through his chariots and his horsemen.
18The Egyptians will know that I am the
LORD[n] when I gain glory through Pharaoh,
his chariots and his horsemen."

19Then the angel of God,[o] who had been
traveling in front of Israel's army, withdrew and went behind them. The pillar of
cloud[p] also moved from in front and stood
behind[q] them, 20coming between the armies of Egypt and Israel. Throughout the
night the cloud brought darkness[r] to the
one side and light to the other side; so neither went near the other all night long.

21Then Moses stretched out his hand[s]
over the sea,[t] and all that night the LORD
drove the sea back with a strong east
wind[u] and turned it into dry land.[v] The
waters were divided,[w] 22and the Israelites
went through the sea[x] on dry ground,[y]
with a wall[z] of water on their right and
on their left.

14:10 [a]Ex 15:25; Jos 24:7; Ne 9:9; Ps 5:2; 34:17; 50:15; 107:6, 28 **14:11** [b]S Ex 5:21; 16:3; 17:3; Nu 11:1; 14:22; 20:4; 21:5; Dt 9:7 **14:12** [c]S Ex 5:21; 15:24; 17:2; Ps 106:7-8 **14:13** [d]S Ge 15:1 [e]1Sa 12:16; 2Ch 20:17 [f]ver 30 **14:14** [g]ver 25; Ex 15:3; Dt 1:30; 3:22; 20:4; Jos 10:14; 23:3, 10; 2Sa 5:24; 2Ch 20:29; Ne 4:20; Ps 24:8; 35:1; Isa 42:13; Jer 41:12 [h]1Sa 12:16; Ps 37:7; 46:10; 116:7; Isa 28:12; 30:15; Zec 2:13 **14:15** [i]Jos 7:10 **14:16** [j]S Ex 4:2 [k]ver 27; Isa 10:26 **14:17** [l]Ex 4:21 [m]S ver 4 **14:18** [n]S Ex 6:2; Eze 32:15 **14:19** [o]S Ge 16:7; Isa 63:9 [p]S Ex 13:21; 1Co 10:1 [q]Isa 26:7; 42:16; 49:10; 52:12; 58:8 **14:20** [r]Jos 24:7 **14:21** [s]S Ex 7:19 [t]S Ex 4:2; Job 26:12; Isa 14:27; 23:11; 51:15; Jer 31:35; Ac 7:36 [u]S Ge 41:6; Ex 15:8; 2Sa 22:16; 1Ki 19:11; Job 38:1; 40:6; Jer 23:19; Na 1:3 [v]S ver 22; S Ge 8:1 [w]2Ki 2:8; Ps 74:13; 78:13; 114:5; 136:13; Isa 63:12 **14:22** [x]ver 16; Nu 33:8; Jos 24:6; Isa 43:16; 63:11; 1Co 10:1 [y]ver 21, 29; S Ex 3:12; 15:19; Dt 31:6-8; Jos 3:16, 17; 4:22; Ne 9:11; Ps 66:6; 77:19; 106:9; Isa 11:15; 41:10; 43:5; 44:27; 50:2; 51:10; 63:13; Jer 46:28; Na 1:4; Heb 11:29 [z]Ex 15:8; Jos 3:13; Ps 78:13

23The Egyptians pursued them, and all
Pharaoh's horses and chariots and horsemen[a] followed them into the sea. 24During
the last watch of the night the LORD looked
down from the pillar of fire and cloud[b] at
the Egyptian army and threw it into confusion.[c] 25He made the wheels of their chariots come off[a] so that they had difficulty
driving. And the Egyptians said, "Let's get
away from the Israelites! The LORD is fighting[d] for them against Egypt."[e]

26Then the LORD said to Moses, "Stretch
out your hand over the sea so that the
waters may flow back over the Egyptians and their chariots and horsemen."
27Moses stretched out his hand over the
sea, and at daybreak the sea went back
to its place.[f] The Egyptians were fleeing
toward[b] it, and the LORD swept them into
the sea.[g] 28The water flowed back and
covered the chariots and horsemen — the
entire army of Pharaoh that had followed
the Israelites into the sea.[h] Not one of
them survived.[i]

29But the Israelites went through the sea
on dry ground,[j] with a wall[k] of water on
their right and on their left. 30That day the
LORD saved[l] Israel from the hands of the
Egyptians, and Israel saw the Egyptians
lying dead on the shore. 31And when the
Israelites saw the great power[m] the LORD
displayed against the Egyptians, the people feared[n] the LORD and put their trust[o] in
him and in Moses his servant.

[a] 25 Or *He jammed the wheels of their chariots* (see Samaritan Pentateuch, Septuagint and Syriac)
[b] 27 Or *from*

14:23 [a]ver 7 **14:24** [b]S Ex 13:21; 1Co 10:1 [c]Ex 23:27; Jos 10:10; 1Sa 5:9; 7:10; 14:15; 2Sa 5:24; 2Ki 7:6; 19:7 **14:25** [d]S ver 14 [e]S ver 9; Dt 32:31; 1Sa 2:2; 4:8 **14:27** [f]Jos 4:18 [g]ver 28; Ex 15:1, 21; Dt 1:40; 2:1; 11:4; Ps 78:53; 106:11; 136:15; Heb 11:29 **14:28** [h]ver 23; Ex 15:19; Jos 24:7 [i]S ver 27; Ex 15:5; Jdg 4:16; Ne 9:11 **14:29** [j]ver; 21, S 22; Jos 24:11; 2Ki 2:8; Ps 74:15 [k]Ps 78:13 **14:30** [l]ver 29; 1Sa 14:23; 1Ch 11:14; Ps 44:7; 106:8, 10, 21; Isa 43:3; 50:2; 51:9-10; 60:16; 63:8, 11 **14:31** [m]S Ex 9:16; Ps 147:5 [n]Ex 20:18; Dt 31:13; Jos 4:24; 1Sa 12:18; Ps 76:7; 112:1 [o]S Ex 4:5; Ps 22:4; 40:3; 106:12; Jn 2:11; 11:45

14:14 *The LORD will fight for you.* A necessary reminder that although Israel was "armed for battle" (13:18) and "marching out boldly" (v. 8), the victory would be won by God alone.

14:19 *angel of God.* See note on Ge 16:7; here associated with the cloud (see 13:21 and note).

14:20 *coming between the armies of Egypt and Israel.* The pillar of cloud (signifying the Lord's presence) protected Israel (see Ps 105:39 and note).

14:21 *strong east wind.* See 10:13 and note on 10:4. In 15:8 the poet praises the Lord and calls the wind the "blast of your nostrils," affirming (as here) that the miracle occurred in accordance with God's timing and under his direction (see 15:10).

14:22 *through the sea on dry ground.* In later times, psalmists and prophets reminded Israel of what God had done for them (see Ps 66:6; 106:9; 136:13–14; Isa 51:10; 63:11–13). *wall of water.* See v. 29. The waters were "piled up" (15:8) on both sides.

14:24 *last watch of the night.* Often the time for surprise attack (see Jos 10:9; 1Sa 11:11 and notes). *the LORD looked down from the pillar.* See note on 13:21.

14:25 *The LORD is fighting for them.* See note on v. 14.

14:27 *the LORD swept them into the sea.* As he had done with the locusts of the eighth plague (see 10:19).

14:31 *feared the LORD.* See note on Ge 20:11. *put their trust in him and in Moses.* Faith in God's mighty power and confidence in Moses' leadership (cf. 1Sa 2:26; 3:19; 12:18 and notes). *his servant.* Here refers to one who has the status of a high official in the Lord's kingly administration (see notes on Nu 12:6–8; Dt 34:5). See also the same title applied to Joshua (Jos 24:29), Samuel (1Sa 3:10), David (2Sa 3:18) and Elijah (2Ki 9:36).

The Song of Moses and Miriam

15 Then Moses and the Israelites sang
this song[p] to the LORD:

"I will sing[q] to the LORD,
for he is highly exalted.
The horse and its rider[r]
he has hurled into the sea.[s]
2 The LORD is my strength[t] and my song;
he has become my salvation.[u]
He is my God,[v] and I will praise him,
my father's God, and I will exalt[w]
him.
3 The LORD is a warrior;[x]
the LORD is his name.[y]
4 Pharaoh's chariots and his army[z]
he has hurled into the sea.
The best of Pharaoh's officers
are drowned in the Red Sea.[a]
5 The deep waters[a] have covered them;
they sank to the depths like a stone.[b]
6 "Your right hand,[c] O LORD,
was majestic in power.
Your right hand,[d] O LORD,
shattered[e] the enemy.
7 In the greatness of your majesty[f]
you threw down those who opposed
you.
You unleashed your burning anger;[g]
it consumed[h] them like stubble.
8 By the blast of your nostrils[i]
the waters piled up.[j]
The surging waters stood firm like a
wall;[k]
the deep waters congealed in the
heart of the sea.[l]
9 "The enemy boasted,
'I will pursue,[m] I will overtake them.
I will divide the spoils;[n]
I will gorge myself on them.
I will draw my sword
and my hand will destroy them.'
10 But you blew with your breath,[o]
and the sea covered them.
They sank like lead
in the mighty waters.[p]
11 "Who among the gods is like you,[q]
O LORD?
Who is like you —
majestic in holiness,[r]
awesome in glory,[s]
working wonders?[t]
12 You stretched out[u] your right hand
and the earth swallowed them.[v]
13 "In your unfailing love you will lead[w]
the people you have redeemed.[x]
In your strength you will guide them
to your holy dwelling.[y]
14 The nations will hear and tremble;[z]
anguish[a] will grip the people of
Philistia.[b]
15 The chiefs[c] of Edom[d] will be terrified,
the leaders of Moab will be seized
with trembling,[e]
the people[b] of Canaan will melt[f] away;

[a] *4* Hebrew *Yam Suph*; that is, Sea of Reeds; also in verse 22 [b] *15* Or *rulers*

15:1 [p] Nu 21:17; Jdg 5:1; 2Sa 22:1; 1Ch 16:9; Job 36:24; Ps 59:16; 105:2; Rev 15:3 [q] Jdg 5:3; Ps 13:6; 21:13; 27:6; 61:8; 104:33; 106:12; Isa 12:5,6; 42:10; 44:23 [r] Dt 11:4; Ps 76:6; Jer 51:21 [s] S Ex 14:27 **15:2** [t] Ps 18:1; 59:17 [u] S Ge 45:7; Ex 14:13; Ps 18:2,46; 25:5; 27:1; 62:2; 118:14; Isa 12:2; 33:2; Jnh 2:9; Hab 3:18 [v] S Ge 28:21 [w] Dt 10:21; 2Sa 22:47; Ps 22:3; 30:1; 34:3; 35:27; 99:5; 103:19; 107:32; 108:5; 109:1; 118:28; 145:11; 148:14; Isa 24:15; 25:1; Jer 17:14; Da 4:37 **15:3** [x] S Ex 14:14; Rev 19:11 [y] S Ex 3:15 **15:4** [z] Ex 14:6-7; Jer 51:21 **15:5** [a] S Ex 14:28 [b] ver 10; Ne 9:11 **15:6** [c] Ps 16:11; 17:7; 21:8; 63:8; 74:11; 77:10; 89:13; 98:1; 118:15; 138:7 [d] S Ex 3:20; S Job 40:14 [e] Nu 24:8; 1Sa 2:10; Ps 2:9 **15:7** [f] Dt 33:26; Ps 150:2 [g] Ps 2:5; 78:49-50; Jer 12:13; 25:38 [h] Ex 24:17; Dt 4:24; 9:3; Ps 18:8; 59:13; Heb 12:29

15:8 [i] S Ex 14:21; Ps 18:15 [j] Jos 3:13; Ps 78:13; Isa 43:16 [k] S Ex 14:22 [l] Ps 46:2 **15:9** [m] Ex 14:5-9; Dt 28:45; Ps 7:5; La 1:3 [n] Jdg 5:30; Isa 9:3; 53:12; Lk 11:22 **15:10** [o] Job 4:9; 15:30; Isa 11:4; 30:33; 40:7 [p] ver 5; Ne 9:11; Ps 29:3; 32:6; 77:19 **15:11** [q] S Ex 8:10; Ps 77:13; S Isa 46:5 [r] Lev 19:2; 1Sa 2:2; 1Ch 16:29; Ps 99:3; 110:3; Isa 6:3; Rev 4:8 [s] S Ex 14:4; Ps 4:2; 8:1; 26:8; Isa 35:2; 40:5 [t] S Ex 3:20 **15:12** [u] S Ex 7:5 [v] Nu 16:32; 26:10; Dt 11:6; Ps 106:17 **15:13** [w] Ne 9:12; Ps 77:20 [x] S Ex 6:6; Job 33:28; Ps 71:23; 106:10; Isa 1:27; 41:14; 43:14; 44:22-24; 51:10; 63:9; Tit 2:14 [y] ver 17; Ps 68:16; 76:2; 78:54 **15:14** [z] ver 16; Ex 23:27; Dt 2:25; Jos 2:9; 5:1; 9:24; 1Sa 4:7; Est 8:17; Ps 48:6; 96:9; 99:1; 114:7; Eze 38:20 [a] Isa 13:8 [b] Ps 83:7 **15:15** [c] S Ge 36:15 [d] Dt 2:4 [e] Nu 22:3; Ps 114:7 [f] Jos 2:9,24

15:1–18 A hymn celebrating God's spectacular victory over the pharaoh and his army. The focus of the song is God himself (see v. 11 and note); the divine name Yahweh ("the LORD") appears ten times. The first two stanzas (vv. 2–6, 7–11) retell the story of the "deliverance" (14:13) at the Red Sea, and the final stanza (vv. 12–17) anticipates the future approach to and conquest of Canaan (the promised land).
15:1 *Moses and the Israelites sang.* As though one person, the whole community praises God. *I will sing … into the sea.* Together with v. 18, this opening couplet frames the song and concentrates its dominant theme. *I will sing.* A common way to begin a hymn of praise (see Jdg 5:3; Ps 89:1; 101:1; 108:1).
15:2–6 The Lord's victory over the pharaoh was decisive.
15:2 The first half of the verse is echoed in Ps 118:14 (see Isa 12:2 and note).
15:3 *The LORD is a warrior.* See note on 14:14. God is often pictured as a king leading his people into battle (see, e.g., Dt 1:30; Jdg 4:14 and note; 2Sa 5:24; 2Ch 20:17–18).
15:4 *officers.* See note on 14:7.
15:5 *sank … like a stone.* See v. 10. Babylon is similarly described in Jer 51:63–64.
15:6 *right hand.* See Isa 41:10 and note.
15:7–8 The Lord's overwhelming victory marks him as incomparable among the gods.
15:8 See note on 14:22. *blast of your nostrils.* See note on 14:21; see also Ps 18:15.
15:10 *you blew with your breath.* See note on 14:21. *sank like lead.* See v. 5.
15:11 *Who is like you … ?* See Ps 35:10; 71:19; 89:6; 113:5; Isa 40:18,25; 46:5; Mic 7:18 and note. The Lord, who tolerates no rivals (see 20:3 and note), has defeated all the gods of Egypt and their worshipers (see note on 12:12).
15:12–17 The Lord's victorious right hand will surely establish his people in the promised land.
15:12 *earth.* Perhaps refers to Sheol or the grave (see Ps 63:9; 71:20 and notes), the "realm of death below" (Dt 32:22; see note there), since it was the sea that swallowed the Egyptians.
15:13 *unfailing love.* See note on Ps 6:4. *people you have redeemed.* See note on 6:6. *your holy dwelling.* Perhaps a reference to the house of worship at Shiloh (see Jer 7:12 and note), and ultimately the temple on Mount Zion (see Ps 76:2), the "place" God would "choose" (Dt 12:14,18,26; 14:25; 16:7,15–16; 17:8,10; 18:6; 31:11) to put "his Name" (Dt 12:5,11,21; 14:23–24; 16:2,6,11; 26:2). But the phrase may refer to the promised land, which is called "your dwelling" and "the sanctuary … your hands established" in v. 17. *holy.* See notes on 3:5; Ge 2:3.
15:14–15 *Philistia … Edom … Moab … Canaan.* Israel's potential enemies. The order is roughly that along the route Israel would follow from Mount Sinai to the promised land.
15:15 *chiefs.* The term used earlier of the Edomite rulers (see Ge 36:15–19,21,29–30,40,43).

16 terror[g] and dread will fall upon
them.
By the power of your arm
they will be as still as a stone[h]—
until your people pass by, O LORD,
until the people you bought[a][i]
pass by.[j]
17 You will bring[k] them in and plant[l]
them
on the mountain[m] of your
inheritance—
the place, O LORD, you made for your
dwelling,[n]
the sanctuary,[o] O Lord, your hands
established.
18 The LORD will reign
for ever and ever."[p]

19 When Pharaoh's horses, chariots and
horsemen[b] went into the sea,[q] the LORD
brought the waters of the sea back over
them, but the Israelites walked through
the sea on dry ground.[r] 20 Then Miriam[s]
the prophetess,[t] Aaron's sister, took a tambourine in her hand, and all the women
followed her, with tambourines[u] and dancing.[v] 21 Miriam sang[w] to them:

"Sing to the LORD,
for he is highly exalted.
The horse and its rider[x]
he has hurled into the sea."[y]

The Waters of Marah and Elim

22 Then Moses led Israel from the Red Sea
and they went into the Desert[z] of Shur.[a]
For three days they traveled in the desert
without finding water.[b] 23 When they came
to Marah, they could not drink its water
because it was bitter. (That is why the
place is called Marah.[c]) 24 So the people
grumbled[d] against Moses, saying, "What
are we to drink?"[e]
25 Then Moses cried out[f] to the LORD,
and the LORD showed him a piece of wood.
He threw[g] it into the water, and the water
became sweet.
There the LORD made a decree and a law
for them, and there he tested[h] them. 26 He
said, "If you listen carefully to the voice of
the LORD your God and do what is right in
his eyes, if you pay attention to his commands and keep[i] all his decrees,[j] I will not
bring on you any of the diseases[k] I brought
on the Egyptians, for I am the LORD, who
heals[l] you."
27 Then they came to Elim, where there
were twelve springs and seventy palm
trees, and they camped[m] there near the
water.

Manna and Quail

16 The whole Israelite community set
out from Elim and came to the Desert of Sin,[n] which is between Elim and
Sinai, on the fifteenth day of the second
month after they had come out of Egypt.[o]
2 In the desert the whole community grumbled[p] against Moses and Aaron. 3 The Israelites said to them, "If only we had died
by the LORD's hand in Egypt![q] There we sat

15:16 [g] S ver 14; S Ge 35:5 [h] 1Sa 25:37 [i] Ps 74:2; 2Pe 2:1 [j] Dt 2:4 **15:17** [k] Ex 23:20; 32:34; 33:12 [l] 2Sa 7:10; Ps 44:2; 80:8, 15; Isa 5:2; 60:21; Jer 2:21; 11:17; 24:6; Am 9:15 [m] Dt 33:19; Ps 2:6; 3:4; 15:1; 78:54, 68; 133:3; Da 9:16; Joel 2:1; Ob 1:16; Zep 3:11 [n] S ver 13; Ps 132:13-14 [o] Ps 78:69; 114:2 **15:18** [p] S Ge 21:33; Ps 9:7; 29:10; 55:19; 66:7; 80:1; 102:12; 145:13; La 5:19 **15:19** [q] S Ex 14:28 [r] S Ex 14:22 **15:20** [s] ver 21; Ex 2:4; Nu 12:1; 20:1; 26:59; 1Ch 4:17; 6:3 [t] Jdg 4:4; 2Ki 22:14; 2Ch 34:22; Ne 6:14; Isa 8:3; Eze 13:17 [u] S Ge 31:27; 1Sa 18:6; Ps 81:2; Isa 30:32 [v] S Ge 4:21; Jdg 11:34; 21:21; 1Sa 18:6; 2Sa 6:5, 14, 16; Ps 30:11; 149:3; 150:4; SS 6:13; Jer 31:4, 13 **15:21** [w] 1Sa 18:7 [x] Am 2:15; Hag 2:22 [y] S Ex 14:27 **15:22** [z] Ps 78:52 [a] S Ge 16:7 [b] Ex 17:1, 3; Nu 20:2, 5; 33:14; Ps 107:5 **15:23** [c] Nu 33:8; Ru 1:20 **15:24** [d] S Ex 14:12; 16:2; 7:3; Nu 14:2; Jos 9:18; Ps 78:18, 42; 106:13, 25; Eze 16:43 [e] Mt 6:31 **15:25** [f] S Ex 14:10 [g] 2Ki 2:21; 4:41; 6:6 [h] S Ge 22:1; Jdg 3:4; Job 23:10; Ps 81:7; Isa 48:10 **15:26** [i] Ex 23:22; Dt 11:13; 15:5; 28:1; Jer 11:6 [j] Ex 19:5-6; 20:2-17; Dt 7:12 [k] Dt 7:15; 28:27, 58-60; 32:39; 1Sa 5:6; Ps 30:2; 41:3-4; 103:3 [l] Ex 23:25-26; 2Ki 20:5; Ps 25:11; 103:3; 107:20; Jer 30:17; Hos 11:3 **15:27** [m] Nu 33:9 **16:1** [n] Ex 17:1; Nu 33:11, 12 [o] S Ex 6:6; 12:1-2 **16:2** [p] S Ex 15:24; 1Co 10:10 **16:3** [q] Ex 17:3; Nu 14:2; 20:3

[a] 16 Or *created* [b] 19 Or *charioteers* [c] 23 *Marah* means *bitter.*

15:16 *dread will fall upon them.* See note on 1Ch 14:17. *bought.* See NIV text note; see also Dt 32:6 and NIV text note. In Ps 74:2 the meaning "bought" or "purchased" is found in context with "redeemed" (see note on 13:13).
15:17 *inheritance.* The promised land (see 1Sa 26:19; Ps 79:1 and notes).
15:18 See note on v. 1.
15:20 *prophetess.* See Nu 12:1–2 for a statement by Miriam concerning her prophetic gift (see note on 7:1–2). Other female prophets in the Bible were Deborah (Jdg 4:4), Isaiah's wife (Isa 8:3, but see note there), Huldah (2Ki 22:14), Noadiah (Ne 6:14), Anna (Lk 2:36) and Philip's daughters (Ac 21:9). *women followed her, with tambourines and dancing.* Such celebration was common after victory in battle (see 1Sa 18:6; 2Sa 1:20).
15:21 Miriam repeats the first four lines of the victory hymn (see v. 1), changing only the form of the first verb.
15:22—18:27 The story of Israel's journey from the Red Sea to Mount Sinai (see Introduction: Outline).
15:22 *Desert of Shur.* Located east of Egypt (see Ge 25:18; 1Sa 15:7) in the northwestern part of the Sinai peninsula. In Nu 33:8 it is called the "Desert of Etham." Shur and Etham both mean "fortress wall" (Shur in Hebrew, Etham in Egyptian).
15:23 *Marah.* Probably modern Ain Hawarah, inland from the western arm of the Red Sea, about 50 miles south of its northern end.
15:24 *grumbled.* During their desert wanderings, the Israelites grumbled against Moses and Aaron whenever they faced a crisis (see 16:2; 17:3; Nu 14:2,29 and note; 16:11,41). In reality, however, they were grumbling "against the LORD" (16:8). Paul warns us not to follow their example (see 1Co 10:10 and note). Cf. also note on Nu 11:1.
15:25 *He threw it into the water, and the water became sweet.* For a similar occurrence see 2Ki 2:19–22. *a decree and a law.* Technical terms presumably referring to what follows in v. 26. *tested.* See note on Ge 22:1. God tested Israel also in connection with his provision of manna (see 16:4; Dt 8:2–3) and the giving of the Ten Commandments (see 20:20).
15:27 *Elim.* Seven miles south of Ain Hawarah (see note on v. 23) in the well-watered valley of Gharandel. *palm trees.* Elim means "large trees."
16:1 *from Elim ... to the Desert of Sin.* See Nu 33:10–11. The Desert of Sin was in southwestern Sinai ("Sin" is probably derived from "Sinai"). *fifteenth day of the second month.* Exactly one month had passed since Israel's exodus from Egypt (see 12:2,6,29,31).
16:2 *grumbled.* See note on 15:24.
16:3 *meat.* Nu 11:5 lists additional items of food from Egypt that the Israelites craved.

around pots of meat and ate all the food[r]
we wanted, but you have brought us out
into this desert to starve this entire assembly to death."[s]
4Then the LORD said to Moses, "I will
rain down bread from heaven[t] for you.
The people are to go out each day and
gather enough for that day. In this way I
will test[u] them and see whether they will
follow my instructions. 5On the sixth day
they are to prepare what they bring in, and
that is to be twice[v] as much as they gather
on the other days."
6So Moses and Aaron said to all the Israelites, "In the evening you will know
that it was the LORD who brought you out
of Egypt,[w] 7and in the morning you will
see the glory[x] of the LORD, because he has
heard your grumbling[y] against him. Who
are we, that you should grumble against
us?"[z] 8Moses also said, "You will know
that it was the LORD when he gives you
meat to eat in the evening and all the bread
you want in the morning, because he has
heard your grumbling[a] against him. Who
are we? You are not grumbling against us,
but against the LORD."[b]
9Then Moses told Aaron, "Say to the entire Israelite community, 'Come before the
LORD, for he has heard your grumbling.' "
10While Aaron was speaking to the
whole Israelite community, they looked toward the desert, and there was the glory[c]
of the LORD appearing in the cloud.[d]
11The LORD said to Moses, 12"I have
heard the grumbling[e] of the Israelites.
Tell them, 'At twilight you will eat meat,
and in the morning you will be filled with
bread. Then you will know that I am the
LORD your God.' "[f]
13That evening quail[g] came and covered
the camp, and in the morning there was
a layer of dew[h] around the camp. 14When
the dew was gone, thin flakes like frost[i] on
the ground appeared on the desert floor.
15When the Israelites saw it, they said to
each other, "What is it?" For they did not
know[j] what it was.

16:3 [r]Nu 11:4,34; Dt 12:20; Ps 78:18; 106:14; Jer 44:17 [s]S Ge 47:15; Dt 8:3 **16:4** [t]ver 14-15; Dt 8:3; Ne 9:15; Ps 78:24; 105:40; S Jn 6:31* [u]S Ge 22:1 **16:5** [v]ver 22; Lev 25:21 **16:6** [w]S Ex 6:6 **16:7** [x]ver 10; Ex 24:16; 29:43; 33:18,22; 40:34; Lev 9:6; Nu 16:19,42; Dt 5:24; 1Ki 8:11; Ps 63:2; Isa 6:3; 35:2; 40:5; 44:23; 60:1; 66:18; Eze 1:28; 10:4; 43:5; Hab 2:14; Hag 2:7; Jn 11:40 [y]ver 12; Nu 11:1,18; 14:2,27,28; 17:5 [z]Nu 16:11 **16:8** [a]ver 7 [b]Nu 23:21; Dt 33:5; Jdg 8:23; 1Sa 8:7; 12:12; S Mt 10:40; Ro 13:2; 1Th 4:8 **16:10** [c]S ver 7; Jn 11:4 [d]Ex 13:21; 40:34-35; 1Ki 8:10; 2Ch 7:1; Eze 10:4 **16:12** [e]S ver 7 [f]S Ex 6:2; S 20:2 **16:13** [g]Nu 11:31; Ps 78:27-28; 105:40; 106:15 [h]Nu 11:9 **16:14** [i]ver 31; Nu 11:7-9; Dt 8:3,16; Ps 105:40 **16:15** [j]Dt 8:16 [k]S ver 4; Ne 9:20; S Jn 6:31 **16:16** [l]ver 32,36 **16:18** [m]2Co 8:15* **16:19** [n]ver 23; Ex 12:10 **16:20** [o]ver 24 [p]Ex 32:19 **16:22** [q]S ver 5 [r]Ex 34:31 **16:23** [s]S Ge 2:3; S Ex 20:8; Dt 5:13-14 **16:26** [t]ver 23

Moses said to them, "It is the bread[k] the
LORD has given you to eat. 16This is what
the LORD has commanded: 'Each one is
to gather as much as he needs. Take an
omer[a][l] for each person you have in your
tent.' "
17The Israelites did as they were told;
some gathered much, some little. 18And
when they measured it by the omer, he
who gathered much did not have too
much, and he who gathered little did not
have too little.[m] Each one gathered as
much as he needed.
19Then Moses said to them, "No one is
to keep any of it until morning."[n]
20However, some of them paid no attention to Moses; they kept part of it until
morning, but it was full of maggots and
began to smell.[o] So Moses was angry[p]
with them.
21Each morning everyone gathered as
much as he needed, and when the sun
grew hot, it melted away. 22On the sixth
day, they gathered twice[q] as much—two
omers[b] for each person—and the leaders of the community[r] came and reported
this to Moses. 23He said to them, "This is
what the LORD commanded: 'Tomorrow
is to be a day of rest, a holy Sabbath[s]
to the LORD. So bake what you want to
bake and boil what you want to boil.
Save whatever is left and keep it until
morning.' "
24So they saved it until morning, as Moses commanded, and it did not stink or get
maggots in it. 25"Eat it today," Moses said,
"because today is a Sabbath to the LORD.
You will not find any of it on the ground
today. 26Six days you are to gather it, but
on the seventh day, the Sabbath,[t] there
will not be any."
27Nevertheless, some of the people went
out on the seventh day to gather it, but

[a] *16* That is, probably about 2 quarts (about 2 liters); also in verses 18, 32, 33 and 36 [b] *22* That is, probably about 4 quarts (about 4.5 liters)

16:4 *bread from heaven.* That the God of Israel could provide food in the desert for his people for 40 years was one of the great signs that Israel's God was the true God, the Lord of creation (see note on v. 31). Jesus called himself "the true bread from heaven" (Jn 6:32; see notes on 6:31–33), "the bread of God" (Jn 6:33), "the bread of life" (Jn 6:35,48), "the living bread that came down from heaven" (Jn 6:51)—all in the spiritual sense (Jn 6:63). For a similar application see Dt 8:3 and Jesus' quotation of it in Mt 4:4 (see also note there). *go out each day and gather enough for that day.* Probably the background for Jesus' model petition in Mt 6:11; Lk 11:3. *test.* See notes on 15:25; Ge 22:1.

16:5 *sixth day ... twice as much as they gather on the other days.* To provide for "the seventh day, the Sabbath" (v. 26), "a day of rest" (v. 23). See v. 29.

16:6 *know.* See note on 6:3.

16:8 *meat ... in the evening and ... bread ... in the morning.* See vv. 13–14.

16:10 *glory of the LORD appearing in the cloud.* See 24:15–17; see also notes on 13:21; 40:34; Ps 26:8.

16:12 *twilight.* See note on 12:6.

16:13 *quail came.* For a similar incident see Nu 11:31–33 and note on 11:31–32.

16:14 *thin flakes like frost.* See note on v. 31.

16:15 *What is it?* See v. 31 and NIV text note.

16:18 See 2Co 8:15, where Paul quotes the heart of the verse to describe Christians who share with each other what they possess (see also note on 2Co 8:13–15).

16:23 *Sabbath.* The first occurrence of the word itself, though the principle of the seventh day as a day of rest and holiness is set forth in the account of creation (see note on Ge 2:3).

they found none. 28Then the LORD said
to Moses, "How long will you[a] refuse to
keep my commands[u] and my instructions?
29Bear in mind that the LORD has given you
the Sabbath; that is why on the sixth day
he gives you bread for two days. Everyone
is to stay where he is on the seventh day;
no one is to go out." 30So the people rested
on the seventh day.

31The people of Israel called the bread
manna.[b][v] It was white like coriander seed
and tasted like wafers made with honey.
32Moses said, "This is what the LORD has
commanded: 'Take an omer of manna and
keep it for the generations to come, so
they can see the bread I gave you to eat
in the desert when I brought you out of
Egypt.'"

33So Moses said to Aaron, "Take a jar
and put an omer of manna[w] in it. Then
place it before the LORD to be kept for the
generations to come."

34As the LORD commanded Moses, Aaron put the manna in front of the Testimony,[x] that it might be kept. 35The Israelites ate manna[y] forty years,[z] until they
came to a land that was settled; they ate
manna until they reached the border of
Canaan.[a]

36(An omer[b] is one tenth of an ephah.)[c]

Water From the Rock

17 The whole Israelite community set
out from the Desert of Sin,[d] traveling
from place to place as the LORD commanded. They camped at Rephidim,[e] but there
was no water[f] for the people to drink. 2So
they quarreled with Moses and said, "Give
us water[g] to drink."[h]

Moses replied, "Why do you quarrel
with me? Why do you put the LORD to the
test?"[i]

3But the people were thirsty[j] for water
there, and they grumbled[k] against Moses.
They said, "Why did you bring us up out
of Egypt to make us and our children and
livestock die[l] of thirst?"

4Then Moses cried out to the LORD,
"What am I to do with these people? They
are almost ready to stone[m] me."

5The LORD answered Moses, "Walk on
ahead of the people. Take with you some
of the elders of Israel and take in your
hand the staff[n] with which you struck
the Nile,[o] and go. 6I will stand there before you by the rock at Horeb.[p] Strike[q] the
rock, and water[r] will come out of it for
the people to drink." So Moses did this in
the sight of the elders of Israel. 7And he
called the place Massah[c][s] and Meribah[d][t]
because the Israelites quarreled and because they tested the LORD saying, "Is the
LORD among us or not?"

[a] *28* The Hebrew is plural. [b] *31* *Manna* means *What is it?* (see verse 15). [c] *7* *Massah* means *testing.* [d] *7* *Meribah* means *quarreling.*

16:28 [u] Jos 9:14; Ps 78:10; 106:13; 107:11; 119:1; Jer 32:23 **16:31** [v] S ver 14 **16:33** [w] Heb 9:4; Rev 2:17 **16:34** [x] Ex 25:16,21,22; 27:21; 31:18; 40:20; Lev 16:13; Nu 1:50; 7:89; 10:11; 17:4,10; Dt 10:2; 1Ki 8:9; 2Ch 5:10 **16:35** [y] Jn 6:31,49 [z] Nu 14:33; 33:38; Dt 1:3; 2:7; 8:2-4; Jos 5:6; Jdg 3:11; Ne 9:21; Ps 95:10; Am 5:25 [a] Jos 5:12 **16:36** [b] S ver 16 [c] Lev 5:11; 6:20; Nu 5:15; 15:4; 28:5 **17:1** [d] S Ex 16:1 [e] ver 8; Ex 19:2; Nu 33:15 [f] Nu 20:5; 21:5; 33:14 **17:2** [g] Nu 20:2; 33:14; Ps 107:5 [h] S Ex 14:12 [i] Dt 6:16; Ps 78:18,41; 106:14; Mt 4:7; 1Co 10:9 **17:3** [j] S Ex 15:22 [k] S Ex 15:24 [l] S Ex 14:11 **17:4** [m] Nu 14:10; 1Sa 30:6; S Jn 8:59 **17:5** [n] S Ex 4:2; S 10:12-13 [o] Ex 7:20 **17:6** [p] S Ex 3:1 [q] Nu 20:8 [r] Nu 20:11; Dt 8:15; Jdg 15:19; 2Ki 3:20; Ne 9:15; Ps 74:15; 78:15-16; 105:41; 107:35; 114:8; Isa 30:25; 35:6; 43:19; 48:21; 1Co 10:4 **17:7** [s] Dt 6:16; 9:22; 33:8; Ps 95:8 [t] Nu 20:13,24; 27:14; Ps 81:7; 106:32

For its importance in the life of the Israelites see 20:8 – 10 and note on 20:10.

16:29 See note on v. 5.

16:31 *manna.* Several naturalistic explanations for the manna have been given. For example, some equate it with the sticky and often granular honeydew that is excreted in Sinai in early June by various scale insects and that solidifies rapidly through evaporation. But no naturally occurring substance fits all the data of the text, and several factors suggest that manna was in fact the Lord's unique provision for his people in the desert: (1) The meaning of the Hebrew word for "manna" suggests that it was something unknown by the people at the time (see NIV text note). (2) The appearance and taste of the manna suggest that it is not something experienced by other peoples in other times. (3) The daily abundance of the manna and its regular periodic surge and slump (double amounts on the sixth day but none on the seventh day, vv. 22,27) hardly fit a natural phenomenon. (4) Its availability in ample supply for the entire desert experience, no matter where the people were (v. 35), argues against a natural substance. (5) The keeping of a sample of the manna in the ark for future generations (vv. 33 – 34) suggests that it was a unique food.

16:33 *jar.* Said in Heb 9:4 to be made of gold.

16:34 *Testimony.* Reference is to the two tablets of the covenant law; the present language anticipates the later references to the "two tablets of the Testimony" (31:18; 32:15; 34:29), which gave their name to the "ark of the Testimony" (25:22; 26:33) in which they were placed (see 25:16,21 and note on 25:16) along with the jar of manna (see Heb 9:4; see also Rev 2:17 and note).

16:35 *ate manna forty years ... until they reached ... Canaan.* The manna stopped at the time the Israelites celebrated their first Passover in Canaan (see Jos 5:10 – 12 and note on 5:12).

17:1 *traveling from place to place.* For a list of specific sites see Nu 33:12 – 14. *Rephidim.* Probably either the Wadi Refayid or the Wadi Feiran, both near Jebel Musa (see note on 3:1) in southern Sinai.

17:2 *put the LORD to the test.* Israel fails the Lord's testing of her (see 16:4) by putting the Lord to the test.

17:3 *grumbled.* See note on 15:24.

17:4 *these people.* The same note of distance and alienation ("these people" instead of "my people") in such situations (see also the interplay in 32:7,9 – 11; 33:13) is found often in the prophets (see, e.g., Isa 6:9 – 10 and note; Hag 1:2).

17:6 *I will stand there ... by the rock.* Paul may have had this incident in mind when he spoke of Christ as "the spiritual rock that accompanied" Israel (see 1Co 10:4 and note; see also Heb 11:24 – 26). *Horeb.* See note on 3:1. *Strike the rock, and water will come out.* The event was later celebrated by Israel's hymn writers and prophets (see Ps 78:15 – 16,20; 105:41; 114:8; Isa 48:21).

17:7 *Massah and Meribah.* Heb 3:7 – 8,15 (quoting Ps 95:7 – 8) gives the meaning "testing" for Massah and "rebellion" for Meribah. Another Meribah, where a similar incident occurred near Kadesh Barnea (see note on Ge 14:7), is referred to in Nu 20:13 (see note there), 24; 27:14; Dt 32:51; 33:8; Ps 81:7; 106:32; Eze 47:19; 48:28.

The Amalekites Defeated

8The Amalekites[u] came and attacked
the Israelites at Rephidim.[v] 9Moses said to
Joshua,[w] "Choose some of our men and
go out to fight the Amalekites. Tomorrow I
will stand on top of the hill with the staff[x]
of God in my hands."
10So Joshua fought the Amalekites as
Moses had ordered, and Moses, Aaron
and Hur[y] went to the top of the hill. 11As
long as Moses held up his hands, the Israelites were winning,[z] but whenever he
lowered his hands, the Amalekites were
winning. 12When Moses' hands grew tired,
they took a stone and put it under him
and he sat on it. Aaron and Hur held his
hands up—one on one side, one on the
other—so that his hands remained steady
till sunset.[a] 13So Joshua overcame the Amalekite[b] army with the sword.
14Then the LORD said to Moses, "Write[c]
this on a scroll as something to be remembered and make sure that Joshua
hears it, because I will completely blot
out[d] the memory of Amalek[e] from under
heaven."
15Moses built an altar[f] and called[g] it The
LORD is my Banner. 16He said, "For hands
were lifted up to the throne of the LORD.
The[a] LORD will be at war against the Amalekites[h] from generation to generation."[i]

Jethro Visits Moses

18 Now Jethro,[j] the priest of Midian[k]
and father-in-law of Moses, heard of
everything God had done for Moses and
for his people Israel, and how the LORD
had brought Israel out of Egypt.[l]
2After Moses had sent away his wife
Zipporah,[m] his father-in-law Jethro received her 3and her two sons.[n] One son
was named Gershom,[b] for Moses said, "I
have become an alien in a foreign land";[o]
4and the other was named Eliezer,[c p] for he
said, "My father's God was my helper;[q] he
saved me from the sword of Pharaoh."
5Jethro, Moses' father-in-law, together
with Moses' sons and wife, came to him
in the desert, where he was camped near
the mountain[r] of God. 6Jethro had sent
word to him, "I, your father-in-law Jethro,
am coming to you with your wife and her
two sons."
7So Moses went out to meet his father-
in-law and bowed down[s] and kissed[t] him.
They greeted each other and then went
into the tent. 8Moses told his father-in-
law about everything the LORD had done
to Pharaoh and the Egyptians for Israel's
sake and about all the hardships[u] they had
met along the way and how the LORD had
saved[v] them.
9Jethro was delighted to hear about all
the good things[w] the LORD had done for
Israel in rescuing them from the hand of
the Egyptians. 10He said, "Praise be to the
LORD,[x] who rescued you from the hand of
the Egyptians and of Pharaoh, and who
rescued the people from the hand of the
Egyptians. 11Now I know that the LORD is
greater than all other gods,[y] for he did this
to those who had treated Israel arrogantly."[z]

17:8 [u] S Ge 36:12 [v] S ver 1 **17:9** [w] Ex 24:13; 32:17; 33:11; Nu 11:28; 27:22; Dt 1:38; Jos 1:1; Ac 7:45 [x] S Ex 4:17 **17:10** [y] ver 10-12; Ex 24:14; 31:2 **17:11** [z] Jas 5:16 **17:12** [a] Jos 8:26 **17:13** [b] ver 8 **17:14** [c] Ex 24:4; 34:27; Nu 33:2; Dt 31:9; Job 19:23; Isa 30:8; Jer 36:2; 45:1; 51:60 [d] Ex 32:33; Dt 29:20; Job 18:17; Ps 9:5; 34:16; 109:15; Eze 18:4 [e] ver 13; S Ge 36:12; Nu 24:7; Jdg 3:13; 1Sa 30:17-18; Ps 83:7 **17:15** [f] S Ge 8:20 [g] S Ge 22:14 **17:16** [h] Nu 24:7; 1Sa 15:8, 32; 1Ch 4:43; Est 3:1; 8:3; 9:24 [i] Est 9:5 **18:1** [j] S Ex 2:18 [k] S Ex 2:16 [l] S Ex 6:6 **18:2** [m] S Ex 2:21 **18:3** [n] S Ex 4:20; Ac 7:29 [o] Ex 2:22 **18:4** [p] 1Ch 23:15 [q] S Ge 49:25; S Dt 33:29 **18:5** [r] S Ex 3:1 **18:7** [s] S Ge 17:3; S 43:28 [t] S Ge 29:13 **18:8** [u] Nu 20:14; Ne 9:32 [v] Ex 15:6, 16; Ps 81:7

[a] 16 Or *"Because a hand was against the throne of the LORD, the* [b] 3 *Gershom* sounds like the Hebrew for *an alien there.* [c] 4 *Eliezer* means *my God is helper.*

18:9 [w] Jos 21:45; 1Ki 8:66; Ne 9:25; Ps 145:7; Isa 63:7 **18:10** [x] S Ge 9:26; S 24:27 **18:11** [y] S Ex 12:12; S 1Ch 16:25 [z] S Ex 1:10; S Lk 1:51

17:8 *Amalekites.* See note on Ge 14:7.

17:9 *Joshua.* The name given by Moses to Hoshea son of Nun (see Nu 13:16 and note). "Hoshea" means "salvation," while "Joshua" means "The LORD saves." The Greek form of the name Joshua is the same as that of the name Jesus, for the meaning of which see NIV text note on Mt 1:21. Joshua was from the tribe of Ephraim (Nu 13:8), one of the most powerful of the 12 tribes (see notes on Ge 48:6,19). *fight the Amalekites.* Joshua's military prowess uniquely suited him to be the conqueror of Canaan 40 years later, while his faith in God and loyalty to Moses suited him to be Moses' "aide" (24:13; 33:11) and successor (see Dt 1:38; 3:28; 31:14; 34:9; Jos 1:5).

17:10 *Hur.* Perhaps the same Hur who was the son of Caleb and the grandfather of Bezalel (see 1Ch 2:19–20), one of the builders of the tabernacle (see 31:2–5).

17:11 *held up his hands.* A symbol of appeal to God for help and enablement (see note on 9:29; see also 9:22; 10:12; 14:16).

17:14 *Write.* See 24:4; 34:27–28; Nu 33:2; Dt 28:58; 29:20,21,27; 30:10; 31:9,19,22,24; see also Introduction: Author and Date of Writing. *scroll.* A long strip of leather or papyrus on which scribes wrote in columns (see Jer 36:23) with pen (see Isa 8:1) and ink (see Jer 36:18 and note), sometimes on both sides (see Eze 2:10; Rev 5:1). After being rolled up, a scroll was often sealed (see Isa 29:11; Da 12:4; Rev 5:1–2,5,9) to protect its contents. Scrolls were of various sizes (see Isa 8:1; Rev 10:2,9–10). Certain Egyptian examples reached lengths of over 100 feet; Biblical scrolls, however, rarely exceeded 30 feet in length, as in the case of a book like Isaiah (see Lk 4:17). Reading the contents of a scroll involved the awkward procedure of unrolling it with one hand while rolling it up with the other (see Isa 34:4; Eze 2:10; Lk 4:17,20; Rev 6:14). Shortly after the time of Christ the scroll gave way to the book form still used today.

17:15 *my Banner.* Recalling Moses' petition with upraised hands (see vv. 11–12,16) and testifying to the power of God displayed in defense of his people.

18:1 *Jethro, the priest of Midian.* See note on 2:16.

18:2 *sent away his wife.* Apparently Moses sent Zipporah to her father with the news that the Lord had blessed his mission (see v. 1) and that he was in the vicinity of Mount Sinai with Israel.

18:5 *mountain of God.* See 3:1 and note.

18:7–12 A striking example of how the God of Israel manifested himself, not only to Israel but also to non-Israelites, by his mighty acts in behalf of his people, to be the only true God. See the similar responses of Rahab (see Jos 2:9–11 and note) and the Gibeonites (Jos 9:9–10); see also notes on Ge 12:1; Ex 16:4.

18:11 *Now I know that the LORD is greater than all other gods.* See the similar confession of Naaman in 2Ki 5:15 (see also note there).

12Then Jethro, Moses' father-in-law,[a]
brought a burnt offering[b] and other sacrifices[c] to God, and Aaron came with all the
elders of Israel to eat bread[d] with Moses'
father-in-law in the presence[e] of God.
13The next day Moses took his seat to
serve as judge for the people, and they
stood around him from morning till evening. 14When his father-in-law saw all that
Moses was doing for the people, he said,
"What is this you are doing for the people?
Why do you alone sit as judge, while all
these people stand around you from morning till evening?"
15Moses answered him, "Because the
people come to me to seek God's will.[f]
16Whenever they have a dispute,[g] it is
brought to me, and I decide between the
parties and inform them of God's decrees
and laws."[h]
17Moses' father-in-law replied, "What
you are doing is not good. 18You and these
people who come to you will only wear
yourselves out. The work is too heavy for
you; you cannot handle it alone.[i] 19Listen
now to me and I will give you some advice,
and may God be with you.[j] You must be
the people's representative before God and
bring their disputes[k] to him. 20Teach them
the decrees and laws,[l] and show them the
way to live[m] and the duties they are to perform.[n] 21But select capable men[o] from all
the people—men who fear[p] God, trustworthy men who hate dishonest gain[q]—and
appoint them as officials[r] over thousands,
hundreds, fifties and tens. 22Have them
serve as judges for the people at all times,
but have them bring every difficult case[s]
to you; the simple cases they can decide
themselves. That will make your load lighter, because they will share[t] it with you. 23If
you do this and God so commands, you
will be able to stand the strain, and all
these people will go home satisfied."
24Moses listened to his father-in-law and
did everything he said. 25He chose capable
men from all Israel and made them leaders[u] of the people, officials over thousands,
hundreds, fifties and tens.[v] 26They served
as judges[w] for the people at all times. The
difficult cases[x] they brought to Moses, but
the simple ones they decided themselves.[y]
27Then Moses sent his father-in-law on
his way, and Jethro returned to his own
country.[z]

At Mount Sinai

19 In the third month after the Israelites
left Egypt[a]—on the very day—they
came to the Desert of Sinai.[b] 2After they
set out from Rephidim,[c] they entered the
Desert of Sinai, and Israel camped there in
the desert in front of the mountain.[d]
3Then Moses went up to God,[e] and the
LORD called[f] to him from the mountain
and said, "This is what you are to say to
the house of Jacob and what you are to
tell the people of Israel: 4'You yourselves
have seen what I did to Egypt,[g] and how I
carried you on eagles' wings[h] and brought
you to myself.[i] 5Now if you obey me fully[j] and keep my covenant,[k] then out of all
nations you will be my treasured possession.[l] Although the whole earth[m] is mine,
6you[a] will be for me a kingdom of priests[n]
and a holy nation.'[o] These are the words
you are to speak to the Israelites."

[a] 5,6 Or *possession, for the whole earth is mine.* 6*You*

18:12 [a]S Ex 3:1 [b]Ex 10:25; 20:24; Lev 1:2-9 [c]Ge 31:54; Ex 24:5 [d]S Ge 26:30 [e]Dt 12:7 **18:15** [f]S ver 19; S Ge 25:22 **18:16** [g]Ex 24:14 [h]ver 15; Lev 24:12; Nu 15:34; Dt 1:17; 2Ch 19:7; Pr 24:23; Mal 2:9 **18:18** [i]Nu 11:11,14,17; Dt 1:9,12 **18:19** [j]Ex 3:12 [k]ver 15; Nu 27:5 **18:20** [l]Dt 4:1, 5; 5:1; Ps 119:12, 26,68 [m]Ps 143:8 [n]S Ge 39:11 **18:21** [o]S Ge 47:6; Ac 6:3 [p]S Ge 22:12 [q]Ex 23:8; Dt 16:19; 1Sa 12:3; Ps 15:5; Pr 17:23; 28:8; Ecc 7:7; Eze 18:8; 22:12 [r]Nu 1:16; 7:2; 10:4; Dt 16:18; Ezr 7:25 **18:22** [s]Lev 24:11; Dt 1:17-18 [t]Nu 11:17; Dt 1:9 **18:25** [u]Nu 1:16; 7:2; 11:16; Dt 16:18 [v]Dt 1:13-15 **18:26** [w]Dt 16:18; 2Ch 19:5; Ezr 7:25 [x]Dt 1:17 [y]ver 22 **18:27** [z]Nu 10:29-30 **19:1** [a]S Ex 6:6 [b]Nu 1:1; 3:14; 33:15 **19:2** [c]S Ex 17:1 [d]S ver 17; S Ex 3:1; Dt 5:2-4 **19:3** [e]Ex 20:21 [f]S Ex 3:4; S 25:22; Ac 7:38 **19:4** [g]Dt 29:2; Jos 24:7 [h]Dt 32:11; Ps 103:5; Isa 40:31; Jer 4:13; 48:40; Rev 12:14 [i]Dt 33:12; Isa 31:5; Eze 16:6 **19:5** [j]Ex 15:26; Dt 6:3; Ps 78:10; Jer 7:23 [k]S Ge 17:9; S Ex 3:1 [l]S Ex 8:22; S 34:9; S Dt 8:1; S Tit 2:14 [m]S Ex 9:29; 1Co 10:26 **19:6** [n]Isa 61:6; 66:21; S 1Pe 2:5 [o]Ge 18:19; Lev 11:44-45; Dt 4:37; 7:6; 26:19; 28:9; 29:13; 33:3; Isa 4:3; 62:12; Jer 2:3; Am 3:2

18:12 *brought.* The verb means "provided" an animal for sacrifice (see, e.g., 25:2; Lev 12:8), not "officiated at" a sacrifice. *eat bread with.* A token of friendship (contrast the hostility of the Amalekites, 17:8–16). Such a meal often climaxed the establishment of a treaty (see Ge 31:54; Ex 24:11 and notes).

18:16 *God's decrees and laws.* The process of compiling and systematizing the body of divine law that would govern the newly formed nation of Israel may have already begun (see 15:25–26).

18:21 *men who fear God.* See note on Ge 20:11.

19:1 The arrival at Sinai marked a significant milestone in Israel's life. Having been delivered by God from Egyptian bondage and having experienced his care and provision, they would at Sinai be brought into a national covenantal relationship with the Lord. In the ancient Near East the relationship between a king and his subjects was commonly governed by a covenant—rather than by a constitution (see note on 20:2).

19:2 *Desert of Sinai.* Located in the southeast region of the peninsula (see note on 3:1). The narrator locates there the events recorded in the rest of Exodus, all of Leviticus, and Nu 1:1—10:10.

19:3—24:18 The Sinaitic covenant. It was cast in the form of ancient Near Eastern suzerainty-vassal treaties of the second millennium B.C. It contained the Lord's pledge to be Israel's Suzerain-Protector if they would be faithful to him as their covenant Lord and obedient to the stipulations of the covenant as the vassal-people of his kingdom. The covenant had several later renewals, including ch. 34, the whole book of Deuteronomy, and Jos 24. See chart, p. 19; see also note on Jer 31:32.

19:3 *Jacob ... Israel.* See note on 1:1.

19:4 *I carried you on eagles' wings.* The description best fits the female golden eagle.

19:5 *if ... then.* The covenant between God and Israel at Mount Sinai is the outgrowth and extension of the Lord's covenant with Abraham and his descendants 600 years earlier. Participation in the divine blessings is conditioned on obedience added to faith (see note on Ge 17:9). *my covenant.* See note on Ge 9:9. *out of all nations ... my treasured possession.* The equivalent phrases used of Christians in 1Pe 2:9 are "chosen people" and "people belonging to God" (see Dt 7:6; 14:2; 26:18; Ps 135:4; Mal 3:17; cf. Tit 2:14). *the whole earth is mine.* The God of Israel is the Creator and Possessor of the earth and everything in it (see Ge 14:19,22; Ps 24:1–2 and note).

19:6 *kingdom of priests.* The Israelites were to constitute the Lord's kingdom (the people who acknowledged him as their King) and, like priests, were to be wholly consecrated to his service (see Isa 61:6 and note; cf. 1Pe 2:5 and note;

7 So Moses went back and summoned the
elders[p] of the people and set before them
all the words the LORD had commanded
him to speak.[q] 8 The people all responded
together, "We will do everything the LORD
has said."[r] So Moses brought their answer
back to the LORD.
9 The LORD said to Moses, "I am going to
come to you in a dense cloud,[s] so that the
people will hear me speaking[t] with you
and will always put their trust[u] in you."
Then Moses told the LORD what the people had said.
10 And the LORD said to Moses, "Go to the
people and consecrate[v] them today and tomorrow. Have them wash their clothes[w]
11 and be ready by the third day,[x] because
on that day the LORD will come down[y] on
Mount Sinai[z] in the sight of all the people. 12 Put limits[a] for the people around the
mountain and tell them, 'Be careful that
you do not go up the mountain or touch
the foot of it. Whoever touches the mountain shall surely be put to death. 13 He shall
surely be stoned[b] or shot with arrows; not
a hand is to be laid on him. Whether man
or animal, he shall not be permitted to live.'
Only when the ram's horn[c] sounds a long
blast may they go up to the mountain."[d]
14 After Moses had gone down the mountain to the people, he consecrated them, and
they washed their clothes.[e] 15 Then he said
to the people, "Prepare yourselves for the
third day. Abstain[f] from sexual relations."
16 On the morning of the third day there
was thunder[g] and lightning, with a thick
cloud[h] over the mountain, and a very loud
trumpet blast.[i] Everyone in the camp trembled.[j] 17 Then Moses led the people out of
the camp to meet with God, and they stood
at the foot of the mountain.[k] 18 Mount Sinai was covered with smoke,[l] because the
LORD descended on it in fire.[m] The smoke
billowed up from it like smoke from a furnace,[n] the whole mountain[a] trembled[o]
violently, 19 and the sound of the trumpet
grew louder and louder. Then Moses spoke
and the voice[p] of God answered[q] him.[b]
20 The LORD descended to the top of
Mount Sinai[r] and called Moses to the top
of the mountain. So Moses went up 21 and
the LORD said to him, "Go down and warn
the people so they do not force their way
through to see[s] the LORD and many of them
perish.[t] 22 Even the priests, who approach[u]
the LORD, must consecrate[v] themselves, or
the LORD will break out against them."[w]
23 Moses said to the LORD, "The people
cannot come up Mount Sinai,[x] because you
yourself warned us, 'Put limits[y] around the
mountain and set it apart as holy.'"
24 The LORD replied, "Go down and
bring Aaron[z] up with you. But the priests
and the people must not force their way
through to come up to the LORD, or he will
break out against them."[a]
25 So Moses went down to the people
and told them.

The Ten Commandments

20:1-17pp — Dt 5:6-21

20 And God spoke[b] all these words:[c]
2 "I am the LORD your God,[d] who

[a] *18* Most Hebrew manuscripts; a few Hebrew manuscripts and Septuagint *all the people*
[b] *19* Or *and God answered him with thunder*

19:7 [p] Ex 18:12; Lev 4:15; 9:1; Nu 16:25 [q] Ex 4:30; 1Sa 8:10 **19:8** [r] Ex 24:3,7; Dt 5:27; 26:17 **19:9** [s] ver 16; Ex 20:21; 24:15-16; 33:9; 34:5; Dt 4:11; 2Sa 22:10,12; 2Ch 6:1; Ps 18:11; 97:2; 99:7; Mt 17:5 [t] Dt 4:12,36; Jn 12:29-30 [u] S Ex 4:5 **19:10** [v] ver 14,22; Lev 11:44; Nu 11:18; 1Sa 16:5; Joel 2:16; Heb 10:22 [w] S Ge 35:2; Rev 22:14 **19:11** [x] ver 16 [y] S Ge 11:5 [z] ver 3,20; S Ex 3:1; 24:16; 31:18; 34:2,4,29,32; Lev 7:38; 26:46; 27:34; Nu 3:1; Dt 10:5; Ne 9:13; Gal 4:24-25 **19:12** [a] ver 23 **19:13** [b] Heb 12:20* [c] Jos 6:4; 1Ch 15:28; Ps 81:3; 98:6 [d] ver 21; Ex 34:3 **19:14** [e] S Ge 35:2 **19:15** [f] 1Sa 21:4; 1Co 7:5 **19:16** [g] 1Sa 2:10; Isa 29:6 [h] S ver 9 [i] Heb 12:18-19; Rev 4:1 [j] S Ge 3:10; 1Sa 13:7; 14:15; 28:5; Ps 99:1; Heb 12:21 **19:17** [k] S ver 2; Dt 4:11 **19:18** [l] Ex 20:18; Ps 104:32; Isa 6:4; Rev 15:8 [m] S Ex 3:2; 24:17; Lev 9:24; Dt 4:11,24,33,36; 5:4; 9:3; 1Ki 18:24,38; 1Ch 21:26; 2Ch 7:1; Ps 18:8; Heb 12:18 [n] S Ge 19:28; Rev 9:2 [o] Jdg 5:5; 2Sa 22:8; Ps 18:7; 68:8; Isa 2:19; 5:25; 41:15; 64:1; Jer 4:24; 10:10; Mic 1:4; Na 1:5; Hab 3:6,10; Hag 2:6 **19:19** [p] S ver 9; Dt 4:33; Ne 9:13 [q] Ps 81:7 **19:20** [r] S ver 11 **19:21** [s] Ex 24:10-11; Nu 4:20; 1Sa 6:19 [t] S ver 13 **19:22** [u] Lev 10:3 [v] 1Sa 16:5; 2Ch 29:5; Joel 2:16 [w] ver 24; 2Sa 6:7 **19:23** [x] ver 11 [y] ver 12 **19:24** [z] Ex 24:1,9 [a] ver 22 **20:1** [b] Dt 10:4 [c] Ne 9:13; Ps 119:9; 147:19; Mal 4:4 **20:2** [d] S Ge 17:7; Ex 16:12; Lev 19:2; 20:7; Isa 43:3; Eze 20:19

Rev 1:6; 5:10; 20:6). In their priestly role, the Israelites were to be channels of God's grace to the nations (see notes on Ge 12:2–3; Isa 42:1–4; 49:6). *holy nation.* See 1Pe 2:9. God's people, both individually and collectively, are to be "set apart" (see note on 3:5) to do his will (see Dt 7:6 and note; 14:2,21; 26:19; Isa 62:12).

19:8 *We will do everything the LORD has said.* The people promised to obey the terms of the covenant (see 24:3,7; Dt 5:27).

19:9 *dense cloud.* See 13:21 and note. *the people will hear me speaking.* See Dt 4:33. *put their trust in you.* See 14:31 and note.

19:10–11 Outward preparation to meet God symbolizes the inward consecration God requires of his people.

19:12–13 The whole mountain becomes holy because of God's presence (see 3:5 and note). Israel must keep itself from the mountain even as it is to keep itself from the tabernacle (see Nu 3:10 and note).

19:15 *Abstain from sexual relations.* Not because sex is sinful but because it may leave the participants ceremonially unclean (see Lev 15:18; see also 1Sa 21:4–5 and notes).

19:16 *thunder ... lightning ... trumpet blast.* God's appearance was often accompanied by an impressive display of meteorological sights and sounds (see, e.g., 1Sa 7:10; 12:18; Job 38:1; 40:6; Ps 18:13–14). *thick cloud.* See 13:21 and note.

19:18 *fire ... smoke from a furnace.* See Ge 15:17 and note.

19:22 *priests.* See also v. 24. Before the Aaronic priesthood was established (see 28:1), priestly functions were performed either by the elders (see note on 3:16; see also 3:18; 12:21; 18:12) or by designated younger men (see 24:5). But perhaps the verse anticipates the regulations for the Aaronic priests who will be appointed. *who approach the LORD.* To officiate at sacrifices (see 40:32; Lev 21:23).

19:23 *set it apart as holy.* See note on 3:5.

20:1–17 See Dt 5:6–21 and note; see also Mt 5:21,27 and note on 5:21; 19:17–19; Mk 10:19; Lk 18:20; Ro 13:9–10 and notes; Eph 6:2–3; Jas 2:10–11.

20:1 *words.* A technical term for "(covenant) stipulations" in the ancient Near East (e.g., among the Hittites; see also 24:3,8; 34:28). The basic code in Israel's divine law is found in vv. 2–17, elsewhere called the "Ten Commandments" (34:28; Dt 4:13; 10:4), the Hebrew words for which mean lit. "Ten Words." "Decalogue," a term of Greek origin often used as a synonym for the Ten Commandments, also means lit. "Ten Words."

20:2 *I am the LORD your God, who brought you out.* The Decalogue reflects the structure of the contemporary royal treaties (see note on Ge 15:7). On the basis of (1) a pre-

brought you out[e] of Egypt,[f] out
of the land of slavery.[g]
3 "You shall have no other gods before[a] me.[h]
4 "You shall not make for yourself an
idol[i] in the form of anything in
heaven above or on the earth
beneath or in the waters below. 5 You shall not bow down
to them or worship[j] them; for I,
the LORD your God, am a jealous
God,[k] punishing the children for
the sin of the fathers[l] to the third
and fourth generation[m] of those
who hate me, 6 but showing love
to a thousand[n] ⌞generations⌟ of
those who love me and keep my
commandments.
7 "You shall not misuse the name of the
LORD your God, for the LORD will
not hold anyone guiltless who
misuses his name.[o]
8 "Remember the Sabbath[p] day by keeping it holy. 9 Six days you shall labor and do all your work,[q] 10 but
the seventh day is a Sabbath[r] to
the LORD your God. On it you
shall not do any work, neither
you, nor your son or daughter,
nor your manservant or maidservant, nor your animals, nor the
alien within your gates. 11 For in
six days the LORD made the heavens and the earth,[s] the sea, and
all that is in them, but he rested[t]
on the seventh day.[u] Therefore
the LORD blessed the Sabbath day
and made it holy.
12 "Honor your father and your mother,[v]
so that you may live long[w] in the
land[x] the LORD your God is giving you.
13 "You shall not murder.[y]

[a] 3 Or *besides*

20:2 [e] S Ge 15:7 [f] S Ex 6:6 [g] Ex 13:3; Eze 20:6 **20:3** [h] ver 23; Ex 34:14; Dt 6:14; 13:10; 2Ki 17:35; Ps 44:20; 81:9; Jer 1:16; 7:6,9; 11:13; 19:4; 25:6; 35:15 **20:4** [i] ver 5,23; Ex 32:8; 34:17; Lev 19:4; 26:1; Dt 4:15-19,23; 27:15; 2Sa 7:22; 1Ki 14:9; 2Ki 17:12; Isa 40:19; 42:8; 44:9 **20:5** [j] Ex 23:13, 24; Jos 23:7; Jdg 6:10; 2Ki 17:35; Isa 44:15,17,19; 46:6 [k] Ex 34:14; Dt 4:24; Jos 24:19; Na 1:2 [l] S Ge 9:25; S Lev 26:39 [m] Ex 34:7; Nu 14:18; Jer 32:18 **20:6** [n] Ex 34:7; Nu 14:18; Dt 7:9; Jer 32:18; Lk 1:50; Ro 11:28 **20:7** [o] Ex 22:28; Lev 18:21; 19:12; 22:2; 24:11,16; Dt 6:13; 10:20; Job 2:5,9; Ps 63:11; Isa 8:21; Eze 20:39; 39:7; S Mt 5:33 **20:8** [p] S Ex 16:23; 31:13-16; 35:3; Lev 19:3,30; 26:2; Isa 56:2; Jer 17:21-27; Eze 22:8 **20:9** [q] Ex 23:12; 31:13-17; 34:21; 35:2-3; Lev 23:3; Lk 13:14 **20:10** [r] S Ge 2:3; Ex 31:14; Lev 23:38; Nu 28:9; Isa 56:2; Eze 20:12,20 **20:11** [s] Ge 1:3-2:1 [t] S Ge 2:2 [u] Ex 31:17; Heb 4:4 **20:12** [v] S Ge 31:35; S Dt 5:16; Mt 15:4*; 19:19*; Mk 7:10*; 10:19*; Lk 18:20*; Eph 6:2 [w] Dt 6:2; Eph 6:3 [x] Dt 11:9; 25:15; Jer 35:7 **20:13** [y] S Ge 4:23; Mt 5:21*; 19:18*; Mk 10:19*; Lk 18:20*; Ro 13:9*; Jas 2:11*

amble, in which the great king identified himself ("I am the LORD your God"), and (2) a historical prologue, in which he sketched his previous gracious acts toward the subject king or people ("who brought you out ..."), the Lord then set forth (3) the treaty (covenant) stipulations (see Dt 5:1–3,7–21) to be obeyed (in this case, ten in number: vv. 3–17). Use of this ancient royal treaty pattern shows that the Lord is here formally acknowledged as Israel's King and that Israel is his subject people. As his subjects, his covenant people are to render complete submission, allegiance and obedience to him out of gratitude for his mercies, reverence for his sovereignty, and trust in his continuing care. See chart, p. 19.

20:3 *before.* The Hebrew for this word is translated "in hostility toward" in Ge 16:12; 25:18. Something of that sense may be intended here. In any event, no deity is to rival the one true God in Israel's heart and life (see vv. 22–26 and note on v. 23).

20:4 *idol in the form of anything.* Because God has no visible form, any idol intended to resemble him would be a sinful misrepresentation of him (see Dt 4:12,15–18). Since other gods are not to be worshiped (see v. 5), making idols of them would be equally sinful (see Dt 4:19,23–28). Cf. Jn 4:23–24 and note on 4:24.

20:5 *jealous God.* God will not put up with rivalry or unfaithfulness. Usually his "jealousy" concerns Israel and assumes the covenant relationship (analogous to marriage) and the Lord's exclusive right to possess Israel and to claim her love and allegiance. Actually, jealousy is part of the vocabulary of love. The "jealousy" of God (1) demands exclusive devotion to himself (see 34:14; Dt 4:24; 32:16,21; Jos 24:19; Ps 78:58; 1Co 10:22; Jas 4:5 and NIV text note), (2) delivers to judgment all who oppose him (see Dt 29:20; 1Ki 14:22; Ps 79:5; Isa 42:13; 59:17; Eze 5:13; 16:38; 23:25; 36:5–6; Na 1:2; Zep 1:18; 3:8) and (3) vindicates his people (see 2Ki 19:31; Isa 9:7; 26:11; Eze 39:25; Joel 2:18 and note; Zec 1:14 and note; 8:2). In some of these passages the meaning is closer to "zeal" (the same Hebrew word may be translated either way, depending on context). *to the third and fourth generation of those who hate me.* Those Israelites who blatantly violate God's covenant and thus show that they reject the Lord as their King will bring down judgment on themselves and their households (see, e.g., Nu 16:31–34; Jos 7:24 and note)—households were usually extended to "three or four" generations. See note on Ps 109:12. *hate.* In covenant contexts the terms "hate" and "love" (v. 6) were conventionally used to indicate rejection of or loyalty to the covenant Lord.

20:6 *a thousand ⌞generations⌟ of those.* See Dt 7:9; 1Ch 16:15; Ps 105:8. *love me and keep my commandments.* See Dt 5:10; 6:5; 7:9,12 and note; Ne 1:5; Da 9:4; Jn 14:15; 1Jn 5:3. In the treaty language of the ancient Near East the "love" owed to the great king was a conventional term for total allegiance and implicit trust expressing itself in obedient service.

20:7 *misuse the name of the LORD.* By profaning God's name—e.g., by swearing falsely by it (see Lev 19:12; see also Jer 7:9 and note and NIV text note), as on the witness stand in court. Jesus elaborates on oath-taking in Mt 5:33–37 (see note there).

20:8 See Ge 2:3 and note. *Sabbath.* See note on 16:23. *holy.* See note on 3:5.

20:9 *Six days.* The question of a shorter work week in a modern industrialized culture is not in view.

20:10 *On it you shall not do any work.* Two reasons (one here and one in Deuteronomy) are given: (1) Having completed his work of creation God "rested on the seventh day" (v. 11), and the Israelites are to observe the same pattern in their service of God in the creation; (2) the Israelites must cease all labor so that their servants can also participate in the Sabbath-rest—just as God had delivered his people from the burden of slavery in Egypt (see Dt 5:14–15). The Sabbath thus became a "sign" of the covenant between God and Israel at Mount Sinai (see 31:12–17 and note on 31:16–17; see also note on Ge 9:12).

20:12 *Honor.* (1) Prize highly (see Pr 4:8), (2) care for (see Ps 91:15), (3) show respect for (see Lev 19:3; 20:9), and (4) obey (see Dt 21:18–21; cf. Eph 6:1). *so that you may live long.* "The first commandment with a promise" (Eph 6:2). See also note on Dt 6:2. Honoring those in authority is essential for social stability.

20:13 See Mt 5:21–26 and notes. *murder.* The Hebrew for this verb usually refers to a premeditated and deliberate act.

14 "You shall not commit adultery.[z]
15 "You shall not steal.[a]
16 "You shall not give false testimony[b]
against your neighbor.[c]
17 "You shall not covet[d] your neighbor's
house. You shall not covet your
neighbor's wife, or his manservant or maidservant, his ox or
donkey, or anything that belongs
to your neighbor."

18 When the people saw the thunder and
lightning and heard the trumpet[e] and saw
the mountain in smoke,[f] they trembled
with fear.[g] They stayed at a distance 19 and
said to Moses, "Speak to us yourself and
we will listen. But do not have God speak[h]
to us or we will die."[i]
20 Moses said to the people, "Do not be
afraid.[j] God has come to test[k] you, so that
the fear[l] of God will be with you to keep
you from sinning."[m]
21 The people remained at a distance,
while Moses approached the thick darkness[n] where God was.

Idols and Altars

22 Then the LORD said to Moses, "Tell the
Israelites this: 'You have seen for yourselves that I have spoken to you from
heaven:[o] 23 Do not make any gods to be
alongside me;[p] do not make for yourselves
gods of silver or gods of gold.[q]
24 " 'Make an altar[r] of earth for me and
sacrifice on it your burnt offerings[s] and
fellowship offerings,[a] your sheep and
goats and your cattle. Wherever I cause
my name[t] to be honored, I will come to
you and bless[u] you. 25 If you make an altar of stones for me, do not build it with
dressed stones, for you will defile it if you
use a tool[v] on it. 26 And do not go up to
my altar on steps, lest your nakedness[w] be
exposed on it.'

21 "These are the laws[x] you are to set
before them:

[a] *24* Traditionally *peace offerings*

20:14 [z] Lev 18:20; 20:10; Nu 5:12, 13, 29; Pr 6:29, 32; Mt 5:27*; 19:18*; Mk 10:19*; Lk 18:20*; Ro 13:9*; Jas 2:11* **20:15** [a] Lev 19:11, 13; Eze 18:7; Mt 19:18*; Mk 10:19*; Lk 18:20*; Ro 13:9* **20:16** [b] Lev 19:11; Jer 9:3, 5 [c] Ex 23:1, 7; Lev 19:18; Ps 50:20; 101:5; 119:29; Mt 19:18*; Mk 10:19; Lk 3:14*; 18:20* **20:17** [d] Lk 12:15; Ro 7:7*; 13:9*; Eph 5:3; Heb 13:5 **20:18** [e] Ex 19:16-19; Dt 4:36; Isa 58:1; Jer 6:17; Eze 33:3; Heb 12:18-19; Rev 1:10 [f] S Ex 19:18 [g] S Ge 3:10; S Ex 14:31; S 19:16 **20:19** [h] Job 37:4, 5; 40:9; Ps 29:3-4 [i] Dt 5:5, 23-27; 18:16; Gal 3:19 **20:20** [j] S Ge 15:1 [k] S Ge 22:1 [l] Dt 4:10; 6:2, 24; 10:12; Ps 111:10; 128:1; Pr 1:7; Ecc 12:13; Isa 8:13 [m] Job 1:8; 2:3; 28:28; Pr 3:7; 8:13; 14:16; 16:6 **20:21** [n] S Ex 19:9; Dt 5:22; Ps 18:9; 68:4; 97:2; Isa 19:1 **20:22** [o] Dt 5:24, 26; Ne 9:13 **20:23** [p] S ver 3 [q] Ex 22:20; 32:4, 8, 31; 34:17; Dt 29:17-18; Ne 9:18 **20:24** [r] Ex 27:1; 40:29; Nu 16:38; Dt 27:5; Jos 8:30; 2Ki 16:14; 2Ch 4:1; Ezr 3:2; Eze 43:13 [s] S Ge 8:20; S Ex 18:12 [t] Dt 12:5; 16:6, 11; 26:2; 1Ki 9:3; 2Ki 21:4, 7; 2Ch 6:6; 12:13; Ezr 6:12 [u] S Ge 12:2; 22:17 **20:25** [v] Jos 8:31; 1Ki 6:7 **20:26** [w] Eze 43:17 **21:1** [x] Ex 24:3; 34:32; Dt 4:14; 6:1

20:14 See Mt 5:27–30 and notes on 5:28–30. *adultery.* A sin "against God" (Ge 39:9; see note there) as well as against the marriage partner. "Marriage should be honored by all, and the marriage bed kept pure" (Heb 13:4).

20:15 *steal.* Stealing deprives others of what God has entrusted to them (see 22:1–15 and notes).

20:16 *false testimony.* Violates others' reputation and deprives them of their rights (see Ps 24:4; Pr 6:19; Jer 5:2 and notes).

20:17 *covet.* Desire something with evil motivation (see Mt 15:19 and note on Mk 7:20). To break God's commandments inwardly is equivalent to breaking them outwardly (see Mt 5:21–30; cf. Col 3:5).

20:18–21 Concludes the account of the giving of the Decalogue. The order of the narrative appears to be different from the order of events, since v. 18 is most likely a continuation of 19:25. On this reading, the proclamation of the Decalogue took place after Moses approached God (v. 21). Biblical writers often did not follow chronological sequence in their narratives for various literary reasons. The purpose of chronological displacement here may have been either (1) to keep the Decalogue distinct from the "Book of the Covenant" (24:7) that follows (20:22—23:19), or (2) to conclude the account with the formal institution of Moses' office as covenant mediator—or both.

20:19 See Heb 12:19–20. Israel requests a mediator to stand between them and God, a role fulfilled by Moses and subsequently by priests, prophets and kings—and ultimately by Jesus Christ (see 1Ti 2:5 and note).

20:20 *Do not be afraid.* Do not think that God's display of his majesty is intended simply to fill you with abject fear. He has come to enter into covenant with you as your heavenly King. *test.* See note on Ge 22:1. *fear of God.* See note on Ge 20:11.

20:22—23:19 The stipulations of the "Book of the Covenant" (24:7), consisting largely of expansions on and expositions of the Ten Commandments. See chart, p. 268.

20:22–26 Initial stipulations governing Israel's basic relationship with God (cf. v. 3 and note).

20:22 *heaven.* God's dwelling place. Even on "top of Mount Sinai" (19:20) God spoke from heaven.

20:23 See vv. 3–4. The contrast between the one true God "in heaven," who "does whatever pleases him" (Ps 115:3), and idols of silver or gold, who can do nothing at all (see Ps 115:3–8 and notes; see also Ps 135:5–7,15–18 and notes), is striking indeed.

20:24 *altar of earth.* Such an altar, with dimensions the same as those of the altar in the tabernacle (see 27:1), has been found in the excavated ruins of a small Iron Age (10th, or possibly 11th, century B.C.) Israelite temple at Arad in southern Israel. *burnt offerings.* See note on Lev 1:3. *fellowship offerings.* See note on Lev 3:1. *Wherever.* Not the later central sanctuary at Jerusalem, but numerous temporary places of worship (see, e.g., Jos 8:30–31; Jdg 6:24; 21:4; 1Sa 7:17; 14:35; 2Sa 24:25; 1Ki 18:30).

20:25 *do not build it with dressed stones.* Many ancient altars of undressed stones (from various periods) have been found in the land of Israel. *defile it if you use a tool on it.* For reasons not now clear, but perhaps related to pagan practices.

20:26 *steps.* The oldest stepped altar known in Israel is at Megiddo and dates between 3000 and 2500 B.C. *nakedness be exposed.* Men who ascended to such altars would expose their nakedness in the presence of God. Although Aaron and his descendants served at stepped altars (see Lev 9:22; Eze 43:17 and note), they were instructed to wear linen undergarments (see 28:42–43; Lev 6:10; 16:3–4; Eze 44:17–18).

21:1 This verse functions as the heading for the section 21:2—23:19.

Hebrew Servants

21:2-6pp — Dt 15:12-18
21:2-11Ref — Lev 25:39-55

2“If you buy a Hebrew servant,[y] he is
to serve you for six years. But in the seventh year, he shall go free,[z] without paying
anything. 3If he comes alone, he is to go
free alone; but if he has a wife when he
comes, she is to go with him. 4If his master gives him a wife and she bears him
sons or daughters, the woman and her
children shall belong to her master, and
only the man shall go free.
5“But if the servant declares, ‘I love
my master and my wife and children and
do not want to go free,’[a] 6then his master must take him before the judges.[a b] He
shall take him to the door or the doorpost
and pierce[c] his ear with an awl. Then he
will be his servant for life.[d]
7“If a man sells his daughter as a servant, she is not to go free as menservants
do. 8If she does not please the master who
has selected her for himself,[b] he must
let her be redeemed. He has no right to
sell her to foreigners, because he has broken faith with her. 9If he selects her for
his son, he must grant her the rights of
a daughter. 10If he marries another woman, he must not deprive the first one of
her food, clothing and marital rights.[e] 11If
he does not provide her with these three
things, she is to go free, without any payment of money.

Personal Injuries

12“Anyone who strikes a man and kills
him shall surely be put to death.[f] 13How-
ever, if he does not do it intentionally, but
God lets it happen, he is to flee to a place[g]
I will designate. 14But if a man schemes
and kills another man deliberately,[h] take
him away from my altar and put him to
death.[i]
15“Anyone who attacks[c] his father or his
mother must be put to death.
16“Anyone who kidnaps another and either sells[j] him or still has him when he is
caught must be put to death.[k]
17“Anyone who curses his father or
mother must be put to death.[l]
18“If men quarrel and one hits the other
with a stone or with his fist[d] and he does
not die but is confined to bed, 19the one
who struck the blow will not be held responsible if the other gets up and walks
around outside with his staff; however,
he must pay the injured man for the loss
of his time and see that he is completely
healed.
20“If a man beats his male or female
slave with a rod and the slave dies as a
direct result, he must be punished, 21but
he is not to be punished if the slave gets
up after a day or two, since the slave is
his property.[m]
22“If men who are fighting hit a pregnant woman and she gives birth prematurely[e] but there is no serious injury, the
offender must be fined whatever the woman’s husband demands[n] and the court allows. 23But if there is serious injury, you
are to take life for life,[o] 24eye for eye, tooth
for tooth,[p] hand for hand, foot for foot,
25burn for burn, wound for wound, bruise
for bruise.
26“If a man hits a manservant or maidservant in the eye and destroys it, he must
let the servant go free to compensate for
the eye. 27And if he knocks out the tooth
of a manservant or maidservant, he must

21:2 [y]Ex 22:3 [z]ver 7; Jer 34:8,14 **21:5** [a]Dt 15:16 **21:6** [b]Ex 22:8-9; Dt 17:9; 19:17; 25:1 [c]Ps 40:6 [d]Job 39:9; 41:4 **21:10** [e]1Co 7:3-5 **21:12** [f]ver 15,17; S Ge 4:14,23; Ex 31:15; Lev 20:9,10; 24:16; 27:29; Nu 1:51; 35:16,30-31; Dt 13:5; 19:11; 22:22; 27:16; Job 31:11; Pr 20:20; S Mt 26:52 **21:13** [g]Nu 35:10-34; Dt 4:42; 19:2-13; Jos 20:9 **21:14** [h]Ge 4:8; Nu 35:20; 2Sa 3:27; 20:10; Heb 10:26 [i]Dt 19:11-12; 1Ki 2:28-34 **21:16** [j]Ge 37:28 [k]Ex 22:4; Dt 24:7 **21:17** [l]S ver 12; S Dt 5:16; Mt 15:4*; Mk 7:10* **21:21** [m]Lev 25:44-46 **21:22** [n]ver 30 **21:23** [o]Lev 24:19; Dt 19:21 **21:24** [p]S ver 23; Mt 5:38*

[a] 6 Or *before God* [b] 8 Or *master so that he does not choose her* [c] 15 Or *kills* [d] 18 Or *with a tool* [e] 22 Or *she has a miscarriage*

21:2–11 See Jer 34:8–22. The list begins with laws regulating servitude. No other ancient Near Eastern law collection begins this way. Hammurapi’s law code, e.g., deals with the question of slavery last. The fact that the Lord gives priority to regulating servitude in the Book of the Covenant may reflect his recent deliverance of Israel from a painful period of enslavement in Egypt.
21:2 *Hebrew.* See note on Ge 14:13. *in the seventh year, he shall go free.* The Lord’s servants are not to be anyone’s perpetual slaves (see 20:10 and note).
21:6 *the judges.* See NIV text note; see also 22:8–9,28 and NIV text notes. *pierce his ear with an awl.* See Dt 15:17. Submission to this rite symbolized willing service (see Ps 40:6–8 and note on 40:6).
21:12–15 See 20:13 and note; see also Nu 35:16–34 and note on 35:33; Dt 19:1–13; 21:1–9; 24:7; 27:24–25; Jos 20:1–9 and note.
21:12 See Ge 9:6 and note.
21:13 *does not do it intentionally.* Related terms and expressions are “accidentally” (Nu 35:11), “without hostility” (Nu 35:22), “was not his enemy” (Nu 35:23), “did not intend to harm him” (Nu 35:23) and “without malice aforethought” (Dt 19:4). Premeditated murder is thus distinguished from accidental manslaughter. *God lets it happen.* The event is beyond human control—in modern legal terminology, an “act of God.” *place.* A city of refuge (see Nu 35:6–32; Dt 19:1–13; Jos 20:1–9 and relevant notes; 21:13,21,27,32,38).
21:14 *away from my altar.* Or “even from my altar.” The horns of the altar were a final refuge for those subject to judicial action (see 1Ki 1:50–51; 2:28; Am 3:14 and notes).
21:15 See 20:12 and note.
21:16 See 20:15 and note.
21:17 *curses … father or mother.* Calls down curses on them to effect their destruction.
21:19 *walks around outside with his staff.* Is convalescing in a satisfactory way. *the loss of his time.* Lit. “his sitting,” i.e., his enforced idleness.
21:20–21 Benefit of doubt was granted to the slaveholder where no homicidal intentions could be proved.
21:23–25 See Dt 19:21. The so-called law of retaliation, as its contexts show, was meant to limit the punishment to fit the crime. By invoking the law of love, Jesus corrected the popular misunderstanding of the law of retaliation (see Mt 5:38–42). See note on Lev 24:20.
21:23 *serious injury.* Either to mother or to child.
21:26–27 Humane applications of the law of retaliation.

let the servant go free to compensate for
the tooth.
28"If a bull gores a man or a woman to
death, the bull must be stoned to death,[q]
and its meat must not be eaten. But the
owner of the bull will not be held responsible. 29If, however, the bull has had the
habit of goring and the owner has been
warned but has not kept it penned up[r] and
it kills a man or woman, the bull must be
stoned and the owner also must be put to
death. 30However, if payment is demanded
of him, he may redeem his life by paying
whatever is demanded.[s] 31This law also
applies if the bull gores a son or daughter.
32If the bull gores a male or female slave,
the owner must pay thirty shekels[a][t] of silver to the master of the slave, and the bull
must be stoned.
33"If a man uncovers a pit[u] or digs one
and fails to cover it and an ox or a donkey
falls into it, 34the owner of the pit must
pay for the loss; he must pay its owner,
and the dead animal will be his.
35"If a man's bull injures the bull of another and it dies, they are to sell the live
one and divide both the money and the
dead animal equally. 36However, if it was
known that the bull had the habit of goring, yet the owner did not keep it penned
up,[v] the owner must pay, animal for animal, and the dead animal will be his.

Protection of Property

22 "If a man steals an ox or a sheep and
slaughters it or sells it, he must pay
back[w] five head of cattle for the ox and
four sheep for the sheep.
2"If a thief is caught breaking in[x] and is
struck so that he dies, the defender is not
guilty of bloodshed;[y] 3but if it happens[b]
after sunrise, he is guilty of bloodshed.
"A thief must certainly make restitution,[z] but if he has nothing, he must be
sold[a] to pay for his theft.
4"If the stolen animal is found alive in
his possession[b]—whether ox or donkey or
sheep—he must pay back double.[c]
5"If a man grazes his livestock in a field
or vineyard and lets them stray and they
graze in another man's field, he must
make restitution[d] from the best of his own
field or vineyard.
6"If a fire breaks out and spreads into
thornbushes so that it burns shocks[e] of
grain or standing grain or the whole field,
the one who started the fire must make
restitution.[f]
7"If a man gives his neighbor silver or
goods for safekeeping[g] and they are stolen
from the neighbor's house, the thief, if he
is caught, must pay back double.[h] 8But if
the thief is not found, the owner of the
house must appear before the judges[c][i] to
determine whether he has laid his hands
on the other man's property. 9In all cases
of illegal possession of an ox, a donkey, a
sheep, a garment, or any other lost property about which somebody says, 'This is
mine,' both parties are to bring their cases before the judges.[j] The one whom the
judges declare[d] guilty must pay back double to his neighbor.
10"If a man gives a donkey, an ox, a
sheep or any other animal to his neighbor
for safekeeping[k] and it dies or is injured
or is taken away while no one is looking,
11the issue between them will be settled
by the taking of an oath[l] before the LORD
that the neighbor did not lay hands on the
other person's property. The owner is to
accept this, and no restitution is required.
12But if the animal was stolen from the
neighbor, he must make restitution[m] to
the owner. 13If it was torn to pieces by a
wild animal, he shall bring in the remains
as evidence and he will not be required to
pay for the torn animal.[n]
14"If a man borrows an animal from his
neighbor and it is injured or dies while the
owner is not present, he must make restitution.[o] 15But if the owner is with the animal, the borrower will not have to pay. If
the animal was hired, the money paid for
the hire covers the loss.[p]

21:28 [q] ver 32; Ge 9:5
21:29 [r] ver 36
21:30 [s] ver 22
21:32 [t] Ge 37:28; Zec 11:12-13; Mt 26:15; 27:3,9
21:33 [u] Lk 14:5
21:36 [v] ver 29
22:1 [w] Lev 6:1-7; 2Sa 12:6; Pr 6:31; S Lk 19:8
22:2 [x] Job 24:16; Jer 2:34; Hos 7:1; Mt 6:19-20; 24:43 [y] Nu 35:27
22:3 [z] ver 1 [a] S Ex 21:2; S Mt 18:25
22:4 [b] 1Sa 12:5 [c] S Ge 43:12
22:5 [d] ver 1
22:6 [e] Jdg 15:5 [f] ver 1
22:7 [g] ver 10; Lev 6:2 [h] S Ge 43:12
22:8 [i] S Ex 21:6
22:9 [j] ver 8; Dt 25:1
22:10 [k] S ver 7
22:11 [l] Lev 6:3; 1Ki 8:31; 2Ch 6:22; Heb 6:16
22:12 [m] ver 1
22:13 [n] Ge 31:39
22:14 [o] ver 1
22:15 [p] Lev 19:13; Job 17:5

[a] *32* That is, about 12 ounces (about 0.3 kilogram)
[b] *3* Or *if he strikes him*
[c] *8* Or *before God*; also in verse 9
[d] *9* Or *whom God declares*

21:28–32 The law of the goring bull.
21:28 *the bull must be stoned to death.* By killing someone, the bull becomes accountable for that person's life (see Ge 9:5 and note).
21:30 *if payment is demanded.* If the victim's family is willing to accept a ransom payment instead of demanding the death penalty. *he may redeem his life by paying.* The payment (lit. "ransom," as in Nu 35:31) is not to compensate the victim's family but to save the negligent man's life.
21:32 *thirty shekels of silver.* Apparently the standard price for a slave. It was also the amount Judas was willing to accept as his price for betraying Jesus (see Mt 26:14–15; see also Zec 11:12–13 and notes). *shekels.* See note on Ge 20:16.
21:33–36 Laws concerning injuries to animals.
22:1–15 Laws concerning property rights (see 20:15 and note).
22:1 *must pay back … four sheep for the sheep.* For a memorable reference to this requirement see David's words in 2Sa 12:6 (see also note there).
22:2 An act of self-defense in darkness does not produce bloodguilt.
22:3 Killing an intruder in broad daylight is not justifiable.
22:5 *from the best.* Restitution should always err on the side of quality and generosity.
22:6 *thornbushes.* Often used as hedges (see Mic 7:4) bordering cultivated areas.
22:11 See 20:7 and note. *an oath before the LORD.* The judges were God's representatives in court cases (see 21:6; 22:8–9,28 and NIV text notes).
22:12–13 Similar laws apparently existed as early as the patriarchal period (see Ge 31:39 and note).

Social Responsibility

16“If a man seduces a virgin[q] who is not
pledged to be married and sleeps with her,
he must pay the bride-price,[r] and she shall
be his wife. 17If her father absolutely refuses to give her to him, he must still pay the
bride-price for virgins.
18“Do not allow a sorceress[s] to live.
19“Anyone who has sexual relations with
an animal[t] must be put to death.
20“Whoever sacrifices to any god[u] other
than the LORD must be destroyed.[a][v]
21“Do not mistreat an alien[w] or oppress
him, for you were aliens[x] in Egypt.
22“Do not take advantage of a widow or
an orphan.[y] 23If you do and they cry out[z]
to me, I will certainly hear their cry.[a] 24My
anger will be aroused, and I will kill you
with the sword; your wives will become
widows and your children fatherless.[b]
25“If you lend money to one of my people among you who is needy, do not be
like a moneylender; charge him no interest.[b][c] 26If you take your neighbor’s cloak
as a pledge,[d] return it to him by sunset,
27because his cloak is the only covering he
has for his body. What else will he sleep
in?[e] When he cries out to me, I will hear,
for I am compassionate.[f]
28“Do not blaspheme God[c][g] or curse[h]
the ruler of your people.[i]
29“Do not hold back offerings[j] from your
granaries or your vats.[d]
“You must give me the firstborn of your
sons.[k] 30Do the same with your cattle
and your sheep.[l] Let them stay with their
mothers for seven days, but give them to
me on the eighth day.[m]
31“You are to be my holy people.[n] So do
not eat the meat of an animal torn by wild
beasts;[o] throw it to the dogs.

Laws of Justice and Mercy

23 “Do not spread false reports.[p] Do not
help a wicked man by being a malicious witness.[q]
2“Do not follow the crowd in doing
wrong. When you give testimony in a lawsuit, do not pervert justice[r] by siding with
the crowd,[s] 3and do not show favoritism[t]
to a poor man in his lawsuit.
4“If you come across your enemy’s[u] ox
or donkey wandering off, be sure to take
it back to him.[v] 5If you see the donkey[w] of
someone who hates you fallen down under its load, do not leave it there; be sure
you help him with it.
6“Do not deny justice[x] to your poor people in their lawsuits. 7Have nothing to do
with a false charge[y] and do not put an in-

[a] 20 The Hebrew term refers to the irrevocable giving over of things or persons to the LORD, often by totally destroying them. [b] 25 Or *excessive interest* [c] 28 Or *Do not revile the judges* [d] 29 The meaning of the Hebrew for this phrase is uncertain.

22:16 [q]Dt 22:28 [r]S Ge 34:12 **22:18** [s]S Ex 7:11; Lev 19:26, 31; 20:27; Dt 18:11; 1Sa 28:3; 2Ch 33:6; Isa 57:3 **22:19** [t]Lev 18:23; 20:15; Dt 27:21 **22:20** [u]S Ex 20:23; 34:15; Lev 17:7; Nu 25:2; Dt 32:17; Ps 106:37 [v]Lev 27:29; Dt 13:5; 17:2-5; 18:20; 1Ki 18:40; 19:1; 2Ki 10:25; 23:20; 2Ch 15:13 **22:21** [w]Ex 23:9; Lev 19:33; 24:22; Nu 15:14; Dt 1:16; 24:17; Eze 22:29 [x]Dt 10:19; 27:19; Zec 7:10; Mal 3:5 **22:22** [y]ver 26; Dt 10:18; 24:6, 10, 12, 17; Job 22:6, 9; 24:3, 21; Ps 68:5; 146:9; Pr 23:10; Isa 1:17; Jer 7:5, 6; 21:12; 22:3; Eze 18:5-9, 12; Zec 7:9-10; Mal 3:5; Jas 1:27 **22:23** [z]Lk 18:7 [a]Dt 10:18; 15:9; 24:15; Job 34:28; 35:9; Ps 10:14, 17; 12:5; 18:6; 34:15; Jas 5:4 **22:24** [b]Ps 69:24; 109:9; La 5:3 **22:25** [c]Lev 25:35-37; Dt 15:7-11; 23:20; Ne 5:7, 10; Ps 15:5; Eze 18:8 **22:26** [d]S ver 22; Pr 20:16; Eze 33:15; Am 2:8 **22:27** [e]Dt 24:13, 17; Job 22:6; 24:7; 29:11; 31:19-20; Eze 18:12, 16 [f]Ex 34:6; Dt 4:31; 2Ch 30:9; Ne 9:17; Ps 99:8; 103:8; 116:5; 145:8; Joel 2:13; Jnh 4:2 **22:28** [g]S Ex 20:7 [h]2Sa 16:5, 9; 19:21; 1Ki 21:10; 2Ki 2:23; Ps 102:8 [i]Ecc 10:20; Ac 23:5* **22:29** [j]Ex 23:15, 16, 19; 34:20, 26; Lev 19:24; 23:10; Nu 18:13; 28:26; Dt 18:4; 26:2, 10; 1Sa 6:3; Ne 10:35; Pr 3:9; Mal 3:10 [k]S Ex 13:2; Nu 8:16-17; Lk 2:23 **22:30** [l]Ex 34:19; Dt 15:19 [m]Ge 17:12; Lev 12:3; 22:27 **22:31** [n]Ex 19:6; Lev 19:2; 22:31; Ezr 9:2 [o]Lev 7:24; 17:15; 22:8; Dt 14:21; Eze 4:14; 44:31 **23:1** [p]S Ge 39:17; Mt 19:18; Lk 3:14 [q]S Ex 20:16; Dt 5:20; 19:16-21; Ps 27:12; 35:11; Pr 19:5; Ac 6:11 **23:2** [r]ver 3, 6, 9; Lev 19:15, 33; Dt 1:17; 16:19; 24:17; 27:19; 1Sa 8:3 [s]Job 31:34 **23:3** [t]Dt 1:17 **23:4** [u]Ro 12:20 [v]Lev 6:3; 19:11; Dt 22:1-3 **23:5** [w]Dt 22:4 **23:6** [x]S ver 2; Dt 23:16; Pr 22:22 **23:7** [y]S Ex 20:16; S Eph 4:25

22:16–31 General laws related to social obligations (see chart, p. 268).

22:16 *bride-price.* A gift, usually substantial, given by the prospective groom to the bride’s family as payment for her (see Ge 24:53 and note). The custom is still followed today in parts of the Middle East.

22:18 Dt 18:9–12 strongly condemns sorcery and all such occult practices (see note on Dt 18:9; see also 1Sa 28:9; Isa 47:12–14).

22:19 Ancient myths and epics describe acts of bestiality performed by pagan gods and demigods in Babylonia and Canaan.

22:20 See 20:3–5 and notes. The total destruction (see NIV text note) of the idolatrous Canaanites was later commanded by the Lord (see Dt 7:2; 13:15; 20:17; Jos 6:17 and note; 10:40; 11:12,20).

22:21–27 That the poor, the widow, the orphan, the alien — in fact, all defenseless people — are objects of God’s special concern and providential care is clear from the writings of Moses (see 21:26–27; 23:6–12; Lev 19:9–10 and note; Dt 14:29 and note on 14:22–29; 16:11,14; 24:19–21; 26:12–13), the psalmists (see Ps 10:14,17–18; 68:5–6 and note; 82:3–4 and note; 146:9) and the prophets (see Isa 1:23; 10:2; Jer 7:6; 22:3; Zec 7:10 and note; Mal 3:5) as well as from the teachings of Jesus (see, e.g., Mt 25:34–45) and the apostles (see Ro 15:26; Gal 2:10 and note; Jas 1:27; 2:2–7).

22:25–27 Laws dealing with interest on loans (see Lev 25:35–37; Dt 15:7–11; 23:19–20; see also Ne 5:10 and note; Job 24:9; Ps 15:5; Pr 28:8 and note; Eze 18:13; 22:12). Interest for profit was not to be charged at the expense of the poor. Generosity in such matters was extended even further by Jesus (see Lk 6:34–35).

22:26–27 If all a person had to offer in pledge for a loan was a cloak, that person was among the poorest of the poor (see Am 2:8 and note).

22:28 *Do not … curse the ruler of your people.* A ruler was God’s representative. A penitent Paul quoted this law after he had unwittingly insulted the high priest (see Ac 23:4–5).

22:29 *vats.* See note on Hag 2:16. *give me the firstborn.* See notes on 4:22; 13:2,13; see also 13:15.

22:30 *Do the same with your cattle and your sheep.* See notes on 13:2,13; see also 13:12,15. *give them to me on the eighth day.* The same principle applied in a different way to firstborn sons as well (see note on Ge 17:12).

22:31 Since God’s people were “a kingdom of priests” (see 19:6 and note), they were to obey a law later specified for members of the Aaronic priesthood (see Lev 22:8) as well.

23:1–9 Most of the regulations in this section pertain to 20:16 (see note there).

23:1 See Lev 19:16; Dt 22:13–19; 1Ki 21:10–13.

23:4–5 Those hostile to you are to be shown the same consideration as others (see Dt 22:1–4; Pr 25:21). Jesus teaches that this means “Love your enemies” (Mt 5:44; see note there).

nocent[z] or honest person to death,[a] for I
will not acquit the guilty.[b]
8"Do not accept a bribe,[c] for a bribe
blinds those who see and twists the words
of the righteous.
9"Do not oppress an alien;[d] you yourselves know how it feels to be aliens, because you were aliens in Egypt.

Sabbath Laws

10"For six years you are to sow your
fields and harvest the crops, 11but during
the seventh year let the land lie unplowed
and unused.[e] Then the poor among your
people may get food from it, and the wild
animals may eat what they leave. Do the
same with your vineyard and your olive
grove.
12"Six days do your work,[f] but on the
seventh day do not work, so that your ox
and your donkey may rest and the slave
born in your household, and the alien as
well, may be refreshed.[g]
13"Be careful[h] to do everything I have
said to you. Do not invoke the names of
other gods;[i] do not let them be heard on
your lips.[j]

The Three Annual Festivals

14"Three times[k] a year you are to celebrate a festival to me.
15"Celebrate the Feast of Unleavened
Bread;[l] for seven days eat bread made
without yeast, as I commanded you. Do
this at the appointed time in the month
of Abib,[m] for in that month you came out
of Egypt.
"No one is to appear before me empty-
handed.[n]
16"Celebrate the Feast of Harvest[o] with
the firstfruits[p] of the crops you sow in your
field.
"Celebrate the Feast of Ingathering[q] at
the end of the year, when you gather in
your crops from the field.[r]
17"Three times[s] a year all the men are to
appear before the Sovereign LORD.
18"Do not offer the blood of a sacrifice
to me along with anything containing
yeast.[t]
"The fat of my festival offerings must
not be kept until morning.[u]
19"Bring the best of the firstfruits[v] of
your soil to the house of the LORD your
God.
"Do not cook a young goat in its mother's milk.[w]

God's Angel to Prepare the Way

20"See, I am sending an angel[x] ahead
of you to guard you along the way and to
bring you to the place I have prepared.[y]
21Pay attention to him and listen[z] to what he
says. Do not rebel against him; he will not
forgive[a] your rebellion,[b] since my Name[c]
is in him. 22If you listen carefully to what
he says and do[d] all that I say, I will be an
enemy[e] to your enemies and will oppose
those who oppose you. 23My angel will go
ahead of you and bring you into the land of
the Amorites, Hittites, Perizzites, Canaanites, Hivites and Jebusites,[f] and I will wipe

23:7 [z]Mt 27:4 [a]S Ge 18:23 [b]Ex 34:7; Dt 19:18; 25:1 **23:8** [c]S Ex 18:21; Lev 19:15; Dt 10:17; 27:25; Job 15:34; 36:18; Ps 26:10; Pr 6:35; 15:27; 17:8; Isa 1:23; 5:23; Mic 3:11; 7:3 **23:9** [d]S ver 2; S Ex 22:21; Lev 19:33-34; Eze 22:7 **23:11** [e]Lev 25:1-7; Ne 10:31 **23:12** [f]S Ex 20:9; Lk 13:14 [g]Ge 2:2-3 **23:13** [h]Dt 4:9,23; 1Ti 4:16 [i]ver 32; Dt 12:3; Jos 23:7; Ps 16:4; Zec 13:2 [j]Dt 18:20; Jos 23:7; Ps 16:4; Hos 2:17 **23:14** [k]ver 17; S Ex 12:14; 34:23,24; Dt 16:16; 1Ki 9:25; 2Ch 8:13; Eze 46:9 **23:15** [l]S Ex 12:17; Mt 26:17; Lk 22:1; Ac 12:3 [m]S Ex 12:2 [n]S Ex 22:29 **23:16** [o]Lev 23:15-21; Nu 28:26; Dt 16:9; 2Ch 8:13 [p]S Ex 22:29; S 34:22 [q]Ex 34:22; Lev 23:34,42; Dt 16:16; 31:10; Ezr 3:4; Ne 8:14; Zec 14:16 [r]Lev 23:39; Dt 16:13; Jer 40:10 **23:17** [s]S ver 14 **23:18** [t]Ex 34:25; Lev 2:11 [u]S Ex 12:8 **23:19** [v]S Ex 22:29; S 34:22; S Nu 18:12 [w]Ex 34:26; Dt 14:21 **23:20** [x]S Ge 16:7 [y]Ex 15:17 **23:21** [z]Dt 18:19; Jer 13:15 [a]Dt 29:20; 2Ki 24:4; La 1:17 [b]Nu 17:10; Dt 9:7; 31:27; Jos 24:19; Ps 25:7; 78:8,40,56; 106:33; 107:11; 1Jn 5:16 [c]S Ex 3:15 **23:22** [d]S Ex 15:26 [e]S Ge 12:3; Isa 41:11; Jer 30:20 **23:23** [f]Nu 13:29; 21:21; Jos 3:10; 24:8,11; Ezr 9:1; Ps 135:11

23:8 See Dt 16:19 and note.
23:10–13 Extensions of the principles taught in 20:8–11; Dt 5:12–15 (see notes there).
23:14–19 See 34:18–26; Lev 23:4–44 and notes; Nu 28:16—29:40; Dt 16:1–17; see also chart, pp. 178–179.
23:15 *Feast of Unleavened Bread.* Celebrated from the 15th through the 21st days of the first month (usually about mid-March to mid-April; see note on 12:2) at the beginning of the barley harvest; it commemorated the exodus.
23:16 *Feast of Harvest.* Also called the "Feast of Weeks" (34:22) because it was held seven weeks after the Feast of Unleavened Bread. It was celebrated on the sixth day of the third month (usually about mid-May to mid-June) during the wheat harvest. In later Judaism it came to commemorate the giving of the law on Mount Sinai, though there is no evidence of this significance in the OT. In NT times it was called "(the day of) Pentecost" (Ac 2:1 [see note there]; 20:16; 1Co 16:8), which means "50" (see Lev 23:16). *Feast of Ingathering.* Also called the "Feast of Tabernacles" (Lev 23:34; see note on Zec 14:16) or "Booths" because the Israelites lived in temporary shelters when God brought them out of Egypt (see Lev 23:42–43 and note on 23:42). It was celebrated from the 15th through the 22nd days of the seventh month (usually about mid-September to mid-October) when the produce of the orchards and vines had been harvested; it commemorated the desert wanderings after the exodus. *end of the year.* End of the agricultural year, which began in the fall (see note on 12:2).
23:17 *all the men.* Normally accompanied by their families (see, e.g., 1Sa 1).
23:18 *not … with anything containing yeast.* See note on 12:15. *not be kept until morning.* See 12:9–10.
23:19 *firstfruits.* Representative of the whole harvest. The offering of firstfruits was an acknowledgment that the harvest was from the Lord and belonged wholly to him (see 34:26; Lev 23:9–14; Nu 18:12–13; Dt 18:13). *Do not cook a young goat in its mother's milk.* The reason for this prohibition is uncertain, but it may well be related to the prohibition against slaughtering a cow and its calf, or a mother sheep and its lamb, or a mother goat and its young on the same day (Lev 22:28) and the prohibition against "taking" from a nest both a mother bird and its young for human consumption (Dt 22:6–7). Such acts would be in tension with the especially tender relationship between mother and offspring established by God in his ordering of the creation.
23:20 *angel.* See 14:19; see also note on Ge 16:7. *place I have prepared.* Canaan (cf. the similar statement of Jesus in Jn 14:2–3).
23:21 *Name.* Representing God's presence (see note on Dt 12:5).
23:22 *If.* See note on 19:5.
23:23 See 3:8 and note.

them out. [24]Do not bow down before their
gods or worship[g] them or follow their practices.[h] You must demolish[i] them and break
their sacred stones[j] to pieces. [25]Worship
the LORD your God,[k] and his blessing[l] will
be on your food and water. I will take away
sickness[m] from among you, [26]and none will
miscarry or be barren[n] in your land. I will
give you a full life span.[o]
[27]"I will send my terror[p] ahead of you
and throw into confusion[q] every nation
you encounter. I will make all your enemies
turn their backs and run.[r] [28]I will send the
hornet[s] ahead of you to drive the Hivites,
Canaanites and Hittites[t] out of your way.
[29]But I will not drive them out in a single
year, because the land would become desolate and the wild animals[u] too numerous
for you. [30]Little by little I will drive them
out before you, until you have increased
enough to take possession[v] of the land.
[31]"I will establish your borders from the
Red Sea[a] to the Sea of the Philistines,[b] and
from the desert to the River.[c][w] I will hand
over to you the people who live in the land
and you will drive them out[x] before you.
[32]Do not make a covenant[y] with them or
with their gods. [33]Do not let them live in
your land, or they will cause you to sin
against me, because the worship of their
gods will certainly be a snare[z] to you."

The Covenant Confirmed

24 Then he said to Moses, "Come up
to the LORD, you and Aaron,[a] Nadab
and Abihu,[b] and seventy of the elders[c] of
Israel. You are to worship at a distance,
[2]but Moses alone is to approach[d] the LORD;
the others must not come near. And the
people may not come up with him."
[3]When Moses went and told the people
all the LORD's words and laws,[e] they responded with one voice, "Everything the
LORD has said we will do."[f] [4]Moses then
wrote[g] down everything the LORD had said.
He got up early the next morning and
built an altar[h] at the foot of the mountain
and set up twelve stone pillars[i] representing the twelve tribes of Israel. [5]Then he
sent young Israelite men, and they offered
burnt offerings[j] and sacrificed young bulls
as fellowship offerings[d][k] to the LORD. [6]Mo-
ses[l] took half of the blood[m] and put it in
bowls, and the other half he sprinkled[n] on
the altar. [7]Then he took the Book of the
Covenant[o] and read it to the people. They
responded, "We will do everything the
LORD has said; we will obey."[p]
[8]Moses then took the blood, sprinkled
it on the people[q] and said, "This is the
blood of the covenant[r] that the LORD has

[a] *31* Hebrew *Yam Suph*; that is, Sea of Reeds
[b] *31* That is, the Mediterranean [c] *31* That is, the Euphrates [d] *5* Traditionally *peace offerings*

23:24 [g]S Ex 20:5 [h]Lev 18:3; 20:23; Dt 9:4; 12:30-31; Jer 10:2 [i]Ex 34:13; Nu 33:52; Dt 7:5; 12:3; Jdg 2:2; 2Ki 18:4; 23:14 [j]Lev 26:1; Dt 16:22; 1Ki 14:23; 2Ki 3:2; 10:26; 17:10; 2Ch 14:3; Isa 27:9 **23:25** [k]Mt 4:10 [l]Lev 26:3-13; Dt 7:12-15; 28:1-14 [m]S Ex 15:26 **23:26** [n]Lev 26:3-4; Dt 7:14; 28:4; Mal 3:11 [o]S Ge 15:15; Dt 4:1,40; 32:47; Ps 90:10 **23:27** [p]S Ge 35:5; S Ex 15:14 [q]S Ex 14:24; Dt 7:23 [r]2Sa 22:41; Ps 18:40; 21:12 **23:28** [s]Dt 7:20; Jos 24:12 [t]Ex 33:2; 34:11,24; Nu 13:29; Dt 4:38; 11:23; 18:12; Jos 3:10; 24:11; Ps 78:55 **23:29** [u]Dt 7:22 **23:30** [v]Jos 23:5 **23:31** [w]S Ge 2:14; Dt 34:2; Ezr 4:20 [x]Dt 7:24; 9:3; Jos 21:44; 24:12,18; Ps 80:8 **23:32** [y]S Ge 26:28; Ex 34:12; Dt 7:2; Jos 9:7; Jdg 2:2; 1Sa 11:1; 1Ki 15:19; 20:34; Eze 17:13 **23:33** [z]S Ex 10:7 **24:1** [a]S Ex 19:24 [b]S Ex 6:23 [c]ver 9; Nu 11:16 **24:2** [d]Nu 12:6-8 **24:3** [e]S Ex 21:1; Gal 3:19 [f]S Ex 19:8; Jos 24:24 **24:4** [g]S Ex 17:14 [h]S Ge 8:20 [i]S Ge 28:18; S Dt 27:2 **24:5** [j]Lev 1:3 [k]S Ge 31:54 **24:6** [l]Ex 14:15; 32:31; Ps 99:6 [m]Heb 9:18 [n]Lev 1:11; 3:2,8,13; 5:9; Mt 26:28 **24:7** [o]2Ki 23:2,21; Heb 9:19 [p]Ex 19:8; Jer 40:3; 42:6,21; 43:2 **24:8** [q]Heb 9:19; 1Pe 1:2 [r]Lev 26:3; Dt 5:2-3; Jos 24:25; 2Ki 11:17; Jer 11:4,8; 31:32; 34:13; Zec 9:11; S Mt 26:28; S Lk 22:20; Heb 9:20*

23:25–26 For more expanded lists of God's covenant blessings see Lev 26:3–13; Dt 7:13–15; 28:1–14; 31:1–10 and relevant notes.

23:27 *my terror.* See note on 1Ch 14:17.

23:28 *hornet.* The meaning of the Hebrew for this word is uncertain. The Septuagint (the pre-Christian Greek translation of the OT) renders it "wasp," but the translators may have been guessing. In any event, the Lord promises to send some agent to disable or frighten the peoples of Canaan so that they will not be able to resist Israel's invasion. But probably the word involves concrete imagery and the focus of the statement is on the effects — therefore we are not to look for some historical agent to which the word metaphorically refers (cf. Isa 7:18).

23:30 *Little by little.* See Jdg 1.

23:31 See Ge 15:18; 1Ki 4:21 and note. *Red Sea.* The (south) eastern border (here the modern Gulf of Aqaba; see note on 1Ki 9:26). *Sea of the Philistines.* The western border (see NIV text note). *the desert.* The southern border (northeastern Sinai; see note on Ge 15:18). *the River.* The northern border (see NIV text note).

23:33 *snare.* A symbol of destruction (see 10:7; Job 18:9; Ps 18:5; Pr 13:14; 21:6; Isa 24:17–18).

24:1 *Come up.* The action, temporarily interrupted for the Book of the Covenant (20:22 — 23:33), is resumed from 20:21. Moses and his associates would ascend the mountain after the events of vv. 3–8. *Nadab and Abihu.* Aaron's two oldest sons. Nadab would have succeeded Aaron as high priest, but he and his brother died because they offered unauthorized fire before the Lord (see Lev 10:2; Nu 3:4 and notes). *seventy … elders.* Cf. Nu 11:16; perhaps representing the clans that developed from the 70 descendants of Jacob referred to in 1:5 (see Ge 46:27 and note). *elders.* See note on 3:16. *at a distance.* See 20:21.

24:2 *Moses alone.* As God's chosen mediator between himself and Israel and through whom he would establish his covenant with them. Jesus, who is greater than Moses (see Heb 3:1–6), is the "mediator of a new covenant" (Heb 12:24; see note on Heb 8:6).

24:3 *words.* Probably refers to the Ten Commandments (see 20:1 and note). *laws.* Probably refers to the stipulations of the Book of the Covenant (20:22 — 23:19). *we will do.* See v. 7; see also 19:8 and note.

24:4 *Moses … wrote.* See note on 17:14; see also Introduction: Author and Date of Writing. *twelve stone pillars representing.* See Jos 4:5,20 and note on 4:9; 1Ki 18:31 and note.

24:5 *young Israelite men … offered.* See note on 19:22.

24:6 *half of the blood … the other half.* The division of the blood points to the twofold aspect of the "blood of the covenant" (v. 8): The blood on the altar symbolizes God's forgiveness and his acceptance of the offering; the blood on the people points to an oath that binds them in obedience (see vv. 3,7).

24:7 *Book of the Covenant.* Strictly speaking, 20:22 — 23:19 (see note there) — but here perhaps implying also the stipulations of 20:2–17; 23:20–33. *We will do … we will obey.* See v. 3; see also 19:8 and note.

24:8 *then.* Israel's pledge of full obedience to the Lord's rule (v. 7) was an essential element in the establishment of the covenant between the Lord and Israel (see note on v. 6;

made with you in accordance with all
these words."
9Moses and Aaron, Nadab and Abihu,
and the seventy elders[s] of Israel went up
10and saw[t] the God of Israel. Under his feet
was something like a pavement made of
sapphire,[a u] clear as the sky[v] itself. 11But
God did not raise his hand against these
leaders of the Israelites; they saw[w] God,
and they ate and drank.[x]
12The LORD said to Moses, "Come up to
me on the mountain and stay here, and I
will give you the tablets of stone,[y] with the
law and commands I have written for their
instruction."
13Then Moses set out with Joshua[z] his
aide, and Moses went up on the mountain[a] of God. 14He said to the elders, "Wait
here for us until we come back to you.
Aaron and Hur[b] are with you, and anyone
involved in a dispute[c] can go to them."
15When Moses went up on the mountain, the cloud[d] covered it, 16and the glory[e] of the LORD settled on Mount Sinai.[f]
For six days the cloud covered the mountain, and on the seventh day the LORD
called to Moses from within the cloud.[g]
17To the Israelites the glory of the LORD
looked like a consuming fire[h] on top of
the mountain. 18Then Moses entered the
cloud as he went on up the mountain.
And he stayed on the mountain forty[i] days
and forty nights.[j]

24:9 [s]S ver 1 **24:10** [t]S Ge 16:13; Nu 12:6; Isa 6:1; Eze 1:1; 8:3; 40:2; S Jn 1:18 [u]Job 28:16; Isa 54:11; Eze 1:26; 10:1 [v]Rev 4:3 **24:11** [w]S ver 10; S Ex 3:6; S 19:21 [x]Eze 44:3; Mt 26:29 **24:12** [y]Ex 31:18; 32:15-16; 34:1,28,29; Dt 4:13; 5:22; 8:3; 9:9,10,11; 10:4; 2Co 3:3 **24:13** [z]S Ex 17:9 [a]S Ex 3:1 **24:14** [b]S Ex 17:10 [c]Ex 18:16 **24:15** [d]S Ex 19:9; Mt 17:5 **24:16** [e]S Ex 16:7; Lev 9:23; Nu 14:10; 1Sa 4:21,22; Eze 8:4; 11:22 [f]S Ex 19:11 [g]Ps 99:7 **24:17** [h]S Ex 15:7; S 19:18; Heb 12:18,29 **24:18** [i]1Ki 19:8 [j]S Ge 7:4; Mt 4:2

25:2 [k]Ex 35:21,22,26,27,29; 36:2; 2Ki 12:4;

Offerings for the Tabernacle

25:1-7pp — Ex 35:4-9

25 The LORD said to Moses, 2"Tell the
Israelites to bring me an offering.
You are to receive the offering for me from
each man whose heart prompts[k] him to
give. 3These are the offerings you are to receive from them: gold, silver and bronze;
4blue, purple and scarlet yarn[l] and fine
linen; goat hair; 5ram skins dyed red and
hides of sea cows[b];[m] acacia wood;[n] 6olive
oil[o] for the light; spices for the anointing
oil and for the fragrant incense;[p] 7and onyx
stones and other gems to be mounted on
the ephod[q] and breastpiece.[r]
8"Then have them make a sanctuary[s] for
me, and I will dwell[t] among them. 9Make
this tabernacle and all its furnishings exactly like the pattern[u] I will show you.

The Ark

25:10-20pp — Ex 37:1-9

10"Have them make a chest[v] of acacia
wood — two and a half cubits long, a cu-

[a] *10* Or *lapis lazuli* [b] *5* That is, dugongs

1Ch 29:5,7,9; 2Ch 24:10; 29:31; Ezr 2:68; Ne 7:70-72; 2Co 8:11-12; 9:7 **25:4** [l]Ex 28:4-8 **25:5** [m]Nu 4:6,10 [n]Dt 10:3 **25:6** [o]Ex 27:20; 30:22-32; 35:28; 39:37; Nu 4:16 [p]Ex 30:1,7,35; 31:11; 35:28; Lev 16:12; Nu 4:16; 7:14; 2Ch 13:11 **25:7** [q]Ex 28:4,6-14; 29:5; Jdg 8:27; Hos 3:4 [r]Lev 8:8 **25:8** [s]Ex 36:1-5; Lev 4:6; 10:4,7; 21:12,23; Nu 3:28; Heb 9:1-2 [t]Ex 29:45; Lev 26:11-12; Nu 5:3; Dt 12:11; 1Ki 6:13; Zec 2:10; 2Co 6:16 **25:9** [u]ver 40; Ex 26:30; 27:8; 31:11; 39:32,42,43; Nu 8:4; 1Ch 28:11,19; Ac 7:44; Heb 8:5 **25:10** [v]Dt 10:1-5; 1Ki 6:19; Heb 9:4

see also Ge 17:9 – 10 and notes). *blood of the covenant.* See Mk 14:24 and note.

24:9 *went up.* See v. 1 and note.

24:10 *saw … God.* But not in the fullness of his glory (see 33:20; see also notes on 3:6; Ge 16:13; Nu 12:8; Eze 1:28). *sapphire.* See NIV text note. *sky.* Symbolized by the blue color of the "sapphire" (see Eze 1:26).

24:11 *raise his hand against.* See 9:15. *leaders.* Lit. "corners," "corner supports"; used in the sense of "leaders" only here. Cf. Gal 2:9 and note. *ate and drank.* A covenant meal (cf. Ge 26:30; 31:54 and notes), celebrating the sealing of the covenant described in vv. 3 – 8. It foreshadows the Lord's Supper, which celebrates the new covenant sealed by Christ's death (see 1Co 11:25 – 26 and notes).

24:12 *Come up.* See note on v. 1. *tablets of stone.* See note on 31:18. *their.* The people's. *instruction.* As instruction from the covenant Lord, the laws were divine directives.

24:13 *Joshua his aide.* See note on 17:9.

24:14 *Hur.* See note on 17:10.

24:17 *glory of the LORD.* See v. 10; 16:10 and notes.

24:18 *stayed on the mountain.* Moses did not come down until he had received instructions concerning the tabernacle and its furnishings (see 32:15). *forty days and forty nights.* Jesus, the new Moses (see note on v. 2), fasted for the same length of time (see Mt 4:2 and note).

25:2 *offering.* Here refers to a voluntary contribution.

25:4 *blue, purple and scarlet.* Royal colors. *blue, purple.* Dyes derived from various shellfish (primarily the *murex*) that swarm in the waters of the northeast Mediterranean. See note on Ge 10:6. *scarlet.* Derived from the eggs and carcasses of the worm *Coccus ilicis,* which attaches itself to the leaves of the holly plant. *fine linen.* A very high quality cloth (often used by Egyptian royalty) made from thread spun from the fibers of flax straw. The Hebrew for this term derives ultimately from Egyptian. Excellent examples of unusually white, tightly woven linen have been found in ancient Egyptian tombs. Some are so finely woven that they cannot be distinguished from silk without the use of a magnifying glass. *goat hair.* From long-haired goats. Coarse and black (cf. SS 1:5 and note; 6:5), it was often used to weave cloth for tents.

25:5 *ram skins dyed red.* After all the wool had been removed from the skins. The final product was similar to present-day morocco leather. *sea cows.* Native to the Red Sea. *acacia.* The wood is darker and harder than oak and is avoided by wood-eating insects. It is still common in the Sinai peninsula.

25:6 *spices.* Those used in the anointing oil are identified in 30:23 – 24 as myrrh (balsam sap), cinnamon (bark of the cinnamon tree, a species of laurel), cane (pith from the root of a reed plant) and cassia (made from dried flowers of the cinnamon tree). Those used in the fragrant incense are identified in 30:34 as gum resin (a powder taken from the middle of hardened drops of myrrh — rare and very valuable), onycha (made from mollusk shells) and galbanum (a rubbery resin taken from the roots of a flowering plant that thrives in Syria and Persia).

25:7 *other gems.* See 28:17 – 20. *ephod.* See 28:6 and note. *breastpiece.* See 28:15 – 30.

25:8 *sanctuary.* Lit. "holy place," "place set apart." See note on 3:5.

25:9 *tabernacle.* Lit. "dwelling place." The word is rarely used of human dwellings; it almost always signifies the place where God dwells among his people (see v. 8; 29:45 – 46; Lev 26:11; Eze 37:27; cf. Jn 1:14; Rev 21:3). *pattern.* See note on v. 40.

25:10 *chest.* See v. 14. Such was its form and function. The Hebrew for this word is translated by the more traditional term "ark" throughout the rest of Exodus (see note on

bit and a half wide, and a cubit and a half high.[a] 11Overlay[w] it with pure gold, both inside and out, and make a gold molding around it. 12Cast four gold rings for it and fasten them to its four feet, with two rings[x] on one side and two rings on the other. 13Then make poles of acacia wood and overlay them with gold.[y] 14Insert the poles[z] into the rings on the sides of the chest to carry it. 15The poles are to remain in the rings of this ark; they are not to be removed.[a] 16Then put in the ark the Testimony,[b] which I will give you.

17"Make an atonement cover[b][c] of pure gold—two and a half cubits long and a cubit and a half wide.[c] 18And make two cherubim[d] out of hammered gold at the ends of the cover. 19Make one cherub on one end and the second cherub on the other; make the cherubim of one piece with the cover, at the two ends. 20The cherubim[e] are to have their wings spread upward, overshadowing[f] the cover with them. The cherubim are to face each other, looking toward the cover. 21Place the cover on top of the ark[g] and put in the ark the Testimony,[h] which I will give you. 22There, above the cover between the two cherubim[i] that are over the ark of the Testimony, I will meet[j] with you and give you all my commands for the Israelites.[k]

The Table

25:23-29pp — Ex 37:10-16

23"Make a table[l] of acacia wood—two cubits long, a cubit wide and a cubit and a half high.[d] 24Overlay it with pure gold and make a gold molding around it. 25Also make around it a rim a handbreadth[e] wide and put a gold molding on the rim. 26Make four gold rings for the table and fasten them to the four corners, where the four legs are. 27The rings are to be close to the rim to hold the poles used in carrying the table. 28Make the poles of acacia wood, overlay them with gold[m] and carry the table with them. 29And make its plates and dishes of pure gold, as well as its pitchers and bowls for the pouring out of offerings.[n] 30Put the bread of the Presence[o] on this table to be before me at all times.

The Lampstand

25:31-39pp — Ex 37:17-24

31"Make a lampstand[p] of pure gold and hammer it out, base and shaft; its flowerlike cups, buds and blossoms shall be of one piece with it. 32Six branches are to extend from the sides of the lampstand—three on one side and three on the other. 33Three cups shaped like almond flowers with buds and blossoms are to be on one branch, three on the next branch, and the same for all six branches extending from the lampstand. 34And on the lampstand there are to be four cups

25:11 [w] ver 24; Ex 30:3 **25:12** [x] ver 26; Ex 30:4 **25:13** [y] ver 28; Ex 27:6; 30:5; 37:28 **25:14** [z] Ex 27:7; 40:20; 1Ch 15:15 **25:15** [a] 1Ki 8:8 **25:16** [b] S Ex 16:34; Heb 9:4 **25:17** [c] ver 21; Lev 16:13; Ro 3:25 **25:18** [d] Ex 26:1, 31; 36:35; 1Ki 6:23, 27; 8:6; 2Ch 3:10-13; Heb 9:5 **25:20** [e] S Ge 3:24 [f] Ex 37:9; 1Ki 8:7; 1Ch 28:18; Heb 9:5 **25:21** [g] ver 10-15; Ex 26:34; 40:20; Dt 10:5 [h] S Ex 16:34; Heb 9:4 **25:22** [i] Nu 7:89; 1Sa 4:4; 2Sa 6:2; 22:11; 2Ki 19:15; 1Ch 13:6; 28:18; Ps 18:10; 80:1; 99:1; Isa 37:16 [j] S Ex 19:3; 29:42; 30:6, 36; Lev 1:1; 16:2; Nu 17:4 [k] Jer 3:16 **25:23** [l] ver 30; Ex 26:35; 40:4, 22; Lev 24:6; Nu 3:31; 1Ki 7:48; 1Ch 28:16; 2Ch 4:8, 19; Eze 41:22; 44:16; Heb 9:2 **25:28** [m] S ver 13 **25:29** [n] Nu 4:7 **25:30** [o] Ex 35:13; 39:36; 40:4, 23; Lev 24:5-9; Nu 4:7; 1Sa 21:4-6; 1Ki 7:48; 1Ch 23:29 **25:31** [p] Ex 26:35; 31:8; 35:14; 39:37; 40:4, 24; Lev 24:4; Nu 3:31; 1Ki 7:49; 2Ch 4:7; Zec 4:2; Heb 9:2; Rev 1:12

[a] *10* That is, about 3 3/4 feet (about 1.1 meters) long and 2 1/4 feet (about 0.7 meter) wide and high [b] *17* Traditionally *a mercy seat* [c] *17* That is, about 3 3/4 feet (about 1.1 meters) long and 2 1/4 feet (about 0.7 meter) wide [d] *23* That is, about 3 feet (about 0.9 meter) long and 1 1/2 feet (about 0.5 meter) wide and 2 1/4 feet (about 0.7 meter) high [e] *25* That is, about 3 inches (about 8 centimeters)

Dt 10:1–3); it is different from that used to refer to Noah's ark and to the reed basket in which the infant Moses was placed (see note on 2:3). Of all the tabernacle furnishings, the ark is mentioned first probably because it symbolized the throne of the Lord (see 1Sa 4:4 and note; 2Sa 6:2), the great King, who chose to dwell among his people (see note on v. 9).

25:11 *pure gold.* Uncontaminated by silver or other impurities.

25:16 *Testimony.* The two tablets on which were inscribed the Ten Commandments as the basic stipulations of the Sinai covenant (see 20:1–17; 31:18). The Hebrew word for "Testimony" is related to a Babylonian word meaning "covenant stipulations." See also notes on v. 22; 16:34.

25:17 *atonement.* Reconciliation, the divine act of grace whereby God draws to himself and makes "at one" with him those who were once alienated from him. In the OT, the shed blood of sacrificial offerings effected atonement (see Lev 17:11 and note); in the NT, the blood of Jesus, shed once for all time (see Heb 9:12 and note), does the same (see Ro 3:25; 1Jn 2:2 and notes). *atonement cover.* See NIV text note; see also Lev 16:2 and note. That God's symbolic throne was capped with an atonement cover signified his great mercy toward his people—only such a God can be revered (see Ps 130:3–4).

25:18 *cherubim.* Probably similar to the carvings of winged sphinxes that adorned the armrests of royal thrones (see note on v. 10) in many parts of the ancient Near East (see also note on Ge 3:24). In the OT the cherubim were symbolic attendants that marked the place of the Lord's "enthronement" in his earthly kingdom (see 1Sa 4:4 and note; 2Sa 6:2; 2Ki 19:15; Ps 99:1). From the cover of the ark (God's symbolic throne) the Lord gave directions to Moses (see v. 22; Nu 7:89 and note). Later the ark's presence in the temple at Jerusalem would designate it as God's earthly royal city (see Ps 9:11 and note).

25:21 *put in the ark the Testimony.* See note on 31:18, but see also Dt 31:26.

25:22 *ark of the Testimony.* Called this because it contained the Testimony (see note on v. 16). The phrase "ark of the Testimony" is a synonym of the more familiar phrase "ark of the covenant" (see, e.g., Nu 10:33). *I will meet with you.* See note on 27:21.

25:30 *bread of the Presence.* Traditionally "showbread." In this phrase, "Presence" refers to the presence of God himself (as in 33:14–15; Isa 63:9). The bread (twelve loaves, one for each tribe) represented a perpetual bread offering to the Lord by which Israel declared that it consecrated to God the fruits of its labors, and by which the nation at the same time acknowledged that all such fruit had been provided only by God's blessing. See Lev 24:5–9 and note on 24:8.

25:31 *flowerlike cups, buds and blossoms.* The design is patterned after an almond tree (see v. 33), the first of the trees in the Near East to blossom in spring. The cups of the lampstand resemble either the outer covering of the almond flower or the almond nut.

shaped like almond flowers with buds and
blossoms. 35One bud shall be under the
first pair of branches extending from the
lampstand, a second bud under the second pair, and a third bud under the third
pair—six branches in all. 36The buds and
branches shall all be of one piece with the
lampstand, hammered out of pure gold.[q]
37"Then make its seven lamps[r] and set
them up on it so that they light the space
in front of it. 38Its wick trimmers and trays[s]
are to be of pure gold. 39A talent[a] of pure
gold is to be used for the lampstand and
all these accessories. 40See that you make
them according to the pattern[t] shown you
on the mountain.

The Tabernacle

26:1-37pp — Ex 36:8-38

26 "Make the tabernacle[u] with ten curtains of finely twisted linen and blue,
purple and scarlet yarn, with cherubim[v]
worked into them by a skilled craftsman.

[a] *39* That is, about 75 pounds (about 34 kilograms)

25:36 [q]ver 18; Nu 8:4 **25:37** [r]Ex 27:21; 30:8; Lev 24:3-4; Nu 8:2; 1Sa 3:3; 2Ch 13:11 **25:38** [s]S ver 37; Nu 4:9 **25:40** [t]S ver 9; Ac 7:44; Heb 8:5* **26:1** [u]Ex 29:42; 40:2; Lev 8:10; Nu 1:50; Jos 22:19,29; 2Sa 7:2; 1Ki 1:39; Ac 7:44; Heb 8:2,5; 13:10; S Rev 21:3 [v]S Ex 25:18

25:37 *seven.* Signifying completeness. *lamps.* The ancient lamp was a small clay saucer with part of its rim pinched together to form a spout from which protruded the top of a wick fed by oil contained in the saucer. (Examples of seven-spouted lamps come from the time of Moses.) The ruins of Beth Shan and Megiddo have yielded examples of a metal pedestal topped by a ledge designed to carry a lamp. The classic representation of the shape of the tabernacle lampstand comes from the time of Herod the Great and may be seen on the Arch of Titus in Rome. The lamps were to burn all night in the tabernacle, tended by the priests. Oil for the lamps was to be supplied by the people; the light from the lamps represented the glory of the Lord reflected in the consecrated lives of the Israelites—Israel's glory answering to God's glory in the tabernacle (see 29:43 and note; see also 27:20–21 and note on 27:21).

25:40 Quoted in Heb 8:5 (see note there) in order to contrast the "shadow" (the symbolic physical objects used in the ceremonies of old covenant worship) with the reality (the Christ of the new covenant). See also Heb 10:1 and note.

26:1 *tabernacle.* See note on 25:9; see also diagram, p. 126. Its basic structure was to be 15 feet wide by 45 feet long by 15 feet high. Over an inner lining of embroidered linen (vv. 1–6), it was to have a covering woven of goat hair (vv. 7–13) and two additional coverings of leather, one made from ram skins dyed red and one from the hides of sea cows (v. 14). Internally, the ceiling was probably flat, but whether

The Tabernacle

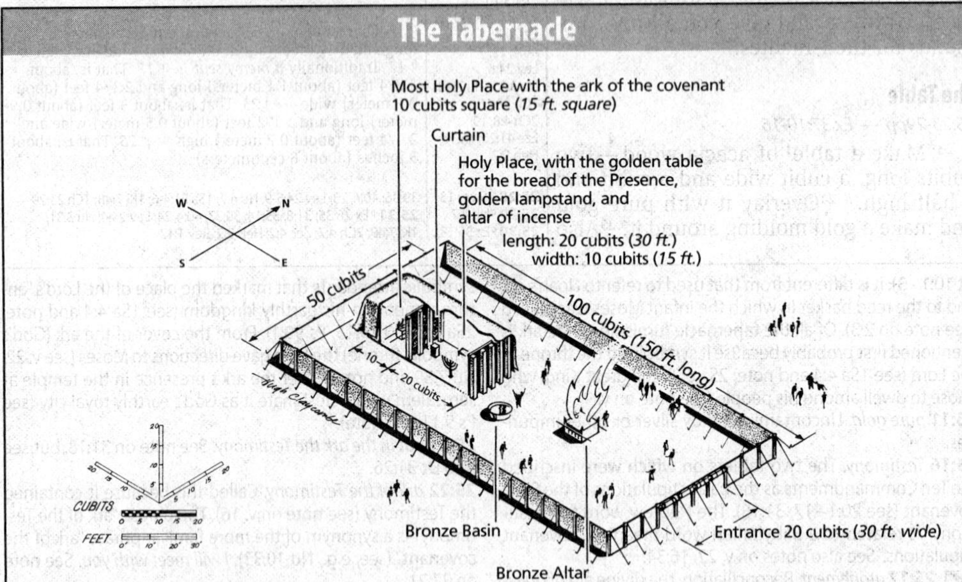

The new religious observances taught by Moses in the desert centered on rituals connected with the tabernacle, and amplified Israel's sense of separateness, purity and oneness under the Lordship of Yahweh.

A few desert shrines have been found in Sinai, notably at Serabit el-Khadem and at Timnah in the Negev, and show marked Egyptian influence.

Specific cultural antecedents to portable shrines carried on poles and covered with thin sheets of gold can be found in ancient Egypt as early as the Old Kingdom (2800–2250 B.C.), but were especially prominent in the 18th and 19th dynasties (1570–1180). The best examples come from the fabulous tomb of Tutankhamun, c. 1350.

Comparisons of construction details in the text of Ex 25–40 with the frames, shrines, poles, sheathing, draped fabric covers, gilt rosettes, and winged protective figures from the shrine of Tutankhamun are instructive. The period, the Late Bronze Age, is equivalent in all dating systems to the era of Moses and the exodus.

²All the curtains are to be the same
size[w] — twenty-eight cubits long and four
cubits wide.[a] ³Join five of the curtains together, and do the same with the other
five. ⁴Make loops of blue material along
the edge of the end curtain in one set, and
do the same with the end curtain in the
other set. ⁵Make fifty loops on one curtain and fifty loops on the end curtain of
the other set, with the loops opposite each
other. ⁶Then make fifty gold clasps and
use them to fasten the curtains together
so that the tabernacle is a unit.[x]
⁷"Make curtains of goat hair for the tent
over the tabernacle — eleven altogether.
⁸All eleven curtains are to be the same
size[y] — thirty cubits long and four cubits
wide.[b] ⁹Join five of the curtains together
into one set and the other six into another
set. Fold the sixth curtain double at the
front of the tent. ¹⁰Make fifty loops along
the edge of the end curtain in one set and
also along the edge of the end curtain in
the other set. ¹¹Then make fifty bronze
clasps and put them in the loops to fasten the tent together as a unit.[z] ¹²As for
the additional length of the tent curtains,
the half curtain that is left over is to hang
down at the rear of the tabernacle. ¹³The
tent curtains will be a cubit[c] longer on
both sides; what is left will hang over
the sides of the tabernacle so as to cover
it. ¹⁴Make for the tent a covering[a] of ram
skins dyed red, and over that a covering of
hides of sea cows.[d][b]

26:2 [w] ver 8
26:6 [x] ver 11
26:8 [y] ver 2
26:11 [z] ver 6
26:14 [a] Nu 3:25 [b] Nu 4:25

[a] *2* That is, about 42 feet (about 12.5 meters) long and 6 feet (about 1.8 meters) wide [b] *8* That is, about 45 feet (about 13.5 meters) long and 6 feet (about 1.8 meters) wide [c] *13* That is, about 1 1/2 feet (about 0.5 meter) [d] *14* That is, dugongs

the leather coverings had a ridge line with sloping sides (like a tent) is not known. The tabernacle represented God's royal tent. Its form and adornment (like those of the later temples that replaced it) marked it as a symbolic representation of the created cosmos over which God is sovereign as Creator and Lord. As such, it stood for the center of the cosmos from which the Creator reigns, the place where the heavenly and earthly realms converge. There God "lived" among his people (Immanuel, "God with us"), and his people could come near to him (see note on Ge 26:3). At this sanctuary Israel lived symbolically at the gate of Paradise — very near though still outside, awaiting the fulfillment of God's redemptive program (see vv. 31 – 35; Ge 3:24 and notes; see also Rev 21:1 — 22:6 and notes). *finely twisted linen and blue, purple and scarlet yarn.* See note on 25:4. *cherubim.* Signifying a royal chamber (see 25:18 and note).

26:7 *goat hair.* See note on 25:4.

26:14 *ram skins dyed red . . . sea cows.* See note on 25:5.

Tabernacle Furnishings

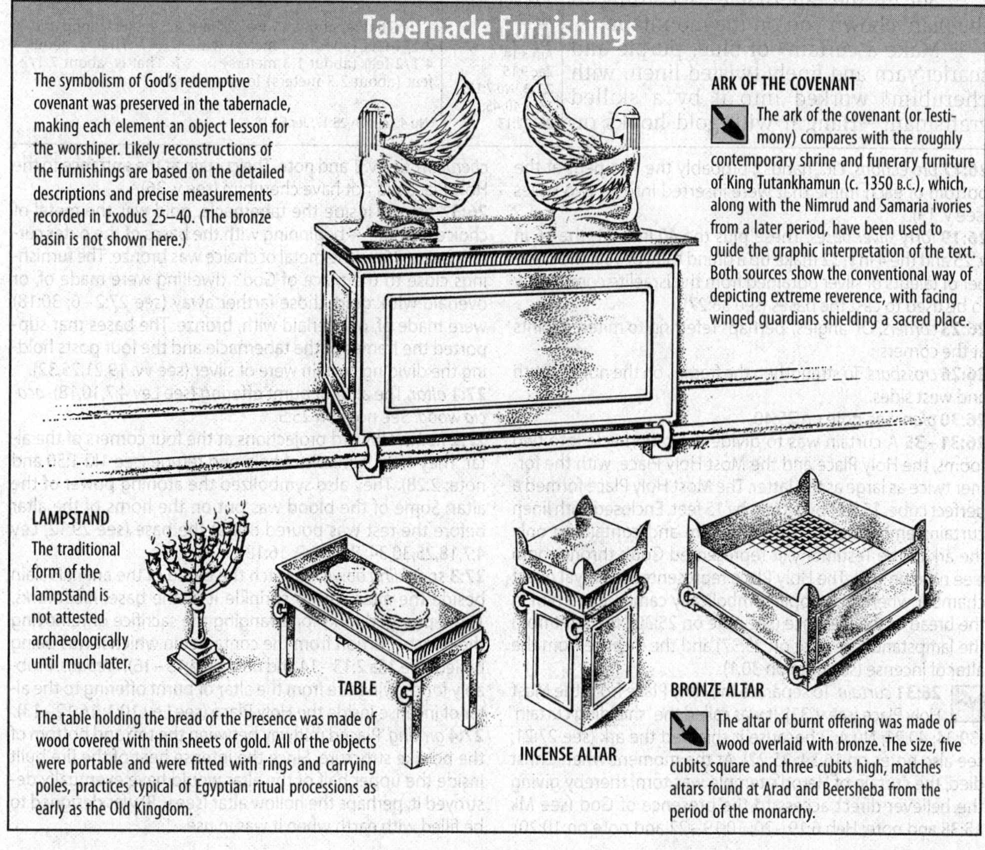

The symbolism of God's redemptive covenant was preserved in the tabernacle, making each element an object lesson for the worshiper. Likely reconstructions of the furnishings are based on the detailed descriptions and precise measurements recorded in Exodus 25–40. (The bronze basin is not shown here.)

ARK OF THE COVENANT

The ark of the covenant (or Testimony) compares with the roughly contemporary shrine and funerary furniture of King Tutankhamun (c. 1350 B.C.), which, along with the Nimrud and Samaria ivories from a later period, have been used to guide the graphic interpretation of the text. Both sources show the conventional way of depicting extreme reverence, with facing winged guardians shielding a sacred place.

LAMPSTAND

The traditional form of the lampstand is not attested archaeologically until much later.

TABLE

The table holding the bread of the Presence was made of wood covered with thin sheets of gold. All of the objects were portable and were fitted with rings and carrying poles, practices typical of Egyptian ritual processions as early as the Old Kingdom.

INCENSE ALTAR

BRONZE ALTAR

The altar of burnt offering was made of wood overlaid with bronze. The size, five cubits square and three cubits high, matches altars found at Arad and Beersheba from the period of the monarchy.

15“Make upright frames of acacia wood
for the tabernacle. 16Each frame is to be
ten cubits long and a cubit and a half
wide,[a] 17with two projections set parallel to each other. Make all the frames of
the tabernacle in this way. 18Make twenty frames for the south side of the tabernacle 19and make forty silver bases[c] to go
under them—two bases for each frame,
one under each projection. 20For the other side, the north side of the tabernacle,
make twenty frames 21and forty silver bases[d]—two under each frame. 22Make six
frames for the far end, that is, the west end
of the tabernacle, 23and make two frames
for the corners at the far end. 24At these
two corners they must be double from the
bottom all the way to the top, and fitted
into a single ring; both shall be like that.
25So there will be eight frames and sixteen
silver bases—two under each frame.
26“Also make crossbars of acacia wood:
five for the frames on one side of the tabernacle, 27five for those on the other side, and
five for the frames on the west, at the far
end of the tabernacle. 28The center crossbar
is to extend from end to end at the middle
of the frames. 29Overlay the frames with
gold and make gold rings to hold the crossbars. Also overlay the crossbars with gold.
30“Set up the tabernacle[e] according to
the plan[f] shown you on the mountain.
31“Make a curtain[g] of blue, purple and
scarlet yarn and finely twisted linen, with
cherubim[h] worked into it by a skilled
craftsman. 32Hang it with gold hooks on
four posts of acacia wood overlaid with
gold and standing on four silver bases.[i]
33Hang the curtain from the clasps and
place the ark of the Testimony behind the
curtain.[j] The curtain will separate the Holy
Place from the Most Holy Place.[k] 34Put the
atonement cover[l] on the ark of the Testimony in the Most Holy Place. 35Place the
table[m] outside the curtain on the north
side of the tabernacle and put the lampstand[n] opposite it on the south side.
36“For the entrance to the tent make a
curtain[o] of blue, purple and scarlet yarn
and finely twisted linen—the work of an
embroiderer.[p] 37Make gold hooks for this
curtain and five posts of acacia wood overlaid with gold. And cast five bronze bases
for them.

The Altar of Burnt Offering

27:1-8pp — Ex 38:1-7

27 “Build an altar[q] of acacia wood, three
cubits[b] high; it is to be square, five
cubits long and five cubits wide.[c] 2Make a
horn[r] at each of the four corners, so that
the horns and the altar are of one piece,
and overlay the altar with bronze. 3Make
all its utensils of bronze—its pots to remove the ashes, and its shovels, sprinkling
bowls,[s] meat forks and firepans.[t] 4Make a

26:19 [c]ver 21,25,32; Ex 38:27
26:21 [d]S ver 19
26:30 [e]Ex 40:2; Nu 9:15 [f]S Ex 25:9
26:31 [g]Nu 4:5; 2Ch 3:14; Mt 27:51; Lk 23:45; Heb 9:3 [h]S Ex 25:18
26:32 [i]S ver 19
26:33 [j]Ex 27:21; 35:12; 40:3,21; Lev 16:2; Nu 3:31; 4:5; 2Ch 3:14 [k]Lev 16:2,16; 1Ki 6:16; 7:50; 8:6; 2Ch 3:8; 5:7; Eze 41:4; Heb 9:2-3
26:34 [l]Ex 25:21; 30:6; 37:6; Lev 16:2; Heb 9:5
26:35 [m]S Ex 25:23; Heb 9:2 [n]S Ex 25:31
26:36 [o]Ex 35:15; 40:5,28 [p]Ps 45:14; Eze 16:10; 26:16; 27:7
27:1 [q]S Ex 20:24; S 40:6; S 1Ki 8:64
27:2 [r]Ex 29:12; 30:2; 37:25; Lev 4:7; 1Ki 1:50; 2:28; Ps 118:27; Jer 17:1; Eze 43:15; Am 3:14; Zec 9:15
27:3 [s]Nu 7:13; 1Ki 7:40,45; 2Ki 12:13 [t]Nu 4:14; 1Ch 28:17; Jer 52:18

[a] *16* That is, about 15 feet (about 4.5 meters) long and 2 1/4 feet (about 0.7 meter) wide [b] *1* That is, about 4 1/2 feet (about 1.3 meters) [c] *1* That is, about 7 1/2 feet (about 2.3 meters) long and wide

26:17 *projections.* Lit. "hands"; probably the two pegs at the bottom of each frame that were inserted into its two bases (see v. 19).
26:19 *forty silver bases.* These plus the 40 in v. 21, the 16 in v. 25 and the 4 in v. 32 make up a grand total of 100, the number of talents of silver obtained from the Israelite community to be used to cast the bases (see 38:27).
26:23 *corners.* Or "angles," perhaps referring to mitered joints at the corners.
26:26 *crossbars.* To strengthen the frames on the north, south and west sides.
26:30 *plan.* See note on 25:40.
26:31 – 35 A curtain was to divide the tabernacle into two rooms, the Holy Place and the Most Holy Place, with the former twice as large as the latter. The Most Holy Place formed a perfect cube, 15 feet by 15 feet by 15 feet. Enclosed with linen curtains embroidered with cherubim and containing only the ark of the Testimony, it represented God's throne room (see note on v. 1). The Holy Place represented his royal guest chamber where his people symbolically came before him in the bread of the Presence (see note on 25:30), the light from the lampstand (see note on 25:37) and the incense from the altar of incense (see note on 30:1).
26:31 *curtain.* To separate the Holy Place from the Most Holy Place (see v. 33). It was called the "shielding curtain" (39:34; 40:21; Nu 4:5) because it shielded the ark (see 27:21; see also notes on 16:34; 25:22). At the moment when Christ died, the curtain of Herod's temple was torn, thereby giving the believer direct access to the presence of God (see Mk 15:38 and note; Heb 6:19 – 20; 10:19 – 22 and note on 10:20). *cherubim.* See v. 1 and note. The curtain at the entrance to the Holy Place did not have cherubim (see v. 36).
26:37 *bronze.* Inside the tabernacle, gold was the metal of choice; outside — beginning with the bases of the outer curtain (see v. 36) — the metal of choice was bronze. The furnishings close to the place of God's dwelling were made of, or overlaid with, gold; those farther away (see 27:2 – 6; 30:18) were made of, or overlaid with, bronze. The bases that supported the frames of the tabernacle and the four posts holding the dividing curtain were of silver (see vv. 19,21,25,32).
27:1 *altar.* The altar of burnt offering (see Lev 4:7,10,18). *acacia wood.* See note on 25:5.
27:2 *horns.* Upward projections at the four corners of the altar. They were symbols of help and refuge (see 1Ki 1:50 and note; 2:28). They also symbolized the atoning power of the altar: Some of the blood was put on the horns of the altar before the rest was poured out at the base (see 29:12; Lev 4:7,18,25,30,34; 8:15; 9:9; 16:18).
27:3 *sprinkling bowls.* To catch the blood of the animals slain beside the altar and to sprinkle it at the base. *meat forks.* Three-pronged forks for arranging the sacrifice or removing the priests' portion from the container in which it was being boiled (see 1Sa 2:13 – 14 and note on 2:13 – 16). *firepans.* Probably for carrying fire from the altar of burnt offering to the altar of incense inside the Holy Place (see Lev 10:1; 16:12 – 13).
27:4 *grating.* Placed midway between the top and bottom of the boxlike structure. Since the intense heat of the fire built inside the upper half of the altar would have eventually destroyed it, perhaps the hollow altar (see v. 8) was designed to be filled with earth when it was in use.

grating for it, a bronze network, and make a bronze ring at each of the four corners of the network. 5Put it under the ledge of the altar so that it is halfway up the altar. 6Make poles of acacia wood for the altar and overlay them with bronze.[u] 7The poles are to be inserted into the rings so they will be on two sides of the altar when it is carried.[v] 8Make the altar hollow, out of boards. It is to be made just as you were shown[w] on the mountain.

The Courtyard

27:9-19pp — Ex 38:9-20

9"Make a courtyard[x] for the tabernacle. The south side shall be a hundred cubits[a] long and is to have curtains of finely twisted linen, 10with twenty posts and twenty bronze bases and with silver hooks and bands on the posts. 11The north side shall also be a hundred cubits long and is to have curtains, with twenty posts and twenty bronze bases and with silver hooks and bands on the posts.

12"The west end of the courtyard shall be fifty cubits[b] wide and have curtains, with ten posts and ten bases. 13On the east end, toward the sunrise, the courtyard shall also be fifty cubits wide. 14Curtains fifteen cubits[c] long are to be on one side of the entrance, with three posts and three bases, 15and curtains fifteen cubits long are to be on the other side, with three posts and three bases.

16"For the entrance to the courtyard, provide a curtain[y] twenty cubits[d] long, of blue, purple and scarlet yarn and finely twisted linen — the work of an embroiderer[z] — with four posts and four bases. 17All the posts around the courtyard are to have silver bands and hooks, and bronze bases. 18The courtyard shall be a hundred cubits long and fifty cubits wide,[e] with curtains of finely twisted linen five cubits[f] high, and with bronze bases. 19All the other articles used in the service of the tabernacle, whatever their function, including all the tent pegs for it and those for the courtyard, are to be of bronze.

Oil for the Lampstand

27:20-21pp — Lev 24:1-3

20"Command the Israelites to bring you clear oil[a] of pressed olives for the light so that the lamps may be kept burning. 21In the Tent of Meeting,[b] outside the curtain that is in front of the Testimony,[c] Aaron and his sons are to keep the lamps[d] burning before the LORD from evening till morning. This is to be a lasting ordinance[e] among the Israelites for the generations to come.

The Priestly Garments

28 "Have Aaron[f] your brother brought to you from among the Israelites, along with his sons Nadab and Abihu,[g] Eleazar and Ithamar,[h] so they may serve me as priests.[i] 2Make sacred garments[j] for your brother Aaron, to give him dignity and honor.[k] 3Tell all the skilled men[l] to whom I have given wisdom[m] in such matters that they are to make garments for Aaron, for his consecration, so he may serve me as priest. 4These are the garments they are to make: a breastpiece,[n] an ephod,[o] a robe,[p] a woven tunic,[q] a turban[r] and a sash. They are to make these sacred garments for your brother Aaron and his sons, so they may serve me as priests. 5Have them use gold, and blue, purple and scarlet yarn, and fine linen.[s]

The Ephod

28:6-14pp — Ex 39:2-7

6"Make the ephod[t] of gold, and of blue, purple and scarlet yarn, and of finely twisted

[a] *9* That is, about 150 feet (about 46 meters); also in verse 11 [b] *12* That is, about 75 feet (about 23 meters); also in verse 13 [c] *14* That is, about 22 1/2 feet (about 6.9 meters); also in verse 15 [d] *16* That is, about 30 feet (about 9 meters) [e] *18* That is, about 150 feet (about 46 meters) long and 75 feet (about 23 meters) wide [f] *18* That is, about 7 1/2 feet (about 2.3 meters)

27:6 [u]S Ex 25:13 **27:7** [v]Ex 25:14, 28 **27:8** [w]S Ex 25:9 **27:9** [x]Ex 35:17; 40:8,33; Lev 6:16,26; Eze 40:14; 42:1 **27:16** [y]Ex 40:33 [z]Ex 36:37
27:20 [a]S Ex 25:6 **27:21** [b]Ex 28:43; 29:42; 30:36; 33:7; Lev 1:1; 6:26; 8:3,31; Nu 1:1; 31:54; Jos 18:1; 1Ki 1:39 [c]S Ex 16:34 [d]S Ex 25:37 [e]Ex 29:9; 30:21; Lev 3:17; 16:34; 17:7; Nu 18:23; 19:21; 1Sa 30:25 **28:1** [f]Lev 8:30; Ps 99:6; Heb 5:4 [g]S Ex 6:23; 24:9 [h]S Ex 6:23 [i]Lev 8:2; 21:1; Nu 18:1-7; Dt 18:5; 1Sa 2:28; Heb 5:1 **28:2** [j]Ex 29:5,29; 31:10; 35:19; 39:1; Lev 8:7-9,30; 16:32; Nu 20:26-28 [k]ver 40 **28:3** [l]Ex 31:6; 35:10,25,35; 36:1 [m]Ex 31:3; Dt 34:9; Isa 11:2; 1Co 12:8; S Eph 1:17 **28:4** [n]ver 15-30 [o]S Ex 25:7 [p]ver 31-35 [q]ver 39; Lev 10:5 [r]ver 37 **28:5** [s]Ex 25:4 **28:6** [t]S Ex 25:7

27:12-13 *west end ... east end.* The courtyard is described as having two equal parts. The Most Holy Place probably occupied the central position in the western half, the altar of burnt offering the central position in the eastern half.
27:13-14 *toward the sunrise ... the entrance.* The entrance to the tabernacle courtyard faced east, as did that of Solomon's temple (see Eze 8:16 and note) and of Herod's temple.
27:18 *five cubits.* See NIV text note; high enough to block the view of people standing outside the courtyard, thus protecting the sanctity of the ceremonies taking place inside.
27:20 *clear oil of pressed olives.* Unripe olives were crushed in a mortar. The pulpy mass was then placed in a cloth basket through the bottom of which the oil dripped, producing a clear fuel that burned with little or no smoke.
27:21 *Tent of Meeting.* The tabernacle; it was not a tent in which God's people gathered to worship but one where God presented himself to his people when he chose to (see 29:42-43). *curtain that is in front of the Testimony.* See note on 26:31. *lamps burning ... from evening till morning.* The lamps were lit in the evening (see 30:8) and apparently extinguished in the morning (see 1Sa 3:3 and note).
28:1 *Nadab and Abihu.* See note on 24:1. *serve me as priests.* In order "to offer gifts and sacrifices for sins" and "to deal gently with those who are ignorant and are going astray" (Heb 5:1-2). Another important function of the priests was to read the law of Moses to the people and remind them of their covenant obligations (see Dt 31:9-13 and note on 31:11; Ne 8:2-3 and note on 8:3; Jer 18:18 and note; Mal 2:5-8 and note on 2:6-7).
28:2 *to give him dignity and honor.* The garments were to exalt the office and functions of the regular priests (see v. 40) as well as of the high priest.
28:6 *ephod.* A sleeveless vestment worn by the high priest. Sometimes the word refers to an otherwise unidentified object of worship (see, e.g., Jdg 8:27 and note; 18:17; Hos 3:4 and note).

linen—the work of a skilled craftsman. 7It
is to have two shoulder pieces attached to
two of its corners, so it can be fastened. 8Its
skillfully woven waistband[u] is to be like
it—of one piece with the ephod and made
with gold, and with blue, purple and scarlet yarn, and with finely twisted linen.
9"Take two onyx stones and engrave[v] on
them the names of the sons of Israel 10in
the order of their birth—six names on one
stone and the remaining six on the other.
11Engrave the names of the sons of Israel
on the two stones the way a gem cutter
engraves a seal. Then mount the stones in
gold filigree settings 12and fasten them on
the shoulder pieces of the ephod as memorial stones for the sons of Israel. Aaron
is to bear the names on his shoulders[w] as
a memorial[x] before the LORD. 13Make gold
filigree settings 14and two braided chains
of pure gold, like a rope, and attach the
chains to the settings.

The Breastpiece

28:15-28pp — Ex 39:8-21

15"Fashion a breastpiece[y] for making
decisions—the work of a skilled craftsman. Make it like the ephod: of gold, and
of blue, purple and scarlet yarn, and of
finely twisted linen. 16It is to be square—a
span[a] long and a span wide—and folded
double. 17Then mount four rows of precious stones[z] on it. In the first row there
shall be a ruby, a topaz and a beryl; 18in
the second row a turquoise, a sapphire[b]
and an emerald; 19in the third row a jacinth, an agate and an amethyst; 20in the
fourth row a chrysolite,[a] an onyx and a
jasper.[c] Mount them in gold filigree settings. 21There are to be twelve stones, one
for each of the names of the sons of Israel,[b] each engraved like a seal with the
name of one of the twelve tribes.[c]
22"For the breastpiece make braided
chains of pure gold, like a rope. 23Make
two gold rings for it and fasten them to
two corners of the breastpiece. 24Fasten the
two gold chains to the rings at the corners
of the breastpiece, 25and the other ends of
the chains to the two settings, attaching
them to the shoulder pieces of the ephod
at the front. 26Make two gold rings and attach them to the other two corners of the
breastpiece on the inside edge next to the
ephod. 27Make two more gold rings and
attach them to the bottom of the shoulder
pieces on the front of the ephod, close to
the seam just above the waistband of the
ephod. 28The rings of the breastpiece are
to be tied to the rings of the ephod with
blue cord, connecting it to the waistband,
so that the breastpiece will not swing out
from the ephod.
29"Whenever Aaron enters the Holy
Place,[d] he will bear the names of the sons
of Israel over his heart on the breastpiece
of decision as a continuing memorial before the LORD. 30Also put the Urim and
the Thummim[e] in the breastpiece, so they
may be over Aaron's heart whenever he
enters the presence of the LORD. Thus Aaron will always bear the means of making
decisions for the Israelites over his heart
before the LORD.

Other Priestly Garments

28:31-43pp — Ex 39:22-31

31"Make the robe of the ephod entirely
of blue cloth, 32with an opening for the
head in its center. There shall be a woven
edge like a collar[d] around this opening, so
that it will not tear. 33Make pomegranates[f]
of blue, purple and scarlet yarn around the
hem of the robe, with gold bells between
them. 34The gold bells and the pomegranates are to alternate around the hem of the
robe. 35Aaron must wear it when he ministers. The sound of the bells will be heard
when he enters the Holy Place before the
LORD and when he comes out, so that he
will not die.
36"Make a plate[g] of pure gold and engrave on it as on a seal: HOLY TO THE LORD.[h]

28:8 [u] Ex 29:5 **28:9** [v] SS 8:6; Isa 49:16; Hag 2:23 **28:12** [w] Dt 33:12; Job 31:36 [x] ver 29; Ex 30:16; Nu 10:10; 31:54; Jos 4:7; Zec 6:14 **28:15** [y] S Ex 25:7 **28:17** [z] Eze 28:13; Rev 21:19-20 **28:20** [a] Eze 1:16; 10:9; Da 10:6 **28:21** [b] Jos 4:8 [c] Rev 21:12

28:29 [d] ver 43 **28:30** [e] Lev 8:8; Nu 27:21; Dt 33:8; 1Sa 28:6; Ezr 2:63; Ne 7:65 **28:33** [f] Nu 13:23; 1Sa 14:2; 1Ki 7:18; SS 4:3; Jer 52:22; Joel 1:12; Hag 2:19 **28:36** [g] ver 37; Ex 29:6; Lev 8:9 [h] Zec 14:20

[a] *16* That is, about 9 inches (about 22 centimeters)
[b] *18* Or *lapis lazuli* [c] *20* The precise identification of some of these precious stones is uncertain.
[d] *32* The meaning of the Hebrew for this word is uncertain.

28:8 *waistband.* Apparently to hold the front and the back of the ephod to the priest's body.
28:12 *Aaron is to bear the names on his shoulders.* To symbolize the fact that the high priest represents all Israel when he ministers in the tabernacle.
28:15 *for making decisions.* By means of the Urim and Thummim (see note on v. 30).
28:29 *Aaron … will bear the names … over his heart.* Thus the nation was doubly represented before the Lord (see v. 12 and note).
28:30 *the Urim and the Thummim.* The Hebrew for this phrase probably means "the curses [traditionally 'lights'] and the perfections." The Hebrew word *Urim* begins with the first letter of the Hebrew alphabet (*aleph*) and *Thummim* begins with the last letter (*taw*). They were sacred lots and were often used in times of crisis to determine the will of God (see Nu 27:21). It has been suggested that if Urim ("curses") dominated when the lots were cast the answer was "no," but if Thummim ("perfections") dominated it was "yes." In any event, their "every decision" was "from the LORD" (Pr 16:33; see note there).
28:31 *robe.* Worn under the ephod.
28:35 According to Jewish tradition, one end of a length of rope was tied to the high priest's ankle and the other end remained outside the tabernacle. If the bells on his robe stopped tinkling while he was in the Holy Place, the assumption that he had died could be tested by pulling gently on the rope.
28:36 *HOLY TO THE LORD.* See 3:5 and note; 39:30; Zec 14:20 and note.

37 Fasten a blue cord to it to attach it to the turban; it is to be on the front of the turban. 38 It will be on Aaron's forehead, and he will bear the guilt[i] involved in the sacred gifts the Israelites consecrate, whatever their gifts may be. It will be on Aaron's forehead continually so that they will be acceptable[j] to the LORD.

39 "Weave the tunic[k] of fine linen and make the turban[l] of fine linen. The sash is to be the work of an embroiderer. 40 Make tunics, sashes and headbands for Aaron's sons,[m] to give them dignity and honor.[n] 41 After you put these clothes[o] on your brother Aaron and his sons, anoint[p] and ordain them. Consecrate them so they may serve me as priests.[q]

42 "Make linen undergarments[r] as a covering for the body, reaching from the waist to the thigh. 43 Aaron and his sons must wear them whenever they enter the Tent of Meeting[s] or approach the altar to minister in the Holy Place,[t] so that they will not incur guilt and die.[u]

"This is to be a lasting ordinance[v] for Aaron and his descendants.

Consecration of the Priests

29:1-37pp — Lev 8:1-36

29 "This is what you are to do to consecrate[w] them, so they may serve me as priests: Take a young bull and two rams without defect.[x] 2 And from fine wheat flour, without yeast, make bread, and cakes mixed with oil, and wafers spread with oil.[y] 3 Put them in a basket and present them in it—along with the bull and the two rams.[z] 4 Then bring Aaron and his sons to the entrance to the Tent of Meeting and wash them with water.[a] 5 Take the garments[b] and dress Aaron with the tunic, the robe of the ephod, the ephod itself and the breastpiece. Fasten the ephod on him by its skillfully woven waistband.[c] 6 Put the turban[d] on his head and attach the sacred diadem[e] to the turban. 7 Take the anointing oil[f] and anoint him by pouring it on his head. 8 Bring his sons and dress them in tunics[g] 9 and put headbands on them. Then tie sashes on Aaron and his sons.[a][h] The priesthood is theirs by a lasting ordinance.[i] In this way you shall ordain Aaron and his sons.

10 "Bring the bull to the front of the Tent of Meeting, and Aaron and his sons shall lay their hands on its head.[j] 11 Slaughter it in the LORD's presence[k] at the entrance to the Tent of Meeting. 12 Take some of the bull's blood and put it on the horns[l] of the altar with your finger, and pour out the rest of it at the base of the altar.[m] 13 Then take all the fat[n] around the inner parts,[o] the covering of the liver, and both kidneys with the fat on them, and burn them on the altar. 14 But burn the bull's flesh and its hide and its offal[p] outside the camp.[q] It is a sin offering.

15 "Take one of the rams,[r] and Aaron and his sons shall lay their hands on its head.[s] 16 Slaughter it and take the blood and sprinkle it against the altar on all sides. 17 Cut the ram into pieces and wash[t] the inner parts and the legs, putting them with the head and the other pieces. 18 Then burn the entire ram on the altar. It is a burnt offering to the LORD, a pleasing aroma,[u] an offering made to the LORD by fire.

19 "Take the other ram,[v] and Aaron and his sons shall lay their hands on its head.[w] 20 Slaughter it, take some of its blood and put it on the lobes of the right ears of Aaron and his sons, on the thumbs of their right hands, and on the big toes of their right feet.[x] Then sprinkle blood against the altar on all sides.[y] 21 And take some of the blood[z] on the altar and some of the anointing oil[a] and sprinkle it on Aaron and his garments and on his sons and their garments. Then he and his sons and their garments will be consecrated.[b]

[a] 9 Hebrew; Septuagint *on them*

28:38 [i] Lev 5:1; 10:17; 16:22; 22:9,16; Nu 18:1; Isa 53:5,6,11; Eze 4:4-6; Heb 9:28; 1Pe 2:24 [j] S Ge 32:20; Lev 22:20,27; 23:11; Isa 56:7 **28:39** [k] ver 4 [l] Ex 29:6; Lev 16:4; Eze 24:17,23; 44:18 **28:40** [m] ver 4; Ex 29:8-9; 39:41; 40:14; Lev 8:13 [n] ver 2 **28:41** [o] Ex 40:13 [p] Ex 29:7; Lev 6:20; 10:7; 21:12; Nu 35:25 [q] Ex 29:7-9; 30:30; 40:15; Lev 4:3; 6:22; 8:1-36; Nu 3:3; Heb 7:28 **28:42** [r] Lev 6:10; 16:4,23; Eze 44:18 **28:43** [s] S Ex 27:21 [t] ver 29 [u] Ex 30:20,21; Lev 16:13; 22:9; Nu 1:51; 4:15,20; 18:22 [v] S Ex 27:21 **29:1** [w] ver 21,44; Lev 20:7; Jos 3:5; 1Ch 15:12 [x] Eze 43:23 **29:2** [y] ver 23; Lev 2:1,4; 6:19-23; Nu 6:15 **29:3** [z] ver 15,19 **29:4** [a] Ex 40:12; Lev 14:8; 16:4; Heb 10:22 **29:5** [b] S Ex 28:2 [c] Ex 28:8 **29:6** [d] Ex 28:39; Isa 3:23; Zec 3:5 [e] S Ex 28:36 **29:7** [f] ver 21; S Ex 28:41; 30:25,30,31; 37:29; 40:9; Lev 21:10; 1Sa 10:1; 1Ki 1:39; Ps 89:20; 133:2; 141:5 **29:8** [g] S Ex 28:4; Lev 16:4 **29:9** [h] Ex 28:40 [i] S Ex 27:21; 40:15; Nu 3:10; 18:7; 25:13; Dt 18:5; Jdg 17:5; 1Sa 2:30; 1Ki 12:31 **29:10** [j] ver 19; Lev 1:4; 4:15; 16:21; Nu 8:12 **29:11** [k] Lev 1:5,11; 4:24; 6:16,25; 14:13 **29:12** [l] S Ex 27:2 [m] Lev 4:7; 9:9 **29:13** [n] ver 22; Lev 1:8; 3:3,5,9; 4:10; 6:12; 7:3,5,31; 9:10; Nu 18:17; 1Sa 2:15; 1Ki 8:64; 2Ch 7:7; 29:35; 35:14; Isa 43:24; Eze 44:15 [o] S Ex 12:9 **29:14** [p] Na 3:6; Mal 2:3 [q] Lev 4:12,21; 16:27; Nu 19:3-5; Heb 13:11 **29:15** [r] S ver 3 [s] ver 10; Lev 3:2; 2Ch 29:23 **29:17** [t] Lev 1:9,13 **29:18** [u] S Ge 8:21; 2Co 2:15 **29:19** [v] S ver 3 [w] S ver 10 **29:20** [x] Lev 14:14,25 [y] ver 16; Lev 1:5,11; 3:2 **29:21** [z] Heb 9:22 [a] S ver 7 [b] S ver 1

28:38 *bear the guilt.* Symbolically.
28:39 *tunic.* Worn under the robe.
28:40 *to give them dignity and honor.* See note on v. 2.
28:42–43 See note on 20:26.
28:43 *Tent of Meeting.* See note on 27:21.
29:1 *consecrate them.* See note on 19:10–11. *without defect.* See note on 12:5.

29:4 *Tent of Meeting.* See note on 27:21. *wash them with water.* Symbolizing the removal of ceremonial uncleanness (cf. Heb 10:22 and note) and thus signifying the purity that must characterize them.

29:7 *anoint him.* Symbolizing spiritual endowment for serving God (see 28:41; Isa 61:1 and note).

29:10 *Bring the bull.* As a sin offering (see v. 14) to atone for the past sins of Aaron and his sons (see Lev 4:3 and note). *lay their hands on its head.* As a symbol of (1) the animal's becoming their substitute and (2) transferring their sins to the sin-bearer (see Lev 16:20–22 and note).
29:12 *horns of the altar.* See note on 27:2.
29:13 *fat.* The most select parts of the bull (see Lev 3:3–5,16 and note on 3:16) were burned on the altar as a sacrifice to the Lord.
29:14 *flesh … hide … offal.* Thought of as bearing sin, and thus burned outside the camp (see Heb 13:11–13 and notes).

29:18 *burn the entire ram.* Symbolizing total dedication (see note on Lev 1:3).

29:20 *right ears.* Symbolizing sensitivity to God and his word. *right hands … right feet.* Symbolizing a life of service to others on God's behalf.

22 "Take from this ram the fat,[c] the fat tail, the fat around the inner parts, the covering of the liver, both kidneys with the fat on them, and the right thigh. (This is the ram for the ordination.) 23 From the basket of bread made without yeast, which is before the LORD, take a loaf, and a cake made with oil, and a wafer. 24 Put all these in the hands of Aaron and his sons and wave them before the LORD as a wave offering.[d] 25 Then take them from their hands and burn them on the altar along with the burnt offering for a pleasing aroma to the LORD, an offering made to the LORD by fire.[e] 26 After you take the breast of the ram for Aaron's ordination, wave it before the LORD as a wave offering, and it will be your share.[f]

27 "Consecrate those parts of the ordination ram that belong to Aaron and his sons:[g] the breast that was waved and the thigh that was presented. 28 This is always to be the regular share from the Israelites for Aaron and his sons. It is the contribution the Israelites are to make to the LORD from their fellowship offerings.[a][h]

29 "Aaron's sacred garments[i] will belong to his descendants so that they can be anointed and ordained in them.[j] 30 The son[k] who succeeds him as priest and comes to the Tent of Meeting to minister in the Holy Place is to wear them seven days.

31 "Take the ram[l] for the ordination and cook the meat in a sacred place.[m] 32 At the entrance to the Tent of Meeting, Aaron and his sons are to eat the meat of the ram and the bread[n] that is in the basket. 33 They are to eat these offerings by which atonement was made for their ordination and consecration. But no one else may eat[o] them, because they are sacred. 34 And if any of the meat of the ordination ram or any bread is left over till morning,[p] burn it up. It must not be eaten, because it is sacred.

35 "Do for Aaron and his sons everything I have commanded you, taking seven days to ordain them. 36 Sacrifice a bull each day[q] as a sin offering to make atonement[r]. Purify the altar by making atonement for it, and anoint it to consecrate[s] it. 37 For seven days make atonement for the altar and consecrate it. Then the altar will be most holy, and whatever touches it will be holy.[t]

38 "This is what you are to offer on the altar regularly each day:[u] two lambs a year old. 39 Offer one in the morning and the other at twilight.[v] 40 With the first lamb offer a tenth of an ephah[b] of fine flour mixed with a quarter of a hin[c] of oil[w] from pressed olives, and a quarter of a hin of wine as a drink offering.[x] 41 Sacrifice the other lamb at twilight[y] with the same grain offering[z] and its drink offering as in the morning—a pleasing aroma, an offering made to the LORD by fire.

42 "For the generations to come[a] this burnt offering is to be made regularly[b] at the entrance to the Tent of Meeting[c] before the LORD. There I will meet you and speak to you;[d] 43 there also I will meet with the Israelites, and the place will be consecrated by my glory.[e]

44 "So I will consecrate the Tent of Meeting and the altar and will consecrate Aaron and his sons to serve me as priests.[f] 45 Then I will dwell[g] among the Israelites and be their God.[h] 46 They will know that I am the LORD their God, who brought them out of Egypt[i] so that I might dwell among them. I am the LORD their God.[j]

The Altar of Incense

30:1-5pp — Ex 37:25-28

30 "Make an altar[k] of acacia wood for burning incense.[l] 2 It is to be square, a cubit long and a cubit wide, and two cubits high[d]—its horns[m] of one piece with it. 3 Overlay the top and all the sides and the horns with pure gold, and make a gold

a 28 Traditionally *peace offerings* *b 40* That is, probably about 2 quarts (about 2 liters) *c 40* That is, probably about 1 quart (about 1 liter) *d 2* That is, about 1 1/2 feet (about 0.5 meter) long and wide and about 3 feet (about 0.9 meter) high

29:22 [c]S ver 13 **29:24** [d]Lev 7:30; 9:21; 10:15; 14:12; 23:11, 20; Nu 6:20; 8:11, 13, 15 **29:25** [e]ver 18 **29:26** [f]Lev 7:31-34 **29:27** [g]Ex 22:29; Lev 7:31, 34; Nu 18:11, 12; Dt 18:3 **29:28** [h]ver 22-27; Lev 7:30, 34; 10:15 **29:29** [i]S Ex 28:2; S Lev 16:4 [j]Nu 20:28 **29:30** [k]Lev 6:22; Nu 3:3; 20:28 **29:31** [l]Lev 7:37; 2Ch 13:9 [m]Lev 10:14; Nu 19:9; Eze 42:13 **29:32** [n]Mt 12:4 **29:33** [o]Lev 22:10, 13 **29:34** [p]S Ex 12:10 **29:36** [q]Heb 10:11 [r]ver 33, 37; Ex 30:10; Lev 1:4; 4:20; 16:16; Nu 6:11; 8:12, 19; 16:46; 25:13; 2Ch 29:24 [s]Ex 40:10; Nu 7:10 **29:37** [t]Ex 30:28-29; 40:10; Eze 43:25; Mt 23:19 **29:38** [u]Lev 23:2; Nu 28:3-8; 1Ch 16:40; 2Ch 8:13; Eze 46:13-15; Da 12:11 **29:39** [v]Nu 28:4, 8; 1Ki 18:36; 2Ch 13:11; Ezr 3:3; Ps 141:2; Da 9:21 **29:40** [w]Ex 30:24; Nu 15:4; 28:5 [x]S Ge 35:14; Lev 23:37; 2Ki 16:13 **29:41** [y]1Ki 18:29, 36; 2Ki 3:20; 16:15; Ezr 9:4, 5; Ps 141:2; Da 9:21 [z]Lev 2:1; 5:13; 10:12; Nu 4:16; 6:17; 1Ki 8:64; Isa 43:23 **29:42** [a]Ex 30:8, 10, 21, 31; 31:13 [b]Eze 46:15 [c]S Ex 26:1; S 27:21 [d]ver 43; Ex 25:22; 33:9, 11; Nu 7:89 **29:43** [e]Ex 33:18; 40:34; Lev 9:6; 1Ki 8:11; 2Ch 5:14; 7:2; Ps 26:8; 85:9; Eze 1:28; 43:5; Hag 1:8; 2:7 **29:44** [f]S ver 1 **29:45** [g]S Ex 25:8; Nu 35:34; Jn 14:17; S Ro 8:10 [h]S Ge 17:7; 2Co 6:16 **29:46** [i]S Ex 6:6; 19:4-6; Dt 5:6; Ps 114:1; Hag 2:5 [j]S Ge 17:7 **30:1** [k]Ex 40:5, 26; Nu 4:11; 1Ki 6:20; Eze 41:22 [l]S Ex 25:6; 37:29; Lk 1:11; Heb 9:4; Rev 8:3 **30:2** [m]S Ex 27:2; Rev 9:13

29:24 *wave offering.* See note on Lev 7:30–32.

29:28 *regular share … for Aaron and his sons.* Parts of certain sacrificial animals were set aside as food for the priests and their families (see Lev 10:14).

29:31 *a sacred place.* Probably the tabernacle courtyard.

29:36 *making atonement for it.* Because the altar was corrupted by the sins of the people (see Lev 16:16; Heb 9:21–22).

29:37 *holy … holy.* Set apart as consecrated to the Lord (see note on 3:5).

29:38–39 Institution of the daily morning and evening offerings—sometimes observed even during days of apostasy (see 2Ki 16:15).

29:42–43 *I will meet.* See note on 27:21.

29:43 *my glory.* Symbolic of God's presence over the ark of the covenant (see note on 25:10; see also 40:34–35 and note on 40:34; 1Ki 8:10–13 and note on 8:10).

29:45–46 *dwell among.* See note on 25:9.

29:45 *I will … be their God.* Commonly denotes the essence of the divine promise pledged in his covenant with his people (see note on 6:7).

29:46 *I am the LORD … who brought them out.* See note on 20:2.

30:1 *incense.* Its fragrant smoke symbolized the prayers of God's people (see Ps 141:2; Lk 1:9–10; Rev 5:8 and note; 8:3–4).

30:3 *gold.* See note on 26:37.

molding around it.[n] 4 Make two gold rings[o] for the altar below the molding — two on opposite sides — to hold the poles used to carry it. 5 Make the poles of acacia wood and overlay them with gold.[p] 6 Put the altar in front of the curtain that is before the ark of the Testimony — before the atonement cover[q] that is over the Testimony — where I will meet with you.

7 "Aaron must burn fragrant incense[r] on the altar every morning when he tends the lamps. 8 He must burn incense again when he lights the lamps at twilight so incense will burn regularly before the LORD for the generations to come.[s] 9 Do not offer on this altar any other incense[t] or any burnt offering or grain offering, and do not pour a drink offering on it. 10 Once a year[u] Aaron shall make atonement[v] on its horns. This annual atonement must be made with the blood of the atoning sin offering[w] for the generations to come.[x] It is most holy to the LORD."

Atonement Money

11 Then the LORD said to Moses, 12 "When you take a census[y] of the Israelites to count them, each one must pay the LORD a ransom[z] for his life at the time he is counted. Then no plague[a] will come on them when you number them. 13 Each one who crosses over to those already counted is to give a half shekel,[a] according to the sanctuary shekel,[b] which weighs twenty gerahs. This half shekel is an offering to the LORD. 14 All who cross over, those twenty years old or more,[c] are to give an offering to the LORD. 15 The rich are not to give more than a half shekel and the poor are not to give less[d] when you make the offering to the LORD to atone for your lives. 16 Receive the atonement[e] money from the Israelites and use it for the service of the Tent of Meeting.[f] It will be a memorial[g] for the Israelites before the LORD, making atonement for your lives."

Basin for Washing

17 Then the LORD said to Moses, 18 "Make a bronze basin,[h] with its bronze stand, for washing. Place it between the Tent of Meeting and the altar, and put water in it. 19 Aaron and his sons are to wash their hands and feet[i] with water[j] from it. 20 Whenever they enter the Tent of Meeting, they shall wash with water so that they will not die.[k] Also, when they approach the altar to minister by presenting an offering made to the LORD by fire, 21 they shall wash their hands and feet so that they will not die. This is to be a lasting ordinance[l] for Aaron and his descendants for the generations to come."[m]

Anointing Oil

22 Then the LORD said to Moses, 23 "Take the following fine spices:[n] 500 shekels[b] of liquid myrrh,[o] half as much (that is, 250 shekels) of fragrant cinnamon,[p] 250 shekels of fragrant cane,[q] 24 500 shekels[r] of cassia[s] — all according to the sanctuary shekel — and a hin[c] of olive oil. 25 Make these into a sacred anointing oil, a fragrant blend, the work of a perfumer.[t] It will be the sacred anointing oil.[u] 26 Then use it to anoint[v] the Tent of Meeting, the ark of the Testimony, 27 the table and all its articles, the lampstand and its accessories, the altar of incense, 28 the altar of burnt offering and all its utensils, and the basin with its stand. 29 You shall consecrate them[w] so they will be most holy, and whatever touches them will be holy.[x]

30 "Anoint Aaron and his sons and consecrate[y] them so they may serve me as priests.[z] 31 Say to the Israelites, 'This is to be my sacred anointing oil[a] for the generations to come.[b] 32 Do not pour it on men's bodies and do not make any oil with the same formula. It is sacred, and you are to consider it sacred.[c] 33 Whoever makes perfume like it and whoever puts it on anyone other than a priest must be cut off[d] from his people.' "

a 13 That is, about 1/5 ounce (about 6 grams); also in verse 15 *b* 23 That is, about 12 1/2 pounds (about 6 kilograms) *c* 24 That is, probably about 4 quarts (about 4 liters)

30:3 [n]S Ex 25:11 **30:4** [o]S Ex 25:12 **30:5** [p]S Ex 25:13 **30:6** [q]Ex 25:22; S 26:34 **30:7** [r]S Ex 25:6; 40:27; Nu 3:10; Dt 33:10; 1Sa 2:28; 1Ch 6:49; 2Ch 2:4; 26:18; 29:7 **30:8** [s]S Ex 25:37; S 29:42 **30:9** [t]Lev 10:1; Nu 16:7,40 **30:10** [u]Lev 16:2 [v]Lev 9:7; 16:18-19,30; 23:27,28; 25:9 [w]Ex 29:14; Lev 4:3; 6:25; 7:7; 8:2,14; Nu 6:11 [x]S Ex 29:42 **30:12** [y]Ex 38:25; Nu 1:2,49; 4:2,29; 14:29; 26:2; 31:26; 2Sa 24:1; 2Ki 12:4 [z]Ex 38:26; Nu 31:50; S Mt 20:28 [a]Nu 14:12; Dt 28:58-61; 2Sa 24:13; 1Ki 8:37 **30:13** [b]ver 24; Ex 38:24,26; Lev 5:15; 27:3,25; Nu 3:47; 7:13; 18:16; Eze 4:10; 45:12; Mt 17:24 **30:14** [c]Ex 38:26; Nu 1:3,18; 14:29; 26:2; 32:11; 2Ch 25:5 **30:15** [d]Pr 22:2; Eph 6:9 **30:16** [e]ver 12 [f]Ex 38:25-28; 2Ch 24:5 [g]Nu 31:54 **30:18** [h]Ex 31:9; 35:16; 38:8; 39:39; 40:7,30; 1Ki 7:38; 2Ch 4:6 **30:19** [i]Ex 40:31-32; Jn 13:10 [j]Ex 29:4; 40:12; Lev 8:6; Ps 26:6; Heb 10:22 **30:20** [k]S Ex 28:43 **30:21** [l]S Ex 27:21 [m]Ex 29:42 **30:23** [n]S Ge 43:11 [o]S Ge 37:25 [p]Pr 7:17; SS 4:14 [q]SS 4:14; Isa 43:24; Jer 6:20 **30:24** [r]S ver 13 [s]Ps 45:8; Eze 27:19 **30:25** [t]ver 35; Ex 37:29; 1Ch 9:30 [u]S Ex 29:7; S 1Sa 9:16 **30:26** [v]Ex 40:9; Lev 8:10; Nu 7:1 **30:29** [w]Lev 8:10-11 [x]Ex 29:37; Lev 6:18,27; Mt 23:17 **30:30** [y]Ex 29:7; Lev 8:2,12,30; 10:7; 16:32; 21:10,12; 1Ch 15:12; Ps 133:2 [z]S Ex 28:41 **30:31** [a]S Ex 29:7 [b]S Ex 29:42 **30:32** [c]ver 25,37 **30:33** [d]ver 38; S Ge 17:14

30:6 *curtain that is before the ark of the Testimony.* See notes on 25:16,22; 26:31.
30:10 *annual atonement.* See Lev 16:34 and note. *holy to the LORD.* See 29:37 and note.
30:12 *take a census.* Perhaps such censuses were taken on various occasions (and at stated intervals) to enter the Israelites into an official roll for public duties in the Lord's service (see Nu 1:2 and note; 26:2). *pay … a ransom for his life.* An extension of the principle stated in 13:13,15 (see note on 13:13). Jesus gave "his life as a ransom for many" (see Mt 20:28; Mk 10:45 and notes; cf. 1Ti 2:5–6 and notes).
30:13 *shekel.* A unit of weight, not a coin (see note on Ge 20:16). *according to the sanctuary shekel.* In keeping with the standard weights used at the tabernacle. They may have differed slightly from those used in the marketplace.
30:14 *twenty years old or more.* Of military age (see Nu 1:3).
30:16 *Tent of Meeting.* See note on 27:21. *atonement.* See note on 25:17.
30:18 *basin.* Made from bronze obtained by melting the bronze mirrors contributed by Israelite women (see 38:8 and note). *washing.* See note on 29:4.
30:23–24 *myrrh … cinnamon … cane … cassia.* See note on 25:6.
30:29 *holy … holy.* See 29:37 and note.
30:33 *cut off from his people.* See note on 12:15.

Incense

34 Then the LORD said to Moses, "Take
fragrant spices[e]—gum resin, onycha and
galbanum—and pure frankincense, all
in equal amounts, 35 and make a fragrant
blend of incense,[f] the work of a perfumer.[g] It is to be salted and pure and sacred.
36 Grind some of it to powder and place it in
front of the Testimony in the Tent of Meeting, where I will meet[h] with you. It shall
be most holy[i] to you. 37 Do not make any
incense with this formula for yourselves;
consider it holy[j] to the LORD. 38 Whoever
makes any like it to enjoy its fragrance
must be cut off[k] from his people."

Bezalel and Oholiab

31:2-6pp — Ex 35:30-35

31 Then the LORD said to Moses, 2 "See,
I have chosen Bezalel[l] son of Uri, the
son of Hur,[m] of the tribe of Judah, 3 and
I have filled him with the Spirit of God,
with skill, ability and knowledge[n] in all
kinds of crafts[o]— 4 to make artistic designs for work in gold, silver and bronze,
5 to cut and set stones, to work in wood,
and to engage in all kinds of craftsmanship. 6 Moreover, I have appointed Oholiab[p] son of Ahisamach, of the tribe of
Dan,[q] to help him. Also I have given skill
to all the craftsmen[r] to make everything I
have commanded you: 7 the Tent of Meeting,[s] the ark of the Testimony[t] with the
atonement cover[u] on it, and all the other
furnishings of the tent— 8 the table[v] and
its articles, the pure gold lampstand[w] and
all its accessories, the altar of incense,[x]
9 the altar of burnt offering[y] and all its
utensils, the basin[z] with its stand— 10 and
also the woven garments[a], both the sacred garments for Aaron the priest and the
garments for his sons when they serve as
priests, 11 and the anointing oil[b] and fragrant incense[c] for the Holy Place. They
are to make them just as I commanded[d]
you."

The Sabbath

12 Then the LORD said to Moses, 13 "Say to
the Israelites, 'You must observe my Sabbaths.[e] This will be a sign[f] between me
and you for the generations to come,[g] so
you may know that I am the LORD, who
makes you holy.[a][h]

14 " 'Observe the Sabbath, because it is
holy to you. Anyone who desecrates it
must be put to death;[i] whoever does any
work on that day must be cut off from his
people. 15 For six days, work[j] is to be done,
but the seventh day is a Sabbath of rest,[k]
holy to the LORD. Whoever does any work
on the Sabbath day must be put to death.
16 The Israelites are to observe the Sabbath,[l] celebrating it for the generations to
come as a lasting covenant. 17 It will be a
sign[m] between me and the Israelites forever, for in six days the LORD made the heavens and the earth, and on the seventh day
he abstained from work and rested.[n]' "[o]

18 When the LORD finished speaking to
Moses on Mount Sinai,[p] he gave him the
two tablets of the Testimony, the tablets of
stone[q] inscribed by the finger of God.[r]

The Golden Calf

32 When the people saw that Moses
was so long in coming down from
the mountain,[s] they gathered around Aaron and said, "Come, make us gods[b] who
will go before[t] us. As for this fellow Moses
who brought us up out of Egypt, we don't
know what has happened to him."[u]

2 Aaron answered them, "Take off the
gold earrings[v] that your wives, your sons

a 13 Or *who sanctifies you*; or *who sets you apart as holy*
b 1 Or *a god*; also in verses 23 and 31

30:34 [e] SS 3:6 **30:35** [f] S Ex 25:6 [g] S ver 25 **30:36** [h] S Ex 25:22 [i] ver 32; Ex 29:37; Lev 2:3 **30:37** [j] S ver 32 **30:38** [k] S ver 33 **31:2** [l] Ex 36:1,2; 37:1; 38:22; 1Ch 2:20; 2Ch 1:5 [m] S Ex 17:10 **31:3** [n] S Ex 28:3 [o] 1Ki 7:14; 1Co 12:4 **31:6** [p] Ex 36:1,2; 38:23 [q] 1Ki 7:14; 2Ch 2:14 [r] S Ex 28:3 **31:7** [s] Ex 36:8-38 [t] Ex 37:1-5 [u] Ex 37:6; 40:20 **31:8** [v] Ex 37:10-16 [w] Ex 37:17-24; Lev 24:4 [x] Ex 37:25-28 **31:9** [y] Ex 38:3; Nu 4:14 [z] S Ex 30:18 **31:10** [a] S Ex 28:2 **31:11** [b] Ex 30:22-32; 37:29 [c] S Ex 25:6 [d] S Ex 25:9 **31:13** [e] S Ex 20:8 [f] ver 17; Isa 56:4; Eze 20:12,20 [g] S Ex 29:42 [h] Lev 11:44; 20:8; 21:8; Eze 37:28 **31:14** [i] Ex 35:2; Nu 15:32-36 **31:15** [j] S Ex 20:8-11; 35:2; Lev 16:29; 23:3; Nu 29:7 [k] S Ge 2:3 **31:16** [l] S Ex 20:8 **31:17** [m] S ver 13 [n] S Ge 2:2-3 [o] S Ge 2:2; S Ex 20:9; Isa 56:2; 58:13; 66:23; Jer 17:21-22; Eze 20:12,20 **31:18** [p] S Ex 19:11 [q] S Ex 24:12; 2Co 3:3; Heb 9:4 [r] Ex 32:15-16; 34:1,28; Dt 4:13; 9:10 **32:1** [s] S Ge 7:4; Dt 9:9-12 [t] S Ex 13:21 [u] ver 23; Ac 7:40* **32:2** [v] Jdg 8:24-27

30:34 *gum resin, onycha and galbanum.* See note on 25:6. *frankincense.* A resin from the bark of *Boswellia carteri*, which grows in southern Arabia.

31:2 *Bezalel.* Means "in the shadow/protection of God." *Hur.* See note on 17:10.

31:3 *filled him with the Spirit of God.* Ability to work skillfully in all kinds of crafts was a spiritual gift, equipping a person for special service to God. *skill.* See Pr 1:2 and note.

31:6 *Oholiab.* Means "The (divine) father is my tent/tabernacle." The names of Bezalel (see note on v. 2) and Oholiab were appropriate for the chief craftsmen working on the tabernacle.

31:7 *Tent of Meeting.* See note on 27:21.

31:13 *observe my Sabbaths.* Instructions for building the tabernacle and making the priestly garments are concluded by impressing on the Israelites the importance and necessity of keeping the Sabbath even while carrying out this special task. *makes you holy.* See 19:6; 29:37 and notes.

31:14 *cut off from his people.* See note on 12:15.

31:16–17 *covenant ... sign.* In their rhythm of work and rest in the service of God, Israel is to emulate God's pattern in creation as an ever-renewed sign of their covenant with God (see note on Ge 9:12).

31:18 *two tablets.* In keeping with ancient Near Eastern practice, these were probably duplicates of the covenant document, not two sections of the Ten Commandments. One copy belonged to each party of the covenant. Since Israel's copy was to be laid up in the presence of God (according to custom), both covenant tablets (God's and Israel's) were placed in the ark (see 25:21 and note). *Testimony.* See notes on 16:34; 25:16. *inscribed by the finger of God.* Because it was God's covenant (see 19:5–6 and notes), and the stipulations of the covenant (20:1–17) were his.

32:1 *so long.* Forty days and forty nights (see 24:18 and note). *they.* Probably the tribe and clan leaders. *gods.* See NIV text note. *Moses who brought us up out of Egypt.* A rebellious contrast to the gracious statement of Israel's covenant Lord (see 20:2 and note; 29:46).

32:2 *gold earrings.* Probably part of the plunder brought from Egypt (see 3:21–22 and note on 3:21; 11:2–3; 12:35–36).

and your daughters are wearing, and bring
them to me." [3]So all the people took off
their earrings and brought them to Aaron.
[4]He took what they handed him and made
it into an idol[w] cast in the shape of a calf,[x]
fashioning it with a tool. Then they said,
"These are your gods,[a][y] O Israel, who
brought you up out of Egypt."[z]
[5]When Aaron saw this, he built an altar in front of the calf and announced,
"Tomorrow there will be a festival[a] to the
LORD." [6]So the next day the people rose
early and sacrificed burnt offerings and
presented fellowship offerings.[b][b] Afterward they sat down to eat and drink[c] and
got up to indulge in revelry.[d]
[7]Then the LORD said to Moses, "Go
down, because your people, whom you
brought up out of Egypt,[e] have become
corrupt.[f] [8]They have been quick to turn
away[g] from what I commanded them
and have made themselves an idol[h] cast
in the shape of a calf.[i] They have bowed
down to it and sacrificed[j] to it and have
said, 'These are your gods, O Israel, who
brought you up out of Egypt.'[k]
[9]"I have seen these people," the LORD
said to Moses, "and they are a stiff-necked[l]
people. [10]Now leave me alone[m] so that my
anger may burn against them and that I
may destroy[n] them. Then I will make you
into a great nation."[o]
[11]But Moses sought the favor[p] of the
LORD his God. "O LORD," he said, "why
should your anger burn against your people, whom you brought out of Egypt with
great power and a mighty hand?[q] [12]Why
should the Egyptians say, 'It was with
evil intent that he brought them out, to
kill them in the mountains and to wipe
them off the face of the earth'?[r] Turn from
your fierce anger; relent and do not bring
disaster[s] on your people. [13]Remember[t]
your servants Abraham, Isaac and Israel,
to whom you swore by your own self:[u] 'I
will make your descendants as numerous as the stars[v] in the sky and I will give
your descendants all this land[w] I promised
them, and it will be their inheritance forever.'" [14]Then the LORD relented[x] and did
not bring on his people the disaster he had
threatened.
[15]Moses turned and went down the
mountain with the two tablets of the Testimony[y] in his hands.[z] They were inscribed[a]
on both sides, front and back. [16]The tablets
were the work of God; the writing was the
writing of God, engraved on the tablets.[b]
[17]When Joshua[c] heard the noise of the
people shouting, he said to Moses, "There
is the sound of war in the camp."
[18]Moses replied:

"It is not the sound of victory,
it is not the sound of defeat;
it is the sound of singing that I
hear."

[a] 4 Or *This is your god*; also in verse 8
[b] 6 Traditionally *peace offerings*

32:4 [w]S Ex 20:23; Jdg 17:3-4; Isa 30:22 [x]ver 8, 24, 35; Dt 9:16; Ne 9:18; Ps 106:19; Ac 7:41 [y]Ex 20:23; Isa 42:17 [z]1Ki 12:28; 14:9; 2Ki 10:29; 17:16; 2Ch 13:8; Hos 8:6; 10:5 **32:5** [a]Lev 23:2, 37; 2Ki 10:20; Joel 2:15 **32:6** [b]Ex 20:24; 34:15; Lev 3:1; 4:10; 6:12; 9:4; 22:21; Nu 6:14; 25:2; Dt 27:7; Jdg 20:26; Eze 43:27; Ac 7:41 [c]Jdg 19:4; Ru 3:3; 1Sa 1:9; 2Sa 11:11; 1Ki 13:23; 18:42; Ne 8:12; Job 1:4; Ecc 5:18; 8:15; Jer 16:8 [d]ver 17-19; 1Co 10:7* **32:7** [e]ver 4, 11; Ex 33:1 [f]S Ge 6:11-12; Eze 20:8 **32:8** [g]Jer 7:26; 16:12; Mal 2:8; 3:7 [h]S Ex 20:4 [i]S ver 4 [j]Ex 22:20 [k]1Ki 12:28; Eze 23:8 **32:9** [l]Ex 33:3, 5; 34:9; Dt 9:6, 13; 10:16; 31:27; Jdg 2:19; 2Ki 17:14; 2Ch 30:8; 36:13; Ne 9:16; Ps 78:8; Pr 29:1; Isa 46:12; 48:4; Jer 7:26; Eze 2:4; Hos 4:16; Ac 7:51

32:10 [m]1Sa 2:25; Jer 7:16; 11:14; 14:11 [n]Ex 22:24; 33:3, 5; Nu 16:21, 45; Dt 9:14, 19; Ps 106:23; Jer 14:12; Eze 20:13 [o]Nu 14:12; Dt 9:14 **32:11** [p]Dt 9:18; 2Sa 21:1; 2Ch 15:2; Ps 9:10; 34:4; 106:23; Isa 9:13; Jer 15:1 [q]ver 13; Dt 9:26; 1Sa 7:9; Ne 1:10; Ps 136:12 **32:12** [r]Nu 14:13-16; Dt 9:28 [s]ver 14; Ex 33:13 **32:13** [t]S Ex 2:24; 33:13 [u]S Ge 22:16; Heb 6:13 [v]Ge 15:5; 22:17 [w]S Ge 12:7 **32:14** [x]Dt 9:19; 1Sa 15:11; 2Sa 24:16; 1Ki 21:29; 1Ch 21:15; Ps 106:45; Jer 18:8; 26:3, 19; Am 7:3, 6; Jnh 3:10 **32:15** [y]Ex 31:18; Heb 9:4 [z]S Ex 19:18; 34:4, 29; Dt 9:15 [a]2Co 3:3 **32:16** [b]S Ex 24:12 **32:17** [c]S Ex 17:9

32:4 *cast in the shape of a calf.* Either gold plating over a carved wooden calf (it was later burned, v. 20) or crudely cast in solid gold and then further shaped with a tool, later to be melted down in the fire. The calf was probably similar to representations of the Egyptian bull-god Apis (see note on Jer 46:15). Its manufacture was a flagrant violation of the second commandment (20:4 – 5; see notes there). *they.* The leaders among the people (see note on v. 1). *These are your gods … up out of Egypt.* A parody of 20:2 (see note on v. 1). Centuries later, King Jeroboam echoed these words when he set up two golden calves in the northern kingdom of Israel (see 1Ki 12:28 – 29 and notes).

32:5 *altar in front of the calf … festival to the LORD.* Apparently Aaron recognized the idolatrous consequences of his deed and acted quickly to keep the people from turning completely away from the Lord.

32:6 *they sat down … indulge in revelry.* A pagan symbol evoked pagan religious practices. Paul quotes this sentence as a vivid example of Israel's tendency toward idolatry (see 1Co 10:7 and note). The Hebrew verb translated "indulge in revelry" often has sexual connotations (see, e.g., "caressing," Ge 26:8). Sexual orgies frequently accompanied pagan worship in ancient times (see notes on Ge 15:16; Nu 25:1; Hos 4:13 – 14).

32:7,9 *your people … these people.* By not calling Israel "my people" (as, e.g., in 3:10), God indicates that he is disowning them for breaking his covenant with them (see note on 17:4).

32:7 *corrupt.* And therefore ripe for destruction (see v. 10; Ge 6:11 – 13).

32:9 *stiff-necked.* Like unresponsive oxen or horses (see Jer 27:11 – 12; see also note on Ne 3:5).

32:10 *I will make you into a great nation.* After Israel — Abraham's descendants — has been destroyed, God will transfer to Moses the pledge originally given to Abraham (see Ge 12:2).

32:11 *your people.* Using God's own words (see v. 7 and note on vv. 7,9), Moses appeals to God's special relationship to Israel, then to God's need to vindicate his name in the eyes of the Egyptians (see v. 12), and finally to the great patriarchal promises (see v. 13).

32:13 *Israel.* Jacob (see 33:1; see also Ge 32:28 and note).

32:14 *the LORD relented.* See note on Jer 18:7 – 10; see also 2Sa 24:16; Ps 106:45; Am 7:1 – 6; cf. Jas 5:16.

32:15 *went down the mountain.* See note on 24:18. *two tablets.* See note on 31:18. *Testimony.* See notes on 16:34; 25:16. *inscribed on both sides.* See note on 31:18. Elsewhere note is taken of scrolls written on both sides (see Eze 2:10 and note; Zec 5:3; Rev 5:1); in each case what is written pertains to God's sovereign involvement in human history, especially his coming judgment.

32:16 *work of God … writing of God.* See 31:18 and note.

32:17 *Joshua.* Perhaps he had accompanied Moses part of the way up the mountain (see 24:13).

19When Moses approached the camp and
saw the calf[d] and the dancing,[e] his anger
burned[f] and he threw the tablets out of his
hands, breaking them to pieces[g] at the foot
of the mountain. 20And he took the calf
they had made and burned[h] it in the fire;
then he ground it to powder,[i] scattered it on
the water[j] and made the Israelites drink it.
21He said to Aaron, "What did these
people do to you, that you led them into
such great sin?"
22"Do not be angry,[k] my lord," Aaron answered. "You know how prone these people are to evil.[l] 23They said to me, 'Make
us gods who will go before us. As for this
fellow Moses who brought us up out of
Egypt, we don't know what has happened
to him.'[m] 24So I told them, 'Whoever has
any gold jewelry, take it off.' Then they
gave me the gold, and I threw it into the
fire, and out came this calf!"[n]
25Moses saw that the people were running wild and that Aaron had let them get
out of control and so become a laughingstock[o] to their enemies. 26So he stood at
the entrance to the camp and said, "Whoever is for the LORD, come to me." And all
the Levites rallied to him.
27Then he said to them, "This is what
the LORD, the God of Israel, says: 'Each
man strap a sword to his side. Go back
and forth through the camp from one end
to the other, each killing his brother and
friend and neighbor.'"[p] 28The Levites did
as Moses commanded, and that day about
three thousand of the people died. 29Then
Moses said, "You have been set apart to
the LORD today, for you were against your
own sons and brothers, and he has blessed
you this day."
30The next day Moses said to the people, "You have committed a great sin.[q] But
now I will go up to the LORD; perhaps I can
make atonement[r] for your sin."
31So Moses went back to the LORD and
said, "Oh, what a great sin these people
have committed![s] They have made themselves gods of gold.[t] 32But now, please forgive their sin[u]—but if not, then blot me[v]
out of the book[w] you have written."
33The LORD replied to Moses, "Whoever
has sinned against me I will blot out[x] of
my book. 34Now go, lead[y] the people to
the place[z] I spoke of, and my angel[a] will
go before you. However, when the time
comes for me to punish,[b] I will punish
them for their sin."
35And the LORD struck the people with a
plague because of what they did with the
calf[c] Aaron had made.

33 Then the LORD said to Moses, "Leave
this place, you and the people you
brought up out of Egypt, and go up to the
land I promised on oath[d] to Abraham,
Isaac and Jacob, saying, 'I will give it to
your descendants.'[e] 2I will send an angel[f]
before you and drive out the Canaanites,
Amorites, Hittites, Perizzites, Hivites and
Jebusites.[g] 3Go up to the land flowing with
milk and honey.[h] But I will not go with
you, because you are a stiff-necked[i] people and I might destroy[j] you on the way."

32:19 [d]Dt 9:16 [e]ver 6; 1Co 10:7 [f]Ezr 9:3; Ps 119:53,158 [g]Ex 34:1; Dt 9:17 **32:20** [h]Dt 7:25; 12:3; Jos 7:1; 2Ki 23:6; 1Ch 14:12 [i]2Ch 34:7; Mic 1:7 [j]Dt 9:21 **32:22** [k]S Ge 18:30 [l]Dt 9:24; 28:20; 2Ki 21:15; Ezr 9:13; Ne 9:28; Jer 4:4; 44:3; Eze 6:9 **32:23** [m]S ver 1; Ac 7:40 **32:24** [n]S ver 4 **32:25** [o]S Ge 38:23 **32:27** [p]Nu 25:3,5; Dt 33:9; Eze 9:5 **32:30** [q]1Sa 12:20; Ps 25:11; 85:2 [r]Lev 1:4; 4:20,26; 5:6,10,13; 6:7 **32:31** [s]Ex 34:9; Dt 9:18 [t]S Ex 20:23 **32:32** [u]Nu 14:19 [v]Ro 9:3 [w]Ps 69:28; Eze 13:9; Da 7:10; 12:1; Mal 3:16; S Lk 10:20 **32:33** [x]S Ex 17:14; S Job 21:20; Rev 3:5 **32:34** [y]S Ex 15:17 [z]Ex 3:17 [a]S Ex 14:19 [b]S Ge 50:19; Dt 32:35; Ps 89:32; 94:23; 99:8; 109:20; Isa 27:1; Jer 5:9; 11:22; 23:2; 44:13,29; Hos 12:2; Ro 2:5-6 **32:35** [c]S ver 4 **33:1** [d]S Ex 13:11; S Nu 14:23; Heb 6:13 [e]S Ge 12:7 **33:2** [f]S Ex 14:19 [g]S Ex 23:28 **33:3** [h]S Ex 3:8 [i]Ex 32:9; Ac 7:51 [j]S Ex 32:10

32:19 *breaking them to pieces.* Thus testifying against Israel that they had broken the covenant.

32:20 *burned it ... ground it to powder.* King Jeroboam's altar (see note on v. 4) at Bethel received the same treatment (see 2Ki 23:15).

32:21 *great sin.* See Ge 20:9 and note.

32:22–24 In his desperation, Aaron blamed the people (cf. Ge 3:12–13 and notes), but the Lord held him accountable. Only through Moses' intercession was Aaron spared (see Dt 9:20).

32:24 *out came this calf.* Aaron could hardly have thought that Moses would believe such an incredible story (see v. 4).

32:25 *were running wild ... get out of control.* The same Hebrew root underlies both phrases and is found also in Pr 29:18 ("cast off restraint"). Anarchy reigns among people who refuse to obey and worship the Lord.

32:26 *Whoever is for the LORD, come to me.* See Jos 24:15; 1Ki 18:21 and notes; Mt 6:24. *all.* Perhaps a generalization since Dt 33:9 may imply that some of the Levites were also slain. *Levites.* The descendants of Levi (Ge 29:34). For the special role later assigned them in the life of the covenant community see Nu 3:5–39 and note on 3:5–10.

32:27 *killing his brother and friend and neighbor.* See Mt 10:37; Lk 14:26 and note.

32:28 *The Levites did as Moses commanded.* Their zeal for the Lord is later matched by Aaron's grandson Phinehas, resulting in a perpetual covenant of the priesthood (see Nu 25:7–13 and note on 25:11).

32:29 *You have been set apart to the LORD today.* Because of their zeal for the Lord the Levites were set apart to be caretakers of the tabernacle and aides to the priests (see Nu 1:47–53; 3:5–9,12,41,45 and note on 3:5–10; 4:2–3).

32:30 *make atonement for your sin.* By making urgent intercession before God, as the mediator God had appointed between himself and Israel. No sacrifice that Israel or Moses might bring could atone for this sin. But Moses so identified himself with Israel that he made his own death the condition for God's destruction of the nation (see v. 32). Jesus Christ, the great Mediator, offered himself on the cross to make atonement for his people.

32:32 *blot me out.* Paul made a similar statement (see Ro 9:3 and note). *book you have written.* See notes on Ps 9:5; 51:1; 69:28.

32:33 *Whoever has sinned ... I will blot out.* Moses' gracious offer is refused, because the individuals who sin are responsible for their own sin (see Dt 24:16; Eze 18:4 and note).

32:34 *Now go, lead the people.* Thus Moses received assurance that the Lord will continue his covenant with wayward Israel and fulfill his promise concerning the land. *the place I spoke of.* Canaan (see 33:1). *my angel.* See 23:23; 33:2.

33:2 *Canaanites ... Jebusites.* See note on 3:8.

33:3 *land flowing with milk and honey.* See note on 3:8. *I will*

4When the people heard these distress-
ing words, they began to mourn[k] and no
one put on any ornaments. 5For the LORD
had said to Moses, "Tell the Israelites, 'You
are a stiff-necked people.[l] If I were to go
with you even for a moment, I might destroy[m] you. Now take off your ornaments
and I will decide what to do with you.' "
6So the Israelites stripped off their ornaments at Mount Horeb.[n]

The Tent of Meeting

7Now Moses used to take a tent and
pitch it outside the camp some distance
away, calling it the "tent of meeting."[o]
Anyone inquiring[p] of the LORD would go
to the tent of meeting outside the camp.
8And whenever Moses went out to the
tent, all the people rose and stood at the
entrances to their tents,[q] watching Moses
until he entered the tent. 9As Moses went
into the tent, the pillar of cloud[r] would
come down and stay at the entrance, while
the LORD spoke[s] with Moses. 10Whenever
the people saw the pillar of cloud standing
at the entrance to the tent, they all stood
and worshiped, each at the entrance to his
tent.[t] 11The LORD would speak to Moses
face to face,[u] as a man speaks with his
friend. Then Moses would return to the
camp, but his young aide Joshua[v] son of
Nun did not leave the tent.

Moses and the Glory of the LORD

12Moses said to the LORD, "You have been
telling me, 'Lead these people,'[w] but you
have not let me know whom you will send
with me. You have said, 'I know you by
name[x] and you have found favor[y] with me.'
13If you are pleased with me, teach me
your ways[z] so I may know you and continue to find favor with you. Remember
that this nation is your people."[a]
14The LORD replied, "My Presence[b] will
go with you, and I will give you rest."[c]
15Then Moses said to him, "If your Presence[d] does not go with us, do not send
us up from here. 16How will anyone know
that you are pleased with me and with
your people unless you go with us?[e] What
else will distinguish me and your people
from all the other people on the face of
the earth?"[f]
17And the LORD said to Moses, "I will do
the very thing you have asked,[g] because I
am pleased with you and I know you by
name."[h]
18Then Moses said, "Now show me your
glory."[i]
19And the LORD said, "I will cause all my
goodness to pass[j] in front of you, and I
will proclaim my name,[k] the LORD, in your
presence. I will have mercy on whom I
will have mercy, and I will have compassion on whom I will have compassion.[l]
20But," he said, "you cannot see my face,
for no one may see[m] me and live."
21Then the LORD said, "There is a place
near me where you may stand on a rock.
22When my glory passes by, I will put you
in a cleft in the rock[n] and cover you with
my hand[o] until I have passed by. 23Then I
will remove my hand and you will see my
back; but my face must not be seen."

33:4 [k]Nu 14:39; Ezr 9:3; Est 4:1; Ps 119:53 **33:5** [l]S Ex 32:9 [m]S Ex 32:10 **33:6** [n]S Ex 3:1 **33:7** [o]S Ex 27:21 [p]S Ge 25:22; S 1Ki 22:5 **33:8** [q]ver 10; Nu 16:27 **33:9** [r]Ex 13:21; S 19:9; Dt 31:15; 1Co 10:1 [s]S Ex 29:42; 31:18; Ps 99:7 **33:10** [t]S ver 8 **33:11** [u]Nu 12:8; Dt 5:4; 34:10 [v]S Ex 17:9 **33:12** [w]Ex 3:10; S 15:17 [x]ver 17; Isa 43:1; 45:3; 49:1; Jn 10:14-15; 2Ti 2:19 [y]S Ge 6:8 **33:13** [z]Ps 25:4; 27:11; 51:13; 86:11; 103:7; 143:8 [a]Ex 3:7; Dt 9:26, 29; Ps 77:15 **33:14** [b]S Ex 13:21; Dt 4:37; Isa 63:9; Hag 1:13; 2:4 [c]Dt 12:9, 10; 25:19; Jos 1:13; 11:23; 21:44; 22:4; 23:1; 1Ki 8:56; Isa 63:14; Jer 31:2; Mt 11:28; Heb 4:1-11 **33:15** [d]ver 3; Ex 34:9; 2Ki 13:23; 17:18; 23:27; 24:20; Ps 51:11; 80:3, 7, 19; Jer 7:15; 52:3 **33:16** [e]Ex 34:5; 40:34, 35; Nu 9:15; 14:14 [f]Ex 34:10; Lev 20:24, 26; Nu 23:9; Dt 4:7, 32, 34; 32:9; 33:28 **33:17** [g]Ex 34:28; Dt 9:18, 25; 10:10; Jas 5:16 [h]S Ge 6:8 **33:18** [i]S Ex 16:7; Jn 1:14; 12:41; 1Ti 6:16; Rev 15:8 **33:19** [j]1Ki 19:11 [k]Ex 6:3; 34:5-7 [l]Ro 9:15* **33:20** [m]S Ge 16:13; S Ex 3:6; S Dt 5:26; S Jn 1:18 **33:22** [n]Ge 49:24; 1Ki 19:9; Ps 27:5; 31:20; 62:7; 91:1; Isa 2:21; Jer 4:29 [o]Ps 91:4; Isa 49:2; 51:16

not go with you. The Lord's presence, earlier assured to his people (see 23:21 and note), is now temporarily withdrawn because of sin. *stiff-necked.* See note on 32:9.

33:6 *stripped off their ornaments.* As a sign of mourning (see Eze 26:16–17).

33:7 *tent of meeting outside the camp.* Not the tabernacle (contrast 27:21), which occupied a central location within the Israelite camp, but a temporary structure where the people could consult the Lord until the more durable tabernacle was completed.

33:9 *pillar of cloud would come down.* Symbolizing God's communication with Moses "as a man speaks with his friend" (v. 11). Later, a similar descent crowned the completion of the tabernacle (see 40:33–34; see also note on 13:21).

33:11 *The LORD would speak to Moses face to face.* God communicated with him directly—but without visually showing his "face." As the OT mediator, Moses was unique among the prophets (see Nu 12:6–8; Dt 34:10,12 and notes). *Joshua ... did not leave the tent.* Probably his task was to guard the tent against intrusion by others.

33:12 *you have not let me know whom you will send with me.* See note on v. 3. Moses objects that a mere angel is no substitute for God's own presence. *I know you by name.* I have chosen you for my special purpose (see Jer 1:5 and note).

33:13 *teach me your ways.* A prayer that is answered in 34:6–7.

33:14 *My Presence.* Lit. "My face." The Lord will not "hide" his face from his people but will cause it to "shine" on them (see Nu 6:25; Ps 13:1 and notes). See also note on v. 12.

33:17 *because I am pleased with you.* How much more does God hear the prayers of his Son Jesus Christ (see Mt 17:5; Heb 3:1–6 and notes)!

33:18 *show me your glory.* All that God has done for Israel through Moses has made him very bold. At his first meeting with God he was "afraid to look at God" in the small display of God's glory in the burning bush (see 3:6 and note), and he inquired concerning God's name (3:13). Now he asks to be shown God's glory unveiled and is told he has asked too much, that he must be content with the fuller proclamation of God's name (see vv. 19,22 and note on v. 19; 34:5–7 and notes).

33:19 *goodness.* God's nature and character. *name.* A further symbol of God's nature, character and person (see Ps 20:1; Jn 1:12; 17:6 and note). Here his name implies his mercy (grace) and his compassion (as it does also in 34:6). *I will have mercy on whom ... compassion.* Paul quotes these words in Ro 9:15 (see note there) to defend his view of God's sovereignty.

33:20 *no one may see me and live.* See note on Ge 16:13; see also Jn 1:18 and note; 6:46; 1Ti 1:17; 1Jn 4:12 and note.

33:21–23 God speaks of himself in human language. See 34:5–7 for the fulfillment of his promise.

The New Stone Tablets

34 The LORD said to Moses, "Chisel
out two stone tablets like the first
ones,[p] and I will write on them the words
that were on the first tablets,[q] which you
broke.[r] 2Be ready in the morning, and then
come up on Mount Sinai.[s] Present yourself to me there on top of the mountain.
3No one is to come with you or be seen
anywhere on the mountain;[t] not even the
flocks and herds may graze in front of the
mountain."

4So Moses chiseled[u] out two stone tablets like the first ones and went up Mount
Sinai early in the morning, as the LORD
had commanded him; and he carried the
two stone tablets in his hands.[v] 5Then the
LORD came down in the cloud[w] and stood
there with him and proclaimed his name,
the LORD.[x] 6And he passed in front of Moses, proclaiming, "The LORD, the LORD, the
compassionate[y] and gracious God, slow
to anger,[z] abounding in love[a] and faithfulness,[b] 7maintaining love to thousands,[c]
and forgiving wickedness, rebellion and
sin.[d] Yet he does not leave the guilty unpunished;[e] he punishes the children and
their children for the sin of the fathers to
the third and fourth generation."[f]

8Moses bowed to the ground at once
and worshiped. 9"O Lord, if I have found
favor[g] in your eyes," he said, "then let
the Lord go with us.[h] Although this is a
stiff-necked[i] people, forgive our wickedness and our sin,[j] and take us as your inheritance."[k]

10Then the LORD said: "I am making a
covenant[l] with you. Before all your people I will do wonders[m] never before done
in any nation in all the world.[n] The people
you live among will see how awesome is
the work that I, the LORD, will do for you.
11Obey what I command[o] you today. I will
drive out before you the Amorites, Canaanites, Hittites, Perizzites, Hivites and Jebusites.[p] 12Be careful not to make a treaty[q]
with those who live in the land where you
are going, or they will be a snare[r] among
you. 13Break down their altars, smash their
sacred stones and cut down their Asherah
poles.[a][s] 14Do not worship any other god,[t]
for the LORD, whose name[u] is Jealous, is a
jealous God.[v]

15"Be careful not to make a treaty[w] with
those who live in the land; for when they
prostitute[x] themselves to their gods and
sacrifice to them, they will invite you and
you will eat their sacrifices.[y] 16And when
you choose some of their daughters as
wives[z] for your sons and those daughters
prostitute themselves to their gods,[a] they
will lead your sons to do the same.

17"Do not make cast idols.[b]

18"Celebrate the Feast of Unleavened
Bread.[c] For seven days eat bread made
without yeast,[d] as I commanded you. Do
this at the appointed time in the month
of Abib,[e] for in that month you came out
of Egypt.

19"The first offspring[f] of every womb

[a] *13* That is, wooden symbols of the goddess Asherah

34:1 [p] S Ex 24:12 [q] Dt 10:2,4 [r] S Ex 32:19 **34:2** [s] S Ex 19:11 **34:3** [t] S Ex 19:13 **34:4** [u] Dt 10:3 [v] S Ex 32:15 **34:5** [w] S Ex 13:21; S 19:9 [x] Ex 6:3; 33:19 **34:6** [y] S Ex 22:27; S Nu 14:20; S Ps 86:15 [z] Nu 14:18; Ps 78:38; Jer 15:15; Ro 2:4 [a] S Ge 19:16 [b] Ps 61:7; 108:4; 115:1; 138:2; 143:1; La 3:23; Jas 5:11 **34:7** [c] S Ex 20:6; Dt 5:10 [d] 1Ki 8:30; Ps 86:5; 103:3; 130:4,8; Isa 43:25; Da 9:9; 1Jn 1:9 [e] Ex 23:7; Jos 24:19; Job 7:20-21; 9:28; 10:14; Mic 6:1-16; Na 1:3 [f] S Ex 20:5 **34:9** [g] Ex 33:13; Nu 11:15 [h] S Ex 33:15 [i] Ex 32:9 [j] Nu 14:19; 1Ki 8:30; 2Ch 6:21; Ps 19:12; 25:11; Jer 33:8; Hos 14:2 [k] S Ex 6:7; 19:5; Dt 4:20; 7:6; 9:26,29; 14:2; 26:18; 32:9; 1Sa 10:1; 2Sa 14:16; 1Ki 8:51,53; Ps 28:9; 33:12; 74:2; 79:1; 94:14; 106:5,40; Isa 19:25; 63:17; Jer 10:16; 51:19; Mic 7:18; Zec 2:12 **34:10** [l] S Ge 6:18; S 9:15; S 15:18; Dt 5:2-3 [m] S Ex 3:20 [n] S Ex 33:16 **34:11** [o] Dt 6:25; Jos 11:15 [p] S Ex 23:28 **34:12** [q] Jdg 2:2 [r] S Ex 10:7 **34:13** [s] S Ex 23:24; Nu 33:52; Dt 7:5; 12:3; Jdg 6:26; 1Ki 15:13; 2Ch 15:16; 17:6; 34:3-4; Mic 5:14 **34:14** [t] S Ex 20:3 [u] Isa 9:6 [v] S Ex 20:5 **34:15** [w] ver 12; Dt 23:6; Ezr 9:12 [x] Ex 22:20; 32:8; Dt 31:16; Jdg 2:17; 2Ki 17:8; 1Ch 5:25; 2Ch 11:15; Am 2:4 [y] S Ex 32:6; 1Co 8:4 **34:16** [z] Dt 7:3; 17:17; Jos 23:12; Jdg 3:6; 14:3; 1Ki 11:1,2; 16:31; Ezr 9:2; 10:3; Ne 10:30; 13:25,26 [a] Dt 7:4; 12:31; 20:18; 1Ki 11:4; 2Ki 21:3-15; Ps 106:34-41; Mal 2:11 **34:17** [b] S Ex 20:4 **34:18** [c] S Ex 12:17; Mt 26:17; Lk 22:1; Ac 12:3 [d] S Ex 12:15 [e] S Ex 12:2 **34:19** [f] Ex 13:2

34:1 *two stone tablets ... I will write on them.* See note on 31:18. *words.* See note on 20:1.

34:5 *name.* See note on 33:19.

34:6–7 See 33:19 and note. The Lord's proclamation of the meaning and implications of his name in these verses became a classic exposition that was frequently recalled elsewhere in the OT (see Nu 14:17–19 and note; Ne 9:17; Ps 86:15; 103:8; 145:8; Joel 2:13 and note; Jnh 4:2). See also notes on 3:14–15; 6:2–3.

34:7 *thousands.* Or "a thousand generations" (see 20:6). *wickedness, rebellion and sin.* See Isa 59:12 and note.

34:10 *making a covenant.* Renewing the covenant he had earlier made (chs. 19–24). Verses 10–26, many of which are quoted almost verbatim from previous sections of Exodus (compare especially vv. 18–26 with 23:14–19), are sometimes referred to as the Ritual Decalogue since they can be convincingly divided into ten sections (see, e.g., the NIV paragraphing of vv. 15–26). *wonders.* The same word used for the plagues sent on Egypt (3:20). Here it probably refers to the miracles God performed during the desert wanderings and the conquest of Canaan (see Ps 9:1 and note).

34:12 *not to make a treaty with those who live in the land.* Israel is not to make a treaty of peace with any of the people of Canaan to let them live in the land. *treaty.* The Hebrew for this word is the same as that for "covenant" in v. 10 (see also v. 15).

34:13 *Asherah poles.* Asherah was the name of the wife of El, the chief Canaanite god. Wooden poles, perhaps carved in her image, were often set up in her honor and placed near other pagan objects of worship (see, e.g., Jdg 6:25).

34:14 *whose name is Jealous.* See note on 20:5.

34:15 *prostitute themselves.* A metaphor widely used in the OT to refer to Israel's unfaithfulness to her covenant Lord, who, according to a related metaphor, had become Israel's "husband" (with all that that implied in the ancient social world) when he established his special covenant with her (see Isa 54:5–6; Jer 3:14 and note; 31:32; Hos 2:2,7,16 and note on 2:16–17; cf. Jer 2:2; 3:1,20 and note on 3:14; Eze 16:8,32,45 and note on 16:32; 23:4,37). Such unfaithfulness took various forms, but most commonly outright idolatry (worshiping other gods and looking to them for fertility of wombs, fields and flocks, for healing wounds and diseases, for deliverance or security from enemies—thus treating the false gods as their "lovers"). *eat their sacrifices.* Partaking of food sacrificed to a pagan deity symbolized attachment to that deity (for an example see Nu 25:1–3; cf. 1Co 8; 10:18–21).

34:17 *Do not make cast idols.* As Aaron had done when he made the golden calf (see 32:4).

34:18–26 See notes on 23:14–19.

belongs to me, including all the firstborn males of your livestock, whether from herd or flock. 20Redeem the firstborn donkey with a lamb, but if you do not redeem it, break its neck.[g] Redeem all your firstborn sons.[h]

"No one is to appear before me empty-handed.[i]

21"Six days you shall labor, but on the seventh day you shall rest;[j] even during the plowing season and harvest[k] you must rest.

22"Celebrate the Feast of Weeks with the firstfruits[l] of the wheat harvest, and the Feast of Ingathering[m] at the turn of the year.[a] 23Three times[n] a year all your men are to appear before the Sovereign LORD, the God of Israel. 24I will drive out nations[o] before you and enlarge your territory,[p] and no one will covet your land when you go up three times each year to appear before the LORD your God.

25"Do not offer the blood of a sacrifice to me along with anything containing yeast,[q] and do not let any of the sacrifice from the Passover Feast remain until morning.[r]

26"Bring the best of the firstfruits[s] of your soil to the house of the LORD your God.

"Do not cook a young goat in its mother's milk."[t]

27Then the LORD said to Moses, "Write[u] down these words, for in accordance with these words I have made a covenant[v] with you and with Israel." 28Moses was there with the LORD forty days and forty nights[w] without eating bread or drinking water.[x] And he wrote on the tablets[y] the words of the covenant—the Ten Commandments.[z]

The Radiant Face of Moses

29When Moses came down from Mount Sinai[a] with the two tablets of the Testimony in his hands,[b] he was not aware that his face was radiant[c] because he had spoken with the LORD. 30When Aaron and all the Israelites saw Moses, his face was radiant, and they were afraid to come near him. 31But Moses called to them; so Aaron and all the leaders of the community[d] came back to him, and he spoke to them. 32Afterward all the Israelites came near him, and he gave them all the commands[e] the LORD had given him on Mount Sinai.

33When Moses finished speaking to them, he put a veil[f] over his face. 34But whenever he entered the LORD's presence to speak with him, he removed the veil until he came out. And when he came out and told the Israelites what he had been commanded, 35they saw that his face was radiant.[g] Then Moses would put the veil back over his face until he went in to speak with the LORD.

Sabbath Regulations

35 Moses assembled the whole Israelite community and said to them, "These are the things the LORD has commanded[h] you to do: 2For six days, work is to be done, but the seventh day shall be your holy day, a Sabbath[i] of rest to the LORD. Whoever does any work on it must be put to death.[j] 3Do not light a fire in any of your dwellings on the Sabbath day.[k]"

Materials for the Tabernacle

35:4-9pp — Ex 25:1-7
35:10-19pp — Ex 39:32-41

4Moses said to the whole Israelite community, "This is what the LORD has commanded: 5From what you have, take an offering for the LORD. Everyone who is

34:20 [g]S Ex 13:13 [h]S Ex 13:2 [i]S Ex 22:29; Dt 16:16; Eze 46:9 **34:21** [j]Ge 2:2-3 [k]Ne 13:15; Isa 56:2; 58:13 **34:22** [l]ver 26; Ex 23:19; Lev 2:12,14; 7:13; 23:10,17; Nu 28:26 [m]S Ex 23:16 **34:23** [n]S Ex 23:14 **34:24** [o]S Ex 23:28 [p]Dt 12:20; 19:8; Job 12:23 **34:25** [q]S Ex 23:18 [r]S Ex 12:8 **34:26** [s]S Ex 22:29; S Nu 18:12 [t]S Ex 23:19 **34:27** [u]S Ex 17:14 [v]S Ge 6:18; S 15:18 **34:28** [w]S Ge 7:4; Mt 4:2; Lk 4:2 [x]Dt 9:9,18; Ezr 10:6 [y]ver 1; Ex 31:18 [z]Dt 4:13; 10:4 **34:29** [a]S Ex 19:11 [b]S Ex 32:15 [c]ver 35; Ps 34:5; Isa 60:5; Mt 17:2; 2Co 3:7,13 **34:31** [d]Ex 16:22 **34:32** [e]S Ex 21:1; 35:1,4 **34:33** [f]2Co 3:13 **34:35** [g]S ver 29 **35:1** [h]S Ex 34:32 **35:2** [i]S Ge 2:3; Ex 34:21; Dt 5:13-14 [j]S Ex 31:14 **35:3** [k]Ex 16:23

[a] 22 That is, in the fall

34:21 *even during the plowing season and harvest you must rest.* Just as they were also to rest while building the tabernacle (see notes on 31:13,16–17).

34:24 *no one will covet your land.* The Lord promises to protect the Israelite pilgrim's ownership of his land while he is away attending the three annual feasts that required his presence (see Dt 16:16 and note).

34:26 *firstfruits.* See 23:19 and note. *Do not cook a young goat in its mother's milk.* See note on 23:19.

34:27 *Write down these words.* As he had earlier written down similar words (see 24:4).

34:28 *he wrote.* Here the Lord, rather than Moses, is probably the subject (see v. 1). *the words of the covenant—the Ten Commandments.* The two phrases are synonymous (see note on 20:1).

34:29 *Testimony.* See notes on 16:34; 25:16. *was radiant.* He who had asked to see God's glory (see 33:18 and note) now, quite unawares, reflects the divine glory. The Hebrew for "was radiant" is related to the Hebrew noun for "horn." The meaning of the phrase was therefore misunderstood by the Vulgate (the Latin translation), and thus European medieval art often showed horns sprouting from Moses' head.

34:33 *he put a veil over his face.* So that the Israelites would not see the fading away of the radiance but would continue to honor Moses as the one who represented God. For a NT reflection on Moses' action see 2Co 3:7–18 and notes.

35:1–3 Just as the Israelites had been reminded of the importance of Sabbath observance immediately after the instructions for building the tabernacle and making the priestly garments (see note on 31:13), so now—just before the fulfilling of those instructions—the people are given the same reminder.

35:4—39:43 For the most part repeated from chs. 25–28; 30:1–5; 31:1–11 (see notes on those passages), sometimes verbatim, but with the verbs primarily in the past rather than the future tense and with the topics arranged in a different order. Such repetition was a common feature of ancient Near Eastern literature and was intended to fix the details of a narrative in the reader's mind (see note on Ge 24:34–49).

35:5 *Everyone who is willing.* The voluntary motivation behind the offering of materials and services for the tabernacle is stressed (see vv. 21–22,26,29; 36:2–3).

willing is to bring to the LORD an offering of gold, silver and bronze; 6blue, purple and scarlet yarn and fine linen; goat hair; 7ram skins dyed red and hides of sea cows[a]; acacia wood; 8olive oil[l] for the light; spices for the anointing oil and for the fragrant incense; 9and onyx stones and other gems to be mounted on the ephod and breastpiece.

10"All who are skilled among you are to come and make everything the LORD has commanded:[m] 11the tabernacle[n] with its tent and its covering, clasps, frames, crossbars, posts and bases; 12the ark[o] with its poles and the atonement cover and the curtain[p] that shields it; 13the table[q] with its poles and all its articles and the bread of the Presence; 14the lampstand[r] that is for light with its accessories, lamps and oil for the light; 15the altar[s] of incense with its poles, the anointing oil[t] and the fragrant incense;[u] the curtain for the doorway at the entrance to the tabernacle;[v] 16the altar[w] of burnt offering with its bronze grating, its poles and all its utensils; the bronze basin[x] with its stand; 17the curtains of the courtyard with its posts and bases, and the curtain for the entrance to the courtyard;[y] 18the tent pegs[z] for the tabernacle and for the courtyard, and their ropes; 19the woven garments worn for ministering in the sanctuary—both the sacred garments[a] for Aaron the priest and the garments for his sons when they serve as priests."

20Then the whole Israelite community withdrew from Moses' presence, 21and everyone who was willing and whose heart moved him came and brought an offering to the LORD for the work on the Tent of Meeting, for all its service, and for the sacred garments. 22All who were willing, men and women alike, came and brought gold jewelry of all kinds: brooches, earrings, rings and ornaments. They all presented their gold as a wave offering to the LORD. 23Everyone who had blue, purple or scarlet yarn[b] or fine linen, or goat hair, ram skins dyed red or hides of sea cows brought them. 24Those presenting an offering of silver or bronze brought it as an offering to the LORD, and everyone who had acacia wood for any part of the work brought it. 25Every skilled woman[c] spun with her hands and brought what she had spun—blue, purple or scarlet yarn or fine linen. 26And all the women who were willing and had the skill spun the goat hair. 27The leaders[d] brought onyx stones and other gems[e] to be mounted on the ephod and breastpiece. 28They also brought spices and olive oil for the light and for the anointing oil and for the fragrant incense.[f] 29All the Israelite men and women who were willing[g] brought to the LORD freewill offerings[h] for all the work the LORD through Moses had commanded them to do.

Bezalel and Oholiab

35:30-35pp — Ex 31:2-6

30Then Moses said to the Israelites, "See, the LORD has chosen Bezalel son of Uri, the son of Hur, of the tribe of Judah, 31and he has filled him with the Spirit of God, with skill, ability and knowledge in all kinds of crafts[i]— 32to make artistic designs for work in gold, silver and bronze, 33to cut and set stones, to work in wood and to engage in all kinds of artistic craftsmanship. 34And he has given both him and Oholiab[j] son of Ahisamach, of the tribe of Dan, the ability to teach[k] others. 35He has filled them with skill to do all kinds of work[l] as craftsmen, designers, embroiderers in blue, purple and scarlet yarn and fine linen, and weavers—all of them master craftsmen and designers.

36 1So Bezalel, Oholiab and every skilled person[m] to whom the LORD has given skill and ability to know how to carry out all the work of constructing the sanctuary[n] are to do the work just as the LORD has commanded."

2Then Moses summoned Bezalel[o] and Oholiab[p] and every skilled person to whom the LORD had given ability and who was willing[q] to come and do the work. 3They received from Moses all the offerings[r] the Israelites had brought to carry out the work of constructing the sanctuary. And the people continued to bring freewill offerings morning after morning. 4So all the skilled craftsmen who were doing all the work on the sanctuary left their work 5and said to Moses, "The people are bringing more than enough[s] for doing the work the LORD commanded to be done."

6Then Moses gave an order and they sent this word throughout the camp: "No man or woman is to make anything else as an offering for the sanctuary." And so the people were restrained from bringing more, 7because what they already had was more[t] than enough to do all the work.

The Tabernacle

36:8-38pp — Ex 26:1-37

8All the skilled men among the workmen made the tabernacle with ten curtains of finely twisted linen and blue, purple and scarlet yarn, with cherubim worked into them by a skilled craftsman. 9All the curtains were the same size—twenty-eight

35:8 [l]S Ex 25:6 **35:10** [m]Ex 31:6; 39:43 **35:11** [n]Ex 26:1-37; 36:8-38 **35:12** [o]Ex 25:10-22; 37:1-9 [p]S Ex 26:33 **35:13** [q]Ex 25:23-30; 37:10-16 **35:14** [r]S Ex 25:31 **35:15** [s]Ex 30:1-6; 37:25-28 [t]Ex 30:25 [u]Ex 30:34-38 [v]S Ex 26:36 **35:16** [w]Ex 27:1-8; 38:1-7 [x]S Ex 30:18 **35:17** [y]S Ex 27:9; 38:9-20 **35:18** [z]Ex 27:19; 38:20 **35:19** [a]S Ex 28:2 **35:23** [b]Ex 39:1 **35:25** [c]S Ex 28:3 **35:27** [d]S Ex 25:2; 1Ch 29:6 [e]1Ch 29:8

35:28 [f]S Ex 25:6 **35:29** [g]S Ex 25:2 [h]ver 4-9; Ex 25:1-7; 36:3; 2Ki 12:4 **35:31** [i]ver 35; 2Ch 2:7,14 **35:34** [j]S Ex 31:6 [k]2Ch 2:14 **35:35** [l]ver 31 **36:1** [m]S Ex 28:3 [n]Ex 25:8 **36:2** [o]S Ex 31:2 [p]S Ex 31:6 [q]S Ex 25:2 **36:3** [r]S Ex 35:29 **36:5** [s]2Ch 24:14; 31:10; 2Co 8:2-3 **36:7** [t]1Ki 7:47

[a] 7 That is, dugongs; also in verse 23

35:21 *Tent of Meeting.* See note on 27:21.

36:1–38 See note on 35:4—39:43.

cubits long and four cubits wide.[a] 10They joined five of the curtains together and did the same with the other five. 11Then they made loops of blue material along the edge of the end curtain in one set, and the same was done with the end curtain in the other set. 12They also made fifty loops on one curtain and fifty loops on the end curtain of the other set, with the loops opposite each other. 13Then they made fifty gold clasps and used them to fasten the two sets of curtains together so that the tabernacle was a unit.[u]

14They made curtains of goat hair for the tent over the tabernacle—eleven altogether. 15All eleven curtains were the same size—thirty cubits long and four cubits wide.[b] 16They joined five of the curtains into one set and the other six into another set. 17Then they made fifty loops along the edge of the end curtain in one set and also along the edge of the end curtain in the other set. 18They made fifty bronze clasps to fasten the tent together as a unit.[v] 19Then they made for the tent a covering of ram skins dyed red, and over that a covering of hides of sea cows.[c]

20They made upright frames of acacia wood for the tabernacle. 21Each frame was ten cubits long and a cubit and a half wide,[d] 22with two projections set parallel to each other. They made all the frames of the tabernacle in this way. 23They made twenty frames for the south side of the tabernacle 24and made forty silver bases to go under them—two bases for each frame, one under each projection. 25For the other side, the north side of the tabernacle, they made twenty frames 26and forty silver bases—two under each frame. 27They made six frames for the far end, that is, the west end of the tabernacle, 28and two frames were made for the corners of the tabernacle at the far end. 29At these two corners the frames were double from the bottom all the way to the top and fitted into a single ring; both were made alike. 30So there were eight frames and sixteen silver bases—two under each frame.

31They also made crossbars of acacia wood: five for the frames on one side of the tabernacle, 32five for those on the other side, and five for the frames on the west, at the far end of the tabernacle. 33They made the center crossbar so that it extended from end to end at the middle of the frames. 34They overlaid the frames with gold and made gold rings to hold the crossbars. They also overlaid the crossbars with gold.

35They made the curtain[w] of blue, purple and scarlet yarn and finely twisted linen, with cherubim worked into it by a skilled craftsman. 36They made four posts of acacia wood for it and overlaid them with gold. They made gold hooks for them and cast their four silver bases. 37For the entrance to the tent they made a curtain of blue, purple and scarlet yarn and finely twisted linen—the work of an embroiderer;[x] 38and they made five posts with hooks for them. They overlaid the tops of the posts and their bands with gold and made their five bases of bronze.

The Ark

37:1-9pp — Ex 25:10-20

37 Bezalel[y] made the ark[z] of acacia wood—two and a half cubits long, a cubit and a half wide, and a cubit and a half high.[e] 2He overlaid it with pure gold,[a] both inside and out, and made a gold molding around it. 3He cast four gold rings for it and fastened them to its four feet, with two rings on one side and two rings on the other. 4Then he made poles of acacia wood and overlaid them with gold. 5And he inserted the poles into the rings on the sides of the ark to carry it.

6He made the atonement cover[b] of pure gold—two and a half cubits long and a cubit and a half wide.[f] 7Then he made two cherubim[c] out of hammered gold at the ends of the cover. 8He made one cherub on one end and the second cherub on the other; at the two ends he made them of one piece with the cover. 9The cherubim had their wings spread upward, overshadowing[d] the cover with them. The cherubim faced each other, looking toward the cover.[e]

The Table

37:10-16pp — Ex 25:23-29

10They[g] made the table[f] of acacia wood—two cubits long, a cubit wide, and a cubit and a half high.[h] 11Then they overlaid it with pure gold[g] and made a gold molding around it. 12They also made around it a rim a handbreadth[i] wide and

36:13 [u] ver 18
36:18 [v] ver 13
36:35 [w] Ex 39:38; Mt 27:51; Lk 23:45; Heb 9:3
36:37 [x] Ex 27:16
37:1 [y] S Ex 31:2 [z] Ex 30:6; 39:35; Dt 10:3
37:2 [a] ver 11, 26
37:6 [b] S Ex 26:34; S 31:7; Heb 9:5
37:7 [c] Eze 41:18
37:9 [d] Heb 9:5 [e] Dt 10:3
37:10 [f] Heb 9:2
37:11 [g] S ver 2

[a] *9* That is, about 42 feet (about 12.5 meters) long and 6 feet (about 1.8 meters) wide [b] *15* That is, about 45 feet (about 13.5 meters) long and 6 feet (about 1.8 meters) wide [c] *19* That is, dugongs [d] *21* That is, about 15 feet (about 4.5 meters) long and 2 1/4 feet (about 0.7 meter) wide [e] *1* That is, about 3 3/4 feet (about 1.1 meters) long and 2 1/4 feet (about 0.7 meter) wide and high [f] *6* That is, about 3 3/4 feet (about 1.1 meters) long and 2 1/4 feet (about 0.7 meter) wide [g] *10* Or *He*; also in verses 11-29 [h] *10* That is, about 3 feet (about 0.9 meter) long, 1 1/2 feet (about 0.5 meter) wide, and 2 1/4 feet (about 0.7 meter) high [i] *12* That is, about 3 inches (about 8 centimeters)

37:1–29 See note on 35:4—39:43.

37:1 *Bezalel made the ark.* The chief craftsman (see 31:2–3 and notes) was given the honor of making the object that was most sacred (see 25:10 and note) among the furnishings for the tabernacle.

put a gold molding on the rim. [13]They cast four gold rings for the table and fastened them to the four corners, where the four legs were. [14]The rings[h] were put close to the rim to hold the poles used in carrying the table. [15]The poles for carrying the table were made of acacia wood and were overlaid with gold. [16]And they made from pure gold the articles for the table—its plates and dishes and bowls and its pitchers for the pouring out of drink offerings.

The Lampstand

37:17-24pp — Ex 25:31-39

[17]They made the lampstand[i] of pure gold and hammered it out, base and shaft; its flowerlike cups, buds and blossoms were of one piece with it. [18]Six branches extended from the sides of the lampstand—three on one side and three on the other. [19]Three cups shaped like almond flowers with buds and blossoms were on one branch, three on the next branch and the same for all six branches extending from the lampstand. [20]And on the lampstand were four cups shaped like almond flowers with buds and blossoms. [21]One bud was under the first pair of branches extending from the lampstand, a second bud under the second pair, and a third bud under the third pair—six branches in all. [22]The buds and the branches were all of one piece with the lampstand, hammered out of pure gold.[j]

[23]They made its seven lamps,[k] as well as its wick trimmers and trays, of pure gold. [24]They made the lampstand and all its accessories from one talent[a] of pure gold.

The Altar of Incense

37:25-28pp — Ex 30:1-5

[25]They made the altar of incense[l] out of acacia wood. It was square, a cubit long and a cubit wide, and two cubits high[b]—its horns[m] of one piece with it. [26]They overlaid the top and all the sides and the horns with pure gold, and made a gold molding around it. [27]They made two gold rings[n] below the molding—two on opposite sides—to hold the poles used to carry it. [28]They made the poles of acacia wood and overlaid them with gold.[o]

[29]They also made the sacred anointing oil[p] and the pure, fragrant incense[q]—the work of a perfumer.

The Altar of Burnt Offering

38:1-7pp — Ex 27:1-8

38 They[c] built the altar of burnt offering of acacia wood, three cubits[d] high; it was square, five cubits long and five cubits wide.[e] [2]They made a horn at each of the four corners, so that the horns and the altar were of one piece, and they overlaid the altar with bronze.[r] [3]They made all its utensils[s] of bronze—its pots, shovels, sprinkling bowls, meat forks and firepans. [4]They made a grating for the altar, a bronze network, to be under its ledge, halfway up the altar. [5]They cast bronze rings to hold the poles for the four corners of the bronze grating. [6]They made the poles of acacia wood and overlaid them with bronze. [7]They inserted the poles into the rings so they would be on the sides of the altar for carrying it. They made it hollow, out of boards.

Basin for Washing

[8]They made the bronze basin[t] and its bronze stand from the mirrors of the women[u] who served at the entrance to the Tent of Meeting.

The Courtyard

38:9-20pp — Ex 27:9-19

[9]Next they made the courtyard. The south side was a hundred cubits[f] long and had curtains of finely twisted linen, [10]with twenty posts and twenty bronze bases, and with silver hooks and bands on the posts. [11]The north side was also a hundred cubits long and had twenty posts and twenty bronze bases, with silver hooks and bands on the posts.

[12]The west end was fifty cubits[g] wide and had curtains, with ten posts and ten bases, with silver hooks and bands on the posts. [13]The east end, toward the sunrise, was also fifty cubits wide. [14]Curtains fifteen cubits[h] long were on one side of the entrance, with three posts and three bases, [15]and curtains fifteen cubits long were on the other side of the entrance to the courtyard, with three posts and three bases. [16]All the curtains around the courtyard were of finely twisted linen. [17]The bases for the posts were bronze. The hooks and bands on the posts were silver, and their tops were overlaid with silver; so all the posts of the courtyard had silver bands.

[18]The curtain for the entrance to the courtyard was of blue, purple and scarlet

37:14 [h]ver 27
37:17 [i]Heb 9:2; Rev 1:12
37:22 [j]ver 17; Nu 8:4
37:23 [k]Ex 40:4,25
37:25 [l]Ex 30:34-36; Lk 1:11; Heb 9:4; Rev 8:3 [m]S Ex 27:2; Rev 9:13
37:27 [n]ver 14
37:28 [o]S Ex 25:13
37:29 [p]S Ex 31:11 [q]Ex 30:1,25; 39:38
38:2 [r]2Ch 1:5
38:3 [s]S Ex 31:9
38:8 [t]S Ex 30:18; S 40:7 [u]Dt 23:17; 1Sa 2:22; 1Ki 14:24

[a] *24* That is, about 75 pounds (about 34 kilograms)
[b] *25* That is, about 1 1/2 feet (about 0.5 meter) long and wide, and about 3 feet (about 0.9 meter) high
[c] *1* Or *He*; also in verses 2-9
[d] *1* That is, about 4 1/2 feet (about 1.3 meters)
[e] *1* That is, about 7 1/2 feet (about 2.3 meters) long and wide
[f] *9* That is, about 150 feet (about 46 meters)
[g] *12* That is, about 75 feet (about 23 meters)
[h] *14* That is, about 22 1/2 feet (about 6.9 meters)

38:1-31 See note on 35:4—39:43.
38:8 *bronze ... mirrors.* See note on 30:18. Mirrored glass was unknown in ancient times, but highly polished bronze gave adequate reflection (cf. 1Co 13:12 and note). *Tent of Meeting.* See note on 27:21.

yarn and finely twisted linen—the work
of an embroiderer. It was twenty cubits[a]
long and, like the curtains of the courtyard, five cubits[b] high, 19with four posts
and four bronze bases. Their hooks and
bands were silver, and their tops were
overlaid with silver. 20All the tent pegs[v]
of the tabernacle and of the surrounding
courtyard were bronze.

The Materials Used

21These are the amounts of the materials used for the tabernacle, the tabernacle
of the Testimony,[w] which were recorded
at Moses' command by the Levites under
the direction of Ithamar[x] son of Aaron,
the priest. 22(Bezalel[y] son of Uri, the son
of Hur, of the tribe of Judah, made everything the LORD commanded Moses; 23with
him was Oholiab[z] son of Ahisamach, of
the tribe of Dan—a craftsman and designer, and an embroiderer in blue, purple and
scarlet yarn and fine linen.) 24The total
amount of the gold from the wave offering
used for all the work on the sanctuary[a]
was 29 talents and 730 shekels,[c] according
to the sanctuary shekel.[b]

25The silver obtained from those of the
community who were counted in the census[c] was 100 talents and 1,775 shekels,[d]
according to the sanctuary shekel— 26one
beka per person,[d] that is, half a shekel,[e]
according to the sanctuary shekel,[e] from
everyone who had crossed over to those
counted, twenty years old or more,[f] a total
of 603,550 men.[g] 27The 100 talents[f] of silver
were used to cast the bases[h] for the sanctuary and for the curtain—100 bases from
the 100 talents, one talent for each base.
28They used the 1,775 shekels[g] to make the
hooks for the posts, to overlay the tops of
the posts, and to make their bands.

29The bronze from the wave offering
was 70 talents and 2,400 shekels.[h] 30They
used it to make the bases for the entrance
to the Tent of Meeting, the bronze altar
with its bronze grating and all its utensils,
31the bases for the surrounding courtyard
and those for its entrance and all the tent
pegs for the tabernacle and those for the
surrounding courtyard.

The Priestly Garments

39 From the blue, purple and scarlet
yarn[i] they made woven garments for
ministering in the sanctuary.[j] They also
made sacred garments[k] for Aaron, as the
LORD commanded Moses.

The Ephod

39:2-7pp — Ex 28:6-14

2They[i] made the ephod of gold, and
of blue, purple and scarlet yarn, and of
finely twisted linen. 3They hammered
out thin sheets of gold and cut strands
to be worked into the blue, purple and
scarlet yarn and fine linen—the work of
a skilled craftsman. 4They made shoulder pieces for the ephod, which were attached to two of its corners, so it could be
fastened. 5Its skillfully woven waistband
was like it—of one piece with the ephod
and made with gold, and with blue, purple and scarlet yarn, and with finely
twisted linen, as the LORD commanded
Moses.

6They mounted the onyx stones in gold
filigree settings and engraved them like a
seal with the names of the sons of Israel.
7Then they fastened them on the shoulder
pieces of the ephod as memorial[l] stones
for the sons of Israel, as the LORD commanded Moses.

The Breastpiece

39:8-21pp — Ex 28:15-28

8They fashioned the breastpiece[m]—the
work of a skilled craftsman. They made it
like the ephod: of gold, and of blue, purple and scarlet yarn, and of finely twisted
linen. 9It was square—a span[j] long and
a span wide—and folded double. 10Then
they mounted four rows of precious stones
on it. In the first row there was a ruby,
a topaz and a beryl; 11in the second row
a turquoise, a sapphire[k] and an emerald;
12in the third row a jacinth, an agate and
an amethyst; 13in the fourth row a chrysolite, an onyx and a jasper.[l] They were
mounted in gold filigree settings. 14There
were twelve stones, one for each of the
names of the sons of Israel, each engraved
like a seal with the name of one of the
twelve tribes.[n]

15For the breastpiece they made braided

38:20 [v]S Ex 35:18 **38:21** [w]Nu 1:50,53; 8:24; 9:15; 10:11; 17:7; 1Ch 23:32; 2Ch 24:6; Ac 7:44; Rev 15:5 [x]Nu 4:28,33 **38:22** [y]S Ex 31:2 **38:23** [z]S Ex 31:6 **38:24** [a]S Ex 30:16 [b]S Ex 30:13 **38:25** [c]S Ex 30:12 **38:26** [d]S Ex 30:12 [e]S Ex 30:13 [f]S Ex 30:14 [g]S Ex 12:37 **38:27** [h]S Ex 26:19 **39:1** [i]Ex 35:23 [j]Ex 35:19 [k]ver 41; Ex 28:2

39:7 [l]Lev 24:7; Jos 4:7 **39:8** [m]Lev 8:8 **39:14** [n]Rev 21:12

[a] *18* That is, about 30 feet (about 9 meters)
[b] *18* That is, about 7 1/2 feet (about 2.3 meters)
[c] *24* The weight of the gold was a little over one ton (about 1 metric ton).
[d] *25* The weight of the silver was a little over 3 3/4 tons (about 3.4 metric tons).
[e] *26* That is, about 1/5 ounce (about 5.5 grams)
[f] *27* That is, about 3 3/4 tons (about 3.4 metric tons)
[g] *28* That is, about 45 pounds (about 20 kilograms)
[h] *29* The weight of the bronze was about 2 1/2 tons (about 2.4 metric tons).
[i] *2* Or *He;* also in verses 7, 8 and 22
[j] *9* That is, about 9 inches (about 22 centimeters)
[k] *11* Or *lapis lazuli*
[l] *13* The precise identification of some of these precious stones is uncertain.

38:25 *100 talents and 1,775 shekels.* Since there are 3,000 shekels in a talent, 100 talents equals 300,000 shekels, which, when added to the 1,775 shekels, gives a grand total of 301,775—half a shekel for each of the 603,550 men of military age (v. 26).

38:26 *603,550 men.* See Introduction to Numbers: Special Problem; see also Nu 1:46 and note.

38:27 *one talent for each base.* See note on 26:19.

39:1-43 See note on 35:4—39:43.

chains of pure gold, like a rope. 16They made two gold filigree settings and two gold rings, and fastened the rings to two of the corners of the breastpiece. 17They fastened the two gold chains to the rings at the corners of the breastpiece, 18and the other ends of the chains to the two settings, attaching them to the shoulder pieces of the ephod at the front. 19They made two gold rings and attached them to the other two corners of the breastpiece on the inside edge next to the ephod. 20Then they made two more gold rings and attached them to the bottom of the shoulder pieces on the front of the ephod, close to the seam just above the waistband of the ephod. 21They tied the rings of the breastpiece to the rings of the ephod with blue cord, connecting it to the waistband so that the breastpiece would not swing out from the ephod — as the LORD commanded Moses.

Other Priestly Garments

39:22-31pp — Ex 28:31-43

22They made the robe of the ephod entirely of blue cloth — the work of a weaver — 23with an opening in the center of the robe like the opening of a collar,[a] and a band around this opening, so that it would not tear. 24They made pomegranates of blue, purple and scarlet yarn and finely twisted linen around the hem of the robe. 25And they made bells of pure gold and attached them around the hem between the pomegranates. 26The bells and pomegranates alternated around the hem of the robe to be worn for ministering, as the LORD commanded Moses.

27For Aaron and his sons, they made tunics of fine linen[o] — the work of a weaver — 28and the turban[p] of fine linen, the linen headbands and the undergarments of finely twisted linen. 29The sash was of finely twisted linen and blue, purple and scarlet yarn — the work of an embroiderer — as the LORD commanded Moses.

30They made the plate, the sacred diadem, out of pure gold and engraved on it, like an inscription on a seal: HOLY TO THE LORD.[q] 31Then they fastened a blue cord to it to attach it to the turban,[r] as the LORD commanded Moses.

Moses Inspects the Tabernacle

39:32-41pp — Ex 35:10-19

32So all the work on the tabernacle, the Tent of Meeting, was completed. The Israelites did everything just as the LORD commanded Moses.[s] 33Then they brought the tabernacle[t] to Moses: the tent and all its furnishings, its clasps, frames, crossbars, posts and bases; 34the covering of ram skins dyed red, the covering of hides of sea cows[b] and the shielding curtain; 35the ark of the Testimony[u] with its poles and the atonement cover; 36the table[v] with all its articles and the bread of the Presence;[w] 37the pure gold lampstand[x] with its row of lamps and all its accessories,[y] and the oil[z] for the light; 38the gold altar,[a] the anointing oil,[b] the fragrant incense,[c] and the curtain[d] for the entrance to the tent; 39the bronze altar[e] with its bronze grating, its poles and all its utensils; the basin[f] with its stand; 40the curtains of the courtyard with its posts and bases, and the curtain for the entrance to the courtyard;[g] the ropes and tent pegs for the courtyard; all the furnishings for the tabernacle, the Tent of Meeting; 41and the woven garments[h] worn for ministering in the sanctuary, both the sacred garments for Aaron the priest and the garments for his sons when serving as priests.

42The Israelites had done all the work just as the LORD had commanded Moses.[i] 43Moses inspected the work and saw that they had done it just as the LORD had commanded.[j] So Moses blessed[k] them.

Setting Up the Tabernacle

40 Then the LORD said to Moses: 2"Set up[l] the tabernacle, the Tent of Meeting,[m] on the first day of the first month.[n] 3Place the ark[o] of the Testimony in it and shield the ark with the curtain. 4Bring in the table[p] and set out what belongs on it.[q] Then bring in the lampstand[r] and set up its lamps. 5Place the gold altar[s] of incense in front of the ark of the Testimony and put the curtain at the entrance to the tabernacle.

6"Place the altar[t] of burnt offering in

39:27 [o] Lev 6:10; 8:2 **39:28** [p] ver 31; S Ex 28:4; Lev 8:9; Isa 61:10 **39:30** [q] Isa 23:18; Zec 14:20 **39:31** [r] S ver 28 **39:32** [s] S Ex 25:9 **39:33** [t] Ex 25:8-40; 36:8-38 **39:35** [u] S Ex 37:1 **39:36** [v] Ex 25:23-30; 37:10-16 [w] S Ex 25:30 **39:37** [x] S Ex 25:31 [y] Ex 25:31-39 [z] S Ex 25:6 **39:38** [a] Ex 30:1-10 [b] Ex 30:22-32; 37:29 [c] Ex 30:34-38; S 37:29 [d] S Ex 36:35 **39:39** [e] Ex 27:1-8; 38:1-7 [f] S Ex 30:18 **39:40** [g] Ex 27:9-19; 38:9-20 **39:41** [h] S ver 1 **39:42** [i] S Ex 25:9 **39:43** [j] S Ex 25:9; S 35:10 [k] Ge 31:55; Lev 9:22,23; Nu 6:23-27; Dt 21:5; 26:15; 2Sa 6:18; 1Ki 8:14,55; 1Ch 16:2; 2Ch 30:27 **40:2** [l] S Ex 26:30 [m] ver 34,35; Lev 1:1; 3:2; 6:26; 9:23; 16:16; Nu 1:1; 7:89; 11:16; 17:4; 20:6; Jos 18:1; 19:51; Jer 7:12 [n] ver 17; S Ex 12:2; Nu 9:1 **40:3** [o] S Ex 26:33 **40:4** [p] S Ex 25:23 [q] S Ex 25:30 [r] S Ex 25:31 **40:5** [s] S Ex 30:1 **40:6** [t] S Ex 27:1; 2Ki 16:14; 2Ch 4:1

[a] *23* The meaning of the Hebrew for this word is uncertain. [b] *34* That is, dugongs

39:30 *sacred diadem.* An official designation (not found in 28:36–37) for the plate of the turban. *HOLY TO THE LORD.* See 28:36 and note.

39:32 *all the work on the tabernacle ... was completed.* Reminiscent of the concluding words of the creation narrative (see Ge 2:1–3). Thus the end of Exodus links with the beginning (see 1:7 and note), marking the complex of events narrated in the book as the beginning of the restoration of the creation order and of the realization of God's redemptive purposes in history (see also note on 26:1).

39:34 *shielding curtain.* See note on 26:31.

39:43 *Moses blessed them.* For the faithfulness with which the Israelites had donated their gifts, time and talents in building the tabernacle and all its furnishings — faithfulness in service brings divine benediction.

40:2 *first day of the first month.* The tabernacle was set up almost a year after the institution of the Passover (see v. 17; 12:2,6 and note on 12:2).

front of the entrance to the tabernacle, the
Tent of Meeting; 7place the basin[u] between
the Tent of Meeting and the altar and put
water in it. 8Set up the courtyard[v] around
it and put the curtain at the entrance to
the courtyard.
9"Take the anointing oil and anoint[w] the
tabernacle and everything in it; consecrate
it and all its furnishings,[x] and it will be
holy. 10Then anoint the altar of burnt offering and all its utensils; consecrate[y] the
altar, and it will be most holy. 11Anoint the
basin and its stand and consecrate them.
12"Bring Aaron and his sons to the entrance to the Tent of Meeting[z] and wash
them with water.[a] 13Then dress Aaron in
the sacred garments,[b] anoint him and consecrate[c] him so he may serve me as priest.
14Bring his sons and dress them in tunics.[d]
15Anoint them just as you anointed their
father, so they may serve me as priests.
Their anointing will be to a priesthood
that will continue for all generations to
come.[e]" 16Moses did everything just as the
LORD commanded[f] him.
17So the tabernacle[g] was set up on the
first day of the first month[h] in the second
year. 18When Moses[i] set up the tabernacle, he put the bases in place, erected the
frames,[j] inserted the crossbars and set up
the posts. 19Then he spread the tent over
the tabernacle and put the covering[k] over
the tent, as the LORD commanded[l] him.
20He took the Testimony[m] and placed
it in the ark,[n] attached the poles to the
ark and put the atonement cover[o] over it.
21Then he brought the ark into the tabernacle and hung the shielding curtain[p] and
shielded the ark of the Testimony, as the
LORD commanded[q] him.
22Moses placed the table[r] in the Tent of
Meeting on the north side of the tabernacle outside the curtain 23and set out the
bread[s] on it before the LORD, as the LORD
commanded[t] him.
24He placed the lampstand[u] in the Tent
of Meeting opposite the table on the south
side of the tabernacle 25and set up the
lamps[v] before the LORD, as the LORD commanded[w] him.
26Moses placed the gold altar[x] in the
Tent of Meeting in front of the curtain
27and burned fragrant incense on it, as the
LORD commanded[y] him. 28Then he put up
the curtain[z] at the entrance to the tabernacle.
29He set the altar[a] of burnt offering near
the entrance to the tabernacle, the Tent of
Meeting, and offered on it burnt offerings
and grain offerings,[b] as the LORD commanded[c] him.
30He placed the basin[d] between the Tent
of Meeting and the altar and put water in
it for washing, 31and Moses and Aaron and
his sons used it to wash[e] their hands and
feet. 32They washed whenever they entered the Tent of Meeting or approached
the altar,[f] as the LORD commanded[g] Moses.
33Then Moses set up the courtyard[h]
around the tabernacle and altar and put
up the curtain[i] at the entrance to the courtyard. And so Moses finished the work.

The Glory of the LORD

34Then the cloud[j] covered the Tent of
Meeting, and the glory[k] of the LORD filled
the tabernacle. 35Moses could not enter
the Tent of Meeting because the cloud had
settled upon it, and the glory[l] of the LORD
filled the tabernacle.[m]
36In all the travels of the Israelites,
whenever the cloud lifted from above
the tabernacle, they would set out;[n] 37but
if the cloud did not lift, they did not set
out — until the day it lifted. 38So the cloud[o]
of the LORD was over the tabernacle by
day, and fire was in the cloud by night, in
the sight of all the house of Israel during
all their travels.

40:7 [u]Ex 30:18
40:8 [v]S Ex 27:9
40:9 [w]S Ex 30:26 [x]Nu 7:1
40:10 [y]S Ex 29:36
40:12 [z]Nu 8:9 [a]S Ex 29:4; S 30:19
40:13 [b]S Ex 28:41 [c]Lev 8:12
40:14 [d]S Ex 28:40; Lev 10:5
40:15 [e]S Ex 29:9
40:16 [f]S Ge 6:22
40:17 [g]Nu 7:1 [h]S ver 2
40:18 [i]2Ch 1:3 [j]Ex 36:20-34
40:19 [k]Ex 36:19 [l]S Ge 6:22
40:20 [m]S Ex 16:34; Heb 9:4 [n]S Ex 25:21 [o]Ex 25:17-22; S 26:34; S 31:7
40:21 [p]S Ex 26:33 [q]S Ge 6:22
40:22 [r]S Ex 25:23
40:23 [s]S Ex 25:30; Lev 24:5-8 [t]S Ge 6:22
40:24 [u]S Ex 25:31
40:25 [v]S Ex 37:23 [w]S Ge 6:22
40:26 [x]S Ex 30:1
40:27 [y]S Ge 6:22
40:28 [z]S Ex 26:36
40:29 [a]S Ex 20:24 [b]Ex 29:38-42 [c]S Ge 6:22
40:30 [d]S ver 7; S Ex 30:18
40:31 [e]Ex 30:19-21
40:32 [f]Ex 30:20 [g]S Ge 6:22
40:33 [h]S Ex 27:9; 38:9-20 [i]Ex 27:16
40:34 [j]Ex 19:16; Lev 16:2; Nu 9:15-23; 1Ki 8:12; 2Ch 5:13; Isa 6:4; Eze 10:4 [k]S Ex 16:7; Jn 1:14; 12:41; Rev 15:8
40:35 [l]S Ex 16:10 [m]1Ki 8:11; 2Ch 5:13-14; 7:2
40:36 [n]Nu 9:17-23; 10:13
40:38 [o]S Ex 13:21; 1Co 10:1

40:9 – 10 *holy ... most holy.* See 3:5; 29:37 and notes.

40:16 *Moses did ... just as the LORD commanded.* Moses' obedience to God's command is a key theme of the final chapter of Exodus (see vv. 19,21,23,25,27,29,32). The people provided all the resources and made all the components, but only the Lord's servant Moses was authorized to erect the tabernacle and prepare it for the Lord's entry.

40:33 *Moses finished the work.* See note on 39:32.

40:34 With the glory of the Lord entering the tabernacle (cf. 1Ki 8:10 – 11 and note on 8:10), the great series of events that began with the birth of Moses and his rescue from the Nile, foreshadowing the deliverance of Israel from Egypt, comes to a grand climax. From now on, the Israelites march through the desert, and through history, with the Lord tenting among them and leading them to the land of fulfilled promises.

40:38 See note on 13:21.

Leviticus

I N T R O D U C T I O N

Author and Date

See note on 1:1; see also Introduction to Genesis: Author and Date of Writing.

Title

Leviticus receives its name from the Septuagint (the pre-Christian Greek translation of the OT) and means "relating to the Levites." Its Hebrew title, *wayyiqra',* is the first word in the Hebrew text of the book and means "And he [i.e., the LORD] called." Although Leviticus does not deal only with the special duties of the Levites, it is so named because it concerns mainly the service of worship at the tabernacle, which was conducted by the priests who were the sons of Aaron, assisted by many from the rest of the tribe of Levi. Exodus gave the directions for building the tabernacle, and now Leviticus gives the laws and regulations for worship there, including instructions on ceremonial cleanness, moral laws, holy days, the sabbath year and the Year of Jubilee. These laws were given, at least for the most part, during the year that Israel camped at Mount Sinai, when God directed Moses in organizing Israel's worship, government and military forces. The book of Numbers continues the history with preparations for moving on from Sinai to Canaan.

Theological Themes

Leviticus is a manual of regulations enabling the holy King to set up his earthly throne among the people of his kingdom. It explains how they are to be his holy people and to worship him in a holy manner. Holiness in this sense means to be separated from sin and set apart exclusively to the Lord for his purpose, in his service and for his glory. So the key thought of the book is holiness (see notes on 11:44; Ex 3:5) — the holiness of God and his people (they must revere him in "holiness"). In Leviticus spiritual holiness is symbolized by physical perfection. Therefore the book demands perfect animals for its many sacrifices (chs. 1 – 7) and requires priests without deformity (chs. 8 – 10). A woman's hemorrhaging after giving birth (ch. 12); sores, burns or baldness (chs. 13 – 14); a man's bodily discharge (15:1 – 18); specific activities during a woman's monthly period (15:19 – 33) — all may be signs of blemish (a lack of perfection) and may symbolize human spiritual defects, which break spiritual wholeness. The person with visible skin disease must be banished from the camp,

Leviticus explains how the Israelites are to be the Lord's holy people and are to worship him in a holy manner.

the place of God's special presence, just as Adam and Eve were banished from the Garden of Eden. Such people can return to the camp (and therefore to God's presence) when they are pronounced whole again by the examining priests. Before they can reenter the camp, however, they must offer the prescribed, perfect sacrifices (symbolizing the perfect, whole sacrifice of Christ).

After the establishment of the covenant at Sinai, Israel represented God's kingdom on earth (the theocracy), and, as its King, the Lord imposed his administration over all of Israel's life. He so regulated Israel's religious, communal and personal life as to establish them as his holy people and to instruct them in holiness. In Leviticus, special attention is given to Israel's religious ceremonies and rituals. Their sacrifices were to be offered only at the appointed sanctuary, which symbolized both God's holiness and his compassion. Only the appointed priests were to officiate at Israel's sacrifices, and it was the duty of the priests also to instruct the people concerning the proper form and meaning of each sacrifice. For more information on the meaning of sacrifice in general, see the solemn ritual of the Day of Atonement (ch. 16; see note on 16:1 – 34). For the meaning of the blood of the offering, see 17:11; Ge 9:4 and notes. For the emphasis on substitution, see 1:5; 4:4; 16:20 – 22 and notes.

Some suppose that the OT sacrifices were carryovers and adaptations of an older sacrificial system developed by agricultural peoples who thought that humans needed to please the gods by feeding them from their crops, flocks and herds. But the OT sacrifices Israel was to bring were specifically prescribed by God and received their meaning from the Lord's covenant relationship with Israel — whatever their superficial resemblances to pagan sacrifices may have been. They did indeed include the idea of gift, but this is accompanied by such other values as dedication, communion, propitiation (appeasing God's judicial wrath against sin) and restitution. The various offerings have differing functions, the primary ones being atonement (see note on Ex 25:17) and worship (see chart, p. 153).

A Quick Look

Author:
Moses

Audience:
God's chosen people, the Israelites

Date:
Between 1446 and 1406 B.C.

Theme:
The Israelites receive instructions from God at the base of Mount Sinai concerning how to live as God's holy people.

Outline

The subjects treated in Leviticus, as in any book of laws and regulations, cover several categories:

- I. The Five Main Offerings (chs. 1 – 7)
  - A. The Burnt Offering (ch. 1)
  - B. The Grain Offering (ch. 2)
  - C. The Fellowship Offering (ch. 3)
  - D. The Sin Offering (4:1 — 5:13)
  - E. The Guilt Offering (5:14 — 6:7)
  - F. Additional Regulations for the Offerings (6:8 — 7:38)
- II. The Installation and Ministry of Aaron and His Sons (chs. 8 – 10)
  - A. The Ordination of Aaron and His Sons (ch. 8)
  - B. The Ministry of the Priests (ch. 9)
  - C. The Death of Nadab and Abihu and Attendant Regulations (ch. 10)
- III. The Distinction Between Clean and Unclean (chs. 11 – 15)
  - A. Clean and Unclean Food (ch. 11)
  - B. Purification After Childbirth (ch. 12)
  - C. Regulations for Skin Diseases (13:1 – 46)
  - D. Regulations for Mildew (13:47 – 59)
  - E. Cleansing from Skin Diseases (14:1 – 32)

- F. Cleansing from Mildew (14:33 – 57)
- G. Discharges That Cause Uncleanness (ch. 15)

IV. The Annual Day of Atonement (ch. 16)

V. Holy Living (chs. 17 – 26)

- A. Eating Blood Prohibited (ch. 17)
- B. Unlawful Sexual Relations (ch. 18)
- C. Various Laws for Holy Living (ch. 19)
- D. Punishments for Sin (ch. 20)
- E. Regulations for Priests (21:1 — 22:16)
- F. Acceptable and Unacceptable Sacrifices (22:17 – 33)
- G. The Annual Feasts (ch. 23)
- H. Rules for Oil and Bread in the Tabernacle (24:1 – 9)
- I. Punishment for Blasphemy (24:10 – 23)
- J. The Sabbath and Jubilee Years (ch. 25)
- K. Covenant Blessings and Curses (ch. 26)

VI. Regulations for Offerings Vowed to the Lord (ch. 27)

The Burnt Offering

1 The LORD called to Moses[a] and spoke to him from the Tent of Meeting.[b] He said, 2"Speak to the Israelites and say to them: 'When any of you brings an offering to the LORD,[c] bring as your offering an animal from either the herd or the flock.[d]

3" 'If the offering is a burnt offering[e] from the herd,[f] he is to offer a male without defect.[g] He must present it at the entrance to the Tent[h] of Meeting so that it[a] will be acceptable[i] to the LORD. 4He is to lay his hand on the head[j] of the burnt offering,[k] and it will be accepted[l] on his behalf to make atonement[m] for him. 5He is to slaughter[n] the young bull[o] before the LORD, and then Aaron's sons[p] the priests shall bring the blood and sprinkle it against the altar on all sides[q] at the entrance to the Tent of Meeting. 6He is to skin[r] the burnt offering and cut it into pieces.[s] 7The sons of Aaron the priest are to put fire on the altar and arrange wood[t] on the fire. 8Then Aaron's sons the priests shall arrange the pieces, including the head and the fat,[u] on the burning wood[v] that is on the altar. 9He is to wash the inner parts and the legs with water,[w] and the priest is to burn all of it[x] on the altar.[y] It is a burnt offering,[z] an offering made by fire,[a] an aroma pleasing to the LORD.[b]

10" 'If the offering is a burnt offering from the flock, from either the sheep[c] or the goats,[d] he is to offer a male without defect. 11He is to slaughter it at the north side of the altar[e] before the LORD, and Aaron's sons the priests shall sprinkle its blood against the altar on all sides.[f] 12He is to cut it into pieces, and the priest shall arrange them, including the head and the fat,[g] on the burning wood that is on the altar. 13He is to wash the inner parts and the legs with water,[h] and the priest is to bring all of it and burn it[i] on the altar.[j] It is a burnt offering,[k] an offering made by fire, an aroma pleasing to the LORD.

14" 'If the offering to the LORD is a burnt offering of birds, he is to offer a dove or a young pigeon.[l] 15The priest shall bring it to the altar, wring off the head[m] and burn it on the altar; its blood shall be drained out

[a] 3 Or *he*

1:1 [a]S Ex 3:4; S 25:22 [b]S Ex 27:21; S 40:2 **1:2** [c]Lev 7:16, 38; 22:21; 23:38; 27:9 [d]Lev 22:18-19; Nu 15:3 **1:3** [e]S Ge 8:20 [f]ver 10; Lev 22:27; Ezr 8:35; Mal 1:8 [g]S ver 5; S Ex 12:5; S Lev 22:19, 20; Heb 9:14; 1Pe 1:19 [h]Lev 6:25; 17:9; Nu 6:16; Dt 12:5-6, 11 [i]Isa 58:5 **1:4** [j]S Ex 29:10, 15 [k]ver 3; Lev 4:29; 6:25; Eze 45:15 [l]S Ge 32:20 [m]S Ex 29:36; S 32:30 **1:5** [n]Ex 29:11; Lev 3:2, 8 [o]S ver 3; Ex 29:1; Nu 15:8; Dt 18:3; Ps 50:9; 69:31 [p]Lev 8:2; 10:6; 21:1 [q]S Ex 29:20; Heb 12:24; 1Pe 1:2 **1:6** [r]Lev 7:8 [s]Ex 29:17 **1:7** [t]ver 17; S Ge 22:9; Lev 3:5; 6:12 **1:8** [u]ver 12; S Ex 29:13; Lev 8:20 [v]Lev 9:13 **1:9** [w]S Ex 29:17 [x]Lev 6:22 [y]ver 13; Ex 29:18; Lev 9:14 [z]ver 3 [a]Lev 23:8, 25, 36; Nu 28:6, 19 [b]ver 13; Ge 8:21; Lev 2:2; 3:5, 16; 17:6; Nu 18:17; 28:11-13; Eph 5:2 **1:10** [c]S Ge 22:7 [d]S ver 3; Ex 12:5; Lev 3:12; 4:23, 28; 5:6; Nu 15:11 **1:11** [e]S Ex 29:11 [f]S Ex 29:20 **1:12** [g]S ver 8 **1:13** [h]S Ex 29:17 [i]Lev 6:22 [j]S ver 9 [k]Dt 12:27 **1:14** [l]S Ge 15:9; Lk 2:24 **1:15** [m]Lev 5:8

1:1—7:38 Regulations for the five main offerings: burnt, grain, fellowship, sin and guilt offerings.

1:1 Emphasizes that the contents of Leviticus were given to Moses by God at Mount Sinai. Cf. also the concluding verse (27:34). In more than 50 places it is said that the Lord spoke to Moses. Modern criticism has attributed practically the whole book to priestly legislation written during or after the exile. But this is without objective evidence, is against the repeated claim of the book to be Mosaic, is against the traditional Jewish view, and runs counter to other OT and NT witness (Ro 10:5). Many items in Leviticus are now seen to be best explained in terms of a second-millennium B.C. date, which is also the most likely time for Moses to have written the Pentateuch (see Introduction to Genesis: Author and Date of Writing). There is no convincing reason not to take at face value the many references to Moses and his work. *Tent of Meeting.* The tabernacle, where God met with Israel (see note on Ex 27:21).

1:2 *brings an offering.* The Hebrew word for "offering" used here (*qorban*) comes from the verb translated "brings." An "offering" is something that someone "brings" to God as a gift (most offerings were voluntary, such as the burnt offering). This word for "offering" is also used in Mk 7:11 (Corban), where Mark explains its meaning as "gift devoted to God" (see note there).

1:3 *burnt offering.* See further priestly regulations in 6:8–13 (see also chart, p. 153). A burnt offering was offered every morning and evening for all Israel (Ex 29:39–42). Double burnt offerings were brought on the Sabbath (Nu 28:9–10) and extra ones on feast days (Nu 28–29). In addition, anyone could offer special burnt offerings to express devotion to the Lord. *male.* The burnt offering had to be a male animal because of its greater value, and also perhaps because it was thought to better represent vigor and fertility. It was usually a young sheep or goat (for the average individual), but bulls (for the wealthy) and doves or pigeons (for the poor) were also specified. *without defect.* The animal had to be unblemished (cf. Mal 1:8; 1Pe 1:19 and note). As in all offerings, the offerers were to lay their hands on the head of the animal to express identification between themselves and the animal (see 16:20–22 and note), whose death would then be accepted in "atonement" (v. 4). The blood was sprinkled on the sides of the great altar (located outside the tabernacle—later the temple—in the eastern half of the courtyard), where the fire of sacrifice was never to go out (see 6:13 and note). The whole sacrifice was to be burned up (v. 9), including the head, legs, fat and internal organs. It is therefore sometimes called a holocaust offering (*holo* means "whole," and *caust* means "burnt"). When a bull was offered, however, the officiating priest could keep its hide (7:8). The burnt offering may have been the usual sacrifice offered by the patriarchs. It was the most comprehensive in its meaning. Its Hebrew name means "going up," perhaps symbolizing worship and prayer as its aroma ascended to the Lord (v. 17). The completeness of its burning also speaks of total dedication on the part of the worshiper. *entrance to the Tent of Meeting.* Where the altar of burnt offering was (see Ex 40:29). *acceptable to the LORD.* See Ro 12:1; Php 4:18 and note.

1:4 *lay his hand on.* See notes on v. 3; Ex 29:10. *atonement.* See notes on 16:20–22; 17:11; Ex 25:17.

1:5 Only after the offerer killed the animal (symbolizing substitution of a perfect animal sacrifice for a sinful human life) did the priestly work begin. *blood.* See notes on 17:11; Heb 9:18. *sprinkle it against the altar.* See Ex 24:6; Heb 9:19–22.

1:6 *skin.* The whole animal was burned except the hide, which was given to the priest (7:8).

1:9,13,17 *aroma pleasing to the LORD.* The OT sacrifices foreshadowed Christ, who was a "fragrant offering" (Eph 5:2 [see note there]; cf. Php 4:18 and note).

1:11 *north side.* See diagram, p. 126.

1:14 *birds.* Three categories of sacrifices are mentioned: (1) from the herd (vv. 3–9), (2) from the flock (vv. 10–13) and (3) from birds (vv. 14–17). Sacrifices of birds were allowed for the poor (see 4:23; 12:8 and notes; Lk 2:24 and note on 2:22).

on the side of the altar.[n] 16He is to remove
the crop with its contents[a] and throw it to
the east side of the altar, where the ashes[o]
are. 17He shall tear it open by the wings,
not severing it completely,[p] and then the
priest shall burn it on the wood[q] that is on
the fire on the altar. It is a burnt offering,
an offering made by fire, an aroma pleasing to the LORD.

The Grain Offering

2 " 'When someone brings a grain offering[r] to the LORD, his offering is to be
of fine flour.[s] He is to pour oil[t] on it,[u] put
incense on it[v] 2and take it to Aaron's sons
the priests. The priest shall take a handful
of the fine flour[w] and oil, together with all
the incense,[x] and burn this as a memorial portion[y] on the altar, an offering made
by fire,[z] an aroma pleasing to the LORD.[a]
3The rest of the grain offering belongs to
Aaron and his sons;[b] it is a most holy[c]
part of the offerings made to the LORD by
fire.

4" 'If you bring a grain offering baked
in an oven,[d] it is to consist of fine flour:
cakes made without yeast and mixed with
oil, or[b] wafers[e] made without yeast and
spread with oil.[f] 5If your grain offering is
prepared on a griddle,[g] it is to be made
of fine flour mixed with oil, and without
yeast. 6Crumble it and pour oil on it; it
is a grain offering. 7If your grain offering
is cooked in a pan,[h] it is to be made of
fine flour and oil. 8Bring the grain offering
made of these things to the LORD; present it
to the priest, who shall take it to the altar.
9He shall take out the memorial portion[i]
from the grain offering and burn it on the
altar as an offering made by fire, an aroma pleasing to the LORD.[j] 10The rest of the
grain offering belongs to Aaron and his
sons;[k] it is a most holy part of the offerings made to the LORD by fire.[l]

11" 'Every grain offering you bring to the
LORD must be made without yeast,[m] for
you are not to burn any yeast or honey in
an offering made to the LORD by fire. 12You
may bring them to the LORD as an offering
of the firstfruits,[n] but they are not to be
offered on the altar as a pleasing aroma.
13Season all your grain offerings with salt.[o]
Do not leave the salt of the covenant[p] of
your God out of your grain offerings; add
salt to all your offerings.

14" 'If you bring a grain offering of firstfruits[q] to the LORD, offer crushed heads of
new grain roasted in the fire. 15Put oil and
incense[r] on it; it is a grain offering. 16The
priest shall burn the memorial portion[s]
of the crushed grain and the oil, together
with all the incense,[t] as an offering made
to the LORD by fire.[u]

The Fellowship Offering

3 " 'If someone's offering is a fellowship
offering,[c][v] and he offers an animal from
the herd, whether male or female, he is to
present before the LORD an animal with-

[a] *16* Or *crop and the feathers*; the meaning of the Hebrew for this word is uncertain. [b] *4* Or *and* [c] *1* Traditionally *peace offering*; also in verses 3, 6 and 9

1:15 [n]Lev 5:9 **1:16** [o]Lev 4:12; 6:10; Nu 4:13 **1:17** [p]S Ge 15:10 [q]S ver 7 **2:1** [r]S Ex 29:41; Lev 6:14-18 [s]Ex 29:2, 40; Lev 5:11 [t]Nu 15:4; 28:5 [u]S Ex 29:2; Lev 7:12 [v]ver 2, 15, 16; Lev 24:7; Ne 13:9; Isa 43:23 **2:2** [w]Lev 5:11 [x]Lev 6:15; Isa 1:13; 65:3; 66:3 [y]ver 9, 16; Lev 5:12; 6:15; 24:7; Nu 5:26; 18:8; Ps 16:5; 73:26; Isa 53:12 [z]ver 16 [a]S Lev 1:9 **2:3** [b]ver 10; Lev 6:16; 10:12, 13 [c]S Ex 30:36 **2:4** [d]Lev 7:9; 26:26 [e]Lev 7:12; 8:26 [f]S Ex 29:2 **2:5** [g]Lev 6:21; 7:9; Eze 4:3 **2:7** [h]Lev 7:9 **2:9** [i]S ver 2 [j]S Ge 8:21 **2:10** [k]ver 3 [l]Ezr 2:63 **2:11** [m]S Ex 23:18; Lev 6:16 **2:12** [n]S Ex 34:22 **2:13** [o]Mk 9:49 [p]Nu 18:19; 2Ch 13:5; Eze 43:24 **2:14** [q]S Ex 34:22; Nu 15:20; Dt 16:13; 26:2; Ru 3:2 **2:15** [r]S ver 1 **2:16** [s]S ver 2 [t]S ver 1 [u]Nu 4:16; Jer 14:12 **3:1** [v]S ver 6; S Ex 32:6; Lev 7:11-34; S 17:5

1:17 *not severing it completely.* See note on Ge 15:10.

2:1 *grain offering.* See further priestly regulations in 6:14–23; 7:9–10. It was made of grain or finely-milled flour. If baked or cooked, it consisted of cakes or wafers made in a pan or oven or on a griddle. It was the only bloodless offering, but it was to accompany the burnt offering (see Nu 28:3–6), sin offering (see Nu 6:14–15) and fellowship offering (see 9:4; Nu 6:17). The amounts of grain offering ingredients specified to accompany a bull, ram or lamb sacrificed as a burnt offering are given in Nu 28:12–13. A representative handful of flour was to be burned on the altar with the accompanying offerings, and the balance was to be baked without yeast and eaten by the priests in their holy meals (6:14–17). The flour that was burned on the altar was mixed with olive oil for shortening, salted for taste and accompanied by incense, but it was to have no yeast or honey—neither of which was allowed on the altar (vv. 11–13). The cooked product was similar to pie crust. The worshiper was not to eat any of the grain offering, and the priests were not to eat any of their own grain offerings, which were to be totally burned (6:22–23). The Hebrew word for grain offering can mean "present" or "gift" and is often used in that way (see Ge 43:11). The sacred gifts expressed devotion to God (see v. 2). *fine flour.* Grain that was milled and sifted. *oil.* Olive oil is often mentioned in connection with grain and new wine as fresh products of the harvest (see Dt 7:13 and note). Used extensively in cooking, it was a suitable part of the worshiper's gift. *incense.* Frankincense was the chief ingredient (see Ex 30:34–35 and note on 30:34).

2:2,9,16 *memorial portion.* Either (1) to remind the worshiper that all good things come from the Lord (cf. Jas 1:17), or (2) to cause the Lord to remember and bless the offerer in covenant faithfulness (cf. Ge 9:13–16 and note on 9:13). It may have been a combination of both. See also 5:12; 6:15; 24:7.

2:3 *most holy part.* For this reason, the priests were to eat it in the sanctuary area proper and not feed their families with it (6:16–18). See also v. 10. *holy.* See Ex 29:37 and note.

2:4 *without yeast.* See notes on Ex 12:8,15.

2:5 *griddle.* A clay pan that rested on a stone heated by a fire. Later, iron pans were sometimes used.

2:11 *honey.* It was forbidden on the altar perhaps because of its use in brewing beer (as an aid to fermentation), though some suggest that it was because of its use in Canaanite cultic practice.

2:12 *firstfruits.* See 23:10–11; Ex 23:16,19 and note on 23:19; Nu 15:18–20 and note on 15:20; Dt 18:4–5; 26:1–11.

2:13 *salt of the covenant.* See note on Nu 18:19.

3:1 *fellowship offering.* See further priestly regulations in 7:11–21,28–34. Two basic ideas are included in this offering: peace and fellowship. The traditional translation is "peace offering," a name that comes from the Hebrew word for the offering, which in turn is related to the Hebrew word *shalom,* meaning "peace" or "wholeness." Thus the offering perhaps symbolized peace between God and his people as well as the inward peace that resulted. The fellowship offering was the only sacrifice of which the offerer might eat

out defect.[w] 2He is to lay his hand on the
head[x] of his offering and slaughter it[y] at
the entrance to the Tent of Meeting.[z] Then
Aaron's sons the priests shall sprinkle[a]
the blood against the altar[b] on all sides.[c]
3From the fellowship offering he is to bring
a sacrifice made to the LORD by fire: all the
fat[d] that covers the inner parts[e] or is connected to them, 4both kidneys[f] with the fat
on them near the loins, and the covering
of the liver, which he will remove with the
kidneys. 5Then Aaron's sons[g] are to burn
it on the altar[h] on top of the burnt offering[i] that is on the burning wood,[j] as an
offering made by fire, an aroma pleasing
to the LORD.[k]
6" 'If he offers an animal from the flock as
a fellowship offering[l] to the LORD, he is to
offer a male or female without defect. 7If he
offers a lamb,[m] he is to present it before the
LORD.[n] 8He is to lay his hand on the head of
his offering and slaughter it[o] in front of the
Tent of Meeting. Then Aaron's sons shall
sprinkle its blood against the altar on all
sides. 9From the fellowship offering he is
to bring a sacrifice[p] made to the LORD by
fire: its fat, the entire fat tail cut off close
to the backbone, all the fat that covers the
inner parts or is connected to them, 10both
kidneys with the fat on them near the loins,
and the covering of the liver, which he will
remove with the kidneys. 11The priest shall
burn them on the altar[q] as food,[r] an offering made to the LORD by fire.[s]
12" 'If his offering is a goat,[t] he is to present it before the LORD. 13He is to lay his
hand on its head and slaughter it in front
of the Tent of Meeting. Then Aaron's sons
shall sprinkle[u] its blood against the altar
on all sides.[v] 14From what he offers he is
to make this offering to the LORD by fire:
all the fat that covers the inner parts or
is connected to them, 15both kidneys with
the fat on them near the loins, and the
covering of the liver, which he will remove
with the kidneys.[w] 16The priest shall burn
them on the altar[x] as food,[y] an offering
made by fire, a pleasing aroma.[z] All the
fat[a] is the LORD's.[b]
17" 'This is a lasting ordinance[c] for the
generations to come,[d] wherever you live:[e]
You must not eat any fat or any blood.[f] ' "

The Sin Offering

4 The LORD said to Moses, 2"Say to the
Israelites: 'When anyone sins unintentionally[g] and does what is forbidden in
any of the LORD's commands[h]—
3" 'If the anointed priest[i] sins,[j] bringing guilt on the people, he must bring to
the LORD a young bull[k] without defect[l] as a
sin offering[m] for the sin he has committed.[n]
4He is to present the bull at the entrance to
the Tent of Meeting before the LORD.[o] He
is to lay his hand on its head and slaughter it before the LORD. 5Then the anointed
priest shall take some of the bull's blood[p]
and carry it into the Tent of Meeting.

3:1 [w]S Ex 12:5 **3:2** [x]S Ex 29:15; Nu 8:10 [y]S Lev 1:5 [z]S Ex 40:2 [a]S Ex 24:6 [b]Lev 17:6; Nu 18:17 [c]S Ex 29:20 **3:3** [d]S Ex 29:13 [e]S Ex 12:9 **3:4** [f]ver 10; Ex 29:13; Lev 4:9 **3:5** [g]Lev 7:29-34 [h]ver 11,16 [i]Ex 29:13,38-42; Nu 28:3-10 [j]S Lev 1:7 [k]S Lev 1:9 **3:6** [l]S ver 1; Lev 22:21; Nu 15:3,8 **3:7** [m]Lev 17:3; Nu 15:5; 28:5,7,8 [n]Lev 17:8-9; 1Ki 8:62 **3:8** [o]S Lev 1:5 **3:9** [p]Isa 34:6; Jer 46:10; Eze 39:19; Zep 1:7 **3:11** [q]S ver 5 [r]ver 16; Lev 21:6,17; Nu 28:2 [s]Lev 9:18 **3:12** [t]S Lev 1:10; S 4:3 **3:13** [u]S Ex 24:6 [v]Lev 1:5 **3:15** [w]Lev 7:4 **3:16** [x]S ver 5; Lev 7:31 [y]S ver 11 [z]S Lev 1:9 [a]S Ge 4:4 [b]1Sa 2:16 **3:17** [c]S Ex 12:14; S 27:21 [d]S Ge 9:12 [e]S Ex 12:20 [f]Ge 9:4; Lev 7:25-26; 17:10-16; Dt 12:16; Ac 15:20 **4:2** [g]ver 13,27; Lev 5:15-18; 22:14; Nu 15:24-29; 35:11-15; Jos 20:3,9; Heb 9:7 [h]ver 22; Nu 15:22 **4:3** [i]S Ex 28:41 [j]S Ge 18:23 [k]ver 14; Lev 3:12; 8:14; 10:16; 16:3,5; Nu 15:27; Ps 66:15; Eze 43:19,23 [l]S Ex 12:5 [m]S ver 24; S Ex 30:10; Lev 5:6-13; 9:2-22; Heb 9:13-14 [n]ver 32 **4:4** [o]ver 15,24; Lev 1:3; Nu 8:12 **4:5** [p]ver 16; Lev 16:14

a part. Fellowship was involved because the offerer, on the basis of the sacrifice, had fellowship with God and with the priest, who also ate part of the offering (7:14–15,31–34). This sacrifice—along with others—was offered by the thousands during the three annual festivals in Israel (see Ex 23:14–17; Nu 29:39) because multitudes of people came to the temple to worship and share in a communal meal. During the monarchy, the animals offered by the people were usually supplemented by large numbers given by the king. At the dedication of the temple, Solomon offered 20,000 cattle and 120,000 sheep and goats as fellowship offerings over a period of 14 days (1Ki 8:63–65; see 1Sa 11:15 and note).

3:2 *lay his hand on.* See notes on 1:3; Ex 29:10.

3:5 *on top of the burnt offering.* The burnt offerings for the nation as a whole were offered every morning and evening, and the fellowship offerings were offered on top of them.

3:9 *fat tail.* A breed of sheep still much used in the Middle East has a tail heavy with fat.

3:11,16 *on the altar as food.* Israelite sacrifices were not "food for the gods" (as in other ancient cultures; see Eze 16:20; Ps 50:8–13 and note) but were sometimes called "food" metaphorically (21:6,8,17,21; 22:25) in the sense that they were gifts to God, which he received with delight.

3:16 *All the fat is the LORD's.* Because it signified the best (see 7:23; Ge 4:3–4; Ex 29:13 and notes).

3:17 *not eat any fat or any blood.* See note on 17:11.

4:2 *unintentionally.* See 5:15; contrast Nu 15:30–31 and see note on 15:30. Four classes of people involved in committing unintentional sins are listed: (1) "the anointed priest" (vv. 3–12), (2) the "whole Israelite community" (vv. 13–21), (3) a "leader" (vv. 22–26) and (4) a "member of the community" (vv. 27–35). Heb 9:7 speaks of sins "committed in ignorance" in referring to the Day of Atonement (see note on Heb 5:2).

4:3 *anointed priest.* The high priest (see 6:20,22). *sins.* All high priests sinned except the high priest Jesus Christ (see Heb 5:1–3; 7:26–28 and note on 7:27). *on the people.* The relationship of the priests to the people was so intimate in Israel (as a nation consecrated to God) that the people became guilty when the priest sinned. *must.* Although the burnt, grain and fellowship offerings (chs. 1–3) were voluntary, the sin offering was compulsory (see vv. 14,23,28). *without defect.* A defective sacrifice could not be a substitute for a defective people. The final perfect sacrifice for the sins of God's people was the crucified Christ, who was without any moral defect (Heb 9:13–14; 1Pe 1:19). See Introduction: Theological Themes. *sin offering.* See further priestly regulations in 6:24–30; Nu 15:22–29. As soon as an "anointed priest" (or a person from one of the other classes of people) became aware of unintentional sin, he was to bring his sin offering to the Lord. On the other hand, if the priest or others remained unaware of unintentional sin, this lack was atoned for on the Day of Atonement.

4:4 Three principles of atonement are found in this verse: (1) substitution ("present the bull"), (2) identification ("lay his hand on its head") and (3) the death of the substitute ("slaughter it").

4:5 *blood.* See note on 17:11. There were two types of sin offerings. The first (vv. 3–21) and more important

6He is to dip his finger into the blood and
sprinkle[q] some of it seven times before the
LORD,[r] in front of the curtain of the sanctuary.[s] 7The priest shall then put some of the
blood on the horns[t] of the altar of fragrant
incense that is before the LORD in the Tent
of Meeting. The rest of the bull's blood he
shall pour out at the base of the altar[u] of
burnt offering[v] at the entrance to the Tent
of Meeting. 8He shall remove all the fat[w]
from the bull of the sin offering—the fat
that covers the inner parts or is connected to them, 9both kidneys with the fat on
them near the loins, and the covering of
the liver, which he will remove with the
kidneys[x]— 10just as the fat is removed
from the ox[a][y] sacrificed as a fellowship offering.[b][z] Then the priest shall burn them
on the altar of burnt offering.[a] 11But the
hide of the bull and all its flesh, as well as
the head and legs, the inner parts and offal[b]— 12that is, all the rest of the bull—he
must take outside the camp[c] to a place
ceremonially clean,[d] where the ashes[e] are
thrown, and burn it[f] in a wood fire on the
ash heap.[g]

13" 'If the whole Israelite community
sins unintentionally[h] and does what is
forbidden in any of the LORD's commands,
even though the community is unaware of
the matter, they are guilty. 14When they
become aware of the sin they committed,
the assembly must bring a young bull[i] as a
sin offering[j] and present it before the Tent
of Meeting. 15The elders[k] of the commu-

4:6 [q]Ex 24:8 [r]ver 17; Lev 16:14,19 [s]S Ex 25:8 **4:7** [t]S Ex 27:2 [u]ver 34; S Ex 29:12; Lev 8:15 [v]ver 18,30; Lev 5:9; 9:9; 16:18 **4:8** [w]ver 19 **4:9** [x]S Lev 3:4 **4:10** [y]Lev 9:4 [z]S Ex 32:6 [a]S Ex 29:13 **4:11** [b]Ex 29:14; Lev 8:17; 9:11; Nu 19:5 **4:12** [c]S Ex 29:14; Lev 8:17; 9:11; Heb 13:11 [d]Lev 6:11; 10:14; Nu 19:9 [e]S Lev 1:16 [f]Lev 6:30 [g]Lev 16:3 **4:13** [h]S ver 2 **4:14** [i]S ver 3 [j]Nu 15:24 **4:15** [k]S Ex 3:16; S 19:7 [l]2Ch 29:23 [m]S Ex 29:10; Lev 8:14,22; Nu 8:10 [n]S ver 4 **4:16** [o]S ver 5 **4:17** [p]Nu 19:4,18 [q]S ver 6 **4:18** [r]Lev 8:15; 17:6; 2Ch 29:22 [s]ver 7; Lev 6:30; 10:18 [t]Lev 5:9 **4:19** [u]ver 8 [v]ver 26 **4:20** [w]S Ex 29:36; S 32:30;

nity are to lay their hands[l] on the bull's
head[m] before the LORD, and the bull shall
be slaughtered before the LORD.[n] 16Then
the anointed priest is to take some of the
bull's blood[o] into the Tent of Meeting.
17He shall dip his finger into the blood and
sprinkle[p] it before the LORD[q] seven times
in front of the curtain. 18He is to put some
of the blood[r] on the horns of the altar that
is before the LORD[s] in the Tent of Meeting. The rest of the blood he shall pour
out at the base of the altar[t] of burnt offering at the entrance to the Tent of Meeting.
19He shall remove all the fat[u] from it and
burn it on the altar,[v] 20and do with this
bull just as he did with the bull for the sin
offering. In this way the priest will make
atonement[w] for them, and they will be forgiven.[x] 21Then he shall take the bull outside the camp[y] and burn it as he burned
the first bull. This is the sin offering for
the community.[z]

22" 'When a leader[a] sins unintentionally[b] and does what is forbidden in any
of the commands of the LORD his God, he
is guilty. 23When he is made aware of the
sin he committed, he must bring as his
offering a male goat[c] without defect. 24He
is to lay his hand on the goat's head and

[a] *10* The Hebrew word can include both male and female. [b] *10* Traditionally *peace offering*; also in verses 26, 31 and 35

S Ro 3:25; Heb 10:10-12 [x]ver 26,31,35; Nu 15:25 **4:21** [y]S ver 12 [z]Lev 16:5,15; 2Ch 29:21 **4:22** [a]Nu 31:13 [b]ver 2 **4:23** [c]S ver 3; S Lev 1:10

involved sprinkling the blood in the tabernacle in front of the inner curtain or, in the case of the solemn Day of Atonement (ch. 16), on and in front of the atonement cover (traditionally "mercy seat") itself. This type of sin offering was not eaten. The fat, kidneys and covering of the liver were burned on the great altar, but all the rest was burned outside the camp (v. 12). Heb 13:11–13 clearly draws the parallel to our sin offering, Jesus, who suffered outside the city gate (see note on Heb 13:12). This type of sin offering was offered by and for a priest or by the elders for the whole community. In general, the animal to be sacrificed was a young bull, but on the Day of Atonement the sin offering was to be a goat (16:9).

The second type of sin offering (4:22—5:13) was for a leader of the nation or a private individual. Some of the blood was applied to the horns of the great altar; the rest was poured out at its base. The fat, etc., was burned on the altar, but the rest of the offering was given to the priest and his male relatives as food to be eaten in a holy place (6:29–30; see 10:16–20). The sin offering brought by a private person was to be a female goat or lamb. If such persons were poor, they could bring a dove or young pigeon (5:7–8; 12:6,8; cf. Lk 2:24 and note on 2:22), or even about two quarts of flour (5:11). The offering included confession (see 5:5 and note) and the symbolic transfer of guilt by laying hands on the sacrifice (v. 29; see 16:20–22 and note). Then the priest who offered the sacrifice made atonement for the sin, and the Lord promised forgiveness (5:13). By bringing such a sin offering, a faithful Israelite under conviction of sin sought restoration of fellowship with God.

4:6 *finger.* The right forefinger (see 14:16). *seven.* The number was symbolic of perfection and completeness (see note on Ge 5:5). *curtain.* The great curtain that separated the Holy Place from the Most Holy Place (Ex 26:33).

4:7,30 *horns.* The four horns of the altar (see Ex 30:1–3) were symbols of the atoning power of the sin offering (Ex 30:10).

4:8–10 See 3:3–5.

4:12 *outside the camp.* See note on 13:45–46. So also Jesus was crucified outside Jerusalem (see Heb 13:11–13 and note on 13:12; cf. Lev 9:11; 16:26–28; Nu 19:3; Eze 43:21). *ceremonially clean.* The distinction between clean and unclean was a matter of ritual or religious purity, not a concern for physical cleanliness (see chs. 11–15 for examples; see also Mk 7:1–4). *burn.* Since the sins of the offerer were symbolically transferred to the sacrificial bull, the bull had to be entirely destroyed and not thrown on the ash pile of 1:16.

4:15 *elders.* See note on Ex 3:16.

4:18 *altar.* Of incense (see v. 7).

4:20 *sin offering.* The offering of the priest who had sinned (see v. 3 and note). *will be forgiven.* In 4:20—6:7 this is a key phrase, occurring nine times and referring to forgiveness by God.

4:23 *male goat.* Less valuable animals were sacrificed for those with lesser standing in the community or of lesser economic means. Thus a bull was required for the high priest (v. 3) and the whole community (vv. 13–14), but a male goat for a civic leader (here) and a female goat (v. 28) or lamb (v. 32) for an ordinary Israelite. If an offerer was too poor, then doves and pigeons were sufficient (5:7) or even a handful of fine flour (see 5:11–12 and note on 5:11).

Old Testament Sacrifices

SACRIFICE	OT REFERENCES	ELEMENTS	PURPOSE
Burnt Offering	Lev 1; 6:8-13; 8:18-21; 16:24	Bull, ram or male bird (dove or young pigeon for the poor); wholly consumed; no defect	Voluntary act of worship; atonement for unintentional sin in general; expression of devotion, commitment and complete surrender to God
Grain Offering	Lev 2; 6:14-23	Grain, fine flour, olive oil, incense, baked bread (cakes or wafers), salt; no yeast or honey; accompanied burnt offering and fellowship offering (along with drink offering)	Voluntary act of worship; recognition of God's goodness and provisions; devotion to God
Fellowship Offering	Lev 3; 7:11-34	Any animal without defect from herd or flock; variety of breads	Voluntary act of worship; thanksgiving and fellowship (it included a communal meal)
Sin Offering	Lev 4:1–5:13; 6:24-30; 8:14-17; 16:3-22	1. Young bull: for high priest and congregation 2. Male goat: for leader 3. Female goat or lamb: for common person 4. Dove or pigeon: for the poor 5. Tenth of an ephah of fine flour: for the very poor	Mandatory atonement for specific unintentional sin; confession of sin; forgiveness of sin; cleansing from defilement
Guilt Offering	Lev 5:14–6:7; 7:1-6	Ram	Mandatory atonement for unintentional sin requiring restitution; cleansing from defilement; make restitution; pay 20% fine

When more than one kind of offering was presented (as in Nu 7:13-17), the procedure was usually as follows: (1) sin offering or guilt offering, (2) burnt offering, (3) fellowship offering and grain offering (along with a drink offering). This sequence furnishes part of the spiritual significance of the sacrificial system. First, sin had to be dealt with (sin offering or guilt offering). Second, the worshipers committed themselves completely to God (burnt offering and grain offering). Third, fellowship or communion between the Lord, the priest and the worshiper (fellowship offering) was established. To state it another way, there were sacrifices of expiation (sin offerings and guilt offerings), consecration (burnt offerings and grain offerings) and communion (fellowship offerings—these included vow offerings, thank offerings and freewill offerings).

slaughter it at the place where the burnt
offering is slaughtered before the LORD.[d] It
is a sin offering.[e] 25 Then the priest shall
take some of the blood of the sin offering
with his finger and put it on the horns of
the altar[f] of burnt offering and pour out
the rest of the blood at the base of the
altar.[g] 26 He shall burn all the fat on the
altar as he burned the fat of the fellowship
offering. In this way the priest will make
atonement[h] for the man's sin, and he will
be forgiven.[i]

27 "'If a member of the community sins
unintentionally[j] and does what is forbidden in any of the LORD's commands, he
is guilty. 28 When he is made aware of the
sin he committed, he must bring as his offering[k] for the sin he committed a female
goat[l] without defect. 29 He is to lay his
hand on the head[m] of the sin offering[n] and
slaughter it at the place of the burnt offering.[o] 30 Then the priest is to take some of
the blood with his finger and put it on the
horns of the altar of burnt offering[p] and
pour out the rest of the blood at the base of
the altar. 31 He shall remove all the fat, just
as the fat is removed from the fellowship
offering, and the priest shall burn it on the
altar[q] as an aroma pleasing to the LORD.[r] In
this way the priest will make atonement[s]
for him, and he will be forgiven.[t]

32 "'If he brings a lamb[u] as his sin offering, he is to bring a female without defect.[v] 33 He is to lay his hand on its head
and slaughter it[w] for a sin offering[x] at the
place where the burnt offering is slaughtered.[y] 34 Then the priest shall take some
of the blood of the sin offering with his
finger and put it on the horns of the altar
of burnt offering and pour out the rest of
the blood at the base of the altar.[z] 35 He
shall remove all the fat, just as the fat is
removed from the lamb of the fellowship
offering, and the priest shall burn it on the
altar[a] on top of the offerings made to the
LORD by fire. In this way the priest will
make atonement for him for the sin he has
committed, and he will be forgiven.

5 "'If a person sins because he does
not speak up when he hears a public
charge to testify[b] regarding something he
has seen or learned about, he will be held
responsible.[c]

2 "'Or if a person touches anything ceremonially unclean—whether the carcasses
of unclean wild animals or of unclean livestock or of unclean creatures that move
along the ground[d]—even though he is unaware of it, he has become unclean[e] and
is guilty.

3 "'Or if he touches human uncleanness[f]—anything that would make him
unclean[g]—even though he is unaware of
it, when he learns of it he will be guilty.

4 "'Or if a person thoughtlessly takes
an oath[h] to do anything, whether good or
evil[i]—in any matter one might carelessly
swear about—even though he is unaware
of it, in any case when he learns of it he
will be guilty.

5 "'When anyone is guilty in any of
these ways, he must confess[j] in what way
he has sinned 6 and, as a penalty for the
sin he has committed, he must bring to
the LORD a female lamb or goat[k] from the
flock as a sin offering;[l] and the priest shall
make atonement[m] for him for his sin.

7 "'If he cannot afford[n] a lamb,[o] he is to
bring two doves or two young pigeons[p] to
the LORD as a penalty for his sin—one for
a sin offering and the other for a burnt offering. 8 He is to bring them to the priest,
who shall first offer the one for the sin
offering. He is to wring its head from its
neck,[q] not severing it completely,[r] 9 and is
to sprinkle[s] some of the blood of the sin
offering against the side of the altar;[t] the
rest of the blood must be drained out at
the base of the altar.[u] It is a sin offering.
10 The priest shall then offer the other as a
burnt offering in the prescribed way[v] and
make atonement[w] for him for the sin he
has committed, and he will be forgiven.[x]

11 "'If, however, he cannot afford[y] two
doves or two young pigeons,[z] he is to
bring as an offering for his sin a tenth of
an ephah[a][a] of fine flour[b] for a sin offering.
He must not put oil or incense on it, because it is a sin offering. 12 He is to bring
it to the priest, who shall take a handful
of it as a memorial portion[c] and burn it on
the altar[d] on top of the offerings made
to the LORD by fire. It is a sin offering. 13 In
this way the priest will make atonement[e]

[a] *11* That is, probably about 2 quarts (about 2 liters)

4:24 [d] S ver 4 [e] S ver 3; Lev 6:25 **4:25** [f] Lev 16:18; Eze 43:20,22 [g] Lev 9:9 **4:26** [h] S Ex 32:30 [i] Lev 5:10; 12:8 **4:27** [j] S ver 2 **4:28** [k] Lev 5:6; Eze 40:39; 44:27 [l] S ver 3; S Lev 1:10 **4:29** [m] ver 4,24 [n] S Lev 1:4 [o] S Ge 8:20 **4:30** [p] S ver 7 **4:31** [q] ver 35 [r] S Ge 8:21 [s] Lev 1:4 [t] S ver 20 **4:32** [u] Ex 29:38; Lev 9:3; 14:10 [v] Lev 1:3 **4:33** [w] Lev 1:5 [x] Lev 1:4 [y] ver 29 **4:34** [z] S ver 7 **4:35** [a] ver 31 **5:1** [b] Pr 29:24; Mt 26:63 [c] ver 17; S Ex 28:38; Lev 7:18; 17:16; 19:8; 20:17; 24:15; Nu 5:31; 9:13; 15:31; 19:20; 30:15 **5:2** [d] Lev 11:11, 24-40; Dt 14:8; Isa 52:11 [e] ver 3; Lev 7:21; 11:8,24; 13:45; Nu 19:22; Job 15:16; Ps 51:5; Isa 6:5; 64:6; Eze 36:17; Hag 2:13 **5:3** [f] Nu 19:11-16 [g] Lev 7:20; 11:25; 14:19; 21:1; Nu 5:2; 9:6; 19:7; Eze 44:25 **5:4** [h] Nu 30:6,8 [i] Isa 41:23 **5:5** [j] Lev 16:21; 26:40; Nu 5:7; Jos 7:19; 1Ki 8:47; Pr 28:13 **5:6** [k] S Lev 1:10; S 4:3 [l] S Lev 4:28 [m] S Ex 32:30 **5:7** [n] ver 11; Lev 12:8; 14:21; 27:8 [o] Lev 12:8; 14:22,30 [p] S Ge 15:9; Nu 6:10 **5:8** [q] Lev 1:15 [r] Lev 1:17 **5:9** [s] S Ex 24:6 [t] Lev 1:15 [u] S Lev 4:7 **5:10** [v] Lev 1:14-17; 1Ch 15:13 [w] S Ex 32:30 [x] S Lev 4:26 **5:11** [y] S ver 7 [z] S Ge 15:9 [a] S Ex 16:36 [b] S Lev 2:1 **5:12** [c] S Lev 2:2 [d] Lev 2:9 **5:13** [e] S Ex 32:30

4:25 *priest.* The priest who officiated for the civil authority or the layperson (see vv. 30,34).
4:28 *female goat.* See note on v. 23.
4:29 *lay his hand on.* See notes on 1:3; Ex 29:10.
4:32 *lamb ... female.* See note on v. 23.
4:35 *fat ... of the fellowship offering.* See 3:3–5.
5:1–4 Four examples of the unintentional sins (see 4:2–3,13,22,27) the sin offering covers.
5:2 *ceremonially unclean.* See note on 4:12.
5:3 *human uncleanness.* See chs. 11–15.
5:5 *confess.* The offerers had to acknowledge their sin to God in order to receive forgiveness (cf. Pr 28:13 and note).
5:7 *two doves ... pigeons.* See 4:23; 12:8 and notes.
5:11 *fine flour.* See note on 4:23. Although no blood was used with a flour offering, it was offered "on top of the offerings made to the LORD by fire" (v. 12). Heb 9:22 may refer to such a situation.
5:12 *memorial portion.* See note on 2:2,9,16.

for him for any of these sins he has committed, and he will be forgiven. The rest of the offering will belong to the priest,[f] as in the case of the grain offering.[g]' "

The Guilt Offering

14 The LORD said to Moses: 15 "When a person commits a violation and sins unintentionally[h] in regard to any of the LORD's holy things, he is to bring to the LORD as a penalty[i] a ram[j] from the flock, one without defect and of the proper value in silver, according to the sanctuary shekel.[a][k] It is a guilt offering.[l] 16 He must make restitution[m] for what he has failed to do in regard to the holy things, add a fifth of the value[n] to that and give it all to the priest, who will make atonement for him with the ram as a guilt offering, and he will be forgiven.

17 "If a person sins and does what is forbidden in any of the LORD's commands, even though he does not know it,[o] he is guilty and will be held responsible.[p] 18 He is to bring to the priest as a guilt offering[q] a ram from the flock, one without defect and of the proper value. In this way the priest will make atonement for him for the wrong he has committed unintentionally, and he will be forgiven.[r] 19 It is a guilt offering; he has been guilty of[b] wrongdoing against the LORD."[s]

6 The LORD said to Moses: 2 "If anyone sins and is unfaithful to the LORD[t] by deceiving his neighbor[u] about something entrusted to him or left in his care[v] or stolen, or if he cheats[w] him, 3 or if he finds lost property and lies about it,[x] or if he swears falsely,[y] or if he commits any such sin that people may do— 4 when he thus sins and becomes guilty, he must return[z] what he has stolen or taken by extortion, or what was entrusted to him, or the lost property he found, 5 or whatever it was he swore falsely about. He must make restitution[a] in full, add a fifth of the value to it and give it all to the owner on the day he presents his guilt offering.[b] 6 And as a penalty he must bring to the priest, that is, to the LORD, his guilt offering,[c] a ram from the flock, one without defect and of the proper value.[d] 7 In this way the priest will make atonement[e] for him before the LORD, and he will be forgiven for any of these things he did that made him guilty."

The Burnt Offering

8 The LORD said to Moses: 9 "Give Aaron and his sons this command: 'These are the regulations for the burnt offering[f]: The burnt offering is to remain on the altar hearth throughout the night, till morning, and the fire must be kept burning on the altar.[g] 10 The priest shall then put on his linen clothes,[h] with linen undergarments next to his body,[i] and shall remove the ashes[j] of the burnt offering that the fire has consumed on the altar and place them beside the altar. 11 Then he is to take off these clothes and put on others, and carry the ashes outside the camp to a place that is ceremonially clean.[k] 12 The fire on the altar must be kept burning; it must not go out. Every morning the priest is to add firewood[l] and arrange the burnt offering on the fire and burn the fat[m] of the fellowship offerings[c][n] on it. 13 The fire must be kept burning on the altar continuously; it must not go out.

The Grain Offering

14 " 'These are the regulations for the grain offering:[o] Aaron's sons are to bring it before the LORD, in front of the altar. 15 The priest is to take a handful of fine flour and oil, together with all the incense[p] on the grain offering,[q] and burn the memorial portion[r] on the altar as an aroma pleasing to the LORD. 16 Aaron and his sons[s] shall eat the rest[t] of it, but it is to be eaten without yeast[u] in a holy place;[v] they are to eat it in the courtyard[w] of the Tent of Meeting.[x] 17 It must not be baked with yeast; I have given it as their share[y] of the offerings made to me by fire.[z] Like the sin offering and

[a] 15 That is, about 2/5 ounce (about 11.5 grams)
[b] 19 Or *has made full expiation for his*
[c] 12 Traditionally *peace offerings*

5:13 [f]Lev 2:3 [g]S Ex 29:41 **5:15** [h]S Lev 4:2 [i]Lev 22:14 [j]S Ex 29:3; Lev 6:6; Nu 5:8; 6:14; 15:6; 28:11 [k]S Ex 30:13 [l]ver 16, 18; Lev 6:5, 6; 7:1, 7; 14:12-17; 19:21, 22; Nu 6:12; 18:9; 1Sa 6:3; Ezr 10:19; Isa 53:10 **5:16** [m]Lev 6:4 [n]ver 15; Lev 27:13; Nu 5:7 **5:17** [o]ver 15 [p]S ver 1 **5:18** [q]Lev 6:6; 14:12 [r]S ver 15 **5:19** [s]2Ki 12:16 **6:2** [t]Nu 5:6; Ps 73:27; Ac 5:4; Col 3:9 [u]Lev 19:11; Jer 9:4, 5 [v]S Ex 22:7 [w]S Ge 31:7 **6:3** [x]S Ex 23:4 [y]S Ex 22:11 **6:4** [z]Lev 5:16; Eze 33:15; S Lk 19:8 **6:5** [a]Nu 5:7 [b]S Lev 5:15 **6:6** [c]S Lev 5:15 [d]Nu 5:8 **6:7** [e]S Ex 32:30 **6:9** [f]Lev 7:37 [g]ver 12 **6:10** [h]S Ex 39:27 [i]Ex 28:39-42, 43; 39:28 [j]S Lev 1:16 **6:11** [k]S Lev 4:12 **6:12** [l]S Lev 1:7 [m]S Ex 29:13 [n]S Ex 32:6 **6:14** [o]S Lev 2:1; Nu 6:15; 15:4; 28:13 **6:15** [p]S Lev 2:1 [q]Lev 2:9 [r]S Lev 2:2 **6:16** [s]S Lev 2:3 [t]Eze 44:29 [u]S Lev 2:11 [v]ver 26; S Ex 29:11; Lev 10:13; 16:24; 24:9; Nu 18:10 [w]S Ex 27:9 [x]Ex 29:31; Lev 8:31 **6:17** [y]Nu 5:9 [z]Ex 29:28; Lev 7:7; 10:16-18

5:15 *LORD's holy things.* See note on Ex 3:5. *according to the sanctuary shekel.* See note on Ex 30:13. *guilt offering.* See further priestly regulations in 7:1–6 (see also Isa 53:10 and note, as well as chart, p. 153). Traditionally called the "trespass offering," it was very similar to the sin offering (cf. 7:7), and the Hebrew words for the two were apparently sometimes interchanged. The major difference between the guilt and sin offerings was that the guilt offering was brought in cases where restitution for the sin was possible and therefore required (v. 16). Thus in cases of theft and cheating (6:2–5) the stolen property had to be returned along with 20 percent indemnity. By contrast, the sin offering was prescribed in cases of sin where no restitution was possible. The animal sacrificed as a guilt offering was always a ram.

6:3 *lost property.* See Dt 22:1–3.

6:6 *to the priest, that is, to the LORD.* Sacrifices were brought to the Lord, but priests were his authorized representatives.

6:8—7:36 Further regulations concerning the sacrifices, dealing mainly with the portions to be eaten by the priests or, in the case of the fellowship offering, by the one offering the sacrifice.

6:9 *burnt offering.* See ch. 1; Nu 15:1–16 and notes.

6:13 The perpetual fire on the altar represented uninterrupted offering to and appeal to God on behalf of Israel.

6:14 *grain offering.* See ch. 2 and notes.

6:15 *memorial portion.* See note on 2:2,9,16.

6:16 *in a holy place.* In the sanctuary area. *holy.* See note on Ex 3:5.

the guilt offering, it is most holy.[a] 18 Any
male descendant of Aaron may eat it.[b] It
is his regular share[c] of the offerings made
to the LORD by fire for the generations to
come.[d] Whatever touches them will become holy.[a e]' "
19 The LORD also said to Moses, 20 "This
is the offering Aaron and his sons are to
bring to the LORD on the day he[b] is anointed:[f] a tenth of an ephah[c g] of fine flour[h]
as a regular grain offering,[i] half of it in
the morning and half in the evening. 21 Prepare it with oil on a griddle;[j] bring it well-
mixed and present the grain offering broken[d] in pieces as an aroma pleasing to the
LORD. 22 The son who is to succeed him as
anointed priest[k] shall prepare it. It is the
LORD's regular share and is to be burned
completely.[l] 23 Every grain offering of a
priest shall be burned completely; it must
not be eaten."

The Sin Offering

24 The LORD said to Moses, 25 "Say to Aaron and his sons: 'These are the regulations
for the sin offering:[m] The sin offering is
to be slaughtered before the LORD[n] in the
place[o] the burnt offering is slaughtered;
it is most holy. 26 The priest who offers
it shall eat it; it is to be eaten in a holy
place,[p] in the courtyard[q] of the Tent of
Meeting.[r] 27 Whatever touches any of the
flesh will become holy,[s] and if any of the
blood is spattered on a garment, you must
wash it in a holy place. 28 The clay pot[t] the
meat is cooked in must be broken; but if
it is cooked in a bronze pot, the pot is to
be scoured and rinsed with water. 29 Any
male in a priest's family may eat it;[u] it is
most holy.[v] 30 But any sin offering whose
blood is brought into the Tent of Meeting
to make atonement[w] in the Holy Place[x]
must not be eaten; it must be burned.[y]

The Guilt Offering

7 " 'These are the regulations for the guilt
offering,[z] which is most holy: 2 The guilt
offering is to be slaughtered in the place
where the burnt offering is slaughtered,
and its blood is to be sprinkled against
the altar on all sides. 3 All its fat[a] shall be
offered: the fat tail and the fat that covers
the inner parts, 4 both kidneys with the fat
on them near the loins, and the covering
of the liver, which is to be removed with
the kidneys.[b] 5 The priest shall burn them
on the altar[c] as an offering made to the
LORD by fire. It is a guilt offering. 6 Any
male in a priest's family may eat it,[d] but
it must be eaten in a holy place; it is most
holy.[e]
7 " 'The same law applies to both the sin
offering[f] and the guilt offering:[g] They belong to the priest[h] who makes atonement
with them.[i] 8 The priest who offers a burnt
offering for anyone may keep its hide[j] for
himself. 9 Every grain offering baked in an
oven[k] or cooked in a pan[l] or on a griddle[m]
belongs to the priest who offers it, 10 and
every grain offering, whether mixed with
oil or dry, belongs equally to all the sons
of Aaron.

The Fellowship Offering

11 " 'These are the regulations for the fellowship offering[e] a person may present to
the LORD:
12 " 'If he offers it as an expression of
thankfulness, then along with this thank
offering[n] he is to offer cakes[o] of bread
made without yeast[p] and mixed with oil,
wafers[q] made without yeast and spread
with oil,[r] and cakes of fine flour well-
kneaded and mixed with oil. 13 Along with
his fellowship offering of thanksgiving[s]
he is to present an offering with cakes of
bread made with yeast.[t] 14 He is to bring
one of each kind as an offering, a contribution to the LORD; it belongs to the priest
who sprinkles the blood of the fellowship
offerings. 15 The meat of his fellowship offering of thanksgiving must be eaten on
the day it is offered; he must leave none of
it till morning.[u]

[a] *18* Or *Whoever touches them must be holy*; similarly in verse 27 [b] *20* Or *each* [c] *20* That is, probably about 2 quarts (about 2 liters) [d] *21* The meaning of the Hebrew for this word is uncertain. [e] *11* Traditionally *peace offering*; also in verses 13-37

6:17 [a] ver 29; Ex 40:10; Lev 10:12; 21:22; 24:9; Nu 18:9,10 **6:18** [b] ver 29; Lev 2:3; 7:6; Nu 18:9-10 [c] Nu 5:9 [d] S Ge 9:12 [e] S Ex 30:29 **6:20** [f] S Ex 28:41 [g] S Ex 16:36 [h] Nu 5:15; 28:5 [i] Ex 29:2; Lev 23:13; Nu 4:16 **6:21** [j] Lev 2:5 **6:22** [k] S Ex 28:41; S 29:30 [l] S Lev 1:9 **6:25** [m] S Ex 30:10; S Lev 4:24 [n] S Lev 1:3 [o] S Ex 29:11 **6:26** [p] S ver 16 [q] S Ex 27:9 [r] S Ex 27:21; S 40:2 **6:27** [s] S Ex 29:37; Lev 10:10; Eze 44:19; 46:20; Hag 2:12 **6:28** [t] Lev 11:33; 15:12; Nu 19:15 **6:29** [u] S ver 18 [v] S ver 17; Eze 42:13 **6:30** [w] Eze 45:15 [x] S Lev 4:18 [y] Lev 4:12 **7:1** [z] S Lev 5:15; Eze 40:39

7:3 [a] S Ex 29:13 **7:4** [b] Lev 3:15 **7:5** [c] S Ex 29:13 **7:6** [d] S Lev 6:18 [e] Eze 42:13 **7:7** [f] S Ex 30:10 [g] S Lev 5:15 [h] ver 6; Lev 2:3; 6:17,26; 14:13; 2Ki 12:16; 1Co 9:13; 10:18 [i] Nu 5:8 **7:8** [j] Lev 1:6 **7:9** [k] S Lev 2:4 [l] Lev 2:7 [m] S Lev 2:5 **7:12** [n] ver 13,15; Lev 22:29; Ps 50:14; 54:6; 107:22; 116:17; Jer 33:11 [o] Jer 44:19 [p] Nu 6:19 [q] S Lev 2:4 [r] S Lev 2:1 **7:13** [s] S ver 12; S Ex 34:22 [t] Lev 23:17; Am 4:5 **7:15** [u] S Ex 12:10

6:18 *will become holy.* See Ex 29:37 and note.
6:25 *sin offering.* See 4:1—5:13 and notes.
6:28 *clay.* Ordinary kitchen utensils and domestic ware were made of clay, usually fired in a kiln and often painted or burnished.
7:1 *holy.* See note on Ex 3:5.
7:2 *guilt offering.* See 5:14—6:7 and notes. *place.* On the north side of the altar of burnt offering in front of the tabernacle (1:11; see note there).
7:3 *fat tail.* See note on 3:9.
7:7–10 See Nu 18:8–20; 1Co 9:13 and notes.
7:11–36 This section supplements ch. 3, adding regulations about (1) three types of fellowship offerings (thank, vv. 12–15; vow, v. 16; freewill, v. 16), (2) prohibition of eating fat and blood (vv. 22–27) and (3) the priests' share (vv. 28–36).
7:12–15 Thank offerings were given in gratitude for deliverance from sickness (Ps 116:17), trouble (Ps 107:22) or death (Ps 56:12–13), or for a blessing received.
7:13 *with yeast.* This regulation was not against the prohibition of 2:11 or Ex 23:18 since the offering here was not burned on the altar.
7:15–18 See 19:5–8. All meat had to be eaten promptly (in the case of the thank offering on the same day, and in the case of the vow and freewill offerings within two days). One reason may have been that in Canaan meat spoiled quickly and thus became ceremonially impure (v. 18) because it was not then perfect (1:3; see 21:16–23 and note on 21:17). The prohibition applied also to the Passover (Ex 12:10).

16“ ‘If, however, his offering is the result
of a vow[v] or is a freewill offering,[w] the sacrifice shall be eaten on the day he offers
it, but anything left over may be eaten on
the next day.[x] 17Any meat of the sacrifice
left over till the third day must be burned
up.[y] 18If any meat of the fellowship offering[z] is eaten on the third day, it will not
be accepted.[a] It will not be credited[b] to the
one who offered it, for it is impure; the
person who eats any of it will be held responsible.[c]
19“ ‘Meat that touches anything ceremonially unclean must not be eaten; it must
be burned up. As for other meat, anyone
ceremonially clean may eat it. 20But if anyone who is unclean[d] eats any meat of the
fellowship offering belonging to the LORD,
that person must be cut off from his people.[e] 21If anyone touches something unclean[f]—whether human uncleanness or
an unclean animal or any unclean, detestable thing—and then eats any of the meat
of the fellowship offering belonging to the
LORD, that person must be cut off from his
people.’ ”

Eating Fat and Blood Forbidden

22The LORD said to Moses, 23“Say to the
Israelites: ‘Do not eat any of the fat of cattle, sheep or goats.[g] 24The fat of an animal
found dead or torn by wild animals[h] may
be used for any other purpose, but you
must not eat it. 25Anyone who eats the fat
of an animal from which an offering by fire
may be[a] made to the LORD must be cut off
from his people. 26And wherever you live,
you must not eat the blood[i] of any bird or
animal. 27If anyone eats blood,[j] that person must be cut off from his people.’ ”

The Priests’ Share

28The LORD said to Moses, 29“Say to the
Israelites: ‘Anyone who brings a fellowship offering to the LORD is to bring part
of it as his sacrifice to the LORD. 30With
his own hands he is to bring the offering
made to the LORD by fire; he is to bring the
fat, together with the breast, and wave the
breast before the LORD as a wave offering.[k]
31The priest shall burn the fat on the altar,[l]
but the breast belongs to Aaron and his
sons.[m] 32You are to give the right thigh of
your fellowship offerings to the priest as a
contribution.[n] 33The son of Aaron who offers the blood and the fat of the fellowship
offering shall have the right thigh as his
share. 34From the fellowship offerings of
the Israelites, I have taken the breast that
is waved and the thigh[o] that is presented
and have given them to Aaron the priest
and his sons[p] as their regular share from
the Israelites.’ ”
35This is the portion of the offerings
made to the LORD by fire that were allotted to Aaron and his sons on the day
they were presented to serve the LORD as
priests. 36On the day they were anointed,[q]
the LORD commanded that the Israelites
give this to them as their regular share for
the generations to come.
37These, then, are the regulations for
the burnt offering,[r] the grain offering,[s] the
sin offering, the guilt offering, the ordination offering[t] and the fellowship offering,
38which the LORD gave Moses[u] on Mount
Sinai[v] on the day he commanded the Israelites to bring their offerings to the LORD,[w]
in the Desert of Sinai.

The Ordination of Aaron and His Sons

8:1-36pp — Ex 29:1-37

8 The LORD said to Moses, 2“Bring Aaron and his sons,[x] their garments,[y] the
anointing oil,[z] the bull for the sin offering,[a] the two rams[b] and the basket containing bread made without yeast,[c] 3and
gather the entire assembly[d] at the entrance

7:16 [v]S Ge 28:20; S Lev 1:2; Dt 23:21-23 [w]Ex 35:29; Lev 22:18,21; 23:38; Nu 15:3; 29:39; Dt 12:6; Ps 54:6; Eze 46:12 [x]Lev 19:5-8 **7:17** [y]Ex 12:10; Lev 19:6 **7:18** [z]2Ch 33:16 [a]Lev 19:7 [b]Nu 18:27 [c]S Lev 5:1 **7:20** [d]S Lev 5:3 [e]S Ge 17:14; Lev 22:3-7 **7:21** [f]S Lev 5:2 **7:23** [g]Lev 17:13-14; Dt 14:4 **7:24** [h]S Ex 22:31 **7:26** [i]S Ge 9:4 **7:27** [j]S Ge 9:4 **7:30** [k]S Ex 29:24 **7:31** [l]S Ex 29:13 [m]S Ex 29:27 **7:32** [n]Ex 29:27; Lev 10:14,15; Nu 5:9; 6:20; 18:18 **7:34** [o]Ex 29:22; Lev 10:15; Nu 6:20; 1Sa 9:24 [p]S Ex 29:27 **7:36** [q]Lev 8:12,30 **7:37** [r]Lev 6:9 [s]Lev 6:14 [t]S Ex 29:31 **7:38** [u]Lev 26:46; Nu 36:13; Dt 4:5; 29:1 [v]S Ex 19:11 [w]S Lev 1:2 **8:2** [x]S Ex 28:1; S Lev 1:5 [y]Ex 28:2,4,43; S 39:27 [z]Ex 30:23-25,30 [a]S Ex 30:10 [b]ver 18,22 [c]Ex 29:2-3 **8:3** [d]Nu 8:9

[a] 25 Or *fire is*

7:16 *vow.* See 22:18–23. A vow was a solemn promise to offer a gift to God in response to a divine deliverance or blessing. Such vows often accompanied prayers for deliverance or blessing (see note on Ps 7:17). *freewill offering.* See 22:18–23.

7:19 *ceremonially unclean.* See note on 4:12.

7:20 *cut off from his people.* Removed from the covenant people through direct divine judgment (see Ge 17:14 and note), or (as here and in vv. 21,25,27; 17:4,9–10,14; 18:29; 19:8; 20:3,5–6,17–18; 23:29) through execution (see, e.g., 20:2–3; Ex 31:14), or possibly sometimes through banishment (see note on Ex 12:15).

7:21 *detestable.* The penalty for doing things the Lord especially detested was severe (see note on v. 20; see also 18:29; 20:13).

7:22–27 See note on 17:11.

7:23 *fat.* The prohibition of fat for food was as strict as that of blood, but the reason was different. The fat of the fellowship offerings was the Lord’s and was to be burned on the altar (see 3:16 and note). There was no explicit prohibition of eating the fat of hunted animals like the gazelle or deer, but probably that was included (see 3:17; Dt 12:15–22).

7:26 *not eat the blood.* See note on 17:11; see also 3:17; 19:26; Ge 9:4–6; Dt 12:16,23–25; 15:23; 1Sa 14:32–34 and note on 14:33; Eze 33:25.

7:28–36 See 10:12–15; Nu 18:8–20 and notes on 18:8,11–12; Dt 18:1–5.

7:30–32 *breast ... right thigh.* The breast and right thigh given to the priest were first presented to the Lord with gestures described as waving the breast and presenting the thigh (v. 34). See 8:25–29; 9:21; 10:14–15; Ex 29:26–27; Nu 6:20; 18:11,18.

7:37–38 A summary of chs. 1–7.

7:37 *ordination offering.* See 8:14–36; Ex 29:1–35.

8:1—10:20 The ordination, installation and ministry of Aaron and his sons, and the death of Nadab and Abihu and attendant regulations.

8:2 *their garments.* See Ex 39:1–31; 40:12–16. The garments that the high priest was to wear when he ministered are detailed in Ex 28:4–43 (see notes there). *anointing oil.* See note

to the Tent of Meeting." 4Moses did as the LORD commanded him, and the assembly gathered at the entrance to the Tent of Meeting.

5Moses said to the assembly, "This is what the LORD has commanded to be done.[e]" 6Then Moses brought Aaron and his sons forward and washed them with water.[f] 7He put the tunic on Aaron, tied the sash around him, clothed him with the robe and put the ephod on him. He also tied the ephod to him by its skillfully woven waistband; so it was fastened on him.[g] 8He placed the breastpiece[h] on him and put the Urim and Thummim[i] in the breastpiece. 9Then he placed the turban[j] on Aaron's head and set the gold plate, the sacred diadem,[k] on the front of it, as the LORD commanded Moses.[l]

10Then Moses took the anointing oil[m] and anointed[n] the tabernacle[o] and everything in it, and so consecrated them. 11He sprinkled some of the oil on the altar seven times, anointing the altar and all its utensils and the basin with its stand, to consecrate them.[p] 12He poured some of the anointing oil on Aaron's head and anointed[q] him to consecrate him.[r] 13Then he brought Aaron's sons[s] forward, put tunics[t] on them, tied sashes around them and put headbands on them, as the LORD commanded Moses.[u]

14He then presented the bull[v] for the sin offering,[w] and Aaron and his sons laid their hands on its head.[x] 15Moses slaughtered the bull and took some of the blood,[y] and with his finger he put it on all the horns of the altar[z] to purify the altar.[a] He poured out the rest of the blood at the base of the altar. So he consecrated it to make atonement for it.[b] 16Moses also took all the fat around the inner parts, the covering of the liver, and both kidneys and their fat, and burned it on the altar. 17But the bull with its hide and its flesh and its offal[c] he burned up outside the camp,[d] as the LORD commanded Moses.

18He then presented the ram[e] for the burnt offering, and Aaron and his sons laid their hands on its head. 19Then Moses slaughtered the ram and sprinkled the blood against the altar on all sides. 20He cut the ram into pieces and burned the head, the pieces and the fat.[f] 21He washed the inner parts and the legs with water and burned the whole ram on the altar as a burnt offering, a pleasing aroma, an offering made to the LORD by fire, as the LORD commanded Moses.

22He then presented the other ram, the ram for the ordination,[g] and Aaron and his sons laid their hands on its head.[h] 23Moses slaughtered the ram and took some of its blood and put it on the lobe of Aaron's right ear, on the thumb of his right hand and on the big toe of his right foot.[i] 24Moses also brought Aaron's sons forward and put some of the blood on the lobes of their right ears, on the thumbs of their right hands and on the big toes of their right feet. Then he sprinkled blood against the altar on all sides.[j] 25He took the fat[k], the fat tail, all the fat around the inner parts, the covering of the liver, both kidneys and their fat and the right thigh. 26Then from the basket of bread made without yeast, which was before the LORD, he took a cake of bread, and one made with oil, and a wafer;[l] he put these on the fat portions and on the right thigh. 27He put all these in the hands of Aaron and his sons and waved them before the LORD[m] as a wave offering. 28Then Moses took them from their hands and burned them on the altar on top of the burnt offering as an ordination offering, a pleasing aroma, an offering made to the LORD by fire. 29He also took the breast—Moses' share of the ordination ram[n]—and waved it before the LORD as a wave offering, as the LORD commanded Moses.

30Then Moses[o] took some of the anointing oil and some of the blood from the altar and sprinkled them on Aaron and his garments[p] and on his sons and their garments. So he consecrated[q] Aaron and his garments and his sons and their garments.

31Moses then said to Aaron and his sons, "Cook the meat at the entrance to the Tent

8:5 [e]Ex 29:1
8:6 [f]S Ex 29:4; S 30:19; S Ac 22:16
8:7 [g]Ex 28:4
8:8 [h]S Ex 25:7 [i]S Ex 28:30
8:9 [j]S Ex 39:28 [k]S Ex 28:36 [l]S Ex 28:2; Lev 21:10
8:10 [m]ver 2 [n]S Ex 30:26 [o]S Ex 26:1
8:11 [p]S Ex 30:29
8:12 [q]S Lev 7:36 [r]S Ex 30:30
8:13 [s]S Ex 28:40 [t]S Ex 28:4,39; 39:27 [u]Lev 21:10
8:14 [v]S Lev 4:3 [w]S Ex 30:10 [x]S Lev 4:15
8:15 [y]S Lev 4:18 [z]S Lev 4:7 [a]Heb 9:22 [b]Eze 43:20
8:17 [c]S Lev 4:11 [d]S Lev 4:12
8:18 [e]S ver 2
8:20 [f]S Lev 1:8
8:22 [g]S ver 2 [h]S Lev 4:15
8:23 [i]Lev 14:14,25
8:24 [j]Heb 9:18-22
8:25 [k]Lev 3:3-5
8:26 [l]S Lev 2:4
8:27 [m]Nu 5:25
8:29 [n]Lev 7:31-34
8:30 [o]S Ex 28:1 [p]S Ex 28:2 [q]S Lev 7:36

on Ex 25:6. The oil was used to anoint the tabernacle, sacred objects and consecrated priests (vv. 10–12,30). It was later used to anoint leaders and kings (1Sa 10:1; 16:13). See also note on Ex 29:7.

8:6 *washed them with water.* In the bronze basin (see v. 11) in the courtyard of the tabernacle (see Ex 30:17–21).

8:7 *ephod.* See note on Ex 28:6.

8:8 *Urim and Thummim.* See notes on Ex 28:30; 1Sa 2:28.

8:9 *sacred diadem.* See note on Ex 39:30.

8:11 *seven times.* See note on 4:6.

8:12 *oil on Aaron's head.* See Ps 133 and note on 133:2.

8:14 *sin offering.* See 4:3–11 and notes. The consecration service included a sin offering for atonement, a burnt offering for worship (v. 18) and a "ram for ordination" (v. 22), whose blood was applied to the high priest on his right ear, thumb and toe (v. 23). After this was done, Aaron offered sacrifices for the people (9:15–21). Then he blessed the people in his capacity as priest, and the Lord accepted his ministry with the sign of miraculous fire (9:23–24). *laid their hands on.* See notes on 1:3; Ex 29:10.

8:15 *make atonement for it.* See 16:16; see also note on Ex 29:36.

8:17 *outside the camp.* See notes on 4:5,12; 13:45–46; Eze 43:21; Heb 13:12–13.

8:23 Putting some of the blood on Aaron's extremities signified his complete consecration to the Lord's service (cf. note on v. 14).

8:27 *wave offering.* See note on 7:30–32.

8:28 *on top of the burnt offering.* See note on 3:5.

8:31 *saying, 'Aaron and his sons are to eat it.'* Quoted from Ex 29:32 (but see NIV text note here).

of Meeting[r] and eat it there with the bread from the basket of ordination offerings, as I commanded, saying,[a] 'Aaron and his sons are to eat it.' 32Then burn up the rest of the meat and the bread. 33Do not leave the entrance to the Tent of Meeting for seven days, until the days of your ordination are completed, for your ordination will last seven days.[s] 34What has been done today was commanded by the LORD[t] to make atonement for you. 35You must stay at the entrance to the Tent of Meeting day and night for seven days and do what the LORD requires,[u] so you will not die; for that is what I have been commanded." 36So Aaron and his sons did everything the LORD commanded through Moses.

The Priests Begin Their Ministry

9 On the eighth day[v] Moses summoned Aaron and his sons and the elders[w] of Israel. 2He said to Aaron, "Take a bull calf for your sin offering and a ram for your burnt offering, both without defect, and present them before the LORD. 3Then say to the Israelites: 'Take a male goat[x] for a sin offering,[y] a calf[z] and a lamb[a]—both a year old and without defect—for a burnt offering, 4and an ox[b][b] and a ram for a fellowship offering[c][c] to sacrifice before the LORD, together with a grain offering mixed with oil. For today the LORD will appear to you.[d]'"

5They took the things Moses commanded to the front of the Tent of Meeting, and the entire assembly came near and stood before the LORD. 6Then Moses said, "This is what the LORD has commanded you to do, so that the glory of the LORD[e] may appear to you."

7Moses said to Aaron, "Come to the altar and sacrifice your sin offering and your burnt offering and make atonement for yourself and the people;[f] sacrifice the offering that is for the people and make atonement for them, as the LORD has commanded.[g]"

8So Aaron came to the altar and slaughtered the calf as a sin offering[h] for himself. 9His sons brought the blood to him,[i] and he dipped his finger into the blood and put it on the horns of the altar; the rest of the blood he poured out at the base of the altar.[j][k] 10On the altar he burned the fat, the kidneys and the covering of the liver from the sin offering, as the LORD commanded Moses; 11the flesh and the hide[l] he burned up outside the camp.[m]

12Then he slaughtered the burnt offering.[n] His sons handed him the blood,[o] and he sprinkled it against the altar on all sides. 13They handed him the burnt offering piece by piece, including the head, and he burned them on the altar.[p] 14He washed the inner parts and the legs and burned them on top of the burnt offering on the altar.[q]

15Aaron then brought the offering that was for the people.[r] He took the goat for the people's sin offering and slaughtered it and offered it for a sin offering as he did with the first one.

16He brought the burnt offering and offered it in the prescribed way.[s] 17He also brought the grain offering, took a handful of it and burned it on the altar in addition to the morning's burnt offering.[t]

18He slaughtered the ox and the ram as the fellowship offering for the people.[u] His sons handed him the blood, and he sprinkled it against the altar on all sides. 19But the fat portions of the ox and the ram—the fat tail, the layer of fat, the kidneys and the covering of the liver— 20these they laid on the breasts, and then Aaron burned the fat on the altar. 21Aaron waved the breasts and the right thigh before the LORD as a wave offering,[v] as Moses commanded.

22Then Aaron lifted his hands toward the people and blessed them.[w] And having sacrificed the sin offering, the burnt offering and the fellowship offering, he stepped down.

23Moses and Aaron then went into the Tent of Meeting.[x] When they came out, they blessed the people; and the glory of the LORD[y] appeared to all the people. 24Fire[z] came out from the presence of the LORD and consumed the burnt offering and the fat portions on the altar. And when all the people saw it, they shouted for joy and fell facedown.[a]

8:31 [r] S Lev 6:16
8:33 [s] Lev 14:8; 15:13,28; Nu 19:11; Eze 43:25
8:34 [t] Heb 7:16
8:35 [u] Lev 18:30; 22:9; Nu 3:7; 9:19; Dt 11:1; 1Ki 2:3; Eze 48:11; Zec 3:7
9:1 [v] Eze 43:27 [w] S Lev 4:15
9:3 [x] S Lev 4:3 [y] ver 15; Lev 10:16 [z] ver 8 [a] S Lev 4:32
9:4 [b] Lev 4:10 [c] S Ex 32:6 [d] Ex 29:43
9:6 [e] S Ex 16:7
9:7 [f] Lev 16:6 [g] S Ex 30:10; Heb 5:1,3; 7:27
9:8 [h] Lev 4:1-12; 10:19
9:9 [i] ver 12,18 [j] S Ex 29:12 [k] Eze 43:20
9:11 [l] S Lev 4:11 [m] S Lev 4:12
9:12 [n] Lev 10:19 [o] S ver 9
9:13 [p] S Lev 1:8
9:14 [q] S Lev 1:9
9:15 [r] Lev 4:27-31
9:16 [s] Lev 1:1-13
9:17 [t] Lev 3:5
9:18 [u] Lev 3:1-11
9:21 [v] S Ex 29:24,26
9:22 [w] S Ge 48:20; S Ex 39:43; Lk 24:50
9:23 [x] S Ex 40:2 [y] S Ex 24:16
9:24 [z] S Ex 19:18; Jdg 6:21; 13:20 [a] 1Ki 18:39

[a] 31 Or *I was commanded:*
[b] 4 The Hebrew word can include both male and female; also in verses 18 and 19.
[c] 4 Traditionally *peace offering*; also in verses 18 and 22

9:1 *eighth day.* After the seven days of ordination (8:33).
9:2 *sin offering.* See notes on 4:3,5. *burnt offering.* See note on 1:3.
9:4 *fellowship offering.* See note on 3:1. *grain offering.* See note on 2:1. *LORD will appear.* See vv. 6,23; see also note on Ge 12:7.
9:6,23 *glory of the LORD.* See Ex 16:7; see also notes on Ex 40:34; Ps 26:8; Eze 1:28.
9:8 *sin offering for himself.* Contrast Jesus in Heb 7:26–28 (see notes there).
9:11 *outside the camp.* See note on 8:17.
9:17 *morning's burnt offering.* See Ex 29:38–42.
9:21 *wave offering.* See note on 7:30–32.
9:22 *blessed.* The Aaronic benediction, a threefold blessing, is given in Nu 6:24–26 (see note there). Cf. the threefold apostolic benediction in 2Co 13:14.
9:23 *glory of the LORD.* See v. 6; cf. the display of the Lord's glory at the erection of the tabernacle (Ex 40:34–35); cf. also God's acceptance of sacrifices at the dedication of Solomon's temple (see 2Ch 7:1 and note on 2Ch 5:14).
9:24 *Fire came out from the presence of the LORD.* See 10:2; 1Ki 18:38.

The Death of Nadab and Abihu

10 Aaron's sons Nadab and Abihu[b] took
their censers,[c] put fire in them[d] and
added incense;[e] and they offered unauthorized fire before the LORD,[f] contrary to his
command.[g] 2So fire came out[h] from the
presence of the LORD and consumed them,[i]
and they died before the LORD.[j] 3Moses
then said to Aaron, "This is what the LORD
spoke of when he said:

"'Among those who approach me[k]
I will show myself holy;[l]
in the sight of all the people
I will be honored.[m]'"

Aaron remained silent.
4Moses summoned Mishael and Elzaphan,[n] sons of Aaron's uncle Uzziel,[o] and
said to them, "Come here; carry your cousins outside the camp,[p] away from the front
of the sanctuary.[q]" 5So they came and carried them, still in their tunics,[r] outside the
camp, as Moses ordered.
6Then Moses said to Aaron and his sons
Eleazar and Ithamar,[s] "Do not let your hair
become unkempt,[a][t] and do not tear your
clothes,[u] or you will die and the LORD will
be angry with the whole community.[v] But
your relatives, all the house of Israel, may
mourn[w] for those the LORD has destroyed
by fire. 7Do not leave the entrance to the
Tent of Meeting[x] or you will die, because
the LORD's anointing oil[y] is on you." So
they did as Moses said.
8Then the LORD said to Aaron, 9"You and
your sons are not to drink wine[z] or other fermented drink[a] whenever you go into
the Tent of Meeting, or you will die. This
is a lasting ordinance[b] for the generations
to come. 10You must distinguish between
the holy and the common, between the
unclean and the clean,[c] 11and you must
teach[d] the Israelites all the decrees the
LORD has given them through Moses.[e]"
12Moses said to Aaron and his remaining sons, Eleazar and Ithamar, "Take the
grain offering[f] left over from the offerings
made to the LORD by fire and eat it prepared without yeast beside the altar,[g] for
it is most holy. 13Eat it in a holy place,[h] because it is your share and your sons' share
of the offerings made to the LORD by fire;
for so I have been commanded.[i] 14But you
and your sons and your daughters may eat
the breast[j] that was waved and the thigh
that was presented. Eat them in a ceremonially clean place;[k] they have been given
to you and your children as your share of
the Israelites' fellowship offerings.[b] 15The
thigh[l] that was presented and the breast
that was waved must be brought with the
fat portions of the offerings made by fire,
to be waved before the LORD as a wave
offering.[m] This will be the regular share
for you and your children, as the LORD has
commanded."
16When Moses inquired about the goat
of the sin offering[n] and found that it had
been burned up, he was angry with Eleazar and Ithamar, Aaron's remaining sons,
and asked, 17"Why didn't you eat the sin
offering[o] in the sanctuary area? It is most
holy; it was given to you to take away the
guilt[p] of the community by making atonement for them before the LORD. 18Since its
blood was not taken into the Holy Place,[q]
you should have eaten the goat in the
sanctuary area, as I commanded.[r]"
19Aaron replied to Moses, "Today they
sacrificed their sin offering and their burnt

[a] 6 Or *Do not uncover your heads* [b] 14 Traditionally *peace offerings*

10:1 [b] Ex 6:23; 24:1; 28:1; Nu 3:2-4; 26:61; 1Ch 6:3 [c] Nu 16:46; 1Ki 7:50; 2Ki 25:15; 2Ch 4:22; Jer 52:19; Eze 8:11 [d] Lev 16:12; Nu 16:7, 18; Isa 6:6 [e] S Ex 30:9 [f] ver 2; Lev 16:1 [g] Ex 30:9 **10:2** [h] Ps 106:18 [i] Nu 11:1; 16:35; Ps 2:12; 50:3; Isa 29:6 [j] S Ge 19:24; S 38:7; Nu 16:35; 1Ch 24:2; Job 1:16 **10:3** [k] Ex 19:22 [l] Ex 30:29; Lev 21:6; 22:32; Nu 16:5; 20:13; Isa 5:16; Eze 28:22; 38:16 [m] Ex 14:4; Isa 44:23; 49:3; 55:5; 60:21 **10:4** [n] S Ex 6:22 [o] Ex 6:18 [p] Ac 5:6, 9, 10 [q] S Ex 25:8 **10:5** [r] S Lev 8:13 **10:6** [s] S Ex 6:23 [t] Lev 13:45; 21:10; Nu 5:18 [u] Jer 41:5; S Mk 14:63 [v] Nu 1:53; 16:22; Jos 7:1; 22:18 [w] Ge 50:3, 10; Nu 20:29; 1Sa 25:1 **10:7** [x] S Ex 25:8 [y] S Ex 28:41 **10:9** [z] Ge 9:21; Ex 29:40; Lev 23:13; Nu 15:5; Dt 28:39; Isa 5:22; 22:13; 28:1; 29:9; 56:12; Jer 35:6; Hos 4:11; Hab 2:15-16 [a] Nu 6:3; 28:7; Dt 14:26; 29:6; Jdg 13:4; Pr 20:1; 23:29-35; 31:4-7; Isa 28:7; Eze 44:21; Mic 2:11; Lk 1:15; S Eph 5:18; 1Ti 3:3; Tit 1:7 [b] S Ex 12:14 **10:10** [c] S Ge 7:2; S Lev 6:27; 14:57; 20:25; Eze 22:26 **10:11** [d] 2Ch 15:3; 17:7; Ezr 7:25; Ne 8:7; Mal 2:7 [e] Dt 17:10, 11; 24:8; 25:1; 33:10; Pr 4:27; Hag 2:11; Mal 2:7 **10:12** [f] S Ex 29:41 [g] Lev 6:14-18 **10:13** [h] S Lev 6:16 [i] Eze 42:13 **10:14** [j] Nu 5:9 [k] S Ex 29:31; S Lev 4:12 **10:15** [l] S Lev 7:34 [m] S Ex 29:28 **10:16** [n] S Lev 9:3 **10:17** [o] Lev 6:24-30; Eze 42:13 [p] S Ex 28:38 **10:18** [q] S Lev 4:18; 6:26 [r] S Lev 6:17

10:1 *censers.* Ceremonial vessels containing hot coals and used for burning incense (see 16:12–13; 2Ch 26:19; Rev 8:3–4).

10:2 *died before the LORD.* Aaron's older sons are mentioned also in Ex 6:23; 24:1,9 (see note on 24:1); 28:1; Nu 3:2–4 (see note on 3:4); 26:60–61; 1Ch 6:3; 24:1–2. They are regularly remembered as having died before the Lord and as having had no sons. Their death was tragic and at first seems harsh, but no more so than that of Ananias and Sapphira (Ac 5:1–11; see notes on 5:1,9). In both cases a new era was being inaugurated (cf. also the judgment on Achan, Jos 7, and on Uzzah, 2Sa 6:1–7). The new community had to be made aware that it existed for God, not vice versa.

10:3 The quotation reflects the spirit and substance of passages like Ex 14:4; 19:22; 29:1,44; 30:29. *show myself holy.* Act so as to publicly display my holiness (see 11:44 and note; see also Nu 20:13; Isa 5:16; Eze 20:41; 28:22,25; 36:23; 38:16; 39:27). *holy.* See Introduction: Theological Themes.

10:4 *outside the camp.* See note on 8:17.

10:6 *do not tear your clothes.* See 21:10; see also note on Ge 44:13.

10:7 *Do not leave.* To join the mourners (see 21:11–12 and note on 21:1).

10:10 *between the holy and the common.* The distinction between what was holy (sacred; see note on Ex 3:5) and what was common (not associated with the sacred) was carefully maintained (see Eze 22:26 and note; 42:20; 44:23 and note; 48:14–15).

10:12–15 See 7:28–36; Nu 18:8–20; Dt 18:1–5.

10:18 *Since its blood was not taken into the Holy Place, you should have eaten.* There were two types of sin offerings: (1) those in which the blood was sprinkled within the tabernacle, and (2) those in which it was sprinkled only on the great altar. Portions of the second type normally should have been eaten (see note on 4:5). But Moses was satisfied when he learned that Aaron had acted sincerely and not in negligence or rebellion (vv. 19–20).

10:19 *such things as this have happened to me.* Probably referring to the death of his two oldest sons (v. 2), for which he mourned by fasting. Or possibly something had occurred that made him ceremonially unclean.

offering[s] before the LORD, but such things
as this have happened to me. Would the
LORD have been pleased if I had eaten the
sin offering today?" 20When Moses heard
this, he was satisfied.

Clean and Unclean Food

11:1-23pp — Dt 14:3-20

11 The LORD said to Moses and Aaron,
2"Say to the Israelites: 'Of all the animals that live on land, these are the ones
you may eat:[t] 3You may eat any animal
that has a split hoof completely divided
and that chews the cud.
4" 'There are some that only chew the
cud or only have a split hoof, but you
must not eat them.[u] The camel, though it
chews the cud, does not have a split hoof;
it is ceremonially unclean for you. 5The
coney,[a] though it chews the cud, does not
have a split hoof; it is unclean for you.
6The rabbit, though it chews the cud, does
not have a split hoof; it is unclean for you.
7And the pig,[v] though it has a split hoof
completely divided, does not chew the
cud; it is unclean for you. 8You must not
eat their meat or touch their carcasses;
they are unclean for you.[w]
9" 'Of all the creatures living in the water of the seas and the streams, you may
eat any that have fins and scales. 10But all
creatures in the seas or streams that do
not have fins and scales — whether among
all the swarming things or among all the
other living creatures in the water — you
are to detest.[x] 11And since you are to detest
them, you must not eat their meat and you
must detest their carcasses.[y] 12Anything
living in the water that does not have fins
and scales is to be detestable to you.[z]
13" 'These are the birds you are to detest
and not eat because they are detestable:
the eagle, the vulture, the black vulture,
14the red kite, any kind[a] of black kite,
15any kind of raven,[b] 16the horned owl, the
screech owl, the gull, any kind of hawk,
17the little owl, the cormorant, the great
owl, 18the white owl,[c] the desert owl, the
osprey, 19the stork,[d] any kind[e] of heron,
the hoopoe and the bat.[b][f]
20" 'All flying insects that walk on all
fours are to be detestable to you.[g] 21There
are, however, some winged creatures that
walk on all fours that you may eat: those
that have jointed legs for hopping on the
ground. 22Of these you may eat any kind
of locust,[h] katydid, cricket or grasshopper.
23But all other winged creatures that have
four legs you are to detest.
24" 'You will make yourselves unclean
by these;[i] whoever touches their carcasses will be unclean till evening.[j] 25Whoever
picks up one of their carcasses must wash
his clothes,[k] and he will be unclean till
evening.[l]
26" 'Every animal that has a split hoof
not completely divided or that does not
chew the cud is unclean for you; whoever touches ⌊the carcass of⌋ any of them
will be unclean. 27Of all the animals that
walk on all fours, those that walk on
their paws are unclean for you; whoever
touches their carcasses will be unclean
till evening. 28Anyone who picks up their
carcasses must wash his clothes, and he
will be unclean till evening.[m] They are unclean for you.
29" 'Of the animals that move about on
the ground, these are unclean for you:[n]
the weasel, the rat,[o] any kind of great lizard, 30the gecko, the monitor lizard, the
wall lizard, the skink and the chameleon.
31Of all those that move along the ground,
these are unclean for you. Whoever touches them when they are dead will be unclean till evening. 32When one of them
dies and falls on something, that article,
whatever its use, will be unclean, whether
it is made of wood, cloth, hide or sackcloth.[p] Put it in water; it will be unclean
till evening, and then it will be clean. 33If
one of them falls into a clay pot, everything in it will be unclean, and you must
break the pot.[q] 34Any food that could be
eaten but has water on it from such a pot
is unclean, and any liquid that could be
drunk from it is unclean. 35Anything that
one of their carcasses falls on becomes
unclean; an oven or cooking pot must be

[a] 5 That is, the hyrax or rock badger [b] 19 The precise identification of some of the birds, insects and animals in this chapter is uncertain.

10:19 [s] Lev 9:12
11:2 [t] Ac 10:12-14
11:4 [u] Ac 10:14
11:7 [v] Isa 65:4; 66:3, 17
11:8 [w] S Lev 5:2; Heb 9:10
11:10 [x] ver 12
11:11 [y] S Lev 5:2
11:12 [z] ver 10
11:14 [a] S Ge 1:11
11:15 [b] S Ge 8:7
11:18 [c] Isa 13:21; 14:23; 34:11, 13; Zep 2:14
11:19 [d] Zec 5:9 [e] S Ge 1:11 [f] Isa 2:20
11:20 [g] Ac 10:14
11:22 [h] Mt 3:4; Mk 1:6
11:24 [i] S Lev 5:2 [j] ver 27-40; Lev 13:3; 14:46; 15:5; 22:6; Nu 19:7, 19
11:25 [k] ver 28; S Ex 19:10; Lev 13:6; 14:8, 47; 15:5; 16:26; Nu 8:7; 19:7 [l] Lev 13:34; Nu 19:8; 31:24
11:28 [m] Heb 9:10
11:29 [n] ver 41 [o] Isa 66:17
11:32 [p] Lev 15:12; Nu 19:18; 31:20
11:33 [q] S Lev 6:28

11:1—15:33 The distinction between clean and unclean (see note on 11:2).

11:2 *the ones you may eat.* Ch. 11 is closely paralleled in Dt 14:3–21 but is more extensive. The animals acceptable for human consumption were those that chewed the cud and had a split hoof (v. 3). Of marine life, only creatures with fins and scales were permissible (v. 9). Birds and insects are also covered in the instructions (vv. 13–23). Some distinction between clean and unclean food was as old as the time of Noah (see Ge 7:2 and note). The Hittites also had a system of clean and unclean animals. The main reason for the laws concerning clean and unclean food is the same as for other laws concerning the clean and unclean — to preserve the sanctity of Israel as God's holy people (see v. 44 and note). Some hold that certain animal life was considered unclean for health considerations, but it is difficult to substantiate this idea. Notably, as a broad generalization, animals and birds that hunted other animals and birds, or that ate carrion, were counted among the unclean. For the uncleanness of disease and bodily discharges see chs. 13–15.

11:6 *rabbit.* Although it does not technically "chew the cud," a rabbit's chewing-like movements caused it to be classified popularly with cud chewers.

11:20 *all fours.* Although insects have six legs, perhaps people in ancient times did not count as ordinary legs the two large hind legs used for jumping.

broken up. They are unclean, and you are
to regard them as unclean. 36A spring,
however, or a cistern for collecting water
remains clean, but anyone who touches
one of these carcasses is unclean. 37If a
carcass falls on any seeds that are to be
planted, they remain clean. 38But if water
has been put on the seed and a carcass
falls on it, it is unclean for you.

39" 'If an animal that you are allowed to
eat dies,[r] anyone who touches the carcass[s]
will be unclean till evening. 40Anyone who
eats some of the carcass[t] must wash his
clothes, and he will be unclean till evening.[u] Anyone who picks up the carcass
must wash his clothes, and he will be unclean till evening.

41" 'Every creature that moves about on
the ground is detestable; it is not to be eat-
en. 42You are not to eat any creature that
moves about on the ground, whether it
moves on its belly or walks on all fours or
on many feet; it is detestable. 43Do not defile yourselves by any of these creatures.[v]
Do not make yourselves unclean by means
of them or be made unclean by them. 44I
am the LORD your God;[w] consecrate yourselves[x] and be holy,[y] because I am holy.[z]
Do not make yourselves unclean by any
creature that moves about on the ground.[a]
45I am the LORD who brought you up out of
Egypt[b] to be your God;[c] therefore be holy,
because I am holy.[d]

46" 'These are the regulations concerning animals, birds, every living thing that
moves in the water and every creature
that moves about on the ground. 47You
must distinguish between the unclean
and the clean, between living creatures
that may be eaten and those that may not
be eaten.[e] ' "

Purification After Childbirth

12 The LORD said to Moses, 2"Say to the
Israelites: 'A woman who becomes
pregnant and gives birth to a son will be
ceremonially unclean for seven days, just
as she is unclean during her monthly period.[f] 3On the eighth day[g] the boy is to be
circumcised.[h] 4Then the woman must wait
thirty-three days to be purified from her
bleeding. She must not touch anything sacred or go to the sanctuary until the days
of her purification are over. 5If she gives
birth to a daughter, for two weeks the
woman will be unclean, as during her period. Then she must wait sixty-six days to
be purified from her bleeding.

6" 'When the days of her purification for
a son or daughter are over,[i] she is to bring
to the priest at the entrance to the Tent of
Meeting a year-old lamb[j] for a burnt offering and a young pigeon or a dove for a sin
offering.[k] 7He shall offer them before the
LORD to make atonement for her, and then
she will be ceremonially clean from her
flow of blood.

" 'These are the regulations for the
woman who gives birth to a boy or a girl.
8If she cannot afford a lamb, she is to
bring two doves or two young pigeons,[l]
one for a burnt offering and the other for
a sin offering.[m] In this way the priest will
make atonement for her, and she will be
clean.[n] ' "

Regulations About Infectious Skin Diseases

13 The LORD said to Moses and Aaron,
2"When anyone has a swelling[o] or a
rash or a bright spot[p] on his skin that may

11:39 [r] Lev 17:15; 22:8; Dt 14:21; Eze 4:14; 44:31 [s] ver 40; Lev 22:4; Nu 19:11 **11:40** [t] S ver 39 [u] ver 25; Lev 14:8; 17:15; 22:8; Eze 44:31; Heb 9:10 **11:43** [v] ver 44; Lev 20:25; 22:5 **11:44** [w] S Ex 6:2, 7; 20:2; Isa 43:3; 51:15; Eze 20:5 [x] S Ex 19:10; Lev 20:7; Nu 15:40; Jos 3:5; 7:13; 1Ch 15:12; 2Ch 29:5; 35:6 [y] S Ex 22:31; S Dt 14:2 [z] S Ex 31:13; Lev 19:2; 20:7; Jos 24:19; 1Sa 2:2; Job 6:10; Ps 99:3; Eph 1:4; 1Th 4:7; 1Pe 1:15, 16* [a] S ver 43 **11:45** [b] Lev 25:38, 55 [c] S Ge 17:7 [d] S Ex 19:6; 1Pe 1:16* **11:47** [e] Lev 10:10 **12:2** [f] Lev 15:19; 18:19; Isa 64:6; Eze 18:6; 22:10; 36:17 **12:3** [g] S Ex 22:30 [h] S Ge 17:10; S Lk 1:59 **12:6** [i] Lk 2:22 [j] Ex 29:38; Lev 23:12; Nu 6:12, 14; 7:15 [k] Lev 5:7 **12:8** [l] S Ge 15:9; Lev 14:22 [m] Lev 5:7; Lk 2:22-24* [n] S Lev 4:26 **13:2** [o] ver 10, 19, 28, 43 [p] ver 4, 38, 39; Lev 14:56

11:36 *cistern for collecting water.* The use of waterproof plaster for lining cisterns dug in the ground was an important factor in helping the Israelites to settle the dry areas of Canaan after the conquest (cf. 2Ch 26:10 and note).

11:41 *ground.* Verses 29–30 identify the animals that move about (or swarm) on the ground.

11:44 *be holy.* Quoted in 1Pe 1:16 (see note there; see also Introduction to Leviticus: Theological Themes). Holiness is the key theme of Leviticus, ringing like a refrain in various forms throughout the book (e.g., v. 45; 19:2; 20:7,26; 21:8,15; 22:9,16,32). The word "holy" appears more often in Leviticus than in any other book of the Bible. Israel was to be totally consecrated to God. Her holiness was to be expressed in every aspect of her life, to the extent that all of life had a certain ceremonial quality. Because of who God is and what he has done (v. 45), his people must dedicate themselves fully to him and praise him (see Ps 150:2 and note; cf. Mt 5:48; Ro 12:1; 1Co 1:2 and notes). *I am holy.* When God's holiness is spoken of in the Bible, reference is to (1) his incomparably awesome majesty (the mysterious, overwhelming presence of his infinite power, before which the whole creation trembles), and (2) his absolute moral virtue (a presence so infinitely pure that it unmasks and judges every moral flaw or fault). Sometimes one of these aspects is foregrounded, sometimes the other, but often both are evoked together (as in Isa 6:3–5).

11:45 *brought ... out of Egypt.* A refrain found 8 more times in Leviticus (19:36; 22:33; 23:43; 25:38,42,55; 26:13,45) and nearly 60 times in 18 other books of the OT.

11:46–47 A summary of ch. 11.

12:2 *unclean.* The uncleanness came from the bleeding (vv. 4–5,7), not from the birth. It is not clear why the period of uncleanness after the birth of a baby boy (40 days) was half the period for a girl (80 days). *monthly period.* See 15:19–24.

12:3 See notes on Ge 17:10,12.

12:6 *burnt offering.* See note on 1:3. *sin offering.* See notes on 4:3,5.

12:7 The last sentence in this verse is a summary of ch. 12.

12:8 An appendix prescribing alternative sacrifices for people who were poor. See 1:14–17 and note on 1:14; see also 5:7–10; 14:21–22; and especially Lk 2:24 (Mary's offering for Jesus).

13:1–46 This section deals with preliminary symptoms of skin diseases (vv. 1–8) and then with the symptoms of (1) raw flesh (vv. 9–17), (2) boils (vv. 18–23), (3) burns (vv. 24–28), (4) sores on the head or chin (vv. 29–37), (5) white spots (vv. 38–39) and (6) skin diseases on the head that cause baldness (vv. 40–44).

13:2 *infectious skin disease.* Occurs often in chs. 13–14; see also 22:4; Nu 5:2. Since it is unlikely that ancient people would have understood the concept of infectiousness, this render-

become an infectious skin disease,[a][q] he
must be brought to Aaron the priest[r] or
to one of his sons[b] who is a priest. 3The
priest is to examine the sore on his skin,
and if the hair in the sore has turned white
and the sore appears to be more than skin
deep,[c] it is an infectious skin disease.
When the priest examines him, he shall
pronounce him ceremonially unclean.[s] 4If
the spot[t] on his skin is white but does not
appear to be more than skin deep and the
hair in it has not turned white, the priest
is to put the infected person in isolation
for seven days.[u] 5On the seventh day[v]
the priest is to examine him,[w] and if he
sees that the sore is unchanged and has
not spread in the skin, he is to keep him
in isolation another seven days. 6On the
seventh day the priest is to examine him
again, and if the sore has faded and has
not spread in the skin, the priest shall pronounce him clean;[x] it is only a rash. The
man must wash his clothes,[y] and he will
be clean.[z] 7But if the rash does spread in
his skin after he has shown himself to the
priest to be pronounced clean, he must appear before the priest again.[a] 8The priest is
to examine him, and if the rash has spread
in the skin, he shall pronounce him unclean; it is an infectious disease.

9"When anyone has an infectious skin
disease, he must be brought to the priest.
10The priest is to examine him, and if there
is a white swelling in the skin that has
turned the hair white and if there is raw
flesh in the swelling, 11it is a chronic skin
disease[b] and the priest shall pronounce
him unclean. He is not to put him in isolation, because he is already unclean.

12"If the disease breaks out all over his
skin and, so far as the priest can see, it
covers all the skin of the infected person from head to foot, 13the priest is to
examine him, and if the disease has covered his whole body, he shall pronounce
that person clean. Since it has all turned
white, he is clean. 14But whenever raw
flesh appears on him, he will be unclean.
15When the priest sees the raw flesh, he
shall pronounce him unclean. The raw
flesh is unclean; he has an infectious disease.[c] 16Should the raw flesh change and
turn white, he must go to the priest. 17The
priest is to examine him, and if the sores
have turned white, the priest shall pronounce the infected person clean;[d] then
he will be clean.

18"When someone has a boil[e] on his
skin and it heals, 19and in the place where
the boil was, a white swelling or reddish-
white[f] spot[g] appears, he must present himself to the priest. 20The priest is to examine
it, and if it appears to be more than skin
deep and the hair in it has turned white,
the priest shall pronounce him unclean.
It is an infectious skin disease[h] that has
broken out where the boil was. 21But if,
when the priest examines it, there is no
white hair in it and it is not more than
skin deep and has faded, then the priest is
to put him in isolation for seven days. 22If
it is spreading in the skin, the priest shall
pronounce him unclean; it is infectious.
23But if the spot is unchanged and has not
spread, it is only a scar from the boil, and
the priest shall pronounce him clean.[i]

24"When someone has a burn on his
skin and a reddish-white or white spot appears in the raw flesh of the burn, 25the
priest is to examine the spot, and if the
hair in it has turned white, and it appears
to be more than skin deep, it is an infectious disease that has broken out in the
burn. The priest shall pronounce him
unclean; it is an infectious skin disease.[j]
26But if the priest examines it and there is
no white hair in the spot and if it is not
more than skin deep and has faded, then
the priest is to put him in isolation for sev-
en days.[k] 27On the seventh day the priest
is to examine him,[l] and if it is spreading
in the skin, the priest shall pronounce him
unclean; it is an infectious skin disease.
28If, however, the spot is unchanged and
has not spread in the skin but has faded, it
is a swelling from the burn, and the priest
shall pronounce him clean; it is only a scar
from the burn.[m]

29"If a man or woman has a sore on
the head[n] or on the chin, 30the priest is to
examine the sore, and if it appears to be
more than skin deep and the hair in it is
yellow and thin, the priest shall pronounce
that person unclean; it is an itch, an infectious disease of the head or chin. 31But
if, when the priest examines this kind of
sore, it does not seem to be more than skin
deep and there is no black hair in it, then
the priest is to put the infected person in
isolation for seven days.[o] 32On the seventh
day the priest is to examine the sore,[p] and

13:2 [q] ver 3,9, 15; S Ex 4:6; Lev 14:3,32; Nu 5:2; Dt 24:8 [r] Dt 24:8
13:3 [s] ver 8,11,20,30; Lev 21:1; Nu 9:6
13:4 [t] S ver 2 [u] ver 5,21,26, 33,46; Lev 14:38; Nu 12:14,15; Dt 24:9
13:5 [v] Lev 14:9 [w] ver 27,32, 34,51
13:6 [x] ver 13,17, 23,28,34; Mt 8:3; Lk 5:12-14 [y] S Lev 11:25 [z] Lev 11:25; 14:8,9,20,48; 15:8; Nu 8:7
13:7 [a] Lk 5:14
13:11 [b] S Ex 4:6; S Lev 14:8; S Nu 12:10; Mt 8:2
13:15 [c] S ver 2
13:17 [d] S ver 6
13:18 [e] S Ex 9:9
13:19 [f] ver 24, 42; Lev 14:37 [g] S ver 2
13:20 [h] ver 2
13:23 [i] S ver 6
13:25 [j] ver 11
13:26 [k] S ver 4
13:27 [l] S ver 5
13:28 [m] S ver 2
13:29 [n] ver 43,44
13:31 [o] ver 4
13:32 [p] S ver 5

[a] 2 Traditionally *leprosy*; the Hebrew word was used for various diseases affecting the skin — not necessarily leprosy; also elsewhere in this chapter.
[b] 2 Or *descendants* [c] 3 Or *be lower than the rest of the skin*; also elsewhere in this chapter

ing is questionable; the Hebrew should perhaps be translated "defiling skin disease." Such diseases show visible defects that could function aptly as a symbol for defilement — as could mildew (cf. vv. 47–59). *disease.* See NIV text note; see also 22:4–8; Nu 5:2–4; Dt 24:8–9. The symptoms described, and the fact that they may rapidly change (vv. 6,26–27,32–37), show that the disease was not true leprosy (Hansen's disease). They apply also to a number of other diseases, as well as to rather harmless skin eruptions. The Hebrew word translated "infectious skin disease" can also mean "mildew" (v. 47; 14:34; and especially 14:57).

if the itch has not spread and there is no yellow hair in it and it does not appear to be more than skin deep, 33he must be shaved except for the diseased area, and the priest is to keep him in isolation another seven days. 34On the seventh day the priest is to examine the itch,[q] and if it has not spread in the skin and appears to be no more than skin deep, the priest shall pronounce him clean. He must wash his clothes, and he will be clean.[r] 35But if the itch does spread in the skin after he is pronounced clean, 36the priest is to examine him, and if the itch has spread in the skin, the priest does not need to look for yellow hair; the person is unclean.[s] 37If, however, in his judgment it is unchanged and black hair has grown in it, the itch is healed. He is clean, and the priest shall pronounce him clean.

38"When a man or woman has white spots on the skin, 39the priest is to examine them, and if the spots are dull white, it is a harmless rash that has broken out on the skin; that person is clean.

40"When a man has lost his hair and is bald,[t] he is clean. 41If he has lost his hair from the front of his scalp and has a bald forehead, he is clean. 42But if he has a reddish-white sore on his bald head or forehead, it is an infectious disease breaking out on his head or forehead. 43The priest is to examine him, and if the swollen sore on his head or forehead is reddish-white like an infectious skin disease, 44the man is diseased and is unclean. The priest shall pronounce him unclean because of the sore on his head.

45"The person with such an infectious disease must wear torn clothes,[u] let his hair be unkempt,[a] cover the lower part of his face[v] and cry out, 'Unclean! Unclean!'[w] 46As long as he has the infection he remains unclean. He must live alone; he must live outside the camp.[x]

Regulations About Mildew

47"If any clothing is contaminated with mildew — any woolen or linen clothing, 48any woven or knitted material of linen or wool, any leather or anything made of leather — 49and if the contamination in the clothing, or leather, or woven or knitted material, or any leather article, is greenish or reddish, it is a spreading mildew and must be shown to the priest.[y] 50The priest is to examine the mildew[z] and isolate the affected article for seven days. 51On the seventh day he is to examine it,[a] and if the mildew has spread in the clothing, or the woven or knitted material, or the leather, whatever its use, it is a destructive mildew; the article is unclean.[b] 52He must burn up the clothing, or the woven or knitted material of wool or linen, or any leather article that has the contamination in it, because the mildew is destructive; the article must be burned up.[c]

53"But if, when the priest examines it, the mildew has not spread in the clothing, or the woven or knitted material, or the leather article, 54he shall order that the contaminated article be washed. Then he is to isolate it for another seven days. 55After the affected article has been washed, the priest is to examine it, and if the mildew has not changed its appearance, even though it has not spread, it is unclean. Burn it with fire, whether the mildew has affected one side or the other. 56If, when the priest examines it, the mildew has faded after the article has been washed, he is to tear the contaminated part out of the clothing, or the leather, or the woven or knitted material. 57But if it reappears in the clothing, or in the woven or knitted material, or in the leather article, it is spreading, and whatever has the mildew must be burned with fire. 58The clothing, or the woven or knitted material, or any leather article that has been washed and is rid of the mildew, must be washed again, and it will be clean."

59These are the regulations concerning contamination by mildew in woolen or linen clothing, woven or knitted material, or any leather article, for pronouncing them clean or unclean.

Cleansing From Infectious Skin Diseases

14 The LORD said to Moses, 2"These are the regulations for the diseased person at the time of his ceremonial cleansing, when he is brought to the priest:[d]

13:34 [q] S ver 5 [r] S Lev 11:25 **13:36** [s] ver 30 **13:40** [t] Lev 21:5; 2Ki 2:23; Isa 3:24; 15:2; 22:12; Eze 27:31; 29:18; Am 8:10; Mic 1:16 **13:45** [u] S Lev 10:6 [v] Eze 24:17,22; Mic 3:7 [w] S Lev 5:2; La 4:15; Lk 17:12 **13:46** [x] Nu 5:1-4; 12:14; 2Ki 7:3; 15:5 **13:49** [y] Mk 1:44 **13:50** [z] Eze 44:23 **13:51** [a] S ver 5 [b] Lev 14:44 **13:52** [c] ver 55,57 **14:2** [d] Lev 13:57; Dt 24:8; Mt 8:2-4; Mk 1:40-44; Lk 5:12-14; 17:14

[a] 45 Or *clothes, uncover his head*

13:45 – 46 The ceremonially unclean were excluded from the camp (the area around the tabernacle and courtyard), where the Israelites lived in tents. (Later, no unclean persons were allowed in the temple area.) Not only was God present in the tabernacle in a special way, but also in the camp (see Nu 5:3 and note; Dt 23:14). Therefore unclean people were not to be in the camp (see Nu 5:1 – 4; 12:14 – 15, Miriam; 31:19 – 24; see also Lev 10:4 – 5; Nu 15:35 – 36; 2Ki 7:3 – 4 and note on 7:3; 2Ch 26:21, Uzziah). As a result of their separation from God, they were to exhibit their grief by tearing their clothes, by having unkempt hair and by partially covering their faces (v. 45).

13:47 *mildew.* During Israel's rainy season (October through March), this was especially a problem along the coast and by the Sea of Galilee, where it is very humid.

13:54 *washed.* See vv. 34,55 – 56,58. The treatment of disorders commonly included washing.

13:59 A summary of ch. 13.

14:1 – 32 The ritual after the skin disease had been cured had three parts: (1) ritual for the first week (outside the camp, vv. 1 – 7), (2) ritual for the second week (inside the camp, vv. 8 – 20) and (3) special permission for the poor (vv. 21 – 32).

3The priest is to go outside the camp and examine him.[e] If the person has been healed of his infectious skin disease,[a][f] 4the priest shall order that two live clean birds and some cedar wood, scarlet yarn and hyssop[g] be brought for the one to be cleansed.[h] 5Then the priest shall order that one of the birds be killed over fresh water in a clay pot.[i] 6He is then to take the live bird and dip it, together with the cedar wood, the scarlet yarn and the hyssop, into the blood of the bird that was killed over the fresh water.[j] 7Seven times[k] he shall sprinkle[l] the one to be cleansed of the infectious disease and pronounce him clean. Then he is to release the live bird in the open fields.[m]

8"The person to be cleansed must wash his clothes,[n] shave off all his hair and bathe with water;[o] then he will be ceremonially clean.[p] After this he may come into the camp,[q] but he must stay outside his tent for seven days. 9On the seventh day[r] he must shave off all his hair;[s] he must shave his head, his beard, his eyebrows and the rest of his hair. He must wash his clothes and bathe himself with water, and he will be clean.[t]

10"On the eighth day[u] he must bring two male lambs and one ewe lamb[v] a year old, each without defect, along with three-tenths of an ephah[b][w] of fine flour mixed with oil for a grain offering,[x] and one log[c] of oil.[y] 11The priest who pronounces him clean shall present[z] both the one to be cleansed and his offerings before the LORD at the entrance to the Tent of Meeting.[a]

12"Then the priest is to take one of the male lambs and offer it as a guilt offering,[b] along with the log of oil; he shall wave them before the LORD as a wave offering.[c] 13He is to slaughter the lamb in the holy place[d] where the sin offering and the burnt offering are slaughtered. Like the sin offering, the guilt offering belongs to the priest;[e] it is most holy. 14The priest is to take some of the blood of the guilt offering and put it on the lobe of the right ear of the one to be cleansed, on the thumb of his right hand and on the big toe of his right foot.[f] 15The priest shall then take some of the log of oil, pour it in the palm of his own left hand,[g] 16dip his right forefinger into the oil in his palm, and with his finger sprinkle some of it before the LORD seven times.[h] 17The priest is to put some of the oil remaining in his palm on the lobe of the right ear of the one to be cleansed, on the thumb of his right hand and on the big toe of his right foot, on top of the blood of the guilt offering.[i] 18The rest of the oil in his palm the priest shall put on the head of the one to be cleansed[j] and make atonement for him before the LORD.

19"Then the priest is to sacrifice the sin offering and make atonement for the one to be cleansed from his uncleanness.[k] After that, the priest shall slaughter the burnt offering 20and offer it on the altar, together with the grain offering, and make atonement for him,[l] and he will be clean.[m]

21"If, however, he is poor[n] and cannot afford these,[o] he must take one male lamb as a guilt offering to be waved to make atonement for him, together with a tenth of an ephah[d] of fine flour mixed with oil for a grain offering, a log of oil, 22and two doves or two young pigeons,[p] which he can afford, one for a sin offering and the other for a burnt offering.[q]

23"On the eighth day he must bring them for his cleansing to the priest at the entrance to the Tent of Meeting,[r] before the LORD.[s] 24The priest is to take the lamb for the guilt offering,[t] together with the log of oil,[u] and wave them before the LORD as a wave offering.[v] 25He shall slaughter the lamb for the guilt offering and take some of its blood and put it on the lobe of the right ear of the one to be cleansed, on the thumb of his right hand and on the big toe of his right foot.[w] 26The priest is to pour some of the oil into the palm of his own left hand,[x] 27and with his right forefinger sprinkle some of the oil from his palm

14:3 [e]Lev 13:46 [f]S Lev 13:2
14:4 [g]S Ex 12:22 [h]ver 6,49,51,52; Nu 19:6; Ps 51:7
14:5 [i]ver 50
14:6 [j]S ver 4
14:7 [k]ver 51 [l]2Ki 5:10,14; Isa 52:15; Eze 36:25 [m]ver 53
14:8 [n]S Lev 11:25 [o]ver 9; S Ex 29:4; Lev 15:5; 17:15; 22:6; Nu 19:7,8 [p]ver 20 [q]S Lev 13:11; Nu 5:2,3; 12:14,15; 19:20; 31:24; 2Ch 26:21
14:9 [r]S Lev 13:5 [s]Nu 6:9; Dt 21:12 [t]S Lev 13:6
14:10 [u]Nu 6:10; Mt 8:4; Mk 1:44; Lk 5:14 [v]S Lev 4:32 [w]Nu 15:9; 28:20 [x]Lev 2:1 [y]ver 12,15,21,24
14:11 [z]Nu 6:16 [a]Nu 6:10
14:12 [b]S Lev 5:18 [c]S Ex 29:24
14:13 [d]S Ex 29:11 [e]Lev 6:24-30; S 7:7
14:14 [f]S Ex 29:20
14:15 [g]ver 26
14:16 [h]ver 27
14:17 [i]ver 28
14:18 [j]ver 31; Lev 15:15
14:19 [k]ver 31; S Lev 5:3; 15:15
14:20 [l]Lev 15:30 [m]ver 8
14:21 [n]S Lev 5:7 [o]ver 22,32
14:22 [p]S Lev 5:7 [q]Lev 15:30
14:23 [r]Lev 15:14,29 [s]S ver 10,11
14:24 [t]Nu 6:14 [u]S ver 10 [v]ver 12
14:25 [w]S Ex 29:20
14:26 [x]ver 15

[a] *3* Traditionally *leprosy*; the Hebrew word was used for various diseases affecting the skin—not necessarily leprosy; also elsewhere in this chapter. [b] *10* That is, probably about 6 quarts (about 6.5 liters) [c] *10* That is, probably about 2/3 pint (about 0.3 liter); also in verses 12, 15, 21 and 24 [d] *21* That is, probably about 2 quarts (about 2 liters)

14:4 *hyssop.* A plant used in ceremonial cleansing (see note on Ex 12:22).

14:5 *killed.* Diseases and disorders were a symbol of sin and rendered a person or object ceremonially unclean. The prescribed cleansing included sacrifice as well as washing (see note on 13:54).

14:6 *cedar ... yarn ... hyssop.* Also used for cleansing in vv. 51–52; Nu 19:6 (see note there).

14:7,16,51 *Seven times.* See note on 4:6.

14:7 *clean.* Perhaps the yarn and cedar stick were used as well as the hyssop plant to sprinkle the blood for cleansing (see Ps 51:7 and note). Further sacrifices are specified in vv. 10–31. *release the live bird.* Cf. 16:22; see note on 16:5.

14:8 The Levites were similarly cleansed (see Nu 8:7 and note).

14:10 *grain offering.* See note on 2:1.

14:12 *guilt offering.* See 5:14—6:7 and note on 5:15. *wave offering.* See note on 7:30–32.

14:13 *most holy.* See note on Ex 3:5.

14:14 See note on 8:14.

14:18–21,29,31 *atonement.* See notes on 16:20–22; 17:11; Ex 25:17; cf. note on Ro 3:25.

14:19 *sin offering.* See 4:1—5:13 and notes on 4:3,5. *burnt offering.* See note on 1:3.

14:20 *grain offering.* See note on 2:1.

seven times before the LORD. 28Some of the
oil in his palm he is to put on the same
places he put the blood of the guilt offering—on the lobe of the right ear of the
one to be cleansed, on the thumb of his
right hand and on the big toe of his right
foot. 29The rest of the oil in his palm the
priest shall put on the head of the one to
be cleansed, to make atonement for him
before the LORD.[y] 30Then he shall sacrifice
the doves or the young pigeons, which
the person can afford,[z] 31one[a] as a sin offering and the other as a burnt offering,[a]
together with the grain offering. In this
way the priest will make atonement before the LORD on behalf of the one to be
cleansed.[b]"
32These are the regulations for anyone
who has an infectious skin disease[c] and
who cannot afford the regular offerings[d]
for his cleansing.

Cleansing From Mildew

33The LORD said to Moses and Aaron,
34"When you enter the land of Canaan,[e]
which I am giving you as your possession,[f] and I put a spreading mildew in
a house in that land, 35the owner of the
house must go and tell the priest, 'I have
seen something that looks like mildew
in my house.' 36The priest is to order the
house to be emptied before he goes in to
examine the mildew, so that nothing in the
house will be pronounced unclean. After
this the priest is to go in and inspect the
house. 37He is to examine the mildew on
the walls, and if it has greenish or reddish[g]
depressions that appear to be deeper than
the surface of the wall, 38the priest shall go
out the doorway of the house and close it
up for seven days.[h] 39On the seventh day[i]
the priest shall return to inspect the house.
If the mildew has spread on the walls, 40he
is to order that the contaminated stones
be torn out and thrown into an unclean
place outside the town.[j] 41He must have all
the inside walls of the house scraped and
the material that is scraped off dumped
into an unclean place outside the town.
42Then they are to take other stones to replace these and take new clay and plaster
the house.
43"If the mildew reappears in the house
after the stones have been torn out and the
house scraped and plastered, 44the priest is
to go and examine it and, if the mildew
has spread in the house, it is a destructive
mildew; the house is unclean.[k] 45It must
be torn down—its stones, timbers and all
the plaster—and taken out of the town to
an unclean place.
46"Anyone who goes into the house
while it is closed up will be unclean till
evening.[l] 47Anyone who sleeps or eats in
the house must wash his clothes.[m]
48"But if the priest comes to examine it
and the mildew has not spread after the
house has been plastered, he shall pronounce the house clean,[n] because the mildew is gone. 49To purify the house he is
to take two birds and some cedar wood,
scarlet yarn and hyssop.[o] 50He shall kill
one of the birds over fresh water in a clay
pot.[p] 51Then he is to take the cedar wood,
the hyssop,[q] the scarlet yarn and the live
bird, dip them into the blood of the dead
bird and the fresh water, and sprinkle
the house seven times.[r] 52He shall purify the house with the bird's blood, the
fresh water, the live bird, the cedar wood,
the hyssop and the scarlet yarn. 53Then
he is to release the live bird in the open
fields[s] outside the town. In this way he
will make atonement for the house, and it
will be clean.[t]"
54These are the regulations for any infectious skin disease,[u] for an itch, 55for
mildew[v] in clothing or in a house, 56and
for a swelling, a rash or a bright spot,[w]
57to determine when something is clean
or unclean.
These are the regulations for infectious
skin diseases and mildew.[x]

Discharges Causing Uncleanness

15 The LORD said to Moses and Aaron,
2"Speak to the Israelites and say to
them: 'When any man has a bodily discharge,[y] the discharge is unclean. 3Wheth-
er it continues flowing from his body or is
blocked, it will make him unclean. This
is how his discharge will bring about uncleanness:
4" 'Any bed the man with a discharge
lies on will be unclean, and anything he
sits on will be unclean. 5Anyone who
touches his bed must wash his clothes[z]

[a] 31 Septuagint and Syriac; Hebrew *31such as the person can afford, one*

14:29 [y]ver 18
14:30 [z]S Lev 5:7
14:31 [a]ver 22; Lev 5:7; 15:15,30 [b]S ver 18,19
14:32 [c]S Lev 13:2 [d]S ver 21
14:34 [e]Ge 12:5; Ex 6:4; Nu 13:2 [f]Ge 17:8; 48:4; Nu 27:12; 32:22; Dt 3:27; 7:1; 32:49
14:37 [g]S Lev 13:19
14:38 [h]S Lev 13:4
14:39 [i]Lev 13:5
14:40 [j]ver 45
14:44 [k]Lev 13:51
14:46 [l]S Lev 11:24
14:47 [m]S Lev 11:25
14:48 [n]S Lev 13:6
14:49 [o]ver 4; 1Ki 4:33
14:50 [p]ver 5
14:51 [q]ver 6; Ps 51:7 [r]S ver 4,7
14:53 [s]S ver 7 [t]ver 20
14:54 [u]Lev 13:2
14:55 [v]Lev 13:47-52
14:56 [w]Lev 13:2
14:57 [x]S Lev 10:10
15:2 [y]ver 16,32; Lev 22:4; Nu 5:2; 2Sa 3:29; Mt 9:20
15:5 [z]S Lev 11:25

14:33–53 There are many similarities between this section and the previous one, particularly in the manner of restoration.

14:45 *torn down.* A house desecrated by mildew, mold or fungus would be a defiled place to live in, so drastic measures had to be taken.

14:54–57 A summary of chs. 13; 14.

15:1–33 The chapter deals with (1) male uncleanness caused by bodily discharge (vv. 2–15) or emission of semen (vv. 16–18); (2) female uncleanness caused by her monthly period (vv. 19–24) or lengthy hemorrhaging (vv. 25–30); (3) summary (vv. 31–33).

15:2 *bodily discharge.* Probably either diarrhea or urethral discharge (various kinds of infections). The contamination of anything under the man (v. 10), whether he sat (vv. 4,6,9) or lay (v. 4) on it, indicates that the bodily discharge had to do with the buttocks or genitals.

15:4 *bed.* Something like a mat (cf. 2Sa 11:13).

and bathe with water,[a] and he will be unclean till evening.[b] 6Whoever sits on anything that the man with a discharge sat on
must wash his clothes and bathe with water, and he will be unclean till evening.
7" 'Whoever touches the man[c] who has
a discharge[d] must wash his clothes and
bathe with water, and he will be unclean
till evening.
8" 'If the man with the discharge spits[e]
on someone who is clean, that person
must wash his clothes and bathe with water, and he will be unclean till evening.
9" 'Everything the man sits on when riding will be unclean, 10and whoever touches any of the things that were under him
will be unclean till evening; whoever picks
up those things[f] must wash his clothes
and bathe with water, and he will be unclean till evening.
11" 'Anyone the man with a discharge
touches without rinsing his hands with water must wash his clothes and bathe with
water, and he will be unclean till evening.
12" 'A clay pot[g] that the man touches
must be broken, and any wooden article[h]
is to be rinsed with water.
13" 'When a man is cleansed from his
discharge, he is to count off seven days[i] for
his ceremonial cleansing; he must wash his
clothes and bathe himself with fresh water, and he will be clean.[j] 14On the eighth
day he must take two doves or two young
pigeons[k] and come before the LORD to the
entrance to the Tent of Meeting and give
them to the priest. 15The priest is to sacrifice them, the one for a sin offering[l] and
the other for a burnt offering.[m] In this way
he will make atonement before the LORD
for the man because of his discharge.[n]
16" 'When a man has an emission of semen,[o] he must bathe his whole body with
water, and he will be unclean till evening.[p]
17Any clothing or leather that has semen
on it must be washed with water, and it
will be unclean till evening. 18When a man
lies with a woman and there is an emission of semen,[q] both must bathe with water, and they will be unclean till evening.
19" 'When a woman has her regular flow
of blood, the impurity of her monthly period[r] will last seven days, and anyone who
touches her will be unclean till evening.
20" 'Anything she lies on during her period will be unclean, and anything she sits
on will be unclean. 21Whoever touches her
bed must wash his clothes and bathe with
water, and he will be unclean till evening.[s]
22Whoever touches anything she sits on
must wash his clothes and bathe with water, and he will be unclean till evening.
23Whether it is the bed or anything she
was sitting on, when anyone touches it,
he will be unclean till evening.
24" 'If a man lies with her and her
monthly flow[t] touches him, he will be unclean for seven days; any bed he lies on
will be unclean.
25" 'When a woman has a discharge of
blood for many days at a time other than
her monthly period[u] or has a discharge
that continues beyond her period, she
will be unclean as long as she has the discharge, just as in the days of her period.
26Any bed she lies on while her discharge
continues will be unclean, as is her bed
during her monthly period, and anything
she sits on will be unclean, as during her
period. 27Whoever touches them will be
unclean; he must wash his clothes and
bathe with water, and he will be unclean
till evening.
28" 'When she is cleansed from her discharge, she must count off seven days, and
after that she will be ceremonially clean.
29On the eighth day she must take two
doves or two young pigeons[v] and bring
them to the priest at the entrance to the
Tent of Meeting. 30The priest is to sacrifice
one for a sin offering and the other for a
burnt offering. In this way he will make
atonement for her before the LORD for the
uncleanness of her discharge.[w]
31" 'You must keep the Israelites separate from things that make them unclean,
so they will not die in their uncleanness
for defiling my dwelling place,[a][x] which is
among them.' "
32These are the regulations for a man
with a discharge, for anyone made unclean

[a] 31 Or *my tabernacle*

15:5 [a] Lev 14:8 [b] S Lev 11:24 **15:7** [c] ver 19; Lev 22:5 [d] ver 16; Lev 22:4 **15:8** [e] Nu 12:14 **15:10** [f] Nu 19:10 **15:12** [g] S Lev 6:28 [h] S Lev 11:32 **15:13** [i] S Lev 8:33 [j] ver 5 **15:14** [k] Lev 14:22 **15:15** [l] Lev 5:7 [m] Lev 14:31 [n] S Lev 14:18, 19 **15:16** [o] S ver 2; Dt 23:10 [p] ver 5; Dt 23:11 **15:18** [q] 1Sa 21:4 **15:19** [r] S ver 24 **15:21** [s] ver 27 **15:24** [t] ver 19; Lev 12:2; 18:19; 20:18; Eze 18:6 **15:25** [u] Mt 9:20; Mk 5:25; Lk 8:43 **15:29** [v] Lev 14:22 **15:30** [w] Lev 5:10; 14:20, 31; 18:19; 2Sa 11:4; Mk 5:25; Lk 8:43 **15:31** [x] Lev 20:3; Nu 5:3; 19:13, 20; 2Sa 15:25; 2Ki 21:7; Ps 33:14; 74:7; 76:2; Eze 5:11; 23:38

15:13 *cleansed.* God brought about the healing; the priest could only ascertain that a person was already healed.

15:16 *semen.* Normal sexual activity and a woman's menstruation required no sacrifices but only washing and a minimal period of uncleanness.

15:19 *seven days.* See 12:2. This regulation is the background of 2Sa 11:4 (Bathsheba; see note there).

15:20 See note on Ge 31:35.

15:24 *flow.* During her period a woman was protected from sexual activity. No offering was required for uncleanness contracted by a man in this way, but the uncleanness lasted seven days.

15:25 *discharge of blood for many days.* As, e.g., the woman in Mk 5:25 (see note there). *beyond her period.* An unnatural discharge, possibly caused by disease, was treated like a sickness and required an offering upon recovery (vv. 28–30; see vv. 14–15).

15:31 Addressed to the priests, thus emphasizing the importance of the regulations. Since God dwelt in the tabernacle, any unholiness, symbolized by the discharges of ch. 15, could result in death if the people came into his presence. Sin separates all people from a holy God and results in their death, unless atonement is made (see the next chapter).

15:32–33 A summary of ch. 15.

by an emission of semen,[y] 33 for a woman in her monthly period, for a man or a woman with a discharge, and for a man who lies with a woman who is ceremonially unclean.[z]

The Day of Atonement

16:2-34pp — Lev 23:26-32; Nu 29:7-11

16 The LORD spoke to Moses after the death of the two sons of Aaron who died when they approached the LORD.[a] 2 The LORD said to Moses: "Tell your brother Aaron not to come whenever he chooses[b] into the Most Holy Place[c] behind the curtain[d] in front of the atonement cover[e] on the ark, or else he will die, because I appear[f] in the cloud[g] over the atonement cover.

3 "This is how Aaron is to enter the sanctuary area:[h] with a young bull[i] for a sin offering and a ram for a burnt offering.[j] 4 He is to put on the sacred linen tunic,[k] with linen undergarments next to his body; he is to tie the linen sash around him and put on the linen turban.[l] These are sacred garments;[m] so he must bathe himself with water[n] before he puts them on.[o] 5 From the Israelite community[p] he is to take two male goats[q] for a sin offering and a ram for a burnt offering.

6 "Aaron is to offer the bull for his own sin offering to make atonement for himself and his household.[r] 7 Then he is to take the two goats and present them before the LORD at the entrance to the Tent of Meeting. 8 He is to cast lots[s] for the two goats—one lot for the LORD and the other for the scapegoat.[a][t] 9 Aaron shall bring the goat whose lot falls to the LORD and sacrifice it for a sin offering. 10 But the goat chosen by lot as the scapegoat shall be presented alive before the LORD to be used for making atonement[u] by sending it into the desert as a scapegoat.

11 "Aaron shall bring the bull for his own sin offering to make atonement for himself and his household,[v] and he is to slaughter the bull for his own sin offering. 12 He is to take a censer full of burning coals[w] from the altar before the LORD and two handfuls of finely ground fragrant incense[x] and take them behind the curtain. 13 He is to put the incense on the fire before the LORD, and the smoke of the incense will conceal the atonement cover[y] above the Testimony, so that he will not die.[z] 14 He is to take

[a] *8* That is, the goat of removal; Hebrew *azazel*; also in verses 10 and 26

15:32 [y]S ver 2 **15:33** [z]ver 19,24,25 **16:1** [a]S Lev 10:1 **16:2** [b]Ex 30:10; Heb 9:7 [c]S Ex 26:33; Heb 9:25; 10:19 [d]S Ex 26:33; Heb 6:19 [e]S Ex 26:34 [f]S Ex 25:22 [g]S Ex 40:34; S 2Sa 22:10 **16:3** [h]ver 6; Lev 4:1-12; Heb 9:24,25 [i]S Lev 4:3 [j]ver 5 **16:4** [k]S Lev 8:13 [l]S Ex 28:39 [m]ver 32; S Ex 28:42; 29:29,30; Lev 21:10; Nu 20:26,28 [n]S Ex 29:4; Heb 10:22 [o]Eze 9:2; 44:17-18 **16:5** [p]S Lev 4:13-21 [q]ver 20; S Lev 4:3; 2Ch 29:23; Ps 50:9 **16:6** [r]Lev 9:7; Heb 7:27; 9:7,12 **16:8** [s]Nu 26:55,56; 33:54; 34:13; Jos 14:2; 18:6; Jdg 20:9; Ne 10:34; Est 3:7; 9:24; Ps 22:18; Pr 16:33 [t]ver 10,26 **16:10** [u]Isa 53:4-10; S Ro 3:25 **16:11** [v]S ver 6,24,33 **16:12** [w]S Lev 10:1; Rev 8:5 [x]S Ex 25:6; 30:34-38 **16:13** [y]S Ex 25:17 [z]S Ex 28:43

16:1–34 See 23:26–32 and note on 23:27; 25:9; Ex 30:10; Nu 29:7–11; Heb 9:7. The order of ritual for the Day of Atonement was as follows: (1) The high priest went to the basin in the courtyard, removed his regular garments, washed himself and went into the Holy Place to put on the special garments for the Day of Atonement (v. 4). (2) He went out to sacrifice a bull at the altar of burnt offering as a sin offering for himself and the other priests (v. 11). (3) He went into the Most Holy Place with some of the bull's blood, with incense and with coals from the altar of burnt offering (vv. 12–13). The incense was placed on the burning coals, and the smoke of the incense hid the ark from view. (4) He sprinkled some of the bull's blood on and in front of the atonement cover of the ark (v. 14). (5) He went outside the tabernacle and cast lots for two goats to see which was to be sacrificed and which was to be the scapegoat (vv. 7–8). (6) At the altar of burnt offering the high priest killed the goat for the sin offering for the people, and for a second time he went into the Most Holy Place, this time to sprinkle the goat's blood in front of and on the atonement cover (vv. 5,9,15–16a). (7) He returned to the Holy Place (called "Tent of Meeting" in v. 16) and sprinkled the goat's blood there (v. 16b). (8) He went outside to the altar of burnt offering and sprinkled it (vv. 18–19) with the blood of the bull (for himself, v. 11) and of the goat (for the people, v. 15). (9) While in the courtyard, he laid both hands on the second goat, thus symbolizing the transfer of Israel's sin, and sent it out into the desert (vv. 20–22). (10) The man who took the goat away, after he accomplished his task, washed himself and his clothes outside the camp (v. 26) before rejoining the people. (11) The high priest entered the Holy Place to remove his special garments (v. 23). (12) He went out to the basin to wash and put on his regular priestly clothes (v. 24). (13) As a final sacrifice he went out to the great altar and offered a ram (v. 3) as a burnt offering for himself, and another ram (v. 5) for the people (v. 24). (14) The conclusion of the entire day was the removal of the sacrifices for the sin offerings to a place outside the camp, where they were burned, and there the man who performed this ritual bathed and washed his clothes (vv. 27–28) before rejoining the people.

16:1 *sons of Aaron who died.* See 10:1–3.

16:2 *atonement cover.* See Ex 25:17 and note. Blood sprinkled on the lid of the ark made atonement for Israel on the Day of Atonement (vv. 15–17). In the Septuagint (the pre-Christian Greek translation of the OT) the word for "atonement cover" is the same one used of Christ and translated "sacrifice of atonement" in Ro 3:25 (see note there).

16:3 *sanctuary area.* The Most Holy Place (see v. 2). *bull.* For Aaron's cleansing (vv. 6,11). Before Aaron could minister in the Most Holy Place for the nation, he himself had to be cleansed (Heb 5:1–3); not so Christ, who is our high priest and whom Aaron's priesthood foreshadowed (see Heb 7:26–28 and notes).

16:5 *two male goats for a sin offering.* One was the usual sin offering (see notes on 4:3,5) and the other a scapegoat. No single offering could symbolically foreshadow the full significance of Christ's atonement. The one goat was killed, its blood sprinkled in the Most Holy Place and its body burned outside the camp (vv. 15,27), symbolizing the payment of the price of Christ's atonement. The other goat, sent away alive and bearing the sins of the nation (v. 21), symbolized the removal of sin and its guilt. *ram.* For the sins of the people; the one in v. 3 was for the sins of the high priest. Both were sacrificed at the end of the ceremony (v. 24).

16:6–10 An outline of vv. 11–22.

16:8 *scapegoat.* See NIV text note; the meaning of Hebrew *'azazel* is uncertain.

16:11 *make atonement for himself.* See note on v. 3.

16:13 *smoke of the incense.* Covered the ark so that the high priest would not see the glorious presence of God (v. 2) and thus die (see Ex 33:20). *Testimony.* See note on Ex 25:22.

16:14 *atonement cover.* See Ro 3:25 and note. *seven times.* See note on 4:6.

some of the bull's blood[a] and with his finger sprinkle it on the front of the atonement cover; then he shall sprinkle some
of it with his finger seven times before the
atonement cover.[b]
15"He shall then slaughter the goat for
the sin offering for the people[c] and take
its blood behind the curtain[d] and do with
it as he did with the bull's blood: He shall
sprinkle[e] it on the atonement cover and in
front of it. 16In this way he will make atonement[f] for the Most Holy Place[g] because of
the uncleanness and rebellion of the Israelites, whatever their sins have been. He
is to do the same for the Tent of Meeting,[h]
which is among them in the midst of their
uncleanness. 17No one is to be in the Tent
of Meeting from the time Aaron goes in to
make atonement in the Most Holy Place
until he comes out, having made atonement for himself, his household and the
whole community of Israel.
18"Then he shall come out to the altar[i]
that is before the LORD and make atonement for it. He shall take some of the
bull's blood and some of the goat's blood
and put it on all the horns of the altar.[j]
19He shall sprinkle some of the blood on
it with his finger seven times to cleanse it
and to consecrate it from the uncleanness
of the Israelites.[k]
20"When Aaron has finished making
atonement for the Most Holy Place, the
Tent of Meeting and the altar, he shall
bring forward the live goat.[l] 21He is to lay
both hands on the head of the live goat[m]
and confess[n] over it all the wickedness
and rebellion of the Israelites—all their
sins—and put them on the goat's head.
He shall send the goat away into the desert in the care of a man appointed for the
task. 22The goat will carry on itself all their
sins[o] to a solitary place; and the man shall
release it in the desert.
23"Then Aaron is to go into the Tent of
Meeting and take off the linen garments[p]
he put on before he entered the Most Holy
Place, and he is to leave them there.[q] 24He
shall bathe himself with water in a holy
place[r] and put on his regular garments.[s]
Then he shall come out and sacrifice the
burnt offering for himself and the burnt
offering for the people,[t] to make atonement for himself and for the people.[u] 25He
shall also burn the fat of the sin offering
on the altar.
26"The man who releases the goat as a
scapegoat[v] must wash his clothes[w] and
bathe himself with water;[x] afterward he
may come into the camp. 27The bull and
the goat for the sin offerings, whose blood
was brought into the Most Holy Place to
make atonement, must be taken outside
the camp;[y] their hides, flesh and offal are
to be burned up. 28The man who burns
them must wash his clothes and bathe
himself with water; afterward he may
come into the camp.[z]
29"This is to be a lasting ordinance[a]
for you: On the tenth day of the seventh
month[b] you must deny yourselves[a][c] and
not do any work[d]—whether native-born[e]
or an alien living among you— 30because
on this day atonement will be made[f] for
you, to cleanse you. Then, before the
LORD, you will be clean from all your sins.[g]
31It is a sabbath of rest, and you must deny
yourselves;[h] it is a lasting ordinance.[i] 32The
priest who is anointed and ordained[j] to
succeed his father as high priest is to make
atonement. He is to put on the sacred lin-
en garments[k] 33and make atonement for
the Most Holy Place, for the Tent of Meeting and the altar, and for the priests and
all the people of the community.[l]
34"This is to be a lasting ordinance[m] for
you: Atonement is to be made once a year[n]
for all the sins of the Israelites."
And it was done, as the LORD commanded Moses.

Eating Blood Forbidden

17 The LORD said to Moses, 2"Speak to
Aaron and his sons[o] and to all the Is-
raelites and say to them: 'This is what the
LORD has commanded: 3Any Israelite who

16:14 [a]S Lev 4:5; Heb 9:7,13,25 [b]S Lev 4:6 **16:15** [c]S Lev 4:13-21; Heb 7:27; 9:7,12; 13:11 [d]Heb 9:3 [e]S Lev 4:17; Nu 19:19; Isa 52:15; Eze 36:25 **16:16** [f]S Ex 29:36; S Ro 3:25 [g]S Ex 26:33; Heb 9:25 [h]Ex 29:4; S 40:2 **16:18** [i]S Lev 4:7 [j]S Lev 4:25 **16:19** [k]Eze 43:20 **16:20** [l]S ver 5 **16:21** [m]S Ex 29:10 [n]S Lev 5:5 **16:22** [o]S Ex 28:38; Isa 53:12 **16:23** [p]S Ex 28:42 [q]Eze 42:14 **16:24** [r]S Lev 6:16 [s]ver 3-5 [t]Lev 1:3 [u]S ver 11 **16:26** [v]S ver 8 [w]S Lev 11:25 [x]Lev 14:8 **16:27** [y]S Ex 29:14 **16:28** [z]Nu 19:8,10 **16:29** [a]S Ex 12:14 [b]Lev 25:9 [c]ver 31; Lev 23:27,32; Nu 29:7; Isa 58:3 [d]S Ex 31:15; S Lev 23:28 [e]Ex 12:19 **16:30** [f]S Ex 30:10 [g]Ps 51:2; Jer 33:8; Eze 36:33; Zec 13:1; Eph 5:26 **16:31** [h]Ezr 8:21; Isa 58:3,5; Da 10:12 [i]Ac 27:9 **16:32** [j]S Ex 30:30 [k]S ver 4; S Ex 28:2

[a] 29 Or *must fast*; also in verse 31

16:33 [l]S ver 11,16-18; Eze 45:18 **16:34** [m]S Ex 27:21 [n]Heb 9:7,25 **17:2** [o]Lev 10:6,12

16:16 *Tent of Meeting.* Here and in vv. 17,20,33 the term refers to the Holy Place.

16:20–22 A summary description of substitutionary atonement. The sin of the worshipers was confessed and symbolically transferred to the sacrificial animal, on which hands were laid (see notes on 1:3; Ex 29:10; see also Lev 1:4; 3:8; 4:4; cf. Isa 53:6 and note; Jn 1:29; 1Pe 2:24).

16:24 *holy place.* Cf. 6:16,26 and note on 6:16. *burnt offering … burnt offering.* The two rams mentioned in vv. 3,5.

16:25 *fat of the sin offering.* See 4:8–10.

16:27 *outside the camp.* See note on 4:12.

16:29,31 *deny yourselves.* See NIV text note; more lit. "humble (or afflict) yourselves." The expression came to be used of fasting (Ps 35:13). The Day of Atonement was the only regular fast day stipulated in the OT (see 23:27,29,32 and NIV text note), though tradition later added other fast days to the Jewish calendar (see Zec 7:5; 8:19; Lk 18:12 and notes).

16:29 *seventh month.* Tishri, the seventh month, begins with the Feast of Trumpets (see note on 23:24). The Day of Atonement follows on the 10th day, and on the 15th day the Feast of Tabernacles begins (see 23:23–36). See chart, pp. 178–179.

16:30 *clean from all your sins.* On the Day of Atonement the repentant Israelite was assured of sins forgiven.

16:34 *once a year.* Heb 9:11—10:14 repeatedly contrasts this with Christ's "once for all" sacrifice (see note on Heb 9:12).

17:1—26:46 Sometimes called the "Holiness Code," these

sacrifices an ox,[a] a lamb[p] or a goat[q] in the
camp or outside of it 4instead of bringing
it to the entrance to the Tent of Meeting[r]
to present it as an offering to the LORD in
front of the tabernacle of the LORD[s]—that
man shall be considered guilty of bloodshed; he has shed blood and must be cut
off from his people.[t] 5This is so the Israelites will bring to the LORD the sacrifices
they are now making in the open fields.
They must bring them to the priest, that
is, to the LORD, at the entrance to the Tent
of Meeting and sacrifice them as fellowship offerings.[b][u] 6The priest is to sprinkle
the blood against the altar[v] of the LORD[w]
at the entrance to the Tent of Meeting and
burn the fat as an aroma pleasing to the
LORD.[x] 7They must no longer offer any of
their sacrifices to the goat idols[c][y] to whom
they prostitute themselves.[z] This is to be
a lasting ordinance[a] for them and for the
generations to come.'[b]

8"Say to them: 'Any Israelite or any alien
living among them who offers a burnt offering or sacrifice 9and does not bring it
to the entrance to the Tent[c] of Meeting[d] to
sacrifice it to the LORD[e]—that man must
be cut off from his people.

10" 'Any Israelite or any alien living
among them who eats any blood—I will
set my face against that person who eats
blood[f] and will cut him off from his people. 11For the life of a creature is in the
blood,[g] and I have given it to you to make
atonement for yourselves on the altar; it is
the blood that makes atonement for one's
life.[h] 12Therefore I say to the Israelites,
"None of you may eat blood, nor may an
alien living among you eat blood."

13" 'Any Israelite or any alien living
among you who hunts any animal or bird
that may be eaten must drain out the blood
and cover it with earth,[i] 14because the life
of every creature is its blood. That is why
I have said to the Israelites, "You must not
eat the blood of any creature, because the
life of every creature is its blood; anyone
who eats it must be cut off."[j]

15" 'Anyone, whether native-born or
alien, who eats anything[k] found dead
or torn by wild animals[l] must wash his
clothes and bathe with water,[m] and he will
be ceremonially unclean till evening;[n] then
he will be clean. 16But if he does not wash
his clothes and bathe himself, he will be
held responsible.[o]' "

Unlawful Sexual Relations

18 The LORD said to Moses, 2"Speak to
the Israelites and say to them: 'I am
the LORD your God.[p] 3You must not do as
they do in Egypt, where you used to live,
and you must not do as they do in the land
of Canaan, where I am bringing you. Do
not follow their practices.[q] 4You must obey
my laws[r] and be careful to follow my decrees.[s] I am the LORD your God.[t] 5Keep my
decrees and laws,[u] for the man who obeys
them will live by them.[v] I am the LORD.

6" 'No one is to approach any close relative to have sexual relations. I am the
LORD.

7" 'Do not dishonor your father[w] by having sexual relations with your mother.[x]
She is your mother; do not have relations
with her.

[a] 3 The Hebrew word can include both male and female.
[b] 5 Traditionally *peace offerings* [c] 7 Or *demons*

17:3 [p]S Lev 3:7 [q]S Lev 7:23 **17:4** [r]ver 9; 1Ki 8:4; 2Ch 1:3 [s]Dt 12:5-21 [t]S Ge 17:14 **17:5** [u]S Lev 3:1; Eze 43:27 **17:6** [v]S Lev 4:18 [w]S Lev 3:2 [x]S Lev 1:9 **17:7** [y]S Ex 22:20 [z]S Ex 34:15; Jer 3:6,9; Eze 23:3; 1Co 10:20 [a]S Ex 12:14 [b]S Ge 9:12 **17:9** [c]S Lev 1:3 [d]S ver 4 [e]S Lev 3:7 **17:10** [f]S Ge 9:4 **17:11** [g]ver 14 [h]Heb 9:22 **17:13** [i]Lev 7:26; Eze 24:7; 33:25; Ac 15:20 **17:14** [j]S Ge 9:4 **17:15** [k]S Lev 7:24 [l]S Ex 22:31 [m]S Lev 14:8 [n]S Lev 11:40 **17:16** [o]S Lev 5:1 **18:2** [p]S Ge 17:7 **18:3** [q]ver 24-30; S Ex 23:24; Dt 18:9; 2Ki 16:3; 17:8; 1Ch 5:25 **18:4** [r]S Ge 26:5 [s]Dt 4:1; 1Ki 11:11; Jer 44:10,23; Eze 11:12 [t]ver 2 **18:5** [u]S Ge 26:5 [v]Dt 4:1; Ne 9:29; Isa 55:3; Eze 18:9; 20:11; Am 5:4-6; Mt 19:17; S Ro 10:5*; Gal 3:12* **18:7** [w]ver 8; Lev 20:11; Dt 27:20 [x]Eze 22:10

chapters deal with regulations for holy living and holy practices in various areas (see Introduction: Theological Themes; Outline; see also note on 11:44).

17:4 *tabernacle of the LORD.* The people, with few exceptions (e.g., Dt 12:15,20–21), were directed to sacrifice only at the central sanctuary (see Dt 12:5–6 and notes on 12:5,13). Sennacherib's representative referred to Hezekiah's requiring worship only in Jerusalem (2Ki 18:22). One reason for such a regulation was to keep the Israelites from becoming corrupted by the Canaanites' pagan worship. *cut off from his people.* See note on 7:20.

17:5 *to the priest, that is, to the LORD.* See note on 6:6.

17:7 *prostitute themselves.* See Ex 34:15 and note.

17:11 *the life of a creature is in the blood.* See note on Ge 9:4. The blood shed in the sacrifices was sacred. It epitomized the life of the sacrificial victim. Since life was sacred, blood (a symbol of life) had to be treated with respect (see Ge 9:5–6 and notes). Eating blood was therefore strictly forbidden (see 7:26–27; Dt 12:16,23–25; 15:23; 1Sa 14:32–34). *blood ... makes atonement.* Practically every sacrifice included the sprinkling or smearing of blood on the altar or within the tabernacle (v. 6; 1:5; 3:2; 4:6,25; 7:2), thus teaching that atonement involves the substitution of life for life. The blood of the OT sacrifice pointed forward to the blood of the Lamb of God, who obtained for his people "eternal redemption" (Heb 9:12). "Without the shedding of blood there is no forgiveness" (Heb 9:22).

17:15 *found dead or torn.* Such animals would not have had the blood drained from them and therefore would be forbidden.

18:1—20:27 Here God's people are given instructions concerning interpersonal relations and a morality reflecting God's holiness. Israel was thereby prepared for a life different from the Canaanites, whose lifestyle was deplorably immoral. Ch. 18 marks the boundaries for marriage and sexual relations (but see also v. 21 and note), ch. 19 provides specific moral guidance on a variety of matters, many of which are implicitly covered by the Ten Commandments, and ch. 20 specifies the penalties for violating God's standard of morality. See chart, p. 268.

18:2 In chs. 18–26 the phrase "I am the LORD" occurs 47 times. The Lord's name (i.e., his revealed character as Yahweh, "the LORD") is the authority that stands behind his instructions. See note on Ex 3:15.

18:3 Six times in this chapter Israel is warned not to follow the example of pagans (here, two times; see also vv. 24,26–27,30).

18:5 *live.* With God's full blessing. The law was the way of life for the redeemed (see Dt 6:2; 8:2–3; 30:20 and notes; 32:47; Eze 20:11,13,21), not a way of salvation for the lost (see Ro 10:5 and note; Gal 3:12).

18:6 A summary of the laws against incest (vv. 7–18). Penalties for incestuous relations are given in ch. 20. (Cf. 1Co 5.)

18:7 This prohibition applied also after the father's death.

8 “ ‘Do not have sexual relations with
your father’s wife;[y] that would dishonor
your father.[z]
9 “ ‘Do not have sexual relations with
your sister,[a] either your father’s daughter or your mother’s daughter, whether
she was born in the same home or elsewhere.[b]
10 “ ‘Do not have sexual relations with
your son’s daughter or your daughter’s
daughter; that would dishonor you.
11 “ ‘Do not have sexual relations with
the daughter of your father’s wife, born to
your father; she is your sister.
12 “ ‘Do not have sexual relations with
your father’s sister;[c] she is your father’s
close relative.
13 “ ‘Do not have sexual relations with
your mother’s sister,[d] because she is your
mother’s close relative.
14 “ ‘Do not dishonor your father’s brother by approaching his wife to have sexual
relations; she is your aunt.[e]
15 “ ‘Do not have sexual relations with
your daughter-in-law.[f] She is your son’s
wife; do not have relations with her.[g]
16 “ ‘Do not have sexual relations with
your brother’s wife;[h] that would dishonor
your brother.
17 “ ‘Do not have sexual relations with
both a woman and her daughter.[i] Do not
have sexual relations with either her son’s
daughter or her daughter’s daughter; they
are her close relatives. That is wickedness.
18 “ ‘Do not take your wife’s sister[j] as a
rival wife and have sexual relations with
her while your wife is living.
19 “ ‘Do not approach a woman to have
sexual relations during the uncleanness[k]
of her monthly period.[l]
20 “ ‘Do not have sexual relations with
your neighbor’s wife[m] and defile yourself
with her.
21 “ ‘Do not give any of your children[n] to
be sacrificed[a] to Molech,[o] for you must
not profane the name of your God.[p] I am
the LORD.[q]
22 “ ‘Do not lie with a man as one lies
with a woman;[r] that is detestable.[s]
23 “ ‘Do not have sexual relations with an
animal and defile yourself with it. A woman must not present herself to an animal
to have sexual relations with it; that is a
perversion.[t]
24 “ ‘Do not defile yourselves in any of
these ways, because this is how the nations that I am going to drive out before
you[u] became defiled.[v] 25 Even the land was
defiled;[w] so I punished it for its sin,[x] and
the land vomited out its inhabitants.[y] 26 But
you must keep my decrees and my laws.[z]
The native-born and the aliens living
among you must not do any of these detestable things, 27 for all these things were
done by the people who lived in the land
before you, and the land became defiled.
28 And if you defile the land,[a] it will vomit
you out[b] as it vomited out the nations that
were before you.
29 “ ‘Everyone who does any of these detestable things—such persons must be
cut off from their people. 30 Keep my requirements[c] and do not follow any of the
detestable customs that were practiced before you came and do not defile yourselves
with them. I am the LORD your God.[d]’ ”

Various Laws

19 The LORD said to Moses, 2 “Speak to
the entire assembly of Israel[e] and say
to them: ‘Be holy because I, the LORD your
God,[f] am holy.[g]

[a] 21 Or *to be passed through ⌞the fire⌟*

18:8 [y] 1Co 5:1 [z] Ge 35:22; Lev 20:11; Dt 22:30; 27:20 **18:9** [a] ver 11; Lev 20:17; Dt 27:22 [b] Lev 20:17; Dt 27:22; 2Sa 13:13; Eze 22:11 **18:12** [c] ver 13; Lev 20:19 **18:13** [d] S ver 12,14; Lev 20:20 **18:14** [e] S ver 13 **18:15** [f] S Ge 11:31; S 38:16 [g] Eze 22:11 **18:16** [h] Lev 20:21; Mt 14:4; Mk 6:18 **18:17** [i] Lev 20:14; Dt 27:23 **18:18** [j] S Ge 30:1 **18:19** [k] S Lev 15:25-30 [l] S Lev 15:24 **18:20** [m] S Ex 20:14; Mt 5:27,28; 1Co 6:9; Heb 13:4 **18:21** [n] Dt 12:31; 18:10; 2Ki 16:3; 17:17; 21:6; 23:10; 2Ch 28:1-4; 33:6; Ps 106:37,38; Isa 57:5; Jer 7:30,31; 19:5; 32:35; Eze 16:20; Mic 6:7 [o] Lev 20:2-5; Dt 9:4; 1Ki 11:5,7,33; Isa 57:9; Jer 32:35; 49:1; Zep 1:5 [p] Lev 19:12; 21:6; Isa 48:11; Eze 22:26; 36:20; Am 2:7; Mal 1:12 [q] S Ex 6:2 **18:22** [r] Lev 20:13; Dt 23:18; Ro 1:27; 1Co 6:9 [s] S Ge 19:5 **18:23** [t] Ex 22:19; Lev 20:15; Dt 27:21 **18:24** [u] ver 3,27,30; Lev 20:23 [v] Dt 9:4; 18:12 **18:25** [w] Nu 35:34; Dt 21:23 [x] Lev 20:23; Dt 9:5; 12:31; 18:12 [y] ver 28; Lev 20:22; Job 20:15; Jer 51:34 **18:26** [z] S Ge 26:5 **18:28** [a] Lev 20:22; Ezr 9:11; La 1:17 [b] S ver 25 **18:30** [c] S Lev 8:35 [d] ver 2 **19:2** [e] Nu 14:5; Ps 68:26 [f] S Ex 20:2 [g] S Ex 15:11; 1Pe 1:16*; S Lev 11:44; S 20:26

18:8 *your father’s wife.* Other than your mother—assuming there is more than one wife.
18:11 *sister.* There would be many half-sisters in a polygamous society. Tamar claimed that an exception to this prohibition could be made (2Sa 13:12–13; but see notes there).
18:14 *your aunt.* See 20:20. If the father’s brother was alive, the act would be adulterous. If he was dead, one could rationalize such a marriage because the aunt was not a blood relative—but it was forbidden.
18:15 Cf. the account of Judah and Tamar (Ge 38:18).
18:16 *your brother’s wife.* The law also applied to a time after divorce or the brother’s death. To marry one’s brother’s widow was not immoral but might damage the brother’s inheritance (cf. Ru 4:6 and note). The levirate law of Dt 25:5–6 (see note there) offered an exception that preserved the dead brother’s inheritance and continued his line.
18:17 *daughter.* Stepdaughter (granddaughter-in-law is also covered in the verse). The law applied even after the mother’s death.
18:18 Cf. the account of Jacob with Leah and Rachel (Ge 29:23–30).
18:19 See Eze 18:6 and note; 22:10.
18:20 See note on Ex 20:14.
18:21 *Molech.* The god of the Ammonites (see 20:2–5; 1Ki 11:5 and note). The detestable practice of sacrificing children to Molech was common in Phoenicia and other surrounding countries. Cf. 2Ki 3:26–27 and note on 3:27. King Manasseh evidently sacrificed his sons to Molech (2Ch 33:6; see 2Ki 23:10). Jer 32:35 protests the practice (see note on Jer 7:31). *profane the name of your God.* Whatever blatantly violates God’s revealed will desecrates his name (see note on Ps 5:11) because it fails to honor his holiness (see note on Lev 11:44).
18:22 *lie with a man.* See 20:13, where the penalty for homosexual acts is death.
18:29 *detestable.* See note on 7:21. *cut off from their people.* See note on 7:20.
19:1 See note on 18:1—20:27.
19:2 *Be holy.* See note on 11:44.

[3]“ ‘Each of you must respect his mother and father,[h] and you must observe my
Sabbaths.[i] I am the LORD your God.[j]
[4]“ ‘Do not turn to idols or make gods of
cast metal for yourselves.[k] I am the LORD
your God.[l]
[5]“ ‘When you sacrifice a fellowship offering[a] to the LORD, sacrifice it in such a way
that it will be accepted on your behalf. [6]It
shall be eaten on the day you sacrifice it
or on the next day; anything left over until
the third day must be burned up.[m] [7]If any
of it is eaten on the third day, it is impure
and will not be accepted.[n] [8]Whoever eats
it will be held responsible[o] because he has
desecrated what is holy[p] to the LORD; that
person must be cut off from his people.[q]
[9]“ ‘When you reap the harvest of your
land, do not reap to the very edges[r] of
your field or gather the gleanings of your
harvest.[s] [10]Do not go over your vineyard
a second time[t] or pick up the grapes that
have fallen.[u] Leave them for the poor and
the alien.[v] I am the LORD your God.
[11]“ ‘Do not steal.[w]
“ ‘Do not lie.[x]
“ ‘Do not deceive one another.[y]
[12]“ ‘Do not swear falsely[z] by my name[a]
and so profane[b] the name of your God. I
am the LORD.
[13]“ ‘Do not defraud your neighbor[c] or
rob[d] him.[e]
“ ‘Do not hold back the wages of a hired
man[f] overnight.[g]
[14]“ ‘Do not curse the deaf or put a stumbling block in front of the blind,[h] but fear
your God.[i] I am the LORD.
[15]“ ‘Do not pervert justice;[j] do not show
partiality[k] to the poor or favoritism to the
great,[l] but judge your neighbor fairly.[m]
[16]“ ‘Do not go about spreading slander[n]
among your people.
“ ‘Do not do anything that endangers
your neighbor’s life.[o] I am the LORD.
[17]“ ‘Do not hate your brother in your
heart.[p] Rebuke your neighbor frankly[q] so
you will not share in his guilt.

19:3 [h]Ex 20:12 [i]S Ex 20:8 [j]Lev 11:44 **19:4** [k]S Ex 20:4; Jdg 17:3; Ps 96:5; 115:4-7; 135:15 [l]Lev 11:44 **19:6** [m]Lev 7:16-17 **19:7** [n]Lev 7:18 **19:8** [o]S Lev 5:1 [p]Lev 22:2, 15, 16; Nu 18:32 [q]S Ge 17:14 **19:9** [r]Ru 2:2, 3, 7, 16, 17 [s]Lev 23:10, 22; Dt 24:19-22; Job 24:10 **19:10** [t]Dt 24:20 [u]ver 9 [v]Dt 24:19, 21 **19:11** [w]Ex 20:15; S 23:4; Lk 3:14 [x]S Ex 20:16; S Eph 4:25 [y]S Lev 6:2 **19:12** [z]Jer 5:2; 7:9; Mal 3:5 [a]Ex 3:13; 20:7; Dt 18:19; Pr 18:10; Isa 42:8; Jer 44:16, 26; S Mt 5:33 [b]Jer 34:16 **19:13** [c]Lev 25:14, 17 [d]S Ex 20:15 [e]S Ex 22:15, 25-27 [f]Job 7:2; 24:12; 31:39; Isa 16:14; Mal 3:5 [g]Dt 24:15; Jer 22:13; Mt 20:8; 1Ti 5:18; Jas 5:4 **19:14** [h]S Ex 4:11; Lev 21:18; Dt 27:18 [i]ver 32; Lev 25:17, 36 **19:15** [j]S Ex 23:2; Ex 23:2, 6 [k]Dt 24:17; Job 13:8, 10; 32:21; Pr 28:21 [l]Job 34:19 [m]S Ex 23:8; Pr 24:23; Mal 2:9; Jas 2:1-4 **19:16** [n]Ps 15:3; 31:13; 41:6; 101:5; Jer 6:28; 9:4; Eze 22:9 [o]Ex 23:7; Dt 10:17; 27:25; Ps 15:5;

[18]“ ‘Do not seek revenge[r] or bear a grudge[s]
against one of your people,[t] but love your
neighbor[u] as yourself.[v] I am the LORD.
[19]“ ‘Keep my decrees.[w]
“ ‘Do not mate different kinds of animals.
“ ‘Do not plant your field with two kinds
of seed.[x]
“ ‘Do not wear clothing woven of two
kinds of material.[y]
[20]“ ‘If a man sleeps with a woman who is
a slave girl promised to another man[z] but
who has not been ransomed or given her
freedom, there must be due punishment.
Yet they are not to be put to death, because she had not been freed. [21]The man,
however, must bring a ram to the entrance
to the Tent of Meeting for a guilt offering
to the LORD.[a] [22]With the ram of the guilt
offering the priest is to make atonement
for him before the LORD for the sin he has
committed, and his sin will be forgiven.[b]
[23]“ ‘When you enter the land and plant
any kind of fruit tree, regard its fruit as forbidden.[b] For three years you are to consider it forbidden[b]; it must not be eaten. [24]In
the fourth year all its fruit will be holy,[c] an
offering of praise to the LORD. [25]But in the
fifth year you may eat its fruit. In this way
your harvest will be increased. I am the
LORD your God.
[26]“ ‘Do not eat any meat with the blood
still in it.[d]
“ ‘Do not practice divination[e] or sorcery.[f]
[27]“ ‘Do not cut the hair at the sides of
your head or clip off the edges of your
beard.[g]
[28]“ ‘Do not cut[h] your bodies for the dead

[a] 5 Traditionally *peace offering* [b] 23 Hebrew *uncircumcised*

Eze 22:12 **19:17** [p]S 1Jn 2:9 [q]S Mt 18:15 **19:18** [r]S Ge 4:23; Ro 12:19; Heb 10:30 [s]Ps 103:9 [t]S Ex 12:48 [u]S Ex 20:16 [v]ver 34; S Mt 5:43*; 19:16*; 22:39*; Mk 12:31*; Lk 10:27*; Jn 13:34; Ro 13:9*; Gal 5:14*; Jas 2:8* **19:19** [w]S Ge 26:5 [x]Dt 22:9 [y]Dt 22:11 **19:20** [z]Dt 22:23-27 **19:21** [a]S Lev 5:15 **19:22** [b]S Lev 5:15 **19:24** [c]S Ex 22:29 **19:26** [d]S Ge 9:4 [e]S Ge 30:27; S Isa 44:25 [f]S Ex 22:18; 2Ki 17:17 **19:27** [g]Lev 21:5; Dt 14:1; 2Sa 10:4-5; Jer 41:5; 48:37; Eze 5:1-5 **19:28** [h]Lev 21:5; Dt 14:1; 1Ki 18:28; Jer 16:6; 41:5; 47:5

19:3–4 See v. 30; see also Ex 20:4–6,8–12 and notes; and see chart, p. 268.
19:5 *fellowship offering.* See note on 3:1.
19:6 *third day.* See note on 7:15–18.
19:8 *what is holy to the LORD.* See note on Ex 3:5. *cut off from his people.* See note on 7:20.
19:9–10 See 23:22; see also Dt 24:19–21. Ru 2 gives an example of the application of the law of gleaning.
19:11–12 See Ex 20:7,15–16 and notes.
19:13 *wages of a hired man.* See Dt 24:14–15; Mt 20:8 and note.
19:17 *Do not hate your brother.* Cf. 1Jn 2:9,11; 3:15; 4:20.
19:18 *love your neighbor as yourself.* Quoted by Jesus (see Mk 12:31 and note; Lk 10:27), Paul (see Ro 13:9; Gal 5:14 and notes) and James (see Jas 2:8 and note). The stricter Pharisees (school of Shammai) added to this command what they thought it implied: “Hate your enemy” (Mt 5:43; see note there). Jesus’ reaction, “Love your enemies,” was in line with true OT teaching (see vv. 17,34) and was more in agreement with the middle-of-the-road Pharisees. Rabbi Nahmanides (13th century) caught their sentiments: “One should place no limitations upon the love for the neighbor, but instead a person should love to do an abundance of good for his fellow being as he does for himself.” “Neighbor” does not merely mean one who lives nearby, but anyone with whom one comes in contact (see Lk 10:25–36 and notes).
19:19 *Do not mate ... plant ... wear.* Such mixing symbolically violated the distinction God established in the creation order.
19:21–22 *guilt offering.* See 5:14—6:7 and note on 5:15.
19:26 *meat with the blood.* See note on 17:11. *sorcery.* See v. 31; Ex 22:18 and note; Dt 18:10,14; 1Sa 28:9 and note; Isa 47:12–14.
19:27 *Do not cut the hair at the sides of your head.* A prohibition still followed by orthodox Jews.
19:28 There was to be no disfiguring of the body, after the manner of the pagans (see note on 21:5).

or put tattoo marks on yourselves. I am the LORD.

[29]" 'Do not degrade your daughter by making her a prostitute,[i] or the land will turn to prostitution and be filled with wickedness.[j]

[30]" 'Observe my Sabbaths[k] and have reverence for my sanctuary. I am the LORD.[l]

[31]" 'Do not turn to mediums[m] or seek out spiritists,[n] for you will be defiled by them. I am the LORD your God.

[32]" 'Rise in the presence of the aged, show respect[o] for the elderly[p] and revere your God.[q] I am the LORD.[r]

[33]" 'When an alien lives with you in your land, do not mistreat him. [34]The alien living with you must be treated as one of your native-born.[s] Love him as yourself,[t] for you were aliens[u] in Egypt.[v] I am the LORD your God.

[35]" 'Do not use dishonest standards when measuring length, weight or quantity.[w] [36]Use honest scales[x] and honest weights, an honest ephah[a][y] and an honest hin.[b][z] I am the LORD your God, who brought you out of Egypt.[a]

[37]" 'Keep all my decrees[b] and all my laws[c] and follow them. I am the LORD.' "

Punishments for Sin

20 The LORD said to Moses, [2]"Say to the Israelites: 'Any Israelite or any alien living in Israel who gives[c] any of his children to Molech must be put to death.[d] The people of the community are to stone him.[e] [3]I will set my face against that man and I will cut him off from his people;[f] for by giving his children to Molech, he has defiled[g] my sanctuary[h] and profaned my holy name.[i] [4]If the people of the community close their eyes when that man gives one of his children to Molech and they fail to put him to death,[j] [5]I will set my face against that man and his family and will cut off from their people both him and all who follow him in prostituting themselves to Molech.

[6]" 'I will set my face against the person who turns to mediums and spiritists to prostitute himself by following them, and I will cut him off from his people.[k]

[7]" 'Consecrate yourselves[l] and be holy,[m] because I am the LORD your God.[n] [8]Keep my decrees[o] and follow them. I am the LORD, who makes you holy.[d][p]

[9]" 'If anyone curses his father[q] or mother,[r] he must be put to death.[s] He has cursed his father or his mother, and his blood will be on his own head.[t]

[10]" 'If a man commits adultery with another man's wife[u]—with the wife of his neighbor—both the adulterer and the adulteress must be put to death.[v]

[11]" 'If a man sleeps with his father's wife, he has dishonored his father.[w] Both the man and the woman must be put to death; their blood will be on their own heads.[x]

[12]" 'If a man sleeps with his daughter-in-law,[y] both of them must be put to death. What they have done is a perversion; their blood will be on their own heads.

[13]" 'If a man lies with a man as one lies with a woman, both of them have done what is detestable.[z] They must be put to death; their blood will be on their own heads.

[14]" 'If a man marries both a woman and her mother,[a] it is wicked. Both he and they must be burned in the fire,[b] so that no wickedness will be among you.[c]

[15]" 'If a man has sexual relations with an animal,[d] he must be put to death,[e] and you must kill the animal.

[16]" 'If a woman approaches an animal to have sexual relations with it, kill both the woman and the animal. They must be put to death; their blood will be on their own heads.

[a] 36 An ephah was a dry measure. [b] 36 A hin was a liquid measure. [c] 2 Or *sacrifices*; also in verses 3 and 4 [d] 8 Or *who sanctifies you*; or *who sets you apart as holy*

19:29 [i]Lev 21:9; Dt 23:18 [j]Ge 34:7; Lev 21:9 **19:30** [k]S Ex 20:8 [l]Lev 26:2 **19:31** [m]S Ex 22:18; 1Sa 28:7-20; 1Ch 10:13 [n]Lev 20:6; 2Ki 21:6; 23:24; Isa 8:19; 19:3; 29:4; 47:12; 65:4 **19:32** [o]1Ki 12:8 [p]Job 32:4; Pr 23:22; La 5:12; 1Ti 5:1 [q]S ver 14; Job 29:8 [r]Lev 11:44; 25:17 **19:34** [s]S Ex 12:48 [t]S ver 18 [u]S Ex 22:21 [v]Ex 23:9; Dt 10:19; 23:7; Ps 146:9 **19:35** [w]Dt 25:13-16 **19:36** [x]Job 31:6; Pr 11:1; Hos 12:7; Mic 6:11 [y]Jdg 6:19; Ru 2:17; 1Sa 1:24; 17:17; Eze 45:10 [z]Dt 25:13-15; Pr 20:10; Eze 45:11 [a]S Ex 12:17 **19:37** [b]2Ki 17:37; 2Ch 7:17; Ps 119:5; Eze 18:9 [c]S Ge 26:5 **20:2** [d]ver 10; Ge 26:11; Ex 19:12 [e]ver 27; Lev 24:14; Nu 15:35,36; Dt 21:21; Jos 7:25 **20:3** [f]ver 5,6; Lev 23:30 [g]Ps 74:7; 79:1; Jer 7:30; Eze 5:11 [h]S Lev 15:31 [i]S Lev 18:21 **20:4** [j]Dt 17:2-5 **20:6** [k]S ver 3; S Lev 19:31 **20:7** [l]S Lev 11:44 [m]S Ex 29:1; 31:13; Lev 11:45; Eph 1:4; 1Pe 1:16* [n]S Ex 6:2; S 20:2 **20:8** [o]S Ge 26:5 [p]S Ex 31:13; Eze 20:12 **20:9** [q]Ex 20:12; Jer 35:16; Mal 1:6; 2:10 [r]S Ex 20:12; Dt 27:16; Eze 22:7 [s]Ex 21:17; Dt 21:20-21; Mt 15:4*; Mk 7:10* [t]ver 11; Dt 22:30; Jos 2:19; 2Sa 1:16; 3:29; 1Ki 2:37; Eze 18:13; 33:4,5 **20:10** [u]Ex 20:14; Dt 5:18; 22:22; Jn 8:5 [v]S Ge 38:24; S Ex 21:12 **20:11** [w]S Lev 18:7 [x]S ver 9; S Lev 18:8 **20:12** [y]S Ge 11:31; S 38:16 **20:13** [z]Lev 18:22 **20:14** [a]S Lev 18:17 [b]Lev 21:9; Nu 16:39; Jdg 14:15; 15:6 [c]S Lev 18:8; Dt 27:23 **20:15** [d]S Ex 22:19 [e]ver 10

19:31 See 20:6; 2Sa 28:7 and notes.

19:34 *you were aliens in Egypt.* See Dt 5:15.

19:35 *dishonest standards.* In a culture with no bureau of weights and measures, cheating in business transactions by falsification of standards was common (see Dt 25:13–16; Pr 11:1 and note; 16:11 and note; 20:10,23). The prophets also condemned such sin (Am 8:5; Mic 6:10–11).

20:1–27 In ch. 20 many of the same sins listed in ch. 18 are mentioned again, but this time usually with the death penalty specified. Israel's God is a jealous God and tolerates no rivals (see note on Ex 20:5). He requires exclusive allegiance (see Ex 20:3 and note). See note on 18:1—20:27.

20:2–5 *Molech.* See note on 18:21.

20:3 *cut him off from his people.* See note on 7:20.

20:5 *prostituting themselves.* See Ex 34:15 and note.

20:6 *mediums and spiritists.* Practitioners of the occult; consulting a medium was no less a sin than being one (v. 27; 19:31). See Dt 18:10–11 and note on 18:9; Isa 3:2–3 and note. Only God was to be consulted—through either the priest or a prophet (see Isa 8:19–20 and notes).

20:7 *be holy.* See note on 11:44.

20:8 *who makes … holy.* This phrase and the expression, "I am the LORD (your God)," are characteristic of chs. 18–26. See also NIV text note.

20:9 Cf. the penalty of a profligate son in Dt 21:20–21.

20:10 See 18:20.

20:12 See 18:15.

20:13 *detestable.* See note on 7:21.

20:15–16 See 18:23.

17“ ‘If a man marries his sister[f], the daughter of either his father or his mother, and they have sexual relations, it is a disgrace. They must be cut off before the eyes[g] of their people. He has dishonored his sister and will be held responsible.[h]

18“ ‘If a man lies with a woman during her monthly period[i] and has sexual relations with her, he has exposed the source of her flow, and she has also uncovered it. Both of them must be cut off from their people.[j]

19“ ‘Do not have sexual relations with the sister of either your mother or your father,[k] for that would dishonor a close relative; both of you would be held responsible.

20“ ‘If a man sleeps with his aunt,[l] he has dishonored his uncle. They will be held responsible; they will die childless.[m]

21“ ‘If a man marries his brother’s wife,[n] it is an act of impurity; he has dishonored his brother. They will be childless.[o]

22“ ‘Keep all my decrees and laws[p] and follow them, so that the land[q] where I am bringing you to live may not vomit you out. 23You must not live according to the customs of the nations[r] I am going to drive out before you.[s] Because they did all these things, I abhorred them.[t] 24But I said to you, “You will possess their land; I will give it to you as an inheritance, a land flowing with milk and honey.”[u] I am the LORD your God, who has set you apart from the nations.[v]

25“ ‘You must therefore make a distinction between clean and unclean animals and between unclean and clean birds.[w] Do not defile yourselves by any animal or bird or anything that moves along the ground—those which I have set apart as unclean for you. 26You are to be holy to me[a x] because I, the LORD, am holy,[y] and I have set you apart from the nations[z] to be my own.

27“ ‘A man or woman who is a medium[a] or spiritist among you must be put to death.[b] You are to stone them;[c] their blood will be on their own heads.’ ”

20:17 [f]S Lev 18:9 [g]S Ge 17:14 [h]S Lev 5:1 **20:18** [i]S Lev 15:24 [j]Eze 18:6 **20:19** [k]S Lev 18:12 **20:20** [l]S Lev 18:13 [m]ver 21; Ge 15:2 **20:21** [n]S Lev 18:16; Mt 14:4; Mk 6:18 [o]S ver 20 **20:22** [p]S Ge 26:5 [q]S Lev 18:25-28 **20:23** [r]S Lev 18:3 [s]S Lev 18:24 [t]S Lev 18:25 **20:24** [u]S Ex 3:8; Nu 14:8; 16:14 [v]S Ex 33:16 **20:25** [w]Lev 10:10; Dt 14:3-21; Ac 10:14 **20:26** [x]Dt 14:2 [y]ver 8; Lev 19:2; Jos 24:19; 2Ki 19:22; Ps 99:3 [z]S Ex 33:16 **20:27** [a]S Ex 22:18 [b]S Lev 19:31 [c]S ver 2; S Lev 24:14

21:1 [d]S Ex 28:1; S Lev 1:5 [e]S Lev 5:3; S 13:3 [f]ver 11; Nu 5:2; 6:6; 19:11; 31:19 **21:2** [g]ver 11 **21:3** [h]Nu 6:6 **21:5** [i]S Lev 13:40; Jer 7:29; 16:6 [j]Eze 5:1; 44:20 [k]S Lev 19:28 **21:6** [l]ver 8; Ezr 8:28 [m]Lev 18:21 [n]S Lev 3:11 [o]ver 17, 22; Lev 22:25 [p]S Ex 19:22; S Lev 10:3 **21:7** [q]ver 13, 14 [r]Eze 44:22 **21:8** [s]ver 6 [t]Lev 3:11 [u]S Ex 31:13 **21:9** [v]S Ge 38:24;

Rules for Priests

21 The LORD said to Moses, “Speak to the priests, the sons of Aaron,[d] and say to them: ‘A priest must not make himself ceremonially unclean[e] for any of his people who die,[f] 2except for a close relative, such as his mother or father,[g] his son or daughter, his brother, 3or an unmarried sister who is dependent on him since she has no husband—for her he may make himself unclean.[h] 4He must not make himself unclean for people related to him by marriage,[b] and so defile himself.

5“ ‘Priests must not shave[i] their heads or shave off the edges of their beards[j] or cut their bodies.[k] 6They must be holy to their God[l] and must not profane the name of their God.[m] Because they present the offerings made to the LORD by fire,[n] the food of their God,[o] they are to be holy.[p]

7“ ‘They must not marry women defiled by prostitution or divorced from their husbands,[q] because priests are holy to their God.[r] 8Regard them as holy,[s] because they offer up the food of your God.[t] Consider them holy, because I the LORD am holy—I who make you holy.[c u]

9“ ‘If a priest’s daughter defiles herself by becoming a prostitute, she disgraces her father; she must be burned in the fire.[v]

10“ ‘The high priest, the one among his brothers who has had the anointing oil poured on his head[w] and who has been ordained to wear the priestly garments,[x] must not let his hair become unkempt[d] or tear his clothes.[y] 11He must not enter a place where there is a dead body.[z] He must not make himself unclean,[a] even for his father or mother,[b] 12nor leave the sanctuary[c] of his God or desecrate it, because he has been dedicated by the anointing oil[d] of his God. I am the LORD.

[a] *26* Or *be my holy ones* [b] *4* Or *unclean as a leader among his people* [c] *8* Or *who sanctify you*; or *who set you apart as holy* [d] *10* Or *not uncover his head*

S Lev 19:29 **21:10** [w]S Ex 29:7 [x]S Lev 8:7-9,13; S 16:4 [y]S Lev 10:6 **21:11** [z]Nu 5:2; 6:6; 9:6; 19:11,13,14; 31:19 [a]Lev 19:28 [b]ver 2 **21:12** [c]S Ex 25:8 [d]S Ex 28:41

20:18 See 18:19.

20:20 See 18:14 and note.

20:21 See 18:16 and note.

20:24 *flowing with milk and honey.* A common phrase in Exodus, Numbers and Deuteronomy (see notes on Ex 3:8; Dt 6:3; see also Jos 5:6; Jer 11:5; 32:22; Eze 20:6,15).

20:25 See ch. 11 and notes.

20:26 See 11:44 and note.

20:27 See note on v. 6.

21:1—22:33 Directions for the priests’ conduct, especially about separation from ceremonial uncleanness.

21:1 *for any ... who die.* Touching a corpse (Nu 19:11) or entering the home of a person who had died (Nu 19:14) made one unclean. A priest was only to contract such uncleanness at the death of a close relative (vv. 2–3), and the regulations for the high priest denied him even this (vv. 11–12).

21:5 *cut their bodies.* See 19:27–28 and note on 19:28. Such lacerations and disfigurement were common among pagans as signs of mourning and to secure the attention of their deity (see 1Ki 18:28 and note). Israelite faith had a much less grotesque view of death (see, e.g., vv. 1–4; Ge 5:24 and note; 2Sa 12:23; Heb 11:19).

21:6 *They must be holy to their God.* As those especially set apart for service at God’s sanctuary and who represent him in a special way, the priests must be especially careful to retain ceremonial and moral purity (see 11:44; Ex 3:5 and notes). *food of their God.* See note on 3:11,16.

21:8 *I ... am holy.* See note on 11:44.

21:9 See Ge 38:24 and note.

21:11–12 See note on v. 1.

13“ ‘The woman he marries must be a
virgin.[e] 14He must not marry a widow, a
divorced woman, or a woman defiled by
prostitution, but only a virgin from his
own people, 15so he will not defile his offspring among his people. I am the LORD,
who makes him holy.[a]’ ”
16The LORD said to Moses, 17“Say to Aaron: ‘For the generations to come none of
your descendants who has a defect[f] may
come near to offer the food of his God.[g]
18No man who has any defect[h] may come
near: no man who is blind[i] or lame,[j] disfigured or deformed; 19no man with a
crippled foot or hand, 20or who is hunch-
backed or dwarfed, or who has any eye
defect, or who has festering or running
sores or damaged testicles.[k] 21No descendant of Aaron the priest who has any defect[l] is to come near to present the offerings made to the LORD by fire.[m] He has a
defect; he must not come near to offer the
food of his God.[n] 22He may eat the most
holy food of his God,[o] as well as the holy
food; 23yet because of his defect,[p] he must
not go near the curtain or approach the altar, and so desecrate my sanctuary.[q] I am
the LORD, who makes them holy.[b][r]’ ”
24So Moses told this to Aaron and his
sons and to all the Israelites.

22 The LORD said to Moses, 2“Tell Aaron
and his sons to treat with respect the
sacred offerings[s] the Israelites consecrate
to me, so they will not profane my holy
name.[t] I am the LORD.[u]
3“Say to them: ‘For the generations to
come, if any of your descendants is ceremonially unclean and yet comes near the
sacred offerings that the Israelites consecrate to the LORD,[v] that person must be cut
off from my presence.[w] I am the LORD.
4“ ‘If a descendant of Aaron has an infectious skin disease[c] or a bodily discharge,[x]
he may not eat the sacred offerings until he
is cleansed. He will also be unclean if he
touches something defiled by a corpse[y] or
by anyone who has an emission of semen,
5or if he touches any crawling thing[z] that
makes him unclean, or any person[a] who
makes him unclean, whatever the uncleanness may be. 6The one who touches
any such thing will be unclean[b] till evening.[c] He must not eat any of the sacred
offerings unless he has bathed himself
with water.[d] 7When the sun goes down,
he will be clean, and after that he may eat
the sacred offerings, for they are his food.[e]
8He must not eat anything found dead[f] or
torn by wild animals,[g] and so become unclean[h] through it. I am the LORD.[i]
9“ ‘The priests are to keep my requirements[j] so that they do not become guilty[k]
and die[l] for treating them with contempt. I
am the LORD, who makes them holy.[d][m]
10“ ‘No one outside a priest’s family may
eat the sacred offering, nor may the guest
of a priest or his hired worker eat it.[n] 11But
if a priest buys a slave with money, or if a
slave is born in his household, that slave
may eat his food.[o] 12If a priest’s daughter
marries anyone other than a priest, she
may not eat any of the sacred contributions. 13But if a priest’s daughter becomes
a widow or is divorced, yet has no children, and she returns to live in her father’s
house as in her youth, she may eat of her
father’s food. No unauthorized person,
however, may eat any of it.
14“ ‘If anyone eats a sacred offering by
mistake,[p] he must make restitution to the
priest for the offering and add a fifth of
the value[q] to it. 15The priests must not desecrate the sacred offerings[r] the Israelites
present to the LORD[s] 16by allowing them to
eat[t] the sacred offerings and so bring upon
them guilt[u] requiring payment.[v] I am the
LORD, who makes them holy.[w]’ ”

Unacceptable Sacrifices

17The LORD said to Moses, 18“Speak to
Aaron and his sons and to all the Israelites
and say to them: ‘If any of you—either an
Israelite or an alien living in Israel[x]—presents a gift[y] for a burnt offering to the
LORD, either to fulfill a vow[z] or as a freewill offering,[a] 19you must present a male
without defect[b] from the cattle, sheep or
goats in order that it may be accepted on
your behalf.[c] 20Do not bring anything with

21:13 [e]Eze 44:22 **21:17** [f]ver 18,21,23 [g]S ver 6 **21:18** [h]Lev 22:19-25 [i]S Lev 19:14 [j]2Sa 4:4; 9:3; 19:26 **21:20** [k]Lev 22:24; Dt 23:1; Isa 56:3 **21:21** [l]S ver 17 [m]S Lev 3:11 [n]Lev 22:19 **21:22** [o]1Co 9:13 **21:23** [p]S ver 17 [q]S Ex 25:8 [r]Lev 20:8 **22:2** [s]S Lev 19:8 [t]S Ex 20:7; S Mt 5:33 [u]Eze 44:8 **22:3** [v]Ezr 8:28 [w]Lev 7:20,21; Nu 19:13 **22:4** [x]Lev 15:2-15 [y]Lev 11:24-28,39 **22:5** [z]Lev 11:24-28,43 [a]S Lev 15:7 **22:6** [b]Hag 2:13 [c]S Lev 11:24 [d]S Lev 14:8 **22:7** [e]Nu 18:11 **22:8** [f]S Lev 11:39 [g]S Ex 22:31 [h]S Lev 11:40 [i]Lev 11:44 **22:9** [j]S Lev 8:35 [k]S Ex 28:38 [l]ver 16; S Ex 28:43 [m]Lev 20:8 **22:10** [n]ver 13; Ex 12:45; 29:33 **22:11** [o]Ge 17:13; Ex 12:44 **22:14** [p]S Lev 4:2 [q]Lev 5:15 **22:15** [r]S Lev 19:8 [s]Nu 18:32 **22:16** [t]Nu 18:11 [u]S Ex 28:38 [v]S ver 9 [w]Lev 20:8 **22:18** [x]Nu 15:16; 19:10; Jos 8:33 [y]S Lev 1:2 [z]ver 21; S Ge 28:20; Nu 15:8; Ps 22:25; 76:11; 116:18 [a]S Lev 7:16 **22:19** [b]S Lev 1:3; 21:18-21; Nu 28:11; Dt 15:21 [c]S Lev 1:2

[a] 15 Or *who sanctifies him*; or *who sets him apart as holy* [b] 23 Or *who sanctifies them*; or *who sets them apart as holy* [c] 4 Traditionally *leprosy*; the Hebrew word was used for various diseases affecting the skin—not necessarily leprosy. [d] 9 Or *who sanctifies them*; or *who sets them apart as holy*; also in verse 16

21:17 *defect.* Just as the sacrifices had to be without defect, so the priests who officiated at the sacrifices had to be without defect (cf. Heb 7:26,28 and note on 7:28).
21:23 *curtain.* Between the Holy Place and the Most Holy Place (see Ex 26:33).
22:3 *cut off from my presence.* Excluded from the worshiping community.
22:4 See 13:1–46 and note on 13:45–46; 15:1–18 and notes; 21:11.
22:5 See 11:29–31.
22:8 See 17:15 and note.
22:9 *die for treating them with contempt.* The laws of cleanness were the same for priests and people, but the penalties were far more severe for the priests, who had greater responsibility. Cf. Nadab and Abihu (10:1–3) and the faithless priests of Malachi's day (Mal 1:6—2:9). *holy.* See note on 11:44.
22:14 *make restitution ... add a fifth.* Cf. 5:16 and note on 5:15; cf. also chart, p. 153 ("Guilt Offering").
22:16 *holy.* See note on 11:44.
22:18 *burnt offering.* See note on 1:3.
22:20–22 See Mal 1:8 and note.

a defect,[d] because it will not be accepted on your behalf.[e] 21When anyone brings from the herd or flock[f] a fellowship offering[a][g] to the LORD to fulfill a special vow or as a freewill offering,[h] it must be without defect or blemish[i] to be acceptable.[j] 22Do not offer to the LORD the blind, the injured or the maimed, or anything with warts or festering or running sores. Do not place any of these on the altar as an offering made to the LORD by fire. 23You may, however, present as a freewill offering an ox[b] or a sheep that is deformed or stunted, but it will not be accepted in fulfillment of a vow. 24You must not offer to the LORD an animal whose testicles are bruised, crushed, torn or cut.[k] You must not do this in your own land, 25and you must not accept such animals from the hand of a foreigner and offer them as the food of your God.[l] They will not be accepted on your behalf, because they are deformed and have defects.[m]' "

26The LORD said to Moses, 27"When a calf, a lamb or a goat[n] is born, it is to remain with its mother for seven days.[o] From the eighth day[p] on, it will be acceptable[q] as an offering made to the LORD by fire. 28Do not slaughter a cow or a sheep and its young on the same day.[r]

29"When you sacrifice a thank offering[s] to the LORD, sacrifice it in such a way that it will be accepted on your behalf. 30It must be eaten that same day; leave none of it till morning.[t] I am the LORD.[u]

31"Keep[v] my commands and follow them.[w] I am the LORD. 32Do not profane my holy name.[x] I must be acknowledged as holy by the Israelites.[y] I am the LORD, who makes[c] you holy[d][z] 33and who brought you out of Egypt[a] to be your God.[b] I am the LORD."

23 The LORD said to Moses, 2"Speak to the Israelites and say to them: 'These are my appointed feasts,[c] the appointed feasts of the LORD, which you are to proclaim as sacred assemblies.[d]

22:20 [d]S Lev 1:3; Dt 15:21; 17:1; Eze 43:23; 45:18; 46:6; Mal 1:8; Heb 9:14; 1Pe 1:19 [e]S Ex 28:38 **22:21** [f]S Lev 1:2 [g]S Ex 32:6; S Lev 3:6 [h]S Lev 7:16 [i]S Ex 12:5; Mal 1:14 [j]Am 4:5 **22:24** [k]S Lev 21:20 **22:25** [l]S Lev 21:6 [m]S Lev 1:3; S 3:1; Nu 19:2 **22:27** [n]S Lev 1:3 [o]S Ex 22:30 [p]S Ex 22:30 [q]S Ex 28:38 **22:28** [r]Dt 22:6,7 **22:29** [s]S Lev 7:12 **22:30** [t]Lev 7:15 [u]Lev 11:44 **22:31** [v]Dt 4:2,40; Ps 105:45 [w]S Ex 22:31 **22:32** [x]Lev 18:21 [y]S Lev 10:3 [z]Lev 20:8 **22:33** [a]S Ex 6:6 [b]S Ge 17:7 **23:2** [c]ver 4,37,44; Nu 29:39; Eze 44:24; Col 2:16 [d]ver 21,27

23:3 [e]Ex 20:9 [f]S Ex 20:10; Heb 4:9,10 [g]ver 7,21,35; Nu 28:26 **23:4** [h]Na 1:15 **23:5** [i]S Ex 12:11 [j]S Ex 12:6 **23:6** [k]Ex 12:17 [l]S Ex 12:19 **23:7** [m]ver 3,8 **23:8** [n]S Lev 1:9 **23:10** [o]Nu 15:2,18 [p]S Lev 19:9 [q]S Lev 19:9 [r]S Ex 22:29; S 34:22; Ro 11:16 **23:11** [s]S Ex 29:24 [t]S Ex 28:38

The Sabbath

3" 'There are six days when you may work,[e] but the seventh day is a Sabbath of rest,[f] a day of sacred assembly. You are not to do any work;[g] wherever you live, it is a Sabbath to the LORD.

The Passover and Unleavened Bread

23:4-8pp — Ex 12:14-20; Nu 28:16-25; Dt 16:1-8

4" 'These are the LORD's appointed feasts, the sacred assemblies you are to proclaim at their appointed times:[h] 5The LORD's Passover[i] begins at twilight on the fourteenth day of the first month.[j] 6On the fifteenth day of that month the LORD's Feast of Unleavened Bread[k] begins; for seven days[l] you must eat bread made without yeast. 7On the first day hold a sacred assembly[m] and do no regular work. 8For seven days present an offering made to the LORD by fire.[n] And on the seventh day hold a sacred assembly and do no regular work.' "

Firstfruits

9The LORD said to Moses, 10"Speak to the Israelites and say to them: 'When you enter the land I am going to give you[o] and you reap its harvest,[p] bring to the priest a sheaf[q] of the first grain you harvest.[r] 11He is to wave the sheaf before the LORD[s] so it will be accepted[t] on your behalf; the priest is to wave it on the day after the Sabbath. 12On the day you wave the sheaf, you must sacrifice as a burnt offering to the LORD a lamb a year old[u] without defect,[v] 13together with its grain offering[w] of two-tenths of an ephah[e][x] of fine flour mixed with oil—an offering made to the LORD by fire, a pleasing aroma—and its drink

[a] *21* Traditionally *peace offering* [b] *23* The Hebrew word can include both male and female. [c] *32* Or *made* [d] *32* Or *who sanctifies you*; or *who sets you apart as holy* [e] *13* That is, probably about 4 quarts (about 4.5 liters); also in verse 17

23:12 [u]S Lev 12:6 [v]S Ex 12:5 **23:13** [w]Lev 2:14-16; S 6:20 [x]ver 17; Lev 24:5; Nu 15:6; 28:9

22:21 *fellowship offering.* See note on 3:1.

22:24 *bruised, crushed, torn or cut.* Castrated animals were not acceptable offerings.

22:28 See note on Ex 23:19.

22:30 *that same day.* The rule applied also to the Passover (Ex 34:25); however, the fellowship offering could be saved and eaten on the following day (7:16).

22:32 *holy ... holy ... holy.* See 11:44; 18:21 and notes.

23:2 *appointed feasts.* See Ex 23:14–19 and notes; 34:18–26; Nu 28–29; Dt 16:1–17. The parallel in Numbers (the fullest and closest to Leviticus) specifies in great detail the offerings to be made at each feast. See chart, pp. 178–179.

23:3 *Sabbath.* See notes on Ex 16:23; 20:9–10. The Sabbath is associated with the annual feasts also in Ex 23:12,14. Two additional lambs were to be sacrificed as a burnt offering every weekly Sabbath (Nu 28:9–10).

23:5 *Passover.* See notes on Ex 12:11,14,21. *first month.* See note on Ex 12:2. The Israelites had three systems of referring to months. In one, the months were simply numbered (as here and in v. 24). In another, the Canaanite names were used (Abib, Bul, etc.), of which only four are known. In the third system, the Babylonian names (Nisan, Adar, Tishri, Kislev, etc.) were used—in the exilic and postexilic books only—and are still used today. See chart, p. 104.

23:6 *Feast of Unleavened Bread.* See note on Ex 23:15. During the Feast the first sheaf of the barley harvest was brought (see vv. 10–11).

23:9–14 Feast of Firstfruits (see notes on Ex 23:19; Nu 15:20; Ne 10:35).

23:10 *first grain you harvest.* That is, barley (see Ru 1:22); wheat harvest followed (see Ru 2:23).

offering[y] of a quarter of a hin[a] of wine.[z] 14 You must not eat any bread, or roasted or new grain,[a] until the very day you bring this offering to your God.[b] This is to be a lasting ordinance for the generations to come,[c] wherever you live.[d]

Feast of Weeks

23:15-22pp — Nu 28:26-31; Dt 16:9-12

15 "'From the day after the Sabbath, the day you brought the sheaf of the wave offering, count off seven full weeks. 16 Count off fifty days up to the day after the seventh Sabbath,[e] and then present an offering of new grain to the LORD. 17 From wherever you live, bring two loaves made of two-tenths of an ephah[f] of fine flour, baked with yeast, as a wave offering of firstfruits[g] to the LORD. 18 Present with this bread seven male lambs, each a year old and without defect, one young bull and two rams. They will be a burnt offering to the LORD, together with their grain offerings and drink offerings[h]—an offering made by fire, an aroma pleasing to the LORD. 19 Then sacrifice one male goat for a sin offering and two lambs, each a year old, for a fellowship offering.[b] 20 The priest is to wave the two lambs before the LORD as a wave offering,[i] together with the bread of the firstfruits. They are a sacred offering to the LORD for the priest. 21 On that same day you are to proclaim a sacred assembly[j] and do no regular work.[k] This is to be a lasting ordinance for the generations to come, wherever you live.

22 "'When you reap the harvest[l] of your land, do not reap to the very edges of your field or gather the gleanings of your harvest.[m] Leave them for the poor and the alien.[n] I am the LORD your God.'"

Feast of Trumpets

23:23-25pp — Nu 29:1-6

23 The LORD said to Moses, 24 "Say to the Israelites: 'On the first day of the seventh month you are to have a day of rest, a sacred assembly[o] commemorated with trumpet blasts.[p] 25 Do no regular work,[q] but present an offering made to the LORD by fire.[r]'"

23:13 [y] S Ge 35:14 [z] S Lev 10:9 **23:14** [a] Jos 5:11; Ru 2:14; 1Sa 17:17; 25:18; 2Sa 17:28 [b] Ex 34:26 [c] Lev 3:17; Nu 10:8; 15:21 [d] Jer 2:3 **23:16** [e] Ac 2:1; 20:16 **23:17** [f] S ver 13 [g] S Ex 34:22 **23:18** [h] ver 13; Ex 29:41; 30:9; 37:16; Jer 19:13; 44:18 **23:20** [i] S Ex 29:24 **23:21** [j] S ver 2; Ex 32:5 [k] S ver 3 **23:22** [l] S Lev 19:9 [m] S Lev 19:10; Dt 24:19-21; Ru 2:15 [n] Ru 2:2 **23:24** [o] ver 27,36; Ezr 3:1 [p] Lev 25:9; Nu 10:9,10; 29:1; 31:6; 2Ki 11:14; 2Ch 13:12; Ps 98:6 **23:25** [q] ver 21 [r] S Lev 1:9

23:27 [s] S Lev 16:29 [t] S Ex 30:10 [u] S ver 2, S 24 **23:28** [v] ver 31 **23:29** [w] Ge 17:14; Lev 7:20; Nu 5:2 **23:30** [x] S Lev 20:3 **23:31** [y] Lev 3:17 **23:32** [z] S Lev 16:31 [a] Ne 13:19 **23:34** [b] 1Ki 8:2; Hag 2:1 [c] S Ex 23:16; Jn 7:2 **23:35** [d] ver 2 [e] ver 3 **23:36** [f] S ver 24; 1Ki 8:2; 2Ch 7:9; Ne 8:18; Jn 7:37 [g] S Lev 1:9 **23:37** [h] ver 13 **23:38** [i] S Lev 1:2 [j] S Ex 20:10; 2Ch 2:4; Eze 45:17 [k] S Lev 7:16

Day of Atonement

23:26-32pp — Lev 16:2-34; Nu 29:7-11

26 The LORD said to Moses, 27 "The tenth day of this seventh month[s] is the Day of Atonement.[t] Hold a sacred assembly[u] and deny yourselves,[c] and present an offering made to the LORD by fire. 28 Do no work[v] on that day, because it is the Day of Atonement, when atonement is made for you before the LORD your God. 29 Anyone who does not deny himself on that day must be cut off from his people.[w] 30 I will destroy from among his people[x] anyone who does any work on that day. 31 You shall do no work at all. This is to be a lasting ordinance[y] for the generations to come, wherever you live. 32 It is a sabbath of rest[z] for you, and you must deny yourselves. From the evening of the ninth day of the month until the following evening you are to observe your sabbath."[a]

Feast of Tabernacles

23:33-43pp — Nu 29:12-39; Dt 16:13-17

33 The LORD said to Moses, 34 "Say to the Israelites: 'On the fifteenth day of the seventh[b] month the LORD's Feast of Tabernacles[c] begins, and it lasts for seven days. 35 The first day is a sacred assembly;[d] do no regular work.[e] 36 For seven days present offerings made to the LORD by fire, and on the eighth day hold a sacred assembly[f] and present an offering made to the LORD by fire.[g] It is the closing assembly; do no regular work.

37 ("'These are the LORD's appointed feasts, which you are to proclaim as sacred assemblies for bringing offerings made to the LORD by fire—the burnt offerings and grain offerings, sacrifices and drink offerings[h] required for each day. 38 These offerings[i] are in addition to those for the LORD's Sabbaths[j] and[d] in addition to your gifts and whatever you have vowed and all the freewill offerings[k] you give to the LORD.)

39 "'So beginning with the fifteenth day of the seventh month, after you have gathered the crops of the land, celebrate the

[a] 13 That is, probably about 1 quart (about 0.9 liter) [b] 19 Traditionally *peace offering* [c] 27 Or *and fast*; also in verses 29 and 32 [d] 38 Or *These feasts are in addition to the LORD's Sabbaths, and these offerings are*

23:15 *seven full weeks.* See note on Ex 23:16.
23:16 *fifty days.* The NT name for the Feast of Weeks was Pentecost (see Ac 2:1 and note; 20:16; 1Co 16:8), meaning "fifty." *new grain.* That is, wheat (see note on v. 10).
23:22 See note on 19:9–10.
23:24 *first day of the seventh month.* Today known as the Jewish New Year (*Rosh Hashanah*, "the beginning of the year"), but not so called in the Bible (the Hebrew expression is only used in Eze 40:1 in a date formula; see note there). *trumpet blasts.* Trumpets were blown on the first of every month (see Ps 81:3 and note). With no calendars available, the trumpets sounding across the land were an important signal of the beginning of the new season, the end of the agricultural year. See note on 16:29; see also chart, p. 104.
23:27 *Day of Atonement.* For details see notes on 16:1–34. Aaron was to enter the Most Holy Place only once a year (16:29–34) on this day. Modern Jews call it *Yom Kippur.* The day was typological, foreshadowing the atoning work of Christ, our high priest (see Heb 9:7; 13:10–13 and notes). *deny yourselves.* See note on 16:29,31.
23:29 *cut off from his people.* See note on 7:20.
23:34 *Feast of Tabernacles.* See notes on Ex 23:16; Zec 14:16; Jn 7:37–39. Tabernacles was the last of the three annual pilgrimage festivals (see Ex 23:14–17; Dt 16:16 and notes).

festival[l] to the LORD for seven days;[m] the
first day is a day of rest, and the eighth
day also is a day of rest. 40On the first
day you are to take choice fruit from the
trees, and palm fronds, leafy branches[n]
and poplars,[o] and rejoice[p] before the LORD
your God for seven days. 41Celebrate this
as a festival to the LORD for seven days
each year. This is to be a lasting ordinance
for the generations to come; celebrate it
in the seventh month. 42Live in booths[q]
for seven days: All native-born Israelites
are to live in booths 43so your descendants
will know[r] that I had the Israelites live in
booths when I brought them out of Egypt.
I am the LORD your God.' "
44So Moses announced to the Israelites
the appointed feasts of the LORD.

23:39 [l]Isa 62:9 [m]S Ex 23:16 **23:40** [n]Ps 118:27 [o]Ne 8:14-17; Ps 137:2; Isa 44:4 [p]Dt 12:7; 14:26; 28:47; Ne 8:10; Ps 9:2; 66:6; 105:43; Joel 2:26 **23:42** [q]S Ex 23:16 **23:43** [r]Ps 78:5

Oil and Bread Set Before the LORD

24:1-3pp — Ex 27:20-21

24 The LORD said to Moses, 2"Command
the Israelites to bring you clear oil of
pressed olives for the light so that the lamps
may be kept burning continually. 3Outside
the curtain of the Testimony in the Tent of
Meeting, Aaron is to tend the lamps before
the LORD from evening till morning, continually. This is to be a lasting ordinance[s]
for the generations to come. 4The lamps on
the pure gold lampstand[t] before the LORD
must be tended continually.
5"Take fine flour and bake twelve loaves
of bread,[u] using two-tenths of an ephah[a v]
for each loaf. 6Set them in two rows, six in

[a] 5 That is, probably about 7 pounds (about 3.2 kilograms)

24:3 [s]S Ex 12:14 **24:4** [t]S Ex 25:31 **24:5** [u]S Ex 25:30; Heb 9:2 [v]S Lev 23:13

23:42 *booths.* The Hebrew for this word is *Sukkoth* and is also translated "Tabernacles" (as in v. 34), giving the feast its name. Even today, orthodox Jews construct small booths (see Ne 8:13–17) to remind them of the booths they lived in when God brought them out of Egypt at the time of the exodus (v. 43).

24:2–4 See Ex 27:20–21.
24:3 *Testimony.* See note on Ex 25:22. *continually.* Every night without interruption, but not throughout the day. See 1Sa 3:3 and note.
24:5 *two-tenths of an ephah.* See NIV text note. Either the

Old Testament Feasts and Other Sacred Days

NAME	OLD TESTAMENT REFERENCES	OT TIME	MODERN EQUIVALENT
Sabbath	Ex 20:8-11; 31:12-17; Lev 23:3; Dt 5:12-15	7th day	Same
Sabbath Year	Ex 23:10-11; Lev 25:1-7	7th year	Same
Year of Jubilee	Lev 25:8-55; 27:17-24; Nu 36:4	50th year	Same
Passover	Ex 12:1-14; Lev 23:5; Nu 9:1-14; 28:16; Dt 16:1-3a,4b-7	1st month (Abib) 14	Mar.–Apr.
Unleavened Bread	Ex 12:15-20; 13:3-10; 23:15; 34:18; Lev 23:6-8; Nu 28:17-25; Dt 16:3b,4a,8	1st month (Abib) 15-21	Mar.–Apr.
Firstfruits	Lev 23:9-14	1st month (Abib) 16	Mar.–Apr.
Weeks (Pentecost) (Harvest)	Ex 23:16a; 34:22a; Lev 23:15-21; Nu 28:26-31; Dt 16:9-12	3rd month (Sivan) 6	May–June
Trumpets (later: Rosh Hashanah–New Year's Day)	Lev 23:23-25; Nu 29:1-6	7th month (Tishri) 1	Sept.–Oct.
Day of Atonement (Yom Kippur)	Lev 16; 23:26-32; Nu 29:7-11	7th month (Tishri) 10	Sept.–Oct.
Tabernacles (Booths) (Ingathering)	Ex 23:16b; 34:22b; Lev 23:33-36a,39-43; Nu 29:12-34; Dt 16:13-15; Zec 14:16-19	7th month (Tishri) 15-21	Sept.–Oct.
Sacred Assembly	Lev 23:36b; Nu 29:35-38	7th month (Tishri) 22	Sept.–Oct.
Purim	Est 9:18-32	12th month (Adar) 14,15	Feb.–Mar.

On Kislev 25 (mid-December) Hanukkah, the feast of dedication or festival of lights, commemorated the purification of the temple and altar in the Maccabean period (165/4 B.C.). This feast is mentioned in Jn 10:22 (see note there).

each row, on the table of pure gold[w] before
the LORD. 7Along each row put some pure
incense[x] as a memorial portion[y] to represent the bread and to be an offering made
to the LORD by fire. 8This bread is to be
set out before the LORD regularly,[z] Sabbath
after Sabbath,[a] on behalf of the Israelites,
as a lasting covenant. 9It belongs to Aaron
and his sons,[b] who are to eat it in a holy
place,[c] because it is a most holy[d] part of
their regular share of the offerings made to
the LORD by fire."

A Blasphemer Stoned

10Now the son of an Israelite mother
and an Egyptian father went out among
the Israelites, and a fight broke out in the
camp between him and an Israelite. 11The
son of the Israelite woman blasphemed
the Name[e] with a curse;[f] so they brought
him to Moses.[g] (His mother's name was
Shelomith, the daughter of Dibri the Danite.)[h] 12They put him in custody until the
will of the LORD should be made clear to
them.[i]

13Then the LORD said to Moses: 14"Take
the blasphemer outside the camp. All
those who heard him are to lay their

24:6 [w]Ex 25:23-30; Nu 4:7 **24:7** [x]S Lev 2:1 [y]S Lev 2:2 **24:8** [z]Ex 25:30; Nu 4:7; 1Ch 9:32; 2Ch 2:4 [a]Mt 12:5 **24:9** [b]Mt 12:4; Mk 2:26; Lk 6:4 [c]S Lev 6:16 [d]S Lev 6:17 **24:11** [e]S Ex 3:15 [f]S Ex 20:7; S 2Ki 6:33; S Job 1:11 [g]S Ex 18:22 [h]Ex 31:2; Nu 1:4; 7:2; 10:15; 13:2; 17:2; Jos 7:18; 1Ki 7:14 **24:12** [i]S Ex 18:16

loaves were quite large or a smaller unit of measurement is intended. The Hebrew word *ephah* is not expressed, but since the ephah was the standard measure of capacity (see table, p. 1993), it is the measure most likely implied here.

24:7 *pure incense.* Not used as a condiment for the bread, but burned either in piles on the table or in small receptacles alongside the rows of bread. *memorial portion.* See note on 2:2,9,16.

24:8 *This bread.* Often called the "bread of the Presence" (see Ex 25:30 and note). It represented a gift from the 12 tribes and signified the fact that God sustained his people. It was eaten by the priests (v. 9).

24:9 See 1Sa 21:4–6 and note on 21:4.

24:10 *Egyptian father.* An alien. The laws, at least in the judicial sphere, applied equally to both the alien and the native-born Israelite (v. 22; see Ex 12:49).

24:11 *blasphemed.* See Ex 20:7 and note.

DESCRIPTION	PURPOSE	NEW TESTAMENT REFERENCES
Day of rest; no work	Rest for people and animals	Mt 12:1-14; 28:1; Lk 4:16; Jn 5:9–10; Ac 13:42; Col 2:16; Heb 4:1-11
Year of rest; fallow fields	Rest for land	
Canceled debts; liberation of slaves and indentured servants; land returned to original family owners	Help for poor; stabilize society	
Slaying and eating a lamb, together with bitter herbs and bread made without yeast, in every household	Remember Israel's deliverance from Egypt	Mt 26:17; Mk 14:12-26; Jn 2:13; 11:55; 1Co 5:7; Heb 11:28
Eating bread made without yeast; holding several assemblies; making designated offerings	Remember how the Lord brought the Israelites out of Egypt in haste	Mk 14:1; Ac 12:3; 1Co 5:6-8
Presenting a sheaf of the first of the barley harvest as a wave offering; making a burnt offering and a grain offering	Recognize the Lord's bounty in the land	Ro 8:23; 1Co 15:20-23
A festival of joy; mandatory and voluntary offerings, including the firstfruits of the wheat harvest	Show joy and thankfulness for the Lord's blessing of harvest	Ac 2:1-4; 20:16; 1Co 16:8
An assembly on a day of rest commemorated with trumpet blasts and sacrifices	Present Israel before the Lord for his favor	
A day of rest, fasting and sacrifices of atonement for priests and people and atonement for the tabernacle and altar	Atone for the sins of priests and people and purify the Holy Place	Ro 3:24-26; Heb 9:7; 10:3,19-22
A week of celebration for the harvest; living in booths and offering sacrifices	Memorialize the journey from Egypt to Canaan; give thanks for the productivity of Canaan	Jn 7:2,37
A day of convocation, rest and offering sacrifices	Commemorate the closing of the cycle of feasts	
A day of joy and feasting and giving presents	Remind the Israelites of their national deliverance in the time of Esther	
In addition, New Moon festivals were prescribed (See Nu 28:11-15; 1 Sa 20:5; Isa 1:14 and notes; see also 1Ch 23:31; Ezr 3:5; Ne 10:33; Ps 81:3; Hos 5:7; Am 8:5; Col 2:16).		

hands on his head, and the entire assembly is to stone him.[j] 15Say to the Israelites:
'If anyone curses his God,[k] he will be held
responsible;[l] 16anyone who blasphemes[m]
the name of the LORD must be put to
death.[n] The entire assembly must stone
him. Whether an alien or native-born,
when he blasphemes the Name, he must
be put to death.
17" 'If anyone takes the life of a human
being, he must be put to death.[o] 18Anyone
who takes the life of someone's animal
must make restitution[p]—life for life. 19If
anyone injures his neighbor, whatever he
has done must be done to him: 20fracture
for fracture, eye for eye, tooth for tooth.[q]
As he has injured the other, so he is to be
injured. 21Whoever kills an animal must
make restitution,[r] but whoever kills a man
must be put to death.[s] 22You are to have
the same law for the alien[t] and the native-
born.[u] I am the LORD your God.' "
23Then Moses spoke to the Israelites,
and they took the blasphemer outside the
camp and stoned him.[v] The Israelites did
as the LORD commanded Moses.

The Sabbath Year

25 The LORD said to Moses on Mount
Sinai,[w] 2"Speak to the Israelites and
say to them: 'When you enter the land I
am going to give you, the land itself must
observe a sabbath to the LORD. 3For six
years sow your fields, and for six years
prune your vineyards and gather their
crops.[x] 4But in the seventh year the land
is to have a sabbath of rest,[y] a sabbath to
the LORD. Do not sow your fields or prune
your vineyards.[z] 5Do not reap what grows
of itself[a] or harvest the grapes[b] of your untended vines.[c] The land is to have a year of
rest. 6Whatever the land yields during the
sabbath year[d] will be food for you—for
yourself, your manservant and maidservant, and the hired worker and temporary
resident who live among you, 7as well as
for your livestock and the wild animals[e]
in your land. Whatever the land produces
may be eaten.

The Year of Jubilee

25:8-38Ref — Dt 15:1-11
25:39-55Ref — Ex 21:2-11; Dt 15:12-18

8" 'Count off seven sabbaths of years—
seven times seven years—so that the sev-
en sabbaths of years amount to a period of
forty-nine years. 9Then have the trumpet[f]
sounded everywhere on the tenth day of
the seventh month;[g] on the Day of Atonement[h] sound the trumpet throughout your
land. 10Consecrate the fiftieth year and proclaim liberty[i] throughout the land to all its
inhabitants. It shall be a jubilee[j] for you;
each one of you is to return to his family
property[k] and each to his own clan. 11The
fiftieth year shall be a jubilee[l] for you; do
not sow and do not reap what grows of itself or harvest the untended vines.[m] 12For
it is a jubilee and is to be holy for you;
eat only what is taken directly from the
fields.
13" 'In this Year of Jubilee[n] everyone is to
return to his own property.
14" 'If you sell land to one of your countrymen or buy any from him, do not take
advantage of each other.[o] 15You are to buy
from your countryman on the basis of the
number of years[p] since the Jubilee. And he
is to sell to you on the basis of the number

24:14 [j]ver 23; S Lev 20:2; Dt 13:9; 17:5,7; Ac 7:58 **24:15** [k]S Ex 22:28 [l]S Lev 5:1 **24:16** [m]S Ex 22:28 [n]S Ex 21:12; 1Ki 21:10,13; Mt 26:66; Mk 14:64; Jn 10:33; 19:7; Ac 7:58 **24:17** [o]ver 21; Ge 9:6; S Ex 21:12; Dt 27:24 **24:18** [p]ver 21 **24:20** [q]S Ex 21:24; Mt 5:38* **24:21** [r]S ver 18 [s]S ver 17 **24:22** [t]S Ex 12:49; S 22:21; Eze 47:22 [u]Nu 9:14 **24:23** [v]S ver 14 **25:1** [w]Ex 19:11 **25:3** [x]Ex 23:10 **25:4** [y]ver 5,6,20; Lev 26:35; 2Ch 36:21 [z]Isa 36:16; 37:30 **25:5** [a]2Ki 19:29 [b]Ge 40:10; Nu 6:3; 13:20; Dt 23:24; Ne 13:15; Isa 5:2 [c]ver 4,11 **25:6** [d]S ver 4 **25:7** [e]Ex 23:11 **25:9** [f]Lev 23:24; Nu 10:8; Jos 6:4; Jdg 3:27; 7:16; 1Sa 13:3; Isa 27:13; Zec 9:14 [g]S Lev 16:29 [h]S Ex 30:10 **25:10** [i]Isa 61:1; Jer 34:8,15,17; S Lk 4:19 [j]ver 11,28,50; Lev 27:17,21; Nu 36:4; Eze 46:17 [k]ver 27 **25:11** [l]S ver 10 [m]S ver 5 **25:13** [n]ver 10 **25:14** [o]S Lev 19:13; 1Sa 12:3,4; 1Co 6:8 **25:15** [p]ver 27; Lev 27:18,23

24:16 *the Name.* See note on Dt 12:5.
24:17,21 See Ge 9:6 and note.
24:20 *eye for eye, tooth for tooth.* See note on Ex 21:23–25. This represents a statement of principle: The penalty is to fit the crime, not exceed it. An actual eye or tooth was not to be required, nor is there evidence that such a penalty was ever exacted. A similar law of retaliation is found in the Code of Hammurapi (see chart, p. xxii), which also seems not to have been literally applied. Christ, like the middle-of-the-road Pharisees (school of Hillel), objected to an extremist use of this judicial principle to excuse private vengeance, such as by the strict Pharisees (school of Shammai); see Mt 5:38–42.
24:22 See note on v. 10.
25:4 *land is to have a sabbath.* See Ex 23:10–11. The Israelites did not practice crop rotation, but the fallow year (when the crops were not planted) served somewhat the same purpose. And just as the land was to have a sabbath year, so the servitude of a Hebrew slave was limited to six years, apparently whether or not the year he was freed was a sabbath year (see Ex 21:2 and note). Dt 15:1–11 specifies that debts were also to be canceled in the sabbath year. The care for the poor in the laws of Israel (see Ex 23:11) is noteworthy. See 23:7,35; Dt 31:10; Ne 10:31.
25:9 *Day of Atonement.* See notes on 16:1–34; see also 23:27 and note.
25:10 *fiftieth year.* Possibly a fallow year in addition to the seventh sabbath year, or perhaps the same as the 49th year (counting the first and last years). Jewish sources from the period between the Testaments favor the latter interpretation. *proclaim liberty ... inhabitants.* See vv. 39–43,47–55. The Liberty Bell in Philadelphia is so named because this statement was written on it. Cf. Isa 61:1 and note; Lk 4:16–21 and note on 4:19. *jubilee.* The Hebrew for this word is the same as and may be related to one of the Hebrew words for "[ram's] horn," "trumpet" (see, e.g., Ex 19:13), though in v. 9 a different Hebrew word for "trumpet" is used. Trumpets were blown at the close of the Day of Atonement to inaugurate the Year of Jubilee. Cf. 23:24.
25:13 *return to his own property.* See v. 10. The Lord prohibited the accumulation of property to the detriment of the poor. "The land is mine," said the Lord (v. 23). God's people are only tenants (see 1Ch 29:15; Heb 11:13 and note).
25:15 *number of years left for harvesting.* In a way, the sale of land in Israel was a lease until the Year of Jubilee (see 27:18,23).

of years left for harvesting crops. 16When
the years are many, you are to increase the
price, and when the years are few, you are
to decrease the price,[q] because what he is
really selling you is the number of crops.
17Do not take advantage of each other,[r] but
fear your God.[s] I am the LORD your God.[t]

18" 'Follow my decrees and be careful to
obey my laws,[u] and you will live safely
in the land.[v] 19Then the land will yield its
fruit,[w] and you will eat your fill and live
there in safety.[x] 20You may ask, "What will
we eat in the seventh year[y] if we do not
plant or harvest our crops?" 21I will send
you such a blessing[z] in the sixth year that
the land will yield enough for three years.[a]
22While you plant during the eighth year,
you will eat from the old crop and will
continue to eat from it until the harvest of
the ninth year comes in.[b]

23" 'The land[c] must not be sold permanently, because the land is mine[d] and you
are but aliens[e] and my tenants. 24Through-
out the country that you hold as a possession, you must provide for the redemption[f] of the land.

25" 'If one of your countrymen becomes
poor and sells some of his property, his
nearest relative[g] is to come and redeem[h]
what his countryman has sold. 26If, however, a man has no one to redeem it for
him but he himself prospers[i] and acquires
sufficient means to redeem it, 27he is to
determine the value for the years[j] since he
sold it and refund the balance to the man
to whom he sold it; he can then go back
to his own property.[k] 28But if he does not
acquire the means to repay him, what he
sold will remain in the possession of the
buyer until the Year of Jubilee. It will be
returned[l] in the Jubilee, and he can then
go back to his property.[m]

29" 'If a man sells a house in a walled
city, he retains the right of redemption a
full year after its sale. During that time he
may redeem it. 30If it is not redeemed before a full year has passed, the house in
the walled city shall belong permanently
to the buyer and his descendants. It is not
to be returned in the Jubilee. 31But houses
in villages without walls around them are
to be considered as open country. They
can be redeemed, and they are to be returned in the Jubilee.

32" 'The Levites always have the right
to redeem their houses in the Levitical
towns,[n] which they possess. 33So the property of the Levites is redeemable—that is,
a house sold in any town they hold—and
is to be returned in the Jubilee, because
the houses in the towns of the Levites are
their property among the Israelites. 34But
the pastureland belonging to their towns
must not be sold; it is their permanent
possession.[o]

35" 'If one of your countrymen becomes
poor[p] and is unable to support himself
among you, help him[q] as you would an
alien or a temporary resident, so he can
continue to live among you. 36Do not take
interest[r] of any kind[a] from him, but fear
your God,[s] so that your countryman may
continue to live among you. 37You must
not lend him money at interest[t] or sell him
food at a profit. 38I am the LORD your God,
who brought you out of Egypt to give you
the land of Canaan[u] and to be your God.[v]

39" 'If one of your countrymen becomes
poor among you and sells himself to you,
do not make him work as a slave.[w] 40He is
to be treated as a hired worker[x] or a temporary resident among you; he is to work
for you until the Year of Jubilee. 41Then he
and his children are to be released, and
he will go back to his own clan and to the
property[y] of his forefathers.[z] 42Because the
Israelites are my servants, whom I brought
out of Egypt,[a] they must not be sold as
slaves. 43Do not rule over them ruthlessly,[b]
but fear your God.[c]

44" 'Your male and female slaves are to
come from the nations around you; from
them you may buy slaves. 45You may also
buy some of the temporary residents living among you and members of their clans
born in your country, and they will become your property. 46You can will them
to your children as inherited property and
can make them slaves for life, but you
must not rule over your fellow Israelites
ruthlessly.

47" 'If an alien or a temporary resident
among you becomes rich and one of your
countrymen becomes poor and sells himself[d] to the alien living among you or to
a member of the alien's clan, 48he retains
the right of redemption[e] after he has sold
himself. One of his relatives[f] may redeem
him: 49An uncle or a cousin or any blood

[a] 36 Or *take excessive interest*; similarly in verse 37

25:16 [q]ver 27,51,52 **25:17** [r]S Lev 19:13; Job 31:16; Pr 22:22; Jer 7:5,6; 21:12; 22:3,15; Zec 7:9-10; 1Th 4:6 [s]S Lev 19:14 [t]S Lev 19:32 **25:18** [u]S Ge 26:5 [v]ver 19; Lev 26:4,5; Dt 12:10; 33:28; Job 5:22; Ps 4:8; Jer 23:6; 30:10; 32:37; 33:16; Eze 28:26; 34:25; 38:14 **25:19** [w]Lev 26:4; Dt 11:14; 28:12; Isa 55:10 [x]S ver 18 **25:20** [y]S ver 4 **25:21** [z]Dt 28:8,12; Ps 133:3; 134:3; 147:13; Eze 44:30; Hag 2:19; Mal 3:10 [a]S Ex 16:5 **25:22** [b]Lev 26:10 **25:23** [c]Nu 36:7; 1Ki 21:3; Eze 46:18 [d]Ex 19:5 [e]S Ge 23:4; S Heb 11:13 **25:24** [f]ver 29,48; Ru 4:7 **25:25** [g]ver 48; Ru 2:20; Jer 32:7 [h]Lev 27:13,19,31; Ru 4:4 **25:26** [i]ver 49 **25:27** [j]S ver 15 [k]ver 10 **25:28** [l]Lev 27:24 [m]S ver 10 **25:32** [n]Nu 35:1-8; Jos 21:2 **25:34** [o]Nu 35:2-5; Eze 48:14 **25:35** [p]Dt 24:14,15 [q]Dt 15:8; Ps 37:21,26; Pr 21:26; Lk 6:35 **25:36** [r]S Ex 22:25; Jer 15:10 [s]S Lev 19:32 **25:37** [t]S Ex 22:25 **25:38** [u]S Ge 10:19 [v]S Ge 17:7 **25:39** [w]1Ki 5:13; 9:22; Jer 34:14 **25:40** [x]ver 53 **25:41** [y]ver 28 [z]Jer 34:8 **25:42** [a]ver 38 **25:43** [b]S Ex 1:13; Eze 34:4; Col 4:1 [c]S Ge 42:18 **25:47** [d]Ne 5:5; Job 24:9 **25:48** [e]S ver 24 [f]S ver 25

25:24 *redemption of the land.* That is, the right to repurchase the land by (or for) the original family.
25:25 *nearest relative is to come and redeem.* See Jer 32:6–15 and note on 32:7. This is apparently what the nearest relative was to do for Naomi and Ruth (Ru 4:1–4).
25:33 *towns of the Levites.* See Nu 35:1–15 and notes; Jos 21:1–42.
25:35–38 See notes on Ex 22:21–27; Ne 5:10; Pr 28:8.
25:36 *not take interest.* The main idea was that no one should profit in any way from another's poverty; rather, the poor should be given assistance.
25:43 *fear your God.* See note on Ge 20:11.

relative in his clan may redeem him. Or if
he prospers,[g] he may redeem himself. 50He
and his buyer are to count the time from
the year he sold himself up to the Year of
Jubilee.[h] The price for his release is to be
based on the rate paid to a hired man[i] for
that number of years. 51If many years remain, he must pay for his redemption a
larger share of the price paid for him. 52If
only a few years remain until the Year of
Jubilee, he is to compute that and pay for
his redemption accordingly.[j] 53He is to be
treated as a man hired from year to year;
you must see to it that his owner does not
rule over him ruthlessly.[k]
54" 'Even if he is not redeemed in any
of these ways, he and his children are to
be released in the Year of Jubilee, 55for the
Israelites belong to me as servants. They
are my servants, whom I brought out of
Egypt.[l] I am the LORD your God.[m]

Reward for Obedience

26 " 'Do not make idols[n] or set up an
image[o] or a sacred stone[p] for yourselves, and do not place a carved stone[q]
in your land to bow down before it. I am
the LORD your God.
2" 'Observe my Sabbaths[r] and have reverence for my sanctuary.[s] I am the LORD.
3" 'If you follow my decrees and are
careful to obey[t] my commands, 4I will
send you rain[u] in its season,[v] and the
ground will yield its crops and the trees of
the field their fruit.[w] 5Your threshing will
continue until grape harvest and the grape
harvest will continue until planting, and
you will eat all the food you want[x] and live
in safety in your land.[y]
6" 'I will grant peace in the land,[z] and
you will lie down[a] and no one will make
you afraid.[b] I will remove savage beasts[c]
from the land, and the sword will not
pass through your country. 7You will pursue your enemies,[d] and they will fall by
the sword before you. 8Five[e] of you will
chase a hundred, and a hundred of you
will chase ten thousand, and your enemies
will fall by the sword before you.[f]
9" 'I will look on you with favor and
make you fruitful and increase your numbers,[g] and I will keep my covenant[h] with
you. 10You will still be eating last year's
harvest when you will have to move it out
to make room for the new.[i] 11I will put my
dwelling place[a][j] among you, and I will not
abhor you.[k] 12I will walk[l] among you and
be your God,[m] and you will be my people.[n]
13I am the LORD your God,[o] who brought
you out of Egypt[p] so that you would no
longer be slaves to the Egyptians; I broke
the bars of your yoke[q] and enabled you to
walk with heads held high.

Punishment for Disobedience

14" 'But if you will not listen to me and
carry out all these commands,[r] 15and if you
reject my decrees and abhor my laws[s] and
fail to carry out all my commands and so
violate my covenant,[t] 16then I will do this
to you: I will bring upon you sudden terror, wasting diseases and fever[u] that will
destroy your sight and drain away your
life.[v] You will plant seed in vain, because
your enemies will eat it.[w] 17I will set my
face[x] against you so that you will be defeated[y] by your enemies;[z] those who hate
you will rule over you,[a] and you will flee
even when no one is pursuing you.[b]
18" 'If after all this you will not listen to
me,[c] I will punish[d] you for your sins seven
times over.[e] 19I will break down your stubborn pride[f] and make the sky above you

[a] *11* Or *my tabernacle*

25:49 [g]ver 26 **25:50** [h]S ver 10 [i]Job 7:1; 14:6; Isa 16:14; 21:16 **25:52** [j]S ver 16 **25:53** [k]Col 4:1 **25:55** [l]S Lev 11:45 [m]Lev 11:44 **26:1** [n]S Ex 20:4 [o]Ps 97:7; Isa 48:5; Jer 44:19; Hab 2:18 [p]S Ex 23:24 [q]Nu 33:52 **26:2** [r]S Ex 20:8 [s]Lev 19:30 **26:3** [t]S Ge 26:5; S Ex 24:8; Dt 6:17; 7:12; 11:13, 22; 28:1, 9 **26:4** [u]Dt 11:14; 28:12; Ps 68:9; Jer 5:24; Hos 6:3; Joel 2:23; Zec 10:1 [v]Job 5:10; Ps 65:9; 104:13; 147:8; Jer 5:24 [w]S Ex 23:26; S Lev 25:19; S Job 14:9; Ps 67:6 **26:5** [x]Dt 6:11; 11:15; Eze 36:29-30; Joel 2:19, 26 [y]S Lev 25:18 **26:6** [z]Ps 29:11; 37:11; 85:8; 147:14; Isa 26:3; 54:13; 60:18; Hag 2:9 [a]Ps 3:5; 4:8; Pr 3:24 [b]Job 11:18, 19; Isa 17:2; Jer 30:10; Mic 4:4; Zep 3:13 [c]S ver 22; S Ge 37:20 **26:7** [d]Ps 18:37; 44:5 **26:8** [e]Isa 30:17 [f]Dt 28:7; 32:30; Jos 23:10; Jdg 15:15; 1Ch 12:14 **26:9** [g]S Ge 1:22; S 17:6; Ne 9:23 [h]S Ge 17:7 **26:10** [i]Lev 25:22 **26:11** [j]Ex 25:8; Ps 74:7; 76:2; Eze 37:27 [k]ver 15, 43, 44; Dt 31:6; 1Sa 12:22; 1Ki 6:13; 2Ki 17:15 **26:12** [l]S Ge 3:8 [m]S Ge 17:7 [n]Ex 6:7; Jer 7:23; 11:4; 24:7; 30:22; 31:1; Zec 13:9; 2Co 6:16* **26:13** [o]Lev 11:44 [p]S Ex 6:6; S 13:3 [q]Isa 10:27; Jer 2:20; 27:2; 28:10; 30:8; Eze 30:18; 34:27; Hos 11:4 **26:14** [r]Dt 28:15-68; Mal 2:2 **26:15** [s]S ver 11 [t]S Ge 17:7 **26:16** [u]Dt 28:22, 35; Ps 78:33 [v]ver 39; 1Sa 2:33; Ps 107:17; Eze 4:17; 24:23; 33:10 [w]Jdg 6:3-6; Job 31:8 **26:17** [x]Lev 17:10; Eze 15:7 [y]Dt 28:48; Jos 7:12; Jdg 2:15; 1Ki 8:33; 2Ch 6:24 [z]Jos 7:4; Jer 19:7; 21:7 [a]Ps 106:41 [b]ver 36, 37; Dt 28:7, 25; Ps 53:5; Pr 28:1; Isa 30:17 **26:18** [c]ver 14 [d]Ps 99:8; Jer 21:14; Am 3:14 [e]ver 21 **26:19** [f]Ps 10:4; 73:6; Isa 16:6; 25:11; 28:1-3; Jer 13:9; 48:29; Eze 24:21; Am 6:8; Zep 3:11

25:55 *servants.* Here to be understood as covenant terminology, referring to those who have submitted themselves in covenant to live under the Lord's rule (see chart, p. 19).

26:1 Forbids representing God in any material form (see Ex 20:4 and note). "God is spirit" (Jn 4:24; see Dt 4:15–19).

26:3 *obey my commands.* Obedience is the key to blessing (see Gal 6:7–10; Jas 1:22–25 and note on 1:25). Compare the blessings promised in vv. 3–13 with those in Dt 28:1–14.

26:4 *I will send you rain.* One of the blessings for faithful obedience to the Sinaitic covenant (see Dt 28:12; see also Dt 11:14; Isa 30:23; Jer 14:22; Zec 10:1 and notes). On the other hand, one of the curses for covenant disobedience was God's withholding of rain (v. 19; Dt 28:23–24; see also Dt 11:17; 1Ki 8:35; Isa 5:6; Jer 3:3; 14:4; Zec 14:17–18 and notes).

26:9 *fruitful and increase.* See note on Ge 1:22; contrast Lev 26:22.

26:12 *your God … my people.* Covenantal terms, later famously utilized by the prophet Hosea (1:9–10; 2:23). See Jer 31:33; Zec 8:8 and note; Heb 8:10.

26:14 *if you will not listen.* The list of curses for covenant disobedience (see vv. 14–39) is usually much longer than that of blessings for obedience (as in vv. 3–13; see Dt 28:15—29:28; cf. Dt 28:1–14), as demonstrated also in covenants and treaties elsewhere in the ancient Near East.

26:16 *You will plant seed … your enemies will eat it.* See note on Hag 1:6.

26:17 See v. 36.

26:18,21,24,28 *seven times over.* Thoroughly (cf. note on 4:6).

26:19 *sky … like iron … ground … like bronze.* See note on Dt 28:23.

like iron and the ground beneath you like
bronze.[g] 20Your strength will be spent in
vain,[h] because your soil will not yield its
crops, nor will the trees of the land yield
their fruit.[i]
21" 'If you remain hostile[j] toward me
and refuse to listen to me, I will multiply
your afflictions seven times over,[k] as your
sins deserve. 22I will send wild animals[l]
against you, and they will rob you of your
children, destroy your cattle and make
you so few[m] in number that your roads
will be deserted.[n]
23" 'If in spite of these things you do
not accept my correction[o] but continue to be hostile toward me, 24I myself
will be hostile[p] toward you and will afflict you for your sins seven times over.
25And I will bring the sword[q] upon you
to avenge[r] the breaking of the covenant.
When you withdraw into your cities, I
will send a plague[s] among you, and you
will be given into enemy hands. 26When
I cut off your supply of bread,[t] ten wom-
en will be able to bake your bread in one
oven, and they will dole out the bread by
weight. You will eat, but you will not be
satisfied.
27" 'If in spite of this you still do not
listen to me[u] but continue to be hostile toward me, 28then in my anger[v] I will be hostile[w] toward you, and I myself will punish
you for your sins seven times over.[x] 29You
will eat[y] the flesh of your sons and the
flesh of your daughters.[z] 30I will destroy
your high places,[a] cut down your incense
altars[b] and pile your dead bodies on the
lifeless forms of your idols,[c] and I will
abhor[d] you. 31I will turn your cities into
ruins[e] and lay waste[f] your sanctuaries,[g]
and I will take no delight in the pleasing aroma of your offerings.[h] 32I will lay
waste the land,[i] so that your enemies who
live there will be appalled.[j] 33I will scatter[k] you among the nations[l] and will draw
out my sword[m] and pursue you. Your land
will be laid waste,[n] and your cities will
lie in ruins.[o] 34Then the land will enjoy
its sabbath years all the time that it lies
desolate[p] and you are in the country of
your enemies;[q] then the land will rest and
enjoy its sabbaths. 35All the time that it
lies desolate, the land will have the rest[r]
it did not have during the sabbaths you
lived in it.
36" 'As for those of you who are left, I
will make their hearts so fearful in the
lands of their enemies that the sound of
a windblown leaf[s] will put them to flight.[t]
They will run as though fleeing from the
sword, and they will fall, even though no
one is pursuing them.[u] 37They will stumble
over one another[v] as though fleeing from
the sword, even though no one is pursuing them. So you will not be able to stand
before your enemies.[w] 38You will perish[x]
among the nations; the land of your enemies will devour you.[y] 39Those of you who
are left will waste away in the lands of
their enemies because of their sins; also
because of their fathers'[z] sins they will
waste away.[a]
40" 'But if they will confess[b] their sins[c]
and the sins of their fathers[d]—their
treachery against me and their hostility
toward me, 41which made me hostile[e] toward them so that I sent them into the
land of their enemies—then when their
uncircumcised hearts[f] are humbled[g] and
they pay[h] for their sin, 42I will remember
my covenant with Jacob[i] and my covenant with Isaac[j] and my covenant with
Abraham,[k] and I will remember the land.
43For the land will be deserted[l] by them
and will enjoy its sabbaths while it lies
desolate without them. They will pay for
their sins because they rejected[m] my laws
and abhorred my decrees.[n] 44Yet in spite
of this, when they are in the land of their
enemies,[o] I will not reject them or abhor[p]
them so as to destroy them completely,[q]
breaking my covenant[r] with them. I am
the LORD their God. 45But for their sake I
will remember[s] the covenant with their
ancestors whom I brought out of Egypt[t] in
the sight of the nations to be their God. I
am the LORD.' "
46These are the decrees, the laws and
the regulations that the LORD established
on Mount Sinai[u] between himself and the
Israelites through Moses.[v]

26:19 [g]Dt 28:23; Job 38:38 **26:20** [h]Dt 28:38; Ps 127:1; Isa 17:11; 49:4; Jer 12:13; Mic 6:15; Hag 1:6 [i]Dt 11:17; 28:24 **26:21** [j]ver 41 [k]ver 18; S Ge 4:15 **26:22** [l]S Ge 37:20 [m]Dt 28:62; Jer 42:2 [n]Jer 5:6; 14:16; 15:3; 16:4; Eze 14:15 **26:23** [o]Jer 2:30; 5:3; 7:28; 17:23; 32:33; Zep 3:2 **26:24** [p]2Sa 22:27 **26:25** [q]Jer 5:17; 15:3; 47:6; Eze 11:8; 14:17; 21:4; 33:2 [r]Jer 50:28; 51:6, 11 [s]S Ex 5:3; S 9:3; Nu 16:46; 1Ki 8:37; Hab 3:5 **26:26** [t]1Ki 8:37; 18:2; 2Ki 4:38; 6:25; 8:1; 25:3; Ps 105:16; Isa 3:1; 9:20; Jer 37:21; 52:6; Eze 4:16, 17; 5:16; 14:13; Hos 4:10; Mic 6:14 **26:27** [u]ver 14 **26:28** [v]Dt 32:19; Jdg 2:14; Ps 78:59; 106:40 [w]Dt 7:10; Job 34:11; Isa 59:18; 65:6-7; 66:6; Jer 17:10; 25:29; Joel 3:4 [x]ver 18 **26:29** [y]2Ki 6:29; Jer 19:9; La 4:10; Eze 5:10 [z]Dt 28:53 **26:30** [a]Dt 12:2; 1Sa 9:12; 10:5; 1Ki 3:2, 4; 12:31; 13:2, 32; 2Ki 17:29; 23:20; 2Ch 34:3; Ps 78:58; Eze 6:3; 16:16; Am 7:9 [b]2Ch 34:4; Isa 17:8; 27:9; Eze 6:6 [c]Isa 21:9; Jer 50:2; Eze 6:13 [d]Ps 106:40; Am 6:8 **26:31** [e]Ne 1:3; Isa 1:7; 3:8, 26; 6:11; 24:12; 61:4; Jer 4:7; 9:11; 25:11; 34:22; 44:2, 6, 22; Eze 36:33; Mic 2:4; 3:12; Zep 2:5; 3:6 [f]2Ki 22:19 [g]Ps 74:3-7; Isa 63:18; 64:11; La 2:7; Eze 24:21; Am 7:9 [h]Am 5:21, 22; 8:10 **26:32** [i]Isa 5:6; Jer 9:11; 12:11; 25:11; 26:9; 33:10; 34:22; 44:22 [j]1Ki 9:8; 2Ch 29:8; Isa 52:14; Jer 18:16; 19:8; 48:39; Eze 5:14; 26:16; 27:35; 28:19 **26:33** [k]Jer 40:15; 50:17; Eze 34:6; Joel 3:2 [l]Dt 4:27; 28:64; Ne 1:8; Ps 44:11; 106:27; Jer 4:11; 9:16; 13:24; 31:10; Eze 5:10; 12:15; 17:21; 20:23; 22:15; Zec 7:14 [m]Jer 42:16; Am 9:4 [n]Isa 49:19; Jer 7:34 [o]ver 31; 1Sa 15:22; Job 36:11; Jer 40:3 **26:34** [p]Isa 1:7; Jer 7:34; 25:11; 44:6; Eze 33:29 [q]ver 43; 2Ch 36:21 **26:35** [r]S Lev 25:4 **26:36** [s]Job 13:25 [t]2Ki 25:5; Ps 58:7; La 1:3, 6; 4:19; Eze 21:7 [u]S ver 17 **26:37** [v]Jer 6:21; 13:16; 46:16; Eze 3:20; Na 3:3 [w]Jos 7:12 **26:38** [x]Job 4:9; 36:12; Ps 1:6; Isa 1:28; Jer 16:4; 44:27 [y]Dt 4:26 **26:39** [z]Ex 20:5; Isa 14:21 [a]S ver 16; Isa 24:16 **26:40** [b]S Lev 5:5 [c]Ps 32:5; 38:18 [d]Ne 9:2; Ps 106:6; Jer 3:12-15; 14:20; Hos 5:15; Lk 15:18; 1Jn 1:9 **26:41** [e]S ver 21 [f]Dt 10:16; 30:6; Jer 4:4; 9:25, 26; Eze 44:7, 9; Ac 7:51 [g]2Ch 7:14; 12:6; Eze 20:43 [h]Isa 6:7; 33:24; 40:2; 53:5, 6, 11 **26:42** [i]Ge 28:15; 35:11-12 [j]S Ge 26:5 [k]S Ex 2:24 **26:43** [l]Ps 69:25; Isa 6:11; 32:14; 62:4; Jer 2:15; 44:2; La 1:1; Eze 36:4 [m]Nu 11:20; 14:31; 1Sa 8:7; Ps 106:24 [n]S ver 11; Eze 20:13 **26:44** [o]S ver 33; 2Ki 17:20; 25:11; 2Ch 6:36; 36:20 [p]S ver 11; Ro 11:2 [q]Dt 4:31; Jer 4:27; 5:10; 30:11 [r]Jdg 2:1; Jer 31:37; 33:26; 51:5 **26:45** [s]Dt 4:31 [t]Ex 6:8; Lev 25:38 **26:46** [u]S Ex 19:11 [v]S Lev 7:38; 27:34

26:30 *high places.* See note on 1Sa 9:12. *idols.* The Hebrew term means something like "piles of dung."
26:34 Fulfilled during the Babylonian exile (see note on 2Ch 36:20–21).
26:40 *confess their sins.* See notes on Pr 28:13; 1Jn 1:19.
26:41 *uncircumcised hearts.* See note on Ge 17:10.
26:44 *not reject them.* See Jer 31:37; 33:25–26; Ro 11:1–29 and notes.
26:46 A summary statement concerning chs. 1–26.

Redeeming What Is the LORD's

27 The LORD said to Moses, 2 "Speak to
the Israelites and say to them: 'If
anyone makes a special vow[w] to dedicate
persons to the LORD by giving equivalent
values, 3 set the value of a male between
the ages of twenty and sixty at fifty shekels[a] of silver, according to the sanctuary
shekel[b];[x] 4 and if it is a female, set her value at thirty shekels.[c] 5 If it is a person between the ages of five and twenty, set the
value of a male at twenty shekels[d][y] and
of a female at ten shekels.[e] 6 If it is a person between one month and five years, set
the value of a male at five shekels[f][z] of silver and that of a female at three shekels[g]
of silver. 7 If it is a person sixty years old
or more, set the value of a male at fifteen
shekels[h] and of a female at ten shekels.
8 If anyone making the vow is too poor to
pay[a] the specified amount, he is to present
the person to the priest, who will set the
value[b] for him according to what the man
making the vow can afford.

9 " 'If what he vowed is an animal that
is acceptable as an offering to the LORD,[c]
such an animal given to the LORD becomes
holy.[d] 10 He must not exchange it or substitute a good one for a bad one, or a bad one
for a good one;[e] if he should substitute one
animal for another, both it and the substitute become holy. 11 If what he vowed
is a ceremonially unclean animal[f]—one
that is not acceptable as an offering to the
LORD—the animal must be presented to
the priest, 12 who will judge its quality as
good or bad. Whatever value the priest
then sets, that is what it will be. 13 If the
owner wishes to redeem[g] the animal, he
must add a fifth to its value.[h]

14 " 'If a man dedicates his house as
something holy to the LORD, the priest will
judge its quality as good or bad. Whatever
value the priest then sets, so it will remain.
15 If the man who dedicates his house redeems it,[i] he must add a fifth to its value,
and the house will again become his.

16 " 'If a man dedicates to the LORD part
of his family land, its value is to be set according to the amount of seed required for
it—fifty shekels of silver to a homer[i] of
barley seed. 17 If he dedicates his field during the Year of Jubilee, the value that has
been set remains. 18 But if he dedicates his
field after the Jubilee,[j] the priest will determine the value according to the number
of years that remain[k] until the next Year of
Jubilee, and its set value will be reduced.
19 If the man who dedicates the field wishes to redeem it,[l] he must add a fifth to
its value, and the field will again become
his. 20 If, however, he does not redeem the
field, or if he has sold it to someone else,
it can never be redeemed. 21 When the field
is released in the Jubilee,[m] it will become
holy,[n] like a field devoted to the LORD;[o] it
will become the property of the priests.[j]

22 " 'If a man dedicates to the LORD a field
he has bought, which is not part of his
family land, 23 the priest will determine
its value up to the Year of Jubilee,[p] and
the man must pay its value on that day as
something holy to the LORD. 24 In the Year
of Jubilee the field will revert to the person
from whom he bought it,[q] the one whose
land it was. 25 Every value is to be set according to the sanctuary shekel,[r] twenty
gerahs[s] to the shekel.

26 " 'No one, however, may dedicate the
firstborn of an animal, since the firstborn
already belongs to the LORD;[t] whether an
ox[k] or a sheep, it is the LORD's. 27 If it is
one of the unclean animals,[u] he may buy
it back at its set value, adding a fifth of the
value to it. If he does not redeem it, it is to
be sold at its set value.

28 " 'But nothing that a man owns and
devotes[l][v] to the LORD—whether man or
animal or family land—may be sold or

27:2 [w] S Ge 28:20 **27:3** [x] S Ex 30:13 **27:5** [y] S Ge 37:28 **27:6** [z] Nu 3:47; 18:16 **27:8** [a] S Lev 5:11 [b] ver 12,14 **27:9** [c] S Ge 28:20; S Lev 1:2 [d] ver 21,26,28; Ex 40:9; Nu 6:20; 18:17; Dt 15:19 **27:10** [e] ver 33 **27:11** [f] ver 27; S Ex 13:13; Nu 18:15 **27:13** [g] S Lev 25:25 [h] S Lev 5:16 **27:15** [i] ver 13,20 **27:18** [j] Lev 25:10 [k] Lev 25:15 **27:19** [l] S Lev 25:25 **27:21** [m] S Lev 25:10 [n] S ver 9 [o] ver 28; Nu 18:14; Eze 44:29 **27:23** [p] S Lev 25:15 **27:24** [q] Lev 25:28 **27:25** [r] S Ex 30:13 [s] Nu 3:47; Eze 45:12 **27:26** [t] S Ex 13:12 **27:27** [u] S ver 11 **27:28** [v] Nu 18:14; Jos 6:17-19

[a] *3* That is, about 1 1/4 pounds (about 0.6 kilogram); also in verse 16 [b] *3* That is, about 2/5 ounce (about 11.5 grams); also in verse 25 [c] *4* That is, about 12 ounces (about 0.3 kilogram) [d] *5* That is, about 8 ounces (about 0.2 kilogram) [e] *5* That is, about 4 ounces (about 110 grams); also in verse 7 [f] *6* That is, about 2 ounces (about 55 grams) [g] *6* That is, about 1 1/4 ounces (about 35 grams) [h] *7* That is, about 6 ounces (about 170 grams) [i] *16* That is, probably about 6 bushels (about 220 liters) [j] *21* Or *priest* [k] *26* The Hebrew word can include both male and female. [l] *28* The Hebrew term refers to the irrevocable giving over of things or persons to the LORD.

27:1–34 This final chapter concerns things promised to the Lord in kind—servants, animals, houses or lands. But provisions were made to give money instead of the item, in which case usually the adding of a fifth of its value was required. Such vows were expressions of special thanksgiving (cf. Hannah, 1Sa 1:28) and were given over and above the expected sacrifices.
27:2 *to dedicate persons.* Possibly to give slaves to the service of the temple, but more likely to offer oneself or a member of one's family. Since only Levites were acceptable for most work of this kind, other people gave the monetary equivalent—but see 1Sa 1:11 and note.
27:3,25 *according to the sanctuary shekel.* See note on Ex 30:13.
27:9 *becomes holy.* See note on Ex 3:5. An animal given for a sacrifice could not be exchanged for another (v. 10). The people of Malachi's day chose the poorest animals after having vowed to offer good ones (see Mal 1:13–14 and notes). If an unclean animal was given, it could be redeemed with the 20 percent penalty (vv. 11–13).
27:18 See note on 25:15.
27:28 *devotes to the LORD.* See NIV text note. Devoting something was far more serious than dedicating it to sacred use. The devoted thing became totally the Lord's. Achan's sin was the greater because he stole what had been devoted to the Lord (Jos 7:11). Persons devoted to destruction were usually the captives in the wars of Canaan (cf. 1Sa 15:3,18 and note on 15:3).

redeemed; everything so devoted is most
holy[w] to the LORD.
29 " 'No person devoted to destruction[a]
may be ransomed; he must be put to
death.[x]
30 " 'A tithe[y] of everything from the land,
whether grain from the soil or fruit from
the trees, belongs to the LORD; it is holy[z]
to the LORD. 31 If a man redeems[a] any of
his tithe, he must add a fifth of the value[b] to it. 32 The entire tithe of the herd and
flock—every tenth animal that passes under the shepherd's rod[c]—will be holy to
the LORD. 33 He must not pick out the good
from the bad or make any substitution.[d]
If he does make a substitution, both the
animal and its substitute become holy and
cannot be redeemed.[e] ' "

34 These are the commands the LORD gave
Moses on Mount Sinai[f] for the Israelites.[g]

27:28 [w] S ver 9 **27:29** [x] Dt 7:26 **27:30** [y] Nu 18:26; Dt 12:6, 17; 14:22, 28; 2Ch 31:6; Ne 10:37; 12:44; 13:5; Mal 3:8 [z] Dt 7:6; Ezr 9:2; Isa 6:13 **27:31** [a] S Lev 25:25 [b] Lev 5:16 **27:32** [c] Ps 89:32; Jer 33:13; Eze 20:37

[a] *29* The Hebrew term refers to the irrevocable giving over of things or persons to the LORD, often by totally destroying them.

27:33 [d] ver 10 [e] Nu 18:21 **27:34** [f] S Ex 19:11 [g] S Lev 7:38; Ac 7:38

27:29 Saul sinned in this regard when he did not totally destroy the Amalekites (1Sa 15).
27:30 *tithe.* A tenth (see Nu 18:21 – 29 and note on 18:26 – 32; Dt 12:6 – 18; 14:22 – 29 and note; 26:12). From these passages it appears that Israel actually had three tithes: (1) the general tithe (here), paid to the Levites (Nu 18:21), who in turn had to give a tenth of that to the priests (Nu 18:26); (2) the tithe associated with the sacred meal involving offerer and Levite (Dt 14:22 – 27); (3) the tithe paid every three years to the poor (Dt 14:28 – 29).
27:34 *the LORD gave Moses.* See 1:1 and note; 7:37 – 38; 25:1; 26:46.

Numbers

I N T R O D U C T I O N

Title

The English name of the book comes from the Septuagint (the pre-Christian Greek translation of the OT) and is based on the census lists found in chs. 1; 26. The Hebrew title of the book (*bemidbar,* "in the Desert of," 1:1) is more descriptive of its contents. Numbers presents an account of the 38-year period of Israel's wandering in the desert following the establishment of the covenant of Sinai (compare 1:1 with Dt 1:1).

> **A Quick Look**
>
> **Author:**
> Moses
>
> **Audience:**
> God's chosen people, the Israelites
>
> **Date:**
> Probably between 1446 and 1406 B.C.
>
> **Theme:**
> Because the Israelites are unwilling to enter the land of Canaan, their entire generation is forced to wander in the Desert of Sinai for 38 years.

Author and Date

The book has traditionally been ascribed to Moses. This conclusion is based on (1) statements concerning Moses' writing activity (see, e.g., 33:1–2; Ex 17:14 and note; 24:4; 34:27–28) and (2) the assumption that the first five books of the Bible, the Pentateuch, are a unit and come from one author. See Introduction to Genesis: Author and Date of Writing.

It is not necessary, however, to claim that Numbers came from Moses' hand complete and in final form. Portions of the book were probably added by scribes or editors from later periods of Israel's history. For example, the protestation of the humility of Moses (12:3) would hardly be convincing if it came from his own mouth. But it seems reasonable to assume that Moses wrote the essential content of the book.

Contents

Numbers relates the story of Israel's journey from Mount Sinai to the plains of Moab on the border of Canaan. Much of its legislation for people and priests is similar to that in Exodus, Leviticus and Deuteronomy. The book tells of the murmuring and rebellion of the people of God and of their subsequent judgment. Those whom God had redeemed from slavery in Egypt and with whom he had made a covenant at Mount Sinai responded not with faith, gratitude and obedience but with unbelief, ingratitude and repeated acts of rebellion, which came to extreme expression in their refusal to undertake the conquest of Canaan (ch. 14). The community of the redeemed forfeited their part in the promised land. They were condemned to live out their lives in the desert; only their children would enjoy the fulfillment of the promise that had originally been theirs (cf. Heb 3:7—4:11 and notes).

Theological Teaching

In telling the story of Israel's desert wanderings, Numbers offers much that is theologically significant. During the first year after Israel's deliverance from Egypt, the nation entered into covenant with the Lord at Sinai to be the people of his kingdom, among whom he pitched his royal tent (the tabernacle)—this is the story of Exodus. As the account of Numbers begins, the Lord organizes Israel into a military camp. Leaving Sinai, they march forth as his conquering army, with the Lord at the head, to establish his kingdom in the promised land in the midst of the nations. The book graphically portrays Israel's identity as the Lord's redeemed covenant people and its vocation as the servant people of God, charged with establishing his kingdom on earth. God's purpose in history is implicitly disclosed: to invade the arena of fallen humanity and effect the redemption of his creation—the mission in which his people are also to be totally engaged.

The book of Numbers tells of the murmuring and rebellion of the people of God, those whom he had redeemed from slavery in Egypt.

Numbers also presents the chastening wrath of God against his disobedient people. Because of their rebellion (and especially the nation's refusal to undertake the conquest of Canaan), Israel was in breach of covenant. The fourth book of the Pentateuch presents a sobering reality: The God who had entered into covenant with Abraham (Ge 15; 17), who had delivered his people from bondage in the exodus (Ex 14–15), who had brought Israel into covenant with himself as his "treasured possession" (Ex 19; see especially Ex 19:5 and note) and who had revealed his holiness and the gracious means of approaching him (Lev 1–7) was also a God of wrath. His wrath extended to his errant children as well as to the enemy nations of Egypt and Canaan.

Even Moses, the great prophet and servant of the Lord, was not exempt from God's wrath when he disobeyed God. Ch. 20, which records his error, begins with the notice of Miriam's death (20:1) and concludes with the record of Aaron's death (20:22–29). Here is the passing of the old guard. Those whom God has used to establish the nation are dying before the nation has come into its own.

The questions arise: Is God finished with the nation as a whole (cf. Ro 11:1)? Are his promises a thing of the past? In one of the most remarkable sections of the Bible—the account of Balaam, the pagan diviner (chs. 22–24)—the reply is given. The Lord, working in a providential and direct way, proclaims his continued faithfulness to his purpose for his people despite their unfaithfulness to him.

Balaam is Moab's answer to Moses, the man of God. He is an internationally known prophet who shares the pagan belief that the God of Israel is like any other deity who might be manipulated by acts of magic or sorcery. But from the early part of the narrative, when Balaam first encounters the one true God in visions, and in the narrative of the journey on the donkey (ch. 22), he begins to learn that dealing with the true God is fundamentally different from anything he has ever known. When he attempts to curse Israel at the instigation of Balak king of Moab, Balaam finds his mouth unable to express the curse he desires to pronounce. Instead, from his lips come blessings on Israel and curses on its enemies (chs. 23–24).

In his seven prophetic oracles, Balaam proclaims God's great blessing for his people (see 23:20). Though the immediate enjoyment of this blessing will always depend on the faithfulness of his people, the ultimate realization of God's blessing is sure—because of the character of God (see 23:19 and note). Thus Numbers reaffirms the ongoing purposes of God. Despite his judgment on his rebellious people, God is still determined to bring Israel into the land of promise. His blessing to Israel rests in his sovereign will.

The teaching of the book has lasting significance for Israel and for the church (cf. Ro 15:4; 1Co 10:6,11 and notes). God does display his wrath even against his errant people, but his grace is renewed as surely as is the dawn and his redemptive purpose will not be thwarted.

Special Problem

The large numbers of men conscripted into Israel's army (see, e.g., the figures in 1:46; 26:51) have puzzled many interpreters. The numbers of men mustered for warfare seem to demand a total population in excess of 2,000,000. Such numbers appear to be exceedingly large for the times, for the locale, for the desert wanderings, and in comparison with the inhabitants of Canaan. See note on 3:43.

Those whom God has used to establish the nation are dying before the nation has come into its own.

Various possibilities have been suggested to solve this problem. Some have thought that the numbers may have been corrupted in transmission. The present text, however, does not betray textual difficulties with the numbers.

Others have felt that the Hebrew word for "thousand" might have a different meaning here from its usual numerical connotation. In some passages, for example, the word is a technical term for a company of men that may or may not equal 1,000 (e.g., Jos 22:14, "family division"; 1Sa 23:23, "clans"). Further, some have postulated that this Hebrew word means "chief" (as in Ge 36:15). In this way the figure 53,400 (26:47) would mean "53 chiefs plus 400 men." Such a procedure would yield a greatly reduced total, but it would be at variance with the fact that the Hebrew text adds the "thousands" in the same way it adds the "hundreds" for a large total. Also, this would make the proportion of chiefs to fighting men top-heavy (59 chiefs for 300 men in Simeon).

Another option is to read the Hebrew word for "thousand" with a dual meaning of "chief" and "1,000," with the chiefs numbering one less than the stated figure. For example, the 46,500 of Reuben (1:20) is read as 45 chiefs and 1,500 fighting men, the 59,300 of Simeon (1:23) is read as 58 chiefs and 1,300 fighting men, etc. But in this case, as in the former, the totals of 1:46 and 2:32 must then be regarded as errors of understanding (perhaps by later scribes).

Still another approach is to regard the numbers as symbolic figures rather than as strictly mathematical. The numerical value of the Hebrew letters in the expression *bene yisra'el* ("the Israelite community," 1:2) equals 603 (the number of the thousands of the fighting men, 1:46); the remaining 550 (plus 1 for Moses) might come from the numerical equivalent of the Hebrew letters in the expression "all the men ... who are able to serve in the army" (1:3). This symbolic use of numbers (called "gematria") is not unknown in the Bible (see Rev 13:18), but it is not likely in Numbers, where there are no literary clues pointing in that direction. (For one more option [hyperbole] see note on 1Ch 12:23–37.)

While the problem of the large numbers has not been satisfactorily solved, the Bible does point to a remarkable increase of Jacob's descendants during the four centuries of their sojourn in Egypt (see Ex 1:7–12). With all their difficulties, these numbers also point to the great role of providence and miracles in God's dealings with his people during their life in the desert (see note on 1:46).

Structure and Outline

The book has three major divisions, based on Israel's geographical locations. Each of the three divisions has two parts, as the following breakdown demonstrates: (1) Israel at Sinai, preparing to depart for the land of promise (1:1—10:10), followed by the journey from Sinai to Kadesh (10:11—12:16); (2) Israel at Kadesh, delayed as a result of rebellion (13:1—20:13), followed by the journey from Kadesh to the plains of Moab (20:14—22:1); (3) Israel on the plains of Moab, anticipating the conquest of the land of promise (22:2—32:42), followed by appendixes dealing with various matters (chs. 33–36).

I. Israel at Sinai, Preparing to Depart for the Promised Land (1:1 — 10:10)
   A. The Commands for the Census of the People (chs. 1 – 4)
      1. The numbers of men from each tribe mustered for war (ch. 1)
      2. The placement of the tribes around the tabernacle and their order for march (ch. 2)
      3. The placement of the Levites around the tabernacle, and the numbers of the Levites and the firstborn of Israel (ch. 3)
      4. The numbers of the Levites in their tabernacle service for the Lord (ch. 4)
   B. The Commands for Purity of the People (5:1 — 10:10)
      1. The test for purity in the law of jealousy (ch. 5)
      2. The Nazirite vow and the Aaronic benediction (ch. 6)
      3. The offerings of the 12 leaders at the dedication of the tabernacle (ch. 7)
      4. The setting up of the lamps and the separation of the Levites (ch. 8)
      5. The observance of the Passover (9:1 – 14)
      6. The covering cloud and the silver trumpets (9:15 — 10:10)

II. The Journey from Sinai to Kadesh (10:11 — 12:16)
   A. The Beginning of the Journey (10:11 – 36)
   B. The Beginning of the Sorrows: Fire and Quail (ch. 11)
   C. The Opposition of Miriam and Aaron (ch. 12)

III. Israel at Kadesh, the Delay Resulting from Rebellion (13:1 — 20:13)
   A. The 12 Spies and Their Mixed Report of the Good Land (ch. 13)
   B. The People's Rebellion against God's Commission, and Their Defeat (ch. 14)
   C. A Collection of Laws on Offerings, the Sabbath and Tassels on Garments (ch. 15)
   D. The Rebellion of Korah and His Allies (ch. 16)
   E. The Budding of Aaron's Staff: A Sign for Rebels (ch. 17)
   F. Concerning Priests, Their Duties and Their Support (ch. 18)
   G. The Red Heifer and the Cleansing Water (ch. 19)
   H. The Sin of Moses (20:1 – 13)

IV. The Journey from Kadesh to the Plains of Moab (20:14 — 22:1)
   A. The Resistance of Edom (20:14 – 21)
   B. The Death of Aaron (20:22 – 29)
   C. The Destruction of Arad (21:1 – 3)
   D. The Bronze Snake (21:4 – 9)
   E. The Song of the Well and the Journey to Moab (21:10 – 20)
   F. The Defeat of Sihon and Og (21:21 – 35)
   G. Israel Returns to Moab (22:1)

V. Israel on the Plains of Moab, in Anticipation of Taking the Promised Land (22:2 — 32:42)
   A. Balak of Moab Hires Balaam to Curse Israel (22:2 – 41)
   B. Balaam Blesses Israel in Seven Oracles (chs. 23 – 24)
   C. The Baal of Peor and Israel's Apostasy (ch. 25)
   D. The Second Census (ch. 26)
   E. Instructions for the New Generation (chs. 27 – 30)
      1. The inheritance for women (27:1 – 11)
      2. The successor to Moses (27:12 – 23)
      3. Commands regarding offerings (28:1 – 15)
      4. Commands regarding festivals (28:16 — 29:40)
      5. Commands regarding vows (ch. 30)
   F. The War against Midian (ch. 31)
   G. The Settlement of the Transjordan Tribes (ch. 32)

VI. Appendixes Dealing with Various Matters (chs. 33 – 36)
   A. The Stages of the Journey (ch. 33)
   B. The Land of Inheritance (chs. 34 – 35)
   C. The Inheritance for Women (ch. 36)

The Census

1 The LORD spoke to Moses in the Tent
of Meeting[a] in the Desert of Sinai[b] on
the first day of the second month[c] of the
second year after the Israelites came out
of Egypt.[d] He said: 2“Take a census[e] of the
whole Israelite community by their clans
and families,[f] listing every man by name,[g]
one by one. 3You and Aaron[h] are to number by their divisions all the men in Israel
twenty years old or more[i] who are able to
serve in the army.[j] 4One man from each
tribe,[k] each the head of his family,[l] is to
help you.[m] 5These are the names[n] of the
men who are to assist you:

from Reuben,[o] Elizur son of Shedeur;[p]
6from Simeon,[q] Shelumiel son of Zurishaddai;[r]
7from Judah,[s] Nahshon son of Amminadab;[t]
8from Issachar,[u] Nethanel son of Zuar;[v]
9from Zebulun,[w] Eliab son of Helon;[x]
10from the sons of Joseph:
from Ephraim,[y] Elishama son of
Ammihud;[z]
from Manasseh,[a] Gamaliel son of
Pedahzur;[b]
11from Benjamin,[c] Abidan son of Gideoni;[d]
12from Dan,[e] Ahiezer son of Ammishaddai;[f]
13from Asher,[g] Pagiel son of Ocran;[h]
14from Gad,[i] Eliasaph son of Deuel;[j]
15from Naphtali,[k] Ahira son of Enan.[l]”

16These were the men appointed from
the community, the leaders[m] of their ancestral tribes.[n] They were the heads of the
clans of Israel.[o]

17Moses and Aaron took these men
whose names had been given, 18and they
called the whole community together on
the first day of the second month.[p] The
people indicated their ancestry[q] by their
clans and families,[r] and the men twenty
years old or more[s] were listed by name,
one by one, 19as the LORD commanded Moses. And so he counted[t] them in the Desert
of Sinai:

20From the descendants of Reuben[u] the
firstborn son[v] of Israel:
All the men twenty years old or
more who were able to serve in
the army were listed by name, one
by one, according to the records
of their clans and families. 21The
number from the tribe of Reuben[w]
was 46,500.

22From the descendants of Simeon:[x]
All the men twenty years old or
more who were able to serve in
the army were counted and listed
by name, one by one, according to
the records of their clans and families. 23The number from the tribe of
Simeon was 59,300.[y]

24From the descendants of Gad:[z]
All the men twenty years old or
more who were able to serve in the
army were listed by name, according to the records of their clans and

1:1 [a]S Ex 27:21; S 40:2 [b]S Ex 19:1 [c]ver 18 [d]S Ex 6:14 **1:2** [e]Ex 30:11-16 [f]ver 18 [g]Nu 3:40 **1:3** [h]Ex 4:14; Nu 17:3 [i]S Ex 30:14 [j]ver 20; Nu 26:2; Jos 5:4; 1Ch 5:18 **1:4** [k]S Lev 24:11; S Jos 7:1 [l]ver 16; Nu 7:2; 30:1; 31:26 [m]Ex 18:21; Nu 34:18; Dt 1:15; Jos 22:14 **1:5** [n]Nu 17:2 [o]S Ge 29:32; Rev 7:5 [p]Nu 2:10; 7:30; 10:18 **1:6** [q]ver 22; Nu 25:14 [r]Nu 2:12; 7:36,41; 10:19 **1:7** [s]ver 26; S Ge 29:35; Ps 78:68 [t]Ex 6:23; Nu 7:12; Ru 4:20; 1Ch 2:10; Mt 1:4; Lk 3:32 **1:8** [u]S Ge 30:18; Nu 10:15 [v]Nu 2:5; 7:18 **1:9** [w]ver 30; Nu 10:16 [x]Nu 2:7; 7:24 **1:10** [y]ver 32 [z]Nu 2:18; 7:48,53; 10:22 [a]ver 34; Nu 10:23 [b]Nu 2:20; 7:54 **1:11** [c]Nu 10:24 [d]Nu 2:22; 7:60; Ps 68:27 **1:12** [e]ver 38 [f]Nu 2:25; 7:66; 10:25 **1:13** [g]ver 40; Nu 10:26 [h]Nu 2:27; 7:72 **1:14** [i]ver 24; Nu 10:20 [j]Nu 2:14; 7:42 **1:15** [k]ver 42; Nu 10:27 [l]Nu 2:29; 7:78 **1:16** [m]S Ex 18:25 [n]Nu 32:28 [o]S ver 4 **1:18** [p]ver 1 [q]Ezr 2:59; Heb 7:3 [r]ver 2 [s]S Ex 30:14 **1:19** [t]Ex 30:12; Nu 26:63; 31:49 **1:20** [u]S Ge 29:32; S 46:9; Rev 7:5 [v]S Ge 10:15 **1:21** [w]Nu 26:7 **1:22** [x]S Ge 29:33; Rev 7:7 **1:23** [y]Nu 26:14 **1:24** [z]S Ge 30:11; S Jos 13:24-28; Rev 7:5

1:1 *The LORD spoke to Moses.* One of the most pervasive emphases in Numbers is the fact that the Lord spoke to Moses and through Moses to Israel. From the opening words to the closing words (36:13), this is stated over 150 times and in more than 20 ways. The Lord's use of Moses as his prophet is described in 12:6–8 (see notes there). One of the Hebrew names for the book is *wayedabber* ("And he [the LORD] spoke"), from the first word in the Hebrew text. *Tent of Meeting.* The tabernacle. *Desert of Sinai.* The more common Hebrew name for Numbers is *bemidbar* ("in the Desert of"), the fifth word in the Hebrew text. The events of Numbers cover a period of 38 years and nine or ten months, i.e., the period of Israel's desert wanderings. *first day ... second month ... second year.* Thirteen months after the exodus, Numbers begins. Israel had spent the previous year in the region of Mount Sinai receiving the law and erecting the tabernacle. Now the people were to be mustered as a military force for an orderly march. Dating events from the exodus (for another example see 1Ki 6:1 and note) is similar to the Christian practice of dating years in reference to the incarnation of Christ (B.C. and A.D.). The exodus was God's great act of deliverance of his people from bondage.

1:2 *Take.* The Hebrew for this word is plural, indicating that Moses and Aaron were to complete this task together (see v. 3, "You and Aaron"), but the primary responsibility lay with Moses. *census.* Its main purpose was to form a military roster, not a social, political or taxing document.

1:3 *able to serve in the army.* Refers to the principal military purpose of the census. The phrase occurs 14 times in ch. 1 and again in 26:2 (see note on 26:1–51).

1:4 *One man from each tribe.* By having a representative from each tribe assist Moses and Aaron, the count would be regarded as legitimate by all.

1:5–16 The names of these men occur again in chs. 2; 7; 10. Most contain within them a reference to the name of God. Levi is not represented in the list (see vv. 47–53 and notes).

1:19 *And so he counted them in the Desert of Sinai.* A summary statement; vv. 20–43 provide the details.

1:20–43 For each tribe there are two verses in repetitive formulaic structure, giving: (1) the name of the tribe, (2) the specifics of those numbered, (3) the name of the tribe again and (4) the total count for that tribe. The numbers for each tribe are probably rounded off to the hundred (but Gad to the 50, v. 25). The same numbers are given for each tribe in ch. 2, where there are four triads of tribes. A peculiarity in the numbers that leads some to believe that they are symbolic is that the hundreds are grouped between 200 and 700. Also, various speculations have arisen regarding the meaning of the Hebrew word for "thousand" (see Introduction: Special Problem). In this chapter, the word has been used to mean 1,000 in order for the totals to be achieved.

families. 25The number from the
tribe of Gad[a] was 45,650.

26From the descendants of Judah:[b]
All the men twenty years old or
more who were able to serve in the
army were listed by name, according to the records of their clans and
families. 27The number from the
tribe of Judah[c] was 74,600.

28From the descendants of Issachar:[d]
All the men twenty years old or
more who were able to serve in the
army were listed by name, according to the records of their clans and
families. 29The number from the
tribe of Issachar[e] was 54,400.[f]

30From the descendants of Zebulun:[g]
All the men twenty years old or
more who were able to serve in the
army were listed by name, according to the records of their clans and
families. 31The number from the
tribe of Zebulun was 57,400.[h]

32From the sons of Joseph:[i]
From the descendants of Ephraim:[j]
All the men twenty years old or
more who were able to serve in the
army were listed by name, according to the records of their clans and
families. 33The number from the
tribe of Ephraim[k] was 40,500.
34From the descendants of Manasseh:[l]
All the men twenty years old or
more who were able to serve in the
army were listed by name, according to the records of their clans and
families. 35The number from the
tribe of Manasseh was 32,200.

36From the descendants of Benjamin:[m]
All the men twenty years old or
more who were able to serve in the
army were listed by name, according to the records of their clans and
families. 37The number from the
tribe of Benjamin[n] was 35,400.

38From the descendants of Dan:[o]
All the men twenty years old or
more who were able to serve in the
army were listed by name, according to the records of their clans and
families. 39The number from the
tribe of Dan was 62,700.[p]

40From the descendants of Asher:[q]
All the men twenty years old or
more who were able to serve in the
army were listed by name, according to the records of their clans and
families. 41The number from the
tribe of Asher[r] was 41,500.

42From the descendants of Naphtali:[s]
All the men twenty years old or
more who were able to serve in the
army were listed by name, according to the records of their clans and
families. 43The number from the
tribe of Naphtali[t] was 53,400.[u]

44These were the men counted by Moses
and Aaron[v] and the twelve leaders of Israel, each one representing his family. 45All
the Israelites twenty years old or more[w]
who were able to serve in Israel's army
were counted according to their families.[x]
46The total number was 603,550.[y]

47The families of the tribe of Levi,[z] however, were not counted[a] along with the
others. 48The LORD had said to Moses:
49"You must not count the tribe of Levi or
include them in the census of the other
Israelites. 50Instead, appoint the Levites to
be in charge of the tabernacle[b] of the Testimony[c]—over all its furnishings[d] and everything belonging to it. They are to carry
the tabernacle and all its furnishings; they
are to take care of it and encamp around
it. 51Whenever the tabernacle[e] is to move,[f]
the Levites are to take it down, and whenever the tabernacle is to be set up, the

1:25 [a]Ge 46:16; Nu 26:18; 1Ch 5:11 **1:26** [b]S ver 7; Mt 1:2; Rev 7:5 **1:27** [c]Nu 26:22 **1:28** [d]S Ge 30:18; Rev 7:7 **1:29** [e]S Ge 30:18 [f]Nu 26:25 **1:30** [g]S Ge 30:20; Rev 7:8 **1:31** [h]Nu 26:27 **1:32** [i]Ge 49:26 [j]S Ge 41:52 **1:33** [k]Nu 26:37; 1Ch 7:20 **1:34** [l]S Ge 41:51; Rev 7:6 **1:36** [m]S Ge 35:18; 2Ch 17:17; Jer 32:44; Ob 1:19; Rev 7:8 **1:37** [n]Nu 26:41 **1:38** [o]Ge 30:6; Dt 33:22 **1:39** [p]Nu 26:43 **1:40** [q]S Ge 30:13; Nu 26:44; Rev 7:6 **1:41** [r]Nu 26:47 **1:42** [s]S Ge 30:8; Rev 7:6 **1:43** [t]Nu 26:50 [u]S Ex 1:1-4 **1:44** [v]Nu 26:64 **1:45** [w]ver 3; Nu 14:29 [x]Nu 2:32 **1:46** [y]S Ex 12:37; 2Sa 24:9 **1:47** [z]S Nu 3:17-20 [a]Nu 4:3,49 **1:50** [b]Ex 25:9; S 26:1 [c]S 16:34; Ac 7:44; Rev 15:5 [d]Nu 3:31 **1:51** [e]S Ex 26:1 [f]Nu 4:5

1:32–35 Because the descendants of Levi were excluded from the census (see note on v. 47), the descendants of Joseph are listed according to the families of his two sons, Ephraim (vv. 32–33) and Manasseh (vv. 34–35). In this way the traditional tribal number of 12 is maintained, and Joseph is given the "double portion" of the ranking heir (cf. Ge 49:22–26; Dt 33:13–17; 2Ki 2:9 and relevant notes).

1:46 *603,550.* Except for Joshua and Caleb, all these died in the desert. The mathematics of these numbers is accurate and complex. It is complex in that the totals are reached in two ways: (1) a linear listing of 12 units (vv. 20–43), with the total given (v. 46); (2) four sets of triads, each with a subtotal, and then the grand total (2:3–32). These figures are also consistent with those in Ex 12:37; 38:26. This large number of men conscripted for the army suggests a population for the entire community in excess of 2,000,000 (see Introduction: Special Problem). Ex 1:7 describes the remarkable growth of the Hebrew people in Egypt during the 400-year sojourn. They had become so numerous that they were regarded as a grave threat to the security of Egypt (Ex 1:9–10,20). Israel's amazing growth from the 70 who entered Egypt (Ex 1:5) was an evidence of God's great blessing and his faithfulness to his covenant with Abraham (Ge 12:2; 15:5; 17:4–6; 22:17).

1:47 Because of their special tasks, the Levites were excluded from this military count. They too had to perform service to the Lord, but they were to be engaged in the ceremonies and maintenance of the tabernacle (see note on vv. 32–35).

1:50,53 *Testimony.* The Ten Commandments written on stone tablets (see Ex 31:18; 32:15; 34:29), which were placed in the ark (Ex 25:16,21; 40:20), leading to the phrase the "ark of the Testimony" (Ex 25:22; 26:33,34). See notes on Ex 16:34; 25:16,22.

1:51 *Anyone else.* The Hebrew for this phrase is often translated "stranger," "alien" or "foreigner" (e.g., Isa 1:7; Hos 7:9). Thus a non-Levite Israelite was considered an alien to the religious duties of the tabernacle (see Ex 29:33; 30:33; Lev 22:12). *death.* See 3:10,38; 18:7; cf. 16:31–33; 1Sa 6:19.

Levites shall do it.[g] Anyone else who goes
near it shall be put to death.[h] 52The Israelites are to set up their tents by divisions,
each man in his own camp under his own
standard.[i] 53The Levites, however, are to
set up their tents around the tabernacle[j] of
the Testimony so that wrath will not fall[k]
on the Israelite community. The Levites
are to be responsible for the care of the
tabernacle of the Testimony.[l]"
54The Israelites did all this just as the
LORD commanded Moses.

The Arrangement of the Tribal Camps

2 The LORD said to Moses and Aaron:
2"The Israelites are to camp around
the Tent of Meeting some distance from
it, each man under his standard[m] with the
banners of his family."

3On the east, toward the sunrise,
the divisions of the camp of Judah
are to encamp under their standard.
The leader of the people of Judah is
Nahshon son of Amminadab.[n] 4His
division numbers 74,600.
5The tribe of Issachar[o] will camp
next to them. The leader of the people
of Issachar is Nethanel son of Zuar.[p]
6His division numbers 54,400.
7The tribe of Zebulun will be next.
The leader of the people of Zebulun
is Eliab son of Helon.[q] 8His division
numbers 57,400.
9All the men assigned to the camp
of Judah, according to their divisions,
number 186,400. They will set out
first.[r]

10On the south[s] will be the divisions of the camp of Reuben under
their standard. The leader of the people of Reuben is Elizur son of Shedeur.[t] 11His division numbers 46,500.
12The tribe of Simeon[u] will camp
next to them. The leader of the people of Simeon is Shelumiel son of Zurishaddai.[v] 13His division numbers
59,300.
14The tribe of Gad[w] will be next.
The leader of the people of Gad is Eliasaph son of Deuel.[a][x] 15His division
numbers 45,650.
16All the men assigned to the camp
of Reuben,[y] according to their divisions, number 151,450. They will set
out second.

17Then the Tent of Meeting and the
camp of the Levites[z] will set out in
the middle of the camps. They will
set out in the same order as they encamp, each in his own place under
his standard.

18On the west[a] will be the divisions
of the camp of Ephraim[b] under their
standard. The leader of the people of

1:51 [g]Nu 3:38; 4:15 [h]S Ex 21:12
1:52 [i]Nu 10:14; Ps 20:5; SS 2:4; 6:4
1:53 [j]Nu 2:10; 3:23,29,38 [k]Lev 10:6; Nu 16:46; 18:5; Dt 9:22 [l]S Ex 38:21; Nu 18:2-4
2:2 [m]Ps 74:4; Isa 31:9; Jer 4:21
2:3 [n]S Ex 6:23
2:5 [o]Nu 10:15 [p]S Nu 1:8
2:7 [q]Nu 1:9; 10:16
2:9 [r]Nu 10:14; Jdg 1:1
2:10 [s]S Nu 1:53 [t]Nu 1:5
2:12 [u]Nu 10:19 [v]S Nu 1:6
2:14 [w]Nu 10:20 [x]Nu 1:14; 10:20
2:16 [y]Nu 10:18
2:17 [z]Nu 1:50; 10:21
2:18 [a]S Nu 1:53 [b]S Ge 48:20; Jer 31:18-20

[a] 14 Many manuscripts of the Masoretic Text, Samaritan Pentateuch and Vulgate (see also Num. 1:14); most manuscripts of the Masoretic Text *Reuel*

1:53 *their tents around the tabernacle.* See 3:21–38. *wrath.* The Levites formed a protective hedge against trespassing by the non-Levites to keep them from experiencing divine wrath.

1:54 *as the LORD commanded Moses.* In view of Israel's great disobedience in the later chapters of Numbers, these words of initial compliance have a special poignancy.

2:1–34 This chapter is symmetrically structured:

- Summary command (vv. 1–2)
  - Details of execution (vv. 3–33)
    - Eastern camp (vv. 3–9)
    - Southern camp (vv. 10–16)
      - Tent and Levites (v. 17)
    - Western camp (vv. 18–24)
    - Northern camp (vv. 25–31)
      - Summary totals (vv. 32–33)
- Summary conclusion (v. 34)

In ch. 1 the nation is mustered, and the genealogical relationships are clarified. In ch. 2 the nation is put in structural order, and the line of march and place of encampment are established. The numbers of ch. 1 are given in a new pattern, and the same leaders are named here again.

2:2 *some distance from it.* See 1:52–53. *each man.* Each was to know his exact position within the camp. *standard ... banners.* Each tribe had its banner, and each triad of tribes had its standard. Jewish tradition suggests that the tribal banners corresponded in color to the 12 stones in the breastpiece of the high priest (Ex 28:15–21). Tradition also holds that the standard of the triad led by Judah had the figure of a lion, that of Reuben the figure of a man, that of Ephraim the figure of an ox and that of Dan the figure of an eagle (see the four living creatures described by Eze 1:10; cf. Rev 4:7). But these traditions are not otherwise substantiated. See diagram, p. 193.

2:3–7 *Judah ... Issachar ... Zebulun.* The fourth, fifth and sixth sons of Jacob and Leah. It is somewhat surprising to have these three tribes first in the order of march, since Reuben is regularly noted as Jacob's firstborn son (1:20). However, because of the failure of the older brothers (Reuben, Simeon and Levi; see Ge 49:3–7), Judah is granted pride of place among his brothers (see Ge 43:3; 49:8 and notes). Judah produced the royal line from which the Messiah came (see Ge 49:10; Ru 4:18–22; Mt 1:1–16 and notes).

2:10–12 *Reuben ... Simeon.* The first and second sons of Jacob and Leah.

2:14 *Gad.* The first son of Jacob and Zilpah (Leah's servant). Levi, Leah's third son, is not included with the divisions of the congregation. *Deuel.* See NIV text note. The Hebrew letters for *d* and *r* were easily confused by scribes (copyists) because of their similarity in form (see NIV text note on Ge 10:4).

2:17 *Tent of Meeting.* Representing God's presence in the heart of the camp (see 1:1 and note). *Levites.* In the line of march, the Judah and Reuben triads would lead the community, then would come the tabernacle with the attendant protective hedge of Levites (see note on 1:53), and last would come the Ephraim and Dan triads.

2:18–22 The Rachel tribes (Joseph and Benjamin) were on the west. Joseph's two sons Manasseh and Ephraim received a special blessing from their grandfather Jacob, but the younger son, Ephraim, was given precedence over Manasseh (see Ge 48:5–20 and notes). Here, true to Jacob's words, Ephraim is ahead of Manasseh. Last comes Benjamin, the last son born to Jacob.

Ephraim is Elishama son of Ammihud.[c] 19His division numbers 40,500.
20The tribe of Manasseh[d] will be
next to them. The leader of the people of Manasseh is Gamaliel son of
Pedahzur.[e] 21His division numbers
32,200.
22The tribe of Benjamin[f] will be
next. The leader of the people of Benjamin is Abidan son of Gideoni.[g] 23His
division numbers 35,400.
24All the men assigned to the camp
of Ephraim,[h] according to their divisions, number 108,100. They will set
out third.[i]

25On the north[j] will be the divisions of the camp of Dan, under their
standard.[k] The leader of the people of
Dan is Ahiezer son of Ammishaddai.[l]
26His division numbers 62,700.
27The tribe of Asher will camp next
to them. The leader of the people of
Asher is Pagiel son of Ocran.[m] 28His
division numbers 41,500.
29The tribe of Naphtali[n] will be next.
The leader of the people of Naphtali
is Ahira son of Enan.[o] 30His division
numbers 53,400.
31All the men assigned to the camp
of Dan number 157,600. They will set
out last,[p] under their standards.

32These are the Israelites, counted
according to their families.[q] All those
in the camps, by their divisions, number 603,550.[r] 33The Levites, however,
were not counted[s] along with the other Israelites, as the LORD commanded
Moses.
34So the Israelites did everything the
LORD commanded Moses; that is the way
they encamped under their standards, and
that is the way they set out, each with his
clan and family.

The Levites

3 This is the account of the family of
Aaron and Moses[t] at the time the LORD
talked with Moses on Mount Sinai.[u]
2The names of the sons of Aaron were
Nadab the firstborn[v] and Abihu, Eleazar
and Ithamar.[w] 3Those were the names of

2:18 [c] Nu 1:10
2:20 [d] S Ge 48:20 [e] S Nu 1:10
2:22 [f] Nu 10:24 [g] S Nu 1:11
2:24 [h] Nu 10:22 [i] Ps 80:2
2:25 [j] S Nu 1:53 [k] Nu 10:25 [l] S Nu 1:12
2:27 [m] Nu 1:13; 10:26
2:29 [n] Nu 10:27 [o] Nu 1:15; 10:27
2:31 [p] Nu 10:25; Jos 6:9
2:32 [q] Nu 1:45 [r] S Ex 12:37
2:33 [s] Nu 1:47; 26:57-62
3:1 [t] S Ex 6:27 [u] S Ex 19:11
3:2 [v] Nu 1:20 [w] S Ex 6:23

2:25 *Dan.* The first son of Bilhah, Rachel's servant.
2:27 *Asher.* The second son of Zilpah, Leah's servant.
2:29 *Naphtali.* The second son of Bilhah.
2:32 *603,550.* See 1:46 and note.
2:33 *Levites.* See notes on 1:47,53.
2:34 *did everything the LORD commanded Moses.* As in 1:54 (see note there), these words of absolute compliance contrast with Israel's later folly. *under their standards ... each with his clan and family.* A major accomplishment for a people so numerous, so recently enslaved and more recently a mob in disarray. It may have been the orderliness of this encampment that led Balaam to say: "How beautiful are your tents, O Jacob, your dwelling places, O Israel!" (24:5).
3:1 *Aaron and Moses.* At first glance, the names seem out of order, but the emphasis is correct: It is the family of Aaron that is about to be described (see v. 2).
3:3 *anointed priests.* Ex 28:41 records God's command to Moses to anoint his brother Aaron and his sons as priests of the Lord (see Ex 30:30; Lev 8:30). By this solemn act they were consecrated in a special way to the Lord. Kings (see 1Sa 16:13 and note) were also anointed with oil for special service to God. Physical objects could be anointed as well (see Ge 28:18 and note; Ex 29:36). The Hebrew term for "anointed" (*mashiah*) later became the specific term for the Messiah (Christ); see NIV text note on Mt 1:17. *ordained.* The Hebrew for this word means lit. "fill the hand of." By this

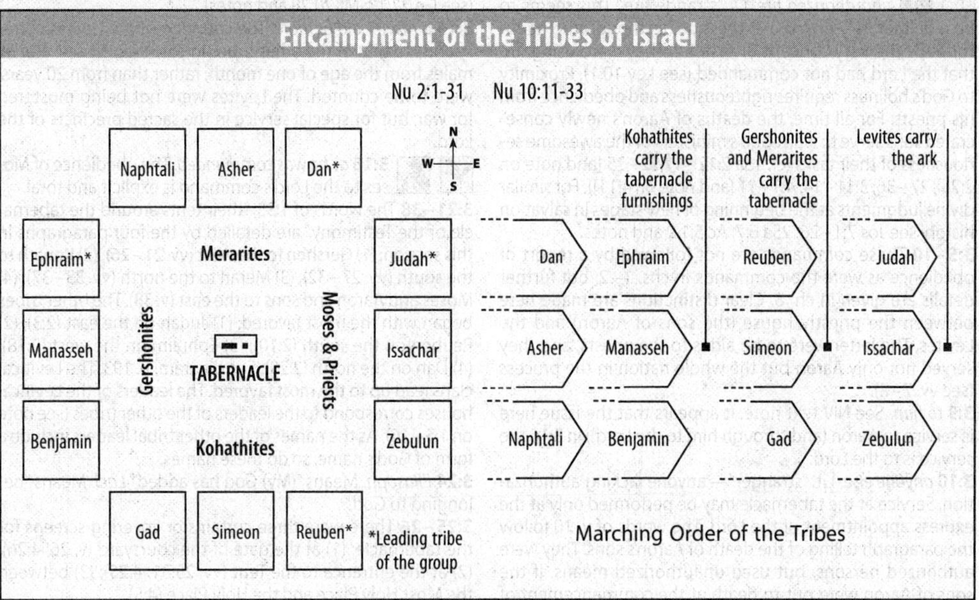

Aaron's sons, the anointed priests,[x] who
were ordained to serve as priests. 4Nadab
and Abihu, however, fell dead before the
LORD[y] when they made an offering with
unauthorized fire before him in the Desert
of Sinai.[z] They had no sons; so only Eleazar and Ithamar[a] served as priests during
the lifetime of their father Aaron.[b]
5The LORD said to Moses, 6"Bring the
tribe of Levi[c] and present them to Aaron the priest to assist him.[d] 7They are to
perform duties for him and for the whole
community[e] at the Tent of Meeting by doing the work[f] of the tabernacle. 8They are
to take care of all the furnishings of the
Tent of Meeting, fulfilling the obligations
of the Israelites by doing the work of the
tabernacle. 9Give the Levites to Aaron and
his sons;[g] they are the Israelites who are to
be given wholly to him.[a] 10Appoint Aaron[h]
and his sons to serve as priests;[i] anyone
else who approaches the sanctuary must
be put to death."[j]
11The LORD also said to Moses, 12"I have
taken the Levites[k] from among the Israelites in place of the first male offspring[l]
of every Israelite woman. The Levites are
mine,[m] 13for all the firstborn are mine.[n]
When I struck down all the firstborn in
Egypt, I set apart for myself every firstborn
in Israel, whether man or animal. They are
to be mine. I am the LORD."[o]
14The LORD said to Moses in the Desert
of Sinai,[p] 15"Count[q] the Levites by their
families and clans. Count every male a
month old or more."[r] 16So Moses counted
them, as he was commanded by the word
of the LORD.
17These were the names of the sons of

Levi:[s]

Gershon,[t] Kohath[u] and Merari.[v]

18These were the names of the Gershonite clans:

Libni and Shimei.[w]

19The Kohathite clans:

Amram, Izhar, Hebron and Uzziel.[x]

20The Merarite clans:[y]

Mahli and Mushi.[z]

These were the Levite clans, according
to their families.

21To Gershon[a] belonged the clans of the
Libnites and Shimeites;[b] these were
the Gershonite clans. 22The number of all
the males a month old or more who were
counted was 7,500. 23The Gershonite clans
were to camp on the west, behind the tabernacle.[c] 24The leader of the families of the
Gershonites was Eliasaph son of Lael. 25At
the Tent of Meeting the Gershonites were
responsible for the care of the tabernacle[d]
and tent, its coverings,[e] the curtain at the
entrance[f] to the Tent of Meeting,[g] 26the curtains of the courtyard[h], the curtain at the
entrance to the courtyard surrounding the

[a] 9 Most manuscripts of the Masoretic Text; some manuscripts of the Masoretic Text, Samaritan Pentateuch and Septuagint (see also Num. 8:16) *to me*

3:3 [x]S Ex 28:41; S 29:30 **3:4** [y]S Lev 10:2 [z]S Lev 10:1 [a]Lev 10:6,12; Nu 4:28 [b]1Ch 24:1 **3:6** [c]Dt 10:8; 31:9; 1Ch 15:2 [d]Nu 8:6-22; 18:1-7; 2Ch 29:11 **3:7** [e]Nu 1:53; 8:19 [f]S Lev 8:35 **3:9** [g]ver 12,45; Nu 8:19; 18:6 **3:10** [h]S Ex 30:7 [i]S Ex 29:9 [j]Nu 1:51 **3:12** [k]Ne 13:29; Mal 2:4 [l]ver 41; Nu 8:16,18 [m]S ver 9; Ex 13:2; Nu 8:14; 16:9 **3:13** [n]S Ex 13:12 [o]Lev 11:44 **3:14** [p]S Ex 19:1 **3:15** [q]ver 39; S Nu 1:19 [r]ver 22; Nu 18:16; 26:62 **3:17** [s]S Ge 29:34; S 46:11; Nu 1:47; 1Ch 15:4; 23:6; 2Ch 29:12 [t]Jos 21:6 [u]Jos 21:4 [v]S Ex 6:16 **3:18** [w]Ex 6:17 **3:19** [x]S Ex 6:18 **3:20** [y]S Ge 46:11 [z]S Ex 6:19 **3:21** [a]S Ge 46:11 [b]Ex 6:17 **3:23** [c]S Nu 2:18 **3:25** [d]Ex 25:9; Nu 7:1 [e]Ex 26:14 [f]Ex 26:36; Nu 4:25 [g]Ex 40:2 **3:26** [h]Ex 27:9

act there was an investing of authority, a consecration and a setting apart (cf. Ex 32:29, where the same Hebrew idiom is translated "set apart"; cf. also note there).

3:4 *Nadab and Abihu.* See Lev 10:1–3 and notes. *unauthorized fire.* Or "strange fire." This seems to be a deliberately obscure expression, as though the narrator finds the very concept distasteful. They were using fire that the Lord had not commanded (see Lev 10:1). Proximity to God's holiness requires righteousness and obedience from his priests. For all time, the deaths of Aaron's newly consecrated sons serve to warn God's ministers of the awesome seriousness of their tasks (cf. 1Sa 2:12–17,22–25 [and note on 2:25], 27–36; 3:11–14; 4:1–11 [and note on 4:11]). For similar divine judgments at the beginning of new stages in salvation history see Jos 7:1–26; 2Sa 6:7; Ac 5:1,9 and notes.

3:5–10 These commands are not followed by a report of obedience as were the commands in chs. 1–2, but further details are given in ch. 8. Clear distinctions are made here between the priestly house (the sons of Aaron) and the Levites. The latter were to be aides to the priests, and they served not only Aaron but the whole nation in the process (see vv. 7–8).

3:9 *to him.* See NIV text note. It appears that the issue here is service to Aaron (and through him to the Lord); in 8:16 the service is to the Lord.

3:10 *anyone else.* Lit. "stranger"—anyone lacking authorization. Service at the tabernacle may be performed only at the express appointment of the Lord. The words of v. 10 follow the paragraph telling of the death of Aaron's sons. They were authorized persons, but used unauthorized means. If the sons of Aaron were put to death at the commencement of their duties, how dare an unauthorized person even think to trespass! See v. 38; 18:1–7 and notes.

3:12–13 See note on Ex 13:2. *mine.* Repeated for emphasis.

3:12 *in place of.* An example of the practice of substitution (see Ge 22:13; Mt 20:28 and notes).

3:15 *a month old or more.* The counting of the Levites corresponds to that of the other tribes in chs. 1–2, except that all males from the age of one month, rather than from 20 years, were to be counted. The Levites were not being mustered for war, but for special service in the sacred precincts of the Lord.

3:16 *as he was commanded.* The obedience of Moses to the Lord's command is explicit and total.

3:21–38 The words of 1:53, "their tents around the tabernacle of the Testimony," are detailed by the four paragraphs in this section: (1) Gershon to the west (vv. 21–26); (2) Kohath to the south (vv. 27–32); (3) Merari to the north (vv. 33–37); (4) Moses and Aaron and sons to the east (v. 38). The other tribes began with the most favored: (1) Judah on the east (2:3); (2) Reuben on the south (2:10); (3) Ephraim on the west (2:18); (4) Dan on the north (2:25). See diagram, p. 193. The Levitical clans lead up to the most favored. The leaders of the Levitical houses correspond to the leaders of the other tribes (see note on 1:5–16). As the names of the other tribal leaders include a form of God's name, so do these names.

3:24 *Eliasaph.* Means "(My) God has added." *Lael.* Means "belonging to God."

3:25–26 There were three curtains or covering screens for the tabernacle: (1) at the gate of the courtyard (v. 26; 4:26); (2) at the entrance to the Tent (vv. 25,31; 4:25); (3) between the Most Holy Place and the Holy Place (4:5).

tabernacle and altar,[i] and the ropes[j]—and everything[k] related to their use.

27To Kohath[l] belonged the clans of the Amramites, Izharites, Hebronites and Uzzielites;[m] these were the Kohathite[n] clans. 28The number of all the males a month old or more[o] was 8,600.[a] The Kohathites were responsible[p] for the care of the sanctuary.[q] 29The Kohathite clans were to camp on the south side[r] of the tabernacle. 30The leader of the families of the Kohathite clans was Elizaphan[s] son of Uzziel. 31They were responsible for the care of the ark,[t] the table,[u] the lampstand,[v] the altars,[w] the articles[x] of the sanctuary used in ministering, the curtain,[y] and everything related to their use.[z] 32The chief leader of the Levites was Eleazar[a] son of Aaron, the priest. He was appointed over those who were responsible[b] for the care of the sanctuary.[c]

33To Merari belonged the clans of the Mahlites and the Mushites;[d] these were the Merarite clans.[e] 34The number of all the males a month old or more[f] who were counted was 6,200. 35The leader of the families of the Merarite clans was Zuriel son of Abihail; they were to camp on the north side of the tabernacle.[g] 36The Merarites were appointed[h] to take care of the frames of the tabernacle,[i] its crossbars,[j] posts,[k] bases, all its equipment, and everything related to their use,[l] 37as well as the posts of the surrounding courtyard[m] with their bases, tent pegs[n] and ropes.

38Moses and Aaron and his sons were to camp to the east[o] of the tabernacle, toward the sunrise, in front of the Tent of Meeting.[p] They were responsible for the care of the sanctuary[q] on behalf of the Israelites. Anyone else who approached the sanctuary was to be put to death.[r]

3:26 [i]ver 31 [j]Ex 35:18 [k]Nu 4:26
3:27 [l]S Ge 46:11; S Ex 6:18 [m]Ex 6:18; 1Ch 26:23 [n]Nu 4:15,37
3:28 [o]ver 15 [p]Nu 4:4,15 [q]S Ex 25:8; 30:13; 2Ch 30:19; Ps 15:1; 20:2; Eze 44:27
3:29 [r]S Nu 1:53
3:30 [s]S Ex 6:22
3:31 [t]S Ex 25:10-22; Dt 10:1-8; 2Ch 5:2; Jer 3:16 [u]S Ex 25:23 [v]S Ex 25:31; 1Ch 28:15; Jer 52:19 [w]ver 26 [x]Nu 1:50 [y]S Ex 26:33; Nu 4:5 [z]Nu 4:15; 18:3
3:32 [a]S Ex 6:23 [b]ver 28 [c]Nu 4:19; 18:3
3:33 [d]S Ex 6:19 [e]S Ge 46:11
3:34 [f]ver 15
3:35 [g]S Nu 2:25
3:36 [h]Nu 4:32 [i]Ex 26:15-25; 35:20-29 [j]Ex 26:26-29 [k]Ex 36:36 [l]Nu 18:3
3:37 [m]Ex 27:10-17 [n]Ex 27:19
3:38 [o]Nu 2:3 [p]S Nu 1:53; 1Ch 9:27; 23:32 [q]ver 7; Nu 18:5 [r]ver 10; Nu 1:51
3:39 [s]S ver 15 [t]Nu 26:62
3:40 [u]ver 15 [v]Nu 1:2
3:41 [w]ver 12 [x]Lev 11:44
3:43 [y]ver 15 [z]ver 39
3:45 [a]S ver 9 [b]Lev 11:44
3:46 [c]Ex 13:13; Nu 18:15
3:47 [d]S Lev 27:6

39The total number of Levites counted[s] at the LORD's command by Moses and Aaron according to their clans, including every male a month old or more, was 22,000.[t]

40The LORD said to Moses, "Count all the firstborn Israelite males who are a month old or more[u] and make a list of their names.[v] 41Take the Levites for me in place of all the firstborn of the Israelites,[w] and the livestock of the Levites in place of all the firstborn of the livestock of the Israelites. I am the LORD."[x]

42So Moses counted all the firstborn of the Israelites, as the LORD commanded him. 43The total number of firstborn males a month old or more,[y] listed by name, was 22,273.[z]

44The LORD also said to Moses, 45"Take the Levites in place of all the firstborn of Israel, and the livestock of the Levites in place of their livestock. The Levites are to be mine.[a] I am the LORD.[b] 46To redeem[c] the 273 firstborn Israelites who exceed the number of the Levites, 47collect five shekels[b][d] for each one, according to the sanctuary shekel,[e] which weighs twenty gerahs.[f] 48Give the money for the redemption[g] of the additional Israelites to Aaron and his sons."[h]

49So Moses collected the redemption money[i] from those who exceeded the number redeemed by the Levites. 50From the firstborn of the Israelites[j] he collected silver weighing 1,365 shekels,[c][k] according to the sanctuary shekel. 51Moses gave the redemption money to Aaron and his sons, as he was commanded by the word of the LORD.

[a] 28 Hebrew; some Septuagint manuscripts *8,300*
[b] 47 That is, about 2 ounces (about 55 grams)
[c] 50 That is, about 35 pounds (about 15.5 kilograms)

[e]S Ex 30:13 [f]S Lev 27:25 **3:48** [g]ver 51 [h]ver 50 **3:49** [i]ver 48 **3:50** [j]ver 41,45 [k]S ver 46-48

3:27 *Amramites.* Aaron was an Amramite (see Ex 6:20 and note); thus he and Moses were from the family of Kohath. To the Kohathites was given the care of the most holy things (see 4:4–18).
3:28 *8,600.* The total number of Levites given in v. 39 is 22,000—300 less than the totals of 7,500 Gershonites (v. 22), 8,600 Kohathites (here) and 6,200 Merarites (v. 34). Many believe that a copyist may have made a mistake here, and that the correct number is 8,300 (see NIV text note).
3:30 *Elizaphan.* Means "(My) God has protected." *Uzziel.* Means "My strength is God."
3:35 *Zuriel.* Means "My Rock is God." *Abihail.* Means "My (divine) Father is powerful."
3:38 *toward the sunrise.* The most honored location, but Moses and Aaron were placed there for a representative ministry (on behalf of the Israelites). *Anyone else ... was to be put to death.* Service in the tabernacle was an act of mercy, a means for the people to come before God. Yet it was marked by strict discipline—it had to be done in God's way. The sovereignty of God was evident in his limitations on the means to approach him (see v. 10; 1:51; 18:1–7 and notes).
3:41 *I am the LORD.* What is being commanded conforms to God's character as Yahweh ("the LORD"; see note on Ex 3:14).
3:43 *22,273.* Seems too small for a population in excess of 2,000,000, and is used as an argument for attempting to find a means of reducing the total number of the people (calculations based on this number suggest a total population of about 250,000). Some suggest that the 22,273 firstborn of Israel were those born since the exodus, all the firstborn at the time of the exodus having already been set apart for the Lord at the first Passover (see Ex 12:22–23). This, however, creates a new problem since nowhere is that allegedly distinct group assigned any special service of the Lord. See Introduction: Special Problem.
3:47,50 *according to the sanctuary shekel.* See note on Ex 30:13.

The Kohathites

4 The LORD said to Moses and Aaron: 2“Take a census[l] of the Kohathite branch of the Levites by their clans and families. 3Count[m] all the men from thirty to fifty years of age[n] who come to serve in the work in the Tent of Meeting.

4“This is the work[o] of the Kohathites[p] in the Tent of Meeting: the care of the most holy things.[q] 5When the camp is to move,[r] Aaron and his sons are to go in and take down the shielding curtain[s] and cover the ark of the Testimony with it.[t] 6Then they are to cover this with hides of sea cows,[a][u] spread a cloth of solid blue over that and put the poles[v] in place.

7“Over the table of the Presence[w] they are to spread a blue cloth and put on it the plates, dishes and bowls, and the jars for drink offerings;[x] the bread that is continually there[y] is to remain on it. 8Over these they are to spread a scarlet cloth, cover that with hides of sea cows and put its poles[z] in place.

9“They are to take a blue cloth and cover the lampstand that is for light, together with its lamps, its wick trimmers and trays,[a] and all its jars for the oil used to supply it. 10Then they are to wrap it and all its accessories in a covering of hides of sea cows and put it on a carrying frame.[b]

11“Over the gold altar[c] they are to spread a blue cloth and cover that with hides of sea cows and put its poles[d] in place.

12“They are to take all the articles[e] used for ministering in the sanctuary, wrap them in a blue cloth, cover that with hides of sea cows and put them on a carrying frame.[f]

13“They are to remove the ashes[g] from the bronze altar[h] and spread a purple cloth over it. 14Then they are to place on it all the utensils[i] used for ministering at the altar, including the firepans,[j] meat forks,[k] shovels[l] and sprinkling bowls.[m] Over it they are to spread a covering of hides of sea cows and put its poles[n] in place.

15“After Aaron and his sons have finished covering the holy furnishings and all the holy articles, and when the camp is ready to move,[o] the Kohathites[p] are to come to do the carrying.[q] But they must not touch the holy things[r] or they will die.[s][t] The Kohathites are to carry those things that are in the Tent of Meeting.

16“Eleazar[u] son of Aaron, the priest, is to have charge of the oil for the light,[v] the fragrant incense,[w] the regular grain offering[x] and the anointing oil. He is to be in charge of the entire tabernacle and everything in it, including its holy furnishings and articles.”

17The LORD said to Moses and Aaron, 18“See that the Kohathite tribal clans are not cut off from the Levites. 19So that they may live and not die when they come near the most holy things,[y] do this for them: Aaron and his sons[z] are to go into the sanctuary and assign to each man his work and what he is to carry.[a] 20But the Kohathites must not go in to look[b] at the holy things, even for a moment, or they will die.”

The Gershonites

21The LORD said to Moses, 22“Take a census also of the Gershonites by their families and clans. 23Count all the men from thirty to fifty years of age[c] who come to serve in the work at the Tent of Meeting.

24“This is the service of the Gershonite clans as they work and carry burdens: 25They are to carry the curtains of the tabernacle,[d] the Tent of Meeting,[e] its covering[f] and the outer covering of hides of sea cows, the curtains for the entrance to the Tent of Meeting, 26the curtains of the courtyard surrounding the tabernacle and altar,[g] the curtain for the entrance,[h] the ropes and all the equipment[i] used in its service. The Gershonites are to do all that needs to be done with these things. 27All their service, whether carrying or doing other work, is to be done under the direction of Aaron and his sons.[j] You shall assign to them as their responsibility[k] all they are to carry. 28This is the service of the Gershonite clans[l] at the Tent of Meeting. Their duties are to be under the direction of Ithamar[m] son of Aaron, the priest.

The Merarites

29“Count[n] the Merarites by their clans and families.[o] 30Count all the men from thirty to fifty years of age who come to serve in the work at the Tent of Meeting. 31This is their duty as they perform ser-

4:2 [l] S Ex 30:12 **4:3** [m] S Nu 1:47 [n] ver 23; Nu 8:25; 1Ch 23:3, 24, 27; Ezr 3:8 **4:4** [o] S Nu 3:28 [p] Nu 7:9 [q] ver 19 **4:5** [r] Nu 1:51 [s] S Ex 26:31, 33 [t] 1Ch 23:26 **4:6** [u] S Ex 25:5 [v] S Ex 25:13-15; 1Ki 8:7; 2Ch 5:8 **4:7** [w] S Lev 24:6 [x] Ex 39:36; Jer 52:19 [y] S Ex 25:30 **4:8** [z] Ex 26:26-28 **4:9** [a] S Ex 25:38 **4:10** [b] ver 12 **4:11** [c] S Ex 30:1 [d] Ex 30:4 **4:12** [e] Nu 3:31 [f] ver 10 **4:13** [g] S Lev 1:16 [h] Ex 27:1-8; Nu 3:31 **4:14** [i] S Ex 31:9 [j] S Ex 27:3 [k] 1Ch 28:17; 2Ch 4:16 [l] 2Ch 4:11 [m] Ex 27:3; Nu 7:84; 2Ch 4:8; Jer 52:18 [n] Ex 27:6 **4:15** [o] ver 5 [p] S Nu 3:27 [q] Nu 7:9 [r] ver 4 [s] S Ex 28:43 [t] Nu 1:51; 2Sa 6:6, 7

4:16 [u] Lev 10:6; Nu 3:32 [v] S Ex 25:6 [w] S Ex 25:6 [x] S Ex 29:41; Lev 6:14-23 **4:19** [y] S ver 15 [z] ver 27 [a] S Nu 3:32 **4:20** [b] S Ex 19:21 **4:23** [c] S ver 3 **4:25** [d] Ex 27:10-18 [e] Nu 3:25 [f] Ex 26:14 **4:26** [g] Ex 27:9 [h] Ex 27:16 [i] Nu 3:26 **4:27** [j] ver 19 [k] Nu 3:25, 26 **4:28** [l] Nu 7:7 [m] S Ex 6:23 **4:29** [n] S Ex 30:12 [o] S Ge 46:11

[a] 6 That is, dugongs; also in verses 8, 10, 11, 12, 14 and 25

4:3 *thirty to fifty years.* Ch. 3 listed all males over the age of one month (3:15). Ch. 4 lists those Levites who were of age to serve in the tabernacle. Of the 22,000 Levite males (3:39), 8,580 were of age for service (v. 48). From 8:24 we learn that the beginning age for service was 25; perhaps the first 5 years were something of an apprenticeship.

4:4 *most holy things.* See note on Ex 3:5. Despite the fact that the primary care of these holy things was given to the Kohathites, they were forbidden to touch them (v. 15) or even to look at them (v. 20), on pain of death. All the work of the Kohathites was to be strictly supervised by Aaron and his sons, and only the priests were able to touch and look at the unveiled holy things.

4:5 *Testimony.* See note on Ex 25:22.

4:6 *sea cows.* Native to the Red Sea.

4:7 *table of the Presence.* See note on Ex 25:30.

4:16 *Eleazar …, the priest, is to have charge.* The high priest could draw near to the most holy things on behalf of the people. If he had not been able to do so, there could have been no worship by the community.

vice at the Tent of Meeting: to carry the
frames of the tabernacle, its crossbars,
posts and bases,[p] 32as well as the posts of
the surrounding courtyard with their bases, tent pegs, ropes,[q] all their equipment
and everything related to their use. Assign
to each man the specific things he is to
carry. 33This is the service of the Merarite
clans as they work at the Tent of Meeting
under the direction of Ithamar[r] son of Aaron, the priest."

The Numbering of the Levite Clans

34Moses, Aaron and the leaders of the
community counted the Kohathites[s] by
their clans and families. 35All the men
from thirty to fifty years of age[t] who came
to serve in the work in the Tent of Meeting, 36counted by clans, were 2,750. 37This
was the total of all those in the Kohathite
clans[u] who served in the Tent of Meeting.
Moses and Aaron counted them according
to the LORD's command through Moses.
38The Gershonites[v] were counted by
their clans and families. 39All the men
from thirty to fifty years of age who came
to serve in the work at the Tent of Meeting,
40counted by their clans and families, were
2,630. 41This was the total of those in the
Gershonite clans who served at the Tent of
Meeting. Moses and Aaron counted them
according to the LORD's command.
42The Merarites were counted by their
clans and families. 43All the men from thirty to fifty years of age[w] who came to serve
in the work at the Tent of Meeting, 44count-
ed by their clans, were 3,200. 45This was
the total of those in the Merarite clans.[x]
Moses and Aaron counted them according
to the LORD's command through Moses.
46So Moses, Aaron and the leaders of Israel counted[y] all the Levites by their clans
and families. 47All the men from thirty to
fifty years of age[z] who came to do the work
of serving and carrying the Tent of Meeting
48numbered 8,580.[a] 49At the LORD's command through Moses, each was assigned
his work and told what to carry.
Thus they were counted,[b] as the LORD
commanded Moses.

The Purity of the Camp

5 The LORD said to Moses, 2"Command
the Israelites to send away from the
camp anyone who has an infectious skin
disease[a][c] or a discharge[d] of any kind, or
who is ceremonially unclean[e] because of
a dead body.[f] 3Send away male and female
alike; send them outside the camp so they
will not defile their camp, where I dwell
among them.[g]" 4The Israelites did this;
they sent them outside the camp. They did
just as the LORD had instructed Moses.

Restitution for Wrongs

5The LORD said to Moses, 6"Say to the
Israelites: 'When a man or woman wrongs
another in any way[b] and so is unfaithful[h]
to the LORD, that person is guilty[i] 7and
must confess[j] the sin he has committed.
He must make full restitution[k] for his
wrong, add one fifth to it and give it all
to the person he has wronged. 8But if that
person has no close relative to whom restitution can be made for the wrong, the
restitution belongs to the LORD and must
be given to the priest, along with the ram[l]
with which atonement is made for him.[m]
9All the sacred contributions the Israelites bring to a priest will belong to him.[n]
10Each man's sacred gifts are his own, but
what he gives to the priest will belong to
the priest.[o]'"

The Test for an Unfaithful Wife

11Then the LORD said to Moses, 12"Speak
to the Israelites and say to them: 'If a
man's wife goes astray[p] and is unfaithful

4:31 [p] Nu 3:36 **4:32** [q] Nu 3:37 **4:33** [r] S Ex 38:21 **4:34** [s] ver 2 **4:35** [t] ver 3 **4:37** [u] S Nu 3:27 **4:38** [v] S Ge 46:11 **4:43** [w] ver 3 **4:45** [x] ver 29 **4:46** [y] Nu 1:19 **4:47** [z] ver 3 **4:48** [a] Nu 3:39
4:49 [b] S Nu 1:47 **5:2** [c] S Lev 13:2 [d] S Lev 15:2; Mt 9:20 [e] Lev 13:3; Nu 9:6-10 [f] S Lev 21:11 **5:3** [g] S Ex 29:45; Lev 26:12; 2Co 6:16 **5:6** [h] S Lev 6:2 [i] Lev 5:14-6:7 **5:7** [j] S Lev 5:5; S Lk 19:8 [k] S Lev 5:16 **5:8** [l] S Lev 5:15 [m] Lev 6:6,7 **5:9** [n] Lev 6:17 **5:10** [o] Lev 7:29-34 **5:12** [p] ver 19-21; S Ex 20:14

[a] 2 Traditionally *leprosy*; the Hebrew word was used for various diseases affecting the skin—not necessarily leprosy. [b] 6 Or *woman commits any wrong common to mankind*

5:2 *infectious skin disease.* See NIV text note; see also note on Lev 13:2; cf. Lk 5:12–16; 17:11–19. *discharge of any kind.* See note on Lev 15:2. Such discharges were primarily from the sexual organs and were chronic in nature (cf. Lk 8:43–48). The people who suffered from them became living object lessons to the whole camp on the necessity for all people to be "clean" in their approach to God. *unclean.* Ceremonially unfit to be with the community, and a possible contaminant to the tabernacle and the pure worship of the Lord. Aspects of uncleanness were not left in the abstract or theoretical; the focus was on tangible issues, such as clearly evident skin diseases and discharges. *dead body.* The ultimate tangible sign of uncleanness. Processes of decay and disease in dead flesh were evident to all. Physical contact with a corpse was a sure mark of uncleanness; normal contacts with the living would have to be curtailed until proper cleansing had been made. See note on 6:6 for application to the Nazirite vow. Jesus reached out to the dead as well as to the living; his raising of Jairus's daughter began with holding her limp hand (Lk 8:54).

5:3 *male and female alike.* The concept of clean versus unclean cuts across gender lines. The essential issue was the presence of the Lord in the camp; there can be no uncleanness where he dwells. In the new Jerusalem (Rev 21:2–3) the dwelling of God with his people will be uncompromised by any form of uncleanness (Rev 21:27).

5:5–10 The connection of these verses (on personal wrongs) with the first paragraph (on ritual uncleanness) may be that of moving from the outward, visible defects to the inward, more secret faults that mar the purity of the community. Those with evident marks of uncleanness are to be expelled for the duration of their malady. But more insidious are those who have overtly sinned against others in the community, and who think that they may continue to function as though they had done nothing wrong.

5:8 *atonement.* See notes on Ex 25:17; Lev 17:11; Ro 3:25.

5:11–31 Again, the connection with the preceding two paragraphs seems to be a movement from the more open, obvious sins to the more personal, hidden ones. Issues of

to him 13by sleeping with another man,[q]
and this is hidden from her husband and
her impurity is undetected (since there is
no witness against her and she has not
been caught in the act), 14and if feelings of
jealousy[r] come over her husband and he
suspects his wife and she is impure — or if
he is jealous and suspects her even though
she is not impure — 15then he is to take
his wife to the priest. He must also take an
offering of a tenth of an ephah[a s] of barley
flour[t] on her behalf. He must not pour oil
on it or put incense on it, because it is a
grain offering for jealousy,[u] a reminder[v] offering to draw attention to guilt.

16" 'The priest shall bring her and have
her stand before the LORD. 17Then he shall
take some holy water in a clay jar and put
some dust from the tabernacle floor into
the water. 18After the priest has had the
woman stand before the LORD, he shall
loosen her hair[w] and place in her hands
the reminder offering, the grain offering
for jealousy,[x] while he himself holds the
bitter water that brings a curse.[y] 19Then
the priest shall put the woman under oath
and say to her, "If no other man has slept
with you and you have not gone astray[z]
and become impure while married to
your husband, may this bitter water that
brings a curse[a] not harm you. 20But if
you have gone astray[b] while married to
your husband and you have defiled yourself by sleeping with a man other than
your husband"— 21here the priest is to
put the woman under this curse of the
oath[c]— "may the LORD cause your people to curse and denounce you when he
causes your thigh to waste away and your
abdomen to swell.[b] 22May this water[d]
that brings a curse[e] enter your body so
that your abdomen swells and your thigh
wastes away.[c]"

" 'Then the woman is to say, "Amen. So
be it.[f]"

23" 'The priest is to write these curses on a scroll[g] and then wash them off
into the bitter water. 24He shall have the
woman drink the bitter water that brings
a curse, and this water will enter her and
cause bitter suffering. 25The priest is to
take from her hands the grain offering
for jealousy, wave it before the LORD[h] and
bring it to the altar. 26The priest is then
to take a handful of the grain offering as
a memorial offering[i] and burn it on the
altar; after that, he is to have the woman
drink the water. 27If she has defiled herself and been unfaithful to her husband,
then when she is made to drink the water
that brings a curse, it will go into her and
cause bitter suffering; her abdomen will
swell and her thigh waste away,[d] and she
will become accursed[j] among her people.
28If, however, the woman has not defiled
herself and is free from impurity, she will
be cleared of guilt and will be able to have
children.

29" 'This, then, is the law of jealousy
when a woman goes astray[k] and defiles
herself while married to her husband,
30or when feelings of jealousy[l] come over
a man because he suspects his wife. The

5:13 [q]S Ex 20:14 **5:14** [r]ver 30; Pr 6:34; 27:4; SS 8:6 **5:15** [s]S Ex 16:36 [t]S Lev 6:20 [u]ver 18,25 [v]Eze 21:23; 29:16 **5:18** [w]S Lev 10:6; 1Co 11:6 [x]ver 15 [y]ver 19 **5:19** [z]ver 12,29 [a]ver 18 **5:20** [b]ver 12 **5:21** [c]Jos 6:26; 1Sa 14:24; Ne 10:29 **5:22** [d]Ps 109:18 [e]ver 18 [f]Dt 27:15 **5:23** [g]Jer 45:1 **5:25** [h]Lev 8:27 **5:26** [i]S Lev 2:2 **5:27** [j]Isa 43:28; 65:15; Jer 26:6; 29:18; 42:18; 44:12,22; Zec 8:13 **5:29** [k]S ver 19 **5:30** [l]S ver 14

[a] *15* That is, probably about 2 quarts (about 2 liters) [b] *21 Or causes you to have a miscarrying womb and barrenness* [c] *22 Or body and cause you to be barren and have a miscarrying womb* [d] *27 Or suffering; she will have barrenness and a miscarrying womb*

purity begin with physical marks (vv. 1–4), are expanded to interpersonal relationships (vv. 5–10), and then intrude into the most intimate of relationships — the purity of a man and woman in their marriage bed (cf. Ex 20:14 and note). A test for marital fidelity is far more difficult to prove than a test for a skin disorder; hence, the larger part of the chapter is given to this most sensitive of issues.

5:14 *feelings of jealousy.* These may have been provoked on the basis of good cause, and the issue must be faced. The concern is not just for the bruised feelings of the husband but is ultimately based on the reality of God's dwelling among his people (see v. 3 and note). Yet the chapter is designed to prevent unfounded charges of unfaithfulness. This text was not to be used by a capricious, petty or malevolent husband to badger an innocent woman. *impure.* The subject of the chapter is consistent; the purity of the camp where God dwells (v. 3) is the burden of the passage.

5:15–28 The actions presented here seem severe and harsh. But the consequences would have been worse for a woman charged with adultery by an angry husband if there was no provision for her guilt or innocence to be demonstrated. That she was taken to the priest (v. 15) is finally an act of mercy. The gravity of the ritual for a suspected unfaithful wife shows that the law regards marital infidelity most seriously. This was not just a concern of a jealous husband. The entire community was affected by this breach of faith; hence, the judgment was in the context of the community.

5:15,18 *reminder offering.* A grain offering apparently designed to stimulate reflection on sin and guilt.

5:17 *holy water.* Pure water perhaps taken from the bronze basin (Ex 38:8) and placed in a consecrated vessel and dedicated to God's service. This rendered it ritually clean for use in this ceremony.

5:18 *loosen her hair.* A sign of openness; for the guilty, an expectation of judgment and mourning. *bitter water that brings a curse.* Or "curse-bringing water of bitterness." It is not just that the water was bitter tasting but that the water had the potential of bringing with it a bitter curse. The Lord's role in the proceedings (vv. 16,21,25) is emphasized repeatedly to show that this potion was neither simply a tool of magic nor merely a psychological device to determine stress. The verdict with respect to the woman was precipitated by her physiological and psychological responses to the bitter water, but the judgment was from the Lord.

5:21 *your thigh to waste away and your abdomen to swell.* See NIV text note. The figurative language here (and in vv. 22,27) speaks of the loss of the capacity for childbearing (and, if pregnant, the miscarriage of the child). This is demonstrated by the determination of the fate of a woman wrongly charged (v. 28). For a woman in the ancient Near East to be denied the ability to bear children was a personal loss of inestimable proportions. Since it was in the bearing of children that a woman's worth was realized in the ancient world, this was a grievous punishment indeed.

priest is to have her stand before the LORD and is to apply this entire law to her. 31 The husband will be innocent of any wrongdoing, but the woman will bear the consequences[m] of her sin.' "

The Nazirite

6 The LORD said to Moses, 2 "Speak to the Israelites and say to them: 'If a man or woman wants to make a special vow[n], a vow of separation[o] to the LORD as a Nazirite,[p] 3 he must abstain from wine[q] and other fermented drink and must not drink vinegar[r] made from wine or from other fermented drink. He must not drink grape juice or eat grapes[s] or raisins. 4 As long as he is a Nazirite, he must not eat anything that comes from the grapevine, not even the seeds or skins.

5 " 'During the entire period of his vow of separation no razor[t] may be used on his head.[u] He must be holy until the period of his separation to the LORD is over; he must let the hair of his head grow long. 6 Throughout the period of his separation to the LORD he must not go near a dead body.[v] 7 Even if his own father or mother or brother or sister dies, he must not make himself ceremonially unclean[w] on account of them, because the symbol of his separation to God is on his head. 8 Throughout the period of his separation he is consecrated to the LORD.

9 " 'If someone dies suddenly in his presence, thus defiling the hair he has dedicated,[x] he must shave his head on the day of his cleansing[y]—the seventh day. 10 Then on the eighth day[z] he must bring two doves or two young pigeons[a] to the priest at the entrance to the Tent of Meeting.[b] 11 The priest is to offer one as a sin offering[c] and the other as a burnt offering[d] to make atonement[e] for him because he sinned by being in the presence of the dead body. That same day he is to consecrate his head. 12 He must dedicate himself to the LORD for the period of his separation and must bring a year-old male lamb[f] as a guilt offering.[g] The previous days do not count, because he became defiled during his separation.

13 " 'Now this is the law for the Nazirite when the period of his separation is over.[h] He is to be brought to the entrance to the Tent of Meeting.[i] 14 There he is to present his offerings to the LORD: a year-old male lamb without defect[j] for a burnt offering, a year-old ewe lamb without defect for a sin offering,[k] a ram[l] without defect for a fellowship offering,[a] [m] 15 together with their grain offerings[n] and drink offerings,[o] and a basket of bread made without yeast—cakes made of fine flour mixed with oil, and wafers spread with oil.[p]

16 " 'The priest is to present them[q] before the LORD[r] and make the sin offering and the burnt offering.[s] 17 He is to present the basket of unleavened bread and is to sacrifice the ram as a fellowship offering[t] to the LORD, together with its grain offering[u] and drink offering.[v]

18 " 'Then at the entrance to the Tent of Meeting, the Nazirite must shave off the hair that he dedicated.[w] He is to take the hair and put it in the fire that is under the sacrifice of the fellowship offering.

19 " 'After the Nazirite has shaved off the hair of his dedication, the priest is to place in his hands a boiled shoulder of the ram, and a cake and a wafer from the basket, both made without yeast.[x] 20 The priest shall then wave them before the LORD as a wave offering;[y] they are holy[z] and belong to the priest, together with the breast that was waved and the thigh that was presented.[a] After that, the Nazirite may drink wine.[b]

21 " 'This is the law of the Nazirite[c] who vows his offering to the LORD in accordance with his separation, in addition to whatever else he can afford. He must fulfill the vow[d] he has made, according to the law of the Nazirite.' "

5:31 [m]S Lev 5:1 **6:2** [n]ver 5; S Ge 28:20; Ac 21:23 [o]ver 6 [p]Jdg 13:5; 16:17 **6:3** [q]S Lev 10:9; S Lk 1:15 [r]Ru 2:14; Ps 69:21; Pr 10:26 [s]S Lev 25:5 **6:5** [t]Ps 52:2; 57:4; 59:7; Isa 7:20; Eze 5:1 [u]1Sa 1:11 **6:6** [v]S Lev 21:1-3; Nu 19:11-22 **6:7** [w]Nu 9:6 **6:9** [x]ver 18 [y]S Lev 14:9 **6:10** [z]S Lev 14:10 [a]S Lev 5:7 [b]Lev 14:11 **6:11** [c]S Ex 30:10 [d]S Ge 8:20 [e]S Ex 29:36 **6:12** [f]S Lev 12:6 [g]S Lev 5:15 **6:13** [h]Ac 21:26 [i]Lev 14:11 **6:14** [j]S Ex 12:5 [k]ver 11; Lev 4:3; 14:10 [l]S Lev 5:15 [m]Lev 3:1 **6:15** [n]Lev 2:1; S 6:14 [o]S Ge 35:14 [p]S Ex 29:2 **6:16** [q]Lev 1:3 [r]ver 10 [s]ver 11 **6:17** [t]Lev 3:1 [u]S Ex 29:41 [v]Lev 23:13 **6:18** [w]ver 9; Ac 21:24 **6:19** [x]Lev 7:12 **6:20** [y]Lev 7:30 [z]S Lev 27:9 [a]S Lev 7:34 [b]Ecc 9:7 **6:21** [c]ver 13 [d]ver 2

[a] *14* Traditionally *peace offering*; also in verses 17 and 18

6:2 *man or woman.* See ch. 30 for the differences between the vows of men and women. *vow ... Nazirite.* Involved separation or consecration for a specific period of special devotion to God—on occasion even for life (see notes on Jdg 13:5; 1Sa 1:11). Attention is usually given to the prohibitions for the Nazirite; more important to the Lord is the positive separation (see v. 8). This was not just a vow of personal self-discipline; it was an act of total devotion to the Lord.

6:4 *anything that comes from the grapevine.* Not only was the fermented beverage forbidden, but even the seed and skin of the grape. During the period of a Nazirite's vow, three areas of his (or her) life were governed: (1) diet, (2) appearance and (3) associations. Every Israelite was regulated in these areas, but for the Nazirite each regulation was heightened.

6:5 *no razor.* See Jdg 13:5. The unusually long hair of a Nazirite would become a physical mark of his (or her) vow of special devotion to the Lord. Cf. Lev 21:5. *He must be holy.* See note on Ex 3:5.

6:6 *dead body.* See note on 5:2. For the Nazirite, the prohibition of contact with dead bodies extended even to the deceased within his (or her) own family (v. 7; contrast Lev 21:1–3).

6:9–12 The provisions of the Nazirite vow concerned areas where he (or she) was able to make conscious decisions. This section deals with the unexpected and the unplanned events of daily living.

6:13–20 The offerings of the Nazirite at the completion of the period of the vow were extensive, expensive and expressive of the spirit of total commitment to the Lord during this time of special devotion. In addition to these several offerings the Nazirite burned his (or her) hair (the sign of the vow).

6:21 A summary of vv. 1–20.

The Priestly Blessing

22The LORD said to Moses, 23"Tell Aaron and his sons, 'This is how you are to
bless[e] the Israelites. Say to them:

24" ' "The LORD bless you[f]
and keep you;[g]
25the LORD make his face shine upon
you[h]
and be gracious to you;[i]
26the LORD turn his face[j] toward you
and give you peace.[k]" '

27"So they will put my name[l] on the Israelites, and I will bless them."

Offerings at the Dedication of the Tabernacle

7 When Moses finished setting up the
tabernacle,[m] he anointed[n] it and consecrated it and all its furnishings.[o] He also
anointed and consecrated the altar and
all its utensils.[p] 2Then the leaders of Israel,[q] the heads of families who were the
tribal leaders in charge of those who were
counted,[r] made offerings. 3They brought
as their gifts before the LORD six covered
carts[s] and twelve oxen—an ox from each
leader and a cart from every two. These
they presented before the tabernacle.
4The LORD said to Moses, 5"Accept these
from them, that they may be used in the
work at the Tent of Meeting. Give them to
the Levites as each man's work requires."
6So Moses took the carts and oxen and
gave them to the Levites. 7He gave two
carts and four oxen to the Gershonites,[t]
as their work required, 8and he gave four
carts and eight oxen to the Merarites,[u] as
their work required. They were all under
the direction of Ithamar son of Aaron, the
priest. 9But Moses did not give any to the
Kohathites,[v] because they were to carry on
their shoulders[w] the holy things, for which
they were responsible.
10When the altar was anointed,[x] the
leaders brought their offerings for its dedication[y] and presented them before the
altar. 11For the LORD had said to Moses,
"Each day one leader is to bring his offering for the dedication of the altar."
12The one who brought his offering on the
first day was Nahshon[z] son of Amminadab
of the tribe of Judah.
13His offering was one silver plate
weighing a hundred and thirty shekels,[a] and one silver sprinkling bowl[a]
weighing seventy shekels,[b b] both according to the sanctuary shekel,[c] each
filled with fine flour mixed with oil
as a grain offering;[d] 14one gold dish[e]
weighing ten shekels,[c f] filled with incense;[g] 15one young bull,[h] one ram
and one male lamb a year old, for a
burnt offering;[i] 16one male goat for
a sin offering;[j] 17and two oxen, five
rams, five male goats and five male
lambs a year old, to be sacrificed as
a fellowship offering.[d k] This was the
offering of Nahshon son of Amminadab.[l]

18On the second day Nethanel son of
Zuar,[m] the leader of Issachar, brought his
offering.
19The offering he brought was one
silver plate weighing a hundred and
thirty shekels, and one silver sprinkling bowl weighing seventy shekels,
both according to the sanctuary shekel, each filled with fine flour mixed
with oil as a grain offering; 20one
gold dish[n] weighing ten shekels, filled
with incense; 21one young bull, one
ram and one male lamb a year old,
for a burnt offering; 22one male goat
for a sin offering; 23and two oxen, five
rams, five male goats and five male

6:23 [e] Dt 21:5; 1Ch 23:13
6:24 [f] S Ge 28:3; Dt 28:3-6; Ps 28:9; 128:5 [g] 1Sa 2:9; Ps 17:8
6:25 [h] Job 29:24; Ps 4:6; 31:16; 80:3; 119:135 [i] Ge 43:29; Ps 25:16; 86:16; 119:29
6:26 [j] Ps 4:6; 44:3 [k] Ps 4:8; 29:11; 37:11,37; 127:2; Isa 14:7; Jer 33:6; Jn 14:27
6:27 [l] Dt 28:10; 2Sa 7:23; 2Ch 7:14; Ne 9:10; Jer 25:29; Eze 36:23
7:1 [m] Ex 40:17 [n] S Ex 30:26 [o] S Ex 40:9 [p] ver 84,88; Ex 40:10; 2Ch 7:9
7:2 [q] Nu 1:5-16 [r] Nu 1:19
7:3 [s] Ge 45:19; 1Sa 6:7-14; 1Ch 13:7
7:7 [t] Nu 4:24-26,28
7:8 [u] Nu 4:31-33
7:9 [v] Nu 4:4 [w] Nu 4:15
7:10 [x] ver 1; S Ex 29:36 [y] 2Ch 7:9
7:12 [z] S Nu 1:7
7:13 [a] S Ex 27:3 [b] ver 85 [c] S Ex 30:13; Lev 27:3-7 [d] Lev 2:1; Nu 6:15; 15:4
7:14 [e] ver 20; 1Ki 7:50; 2Ki 25:14; 2Ch 4:22; 24:14 [f] ver 86 [g] S Ex 25:6
7:15 [h] Ex 24:5; 29:3; Nu 28:11 [i] Lev 1:3
7:16 [j] Lev 4:3
7:17 [k] Lev 3:1 [l] Nu 1:7
7:18 [m] S Nu 1:8
7:20 [n] S ver 14

[a] *13* That is, about 3 1/4 pounds (about 1.5 kilograms); also elsewhere in this chapter [b] *13* That is, about 1 3/4 pounds (about 0.8 kilogram); also elsewhere in this chapter [c] *14* That is, about 4 ounces (about 110 grams); also elsewhere in this chapter [d] *17* Traditionally *peace offering*; also elsewhere in this chapter

6:24–26 The Aaronic benediction. The threefold repetition of the divine name Yahweh ("the LORD") is for emphasis and gives force to the expression in v. 27: "So they will put my name on the Israelites." Each verse conveys two elements of benediction, and the verses are progressively longer (in the Hebrew text, the first verse has three words, the second has five and the third has seven). This benediction is echoed in Ps 67:1 (see note there). In 1979 a condensed version of these verses was found in a burial cave in Jerusalem. The words were inscribed in Hebrew on two silver amulets dating to the seventh century B.C.

6:25 *make his face shine upon you.* In acceptance and favor.

6:26 *peace.* The Hebrew for this word is *shalom,* here seen in its most expressive fullness—not the absence of war, but a positive state of rightness and well-being. Such peace comes only from the Lord (cf. Jn 14:27 and note).

7:1–89 See Ex 40, which describes the setting up of the tabernacle and ends with the report of the cloud covering and the presence of the Lord filling the tabernacle. With much repetition of language, this chapter (the longest in the Pentateuch) records the magnificent (and identical) gifts to the Lord for tabernacle service from the leaders of the 12 tribes. The fact that the record of these gifts follows the text of the Aaronic benediction (6:24–26) seems fitting: In response to God's promise to bless his people, they bring gifts to him in 12 sequential days of celebrative pageantry.

7:12–78 The leaders of the 12 tribes have already been named in 1:5–15; 2:3–32. The order of the presentation of their offerings to the Lord is the same as the order of march: first, the triad of tribes camped east of the tabernacle (Judah, Issachar and Zebulun: 2:3–9; 7:12,18,24); second, the triad camped to the south (Reuben, Simeon and Gad: 2:10–16; 7:30,36,42); third, the triad to the west (Ephraim, Manasseh and Benjamin: 2:18–24; 7:48,54,60); finally, those to the north (Dan, Asher and Naphtali: 2:25–31; 7:66,72,78). See diagram, p. 193.

7:17,23 *fellowship offering.* See note on Lev 3:1.

7:19 *according to the sanctuary shekel.* See note on Ex 30:13.

lambs a year old, to be sacrificed as a fellowship offering. This was the offering of Nethanel son of Zuar.

24On the third day, Eliab son of Helon,[o] the leader of the people of Zebulun, brought his offering.

25His offering was one silver plate weighing a hundred and thirty shekels, and one silver sprinkling bowl weighing seventy shekels, both according to the sanctuary shekel, each filled with fine flour mixed with oil as a grain offering; 26one gold dish weighing ten shekels, filled with incense; 27one young bull, one ram and one male lamb a year old, for a burnt offering; 28one male goat for a sin offering; 29and two oxen, five rams, five male goats and five male lambs a year old, to be sacrificed as a fellowship offering. This was the offering of Eliab son of Helon.

30On the fourth day Elizur son of Shedeur,[p] the leader of the people of Reuben, brought his offering.

31His offering was one silver plate weighing a hundred and thirty shekels, and one silver sprinkling bowl weighing seventy shekels, both according to the sanctuary shekel, each filled with fine flour mixed with oil as a grain offering; 32one gold dish weighing ten shekels, filled with incense; 33one young bull, one ram and one male lamb a year old, for a burnt offering; 34one male goat for a sin offering; 35and two oxen, five rams, five male goats and five male lambs a year old, to be sacrificed as a fellowship offering. This was the offering of Elizur son of Shedeur.

36On the fifth day Shelumiel son of Zurishaddai,[q] the leader of the people of Simeon, brought his offering.

37His offering was one silver plate weighing a hundred and thirty shekels, and one silver sprinkling bowl weighing seventy shekels, both according to the sanctuary shekel, each filled with fine flour mixed with oil as a grain offering; 38one gold dish weighing ten shekels, filled with incense; 39one young bull, one ram and one male lamb a year old, for a burnt offering; 40one male goat for a sin offering; 41and two oxen, five rams, five male goats and five male lambs a year old, to be sacrificed as a fellowship offering. This was the offering of Shelumiel son of Zurishaddai.

42On the sixth day Eliasaph son of Deuel,[r] the leader of the people of Gad, brought his offering.

43His offering was one silver plate weighing a hundred and thirty shekels, and one silver sprinkling bowl weighing seventy shekels, both according to the sanctuary shekel, each filled with fine flour mixed with oil as a grain offering; 44one gold dish weighing ten shekels, filled with incense; 45one young bull, one ram and one male lamb a year old, for a burnt offering; 46one male goat for a sin offering; 47and two oxen, five rams, five male goats and five male lambs a year old, to be sacrificed as a fellowship offering. This was the offering of Eliasaph son of Deuel.

48On the seventh day Elishama son of Ammihud,[s] the leader of the people of Ephraim, brought his offering.

49His offering was one silver plate weighing a hundred and thirty shekels, and one silver sprinkling bowl weighing seventy shekels, both according to the sanctuary shekel, each filled with fine flour mixed with oil as a grain offering; 50one gold dish weighing ten shekels, filled with incense; 51one young bull, one ram and one male lamb a year old, for a burnt offering; 52one male goat for a sin offering; 53and two oxen, five rams, five male goats and five male lambs a year old, to be sacrificed as a fellowship offering. This was the offering of Elishama son of Ammihud.[t]

54On the eighth day Gamaliel son of Pedahzur,[u] the leader of the people of Manasseh, brought his offering.

55His offering was one silver plate weighing a hundred and thirty shekels, and one silver sprinkling bowl weighing seventy shekels, both according to the sanctuary shekel, each filled with fine flour mixed with oil as a grain offering; 56one gold dish weighing ten shekels, filled with incense; 57one young bull, one ram and one male lamb a year old, for a burnt offering; 58one male goat for a sin offering; 59and two oxen, five rams, five male goats and five male lambs a year old, to be sacrificed as a fellowship offering. This was the offering of Gamaliel son of Pedahzur.

60On the ninth day Abidan son of Gideoni,[v] the leader of the people of Benjamin, brought his offering.

61His offering was one silver plate weighing a hundred and thirty shekels, and one silver sprinkling bowl weighing seventy shekels, both according to the sanctuary shekel, each filled with fine flour mixed with oil

7:24 [o] S Nu 1:9
7:30 [p] S Nu 1:5
7:36 [q] S Nu 1:6
7:42 [r] S Nu 1:14
7:48 [s] S Nu 1:10
7:53 [t] S Nu 1:10
7:54 [u] S Nu 1:10
7:60 [v] S Nu 1:11

as a grain offering; 62 one gold dish weighing ten shekels, filled with incense; 63 one young bull, one ram and one male lamb a year old, for a burnt offering; 64 one male goat for a sin offering; 65 and two oxen, five rams, five male goats and five male lambs a year old, to be sacrificed as a fellowship offering. This was the offering of Abidan son of Gideoni.

66 On the tenth day Ahiezer son of Ammishaddai,[w] the leader of the people of Dan, brought his offering.

67 His offering was one silver plate weighing a hundred and thirty shekels, and one silver sprinkling bowl weighing seventy shekels, both according to the sanctuary shekel, each filled with fine flour mixed with oil as a grain offering; 68 one gold dish weighing ten shekels, filled with incense; 69 one young bull, one ram and one male lamb a year old, for a burnt offering; 70 one male goat for a sin offering; 71 and two oxen, five rams, five male goats and five male lambs a year old, to be sacrificed as a fellowship offering. This was the offering of Ahiezer son of Ammishaddai.

72 On the eleventh day Pagiel son of Ocran,[x] the leader of the people of Asher, brought his offering.

73 His offering was one silver plate weighing a hundred and thirty shekels, and one silver sprinkling bowl weighing seventy shekels, both according to the sanctuary shekel, each filled with fine flour mixed with oil as a grain offering; 74 one gold dish weighing ten shekels, filled with incense; 75 one young bull, one ram and one male lamb a year old, for a burnt offering; 76 one male goat for a sin offering; 77 and two oxen, five rams, five male goats and five male lambs a year old, to be sacrificed as a fellowship offering. This was the offering of Pagiel son of Ocran.

78 On the twelfth day Ahira son of Enan,[y] the leader of the people of Naphtali, brought his offering.

79 His offering was one silver plate weighing a hundred and thirty shekels, and one silver sprinkling bowl weighing seventy shekels, both according to the sanctuary shekel, each filled with fine flour mixed with oil as a grain offering; 80 one gold dish weighing ten shekels, filled with incense; 81 one young bull, one ram and one male lamb a year old, for a burnt offering; 82 one male goat for a sin offering; 83 and two oxen, five rams, five male goats and five male lambs a year old, to be sacrificed as a fellowship offering. This was the offering of Ahira son of Enan.

84 These were the offerings of the Israelite leaders for the dedication of the altar when it was anointed:[z] twelve silver plates, twelve silver sprinkling bowls[a] and twelve gold dishes.[b] 85 Each silver plate weighed a hundred and thirty shekels, and each sprinkling bowl seventy shekels. Altogether, the silver dishes weighed two thousand four hundred shekels,[a] according to the sanctuary shekel.[c] 86 The twelve gold dishes filled with incense weighed ten shekels each, according to the sanctuary shekel.[d] Altogether, the gold dishes weighed a hundred and twenty shekels.[b] 87 The total number of animals for the burnt offering[e] came to twelve young bulls, twelve rams and twelve male lambs a year old, together with their grain offering.[f] Twelve male goats were used for the sin offering.[g] 88 The total number of animals for the sacrifice of the fellowship offering[h] came to twenty-four oxen, sixty rams, sixty male goats and sixty male lambs[i] a year old. These were the offerings for the dedication of the altar after it was anointed.[j]

89 When Moses entered the Tent of Meeting[k] to speak with the LORD,[l] he heard the voice speaking to him from between the two cherubim above the atonement cover[m] on the ark of the Testimony.[n] And he spoke with him.

Setting Up the Lamps

8 The LORD said to Moses, 2 "Speak to Aaron and say to him, 'When you set up the seven lamps, they are to light the area in front of the lampstand.[o]' "

3 Aaron did so; he set up the lamps so that they faced forward on the lampstand, just as the LORD commanded Moses. 4 This is how the lampstand was made: It was made of hammered gold[p]—from its base to its blossoms. The lampstand was made exactly like the pattern[q] the LORD had shown Moses.

The Setting Apart of the Levites

5 The LORD said to Moses: 6 "Take the Levites from among the other Israelites

7:66 [w] S Nu 1:12
7:72 [x] S Nu 1:13
7:78 [y] S Nu 1:15
7:84 [z] ver 1, 10 [a] S Nu 4:14 [b] ver 14
7:85 [c] ver 13
7:86 [d] ver 13
7:87 [e] ver 15 [f] ver 13 [g] ver 16
7:88 [h] ver 17 [i] Ge 32:14 [j] S ver 1, 10
7:89 [k] S Ex 40:2 [l] S Ex 29:42 [m] S Ex 16:34; Ps 80:1; 99:1 [n] Nu 3:31
8:2 [o] Ex 25:37
8:4 [p] S Ex 25:18, 36 [q] S Ex 25:9

[a] *85* That is, about 60 pounds (about 28 kilograms)
[b] *86* That is, about 3 pounds (about 1.4 kilograms)

7:84–88 The totals of the 12 sets of gifts.
7:89 The climax: Communion is established between the Lord and his prophet. The people have an advocate with God. *Testimony.* See note on Ex 25:16.

8:2 *area in front of the lampstand.* The Holy Place in the tabernacle (see Ex 25:37; 26:31–35; 27:21 and notes).
8:5–26 Describes the cleansing of the Levites and may be compared with the account of the ordination of Aaron and

and make them ceremonially clean.[r] [7]To
purify them, do this: Sprinkle the water
of cleansing[s] on them; then have them
shave their whole bodies[t] and wash their
clothes,[u] and so purify themselves.[v] [8]Have
them take a young bull with its grain offering of fine flour mixed with oil;[w] then you
are to take a second young bull for a sin
offering.[x] [9]Bring the Levites to the front
of the Tent of Meeting[y] and assemble the
whole Israelite community.[z] [10]You are to
bring the Levites before the LORD, and the
Israelites are to lay their hands on them.[a]
[11]Aaron is to present the Levites before the
LORD as a wave offering[b] from the Israelites, so that they may be ready to do the
work of the LORD.

[12]"After the Levites lay their hands on
the heads of the bulls,[c] use the one for
a sin offering[d] to the LORD and the other
for a burnt offering,[e] to make atonement[f]
for the Levites. [13]Have the Levites stand
in front of Aaron and his sons and then
present them as a wave offering[g] to the
LORD. [14]In this way you are to set the Levites apart from the other Israelites, and
the Levites will be mine.[h]

[15]"After you have purified the Levites
and presented them as a wave offering,[i]
they are to come to do their work at the
Tent of Meeting.[j] [16]They are the Israelites
who are to be given wholly to me. I have
taken them as my own in place of the firstborn,[k] the first male offspring[l] from every
Israelite woman. [17]Every firstborn male in
Israel, whether man or animal,[m] is mine.
When I struck down all the firstborn in
Egypt, I set them apart for myself.[n][o] [18]And
I have taken the Levites in place of all the
firstborn sons in Israel.[p] [19]Of all the Israelites, I have given the Levites as gifts to
Aaron and his sons[q] to do the work at the
Tent of Meeting on behalf of the Israelites[r]
and to make atonement for them[s] so that
no plague will strike the Israelites when
they go near the sanctuary."

[20]Moses, Aaron and the whole Israelite community did with the Levites just
as the LORD commanded Moses. [21]The
Levites purified themselves and washed
their clothes.[t] Then Aaron presented
them as a wave offering before the LORD
and made atonement[u] for them to purify
them.[v] [22]After that, the Levites came to
do their work[w] at the Tent of Meeting under the supervision of Aaron and his sons.
They did with the Levites just as the LORD
commanded Moses.

[23]The LORD said to Moses, [24]"This applies to the Levites: Men twenty-five
years old or more[x] shall come to take
part in the work at the Tent of Meeting,[y]
[25]but at the age of fifty,[z] they must retire
from their regular service and work no
longer. [26]They may assist their brothers
in performing their duties at the Tent of
Meeting, but they themselves must not
do the work.[a] This, then, is how you are
to assign the responsibilities of the Levites."

The Passover

9 The LORD spoke to Moses in the Desert
of Sinai in the first month[b] of the second year after they came out of Egypt.[c]
He said, [2]"Have the Israelites celebrate
the Passover[d] at the appointed time.[e] [3]Cel-
ebrate it at the appointed time, at twilight

8:6 [r] Lev 22:2; Isa 1:16; 52:11
8:7 [s] Nu 19:9,17; 31:23 [t] S Lev 14:9; Nu 6:9; Dt 21:12 [u] S Ge 35:2; Lev 14:8 [v] S Ge 35:2
8:8 [w] Lev 2:1; Nu 15:8-10 [x] Lev 4:3
8:9 [y] Ex 40:12 [z] Lev 8:3
8:10 [a] S Lev 3:2; Ac 6:6
8:11 [b] S Ex 29:24
8:12 [c] S Ex 29:10 [d] Lev 4:3; Nu 6:11 [e] Lev 1:3 [f] S Ex 29:36
8:13 [g] S Ex 29:24
8:14 [h] S Nu 3:12
8:15 [i] S Ex 29:24 [j] Ex 40:2
8:16 [k] Nu 1:20 [l] S Nu 3:12
8:17 [m] S Ex 4:23 [n] S Ex 22:29 [o] S Ex 13:2
8:18 [p] S Nu 3:12
8:19 [q] S Nu 3:9 [r] S Nu 3:7 [s] Nu 16:46
8:21 [t] ver 7; S Ge 35:2 [u] Nu 16:47 [v] ver 12
8:22 [w] ver 11
8:24 [x] 1Ch 23:3 [y] S Ex 38:21
8:25 [z] S Nu 4:3
8:26 [a] ver 11
9:1 [b] S Ex 40:2 [c] Nu 1:1
9:2 [d] S Ex 12:11 [e] ver 7

his sons to the priesthood (Lev 8). The Levites are helpers to the priests, and the language describing their consecration is somewhat different from that of the priests. The priests were made holy, the Levites clean; the priests were anointed and washed, the Levites sprinkled; the priests were given new garments, the Levites washed theirs; blood was applied to the priests, it was waved over the Levites.

8:7 *shave their whole bodies.* Symbolic of the completeness of their cleansing, as in the case of the ritual cleansing of one cured of skin disease (see Lev 14:8 and note).

8:10 *Israelites are to lay their hands on them.* The Levites were substitutes for the nation; by laying hands on them, the other people of the nation were acknowledging this substitutionary act (see vv. 16–18).

8:16 *to me.* See note on 3:9.

8:19 *I have given the Levites as gifts to Aaron and his sons.* The Levites were given to the Lord for his exclusive use (see v. 14). Now the Lord gives his Levites to the priests as their aides for the work of ministry in the tabernacle worship. *so that no plague will strike the Israelites.* The Levites were a protective hedge for the community against trespassing in the sacred precincts of the tabernacle (see note on 1:53).

8:20 *as the LORD commanded Moses.* See vv. 4,22; 1:54; 2:34; 3:16,51; 4:49; 5:4; 9:5,23. The implicit obedience of Moses and the Israelites to God's commands in the areas of ritual and regimen stands in sharp contrast to the people's complaints against the Lord's loving character and to their breaches of faith that begin in ch. 11.

8:24 *twenty-five years old.* See note on 4:3. The age at which the Levites entered service was reduced to 20 by David (see 1Ch 23:3,24,27 and note on 23:3), as the circumstances of their work had greatly changed by the time of the monarchy (see 1Ch 23:26). It is difficult to imagine a change in circumstances between 4:3 and this verse, however. Therefore the Rabbinical suggestion that these two verses indicate a five-year period of apprenticeship seems reasonable.

8:26 *They may assist.* After a Levite had reached the mandatory retirement age of 50 (see v. 25), he was still free to assist his younger coworkers (perhaps at festivals), but he was no longer to do the difficult work he had done in his prime.

9:1–14 This unit is in four parts: (1) the command to keep the Passover (vv. 1–5); (2) the question concerning those ceremonially unclean (vv. 6–8); (3) the response of the Lord—giving permission for legitimate delay, but judgment for willful neglect (vv. 9–13); (4) the rights of the alien at Passover (v. 14). The first Passover was held in Egypt (see Ex 12). The second is here at Sinai a year later. Because of Israel's rebellion and God's judgment on her (ch. 14), Israel would not celebrate the Passover again until she entered the promised land (see Jos 5:10 and note).

9:1 *first month of the second year.* The events of this chapter preceded the beginning of the census in ch. 1 (see 1:1 and note).

9:3 *twilight.* Traditional Jewish practice regards this period as the end of one day and the beginning of the next.

on the fourteenth day of this month,[f] in
accordance with all its rules and regulations.[g]"
4So Moses told the Israelites to celebrate
the Passover,[h] 5and they did so in the Desert of Sinai[i] at twilight on the fourteenth
day of the first month.[j] The Israelites did
everything just as the LORD commanded
Moses.[k]
6But some of them could not celebrate
the Passover on that day because they
were ceremonially unclean[l] on account of
a dead body.[m] So they came to Moses and
Aaron[n] that same day 7and said to Moses, "We have become unclean because
of a dead body, but why should we be
kept from presenting the LORD's offering
with the other Israelites at the appointed
time?[o]"
8Moses answered them, "Wait until I
find out what the LORD commands concerning you."[p]
9Then the LORD said to Moses, 10"Tell the
Israelites: 'When any of you or your descendants are unclean because of a dead
body[q] or are away on a journey, they may
still celebrate[r] the LORD's Passover. 11They
are to celebrate it on the fourteenth day
of the second month[s] at twilight. They
are to eat the lamb, together with unleavened bread and bitter herbs.[t] 12They must
not leave any of it till morning[u] or break
any of its bones.[v] When they celebrate the
Passover, they must follow all the regulations.[w] 13But if a man who is ceremonially clean and not on a journey fails to
celebrate the Passover, that person must
be cut off from his people[x] because he did
not present the LORD's offering at the appointed time. That man will bear the consequences of his sin.
14" 'An alien[y] living among you who
wants to celebrate the LORD's Passover
must do so in accordance with its rules and
regulations. You must have the same regulations for the alien and the native-born.' "

The Cloud Above the Tabernacle

15On the day the tabernacle, the Tent of
the Testimony,[z] was set up,[a] the cloud[b]
covered it. From evening till morning
the cloud above the tabernacle looked
like fire.[c] 16That is how it continued to
be; the cloud covered it, and at night it
looked like fire.[d] 17Whenever the cloud
lifted from above the Tent, the Israelites set out;[e] wherever the cloud settled,
the Israelites encamped.[f] 18At the LORD's
command the Israelites set out, and at his
command they encamped. As long as the
cloud stayed over the tabernacle, they remained[g] in camp. 19When the cloud remained over the tabernacle a long time,
the Israelites obeyed the LORD's order[h]
and did not set out.[i] 20Sometimes the
cloud was over the tabernacle only a few
days; at the LORD's command they would
encamp, and then at his command they
would set out. 21Sometimes the cloud
stayed only from evening till morning,
and when it lifted in the morning, they set
out. Whether by day or by night, whenever the cloud lifted, they set out. 22Whether
the cloud stayed over the tabernacle for
two days or a month or a year, the Israelites would remain in camp and not set
out; but when it lifted, they would set out.
23At the LORD's command they encamped,
and at the LORD's command they set out.
They obeyed the LORD's order, in accordance with his command through Moses.

The Silver Trumpets

10 The LORD said to Moses: 2"Make two
trumpets[j] of hammered silver, and
use them for calling the community[k] together and for having the camps set out.[l]

9:3 [f]S Ex 12:6,42 [g]Ex 12:2-11, 43-49; Lev 23:5-8; Dt 16:1-8 **9:4** [h]ver 2; S Ex 12:11 **9:5** [i]ver 1 [j]S Ex 12:6 [k]ver 3 **9:6** [l]S Lev 5:3; S 13:3 [m]S Lev 21:11 [n]Ex 18:15; Nu 27:2 **9:7** [o]ver 2 **9:8** [p]Ex 18:15; Lev 24:12; Nu 15:34; 27:5,21; Ps 85:8 **9:10** [q]ver 6 [r]2Ch 30:2 **9:11** [s]S Ex 12:6 [t]Ex 12:8 **9:12** [u]S Ex 12:8 [v]S Ex 12:46; Jn 19:36* [w]ver 3 **9:13** [x]S Ge 17:14 **9:14** [y]S Ex 12:19,43 **9:15** [z]S Ex 38:21 [a]S Ex 26:30 [b]S Ex 33:16 [c]Ex 13:21 **9:16** [d]S Ex 40:38 **9:17** [e]ver 21 [f]1Co 10:1 **9:18** [g]Ex 40:37 **9:19** [h]S Lev 8:35 [i]Ex 40:37 **10:2** [j]ver 8,9; Nu 31:6; Ne 12:35; Ps 47:5; 98:6; 150:3 [k]Ne 4:18; Jer 4:5,19; 6:1; Hos 5:8; 8:1; Joel 2:1,15; Am 3:6 [l]Nu 33:3

9:7 *why should we be kept from presenting the LORD's offering ...?* Those with ceremonial uncleanness had a keen desire to worship the Lord "in spirit and in truth" (Jn 4:24; see note there).

9:10 *they may still celebrate.* God's gracious provision for these people was an alternative day one month later (v. 11) so that they would not be excluded totally from the Passover celebration. The Lord thus demonstrates the reality of the distance that uncleanness brings between a believer and his or her participation in the worship of the community, but he also provides a merciful alternative.

9:12 *not ... break any of its bones.* When Jesus ("our Passover lamb," 1Co 5:7; cf. Jn 1:29) was crucified, it was reported that none of his bones was broken, in fulfillment of Scripture (Jn 19:36). See also Ex 12:46; Ps 34:20 and note.

9:13 *fails to celebrate ... cut off.* The NT also issues grave warnings concerning the abuse or the misuse of the celebration of the Lord's Supper (see 1Co 11:28–30 and notes). See note on Ex 12:15.

9:14 *alien.* Must first be circumcised before participating in the Passover celebration (see Ex 12:48 and note).

9:15 *Testimony.* See note on Ex 25:16. *cloud covered it.* See notes on Ex 13:21; 40:34. The cloud was the visible symbol of the Lord's presence hovering above the tabernacle. That this was no ordinary cloud is attested not only by its spontaneous appearance at the completion of the setting up of the tabernacle, but also by the fact that at night it had the appearance of fire. The Lord also directed the movements of his people by means of the cloud (vv. 17–18).

9:18 *At the LORD's command.* The lifting and settling of the cloud are identified with the Lord's command.

9:23 *obeyed the LORD's order.* The repetitious nature of vv. 15–23 enhances the expectation of continued complete obedience to the Lord's direction of Israel's movements through the desert. The role of Moses is mentioned for balance: Moses was the Lord's agent, who interpreted the movement of the cloud as signaling the movement of the people. The tragedy of their subsequent disobedience (ch. 11) is heightened by this paragraph on their obedience.

10:2 *trumpets.* Long, straight, slender metal tubes with flared ends. They were blown for order and discipline.

3When both are sounded, the whole community is to assemble before you at the
entrance to the Tent of Meeting. 4If only
one is sounded, the leaders[m]—the heads
of the clans of Israel—are to assemble before you. 5When a trumpet blast is sounded, the tribes camping on the east are to
set out.[n] 6At the sounding of a second
blast, the camps on the south are to set
out.[o] The blast will be the signal for setting out. 7To gather the assembly, blow the
trumpets,[p] but not with the same signal.[q]
8"The sons of Aaron, the priests, are to
blow the trumpets. This is to be a lasting ordinance for you and the generations to come.[r] 9When you go into battle
in your own land against an enemy who
is oppressing you,[s] sound a blast on the
trumpets.[t] Then you will be remembered[u]
by the LORD your God and rescued from
your enemies.[v] 10Also at your times of rejoicing—your appointed feasts and New
Moon festivals[w]—you are to sound the
trumpets[x] over your burnt offerings[y] and
fellowship offerings,[a z] and they will be a
memorial for you before your God. I am
the LORD your God.[a]"

The Israelites Leave Sinai

11On the twentieth day of the second
month of the second year,[b] the cloud lifted[c] from above the tabernacle of the Testimony.[d] 12Then the Israelites set out from
the Desert of Sinai and traveled from place
to place until the cloud came to rest in
the Desert of Paran.[e] 13They set out, this
first time, at the LORD's command through
Moses.[f]
14The divisions of the camp of Judah
went first, under their standard.[g] Nahshon
son of Amminadab[h] was in command.
15Nethanel son of Zuar was over the division of the tribe[i] of Issachar,[j] 16and Eliab
son of Helon[k] was over the division of the
tribe of Zebulun.[l] 17Then the tabernacle
was taken down, and the Gershonites and
Merarites, who carried it, set out.[m]
18The divisions of the camp of Reuben[n]
went next, under their standard.[o] Elizur
son of Shedeur[p] was in command. 19Shelu-
miel son of Zurishaddai was over the division of the tribe of Simeon,[q] 20and Eliasaph
son of Deuel was over the division of the
tribe of Gad.[r] 21Then the Kohathites[s] set
out, carrying the holy things.[t] The tabernacle was to be set up before they arrived.[u]
22The divisions of the camp of Ephraim[v]
went next, under their standard. Elishama son of Ammihud[w] was in command.
23Gamaliel son of Pedahzur was over the
division of the tribe of Manasseh,[x] 24and
Abidan son of Gideoni was over the division of the tribe of Benjamin.[y]
25Finally, as the rear guard[z] for all the
units, the divisions of the camp of Dan set
out, under their standard. Ahiezer son of
Ammishaddai[a] was in command. 26Pagiel
son of Ocran was over the division of the
tribe of Asher,[b] 27and Ahira son of Enan
was over the division of the tribe of Naphtali.[c] 28This was the order of march for the
Israelite divisions as they set out.
29Now Moses said to Hobab[d] son of Reuel[e] the Midianite, Moses' father-in-law,[f] "We
are setting out for the place about which
the LORD said, 'I will give it to you.'[g] Come
with us and we will treat you well, for the
LORD has promised good things to Israel."
30He answered, "No, I will not go;[h] I am
going back to my own land and my own
people.[i]"
31But Moses said, "Please do not leave
us. You know where we should camp in

[a] 10 Traditionally *peace offerings*

10:4 [m]S Ex 18:21 **10:5** [n]ver 14 **10:6** [o]ver 18 **10:7** [p]Jer 4:5; 6:1; Eze 33:3; Joel 2:1 [q]1Co 14:8 **10:8** [r]S Ge 9:12; Nu 15:14; 35:29 **10:9** [s]Ex 3:9; Jdg 2:18; 6:9; 1Sa 10:18; 2Ki 13:4; Ps 106:42 [t]S Lev 23:24 [u]S Ge 8:1 [v]2Ch 13:12; Ps 106:4 **10:10** [w]Nu 28:11; 1Sa 20:5,24; 2Ki 4:23; 2Ch 8:13; Ps 81:3; Isa 1:13; Eze 45:17; 46:6; Am 8:5 [x]S Lev 23:24 [y]Lev 1:3 [z]Lev 3:1; Nu 6:14 [a]Lev 11:44 **10:11** [b]Ex 40:17 [c]Nu 9:17 [d]S Ex 38:21 **10:12** [e]S Ge 14:6; Dt 1:1; 33:2 **10:13** [f]Dt 1:6 **10:14** [g]S Nu 1:52; S 2:3-9 [h]Nu 1:7 **10:15** [i]S Lev 24:11 [j]S Nu 1:8 **10:16** [k]S Nu 2:7 [l]S Nu 1:9 **10:17** [m]ver 21; Nu 4:21-32 **10:18** [n]Nu 2:16 [o]Nu 2:10-16 [p]S Nu 1:5 **10:19** [q]Nu 1:6 **10:20** [r]S Nu 1:14 **10:21** [s]S Nu 2:17 [t]Nu 4:20 [u]S ver 17 **10:22** [v]Nu 2:24 [w]S Nu 1:10 **10:23** [x]S Nu 1:10 **10:24** [y]Nu 1:11 **10:25** [z]S Nu 2:31 [a]S Nu 1:12 **10:26** [b]S Nu 1:13 **10:27** [c]S Nu 1:15 **10:29** [d]Jdg 4:11 [e]S Ex 2:18 [f]S Ex 3:1 [g]S Ge 12:7; S 15:14 **10:30** [h]Mt 21:29 [i]S Ex 18:27

10:3 *sounded.* Not only for assembling but also for marching (vv. 5–6), battle (v. 9) and festivals (v. 10). Since different signals were used (v. 7), a guild of priestly musicians was developed (v. 8). See Jos 6:4 (see also note there) for the use of seven trumpets of rams' horns (Hebrew *shophar*) in the battle of Jericho.
10:10 *at your ... appointed feasts ... sound the trumpets.* To prepare the people for communion with God. Later, David expanded the instruments to include the full orchestra in the worship of the Lord (see, e.g., 1Ch 25), but he maintained the playing of the silver trumpets regularly before the ark of the covenant (1Ch 16:6).
10:11—22:1 The sordid account of the Israelites' long trek from Sinai to Kadesh (13:26) to the plains of Moab (see Introduction: Structure and Outline).
10:11–28 The structure of this section is: (1) v. 11, time frame; (2) vv. 12–13, introductory summary of setting out; (3) vv. 14–17, setting out of the tribes led by Judah (see 2:3–9); (4) vv. 18–21, setting out of the tribes led by Reuben (see 2:10–16); (5) vv. 22–24, setting out of the tribes led by Ephraim (see 2:18–24); (6) vv. 25–27, setting out of the tribes led by Dan (see 2:25–31); (7) v. 28, concluding summary of the line of march (see diagram, p. 193).
10:11 *twentieth day of the second month.* After 11 months in the region of Mount Sinai, the people set out for the promised land, led by the cloud (see note on 9:15). Israel leaves on a journey that in a few months should have led to the conquest of Canaan. *Testimony.* See note on Ex 25:16.
10:14–27 The names of the leaders of the 12 tribes are given for the fourth time in the book (see 1:5–15; 2:3–31; 7:12–83). The order of the line of march is essentially the same as that in ch. 2. The new details are that the Gershonites and Merarites, who carry the tabernacle, follow the triad of the Judah tribes (v. 17), and the Kohathites, who carry the holy things, follow the triad of the Reuben tribes (v. 21) (see diagram, p. 193).
10:14 *standard.* As in 2:3,10,18,25, each of the four triads of tribes had a standard or banner for rallying and organization.
10:29 *Hobab son of Reuel.* Thus Hobab was Moses' brother-in-law. *Reuel.* Jethro (see Ex 2:16 and note; 3:1).
10:31 *be our eyes.* Jdg 1:16 indicates that Hobab acceded to Moses' request.

the desert, and you can be our eyes.[j] 32If
you come with us, we will share with you[k]
whatever good things the LORD gives us.[l]"
33So they set out[m] from the mountain of
the LORD and traveled for three days. The
ark of the covenant of the LORD[n] went before them during those three days to find
them a place to rest.[o] 34The cloud of the
LORD was over them by day when they set
out from the camp.[p]
35Whenever the ark set out, Moses
said,

"Rise up,[q] O LORD!
May your enemies be scattered;[r]
may your foes flee before you.[s]"[t]

36Whenever it came to rest, he said,

"Return,[u] O LORD,
to the countless thousands of Israel.[v]"

Fire From the LORD

11 Now the people complained[w] about
their hardships in the hearing of the
LORD,[x] and when he heard them his anger was aroused.[y] Then fire from the LORD
burned among them[z] and consumed[a] some
of the outskirts of the camp. 2When the
people cried out to Moses, he prayed[b] to
the LORD[c] and the fire died down. 3So that
place was called Taberah,[a][d] because fire
from the LORD had burned among them.[e]

Quail From the LORD

4The rabble with them began to crave
other food,[f] and again the Israelites started wailing[g] and said, "If only we had meat
to eat! 5We remember the fish we ate in
Egypt at no cost—also the cucumbers,
melons, leeks, onions and garlic.[h] 6But
now we have lost our appetite; we never
see anything but this manna![i]"
7The manna was like coriander seed[j]
and looked like resin.[k] 8The people went
around gathering it,[l] and then ground it
in a handmill or crushed it in a mortar.
They cooked it in a pot or made it into
cakes. And it tasted like something made
with olive oil. 9When the dew[m] settled on
the camp at night, the manna also came
down.
10Moses heard the people of every family wailing,[n] each at the entrance to his
tent. The LORD became exceedingly angry,
and Moses was troubled. 11He asked the
LORD, "Why have you brought this trouble[o] on your servant? What have I done to
displease you that you put the burden of
all these people on me?[p] 12Did I conceive
all these people? Did I give them birth?
Why do you tell me to carry them in my
arms, as a nurse carries an infant,[q] to the
land you promised on oath[r] to their forefathers?[s] 13Where can I get meat for all these
people?[t] They keep wailing to me, 'Give
us meat to eat!' 14I cannot carry all these

[a] 3 *Taberah* means *burning*.

10:31 [j]Job 29:15 **10:32** [k]S Ex 12:48; Dt 10:18 [l]Ps 22:27-31; 67:5-7 **10:33** [m]ver 12; Dt 1:33 [n]Dt 10:8; 31:9; Jos 3:3; Jdg 20:27; 2Sa 15:24 [o]Jer 31:2 **10:34** [p]Nu 9:15-23 **10:35** [q]2Ch 6:41; Ps 17:13; 44:26; 94:2; 132:8 [r]Jdg 5:31; 1Sa 2:1; Ps 68:1; 92:9 [s]Dt 5:9; 7:10; 32:41; Ps 68:2; Isa 17:12-14 [t]Isa 59:18 **10:36** [u]Isa 52:8; 63:17 [v]Ge 15:5; 26:4; Dt 1:10; 10:22; Ne 9:23 **11:1** [w]S Ex 14:11; S 16:7; La 3:39 [x]Nu 12:2; Dt 1:34 [y]S Ex 4:14 [z]S Lev 10:2 [a]Nu 21:28; Ps 78:63; Isa 26:11 **11:2** [b]Dt 9:19; 1Sa 2:25; 12:23; Ps 106:23 [c]S Ge 20:7; Nu 21:7; Dt 9:20; Jnh 2:1 **11:3** [d]Dt 9:22 [e]Nu 16:35; Job 1:16; Isa 10:17 **11:4** [f]S Ex 16:3 [g]ver 18 **11:5** [h]S Ex 16:3; Nu 21:5 **11:6** [i]Ex 16:14 **11:7** [j]S Ex 16:31 [k]Ge 2:12 **11:8** [l]Ex 16:16 **11:9** [m]Ex 16:13 **11:10** [n]ver 4 **11:11** [o]S Ge 34:30 [p]S Ex 5:22; S 18:18 **11:12** [q]Isa 40:11; 49:23; 66:11,12 [r]Nu 14:16 [s]S Ge 12:7; Ex 13:5 **11:13** [t]S Ex 12:37; Jn 6:5-9

10:33 *three days.* Because of the huge numbers of people in the tribes of Israel, and because this was their first organized march, it is not likely that this first journey covered much territory (cf. note on Ge 22:4).

10:35–36 Reinforces the portrayal of Israel as the Lord's army on the march, with the Lord in the vanguard.

10:35 Later used in the opening words of a psalm celebrating God's triumphal march from Sinai to Jerusalem (see Ps 68:1 and note on 68:1–3).

11:1 *people complained.* The first ten chapters of Numbers repeatedly emphasize the complete obedience of Moses and the people to the dictates of the Lord. But only three days into their march, the people reverted to disloyal complaints. They had expressed the same complaints a year earlier only three days after their deliverance at the waters of the "Red Sea" (see Ex 15:22–27 and note on 15:24) and subsequently had complained about manna (Ex 16) and a lack of water (Ex 17:1–7). *fire from the LORD.* By God's mercy, this purging fire was limited to the outskirts of the camp. The phrase sometimes refers to fire ignited by lightning (as probably in 1Ki 18:38; see note on 18:24).

11:3 *Taberah.* See NIV text note.

11:4 *rabble.* An apt term for the non-Israelite mixed group of people who followed the Israelites out of Egypt, pointing to a recurring source of complaints and trouble in the camp. Those who did not know the Lord and his mercies incited those who did know him to rebel against him. *If only we had meat to eat!* As in Ex 16, the people began to complain about their diet, forgetting what God had done for them (see Ps 106:14). Certainly meat was not their common fare when they were slaves in Egypt. Now that they were in a new type of distress, the people romanticized the past and minimized its discomforts.

11:5 *fish ... cucumbers ... garlic.* Suggestive of the varieties of foods available in Egypt, in contrast to the diet of manna in the desert.

11:7 *manna.* See note on Ex 16:31.

11:10 *The LORD became exceedingly angry.* The rejection of his gracious gift of heavenly food (called "bread from heaven" in Ex 16:4) angered the Lord. God had said that the reception of the manna by the people would be a significant test of their obedience (see Ex 16:4 and note). In view of the good things he was to give them (10:32), the people were expected to receive each day's supply of manna as a gracious gift of a merciful God, and a promise of abundance to come. In spurning the manna, the people had spurned the Lord. They had failed the test of faith. *Moses was troubled.* The people's reaction to God's provision of manna was troubling to Moses as well. Instead of asking the Lord to understand the substance of their complaint, Moses asked him why he was given such an ungrateful people to lead.

11:11–15 A prayer of distress and complaint, filled with urgency, irony and passion.

11:12 *Did I conceive all these people?* The implication is that the Lord conceived the people of Israel, that he was their nurse and that their promises were his. Moses asks that he be relieved of his mediatorial office, for "the burden is too heavy for me" (v. 14; cf. Elijah, 1Ki 19). Even death, Moses asserts (v. 15), would be preferable to facing the continuing complaints of the people.

people by myself; the burden is too heavy
for me.[u] 15If this is how you are going to
treat me, put me to death[v] right now[w]—if
I have found favor in your eyes—and do
not let me face my own ruin."
16The LORD said to Moses: "Bring me
seventy of Israel's elders[x] who are known
to you as leaders and officials among the
people.[y] Have them come to the Tent of
Meeting,[z] that they may stand there with
you. 17I will come down and speak with
you[a] there, and I will take of the Spirit
that is on you and put the Spirit on them.[b]
They will help you carry the burden of the
people so that you will not have to carry
it alone.[c]
18"Tell the people: 'Consecrate yourselves[d] in preparation for tomorrow, when
you will eat meat. The LORD heard you
when you wailed,[e] "If only we had meat
to eat! We were better off in Egypt!"[f] Now
the LORD will give you meat,[g] and you
will eat it. 19You will not eat it for just one
day, or two days, or five, ten or twenty
days, 20but for a whole month—until it
comes out of your nostrils and you loathe
it[h]—because you have rejected the LORD,[i]
who is among you, and have wailed before him, saying, "Why did we ever leave
Egypt?" ' "[j]
21But Moses said, "Here I am among
six hundred thousand men[k] on foot, and
you say, 'I will give them meat to eat for a
whole month!' 22Would they have enough
if flocks and herds were slaughtered for
them? Would they have enough if all the
fish in the sea were caught for them?"[l]
23The LORD answered Moses, "Is the
LORD's arm too short?[m] You will now see
whether or not what I say will come true
for you.[n]"
24So Moses went out and told the people what the LORD had said. He brought
together seventy of their elders and had
them stand around the Tent. 25Then the
LORD came down in the cloud[o] and spoke
with him,[p] and he took of the Spirit[q] that
was on him and put the Spirit on the seventy elders.[r] When the Spirit rested on
them, they prophesied,[s] but they did not
do so again.[a]
26However, two men, whose names
were Eldad and Medad, had remained in
the camp. They were listed among the elders, but did not go out to the Tent. Yet
the Spirit also rested on them,[t] and they
prophesied in the camp. 27A young man
ran and told Moses, "Eldad and Medad are
prophesying in the camp."
28Joshua son of Nun,[u] who had been
Moses' aide[v] since youth, spoke up and
said, "Moses, my lord, stop them!"[w]
29But Moses replied, "Are you jealous
for my sake? I wish that all the LORD's
people were prophets[x] and that the LORD
would put his Spirit[y] on them!"[z] 30Then
Moses and the elders of Israel returned to
the camp.
31Now a wind went out from the LORD
and drove quail[a] in from the sea. It
brought them[b] down all around the camp
to about three feet[c] above the ground, as
far as a day's walk in any direction. 32All
that day and night and all the next day
the people went out and gathered quail.
No one gathered less than ten homers.[d]
Then they spread them out all around the
camp. 33But while the meat was still between their teeth[b] and before it could be
consumed, the anger[c] of the LORD burned

[a] 25 Or *prophesied and continued to do so*
[b] 31 Or *They flew* [c] 31 Hebrew *two cubits* (about 1 meter) [d] 32 That is, probably about 60 bushels (about 2.2 kiloliters)

11:14 [u] S Ex 18:18 **11:15** [v] Ex 32:32 [w] 1Ki 19:4; Job 6:9; 7:15-16; 9:21; 10:1; Isa 38:12; Jnh 4:3 **11:16** [x] S Ex 3:16 [y] S Ex 18:25 [z] S Ex 40:2 **11:17** [a] Ex 19:20 [b] ver 25,29; 1Sa 10:6; 2Ki 2:9,15; 3:12; Isa 32:15; 40:5; 63:11; Joel 2:28; Hag 2:5 [c] S Ex 18:18; Jer 19:1 **11:18** [d] S Ex 19:10 [e] S Ex 16:7 [f] ver 5; Ac 7:39 [g] Ps 78:20 **11:20** [h] Ps 78:29; 106:14,15 [i] S Lev 26:43; Jos 24:27; Jdg 8:23; 1Sa 10:19; Job 31:28; Isa 59:13; Hos 13:11 [j] ver 33; Job 20:13,23 **11:21** [k] S Ex 12:37 **11:22** [l] Mt 15:33 **11:23** [m] Isa 50:2; 59:1 [n] Nu 23:19; 1Sa 15:29; Eze 12:25; 24:14 **11:25** [o] S Ex 19:9; Nu 12:5 [p] ver 17 [q] ver 29; 1Sa 10:6; 19:23 [r] S Ac 2:17 [s] ver 26; Nu 24:2; Jdg 3:10; 1Sa 10:10; 19:20; 2Ch 15:1 **11:26** [t] S ver 25; 1Ch 12:18; Rev 1:10 **11:28** [u] Ex 17:9; Nu 13:8; 26:65; Jos 14:10 [v] Ex 33:11; Jos 1:1 [w] Mk 9:38-40 **11:29** [x] 1Sa 10:5; 19:20; 2Ch 24:19; Jer 7:25; 44:4; 1Co 14:5 [y] S ver 17 [z] Nu 27:18 **11:31** [a] S Ex 16:13; Ps 78:26-28 **11:33** [b] Ps 78:30 [c] Nu 14:18; Dt 9:7; Jdg 2:12; 2Ki 22:17; Ps 106:29; Jer 44:3; Eze 8:17

11:16–34 The Lord's response to the great distress of his prophet was twofold—mercy and curse: (1) There was mercy to Moses in that his responsibility was now to be shared by 70 leaders (vv. 16–17). (2) There was a curse on the people that was analogous to their complaint: They asked for meat and would now become sick with meat (vv. 18–34).

11:18 *you will eat meat.* Their distress at the lack of variety in the daily manna had led the people to challenge the Lord's goodness. They had wailed for meat. Now they were going to get their fill of meat, so much that it would make them physically ill (v. 20).

11:20 *you have rejected the LORD.* The principal issue was not meat at all, but a failure to demonstrate proper gratitude to the Lord, who was in their midst and who was their constant source of good.

11:21 *six hundred thousand men on foot.* The numbers are consistent: A marching force of this size suggests a total population of over 2,000,000 (see note on 1:46). Moses' distress at providing meat for this immense number of people (v. 22) is nearly comical—the task is impossible.

11:23 *Is the LORD's arm too short?* The human impossibility is an occasion for demonstrating the Lord's power (see Isa 59:1).

11:25 *the Spirit.* God's empowering presence (cf. Jdg 3:10 and note). *they prophesied.* Probably means that they gave ecstatic expression to an intense religious experience (see 1Sa 10:5; 18:10; 19:20,24; 1Ki 18:29 and notes). *but they did not do so again.* It seems that the temporary gift of prophecy to the elders was primarily to establish their credentials as Spirit-empowered leaders.

11:29 *Are you jealous for my sake?* Here the true spirit of Moses is demonstrated. Rather than being threatened by the public demonstration of the gifts of the Spirit by Eldad and Medad, Moses desired that all God's people might have the full gifts of the Spirit (cf. Joel 2:28 and note; Php 1:15–18). This verse is a fitting introduction to the inexcusable challenge to Moses' leadership in ch. 12.

11:31–32 Cf. the great provision of Jesus in the feeding of the 5,000 (Jn 6:5–13) and the 4,000 (Mt 15:29–39). In those cases the feeding was a demonstration of God's grace; in this instance it was accompanied by God's wrath.

against the people, and he struck them with a severe plague.[d] 34Therefore the place was named Kibroth Hattaavah,[a][e] because there they buried the people who had craved other food.

35From Kibroth Hattaavah the people traveled to Hazeroth[f] and stayed there.

Miriam and Aaron Oppose Moses

12 Miriam[g] and Aaron began to talk against Moses because of his Cushite wife,[h] for he had married a Cushite. 2"Has the LORD spoken only through Moses?" they asked. "Hasn't he also spoken through us?"[i] And the LORD heard this.[j]

3(Now Moses was a very humble man,[k] more humble than anyone else on the face of the earth.)

4At once the LORD said to Moses, Aaron and Miriam, "Come out to the Tent of Meeting, all three of you." So the three of them came out. 5Then the LORD came down in a pillar of cloud;[l] he stood at the entrance to the Tent and summoned Aaron and Miriam. When both of them stepped forward, 6he said, "Listen to my words:

"When a prophet of the LORD is among
you,
I reveal[m] myself to him in visions,[n]
I speak to him in dreams.[o]
7But this is not true of my servant
Moses;[p]
he is faithful in all my house.[q]
8With him I speak face to face,
clearly and not in riddles;[r]
he sees the form of the LORD.[s]
Why then were you not afraid
to speak against my servant
Moses?"[t]

9The anger of the LORD burned against them,[u] and he left them.[v]

10When the cloud lifted from above the Tent,[w] there stood Miriam—leprous,[b] like snow.[x] Aaron turned toward her and saw that she had leprosy;[y] 11and he said to Moses, "Please, my lord, do not hold against us the sin we have so foolishly committed.[z] 12Do not let her be like a stillborn infant coming from its mother's womb with its flesh half eaten away."

13So Moses cried out to the LORD, "O God, please heal her![a]"

14The LORD replied to Moses, "If her father had spit in her face,[b] would she not have been in disgrace for seven days? Confine her outside the camp[c] for seven days; after that she can be brought back." 15So Miriam was confined outside the camp[d] for seven days,[e] and the people did not move on till she was brought back.

16After that, the people left Hazeroth[f] and encamped in the Desert of Paran.[g]

[a] 34 *Kibroth Hattaavah* means *graves of craving.*
[b] 10 The Hebrew word was used for various diseases affecting the skin—not necessarily leprosy.

11:33 [d]S ver 18-20; Ps 106:15; Isa 10:16 **11:34** [e]Nu 33:16; Dt 9:22 **11:35** [f]Nu 33:17 **12:1** [g]S Ex 15:20 [h]S Ex 2:21 **12:2** [i]Nu 16:3 [j]S Nu 11:1 **12:3** [k]Mt 11:29 **12:5** [l]S Ex 13:21; S Nu 11:25 **12:6** [m]1Sa 3:7,21 [n]S Ge 15:1 [o]S Ge 20:3; S Mt 27:19; Heb 1:1 **12:7** [p]Dt 34:5; Jos 1:1-2; Ps 105:26 [q]Heb 3:2,5 **12:8** [r]Jdg 14:12; 1Ki 10:1; Ps 49:4; Pr 1:6; Da 5:12 [s]Ex 20:4; Job 19:26; Ps 17:15; 140:13; Isa 6:1 [t]Ex 24:2 **12:9** [u]S Ex 4:14 [v]S Ge 17:22 **12:10** [w]Ex 40:2 [x]S Ex 4:6; Dt 24:9 [y]S Lev 13:11; 2Ki 5:1,27; 2Ch 16:12; 21:12-15; 26:19 **12:11** [z]2Sa 19:19; 24:10 **12:13** [a]Ex 15:26; Ps 6:2; 147:3; Isa 1:6; 30:26; 53:5; Jer 17:14; Hos 6:1 **12:14** [b]Dt 25:9; Job 17:6; 30:9-10; Isa 50:6 [c]S Lev 13:46 **12:15** [d]S Lev 14:8 [e]S Lev 13:4 **12:16** [f]Nu 11:35 [g]Ge 21:21; Nu 10:12; 15:32

11:34 *Kibroth Hattaavah.* See NIV text note. These graves marked the death camp of those who had turned against the food of the Lord's mercy.

12:1 *his Cushite wife.* Ham had a son named Cush. His descendants, as named in Ge 10:7, were all located in Arabia (see note on Ge 10:7). Nimrod, a descendant of perhaps another Cush, is identified as a great empire builder in lower Mesopotamia (Ge 10:8–12; see note on 10:8). Elsewhere "Cush" also frequently refers to a region lying just south of Egypt (ancient Nubia, modern Sudan; see note on Ge 10:6). Because of this diversity, we cannot know with any certainty the ethnic identity of Moses' wife here referred to. Perhaps Hab 3:7 provides a better clue. There "the tents of Cushan" appear to be identified with "the dwellings of Midian." It is possible that one from "the tents of Cushan" could be referred to as "a Cushite." In that case, the wife of Moses in question is Zipporah, a daughter of the Midianite priest Jethro (Ex 3:1; see note there). The attack on Moses because of his Cushite wife was a pretext; its focus was the prophetic gift of Moses and his special relationship with the Lord (v. 2).

12:2 *Hasn't he also spoken through us?* Of course he had. Mic 6:4 speaks of Moses, Aaron and Miriam as God's gracious provision for Israel. The prophetic gifting of the 70 elders (11:24–30) seems to have been the immediate provocation for the attack of Miriam and Aaron on their brother.

12:3 Perhaps a later addition to the text, alerting the reader to the great unfairness of the charge of arrogance against Moses.

12:5 *came down.* Often used of divine manifestations. In 11:25 the Lord came down in grace; here and in Ge 11:5 he came down in judgment. In a sense every theophany (appearance of God) is a picture and promise of the grand theophany, the incarnation of Jesus, both in grace and in judgment.

12:6–8 The poetic cast of these words adds a sense of solemnity to them. The point of the poem is clear: All true prophetic vision is from the Lord, but in the case of Moses his position and faithfulness enhance his special relationship with the Lord.

12:7 *my servant.* See notes on Ex 14:31; Ps 18 title; Isa 41:8–9; 42:1. *my house.* The household of God's people Israel (see notes on Heb 3:5–6).

12:8 *clearly and not in riddles.* God's revelation does not come with equal clarity to his servants. There may be oracles of the Lord that a prophet might not fully understand at the time; to him they may be riddles and mysteries (cf. 1Pe 1:10–11 and note on 1:10). But to Moses, God spoke with special clarity, as though "face to face" (see also Dt 34:10 and note).

12:10 *leprous.* See NIV text note. Miriam, the principal offender against her brother Moses, has become an outcast, as she now suffers from a skin disease that would exclude her from the community of Israel (see 5:1–4).

12:14 *disgrace for seven days.* An act of public rebuke (see Dt 25:9) demands a period of public shame. A period of seven days was a standard time for uncleanness occasioned by being in contact with a dead body (see 19:11,14,16).

12:16 *Desert of Paran.* The southernmost region of the promised land. The people's opportunity to conquer the land was soon to come.

Exploring Canaan

13 The LORD said to Moses, 2"Send some
men to explore[h] the land of Canaan,[i]
which I am giving to the Israelites.[j] From
each ancestral tribe[k] send one of its leaders."
3So at the LORD's command Moses sent
them out from the Desert of Paran. All of
them were leaders of the Israelites.[l] 4These
are their names:

from the tribe of Reuben, Shammua
son of Zaccur;
5from the tribe of Simeon, Shaphat son
of Hori;
6from the tribe of Judah, Caleb son of
Jephunneh;[m]
7from the tribe of Issachar, Igal son of
Joseph;
8from the tribe of Ephraim, Hoshea
son of Nun;[n]
9from the tribe of Benjamin, Palti son
of Raphu;
10from the tribe of Zebulun, Gaddiel
son of Sodi;
11from the tribe of Manasseh (a tribe of
Joseph), Gaddi son of Susi;
12from the tribe of Dan, Ammiel son of
Gemalli;
13from the tribe of Asher, Sethur son of
Michael;
14from the tribe of Naphtali, Nahbi son
of Vophsi;
15from the tribe of Gad, Geuel son of
Maki.

16These are the names of the men Moses
sent to explore[o] the land. (Moses gave Hoshea son of Nun[p] the name Joshua.)[q]
17When Moses sent them to explore Canaan,[r] he said, "Go up through the Negev[s] and on into the hill country.[t] 18See
what the land is like and whether the
people who live there are strong or weak,
few or many. 19What kind of land do they
live in? Is it good or bad? What kind of
towns do they live in? Are they unwalled
or fortified? 20How is the soil? Is it fertile
or poor? Are there trees on it or not? Do
your best to bring back some of the fruit of
the land."[u] (It was the season for the first
ripe grapes.)[v]
21So they went up and explored the land
from the Desert of Zin[w] as far as Rehob,[x]
toward Lebo[a] Hamath.[y] 22They went up
through the Negev and came to Hebron,[z]
where Ahiman, Sheshai and Talmai,[a] the
descendants of Anak,[b] lived. (Hebron had
been built seven years before Zoan in
Egypt.)[c] 23When they reached the Valley
of Eshcol,[b][d] they cut off a branch bearing a single cluster of grapes. Two of them
carried it on a pole between them, along
with some pomegranates[e] and figs.[f] 24That
place was called the Valley of Eshcol because of the cluster of grapes the Israelites
cut off there. 25At the end of forty days[g]
they returned from exploring the land.[h]

Report on the Exploration

26They came back to Moses and Aaron
and the whole Israelite community at Kadesh[i] in the Desert of Paran.[j] There they
reported to them[k] and to the whole assembly and showed them the fruit of the land.[l]
27They gave Moses this account: "We went
into the land to which you sent us, and it

13:2 [h]ver 16; Dt 1:22 [i]S Lev 14:34 [j]Jos 1:3 [k]S Lev 24:11 **13:3** [l]Nu 1:16 **13:6** [m]ver 30; Nu 14:6, 24; 34:19; Dt 1:36; Jdg 1:12-15 **13:8** [n]S Nu 11:28 **13:16** [o]S ver 2 [p]ver 8 [q]Dt 32:44 **13:17** [r]ver 2; Jos 14:7 [s]S Ge 12:9 [t]Dt 1:7; Jos 9:1; Jdg 1:9 **13:20** [u]Dt 1:25 [v]S Lev 25:5 **13:21** [w]Nu 20:1; 27:14; 33:36; Dt 32:51; Jos 15:1 [x]Jos 19:28; Jdg 1:31; 18:28; 2Sa 10:6; 1Ch 6:75 [y]Nu 34:8; Jos 13:5; Jdg 3:3; 1Ki 8:65; 2Ki 14:25; 1Ch 13:5; 2Ch 7:8; Jer 52:9; Eze 47:16, 20; Am 6:14 **13:22** [z]S Ge 13:18; S 23:19 [a]Jos 15:14; Jdg 1:10 [b]ver 28; Dt 2:10; 9:2; Jos 11:21; 15:13; Jdg 1:20 [c]Ps 78:12, 43; Isa 19:11, 13; 30:4; Eze 30:14 **13:23** [d]S Ge 14:13 [e]S Ex 28:33 [f]Ge 3:7; Nu 20:5; Dt 8:8; 2Ki 18:31; Ne 13:15 **13:25** [g]S Ge 7:4 [h]Nu 14:34 **13:26** [i]S Ge 14:7 [j]S Ge 14:6 [k]Nu 32:8 [l]Dt 1:25

[a] 21 Or *toward the entrance to* [b] 23 *Eshcol* means *cluster*; also in verse 24.

13:2 *Send some men to explore the land of Canaan.* The use of spies was a common practice in the ancient Near East (see note on Jos 2:1–24). From Dt 1:22–23 it appears that this directive of the Lord was in response to the people's request.

13:4–15 The names listed here are different from those in chs. 1–2; 7; 10. Presumably the tribal leaders in the four earlier lists were older men. The task for the spies called for men who were younger and more robust, but no less respected by their peers.

13:6 Although Caleb was not a native Israelite since he was a Kenizzite (32:12) and Kenaz was an Edomite (Ge 36:6,9,11), he became associated with the tribe of Judah. See note on 14:24.

13:16 *Moses gave Hoshea son of Nun the name Joshua.* A parenthetical statement anticipating the later prominence of Joshua. The reader is alerted to the significance of this name in the list of the spies; here is a man of destiny. Hoshea means "salvation"; Joshua means "The LORD saves" (see NIV text note on Mt 1:21).

13:17–20 Moses' instruction to the 12 spies was comprehensive; a thorough report of the land and its produce and the peoples and their towns was required in their reconnaissance mission.

13:21 *explored the land.* The journey of the spies began in the southernmost extremity of the land (the Desert of Zin) and took them to the northernmost point (Rehob, near Lebo Hamath; see 34:8). This journey of about 250 miles each way took them 40 days (v. 25), perhaps a round number.

13:22 *Hebron.* The first city the spies came to in Canaan. The parenthetical comment about the city's being built seven years before Zoan in Egypt (see note on Ps 78:12) may have been prompted by their amazement at the size and fortifications of the city that was so closely associated with the lives of their ancestors four centuries before this time (see Ge 13:14–18; 14:13; 23:2; 25:9; 35:27–29; 50:13). In the stories of the ancestors of their people, Hebron had not been a great city, but a dwelling and trading place for shepherds and herdsmen. *descendants of Anak.* The Anakites were men of great stature; their physical size brought fear to the people (see vv. 32–33). In a later day of faith, Caleb was to drive them from their city (Jos 15:14; Jdg 1:10).

13:23 *Valley of Eshcol.* See NIV text note. This valley is near Hebron. The size of the grape cluster should have indicated the goodness of the land God was giving them.

13:26–29 The first part of the spies' report was truthful, but the goodness of the land was offset in their fearful eyes by the powerful peoples who lived there.

13:26 *Kadesh.* See note on Ge 14:7.

13:27 *flow with milk and honey.* See notes on Ex 3:8; Dt 6:3.

does flow with milk and honey![m] Here is its fruit.[n] 28But the people who live there are powerful, and the cities are fortified and very large.[o] We even saw descendants of Anak[p] there.[q] 29The Amalekites[r] live in the Negev; the Hittites,[s] Jebusites[t] and Amorites[u] live in the hill country;[v] and the Canaanites[w] live near the sea and along the Jordan.[x]"

30Then Caleb[y] silenced the people before Moses and said, "We should go up and take possession of the land, for we can certainly do it."

31But the men who had gone up with him said, "We can't attack those people; they are stronger than we are."[z] 32And they spread among the Israelites a bad report[a] about the land they had explored. They said, "The land we explored devours[b] those living in it. All the people we saw there are of great size.[c] 33We saw the Nephilim[d] there (the descendants of Anak[e] come from the Nephilim). We seemed like grasshoppers[f] in our own eyes, and we looked the same to them."

The People Rebel

14 That night all the people of the community raised their voices and wept aloud.[g] 2All the Israelites grumbled[h] against Moses and Aaron, and the whole assembly said to them, "If only we had died in Egypt![i] Or in this desert![j] 3Why is the LORD bringing us to this land only to let us fall by the sword?[k] Our wives and children[l] will be taken as plunder.[m] Wouldn't it be better for us to go back to Egypt?[n]" 4And they said to each other, "We should choose a leader and go back to Egypt.[o]"

5Then Moses and Aaron fell facedown[p] in front of the whole Israelite assembly[q] gathered there. 6Joshua son of Nun[r] and Caleb son of Jephunneh, who were among those who had explored the land, tore their clothes[s] 7and said to the entire Israelite assembly, "The land we passed through and explored is exceedingly good.[t] 8If the LORD is pleased with us,[u] he will lead us into that land, a land flowing with milk and honey,[v] and will give it to us.[w] 9Only do not rebel[x] against the LORD. And do not be afraid[y] of the people of the land,[z] because we will swallow them up. Their protection is gone, but the LORD is with[a] us.[b] Do not be afraid of them."[c]

10But the whole assembly talked about stoning[d] them. Then the glory of the LORD[e] appeared at the Tent of Meeting to all the Israelites. 11The LORD said to Moses, "How long will these people treat me with contempt?[f] How long will they refuse to believe in me,[g] in spite of all the miraculous signs[h] I have performed among them? 12I will strike them down with a plague[i] and destroy them, but I will make you into a nation[j] greater and stronger than they."[k]

13Moses said to the LORD, "Then the Egyptians will hear about it! By your power you brought these people up from among them.[l] 14And they will tell the inhabitants of this land about it. They have already heard[m] that you, O LORD, are with these people[n] and that you, O LORD, have been seen face to face,[o] that your cloud stays over them,[p] and that you go before them in a pillar of cloud by day and a pillar of fire by night.[q] 15If you put these peo-

13:27 [m]S Ex 3:8 [n]Dt 1:25; Jer 2:7 **13:28** [o]Dt 1:28; 9:1,2 [p]S ver 22 [q]Jos 14:12 **13:29** [r]S Ge 14:7 [s]S Ge 10:15; Dt 7:1; 20:17; 1Ki 9:20; 10:29; 2Ki 7:6 [t]S Ex 3:8 [u]S Ge 10:16 [v]ver 17 [w]Ge 10:18 [x]S Ge 13:10; Nu 22:1; 32:5; Dt 1:1; Jos 1:2; Jdg 3:28; Ps 42:6 **13:30** [y]S ver 6 **13:31** [z]Dt 9:1; Jos 14:8 **13:32** [a]Nu 14:36,37 [b]Eze 36:13,14 [c]Dt 1:28; Am 2:9 **13:33** [d]Ge 6:4 [e]ver 28; Dt 1:28; Jos 11:22; 14:12 [f]Ecc 12:5; Isa 40:22 **14:1** [g]S Ge 27:38; Ex 33:4; Nu 25:6; Dt 1:45; Jdg 20:23,26; 2Sa 3:32; Job 31:29 **14:2** [h]S Ex 15:24; Heb 3:16 [i]S Ex 16:3 [j]S Nu 11:1; 16:13; 20:4; 21:5 **14:3** [k]S Ex 5:21 [l]ver 31 [m]S Ge 34:29; Dt 1:39; Ps 109:11; Isa 33:4; Eze 7:21; 25:7; 26:5 [n]Ac 7:39 **14:4** [o]Ne 9:17 **14:5** [p]S Lev 9:24; Nu 16:4,22,45; 20:6; Jos 5:14; 2Sa 14:4; 1Ch 21:16; Eze 1:28 [q]S Lev 19:2 **14:6** [r]Nu 11:28 [s]S Ge 37:29,34; Jdg 11:35; 2Sa 13:31; 2Ki 19:1; Ezr 9:3; Est 4:1; S Mk 14:63 **14:7** [t]Nu 13:27; Dt 1:25 **14:8** [u]Dt 7:8; 10:15; Ps 18:19; 22:8; 37:23; 41:11; 56:9; 147:11; Pr 11:20; Isa 62:4; Mal 2:17 [v]Nu 13:27 [w]Dt 1:21 **14:9** [x]Dt 1:26; 9:7,23,24 [y]Ge 26:24; 2Ch 32:7; Ps 118:6; Jer 41:18; 42:11 [z]Dt 1:21; 7:18; 20:1 [a]Hag 2:4 [b]S Ge 21:22; Dt 1:30; 2Ch 13:12; Jer 15:20; 46:28; Hag 1:13 [c]ver 24 **14:10** [d]S Ex 17:4 [e]S Ex 24:16 **14:11** [f]Ex 23:21; Nu 15:31; 16:30; 1Sa 2:17; Eze 31:14; Mal 1:13 [g]Dt 1:32; Ps 78:22; 106:24; Jn 3:15 [h]S Ex 3:20; S 4:17; S 10:1 **14:12** [i]S Ex 5:3; S 30:12 [j]S Ex 32:10 [k]Dt 9:14; 29:20; 32:26; Ps 109:13 **14:13** [l]Ex 32:11-14; Ps 106:23 **14:14** [m]Ex 15:14 [n]Nu 5:3; 16:3; Jos 2:9 [o]Dt 5:4; 34:10 [p]S Ex 33:16 [q]S Ex 13:21

13:29 *Amalekites.* See note on Ge 14:7.

13:30 *Caleb silenced the people.* Only Caleb and Joshua gave a report prompted by faith in God.

13:32 *bad report about the land.* The promised land was a good land, a gracious gift from God (cf. 10:29). By speaking bad things about it, the faithless spies were speaking evil of the Lord.

13:33 Their words became exaggerations and distortions. The Anakites were now said to be Nephilim (see note on Ge 6:4). The reference to the Nephilim seems deliberately intended to evoke fear. The exaggeration of the faithless led to their final folly: "We seemed like grasshoppers."

14:1 *all the people ... wept.* The frightening words of the faithless spies led to mourning by the entire community and to their great rebellion against the Lord. They forgot all the miracles the Lord had done for them, they despised his mercies, and they spurned his might. In their ingratitude they preferred death (v. 2).

14:2,29 *grumbled.* See Introduction: Contents; see also note on Ex 15:24.

14:3 *children.* The most reprehensible charge against God's grace was that concerning their children. Only their children would survive (see vv. 31–33).

14:8 *flowing with milk and honey.* See notes on Ex 3:8; Dt 6:3.

14:9 *the LORD is with us.* There are no walls, no fortifications, no factors of size or bearing, and certainly no gods that can withstand the onslaught of God's people when the Lord is with them.

14:10 *glory of the LORD appeared.* This manifestation of God must have been staggering in its sudden and intense display of his majesty and wrath (see vv. 21–22; see also notes on Ps 26:8; Eze 1:28).

14:11 *treat me with contempt.* By refusing to believe in the Lord's power, especially in view of all the wonders they had experienced, the people of Israel were holding him in contempt.

14:12 *I will make you into a nation.* For the second time since the exodus, God speaks of starting over with Moses in creating a people faithful to himself (see Ex 32:10 and note).

14:13 *Egyptians will hear about it!* Moses desires to protect the Lord's reputation. The enemies of God's people will charge the Lord with inability to complete his deliverance and will be contemptuous of his power.

ple to death all at one time, the nations
who have heard this report about you will
say, 16‘The LORD was not able to bring
these people into the land he promised
them on oath;[r] so he slaughtered them in
the desert.’[s]
17“Now may the Lord’s strength be displayed, just as you have declared: 18‘The
LORD is slow to anger, abounding in love
and forgiving sin and rebellion.[t] Yet he
does not leave the guilty unpunished; he
punishes the children for the sin of the fathers to the third and fourth generation.’[u]
19In accordance with your great love, forgive[v] the sin of these people,[w] just as you
have pardoned them from the time they
left Egypt until now.”[x]
20The LORD replied, “I have forgiven
them,[y] as you asked. 21Nevertheless, as
surely as I live[z] and as surely as the glory
of the LORD[a] fills the whole earth,[b] 22not
one of the men who saw my glory and
the miraculous signs[c] I performed in Egypt
and in the desert but who disobeyed me
and tested me ten times[d]— 23not one of
them will ever see the land I promised on
oath[e] to their forefathers. No one who has
treated me with contempt[f] will ever see
it.[g] 24But because my servant Caleb[h] has a
different spirit and follows me wholeheartedly,[i] I will bring him into the land he
went to, and his descendants will inherit
it.[j] 25Since the Amalekites[k] and Canaanites[l] are living in the valleys, turn[m] back
tomorrow and set out toward the desert
along the route to the Red Sea.[a][n]”
26The LORD said to Moses and Aaron:
27“How long will this wicked community grumble against me? I have heard the
complaints of these grumbling Israelites.[o]
28So tell them, ‘As surely as I live,[p] declares the LORD, I will do to you[q] the very
things I heard you say: 29In this desert
your bodies will fall[r]—every one of you
twenty years old or more[s] who was counted in the census[t] and who has grumbled
against me. 30Not one of you will enter
the land[u] I swore with uplifted hand[v] to
make your home, except Caleb son of Jephunneh[w] and Joshua son of Nun.[x] 31As
for your children that you said would be
taken as plunder, I will bring them in to
enjoy the land you have rejected.[y] 32But
you—your bodies will fall[z] in this desert.
33Your children will be shepherds here for
forty years,[a] suffering for your unfaithfulness, until the last of your bodies lies in
the desert. 34For forty years[b]—one year for
each of the forty days you explored the
land[c]—you will suffer for your sins and
know what it is like to have me against
you.’ 35I, the LORD, have spoken, and I will
surely do these things[d] to this whole wicked community, which has banded together
against me. They will meet their end in
this desert; here they will die.[e]”
36So the men Moses had sent[f] to explore the land, who returned and made
the whole community grumble[g] against
him by spreading a bad report[h] about it—
37these men responsible for spreading the
bad report[i] about the land were struck
down and died of a plague[j] before the
LORD. 38Of the men who went to explore
the land,[k] only Joshua son of Nun and Caleb son of Jephunneh survived.[l]
39When Moses reported this[m] to all the
Israelites, they mourned[n] bitterly. 40Early
the next morning they went up toward

[a] *25* Hebrew *Yam Suph*; that is, Sea of Reeds

14:16 [r]Nu 11:12 [s]Ex 32:12; Jos 7:7 **14:18** [t]S Ex 20:6; 34:6; Ps 145:8; Jnh 4:2; Jas 5:11 [u]Ex 20:5 **14:19** [v]S Ex 34:9; 1Ki 8:34; Ps 85:2; 103:3 [w]Ps 106:45 [x]Ps 78:38 **14:20** [y]Ex 34:6; Ps 99:8; 106:23; Mic 7:18-20 **14:21** [z]ver 28; Dt 32:40; Jdg 8:19; Ru 3:13; 1Sa 14:39; 19:6; Isa 49:18; Jer 4:2; Eze 5:11; Zep 2:9 [a]Lev 9:6 [b]Ps 72:19; Isa 6:3; 40:5; Hab 2:14 **14:22** [c]ver 11 [d]S Ex 14:11; 17:7; 32:1; Ps 81:7; 1Co 10:5 **14:23** [e]ver 16; S Ex 33:1; Nu 32:11; Dt 1:34; Ps 95:11; 106:26 [f]ver 11 [g]Heb 3:18 **14:24** [h]Nu 13:6 [i]ver 6-9; Dt 1:36; Jos 14:8, 14 [j]Nu 26:65; 32:12; Ps 25:13; 37:9, 11 **14:25** [k]S Ge 14:7 [l]S Ge 10:18 [m]Dt 1:40 [n]Ex 23:31; Nu 21:4; 1Ki 9:26 **14:27** [o]Ex 16:12; Dt 1:34, 35 **14:28** [p]S ver 21 [q]Nu 33:56 **14:29** [r]ver 23, 30, 32; Nu 26:65; 32:13; 1Co 10:5; Heb 3:17; Jude 1:5 [s]S Nu 1:45 [t]S Ex 30:12 **14:30** [u]S ver 29 [v]Ex 6:8; Dt 32:40; Ne 9:15; Ps 106:26; Eze 20:5; 36:7 [w]Nu 13:6 [x]Nu 11:28 **14:31** [y]S Lev 26:43 **14:32** [z]S ver 29, 35 **14:33** [a]ver 34; S Ex 16:35; Ac 13:18; Heb 3:9 **14:34** [b]S ver 33 [c]Nu 13:25 **14:35** [d]Nu 23:19 [e]S ver 32 **14:36** [f]Nu 13:4-16 [g]ver 2 [h]S Nu 13:32 **14:37** [i]S Nu 13:32; 1Co 10:10; Heb 3:17 [j]Nu 16:49; 5:9; 26:1; 31:16; Dt 4:3 **14:38** [k]ver 30; Nu 13:4-16 [l]ver 24; Jos 14:6 **14:39** [m]ver 28-35 [n]S Ex 33:4

14:17–19 Moses now moves from the Lord’s reputation to his character, presenting a composite quotation of his own words of loyal love for and faithful discipline of his people (see Ex 20:6; 34:6–7 and notes).

14:22 *ten times.* Perhaps to be enumerated as follows: (1) Ex 14:10–12; (2) Ex 15:22–24; (3) Ex 16:1–3; (4) Ex 16:19–20; (5) Ex 16:27–30; (6) Ex 17:1–4; (7) Ex 32:1–35; (8) Nu 11:1–3; (9) 11:4–34; (10) 14:3. But “ten times” may also be a way of saying “many times.”

14:24 *Caleb . . . follows me wholeheartedly.* Caleb may be singled out—even from Joshua—because although he was not a native Israelite (see note on 13:6), he was faithful to the Lord. His ultimate vindication came 45 years later (see note on 13:22; see also Jos 14:10–14).

14:25 *Amalekites.* See note on Ge 14:7.

14:28 *I will do to you the very things I heard you say.* The people of Israel brought upon themselves their punishment. They had said that they would rather die in the desert (v. 2) than be led into Canaan to die by the sword. All those 20 years old or more, who were counted in the census, were to die in the desert (v. 29). The only exceptions would be Joshua and Caleb (v. 30). Only the people’s children would survive (v. 31)—the children they said God would allow to die in the desert (see v. 3 and note).

14:32 See Heb 3:17 and note on 3:16–19.

14:34 The 40 days of the travels of the spies became the numerical pattern for their suffering: one year for one day—for 40 years they would recount their misjudgment, and for 40 years the people 20 years old or more would be dying, so that only the young generation might enter the land. Significantly, Israel’s refusal to carry out the Lord’s commission to conquer his land is the climactic act of rebellion for which God condemns Israel to die in the desert.

14:37 *these men responsible for spreading the bad report . . . were struck down.* The judgment on the ten evil spies was immediate; the generation that they influenced would live out their lives in the desert.

14:40 *We will go up.* Now, too late, the people determine to go up to the land they had refused. Such a course of action was doomed to failure. Not only was the Lord not with them; he was against them (v. 41). Their subsequent defeat (v. 45) was another judgment the rebellious people brought down upon their own heads (see Eze 16:43 and note).

the high hill country.[o] "We have sinned[p]," they said. "We will go up to the place the LORD promised."

41But Moses said, "Why are you disobeying the LORD's command? This will not succeed![q] 42Do not go up, because the LORD is not with you. You will be defeated by your enemies,[r] 43for the Amalekites[s] and Canaanites[t] will face you there. Because you have turned away from the LORD, he will not be with you[u] and you will fall by the sword."

44Nevertheless, in their presumption they went up[v] toward the high hill country, though neither Moses nor the ark of the LORD's covenant moved from the camp.[w] 45Then the Amalekites and Canaanites[x] who lived in that hill country[y] came down and attacked them and beat them down all the way to Hormah.[z]

Supplementary Offerings

15 The LORD said to Moses, 2"Speak to the Israelites and say to them: 'After you enter the land I am giving you[a] as a home 3and you present to the LORD offerings made by fire, from the herd or the flock,[b] as an aroma pleasing to the LORD[c]—whether burnt offerings[d] or sacrifices, for special vows or freewill offerings[e] or festival offerings[f]— 4then the one who brings his offering shall present to the LORD a grain offering[g] of a tenth of an ephah[a] of fine flour[h] mixed with a quarter of a hin[b] of oil. 5With each lamb[i] for the burnt offering or the sacrifice, prepare a quarter of a hin of wine[j] as a drink offering.[k]

6" 'With a ram[l] prepare a grain offering[m] of two-tenths of an ephah[c][n] of fine flour mixed with a third of a hin[d] of oil,[o] 7and a third of a hin of wine[p] as a drink offering.[q] Offer it as an aroma pleasing to the LORD.[r]

8" 'When you prepare a young bull[s] as a burnt offering or sacrifice, for a special vow[t] or a fellowship offering[e][u] to the LORD, 9bring with the bull a grain offering[v] of three-tenths of an ephah[f][w] of fine flour mixed with half a hin[g] of oil. 10Also bring half a hin of wine[x] as a drink offering.[y] It will be an offering made by fire, an aroma pleasing to the LORD.[z] 11Each bull or ram, each lamb or young goat, is to be prepared in this manner. 12Do this for each one, for as many as you prepare.[a]

13" 'Everyone who is native-born[b] must do these things in this way when he brings an offering made by fire as an aroma pleasing to the LORD.[c] 14For the generations to come,[d] whenever an alien[e] or anyone else living among you presents an offering[f] made by fire[g] as an aroma pleasing to the LORD, he must do exactly as you do. 15The community is to have the same rules for you and for the alien living among you; this is a lasting ordinance for the generations to come.[h] You and the alien shall be the same before the LORD: 16The same laws and regulations will apply both to you and to the alien living among you.[i]' "

17The LORD said to Moses, 18"Speak to the Israelites and say to them: 'When you enter the land to which I am taking you[j] 19and you eat the food of the land,[k] present a portion as an offering to the LORD.[l] 20Present a cake from the first of your ground meal[m] and present it as an offering from the threshing floor.[n][o] 21Throughout the generations to come[p] you are to give this offering to the LORD from the first of your ground meal.[q]

Offerings for Unintentional Sins

22" 'Now if you unintentionally fail to keep any of these commands the LORD gave Moses[r]— 23any of the LORD's com-

a 4 That is, probably about 2 quarts (about 2 liters) *b* 4 That is, probably about 1 quart (about 1 liter); also in verse 5 *c* 6 That is, probably about 4 quarts (about 4.5 liters) *d* 6 That is, probably about 1 1/4 quarts (about 1.2 liters); also in verse 7 *e* 8 Traditionally *peace offering* *f* 9 That is, probably about 6 quarts (about 6.5 liters) *g* 9 That is, probably about 2 quarts (about 2 liters); also in verse 10

14:40 [o]ver 45; Nu 13:17 [p]S Ex 9:27 **14:41** [q]2Ch 24:20 **14:42** [r]Dt 1:42 **14:43** [s]Jdg 3:13 [t]ver 45; Nu 13:29 [u]S Ge 39:23; Dt 31:8; Jos 6:27; Jdg 1:19; 6:16; 1Sa 3:19; 18:14; 2Ch 1:1 **14:44** [v]Dt 1:43 [w]Nu 31:6 **14:45** [x]S ver 43 [y]S ver 40 [z]Nu 21:3; Dt 1:44; Jos 12:14; 15:30; 19:4; Jdg 1:17; 1Sa 30:30; 1Ch 4:30 **15:2** [a]S Lev 23:10 **15:3** [b]S Lev 1:2 [c]ver 24; S Lev 1:9 [d]Lev 1:3; Nu 28:13 [e]S Lev 7:16; S Ezr 1:4 [f]Lev 23:1-44 **15:4** [g]S Lev 6:14 [h]S Ex 16:36 **15:5** [i]S Lev 3:7 [j]S Lev 10:9 [k]S Ge 35:14 **15:6** [l]S Lev 5:15 [m]Nu 28:12; 29:14 [n]S Lev 23:13 [o]Eze 46:14 **15:7** [p]ver 5 [q]Lev 23:13; Nu 28:14; 29:18 [r]S Lev 1:9 **15:8** [s]S Ex 12:5; S Lev 1:5 [t]S Lev 22:18 [u]S Lev 3:6 **15:9** [v]Lev 2:1 [w]S Lev 14:10 **15:10** [x]Nu 28:14 [y]Lev 23:13 [z]Lev 1:9 **15:12** [a]Ezr 7:17 **15:13** [b]S Lev 16:29 [c]Lev 1:9 **15:14** [d]Lev 3:17; Nu 10:8 [e]S Ex 12:19,43; S 22:21 [f]S Lev 22:18 [g]ver 25 **15:15** [h]ver 14,21 **15:16** [i]Ex 12:49; S Lev 22:18; Nu 9:14 **15:18** [j]S Lev 23:10 **15:19** [k]Jos 5:11,12 [l]Nu 18:8 **15:20** [m]S Lev 23:14 [n]S Lev 2:14; S Nu 18:27 [o]S Ge 50:10 **15:21** [p]S Lev 23:14 [q]Eze 44:30; Ro 11:16 **15:22** [r]S Lev 4:2

14:43 *Amalekites.* See note on v. 25.

15:1 – 41 This chapter is divided into three units, each introduced by the phrase, "The LORD said to Moses" (vv. 1,17,37). The people were under terrible judgment because they had disobeyed the specific commands of the Lord and had despised his character.

15:2 *After you enter the land.* The juxtaposition of this clause with the sad ending of ch. 14 is dramatic. The sins of the people were manifold; they would be judged. The grace and mercy of the Lord are magnified as he points to the ultimate realization of his ancient promise to Abraham (Ge 12:7), as well as to his continuing promise to the nation that they would indeed enter the land.

15:3 – 12 Grain and wine offerings were to accompany the offerings by fire; the grain was to be mixed with olive oil. The offerings increased in amounts with the increase of size of the sacrificial animal (vv. 6 – 12).

15:14 *alien.* As in the case of the celebration of the Passover (see note on 9:14), the alien had the same regulations as the native-born Israelite. The commonwealth of Israel would always be open to proselytes. Indeed, God's promise to Abraham embraces all peoples of the earth (see note on Ge 12:2 – 3).

15:20 *Present a cake from the first.* This law also looks forward to the time when the Israelites would be in the land. The first of the threshed grain was to be made into a cake and presented to the Lord. This concept of the firstfruits is a symbol that all blessing is from the Lord and all produce belongs to him.

15:22 *unintentionally fail.* Sins may be unintentional, but they still need to be dealt with (see note on Lev 4:2). Such unintentional sins may be committed by the people as a whole (vv. 22 – 26) or by an individual (vv. 27 – 29).

mands to you through him, from the
day the LORD gave them and continuing
through the generations to come[s]— 24 and
if this is done unintentionally[t] without the
community being aware of it,[u] then the
whole community is to offer a young bull
for a burnt offering[v] as an aroma pleasing to the LORD,[w] along with its prescribed
grain offering[x] and drink offering,[y] and a
male goat for a sin offering.[z] 25 The priest
is to make atonement for the whole Israelite community, and they will be forgiven,[a]
for it was not intentional[b] and they have
brought to the LORD for their wrong an offering made by fire[c] and a sin offering.[d]
26 The whole Israelite community and the
aliens living among them will be forgiven,
because all the people were involved in
the unintentional wrong.[e]

27 " 'But if just one person sins unintentionally,[f] he must bring a year-old female
goat for a sin offering.[g] 28 The priest is to
make atonement[h] before the LORD for the
one who erred by sinning unintentionally, and when atonement has been made
for him, he will be forgiven.[i] 29 One and
the same law applies to everyone who
sins unintentionally, whether he is a native-born Israelite or an alien.[j]

30 " 'But anyone who sins defiantly,[k]
whether native-born or alien,[l] blasphemes
the LORD,[m] and that person must be cut
off from his people.[n] 31 Because he has despised[o] the LORD's word and broken his
commands,[p] that person must surely be
cut off; his guilt remains on him.[q] ' "

The Sabbath-Breaker Put to Death

32 While the Israelites were in the desert,[r] a man was found gathering wood
on the Sabbath day.[s] 33 Those who found
him gathering wood brought him to Moses and Aaron and the whole assembly,
34 and they kept him in custody, because
it was not clear what should be done to
him.[t] 35 Then the LORD said to Moses, "The
man must die.[u] The whole assembly must
stone him outside the camp.[v]" 36 So the
assembly took him outside the camp and
stoned him[w] to death,[x] as the LORD commanded Moses.[y]

Tassels on Garments

37 The LORD said to Moses, 38 "Speak to
the Israelites and say to them: 'Throughout the generations to come[z] you are to
make tassels on the corners of your garments,[a] with a blue cord on each tassel.
39 You will have these tassels to look at and
so you will remember[b] all the commands
of the LORD, that you may obey them and
not prostitute yourselves[c] by going after
the lusts of your own hearts[d] and eyes.
40 Then you will remember to obey all my
commands[e] and will be consecrated to
your God.[f] 41 I am the LORD your God, who
brought you out of Egypt to be your God.[g]
I am the LORD your God.[h] ' "

Korah, Dathan and Abiram

16 Korah[i] son of Izhar, the son of Kohath, the son of Levi, and certain
Reubenites—Dathan and Abiram[j], sons
of Eliab,[k] and On son of Peleth—became
insolent[a] 2 and rose up against Moses.[l]
With them were 250 Israelite men, well-
known community leaders who had been
appointed members of the council.[m] 3 They
came as a group to oppose Moses and Aaron[n] and said to them, "You have gone too
far! The whole community is holy,[o] every
one of them, and the LORD is with them.[p]
Why then do you set yourselves above the
LORD's assembly?"[q]

[a] 1 Or *Peleth—took* ⌞*men*⌟

15:23 [s]ver 21 **15:24** [t]ver 25,26 [u]S Lev 5:15 [v]Lev 4:14 [w]S ver 3 [x]Lev 2:1 [y]Lev 23:13; Nu 6:15 [z]Lev 4:3 **15:25** [a]Lev 4:20; S Ro 3:25 [b]ver 22, S 24 [c]ver 14 [d]Lev 4:3 **15:26** [e]S ver 24 **15:27** [f]Lev 4:27 [g]Lev 4:3; Nu 6:14 **15:28** [h]Nu 8:12; 28:22 [i]Lev 4:20 **15:29** [j]S Ex 12:49 **15:30** [k]Nu 14:40-44; Dt 1:43; 17:13; Ps 19:13 [l]ver 14 [m]2Ki 19:6,20; Isa 37:6,23; Eze 20:27 [n]S Ge 17:14; S Job 31:22 **15:31** [o]S Nu 14:11 [p]1Sa 15:23,26; 2Sa 11:27; 12:9; Ps 119:126; Pr 13:13 [q]S Lev 5:1; Eze 18:20 **15:32** [r]S Nu 12:16 [s]Ex 31:14,15; 35:2,3 **15:34** [t]Nu 9:8 **15:35** [u]Ex 31:14,15 [v]S Lev 20:2; Lk 4:29; Ac 7:58 **15:36** [w]S Lev 20:2 [x]S Ex 31:14 [y]Jer 17:21 **15:38** [z]Lev 3:17; Nu 10:8 [a]Dt 22:12; Mt 23:5 **15:39** [b]Dt 4:23; 6:12; Ps 73:27 [c]S Lev 17:7; Jdg 2:17; Ps 106:39; Jer 3:2; Hos 4:12 [d]Ps 78:37; Jer 7:24; Eze 20:16

15:40 [e]S Ge 26:5; Dt 11:13; Ps 103:18; 119:56 [f]S Lev 11:44; Ro 12:1; Col 1:22; 1Pe 1:15 **15:41** [g]S Ge 17:7 [h]S Ex 20:2 **16:1** [i]S Ex 6:24; Jude 1:11 [j]ver 24; Ps 106:17 [k]Nu 26:8; Dt 11:6 **16:2** [l]Nu 27:3 [m]Nu 1:16; 26:9 **16:3** [n]ver 7; Ps 106:16 [o]Ex 19:6 [p]S Nu 14:14 [q]Nu 12:2

15:30 *defiantly.* Lit. "with a high hand." Unlike unintentional sins, for which there are provisions of God's mercy, one who sets his hand defiantly to despise the word of God and to blaspheme his name must be punished. This was the experience of the nation in ch. 14, and it is described in the case of an individual here in vv. 32–36. *cut off from his people.* See note on Ex 12:15.

15:32 *gathering wood on the Sabbath day.* The penalty for breaking the Sabbath was death (v. 36; Ex 31:15; 35:2). As in the case of the willful blasphemer (Lev 24:10–16), the Sabbath-breaker was guilty of high-handed rebellion (see note on v. 30) and was judged with death. By the time of Christ, Sabbath-keeping had become distorted to the point that its regulations were regarded as more important than the needs of people. Jesus confronted the Pharisees on this issue on several occasions (see, e.g., Mt 12:1–14). From their point of view, these regulations (vv. 32–36) gave them reasons to seek his death (see Mk 3:6 and note).

15:38 *tassels on the corners of your garments.* As one would walk along, the tassels would swirl about at the edge of one's garment (cf. v. 39), serving as excellent memory prods to obey God's commands (cf. Dt 6:4–9 and notes).

15:39 *prostitute yourselves.* See Ex 34:15 and note.

15:41 *I am the LORD your God, who brought you out.* The demands that God made upon his people were grounded in his act of redemption (see Ex 20:2 and note).

16:1–7 Earlier, Miriam and Aaron had led a rebellion against the leadership of Moses (ch. 12). Now Korah and his allies attack the leadership of Moses and Aaron. Korah was descended from Levi through Kohath. As a Kohathite, he had high duties in the service of the Lord at the tabernacle (see 4:1–20), but he desired more. His passion was to assume the role of priest, and he used deception to advance his claim. Korah was joined by the Reubenites, Dathan, Abiram and On, and about 250 other leaders of Israel who had their own complaints. Their charge was that Moses had "gone too far" (v. 3) in taking the role of spiritual leadership of the people; "the whole community is holy" (v. 3). To this abusive charge Moses retorts, "You Levites have gone too far!" (v. 7), and sets up a trial by fire.

16:3 *The whole community is holy.* See notes on Ex 3:5; 19:6.

4When Moses heard this, he fell facedown.[r] 5Then he said to Korah and all his followers: "In the morning the LORD will show who belongs to him and who is holy,[s] and he will have that person come near him.[t] The man he chooses[u] he will cause to come near him. 6You, Korah, and all your followers[v] are to do this: Take censers[w] 7and tomorrow put fire[x] and incense[y] in them before the LORD. The man the LORD chooses[z] will be the one who is holy.[a] You Levites have gone too far!"

8Moses also said to Korah, "Now listen, you Levites! 9Isn't it enough[b] for you that the God of Israel has separated you from the rest of the Israelite community and brought you near himself to do the work at the LORD's tabernacle and to stand before the community and minister to them?[c] 10He has brought you and all your fellow Levites near himself, but now you are trying to get the priesthood too.[d] 11It is against the LORD that you and all your followers have banded together. Who is Aaron that you should grumble[e] against him?[f]"

12Then Moses summoned Dathan and Abiram,[g] the sons of Eliab. But they said, "We will not come![h] 13Isn't it enough that you have brought us up out of a land flowing with milk and honey[i] to kill us in the desert?[j] And now you also want to lord it over us?[k] 14Moreover, you haven't brought us into a land flowing with milk and honey[l] or given us an inheritance of fields and vineyards.[m] Will you gouge out the eyes of[a] these men?[n] No, we will not come![o]"

15Then Moses became very angry[p] and said to the LORD, "Do not accept their offering. I have not taken so much as a donkey[q] from them, nor have I wronged any of them."

16Moses said to Korah, "You and all your followers are to appear before the LORD tomorrow—you and they and Aaron.[r] 17Each man is to take his censer and put incense in it—250 censers in all—and present it before the LORD. You and Aaron are to present your censers also.[s]"

16:4 [r]Nu 14:5 **16:5** [s]S Lev 10:3; 2Ti 2:19* [t]Jer 30:21 [u]Nu 17:5; Ps 65:4; 105:26; Jer 50:44 **16:6** [v]ver 7,16 [w]S Lev 10:1; Rev 8:3 **16:7** [x]S Lev 10:1 [y]S Ex 30:9 [z]S ver 6 [a]ver 5 **16:9** [b]S Ge 30:15 [c]Nu 3:6; Dt 10:8; 17:12; 21:5; 1Sa 2:11; Ps 134:1; Eze 44:11 **16:10** [d]Nu 3:10; 18:7; Jdg 17:5,12 **16:11** [e]ver 41; 1Co 10:10 [f]S Ex 16:7 **16:12** [g]S ver 1,27 [h]ver 14 **16:13** [i]Nu 13:27 [j]Nu 14:2 [k]S Ge 13:8; Ac 7:27,35 **16:14** [l]S Lev 20:24 [m]Ex 22:5; 23:11; Nu 20:5; 1Ki 4:25; Ne 13:15; Ps 105:33; Jer 5:17; Hos 2:12; Joel 2:22; Hag 2:19; Zec 3:10 [n]Jdg 16:21; 1Sa 11:2; Jer 39:7 [o]ver 12 **16:15** [p]S Ex 4:14 [q]1Sa 12:3 **16:16** [r]S ver 6 **16:17** [s]Eze 8:11 **16:18** [t]Lev 10:1 **16:19** [u]ver 42; Nu 20:2 [v]S Ex 16:7; Nu 14:10; 20:6 **16:21** [w]ver 24 [x]S Ge 19:14; S Ex 32:10 **16:22** [y]S Nu 14:5 [z]Nu 27:16; Job 12:10; 27:8; 33:4; 34:14; Jer 32:27; Eze 18:4; Heb 12:9 [a]S Lev 10:6 [b]S Ge 18:23; S Job 21:20

18So each man took his censer,[t] put fire and incense in it, and stood with Moses and Aaron at the entrance to the Tent of Meeting. 19When Korah had gathered all his followers in opposition to them[u] at the entrance to the Tent of Meeting, the glory of the LORD[v] appeared to the entire assembly. 20The LORD said to Moses and Aaron, 21"Separate yourselves[w] from this assembly so I can put an end to them at once."[x]

22But Moses and Aaron fell facedown[y] and cried out, "O God, God of the spirits of all mankind,[z] will you be angry with the entire assembly[a] when only one man sins?"[b]

23Then the LORD said to Moses, 24"Say to the assembly, 'Move away from the tents of Korah, Dathan and Abiram.'"

25Moses got up and went to Dathan and Abiram, and the elders of Israel[c] followed him. 26He warned the assembly, "Move back from the tents of these wicked men![d] Do not touch anything belonging to them, or you will be swept away[e] because of all their sins.[f]" 27So they moved away from the tents of Korah, Dathan and Abiram.[g] Dathan and Abiram had come out and were standing with their wives, children[h] and little ones at the entrances to their tents.[i]

28Then Moses said, "This is how you will know[j] that the LORD has sent me[k] to do all these things and that it was not my idea: 29If these men die a natural death and experience only what usually happens to men, then the LORD has not sent me.[l] 30But if the LORD brings about something totally new, and the earth opens its mouth[m] and swallows them, with everything that belongs to them, and they go down alive into the grave,[b][n] then you will know that these men have treated the LORD with contempt.[o]"

[a] 14 Or *you make slaves of*; or *you deceive*
[b] 30 Hebrew *Sheol*; also in verse 33

16:25 [c]S Ex 19:7 **16:26** [d]Isa 52:11 [e]S Ge 19:15 [f]Jer 51:6 **16:27** [g]S ver 12 [h]ver 32; Jos 7:24; Isa 13:16; 14:21 [i]S Ex 33:8 **16:28** [j]1Ki 18:36 [k]Ex 3:12; Jn 5:36; 6:38 **16:29** [l]Nu 24:13; Job 31:2; Ecc 3:19 **16:30** [m]Ps 141:7; Isa 5:14 [n]ver 33; S Ge 37:35; 1Sa 2:6; Job 5:26; 21:13; Ps 9:17; 16:10; 55:15; Isa 14:11; 38:18 [o]S Nu 14:11; S Eze 26:20

16:6 *censers.* See note on Lev 10:1.

16:12 *Dathan and Abiram.* Their charge against Moses was that he had not led them into the land of promise. They claimed that Moses had in fact led the people "out of a land flowing with milk and honey" (v. 13). By this strange alchemy, in their minds the land of Egypt has been transformed from prison to paradise.

16:13–14 *flowing with milk and honey.* See notes on Ex 3:8; Dt 6:3.

16:15 *nor have I wronged any of them.* Moses' humanity is seen in his plea of innocence.

16:18–21 The trial was to be by fire: Which men would the Lord accept as his priests in the holy tabernacle? The 250 men allied with Korah came with arrogance to withstand Moses and Aaron at the entrance to the Tent of Meeting. The revelation of the Lord's glory was sure and sudden (v. 19), with words of impending doom for the rebellious people (v. 21). The punishment was fittingly ironic. Those 250 men who dared to present themselves as priests before the Lord with fire in their censers were themselves put to death by fire (perhaps lightning) from the Lord (see v. 35).

16:19,42 *glory of the LORD.* See note on 14:10.

16:24 *Move away.* God's judgment was going to be severe, but he did not want to lash out against bystanders. It appears that Korah himself had left the 250 false priests and was standing with Dathan and Abiram to continue their opposition to Moses.

16:30 *something totally new.* Moses wished to assure the people that the imminent judgment was the direct work of the Lord and not a chance event that might be interpreted

31 As soon as he finished saying all this, the ground under them split apart[p] 32 and the earth opened its mouth and swallowed them,[q] with their households and all Korah's men and all their possessions. 33 They went down alive into the grave,[r] with everything they owned; the earth closed over them, and they perished and were gone from the community. 34 At their cries, all the Israelites around them fled, shouting, "The earth is going to swallow us too!"

35 And fire came out from the LORD[s] and consumed[t] the 250 men who were offering the incense.

36 The LORD said to Moses, 37 "Tell Eleazar[u] son of Aaron, the priest, to take the censers[v] out of the smoldering remains and scatter the coals some distance away, for the censers are holy— 38 the censers of the men who sinned at the cost of their lives.[w] Hammer the censers into sheets to overlay the altar,[x] for they were presented before the LORD and have become holy. Let them be a sign[y] to the Israelites."

39 So Eleazar the priest[z] collected the bronze censers brought by those who had been burned up,[a] and he had them hammered out to overlay the altar, 40 as the LORD directed him through Moses. This was to remind the Israelites that no one except a descendant of Aaron should come to burn incense[b] before the LORD,[c] or he would become like Korah and his followers.[d]

41 The next day the whole Israelite community grumbled against Moses and Aaron. "You have killed the LORD's people," they said.

42 But when the assembly gathered in opposition[e] to Moses and Aaron and turned toward the Tent of Meeting, suddenly the cloud covered it and the glory of the LORD[f] appeared. 43 Then Moses and Aaron went to the front of the Tent of Meeting, 44 and the LORD said to Moses, 45 "Get away from this assembly so I can put an end[g] to them at once." And they fell facedown.

46 Then Moses said to Aaron, "Take your censer[h] and put incense in it, along with fire from the altar, and hurry to the assembly[i] to make atonement[j] for them. Wrath has come out from the LORD;[k] the plague[l] has started." 47 So Aaron did as Moses said, and ran into the midst of the assembly. The plague had already started among the people,[m] but Aaron offered the incense and made atonement for them. 48 He stood between the living and the dead, and the plague stopped.[n] 49 But 14,700 people died from the plague, in addition to those who had died because of Korah.[o] 50 Then Aaron returned to Moses at the entrance to the Tent of Meeting, for the plague had stopped.

The Budding of Aaron's Staff

17 The LORD said to Moses, 2 "Speak to the Israelites and get twelve staffs[p] from them, one from the leader of each of their ancestral tribes.[q] Write the name of each man on his staff. 3 On the staff of Levi write Aaron's name,[r] for there must be one staff for the head of each ancestral tribe. 4 Place them in the Tent of Meeting[s] in front of the Testimony,[t] where I meet with you.[u] 5 The staff belonging to the man I choose[v] will sprout,[w] and I will rid myself of this constant grumbling[x] against you by the Israelites."

6 So Moses spoke to the Israelites, and their leaders gave him twelve staffs, one for the leader of each of their ancestral tribes, and Aaron's staff was among them. 7 Moses placed the staffs before the LORD in the Tent of the Testimony.[y]

8 The next day Moses entered the Tent of the Testimony[z] and saw that Aaron's staff,[a] which represented the house of Levi, had not only sprouted but had budded, blossomed and produced almonds.[b] 9 Then Moses brought out all the staffs[c]

16:31 [p] Isa 64:1-2; Eze 47:1-12; Mic 1:3-4; Zec 14:4 **16:32** [q] S Ex 15:12 **16:33** [r] S ver 30; S Ecc 9:10 **16:35** [s] S Nu 11:1-3; 26:10; Rev 11:5 [t] S Lev 10:2 **16:37** [u] S Ex 6:23 [v] ver 6 **16:38** [w] Lev 10:1; Pr 20:2 [x] S Ex 20:24; 38:1-7 [y] Nu 26:10; Dt 28:46; Jer 44:29; Eze 14:8; 2Pe 2:6 **16:39** [z] 2Ch 26:18 [a] S Lev 20:14 **16:40** [b] S Ex 30:1; 2Ki 12:3; Isa 1:13; 66:3; Jer 41:5; 44:3 [c] S Ex 30:9; 2Ch 26:18 [d] S Nu 3:10 **16:42** [e] S ver 19 [f] Ex 16:7; Nu 14:10 **16:45** [g] S Ex 32:10 **16:46** [h] S Lev 10:1 [i] Lev 10:6 [j] S Ex 29:36 [k] S Nu 1:53 [l] S Lev 26:25; Nu 8:19; Ps 106:29 **16:47** [m] Nu 25:6-8 **16:48** [n] Nu 25:8; Ps 106:30 **16:49** [o] ver 32 **17:2** [p] S Ge 32:10; S Ex 4:2 [q] Nu 1:4 **17:3** [r] S Nu 1:3 **17:4** [s] S Ex 40:2 [t] ver 7; Ex 16:34 [u] Ex 25:22 **17:5** [v] S Nu 16:5 [w] ver 8 [x] S Ex 16:7 **17:7** [y] S Ex 38:21 **17:8** [z] ver 7; Nu 1:50 [a] ver 2, 10 [b] Eze 17:24; Heb 9:4 **17:9** [c] ver 2

differently. The opening of the earth to swallow the rebels was a sure sign of the wrath of God and the vindication of Moses and Aaron. *grave.* See v. 33; see also note on Ge 37:35.

16:32 *swallowed them, with their households.* The sons of Korah did not die (26:11); apparently they did not join their father in his rash plan. The households of the other rebels died with them. Cf. Jos 7:24 and note.

16:37 *take the censers.* The true priests took the censers of the 250 deceased impostors from their charred remains and hammered them into bronze sheets for the altar as a memorial of the folly of a self-proclaimed priest (v. 40).

16:41 *the whole Israelite community grumbled.* Again the community attacked Moses, unfairly charging him with the death of the Lord's people. Except for the intervention of Moses and Aaron (see vv. 4,22), the entire nation might have been destroyed because of their continued rebellion (see v. 45).

16:49 *14,700 people died.* The number makes sense only if the community is as large as the census lists of ch. 2 suggest.

17:1 – 13 This story follows the account of the divine judgment of Korah (16:1 – 35) and the narrative of the symbolic use given to the censers of the rebels and its aftermath (16:36 – 50). Ch. 17 is thus the third in a series of accounts vindicating the Aaronic priesthood against all opposition. The selection of 12 staffs, one from each tribe, was a symbolic act whereby the divine choice of Aaron would be indicated again.

17:3 *On the staff of Levi write Aaron's name.* The test needed to be unequivocal because of the wide support given to Korah's rebellion. The 250 who had joined with Korah were from many, perhaps all, of the tribes.

17:4 *in front of the Testimony.* In front of the ark, with the Ten Commandments, thus probably in the Holy Place, near the altar of incense (see vv. 7 – 8,10; see also note on Ex 25:22).

17:8 *had not only sprouted but had budded, blossomed and produced almonds.* God exceeded the demands of the test so that there might be no uncertainty as to who had acted or what he intended by his action.

from the LORD's presence to all the Israelites. They looked at them, and each man
took his own staff.
10The LORD said to Moses, "Put back
Aaron's staff[d] in front of the Testimony, to
be kept as a sign to the rebellious.[e] This
will put an end to their grumbling against
me, so that they will not die." 11Moses did
just as the LORD commanded him.
12The Israelites said to Moses, "We will
die! We are lost, we are all lost![f] 13Anyone
who even comes near the tabernacle of the
LORD will die.[g] Are we all going to die?"

Duties of Priests and Levites

18 The LORD said to Aaron, "You, your
sons and your father's family are to
bear the responsibility for offenses against
the sanctuary,[h] and you and your sons
alone are to bear the responsibility for offenses against the priesthood. 2Bring your
fellow Levites from your ancestral tribe
to join you and assist you when you and
your sons minister[i] before the Tent of the
Testimony. 3They are to be responsible to
you[j] and are to perform all the duties of
the Tent,[k] but they must not go near the
furnishings of the sanctuary or the altar,
or both they and you will die.[l] 4They are
to join you and be responsible for the care
of the Tent of Meeting—all the work at
the Tent—and no one else may come near
where you are.[m]
5"You are to be responsible for the care
of the sanctuary and the altar,[n] so that
wrath will not fall on the Israelites again.
6I myself have selected your fellow Levites
from among the Israelites as a gift to you,[o]
dedicated to the LORD to do the work at the
Tent of Meeting.[p] 7But only you and your
sons may serve as priests in connection
with everything at the altar and inside the
curtain.[q] I am giving you the service of
the priesthood as a gift.[r] Anyone else who
comes near the sanctuary must be put to
death.[s]"

Offerings for Priests and Levites

8Then the LORD said to Aaron, "I myself have put you in charge of the offerings
presented to me; all the holy offerings the
Israelites give me I give to you and your
sons as your portion[t] and regular share.[u]
9You are to have the part of the most holy
offerings[v] that is kept from the fire. From
all the gifts they bring me as most holy
offerings, whether grain[w] or sin[x] or guilt
offerings,[y] that part belongs to you and
your sons. 10Eat it as something most holy;
every male shall eat it.[z] You must regard
it as holy.[a]
11"This also is yours: whatever is set
aside from the gifts of all the wave offerings[b] of the Israelites. I give this to you
and your sons and daughters as your regular share.[c] Everyone in your household
who is ceremonially clean[d] may eat it.
12"I give you all the finest olive oil and
all the finest new wine and grain[e] they
give the LORD[f] as the firstfruits of their harvest.[g] 13All the land's firstfruits that they
bring to the LORD will be yours.[h] Everyone
in your household who is ceremonially
clean may eat it.[i]
14"Everything in Israel that is devoted[a]
to the LORD[j] is yours. 15The first offspring
of every womb, both man and animal, that
is offered to the LORD is yours.[k] But you

[a] *14* The Hebrew term refers to the irrevocable giving over of things or persons to the LORD.

17:10 [d] S ver 8 [e] S Ex 23:21; Dt 9:24; Ps 66:7; 68:18; Pr 24:21
17:12 [f] Jdg 13:22; Isa 6:5; 15:1
17:13 [g] Nu 1:51
18:1 [h] S Ex 28:38
18:2 [i] Nu 3:10
18:3 [j] S Nu 3:32 [k] Nu 1:51 [l] ver 7
18:4 [m] S Nu 3:38
18:5 [n] ver 3; Lev 6:12
18:6 [o] S Nu 3:9 [p] Nu 3:8
18:7 [q] Heb 9:3,6 [r] ver 20; Ex 29:9; 40:13; Heb 5:4 [s] ver 3; Nu 3:10
18:8 [t] S Lev 2:2 [u] Lev 6:16; 7:6,31-34,36; Dt 18:1; 2Ch 31:4
18:9 [v] S Lev 6:17 [w] Lev 2:1 [x] Lev 6:25 [y] S Lev 5:15
18:10 [z] S Lev 6:16 [a] Lev 6:17,18
18:11 [b] Ex 29:26; Lev 7:30; Nu 6:20 [c] Lev 7:31-34 [d] Lev 13:3; 22:1-16
18:12 [e] Dt 7:13; 11:14; 12:17; 28:51; 2Ki 18:32; 2Ch 31:5; Ne 10:37; Jer 31:12; Eze 23:41; Hos 2:8; Joel 1:10; Hag 1:11 [f] S Ge 4:3 [g] Ex 23:19; 34:26; Ne 10:35
18:13 [h] S Ex 29:27 [i] ver 11
18:14 [j] S Lev 27:21; Jos 6:17-19
18:15 [k] Ex 13:2

17:10 *in front of the Testimony.* Aaron's rod joined the stone tablets of the law of Moses (see note on Ex 25:16) and the jar of manna (Ex 16:33–34) within or near the ark of the covenant (see Heb 9:4 and note). These holy symbols were ever before the Lord as memorials of his special deeds in behalf of his people. Moreover, if anyone of a later age should dare to question the unique and holy place of the Aaronic priests in the Lord's service, this symbolic memorial of God's choice of Aaron would stand in opposition to their audacity. It is difficult to overestimate the importance of the role of Aaron and his sons in the worship of Israel (see note on 18:1–7).

17:12 *We will die!* At last the people realized the sin of their arrogance in challenging Aaron's role. The appropriate ways of approaching the Lord are detailed in chs. 18–19.

18:1–7 Aaron and his family, chosen by the Lord to be the true priests of holy worship, faced a burdensome task. The lament of the people in 17:12–13 was real; grievous sins against the holy meeting place of the Lord and his people would be judged by death. The Lord's mercy in providing a legitimate priesthood was actually an aspect of his grace (cf. Ps 99:6–7 and note), because it was the people's only hope for deliverance from judgment.

18:2 *Bring your fellow Levites.* The Aaronic priests were to be assisted by the others in the tribe of Levi, but the assistants were not to go beyond their serving role. If they did so, not only would they die, but so would the priests who were responsible (v. 3). *Testimony.* See note on Ex 25:16.

18:7 *the service of the priesthood as a gift.* Of all men, the priests were privileged to approach the Holy Place and minister before the Lord. The priesthood was a gift of God's grace to both priests and people.

18:8 *your portion and regular share.* The priests were to be supported in their work of ministry (see Lev 6:14—7:36). Since the Levites as a whole and the priests in particular had no part in the land that God was going to give them, it was necessary that the means for their provision be spelled out fully. They were not to have a part in the land; their share was the Lord himself (v. 20).

18:11 *your sons and daughters.* Provision was made not only for the priests, but for their families as well. Only family members who were ceremonially unclean were forbidden to eat the gifts and offerings of the people (see v. 13). Provisions for cleansing were stated in Lev 22:4–8.

18:12 *finest olive oil ... finest new wine and grain.* Since the best items of produce were to be given to the Lord, these became the special foods of the priests and their families. The NT writers similarly argue that those who minister the word of God in the present period should also be paid suitably for their work (see, e.g., 1Co 9:4–11 and notes).

18:13 *firstfuits.* See Ex 23:19 and note.

must redeem[l] every firstborn[m] son and
every firstborn male of unclean animals.[n]
16 When they are a month old,[o] you must
redeem them at the redemption price set
at five shekels[a][p] of silver, according to the
sanctuary shekel,[q] which weighs twenty
gerahs.[r]
17 "But you must not redeem the firstborn of an ox, a sheep or a goat; they are
holy.[s] Sprinkle their blood[t] on the altar
and burn their fat[u] as an offering made
by fire, an aroma pleasing to the LORD.[v]
18 Their meat is to be yours, just as the
breast of the wave offering[w] and the right
thigh are yours.[x] 19 Whatever is set aside
from the holy[y] offerings the Israelites present to the LORD I give to you and your
sons and daughters as your regular share.
It is an everlasting covenant of salt[z] before the LORD for both you and your offspring."
20 The LORD said to Aaron, "You will
have no inheritance in their land, nor will
you have any share among them;[a] I am
your share and your inheritance[b] among
the Israelites.
21 "I give to the Levites all the tithes[c] in
Israel as their inheritance[d] in return for
the work they do while serving at the Tent
of Meeting.[e] 22 From now on the Israelites
must not go near the Tent of Meeting, or
they will bear the consequences of their
sin and will die.[f] 23 It is the Levites who are
to do the work at the Tent of Meeting and
bear the responsibility for offenses against
it. This is a lasting ordinance[g] for the generations to come.[h] They will receive no inheritance[i] among the Israelites.[j] 24 Instead,
I give to the Levites as their inheritance
the tithes that the Israelites present as an
offering to the LORD.[k] That is why I said
concerning them: 'They will have no inheritance among the Israelites.' "
25 The LORD said to Moses, 26 "Speak to
the Levites and say to them: 'When you
receive from the Israelites the tithe I give
you[l] as your inheritance, you must present

18:15 [l] S Nu 3:46 [m] S Ge 10:15 [n] S Ex 13:13 **18:16** [o] S Nu 3:15 [p] S Lev 27:6 [q] S Ex 30:13 [r] Nu 3:47 **18:17** [s] S Lev 27:9 [t] S Lev 3:2 [u] S Ex 29:13 [v] S Lev 1:9 **18:18** [w] Lev 7:30 [x] ver 11 **18:19** [y] 2Ki 12:4 [z] S Lev 2:13 **18:20** [a] Nu 26:62; Dt 12:12 [b] ver 24; Dt 10:9; 14:27; 18:1-2; Jos 13:33; Eze 44:28 **18:21** [c] ver 24; S Ge 28:22; Nu 31:28; Dt 14:22; Ne 10:37; 13:5; Mal 3:8 [d] Lev 27:30-33; Heb 7:5 [e] Nu 1:53 **18:22** [f] S Ex 28:43 **18:23** [g] S Ex 12:14; S 27:21 [h] Nu 10:8 [i] ver 20; Nu 26:62; Dt 10:9 [j] Eze 44:10 **18:24** [k] Lev 27:30; Dt 26:12 **18:26** [l] ver 21

[m] ver 28; Ne 10:38 **18:27** [n] Lev 7:18 [o] Ge 50:10; Dt 15:14; Jdg 6:37; Ru 3:3,6,14; 1Sa 23:1 [p] ver 12,30 **18:28** [q] Mal 3:8 **18:30** [r] S ver 27 **18:31** [s] ver 23 **18:32** [t] Lev 22:15 [u] ver 29 [v] S Lev 19:8 **19:2** [w] S Ge 15:9; Heb 9:13 [x] S Lev 22:19-25 [y] Dt 21:3; 1Sa 6:7

a tenth of that tithe as the LORD's offering.[m] 27 Your offering will be reckoned[n] to
you as grain from the threshing floor[o] or
juice from the winepress.[p] 28 In this way
you also will present an offering to the
LORD from all the tithes[q] you receive from
the Israelites. From these tithes you must
give the LORD's portion to Aaron the priest.
29 You must present as the LORD's portion
the best and holiest part of everything giv-
en to you.'
30 "Say to the Levites: 'When you present the best part, it will be reckoned to
you as the product of the threshing floor
or the winepress.[r] 31 You and your households may eat the rest of it anywhere, for
it is your wages for your work at the Tent
of Meeting.[s] 32 By presenting the best part[t]
of it you will not be guilty in this matter;[u]
then you will not defile the holy offerings[v]
of the Israelites, and you will not die.' "

The Water of Cleansing

19 The LORD said to Moses and Aaron:
2 "This is a requirement of the law
that the LORD has commanded: Tell the
Israelites to bring you a red heifer[w] without defect or blemish[x] and that has never
been under a yoke.[y] 3 Give it to Eleazar[z]
the priest; it is to be taken outside the
camp[a] and slaughtered in his presence.
4 Then Eleazar the priest is to take some
of its blood on his finger and sprinkle[b] it
seven times toward the front of the Tent
of Meeting. 5 While he watches, the heifer is to be burned—its hide, flesh, blood
and offal.[c] 6 The priest is to take some cedar wood, hyssop[d] and scarlet wool[e] and
throw them onto the burning heifer. 7 After
that, the priest must wash his clothes and
bathe himself with water.[f] He may then
come into the camp, but he will be ceremonially unclean till evening. 8 The man

[a] *16* That is, about 2 ounces (about 55 grams)

19:3 [z] Nu 3:4 [a] S Ex 29:14 **19:4** [b] S Lev 4:17 **19:5** [c] S Ex 29:14 **19:6** [d] ver 18; Ps 51:7 [e] S Lev 14:4 **19:7** [f] S Lev 11:25; S 14:8

18:16 *according to the sanctuary shekel.* See note on Ex 30:13.

18:19 *everlasting covenant of salt.* A permanent provision for the priests. The phrase "covenant of salt" (see 2Ch 13:5) remains obscure. In Lev 2:13 the salt that must accompany grain offerings is called the "salt of the covenant." According to Eze 43:24, salt is also to be sprinkled on burnt offerings, and Ex 30:35 specifies salt as one of the ingredients in the special incense compounded for the sanctuary. A "covenant of salt" is perhaps an allusion to the salt used in the sacrificial meal that commonly accompanied the making of a covenant (see Ge 31:54; Ex 24:5–11; Ps 50:5 and note).

18:26–32 Although the Levites were the recipients of the tithe given to the Lord, they were not themselves exempt from tithing. They in turn were to give a tenth of their income to Aaron (v. 28) and were to be sure that the best part was given as the Lord's portion (v. 29). By obedient compliance the Levites would escape judicial death (v. 32).

19:2 *red heifer.* The qualifying words, "without defect or blemish," are familiar in contexts of sacrificial worship in the OT. But this is not a sacrificial animal. It is a cow, not an ox; it is to be slaughtered, not sacrificed; and it is to be killed outside the camp, not at the holy altar. The ashes of the red heifer (v. 9) are the primary focus of this act, for they will be used in the ritual of the water of cleansing. The burning of the animal with its "blood and offal" (v. 5) is unprecedented in the OT. The normal pattern for the sacrifice of the burnt offering is given in Lev 1:3–9. In every respect the killing of the red heifer is distinct: A female animal was taken outside the camp to be killed; the priest had to be present, but he did not identify himself with it; and a bit of the heifer's blood was sprinkled from the priest's finger toward the tabernacle seven times, but the rest of the animal was to be burned in its entirety, without the draining of its blood or the cleansing of its offal.

19:6 *cedar wood, hyssop and scarlet wool.* Associated with the cleansing properties of the ashes of the red heifer.

who burns it must also wash his clothes
and bathe with water, and he too will be
unclean till evening.
9“A man who is clean shall gather up
the ashes of the heifer[g] and put them in
a ceremonially clean place[h] outside the
camp. They shall be kept by the Israelite
community for use in the water of cleansing;[i] it is for purification from sin.[j] 10The
man who gathers up[k] the ashes of the heifer must also wash his clothes, and he too
will be unclean till evening.[l] This will be
a lasting ordinance[m] both for the Israelites
and for the aliens living among them.[n]
11“Whoever touches the dead body[o] of
anyone will be unclean for seven days.[p]
12He must purify himself with the water
on the third day and on the seventh day;[q]
then he will be clean. But if he does not
purify himself on the third and seventh
days, he will not be clean.[r] 13Whoever
touches the dead body[s] of anyone and fails
to purify himself defiles the LORD's tabernacle.[t] That person must be cut off from
Israel.[u] Because the water of cleansing has
not been sprinkled on him, he is unclean;[v]
his uncleanness remains on him.
14“This is the law that applies when a
person dies in a tent: Anyone who enters
the tent and anyone who is in it will be
unclean for seven days, 15and every open
container[w] without a lid fastened on it will
be unclean.
16“Anyone out in the open who touches someone who has been killed with a
sword or someone who has died a natural
death,[x] or anyone who touches a human
bone[y] or a grave,[z] will be unclean for sev-
en days.[a]
17“For the unclean person, put some
ashes[b] from the burned purification offering into a jar and pour fresh water[c] over
them. 18Then a man who is ceremonially
clean is to take some hyssop,[d] dip it in
the water and sprinkle[e] the tent and all
the furnishings and the people who were
there. He must also sprinkle anyone who
has touched a human bone or a grave[f] or
someone who has been killed or someone
who has died a natural death. 19The man
who is clean is to sprinkle[g] the unclean
person on the third and seventh days, and
on the seventh day he is to purify him.[h]
The person being cleansed must wash his
clothes[i] and bathe with water, and that
evening he will be clean. 20But if a person
who is unclean does not purify himself,
he must be cut off from the community,
because he has defiled[j] the sanctuary of
the LORD.[k] The water of cleansing has not
been sprinkled on him, and he is unclean.[l]
21This is a lasting ordinance[m] for them.
“The man who sprinkles the water of
cleansing must also wash his clothes, and
anyone who touches the water of cleansing will be unclean till evening. 22Anything
that an unclean[n] person touches becomes
unclean, and anyone who touches it becomes unclean till evening.”

Water From the Rock

20 In the first month the whole Israelite
community arrived at the Desert of
Zin,[o] and they stayed at Kadesh.[p] There
Miriam[q] died and was buried.
2Now there was no water[r] for the community,[s] and the people gathered in opposition[t] to Moses and Aaron. 3They quarreled[u] with Moses and said, “If only we
had died when our brothers fell dead[v] before the LORD![w] 4Why did you bring the
LORD's community into this desert,[x] that
we and our livestock should die here?[y]

19:9 [g]Heb 9:13 [h]S Ex 29:31; S Lev 4:12 [i]ver 13; Nu 8:7 [j]S Ge 35:2 **19:10** [k]Lev 15:10 [l]Lev 14:46 [m]Lev 3:17 [n]S Lev 22:18 **19:11** [o]S Lev 21:1 [p]S Lev 8:33; Nu 31:19 **19:12** [q]ver 19; Nu 31:19 [r]ver 20; 2Ch 26:21 **19:13** [s]S Lev 21:11 [t]S Lev 15:31; 2Ch 36:14; Ps 79:1 [u]Lev 7:20; 22:3 [v]ver 22; Hag 2:13 **19:15** [w]S Lev 6:28 **19:16** [x]Nu 31:19 [y]1Ki 13:2; 2Ki 23:14; Eze 6:5 [z]2Ki 23:6; Mt 23:27 [a]S Lev 5:3 **19:17** [b]ver 9 [c]S Nu 8:7 **19:18** [d]S ver 6; S Ex 12:22 [e]S Lev 4:17 [f]ver 16 **19:19** [g]S Lev 16:14-15 [h]Nu 31:19; Eze 36:25; Heb 10:22 [i]S Ge 35:2 **19:20** [j]Ps 74:7 [k]S Lev 15:31 [l]S ver 12; S Lev 14:8 **19:21** [m]S Ex 27:21 **19:22** [n]S Lev 5:2; 15:4-12 **20:1** [o]Nu 13:21 [p]ver 14; Nu 13:26; 33:36; Dt 1:46; Jdg 11:17; Ps 29:8

[q]S Ex 15:20 **20:2** [r]S Ex 15:22 [s]Ex 17:1 [t]S Nu 16:19 **20:3** [u]ver 13; S Ge 13:7; Ex 17:2; 21:18 [v]S Ex 5:21 [w]S Nu 14:2; 16:31-35 **20:4** [x]S Nu 14:2 [y]S Ex 14:11; Nu 14:3; 16:13

19:12 *purify himself with the water.* The ashes from the red heifer were kept outside the camp and would be mixed as needed with water to provide a means of cleansing after contact with dead bodies.

19:13 *defiles the LORD's tabernacle.* Willful neglect of the provision for cleansing brought not only judgment on the person, but also a pollution of the tabernacle itself. *cut off from Israel.* See note on Ex 12:15.

19:14 *anyone who is in it.* There would be many occasions in which a person would become unclean, not because of deliberate contact with a dead body, but just by being in the proximity of one who died.

19:18 *hyssop, dip it in the water and sprinkle.* Here the method of the cleansing ritual is explained. A ceremonially clean person had to sprinkle the ceremonially unclean person or thing. The cleansing power of the blood of Christ is specifically contrasted ("much more," Heb 9:13–14; see note there) with the cleansing effectiveness of the water of the ashes of the red heifer.

20:1–29 This chapter begins with the death of Miriam (v. 1), concludes with the death of Aaron (v. 28), includes the record of the conflict with Edom (vv. 14–21) and centers on the tragic sin of Moses (vv. 11–12). Such was the sad beginning of Israel's last year in the desert.

20:1 *first month.* The year is not given, but a comparison of vv. 22–29 with 33:38 leads to the conclusion that this chapter begins in the 40th year after the exodus (see notes on 1:1; 9:1). Most of the people 20 years old or more at the time of the rebellion at Kadesh (chs. 13–14) would already have died. *at Kadesh.* See note on Ge 14:7. The larger part of the desert wandering (see 32:13) is left without record. The people may have traveled about, seeking the water sources and the sparse vegetation, supported primarily by manna. But their circuits would bring them back to the central camp at Kadesh, the scene of their great rebellion (chs. 13–14). They have now come full circle; the land of promise lies before them again.

20:2 *no water.* Forty years earlier, the Lord had instructed Moses to take the staff he had used to strike the Nile (Ex 7:17) and to strike the rock at Horeb to initiate a flow of water (Ex 17:1–7). Now, 40 years later, at the place of Israel's worst acts of rebellion, the scene was recurring. The children of the rebellious nation now desire to die with their parents; the parents' complaints about the bread from heaven are repeated by the children.

5 Why did you bring us up out of Egypt to
this terrible place? It has no grain or figs,
grapevines or pomegranates.[z] And there is
no water to drink![a]"
6 Moses and Aaron went from the assembly to the entrance to the Tent of Meeting[b]
and fell facedown,[c] and the glory of the
LORD[d] appeared to them. 7 The LORD said to
Moses, 8 "Take the staff,[e] and you and your
brother Aaron gather the assembly together. Speak to that rock before their eyes and
it will pour out its water.[f] You will bring
water out of the rock for the community
so they and their livestock can drink."
9 So Moses took the staff[g] from the
LORD's presence,[h] just as he commanded
him. 10 He and Aaron gathered the assembly together[i] in front of the rock and Moses
said to them, "Listen, you rebels, must we
bring you water out of this rock?"[j] 11 Then
Moses raised his arm and struck the rock
twice with his staff. Water[k] gushed out,
and the community and their livestock
drank.
12 But the LORD said to Moses and Aaron,
"Because you did not trust in me enough
to honor me as holy[l] in the sight of the Israelites, you will not bring this community
into the land I give them."[m]
13 These were the waters of Meribah,[a][n]
where the Israelites quarreled[o] with the
LORD and where he showed himself holy
among them.[p]

Edom Denies Israel Passage

14 Moses sent messengers from Kadesh[q]
to the king of Edom,[r] saying:

"This is what your brother Israel
says: You know[s] about all the hardships[t] that have come upon us. 15 Our
forefathers went down into Egypt,[u]
and we lived there many years.[v] The
Egyptians mistreated[w] us and our fathers, 16 but when we cried out to the
LORD, he heard our cry[x] and sent an
angel[y] and brought us out of Egypt.[z]
"Now we are here at Kadesh, a town
on the edge of your territory.[a] 17 Please
let us pass through your country. We
will not go through any field or vineyard, or drink water from any well.
We will travel along the king's highway and not turn to the right or to
the left until we have passed through
your territory.[b]"

18 But Edom[c] answered:

"You may not pass through here; if
you try, we will march out and attack
you with the sword.[d]"

19 The Israelites replied:

"We will go along the main road,
and if we or our livestock[e] drink any
of your water, we will pay for it.[f]
We only want to pass through on
foot—nothing else."

20 Again they answered:

"You may not pass through.[g]"

Then Edom[h] came out against them
with a large and powerful army. 21 Since
Edom refused to let them go through their
territory,[i] Israel turned away from them.[j]

The Death of Aaron

22 The whole Israelite community set
out from Kadesh[k] and came to Mount
Hor.[l] 23 At Mount Hor, near the border of
Edom,[m] the LORD said to Moses and Aaron,

20:5 [z] Nu 13:23; 16:14 [a] S Ex 17:1 **20:6** [b] S Ex 40:2 [c] Nu 14:5 [d] S Nu 16:19 **20:8** [e] S Ex 4:2; S 10:12-13 [f] Ex 17:6; Isa 41:18; 43:20; Jer 31:9 **20:9** [g] Nu 17:2 [h] Nu 17:10 **20:10** [i] ver 8 [j] Ps 106:32,33 **20:11** [k] S Ex 17:6; S Isa 33:21 **20:12** [l] Nu 27:14; Dt 32:51; Isa 5:16; 8:13 [m] ver 24; Dt 1:37; 3:27 **20:13** [n] S Ex 17:7 [o] S ver 3 [p] S Lev 10:3 **20:14** [q] S ver 1 [r] S ver 16; S Ge 25:30; S 36:16 [s] Ge 24:3; Dt 4:39; Jos 2:11; 9:9 [t] S Ex 18:8 **20:15** [u] S Ge 46:6 [v] S Ge 15:13 [w] S Ex 1:14 **20:16** [x] S Ge 16:11; S 21:17; S Ex 2:23 [y] Ex 14:19 [z] Ex 12:42; Dt 26:8 [a] ver 14,23; Nu 33:37 **20:17** [b] ver 20; Nu 21:22; Dt 2:27; Jdg 11:17 **20:18** [c] ver 14 [d] Nu 21:23 **20:19** [e] Ex 12:38 [f] Dt 2:6,28 **20:20** [g] S ver 17,18 [h] ver 14 **20:21** [i] Nu 21:23 [j] Nu 21:4; Dt 2:8; Jdg 11:18 **20:22** [k] Dt 1:46 [l] Nu 33:37; 34:7; Dt 32:50 **20:23** [m] S ver 16

[a] 13 *Meribah* means *quarreling.*

20:6 *glory of the LORD.* See note on 14:10.
20:8 *Speak to that rock.* Moses was told to take his staff, through which God had performed wonders in Egypt and in the desert all these years, but this time he was merely to speak to the rock and it would pour out its water for the people. Cf. Ps 114:8 and note.
20:10 *Listen, you rebels.* At once the accumulated anger, exasperation and frustration of 40 years came to expression (see Ps 106:33 and note).
20:11 *struck the rock twice with his staff.* In his rage Moses disobeyed the Lord's instruction to speak to the rock (v. 8). Moses' rash action brought a stern rebuke from the Lord (v. 12). The nature of Moses' offense is not clearly stated in this text, but these factors appear to be involved: (1) Moses' action was a lack of trust in God (v. 12), as though he believed that a word alone would not suffice. (2) God's holiness was offended by Moses' rash action (v. 12), for he had not shown proper deference to God's presence (see v. 24; 27:14; Dt 1:37 and note; Ps 106:32–33).
20:12 *to honor me as holy.* See note on Lev 11:44. *you will not bring this community into the land.* The end result of Moses' action is sure: Neither Aaron nor Moses would enter the land of promise. Of their contemporaries only Joshua and Caleb would survive to enter the land. The inclusion of Aaron demonstrates his partnership with his brother in the breach against God's holiness.
20:13 *Meribah.* See NIV text note. The same name was used 40 years earlier at the first occasion of bringing water from the rock (Ex 17:7, where it is also called Massah, "testing"; see note there). Ps 95:8 (see note there) laments the rebellion at Meribah and Massah. *showed himself holy.* See Lev 10:3 and note.
20:14–21 Moses' attempt to pass through the territory of Edom by peaceful negotiation and payment for services rendered is met by arrogant rebuff.
20:14 *your brother Israel.* The people of Edom were descended from Esau, the brother of Jacob (see Ge 36:1; Ob 10 and notes).
20:17 *king's highway.* The major north-south trade route in Transjordan, extending from Arabia to Damascus.
20:20 *large and powerful army.* The show of force by Edom caused Israel to turn away so as not to risk conflict with this brother nation. Israel was forbidden by the Lord to take even a foothold in Edom (see Dt 2:4–6 and note on 2:5).
20:22 *Mount Hor.* Somewhere near the border of Edom (v. 23).

24“Aaron will be gathered to his people.[n]
He will not enter the land I give the Israelites, because both of you rebelled against
my command[o] at the waters of Meribah.[p]
25Get Aaron and his son Eleazar and take
them up Mount Hor.[q] 26Remove Aaron’s
garments[r] and put them on his son Eleazar, for Aaron will be gathered to his people;[s] he will die there.”
27Moses did as the LORD commanded:
They went up Mount Hor[t] in the sight of
the whole community. 28Moses removed
Aaron’s garments and put them on his
son Eleazar.[u] And Aaron died there[v] on
top of the mountain. Then Moses and Eleazar came down from the mountain, 29and
when the whole community learned that
Aaron had died,[w] the entire house of Israel
mourned for him[x] thirty days.

Arad Destroyed

21 When the Canaanite king of Arad,[y]
who lived in the Negev,[z] heard that
Israel was coming along the road to Ath-
arim, he attacked the Israelites and captured some of them. 2Then Israel made
this vow[a] to the LORD: “If you will deliver these people into our hands, we will
totally destroy[a][b] their cities.” 3The LORD
listened to Israel’s plea and gave the Canaanites[c] over to them. They completely
destroyed them[d] and their towns; so the
place was named Hormah.[b][e]

The Bronze Snake

4They traveled from Mount Hor[f] along
the route to the Red Sea,[c][g] to go around
Edom.[h] But the people grew impatient
on the way;[i] 5they spoke against God[j]

20:24 [n]S Ge 25:8 [o]S ver 10 [p]S Ex 17:7 **20:25** [q]Nu 33:38 **20:26** [r]Ex 28:1-4; 40:13; S Lev 16:4 [s]ver 24; Nu 27:13; 31:2 **20:27** [t]Nu 33:38 **20:28** [u]S Ex 29:29 [v]ver 26; Nu 33:38; Dt 10:6; 32:50 **20:29** [w]Dt 32:50 [x]S Ge 27:41; S Lev 10:6; S Dt 34:8 **21:1** [y]Nu 33:40; Jos 12:14 [z]S Ge 12:9; Nu 13:17; Dt 1:7; Jdg 1:9,16 **21:2** [a]Lev 7:16 [b]ver 3; Ex 22:20; Dt 2:34; Jos 2:10; 8:26; Jer 25:9; 50:21 **21:3** [c]S Ge 10:18 [d]S ver 2 [e]S Nu 14:45 **21:4** [f]Nu 20:22 [g]Nu 14:25; Dt 2:1; 11:4 [h]S Nu 20:21 [i]Dt 2:8; Jdg 11:18 **21:5** [j]Ps 78:19 [k]Nu 11:20 [l]S Ex 14:11; Nu 14:2,3 [m]Nu 20:5 [n]S Nu 11:5 **21:6** [o]ver 7; Dt 8:15; 32:33; Job 20:14; Ps 58:4; 140:3; Jer 8:17 [p]1Co 10:9 **21:7** [q]Ps 78:34; Hos 5:15 [r]Nu 14:40

and against Moses, and said, “Why have
you brought us up out of Egypt[k] to die in
the desert?[l] There is no bread! There is
no water![m] And we detest this miserable
food!”[n]
6Then the LORD sent venomous snakes[o]
among them; they bit the people and
many Israelites died.[p] 7The people came
to Moses[q] and said, “We sinned[r] when we
spoke against the LORD and against you.
Pray that the LORD[s] will take the snakes
away from us.” So Moses prayed[t] for the
people.
8The LORD said to Moses, “Make a snake
and put it up on a pole;[u] anyone who is
bitten can look at it and live.” 9So Moses
made a bronze snake[v] and put it up on a
pole. Then when anyone was bitten by a
snake and looked at the bronze snake, he
lived.[w]

The Journey to Moab

10The Israelites moved on and camped
at Oboth.[x] 11Then they set out from Oboth
and camped in Iye Abarim, in the desert that faces Moab[y] toward the sunrise.
12From there they moved on and camped
in the Zered Valley.[z] 13They set out from
there and camped alongside the Arnon[a],
which is in the desert extending into Amorite territory. The Arnon is the border of

[a] *2* The Hebrew term refers to the irrevocable giving over of things or persons to the LORD, often by totally destroying them; also in verse 3. [b] *3* *Hormah* means *destruction.* [c] *4* Hebrew *Yam Suph*; that is, Sea of Reeds

[s]Ex 8:8; 1Sa 7:8; Jer 27:18; 37:3; Ac 8:24 [t]S Nu 11:2 **21:8** [u]Jn 3:14 **21:9** [v]2Ki 18:4 [w]Jn 3:14-15 **21:10** [x]Nu 33:43 **21:11** [y]S Ge 36:35; Nu 33:44; Dt 34:8; Jer 40:11 **21:12** [z]Dt 2:13,14 **21:13** [a]Nu 22:36; Dt 2:24; Jos 12:1; Jdg 11:13,18; 2Ki 10:33; Isa 16:2; Jer 48:20

20:24 *gathered to his people.* A euphemism for death (see, e.g., Ge 25:8,17 and note on 25:8; 35:29). *both of you.* Aaron had joined Moses in rebellion against God (see v. 12 and note); his impending death was a precursor of Moses' death as well (see Dt 34).

20:25 *Aaron and his son Eleazar.* There was no doubt about Aaron's successor, just as there was no doubt about Moses' successor (see Dt 34).

20:26–28 While Aaron was still alive, his garments were to be placed on his son; only then did he die.

20:29 *mourned for him.* His death (and that of Moses) marked the passing of a generation. The old generation was now nearly gone; in 40 years there had been almost a complete turnover of the people 20 years old or more.

21:1–3 The first battle of the new community against the Canaanites was provoked by the king of Arad, perhaps as he was raiding them. The result was a complete victory for the Israelites—a new day for them, since they had been defeated by the Amalekites and Canaanites a generation before (14:41–45).

21:1 *Negev.* See note on Ge 12:9.

21:2 *totally destroy.* See NIV text note.

21:3 *Hormah.* See NIV text note; the association with Israel's earlier defeat is made certain by the use of this place-name (cf. 14:45).

21:4 With Moses' determination not to engage Edom in battle (see note on 20:20), the people became impatient with him and with the direction the Lord was taking them. Flush with victory, they were confident in themselves. They forgot that their victory over Arad was granted by the Lord in response to their solemn pledge (v. 2); now they were ready to rebel again.

21:5 *we detest this miserable food!* The people's impatience (v. 4) led them to blaspheme God, to reject his servant Moses and to despise the "bread from heaven" (Ex 16:4; see note there). This is the most bitter of their several attacks on the manna (see note on 11:7). Just as Moses' attack on the rock was more than it appeared to be (see note on 20:11), so the people's contempt for the heavenly bread was more serious than one might think. Rejecting the heavenly manna was tantamount to spurning God's grace (cf. Jn 6:32–35,48–51,58 and notes on 6:32–35).

21:8–9 In response to the people's confession of sin (v. 7), God directed Moses to make an image of a snake and put it on a pole, so that anyone who had been bitten could look at it and live. See the typological use of this incident in Jn 3:14–15.

21:10–13 The people skirt Edom and make their way to the Arnon, the river that serves as the border between Moab and the region of the Amorites and that flows west into the midpoint of the Dead Sea.

21:12 *Zered.* See note on Dt 2:13.

Moab, between Moab and the Amorites.[b]
14 That is why the Book of the Wars[c] of the
LORD says:

"... Waheb in Suphah[a] and the
ravines,
the Arnon 15 and[b] the slopes of the
ravines
that lead to the site of Ar[d]
and lie along the border of Moab."

16 From there they continued on to Beer,[e]
the well where the LORD said to Moses,
"Gather the people together and I will give
them water."
17 Then Israel sang this song:[f]

"Spring up, O well!
Sing about it,
18 about the well that the princes dug,
that the nobles of the people sank—
the nobles with scepters and staffs."

Then they went from the desert to Mattanah, 19 from Mattanah to Nahaliel, from
Nahaliel to Bamoth, 20 and from Bamoth to
the valley in Moab where the top of Pisgah[g] overlooks the wasteland.

Defeat of Sihon and Og

21 Israel sent messengers[h] to say to Sihon[i] king of the Amorites:[j]

22 "Let us pass through your country. We will not turn aside into any
field or vineyard, or drink water from
any well. We will travel along the
king's highway until we have passed
through your territory.[k]"

23 But Sihon would not let Israel pass
through his territory.[l] He mustered his entire army and marched out into the desert
against Israel. When he reached Jahaz,[m]
he fought with Israel.[n] 24 Israel, however,
put him to the sword[o] and took over his
land[p] from the Arnon to the Jabbok,[q] but
only as far as the Ammonites,[r] because
their border was fortified. 25 Israel captured
all the cities of the Amorites[s] and occupied them,[t] including Heshbon[u] and all its
surrounding settlements. 26 Heshbon was
the city of Sihon[v] king of the Amorites,[w]
who had fought against the former king of

21:13 [b]S Ge 10:16
21:14 [c]1Sa 17:47; 18:17; 25:28
21:15 [d]ver 28; Dt 2:9, 18; Isa 15:1
21:16 [e]Nu 25:1; 33:49; Jdg 9:21; Isa 15:8
21:17 [f]S Ex 15:1
21:20 [g]Nu 23:14; Dt 3:17, 27; 34:1; Jos 12:3; 13:20
21:21 [h]S Ge 32:3 [i]Nu 32:33; Dt 1:4; Jos 2:10; 12:2, 4; 13:10; Jdg 11:19-21; 1Ki 4:19; Ne 9:22; Ps 135:11; 136:19; Jer 48:45 [j]S Ex 23:23
21:22 [k]S Nu 20:17
21:23 [l]Nu 20:21 [m]Dt 2:32; Jos 13:18; 21:36; Jdg 11:20; Isa 15:4; Jer 48:21, 34 [n]Nu 20:18
21:24 [o]Dt 2:33; 3:3; 29:7; Ps 135:10-11; Am 2:9 [p]ver 35; Dt 3:4 [q]S Ge 32:22; Nu 32:33; Jdg 11:13, 22 [r]S Ge 19:38; Dt 2:37; Jos 13:10
21:25 [s]Nu 13:29; Jdg 10:11; Am 2:10 [t]Jdg 11:26 [u]ver 30; Nu 32:3; Dt 1:4; 29:7; Jos 9:10; 12:2; Isa 15:4; 16:8; Jer 48:2, 34
21:26 [v]ver 21; Dt 29:7; Ps 135:11 [w]Nu 13:29
[x]ver 11 [y]ver 13
21:28 [z]Jer 48:45 [a]S Nu 11:1 [b]S ver 15 [c]Nu 22:41; Dt 12:2; Jos 13:17; Isa 15:2; Jer 19:5
21:29 [d]Nu 24:17; 2Sa 8:2;

Moab[x] and had taken from him all his land
as far as the Arnon.[y]
27 That is why the poets say:

"Come to Heshbon and let it be rebuilt;
let Sihon's city be restored.
28 "Fire went out from Heshbon,
a blaze from the city of Sihon.[z]
It consumed[a] Ar[b] of Moab,
the citizens of Arnon's heights.[c]
29 Woe to you, O Moab![d]
You are destroyed, O people of
Chemosh![e]
He has given up his sons as fugitives[f]
and his daughters as captives[g]
to Sihon king of the Amorites.
30 "But we have overthrown them;
Heshbon is destroyed all the way to
Dibon.[h]
We have demolished them as far as
Nophah,
which extends to Medeba.[i]"

31 So Israel settled in the land of the Amorites.[j]
32 After Moses had sent spies[k] to Jazer,[l]
the Israelites captured its surrounding settlements and drove out the Amorites who
were there. 33 Then they turned and went
up along the road toward Bashan[m],[n] and Og
king of Bashan and his whole army marched
out to meet them in battle at Edrei.[o]
34 The LORD said to Moses, "Do not be
afraid of him, for I have handed him over
to you, with his whole army and his land.
Do to him what you did to Sihon king of
the Amorites, who reigned in Heshbon.[p]"
35 So they struck him down, together
with his sons and his whole army, leaving
them no survivors.[q] And they took possession of his land.[r]

[a] *14* The meaning of the Hebrew for this phrase is uncertain. [b] *14,15* Or *"I have been given from Suphah and the ravines / of the Arnon* [15] *to*

1Ch 18:2; Ps 60:8; Isa 25:10; Jer 48:46 [e]Jdg 10:6; 11:24; Ru 1:15; 1Ki 11:7, 33; 2Ki 23:13; Jer 48:7, 46 [f]Isa 15:5 [g]Isa 16:2 **21:30** [h]Nu 32:3; Jos 13:9, 17; Ne 11:25; Isa 15:2; Jer 48:18, 22 [i]Jos 13:16; 1Ch 19:7 **21:31** [j]Nu 13:29 **21:32** [k]Jos 2:1; 6:22; 7:2; Jdg 18:2; 2Sa 10:3; 1Ch 19:3 [l]Nu 32:1, 3, 35; Jos 13:25; 2Sa 24:5; 1Ch 6:81; Isa 16:8; Jer 48:32 **21:33** [m]Nu 32:33; Dt 3:3; 31:4; Jos 2:10; 12:4; 13:30; 1Ki 4:19; Ne 9:22; Ps 135:11; 136:20 [n]Dt 3:4; 32:14; Jos 9:10; 1Ki 4:13 [o]Dt 1:4; 3:1, 10; Jos 12:4; 13:12, 31; 19:37 **21:34** [p]Dt 3:2 **21:35** [q]Jos 9:10 [r]S ver 24

21:14 *Book of the Wars of the LORD.* Mentioned only here in the OT. This is not in existence today; it was presumably an ancient collection of songs of war in praise of God (see note on 10:3 for music in war). Cf. the "Book of Jashar" (Jos 10:13 [see note there]; 2Sa 1:18 and note).

21:16 *I will give them water.* The quest for water had been a constant problem during the desert experience (see ch. 20; Ex 17).

21:17–18 The song about the well may also come from the "Book of the Wars of the LORD" (v. 14).

21:21–26 As they had done with Edom (20:14–19), Israel requested freedom to pass through the land of the Amorites. When Sihon their king tried to meet Israel with a show of force, he suffered an overwhelming defeat. The land of the Amorites referred to here was in Transjordan, extending from the Arnon River (at the midpoint of the Dead Sea) to the Jabbok River (v. 24), which flows into the Jordan some 24 miles north of the Dead Sea.

21:27–30 This third ancient poem in ch. 21 was an Amorite taunt song about their earlier victory over Moab (v. 29). Perhaps the song about Heshbon was also preserved in the "Book of the Wars of the LORD" (v. 14).

21:33 *Bashan.* The region northeast of the Sea of Galilee.

21:35 *struck him down.* By defeating Og, Israel now controlled Transjordan from Moab to the heights of Bashan in the vicinity of Mount Hermon. The victory over Sihon and Og became

Balak Summons Balaam

22 Then the Israelites traveled to the
plains of Moab[s] and camped along
the Jordan[t] across from Jericho.[a u]
2Now Balak son of Zippor[v] saw all that
Israel had done to the Amorites, 3and
Moab was terrified because there were
so many people. Indeed, Moab was filled
with dread[w] because of the Israelites.
4The Moabites[x] said to the elders of
Midian,[y] "This horde is going to lick up
everything[z] around us, as an ox licks up
the grass of the field.[a]"
So Balak son of Zippor, who was king
of Moab at that time, 5sent messengers to
summon Balaam son of Beor,[b] who was at
Pethor, near the River,[b c] in his native land.
Balak said:

> "A people has come out of Egypt;[d]
> they cover the face of the land and
> have settled next to me. 6Now come
> and put a curse[e] on these people, be-
> cause they are too powerful for me.
> Perhaps then I will be able to defeat
> them and drive them out of the coun-
> try.[f] For I know that those you bless
> are blessed, and those you curse are
> cursed."

7The elders of Moab and Midian left,
taking with them the fee for divination.[g]
When they came to Balaam, they told him
what Balak had said.
8"Spend the night here," Balaam said to
them, "and I will bring you back the answer the LORD gives me.[h]" So the Moabite
princes stayed with him.
9God came to Balaam[i] and asked,[j] "Who
are these men with you?"
10Balaam said to God, "Balak son of Zippor, king of Moab, sent me this message:
11'A people that has come out of Egypt covers the face of the land. Now come and
put a curse on them for me. Perhaps then
I will be able to fight them and drive them
away.'"
12But God said to Balaam, "Do not go
with them. You must not put a curse on
those people, because they are blessed.[k]"
13The next morning Balaam got up and
said to Balak's princes, "Go back to your
own country, for the LORD has refused to
let me go with you."
14So the Moabite princes returned to
Balak and said, "Balaam refused to come
with us."
15Then Balak sent other princes, more
numerous and more distinguished than the
first. 16They came to Balaam and said:

> "This is what Balak son of Zip-
> por says: Do not let anything keep
> you from coming to me, 17because I
> will reward you handsomely[l] and do
> whatever you say. Come and put a
> curse[m] on these people for me."

18But Balaam answered them, "Even if
Balak gave me his palace filled with silver
and gold, I could not do anything great or
small to go beyond the command of the
LORD my God.[n] 19Now stay here tonight as
the others did, and I will find out what
else the LORD will tell me.[o]"
20That night God came to Balaam[p] and
said, "Since these men have come to summon you, go with them, but do only what
I tell you."[q]

22:1 [s] S Nu 21:11 [t] S Nu 13:29; S Jos 2:7 [u] Nu 31:12; 33:48; Dt 32:49; Jos 2:1
22:2 [v] Nu 23:1-3; Jos 24:9; Jdg 11:25; Mic 6:5; Rev 2:14
22:3 [w] S Ex 15:15
22:4 [x] S Ge 19:37 [y] S Ge 25:2 [z] Nu 32:17, 18, 29 [a] Job 5:25; Ps 72:16
22:5 [b] ver 7; Nu 24:25; 31:8, 16; Dt 23:4; Jos 13:22; Ne 13:2; Mic 6:5; S 2Pe 2:15 [c] S Ge 2:14 [d] S Ex 13:3
22:6 [e] ver 12, 17; Nu 23:7, 11, 13; 24:9, 10 [f] ver 11
22:7 [g] S Ge 30:27
22:8 [h] ver 19
22:9 [i] S Ge 20:3 [j] ver 20; Nu 23:5; 24:4, 16
22:12 [k] S Ge 12:2
22:17 [l] ver 37; Nu 24:11 [m] S ver 6
22:18 [n] ver 38; Nu 23:12, 26; 24:13; 1Ki 22:14; 2Ch 18:13; Jer 42:4
22:19 [o] ver 8
22:20 [p] S Ge 20:3 [q] ver 35, 38; Nu 23:5, 12, 16, 26; 24:13; 2Ch 18:13

[a] *1* Hebrew *Jordan of Jericho*; possibly an ancient name for the Jordan River [b] *5* That is, the Euphrates

a subject of song (Ps 135:11; 136:19–20), and is now a regular part of the commemoration of the works of the Lord in the Passover celebration.

22:1 *plains of Moab.* Israel now marched back to their staging area east of the Jordan and just north of the Dead Sea. From this point they would launch their attack on Canaan, beginning with the ancient city of Jericho. Moab did not trust Israel's intentions, however. Moab's fear leads to a remarkable interval in the story of Israel: the account of Balak and Balaam (chs. 22–24).

22:3 *Moab was terrified.* Balak king of Moab did not know that Israel had no plans against him.

22:4 *said to the elders of Midian.* Balak made an alliance with the Midianites to oppose Israel (see v. 7). *as an ox licks up the grass of the field.* A proverbial simile particularly fitting for a pastoral people.

22:5 *summon Balaam.* Since Balak believed that there was no military way to withstand Israel, he sought to oppose them through pagan divination (vv. 6–7), sending for a diviner with an international reputation. (One of Balaam's non-Biblical prophecies is preserved in an Aramaic [or, according to some, a dialect of Hebrew] inscription from Deir 'Alla—east of the Jordan River just north of the Jabbok River—dating to the seventh century B.C.) *Pethor.* Located in Northwest Mesopotamia and mentioned in Assyrian inscriptions.

22:6 *put a curse on these people.* See note on Ge 12:3.

22:8 *the answer the LORD gives me.* The language here and in v. 18 ("the LORD my God") has led some to believe that Balaam was a believer in Yahweh ("the LORD"), God of Israel. Based on the subsequent narrative, however, it seems best to take Balaam's words as claiming to be the spokesman for any god. Balaam is universally condemned in Scripture for moral, ethical and religious faults (see 31:7–8,15–16 and note on 31:8; Dt 23:3–6; Jos 13:22 and note; 24:9–10 and note on 24:10; Ne 13:1–3; Mic 6:5; 2Pe 2:15–16; Jude 11; Rev 2:14 and note).

22:9 That God spoke to Balaam is not to be denied, but Balaam did not yet realize that the God of Israel was unlike the supposed deities that he usually schemed against.

22:12 *they are blessed.* Israel was under the Lord's blessing promised to Abraham (see note on Ge 12:2–3).

22:20 *go with them.* There appears to be a contradiction between the permission God grants Balaam here and the prohibition he had given earlier (v. 12), and then the anger the Lord displayed against Balaam on his journey (v. 22). The difficulty is best understood as lying in the contrary character of Balaam. God had forbidden him to go to curse Israel. He then allowed Balaam to go, but only if he would follow the Lord's direction. But Balaam's real intentions were known to the Lord, and so with severe displeasure he confronted the pagan prophet.

Balaam's Donkey

21 Balaam got up in the morning, saddled his donkey and went with the princes of Moab. 22 But God was very angry[r] when he went, and the angel of the LORD[s] stood in the road to oppose him. Balaam was riding on his donkey, and his two servants were with him. 23 When the donkey saw the angel of the LORD standing in the road with a drawn sword[t] in his hand, she turned off the road into a field. Balaam beat her[u] to get her back on the road.

24 Then the angel of the LORD stood in a narrow path between two vineyards, with walls on both sides. 25 When the donkey saw the angel of the LORD, she pressed close to the wall, crushing Balaam's foot against it. So he beat her again.

26 Then the angel of the LORD moved on ahead and stood in a narrow place where there was no room to turn, either to the right or to the left. 27 When the donkey saw the angel of the LORD, she lay down under Balaam, and he was angry[v] and beat her with his staff. 28 Then the LORD opened the donkey's mouth,[w] and she said to Balaam, "What have I done to you to make you beat me these three times?[x]"

29 Balaam answered the donkey, "You have made a fool of me! If I had a sword in my hand, I would kill you right now.[y]"

30 The donkey said to Balaam, "Am I not your own donkey, which you have always ridden, to this day? Have I been in the habit of doing this to you?"

"No," he said.

31 Then the LORD opened Balaam's eyes,[z] and he saw the angel of the LORD standing in the road with his sword drawn. So he bowed low and fell facedown.

32 The angel of the LORD asked him, "Why have you beaten your donkey these three times? I have come here to oppose you because your path is a reckless one before me.[a] 33 The donkey saw me and turned away from me these three times. If she had not turned away, I would certainly have killed you by now,[a] but I would have spared her."

34 Balaam said to the angel of the LORD, "I have sinned.[b] I did not realize you were standing in the road to oppose me. Now if you are displeased, I will go back."

35 The angel of the LORD said to Balaam, "Go with the men, but speak only what I tell you." So Balaam went with the princes of Balak.

36 When Balak[c] heard that Balaam was coming, he went out to meet him at the Moabite town on the Arnon[d] border, at the edge of his territory. 37 Balak said to Balaam, "Did I not send you an urgent summons? Why didn't you come to me? Am I really not able to reward you?"

38 "Well, I have come to you now," Balaam replied. "But can I say just anything? I must speak only what God puts in my mouth."[e]

39 Then Balaam went with Balak to Kiriath Huzoth. 40 Balak sacrificed cattle and sheep,[f] and gave some to Balaam and the princes who were with him. 41 The next morning Balak took Balaam up to Bamoth Baal,[g] and from there he saw part of the people.[h]

Balaam's First Oracle

23 Balaam said, "Build me seven altars here, and prepare seven bulls and seven rams[i] for me." 2 Balak did as Balaam said, and the two of them offered a bull and a ram on each altar.[j]

3 Then Balaam said to Balak, "Stay here beside your offering while I go aside. Perhaps the LORD will come to meet with me.[k] Whatever he reveals to me I will tell you." Then he went off to a barren height.

4 God met with him,[l] and Balaam said, "I have prepared seven altars, and on each altar I have offered a bull and a ram."

5 The LORD put a message in Balaam's mouth[m][n] and said, "Go back to Balak and give him this message."[o]

6 So he went back to him and found him standing beside his offering, with all the

22:22 [r] S Ex 4:14 [s] S Ge 16:7; Jdg 13:3,6,13 **22:23** [t] Jos 5:13 [u] ver 25,27 **22:27** [v] Nu 11:1; Jas 1:19 **22:28** [w] 2Pe 2:16 [x] ver 32 **22:29** [y] ver 33; Dt 25:4; Pr 12:10; 27:23-27; Mt 15:19 **22:31** [z] Ge 21:19 **22:33** [a] S ver 29
22:34 [b] Ge 39:9; Nu 14:40; 1Sa 15:24,30; 2Sa 12:13; 24:10; Job 33:27; Ps 51:4 **22:36** [c] ver 2 [d] S Nu 21:13 **22:38** [e] Nu 23:5,16,26 **22:40** [f] Nu 23:1,14,29; Eze 45:23 **22:41** [g] S Nu 21:28 [h] Nu 23:13 **23:1** [i] S Nu 22:40 **23:2** [j] ver 14,30 **23:3** [k] ver 15 **23:4** [l] ver 16 **23:5** [m] S Ex 4:12; Isa 59:21 [n] S Ex 4:15 [o] S Nu 22:20

[a] 32 The meaning of the Hebrew for this clause is uncertain.

22:23 *the donkey saw the angel of the LORD.* As a pagan prophet, Balaam was a specialist in animal divination, but his dumb beast saw what Balaam was blind to observe.
22:29 *If I had a sword.* A ridiculous picture of the hapless Balaam. A sword was nearby (see vv. 23,31 – 33), but its victim was not going to be the donkey.
22:31 *Then the LORD opened Balaam's eyes.* The language follows the same structure as the opening words of v. 28. In some ways, the opening of the eyes of the pagan prophet to see the reality of the angel was the greater miracle.
22:35 *speak only what I tell you.* The one great gain was that Balaam was now more aware of the seriousness of the task before him; he would not be able to change the word the Lord would give him (see 23:12,20,26).
22:37 *Did I not send you an urgent summons?* The comic element of the story is seen not only in the hapless Balaam but also in the frustrated Balak (see 23:11,25; 24:10).
22:40 The pieces given to Balaam would have included the livers, for, as a pagan diviner, Balaam was a specialist in liver divination. Balaam subsequently gave up his acts of sorcery as the power of the Lord's word came upon him (24:1).
23:1 *seven altars ... seven bulls and seven rams.* These sacrifices were prepared as a part of Balaam's pagan actions. The number seven (signifying completeness) was held in high regard among Semitic peoples in general. The many animals would provide abundant liver and other organ materials for the diviner from Northwest Mesopotamia.
23:2 *Balak did as Balaam said.* Balaam is in charge; Balak is now his subordinate.

princes of Moab.[p] 7Then Balaam[q] uttered
his oracle:[r]

"Balak brought me from Aram,[s]
the king of Moab from the eastern
mountains.[t]
'Come,' he said, 'curse Jacob for me;
come, denounce Israel.'[u]
8How can I curse
those whom God has not cursed?[v]
How can I denounce
those whom the LORD has not
denounced?[w]
9From the rocky peaks I see them,
from the heights I view them.[x]
I see a people who live apart
and do not consider themselves one
of the nations.[y]
10Who can count the dust of Jacob[z]
or number the fourth part of Israel?
Let me die the death of the righteous,[a]
and may my end be like theirs![b]"

11Balak said to Balaam, "What have you
done to me? I brought you to curse my
enemies,[c] but you have done nothing but
bless them!"[d]

12He answered, "Must I not speak what
the LORD puts in my mouth?"[e]

Balaam's Second Oracle

13Then Balak said to him, "Come with
me to another place[f] where you can see
them; you will see only a part but not all
of them.[g] And from there, curse them for
me.[h]" 14So he took him to the field of Zo-
phim on the top of Pisgah,[i] and there he
built seven altars and offered a bull and a
ram on each altar.[j]

15Balaam said to Balak, "Stay here beside your offering while I meet with him
over there."

16The LORD met with Balaam and put a
message in his mouth[k] and said, "Go back
to Balak and give him this message."

17So he went to him and found him
standing beside his offering, with the
princes of Moab.[l] Balak asked him, "What
did the LORD say?"

18Then he uttered his oracle:[m]

"Arise, Balak, and listen;
hear me, son of Zippor.[n]
19God is not a man,[o] that he should
lie,[p]
nor a son of man, that he should
change his mind.[q]
Does he speak and then not act?
Does he promise[r] and not fulfill?
20I have received a command to bless;[s]
he has blessed,[t] and I cannot
change it.[u]

21"No misfortune is seen in Jacob,[v]
no misery observed in Israel.[a][w]
The LORD their God is with them;[x]
the shout of the King[y] is among
them.
22God brought them out of Egypt;[z]
they have the strength of a wild ox.[a]
23There is no sorcery against Jacob,
no divination[b] against Israel.
It will now be said of Jacob
and of Israel, 'See what God has
done!'
24The people rise like a lioness;[c]
they rouse themselves like a lion[d]
that does not rest till he devours his
prey
and drinks the blood[e] of his
victims."

25Then Balak said to Balaam, "Neither
curse them at all nor bless them at all!"

26Balaam answered, "Did I not tell you I
must do whatever the LORD says?"[f]

[a] 21 Or *He has not looked on Jacob's offenses / or on the wrongs found in Israel.*

23:6 [p]ver 17 **23:7** [q]Nu 22:5; Jos 24:9 [r]ver 18; Nu 24:3, 21; 2Sa 23:1 [s]2Ki 5:1 [t]S Ge 24:10 [u]S Nu 22:6; Ne 13:2 **23:8** [v]Nu 22:12 [w]ver 20; Isa 43:13 **23:9** [x]Nu 22:41 [y]S Ex 33:16; S Dt 32:8 **23:10** [z]S Ge 13:16 [a]Ps 16:3; 116:15; Isa 57:1 [b]Ps 37:37 **23:11** [c]S Nu 22:6 [d]Nu 24:10; Jos 24:10; Ne 13:2 **23:12** [e]S Nu 22:18, 20 **23:13** [f]ver 27 [g]Nu 22:41 [h]S Nu 22:6 **23:14** [i]S Nu 21:20; 27:12 [j]S ver 2 **23:16** [k]S Ex 4:15; S Nu 22:38 **23:17** [l]ver 6 **23:18** [m]S ver 7 [n]Nu 22:2 **23:19** [o]Job 9:32; Isa 55:9; Hos 11:9 [p]S Nu 11:23 [q]1Sa 15:29; Job 12:13; 36:5; Ps 33:11; 89:34; 102:27; 110:4; Jer 4:28; 7:16; Mal 3:6; Tit 1:2; Heb 6:18; 7:21; Jas 1:17 [r]2Sa 7:25; Ps 119:38 **23:20** [s]ver 5, 16; Nu 24:1 [t]Ge 22:17; Nu 22:12 [u]S ver 8; S Job 9:12 **23:21** [v]Ps 32:2, 5; 85:2; Ro 4:7-8 [w]Isa 33:24; 40:2; Jer 50:20 [x]S Ge 26:3; Ex 29:45, 46; Dt 4:7; Ps 34:17-18; 145:18; Zec 2:10 [y]Dt 32:15; 33:5; Ps 89:15-18; Isa 44:2 **23:22** [z]Nu 24:8; Jos 2:10; 9:9 [a]Dt 33:17; Job 39:9; Ps 22:21; 29:6; 92:10; Isa 34:7 **23:23** [b]ver 3; S Ge 30:27; Nu 24:1 **23:24** [c]Nu 24:9; Eze 19:2; Na 2:11 [d]S Ge 49:9 [e]Isa 49:26 **23:26** [f]S Nu 22:18, 20

23:7 — 24:24 There are seven poetic oracles here: The first four are longer, have introductory narrative bridges and are written in exquisite poetry (23:7 – 10; 23:18 – 24; 24:3 – 9; 24:15 – 19). The last three are brief, are much more difficult to understand, and follow one another in a staccato pattern (24:20, 21 – 22, 23 – 24).

23:7 *oracle.* Hebrew *mashal,* usually translated "proverb," but here "oracle" is appropriate. By this word the distinctive nature of Balaam's prophecies is established; none of the prophecies of Israel's true prophets is described by this term.

23:8 *How can I curse those whom God has not cursed?* That which Balaam had been hired to do he was unable to do. God kept him from pronouncing a curse on his people, who were unlike the nations of the world (v. 9).

23:10 *Let me die the death of the righteous.* A wish not granted (see 31:8,16 and note on 31:8). *may my end be like theirs!* He who had come to curse desired to share in Israel's blessing.

23:13 *a part but not all.* Balak attempted to reduce Israel's power by selecting a point where their immense numbers would be obscured. Unfortunately for Balak, the oracle that followed (vv. 18 – 24) exceeded the first in its blessing on Israel.

23:19 *God is not a man, that he should lie.* These sublime words describe the immutability of the Lord and the integrity of his word. Balaam is a foil to God — constantly shifting, prevaricating, equivocating, changing — a prime example of the distinction between God and human beings.

23:21 *the shout of the King is among them.* That the first explicit declaration of the Lord's kingship in the Pentateuch was made by Balaam is a suitable improbability. Because God is King (Sovereign), he was able to use Balaam for his own ends — to bless his people in a new and wonderful manner.

23:22 *wild ox.* Or "aurochs," a traditional image of power in the ancient Near East (see also 24:8); or possibly "oryx," a large, straight-horned antelope.

23:23 *no sorcery against Jacob.* Balaam speaks from his frightful experience. He had no means in his bag of tricks to withstand God's blessing of Israel.

23:24 *like a lioness.* Israel was about to arise and devour its foes, like a lioness on the hunt (see 24:9; Ge 49:9 and note).

Balaam's Third Oracle

27Then Balak said to Balaam, "Come, let
me take you to another place.[g] Perhaps it
will please God to let you curse them for
me[h] from there." 28And Balak took Balaam
to the top of Peor,[i] overlooking the wasteland.
29Balaam said, "Build me seven altars
here, and prepare seven bulls and seven
rams for me." 30Balak did as Balaam had
said, and offered a bull and a ram on each
altar.[j]

24 Now when Balaam saw that it pleased
the LORD to bless Israel,[k] he did not resort to sorcery[l] as at other times, but turned
his face toward the desert.[m] 2When Balaam
looked out and saw Israel encamped tribe
by tribe, the Spirit of God came upon him[n]
3and he uttered his oracle:

"The oracle of Balaam son of Beor,
the oracle of one whose eye sees
clearly,[o]
4the oracle of one who hears the words
of God,[p]
who sees a vision from the
Almighty,[a][q]
who falls prostrate, and whose eyes
are opened:

5"How beautiful are your tents,[r]
O Jacob,
your dwelling places, O Israel!

6"Like valleys they spread out,
like gardens beside a river,[s]
like aloes[t] planted by the LORD,
like cedars beside the waters.[u]
7Water will flow from their buckets;
their seed will have abundant water.

"Their king will be greater than Agag;[v]
their kingdom will be exalted.[w]

8"God brought them out of Egypt;
they have the strength of a wild ox.
They devour hostile nations
and break their bones in pieces;[x]
with their arrows they pierce them.[y]
9Like a lion they crouch and lie down,
like a lioness[z]—who dares to rouse
them?

"May those who bless you be blessed[a]
and those who curse you be
cursed!"[b]

10Then Balak's anger burned[c] against
Balaam. He struck his hands together[d] and
said to him, "I summoned you to curse
my enemies,[e] but you have blessed them[f]
these three times.[g] 11Now leave at once
and go home![h] I said I would reward you
handsomely,[i] but the LORD has kept you
from being rewarded."
12Balaam answered Balak, "Did I not
tell the messengers you sent me,[j] 13'Even
if Balak gave me his palace filled with silver and gold, I could not do anything of
my own accord, good or bad, to go beyond
the command of the LORD[k]—and I must
say only what the LORD says'?[l] 14Now I am
going back to my people, but come, let me
warn you of what this people will do to
your people in days to come."[m]

Balaam's Fourth Oracle

15Then he uttered his oracle:

"The oracle of Balaam son of Beor,
the oracle of one whose eye sees
clearly,
16the oracle of one who hears the words[n]
of God,
who has knowledge from the Most
High,[o]
who sees a vision from the Almighty,
who falls prostrate, and whose eyes
are opened:

17"I see him, but not now;
I behold him, but not near.[p]
A star will come out of Jacob;[q]
a scepter will rise out of Israel.[r]

[a] 4 Hebrew *Shaddai*; also in verse 16

23:27 [g]ver 13 [h]Nu 24:10 **23:28** [i]Nu 25:3, 18; 31:16; Dt 3:29; 4:3; Jos 22:17; Ps 106:28; Hos 9:10 **23:30** [j]S ver 2 **24:1** [k]S Nu 23:20 [l]S Nu 23:23 [m]Nu 23:28 **24:2** [n]S Nu 11:25, 26 **24:3** [o]ver 15 **24:4** [p]S Nu 22:9 [q]S Ge 15:1 **24:5** [r]Jer 4:20; 30:18; Mal 2:12 **24:6** [s]S Ge 2:10 [t]Ps 45:8; SS 4:14 [u]Job 29:19; Ps 1:3; 104:16; Eze 31:5 **24:7** [v]S Ex 17:8-16 [w]Dt 28:1; 2Sa 5:12; 1Ch 14:2; Ps 89:27; 145:11-13 **24:8** [x]S Ex 15:6; Jer 50:17 [y]2Sa 18:14; Ps 45:5 **24:9** [z]S Nu 23:24 [a]S Ge 12:2 [b]S Ge 12:3 **24:10** [c]S Ex 4:14 [d]Job 27:23; 34:37; La 2:15; Eze 21:14; 22:13; 25:6 [e]S Nu 22:6 [f]S Nu 23:11; S Dt 23:5 [g]ver 3-9; Nu 23:7-10, 18-24 **24:11** [h]ver 14, 25 [i]S Nu 22:17 **24:12** [j]Nu 22:18 **24:13** [k]S Nu 22:18 [l]S Nu 22:20 **24:14** [m]S Ge 49:1; Nu 31:8, 16; Mic 6:5 **24:16** [n]S Nu 22:9 [o]Ge 14:18; Isa 14:14 **24:17** [p]Rev 1:7 [q]Mt 2:2 [r]S Ge 49:10

24:1 *sorcery as at other times.* Balaam's magic and sorcery are identified here (see notes on 22:40; 23:1).
24:2 *the Spirit of God came upon him.* This unexpected language indicates that God has overpowered the pagan prophet for his own purposes. Cf. note on Jdg 3:10.
24:3–4 The extensive introduction of this oracle describes Balaam's experience in the Lord's presence. Now Balaam's eyes were opened (see note on 22:31).
24:6–7 Balaam speaks here in general, but luxuriant, terms of the blessings that will come to the Israelites as they settle in their new land. The lushness of their blessing from the Lord is reminiscent of Eden.
24:7 *Agag.* Possibly a throne name for the king of the Amalekites (cf. 1Sa 15:32–33). The allusion here may be to the Amalekites who attacked Israel when they came out of Egypt (see Ex 17:8–13) and again when they first approached Canaan (see 14:45).
24:8 *God brought them out of Egypt.* These central words about Israel's salvation are recited by one who was a hostile outsider (see notes on 23:21; 25:1–18).
24:9 *May those who bless you be blessed . . . cursed!* The theology of blessing and cursing in the promises made to Abraham (Ge 12:2–3; see notes there) is now a part of this oracle of blessing. Perhaps here Balaam was reasserting his desire to be a part of Israel's blessing (see 23:10–11 and note on 23:10).
24:11 *the LORD has kept you from being rewarded.* In his disgust with Balaam's failure to curse Israel, Balak now dismisses him without pay—the ultimate insult to his greed (see 2Pe 2:15 and note).
24:14 *in days to come.* The distant (Messianic) future is usually indicated by this expression (see, e.g., Jer 48:47 and note).
24:15–16 As in the third oracle (see vv. 3–4), the introduction to the fourth oracle is lengthy, helping to prepare the reader for the startling words of the prophecy.

24:17 *star . . . scepter.* Perhaps fulfilled initially in David, but ultimately in the coming Messianic

He will crush the foreheads of Moab,[s]
the skulls[a][t] of[b] all the sons of
Sheth.[c]
18 Edom[u] will be conquered;
Seir,[v] his enemy, will be conquered,[w]
but Israel[x] will grow strong.
19 A ruler will come out of Jacob[y]
and destroy the survivors of the
city."

Balaam's Final Oracles

20 Then Balaam saw Amalek[z] and uttered his oracle:

"Amalek was first among the nations,
but he will come to ruin at last."[a]

21 Then he saw the Kenites[b] and uttered his oracle:

"Your dwelling place is secure,[c]
your nest is set in a rock;
22 yet you Kenites will be destroyed
when Asshur[d] takes you captive."

23 Then he uttered his oracle:

"Ah, who can live when God does
this?[d]
24 Ships will come from the shores of
Kittim;[e]
they will subdue Asshur[f] and Eber,[g]
but they too will come to ruin."[h]

25 Then Balaam[i] got up and returned home and Balak went his own way.

Moab Seduces Israel

25 While Israel was staying in Shittim,[j]
the men began to indulge in sexual
immorality[k] with Moabite[l] women,[m] 2 who
invited them to the sacrifices[n] to their
gods.[o] The people ate and bowed down
before these gods. 3 So Israel joined in worshiping[p] the Baal of Peor.[q] And the LORD's
anger burned against them.
4 The LORD said to Moses, "Take all the
leaders[r] of these people, kill them and expose[s] them in broad daylight before the
LORD,[t] so that the LORD's fierce anger[u] may
turn away from Israel."
5 So Moses said to Israel's judges, "Each
of you must put to death[v] those of your
men who have joined in worshiping the
Baal of Peor."[w]
6 Then an Israelite man brought to his
family a Midianite[x] woman right before the
eyes of Moses and the whole assembly of
Israel while they were weeping[y] at the entrance to the Tent of Meeting. 7 When Phinehas[z] son of Eleazar, the son of Aaron, the
priest, saw this, he left the assembly, took
a spear[a] in his hand 8 and followed the Israelite into the tent. He drove the spear
through both of them — through the Israelite and into the woman's body. Then the
plague against the Israelites was stopped;[b]
9 but those who died in the plague[c] numbered 24,000.[d]
10 The LORD said to Moses, 11 "Phinehas son of Eleazar, the son of Aaron, the

24:17 [s] S Ge 19:37; S Nu 21:29; S Dt 23:6; Isa 15:1-16:14 [t] Jer 48:45 **24:18** [u] 2Sa 8:12; 1Ch 18:11; Ps 60:8; Isa 11:14; Am 9:12 [v] S Ge 14:6; Dt 1:44; Jos 12:7; 15:10; Jdg 5:4 [w] Ob 1:2 [x] S Ge 9:25 **24:19** [y] S Ge 49:10; Mic 5:2 **24:20** [z] S Ge 14:7; S Ex 17:14 [a] Dt 25:19; 1Sa 15:20; 30:17-20; 2Sa 8:12; 1Ch 18:11 **24:21** [b] S Ge 15:19 [c] Ps 37:27; Pr 1:33; Isa 32:18; Eze 34:27 **24:22** [d] S Ge 10:22 **24:24** [e] S Ge 10:4 [f] ver 22 [g] S Ge 10:21 [h] ver 20 **24:25** [i] S Nu 22:5 **25:1** [j] S Nu 21:16; Jos 2:1; Isa 66:11; Joel 3:18; Mic 6:5 [k] Jer 5:7; 7:9; 9:2; 1Co 10:8; Rev 2:14 [l] S Ge 19:37 [m] Nu 31:16 **25:2** [n] S Ex 32:6 [o] Ex 20:5; Dt 32:38; 1Co 10:20 **25:3** [p] Dt 4:19; Jdg 2:19; 1Ki 9:9; Jer 1:16; 44:3 [q] S Nu 23:28 **25:4** [r] Nu 7:2; 13:3 [s] 2Sa 21:6 [t] Dt 4:3 [u] Ex 32:12; Dt 13:17; Jos 7:26; 2Ki 23:26; 2Ch 28:11; 29:10; 30:8; Ezr 10:14; Jer 44:3 **25:5** [v] S Ex 32:27 [w] Hos 9:10 **25:6** [x] S Ge 25:2 [y] S Nu 14:1; Jdg 2:4; Ru 1:9; 1Sa 11:4; 2Sa 15:30; Ezr 10:1; Ps 126:6; Jer 41:6 **25:7** [z] S Ex 6:25; Jos 22:13; Jdg 20:28 [a] Jdg 5:8; 1Sa 13:19,22; 1Ki 18:28; Ps 35:3; 46:9; Joel 3:10; Mic 4:3 **25:8** [b] Ps 106:30 **25:9** [c] S Nu 14:37; 1Co 10:8 [d] Nu 31:16

[a] *17* Samaritan Pentateuch (see also Jer. 48:45); the meaning of the word in the Masoretic Text is uncertain. [b] *17* Or possibly *Moab, / batter* [c] *17* Or *all the noisy boasters* [d] *23* Masoretic Text; with a different word division of the Hebrew *A people will gather from the north.*

ruler. Israel's future Deliverer will be like a star (cf. 2Pe 1:19; Rev 22:16); he will wield a royal scepter (see Ge 49:10 and note) and bring victory over the enemies of his people (see v. 19). *Sheth.* Possibly the early inhabitants of Moab known as the Shutu people in ancient Egyptian documents (but see NIV text note; see also Jer 48:45 – 46 and note).

24:20 *Amalek was first.* The first to attack Israel and oppose the Lord's purpose with his people (see Ex 17:8 – 13; see also note on Ge 14:7).

24:21 *Kenites.* The name suggests a tribe of metal workers. In other passages the Kenites are allied with Israel (see, e.g., Jdg 1:16; see also Jdg 4:11; 1Sa 15:6 and notes). Since Moses' father-in-law was a Kenite but also associated with Midian (see Ex 2:16), it may be that Balaam's reference is to Midianites (see 22:4,7). *nest.* Hebrew *qen*, a wordplay on the word for Kenites (Hebrew *qeni*).

24:22 *Asshur.* Assyria.

24:24 *Kittim.* Probably ancient Kition in Cyprus. *they will subdue Asshur and Eber, but … ruin.* One nation will rise and supplant another, only to face its own doom. By contrast, there is the implied ongoing blessing on Israel, and their sure promise of a future deliverer who will have the final victory (vv. 17 – 19).

25:1 – 18 It is not until 31:8,16 (see note on 31:8) that we learn that the principal instigator of Israel's apostasy here was Balaam (see notes on 22:5,8). Failing to destroy Israel by means of a curse, Balaam seduced Israel by the Canaanite fertility rites of Baal.

25:1 *Shittim.* Another name for the region of Israel's staging for the conquest of Canaan; it was across the Jordan River opposite the ancient city of Jericho (see Jos 2:1 and note). *indulge in sexual immorality.* Israel's engagement in the fertility rites of Baal involved not only the evil of sexual immorality. It was also a breach of covenant with the Lord (see Ex 20:3 – 4 and notes), a worship of the gods of the land (vv. 2 – 3) and a foretaste of the people's ruin in the unfolding of their history.

25:4 *kill them and expose them in broad daylight.* The special display of the corpses would warn survivors of the consequences of sin.

25:6 *brought to his family a Midianite woman.* The contempt for the holy things and the word of the Lord shown by Zimri (v. 14) and his lover Cozbi (v. 15) is unimaginable.

25:9 *24,000.* The number of those who died because of the flagrant actions of the people in their worship of Baal exceeded even those who died in the rebellion of Korah and his allies (14,700; see 16:49 and note). Again, the large number of those who died fits well with the immense number of the people stated in the first census (see 1:46 and note) and the second (see 26:51 and note).

25:11 *he was as zealous as I am for my honor.* Cf. Ex 20:4 – 6. The zeal of Phinehas for the Lord's honor became the occa-

priest, has turned my anger away from the
Israelites;[e] for he was as zealous as I am
for my honor[f] among them, so that in my
zeal I did not put an end to them. 12There-
fore tell him I am making my covenant of
peace[g] with him. 13He and his descendants
will have a covenant of a lasting priesthood,[h] because he was zealous[i] for the
honor[j] of his God and made atonement[k]
for the Israelites."[l]

14The name of the Israelite who was
killed with the Midianite woman[m] was
Zimri son of Salu, the leader of a Sime-
onite family.[n] 15And the name of the Midianite woman who was put to death was
Cozbi[o] daughter of Zur, a tribal chief of a
Midianite family.[p]

16The LORD said to Moses,[q] 17"Treat the
Midianites[r] as enemies[s] and kill them,[t]
18because they treated you as enemies
when they deceived you in the affair of
Peor[u] and their sister Cozbi, the daughter
of a Midianite leader, the woman who was
killed when the plague came as a result
of Peor."

The Second Census

26 After the plague[v] the LORD said to
Moses and Eleazar son of Aaron, the
priest, 2"Take a census[w] of the whole Israelite community by families—all those
twenty years old or more who are able to
serve in the army[x] of Israel." 3So on the
plains of Moab[y] by the Jordan across from
Jericho,[a z] Moses and Eleazar the priest
spoke with them and said, 4"Take a census of the men twenty years old or more,
as the LORD commanded Moses."

25:11 [e] Ps 106:30 [f] Ex 20:5; Dt 32:16, 21; Ps 78:58 **25:12** [g] Isa 11:9; 54:10; Eze 34:25; 37:26; Mal 2:4, 5 **25:13** [h] S Ex 29:9 [i] 1Ki 19:10; 2Ki 10:16 [j] ver 11 [k] S Ex 29:36; S Ro 3:25 [l] Ps 106:31; Jer 33:18 **25:14** [m] ver 6 [n] S Nu 1:6 **25:15** [o] ver 18 [p] Nu 31:8; Jos 13:21; Hab 3:7 **25:16** [q] Nu 31:7 **25:17** [r] Nu 31:1-3 [s] Ex 23:22; Jdg 2:16-18; Ne 9:27; Ps 8:2; 21:8; 74:23 [t] Dt 21:1; 1Sa 17:9, 35; 2Ki 9:27; 10:25 **25:18** [u] S Nu 23:28 **26:1** [v] S Nu 14:37; 25:8 **26:2** [w] Ex 30:11-16 [x] S Nu 1:3 **26:3** [y] ver 63; Nu 33:48; Jos 13:32 [z] Nu 22:1
26:4 [a] S Ex 6:14; S 13:3 **26:5** [b] Nu 1:20 [c] S Ge 46:9 [d] 1Ch 5:3 **26:6** [e] 1Ch 5:3 [f] Ge 46:9 **26:9** [g] Nu 16:1 [h] Nu 1:16 [i] S Nu 16:2

These were the Israelites who came out
of Egypt:[a]

5The descendants of Reuben,[b] the firstborn
son of Israel, were:
through Hanoch,[c] the Hanochite clan;
through Pallu,[d] the Palluite clan;
6through Hezron,[e] the Hezronite clan;
through Carmi,[f] the Carmite clan.
7These were the clans of Reuben; those
numbered were 43,730.
8The son of Pallu was Eliab, 9and the
sons of Eliab[g] were Nemuel, Dathan
and Abiram. The same Dathan and Abiram were the community[h] officials who
rebelled against Moses and Aaron and
were among Korah's followers when they
rebelled against the LORD.[i] 10The earth
opened its mouth and swallowed them[j]
along with Korah, whose followers died
when the fire devoured the 250 men.[k] And
they served as a warning sign.[l] 11The line
of Korah,[m] however, did not die out.[n]

12The descendants of Simeon by their
clans were:
through Nemuel,[o] the Nemuelite
clan;
through Jamin,[p] the Jaminite clan;
through Jakin, the Jakinite clan;
13through Zerah,[q] the Zerahite clan;
through Shaul, the Shaulite clan.
14These were the clans of Simeon;[r] there
were 22,200 men.[s]

[a] *3* Hebrew *Jordan of Jericho*; possibly an ancient name for the Jordan River; also in verse 63

26:10 [j] S Ex 15:12 [k] S Nu 16:35 [l] S Ex 3:12; S Nu 16:38 **26:11** [m] Ex 6:24 [n] Nu 16:33; Dt 5:9; 24:16; 2Ki 14:6; 2Ch 25:4; Eze 18:20 **26:12** [o] S Ge 46:10 [p] 1Ch 4:24 **26:13** [q] S Ge 46:10 **26:14** [r] S Ge 46:10 [s] Nu 1:23

sion for the Lord's covenanting with him and his descendants as God's true priests (see note on Ge 9:9; see also v. 12 and chart, p. 19). This son of Eleazar contrasts with the casual wickedness of his uncles, Nadab and Abihu (see Lev 10:1–3 and notes).

25:12 *covenant of peace.* See Ps 106:31; cf. note on Isa 54:10.

25:17 *Treat the Midianites as enemies.* Because of their active participation in the seduction of the Israelites. Midianites had been in league with Balak from the beginning of the confrontation (see 22:4,7) and became the objects of a holy war (see 31:1–24 and note).

26:1–51 The first census of those who were mustered for the war of conquest had been taken over 38 years earlier. That first generation of men 20 years old or more had nearly all died. It was now time for the new generation to be numbered and mustered for the campaign that awaited them. The aged Moses was joined in the task this time by his nephew Eleazar; Aaron was dead (see 20:28). In this second census the prominent clans of each tribe are listed. The numbers of most of the tribes increase. Reuben is one of the tribes that shows a decline. It is possible that the slight reduction of the families of Reuben was brought about by the judgment on their members during the rebellion of Korah and his Reubenite allies (see note on v. 9). In the intervening years the family of Reuben had nearly caught up with its former numbers (see note on v. 14). Note the comparison of the numbers of each tribe from the first census to the second:

Tribe	*First Census*	*Second Census*
Reuben	46,500	43,730
Simeon	59,300	22,200
Gad	45,650	40,500
Judah	74,600	76,500
Issachar	54,400	64,300
Zebulun	57,400	60,500
Ephraim	40,500	32,500
Manasseh	32,200	52,700
Benjamin	35,400	45,600
Dan	62,700	64,400
Asher	41,500	53,400
Naphtali	53,400	45,400
Total	603,550	601,730

26:9 *Dathan and Abiram.* The listing of Reuben's families becomes an occasion to remind the reader of the part that certain of their number had in Korah's rebellion (see 16:1–7 and note; cf. Jude 11 and note).

26:14 *22,200.* The greatest loss was in the tribe of Simeon (down from 59,300). Zimri was from the house of Simeon (25:14). Perhaps most of the 24,000 who died in the plague of that time were from Simeon. The judgment was so recent that the tribe had not had time to recover, as had the tribe of Reuben (see note on vv. 1–51).

15The descendants of Gad by their clans
were:
through Zephon,[t] the Zephonite clan;
through Haggi, the Haggite clan;
through Shuni, the Shunite clan;
16through Ozni, the Oznite clan;
through Eri, the Erite clan;
17through Arodi,[a] the Arodite clan;
through Areli, the Arelite clan.
18These were the clans of Gad;[u] those
numbered were 40,500.
19Er[v] and Onan[w] were sons of Judah, but
they died[x] in Canaan.
20The descendants of Judah by their clans
were:
through Shelah,[y] the Shelanite clan;
through Perez,[z] the Perezite clan;
through Zerah, the Zerahite clan.[a]
21The descendants of Perez[b] were:
through Hezron,[c] the Hezronite
clan;
through Hamul, the Hamulite clan.
22These were the clans of Judah;[d] those
numbered were 76,500.
23The descendants of Issachar by their
clans were:
through Tola,[e] the Tolaite clan;
through Puah, the Puite[b] clan;
24through Jashub,[f] the Jashubite clan;
through Shimron, the Shimronite
clan.
25These were the clans of Issachar;[g] those
numbered were 64,300.
26The descendants of Zebulun[h] by their
clans were:
through Sered, the Seredite clan;
through Elon, the Elonite clan;
through Jahleel, the Jahleelite clan.
27These were the clans of Zebulun;[i] those
numbered were 60,500.
28The descendants of Joseph[j] by their clans
through Manasseh and Ephraim[k] were:
29The descendants of Manasseh:[l]
through Makir,[m] the Makirite clan
(Makir was the father of Gilead[n]);
through Gilead, the Gileadite clan.
30These were the descendants of Gilead:[o]
through Iezer,[p] the Iezerite clan;
through Helek, the Helekite clan;
31through Asriel, the Asrielite clan;
through Shechem, the Shechemite
clan;
32through Shemida, the Shemidaite
clan;
through Hepher, the Hepherite
clan.
33(Zelophehad[q] son of Hepher had
no sons;[r] he had only daughters,
whose names were Mahlah, Noah,
Hoglah, Milcah and Tirzah.)[s]
34These were the clans of Manasseh; those
numbered were 52,700.[t]
35These were the descendants of Ephraim[u]
by their clans:
through Shuthelah, the Shuthelahite
clan;
through Beker, the Bekerite clan;
through Tahan, the Tahanite clan.
36These were the descendants of Shuthelah:
through Eran, the Eranite clan.
37These were the clans of Ephraim;[v] those
numbered were 32,500.
These were the descendants of Joseph by
their clans.
38The descendants of Benjamin[w] by their
clans were:
through Bela, the Belaite clan;
through Ashbel, the Ashbelite clan;
through Ahiram, the Ahiramite clan;
39through Shupham,[c] the Shuphamite
clan;
through Hupham, the Huphamite
clan.
40The descendants of Bela through Ard[x]
and Naaman were:
through Ard,[d] the Ardite clan;
through Naaman, the Naamite
clan.
41These were the clans of Benjamin;[y] those
numbered were 45,600.
42These were the descendants of Dan[z] by
their clans:[a]
through Shuham,[b] the Shuhamite
clan.
These were the clans of Dan: 43All of them
were Shuhamite clans; and those numbered were 64,400.
44The descendants of Asher[c] by their clans
were:
through Imnah, the Imnite clan;

26:15 [t]Ge 46:16
26:18 [u]S Ge 30:11; S Nu 1:25; S Jos 13:24-28
26:19 [v]S Ge 38:3 [w]S Ge 38:4 [x]Ge 38:7
26:20 [y]S Ge 38:5 [z]S Ge 38:29 [a]Jos 7:17
26:21 [b]S Ge 38:29 [c]Ru 4:19; 1Ch 2:9
26:22 [d]Nu 1:27
26:23 [e]S Ge 46:13
26:24 [f]Ge 46:13
26:25 [g]S Ge 30:18
26:26 [h]Nu 1:30
26:27 [i]S Ge 30:20
26:28 [j]Nu 1:32; 36:1 [k]S Ge 41:52
26:29 [l]Nu 1:34 [m]S Ge 50:23 [n]Jdg 11:1
26:30 [o]Nu 27:1; 36:1; 1Ch 7:14,17 [p]Jos 17:2; Jdg 6:11; 8:2
26:33 [q]Nu 27:1; 36:2; Jos 17:3; 1Ch 7:15 [r]Nu 27:3 [s]Nu 36:11
26:34 [t]Nu 1:35
26:35 [u]Nu 1:32
26:37 [v]S Nu 1:33
26:38 [w]Ge 46:21; Nu 1:36; 1Ch 8:40
26:40 [x]S Ge 46:21
26:41 [y]Nu 1:37
26:42 [z]Nu 1:38 [a]Jdg 18:19 [b]Ge 46:23
26:44 [c]S Nu 1:40

[a] *17* Samaritan Pentateuch and Syriac (see also Gen. 46:16); Masoretic Text *Arod* [b] *23* Samaritan Pentateuch, Septuagint, Vulgate and Syriac (see also 1 Chron. 7:1); Masoretic Text *through Puvah, the Punite* [c] *39* A few manuscripts of the Masoretic Text, Samaritan Pentateuch, Vulgate and Syriac (see also Septuagint); most manuscripts of the Masoretic Text *Shephupham* [d] *40* Samaritan Pentateuch and Vulgate (see also Septuagint); Masoretic Text does not have *through Ard.*

26:19 *Er and Onan.* The names of the evil sons of Judah had not been forgotten, but they had no heritage (see Ge 38:1 – 10).
26:20 *Perez.* The line of David and Jesus would be traced through him (see Ru 4:18 – 22 and note; Mt 1:1 – 3).
26:29,35 *Manasseh … Ephraim.* The order of the tribes is the same as in ch. 1, except for the inversion of Ephraim and Manasseh, perhaps due to the much larger relative growth of Manasseh's tribe (see note on vv. 1 – 51; see also note on v. 34).
26:33 *Zelophehad … daughters.* See 27:1 – 11; 36:1 – 13 and notes.
26:34 *52,700.* The greatest gain was in the tribe of Manasseh (up from 32,200). The reason for this increase is not known.

through Ishvi, the Ishvite clan;
through Beriah, the Beriite clan;
45 and through the descendants of Beriah:
through Heber, the Heberite clan;
through Malkiel, the Malkielite clan.
46 (Asher had a daughter named Serah.)
47 These were the clans of Asher;[d] those
numbered were 53,400.

48 The descendants of Naphtali[e] by their
clans were:
through Jahzeel, the Jahzeelite clan;
through Guni, the Gunite clan;
49 through Jezer, the Jezerite clan;
through Shillem, the Shillemite clan.
50 These were the clans of Naphtali;[f] those
numbered were 45,400.[g]

51 The total number of the men of Israel
was 601,730.[h]

52 The LORD said to Moses, 53 "The land
is to be allotted to them as an inheritance
based on the number of names.[i] 54 To a
larger group give a larger inheritance, and
to a smaller group a smaller one; each is to
receive its inheritance according to the
number[j] of those listed.[k] 55 Be sure that
the land is distributed by lot.[l] What each
group inherits will be according to the
names for its ancestral tribe. 56 Each inheritance is to be distributed by lot among the
larger and smaller groups."

57 These were the Levites[m] who were counted by their clans:
through Gershon, the Gershonite clan;
through Kohath, the Kohathite clan;
through Merari, the Merarite clan.
58 These also were Levite clans:
the Libnite clan,
the Hebronite clan,
the Mahlite clan,
the Mushite clan,
the Korahite clan.
(Kohath was the forefather of Amram;[n] 59 the name of Amram's wife was
Jochebed,[o] a descendant of Levi, who
was born to the Levites[a] in Egypt. To
Amram she bore Aaron, Moses[p] and
their sister[q] Miriam.[r] 60 Aaron was the
father of Nadab and Abihu, Eleazar
and Ithamar.[s] 61 But Nadab and Abihu[t] died when they made an offering
before the LORD with unauthorized
fire.)[u]

62 All the male Levites a month old or more
numbered 23,000.[v] They were not counted[w] along with the other Israelites because
they received no inheritance[x] among
them.[y]

63 These are the ones counted[z] by Moses
and Eleazar the priest when they counted
the Israelites on the plains of Moab[a] by the
Jordan across from Jericho.[b] 64 Not one of
them was among those counted[c] by Moses
and Aaron[d] the priest when they counted
the Israelites in the Desert of Sinai. 65 For
the LORD had told those Israelites they
would surely die in the desert,[e] and not
one of them was left except Caleb[f] son of
Jephunneh and Joshua son of Nun.[g]

26:47 [d] Nu 1:41
26:48 [e] S Ge 30:8
26:50 [f] Nu 1:43 [g] Nu 1:42
26:51 [h] S Ex 12:37
26:53 [i] ver 55; Jos 11:23; 14:1; Eze 45:8
26:54 [j] Nu 33:54 [k] Nu 35:8
26:55 [l] S Lev 16:8
26:57 [m] S Ge 46:11
26:58 [n] Ex 6:20
26:59 [o] S Ex 2:1 [p] S Ex 6:20 [q] S Ex 2:4 [r] S Ex 15:20
26:60 [s] Ex 6:23
26:61 [t] S Lev 10:1-2 [u] Nu 3:4
26:62 [v] Nu 3:39 [w] Nu 1:47 [x] S Nu 18:23 [y] S Nu 2:33
26:63 [z] S Nu 1:19 [a] S ver 3 [b] Nu 22:1
26:64 [c] S Nu 14:29 [d] Nu 1:44
26:65 [e] Nu 14:28; 1Co 10:5 [f] Nu 13:6 [g] S Nu 11:28
27:1 [h] S Nu 26:33 [i] Jos 17:2,3 [j] S Nu 26:30 [k] S Ge 50:23; 1Ch 2:21
27:2 [l] Ex 40:2,17 [m] S Nu 9:6 [n] Nu 1:16; 31:13; 32:2; 36:1
27:3 [o] Nu 26:65 [p] Nu 16:2 [q] Nu 26:33
27:5 [r] S Ge 25:22; S Ex 18:19 [s] S Nu 9:8

Zelophehad's Daughters

27:1-11pp — Nu 36:1-12

27 The daughters of Zelophehad[h] son of
Hepher,[i] the son of Gilead,[j] the son
of Makir,[k] the son of Manasseh, belonged
to the clans of Manasseh son of Joseph.
The names of the daughters were Mahlah,
Noah, Hoglah, Milcah and Tirzah. They
approached 2 the entrance to the Tent of
Meeting[l] and stood before Moses,[m] Eleazar the priest, the leaders[n] and the whole
assembly, and said, 3 "Our father died in
the desert.[o] He was not among Korah's followers, who banded together against the
LORD,[p] but he died for his own sin and left
no sons.[q] 4 Why should our father's name
disappear from his clan because he had no
son? Give us property among our father's
relatives."
5 So Moses brought their case[r] before the
LORD[s] 6 and the LORD said to him, 7 "What

[a] 59 Or *Jochebed, a daughter of Levi, who was born to Levi*

26:46 *daughter named Serah.* The listing of this solitary daughter is striking.
26:51 *601,730.* Despite all that the people had been through during the years of desert experience, their total number was nearly the same as that of those who were first numbered. This remarkable fact is to be regarded as the blessing of the Lord, in fulfillment of his many promises to give numerical strength to the people descended from Abraham through Jacob (see note on Ge 12:2–3). This grand total and its parts are in accord with the general pattern of the numbers in the book (see note on 1:46).
26:53–56 Larger tribes would receive larger shares, but decisions of place would be made by lot (see v. 56; 33:54).
26:57 *Levites.* As in the first census (ch. 3), the Levites were counted separately.
27:1–11 The daughters of a man who had no son (see 26:33) were concerned about their rights of inheritance and the preservation of their father's name in the land (v. 4). Their action in approaching Moses, Eleazar and the leaders of the nation was unprecedented, an act of courage and conviction.
27:3 *he died for his own sin.* A particular case from among those who died in the desert (see 26:64–65). These pious women had a sound understanding of the nature of the desert experience and a just claim for their family.
27:5 *Moses brought their case before the LORD.* This verse indicates how case law might have operated in Israel. The general laws would be proclaimed. Then legitimate exceptions or special considerations would come to the elders, and perhaps to Moses himself. He then would await a decision from

Zelophehad’s daughters are saying is right.
You must certainly give them property as
an inheritance[t] among their father’s relatives and turn their father’s inheritance
over to them.[u]
8“Say to the Israelites, ‘If a man dies and
leaves no son, turn his inheritance over to
his daughter. 9If he has no daughter, give
his inheritance to his brothers. 10If he has
no brothers, give his inheritance to his father’s brothers. 11If his father had no brothers, give his inheritance to the nearest relative in his clan, that he may possess it.
This is to be a legal requirement[v] for the Israelites, as the LORD commanded Moses.’ ”

Joshua to Succeed Moses

12Then the LORD said to Moses, “Go up
this mountain[w] in the Abarim range[x] and
see the land[y] I have given the Israelites.[z]
13After you have seen it, you too will be
gathered to your people,[a] as your brother Aaron[b] was, 14for when the community rebelled at the waters in the Desert of
Zin,[c] both of you disobeyed my command
to honor me as holy[d] before their eyes.”
(These were the waters of Meribah[e] Kadesh, in the Desert of Zin.)
15Moses said to the LORD, 16“May the
LORD, the God of the spirits of all mankind,[f] appoint a man over this community
17to go out and come in before them, one
who will lead them out and bring them in,
so the LORD’s people will not be like sheep
without a shepherd.”[g]
18So the LORD said to Moses, “Take Joshua son of Nun, a man in whom is the spirit,[a][h] and lay your hand on him.[i] 19Have
him stand before Eleazar the priest and the
entire assembly and commission him[j] in
their presence.[k] 20Give him some of your
authority so the whole Israelite community
will obey him.[l] 21He is to stand before Eleazar the priest, who will obtain decisions
for him by inquiring[m] of the Urim[n] before
the LORD. At his command he and the entire community of the Israelites will go out,
and at his command they will come in.”

22Moses did as the LORD commanded
him. He took Joshua and had him stand
before Eleazar the priest and the whole assembly. 23Then he laid his hands on him
and commissioned him,[o] as the LORD instructed through Moses.

Daily Offerings

28 The LORD said to Moses, 2“Give this
command to the Israelites and say
to them: ‘See that you present to me at
the appointed time[p] the food[q] for my offerings made by fire, as an aroma pleasing
to me.’[r] 3Say to them: ‘This is the offering
made by fire that you are to present to the
LORD: two lambs a year old without defect,[s] as a regular burnt offering each day.[t]
4Prepare one lamb in the morning and the
other at twilight,[u] 5together with a grain
offering[v] of a tenth of an ephah[b] of fine
flour[w] mixed with a quarter of a hin[c] of
oil[x] from pressed olives. 6This is the regular burnt offering[y] instituted at Mount
Sinai[z] as a pleasing aroma, an offering
made to the LORD by fire.[a] 7The accompanying drink offering[b] is to be a quarter of
a hin of fermented drink[c] with each lamb.
Pour out the drink offering to the LORD at
the sanctuary.[d] 8Prepare the second lamb
at twilight,[e] along with the same kind of
grain offering and drink offering that you
prepare in the morning.[f] This is an offering made by fire, an aroma pleasing to the
LORD.[g]

Sabbath Offerings

9“ ‘On the Sabbath[h] day, make an offering of two lambs a year old without defect,[i] together with its drink offering and a
grain offering of two-tenths of an ephah[d][j]
of fine flour mixed with oil.[k] 10This is the

[a] 18 Or *Spirit* [b] 5 That is, probably about 2 quarts (about 2 liters); also in verses 13, 21 and 29 [c] 5 That is, probably about 1 quart (about 1 liter); also in verses 7 and 14 [d] 9 That is, probably about 4 quarts (about 4.5 liters); also in verses 12, 20 and 28

27:7 [t] Job 42:15 [u] ver 8; Jos 17:4 **27:11** [v] Nu 35:29 **27:12** [w] Nu 23:14 [x] Nu 33:47; Jer 22:20 [y] Dt 3:23-27; 32:48-52 [z] S Lev 14:34 **27:13** [a] Nu 20:12; 31:2; Dt 4:22; 31:14; 32:50; 1Ki 2:1 [b] Nu 20:28 **27:14** [c] S Nu 20:1, 2-5 [d] S Nu 20:12 [e] S Ex 17:7 **27:16** [f] S Nu 16:22; S Job 21:20 **27:17** [g] 1Ki 22:17; 2Ch 18:16; Eze 34:5; Zec 10:2; S Mt 9:36 **27:18** [h] S Ge 41:38; Nu 11:25-29 [i] ver 23; Dt 34:9; Ac 6:6 **27:19** [j] ver 23; Dt 3:28; 31:14, 23 [k] Dt 31:7 **27:20** [l] Jos 1:16, 17 **27:21** [m] S Ge 25:22; Jos 9:14; Ps 106:13; Isa 8:19; Hag 1:13; Mal 2:7; 3:1 [n] S Ex 28:30 **27:23** [o] S ver 19 **28:2** [p] Lev 23:1-44 [q] S Lev 3:11 [r] Lev 1:9 **28:3** [s] S Ex 12:5 [t] Ex 29:38; Am 4:4 **28:4** [u] S Ex 29:39 **28:5** [v] Nu 29:6 [w] Lev 6:20 [x] S Lev 2:1 **28:6** [y] Lev 1:3 [z] Ex 19:3 [a] S Lev 1:9 **28:7** [b] Nu 6:15 [c] S Lev 10:9; S 23:13 [d] S Lev 3:7; Nu 3:28 **28:8** [e] S Ex 29:39 [f] S Lev 3:7 [g] ver 2; Lev 1:9 **28:9** [h] S Ex 20:10; Mt 12:5 [i] ver 3 [j] S Lev 23:13 [k] ver 5

the Lord. In this case, the Lord gave a favorable decision for these women. Ch. 36 provides an appendix to this account.

27:12 – 23 The juxtaposition of the story of Zelophehad’s daughters’ request for an inheritance in the land (vv. 1 – 11) and the Lord’s words to Moses about his own exclusion from the land (vv. 12 – 14) is striking. Provisions are made for exceptions and irregularities in the inheritance laws, but there is no provision for Moses. His sin at the waters of Meribah at Kadesh (see 20:1 – 13 and note on 20:11) was always before him.

27:14 *honor me as holy.* See 20:12 and note.

27:16 *appoint a man.* Moses’ reaction to this reassertion of his restriction is a prayer for his successor.

27:18 *Take Joshua.* As Moses and Aaron needed to determine the true successor of Aaron before his death (20:22 – 29), so the true successor of Moses also needed to be established. Joshua and Caleb were the two heroes in the darkest hour of Israel’s apostasy (chs. 13 – 14). It was fitting that the Lord selected one of them (cf. Ex 17:9 – 14 and note on 17:9; 24:13; 32:17; 33:11).

27:20 *Give him some of your authority.* The transition from Moses’ leadership to that of any successor would be difficult. The change would be made smoother by a gradual shift of power while Moses was still alive.

27:21 *Urim.* See notes on Ex 28:30; 1Sa 2:28.

28:1 — 29:40 These chapters attest to the all-pervasiveness of sacrifice in the life of the people and to the enormity of the work of the priests. Perhaps the reason for these passages at this time is to give continuity to the impending transition from the leadership of Moses to that of Joshua (27:12 – 23).

28:1 – 8 See Ex 29:38 – 41; see also Lev 1 – 7 and notes.

28:9 – 10 The Sabbath offerings were in addition to the daily offerings.

burnt offering for every Sabbath,[l] in addition to the regular burnt offering[m] and its drink offering.

Monthly Offerings

11 " 'On the first of every month,[n] present to the LORD a burnt offering of two young bulls,[o] one ram[p] and seven male lambs a year old, all without defect.[q] 12 With each bull there is to be a grain offering[r] of three-tenths of an ephah[a][s] of fine flour mixed with oil; with the ram, a grain offering of two-tenths[t] of an ephah of fine flour mixed with oil; 13 and with each lamb, a grain offering[u] of a tenth[v] of an ephah of fine flour mixed with oil. This is for a burnt offering,[w] a pleasing aroma, an offering made to the LORD[x] by fire. 14 With each bull there is to be a drink offering[y] of half a hin[b] of wine; with the ram, a third of a hin[c]; and with each lamb, a quarter of a hin. This is the monthly burnt offering to be made at each new moon[z] during the year. 15 Besides the regular burnt offering[a] with its drink offering, one male goat[b] is to be presented to the LORD as a sin offering.[c]

The Passover

28:16-25pp — Ex 12:14-20; Lev 23:4-8; Dt 16:1-8

16 " 'On the fourteenth day of the first month the LORD's Passover[d] is to be held. 17 On the fifteenth day of this month there is to be a festival; for seven days[e] eat bread made without yeast.[f] 18 On the first day hold a sacred assembly and do no regular work.[g] 19 Present to the LORD an offering made by fire,[h] a burnt offering of two young bulls, one ram and seven male lambs a year old, all without defect.[i] 20 With each bull prepare a grain offering of three-tenths of an ephah[j] of fine flour mixed with oil; with the ram, two-tenths;[k] 21 and with each of the seven lambs, one-tenth.[l] 22 Include one male goat as a sin offering[m] to make atonement for you.[n] 23 Prepare these in addition to the regular morning burnt offering. 24 In this way prepare the food for the offering made by fire every day for seven days as an aroma pleasing to the LORD;[o] it is to be prepared in addition to the regular burnt offering and its drink offering. 25 On the seventh day hold a sacred assembly and do no regular work.

28:10 [l] S Lev 23:38 [m] ver 3
28:11 [n] S Nu 10:10 [o] S Nu 7:15 [p] S Lev 5:15 [q] Lev 1:3
28:12 [r] S Nu 15:6; S 29:3 [s] Nu 15:9 [t] ver 20
28:13 [u] S Lev 6:14 [v] ver 21 [w] S Nu 15:3 [x] Lev 1:9
28:14 [y] S Nu 15:7 [z] ver 11; 2Ch 2:4; Ezr 3:5
28:15 [a] ver 3, 23, 24 [b] ver 30 [c] Lev 4:3; Nu 29:16, 19
28:16 [d] S Ex 12:11; 2Ch 30:13; 35:1
28:17 [e] S Ex 12:19 [f] S Ex 12:15
28:18 [g] S Ex 12:16
28:19 [h] S Lev 1:9 [i] ver 11
28:20 [j] S Lev 14:10 [k] ver 12
28:21 [l] ver 13
28:22 [m] Lev 4:3; Ro 8:3 [n] S Nu 15:28
28:24 [o] Lev 1:9
28:26 [p] S Ex 34:22 [q] S Ex 23:16 [r] ver 18
28:27 [s] ver 19
28:28 [t] ver 12
28:29 [u] ver 13
28:30 [v] ver 15
28:31 [w] ver 3, 19
29:1 [x] Nu 28:18
29:2 [y] Nu 28:2 [z] Lev 1:9; Nu 28:11 [a] ver 36 [b] Lev 1:3; Nu 28:3
29:3 [c] ver 14; Nu 28:12
29:4 [d] Nu 28:13
29:5 [e] Nu 28:15
29:6 [f] Nu 28:11 [g] Nu 28:3 [h] Nu 28:5 [i] Nu 28:7 [j] Lev 1:9; Nu 28:2

Feast of Weeks

28:26-31pp — Lev 23:15-22; Dt 16:9-12

26 " 'On the day of firstfruits,[p] when you present to the LORD an offering of new grain during the Feast of Weeks,[q] hold a sacred assembly and do no regular work.[r] 27 Present a burnt offering of two young bulls, one ram and seven male lambs a year old as an aroma pleasing to the LORD.[s] 28 With each bull there is to be a grain offering of three-tenths of an ephah of fine flour mixed with oil; with the ram, two-tenths;[t] 29 and with each of the seven lambs, one-tenth.[u] 30 Include one male goat[v] to make atonement for you. 31 Prepare these together with their drink offerings, in addition to the regular burnt offering[w] and its grain offering. Be sure the animals are without defect.

Feast of Trumpets

29:1-6pp — Lev 23:23-25

29 " 'On the first day of the seventh month hold a sacred assembly and do no regular work.[x] It is a day for you to sound the trumpets. 2 As an aroma pleasing to the LORD,[y] prepare a burnt offering[z] of one young bull, one ram and seven male lambs a year old,[a] all without defect.[b] 3 With the bull prepare a grain offering[c] of three-tenths of an ephah[d] of fine flour mixed with oil; with the ram, two-tenths[e]; 4 and with each of the seven lambs, one-tenth.[f][d] 5 Include one male goat[e] as a sin offering to make atonement for you. 6 These are in addition to the monthly[f] and daily burnt offerings[g] with their grain offerings[h] and drink offerings[i] as specified. They are offerings made to the LORD by fire—a pleasing aroma.[j]

Day of Atonement

29:7-11pp — Lev 16:2-34; 23:26-32

7 " 'On the tenth day of this seventh month hold a sacred assembly. You must

[a] 12 That is, probably about 6 quarts (about 6.5 liters); also in verses 20 and 28 [b] 14 That is, probably about 2 quarts (about 2 liters) [c] 14 That is, probably about 1 1/4 quarts (about 1.2 liters) [d] 3 That is, probably about 6 quarts (about 6.5 liters); also in verses 9 and 14 [e] 3 That is, probably about 4 quarts (about 4.5 liters); also in verses 9 and 14 [f] 4 That is, probably about 2 quarts (about 2 liters); also in verses 10 and 15

28:11–15 The sacrifices at the beginning of the month were of great significance. These were times for celebration and blowing of trumpets in worship (see 10:10 and note).

28:16–25 The priests are instructed as to the proper preparation for the Passover in the first month of the year. Passover is also associated with the Feast of Unleavened Bread (see Ex 12:15 and note on 12:17; Lev 23:4–8). The number 7 (and 14, its multiple) recurs frequently in the paragraph.

28:26–31 The Feast of Weeks came 50 days after the Feast of Unleavened Bread (see Lev 23:9–22); from this number the term "Pentecost" (meaning "fifty") was used in the NT (see Ac 2:1 and note).

29:1–6 The Feast of Trumpets came at the beginning of the seventh month, a busy month for the worship of the Lord in holy festivals (see Lev 23:23–25; see also chart, pp. 178–179). Later in Jewish tradition this feast commemorated the New Year (Rosh Hashanah). The trumpet used was the ram's horn (*shophar*).

29:7–11 The Feast of Trumpets leads into the Day of Atonement, a time of confession, contrition and celebration (see Lev 16:1–34 and note; 23:26–32).

deny yourselves[a][k] and do no work.[l] 8Pre-
sent as an aroma pleasing to the LORD a
burnt offering of one young bull, one ram
and seven male lambs a year old, all without defect.[m] 9With the bull prepare a grain
offering[n] of three-tenths of an ephah of
fine flour mixed with oil; with the ram,
two-tenths;[o] 10and with each of the sev-
en lambs, one-tenth.[p] 11Include one male
goat[q] as a sin offering, in addition to the
sin offering for atonement and the regular
burnt offering[r] with its grain offering, and
their drink offerings.[s]

Feast of Tabernacles

29:12-39pp — Lev 23:33-43; Dt 16:13-17

12" 'On the fifteenth day of the seventh[t]
month,[u] hold a sacred assembly and do
no regular work. Celebrate a festival to the
LORD for seven days. 13Present an offering
made by fire as an aroma pleasing to the
LORD,[v] a burnt offering of thirteen young
bulls, two rams and fourteen male lambs
a year old, all without defect.[w] 14With each
of the thirteen bulls prepare a grain offering[x] of three-tenths of an ephah of fine
flour mixed with oil; with each of the two
rams, two-tenths; 15and with each of the
fourteen lambs, one-tenth.[y] 16Include one
male goat as a sin offering,[z] in addition
to the regular burnt offering with its grain
offering and drink offering.[a]
17" 'On the second day[b] prepare twelve
young bulls, two rams and fourteen male
lambs a year old, all without defect.[c]
18With the bulls, rams and lambs, prepare
their grain offerings[d] and drink offerings[e]
according to the number specified.[f] 19In-
clude one male goat as a sin offering,[g]
in addition to the regular burnt offering[h]
with its grain offering, and their drink offerings.[i]
20" 'On the third day prepare eleven
bulls, two rams and fourteen male lambs
a year old, all without defect.[j] 21With the
bulls, rams and lambs, prepare their grain
offerings and drink offerings according to
the number specified.[k] 22Include one male
goat as a sin offering, in addition to the
regular burnt offering with its grain offering and drink offering.
23" 'On the fourth day prepare ten bulls,
two rams and fourteen male lambs a year
old, all without defect. 24With the bulls,
rams and lambs, prepare their grain offerings and drink offerings according to the
number specified. 25Include one male goat
as a sin offering, in addition to the regular
burnt offering with its grain offering and
drink offering.
26" 'On the fifth day prepare nine bulls,
two rams and fourteen male lambs a year
old, all without defect. 27With the bulls,
rams and lambs, prepare their grain offerings and drink offerings according to the
number specified. 28Include one male goat
as a sin offering, in addition to the regular
burnt offering with its grain offering and
drink offering.
29" 'On the sixth day prepare eight bulls,
two rams and fourteen male lambs a year
old, all without defect. 30With the bulls,
rams and lambs, prepare their grain offerings and drink offerings according to the
number specified. 31Include one male goat
as a sin offering, in addition to the regular
burnt offering with its grain offering and
drink offering.
32" 'On the seventh day prepare seven
bulls, two rams and fourteen male lambs
a year old, all without defect. 33With the
bulls, rams and lambs, prepare their grain
offerings and drink offerings according to
the number specified. 34Include one male
goat as a sin offering, in addition to the
regular burnt offering with its grain offering and drink offering.
35" 'On the eighth day hold an assembly[l] and do no regular work. 36Present an
offering made by fire as an aroma pleasing to the LORD,[m] a burnt offering of one
bull, one ram and seven male lambs a year
old,[n] all without defect. 37With the bull,
the ram and the lambs, prepare their grain
offerings and drink offerings according to
the number specified. 38Include one male
goat as a sin offering, in addition to the
regular burnt offering with its grain offering and drink offering.
39" 'In addition to what you vow[o] and
your freewill offerings,[p] prepare these for
the LORD at your appointed feasts:[q] your
burnt offerings,[r] grain offerings, drink offerings and fellowship offerings.[b][s] ' "
40Moses told the Israelites all that the
LORD commanded him.

Vows

30 Moses said to the heads of the tribes
of Israel:[t] "This is what the LORD
commands: 2When a man makes a vow
to the LORD or takes an oath to obligate

29:7 [k] Ac 27:9 [l] S Ex 31:15 **29:8** [m] ver 2 **29:9** [n] S ver 3,18 [o] Nu 28:12 **29:10** [p] Nu 28:13 **29:11** [q] ver 5; Nu 28:15 [r] S Lev 16:3 [s] S ver 6 **29:12** [t] 1Ki 8:2; 12:32 [u] S Lev 23:24 **29:13** [v] ver 2; Nu 28:2 [w] Nu 28:3 **29:14** [x] S ver 3; S Nu 15:6 **29:15** [y] ver 4; Nu 28:13 **29:16** [z] ver 5; S Nu 28:15 [a] ver 6 **29:17** [b] Lev 23:36 [c] ver 2; Nu 28:3 **29:18** [d] S ver 9 [e] Nu 28:7 [f] Nu 15:4-12 **29:19** [g] S Nu 28:15 [h] Nu 28:3 [i] ver 6 **29:20** [j] S ver 17 **29:21** [k] S ver 18 **29:35** [l] S Lev 23:36 **29:36** [m] Lev 1:9 [n] ver 2 **29:39** [o] Nu 6:2 [p] S Lev 7:16 [q] S Lev 23:2 [r] Lev 1:3; 1Ch 23:31; 2Ch 31:3 [s] Lev 3:1 **30:1** [t] S Nu 1:4

[a] 7 Or *must fast* [b] 39 Traditionally *peace offerings*

29:12–34 In the seventh month the Feast of Trumpets took place on the first day, the Day of Atonement occurred on the tenth day, and the Feast of Tabernacles began on the 15th day and lasted for seven days (see Lev 23:33–44). Each day of the Feast of Tabernacles had its own order for sacrifice (see note on Zec 14:16).

29:40 *Moses told the Israelites.* The recapitulation of these festivals was a necessary part of the transfer of power from Moses to Joshua.

30:1–16 The principal OT passage on vows (see Dt 23:21–23). A vow is not to be made rashly (cf. Ecc 5:1–7), and a vow to the Lord must be kept (see Jdg 11:30,35 and notes).

himself by a pledge, he must not break his
word but must do everything he said.[u]
3"When a young woman still living in
her father's house makes a vow to the
LORD or obligates herself by a pledge 4and
her father hears about her vow or pledge
but says nothing to her, then all her vows
and every pledge by which she obligated
herself will stand.[v] 5But if her father forbids her[w] when he hears about it, none
of her vows or the pledges by which she
obligated herself will stand; the LORD will
release her because her father has forbidden her.
6"If she marries after she makes a vow[x]
or after her lips utter a rash promise by
which she obligates herself 7and her husband hears about it but says nothing to
her, then her vows or the pledges by which
she obligated herself will stand. 8But if her
husband[y] forbids her when he hears about
it, he nullifies the vow that obligates her
or the rash promise by which she obligates
herself, and the LORD will release her.[z]
9"Any vow or obligation taken by a widow or divorced woman will be binding on
her.
10"If a woman living with her husband
makes a vow or obligates herself by a
pledge under oath 11and her husband hears
about it but says nothing to her and does
not forbid her, then all her vows or the
pledges by which she obligated herself will
stand. 12But if her husband nullifies them
when he hears about them, then none of
the vows or pledges that came from her
lips will stand.[a] Her husband has nullified
them, and the LORD will release her. 13Her
husband may confirm or nullify any vow
she makes or any sworn pledge to deny
herself. 14But if her husband says nothing
to her about it from day to day, then he
confirms all her vows or the pledges binding on her. He confirms them by saying
nothing to her when he hears about them.
15If, however, he nullifies them[b] some time
after he hears about them, then he is responsible for her guilt."
16These are the regulations the LORD
gave Moses concerning relationships between a man and his wife, and between a
father and his young daughter still living
in his house.

Vengeance on the Midianites

31 The LORD said to Moses, 2"Take vengeance on the Midianites[c] for the Israelites. After that, you will be gathered to
your people.[d]"
3So Moses said to the people, "Arm
some of your men to go to war against
the Midianites and to carry out the LORD's
vengeance[e] on them. 4Send into battle a
thousand men from each of the tribes of
Israel." 5So twelve thousand men armed
for battle,[f] a thousand from each tribe,
were supplied from the clans of Israel.
6Moses sent them into battle,[g] a thousand
from each tribe, along with Phinehas[h] son
of Eleazar, the priest, who took with him
articles from the sanctuary[i] and the trumpets[j] for signaling.
7They fought against Midian, as the
LORD commanded Moses,[k] and killed every
man.[l] 8Among their victims were Evi, Rekem, Zur, Hur and Reba[m]—the five kings
of Midian.[n] They also killed Balaam son of
Beor[o] with the sword.[p] 9The Israelites captured the Midianite women[q] and children
and took all the Midianite herds, flocks and
goods as plunder.[r] 10They burned[s] all the
towns where the Midianites had settled, as
well as all their camps.[t] 11They took all the
plunder and spoils, including the people
and animals,[u] 12and brought the captives,
spoils[v] and plunder to Moses and Eleazar

30:2 [u]Dt 23:21-23; Jdg 11:35; Job 22:27; Ps 22:25; 50:14; 61:5,8; 76:11; 116:14; Pr 20:25; Ecc 5:4,5; Isa 19:21; Jnh 1:16; 2:9 **30:4** [v]ver 7 **30:5** [w]ver 8,12,15 **30:6** [x]S Lev 5:4 **30:8** [y]S Ge 3:16 [z]ver 5 **30:12** [a]Eph 5:22; Col 3:18 **30:15** [b]S ver 5 **31:2** [c]S Ge 25:2 [d]S Nu 20:26 **31:3** [e]Jdg 11:36; 1Sa 24:12; 2Sa 4:8; 22:48; Ps 94:1; 149:7; Isa 34:8; Jer 11:20; 46:10; Eze 25:17 **31:5** [f]ver 6,21 **31:6** [g]S ver 5 [h]S Ex 6:25 [i]Nu 14:44 [j]S Nu 10:2 **31:7** [k]Nu 25:16 [l]Dt 20:13; Jdg 21:11; 1Ki 11:15,16 **31:8** [m]Jos 13:21 [n]S Nu 25:15 [o]S Nu 22:5; S 24:14 [p]Jos 13:22 **31:9** [q]ver 15 [r]S Ge 34:29 **31:10** [s]Jos 6:24; 8:28; 11:11; Jdg 18:27 [t]Ge 25:16; 1Ch 6:54; Ps 69:25; Eze 25:4 **31:11** [u]ver 26; Dt 20:14; 2Ch 28:8 **31:12** [v]ver 32, 53; Ge 49:27; Ex 15:9

30:3–8 In Near Eastern society, women were subject to the authority of their fathers (vv. 3–5) or husbands (vv. 6–8), who could disallow the carrying out of a vow.
30:9 *widow or divorced woman.* Such women remained responsible for the vows they made.
30:10–15 Further examples of the complications that come in the making of vows within the husband-wife relationship. Such complications may have come up much as in the case of Zelophehad's daughters (see 27:1–11 and note). One case after another presented itself, resulting in this final codification. Presumably, in the centuries leading up to the NT, the legal decisions on vows became even more complex. The words of Jesus that one is to avoid complications connected with oaths (Mt 5:33–37) are liberating.
31:1–24 The Lord declares war (see essay, p. 286) against the Midianites as one of Moses' last actions before the end of his life. Moses was not motivated by petty jealousy; rather, the war was "the LORD's vengeance" (v. 3) for the Midianites' part in seducing the Israelites to engage in sexual immorality and to worship the Baal of Peor. (See 25:16–18, where the specific mention of Cozbi, a Midianite woman, heightens the anger expressed in ch. 31.)
31:2 *be gathered to your people.* In death (see note on Ge 25:8).
31:4 *a thousand men from each of the tribes of Israel.* The burden of the Lord's war had to be shared equally among the tribes.
31:6 *Phinehas.* His zeal for the Lord's honor led him to execute Zimri and Cozbi (25:8). Now he leads in the sacred aspects of the battle to demonstrate that this is the Lord's war. *trumpets.* See note on 10:3.
31:8 *They also killed Balaam.* Ch. 25 lacks the name of the principal instigator of the seduction of the Israelite men to the depraved worship of Baal. But here he is found among the dead. What Balaam had been unable to accomplish through acts of magic or sorcery (chs. 22–24) he was almost able to achieve by his advice to the Midianites (v. 16).
31:9–18 While the troops killed the men of Midian, they spared the women and children as plunder. Moses commanded that only the virgin women (who were thus innocent of the indecencies at Peor) could be spared; the guilty women and the boys (who might endanger the inheritance rights of Israelite men) were to be put to death (vv. 15–17).

the priest and the Israelite assembly[w] at their camp on the plains of Moab, by the Jordan across from Jericho.[a x]

[13]Moses, Eleazar the priest and all the leaders of the community went to meet them outside the camp. [14]Moses was angry with the officers of the army[y]—the commanders of thousands and commanders of hundreds—who returned from the battle.

[15]"Have you allowed all the women to live?" he asked them. [16]"They were the ones who followed Balaam's advice[z] and were the means of turning the Israelites away from the LORD in what happened at Peor,[a] so that a plague[b] struck the LORD's people. [17]Now kill all the boys. And kill every woman who has slept with a man,[c] [18]but save for yourselves every girl who has never slept with a man.

[19]"All of you who have killed anyone or touched anyone who was killed[d] must stay outside the camp seven days.[e] On the third and seventh days you must purify yourselves[f] and your captives. [20]Purify every garment[g] as well as everything made of leather, goat hair or wood.[h]"

[21]Then Eleazar the priest said to the soldiers who had gone into battle,[i] "This is the requirement of the law that the LORD gave Moses: [22]Gold, silver, bronze, iron,[j] tin, lead [23]and anything else that can withstand fire must be put through the fire,[k] and then it will be clean. But it must also be purified with the water of cleansing.[l] And whatever cannot withstand fire must be put through that water. [24]On the seventh day wash your clothes and you will be clean.[m] Then you may come into the camp.[n]"

Dividing the Spoils

[25]The LORD said to Moses, [26]"You and Eleazar the priest and the family heads[o] of the community are to count all the people[p] and animals that were captured.[q] [27]Divide[r] the spoils between the soldiers who took part in the battle and the rest of the community. [28]From the soldiers who fought in the battle, set apart as tribute for the LORD[s] one out of every five hundred, whether persons, cattle, donkeys, sheep or goats. [29]Take this tribute from their half share and give it to Eleazar the priest as the LORD's part. [30]From the Israelites' half, select one out of every fifty, whether persons, cattle, donkeys, sheep, goats or other animals. Give them to the Levites, who are responsible for the care of the LORD's tabernacle.[t]" [31]So Moses and Eleazar the priest did as the LORD commanded Moses.

[32]The plunder remaining from the spoils[u] that the soldiers took was 675,000 sheep, [33]72,000 cattle, [34]61,000 donkeys [35]and 32,000 women who had never slept with a man.

[36]The half share of those who fought in the battle was:

337,500 sheep, [37]of which the tribute for the LORD[v] was 675;

[38]36,000 cattle, of which the tribute for the LORD was 72;

[39]30,500 donkeys, of which the tribute for the LORD was 61;

[40]16,000 people, of which the tribute for the LORD was 32.

[41]Moses gave the tribute to Eleazar the priest as the LORD's part,[w] as the LORD commanded Moses.[x]

[42]The half belonging to the Israelites, which Moses set apart from that of the fighting men— [43]the community's half—was 337,500 sheep, [44]36,000 cattle, [45]30,500 donkeys [46]and 16,000 people. [47]From the Israelites' half, Moses selected one out of every fifty persons and animals, as the LORD commanded him, and gave them to the Levites, who were responsible for the care of the LORD's tabernacle.

[48]Then the officers[y] who were over the units of the army—the commanders of thousands and commanders of hundreds—went to Moses [49]and said to him, "Your servants have counted[z] the soldiers under our command, and not one is missing.[a] [50]So we have brought as an offering to the LORD the gold articles each of us acquired—armlets, bracelets, signet rings, earrings and necklaces—to make atonement for ourselves[b] before the LORD."

[51]Moses and Eleazar the priest accepted from them the gold—all the crafted articles. [52]All the gold from the commanders of thousands and commanders of hundreds that Moses and Eleazar presented as a gift to the LORD weighed 16,750 shekels.[b] [53]Each soldier had taken plunder[c] for himself. [54]Moses and Eleazar the priest accepted the gold from the commanders of thousands and commanders of hundreds and brought it into the Tent of Meeting[d] as a memorial[e] for the Israelites before the LORD.

31:12 [w] S Nu 27:2 [x] Nu 22:1
31:14 [y] ver 48; Ex 18:21; Dt 1:15; 2Sa 18:1
31:16 [z] S Nu 22:5; S 24:14; S 2Pe 2:15 [a] S Nu 23:28; 25:1-9 [b] S Nu 14:37
31:17 [c] Dt 7:2; 20:16-18; Jdg 21:11
31:19 [d] Nu 19:16 [e] S Lev 21:1 [f] Nu 19:12
31:20 [g] Nu 19:19 [h] S Lev 11:32
31:21 [i] S ver 5
31:22 [j] Jos 6:19; 22:8
31:23 [k] S 1Co 3:13 [l] S Nu 8:7
31:24 [m] S Lev 11:25 [n] S Lev 14:8
31:26 [o] S Nu 1:4 [p] S Nu 1:19 [q] S ver 11,12
31:27 [r] Jos 22:8; 1Sa 25:13; 30:24
31:28 [s] ver 37-41; S Nu 18:21
31:30 [t] Nu 3:7; 18:3
31:32 [u] S ver 12
31:37 [v] ver 38-41
31:41 [w] Nu 5:9; 18:8 [x] ver 21,28
31:48 [y] S ver 14
31:49 [z] S Nu 1:19 [a] Jer 23:4
31:50 [b] S Ex 30:16
31:53 [c] S Ge 34:29; Dt 20:14
31:54 [d] S Ex 27:21; 40:2 [e] S Ex 28:12

[a] *12* Hebrew *Jordan of Jericho*; possibly an ancient name for the Jordan River [b] *52* That is, about 420 pounds (about 190 kilograms)

31:16 *what happened at Peor.* See notes on v. 8; 25:1–18.

31:19–24 Since this was the Lord's war, both people (vv. 19–20) and things (vv. 21–24) had to be cleansed (cf. 19:11–13).

31:26–35 Another aspect of the Lord's war was the fair distribution of the spoils of war, both among those who fought in the battle and among those who stayed with the community, with appropriate shares to be given to the Lord, whose battle it was (v. 28).

The Transjordan Tribes

32 The Reubenites and Gadites, who
had very large herds and flocks,[f] saw
that the lands of Jazer[g] and Gilead[h] were
suitable for livestock.[i] 2So they came to
Moses and Eleazar the priest and to the
leaders of the community,[j] and said, 3"Ataroth,[k] Dibon,[l] Jazer,[m] Nimrah,[n] Heshbon,[o]
Elealeh,[p] Sebam,[q] Nebo[r] and Beon[s]— 4the
land the LORD subdued[t] before the people
of Israel—are suitable for livestock,[u] and
your servants have livestock. 5If we have
found favor in your eyes," they said, "let
this land be given to your servants as our
possession. Do not make us cross the Jordan.[v]"

6Moses said to the Gadites and Reubenites, "Shall your countrymen go to war
while you sit here? 7Why do you discourage the Israelites from going over into the
land the LORD has given them?[w] 8This is
what your fathers did when I sent them
from Kadesh Barnea to look over the land.[x]
9After they went up to the Valley of Eshcol[y] and viewed the land, they discouraged
the Israelites from entering the land the
LORD had given them. 10The LORD's anger
was aroused[z] that day and he swore this
oath:[a] 11'Because they have not followed
me wholeheartedly, not one of the men
twenty years old or more[b] who came up
out of Egypt[c] will see the land I promised
on oath[d] to Abraham, Isaac and Jacob[e]—
12not one except Caleb son of Jephunneh
the Kenizzite and Joshua son of Nun, for
they followed the LORD wholeheartedly.'[f]
13The LORD's anger burned against Israel[g]
and he made them wander in the desert
forty years, until the whole generation of
those who had done evil in his sight was
gone.[h]

14"And here you are, a brood of sinners,
standing in the place of your fathers and
making the LORD even more angry with
Israel.[i] 15If you turn away from following
him, he will again leave all this people in
the desert, and you will be the cause of
their destruction.[j]"

16Then they came up to him and said,
"We would like to build pens[k] here for our
livestock[l] and cities for our women and
children. 17But we are ready to arm ourselves and go ahead of the Israelites[m] until we have brought them to their place.[n]
Meanwhile our women and children will
live in fortified cities, for protection from
the inhabitants of the land. 18We will not
return to our homes until every Israelite
has received his inheritance.[o] 19We will
not receive any inheritance with them on
the other side of the Jordan, because our
inheritance[p] has come to us on the east
side of the Jordan."[q]

20Then Moses said to them, "If you will
do this—if you will arm yourselves before
the LORD for battle,[r] 21and if all of you will
go armed over the Jordan before the LORD
until he has driven his enemies out before
him[s]— 22then when the land is subdued
before the LORD, you may return[t] and be
free from your obligation to the LORD and
to Israel. And this land will be your possession[u] before the LORD.[v]

23"But if you fail to do this, you will be
sinning against the LORD; and you may
be sure that your sin will find you out.[w]
24Build cities for your women and children, and pens for your flocks,[x] but do
what you have promised.[y]"

25The Gadites and Reubenites said
to Moses, "We your servants will do as
our lord commands.[z] 26Our children and
wives, our flocks and herds will remain
here in the cities of Gilead.[a] 27But your
servants, every man armed for battle, will
cross over to fight[b] before the LORD, just as
our lord says."

28Then Moses gave orders about them[c]
to Eleazar the priest and Joshua son of
Nun[d] and to the family heads of the Israelite tribes.[e] 29He said to them, "If the
Gadites and Reubenites, every man armed
for battle, cross over the Jordan with you
before the LORD, then when the land is
subdued before you,[f] give them the land
of Gilead as their possession.[g] 30But if they
do not cross over[h] with you armed, they
must accept their possession with you in
Canaan.[i]"

31The Gadites and Reubenites answered,
"Your servants will do what the LORD has
said.[j] 32We will cross over before the LORD
into Canaan armed,[k] but the property we
inherit will be on this side of the Jordan.[l]"

32:1 [f] ver 24,36; Jdg 5:16 [g] S Nu 21:32 [h] S Ge 31:21 [i] Ex 12:38 **32:2** [j] Lev 4:22; Nu 27:2 **32:3** [k] ver 34; Jos 16:2,7; 18:13 [l] ver 34; S Nu 21:30 [m] ver 1 [n] ver 36; Jos 13:27 [o] Nu 21:25 [p] ver 37; Isa 15:4; 16:9; Jer 48:34 [q] Jos 13:19; Isa 16:8,9; Jer 48:32 [r] Nu 33:47; Dt 32:49; 34:1; 1Ch 5:8 [s] ver 38; Jos 13:17; Eze 25:9 **32:4** [t] Nu 21:34 [u] Ex 12:38 **32:5** [v] S Nu 13:29 **32:7** [w] Nu 13:27-14:4 **32:8** [x] Nu 13:3,26; Dt 1:19-25 **32:9** [y] Nu 13:23; Dt 1:24 **32:10** [z] Nu 11:1 [a] S Nu 14:20-23 **32:11** [b] S Ex 30:14 [c] Nu 1:1 [d] S Nu 14:23 [e] Nu 14:28-30 **32:12** [f] Nu 14:24,30 **32:13** [g] S Ex 4:14 [h] Nu 14:28-35; 26:64,65 **32:14** [i] S ver 10; Dt 1:34; Ps 78:59 **32:15** [j] Dt 30:17-18; 2Ch 7:20 **32:16** [k] ver 24,36; 1Sa 24:3; Ps 50:9; 78:70 [l] Ex 12:38; Dt 3:19 **32:17** [m] Dt 3:18; Jos 4:12,13 [n] S Nu 22:4; Dt 3:20 **32:18** [o] Jos 22:1-4 **32:19** [p] ver 22,29 [q] Nu 21:33; Jos 12:1; 22:7 **32:20** [r] ver 17 **32:21** [s] ver 17 **32:22** [t] Jos 22:4 [u] S Lev 14:34 [v] Dt 3:18-20 **32:23** [w] S Ge 4:7; S Isa 3:9 **32:24** [x] S ver 1,16 [y] Nu 30:2 **32:25** [z] ver 29; Jos 1:16,18; 22:2 **32:26** [a] ver 16,24; Jos 1:14; 12:2; 22:9; 2Sa 2:9; 1Ch 5:9 **32:27** [b] ver 17,21 **32:28** [c] ver 29; Dt 3:18-20; Jos 1:13 [d] Nu 11:28 [e] Nu 1:16 **32:29** [f] S Nu 22:4 [g] S ver 19 **32:30** [h] ver 23 [i] ver 29,32 **32:31** [j] ver 29 **32:32** [k] ver 17 [l] S ver 30; Jos 12:6

32:1 *Reubenites and Gadites.* The abundance of fertile grazing land in Transjordan prompted the leaders of these two tribes to request that they be allowed to settle there and not cross the Jordan. This area too was a gift of God won by conquest. **32:8** *This is what your fathers did.* Moses' fear was that the failure of these two tribes to stay with the whole community in conquering Canaan would be the beginning of a general revolt against entering the land. It would be the failure of Kadesh (chs. 13–14) all over again. Moreover, the conquest of Canaan was a commission to all Israel.

32:12 *followed the LORD wholeheartedly.* See note on 14:24.
32:17 *we are ready to arm ourselves.* The leaders of Reuben and Gad sought to assure Moses that they did not wish to shirk their duty to serve in the Lord's army in conquering the land. They would join their brothers in battle but wished to leave their families and livestock behind in the territory of their choosing.

32:23 *your sin will find you out.* The bargain was struck, but not without strong warnings if they failed to live up to their word.

33 Then Moses gave to the Gadites,[m] the
Reubenites and the half-tribe of Manasseh[n] son of Joseph the kingdom of Sihon
king of the Amorites[o] and the kingdom of
Og king of Bashan[p]—the whole land with
its cities and the territory around them.[q]
34 The Gadites built up Dibon, Ataroth,
Aroer,[r] 35 Atroth Shophan, Jazer,[s] Jogbehah,[t] 36 Beth Nimrah[u] and Beth Haran as
fortified cities, and built pens for their
flocks.[v] 37 And the Reubenites rebuilt Heshbon,[w] Elealeh[x] and Kiriathaim,[y] 38 as well
as Nebo[z] and Baal Meon (these names
were changed) and Sibmah.[a] They gave
names to the cities they rebuilt.
39 The descendants of Makir[b] son of Manasseh went to Gilead,[c] captured it and
drove out the Amorites[d] who were there.
40 So Moses gave Gilead to the Makirites,[e]
the descendants of Manasseh, and they
settled there. 41 Jair,[f] a descendant of Manasseh, captured their settlements and
called them Havvoth Jair.[a][g] 42 And Nobah
captured Kenath[h] and its surrounding settlements and called it Nobah[i] after himself.[j]

Stages in Israel's Journey

33 Here are the stages in the journey[k] of
the Israelites when they came out of
Egypt[l] by divisions under the leadership
of Moses and Aaron.[m] 2 At the LORD's command Moses recorded[n] the stages in their
journey[o]. This is their journey by stages:

3 The Israelites set out[p] from Rameses[q] on the fifteenth day of the first
month, the day after the Passover.[r]
They marched out boldly[s] in full
view of all the Egyptians, 4 who were
burying all their firstborn,[t] whom the
LORD had struck down among them;
for the LORD had brought judgment[u]
on their gods.[v]
5 The Israelites left Rameses and
camped at Succoth.[w]
6 They left Succoth and camped at
Etham, on the edge of the desert.[x]
7 They left Etham, turned back to Pi
Hahiroth, to the east of Baal Zephon,[y]
and camped near Migdol.[z]
8 They left Pi Hahiroth[b][a] and passed
through the sea[b] into the desert, and
when they had traveled for three days
in the Desert of Etham, they camped
at Marah.[c]
9 They left Marah and went to Elim,
where there were twelve springs and
seventy palm trees, and they camped[d]
there.
10 They left Elim[e] and camped by
the Red Sea.[c]
11 They left the Red Sea and camped
in the Desert of Sin.[f]
12 They left the Desert of Sin and
camped at Dophkah.
13 They left Dophkah and camped at
Alush.
14 They left Alush and camped at
Rephidim, where there was no water
for the people to drink.[g]
15 They left Rephidim[h] and camped
in the Desert of Sinai.[i]
16 They left the Desert of Sinai and
camped at Kibroth Hattaavah.[j]
17 They left Kibroth Hattaavah and
camped at Hazeroth.[k]
18 They left Hazeroth and camped at
Rithmah.
19 They left Rithmah and camped at
Rimmon Perez.
20 They left Rimmon Perez and
camped at Libnah.[l]
21 They left Libnah and camped at
Rissah.
22 They left Rissah and camped at
Kehelathah.
23 They left Kehelathah and camped
at Mount Shepher.
24 They left Mount Shepher and
camped at Haradah.
25 They left Haradah and camped at
Makheloth.
26 They left Makheloth and camped
at Tahath.

32:33 [m] Jos 13:24-28; 1Sa 13:7 [n] Jos 1:12 [o] Nu 21:21; Dt 2:26 [p] S ver 19; S Jos 12:5 [q] S Nu 21:24; 34:14; Dt 2:36; Jos 12:6 **32:34** [r] Dt 2:36; 3:12; 4:48; Jos 12:2; 13:9; Jdg 11:26; 1Sa 30:28; 1Ch 5:8; Jer 48:19 **32:35** [s] ver 3 [t] Jdg 8:11 **32:36** [u] S ver 3 [v] S ver 1 **32:37** [w] Nu 21:25 [x] S ver 3 [y] Jos 13:19; 1Ch 6:76; Jer 48:1,23; Eze 25:9 **32:38** [z] S ver 3; Isa 15:2; Jer 48:1,22 [a] S ver 3 **32:39** [b] S Ge 50:23 [c] Nu 26:29; Dt 2:36 [d] S Ge 10:16 **32:40** [e] S Ge 50:23; Dt 3:15 **32:41** [f] 1Ki 4:13 [g] Dt 3:14; Jos 13:30; Jdg 10:4; 1Ch 2:23 **32:42** [h] 1Ch 2:23 [i] Jdg 8:11 [j] 1Sa 15:12; 2Sa 18:18; Ps 49:11; Isa 22:16; 56:5 **33:1** [k] Ex 17:1; 40:36 [l] Nu 1:1 [m] S Ex 4:16; 6:26 **33:2** [n] S Ex 17:14 [o] S ver 1 **33:3** [p] Nu 10:2 [q] S Ge 47:11 [r] Jos 5:10 [s] S Ex 14:8 **33:4** [t] S Ex 4:23 [u] 2Ch 24:24; Jer 15:3; Eze 14:21 [v] S Ex 12:12 **33:5** [w] Ex 12:37 **33:6** [x] Ex 13:20 **33:7** [y] Ex 14:9 [z] S Ex 14:2 **33:8** [a] Ex 14:2 [b] S Ex 14:22 [c] S Ex 15:23

[a] 41 Or *them the settlements of Jair* [b] 8 Many manuscripts of the Masoretic Text, Samaritan Pentateuch and Vulgate; most manuscripts of the Masoretic Text *left from before Hahiroth* [c] 10 Hebrew *Yam Suph*; that is, Sea of Reeds; also in verse 11

33:9 [d] Ex 15:27 **33:10** [e] Ex 16:1 **33:11** [f] S Ex 16:1 **33:14** [g] S Ex 15:22; S 17:2 **33:15** [h] S Ex 17:1 [i] S Ex 19:1 **33:16** [j] S Nu 11:34 **33:17** [k] Nu 11:35 **33:20** [l] Jos 10:29; 12:15; 15:42; 21:13; 2Ki 8:22; 19:8; 23:31; 1Ch 6:57; 2Ch 21:10; Isa 37:8; Jer 52:1

32:33 *and the half-tribe of Manasseh.* It appears that after the requirements for Transjordan settlement were established with the tribes of Reuben and Gad, half the tribe of Manasseh joined with them.

33:1–49 The numerous places (significantly, 40 in number between Rameses and the plains of Moab) in Israel's desert experience are listed. Unfortunately, most of the sites were desert encampments, not cities with lasting archaeological records; so they are difficult to locate. Many of the places (e.g., in vv. 19–29) are not recorded elsewhere in Exodus and Numbers. Some of the places mentioned elsewhere (e.g., Taberah, 11:3; see 21:19) are missing here. The data warrant these conclusions: (1) Moses recorded the list at the Lord's command (v. 2). (2) The list should be taken seriously, as an accurate recapitulation of the stages of the journey, despite difficulty in locating many of the sites. (3) The numerical factor of 40 sites between Rameses and the plains of Moab suggests some styling of the list, which helps to account for the sites not included. (4) As in the case of genealogies in the Pentateuch, some factors of ancient significance may not be clear to us today. (5) Ultimately the record is a recital of the Lord's blessing on his people for the extended period of their desert experience. Although certainly not without geographical importance, the listing of the stages of Israel's experience in the desert is fundamentally a religious document, a litany of the Lord's deliverance of his people.

27They left Tahath and camped at
Terah.
28They left Terah and camped at
Mithcah.
29They left Mithcah and camped at
Hashmonah.
30They left Hashmonah and camped
at Moseroth.[m]
31They left Moseroth and camped at
Bene Jaakan.[n]
32They left Bene Jaakan and camped
at Hor Haggidgad.
33They left Hor Haggidgad and
camped at Jotbathah.[o]
34They left Jotbathah and camped
at Abronah.
35They left Abronah and camped at
Ezion Geber.[p]
36They left Ezion Geber and camped
at Kadesh, in the Desert of Zin.[q]
37They left Kadesh and camped at
Mount Hor,[r] on the border of Edom.[s]
38At the LORD's command Aaron the
priest went up Mount Hor, where
he died[t] on the first day of the fifth
month of the fortieth year[u] after the
Israelites came out of Egypt.[v] 39Aar-
on was a hundred and twenty-three
years old when he died on Mount
Hor.
40The Canaanite king[w] of Arad,[x]
who lived in the Negev[y] of Canaan,
heard that the Israelites were coming.
41They left Mount Hor and camped
at Zalmonah.
42They left Zalmonah and camped
at Punon.
43They left Punon and camped at
Oboth.[z]
44They left Oboth and camped at
Iye Abarim, on the border of Moab.[a]
45They left Iyim[a] and camped at Dibon Gad.
46They left Dibon Gad and camped
at Almon Diblathaim.
47They left Almon Diblathaim and
camped in the mountains of Abarim,[b]
near Nebo.[c]
48They left the mountains of Abarim[d] and camped on the plains of
Moab[e] by the Jordan[f] across from Jericho.[b][g] 49There on the plains of Moab
they camped along the Jordan from
Beth Jeshimoth[h] to Abel Shittim.[i]

50On the plains of Moab by the Jordan
across from Jericho[j] the LORD said to Moses, 51"Speak to the Israelites and say to
them: 'When you cross the Jordan into Canaan,[k] 52drive out all the inhabitants of the
land before you. Destroy all their carved
images and their cast idols, and demolish
all their high places.[l] 53Take possession of
the land and settle in it, for I have given
you the land to possess.[m] 54Distribute the
land by lot,[n] according to your clans.[o] To a
larger group give a larger inheritance, and
to a smaller group a smaller one.[p] Whatever falls to them by lot will be theirs.
Distribute it according to your ancestral
tribes.[q]
55" 'But if you do not drive out the inhabitants of the land, those you allow to
remain will become barbs in your eyes and
thorns[r] in your sides. They will give you
trouble in the land where you will live.
56And then I will do to you what I plan to
do to them.[s]' "

Boundaries of Canaan

34 The LORD said to Moses, 2"Command
the Israelites and say to them: 'When
you enter Canaan,[t] the land that will be allotted to you as an inheritance[u] will have
these boundaries:[v]
3" 'Your southern side will include some
of the Desert of Zin[w] along the border of
Edom. On the east, your southern boundary will start from the end of the Salt Sea,[c][x]
4cross south of Scorpion[d] Pass,[y] continue
on to Zin and go south of Kadesh Barnea.[z]
Then it will go to Hazar Addar and over to
Azmon,[a] 5where it will turn, join the Wadi
of Egypt[b] and end at the Sea.[e]
6" 'Your western boundary will be the
coast of the Great Sea.[c] This will be your
boundary on the west.[d]
7" 'For your northern boundary,[e] run
a line from the Great Sea to Mount Hor[f]
8and from Mount Hor to Lebo[f] Hamath.[g]
Then the boundary will go to Zedad,
9continue to Ziphron and end at Hazar
Enan. This will be your boundary on the
north.
10" 'For your eastern boundary,[h] run a
line from Hazar Enan to Shepham. 11The

[a] 45 That is, Iye Abarim [b] 48 Hebrew *Jordan of Jericho*; possibly an ancient name for the Jordan River; also in verse 50 [c] 3 That is, the Dead Sea; also in verse 12 [d] 4 Hebrew *Akrabbim* [e] 5 That is, the Mediterranean; also in verses 6 and 7 [f] 8 Or *to the entrance to*

33:30 [m] Dt 10:6 **33:31** [n] Dt 10:6 **33:33** [o] Dt 10:7 **33:35** [p] Dt 2:8; 1Ki 9:26; 22:48 **33:36** [q] S Nu 13:21 **33:37** [r] S Nu 20:22 [s] S Ge 36:16; S Nu 20:16 **33:38** [t] S Nu 27:13 [u] S Ex 16:35 [v] Nu 20:25-28 **33:40** [w] S Ge 10:18 [x] S Nu 21:1 [y] S Ge 12:9 **33:43** [z] Nu 21:10 **33:44** [a] S Nu 21:11 **33:47** [b] Nu 27:12 [c] Nu 32:3 **33:48** [d] Nu 27:12 [e] S Nu 26:3 [f] S Ge 13:10 [g] Nu 22:1; Jos 12:9 **33:49** [h] Jos 12:3; 13:20; Eze 25:9 [i] S Nu 21:16 **33:50** [j] ver 48 **33:51** [k] Nu 34:2; Jos 3:17 **33:52** [l] 34:13; S Lev 26:1; Ps 106:34-36 **33:53** [m] Dt 11:31; 17:14; Jos 1:11; 21:43 **33:54** [n] S Lev 16:8; Nu 36:2 [o] Nu 26:54 [p] Nu 35:8 [q] Jos 18:10 **33:55** [r] Jos 23:13; Jdg 2:3; Ps 106:36; Isa 55:13; Eze 2:6; 28:24; Mic 7:4; 2Co 12:7 **33:56** [s] Nu 14:28 **34:2** [t] S Nu 33:51 [u] Ge 17:8; Dt 1:7-8; Jos 23:4; Ps 78:54-55; 105:11 [v] Eze 47:15 **34:3** [w] Nu 13:21; Jos 15:1-3 [x] S Ge 14:3 **34:4** [y] Jos 15:3; Jdg 1:36 [z] Nu 32:8 [a] Jos 15:4 **34:5** [b] Ge 15:18 **34:6** [c] Jos 1:4; 9:1; 15:12,47; 23:4; Eze 47:10,15; 48:28 [d] Eze 47:19-20 **34:7** [e] Eze 47:15-17 [f] S Nu 20:22 **34:8** [g] Nu 13:21; Jos 13:5 **34:10** [h] Jos 15:5

33:40 *Negev.* See note on Ge 12:9.
33:50—36:13 A summary statement dealing with matters of land and other property in the promised land. The first and last verses—with their several verbal links—frame the section.
33:52 *drive out all the inhabitants of the land ... Destroy all their ... idols.* What Israel had accomplished in the war against the Midianites (ch. 31) was now to be extended to all the inhabitants of Canaan. Particularly important was the command to destroy all symbols of the pagan religious system of the Canaanites.
33:54 See note on 26:53–56.
34:3–12 The listing of the four boundaries displays the dimensions of God's great gift to his people.

boundary will go down from Shepham to
Riblah[i] on the east side of Ain[j] and con-
tinue along the slopes east of the Sea of
Kinnereth.[a][k] 12Then the boundary will go
down along the Jordan and end at the Salt
Sea.

"'This will be your land, with its boundaries on every side.'"

13Moses commanded the Israelites: "Assign this land by lot[l] as an inheritance.[m]
The LORD has ordered that it be given to
the nine and a half tribes, 14because the
families of the tribe of Reuben, the tribe of
Gad and the half-tribe of Manasseh have
received their inheritance.[n] 15These two
and a half tribes have received their inheritance on the east side of the Jordan of
Jericho,[b] toward the sunrise."

16The LORD said to Moses, 17"These are
the names of the men who are to assign
the land for you as an inheritance: Eleazar the priest and Joshua[o] son of Nun.
18And appoint one leader from each tribe
to help[p] assign the land.[q] 19These are their
names:[r]

Caleb[s] son of Jephunneh,
from the tribe of Judah;[t]
20Shemuel son of Ammihud,
from the tribe of Simeon;[u]
21Elidad son of Kislon,
from the tribe of Benjamin;[v]
22Bukki son of Jogli,
the leader from the tribe of Dan;
23Hanniel son of Ephod,
the leader from the tribe of Manasseh[w] son of Joseph;
24Kemuel son of Shiphtan,
the leader from the tribe of Ephraim[x] son of Joseph;
25Elizaphan son of Parnach,
the leader from the tribe of Zebulun;[y]
26Paltiel son of Azzan,
the leader from the tribe of Issachar;
27Ahihud son of Shelomi,
the leader from the tribe of Asher;[z]
28Pedahel son of Ammihud,
the leader from the tribe of Naphtali."

29These are the men the LORD commanded to assign the inheritance to the Israelites in the land of Canaan.[a]

34:11 [i]2Ki 23:33; 25:6,21; Jer 39:5; 52:9,27 [j]Jos 15:32; 21:16; 1Ch 4:32 [k]Dt 3:17; Jos 11:2; 13:27
34:13 [l]S Lev 16:8; Jos 18:10; Mic 2:5 [m]Jos 13:6; 14:1-5; Isa 49:8; 65:9; Eze 45:1
34:14 [n]Nu 32:19; Dt 33:21; Jos 14:3
34:17 [o]Nu 11:28; Dt 1:38
34:18 [p]S Nu 1:4 [q]Jos 14:1
34:19 [r]ver 29 [s]S Nu 26:65 [t]Ge 29:35; Dt 33:7; Ps 60:7
34:20 [u]S Ge 29:33
34:21 [v]Ge 49:27; Jdg 5:14; Ps 68:27
34:23 [w]Nu 1:34
34:24 [x]Nu 1:32
34:25 [y]S Ge 30:20
34:27 [z]Nu 1:40
34:29 [a]ver 19
35:1 [b]Nu 22:1
35:2 [c]Lev 25:32-34; Jos 14:3,4 [d]Jos 21:1-42
35:3 [e]Dt 18:6; Jos 14:4; 21:2
35:5 [f]Jos 3:4 [g]Lev 25:34; 2Ch 11:14; 13:9; 23:2; 31:19
35:6 [h]ver 11; Jos 21:13
35:8 [i]Nu 26:54; 33:54
35:10 [j]Nu 33:51; Dt 9:1; Jos 1:2,11
35:11 [k]ver 22-25 [l]S Ex 21:13
35:12 [m]ver 19; Dt 19:6; Jos 20:3; 2Sa 14:11 [n]ver 26,27,28 [o]ver 24,25
35:13 [p]ver 6,14

Towns for the Levites

35 On the plains of Moab by the Jordan across from Jericho,[c][b] the LORD
said to Moses, 2"Command the Israelites
to give the Levites towns to live in[c] from
the inheritance the Israelites will possess.
And give them pasturelands[d] around the
towns. 3Then they will have towns to live
in and pasturelands for their cattle, flocks
and all their other livestock.[e]

4"The pasturelands around the towns
that you give the Levites will extend out
fifteen hundred feet[d] from the town wall.
5Outside the town, measure three thousand
feet[e][f] on the east side, three thousand on
the south side, three thousand on the west
and three thousand on the north, with the
town in the center. They will have this
area as pastureland for the towns.[g]

Cities of Refuge

35:6-34Ref — Dt 4:41-43; 19:1-14; Jos 20:1-9

6"Six of the towns you give the Levites
will be cities of refuge, to which a person
who has killed someone may flee.[h] In addition, give them forty-two other towns.
7In all you must give the Levites forty-
eight towns, together with their pasturelands. 8The towns you give the Levites
from the land the Israelites possess are to
be given in proportion to the inheritance
of each tribe: Take many towns from a
tribe that has many, but few from one that
has few."[i]

9Then the LORD said to Moses: 10"Speak
to the Israelites and say to them: 'When
you cross the Jordan into Canaan,[j] 11select
some towns to be your cities of refuge, to
which a person who has killed someone[k]
accidentally[l] may flee. 12They will be places of refuge from the avenger,[m] so that a
person accused of murder[n] may not die
before he stands trial before the assembly.[o] 13These six towns you give will be
your cities of refuge.[p] 14Give three on this
side of the Jordan and three in Canaan as
cities of refuge. 15These six towns will be
a place of refuge for Israelites, aliens and

[a] *11* That is, Galilee [b] *15* *Jordan of Jericho* was possibly an ancient name for the Jordan River. [c] *1* Hebrew *Jordan of Jericho*; possibly an ancient name for the Jordan River [d] *4* Hebrew *a thousand cubits* (about 450 meters) [e] *5* Hebrew *two thousand cubits* (about 900 meters)

34:13–15 The new realities that the settlement of Reuben, Gad and the half-tribe of Manasseh in Transjordan brought about (see ch. 32).

34:16–29 The listing of the new tribal leaders recalls the listing of the leaders of the first generation (1:5–16). This time the promise will be realized; these new leaders will assist Eleazar and Joshua in actually allotting the land.

34:19 *Caleb ... Judah.* See note on 13:6.

35:1–5 Since the Levites would not receive an allotment with the other tribes in the land (1:47–53), they would need towns in which to live and to raise their families and care for their livestock. The Levites were to be spread throughout the land (see Ge 49:5,7 and notes), not in an isolated encampment. Jos 21 presents the fulfillment of this command.

35:6–15 Six Levitical cities were to be stationed strategically in the land—three in Transjordan and three in Canaan proper—as cities of refuge, where a person guilty of unintentional manslaughter might escape blood revenge. Jos 20 describes the sites that were chosen. See map, p. 239 and accompanying text.

any other people living among them, so
that anyone who has killed another accidentally can flee there.
16" 'If a man strikes someone with an
iron object so that he dies, he is a murderer; the murderer shall be put to death.[q]
17Or if anyone has a stone in his hand that
could kill, and he strikes someone so that
he dies, he is a murderer; the murderer
shall be put to death. 18Or if anyone has
a wooden object in his hand that could
kill, and he hits someone so that he dies,
he is a murderer; the murderer shall be
put to death. 19The avenger of blood[r] shall
put the murderer to death; when he meets
him, he shall put him to death.[s] 20If anyone with malice aforethought shoves another or throws something at him intentionally[t] so that he dies 21or if in hostility
he hits him with his fist so that he dies,
that person shall be put to death;[u] he is
a murderer. The avenger of blood[v] shall
put the murderer to death when he meets
him.
22" 'But if without hostility someone
suddenly shoves another or throws something at him unintentionally[w] 23or, without seeing him, drops a stone on him that
could kill him, and he dies, then since he
was not his enemy and he did not intend
to harm him, 24the assembly[x] must judge
between him and the avenger of blood according to these regulations. 25The assembly must protect the one accused of murder from the avenger of blood and send
him back to the city of refuge to which he
fled. He must stay there until the death of
the high priest,[y] who was anointed[z] with
the holy oil.[a]
26" 'But if the accused ever goes outside
the limits of the city of refuge to which he
has fled 27and the avenger of blood finds
him outside the city, the avenger of blood
may kill the accused without being guilty
of murder. 28The accused must stay in his
city of refuge until the death of the high
priest; only after the death of the high
priest may he return to his own property.
29" 'These are to be legal requirements[b]
for you throughout the generations to
come,[c] wherever you live.[d]
30" 'Anyone who kills a person is to be
put to death as a murderer only on the
testimony of witnesses. But no one is to
be put to death on the testimony of only
one witness.[e]

35:16 [q]S Ex 21:12 **35:19** [r]S ver 12 [s]ver 21 **35:20** [t]S Ex 21:14 **35:21** [u]Ex 21:14 [v]ver 19 **35:22** [w]S Ex 21:13 **35:24** [x]S ver 12 **35:25** [y]ver 32 [z]S Ex 28:41 [a]S Ex 29:7 **35:29** [b]Nu 27:11 [c]Nu 10:8 [d]S Ex 12:20 **35:30** [e]Dt 17:6; 19:15; S Mt 18:16; Jn 7:51

35:16–21 Various descriptions of willful murder.
35:21 *avenger of blood.* See note on Jos 20:3.
35:22 *without hostility.* The cities of refuge were to be established for the person who had committed an act of involuntary manslaughter.
35:24 *according to these regulations.* Any gracious provision is subject to abuse. For this reason the case of the involuntary slayer had to be determined by the judges. Further, the accused had to stay in the city of refuge until the death of the high priest, which probably atoned for the act of manslaughter. Any person accused who left the city of refuge would become fair game again for the avenger of blood.
35:25–28 See note on Jos 20:6.
35:25 *send him back.* The trial of the accused apparently took place outside the city of refuge.
35:30 *witnesses.* To avoid the possibility of an innocent party being accused and sentenced to death on insufficient evidence.

Cities of Refuge

The idea of providing cities of refuge (see Jos 20:1-9 and notes) for capital offenses is rooted in the tension between customary tribal law (retaliation or revenge, in which the blood relative is obligated to execute vengeance) and civil law (carried out less personally by an assembly according to a standard code of justice).

Blood feuds are usually associated with nomadic groups; legal procedures, with villages and towns. Israel, a society in the process of sedentarization, found it necessary to adopt an intermediate step regulating manslaughter, so that an innocent person would not be killed before standing trial. Absolution was possible only by being cleared by the assembly, and by the eventual death of the high priest (when there would be general amnesty).

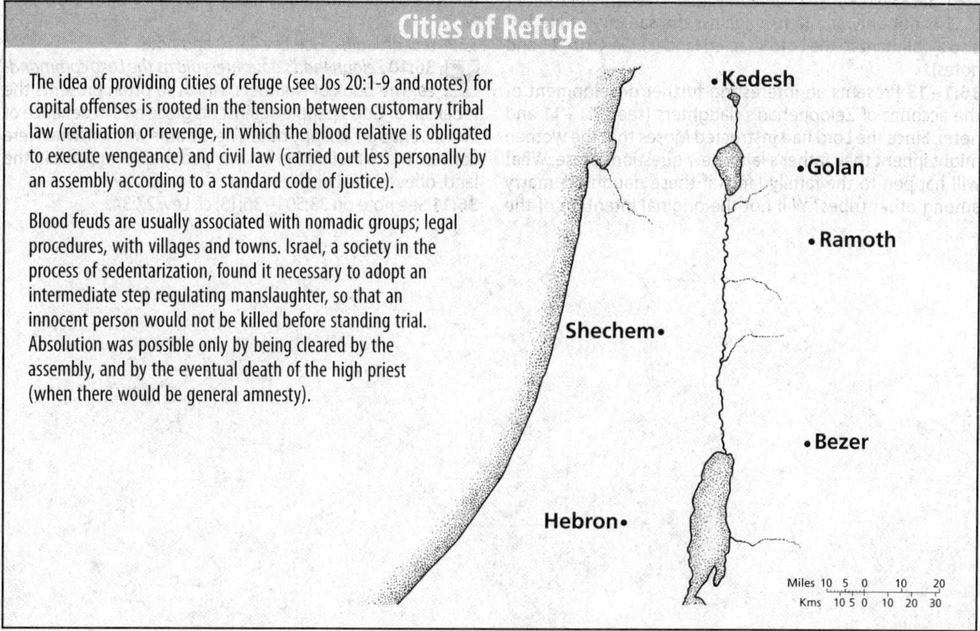

31"'Do not accept a ransom[f] for the life
of a murderer, who deserves to die. He
must surely be put to death.
32"'Do not accept a ransom for anyone
who has fled to a city of refuge and so allow him to go back and live on his own
land before the death of the high priest.
33"'Do not pollute the land where you
are. Bloodshed pollutes the land,[g] and
atonement cannot be made for the land
on which blood has been shed, except by
the blood of the one who shed it. 34Do not
defile the land[h] where you live and where
I dwell,[i] for I, the LORD, dwell among the
Israelites.'"

Inheritance of Zelophehad's Daughters

36:1-12pp — Nu 27:1-11

36 The family heads of the clan of Gilead[j] son of Makir,[k] the son of Manasseh, who were from the clans of the
descendants of Joseph,[l] came and spoke
before Moses and the leaders,[m] the heads
of the Israelite families. 2They said, "When
the LORD commanded my lord to give the
land as an inheritance to the Israelites by
lot,[n] he ordered you to give the inheritance of our brother Zelophehad[o] to his
daughters. 3Now suppose they marry men
from other Israelite tribes; then their inheritance will be taken from our ancestral
inheritance and added to that of the tribe
they marry into. And so part of the inheritance allotted to us will be taken away.
4When the Year of Jubilee[p] for the Israelites comes, their inheritance will be added
to that of the tribe into which they marry,
and their property will be taken from the
tribal inheritance of our forefathers."
5Then at the LORD's command Moses
gave this order to the Israelites: "What the
tribe of the descendants of Joseph is saying is right. 6This is what the LORD commands for Zelophehad's daughters: They
may marry anyone they please as long as
they marry within the tribal clan of their
father. 7No inheritance[q] in Israel is to pass
from tribe to tribe, for every Israelite shall
keep the tribal land inherited from his forefathers. 8Every daughter who inherits land
in any Israelite tribe must marry someone
in her father's tribal clan,[r] so that every
Israelite will possess the inheritance of his
fathers. 9No inheritance may pass from
tribe to tribe, for each Israelite tribe is to
keep the land it inherits."
10So Zelophehad's daughters did as the
LORD commanded Moses. 11Zelophehad's
daughters—Mahlah, Tirzah, Hoglah, Milcah and Noah[s]—married their cousins on
their father's side. 12They married within
the clans of the descendants of Manasseh
son of Joseph, and their inheritance remained in their father's clan and tribe.[t]
13These are the commands and regulations the LORD gave through Moses[u] to the
Israelites on the plains of Moab by the Jordan across from Jericho.[a][v]

[a] 13 Hebrew *Jordan of Jericho*; possibly an ancient name for the Jordan River

35:31 [f] Ex 21:30; Job 6:22; Ps 49:8; Pr 13:8 **35:33** [g] S Ge 4:10 **35:34** [h] Lev 18:24,25 [i] S Ex 29:45 **36:1** [j] S Nu 26:30 [k] S Ge 50:23 [l] S Nu 26:28 [m] S Nu 27:2 **36:2** [n] S Nu 33:54 [o] S Nu 26:33 **36:4** [p] S Lev 25:10 **36:7** [q] S Lev 25:23 **36:8** [r] 1Ch 23:22 **36:11** [s] Nu 26:33 **36:12** [t] 1Ch 7:15 **36:13** [u] S Lev 7:38; S 27:34 [v] Nu 22:1

35:32 Not even an involuntary slayer could leave the city of refuge on the payment of a ransom.

35:33 *Bloodshed pollutes the land.* The crime of murder is not only an offense against the sanctity of life but also a pollutant to the Lord's sacred land (cf. Ge 4:10–11 and notes).

36:1–13 Presents an interesting further development of the account of Zelophehad's daughters (see 27:1–11 and note). Since the Lord had instructed Moses that the women might inherit their father's land, new questions arose: What will happen to the family lands if these daughters marry among other tribes? Will not the original intention of the first provision be frustrated? Such questions led to the decision that marriage is to be kept within one's own tribe, so that the family allotments will not "pass from tribe to tribe" (v. 9).

36:4 *Year of Jubilee.* See Lev 25:10 and note.

36:10 *Zelophehad's daughters did as the LORD commanded.* The book of Numbers, which so often presents the rebellion of God's people against his grace and in defiance of his will, ends on a happy note. These noble women, who were concerned for their father's name and their own place in the land, obeyed the Lord.

36:11 See note on 33:50—36:13; cf. Lev. 27:34.

Deuteronomy

I N T R O D U C T I O N

Title

The Hebrew name of the book is *'elleh haddebarim* ("These are the words") or, more simply, *debarim* ("words"; see 1:1). The word "Deuteronomy" (meaning "repetition of the law") arose from a mistranslation in the Septuagint (the pre-Christian Greek translation of the OT) and the Latin Vulgate of a phrase in Dt 17:18, which in Hebrew means "copy of this law." The error is not serious, however, since Deuteronomy is, in a certain sense, a "repetition of the law" (see Structure and Outline).

Author and Date of Writing

The book itself ascribes most of its content to Moses (see 1:1,5; 31:24 and notes). For that reason, the OT elsewhere ascribes the bulk of Deuteronomy and other Pentateuchal legislation to Moses (see, e.g., Jos 1:7–8; 23:6; 1Ki 2:3; 8:53; Mal 4:4). Similarly Jesus attributed Dt 24:1 to Moses (Mt 19:7–8; Mk 10:3–5), Peter attributed Dt 18:15,18–19 to Moses (Ac 3:22–23), as did Stephen (see Ac 7:37–38 and note on 7:38), and Paul attributed Dt 32:21 to Moses (Ro 10:19). See also Mt 22:24 and note; Mk 12:18–19 and note on 12:18; Lk 20:27–28. At the same time, it seems clear that the narrative framework within which the Mosaic material is placed (e.g., the preamble [1:1–5] and the conclusion [ch. 34]; see also 5:1; 27:1,9,11; 29:1–2; 31:1,7,9–10,14–25,30; 32:44–46,48; 33:1–2) comes from another—and unknown—hand. See Introduction to Genesis: Author and Date of Writing.

> **A Quick Look**
>
> **Author:**
> Moses
>
> **Audience:**
> God's chosen people, the Israelites
>
> **Date:**
> Just before the Israelites entered Canaan, probably about 1406 B.C.
>
> **Theme:**
> In a series of farewell messages, Moses exhorts the new generation of Israelites to live as his obedient people in the promised land.

Historical Setting

Deuteronomy locates Moses and the Israelites in the territory of Moab in the area where the Jordan flows into the Dead Sea (1:5). As his final act at this important time of transferring leadership to Joshua, Moses delivered his farewell addresses to prepare the people for their entrance into Canaan. In them, Moses emphasized the laws that were especially needed at such a time, and he presented them in a way appropriate to the situation. In contrast to the matter-of-fact narratives of Leviticus and Numbers, here Moses, as the servant of the Lord, makes an urgent appeal to the Israelites to obey God's law and to honor all his claims on them as the people he redeemed from Egyptian bondage and made covenant with at Mount Horeb (Sinai).

Special Function in the Bible

The trajectory of the story that unfolds in Genesis – Numbers seems to call for an account of the conquest of Canaan as found in Joshua to bring closure to the movement from promise to fulfillment (see Introduction to Joshua: Title and Theological Theme). But Deuteronomy intervenes as a massive interruption. Here there is very little forward movement. At the end of Numbers, Israel is "on the plains of Moab by the Jordan across from Jericho" (Nu 36:13) and at the end of Deuteronomy, the people are still there (Dt 34:8) waiting to cross the Jordan (see Jos 1:2). All that has happened is the transition from the ministry of Moses as God's spokesman and official representative to that of Joshua in his place (Dt 34:9; see Jos 1:1 – 2 and notes). But Moses' final acts as the Lord's appointed servant for dealing with Israel are so momentous that Deuteronomy's account of them marks the conclusion to the Pentateuch, while the book of Joshua, which narrates the initial fulfillment of the promises made to the patriarchs and the conclusion to the mission on which Moses had been sent (see Nu 27:15 – 23; Jos 21:43 – 45), serves as the introduction to the Former Prophets.

So Deuteronomy creates a long pause in the advancement of the story of redemption:

(1) of deliverance from bondage to a world power (Egypt) to a place in the earth where Israel can be a free people under the rule of God;
(2) of deliverance from rootlessness in the post-Babel world (Abraham, Isaac and Jacob) to security and "rest" (see Dt 3:20 and note; 12:10; 25:19) in the promised land;
(3) of deliverance from a life of banishment from God's garden (Ge 3) to a life in the Lord's own land where he has pitched his tent (Jos 22:19).

But in that long pause on the threshold of the promised land, Moses, in this renewal of the Sinaitic covenant, reminded Israel at length of what the Lord required of them as his people if they were to cross the Jordan, take possession of the promised land and there enjoy the promised "rest" in fellowship with him. It was a word that Israel needed to hear over and over again. Upon reading the Pentateuch, Israel was brought ever anew to the threshold of the promised land and its promised "rest" to hear again this final word from God through his servant Moses (see also Ps 95:7b – 11). For this reason, all the history of Israel in Canaan as narrated in the Former Prophets is brought under the judgment of this word.

Theological Teaching and Purpose

The book of Deuteronomy was cast in the form of ancient Near Eastern suzerainty-vassal treaties of the second millennium B.C. It contained the Great King's pledge to be Israel's Suzerain and Protector if they would be faithful to him as their covenant Lord and obedient to the covenant stipulations as the vassal people of his kingdom. There would be blessings for such obedience, but curses for disobedience (chs. 27 – 30). Deuteronomy's purpose was to prepare the new generation of the Lord's chosen people to be his kingdom representatives in the land he had unconditionally promised them in the Abrahamic covenant (see Structure and Outline on p. 243; see also notes on 3:27; 17:14,18).

The love relationship of the Lord to his people, and that of the people to the Lord as their sovereign God, pervade the whole book of Deuteronomy.

The love relationship of the Lord to his people, and that of the people to the Lord as their sovereign God, pervade the whole book of Deuteronomy. Its spiritual emphasis and its call to total commitment to the Lord in worship and obedience inspired references to its message throughout the rest of Scripture. In particular, the division of the Hebrew Bible called the Former Prophets (Joshua, Judges, Samuel, Kings) is thoroughly imbued with the style, themes and motifs of Deuteronomy. Among the Latter Prophets, Jeremiah also reflects strong influence from this book.

Structure and Outline

Deuteronomy's literary structure supports its historical setting. By its interpretive, repetitious, reminiscent and somewhat irregular style it shows that it is a series of more or less extemporaneous addresses, sometimes describing events in nonchronological order (see, e.g., 10:3 and note). But it also bears in its structure clear reflections of the suzerain-vassal treaties (see chart, p. 19) of the preceding and then-current Near Eastern states, a structure that lends itself to the Biblical emphasis on the covenant between the Lord and his people. In this sense Deuteronomy is a covenant renewal document, as the following outline shows:

I. Preamble (1:1–5)
II. Historical Prologue (1:6—4:43)
III. Stipulations of the Covenant (4:44—26:19)
  A. The Great Commandment: The Demand for Absolute Allegiance (4:44—11:32)
    1. God's covenant Lordship (4:44—5:33)
    2. The principle of consecration (ch. 6)
    3. The program for conquering Canaan (ch. 7)
    4. A call to commitment in the new land (ch. 8)
    5. The lesson of the broken tablets (9:1—10:11)
    6. Another call to commitment (10:12—11:32)
  B. Supplementary Requirements (chs. 12–26)
    1. Ceremonial consecration (12:1—16:17)
    2. Human leaders in God's righteous kingdom (16:18—21:21)
    3. Sanctity of God's kingdom (21:22—25:19)
    4. Confessions of God as Redeemer-King (ch. 26)
IV. Ratification; Curses and Blessings (chs. 27–30)
V. Leadership Succession under the Covenant (chs. 31–34)
  A. Change of Leadership (31:1–29)
  B. Song of Moses (31:30—32:47)
  C. Moses' Testamental Blessing on the Tribes (32:48—33:29)
  D. Death of Moses and Succession of Joshua (ch. 34)

The Command to Leave Horeb

1 These are the words Moses spoke to
all Israel in the desert east of the Jordan[a]—that is, in the Arabah[b]—opposite
Suph, between Paran[c] and Tophel, Laban,
Hazeroth and Dizahab. 2(It takes eleven
days to go from Horeb[d] to Kadesh Barnea[e]
by the Mount Seir[f] road.)[g]
3In the fortieth year,[h] on the first day of
the eleventh month,[i] Moses proclaimed[j] to
the Israelites all that the LORD had commanded him concerning them. 4This was
after he had defeated Sihon[k] king of the
Amorites,[l] who reigned in Heshbon,[m] and
at Edrei had defeated Og[n] king of Bashan,
who reigned in Ashtaroth.[o]
5East of the Jordan in the territory of
Moab,[p] Moses began to expound this law,
saying:

6The LORD our God said to us[q] at Horeb,[r] "You have stayed long enough[s] at
this mountain. 7Break camp and advance
into the hill country of the Amorites;[t] go to
all the neighboring peoples in the Arabah,[u]
in the mountains, in the western foothills,
in the Negev[v] and along the coast, to the
land of the Canaanites[w] and to Lebanon,[x]
as far as the great river, the Euphrates.[y]
8See, I have given you this land[z].[a] Go in
and take possession of the land that the
LORD swore[b] he would give to your fathers—to Abraham, Isaac and Jacob—
and to their descendants after them."

The Appointment of Leaders

9At that time I said to you, "You are too
heavy a burden[c] for me to carry alone.[d]
10The LORD your God has increased[e] your
numbers[f] so that today you are as many[g]
as the stars in the sky.[h] 11May the LORD, the
God of your fathers, increase[i] you a thousand times and bless you as he has promised![j] 12But how can I bear your problems
and your burdens and your disputes all by
myself?[k] 13Choose some wise, understanding and respected men[l] from each of your
tribes, and I will set them over you."
14You answered me, "What you propose
to do is good."
15So I took[m] the leading men of your
tribes,[n] wise and respected men,[o] and
appointed them to have authority over
you—as commanders[p] of thousands, of
hundreds, of fifties and of tens and as tribal officials.[q] 16And I charged your judges
at that time: Hear the disputes between
your brothers and judge[r] fairly,[s] whether
the case is between brother Israelites or
between one of them and an alien.[t] 17Do
not show partiality[u] in judging; hear both
small and great alike. Do not be afraid of
any man,[v] for judgment belongs to God.
Bring me any case too hard for you, and I
will hear it.[w] 18And at that time I told you
everything you were to do.[x]

Spies Sent Out

19Then, as the LORD our God commanded us, we set out from Horeb and went
toward the hill country of the Amorites[y]

1:1 [a]S Nu 13:29; Dt 4:46 [b]ver 7; Dt 2:8; 3:17; Jos 3:16; 8:14; 11:2; Eze 47:8 [c]S Nu 10:12 **1:2** [d]S Ex 3:1 [e]S Ge 14:7; Dt 2:14; 9:23; Jos 15:3 [f]S Nu 24:18 [g]ver 19 **1:3** [h]Nu 14:33; 32:13; Dt 8:2; Heb 3:7-9 [i]Ge 50:3; Dt 34:8; Jos 4:19 [j]Dt 4:1-2 **1:4** [k]Nu 21:21-26 [l]S Ge 10:16; S 14:7 [m]S Nu 21:25 [n]Nu 21:33-35; Dt 3:10 [o]Jos 9:10; 12:4; 1Ch 11:44 **1:5** [p]S Nu 21:11 **1:6** [q]Nu 10:13 [r]S Ex 3:1 [s]Dt 2:3 **1:7** [t]ver 19; Dt 2:24; 7:1; Jos 10:5 [u]S ver 1 [v]S Nu 21:1; Jos 11:16; 12:8; 2Sa 24:7 [w]S Ge 10:18 [x]Dt 11:24 [y]S Ge 2:14 **1:8** [z]S Jos 23:13 [a]S Nu 34:2 [b]S Ex 13:11; S Nu 14:23; Heb 6:13-14 **1:9** [c]S Nu 11:14; Ps 38:4 [d]S Ex 18:18 **1:10** [e]ver 11; Eze 16:7 [f]S Dt 7:13 [g]S Ge 15:5; Isa 51:2; 60:22; Eze 33:24 [h]S Ge 22:17; S Nu 10:36 **1:11** [i]S ver 10 [j]ver 8; Ex 32:13; 2Sa 24:3; 1Ch 21:3 **1:12** [k]S Ex 5:22; S 18:18 **1:13** [l]S Ge 47:6 **1:15** [m]Ex 18:25 [n]Ex 5:14; Nu 11:16; Jos 1:10; 3:2 [o]S Ge 47:6 [p]Nu 31:14; 1Sa 8:12; 22:7; 1Ki 14:27 [q]S Nu 1:4 **1:16** [r]1Ki 3:9; Ps 72:1; Pr 2:9 [s]S Ge 31:37; Jn 7:24 [t]S Ex 12:19,49; S 22:21 **1:17** [u]S Ex 18:16; S Lev 19:15; Ac 10:34; Jas 2:1 [v]Pr 29:25 [w]Ex 18:26 **1:18** [x]S Ge 39:11 **1:19** [y]S ver 7

1:1–5 The preamble gives the historical setting for the entire book and introduces Moses, the Great King's covenant mediator.

1:1 *Moses spoke.* Almost all of Deuteronomy is presented as speeches by Moses during the final months of his life, just before the Israelites crossed the Jordan to enter Canaan. *Arabah.* Includes the valley of the Jordan (from the Sea of Galilee to the southern end of the Dead Sea) and the valley extending down to the Gulf of Aqaba. *Suph ... Paran ... Tophel, Laban, Hazeroth and Dizahab.* Places along the route from Sinai to the territory of Moab (see Nu 33:16–49 and note on 33:1–49).

1:2 *Horeb.* The usual name for Mount Sinai in Deuteronomy (the only exception is in 33:2). *Kadesh Barnea.* See notes on Ge 14:7; Nu 20:1. *Seir.* See notes on Ge 36:8; Eze 35:2.

1:3 *fortieth year.* After leaving Egypt. The Lord had condemned Israel to 40 years of wandering in Sinai as punishment for not entering Canaan as he had commanded them to do at Kadesh (Nu 14:33–34). The 40 years included the time spent at Sinai and on the journey to Kadesh as well as the next 38 years (see 2:14). See 8:2–5; 29:5–6; Nu 14:29–35; 32:13; Ac 7:36; Heb 3:7–19. *eleventh month.* January-February.

1:4 *Sihon ... Og.* See notes on Nu 21:21–26,35. *Heshbon.* See note on Isa 15:4.

1:5 *this law.* The Ten Commandments and other laws given at Mount Sinai and recorded in Ex 20–24, Leviticus and Numbers. In Deuteronomy the laws are summarized and interpreted, and adjusted to the new, specific situation Israel would face in Canaan. Thus Deuteronomy is, in essence, a covenant renewal (and updating) document (see Introduction: Theological Teaching and Purpose; Structure and Outline).

1:6 *The LORD our God.* Together with "the LORD your God," this title occurs almost 300 times in Deuteronomy in addition to the many times that "LORD" is used alone or in other combinations (see notes on 28:58; Ge 2:4; Ex 3:14–15; 6:3,6; Lev 18:2).

1:7 See Jos 1:4 and note. The land is described by its various geographical areas (see map No. 2 at the end of this study Bible). *Arabah.* See note on v. 1. *mountains.* The midsection running north and south. *western foothills.* Sloping toward the Mediterranean. *Negev.* See note on Ge 12:9. *coast.* The Mediterranean coastal strip. The "land of the Canaanites" and "Lebanon, as far as ... the Euphrates" make up the northern sector. The "hill country of the Amorites" is, in general, the central and southern mountains. This description of the land agrees with that in the promise (see v. 8) to Abraham in Ge 15:18–21, a promise later limited to Isaac's descendants (Ge 26:2–4) and still later to the descendants of Jacob (Ge 35:11–12).

1:8 See note on Ge 12:1.

1:9–18 Cf. 16:18–20; Ex 18:13–26.

1:10 *as the stars in the sky.* See 10:22; 28:62; Ge 13:16 and note; 15:5 and note; 22:17; 26:4; Ex 32:13.

1:19–46 See Nu 13–14 and notes.

through all that vast and dreadful desert[z]
that you have seen, and so we reached Kadesh Barnea.[a] 20Then I said to you, "You
have reached the hill country of the Amorites, which the LORD our God is giving us.
21See, the LORD your God has given you
the land. Go up and take possession[b] of it
as the LORD, the God of your fathers, told
you. Do not be afraid;[c] do not be discouraged."[d]
22Then all of you came to me and said,
"Let us send men ahead to spy[e] out the
land[f] for us and bring back a report about
the route we are to take and the towns we
will come to."
23The idea seemed good to me; so I
selected[g] twelve of you, one man from
each tribe. 24They left and went up into
the hill country, and came to the Valley
of Eshcol[h] and explored it. 25Taking with
them some of the fruit of the land, they
brought it down to us and reported,[i] "It
is a good land[j] that the LORD our God is
giving us."[k]

Rebellion Against the LORD

26But you were unwilling to go up;[l] you
rebelled[m] against the command of the
LORD your God. 27You grumbled[n] in your
tents and said, "The LORD hates us; so he
brought us out of Egypt to deliver us into
the hands of the Amorites to destroy us.
28Where can we go? Our brothers have
made us lose heart. They say, 'The people
are stronger and taller[o] than we are; the
cities are large, with walls up to the sky.
We even saw the Anakites[p] there.'"
29Then I said to you, "Do not be terrified; do not be afraid[q] of them.[r] 30The LORD
your God, who is going before you, will
fight[s] for you, as he did for you in Egypt,
before your very eyes, 31and in the desert. There you saw how the LORD your God
carried[t] you, as a father carries his son, all
the way you went until you reached this
place."[u]
32In spite of this,[v] you did not trust[w] in
the LORD your God, 33who went ahead of
you on your journey, in fire by night and
in a cloud by day,[x] to search[y] out places
for you to camp and to show you the way
you should go.
34When the LORD heard[z] what you said,
he was angry[a] and solemnly swore:[b]
35"Not a man of this evil generation shall
see the good land[c] I swore to give your
forefathers, 36except Caleb[d] son of Jephunneh. He will see it, and I will give him and
his descendants the land he set his feet
on, because he followed the LORD wholeheartedly.[e]"
37Because of you the LORD became angry[f] with me also and said, "You shall
not enter[g] it, either. 38But your assistant,
Joshua[h] son of Nun, will enter it. Encourage[i] him, because he will lead[j] Israel to
inherit[k] it. 39And the little ones that you
said would be taken captive,[l] your children who do not yet know[m] good from
bad—they will enter the land. I will give
it to them and they will take possession
of it. 40But as for you, turn around and set
out toward the desert along the route to
the Red Sea.[a][n]"
41Then you replied, "We have sinned
against the LORD. We will go up and fight,
as the LORD our God commanded us."
So every one of you put on his weapons, thinking it easy to go up into the hill
country.
42But the LORD said to me, "Tell them,
'Do not go up and fight, because I will not
be with you. You will be defeated by your
enemies.'"[o]
43So I told you, but you would not listen.
You rebelled against the LORD's command
and in your arrogance you marched up

[a] 40 Hebrew *Yam Suph*; that is, Sea of Reeds

1:19 [z] Dt 2:7; 8:15; 32:10; Ps 136:16; Jer 2:2,6; Hos 13:5 [a] ver 2; Nu 13:26 **1:21** [b] Dt 9:23 [c] S Nu 14:9; Jos 1:6,9,18; 2Sa 10:12; Ps 27:14 [d] Dt 7:18; Jos 8:1; 10:8 **1:22** [e] Nu 13:1-3 [f] S Ge 42:9 **1:23** [g] Nu 13:1-3 **1:24** [h] Nu 13:21-25; S 32:9 **1:25** [i] S Nu 13:27 [j] S Nu 14:7 [k] Jos 1:2 **1:26** [l] Nu 14:1-4 [m] S Nu 14:9 **1:27** [n] Dt 9:28; Ps 106:25 **1:28** [o] S Nu 13:32 [p] S Nu 13:33; Dt 9:1-3 **1:29** [q] Dt 3:22; 20:3; Ne 4:14 [r] Dt 7:18; 20:1; 31:6 **1:30** [s] S Ex 14:14 **1:31** [t] Ex 19:4; Dt 32:10-12; Ps 28:9; Isa 46:3-4; 63:9; Hos 11:3; Ac 13:18 [u] Jer 31:32 **1:32** [v] S Nu 14:11 [w] Dt 9:23; Ps 78:22; 106:24; Zep 3:2; Heb 3:19; Jude 1:5 **1:33** [x] Ex 13:21; Nu 9:15-23; Ne 9:12; Ps 78:14 [y] S Nu 10:33 **1:34** [z] S Nu 11:1 [a] S Nu 32:14 [b] S Nu 14:23, 28-30; Eze 20:15; Heb 3:11 **1:35** [c] S Nu 14:29 **1:36** [d] S Nu 13:6 [e] S Nu 14:24 **1:37** [f] Ps 106:32 [g] S Nu 27:13 **1:38** [h] S Nu 11:28 [i] Dt 31:7 [j] Dt 3:28 [k] Jos 11:23; Ps 78:55; 136:21 **1:39** [l] S Nu 14:3 [m] Isa 7:15-16 **1:40** [n] S Ex 14:27; Jdg 11:16 **1:42** [o] S Nu 14:41-43

1:21 *as the LORD … told you.* The promise of the land (see note on v. 7) was reaffirmed to Moses (v. 8) at the burning bush (Ex 3:8,17). Now the Israelites are told to enter the land and conquer it. *Do not be afraid … discouraged.* See 31:8; Jos 1:9; 8:1; 10:25; cf. Ps 56:3–4; Isa 41:10.

1:23 *twelve.* They are named in Nu 13:4–15.

1:24 *Eshcol.* See note on Nu 13:23.

1:27 *grumbled.* See note on Ex 15:24. *The LORD hates us.* The people's statement is ironic indeed in the light of Deuteronomy's major theme of love (see Introduction: Theological Teaching and Purpose).

1:28 *Anakites.* Earlier inhabitants of Canaan, described as giants (see 2:10,21; 9:2; see also Nu 13:32–33 and notes).

1:29 *Do not be terrified … afraid.* See notes on v. 21; Isa 41:10,13; 43:2.

1:30 *as he did for you in Egypt.* See Ex 14:1—15:19.

1:31 *God carried you.* Cf. Isa 40:11; Jer 31:10; cf. also Eze 34:11–16 and notes.

1:33 *in fire by night and in a cloud by day.* The presence of the Lord was in the cloud over the tabernacle to guide the Israelites throughout their desert journeys (see Ex 13:21 and note; 40:34–38 and note on 40:34).

1:36 *Caleb.* See Nu 13:30—14:38; Jos 14:6–15. *followed the LORD wholeheartedly.* See note on Nu 14:24.

1:37 *Because of you.* See 3:26; 4:21. God was angry with Moses who, failing to honor the Lord as holy, struck the rock at Meribah to get water (see Nu 20:9–13 and note on 20:11; 27:12–14). And since it was the Israelites who had incited him to sin, God was angry with them too. This event (v. 37) occurred almost 40 years after that of the preceding verses (vv. 34–36), but Moses, interested in telling about the Israelites' sin and his own, brings the two events together.

1:39 *do not yet know good from bad.* See notes on Ge 2:9; Isa 7:15; cf. Jnh 4:11 and note.

1:41 *We will go up.* See v. 26; Nu 14:40 and note.

1:43 *You rebelled against the LORD's command.* The same charge as in v. 26. First the people rebelled against the

into the hill country. 44The Amorites who
lived in those hills came out against you;
they chased you like a swarm of bees[p] and
beat you down from Seir[q] all the way to
Hormah.[r] 45You came back and wept before the LORD,[s] but he paid no attention[t]
to your weeping and turned a deaf ear[u] to
you. 46And so you stayed in Kadesh[v] many
days—all the time you spent there.

Wanderings in the Desert

2 Then we turned back and set out toward the desert along the route to the
Red Sea,[a][w] as the LORD had directed me.
For a long time we made our way around
the hill country of Seir.[x]
2Then the LORD said to me, 3"You have
made your way around this hill country
long enough;[y] now turn north. 4Give the
people these orders:[z] 'You are about to
pass through the territory of your brothers the descendants of Esau,[a] who live in
Seir.[b] They will be afraid[c] of you, but be
very careful. 5Do not provoke them to war,
for I will not give you any of their land,
not even enough to put your foot on. I
have given Esau the hill country of Seir as
his own.[d] 6You are to pay them in silver
for the food you eat and the water you
drink.' "
7The LORD your God has blessed you
in all the work of your hands. He has
watched[e] over your journey through this
vast desert.[f] These forty years[g] the LORD
your God has been with you, and you
have not lacked anything.[h]
8So we went on past our brothers the
descendants of Esau, who live in Seir.
We turned from[i] the Arabah[j] road, which
comes up from Elath and Ezion Geber,[k]
and traveled along the desert road of
Moab.[l]
9Then the LORD said to me, "Do not harass the Moabites or provoke them to war,
for I will not give you any part of their
land. I have given Ar[m] to the descendants
of Lot[n] as a possession."
10(The Emites[o] used to live there—a
people strong and numerous, and as tall
as the Anakites.[p] 11Like the Anakites, they
too were considered Rephaites,[q] but the
Moabites called them Emites. 12Horites[r]
used to live in Seir, but the descendants
of Esau drove them out. They destroyed
the Horites from before them and settled
in their place, just as Israel did[s] in the land
the LORD gave them as their possession.)
13And the LORD said, "Now get up and
cross the Zered Valley.[t]" So we crossed the
valley.
14Thirty-eight years[u] passed from the
time we left Kadesh Barnea[v] until we
crossed the Zered Valley. By then, that
entire generation[w] of fighting men had
perished from the camp, as the LORD had
sworn to them.[x] 15The LORD's hand was
against them until he had completely eliminated[y] them from the camp.
16Now when the last of these fighting
men among the people had died, 17the
LORD said to me, 18"Today you are to pass
by the region of Moab at Ar.[z] 19When you
come to the Ammonites,[a] do not harass
them or provoke them to war,[b] for I will
not give you possession of any land belonging to the Ammonites. I have given
it as a possession to the descendants of
Lot.[c]"
20(That too was considered a land of the
Rephaites,[d] who used to live there; but the
Ammonites called them Zamzummites.
21They were a people strong and numerous, and as tall as the Anakites.[e] The LORD
destroyed them from before the Ammonites, who drove them out and settled in
their place. 22The LORD had done the same
for the descendants of Esau, who lived in
Seir,[f] when he destroyed the Horites from
before them. They drove them out and

[a] *1* Hebrew *Yam Suph*; that is, Sea of Reeds

1:44 [p] Ps 118:12 [q] S Nu 24:18 [r] S Nu 14:45
1:45 [s] S Nu 14:1 [t] Job 27:9; 35:13; Ps 18:41; 66:18; Pr 1:28; Isa 1:15; Jer 14:12; La 3:8; Mic 3:4; S Jn 9:31 [u] Ps 28:1; 39:12; Pr 28:9
1:46 [v] S Nu 20:1
2:1 [w] S Ex 14:27; S Nu 21:4 [x] S Nu 24:18
2:3 [y] Dt 1:6
2:4 [z] Nu 20:14-21 [a] Ge 36:8 [b] ver 1 [c] Ex 15:16
2:5 [d] Jos 24:4
2:7 [e] Dt 8:2-4 [f] S Ex 13:21; S Dt 1:19 [g] ver 14; S Nu 14:33; 32:13; Jos 5:6 [h] Ne 9:21; Am 2:10
2:8 [i] S Nu 20:21 [j] S Dt 1:1 [k] Nu 33:35; 1Ki 9:26 [l] S Nu 21:4
2:9 [m] S Nu 21:15 [n] Ge 19:38; Ps 83:8
2:10 [o] Ge 14:5 [p] S Nu 13:22,33
2:11 [q] S Ge 14:5
2:12 [r] S Ge 14:6 [s] Nu 21:25,35
2:13 [t] S Nu 21:12
2:14 [u] S ver 7 [v] S Dt 1:2 [w] Nu 14:29-35 [x] Dt 1:34-35; Jos 5:6
2:15 [y] Ps 106:26; Jude 1:5
2:18 [z] S Nu 21:15
2:19 [a] S Ge 19:38 [b] 2Ch 20:10 [c] S ver 9
2:20 [d] S Ge 14:5
2:21 [e] ver 10
2:22 [f] S Ge 14:6

Lord's command to go into the land, then against his command not to enter the land. After their first rebellion the Lord would not go with them. His presence was essential, and Israel needed to learn that lesson.

1:44 *bees.* See note on Ex 23:28.

1:45 *before the LORD.* At the tabernacle.

2:1—3:11 See Nu 20:14—21:35 and notes.

2:1 *Red Sea.* Here probably the Gulf of Aqaba (see note on 1Ki 9:26). *hill country of Seir.* The mountainous area south of the Dead Sea (Edom).

2:5 *I will not give you any of their land.* See vv. 9,19. The Lord told Moses to bypass Edom, Moab and Ammon because of their blood relationship to Israel. The Israelites were to take over only those lands east of the Jordan that were in the hands of the Amorites (see v. 24; 3:2). *I have given.* See vv. 9,19. The Lord had given the descendants of Esau (Edomites) and Lot (Moabites and Ammonites) their lands, just as he was giving the Israelites the territories of Transjordan and Canaan.

2:6,28 *silver.* See note on 14:25.

2:8 *Elath and Ezion Geber.* Towns at the head of the Gulf of Aqaba. The "Arabah road" ran from the head of the gulf northward and to the east of Moab.

2:10 *Anakites.* See note on 1:28.

2:11 *Rephaites.* People of large stature (see 3:11; 1Ch 20:4 and note).

2:12 *Horites.* See note on Ge 14:6. *the land the LORD gave them.* Either (1) the Transjordan regions (see 2:24—3:20), (2) Canaan itself or (3) Transjordan and Canaan. If either (2) or (3) is intended, editorial updating is involved (see note on Ge 14:14).

2:13 *Zered.* The main stream (intermittent) that flows into the southern end of the Dead Sea from the east. It marked the border between Edom and Moab (see map No. 4 at the end of this study Bible).

2:14 *Thirty-eight years.* See note on 1:3.

2:20 *Zamzummites.* Perhaps to be identified with the Zuzites of Ge 14:5.

have lived in their place to this day. 23And
as for the Avvites[g] who lived in villages as
far as Gaza,[h] the Caphtorites[i] coming out
from Caphtor[a][j] destroyed them and settled
in their place.)

Defeat of Sihon King of Heshbon

24"Set out now and cross the Arnon
Gorge.[k] See, I have given into your hand
Sihon the Amorite,[l] king of Heshbon,
and his country. Begin to take possession
of it and engage[m] him in battle. 25This
very day I will begin to put the terror[n]
and fear[o] of you on all the nations under
heaven. They will hear reports of you and
will tremble[p] and be in anguish because
of you."

26From the desert of Kedemoth[q] I sent
messengers to Sihon[r] king of Heshbon offering peace[s] and saying, 27"Let us pass
through your country. We will stay on the
main road; we will not turn aside to the
right or to the left.[t] 28Sell us food to eat[u]
and water to drink for their price in silver.
Only let us pass through on foot[v]— 29as
the descendants of Esau, who live in Seir,
and the Moabites, who live in Ar, did for
us — until we cross the Jordan into the
land the LORD our God is giving us." 30But
Sihon king of Heshbon refused to let us
pass through. For the LORD[w] your God had
made his spirit stubborn[x] and his heart
obstinate[y] in order to give him into your
hands,[z] as he has now done.

31The LORD said to me, "See, I have begun to deliver Sihon and his country over
to you. Now begin to conquer and possess
his land."[a]

32When Sihon and all his army came out
to meet us in battle[b] at Jahaz, 33the LORD
our God delivered[c] him over to us and we
struck him down,[d] together with his sons
and his whole army. 34At that time we took
all his towns and completely destroyed[b][e]
them — men, women and children. We left
no survivors. 35But the livestock[f] and the
plunder[g] from the towns we had captured
we carried off for ourselves. 36From Aroer[h]
on the rim of the Arnon Gorge, and from
the town in the gorge, even as far as Gilead,[i] not one town was too strong for us.
The LORD our God gave[j] us all of them.
37But in accordance with the command of
the LORD our God,[k] you did not encroach
on any of the land of the Ammonites,[l]
neither the land along the course of the
Jabbok[m] nor that around the towns in the
hills.

Defeat of Og King of Bashan

3 Next we turned and went up along the
road toward Bashan, and Og king of Bashan[n] with his whole army marched out to
meet us in battle at Edrei.[o] 2The LORD said
to me, "Do not be afraid[p] of him, for I have
handed him over to you with his whole
army and his land. Do to him what you
did to Sihon king of the Amorites, who
reigned in Heshbon."

3So the LORD our God also gave into our
hands Og king of Bashan and all his army.
We struck them down,[q] leaving no survivors.[r] 4At that time we took all his cities.[s]
There was not one of the sixty cities that
we did not take from them — the whole region of Argob, Og's kingdom[t] in Bashan.[u]
5All these cities were fortified with high
walls and with gates and bars, and there
were also a great many unwalled villages.
6We completely destroyed[b] them, as we
had done with Sihon king of Heshbon, destroying[b][v] every city — men, women and
children. 7But all the livestock[w] and the
plunder from their cities we carried off for
ourselves.

8So at that time we took from these two
kings of the Amorites[x] the territory east of
the Jordan, from the Arnon Gorge as far as

2:23 [g] Jos 13:3; 18:23; 2Ki 17:31 [h] S Ge 10:19 [i] S Ge 10:14 [j] Jer 47:4; Am 9:7 **2:24** [k] Nu 21:13-14; Jdg 11:13,18 [l] S Dt 1:7 [m] Dt 3:6 **2:25** [n] S Ge 35:5; Dt 11:25 [o] Jos 2:9,11; 1Ch 14:17; 2Ch 14:14; 17:10; 20:29; Isa 2:19; 13:13; 19:16 [p] Ex 15:14-16 **2:26** [q] Jos 13:18; 1Ch 6:79 [r] Dt 1:4; Jdg 11:21-22 [s] Dt 20:10; Jdg 21:13; 2Sa 20:19 **2:27** [t] Nu 21:21-22 **2:28** [u] Dt 23:4 [v] S Nu 20:19 **2:30** [w] Jdg 14:4; 1Ki 12:15 [x] S Ex 4:21; Ro 9:18 [y] S Ex 14:17 [z] La 3:65 **2:31** [a] S Ge 12:7 **2:32** [b] S Nu 21:23 **2:33** [c] Ex 23:31; Dt 7:2; 31:5 [d] S Nu 21:24 **2:34** [e] S Nu 21:2; Dt 3:6; 7:2; Ps 106:34 **2:35** [f] Dt 3:7 [g] S Ge 34:29; S 49:27 **2:36** [h] S Nu 32:34 [i] S Nu 32:39 [j] Ps 44:3 **2:37** [k] ver 18-19 [l] S Nu 21:24 [m] S Ge 32:22 **3:1** [n] S Nu 32:19 [o] S Nu 21:33 **3:2** [p] Jos 10:8; 2Ki 19:6; Isa 7:4 **3:3** [q] S Nu 21:24 [r] Nu 21:35 **3:4** [s] S Nu 21:24 [t] ver 13 [u] S Nu 21:33 **3:6** [v] Dt 2:24 **3:7** [w] Dt 2:35 **3:8** [x] Nu 32:33; Jos 13:8-12

[a] *23* That is, Crete [b] *34,6* The Hebrew term refers to the irrevocable giving over of things or persons to the LORD, often by totally destroying them.

2:23 *Avvites.* Pre-Philistine people otherwise unknown (Jos 13:3). *Caphtorites.* See note on Ge 10:14.
2:24 *Arnon.* See note on Nu 21:10–13. *Sihon . . . Heshbon.* See 1:4 and note.
2:26 *Kedemoth.* Means "eastern regions."
2:30 *God had made his spirit stubborn and his heart obstinate.* In the OT, actions are often attributed to God without the mention of mediate or contributing situations or persons. Sihon by his own conscious will refused Israel passage, but it was God who would give Sihon's land to Israel (see note on Ex 4:21).
2:32 *Jahaz.* See Nu 21:23; see also note on Isa 15:4.
2:34 *completely destroyed.* See NIV text note. The Hebrew for this expression usually refers to the destruction of everyone and everything that could be destroyed. Objects like gold, silver and bronze, not subject to destruction, were put in a secure place as God's possession. Destruction of people and things made them useless to the conquerors but put them in the hands of God. So the word is sometimes translated "destroyed" and sometimes "devoted" (see, e.g., Nu 18:14; Jos 6:17 and note). God sometimes permitted exclusion from this practice, as when he assigned captured livestock and other plunder to his people as recompense for service in his army (see v. 35; 3:7; Jos 8:2).
2:36 *Aroer.* See note on Isa 17:2. *Gilead.* See note on Ge 31:21.
2:37 *Jabbok.* See note on Ge 32:22.
3:3 *gave into our hands Og.* As in 2:26–37. See 1:4 and note.
3:4 *sixty cities.* These were "large walled cities" (1Ki 4:13), implying a heavily populated territory (see v. 5). *region of Argob.* An otherwise unidentified area in Bashan (see vv. 13–14; 1Ki 4:13), which was northeast of the Sea of Galilee.
3:6–7 See note on 2:34.
3:8 *Mount Hermon.* Rising to a height of over 9,200 feet and snowcapped throughout the year, it is one of the most prominent and beautiful mountains in Lebanon.

Mount Hermon.[y] 9(Hermon is called Sirion[z] by the Sidonians; the Amorites call it Senir.)[a] 10We took all the towns on the plateau, and all Gilead, and all Bashan as far as Salecah[b] and Edrei, towns of Og's kingdom in Bashan. 11(Only Og king of Bashan was left of the remnant of the Rephaites.[c] His bed[a] was made of iron and was more than thirteen feet long and six feet wide.[b] It is still in Rabbah[d] of the Ammonites.)

Division of the Land

12Of the land that we took over at that time, I gave the Reubenites and the Gadites the territory north of Aroer[e] by the Arnon Gorge, including half the hill country of Gilead, together with its towns. 13The rest of Gilead and also all of Bashan, the kingdom of Og, I gave to the half-tribe of Manasseh.[f] (The whole region of Argob in Bashan used to be known as a land of the Rephaites.[g] 14Jair,[h] a descendant of Manasseh, took the whole region of Argob as far as the border of the Geshurites and the Maacathites;[i] it was named[j] after him, so that to this day Bashan is called Havvoth Jair.[c]) 15And I gave Gilead to Makir.[k] 16But to the Reubenites and the Gadites I gave the territory extending from Gilead down to the Arnon Gorge (the middle of the gorge being the border) and out to the Jabbok River,[l] which is the border of the Ammonites. 17Its western border was the Jordan in the Arabah,[m] from Kinnereth[n] to the Sea of the Arabah[o] (the Salt Sea[d][p]), below the slopes of Pisgah.

18I commanded you at that time: "The LORD your God has given[q] you this land to take possession of it. But all your able-bodied men, armed for battle, must cross over ahead of your brother Israelites.[r] 19However, your wives,[s] your children and your livestock[t] (I know you have much livestock) may stay in the towns I have given you, 20until the LORD gives rest to your brothers as he has to you, and they too have taken over the land that the LORD your God is giving them, across the Jordan. After that, each of you may go back to the possession I have given you."

Moses Forbidden to Cross the Jordan

21At that time I commanded Joshua: "You have seen with your own eyes all that the LORD your God has done to these two kings. The LORD will do the same to all the kingdoms over there where you are going. 22Do not be afraid[u] of them;[v] the LORD your God himself will fight[w] for you."

23At that time I pleaded[x] with the LORD: 24"O Sovereign LORD, you have begun to show to your servant your greatness[y] and your strong hand. For what god[z] is there in heaven or on earth who can do the deeds and mighty works[a] you do?[b] 25Let me go over and see the good land[c] beyond the Jordan—that fine hill country and Lebanon.[d]"

26But because of you the LORD was angry[e] with me and would not listen to me. "That is enough," the LORD said. "Do not speak to me anymore about this matter. 27Go up to the top of Pisgah[f] and look west and north and south and east.[g] Look at

[a] 11 Or *sarcophagus* [b] 11 Hebrew *nine cubits long and four cubits wide* (about 4 meters long and 1.8 meters wide) [c] 14 Or *called the settlements of Jair* [d] 17 That is, the Dead Sea

3:8 [y] Dt 4:48; Jos 11:3, 17; 12:1; 13:5; Jdg 3:3; 1Ch 5:23; Ps 42:6; 89:12; 133:3; SS 4:8 **3:9** [z] Ps 29:6 [a] 1Ch 5:23; SS 4:8; Eze 27:5 **3:10** [b] Jos 12:5; 1Ch 5:11 **3:11** [c] Ge 14:5 [d] Jos 13:25; 15:60; 2Sa 11:1; 12:26; 17:27; 1Ch 20:1; Jer 49:2; Eze 21:20; 25:5; Am 1:14 **3:12** [e] Dt 2:36 **3:13** [f] Dt 29:8 [g] S Ge 14:5 **3:14** [h] S Nu 32:41 [i] Jos 12:5; 13:11, 13; 2Sa 10:6; 23:34; 2Ki 25:23; 1Ch 4:19; Jer 40:8 [j] Jos 19:47; Ps 49:11 **3:15** [k] S Ge 50:23; Nu 32:39-40 **3:16** [l] S Nu 21:24 **3:17** [m] 2Sa 2:29; 4:7; Eze 47:8 [n] S Nu 34:11 [o] S Dt 1:1 [p] S Ge 14:3 **3:18** [q] Jos 1:13 [r] S Nu 32:17 **3:19** [s] Jos 1:14 [t] S Nu 32:16 **3:22** [u] S Dt 1:29 [v] Dt 7:18; 20:1; 31:6; 2Ch 32:8; Ps 23:4; Isa 41:10 [w] S Ex 14:14 **3:23** [x] Dt 1:37; 31:2; 32:52; 34:4 **3:24** [y] Dt 5:24; 11:2; 32:3 [z] S Ex 8:10 [a] Ps 71:16; 106:2; 145:12; 150:2 [b] 2Sa 7:22 **3:25** [c] Dt 4:22 [d] Dt 1:7; Jos 1:4; 9:1; 11:17; 12:7; 13:5; Jdg 3:3; 9:15; 1Ki 4:33 **3:26** [e] ver 27; Dt 1:37; 31:2 **3:27** [f] S Nu 21:20 [g] S Ge 13:14

3:9 *Sirion.* This name for Mount Hermon is found also in a Canaanite document contemporary with Moses. *Senir.* This name for Mount Hermon is also found in Assyrian sources.

3:10 *Salecah.* A city marking the eastern boundary of Bashan (see Jos 13:11).

3:11 *bed ... of iron.* Possibly a sarcophagus made of black basalt. Such sarcophagi (stone coffins) have been found in Bashan, and the Hebrew for "bed" (see NIV text note) and "iron" may reflect this. If an actual bed, it was probably made of wood but with certain iron fixtures, as were the "iron chariots" (see note on Jos 17:16). *Rabbah of the Ammonites.* Called Philadelphia in NT times, Rabbah was the capital of ancient Ammon (Am 1:13–14). Today its name is Amman, the capital of the kingdom of Jordan.

3:12–20 See Nu 32; 34:13–15 and notes.

3:14 *Jair ... Havvoth Jair.* See NIV text note; see also note on Jdg 10:3. *the Geshurites and the Maacathites.* Two comparatively small kingdoms, Geshur was east of the Sea of Galilee and Maacah was east of the Waters of Merom (see note on Jos 11:5) and north of Geshur.

3:15 *Makir.* See note on Ge 50:23.

3:17 *Kinnereth.* See note on Mk 1:16. The Hebrew word *kinnor* means "harp"; the Sea of Galilee is a harp-shaped lake. Or reference may be to the town on the northwestern shore of the Sea of Galilee that gave its name to the sea. *Pisgah.* On the edge of the high plateau overlooking the Dead Sea from the east (see Nu 21:20).

3:18 *you.* The tribes of Reuben and Gad and the half-tribe of Manasseh.

3:20 *rest.* A peaceful situation—free from external threat and oppression, and untroubled within by conflict, famine or plague (see 12:9–10; 25:19; see also notes on Jos 1:13; 1Ki 5:4; Heb 4:1–11).

3:22 *God himself.* The conquest narratives emphasize the truth that without the Lord's help Israel's victory would be impossible. The Lord's power, not Israel's unaided strength, achieved victory. Moses bolstered Israel's resolve and faith by giving this assurance (see 1:30; 2:21–22,31; 20:4).

3:23–25 Moses' final plea to be allowed to enter the land (see 1:37; 31:2 and notes).

3:26 *because of you.* See note on 1:37.

3:27 *Go up to the top of Pisgah.* Moses did so after he had expounded the law to the Israelites to prepare them for life in the promised land (see 32:48–52; 34:1–6). *Pisgah.* See note on v. 17. *look west and north and south and east.* Like Abraham (see Ge 13:14 and note), Moses would inherit the promised land only through his descendants (see 34:1–4).

the land with your own eyes, since you
are not going to cross[h] this Jordan.[i] 28But
commission[j] Joshua, and encourage[k] and
strengthen him, for he will lead this people across[l] and will cause them to inherit
the land that you will see." 29So we stayed
in the valley near Beth Peor.[m]

Obedience Commanded

4 Hear now, O Israel, the decrees[n] and
laws I am about to teach[o] you. Follow
them so that you may live[p] and may go in
and take possession of the land that the
LORD, the God of your fathers, is giving
you. 2Do not add[q] to what I command you
and do not subtract[r] from it, but keep[s] the
commands[t] of the LORD your God that I
give you.
3You saw with your own eyes what the
LORD did at Baal Peor.[u] The LORD your God
destroyed from among you everyone who
followed the Baal of Peor, 4but all of you
who held fast to the LORD your God are still
alive today.
5See, I have taught[v] you decrees and
laws[w] as the LORD my God commanded[x]
me, so that you may follow them in the
land you are entering[y] to take possession
of it. 6Observe[z] them carefully, for this will
show your wisdom[a] and understanding to
the nations, who will hear about all these
decrees and say, "Surely this great nation is
a wise and understanding people."[b] 7What
other nation is so great[c] as to have their
gods near[d] them the way the LORD our God
is near us whenever we pray to him? 8And
what other nation is so great as to have such
righteous decrees and laws[e] as this body of
laws I am setting before you today?
9Only be careful,[f] and watch yourselves
closely so that you do not forget the things
your eyes have seen or let them slip from
your heart as long as you live. Teach[g]
them to your children[h] and to their children after them. 10Remember the day you
stood before the LORD your God at Horeb,[i]
when he said to me, "Assemble the people before me to hear my words so that
they may learn[j] to revere[k] me as long as
they live in the land[l] and may teach[m] them
to their children." 11You came near and
stood at the foot of the mountain[n] while
it blazed with fire[o] to the very heavens,
with black clouds and deep darkness.[p]
12Then the LORD spoke[q] to you out of the
fire. You heard the sound of words but saw
no form;[r] there was only a voice.[s] 13He declared to you his covenant,[t] the Ten Commandments,[u] which he commanded you
to follow and then wrote them on two
stone tablets. 14And the LORD directed me
at that time to teach you the decrees and
laws[v] you are to follow in the land that
you are crossing the Jordan to possess.

Idolatry Forbidden

15You saw no form[w] of any kind the day
the LORD spoke to you at Horeb[x] out of the
fire. Therefore watch yourselves very carefully,[y] 16so that you do not become corrupt[z] and make for yourselves an idol,[a] an
image of any shape, whether formed like
a man or a woman, 17or like any animal
on earth or any bird that flies in the air,[b]
18or like any creature that moves along the
ground or any fish in the waters below.
19And when you look up to the sky and
see the sun,[c] the moon and the stars[d]—all
the heavenly array[e]—do not be enticed[f]
into bowing down to them and worshiping[g] things the LORD your God has apportioned to all the nations under heav-
en. 20But as for you, the LORD took you
and brought you out of the iron-smelting

3:27 [h]S ver 26; S Nu 20:12; Dt 32:52 [i]S Nu 27:12 **3:28** [j]Nu 27:18-23 [k]Dt 31:7 [l]Dt 1:38; 31:3,23 **3:29** [m]S Nu 23:28; Dt 4:46; 34:6; Jos 13:20 **4:1** [n]S Lev 18:4 [o]Dt 1:3 [p]S Lev 18:5; Dt 30:15-20; S Ro 10:5 **4:2** [q]Dt 12:32; Jos 1:7; Pr 30:6; Rev 22:18-19 [r]Jer 26:2 [s]S Lev 22:31 [t]Dt 10:12-13; Ecc 12:13 **4:3** [u]Nu 25:1-9; Ps 106:28 **4:5** [v]Ps 71:17; 119:102; Jer 32:33 [w]S Ex 18:20 [x]S Lev 27:34 [y]Ezr 9:11 **4:6** [z]Dt 29:9; 1Ki 2:3 [a]Dt 30:19-20; 32:46-47; Ps 19:7; 119:98; Pr 1:7; 2Ti 3:15 [b]Job 1:1; 28:28; Ps 111:10; Pr 2:5; 3:7; 9:10; Ecc 12:13; Eze 5:5 **4:7** [c]ver 32-34; 2Sa 7:23 [d]S Nu 23:21; S Ps 46:1; Ac 17:27 **4:8** [e]Ps 89:14; 97:2; 119:7,62, 144,160,172; Ro 3:2 **4:9** [f]S Ex 23:13 [g]S Ge 14:14; 18:19; Dt 6:20-25; Eph 6:4 [h]S Ex 10:2 **4:10** [i]S Ex 3:1 [j]Dt 14:23; 17:19; 31:12-13; Ps 2:11; 111:10; 147:11; Isa 8:13; Jer 32:40 [k]S Ex 20:20 [l]Dt 12:1 [m]ver 9 **4:11** [n]S Ex 3:1; S 19:17 [o]S Ex 19:18 [p]S Ex 19:9; Ps 18:11; 97:2 **4:12** [q]Ex 20:22; Dt 5:4,22; S Mt 3:17; Heb 12:19 [r]Jn 5:37 [s]S Ex 19:9 **4:13** [t]Dt 9:9; Ro 9:4 [u]S Ex 24:12 **4:14** [v]S Ex 21:1 **4:15** [w]Isa 40:18; 41:22-24 [x]S Ex 3:1 [y]Jos 23:11; Mal 2:15 **4:16** [z]S Ge 6:11-12; Dt 9:12; 31:29; 32:5; Jdg 2:19 [a]Ex 20:4-5; Ro 1:23 **4:17** [b]Ro 1:23 **4:19** [c]Dt 17:3; 2Ki 23:11; Job 31:26; Jer 8:2; 43:13; Eze 8:16 [d]S Ge 1:16 [e]S Ge 2:1; S 37:9; Ro 1:25 [f]Dt 13:5 [g]S Nu 25:3

3:28 *commission Joshua.* See 31:7–8.

3:29 *Beth Peor.* Means "house/sanctuary of Peor." Very likely, reference is to the place where the Baal of Peor was worshiped (see Nu 23:28; 25:3,5).

4:1 *Hear … O Israel.* God's call to his people to hear and obey is a frequent theme in Deuteronomy (see, e.g., 5:1; 6:3–4; 9:1; 20:3) and elsewhere in the OT. See also note on 6:4–9.

4:2 *Do not add … do not subtract.* The revelation the Lord gives is sufficient. All of it must be obeyed, and anything that adulterates or contradicts it cannot be tolerated (see 12:32; Pr 30:6 and note; Gal 3:15; Rev 22:18–19 and note).

4:4 *held fast.* See note on 10:20.

4:7 *near us whenever we pray.* The Israelites always had access to the Lord in prayer. His presence was symbolized by the tabernacle in the center of the camp, and by the pillar of cloud over the tabernacle (see Ex 40:34–38 and note on 40:34; Nu 23:21).

4:9 *Teach them to your children.* See v. 10; 6:7; 11:19; Ps 78:4–8; cf. Ex 12:26–27.

4:10–14 See Ex 19–24 and notes.

4:10 *Remember.* The divine call to Israel to remember the Lord's past redemptive acts—especially how he delivered them from slavery in Egypt—is a common theme in Deuteronomy (5:15; 7:18; 8:2,18; 9:7,27; 11:2; 15:15; 16:3,12; 24:9,18,22; 25:17) and is summarized in 32:7: "Remember the days of old."

4:12 *no form.* See v. 15; see also note on Ex 20:4. "God is spirit" (Jn 4:24; cf. Isa 31:3 and note). *only a voice.* See v. 36; 5:23–26; Nu 7:89; 1Ki 19:13.

4:13 *his covenant, the Ten Commandments.* See notes on Ex 20:1; 34:28. *two stone tablets.* See note on Ex 31:18.

4:15–18 See note on Ex 20:4.

4:19 Cf. 17:3. *do not be enticed.* As kings of Judah would be later (see 2Ki 17:16 and note; 21:3,5; 23:4–5).

4:20 *iron-smelting furnace.* The period in Egypt was a time of affliction for the Israelites (see 1Ki 8:51; Jer 11:4; see also Isa 48:10 and note).

furnace,[h] out of Egypt,[i] to be the people of
his inheritance,[j] as you now are.
21 The LORD was angry with me[k] because of you, and he solemnly swore that
I would not cross the Jordan and enter
the good land the LORD your God is giving
you as your inheritance. 22 I will die in this
land;[l] I will not cross the Jordan; but you
are about to cross over and take possession of that good land.[m] 23 Be careful not
to forget the covenant[n] of the LORD your
God that he made with you; do not make
for yourselves an idol[o] in the form of anything the LORD your God has forbidden.
24 For the LORD your God is a consuming
fire,[p] a jealous God.[q]
25 After you have had children and grandchildren and have lived in the land a long
time—if you then become corrupt[r] and
make any kind of idol,[s] doing evil[t] in the
eyes of the LORD your God and provoking
him to anger, 26 I call heaven and earth as
witnesses[u] against you[v] this day that you
will quickly perish[w] from the land that you
are crossing the Jordan to possess. You
will not live there long but will certainly
be destroyed. 27 The LORD will scatter[x] you
among the peoples, and only a few of you
will survive[y] among the nations to which
the LORD will drive you. 28 There you will
worship man-made gods[z] of wood and
stone,[a] which cannot see or hear or eat or
smell.[b] 29 But if from there you seek[c] the
LORD your God, you will find him if you
look for him with all your heart[d] and with
all your soul.[e] 30 When you are in distress[f]
and all these things have happened to you,
then in later days[g] you will return[h] to the
LORD your God and obey him. 31 For the
LORD your God is a merciful[i] God; he will
not abandon[j] or destroy[k] you or forget[l] the
covenant with your forefathers, which he
confirmed to them by oath.

The LORD Is God

32 Ask[m] now about the former days,
long before your time, from the day God
created man on the earth;[n] ask from one
end of the heavens to the other.[o] Has anything so great[p] as this ever happened, or
has anything like it ever been heard of?
33 Has any other people heard the voice of
God[a] speaking out of fire, as you have,
and lived?[q] 34 Has any god ever tried to
take for himself one nation out of another
nation,[r] by testings,[s] by miraculous signs[t]
and wonders,[u] by war, by a mighty hand
and an outstretched arm,[v] or by great and
awesome deeds,[w] like all the things the
LORD your God did for you in Egypt before
your very eyes?
35 You were shown these things so that
you might know that the LORD is God; besides him there is no other.[x] 36 From heav-
en he made you hear his voice[y] to discipline[z] you. On earth he showed you his
great fire, and you heard his words from
out of the fire. 37 Because he loved[a] your
forefathers and chose their descendants
after them, he brought you out of Egypt
by his Presence and his great strength,[b]
38 to drive out before you nations greater
and stronger than you and to bring you
into their land to give it to you for your
inheritance,[c] as it is today.
39 Acknowledge[d] and take to heart this
day that the LORD is God in heaven above
and on the earth below. There is no other.[e]
40 Keep[f] his decrees and commands,[g] which
I am giving you today, so that it may go
well[h] with you and your children after you
and that you may live long[i] in the land the
LORD your God gives you for all time.

[a] 33 Or *of a god*

4:20 [h] S Ex 1:13 [i] S Ex 3:10 [j] S Ge 17:7; S Ex 8:22; S 34:9; Tit 2:14 **4:21** [k] Nu 20:12; Dt 1:37 **4:22** [l] Nu 27:13-14 [m] Dt 3:25 **4:23** [n] ver 9 [o] S Ex 20:4 **4:24** [p] S Ex 15:7; S 19:18; Heb 12:29 [q] S Ex 20:5 **4:25** [r] ver 16 [s] ver 23 [t] 1Ki 11:6; 15:26; 16:25,30; 2Ki 17:2,17; 21:2 **4:26** [u] Ge 31:50; Pr 14:5 [v] Dt 30:18-19; 31:28; 32:1; Ps 50:4; Isa 1:2; 34:1; Jer 6:19; Mic 6:2 [w] Dt 6:15; 7:4 **4:27** [x] S Lev 26:33; Dt 28:36,64; 29:28; 1Ki 8:46; 2Ki 17:6; Ps 44:11; 106:27; Jer 3:8; Mic 1:16 [y] Isa 17:6; 21:17; Ob 1:5 **4:28** [z] Dt 13:2; 28:36,64; 1Sa 26:19; Jer 5:19; 16:13; Ac 19:26 [a] Dt 29:17 [b] Ps 115:4-8; 135:15-18; Isa 8:19; 26:14; 44:17-20; Rev 9:20 **4:29** [c] 1Sa 13:12; 2Ki 13:4; 2Ch 7:14; 15:4; 33:12; Ps 78:34; 119:58; Isa 45:19,22; 55:6; Jer 26:19; Da 9:13; Hos 3:5; Am 5:4 [d] 1Sa 7:3; 1Ki 8:48; Jer 29:13 [e] Dt 6:5; 30:1-3,10 **4:30** [f] Lev 26:41; Dt 31:17,21; Ps 4:1; 18:6; 46:1; 59:16; 107:6 [g] Dt 31:29; Jer 23:20; Hos 3:5; Heb 1:2 [h] Dt 30:2; 1Ki 8:48; Ne 1:9; Jer 3:1,12,22; 4:1; 18:11; Joel 2:12 **4:31** [i] Ex 34:6; Ne 9:31; Ps 111:4 [j] Dt 31:6,8; Jos 1:5; 1Ki 8:57; 1Ch 28:9,20; Ps 9:10; 27:9; 71:9; Isa 42:16; Heb 13:5 [k] S Lev 26:44 [l] Lev 26:45 **4:32** [m] Dt 32:7 [n] S Ge 1:27; Isa 45:12 [o] Dt 28:64; 30:1; Jer 9:16; Mt 24:31 [p] ver 7; 2Sa 7:23 **4:33** [q] Ex 20:22; Dt 5:24-26 **4:34** [r] Ex 14:30 [s] Isa 7:12 [t] S Ex 4:17 [u] Dt 7:19; 26:8; 29:3; 1Ch 16:12; Ps 9:1; 40:5; Jer 32:20 [v] S Ex 3:20; Dt 5:15; 6:21; 15:15 [w] Ex 15:11; Dt 34:12; Ps 45:4; 65:5 **4:35** [x] ver 39; Ex 8:10; Dt 7:9; 32:4,12; 1Sa 2:2; 1Ki 8:60; 2Ki 19:19; Isa 43:10; Mk 12:32 **4:36** [y] S Ex 19:19; Heb 12:25 [z] Dt 8:5 **4:37** [a] Dt 7:8; 10:15; 23:5; 33:3; Ps 44:3; Jer 31:3; Hos 11:1; Mal 1:2; 2:11 [b] S Ex 3:20; S 33:14 **4:38** [c] Nu 34:14-15; Dt 7:1; 9:5 **4:39** [d] Ex 8:10 [e] S ver 35; Ex 15:11 **4:40** [f] S Lev 22:31 [g] ver 1; S Ge 26:5; Dt 5:29; 11:1; Ps 105:45; Isa 48:18 [h] Dt 5:16; 12:25; Isa 3:10 [i] S Ex 23:26; Eph 6:2-3

4:21 *because of you.* See note on 1:37.
4:24 *consuming fire.* See 9:3; Ex 24:17; see also Isa 33:14 and note; Heb 12:29. *jealous God.* See 5:9; 6:15; see also note on Ex 20:5.
4:25 *After you ... have lived in the land.* The pattern of Israel's rebellion, resulting in expulsion from the land, and then their repentance, leading to restoration to the land, is prominent in Deuteronomy (see, e.g., the blessing and curse formulas in chs. 27–28).
4:26 *heaven and earth as witnesses.* See notes on 30:19; Ps 50:1; Isa 1:2; cf. Mic 6:1–2 and note.
4:27 *will scatter you.* See note on 28:64.
4:29 *with all your heart and ... soul.* Indicates total involvement and commitment. The phrase is applied not only to how the Lord's people should seek him, but also to how they should fear (revere) him, live in obedience to him, love and serve him (see 6:5 and note; 10:12; 11:13; 13:3; 30:6), and, after forsaking him, renew their allegiance and commitment (26:16; 30:2,10).
4:31 *covenant ... confirmed ... by oath.* See notes on Ge 21:23; 22:16; Ex 19:5; Heb 6:13,18. In ancient times, parties to a covenant were expected to confirm their intentions by means of a self-maledictory oath (see note on Ge 15:17).
4:35 *so that you might know.* See v. 10. *besides him there is no other.* See v. 39; 5:7; 6:4 and note; 32:39. Moses insists that there is only one God (see also note on Ge 1:1).
4:37 *he loved.* The first reference in Deuteronomy to God's love for his people (see Introduction: Theological Teaching and Purpose). See 5:10; 7:9,12 and note; 10:15; 23:5. The corollary truth is that his people should love him (see note on 6:5). *Presence.* See notes on Ex 25:30; 33:14.
4:39 See v. 35 and note.
4:40 *it may go well with you.* That is, you will receive the covenant benefits. This assurance occurs ten times in Deuter-

Cities of Refuge

4:41-43Ref — Nu 35:6-34; Dt 19:1-14; Jos 20:1-9

41Then Moses set aside three cities east of the Jordan, 42to which anyone who had killed a person could flee if he had unintentionally[j] killed his neighbor without malice aforethought. He could flee into one of these cities and save his life. 43The cities were these: Bezer in the desert plateau, for the Reubenites; Ramoth[k] in Gilead, for the Gadites; and Golan in Bashan, for the Manassites.

Introduction to the Law

44This is the law Moses set before the Israelites. 45These are the stipulations, decrees and laws Moses gave them when they came out of Egypt 46and were in the valley near Beth Peor east of the Jordan, in the land of Sihon[l] king of the Amorites, who reigned in Heshbon and was defeated by Moses and the Israelites as they came out of Egypt. 47They took possession of his land and the land of Og king of Bashan, the two Amorite kings east of the Jordan. 48This land extended from Aroer[m] on the rim of the Arnon Gorge to Mount Siyon[a n] (that is, Hermon[o]), 49and included all the Arabah east of the Jordan, as far as the Sea of the Arabah,[b] below the slopes of Pisgah.

The Ten Commandments

5:6-21pp — Ex 20:1-17

5 Moses summoned all Israel and said: Hear, O Israel, the decrees and laws[p] I declare in your hearing today. Learn them and be sure to follow them. 2The LORD our God made a covenant[q] with us at Horeb.[r] 3It was not with our fathers that the LORD made this covenant, but with us,[s] with all of us who are alive here today.[t] 4The LORD spoke[u] to you face to face[v] out of the fire[w] on the mountain. 5(At that time I stood between[x] the LORD and you to declare to you the word of the LORD, because you were afraid[y] of the fire and did not go up the mountain.) And he said:

6"I am the LORD your God, who brought you out of Egypt,[z] out of the land of slavery.[a]

7"You shall have no other gods before[c] me.

8"You shall not make for yourself an idol in the form of anything in heaven above or on the earth beneath or in the waters below.[b] 9You shall not bow down to them or worship them; for I, the LORD your God, am a jealous God, punishing the children for the sin of the fathers[c] to the third and fourth generation of those who hate me,[d] 10but showing love to a thousand[e] ⌊generations⌋ of those who love me and keep my commandments.[f]

11"You shall not misuse the name[g] of the LORD your God, for the LORD will not hold anyone guiltless who misuses his name.[h]

12"Observe the Sabbath day by keeping it holy,[i] as the LORD your God has commanded you. 13Six days you shall labor and do all your work, 14but the seventh day[j] is a Sabbath to the LORD your God. On it you shall not do any work, neither you, nor your son or daughter, nor your manservant or maidservant,[k] nor your ox, your donkey or any of your animals, nor the alien within your gates, so that your manservant and maidservant may rest, as you do.[l] 15Remember that you were slaves[m] in Egypt and that the LORD your God brought you

4:42 [j]S Ex 21:13 **4:43** [k]Jos 21:38; 1Ki 22:3; 2Ki 8:28; 9:14 **4:46** [l]Nu 21:26 **4:48** [m]Dt 2:36 [n]Dt 3:9 [o]S Dt 3:8 **5:1** [p]S Ex 18:20 **5:2** [q]Ex 19:5; Jer 11:2; Heb 9:15; 10:15-17 [r]S Ge 17:9; S Ex 3:1 **5:3** [s]Dt 11:2-7 [t]Nu 26:63-65; Heb 8:9 **5:4** [u]S Dt 4:12 [v]S Nu 14:14 [w]S Ex 19:18 **5:5** [x]Gal 3:19 [y]S Ge 3:10; Heb 12:18-21 **5:6** [z]S Ex 13:3; S 29:46 [a]Lev 26:1; Dt 6:4; Ps 81:10 **5:8** [b]Lev 26:1; Dt 4:15-18; Ps 78:58; 97:7 **5:9** [c]S Nu 26:11 [d]Ex 34:7; S Nu 10:35; 14:18 **5:10** [e]S Ex 34:7 [f]Nu 14:18; Dt 7:9; Ne 1:5; Jer 32:18; Da 9:4 **5:11** [g]Ps 139:20 [h]Lev 19:12; Dt 10:20; Mt 5:33-37 **5:12** [i]Ex 16:23-30; 31:13-17; Mk 2:27-28 **5:14** [j]S Ge 2:2; Mt 12:2; Mk 2:27; Heb 4:4 [k]Job 31:13; Jer 34:9-11 [l]Jer 17:21,24 **5:15** [m]S Ge 15:13

[a] *48* Hebrew; Syriac (see also Deut. 3:9) *Sirion*
[b] *49* That is, the Dead Sea
[c] *7* Or *besides*

onomy (here; 5:16,29; 6:3,18; 8:16; 12:25,28; 19:13; 22:7). Cf. also 28:1–14; 30:1–10.

4:41–43 See 19:1–13; Nu 35:9–28; Jos 20 and notes.

4:43 *Bezer ... Ramoth ... Golan.* See map, p. 239.

5:1 *Hear, O Israel.* See note on 4:1.

5:2 *covenant with us at Horeb.* See notes on Ex 19:3—24:18 and 19:5. God's covenant with Israel, given at Mount Horeb (Sinai) and now being confirmed, bound Israel to the Lord as their absolute Sovereign, and to his laws and regulations as their way of life. Adherence to the covenant would bring to Israel the blessings of the Lord, while breaking the covenant would bring against them the punishments described as "curses" (see, e.g., 28:15–20). Jer 31:31–34 (see note there) predicted the establishing of a new covenant, which made the Sinaitic covenant obsolete (see Heb 7:18–22; see also Heb 8:6–13; 10:15–18 and notes). See chart, p. 19.

5:3 *not with our fathers ... but with us.* The covenant was made with those who were present at Sinai, but since they were representatives of the nation, it was made with all succeeding generations as well.

5:5 See vv. 23–27; Ex 20:18–21.

5:6–21 The Ten Commandments are the central stipulations of God's covenant with Israel made at Sinai. It is almost impossible to exaggerate their effect on subsequent history. They constitute the basis of the moral principles found throughout the Western world, and they summarize what the one true God expects of his people in terms of faith, worship and conduct (see notes on Ex 20:2–17; Jer 16:2).

5:7 See 6:4 and note.

5:12 *as the LORD your God has commanded you.* Missing from the parallel verse in Exodus (20:8), this clause reminds the people of the divine origin of the Ten Commandments 40 years earlier at Mount Sinai (see vv. 15–16).

5:14 *so that your manservant and maidservant may rest.* See v. 15; see also note on Ex 20:10.

5:15 *Remember.* See note on 4:10.

out of there with a mighty hand[n]
and an outstretched arm.[o] Therefore the LORD your God has commanded you to observe the Sabbath day.
16 "Honor your father[p] and your mother,[q] as the LORD your God has
commanded you, so that you
may live long[r] and that it may
go well with you in the land the
LORD your God is giving you.
17 "You shall not murder.[s]
18 "You shall not commit adultery.[t]
19 "You shall not steal.[u]
20 "You shall not give false testimony
against your neighbor.[v]
21 "You shall not covet your neighbor's
wife. You shall not set your desire on your neighbor's house or
land, his manservant or maidservant, his ox or donkey, or anything that belongs to your neighbor."[w]

22 These are the commandments the LORD
proclaimed in a loud voice to your whole
assembly there on the mountain from out
of the fire, the cloud and the deep darkness;[x] and he added nothing more. Then
he wrote them on two stone tablets[y] and
gave them to me.
23 When you heard the voice out of the
darkness, while the mountain was ablaze
with fire, all the leading men of your tribes
and your elders[z] came to me. 24 And you
said, "The LORD our God has shown us[a]
his glory and his majesty,[b] and we have
heard his voice from the fire. Today we
have seen that a man can live even if God
speaks with him.[c] 25 But now, why should
we die? This great fire will consume us,
and we will die if we hear the voice of the
LORD our God any longer.[d] 26 For what mortal man has ever heard the voice of the living God speaking out of fire, as we have,
and survived?[e] 27 Go near and listen to all
that the LORD our God says.[f] Then tell us
whatever the LORD our God tells you. We
will listen and obey."[g]
28 The LORD heard you when you spoke
to me and the LORD said to me, "I have
heard what this people said to you. Everything they said was good.[h] 29 Oh, that their
hearts would be inclined to fear me[i] and
keep all my commands[j] always, so that it
might go well with them and their children forever![k]
30 "Go, tell them to return to their tents.
31 But you stay here[l] with me so that I may
give you all the commands, decrees and
laws you are to teach them to follow in the
land I am giving them to possess."
32 So be careful to do what the LORD your
God has commanded you;[m] do not turn
aside to the right or to the left.[n] 33 Walk
in all the way that the LORD your God has
commanded you,[o] so that you may live
and prosper and prolong your days[p] in the
land that you will possess.

Love the LORD Your God

6 These are the commands, decrees and
laws the LORD your God directed me to
teach you to observe in the land that you
are crossing the Jordan to possess, 2 so that
you, your children and their children after
them may fear[q] the LORD your God as long
as you live[r] by keeping all his decrees and
commands[s] that I give you, and so that
you may enjoy long life.[t] 3 Hear, O Israel,
and be careful to obey[u] so that it may go
well with you and that you may increase
greatly[v] in a land flowing with milk and
honey,[w] just as the LORD, the God of your
fathers, promised[x] you.
4 Hear, O Israel: The LORD our God, the

5:15 [n] Ex 6:1; Ps 108:6; Jer 32:21 [o] S Dt 4:34 **5:16** [p] Mal 1:6 [q] Ex 21:17; Lev 19:3; Eze 22:7; Mt 15:4*; 19:19*; Mk 7:10*; 10:19*; Lk 18:20*; Eph 6:2-3* [r] S Dt 4:40; 11:9; Pr 3:1-2 **5:17** [s] Ge 9:6; Lev 24:17; Ecc 3:3; Jer 40:15; 41:3; Mt 5:21-22*; 19:19*; Mk 10:19*; Lk 18:20*; Ro 13:9*; Jas 2:11* **5:18** [t] Lev 20:10; Mt 5:27-30; 19:18*; Mk 10:19*; Lk 18:20*; Ro 13:9*; Jas 2:11* **5:19** [u] Lev 19:11; Mt 19:19*; Mk 10:19*; Lk 18:20*; Ro 13:9* **5:20** [v] S Ex 23:1; Mt 19:18*; Mk 10:19*; Lk 18:20* **5:21** [w] Ro 7:7*; 13:9* **5:22** [x] S Ex 20:21 [y] S Ex 24:12 **5:23** [z] S Ex 3:16 **5:24** [a] Dt 4:34; 8:5; 11:2; Isa 53:4 [b] S Dt 3:24 [c] Ex 19:19 **5:25** [d] Ex 20:18-19; Dt 18:16; Heb 12:19 **5:26** [e] S Ex 33:20; Dt 4:33; Jdg 6:22-23; 13:22; Isa 6:5 **5:27** [f] S Ex 19:8 [g] S Ex 24:7 **5:28** [h] Dt 18:17 **5:29** [i] Ps 81:8, 13 [j] Jos 22:5; Ps 78:7 [k] ver 33; S Dt 4:1, 40; 12:25; 22:7 **5:31** [l] Ex 24:12 **5:32** [m] S Dt 4:29; 10:12 [n] Dt 17:11, 20; 28:14; Jos 1:7; 1Ki 15:5; 2Ki 22:2; Pr 4:27 **5:33** [o] Isa 3:10; Jer 7:23; 38:20; S Lk 1:6 [p] S ver 29 **6:2** [q] S Ex 20:20; S 1Sa 12:24 [r] Dt 4:9 [s] S Ge 26:5 [t] S Ex 20:12 **6:3** [u] S Ex 19:5 [v] Ge 15:5; Dt 5:33 [w] S Ex 3:8; Dt 32:13-14 [x] Ex 13:5

5:16–21 The NT quotes often from this section of the Ten Commandments (see cross references on these verses).
5:16 *that it may go well with you.* Missing from the parallel in Ex 20:12, this clause explains that the life the Lord desires for his people is not to be measured merely in terms of longevity (see note on 4:40).
5:20 See 19:18–19; Lev. 19:11–13; 1Ki 21:10,13.
5:22 *commandments.* Lit. "words" (see note on Ex 20:1). *two stone tablets.* See note on Ex 31:18.
5:25 *we will die.* See notes on Ge 16:13; 32:30.
5:27 *We will listen and obey.* See note on Ex 19:8.
6:2 *fear the LORD.* See note on Ge 20:11. *enjoy long life.* See 4:40; 5:16 and note. By obeying the Lord and keeping his decrees, individual Israelites would enjoy long life in the land, and the people as a whole would enjoy a long national existence in the land.
6:3–4 *Hear, O Israel.* See note on 4:1.
6:3 *land flowing with milk and honey.* See note on Ex 3:8. The phrase is used 14 times from Exodus through Deuteronomy and 5 times elsewhere in the OT.

6:4–9 See Mk 12:29–30 and note on 12:29; see also Mt 22:37–38; Lk 10:27. This passage in Deuteronomy is known as the *Shema* (Hebrew for "Hear"). It has become the Jewish confession of faith, recited daily by the pious and every Sabbath day in the synagogue.
6:4 *the LORD is one.* The truth revealed to Israel that God is one and that this one God created all things, sustains all things and governs all things stood in radical opposition to all the religions of the ancient Near Eastern world. All of Israel's neighbors had to come to terms in their daily lives with scores of gods, each with its own sphere of influence, its own limitations, its own petty self-interests and its own morally erratic ways. But Israel could live serenely in the knowledge that all things and all times were under the rule of one divine King, whose ways are righteous and whose purpose with her and through her (as Yahweh, her God) is salvation for humankind—from sin and judgment and every evil that has burdened human life. Such serenity in the midst of the ragings of history and all its seeming chaos remains the precious gift of faith for all who know and trust the God of Israel.

LORD is one.[a][y] 5Love[z] the LORD your God
with all your heart[a] and with all your soul
and with all your strength.[b] 6These commandments that I give you today are to be
upon your hearts.[c] 7Impress them on your
children. Talk about them when you sit at
home and when you walk along the road,
when you lie down and when you get
up.[d] 8Tie them as symbols on your hands
and bind them on your foreheads.[e] 9Write
them on the doorframes of your houses
and on your gates.[f]
10When the LORD your God brings you
into the land he swore to your fathers, to
Abraham, Isaac and Jacob, to give you — a
land with large, flourishing cities you did
not build,[g] 11houses filled with all kinds
of good things you did not provide, wells
you did not dig,[h] and vineyards and olive
groves you did not plant — then when you
eat and are satisfied,[i] 12be careful that you
do not forget[j] the LORD, who brought you
out of Egypt, out of the land of slavery.
13Fear the LORD[k] your God, serve him
only[l] and take your oaths[m] in his name.[n]
14Do not follow other gods, the gods of the
peoples around you; 15for the LORD your
God[o], who is among you, is a jealous God
and his anger will burn against you, and
he will destroy you from the face of the
land. 16Do not test the LORD your God[p]
as you did at Massah. 17Be sure to keep[q]
the commands of the LORD your God and
the stipulations and decrees he has given
you.[r] 18Do what is right and good in the
LORD's sight,[s] so that it may go well[t] with
you and you may go in and take over the
good land that the LORD promised on oath
to your forefathers, 19thrusting out all your
enemies[u] before you, as the LORD said.
20In the future, when your son asks you,[v]
"What is the meaning of the stipulations,
decrees and laws the LORD our God has
commanded you?" 21tell him: "We were
slaves of Pharaoh in Egypt, but the LORD
brought us out of Egypt with a mighty
hand.[w] 22Before our eyes the LORD sent miraculous signs and wonders — great and
terrible — upon Egypt and Pharaoh and his
whole household. 23But he brought us out
from there to bring us in and give us the
land that he promised on oath to our forefathers. 24The LORD commanded us to obey
all these decrees and to fear the LORD our
God,[x] so that we might always prosper and
be kept alive, as is the case today.[y] 25And if
we are careful to obey all this law[z] before
the LORD our God, as he has commanded
us, that will be our righteousness.[a]"

Driving Out the Nations

7 When the LORD your God brings you
into the land you are entering to possess[b] and drives out before you many
nations[c] — the Hittites,[d] Girgashites,[e]
Amorites,[f] Canaanites, Perizzites,[g] Hivites[h] and Jebusites,[i] seven nations larger

[a] 4 Or *The LORD our God is one LORD*; or *The LORD is our God, the LORD is one*; or *The LORD is our God, the LORD alone*

6:4 [y]Dt 4:35,39; Ne 9:6; Ps 86:10; Isa 44:6; Zec 14:9; Mk 12:29*; Jn 10:30; 1Co 8:4; Eph 4:6; Jas 2:19 **6:5** [z]Dt 11:1,22; Mt 22:37*; Mk 12:30*; Lk 10:27* [a]1Sa 12:24 [b]Dt 4:29; 10:12; Jos 22:5 **6:6** [c]ver 8; Dt 11:18; 30:14; 32:46; Ps 26:2; 37:31; 40:8; 119:11; Pr 3:3; Isa 51:7; Jer 17:1; 31:33; Eze 40:4 **6:7** [d]Dt 4:9; 11:19; Pr 22:6; Eph 6:4 **6:8** [e]S ver 6; S Ex 13:9; Mt 23:5 **6:9** [f]Dt 11:20 **6:10** [g]S Ge 11:4; Dt 12:29; 19:1; Jos 24:13; Ps 105:44 **6:11** [h]Jer 2:13 [i]S Lev 26:5; Dt 8:10; 14:29; 31:20 **6:12** [j]Dt 4:9,23; 2Ki 17:38; Ps 44:17; 78:7; 103:2 **6:13** [k]Ps 33:8; 34:9 [l]Dt 13:4; 1Sa 7:3; Jer 44:10; Mt 4:10*; Lk 4:4*; 4:8* [m]1Sa 20:3 [n]S Ex 20:7; S Mt 5:33 **6:15** [o]Dt 4:24; 5:9 **6:16** [p]S Ex 17:2; Mt 4:7*; Lk 4:12* **6:17** [q]S Lev 26:3 [r]Dt 11:22; Ps 119:4,56,100,134,168 **6:18** [s]2Ki 18:6; Isa 36:7; 38:3 [t]Dt 4:40 **6:19** [u]Ex 23:27; Jos 21:44; Ps 78:53; 107:2; 136:24 **6:20** [v]S Ex 10:2 **6:21** [w]S Dt 4:34 **6:24** [x]Dt 10:12; 30:6; Ps 86:11; Jer 32:39 [y]Ps 27:12; 41:2; S Ro 10:5 **6:25** [z]Ps 103:18; 119:34,55 [a]Dt 24:13; S Ro 9:31; Ro 10:3,5 **7:1** [b]S Lev 14:34; S Dt 4:38 [c]Dt 20:16-18; 31:3 [d]Ge 15:20 [e]S Ge 10:16 [f]S Dt 1:7 [g]Ge 13:7 [h]S Ge 10:17 [i]Jos 3:10

6:5 *Love the LORD.* See notes on Ex 20:5 – 6. Primarily in view here is the love shown by a subject to a king. To love King Yahweh is to be his loyal and obedient servant (Israel was the Lord's kingdom people). Love for God and neighbor (see Lev 19:18 and note) is built on the love that the Lord has for his people (see 4:37 and note; 7:8 – 9,13; 23:5; 1Jn 4:19 – 21) and on his identification with them. Such love is to be total, involving one's whole being (see notes on 4:29; Jos 22:5).

6:6 *commandments ... upon your hearts.* A feature that would especially characterize the "new covenant" (see Jer 31:31 – 33 and note on 31:33; 2Co 3:3 and note).

6:8 – 9 Many Jews take these verses literally and tie phylacteries (see note on Mt 23:5) to their foreheads and left arms. They also attach mezuzoth (small wooden or metal containers in which passages of Scripture are placed) to the doorframes of their houses. But a figurative interpretation is supported by 11:18 – 20; Ex 13:9,16 (see note on Ex 13:9).

6:10 – 12 Because the emphasis in Scripture is always on what God does and not on what his people achieve, they are never to forget what he has done for them. See note on 4:10.

6:13 Quoted in part by Jesus in response to Satan's temptation (Mt 4:10; Lk 4:8). Jesus quoted from Deuteronomy in response to the devil's other two temptations as well (see notes on v. 16; 8:3). *Fear the LORD.* See note on Ge 20:11. *take your oaths in his name.* In ancient Israel's world, when people appealed to the gods to affirm and uphold their oaths, they singled out the divine power or powers they most revered. For this reason, to take an oath in the Lord's name was a key sign of loyalty to and trust in him and of the rejection of all other gods, even an implicit denial that they amounted to anything or even existed. The Israelites were to swear oaths in no other name.

6:15 *jealous God.* See 4:24; 5:9; see also note on Ex 20:5.

6:16 Quoted in part by Jesus in Mt 4:7; Lk 4:12 (see note there; see also note on v. 13 here). *as you did at Massah.* See 9:22; 33:8; see also note on Ex 17:7.

6:20 See Ex 12:26 and note.

6:23 *brought us out ... to bring us in.* See note on Ex 6:7 – 8.

6:25 *righteousness.* Probably here refers to a true, personal relationship with the covenant Lord that manifests itself in the daily lives of God's people (see 24:13 [note "righteous act"] and note on 24:10 – 13; cf. Mt 6:1 and note).

7:1 – 6 When this passage is carefully examined together with 1Ki 11:1 – 13 (see note there); Ezr 9:1 – 2,10 – 12,14, it seems clear that what was prohibited was intermarriage with idolatrous and immoral foreigners. On the other hand, outsiders who placed themselves under the Lord's rule and thus became affiliated with the covenant community were treated for the most part just like ordinary Israelites (see Ex 12:48 – 49; Lev 17:8 – 9; 19:33 – 34; Nu 9:14; 15:13 – 16,26 – 31; Dt 16:11 – 14; cf. Mal 2:11 and note; see also Rahab [Jos 2; 6:17,22 – 25] and Ruth [the book of Ruth]; see further Isa 56:3 and note; Mt 1:5 and note on 1:3).

7:1 *Hittites ... Jebusites.* See 20:17; see also notes on Ge 10:6,15 – 18; 13:7; Jos 9:7. *seven nations.* See note on Ex 3:8.

and stronger than you— 2and when the
LORD your God has delivered[j] them over
to you and you have defeated them, then
you must destroy[k] them totally.[a][l] Make
no treaty[m] with them, and show them no
mercy.[n] 3Do not intermarry with them.[o]
Do not give your daughters to their sons
or take their daughters for your sons, 4for
they will turn your sons away from following me to serve other gods,[p] and the
LORD's anger will burn against you and
will quickly destroy[q] you. 5This is what
you are to do to them: Break down their
altars, smash their sacred stones, cut down
their Asherah poles[b][r] and burn their idols
in the fire.[s] 6For you are a people holy[t] to
the LORD your God.[u] The LORD your God
has chosen[v] you out of all the peoples on
the face of the earth to be his people, his
treasured possession.[w]

7The LORD did not set his affection on
you and choose you because you were
more numerous[x] than other peoples, for
you were the fewest[y] of all peoples.[z] 8But it
was because the LORD loved[a] you and kept
the oath he swore[b] to your forefathers that
he brought you out with a mighty hand[c]
and redeemed[d] you from the land of slavery,[e] from the power of Pharaoh king of
Egypt. 9Know therefore that the LORD your
God is God;[f] he is the faithful God,[g] keeping his covenant of love[h] to a thousand
generations[i] of those who love him and
keep his commands.[j] 10But

> those who hate him he will repay to
> their face by destruction;
> he will not be slow to repay to their
> face those who hate him.[k]

11Therefore, take care to follow the commands, decrees and laws I give you today.

12If you pay attention to these laws
and are careful to follow them, then the
LORD your God will keep his covenant of
love with you, as he swore to your forefathers.[l] 13He will love you and bless
you[m] and increase your numbers.[n] He will
bless the fruit of your womb,[o] the crops
of your land—your grain, new wine[p] and
oil[q]—the calves of your herds and the
lambs of your flocks in the land that he
swore to your forefathers to give you.[r]
14You will be blessed more than any other people; none of your men or women
will be childless, nor any of your livestock
without young.[s] 15The LORD will keep you
free from every disease.[t] He will not inflict
on you the horrible diseases you knew in
Egypt,[u] but he will inflict them on all who
hate you.[v] 16You must destroy all the peoples the LORD your God gives over to you.[w]
Do not look on them with pity[x] and do not
serve their gods,[y] for that will be a snare[z]
to you.

17You may say to yourselves, "These
nations are stronger than we are. How
can we drive them out?[a]" 18But do not
be afraid[b] of them; remember well what
the LORD your God did to Pharaoh and
to all Egypt.[c] 19You saw with your own
eyes the great trials, the miraculous signs
and wonders, the mighty hand[d] and outstretched arm, with which the LORD your
God brought you out. The LORD your God
will do the same to all the peoples you
now fear.[e] 20Moreover, the LORD your
God will send the hornet[f] among them
until even the survivors who hide from
you have perished. 21Do not be terrified
by them, for the LORD your God, who is
among you,[g] is a great and awesome God.[h]

[a] *2* The Hebrew term refers to the irrevocable giving over of things or persons to the LORD, often by totally destroying them; also in verse 26. [b] *5* That is, wooden symbols of the goddess Asherah; here and elsewhere in Deuteronomy

7:2 [j]S Dt 2:33 [k]S Dt 2:34 [l]Nu 31:17; Dt 33:27; Jos 11:11 [m]S Ex 23:32 [n]ver 16; Dt 13:8; 19:13; 25:12 **7:3** [o]Ex 34:15-16; Jos 22:16; Da 9:7 **7:4** [p]Jdg 3:6 [q]S Dt 4:26 **7:5** [r]S Ex 34:13; Dt 16:21 [s]S Ex 23:24 **7:6** [t]Ex 19:6; S Lev 27:30 [u]Dt 26:19; Ps 30:4; 37:28; 50:5; 52:9 [v]Dt 14:2; 1Ki 3:8; Isa 41:9; Eze 20:5 [w]S Ge 17:7; S Ex 8:22; S 34:9; Isa 43:1; Ro 9:4; Tit 2:14 **7:7** [x]S Ge 22:17 [y]Ge 34:30 [z]Dt 4:37; 10:22 **7:8** [a]S Dt 4:37; 1Ki 10:9; 2Ch 2:11; Ps 44:3 [b]Ex 32:13; S Nu 14:8; Ro 11:28 [c]S Ex 3:20 [d]S Ex 6:6 [e]S Ex 13:14 **7:9** [f]S Dt 4:35 [g]Ps 18:25; 33:4; 108:4; 145:13; 146:6; Isa 49:7; Jer 42:5; Hos 11:12; S 1Co 1:9 [h]ver 12; 1Ki 8:23; 2Ch 6:14; Ne 1:5; 9:32 [i]S Ex 20:6 [j]S Dt 5:10 **7:10** [k]S Lev 26:28; S Nu 10:35; Na 1:2 **7:12** [l]Lev 26:3-13; Dt 28:1-14; Ps 105:8-9; Mic 7:20 **7:13** [m]Ps 11:5; 146:8; Pr 15:9; Isa 51:1; Jn 14:21 [n]S Ge 17:6; Ex 1:7; Dt 1:10; 13:17; 30:5; Ps 107:38 [o]S Ge 49:25 [p]S Ge 27:28 [q]S Nu 18:12 [r]Dt 28:4 **7:14** [s]Ex 23:26 **7:15** [t]S Ex 15:26 [u]S Ex 9:9 [v]S Ex 23:25; Dt 30:8-10 **7:16** [w]ver 24; Jos 6:2; 10:26 [x]S ver 2 [y]Jdg 3:6; Ezr 9:1; Ps 106:36 [z]ver 25; S Ex 10:7 **7:17** [a]Nu 33:53 **7:18** [b]S Nu 14:9; S Dt 1:21,29 [c]Ps 105:5; 119:52 **7:19** [d]Ps 136:12 [e]Dt 4:34 **7:20** [f]S Ex 23:28 **7:21** [g]S Ge 17:7; Jos 3:10 [h]Dt 10:17; Ne 1:5; 9:32; Ps 47:2; 66:3; 68:35; Isa 9:6; Da 9:4

7:2–5 *Make no treaty ... Do not intermarry ... Break down their altars.* Israel was to have no association—political, social or religious—with the idol worshipers of Canaan (see v. 16; cf. Mal 2:11 and note).

7:2 *destroy them totally.* See note on 2:34.

7:4 *turn your sons away ... to serve other gods.* The Lord's command against intermarriage with foreigners was not racially motivated but was intended to prevent spiritual contamination and apostasy (see, e.g., 1Ki 11:1–11; Ne 13:25–27).

7:5 *altars ... sacred stones ... Asherah poles.* Objects of Canaanite idolatrous worship (see 12:3; 16:21–22). See also NIV text note; Ex 34:13 and note.

7:6 *holy.* Separated from all corrupting people or things and consecrated totally to the Lord (see note on Ex 3:5). *treasured possession.* See note on Ex 19:5.

7:8 *because the LORD loved you.* See 4:37 and note.

7:9,12 *his covenant of love.* See 1Ki 8:23; 1Ch 6:14; Ne 1:5; 9:32; Da 9:4; cf. Ps 89:28; 106:45; Isa 54:10; 55:3; i.e., the covenant in which God pledges on oath to show Israel his unfailing love (kindness, mercy; see note on Ps 6:4) in all his ways with them through the vicissitudes of their history so that all his particular promises to them (see vv. 13–15; 19:24; 28:1–14; 30:1–10; see also Ge 22:17–18; Lev 26:3–13) will be fulfilled. A closely related phrase is "covenant of peace" (Nu 25:12; Isa 54:10 [see note there]; Eze 34:25; 37:26).

7:9 *Know ... that the LORD ... is God.* See 11:28; Ps 100:3 and notes. *thousand generations ... keep his commands.* See note on Ex 20:6.

7:12–15 The blessings are stated more fully in 28:1–14; 30:1–10.

7:13 *grain, new wine and oil.* A common OT summary of the produce of field, vineyard and olive grove (see, e.g., 11:14; 14:23; 18:4; 28:51).

7:15 *not inflict ... diseases.* See note on 28:60.

7:16 See essay, p. 286.

7:18 *remember.* See note on 4:10.

7:20 *hornet.* See note on Ex 23:28.

22The LORD your God will drive out those
nations before you, little by little.[i] You
will not be allowed to eliminate them all
at once, or the wild animals will multiply around you. 23But the LORD your God
will deliver them over to you, throwing
them into great confusion until they are
destroyed.[j] 24He will give their kings[k] into
your hand,[l] and you will wipe out their
names from under heaven. No one will
be able to stand up against you;[m] you will
destroy them.[n] 25The images of their gods
you are to burn[o] in the fire. Do not covet[p] the silver and gold on them, and do
not take it for yourselves, or you will be
ensnared[q] by it, for it is detestable[r] to the
LORD your God. 26Do not bring a detestable thing into your house or you, like it,
will be set apart for destruction.[s] Utterly
abhor and detest it, for it is set apart for
destruction.

Do Not Forget the LORD

8 Be careful to follow every command I
am giving you today, so that you may
live[t] and increase and may enter and possess the land that the LORD promised on
oath to your forefathers.[u] 2Remember how
the LORD your God led[v] you all the way in
the desert these forty years, to humble you
and to test[w] you in order to know what
was in your heart, whether or not you
would keep his commands. 3He humbled[x]
you, causing you to hunger and then feeding you with manna,[y] which neither you
nor your fathers had known, to teach[z] you
that man does not live on bread[a] alone
but on every word that comes from the
mouth[b] of the LORD.[c] 4Your clothes did not
wear out and your feet did not swell during these forty years.[d] 5Know then in your
heart that as a man disciplines his son, so
the LORD your God disciplines you.[e]
6Observe the commands of the LORD
your God, walking in his ways[f] and revering him.[g] 7For the LORD your God is
bringing you into a good land[h]—a land
with streams and pools of water, with
springs flowing in the valleys and hills;[i]
8a land with wheat and barley,[j] vines[k]
and fig trees,[l] pomegranates, olive oil and
honey;[m] 9a land where bread[n] will not be
scarce and you will lack nothing;[o] a land
where the rocks are iron and you can dig
copper out of the hills.[p]
10When you have eaten and are satisfied,[q] praise the LORD your God for the
good land he has given you. 11Be careful
that you do not forget[r] the LORD your God,
failing to observe his commands, his laws
and his decrees that I am giving you this
day. 12Otherwise, when you eat and are
satisfied, when you build fine houses and
settle down,[s] 13and when your herds and
flocks grow large and your silver and gold
increase and all you have is multiplied,
14then your heart will become proud and
you will forget[t] the LORD your God, who
brought you out of Egypt, out of the land
of slavery. 15He led you through the vast
and dreadful desert,[u] that thirsty and waterless land, with its venomous snakes[v]
and scorpions. He brought you water out
of hard rock.[w] 16He gave you manna[x] to eat
in the desert, something your fathers had
never known,[y] to humble and to test[z] you
so that in the end it might go well with
you. 17You may say to yourself,[a] "My power and the strength of my hands[b] have produced this wealth for me." 18But remember
the LORD your God, for it is he who gives
you the ability to produce wealth,[c] and so
confirms his covenant, which he swore to
your forefathers, as it is today.
19If you ever forget the LORD your God
and follow other gods[d] and worship and

7:22 [i]Ex 23:28-30 **7:23** [j]Ex 23:27; Jos 10:10 **7:24** [k]Jos 10:24; Ps 110:5 [l]S ver 16 [m]S Ex 23:31; Dt 11:25; Jos 1:5; 10:8; 23:9 [n]Jos 21:44 **7:25** [o]S Ex 4:14; S 32:20 [p]Ex 20:17; Jos 7:21 [q]S ver 16 [r]Dt 17:1 **7:26** [s]Lev 27:28-29 **8:1** [t]Dt 4:1 [u]S Ex 19:5; Job 36:11; Ps 16:11; Eze 20:19 **8:2** [v]Dt 29:5; Ps 136:16; Am 2:10 [w]S Ge 22:1 **8:3** [x]2Ch 36:12; Ps 44:9; Pr 18:12; Isa 2:11; Jer 44:10 [y]S Ex 16:4 [z]1Ki 8:36; Ps 25:5; 94:12; 119:171 [a]ver 9; S Ge 3:19; Job 23:12; Ps 104:15; Pr 28:21; Isa 51:14; Jer 42:14 [b]Job 22:22; Ps 119:13; 138:4 [c]S Ex 16:2-3; Mt 4:4*; Lk 4:4* **8:4** [d]Dt 29:5; Ne 9:21 **8:5** [e]Dt 4:36; 2Sa 7:14; Job 5:17; 33:19; Pr 3:11-12; Heb 12:5-11; Rev 3:19 **8:6** [f]S Ex 33:13; 1Ki 3:14; Ps 81:13; 95:10 [g]Dt 5:33 **8:7** [h]Ps 106:24; Jer 3:19; Eze 20:6 [i]Dt 11:9-12; Jer 2:7 **8:8** [j]S Ex 9:31 [k]S Ge 49:11 [l]S Nu 13:23; S 1Ki 4:25 [m]Dt 32:13; Ps 81:16 **8:9** [n]S ver 3 [o]Jdg 18:10 [p]Job 28:2 **8:10** [q]Dt 6:10-12 **8:11** [r]Dt 4:9 **8:12** [s]Pr 30:9; Hos 13:6 **8:14** [t]ver 11; Ps 78:7; 106:21 **8:15** [u]S Dt 1:19; S 32:10 [v]Nu 21:6; Isa 14:29; 30:6 [w]Ex 17:6; Dt 32:13; Job 28:9; Ps 78:15; 114:8 **8:16** [x]S Ex 16:14 [y]Ex 16:15 [z]S Ge 22:1 **8:17** [a]Dt 9:4,7,24; 31:27 [b]Jdg 7:2; Ps 44:3; Isa 10:13 **8:18** [c]Ge 26:13; Dt 26:10; 28:4; 1Sa 2:7; Ps 25:13; 112:3; Pr 8:18; 10:22; Ecc 9:11; Hos 2:8 **8:19** [d]Dt 6:14; Ps 16:4; Jer 7:6; 13:10; 25:6

7:22 *God will drive out.* See note on 3:22. *wild animals will multiply.* The rapid expulsion of the Canaanites would leave much of the land deserted and therefore open to wild animals.
7:25–26 Cf. the story of Achan (see Jos 6:17–19 and notes on 6:17–18; 7:1,20–25).
7:26 *set apart for destruction.* See note on 2:34.
8:2 *Remember.* See note on 4:10. *test.* See v. 16; see also note on Ge 22:1.
8:3 *manna.* See v. 16; see also note on Ex 16:31. *man does not live on bread alone.* See note on 6:13; quoted by Jesus in response to the devil's temptation (see Mt 4:4 and note; Lk 4:4). Bread sustains but does not guarantee life, which is God's gift to those who trust in and live by his word: his commands and promises (see vv. 1,18). God's "discipline" (v. 5) of his people by bringing them through the desert taught them this fundamental truth. There they were humbled (v. 16; cf. v. 14) by being cast on the Lord in total dependence.
8:7–9 A concise description of the rich and fertile land of promise that the Israelites were about to enter and possess (see 11:8–12; see also Ne 9:25 and note). See map No. 2 at the end of this study Bible.
8:9 *iron ... copper.* The mountains of southern Lebanon and the regions east of the Sea of Galilee and south of the Dead Sea contain iron. Both copper and iron were plentiful in the part of the Arabah south of the Dead Sea. Some of the copper mines date to the time of Solomon and earlier. Zarethan, located in the Jordan Valley north of the Dead Sea, was a center for bronze works in Solomon's time (see 1Ki 7:45–46 and note on 7:46). Some bronze objects from this site precede the Solomonic period, and today there are copper works at Timnah in the Negev.
8:11 *not forget.* See note on 4:10; cf. 8:14,19.
8:15 *water out of hard rock.* See Ex 17:6 and note.
8:16 *test.* See v. 2; see also note on Ge 22:1.
8:17–18 See Zec 4:6 and note.
8:18 *remember.* See note on 4:10.

bow down to them, I testify against you today that you will surely be destroyed.[e] 20Like the nations[f] the LORD destroyed before you, so you will be destroyed for not obeying the LORD your God.[g]

Not Because of Israel's Righteousness

9 Hear, O Israel. You are now about to cross the Jordan[h] to go in and dispossess nations greater and stronger than you,[i] with large cities[j] that have walls up to the sky.[k] 2The people are strong and tall — Anakites! You know about them and have heard it said: "Who can stand up against the Anakites?"[l] 3But be assured today that the LORD your God is the one who goes across ahead of you[m] like a devouring fire.[n] He will destroy them; he will subdue them before you. And you will drive them out and annihilate them quickly,[o] as the LORD has promised you.

4After the LORD your God has driven them out before you, do not say to yourself,[p] "The LORD has brought me here to take possession of this land because of my righteousness." No, it is on account of the wickedness[q] of these nations[r] that the LORD is going to drive them out before you. 5It is not because of your righteousness or your integrity[s] that you are going in to take possession of their land; but on account of the wickedness[t] of these nations,[u] the LORD your God will drive them out[v] before you, to accomplish what he swore[w] to your fathers, to Abraham, Isaac and Jacob.[x] 6Understand, then, that it is not because of your righteousness that the LORD your God is giving you this good land to possess, for you are a stiff-necked people.[y]

The Golden Calf

7Remember this and never forget how you provoked[z] the LORD your God to anger in the desert. From the day you left Egypt until you arrived here, you have been rebellious[a] against the LORD.[b] 8At Horeb you aroused the LORD's wrath[c] so that he was angry enough to destroy you.[d] 9When I went up on the mountain to receive the tablets of stone, the tablets of the covenant[e] that the LORD had made with you, I stayed on the mountain forty days[f] and forty nights; I ate no bread and drank no water.[g] 10The LORD gave me two stone tablets inscribed by the finger of God.[h] On them were all the commandments the LORD proclaimed to you on the mountain out of the fire, on the day of the assembly.[i]

11At the end of the forty days and forty nights,[j] the LORD gave me the two stone tablets,[k] the tablets of the covenant. 12Then the LORD told me, "Go down from here at once, because your people whom you brought out of Egypt have become corrupt.[l] They have turned away quickly[m] from what I commanded them and have made a cast idol for themselves."

13And the LORD said to me, "I have seen this people[n], and they are a stiff-necked people indeed! 14Let me alone,[o] so that I may destroy them and blot out[p] their name from under heaven.[q] And I will make you into a nation stronger and more numerous than they."

15So I turned and went down from the mountain while it was ablaze with fire. And the two tablets of the covenant were in my hands.[a][r] 16When I looked, I saw that you had sinned against the LORD your God; you had made for yourselves an idol cast in the shape of a calf.[s] You had turned aside quickly from the way that the LORD had commanded you. 17So I took the two tablets and threw them out of my hands, breaking them to pieces before your eyes.

18Then once again I fell[t] prostrate before the LORD for forty days and forty nights; I ate no bread and drank no water,[u] because of all the sin you had committed,[v] doing what was evil in the LORD's sight and so provoking him to anger. 19I feared the anger and wrath of the LORD, for he was angry enough with you to destroy you.[w] But again the LORD listened to me.[x] 20And the LORD was angry enough with Aaron to destroy him, but at that time I prayed for Aaron too. 21Also I took that sinful thing of yours, the calf you had made, and burned

[a] 15 Or *And I had the two tablets of the covenant with me, one in each hand*

8:19 [e]Dt 4:26; 30:18
8:20 [f]2Ki 21:2; Ps 10:16 [g]Eze 5:5-17
9:1 [h]S Nu 35:10 [i]Dt 4:38 [j]S Nu 13:28 [k]S Ge 11:4
9:2 [l]Nu 13:22; Jos 11:22
9:3 [m]Dt 31:3; Jos 3:11 [n]S Ex 15:7; S 19:18; Heb 12:29 [o]S Ex 23:31
9:4 [p]S Dt 8:17 [q]2Ki 16:3; 17:8; 21:2; Ezr 9:11 [r]S Ex 23:24; S Lev 18:21, 24-30; Dt 18:9-14
9:5 [s]S Eph 2:9 [t]Dt 18:9 [u]S Lev 18:25 [v]Dt 4:38; 11:23 [w]S Ge 12:7 [x]Eze 36:32
9:6 [y]S Ex 32:9; Ac 7:51
9:7 [z]S Nu 11:33 [a]S Ex 23:21 [b]S Ex 14:11
9:8 [c]Nu 16:46; 1Sa 28:18; Job 20:28; Ps 2:12; 7:11; 69:24; 110:5; Isa 9:19; Eze 20:13 [d]Ex 32:7-10; Ezr 9:14; Ps 106:19
9:9 [e]S Dt 4:13 [f]S Ge 7:4 [g]S Ex 24:12
9:10 [h]S Ex 31:18 [i]Dt 10:4; 18:16
9:11 [j]S Ge 7:4 [k]S Ex 24:12
9:12 [l]S Dt 4:16 [m]Jdg 2:17
9:13 [n]ver 6; Dt 10:16
9:14 [o]Ex 32:10 [p]S Nu 14:12 [q]Jer 7:16
9:15 [r]S Ex 32:15
9:16 [s]S Ex 32:4
9:18 [t]S Ex 34:28 [u]ver 9 [v]S Ex 32:31
9:19 [w]S Ex 32:14; Heb 12:21* [x]ver 26; Ex 34:10; S Nu 11:2; 1Sa 7:9; Jer 15:1

9:1 *Hear, O Israel.* See note on 4:1.
9:2 *Anakites.* See note on 1:28.
9:3 *devouring fire.* See 4:24 and note. *he will subdue them before you ... you will drive them out.* The Lord not only went ahead of the Israelites, but he also exerted his power alongside them and through them to assure victory. The Lord's involvement, together with that of the Israelite armies, continues throughout Deuteronomy and the conquest narratives.
9:4 *because of my righteousness.* See note on 7:8. *wickedness of these nations.* See note on Ge 15:16.
9:6,13 *stiff-necked.* See 10:16; 31:27; see also note on Ex 32:9.
9:7,27 *Remember.* See note on 4:10.
9:9 *tablets of the covenant.* See notes on Ex 20:1; 34:28.
9:10 *two stone tablets ... finger of God.* See Ex 31:18 and note; see also note on Ex 8:19.
9:11–21 See Ex 31:18—32:20 and notes.
9:12–13 *your people ... this people.* See note on Ex 17:4.
9:14 *blot out their name.* The Phoenician cognate of the Hebrew for this phrase appears in a ninth-century B.C. inscription on a gateway: "If ... a man ... blots out the name of Azitawadda from this gate ... may (the gods) wipe out ... that man!"
9:19 *But again the LORD listened to me.* Moses' intercessory prayer on this occasion (vv. 26–29) ranks among the great prayers for Israel's national survival (see Ex 32:11–13 and note on 32:11; see also Ezr 9:6–15; Ne 9:5–37 and note; Da 9:4–19).

it in the fire. Then I crushed it and ground
it to powder as fine as dust[y] and threw the
dust into a stream that flowed down the
mountain.[z]
22You also made the LORD angry[a] at Taberah,[b] at Massah[c] and at Kibroth Hattaavah.[d]
23And when the LORD sent you out from
Kadesh Barnea,[e] he said, "Go up and take
possession[f] of the land I have given you."
But you rebelled[g] against the command of
the LORD your God. You did not trust[h] him
or obey him. 24You have been rebellious
against the LORD ever since I have known
you.[i]
25I lay prostrate before the LORD those
forty days and forty nights[j] because the
LORD had said he would destroy you.[k] 26I
prayed to the LORD and said, "O Sovereign
LORD, do not destroy your people,[l] your
own inheritance[m] that you redeemed[n] by
your great power and brought out of Egypt
with a mighty hand.[o] 27Remember your
servants Abraham, Isaac and Jacob. Overlook the stubbornness[p] of this people, their
wickedness and their sin. 28Otherwise, the
country[q] from which you brought us will
say, 'Because the LORD was not able to take
them into the land he had promised them,
and because he hated them,[r] he brought
them out to put them to death in the desert.'[s] 29But they are your people,[t] your inheritance[u] that you brought out by your
great power and your outstretched arm.[v]"

Tablets Like the First Ones

10 At that time the LORD said to me,
"Chisel out two stone tablets[w] like
the first ones and come up to me on the
mountain. Also make a wooden chest.[a]
2I will write on the tablets the words that
were on the first tablets, which you broke.
Then you are to put them in the chest."[x]
3So I made the ark out of acacia wood[y]
and chiseled[z] out two stone tablets like the
first ones, and I went up on the mountain
with the two tablets in my hands. 4The
LORD wrote on these tablets what he had
written before, the Ten Commandments[a]
he had proclaimed[b] to you on the mountain, out of the fire, on the day of the assembly.[c] And the LORD gave them to me.
5Then I came back down the mountain[d]
and put the tablets in the ark[e] I had made,[f]
as the LORD commanded me, and they are
there now.[g]
6(The Israelites traveled from the wells
of the Jaakanites to Moserah.[h] There Aaron
died[i] and was buried, and Eleazar[j] his son
succeeded him as priest.[k] 7From there they
traveled to Gudgodah and on to Jotbathah,
a land with streams of water.[l] 8At that time
the LORD set apart the tribe of Levi[m] to carry the ark of the covenant[n] of the LORD, to
stand before the LORD to minister[o] and to
pronounce blessings[p] in his name, as they
still do today.[q] 9That is why the Levites
have no share or inheritance among their
brothers; the LORD is their inheritance,[r] as
the LORD your God told them.)
10Now I had stayed on the mountain forty days and nights, as I did the first time,
and the LORD listened to me at this time
also. It was not his will to destroy you.[s]
11"Go," the LORD said to me, "and lead the
people on their way, so that they may enter and possess the land that I swore to
their fathers to give them."

Fear the LORD

12And now, O Israel, what does the LORD
your God ask of you[t] but to fear[u] the LORD
your God, to walk[v] in all his ways, to love
him,[w] to serve the LORD[x] your God with all
your heart[y] and with all your soul,[z] 13and
to observe the LORD's commands[a] and decrees that I am giving you today for your
own good?[b]
14To the LORD your God belong the heavens,[c][d][e] even the highest heavens,[f][g] the
earth and everything in it.[h] 15Yet the LORD
set his affection on your forefathers and
loved[i] them, and he chose you,[j] their descendants, above all the nations, as it is
today.[k] 16Circumcise[l] your hearts,[m] there-

[a] *1* That is, an ark

9:21 [y]Ps 18:42; Isa 29:5; 40:15 [z]Ex 32:20; Isa 2:18; Mic 1:7 **9:22** [a]S Nu 1:53 [b]Nu 11:3 [c]S Ex 17:7 [d]Nu 11:34 **9:23** [e]S Dt 1:2 [f]Dt 1:21 [g]S Nu 14:9 [h]S Dt 1:32; Ps 106:24 **9:24** [i]S Dt 8:17 **9:25** [j]S Ge 7:4 [k]ver 18; S Ex 33:17 **9:26** [l]S Ex 33:13 [m]S Ex 34:9 [n]S Ex 6:6; Dt 15:15; 2Sa 7:23; Ps 78:35 [o]S ver 19; S Ex 32:11 **9:27** [p]ver 6; S Ex 32:9 **9:28** [q]Dt 32:27 [r]S Dt 1:27 [s]S Ex 32:12; Jos 7:9 **9:29** [t]S Ex 33:13 [u]S Ex 34:9; Dt 32:9 [v]Dt 4:34; Ne 1:10; Jer 27:5; 32:17 **10:1** [w]Ex 34:1-2 **10:2** [x]Ex 25:16,21; 2Ch 5:10; 6:11 **10:3** [y]Ex 37:1-9 [z]Ex 34:4 **10:4** [a]S Ex 24:12; S 34:28 [b]Ex 20:1 [c]S Dt 9:10 **10:5** [d]S Ex 19:11 [e]S Ex 25:10; S 1Sa 3:3 [f]S Ex 25:21 [g]1Ki 8:9 **10:6** [h]Nu 33:30 [i]S Nu 27:13 [j]S Ex 6:23 [k]S Nu 20:25-28 **10:7** [l]Nu 33:32-34; Ps 42:1; SS 5:12; Isa 32:2 **10:8** [m]S Nu 3:6 [n]S Nu 10:33 [o]S Nu 16:9 [p]S Ge 48:20 [q]1Ch 23:26 **10:9** [r]S Nu 18:20 **10:10** [s]S Ex 33:17 **10:12** [t]Mic 6:8 [u]S Ex 20:20 [v]1Ki 2:3; 3:3; 9:4 [w]Dt 5:33; 6:13; Mt 22:37; 1Ti 1:5 [x]Dt 11:13; 28:47; Ps 100:2 [y]S Dt 6:5; Ps 119:2 [z]S Dt 5:32 **10:13** [a]S Dt 4:2 [b]Dt 5:33; 6:24 **10:14** [c]Ps 148:4; Isa 19:1; Hab 3:8 [d]Ne 9:6; Job 35:5; Ps 8:3; 89:11; 104:3 [e]Dt 33:26 [f]Ps 115:16 [g]1Ki 8:27 [h]Ex 19:5; Ps 24:1; Ac 17:24 **10:15** [i]S Dt 4:37 [j]Ps 105:6; 135:4 [k]S Nu 14:8; Ro 11:28; 1Pe 2:9 **10:16** [l]S Ge 17:11 [m]S Lev 26:41; Dt 30:6; Jer 32:39

9:22 *Taberah.* See Nu 11:3 and NIV text note. *Massah.* See 6:16; 33:8; see also note on Ex 17:7. *Kibroth Hattaavah.* See Nu 11:34 and note.
9:23 *Kadesh Barnea.* See notes on Ge 14:7; Nu 20:1.
9:27 *Overlook.* See note on Ac 17:30.
10:1–3 *chest ... ark.* Both words translate the same Hebrew word, which means "chest" or "box." After initially translating "chest" for clarity, the NIV reverts to the more traditional and familiar rendering "ark." See NIV text note; see also note on Ex 25:10.
10:1 *two stone tablets.* See note on Ex 31:18.
10:2 *put them in the chest.* See notes on Ex 16:34; 25:16.
10:3 The order of events here is different from that in Exodus 34–37 (see Introduction to Deuteronomy: Structure and Outline).
10:6–9 A historical parenthesis, apparently stemming from Moses' prayer for Aaron and the Israelites (9:26–29) and the reference to the ark (vv. 1–5).
10:8 *carry the ark.* See Nu 1:50 and note on 1:51. *to minister ... to pronounce blessings.* See note on 21:5.
10:9 See 12:12 and note.
10:12 *what does the LORD ... ask of you ...?* See Mic 6:8 and note. *fear the LORD.* See note on Ge 20:11. *love him.* See notes on 4:29,37; 6:5.
10:13 *for your own good.* See 6:24; see also note on 6:2.
10:15 *set his affection ... loved.* See 7:7–8 and notes on 7:8 and 7:9,12. *forefathers.* The patriarchs (cf. v. 22).
10:16 *Circumcise your hearts.* See note on Ge 17:10. *stiff-necked.* See 9:6,13; 31:27; see also note on Ex 32:9.

fore, and do not be stiff-necked[n] any longer. 17For the LORD your God is God of
gods[o] and Lord of lords,[p] the great God,
mighty and awesome,[q] who shows no
partiality[r] and accepts no bribes.[s] 18He defends the cause of the fatherless and the
widow,[t] and loves the alien, giving him
food and clothing.[u] 19And you are to love[v]
those who are aliens,[w] for you yourselves
were aliens in Egypt.[x] 20Fear the LORD your
God and serve him.[y] Hold fast[z] to him and
take your oaths in his name.[a] 21He is your
praise;[b] he is your God, who performed
for you those great[c] and awesome wonders[d] you saw with your own eyes. 22Your
forefathers who went down into Egypt
were seventy in all,[e] and now the LORD
your God has made you as numerous as
the stars in the sky.[f]

Love and Obey the LORD

11 Love[g] the LORD your God and keep
his requirements, his decrees, his
laws and his commands always.[h] 2Re-
member today that your children[i] were
not the ones who saw and experienced the
discipline of the LORD your God:[j] his majesty,[k] his mighty hand, his outstretched
arm;[l] 3the signs he performed and the
things he did in the heart of Egypt, both
to Pharaoh king of Egypt and to his whole
country;[m] 4what he did to the Egyptian
army, to its horses and chariots,[n] how he
overwhelmed them with the waters of
the Red Sea[a][o] as they were pursuing you,
and how the LORD brought lasting ruin on
them. 5It was not your children who saw
what he did for you in the desert until
you arrived at this place, 6and what he
did[p] to Dathan and Abiram, sons of Eliab
the Reubenite, when the earth opened[q]
its mouth right in the middle of all Israel
and swallowed them up with their households, their tents and every living thing
that belonged to them. 7But it was your
own eyes that saw all these great things
the LORD has done.[r]
8Observe therefore all the commands[s]
I am giving you today, so that you may
have the strength to go in and take over
the land that you are crossing the Jordan
to possess,[t] 9and so that you may live
long[u] in the land that the LORD swore[v] to
your forefathers to give to them and their
descendants, a land flowing with milk and
honey.[w] 10The land you are entering to take
over is not like the land of Egypt,[x] from
which you have come, where you planted
your seed and irrigated it by foot as in a
vegetable garden. 11But the land you are
crossing the Jordan to take possession of
is a land of mountains and valleys[y] that
drinks rain from heaven.[z] 12It is a land the
LORD your God cares for; the eyes[a] of the
LORD your God are continually on it from
the beginning of the year to its end.
13So if you faithfully obey[b] the commands I am giving you today—to love[c]
the LORD your God and to serve him with
all your heart and with all your soul[d]—
14then I will send rain[e] on your land in its
season, both autumn and spring rains,[f] so
that you may gather in your grain, new
wine and oil. 15I will provide grass[g] in the
fields for your cattle, and you will eat and
be satisfied.[h]
16Be careful, or you will be enticed to
turn away and worship other gods and
bow down to them.[i] 17Then the LORD's
anger[j] will burn against you, and he will
shut[k] the heavens so that it will not rain
and the ground will yield no produce,[l] and
you will soon perish[m] from the good land
the LORD is giving you. 18Fix these words of
mine in your hearts and minds; tie them as
symbols on your hands and bind them on
your foreheads.[n] 19Teach them to your children,[o] talking about them when you sit at
home and when you walk along the road,
when you lie down and when you get up.[p]
20Write them on the doorframes of your

[a] 4 Hebrew *Yam Suph*; that is, Sea of Reeds

10:16 [n]S Ex 32:9; S Dt 9:13 **10:17** [o]Jos 22:22; Ps 135:5; 136:2; Da 2:47; 11:36 [p]Ps 136:3; S 1Ti 6:15 [q]S Dt 7:21 [r]Dt 1:17; Mal 2:9 [s]S Ex 23:8; S Lev 19:16 **10:18** [t]Ex 22:21,22-24; 23:9; Lev 19:33; Dt 27:19; Job 29:13; Ps 94:6; Isa 10:2; Jer 49:11 [u]S Nu 10:32 **10:19** [v]Dt 7:12 [w]S Ex 22:21; S Dt 24:19 [x]S Lev 19:34; Eze 47:22-23 **10:20** [y]Mt 4:10 [z]Dt 11:22; 13:4; 30:20; Jos 23:8; Ru 1:14; 2Ki 18:6; Ps 119:31; Isa 38:3 [a]S Ex 20:7 **10:21** [b]S Ex 15:2 [c]1Sa 12:24; Ps 126:2 [d]2Sa 7:23 **10:22** [e]S Ge 34:30; S 46:26; Ac 7:14 [f]S Ge 12:2; S Nu 10:36 **11:1** [g]S Dt 6:5 [h]S Lev 8:35 **11:2** [i]Dt 31:13; Ps 78:6 [j]S Dt 5:24 [k]S Dt 3:24 [l]Ps 136:12 **11:3** [m]Ex 7:8-21 **11:4** [n]S Ex 15:1 [o]S Ex 14:27; S Nu 21:4 **11:6** [p]Nu 16:1-35; Ps 106:16-18 [q]Isa 24:19 **11:7** [r]Dt 5:3 **11:8** [s]Ezr 9:10 [t]Dt 31:6-7,23; Jos 1:7 **11:9** [u]S Dt 5:16 [v]Dt 9:5 [w]S Ex 3:8 **11:10** [x]Isa 11:15; 37:25 **11:11** [y]Eze 36:4 [z]Dt 8:7; Ne 9:25 **11:12** [a]1Ki 8:29; 9:3 **11:13** [b]S Dt 6:17 [c]S Dt 10:12 [d]Dt 4:29; Jer 17:24 **11:14** [e]S Lev 26:4; Ac 14:17 [f]Ps 147:8; Jer 3:3; 5:24; Joel 2:23; Jas 5:7 **11:15** [g]Ps 104:14 [h]S Lev 26:5 **11:16** [i]Dt 4:19; 8:19; 29:18; Job 31:9,27 **11:17** [j]Dt 6:15; 9:19 [k]1Ki 17:1; 2Ch 6:26; 7:13 [l]S Lev 26:20 [m]Dt 4:26; 28:12,24 **11:18** [n]S Ex 13:9; Dt 6:6-8 **11:19** [o]S Ex 12:26; Dt 6:7; Ps 145:4; Isa 38:19; Jer 32:39 [p]Dt 4:9-10

10:20 *Hold fast.* As a man is "united" to his wife (Ge 2:24), and as Ruth "clung" to Naomi (Ru 1:14). See 4:4; 11:22; 13:4; 30:20.
10:21 *He is your praise.* He is the one you praise. See Ps 22:3 and note.
10:22 *seventy.* See notes on Ge 10:2; 46:26–27; see also Ex 1:5. *as the stars in the sky.* See note on 1:10.
11:1 *Love.* See note on 6:5. *keep.* Love and obedience are frequently linked in Scripture (e.g., 6:5–6; Jn 14:15; 1Jn 5:3; see note on Ex 20:2).
11:2–7 Moses continually emphasizes the involvement of his listeners in the Lord's works of providence and deliverance. In 5:3 it was not the patriarchs but they themselves with whom the covenant was made at Sinai. Here it is not their children (vv. 2–6) but they themselves who saw God's great deeds (v. 7).
11:2 *Remember.* See note on 4:10.
11:8–12 See note on 8:7–9.
11:9 *live long.* See note on 6:2.
11:10 *irrigated it by foot.* Irrigation channels dug by foot and/or fed by devices powered by foot brought the water of the Nile to the gardens in Egypt, in contrast to the rains that watered Canaan (v. 11).
11:13 See note on 4:29.
11:14 *autumn and spring rains.* The rainy season in Israel begins in October and ends in April.
11:17 *shut the heavens.* The all-important seasonal rains (see v. 14) were controlled by the Lord—not by Baal, as the inhabitants of Canaan thought (cf. Jer 14:22; Hos 2:8; Zec 10:1 and notes).
11:18–20 See note on 6:8–9.

houses and on your gates,[q] 21so that your
days and the days of your children may be
many[r] in the land that the LORD swore to
give your forefathers, as many as the days
that the heavens are above the earth.[s]
22If you carefully observe[t] all these commands I am giving you to follow — to love[u]
the LORD your God, to walk in all his ways
and to hold fast[v] to him — 23then the LORD
will drive out[w] all these nations[x] before
you, and you will dispossess nations larger and stronger than you.[y] 24Every place
where you set your foot will be yours:[z]
Your territory will extend from the desert to
Lebanon, and from the Euphrates River[a]
to the western sea.[a] 25No man will be able
to stand against you. The LORD your God,
as he promised you, will put the terror[b]
and fear of you on the whole land, wherever you go.[c]
26See, I am setting before you today a
blessing[d] and a curse[e] — 27the blessing[f] if
you obey the commands of the LORD your
God that I am giving you today; 28the curse
if you disobey[g] the commands of the LORD
your God and turn from the way that I command you today by following other gods,[h]
which you have not known. 29When the
LORD your God has brought you into the
land you are entering to possess, you are
to proclaim on Mount Gerizim[i] the blessings, and on Mount Ebal[j] the curses.[k] 30As
you know, these mountains are across the
Jordan, west of the road,[b] toward the setting sun, near the great trees of Moreh,[l] in
the territory of those Canaanites living in
the Arabah in the vicinity of Gilgal.[m] 31You
are about to cross the Jordan to enter and
take possession[n] of the land the LORD your
God is giving[o] you. When you have taken
it over and are living there, 32be sure that
you obey all the decrees and laws I am
setting before you today.

11:20 [q] Dt 6:9
11:21 [r] Job 5:26; Pr 3:2; 4:10; 9:11 [s] Ps 72:5
11:22 [t] S Dt 6:17 [u] S Dt 6:5 [v] S Dt 10:20
11:23 [w] S Dt 9:5 [x] S Ex 23:28 [y] Dt 9:1
11:24 [z] Ge 15:18; Dt 1:36; 12:20; 19:8; Jos 1:3; 14:9 [a] S Ge 2:14
11:25 [b] S Dt 2:25 [c] Ex 23:27; Dt 7:24
11:26 [d] Ps 24:5 [e] Lev 26:14-17; Dt 27:13-26; 30:1, 15, 19; La 2:17; Da 9:11; Hag 1:11; Mal 2:2; 3:9; 4:6
11:27 [f] Dt 28:1-14; Ps 24:5
11:28 [g] 2Ch 24:20; Jer 42:13; 44:16 [h] S Dt 4:28; 13:6, 13; 29:26; 1Sa 26:19
11:29 [i] Jdg 9:7 [j] Dt 27:4; Jos 8:30 [k] Dt 27:12-13; Jos 8:33; Jn 4:20
11:30 [l] S Ge 12:6 [m] Jos 4:19; 5:9; 9:6; 10:6; 14:6; 15:7; Jdg 2:1; 2Ki 2:1; Mic 6:5
11:31 [n] S Nu 33:53 [o] Dt 12:10; Jos 11:23

The One Place of Worship

12 These are the decrees[p] and laws you
must be careful to follow in the land
that the LORD, the God of your fathers,
has given you to possess — as long as you
live in the land.[q] 2Destroy completely all
the places on the high mountains[r] and on
the hills and under every spreading tree[s]
where the nations you are dispossessing
worship their gods. 3Break down their altars, smash[t] their sacred stones and burn[u]
their Asherah[v] poles in the fire; cut down
the idols of their gods and wipe out their
names[w] from those places.
4You must not worship the LORD your
God in their way.[x] 5But you are to seek the
place the LORD your God will choose from
among all your tribes to put his Name[y]
there for his dwelling.[z] To that place you
must go; 6there bring your burnt offerings
and sacrifices, your tithes[a] and special
gifts, what you have vowed[b] to give and
your freewill offerings, and the firstborn
of your herds and flocks.[c] 7There, in the
presence[d] of the LORD your God, you and
your families shall eat and shall rejoice[e]
in everything you have put your hand to,
because the LORD your God has blessed
you.
8You are not to do as we do here today,
everyone as he sees fit,[f] 9since you have
not yet reached the resting place[g] and the
inheritance[h] the LORD your God is giving
you. 10But you will cross the Jordan and

[a] *24* That is, the Mediterranean [b] *30* Or *Jordan, westward*

12:1 [p] Ps 119:5 [q] Dt 4:9-10; 6:15; 1Ki 8:40; Eze 20:19
12:2 [r] S Nu 21:28 [s] 1Ki 14:23; 2Ki 17:10; Isa 57:5; Jer 2:20; 3:6, 13
12:3 [t] 2Ki 11:18 [u] S Ex 32:20 [v] Ex 34:13; 1Ki 14:15, 23 [w] S Ex 23:13
12:4 [x] ver 30; 2Ki 17:15; Jer 10:2
12:5 [y] S Ex 20:24; S 2Sa 7:13 [z] ver 11, 13; Dt 14:23; 15:20; 16:2, 11; 18:6; 26:2; 1Sa 2:29; 1Ki 5:5; 8:16; 9:3; 2Ch 2:4; 6:6; 7:12, 16; Ezr 6:12; 7:15; Ps 26:8; 78:68; Zec 2:12
12:6 [a] S Lev 27:30 [b] S Ge 28:20 [c] Jos 22:27; Isa 66:20
12:7 [d] S Ex 18:12 [e] S Lev 23:40; Ecc 3:12-13; 5:18-20; S Isa 62:9
12:8 [f] Jdg 17:6; 21:25
12:9 [g] S Ex 33:14; Dt 3:20; Ps 95:11; Mic 2:10 [h] Dt 4:21

11:21 *as many as the days ... earth.* That is, as long as the present creation endures.

11:22 *hold fast.* See note on 10:20.

11:24 *Every place where you set your foot.* See 1:7 and note; Jos 1:3.

11:26 – 30 The blessings and curses proclaimed on Mount Gerizim and Mount Ebal are detailed in chs. 27 – 28.

11:28 *known.* Experienced or acknowledged (see 13:2,6,13; 28:64; 29:26; 32:17; see also note on Ex 6:3).

11:30 *road.* Probably the north-south road that ran parallel to the Jordan between the Sea of Galilee and the Dead Sea. *great trees of Moreh.* See note on Ge 12:6. *Arabah.* See note on 1:1. The Canaanites who lived there controlled the territory around Gerizim and Ebal. *Gilgal.* See Jos 4:19 and note.

12:2 *under every spreading tree.* See note on 2Ki 16:4.

12:3 *altars ... sacred stones ... Asherah poles.* See note on 7:5.

12:4 *in their way.* The rituals and accessories of idolatrous worship were not to be used to worship the Lord, the one true God (cf. vv. 29 – 31). Everything that does not honor him must be eliminated from his people's worship (see Mic 5:10 – 15 and note).

12:5 *the place the LORD ... will choose ... to put his Name.* The tabernacle, the Lord's dwelling place during the desert journey, will be located in the city in Canaan where the Lord would choose to dwell. Moses stresses the importance of centralizing the place of worship as he prepares the people for settlement in the promised land, where the Canaanites had established many places of worship. See vv. 11,14,18,21,26; 14:23 – 24; 16:2,6,11; 26:2. *his Name.* Since in the ancient Semitic world "name" often stood for the essence of the thing named, God's "Name" is equivalent to "his presence" (see notes on Ex 3:13 – 15; 23:21; 2Sa 7:13; 1Ki 5:5).

12:6 See v. 11 and chart, p. 153.

12:7 *rejoice in everything you have put your hand to.* The Lord wants his people to enjoy the fruit of their labor, because it is the result of his blessing (see v. 18; cf. Ecc 2:24 – 25 and note; 5:18 – 20).

12:8 *as we do here today.* Israel was not able to follow all the procedures of the sacrificial system during the desert wandering and conquest periods. Moses was giving directives for their worship and way of life when settled in the land (vv. 10 – 14). *as he sees fit.* See note on Jdg 17:6.

12:9 *resting place.* See note on 3:20.

settle in the land the LORD your God is
giving[i] you as an inheritance, and he will
give you rest[j] from all your enemies around
you so that you will live in safety. 11Then
to the place the LORD your God will choose
as a dwelling for his Name[k]—there you
are to bring everything I command you:
your burnt offerings and sacrifices, your
tithes and special gifts, and all the choice
possessions you have vowed to the LORD.[l]
12And there rejoice[m] before the LORD your
God, you, your sons and daughters, your
menservants and maidservants, and the
Levites[n] from your towns, who have no allotment or inheritance[o] of their own. 13Be
careful not to sacrifice your burnt offerings anywhere you please.[p] 14Offer them
only at the place the LORD will choose[q] in
one of your tribes, and there observe everything I command you.
15Nevertheless, you may slaughter your
animals in any of your towns and eat as
much of the meat as you want, as if it were
gazelle or deer,[r] according to the blessing
the LORD your God gives you. Both the
ceremonially unclean and the clean may
eat it. 16But you must not eat the blood;[s]
pour[t] it out on the ground like water.[u]
17You must not eat in your own towns the
tithe[v] of your grain and new wine and oil,[w]
or the firstborn of your herds and flocks,
or whatever you have vowed to give,[x] or
your freewill offerings or special gifts.[y]
18Instead, you are to eat[z] them in the presence of the LORD your God at the place the
LORD your God will choose[a]—you, your
sons and daughters, your menservants
and maidservants, and the Levites from
your towns—and you are to rejoice[b] before the LORD your God in everything you
put your hand to. 19Be careful not to neglect the Levites[c] as long as you live in
your land.[d]
20When the LORD your God has enlarged
your territory[e] as he promised[f] you, and
you crave meat[g] and say, "I would like
some meat," then you may eat as much
of it as you want. 21If the place where the
LORD your God chooses to put his Name[h]
is too far away from you, you may slaughter animals from the herds and flocks the
LORD has given you, as I have commanded you, and in your own towns you may
eat as much of them as you want.[i] 22Eat
them as you would gazelle or deer.[j] Both
the ceremonially unclean and the clean
may eat. 23But be sure you do not eat the
blood,[k] because the blood is the life, and
you must not eat the life with the meat.[l]
24You must not eat the blood; pour it out
on the ground like water.[m] 25Do not eat it,
so that it may go well[n] with you and your
children after you, because you will be doing what is right[o] in the eyes of the LORD.
26But take your consecrated things and
whatever you have vowed to give,[p] and go
to the place the LORD will choose. 27Pre-
sent your burnt offerings[q] on the altar of
the LORD your God, both the meat and the
blood. The blood of your sacrifices must
be poured beside the altar of the LORD
your God, but you may eat[r] the meat. 28Be
careful to obey all these regulations I am
giving you, so that it may always go well[s]
with you and your children after you, because you will be doing what is good and
right in the eyes of the LORD your God.
29The LORD your God will cut off[t] before you the nations you are about to invade and dispossess. But when you have
driven them out and settled in their land,[u]
30and after they have been destroyed before you, be careful not to be ensnared[v] by
inquiring about their gods, saying, "How
do these nations serve their gods? We will
do the same."[w] 31You must not worship the
LORD your God in their way, because in
worshiping their gods, they do all kinds
of detestable things the LORD hates.[x] They
even burn their sons[y] and daughters in the
fire as sacrifices to their gods.[z]
32See that you do all I command you; do
not add[a] to it or take away from it.

Worshiping Other Gods

13 If a prophet,[b] or one who foretells by
dreams,[c] appears among you and announces to you a miraculous sign or wonder, 2and if the sign[d] or wonder of which
he has spoken takes place, and he says,
"Let us follow other gods"[e] (gods you have
not known) "and let us worship them,"
3you must not listen to the words of that
prophet[f] or dreamer.[g] The LORD your God

12:10 [i]S Dt 11:31 [j]S Ex 33:14 **12:11** [k]S ver 5 [l]S Lev 1:3; Jos 22:23 **12:12** [m]ver 7 [n]Dt 26:11-13 [o]S Nu 18:20 **12:13** [p]S ver 5 **12:14** [q]ver 11 **12:15** [r]ver 22; Dt 14:5; 15:22 **12:16** [s]S Ge 9:4; Ac 15:20 [t]ver 23-24; S Ge 35:14; 1Ch 11:18; Jer 7:18 [u]S Lev 17:13; S Dt 15:23; Jn 19:34 **12:17** [v]S Lev 27:30 [w]S Nu 18:12 [x]ver 26; Nu 18:19 [y]Dt 14:23; 15:20 **12:18** [z]Dt 14:23; 15:20 [a]ver 5 [b]ver 7,12; Dt 14:26; Ne 8:10; Ecc 3:12-13; 5:18-20 **12:19** [c]ver 12; Dt 14:27; Ne 13:10 [d]Mal 3:8 **12:20** [e]S Ex 34:24 [f]S Ge 15:8; S Dt 11:24 [g]S Ex 16:3 **12:21** [h]Dt 14:24 [i]Lev 17:4 **12:22** [j]S ver 15 **12:23** [k]Ge 9:4; S Lev 7:26 [l]Eze 33:25 **12:24** [m]ver 16 **12:25** [n]S Dt 4:40 [o]ver 28; Ex 15:26; Dt 13:18; 1Ki 11:38; 2Ki 12:2 **12:26** [p]S ver 17; Nu 5:9-10 **12:27** [q]S Lev 1:13 [r]Lev 3:1-17 **12:28** [s]Dt 4:40; Ecc 8:12 **12:29** [t]Jos 23:4 [u]S Dt 6:10 **12:30** [v]S Ex 10:7 [w]S ver 4 **12:31** [x]S Lev 18:25 [y]S Lev 18:21 [z]S 2Ki 3:27 **12:32** [a]S Dt 4:2; Rev 22:18-19 **13:1** [b]Mt 24:24; Mk 13:22; 2Th 2:9 [c]S Ge 20:3; Jer 23:25; 27:9; 29:8 **13:2** [d]Dt 18:22; 1Sa 2:34; 10:9; 2Ki 19:29; 20:9; Isa 7:11 [e]S Dt 11:28 **13:3** [f]2Pe 2:1 [g]1Sa 28:6,15

12:11 *dwelling for his Name.* See note on v. 5.

12:12 *rejoice before the LORD.* Joy, based on the Lord's blessings, was to be a major feature of Hebrew life and worship in the promised land (vv. 7,18). *Levites ... have no ... inheritance.* See 10:9; Nu 18:1–8 and note on 18:8; 18:20,24.

12:13 *not ... anywhere you please.* Sacrifices and offerings to the Lord were to be brought only to the central sanctuary, not to the various Canaanite worship sites (see v. 5 and note).

12:15,22 *ceremonially unclean.* See notes on Lev 4:12; 11:2.

12:16,24 *you must not eat the blood.* See notes on Ge 9:4; Lev 17:11.

12:31 *burn ... sons and daughters ... as sacrifices.* See 18:10; see also note on Lev 18:21.

12:32 *do not add ... or take away.* See note on 4:2.

13:1–5 Eventual fulfillment is one test of true prophecy (18:21–22), but the more stringent rule given here guards against intelligent foresight masquerading as prophecy and against coincidental fulfillment of the predictions of false prophets (cf. Isa 8:20).

13:3 *testing.* See note on Ge 22:1. *all your heart.* See note on 4:29.

is testing[h] you to find out whether you love[i] him with all your heart and with all your soul. 4It is the LORD your God you must follow,[j] and him you must revere.[k] Keep his commands and obey him; serve him and hold fast[l] to him. 5That prophet or dreamer must be put to death,[m] because he preached rebellion against the LORD your God, who brought you out of Egypt and redeemed you from the land of slavery; he has tried to turn[n] you from the way the LORD your God commanded you to follow. You must purge the evil[o] from among you.

6If your very own brother, or your son or daughter, or the wife you love, or your closest friend secretly entices[p] you, saying, "Let us go and worship other gods"[q] (gods that neither you nor your fathers have known, 7gods of the peoples around you, whether near or far, from one end of the land to the other), 8do not yield[r] to him or listen to him. Show him no pity.[s] Do not spare him or shield him. 9You must certainly put him to death.[t] Your hand[u] must be the first in putting him to death, and then the hands of all the people. 10Stone him to death, because he tried to turn you away[v] from the LORD your God, who brought you out of Egypt, out of the land of slavery. 11Then all Israel will hear and be afraid,[w] and no one among you will do such an evil thing again.

12If you hear it said about one of the towns the LORD your God is giving you to live in 13that wicked men[x] have arisen among you and have led the people of their town astray, saying, "Let us go and worship other gods" (gods you have not known), 14then you must inquire, probe and investigate it thoroughly.[y] And if it is true and it has been proved that this detestable thing has been done among you,[z] 15you must certainly put to the sword all who live in that town. Destroy it completely,[a][a] both its people and its livestock.[b] 16Gather all the plunder of the town into the middle of the public square and completely burn the town[c] and all its plunder as a whole burnt offering to the LORD your God.[d] It is to remain a ruin[e] forever, never to be rebuilt. 17None of those condemned things[a] shall be found in your hands, so that the LORD will turn from his fierce anger;[f] he will show you mercy,[g] have compassion[h] on you, and increase your numbers,[i] as he promised[j] on oath to your forefathers, 18because you obey the LORD your God, keeping all his commands that I am giving you today and doing what is right[k] in his eyes.

13:3 [h]S Ge 22:1; 1Ki 13:18; 22:22-23; Jer 29:31; 43:2; Eze 13:9; 1Co 11:19 [i]Dt 6:5 13:4 [j]2Ki 23:3; 2Ch 34:31; 2Jn 1:6 [k]S Dt 6:13; S Ps 5:7 [l]S Dt 10:20 13:5 [m]S Ex 21:12; S 22:20 [n]ver 10; Dt 4:19 [o]Dt 17:7,12; 19:19; 24:7; Jdg 20:13; S 1Co 5:13 13:6 [p]Dt 17:2-7; 29:18 [q]S Dt 11:28 13:8 [r]Pr 1:10 [s]S Dt 7:2 13:9 [t]ver 5 [u]S Lev 24:14 13:10 [v]S Ex 20:3 13:11 [w]Dt 17:13; 19:20; 21:21; 1Ti 5:20 13:13 [x]ver 2,6; Jdg 19:22; 20:13; 1Sa 2:12; 10:27; 11:12; 25:17; 1Ki 21:10 13:14 [y]Jdg 20:12 [z]Dt 17:4 13:15 [a]Isa 24:6; 34:5; 43:28; 47:6; La 2:6; Da 9:11; Zec 8:13; Mal 4:6 [b]Ex 22:20 13:16 [c]2Ki 25:9; Jer 39:8; 52:13; Eze 16:41 [d]Dt 7:25,26; Jos 6:24 [e]Jos 8:28; Isa 7:16; 17:1; 24:10; 25:2; 27:10; 32:14,19; 37:26; Jer 49:2; Mic 1:6 13:17 [f]Ex 32:12; Nu 25:4 [g]S Ge 43:14 [h]Dt 30:3 [i]S Dt 7:13 [j]S Ge 12:2; S 13:14; S 26:24 13:18 [k]S Dt 12:25 14:1 [l]19:28; S Jn 1:12; S Ro 8:14; 9:8 14:2 [m]S Ge 28:14; Ex 22:31;

Clean and Unclean Food

14:3-20pp — Lev 11:1-23

14 You are the children[l] of the LORD your God. Do not cut yourselves or shave the front of your heads for the dead, 2for you are a people holy[m] to the LORD your God.[n] Out of all the peoples on the face of the earth, the LORD has chosen you to be his treasured possession.[o]

3Do not eat any detestable thing.[p] 4These are the animals you may eat:[q] the ox, the sheep, the goat,[r] 5the deer,[s] the gazelle, the roe deer, the wild goat,[t] the ibex, the antelope and the mountain sheep.[b] 6You may eat any animal that has a split hoof divided in two and that chews the cud. 7However, of those that chew the cud or that have a split hoof completely divided you may not eat the camel, the rabbit or the coney.[c] Although they chew the cud, they do not have a split hoof; they are ceremonially unclean for you. 8The pig is also unclean; although it has a split hoof, it does not chew the cud. You are not to eat their meat or touch their carcasses.[u]

9Of all the creatures living in the water, you may eat any that has fins and scales. 10But anything that does not have fins and scales you may not eat; for you it is unclean.

[a] *15,17* The Hebrew term refers to the irrevocable giving over of things or persons to the LORD, often by totally destroying them. [b] *5* The precise identification of some of the birds and animals in this chapter is uncertain. [c] *7* That is, the hyrax or rock badger

Isa 6:13; Mal 2:15 [n]S Lev 20:26; Ro 12:1 [o]S Ex 8:22; S Dt 7:6 14:3 [p]Eze 4:14 14:4 [q]Ac 10:14 [r]S Lev 7:23 14:5 [s]S Dt 12:15 [t]Job 39:1; Ps 104:18 14:8 [u]S Lev 5:2

13:4 *hold fast.* See note on 10:20.

13:5 *prophet ... must be put to death.* See 18:20; Jer 28:15–17 and note on 28:16; Zec 13:3 and note. *You must purge the evil from among you.* Repeated in 17:7; 19:19; 21:21; 22:21,24; 24:7, and quoted in 1Co 5:13. The purpose was to eliminate the evildoers as well as the evil itself.

13:13 *wicked.* See 1Sa 1:16; 2:12; 25:17. The same Hebrew word is also used, e.g., in 1Sa 10:27; 30:22 ("troublemakers"); 1Ki 21:10,13 ("scoundrels"); Job 34:18 ("worthless"); Pr 6:12 ("scoundrel"). Later, this word (*beliyya'al* in Hebrew) was used as a name for Satan (2Co 6:15, *Belial* in Greek), who is the personification of wickedness and lawlessness.

13:15 *Destroy it completely.* See NIV text note and note on 2:34.

14:1 *cut yourselves.* A pagan religious custom (see 1Ki 18:28 and note). *shave the front of your heads.* Shaving the forehead was a practice of mourners in Canaan.

14:2,21 *holy to the LORD.* See note on Lev 11:44. The regulations regarding clean and unclean foods were intended to separate Israel from things the Lord had identified as detestable and ceremonially unclean.

14:2 *a people holy to the LORD.* See Ex 3:5; 19:6 and notes. *treasured possession.* See note on Ex 19:5.

14:3–21 The subject of clean and unclean food is discussed in greater detail in Lev 11 (see notes there).

14:7 *ceremonially unclean.* See notes on Lev 4:12; 11:2.

11You may eat any clean bird. 12But these
you may not eat: the eagle, the vulture, the
black vulture, 13the red kite, the black kite,
any kind[v] of falcon,[w] 14any kind of raven,[x]
15the horned owl, the screech owl, the
gull, any kind of hawk, 16the little owl, the
great owl, the white owl, 17the desert owl,[y]
the osprey, the cormorant, 18the stork, any
kind of heron, the hoopoe and the bat.
19All flying insects that swarm are unclean to you; do not eat them. 20But any
winged creature that is clean you may
eat.[z]
21Do not eat anything you find already
dead.[a] You may give it to an alien living in
any of your towns, and he may eat it, or
you may sell it to a foreigner. But you are a
people holy to the LORD your God.[b]
Do not cook a young goat in its mother's milk.[c]

Tithes

22Be sure to set aside a tenth[d] of all that
your fields produce each year. 23Eat[e] the
tithe of your grain, new wine[f] and oil, and
the firstborn of your herds and flocks in
the presence of the LORD your God at the
place he will choose as a dwelling for his
Name,[g] so that you may learn[h] to revere[i]
the LORD your God always. 24But if that
place is too distant and you have been
blessed by the LORD your God and cannot
carry your tithe (because the place where
the LORD will choose to put his Name is
so far away), 25then exchange[j] your tithe
for silver, and take the silver with you and
go to the place the LORD your God will
choose. 26Use the silver to buy whatever you like: cattle, sheep, wine or other
fermented drink,[k] or anything you wish.
Then you and your household shall eat
there in the presence of the LORD your God
and rejoice.[l] 27And do not neglect the Levites[m] living in your towns, for they have
no allotment or inheritance of their own.[n]
28At the end of every three years, bring
all the tithes[o] of that year's produce and
store it in your towns,[p] 29so that the Levites (who have no allotment[q] or inheritance[r] of their own) and the aliens,[s] the fatherless and the widows who live in your
towns may come and eat and be satisfied,[t]
and so that the LORD your God may bless[u]
you in all the work of your hands.

The Year for Canceling Debts

15:1-11Ref — Lev 25:8-38

15 At the end of every seven years you
must cancel debts.[v] 2This is how it is
to be done: Every creditor shall cancel the
loan he has made to his fellow Israelite.
He shall not require payment from his fellow Israelite or brother, because the LORD's
time for canceling debts has been proclaimed. 3You may require payment from
a foreigner,[w] but you must cancel any debt
your brother owes you. 4However, there
should be no poor among you, for in the
land the LORD your God is giving you to
possess as your inheritance, he will richly bless[x] you, 5if only you fully obey the
LORD your God and are careful to follow[y]
all these commands I am giving you today. 6For the LORD your God will bless you
as he has promised, and you will lend to
many nations but will borrow from none.
You will rule over many nations but none
will rule over you.[z]
7If there is a poor man[a] among your
brothers in any of the towns of the land
that the LORD your God is giving you, do
not be hardhearted or tightfisted[b] toward
your poor brother. 8Rather be openhanded[c]
and freely lend him whatever he needs. 9Be
careful not to harbor this wicked thought:
"The seventh year, the year for canceling
debts,[d] is near," so that you do not show ill
will[e] toward your needy brother and give
him nothing. He may then appeal to the
LORD against you, and you will be found
guilty of sin.[f] 10Give generously to him and
do so without a grudging heart;[g] then be-

14:13 [v]S Ge 1:11 [w]Isa 34:15 **14:14** [x]S Ge 8:7 **14:17** [y]Ps 102:6; Isa 13:21; 14:23; 34:11; Zep 2:14 **14:20** [z]S Lev 20:25 **14:21** [a]S Lev 11:39 [b]ver 2 [c]S Ex 23:19 **14:22** [d]S Ge 14:20; S Lev 27:30; S Nu 18:21 **14:23** [e]S Dt 12:17,18 [f]Ps 4:7 [g]S Dt 12:5; 1Ki 3:2 [h]S Dt 4:10 [i]Ps 22:23; 33:8; Mal 2:5 **14:25** [j]Mt 21:12; Jn 2:14 **14:26** [k]S Lev 10:9; Ecc 10:16-17 [l]S Lev 23:40; S Dt 12:18 **14:27** [m]S Dt 12:19 [n]S Nu 18:20; 26:62; Dt 18:1-2 **14:28** [o]S Lev 27:30 [p]Dt 26:12 **14:29** [q]Ge 47:22 [r]Nu 26:62 [s]Dt 16:11; 24:19-21; Ps 94:6; Isa 1:17; 58:6 [t]S Dt 6:11 [u]Dt 15:10; Ps 41:1; Pr 22:9; Mal 3:10 **15:1** [v]Dt 31:10; Ne 10:31 **15:3** [w]S Ge 31:15; Dt 23:20; 28:12; Ru 2:10 **15:4** [x]Dt 28:8 **15:5** [y]S Ex 15:26; Dt 7:12; 28:1 **15:6** [z]Dt 28:12-13,44 **15:7** [a]ver 11; Mt 26:11 [b]1Jn 3:17 **15:8** [c]Mt 5:42; Lk 6:34; S Ac 24:17 **15:9** [d]ver 1 [e]Mt 20:15 [f]S Ex 22:23; S Job 5:15; Jas 5:4 **15:10** [g]2Co 9:5

14:21 *Do not eat ... already dead.* Because of the prohibition against eating blood, since the dead animal's blood would not be properly drained (see 12:16,24; see also notes on Ge 9:4; Lev 17:11). *Do not cook a young goat in its mother's milk.* See note on Ex 23:19.

14:22–29 See Nu 18:21–29. Taken together, the two passages suggest the following: (1) Annually, a tenth of all Israelite produce was to be taken to the city of the central sanctuary for distribution to the Levites. (2) At that time, at an initial festival, all Israelites ate part of the tithe. (3) The rest, which would be by far the major part of it, belonged to the Levites. (4) Every third year the tithe was gathered in the towns and stored for distribution to the Levites and the less fortunate: aliens, fatherless and widows (see 26:12). (5) The Levites were to present to the Lord a tenth of their tithe. See note on Lev 27:30.

14:22 *set aside a tenth.* See notes on Ge 14:20; 28:22.

14:23 *dwelling for his Name.* See note on 12:5.

14:25 *silver.* Pieces of silver of various weights were a common medium of exchange, but not in the form of coins (see note on Ge 20:16).

15:1 *every seven years.* See Ex 23:10–11; Lev 25:1–7 and note on 25:4.

15:3 *require payment from a foreigner.* Since he was not subject to the command to allow his fields to lie fallow during the seventh year, a foreigner would probably be financially able to pay his debts if asked to do so.

15:4 *there should be no poor among you.* Because of the Lord's reward for obedience (vv. 4–6), and because of the sabbath-year arrangement (vv. 7–11). This "year for canceling debts" (v. 9) gave Israelites who had experienced economic reverses a way to gain release from indebtedness and so, in a measure, a way to equalize wealth. Cf. the provisions of the Year of Jubilee (see Lev 25:8–38 and notes).

15:6 *you will lend.* If Israel failed to follow the Lord's commands, the reverse would be true (see 28:43–44).

cause of this the LORD your God will bless[h]
you in all your work and in everything you
put your hand to. 11There will always be
poor people[i] in the land. Therefore I command you to be openhanded toward your
brothers and toward the poor and needy
in your land.[j]

Freeing Servants

15:12-18pp — Ex 21:2-6
15:12-18Ref — Lev 25:38-55

12If a fellow Hebrew, a man or a woman, sells himself to you and serves you
six years, in the seventh year you must
let him go free.[k] 13And when you release
him, do not send him away empty-handed. 14Supply him liberally from your flock,
your threshing floor[l] and your winepress.
Give to him as the LORD your God has
blessed you. 15Remember that you were
slaves[m] in Egypt and the LORD your God
redeemed you.[n] That is why I give you this
command today.

16But if your servant says to you, "I
do not want to leave you," because he
loves you and your family and is well off
with you, 17then take an awl and push it
through his ear lobe into the door, and he
will become your servant for life. Do the
same for your maidservant.

18Do not consider it a hardship to set
your servant free, because his service to
you these six years has been worth twice
as much as that of a hired hand. And the
LORD your God will bless you in everything
you do.

The Firstborn Animals

19Set apart for the LORD[o] your God every firstborn male[p] of your herds and
flocks.[q] Do not put the firstborn of your
oxen to work, and do not shear the firstborn of your sheep.[r] 20Each year you and
your family are to eat them in the presence of the LORD your God at the place
he will choose.[s] 21If an animal has a defect,[t] is lame or blind, or has any serious
flaw, you must not sacrifice it to the LORD
your God.[u] 22You are to eat it in your own
towns. Both the ceremonially unclean and
the clean may eat it, as if it were gazelle
or deer.[v] 23But you must not eat the blood;
pour it out on the ground like water.[w]

Passover

16:1-8pp — Ex 12:14-20; Lev 23:4-8; Nu 28:16-25

16 Observe the month of Abib[x] and celebrate the Passover[y] of the LORD your
God, because in the month of Abib he
brought you out of Egypt by night. 2Sacri-
fice as the Passover to the LORD your God
an animal from your flock or herd at the
place the LORD will choose as a dwelling
for his Name.[z] 3Do not eat it with bread
made with yeast, but for seven days eat
unleavened bread, the bread of affliction,[a]
because you left Egypt in haste[b]—so that
all the days of your life you may remember
the time of your departure from Egypt.[c]
4Let no yeast be found in your possession
in all your land for seven days. Do not let
any of the meat you sacrifice on the evening[d] of the first day remain until morning.[e]

5You must not sacrifice the Passover in
any town the LORD your God gives you 6ex-
cept in the place he will choose as a dwelling for his Name. There you must sacrifice
the Passover in the evening, when the sun
goes down, on the anniversary[a][f] of your
departure from Egypt. 7Roast[g] it and eat it
at the place the LORD your God will choose.
Then in the morning return to your tents.
8For six days eat unleavened bread and on
the seventh day hold an assembly[h] to the
LORD your God and do no work.[i]

Feast of Weeks

16:9-12pp — Lev 23:15-22; Nu 28:26-31

9Count off seven weeks[j] from the time
you begin to put the sickle to the standing grain.[k] 10Then celebrate the Feast of

[a] 6 Or *down, at the time of day*

15:10 [h] S Dt 14:29
15:11 [i] S ver 7 [j] Mt 26:11; Mk 14:7; Jn 12:8
15:12 [k] Jer 34:14
15:14 [l] S Nu 18:27
15:15 [m] Ex 13:3; Jer 34:13 [n] Ex 20:2; S Dt 4:34; S 9:26; 16:12; 24:18; Jer 16:14; 23:7
15:19 [o] S Lev 27:9 [p] S Ex 13:2 [q] S Ge 4:4 [r] S Ex 22:30
15:20 [s] S Lev 7:15-18; Dt 12:5-7,17,18
15:21 [t] S Ex 12:5 [u] S Lev 22:19-25; Dt 17:1; Mal 1:8,13
15:22 [v] S Dt 12:15
15:23 [w] S Ge 9:4; Dt 12:16; Eze 33:25
16:1 [x] S Ex 12:2 [y] S Ex 12:11; 2Ki 23:21; Mt 26:17-29
16:2 [z] Dt 12:5,26
16:3 [a] Ex 12:8,39; 34:18; 1Co 5:8 [b] S Ex 12:11 [c] Dt 4:9
16:4 [d] S Ex 12:6 [e] S Ex 12:8; Mk 14:12
16:6 [f] S Ex 12:42
16:7 [g] S Ex 12:8
16:8 [h] 13:6; S Lev 23:8 [i] Mt 26:17; Lk 2:41; 22:7; Jn 2:13
16:9 [j] Ac 2:1 [k] S Ex 23:16

15:11 *There will always be poor people.* See Jesus' statement in Mk 14:7 (see also note there). Even in the best of societies under the most enlightened laws, the uncertainties of life and the variations among citizens result in some people becoming poor. In such cases the Lord commands that generosity and kindness be extended to them.
15:15 *Remember.* See note on 4:10.
15:16 *because he loves you.* In Ex 21:5 an additional reason is given: The servant may want to stay with his family.
15:17 *take an awl and push it through his ear lobe.* See note on Ex 21:6.
15:18 *worth twice as much.* A Hebrew servant worked twice as many years as the Code of Hammurapi, e.g., required for release from debt (see chart, p. xxii). Other ancient legal texts, however, support "equivalent to" as a possible translation of the phrase.
15:19 *Set apart ... every firstborn male.* Because the Lord saved his people from the plague of death on the firstborn in Egypt (see Ex 12:12,29; 13:2 and note; 13:15).
15:21 *If an animal has a defect ... you must not sacrifice it.* See note on Lev 1:3.
15:22 *ceremonially unclean.* See notes on Lev 4:12; 11:2.
15:23 See 12:16,24; see also notes on Ge 9:4; Lev 17:11.
16:1 – 17 See chart, pp. 178 – 179; see also Ex 23:14 – 19; 34:18 – 26; Lev 23:4 – 44; Nu 28:16 — 29:34 and notes.
16:1 – 8 See Ex 12:2 – 27; 13:2 – 16 and notes.
16:1 *Abib.* See chart, p. 104.
16:3,12 *remember.* See note on 4:10.
16:7 *to your tents.* To wherever they were staying while at the festival, whether in permanent or temporary quarters.
16:8 *assembly.* That is, the closing assembly (see Lev 23:36).
16:9 *seven weeks.* Symbolizing the full season of grain harvest.
16:10 *giving ... in proportion to.* See v. 17; cf. 1Co 16:2; 2Co 8:12 and notes.

Weeks to the LORD your God by giving a
freewill offering in proportion to the blessings the LORD your God has given you.
11 And rejoice[l] before the LORD your God
at the place he will choose as a dwelling for his Name[m] — you, your sons and
daughters, your menservants and maidservants, the Levites[n] in your towns, and
the aliens,[o] the fatherless and the widows
living among you.[p] 12 Remember that you
were slaves in Egypt,[q] and follow carefully
these decrees.

Feast of Tabernacles

16:13-17pp — Lev 23:33-43; Nu 29:12-39

13 Celebrate the Feast of Tabernacles
for seven days after you have gathered
the produce of your threshing floor[r] and
your winepress.[s] 14 Be joyful[t] at your
Feast — you, your sons and daughters,
your menservants and maidservants, and
the Levites, the aliens, the fatherless and
the widows who live in your towns. 15 For
seven days celebrate the Feast to the LORD
your God at the place the LORD will choose.
For the LORD your God will bless you in all
your harvest and in all the work of your
hands, and your joy[u] will be complete.
16 Three times a year all your men must
appear[v] before the LORD your God at the
place he will choose: at the Feast of Unleavened Bread,[w] the Feast of Weeks and
the Feast of Tabernacles.[x] No man should
appear before the LORD empty-handed:[y]
17 Each of you must bring a gift in proportion to the way the LORD your God has
blessed you.

Judges

18 Appoint judges[z] and officials for each
of your tribes in every town the LORD your
God is giving you, and they shall judge the
people fairly.[a] 19 Do not pervert justice[b] or
show partiality.[c] Do not accept a bribe,[d]
for a bribe blinds the eyes of the wise and
twists the words of the righteous. 20 Follow
justice and justice alone, so that you may
live and possess the land the LORD your
God is giving you.

Worshiping Other Gods

21 Do not set up any wooden Asherah
pole[a][e] beside the altar you build to the
LORD your God,[f] 22 and do not erect a sacred stone,[g] for these the LORD your God
hates.

17 Do not sacrifice to the LORD your God
an ox or a sheep that has any defect[h]
or flaw in it, for that would be detestable[i]
to him.[j]
2 If a man or woman living among you
in one of the towns the LORD gives you is
found doing evil in the eyes of the LORD
your God in violation of his covenant,[k]
3 and contrary to my command[l] has worshiped other gods,[m] bowing down to them
or to the sun[n] or the moon or the stars of
the sky,[o] 4 and this has been brought to
your attention, then you must investigate
it thoroughly. If it is true[p] and it has been
proved that this detestable thing has been
done in Israel,[q] 5 take the man or woman
who has done this evil deed to your city
gate and stone that person to death.[r] 6 On
the testimony of two or three witnesses
a man shall be put to death, but no one
shall be put to death on the testimony of
only one witness.[s] 7 The hands of the witnesses must be the first in putting him to
death,[t] and then the hands of all the people.[u] You must purge the evil[v] from among
you.

Law Courts

8 If cases come before your courts that
are too difficult for you to judge[w] — whether bloodshed, lawsuits or assaults[x] — take
them to the place the LORD your God will
choose.[y] 9 Go to the priests, who are Levites,[z] and to the judge[a] who is in office
at that time. Inquire of them and they will
give you the verdict.[b] 10 You must act according to the decisions they give you at
the place the LORD will choose. Be careful to do everything they direct you to do.
11 Act according to the law they teach you
and the decisions they give you. Do not
turn aside from what they tell you, to the
right or to the left.[c] 12 The man who shows
contempt[d] for the judge or for the priest
who stands ministering[e] there to the LORD
your God must be put to death.[f] You must
purge the evil from Israel.[g] 13 All the people will hear and be afraid, and will not be
contemptuous again.[h]

[a] 21 Or *Do not plant any tree dedicated to Asherah*

16:11 [l] Dt 12:7 [m] S Ex 20:24; S 2Sa 7:13 [n] Dt 12:12 [o] S Dt 14:29 [p] Ne 8:10
16:12 [q] S Dt 15:15
16:13 [r] S Lev 2:14 [s] S Ge 27:37; S Ex 23:16
16:14 [t] ver 11
16:15 [u] Job 38:7; Ps 4:7; 28:7; 30:11
16:16 [v] Dt 31:11; Ps 84:7 [w] S Ex 12:17 [x] S Ex 23:14, 16; Ezr 3:4 [y] S Ex 34:20
16:18 [z] S Ex 18:21, 26 [a] S Ge 31:37
16:19 [b] S Ex 23:2 [c] S Lev 19:15 [d] S Ex 18:21; S 1Sa 8:3
16:21 [e] S Dt 7:5 [f] Ex 34:13; 1Ki 14:15; 2Ki 17:16; 21:3; 2Ch 33:3
16:22 [g] S Ex 23:24
17:1 [h] S Ex 12:5; S Lev 22:20 [i] Dt 7:25 [j] S Dt 15:21
17:2 [k] Dt 13:6-11
17:3 [l] Jer 7:31 [m] Ex 22:20 [n] S Ge 1:16 [o] S Ge 2:1; S 37:9
17:4 [p] Dt 22:20 [q] Dt 13:12-14
17:5 [r] S Lev 24:14
17:6 [s] Nu 35:30; Dt 19:15; S Mt 18:16
17:7 [t] Jn 8:7 [u] S Lev 24:14; Ac 7:58 [v] S Dt 13:5; 1Co 5:13*
17:8 [w] Ex 21:6 [x] 2Ch 19:10 [y] Dt 12:5; Ps 122:3-5
17:9 [z] Dt 24:8; 27:9 [a] S Ex 21:6 [b] S Ge 25:22; Dt 19:17; Eze 44:24; Hag 2:11
17:11 [c] S Lev 10:11; S Dt 5:32
17:12 [d] Nu 15:30 [e] S Nu 16:9 [f] ver 13; S Ge 17:14; Dt 13:11; 18:20; 19:20; 1Ki 18:40; Jer 14:14; Hos 4:4; Zec 13:3 [g] S Dt 13:5
17:13 [h] S ver 12

16:15 *your joy will be complete.* As a result of God's blessing (see 12:12 and note; cf. Jn 3:29; 15:11 and note; 16:24; Php 2:2; 1Jn 1:4 and note; 2Jn 12).
16:16 *Three times a year.* The three annual pilgrimage festivals (see Ex 23:14,17; 34:23; see also chart, p. 104).
16:18 – 20 Cf. 1:9 – 18; Ex 18:13 – 26.
16:19 Israel must emulate the Lord in these matters (see 10:17; see also Ex 23:8 and note).
16:21 – 22 *Asherah pole ... sacred stone.* See note on 7:5.
17:1 *defect or flaw.* See note on Lev 1:3.
17:3 *bowing down to ... the sun or the moon or the stars.* See 4:19 and note.
17:6 *two or three witnesses.* A further specification of the law set forth in Nu 35:30 (see note there). See 19:15; cf. Mt 18:16; 2Co 13:1; 1Ti 5:19; Heb 10:28.
17:7 *You must purge the evil from among you.* See v. 12; see also note on 13:5.

The King

14 When you enter the land the LORD your God is giving you and have taken possession[i] of it and settled in it,[j] and you say, "Let us set a king over us like all the nations around us,"[k] 15 be sure to appoint[l] over you the king the LORD your God chooses. He must be from among your own brothers.[m] Do not place a foreigner over you, one who is not a brother Israelite. 16 The king, moreover, must not acquire great numbers of horses[n] for himself[o] or make the people return to Egypt[p] to get more of them,[q] for the LORD has told you, "You are not to go back that way again."[r] 17 He must not take many wives,[s] or his heart will be led astray.[t] He must not accumulate[u] large amounts of silver and gold.[v]

18 When he takes the throne[w] of his kingdom, he is to write[x] for himself on a scroll a copy[y] of this law, taken from that of the priests, who are Levites. 19 It is to be with him, and he is to read it all the days of his life[z] so that he may learn to revere the LORD his God and follow carefully all the words of this law and these decrees[a] 20 and not consider himself better than his brothers and turn from the law[b] to the right or to the left.[c] Then he and his descendants will reign a long time over his kingdom in Israel.[d]

Offerings for Priests and Levites

18 The priests, who are Levites[e]—indeed the whole tribe of Levi—are to have no allotment or inheritance with Israel. They shall live on the offerings[f] made to the LORD by fire, for that is their inheritance.[g] 2 They shall have no inheritance among their brothers; the LORD is their inheritance,[h] as he promised them.[i]

3 This is the share due the priests[j] from the people who sacrifice a bull[k] or a sheep: the shoulder, the jowls and the inner parts.[l] 4 You are to give them the firstfruits of your grain, new wine and oil, and the first wool from the shearing of your sheep,[m] 5 for the LORD your God has chosen them[n] and their descendants out of all your tribes to stand and minister[o] in the LORD's name always.[p]

6 If a Levite moves from one of your towns anywhere in Israel where he is living, and comes in all earnestness to the place the LORD will choose,[q] 7 he may minister in the name[r] of the LORD his God like all his fellow Levites who serve there in the presence of the LORD. 8 He is to share equally in their benefits, even though he has received money from the sale of family possessions.[s]

Detestable Practices

9 When you enter the land the LORD your God is giving you, do not learn to imitate[t] the detestable ways[u] of the nations there. 10 Let no one be found among you who sacrifices his son or daughter in[a] the fire,[v] who practices divination[w] or sorcery,[x] interprets omens, engages in witchcraft,[y] 11 or casts spells,[z] or who is a medium or spiritist[a] or who consults the dead. 12 Anyone who does these things is detestable to the LORD, and because of these detestable practices the LORD your God will drive out those nations before you.[b] 13 You must be blameless[c] before the LORD your God.[d]

The Prophet

14 The nations you will dispossess listen to those who practice sorcery or divination.[e] But as for you, the LORD your God

[a] 10 Or *who makes his son or daughter pass through*

17:14 [i] S Nu 33:53 [j] Jos 21:43 [k] 1Sa 8:5, 19-20; 10:19 **17:15** [l] 1Sa 16:3; 2Sa 5:3 [m] Jer 30:21 **17:16** [n] Isa 2:7; 30:16 [o] 1Sa 8:11; 1Ki 4:26; 9:19; 10:26; 2Ch 1:14; Ps 20:7 [p] 1Ki 10:29; Isa 31:1; Jer 42:14 [q] 1Ki 10:28; Isa 31:1; Eze 17:15 [r] S Ex 13:17 **17:17** [s] S Ex 34:16; 2Sa 5:13; 12:11; 1Ki 11:3; 2Ch 11:21 [t] 1Ki 11:2; Pr 31:3 [u] 1Ki 10:27 [v] 2Ch 1:11; Isa 2:7 **17:18** [w] 1Ki 1:46; 1Ch 29:23 [x] Dt 31:22, 24; Jos 24:26; 1Sa 10:25 [y] 2Ch 23:11 **17:19** [z] Dt 4:9-10; Jos 1:8 [a] Dt 11:13; 1Ki 3:3; 11:38; 2Ki 22:2 **17:20** [b] Jos 23:6; Job 23:12; Ps 119:102 [c] S Dt 5:32; S 1Ki 9:4 [d] 1Sa 8:5; 10:25; 1Ki 2:3; 1Ch 28:8 **18:1** [e] Jer 33:18, 21 [f] S Nu 18:8 [g] S Nu 18:20; 1Co 9:13 **18:2** [h] Nu 18:20 [i] Jos 13:14 **18:3** [j] S Ex 29:27 [k] S Lev 1:5 [l] Lev 7:28-34; Nu 18:12 **18:4** [m] Ex 22:29; Nu 18:12 **18:5** [n] S Ex 28:1 [o] Dt 10:8 [p] S Ex 29:9

18:6 [q] S Nu 35:2-3; S Dt 12:5 **18:7** [r] ver 19; 1Ki 18:32; 22:16; Ps 118:26 **18:8** [s] Nu 18:24; 2Ch 31:4; Ne 12:44, 47; 13:12 **18:9** [t] Dt 9:5; 12:29-31 [u] S Lev 18:3; 2Ki 21:2; 2Ch 28:3; 33:2; 34:33; Ezr 6:21; 9:11; Jer 44:4 **18:10** [v] S Lev 18:21 [w] 1Sa 15:23 [x] S Ex 7:11 [y] S Lev 19:31 **18:11** [z] Isa 47:9 [a] S Ex 22:18; S 1Sa 28:13 **18:12** [b] S Lev 18:24 **18:13** [c] S Ge 6:9; Ps 119:1 [d] Mt 5:48 **18:14** [e] 2Ki 21:6

17:14 *a king … like all the nations around us.* Moses, Joshua and a succession of judges were chosen directly by the Lord to govern Israel on his behalf. As Gideon later said, "The LORD will rule over you" (Jdg 8:23; see note there). Moses here, however, anticipates a time when the people would ask for a king (see 1Sa 8:4–9) contrary to the Lord's ideal for them (see notes on 7:2–5; 1Sa 8:1—12:25; see also Lev 20:23). So Moses gives guidance concerning the eventual selection of a king (vv. 14–20).

17:16–17 The very things that later kings were guilty of, beginning especially with Solomon (see 1Ki 4:26; 10:14–22; see also 1Ki 11:1–13 and notes)—except that they did not make Israel return to Egypt (but see Jer 42:13—43:7).

17:18 *write for himself … a copy of this law.* As a sign of submission to the Lord as his King, and as a guide for his rule in obedience to his heavenly Suzerain. This was required procedure for vassal kings under the suzerainty treaties among the Hittites and others before and during this period (see note on 31:9). See chart, p. 19. *copy of this law.* See Introduction: Title.

17:20 *not consider himself better.* The king was not above God's law, any more than were the humblest of his subjects.

18:1 *no allotment or inheritance.* No private ownership of land. Towns and surrounding pasturelands were set aside for the use of the Levites (Jos 21:41–42), as were the tithes and parts of sacrifices (see 14:22–29; Lev 27:30 and notes; Nu 18:21–29).

18:4 *firstfruits.* See Ex 23:19 and note; 34:26; Lev 23:10–11; Nu 15:18–20 and note on 15:20; 18:12–13.

18:5 See note on 21:5.

18:9 *detestable ways of the nations.* What follows is the most complete list of magical or spiritistic arts in the OT. All were practiced in Canaan, and all are condemned and prohibited. The people are not to resort to such sources for their information, guidance or revelation. Rather, they are to listen to the Lord's true prophets (see vv. 14–22; Isa 8:19–20).

18:10 *sacrifices his son or daughter.* See 12:31; see also note on Lev 18:21.

has not permitted you to do so. 15 The LORD
your God will raise up for you a prophet
like me from among your own brothers.[f]
You must listen to him. 16 For this is what
you asked of the LORD your God at Horeb
on the day of the assembly when you said,
"Let us not hear the voice of the LORD our
God nor see this great fire anymore, or we
will die."[g]
17 The LORD said to me: "What they say
is good. 18 I will raise up for them a prophet[h] like you from among their brothers;
I will put my words[i] in his mouth,[j] and
he will tell them everything I command
him.[k] 19 If anyone does not listen[l] to my
words that the prophet speaks in my
name,[m] I myself will call him to account.[n]
20 But a prophet who presumes to speak in
my name anything I have not commanded him to say, or a prophet who speaks
in the name of other gods,[o] must be put
to death."[p]
21 You may say to yourselves, "How can
we know when a message has not been
spoken by the LORD?" 22 If what a prophet
proclaims in the name of the LORD does
not take place or come true,[q] that is a
message the LORD has not spoken.[r] That
prophet has spoken presumptuously.[s] Do
not be afraid of him.

Cities of Refuge

19:1-14Ref — Nu 35:6-34; Dt 4:41-43; Jos 20:1-9

19 When the LORD your God has destroyed the nations whose land he
is giving you, and when you have driven
them out and settled in their towns and
houses,[t] 2 then set aside for yourselves
three cities centrally located in the land
the LORD your God is giving you to possess. 3 Build roads to them and divide into
three parts the land the LORD your God is
giving you as an inheritance, so that anyone who kills a man may flee there.
4 This is the rule concerning the man
who kills another and flees there to save
his life—one who kills his neighbor unintentionally, without malice aforethought.
5 For instance, a man may go into the forest with his neighbor to cut wood, and as
he swings his ax to fell a tree, the head
may fly off and hit his neighbor and kill
him. That man may flee to one of these
cities and save his life. 6 Otherwise, the
avenger of blood[u] might pursue him in a
rage, overtake him if the distance is too
great, and kill him even though he is not
deserving of death, since he did it to his
neighbor without malice aforethought.
7 This is why I command you to set aside
for yourselves three cities.
8 If the LORD your God enlarges your territory,[v] as he promised[w] on oath to your
forefathers, and gives you the whole land
he promised them, 9 because you carefully follow all these laws I command you
today—to love the LORD your God and to
walk always in his ways[x]—then you are
to set aside three more cities. 10 Do this
so that innocent blood[y] will not be shed
in your land, which the LORD your God
is giving you as your inheritance, and
so that you will not be guilty of bloodshed.[z]
11 But if a man hates his neighbor and
lies in wait for him, assaults and kills
him,[a] and then flees to one of these cities, 12 the elders of his town shall send for
him, bring him back from the city, and
hand him over to the avenger of blood to
die. 13 Show him no pity.[b] You must purge
from Israel the guilt of shedding innocent
blood,[c] so that it may go well with you.
14 Do not move your neighbor's boundary stone set up by your predecessors in
the inheritance you receive in the land the
LORD your God is giving you to possess.[d]

Witnesses

15 One witness is not enough to convict
a man accused of any crime or offense
he may have committed. A matter must
be established by the testimony of two or
three witnesses.[e]
16 If a malicious witness[f] takes the stand
to accuse a man of a crime, 17 the two men
involved in the dispute must stand in the
presence of the LORD before the priests and
the judges[g] who are in office at the time.
18 The judges must make a thorough investigation,[h] and if the witness proves to be
a liar, giving false testimony against his

18:15 [f] S Mt 21:11; Lk 2:25-35; Jn 1:21; Ac 3:22*; 7:37*
18:16 [g] S Ex 20:19; Dt 5:23-27
18:18 [h] S Ge 20:7 [i] Isa 2:3; 26:8; 51:4; Mic 4:2 [j] S Ex 4:12 [k] Jn 4:25-26; S 14:24; Ac 3:22*
18:19 [l] S Ex 23:21 [m] S ver 7; S Lev 19:12; 2Ki 2:24 [n] Jos 22:23; Ac 3:23*; Heb 12:25
18:20 [o] S Ex 23:13 [p] Dt 13:1-5; S 17:12
18:22 [q] S Dt 13:2; 1Sa 3:20 [r] 1Ki 22:28; Jer 28:9 [s] ver 20
19:1 [t] Dt 6:10-11
19:6 [u] S Nu 35:12
19:8 [v] S Ex 34:24 [w] S Ge 15:8; S Dt 11:24
19:9 [x] Dt 6:5
19:10 [y] Pr 6:17; Jer 7:6; 26:15 [z] Dt 21:1-9
19:11 [a] S Ex 21:12; 1Jn 3:15
19:13 [b] Dt 7:2 [c] Dt 21:9; 1Ki 2:31
19:14 [d] Dt 27:17; Job 24:2; Ps 16:6; Pr 15:25; 22:28; 23:10; Isa 1:23; Hos 5:10
19:15 [e] S Dt 17:6; S Mt 18:16*; 26:60; 2Co 13:1*
19:16 [f] Ex 23:1; Pr 6:19
19:17 [g] S Ex 21:6
19:18 [h] S Ex 23:7

18:15 *prophet like me.* See 34:10–12 and note on 34:12. Verses 16–19, as well as the general context (especially vv. 20–22), indicate that a series of prophets is meant. At Mount Horeb the people requested that Moses take the message from God and deliver it to them (see Ex 20:19 and note). But now that Moses is to leave them, he says that another spokesman will take his place, and then another will be necessary for the next generation. This is therefore a collective reference to the prophets who will follow. As such, it is also the basis for later Messianic expectation and receives a unique fulfillment in Jesus (see Jn 1:21,25,45 and notes; 5:46; 6:14 and note; 7:40; Ac 3:22–26; 7:37).

18:16 See Ex 20:18–21; Heb 12:18–21 and notes.

18:18 *my words in his mouth.* See Ex 4:15–16; see also notes on Ex 7:1–2; Jer 1:9.

18:20 *prophet who presumes to speak.* See note on 13:1–5. *must be put to death.* See 13:5; Jer 28:15–17.

18:21–22 See note on 13:1–5.

19:1–13 See 4:41–43; Nu 35:9–28; Jos 20 and notes.

19:14 *boundary stone.* Such stones were set up to indicate the perimeters of fields and landed estates. Moving them illegally to increase one's own holdings was considered a serious crime (see 27:17).

19:15 See note on 17:6.

19:18 *giving false testimony.* See 5:20 and note on Ex 20:16; Lev 19:11–12; 1Ki 21:10,13.

brother, 19then do to him as he intended to do to his brother.[i] You must purge the evil from among you. 20The rest of the people will hear of this and be afraid,[j] and never again will such an evil thing be done among you. 21Show no pity:[k] life for life, eye for eye, tooth for tooth, hand for hand, foot for foot.[l]

Going to War

20 When you go to war against your enemies and see horses and chariots and an army greater than yours,[m] do not be afraid[n] of them,[o] because the LORD your God, who brought you up out of Egypt, will be with[p] you. 2When you are about to go into battle, the priest shall come forward and address the army. 3He shall say: "Hear, O Israel, today you are going into battle against your enemies. Do not be fainthearted[q] or afraid; do not be terrified or give way to panic before them. 4For the LORD your God is the one who goes with you[r] to fight[s] for you against your enemies to give you victory.[t]"

5The officers shall say to the army: "Has anyone built a new house and not dedicated[u] it? Let him go home, or he may die in battle and someone else may dedicate it. 6Has anyone planted[v] a vineyard and not begun to enjoy it?[w] Let him go home, or he may die in battle and someone else enjoy it. 7Has anyone become pledged to a woman and not married her? Let him go home, or he may die in battle and someone else marry her.[x]" 8Then the officers shall add, "Is any man afraid or fainthearted? Let him go home so that his brothers will not become disheartened too."[y] 9When the officers have finished speaking to the army, they shall appoint commanders over it.

10When you march up to attack a city, make its people an offer of peace.[z] 11If they accept and open their gates, all the people in it shall be subject[a] to forced labor[b] and shall work for you. 12If they refuse to make peace and they engage you in battle, lay siege to that city. 13When the LORD your God delivers it into your hand, put to the sword all the men in it.[c] 14As for the women, the children, the livestock[d] and everything else in the city,[e] you may take these as plunder[f] for yourselves. And you may use the plunder the LORD your God gives you from your enemies. 15This is how you are to treat all the cities that are at a distance[g] from you and do not belong to the nations nearby.

16However, in the cities of the nations the LORD your God is giving you as an inheritance, do not leave alive anything that breathes.[h] 17Completely destroy[a] them—the Hittites, Amorites, Canaanites, Perizzites, Hivites and Jebusites—as the LORD your God has commanded you. 18Otherwise, they will teach you to follow all the detestable things they do in worshiping their gods,[i] and you will sin[j] against the LORD your God.

19When you lay siege to a city for a long time, fighting against it to capture it, do not destroy its trees by putting an ax to them, because you can eat their fruit. Do not cut them down. Are the trees of the field people, that you should besiege them?[b] 20However, you may cut down trees that you know are not fruit trees[k] and use them to build siege works until the city at war with you falls.

Atonement for an Unsolved Murder

21 If a man is found slain, lying in a field in the land the LORD your God is giving you to possess, and it is not known who killed him,[l] 2your elders and judges shall go out and measure the distance from the body to the neighboring towns. 3Then the elders of the town nearest the body shall take a heifer that has never been worked and has never worn a yoke[m] 4and lead her down to a valley that has not been plowed or planted and where there is a flowing stream. There in the valley they are to break the heifer's neck. 5The priests, the sons of Levi, shall step forward, for the LORD your God has chosen them to minister

[a] *17* The Hebrew term refers to the irrevocable giving over of things or persons to the LORD, often by totally destroying them. [b] *19* Or *down to use in the siege, for the fruit trees are for the benefit of man.*

19:19 [i] Pr 19:5,9; 1Co 5:13* **19:20** [j] S Dt 13:11 **19:21** [k] ver 13 [l] S Ex 21:24; Mt 5:38* **20:1** [m] Ps 20:7; Isa 31:1 [n] S Nu 14:9 [o] S Dt 3:22; S 1Sa 17:45 [p] Isa 41:10 **20:3** [q] 1Sa 17:32; Job 23:16; Ps 22:14; Isa 7:4; 35:4; Jer 51:46 **20:4** [r] 2Ch 20:14-22 [s] S Ex 14:14; 1Ch 5:22; Ne 4:20 [t] Jdg 12:3; 15:18; Ps 44:7; 144:10 **20:5** [u] Ne 12:27 **20:6** [v] Jer 31:5; Eze 28:26; Mic 1:6 [w] 1Co 9:7 **20:7** [x] Dt 24:5; Pr 5:18 **20:8** [y] Jdg 7:3 **20:10** [z] S Dt 2:26; Lk 14:31-32 **20:11** [a] ver 15; 2Ki 6:22 [b] 1Ki 9:21; 1Ch 22:2; Isa 31:8 **20:13** [c] Nu 31:7 **20:14** [d] Jos 8:2; 22:8 [e] S Nu 31:11 [f] S Nu 31:53 **20:15** [g] S ver 11; Jos 9:9 **20:16** [h] Ex 23:31-33; Nu 21:2-3; S Dt 7:2; Jos 6:21; 10:1; 11:14 **20:18** [i] S Ex 34:16 [j] S Ex 10:7 **20:20** [k] Jer 6:6 **21:1** [l] S Nu 25:17 **21:3** [m] S Nu 19:2

19:19 *You must purge the evil from among you.* See note on 13:5.
19:21 *life for life.* See notes on Ex 21:23–25; Lev 24:20; see also Mt 5:38–42.
20:2 *priest shall … address.* Priests sometimes accompanied the army when it went into battle (see, e.g., Jos 6:4–21; 2Ch 20:14–22).
20:3 *Hear, O Israel.* See note on 4:1.
20:4 See note on 3:22.
20:5–8 Cf. the curses in 28:30. *Let him go home.* Israel was not to trust in the size of its army but in the Lord (see notes on 2Sa 24:1; Ps 30:6–7). The number of exemptions from military duty was sometimes extensive (see, e.g., Jdg 7:1–8 and note).
20:10–15 Rules regarding warfare against nations outside the promised land.
20:11 *subject to forced labor.* A fulfillment of Noah's curse on Canaan (see Ge 9:25 and note).
20:17 *Hittites … Jebusites.* See 7:1; see also notes on Ge 10:6,15–18; 13:7; Jos 9:7.
20:19 *do not destroy its trees.* The failure of later armies to follow this wise rule stripped bare much of the land (though the absence of woodlands there today is of relatively recent origin).
21:5 *to minister.* To officiate at the place of worship before the Lord on behalf of the people (see 10:8; 18:5).

and to pronounce blessings[n] in the name
of the LORD and to decide all cases of dispute and assault.[o] 6Then all the elders of
the town nearest the body shall wash their
hands[p] over the heifer whose neck was
broken in the valley, 7and they shall declare: "Our hands did not shed this blood,
nor did our eyes see it done. 8Accept this
atonement for your people Israel, whom
you have redeemed, O LORD, and do not
hold your people guilty of the blood of an
innocent man." And the bloodshed will
be atoned for.[q] 9So you will purge[r] from
yourselves the guilt of shedding innocent
blood, since you have done what is right
in the eyes of the LORD.

21:5 [n]S Ge 48:20; S Ex 39:43 [o]Dt 17:8-11
21:6 [p]Mt 27:24
21:8 [q]Nu 35:33-34
21:9 [r]Dt 19:13
21:10 [s]Jos 21:44 [t]1Ki 8:46; 1Ch 9:1; Ezr 5:12; Jer 40:1; Eze 1:1; 17:12; Da 2:25; Mic 4:10
21:11 [u]Ge 6:2 [v]S Ge 34:8
21:12 [w]S Lev 14:9; S Nu 8:7; 1Co 11:5
21:13 [x]Ps 45:10

Marrying a Captive Woman

10When you go to war against your enemies and the LORD your God delivers them
into your hands[s] and you take captives,[t]
11if you notice among the captives a beautiful[u] woman and are attracted to her,[v] you
may take her as your wife. 12Bring her into
your home and have her shave her head,[w]
trim her nails 13and put aside the clothes
she was wearing when captured. After she
has lived in your house and mourned her
father and mother for a full month,[x] then
you may go to her and be her husband
and she shall be your wife. 14If you are
not pleased with her, let her go wherever

21:5 *to pronounce blessings.* See Nu 6:24–26 and notes.
21:6 *wash their hands.* Symbolic of a declaration of innocence (v. 7; see Mt 27:24).
21:10 *take captives.* The enemies here were those outside Canaan (see 20:14–15); so they were not subject to total destruction (see 20:17 and NIV text note there).
21:12 *shave her head.* Indicative of leaving her former life and beginning a new life, or perhaps symbolic of mourning (v. 13; see, e.g., Jer 47:5; Mic 1:16) or of humiliation (see note on Isa 7:20). For cleansing rites see Lev 14:8; Nu 8:7 and note; cf. 2Sa 19:24.
21:14 *dishonored.* Twelve other times the Hebrew for this word is used of men forcing women to have sexual intercourse with them (22:24,29; Ge 34:2; Jdg 19:24; 20:5; 2Sa 13:12,14,22,32; La 5:11; Eze 22:10–11). In most of these other passages the Hebrew is rendered "violate" or "rape."

Major Social Concerns in the Covenant

1. **Personhood**
Everyone's person is to be secure (Ex 20:13; Dt 5:17; Ex 21:16-21,26-32; Lev 19:14; Dt 24:7; 27:18).

2. **False Accusation**
Everyone is to be secure against slander and false accusation (Ex 20:16; Dt 5:20; Ex 23:1-3,6-8; Lev 19:16; Dt 19:15-21).

3. **Women**
No woman is to be taken advantage of within her subordinate status in society (Ex 21:7-11,20,26-32; 22:16-17; Dt 21:10-14; 22:13-30; 24:1-5).

4. **Punishment**
Punishment for wrongdoing shall not be excessive so that the culprit is dehumanized (Dt 25:1-3).

5. **Dignity**
Every Israelite's dignity and right to be God's servant are to be honored and safeguarded (Ex 21:2,5-6; Lev 25; Dt 15:12-18).

6. **Inheritance**
Every Israelite's inheritance in the promised land is to be secure (Lev 25; Nu 27:5-7; 36:1-9; Dt 25:5-10).

7. **Property**
Everyone's property is to be secure (Ex 20:15; Dt 5:19; Ex 21:33-36; 22:1-15; 23:4-5; Lev 19:35-36; Dt 22:1-4; 25:13-15).

8. **Fruit of Labor**
Everyone is to receive the fruit of their labors (Lev 19:13; Dt 24:14; 25:4).

9. **Fruit of the Ground**
Everyone is to share the fruit of the ground (Ex 23:10-11; Lev 19:9-10; 23:22; 25:3-55; Dt 14:28-29; 24:19-21).

10. **Rest on Sabbath**
Everyone, down to the humblest servant and the resident alien, is to share in the weekly rest of God's Sabbath (Ex 20:8-11; Dt 5:12-15; Ex 23:12).

11. **Marriage**
The marriage relationship is to be kept inviolate (Ex 20:14; Dt 5:18; see also Lev 18:6-23; 20:10-21; Dt 22:13-30).

12. **Exploitation**
No one, however disabled, impoverished or powerless, is to be oppressed or exploited (Ex 22:21-27; Lev 19:14,33-34; 25:35-36; Dt 23:19; 24:6,12-15,17; 27:18).

13. **Fair Trial**
Everyone is to have free access to the courts and is to be afforded a fair trial (Ex 23:6-8; Lev 19:15; Dt 1:17; 10:17-18; 16:18-20; 17:8-13; 19:15-21).

14. **Social Order**
Every person's God-given place in the social order is to be honored (Ex 20:12; Dt 5:16; Ex 21:15,17; 22:28; Lev 19:3,32; 20:9; Dt 17:8-13; 21:15-21; 27:16).

15. **Law**
No one shall be above the law, not even the king (Dt 17:18-20).

16. **Animals**
Concern for the welfare of other creatures is to be extended to the animal world (Ex 23:5,11; Lev 25:7; Dt 22:4,6-7; 25:4).

she wishes. You must not sell her or treat
her as a slave, since you have dishonored
her.[y]

The Right of the Firstborn

15If a man has two wives,[z] and he loves
one but not the other, and both bear him
sons but the firstborn is the son of the
wife he does not love,[a] 16when he wills
his property to his sons, he must not give
the rights of the firstborn to the son of the
wife he loves in preference to his actual
firstborn, the son of the wife he does not
love.[b] 17He must acknowledge the son of
his unloved wife as the firstborn by giving him a double[c] share of all he has.
That son is the first sign of his father's
strength.[d] The right of the firstborn belongs to him.[e]

A Rebellious Son

18If a man has a stubborn and rebellious[f] son[g] who does not obey his father
and mother[h] and will not listen to them
when they discipline him, 19his father and
mother shall take hold of him and bring
him to the elders at the gate of his town.
20They shall say to the elders, "This son
of ours is stubborn and rebellious. He
will not obey us. He is a profligate and a
drunkard." 21Then all the men of his town
shall stone him to death.[i] You must purge
the evil[j] from among you. All Israel will
hear of it and be afraid.[k]

Various Laws

22If a man guilty of a capital offense[l] is
put to death and his body is hung on a
tree, 23you must not leave his body on the
tree overnight.[m] Be sure to bury[n] him that
same day, because anyone who is hung on
a tree is under God's curse.[o] You must not
desecrate[p] the land the LORD your God is
giving you as an inheritance.

21:14 [y]S Ge 34:2
21:15 [z]S Ge 4:19 [a]Ge 29:33
21:16 [b]1Ch 26:10
21:17 [c]2Ki 2:9; Isa 40:2; 61:7; Zec 9:12 [d]S Ge 49:3 [e]Ge 25:31; Lk 15:12
21:18 [f]Ps 78:8; Jer 5:23; Zep 3:1 [g]Pr 30:17 [h]S Ge 31:35; Pr 1:8; Isa 30:1; Eph 6:1-3
21:21 [i]S Lev 20:9 [j]Dt 19:19; 1Co 5:13* [k]S Dt 13:11
21:22 [l]Dt 22:26; Mt 26:66; Mk 14:64; Ac 23:29
21:23 [m]Jos 8:29; 10:27; Jn 19:31 [n]Eze 39:12 [o]Ezr 6:11; Est 2:23; 7:9; 8:7; 9:13,25; Isa 50:11; Gal 3:13* [p]S Lev 18:25
22:1 [q]Ex 23:4-5; Pr 27:10; Zec 7:9
22:4 [r]Ex 23:5 [s]1Co 9:9
22:6 [t]Lev 22:28
22:7 [u]S Lev 22:28 [v]S Dt 5:29
22:8 [w]Jos 2:8; 1Sa 9:25; 2Sa 11:2
22:9 [x]Lev 19:19
22:10 [y]2Co 6:14
22:11 [z]Lev 19:19
22:12 [a]Nu 15:37-41; Mt 23:5
22:13 [b]Dt 24:1

22 If you see your brother's ox or sheep
straying, do not ignore it but be sure
to take it back to him.[q] 2If the brother does
not live near you or if you do not know
who he is, take it home with you and keep
it until he comes looking for it. Then give
it back to him. 3Do the same if you find
your brother's donkey or his cloak or anything he loses. Do not ignore it.
4If you see your brother's donkey[r] or
his ox fallen on the road, do not ignore it.
Help him get it to its feet.[s]
5A woman must not wear men's clothing, nor a man wear women's clothing,
for the LORD your God detests anyone who
does this.
6If you come across a bird's nest beside
the road, either in a tree or on the ground,
and the mother is sitting on the young or
on the eggs, do not take the mother with
the young.[t] 7You may take the young, but
be sure to let the mother go,[u] so that it
may go well with you and you may have
a long life.[v]
8When you build a new house, make a
parapet around your roof so that you may
not bring the guilt of bloodshed on your
house if someone falls from the roof.[w]
9Do not plant two kinds of seed in your
vineyard;[x] if you do, not only the crops
you plant but also the fruit of the vineyard
will be defiled.[a]
10Do not plow with an ox and a donkey
yoked together.[y]
11Do not wear clothes of wool and linen
woven together.[z]
12Make tassels on the four corners of the
cloak you wear.[a]

Marriage Violations

13If a man takes a wife and, after lying
with her[b], dislikes her 14and slanders her
and gives her a bad name, saying, "I married

[a] 9 *Or be forfeited to the sanctuary*

21:15 *two wives.* See notes on Ge 4:19; 25:6.
21:16 *in preference to.* The order of birth rather than parental favoritism governed succession, though the rule was sometimes set aside with divine approval (cf., e.g., Jacob [Ge 25:19–26; see note on 25:23] or Solomon [1Ki 1:5,13; see notes there]; see also Introduction to Genesis: Literary Features).
21:17 *double share.* In Israel the oldest son enjoyed a double share of the inheritance. Parallels to this practice come from Nuzi, Larsa in the Old Babylonian period, and Assyria in the Middle Assyrian period (see chart, p. xxiii). Receiving a double portion of an estate was also tantamount to succession. Thus Elisha succeeded Elijah (see 2Ki 2:9 and note). *first sign of his father's strength.* The first result of a man's procreative ability.
21:18 *stubborn and rebellious … does not obey.* In wicked defiance of the fifth commandment (see 5:16; Ex 20:12 and note).
21:21 *stone him to death.* See 5:16; 27:16; Ex 21:15,17. *You must purge the evil from among you.* See note on 13:5.
21:22 *put to death and … hung on a tree.* The offender was first executed, then "hung on a tree" (see Ge 40:19), or, as the Hebrew for this phrase doubtless intends, "impaled on a pole" (see Ge 40:19 and NIV text note; Est 2:23 and note).
21:23 *not leave his body on the tree overnight.* Prolonged exposure gives undue attention to the crime and the criminal. *under God's curse.* God had condemned murder, and hanging on a tree symbolized divine judgment and rejection. Christ accepted the full punishment of our sins, thus becoming "a curse for us" (Gal 3:13; see note there).
22:1 *do not ignore it.* See vv. 3–4; see also chart, p. 268.
22:5 Probably intended to prohibit such perversions as transvestism and homosexual practices, especially under religious auspices. The God-created differences between men and women are not to be disregarded (see Lev 18:22; 20:13).
22:6–7 See note on Ex 23:19.
22:9–11 See note on Lev 19:19.
22:12 *tassels.* See note on Nu 15:38; cf. Mt 23:5.
22:14 *proof of her virginity.* A blood-stained cloth or garment (see vv. 15,17,20).

this woman, but when I approached her, I did not find proof of her virginity," [15]then the girl's father and mother shall bring proof that she was a virgin to the town elders at the gate.[c] [16]The girl's father will say to the elders, "I gave my daughter in marriage to this man, but he dislikes her. [17]Now he has slandered her and said, 'I did not find your daughter to be a virgin.' But here is the proof of my daughter's virginity." Then her parents shall display the cloth before the elders of the town, [18]and the elders[d] shall take the man and punish him. [19]They shall fine him a hundred shekels of silver[a] and give them to the girl's father, because this man has given an Israelite virgin a bad name. She shall continue to be his wife; he must not divorce her as long as he lives.

[20]If, however, the charge is true[e] and no proof of the girl's virginity can be found, [21]she shall be brought to the door of her father's house and there the men of her town shall stone her to death. She has done a disgraceful thing[f] in Israel by being promiscuous while still in her father's house. You must purge the evil from among you.

[22]If a man is found sleeping with another man's wife, both the man who slept[g] with her and the woman must die.[h] You must purge the evil from Israel.

[23]If a man happens to meet in a town a virgin pledged to be married and he sleeps with her, [24]you shall take both of them to the gate of that town and stone them to death—the girl because she was in a town and did not scream for help, and the man because he violated another man's wife. You must purge the evil from among you.[i]

[25]But if out in the country a man happens to meet a girl pledged to be married and rapes her, only the man who has done this shall die. [26]Do nothing to the girl; she has committed no sin deserving death. This case is like that of someone who attacks and murders his neighbor, [27]for the man found the girl out in the country, and though the betrothed girl screamed,[j] there was no one to rescue her.

[28]If a man happens to meet a virgin who is not pledged to be married and rapes her and they are discovered,[k] [29]he shall pay the girl's father fifty shekels of silver.[b] He must marry the girl, for he has violated her. He can never divorce her as long as he lives.

[30]A man is not to marry his father's wife; he must not dishonor his father's bed.[l]

Exclusion From the Assembly

23 No one who has been emasculated[m] by crushing or cutting may enter the assembly of the LORD.

[2]No one born of a forbidden marriage[c] nor any of his descendants may enter the assembly of the LORD, even down to the tenth generation.

[3]No Ammonite[n] or Moabite or any of his descendants may enter the assembly of the LORD, even down to the tenth generation.[o] [4]For they did not come to meet you with bread and water[p] on your way when you came out of Egypt, and they hired Balaam[q] son of Beor from Pethor in Aram Naharaim[d][r] to pronounce a curse on you.[s] [5]However, the LORD your God would not listen to Balaam but turned the curse[t] into a blessing for you, because the LORD your God loves[u] you. [6]Do not seek a treaty[v] of friendship with them as long as you live.[w]

[7]Do not abhor an Edomite,[x] for he is your brother.[y] Do not abhor an Egyptian, because you lived as an alien in his country.[z] [8]The third generation of children born to them may enter the assembly of the LORD.

Uncleanness in the Camp

[9]When you are encamped against your enemies, keep away from everything impure.[a]

22:15 [c]S Ge 23:10
22:18 [d]Ex 18:21; Dt 1:9-18
22:20 [e]Dt 17:4
22:21 [f]S Ge 34:7; S 38:24; S Lev 19:29; Dt 23:17-18; 1Co 5:13*
22:22 [g]2Sa 11:4 [h]S Ge 38:24; S Ex 21:12; Mt 5:27-28; Jn 8:5; 1Co 6:9; Heb 13:4
22:24 [i]1Co 5:13*
22:27 [j]S Ge 39:14
22:28 [k]Ex 22:16
22:30 [l]S Ge 29:29; S Lev 18:8; S 20:9; 1Co 5:1
23:1 [m]S Lev 21:20
23:3 [n]S Ge 19:38 [o]ver 4; Ne 13:2
23:4 [p]Dt 2:28 [q]S Nu 23:7; S 2Pe 2:15 [r]S Ge 24:10 [s]S ver 3
23:5 [t]Nu 24:10; Jos 24:10; Pr 26:2 [u]S Dt 4:37
23:6 [v]S Nu 24:17; Isa 15:1; 25:10; Jer 25:21; 27:3; 48:1; Eze 25:8; Zep 2:9 [w]Ezr 9:12; Mt 5:43
23:7 [x]S Ge 25:30 [y]S Ge 25:26 [z]S Lev 19:34
23:9 [a]Lev 15:1-33

[a] *19* That is, about 2 1/2 pounds (about 1 kilogram)
[b] *29* That is, about 1 1/4 pounds (about 0.6 kilogram)
[c] *2* Or *one of illegitimate birth*
[d] *4* That is, Northwest Mesopotamia

22:15 *elders at the gate.* See 21:19; 25:7; see also notes on Ge 19:1; Ru 4:1; La 5:14.

22:19 *hundred shekels of silver.* A heavy fine—several times what Hosea paid to buy Gomer back (Hos 3:2) or what Jeremiah paid for the field at Anathoth (Jer 32:9). It may have been about twice the average bride-price (see note on v. 29). The high fine, in addition to the no-divorce rule, was intended to restrain not only a husband's charges against his wife but also easy divorce. *shekels.* See note on Ge 20:16.

22:21,24 *You must purge the evil from among you.* See v. 22; see also note on 13:5.

22:22 See Lev 20:10.

22:29 *fifty shekels of silver.* Probably equaled the average bride-price, which must have varied with the economic status of the participants (see note on Ex 22:16).

22:30 *his father's wife.* Refers to a wife other than his mother (see 27:20). *dishonor his father's bed.* Lit. "uncover the corner of his father's garment" (cf. notes on Ru 3:9; Eze 16:8).

23:1 For blessings on eunuchs in later times see Isa 56:4-5 and note on 56:3; Ac 8:26-39.

23:2-3 *down to the tenth generation.* Perhaps forever, since ten is symbolic of completeness or finality. In v. 6 the equivalent expression is "as long as you live" (lit. "all your days forever").

23:4 *Balaam son of Beor.* See Nu 22:4—24:25 and notes.

23:6 See the prophets' denunciation of Moab and Ammon (Isa 15-16; Jer 48:1—49:6; Eze 25:1-11; Am 1:13—2:3; Zep 2:8-11).

23:7 *Edomite ... your brother.* Edom (Esau) is often condemned for his hostility against his "brother" Jacob (Israel; see Am 1:11; Ob 10 and notes; see also notes on Ge 25:22,26).

23:9-14 Sanitary rules for Israel's military camps. For similar rules for the people in general see Lev 15 and notes.

10If one of your men is unclean because of
a nocturnal emission, he is to go outside
the camp and stay there.[b] 11But as evening
approaches he is to wash himself, and at
sunset[c] he may return to the camp.[d]
12Designate a place outside the camp
where you can go to relieve yourself. 13As
part of your equipment have something to
dig with, and when you relieve yourself,
dig a hole and cover up your excrement.
14For the LORD your God moves[e] about in
your camp to protect you and to deliver
your enemies to you. Your camp must be
holy,[f] so that he will not see among you
anything indecent and turn away from
you.

Miscellaneous Laws

15If a slave has taken refuge[g] with you,
do not hand him over to his master.[h] 16Let
him live among you wherever he likes and
in whatever town he chooses. Do not oppress[i] him.
17No Israelite man[j] or woman is to become a shrine prostitute.[k] 18You must not
bring the earnings of a female prostitute or
of a male prostitute[a] into the house of the
LORD your God to pay any vow, because
the LORD your God detests them both.[l]
19Do not charge your brother interest, whether on money or food or anything else that may earn interest.[m] 20You
may charge a foreigner[n] interest, but not
a brother Israelite, so that the LORD your
God may bless[o] you in everything you put
your hand to in the land you are entering
to possess.
21If you make a vow to the LORD your
God, do not be slow to pay it,[p] for the
LORD your God will certainly demand it of
you and you will be guilty of sin.[q] 22But if
you refrain from making a vow, you will
not be guilty.[r] 23Whatever your lips utter
you must be sure to do, because you made
your vow freely to the LORD your God with
your own mouth.
24If you enter your neighbor's vineyard,
you may eat all the grapes you want, but
do not put any in your basket. 25If you enter
your neighbor's grainfield, you may pick
kernels with your hands, but you must not
put a sickle to his standing grain.[s]

24 If a man marries a woman who becomes displeasing to him[t] because he
finds something indecent about her, and he
writes her a certificate of divorce,[u] gives it
to her and sends her from his house, 2and
if after she leaves his house she becomes
the wife of another man, 3and her second husband dislikes her and writes her
a certificate of divorce, gives it to her and
sends her from his house, or if he dies,
4then her first husband, who divorced her,
is not allowed to marry her again after she
has been defiled. That would be detestable
in the eyes of the LORD. Do not bring sin
upon the land the LORD[v] your God is giving
you as an inheritance.
5If a man has recently married, he must
not be sent to war or have any other duty
laid on him. For one year he is to be free
to stay at home and bring happiness to the
wife he has married.[w]
6Do not take a pair of millstones—not
even the upper one—as security for a
debt, because that would be taking a
man's livelihood as security.[x]
7If a man is caught kidnapping one of
his brother Israelites and treats him as
a slave or sells him, the kidnapper must
die.[y] You must purge the evil from among
you.[z]
8In cases of leprous[b] diseases be very
careful to do exactly as the priests, who
are Levites,[a] instruct you. You must follow
carefully what I have commanded them.[b]
9Remember what the LORD your God did
to Miriam along the way after you came
out of Egypt.[c]
10When you make a loan of any kind to
your neighbor, do not go into his house to
get what he is offering as a pledge.[d] 11Stay
outside and let the man to whom you are
making the loan bring the pledge out to
you. 12If the man is poor, do not go to sleep
with his pledge[e] in your possession. 13Re-
turn his cloak to him by sunset[f] so that he

[a] 18 Hebrew *of a dog* [b] 8 The Hebrew word was used for various diseases affecting the skin—not necessarily leprosy.

23:10 [b] Lev 15:16 **23:11** [c] S Lev 15:16 [d] 1Sa 21:5 **23:14** [e] S Ge 3:8 [f] Ex 3:5 **23:15** [g] 2Sa 22:3; Ps 2:12; 71:1 [h] 1Sa 30:15 **23:16** [i] Ex 22:21; S 23:6 **23:17** [j] 1Ki 14:24; 15:12; 22:46; 2Ki 23:7; Job 36:14 [k] S Ge 38:21 **23:18** [l] S Ge 19:5; S Lev 20:13; Rev 22:15 **23:19** [m] S Lev 25:35-37; Ne 5:2-7 **23:20** [n] S Ge 31:15; S Dt 15:3 [o] Dt 15:10 **23:21** [p] S Nu 6:21; Jdg 11:35; Ps 15:4 [q] Nu 30:1-2; Job 22:27; Ps 61:8; 65:1; 76:11; Isa 19:21; S Mt 5:33; Ac 5:3 **23:22** [r] Ac 5:4 **23:25** [s] Mt 12:1; Mk 2:23; Lk 6:1 **24:1** [t] Dt 22:13 [u] ver 3; 2Ki 17:6; Isa 50:1; Jer 3:8; Mal 2:16; Mt 1:19; 5:31*; 19:7-9; Mk 10:4-5 **24:4** [v] Jer 3:1 **24:5** [w] S Dt 20:7 **24:6** [x] S Ex 22:22 **24:7** [y] S Ex 21:16 [z] 1Co 5:13* **24:8** [a] S Dt 17:9 [b] Lev 13:1-46; S 14:2 **24:9** [c] S Nu 12:10 **24:10** [d] Ex 22:25-27 **24:12** [e] S Ex 22:26 **24:13** [f] Ex 22:26

23:14 *Your camp must be holy.* Even as the Lord is holy (see Lev 11:44 and note).
23:15 *If a slave has taken refuge.* A foreign slave seeking freedom in Israel.
23:17–18 See notes on Ge 38:21; Ex 34:15; 1Ki 14:24; Mic 1:7.
23:18 *male prostitute.* Lit. "dog" (see NIV text note), a word often associated with moral or spiritual impurity (cf. Mt 7:6; Php 3:2; Rev 22:15 and notes; cf. also Mt 15:26).
23:19 *interest.* See note on Ex 22:25–27.
23:20 *charge a foreigner.* A foreign merchant would come into Israel for financial advantage and so would be subject to paying interest.
23:21–23 See notes on Nu 30; Ecc 5:1–7.
24:1–4 In the books of Moses divorce was permitted and regulated (see Lev 21:7,14; 22:13; Nu 30:9). Jesus commented on the law of 24:1 in the Sermon on the Mount (Mt 5:31–32; see note on Mt 19:3). On another occasion, he cited the higher law of creation (Mt 19:3–9).
24:5 *happiness.* Marital bliss was held in high regard (cf. Pr 5:18; Ecc 9:9).
24:6 *millstones.* Used for grinding grain for flour and daily food (see note on Jdg 9:53).
24:7 *as a slave.* Cf. 23:15. *You must purge the evil from among you.* See note on 13:5.
24:8 *leprous.* See NIV text note; see also note on Lev 13:2.
24:9,18,22 *Remember.* See note on 4:10.
24:10–13 See notes on 6:25; Ex 22:21–27.

may sleep in it.[g] Then he will thank you,
and it will be regarded as a righteous act
in the sight of the LORD your God.[h]
14Do not take advantage of a hired man
who is poor and needy, whether he is a
brother Israelite or an alien living in one
of your towns.[i] 15Pay him his wages each
day before sunset, because he is poor[j] and
is counting on it.[k] Otherwise he may cry
to the LORD against you, and you will be
guilty of sin.[l]
16Fathers shall not be put to death for
their children, nor children put to death
for their fathers; each is to die for his own
sin.[m]
17Do not deprive the alien or the fatherless[n] of justice,[o] or take the cloak of the
widow as a pledge. 18Remember that you
were slaves in Egypt[p] and the LORD your
God redeemed you from there. That is why
I command you to do this.
19When you are harvesting in your field
and you overlook a sheaf, do not go back
to get it.[q] Leave it for the alien,[r] the fatherless and the widow,[s] so that the LORD
your God may bless[t] you in all the work
of your hands. 20When you beat the olives from your trees, do not go over the
branches a second time.[u] Leave what remains for the alien, the fatherless and the
widow. 21When you harvest the grapes in
your vineyard, do not go over the vines
again. Leave what remains for the alien,
the fatherless and the widow. 22Remember
that you were slaves in Egypt. That is why
I command you to do this.[v]

25 When men have a dispute, they are
to take it to court and the judges[w]
will decide the case,[x] acquitting[y] the innocent and condemning the guilty.[z] 2If
the guilty man deserves to be beaten,[a] the
judge shall make him lie down and have
him flogged in his presence with the number of lashes his crime deserves, 3but he
must not give him more than forty lashes.[b]
If he is flogged more than that, your brother will be degraded in your eyes.[c]
4Do not muzzle an ox while it is treading out the grain.[d]
5If brothers are living together and one
of them dies without a son, his widow
must not marry outside the family. Her
husband's brother shall take her and marry
her and fulfill the duty of a brother-in-law
to her.[e] 6The first son she bears shall carry
on the name of the dead brother so that his
name will not be blotted out from Israel.[f]
7However, if a man does not want to
marry his brother's wife,[g] she shall go to
the elders at the town gate[h] and say, "My
husband's brother refuses to carry on his
brother's name in Israel. He will not fulfill
the duty of a brother-in-law to me."[i] 8Then
the elders of his town shall summon him
and talk to him. If he persists in saying, "I
do not want to marry her," 9his brother's
widow shall go up to him in the presence
of the elders, take off one of his sandals,[j]
spit in his face[k] and say, "This is what is
done to the man who will not build up his
brother's family line." 10That man's line
shall be known in Israel as The Family of
the Unsandaled.
11If two men are fighting and the wife of
one of them comes to rescue her husband
from his assailant, and she reaches out
and seizes him by his private parts, 12you
shall cut off her hand. Show her no pity.[l]
13Do not have two differing weights in
your bag—one heavy, one light.[m] 14Do
not have two differing measures in your
house—one large, one small. 15You must
have accurate and honest weights and
measures, so that you may live long[n] in
the land the LORD your God is giving you.
16For the LORD your God detests anyone
who does these things, anyone who deals
dishonestly.[o]
17Remember what the Amalekites[p] did
to you along the way when you came out
of Egypt. 18When you were weary and
worn out, they met you on your journey
and cut off all who were lagging behind;
they had no fear of God.[q] 19When the LORD
your God gives you rest[r] from all the enemies[s] around you in the land he is giving

24:13 [g]S Ex 22:27 [h]Dt 6:25; Ps 106:31; Da 4:27 **24:14** [i]Lev 19:13; 25:35-43; Dt 15:12-18; Job 24:4; Pr 14:31; 19:17; Am 4:1; 1Ti 5:18 **24:15** [j]S Lev 25:35 [k]S Lev 19:13; Mt 20:8 [l]S Ex 22:23; S Job 12:19; Jas 5:4 **24:16** [m]S Nu 26:11; Jer 31:29-30 **24:17** [n]Ex 22:22; Job 6:27; 24:9; 29:12; Ps 10:18; 82:3; Pr 23:10; Eze 22:7 [o]S Ex 22:21; S 23:2; S Dt 10:18 **24:18** [p]S Dt 15:15 **24:19** [q]S Lev 19:9 [r]Dt 10:19; 27:19; Eze 47:22; Zec 7:10; Mal 3:5 [s]ver 20; Dt 14:29 [t]S Dt 14:29; Pr 19:17; 28:27; Ecc 11:1 **24:20** [u]Lev 19:10 **24:22** [v]ver 18 **25:1** [w]S Ex 21:6 [x]Dt 17:8-13; 19:17; Ac 23:3 [y]1Ki 8:32 [z]S Ex 23:7; Dt 1:16-17 **25:2** [a]Pr 10:13; 19:29; Lk 12:47-48 **25:3** [b]Mt 27:26; Jn 19:1; 2Co 11:24 [c]Jer 20:2 **25:4** [d]S Nu 22:29; 1Co 9:9*; 1Ti 5:18* **25:5** [e]Ru 4:10, 13; Mt 22:24; Mk 12:19; Lk 20:28 **25:6** [f]Ge 38:9; Ru 4:5, 10 **25:7** [g]Ru 1:15 [h]S Ge 23:10 [i]Ru 4:1-2, 5-6 **25:9** [j]Jos 24:22; Ru 4:7-8, 11 [k]Nu 12:14; Job 17:6; 30:10; Isa 50:6 **25:12** [l]S Dt 7:2 **25:13** [m]Pr 11:1; 20:23; Mic 6:11 **25:15** [n]S Ex 20:12 **25:16** [o]Pr 11:1 **25:17** [p]S Ge 36:12 **25:18** [q]Ps 36:1; Ro 3:18 **25:19** [r]S Ex 33:14; Heb 3:18-19 [s]Est 9:16

24:16 *each is to die for his own sin.* See Eze 18:4 and note.

24:17–18 See 10:18–19. When the Israelites were in trouble, the Lord helped them. Therefore they were not to take advantage of others in difficulty.

24:19–21 See note on Lev 19:9–10.

25:3 *not … more than forty lashes.* Beating could subject the culprit to excessive abuse, so the law kept the punishment from becoming inhumane. Cf. Paul's experience (see 2Co 11:24–25 and note).

25:4 Applied to those appointed to proclaim the gospel of Christ (see 1Co 9:9–10 and note on 9:9; 1Ti 5:17–18). *treading out the grain.* See notes on Ge 50:10; Ru 1:22.

25:5–6 The continuity of each family and the decentralized control of land through family ownership were basic to the Mosaic economy (see note on Ge 38:8).

25:7 *if a man does not want to marry his brother's wife.* See vv. 8–10; note the experiences, with some variations, described in Ge 38:8–10; Ru 4:1–12. *elders at the town gate.* See 21:19; 22:15; see also notes on Ge 19:1; Ru 4:1.

25:11–12 Cf. Ex 21:22–25 and note on 21:23–25.

25:13–16 See note on Lev 19:35.

25:14 *measures.* Of quantity.

25:17 *Remember.* See note on 4:10. *Amalekites.* See note on Ge 14:7; see also Ex 17:8–16; Nu 14:45; 1Sa 15:2–3 and note on 15:2; 30:1–20.

25:18 *fear of God.* See note on Ge 20:11.

25:19 *rest.* See note on 3:20.

you to possess as an inheritance, you shall
blot out the memory of Amalek[t] from under heaven. Do not forget!

Firstfruits and Tithes

26 When you have entered the land the
LORD your God is giving you as an
inheritance and have taken possession of
it and settled in it, 2take some of the firstfruits[u] of all that you produce from the soil
of the land the LORD your God is giving
you and put them in a basket. Then go to
the place the LORD your God will choose as
a dwelling for his Name[v] 3and say to the
priest in office at the time, "I declare today
to the LORD your God that I have come to
the land the LORD swore to our forefathers
to give us." 4The priest shall take the basket from your hands and set it down in
front of the altar of the LORD your God.
5Then you shall declare before the LORD
your God: "My father was a wandering[w]
Aramean,[x] and he went down into Egypt
with a few people[y] and lived there and became a great nation,[z] powerful and numerous. 6But the Egyptians mistreated us and
made us suffer,[a] putting us to hard labor.[b]
7Then we cried out to the LORD, the God of
our fathers, and the LORD heard our voice[c]
and saw[d] our misery,[e] toil and oppression.[f]
8So the LORD brought us out of Egypt[g] with
a mighty hand and an outstretched arm,[h]
with great terror and with miraculous
signs and wonders.[i] 9He brought us to this
place and gave us this land, a land flowing
with milk and honey;[j] 10and now I bring
the firstfruits of the soil that you, O LORD,
have given me.[k]" Place the basket before
the LORD your God and bow down before
him. 11And you and the Levites[l] and the
aliens among you shall rejoice[m] in all the
good things the LORD your God has given
to you and your household.

12When you have finished setting aside
a tenth[n] of all your produce in the third
year, the year of the tithe,[o] you shall give
it to the Levite, the alien, the fatherless
and the widow, so that they may eat in
your towns and be satisfied. 13Then say
to the LORD your God: "I have removed
from my house the sacred portion and
have given it to the Levite, the alien, the
fatherless and the widow, according to all
you commanded. I have not turned aside
from your commands nor have I forgotten
any of them.[p] 14I have not eaten any of the
sacred portion while I was in mourning,
nor have I removed any of it while I was
unclean,[q] nor have I offered any of it to
the dead. I have obeyed the LORD my God;
I have done everything you commanded
me. 15Look down from heaven,[r] your holy
dwelling place, and bless[s] your people Israel and the land you have given us as you
promised on oath to our forefathers, a land
flowing with milk and honey."

Follow the LORD's Commands

16The LORD your God commands you
this day to follow these decrees and laws;
carefully observe them with all your heart
and with all your soul.[t] 17You have declared this day that the LORD is your God
and that you will walk in his ways, that
you will keep his decrees, commands and
laws, and that you will obey him.[u] 18And
the LORD has declared this day that you are
his people, his treasured possession[v] as he
promised, and that you are to keep all his
commands. 19He has declared that he will
set you in praise,[w] fame and honor high
above all the nations[x] he has made and
that you will be a people holy[y] to the LORD
your God, as he promised.

The Altar on Mount Ebal

27 Moses and the elders of Israel commanded the people: "Keep all these
commands[z] that I give you today. 2When
you have crossed the Jordan[a] into the land
the LORD your God is giving you, set up
some large stones[b] and coat them with
plaster.[c] 3Write on them all the words of
this law when you have crossed over to
enter the land the LORD your God is giving
you, a land flowing with milk and honey,[d] just as the LORD, the God of your fathers, promised you. 4And when you have

25:19 [t]S Ge 36:12 **26:2** [u]S Ex 22:29 [v]S Ex 20:24; S Dt 12:5 **26:5** [w]S Ge 20:13 [x]S Ge 25:20 [y]S Ge 34:30; 43:14 [z]S Ge 12:2 **26:6** [a]S Nu 20:15 [b]S Ex 1:13 **26:7** [c]S Ge 21:17 [d]Ex 3:9; 2Ki 13:4; 14:26 [e]S Ge 16:11 [f]Ps 42:9; 44:24; 72:14 **26:8** [g]S Nu 20:16 [h]S Ex 3:20 [i]S Dt 4:34; 34:11-12 **26:9** [j]S Ex 3:8 **26:10** [k]S Dt 8:18 **26:11** [l]Dt 12:12 [m]S Dt 16:11 **26:12** [n]S Ge 14:20 [o]S Nu 18:24; Dt 14:28-29; Heb 7:5,9 **26:13** [p]Ps 119:141, 153,176 **26:14** [q]Lev 7:20; Hos 9:4 **26:15** [r]Ps 68:5; 80:14; 102:19; Isa 63:15; Zec 2:13 [s]S Ex 39:43 **26:16** [t]Dt 4:29 **26:17** [u]Ex 19:8; Ps 48:14 **26:18** [v]Ex 6:7; Dt 7:6 **26:19** [w]Isa 62:7; Zep 3:20 [x]Dt 4:7-8; 28:1,13,44; 1Ch 14:2; Ps 148:14; Isa 40:11 [y]S Dt 7:6 **27:1** [z]Ps 78:7 **27:2** [a]Jos 4:1 [b]Ex 24:4; Jos 24:26; 1Sa 7:12 [c]Jos 8:31 **27:3** [d]S Ex 3:8

26:1 *inheritance.* See note on Ex 15:17.
26:2 *firstfruits.* The offering described here occurred only once and must not be confused with the annual offerings of firstfruits (see 18:4 and note). *the place the LORD ... will choose as a dwelling for his Name.* See note on 12:5.
26:5 *wandering Aramean.* A reference to Jacob, who had wandered from southern Canaan to Haran in Aram (see note on Ge 10:22 and maps, pp. 22, 56, 497) and back (Ge 27–35) and who later migrated to Egypt (see Ge 46:3–7). He also married two Aramean women (see Ge 28:5; 29:16,28). The Arameans were a Semitic people who spoke a form of the Aramaic language (see also Ge 22:23–24 and note; 25:20; 31:20,24; 1Ch 18:5 and note). *with a few people ... became a great nation.* See Ex 1:5,7 and note on 1:7.
26:11 *rejoice.* See note on 12:12.
26:12 See note on 14:22–29.
26:16 *with all your heart ... soul.* See note on 4:29.
26:17 The terminology is covenantal, involving a renewal of Israel's vow that the Lord was God and that they would obey him (see 5:27; see also note on Ex 19:8).
26:18 *treasured possession.* See note on Ex 19:5.
26:19 *a people holy to the LORD.* See 14:2 and note.
27:2–8 Setting up stones inscribed with messages to be remembered was a common practice in the ancient Near East.
27:2,4 *coat them with plaster.* So that the writing inscribed on them would stand out clearly (see v. 8).
27:3,8 *all the words of this law.* The stipulations (see note on Ex 20:1) of the covenant that Moses' reaffirmation contained.
27:4 *Mount Ebal.* See note on Jos 8:30.

crossed the Jordan, set up these stones on
Mount Ebal,[e] as I command you today,
and coat them with plaster. 5Build there
an altar[f] to the LORD your God, an altar
of stones. Do not use any iron tool[g] upon
them. 6Build the altar of the LORD your
God with fieldstones and offer burnt offerings on it to the LORD your God. 7Sac-
rifice fellowship offerings[a][h] there, eating
them and rejoicing[i] in the presence of the
LORD your God.[j] 8And you shall write very
clearly all the words of this law on these
stones[k] you have set up."[l]

Curses From Mount Ebal

9Then Moses and the priests, who are
Levites,[m] said to all Israel, "Be silent, O Israel, and listen! You have now become the
people of the LORD your God.[n] 10Obey the
LORD your God and follow his commands
and decrees that I give you today."
11On the same day Moses commanded
the people:
12When you have crossed the Jordan,
these tribes shall stand on Mount Gerizim[o]
to bless the people: Simeon, Levi, Judah,
Issachar,[p] Joseph and Benjamin.[q] 13And
these tribes shall stand on Mount Ebal[r]
to pronounce curses: Reuben, Gad, Asher,
Zebulun, Dan and Naphtali.
14The Levites shall recite to all the people of Israel in a loud voice:
15"Cursed is the man who carves
an image or casts an idol[s]—a thing
detestable[t] to the LORD, the work of
the craftsman's hands—and sets it
up in secret."
Then all the people shall say,
"Amen!"[u]
16"Cursed is the man who dishonors his father or his mother."[v]
Then all the people shall say,
"Amen!"
17"Cursed is the man who moves
his neighbor's boundary stone."[w]
Then all the people shall say,
"Amen!"
18"Cursed is the man who leads the
blind astray on the road."[x]
Then all the people shall say,
"Amen!"
19"Cursed is the man who withholds justice from the alien,[y] the fatherless or the widow."[z]
Then all the people shall say,
"Amen!"
20"Cursed is the man who sleeps
with his father's wife, for he dishonors his father's bed."[a]
Then all the people shall say,
"Amen!"
21"Cursed is the man who has sexual relations with any animal."[b]
Then all the people shall say,
"Amen!"
22"Cursed is the man who sleeps
with his sister, the daughter of his father or the daughter of his mother."[c]
Then all the people shall say,
"Amen!"
23"Cursed is the man who sleeps
with his mother-in-law."[d]
Then all the people shall say,
"Amen!"
24"Cursed is the man who kills[e] his
neighbor secretly."[f]
Then all the people shall say,
"Amen!"
25"Cursed is the man who accepts a
bribe to kill an innocent person."[g]
Then all the people shall say,
"Amen!"
26"Cursed is the man who does not
uphold the words of this law by carrying them out."[h]
Then all the people shall say,
"Amen!"[i]

Blessings for Obedience

28 If you fully obey the LORD your God
and carefully follow[j] all his commands[k] I give you today, the LORD your
God will set you high above all the na-

27:4 [e] S Dt 11:29
27:5 [f] S Ex 20:24 [g] Ex 20:25
27:7 [h] S Ex 32:6 [i] S Dt 16:11 [j] Jos 8:31
27:8 [k] Isa 8:1; 30:8; Hab 2:2 [l] Jos 8:32
27:9 [m] S Dt 17:9 [n] Dt 26:18
27:12 [o] S Dt 11:29 [p] S Ge 30:18 [q] Jos 8:35
27:13 [r] S Dt 11:29
27:15 [s] S Ex 20:4 [t] 1Ki 11:5,7; 2Ki 23:13; Isa 44:19; 66:3 [u] Nu 5:22; S 1Co 14:16
27:16 [v] S Ge 31:35; S Ex 21:12; S Dt 5:16
27:17 [w] S Dt 19:14
27:18 [x] S Lev 19:14
27:19 [y] S Ex 22:21; S Dt 24:19 [z] S Ex 23:2; S Dt 10:18
27:20 [a] S Ge 34:5; S Lev 18:7
27:21 [b] S Ex 22:19
27:22 [c] S Lev 18:9
27:23 [d] S Lev 20:14
27:24 [e] S Ge 4:23 [f] Ex 21:12
27:25 [g] Ex 23:7-8; S Lev 19:16
27:26 [h] S Lev 26:14; Dt 28:15; Ps 119:21; Jer 11:3; Gal 3:10* [i] Jer 11:5
28:1 [j] S Dt 15:5 [k] S Lev 26:3

[a] 7 Traditionally *peace offerings*

27:5 *Build ... an altar of stones.* Different from the altars of the tabernacle, both in form and in use (see note on Ex 20:25).
27:9 *You have now become the people of the LORD.* The language of covenant renewal.
27:12 *these tribes shall stand on Mount Gerizim.* All six were descendants of Jacob by Leah and Rachel (see Ge 35:23–24). See 11:30 and note. *Mount Gerizim.* See note on Jn 4:20. *to bless.* No blessings appear in vv. 15–26, which consist entirely of 12 curses (see 28:15–68). Blessings, however, are listed and described in 28:1–14.
27:13 *these tribes shall stand on Mount Ebal.* Reuben and Zebulun were descendants of Jacob by Leah; the rest were his descendants by the female servants Zilpah and Bilhah (see Ge 35:23,25–26).
27:15 *carves an image ... casts an idol.* In violation of the first and second commandments of the Decalogue (see notes on Ex 20:3–4). See 4:28; 5:6–10; 31:29 and note; Isa 40:18–20 and note; 41:7; 44:9–20 and notes; 45:16; Jer 10:3–9; Hos 8:4–6 and note on 8:6; 13:2. *Amen!* Not simply approval but a solemn, formal assertion that the people accept and agree to the covenant with its curses and blessings (see vv. 16–26).
27:16 See 5:16; Ex 20:12 and note.
27:17 See note on 19:14.
27:19 See 24:17–18 and note.
27:20 See 22:30; Lev 18:8 and notes.
27:21 See Ex 22:19 and note; Lev 18:23; 20:15–16.
27:22 See Lev 18:9,11 and note on 18:11.
27:24–25 See 5:17; Ex 20:13 and note; 21:12; Lev 24:17,21.
27:26 Quoted in Gal 3:10 to prove that humankind is under a curse because no one follows the law of God fully (cf. Jas 2:10 and note; 1Jn 1:8,10).
28:1–14 These blessings are the opposites of the curses in vv. 15–44 (compare especially vv. 3–6 with vv. 16–19).

tions on earth.[l] 2All these blessings will come upon you[m] and accompany you if you obey the LORD your God:

3You will be blessed[n] in the city and
blessed in the country.[o]
4The fruit of your womb will be
blessed, and the crops of your land
and the young of your livestock—the
calves of your herds and the lambs of
your flocks.[p]
5Your basket and your kneading
trough will be blessed.
6You will be blessed when you come
in and blessed when you go out.[q]

7The LORD will grant that the enemies[r] who rise up against you will be defeated before you. They will come at you from one direction but flee from you in seven.[s]
8The LORD will send a blessing on your barns and on everything you put your hand to. The LORD your God will bless[t] you in the land he is giving you.
9The LORD will establish you as his holy people,[u] as he promised you on oath, if you keep the commands[v] of the LORD your God and walk in his ways. 10Then all the peoples on earth will see that you are called by the name[w] of the LORD, and they will fear you. 11The LORD will grant you abundant prosperity—in the fruit of your womb, the young of your livestock[x] and the crops of your ground—in the land he swore to your forefathers to give you.[y]
12The LORD will open the heavens, the storehouse[z] of his bounty,[a] to send rain[b] on your land in season and to bless[c] all the work of your hands. You will lend to many nations but will borrow from none.[d]
13The LORD will make you the head, not the tail. If you pay attention to the commands of the LORD your God that I give you this day and carefully follow[e] them, you will always be at the top, never at the bottom.[f] 14Do not turn aside from any of the commands I give you today, to the right or to the left,[g] following other gods and serving them.

Curses for Disobedience

15However, if you do not obey[h] the LORD your God and do not carefully follow all his commands and decrees I am giving you today,[i] all these curses will come upon you and overtake you:[j]

16You will be cursed in the city and
cursed in the country.[k]
17Your basket and your kneading
trough will be cursed.[l]
18The fruit of your womb will be
cursed, and the crops of your land,
and the calves of your herds and the
lambs of your flocks.[m]
19You will be cursed when you
come in and cursed when you go
out.[n]

20The LORD will send on you curses,[o] confusion and rebuke[p] in everything you put your hand to, until you are destroyed and come to sudden ruin[q] because of the evil[r] you have done in forsaking him.[a] 21The LORD will plague you with diseases until he has destroyed you from the land you are entering to possess.[s] 22The LORD will strike you with wasting disease,[t] with fever and inflammation, with scorching heat and drought,[u] with blight[v] and mildew, which will plague[w] you until you perish.[x] 23The sky over your head will be bronze, the ground beneath you iron.[y] 24The LORD will turn the rain[z] of your country into dust and powder; it will come down from the skies until you are destroyed.
25The LORD will cause you to be defeated[a] before your enemies. You will come at them from one direction but flee from them in seven,[b] and you will become a thing of horror[c] to all the kingdoms on earth.[d] 26Your carcasses will be food for all the birds of the air[e] and the beasts of the earth, and there will be no one to frighten them away.[f] 27The LORD will afflict you with the boils of Egypt[g] and with tumors, festering sores and the itch, from which you cannot be cured. 28The LORD will afflict you with madness, blindness and confusion of mind. 29At midday you will grope[h] about like a blind man in the dark. You will be unsuccessful in everything you do; day after day you will be oppressed and robbed, with no one to rescue[i] you.

[a] 20 Hebrew *me*

28:1 [l]S Nu 24:7; S Dt 26:19 **28:2** [m]Jer 32:24; Zec 1:6 **28:3** [n]Ps 144:15 [o]S Ge 39:5 **28:4** [p]S Ge 49:25; S Dt 8:18 **28:6** [q]Ps 121:8 **28:7** [r]2Ch 6:34 [s]S Lev 26:8, 17 **28:8** [t]Dt 15:4 **28:9** [u]S Ex 19:6 [v]S Lev 26:3 **28:10** [w]S Nu 6:27; 1Ki 8:43; Jer 25:29; Da 9:18 **28:11** [x]S Ge 30:27 [y]ver 4; Dt 30:9 **28:12** [z]Job 38:22; Ps 135:7; Jer 10:13; 51:16 [a]Ps 65:11; 68:10; Jer 31:12 [b]S Lev 26:4; 1Ki 8:35-36; 18:1; Ps 104:13; Isa 5:6; 30:23; 32:20 [c]Isa 61:9; 65:23; Jer 32:38-41; Mal 3:12 [d]ver 44; S Lev 25:19; S Dt 15:3, 6; Eze 34:26 **28:13** [e]Jer 11:6 [f]S Dt 26:19 **28:14** [g]S Dt 5:32; Jos 1:7 **28:15** [h]1Ki 9:6; 2Ch 7:19 [i]S Dt 27:26 [j]Dt 29:27; Jos 23:15; 2Ch 12:5; Da 9:11; Mal 2:2
28:16 [k]ver 3 **28:17** [l]ver 5 **28:18** [m]ver 4 **28:19** [n]ver 6 **28:20** [o]ver 8, 15; Lev 26:16; Jer 42:18; Mal 2:2; 3:9; 4:6 [p]Ps 39:11; 76:6; 80:16; Isa 17:13; 51:20; 54:9; 66:15; Eze 5:15 [q]Dt 4:26 [r]S Ex 32:22 **28:21** [s]Lev 26:25; Nu 14:12; Jer 24:10; Am 4:10 **28:22** [t]ver 48; Dt 32:24 [u]Lev 26:16; 2Ki 8:1; Job 12:15; Ps 105:16; Jer 14:1; Hag 1:11; Mal 3:9 [v]Hag 2:17 [w]S Lev 26:25 [x]Dt 4:26; Am 4:9 **28:23** [y]S Lev 26:19 **28:24** [z]Lev 26:19; Dt 11:17; 1Ki 8:35; 17:1; Isa 5:6; Jer 14:1; Hag 1:10 **28:25** [a]1Sa 4:10; Ps 78:62 [b]S Lev 26:17 [c]ver 37 [d]2Ch 29:8; 30:7; Jer 15:4; 24:9; 26:6; 29:18; 44:12; Eze 23:46 **28:26** [e]S Ge 40:19 [f]Ps 79:2; Isa 18:6; Jer 7:33; 12:9; 15:2; 16:4; 19:7; 34:20 **28:27** [g]Dt 7:15 **28:29** [h]Ge 19:11; Ex 10:21; Job 5:14; 12:25; 24:13; 38:15; Isa 59:10 [i]Jdg 3:9; 2Ki 13:5; Est 4:14; Isa 19:20; 43:11; Hos 13:4; Ob 1:21

28:5,17 *basket … kneading trough.* Used for storage and for the preparation of foods, particularly bread.
28:7 For the reverse see v. 25.
28:9 *establish you as his holy people.* See 7:6 and note.
28:12 *the heavens, the storehouse.* For the heavens as the storehouse of rain, snow, hail and wind see Job 38:22; Ps 135:7; Jer 10:13; 51:16. *You will lend.* For the opposite see v. 44; see also note on 15:6.
28:13 *the head, not the tail.* For the reverse see v. 44.
28:16–19 The opposites of vv. 3–6 (see note on vv. 1–14).
28:23 *sky … bronze … ground … iron.* No rain would fall from the sky or penetrate the ground (see v. 22).
28:25 For the reverse see v. 7.
28:27 *boils of Egypt.* See note on Ex 9:9.

30You will be pledged to be married to
a woman, but another will take her and
ravish her.[j] You will build a house, but you
will not live in it.[k] You will plant a vineyard, but you will not even begin to enjoy
its fruit.[l] 31Your ox will be slaughtered before your eyes, but you will eat none of it.
Your donkey will be forcibly taken from
you and will not be returned. Your sheep
will be given to your enemies, and no one
will rescue them. 32Your sons and daughters will be given to another nation,[m] and
you will wear out your eyes watching for
them day after day, powerless to lift a
hand. 33A people that you do not know
will eat what your land and labor produce, and you will have nothing but cruel oppression[n] all your days.[o] 34The sights
you see will drive you mad.[p] 35The LORD
will afflict your knees and legs with painful boils[q] that cannot be cured, spreading
from the soles of your feet to the top of
your head.[r]
36The LORD will drive you and the king[s]
you set over you to a nation unknown to
you or your fathers.[t] There you will worship other gods, gods of wood and stone.[u]
37You will become a thing of horror[v] and
an object of scorn[w] and ridicule[x] to all the
nations where the LORD will drive you.[y]
38You will sow much seed in the field but
you will harvest little,[z] because locusts[a]
will devour[b] it. 39You will plant vineyards
and cultivate them but you will not drink
the wine[c] or gather the grapes, because
worms will eat[d] them.[e] 40You will have olive trees throughout your country but you
will not use the oil, because the olives will
drop off.[f] 41You will have sons and daughters but you will not keep them, because
they will go into captivity.[g] 42Swarms of
locusts[h] will take over all your trees and
the crops of your land.
43The alien who lives among you will
rise above you higher and higher, but you
will sink lower and lower.[i] 44He will lend
to you, but you will not lend to him.[j] He
will be the head, but you will be the tail.[k]
45All these curses will come upon you.
They will pursue you and overtake you[l]
until you are destroyed,[m] because you did
not obey the LORD your God and observe
the commands and decrees he gave you.
46They will be a sign and a wonder to you
and your descendants forever.[n] 47Because
you did not serve[o] the LORD your God joyfully and gladly[p] in the time of prosperity,
48therefore in hunger and thirst,[q] in nakedness and dire poverty, you will serve the
enemies the LORD sends against you. He
will put an iron yoke[r] on your neck[s] until
he has destroyed you.
49The LORD will bring a nation against
you[t] from far away, from the ends of the
earth,[u] like an eagle[v] swooping down, a
nation whose language you will not understand,[w] 50a fierce-looking nation without
respect for the old[x] or pity for the young.
51They will devour the young of your livestock and the crops of your land until
you are destroyed. They will leave you no
grain, new wine[y] or oil,[z] nor any calves
of your herds or lambs of your flocks until you are ruined.[a] 52They will lay siege[b]
to all the cities throughout your land until
the high fortified walls in which you trust
fall down. They will besiege all the cities
throughout the land the LORD your God is
giving you.[c]
53Because of the suffering that your enemy will inflict on you during the siege,
you will eat the fruit of the womb, the
flesh of the sons and daughters the LORD
your God has given you.[d] 54Even the most
gentle and sensitive man among you will
have no compassion on his own brother
or the wife he loves or his surviving children, 55and he will not give to one of them
any of the flesh of his children that he is
eating. It will be all he has left because
of the suffering your enemy will inflict on
you during the siege of all your cities.[e]
56The most gentle and sensitive[f] woman
among you—so sensitive and gentle that
she would not venture to touch the ground
with the sole of her foot—will begrudge
the husband she loves and her own son or
daughter[g] 57the afterbirth from her womb
and the children she bears. For she intends
to eat them[h] secretly during the siege and

28:30 [j]Job 31:10 [k]Isa 65:22; Am 5:11 [l]Jer 12:13 **28:32** [m]ver 41 **28:33** [n]Jer 6:6; 22:17 [o]Jer 5:15-17; Eze 25:4 **28:34** [p]ver 67 **28:35** [q]Dt 7:15; Rev 16:2 [r]Job 2:7; 7:5; 13:28; 30:17, 30; Isa 1:6 **28:36** [s]1Sa 12:25 [t]S Dt 4:27; 2Ki 24:14; 25:7, 11; 2Ch 33:11; 36:21; Ezr 5:12; Jer 15:14; 16:13; 27:20; 39:1-9; 52:28; La 1:3 [u]S Dt 4:28 **28:37** [v]ver 25; Jer 42:18; Eze 5:15 [w]Ps 22:7; 39:8; 44:13; 64:8; Jer 18:16; 48:27; Mic 6:16 [x]2Ch 7:20; Ezr 9:7; Jer 44:8 [y]1Ki 9:7; Ps 44:14; Jer 19:8; 24:9; 25:9, 18; 29:18; La 2:15 **28:38** [z]Lev 26:20; Ps 129:7; Isa 5:10; Jer 12:13; Hos 8:7; Mic 6:15; Hag 1:6, 9; 2:16 [a]S Ex 10:4 [b]S Ex 10:15 **28:39** [c]S Lev 10:9 [d]Joel 1:4; 2:25; Mal 3:11 [e]Isa 5:10; 17:10-11; Zep 1:13 **28:40** [f]Jer 11:16; Mic 6:15 **28:41** [g]ver 32 **28:42** [h]ver 38; Jdg 6:5; 7:12; Jer 46:23 **28:43** [i]ver 13 **28:44** [j]S ver 12 [k]S Dt 26:19 **28:45** [l]S Ex 15:9 [m]ver 15; Dt 4:25-26 **28:46** [n]S Nu 16:38; Ps 71:7; Isa 8:18; 20:3; Eze 5:15; Zec 3:8 **28:47** [o]S Dt 10:12 [p]S Lev 23:40; Ne 9:35 **28:48** [q]Jer 14:3; La 4:4 [r]Jer 28:13-14; La 1:14 [s]Ge 49:8 **28:49** [t]S Lev 26:44 [u]Isa 5:26-30, 26; 7:18-20; 39:3; Jer 4:16; 5:15; 6:22; 25:32; 31:8; Hab 1:6 [v]2Sa 1:23; Jer 4:13; 48:40; 49:22; La 4:19; Eze 17:3 [w]S Ge 11:7; 1Co 14:21* **28:50** [x]Isa 47:6 **28:51** [y]Ps 4:7; Isa 36:17; Hag 1:11 [z]S Nu 18:12 [a]ver 33; Jdg 6:4 **28:52** [b]2Ki 6:24 [c]Jer 10:18; Eze 6:10; Zep 1:14-16, 17 **28:53** [d]ver 57; Lev 26:29; 2Ki 6:28-29; La 2:20 **28:55** [e]2Ki 6:29 **28:56** [f]Isa 47:1 [g]La 4:10 **28:57** [h]S ver 53

28:30–33 See Mic 6:14–15; Hag 1:6 and note.
28:30 See 20:5–8 and note; contrast Isa 65:21–22 (see note there).
28:35 See note on Ex 9:11.
28:44 See notes on vv. 12–13.
28:49 *ends of the earth.* An indefinite figurative expression meaning "far away"—anywhere from the visible horizon to the outer perimeter of the then-known world. *eagle swooping down.* Later used to symbolize the speed and power of the Assyrians (see Hos 8:1) and Babylonians (see Jer 48:40; 49:22). *whose language you will not understand.* The Lord's threat was fulfilled through the actions of Assyria and Babylonia whose languages, though related to Hebrew, were not understood by the average Israelite (see Isa 28:11; 33:19 and note; cf. 1Co 14:21–22 and note).
28:53 *suffering that your enemy will inflict on you during the siege.* See vv. 55,57. The repetition of the clause emphasizes the distress that the Israelites would suffer if they refused to obey the Lord. *you will eat … sons and daughters.* For the actualizing of this curse see 2Ki 6:24–29; La 2:20; 4:10; cf. Zec 11:9 and note.

in the distress that your enemy will inflict
on you in your cities.
58If you do not carefully follow all the
words of this law,[i] which are written in
this book, and do not revere[j] this glorious and awesome name[k] — the LORD
your God — 59the LORD will send fearful
plagues on you and your descendants,
harsh and prolonged disasters, and severe and lingering illnesses. 60He will
bring upon you all the diseases of Egypt[l]
that you dreaded, and they will cling to
you. 61The LORD will also bring on you
every kind of sickness and disaster not
recorded in this Book of the Law,[m] until
you are destroyed.[n] 62You who were as
numerous as the stars in the sky[o] will be
left but few[p] in number, because you did
not obey the LORD your God. 63Just as it
pleased[q] the LORD to make you prosper
and increase in number, so it will please[r]
him to ruin and destroy you.[s] You will be
uprooted[t] from the land you are entering
to possess.
64Then the LORD will scatter[u] you among
all nations,[v] from one end of the earth to
the other.[w] There you will worship other
gods — gods of wood and stone, which
neither you nor your fathers have known.[x]
65Among those nations you will find no
repose, no resting place[y] for the sole of
your foot. There the LORD will give you an
anxious mind, eyes[z] weary with longing,
and a despairing heart.[a] 66You will live in
constant suspense, filled with dread both
night and day, never sure of your life. 67In
the morning you will say, "If only it were
evening!" and in the evening, "If only it
were morning!" — because of the terror
that will fill your hearts and the sights that
your eyes will see.[b] 68The LORD will send
you back in ships to Egypt on a journey I
said you should never make again.[c] There
you will offer yourselves for sale to your
enemies as male and female slaves, but no
one will buy you.

28:58 [i] Dt 31:24 [j] Ps 96:4; Jer 5:22; Mal 1:14; 2:5; 3:5, 16; 4:2 [k] S Ex 3:15; S Jos 7:9 **28:60** [l] Ex 15:26 **28:61** [m] Dt 29:21; 30:10; 31:26; Jos 1:8; 8:34; 23:6; 24:26; 2Ki 14:6; 22:8; 2Ch 17:9; 25:4; Ne 8:1, 18; Mal 4:4 [n] Dt 4:25-26 **28:62** [o] S Ge 22:17; Dt 4:27; 10:22 [p] S Lev 26:22 **28:63** [q] Dt 30:9; Isa 62:5; 65:19; Jer 32:41; Zep 3:17 [r] Pr 1:26 [s] S Ge 6:7 [t] Ps 52:5; Jer 12:14; 31:28; 45:4 **28:64** [u] S Dt 4:27; Ezr 9:7; Isa 6:12; Jer 32:23; 43:11; 52:27 [v] Ne 1:8; Ps 44:11; Jer 13:24; 18:17; 22:22 [w] S Dt 4:32; S Jer 8:19 [x] Dt 11:28; 32:17 **28:65** [y] La 1:3 [z] Job 11:20 [a] Lev 26:16, 36; Hos 9:17 **28:67** [b] ver 34 **28:68** [c] S Ex 13:14

29:1 [d] S Lev 7:38 [e] S Ex 3:1 **29:2** [f] Ex 19:4 **29:3** [g] S Dt 4:34 **29:4** [h] Isa 6:10; 32:3; 48:8; Jer 5:21; Eze 12:2; S Mt 13:15; Eph 4:18 **29:5** [i] S Dt 8:2 [j] S Dt 8:4 **29:6** [k] S Lev 10:9 [l] Dt 8:3 **29:7** [m] S Nu 21:26 [n] S Nu 21:25 [o] Nu 21:21-24, 33-35; Dt 2:26-3:11 **29:8** [p] Ps 78:55; 135:12; 136:22 [q] Nu 32:33; Dt 3:12-13 **29:9** [r] S Dt 4:6; S Jos 1:7 [s] Ex 19:5; Ps 25:10; 103:18 [t] Jos 1:8; 2Ch 31:21 **29:11** [u] Jos 9:21, 23, 27; 1Ch 20:3 **29:13** [v] S Ge 6:18; S Ex 19:6

Renewal of the Covenant

29 These are the terms of the covenant
the LORD commanded Moses to make
with the Israelites in Moab,[d] in addition
to the covenant he had made with them
at Horeb.[e]
2Moses summoned all the Israelites and
said to them:
Your eyes have seen all that the LORD
did in Egypt to Pharaoh, to all his officials
and to all his land.[f] 3With your own eyes
you saw those great trials, those miraculous signs and great wonders.[g] 4But to this
day the LORD has not given you a mind
that understands or eyes that see or ears
that hear.[h] 5During the forty years that I
led[i] you through the desert, your clothes
did not wear out, nor did the sandals on
your feet.[j] 6You ate no bread and drank no
wine or other fermented drink.[k] I did this
so that you might know that I am the LORD
your God.[l]
7When you reached this place, Sihon[m]
king of Heshbon[n] and Og king of Bashan
came out to fight against us, but we defeated them.[o] 8We took their land and gave
it as an inheritance[p] to the Reubenites, the
Gadites and the half-tribe of Manasseh.[q]
9Carefully follow[r] the terms of this covenant,[s] so that you may prosper in everything you do.[t] 10All of you are standing
today in the presence of the LORD your
God — your leaders and chief men, your
elders and officials, and all the other men
of Israel, 11together with your children and
your wives, and the aliens living in your
camps who chop your wood and carry your
water.[u] 12You are standing here in order to
enter into a covenant with the LORD your
God, a covenant the LORD is making with
you this day and sealing with an oath, 13to
confirm you this day as his people,[v] that

28:58 *words of this law.* See note on 31:24. *this glorious and awesome name — the LORD.* See note and NIV text note on Ex 3:15. One of the oddities of history is the loss of the proper pronunciation of the Hebrew word *YHWH,* the personal and covenant name of God in the OT (see note on Ge 2:4). "Jehovah" is a spelling that developed from combining the consonants of the name with the vowels of a word for "Lord" (*Adonai*). "Yahweh" is probably the original pronunciation. The name eventually ceased to be pronounced because later Jews thought it too holy to be uttered and feared violating Ex 20:7; Lev 24:16. It is translated "LORD" in this version (see Preface to the NIV).
28:60 *diseases of Egypt.* Those brought on the Egyptians during the plagues (see 7:15; Ex 15:26).
28:61 *Book of the Law.* See note on 31:24.
28:62 *as the stars in the sky.* See 1:10 and note.
28:64 *will scatter you.* Experienced by Israel in the Assyrian (722 – 721 B.C.) and Babylonian (586 B.C.) exiles (see 2Ki 17:6; 25:21 and notes).
28:68 *a journey I said you should never make again.* See 17:16; Ex 13:17; Nu 14:3 – 4.
29:1 See notes on 5:2 – 3.
29:2 *Your eyes have seen.* Only those who were less than 20 years old (see Nu 14:29 and note on 14:28) when Israel followed the majority spy report at Kadesh Barnea and refused to enter Canaan would have actually experienced life in Egypt before the exodus. But Moses is speaking to the people as a nation and referring to the national experience (see note on 5:3).
29:4 Quoted in Ro 11:8 (see note there) and applied to hardened Israel.
29:7 *Sihon . . . Og.* See 1:4 and note.
29:8 *gave it as an inheritance.* See 3:12 – 17.
29:9 – 15 A clear summary of the nature of covenant reaffirmation.
29:13 *his people . . . your God.* See note on Zec 8:8.

he may be your God[w] as he promised you and as he swore to your fathers, Abraham, Isaac and Jacob. 14 I am making this covenant,[x] with its oath, not only with you 15 who are standing here with us today in the presence of the LORD our God but also with those who are not here today.[y]

16 You yourselves know how we lived in Egypt and how we passed through the countries on the way here. 17 You saw among them their detestable images and idols of wood and stone, of silver and gold.[z] 18 Make sure there is no man or woman, clan or tribe among you today whose heart turns[a] away from the LORD our God to go and worship the gods of those nations; make sure there is no root among you that produces such bitter poison.[b]

19 When such a person hears the words of this oath, he invokes a blessing[c] on himself and therefore thinks, "I will be safe, even though I persist in going my own way."[d] This will bring disaster on the watered land as well as the dry.[a] 20 The LORD will never be willing to forgive[e] him; his wrath and zeal[f] will burn[g] against that man. All the curses written in this book will fall upon him, and the LORD will blot[h] out his name from under heaven. 21 The LORD will single him out from all the tribes of Israel for disaster,[i] according to all the curses of the covenant written in this Book of the Law.[j]

22 Your children who follow you in later generations and foreigners who come from distant lands will see the calamities that have fallen on the land and the diseases with which the LORD has afflicted it.[k] 23 The whole land will be a burning waste[l] of salt[m] and sulfur—nothing planted, nothing sprouting, no vegetation growing on it. It will be like the destruction of Sodom and Gomorrah,[n] Admah and Zeboiim, which the LORD overthrew in fierce anger.[o] 24 All the nations will ask: "Why has the LORD done this to this land?[p] Why this fierce, burning anger?"

25 And the answer will be: "It is because this people abandoned the covenant of the LORD, the God of their fathers, the covenant he made with them when he brought them out of Egypt.[q] 26 They went off and worshiped other gods and bowed down to them, gods they did not know, gods he had not given them. 27 Therefore the LORD's anger burned against this land, so that he brought on it all the curses written in this book.[r] 28 In furious anger and in great wrath[s] the LORD uprooted[t] them from their land and thrust them into another land, as it is now."

29 The secret things belong to the LORD our God,[u] but the things revealed belong to us and to our children forever, that we may follow all the words of this law.[v]

Prosperity After Turning to the LORD

30 When all these blessings and curses[w] I have set before you come upon you and you take them to heart wherever the LORD your God disperses you among the nations,[x] 2 and when you and your children return[y] to the LORD your God and obey him with all your heart[z] and with all your soul according to everything I command you today, 3 then the LORD your God will restore your fortunes[b][a] and have compassion[b] on you and gather[c] you again from all the nations where he scattered[d] you.[e] 4 Even if you have been banished to the most distant land under the heavens,[f] from there the LORD your God will gather[g] you and bring you back.[h] 5 He will bring[i] you to the land that belonged to your fathers, and you will take possession of it. He will make you more prosperous and numerous[j] than your fathers. 6 The LORD your God will circumcise your hearts and the hearts of your descendants,[k] so that you may love[l] him with all your heart and with all your soul, and live. 7 The LORD your God will put all

[a] 19 Or *way, in order to add drunkenness to thirst."*
[b] 3 Or *will bring you back from captivity*

29:13 [w] S Ge 17:7 **29:14** [x] Ex 19:5; Isa 59:21; Jer 31:31; 32:40; 50:5; Eze 16:62; 37:26; Heb 8:7-8 **29:15** [y] S Ge 6:18; Ac 2:39 **29:17** [z] Ex 20:23; Dt 4:28 **29:18** [a] S Dt 13:6 [b] S Dt 11:16; Heb 12:15 **29:19** [c] Ps 72:17; Isa 65:16 [d] Ps 36:2 **29:20** [e] S Ex 23:21 [f] Ex 34:14; Eze 23:25; Zep 1:18 [g] Ps 74:1; 79:5; 80:4; Eze 36:5 [h] 2Ki 13:23; 14:27; Rev 3:5 **29:21** [i] Dt 32:23; Eze 7:26 [j] S Dt 28:61 **29:22** [k] Jer 19:8; 49:17; 50:13 **29:23** [l] Isa 1:7; 6:11; 9:18; 64:10; Jer 12:11; 44:2,6; Mic 5:11 [m] S Ge 13:10; Eze 47:11 [n] S Ge 19:24,25; Zep 2:9; S Mt 10:15; Ro 9:29 [o] S Ge 14:8 **29:24** [p] 1Ki 9:8; 2Ch 36:19; Jer 16:10; 22:8-9; 52:13 **29:25** [q] 2Ki 17:23; 2Ch 36:21 **29:27** [r] S Dt 28:15 **29:28** [s] Ps 7:11 [t] 1Ki 14:15; 2Ch 7:20; Ps 9:6; 52:5; Pr 2:22; Jer 12:14; 31:28; 42:10; Eze 19:12 **29:29** [u] Ac 1:7 [v] Jn 5:39; Ac 17:11; 2Ti 3:16 **30:1** [w] S Dt 11:26 [x] Lev 26:40-45; S Dt 4:32; 29:28 **30:2** [y] S Dt 4:30 [z] Dt 4:29; Ps 119:2 **30:3** [a] Ps 14:7; 53:6; 85:1; 126:4; Jer 30:18; 33:11; Eze 16:53; Joel 3:1; Zep 2:7 [b] Dt 13:17 [c] S Ge 48:21 [d] S Ge 11:4; Dt 4:27 [e] Isa 11:11; Jer 12:15; 16:15; 24:6; 29:14; 48:47; 49:6 **30:4** [f] Ps 19:6 [g] Isa 17:6; 24:13; 27:12; 40:11; 49:5; 56:8; Eze 20:34,41; 34:13 [h] Ne 1:8-9; Isa 11:12; 41:5; 42:10; 43:6; 48:20; 62:11; Jer 31:8,10; 50:2 **30:5** [i] Jer 29:14 [j] S Dt 7:13 **30:6** [k] S Dt 6:24; S 10:16 [l] Dt 6:5

29:17 *idols.* See note on Lev 26:30.

29:18 *root . . . that produces such bitter poison.* The poison of idolatry, involving the rejection of the Lord (see Ex 20:3–4 and notes).

29:19 *oath.* God's covenant with his people (vv. 12–14). *watered land . . . dry.* It is unclear whether the language used here should be understood literally or metaphorically (see NIV text note). In either case, a disaster of major proportions is indicated (vv. 20–21).

29:20 *The LORD will never be willing to forgive him.* Not to be taken as contradictory to 2Pe 3:9 ("not wanting anyone to perish"). Peter, too, says that those who deny the "sovereign Lord" bring "swift destruction on themselves" (2Pe 2:1). See note on 2Pe 3:9. *this book.* See note on 31:24. *blot out his name.* See 9:14 and note.

29:21 *Book of the Law.* See note on 31:24.

29:23 *destruction of Sodom.* See Ge 19:24–25; see also notes on Ge 10:19; 13:10.

29:27 *this book.* See note on 31:24.

29:28 *as it is now.* This would be said when Israel was in exile (see vv. 22–25).

29:29 *secret things.* The hidden events of Israel's future relative to the blessings and curses; but the phrase can also have wider application. *things revealed.* Primarily the "words of this law."

30:2,6,10 *with all your heart and . . . soul.* See note on 4:29.

30:3 *restore your fortunes.* See NIV text note.

30:6 *circumcise your hearts.* See 10:16; see also note on Ge 17:10.

30:7 *curses on your enemies.* Cf. Ge 12:3 and note.

these curses[m] on your enemies who hate and persecute you.[n] 8You will again obey the LORD and follow all his commands I am giving you today. 9Then the LORD your God will make you most prosperous in all the work of your hands and in the fruit of your womb, the young of your livestock and the crops of your land.[o] The LORD will again delight[p] in you and make you prosperous, just as he delighted in your fathers, 10if you obey the LORD your God and keep his commands and decrees that are written in this Book of the Law[q] and turn to the LORD your God with all your heart and with all your soul.[r]

The Offer of Life or Death

11Now what I am commanding you today is not too difficult for you or beyond your reach.[s] 12It is not up in heaven, so that you have to ask, "Who will ascend into heaven[t] to get it and proclaim it to us so we may obey it?"[u] 13Nor is it beyond the sea,[v] so that you have to ask, "Who will cross the sea to get it and proclaim it to us so we may obey it?"[w] 14No, the word is very near you; it is in your mouth and in your heart so you may obey it.[x]

15See, I set before you today life[y] and prosperity,[z] death[a] and destruction.[b] 16For I command you today to love[c] the LORD your God, to walk in his ways, and to keep his commands, decrees and laws; then you will live[d] and increase, and the LORD your God will bless you in the land you are entering to possess.

17But if your heart turns away and you are not obedient, and if you are drawn away to bow down to other gods and worship them, 18I declare to you this day that you will certainly be destroyed.[e] You will not live long in the land you are crossing the Jordan to enter and possess.

19This day I call heaven and earth as witnesses against you[f] that I have set before you life and death, blessings and curses.[g] Now choose life, so that you and your children may live 20and that you may love[h] the LORD your God, listen to his voice, and hold fast to him. For the LORD is your life,[i] and he will give[j] you many years in the land[k] he swore to give to your fathers, Abraham, Isaac and Jacob.

Joshua to Succeed Moses

31 Then Moses went out and spoke these words to all Israel: 2"I am now a hundred and twenty years old[l] and I am no longer able to lead you.[m] The LORD has said to me, 'You shall not cross the Jordan.'[n] 3The LORD your God himself will cross[o] over ahead of you.[p] He will destroy these nations[q] before you, and you will take possession of their land. Joshua also will cross[r] over ahead of you, as the LORD said. 4And the LORD will do to them what he did to Sihon and Og,[s] the kings of the Amorites, whom he destroyed along with their land. 5The LORD will deliver[t] them to you, and you must do to them all that I have commanded you. 6Be strong and courageous.[u] Do not be afraid or terrified[v] because of them, for the LORD your God goes with you;[w] he will never leave you[x] nor forsake[y] you."

7Then Moses summoned Joshua and said[z] to him in the presence of all Israel, "Be strong and courageous, for you must go with this people into the land that the LORD swore to their forefathers to give them,[a] and you must divide it among them as their inheritance. 8The LORD himself goes before you and will be with you;[b] he will never leave you nor forsake you.[c] Do not be afraid; do not be discouraged."

The Reading of the Law

9So Moses wrote[d] down this law and gave it to the priests, the sons of Levi,

30:7 [m]S Ge 12:3 [n]Dt 7:15 **30:9** [o]Jer 1:10; 24:6; 31:28; 32:41; 42:10; 45:4 [p]S Dt 28:63 **30:10** [q]S Dt 28:61 [r]S Dt 4:29 **30:11** [s]Ps 19:8; Isa 45:19,23; 63:1 **30:12** [t]Pr 30:4 [u]Ro 10:6* **30:13** [v]Job 28:14 [w]Ro 10:7* **30:14** [x]S Dt 6:6; Ro 10:8* **30:15** [y]Pr 10:16; 11:19; 12:28; Jer 21:8 [z]Dt 28:11; Job 36:11; Ps 25:13; 106:5; Pr 3:1-2 [a]S Ge 2:17 [b]S Dt 11:26 **30:16** [c]Dt 6:5 [d]ver 19; Dt 4:1; 32:47; Ne 9:29 **30:18** [e]S Dt 8:19 **30:19** [f]Dt 4:26 [g]S Dt 11:26 **30:20** [h]Dt 6:5 [i]Dt 4:1; S 8:3; 32:47; Ps 27:1; Pr 3:22; S Jn 5:26; Ac 17:28 [j]Ge 12:7 [k]Ps 37:3 **31:2** [l]S Ex 7:7 [m]Nu 27:17; 1Ki 3:7 [n]S Dt 3:23,26 **31:3** [o]Nu 27:18 [p]S Dt 9:3 [q]S Dt 7:1 [r]S Dt 3:28 **31:4** [s]S Nu 21:33 **31:5** [t]S Dt 2:33 **31:6** [u]ver 7,23; Jos 1:6,9,18; 10:25; 1Ch 22:13; 28:20; 2Ch 32:7 [v]Jer 1:8,17; Eze 2:6 [w]S Ge 28:15; S Dt 1:29; 20:4; S Mt 28:20 [x]Ps 56:9; 118:6 [y]S Dt 4:31; 1Sa 12:22; 1Ki 6:13; Ps 94:14; Isa 41:17; Heb 13:5* **31:7** [z]ver 23; Nu 27:23 [a]Jos 1:6 **31:8** [b]S Ex 13:21 [c]S Ge 28:15; S Dt 4:31 **31:9** [d]S Ex 17:14

30:9 *your fathers.* The patriarchs (see v. 20).
30:10 *Book of the Law.* See note on 31:24.
30:12,14 *It is not up in heaven ... the word is very near you.* Moses declares that understanding, believing and obeying the covenant were not beyond them. Paul applies this passage to the availability of the "word of faith" (Ro 10:6–10; see notes on 10:6–8).
30:16 *love ... keep.* See notes on 6:5; 11:1.
30:19 *I call heaven and earth as witnesses.* The typical ancient covenant outside the OT contained a list of gods who served as "witnesses" to its provisions. The covenant in Deuteronomy was "witnessed" by heaven and earth (see 31:28; 32:1; see also notes on Ps 50:1; Isa 1:2).
30:20 *hold fast.* See note on 10:20. *the LORD is your life.* When they chose the Lord, they chose life (v. 19). In 32:46–47 "all the words of this law" are said to be their life. The law, the Lord and life are bound together. "Life" in this context refers to all that makes life rich, full and productive—as God created it to be (cf. Lev 18:5; Jn 10:10 and notes).
31:2 *no longer able to lead.* Not a reference to physical disability (see 34:7). The Lord did not allow Moses to lead the people into Canaan because of his sin (see 1:37; 3:23–27; 4:21–22; 32:48–52; Nu 20:2–13 and relevant notes).
31:4 *what he did to Sihon and Og.* See 2:24—3:11; see also note on 1:4.
31:6 *Be strong and courageous.* The Lord's exhortation, often through his servants, to the people of Israel (Jos 10:25), to Joshua (vv. 7,23; see Jos 1:6–7,9,18 and note on 1:18), to Solomon (1Ch 22:13; 28:20) and to Hezekiah's military officers (2Ch 32:7). By trusting in the Lord and obeying him, his followers would be victorious in spite of great obstacles. *he will never leave you nor forsake you.* See v. 8; Jos 1:5; 1Ki 8:57; see also note on Ge 28:15. The clause is quoted in the first person in Heb 13:5 and applied to God's faithfulness in providing for the material needs of his people.
31:9 *wrote down this law and gave it to the priests.* Ancient treaties specified that a copy of the treaty was to be placed before the gods at the religious centers of the

who carried[e] the ark of the covenant of the LORD, and to all the elders of Israel. 10Then Moses commanded them: "At the end of every seven years, in the year for canceling debts,[f] during the Feast of Tabernacles,[g] 11when all Israel comes to appear[h] before the LORD your God at the place he will choose,[i] you shall read this law[j] before them in their hearing. 12Assemble the people—men, women and children, and the aliens living in your towns—so they can listen and learn[k] to fear[l] the LORD your God and follow carefully all the words of this law. 13Their children,[m] who do not know this law, must hear it and learn to fear the LORD your God as long as you live in the land you are crossing the Jordan to possess."

Israel's Rebellion Predicted

14The LORD said to Moses, "Now the day of your death[n] is near. Call Joshua[o] and present yourselves at the Tent of Meeting, where I will commission him.[p]" So Moses and Joshua came and presented themselves at the Tent of Meeting.[q]

15Then the LORD appeared at the Tent in a pillar of cloud, and the cloud stood over the entrance to the Tent.[r] 16And the LORD said to Moses: "You are going to rest with your fathers,[s] and these people will soon prostitute[t] themselves to the foreign gods of the land they are entering. They will forsake[u] me and break the covenant I made with them. 17On that day I will become angry[v] with them and forsake[w] them; I will hide[x] my face[y] from them, and they will be destroyed. Many disasters[z] and difficulties will come upon them, and on that day they will ask, 'Have not these disasters come upon us because our God is not with us?'[a] 18And I will certainly hide my face on that day because of all their wickedness in turning to other gods.

19"Now write[b] down for yourselves this song and teach it to the Israelites and have them sing it, so that it may be a witness[c] for me against them. 20When I have brought them into the land flowing with milk and honey, the land I promised on oath to their forefathers,[d] and when they eat their fill and thrive, they will turn to other gods[e] and worship them,[f] rejecting me and breaking my covenant.[g] 21And when many disasters and difficulties come upon them,[h] this song will testify against them, because it will not be forgotten by their descendants. I know what they are disposed to do,[i] even before I bring them into the land I promised them on oath." 22So Moses wrote[j] down this song that day and taught it to the Israelites.

23The LORD gave this command[k] to Joshua son of Nun: "Be strong and courageous,[l] for you will bring the Israelites into the land I promised them on oath, and I myself will be with you."

24After Moses finished writing[m] in a book the words of this law[n] from beginning to end, 25he gave this command to the Levites who carried[o] the ark of the covenant of the LORD: 26"Take this Book of the Law and place it beside the ark of the covenant of the LORD your God. There it will remain as a witness against you.[p] 27For I know how rebellious[q] and stiff-necked[r] you are. If you have been rebellious against the LORD while I am still alive and with you, how much more will you rebel after I die! 28Assemble before me all the elders of your tribes and all your officials, so that I can speak these words in their hearing and call heaven and earth to testify against them.[s] 29For I know that after my death you are sure to become utterly corrupt[t] and to turn from the way I have commanded you. In days to come, disaster[u] will fall upon you because you will do evil in the sight of the LORD and provoke him to anger by what your hands have made."

The Song of Moses

30And Moses recited the words of this song from beginning to end in the hearing of the whole assembly of Israel:

31:9 [e]ver 25; 1Ch 15:2 **31:10** [f]S Dt 15:1 [g]S Ex 23:16; Dt 16:13 **31:11** [h]S Dt 16:16 [i]Dt 12:5 [j]Jos 8:34-35; 2Ki 23:2; Ne 8:2 **31:12** [k]Dt 4:10 [l]Hag 1:12; Mal 1:6; 3:5,16 **31:13** [m]S Dt 11:2 **31:14** [n]S Ge 25:8; S Nu 27:13 [o]Nu 27:23; Dt 34:9; Jos 1:1-9 [p]S Nu 27:19 [q]Ex 33:9-11 **31:15** [r]S Ex 33:9 **31:16** [s]S Ge 15:15 [t]S Ex 34:15; Dt 4:25-28; Jdg 2:12 [u]Jdg 10:6,13; 1Ki 9:9; 18:18; 19:10; Jer 2:13; 5:19; 19:4 **31:17** [v]Dt 32:16; Jdg 2:14,20; 10:7; 2Ki 13:3; 22:13; Ps 106:29,40; Jer 7:18; 21:5; 36:7 [w]Jdg 6:13; 2Ch 15:2; 24:20; Ezr 8:22; Ps 44:9; Isa 2:6 [x]Dt 32:20; Isa 1:15; 45:15; 53:3; 54:8 [y]Job 13:24; Ps 13:1; 27:9; 30:7; 104:29; Isa 50:6; Jer 33:5; Eze 39:29; Mic 3:4 [z]Jer 4:20; Eze 7:26 [a]Nu 14:42; Hos 9:12 **31:19** [b]ver 22 [c]S Ge 31:50 **31:20** [d]Dt 6:10-12 [e]Ps 4:2; 16:4; 40:4; Jer 13:25; Da 3:28; Am 2:4 [f]Dt 8:19; 11:16-17 [g]ver 16 **31:21** [h]S Dt 4:30 [i]1Ch 28:9; Hos 5:3; Jn 2:24-25 **31:22** [j]ver 19 **31:23** [k]S ver 7 [l]Jos 1:6 **31:24** [m]Dt 17:18; 2Ki 22:8 [n]Dt 28:58 **31:25** [o]S ver 9 **31:26** [p]ver 19 **31:27** [q]S Ex 23:21 [r]S Dt 9:27 **31:28** [s]Dt 4:26; 30:19; 32:1; Job 20:27; Isa 26:21 **31:29** [t]S Dt 4:16; Rev 9:20 [u]1Ki 9:9; 22:23; 2Ki 22:16

nations involved. For Israel, that meant to place it in the ark of the covenant (but see v. 26; see also notes on 33:9; Ex 16:34; 31:18).

31:10 *every seven years.* See 15:4 and note; Ex 23:10–11; Lev 25:1–7 and note on 25:4; see also chart, pp. 178–179.

31:11 *place he will choose.* See note on 12:5. *read this law before them.* Reading the law to the Israelites (and teaching it to them) was one of the main duties of the priests (see 33:10; Mal 2:4–9 and note on 2:6–7).

31:12 *fear the LORD.* See notes on Ge 20:11; Ps 34:8–14. *words of this law.* See note on v. 24.

31:14 *I will commission him.* See v. 23; cf. Nu 27:18–23 and notes on 27:18,20.

31:16 *prostitute themselves.* See Ex 34:15 and note.

31:17–18 *hide my face.* See 32:20; see also note on Ps 13:1.

31:19 *write down ... this song and teach it.* See v. 22; 31:30—32:44 and note.

31:23 *Be strong and courageous.* See note on v. 6.

31:24 *words of this law from beginning to end.* The book of Deuteronomy up to this place (see note on v. 9).

31:26 *place it beside the ark.* See note on v. 9.

31:27 *stiff-necked.* See 9:6,13; 10:16; see also note on Ex 32:9.

31:28 *heaven and earth to testify.* See note on 30:19.

31:29 *what your hands have made.* A reference to idols (see 4:28; 27:15 and note).

31:30—32:44 The song of Moses (see notes on Ex 15:1–18; Rev 15:3) set within the narrative frame of 31:30 and 32:44. The song may be outlined as follows: (1) summoning of covenant witnesses and description of the

32 Listen,[v] O heavens,[w] and I will
speak;
hear, O earth, the words of my
mouth.[x]
2 Let my teaching fall like rain[y]
and my words descend like dew,[z a]
like showers[b] on new grass,
like abundant rain on tender plants.
3 I will proclaim[c] the name of the LORD.[d]
Oh, praise the greatness[e] of our God!
4 He is the Rock,[f] his works are perfect,[g]
and all his ways are just.
A faithful God[h] who does no wrong,
upright[i] and just is he.[j]
5 They have acted corruptly toward him;
to their shame they are no longer his
children,
but a warped and crooked
generation.[a k]
6 Is this the way you repay[l] the LORD,
O foolish[m] and unwise people?[n]
Is he not your Father,[o] your Creator,[b]
who made you and formed you?[p]
7 Remember the days of old;[q]
consider the generations long past.[r]
Ask your father and he will tell you,
your elders, and they will explain to
you.[s]
8 When the Most High[t] gave the nations
their inheritance,
when he divided all mankind,[u]
he set up boundaries[v] for the peoples
according to the number of the sons
of Israel.[c w]
9 For the LORD's portion[x] is his people,
Jacob his allotted inheritance.[y]
10 In a desert[z] land he found him,
in a barren and howling waste.[a]
He shielded[b] him and cared for him;
he guarded him as the apple of his
eye,[c]
11 like an eagle that stirs up its nest
and hovers over its young,[d]
that spreads its wings to catch them
and carries them on its pinions.[e]
12 The LORD alone led[f] him;[g]
no foreign god was with him.[h]
13 He made him ride on the heights[i] of
the land
and fed him with the fruit of the
fields.
He nourished him with honey from the
rock,[j]
and with oil[k] from the flinty crag,
14 with curds and milk from herd and
flock
and with fattened lambs and goats,
with choice rams of Bashan[l]
and the finest kernels of wheat.[m]
You drank the foaming blood of the
grape.[n]
15 Jeshurun[d o] grew fat[p] and kicked;
filled with food, he became heavy
and sleek.
He abandoned[q] the God who made
him
and rejected the Rock[r] his Savior.
16 They made him jealous[s] with their
foreign gods
and angered[t] him with their
detestable idols.
17 They sacrificed[u] to demons,[v] which are
not God—
gods they had not known,[w]
gods that recently appeared,[x]
gods your fathers did not fear.
18 You deserted the Rock, who fathered
you;
you forgot[y] the God who gave you
birth.

[a] 5 Or *Corrupt are they and not his children, / a generation warped and twisted to their shame*
[b] 6 Or *Father, who bought you*
[c] 8 Masoretic Text; Dead Sea Scrolls (see also Septuagint) *sons of God*
[d] 15 *Jeshurun* means *the upright one*, that is, Israel.

32:1 [v] Ps 49:1; Mic 1:2 [w] Jer 2:12 [x] S Dt 4:26 **32:2** [y] 2Sa 23:4 [z] Ps 107:20; Isa 9:8; 55:11 [a] Mic 5:7 [b] Ps 65:10; 68:9; 72:6; 147:8 **32:3** [c] Ps 118:17; 145:6 [d] Ex 33:19; 34:5-6 [e] S Dt 3:24 **32:4** [f] S Ge 49:24 [g] 2Sa 22:31; Ps 18:30; 19:7 [h] S Dt 4:35 [i] Ps 92:15 [j] S Ge 18:25 **32:5** [k] ver 20; Mt 17:17; Lk 9:41; Ac 2:40 **32:6** [l] Ps 116:12 [m] Ps 94:8; Jer 5:21 [n] ver 28 [o] S Ex 4:22; 2Sa 7:24 [p] ver 15 **32:7** [q] Ps 44:1; 74:2; 77:5; Isa 51:9; 63:9 [r] Dt 4:32; Job 8:8; 20:4; Ps 78:4; Isa 46:9 [s] S Ex 10:2; Job 15:18 **32:8** [t] Ps 7:8 [u] S Ge 11:8; Ac 8:1 [v] Ps 74:17 [w] Nu 23:9; Dt 33:12, 28; Jer 23:6 **32:9** [x] Ps 16:5; 73:26; 119:57; 142:5; Jer 10:16 [y] S Dt 9:29; S 1Sa 26:19 **32:10** [z] S Dt 1:19 [a] Dt 8:15; Job 12:24; Ps 107:40 [b] Ps 32:10; Jer 31:22 [c] Ps 17:8; Pr 7:2; Hos 13:5; Zec 2:8 **32:11** [d] S Ex 19:4 [e] Ps 17:8; 18:10-19; 61:4 **32:12** [f] Ps 106:9; Isa 63:13; Jer 31:32 [g] Dt 4:35 [h] ver 39; Jdg 2:12; Ps 18:31; 81:9; Isa 43:12; 45:5 **32:13** [i] Dt 33:29; 2Sa 22:34; Ps 18:33; Isa 33:16; 58:14; Eze 36:2; Hab 3:19 [j] S Dt 8:8 [k] Dt 33:24; Job 29:6 **32:14** [l] S Nu 21:33 [m] Ps 65:9; 81:16; 147:14 [n] S Ge 49:11 **32:15** [o] Dt 33:5, 26; Isa 44:2 [p] Dt 31:20; Jer 5:28 [q] Dt 31:16; Isa 1:4, 28; 58:2; 65:11; Jer 15:6; Eze 14:5 [r] S Ge 49:24 **32:16** [s] S Nu 25:11; S 1Co 10:22 [t] S Dt 31:17; S 1Ki 14:9 **32:17** [u] S Ex 32:8 [v] S Ex 22:20; 1Co 10:20 [w] S Dt 28:64 [x] Jdg 5:8 **32:18** [y] Jdg 3:7; 1Sa 12:9; Ps 44:17, 20; 106:21; Jer 2:32; Eze 23:35; Hos 8:14; 13:6

covenant God (32:1–4), (2) charges against the people (32:5–6), (3) review of God's covenant benefits (32:7–14), (4) the people's disobedience to the covenant stipulations (32:15–18), (5) covenant curses for such disobedience (32:19–27), (6) the impotence of false gods (32:28–38) and (7) the Lord's vindication and vengeance (32:39–43).

32:1 *Listen, O heavens.* For similar introductions see Isa 1:2 and note; 34:1; Mic 1:2; 6:1–2 and note.

32:4 *He is the Rock.* A major theme of the song of Moses (see vv. 15,18,30–31; see also notes on Ge 49:24; Ps 18:2). *perfect ... just ... upright ... just.* See note on Ps 119:121.

32:5 *warped and crooked generation.* See Php 2:15 and note.

32:6 *Father.* See Isa 63:16; 64:8.

32:7 *Remember the days of old.* See note on 4:10.

32:8 *Most High.* The only occurrence in Deuteronomy of this name for God (see note on Ge 14:19). It emphasizes the Lord's sovereignty over all creation. *gave the nations their inheritance.* See Ge 10. *according to the number of the sons of Israel.* Perhaps referring to the number (70; see 10:22 and note) of the sons of Jacob (Israel) who went down to Egypt (see Ge 46:27 and note; Ex 1:5; see also note on Ge 10:2). But see NIV text note.

32:10 *apple of his eye.* Referring to the pupil, a delicate part of the eye that is essential for vision and that therefore must be protected at all costs.

32:11 *hovers over.* See note on Ge 1:2.

32:13 *honey from the rock.* See Ps 81:16. In Canaan, bees sometimes built their hives in crevices in the rocks (cf. Isa 7:18–19). *oil from the flinty crag.* Olive trees often grew on rocky hillsides, as on the Mount of Olives east of Jerusalem.

32:14 *choice rams of Bashan.* See note on Eze 39:18. *foaming blood of the grape.* Red wine (see Ge 49:11).

32:15 *Jeshurun.* See NIV text note; see also Isa 44:2 and note. *Rock.* See v. 18 and note on v. 4.

32:17 *demons.* See Ps 106:37 and note.

19 The LORD saw this and rejected them[z]
because he was angered by his sons
and daughters.[a]
20 "I will hide my face[b] from them," he
said,
"and see what their end will be;
for they are a perverse generation,[c]
children who are unfaithful.[d]
21 They made me jealous[e] by what is no
god
and angered me with their worthless
idols.[f]
I will make them envious by those
who are not a people;
I will make them angry by a nation
that has no understanding.[g]
22 For a fire has been kindled by my
wrath,[h]
one that burns to the realm of
death[a] below.[i]
It will devour[j] the earth and its
harvests[k]
and set afire the foundations of the
mountains.[l]

23 "I will heap calamities[m] upon them
and spend my arrows[n] against them.
24 I will send wasting famine[o] against
them,
consuming pestilence[p] and deadly
plague;[q]
I will send against them the fangs of
wild beasts,[r]
the venom of vipers[s] that glide in the
dust.[t]
25 In the street the sword will make them
childless;
in their homes terror[u] will reign.[v]
Young men and young women will
perish,
infants and gray-haired men.[w]
26 I said I would scatter[x] them
and blot out their memory from
mankind,[y]
27 but I dreaded the taunt of the enemy,
lest the adversary misunderstand[z]
and say, 'Our hand has triumphed;
the LORD has not done all this.' "[a]

28 They are a nation without sense,
there is no discernment[b] in them.
29 If only they were wise and would
understand this[c]
and discern what their end will be![d]

30 How could one man chase a thousand,
or two put ten thousand to flight,[e]
unless their Rock had sold them,[f]
unless the LORD had given them up?[g]
31 For their rock is not like our Rock,[h]
as even our enemies concede.[i]
32 Their vine comes from the vine of
Sodom[j]
and from the fields of Gomorrah.
Their grapes are filled with poison,[k]
and their clusters with bitterness.[l]
33 Their wine is the venom of serpents,
the deadly poison of cobras.[m]

34 "Have I not kept this in reserve
and sealed it in my vaults?[n]
35 It is mine to avenge;[o] I will repay.[p]
In due time their foot will slip;[q]
their day of disaster is near
and their doom rushes upon them.[r]"

36 The LORD will judge his people[s]
and have compassion[t] on his servants[u]
when he sees their strength is gone
and no one is left, slave[v] or free.
37 He will say: "Now where are their
gods,
the rock they took refuge in,[w]
38 the gods who ate the fat of their
sacrifices
and drank the wine of their drink
offerings?[x]
Let them rise up to help you!
Let them give you shelter!

39 "See now that I myself am He![y]
There is no god besides me.[z]
I put to death[a] and I bring to life,[b]
I have wounded and I will heal,[c]
and no one can deliver out of my
hand.[d]
40 I lift my hand[e] to heaven and declare:
As surely as I live forever,[f]

[a] 22 Hebrew *to Sheol*

32:19 [z] Lev 26:30; Ps 78:59 [a] Am 6:8 **32:20** [b] Dt 31:17, 29; Ps 4:6; 44:24 [c] S ver 5 [d] Dt 9:23 **32:21** [e] S Nu 25:11; S 1Co 10:22 [f] ver 17; 1Ki 16:13, 26; 2Ki 17:15; Ps 31:6; Jer 2:5; 8:19; 10:8; 16:19; Jnh 2:8 [g] Ro 10:19* **32:22** [h] Ps 7:11 [i] Nu 16:31-35; Ps 18:7-8; Jer 15:14; La 4:11 [j] Am 7:4 [k] Lev 26:20 [l] Ps 83:14 **32:23** [m] S Dt 29:21 [n] ver 42; 2Sa 22:15; Job 6:4; Ps 7:13; 18:14; 45:5; 77:17; 120:4; Isa 5:28; 49:2; Eze 5:16; Hab 3:9, 11 **32:24** [o] Ge 26:1; S 41:55; 42:5; 2Sa 24:13; 1Ch 21:12 [p] S Dt 28:22 [q] Ps 91:6 [r] S Ge 37:20 [s] ver 33; Job 20:16; Ps 58:4; Jer 8:17; Am 5:18-19; Mic 7:17 [t] Job 20:16 **32:25** [u] Isa 24:17 [v] Jer 14:18; La 1:20; Eze 7:15; 2Co 7:5 [w] 2Ch 36:17; Isa 13:18; Jer 4:31; La 2:21 **32:26** [x] Dt 4:27 [y] S Nu 14:12; Job 18:17; Ps 34:16; 37:28; 109:15; Isa 14:20 **32:27** [z] Dt 9:26-28 [a] Ps 140:8; Isa 10:13; Jer 40:2-3 **32:28** [b] Isa 1:3; 5:13; 27:11; Jer 8:7 **32:29** [c] Dt 5:29; Ps 81:13 [d] Isa 47:7; La 1:9 **32:30** [e] S Lev 26:8 [f] Jdg 2:14; 3:8; 4:2; 10:7; 1Sa 12:9 [g] Nu 21:34; 1Sa 23:7; Ps 31:8; 44:12; 106:41; Isa 50:1; 54:6 **32:31** [h] S Ge 49:24 [i] S Ex 14:25 **32:32** [j] Jer 23:14 [k] Job 6:4; 20:16 [l] Dt 29:18 **32:33** [m] S ver 24 **32:34** [n] Job 14:17; Jer 2:22; Hos 13:12 **32:35** [o] S ver 41; S Ge 4:24; S Jer 51:6 [p] S Ge 30:2; S Ex 32:34; S Ps 54:5; S Ro 12:19*; Heb 10:30* [q] Ps 17:5; 35:6; 37:31; 38:16; 66:9; 73:2, 18; 94:18; 121:3; Pr 4:19; Jer 23:12 [r] Eze 7:8-9 **32:36** [s] Heb 10:30* [t] Am 7:3 [u] Lev 26:43-45; Dt 30:1-3; Jdg 2:18; Ps 90:13; 102:13; 103:13; 106:45; 135:14; Joel 2:14 [v] 1Ki 14:10; 21:21; 2Ki 9:8 **32:37** [w] Jdg 10:14; Jer 2:28; 11:12 **32:38** [x] Nu 25:1-2; Jer 11:12; 44:8, 25 **32:39** [y] Isa 41:4; 43:10; 44:7; 46:4; 48:12 [z] S ver 12 [a] 1Sa 2:6 [b] 1Sa 2:6; 2Ki 5:7; Ps 68:20; Jn 11:25-26 [c] Ex 15:26; Job 5:18; 15:11; Ps 147:3; Isa 6:10; 19:22; 30:26; 53:5; 57:18; Jer 33:6; Hos 6:1; Mal 4:2; 1Pe 2:24 [d] Job 9:12; 10:7; Ps 7:2; 50:22; Isa 43:13; Da 4:35; Hos 5:14 **32:40** [e] S Ge 14:22 [f] S Ge 21:33; Rev 1:18

32:20 *hide my face.* See note on 31:17 – 18.

32:21 Quoted in part in Ro 10:19 to illustrate Israel's failure to understand the good news about Christ. See also v. 16. *those who are not a people.* See note on Ro 10:19.

32:22 *realm of death below.* See notes on Ge 37:35; Job 17:16; Ps 6:5; Pr 15:11; Am 9:2 – 4; see also Job 3:13 – 19; 11:8; 26:6; Ps 139:8; Pr 23:14; 27:20; Isa 7:11; 14:9 – 11,15 – 20; 38:10.

32:26 *I said I would scatter them.* See 28:64 and note; see also 4:27. *blot out their memory.* See 9:14 and note; cf. 25:19.

32:30 *their Rock.* Israel's God (see note on v. 4).

32:31 *their rock.* The god of Israel's enemy.

32:34 *sealed it in my vaults.* The Lord's plans for the future are fixed and certain. Sin will be punished in due time.

32:35 – 36 Quoted in part in Heb 10:30 as a warning against rejecting the Son of God.

32:35 *It is mine to avenge; I will repay.* Quoted in Ro 12:19 to affirm that avenging is God's prerogative, not ours.

32:39 *I myself am He.* See Ex 3:12 – 15 and notes; cf. Jn 4:26 and note. *no god besides me.* See note on 4:35. *I put to death and I bring to life.* See note on 1Sa 2:6 – 8.

32:40 *lift my hand.* See Ge 14:22 and note.

41 when I sharpen my flashing sword[g]
and my hand grasps it in judgment,
I will take vengeance[h] on my
adversaries
and repay those who hate me.[i]
42 I will make my arrows drunk with
blood,[j]
while my sword devours flesh:[k]
the blood of the slain and the captives,
the heads of the enemy leaders."

43 Rejoice,[l] O nations, with his people,[a, b]
for he will avenge the blood of his
servants;[m]
he will take vengeance on his
enemies[n]
and make atonement for his land
and people.[o]

44 Moses came with Joshua[c p] son of Nun
and spoke all the words of this song in
the hearing of the people. 45 When Moses
finished reciting all these words to all Israel, 46 he said to them, "Take to heart all
the words I have solemnly declared to you
this day,[q] so that you may command[r] your
children to obey carefully all the words of
this law. 47 They are not just idle words for
you—they are your life.[s] By them you will
live long[t] in the land you are crossing the
Jordan to possess."

Moses to Die on Mount Nebo

48 On that same day the LORD told Moses,[u] 49 "Go up into the Abarim[v] Range to
Mount Nebo[w] in Moab, across from Jericho,[x] and view Canaan,[y] the land I am giving the Israelites as their own possession.
50 There on the mountain that you have
climbed you will die[z] and be gathered to
your people, just as your brother Aaron
died[a] on Mount Hor[b] and was gathered to
his people. 51 This is because both of you
broke faith with me in the presence of the
Israelites at the waters of Meribah Kadesh[c]
in the Desert of Zin[d] and because you did
not uphold my holiness among the Israelites.[e] 52 Therefore, you will see the land
only from a distance;[f] you will not enter[g]
the land I am giving to the people of Israel."

32:41 [g] Jdg 7:20; Ps 7:12; 45:3; Isa 27:1; 34:6; 66:16; Jer 12:12; Eze 21:9-10 [h] ver 35; Ps 149:7; Jer 46:10; Na 1:2 [i] Ps 137:8; Jer 25:14; 50:29; 51:24, 56
32:42 [j] S ver 23 [k] 2Sa 2:26; Jer 12:12; 44:1; 46:10, 14
32:43 [l] Ps 137:6; Isa 25:9; 65:18; 66:10; Ro 15:10* [m] 2Ki 9:7; S Rev 6:10 [n] Isa 1:24; Jer 9:9 [o] Ps 65:3; 79:9
32:44 [p] Nu 13:8, 16
32:46 [q] S Dt 6:6; Jn 1:17; 7:19 [r] Dt 6:7
32:47 [s] S Dt 30:20 [t] S Ex 23:26; Dt 33:25; Isa 65:22
32:48 [u] Nu 27:12
32:49 [v] Nu 27:12 [w] S Nu 32:3 [x] S Nu 22:1 [y] S Lev 14:34
32:50 [z] S Ge 25:8; S Nu 27:13 [a] Nu 20:29 [b] S Nu 20:22
32:51 [c] Eze 47:19 [d] S Nu 13:21; 20:11-13 [e] Nu 27:14
32:52 [f] Dt 34:1-3 [g] S Dt 3:27

33:1 [h] S Ge 27:4 [i] Jos 14:6; 1Sa 2:27; 9:6; 1Ki 12:22; 13:1; 2Ki 1:9-13; 5:8; Jer 35:4
33:2 [j] Ex 19:18; Ps 68:8 [k] Jos 11:17; Jdg 5:4 [l] Ps 50:2; 80:1; 94:1 [m] S Nu 10:12 [n] Ps 89:7; Da 4:13; 7:10; 8:13; Zec 14:5; Ac 7:53; Gal 3:19; Heb 2:2; Rev 5:11
33:3 [o] S Dt 4:37 [p] Dt 7:6 [q] Lk 10:39; Rev 4:10

Moses Blesses the Tribes

33:1-29Ref — Ge 49:1-28

33 This is the blessing[h] that Moses the
man of God[i] pronounced on the Israelites before his death. 2 He said:

"The LORD came from Sinai[j]
and dawned over them from Seir;[k]
he shone forth[l] from Mount
Paran.[m]
He came with[d] myriads of holy ones[n]
from the south, from his mountain
slopes.[e]
3 Surely it is you who love[o] the people;
all the holy ones are in your hand.[p]
At your feet they all bow down,[q]
and from you receive instruction,
4 the law that Moses gave us,[r]
the possession of the assembly of
Jacob.[s]
5 He was king[t] over Jeshurun[f u]
when the leaders of the people
assembled,
along with the tribes of Israel.

6 "Let Reuben live and not die,
nor[g] his men be few."[v]

7 And this he said about Judah:[w]

"Hear, O LORD, the cry of Judah;
bring him to his people.
With his own hands he defends his
cause.
Oh, be his help against his foes!"

8 About Levi[x] he said:

"Your Thummim and Urim[y] belong
to the man you favored.[z]
You tested[a] him at Massah;
you contended with him at the
waters of Meribah.[b]

[a] 43 Or *Make his people rejoice, O nations*
[b] 43 Masoretic Text; Dead Sea Scrolls (see also Septuagint) *people, / and let all the angels worship him /*
[c] 44 Hebrew *Hoshea,* a variant of *Joshua*
[d] 2 Or *from*
[e] 2 The meaning of the Hebrew for this phrase is uncertain.
[f] 5 *Jeshurun* means *the upright one,* that is, Israel; also in verse 26.
[g] 6 Or *but let*

33:4 [r] Dt 4:2; Jn 1:17; 7:19 [s] Ps 119:111 **33:5** [t] S Ex 16:8; 1Sa 10:19; Ps 10:16; 149:2 [u] S Nu 23:21; S Dt 32:15 **33:6** [v] S Ge 34:5 **33:7** [w] S Ge 49:10 **33:8** [x] S Ge 29:34 [y] Ex 28:30 [z] Ps 106:16 [a] S Nu 14:22 [b] S Ex 17:7

32:43 *Rejoice, O nations, with his people.* One of the Dead Sea Scrolls adds a clause in Deuteronomy (see NIV text note), and the clause is quoted in Ro 15:10; Heb 1:6 (see note there).
32:47 *they are your life.* See note on 30:20.
32:50 *gathered to your people.* See note on Ge 25:8. *Aaron died on Mount Hor.* See 10:6; see also Nu 20:22–29 and notes.
32:51 *you broke faith with me.* See 1:37; 3:23–27; 4:21–22; 31:2; Nu 20:11–12 and notes. *Meribah Kadesh in the Desert of Zin.* See 33:8; see also notes on Ex 17:7; Nu 20:13.
33:1 *blessing.* See Ge 12:1–3 and notes; 22:15–18; 27:27–29; 28:10–15. Moses' blessings on the tribes (vv. 6–25) should be compared particularly with Jacob's blessings on his sons in Ge 49:3–27. *man of God.* The first occurrence of this title. It appears next in Jos 14:6 (also of Moses; see Ps 90 title). Later it designates other messengers of God (see note on 1Sa 2:27).
33:2 *Sinai ... Seir ... Paran.* Mountains associated with the giving of the law (see Ge 21:21 and note; Jdg 5:4–5; Hab 3:3 and note). *holy ones.* Angels.
33:3 *holy ones.* Israelites (see 7:6 and note; 14:2; 26:19; 28:9).
33:5 *king.* The Lord, not an earthly monarch, was to be king over Israel (see Jdg 8:23 and note). *Jeshurun.* See NIV text note; see also Isa 44:2 and note.
33:6 *Reuben.* For the boundaries of the tribal territories see map No. 4 at the end of this study Bible.
33:8 *Thummim and Urim.* See note on Ex 28:30. *Massah.* See 6:16; 9:22; see also note on Ex 17:7. *Meribah.* See note on 32:51.

9He said of his father and mother,[c]
'I have no regard for them.'
He did not recognize his brothers
or acknowledge his own children,
but he watched over your word
and guarded your covenant.[d]
10He teaches[e] your precepts to Jacob
and your law to Israel.[f]
He offers incense before you[g]
and whole burnt offerings on your
altar.[h]
11Bless all his skills, O LORD,
and be pleased with the work of
his hands.[i]
Smite the loins of those who rise up
against him;
strike his foes till they rise no
more."

12About Benjamin[j] he said:

"Let the beloved of the LORD rest
secure in him,[k]
for he shields him all day long,[l]
and the one the LORD loves[m] rests
between his shoulders.[n]"

13About Joseph[o] he said:

"May the LORD bless his land
with the precious dew from heaven
above
and with the deep waters that lie
below;[p]
14with the best the sun brings forth
and the finest the moon can yield;
15with the choicest gifts of the ancient
mountains[q]
and the fruitfulness of the
everlasting hills;
16with the best gifts of the earth and
its fullness
and the favor of him who dwelt in
the burning bush.[r]
Let all these rest on the head of
Joseph,
on the brow of the prince among[a]
his brothers.[s]
17In majesty he is like a firstborn
bull;
his horns[t] are the horns of a
wild ox.[u]
With them he will gore[v] the nations,
even those at the ends of the earth.
Such are the ten thousands of
Ephraim;[w]
such are the thousands of
Manasseh.[x]"

18About Zebulun[y] he said:

"Rejoice, Zebulun, in your going
out,
and you, Issachar,[z] in your tents.
19They will summon peoples to the
mountain[a]
and there offer sacrifices of
righteousness;[b]
they will feast on the abundance of
the seas,[c]
on the treasures hidden in the sand."

20About Gad[d] he said:

"Blessed is he who enlarges Gad's
domain![e]
Gad lives there like a lion,
tearing at arm or head.
21He chose the best land for himself;[f]
the leader's portion was kept for
him.[g]
When the heads of the people
assembled,
he carried out the LORD's righteous
will,[h]
and his judgments concerning
Israel."

22About Dan[i] he said:

"Dan is a lion's cub,
springing out of Bashan."

23About Naphtali[j] he said:

"Naphtali is abounding with the favor
of the LORD
and is full of his blessing;
he will inherit southward to the
lake."

24About Asher[k] he said:

"Most blessed of sons is Asher;
let him be favored by his brothers,
and let him bathe his feet in oil.[l]
25The bolts of your gates will be iron and
bronze,[m]
and your strength will equal your
days.[n]

[a] 16 Or *of the one separated from*

33:9 [c]Ex 32:26-29 [d]Ps 61:5; Mal 2:5 **33:10** [e]Ezr 7:10; Ne 8:18; Ps 119:151; Jer 23:22; Mal 2:6 [f]S Lev 10:11; Dt 17:8-11; 31:9-13 [g]S Ex 30:7; Lev 16:12-13 [h]Ps 51:19 **33:11** [i]2Sa 24:23; Ps 20:3; 51:19 **33:12** [j]S Ge 35:18 [k]Dt 4:37-38; 12:10; S 32:8 [l]S Ex 19:4 [m]Ps 60:5; 127:2; Isa 5:1 [n]S Ex 28:12 **33:13** [o]S Ge 30:24 [p]Ge 27:28; Ps 148:7 **33:15** [q]Hab 3:6 **33:16** [r]S Ex 3:2 [s]S Ge 37:8 **33:17** [t]1Sa 2:10; 2Sa 22:3; Eze 34:21 [u]S Nu 23:22 [v]1Ki 22:11; Ps 44:5 [w]S Ge 41:52 [x]S Ge 41:51 **33:18** [y]S Ge 30:20 [z]S Ge 30:18 **33:19** [a]S Ex 15:17; Ps 48:1; Isa 2:3; 65:11; 66:20; Jer 31:6 [b]Ps 4:5; 51:19 [c]Isa 18:7; 23:18; 45:14; 60:5, 11; 61:6; Hag 2:7; Zec 14:14 **33:20** [d]Ge 30:11 [e]Dt 3:12-17 **33:21** [f]Nu 32:1-5, 31-32 [g]S Nu 34:14 [h]Jos 22:1-3 **33:22** [i]Ge 49:16; S Nu 1:38 **33:23** [j]S Ge 30:8 **33:24** [k]S Ge 30:13 [l]S Ge 49:20; S Dt 32:13 **33:25** [m]Ne 3:3; 7:3; Ps 147:13 [n]S Dt 32:47

33:9 *he watched over your word.* The Levites had charge of the tabernacle with its ark, in which the Book of the Law was placed (see note on 31:9).
33:10 *teaches your precepts to Jacob.* See note on 31:11.
33:12 *between his shoulders.* See Isa 49:22; cf. Dt 33:27.
33:13 *About Joseph.* Moses included the blessing on the two tribes of Ephraim and Manasseh (v. 17), Joseph's sons, with that of Joseph himself. *dew from heaven ... deep waters.* See note on Ge 49:25.
33:15–16 See Ge 49:26 and note.
33:16 *best gifts of the earth.* Under the Lord's blessing, Joseph's land in the central part of Canaan was to be unusually fertile and productive. *who dwelt in the burning bush.* See Ex 3:1–6 and notes.
33:19 *abundance of the seas ... treasures hidden in the sand.* References to maritime wealth (see note on Ge 49:13).
33:21 *He chose the best land.* For his livestock (see 3:12–20 and notes).
33:22 *springing out of Bashan.* The lion's cub, not Dan, is the subject. Another possible translation is "keeping away from the viper." Although someday he would be like a viper himself (see Ge 49:17 and note), the early history of Dan pictured him as being somewhat more timid (see Jdg 18 and note on 18:1).
33:23 *lake.* The Sea of Galilee.

26 "There is no one like the God of
Jeshurun,[o]
who rides[p] on the heavens to help
you[q]
and on the clouds[r] in his majesty.[s]
27 The eternal[t] God is your refuge,[u]
and underneath are the everlasting[v]
arms.
He will drive out your enemy before
you,[w]
saying, 'Destroy him!'[x]
28 So Israel will live in safety alone;[y]
Jacob's spring is secure
in a land of grain and new wine,
where the heavens drop dew.[z]
29 Blessed are you, O Israel![a]
Who is like you,[b]
a people saved by the LORD?[c]
He is your shield and helper[d]
and your glorious sword.
Your enemies will cower before you,
and you will trample down their
high places.[a][e]"

The Death of Moses

34 Then Moses climbed Mount Nebo[f]
from the plains of Moab to the top of
Pisgah,[g] across from Jericho.[h] There the
LORD showed[i] him the whole land—from
Gilead to Dan,[j] 2 all of Naphtali, the territory of Ephraim and Manasseh, all the land
of Judah as far as the western sea,[b][k] 3 the
Negev[l] and the whole region from the Valley of Jericho, the City of Palms,[m] as far as
Zoar.[n] 4 Then the LORD said to him, "This is
the land I promised on oath[o] to Abraham,
Isaac and Jacob[p] when I said, 'I will give
it[q] to your descendants.' I have let you see
it with your eyes, but you will not cross[r]
over into it."
5 And Moses the servant of the LORD[s]
died[t] there in Moab, as the LORD had said.
6 He buried him[c] in Moab, in the valley opposite Beth Peor,[u] but to this day no one
knows where his grave is.[v] 7 Moses was a
hundred and twenty years old[w] when he
died, yet his eyes were not weak[x] nor his
strength gone.[y] 8 The Israelites grieved for
Moses in the plains of Moab[z] thirty days,[a]
until the time of weeping and mourning[b]
was over.
9 Now Joshua son of Nun was filled with
the spirit[d] of wisdom[c] because Moses had
laid his hands on him.[d] So the Israelites
listened to him and did what the LORD had
commanded Moses.
10 Since then, no prophet[e] has risen in
Israel like Moses,[f] whom the LORD knew
face to face,[g] 11 who did all those miraculous signs and wonders[h] the LORD sent him
to do in Egypt—to Pharaoh and to all his
officials[i] and to his whole land. 12 For no
one has[j] ever shown the mighty power or
performed the awesome deeds[k] that Moses
did in the sight of all Israel.

[a] 29 Or *will tread upon their bodies* [b] 2 That is, the Mediterranean [c] 6 Or *He was buried* [d] 9 Or *Spirit*

33:26 [o] S Dt 32:15 [p] Ps 18:10; 68:33 [q] S Dt 10:14; S Ps 104:3 [r] 2Sa 22:10; Ps 18:9; 68:4; Da 7:13 [s] S Ex 15:7 **33:27** [t] Ex 15:18; Isa 40:28; 57:15 [u] Ps 9:9; 84:1; 90:1; 91:9 [v] S Ge 21:33 [w] Ex 34:11; Jos 24:18 [x] S Dt 7:2 **33:28** [y] S Ex 33:16; S Lev 25:18; S Dt 32:8; Ps 16:9; Pr 1:33; Isa 14:30 [z] ver 13; Ge 27:28 **33:29** [a] Ps 1:1; 32:1-2; 144:15 [b] 2Sa 22:45; Ps 18:44; 66:3; 81:15 [c] Dt 4:7 [d] Ge 15:1; Ex 18:4; Ps 10:14; 18:1; 27:1, 9; 30:10; 54:4; 70:5; 115:9-11; 118:7; Isa 45:24; Hos 13:9; Hab 3:19 [e] S Nu 33:52; S Dt 32:13 **34:1** [f] S Nu 32:3 [g] S Nu 21:20 [h] Dt 32:49 [i] Dt 32:52 [j] S Ge 14:14 **34:2** [k] S Ex 23:31 **34:3** [l] S Ge 12:9 [m] Jdg 1:16; 3:13; 2Ch 28:15 [n] S Ge 13:10 **34:4** [o] Ge 28:13 [p] Jos 21:43 [q] Ge 12:7 [r] S Dt 3:23 **34:5** [s] S Nu 12:7 [t] S Ge 25:8 **34:6** [u] S Dt 3:29 [v] Jude 1:9 **34:7** [w] S Ex 7:7 [x] S Ge 27:1 [y] S Ge 15:15 **34:8** [z] S Nu 21:11 [a] S Ge 37:34; S Dt 1:3 [b] 2Sa 11:27 **34:9** [c] S Ge 41:38; S Ex 28:3; Isa 11:2 [d] S Dt 31:14; Ac 6:6 **34:10** [e] S Ge 20:7 [f] Dt 18:15, 18 [g] S Ex 33:11 **34:11** [h] Dt 4:34 [i] S Ex 11:3 **34:12** [j] Heb 3:1-6 [k] S Dt 4:34

33:26 *Jeshurun.* See note on 32:15. *rides … on the clouds.* See note on Ps 68:4.

33:27 *underneath are the everlasting arms.* See v. 12 and note.

33:29 *shield.* See note on Ge 15:1. *trample down their high places.* Or "tread on their heights" (see Mic 1:3 and note; cf. Dt 32:13). But see also NIV text note.

34:1 *Moses climbed Mount Nebo.* In obedience to the Lord's command in 32:48–52.

34:3 *Negev.* See note on Ge 12:9. *as far as Zoar.* See Isa 15:5 and note.

34:4 *land I promised.* See 1:8; Ge 12:1; 15:18 and note; Ex 33:1.

34:5 *servant of the LORD.* A special title used to refer to those whom the Lord, as the Great King, has taken into his service; they serve as members of God's royal administration. For example, it was used especially of Abraham (Ge 26:24), Moses (Ex 14:31; Jos 1:1), Joshua (Jos 24:29), David (2Sa 3:18; 7:5), the prophets (2Ki 9:7), Israel collectively (Isa 41:8–9), and even a foreign king the Lord used to carry out his purposes (Jer 25:9). See notes on Ex 14:31; Isa 41:8–9; 42:1–4.

34:6 *Beth Peor.* See note on 3:29.

34:7 *a hundred and twenty years old.* See 31:2; perhaps a round number, indicating three generations of about 40 years each (see Ac 7:23 and note).

34:8 *grieved … thirty days.* See Ge 50:3 and note.

34:10 *no prophet has risen in Israel like Moses.* See note on 18:15. *face to face.* See Nu 12:8 and note.

34:12 *no one has ever.* Until Jesus came, no one was superior to Moses. See Heb 3:1–6, where Moses the "*servant in* all God's house" (v. 5) is contrasted with Christ the "*son over* God's house" (v. 6).

The Conquest and the Ethical Question of War

Many readers of Joshua (and other OT books) are deeply troubled by the role that warfare plays in this account of God's dealings with his people. Not a few relieve their ethical scruples by ascribing the author's perspective to a pre-Christian (and sub-Christian) stage of moral development that the Christian, in the light of Christ's teaching, must repudiate and transcend. Hence the main thread of the narrative line of Joshua is an offense to them.

It must be remembered, however, that the book of Joshua does not address itself to the abstract ethical question of war as a means for gaining human ends. It can only be understood in the context of the history of redemption unfolding in the Pentateuch, with its interplay of divine grace and judgment. Of that story it is the direct continuation.

Joshua is not an epic account of Israel's heroic generation or the story of Israel's conquest of Canaan with the aid of her national deity. It is rather the story of how God, to whom the whole world belongs, at one stage in the history of redemption reconquered a portion of the earth from the powers of this world that had claimed it for themselves, defending their claims by force of arms and reliance on their false gods. It tells how God commissioned his people to serve as his army under the leadership of his servant Joshua, to take Canaan in his name out of the hands of the idolatrous and dissolute Canaanites (whose measure of sin was now full; see Ge 15:16 and note). It further tells how he aided them in the enterprise and gave them conditional tenancy in his land in fulfillment of the ancient pledge he had made to Israel's ancestors, Abraham, Isaac and Jacob (see note on Ge 12:1).

Joshua is the story of the kingdom of God breaking into the world of nations at a time when national and political entities were viewed as the creation of the gods and living proofs of their power. Thus the Lord's triumph over the Canaanites testified to the world that the God of Israel is the one true and living God, whose claim on the world is absolute. It was also a warning to the nations that the irresistible advance of the kingdom of God would ultimately disinherit all those who opposed it, giving place in the earth only to those who acknowledge and serve the Lord. At once an act of redemption and judgment, it gave notice of the outcome of history and anticipated the final destiny of humankind and the creation.

The battles for Canaan were therefore the Lord's war, undertaken at a particular time in the program of redemption. God gave his people under Joshua no commission or license to conquer the world with the sword but a particular, limited mission. The conquered land itself would not become Israel's national possession by right of conquest, but it belonged to the Lord. So the land had to be cleansed of all remnants of paganism. Its people and their wealth were not for Israel to seize as the booty of war from which to enrich themselves (as Achan tried to do, ch. 7) but were placed under God's ban (were to be devoted to God to dispense with as he pleased). On that land Israel was to establish a commonwealth faithful to the righteous rule of God and thus be a witness (and a blessing) to the nations. If Israel became unfaithful and conformed to Canaanite culture and practice, it would in turn lose its place in the Lord's land — as Israel almost did in the days of the judges, and as it eventually did in the exile.

War is a terrible curse that the human race brings on itself as it seeks to possess the earth by its own unrighteous ways. But it pales before the curse that awaits all those who do not heed God's testimony to himself or his warnings — those who oppose the rule of God and reject his offer of grace. The God of the second Joshua (Jesus) is the God of the first Joshua also. Although now for a time he reaches out to the whole world with the gospel (and commissions his people urgently to carry his offer of peace to all nations), the sword of his judgment waits in the wings — and his second Joshua will wield it (Rev 19:11 – 16; see notes there).

Joshua

INTRODUCTION

Title and Theological Theme

Joshua is a story of conquest and fulfilled promise for the people of God. After many years of slavery in Egypt and 40 years in the desert, the Israelites were finally allowed to enter the land promised to their fathers. Abraham, always a migrant, never possessed the country to which he was sent, but he left to his children the legacy of God's covenant that made them the eventual heirs of all of Canaan (see Ge 15:13,16,18; 17:8 and note). Joshua was appointed to turn that promise into reality.

Where Deuteronomy ends, the book of Joshua begins: The tribes of Israel are still camped on the east side of the Jordan River. The narrative opens with God's command to move forward and pass through the river on dry land. Then it relates the series of victories in central, southern and northern Canaan that gave the Israelites control of all the hill country and the Negev. It continues with a description of the tribal allotments and ends with Joshua's final addresses to the people. The theme of the book, therefore, is the establishment of God's people Israel in the Lord's land, the land he had promised to give them as their place of "rest" in the earth (see 1:13,15 and note; 21:44; 22:4; 23:1; see also Dt 3:20 and note; 12:9–10; 25:19; 1Ki 5:4 and note; 8:56). So the Great King's promise to the patriarchs and Moses to give the land of Canaan to the chosen people of his kingdom is now historically fulfilled (see 1:1–6; 21:43–45 and note).

A Quick Look

Author:

Unknown, though certain sections may derive from Joshua himself

Audience:

God's chosen people, the Israelites

Date:

Probably about 1390 B.C.

Theme:

Joshua leads the armies of Israel to victory over the Canaanites in the promised land.

In the story the book tells, three primary actors play a part: "the LORD" (as Israel's God), his servant Joshua, and his people Israel (the last a collective "character" in the story). We meet all three immediately in ch. 1, where all three are clearly presented in the distinctive roles they will play in the story that follows (see note on 1:1–18). Ch. 1 also introduces the reader to the main concern of the book as a whole.

The role of the central human actor in the events narrated here is reinforced by the name he bears. Earlier in his life Joshua was called simply Hoshea (Nu 13:8,16), meaning "salvation." But later

Moses changed his name to Joshua, meaning "The LORD saves" (or "The LORD gives victory"). When this same name (the Greek form of which is Jesus; see NIV text note on Mt 1:21) was given to Mary's firstborn son, it identified him as the servant of God who would complete what God did for Israel in a preliminary way through the first Joshua, namely, overcome all powers of evil in the world and bring God's people into their eternal "rest" (see Heb 4:1 – 11 and notes).

The theme of the book, therefore, is the establishment of God's people Israel in the Lord's land, the land he had promised to give them as their place of "rest" in the earth.

In the Hebrew Bible the book of Joshua initiates a division called the Former Prophets, including also Judges, Samuel and Kings. These are all historical in content but are written from a prophetic standpoint. They do more than merely record the nation's history from Moses to the fall of Judah in 586 B.C. They prophetically interpret God's covenant ways with Israel in history — how he fulfills and remains true to his promises (especially through his servants such as Joshua, the judges, Samuel and David) and how he deals with the waywardness of the Israelites. In Joshua it was the Lord who won the victories and "gave Israel all the land he had sworn to give their forefathers" (21:43).

Author and Date

In the judgment of many scholars Joshua was not written until the end of the period of the kings, some 800 years after the actual events. But there are significant reasons to question this conclusion and to place the time of composition much earlier. The earliest Jewish traditions (Talmud) claim that Joshua wrote his own book except for the final section about his funeral, which is attributed to Eleazar son of Aaron (the last verse must have been added by a later editor).

On at least two occasions the text reports writing at Joshua's command or by Joshua himself. We are told that when the tribes received their territories, Joshua instructed his men to "make a survey of the land and write a description of it" (18:8). Then in the last scene of the book, when Joshua led Israel in a renewal of the covenant with the Lord, it is said that "he drew up for them decrees and laws" (24:25). On another occasion the narrator speaks as if he had been a participant in the event; he uses the pronouns "we" and "us" (5:1,6).

Moreover, the author seems to be familiar with ancient names of cities, such as "the Jebusite city" (15:8; 18:16,28) for Jerusalem, Kiriath Arba (14:15; 15:54; 20:7; 21:11) for Hebron, and Greater Sidon (11:8; 19:28) for what later became simply Sidon. And Tyre is never mentioned, probably because in Joshua's day it had not yet developed into a port of major importance.

But if some features suggest an author of Joshua's own lifetime, others point to a writer of a somewhat later period. The account of the long day when the sun stood still at Aijalon is substantiated by a quotation from another source, the Book of Jashar (see 10:13 and note). This would hardly be natural for an eyewitness of the miracle who was writing shortly after it happened. Also, there are 12 instances where the phrase "until this day" occurs.

It seems safe to conclude that the book draws on early sources. It may date from the beginning of the monarchy. Some think that Samuel may have had a hand in shaping or compiling the materials of the book, but in fact we are unsure who the final author or editor was.

The Life of Joshua

Joshua's remarkable life was filled with excitement, variety, success and honor. He was known for his deep trust in God and as "a man in whom is the spirit" (Nu 27:18). As a youth he lived through the bitter realities of slavery in Egypt, but he also witnessed the supernatural plagues and the miracle of Israel's escape from the army of the Egyptians when the waters of the sea opened before them. In the Sinai peninsula it was Joshua who led the troops of Israel to victory over the Amalekites (Ex 17:8 – 13). He alone was allowed to accompany Moses up the holy mountain where the tablets of the law were received (Ex 24:13 – 14 [but see v. 18]). And it was he who stood watch at the temporary tent of meeting Moses set up before the tabernacle was erected (see Ex 33:11 and note).

Joshua was elected to represent his own tribe of Ephraim when the 12 spies were sent into Canaan to look over the land. Only Joshua and Caleb, representing the tribe of Judah, were ready to follow God's will and take immediate possession of the land (see Nu 14:26–34 and note on 14:28). The rest of the Israelites of that generation were condemned to die in the desert. Even Moses died short of the goal and was told to turn everything over to Joshua. God promised to guide and strengthen Joshua, just as he had Moses (Dt 31:23; cf. Jos 1:5 and note).

Joshua was God's chosen servant (see 24:29 and note on Dt 34:5) to bring Moses' work to completion and establish Israel in the promised land. To that special divine appointment he was faithful — as the leader of God's army, as the administrator of God's division of the land and as God's spokesman for promoting Israel's covenant faithfulness. In all this he was a striking OT type (foreshadowing) of Christ (see notes on Heb 4:1,6–8).

Historical Setting

At the time of the Israelite migration into Canaan the superpowers of the ancient Near East were relatively weak. The Hittites had virtually faded from the scene. Neither Babylon nor Egypt could maintain a standing military presence in Canaan, and the Assyrians would not send in their armies until centuries later.

As the tribes circled east of the Dead Sea, the Edomites refused them passage, so Israel bypassed them to the east. However, when Sihon and Og, two regional Amorite kings of Transjordan, tried to stop the Israelites, they were easily defeated and their lands occupied. Moab was forced to let Israel pass through her territory and camp in her plains. Also the Midianites were dealt a severe blow.

Biblical archaeologists call this period the Late Bronze Age (1550–1200 B.C.). Today thousands of artifacts give testimony to the richness of the Canaanite material culture, which was in many ways superior to that of the Israelites. When the ruins of the ancient kingdom of Ugarit were discovered at modern Ras Shamra on the northern coast of Syria (see chart, p. xxiii), a wealth of new information came to light concerning the domestic, commercial and religious life of the Canaanites. From a language close to Hebrew came stories of ancient kings and gods that revealed their immoral behavior and cruelty. In addition, pagan temples, altars, tombs and ritual vessels have been uncovered, throwing more light on the culture and customs of the peoples surrounding Israel.

Excavations at the ancient sites of Megiddo, Beth Shan and Gezer show how powerfully fortified these cities were and why they were not captured and occupied by Israel in Joshua's day. Many other fortified towns were taken, however, so that Israel became firmly established in the land as the dominant power. Apart from Jericho and Ai, Joshua is reported to have burned only Hazor (11:13), so attempts to date these events by destruction levels in the mounds of Canaan's ancient cities are questionable undertakings. It must also be remembered that other groups were involved in campaigns in the region about this time, among whom were Egyptian rulers and the Sea Peoples (including the Philistines). There had also been much intercity warfare among the Canaanites, and afterward the period of the judges was marked by general turbulence.

Only Joshua and Caleb were ready to follow God's will and take immediate possession of the land. The rest of the Israelites of that generation were condemned to die in the desert.

Much of the data from archaeology appears to support a date for Joshua's invasion c. 1250 B.C. This fits well with an exodus that would then have taken place 40 years earlier under the famous Rameses II, who ruled from the Nile delta at a city with the same name (Ex 1:11; see note on Ge 47:11). It also places Joseph in Egypt in a favorable situation. Four hundred years before Rameses II the pharaohs were the Semitic Hyksos, who also ruled from the delta near the land of Goshen.

On the other hand, a good case can be made for the traditional viewpoint that the invasion occurred c. 1406 B.C. The oppression would have taken place under Amunhotep II after the death of his father Thutmose III, who is known to have used slave labor in his building projects. The earlier date also fits better with the two numbers found in Jdg 11:26 and 1Ki 6:1, since it allows for an additional 150 years between Moses and the monarchy. See also Introductions to Genesis: Author and Date of Writing; Exodus: Chronology; Judges: Background; and note on 1Ki 6:1.

Outline

- I. The Entrance into the Land (1:1 — 5:12)
  - A. The Exhortations to Conquer (ch. 1)
  - B. The Reconnaissance of Jericho (ch. 2)
  - C. The Crossing of the Jordan (chs. 3 – 4)
  - D. The Consecration at Gilgal (5:1 – 12)
- II. The Conquest of the Land (5:13 — 12:24)
  - A. The Initial Battles (5:13 — 8:35)
    1. The victory at Jericho (5:13 — 6:27)
    2. The failure at Ai because of Achan's sin (ch. 7)
    3. The victory at Ai (8:1 – 29)
    4. The covenant renewed at Shechem (8:30 – 35)
  - B. The Campaign in the South (chs. 9 – 10)
    1. The treaty with the Gibeonites (ch. 9)
    2. The long day of Joshua (10:1 – 15)
    3. The southern cities conquered (10:16 – 43)
  - C. The Campaign in the North (ch. 11)
  - D. The Defeated Kings of Canaan (ch. 12)
- III. The Distribution of the Land (chs. 13 – 21)
  - A. The Areas Yet to Be Conquered (13:1 – 7)
  - B. The Land Assigned by Moses to the Tribes in Transjordan (13:8 – 33)
  - C. The Division of the Land of Canaan (chs. 14 – 19)
    1. Introduction (14:1 – 5)
    2. The town given to Caleb (14:6 – 15)
    3. The lands given to Judah and "Joseph" at Gilgal (chs. 15 – 17)
    4. The allotments for Benjamin, Simeon, Zebulun, Issachar, Asher, Naphtali and Dan (18:1 — 19:48)
    5. The town given to Joshua (19:49 – 51)
  - D. The Cities Assigned to the Levites (chs. 20 – 21)
    1. The 6 cities of refuge (ch. 20)
    2. The 48 cities of the priests and other Levites (ch. 21)
- IV. Epilogue: Tribal Unity and Loyalty to the Lord (chs. 22 – 24)
  - A. The Altar of Witness by the Jordan (ch. 22)
  - B. Joshua's Farewell Exhortation (ch. 23)
  - C. The Renewal of the Covenant at Shechem (24:1 – 28)
  - D. The Death and Burial of Joshua and Eleazar (24:29 – 33)

The LORD Commands Joshua

1 After the death of Moses the servant of the LORD,[a] the LORD said to Joshua[b] son of Nun, Moses' aide: 2"Moses my servant is dead. Now then, you and all these people, get ready to cross the Jordan River[c][d] into the land[e] I am about to give to them[f]—to the Israelites. 3I will give you every place where you set your foot,[g] as I promised Moses.[h] 4Your territory will extend from the desert to Lebanon,[i] and from the great river, the Euphrates[j]—all the Hittite[k] country—to the Great Sea[a] on the west.[l] 5No one will be able to stand up against you[m] all the days of your life. As I was with[n] Moses, so I will be with you; I will never leave you nor forsake[o] you.

6"Be strong[p] and courageous,[q] because you will lead these people to inherit the land I swore to their forefathers[r] to give them. 7Be strong and very courageous. Be careful to obey[s] all the law[t] my servant Moses[u] gave you; do not turn from it to the right or to the left,[v] that you may be successful wherever you go.[w] 8Do not let this Book of the Law[x] depart from your mouth;[y] meditate[z] on it day and night, so that you may be careful to do everything written in it. Then you will be prosperous and successful.[a] 9Have I not commanded you? Be strong and courageous. Do not be terrified;[b] do not be discouraged,[c] for the LORD your God will be with you wherever you go."[d]

10So Joshua ordered the officers of the people:[e] 11"Go through the camp[f] and tell the people, 'Get your supplies[g] ready. Three days[h] from now you will cross the Jordan[i] here to go in and take possession[j] of the land the LORD your God is giving you for your own.'"

12But to the Reubenites, the Gadites and the half-tribe of Manasseh,[k] Joshua said, 13"Remember the command that Moses the servant of the LORD gave you: 'The LORD your God is giving you rest[l] and has granted you this land.' 14Your wives,[m] your children and your livestock may stay in the land[n] that Moses gave you east of the Jordan, but all your fighting men, fully armed,[o] must cross over ahead of your brothers.[p] You are to help your brothers 15until the LORD gives them rest, as he has

[a] 4 That is, the Mediterranean

1:1 [a] Ex 14:31; Dt 34:5; Rev 15:3 [b] S Ex 17:9 **1:2** [c] S Nu 13:29 [d] S Nu 35:10 [e] S Ge 15:14 [f] Ge 12:7; Dt 1:25 **1:3** [g] S Dt 11:24 [h] Ge 50:24; Nu 13:2; Dt 1:8 **1:4** [i] S Dt 3:25 [j] S Ge 2:14 [k] S Ge 10:15; 23:10; Ex 3:8 [l] Nu 34:2-12; Ezr 4:20 **1:5** [m] S Dt 7:24 [n] ver 17; S Ge 26:3; S 39:2; Jdg 6:12; 1Sa 10:7; Jer 1:8; 30:11 [o] S Ge 28:15; S Dt 4:31 **1:6** [p] 2Sa 2:7; 1Ki 2:2; Isa 41:6; Joel 3:9-10 [q] S Dt 1:21; S 31:6; S Jdg 5:21 [r] Jer 3:18; 7:7 **1:7** [s] Dt 29:9; 1Ki 2:3; 3:3 [t] Ezr 7:26; Ps 78:10; 119:136; Isa 42:24; Jer 26:4-6; 32:23; 44:10 [u] ver 2, 15; S Nu 12:7; Job 1:8; 42:7 [v] S Dt 5:32; Jos 23:6 [w] ver 9; S Dt 4:2; 5:33; S 11:8; Jos 11:15 **1:8** [x] S Dt 28:61; S Ps 147:19 [y] S Ex 4:15; Isa 59:21 [z] S Ge 24:63 [a] Dt 29:9; 1Sa 18:14; Ps 1:1-3; Isa 52:13; 53:10; Jer 23:5 **1:9** [b] S Dt 31:6; Jos 10:8; 2Ki 19:6; Isa 35:4; 37:6 [c] S Dt 1:21; Job 4:5 [d] S ver 7; Dt 31:7-8; Jer 1:8 **1:10** [e] S Dt 1:15 **1:11** [f] Jos 3:2 [g] 1Sa 17:22; Isa 10:28 [h] S Ge 40:13 [i] S Nu 35:10 [j] S Nu 33:53 **1:12** [k] Nu 32:33 **1:13** [l] S Ex 33:14; Ps 55:6; Isa 11:10; 28:12; 30:15; 32:18; 40:31; Jer 6:16; 45:3; La 5:5 **1:14** [m] Dt 3:19 [n] S Nu 32:26 [o] S Ex 13:18 [p] Jos 4:12

1:1–18 The Lord initiates the action by charging Joshua, his chosen replacement for Moses (see Dt 31:1–8), to lead Israel across the Jordan and take possession of the promised land. He urges courage and promises success—but only if Israel obeys the law of God that Moses has given them. The chapter consists of speeches significant in their content and order: The Lord commands Joshua as his appointed leader over his people (vv. 1–9); Joshua, as the Lord's representative, addresses Israel (vv. 10–15); Israel responds to Joshua as the Lord's representative and successor to Moses (vv. 16–18). Thus the events of the book are set in motion and the roles of the main actors indicated (see Introduction: Title and Theological Theme).

1:1 *After the death of Moses.* Immediately the time and occasion of the action are set forth, showing that the story will continue where Deuteronomy ended, with the death of Moses. Cf. "After the death of Joshua" (Jdg 1:1; see note there). *servant of the LORD.* See notes on Ex 14:31; Dt 34:5; Ps 18 title; Isa 41:8–9; 42:1. *Moses' aide.* The title by which Joshua served for many years as second in command (see Nu 11:28; see also Ex 17:9 and note; 24:13; 33:11; Dt 1:38).

1:2 *Jordan River.* The flow of the Jordan near Jericho was not large during most of the year (less than 100 feet wide), but at flood stage in the spring it filled its wider bed, which at places was a mile wide and far more treacherous to cross (see 3:15 and note). *land I am about to give to them.* A central theme of the Pentateuch (see Ge 12:1; 15:18 and notes; 50:24; Ex 3:8; 23:31; Dt 1:8). The book of Joshua relates the fulfillment of this promise of God.

1:3–5 See Dt 11:24–25.

1:4 The dimensions of the land promised to Israel vary (compare this text and Ge 15:18 with Dt 34:1–4), but these are the farthest limits—conquered and held only by David and Solomon. Canaan was still called "Hatti-land" centuries after the Hittites had withdrawn to the north. But Joshua was to take all he set out to conquer; wherever he set his foot was his (v. 3). His victories gave the 12 tribes control over most of the central hill country and much of the Negev.

1:5 *I will be with you.* To direct, sustain and assure success (see notes on Ge 26:3; Jer 1:8).

1:6 *land I swore to their forefathers.* The long-awaited inheritance pledged to the descendants of Abraham (Ge 15:7,8–21) and of Jacob (Ge 28:13).

1:7 *Be careful to obey.* Success was not guaranteed unconditionally (see Dt 8:1; 11:8–9,22–25).

1:8 See note on Ge 12:1. *Book of the Law.* See Dt 28:58,61; 29:20–21,27; 30:10; 31:24. *mouth; meditate.* See Ps 1:2. In the ancient world, reading written texts and even meditating on them were rarely completely silent (see Ex 13:9; Dt 30:14; Ps 19:14; 119:13; Ac 8:30 and note). *day and night.* See Ps 1:2.

1:9 *Have I not commanded you?* A rhetorical question that emphasizes the authority of the speaker.

1:10 *Joshua ordered.* At this point Joshua assumes full command. *officers.* May refer to those whom Moses had appointed over the divisions within the tribes (Ex 18:21; Dt 1:15).

1:11 *supplies.* Foodstuffs needed for the next several days' march.

1:12–15 The threat from the two kings of Transjordan was overcome by military victory and the occupation of the lands north of Moab and east of the Jordan River. The two and a half tribes who asked to remain had been ordered by Moses to send their fighting men across with the rest to conquer Canaan (Nu 21:21–35; 32:1–27). The conquest of the promised land must be an undertaking by all Israel.

1:13,15 *rest.* An important OT concept (see notes on Dt 3:20; 2Sa 7:1,11), implying secure borders, peace with neighboring countries and absence of threat to life and wellbeing within the land (see 1Ki 5:4; 8:56 and notes).

1:14 *your fighting men.* Those 20 years old or more (see Nu 1:3,18–45; 26:1–4) who were fit for the rigors of war.

done for you, and until they too have tak-
en possession of the land that the LORD
your God is giving them. After that, you
may go back and occupy your own land,
which Moses the servant of the LORD gave
you east of the Jordan toward the sunrise."[q]
16Then they answered Joshua, "Whatever you have commanded us we will do,
and wherever you send us we will go.[r]
17Just as we fully obeyed Moses, so we
will obey you.[s] Only may the LORD your
God be with you as he was with Moses.
18Whoever rebels against your word and
does not obey[t] your words, whatever you
may command them, will be put to death.
Only be strong and courageous![u]"

Rahab and the Spies

2 Then Joshua son of Nun secretly sent
two spies[v] from Shittim.[w] "Go, look
over[x] the land," he said, "especially Jericho.[y]" So they went and entered the house
of a prostitute[a] named Rahab[z] and stayed
there.
2The king of Jericho was told, "Look!
Some of the Israelites have come here tonight to spy out the land." 3So the king
of Jericho sent this message to Rahab:[a]
"Bring out the men who came to you and
entered your house, because they have
come to spy out the whole land."
4But the woman had taken the two men[b]
and hidden them.[c] She said, "Yes, the men
came to me, but I did not know where they
had come from. 5At dusk, when it was
time to close the city gate,[d] the men left. I
don't know which way they went. Go after them quickly. You may catch up with
them."[e] 6(But she had taken them up to
the roof and hidden them under the stalks
of flax[f] she had laid out on the roof.)[g] 7So
the men set out in pursuit of the spies on
the road that leads to the fords of the Jordan,[h] and as soon as the pursuers[i] had
gone out, the gate was shut.
8Before the spies lay down for the night,
she went up on the roof[j] 9and said to them,
"I know that the LORD has given this land
to you and that a great fear[k] of you has
fallen on us, so that all who live in this
country are melting in fear because of you.
10We have heard how the LORD dried up[l]
the water of the Red Sea[b] for you when
you came out of Egypt,[m] and what you
did to Sihon and Og,[n] the two kings of the
Amorites[o] east of the Jordan,[p] whom you
completely destroyed.[c q] 11When we heard
of it, our hearts melted[r] and everyone's
courage failed[s] because of you,[t] for the
LORD your God[u] is God in heaven above
and on the earth[v] below. 12Now then,
please swear to me[w] by the LORD that you
will show kindness[x] to my family, because
I have shown kindness to you. Give me a

[a] *1* Or possibly *an innkeeper* [b] *10* Hebrew *Yam Suph*; that is, Sea of Reeds [c] *10* The Hebrew term refers to the irrevocable giving over of things or persons to the LORD, often by totally destroying them.

1:15 [q] Nu 32:20-22; Jos 22:1-4 **1:16** [r] S Nu 27:20; S 32:25 **1:17** [s] S Nu 27:20 **1:18** [t] S Nu 32:25 [u] S Dt 1:21; S 31:6 **2:1** [v] S ver 4; S Ge 42:9 [w] S Nu 25:1; Jos 3:1; Joel 3:18 [x] S Nu 21:32; Jdg 18:2 [y] S Nu 33:48 [z] Jos 6:17, 25; S Heb 11:31 **2:3** [a] Jos 6:23 **2:4** [b] ver 1; Jos 6:22 [c] Jos 6:17 **2:5** [d] Jdg 5:8; 9:35; 16:2 [e] S Heb 11:31 **2:6** [f] Jdg 15:14; Pr 31:13; Isa 19:9 [g] S Ex 1:17, 19; Jos 6:25; 2Sa 17:19 **2:7** [h] Nu 22:1; Jdg 3:28; 7:24; 12:5, 6; Isa 16:2 [i] ver 16, 22 **2:8** [j] S Dt 22:8; Jdg 16:27; 2Sa 16:22; Ne 8:16; Isa 15:3; 22:1; Jer 32:29 **2:9** [k] S Ge 35:5; S Ex 15:14 **2:10** [l] S Ge 8:1; Ex 14:21; Jos 3:17; Ps 74:15 [m] S Nu 23:22 [n] S Nu 21:21 [o] S Ge 10:16; S 14:7 [p] Jos 9:10 [q] S Nu 21:2 **2:11** [r] S Ge 42:28 [s] S Dt 2:25; Ps 107:26; Jnh 1:5 [t] Ex 15:14; Jos 5:1; 7:5; 2Sa 4:1; Ps 22:14; Isa 13:7; 19:1; Jer 51:30; Na 2:10 [u] 2Ki 5:15; 19:15; Da 6:26 [v] S Ge 14:19; S Nu 20:14 **2:12** [w] S Ge 24:8; S 47:31 [x] S Ge 24:12; Ru 3:10

1:18 *Whoever rebels.* Having just taken the oath of allegiance to Joshua, they now agree to the death penalty for any rebellious act (e.g., the sin of Achan, 7:15; see note there). *be strong and courageous.* The people's words of encouragement to Joshua echo and reinforce those from the Lord (vv. 6–7,9).

2:1–24 The mission of the two spies and the account of Rahab. The practice of reconnaissance and espionage is as old as war itself (cf. Jdg 7:10–11; 1Sa 26:6–12). Rahab became a convert to the God of Israel and a famous woman among the Hebrews. She is honored in the NT for her faith (Heb 11:31) and good works (see Jas 2:25 and note).

In this first encounter of the Israelites (represented by the two spies) and the Canaanites (represented by Rahab and the men sent by the king of Jericho) the outcome of the mission on which God had sent his army under Joshua (ch.1) is foreshadowed, and God's assurances of success (1:5) are confirmed.

2:1 *sent ... from Shittim.* The invasion point was in the plains of Moab facing toward the Jordan and Jericho (Nu 33:48–49). The Hebrew word *Shittim* means "acacia trees," which grow in the semi-arid conditions of the desert. *especially Jericho.* The primary focus of the spies. It was a fortified city, was well supplied with water by strong springs and was located just five miles west of the Jordan (see note on 6:1). *prostitute.* Josephus and other early sources refer to Rahab as an "innkeeper" (see NIV text note), but see Heb 11:31; Jas 2:25.

2:2 *king of Jericho.* The major cities of Canaan were in reality small kingdoms, each ruled by a local king (attested also in the Amarna letters of the 14th century B.C.; see chart, p. xxii).

2:6 *hidden ... under the stalks of flax.* Rooftops in the Near East are still used for drying grain or stalks. Rahab's cunning saved the lives of the two Israelites but put her own life in jeopardy.

2:7 *fords of the Jordan.* Shallow crossings of the Jordan, where the depth of normal flow averages only three feet.

2:9–11 Rahab's confession has a significant concentric structure:

a. "I know";
 b. "a great fear ... has fallen on us ... all who live in this country";
  c. "We have heard";
 bb. "our hearts melted and everyone's courage failed";
aa. "the LORD your God is God."

Rahab's personal confession forms the outer frame (a.-aa.); the inner frame (b.-bb.) offers the military intelligence that the spies report back to Joshua; the center (c., v. 10) sums up the news about the Lord that occasioned both the Canaanite fear and Rahab's abandonment of Canaan and its gods to side with the Lord and Israel. That the hearts of the Canaanites were "melting in fear" (v. 9) was vital information to the spies. Rahab's word is the decisive turning point in the narrator's account of this event. The whole outcome of the spies' venture into Jericho hinges on her actions.

2:10 *completely destroyed.* See NIV text note.

2:12 *show kindness to my family.* The Hebrew for "kindness" is frequently translated "love" or "unfailing love" and often summarizes God's covenant favor toward his people or the love

sure sign[y] 13that you will spare the lives
of my father and mother, my brothers and
sisters, and all who belong to them,[z] and
that you will save us from death."
14"Our lives for your lives!"[a] the men
assured her. "If you don't tell what we are
doing, we will treat you kindly and faithfully[b] when the LORD gives us the land."
15So she let them down by a rope[c]
through the window,[d] for the house she
lived in was part of the city wall. 16Now
she had said to them, "Go to the hills[e] so
the pursuers[f] will not find you. Hide yourselves there three days[g] until they return,
and then go on your way."[h]
17The men said to her, "This oath[i] you
made us swear will not be binding on us
18unless, when we enter the land, you
have tied this scarlet cord[j] in the window[k]
through which you let us down, and unless you have brought your father and
mother, your brothers and all your family[l] into your house. 19If anyone goes outside your house into the street, his blood
will be on his own head;[m] we will not be
responsible. As for anyone who is in the
house with you, his blood will be on our
head[n] if a hand is laid on him. 20But if you
tell what we are doing, we will be released
from the oath you made us swear.[o]"
21"Agreed," she replied. "Let it be as you
say." So she sent them away and they departed. And she tied the scarlet cord[p] in
the window.[q]

22When they left, they went into the
hills and stayed there three days,[r] until
the pursuers[s] had searched all along the
road and returned without finding them.
23Then the two men started back. They
went down out of the hills, forded the river and came to Joshua son of Nun and
told him everything that had happened to
them. 24They said to Joshua, "The LORD
has surely given the whole land into our
hands;[t] all the people are melting in fear[u]
because of us."

Crossing the Jordan

3 Early in the morning Joshua and all
the Israelites set out from Shittim[v] and
went to the Jordan,[w] where they camped
before crossing over. 2After three days[x]
the officers[y] went throughout the camp,[z]
3giving orders to the people: "When you
see the ark of the covenant[a] of the LORD
your God, and the priests,[b] who are Levites,[c] carrying it, you are to move out
from your positions and follow it. 4Then
you will know which way to go, since
you have never been this way before.
But keep a distance of about a thousand
yards[a d] between you and the ark; do not
go near it."
5Joshua told the people, "Consecrate

[a] *4* Hebrew *about two thousand cubits* (about 900 meters)

2:12 [y]S Ge 24:14; S Ex 3:12; Jos 4:6; 1Sa 2:34; 2Ki 19:29 **2:13** [z]ver 18; Jos 6:23 **2:14** [a]1Ki 20:39,42; 2Ki 10:24 [b]S Ge 47:29 **2:15** [c]Jer 38:6,11 [d]ver 18,21; Ge 26:8; Jdg 5:28; 1Sa 19:12 **2:16** [e]S Ge 14:10 [f]S ver 7 [g]ver 22 [h]S Heb 11:31 **2:17** [i]S Ge 24:8 **2:18** [j]ver 21 [k]S ver 15 [l]S ver 13 **2:19** [m]S Lev 20:9 [n]Mt 27:25 **2:20** [o]S Ge 24:8; S 47:31 **2:21** [p]ver 18 [q]S ver 15 **2:22** [r]ver 16 [s]S ver 7 **2:24** [t]Jos 10:8; 11:6; Jdg 3:28; 7:9,14; 20:28; 1Sa 14:10 [u]S Ex 15:15 **3:1** [v]S Jos 2:1 [w]S Ge 13:10; Job 40:23 **3:2** [x]S Ge 40:13; Jos 2:16 [y]S Dt 1:15 [z]Jos 1:11 **3:3** [a]S Nu 10:33 [b]ver 8,17; Nu 4:15; Dt 31:9; 1Ki 8:3 [c]1Sa 6:15 **3:4** [d]Nu 35:5

that people are to show to others. Rahab had acted toward the spies as a friend of Israel, and now she asks that Israel treat her and her family similarly. *sure sign.* They gave her their oath to spare her whole family (v. 14).

2:14 *kindly and faithfully.* The terms of the pledge made by the spies echo Rahab's request (v. 12). *when the LORD gives us the land.* Rahab's words had added to their assurance of the inevitable victory of the Israelites over Jericho.

2:15 *the house … was part of the city wall.* There is archaeological evidence that the people of Jericho would occasionally integrate living quarters into the city wall. Although this evidence predates the time of Joshua, it may still serve to illumine this verse. The Late Bronze fortifications at Jericho may have included a casemate wall (a hollow wall with partitions), and Rahab may have occupied one or more rooms inside it.

2:16 *Go to the hills.* The opposite direction from the fords of the Jordan where the spies' pursuers had gone (see v. 7).

2:18 *scarlet cord in the window.* The function of the red marker was similar to that of the blood of the Passover lamb when the Lord struck down the firstborn of Egypt (see Ex 12:13,22–23 and notes). The early church viewed the blood-colored cord as a type (symbol) of Christ's atonement.

2:19 *his blood will be on our head.* A vow that accepted responsibility for the death of another, with its related guilt and the retribution meted out by either relatives or the state.

2:22 *into the hills.* Directly west of ancient Jericho were the high, rugged hills of the central mountain ridge in Canaan. They are honeycombed with caves, making the concealment and escape of the two spies relatively easy.

2:24 The spies' mission (see v. 1) concludes with a reassuring word to Joshua (cf. Nu 13:26–33).

3:1—4:24 Details of the river crossing and the memorial of 12 stones set up in the camp at Gilgal. The great significance of this account can hardly be overemphasized, since it marks the crossing of the boundary into the promised land and parallels the miracle of the Red Sea crossing in the exodus (Ex 14–15). The Israelites' faith in the God of their ancestors was renewed and strengthened when it was about to be most severely challenged, while at the same time the Canaanites' fear was greatly increased (5:1). In this account the author uses an overlay technique in which, having narrated the crossing to its conclusion (ch. 3), he returns to various points in the event to enlarge on several details: the stones for a memorial (4:1–9); the successful crossing by all Israel (4:10–14); the renewed flow of the river after the crossing was completed (4:15–18). The final paragraph of ch. 4 (vv. 19–24) picks up the story again from 3:17 and completes the account by noting Israel's encampment at Gilgal and the erecting of the stone memorial.

3:3 *ark of the covenant.* The most sacred of the tabernacle furnishings (see Ex 25:10–22 and notes). Since it signified the Lord's throne, the Lord himself went into the Jordan ahead of his people as he led them into the land of rest (see Nu 10:33–36 and note on 10:35–36; Dt 31:7).

3:4 *distance of about a thousand yards.* There was evidently a line of march, with the priests and ark leading the way. Respect for the sacred symbol of the Lord's holy presence accounts for this gap between the people and the priests bearing the ark.

3:5 *Consecrate yourselves.* Before their meeting with God at Sinai this had involved washing all their garments as well as their bodies, and also abstinence from sexual intercourse (see Ex 19:10,14–15 and note on 19:15).

yourselves,[e] for tomorrow the LORD will do amazing things[f] among you."

6 Joshua said to the priests, "Take up the ark of the covenant and pass on ahead of the people." So they took it up and went ahead of them.

7 And the LORD said to Joshua, "Today I will begin to exalt you[g] in the eyes of all Israel, so they may know that I am with you as I was with Moses.[h] 8 Tell the priests[i] who carry the ark of the covenant: 'When you reach the edge of the Jordan's waters, go and stand in the river.' "

9 Joshua said to the Israelites, "Come here and listen to the words of the LORD your God. 10 This is how you will know that the living God[j] is among you[k] and that he will certainly drive out before you the Canaanites, Hittites,[l] Hivites, Perizzites,[m] Girgashites, Amorites and Jebusites.[n] 11 See, the ark of the covenant of the Lord of all the earth[o] will go into the Jordan ahead of you.[p] 12 Now then, choose twelve men[q] from the tribes of Israel, one from each tribe. 13 And as soon as the priests who carry the ark of the LORD—the Lord of all the earth[r]—set foot in the Jordan, its waters flowing downstream[s] will be cut off[t] and stand up in a heap.[u]"

14 So when the people broke camp to cross the Jordan, the priests carrying the ark of the covenant[v] went ahead[w] of them. 15 Now the Jordan[x] is at flood stage[y] all during harvest.[z] Yet as soon as the priests who carried the ark reached the Jordan and their feet touched the water's edge, 16 the water from upstream stopped flowing.[a] It piled up in a heap[b] a great distance away, at a town called Adam in the vicinity of Zarethan,[c] while the water flowing down[d] to the Sea of the Arabah[e] (the Salt Sea[a][f]) was completely cut off.[g] So the people crossed over opposite Jericho.[h] 17 The priests[i] who carried the ark of the covenant of the LORD stood firm on dry ground in the middle of the Jordan,[j] while all Israel passed by until the whole nation had completed the crossing on dry ground.[k]

4 When the whole nation had finished crossing the Jordan,[l] the LORD said to Joshua, 2 "Choose twelve men[m] from among the people, one from each tribe, 3 and tell them to take up twelve stones[n] from the middle of the Jordan[o] from right where the priests stood and to carry them over with you and put them down at the place where you stay tonight.[p]"

4 So Joshua called together the twelve men[q] he had appointed from the Israelites, one from each tribe, 5 and said to them, "Go over before the ark of the LORD your God into the middle of the Jordan.[r] Each of you is to take up a stone on his shoulder, according to the number of the tribes of the Israelites, 6 to serve as a sign[s] among you. In the future, when your children[t]

3:5 [e] S Ex 29:1; S Lev 11:44 [f] Jdg 6:13; 1Ch 16:9, 24; Ps 26:7; 75:1 **3:7** [g] Jos 4:14; 1Ch 29:25 [h] Jos 1:5 **3:8** [i] S ver 3 **3:10** [j] Dt 5:26; 1Sa 17:26, 36; 2Ki 19:4, 16; Ps 18:46; 42:2; 84:2; Isa 37:4, 17; Jer 10:10; 23:36; Da 6:26; Hos 1:10; S Mt 16:16 [k] S Dt 7:21 [l] S Ge 26:34 [m] Jos 17:15; 24:11; Jdg 1:4; 3:5 [n] S Ex 3:8; S 23:23; S Dt 7:1; Jos 9:1; 11:3; 12:8; Jdg 19:11; 1Ch 11:4 **3:11** [o] ver 13; Ex 19:5; Dt 10:14; Job 9:10; 28:24; 41:11; Ps 50:12; 97:5; Zec 6:5 [p] S Dt 9:3 **3:12** [q] Jos 4:2, 4 **3:13** [r] S ver 11 [s] ver 16 [t] Jos 4:7 [u] S Ex 14:22; S Isa 11:15 **3:14** [v] Ps 132:8 [w] Ac 7:44-45 **3:15** [x] 2Ki 2:6 [y] Jos 4:18; 1Ch 12:15; Isa 8:7 [z] S Ge 8:22 **3:16** [a] Ps 66:6; 74:15; 114:3 [b] Job 38:37; Ps 33:7 [c] 1Ki 4:12; 7:46 [d] ver 13 [e] S Dt 1:1 [f] S Ge 14:3 [g] S Ge 8:1; S Ex 14:22 [h] 2Ki 2:4 **3:17** [i] S ver 3 [j] Jos 4:3, 5, 8, 9, 10 [k] S Ex 14:22; S Jos 2:10 **4:1** [l] Dt 27:2 **4:2** [m] S Jos 3:12 **4:3** [n] ver 20 [o] S Jos 3:17 [p] ver 19 **4:4** [q] S Jos 3:12 **4:5** [r] S Jos 3:17 **4:6** [s] S Jos 2:12 [t] S Ex 10:2

[a] *16* That is, the Dead Sea

3:7 *I will begin to exalt you.* A prime objective for the divine intervention at the Jordan was to validate the leadership of Joshua. With a miraculous event so much like that of the Red Sea crossing, Joshua's position as the Lord's servant would be shown to be comparable to that of Moses.

3:10 *This is how you will know.* The manner by which God is about to bring Israel across the Jordan River, the eastern boundary of the promised land, will bring assurance that the one true God is with them and that he will surely dislodge the present inhabitants of Canaan. Two fundamental issues are at stake: (1) Who is the true and mighty God—the God of Israel or the god on whom the Canaanites depend (Baal, who was believed to reign as king among the gods because he had triumphed over the sea-god)? By opening the way through the flooded Jordan the Lord would show both Israel and the Canaanites that he is Lord over the waters (as he was at the Red Sea, at the flood and at creation) and that he is able to establish his own order in the world. See 1Ki 20:23; 2Ki 18:32–35 and note on 18:33–35. (2) Who has the rightful claim to the land—the Lord or the Canaanites? (For the juridical aspect of such wars see Jdg 11:27.) By passing safely through the Jordan at the head of his army the Lord showed the rightness of his claim on the land. In the ancient Near East a common way for obtaining the judicial verdict of the gods was by compelling the accused to submit to trial by water ordeal. Usually this involved casting them into a river (if the accused drowned, the gods had found them guilty; if not, the gods had declared them innocent). For another form of trial by water ordeal see Nu 5:15–28 and note. Significantly, the Lord would enter the Jordan first and then remain there until his whole army had crossed safely over. Thus his claim to the land was vindicated before the eyes of all who heard about it. And it was his claim, not Israel's; they came through the Jordan only with him and as his army, "baptized" into his service. *Canaanites ... Jebusites.* See notes on Ge 9:25; 10:6,15–16; 13:7; 15:16; 23:3; Ex 3:8; Jdg 3:3; 6:10.

3:12 *choose twelve men.* Joshua seems to anticipate the Lord's instructions concerning a stone monument of the event (see 4:2–3 and note on 4:9).

3:13 *cut off.* Blocked, stopped in its flow. *stand up in a heap.* The Hebrew for "heap" is found here, in v. 16 and also in the poetic accounts of the Red Sea crossing (Ex 15:8; Ps 78:13). It is possible that God used a physical means (such as a landslide) to dam up the Jordan at the place called Adam (v. 16), near the entrance of the Jabbok River. (As recently as 1927 a blockage of the water in this area was recorded that lasted over 20 hours.) But if so, the miraculous element is not diminished (see Ex 14:21 and note).

3:15 *at flood stage.* Because of the spring rains and the melting of snow on Mount Hermon (see 1:2 and note). *harvest.* Grain harvest took place in April and May. *as soon as.* The stoppage nearly 20 miles upstream (v. 16) would have happened several hours earlier to make the events coincide.

3:17 *The priests who carried the ark ... stood firm on dry ground in the middle of the Jordan.* Signifying that the Lord himself remained in the place of danger—under the threat of the waters of judgment—until all Israel had crossed the Jordan.

4:6 *What do these stones mean?* A stone monument was commonly used as a memorial to remind future generations of

ask you, 'What do these stones mean?'[u]
7tell them that the flow of the Jordan was
cut off[v] before the ark of the covenant of
the LORD. When it crossed the Jordan, the
waters of the Jordan were cut off. These
stones are to be a memorial[w] to the people
of Israel forever."
8So the Israelites did as Joshua commanded them. They took twelve stones[x]
from the middle of the Jordan,[y] according to the number of the tribes of the
Israelites, as the LORD had told Joshua;[z]
and they carried them over with them to
their camp, where they put them down.
9Joshua set up the twelve stones[a] that had
been[a] in the middle of the Jordan at the
spot where the priests who carried the ark
of the covenant had stood. And they are
there to this day.[b]
10Now the priests who carried the ark
remained standing in the middle of the
Jordan until everything the LORD had commanded Joshua was done by the people,
just as Moses had directed Joshua. The
people hurried over, 11and as soon as all of
them had crossed, the ark of the LORD and
the priests came to the other side while
the people watched. 12The men of Reuben,[c] Gad[d] and the half-tribe of Manasseh[e] crossed over, armed, in front of the
Israelites,[f] as Moses had directed them.[g]
13About forty thousand armed for battle[h]
crossed over[i] before the LORD to the plains
of Jericho for war.
14That day the LORD exalted[j] Joshua in
the sight of all Israel; and they revered him
all the days of his life, just as they had revered Moses.

4:6 [u]ver 21; Ex 12:26; S 13:14 **4:7** [v]Jos 3:13 [w]S Ex 28:12 **4:8** [x]Ex 28:21 [y]S Jos 3:17 [z]ver 20 **4:9** [a]S Ge 28:18; Jos 24:26; 1Sa 7:12 [b]S Ge 35:20 **4:12** [c]S Ge 29:32 [d]S Ge 30:11 [e]S Ge 41:51 [f]S Nu 32:27 [g]Nu 32:29 **4:13** [h]S Ex 13:18 [i]S Nu 32:17 **4:14** [j]S Jos 3:7 **4:16** [k]Ex 25:22 **4:18** [l]Ex 14:27 [m]S Jos 3:15 **4:19** [n]S Dt 11:30 **4:20** [o]ver 3,8 **4:21** [p]S ver 6 **4:22** [q]S Ex 14:22 **4:23** [r]Ex 14:19-22 **4:24** [s]1Ki 8:60; 18:36; 2Ki 5:15; Ps 67:2; 83:18; 106:8; Isa 37:20; 52:10 [t]Ex 15:16; 1Ch 29:12; Ps 44:3; 89:13; 98:1; 118:15-16 [u]S Ex 14:31 **5:1** [v]S Nu 13:29

15Then the LORD said to Joshua, 16"Command the priests carrying the ark of the
Testimony[k] to come up out of the Jordan."
17So Joshua commanded the priests,
"Come up out of the Jordan."
18And the priests came up out of the
river carrying the ark of the covenant of
the LORD. No sooner had they set their feet
on the dry ground than the waters of the
Jordan returned to their place[l] and ran at
flood stage[m] as before.
19On the tenth day of the first month
the people went up from the Jordan and
camped at Gilgal[n] on the eastern border of
Jericho. 20And Joshua set up at Gilgal the
twelve stones[o] they had taken out of the
Jordan. 21He said to the Israelites, "In the
future when your descendants ask their fathers, 'What do these stones mean?'[p] 22tell
them, 'Israel crossed the Jordan on dry
ground.'[q] 23For the LORD your God dried
up the Jordan before you until you had
crossed over. The LORD your God did to
the Jordan just what he had done to the
Red Sea[b] when he dried it up before us
until we had crossed over.[r] 24He did this
so that all the peoples of the earth might
know[s] that the hand of the LORD is powerful[t] and so that you might always fear the
LORD your God.[u]"

Circumcision at Gilgal

5 Now when all the Amorite kings west
of the Jordan and all the Canaanite
kings along the coast[v] heard how the LORD

[a] 9 Or *Joshua also set up twelve stones* [b] 23 Hebrew *Yam Suph*; that is, Sea of Reeds

what had happened at a particular place (see v. 9; 24:26 and notes; 1Sa 7:12).
4:9 *Joshua set up the twelve stones.* Each tribe brought a stone for the monument from the riverbed to the new campsite at Gilgal, and Joshua constructed the monument there (see v. 20). An alternative translation suggests that Joshua set up a second pile in the middle of the river (see NIV text note; but see also note on 3:1 — 4:24). The monument at Gilgal was the first of many others that came to dot the countryside as memorials to how Israel came to be established in the promised land: the ruins of Jericho (6:26), the pile of rocks raised over Achan's body (see 7:26 and note), the pile of rocks raised over the body of the king of Ai (see 8:29 and note), the altar of covenant renewal on Mount Ebal (8:30 – 31), the pile of rocks that closed the cave where five Canaanite kings were buried (see 10:27 and note), the altar built in the Jordan Valley as a witness to the tribes west of the Jordan that those east of the Jordan had equal share in the Lord (see 22:26 – 28 and note on 22:27) and the stone of covenant witness that Joshua set up at Shechem (see 24:26 – 27 and note on 24:26).
4:13 *About forty thousand.* Seems too few for the number of men listed in Nu 26 for Reuben, Gad and half of Manasseh; the contingents were very likely representative since it would have been imprudent to leave the people undefended who settled in Transjordan (cf. 22:8, "brothers"; Nu 32:17 and note).
4:14 See 3:7 and note.
4:19 *tenth day of the first month.* The day the Passover lamb was to be selected (Ex 12:3). *Gilgal.* Usually identified with the ruins at Khirbet el-Mafjer, two miles northeast of Jericho.
4:22 *Israel crossed the Jordan.* Earlier Joshua had instructed Israel to answer that the waters of the Jordan were "cut off" so that "the ark of the covenant of the LORD" could cross the Jordan (vv. 6 – 7). That was the primary fact to be remembered: God crossed the Jordan to take possession of Canaan as the place in his creation where he would establish his kingdom — and he brought Israel as his people (army) with him.
4:23 *God dried up the Jordan.* Still another descriptive phrase for the miracle, along with "the water ... cut off," "piled up in a heap" and "stopped flowing" (3:16).
4:24 *so that all ... might know.* The Lord's revelation of his power to the Israelites was a public event that all the Canaanites heard about (see 5:1 and note), just as they had heard of the crossing of the Red Sea and defeat of Sihon and Og (2:10). *fear the LORD.* Worship and serve him according to his commandments (see note on Ge 20:11).
5:1 – 12 Circumcision and the celebration of the Passover, the two basic covenant rites, were resumed at Gilgal. Both were significant preparations for the conquest of the promised land. Only as a people who had consecrated themselves to God (circumcision; see note on Ge 17:10) and who remembered that God had set them free from Egyptian bondage to be his people (Passover; see Ex 12:11,17 and notes) could Israel expect to be given possession of Canaan.
5:1 *Amorite ... Canaanite.* Usually interchangeable, these general names included the many smaller nations in the

had dried up the Jordan before the Israelites until we had crossed over, their hearts
melted[w] and they no longer had the courage to face the Israelites.
2At that time the LORD said to Joshua,
"Make flint knives[x] and circumcise[y] the
Israelites again." 3So Joshua made flint
knives and circumcised the Israelites at
Gibeath Haaraloth.[a]
4Now this is why he did so: All those
who came out of Egypt—all the men of
military age[z]—died in the desert on the
way after leaving Egypt.[a] 5All the people
that came out had been circumcised, but
all the people born in the desert during
the journey from Egypt had not. 6The Israelites had moved about in the desert[b]
forty years[c] until all the men who were
of military age when they left Egypt had
died, since they had not obeyed the LORD.
For the LORD had sworn to them that they
would not see the land that he had solemnly promised their fathers to give us,[d]
a land flowing with milk and honey.[e] 7So
he raised up their sons in their place, and
these were the ones Joshua circumcised.
They were still uncircumcised because
they had not been circumcised on the way.
8And after the whole nation had been circumcised, they remained where they were
in camp until they were healed.[f]
9Then the LORD said to Joshua, "Today
I have rolled away the reproach of Egypt
from you." So the place has been called
Gilgal[b][g] to this day.
10On the evening of the fourteenth day
of the month,[h] while camped at Gilgal on
the plains of Jericho, the Israelites celebrated the Passover.[i] 11The day after the
Passover, that very day, they ate some
of the produce of the land:[j] unleavened
bread[k] and roasted grain.[l] 12The manna
stopped the day after[c] they ate this food
from the land; there was no longer any
manna for the Israelites, but that year they
ate of the produce of Canaan.[m]

The Fall of Jericho

13Now when Joshua was near Jericho,
he looked up and saw a man[n] standing in
front of him with a drawn sword[o] in his
hand. Joshua went up to him and asked,
"Are you for us or for our enemies?"
14"Neither," he replied, "but as commander of the army of the LORD I have
now come." Then Joshua fell facedown[p]
to the ground[q] in reverence, and asked
him, "What message does my Lord[d] have
for his servant?"
15The commander of the LORD's army replied, "Take off your sandals, for the place

[a] *3 Gibeath Haaraloth* means *hill of foreskins.*
[b] *9 Gilgal* sounds like the Hebrew for *roll.*
[c] *12* Or *the day*
[d] *14* Or *lord*

5:1 [w]S Ge 42:28 **5:2** [x]S Ex 4:25 [y]S Ge 17:10, 12,14 **5:4** [z]S Nu 1:3 [a]Dt 2:14 **5:6** [b]Nu 32:13; Jos 14:10; Ps 107:4 [c]S Ex 16:35 [d]Nu 14:23,29-35; Dt 2:14 [e]S Ex 3:8 **5:8** [f]Ge 34:25 **5:9** [g]S Dt 11:30 **5:10** [h]S Ex 12:6 [i]S Ex 12:11 **5:11** [j]S Nu 15:19 [k]Ex 12:15 [l]S Lev 23:14 **5:12** [m]Ex 16:35 **5:13** [n]S Ge 18:2 [o]Nu 22:23 **5:14** [p]S Ge 17:3 [q]S Ge 19:1

land. Amorite meant "westerner," and Canaanite referred to the people living along the Mediterranean coast. This verse perhaps concludes the account of the crossing since it notes the effect of that event on the peoples of Canaan (see note on 3:10).

5:2 *flint knives.* Metal knives were available, but flint made a more efficient surgical tool, as modern demonstrations have shown (see Ex 4:25 and note). *circumcise.* Circumcision marked every male as a son of Abraham (Ge 17:10–11) bound to the service of the Lord, and it was a prerequisite for the Passover (see Ex 12:48 and note). *again.* Explained in vv. 4–9.

5:3 *Gibeath Haaraloth.* See NIV text note.

5:6 *forty years.* The time between their departure from Egypt and the crossing of the Jordan. Only 38 years had passed since they turned back at Kadesh Barnea (Nu 14:20–22; Dt 2:14). *milk and honey.* See notes on Ex 3:8; Dt 6:3.

5:9 *reproach of Egypt.* Although the reference may be to Egypt's enslavement of Israel, it is much more likely that the author had in mind the reproach the Egyptians would have cast upon them and their God if they had perished in the desert (see Ex 32:12; Nu 14:13 and note; Dt 9:28). Now that the desert journey is over and Israel is safely in the promised land as his special people consecrated to him by circumcision, the reproach of Egypt is rolled away.

5:10 *Passover.* The ceremonies took place in the month of Abib, the first month of the year (see Ex 12:2 and note). At twilight on the 14th day of the month the Passover lamb was to be slaughtered, then roasted and eaten that same night (Ex 12:5–8). Israel had not celebrated Passover since Sinai, one year after their release from Egypt (see Nu 9:1–5 and note on 9:1–14). Before the next season they had rebelled at the border of Canaan, and the generation of the exodus had been condemned to die in the desert (Nu 14:21–23,29–35). For that generation the celebration of Passover (deliverance from the judgment that God brought on Egypt; see Ex 12:12–13,23 and notes) could have had little meaning.

5:11 *unleavened bread.* Bread baked without yeast. It was to be eaten during the seven feast days that followed (see Ex 12:15 and note; Lev 23:6).

5:12 *manna stopped.* This transition from eating manna to eating the "produce of the land" (v. 11) ended 40 years of dependence on God's special provision. Manna was God's gift for the desert journey; from now on he provided Israel with food from the promised land.

5:13–15 The narration of the conquest of Jericho (5:13—6:27) is introduced by the sudden appearance of a heavenly figure who calls himself the "commander of the army of the LORD" (5:14).

5:13 *Joshua was near Jericho.* The leader of God's army went to scout the nearest Canaanite stronghold, but another warrior was already on the scene. *a man standing.* The experience is taken by many to be an encounter with God in human form (theophany), or with Christ (Christophany). But angels also were sent on missions of this kind (Jdg 6:11; 13:3), and some were identified as captains over the heavenly armies (Da 10:5,20; 12:1).

5:14 *Neither.* Joshua and Israel must know their place—it is not that God is on their side; rather, they must fight God's battles. *commander of the army of the LORD.* God has sent the commander of his heavenly armies to take charge of the battle on earth. Joshua must take orders from him (see 6:2–5 and note on 6:2), and he can also know that the armies of heaven are committed to this war—as later events confirm. *my Lord.* A term of respect for a superior (see NIV text note).

5:15 Joshua is commissioned to undertake the Lord's battles for Canaan, just as Moses had been commis-

where you are standing is holy."[r] And
Joshua did so.

6 Now Jericho[s] was tightly shut up because of the Israelites. No one went out
and no one came in.
2Then the LORD said to Joshua, "See, I
have delivered[t] Jericho into your hands,
along with its king and its fighting men.
3March around the city once with all the
armed men. Do this for six days. 4Have
seven priests carry trumpets of rams'
horns[u] in front of the ark. On the seventh
day, march around the city seven times,
with the priests blowing the trumpets.[v]
5When you hear them sound a long blast[w]
on the trumpets, have all the people give
a loud shout;[x] then the wall of the city will
collapse and the people will go up, every
man straight in."
6So Joshua son of Nun called the priests
and said to them, "Take up the ark of
the covenant of the LORD and have seven
priests carry trumpets in front of it."[y] 7And
he ordered the people, "Advance[z]! March
around the city, with the armed guard going ahead of the ark[a] of the LORD."
8When Joshua had spoken to the people, the seven priests carrying the seven
trumpets before the LORD went forward,
blowing their trumpets, and the ark of
the LORD's covenant followed them. 9The
armed guard marched ahead of the priests
who blew the trumpets, and the rear
guard[b] followed the ark. All this time the
trumpets were sounding. 10But Joshua
had commanded the people, "Do not give
a war cry, do not raise your voices, do not
say a word until the day I tell you to shout.
Then shout![c]" 11So he had the ark of the
LORD carried around the city, circling it
once. Then the people returned to camp
and spent the night there.
12Joshua got up early the next morning
and the priests took up the ark of the LORD.
13The seven priests carrying the seven
trumpets went forward, marching before
the ark of the LORD and blowing the trumpets. The armed men went ahead of them
and the rear guard followed the ark of
the LORD, while the trumpets kept sounding. 14So on the second day they marched
around the city once and returned to the
camp. They did this for six days.
15On the seventh day, they got up at daybreak and marched around the city seven
times in the same manner, except that on
that day they circled the city seven times.[d]
16The seventh time around, when the
priests sounded the trumpet blast, Joshua
commanded the people, "Shout! For the
LORD has given you the city![e] 17The city
and all that is in it are to be devoted[a][f] to
the LORD. Only Rahab the prostitute[b][g] and
all who are with her in her house shall be

5:15 [r]S Ge 28:17; Ex 3:5; Ac 7:33 **6:1** [s]Jos 24:11 **6:2** [t]ver 16; Dt 7:24; Jos 8:1 **6:4** [u]S Ex 19:13 [v]S Lev 25:9 **6:5** [w]Ex 19:13 [x]ver 20; 1Sa 4:5; 2Sa 6:15; Ezr 3:11; 10:12; Ps 42:4; 95:1; Isa 8:9; 42:13 **6:6** [y]ver 4 **6:7** [z]Ex 14:15 [a]Nu 10:35; 1Sa 4:3; 7:1 **6:9** [b]ver 13; S Nu 2:31; Isa 52:12 **6:10** [c]ver 20; 1Sa 4:5; Ezr 3:11 **6:15** [d]1Ki 18:44; 2Ki 4:35; 5:14 **6:16** [e]S ver 2 **6:17** [f]ver 21; Lev 27:28; Dt 20:17; Isa 13:5; 24:1; 34:2,5; Mal 4:6 [g]S Jos 2:1

[a] *17* The Hebrew term refers to the irrevocable giving over of things or persons to the LORD, often by totally destroying them; also in verses 18 and 21.
[b] *17* Or possibly *innkeeper*; also in verses 22 and 25

sioned to confront the pharaoh (Ex 3:5,10). *place ... is holy.* See Ex 3:5 and note.

6:1 *Jericho.* Modern Tell es-Sultan. Archaeological excavations have revealed that Jericho may have been the first site of village settlement in Canaan. (People who moved about and lived by hunting and gathering had been present in the area for thousands of years.) The earliest settled occupation dates from c. 7000 B.C. By Joshua's day, more than two dozen cities had already been built and destroyed on the site, one above the other, over a period of some 5,000 years. Many of them had powerful double walls. The present-day tell (mound) is roughly 400 by 200 yards in size, and about 65 feet high. Jericho may have been a center for the worship of the moon-god (Jericho probably means "moon city"). If so, God was destroying not only Canaanite cities, but also Canaanite religion. See map No. 3 at the end of this study Bible; see also maps, pp. 310–311.

6:2 *the LORD.* The Lord's command no doubt comes to Joshua through the "commander of the army of the LORD" (5:14), who orders the first conquest of a Canaanite city.

6:3 *March around the city.* A ritual act, signifying a siege of the city, that was to be repeated for six days.

6:4 *trumpets of rams' horns.* Instruments not of music but of signaling, in both religious and military contexts (which appear to come together here). The trumpets were to be sounded (v. 8), as on the seventh day, announcing the presence of the Lord (see 2Sa 6:15; 1Ch 15:28; Zec 9:14, but see note there). *ark.* Signified that the Lord was laying siege to the city. *seventh day.* No note is taken of the Sabbath during this seven-day siege, but perhaps that was the day the Lord gave the city to Israel as the first pledge of the land of rest. To arrive at the goal of a long march on the seventh day is a motif found also in other ancient Near Eastern literature. In any event, the remarkable constellation of sevens (seven priests with trumpets, seven days, seven encirclements on the seventh day) underscores the sacred significance of the event and is, perhaps, a deliberate evoking of the seven days of creation to signal the beginning of God's new order in the world.

6:5 *long blast ... loud shout.* Signaling the onset of the attack—psychological warfare, intended to create panic and confusion (see Jdg 7). In the Dead Sea Scroll of "The War of the Sons of Light against the Sons of Darkness," the Levites are instructed to blow in unison a great battle fanfare to melt the heart of the enemy. (For Dead Sea Scrolls see essay, pp. 1452–1453.) *every man straight in.* Not a breach here and there but a general collapse of the walls, giving access to the city from all sides.

6:7 *armed guard.* The Hebrew for this term differs from that in v. 3 but may be synonymous with it. It is to be expected that the ark led the procession. If so, the present reference may be to a kind of royal guard (but see v. 9 and note).

6:8–14 Throughout these verses the ark of the Lord is made the center of focus (as it was in the account of the crossing of the Jordan), highlighting the fact that the Lord himself besieged the city.

6:9 *rear guard.* If the rear guard was made up of the final contingents of the army (see Nu 10:25), the armed guard of vv. 7,9 constituted the main body of troops.

6:12–14 Literary repetition reflects repetition in action, a common feature in ancient Near Eastern literature.

6:17 *devoted.* See NIV text note. The ban placed all of Jericho's inhabitants under the curse of death and all of the city's treasures that could not be destroyed under consignment to the

spared, because she hid[h] the spies we sent.
[18]But keep away from the devoted things,[i]
so that you will not bring about your own
destruction by taking any of them. Otherwise you will make the camp of Israel
liable to destruction[j] and bring trouble[k] on
it. [19]All the silver and gold and the articles
of bronze and iron[l] are sacred to the LORD
and must go into his treasury."
[20]When the trumpets sounded,[m] the
people shouted, and at the sound of the
trumpet, when the people gave a loud
shout,[n] the wall collapsed; so every man
charged straight in, and they took the
city.[o] [21]They devoted[p] the city to the LORD
and destroyed[q] with the sword every living thing in it—men and women, young
and old, cattle, sheep and donkeys.
[22]Joshua said to the two men[r] who had
spied out[s] the land, "Go into the prostitute's house and bring her out and all who
belong to her, in accordance with your
oath to her.[t]" [23]So the young men who had
done the spying went in and brought out
Rahab, her father and mother and brothers and all who belonged to her.[u] They
brought out her entire family and put them
in a place outside the camp of Israel.
[24]Then they burned the whole city[v] and
everything in it, but they put the silver and
gold and the articles of bronze and iron[w]
into the treasury of the LORD's house.[x]
[25]But Joshua spared[y] Rahab the prostitute,[z]
with her family and all who belonged to
her, because she hid the men Joshua had
sent as spies to Jericho[a]—and she lives
among the Israelites to this day.
[26]At that time Joshua pronounced this
solemn oath:[b] "Cursed[c] before the LORD is
the man who undertakes to rebuild this
city, Jericho:

"At the cost of his firstborn son
will he lay its foundations;
at the cost of his youngest
will he set up its gates."[d]

[27]So the LORD was with Joshua,[e] and his
fame spread[f] throughout the land.

Achan's Sin

7 But the Israelites acted unfaithfully in
regard to the devoted things[a];[g] Achan[h]
son of Carmi, the son of Zimri,[b] the son of
Zerah,[i] of the tribe of Judah,[j] took some of
them. So the LORD's anger burned[k] against
Israel.[l]
[2]Now Joshua sent men from Jericho to
Ai,[m] which is near Beth Aven[n] to the east
of Bethel,[o] and told them, "Go up and spy
out[p] the region." So the men went up and
spied out Ai.
[3]When they returned to Joshua, they
said, "Not all the people will have to go
up against Ai. Send two or three thousand men to take it and do not weary all
the people, for only a few men are there."
[4]So about three thousand men went up;
but they were routed by the men of Ai,[q]
[5]who killed about thirty-six[r] of them. They

[a] *1* The Hebrew term refers to the irrevocable giving over of things or persons to the LORD, often by totally destroying them; also in verses 11, 12, 13 and 15.
[b] *1* See Septuagint and 1 Chron. 2:6; Hebrew *Zabdi*; also in verses 17 and 18.

6:17 [h]ver 25; Jos 2:4 **6:18** [i]Jos 7:1; 1Ch 2:7 [j]Jos 7:12 [k]Jos 7:25, 26 **6:19** [l]ver 24; Nu 31:22 **6:20** [m]Lev 25:9; Jdg 6:34; 7:22; 1Ki 1:41; Isa 18:3; 27:13; Jer 4:21; 42:14; Am 2:2 [n]S ver 5; S ver 10 [o]Heb 11:30 **6:21** [p]S ver 17 [q]S Dt 20:16 **6:22** [r]S Ge 42:9; S Jos 2:4 [s]S Nu 21:32 [t]Jos 2:14; Heb 11:31 **6:23** [u]S Jos 2:13 **6:24** [v]S Nu 31:10 [w]S ver 19 [x]S Dt 13:16 **6:25** [y]Jdg 1:25 [z]S Jos 2:1 [a]S ver 17; S Jos 2:6 **6:26** [b]1Sa 14:24 [c]S Nu 5:21 [d]1Ki 16:34 **6:27** [e]S Ge 39:2; S Nu 14:43 [f]Jos 9:1; 1Ch 14:17 **7:1** [g]S Jos 6:18 [h]ver 26; 1Ch 2:7 [i]Jos 22:20 [j]ver 18; Nu 1:4 [k]S Ex 4:14; S 32:20 [l]S Lev 10:6 **7:2** [m]S Ge 12:8; S Jos 8:1, 28 [n]Jos 18:12; 1Sa 13:5; 14:23; Hos 4:15; 5:8; 10:5 [o]Ge 12:8; Jos 12:16; 16:1; Jdg 1:22; 1Sa 30:27; 2Ki 23:15; Jer 48:13; Am 3:14; 4:4; 5:5-6; 7:10, 13 [p]S Nu 21:32 **7:4** [q]S Lev 26:17; S Dt 28:25 **7:5** [r]Jos 22:20

Lord's house (v. 19). According to the law of Moses this ban could be applied to animals for sacrifice, to property given to God, or to any person found worthy of death (see Lev 27:28–29 and note on 27:28). It was Moses himself who ruled that all the inhabitants of Canaan be "devoted" by execution for their idolatry and all its accompanying moral corruption (Dt 20:16–18). See note on Dt 2:34. *Rahab ... and ... her house shall be spared.* Honoring the pledge made by the two spies (see 2:14 and note).

6:18 *your own destruction.* See NIV text note on v. 17. If Israel took for themselves anything that was under God's ban, they themselves would fall under the ban.

6:25 *she lives among the Israelites.* Rahab became the wife of Salmon, the father of Boaz, who married Ruth (see Ru 4:20–21; 1Ch 2:11; Mt 1:5 and note; see also note on Mt 1:3). Rahab's faith is noted twice in the NT (see Heb 11:31; Jas 2:25 and note).

6:26 *Cursed ... is the man.* Jericho itself was to be devoted to the Lord as a perpetual sign of God's judgment on the wicked Canaanites (a second memorial in the land; see note on 4:9) and as a firstfruits offering of the land. This was a way of signifying that the conquered land belonged to the Lord. The curse was fulfilled in the rebellious days of King Ahab (see 1Ki 16:34 and note).

7:1–26 The tragic story of Achan, which stands in sharp contrast to the story of Rahab. In the earlier event a Canaanite prostitute, because of her courageous allegiance to Israel and her acknowledgment of the Lord, was spared, together with all her extended family, and received into Israel. She abandoned Canaan and its gods on account of the Lord and Israel, and so received Canaan back. In the case of Achan, an Israelite (of the tribe of Judah, no less), because of his disloyalty to the Lord and Israel, was destroyed just as the inhabitants of Jericho had been—he and his whole household. He stole the riches of Canaan from the Lord, and so lost his inheritance in the promised land. This is also a story of how one man's sin adversely affected the entire nation. Throughout this account (as often in the OT) Israel is considered a corporate unity in covenant with and in the service of the Lord. Thus even in the acts of one (Achan) or a few (the 3,000 defeated at Ai) all Israel is involved (see vv. 1,11; 22:20).

7:2 *from Jericho to Ai.* An uphill march of some 15 miles through a ravine to the top of the central Canaanite ridge. Strategically, an advance from Gilgal to Ai would bring Israel beyond the Jordan Valley and provide them a foothold in the central highlands. Ai in Hebrew means "the ruin." It is usually identified with et-Tell (meaning "the ruin" in Arabic), just two miles east of Bethel, but some dispute this precise identification. *Beth Aven.* Means "house of wickedness," a derogatory designation of either Bethel itself or a pagan shrine nearby (see 1Sa 13:5; Hos 4:15 and note; Am 5:5 and NIV text note). *spy out the region.* See note on 2:1–24.

7:5 *stone quarries.* Or possibly a place called Shebarim (see NIV text note), meaning "breaks," a fitting term for the rocky bluffs overlooking the Jordan Valley.

chased the Israelites from the city gate as
far as the stone quarries[a] and struck them
down on the slopes. At this the hearts of
the people melted[s] and became like water.
6Then Joshua tore his clothes[t] and
fell facedown[u] to the ground before the
ark of the LORD, remaining there till evening.[v] The elders of Israel[w] did the same,
and sprinkled dust[x] on their heads. 7And
Joshua said, "Ah, Sovereign LORD, why[y]
did you ever bring this people across the
Jordan to deliver us into the hands of the
Amorites to destroy us?[z] If only we had
been content to stay on the other side of
the Jordan! 8O Lord, what can I say, now
that Israel has been routed by its enemies?
9The Canaanites and the other people of
the country will hear about this and they
will surround us and wipe out our name
from the earth.[a] What then will you do for
your own great name?[b]"
10The LORD said to Joshua, "Stand up!
What are you doing down on your face?
11Israel has sinned;[c] they have violated
my covenant,[d] which I commanded them
to keep. They have taken some of the devoted things; they have stolen, they have
lied,[e] they have put them with their own
possessions.[f] 12That is why the Israelites
cannot stand against their enemies;[g] they
turn their backs[h] and run[i] because they
have been made liable to destruction.[j] I
will not be with you anymore[k] unless you
destroy whatever among you is devoted to
destruction.
13"Go, consecrate the people. Tell them,
'Consecrate yourselves[l] in preparation for
tomorrow; for this is what the LORD, the
God of Israel, says: That which is devoted
is among you, O Israel. You cannot stand
against your enemies until you remove it.
14" 'In the morning, present[m] yourselves
tribe by tribe. The tribe that the LORD
takes[n] shall come forward clan by clan;
the clan that the LORD takes shall come
forward family by family; and the family that the LORD takes shall come forward
man by man. 15He who is caught with the
devoted things[o] shall be destroyed by fire,[p]
along with all that belongs to him.[q] He has
violated the covenant[r] of the LORD and has
done a disgraceful thing in Israel!' "[s]
16Early the next morning Joshua had
Israel come forward by tribes, and Judah
was taken. 17The clans of Judah came forward, and he took the Zerahites.[t] He had
the clan of the Zerahites come forward by
families, and Zimri was taken. 18Joshua
had his family come forward man by man,
and Achan son of Carmi, the son of Zimri,
the son of Zerah, of the tribe of Judah,[u]
was taken.[v]
19Then Joshua said to Achan, "My son,
give glory[w] to the LORD,[b] the God of Israel,
and give him the praise.[c] Tell[x] me what
you have done; do not hide it from me."
20Achan replied, "It is true! I have
sinned against the LORD, the God of Israel.
This is what I have done: 21When I saw in
the plunder[y] a beautiful robe from Babylonia,[d] two hundred shekels[e] of silver and
a wedge of gold weighing fifty shekels,[f]
I coveted[z] them and took them. They are
hidden in the ground inside my tent, with
the silver underneath."
22So Joshua sent messengers, and they
ran to the tent, and there it was, hidden in
his tent, with the silver underneath. 23They
took the things from the tent, brought
them to Joshua and all the Israelites and
spread them out before the LORD.

7:5 [s]S Ge 42:28; Ps 22:14; Isa 13:7; Eze 21:7; Na 2:10 **7:6** [t]S Ge 37:29 [u]S Ge 17:3; 1Ch 21:16; Eze 9:8 [v]Jdg 20:23 [w]Jos 8:10; 9:11; 20:4; 23:2 [x]1Sa 4:12; 2Sa 13:19; 15:32; Ne 9:1; Job 2:12; La 2:10; Eze 27:30; Rev 18:19 **7:7** [y]1Sa 4:3 [z]S Ex 5:22; S Nu 14:16 **7:9** [a]Ex 32:12; S Dt 9:28 [b]Dt 28:58; 1Sa 12:22; Ps 48:10; 106:8; Jer 14:21 **7:11** [c]S Ex 9:27; Dt 29:27; Jos 24:16-27; 2Ki 17:7; Hos 10:9 [d]ver 15; Jos 6:17-19; 23:16; Jdg 2:20; 1Sa 15:24; Ps 78:10 [e]Ac 5:1-2 [f]ver 21 **7:12** [g]Lev 26:37 [h]Ps 18:40; 21:12 [i]S Lev 26:17 [j]Jos 6:18 [k]Ps 44:9; 60:10 **7:13** [l]S Lev 11:44 **7:14** [m]1Sa 10:19 [n]Pr 16:33 **7:15** [o]Jos 6:18 [p]Dt 7:25; 2Ki 25:9; 1Ch 14:12; Isa 37:19; Jer 43:12; Eze 30:16 [q]1Sa 14:39 [r]S ver 11 [s]Ge 34:7 **7:17** [t]Nu 26:20 **7:18** [u]S ver 1; S Lev 24:11 [v]Jnh 1:7 **7:19** [w]Ex 14:17; 1Sa 6:5; Ps 96:8; Isa 42:12; Jer 13:16; Jn 9:24* [x]S Lev 5:5; 1Sa 14:43 **7:21** [y]S Ge 34:29; S 49:27 [z]S Dt 7:25; Eph 5:5; 1Ti 6:10

[a] *5* Or *as far as Shebarim* [b] *19* A solemn charge to tell the truth [c] *19* Or *and confess to him* [d] *21* Hebrew *Shinar* [e] *21* That is, about 5 pounds (about 2.3 kilograms) [f] *21* That is, about 1 1/4 pounds (about 0.6 kilogram)

7:6 *Joshua tore his clothes.* A sign of great distress (see Ge 37:34 and note; 44:13; Jdg 11:35 and note). Joshua's dismay (and that of the people), as indicated by his prayer, arose from his recognition that the Lord had not been with Israel's troops in the battle. And without the Lord the whole venture for which Israel had crossed the Jordan would be impossible. Moreover, the Canaanites would now judge that Israel and their God were not invincible. They would pour out of their fortified cities, combine forces and descend on Israel in the Jordan Valley, from which Israel could not escape across the flooding Jordan. *sprinkled dust on their heads.* See Job 2:12; La 2:10 and notes.

7:9 *your own great name.* Joshua pleads, as Moses had (see Nu 14:13–16 and note on 14:13; Dt 9:28–29), that God's honor in the eyes of all the world was at stake in the fortunes of his people.

7:11 *Israel has sinned.* One soldier's theft of the devoted goods brought collective guilt on the entire nation (see 22:20). *violated my covenant.* See v. 15 and note. This is the main indictment; what follows is further specification.

7:12 *devoted to destruction.* See note on 6:18.

7:13 *Consecrate yourselves.* A series of purifications to be undertaken by every Israelite in preparation for meeting with God, as before a solemn religious feast or a special assembly called by the Lord (see note on 3:5). Here God summons his people before him for his judgment.

7:14 *tribe that the LORD takes.* When the lots are cast, one of the tribes is taken by the Lord so that the search is narrowed until the Lord exposes the guilty persons. The lots may have been the Urim and Thummim from the ephod of the high priest (see notes on Ex 28:30; 1Sa 2:28; see also NIV text note on 1Sa 14:41).

7:15 *disgraceful thing in Israel.* An act that within Israel, as the covenant people of the Lord, is an outrage of utter folly (see Dt 22:21; see also Jdg 19:23–24 and notes; 20:6,10; 2Sa 13:12).

7:19 *My son.* Joshua took a fatherly attitude toward Achan. *give glory to the LORD.* See NIV text note. *give him the praise.* See NIV text note.

7:21 *robe from Babylonia.* A valuable import. *two hundred shekels ... fifty shekels.* See NIV text notes.

7:23 *before the LORD.* Who is here the Judge.

[24]Then Joshua, together with all Israel, took Achan son of Zerah, the silver,
the robe, the gold wedge, his sons[a] and
daughters, his cattle, donkeys and sheep,
his tent and all that he had, to the Valley
of Achor.[b] [25]Joshua said, "Why have you
brought this trouble[c] on us? The LORD will
bring trouble on you today."

Then all Israel stoned him,[d] and after
they had stoned the rest, they burned
them.[e] [26]Over Achan they heaped[f] up a
large pile of rocks, which remains to this
day.[g] Then the LORD turned from his fierce
anger.[h] Therefore that place has been
called the Valley of Achor[a][i] ever since.

Ai Destroyed

8 Then the LORD said to Joshua, "Do not
be afraid;[j] do not be discouraged.[k] Take
the whole army[l] with you, and go up and
attack Ai.[m] For I have delivered[n] into your
hands the king of Ai, his people, his city
and his land. [2]You shall do to Ai and its
king as you did to Jericho and its king,
except that you may carry off their plunder[o] and livestock for yourselves.[p] Set an
ambush[q] behind the city."

[3]So Joshua and the whole army moved
out to attack Ai. He chose thirty thousand
of his best fighting men and sent them out
at night [4]with these orders: "Listen carefully. You are to set an ambush behind the
city. Don't go very far from it. All of you be
on the alert. [5]I and all those with me will
advance on the city, and when the men
come out against us, as they did before,
we will flee from them. [6]They will pursue
us until we have lured them away from
the city, for they will say, 'They are running away from us as they did before.' So
when we flee from them, [7]you are to rise
up from ambush and take the city. The
LORD your God will give it into your hand.[r]
[8]When you have taken the city, set it on
fire.[s] Do what the LORD has commanded.[t]
See to it; you have my orders."

[9]Then Joshua sent them off, and they
went to the place of ambush[u] and lay in
wait between Bethel and Ai, to the west
of Ai—but Joshua spent that night with
the people.

[10]Early the next morning[v] Joshua mustered his men, and he and the leaders of
Israel[w] marched before them to Ai. [11]The
entire force that was with him marched
up and approached the city and arrived
in front of it. They set up camp north of
Ai, with the valley between them and the
city. [12]Joshua had taken about five thousand men and set them in ambush between Bethel and Ai, to the west of the
city. [13]They had the soldiers take up their
positions—all those in the camp to the
north of the city and the ambush to the
west of it. That night Joshua went into the
valley.

[14]When the king of Ai saw this, he and
all the men of the city hurried out early
in the morning to meet Israel in battle at
a certain place overlooking the Arabah.[x]
But he did not know[y] that an ambush
had been set against him behind the city.
[15]Joshua and all Israel let themselves be
driven back[z] before them, and they fled toward the desert.[a] [16]All the men of Ai were
called to pursue them, and they pursued
Joshua and were lured away[b] from the
city. [17]Not a man remained in Ai or Bethel
who did not go after Israel. They left the
city open and went in pursuit of Israel.

[18]Then the LORD said to Joshua, "Hold
out toward Ai the javelin[c] that is in your
hand,[d] for into your hand I will deliver the
city." So Joshua held out his javelin[e] toward Ai. [19]As soon as he did this, the men
in the ambush rose quickly[f] from their position and rushed forward. They entered
the city and captured it and quickly set
it on fire.[g]

[20]The men of Ai looked back and saw
the smoke of the city rising against the
sky,[h] but they had no chance to escape in
any direction, for the Israelites who had

[a] *26* *Achor* means *trouble.*

7:24 [a]S Nu 16:27 [b]ver 26; Jos 15:7; Isa 65:10; Hos 2:15 **7:25** [c]S Jos 6:18 [d]S Lev 20:2; Dt 17:5; 1Ki 12:18; 2Ch 10:18; 24:21; Ne 9:26 [e]S Ge 38:24 **7:26** [f]2Sa 18:17 [g]S Ge 35:20 [h]S Nu 25:4 [i]S ver 24 **8:1** [j]Ge 26:24; Dt 31:6 [k]S Nu 14:9; S Dt 1:21 [l]Jos 10:7 [m]Jos 7:2; 9:3; 10:1; 12:9 [n]S Jos 6:2 **8:2** [o]S Ge 49:27 [p]ver 27; Dt 20:14 [q]ver 4,12; Jdg 9:43; 20:29 **8:7** [r]Jdg 7:7; 1Sa 23:4 **8:8** [s]Jdg 20:29-38 [t]ver 19 **8:9** [u]2Ch 13:13 **8:10** [v]Ge 22:3 [w]S Jos 7:6 **8:14** [x]S Dt 1:1 [y]Jdg 20:34 **8:15** [z]Jdg 20:36 [a]Jos 15:61; 16:1; 18:12 **8:16** [b]Jdg 20:31 **8:18** [c]Job 41:26; Ps 35:3 [d]S Ex 4:2; 17:9-12 [e]ver 26 **8:19** [f]Jdg 20:33 [g]S ver 8 **8:20** [h]Jdg 20:40

7:24 *Joshua ... all Israel.* Joshua and all Israel were God's agents for executing his judgment on both the Canaanites and this violator of the covenant. *all that he had.* As the head of (and example for) his family, Achan involved his whole household in his guilt and punishment. This is in accordance with the principle of corporate solidarity—the whole community is represented in one member (especially the head of that community). See Pr 15:27 and note.

7:25 *stoned him.* Because he had been found guilty of violating the covenant of the holy Lord (see Ex 19:13; Lev 24:23; Nu 15:36 and note on 15:32). Afterward the bodies were burned to purge the land of the evil.

7:26 *large pile of rocks.* A third monument in the land to the events of the conquest (see note on 4:9). *Achor.* See NIV text note. Achor was also another form of Achan's name (see 1Ch 2:7, "Achar," and NIV text note there).

8:1–29 Renewal of the conquest and the taking of Ai.

8:1 *Do not be afraid.* Now that Israel is purged, the Lord reassures Joshua once more (see 1:3–5; 3:11–13; 6:2–5).

8:2 *you may carry off their plunder.* The Lord now assigns the wealth of Canaan to his troops who fight his battles. *Set an ambush.* Still in command, the Lord directs the attack.

8:12 *five thousand.* Verse 3 speaks of a contingent of 30,000 assigned to the ambush. Perhaps Joshua assigned two different units to the task to assure success. Or from the original 30,000 a unit of 5,000 may have been designated to attack Ai itself while the remaining 25,000 served as a covering force to block the threat from Bethel (see v. 17).

8:13 *the camp to the north.* In full visibility Joshua's main force moved north of the city, then pretended to flee to the east, drawing out the entire army of defenders.

8:14 *Arabah.* See note on Dt 1:1.

8:17 *Ai or Bethel.* Their joint action indicates that the two cities were closely allied, though each is said to have had a king (12:9,16).

been fleeing toward the desert had turned
back against their pursuers. 21 For when
Joshua and all Israel saw that the ambush
had taken the city and that smoke was going up from the city, they turned around[i]
and attacked the men of Ai. 22 The men
of the ambush also came out of the city
against them, so that they were caught in
the middle, with Israelites on both sides.
Israel cut them down, leaving them neither survivors nor fugitives.[j] 23 But they
took the king of Ai alive[k] and brought him
to Joshua.
24 When Israel had finished killing all
the men of Ai in the fields and in the
desert where they had chased them, and
when every one of them had been put
to the sword, all the Israelites returned
to Ai and killed those who were in it.
25 Twelve thousand men and women fell
that day—all the people of Ai.[l] 26 For Joshua did not draw back the hand that held
out his javelin[m] until he had destroyed[a n]
all who lived in Ai.[o] 27 But Israel did carry
off for themselves the livestock and plunder of this city, as the LORD had instructed
Joshua.[p]
28 So Joshua burned[q] Ai[r] and made it a
permanent heap of ruins,[s] a desolate place
to this day.[t] 29 He hung the king of Ai on
a tree and left him there until evening.
At sunset,[u] Joshua ordered them to take
his body from the tree and throw it down
at the entrance of the city gate. And they
raised a large pile of rocks[v] over it, which
remains to this day.

8:21 [i] Jdg 20:41 **8:22** [j] Dt 7:2; Jos 10:1 **8:23** [k] 1Sa 15:8 **8:25** [l] Dt 20:16-18 **8:26** [m] ver 18 [n] S Nu 21:2 [o] Ex 17:12 **8:27** [p] S ver 2 **8:28** [q] S Nu 31:10 [r] Jos 7:2; Jer 49:3 [s] S Dt 13:16; Jos 10:1 [t] S Ge 35:20 **8:29** [u] S Dt 21:23; Jn 19:31 [v] 2Sa 18:17

8:30 [w] ver 33; S Dt 11:29 [x] S Ex 20:24 **8:31** [y] S Ex 20:25 [z] Dt 27:6-7 **8:32** [a] Dt 27:8 **8:33** [b] S Lev 16:29 [c] Dt 31:12 [d] Dt 11:29; Jn 4:20 **8:34** [e] S Dt 28:61; 31:11 **8:35** [f] S Ex 12:38; Dt 31:12

The Covenant Renewed at Mount Ebal

30 Then Joshua built on Mount Ebal[w]
an altar[x] to the LORD, the God of Israel,
31 as Moses the servant of the LORD had
commanded the Israelites. He built it according to what is written in the Book
of the Law of Moses—an altar of uncut
stones, on which no iron tool[y] had been
used. On it they offered to the LORD burnt
offerings and sacrificed fellowship offerings.[b z] 32 There, in the presence of the Israelites, Joshua copied on stones the law
of Moses, which he had written.[a] 33 All
Israel, aliens and citizens[b] alike, with
their elders, officials and judges, were
standing on both sides of the ark of the
covenant of the LORD, facing those who
carried it—the priests, who were Levites.[c] Half of the people stood in front of
Mount Gerizim and half of them in front
of Mount Ebal,[d] as Moses the servant of
the LORD had formerly commanded when
he gave instructions to bless the people
of Israel.
34 Afterward, Joshua read all the words
of the law—the blessings and the curses—just as it is written in the Book of the
Law.[e] 35 There was not a word of all that
Moses had commanded that Joshua did
not read to the whole assembly of Israel,
including the women and children, and
the aliens who lived among them.[f]

a 26 The Hebrew term refers to the irrevocable giving over of things or persons to the LORD, often by totally destroying them. *b 31* Traditionally *peace offerings*

8:26 *he had destroyed.* For the second time Joshua ordered the holy ban on the inhabitants of a Canaanite city (see NIV text note).

8:28 *burned Ai.* As he had Jericho (6:24) and would later do to Hazor (see 11:11 and note on 11:10).

8:29 *hung the king of Ai on a tree.* The Israelites did not execute by hanging. "Tree" may refer to a pole on which the king's body was impaled after execution (see note on Dt 21:22). *until evening.* According to Mosaic instructions (see Dt 21:22–23). *large pile of rocks.* A fourth monument in the land memorializing the conquest (see note on 4:9).

8:30–35 The renewal of the covenant with the Lord as Moses had ordered (see Dt 11:26–30 and note; 27:1–8) concludes the account of the initial battles (see Introduction: Outline). The conquest of Canaan has already been put into rich theological perspective. This final event (see also Joshua's final official act, ch. 24) underscores Israel's servant relationship to the Lord (see Introduction to Deuteronomy: Theological Teaching and Purpose). In conquest and occupation they must faithfully acknowledge their unique identity as the people of the kingdom of God, subject to his commission and rule (see note on 5:14).

How Israel could assemble peacefully between Mount Ebal and Mount Gerizim without further conquest is a worrisome question—and has led to some radical reconstructions of Israel's history. It must be noted, however, that Biblical narrators at times followed a thematic rather than a strictly chronological order of events. That may be the case here, since it is clear that the story of the Gibeonite deception and submission (ch. 9) is included in the thematic development of how Israel came into possession of the rest of Canaan (see the author's introduction in 9:1–2). The Shechemites (Shechem was a major city lying between the two mountains mentioned) were Hivites (or were under Hivite domination; see Ge 34:2) and thus were related to the people of the Gibeonite cities (9:7; 11:19). Also, there was no important town between Gibeon and Shechem (Bethel and Ai had been subdued). Perhaps the treaty of submission established between Israel and the Gibeonites (ch. 9) applied also to the Hivites of Shechem, and the covenant renewal ceremony that concludes ch. 8 (and the previous narrative section) actually took place chronologically after the events narrated in ch. 9. If this suggestion is correct, the Gibeonites or their representatives would have been among the "aliens" who participated with Israel in the covenant event (vv. 33,35).

8:30 *Mount Ebal.* At the foot of this peak was the fortress city of Shechem, where Abraham had built an altar (Ge 12:6–7).

8:31 *burnt offerings.* See Lev 1:1–17 and note on 1:3. *fellowship offerings.* See Lev 3:1–17 and note on 3:1; 7:11–18; see also chart, p. 153.

8:32 *copied on stones.* Moses had ordered the people first to plaster the stones, then to inscribe on them the words of the law (see Dt 27:2–4 and note on 27:3,8). These stones are a fifth monument in the land (see note on 4:9).

8:33 *aliens and citizens alike.* Israel now included the "other people" (Ex 12:38) who had come out of Egypt, plus those who had joined them during the desert wanderings (see note on vv. 30–35).

8:34 *the blessings and the curses.* See Dt 27–28 and notes.

The Gibeonite Deception

9 Now when all the kings west of the Jordan heard about these things—those
in the hill country,[g] in the western foothills, and along the entire coast of the
Great Sea[a][h] as far as Lebanon[i] (the kings
of the Hittites, Amorites, Canaanites, Perizzites,[j] Hivites[k] and Jebusites)[l]—2they
came together to make war against Joshua
and Israel.
3However, when the people of Gibeon[m]
heard what Joshua had done to Jericho and
Ai,[n] 4they resorted to a ruse: They went as
a delegation whose donkeys were loaded[b]
with worn-out sacks and old wineskins,
cracked and mended. 5The men put worn
and patched sandals on their feet and wore
old clothes. All the bread of their food supply was dry and moldy. 6Then they went
to Joshua in the camp at Gilgal[o] and said
to him and the men of Israel, "We have
come from a distant country;[p] make a treaty[q] with us."
7The men of Israel said to the Hivites,[r]
"But perhaps you live near us. How then
can we make a treaty[s] with you?"
8"We are your servants,[t]" they said to
Joshua.
But Joshua asked, "Who are you and
where do you come from?"
9They answered: "Your servants have
come from a very distant country[u] because of the fame of the LORD your God.
For we have heard reports[v] of him: all that
he did in Egypt,[w] 10and all that he did to
the two kings of the Amorites east of the
Jordan—Sihon king of Heshbon,[x] and Og
king of Bashan,[y] who reigned in Ashtaroth.[z] 11And our elders and all those living
in our country said to us, 'Take provisions
for your journey; go and meet them and
say to them, "We are your servants; make
a treaty with us."' 12This bread of ours was
warm when we packed it at home on the
day we left to come to you. But now see
how dry and moldy it is. 13And these
wineskins that we filled were new, but
see how cracked they are. And our clothes
and sandals are worn out by the very long
journey."
14The men of Israel sampled their provisions but did not inquire[a] of the LORD.
15Then Joshua made a treaty of peace[b]
with them to let them live,[c] and the leaders of the assembly ratified it by oath.
16Three days after they made the treaty
with the Gibeonites, the Israelites heard
that they were neighbors, living near[d] them.
17So the Israelites set out and on the third
day came to their cities: Gibeon, Kephirah,
Beeroth[e] and Kiriath Jearim.[f] 18But the Israelites did not attack them, because the
leaders of the assembly had sworn an oath[g]
to them by the LORD, the God of Israel.
The whole assembly grumbled[h] against
the leaders, 19but all the leaders answered,
"We have given them our oath by the
LORD, the God of Israel, and we cannot
touch them now. 20This is what we will
do to them: We will let them live, so that
wrath will not fall on us for breaking the
oath[i] we swore to them." 21They continued, "Let them live,[j] but let them be
woodcutters and water carriers[k] for the entire community." So the leaders' promise
to them was kept.
22Then Joshua summoned the Gibeonites and said, "Why did you deceive us
by saying, 'We live a long way[l] from you,'
while actually you live near[m] us? 23You are
now under a curse:[n] You will never cease

[a] *1* That is, the Mediterranean [b] *4* Most Hebrew manuscripts; some Hebrew manuscripts, Vulgate and Syriac (see also Septuagint) *They prepared provisions and loaded their donkeys*

9:1 [g]S Nu 13:17 [h]S Nu 34:6 [i]S Dt 3:25 [j]Ge 13:7; S Jos 3:10 [k]ver 7; Jos 11:19 [l]S Jos 3:10 **9:3** [m]ver 17; Jos 10:10; 11:19; 18:25; 21:17; 2Sa 2:12; 5:25; 20:8; 1Ki 3:4; 9:2; 1Ch 8:29; 14:16; 16:39; 21:29; 2Ch 1:3; Ne 3:7; Isa 28:21; Jer 28:1; 41:12 [n]Ge 12:8; S Jos 8:1 **9:6** [o]S Dt 11:30 [p]ver 22 [q]S Ge 26:28 **9:7** [r]S ver 1 [s]S Ex 23:32; S 1Ki 5:12 **9:8** [t]2Ki 10:5 **9:9** [u]S Dt 20:15 [v]ver 24 [w]S Nu 23:22 **9:10** [x]S Nu 21:25 [y]S Nu 21:33 [z]S Nu 21:24,35; Jos 2:10 **9:14** [a]S Ex 16:28; S Nu 27:21 **9:15** [b]S ver 3,7; Jos 10:1,4; 11:19; 2Sa 21:2; 24:1 [c]ver 21; Jdg 1:21; Ps 106:34 **9:16** [d]ver 22 **9:17** [e]Jos 18:25; 2Sa 4:2; 23:37 [f]Jos 15:9,60; 18:14,15; Jdg 18:12; 1Sa 6:21; 7:2; Ps 132:6; Jer 26:20 **9:18** [g]ver 15; Jdg 21:1,7,18; 1Sa 20:17; Ps 15:4 [h]S Ex 15:24 **9:20** [i]S Ge 24:8 **9:21** [j]S ver 15 [k]S Dt 29:11 **9:22** [l]ver 6 [m]ver 16 **9:23** [n]S Ge 9:25

9:1–27 The account of how the Gibeonites deceived the leaders of the tribes and obtained a treaty of submission to Israel. It is the first of three sections telling how Israel came into possession of the bulk of the land. Verses 1–2 introduce the three units.

9:1 *kings west of the Jordan.* Small, independent city-kingdoms were scattered over Canaan, inhabited by a variety of peoples who had come earlier from outside the land (compare vv. 1–2 with Ge 15:19; see also note on Ex 3:8).

9:3 *Gibeon.* A site just north of Jerusalem, today called el-Jib, showing the remains of a Late Bronze Age city with an excellent water supply (see map, p. 572). The Gibeonites were in league with a number of neighboring towns (v. 17) but seem to have been dominant in the confederation.

9:4 *they resorted to a ruse.* Motivated by their fear of Israel's God, the Gibeonites used pretense to trick Joshua into a treaty that would allow them to live.

9:6 *make a treaty with us.* In this request they were offering to submit themselves by treaty to be subjects of the Israelites (see v. 11, where they call themselves "your servants"—unmistakable language in the international diplomacy of that day). They chose submission rather than certain death (v. 24).

9:7 *Hivites.* Possibly Horites, an ethnic group living in Canaan related to the Hurrians of northern Mesopotamia (see 11:3,19; Ge 10:17; 34:2; 36:2; Ex 23:23; Jdg 3:3 and note; see also note on Jos 8:30–35).

9:9 *heard reports of him.* The same reports that had been heard in Jericho (see 2:10 and note on 2:9–11).

9:14 *did not inquire of the LORD.* Did not consult their King, whose mission they were on.

9:15 *treaty of peace.* A covenant to let them live was sworn by the heads of the tribes—i.e., an oath was taken in the holy name of God. All such oaths were binding in Israel (see Ex 20:7 and note; Lev 19:12; 1Sa 14:24).

9:18 *The whole assembly grumbled.* Perhaps the people feared the consequences of not following through on the earlier divine order to destroy all the Canaanites, but more likely they grumbled because they could not take over the Gibeonite cities and possessions.

9:21 *woodcutters and water carriers.* A conventional phrase for household servants (see Dt 29:11).

9:23 *under a curse.* Noah's prediction that Canaan would someday "be the slave of Shem" (Ge 9:25–26) has part of its fulfillment in this event (see note on Ge 9:25). *for the house of*

to serve as woodcutters and water carriers
for the house of my God."
[24]They answered Joshua, "Your servants
were clearly told[o] how the LORD your God
had commanded his servant Moses to give
you the whole land and to wipe out all its
inhabitants from before you. So we feared
for our lives because of you, and that is
why we did this. [25]We are now in your
hands.[p] Do to us whatever seems good
and right[q] to you."
[26]So Joshua saved them from the Israelites, and they did not kill them. [27]That day
he made the Gibeonites[r] woodcutters and
water carriers[s] for the community and for
the altar of the LORD at the place the LORD
would choose.[t] And that is what they are
to this day.

The Sun Stands Still

10 Now Adoni-Zedek[u] king of Jerusalem[v] heard that Joshua had taken Ai[w]
and totally destroyed[a][x] it, doing to Ai and
its king as he had done to Jericho and its
king, and that the people of Gibeon[y] had
made a treaty of peace[z] with Israel and
were living near them. [2]He and his people were very much alarmed at this, because Gibeon was an important city, like
one of the royal cities; it was larger than
Ai, and all its men were good fighters. [3]So
Adoni-Zedek king of Jerusalem appealed
to Hoham king of Hebron,[a] Piram king of
Jarmuth,[b] Japhia king of Lachish[c] and Debir[d] king of Eglon.[e] [4]"Come up and help
me attack Gibeon," he said, "because it
has made peace[f] with Joshua and the Israelites."
[5]Then the five kings[g] of the Amorites[h]—
the kings of Jerusalem, Hebron, Jarmuth, Lachish and Eglon—joined forces.
They moved up with all their troops and
took up positions against Gibeon and attacked it.
[6]The Gibeonites then sent word to Joshua in the camp at Gilgal:[i] "Do not abandon your servants. Come up to us quickly and save us! Help us, because all the
Amorite kings from the hill country have
joined forces against us."
[7]So Joshua marched up from Gilgal with
his entire army,[j] including all the best
fighting men. [8]The LORD said to Joshua,
"Do not be afraid[k] of them; I have given
them into your hand.[l] Not one of them
will be able to withstand you."[m]
[9]After an all-night march from Gilgal,
Joshua took them by surprise. [10]The LORD
threw them into confusion[n] before Israel,[o] who defeated them in a great victory at Gibeon.[p] Israel pursued them along
the road going up to Beth Horon[q] and cut
them down all the way to Azekah[r] and
Makkedah.[s] [11]As they fled before Israel on the road down from Beth Horon to
Azekah, the LORD hurled large hailstones[t]
down on them from the sky,[u] and more of
them died from the hailstones than were
killed by the swords of the Israelites.
[12]On the day the LORD gave the Amorites[v] over to Israel, Joshua said to the
LORD in the presence of Israel:

[a] *1* The Hebrew term refers to the irrevocable giving over of things or persons to the LORD, often by totally destroying them; also in verses 28, 35, 37, 39 and 40.

9:24 [o]ver 9 **9:25** [p]Ge 16:6 [q]Jer 26:14 **9:27** [r]S Ex 1:11 [s]S Dt 29:11 [t]Dt 12:5 **10:1** [u]ver 3 [v]Jos 12:10; 15:8, 63; 18:28; Jdg 1:7 [w]S Jos 8:1 [x]S Dt 20:16; S Jos 8:22 [y]Jos 9:3 [z]S Jos 9:15 **10:3** [a]S Ge 13:18 [b]ver 5; Jos 12:11; 15:35; 21:29; Ne 11:29 [c]ver 5, 31; Jos 12:11; 15:39; 2Ki 14:19; 2Ch 11:9; 25:27; 32:9; Ne 11:30; Isa 36:2; 37:8; Jer 34:7; Mic 1:13 [d]ver 38; Jos 11:21; 12:13; 13:26; 15:7, 49; 21:15; Jdg 1:11; 1Ch 6:58 [e]ver 23, 34, 36; Jos 12:12; 15:39 **10:4** [f]S Jos 9:15 **10:5** [g]ver 16 [h]Nu 13:29; S Dt 1:7 **10:6** [i]S Dt 11:30 **10:7** [j]Jos 8:1 **10:8** [k]S Dt 3:2; S Jos 1:9 [l]S Jos 2:24 [m]S Dt 7:24 **10:10** [n]S Ex 14:24 [o]S Dt 7:23 [p]S Jos 9:3 [q]Jos 16:3, 5; 18:13, 14; 21:22; 1Sa 13:18; 1Ki 9:17; 1Ch 6:68; 7:24; 2Ch 8:5; 25:13 [r]Jos 15:35; 1Sa 17:1; 2Ch 11:9; Ne 11:30; Jer 34:7 [s]ver 16, 17, 21; Jos 12:16; 15:41 **10:11** [t]S Ex 9:18; Ps 18:12; Isa 28:2, 17; 32:19; Eze 13:11, 13 [u]Jdg 5:20 **10:12** [v]Am 2:9

my God. Probably specifies how the Gibeonites were to serve "the entire community" (v. 21). Worship at the tabernacle (and later at the temple) required much wood and water (for sacrifices and washing) and consequently a great deal of menial labor. From now on, that labor was to be supplied by the Gibeonites, perhaps on a rotating basis. In this way they entered the Lord's service. When Solomon became king, the tabernacle and the altar of burnt offering were at Gibeon (2Ch 1:3,5).

9:27 *place the LORD would choose.* Joshua moved the tabernacle (and its altar) to Shiloh, and there it would reside at least until the days of Samuel (1Sa 4:3). Later, the Lord chose Jerusalem (1Ki 9:3).

10:1–43 The army under Joshua comes to the defense of Gibeon and defeats the coalition of southern kings at Aijalon, then subdues all the southern cities of Judah and the Negev.

10:1 *Adoni-Zedek.* Means "lord of righteousness" or "My (divine) lord is righteous." An earlier king of Jerusalem had a similar name (Melchizedek; see Ge 14:18 and note). *Jerusalem.* City of the Jebusites.

10:2 *important city.* Gibeon was not only larger in size than Bethel or Ai, but also closer to Jerusalem. With Bethel and Ai conquered and the Gibeonite league in submission, the Israelites were well established in the central highlands, virtually cutting the land in two. Naturally the king of Jerusalem felt threatened, and he wanted to reunite all the Canaanites against Israel. Perhaps he also held (or claimed) some political dominion over the Gibeonite cities and viewed their submission to Israel as rebellion. *good fighters.* Men known to be effective in battle. Yet they were wise enough to have made peace with the Israelites.

10:5 *five kings of the Amorites.* Rulers over five of the major cities in the southern hill country. The Amorites of the hills are here distinguished from the Canaanites along the coast.

10:6 *Come ... and save us!* An urgent appeal for deliverance to a man whose name means "The LORD saves." A treaty such as Joshua had made with the Gibeonites usually obliged the ruling nation to come to the aid of the subject peoples if they were attacked (see chart, p. 19, under "SUZERAIN-VASSAL").

10:9 *all-night march.* Gilgal was about 20 miles east of Gibeon, a steep uphill climb for Joshua's men. *by surprise.* Joshua attacked early in the morning, perhaps while the moon was still up (v. 12).

10:10 *confusion.* The Hebrew for this word implies terror or panic.

10:11 *down from Beth Horon.* A long descent to the plain of Aijalon below, following the main east-west crossroad just north of Jerusalem. *large hailstones.* For the Lord's use of the elements of nature as his armaments see Jdg 5:20 and note; 1Sa 7:10; Job 38:22–23; Ps 18:12–14.

"O sun, stand still over Gibeon,
O moon, over the Valley of
Aijalon.[w]"
13So the sun stood still,[x]
and the moon stopped,
till the nation avenged itself on[a] its
enemies,

as it is written in the Book of Jashar.[y]

The sun stopped[z] in the middle of the sky and delayed going down about a full day. 14There has never been a day like it before or since, a day when the LORD listened to a man. Surely the LORD was fighting[a] for Israel!

15Then Joshua returned with all Israel to the camp at Gilgal.[b]

Five Amorite Kings Killed

16Now the five kings had fled[c] and hidden in the cave at Makkedah. 17When Joshua was told that the five kings had been found hiding in the cave at Makkedah, 18he said, "Roll large rocks up to the mouth of the cave, and post some men there to guard it. 19But don't stop! Pursue your enemies, attack them from the rear and don't let them reach their cities, for the LORD your God has given them into your hand."

20So Joshua and the Israelites destroyed them completely[d]—almost to a man—but the few who were left reached their fortified cities.[e] 21The whole army then returned safely to Joshua in the camp at Makkedah, and no one uttered a word against the Israelites.

22Joshua said, "Open the mouth of the cave and bring those five kings out to me." 23So they brought the five kings out of the cave—the kings of Jerusalem, Hebron, Jarmuth, Lachish and Eglon. 24When they had brought these kings[f] to Joshua, he summoned all the men of Israel and said to the army commanders who had come with him, "Come here and put your feet[g] on the necks of these kings." So they came forward and placed their feet[h] on their necks.

10:12 [w] Jos 19:42; 21:24; Jdg 1:35; 12:12; 1Sa 14:31; 1Ch 6:69; 8:13; 2Ch 11:10; 28:18
10:13 [x] Hab 3:11 [y] 2Sa 1:18 [z] Isa 38:8
10:14 [a] ver 42; S Ex 14:14; Ps 106:43; 136:24; Isa 63:10; Jer 21:5
10:15 [b] ver 43
10:16 [c] Ps 68:12
10:20 [d] Dt 20:16 [e] 2Ch 11:10; Jer 4:5; 5:17; 8:14; 35:11
10:24 [f] S Dt 7:24 [g] Mal 4:3 [h] 2Sa 22:40; Ps 110:1; Isa 51:23
10:25 [i] S Dt 31:6
10:27 [j] S Dt 21:23 [k] S Ge 35:20
10:28 [l] Dt 20:16 [m] ver 30, 32, 35, 39; Jos 6:21
10:29 [n] S Nu 33:20
10:31 [o] S ver 3
10:33 [p] Jos 12:12; 16:3, 10; 21:21; Jdg 1:29; 2Sa 5:25; 1Ki 9:15; 1Ch 6:67
10:34 [q] S ver 3

25Joshua said to them, "Do not be afraid; do not be discouraged. Be strong and courageous.[i] This is what the LORD will do to all the enemies you are going to fight." 26Then Joshua struck and killed the kings and hung them on five trees, and they were left hanging on the trees until evening.

27At sunset[j] Joshua gave the order and they took them down from the trees and threw them into the cave where they had been hiding. At the mouth of the cave they placed large rocks, which are there to this day.[k]

28That day Joshua took Makkedah. He put the city and its king to the sword and totally destroyed everyone in it. He left no survivors.[l] And he did to the king of Makkedah as he had done to the king of Jericho.[m]

Southern Cities Conquered

29Then Joshua and all Israel with him moved on from Makkedah to Libnah[n] and attacked it. 30The LORD also gave that city and its king into Israel's hand. The city and everyone in it Joshua put to the sword. He left no survivors there. And he did to its king as he had done to the king of Jericho.

31Then Joshua and all Israel with him moved on from Libnah to Lachish;[o] he took up positions against it and attacked it. 32The LORD handed Lachish over to Israel, and Joshua took it on the second day. The city and everyone in it he put to the sword, just as he had done to Libnah. 33Meanwhile, Horam king of Gezer[p] had come up to help Lachish, but Joshua defeated him and his army—until no survivors were left.

34Then Joshua and all Israel with him moved on from Lachish to Eglon;[q] they took up positions against it and attacked it. 35They captured it that same day and put it to the sword and totally destroyed

[a] 13 Or *nation triumphed over*

10:13 *Book of Jashar.* An early account of Israel's wars (perhaps all in poetic form; see 2Sa 1:18; see also note on Jdg 5:1–31), but now lost. *delayed going down.* Some believe that God extended the hours of daylight for the Israelites to defeat their enemies. Others suggest that the sun remained cool (perhaps as the result of an overcast sky) for an entire day, allowing the fighting to continue through the afternoon. The fact is we do not know what happened, except that it involved divine intervention.

10:16 *Makkedah.* A town near Azekah (v. 10) in the western foothills where Joshua's troops made their camp.

10:19 *Pursue your enemies.* Most of the fighting men defending the southern cities were caught and killed before they could reach the safety of their fortresses.

10:21 *no one uttered a word.* The thought here appears to be that no one dared even to raise his voice against the Israelites anymore.

10:24 *put your feet on the necks.* Public humiliation of defeated enemy chieftains was the usual climax of warfare in the ancient Near East.

10:26 *hung them on five trees.* See note on Dt 21:22.

10:27 *they placed large rocks.* A sixth monument in the land to the events of the conquest (see note on 4:9).

10:28 *totally destroyed everyone.* The holy ban was placed on the people of Makkedah, meaning they were "devoted to death" for their wicked deeds (see NIV text note on v. 1). The same fate came to the other major cities of the south (vv. 29–42).

10:33 *Horam king of Gezer.* An important detail: the defeat of the king of the most powerful city in the area. Gezer was eventually taken over by the Egyptians and given to King Solomon as a wedding gift (see 1Ki 9:16 and note on 3:1).

everyone in it, just as they had done to
Lachish.
36 Then Joshua and all Israel with him
went up from Eglon to Hebron[r] and attacked it. 37 They took the city and put it
to the sword, together with its king, its
villages and everyone[s] in it. They left no
survivors. Just as at Eglon, they totally destroyed it and everyone in it.
38 Then Joshua and all Israel with him
turned around and attacked Debir.[t] 39 They
took the city, its king and its villages, and
put them to the sword. Everyone in it they
totally destroyed. They left no survivors.
They did to Debir and its king as they had
done to Libnah and its king and to Hebron.[u]
40 So Joshua subdued the whole region,
including the hill country, the Negev,[v]
the western foothills and the mountain
slopes,[w] together with all their kings.[x] He
left no survivors. He totally destroyed all
who breathed, just as the LORD, the God
of Israel, had commanded.[y] 41 Joshua subdued them from Kadesh Barnea[z] to Gaza[a]
and from the whole region of Goshen[b] to
Gibeon. 42 All these kings and their lands
Joshua conquered in one campaign, because the LORD, the God of Israel, fought[c]
for Israel.
43 Then Joshua returned with all Israel to
the camp at Gilgal.[d]

Northern Kings Defeated

11 When Jabin[e] king of Hazor[f] heard of
this, he sent word to Jobab king of
Madon, to the kings of Shimron[g] and Acshaph,[h] 2 and to the northern kings who
were in the mountains, in the Arabah[i]
south of Kinnereth,[j] in the western foothills and in Naphoth Dor[a][k] on the west; 3 to
the Canaanites in the east and west; to the
Amorites, Hittites, Perizzites[l] and Jebusites
in the hill country;[m] and to the Hivites[n]
below Hermon[o] in the region of Mizpah.[p]
4 They came out with all their troops and
a large number of horses and chariots—a
huge army, as numerous as the sand on
the seashore.[q] 5 All these kings joined forces[r] and made camp together at the Waters
of Merom,[s] to fight against Israel.
6 The LORD said to Joshua, "Do not be
afraid of them, because by this time tomorrow I will hand all of them over[t] to
Israel, slain. You are to hamstring[u] their
horses and burn their chariots."[v]
7 So Joshua and his whole army came
against them suddenly at the Waters of
Merom and attacked them, 8 and the LORD
gave them into the hand of Israel. They
defeated them and pursued them all the
way to Greater Sidon,[w] to Misrephoth
Maim,[x] and to the Valley of Mizpah on the
east, until no survivors were left. 9 Joshua
did to them as the LORD had directed: He
hamstrung their horses and burned their
chariots.
10 At that time Joshua turned back and
captured Hazor and put its king to the
sword.[y] (Hazor had been the head of all
these kingdoms.) 11 Everyone in it they
put to the sword. They totally destroyed[b]
them,[z] not sparing anything that breathed,[a]
and he burned up[b] Hazor itself.
12 Joshua took all these royal cities and
their kings and put them to the sword.
He totally destroyed them, as Moses the
servant of the LORD had commanded.[c]

[a] 2 Or *in the heights of Dor* [b] 11 The Hebrew term refers to the irrevocable giving over of things or persons to the LORD, often by totally destroying them; also in verses 12, 20 and 21.

10:36 [r] S Ge 13:18; Jos 14:13; 15:13; 20:7; 21:11; Jdg 16:3 **10:37** [s] S ver 28 **10:38** [t] S ver 3 **10:39** [u] S ver 28 **10:40** [v] S Ge 12:9; Jos 12:8; 15:19, 21; 18:25; 19:8; 1Sa 30:27 [w] S Dt 1:7 [x] Dt 7:24 [y] Dt 20:16-17 **10:41** [z] S Ge 14:7 [a] S Ge 10:19 [b] Jos 11:16; 15:51 **10:42** [c] S ver 14 **10:43** [d] ver 15; Jos 5:9; 1Sa 7:16; 10:8; 11:14; 13:12 **11:1** [e] Jdg 4:2, 7, 23; Ps 83:9 [f] ver 10; Jos 12:19; 15:23, 25; 19:36; Jdg 4:2, 17; 1Sa 12:9; 1Ki 9:15; 2Ki 15:29; Ne 11:33; Jer 49:28, 33 [g] Jos 19:15 [h] Jos 12:20; 19:25 **11:2** [i] ver 16; S Dt 1:1; Jos 12:1; 18:18 [j] S Nu 34:11; Dt 3:17; Jos 19:35; 1Ki 15:20 [k] Jos 12:23; 17:11; Jdg 1:27; 1Ki 4:11; 1Ch 7:29 **11:3** [l] S Jos 3:10 [m] Nu 13:17 [n] S Ex 3:8; Dt 7:1; Jdg 3:3, 5; 1Ki 9:20 [o] S Dt 3:8 [p] ver 8; S Ge 31:49; Jos 15:38; 18:26; Jdg 11:11; 20:1; 21:1; 1Sa 7:5, 6; 1Ki 15:22; 2Ki 25:23 **11:4** [q] S Ge 12:2; Jdg 7:12; 1Sa 13:5 **11:5** [r] Jdg 5:19 [s] ver 7 **11:6** [t] S Jos 2:24 [u] S Ge 49:6 [v] ver 9 **11:8** [w] S Ge 10:15; S Jdg 18:7 [x] Jos 13:6 **11:10** [y] Isa 3:25; Jer 41:2; 44:18 **11:11** [z] S Dt 7:2 [a] Dt 20:16-17 [b] S Nu 31:10 **11:12** [c] Nu 33:50-52; Dt 7:2

10:38 *Debir.* Also known as Kiriath Sepher, 15:15. This city was at one time identified with Tell Beit Mirsim. More recently, however, it has been equated with Khirbet Rabud, about five miles southwest of Hebron.

10:41 *Kadesh Barnea to Gaza.* The south-to-north limits in the western part of the region. *Goshen.* A seldom-used name for the eastern Negev, not to be confused with the Goshen in the delta of Egypt; it is also the name of a town (15:51). Goshen and Gibeon mark the south-to-north limits in the eastern part of the region.

11:1–23 Only the northern cities remained to be conquered. The major battle for the hills of Galilee is fought and won against Hazor and the coalition of other northern city-states. A summary follows of all Joshua's victories in the southern and central regions as well.

11:1 *Jabin king of Hazor.* Jabin is perhaps a dynastic name, used again in the days of Deborah (see Jdg 4:2 and note).

11:2 *Kinnereth.* Means "harp"; the Sea of Galilee (but see note on Dt 3:17).

11:3 *Hivites.* See 9:7 and note.

11:4 *as numerous as the sand.* A widely used figure of speech for indicating large numbers (see note on Ge 22:17).

11:5 *All these kings.* Jabin's muster extended as far as the Arabah (v. 2) in the Jordan Valley and as far as Dor on the Mediterranean, south of Mount Carmel. *Merom.* Probably modern Meirun, about eight miles northwest of the Sea of Galilee.

11:6 *hamstring their horses.* Done by cutting the tendon above the hock or ankle, crippling the horse so that it cannot walk again. *burn their chariots.* These advanced implements of war were not used by the armies of Israel until the time of Solomon (see 1Ki 9:22 and note on 4:26; 10:26–29).

11:10 *Joshua ... captured Hazor.* Perhaps his greatest victory. Hazor's armed forces, however, had been defeated earlier at Merom. The archaeological site reveals extensive damage and the burning of the Canaanite city c. 1400 B.C., c. 1300 and again c. 1230. Since the destruction level at c. 1300 probably indicates the burning of the city by Pharaoh Seti I, this leaves the destruction levels at c. 1400 and c. 1230 for Joshua's conquest. Those who hold to the late date of the conquest opt for the 1230 level; those who hold to the early date opt for 1400 (see Introduction: Historical Setting). Once again the ban of total destruction was applied (v. 11).

13Yet Israel did not burn any of the cities
built on their mounds — except Hazor,
which Joshua burned. 14The Israelites carried off for themselves all the plunder and
livestock of these cities, but all the people
they put to the sword until they completely destroyed them, not sparing anyone
that breathed.[d] 15As the LORD commanded
his servant Moses, so Moses commanded
Joshua, and Joshua did it; he left nothing
undone of all that the LORD commanded
Moses.[e]

16So Joshua took this entire land: the hill
country,[f] all the Negev,[g] the whole region
of Goshen, the western foothills,[h] the Arabah and the mountains of Israel with their
foothills, 17from Mount Halak, which rises
toward Seir,[i] to Baal Gad[j] in the Valley of
Lebanon[k] below Mount Hermon.[l] He captured all their kings and struck them down,
putting them to death.[m] 18Joshua waged
war against all these kings for a long time.
19Except for the Hivites[n] living in Gibeon,[o]
not one city made a treaty of peace[p] with
the Israelites, who took them all in battle.
20For it was the LORD himself who hardened their hearts[q] to wage war against Israel, so that he might destroy them totally,
exterminating them without mercy, as the
LORD had commanded Moses.[r]

21At that time Joshua went and destroyed the Anakites[s] from the hill country: from Hebron, Debir[t] and Anab,[u] from
all the hill country of Judah, and from all
the hill country of Israel. Joshua totally
destroyed them and their towns. 22No Anakites were left in Israelite territory; only
in Gaza,[v] Gath[w] and Ashdod[x] did any survive. 23So Joshua took the entire land,[y]
just as the LORD had directed Moses, and
he gave it as an inheritance[z] to Israel according to their tribal divisions.[a b]

Then the land had rest[c] from war.[d]

11:14 [d]S Dt 20:16 **11:15** [e]Ex 34:11; Dt 7:2; S Jos 1:7 **11:16** [f]Nu 13:17 [g]S Dt 1:7 [h]S Jos 10:41 **11:17** [i]S Ge 14:6; S Nu 24:18; S Dt 33:2 [j]Jos 13:5 [k]S Dt 3:25; Jos 12:7 [l]Dt 3:9; Jos 12:8 [m]Dt 7:24 **11:19** [n]S Jos 9:1 [o]S Jos 9:3 [p]S Jos 9:15 **11:20** [q]S Ex 4:21; S 14:17; Ro 9:18 [r]Dt 7:16; Jdg 14:4 **11:21** [s]S Nu 13:22, 33 [t]S Jos 10:3 [u]Jos 15:50 **11:22** [v]S Ge 10:19 [w]Jos 12:17; 19:13; 1Sa 5:8; 17:4; 1Ki 2:39; 2Ki 14:25; 1Ch 8:13; Am 6:2 [x]Jos 15:47; 1Sa 5:1; Isa 20:1 **11:23** [y]Jos 21:43-45; Ne 9:24 [z]S Dt 1:38; 12:9-10; S 25:19; S Jos 13:7 [a]S Nu 26:53 [b]Ps 105:44 [c]S Ex 33:14 [d]Jos 14:15

12:1 [e]Ps 136:21 [f]S Nu 32:19 [g]S Nu 21:13 [h]S Dt 3:8 [i]S Jos 11:2 **12:2** [j]ver 5; S Nu 21:21, 25; Jos 13:10; Jdg 11:19 [k]S Nu 32:34; S Jos 13:16 [l]S Ge 32:22 [m]S Ge 19:38

List of Defeated Kings

12 These are the kings of the land
whom the Israelites had defeated
and whose territory they took[e] over east
of the Jordan,[f] from the Arnon[g] Gorge to
Mount Hermon,[h] including all the eastern
side of the Arabah:[i]

2Sihon king of the Amorites,
who reigned in Heshbon.[j] He ruled
from Aroer[k] on the rim of the Arnon Gorge — from the middle of the
gorge — to the Jabbok River,[l] which is
the border of the Ammonites.[m] This
included half of Gilead.[n] 3He also
ruled over the eastern Arabah from
the Sea of Kinnereth[a o] to the Sea of
the Arabah (the Salt Sea[b p]), to Beth
Jeshimoth,[q] and then southward below the slopes of Pisgah.[r]

4And the territory of Og king of Bashan,[s]
one of the last of the Rephaites,[t] who
reigned in Ashtaroth[u] and Edrei. 5He
ruled over Mount Hermon, Salecah,[v]
all of Bashan[w] to the border of the
people of Geshur[x] and Maacah,[y] and
half of Gilead[z] to the border of Sihon
king of Heshbon.

6Moses, the servant of the LORD, and the
Israelites conquered them.[a] And Moses the
servant of the LORD gave their land to the
Reubenites, the Gadites and the half-tribe
of Manasseh to be their possession.[b]

7These are the kings of the land that
Joshua and the Israelites conquered on

[a] *3* That is, Galilee [b] *3* That is, the Dead Sea

[n]S Ge 31:21; S Nu 32:26; Dt 2:36; S 3:15; Jos 13:11, 25; 17:1; 20:8; 21:38; Jdg 5:17; 7:3; 10:8 **12:3** [o]Jos 11:2 [p]S Ge 14:3 [q]S Nu 33:49; Jos 13:20 [r]S Nu 21:20 **12:4** [s]S Nu 21:21, 33; Jos 13:30 [t]S Ge 14:5 [u]S Dt 1:4 **12:5** [v]S Dt 3:10 [w]Nu 32:33; Jos 17:1; 20:8; 21:27; 22:7 [x]Jos 13:2, 13; 1Sa 27:8 [y]S Dt 3:14 [z]ver 2 **12:6** [a]S Dt 3:8 [b]Nu 32:29, 33; Jos 13:8

11:13 *mounds.* The Hebrew word is *tel* (Arabic *tell*), a hill formed by the accumulated debris of many ancient settlements one on top of another (see notes on 7:2; Jer 30:18).

11:15 *he left nothing undone.* Joshua's success should be measured in the light of the specific orders given by God, which he carried out fully, rather than by the total area that eventually would have to be occupied by Israel.

11:16 *this entire land.* A lesson in the geography of Canaan follows. See map No. 2 at the end of this study Bible; see also maps, pp. 308 – 311.

11:17 *Mount Halak.* A desert peak to the east of Kadesh Barnea marking Israel's southern extremity. *Baal Gad.* The first valley west of Mount Hermon.

11:18 *for a long time.* An estimation of the duration of Joshua's conquests can be made from the life span of Caleb: Seven years had elapsed from the beginning of the conquest (age 78; compare 14:7 with Dt 2:14) until he took Hebron (age 85; see 14:10).

11:19 *Hivites.* See 9:7 and note.

11:20 *the LORD … hardened their hearts.* See notes on Ex 4:21; 7:13.

11:21 *Anakites.* Had been reported by the 12 spies to be a people "of great size" (Nu 13:32), whom the Israelites had feared so much that they had refused to undertake the conquest. They were related to the Nephilim (see note on Ge 6:4) and were named after their forefather, Anak. Joshua shared with Caleb his victory over the Anakites (14:12 – 15).

12:1 – 24 A conclusion to the first section of Joshua, and a summary of the victories of the Israelites and the cities whose kings had been defeated (see map No. 3 at the end of this study Bible; see also maps, pp. 308 – 311).

12:1 *territory … east of the Jordan.* The unity of the nation is reaffirmed by the inclusion of these lands in Transjordan. *Arnon Gorge.* Marked the border with Moab to the south. *Mount Hermon.* The upper limits of Israel's land to the north.

12:4 *Og king of Bashan.* Sihon and Og (v. 2) were defeated by Israel under Moses' leadership, a long-remembered sign of God's mighty power (see Ne 9:22; Ps 135:11).

12:5 *Salecah … Geshur … Maacah.* All of them east of the Sea of Galilee (Kinnereth): Salecah a town in the far east of Bashan (see map, p. 308), Geshur a small city kingdom (see map, p. 497) northeast of Bashan, Maacah a city-state southeast of Mount Hermon (see also 13:11).

12:7 *the land … on the west side.* Canaan proper (9:1; 11:16 – 17; 24:11; Ge 15:18 – 19).

the west side of the Jordan, from Baal Gad
in the Valley of Lebanon[c] to Mount Halak,
which rises toward Seir (their lands Joshua gave as an inheritance to the tribes of
Israel according to their tribal divisions—
8the hill country, the western foothills, the
Arabah, the mountain slopes, the desert
and the Negev[d]—the lands of the Hittites,
Amorites, Canaanites, Perizzites, Hivites
and Jebusites):[e]

9the king of Jericho[f] one
the king of Ai[g] (near Bethel[h]) one
10the king of Jerusalem[i] one
the king of Hebron one
11the king of Jarmuth one
the king of Lachish[j] one
12the king of Eglon[k] one
the king of Gezer[l] one
13the king of Debir[m] one
the king of Geder one
14the king of Hormah[n] one
the king of Arad[o] one
15the king of Libnah[p] one
the king of Adullam[q] one
16the king of Makkedah[r] one
the king of Bethel[s] one
17the king of Tappuah[t] one
the king of Hepher[u] one
18the king of Aphek[v] one
the king of Lasharon one
19the king of Madon one
the king of Hazor[w] one
20the king of Shimron Meron one
the king of Acshaph[x] one
21the king of Taanach[y] one
the king of Megiddo[z] one
22the king of Kedesh[a] one
the king of Jokneam[b] in
Carmel[c] one
23the king of Dor (in Naphoth
Dor[a d]) one
the king of Goyim in Gilgal one
24the king of Tirzah[e] one
thirty-one kings in all.[f]

Land Still to Be Taken

13 When Joshua was old and well advanced in years,[g] the LORD said to
him, "You are very old, and there are still
very large areas of land to be taken over.

2"This is the land that remains: all the
regions of the Philistines[h] and Geshurites:[i] 3from the Shihor River[j] on the
east of Egypt to the territory of Ekron[k] on the north, all of it counted
as Canaanite (the territory of the five
Philistine rulers[l] in Gaza, Ashdod,[m]
Ashkelon,[n] Gath and Ekron—that of
the Avvites);[o] 4from the south, all the
land of the Canaanites, from Arah of
the Sidonians as far as Aphek,[p] the
region of the Amorites,[q] 5the area of
the Gebalites[b];[r] and all Lebanon[s] to
the east, from Baal Gad below Mount
Hermon[t] to Lebo[c] Hamath.[u]

6"As for all the inhabitants of the mountain regions from Lebanon to Misrephoth
Maim,[v] that is, all the Sidonians, I myself
will drive them out[w] before the Israelites.
Be sure to allocate this land to Israel for an
inheritance, as I have instructed you,[x] 7and
divide it as an inheritance[y] among the nine
tribes and half of the tribe of Manasseh."

Division of the Land East of the Jordan

8The other half of Manasseh,[d] the Reubenites and the Gadites had received the inheritance that Moses had given them east
of the Jordan, as he, the servant of the
LORD, had assigned[z] it to them.[a]

9It extended from Aroer[b] on the rim of
the Arnon Gorge, and from the town
in the middle of the gorge, and included the whole plateau[c] of Medeba

12:7 [c]S Jos 11:17 **12:8** [d]S Dt 1:7 [e]S Jos 3:10; S 11:17; Ezr 9:1 **12:9** [f]S Nu 33:48 [g]S Ge 12:8; S Jos 8:1 [h]S Jos 7:2; 8:9; 18:13; Jdg 1:23; 4:5; 20:18; 21:2; Ne 11:31 **12:10** [i]S Jos 10:1 **12:11** [j]S Jos 10:3 **12:12** [k]S Jos 10:3 [l]S Jos 10:33 **12:13** [m]S Jos 10:3 **12:14** [n]S Nu 14:45 [o]S Nu 21:1 **12:15** [p]S Nu 33:20 [q]S Ge 38:1; Jos 15:35; Mic 1:15 **12:16** [r]S Jos 10:10 [s]S Jos 7:2 **12:17** [t]Jos 15:34; 16:8; 17:8 [u]S Jos 11:22; 1Ki 4:10 **12:18** [v]Jos 13:4; 19:30; Jdg 1:31; 1Sa 4:1; 29:1 **12:19** [w]S Jos 11:1 **12:20** [x]S Jos 11:1 **12:21** [y]Jos 17:11; 21:25 [z]Jdg 1:27; 5:19; 1Ki 4:12 **12:22** [a]Jos 15:23; 19:37; 20:7; 21:32; Jdg 4:6,9 [b]Jos 19:11; 21:34 [c]Jos 15:55; 19:26; 1Sa 15:12; 2Sa 23:35 **12:23** [d]S Jos 11:2 **12:24** [e]1Ki 14:17; 15:33; 16:8,23; SS 6:4 [f]Ps 135:11; 136:18 **13:1** [g]Ge 24:1; Jos 14:10; 23:1,2; 1Ki 1:1

[a] 23 Or *in the heights of Dor* [b] 5 That is, the area of Byblos [c] 5 Or *to the entrance to* [d] 8 Hebrew *With it* (that is, with the other half of Manasseh)

13:2 [h]S Ge 10:14; S Jdg 3:31 [i]S Jos 12:5 **13:3** [j]1Ch 13:5; Isa 23:3; Jer 2:18 [k]Jos 15:11,45; 19:43; Jdg 1:18; 1Sa 5:10; 7:14 [l]Jdg 3:3; 16:5,18; 1Sa 6:4,17; Isa 14:29; Jer 25:20; Eze 25:15 [m]S Jos 11:22; Am 3:9 [n]Jdg 1:18; 14:19; 2Sa 1:20 [o]S Dt 2:23 **13:4** [p]S Jos 12:18 [q]S Ge 14:7; S 15:16; Am 2:10 **13:5** [r]1Ki 5:18; Ps 83:7; Eze 27:9 [s]S Jos 11:17 [t]S Dt 3:8 [u]S Nu 13:21; 34:8; Jdg 3:3 **13:6** [v]Jos 11:8 [w]Ps 80:8 [x]Nu 33:54; S 34:13 **13:7** [y]S Jos 11:23; Ps 78:55 **13:8** [z]S Jos 12:6 [a]Jos 18:7 **13:9** [b]ver 16; S Nu 32:34; Dt 2:36; Jdg 11:26; 2Sa 24:5 [c]ver 17,21; Jer 48:8,21

12:12 *king of Gezer.* Had been defeated in the siege of Lachish (see 10:33 and note), but the city itself was not captured by Joshua, nor were the cities of Aphek, Taanach, Megiddo or Dor (vv. 18–23; see Jdg 1:27–31).

13:1–32 The heavenly King, who has conquered the land, begins the administration of his realm by assigning specific territories to the several tribes. Much of chs. 13–21 reads like administrative documents. The account begins by noting the land still to be subdued (but to be allotted) and by recalling the assignments already made by Moses to the two and a half tribes east of the Jordan (see map No. 4 at the end of this study Bible).

13:1 *Joshua was old.* Between 90 and 100 years of age; Caleb was 85 (14:10). *still … large areas … to be taken over.* See note on 18:3.

13:3 *Shihor River.* Elsewhere Shihor apparently refers to a branch of the Nile (see 1Ch 13:5; Isa 23:3 and notes; see also NIV text note on Jer 2:18). Here, however, it appears to be another name for the Wadi el-Arish below Gaza at the eastern entrance to the Sinai ("on the east of Egypt"). *Ekron.* See note on 1Sa 5:10. *rulers.* The Hebrew for this word may be related to the Greek term *tyrannos* (from which comes English "tyrant"). In the OT it is used only of Philistine rulers and so may indicate the Aegean background of the Philistines. See map, p. 331.

13:5 *Gebalites.* Inhabitants of the ancient city of Byblos (see NIV text note) just north of modern Beirut. The Phoenicians and the Philistines held most of the territory still to be occupied by Israel.

13:9 *Aroer.* This town on the Arnon River marked the southern boundary of Israel east of the Jordan. From here the land extended north through Gilead and Bashan to the slopes of Mount Hermon, the territory once dominated by the two kings of the Amorites, Sihon and Og.

as far as Dibon,[d] 10and all the towns
of Sihon king of the Amorites, who
ruled in Heshbon,[e] out to the border
of the Ammonites.[f] 11It also included
Gilead,[g] the territory of the people
of Geshur and Maacah, all of Mount
Hermon and all Bashan as far as Salecah[h]— 12that is, the whole kingdom
of Og in Bashan,[i] who had reigned in
Ashtaroth[j] and Edrei[k] and had survived as one of the last of the Rephaites.[l] Moses had defeated them and
taken over their land.[m] 13But the Israelites did not drive out the people of
Geshur[n] and Maacah,[o] so they continue to live among the Israelites to
this day.[p]

14But to the tribe of Levi he gave no inheritance, since the offerings made by fire
to the LORD, the God of Israel, are their
inheritance, as he promised them.[q]

13:9 [d]S Nu 21:30; S 32:3; Isa 15:2; Jer 48:18,22
13:10 [e]S Jos 12:2 [f]S Nu 21:24
13:11 [g]S Jos 12:2 [h]Jos 12:5
13:12 [i]S Dt 1:4 [j]Jos 12:4 [k]S Nu 21:33 [l]S Ge 14:5 [m]S Dt 3:8
13:13 [n]S Jos 12:5 [o]S Dt 3:14 [p]Dt 3:12
13:14 [q]ver 33; Dt 18:1-2; Jos 14:3
13:16 [r]S ver 9; Jos 12:2; 1Sa 30:28 [s]S Nu 21:30; Isa 15:2
13:17 [t]S ver 9 [u]S Nu 32:3

15This is what Moses had given to the tribe
of Reuben, clan by clan:

16The territory from Aroer[r] on the
rim of the Arnon Gorge, and from
the town in the middle of the gorge,
and the whole plateau past Medeba[s]
17to Heshbon and all its towns on
the plateau,[t] including Dibon,[u] Bamoth Baal,[v] Beth Baal Meon,[w] 18Ja-
haz,[x] Kedemoth,[y] Mephaath,[z] 19Kir-
iathaim,[a] Sibmah,[b] Zereth Shahar
on the hill in the valley, 20Beth Peor,[c]
the slopes of Pisgah, and Beth Jeshimoth— 21all the towns on the plateau[d] and the entire realm of Sihon
king of the Amorites, who ruled at
Heshbon. Moses had defeated him
and the Midianite chiefs,[e] Evi, Re-

[v]Nu 22:41 [w]1Ch 5:8; Jer 48:23; Eze 25:9 **13:18** [x]S Nu 21:23 [y]S Dt 2:26 [z]Jos 21:37; Jer 48:21 **13:19** [a]S Nu 32:37 [b]S Nu 32:3 **13:20** [c]S Dt 3:29 **13:21** [d]S ver 9 [e]S Ge 25:2; S Nu 25:15

13:14 *the offerings . . . are their inheritance.* See Dt 18:1 – 8 and note on 18:1.
13:15 *what Moses had given to . . . Reuben.* The land east of the Dead Sea between the Arnon River (boundary of Moab) and Heshbon (the old royal city of Sihon).

Conquest of Canaan: Entry

ENTRY INTO CANAAN

When the Israelite tribes approached Canaan after four decades of desert existence, they had to overcome the two Amorite kingdoms on the Medeba plateau and in Bashan. Under Moses' leadership, they also subdued the Midianites in order to consolidate their control over the Transjordanian region.

The conquest of Canaan followed a course that in retrospect appears as though it had been planned by a brilliant strategist. Taking Jericho gave Israel control of its strategic plains, fords and roads as a base of operations. When Israel next gained control of the Bethel, Gibeon and Upper Beth Horon region, it dominated the center of the north-south Palestinian ridge. Subsequently, Israel was able to break the power of the allied urban centers in separate campaigns south and north.

kem, Zur, Hur and Reba[f]—princes allied with Sihon—who lived in that country. 22 In addition to those slain in battle, the Israelites had put to the sword Balaam son of Beor,[g] who practiced divination.[h] 23 The boundary of the Reubenites was the bank of the Jordan. These towns and their villages were the inheritance of the Reubenites, clan by clan.[i]

24 This is what Moses had given to the tribe of Gad, clan by clan:

25 The territory of Jazer,[j] all the towns of Gilead[k] and half the Ammonite country as far as Aroer, near Rabbah;[l] 26 and from Heshbon[m] to Ramath Mizpah and Betonim, and from Mahanaim[n] to the territory of Debir;[o] 27 and in the valley, Beth Haram, Beth Nimrah,[p] Succoth[q] and Zaphon[r] with the rest of the realm of Sihon king of Heshbon (the east side of the Jordan, the territory up to the end of the Sea of Kinnereth[a s]). 28 These towns and their villages were the inheritance of the Gadites,[t] clan by clan.

13:21 [f]Nu 31:8 **13:22** [g]S Nu 22:5 [h]S Ge 30:27; S Nu 23:23 **13:23** [i]1Ch 5:7 **13:25** [j]S Nu 21:32; Jos 21:39 [k]S Jos 12:2 [l]S Dt 3:11 **13:26** [m]S Nu 21:25; Jer 49:3 [n]S Ge 32:2 [o]S Jos 10:3 **13:27** [p]S Nu 32:3 [q]S Ge 33:17 [r]Jdg 12:1; Ps 48:2 [s]S Nu 34:11 **13:28** [t]Ge 46:16; S Nu 32:33; Eze 48:27 **13:30** [u]S Ge 32:2 [v]S Nu 21:33 [w]S Jos 12:4 [x]S Nu 32:41 **13:31** [y]Nu 21:33 [z]S Ge 50:23 [a]Jos 17:5 **13:32** [b]S Nu 26:3

29 This is what Moses had given to the half-tribe of Manasseh, that is, to half the family of the descendants of Manasseh, clan by clan:

30 The territory extending from Mahanaim[u] and including all of Bashan,[v] the entire realm of Og king of Bashan[w]—all the settlements of Jair[x] in Bashan, sixty towns, 31 half of Gilead, and Ashtaroth and Edrei (the royal cities of Og in Bashan).[y] This was for the descendants of Makir[z] son of Manasseh—for half of the sons of Makir, clan by clan.[a]

32 This is the inheritance Moses had given when he was in the plains of Moab[b] across the Jordan east of Jericho.[c] 33 But to the tribe of Levi, Moses had given no inheritance;[d] the LORD, the God of Israel, is their inheritance,[e] as he promised them.[f]

a 27 That is, Galilee

[c]S Nu 22:1 **13:33** [d]Nu 26:62 [e]S Nu 18:20 [f]S ver 14; Jos 18:7; Eze 44:28

13:22 *Balaam son of Beor.* The one who supposedly had influence with the gods (Nu 22–24) was slain when the Lord punished the Midianites for trying to seduce Israel into idolatry and sexual immorality (see Nu 25; 31:8 and notes on Nu 22:5,8).
13:24 *what Moses had given to ... Gad.* The central area, beginning near Heshbon on the south and reaching, along the Jordan, to the southern end of the Sea of Galilee. It included most of Gilead, but the exact boundary between Gad and the half-tribe of Manasseh remains somewhat uncertain since not all the places named can now be located.
13:29 *what Moses had given to the half-tribe of Manasseh.* The lands east and north of the Sea of Galilee, but also including the upper part of Gilead. Makir led in the occupation of these lands (see Nu 32:32,39–42).
13:33 *the LORD ... is their inheritance.* See v. 14; see also Dt 18:1–8 and note on 18:1.

Initial Conquests and the Submission of the Gibeonites

The conquest of Jericho and of Ai and Bethel led to the submission of the Gibeonite league (Gibea, Kaphira, Beeroth, Kiriath Jearim). This gave the Israelites control of an east/west corridor across Canaan's hilly spine and cut the area to be conquered into two distinct clusters of cities; those to the south and those to the north.

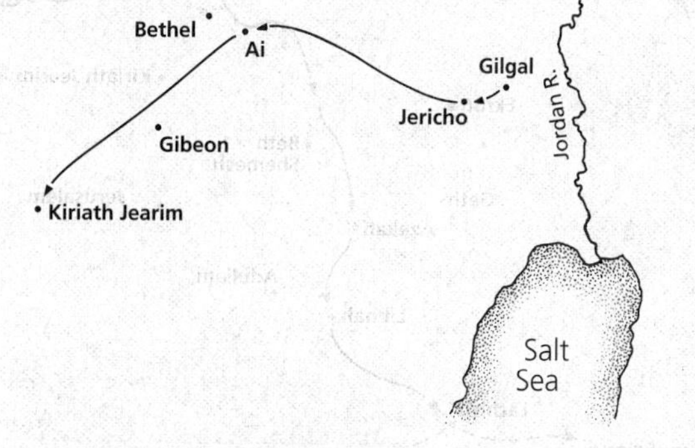

Archaeological evidence for the conquest is mixed, in part because the chronological problems are unsolved. On the one hand, clay tablets containing cuneiform letters to the Egyptian court have been found at Tell el-Amarna in Egypt from c. 1375 B.C. These mention bands of Habiru who threaten many of the cities of Canaan and create fear among the Canaanite inhabitants.

On the other hand, numerous towns were destroyed c. 1230 B.C. by unknown assailants, presumably the "Sea Peoples," but possibly including the Israelites as well. The Biblical chronology based on 1Ki 6:1 seems to demand an even earlier dating, near the end of the 15th century (see Introduction to Joshua: Historical Setting).

Division of the Land West of the Jordan

14 Now these are the areas the Israelites received as an inheritance[g] in the
land of Canaan, which Eleazar[h] the priest,
Joshua son of Nun and the heads of the
tribal clans of Israel[i] allotted[j] to them.[k]
2Their inheritances were assigned by lot[l]
to the nine-and-a-half tribes,[m] as the LORD
had commanded through Moses. 3Moses
had granted the two-and-a-half tribes their
inheritance east of the Jordan[n] but had not
granted the Levites an inheritance among
the rest,[o] 4for the sons of Joseph had become two tribes—Manasseh and Ephraim.[p] The Levites received no share of the
land but only towns to live in, with pasturelands for their flocks and herds.[q] 5So
the Israelites divided the land, just as the
LORD had commanded Moses.[r]

Hebron Given to Caleb

6Now the men of Judah approached
Joshua at Gilgal,[s] and Caleb son of Jephunneh[t] the Kenizzite said to him, "You
know what the LORD said to Moses the
man of God[u] at Kadesh Barnea[v] about you
and me.[w] 7I was forty years old when Moses the servant of the LORD sent me from
Kadesh Barnea[x] to explore the land.[y] And I
brought him back a report according to my
convictions,[z] 8but my brothers who went
up with me made the hearts of the people melt with fear.[a] I, however, followed
the LORD my God wholeheartedly.[b] 9So on
that day Moses swore to me, 'The land on
which your feet have walked will be your
inheritance[c] and that of your children[d] forever, because you have followed the LORD
my God wholeheartedly.'[a]

10"Now then, just as the LORD promised,[e]
he has kept me alive for forty-five years
since the time he said this to Moses, while
Israel moved[f] about in the desert. So here

[a] 9 Deut. 1:36

14:1 [g]S Jos 11:23; Ps 16:6; 136:21 [h]S Ex 6:23 [i]Jos 21:1 [j]S Nu 26:53 [k]Nu 34:17-18; Jos 19:51 **14:2** [l]S Lev 16:8 [m]Nu 34:13 **14:3** [n]S Nu 32:33; S 34:14 [o]S Nu 35:2; S Jos 13:14 **14:4** [p]S Ge 41:52; S Jdg 1:29 [q]S Nu 35:2-3; Jos 21:2 **14:5** [r]S Nu 34:13 **14:6** [s]S Dt 11:30 [t]Nu 13:6; 14:30 [u]S Dt 33:1 [v]Nu 13:26 [w]S Nu 14:38 **14:7** [x]Jos 15:3 [y]S Nu 13:17 [z]Nu 13:30; S 14:6-9 **14:8** [a]S Nu 13:31 [b]S Nu 14:24; S 32:12 **14:9** [c]S Dt 11:24 [d]S Nu 14:24 **14:10** [e]S Nu 11:28; 14:30 [f]S Jos 5:6

14:1–5 An introduction to the allotment of territories in Canaan.
14:1 *Eleazar the priest.* Son of Aaron, Eleazar as high priest was the highest official over the casting of the lots. The Urim and Thummim (see notes on Ex 28:30; 1Sa 2:28) may have been used.
14:4 *Manasseh and Ephraim.* Sons of Joseph. Since Jacob had adopted them as his own sons (see Ge 48:5 and note), they constituted two separate tribes. This made possible the 12-part nation, with the Levite tribe dispersed among them.
14:6–15 Assignment of Hebron to Caleb—in accordance with Moses' pledge to him for his faithful service as one of Israel's spies sent to explore the promised land (see Nu 14:24,30; 32:12 and note on 14:24). Assignment of cities in Canaan to Caleb (Judah) and Joshua (Ephraim) frame the account of territorial divisions west of the Jordan (see 19:49–50 and note on 19:49).
14:6 *what the LORD said.* Caleb now recalls the promise from the Lord 38 years earlier at Kadesh Barnea when he brought back a good report of the land (see Nu 13:30 and note; 14:6–9; Dt 1:34–36).
14:8 *followed … wholeheartedly.* See Nu 14:24 and note; 32:12.

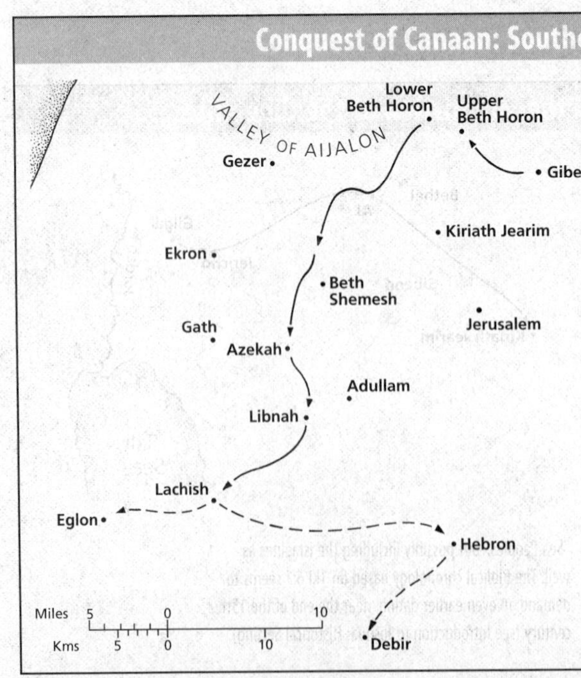

Azekeh, Libnah, Lachish, Eglon, and Debir were all captured by Joshua in his campaign against the southern coalition of Canaanite cities that was led by the king of Jerusalem.

Several of these towns, most notably Lachish, contain destruction evidence that might possibly be correlated with the Israelite conquest, but with Jericho and Ai, the historical implications are not clear.

I am today, eighty-five years old![g] 11I am
still as strong[h] today as the day Moses sent
me out; I'm just as vigorous[i] to go out to
battle now as I was then. 12Now give me
this hill country that the LORD promised me
that day.[j] You yourself heard then that the
Anakites[k] were there and their cities were
large and fortified,[l] but, the LORD helping
me, I will drive them out just as he said."
13Then Joshua blessed[m] Caleb son of
Jephunneh[n] and gave him Hebron[o] as his
inheritance.[p] 14So Hebron has belonged
to Caleb son of Jephunneh the Kenizzite
ever since, because he followed the LORD,
the God of Israel, wholeheartedly.[q] 15(Hebron used to be called Kiriath Arba[r] after
Arba,[s] who was the greatest man among
the Anakites.)
Then the land had rest[t] from war.

14:10 [g]S Jos 13:1 **14:11** [h]S Dt 34:7 [i]S Ge 15:15 **14:12** [j]S Nu 14:24 [k]S Nu 13:33 [l]Nu 13:28 **14:13** [m]Jos 22:6,7 [n]1Sa 25:3; 30:14 [o]S Ge 23:19; S Jos 10:36 [p]Jdg 1:20; 1Ch 6:56 **14:14** [q]S Nu 14:24 **14:15** [r]S Ge 23:2 [s]Jos 15:13 [t]Jos 11:23; Jdg 3:11; 1Ki 4:24; 5:4; 1Ch 22:9 **15:1** [u]Nu 34:3 [v]S Nu 13:21 [w]Jos 18:5 **15:2** [x]S Ge 14:3 **15:3** [y]S Nu 34:4 [z]S Dt 1:2 **15:4** [a]Nu 34:4

Allotment for Judah

15:15-19pp — Jdg 1:11-15

15 The allotment for the tribe of Judah,
clan by clan, extended down to the
territory of Edom,[u] to the Desert of Zin[v] in
the extreme south.[w]
2Their southern boundary started from the bay at the southern end
of the Salt Sea,[a][x] 3crossed south of
Scorpion[b] Pass,[y] continued on to Zin
and went over to the south of Kadesh
Barnea.[z] Then it ran past Hezron up
to Addar and curved around to Karka. 4It then passed along to Azmon[a]

[a] 2 That is, the Dead Sea; also in verse 5 [b] 3 Hebrew *Akrabbim*

14:12 *this hill country.* Hebron is situated high in the Judahite hill country, about 25 miles south of Jerusalem. *Anakites.* See note on 11:21.

14:15 *Kiriath Arba.* Means "the town of Arba" and was named for Arba, the father of the Anakites (15:13; 21:11). It can also mean "the town of four," possibly referring to Anak and his three descendants (see 15:14; Nu 13:22 and note; Jdg 1:20). *Then the land had rest from war.* Since the Judahites and Caleb approached Joshua concerning their territory while he was still headquartered at Gilgal, it may be that they did so shortly before the wars fought under Joshua were ended (see 11:23).

15:1–63 Judah is the first of the west bank tribes to have its territory delineated. First the outer limits are listed, then the area apportioned to Caleb and Othniel; finally the Canaanite cities allotted to the clans of Judah are named region by region.

15:1 *tribe of Judah.* Judah's priority is anchored in the oracle of Jacob (see Ge 49:8–12 and note on 49:8) and upheld in the history of the nation (see Jdg 1:1–2 and note on 1:2; 20:18; 2Ki 17:18; Ps 78:68).

15:4 *southern boundary.* The points listed formed a curved line beginning at the lower tip of the Dead Sea and moving under Kadesh Barnea to join the Mediterranean coast at the mouth of the Wadi el-Arish (see note on 13:3).

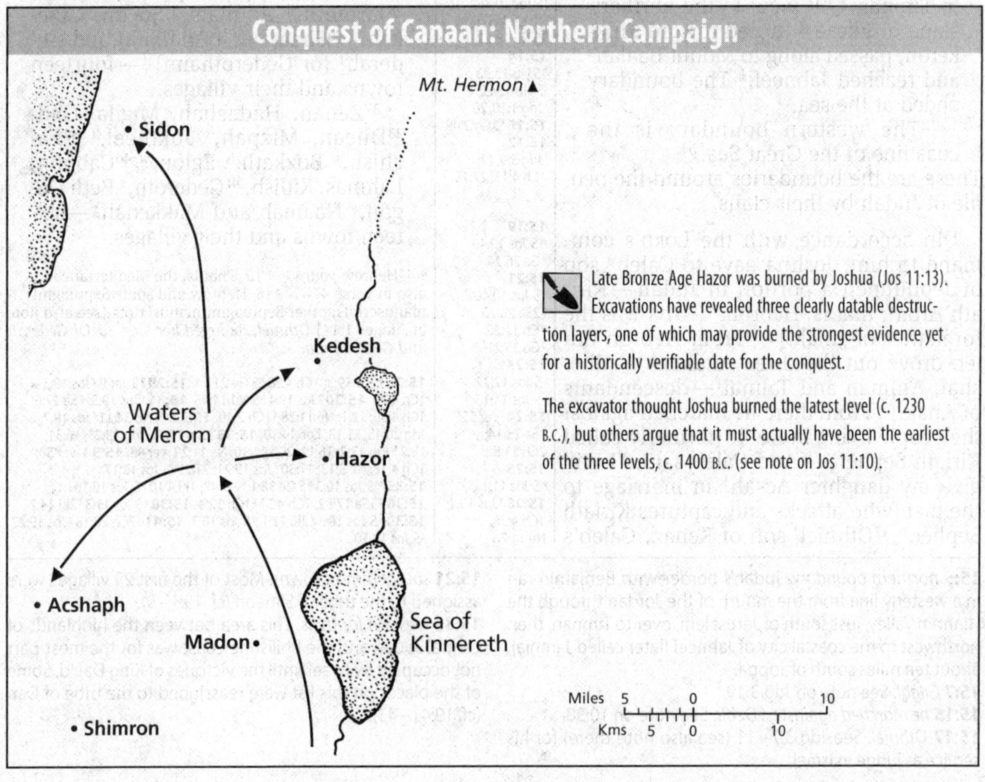
Conquest of Canaan: Northern Campaign
Mt. Hermon
Sidon
Kedesh
Waters of Merom
Hazor
Acshaph
Madon
Sea of Kinnereth
Shimron
Late Bronze Age Hazor was burned by Joshua (Jos 11:13). Excavations have revealed three clearly datable destruction layers, one of which may provide the strongest evidence yet for a historically verifiable date for the conquest.
The excavator thought Joshua burned the latest level (c. 1230 B.C.), but others argue that it must actually have been the earliest of the three levels, c. 1400 B.C. (see note on Jos 11:10).
Miles 5 0 10
Kms 5 0 10

and joined the Wadi of Egypt,[b] ending at the sea. This is their[a] southern boundary.

5 The eastern boundary[c] is the Salt Sea[d] as far as the mouth of the Jordan.

The northern boundary[e] started from the bay of the sea at the mouth of the Jordan, 6 went up to Beth Hoglah[f] and continued north of Beth Arabah[g] to the Stone of Bohan[h] son of Reuben. 7 The boundary then went up to Debir[i] from the Valley of Achor[j] and turned north to Gilgal,[k] which faces the Pass of Adummim south of the gorge. It continued along to the waters of En Shemesh[l] and came out at En Rogel.[m] 8 Then it ran up the Valley of Ben Hinnom[n] along the southern slope of the Jebusite[o] city (that is, Jerusalem[p]). From there it climbed to the top of the hill west of the Hinnom Valley[q] at the northern end of the Valley of Rephaim.[r] 9 From the hilltop the boundary headed toward the spring of the waters of Nephtoah,[s] came out at the towns of Mount Ephron and went down toward Baalah[t] (that is, Kiriath Jearim).[u] 10 Then it curved westward from Baalah[v] to Mount Seir,[w] ran along the northern slope of Mount Jearim (that is, Kesalon), continued down to Beth Shemesh[x] and crossed to Timnah.[y] 11 It went to the northern slope of Ekron,[z] turned toward Shikkeron, passed along to Mount Baalah[a] and reached Jabneel.[b] The boundary ended at the sea.

12 The western boundary is the coastline of the Great Sea.[b][c]

These are the boundaries around the people of Judah by their clans.

13 In accordance with the LORD's command to him, Joshua gave to Caleb[d] son of Jephunneh a portion in Judah—Kiriath Arba[e], that is, Hebron.[f] (Arba was the forefather of Anak.)[g] 14 From Hebron Caleb drove out the three Anakites[h]—Sheshai, Ahiman and Talmai[i]—descendants of Anak.[j] 15 From there he marched against the people living in Debir (formerly called Kiriath Sepher). 16 And Caleb said, "I will give my daughter Acsah[k] in marriage to the man who attacks and captures Kiriath Sepher." 17 Othniel[l] son of Kenaz, Caleb's brother, took it; so Caleb gave his daughter Acsah to him in marriage.

18 One day when she came to Othniel, she urged him[c] to ask her father for a field. When she got off her donkey, Caleb asked her, "What can I do for you?"

19 She replied, "Do me a special favor. Since you have given me land in the Negev,[m] give me also springs of water." So Caleb gave her the upper and lower springs.[n]

20 This is the inheritance of the tribe of Judah, clan by clan:

21 The southernmost towns of the tribe of Judah in the Negev[o] toward the boundary of Edom were:

Kabzeel,[p] Eder,[q] Jagur, 22 Kinah, Dimonah, Adadah, 23 Kedesh,[r] Hazor,[s] Ithnan, 24 Ziph,[t] Telem, Bealoth, 25 Hazor Hadattah, Kerioth Hezron (that is, Hazor),[u] 26 Amam, Shema, Moladah,[v] 27 Hazar Gaddah, Heshmon, Beth Pelet, 28 Hazar Shual,[w] Beersheba,[x] Biziothiah, 29 Baalah,[y] Iim, Ezem,[z] 30 Eltolad,[a] Kesil, Hormah,[b] 31 Ziklag,[c] Madmannah,[d] Sansannah, 32 Lebaoth, Shilhim, Ain[e] and Rimmon[f]—a total of twenty-nine towns and their villages.

33 In the western foothills:

Eshtaol,[g] Zorah,[h] Ashnah,[i] 34 Zanoah,[j] En Gannim,[k] Tappuah,[l] Enam, 35 Jarmuth,[m] Adullam,[n] Socoh,[o] Azekah,[p] 36 Shaaraim,[q] Adithaim and Gederah[r] (or Gederothaim)[d]—fourteen towns and their villages.

37 Zenan, Hadashah, Migdal Gad, 38 Dilean, Mizpah,[s] Joktheel,[t] 39 Lachish,[u] Bozkath,[v] Eglon,[w] 40 Cabbon, Lahmas, Kitlish, 41 Gederoth,[x] Beth Dagon,[y] Naamah and Makkedah[z]—sixteen towns and their villages.

[a] 4 Hebrew *your* [b] 12 That is, the Mediterranean; also in verse 47 [c] 18 Hebrew and some Septuagint manuscripts; other Septuagint manuscripts (see also note at Judges 1:14) *Othniel, he urged her* [d] 36 Or *Gederah and Gederothaim*

15:4 [b] S Ge 15:18 **15:5** [c] Nu 34:10 [d] S Ge 14:3 [e] Jos 18:15-19 **15:6** [f] Jos 18:19,21 [g] ver 61; Jos 18:18 [h] Jos 18:17 **15:7** [i] S Jos 10:3 [j] S Jos 7:24 [k] S Dt 11:30 [l] Jos 18:17 [m] Jos 18:16; 2Sa 17:17; 1Ki 1:9 **15:8** [n] 2Ch 28:3; Jer 19:6 [o] ver 63; Jos 18:16,28; Jdg 1:21; 19:10; 2Sa 5:6; 1Ch 11:4; Ezr 9:1 [p] S Jos 10:1 [q] 2Ki 23:10; Jer 7:31; 19:2 [r] 2Sa 5:18,22; 1Ch 14:9; Isa 17:5 **15:9** [s] Jos 18:15 [t] ver 10,11,29; 2Sa 6:2; 1Ch 13:6 [u] S Jos 9:17 **15:10** [v] S ver 9 [w] S Nu 24:18 [x] Jos 19:22,38; 21:16; Jdg 1:33; 1Sa 6:9; 1Ki 4:9; 2Ki 14:11 [y] S Ge 38:12 **15:11** [z] S Jos 13:3 [a] S ver 9 [b] Jos 19:33 **15:12** [c] S Nu 34:6 **15:13** [d] 1Sa 25:3; 30:14 [e] S Ge 23:2 [f] S Jos 10:36; 21:12; 1Ch 6:56 [g] S Nu 13:22 **15:14** [h] S Nu 13:33 [i] S Nu 13:22 [j] Jdg 1:10,20 **15:16** [k] 1Ch 2:49 **15:17** [l] Jdg 3:9,11; 1Ch 4:13; 27:15 **15:19** [m] S Jos 10:40 [n] Ge 36:24 **15:21** [o] S Jos 10:40 [p] 2Sa 23:20; 1Ch 11:22 [q] Ge 35:21 **15:23** [r] S Jos 12:22 [s] S Jos 11:1 **15:24** [t] ver 55; 1Sa 23:14; 2Ch 11:8 **15:25** [u] S Jos 11:1 **15:26** [v] Jos 19:2; 1Ch 4:28; Ne 11:26

15:28 [w] Jos 19:3; 1Ch 4:28 [x] S Ge 21:14 **15:29** [y] S ver 9 [z] Jos 19:3; 1Ch 4:29 **15:30** [a] Jos 19:4 [b] S Nu 14:45 **15:31** [c] Jos 19:5; 1Sa 27:6; 1Ch 4:30; 12:1; Ne 11:28 [d] 1Ch 2:49 **15:32** [e] S Nu 34:11 [f] Jos 19:7; Jdg 20:45; 21:13; Zec 14:10 **15:33** [g] Jos 19:41; Jdg 13:25; 16:31; 18:2 [h] Jdg 13:2; 18:11; 2Ch 11:10; Ne 11:29 [i] ver 43 **15:34** [j] ver 56; 1Ch 4:18; Ne 3:13; 11:30 [k] Jos 19:21; 21:29 [l] S Jos 12:17 **15:35** [m] S Jos 10:3 [n] S Ge 38:1 [o] ver 48; 1Ki 4:10 [p] S Jos 10:10 **15:36** [q] 1Sa 17:52; 1Ch 4:31 [r] 1Ch 12:4 **15:38** [s] S Jos 11:3 [t] 2Ki 14:7 **15:39** [u] S Jos 10:3 [v] 2Ki 22:1 [w] S Jos 10:3 **15:41** [x] 2Ch 28:18 [y] Jos 19:27 [z] S Jos 10:10

15:5 *northern boundary.* Judah's border with Benjamin ran in a westerly line from the mouth of the Jordan through the Hinnom Valley, just south of Jerusalem, over to Timnah, then northwest to the coastal city of Jabneel (later called Jamnia), about ten miles south of Joppa.

15:7 *Gilgal.* See note on Jdg 3:19.

15:15 *he marched against … Debir.* See note on 10:38.

15:17 *Othniel.* See Jdg 3:7–11 (see also note there) for his service as judge in Israel.

15:21 *southernmost towns.* Most of the first 29 villages were assigned to the tribe of Simeon (cf. 19:1–9).

15:33 *western foothills.* This area between the highlands of central Judah and the Philistine coast was for the most part not occupied by Israel until the victories of King David. Some of the places on this list were reassigned to the tribe of Dan (cf. 19:41–43).

[42]Libnah,[a] Ether, Ashan,[b] [43]Iphtah,
Ashnah,[c] Nezib, [44]Keilah,[d] Aczib[e] and
Mareshah[f]—nine towns and their villages.
[45]Ekron,[g] with its surrounding settlements and villages; [46]west of Ekron, all that were in the vicinity of
Ashdod,[h] together with their villages; [47]Ashdod,[i] its surrounding settlements and villages; and Gaza, its
settlements and villages, as far as the
Wadi of Egypt[j] and the coastline of
the Great Sea.[k]

15:42 [a]S Nu 33:20 [b]Jos 19:7; 1Sa 30:30; 1Ch 4:32; 6:59 **15:43** [c]ver 33 **15:44** [d]1Sa 23:1-2, 1; 1Ch 4:19; Ne 3:17, 18 [e]Jos 19:29; Jdg 1:31; Mic 1:14 [f]Mic 1:15 **15:45** [g]S Jos 13:3 **15:46** [h]Jos 11:22

[48]In the hill country:
Shamir,[l] Jattir,[m] Socoh,[n] [49]Dan-
nah, Kiriath Sannah (that is, Debir[o]),
[50]Anab,[p] Eshtemoh,[q] Anim, [51]Go-
shen,[r] Holon[s] and Giloh[t]—eleven
towns and their villages.
[52]Arab, Dumah,[u] Eshan, [53]Janim,
Beth Tappuah, Aphekah, [54]Humtah,
Kiriath Arba[v] (that is, Hebron) and
Zior—nine towns and their villages.

15:47 [i]S Jos 11:22 [j]S Ge 15:18 [k]S Nu 34:6 **15:48** [l]Jdg 10:1 [m]Jos 21:14; 1Sa 30:27; 1Ch 6:57 [n]S ver 35 **15:49** [o]S Jos 10:3 **15:50** [p]Jos 11:21 [q]Jos 21:14; 1Sa 30:28 **15:51** [r]S Jos 10:41 [s]Jos 21:15; Jer 48:21 [t]2Sa 15:12 **15:52** [u]S Ge 25:14 **15:54** [v]S Ge 35:27

15:48 *hill country.* The high region south of Jerusalem. The Septuagint (the pre-Christian Greek translation of the OT) adds 11 names, including Tekoa and Bethlehem, to this list.

Distances in Miles Between Old Testament Cities

(1 mi = 1.6 km)

	Ashkelon	Babylon	Beersheba	Bethel	Beth Shan	Carchemish	Damascus	Dan	Haran	Hazor	Hebron	Jericho	Jerusalem	Joppa	Lachish	Mari	Megiddo	Memphis	Nineveh	Samaria	Shechem	Sidon	Susa	Thebes	Tyre	Ur
Ashkelon		900	36	48	87	454	178	139	519	117	36	57	44	32	21	653	80	269	726	60	63	155	1118	601	133	1070
Babylon	900		930	869	823	479	724	764	442	783	901	869	880	868	907	251	824	1172	264	845	847	779	218	1504	792	170
Beersheba	36	930		58	104	484	206	166	549	147	28	61	47	62	25	679	116	259	752	80	78	190	1148	591	176	1100
Bethel	48	869	58		47	423	145	105	488	86	31	12	11	32	40	618	50	303	691	26	22	129	1087	635	115	1039
Beth Shan	87	823	104	47		377	92	59	442	40	78	45	57	59	86	572	21	349	645	27	26	82	1041	681	62	993
Carchemish	454	479	484	423	377		278	318	65	337	455	423	434	366	461	228	378	726	285	399	401	333	697	1058	346	649
Damascus	178	724	206	145	92	278		45	343	59	177	134	149	133	181	473	98	441	546	121	123	55	942	773	68	894
Dan	139	764	166	105	59	318	45		383	19	137	105	116	104	142	513	59	408	586	80	82	29	982	740	28	934
Haran	519	442	549	488	442	65	343	383		402	520	488	500	396	526	191	443	791	215	464	466	398	660	1123	411	612
Hazor	117	783	147	86	40	337	59	19	402		118	86	97	85	124	532	41	389	605	62	64	43	1001	721	29	953
Hebron	36	901	28	31	78	455	177	137	520	118		36	21	45	17	650	80	297	723	51	53	161	1119	629	147	1071
Jericho	57	869	61	12	45	423	134	105	488	86	36		15	43	44	618	54	307	691	32	26	129	1087	639	115	1039
Jerusalem	44	880	47	11	57	434	149	116	500	97	21	15		36	29	629	61	292	702	37	33	140	1098	624	126	1050
Joppa	32	868	62	32	59	366	133	104	396	85	45	43	36		37	372	53	301	548	31	36	112	1086	633	89	1038
Lachish	21	907	25	40	86	461	181	142	526	124	17	44	29	37		656	83	281	729	66	62	158	1125	613	136	1077
Mari	653	251	679	618	572	228	473	513	191	532	650	618	629	372	656		573	921	173	594	596	528	469	1253	541	421
Megiddo	80	824	116	50	21	378	98	59	443	41	80	54	61	53	83	573		348	646	25	29	75	1042	680	53	994
Memphis	269	1172	259	303	349	726	441	408	791	389	297	307	292	301	281	921	348		994	329	325	424	1390	332	402	1342
Nineveh	726	264	752	691	645	285	546	586	215	605	723	691	702	548	729	173	646	994		667	669	601	453	1326	614	434
Samaria	60	845	80	26	27	399	121	80	464	62	51	32	37	31	66	594	25	329	667		8	105	1063	661	77	1015
Shechem	63	847	78	22	26	401	123	82	466	64	53	26	33	36	62	596	29	325	669	8		107	1065	657	80	1017
Sidon	155	779	190	129	82	333	55	29	398	43	161	129	140	112	158	528	75	424	601	105	107		997	755	25	949
Susa	1118	218	1148	1087	1041	697	942	982	660	1001	1119	1087	1098	1086	1125	469	1042	1390	453	1063	1065	997		1722	1110	145
Thebes	601	1504	591	635	681	1058	773	740	1123	721	629	639	624	633	613	1253	680	332	1326	661	657	755	1722		733	1674
Tyre	133	792	176	115	62	346	68	28	411	29	147	115	126	89	136	541	53	402	614	77	80	25	1110	733		962
Ur	1070	170	1100	1039	993	649	894	934	612	953	1071	1039	1050	1038	1077	421	994	1342	434	1015	1017	949	145	1674	962	

Note: These distances are meant only as rough estimates. They do not take into account terrain obstacles, although they do, for the most part, follow ancient routes (e.g., around the Fertile Crescent rather than across the desert).

Chronological and Background Charts of the Old Testament, p. 116

55 Maon,[w] Carmel,[x] Ziph,[y] Juttah,[z]
56 Jezreel,[a] Jokdeam, Zanoah,[b] 57 Kain,
Gibeah[c] and Timnah[d]—ten towns
and their villages.
58 Halhul, Beth Zur,[e] Gedor,[f] 59 Ma-
arath, Beth Anoth and Eltekon—six
towns and their villages.
60 Kiriath Baal[g] (that is, Kiriath Jearim[h]) and Rabbah[i]—two towns and
their villages.

61 In the desert:[j]
Beth Arabah,[k] Middin, Secacah,
62 Nibshan, the City of Salt and En
Gedi[l]—six towns and their villages.
63 Judah could not[m] dislodge the Jebusites[n], who were living in Jerusalem;[o] to
this day the Jebusites live there with the
people of Judah.[p]

Allotment for Ephraim and Manasseh

16 The allotment for Joseph began
at the Jordan of Jericho,[a] east
of the waters of Jericho, and went up
from there through the desert[q] into
the hill country of Bethel.[r] 2 It went on
from Bethel (that is, Luz[s]),[b] crossed
over to the territory of the Arkites[t] in
Ataroth,[u] 3 descended westward to the
territory of the Japhletites as far as
the region of Lower Beth Horon[v] and
on to Gezer,[w] ending at the sea.
4 So Manasseh and Ephraim, the descendants of Joseph, received their inheritance.[x]

5 This was the territory of Ephraim, clan
by clan:
The boundary of their inheritance
went from Ataroth Addar[y] in the east
to Upper Beth Horon[z] 6 and continued
to the sea. From Micmethath[a] on the
north it curved eastward to Taanath
Shiloh, passing by it to Janoah[b] on
the east. 7 Then it went down from
Janoah[c] to Ataroth[d] and Naarah,
touched Jericho and came out at the
Jordan. 8 From Tappuah[e] the border
went west to the Kanah Ravine[f] and
ended at the sea. This was the inheritance of the tribe of the Ephraimites,
clan by clan. 9 It also included all the
towns and their villages that were set
aside for the Ephraimites within the
inheritance of the Manassites.[g]
10 They did not dislodge the Canaanites living in Gezer; to this day the Canaanites
live among the people of Ephraim but are
required to do forced labor.[h]

17 This was the allotment for the tribe
of Manasseh[i] as Joseph's firstborn,[j]
that is, for Makir,[k] Manasseh's firstborn.
Makir was the ancestor of the Gileadites,
who had received Gilead[l] and Bashan[m]
because the Makirites were great soldiers.
2 So this allotment was for the rest of the
people of Manasseh[n]—the clans of Abiezer,[o] Helek, Asriel,[p] Shechem, Hepher[q]
and Shemida.[r] These are the other male
descendants of Manasseh son of Joseph
by their clans.
3 Now Zelophehad son of Hepher,[s] the
son of Gilead, the son of Makir, the son of
Manasseh, had no sons but only daughters,[t] whose names were Mahlah, Noah,
Hoglah, Milcah and Tirzah. 4 They went to
Eleazar the priest, Joshua son of Nun, and
the leaders and said, "The LORD commanded Moses to give us an inheritance among
our brothers." So Joshua gave them an inheritance along with the brothers of their
father, according to the LORD's command.[u]
5 Manasseh's share consisted of ten tracts
of land besides Gilead and Bashan east of
the Jordan,[v] 6 because the daughters of the
tribe of Manasseh received an inheritance
among the sons. The land of Gilead belonged to the rest of the descendants of
Manasseh.

[a] 1 *Jordan of Jericho* was possibly an ancient name for the Jordan River. [b] 2 Septuagint; Hebrew *Bethel to Luz*

15:55 [w] Jdg 10:12; 1Sa 23:24,25; 25:1,2; 1Ch 2:45 [x] S Jos 12:22 [y] S ver 24 [z] Jos 21:16 **15:56** [a] Jos 17:16; 19:18; Jdg 6:33; 1Sa 25:43; 1Ki 18:45; 1Ch 3:1; Hos 1:5 [b] S ver 34 **15:57** [c] Jos 18:28; 24:33; Jdg 19:12; 20:4; 2Sa 23:29; 1Ch 11:31 [d] S Ge 38:12 **15:58** [e] 1Ch 2:45; 2Ch 11:7; Ne 3:16 [f] 1Ch 4:39; 12:7 **15:60** [g] ver 9 [h] S Jos 9:17 [i] S Dt 3:11 **15:61** [j] S Jos 8:15 [k] S ver 6 **15:62** [l] 1Sa 23:29; 24:1; Eze 47:10 **15:63** [m] Jos 16:10; 17:12; Jdg 1:21; 1Ki 9:21 [n] S ver 8 [o] S Jos 10:1 [p] Eze 48:7 **16:1** [q] S Jos 8:15 [r] S Jos 12:9 **16:2** [s] S Ge 28:19 [t] 2Sa 15:32 [u] S ver 5; S Nu 32:3 **16:3** [v] S Jos 10:10 [w] S Jos 10:33 **16:4** [x] Jos 18:5 **16:5** [y] ver 2; Jos 18:13 [z] S Jos 10:10 **16:6** [a] Jos 17:7 [b] ver 7; 2Ki 15:29 **16:7** [c] S ver 6 [d] S Nu 32:3 **16:8** [e] S Jos 12:17 [f] Jos 17:9; 19:28 **16:9** [g] Eze 48:5 **16:10** [h] S Jos 15:63; 17:13; Jdg 1:28-29; 1Ki 9:16 **17:1** [i] S Nu 1:34; 1Ch 7:14 [j] S Ge 41:51 [k] S Ge 50:23 [l] S Jos 12:2 [m] S Jos 12:5 **17:2** [n] Jos 22:7 [o] S Nu 26:30; Jdg 6:11,34; 8:2; 1Ch 7:18 [p] 1Ch 7:14 [q] S Nu 27:1 [r] 1Ch 7:19 **17:3** [s] S Nu 27:1 [t] S Nu 26:33 **17:4** [u] Nu 27:5-7 **17:5** [v] Jos 13:30-31

15:61–62 The "desert" is the chalky, dry region east and south of Jerusalem that borders the Dead Sea. Of the places named, only En Gedi can be positively located. However, either Secacah or the City of Salt may have been the ancient name of the site of Qumran, where the scribes who produced the Dead Sea Scrolls lived.
15:63 *Jebusites.* A victory over the city of the Jebusites by the men of Judah is recorded in Jdg 1:8 (see note there), but evidently this did not result in its permanent occupation. Both Benjamin and Judah failed to take the Jebusite fortress of Jerusalem (Jdg 1:21).
16:1—17:18 Two chapters are devoted to the lands given to the "house of Joseph" (Ephraim and the half-tribe of Manasseh that settled west of the Jordan). Following Judah, the Joseph tribes were given priority in the allotting of territory.
16:1 *allotment for Joseph.* The southern border of the Joseph tribes moved west from Jericho past Bethel and down to Gezer and the Mediterranean coast.
16:5 *boundary.* Ephraim's northern border began at the edge of the Jordan Valley and ran west near Shiloh, but south of Shechem, then followed the Wadi Kanah down to the Mediterranean Sea.
16:10 *Gezer.* See note on 10:33. *required to do forced labor.* On projects undertaken by public officials, usually the king (see 2Sa 12:31 and note; 1Ki 9:15,20–21 and note on 9:15).
17:1 *Manasseh as Joseph's firstborn.* A reminder that Manasseh was the firstborn, though Jacob had given priority to Ephraim when he adopted Joseph's two sons (see Ge 48:14,19 and note on 48:19).
17:3 *Zelophehad ... had ... only daughters.* See notes on Nu 27:1–11; 36:1–3.
17:5 *ten tracts of land.* Manasseh's territory was second only to Judah's in size. The ten portions went to the five brothers (minus Hepher) and to the five granddaughters of Hepher.

7The territory of Manasseh extended from Asher[w] to Micmethath[x] east of
Shechem.[y] The boundary ran southward from there to include the people
living at En Tappuah. 8(Manasseh had
the land of Tappuah, but Tappuah[z] itself, on the boundary of Manasseh,
belonged to the Ephraimites.) 9Then
the boundary continued south to the
Kanah Ravine.[a] There were towns belonging to Ephraim lying among the
towns of Manasseh, but the boundary
of Manasseh was the northern side of
the ravine and ended at the sea. 10On
the south the land belonged to Ephraim, on the north to Manasseh. The
territory of Manasseh reached the sea
and bordered Asher[b] on the north and
Issachar[c] on the east.[d]
11Within Issachar[e] and Asher, Manasseh also had Beth Shan,[f] Ibleam[g]
and the people of Dor,[h] Endor,[i] Taanach[j] and Megiddo,[k] together with
their surrounding settlements (the
third in the list is Naphoth[a]).[l]
12Yet the Manassites were not able[m] to occupy these towns, for the Canaanites were
determined to live in that region. 13How-
ever, when the Israelites grew stronger,
they subjected the Canaanites to forced
labor but did not drive them out completely.[n]
14The people of Joseph said to Joshua,
"Why have you given us only one allotment and one portion for an inheritance?
We are a numerous people and the LORD
has blessed us abundantly."[o]
15"If you are so numerous," Joshua answered, "and if the hill country of Ephraim
is too small for you, go up into the forest[p]
and clear land for yourselves there in the
land of the Perizzites[q] and Rephaites.[r]"
16The people of Joseph replied, "The
hill country is not enough for us, and all
the Canaanites who live in the plain have
iron chariots,[s] both those in Beth Shan[t]
and its settlements and those in the Valley
of Jezreel."[u]
17But Joshua said to the house of Joseph — to Ephraim and Manasseh — "You
are numerous and very powerful. You will
have not only one allotment[v] 18but the forested hill country[w] as well. Clear it, and
its farthest limits will be yours; though
the Canaanites have iron chariots[x] and
though they are strong, you can drive
them out."

Division of the Rest of the Land

18 The whole assembly of the Israelites
gathered at Shiloh[y] and set up the
Tent of Meeting[z] there. The country was
brought under their control, 2but there
were still seven Israelite tribes who had
not yet received their inheritance.
3So Joshua said to the Israelites: "How
long will you wait before you begin to
take possession of the land that the LORD,
the God of your fathers, has given you?
4Appoint three men from each tribe. I will
send them out to make a survey of the
land and to write a description of it,[a] according to the inheritance of each.[b] Then
they will return to me. 5You are to divide
the land into seven parts. Judah is to remain in its territory on the south[c] and
the house of Joseph in its territory on the
north.[d] 6After you have written descriptions of the seven parts of the land, bring
them here to me and I will cast lots[e] for
you in the presence of the LORD our God.

[a] *11* That is, Naphoth Dor

17:7 [w] ver 10; Jos 19:24,31; 21:6,30; Jdg 1:31; 5:17; 6:35; 7:23 [x] Jos 16:6 [y] S Ge 12:6; Jos 21:21; 24:25; Jdg 9:1 **17:8** [z] S Jos 12:17 **17:9** [a] S Jos 16:8 **17:10** [b] S ver 7 [c] S Ge 30:18 [d] Eze 48:5 **17:11** [e] ver 10 [f] ver 16; Jdg 1:27; 1Sa 31:10; 2Sa 21:12; 1Ki 4:12; 1Ch 7:29 [g] 2Ki 9:27 [h] S Jos 11:2 [i] 1Sa 28:7; Ps 83:10 [j] S Jos 12:21 [k] 1Ki 9:15 [l] Eze 48:4 **17:12** [m] S Jos 15:63 **17:13** [n] Jdg 1:27-28 **17:14** [o] Nu 26:28-37 **17:15** [p] 2Sa 18:6 [q] S Jos 3:10 [r] S Ge 14:5; Jos 15:8; 18:16; 2Sa 5:18; 23:13; Isa 17:5 **17:16** [s] ver 18; Jdg 1:19; 4:3,13 [t] S ver 11 [u] S Jos 15:56; S 1Sa 29:1 **17:17** [v] Eze 48:5 **17:18** [w] 1Sa 1:1 [x] S ver 16 **18:1** [y] ver 8; Jos 19:51; 21:2; Jdg 18:31; 21:12,19; 1Sa 1:3; 3:21; 4:3; 1Ki 14:2; Ps 78:60; Jer 7:12; 26:6; 41:5 [z] S ver 10; S Ex 27:21; S 40:2; Ac 7:45 **18:4** [a] ver 8 [b] Mic 2:5 **18:5** [c] Jos 15:1 [d] Jos 16:1-4 **18:6** [e] S Lev 16:8

17:11 *Beth Shan ... Megiddo.* These powerfully fortified cities (and others) were not conquered until later. When King Saul died in battle, the victorious Philistines fastened his body to the wall of Beth Shan (see 1Sa 31:10), which suggests that that city was in league with the Philistines.
17:13 *when the Israelites grew stronger.* Possibly referring to the days of David and Solomon (see note on 16:10).
17:14 *people of Joseph ... numerous.* The reference is to both Ephraim and Manasseh (see v. 17, but see also note on v. 15). The allotment to the Joseph tribes is here handled as one (see 16:1,4) — though the two subdivisions are then described separately (16:5 — 17:11).
17:15 *hill country of Ephraim.* The territory of the Joseph tribes — under the name of the legal firstborn (see note on v. 1). *clear land for yourselves.* This region of Canaan was still heavily forested. It seems that the Israelites viewed their assigned territories primarily in terms of the number of cities that had their land cleared for farming and pasturage, not in terms of the size of the region in which these cities were located. The region assigned to the Joseph tribes was at the time not as heavily populated as others. *Perizzites and Rephaites.* Here listed as neighboring peoples, though elsewhere the Perizzites are said to have lived on the west bank in Canaan (3:10; 12:8) and the Rephaites in the Transjordan kingdom of Og (12:4; 13:12). See notes on Ge 13:7; Dt 2:11.
17:16 *in the plain.* Only in the plains were chariots effective. *iron chariots.* Wooden chariots with certain parts made of iron (see note on 2Sa 8:7), perhaps the axles. This use of iron was a new development. Israel did not employ chariots until much later (see note on 11:6).
18:1 — 19:51 Seven tribes remained to be assigned land: Benjamin, Simeon, Zebulun, Issachar, Asher, Naphtali and Dan. Their lots were cast at Shiloh.
18:1 *Shiloh.* About ten miles northeast of Bethel, a little east of the main road from Bethel to Shechem. *Tent of Meeting.* The tabernacle (see note on Ex 27:21) with its sacred ark of the covenant. It would remain at Shiloh until the time of Samuel (1Sa 4:3).
18:3 *take possession.* Conquest had to be followed by settlement, which required a survey, then a fair distribution, and then a full occupation of the land. A distinction must therefore be made between the national wars of conquest (Joshua) and the tribal wars of occupation (see Jdg 1 – 2 and note on 1:1).
18:5 *north.* Relative to the territory of Judah.
18:6 *I will cast lots for you.* See note on 14:1.

7 The Levites, however, do not get a portion
among you, because the priestly service of
the LORD is their inheritance.[f] And Gad,
Reuben and the half-tribe of Manasseh
have already received their inheritance on
the east side of the Jordan. Moses the servant of the LORD gave it to them.[g]"
8 As the men started on their way to map
out the land, Joshua instructed them, "Go
and make a survey of the land and write a
description of it.[h] Then return to me, and
I will cast lots for you here at Shiloh[i] in
the presence of the LORD." 9 So the men left
and went through the land. They wrote its
description on a scroll, town by town, in
seven parts, and returned to Joshua in the
camp at Shiloh. 10 Joshua then cast lots[j]
for them in Shiloh in the presence[k] of the
LORD, and there he distributed the land to
the Israelites according to their tribal divisions.[l]

Allotment for Benjamin

11 The lot came up for the tribe of Benjamin, clan by clan. Their allotted territory
lay between the tribes of Judah and Joseph:
12 On the north side their boundary began at the Jordan, passed the
northern slope of Jericho and headed
west into the hill country, coming out
at the desert[m] of Beth Aven.[n] 13 From
there it crossed to the south slope of
Luz[o] (that is, Bethel[p]) and went down
to Ataroth Addar[q] on the hill south of
Lower Beth Horon.
14 From the hill facing Beth Horon[r]
on the south the boundary turned
south along the western side and
came out at Kiriath Baal (that is, Kiriath Jearim),[s] a town of the people of
Judah. This was the western side.
15 The southern side began at the
outskirts of Kiriath Jearim on the
west, and the boundary came out at
the spring of the waters of Nephtoah.[t] 16 The boundary went down to
the foot of the hill facing the Valley
of Ben Hinnom, north of the Valley of
Rephaim.[u] It continued down the Hinnom Valley[v] along the southern slope
of the Jebusite city and so to En Rogel.[w] 17 It then curved north, went to
En Shemesh, continued to Geliloth,[x]
which faces the Pass of Adummim,[y]
and ran down to the Stone of Bohan[z]
son of Reuben. 18 It continued to the
northern slope of Beth Arabah[a][a] and
on down into the Arabah.[b] 19 It then
went to the northern slope of Beth
Hoglah[c] and came out at the northern
bay of the Salt Sea,[b][d] at the mouth of
the Jordan in the south. This was the
southern boundary.
20 The Jordan formed the boundary
on the eastern side.
These were the boundaries that marked
out the inheritance of the clans of Benjamin on all sides.[e]

21 The tribe of Benjamin, clan by clan, had
the following cities:
Jericho, Beth Hoglah,[f] Emek Keziz,
22 Beth Arabah,[g] Zemaraim,[h] Bethel,[i]
23 Avvim,[j] Parah, Ophrah,[k] 24 Kephar
Ammoni, Ophni and Geba[l]—twelve
towns and their villages.
25 Gibeon,[m] Ramah,[n] Beeroth,[o]
26 Mizpah,[p] Kephirah,[q] Mozah, 27 Rekem, Irpeel, Taralah, 28 Zelah,[r] Hae-
leph, the Jebusite city[s] (that is, Jerusalem[t]), Gibeah[u] and Kiriath—fourteen
towns and their villages.[v]
This was the inheritance of Benjamin for
its clans.[w]

Allotment for Simeon

19:2-10pp — 1Ch 4:28-33

19 The second lot came out for the tribe
of Simeon, clan by clan. Their inheritance lay within the territory of Judah.[x]
2 It included:
Beersheba[y] (or Sheba),[c] Moladah,[z]
3 Hazar Shual,[a] Balah, Ezem,[b] 4 Eltolad,[c] Bethul, Hormah,[d] 5 Ziklag,[e] Beth
Marcaboth, Hazar Susah, 6 Beth Lebaoth and Sharuhen—thirteen towns
and their villages;
7 Ain, Rimmon,[f] Ether and
Ashan[g]—four towns and their villages— 8 and all the villages around
these towns as far as Baalath Beer
(Ramah in the Negev).[h]

[a] 18 Septuagint; Hebrew *slope facing the Arabah*
[b] 19 That is, the Dead Sea [c] 2 Or *Beersheba, Sheba*; 1 Chron. 4:28 does not have *Sheba*.

18:7 [f] S Jos 13:33 [g] Jos 13:8 **18:8** [h] ver 4 [i] S ver 1 **18:10** [j] S Nu 34:13 [k] S ver 1; Jer 7:12 [l] Nu 33:54; Jos 19:51 **18:12** [m] S Jos 8:15 [n] S Jos 7:2 **18:13** [o] S Ge 28:19 [p] S Jos 12:9 [q] S Nu 32:3; S Jos 16:5 **18:14** [r] Jos 10:10 [s] S Jos 9:17 **18:15** [t] Jos 15:9 **18:16** [u] S Jos 17:15 [v] Jos 15:8 [w] S Jos 15:7 **18:17** [x] Jos 22:10 [y] Jos 15:7 [z] Jos 15:6 **18:18** [a] S Jos 15:6 [b] S Jos 11:2 **18:19** [c] S Jos 15:6 [d] S Ge 14:3 **18:20** [e] 1Sa 9:1 **18:21** [f] S Jos 15:6 **18:22** [g] Jos 15:6 [h] 2Ch 13:4 [i] Jos 16:1 **18:23** [j] S Dt 2:23 [k] Jdg 6:11, 24; 8:27, 32; 9:5; 1Sa 13:17 **18:24** [l] Jos 21:17; 1Sa 13:3, 16; 14:5; 1Ki 15:22; 2Ki 23:8; Isa 10:29 **18:25** [m] Jos 9:3 [n] S Jos 10:40; Jdg 4:5; 19:13; Isa 10:29; Jer 31:15; 40:1 [o] S Jos 9:17; Ezr 2:25; Ne 7:29 **18:26** [p] S Jos 11:3 [q] Jos 9:17; Ezr 2:25; Ne 7:29 **18:28** [r] 2Sa 21:14 [s] S Jos 15:8 [t] S Jos 10:1 [u] S Jos 15:57 [v] S Jos 9:17 [w] Eze 48:23 **19:1** [x] S Ge 49:7 **19:2** [y] S Ge 21:14; 1Ki 19:3 [z] S Jos 15:26 **19:3** [a] S Jos 15:28 [b] S Jos 15:29 **19:4** [c] Jos 15:30 [d] S Nu 14:45 **19:5** [e] S Jos 15:31 **19:7** [f] S Jos 15:32 [g] S Jos 15:42 **19:8** [h] S Jos 10:40

18:7 *priestly service of the LORD is their inheritance.* See 13:14; see also Dt 18:1–8 and note on 18:1.
18:9 *scroll.* Presumed form of the document; the Hebrew for this word is not specific.
18:11 *lot ... for ... Benjamin.* Benjamin's northern border was the same as Ephraim's southern border, and Benjamin's southern border was the same as Judah's northern boundary (see note on 15:5). The areas allotted to Benjamin and Dan (19:40–48) constituted a buffer zone between Judah and Ephraim, the two dominant tribes in Israel. The accounts of allotments to Benjamin and Dan frame the account of allotments made at Shiloh. These two tribes and the location of their allotments would play a significant role in the cycles of narratives related in the book of Judges (see Introduction to Judges: Literary Features and notes on Jdg 3:12–30; 13:1—16:31).
18:23 *Avvim.* The people of Ai.
19:1 *second lot ... for ... Simeon.* Cities in the Negev within the borders of Judah (see 15:21; Jdg 1:3; 1Ch 4:24–43 and notes).

This was the inheritance of the tribe of the
Simeonites, clan by clan. 9The inheritance
of the Simeonites was taken from the
share of Judah,[i] because Judah's portion
was more than they needed. So the Simeonites received their inheritance within
the territory of Judah.[j]

Allotment for Zebulun

10The third lot came up for Zebulun,[k] clan
by clan:

The boundary of their inheritance
went as far as Sarid.[l] 11Going west it
ran to Maralah, touched Dabbesheth,
and extended to the ravine near Jokneam.[m] 12It turned east from Sarid[n]
toward the sunrise to the territory of
Kisloth Tabor and went on to Daberath[o] and up to Japhia. 13Then it continued eastward to Gath Hepher[p] and
Eth Kazin; it came out at Rimmon[q]
and turned toward Neah. 14There the
boundary went around on the north
to Hannathon and ended at the Valley
of Iphtah El.[r] 15Included were Kattath,
Nahalal,[s] Shimron,[t] Idalah and Bethlehem.[u] There were twelve towns and
their villages.

16These towns and their villages were the
inheritance of Zebulun,[v] clan by clan.[w]

Allotment for Issachar

17The fourth lot came out for Issachar,[x]
clan by clan. 18Their territory included:

Jezreel,[y] Kesulloth, Shunem,[z]
19Hapharaim, Shion, Anaharath,
20Rabbith, Kishion,[a] Ebez, 21Remeth,
En Gannim,[b] En Haddah and Beth
Pazzez. 22The boundary touched
Tabor,[c] Shahazumah and Beth Shemesh,[d] and ended at the Jordan.
There were sixteen towns and their
villages.

23These towns and their villages were the
inheritance of the tribe of Issachar,[e] clan
by clan.[f]

Allotment for Asher

24The fifth lot came out for the tribe of
Asher,[g] clan by clan. 25Their territory included:

Helkath, Hali, Beten, Acshaph,[h]
26Allammelech, Amad and Mishal.[i]
On the west the boundary touched
Carmel[j] and Shihor Libnath. 27It then
turned east toward Beth Dagon,[k]
touched Zebulun[l] and the Valley of
Iphtah El,[m] and went north to Beth
Emek and Neiel, passing Cabul[n] on
the left. 28It went to Abdon,[a][o] Rehob,[p] Hammon[q] and Kanah,[r] as far as
Greater Sidon.[s] 29The boundary then
turned back toward Ramah[t] and went
to the fortified city of Tyre,[u] turned
toward Hosah and came out at the
sea[v] in the region of Aczib,[w] 30Um-
mah, Aphek[x] and Rehob.[y] There were
twenty-two towns and their villages.

31These towns and their villages were the
inheritance of the tribe of Asher,[z] clan by
clan.

Allotment for Naphtali

32The sixth lot came out for Naphtali, clan
by clan:

33Their boundary went from Heleph
and the large tree in Zaanannim,[a]
passing Adami Nekeb and Jabneel[b]
to Lakkum and ending at the Jordan.
34The boundary ran west through Az-
noth Tabor and came out at Hukkok.[c]
It touched Zebulun[d] on the south,
Asher on the west and the Jordan[b]
on the east. 35The fortified cities were
Ziddim, Zer, Hammath,[e] Rakkath,
Kinnereth,[f] 36Adamah, Ramah,[g] Hazor,[h] 37Kedesh,[i] Edrei,[j] En Hazor,
38Iron, Migdal El, Horem, Beth Anath[k]
and Beth Shemesh.[l] There were nineteen towns and their villages.

39These towns and their villages were the
inheritance of the tribe of Naphtali, clan
by clan.[m]

Allotment for Dan

40The seventh lot came out for the tribe of
Dan, clan by clan. 41The territory of their
inheritance included:

Zorah, Eshtaol,[n] Ir Shemesh, 42Sha-
alabbin, Aijalon,[o] Ithlah, 43Elon, Timnah,[p] Ekron,[q] 44Eltekeh, Gibbethon,[r]
Baalath,[s] 45Jehud, Bene Berak, Gath

19:9 [i]S Ge 49:7 [j]Eze 48:24 **19:10** [k]ver 16,27,34; Jos 21:7,34 [l]ver 12 **19:11** [m]S Jos 12:22 **19:12** [n]ver 10 [o]Jos 21:28; 1Ch 6:72 **19:13** [p]S Jos 11:22 [q]Jos 15:32 **19:14** [r]ver 27 **19:15** [s]Jos 21:35 [t]Jos 11:1 [u]S Ge 35:19 **19:16** [v]S ver 10 [w]Eze 48:26 **19:17** [x]S Ge 30:18 **19:18** [y]S Jos 15:56 [z]1Sa 28:4; 1Ki 1:3; 2Ki 4:8 **19:20** [a]Jos 21:28 **19:21** [b]S Jos 15:34 **19:22** [c]Jdg 4:6,12; 8:18; Ps 89:12; Jer 46:18 [d]S Jos 15:10 **19:23** [e]Jos 17:10 [f]Ge 49:15; Eze 48:25 **19:24** [g]S Jos 17:7 **19:25** [h]S Jos 11:1 **19:26** [i]Jos 21:30 [j]S Jos 12:22; 1Ki 18:19; 2Ki 2:25 **19:27** [k]Jos 15:41 [l]S ver 10 [m]ver 14 [n]1Ki 9:13 **19:28** [o]Jos 21:30; 1Ch 6:74 [p]ver 30; Nu 13:21; Jos 21:31; Jdg 1:31 [q]1Ch 6:76 [r]S Jos 16:8 [s]S Ge 10:19 **19:29** [t]Jos 18:25 [u]2Sa 5:11; 24:7; Ezr 3:7; Ps 45:12; Isa 23:1; Jer 25:22; Eze 26:2 [v]Jdg 5:17 [w]S Jos 15:44 **19:30** [x]S Jos 12:18 [y]S ver 28 **19:31** [z]S Ge 30:13; S Jos 17:7; Eze 48:2 **19:33** [a]Jdg 4:11 [b]Jos 15:11

[a] 28 Some Hebrew manuscripts (see also Joshua 21:30); most Hebrew manuscripts *Ebron* [b] 34 Septuagint; Hebrew *west, and Judah, the Jordan,*

19:34 [c]1Ch 6:75 [d]S ver 10 **19:35** [e]1Ch 2:55 [f]S Jos 11:2 **19:36** [g]Jos 18:25 [h]S Jos 11:1 **19:37** [i]S Jos 12:22 [j]S Nu 21:33 **19:38** [k]Jdg 1:33 [l]S Jos 15:10 **19:39** [m]Eze 48:3 **19:41** [n]S Jos 15:33 **19:42** [o]S Jos 10:12 **19:43** [p]S Ge 38:12 [q]S Jos 13:3 **19:44** [r]Jos 21:23; 1Ki 15:27; 16:15 [s]1Ki 9:18; 2Ch 8:6

19:10 *third lot ... for Zebulun.* To this tribe went a portion of lower Galilee midway between the Sea of Galilee and the Mediterranean.
19:17 *fourth lot ... for Issachar.* Southwest of the Sea of Galilee reaching down to the vicinity of Beth Shan and west to the Jezreel Valley. Mount Tabor marked its northern border.
19:24 *fifth lot ... for ... Asher.* Asher was given the coastal area as far north as Sidon in Phoenicia and as far south as Mount Carmel.
19:32 *sixth lot ... for Naphtali.* An area mostly to the north of the Sea of Galilee, including the mountains bordering on Asher and Zebulun to the west. Its southernmost point was at the southern end of the Sea of Galilee.
19:40 *seventh lot ... for ... Dan.* An elbow of land squeezed between Ephraim and Judah and west of Benjamin (see note on 18:11). The port of Joppa marked the northwestern corner of Dan.

Rimmon,[t] 46Me Jarkon and Rakkon,
with the area facing Joppa.[u]
47(But the Danites had difficulty taking
possession of their territory,[v] so they went
up and attacked Leshem[w], took it, put it
to the sword and occupied it. They settled
in Leshem and named[x] it Dan after their
forefather.)[y]
48These towns and their villages were the
inheritance of the tribe of Dan,[z] clan by
clan.

Allotment for Joshua

49When they had finished dividing the
land into its allotted portions, the Israelites gave Joshua son of Nun an inheritance among them, 50as the LORD had
commanded. They gave him the town he
asked for—Timnath Serah[a][a] in the hill
country of Ephraim. And he built up the
town and settled there.
51These are the territories that Eleazar
the priest, Joshua son of Nun and the
heads of the tribal clans of Israel assigned
by lot at Shiloh in the presence of the LORD
at the entrance to the Tent of Meeting. And
so they finished dividing[b] the land.[c]

Cities of Refuge

20:1-9Ref — Nu 35:9-34; Dt 4:41-43; 19:1-14

20 Then the LORD said to Joshua: 2"Tell
the Israelites to designate the cities
of refuge, as I instructed you through Moses, 3so that anyone who kills a person accidentally and unintentionally[d] may flee
there and find protection from the avenger of blood.[e]
4"When he flees to one of these cities,
he is to stand in the entrance of the city
gate[f] and state his case before the elders[g]
of that city. Then they are to admit him
into their city and give him a place to live
with them. 5If the avenger of blood pursues him, they must not surrender the one
accused, because he killed his neighbor
unintentionally and without malice aforethought. 6He is to stay in that city until he
has stood trial before the assembly[h] and
until the death of the high priest who is
serving at that time. Then he may go back
to his own home in the town from which
he fled."
7So they set apart Kedesh[i] in Galilee in
the hill country of Naphtali, Shechem[j] in
the hill country of Ephraim, and Kiriath
Arba[k] (that is, Hebron[l]) in the hill country
of Judah.[m] 8On the east side of the Jordan of Jericho[b] they designated Bezer[n] in
the desert on the plateau in the tribe of
Reuben, Ramoth in Gilead[o][p] in the tribe
of Gad, and Golan in Bashan[q] in the tribe
of Manasseh. 9Any of the Israelites or any
alien living among them who killed someone accidentally[r] could flee to these designated cities and not be killed by the avenger of blood prior to standing trial before
the assembly.[s]

19:45 [t]Jos 21:24; 1Ch 6:69 **19:46** [u]2Ch 2:16; Ezr 3:7; Jnh 1:3; Ac 9:36 **19:47** [v]Jdg 18:1 [w]Jdg 18:7,14 [x]S Dt 3:14 [y]Jdg 18:27,29 **19:48** [z]S Ge 30:6 **19:50** [a]Jos 24:30; Jdg 2:9 **19:51** [b]Jos 23:4 [c]S Jos 14:1; S 18:10; Ac 13:19 **20:3** [d]S Lev 4:2 [e]S Nu 35:12 **20:4** [f]S Ge 23:10; Jer 38:7 [g]S Jos 7:6 **20:6** [h]S Nu 35:12 **20:7** [i]S Jos 12:22 [j]S Ge 12:6 [k]S Ge 35:27 [l]S Jos 10:36 [m]Lk 1:39 **20:8** [n]Jos 21:36; 1Ch 6:78 [o]1Ch 6:80 [p]S Jos 12:2 [q]S Jos 12:5; 1Ch 6:71 **20:9** [r]S Lev 4:2 [s]S Ex 21:13

[a] 50 Also known as *Timnath Heres* (see Judges 2:9)
[b] 8 *Jordan of Jericho* was possibly an ancient name for the Jordan River.

19:47 *Danites had difficulty.* The Amorites of this area "confined the Danites to the hill country" (Jdg 1:34; see note there), so most of the tribe migrated to the upper Jordan Valley, where they seized the town of Leshem (or Laish, Jdg 18:2–10,27–29; see notes on 18:1,7,29) and renamed it Dan.

19:49 *gave Joshua ... an inheritance.* In the account of the distribution of the promised land (the territory west of the Jordan), the assignment to Caleb is treated first (14:6–15), the assignment to Joshua last. Thus the allotting of inheritance to these two dauntless servants of the Lord from the desert generation (see Nu 13:30; 14:6,24,30 and note on 14:24) frames the whole account—and both received the territory they asked for. Appropriately, Joshua's allotment came last; he was not a king or a warlord but the servant of God commissioned to bring the Lord's people into the promised land.

19:50 *Timnath Serah.* Located in the southwestern corner of Ephraim, facing out to the sea. Here Joshua was also buried (24:30).

20:1–9 Having distributed the land to the tribes, the Lord's next administrative regulation (see note on 13:1–32) provided an elementary system of government, specifically a system of regional courts to deal with capital offenses having to do with manslaughter. Thus this most inflammatory of cases was removed from local jurisdiction, and a safeguard was created against the easy miscarriage of justice (with its potential for endless blood feuds) when retribution for manslaughter was left in the hands of family members. The cities chosen were among those also assigned to the Levites, where ideally the law of Moses would especially be known and honored. See map, p. 239.

20:2 *as I instructed you through Moses.* See Nu 35:6–33 and notes.

20:3 *avenger of blood.* The Hebrew word is also translated "kinsman-redeemer" (see Ru 2:20 and note), or "redeemer" (see Isa 41:14 and note). The avenger was a near relative with the obligation of exacting retribution (see Lev 24:17; Nu 35:16–28).

20:4 *city gate.* Traditional place for trials, where the elders sat to hold court (see Ru 4:1; Job 29:7 and notes).

20:6 *assembly.* Perhaps the assembly in the town where the crime was committed (see Nu 35:24–25). *death of the high priest.* See Nu 35:25–28 and note on 35:24.

20:7 *they set apart Kedesh.* A wordplay in the Hebrew: "they consecrated (the town of) consecration." The other two cities west of the Jordan already had sacred associations: For Shechem see 8:30–35 and note; Ge 12:6–7 and note on 12:6; for Hebron see Ge 23:2 and note; 49:29–32 and note on 49:29. The geographical distribution of the cities was important: one in the north, one in the midlands and one in the south. (See v. 8, where the order of the three cities of refuge that served in Transjordan is reversed: Bezer in the south, Ramoth in the midlands and Golan in the north.) See map, p. 239.

20:9 *or any alien.* Evidence of the equal protection granted to the foreigners living in Israel (cf. Lev 19:33–34; Dt 10:18–19).

Towns for the Levites

21:4-39pp — 1Ch 6:54-80

21 Now the family heads of the Levites
approached Eleazar the priest, Joshua son of Nun, and the heads of the other
tribal families of Israel[t] 2at Shiloh[u] in Canaan and said to them, "The LORD commanded through Moses that you give us
towns[v] to live in, with pasturelands for
our livestock."[w] 3So, as the LORD had commanded, the Israelites gave the Levites the
following towns and pasturelands out of
their own inheritance:

4The first lot came out for the Kohathites,[x] clan by clan. The Levites who were
descendants of Aaron the priest were allotted thirteen towns from the tribes of
Judah, Simeon and Benjamin.[y] 5The rest
of Kohath's descendants were allotted
ten towns from the clans of the tribes of
Ephraim, Dan and half of Manasseh.[z]

6The descendants of Gershon[a] were allotted thirteen towns from the clans of the
tribes of Issachar,[b] Asher,[c] Naphtali and
the half-tribe of Manasseh in Bashan.

7The descendants of Merari,[d] clan by
clan, received twelve[e] towns from the
tribes of Reuben, Gad and Zebulun.[f]

8So the Israelites allotted to the Levites
these towns and their pasturelands, as the
LORD had commanded through Moses.

9From the tribes of Judah and Simeon
they allotted the following towns by name
10(these towns were assigned to the descendants of Aaron who were from the
Kohathite clans of the Levites, because the
first lot fell to them):

11They gave them Kiriath Arba[g]
(that is, Hebron[h]), with its surrounding pastureland, in the hill country
of Judah. (Arba was the forefather
of Anak.) 12But the fields and villages around the city they had given to
Caleb son of Jephunneh as his possession.[i]

13So to the descendants of Aaron
the priest they gave Hebron (a city of
refuge[j] for one accused of murder),
Libnah,[k] 14Jattir,[l] Eshtemoa,[m] 15Ho-
lon,[n] Debir,[o] 16Ain,[p] Juttah[q] and Beth
Shemesh,[r] together with their pasturelands—nine towns from these
two tribes.

17And from the tribe of Benjamin
they gave them Gibeon,[s] Geba,[t] 18An-
athoth[u] and Almon, together with
their pasturelands—four towns.

19All the towns[v] for the priests, the descendants of Aaron, were thirteen, together
with their pasturelands.[w]

20The rest of the Kohathite clans of the Levites were allotted towns from the tribe of
Ephraim:

21In the hill country of Ephraim they
were given Shechem[x] (a city of refuge
for one accused of murder) and Gezer,[y] 22Kibzaim and Beth Horon,[z] together with their pasturelands—four
towns.[a]

23Also from the tribe of Dan they received Eltekeh, Gibbethon,[b] 24Aijalon[c]
and Gath Rimmon,[d] together with
their pasturelands—four towns.

25From half the tribe of Manasseh
they received Taanach[e] and Gath
Rimmon, together with their pasturelands—two towns.

26All these ten towns and their pasturelands were given to the rest of the Kohathite clans.[f]

27The Levite clans of the Gershonites were
given:

from the half-tribe of Manasseh,
Golan in Bashan[g] (a city of refuge
for one accused of murder[h]) and Be
Eshtarah, together with their pasturelands—two towns;

28from the tribe of Issachar,[i]
Kishion,[j] Daberath,[k] 29Jarmuth[l] and
En Gannim,[m] together with their pas-
turelands—four towns;

30from the tribe of Asher,[n]
Mishal,[o] Abdon,[p] 31Helkath and Rehob,[q] together with their pasturelands—four towns;

32from the tribe of Naphtali,
Kedesh[r] in Galilee (a city of refuge for
one accused of murder[s]), Hammoth
Dor and Kartan, together with their
pasturelands—three towns.

33All the towns of the Gershonite[t] clans were
thirteen, together with their pasturelands.

34The Merarite clans (the rest of the Levites) were given:

from the tribe of Zebulun,[u]
Jokneam,[v] Kartah, 35Dimnah and Nahalal,[w] together with their pasturelands—four towns;

21:1 [t]Jos 14:1 **21:2** [u]S Jos 18:1 [v]S Lev 25:32 [w]S Nu 35:2-3; S Jos 14:4 **21:4** [x]Nu 3:17 [y]ver 19 **21:5** [z]ver 26 **21:6** [a]Nu 3:17 [b]S Ge 30:18 [c]S Jos 17:7 **21:7** [d]S Ex 6:16 [e]ver 40 [f]S Jos 19:10 **21:11** [g]S Ge 23:2 [h]S Jos 10:36 **21:12** [i]S Jos 15:13 **21:13** [j]Nu 35:6 [k]S Nu 33:20 **21:14** [l]S Jos 15:48 [m]S Jos 15:50 **21:15** [n]S Jos 15:51 [o]S Jos 10:3 **21:16** [p]S Nu 34:11 [q]Jos 15:55 [r]S Jos 15:10 **21:17** [s]S Jos 9:3 [t]S Jos 18:24; S Ne 11:31 **21:18** [u]2Sa 23:27; 1Ki 2:26; Ezr 2:23; Ne 7:27; 11:32; Isa 10:30; Jer 1:1; 11:21; 32:7 **21:19** [v]2Ch 31:15 [w]ver 4 **21:21** [x]S Jos 17:7 [y]S Jos 10:33 **21:22** [z]S Jos 10:10 [a]1Sa 1:1 **21:23** [b]S Jos 19:44 **21:24** [c]S Jos 10:12 [d]S Jos 19:45 **21:25** [e]S Jos 12:21 **21:26** [f]ver 5 **21:27** [g]S Jos 12:5 [h]Nu 35:6 **21:28** [i]S Ge 30:18 [j]Jos 19:20 [k]S Jos 19:12 **21:29** [l]S Jos 10:3 [m]S Jos 15:34 **21:30** [n]S Jos 17:7 [o]Jos 19:26 [p]S Jos 19:28 **21:31** [q]S Jos 19:28 **21:32** [r]S Jos 12:22 [s]Nu 35:6 **21:33** [t]ver 6 **21:34** [u]S Jos 19:10 [v]S Jos 12:22 **21:35** [w]Jos 19:15

21:1–45 Finally the Levites are allotted their towns and adjoining pasturelands—with the priestly families being given precedence (see v. 10).

21:4 *Kohathites.* The three sons of Levi were Kohath, Gershon and Merari (Ex 6:16; Nu 3:17). *Judah, Simeon and Benjamin.* Tribal areas close to Jerusalem, which would later be the site of the temple. The remaining Kohathites received cities in adjoining tribes.

21:11 *Hebron.* Caleb's city (see 14:13–15 and note on 14:15). The priests and Levites were to be given space in their assigned cities along with the other inhabitants.

21:27 *Gershonites.* Received cities in the northern tribes of Asher, Naphtali and Issachar.

21:34 *Merarite clans.* Their 12 cities were scattered throughout Reuben, Gad and Zebulun.

36from the tribe of Reuben,
Bezer,[x] Jahaz,[y] 37Kedemoth and
Mephaath,[z] together with their pasturelands — four towns;
38from the tribe of Gad,
Ramoth[a] in Gilead[b] (a city of refuge
for one accused of murder), Mahanaim,[c] 39Heshbon and Jazer,[d] together
with their pasturelands — four towns
in all.
40All the towns allotted to the Merarite
clans, who were the rest of the Levites,
were twelve.[e]
41The towns of the Levites in the territory held by the Israelites were forty-eight
in all, together with their pasturelands.[f]
42Each of these towns had pasturelands
surrounding it; this was true for all these
towns.

43So the LORD gave Israel all the land
he had sworn to give their forefathers,[g]
and they took possession[h] of it and settled there.[i] 44The LORD gave them rest[j] on
every side, just as he had sworn to their
forefathers. Not one of their enemies[k]
withstood them; the LORD handed all their
enemies[l] over to them.[m] 45Not one of all
the LORD's good promises[n] to the house of
Israel failed; every one was fulfilled.

Eastern Tribes Return Home

22 Then Joshua summoned the Reubenites, the Gadites and the half-tribe of
Manasseh 2and said to them, "You have
done all that Moses the servant of the LORD
commanded,[o] and you have obeyed me in
everything I commanded. 3For a long time
now — to this very day — you have not deserted your brothers but have carried out
the mission the LORD your God gave you.
4Now that the LORD your God has given
your brothers rest[p] as he promised, return
to your homes[q] in the land that Moses the
servant of the LORD gave you on the other
side of the Jordan.[r] 5But be very careful to
keep the commandment[s] and the law that
Moses the servant of the LORD gave you:
to love the LORD[t] your God, to walk in all
his ways, to obey his commands,[u] to hold
fast to him and to serve him with all your
heart and all your soul.[v]"
6Then Joshua blessed[w] them and sent
them away, and they went to their homes.
7(To the half-tribe of Manasseh Moses had
given land in Bashan,[x] and to the other
half of the tribe Joshua gave land on the
west side[y] of the Jordan with their brothers.) When Joshua sent them home, he
blessed them,[z] 8saying, "Return to your
homes with your great wealth — with
large herds of livestock,[a] with silver, gold,
bronze and iron,[b] and a great quantity of
clothing — and divide[c] with your brothers
the plunder[d] from your enemies."
9So the Reubenites, the Gadites and the
half-tribe of Manasseh left the Israelites
at Shiloh[e] in Canaan to return to Gilead,[f]
their own land, which they had acquired
in accordance with the command of the
LORD through Moses.
10When they came to Geliloth[g] near the
Jordan in the land of Canaan, the Reubenites, the Gadites and the half-tribe of
Manasseh built an imposing altar[h] there
by the Jordan. 11And when the Israelites
heard that they had built the altar on the
border of Canaan at Geliloth near the Jordan on the Israelite side, 12the whole assembly of Israel gathered at Shiloh[i] to go
to war against them.
13So the Israelites sent Phinehas[j] son of
Eleazar,[k] the priest, to the land of Gilead —
to Reuben, Gad and the half-tribe of Manasseh. 14With him they sent ten of the
chief men, one for each of the tribes of
Israel, each the head of a family division
among the Israelite clans.[l]

21:36 [x]S Jos 20:8 [y]S Nu 21:23; Dt 2:32; Jdg 11:20 **21:37** [z]S Jos 13:18 **21:38** [a]S Dt 4:43 [b]S Jos 12:2 [c]S Ge 32:2 **21:39** [d]S Jos 13:25 **21:40** [e]ver 7 **21:41** [f]Nu 35:7 **21:43** [g]Dt 34:4 [h]Dt 11:31 [i]S Dt 17:14 **21:44** [j]S Ex 33:14 [k]S Dt 6:19 [l]S Ex 23:31 [m]Dt 21:10 **21:45** [n]Jos 23:14; Ne 9:8 **22:2** [o]S Nu 32:25 **22:4** [p]S Ex 33:14 [q]Nu 32:22; Dt 3:20 [r]Nu 32:18; S Jos 1:13-15 **22:5** [s]Isa 43:22; Mal 3:14 [t]Jos 23:11 [u]S Dt 5:29 [v]S Dt 6:5 **22:6** [w]S Ge 24:60; S Ex 39:43 **22:7** [x]S Nu 32:19; S Jos 12:5 [y]Jos 17:2 [z]S Jos 14:13; Lk 24:50 **22:8** [a]S Dt 20:14 [b]S Nu 31:22 [c]S Nu 31:27 [d]S Ge 49:27; 1Sa 30:16; 2Sa 1:1; Isa 9:3 **22:9** [e]Jos 18:1 [f]S Nu 32:26 **22:10** [g]Jos 18:17 [h]ver 19,26-27; Isa 19:19; 56:7 **22:12** [i]Jos 18:1 **22:13** [j]S Nu 25:7 [k]Nu 3:32; Jos 24:33 **22:14** [l]ver 32; S Nu 1:4

21:43 – 45 A concluding summary statement of how the Lord had fulfilled his sworn promise to give Israel this land (see Ge 15:18 – 21 and note on 15:18). The occupation of the land was not yet complete (see 23:4 – 5; Jdg 1 – 2), but the national campaign was over and Israel was finally established in the promised land. No power was left in Canaan that could threaten to dislodge her.

21:44 *rest on every side.* See note on 1:13.

21:45 *good promises.* Refers to the good things God had covenanted to give his people (23:14 – 15; 1Ki 8:56; Jer 33:14).

22:1 – 34 The two and a half tribes from east of the Jordan, faithful in battle, are now commended by Joshua and sent to their homes. But their "altar of witness" (see vv. 26 – 27,34 and note on v. 27) was misunderstood, and disciplinary action against them was narrowly averted.

22:2 *all that Moses … commanded.* Moses had ordered them to join the other tribes in the conquest of Canaan (see Nu 32:16 – 27 and note on 32:17; Dt 3:18).

22:5 *love the LORD … serve him with all your heart.* Both Moses and Joshua saw that obedience to the laws of God would require love and service from the heart. In the ancient Near East, "love" was also a political term, indicating truehearted loyalty to one's king (see notes on Dt 6:5; 11:1).

22:8 *divide with your brothers.* Moses also had seen the need for a fair sharing of the spoils of war (see Nu 31:25 – 27 and note on 31:26 – 35).

22:10 *Geliloth.* Understood in the Septuagint (the pre-Christian Greek translation of the OT) to be Gilgal, next to Jericho; more likely it was a site east of Shiloh along the Jordan River (18:17).

22:11 *when the Israelites heard.* Anxiety about apostasy led to hasty conclusions. They thought the altar had been set up as a rival to the true altar at Shiloh.

22:12 *gathered at Shiloh.* In the presence of God at the tabernacle. *to go to war against them.* To take disciplinary action (cf. Dt 13:12 – 18; Jdg 20).

22:13 – 14 A prestigious delegation is sent to try to turn the Transjordan tribes from their (supposed) act of rebellion against the Lord.

15When they went to Gilead—to Reuben, Gad and the half-tribe of Manasseh—they said to them: 16"The whole
assembly of the LORD says: 'How could
you break faith[m] with the God of Israel
like this? How could you turn away from
the LORD and build yourselves an altar in
rebellion[n] against him now? 17Was not
the sin of Peor[o] enough for us? Up to this
very day we have not cleansed ourselves
from that sin, even though a plague fell
on the community of the LORD! 18And are
you now turning away from the LORD?
"'If you rebel against the LORD today, tomorrow he will be angry with the
whole community[p] of Israel. 19If the land
you possess is defiled, come over to the
LORD's land, where the LORD's tabernacle[q]
stands, and share the land with us. But
do not rebel against the LORD or against
us by building an altar[r] for yourselves,
other than the altar of the LORD our God.
20When Achan son of Zerah acted unfaithfully regarding the devoted things,[a][s] did
not wrath[t] come upon the whole community[u] of Israel? He was not the only one
who died for his sin.'"[v]
21Then Reuben, Gad and the half-tribe
of Manasseh replied to the heads of the
clans of Israel: 22"The Mighty One, God,
the LORD! The Mighty One, God,[w] the
LORD![x] He knows![y] And let Israel know!
If this has been in rebellion or disobedience to the LORD, do not spare us this day.
23If we have built our own altar to turn
away from the LORD and to offer burnt offerings and grain offerings,[z] or to sacrifice
fellowship offerings[b] on it, may the LORD
himself call us to account.[a]
24"No! We did it for fear that some
day your descendants might say to ours,
'What do you have to do with the LORD,
the God of Israel? 25The LORD has made
the Jordan a boundary between us and
you—you Reubenites and Gadites! You
have no share in the LORD.' So your descendants might cause ours to stop fearing the LORD.
26"That is why we said, 'Let us get ready
and build an altar—but not for burnt offerings or sacrifices.' 27On the contrary, it
is to be a witness[b] between us and you
and the generations that follow, that we
will worship the LORD at his sanctuary
with our burnt offerings, sacrifices and
fellowship offerings.[c] Then in the future your descendants will not be able
to say to ours, 'You have no share in the
LORD.'
28"And we said, 'If they ever say this
to us, or to our descendants, we will answer: Look at the replica of the LORD's altar, which our fathers built, not for burnt
offerings and sacrifices, but as a witness[d]
between us and you.'
29"Far be it from us to rebel[e] against
the LORD and turn away from him today
by building an altar for burnt offerings,
grain offerings and sacrifices, other than
the altar of the LORD our God that stands
before his tabernacle.[f]"
30When Phinehas the priest and the
leaders of the community—the heads of
the clans of the Israelites—heard what
Reuben, Gad and Manasseh had to say,
they were pleased. 31And Phinehas son of
Eleazar, the priest, said to Reuben, Gad
and Manasseh, "Today we know that the
LORD is with us,[g] because you have not
acted unfaithfully toward the LORD in this
matter. Now you have rescued the Israelites from the LORD's hand."
32Then Phinehas son of Eleazar, the
priest, and the leaders returned to Canaan
from their meeting with the Reubenites
and Gadites in Gilead and reported to the
Israelites.[h] 33They were glad to hear the
report and praised God.[i] And they talked
no more about going to war against them
to devastate the country where the Reubenites and the Gadites lived.
34And the Reubenites and the Gadites
gave the altar this name: A Witness[j] Between Us that the LORD is God.

22:16 [m]S Dt 7:3; 1Sa 13:13; 15:11 [n]Dt 12:13-14 **22:17** [o]S Nu 23:28; 25:1-9 **22:18** [p]S Lev 10:6 **22:19** [q]S Ex 26:1 [r]S ver 10 **22:20** [s]Jos 7:1 [t]Ps 7:11 [u]Lev 10:6 [v]Jos 7:5 **22:22** [w]S Dt 10:17 [x]Ps 50:1 [y]1Sa 2:3; 16:7; 1Ki 8:39; 1Ch 28:9; Ps 11:4; 40:9; 44:21; 139:4; Jer 17:10 **22:23** [z]Jer 41:5 [a]S Dt 12:11; S 18:19; 1Sa 20:16 **22:27** [b]S Ge 21:30; Jos 24:27; Isa 19:20 [c]S Dt 12:6 **22:28** [d]S Ge 21:30 **22:29** [e]Jos 24:16 [f]S Ex 26:1 **22:31** [g]2Ch 15:2 **22:32** [h]S ver 14 **22:33** [i]1Ch 29:20; Da 2:19; Lk 2:28 **22:34** [j]S Ge 21:30

[a] *20* The Hebrew term refers to the irrevocable giving over of things or persons to the LORD, often by totally destroying them. [b] *23* Traditionally *peace offerings*; also in verse 27

22:16 *How could you ...?* The accusations were very grave: You have committed apostasy and rebellion.
22:17 *Peor.* Where some of the Israelites became involved in the Moabite worship of Baal of Peor (see Nu 25:1–5 and notes on 25:1–18 and 25:1).
22:19 *is defiled.* By pagan worship, corrupting its inhabitants. *the LORD's land.* The promised land proper had never included Transjordan territory. Canaan was the land the Lord especially claimed as his own and promised to the descendants of Abraham, Isaac and Jacob.
22:20 *Achan ... the whole community of Israel.* See note on 7:1–26.
22:22 *The Mighty One, God, the LORD!* See note on Ps 50:1. The repetition of the sacred names gives an oath-like quality to this strong denial of any wrongdoing.
22:27 *witness.* The altar, presumably of uncut stone (see 8:31; Ex 20:25 and note), was to serve as a testimony to the commitment of the Transjordan tribes to remain loyal to the Lord, and to their continued right to worship the Lord at the tabernacle—even though they lived outside the land of promise. It constitutes a seventh memorial monument in the land noted by the author of Joshua (see note on 4:9).
22:31 *you have rescued the Israelites.* Their words prevented a terrible punishment that the other tribes were about to inflict as an act of divine judgment (consider the implications of v. 20).

Joshua's Farewell to the Leaders

23 After a long time had passed and the LORD had given Israel rest[k] from all their enemies around them, Joshua, by then old and well advanced in years,[l] 2summoned all Israel—their elders,[m] leaders, judges and officials[n]—and said to them: "I am old and well advanced in years.[o] 3You yourselves have seen everything the LORD your God has done to all these nations for your sake; it was the LORD your God who fought for you.[p] 4Remember how I have allotted[q] as an inheritance[r] for your tribes all the land of the nations that remain—the nations I conquered—between the Jordan and the Great Sea[a][s] in the west. 5The LORD your God himself will drive them out[t] of your way. He will push them out[u] before you, and you will take possession of their land, as the LORD your God promised you.[v]

6"Be very strong; be careful to obey all that is written in the Book of the Law[w] of Moses, without turning aside[x] to the right or to the left.[y] 7Do not associate with these nations that remain among you; do not invoke the names of their gods or swear[z] by them. You must not serve them or bow down[a] to them. 8But you are to hold fast to the LORD[b] your God, as you have until now.

9"The LORD has driven out before you great and powerful nations;[c] to this day no one has been able to withstand you.[d] 10One of you routs a thousand,[e] because the LORD your God fights for you,[f] just as he promised. 11So be very careful[g] to love the LORD[h] your God.

12"But if you turn away and ally yourselves with the survivors of these nations that remain among you and if you intermarry with them[i] and associate with them,[j] 13then you may be sure that the LORD your God will no longer drive out[k] these nations before you. Instead, they will become snares[l] and traps for you, whips on your backs and thorns in your eyes,[m] until you perish from this good land,[n] which the LORD your God has given you.

14"Now I am about to go the way of all the earth.[o] You know with all your heart and soul that not one of all the good promises the LORD your God gave you has failed. Every promise[p] has been fulfilled; not one has failed.[q] 15But just as every good promise[r] of the LORD your God has come true, so the LORD will bring on you all the evil[s] he has threatened, until he has destroyed you[t] from this good land he has given you.[u] 16If you violate the covenant of the LORD your God, which he commanded you, and go and serve other gods and bow down to them, the LORD's anger will burn against you, and you will quickly perish from the good land he has given you.[v]"

The Covenant Renewed at Shechem

24 Then Joshua assembled[w] all the tribes of Israel at Shechem.[x] He summoned[y] the elders,[z] leaders, judges and officials of Israel,[a] and they presented themselves before God.

2Joshua said to all the people, "This is what the LORD, the God of Israel, says: 'Long ago your forefathers, including Terah the father of Abraham and Nahor,[b] lived beyond the River[b] and worshiped other gods.[c] 3But I took your father Abraham from the land beyond the River and

[a] 4 That is, the Mediterranean [b] 2 That is, the Euphrates; also in verses 3, 14 and 15

23:1 [k]S Dt 12:9; Jos 21:44 [l]S Jos 13:1 **23:2** [m]S Jos 7:6 [n]Jos 24:1 [o]S Jos 13:1 **23:3** [p]S Ex 14:14; S Dt 20:4 **23:4** [q]Jos 19:51 [r]S Nu 34:2; Ps 78:55 [s]S Nu 34:6 **23:5** [t]ver 13; Jdg 2:21 [u]Ps 44:5; Jer 46:15 [v]Ex 23:30 **23:6** [w]S Dt 28:61 [x]S Dt 17:20 [y]Jos 1:7 **23:7** [z]Ex 23:13; Jer 5:7; 12:16 [a]S Ex 20:5 **23:8** [b]S Dt 10:20 **23:9** [c]Dt 11:23 [d]Dt 7:24 **23:10** [e]Lev 26:8; Jdg 3:31 [f]S Ex 14:14 **23:11** [g]S Dt 4:15 [h]Jos 22:5 **23:12** [i]S Ge 34:9 [j]S Ex 34:16; Ps 106:34-35 **23:13** [k]S ver 5 [l]S Ex 10:7 [m]S Nu 33:55 [n]Dt 1:8; 1Ki 9:7; 2Ki 25:21 **23:14** [o]1Ki 2:2 [p]Ps 119:140; 145:13 [q]S Jos 21:45 **23:15** [r]1Ki 8:56; Jer 33:14 [s]1Ki 14:10; 2Ki 22:16; Isa 24:6; 34:5; 43:28; Jer 6:19; 11:8; 35:17; 39:16; Mal 4:6 [t]Jos 24:20 [u]Lev 26:17; Dt 28:15; Jer 40:2 **23:16** [v]Dt 4:25-26

24:1 [w]Ge 49:2 [x]S Ge 12:6 [y]1Sa 12:7; 1Ki 8:14 [z]Jos 7:6 [a]Jos 23:2 **24:2** [b]Ge 11:26 [c]Ge 11:32

23:1–16 Joshua, the Lord's servant, delivers a farewell address recalling the victories the Lord has given, but also reminding the people of areas yet to be possessed and of the need to be loyal to God's covenant laws. Their mission remains—to be the people of God's kingdom in the world.

23:1 *rest.* See note on 1:13. *well advanced in years.* Joshua was approaching the age of 110 (24:29).

23:6 *be careful to obey.* Echoing the Lord's instructions at the beginning (1:7–8; see 22:5 and note). *Book of the Law.* See note on 1:8.

23:7 See Dt 6:13 and note.

23:10 *One of you routs a thousand.* See, e.g., Jdg 15:15–16.

23:11 *love the LORD your God.* A concluding summation (see note on 22:5).

23:12 *But if you turn away.* Remaining in the promised land was conditioned on faithfulness to the Lord and separation from the idolaters still around them. Failure to meet these conditions would bring Israel's banishment from the land (cf. vv. 13,15–16; 2Ki 17:7–8; 2Ch 7:14–20). *ally yourselves ... intermarry.* The Lord prohibited alliances, either national or domestic, with the peoples of Canaan because such alliances would tend to compromise Israel's loyalty to the Lord (see Ex 34:15–16 and note on 34:15; Dt 7:2–4 and notes on 7:1–6; 7:2–5; 7:4).

23:13 *snares and traps.* Joshua's warning echoes Ex 23:33; 34:12; Dt 7:16.

23:14 *go the way of all the earth.* To the grave.

24:1–33 Once more Joshua assembled the tribes at Shechem to call Israel to a renewal of the covenant (see 8:30–35 and note). It was his final official act as the Lord's servant, mediator of the Lord's rule over his people. In this he followed the example of Moses, whose final official act was also a call to covenant renewal—of which Deuteronomy is the preserved document.

24:2 *This is what the LORD ... says.* Only a divinely appointed mediator would dare to speak for God with direct discourse, as in vv. 2–13. *Long ago.* In accordance with the common ancient Near Eastern practice of making treaties (covenants), a brief recital of the past history of the relationship precedes the making of covenant commitments. Joshua here focuses on the separation of Abraham from his polytheistic family, the deliverance of Israel from Egypt and the Lord's establishment of his people in Canaan. *the River.* See NIV text note.

led him throughout Canaan[d] and gave him
many descendants.[e] I gave him Isaac,[f] 4 and
to Isaac I gave Jacob and Esau.[g] I assigned
the hill country of Seir[h] to Esau, but Jacob
and his sons went down to Egypt.[i]
5 "'Then I sent Moses and Aaron,[j] and I
afflicted the Egyptians by what I did there,
and I brought you out.[k] 6 When I brought
your fathers out of Egypt, you came to
the sea,[l] and the Egyptians pursued them
with chariots and horsemen[a][m] as far as
the Red Sea.[b][n] 7 But they cried[o] to the LORD
for help, and he put darkness[p] between
you and the Egyptians; he brought the
sea over them and covered them.[q] You
saw with your own eyes what I did to the
Egyptians.[r] Then you lived in the desert
for a long time.[s]
8 "'I brought you to the land of the Amorites[t] who lived east of the Jordan. They
fought against you, but I gave them into
your hands. I destroyed them from before you, and you took possession of their
land.[u] 9 When Balak son of Zippor,[v] the
king of Moab, prepared to fight against Israel, he sent for Balaam son of Beor[w] to
put a curse on you.[x] 10 But I would not listen to Balaam, so he blessed you[y] again
and again, and I delivered you out of his
hand.
11 "'Then you crossed the Jordan[z] and
came to Jericho.[a] The citizens of Jericho
fought against you, as did also the Amorites, Perizzites,[b] Canaanites, Hittites,
Girgashites, Hivites and Jebusites,[c] but I
gave them into your hands.[d] 12 I sent the
hornet[e] ahead of you, which drove them
out[f] before you—also the two Amorite
kings. You did not do it with your own
sword and bow.[g] 13 So I gave you a land[h]
on which you did not toil and cities you
did not build; and you live in them and eat
from vineyards and olive groves that you
did not plant.'[i]
14 "Now fear the LORD[j] and serve him
with all faithfulness.[k] Throw away the
gods[l] your forefathers worshiped beyond
the River and in Egypt,[m] and serve the
LORD. 15 But if serving the LORD seems undesirable to you, then choose for yourselves this day whom you will serve,
whether the gods your forefathers served
beyond the River, or the gods of the Amorites,[n] in whose land you are living. But as
for me and my household,[o] we will serve
the LORD."[p]
16 Then the people answered, "Far be it
from us to forsake[q] the LORD to serve other gods! 17 It was the LORD our God himself
who brought us and our fathers up out of
Egypt, from that land of slavery,[r] and performed those great signs[s] before our eyes.
He protected us on our entire journey and
among all the nations through which we
traveled. 18 And the LORD drove out[t] before
us all the nations,[u] including the Amorites,
who lived in the land.[v] We too will serve
the LORD, because he is our God.[w]"
19 Joshua said to the people, "You are not
able to serve the LORD. He is a holy God;[x]
he is a jealous God.[y] He will not forgive[z]
your rebellion[a] and your sins. 20 If you forsake the LORD[b] and serve foreign gods, he
will turn[c] and bring disaster[d] on you and
make an end of you,[e] after he has been
good to you."
21 But the people said to Joshua, "No!
We will serve the LORD."
22 Then Joshua said, "You are witnesses[f]
against yourselves that you have chosen[g]
to serve the LORD."
"Yes, we are witnesses,[h]" they replied.
23 "Now then," said Joshua, "throw away
the foreign gods[i] that are among you and
yield your hearts[j] to the LORD, the God of
Israel."
24 And the people said to Joshua, "We
will serve the LORD our God and obey
him."[k]
25 On that day Joshua made a covenant[l]
for the people, and there at Shechem[m] he

24:3 [d] S Ge 12:1 [e] S Ge 1:28; S 12:2 [f] S Ge 21:3 **24:4** [g] S Ge 25:26 [h] S Ge 14:6; S Nu 24:18 [i] Ge 46:5-6 **24:5** [j] S Ex 3:10 [k] Ex 12:51 **24:6** [l] S Ex 14:22 [m] S Ex 14:9 [n] Ex 14:23 **24:7** [o] S Ex 14:10 [p] Ex 14:20 [q] S Ex 14:28 [r] S Ex 19:4 [s] Dt 1:46 **24:8** [t] S Ex 23:23 [u] S Nu 21:31 **24:9** [v] Nu 22:2 [w] S Nu 23:7 [x] S Nu 22:6 **24:10** [y] S Nu 23:11; S Dt 23:5 **24:11** [z] S Ex 14:29 [a] Jos 6:1 [b] S Jos 3:10 [c] S Ge 15:18-21 [d] Ex 23:23; Dt 7:1 **24:12** [e] S Ex 23:28; Ps 44:3,6-7 [f] S Ex 23:31 [g] Ps 135:11 **24:13** [h] Ex 6:8 [i] Dt 6:10-11 **24:14** [j] 1Sa 12:14; Job 23:15; Ps 19:9; 119:120 [k] Dt 10:12; 18:13; 1Sa 12:24; 2Co 1:12 [l] ver 23; S Ge 31:19; Ex 12:12; 18:11; 20:3; Nu 25:2; Dt 11:28; Jdg 10:16; Ru 1:15; Isa 55:7 [m] Eze 23:3 **24:15** [n] Jdg 6:10; Ru 1:15 [o] S Ge 35:2 [p] Ru 1:16; 2:12; 1Ki 18:21; Da 3:18 **24:16** [q] Jos 22:29 **24:17** [r] Jdg 6:8 [s] S Ex 10:1 **24:18** [t] S Ex 23:31 [u] S Dt 33:27 [v] Ac 7:45 [w] S Ge 28:21

[a] 6 Or *charioteers* [b] 6 Hebrew *Yam Suph*; that is, Sea of Reeds

24:19 [x] S Lev 11:44; S 20:26 [y] S Ex 20:5 [z] S Ex 34:7 [a] S Ex 23:21 **24:20** [b] 1Ch 28:9,20; 2Ch 24:18 [c] Ac 7:42 [d] 1Sa 12:25; Hos 13:11 [e] Jos 23:15 **24:22** [f] ver 27; Ru 4:10; Isa 8:2; 43:10; 44:8; Jer 42:5; Mal 2:14 [g] Ps 119:30,173 [h] S Dt 25:9 **24:23** [i] S ver 14 [j] 1Ki 8:58; Ps 119:36; 141:4; Jer 31:33 **24:24** [k] Ex 19:8; Jer 42:6 **24:25** [l] S Ex 24:8 [m] S Jos 17:7

24:10 *I would not listen to Balaam.* Not only did the Lord reject Balaam's prayers; he also turned his curse into a blessing (see Nu 23–24; Ne 13:2; see also notes on Nu 22:5,8).

24:12 *hornet.* See note on Ex 23:28.

24:14 *fear the LORD.* Trust, serve and worship him (see note on Ge 20:11). *gods your forefathers worshiped beyond the River and in Egypt.* See v. 2. Joshua appealed to the Israelites to put away the gods their ancestors had worshiped in Mesopotamia and Egypt. In Ur and Haran, Terah's family would have been exposed to the worship of the moon-god, Nanna(r) or Sin. The golden calf of Ex 32:4 may be an example of their worship of the gods of Egypt. It was probably patterned after Apis, the sacred bull of Egypt; see note on Ex 32:4. (Jeroboam's golden calves at Bethel and Dan, on the other hand, probably represented mounts or pedestals for a riding or standing deity; see 1Ki 12:28–29 and notes.)

24:15 *as for me.* Joshua publicly makes his commitment, hoping to elicit the same from Israel.

24:17–18 A confessional statement based on the miraculous events of the exodus.

24:19 *You are not able.* Strong words to emphasize the danger of overconfidence. *He is a holy God.* See Lev 11:44 and note. *he is a jealous God.* See Ex 20:5; Zec 1:14 and notes.

24:22 *witnesses.* See v. 27; a normal part of treaty/covenant-making (see Dt 30:19 and note).

24:23 *foreign gods.* The other gods were represented by idols of wood and metal, which could be thrown away and destroyed.

24:25 *covenant for the people.* Consisting of the pledges they had agreed to and the decrees and laws from God.

drew up for them decrees and laws.[n] 26 And
Joshua recorded[o] these things in the Book
of the Law of God.[p] Then he took a large
stone[q] and set it up there under the oak[r]
near the holy place of the LORD.

27 "See!" he said to all the people. "This
stone[s] will be a witness[t] against us. It has
heard all the words the LORD has said to
us. It will be a witness against you if you
are untrue[u] to your God."[v]

Buried in the Promised Land

24:29-31pp — Jdg 2:6-9

28 Then Joshua sent the people away,
each to his own inheritance.[w]

29 After these things, Joshua son of Nun,
the servant of the LORD, died[x] at the age
of a hundred and ten.[y] 30 And they buried
him in the land of his inheritance, at Timnath Serah[a][z] in the hill country of Ephraim, north of Mount Gaash.[a]

31 Israel served the LORD throughout the
lifetime of Joshua and of the elders[b] who
outlived him and who had experienced everything the LORD had done for Israel.

32 And Joseph's bones,[c] which the Israelites had brought up from Egypt,[d] were
buried at Shechem in the tract of land[e]
that Jacob bought for a hundred pieces of
silver[b] from the sons of Hamor, the father
of Shechem. This became the inheritance
of Joseph's descendants.

33 And Eleazar son of Aaron[f] died and
was buried at Gibeah,[g] which had been
allotted to his son Phinehas[h] in the hill
country[i] of Ephraim.

24:25 [n] Ex 15:25 **24:26** [o] S Dt 17:18 [p] S Dt 28:61; S 31:24 [q] S Ge 28:18; S Dt 27:2 [r] S Ge 12:6; S Jdg 4:11 **24:27** [s] S Ge 28:18; Hab 2:11 [t] S ver 22; S Ge 21:30; S Jos 22:27 [u] S Jos 7:11 [v] S Nu 11:20; S Pr 30:9 **24:28** [w] Jdg 21:23, 24 **24:29** [x] Jdg 1:1 [y] S Ge 50:22 **24:30** [z] S Jos 19:50 [a] 2Sa 23:30 **24:31** [b] Jos 7:6 **24:32** [c] Heb 11:22 [d] S Ge 47:29-30 [e] Ge 33:19; Jn 4:5; Ac 7:16 **24:33** [f] S Jos 22:13 [g] S Jos 15:57 [h] S Ex 6:25 [i] 1Sa 9:4; 1Ki 4:8

[a] *30* Also known as *Timnath Heres* (see Judges 2:9)
[b] *32* Hebrew *hundred kesitahs*; a kesitah was a unit of money of unknown weight and value.

24:26 *Book of the Law of God.* Probably a list of decrees and laws Joshua had drawn up for the people (v. 25). *large stone.* Set up as a witness to the covenant renewal that closed Joshua's ministry, this is the eighth memorial in the land reminding Israel of what the Lord had done for them through his servant (see note on 4:9). Thus the promised land itself bore full testimony to Israel—how they had come into possession of the land and how they would remain in the land only by fulfilling the covenant conditions. The land shouted its own story. *oak.* See note on Ge 12:6.

24:29–33 Three burials. Since it was a deep desire of the ancients to be buried in their homeland, these notices not only mark the conclusion of the story and the close of an era but also underscore the fact that Israel had indeed been established in the promised homeland—the Lord had kept his covenant promises.

24:29 *a hundred and ten.* For the significance of this number see note on Ge 50:26.

24:30 *buried him ... at Timnath Serah.* See 19:50 and note.

24:31 The story told in Joshua is a testimony to Israel's faithfulness in that generation. The author anticipates the quite different story that would follow in Judges.

24:32 *Joseph's bones.* Returning his bones to Shechem was significant not only because of the ancient plot of land Jacob bought from Hamor (Ge 33:19), but also because Shechem was to be the center of the tribes of Ephraim and Manasseh, the two sons of Joseph. Also, the return fulfilled an oath sworn to Joseph on his deathbed (see Ge 50:25 and note; Ex 13:19).

24:33 *Eleazar.* The high priest who served Joshua, as Aaron had served Moses. *Gibeah.* Not the Benjamite city, but a place in Ephraim near Shiloh.

Judges

INTRODUCTION

Title

The title refers to the leaders Israel had from the time of the elders who outlived Joshua until the time of the monarchy. Their principal purpose is best expressed in 2:16: "Then the LORD raised up judges, who saved them out of the hands of … raiders." Since it was God who permitted the oppressions and raised up deliverers, he himself was Israel's ultimate Judge and Deliverer (see 11:27 and note; 8:23, where Gideon, a judge, insists that the Lord is Israel's true ruler; see also note on 8:23).

Author and Date

Although tradition ascribes the book to Samuel, the author is actually unknown. It is possible that Samuel assembled some of the accounts from the period of the judges and that such prophets as Nathan and Gad, both of whom were associated with David's court, had a hand in shaping and editing the material (see 1Ch 29:29).

The date of composition is also unknown, but it was undoubtedly during the monarchy. The frequent expression "In those days Israel had no king" (17:6; 18:1; 19:1; 21:25) suggests a date after the establishment of the monarchy. The observation that the Jebusites still controlled Jerusalem (1:21) has been taken to indicate a time before David's capture of the city c. 1000 B.C. (see 2Sa 5:6–10 and notes). But the new conditions in Israel alluded to in chs. 17–21 suggest a time after the Davidic dynasty had been effectively established (tenth century B.C.).

A Quick Look

Author:
Unknown, though certain sections may derive from the prophet Samuel

Audience:
God's chosen people, the Israelites

Date:
Probably around 1000 B.C.

Theme:
In danger of losing the promised land, the Israelites are delivered again and again by God through leaders known as "judges."

Themes and Theology

The book of Judges depicts the life of Israel in the promised land from the death of Joshua to the rise of the monarchy. On the one hand, Judges is an account of frequent apostasy, provoking divine chastening. On the other hand, it tells about urgent appeals to God in times of crisis, moving him to raise up leaders ("judges") through whom he throws off foreign oppressors and restores the land to peace.

With Israel's conquest of the promised land through the leadership of Joshua, many of the covenant promises God had made to their ancestors were fulfilled (see Jos 21:43–45 and note). The Lord's land, where Israel was to enter into rest, lay under their feet; it remained only for them to occupy it, to displace the Canaanites and to cleanse it of paganism. The time had come for Israel to be the kingdom of God in the form of an established commonwealth on earth.

On the one hand, Judges is an account of frequent apostasy, provoking divine chastening. On the other hand, it tells about urgent appeals to God in times of crisis, moving him to raise up leaders ("judges") through whom he throws off foreign oppressors and restores the land to peace.

But in Canaan, Israel quickly forgot the acts of God that had given them birth and had established them in the land. Consequently they lost sight of their unique identity as God's people, chosen and called to be his army and the loyal citizens of his emerging kingdom. They settled down and attached themselves to Canaan's peoples together with Canaanite morals, gods, and religious beliefs and practices as readily as to Canaan's agriculture and social life.

Throughout Judges the fundamental issue is the lordship of God in Israel, especially Israel's acknowledgment of and loyalty to his rule. His kingship over Israel had been uniquely established by the covenant at Sinai (Ex 19–24), which was later renewed by Moses on the plains of Moab (Dt 29) and by Joshua at Shechem (Jos 24). The author accuses Israel of having rejected the kingship of the Lord again and again. They stopped fighting the Lord's battles, turned to the gods of Canaan to secure the blessings of family, flocks and fields, and abandoned God's laws for daily living. In the very center of the cycle of the judges (see Outline), Gideon had to remind Israel that the Lord was their King (see note on 8:23). The recurring lament, and indictment, of chs. 17–21 (see Outline) is: "In those days Israel had no king; everyone did as he saw fit" (see note on 17:6). The primary reference here is doubtless to the earthly mediators of the Lord's rule (i.e., human kings), but the implicit charge is that Israel did not truly acknowledge or obey her heavenly King either.

Only by the Lord's sovereign use of foreign oppression to chasten his people—thereby implementing the covenant curses (see Lev 26:14–45; Dt 28:15–68)—and by his raising up deliverers when his people cried out to him did he maintain his kingship in Israel and preserve his embryonic kingdom from extinction. Israel's flawed condition was graphically exposed; they continued to need new saving acts by God in order to enter into the promised rest (see note on Jos 1:13,15).

Out of the recurring cycles of disobedience, foreign oppression, cries of distress, and deliverance (see 2:11–19; Ne 9:26–31) emerges another important theme—the covenant faithfulness of the Lord. The amazing patience and long-suffering of God are no better demonstrated than during this unsettled period.

Remarkably, this age of Israel's failure, following directly on the redemptive events that came through Moses and Joshua, is in a special way the OT age of the Spirit. God's Spirit enabled people to accomplish feats of victory in the Lord's war against the powers that threatened his kingdom (see 3:10 and note; 6:34; 11:29; 13:25; 14:6,19; 15:14; see also 1Sa 10:6,10; 11:6; 16:13). This same Spirit, poured out on the church following the redemptive work of the second Joshua (Jesus), empowered the Lord's people to begin the task of preaching the gospel to all nations and of advancing the kingdom of God (see notes on Ac 1:2,8).

Background

Fixing precise dates for the judges is difficult and complex. The dating system followed here is based primarily on 1Ki 6:1, which speaks of an interval of 480 years between the exodus and the fourth year of Solomon's reign. This would place the exodus c. 1446 B.C. and the period of the judges between c. 1380 and the rise of Saul, c. 1050. Jephthah's statement that Israel had occupied Heshbon for 300 years (11:26) generally agrees with these dates. And the reference to "Israel" in the Merneptah Stele demonstrates that Israel was established in Canaan before 1210 B.C. (see chart, p. xxiii).

Some maintain, however, that the number 480 in 1Ki 6:1 is somewhat artificial, arrived at by multiplying 12 (perhaps in reference to the 12 judges) by 40 (a conventional number of years for a generation). They point out the frequent use of the round numbers 10, 20, 40 and 80 in the book of Judges itself. A later date for the exodus would of course require a much shorter period of time for the judges (see Introduction to Exodus: Chronology; see also note on 1Ki 6:1).

Literary Features

Even a quick reading of Judges discloses its basic threefold division: (1) a prologue (1:1—3:6), (2) a main body (3:7—16:31) and (3) an epilogue (chs. 17–21). Closer study brings to light a more complex structure, with interwoven themes that bind the whole into an intricately designed portrayal of the character of an age.

The prologue (1:1—3:6) has two parts, and each serves a different purpose. They are not chronologically related, nor does either offer a strict chronological scheme of the time as a whole. The first part (1:1—2:5) sets the stage historically for the narratives that follow. It describes Israel's occupation of the promised land—from their initial success to their large-scale failure and divine rebuke.

The second part (2:6—3:6) indicates a basic perspective on the period from the time of Joshua to the rise of the monarchy, a time characterized by recurring cycles of apostasy, oppression, cries of distress and gracious divine deliverance. The author summarizes and explains the Lord's dealings with his rebellious people and introduces some of the basic vocabulary and formulas he will use in the later narratives: "did evil in the eyes of the LORD," 2:11 (see note there; see also 3:7,12; 4:1; 6:1; 10:6); "handed them over to," 2:14 (see 6:1; 13:1); and "sold them," 2:14 (see 3:8; 4:2; 10:7).

The main body of the book (3:7—16:31), which gives the actual accounts of the recurring cycles (apostasy, oppression, distress, deliverance), has its own unique design. Each cycle has a similar beginning ("the Israelites did evil in the eyes of the LORD"; see note on 3:7) and a recognizable conclusion ("the land had peace ... years" or "led Israel ... years"; see note on 3:11). The first of these cycles (Othniel; see 3:7–11 and note) provides the "report form" used for each successive story of oppression and deliverance.

The remaining five cycles form the following narrative units, each of which focuses on one of the major judges:

1. Ehud (3:12–30), a lone hero from the tribe of Benjamin who delivers Israel from oppression from the east.

2. Deborah (chs. 4–5), a woman from one of the Joseph tribes (Ephraim, west of the Jordan) who judges at a time when Israel is being overrun by a coalition of Canaanites under Sisera.

3. Gideon and his son Abimelech (chs. 6–9), whose story forms the central account. In many ways Gideon is the ideal judge, evoking memory of Moses, while his son is the very antithesis of a responsible and faithful judge.

4. Jephthah (10:6—12:7), a social outcast from the other Joseph tribe (Manasseh, east of the Jordan) who judges at a time when Israel is being threatened by a coalition of powers under the king of Ammon.

5. Samson (chs. 13–16), a lone hero from the tribe of Dan who delivers Israel from oppression from the west.

The whole design of the book from prologue to epilogue ... clearly portray[s] an age gone awry.

The arrangement of these narrative units is significant. The central accounts of Gideon (the Lord's ideal judge) and Abimelech (the anti-judge) are bracketed by the parallel narratives of the woman Deborah and the social outcast Jephthah—which in turn are framed by the stories of the lone heroes Ehud and Samson. In this way even the structure focuses attention on the crucial issue of the period of the judges: Israel's attraction to the Baals of Canaan (shown by Abimelech; see note on 9:1–57) versus the Lord's kingship over his people (encouraged by Gideon; see note on 8:23).

The epilogue (chs. 17–21) characterizes the era in yet another way, depicting religious and moral corruption on the part of individuals, cities and tribes. Like the introduction, it has two divisions that are neither chronologically related nor expressly dated to the careers of specific judges. The events must have taken place, however, rather early in the period of the judges (see notes on 18:30; 20:1,28).

By dating the events of the epilogue only in relationship to the monarchy (see the recurring refrain in 17:6; 18:1; 19:1; 21:25), the author contrasts the age of the judges with the better time that the monarchy inaugurated, undoubtedly having in view the rule of David and his dynasty (see note on 17:1 — 21:25). The book mentions two instances of the Lord's assigning leadership to the tribe of Judah: (1) in driving out the Canaanites (1:1 – 2), and (2) in disciplining a tribe in Israel (20:18). The author views the ruler from the tribe of Judah as the savior of the nation.

The first division of the epilogue (chs. 17 – 18) relates the story of Micah's development of a paganized place of worship and tells of the tribe of Dan abandoning their allotted territory while adopting Micah's corrupted religion. The second division (chs. 19 – 21) tells the story of a Levite's sad experience at Gibeah in Benjamin and records the disciplinary removal of the tribe of Benjamin because it had defended the degenerate town of Gibeah.

The two divisions have several interesting parallels:

1. Both involve a Levite's passing between Bethlehem (in Judah) and Ephraim across the Benjamin-Dan corridor.
2. Both mention 600 warriors — those who led the tribe of Dan and those who survived from the tribe of Benjamin.
3. Both conclude with the emptying of a tribal area in that corridor (Dan and Benjamin).

Not only are these Benjamin-Dan parallels significant within the epilogue, but they also form a notable link to the main body of the book. The tribe of Benjamin, which in the epilogue undertook to defend gross immorality, setting ties of blood above loyalty to the Lord, was the tribe from which the Lord raised up the deliverer Ehud (3:15). The tribe of Dan, which in the epilogue retreated from its assigned inheritance and adopted pagan religious practices, was the tribe from which the Lord raised up the deliverer Samson (13:2,5). Thus the tribes that in the epilogue depict the religious and moral corruption of Israel are the very tribes from which the deliverers were chosen whose stories frame the central account of the book (Gideon-Abimelech).

The whole design of the book from prologue to epilogue, the unique manner in which each section deals with the age as a whole, and the way the three major divisions are interrelated clearly portray an age gone awry — an age when "Israel had no king" and "everyone did as he saw fit" (see note on 17:6). Of no small significance is the fact that the story is in episodes and cycles. It is given as the story of all Israel, though usually only certain areas are directly involved. The book portrays the centuries after Joshua as a time of Israelite unfaithfulness to the Lord and of their surrender to the allurements of Canaan. Only by the mercies of God was Israel not overwhelmed and absorbed by the pagan nations around them. Meanwhile, however, the history of redemption virtually stood still — awaiting the forward movement that came with the Lord's servant David and the establishment of his dynasty.

Outline

I. Prologue: Incomplete Conquest and Apostasy (1:1 — 3:6)
   - A. Israel's Failure to Purge the Land (1:1 — 2:5)
   - B. God's Dealings with Israel's Rebelliousness (2:6 — 3:6)

II. Oppression and Deliverance (3:7 — 16:31)

Major Judges	*Minor Judges*
A. Othniel Defeats Aram Naharaim (3:7 – 11)	
B. Ehud Defeats Moab (3:12 – 30)	1. Shamgar (3:31)
C. Deborah Defeats Canaan (chs. 4 – 5)	
D. Gideon Defeats Midian (chs. 6 – 8)	
(Abimelech, the anti-judge, ch. 9)	
	2. Tola (10:1 – 2)
	3. Jair (10:3 – 5)
E. Jephthah Defeats Ammon (10:6 — 12:7)	
	4. Ibzan (12:8 – 10)
	5. Elon (12:11 – 12)
	6. Abdon (12:13 – 15)
F. Samson Checks Philistia (chs. 13 – 16)	

III. Epilogue: Religious and Moral Disorder (chs. 17 – 21)
   - A. First Episode (chs. 17 – 18; see 17:6; 18:1)
     1. Micah's corruption of religion (ch. 17)
     2. The Danites' departure from their tribal territory (ch. 18)
   - B. Second Episode (chs. 19 – 21; see 19:1; 21:25)
     1. Gibeah's corruption of morals (ch. 19)
     2. The Benjamites' near removal from their tribal territory (chs. 20 – 21)

Israel Fights the Remaining Canaanites

1:11-15pp — Jos 15:15-19

1 After the death[a] of Joshua, the Israelites asked the LORD, "Who will be the
first[b] to go up and fight for us against the
Canaanites?[c]"
2The LORD answered, "Judah[d] is to go; I
have given the land into their hands.[e]"
3Then the men of Judah said to the Simeonites their brothers, "Come up with us
into the territory allotted to us, to fight
against the Canaanites. We in turn will go
with you into yours." So the Simeonites[f]
went with them.
4When Judah attacked, the LORD gave
the Canaanites and Perizzites[g] into their
hands and they struck down ten thousand
men at Bezek.[h] 5It was there that they
found Adoni-Bezek[i] and fought against
him, putting to rout the Canaanites and
Perizzites. 6Adoni-Bezek fled, but they
chased him and caught him, and cut off
his thumbs and big toes.
7Then Adoni-Bezek said, "Seventy
kings with their thumbs and big toes cut
off have picked up scraps under my table.
Now God has paid me back[j] for what I
did to them." They brought him to Jerusalem,[k] and he died there.
8The men of Judah attacked Jerusalem[l]
also and took it. They put the city to the
sword and set it on fire.
9After that, the men of Judah went
down to fight against the Canaanites living
in the hill country,[m] the Negev[n] and the
western foothills. 10They advanced against
the Canaanites living in Hebron[o] (formerly called Kiriath Arba[p]) and defeated Sheshai, Ahiman and Talmai.[q]
11From there they advanced against the
people living in Debir[r] (formerly called
Kiriath Sepher). 12And Caleb said, "I will
give my daughter Acsah in marriage to
the man who attacks and captures Kiriath
Sepher." 13Othniel son of Kenaz, Caleb's
younger brother, took it; so Caleb gave his
daughter Acsah to him in marriage.
14One day when she came to Othniel,
she urged him[a] to ask her father for a
field. When she got off her donkey, Caleb
asked her, "What can I do for you?"
15She replied, "Do me a special favor.
Since you have given me land in the Negev, give me also springs of water." Then
Caleb gave her the upper and lower
springs.[s]
16The descendants of Moses' father-in-
law,[t] the Kenite,[u] went up from the City
of Palms[b][v] with the men of Judah to live

1:1 [a]Jos 24:29 [b]S Nu 2:3-9; Jdg 20:18; 1Ki 20:14 [c]ver 27; S Ge 10:18; Jdg 3:1-6 **1:2** [d]S Ge 49:10 [e]ver 4; Jdg 3:28; 4:7,14; 7:9 **1:3** [f]ver 17 **1:4** [g]S Ge 13:7; S Jos 3:10 [h]1Sa 11:8 **1:5** [i]ver 6,7 **1:7** [j]Lev 24:19; Jer 25:12 [k]S Jos 10:1 **1:8** [l]ver 21; Jos 15:63; 2Sa 5:6 **1:9** [m]S Nu 13:17 [n]S Ge 12:9; S Nu 21:1; Isa 30:6 **1:10** [o]S Ge 13:18 [p]S Ge 35:27 [q]ver 20; S Nu 13:22; Jos 15:14 **1:11** [r]Jos 10:38 **1:15** [s]S Nu 13:6 **1:16** [t]Nu 10:29 [u]S Ge 15:19 [v]Dt 34:3; Jdg 3:13; 2Ch 28:15

[a] *14* Hebrew; Septuagint and Vulgate *Othniel, he urged her* [b] *16* That is, Jericho

1:1 — 3:6 An introduction in two parts: (1) an account of Israel's failure to lay claim completely to the promised land as the Lord had directed (1:1 - 36; see note there) and of his rebuke for their disloyalty (2:1 - 5; see note there); (2) an overview of the main body of the book (3:7 — 16:31), portraying Israel's rebellious ways in the centuries after Joshua's death and showing how the Lord dealt with her in that period (2:6 — 3:6; see note there). See Introduction: Literary Features.

1:1 - 36 Judah is assigned leadership in occupying the land (see v. 2 and note). Her vigorous efforts (together with those of Simeon) highlight by contrast the sad story of failure that follows. Only Ephraim's success at Bethel (vv. 22 - 26) breaks the monotony of that story.

1:1 *After the death of Joshua.* The book of Judges, like that of Joshua, tells of an era following the death of a leading figure in the history of redemption (see Jos 1:1 and note). Joshua probably died c. 1390 B.C. (but see Introduction: Background). The battles under his leadership broke the power of the Canaanites to drive the Israelites out of the land. The task that now confronted Israel was the actual occupation of Canaanite territory (see notes on Jos 18:3; 21:43 - 45). *asked the LORD.* Probably by the priestly use of Urim and Thummim (see notes on Ex 28:30; 1Sa 2:28). *go up.* The main Israelite encampment was at Gilgal, near Jericho in the Jordan Valley (about 800 feet below sea level), while the Canaanite cities were mainly located in the central hill country (about 2,500 - 3,500 feet above sea level).

1:2 *Judah is to go.* See 20:18. Judah was also the first to be assigned territory west of the Jordan (Jos 15). The leadership role of the tribe of Judah had been anticipated in the blessing of Jacob (see Ge 49:8 - 12 and note on 49:8; see also note on Jos 15:1).

1:3 *Simeonites.* Joshua assigned to Simeon cities within the territory of Judah (see Jos 19:1,9 and note on 19:1; Ge 49:5 - 7 and note on 49:7).

1:4 *Canaanites.* See note on Ge 10:6. *Perizzites.* See note on Ge 13:7. *Bezek.* Saul marshaled his army there before going to rescue Jabesh Gilead (see 1Sa 11:8 and note).

1:5 *Adoni-Bezek.* Means "lord of Bezek."

1:6 *cut off his thumbs and big toes.* Physically mutilating prisoners of war was a common practice in the ancient Near East (see note on 16:21). It rendered them incapable of military service.

1:7 *Seventy kings.* Canaan was made up of many small city-states, each of which was ruled by a king. "Seventy" may be a round number, or it may be symbolic of a large number. *under my table.* Humiliating treatment, like that given to a dog (see Mt 15:27; Lk 16:21). *God has paid me back.* See note on Ex 21:23 - 25.

1:8 *attacked Jerusalem.* Although the city was defeated, it was not occupied by the Israelites at this time (see v. 21). Israel did not permanently control the city until David captured it c. 1000 B.C. (see 2Sa 5:6 - 10 and note on 5:6).

1:10 *Kiriath Arba.* See note on Jos 14:15.

1:11 - 15 Virtually a word-for-word repetition of Jos 15:15 - 19. In Joshua the passage functions as part of the description of the territory allotted to the tribe of Judah. Here it serves as part of the account of Judah's success in taking possession of its tribal territory.

1:11 *Debir.* See note on Jos 10:38.

1:12 *Caleb.* He and Joshua had brought back an optimistic report about the prospects of conquering Canaan (Nu 14:6 - 9). *daughter ... in marriage.* Victory in battle was one way to pay the bride-price for a girl (see 1Sa 18:25 and note).

1:13 *Othniel.* First major judge (see 3:7 - 11 and note).

1:16 *Moses' father-in-law.* See note on Ex 2:16.

among the people of the Desert of Judah
in the Negev near Arad.[w]
17Then the men of Judah went with the
Simeonites[x] their brothers and attacked the
Canaanites living in Zephath, and they totally destroyed[a] the city. Therefore it was
called Hormah.[b][y] 18The men of Judah also
took[c] Gaza,[z] Ashkelon[a] and Ekron—each
city with its territory.
19The LORD was with[b] the men of Judah.
They took possession of the hill country,[c]
but they were unable to drive the people from the plains, because they had
iron chariots.[d] 20As Moses had promised,
Hebron[e] was given to Caleb, who drove
from it the three sons of Anak.[f] 21The Benjamites, however, failed[g] to dislodge the
Jebusites, who were living in Jerusalem;[h]
to this day the Jebusites live there with the
Benjamites.
22Now the house of Joseph[i] attacked
Bethel,[j] and the LORD was with them.

1:16 [w]Nu 21:1; Jos 12:14 **1:17** [x]ver 3 [y]S Nu 14:45 **1:18** [z]Jos 11:22 [a]S Jos 13:3 **1:19** [b]S Nu 14:43 [c]Nu 13:17 [d]S Jos 17:16 **1:20** [e]Jos 10:36 [f]S ver 10; S Jos 14:13 **1:21** [g]S Jos 9:15; S 15:63 [h]S ver 8 **1:22** [i]Jdg 10:9 [j]S Jos 7:2

[a] *17* The Hebrew term refers to the irrevocable giving over of things or persons to the LORD, often by totally destroying them. [b] *17 Hormah* means *destruction.* [c] *18* Hebrew; Septuagint *Judah did not take*

1:17 *men of Judah … Simeonites.* Judah was fulfilling their commitment (v. 3).
1:18 *Gaza, Ashkelon and Ekron.* Three of the five main cities inhabited by the Philistines (see map and accompanying text, p. 331).
1:19 *unable to drive the people from.* Israel failed to comply with God's commands (Dt 7:1–5; 20:16–18) to drive the Canaanites out of the land. Five factors were involved in that failure: (1) The Canaanites possessed superior weapons (here); (2) Israel disobeyed God by making treaties with the Canaanites (2:1–3); (3) Israel took up the worship of the local gods and so violated the covenant the Lord had made with their ancestors (2:20–21); (4) God was testing Israel's faithfulness to obey his commands (2:22–23; 3:4); (5) God was giving Israel, as his army, the opportunity to develop their skills in warfare (see 3:1–2 and note on 3:2). *iron chariots.* Wooden vehicles with certain iron fittings, perhaps axles (see note on Jos 17:16).
1:20 *As Moses had promised.* See Nu 14:24; Dt 1:36; Jos 14:9–14. *Anak.* See notes on Nu 13:22; Jos 14:15.
1:21 *Benjamites … failed to dislodge.* See note on v. 8. Jerusalem lay on the border between Benjamin and Judah but was allotted to Benjamin (Jos 18:28). *Jebusites.* See note on Ge 10:16.
1:22 *house of Joseph.* Ephraim and West Manasseh. *Bethel.* See note on Ge 12:8. There is archaeological evidence of a destruction in the 13th century B.C. that may reflect the battle mentioned in this verse.

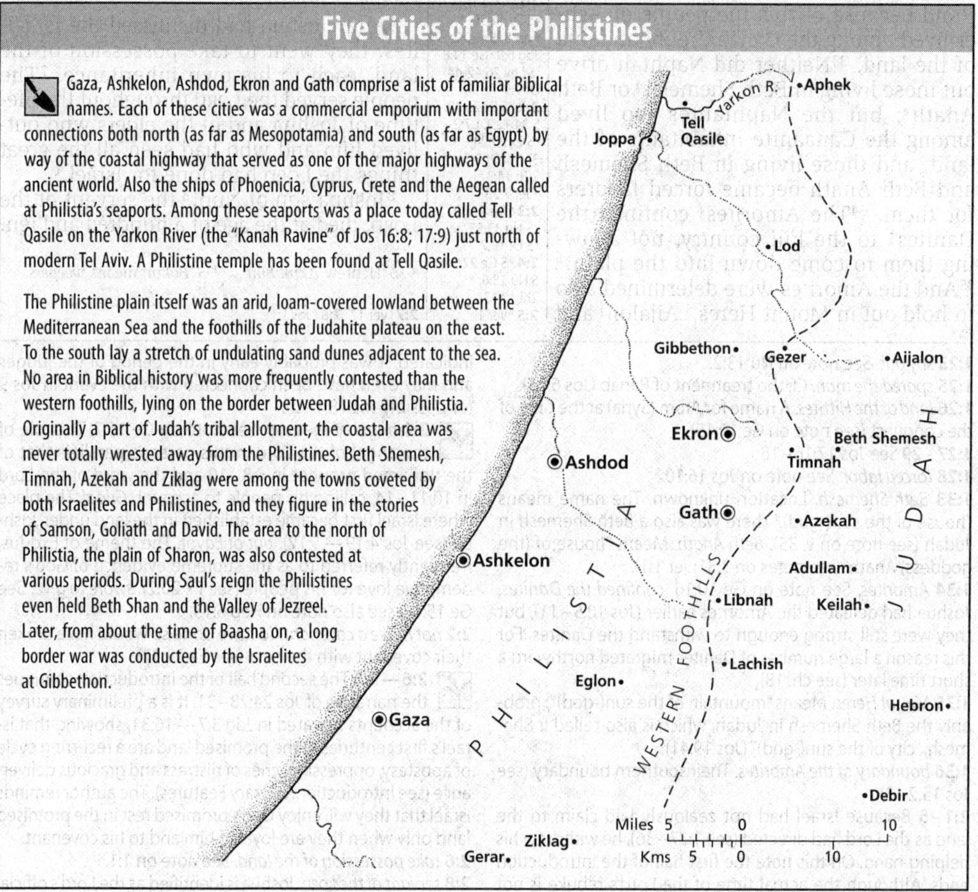

Five Cities of the Philistines

Gaza, Ashkelon, Ashdod, Ekron and Gath comprise a list of familiar Biblical names. Each of these cities was a commercial emporium with important connections both north (as far as Mesopotamia) and south (as far as Egypt) by way of the coastal highway that served as one of the major highways of the ancient world. Also the ships of Phoenicia, Cyprus, Crete and the Aegean called at Philistia's seaports. Among these seaports was a place today called Tell Qasile on the Yarkon River (the "Kanah Ravine" of Jos 16:8; 17:9) just north of modern Tel Aviv. A Philistine temple has been found at Tell Qasile.

The Philistine plain itself was an arid, loam-covered lowland between the Mediterranean Sea and the foothills of the Judahite plateau on the east. To the south lay a stretch of undulating sand dunes adjacent to the sea. No area in Biblical history was more frequently contested than the western foothills, lying on the border between Judah and Philistia. Originally a part of Judah's tribal allotment, the coastal area was never totally wrested away from the Philistines. Beth Shemesh, Timnah, Azekah and Ziklag were among the towns coveted by both Israelites and Philistines, and they figure in the stories of Samson, Goliath and David. The area to the north of Philistia, the plain of Sharon, was also contested at various periods. During Saul's reign the Philistines even held Beth Shan and the Valley of Jezreel. Later, from about the time of Baasha on, a long border war was conducted by the Israelites at Gibbethon.

23When they sent men to spy out Bethel
(formerly called Luz),[k] 24the spies saw a
man coming out of the city and they said
to him, "Show us how to get into the city
and we will see that you are treated well.[l]"
25So he showed them, and they put the
city to the sword but spared[m] the man and
his whole family. 26He then went to the
land of the Hittites,[n] where he built a city
and called it Luz,[o] which is its name to
this day.
27But Manasseh did not[p] drive out the
people of Beth Shan or Taanach or Dor[q] or
Ibleam[r] or Megiddo[s] and their surrounding settlements, for the Canaanites[t] were
determined to live in that land. 28When
Israel became strong, they pressed the
Canaanites into forced labor but never
drove them out completely.[u] 29Nor did
Ephraim[v] drive out the Canaanites living
in Gezer,[w] but the Canaanites continued
to live there among them.[x] 30Neither did
Zebulun drive out the Canaanites living in Kitron or Nahalol, who remained
among them; but they did subject them
to forced labor. 31Nor did Asher[y] drive out
those living in Acco or Sidon[z] or Ahlab or
Aczib[a] or Helbah or Aphek[b] or Rehob,[c]
32and because of this the people of Asher lived among the Canaanite inhabitants
of the land. 33Neither did Naphtali drive
out those living in Beth Shemesh[d] or Beth
Anath[e]; but the Naphtalites too lived
among the Canaanite inhabitants of the
land, and those living in Beth Shemesh
and Beth Anath became forced laborers
for them. 34The Amorites[f] confined the
Danites[g] to the hill country, not allowing them to come down into the plain.[h]
35And the Amorites were determined also
to hold out in Mount Heres,[i] Aijalon[j] and
Shaalbim,[k] but when the power of the
house of Joseph increased, they too were
pressed into forced labor. 36The boundary
of the Amorites was from Scorpion[a] Pass[l]
to Sela[m] and beyond.[n]

The Angel of the LORD at Bokim

2 The angel of the LORD[o] went up from
Gilgal[p] to Bokim[q] and said, "I brought
you up out of Egypt[r] and led you into the
land that I swore to give to your forefathers.[s] I said, 'I will never break my covenant with you,[t] 2and you shall not make
a covenant with the people of this land,[u]
but you shall break down their altars.[v]' Yet
you have disobeyed[w] me. Why have you
done this? 3Now therefore I tell you that I
will not drive them out before you;[x] they
will be ⌊thorns⌋[y] in your sides and their
gods will be a snare[z] to you."
4When the angel of the LORD had spoken these things to all the Israelites, the
people wept aloud,[a] 5and they called that
place Bokim.[b][b] There they offered sacrifices to the LORD.

Disobedience and Defeat

2:6-9pp — Jos 24:29-31

6After Joshua had dismissed the Israelites, they went to take possession of the
land, each to his own inheritance. 7The
people served the LORD throughout the lifetime of Joshua and of the elders who outlived him and who had seen all the great
things the LORD had done for Israel.[c]
8Joshua son of Nun,[d] the servant of the
LORD, died at the age of a hundred and ten.

[a] 36 Hebrew *Akrabbim* [b] 5 *Bokim* means *weepers.*

1:23 [k]S Ge 28:19 **1:24** [l]S Ge 47:29 **1:25** [m]Jos 6:25 **1:26** [n]S Dt 7:1; Eze 16:3 [o]S Ge 28:19 **1:27** [p]1Ki 9:21 [q]S Jos 11:2 [r]S Jos 17:11 [s]S Jos 12:21 [t]S ver 1 **1:28** [u]Jos 17:12-13 **1:29** [v]Jos 14:4; Jdg 5:14 [w]S Jos 10:33 [x]Jos 16:10 **1:31** [y]S Jos 17:7 [z]S Ge 49:13 [a]S Jos 15:44 [b]S Jos 12:18 [c]S Nu 13:21 **1:33** [d]S Jos 15:10 [e]Jos 19:38 **1:34** [f]Nu 13:29; Jdg 10:11; 1Sa 7:14 [g]S Ge 30:6 [h]Jdg 18:1 **1:35** [i]Jdg 8:13 [j]Jos 19:42 [k]1Ki 4:9 **1:36** [l]Jos 15:3 [m]2Ki 14:7; Isa 16:1; 42:11 [n]Ps 106:34 **2:1** [o]S Ge 16:7 [p]S Dt 11:30 [q]ver 5 [r]Ex 20:2; Jdg 6:8 [s]Ge 17:8 [t]S Lev 26:42-44; Dt 7:9 **2:2** [u]S Ex 23:32; S 34:12; Dt 7:2 [v]S Ex 23:24; 34:13; Dt 7:5; 2Ch 14:3 [w]Jer 7:28 **2:3** [x]Jos 23:13 [y]S Nu 33:55 [z]S Ex 10:7 **2:4** [a]S Ge 27:38; S Nu 25:6; 2Ki 17:13 **2:5** [b]ver 1 **2:7** [c]ver 17 **2:8** [d]Jos 1:1

1:23 *spy out.* See note on Nu 13:2.
1:25 *spared the man.* Cf. the treatment of Rahab (Jos 6:25).
1:26 *land of the Hittites.* A name for Aram (Syria) at the time of the conquest (see note on Ge 10:15).
1:27–29 See Jos 17:16–18.
1:28 *forced labor.* See note on Jos 16:10.
1:33 *Beth Shemesh.* Location unknown. The name means "house of the sun(-god)." There was also a Beth Shemesh in Judah (see note on v. 35). *Beth Anath.* Means "house of (the goddess) Anath" (see notes on 3:31; Jer 1:1).
1:34 *Amorites.* See note on Ge 10:16. *confined the Danites.* Joshua had defeated the Amorites earlier (Jos 10:5–11), but they were still strong enough to withstand the Danites. For this reason a large number of Danites migrated northward a short time later (see ch. 18).
1:35 *Mount Heres.* Means "mountain of the sun(-god)"; probably the Beth Shemesh in Judah, which is also called Ir Shemesh, "city of the sun(-god)" (Jos 19:41).
1:36 *boundary of the Amorites.* Their southern boundary (see Jos 15:2–3).
2:1–5 Because Israel had not zealously laid claim to the land as the Lord had directed (see 1:27–36), he withdrew his helping hand. On this note the first half of the introduction ends. Although the actual time of the Lord's rebuke is not indicated, it was probably early in the period of the judges and may even have been connected with the event in Jos 9 (or possibly Jos 18:1–3).
2:1 *angel of the LORD.* See note on Ge 16:7. The role of the angel of the Lord in this passage parallels that of the unnamed prophet in 6:8–10 and the word of the Lord in 10:11–14, calling his people to account. *Gilgal.* The place where Israel first became established in the land under Joshua (see Jos 4:19—5:12). *out of Egypt.* The theme of Exodus, frequently referred to as the supreme evidence of God's redemptive love for his people (see Ex 20:2). *swore to give.* See Ge 15:18; see also note on Heb 6:13.
2:2 *not make a covenant.* To have done so would have broken their covenant with the Lord (see Ex 23:32).
2:6—3:6 The second half of the introduction continues the narrative of Jos 24:28–31. It is a preliminary survey of the accounts narrated in Jdg 3:7—16:31, showing that Israel's first centuries in the promised land are a recurring cycle of apostasy, oppression, cries of distress and gracious deliverance (see Introduction: Literary Features). The author reminds Israel that they will enjoy God's promised rest in the promised land only when they are loyal to him and to his covenant.
2:6 *take possession of the land.* See note on 1:1.
2:8 *servant of the LORD.* Joshua is identified as the Lord's official

9 And they buried him in the land of his
inheritance, at Timnath Heres[a][e] in the hill
country of Ephraim, north of Mount Gaash.
10 After that whole generation had been
gathered to their fathers, another generation grew up, who knew neither the LORD
nor what he had done for Israel.[f] 11 Then
the Israelites did evil[g] in the eyes of the
LORD[h] and served the Baals.[i] 12 They forsook the LORD, the God of their fathers,
who had brought them out of Egypt. They
followed and worshiped various gods[j] of
the peoples around them.[k] They provoked[l]
the LORD to anger[m] 13 because they forsook[n]
him and served Baal and the Ashtoreths.[o]
14 In his anger[p] against Israel the LORD handed them over[q] to raiders who plundered[r]
them. He sold them[s] to their enemies all
around, whom they were no longer able to
resist.[t] 15 Whenever Israel went out to fight,
the hand of the LORD was against them[u] to
defeat them, just as he had sworn to them.
They were in great distress.[v]
16 Then the LORD raised up judges,[b][w]
who saved[x] them out of the hands of these
raiders. 17 Yet they would not listen to their
judges but prostituted[y] themselves to other
gods[z] and worshiped them.[a] Unlike their
fathers, they quickly turned[b] from the way
in which their fathers had walked, the way
of obedience to the LORD's commands.[c]
18 Whenever the LORD raised up a judge for
them, he was with the judge and saved[d]
them out of the hands of their enemies as
long as the judge lived; for the LORD had
compassion[e] on them as they groaned[f]
under those who oppressed and afflicted[g]
them. 19 But when the judge died, the people returned to ways even more corrupt[h]
than those of their fathers,[i] following other gods and serving and worshiping them.[j]
They refused to give up their evil practices
and stubborn[k] ways.
20 Therefore the LORD was very angry[l]
with Israel and said, "Because this nation has violated the covenant[m] that I laid
down for their forefathers and has not listened to me, 21 I will no longer drive out[n]
before them any of the nations Joshua left
when he died. 22 I will use them to test[o]
Israel and see whether they will keep the
way of the LORD and walk in it as their
forefathers did." 23 The LORD had allowed
those nations to remain; he did not drive
them out at once by giving them into the
hands of Joshua.[p]

3

These are the nations the LORD left to
test[q] all those Israelites who had not
experienced any of the wars in Canaan
2 (he did this only to teach warfare to the
descendants of the Israelites who had

[a] *9* Also known as *Timnath Serah* (see Joshua 19:50 and 24:30) [b] *16* Or *leaders*; similarly in verses 17-19

2:9 [e] S Jos 19:50 **2:10** [f] S Ex 5:2; Gal 4:8 **2:11** [g] 1Ki 15:26 [h] Jdg 3:12; 4:1; 6:1; 10:6 [i] Jdg 3:7; 8:33; 1Ki 16:31; 22:53; 2Ki 10:18; 17:16 **2:12** [j] S Dt 32:12; Ps 106:36 [k] S Dt 31:16; Jdg 10:6 [l] S Nu 11:33 [m] Dt 4:25; Ps 78:58; 106:40 **2:13** [n] 1Sa 7:3; 1Ki 11:5,33; 2Ki 23:13 [o] Jdg 3:7; 5:8; 6:25; 8:33; 10:6; 1Sa 31:10; Ne 9:26; Ps 78:56; Jer 11:10 **2:14** [p] S Dt 31:17 [q] Ne 9:27; Ps 106:41 [r] Ps 44:10; 89:41; Eze 34:8 [s] S Dt 32:30; S Jdg 3:8 [t] S Dt 28:25 **2:15** [u] Ru 1:13; Job 19:21; Ps 32:4 [v] Ge 35:3; 2Sa 22:7; 2Ch 15:4; Job 5:5; 20:22; Ps 4:1; 18:6 **2:16** [w] Ru 1:1; 1Sa 4:18; 7:6,15; 2Sa 7:11; 1Ch 17:10; Ac 13:20 [x] 1Sa 11:3; Ps 106:43 **2:17** [y] S Ex 34:15; S Nu 15:39 [z] S Ps 4:2 [a] Ne 9:28; Ps 106:36 [b] Dt 9:12 [c] ver 7 **2:18** [d] 1Sa 7:3; 2Ki 13:5; Isa 19:20; 43:3,11; 45:15,21; 49:26; 60:16; 63:8 [e] S Dt 32:36 [f] S Ex 2:23 [g] S Nu 10:9 **2:19** [h] S Ge 6:11; S Dt 4:16 [i] Dt 32:17; Ne 9:2; Ps 78:57; Jer 44:3,9 [j] Jdg 4:1; 8:33 [k] S Ex 32:9 **2:20** [l] S Dt 31:17; Jos 23:16 [m] S Jos 7:11; S 2Ki 17:15 **2:21** [n] S Jos 23:5 **2:22** [o] S Ge 22:1; S Ex 15:25 **2:23** [p] Jdg 1:1 **3:1** [q] S Ex 15:25

representative (see notes on Ex 14:31; Ps 18 title; Isa 41:8–9; 42:1). *a hundred and ten.* For the significance of this number see note on Ge 50:26.

2:10–15 The Lord withdraws his help because of Israel's apostasy. He "sells" (v. 14) the people he had "bought" (Ex 15:16; see note there) and redeemed (Ex 15:13; cf. Ps 74:2).

2:10 *gathered to their fathers.* See Ge 15:15; see also note on Ge 25:8. *who knew neither the LORD ... Israel.* They had no direct experience of the Lord's acts (see Ex 1:8 and note).

2:11 *did evil in the eyes of the LORD.* The same expression is used in 3:7,12; 4:1; 6:1; 10:6. *Baals.* The many local forms of this Canaanite deity (see note on v. 13).

2:12 *provoked the LORD to anger.* See Dt 4:25; see also note on Zec 1:2.

2:13 *Baal.* Means "lord." Baal, the god worshiped by the Canaanites and Phoenicians, was variously known to them as the son of Dagon and the son of El. In Aram (Syria) he was called Hadad and in Babylonia Adad. Believed to give fertility to the womb and life-giving rain to the soil, he is pictured as standing on a bull, a popular symbol of fertility and strength (see 1Ki 12:28 and note). The storm cloud was his chariot, thunder his voice, and lightning his spear and arrows. The worship of Baal involved sacred prostitution and sometimes even child sacrifice (see Jer 7:31 and note). The stories of Elijah and Elisha (1Ki 17–2Ki 13), as well as many other OT passages, directly or indirectly protest Baalism (see, e.g., introduction to Ps 29; 68:1–4,32–34 and note on 68:4; 93:1–5; 97:1–5; Jer 10:12–16; 14:22 and note; Hos 2:8,16–17 and notes; Am 5:8; Zec 10:1 and note). *Ashtoreths.* Female deities such as Ashtoreth (wife of Baal) and Asherah (wife of El, the chief god of the Canaanite pantheon). Ashtoreth was associated with the evening star and was the beautiful goddess of war and fertility. She was worshiped as Ishtar in Babylonia and as Athtart in Aram. To the Greeks she was Astarte or Aphrodite, and to the Romans, Venus. Worship of the Ashtoreths involved extremely lascivious practices (see 1Ki 14:24 and note; 2Ki 23:7).

2:14 *handed them over to.* The same Hebrew expression is used in 6:1; 13:1. *sold them.* The same expression is used in 3:8; 4:2; 10:7.

2:16–19 The Lord was merciful to his people in times of distress, sending deliverers to save them from oppression. But Israel continually forgot these saving acts, just as they had forgotten those God had performed through Moses and Joshua.

2:16 *judges.* See Introduction: Title. There were six major judges (Othniel, Ehud, Deborah, Gideon, Jephthah and Samson) and six minor ones (Shamgar, Tola, Jair, Ibzan, Elon and Abdon).

2:17 *prostituted themselves.* See Ex 34:15 and note.

2:18 *groaned ... oppressed.* The language of the Egyptian bondage (see Ex 2:24; 3:9; 6:5).

2:20–23 The Lord decided to leave the remaining nations to test Israel's loyalty.

3:1–6 The list of nations the Lord left roughly describes an arc along the western and northern boundaries of the area actually occupied by Israel at the death of Joshua (vv. 1–4). Within Israelite-occupied territory there were large groups of native peoples (v. 5; see 1:27–36) with whom the Israelites intermingled, often adopting their religions (v. 6).

3:2 *only to teach warfare.* As his covenant servant, Israel was the Lord's army for fighting against the powers of the world that were settled in his land. Because of the incomplete

not had previous battle experience): 3the
five[r] rulers of the Philistines,[s] all the Canaanites, the Sidonians, and the Hivites[t]
living in the Lebanon mountains from
Mount Baal Hermon[u] to Lebo[a] Hamath.[v]
4They were left to test[w] the Israelites to
see whether they would obey the LORD's
commands, which he had given their forefathers through Moses.
5The Israelites lived[x] among the Canaanites, Hittites, Amorites, Perizzites,[y] Hivites
and Jebusites.[z] 6They took their daughters[a]
in marriage and gave their own daughters
to their sons, and served their gods.[b c]

Othniel

7The Israelites did evil in the eyes of the
LORD; they forgot the LORD[d] their God and
served the Baals and the Asherahs.[e] 8The
anger of the LORD burned against Israel
so that he sold[f] them into the hands of
Cushan-Rishathaim[g] king of Aram Naharaim,[b h] to whom the Israelites were subject for eight years. 9But when they cried
out[i] to the LORD, he raised up for them a
deliverer,[j] Othniel[k] son of Kenaz, Caleb's
younger brother, who saved them. 10The
Spirit of the LORD came upon him,[l] so that
he became Israel's judge[c] and went to
war. The LORD gave Cushan-Rishathaim[m]
king of Aram[n] into the hands of Othniel,
who overpowered him. 11So the land had
peace[o] for forty years,[p] until Othniel son
of Kenaz[q] died.

Ehud

12Once again the Israelites did evil in
the eyes of the LORD,[r] and because they
did this evil the LORD gave Eglon king of
Moab[s] power over Israel. 13Getting the
Ammonites[t] and Amalekites[u] to join him,
Eglon came and attacked Israel, and they
took possession of the City of Palms.[d v]
14The Israelites were subject to Eglon king
of Moab[w] for eighteen years.
15Again the Israelites cried out to
the LORD, and he gave them a deliverer[x]—Ehud[y], a left-handed[z] man, the son
of Gera the Benjamite. The Israelites sent
him with tribute[a] to Eglon king of Moab.
16Now Ehud[b] had made a double-edged
sword about a foot and a half[e] long, which
he strapped to his right thigh under his
clothing. 17He presented the tribute[c] to
Eglon king of Moab, who was a very fat
man.[d] 18After Ehud had presented the trib-

[a] *3* Or *to the entrance to* [b] *8* That is, Northwest Mesopotamia [c] *10* Or *leader* [d] *13* That is, Jericho [e] *16* Hebrew *a cubit* (about 0.5 meter)

3:3 [r]S Jos 13:3 [s]S Ge 10:14 [t]S Ge 10:17; S Ex 3:8 [u]S Dt 3:8 [v]S Nu 13:21 **3:4** [w]S Ex 15:25 **3:5** [x]Ps 106:35 [y]S Jos 3:10 [z]S Jos 11:3; Ezr 9:1 **3:6** [a]Ezr 10:18; Ne 13:23; Mal 2:11 [b]S Ex 34:16; Dt 7:3-4 [c]S Dt 7:16 **3:7** [d]Dt 4:9; S 32:18; Jdg 8:34; Ps 78:11,42; 106:7; Jer 23:27 [e]S Ex 34:13; S Jdg 2:11,13; 1Ki 16:33; 2Ch 34:7; Isa 17:8 **3:8** [f]Jdg 2:14; Ps 44:12; Isa 50:1; 52:3 [g]ver 10 [h]S Ge 24:10 **3:9** [i]ver 15; Jdg 6:6,7; 10:10; 1Sa 12:10; Ps 106:44; 107:13 [j]S Dt 28:29; Ne 9:27 [k]S Jos 15:17 **3:10** [l]S Nu 11:25,29; Jdg 6:34; 11:29; 13:25; 14:6,19; 15:14; 1Sa 11:6; 16:13; 1Ki 18:46; 1Ch 12:18; 2Ch 24:20; Isa 11:2 [m]ver 8 [n]S Ge 10:22 **3:11** [o]ver 30; S Jos 14:15; Jdg 5:31; 8:28 [p]S Ex 16:35 [q]S Jos 15:17 **3:12** [r]S Jdg 2:11,14 [s]1Sa 12:9 **3:13** [t]S Ge 19:38; Jdg 10:11 [u]S Ge 14:7 [v]S Jdg 1:16 **3:14** [w]Jer 48:1 **3:15** [x]S ver 9 [y]ver 16; Jdg 4:1 [z]Jdg 20:16; 1Ch 12:2 [a]ver 17,18; 2Sa 8:2,6; 1Ki 4:21; 2Ki 17:3; Est 10:1; Ps 68:29; 72:10; 89:22; Ecc 2:8; Isa 60:5; Hos 10:6 **3:16** [b]S ver 15 **3:17** [c]S ver 15 [d]Job 15:27; Ps 73:4

conquest, succeeding generations in Israel needed to become capable warriors. "Only" probably here means "especially."

3:3 *five rulers.* See note on Jos 13:3. These rulers had control of a five-city confederacy (see map, p. 331). At one point Judah defeated three of the cities (1:18) but was unable to hold them. *Sidonians.* Here used collectively of the Phoenicians. *Hivites.* Here identified with a region in northern Canaan reaching all the way to Hamath (see Jos 9:7 and note). *Mount Baal Hermon.* The same as Mount Hermon (see 1Ch 5:23).

3:6 *took their daughters ... and served their gods.* See note on Jos 23:12. The degenerating effect of such intermarriage is well illustrated in Solomon's experience (see 1Ki 11:1–8 and notes on 11:1–2,4–5).

3:7–11 In the account of Othniel's judgeship the author provides the basic literary form he uses in his accounts of the major judges (i.e., beginning statement; cycle of apostasy, oppression, distress, deliverance; recognizable conclusion), filling it out in each case with the materials he considered necessary to his purpose (see Introduction: Literary Features).

3:7 *did evil in the eyes of the LORD.* A recurring expression (see v. 12; 4:1; 6:1; 10:6; 13:1) used to introduce the cycles of the judges (see Introduction: Literary Features). *Baals.* See note on 2:13. *Asherahs.* See notes on 2:13; Ex 34:13.

3:8 *Cushan-Rishathaim.* Probably means "doubly wicked Cushan," perhaps a caricature of his actual name (see note on 10:6 regarding Baal-Zebub). *Aram Naharaim.* See note on Ge 24:10.

3:9 *they cried out to the LORD.* The Israelites' cries of distress occurred in each recurring cycle of the judges (see Introduction: Literary Features). *Othniel.* See 1:13.

3:10 *Spirit of the LORD came upon him.* The Spirit empowered Othniel to deliver his people, as he did Gideon (6:34), Jephthah (11:29), Samson (14:6,19)—and also David (1Sa 16:13). Cf. Nu 11:25–29.

3:11 *the land had peace ... years.* A recognizable conclusion to the cycle of a judge (noted only here and in v. 30; 5:31; 8:28). After the judgeship of Gideon this formula is replaced by "led Israel ... years" (12:7; 15:20; 16:31). See Introduction: Literary Features. *forty years.* A conventional number of years for a generation (see Introduction: Background).

3:12–30 Ehud's triumph over Eglon king of Moab. The left-handed Benjamite was an authentic hero. All alone, and purely by his wits, he cut down the king of Moab, who had established himself in Canaan near Jericho. This account balances that of Samson in the five narrative units central to the book of Judges (see Introduction: Literary Features).

3:12 *Moab.* See note on Ge 19:36–38.

3:13 *Ammonites.* See note on Ge 19:36–38. *Amalekites.* See note on Ge 14:7.

3:14 *Israelites.* Here mainly Benjamin and Ephraim.

3:15 *left-handed man.* Left-handedness was noteworthy among Benjamites (see 20:15–16 and note on 20:16)—which is ironic since Benjamin means "son of (my) right hand." Being left-handed, Ehud could conceal his dagger on the side where it was not expected (see v. 21). *tribute.* An annual payment, perhaps of agricultural products (cf. 2Ki 3:4 and note).

3:16 *made a double-edged sword.* That is, a straight-bladed sword useful for a stabbing thrust, in distinction from the more common sickle sword intended for slashing blows. During the period of the judges, Israelite weapons were often fashioned or improvised for the occasion: Shamgar's oxgoad (v. 31), Jael's tent peg (4:21–22), Gideon's jars and torches (7:20), the woman's millstone (9:53) and Samson's donkey jawbone (15:15). See 1Sa 13:19 and note.

ute, he sent on their way the men who
had carried it. 19At the idols[a] near Gilgal
he himself turned back and said, "I have a
secret message for you, O king."
The king said, "Quiet!" And all his attendants left him.
20Ehud then approached him while he
was sitting alone in the upper room of his
summer palace[b][e] and said, "I have a message from God for you." As the king rose[f]
from his seat, 21Ehud reached with his left
hand, drew the sword[g] from his right thigh
and plunged it into the king's belly. 22Even
the handle sank in after the blade, which
came out his back. Ehud did not pull the
sword out, and the fat closed in over it.
23Then Ehud went out to the porch[c]; he
shut the doors of the upper room behind
him and locked them.
24After he had gone, the servants came
and found the doors of the upper room
locked. They said, "He must be relieving
himself[h] in the inner room of the house."
25They waited to the point of embarrassment,[i] but when he did not open the doors
of the room, they took a key and unlocked
them. There they saw their lord fallen to
the floor, dead.
26While they waited, Ehud got away. He
passed by the idols and escaped to Seirah.
27When he arrived there, he blew a trumpet[j] in the hill country of Ephraim, and the
Israelites went down with him from the
hills, with him leading them.
28"Follow me," he ordered, "for the
LORD has given Moab,[k] your enemy, into
your hands.[l]" So they followed him down
and, taking possession of the fords of the
Jordan[m] that led to Moab, they allowed
no one to cross over. 29At that time they
struck down about ten thousand Moabites, all vigorous and strong; not a man
escaped. 30That day Moab[n] was made subject to Israel, and the land had peace[o] for
eighty years.

Shamgar

31After Ehud came Shamgar son of
Anath,[p] who struck down six hundred[q]
Philistines[r] with an oxgoad. He too saved
Israel.

Deborah

4 After Ehud[s] died, the Israelites once
again did evil[t] in the eyes of the LORD.[u]
2So the LORD sold them[v] into the hands of
Jabin, a king of Canaan, who reigned in
Hazor.[w] The commander of his army was
Sisera,[x] who lived in Harosheth Haggoyim. 3Because he had nine hundred iron
chariots[y] and had cruelly oppressed[z] the
Israelites for twenty years, they cried to
the LORD for help.
4Deborah,[a] a prophetess,[b] the wife of
Lappidoth, was leading[d] Israel at that

3:20 [e]Am 3:15 [f]Ne 8:5
3:21 [g]2Sa 2:16; 3:27; 20:10
3:24 [h]1Sa 24:3
3:25 [i]2Ki 2:17; 8:11
3:27 [j]S Lev 25:9; Jdg 6:34; 7:18; 2Sa 2:28; Isa 18:3; Jer 42:14
3:28 [k]S Ge 19:37 [l]S Jos 2:24; S Jdg 1:2 [m]S Nu 13:29; S Jos 2:7
3:30 [n]S Ge 36:35 [o]S ver 11
3:31 [p]Jdg 5:6 [q]S Jos 23:10 [r]Jos 13:2; Jdg 10:11; 13:1; 1Sa 5:1; 31:1; 2Sa 8:1; Jer 25:20; 47:1
4:1 [s]S Jdg 3:15 [t]S Jdg 2:19 [u]S Jdg 2:11
4:2 [v]S Dt 32:30 [w]S Jos 11:1 [x]1Sa 12:9; Ps 83:9
4:3 [y]S Jos 17:16 [z]Jdg 10:12; Ps 106:42
4:4 [a]Jdg 5:1,7,12,15 [b]S Ex 15:20

[a] 19 Or *the stone quarries*; also in verse 26
[b] 20 The meaning of the Hebrew for this phrase is uncertain.
[c] 23 The meaning of the Hebrew for this word is uncertain.
[d] 4 Traditionally *judging*

3:19 *idols.* Lit. "carved (stone) things," a frequent Hebrew way of referring to stone idols (see NIV text note). But here the reference may be to carved stone statues of Eglon, marking the boundary of the territory he now claims as part of his expanded realm—a common practice in the ancient Near East (see Ge 1:26 and note). *Gilgal.* Perhaps the one mentioned in Jos 15:7, located on the border between Benjamin and Judah, not the well-known one east of Jericho.

3:20 *upper room.* Rooms were built on the flat roofs of houses (2Ki 4:10–11) and palaces (Jer 22:13–14), and had latticed windows (2Ki 1:2) that provided comfort in the heat of summer.

3:22 *which came out his back.* Or "and the offal in his belly came out."

3:28 *taking possession of the fords.* This move enabled the Israelites to cut off the Moabites fleeing Jericho and also prevented the Moabites from sending reinforcements.

3:30 *eighty years.* Round numbers are frequently used in Judges (see Introduction: Background).

3:31 *Shamgar.* The first of six minor judges and a contemporary of Deborah (see 5:6–7). His name is foreign, so he was probably not an Israelite. *son of Anath.* Indicates either that Shamgar came from the town of Beth Anath (see 1:33 and note) or that his family worshiped the goddess Anath. Since Anath, Baal's sister, was a goddess of war who fought for Baal, the expression "son of Anath" may have been a military title, meaning "a warrior." *oxgoad.* A long, wooden rod, sometimes having a metal tip, used for driving draft animals (see 1Sa 13:21).

4:1—5:31 Deborah's triumph over Sisera (commander of a Canaanite army)—first narrated in prose (ch. 4), then celebrated in song (ch. 5). At the time of the Canaanite threat from the north, Israel remained incapable of united action until a woman (Deborah) summoned them to the Lord's battle. Because the warriors of Israel lacked the courage to rise up and face the enemy, the glory of victory went to a woman (Jael)—and she may not have been an Israelite.

4:1–2 Except for the Canaanites, Israel's enemies came from outside the territory they occupied. Nations like Aram Naharaim, Moab, Midian and Ammon were mainly interested in plunder, but the Canaanite uprising of chs. 4–5 was an attempt to restore Canaanite power in the north. The Philistines engaged in continual struggle with Israel for permanent control of the land in the southern and central regions.

4:2 *Jabin.* See Ps 83:9–10. The name was possibly royal rather than personal. Joshua is credited with having earlier slain a king by the same name (Jos 11:1,10). *Hazor.* The original royal city of the Jabin dynasty; it may still have been in ruins (see note on Jos 11:10). Sisera sought to recover the territory once ruled by the kings of Hazor. *Sisera.* His name suggests he was not a Canaanite.

4:3 *nine hundred.* The number probably represents a coalition rather than the chariot force of one city. In the 15th century B.C., Pharaoh Thutmose III boasted of having captured 924 chariots at the battle of Megiddo. *Israelites.* Mainly Zebulun and Naphtali, but West Manasseh, Issachar and Asher were also affected.

4:4 *Deborah.* Means "bee"; cf. Dt 1:44. She is the only judge said to have been a prophet. Other women spoken of as prophets are Miriam (Ex 15:20; see note there), Huldah (2Ki 22:14), Noadiah (Ne 6:14) and Anna (Lk 2:36), but see also Ac 21:9 and note.

time. 5She held court[c] under the Palm of
Deborah between Ramah[d] and Bethel[e] in
the hill country of Ephraim, and the Israelites came to her to have their disputes decided. 6She sent for Barak son of Abinoam[f]
from Kedesh[g] in Naphtali and said to him,
"The LORD, the God of Israel, commands
you: 'Go, take with you ten thousand men
of Naphtali[h] and Zebulun[i] and lead the
way to Mount Tabor.[j] 7I will lure Sisera,
the commander of Jabin's[k] army, with his
chariots and his troops to the Kishon River[l] and give him into your hands.[m]' "
8Barak said to her, "If you go with me,
I will go; but if you don't go with me, I
won't go."
9"Very well," Deborah said, "I will go
with you. But because of the way you are
going about this,[a] the honor will not be
yours, for the LORD will hand Sisera over
to a woman." So Deborah went with Barak to Kedesh,[n] 10where he summoned[o]
Zebulun and Naphtali. Ten thousand men
followed him, and Deborah also went with
him.
11Now Heber the Kenite had left the other Kenites,[p] the descendants of Hobab,[q]
Moses' brother-in-law,[b] and pitched his
tent by the great tree[r] in Zaanannim[s] near
Kedesh.
12When they told Sisera that Barak son
of Abinoam had gone up to Mount Tabor,[t]
13Sisera gathered together his nine hundred iron chariots[u] and all the men with
him, from Harosheth Haggoyim to the Kishon River.[v]
14Then Deborah said to Barak, "Go!
This is the day the LORD has given Sisera
into your hands.[w] Has not the LORD gone
ahead[x] of you?" So Barak went down
Mount Tabor, followed by ten thousand
men. 15At Barak's advance, the LORD routed[y] Sisera and all his chariots and army by
the sword, and Sisera abandoned his chariot and fled on foot. 16But Barak pursued
the chariots and army as far as Harosheth
Haggoyim. All the troops of Sisera fell by
the sword; not a man was left.[z]
17Sisera, however, fled on foot to the
tent of Jael,[a] the wife of Heber the Kenite,[b]
because there were friendly relations between Jabin king of Hazor[c] and the clan
of Heber the Kenite.
18Jael[d] went out to meet Sisera and said
to him, "Come, my lord, come right in.
Don't be afraid." So he entered her tent,
and she put a covering over him.
19"I'm thirsty," he said. "Please give me
some water." She opened a skin of milk,[e]
gave him a drink, and covered him up.
20"Stand in the doorway of the tent," he
told her. "If someone comes by and asks
you, 'Is anyone here?' say 'No.' "
21But Jael,[f] Heber's wife, picked up a
tent peg and a hammer and went quietly

[a] 9 Or *But on the expedition you are undertaking*
[b] 11 Or *father-in-law*

4:5 [c] 1Sa 14:2; 22:6 [d] S Jos 18:25 [e] S Jos 12:9
4:6 [f] Jdg 5:1, 12, 15; 1Sa 12:11; Heb 11:32 [g] S Jos 12:22 [h] S Ge 30:8 [i] Jdg 5:18; 6:35 [j] S Jos 19:22
4:7 [k] S Jos 11:1 [l] ver 13; Jdg 5:21; 1Ki 18:40; Ps 83:9 [m] S Jdg 1:2
4:9 [n] S Jos 12:22
4:10 [o] 2Ch 36:23; Ezr 1:2; Isa 41:2; 42:6; 45:3; 46:11; 48:15
4:11 [p] S Ge 15:19 [q] Nu 10:29 [r] Jos 24:26; Jdg 9:6 [s] Jos 19:33
4:12 [t] S Jos 19:22
4:13 [u] S Jos 17:16 [v] S ver 7; Jdg 5:19
4:14 [w] S Jdg 1:2 [x] Dt 9:3; 1Sa 8:20; 2Sa 5:24; Ps 68:7
4:15 [y] ver 7
4:16 [z] S Ex 14:28; Ps 83:9
4:17 [a] ver 18, 21, 22; Jdg 5:6, 24 [b] S Ge 15:19 [c] S Jos 11:1
4:18 [d] S ver 17
4:19 [e] S Ge 18:8
4:21 [f] S ver 17

4:5 *Palm of Deborah.* The Hebrew word for "honey" refers to both bees' honey and the sweet syrupy juice of dates. Deborah, the Bee, dispensed the sweetness of justice as she held court, not in a city gate where male judges sat, but under the shade of a "honey" tree. See also note on 1Sa 14:2.

4:6 *Barak.* Means "thunderbolt"—which suggests that he is summoned to be the Lord's "flashing sword" (Dt 32:41). He is named among the heroes of faith in Heb 11:32. *Kedesh in Naphtali.* A town affected by the Canaanite oppression. *Naphtali and Zebulun.* Issachar, a near neighbor of these tribes, is not mentioned here but is included in the poetic description of the battle in 5:15. In all, six tribes are mentioned as having participated in the battle. *Mount Tabor.* A mountain about 1,300 feet high, northeast of the battle site.

4:7 With the Israelites encamped on the slopes of Mount Tabor, safe from chariot attack, the Lord's strategy was to draw Sisera into a trap. For the battle site, Sisera cleverly chose the Valley of Jezreel along the Kishon River, where his chariot forces would have ample maneuvering space to range the battlefield and attack in numbers from any quarter. But that was his undoing, for he did not know the power of the Lord, who would fight from heaven for Israel with storm and flood (see 5:20–21 and note on 5:20), as he had done in the days of Joshua (see Jos 10:11–14 and note on 10:11). Even in modern times storms have rendered the plain along the Kishon virtually impassable. In April of 1799 the flooded Kishon River aided Napoleon's victory over a Turkish army.

4:9 *a woman.* Barak's timidity (and that of Israel's other warriors, whom he exemplified) was due to lack of trust in the Lord and was thus rebuked (see note on 9:54).

4:11 *Heber the Kenite.* Since one meaning of Heber's name is "ally," and since "Kenite" identifies him as belonging to a clan of metalworkers, the author hints at the truth that this member of a people allied with Israel since the days of Moses has moved from south to north to ally himself (see v. 17) with the Canaanite king who is assembling a large force of "iron chariots" (v. 3; see note on Jos 17:16). It is no doubt he who informs Sisera of Barak's military preparations. *other Kenites.* Settled in the south not far from Kadesh Barnea in the Negev (see 1:16). *Hobab.* See Nu 10:29 and note.

4:14 *gone ahead of you.* As a king at the head of his army (see 1Sa 8:20). See also Ex 15:3 ("the LORD is a warrior"); Jos 10:10–11; 2Sa 5:24; 2Ch 20:15–17,22–24. *Barak went down Mount Tabor.* The Lord's "thunderbolt" (see note on v. 6) descends the mountain to attack the Canaanite army.

4:15 *routed.* See note on v. 7. The Hebrew for this word is also used of the panic that overcame the Egyptians at the Red Sea (Ex 14:24) and the Philistines at Mizpah (1Sa 7:10).

4:18 *he entered her tent.* Since ancient Near Eastern custom prohibited any man other than a woman's husband or father from entering her tent, Jael seemed to offer Sisera an ideal hiding place.

4:19 *skin.* Containers for liquids were normally made from the skins of goats or lambs. *milk.* See note on 5:25. Jael, whose name means "mountain goat," gave him milk to drink—and it was most likely goat's milk (see Ex 23:19; Pr 27:27).

4:21 *drove the peg through his temple.* The laws of hospitality normally meant that one tried to protect a guest from any harm (see 19:23; Ge 19:8 and note). Jael remained true to her family's previous alliance with Israel (she may not have been an Israelite) and so undid her husband's deliberate breach of faith. Armed only with domestic implements, this dauntless woman destroyed the great warrior whom Barak had earlier feared.

to him while he lay fast asleep,[g] exhausted. She drove the peg through his temple
into the ground, and he died.[h]
22Barak came by in pursuit of Sisera,
and Jael[i] went out to meet him. "Come,"
she said, "I will show you the man you're
looking for." So he went in with her, and
there lay Sisera with the tent peg through
his temple—dead.[j]
23On that day God subdued[k] Jabin,[l] the
Canaanite king, before the Israelites. 24And
the hand of the Israelites grew stronger
and stronger against Jabin, the Canaanite
king, until they destroyed him.[m]

The Song of Deborah

5 On that day Deborah[n] and Barak son of
Abinoam[o] sang this song:[p]

2"When the princes in Israel take the lead,
when the people willingly offer[q] themselves—
praise the LORD![r]

3"Hear this, you kings! Listen, you rulers!
I will sing to[a] the LORD, I will sing;[s]
I will make music to[b] the LORD, the God of Israel.[t]

4"O LORD, when you went out[u] from Seir,[v]
when you marched from the land of Edom,
the earth shook,[w] the heavens poured,
the clouds poured down water.[x]
5The mountains quaked[y] before the LORD, the One of Sinai,
before the LORD, the God of Israel.

6"In the days of Shamgar son of Anath,[z]
in the days of Jael,[a] the roads[b] were abandoned;
travelers took to winding paths.[c]
7Village life[c] in Israel ceased,
ceased until I,[d] Deborah,[d] arose,
arose a mother in Israel.
8When they chose new gods,[e]
war came to the city gates,[f]
and not a shield or spear[g] was seen
among forty thousand in Israel.
9My heart is with Israel's princes,
with the willing volunteers[h] among the people.
Praise the LORD!

10"You who ride on white donkeys,[i]
sitting on your saddle blankets,
and you who walk along the road,
consider 11the voice of the singers[e] at the watering places.
They recite the righteous acts[j] of the LORD,
the righteous acts of his warriors[f] in Israel.

"Then the people of the LORD
went down to the city gates.[k]
12'Wake up,[l] wake up, Deborah![m]
Wake up, wake up, break out in song!
Arise, O Barak![n]
Take captive your captives,[o] O son of Abinoam.'

[a] 3 Or *of* [b] 3 Or / *with song I will praise* [c] 7 Or *Warriors* [d] 7 Or *you* [e] 11 Or *archers*; the meaning of the Hebrew for this word is uncertain. [f] 11 Or *villagers*

4:21 [g]Ge 2:21; 15:12; 1Sa 26:12; Isa 29:10; Jnh 1:5 [h]Jdg 5:26 **4:22** [i]S ver 17 [j]Jdg 5:27 **4:23** [k]Ne 9:24; Ps 18:47; 44:2; 47:3; 144:2 [l]S Jos 11:1 **4:24** [m]Ps 83:9; 106:43 **5:1** [n]S Jdg 4:4 [o]S Jdg 4:6 [p]S Ex 15:1; Ps 32:7 **5:2** [q]2Ch 17:16; Ps 110:3 [r]ver 9 **5:3** [s]S Ex 15:1 [t]Ps 27:6 **5:4** [u]S Ex 13:21 [v]S Nu 24:18; S Dt 33:2 [w]2Sa 22:8; Ps 18:7; 77:18; 82:5; Isa 2:19,21; 13:13; 24:18; 64:3; Jer 10:10; 50:46; 51:29; Joel 3:16; Na 1:5; Hab 3:6 [x]Ps 68:8; 77:17 **5:5** [y]S Ex 19:18; Ps 29:6; 46:3; 77:18; 114:4; Isa 64:3 **5:6** [z]Jdg 3:31 [a]S Jdg 4:17 [b]Lev 26:22; Isa 33:8 [c]Ps 125:5; Isa 59:8 **5:7** [d]S Jdg 4:4 **5:8** [e]Dt 32:17; S Jdg 2:13 [f]ver 11; S Jos 2:5 [g]S Nu 25:7 **5:9** [h]S ver 2 **5:10** [i]S Ge 49:11; Jdg 10:4; 12:14 **5:11** [j]1Sa 12:7; Da 9:16; Mic 6:5 [k]S ver 8 **5:12** [l]Ps 44:23; 57:8; Isa 51:9,17 [m]S Jdg 4:4 [n]S Jdg 4:6 [o]Ps 68:18; Eph 4:8

4:22 *there lay Sisera … dead.* With Sisera dead the kingdom of Jabin was no longer a threat. The land "flowing with milk and honey" had been saved by the courage and faithfulness of "Bee" (see note on v. 4) and "Mountain Goat" (see note on v. 19).

5:1–31 To commemorate a national victory with songs was a common practice (see Ex 15:1–18; Nu 21:27–30; Dt 32:1–43; 1Sa 18:7). The Book of the Wars of the LORD (see note on Nu 21:14) and the Book of Jashar (see note on Jos 10:13) were probably collections of such songs.

The song was probably written by Deborah or a contemporary (see vv. 1,3,7). It highlights some of the central themes of the narrative (cf. Ex 15:1–18; 1Sa 2:1–10; 2Sa 22; 23:1–7; Lk 1:46–55,68–79). In particular, it celebrates before the nations (v. 3) the righteous acts of the Lord and of his warriors (v. 11). The song may be divided into the following sections: (1) the purpose of the song (praise) and the occasion for the deeds it celebrates (vv. 2–9); (2) the exhortation to Israel to act in accordance with their heroic past (vv. 10–11a); (3) the people's appeal to Deborah (vv. 11b–12); (4) the gathering of warriors (vv. 13–18); (5) the battle (vv. 19–23); (6) the crafty triumph of Jael over Sisera (vv. 24–27); (7) the anxious waiting of Sisera's mother (vv. 28–30); and (8) the conclusion (v. 31).

5:4–5 Poetic recalling of the Lord's terrifying appearance in a storm cloud many years before, when he had brought Israel through the desert into Canaan (see Dt 33:2; Ps 68:7–8; Mic 1:3–4; see also Ps 18:7–15 and notes).

5:4 *Seir.* Mt. Seir (in Edom). For a similar association of Seir (and Mount Paran) with Sinai see Dt 33:2. *the heavens poured.* See Ps 68:7–10.

5:5 *the One of Sinai.* See Ps 68:8. An earthquake and thunderstorm occurred when God appeared at Mount Sinai (Ex 19:16–18).

5:6 *Shamgar.* See note on 3:31. *roads were abandoned.* Because of enemy garrisons and marauding bands (see note on 4:1–2) the roads were unsafe.

5:7 *Village life … ceased.* The inhabitants of villages fled to walled towns for protection.

5:8 *not a shield or spear was seen.* Either because Israel had made peace with the native Canaanites (see 3:5–6) or because she had been disarmed (see 1Sa 13:19–22 and note on 13:19).

5:10 *who ride on white donkeys.* An allusion to the nobles and the wealthy (see 10:4; 12:14).

5:11 *voice of the singers.* The leaders are encouraged by the songs of the minstrels at the watering places—songs that rehearse the past heroic achievements of the Lord and his warriors.

5:12 *Wake up.* A plea to take action (see Ps 44:23; Isa 51:9). *Take captive your captives.* The same action is applied to God in Ps 68:18 and to Christ in Eph 4:8 (see notes on those verses).

[13]"Then the men who were left
came down to the nobles;
the people of the LORD
came to me with the mighty.
[14]Some came from Ephraim,[p] whose
roots were in Amalek;[q]
Benjamin[r] was with the people who
followed you.
From Makir[s] captains came down,
from Zebulun those who bear a
commander's staff.
[15]The princes of Issachar[t] were with
Deborah;[u]
yes, Issachar was with Barak,[v]
rushing after him into the valley.
In the districts of Reuben
there was much searching of heart.
[16]Why did you stay among the
campfires[a w]
to hear the whistling for the flocks?[x]
In the districts of Reuben
there was much searching of heart.
[17]Gilead[y] stayed beyond the Jordan.
And Dan, why did he linger by the
ships?
Asher[z] remained on the coast[a]
and stayed in his coves.
[18]The people of Zebulun[b] risked their
very lives;
so did Naphtali[c] on the heights of
the field.[d]

[19]"Kings came[e], they fought;
the kings of Canaan fought
at Taanach by the waters of Megiddo,[f]
but they carried off no silver, no
plunder.[g]
[20]From the heavens[h] the stars fought,
from their courses they fought
against Sisera.

5:14 [p]S Ge 41:52; S Jdg 1:29 [q]Jdg 3:13 [r]S Nu 34:21 [s]S Ge 50:23 **5:15** [t]S Ge 30:18 [u]S Jdg 4:4 [v]S Jdg 4:6 **5:16** [w]S Ge 49:14 [x]S Nu 32:1 **5:17** [y]S Jos 12:2 [z]S Jos 17:7 [a]Jos 19:29 **5:18** [b]S Ge 30:20 [c]S Ge 30:8; Ps 68:27 [d]S Jdg 4:6,10 **5:19** [e]Jos 11:5; S Jdg 4:13; Rev 16:16 [f]S Jos 12:21 [g]ver 30 **5:20** [h]S Jos 10:11

5:21 [i]S Jdg 4:7 [j]Jos 1:6 **5:22** [k]Jer 8:16 **5:24** [l]Lk 1:42 [m]S Jdg 4:17 [n]S Ge 15:19 **5:25** [o]S Ge 18:8 **5:26** [p]Jdg 4:21 **5:27** [q]Jdg 4:22 **5:28** [r]S Jos 2:15 [s]Pr 7:6

[21]The river Kishon[i] swept them away,
the age-old river, the river Kishon.
March on, my soul; be strong![j]
[22]Then thundered the horses' hoofs—
galloping, galloping go his mighty
steeds.[k]
[23]'Curse Meroz,' said the angel of the
LORD.
'Curse its people bitterly,
because they did not come to help
the LORD,
to help the LORD against the
mighty.'

[24]"Most blessed of women[l] be Jael,[m]
the wife of Heber the Kenite,[n]
most blessed of tent-dwelling
women.
[25]He asked for water, and she gave him
milk;[o]
in a bowl fit for nobles she brought
him curdled milk.
[26]Her hand reached for the tent peg,
her right hand for the workman's
hammer.
She struck Sisera, she crushed his
head,
she shattered and pierced his
temple.[p]
[27]At her feet he sank,
he fell; there he lay.
At her feet he sank, he fell;
where he sank, there he fell—
dead[q].

[28]"Through the window[r] peered Sisera's
mother;
behind the lattice she cried out,[s]

[a] 16 Or *saddlebags*

5:13–18 The warriors of the Lord who gathered for the battle. The tribes who came were Ephraim, Benjamin, Manasseh ("Makir" is possibly both East and West Manasseh; see Dt 3:15; Jos 13:29–31; 17:1), Zebulun (vv. 14,18), Issachar (v. 15) and Naphtali (v. 18). Especially involved were Zebulun and Naphtali (v. 18; see 4:10), the tribes most immediately affected by Sisera's tyranny. Reuben (vv. 15–16) and Gad (here referred to as Gilead, v. 17), from east of the Jordan, and Dan and Asher, from along the coast (v. 17), are rebuked for not responding. Judah and Simeon are not even mentioned, perhaps because they were already engaged with the Philistines. Levi is not mentioned because it did not have military responsibilities in the theocracy (kingdom of God).
5:14 *roots ... in Amalek.* Some Amalekites apparently once lived in the hill country of Ephraim (see 12:15; see also note on Ge 14:7). *Makir.* The firstborn son of Manasseh (Jos 17:1). Although the descendants of Makir settled on both sides of the Jordan (see Dt 3:15; Jos 13:29–31; 17:1; 1Ch 7:14–19), reference here is to those west of the Jordan (see v. 17; Jos 17:5).
5:18 *on the heights of the field.* Perhaps connected to Ge 49:21, where Naphtali is described as a "doe set free."
5:19 *Megiddo.* Megiddo and Taanach dominated the main pass that runs northeast through the hill country from the plain of Sharon to the Valley of Jezreel. Because of its strategic location, the "plain of Megiddo" (2Ch 35:22) has been a frequent battleground from the earliest times. There Pharaoh Thutmose III defeated a Canaanite coalition in 1468 B.C., and there in A.D. 1917 the British under General Allenby ended the rule of the Turks in Palestine by vanquishing them in the Valley of Jezreel opposite Megiddo. In Biblical history the forces of Israel under Deborah and Barak crushed the Canaanites "by the waters of Megiddo," and there Judah's good king Josiah died in battle against Pharaoh Neco II in 609 B.C. (2Ki 23:29). See also the reference in Rev 16:16 (as well as note there) to "the place that in Hebrew is called Armageddon" (probably "Mount Megiddo") as the site of the "battle on the great day of God Almighty" (Rev 16:14).
5:20 *stars fought.* A poetic way of saying that the powers of heaven fought in Israel's behalf (see notes on 4:7; Jos 10:11; Ps 18:7–15).
5:21 *swept them away.* See note on 4:7.
5:23 *Meroz.* Because of its refusal to help the army of the Lord, this Israelite town in Naphtali was cursed. Other cities were also punished severely for refusing to participate in the wars of the Lord (see 8:15–17; 21:5–10 and note on 21:5).
5:25 *curdled milk.* Artificially soured milk made by shaking milk in a skin-bottle and then allowing it to ferment (due to bacteria that remained in the skin from previous use).
5:28 This graphic picture of the anxious waiting of Sisera's mother heightens the triumph of Jael over the powerful Canaanite general and presents a contrast between this mother in Canaan and the triumphant Deborah, "a mother in Israel" (v. 7).

'Why is his chariot so long in coming?
Why is the clatter of his chariots delayed?'
29 The wisest of her ladies answer her;
indeed, she keeps saying to herself,
30 'Are they not finding and dividing the spoils:[t]
a girl or two for each man,
colorful garments as plunder for Sisera,
colorful garments embroidered,
highly embroidered garments[u] for my neck—
all this as plunder?'[v]

31 "So may all your enemies perish,[w] O LORD!
But may they who love you be like the sun[x]
when it rises in its strength."[y]

Then the land had peace[z] forty years.

Gideon

6 Again the Israelites did evil in the eyes
of the LORD,[a] and for seven years he
gave them into the hands of the Midianites.[b] 2 Because the power of Midian was so
oppressive,[c] the Israelites prepared shelters
for themselves in mountain clefts, caves[d]
and strongholds.[e] 3 Whenever the Israelites
planted their crops, the Midianites, Amalekites[f] and other eastern peoples[g] invaded the country. 4 They camped on the
land and ruined the crops[h] all the way to
Gaza[i] and did not spare a living thing for
Israel, neither sheep nor cattle nor donkeys. 5 They came up with their livestock
and their tents like swarms of locusts.[j] It
was impossible to count the men and their
camels;[k] they invaded the land to ravage
it. 6 Midian so impoverished the Israelites
that they cried out[l] to the LORD for help.
7 When the Israelites cried[m] to the LORD
because of Midian, 8 he sent them a prophet,[n] who said, "This is what the LORD, the
God of Israel, says: I brought you up out
of Egypt,[o] out of the land of slavery.[p] 9 I
snatched you from the power of Egypt and
from the hand of all your oppressors.[q] I
drove them from before you and gave you
their land.[r] 10 I said to you, 'I am the LORD
your God; do not worship[s] the gods of the
Amorites,[t] in whose land you live.' But
you have not listened to me."
11 The angel of the LORD[u] came and sat
down under the oak in Ophrah[v] that belonged to Joash[w] the Abiezrite,[x] where his
son Gideon[y] was threshing[z] wheat in a
winepress[a] to keep it from the Midianites.
12 When the angel of the LORD appeared to
Gideon, he said, "The LORD is with you,[b]
mighty warrior.[c]"
13 "But sir," Gideon replied, "if the LORD
is with us, why has all this happened to
us? Where are all his wonders[d] that our
fathers told[e] us about when they said, 'Did
not the LORD bring us up out of Egypt?' But
now the LORD has abandoned[f] us and put
us into the hand of Midian."
14 The LORD turned to him and said, "Go
in the strength you have[g] and save[h] Israel

5:30 [t] Ex 15:9; 1Sa 30:24; Ps 68:12 [u] Ps 45:14; Eze 16:10 [v] ver 19; 2Sa 1:24 **5:31** [w] S Nu 10:35 [x] 2Sa 23:4; Job 37:21; Ps 19:4; 89:36; Isa 18:4 [y] 2Sa 18:32 [z] S Jdg 3:11 **6:1** [a] S Jdg 2:11 [b] S Ge 25:2 **6:2** [c] 1Sa 13:6; Isa 5:30; 8:21; 26:16; 37:3 [d] Isa 2:19; Jer 48:28; 49:8, 30 [e] Job 24:8; Jer 41:9; Heb 11:38 **6:3** [f] Nu 13:29 [g] S Ge 25:6; Isa 11:14; Jer 49:28 **6:4** [h] Lev 26:16; Dt 28:30, 51; Isa 10:6; 39:6; 42:22 [i] S Ge 10:19 **6:5** [j] S Dt 28:42 [k] Jdg 8:10; Isa 21:7; 60:6; Jer 49:32 **6:6** [l] S Jdg 3:9 **6:7** [m] S Jdg 3:9 **6:8** [n] Dt 18:15; 1Ki 20:13, 22; 2Ki 17:13, 23; Ne 9:29; Job 36:10; Jer 25:5; Eze 18:30-31 [o] S Jdg 2:1 [p] Jos 24:17 **6:9** [q] S Nu 10:9; Ps 136:24 [r] Ps 44:2 **6:10** [s] S Ex 20:5 [t] S Jos 24:15 **6:11** [u] S Ge 16:7 [v] S Jos 18:23 [w] ver 29; Jdg 7:14; 8:13, 29 [x] S Nu 26:30 [y] Jdg 7:1; 8:1; Heb 11:32 [z] Ru 2:17; 3:2; 1Sa 23:1; 1Ch 21:20 [a] Ne 13:15; Isa 16:10; 63:3; La 1:15; Joel 3:13 **6:12** [b] S Jos 1:5; Ru 2:4; 1Sa 10:7; Ps 129:8 [c] Jdg 11:1 **6:13** [d] S Jos 3:5 [e] 2Sa 7:22; Ps 44:1; 78:3 [f] S Dt 31:17 **6:14** [g] Heb 11:34 [h] ver 36; Jdg 10:1; 2Ki 14:27

5:31 The song ends with a prayer that the present victory would be the pattern for all future battles against the Lord's enemies (see Nu 10:35; Ps 68:1–3 and notes). *your enemies ... they who love you.* The two basic attitudes of people toward the Lord. As Lord of the covenant and royal Head of his people Israel, he demanded their love (see Ex 20:6; Dt 6:5 and notes), just as kings in the ancient Near East demanded the love of their subjects. *forty years.* A conventional number of years for a generation (see Introduction: Background).

6:1—9:57 The Gideon and Abimelech narratives are a literary unit and constitute the center account of the judges. They are bracketed by the stories of Deborah (from Ephraim, a son of Joseph; west of the Jordan) and Jephthah (from Manasseh, the other son of Joseph; east of the Jordan)—which in turn are bracketed by the stories of the heroes Ehud (from Benjamin) and Samson (from Dan). In this center narrative, the crucial issues of the period of the judges are emphasized: the worship of Baal, and the Lord's kingship over his covenant people Israel (see note on 8:23).

6:1 *Midianites.* See notes on Ge 37:25; Ex 2:15. Since they were apparently not numerous enough to wage war against the Israelites alone, they often formed coalitions with surrounding peoples—as with the Moabites (see Nu 22:4–6 and note on 22:4; 25:6–18), the Amalekites and other tribes from the east (v. 3). Their defeat was an event long remembered in Hebrew history (see Ps 83:9; Isa 9:4; 10:26; Hab 3:7).

6:3 *Amalekites.* See note on Ge 14:7. Normally they were a people of the Negev, but they are in coalition here with the Midianites and other eastern peoples, who were nomads from the desert east of Moab and Ammon.

6:5 *swarms of locusts.* A vivid picture of the marauders who swarmed across the land, leaving it stripped bare (see 7:12; Ex 10:13–15; Joel 1:4; see also Introduction to Joel: Theological Message). *camels.* The earliest OT reference to the use of mounted camels in warfare (cf. note on Ge 12:16).

6:7 *cried to the LORD.* The Israelites' cries of distress occurred in each recurring cycle of the judges (see Introduction: Literary Features).

6:8 *prophet.* See notes on 2:1; 10:11. The unnamed prophet rebuked Israel for forgetting that the Lord had saved them from Egyptian bondage and had given them the land (vv. 9–10).

6:10 *Amorites.* Probably here includes all the inhabitants of Canaan (see notes on Ge 10:16; 2Sa 21:2).

6:11 *angel of the LORD.* See note on Ge 16:7. *Ophrah.* To be distinguished from the Benjamite Ophrah (Jos 18:23). *Abiezrite.* The Abiezrites (v. 24) were from the tribe of Manasseh (Jos 17:2). *threshing wheat in a winepress.* Rather than in the usual, exposed area (see note on Ru 1:22). Gideon felt more secure threshing in this better protected but very confined space.

6:12 *mighty warrior.* Apparently Gideon belonged to the upper class, perhaps a kind of landed aristocracy (see v. 27; cf. Barak, Boaz and Nabal), in spite of his disclaimer in v. 15.

6:14 *LORD turned.* See v. 23; see also note on Ge 16:7.

out of Midian's hand. Am I not sending you?"

15"But Lord,[a]" Gideon asked, "how can I save Israel? My clan[i] is the weakest in Manasseh, and I am the least in my family.[j]"

16The LORD answered, "I will be with you[k], and you will strike down all the Midianites together."

17Gideon replied, "If now I have found favor in your eyes, give me a sign[l] that it is really you talking to me. 18Please do not go away until I come back and bring my offering and set it before you."

And the LORD said, "I will wait until you return."

19Gideon went in, prepared a young goat,[m] and from an ephah[b][n] of flour he made bread without yeast. Putting the meat in a basket and its broth in a pot, he brought them out and offered them to him under the oak.[o]

20The angel of God said to him, "Take the meat and the unleavened bread, place them on this rock,[p] and pour out the broth." And Gideon did so. 21With the tip of the staff[q] that was in his hand, the angel of the LORD touched the meat and the unleavened bread.[r] Fire flared from the rock, consuming the meat and the bread. And the angel of the LORD disappeared. 22When Gideon realized[s] that it was the angel of the LORD, he exclaimed, "Ah, Sovereign LORD! I have seen the angel of the LORD face to face!"[t]

23But the LORD said to him, "Peace! Do not be afraid.[u] You are not going to die."[v]

24So Gideon built an altar to the LORD there and called[w] it The LORD is Peace. To this day it stands in Ophrah[x] of the Abiezrites.

25That same night the LORD said to him, "Take the second bull from your father's herd, the one seven years old.[c] Tear down your father's altar to Baal and cut down the Asherah pole[d][y] beside it. 26Then build a proper kind of[e] altar to the LORD your God on the top of this height. Using the wood of the Asherah pole that you cut down, offer the second[f] bull as a burnt offering.[z]"

27So Gideon took ten of his servants and did as the LORD told him. But because he was afraid of his family and the men of the town, he did it at night rather than in the daytime.

28In the morning when the men of the town got up, there was Baal's altar,[a] demolished, with the Asherah pole beside it cut down and the second bull sacrificed on the newly built altar!

29They asked each other, "Who did this?"

When they carefully investigated, they were told, "Gideon son of Joash[b] did it."

30The men of the town demanded of Joash, "Bring out your son. He must die, because he has broken down Baal's altar[c] and cut down the Asherah pole beside it."

31But Joash replied to the hostile crowd around him, "Are you going to plead Baal's cause?[d] Are you trying to save him? Whoever fights for him shall be put to death by morning! If Baal really is a god, he can defend himself when someone breaks down his altar." 32So that day they called Gideon "Jerub-Baal,[g][e]" saying, "Let Baal contend with him," because he broke down Baal's altar.

33Now all the Midianites, Amalekites[f] and other eastern peoples[g] joined forces and crossed over the Jordan and camped in the Valley of Jezreel.[h] 34Then the Spirit of the LORD came upon[i] Gideon, and he blew a trumpet,[j] summoning the Abiezrites[k] to follow him. 35He sent messengers throughout Manasseh, calling them to

6:15 [i] Isa 60:22 [j] 1Sa 9:21
6:16 [k] Ex 3:12; S Nu 14:43; Jos 1:5
6:17 [l] ver 36-37; S Ge 24:14; S Ex 3:12; S 4:8
6:19 [m] Jdg 13:15 [n] S Lev 19:36 [o] Ge 18:7-8
6:20 [p] Jdg 13:19
6:21 [q] S Ex 4:2 [r] S Lev 9:24
6:22 [s] Jdg 13:16,21 [t] Ge 32:30; Jdg 13:22
6:23 [u] Da 10:19 [v] S Ge 16:13; S Dt 5:26
6:24 [w] S Ge 22:14 [x] S Jos 18:23
6:25 [y] ver 26,28,30; Ex 34:13; S Jdg 2:13
6:26 [z] S Ge 8:20
6:28 [a] ver 30; 1Ki 16:32; 2Ki 21:3
6:29 [b] S ver 11
6:30 [c] S ver 28
6:31 [d] 1Sa 24:15; Ps 43:1; Jer 30:13
6:32 [e] Jdg 7:1; 8:29,35; 9:1; 1Sa 12:11
6:33 [f] Nu 13:29 [g] S Ge 25:6 [h] S Jos 15:56; Eze 25:4; Hos 1:5
6:34 [i] S Jdg 3:10 [j] S Jos 6:20; S Jdg 3:27 [k] S Jos 17:2

[a] 15 Or *sir* [b] 19 That is, probably about 3/5 bushel (about 22 liters) [c] 25 Or *Take a full-grown, mature bull from your father's herd* [d] 25 That is, a symbol of the goddess Asherah; here and elsewhere in Judges [e] 26 Or *build with layers of stone an* [f] 26 Or *full-grown*; also in verse 28 [g] 32 *Jerub-Baal* means *let Baal contend.*

6:14 *Go ... Am I not sending you?* Gideon was commissioned to deliver Israel as Moses had been (see Ex 3:7–10).

6:15 *how can I ...?* Cf. Moses and Jeremiah's reactions to God's call to serve (Ex 3:11; 4:10; see Jer 1:6–7 and notes). The Lord usually calls the lowly rather than the mighty to act for him (see Nu 12:3 and notes on Ge 25:23; 1Sa 9:21; cf. 1Co 1:26–31 and notes).

6:17 *give me a sign.* See vv. 36–40; cf. the signs the Lord gave Moses as assurance that he would be with him in his undertaking (see Ex 3:12; 4:1–17).

6:21 *consuming the meat.* Indicating that Gideon's offering was accepted (see Lev 9:24; 1Ki 18:24 and note).

6:23 *not going to die.* See 13:22 and notes on Ge 16:13; 32:30.

6:25 *Tear down ... altar.* Gideon's first task as the Lord's warrior was to tear down his father's altar to Baal (cf. 2:2; Ex 34:13; Dt 7:5). *Baal.* See note on 2:13. *Asherah pole.* See NIV text note; see also notes on 2:13; Ex 34:13.

6:26 *proper kind of altar.* See Ex 20:25 and note.

6:30 *He must die.* The Israelites were so apostate that they were willing to kill one of their own people for the cause of Baal (contrast Dt 13:6–10, where God told Moses that idolaters must be stoned).

6:32 *Jerub-Baal.* See NIV text note. This name later occurs as Jerub-Besheth (2Sa 11:21) by substituting a degrading term (Hebrew *bosheth,* "shameful thing") for the name of Baal (see note on Jer 2:26), as in the change of the names Esh-Baal and Merib-Baal (1Ch 8:33–34) to Ish-Bosheth and Mephibosheth (see notes on 2Sa 2:8; 4:4). *Let Baal contend with him.* Let Baal defend himself against Gideon.

6:33 *Valley of Jezreel.* See note on 5:19.

6:34 *Spirit ... came upon.* Lit. "Spirit ... clothed himself with." This vivid figure, used only three times (here; 1Ch 12:18; 2Ch 24:20), emphasizes that the Spirit of the Lord empowered the human agent and acted through him (see note on 3:10).

6:35 *Manasseh.* West Manasseh. *Asher.* This tribe earlier had failed to answer the call to arms (5:17).

arms, and also into Asher,[l] Zebulun and Naphtali,[m] so that they too went up to meet them.[n]

36 Gideon said to God, "If you will save[o] Israel by my hand as you have promised— 37 look, I will place a wool fleece[p] on the threshing floor.[q] If there is dew only on the fleece and all the ground is dry, then I will know[r] that you will save Israel by my hand, as you said." 38 And that is what happened. Gideon rose early the next day; he squeezed the fleece and wrung out the dew—a bowlful of water.

39 Then Gideon said to God, "Do not be angry with me. Let me make just one more request.[s] Allow me one more test with the fleece. This time make the fleece dry and the ground covered with dew." 40 That night God did so. Only the fleece was dry; all the ground was covered with dew.[t]

Gideon Defeats the Midianites

7 Early in the morning, Jerub-Baal[u] (that is, Gideon[v]) and all his men camped at the spring of Harod.[w] The camp of Midian[x] was north of them in the valley near the hill of Moreh.[y] 2 The LORD said to Gideon, "You have too many men for me to deliver Midian into their hands. In order that Israel may not boast against me that her own strength[z] has saved her, 3 announce now to the people, 'Anyone who trembles with fear may turn back and leave Mount Gilead.[a]'" So twenty-two thousand men left, while ten thousand remained.

4 But the LORD said to Gideon, "There are still too many[b] men. Take them down to the water, and I will sift them for you there. If I say, 'This one shall go with you,' he shall go; but if I say, 'This one shall not go with you,' he shall not go."

5 So Gideon took the men down to the water. There the LORD told him, "Separate those who lap the water with their tongues like a dog from those who kneel down to drink." 6 Three hundred men[c] lapped with their hands to their mouths. All the rest got down on their knees to drink.

7 The LORD said to Gideon, "With the three hundred men that lapped I will save you and give the Midianites into your hands.[d] Let all the other men go, each to his own place."[e] 8 So Gideon sent the rest of the Israelites to their tents but kept the three hundred, who took over the provisions and trumpets of the others.

Now the camp of Midian lay below him in the valley. 9 During that night the LORD said to Gideon, "Get up, go down against the camp, because I am going to give it into your hands.[f] 10 If you are afraid to attack, go down to the camp with your servant Purah 11 and listen to what they are saying. Afterward, you will be encouraged to attack the camp." So he and Purah his servant went down to the outposts of the camp. 12 The Midianites, the Amalekites[g] and all the other eastern peoples had settled in the valley, thick as locusts.[h] Their camels[i] could no more be counted than the sand on the seashore.[j]

13 Gideon arrived just as a man was telling a friend his dream. "I had a dream," he was saying. "A round loaf of barley bread came tumbling into the Midianite camp. It struck the tent with such force that the tent overturned and collapsed."

14 His friend responded, "This can be nothing other than the sword of Gideon son of Joash,[k] the Israelite. God has given the Midianites and the whole camp into his hands."

15 When Gideon heard the dream and its interpretation, he worshiped God.[l] He returned to the camp of Israel and called out, "Get up! The LORD has given the Midianite camp into your hands."[m] 16 Dividing the three hundred men[n] into three companies,[o] he placed trumpets[p] and empty jars[q] in the hands of all of them, with torches[r] inside.

17 "Watch me," he told them. "Follow my lead. When I get to the edge of the camp, do exactly as I do. 18 When I and all who are with me blow our trumpets,[s] then from all around the camp blow yours and shout, 'For the LORD and for Gideon.'"

6:35 [l] S Jos 17:7 [m] S Jdg 4:6 [n] Jdg 7:23 **6:36** [o] S ver 14 **6:37** [p] Job 31:20 [q] S Nu 18:27; 2Sa 6:6; 24:16 [r] S Ge 24:14 **6:39** [s] Ge 18:32 **6:40** [t] Ex 4:3-7; Isa 38:7 **7:1** [u] S Jdg 6:32 [v] S Jdg 6:11 [w] 2Sa 23:25 [x] S Ge 25:2 [y] S Ge 12:6 **7:2** [z] S Dt 8:17; 2Co 4:7 **7:3** [a] Dt 20:8; S Jos 12:2 **7:4** [b] 1Sa 14:6 **7:6** [c] Ge 14:14

7:7 [d] S Jos 8:7 [e] 1Sa 14:6 **7:9** [f] ver 13-15; S Jos 2:24; S Jdg 1:2 **7:12** [g] Nu 13:29 [h] S Dt 28:42; Jer 46:23 [i] Jer 49:29 [j] S Jos 11:4 **7:14** [k] S Jdg 6:11 **7:15** [l] 1Sa 15:31 [m] S ver 9 **7:16** [n] Ge 14:15 [o] Jdg 9:43; 1Sa 11:11; 2Sa 18:2 [p] S Lev 25:9 [q] ver 19; Ge 24:14 [r] S Ge 15:17 **7:18** [s] S Jdg 3:27

6:39 *not be angry … just one more request.* Cf. Abraham's words in Ge 18:32.

7:1–8 As supreme commander of Israel, the Lord reduced the army so that Israel would know that the victory was by his power, not theirs.

7:1 *Harod.* Means "trembling" and may refer to either the timidity of the Israelites (v. 3) or the great panic of the Midianites when Gideon attacked (v. 21). The Hebrew verb form is translated "routing" in 8:12. *valley.* That is, the Valley of Jezreel. *hill of Moreh.* Located across the valley from Harod, approximately four miles from the Israelite army.

7:3 *may turn back.* Those who were afraid to fight the Lord's battle were not to go out with his army so that they would not demoralize the others (Dt 20:8). *Mount Gilead.* Perhaps used here as another name for Mount Gilboa.

7:6 *lapped.* The 300 remained on their feet, prepared for any emergency.

7:8–14 The Lord provided Gideon with encouraging military intelligence for the battle.

7:13–14 Although revelations by dreams are frequently mentioned in the OT, here both dreamer and interpreter are non-Israelite. Contrast Joseph, who interpreted dreams for the Egyptians (Ge 40:1–22; 41:1–32), and Daniel, who interpreted dreams for King Nebuchadnezzar (Da 2:1–45; 4:4–27).

7:13 *round loaf of barley bread.* Since barley was considered an inferior grain and only half the value of wheat (see 2Ki 7:1), it is a fitting symbol for Israel, which was inferior in numbers.

7:16 *three companies.* A strategy adopted by Israel on several occasions (9:43; 1Sa 11:11; 2Sa 18:2). *trumpets.* Rams' horns (see Ex 19:13).

[19]Gideon and the hundred men with him
reached the edge of the camp at the beginning of the middle watch, just after they
had changed the guard. They blew their
trumpets and broke the jars[t] that were in
their hands. [20]The three companies blew the
trumpets and smashed the jars. Grasping
the torches[u] in their left hands and holding
in their right hands the trumpets they were
to blow, they shouted, "A sword[v] for the
LORD and for Gideon!" [21]While each man
held his position around the camp, all the
Midianites ran, crying out as they fled.[w]
[22]When the three hundred trumpets
sounded,[x] the LORD caused the men
throughout the camp to turn on each other[y] with their swords.[z] The army fled to
Beth Shittah toward Zererah as far as the
border of Abel Meholah[a] near Tabbath.
[23]Israelites from Naphtali, Asher[b] and all
Manasseh were called out,[c] and they pursued the Midianites.[d] [24]Gideon sent messengers throughout the hill country of
Ephraim, saying, "Come down against the
Midianites and seize the waters of the Jordan[e] ahead of them as far as Beth Barah."
So all the men of Ephraim were called
out and they took the waters of the Jordan as far as Beth Barah. [25]They also captured two of the Midianite leaders, Oreb

7:19 [t]S ver 16 **7:20** [u]S Ge 15:17 [v]S Dt 32:41 **7:21** [w]2Ki 7:7 **7:22** [x]S Jos 6:20 [y]1Sa 14:20; 2Ch 20:23; Isa 9:21; 19:2; Eze 38:21; Hag 2:22; Zec 14:13 [z]Hab 3:14 [a]1Sa 18:19; 1Ki 4:12; 19:16 **7:23** [b]S Jos 17:7 [c]Jdg 6:35 [d]Ps 83:9 **7:24** [e]S Jos 2:7

7:19 *middle watch.* The Israelites divided the night into three watches (see note on Mt 14:25). The "beginning of the middle watch" would be after the enemy had gone to sleep.
7:22 *three hundred trumpets.* Normally only a comparatively small number of men in an army carried trumpets. *turn on each other.* A similar panic occurred among the Ammonites, Moabites and Edomites (2Ch 20:23) and, on a somewhat smaller scale, among the Philistines at Gibeah (1Sa 14:20). See Eze 38:21; Zec 14:13; see also note on Jdg 4:15. *toward Zererah.* Toward the southeast.
7:23 *were called out.* Encouraged by the turn of events, many of those who had departed now joined the battle.
7:24 *hill country of Ephraim.* Gideon needed the aid of the Ephraimites to cut off the retreat of the Midianites into the Jordan Valley. *waters of the Jordan.* Probably the river crossings in the vicinity of Beth Shan. By controlling the river the Israelites could prevent the escape of the fleeing Midianites (see note on 3:28). *Beth Barah.* Exact location unknown, but it must have been some distance down the river. Gideon's pursuit of the enemy across the river took him to Succoth, a town near the Jabbok River (8:5).
7:25 *Oreb.* Means "raven" (see Isa 10:26). *Zeeb.* Means "wolf." *heads.* Frequently parts of the bodies of dead victims, such as heads, hands (8:6) and foreskins (1Sa 18:25), were cut off and brought back as a kind of body count.

Gideon's Battles

The story of Gideon begins with a graphic portrayal of one of the most striking facts of life in the Fertile Crescent: the periodic migration of nomadic people from the Aramean desert into the settled areas of Canaan. Each spring the tents of the bedouin herdsmen appeared overnight almost as if by magic, scattered on the hills and fields of the farming districts. Conflict between these two ways of life (herdsmen and farmers) was inevitable.

In the Biblical period, the vast numbers and warlike practice of the herdsmen reduced the village people to near vassalage. God's answer was twofold: (1) religious reform, starting with Gideon's own family; and (2) military action, based on a coalition of northern Israelite tribes. The location of Gideon's hometown, "Ophrah of the Abiezrites," is not known with certainty, but probably was ancient Aper (modern Afula) in the Valley of Jezreel.

The battle at the spring of Harod is justly celebrated for its strategic brilliance. Denied the use of the only local water source, the Midianites camped in the valley and fell victim to the small band of Israelites, who attacked them from the heights of the hill of Moreh.

The main battle took place north of the hill near the village of Endor at the foot of Mount Tabor. Fleeing by way of the Jordan Valley, the Midianites were trapped when the Ephraimites seized the fords of the Jordan from below Beth Shan to Beth Barah near Adam.

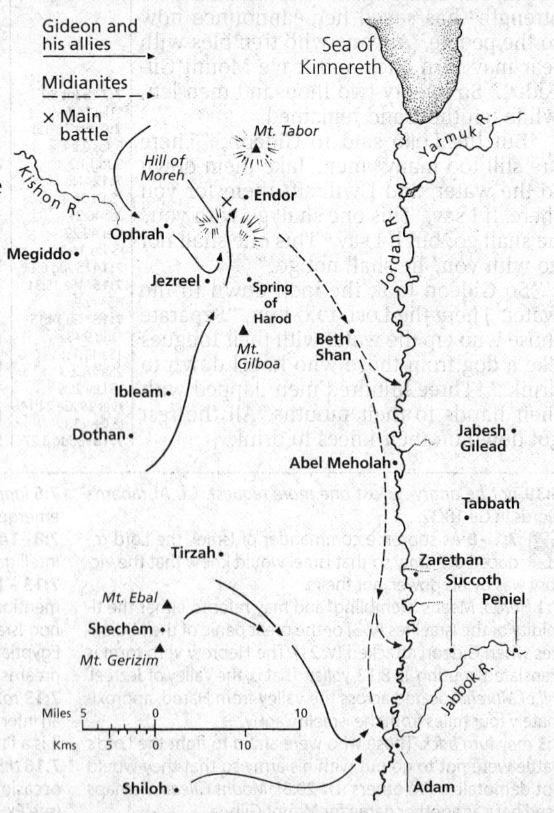

and Zeeb[f]. They killed Oreb at the rock of Oreb,[g] and Zeeb at the winepress of Zeeb. They pursued the Midianites[h] and brought the heads of Oreb and Zeeb to Gideon, who was by the Jordan.[i]

Zebah and Zalmunna

8 Now the Ephraimites asked Gideon,[j] "Why have you treated us like this? Why didn't you call us when you went to fight Midian?[k]"[l] And they criticized him sharply.[m]

2 But he answered them, "What have I accomplished compared to you? Aren't the gleanings of Ephraim's grapes better than the full grape harvest of Abiezer?[n] 3 God gave Oreb and Zeeb,[o] the Midianite leaders, into your hands. What was I able to do compared to you?" At this, their resentment against him subsided.

4 Gideon and his three hundred men, exhausted yet keeping up the pursuit, came to the Jordan[p] and crossed it. 5 He said to the men of Succoth,[q] "Give my troops some bread; they are worn out,[r] and I am still pursuing Zebah and Zalmunna,[s] the kings of Midian."

6 But the officials of Succoth[t] said, "Do you already have the hands of Zebah and Zalmunna in your possession? Why should we give bread[u] to your troops?"[v]

7 Then Gideon replied, "Just for that, when the LORD has given Zebah and Zalmunna[w] into my hand, I will tear your flesh with desert thorns and briers."

8 From there he went up to Peniel[a][x] and made the same request of them, but they answered as the men of Succoth had. 9 So he said to the men of Peniel, "When I return in triumph, I will tear down this tower."[y]

10 Now Zebah and Zalmunna were in Karkor with a force of about fifteen thousand men, all that were left of the armies of the eastern peoples; a hundred and twenty thousand swordsmen had fallen.[z] 11 Gideon went up by the route of the nomads east of Nobah[a] and Jogbehah[b] and fell upon the unsuspecting army. 12 Zebah and Zalmunna, the two kings of Midian, fled, but he pursued them and captured them, routing their entire army.

13 Gideon son of Joash[c] then returned from the battle by the Pass of Heres.[d] 14 He caught a young man of Succoth and questioned him, and the young man wrote down for him the names of the seventy-seven officials of Succoth,[e] the elders[f] of the town. 15 Then Gideon came and said to the men of Succoth, "Here are Zebah and Zalmunna, about whom you taunted me by saying, 'Do you already have the hands of Zebah and Zalmunna in your possession? Why should we give bread to your exhausted men?[g]' " 16 He took the elders of the town and taught the men of Succoth a lesson[h] by punishing them with desert thorns and briers. 17 He also pulled down the tower of Peniel[i] and killed the men of the town.[j]

18 Then he asked Zebah and Zalmunna, "What kind of men did you kill at Tabor?[k]"

"Men like you," they answered, "each one with the bearing of a prince."

19 Gideon replied, "Those were my brothers, the sons of my own mother. As surely as the LORD lives,[l] if you had spared their lives, I would not kill you." 20 Turning to Jether, his oldest son, he said, "Kill them!" But Jether did not draw his sword, because he was only a boy and was afraid.

21 Zebah and Zalmunna said, "Come, do it yourself. 'As is the man, so is his strength.' " So Gideon stepped forward and killed them, and took the ornaments[m] off their camels' necks.

Gideon's Ephod

22 The Israelites said to Gideon, "Rule over us — you, your son and your grandson — because you have saved us out of the hand of Midian."

23 But Gideon told them, "I will not rule over you, nor will my son rule over you.

[a] 8 Hebrew *Penuel,* a variant of *Peniel;* also in verses 9 and 17

7:25 [f] Jdg 8:3; Ps 83:11 [g] Isa 10:26 [h] Isa 9:4 [i] Jdg 8:4; Ps 106:43
8:1 [j] S Jdg 6:11 [k] S Ge 25:2 [l] Jdg 12:1 [m] 2Sa 19:41
8:2 [n] S Nu 26:30
8:3 [o] S Jdg 7:25
8:4 [p] Jdg 7:25
8:5 [q] S Ge 33:17 [r] Job 16:7; Ps 6:6; Jer 45:3 [s] ver 7, 12; Ps 83:11
8:6 [t] ver 14 [u] 1Sa 25:11 [v] ver 15
8:7 [w] S ver 5
8:8 [x] ver 9, 17; Ge 32:30; 1Ki 12:25
8:9 [y] ver 17
8:10 [z] S Jdg 6:5; Isa 9:4
8:11 [a] Nu 32:42 [b] S Nu 32:35
8:13 [c] S Jdg 6:11 [d] Jdg 1:35
8:14 [e] ver 6 [f] S Ex 3:16
8:15 [g] ver 6
8:16 [h] 1Sa 14:12
8:17 [i] S ver 8 [j] ver 9
8:18 [k] S Jos 19:22
8:19 [l] S Nu 14:21
8:21 [m] ver 26; Isa 3:18

8:1 *Ephraimites.* Contrast Gideon, who placates the wrath of this tribe (vv. 2 – 3), with Jephthah, who brings humiliation and defeat to it (12:1 – 6).

8:2 *gleanings.* Leftover grain after the main gathering of the harvest (see note on Ru 1:22). Here Gideon implies that Ephraim has accomplished more than he and all the other forces involved in the initial attack. *Abiezer.* Gideon's clan (see note on 6:11). The name means "My (divine) Father is helper" or "My (divine) Father is strong."

8:3 *their resentment … subsided.* "A gentle answer turns away wrath" (Pr 15:1).

8:5 *kings of Midian.* Zebah and Zalmunna may have belonged to different Midianite tribes (see Nu 31:8).

8:6 *hands.* See note on 7:25. *Why should we give bread … ?* The officials of Succoth doubted Gideon's ability to defeat the Midianite coalition and feared reprisal if they gave his army food.

8:8 *Peniel.* The place where Jacob had wrestled with God (Ge 32:30 – 31).

8:19 *sons of my own mother.* In an age when men often had several wives it was necessary to distinguish between full brothers and half brothers.

8:21 *do it yourself.* Dying at the hands of a boy may have been considered a disgrace (see 1Sa 17:42). *ornaments.* Crescent necklaces, as in Isa 3:18 (see note there).

8:23 *I will not rule … The LORD will rule.* Gideon, like Samuel (1Sa 8:4 – 20), rejected the establishment of a monarchy because he regarded it as a replacement of the Lord's rule. God's rule over Israel (theocracy) is a central issue in Judges.

The LORD will rule[n] over you." 24And he
said, "I do have one request, that each of
you give me an earring[o] from your share
of the plunder.[p]" (It was the custom of the
Ishmaelites[q] to wear gold earrings.)
25They answered, "We'll be glad to give
them." So they spread out a garment, and
each man threw a ring from his plunder
onto it. 26The weight of the gold rings
he asked for came to seventeen hundred
shekels,[a] not counting the ornaments, the
pendants and the purple garments worn
by the kings of Midian or the chains[r]
that were on their camels' necks. 27Gide-
on made the gold into an ephod,[s] which
he placed in Ophrah,[t] his town. All Israel prostituted themselves by worshiping it
there, and it became a snare[u] to Gideon
and his family.[v]

Gideon's Death

28Thus Midian was subdued before the
Israelites and did not raise its head[w] again.
During Gideon's lifetime, the land enjoyed
peace[x] forty years.
29Jerub-Baal[y] son of Joash[z] went back
home to live. 30He had seventy sons[a] of his
own, for he had many wives. 31His concubine,[b] who lived in Shechem, also bore
him a son, whom he named Abimelech.[c]
32Gideon son of Joash died at a good old
age[d] and was buried in the tomb of his father Joash in Ophrah of the Abiezrites.

8:23 [n]S Ex 16:8; S Nu 11:20; 1Sa 12:12 **8:24** [o]S Ge 35:4 [p]S Ge 49:27 [q]S Ge 16:11 **8:26** [r]S ver 21 **8:27** [s]S Ex 25:7; Jdg 17:5; 18:14 [t]S Jos 18:23 [u]S Ex 10:7 [v]S Ex 32:2 **8:28** [w]Ps 83:2 [x]S Jdg 3:11 **8:29** [y]S Jdg 6:32 [z]S Jdg 6:11 **8:30** [a]Jdg 9:2, 5, 18, 24; 12:14; 2Ki 10:1 **8:31** [b]S Ge 22:24 [c]Jdg 9:1; 10:1; 2Sa 11:21 **8:32** [d]S Ge 15:15

8:33 [e]S Jdg 2:11, 13, 19 [f]Jdg 9:4 [g]Jdg 9:27, 46 **8:34** [h]S Jdg 3:7; S Ne 9:17 **8:35** [i]S Jdg 6:32 [j]Jdg 9:16 **9:1** [k]S Jdg 8:31 [l]S Jdg 6:32 **9:2** [m]S Ge 29:14 **9:4** [n]S Jdg 8:33 [o]Jdg 11:3; 1Sa 25:25; 2Ch 13:7; Job 30:8 **9:5** [p]S Jdg 8:30 [q]ver 7, 21, 57

33No sooner had Gideon died than the
Israelites again prostituted themselves to
the Baals.[e] They set up Baal-Berith[f] as
their god[g] 34and did not remember[h] the
LORD their God, who had rescued them
from the hands of all their enemies on every side. 35They also failed to show kindness to the family of Jerub-Baal[i] (that is,
Gideon) for all the good things he had
done for them.[j]

Abimelech

9 Abimelech[k] son of Jerub-Baal[l] went to
his mother's brothers in Shechem and
said to them and to all his mother's clan,
2"Ask all the citizens of Shechem, 'Which
is better for you: to have all seventy of Jerub-Baal's sons rule over you, or just one
man?' Remember, I am your flesh and
blood.[m]"
3When the brothers repeated all this
to the citizens of Shechem, they were inclined to follow Abimelech, for they said,
"He is our brother." 4They gave him seventy shekels[b] of silver from the temple of
Baal-Berith,[n] and Abimelech used it to hire
reckless adventurers,[o] who became his followers. 5He went to his father's home in
Ophrah and on one stone murdered his
seventy brothers,[p] the sons of Jerub-Baal.
But Jotham,[q] the youngest son of Jerub-

[a] *26* That is, about 43 pounds (about 19.5 kilograms)
[b] *4* That is, about 1 3/4 pounds (about 0.8 kilogram)

8:24 *earring.* Or possibly "nose ring" (see Ge 24:47; Eze 16:12 and note). *Ishmaelites.* Related to the Midianites (Ge 25:1–2) and sometimes identified with them (vv. 22,24; Ge 37:25–28; 39:1). See note on Ge 37:25.

8:27 *ephod.* Sometimes a holy garment associated with the priesthood (Ex 28:6–30; 39:2–26; Lev 8:7), at other times a pagan object associated with idols (17:5; 18:14,17). *prostituted themselves.* See Ex 34:15 and note.

8:28 *forty years.* A conventional number of years for a generation (see Introduction: Background).

8:29 *Jerub-Baal.* See note on 6:32.

8:30 *seventy sons.* A sign of power and prosperity (see 12:14; 2Ki 10:1).

8:31 *concubine.* She was originally a slave in his household (9:18; see note on Ge 16:2; see also note on Ge 25:6). *Abimelech.* Appears elsewhere as a royal title (Ge 20:2; 26:1; Ps 34 title) and means "My (divine) Father is King." Gideon, in naming his son, acknowledges that the Lord (here called "Father") is King.

8:32 *at a good old age.* A phrase used elsewhere only of Abraham (Ge 15:15; 25:8) and David (1Ch 29:28).

8:33 *prostituted themselves.* See Ex 34:15 and note. *Baals.* See notes on 2:11,13. *Baal-Berith.* Means "lord of the covenant"; the same deity is called El-Berith ("god of the covenant") in 9:46. There was a temple dedicated to him (see 9:4 and note) in Shechem. The word "covenant" in his name probably refers to a solemn treaty that bound together a league of Canaanite cities whose people worshiped him as their god. Ironically, Shechem (v. 31), near Mount Ebal, was the site at which Joshua had twice renewed the Lord's covenant with Israel after they had entered Canaan (Jos 8:30–35; 24:25–27). See also note on 2:11.

9:1–57 The stories of Gideon and Abimelech form the literary center of Judges (see Introduction: Literary Features). Abimelech, who tried to set himself up like a Canaanite city king with the help of Baal (v. 4), stands in sharp contrast to his father Gideon (Jerub-Baal), who had attacked Baal worship and insisted that the Lord ruled over Israel. Abimelech attempted this Canaanite revival in the very place where Joshua had earlier reaffirmed Israel's allegiance to the Lord (Jos 24:14–27). In every respect Abimelech was the antithesis of the Lord's appointed judges.

9:1 *Shechem.* See note on Ge 33:18. Ruins dating from the Canaanite era give evidence of a sacred area, probably to be associated with the temple of Baal-Berith or El-Berith (vv. 4,46). Archaeological evidence, which is compatible with the destruction of Shechem by Abimelech, indicates that its sacred area was never rebuilt after this time.

9:2 *citizens.* The singular form of the Hebrew for this word is *ba'al.* It means "lord" or "owner" and probably refers here to the aristocracy or landowners of the city. *flesh and blood.* Being half-Canaanite, Abimelech intimated that it was in their best interest to make him king rather than be under the rule of Gideon's 70 sons. The following he gathered was based on this relationship and became a threat to the people of Israel.

9:4 *from the temple.* Ancient temples served as depositories for personal and civic funds. The payments of vows and penalties, as well as gifts, were also part of the temple treasury. The temple of Baal-Berith is probably to be identified with a large building found at Shechem by archaeologists. *reckless adventurers.* Use of mercenaries to accomplish political or military goals was common in ancient times. Others who used them are Jephthah (11:3), David (1Sa 22:1–2), Absalom (2Sa 15:1), Adonijah (1Ki 1:5), Rezon (1Ki 11:23–24) and Jeroboam (2Ch 13:6–7).

9:5 *on one stone.* Abimelech's 70 brothers were slaughtered like sacrificial animals (see 13:19–20; 1Sa 14:33–34). In ef-

Baal, escaped by hiding.[r] 6 Then all the citizens of Shechem and Beth Millo[s] gathered beside the great tree[t] at the pillar in Shechem to crown Abimelech king.

7 When Jotham[u] was told about this, he climbed up on the top of Mount Gerizim[v] and shouted to them, "Listen to me, citizens of Shechem, so that God may listen to you. 8 One day the trees went out to anoint a king for themselves. They said to the olive tree, 'Be our king.'

9 "But the olive tree answered, 'Should I give up my oil, by which both gods and men are honored, to hold sway over the trees?'

10 "Next, the trees said to the fig tree, 'Come and be our king.'

11 "But the fig tree replied, 'Should I give up my fruit, so good and sweet, to hold sway over the trees?'

12 "Then the trees said to the vine, 'Come and be our king.'

13 "But the vine answered, 'Should I give up my wine,[w] which cheers both gods and men, to hold sway over the trees?'

14 "Finally all the trees said to the thornbush, 'Come and be our king.'

15 "The thornbush said to the trees, 'If you really want to anoint me king over you, come and take refuge in my shade;[x] but if not, then let fire come out[y] of the thornbush and consume the cedars of Lebanon!'[z]

16 "Now if you have acted honorably and in good faith when you made Abimelech king, and if you have been fair to Jerub-Baal and his family, and if you have treated him as he deserves— 17 and to think that my father fought for you, risked[a] his life to rescue you from the hand of Midian 18 (but today you have revolted against my father's family, murdered his seventy sons[b] on a single stone, and made Abimelech, the son of his slave girl, king over the citizens of Shechem because he is your brother)— 19 if then you have acted honorably and in good faith toward Jerub-Baal and his family today,[c] may Abimelech be your joy, and may you be his, too! 20 But if you have not, let fire come out[d] from Abimelech and consume you, citizens of Shechem[e] and Beth Millo,[f] and let fire come out from you, citizens of Shechem and Beth Millo, and consume Abimelech!"

21 Then Jotham[g] fled, escaping to Beer,[h] and he lived there because he was afraid of his brother Abimelech.

22 After Abimelech had governed Israel three years, 23 God sent an evil spirit[i] between Abimelech and the citizens of Shechem, who acted treacherously against Abimelech. 24 God did this in order that the crime against Jerub-Baal's seventy sons,[j] the shedding[k] of their blood, might be avenged[l] on their brother Abimelech and on the citizens of Shechem, who had helped him[m] murder his brothers. 25 In opposition to him these citizens of Shechem set men on the hilltops to ambush and rob everyone who passed by, and this was reported to Abimelech.

26 Now Gaal son of Ebed[n] moved with his brothers into Shechem, and its citizens put their confidence in him. 27 After they had gone out into the fields and gathered the grapes and trodden[o] them, they held a festival in the temple of their god.[p] While they were eating and drinking, they cursed Abimelech. 28 Then Gaal son of Ebed[q] said, "Who[r] is Abimelech, and who is Shechem, that we should be subject to him? Isn't he

9:5 [r] 2Ki 11:2; 2Ch 22:9
9:6 [s] ver 20; 2Ki 12:20 [t] S Ge 12:6; S Jdg 4:11
9:7 [u] S ver 5 [v] S Dt 11:29; Jn 4:20
9:13 [w] S Ge 14:18; Ecc 2:3; SS 4:10
9:15 [x] Isa 30:2 [y] ver 20 [z] S Dt 3:25; 1Ki 5:6; Ps 29:5; 92:12; Isa 2:13
9:17 [a] Jdg 12:3; 1Sa 19:5; 28:21; Job 13:14; Ps 119:109
9:18 [b] S Jdg 8:30
9:19 [c] ver 16
9:20 [d] ver 15 [e] ver 45 [f] S ver 6
9:21 [g] S ver 5 [h] Nu 21:16
9:23 [i] 1Sa 16:14, 23; 18:10; 19:9; 1Ki 22:22
9:24 [j] S Jdg 8:30 [k] S Ge 9:6; Nu 35:33; 1Ki 2:32 [l] ver 56-57 [m] Dt 27:25
9:26 [n] ver 28, 31, 41
9:27 [o] Isa 16:10; Am 5:11; 9:13 [p] S Jdg 8:33
9:28 [q] S ver 26 [r] 1Sa 25:10

fect he inaugurated his kingship by using his Israelite half brothers as his coronation sacrifices (see 2Sa 15:10,12; 1Ki 1:5,9; 3:4).

9:6 *Beth Millo.* "Millo" is derived from a Hebrew verb meaning "to fill" and perhaps refers to the earthen fill on which walls and other large structures were built. Beth Millo may be identical to the "stronghold" of v. 46. *great tree.* See Jos 24:25–26; see also note on Ge 12:6.

9:7 *top.* Probably a ledge that overlooked the city.

9:8 *trees went out.* Fables of this type, in which inanimate objects speak and act, were popular among Eastern peoples of that time (see 2Ki 14:9 and note).

9:9–13 The olive tree, the fig tree and the vine were all plants that produced fruit of great importance to the people of the Near East.

9:13 *gods.* It was commonly believed that the gods participated in such human experiences as drinking wine (cf. Ex 29:40).

9:14 *thornbush.* Probably the well-known buckthorn, a scraggly bush common in the hills of Israel and a constant menace to farming. It produced nothing of value except fuel for burning (see Ps 58:9 and note)—an apt figure for Abimelech.

9:15 *shade.* Ironically, in offering shade to the trees, the thornbush symbolized the traditional role of kings as protectors of their subjects (see Isa 30:2–3 and note on 30:2; 32:1–2; La 4:20; Da 4:12). *cedars of Lebanon.* The most valuable of Near Eastern trees, here symbolic of the leading men of Shechem (see v. 20).

9:20 *fire come out ... and consume.* A grim prediction that Abimelech and the people of Shechem would destroy each other. Fire spreads rapidly through bramble bushes and brings about swift destruction (see Ex 22:6; Isa 9:18).

9:21 *Beer.* A very common name, meaning "a well."

9:22 *Israel.* Those Israelites who recognized Abimelech's authority, mainly in the vicinity of Shechem.

9:23 *evil spirit.* Perhaps a "spirit" of distrust and bitterness. The Hebrew for "spirit" is often used to describe an attitude or disposition (cf. 1Sa 16:14 and note; cf. also NIV text note there). *acted treacherously.* The one who founded his kingdom by treachery is himself undone by treachery.

9:26 *put their confidence in him.* Just as the fickle population had followed Abimelech, so they are now swayed by the deceptive proposals of Gaal.

9:27 *held a festival.* The vintage harvest was one of the most joyous times of the year (see Isa 16:9–10; Jer 25:30), but festivals and celebrations held at pagan temples often degenerated into debauched drinking affairs.

9:28 *Hamor.* The Hivite ruler who had founded the city of Shechem (Ge 33:19; 34:2; Jos 24:32).

Jerub-Baal's son, and isn't Zebul his deputy? Serve the men of Hamor,[s] Shechem's
father! Why should we serve Abimelech?
29If only this people were under my command![t] Then I would get rid of him. I
would say to Abimelech, 'Call out your
whole army!' "[a][u]
30When Zebul the governor of the city
heard what Gaal son of Ebed said, he was
very angry. 31Under cover he sent messengers to Abimelech, saying, "Gaal son of
Ebed and his brothers have come to Shechem and are stirring up the city against
you. 32Now then, during the night you and
your men should come and lie in wait[v] in
the fields. 33In the morning at sunrise, advance against the city. When Gaal and his
men come out against you, do whatever
your hand finds to do.[w]"
34So Abimelech and all his troops set out
by night and took up concealed positions
near Shechem in four companies. 35Now
Gaal son of Ebed had gone out and was
standing at the entrance to the city gate[x]
just as Abimelech and his soldiers came
out from their hiding place.[y]
36When Gaal saw them, he said to Zebul, "Look, people are coming down from
the tops of the mountains!"
Zebul replied, "You mistake the shadows of the mountains for men."
37But Gaal spoke up again: "Look, people are coming down from the center of
the land, and a company is coming from
the direction of the soothsayers' tree."
38Then Zebul said to him, "Where is
your big talk now, you who said, 'Who
is Abimelech that we should be subject to
him?' Aren't these the men you ridiculed?[z]
Go out and fight them!"
39So Gaal led out[b] the citizens of Shechem and fought Abimelech. 40Abimelech
chased him, and many fell wounded in the
flight—all the way to the entrance to the
gate. 41Abimelech stayed in Arumah, and
Zebul drove Gaal and his brothers out of
Shechem.
42The next day the people of Shechem
went out to the fields, and this was reported to Abimelech. 43So he took his men,
divided them into three companies[a] and
set an ambush[b] in the fields. When he
saw the people coming out of the city, he
rose to attack them. 44Abimelech and the
companies with him rushed forward to a
position at the entrance to the city gate.
Then two companies rushed upon those in
the fields and struck them down. 45All that
day Abimelech pressed his attack against
the city until he had captured it and killed
its people. Then he destroyed the city[c] and
scattered salt[d] over it.
46On hearing this, the citizens in the
tower of Shechem went into the stronghold of the temple[e] of El-Berith. 47When
Abimelech heard that they had assembled there, 48he and all his men went up
Mount Zalmon.[f] He took an ax and cut
off some branches, which he lifted to his
shoulders. He ordered the men with him,
"Quick! Do what you have seen me do!"
49So all the men cut branches and followed
Abimelech. They piled them against the
stronghold and set it on fire over the people inside. So all the people in the tower
of Shechem, about a thousand men and
women, also died.
50Next Abimelech went to Thebez[g]
and besieged it and captured it. 51Inside
the city, however, was a strong tower, to
which all the men and women—all the
people of the city—fled. They locked
themselves in and climbed up on the tower roof. 52Abimelech went to the tower and
stormed it. But as he approached the entrance to the tower to set it on fire, 53a
woman dropped an upper millstone on his
head and cracked his skull.[h]
54Hurriedly he called to his armor-bearer, "Draw your sword and kill me,[i] so that
they can't say, 'A woman killed him.' " So
his servant ran him through, and he died.
55When the Israelites saw that Abimelech
was dead, they went home.
56Thus God repaid the wickedness that

9:28 [s]S Ge 33:19 **9:29** [t]2Sa 15:4 [u]ver 38 **9:32** [v]Jos 8:2 **9:33** [w]1Sa 10:7 **9:35** [x]S Jos 2:5 [y]Ps 32:7; Isa 28:15,17; Jer 49:10 **9:38** [z]ver 28-29

9:43 [a]S Jdg 7:16 [b]Jos 8:2 **9:45** [c]ver 20 [d]Jer 48:9 **9:46** [e]S Jdg 8:33 **9:48** [f]Ps 68:14 **9:50** [g]2Sa 11:21 **9:53** [h]2Sa 11:21 **9:54** [i]1Sa 31:4; 2Sa 1:9

[a] 29 Septuagint; Hebrew *him." Then he said to Abimelech, "Call out your whole army!"* [b] 39 Or *Gaal went out in the sight of*

9:32 *lie in wait.* Ambush succeeded against Gibeah in Benjamin (20:37) and against Ai (Jos 8:2).
9:34 *four companies.* Smaller segments meant less chance of detection. Also, attack from several directions was a good tactical strategy.
9:37 *center of the land.* See note on Eze 38:12. *soothsayers' tree.* Probably a sacred tree in some way related to the temple of Baal-Berith (see note on Ge 12:6).
9:43 *three companies.* See note on 7:16.
9:45 *scattered salt over it.* To condemn it to perpetual barrenness and desolation (see Dt 29:23; Ps 107:33–34; Jer 17:6; Zep 2:9).
9:46 *stronghold.* Probably the Beth Millo of v. 6. *El-Berith.* Baal-Berith (v. 4).
9:49 *set it on fire.* In fulfillment of Jotham's curse (v. 20).
9:53 *woman.* While the men used bows, arrows and spears, women helped to defend the tower by dropping heavy stones on those who came near it. *upper millstone.* See note on 3:16. The upper, revolving stone of a mill was circular, with a hole in the center. Grinding grain was women's work (see Ex 11:5), usually considered too lowly for men to perform (see 16:21). Abimelech was killed by a woman using a domestic implement (see also 4:21).
9:54 *armor-bearer.* In Israel's earlier years in Canaan, military leaders were usually served by a personal attendant (see 1Sa 14:6; 31:4), but no armor-bearers are mentioned after the time of David. *A woman killed him.* It was considered a disgrace for a soldier to die at the hands of a woman. Abimelech's shameful death was long remembered (2Sa 11:21).
9:56 *God repaid.* God was in control of the events. As Israel's true King, he brought Abimelech's wickedness to a quick and shameful end.

Abimelech had done to his father by murdering his seventy brothers. 57God also
made the men of Shechem pay for all their
wickedness.[j] The curse of Jotham[k] son of
Jerub-Baal came on them.

Tola

10 After the time of Abimelech[l] a man
of Issachar,[m] Tola son of Puah,[n] the
son of Dodo, rose to save[o] Israel. He lived
in Shamir,[p] in the hill country of Ephraim.
2He led[a] Israel twenty-three years; then he
died, and was buried in Shamir.

Jair

3He was followed by Jair[q] of Gilead, who
led Israel twenty-two years. 4He had thirty sons, who rode thirty donkeys.[r] They
controlled thirty towns in Gilead, which to
this day are called Havvoth Jair.[b s] 5When
Jair[t] died, he was buried in Kamon.

Jephthah

6Again the Israelites did evil in the eyes
of the LORD.[u] They served the Baals and
the Ashtoreths,[v] and the gods of Aram,[w]
the gods of Sidon,[x] the gods of Moab, the
gods of the Ammonites[y z] and the gods of
the Philistines.[a] And because the Israelites
forsook the LORD[b] and no longer served
him, 7he became angry[c] with them. He
sold them[d] into the hands of the Philistines and the Ammonites, 8who that year
shattered and crushed them. For eighteen
years they oppressed all the Israelites on
the east side of the Jordan in Gilead,[e] the
land of the Amorites. 9The Ammonites also
crossed the Jordan to fight against Judah,[f]
Benjamin and the house of Ephraim;[g] and
Israel was in great distress. 10Then the Israelites cried[h] out to the LORD, "We have
sinned[i] against you, forsaking our God
and serving the Baals."[j]
11The LORD replied, "When the Egyptians,[k] the Amorites,[l] the Ammonites,[m] the
Philistines,[n] 12the Sidonians, the Amalekites[o] and the Maonites[c p] oppressed you[q]
and you cried to me for help, did I not
save you from their hands? 13But you have
forsaken[r] me and served other gods,[s] so
I will no longer save you. 14Go and cry
out to the gods you have chosen. Let them
save[t] you when you are in trouble![u]"
15But the Israelites said to the LORD, "We
have sinned. Do with us whatever you
think best,[v] but please rescue us now."
16Then they got rid of the foreign gods
among them and served the LORD.[w] And
he could bear Israel's misery[x] no longer.[y]
17When the Ammonites were called to
arms and camped in Gilead, the Israelites
assembled and camped at Mizpah.[z] 18The
leaders of the people of Gilead said to each
other, "Whoever will launch the attack
against the Ammonites will be the head[a]
of all those living in Gilead."

11 Jephthah[b] the Gileadite was a mighty
warrior.[c] His father was Gilead;[d] his
mother was a prostitute.[e] 2Gilead's wife

9:57 [j] ver 24; Ps 94:23 [k] S ver 5 **10:1** [l] S Jdg 8:31 [m] S Ge 30:18 [n] S Ge 46:13 [o] S Jdg 6:14 [p] Jos 15:48 **10:3** [q] S Nu 32:41 **10:4** [r] S Ge 49:11; S 1Ki 1:33 [s] S Nu 32:41 **10:5** [t] S Nu 32:41 **10:6** [u] S Jdg 2:11 [v] S Jdg 2:13 [w] Eze 27:16 [x] S Ge 10:15 [y] S Ge 19:38 [z] S Nu 21:29 [a] S Ge 26:1; S Jdg 2:12 [b] S Dt 32:15 **10:7** [c] S Dt 31:17 [d] S Dt 32:30 **10:8** [e] S Jos 12:2 **10:9** [f] ver 17; Jdg 11:4 [g] Jdg 1:22 **10:10** [h] S Jdg 3:9 [i] S Ex 9:27; Ps 32:5; Jer 3:25; 8:14; 14:20 [j] Jer 2:27 **10:11** [k] Ex 14:30 [l] S Ge 14:7 [m] S Jdg 3:13 [n] S Jdg 3:31 **10:12** [o] S Ge 14:7 [p] S Jos 15:55 [q] S Jdg 4:3 **10:13** [r] S Dt 32:15 [s] Jer 11:10; 13:10 **10:14** [t] Isa 44:17; 57:13 [u] Dt 32:37; Jer 2:28; 11:12; Hab 2:18 **10:15** [v] 1Sa 3:18; 2Sa 10:12; 15:26; Job 1:21; Isa 39:8 **10:16** [w] Jos 24:23; Jer 18:8 [x] Isa 63:9 [y] S Dt 32:36 **10:17** [z] S Ge 31:49; Jdg 11:29 **10:18** [a] Jdg 11:8,9 **11:1** [b] Jdg 12:1; 1Sa 12:11; Heb 11:32 [c] Jdg 6:12 [d] Nu 26:29 [e] S Ge 38:15

[a] 2 Traditionally *judged*; also in verse 3 [b] 4 Or *called the settlements of Jair* [c] 12 Hebrew; some Septuagint manuscripts *Midianites*

9:57 *curse of Jotham.* See v. 20.

10:1 *a man of Issachar, Tola son of Puah.* Tola and Puah bear names of two of the sons of Issachar (Ge 46:13; Nu 26:23; 1Ch 7:1).

10:3 *Jair.* Since Jair came from Gilead (the territory assigned to Manasseh) and since a descendant of Manasseh bore the same name (Nu 32:41; Dt 3:14; 1Ki 4:13), it appears that Jair was a Manassite.

10:4 *thirty sons ... thirty donkeys ... thirty towns.* Evidence of wealth and position. *Havvoth Jair.* See NIV text note.

10:6—12:7 Israel now turned to Jephthah, a social outcast whom they had driven from the land and caused to become an outlaw without an inheritance in Israel. The author notes this to Israel's shame. The account of Jephthah's judgeship balances that of Deborah in the story of the judges (see note on 4:1—5:31; see also Introduction: Literary Features).

10:6 *gods of Aram.* The chief gods were Hadad (Baal), Mot, Anath and Rimmon. *gods of Sidon.* The Sidonians worshiped essentially the same gods as the Canaanites (see notes on 2:11,13). *gods of Moab.* The chief deity of Moab was Chemosh. *gods of the Ammonites.* Molech was the chief Ammonite deity (see 1Ki 11:7) and was sometimes worshiped by the offering of human sacrifice (see Lev 18:21 and note; 20:2–5; 2Ki 23:10 and note). This god is also called Milcom (see NIV text notes on 1Ki 11:5; 2Ki 23:13). Both Molech and Milcom are forms of a Semitic word for "king." *gods of the Philistines.* While the Philistines worshiped most of the Canaanite gods, their most popular deities appear to have been Dagon and Baal-Zebub. The name Dagon is the same as a Hebrew word for "grain," suggesting that he was a vegetation deity. He was worshiped in Babylonia as early as the second millennium B.C. Baal-Zebub was worshiped in Ekron (2Ki 1:2–3,6,16). The name means "lord of the flies," a deliberate change by followers of the Lord (Yahweh) to ridicule and protest the worship of Baal-Zebul ("Baal the Prince"), a name known from ancient Canaanite texts (see Mt 10:25 and note; 12:24 and NIV text note).

10:7 *Philistines.* The account of Philistine oppression is resumed in 13:1.

10:11 *The LORD replied.* See note on 2:1. The Lord rebuked Israel for forgetting that he had delivered them from their oppressors in Canaan (see notes on 2:16–19; 6:8).

10:12 *Amalekites.* See note on Ge 14:7. *Maonites.* See NIV text note; or perhaps the same as the Meunites, who along with the Philistines and Arabs opposed Israel (2Ch 26:7).

10:17 *Mizpah.* Means "watchtower." Several places bore this name. Jephthah's headquarters was a town or fortress in Gilead (11:11) called "Mizpah of Gilead" (11:29). It may have been the same as Ramath Mizpah (Jos 13:26), located about 30 miles east of Beth Shan.

10:18 The Gileadites wanted to resist the Ammonite incursion but lacked the courageous military leadership to press their cause. *people.* Fighting men.

11:1 *his mother was a prostitute.* Therefore Jephthah was a social outcast.

also bore him sons, and when they were
grown up, they drove Jephthah away. "You
are not going to get any inheritance in our
family," they said, "because you are the
son of another woman." 3So Jephthah fled
from his brothers and settled in the land of
Tob,[f] where a group of adventurers[g] gathered around him and followed him.
4Some time later, when the Ammonites[h]
made war on Israel, 5the elders of Gilead
went to get Jephthah from the land of Tob.
6"Come," they said, "be our commander,
so we can fight the Ammonites."
7Jephthah said to them, "Didn't you
hate me and drive me from my father's
house?[i] Why do you come to me now,
when you're in trouble?"
8The elders of Gilead said to him, "Nevertheless, we are turning to you now;
come with us to fight the Ammonites, and
you will be our head[j] over all who live in
Gilead."
9Jephthah answered, "Suppose you take
me back to fight the Ammonites and the
LORD gives them to me—will I really be
your head?"
10The elders of Gilead replied, "The LORD
is our witness;[k] we will certainly do as you
say." 11So Jephthah went with the elders[l] of
Gilead, and the people made him head and
commander over them. And he repeated[m]
all his words before the LORD in Mizpah.[n]
12Then Jephthah sent messengers to the
Ammonite king with the question: "What
do you have against us that you have attacked our country?"
13The king of the Ammonites answered
Jephthah's messengers, "When Israel
came up out of Egypt, they took away my
land from the Arnon[o] to the Jabbok,[p] all
the way to the Jordan. Now give it back
peaceably."
14Jephthah sent back messengers to the
Ammonite king, 15saying:

"This is what Jephthah says: Israel
did not take the land of Moab[q] or the
land of the Ammonites.[r] 16But when
they came up out of Egypt, Israel
went through the desert to the Red
Sea[a][s] and on to Kadesh.[t] 17Then Israel sent messengers[u] to the king of
Edom, saying, 'Give us permission
to go through your country,'[v] but the
king of Edom would not listen. They
sent also to the king of Moab,[w] and he
refused.[x] So Israel stayed at Kadesh.
18"Next they traveled through the
desert, skirted the lands of Edom[y] and
Moab, passed along the eastern side[z]
of the country of Moab, and camped
on the other side of the Arnon.[a] They
did not enter the territory of Moab,
for the Arnon was its border.
19"Then Israel sent messengers[b]
to Sihon king of the Amorites, who
ruled in Heshbon,[c] and said to him,
'Let us pass through your country to
our own place.'[d] 20Sihon, however,
did not trust Israel[b] to pass through
his territory. He mustered all his men
and encamped at Jahaz and fought
with Israel.[e]
21"Then the LORD, the God of Israel,
gave Sihon and all his men into Israel's hands, and they defeated them.
Israel took over all the land of the
Amorites who lived in that country,
22capturing all of it from the Arnon to
the Jabbok and from the desert to the
Jordan.[f]
23"Now since the LORD, the God of
Israel, has driven the Amorites out
before his people Israel, what right
have you to take it over? 24Will you
not take what your god Chemosh[g]
gives you? Likewise, whatever the

11:3 [f] ver 5; 2Sa 10:6,8 [g] S Jdg 9:4 **11:4** [h] S Jdg 10:9 **11:7** [i] S Ge 26:16 **11:8** [j] S Jdg 10:18 **11:10** [k] S Ge 31:50; S Isa 1:2 **11:11** [l] 1Sa 8:4; 2Sa 3:17 [m] Ex 19:9; 1Sa 8:21 [n] S Jos 11:3 **11:13** [o] S Nu 21:13 [p] S Nu 21:24 **11:15** [q] Dt 2:9 [r] Dt 2:19 **11:16** [s] Nu 14:25; S Dt 1:40 [t] S Ge 14:7 **11:17** [u] ver 19; S Ge 32:3; Nu 20:14 [v] S Nu 20:17 [w] Jer 48:1 [x] S Jos 24:9 **11:18** [y] S Nu 20:21 [z] Dt 2:8 [a] S Nu 21:13 **11:19** [b] S ver 17 [c] S Jos 12:2 [d] Nu 21:21-22 **11:20** [e] Nu 21:23 **11:22** [f] Nu 21:21-26; S Dt 2:26 **11:24** [g] S Nu 21:29; S Jos 3:10

[a] 16 Hebrew *Yam Suph*; that is, Sea of Reeds
[b] 20 Or *however, would not make an agreement for Israel*

11:3 *the land of Tob.* The Hebrew name sounds exactly like "the good land," a common way of referring to the promised land in Deuteronomy. The narrator appears to call attention to the irony of this outcast from Israel finding a refuge in "a land of good (things)." The men of Tob were later allied with the Ammonites against David (2Sa 10:6–8). *adventurers.* See note on 9:4.

11:8 *be our head.* In addition to their initial offer of military command during the war with Ammon (v. 6), the Gileadites now also offer to make Jephthah regional head after the fighting is over.

11:11 The proposal of the elders was ratified by the people, a process followed later in the election of Saul (1Sa 11:15), Rehoboam (1Ki 12:1) and Jeroboam (1Ki 12:20). Jephthah's final act here suggests that the agreement reached between himself and the elders had the formal status of a covenant (compare David's covenant with the representatives of the northern tribes, 2Sa 5:3). In any event, Jephthah lays his conditions "before the LORD" as a way of calling on the Lord to enforce the pledge made to him by the elders of Gilead.

11:13 *my land.* When the Israelites had first approached Canaan, this area was ruled by the Amorite king Sihon, who had taken it from the Moabites (Nu 21:29). The Ammonites had since become dominant over Moab and now claimed all previous Moabite territory.

11:14–27 Jephthah responded in accordance with international policies of the time; his letter is a classic example of contemporary international correspondence. It also reflects—and appeals to—the common recognition that the god(s) of a people established and protected their political boundaries and decided all boundary disputes. Jephthah's defense of Israel's claim to the land is threefold: (1) Israel took it from Sihon king of the Amorites, not from the Ammonites (vv. 15–22); (2) the Lord gave the land to Israel (vv. 23–25); (3) Israel had long possessed it (vv. 26–27).

11:16 *Kadesh.* Kadesh Barnea; see note on Nu 20:1.

11:21 *LORD, the God of Israel.* War was viewed not only in military terms but also as a contest between deities (see v. 24; Ex 12:12 and note; Nu 33:4).

11:24 *Chemosh.* The chief deity of the Moabites. At this time either the king of Ammon also ruled Moab, or there was a military confederacy of the two peoples.

LORD our God has given us,[h] we will
possess. 25Are you better than Balak
son of Zippor,[i] king of Moab? Did he
ever quarrel with Israel or fight with
them?[j] 26For three hundred years Israel occupied[k] Heshbon, Aroer,[l] the
surrounding settlements and all the
towns along the Arnon. Why didn't
you retake them during that time?
27I have not wronged you, but you
are doing me wrong by waging war
against me. Let the LORD, the Judge,[a m]
decide[n] the dispute this day between
the Israelites and the Ammonites.[o]"

28The king of Ammon, however, paid no
attention to the message Jephthah sent
him.

29Then the Spirit[p] of the LORD came upon
Jephthah. He crossed Gilead and Manasseh, passed through Mizpah[q] of Gilead,
and from there he advanced against the
Ammonites.[r] 30And Jephthah made a vow[s]
to the LORD: "If you give the Ammonites
into my hands, 31whatever comes out of
the door of my house to meet me when
I return in triumph[t] from the Ammonites
will be the LORD's, and I will sacrifice it as
a burnt offering.[u]"

32Then Jephthah went over to fight the
Ammonites, and the LORD gave them into
his hands. 33He devastated twenty towns
from Aroer to the vicinity of Minnith,[v] as
far as Abel Keramim. Thus Israel subdued
Ammon.

34When Jephthah returned to his home
in Mizpah, who should come out to meet
him but his daughter, dancing[w] to the
sound of tambourines![x] She was an only
child.[y] Except for her he had neither son
nor daughter. 35When he saw her, he tore
his clothes[z] and cried, "Oh! My daughter!
You have made me miserable and wretched, because I have made a vow to the LORD
that I cannot break.[a]"

36"My father," she replied, "you have
given your word to the LORD. Do to me
just as you promised,[b] now that the LORD
has avenged you[c] of your enemies,[d] the
Ammonites. 37But grant me this one request," she said. "Give me two months to
roam the hills and weep with my friends,
because I will never marry."

38"You may go," he said. And he let her
go for two months. She and the girls went
into the hills and wept because she would
never marry. 39After the two months, she
returned to her father and he did to her as
he had vowed. And she was a virgin.

From this comes the Israelite custom
40that each year the young women of Israel go out for four days to commemorate
the daughter of Jephthah the Gileadite.

Jephthah and Ephraim

12 The men of Ephraim called out their
forces, crossed over to Zaphon[e] and
said to Jephthah,[f] "Why did you go to
fight the Ammonites without calling us to
go with you?[g] We're going to burn down
your house over your head."

2Jephthah answered, "I and my people
were engaged in a great struggle with the
Ammonites, and although I called, you
didn't save me out of their hands. 3When I
saw that you wouldn't help, I took my life
in my hands[h] and crossed over to fight the
Ammonites, and the LORD gave me the victory[i] over them. Now why have you come
up today to fight me?"

4Jephthah then called together the men
of Gilead[j] and fought against Ephraim. The
Gileadites struck them down because the
Ephraimites had said, "You Gileadites are
renegades from Ephraim and Manasseh.[k]"
5The Gileadites captured the fords of the
Jordan[l] leading to Ephraim, and whenever

[a] 27 Or *Ruler*

11:24 [h]Dt 2:36
11:25 [i]Nu 22:2
[j]S Jos 24:9
11:26 [k]Nu 21:25
[l]S Nu 32:34;
S Jos 13:9
11:27
[m]S Ge 18:25
[n]S Ge 16:5
[o]2Ch 20:12
11:29
[p]S Jdg 3:10
[q]S Ge 31:49
[r]S Jdg 10:17
11:30
[s]S Ge 28:20;
Nu 30:10;
1Sa 1:11; Pr 31:2
11:31 [t]Ge 28:21
[u]S Ge 8:20;
Lev 1:3;
Jdg 13:16
11:33
[v]Eze 27:17
11:34
[w]S Ex 15:20
[x]S Ge 31:27;
S Ex 15:20
[y]Zec 12:10
11:35
[z]S Nu 14:6
[a]Nu 30:2;
S Dt 23:21;
Ecc 5:2, 4, 5
11:36 [b]Lk 1:38
[c]S Nu 31:3
[d]2Sa 18:19
12:1
[e]S Jos 13:27
[f]S Jdg 11:1
[g]Jdg 8:1
12:3 [h]S Jdg 9:17
[i]S Dt 20:4
12:4 [j]1Ki 17:1
[k]S Ge 46:20;
Isa 9:21; 19:2
12:5 [l]S Jos 2:7

11:25 *Balak.* See Nu 22–24.

11:26 *three hundred years.* For the relevance of this phrase in establishing the time span for Judges see Introduction: Background.

11:27 *Judge.* See 1Sa 24:15. As the divine Judge, the Lord is the final court of appeal. It is significant that in the book of Judges the singular noun "judge" is found only here, where it is used of the Lord, Israel's true Judge.

11:29 *Spirit of the LORD.* See note on 3:10. In the OT the unique empowering of the Spirit was given to individuals primarily to enable them to carry out the special responsibilities God had given them.

11:30 *made a vow.* A common practice among the Israelites (see Ge 28:20; 1Sa 1:11; 2Sa 15:8). Here Jephthah was seeking to assure the outcome of the battle by bargaining for God's help. The precise nature of this vow has been the subject of wide speculation, but v. 31 indicates the promise of a burnt offering and leads to the conclusion that Jephthah probably offered his daughter as a human sacrifice (v. 39). A vow was not to be broken (see Nu 30:2; Dt 23:21–23; see also Ecc 5:4–5).

11:34 *dancing.* It was customary for women to greet armies returning victoriously from battle in this way (see Ex 15:20; 1Sa 18:6).

11:35 *tore his clothes.* A common practice for expressing extreme grief (see Ge 37:34 and note). *a vow to the LORD that I cannot break.* In his determination to secure the position of leadership over his old adversaries, Jephthah had laid their pledge to him "before the LORD" for him to enforce (see v. 11 and note). Now, accordingly, he cannot go back on his own vow (pledge) to the Lord. Thus all his efforts to assure for himself a position of power in Israel by manipulating God backfired. God will not be used!

11:37 *I will never marry.* To be kept from marrying and rearing children was a bitter prospect for an Israelite woman.

11:39 *Israelite custom.* Probably a local custom, since no other mention of it is found in the OT.

12:1 *burn down your house.* The Philistines issued a similar threat to Samson's wife (14:15). See also 20:48.

12:2 *answered.* Again Jephthah tried diplomacy first (see 11:12,14; see also note on 8:1). *I called.* New information on the sequence of events.

a survivor of Ephraim said, "Let me cross
over," the men of Gilead asked him, "Are
you an Ephraimite?" If he replied, "No,"
6they said, "All right, say 'Shibboleth.'" If
he said, "Sibboleth," because he could not
pronounce the word correctly, they seized
him and killed him at the fords of the Jordan. Forty-two thousand Ephraimites were
killed at that time.
7Jephthah led[a] Israel six years. Then
Jephthah the Gileadite died, and was buried in a town in Gilead.

Ibzan, Elon and Abdon

8After him, Ibzan of Bethlehem[m] led Israel. 9He had thirty sons and thirty daughters. He gave his daughters away in marriage to those outside his clan, and for his
sons he brought in thirty young women
as wives from outside his clan. Ibzan led
Israel seven years. 10Then Ibzan died, and
was buried in Bethlehem.
11After him, Elon the Zebulunite led Israel ten years. 12Then Elon died, and was
buried in Aijalon[n] in the land of Zebulun.
13After him, Abdon son of Hillel, from
Pirathon,[o] led Israel. 14He had forty sons
and thirty grandsons,[p] who rode on seventy donkeys.[q] He led Israel eight years.
15Then Abdon son of Hillel died, and was
buried at Pirathon in Ephraim, in the hill
country of the Amalekites.[r]

The Birth of Samson

13 Again the Israelites did evil in the
eyes of the LORD, so the LORD delivered them into the hands of the Philistines[s] for forty years.[t]
2A certain man of Zorah,[u] named Manoah,[v] from the clan of the Danites,[w] had a
wife who was sterile and remained childless.[x] 3The angel of the LORD[y] appeared to
her[z] and said, "You are sterile and childless, but you are going to conceive and
have a son.[a] 4Now see to it that you drink
no wine or other fermented drink[b] and
that you do not eat anything unclean,[c] 5be-
cause you will conceive and give birth to a
son.[d] No razor[e] may be used on his head,
because the boy is to be a Nazirite,[f] set
apart to God from birth, and he will begin[g]
the deliverance of Israel from the hands of
the Philistines."
6Then the woman went to her husband
and told him, "A man of God[h] came to
me. He looked like an angel of God,[i] very
awesome.[j] I didn't ask him where he came
from, and he didn't tell me his name. 7But
he said to me, 'You will conceive and give
birth to a son. Now then, drink no wine[k]
or other fermented drink[l] and do not eat
anything unclean, because the boy will be
a Nazirite of God from birth until the day
of his death.[m]'"

12:8 [m]S Ge 35:19 **12:12** [n]S Jos 10:12 **12:13** [o]ver 15; 2Sa 23:30; 1Ch 11:31; 27:14 **12:14** [p]S Jdg 8:30 [q]S Jdg 5:10 **12:15** [r]Jdg 5:14

13:1 [s]S Jdg 3:31 [t]Jdg 14:4 **13:2** [u]S Jos 15:33 [v]ver 8; Jdg 16:31 [w]S Ge 30:6 [x]S Ge 11:30 **13:3** [y]S Ge 16:7 [z]ver 10 [a]Isa 7:14; Lk 1:13 **13:4** [b]S Lev 10:9 [c]ver 14; Nu 6:2-4; S Lk 1:15 **13:5** [d]S Ge 3:15 [e]1Sa 1:11 [f]S Nu 6:2, 13; Am 2:11, 12 [g]1Sa 7:13 **13:6** [h]ver 8; 1Sa 2:27; 9:6; 1Ki 13:1; 17:18 [i]S Nu 22:22 [j]Ps 66:5 **13:7** [k]Jer 35:6 [l]Lev 10:9 [m]1Sa 1:11, 28

[a] 7 Traditionally *judged*; also in verses 8-14

12:6 *Shibboleth.* Ironically, the word meant "floods" (see, e.g., Ps 69:2,15). Apparently the Israelites east of the Jordan pronounced its initial letter with a strong "sh" sound, while those in Canaan gave it a softer "s" sound. (Peter was similarly betrayed by his accent; see Mt 26:73 and note.)

12:7 *led Israel ... years.* A new formula for closing out the account of a judge (see note on 3:11; see also Introduction: Literary Features).

12:8 *Bethlehem.* Probably the Bethlehem in western Zebulun (see Ge 35:19; 48:7; Jos 19:15).

12:9 *thirty sons and thirty daughters.* See note on 10:4.

12:11 *Elon.* Also the name of a clan in the tribe of Zebulun (Ge 46:14; Nu 26:26).

12:14 *forty sons and thirty grandsons.* A total of 70 (see notes on 8:30; 10:4).

12:15 *hill country of the Amalekites.* See notes on 5:14; 6:3.

13:1—16:31 Samson (from the tribe of Dan), like Ehud (from the tribe of Benjamin), was a loner, whose heroic exploits involved single-handed triumphs over powerful enemies. His story therefore balances that of Ehud (see note on 3:12–30). Significantly, this last of the judges typifies the nation of Israel. Born by special divine provision to a barren woman, consecrated to the Lord from birth and endowed by God's Spirit with unique powers to overcome Israel's enemies, he was forever drawn to Philistine women, which ultimately led to his destruction—just as God's consecrated (by circumcision) and especially empowered (for the conquest of Canaan) people Israel were continually drawn to the gods and ways of the Canaanites to their destruction (see note on Ex 34:15). The story of Samson is the story of Israel in cameo. The author provides a mirror image of Israel in the days of the judges—and of God's unfailing mercies to his wayward people whom he would not abandon.

13:1–25 The account of Samson's birth helps the author to point out the parallels between Samson and Israel that he wanted his readers to see.

13:1 *did evil in the eyes of the LORD.* See note on 3:7.

13:2 *Zorah.* A town first assigned to Judah (Jos 15:33), but later given to Dan (Jos 19:41). It became the point of departure for the Danite migration northward (see 18:2,8,11 and note on 18:1). *Danites.* See 1:34 and note. *sterile ... childless.* The same condition, before divine intervention, as that of Sarah, the mother of Isaac (Ge 11:30; 16:1), and Rebekah, the mother of Jacob (Ge 25:21). Cf. also Hannah, the mother of Samuel (1Sa 1:2), and Elizabeth, the mother of John the Baptist (Lk 1:7).

13:3 *angel of the LORD.* See note on Ge 16:7. *you are going to ... have a son.* See the announcement of Isaac's birth (Ge 18:10). Cf. the announcements of the births of Ishmael (Ge 16:11), Immanuel (Isa 7:14), John the Baptist (Lk 1:13) and Jesus (Lk 1:31).

13:5 *Nazirite.* From a Hebrew word meaning "separated" or "dedicated." For the stipulations of this vow see Nu 6:1–21 and notes. Samson's Nazirite-like consecration was not voluntary—like Israel, he was consecrated to special service by God himself—and his consecration applied to his whole lifetime (v. 7). The same was true of Samuel (1Sa 1:11) and John the Baptist (Lk 1:15). *begin the deliverance ... from ... the Philistines.* The deliverance was continued in the time of Samuel (1Sa 7:10–14) and completed under David (2Sa 5:17–25; 8:1).

13:6 *man of God.* An expression often used of prophets (see Dt 33:1; 1Sa 2:27; 9:6–10; 1Ki 12:22), though it is clear from vv. 3,21 that this messenger was the angel of the Lord.

8Then Manoah[n] prayed to the LORD:
"O Lord, I beg you, let the man of God[o]
you sent to us come again to teach us how
to bring up the boy who is to be born."
9God heard Manoah, and the angel
of God came again to the woman while
she was out in the field; but her husband
Manoah was not with her. 10The woman
hurried to tell her husband, "He's here!
The man who appeared to me[p] the other
day!"
11Manoah got up and followed his wife.
When he came to the man, he said, "Are
you the one who talked to my wife?"
"I am," he said.
12So Manoah asked him, "When your
words are fulfilled, what is to be the rule
for the boy's life and work?"
13The angel of the LORD answered, "Your
wife must do all that I have told her. 14She
must not eat anything that comes from the
grapevine, nor drink any wine or other fermented drink[q] nor eat anything unclean.[r]
She must do everything I have commanded her."
15Manoah said to the angel of the LORD,
"We would like you to stay until we prepare a young goat[s] for you."
16The angel of the LORD replied, "Even
though you detain me, I will not eat any
of your food. But if you prepare a burnt
offering,[t] offer it to the LORD." (Manoah
did not realize[u] that it was the angel of
the LORD.)
17Then Manoah inquired of the angel of
the LORD, "What is your name,[v] so that we
may honor you when your word comes
true?"
18He replied, "Why do you ask my
name?[w] It is beyond understanding.[a]"
19Then Manoah took a young goat, together with the grain offering, and sacrificed it
on a rock[x] to the LORD. And the LORD did
an amazing thing while Manoah and his
wife watched: 20As the flame[y] blazed up
from the altar toward heaven, the angel
of the LORD ascended in the flame. Seeing
this, Manoah and his wife fell with their
faces to the ground.[z] 21When the angel of
the LORD did not show himself again to
Manoah and his wife, Manoah realized[a]
that it was the angel of the LORD.
22"We are doomed[b] to die!" he said to
his wife. "We have seen[c] God!"
23But his wife answered, "If the LORD
had meant to kill us, he would not have
accepted a burnt offering and grain offering from our hands, nor shown us all
these things or now told us this."[d]
24The woman gave birth to a boy and
named him Samson.[e] He grew[f] and the
LORD blessed him,[g] 25and the Spirit of the
LORD began to stir[h] him while he was in
Mahaneh Dan,[i] between Zorah and Eshtaol.

Samson's Marriage

14 Samson[j] went down to Timnah[k] and
saw there a young Philistine woman. 2When he returned, he said to his father and mother, "I have seen a Philistine
woman in Timnah; now get her for me as
my wife."[l]
3His father and mother replied, "Isn't
there an acceptable woman among your
relatives or among all our people?[m] Must
you go to the uncircumcised[n] Philistines
to get a wife?[o]"

13:8 [n]S ver 2 [o]S ver 6 **13:10** [p]ver 3 **13:14** [q]Lev 10:9 [r]S ver 4 **13:15** [s]Jdg 6:19 **13:16** [t]S Jdg 11:31 [u]S Jdg 6:22 **13:17** [v]S Ge 32:29 **13:18** [w]S Ge 32:29 **13:19** [x]Jdg 6:20 **13:20** [y]S Lev 9:24 [z]S Ge 17:3 **13:21** [a]S Jdg 6:22 **13:22** [b]S Nu 17:12; S Dt 5:26 [c]S Ge 16:13; S Ex 3:6; S 24:10; S Jdg 6:22 **13:23** [d]Ps 25:14 **13:24** [e]Jdg 14:1; 15:1; 16:1; Heb 11:32 [f]1Sa 2:21,26; 3:19 [g]Lk 1:80 **13:25** [h]S Jdg 3:10 [i]Jdg 18:12 **14:1** [j]S Jdg 13:24 [k]S Ge 38:12 **14:2** [l]S Ge 21:21 **14:3** [m]S Ge 24:4 [n]S Ge 34:14; S 1Sa 14:6 [o]S Ex 34:16

[a] 18 Or *is wonderful*

13:8 *teach us.* Not the usual parental concern, but a special concern based on the boy's special calling.

13:12 A declaration of faith. To Manoah it was not a matter of whether these events would occur, but of when (v. 17).

13:15 *stay until we prepare a young goat.* Such food was considered a special delicacy. Hospitality of this kind was common in the ancient Near East (see 6:18–19; Ge 18:1–8).

13:17 *What is your name . . . ?* A messenger's identity was considered very important. *when your word comes true.* Fulfilled prophecy was a sign of the authenticity of a prophet (see Dt 13:1–5 and note; 18:21–22; 1Sa 9:6).

13:18 *beyond understanding.* See NIV text note. In Isa 9:6 the Hebrew for this phrase (translated "Wonderful") applies to One who would come as "Mighty God."

13:22 *doomed to die.* See 6:23 and notes on Ge 16:13; 32:30.

13:24 *Samson.* The name is derived from a Hebrew word meaning "sun" or "brightness," and is used here as an expression of joy over the birth of the child. *He grew and the LORD blessed him.* Cf. 1Sa 2:26 (Samuel) and Lk 2:52 (Jesus).

13:25 *began to stir him.* See notes on 3:10; 11:29. *Mahaneh Dan.* Means "Dan's camp" (see NIV text note on 18:12).

14:1—16:31 The account of Samson's extraordinary exploits and flawed character has a literary structure of special note. His first encounter with a Philistine woman (14:1–20) and its aftermath (15:1–8) are closely balanced by the account of his last encounter with a Philistine woman (16:4–22) and its aftermath (16:23–31). And what happens in his first encounter foreshadows what happens in his final encounter. Between these two major cycles are three episodes: (1) Judah's attempt to appease the Philistines by binding Samson over to them (15:9–17), (2) God's rescue of Samson from life-threatening dehydration (15:18–19) and (3) Samson's escape from Gaza, the gates of which he deposits on a hill overlooking Hebron, Judah's main city (16:1–3). The author reminds his readers in the brief centerpiece (15:18–19) that mighty Samson shared in the universal vulnerabilities of human life.

14:1 *Timnah.* Identified as Tell Batash in the Sorek Valley, west of Beth Shemesh (see map, p. 331). Archaeologists have uncovered the Philistine layer of the town. *young Philistine woman.* The disappointment of Samson's parents (v. 3; cf. Esau, Ge 26:35; 27:46; 28:1) is understandable in light of the prohibition against marriage with the pagan peoples of Canaan (see Ex 34:11,16; Dt 7:1–6 and note; see also Jdg 3:5–6 and note on 3:6).

14:2 *get her for me.* See Ge 21:21 and note; 34:4. As the head of the family, the father exercised authority in all matters, often including the choice of wives for his sons (see 12:9; Ge 24:3–9; Ne 10:30).

14:3 *uncircumcised.* A term of scorn, referring to those not bound by covenant to the Lord, used especially of the Philis-

But Samson said to his father, "Get her for me. She's the right one for me." 4(His parents did not know that this was from the LORD,[p] who was seeking an occasion to confront the Philistines;[q] for at that time they were ruling over Israel.)[r] 5Samson went down to Timnah together with his father and mother. As they approached the vineyards of Timnah, suddenly a young lion came roaring toward him. 6The Spirit of the LORD came upon him in power[s] so that he tore the lion apart[t] with his bare hands as he might have torn a young goat. But he told neither his father nor his mother what he had done. 7Then he went down and talked with the woman, and he liked her.

8Some time later, when he went back to marry her, he turned aside to look at the lion's carcass. In it was a swarm of bees and some honey, 9which he scooped out with his hands and ate as he went along. When he rejoined his parents, he gave them some, and they too ate it. But he did not tell them that he had taken the honey from the lion's carcass.

10Now his father went down to see the woman. And Samson made a feast[u] there, as was customary for bridegrooms. 11When he appeared, he was given thirty companions.

12"Let me tell you a riddle,[v]" Samson said to them. "If you can give me the answer within the seven days of the feast,[w] I will give you thirty linen garments and thirty sets of clothes.[x] 13If you can't tell me the answer, you must give me thirty linen garments and thirty sets of clothes."

"Tell us your riddle," they said. "Let's hear it."

14He replied,

"Out of the eater, something to eat;
out of the strong, something sweet."[y]

For three days they could not give the answer.

15On the fourth[a] day, they said to Samson's wife, "Coax[z] your husband into explaining the riddle for us, or we will burn you and your father's household to death.[a] Did you invite us here to rob us?"

16Then Samson's wife threw herself on him, sobbing, "You hate me! You don't really love me.[b] You've given my people a riddle, but you haven't told me the answer."

"I haven't even explained it to my father or mother," he replied, "so why should I explain it to you?" 17She cried the whole seven days[c] of the feast. So on the seventh day he finally told her, because she continued to press him. She in turn explained the riddle to her people.

18Before sunset on the seventh day the men of the town said to him,

"What is sweeter than honey?
What is stronger than a lion?"[d]

Samson said to them,

"If you had not plowed with my heifer,
you would not have solved my riddle."

[a] 15 Some Septuagint manuscripts and Syriac; Hebrew *seventh*

14:4 [p]S Dt 2:30 [q]S Jos 11:20 [r]Jdg 13:1; 15:11 **14:6** [s]S Jdg 3:10 [t]1Sa 17:35 **14:10** [u]S Ge 29:22 **14:12** [v]S Nu 12:8; Eze 17:2; 20:49; 24:3; Hos 12:10 [w]Ge 29:27 [x]S Ge 45:22; S 2Ki 5:5 **14:14** [y]ver 18 **14:15** [z]Jdg 16:5; Ecc 7:26 [a]S Lev 20:14; Jdg 15:6 **14:16** [b]Jdg 16:15 **14:17** [c]Est 1:5 **14:18** [d]ver 14

tines (see note on 1Sa 14:6). *right one for me.* The Hebrew for this expression ("is right in my eyes") is similar to that translated "did as he saw fit" (lit. "did what was right in his own eyes") in 17:6; 21:25. The author anticipates this theme, which recurs in chs. 17–21.

14:4 *this was from the LORD.* See Jos 11:20; 1Ki 12:15 and note. The Lord uses even sinful human weaknesses to accomplish his purposes and bring praise to his name (see Ge 45:8; 50:20 and note; 2Ch 25:20; Ac 2:23 and note; 4:28 and note; Ro 8:28–29).

14:5 *vineyards of Timnah.* The Sorek Valley (in which Timnah was located) and its surrounding areas were noted for their luxuriant vineyards. For anyone under Nazirite vows, vineyards could be a powerful source of temptation (see Nu 6:1–4). *a young lion came roaring toward him.* The author's language anticipates his later "the Philistines came toward him shouting" (15:14). This helps the reader to catch the author's intention to use the lion out of the Philistine vineyards as a symbol of the Philistines themselves, the very enemies of Israel against whom Samson was called to be God's champion (cf. 1Sa 17 for the roles of Goliath and David in a later confrontation between the Philistines and Israel). *young lion.* Lions were once common in southern Canaan (see 1Sa 17:34 and note; 2Sa 23:20; 1Ki 13:24; 20:36).

14:6 *Spirit ... came upon him.* See 13:25; 14:19; 15:14; see also notes on 3:10; 11:29. *tore the lion apart.* With such unique power God's Spirit endowed Samson to overcome the Philistines. Later, David (1Sa 17:34–37) and Benaiah (2Sa 23:20) performed similar feats.

14:8–9 *carcass ... honey, which he scooped out with his hands.* Samson thus violated his Nazirite vows (Nu 6:6–7) in order to delight himself with something sweet.

14:10 *feast.* Such a special feast was common in the ancient Near East (see Ge 29:22 and note) and here lasted seven days (v. 12; see Ge 29:27). Since it would have included drinking wine, Samson may have violated his Nazirite vow (see 13:4,7).

14:11 *companions.* These are the "guests of the bridegroom" (cf. Mt 9:15). They were probably charged with protecting the wedding party against marauders.

14:12 *riddle.* The use of riddles at feasts and special occasions was popular in the ancient world. *sets of clothes.* Mentioned, together with silver, as gifts of great value in Ge 45:22; 2Ki 5:22 (see also Zec 14:14).

14:14 *the eater ... the strong.* Samson refers to the lion he had killed, from the carcass of which he had taken honey to eat. He confidently uses his riddle as his opening shot in a battle of wits with the Philistines. The author, however, uses Samson's riddle to chillingly foreshadow Samson's sorry end. He has just shown us Samson "the eater" (of honey) and Samson "the strong" (killer of a powerful lion). In the end, he shows us blinded Samson grinding grain in prison for his captors (16:21: out of the eater the Philistines get something to eat) and entertaining his captors with feats of strength (16:25: out of the strong the Philistines get something sweet).

14:16 *don't really love me.* Delilah used the same tactics (16:15).

14:18 *sweeter than honey ... stronger than a lion.* The Philistines answer riddle with riddle. And the answer to

19Then the Spirit of the LORD came upon
him in power.[e] He went down to Ashkelon,[f] struck down thirty of their men,
stripped them of their belongings and gave
their clothes to those who had explained
the riddle. Burning with anger,[g] he went
up to his father's house. 20And Samson's
wife was given to the friend[h] who had attended him at his wedding.

Samson's Vengeance on the Philistines

15 Later on, at the time of wheat harvest,[i] Samson[j] took a young goat[k]
and went to visit his wife. He said, "I'm
going to my wife's room."[l] But her father
would not let him go in.
2"I was so sure you thoroughly hated her," he said, "that I gave her to your
friend.[m] Isn't her younger sister more attractive? Take her instead."
3Samson said to them, "This time I have
a right to get even with the Philistines; I
will really harm them." 4So he went out
and caught three hundred foxes[n] and tied
them tail to tail in pairs. He then fastened
a torch[o] to every pair of tails, 5lit the torches[p] and let the foxes loose in the standing
grain of the Philistines. He burned up the
shocks[q] and standing grain, together with
the vineyards and olive groves.
6When the Philistines asked, "Who did
this?" they were told, "Samson, the Tim-
nite's son-in-law, because his wife was
given to his friend.[r]"
So the Philistines went up and burned
her[s] and her father to death.[t] 7Samson said
to them, "Since you've acted like this, I
won't stop until I get my revenge on you."
8He attacked them viciously and slaughtered many of them. Then he went down
and stayed in a cave in the rock[u] of Etam.[v]
9The Philistines went up and camped
in Judah, spreading out near Lehi.[w] 10The
men of Judah asked, "Why have you come
to fight us?"
"We have come to take Samson prisoner," they answered, "to do to him as he
did to us."
11Then three thousand men from Judah
went down to the cave in the rock of Etam
and said to Samson, "Don't you realize
that the Philistines are rulers over us?[x]
What have you done to us?"
He answered, "I merely did to them
what they did to me."
12They said to him, "We've come to tie
you up and hand you over to the Philistines."
Samson said, "Swear to me[y] that you
won't kill me yourselves."
13"Agreed," they answered. "We will
only tie you up and hand you over to
them. We will not kill you." So they bound
him with two new ropes[z] and led him up
from the rock. 14As he approached Lehi,[a]
the Philistines came toward him shouting. The Spirit of the LORD came upon
him in power.[b] The ropes on his arms became like charred flax,[c] and the bindings
dropped from his hands. 15Finding a fresh
jawbone of a donkey, he grabbed it and
struck down a thousand men.[d]

14:19 [e]S Jdg 3:10 [f]S Jos 13:3 [g]1Sa 11:6 **14:20** [h]Jdg 15:2,6; Jn 3:29 **15:1** [i]S Ge 30:14 [j]S Jdg 13:24 [k]S Ge 38:17 [l]Ge 29:21 **15:2** [m]S Jdg 14:20 **15:4** [n]SS 2:15 [o]S Ge 15:17 **15:5** [p]S Ge 15:17 [q]Ex 22:6; 2Sa 14:30-31 **15:6** [r]S Jdg 14:20 [s]S Ge 38:24 [t]S Jdg 14:15 **15:8** [u]Isa 2:21 [v]ver 11 **15:9** [w]ver 14,17,19 **15:11** [x]S Jdg 14:4; Ps 106:40-42 **15:12** [y]S Ge 47:31 **15:13** [z]Jdg 16:11,12 **15:14** [a]S ver 9 [b]S Jdg 3:10 [c]S Jos 2:6 **15:15** [d]S Lev 26:8

their riddle exposes Samson's great weakness. The answer to their riddle is "love," or at least "sexual passion," the very thing that kept drawing Samson to the Philistines — and would ultimately lead to his downfall. Moreover, his downfall is already foreshadowed here where a Philistine girl, the object of Samson's passion, defeats him with her feminine beauty and her feminine wiles. *my heifer.* Samson's wife (see v. 15). Since heifers were not used for plowing, Samson is accusing them of unfairness.

14:19 *Spirit ... came upon him.* See note on 3:10. God's purposes for Samson included humbling the Philistines. *Ashkelon.* One of the five principal cities of the Philistines (see map, p. 331).

14:20 *friend.* See 15:2; probably the young man who had attended Samson (cf. Jn 3:29 and note), in all likelihood one of his 30 companions (v. 11).

15:1 *time of wheat harvest.* Near the end of May or the beginning of June (see note on Ru 1:22). *young goat.* Such a gift was customary, as with Judah and Tamar (Ge 38:17).

15:2 *younger sister.* Samson's father-in-law felt he had to make a counterproposal because he had received the bride-price from Samson. Similar marital transactions were made by Laban and Jacob (Ge 29:16 – 28) and Saul and David (1Sa 18:19 – 21).

15:5 *burned up.* The wheat harvest (v. 1) comes at the end of a long dry season, thus making the fields extremely vulnerable to fire. Samson's burning of the grainfields foreshadows his destruction of the temple of Dagon (whose name means "grain") in his last attack on the Philistines (16:23 – 30; see also note on 10:6).

15:7 *revenge.* A common feature of life in the ancient Near East. Six cities of refuge were designated by the Lord to prevent endless killings (see Jos 20:1 – 9 and note). Samson's act of revenge against the Philistines for murdering the one who had pleased his eyes (see note on 14:3; see also Eze 24:16 and note) foreshadows his act of revenge against them for gouging out his eyes (16:28).

15:9 – 17 See note on 14:1 — 16:31.

15:9 *Lehi.* Means "jawbone." This locality probably did not receive the name until after the events described here; the author uses the name in anticipation of those events — a common device in Hebrew narrative. The exact site of Lehi is not known.

15:11 *three thousand men from Judah.* The only time a force from Judah is explicitly mentioned in connection with any of the judges (but see note on 1:2). The men of Judah were well aware of Samson's capabilities, and even with a large force they did not attempt to tie him up without his consent (vv. 12 – 13). *Philistines are rulers over us.* Much of Judah was under Philistine rule, and the tribe was apparently content to accept it. They mustered a force, not to support Samson, but to capture him for the Philistines. Contrast the role assigned Judah in 1:2 and 20:18.

15:14 *shouting.* A battle cry (see 1Sa 17:52). They came shouting against Samson as the lion had come roaring against him (see 14:5 and note). *Spirit of the LORD.* See notes on 3:10; 11:29; 14:19.

15:15 *struck down a thousand men.* Cf. the exploits of Shamgar, who struck down 600 Philistines with an oxgoad (see 3:16,31 and notes).

16Then Samson said,

"With a donkey's jawbone
I have made donkeys of them.[a][e]
With a donkey's jawbone
I have killed a thousand men."

17When he finished speaking, he threw
away the jawbone; and the place was
called Ramath Lehi.[b][f]
18Because he was very thirsty, he cried
out to the LORD,[g] "You have given your
servant this great victory.[h] Must I now die
of thirst and fall into the hands of the uncircumcised?" 19Then God opened up the
hollow place in Lehi, and water came out
of it. When Samson drank, his strength returned and he revived.[i] So the spring[j] was
called En Hakkore,[c] and it is still there in
Lehi.
20Samson led[d] Israel for twenty years[k] in
the days of the Philistines.

Samson and Delilah

16 One day Samson[l] went to Gaza,[m]
where he saw a prostitute.[n] He went
in to spend the night with her. 2The people
of Gaza were told, "Samson is here!" So
they surrounded the place and lay in wait
for him all night at the city gate.[o] They
made no move during the night, saying,
"At dawn[p] we'll kill him."
3But Samson lay there only until the
middle of the night. Then he got up and
took hold of the doors of the city gate, together with the two posts, and tore them
loose, bar and all. He lifted them to his
shoulders and carried them to the top of
the hill that faces Hebron.[q]
4Some time later, he fell in love[r] with a
woman in the Valley of Sorek whose name
was Delilah.[s] 5The rulers of the Philistines[t]
went to her and said, "See if you can lure[u]
him into showing you the secret of his
great strength[v] and how we can overpower him so we may tie him up and subdue
him. Each one of us will give you eleven
hundred shekels[e] of silver."[w]
6So Delilah[x] said to Samson, "Tell me
the secret of your great strength and how
you can be tied up and subdued."
7Samson answered her, "If anyone ties
me with seven fresh thongs[f] that have not
been dried, I'll become as weak as any
other man."
8Then the rulers of the Philistines
brought her seven fresh thongs that had
not been dried, and she tied him with
them. 9With men hidden in the room,[y] she
called to him, "Samson, the Philistines are
upon you!"[z] But he snapped the thongs as
easily as a piece of string snaps when it
comes close to a flame. So the secret of his
strength was not discovered.
10Then Delilah said to Samson, "You
have made a fool of me;[a] you lied to me.
Come now, tell me how you can be tied."
11He said, "If anyone ties me securely
with new ropes[b] that have never been used,
I'll become as weak as any other man."
12So Delilah took new ropes and tied
him with them. Then, with men hidden
in the room, she called to him, "Samson,
the Philistines are upon you!"[c] But he
snapped the ropes off his arms as if they
were threads.
13Delilah then said to Samson, "Until
now, you have been making a fool of me
and lying to me. Tell me how you can be
tied."

15:16 [e] Jer 22:19 **15:17** [f] S ver 9 **15:18** [g] Jdg 16:28 [h] S Dt 20:4 **15:19** [i] Ge 45:27; 1Sa 30:12; Isa 40:29 [j] S Ex 17:6 **15:20** [k] Jdg 16:31 **16:1** [l] S Jdg 13:24 [m] S Ge 10:19 [n] S Ge 38:15 **16:2** [o] S Jos 2:5 [p] 1Sa 19:11 **16:3** [q] S Jos 10:36 **16:4** [r] S Ge 24:67; S 34:3 [s] ver 6 **16:5** [t] S Jos 13:3 [u] S Ex 10:7; S Jdg 14:15 [v] ver 6, 15 [w] ver 18 **16:6** [x] ver 4 **16:9** [y] ver 12 [z] ver 14 **16:10** [a] ver 13 **16:11** [b] S Jdg 15:13 **16:12** [c] ver 14

[a] 16 Or *made a heap or two*; the Hebrew for *donkey* sounds like the Hebrew for *heap.* [b] 17 *Ramath Lehi* means *jawbone hill.* [c] 19 *En Hakkore* means *caller's spring.* [d] 20 Traditionally *judged* [e] 5 That is, about 28 pounds (about 13 kilograms) [f] 7 Or *bowstrings*; also in verses 8 and 9

15:18–19 See note on 14:1—16:31.
15:18 *Must I now die of thirst . . . ?* Mighty Samson was, after all, only a mortal man.
15:19 *water came out of it.* God provided for Samson as he had for Israel in the desert. See Ex 17:1–7 (Massah and Meribah); Nu 20:2–13 (Meribah).
15:20 *led Israel . . . years.* See note on 12:7. *twenty years.* Round numbers are frequently used in Judges (see Introduction: Background).
16:1–3 See note on 14:1—16:31.
16:1 *Gaza.* An important Philistine seaport on the Mediterranean coast of southwest Canaan. *prostitute.* While Samson certainly possessed physical strength, he lacked moral strength, which ultimately led to his ruin.
16:2 *dawn.* By that time they expected Samson to be exhausted and sleeping soundly.
16:3 *bar.* Probably made of bronze (1Ki 4:13) or iron (Ps 107:16; Isa 45:2). *faces Hebron.* That is, in the direction of Hebron, which was 38 miles away in the hill country. Since Hebron was the chief city of Judah, this must be seen as Samson's response to what the men of Judah had done to him (see 15:11–13).
16:4–31 See note on 14:1—16:31.
16:5 *rulers of the Philistines.* See note on 3:3. *subdue him.* The Philistines were not interested in killing him quickly; they sought revenge by a prolonged period of torture. *eleven hundred shekels.* An extraordinarily generous payment in light of 17:10 (see note there). (The total amount paid by the five Philistines would have been equivalent to the price of 275 slaves, at the rate offered for Joseph centuries earlier; see Ge 37:28.) Micah stole a similar amount of silver from his mother (17:2). *shekels.* See note on Ge 20:16.
16:7 *seven fresh thongs.* The number seven had special significance to the ancients, symbolizing completeness or fullness. Note that Samson's hair was divided into seven braids (v. 13).
16:11 *new ropes.* The Philistines apparently did not know that this method had already been tried and had failed (15:13–14).
16:13 Out of disdain, Samson arrogantly played with his Philistine adversaries. *tighten it with the pin.* Probably from a weaver's shuttle. The details of the account suggest that the loom in question was the vertical type with a crossbeam from which warp threads were suspended. Samson's long hair was woven into the warp and beaten up into the web with the pin, thus forming a tight fabric.

He replied, "If you weave the seven
braids of my head into the fabric ⌞on the
loom⌟ and tighten it with the pin, I'll become as weak as any other man." So while
he was sleeping, Delilah took the seven
braids of his head, wove them into the
fabric 14 and[a] tightened it with the pin.

Again she called to him, "Samson, the
Philistines are upon you!"[d] He awoke from
his sleep and pulled up the pin and the
loom, with the fabric.

15 Then she said to him, "How can you
say, 'I love you,'[e] when you won't confide
in me? This is the third time[f] you have
made a fool of me and haven't told me
the secret of your great strength.[g]" 16 With
such nagging she prodded him day after
day until he was tired to death.

17 So he told her everything.[h] "No razor
has ever been used on my head," he said,
"because I have been a Nazirite[i] set apart
to God since birth. If my head were shaved,
my strength would leave me, and I would
become as weak as any other man."

18 When Delilah saw that he had told her
everything, she sent word to the rulers of
the Philistines[j], "Come back once more; he
has told me everything." So the rulers of
the Philistines returned with the silver in
their hands.[k] 19 Having put him to sleep on
her lap, she called a man to shave off the
seven braids of his hair, and so began to
subdue him.[b] And his strength left him.[l]

20 Then she called, "Samson, the Philistines are upon you!"[m]

He awoke from his sleep and thought,
"I'll go out as before and shake myself
free." But he did not know that the LORD
had left him.[n]

21 Then the Philistines[o] seized him,
gouged out his eyes[p] and took him down
to Gaza.[q] Binding him with bronze shackles, they set him to grinding[r] in the prison.
22 But the hair on his head began to grow
again after it had been shaved.

The Death of Samson

23 Now the rulers of the Philistines assembled to offer a great sacrifice to Dagon[s]
their god and to celebrate, saying, "Our
god has delivered Samson, our enemy,
into our hands."

24 When the people saw him, they
praised their god,[t] saying,

"Our god has delivered our enemy
into our hands,[u]
the one who laid waste our land
and multiplied our slain."

25 While they were in high spirits,[v] they
shouted, "Bring out Samson to entertain
us." So they called Samson out of the prison, and he performed for them.

When they stood him among the pillars, 26 Samson said to the servant who
held his hand, "Put me where I can feel
the pillars that support the temple, so that
I may lean against them." 27 Now the temple was crowded with men and women;
all the rulers of the Philistines were there,
and on the roof[w] were about three thousand men and women watching Samson
perform. 28 Then Samson prayed to the
LORD,[x] "O Sovereign LORD, remember me.
O God, please strengthen me just once
more, and let me with one blow get revenge[y] on the Philistines for my two
eyes." 29 Then Samson reached toward the
two central pillars on which the temple
stood. Bracing himself against them, his
right hand on the one and his left hand on
the other, 30 Samson said, "Let me die with
the Philistines!" Then he pushed with all
his might, and down came the temple on
the rulers and all the people in it. Thus
he killed many more when he died than
while he lived.

16:14 [d] ver 9,20 **16:15** [e] Jdg 14:16 [f] Nu 24:10 [g] S ver 5 **16:17** [h] ver 18; Mic 7:5 [i] S Nu 6:2 **16:18** [j] S Jos 13:3; 1Sa 5:8 [k] ver 5 **16:19** [l] Pr 7:26-27 **16:20** [m] S ver 14 [n] Nu 14:42; Jos 7:12; 1Sa 16:14; 18:12; 28:15 **16:21** [o] Jer 47:1 [p] S Nu 16:14 [q] S Ge 10:19 [r] Job 31:10; Isa 47:2 **16:23** [s] 1Sa 5:2; 1Ch 10:10 **16:24** [t] Da 5:4 [u] 1Sa 31:9; 1Ch 10:9 **16:25** [v] Jdg 9:27; 19:6,9,22; Ru 3:7; Est 1:10 **16:27** [w] S Jos 2:8 **16:28** [x] Jdg 15:18 [y] Jer 15:15

[a] *13,14* Some Septuagint manuscripts; Hebrew *"I can, if you weave the seven braids of my head into the fabric ⌞on the loom⌟." 14So she* [b] *19* Hebrew; some Septuagint manuscripts *and he began to weaken*

16:19–20 *his strength left him ... the LORD had left him.* The source of Samson's strength was ultimately God himself.

16:20 *he did not know.* One of the most tragic statements in the OT. Samson was unaware that he had betrayed his calling. He had permitted a Philistine woman to rob him of the sign of his special consecration to the Lord. The Lord's champion lay asleep and helpless in the arms of his paramour.

16:21 *gouged out his eyes.* Brutal treatment of prisoners of war to humiliate and incapacitate them was common (see 1Sa 11:2 and note; 2Ki 25:7; see also note on Jdg 1:6). *to Gaza.* In shame and weakness, Samson was led to Gaza, the place where he had displayed great strength (vv. 1–3). *set him to grinding.* See notes on 9:53; 14:14.

16:22 *hair ... began to grow again.* The author hints at the great truth that shines through the Samson story and would soon receive its final confirmation for Samson, namely, that God had not and would not abandon his flawed servant—or his flawed people Israel.

16:23 *Dagon.* See notes on 10:6; 15:5. *Our god has delivered.* It was common to attribute a victory to the national deities.

16:25 *to entertain us.* See note on 14:14.

16:27 *on the roof.* The temple complex probably surrounded an open court and had a flat roof where a large number of people had gathered to get a glimpse of the fallen champion.

16:28 *revenge ... for my two eyes.* See note on 15:7.

16:30 *pushed.* Samson pushed the wooden pillars from their stone bases. Archaeologists have discovered a Philistine temple at Tell Qasile with a pair of closely spaced pillar bases (see archaeology note in map, p. 331). *killed many more.* Samson previously had slain well over 1,000 people (see 15:15; see also 14:19; 15:8). Samson's final exploit was a mighty demonstration that the Philistine celebration of their god's victory over the Lord's champion was premature. *when he died.* If the Nazirite vow was violated and the uncut hair marking special dedication to God had become "defiled," that hair had to be cut off and the period of special consecration started all over again. The Nazirite "must dedicate himself

[31]Then his brothers and his father's whole family went down to get him. They brought him back and buried him between Zorah and Eshtaol in the tomb of Manoah[z] his father. He had led[a][a] Israel twenty years.[b]

Micah's Idols

17 Now a man named Micah[c] from the hill country of Ephraim [2]said to his mother, "The eleven hundred shekels[b] of silver that were taken from you and about which I heard you utter a curse—I have that silver with me; I took it."

Then his mother said, "The LORD bless you,[d] my son!"

[3]When he returned the eleven hundred shekels of silver to his mother, she said, "I solemnly consecrate my silver to the LORD for my son to make a carved image and a cast idol.[e] I will give it back to you."

[4]So he returned the silver to his mother, and she took two hundred shekels[c] of silver and gave them to a silversmith, who made them into the image and the idol.[f] And they were put in Micah's house.

[5]Now this man Micah had a shrine,[g] and he made an ephod[h] and some idols[i] and installed[j] one of his sons as his priest.[k] [6]In those days Israel had no king;[l] everyone did as he saw fit.[m]

[7]A young Levite[n] from Bethlehem in Judah,[o] who had been living within the clan of Judah, [8]left that town in search of some other place to stay. On his way[d] he came to Micah's house in the hill country of Ephraim.

[9]Micah asked him, "Where are you from?"

"I'm a Levite from Bethlehem in Judah,[p]" he said, "and I'm looking for a place to stay."

[10]Then Micah said to him, "Live with me and be my father[q] and priest,[r] and I'll give you ten shekels[e] of silver a year, your clothes and your food." [11]So the Levite agreed to live with him, and the young man was to him like one of his sons. [12]Then Micah installed[s] the Levite, and the young man became his priest[t] and lived in his house. [13]And Micah said, "Now I know that the LORD will be good to me, since this Levite has become my priest."[u]

16:31 [z]S Jdg 13:2 [a]Ru 1:1; 1Sa 4:18; 7:6 [b]Jdg 15:20
17:1 [c]Jdg 18:2, 13
17:2 [d]Ru 2:20; 3:10; 1Sa 15:13; 23:21; 2Sa 2:5
17:3 [e]S Ex 20:4
17:4 [f]S Ex 32:4; S Isa 17:8
17:5 [g]Isa 44:13; Eze 8:10 [h]S Jdg 8:27 [i]S Ge 31:19 [j]S Nu 16:10 [k]S Ex 29:9
17:6 [l]Jdg 18:1; 19:1; 21:25 [m]S Dt 12:8
17:7 [n]Jdg 18:3 [o]S Ge 35:19; Mt 2:1
17:9 [p]Ru 1:1
17:10 [q]S Ge 45:8 [r]Jdg 18:19
17:12 [s]S Nu 16:10 [t]Jdg 18:4
17:13 [u]Nu 18:7

[a] *31* Traditionally *judged* [b] *2* That is, about 28 pounds (about 13 kilograms) [c] *4* That is, about 5 pounds (about 2.3 kilograms) [d] *8* Or *To carry on his profession* [e] *10* That is, about 4 ounces (about 110 grams)

to the LORD *again* for the period of his *vowed* separation ... The previous days do not count, because he became defiled during his separation." And he must bring to the Lord "a year-old male lamb as a guilt offering" (Nu 6:9–12). When Samson's hair of dedication was cut off by Delilah, God showed that it had been defiled by Samson's many defiling acts and was not acceptable to him. But when his hair "began to grow again," a new time of Samson's consecration began again (see v. 22 and note). Samson, however, had no lamb to offer God as a guilt offering, and he had no lifetime ("from birth until the day of his death," 13:7) to consecrate to the Lord. But he could offer up his life as God's champion warrior against the Philistines. And that is what he did.

16:31 *went down to get him.* The freedom of his family to secure his body and give it a burial indicates that the Philistines had no intention of further dishonoring him (contrast Saul's death, 1Sa 31:9–10). *led Israel ... years.* See note on 12:7. *twenty years.* Round numbers are frequently used in Judges (see Introduction: Background).

17:1—21:25 Two cycles of events forming an epilogue to the story of the judges (see Introduction: Literary Features). The events narrated evidently took place fairly early in the period of the judges (see notes on 18:30; 20:1,28). They illustrate the religious and moral degeneracy that characterized the age—when "Israel had no king" and "everyone did as he saw fit" (17:6; 21:25). Writing at a time when the monarchy under the Davidic dynasty had brought cohesion and order to the land and had reestablished a center for the worship of the Lord, the author portrays this earlier era of the judges as a dismal period of national decay, from which it was to be rescued by the house of David.

17:1—18:31 The first cycle of events illustrates corruption in Israelite worship by telling of Micah's establishment of a local place of worship in Ephraim, aided by a Levite claiming descent from Moses. This paganized worship of the Lord is taken over by the tribe of Dan when that tribe abandons its appointed inheritance and migrates to Israel's northern frontier.

17:2 *eleven hundred shekels.* See note on 16:5. *I heard you utter a curse.* Fear of the curse seems to have motivated his returning the stolen money. *The LORD bless you.* A blessing to counteract the curse.

17:3 *mother ... son.* With their paganized view of the God of Israel, both were idolaters in disobedience to the law (Ex 20:4,23; Dt 4:16). *a carved image and a cast idol.* The image was probably made of wood overlaid with silver; the idol was made of solid silver or of cheaper metal overlaid with silver.

17:4 *silversmith.* A maker of idols, as in Ac 19:24 (cf. Isa 40:19 and Jer 10:9, where the Hebrew for this word refers to a goldsmith).

17:5 *ephod.* See 8:27 and note on Ex 28:6. *idols.* Household gods, used in this case for divining (cf. Eze 21:21; Zec 10:2). Some of them were in human form (1Sa 19:13).

17:6 *had no king.* See 18:1; 19:1; 21:25; suggests that Judges was written after the establishment of the monarchy (see Introduction: Author and Date). *did as he saw fit.* See note on 14:3. The expression implies that Israel had departed from the covenant standards of conduct found in the law (see Dt 12:8).

17:7 *Levite.* His name was Jonathan (see 18:30 and note). *Bethlehem in Judah.* Not among the 48 designated Levitical cities (Jos 21).

17:8 *left that town.* The failure of the Israelites to obey the law probably resulted in a lack of support for the Levites, which explains the man's wandering in search of his fortune.

17:10 *father.* A term of respect used also for Elijah (2Ki 2:12) and Elisha (2Ki 6:21; 13:14). See Ge 45:8 and note; Mt 23:9. *ten shekels.* See NIV text note. In the light of this remuneration for a year's service, the stated amounts in 16:5 and 17:2 take on special significance. The offer of wages, clothing and food was more than this Levite could resist (v. 11). Clearly material concerns were at the root of his decision, because later he accepts an even more attractive offer (18:19–20).

17:12 *installed the Levite.* An attempt to make his shrine legitimate and give it prestige. Micah probably removed his son (see v. 5).

Danites Settle in Laish

18 In those days Israel had no king.[v]
And in those days the tribe of the
Danites was seeking a place of their own
where they might settle, because they had
not yet come into an inheritance among
the tribes of Israel.[w] 2So the Danites[x] sent
five warriors[y] from Zorah and Eshtaol to
spy out[z] the land and explore it. These
men represented all their clans. They told
them, "Go, explore the land."[a]
The men entered the hill country of
Ephraim and came to the house of Micah,[b] where they spent the night. 3When
they were near Micah's house, they recognized the voice of the young Levite;[c] so
they turned in there and asked him, "Who
brought you here? What are you doing in
this place? Why are you here?"
4He told them what Micah had done for
him, and said, "He has hired me and I am
his priest.[d]"
5Then they said to him, "Please inquire
of God[e] to learn whether our journey will
be successful."
6The priest answered them, "Go in
peace[f]. Your journey has the LORD's approval."
7So the five men[g] left and came to Laish,[h] where they saw that the people were
living in safety, like the Sidonians, unsuspecting and secure.[i] And since their land
lacked nothing, they were prosperous.[a]
Also, they lived a long way from the Sidonians[j] and had no relationship with anyone else.[b]
8When they returned to Zorah and Eshtaol, their brothers asked them, "How did
you find things?"
9They answered, "Come on, let's attack
them! We have seen that the land is very
good. Aren't you going to do something?
Don't hesitate to go there and take it over.[k]
10When you get there, you will find an unsuspecting people and a spacious land that
God has put into your hands, a land that
lacks nothing[l] whatever.[m]"
11Then six hundred men[n] from the clan
of the Danites,[o] armed for battle, set out
from Zorah and Eshtaol. 12On their way
they set up camp near Kiriath Jearim[p] in
Judah. This is why the place west of Kiriath Jearim is called Mahaneh Dan[c][q] to this
day. 13From there they went on to the hill
country of Ephraim and came to Micah's
house.[r]
14Then the five men who had spied out
the land of Laish[s] said to their brothers,
"Do you know that one of these houses
has an ephod,[t] other household gods, a
carved image and a cast idol?[u] Now you
know what to do." 15So they turned in
there and went to the house of the young
Levite at Micah's place and greeted him.
16The six hundred Danites,[v] armed for battle, stood at the entrance to the gate. 17The
five men who had spied out the land went
inside and took the carved image, the
ephod, the other household gods[w] and the
cast idol while the priest and the six hundred armed men[x] stood at the entrance to
the gate.
18When these men went into Micah's
house and took[y] the carved image, the
ephod, the other household gods[z] and the
cast idol, the priest said to them, "What
are you doing?"
19They answered him, "Be quiet![a] Don't
say a word. Come with us, and be our father and priest.[b] Isn't it better that you
serve a tribe and clan[c] in Israel as priest
rather than just one man's household?"
20Then the priest was glad. He took the
ephod, the other household gods and the

18:1 [v]S Jdg 17:6 [w]Jos 19:47; Jdg 1:34 **18:2** [x]S Ge 30:6 [y]ver 17 [z]S Nu 21:32 [a]S Jos 2:1 [b]S Jdg 17:1 **18:3** [c]Jdg 17:7 **18:4** [d]Jdg 17:12 **18:5** [e]S Ge 25:22; Jdg 20:18, 23, 27; 1Sa 14:18; 2Sa 5:19; 2Ki 1:2; 8:8 **18:6** [f]1Ki 22:6 **18:7** [g]ver 17 [h]S Jos 19:47 [i]S Ge 34:25 [j]ver 28; Jos 11:8 **18:9** [k]Nu 13:30; 1Ki 22:3 **18:10** [l]Dt 8:9 [m]1Ch 4:40 **18:11** [n]ver 16, 17 [o]Jdg 13:2 **18:12** [p]S Jos 9:17 [q]Jdg 13:25 **18:13** [r]S Jdg 17:1 **18:14** [s]S Jos 19:47 [t]S Jdg 8:27 [u]S Ge 31:19 **18:16** [v]S ver 11 **18:17** [w]S Ge 31:19; Mic 5:13 [x]ver 11 **18:18** [y]ver 24; Isa 46:2; Jer 43:11; 48:7; 49:3; Hos 10:5 [z]S Ge 31:19 **18:19** [a]Job 13:5; 21:5; 29:9; 40:4; Isa 52:15; Mic 7:16 [b]Jdg 17:10 [c]Nu 26:42

[a] *7* The meaning of the Hebrew for this clause is uncertain. [b] *7* Hebrew; some Septuagint manuscripts *with the Arameans* [c] *12* *Mahaneh Dan* means *Dan's camp.*

18:1 *seeking a place.* The Danite allotment was at the west end of the strip of land between Judah and Ephraim (Jos 19:41–46), but, due to the opposition of the Amorites (Jdg 1:34) and the Philistines, the Danites were unable to occupy that territory (see note on 13:2).
18:2 *spy out.* See 1:23 and note on Nu 13:2.
18:3 *recognized the voice.* Perhaps they recognized him by his dialect or accent.
18:5 *inquire of God.* The request is for an oracle, probably by using the ephod and household gods (see note on 17:5). God had already revealed his will by the allotments given to the various tribes (Jos 14–20). They were searching for an oracle that would guarantee the success of their journey.
18:6 *Go in peace.* The Levite gave them the message they wanted to hear. He was even careful to use the name of the Lord to give the message credibility and authority.
18:7 *Laish.* The journey northward was about 100 miles from Zorah and Eshtaol (v. 2). This town is called Leshem in Jos 19:47 (see note there). After its capture by the Danites, Laish was renamed Dan (v. 29), and it was Israel's northernmost settlement (see 20:1; 1Sa 3:20 and notes; 2Sa 3:10). Excavations there have disclosed that the earliest Israelite occupation of Dan was in the 12th century B.C. and that the first Israelite inhabitants apparently lived in tents or temporary huts. Occupation of the site continued into the Assyrian period, but the town was destroyed and rebuilt many times. A large high place attached to the city was often extensively rebuilt and refurbished and was in use into the Hellenistic period. Cf. note on 1Ki 12:19. *Sidonians.* A peaceful Phoenician people who engaged in commerce throughout the Mediterranean world. *had no relationship.* They did not feel threatened by other powers and therefore sought no treaties for mutual defense.
18:11 *six hundred men.* As leaders of the tribe of Dan, they represented the entire tribe's migration to its new location in the north. Cf. the 600 men who constituted the remnant of the tribe of Benjamin (see 20:47 and note).
18:19 *father.* See note on 17:10. *a tribe and clan.* Only one clan from the tribe of Dan is ever mentioned—Shuham (Nu 26:42; called Hushim in Ge 46:23). The Danites appealed to the Levite's vanity and materialism.

carved image and went along with the
people. 21 Putting their little children, their
livestock and their possessions in front of
them, they turned away and left.
22 When they had gone some distance
from Micah's house, the men who lived
near Micah were called together and overtook the Danites. 23 As they shouted after
them, the Danites turned and said to Micah, "What's the matter with you that you
called out your men to fight?"
24 He replied, "You took[d] the gods I made,
and my priest, and went away. What else
do I have? How can you ask, 'What's the
matter with you?'"
25 The Danites answered, "Don't argue
with us, or some hot-tempered men will
attack you, and you and your family will
lose your lives." 26 So the Danites went
their way, and Micah, seeing that they
were too strong for him,[e] turned around
and went back home.
27 Then they took what Micah had made,
and his priest, and went on to Laish,
against a peaceful and unsuspecting people.[f] They attacked them with the sword
and burned[g] down their city.[h] 28 There was
no one to rescue them because they lived
a long way from Sidon[i] and had no relationship with anyone else. The city was in
a valley near Beth Rehob.[j]
The Danites rebuilt the city and settled there. 29 They named it Dan[k] after
their forefather Dan, who was born to Israel—though the city used to be called
Laish.[l] 30 There the Danites set up for
themselves the idols, and Jonathan son
of Gershom,[m] the son of Moses,[a] and his
sons were priests for the tribe of Dan until the time of the captivity of the land.
31 They continued to use the idols Micah
had made,[n] all the time the house of God[o]
was in Shiloh.[p]

18:24 [d]S ver 17-18
18:26 [e]2Sa 3:39; Ps 18:17; 35:10
18:27 [f]S Ge 34:25 [g]S Nu 31:10 [h]Ge 49:17; S Jos 19:47
18:28 [i]S ver 7; S Ge 10:19 [j]S Nu 13:21
18:29 [k]S Ge 14:14 [l]S Jos 19:47; 1Ki 15:20
18:30 [m]Ex 2:22
18:31 [n]ver 17 [o]Jdg 19:18; 20:18 [p]S Jos 18:1; Jer 7:14

19:1 [q]ver 16, 18 [r]Ru 1:1
19:4 [s]ver 6, 8; S Ex 32:6
19:5 [t]ver 8; Ge 18:5
19:6 [u]S Jdg 16:25
19:10 [v]S Ge 10:16; S Jos 15:8

A Levite and His Concubine

19 In those days Israel had no king.
Now a Levite who lived in a remote
area in the hill country of Ephraim[q] took
a concubine from Bethlehem in Judah.[r]
2 But she was unfaithful to him. She left
him and went back to her father's house
in Bethlehem, Judah. After she had been
there four months, 3 her husband went
to her to persuade her to return. He had
with him his servant and two donkeys.
She took him into her father's house, and
when her father saw him, he gladly welcomed him. 4 His father-in-law, the girl's
father, prevailed upon him to stay; so he
remained with him three days, eating and
drinking,[s] and sleeping there.
5 On the fourth day they got up early and
he prepared to leave, but the girl's father
said to his son-in-law, "Refresh yourself[t]
with something to eat; then you can go."
6 So the two of them sat down to eat and
drink together. Afterward the girl's father
said, "Please stay tonight and enjoy yourself.[u]" 7 And when the man got up to go,
his father-in-law persuaded him, so he
stayed there that night. 8 On the morning
of the fifth day, when he rose to go, the
girl's father said, "Refresh yourself. Wait
till afternoon!" So the two of them ate together.
9 Then when the man, with his concubine and his servant, got up to leave, his
father-in-law, the girl's father, said, "Now
look, it's almost evening. Spend the night
here; the day is nearly over. Stay and enjoy
yourself. Early tomorrow morning you can
get up and be on your way home." 10 But,
unwilling to stay another night, the man
left and went toward Jebus[v] (that is, Jeru-

[a] 30 An ancient Hebrew scribal tradition, some Septuagint manuscripts and Vulgate; Masoretic Text *Manasseh*

18:21 *in front of them.* For protection in case of attack by Micah and his neighbors (cf. Ge 33:2–3, Jacob and Esau).

18:24 *You took the gods.* Micah was concerned about the loss of gods that could not even protect themselves. *What else do I have?* The agonizing cry of one whose faith is centered in helpless gods.

18:28 *Beth Rehob.* Probably the same as Rehob in Nu 13:21 (see note there; see also 2Sa 10:6,8).

18:29 *named it Dan.* For the city's location see map No. 4 at the end of this study Bible; see also map, p. 497.

18:30 *Jonathan.* The Levite is here identified as Jonathan son of Gershom, the son of Moses (Ex 2:22; 18:3; 1Ch 23:14–15). In an effort to prevent desecration of the name of Moses, later scribes modified the name slightly, making it read "Manasseh" (see NIV text note). If Jonathan was the grandson of Moses, the events in this chapter must have occurred early in the period of the judges (see notes on 20:1,28). *captivity of the land.* The date of this captivity has not been determined (see note on v. 7 regarding Laish).

18:31 *all the time the house of God was in Shiloh.* See Jos 18:1 and note. For Shiloh's destruction see Ps 78:60 and note; Jer 7:12,14 and note on 7:12; 26:6. Archaeological work at Shiloh indicates that the site was destroyed c. 1050 B.C. and was left uninhabited for many centuries.

19:1—21:25 The second cycle of events in the epilogue (see note on 17:1—18:31). It illustrates Israel's moral corruption by telling of the degenerate act of the men of Gibeah—an act remembered centuries later (see Hos 9:9 and note; 10:9). Although that town showed itself to be as wicked as any Canaanite town, it was defended by the rest of the tribe of Benjamin against the Lord's discipline through the Israelites, until nearly the whole tribe was destroyed.

19:1–30 An account of an Israelite town (Gibeah) that revived the ways of Sodom (see Ge 19).

19:1 *Levite.* Unlike the Levite of chs. 17–18, this man is not named. *concubine.* See note on Ge 25:6.

19:3 *gladly welcomed him.* The separation of the concubine from the Levite was probably a matter of family disgrace, and so his father-in-law was glad for the prospect of the two being reunited.

19:10 *Jebus.* See 1:21; see also note on Ge 10:16.

salem), with his two saddled donkeys and
his concubine.
11When they were near Jebus and the
day was almost gone, the servant said to
his master, "Come, let's stop at this city
of the Jebusites[w] and spend the night."
12His master replied, "No. We won't go
into an alien city, whose people are not
Israelites. We will go on to Gibeah." 13He
added, "Come, let's try to reach Gibeah
or Ramah[x] and spend the night in one
of those places." 14So they went on, and
the sun set as they neared Gibeah in Benjamin.[y] 15There they stopped to spend
the night.[z] They went and sat in the city
square,[a] but no one took them into his
home for the night.
16That evening[b] an old man from the
hill country of Ephraim,[c] who was living in Gibeah (the men of the place were
Benjamites), came in from his work in
the fields. 17When he looked and saw the
traveler in the city square, the old man
asked, "Where are you going? Where did
you come from?"[d]
18He answered, "We are on our way
from Bethlehem in Judah to a remote
area in the hill country of Ephraim where
I live. I have been to Bethlehem in Judah and now I am going to the house of
the LORD.[e] No one has taken me into his
house. 19We have both straw and fodder[f]
for our donkeys[g] and bread and wine[h] for
ourselves your servants—me, your maidservant, and the young man with us. We
don't need anything."
20"You are welcome at my house," the
old man said. "Let me supply whatever
you need. Only don't spend the night in
the square." 21So he took him into his
house and fed his donkeys. After they
had washed their feet, they had something to eat and drink.[i]
22While they were enjoying themselves,[j] some of the wicked men[k] of the
city surrounded the house. Pounding on
the door, they shouted to the old man
who owned the house, "Bring out the
man who came to your house so we can
have sex with him.[l]"
23The owner of the house went outside[m] and said to them, "No, my friends,
don't be so vile. Since this man is my
guest, don't do this disgraceful thing.[n]
24Look, here is my virgin daughter,[o] and
his concubine. I will bring them out to
you now, and you can use them and do
to them whatever you wish. But to this
man, don't do such a disgraceful thing."
25But the men would not listen to him.
So the man took his concubine and sent
her outside to them, and they raped her[p]
and abused her[q] throughout the night,
and at dawn they let her go. 26At daybreak the woman went back to the house
where her master was staying, fell down
at the door and lay there until daylight.
27When her master got up in the morning and opened the door of the house and
stepped out to continue on his way, there
lay his concubine, fallen in the doorway of the house, with her hands on the
threshold. 28He said to her, "Get up; let's
go." But there was no answer. Then the
man put her on his donkey and set out
for home.
29When he reached home, he took a
knife[r] and cut up his concubine, limb
by limb, into twelve parts and sent them
into all the areas of Israel.[s] 30Everyone
who saw it said, "Such a thing has never been seen or done, not since the day
the Israelites came up out of Egypt.[t]
Think about it! Consider it! Tell us what
to do![u]"

19:11 [w] S Ge 10:16; S Jos 3:10 **19:13** [x] S Jos 18:25 **19:14** [y] Jos 15:57; 1Sa 10:26; 11:4; 13:2; 15:34; Isa 10:29 **19:15** [z] S Ge 24:23 [a] S Ge 19:2 **19:16** [b] Ps 104:23 [c] S ver 1 **19:17** [d] S Ge 29:4 **19:18** [e] S Jdg 18:31 **19:19** [f] Ge 24:25 [g] S Ge 42:27 [h] S Ge 14:18 **19:21** [i] Ge 24:32-33; Lk 7:44 **19:22** [j] S Jdg 16:25 [k] S Dt 13:13 [l] Ge 19:4-5; Jdg 20:5; Ro 1:26-27 **19:23** [m] Ge 19:6 [n] S Ge 34:7; S Lev 19:29; S Jos 7:15; S Jdg 20:6; Ro 1:27 **19:24** [o] Ge 19:8 **19:25** [p] Jdg 20:5 [q] 1Sa 31:4 **19:29** [r] S Ge 22:6 [s] Jdg 20:6; 1Sa 11:7 **19:30** [t] Hos 9:9 [u] Jdg 20:7; Pr 13:10

19:12 *alien city.* With the city under the control of the Jebusites, the Levite was afraid that he would receive no hospitality and might be in mortal danger.
19:14 *Gibeah in Benjamin.* Distinguished from the Gibeah in Judah (Jos 15:20,57) and the Gibeah in the hill country of Ephraim (see Jos 24:33 and note). As the political capital of Saul's kingdom, it is called Gibeah of Saul in 1Sa 11:4; see also 1Sa 13:15 and note on 10:5.
19:15 *took them into his home.* See notes on 13:15; Ge 18:2.
19:18 *house of the LORD.* Apparently the Levite was planning to go to Shiloh (see 18:31 and note; Jos 18:1) to present a thank offering to the Lord or a sin offering for himself and his concubine.
19:21 *washed their feet.* An evidence of hospitality in the ancient Near East, where travelers commonly wore sandals as they walked the dusty roads (see Ge 18:4 and note on 18:2; 24:32; 43:24; Lk 7:44; Jn 13:5–14).
19:22 *wicked men.* The Hebrew for this expression refers to the morally depraved (see note on Dt 13:13). Elsewhere the expression is associated with idolatry (Dt 13:13), drunkenness (1Sa 1:16) and rebellion (1Sa 2:12). Here the reference is to homosexual acts. *Bring out the man.* The sexual perversion of these wicked men is yet another example of the decadence of an age when "everyone did as he saw fit" (17:6; 21:25). A similar request was made by the men of Sodom (Ge 19:5). Homosexual practices were common among the Canaanites.
19:23 *don't be so vile.* An expression of outrage at the willful perversion of what is right and natural (see Ge 19:7; 2Sa 13:12; see also Ro 1:27 and note).
19:24 *my virgin daughter, and his concubine.* The tragedy of this story lies not only in the decadence of Gibeah, but also in the callous selfishness of men who would betray defenseless women to be brutally violated for a whole night. Cf. Ge 19:8, where Lot offered his two daughters to the men of Sodom.
19:25 *took.* Here the Hebrew for this verb suggests taking by force.
19:29 *cut up his concubine.* Dismembering the concubine's body and sending parts to each of the 12 tribes was intended to awaken Israel from its moral lethargy and to marshal the tribes to face up to their responsibility. It is ironic that the one who issued such a call was himself so selfish and insensitive. See also Saul's similar action in 1Sa 11:7.

Israelites Fight the Benjamites

20 Then all the Israelites[v] from Dan to Beersheba[w] and from the land of Gilead came out as one man[x] and assembled[y] before the LORD in Mizpah.[z] 2The leaders of all the people of the tribes of Israel took their places in the assembly of the people of God, four hundred thousand soldiers[a] armed with swords. 3(The Benjamites heard that the Israelites had gone up to Mizpah.) Then the Israelites said, "Tell us how this awful thing happened."

4So the Levite, the husband of the murdered woman, said, "I and my concubine came to Gibeah[b] in Benjamin to spend the night.[c] 5During the night the men of Gibeah came after me and surrounded the house, intending to kill me.[d] They raped my concubine, and she died.[e] 6I took my concubine, cut her into pieces and sent one piece to each region of Israel's inheritance,[f] because they committed this lewd and disgraceful act[g] in Israel. 7Now, all you Israelites, speak up and give your verdict.[h]"

8All the people rose as one man, saying, "None of us will go home. No, not one of us will return to his house. 9But now this is what we'll do to Gibeah: We'll go up against it as the lot directs.[i] 10We'll take ten men out of every hundred from all the tribes of Israel, and a hundred from a thousand, and a thousand from ten thousand, to get provisions for the army. Then, when the army arrives at Gibeah[a] in Benjamin, it can give them what they deserve for all this vileness done in Israel." 11So all the men of Israel got together and united as one man[j] against the city.

12The tribes of Israel sent men throughout the tribe of Benjamin, saying, "What about this awful crime that was committed among you?[k] 13Now surrender those wicked men[l] of Gibeah so that we may put them to death and purge the evil from Israel.[m]"

But the Benjamites would not listen to their fellow Israelites. 14From their towns they came together at Gibeah to fight against the Israelites. 15At once the Benjamites mobilized twenty-six thousand swordsmen from their towns, in addition to seven hundred chosen men from those living in Gibeah. 16Among all these soldiers there were seven hundred chosen men who were left-handed,[n] each of whom could sling a stone at a hair and not miss.

17Israel, apart from Benjamin, mustered four hundred thousand swordsmen, all of them fighting men.

18The Israelites went up to Bethel[b][o] and inquired of God.[p] They said, "Who of us shall go first[q] to fight[r] against the Benjamites?"

The LORD replied, "Judah[s] shall go first."

19The next morning the Israelites got up and pitched camp near Gibeah. 20The men of Israel went out to fight the Benjamites and took up battle positions against them at Gibeah. 21The Benjamites came out of Gibeah and cut down twenty-two thousand Israelites[t] on the battlefield that day. 22But the men of Israel encouraged one another and again took up their positions where they had stationed themselves the first day. 23The Israelites went up and wept

20:1 [v]Jdg 21:5 [w]S Ge 21:14; 1Sa 3:20; 2Sa 3:10; 17:11; 24:15; 1Ki 4:25; 2Ch 30:5 [x]ver 11; 1Sa 11:7 [y]1Sa 7:5 [z]S Jos 11:3 **20:2** [a]1Sa 11:8 **20:4** [b]S Jos 15:57 [c]S Ge 24:23 **20:5** [d]S Jdg 19:22 [e]Jdg 19:25-26 **20:6** [f]S Jdg 19:29 [g]S Jdg 19:23; 2Sa 13:12 **20:7** [h]S Jdg 19:30 **20:9** [i]S Lev 16:8 **20:11** [j]S ver 1 **20:12** [k]Dt 13:14 **20:13** [l]S Dt 13:13 [m]S Dt 13:5; S 1Co 5:13 **20:16** [n]S Jdg 3:15 **20:18** [o]S Jos 12:9; S Jdg 18:31 [p]S Jdg 18:5 [q]S Jdg 1:1 [r]ver 23, 28 [s]S Ge 49:10 **20:21** [t]ver 25

[a] *10* One Hebrew manuscript; most Hebrew manuscripts *Geba,* a variant of *Gibeah* [b] *18* Or *to the house of God*; also in verse 26

20:1–48 All Israel (except Jabesh Gilead; see 21:8–9) assembled before the Lord to deal with the moral outrage committed by the men of Gibeah. Having first inquired of God for divine direction, they marched against Gibeah and the Benjamites as the disciplinary arm of the Lord (see Jos 22:11–34), following him as their King.

20:1 *Dan to Beersheba.* A conventional way of speaking of all Israel from north (Dan) to south (Beersheba); see 1Sa 3:20 and note; 2Sa 3:10; 24:2; 1Ch 21:2; 2Ch 30:5. The use of this expression, however, does not mean that the events of this chapter occurred after Dan's move to the north (18:27–29); rather, it indicates the author's perspective at the time of writing (Judges was probably written after the Davidic dynasty was fully established; see Introduction: Author and Date). Here the expression refers to the disciplinary action of all Israel (except Jabesh Gilead; see 21:8–9) against Gibeah and the rest of the Benjamites. Such a united response must have occurred early in the time of the judges, before the period of foreign domination of various parts of the land. *as one man.* Cf. vv. 8,11; 1Sa 11:7. *assembled … in Mizpah.* A place where the tribes gathered to meet before the Lord also during the days of Saul (see 1Sa 7:5–17 and note on 7:5; 10:17).

20:9 *lot.* Casting lots was a common method of determining the will of God (see notes on Ex 28:30; Jnh 1:7; Ac 1:26).

20:10 *ten men.* Support for the large army had to be well organized and efficient. One man was responsible for providing food for nine men fighting at the front.

20:13 *surrender those wicked men.* The demand of Israel was not unreasonable. They wanted to punish only those directly involved in the crime. *wicked men.* See note on Dt 13:13. *put them to death.* The sin of the men of Gibeah called for the death penalty, and Israel had to punish the sin if she was to avoid guilt herself (see Dt 13:5 and note; 17:7; 19:19–20).

20:16 *left-handed.* The Benjamite Ehud was also left-handed (see 3:15 and note). *sling a stone.* Cf. Zec 9:15. The sling was a very effective weapon, as David later demonstrated in his encounter with Goliath (see 1Sa 17:49 and note on 17:40). A slingstone, weighing one pound or more, could be hurled at 90–100 miles an hour. *miss.* In other contexts the Hebrew for this verb is translated "to sin."

20:18 *Bethel.* At this time the ark of the covenant and the high priest Phinehas were at Bethel (see vv. 26–28). *inquired of God.* Probably by priestly use of Urim and Thummim (see notes on Ex 28:30; 1Sa 2:28). *Who of us shall go first … ?* See 1:1–36. *Judah.* See notes on 1:1–36; 1:2.

20:21 *twenty-two thousand Israelites.* A rousing victory for the Benjamites, who numbered 26,700 (v. 15) and therefore had struck down nearly one man apiece.

before the LORD[u] until evening,[v] and they
inquired of the LORD.[w] They said, "Shall
we go up again to battle[x] against the Benjamites, our brothers?"

The LORD answered, "Go up against
them."

24Then the Israelites drew near to Benjamin the second day. 25This time, when
the Benjamites came out from Gibeah
to oppose them, they cut down another
eighteen thousand Israelites,[y] all of them
armed with swords.

26Then the Israelites, all the people,
went up to Bethel, and there they sat
weeping before the LORD.[z] They fasted[a]
that day until evening and presented
burnt offerings[b] and fellowship offerings[a][c] to the LORD.[d] 27And the Israelites
inquired of the LORD.[e] (In those days the
ark of the covenant of God[f] was there,
28with Phinehas son of Eleazar,[g] the son
of Aaron, ministering before it.)[h] They
asked, "Shall we go up again to battle
with Benjamin our brother, or not?"

The LORD responded, "Go, for tomorrow I will give them into your hands.[i]"

29Then Israel set an ambush[j] around
Gibeah. 30They went up against the Benjamites on the third day and took up positions against Gibeah as they had done
before. 31The Benjamites came out to
meet them and were drawn away[k] from
the city. They began to inflict casualties
on the Israelites as before, so that about
thirty men fell in the open field and on
the roads—the one leading to Bethel[l] and
the other to Gibeah.

32While the Benjamites were saying,
"We are defeating them as before,"[m] the
Israelites were saying, "Let's retreat and
draw them away from the city to the
roads."

33All the men of Israel moved from
their places and took up positions at Baal
Tamar, and the Israelite ambush charged
out of its place[n] on the west[b] of Gibeah.[c] 34Then ten thousand of Israel's finest men made a frontal attack on Gibeah.
The fighting was so heavy that the Benjamites did not realize[o] how near disaster
was.[p] 35The LORD defeated Benjamin[q] before Israel, and on that day the Israelites
struck down 25,100 Benjamites, all armed
with swords. 36Then the Benjamites saw
that they were beaten.

Now the men of Israel had given way[r]
before Benjamin, because they relied on
the ambush[s] they had set near Gibeah.
37The men who had been in ambush
made a sudden dash into Gibeah, spread
out and put the whole city to the sword.[t]
38The men of Israel had arranged with
the ambush that they should send up
a great cloud of smoke[u] from the city,[v]
39and then the men of Israel would turn
in the battle.

The Benjamites had begun to inflict
casualties on the men of Israel (about
thirty), and they said, "We are defeating them as in the first battle."[w] 40But
when the column of smoke began to rise
from the city, the Benjamites turned and
saw the smoke of the whole city going
up into the sky.[x] 41Then the men of Israel turned on them,[y] and the men of
Benjamin were terrified, because they
realized that disaster had come[z] upon
them. 42So they fled before the Israelites
in the direction of the desert, but they
could not escape the battle. And the men
of Israel who came out of the towns cut
them down there. 43They surrounded the
Benjamites, chased them and easily[d]
overran them in the vicinity of Gibeah
on the east. 44Eighteen thousand Benjamites fell, all of them valiant fighters.[a]
45As they turned and fled toward the desert to the rock of Rimmon,[b] the Israelites
cut down five thousand men along the
roads. They kept pressing after the Benjamites as far as Gidom and struck down
two thousand more.

46On that day twenty-five thousand
Benjamite[c] swordsmen fell, all of them
valiant fighters. 47But six hundred men
turned and fled into the desert to the
rock of Rimmon, where they stayed four
months. 48The men of Israel went back
to Benjamin and put all the towns to the
sword, including the animals and everything else they found. All the towns they
came across they set on fire.[d]

20:23 [u]S Nu 14:1 [v]Jos 7:6 [w]S Jdg 18:5 [x]S ver 18 **20:25** [y]ver 21 **20:26** [z]S Nu 14:1 [a]2Sa 12:21 [b]Lev 1:3 [c]S Ex 32:6 [d]Jdg 21:4 **20:27** [e]S Jdg 18:5 [f]S Nu 10:33 **20:28** [g]Nu 25:7 [h]Dt 18:5 [i]S Jos 2:24 **20:29** [j]S Jos 8:2,4 **20:31** [k]Jos 8:16 [l]Jos 16:1 **20:32** [m]ver 39 **20:33** [n]Jos 8:19 **20:34** [o]Jos 8:14 [p]ver 41 **20:35** [q]1Sa 9:21 **20:36** [r]Jos 8:15 [s]Jos 8:2 **20:37** [t]Jos 8:19 **20:38** [u]Jos 8:20 [v]Jos 8:4-8 **20:39** [w]ver 32; Ps 78:9 **20:40** [x]Jos 8:20 **20:41** [y]Jos 8:21 [z]ver 34 **20:44** [a]1Sa 10:26; Ps 76:5 **20:45** [b]S Jos 15:32 **20:46** [c]1Sa 9:21 **20:48** [d]Jdg 21:23

[a] 26 Traditionally *peace offerings* [b] 33 Some Septuagint manuscripts and Vulgate; the meaning of the Hebrew for this word is uncertain. [c] 33 Hebrew *Geba,* a variant of *Gibeah* [d] 43 The meaning of the Hebrew for this word is uncertain.

20:27 *ark.* The only mention of the ark in Judges.

20:28 *Phinehas.* Phinehas was the priest in the tabernacle in the days of Joshua (Jos 22:13), and the fact that he was still serving is further evidence that these events took place early in the days of the judges (see notes on v. 1; 18:30).

20:29 *set an ambush.* See 9:32; Jos 8:2 and notes.

20:33 *Baal Tamar.* Location unknown.

20:35 *25,100.* Apparently 1,000 Benjamites had been killed in the first two battles (see note on v. 21).

20:36b–45 Details of the account in vv. 29–36a.

20:46 *twenty-five thousand.* A round number for 25,100 (v. 35).

20:47 *six hundred men.* If these had not escaped, the tribe of Benjamin would have been annihilated. The same number of Danites went to Laish (see 18:11 and note).

Wives for the Benjamites

21 The men of Israel had taken an oath[e] at Mizpah:[f] "Not one of us will give[g] his daughter in marriage to a Benjamite."

2The people went to Bethel,[a] where they sat before God until evening, raising their voices and weeping bitterly. 3"O LORD, the God of Israel," they cried, "why has this happened to Israel? Why should one tribe be missing[h] from Israel today?"

4Early the next day the people built an altar and presented burnt offerings and fellowship offerings.[b][i]

5Then the Israelites asked, "Who from all the tribes of Israel[j] has failed to assemble before the LORD?" For they had taken a solemn oath that anyone who failed to assemble before the LORD at Mizpah should certainly be put to death.

6Now the Israelites grieved for their brothers, the Benjamites. "Today one tribe is cut off from Israel," they said. 7"How can we provide wives for those who are left, since we have taken an oath[k] by the LORD not to give them any of our daughters in marriage?" 8Then they asked, "Which one of the tribes of Israel failed to assemble before the LORD at Mizpah?" They discovered that no one from Jabesh Gilead[l] had come to the camp for the assembly. 9For when they counted the people, they found that none of the people of Jabesh Gilead were there.

10So the assembly sent twelve thousand fighting men with instructions to go to Jabesh Gilead and put to the sword those living there, including the women and children. 11"This is what you are to do," they said. "Kill every male[m] and every woman who is not a virgin.[n]" 12They found among the people living in Jabesh Gilead four hundred young women who had never slept with a man, and they took them to the camp at Shiloh[o] in Canaan.

13Then the whole assembly sent an offer of peace[p] to the Benjamites at the rock of Rimmon.[q] 14So the Benjamites returned at that time and were given the women of Jabesh Gilead who had been spared. But there were not enough for all of them.

15The people grieved for Benjamin,[r] because the LORD had made a gap in the tribes of Israel. 16And the elders of the assembly said, "With the women of Benjamin destroyed, how shall we provide wives for the men who are left? 17The Benjamite survivors must have heirs," they said, "so that a tribe of Israel will not be wiped out.[s] 18We can't give them our daughters as wives, since we Israelites have taken this oath:[t] 'Cursed be anyone who gives[u] a wife to a Benjamite.' 19But look, there is the annual festival of the LORD in Shiloh,[v] to the north of Bethel[w], and east of the road that goes from Bethel to Shechem,[x] and to the south of Lebonah."

20So they instructed the Benjamites, saying, "Go and hide in the vineyards 21and watch. When the girls of Shiloh come out to join in the dancing,[y] then rush from the vineyards and each of you seize a wife from the girls of Shiloh and go to the land of Benjamin. 22When their fathers or brothers complain to us, we will say to them, 'Do us a kindness by helping them, because

21:1 [e] S Jos 9:18 [f] S Jos 11:3 [g] ver 18,22 **21:3** [h] ver 6,17 **21:4** [i] Jdg 20:26 **21:5** [j] Jdg 20:1 **21:7** [k] S Jos 9:18 **21:8** [l] 1Sa 11:1; 31:11; 2Sa 2:4; 21:12; 1Ch 10:11 **21:11** [m] S Nu 31:7 [n] Nu 31:17-18 **21:12** [o] S Jos 18:1 **21:13** [p] S Dt 2:26 [q] S Jos 15:32 **21:15** [r] ver 6 **21:17** [s] S ver 3 **21:18** [t] S Jos 9:18 [u] S ver 1 **21:19** [v] S Jos 18:1 [w] Jos 16:1 [x] S Jos 17:7 **21:21** [y] S Ex 15:20

[a] 2 Or *to the house of God* [b] 4 Traditionally *peace offerings*

21:1 – 25 Second thoughts about the slaughter of their Benjamite brothers caused the Israelites to grieve over the loss. Only 600 Benjamites were left alive, and the men of Israel decided to provide wives for them in order to keep the tribe from disappearing. After slaughtering most of the people of Jabesh Gilead, the Israelites took 400 young women from the survivors and gave them to 400 Benjamites. Shortly afterward, each of the remaining Benjamites seized a wife from the women of Shiloh, and Benjamin began to be restored.
21:1 *taken an oath.* This vow, probably taken in the name of the Lord, was not an ordinary vow but invoked a curse on oneself if the vow was broken (v. 18; see also Ac 23:12 – 15).
21:2 *Bethel.* See 20:18,26 – 27. *weeping bitterly.* Earlier the Israelites wept because they were defeated by the Benjamites (20:23,26). Now they weep because the disciplinary action against the Benjamites has nearly annihilated one of the tribes (see v. 3).
21:5 *failed to assemble.* The tribes had a mutual responsibility in times of military action (see note on 5:13 – 18). Those who failed to participate were often singled out and sometimes punished (see 5:15 – 17,23 and note on 5:23). *solemn oath.* Complicating the situation for Israel was the fact that they had taken a second oath, calling for the death of those who did not participate in the battle.
21:10 *twelve thousand.* A thousand from each tribe (see Nu 31:6), with 1,000 supplied to represent the tribe of Benjamin.
21:11 *Kill every male.* The punishment of Jabesh Gilead seems brutal, but the covenant bond between the tribes was extremely important. Even though delinquency on some occasions was not punished (5:15 – 17), the nature of the crime in this case, coupled with Benjamin's refusal to turn over the criminals, caused Israel to take this oath (v. 5).
21:12 *in Canaan.* Emphasizes the fact that the women were brought across the Jordan from the east.
21:19 *festival of the LORD.* In light of the mention of vineyards (v. 20), it is likely that this reference is to the Feast of Tabernacles (see note on 1Sa 1:3), though it may have been a local festival. *north of Bethel … south of Lebonah.* This detailed description of Shiloh's location may indicate that this material was written at a time when Shiloh was in ruins, perhaps after its destruction during the battle of Aphek (1Sa 4:1 – 11).
21:21 *seize a wife.* With the Benjamites securing wives in this manner, the other tribes were not actually "giving" their daughters to them (see note on v. 22).
21:22 *When their fathers or brothers complain.* It was customary for the brothers of a young woman who had been abducted to demand satisfaction (see Ge 34:7 – 31; 2Sa 13:20 – 38). It was therefore important that the elders anticipate this response and be prepared to get cooperation from the young women's families.

we did not get wives for them during the
war, and you are innocent, since you did
not give[z] your daughters to them.' "
[23]So that is what the Benjamites did.
While the girls were dancing,[a] each man
caught one and carried her off to be his
wife. Then they returned to their inheritance[b] and rebuilt the towns and settled
in them.[c]
[24]At that time the Israelites left that
place and went home to their tribes and
clans, each to his own inheritance.
[25]In those days Israel had no king; everyone did as he saw fit.[d]

21:22 [z] S ver 1; ver 1,18 **21:23** [a] ver 21 [b] S Jos 24:28 [c] Jdg 20:48 **21:25** [d] S Dt 12:8

21:24 *went home.* These soldiers had probably been away from home at least five months (see 20:47).

21:25 *Israel had no king.* See Introduction: Author and Date; see also note on 17:6. *did as he saw fit.* See note on 17:6; see also Introduction: Themes and Theology; Literary Features.

Ruth

INTRODUCTION

Title

The book is named after one of its main characters, a young woman of Moab, the great-grandmother of David and an ancestress of Jesus (see 4:18 – 22 and note; Mt 1:1,5 and note on 1:3). The only other Biblical book bearing the name of a woman is Esther.

Background

The story is set in the time of the judges, a time characterized in the book of Judges as a period of religious and moral degeneracy, national disunity and frequent foreign oppression. The book of Ruth reflects a time of peace between Israel and Moab (contrast Jdg 3:12 – 30). Like 1Sa 1 – 2, it gives a series of intimate glimpses into the private lives of the members of an Israelite family. It also presents a delightful account of the remnant of true faith and piety in the period of the judges, relieving an otherwise wholly dark picture of that era.

A Quick Look

Author:
Unknown

Audience:
God's chosen people, the Israelites

Date:
Ruth lived during the time of the judges; the book was written sometime after David became king in about 1010 B.C.

Theme:
Ruth, a Moabite woman, proves to be a model of faithfulness in Israel during the period of the judges.

Author and Date of Writing

The author is unknown. Jewish tradition points to Samuel, but it is unlikely that he is the author because the mention of David (4:17,22) implies a later date. Further, the literary style of Hebrew used in Ruth suggests that it was written during the period of the monarchy.

Theme and Theology

The importance of faithful love in human relationships among God's kingdom people is powerfully underscored. The author focuses on Ruth's unswerving and selfless devotion to desolate Naomi (see 1:16 – 17 and notes; 2:11 – 12 and note on 2:11; 3:10; 4:15 and note) and on Boaz's kindness to these two widows (chs. 2 – 4). He thus presents striking examples of lives that embody in their daily affairs the self-giving love that fulfills God's law (see Lev 19:18 and note; cf. Ro 13:10

and note). Such love also reflects God's love, in a marvelous joining of human and divine actions (compare 2:12 with 3:9 and see note on 3:9). In God's benevolence such lives are blessed and are made a blessing.

It may seem surprising that one who reflects God's love so clearly is a Moabite woman (see map, p. 367). Yet her complete loyalty to the Israelite family into which she has been received by marriage and her total devotion to her desolate mother-in-law mark her as a true daughter of Israel and a worthy ancestor of David. She strikingly exemplifies the truth that participation in the coming kingdom of God is decided, not by blood and birth, but by the conformity of one's life to the will of God through the "obedience that comes from faith" (Ro 1:5). Her place in the ancestry of David signifies that all nations will be represented in the kingdom of David's greater Son.

The book is a story of Naomi's transformation from despair to happiness through the selfless, God-blessed acts of Ruth and Boaz. She moves from emptiness to fullness, from destitution to security and hope.

As an episode in the ancestry of David, the book of Ruth sheds light on his role in the history of redemption. Redemption is a key concept throughout the account; the Hebrew word in its various forms occurs 23 times. The book is a story of Naomi's transformation from despair to happiness through the selfless, God-blessed acts of Ruth and Boaz. She moves from emptiness to fullness (1:21; 3:17; see notes on 1:1,3,5–6,12,21–22; 3:17; 4:15), from destitution (1:1–5) to security and hope (see 4:13–17 and note). Similarly, Israel was transformed from national desperation at the death of Eli (see 1Sa 4:18 and note) to peace and prosperity in the early days of Solomon (see 1Ki 4:20–34; 5:4 and note) through the selfless devotion of David, a true descendant of Ruth and Boaz. The author thus reminded Israel that the reign of the house of David, as the means of God's benevolent rule in Israel, held the prospect of God's promised peace and rest. But this rest would continue only so long as those who participated in the kingdom — prince and people alike — reflected in their daily lives the selfless love exemplified by Ruth and Boaz. In Jesus, the great "son of David" (Mt 1:1; see note there), and his redemptive work, the promised blessings of the kingdom of God find their fulfillment.

Literary Features

The book of Ruth is a Hebrew short story, told with consummate skill. Among historical narratives in Scripture it is unexcelled in its compactness, vividness, warmth, beauty and dramatic effectiveness — an exquisitely wrought jewel of Hebrew narrative art.

Marvelously symmetrical throughout (see Outline), the action moves from a briefly sketched account of distress (1:1–5; 71 words in Hebrew) through four episodes to a concluding account of relief and hope that is drawn with equal brevity (4:13–17; 71 words in Hebrew). The crucial turning point occurs exactly midway (see note on 2:20). The opening line of each of the four episodes signals its main development (1:6, the return; 2:1, the meeting with Boaz; 3:1, finding a home for Ruth; 4:1, the decisive event at the gate), while the closing line of each episode facilitates transition to what follows (see notes on 1:22; 2:23; 3:18; 4:12). Contrast is also used to good effect: pleasant (the meaning of "Naomi") and bitter (1:20), full and empty (1:21), and the living and the dead (2:20). Most striking is the contrast between two of the main characters, Ruth and Boaz: The one is a young, alien, destitute widow, while the other is a middle-aged, well-to-do Israelite securely established in his home community. For each there is a corresponding character whose actions highlight, by contrast, his or her selfless acts: Ruth — Orpah; Boaz — the unnamed kinsman.

When movements in space, time and circumstance all correspond in some way, a harmony results that both satisfies the reader's artistic sense and helps open doors to understanding. The author of Ruth keeps his readers from being distracted from the central story — Naomi's passage from emptiness to fullness through the selfless acts of Ruth and Boaz (see Theme and Theology). That passage, or restoration, first takes place in connection with her return from Moab to the promised land and to Bethlehem ("house of food"; see note on 1:1). It then progresses with the harvest season, when the fullness of the land is gathered in. All aspects of the story keep the reader's attention focused on the central issue. Consideration of these and other literary devices (mentioned throughout the notes) will aid understanding of the book of Ruth.

Outline

I. Introduction: Naomi Emptied (1:1–5)
II. Naomi Returns from Moab (1:6–22)
  A. Ruth Clings to Naomi (1:6–18)
  B. Ruth and Naomi Return to Bethlehem (1:19–22)
III. Ruth and Boaz Meet in the Harvest Fields (ch. 2)
  A. Ruth Begins Work (2:1–7)
  B. Boaz Shows Kindness to Ruth (2:8–16)
  C. Ruth Returns to Naomi (2:17–23)
IV. Naomi Sends Ruth to Boaz's Threshing Floor (ch. 3)
  A. Naomi Instructs Ruth (3:1–5)
  B. Boaz Pledges to Secure Redemption (3:6–15)
  C. Ruth Returns to Naomi (3:16–18)
V. Boaz Arranges to Fulfill His Pledge (4:1–12)
  A. Boaz Confronts the Unnamed Kinsman (4:1–8)
  B. Boaz Buys Naomi's Property and Announces His Marriage to Ruth (4:9–12)
VI. Conclusion: Naomi Filled (4:13–17)
VII. Epilogue: Genealogy of David (4:18–22)

Naomi and Ruth

1 In the days when the judges ruled,[a][a]
there was a famine in the land,[b] and a
man from Bethlehem in Judah,[c] together
with his wife and two sons, went to live
for a while[d] in the country of Moab.[e] 2The
man's name was Elimelech,[f] his wife's
name Naomi, and the names of his two
sons were Mahlon and Kilion.[g] They were
Ephrathites[h] from Bethlehem,[i] Judah. And
they went to Moab and lived there.

3Now Elimelech, Naomi's husband,
died, and she was left with her two sons.
4They married Moabite women,[j] one
named Orpah and the other Ruth.[k] After
they had lived there about ten years, 5both
Mahlon and Kilion[l] also died,[m] and Naomi was left without her two sons and her
husband.

6When she heard in Moab[n] that the
LORD had come to the aid of his people[o] by
providing food[p] for them, Naomi and her
daughters-in-law[q] prepared to return home
from there. 7With her two daughters-in-
law she left the place where she had been
living and set out on the road that would
take them back to the land of Judah.

8Then Naomi said to her two daughters-in-law, "Go back, each of you, to your
mother's home.[r] May the LORD show kindness[s] to you, as you have shown to your

1:1 [a]Jdg 2:16-18 [b]S Ge 12:10; 2Ki 6:25; Ps 105:16; Hag 1:11 [c]S Ge 35:19 [d]Ge 47:4 [e]S Ge 36:35 **1:2** [f]ver 3; Ru 2:1; 4:3 [g]ver 5; Ru 4:9 [h]S Ge 35:16 [i]Ge 35:19; 1Sa 16:18 **1:4** [j]1Ki 11:1; 2Ch 24:26; Ezr 9:2; Ne 13:23 [k]ver 14; Ru 4:13; Mt 1:5 **1:5** [l]S ver 2 [m]ver 8; Ru 2:11 **1:6** [n]S Ge 36:35 [o]S Ge 50:24; Ex 4:31; Jer 29:10; Zep 2:7 [p]Ps 132:15; Mt 6:11 [q]S Ge 11:31; S 38:16 **1:8** [r]Ge 38:11 [s]S Ge 19:19; 2Ti 1:16

[a] 1 Traditionally *judged*

1:1 *when the judges ruled.* Probably from c. 1380 to c. 1050 B.C. (see Introduction to Judges: Background). By mentioning the judges, the author calls to mind that period of Israel's apostasy, moral degradation and oppression. *famine.* Not mentioned in Judges. *Bethlehem in Judah.* David's hometown (1Sa 16:18). Bethlehem (the name suggests "house of food") is empty.

1:2 *Elimelech.* Means "(My) God is King" (see note on Jdg 8:23). *Naomi.* See NIV text note on v. 20. *Mahlon.* Ruth's husband (4:10), whose name probably means "weakling" or "sickly person." *Kilion.* Probably means something like "frail person." (Mahlon's and Kilion's names may have been acquired as their conditions became evident.) *Ephrathites.* Ephrathah was a name for the area around Bethlehem (see 4:11; Ge 35:19; 1Sa 17:12; Mic 5:2 and note).

1:3 *Elimelech, Naomi's husband, died.* Naomi's emptying begins (see v. 21 and note).

1:4 *They married.* The prospect of continuing the family line remained. *Moabite women.* See Ge 19:36–37. Marriage with Moabite women was not forbidden, though no Moabite—or his sons to the tenth generation—was allowed to "enter the assembly of the LORD" (Dt 23:3). *Ruth.* The name sounds like the Hebrew for "friendship." Ruth is one of five women in Matthew's genealogy of Jesus. The others are Tamar, Rahab, Bathsheba and Mary (see Mt 1:3,5–6,16; see note on Mt 1:3).

1:5 *Naomi was left.* Naomi's emptiness is complete: She has neither husband nor sons. She has only two young daughters-in-law, both of them foreigners and childless.

1:6–22 Act I in the drama: Naomi's sense of desolation is exposed.

1:6 *the LORD had come to the aid of his people.* At several points in the account, God's sovereign control of events is acknowledged (here; vv. 13,21; 2:20; 4:12–15). *food.* Bethlehem ("house of food") again has food. *prepared to return home.* Empty Naomi returns to the newly filled land of promise.

1:8 *Go back.* Desolate Naomi repeatedly urges her daughters-in-law to return to their original homes in Moab (here; vv. 11–12,15); she has nothing to offer them. *kindness.* See note on Ps 6:4.

The Book of Ruth

Set in the dark and bloody days of the judges, the story of Ruth is silent about the underlying hostility and suspicion the two peoples—Judahites and Moabites—felt for each other. The original onslaught of the invading Israelite tribes against towns that were once Moabite had never been forgotten or forgiven, while the Hebrew prophets denounced Moab's pride and arrogance for trying to bewitch, seduce and oppress Israel from the time of Balaam on. The Mesha Stele (c. 830 B.C.) boasts of the massacre of entire Israelite towns.

Moab encompassed the expansive, grain-rich plateau between the Dead Sea and the eastern desert on both sides of the enormous rift of the Arnon River gorge. Much of eastern Moab was steppeland—semi-arid wastes not profitable for cultivation, but excellent for grazing flocks of sheep and goats. The tribute Moab paid to Israel in the days of Ahab was 100,000 lambs and the wool of 100,000 rams (see 2Ki 3:4 and note).

ISRAEL
Jordan R.
Heshbon
Mt. Nebo
Bethlehem
The main route through Moab was the King's Highway, a road connecting the cities of Heshbon, Dibon and Kir Hareseth with points north and south.
Dead Sea
Dibon
Aroer
Arnon R.
King's Highway
MOAB
Kir Hareseth
Miles 10 5 0 10 20
Kms 10 5 0 10 20 30

dead[t] and to me. 9 May the LORD grant that
each of you will find rest[u] in the home of
another husband."
Then she kissed[v] them and they wept
aloud[w] 10 and said to her, "We will go back
with you to your people."
11 But Naomi said, "Return home, my
daughters. Why would you come with
me? Am I going to have any more sons,
who could become your husbands?[x] 12 Return home, my daughters; I am too old to
have another husband. Even if I thought
there was still hope for me—even if I had
a husband tonight and then gave birth to
sons— 13 would you wait until they grew
up?[y] Would you remain unmarried for
them? No, my daughters. It is more bitter[z]
for me than for you, because the LORD's
hand has gone out against me![a]"
14 At this they wept[b] again. Then Orpah
kissed her mother-in-law[c] good-by,[d] but
Ruth clung to her.[e]
15 "Look," said Naomi, "your sister-in-
law[f] is going back to her people and her
gods.[g] Go back with her."
16 But Ruth replied, "Don't urge me
to leave you[h] or to turn back from you.
Where you go I will go,[i] and where you
stay I will stay. Your people will be my
people[j] and your God my God.[k] 17 Where
you die I will die, and there I will be buried. May the LORD deal with me, be it ever
so severely,[l] if anything but death separates you and me."[m] 18 When Naomi realized that Ruth was determined to go with
her, she stopped urging her.[n]
19 So the two women went on until they
came to Bethlehem.[o] When they arrived in
Bethlehem, the whole town was stirred[p]
because of them, and the women exclaimed, "Can this be Naomi?"
20 "Don't call me Naomi,[a]" she told them.
"Call me Mara,[b] because the Almighty[c][q]
has made my life very bitter.[r] 21 I went
away full, but the LORD has brought me
back empty.[s] Why call me Naomi? The
LORD has afflicted[d] me;[t] the Almighty has
brought misfortune upon me."
22 So Naomi returned from Moab accompanied by Ruth the Moabitess,[u] her daughter-in-law,[v] arriving in Bethlehem as the
barley harvest[w] was beginning.[x]

1:8 [t] S ver 5 **1:9** [u] Ru 3:1 [v] S Ge 27:27; S 29:11 [w] S Ge 27:38; S Nu 25:6 **1:11** [x] Ge 38:11; Dt 25:5 **1:13** [y] Ge 38:11 [z] ver 20; Ex 1:14; 15:23; 1Sa 30:6 [a] S Jdg 2:15; S Job 4:5 **1:14** [b] ver 9 [c] Ru 2:11; 3:1; Mic 7:6 [d] S Ge 31:28 [e] S Dt 10:20 **1:15** [f] Dt 25:7 [g] S Jos 24:14 **1:16** [h] 2Ki 2:2 [i] Ge 24:58 [j] Ps 45:10 [k] S Jos 24:15 **1:17** [l] 1Sa 3:17; 14:44; 20:13; 25:22; 2Sa 3:9,35; 2Sa 19:13; 1Ki 2:23; 19:2; 20:10; 2Ki 6:31 [m] 2Sa 15:21 **1:18** [n] Ac 21:14 **1:19** [o] S Jdg 17:7 [p] Mt 21:10 **1:20** [q] S Ge 15:1; S 17:1; Ps 91:1 [r] S ver 13 **1:21** [s] Job 1:21 [t] Job 30:11; Ps 88:7; Isa 53:4 **1:22** [u] Ru 2:2,6,21; 4:5,10

Ruth Meets Boaz

2 Now Naomi had a relative[y] on her
husband's side, from the clan of Elimelech,[z] a man of standing,[a] whose name
was Boaz.[b]
2 And Ruth the Moabitess[c] said to Naomi,
"Let me go to the fields and pick up the

[a] *20 Naomi* means *pleasant*; also in verse 21.
[b] *20 Mara* means *bitter.* [c] *20* Hebrew *Shaddai*; also in verse 21 [d] *21* Or *has testified against*

[v] S Ge 11:31 [w] S Ex 9:31; S Lev 19:9 [x] 2Sa 21:9 **2:1** [y] Ru 3:2; Pr 7:4 [z] S Ru 1:2 [a] 1Sa 9:1; 1Ki 11:28 [b] Ru 4:21; 1Ch 2:12; Mt 1:5; Lk 3:32 **2:2** [c] S Ru 1:22

1:11 *sons, who could become your husbands?* Naomi alludes to the Israelite law (Dt 25:5–6) regarding levirate marriage (see notes on Ge 38:8; Dt 25:5–7; see also note on Mt 22:24), which was given to protect the widow and guarantee continuance of the family line.

1:12 *I am too old.* Naomi can have no more sons; even her womb is empty.

1:13 *the LORD's hand ... against me.* See notes on vv. 5–6; see also vv. 20–21 and notes.

1:14 Orpah's departure highlights the loyalty and selfless devotion of Ruth to her desolate mother-in-law.

1:15 *her gods.* The chief god of the Moabites was Chemosh.

1:16 This classic expression of loyalty and love discloses Ruth's true character. Her commitment to Naomi is complete, even though it holds no prospect for her except to share in Naomi's desolation. For a similar declaration of devotion see 2Sa 15:21 and note.

1:17 *May the LORD deal with me, be it ever so severely.* See note on 1Sa 3:17. Ruth, a non-Israelite, swears her commitment to Naomi in the name of Israel's God, thus acknowledging him as her God (see v. 16). *if anything but death separates you and me.* Or "if even death separates you and me" (cf. 2Sa 1:23 and note).

1:20 *Naomi ... Mara.* See NIV text notes. In the ancient Near East a person's name was often descriptive. Naomi's choice of name and her explanation for it provide the most poignant disclosure of her sense of desolation—even her God is against her. *Almighty.* See note on Ge 17:1.

1:21 *full ... empty.* These words highlight an important theme of the story—how the empty Naomi becomes full again.

1:22 *Ruth the Moabitess.* Several times the author reminds the reader that Ruth is a foreigner from a despised people (2:2,6,21; 4:5,10; see 2:10). *harvest.* Harvesting grain in ancient Canaan took place in April and May (barley first, wheat a few weeks later; see 2:23 and note). It involved the following steps: (1) cutting the ripened standing grain with hand sickles (Dt 16:9; 23:25; Jer 50:16; Joel 3:13)—usually done by men; (2) binding the grain into sheaves—usually done by women; (3) gleaning, i.e., gathering stalks of grain left behind (2:7); (4) transporting the sheaves to the threshing floor—often by donkey, sometimes by cart (Am 2:13); (5) threshing, i.e., loosening the grain from the straw—usually done by the treading of cattle (Dt 25:4; Hos 10:11), but sometimes by toothed threshing sledges (Isa 41:15; Am 1:3) or the wheels of carts (Isa 28:28); (6) winnowing—done by tossing the grain into the air with winnowing forks (Jer 15:7) so that the wind, which usually came up for a few hours in the afternoon, blew away the straw and chaff (Ps 1:4), leaving the grain at the winnower's feet; (7) sifting the grain (Am 9:9) to remove any residual foreign matter; (8) bagging for transportation and storage (Ge 42–44). Threshing floors, where both threshing and winnowing occurred, were hard, smooth, open places, prepared on either rock or clay and carefully chosen for favorable exposure to the prevailing winds. They were usually on the east side—i.e., downwind—of the village. *was beginning.* Naomi and Ruth arrive in Bethlehem just as the renewed fullness of the land is beginning to be harvested—an early hint that Naomi will be full again. Reference to the barley harvest also prepares the reader for the next major scene in the harvest fields (see Introduction: Literary Features).

2:1–23 Act II in the drama: What is done by Ruth and Boaz awakens hope in Naomi's heart.

2:1 *relative.* A sign of hope (see note on v. 20). *Boaz.* Probably means "In him is strength." Boaz is included in both genealogies of Jesus (Mt 1:5; Lk 3:32).

2:2 *Let me go.* Although Ruth is a foreigner and, as a young

leftover grain[d] behind anyone in whose
eyes I find favor.[e]"
Naomi said to her, "Go ahead, my
daughter." 3So she went out and began to
glean in the fields behind the harvesters.[f]
As it turned out, she found herself working in a field belonging to Boaz, who was
from the clan of Elimelech.[g]
4Just then Boaz arrived from Bethlehem
and greeted the harvesters, "The LORD be
with you![h]"
"The LORD bless you![i]" they called
back.
5Boaz asked the foreman of his harvesters, "Whose young woman is that?"
6The foreman replied, "She is the Moabitess[j] who came back from Moab with
Naomi. 7She said, 'Please let me glean and
gather among the sheaves[k] behind the harvesters.' She went into the field and has
worked steadily from morning till now, except for a short rest[l] in the shelter."
8So Boaz said to Ruth, "My daughter,
listen to me. Don't go and glean in another field and don't go away from here. Stay
here with my servant girls. 9Watch the
field where the men are harvesting, and
follow along after the girls. I have told the
men not to touch you. And whenever you
are thirsty, go and get a drink from the water jars the men have filled."
10At this, she bowed down with her face
to the ground.[m] She exclaimed, "Why have
I found such favor in your eyes that you
notice me[n]—a foreigner?[o]"
11Boaz replied, "I've been told all about
what you have done for your mother-in-law[p] since the death of your husband[q]—how you left your father and
mother and your homeland and came to
live with a people you did not know[r] before.[s] 12May the LORD repay you for what
you have done. May you be richly rewarded by the LORD,[t] the God of Israel,[u] under
whose wings[v] you have come to take refuge.[w]"
13"May I continue to find favor in your
eyes,[x] my lord," she said. "You have giv-
en me comfort and have spoken kindly to
your servant—though I do not have the
standing of one of your servant girls."
14At mealtime Boaz said to her, "Come
over here. Have some bread[y] and dip it in
the wine vinegar."
When she sat down with the harvesters,[z] he offered her some roasted grain.[a]
She ate all she wanted and had some left
over.[b] 15As she got up to glean, Boaz gave
orders to his men, "Even if she gathers
among the sheaves,[c] don't embarrass her.
16Rather, pull out some stalks for her from
the bundles and leave them for her to pick
up, and don't rebuke[d] her."
17So Ruth gleaned in the field until evening. Then she threshed[e] the barley she
had gathered, and it amounted to about
an ephah.[a][f] 18She carried it back to town,
and her mother-in-law saw how much she
had gathered. Ruth also brought out and
gave her what she had left over[g] after she
had eaten enough.
19Her mother-in-law asked her, "Where
did you glean today? Where did you work?
Blessed be the man who took notice of
you![h]"
Then Ruth told her mother-in-law about
the one at whose place she had been working. "The name of the man I worked with
today is Boaz," she said.
20"The LORD bless him![i]" Naomi said to
her daughter-in-law.[j] "He has not stopped
showing his kindness[k] to the living and
the dead." She added, "That man is our
close relative;[l] he is one of our kinsman-
redeemers.[m]"
21Then Ruth the Moabitess[n] said, "He

2:2 [d]S Lev 19:9; S 23:22 [e]S Ge 6:8; S 18:3 **2:3** [f]ver 14; 2Ki 4:18; Jer 9:22; Am 9:13 [g]ver 1 **2:4** [h]S Jdg 6:12; Lk 1:28; 2Th 3:16 [i]S Ge 28:3; S Nu 6:24 **2:6** [j]S Ru 1:22 **2:7** [k]S Ge 37:7; S Lev 19:9 [l]2Sa 4:5 **2:10** [m]S Ge 19:1; S 1Sa 20:41 [n]ver 19; Ps 41:1 [o]S Ge 31:15; S Dt 15:3 **2:11** [p]S Ru 1:14 [q]S Ru 1:5 [r]Isa 55:5 [s]Ru 1:16-17 **2:12** [t]1Sa 24:19; 26:23,25; Ps 18:20; Pr 25:22; Jer 31:16 [u]S Jos 24:15 [v]Ps 17:8; 36:7; 57:1; 61:4; 63:7; 91:4 [w]Ps 71:1 **2:13** [x]S Ge 18:3 **2:14** [y]S Ge 3:19 [z]S ver 3 [a]S Lev 23:14 [b]ver 18 **2:15** [c]S Ge 37:7; S Lev 19:9 **2:16** [d]S Ge 37:10 **2:17** [e]S Jdg 6:11 [f]S Lev 19:36 **2:18** [g]ver 14 **2:19** [h]S ver 10 **2:20** [i]S Jdg 17:2; S 1Sa 23:21 [j]S Ge 11:31 [k]S Ge 19:19 [l]S Lev 25:25 [m]Ru 3:9,12; 4:1,14 **2:21** [n]S Ru 1:22

[a] *17* That is, probably about 3/5 bushel (about 22 liters)

woman alone, obviously quite vulnerable in the harvest fields, she undertakes to provide for her mother-in-law. In 3:1 Naomi undertakes to provide for Ruth. *pick up the leftover grain.* The law of Moses instructed landowners to leave what the harvesters missed so that the poor, the foreigner, the widow and the fatherless could glean for their needs (Lev 19:9; 23:22; Dt 24:19).

2:3 *As it turned out.* Divine providence is at work (vv. 19–20).

2:4 The exchange of greetings between Boaz and his laborers characterizes Boaz as a godly man with a kind spirit.

2:9 *follow along after the girls.* It was customary for the men to cut the grain and for the female servants to go behind them to bind the grain into sheaves. Then Ruth could glean what they had left behind (see note on 1:22). *not to touch you.* This little word from Boaz indicates the risk Ruth had taken and discloses the measure of Boaz's care for her.

2:11 *what you have done for your mother-in-law.* Ruth's commitment to care for her desolate mother-in-law remains the center of attention throughout the book.

2:12 *under whose wings.* A figure of a bird protecting her young under her wings (see Mt 23:37; see also note on 3:9).

2:13 *your servant.* A polite reference to herself.

2:15 *gave orders to his men.* Boaz goes beyond the requirement of the law in making sure that Ruth's labors are abundantly productive (see 3:15 and note).

2:17 *threshed.* See note on 1:22. In Ruth's case, as in that of Gideon (Jdg 6:11), the amount was small and could be threshed by hand simply by beating it with a club or stick. *ephah.* See NIV text note; an unusually large amount for one day's gleaning.

2:20 *He has not stopped showing his kindness.* In 3:10 Boaz credits Ruth with demonstrating this same virtue (see also note on 1:8). *kinsman-redeemers.* Redemption is a key concept in Ruth (see Introduction: Theme and Theology). The kinsman-redeemer was responsible for protecting the interests of needy members of the extended family—e.g., to provide an heir for a brother who had died (Dt 25:5–10), to redeem land that a poor relative had sold outside the family (Lev 25:25–28), to redeem a relative who had been sold into slavery (Lev 25:47–49) and to avenge the

even said to me, 'Stay with my workers until they finish harvesting all my grain.' "
22Naomi said to Ruth her daughter-in-
law, "It will be good for you, my daughter,
to go with his girls, because in someone
else's field you might be harmed."
23So Ruth stayed close to the servant
girls of Boaz to glean until the barley[o] and
wheat harvests[p] were finished. And she
lived with her mother-in-law.

Ruth and Boaz at the Threshing Floor

3 One day Naomi her mother-in-law[q]
said to her, "My daughter, should I not
try to find a home[a][r] for you, where you
will be well provided for? 2Is not Boaz,
with whose servant girls you have been,
a kinsman[s] of ours? Tonight he will be
winnowing barley on the threshing floor.[t]
3Wash[u] and perfume yourself,[v] and put on
your best clothes.[w] Then go down to the
threshing floor, but don't let him know
you are there until he has finished eating
and drinking.[x] 4When he lies down, note
the place where he is lying. Then go and
uncover his feet and lie down. He will tell
you what to do."
5"I will do whatever you say,"[y] Ruth answered. 6So she went down to the threshing floor[z] and did everything her mother-
in-law told her to do.
7When Boaz had finished eating and
drinking and was in good spirits,[a] he went
over to lie down at the far end of the grain
pile.[b] Ruth approached quietly, uncovered
his feet and lay down. 8In the middle of
the night something startled the man, and
he turned and discovered a woman lying
at his feet.
9"Who are you?" he asked.
"I am your servant Ruth," she said.
"Spread the corner of your garment[c] over
me, since you are a kinsman-redeemer.[d]"
10"The LORD bless you,[e] my daughter,"
he replied. "This kindness is greater than
that which you showed earlier:[f] You have
not run after the younger men, whether rich or poor. 11And now, my daughter, don't be afraid. I will do for you all
you ask. All my fellow townsmen know
that you are a woman of noble character.[g] 12Although it is true that I am near of
kin, there is a kinsman-redeemer[h] nearer
than[i] I. 13Stay here for the night, and in
the morning if he wants to redeem,[j] good;
let him redeem. But if he is not willing, as
surely as the LORD lives[k] I will do it.[l] Lie
here until morning."
14So she lay at his feet until morning, but
got up before anyone could be recognized;
and he said, "Don't let it be known that a
woman came to the threshing floor.[m]"[n]
15He also said, "Bring me the shawl[o]
you are wearing and hold it out." When
she did so, he poured into it six measures
of barley and put it on her. Then he[b] went
back to town.

2:23 [o]S Ex 9:31 [p]S Ge 30:14; S 1Sa 6:13 **3:1** [q]Ru 1:14 [r]Ru 1:9 **3:2** [s]S Ru 2:1 [t]S Lev 2:14; S Nu 18:27; S Jdg 6:11 **3:3** [u]2Sa 12:20; 2Ki 5:10; Ps 26:6; 51:2; Isa 1:16; Jer 4:14; Eze 16:9 [v]2Sa 14:2; Isa 61:3 [w]S Ge 41:14 [x]S Ex 32:6; S Ecc 2:3; S Jer 15:17 **3:5** [y]Eph 6:1; Col 3:20 **3:6** [z]S Nu 18:27 **3:7** [a]Jdg 19:6,9,22; 1Sa 25:36; 2Sa 13:28; 1Ki 21:7; Est 1:10 [b]2Ch 31:6; SS 7:2; Jer 50:26; Hag 2:16 **3:9** [c]Eze 16:8 [d]S Ru 2:20 **3:10** [e]S Jdg 17:2 [f]S Jos 2:12 **3:11** [g]Pr 12:4; 14:1; 31:10 **3:12** [h]S Ru 2:20 [i]Ru 4:1 **3:13** [j]Dt 25:5; Ru 4:5; Mt 22:24 [k]S Nu 14:21; Hos 4:15 [l]Ru 4:6 **3:14** [m]S Nu 18:27 [n]Ro 14:16; 2Co 8:21 **3:15** [o]Isa 3:22

[a] *1* Hebrew *find rest* (see Ruth 1:9) [b] *15* Most Hebrew manuscripts; many Hebrew manuscripts, Vulgate and Syriac *she*

killing of a relative (Nu 35:19–21; "avenger" and "kinsman-redeemer" are translations of the same Hebrew word). When Naomi hears about the day's events, she takes courage. This moment of her awakened hope is the crucial turning point of the story (see Introduction: Literary Features).

2:23 *until the barley and wheat harvests were finished.* This phrase rounds out the harvest episode and prepares for the next major scene on the threshing floor (see Introduction: Literary Features).

3:1–18 Act III in the drama: Hopeful Naomi takes the initiative.

3:2 *Tonight he will be winnowing.* See note on 1:22. In the threshing season it was customary for the landowner and his men to spend the night near the threshing floor to protect his grain from theft.

3:3 Ruth is instructed to prepare herself like a bride (see Eze 16:9–12 and notes). *go down to the threshing floor.* At winnowing time the threshing floor was a place for male camaraderie and revelry (v. 14). *eating and drinking.* Harvest was a time of festivity (Isa 9:3; 16:9–10; Jer 48:33).

3:4 *uncover his feet and lie down.* Although Naomi's instructions may appear forward, the moral integrity of Naomi, Ruth and Boaz is never in doubt (see v. 11 and note). Naomi's advice to Ruth is clearly for the purpose of appealing to Boaz's kinsman obligation. Ruth's actions were a request for marriage. Tamar, the mother of Perez (see 4:12 and note), had also laid claim to the provision of the levirate (or kinsman-redeemer) law (Ge 38:13–30).

3:9 *Spread the corner of your garment over me.* A request for marriage (see Dt 22:30 and note); a similar custom is still practiced in some parts of the Middle East today. With a striking play on words Ruth confronts Boaz with his moral obligations. In the harvest field he had wished her well at the hands of the Lord "under whose wings you have come to take refuge" (2:12). Now on the threshing floor Ruth asks him to spread the "wings" (i.e., the corners) of his garment over her. Boaz is vividly reminded that he must serve as the Lord's protective wings over Ruth.

3:10 *kindness ... you showed earlier.* See 2:11–12; see also note on 2:20.

3:11 *woman of noble character.* In Pr 12:4; 31:10, the Hebrew for this phrase is translated "wife of noble character." The Hebrew for "noble character" is the same as that used to describe Boaz in 2:1; thus the author maintains a balance between his descriptions of Ruth and Boaz.

3:12 *a kinsman-redeemer nearer than I.* How Boaz was related to Ruth's former husband (Mahlon) is unknown, but the closest male relative had the primary responsibility to marry a widow. Naomi instructed Ruth to approach Boaz because he had already shown himself willing to be Ruth's protector. Boaz, however, would not bypass the directives of the law, which clearly gave priority to the nearest relative.

3:13 *as surely as the LORD lives.* See Ge 42:15; Job 27:2 and notes. Boaz commits himself by oath (cf. 1:17 and note) to redeem the family property and to arrange Ruth's honorable marriage.

3:15 Boaz goes beyond the requirement of the law in supplying Ruth with grain from the threshing floor (see 2:15–16 and note on 2:15).

16 When Ruth came to her mother-in-
law, Naomi asked, "How did it go, my
daughter?"
Then she told her everything Boaz
had done for her 17 and added, "He gave
me these six measures of barley, saying,
'Don't go back to your mother-in-law
empty-handed.'"
18 Then Naomi said, "Wait, my daughter,
until you find out what happens. For the
man will not rest until the matter is settled
today."[p]

Boaz Marries Ruth

4 Meanwhile Boaz went up to the town
gate[q] and sat there. When the kinsman-
redeemer[r] he had mentioned[s] came along,
Boaz said, "Come over here, my friend,
and sit down." So he went over and sat
down.
2 Boaz took ten of the elders[t] of the town
and said, "Sit here," and they did so.[u]
3 Then he said to the kinsman-redeemer,
"Naomi, who has come back from Moab,
is selling the piece of land that belonged
to our brother Elimelech.[v] 4 I thought I
should bring the matter to your attention
and suggest that you buy it in the presence
of these seated here and in the presence of
the elders of my people. If you will redeem
it, do so. But if you[a] will not, tell me, so I
will know. For no one has the right to do it
except you,[w] and I am next in line."
"I will redeem it," he said.
5 Then Boaz said, "On the day you buy
the land from Naomi and from Ruth the
Moabitess,[x] you acquire[b] the dead man's
widow, in order to maintain the name of
the dead with his property."[y]
6 At this, the kinsman-redeemer said,
"Then I cannot redeem[z] it because I might
endanger my own estate. You redeem it
yourself. I cannot do it."[a]
7 (Now in earlier times in Israel, for the
redemption[b] and transfer of property to
become final, one party took off his sandal[c] and gave it to the other. This was the
method of legalizing transactions[d] in Israel.)[e]
8 So the kinsman-redeemer said to Boaz,
"Buy it yourself." And he removed his
sandal.[f]
9 Then Boaz announced to the elders
and all the people, "Today you are witnesses[g] that I have bought from Naomi
all the property of Elimelech, Kilion and
Mahlon. 10 I have also acquired Ruth the
Moabitess,[h] Mahlon's widow, as my wife,[i]
in order to maintain the name of the dead
with his property, so that his name will
not disappear from among his family or
from the town records.[j] Today you are witnesses![k]"
11 Then the elders and all those at the
gate[l] said, "We are witnesses.[m] May the
LORD make the woman who is coming into
your home like Rachel and Leah,[n] who together built up the house of Israel. May
you have standing in Ephrathah[o] and be
famous in Bethlehem.[p] 12 Through the offspring the LORD gives you by this young

3:18 [p] Ps 37:3-5
4:1 [q] S Ge 18:1; S 23:10 [r] S Ru 2:20 [s] Ru 3:12
4:2 [t] S Ex 3:16 [u] S Dt 25:7
4:3 [v] S Lev 25:25; S Ru 1:2
4:4 [w] S Lev 25:25; Jer 32:7-8
4:5 [x] S Ru 1:22 [y] S Ge 38:8; S Ru 3:13
4:6 [z] Lev 25:25; Ru 3:13 [a] S Dt 25:7
4:7 [b] S Lev 25:24 [c] ver 8 [d] Isa 8:1-2, 16, 20 [e] Dt 25:7-9
4:8 [f] Dt 25:9
4:9 [g] Isa 8:2; Jer 32:10, 44
4:10 [h] S Ru 1:22 [i] S Dt 25:5 [j] S Dt 25:6 [k] S Jos 24:22
4:11 [l] S Ge 23:10 [m] S Dt 25:9 [n] S Ge 4:19; S 29:16 [o] S Ge 35:16 [p] Ru 1:19

[a] 4 Many Hebrew manuscripts, Septuagint, Vulgate and Syriac; most Hebrew manuscripts *he*
[b] 5 Hebrew; Vulgate and Syriac *Naomi, you acquire Ruth the Moabitess,*

3:17 *empty-handed.* Again the empty-full motif (see note on 1:21).

3:18 *Wait.* The Hebrew underlying this word is translated "sat" in 4:1. Thus the author prepares the reader for the next major scene, in which Boaz sits at the town gate to see the matter through.

4:1–12 Act IV in the drama: Boaz arranges to fulfill his pledge to Ruth.

4:1 *town gate.* The "town hall" of ancient Israel, the normal place for business and legal transactions, where witnesses were readily available (vv. 9–12; see note on Ge 19:1). *my friend.* The other kinsman remains unnamed.

4:2 *ten of the elders.* A full court for legal proceedings.

4:3 *selling the piece of land.* See note on 2:20. Two interpretations are possible: (1) Naomi owns the land but is so destitute that she is forced to sell. It was the duty of the kinsman-redeemer to buy any land in danger of being sold outside the family. (2) Naomi does not own the land—it had been sold by Elimelech before the family left for Moab—but by law she retains the right of redemption to buy the land back. Lacking funds to do so herself, she is dependent on a kinsman-redeemer to do it for her. It is the right of redemption that Naomi is "selling." *brother.* Used in the broader sense of "relative."

4:5 *you acquire the dead man's widow.* Now Boaz reveals the other half of the obligation—the acquisition of Ruth. Levirate law (Dt 25:5–6; see note on Lev 25:25) provided that Ruth's firstborn son would keep Mahlon's name alive and retain ownership of the family inheritance.

4:6 *I cannot redeem it.* Possibly he fears that, if he has a son by her and if that son is his only surviving heir, his own property will transfer to the family of Elimelech (see note on Ge 38:9). In that case his risk was no greater than that assumed by Boaz. This kinsman's refusal to assume the kinsman-redeemer's role highlights the kindness and generosity of Boaz toward the two widows—just as Orpah's return to her family highlights Ruth's selfless devotion and loyalty to Naomi.

4:7 *one party took off his sandal.* The process of renouncing one's property rights and passing them to another was publicly attested by taking off a sandal and transferring it to the new owner (cf. Am 2:6; 8:6). The Nuzi documents (see chart, p. xxiii) refer to a similar custom.

4:9 *witnesses.* The role of public witnesses was to attest to all legal transactions and other binding agreements.

4:10 *name of the dead.* See Dt 25:5–7 and notes.

4:11 *Rachel and Leah ... built up the house of Israel.* Cf. Dt 25:9. The Israelite readers of Ruth would have associated the house of Jacob (Israel), built up by Rachel and Leah, with the house of Israel, rebuilt by David, the descendant of Ruth and Boaz, after it had been threatened with extinction (1Sa 4). They also knew that the Lord had covenanted to "build" the house of David as an enduring dynasty, through which Israel's blessed destiny would be assured (see 2Sa 7:27–29). *Ephrathah.* See note on 1:2.

woman, may your family be like that of
Perez,[q] whom Tamar[r] bore to Judah."

The Genealogy of David

4:18-22pp — 1Ch 2:5-15; Mt 1:3-6; Lk 3:31-33

13 So Boaz took Ruth and she became
his wife. Then he went to her, and the
LORD enabled her to conceive,[s] and she
gave birth to a son.[t] 14 The women[u] said
to Naomi: "Praise be to the LORD,[v] who
this day has not left you without a kinsman-redeemer.[w] May he become famous
throughout Israel! 15 He will renew your
life and sustain you in your old age. For
your daughter-in-law,[x] who loves you and
who is better to you than seven sons,[y] has
given him birth."

16 Then Naomi took the child, laid him
in her lap and cared for him. 17 The women
living there said, "Naomi has a son." And
they named him Obed. He was the father
of Jesse,[z] the father of David.[a]

18 This, then, is the family line of Perez[b]:

Perez was the father of Hezron,[c]
19 Hezron the father of Ram,
Ram the father of Amminadab,[d]
20 Amminadab the father of Nahshon,[e]
Nahshon the father of Salmon,[a]
21 Salmon the father of Boaz,[f]
Boaz the father of Obed,
22 Obed the father of Jesse,
and Jesse the father of David.

4:12 [q] S Ge 38:29 [r] Ge 38:6, 24
4:13 [s] S Ge 8:1; S 29:31 [t] S Ge 29:32; S 30:6; Lk 1:57
4:14 [u] Lk 1:58 [v] S Ge 24:27 [w] S Ru 2:20
4:15 [x] S Ge 11:31 [y] 1Sa 1:8; 2:5; Job 1:2
4:17 [z] ver 22; 1Sa 16:1, 18; 17:12, 17, 58; 1Ch 2:12, 13; Ps 72:20 [a] 1Sa 16:13; 1Ch 2:15
4:18 [b] S Ge 38:29 [c] Nu 26:21
4:19 [d] S Ex 6:23
4:20 [e] S Nu 7:12
4:21 [f] S Ru 2:1

[a] *20* A few Hebrew manuscripts, some Septuagint manuscripts and Vulgate (see also verse 21 and Septuagint of 1 Chron. 2:11); most Hebrew manuscripts *Salma*

4:12 *Perez, whom Tamar bore to Judah.* Perez was Boaz's ancestor (vv. 18–21; Mt 1:3; Lk 3:33). His birth to Judah was from a union based on the levirate practice (Ge 38:27–30; see note on 1:11). Perez was therefore an appropriate model within Boaz's ancestry for the blessing the elders gave to Boaz. Moreover, the descendants of Perez had raised the tribe of Judah to a prominent place in Israel. So the blessing of the elders—that, through the offspring Ruth would bear to Boaz, his family would be like that of Perez—was fully realized in David and his dynasty. Thus also v. 12 prepares the reader for the events briefly narrated in the conclusion.

4:13–17 The conclusion of the story balances the introduction (1:1–5): (1) In the Hebrew both have the same number of words; (2) both compress much into a short space; (3) both focus on Naomi; (4) the introduction emphasizes Naomi's emptiness, and the conclusion portrays her fullness.

4:13 *the LORD enabled her to conceive.* See note on 1:6.

4:14 *kinsman-redeemer.* The child Obed, as vv. 15–17 make clear. *May he become famous.* This same wish is expressed concerning Boaz in v. 11.

4:15 *better to you than seven sons.* See 1Sa 1:8. Since seven was considered a number of completeness, to have seven sons was the epitome of all family blessings in Israel (see 1Sa 2:5; Job 1:2; 42:13). Ruth's selfless devotion to Naomi receives its climactic acknowledgment.

4:16 *laid him in her lap.* Possibly symbolizing adoption (see v. 17 and note on Ge 30:3).

4:17 *Naomi has a son.* Through Ruth, aged Naomi, who can no longer bear children, obtains an heir in place of Mahlon. *Obed.* The name means "servant," in its full form possibly "servant of the LORD."

4:18–22 See 1Ch 2:5–15; Mt 1:3–6; Lk 3:31–33. Like the genealogies of Ge 5:3–32; 11:10–26, this genealogy has ten names (see note on Ge 5:5). It brings to mind the reign of David, during which, in contrast to the turbulent period of the judges recalled in 1:1, Israel finally entered into rest in the promised land (see 1Ki 5:4 and note). It signifies that, just as Naomi was brought from emptiness to fullness through the selfless love of Ruth and Boaz, so the Lord brought Israel from unrest to rest through their descendant David, who selflessly gave himself to fight Israel's battles on the Lord's behalf. The ultimate end of this genealogy is Jesus Christ, the great "son of David" (Mt 1:1; see note there), who fulfills prophecy and will bring the Lord's people into final rest (see Introduction to Joshua: Title and Theological Theme; see also Heb. 3:7—4:11 and notes).

1 Samuel

I N T R O D U C T I O N

Title

1 and 2 Samuel are named after the person God used to establish monarchy in Israel. Samuel not only anointed both Saul and David, Israel's first two kings, but he also gave definition to the new order of God's rule over Israel. Samuel's role as God's representative in this period of Israel's history is close to that of Moses (see Ps 99:6; Jer 15:1 and notes) since he, more than any other person, provided for covenant continuity in the transition from the rule of the judges to that of the monarchy.

1 and 2 Samuel were originally one book. It was divided into two parts by the translators of the Septuagint (the pre-Christian Greek translation of the OT)—a division subsequently followed by Jerome (in the Latin Vulgate, c. A.D. 400) and by modern versions. The title of the book has varied from time to time, having been designated "The First and Second Books of Kingdoms" (Septuagint), "First and Second Kings" (Vulgate) and "First and Second Samuel" (Hebrew tradition and most modern versions).

A Quick Look

Author:
Unknown

Audience:
God's chosen people, the Israelites

Date:
Sometime after Israel was divided into the northern and southern kingdoms in about 930 B.C.

Theme:
The nation of Israel transitions from being led by God through "judges" to being led by him through kings.

Literary Features, Authorship and Date

Many questions have arisen pertaining to the literary character, authorship and date of 1,2 Samuel. Certain features of the book suggest that it was compiled with the use of a number of originally independent sources, which the author may have incorporated into his own composition as much as possible in their original, unedited form.

Who the author was cannot be known since the book itself gives no indication of his identity. Whoever he was, he doubtless had access to records of the life and times of Samuel, Saul and David. Explicit reference in the book itself is made to only one such source (the Book of Jashar, 2Sa 1:18), but the writer of Chronicles refers to four others that pertain to this period (the book of the annals of King David, 1Ch 27:24; the records of Samuel the seer; the records of Nathan the prophet; the records of Gad the seer, 1Ch 29:29). For the dates of the period see Chronology, pp. 376 – 377.

Contents and Theme: Kingship and Covenant

1 Samuel relates God's establishment of a political system in Israel headed by a human king. Before the author describes this momentous change in the structure of the theocracy (God's kingly rule over his people), he effectively depicts the complexity of its context. The following events provide both historical and theological background for the beginning of the monarchy:

1. *The birth, youth and call of Samuel (chs. 1 – 3).* In a book dealing for the most part with the reigns of Israel's first two kings, Saul and David, it is significant that the author chose not to include a birth narrative of either of these men, but to describe the birth of their forerunner and anointer, the prophet Samuel. This in itself accentuates the importance the author attached to Samuel's role in the events that follow. He seems to be saying in a subtle way that flesh and blood are to be subordinated to word and Spirit in the process of the establishment of kingship. For this reason chs. 1 – 3 should be viewed as integrally related to what follows, not as a more likely component of the book of Judges or as a loosely attached prefix to the rest of 1,2 Samuel. Kingship is given its birth and then nurtured by the prophetic word and work of the prophet Samuel. Moreover, the events of Samuel's nativity thematically anticipate the story of God's working that is narrated in the rest of the book.

2. *The "ark narratives" (chs. 4 – 6).* This section describes how the ark of God was captured by the Philistines and then, after God wreaked havoc on several Philistine cities, how it was returned to Israel. These narratives reveal the folly of Israel's notion that possession of the ark automatically guaranteed victory over her enemies. They also display the awesome power of the Lord (Yahweh, the God of Israel) and his superiority over the Philistine god Dagon. The Philistines were forced to confess openly their helplessness against God's power by their return of the ark to Israel. The entire ark episode performs a vital function in placing Israel's subsequent sinful desire for a human king in proper perspective.

3. *Samuel as "judge" and deliverer (ch. 7).* When Samuel called Israel to repentance and renewed dedication to the Lord, the Lord intervened mightily in Israel's behalf and gave victory over the Philistines. This narrative reaffirms the authority of Samuel as the divinely ordained leader who in his day of Israel's crisis (see 12:9 – 11 and note) was raised up by God to fulfill a role similar to that of God's servant Moses; at the same time it provides evidence of divine protection and blessing for God's people when they place their confidence in the Lord and live in obedience to their covenant obligations.

All the material in chs. 1 – 7 serves as a necessary preface for the narratives of chs. 8 – 12, which describe the rise and establishment of kingship in Israel. The author has masterfully arranged the stories in chs. 8 – 12 in order to accentuate the serious theological conflict surrounding the historical events. In the study of these chapters, scholars have often noted the presence of a tension or ambivalence in the attitude toward the monarchy: On the one hand, Samuel is commanded by the Lord to give the people a king (8:7,9,22; 9:16 – 17; 10:24; 12:13); on the other hand, their request for a king is considered a sinful rejection of the Lord (8:7; 10:19; 12:12,17,19 – 20). These seemingly conflicting attitudes toward the monarchy must be understood in the context of Israel's covenant relationship with the Lord.

Moses had anticipated Israel's desire for a human king (see Dt 17:14 – 20 and notes), but Israelite kingship was to be compatible with the continued rule of the Lord over his people as their Great King. Instead, when the elders asked Samuel to give them a king (8:5,19 – 20), they rejected the Lord's kingship over them. Their desire was for a king such as the nations around them had — to lead them in battle and give them a sense of national security and unity. The request for a king constituted a denial of their covenant relationship to the Lord, who was their King. Moreover, the Lord not only had promised to be their protector but had also repeatedly demonstrated his power in their behalf, most recently in the ark narratives (chs. 4 – 6), as well as in the great victory won over the Philistines under the leadership of Samuel (ch. 7).

Nevertheless the Lord instructed Samuel to give the people a king. By divine appointment Saul was brought into contact with Samuel, and Samuel was directed to anoint him privately as king (9:1—10:16). Subsequently, Samuel gathered the people at Mizpah, where, after again admonishing them concerning their sin in desiring a king (see 10:18–19 and note on 10:18), he presided over the selection of a king by lot. The lot fell on Saul and publicly designated him as the one whom God had chosen (see 10:24 and note on 10:25). Saul did not immediately assume his royal office, but returned home to work his fields (11:5,7). When the inhabitants of Jabesh Gilead were threatened by Nahash the Ammonite, Saul rose to the challenge, gathered an army and led Israel to victory in battle. His success placed a final seal of divine approval on Saul's selection to be king (cf. 10:24; 11:12–13 and note on 11:13) and occasioned the inauguration of his reign at Gilgal (11:14—12:25).

The question that still needed resolution, then, was not so much whether Israel should have a king (it was clearly the Lord's will to give them a king), but rather how they could maintain their covenant with God (i.e., preserve the theocracy) now that they had a human king. The problem was resolved when Samuel called the people to repentance and renewal of their allegiance to the Lord on the very occasion of the inauguration of Saul as king (see note on 10:25). By establishing kingship in the context of covenant renewal, Samuel placed the monarchy in Israel on a radically different footing from that in surrounding nations. The king in Israel was not to be autonomous in his authority and power; rather, he was to be subject to the law of the Lord and the word of the prophet (10:25; 12:23). This was to be true not only for Saul but also for all the kings who would occupy the throne in Israel in the future. The king was to be an instrument of the Lord's rule over his people, and the people as well as the king were to continue to recognize the Lord as their ultimate Sovereign (see 12:14–15 and notes).

When the elders asked Samuel to give them a king, they rejected the Lord's kingship over them.

Saul soon demonstrated that he was unwilling to submit to the requirements of his theocratic office (chs. 13–15). When he disobeyed the instructions of the prophet Samuel in preparation for battle against the Philistines (see 13:13 and note), and when he refused to totally destroy the Amalekites as he had been commanded to do by the word of the Lord through Samuel (ch. 15), he ceased to be an instrument of the Lord's rule over his people. These abrogations of the requirements of his theocratic office led to his rejection as king (see 15:22–23 and notes).

The remainder of 1 Samuel (chs. 16–31) depicts the Lord's choice of David to be Saul's successor, and then describes the long road by which David is prepared for accession to the throne. Although Saul's rule became increasingly antitheocratic in nature, David refused to usurp the throne by forceful means but left his accession to office in the Lord's hands. Eventually Saul was wounded in a battle with the Philistines and, fearing capture, took his own life. Three of Saul's sons, including David's loyal friend Jonathan, were killed in the same battle (ch. 31).

Chronology

Even though the narratives of 1,2 Samuel contain some statements of chronological import (see, e.g., 1Sa 6:1; 7:2; 8:1,5; 13:1; 25:1; 2Sa 2:10–11; 5:4–5; 14:28; 15:7), the data are insufficient to establish a precise chronology for the major events of this period of Israel's history. Except for the dates of David's birth and the duration of his reign, which are quite firm (see 2Sa 5:4–5), most other dates can only be approximated. The textual problem with the chronological data on the age of Saul when he became king and the length of his reign (see NIV text notes on 1Sa 13:1) contributes to uncertainty concerning the precise time of his birth and the beginning of his reign. No information is given concerning the time of Samuel's birth (1Sa 1:20) or death (25:1). His lifetime probably overlapped that of Samson and that of Obed, son of Ruth and Boaz and grandfather of David. It is indicated that he was well along in years when the elders of Israel asked him to give them a king (see 8:1,5 and note on 8:1). One other factor contributing to chronological uncertainty is that the author has not always arranged his material in strict chronological sequence. It seems clear, e.g., that 2Sa 7 is to be placed chronologically after David's conquests described in 2Sa 8:1 – 14 (see notes on 2Sa 7:1; 8:1). The story of the famine sent by God on Israel during the reign of David because of Saul's violation of a treaty with the Gibeonites is found in 2Sa 21:1 – 14, though chronologically it occurred prior to the time of Absalom's rebellion recorded in 2Sa 15 – 18 (see further the notes on 2Sa 21:1 – 14). The following dates, however, provide an approximate chronological framework for the times of Samuel, Saul and David.

1105 B.C. Birth of Samuel (1Sa 1:20)
1080 Birth of Saul
1050 Saul anointed to be king (1Sa 10:1)
1040 Birth of David
1025 David anointed to be Saul's successor (1Sa 16:1 – 13)
1010 Death of Saul and beginning of David's reign over Judah in Hebron (1Sa 31:4 – 6; 2Sa 2:1,4,11)
1003 Beginning of David's reign over all Israel and capture of Jerusalem (2Sa 5)
997 – 992 David's wars (2Sa 8:1 – 14)
991 Birth of Solomon (2Sa 12:24)
980 David's census (2Sa 24:1 – 9)
970 End of David's reign (2Sa 5:4 – 5; 1Ki 2:10 – 11)

Outline

- I. The Nativity of Samuel and His Authentication as a Prophet "like Moses" (1:1 – 4:1a)
  - A. Samuel's Birth: Hannah's Song (1:1 — 2:11)
  - B. Samuel Contrasted with Eli's Sons (2:12 – 36)
  - C. Samuel's Initiation and Recognition as a Prophet of the Lord (3:1 — 4:1a)
- II. Israel without Faithful Leadership (4:1b — 7:1)
  - A. Israel's Loss of Both the Ark and the Chief Priestly Family (4:1b – 22)
  - B. God's Powerful Presence with His Ark in Philistia (ch. 5)
  - C. The Ark's Return to Israel (6:1 — 7:1)
- III. Samuel's Leadership as Prophet and Judge Characterized Illustratively (7:2 – 17)
- IV. Establishment of the Monarchy in Israel (8:1 — 12:25)
  - A. Israel's Request for a King like the Nations (ch. 8)
  - B. Samuel Anoints Saul (9:1 — 10:8)
  - C. Saul Publicly Chosen by Lot to be King (10:9 – 27)
  - D. Saul's Kingship Confirmed (ch. 11)
  - E. Samuel's Resignation from His Role as Judge (ch. 12)
- V. Saul's Reign Characterized Illustratively (chs. 13 – 14)
- VI. Transition to David's Reign (15:1 — 2Sa 5:5)
  - A. God's Rejection of Saul (ch. 15)
  - B. Saul's Decline; David's Rise (chs. 16 — 2Sa 1)
    1. David's anointing by Samuel (16:1 – 13)
    2. Saul's dependence on David as musician and warrior (16:14 — 17:58)
    3. Saul's alienation from David; his family's protection of David (chs. 18 – 20)
    4. David's flight from Saul (chs. 21 – 22)
    5. Four tests of David's use of his growing power (chs. 23 – 26)
    6. David's flight to Philistia and Saul's final defeat by the Philistines (chs. 27 – 31)
    7. David's reaction to and lament over Saul's death (2Sa 1)
  - C. David Becomes King over Judah (2:1 — 3:5)
  - D. David Becomes King over All Israel (3:6 — 5:5)
- VII. David's Reign Characterized Illustratively (5:6 — 8:18)
  - A. David's Conquest of Jerusalem and His Recognition by the King of Tyre (5:6 – 16)
  - B. David's Crushing of the Philistine Threat (5:17 – 25)
  - C. David's Bringing the Ark (God's Throne) into His Royal City (ch. 6)

- D. God's Covenant with David (ch. 7)
- E. David's Victories that Secure the Boundaries of His Kingdom (ch. 8)

VIII. Threats to David's Reign Overcome (chs. 9 – 20)
- A. David's Kindness to Saul's Remaining Heir (ch. 9)
- B. Defeat of the Ammonite-Aramean Challenge to David's Reign (10:1 – 19; 12:26 – 31)
- C. David's Shameful Abuse of His Royal Power in the Matter of Bathsheba and Uriah (11:1 — 12:25)
- D. Absalom's Challenge to David's Rule (chs. 13 – 20)
  1. Amnon's abuse of power and Absalom's revenge (ch. 13)
  2. Absalom's revolt crushed (chs. 14 – 19)
  3. Absalom's attempt sparks another unsuccessful revolt (ch. 20)

IX. Sidebars to the David Story (Chiastically Arranged) (chs. 21 – 24)
- A. God's Wrath against Israel because of Something Saul Had Done (21:1 – 14)
- B. Exploits of David's Mighty Men in Wars against Philistines (21:15 – 22)
- C. David's Song in Praise of the Lord for Victories Granted (ch. 22)
- C'. David's "Last Song" that Speaks of God's Ways with Him and His House (23:1 – 7)
- B'. David's Mighty Men and Their Exploits, Especially against Philistines (23:8 – 39)
- A'. God's Wrath against Israel because of Something David Did (ch. 24)

The Birth of Samuel

1 There was a certain man from Ramathaim,[a] a Zuphite[a][b] from the hill country[c] of Ephraim,[d] whose name was Elkanah[e] son of Jeroham, the son of Elihu, the son of Tohu, the son of Zuph, an Ephraimite. 2He had two wives;[f] one was called Hannah and the other Peninnah. Peninnah had children, but Hannah had none.

3Year after year[g] this man went up from his town to worship[h] and sacrifice to the LORD Almighty at Shiloh,[i] where Hophni and Phinehas, the two sons of Eli,[j] were priests of the LORD. 4Whenever the day came for Elkanah to sacrifice,[k] he would give portions of the meat to his wife Peninnah and to all her sons and daughters.[l] 5But to Hannah he gave a double portion[m] because he loved her, and the LORD had closed her womb.[n] 6And because the LORD had closed her womb, her rival kept provoking her in order to irritate her.[o] 7This went on year after year. Whenever Hannah went up to the house of the LORD, her rival provoked her till she wept and would not eat.[p] 8Elkanah her husband would say to her, "Hannah, why are you weeping? Why don't you eat? Why are you downhearted? Don't I mean more to you than ten sons?[q]"

9Once when they had finished eating and drinking in Shiloh, Hannah stood up. Now Eli the priest was sitting on a chair by the doorpost of the LORD's temple.[b][r] 10In bitterness of soul[s] Hannah wept much and prayed to the LORD. 11And she made a vow,[t] saying, "O LORD Almighty[u], if you will only look upon your servant's misery and remember[v] me, and not forget your servant but give her a son, then I will give him to the LORD for all the days of his life,[w] and no razor[x] will ever be used on his head."

1:1 [a]S Jos 18:25 [b]1Sa 9:5 [c]Jos 17:17-18 [d]Jos 21:20-22 [e]1Ch 6:27,34 **1:2** [f]S Ge 4:19 **1:3** [g]ver 21; Ex 23:14; 1Sa 2:19; 20:6,29; Lk 2:41 [h]Dt 12:5-7 [i]S Jos 18:1 [j]1Sa 2:31; 14:3 **1:4** [k]Lev 7:15-18; Dt 12:17-18 [l]S Ge 29:34 **1:5** [m]S Ge 37:3 [n]S Ge 11:30; S 29:31 **1:6** [o]S Ge 16:4 **1:7** [p]2Sa 12:17; Ps 102:4 **1:8** [q]S Ru 4:15 **1:9** [r]1Sa 3:3 **1:10** [s]Job 3:20; 7:11; 10:1; 21:25; 23:2; 27:2; Isa 38:15; Jer 20:18 **1:11** [t]S Jdg 11:30 [u]S Ge 17:1; Ps 24:10; 46:7; Isa 1:9 [v]S Ge 8:1 [w]S Jdg 13:7 [x]Nu 6:1-21; Jdg 13:5; Lk 1:15

[a] *1 Or from Ramathaim Zuphim* [b] *9* That is, tabernacle

1:1 — 7:17 The birth of Samuel and his establishment in Israel as a prophet "like Moses" (Dt 18:18). The central thematic focus of 1,2 Samuel is on the author's account of the establishment of the monarchy in Israel and of God's elevation of David to the throne — God's "anointed" who completed the conquest of Canaan begun by Joshua, reinstated God's symbolic throne (the ark) into the center of Israel's life, secured Israel's boundaries on every side and provided for Israel a time of "rest" (see Dt 12:10; Jos 1:13,15 and note; 1Ki 5:4 and note) in the promised land. This account, however, is prefaced by the story of the prophet Samuel, whom God raised up in a time of crisis (see 12:9 – 11 and note) as he had raised up Moses when Israel was under oppression in Egypt. Just as the author of Exodus used his account of Moses' birth and early years to preface his story of God's deliverance of Israel from Egypt in the exodus, because it in many ways foreshadowed the exodus event, so the author of 1,2 Samuel used the story of Samuel's nativity and youth because it foreshadowed — and illumined — much in what was to follow in his account (see notes on 1:27; 2:1 – 10; 2:1).

1:1 *Ramathaim.* The name occurs only here in the OT and appears to be another name for Ramah (see v. 19; 2:11; 7:17; 19:18; 25:1). It is perhaps to be identified with Arimathea (see Mt 27:57 and note; Jn 19:38). *Zuphite.* See NIV text note. It is not clear whether this word refers to the man or the place. If it refers to the man, it indicates his descent from Zuph (see later in this verse; see also 1Ch 6:34 – 35). If it refers to the place, it designates the general area in which Ramathaim was located (see 9:5). *Ephraimite.* Although Elkanah is here called an Ephraimite, he was probably a Levite whose family belonged to the Kohathite clans that had been allotted towns in Ephraim (see Jos 21:20 – 21; 1Ch 6:22 – 27).

1:2 *two wives.* See notes on Ge 4:19; 16:2; 25:6.

1:3 *Year after year this man went up.* Three times a year every Israelite male was required to appear before the Lord at the central sanctuary (see Ex 23:14 – 19 and notes; 34:23; Dt 16:16 – 17 and note on 16:16). The festival referred to here was probably the Feast of Tabernacles, which not only commemorated God's care for his people during the desert journey to Canaan (see Lev 23:43 and note on 23:42) but more especially celebrated, with joy and feasting, God's blessing on the year's crops (see Dt 16:13 – 15). On such festive occasions Hannah's deep sorrow because of her own barrenness was the more poignant. *the LORD Almighty.* Traditionally "the LORD of hosts," a royal title. This is the first time in the Bible that God is so designated. It now becomes prominent at the onset of monarchy in Israel. The Hebrew for "host(s)" can refer to (1) human armies (Ex 7:4, "divisions"; Ps 44:9); (2) the celestial bodies such as the sun, moon and stars (Ge 2:1, "vast array"; Dt 4:19; Isa 40:26); or (3) the heavenly creatures such as angels (Jos 5:14; 1Ki 22:19; Ps 148:2). The title, "the LORD of hosts," is perhaps best understood as a general reference to the sovereignty of God over all powers in the universe (hence the NIV rendering, "the LORD Almighty"). In the account of the establishment of kingship in Israel it became particularly appropriate as a reference to God as the God of armies — both of the heavenly armies (cf. Dt 33:2; Jos 5:14; Ps 68:17; Hab 3:8) and of the armies of Israel (1Sa 17:45). *Shiloh.* The town in Ephraim between Bethel and Shechem where the central sanctuary and the ark of the covenant were located (see 4:3; see also Jos 18:1; Jdg 21:19 and notes).

1:4 *sacrifice.* Here refers to a fellowship offering, a sacrifice that was combined with a festive meal signifying fellowship and communion with the Lord and grateful acknowledgment of his mercies (see Lev 7:11 – 18).

1:5 *the LORD had closed her womb.* The Lord gives and withholds children (see Ge 18:10; 29:31; 30:2,22 and note on 30:2).

1:6 *her rival.* See Ge 16:4 and note.

1:8 *more to you than ten sons.* See 2:5; see also note on Ru 4:15.

1:9 *temple.* Here and in 3:3 the central sanctuary, the tabernacle (see NIV text note), is referred to as "the LORD's temple." It is also called "the house of the LORD" (v. 7; 3:15) and "the Tent of Meeting" (2:22), and the Lord calls it "my dwelling" (2:32). The references to the tabernacle as a "house" and a "temple," as well as references to sleeping quarters and doors (3:2,15), give the impression that at this time the tabernacle was part of a larger, more permanent building complex to which the term "temple" could legitimately be applied (cf. Jer 7:12,14 and note on 7:12; 26:6).

1:11 *vow.* See Ge 28:20 – 22; Nu 21:2; Ps 50:14 and note; 76:11; 116:14,18; 132:2 – 5; Pr 20:25 and note; 31:2. Regulations for the making of vows by women are found in Nu 30. *remember.* To remember is more than simply to recall that Hannah existed. It is to go into action in her behalf (see vv. 19 – 20; see

12As she kept on praying to the LORD, Eli
observed her mouth. 13Hannah was praying in her heart, and her lips were moving
but her voice was not heard. Eli thought
she was drunk 14and said to her, "How
long will you keep on getting drunk? Get
rid of your wine."
15"Not so, my lord," Hannah replied,
"I am a woman who is deeply troubled.[y]
I have not been drinking wine or beer;
I was pouring[z] out my soul to the LORD.
16Do not take your servant for a wicked
woman; I have been praying here out of
my great anguish and grief."[a]
17Eli answered, "Go in peace,[b] and may
the God of Israel grant you what you have
asked of him.[c]"
18She said, "May your servant find favor in your eyes.[d]" Then she went her way
and ate something, and her face was no
longer downcast.[e]
19Early the next morning they arose and
worshiped before the LORD and then went
back to their home at Ramah.[f] Elkanah
lay with Hannah his wife, and the LORD
remembered[g] her. 20So in the course of
time Hannah conceived and gave birth to
a son.[h] She named[i] him Samuel,[a][j] saying,
"Because I asked the LORD for him."

Hannah Dedicates Samuel

21When the man Elkanah went up with
all his family to offer the annual[k] sacrifice
to the LORD and to fulfill his vow,[l] 22Han-
nah did not go. She said to her husband,
"After the boy is weaned, I will take him
and present[m] him before the LORD, and he
will live there always."
23"Do what seems best to you," Elkanah her husband told her. "Stay here until
you have weaned him; only may the LORD
make good[n] his[b] word." So the woman
stayed at home and nursed her son until
she had weaned[o] him.
24After he was weaned, she took the boy
with her, young as he was, along with a
three-year-old bull,[c][p] an ephah[d] of flour
and a skin of wine, and brought him to the
house of the LORD at Shiloh. 25When they
had slaughtered the bull, they brought the
boy to Eli, 26and she said to him, "As surely
as you live, my lord, I am the woman who
stood here beside you praying to the LORD.
27I prayed[q] for this child, and the LORD has
granted me what I asked of him. 28So now
I give him to the LORD. For his whole life[r]
he will be given over to the LORD." And he
worshiped the LORD there.

Hannah's Prayer

2 Then Hannah prayed and said:[s]

"My heart rejoices[t] in the LORD;
in the LORD my horn[e][u] is lifted high.
My mouth boasts[v] over my enemies,[w]
for I delight in your deliverance.

1:15 [y] 2Ki 4:27 [z] Ps 42:4; 62:8; La 2:19 **1:16** [a] Ps 55:2 **1:17** [b] Nu 6:26; 1Sa 20:42; 2Ki 5:19; S Ac 15:33 [c] S Ge 25:21; Ps 20:3-5 **1:18** [d] S Ge 18:3; Ru 2:13 [e] Ro 15:13 **1:19** [f] S Jos 18:25 [g] S Ge 8:1; S 29:31 **1:20** [h] S Ge 17:19; S 29:32; S 30:6 [i] Ex 2:10; Mt 1:21 [j] 1Sa 7:5; 12:23; 1Ch 6:27; Jer 15:1; Heb 11:32 **1:21** [k] S ver 3 [l] S Ge 28:20; Nu 30:2; Dt 12:11 **1:22** [m] Ex 13:2; Lk 2:22 **1:23** [n] S Ge 25:21 [o] Ge 21:8 **1:24** [p] Nu 15:8-10 **1:27** [q] 1Sa 2:20; Ps 66:19-20 **1:28** [r] S Jdg 13:7 **2:1** [s] Lk 1:46-55 [t] Ps 13:5; 33:21; Zec 10:7 [u] Ps 18:2; 89:17,24; 148:14 [v] Ps 6:8 [w] S Nu 10:35; Ps 6:10

[a] *20* *Samuel* sounds like the Hebrew for *heard of God.* [b] *23* Masoretic Text; Dead Sea Scrolls, Septuagint and Syriac *your* [c] *24* Dead Sea Scrolls, Septuagint and Syriac; Masoretic Text *with three bulls* [d] *24* That is, probably about 3/5 bushel (about 22 liters) [e] *1* *Horn* here symbolizes strength; also in verse 10.

also note on Ge 8:1). *your servant.* That is, me (see note on Ge 18:2). *no razor.* Hannah voluntarily vows for her son what God had required of Samson (see Jdg 13:5 and note). Long hair was a symbol of dedication to the service of the Lord and was one of the characteristics of the Nazirite vow, which was normally taken for a limited time rather than for life (see Nu 6:1–21 and notes).

1:13 *drunk.* Eli's mistake suggests that in those days it was not uncommon for drunken people to enter the sanctuary. Further evidence of the religious and moral deterioration of the time is found in the stories of Jdg 17–21.

1:15 *beer.* Written texts from Mesopotamia as early as 2500 B.C. portray the brewing of beer as a major industry.

1:16 *wicked.* See note on Dt 13:13.

1:20 *Samuel.* See NIV text note.

1:21 *annual sacrifice.* See notes on vv. 3–4. *his vow.* Making vows to God was a common feature of OT piety, usually involving thank offerings and praise (see Ps 50:14; 56:12; 116:17–18). Elkanah no doubt annually made vows to the Lord as he prayed for God's blessing on his crops and flocks, and fulfilled those vows at the Feast of Tabernacles (see note on v. 3).

1:22 *weaned.* It was customary in the East to nurse children for three years or longer (in the Apocrypha see 2 Maccabees 7:27) since there was no way to keep milk sweet.

1:23 *his word.* No previous word from God is mentioned, unless this refers to the pronouncement of Eli in v. 17. The Dead Sea Scrolls, Septuagint (the pre-Christian Greek translation of the OT) and Syriac version (see NIV text note) resolve this problem by reading "your word." But "his word" may refer to an earlier, unrecorded word from the Lord.

1:26 *As surely as you live.* A customary way of emphasizing the truthfulness of one's words.

1:27 *I prayed for this child.* In the nativity account of Samuel, which also serves as the nativity account of the monarchy in Israel, Hannah serves as a cameo of Israel. As Hannah in her distress "asked" for a child, so Israel in her distress "asked" for a king, and Hannah's hymnic prayer that follows Samuel's birth (2:1–10) became Israel's hymn of praise as they reflected on the inauguration of the Davidic dynasty.

1:28 *given over.* The unusual Hebrew term used here sounds precisely like the Hebrew for the name Saul. It appears that the author already here hints that Saul, the one "asked for" by Israel, should also have been Saul, the one "given over" to the service of the Lord—that every king in Israel should be a "Saul" in this latter sense.

2:1–10 Hannah's prayer is constructed of two balanced parts (vv. 1–5,6–10). While there is considerable overlapping of themes between the first and second halves, the focus of Hannah's praise shifts from a celebration of the ways of God that "raised up" her "horn" to a celebration of the ways of God that will "exalt" the "horn" of his anointed.

2:1 *prayed.* Hannah's prayer (vv. 1–10) is a song of praise and thanksgiving to God (see Ps 72:20, where the psalms of David are designated "prayers"). This song has sometimes been termed the "Magnificat of the OT" because it is so similar to the Magnificat of the NT (Mary's song, Lk 1:46–55). It also has certain resemblances to the "Benedictus" (Zechariah's song, Lk 1:67–79). Hannah's song of praise

2 "There is no one holy[a][x] like[y] the LORD;
there is no one besides you;
there is no Rock[z] like our God.

3 "Do not keep talking so proudly
or let your mouth speak such
arrogance,[a]
for the LORD is a God who knows,[b]
and by him deeds[c] are weighed.[d]

4 "The bows of the warriors are
broken,[e]
but those who stumbled are armed
with strength.[f]
5 Those who were full hire themselves
out for food,
but those who were hungry[g] hunger
no more.
She who was barren[h] has borne seven
children,
but she who has had many sons
pines away.

6 "The LORD brings death and makes
alive;[i]
he brings down to the grave[b] and
raises up.[j]
7 The LORD sends poverty and
wealth;[k]
he humbles and he exalts.[l]
8 He raises[m] the poor[n] from the dust[o]
and lifts the needy[p] from the ash
heap;
he seats them with princes
and has them inherit a throne of
honor.[q]

"For the foundations[r] of the earth are
the LORD's;
upon them he has set the world.
9 He will guard the feet[s] of his saints,[t]
but the wicked will be silenced in
darkness.[u]

"It is not by strength[v] that one
prevails;
10 those who oppose the LORD will be
shattered.[w]
He will thunder[x] against them from
heaven;
the LORD will judge[y] the ends of the
earth.

2:2 [x]S Ex 15:11; S Lev 11:44 [y]S Ex 8:10; Isa 40:25; 46:5 [z]S Ge 49:24; S Ex 33:22; Dt 32:37; 2Sa 22:2, 32; 23:3; Ps 31:3; 71:3 **2:3** [a]Ps 17:10; 31:18; 73:8; 75:4; 94:4 [b]S Jos 22:22 [c]1Sa 16:7; 1Ki 8:39; 1Ch 28:9; 2Ch 6:30; Pr 15:11; Jer 11:20; 17:10 [d]Pr 16:2; 24:11-12 **2:4** [e]2Sa 1:27; Ps 37:15; 46:9; 76:3 [f]Job 17:9; Isa 40:31; 41:1; 52:1; 57:10 **2:5** [g]Lk 1:53 [h]Ps 113:9; Isa 54:1; Jer 15:9 **2:6** [i]Dt 32:39 [j]Isa 26:19; Eze 37:3, 12 **2:7** [k]S Dt 8:18 [l]Job 5:11; 40:12; Ps 75:7; Isa 2:12; 13:11; 22:19; Da 4:37 **2:8** [m]Ps 113:7-8 [n]Jas 2:5 [o]1Ki 16:2 [p]Ps 72:12; 107:41; 145:14; 146:8; S Mt 23:12 [q]2Sa 7:8; Job 36:7; Isa 22:23; Eze 21:26 [r]Job 15:7; 38:4; Ps 104:5; Pr 8:29; Isa 40:12; Jer 10:12 **2:9** [s]Ps 91:12; 121:3; Pr 3:26 [t]Pr 2:8 [u]Job 10:22; Isa 5:30; 8:22; 59:9; 60:2; Jer 13:16; Am 5:18, 20; Zep 1:14-15; Mt 8:12 [v]1Sa 17:47; Ps 33:16-17; Zec 4:6 **2:10** [w]S Ex 15:6 [x]S Ex 19:16; 1Sa 7:10; 12:17; 2Sa 22:14; Job 37:4, 5; 38:1; Ps 18:13; 29:3; Isa 66:6 [y]Ps 96:13; 98:9; Mt 25:31-32

[a] 2 Or *no Holy One* [b] 6 Hebrew *Sheol*

finds many echoes in David's song near the end of the book (2Sa 22). These two songs frame the main narrative, and their themes highlight the ways of God that the narrative relates—they contain the theology of the book in the form of praise. Hannah speaks prophetically at a time when Israel is about to enter an important new period of its history with the establishment of kingship through her son, Samuel. *rejoices in the LORD.* The supreme source of Hannah's joy is not in the child, but in the God who has answered her prayer. *my horn is lifted high.* See NIV text note; cf. Dt 33:17; Ps 75:4 and note; 92:10; 112:9; Lk 1:69 and note. To have one's horn lifted up by God is to be delivered from disgrace to a position of honor and strength.

2:2 *no one holy like the LORD.* See Lev 11:44 and note. *no one besides you.* See 2Sa 7:22; 22:32; Dt 4:35 and note; Isa 45:6. *Rock.* A metaphor to depict the strength and stability of the God of Israel as the unfailing source of security for his people (see 2Sa 22:2 and note; Ps 19:14; Isa 17:10 and note).

2:3 *so proudly ... such arrogance.* After the manner of Peninnah (and others in the narratives of 1,2 Samuel—Eli's sons, the Philistines, Saul, Nabal, Goliath, Absalom, Shimei and Sheba). *the LORD is a God who knows.* See 16:7; 1Ki 8:39; Ps 139:1–6 and note; Jn 2:24–25.

2:4–5 In a series of examples derived from everyday life Hannah shows that God often works contrary to natural expectations and brings about surprising reversals—seen frequently in the stories that follow.

2:5 *seven children.* See 1:8 and note on Ru 4:15.

2:6–8 Hannah declares that life and death, prosperity and adversity, are determined by the sovereign power of God—thus introducing a theme that is richly illustrated in the following narrative (see also Dt 32:39; 1Ki 17:20–24; 2Ki 4:32–35; Jn 5:21; 11:41–44).

2:6 *grave.* See NIV text note; see also note on Ge 37:35.

2:8 *foundations of the earth.* A common figure in the OT for the solid base on which the earth (the dry land on which people live, not planet earth; Ge 1:10) is founded. The phrase reflects the ancient worldview but does not teach a theory of the structure of the universe (see Job 9:6; 38:6; Ps 24:2 and note; 75:3; 104:5; Zec 12:1).

2:9 *guard the feet.* Travel in ancient Israel was for the most part by foot over trails that were often rocky and dangerous (see Ps 91:11–12; 121:3). *saints.* People who faithfully serve the Lord. The Hebrew root underlying this word is used of both God and his people in 2Sa 22:26 to characterize the nature of their mutual relationship. The word is also translated "godly" (Ps 12:1; 32:6) and "faithful ones" (Pr 2:8). See Ps 4:3 and note.

2:10 *judge.* Impose his righteous rule upon (see Ps 96:13 and note; 98:9). *ends of the earth.* All nations and peoples (see Dt 33:17; Isa 45:22). *his king.* Hannah's prayer is here prophetic, anticipating the establishment of kingship in Israel and the initial realization of the Messianic ideal in David (Lk 1:69). Ultimately her expectation finds fulfillment in Christ and his complete triumph over the enemies of God. *exalt the horn.* The expected king's horn will be "lifted high/exalted" as surely as Hannah's had been (see v. 1). This word about the horns frames the song and highlights its central theme. *anointed.* The first reference in the Bible to the Lord's anointed—i.e., his anointed king. (Priests were also anointed for God's service; see Ex 28:41; Lev 4:3.) The word is often synonymous with "king" (as here) and provides part of the vocabulary basis for the Messianic idea in the Bible. "Anointed" and "Messiah" are the translation and transliteration respectively of the same Hebrew word. The Greek translation of this Hebrew term is *Christos,* from which comes the English word "Christ" (see NIV text note on Mt 1:17). A king (coming from the tribe of Judah) is first prophesied by Jacob (see Ge 49:10 and note); kingship is further anticipated in the oracles of Balaam in Nu 24:7,17 (see note on 24:17). Also Dt 17:14–20 looks forward to the time when the Lord will place a king of his choice over his people after they enter the promised land. 1,2 Samuel shows how this expectation of the theocratic king is realized in the person of David. Hannah's prophetic anticipation of a king at the time of the dedication of her son Samuel, who was to be God's agent for establishing kingship in Israel, is entirely appropriate.

"He will give strength[z] to his king
and exalt the horn[a] of his anointed."

11 Then Elkanah went home to Ramah,[b]
but the boy ministered[c] before the LORD
under Eli the priest.

Eli's Wicked Sons

12 Eli's sons were wicked men; they had
no regard[d] for the LORD. 13 Now it was the
practice[e] of the priests with the people
that whenever anyone offered a sacrifice
and while the meat[f] was being boiled,
the servant of the priest would come with
a three-pronged fork in his hand. 14 He
would plunge it into the pan or kettle or
caldron or pot, and the priest would take
for himself whatever the fork brought up.
This is how they treated all the Israelites
who came to Shiloh. 15 But even before the
fat was burned, the servant of the priest
would come and say to the man who was
sacrificing, "Give the priest some meat to
roast; he won't accept boiled meat from
you, but only raw."
16 If the man said to him, "Let the fat[g]
be burned up first, and then take whatever you want," the servant would then answer, "No, hand it over now; if you don't,
I'll take it by force."
17 This sin of the young men was very
great in the LORD's sight, for they[a] were
treating the LORD's offering with contempt.[h]
18 But Samuel was ministering[i] before
the LORD—a boy wearing a linen ephod.[j]
19 Each year his mother made him a little
robe and took it to him when she went
up with her husband to offer the annual[k]
sacrifice. 20 Eli would bless Elkanah and
his wife, saying, "May the LORD give you
children by this woman to take the place
of the one she prayed[l] for and gave to the
LORD." Then they would go home. 21 And
the LORD was gracious to Hannah;[m] she
conceived and gave birth to three sons
and two daughters. Meanwhile, the boy
Samuel grew[n] up in the presence of the
LORD.
22 Now Eli, who was very old, heard
about everything[o] his sons were doing
to all Israel and how they slept with the
women[p] who served at the entrance to
the Tent of Meeting. 23 So he said to them,
"Why do you do such things? I hear from
all the people about these wicked deeds
of yours. 24 No, my sons; it is not a good
report that I hear spreading among the
LORD's people. 25 If a man sins against another man, God[b] may mediate for him;
but if a man sins against the LORD, who
will[q] intercede[r] for him?" His sons, however, did not listen to their father's rebuke,
for it was the LORD's will to put them to
death.
26 And the boy Samuel continued to
grow[s] in stature and in favor with the LORD
and with men.[t]

2:10 [z] Ps 18:1; 21:1; 59:16 [a] S Dt 33:17; Ps 89:24; S Lk 1:69
2:11 [b] S Jos 18:25 [c] ver 18; S Nu 16:9; 1Sa 3:1
2:12 [d] Jer 2:8; 9:6
2:13 [e] Dt 18:3 [f] Lev 7:35-36
2:16 [g] Lev 3:3,14-16; 7:29-34
2:17 [h] ver 22,29; S Nu 14:11; Jer 7:21; Eze 22:26; Mal 2:7-9
2:18 [i] S ver 11 [j] ver 28; 1Sa 22:18; 23:9; 2Sa 6:14; 1Ch 15:27
2:19 [k] S 1Sa 1:3
2:20 [l] S 1Sa 1:27
2:21 [m] Ge 21:1 [n] S Jdg 13:24; Lk 1:80; 2:40
2:22 [o] S ver 17 [p] S Ex 38:8
2:25 [q] Ex 4:21; Jos 11:20 [r] S Ex 32:10; S Nu 11:2; 1Sa 3:14; 1Ki 13:6; Job 9:33; Ps 106:30; Isa 1:18; 22:14; Jer 15:1; Heb 10:26
2:26 [s] S Jdg 13:24; Lk 2:52 [t] Pr 3:4

[a] 17 Or *men* [b] 25 Or *the judges*

2:11 *ministered.* Performed such services as a boy might render while assisting the high priest. *before the LORD.* At the "house of the LORD" (1:24).

2:12 *wicked.* See 1:16 and note. *had no regard for.* Lit. "did not know." In OT usage, to "know" the Lord is not just intellectual or theoretical recognition. It is to enter into fellowship with him and acknowledge his claims on one's life. The term often has a covenantal connotation (see Jer 31:34; Hos 2:20 and notes).

2:13–16 Apparently vv. 13–14 describe the practice that had come to be accepted for determining the priests' portion of the fellowship offerings (Lev 7:31–36; 10:14–15; Dt 18:1–5)—a tradition presumably based on the assumption that a random thrust of the fork would providentially determine a fair portion. Verses 15–16 then describe how Eli's sons arrogantly violated that custom and the law.

2:15 *before the fat was burned.* On the altar as the Lord's portion, which he was to receive first (see Lev 3:16 and note; 4:10,26,31,35; 7:30–31; 17:6). *roast.* Boiling is the only form of cooking specified in the law for the priests' portion (Nu 6:19–20). Roasting this portion is nowhere expressly forbidden in the law, but it is specified only for the Passover lamb (Ex 12:8–9; Dt 16:7). The present passage seems to imply that for the priests to roast their portion of the sacrifices was unlawful.

2:16 *by force.* Presenting the priests' portion was to be a voluntary act on the part of the worshipers (see Lev 7:28–36; Dt 18:3).

2:18 *But Samuel.* Between 2:12 and 4:1 the author presents a series of sharp contrasts between Samuel and Eli's sons. *linen ephod.* A priestly garment worn by those who served before the Lord at his sanctuary (see 22:18; 2Sa 6:14). Samuel's garment was similar to the ephod worn by the high priest (see note on v. 28; cf. Ex 39:1–7).

2:19 *little robe.* A sleeveless garment reaching to the knees, worn over the undergarment and under the ephod. *annual sacrifice.* See note on 1:3.

2:22 *slept with the women who served.* See Ex 38:8. There is no further reference to such women in the OT. Their service is not to be confused with that of the Levites, which is prescribed in the Pentateuch (Nu 1:50; 3:6–8; 8:15; 16:9; 18:2–3). The immoral acts of Eli's sons are reminiscent of the religious prostitution (fertility rites) at the Canaanite sanctuaries—acts that were an abomination to the Lord and a desecration of his house (see Dt 23:17–18 and notes).

2:23 *he said to them.* Eli rebuked his sons but did not remove them from office. God would do that.

2:25 *God.* See NIV text note. Eli's argument is that when someone commits an offense against another person, there is recourse to a third party to decide the issue (whether this be understood as God or as God's representatives, the judges; see NIV text notes on Ex 22:8–9); but when the offense is against the Lord, there is no recourse, for God is both the one wronged and the judge. *the LORD's will to put them to death.* This comment by the author of the narrative is not intended to excuse Eli's sons, but to indicate that Eli's warning was much too late. Eli's sons had persisted in their evil ways for so long that God's judgment on them was determined (v. 34; see Jos 11:20).

2:26 *grow in stature and in favor with the LORD and with men.* Cf. Luke's description of Jesus (Lk 2:52).

Prophecy Against the House of Eli

27 Now a man of God[u] came to Eli and said to him, "This is what the LORD says: 'Did I not clearly reveal myself to your father's house when they were in Egypt under Pharaoh? 28 I chose[v] your father out of all the tribes of Israel to be my priest, to go up to my altar, to burn incense,[w] and to wear an ephod[x] in my presence. I also gave your father's house all the offerings[y] made with fire by the Israelites. 29 Why do you[a] scorn my sacrifice and offering[z] that I prescribed for my dwelling?[a] Why do you honor your sons more than me by fattening yourselves on the choice parts of every offering made by my people Israel?'

30 "Therefore the LORD, the God of Israel, declares: 'I promised that your house and your father's house would minister before me forever.[b]' But now the LORD declares: 'Far be it from me! Those who honor me I will honor,[c] but those who despise[d] me will be disdained.[e] 31 The time is coming when I will cut short your strength and the strength of your father's house, so that there will not be an old man in your family line[f] 32 and you will see distress[g] in my dwelling. Although good will be done to Israel, in your family line there will never be an old man.[h] 33 Every one of you that I do not cut off from my altar will be spared only to blind your eyes with tears and to grieve your heart, and all your descendants[i] will die in the prime of life.

34 " 'And what happens to your two sons, Hophni and Phinehas, will be a sign[j] to you—they will both die[k] on the same day.[l] 35 I will raise up for myself a faithful priest,[m] who will do according to what is in my heart and mind. I will firmly establish his house, and he will minister before my anointed[n] one always. 36 Then everyone left in your family line will come and bow down before him for a piece of silver and a crust of bread and plead,[o] "Appoint me to some priestly office so I can have food to eat.[p]" ' "

The LORD Calls Samuel

3 The boy Samuel ministered[q] before the LORD under Eli. In those days the word of the LORD was rare;[r] there were not many visions.[s]

2 One night Eli, whose eyes[t] were becoming so weak that he could barely see,[u] was lying down in his usual place. 3 The lamp[v] of God had not yet gone out, and Samuel was lying down in the temple[b][w]

[a] 29 The Hebrew is plural. [b] 3 That is, tabernacle

2:27 [u] S Dt 33:1; S Jdg 13:6 **2:28** [v] S Ex 28:1 [w] S Ex 30:7 [x] 1Sa 22:18; 23:6,9; 30:7 [y] Lev 7:35-36 **2:29** [z] ver 12-17 [a] S Dt 12:5 **2:30** [b] S Ex 29:9 [c] Ps 50:23; 91:15; Pr 8:17 [d] Isa 53:3; Na 3:6; Mal 2:9 [e] Jer 18:10 **2:31** [f] 1Sa 4:11-18; 22:16 **2:32** [g] 1Sa 4:3; 22:17-20; Jer 7:12,14 [h] 1Ki 2:26-27 **2:33** [i] Jer 29:32; Mal 2:12 **2:34** [j] S Dt 13:2 [k] 1Sa 4:11 [l] 1Ki 13:3 **2:35** [m] 2Sa 8:17; 20:25; 1Ki 1:8,32; 2:35; 4:4; 1Ch 16:39; 29:22; Eze 44:15-16 [n] 1Sa 9:16; 10:1; 16:13; 2Sa 2:4; 12:7; 23:1; 1Ki 1:34; Ps 89:20 **2:36** [o] Eze 44:10-14 [p] 1Sa 3:12; 1Ki 2:27 **3:1** [q] S 1Sa 2:11 [r] Ps 74:9; La 2:9; Eze 7:26 [s] Am 8:11 **3:2** [t] 1Sa 4:15 [u] S Ge 27:1 **3:3** [v] Ex 25:31-38; Lev 24:1-4 [w] 1Sa 1:9

2:27 *man of God.* Often a designation for a prophet (see 9:6,9–10; Dt 33:1; Jos 14:6; 1Ki 13:1; 17:24; 2Ki 4:9). *father's house.* The descendants of Aaron.

2:28 *to be my priest.* Three tasks of the priests are mentioned: (1) *to go up to my altar.* To perform the sacrificial rites at the altar of burnt offering in the courtyard of the tabernacle. (2) *to burn incense.* At the altar of incense in the Holy Place (Ex 30:1–10). (3) *to wear an ephod.* See note on v. 18. It would appear that the reference here is to the special ephod of the high priest (see Ex 28:6–14). The breastpiece containing the Urim and Thummim was attached to the ephod. The Urim and Thummim were a divinely ordained means of obtaining guidance from God (see Pr 16:33 and note), placed in the custody of the high priest (see Ex 28:30 and note; see also 1Sa 23:9–12; 30:7–8).

2:30 *I promised.* See Ex 29:9; Lev 8–9; Nu 16–17; 25:13. *Far be it from me!* This is not to say that the promise of the priesthood to Aaron's house has been annulled, but that Eli and his house are to be excluded from participation in this privilege because of their sin. *Those who honor me I will honor.* See v. 29. Spiritual privileges bring responsibilities and obligations; they are not to be treated as irrevocable rights (see 2Sa 22:26–27).

2:31 *strength ... strength.* Lit. "arm ... arm," symbolic of strength. Eli's "arm" and that of his priestly family will be cut off (contrast David, 2Sa 22:35). *not be an old man in your family line.* A prediction of the decimation of Eli's priestly family in the death of his sons (4:11), in the massacre of his descendants by Saul at Nob (22:18–19) and in the removal of Abiathar from his priestly office (1Ki 2:26–27).

2:32 *distress in my dwelling.* Including the capture of the ark by the Philistines (4:1–11), the destruction of Shiloh (see Jer 7:14 and note on 7:12) and the relocation of the tabernacle to Nob (21:1–6; see note on 21:1).

2:33 A reference apparently to Abiathar, who was expelled from office by Solomon (see 1Ki 2:26–27 and note on 2:27) after an unsuccessful attempt to make Adonijah king as the successor to David.

2:34 *a sign to you.* The death of Hophni and Phinehas (4:11) will confirm the longer-term predictions. Such confirmation of a prophetic word was not uncommon (see 10:7–9; 1Ki 13:3 and note; Jer 28:15–17; Lk 1:18–20,64).

2:35 *I will raise up for myself a faithful priest.* Initially fulfilled in the person of Zadok, who served as a priest during the time of David (see 2Sa 8:17 and note; 15:24,35; 20:25) and who eventually replaced Abiathar as high priest in the time of Solomon (see 1Ki 2:35; 1Ch 29:22). *firmly establish his house.* Lit. "build for him a faithful house"; the faithful priest will be given a "faithful" (i.e., enduring) priestly family. See the similar word spoken concerning David (25:28, "lasting dynasty"; see also 2Sa 7:16 and note; 1Ki 11:38). The line of Zadok was continued by his son Azariah (see 1Ki 4:2) and was still on the scene at the time of the exile and return (see 1Ch 6:8–15; Ezr 3:2). It continued in intertestamental times until Antiochus IV Epiphanes (175–164 B.C.) sold the priesthood to Menelaus (in the Apocrypha see 2 Maccabees 4:23–50), who was not of the priestly line. *my anointed one.* David and his successors (see note on v. 10).

3:1 *boy Samuel.* See 2:11,18. Samuel is now no longer a little child (see 2:21,26). The Jewish historian Josephus places his age at 12 years; he may have been older. *the word of the LORD was rare.* See Pr 29:18; Am 8:11 and notes. During the entire period of the judges, apart from the prophet of 2:27–36, we are told of only two prophets (Jdg 4:4; 6:8) and of five revelations (Jdg 2:1–3; 6:11–26; 7:2–11; 10:11–14; 13:3–21). Possibly 2Ch 15:3 also refers to this period. *visions.* Cf. Ge 15:1.

3:3 *The lamp of God had not yet gone out.* The reference is to the golden lampstand, which stood opposite the table of the bread of the Presence (Ex 25:31–40) in the Holy Place. It was still night, but the early morning hours were approach-

of the LORD, where the ark[x] of God was.
4Then the LORD called Samuel.
Samuel answered, "Here I am.[y]" 5And
he ran to Eli and said, "Here I am; you
called me."
But Eli said, "I did not call; go back and
lie down." So he went and lay down.
6Again the LORD called, "Samuel!" And
Samuel got up and went to Eli and said,
"Here I am; you called me."
"My son," Eli said, "I did not call; go
back and lie down."
7Now Samuel did not yet know[z] the
LORD: The word[a] of the LORD had not yet
been revealed[b] to him.
8The LORD called Samuel a third time,
and Samuel got up and went to Eli and
said, "Here I am; you called me."
Then Eli realized that the LORD was calling the boy. 9So Eli told Samuel, "Go and
lie down, and if he calls you, say, 'Speak,
LORD, for your servant is listening.'" So
Samuel went and lay down in his place.
10The LORD came and stood there, calling
as at the other times, "Samuel! Samuel![c]"
Then Samuel said, "Speak, for your servant is listening."
11And the LORD said to Samuel: "See, I
am about to do something in Israel that
will make the ears of everyone who hears
of it tingle.[d] 12At that time I will carry out
against Eli everything[e] I spoke against his
family—from beginning to end. 13For I
told him that I would judge his family forever because of the sin he knew about;
his sons made themselves contemptible,[a]
and he failed to restrain[f] them. 14There-
fore, I swore to the house of Eli, 'The guilt
of Eli's house will never be atoned[g] for by
sacrifice or offering.'"
15Samuel lay down until morning and
then opened the doors of the house of the
LORD. He was afraid to tell Eli the vision,
16but Eli called him and said, "Samuel, my
son."
Samuel answered, "Here I am."
17"What was it he said to you?" Eli
asked. "Do not hide[h] it from me. May God
deal with you, be it ever so severely,[i] if you
hide from me anything he told you." 18So
Samuel told him everything, hiding nothing
from him. Then Eli said, "He is the LORD;
let him do what is good in his eyes."[j]
19The LORD was with[k] Samuel as he
grew[l] up, and he let none[m] of his words
fall to the ground. 20And all Israel from
Dan to Beersheba[n] recognized that Samuel was attested as a prophet of the LORD.[o]
21The LORD continued to appear at Shiloh,
and there he revealed[p] himself to Samuel
through his word.
4 And Samuel's word came to all Israel.

The Philistines Capture the Ark

Now the Israelites went out to fight
against the Philistines. The Israelites
camped at Ebenezer,[q] and the Philistines
at Aphek.[r] 2The Philistines deployed their
forces to meet Israel, and as the battle
spread, Israel was defeated by the Philistines, who killed about four thousand of
them on the battlefield. 3When the soldiers returned to camp, the elders of Israel

3:3 [x]Dt 10:1-5; 1Ki 6:19; 8:1 **3:4** [y]S Ge 22:1; S Ex 3:4 **3:7** [z]1Sa 2:12 [a]Jer 1:2 [b]S Nu 12:6; Am 3:7 **3:10** [c]Ex 3:4 **3:11** [d]2Ki 21:12; Job 15:21; Jer 19:3 **3:12** [e]S 1Sa 2:27-36 **3:13** [f]1Ki 1:6 **3:14** [g]S 1Sa 2:25 **3:17** [h]1Ki 22:14; Jer 23:28; 38:14; 42:4 [i]S Ru 1:17 **3:18** [j]S Jdg 10:15 **3:19** [k]S Ge 21:22; S Nu 14:43 [l]S Jdg 13:24 [m]1Sa 9:6 **3:20** [n]S Jdg 20:1 [o]S Dt 18:22; Eze 33:33 **3:21** [p]S Nu 12:6 **4:1** [q]1Sa 5:1; 7:12 [r]Jos 12:18; 1Sa 29:1; 1Ki 20:26

[a] *13* Masoretic Text; an ancient Hebrew scribal tradition and Septuagint *sons blasphemed God*

ing when the flame grew dim or went out (see Ex 27:20–21; 30:7–8; Lev 24:3–4; 2Ch 13:11; Pr 31:18). For the lamp to be permitted to go out before morning was a violation of the Pentateuchal regulations (see Lev 24:1–4 and note on 24:3). *temple.* See NIV text note and note on 1:9.

3:4 *Here I am.* See note on Ge 22:1.

3:7 *did not yet know the LORD.* In the sense of having a direct experience of him (see Ex 1:8), such as receiving a revelation from him (see the last half of the verse).

3:10 *Samuel! Samuel!* See note on Ge 22:11.

3:11–14 The Lord's first revelation to Samuel summarizes the message Eli had already received from the "man of God" (2:27–36), thus confirming the fact that the youth had indeed received a revelation from God.

3:11 *make the ears … tingle.* See note on Jer 19:3.

3:13 *contemptible.* See NIV text note and Lev 24:14–16.

3:15 *doors of the house of the LORD.* See note on 1:9. *vision.* See notes on vv. 1,11–14.

3:17 *May God deal with you, be it ever so severely.* A curse formula (see 14:44; 20:13; 25:22; 2Sa 3:9,35; 19:13; Ru 1:17; 1Ki 2:23; 2Ki 6:31), usually directed against the speaker but here used by Eli against Samuel if he conceals anything the Lord said (see also note on 14:24).

3:18 *let him do what is good in his eyes.* Eli bows before God, accepting the judgment as righteous (see Ex 34:5–7).

3:19 *The LORD was with Samuel.* As he had been with Moses (see Ex 3:12 and note on Ge 26:3). *he let none of his words fall to the ground.* Because none of Samuel's words proved unreliable, he was recognized as a prophet who spoke the word of the Lord (see vv. 20–21; 9:6).

3:20 *Dan to Beersheba.* A conventional expression often used in Samuel, Kings and Chronicles to denote the entire land (Dan was located in the far north and Beersheba in the far south).

3:21 *continued to appear at Shiloh.* But not after the events narrated in chs. 4–6 (see Jer 7:12–14 and note on 7:12; 26:6).

4:1 *Samuel's word came to all Israel.* Contrast 3:1. *Ebenezer.* Means "stone of help." The precise location is unknown, but it was probably a short distance (see v. 6) to the east of Aphek—not to be confused with the location of the stone named Ebenezer that was later erected by Samuel between Mizpah and Shen (see 7:12) to commemorate a victory over the Philistines. *Aphek.* A town about 12 miles northeast of the coastal city of Joppa (see map, p. 418). Philistine presence this far north suggests an attempt to spread their control over the Israelite tribes of central Canaan (see v. 9; Jdg 15:11 and note).

4:1b—7:1 Israel's loss of faithful leadership, underscored by the "exile" of the ark to Philistia and its return to a fringe of Israel.

4:3 *Why did the LORD bring defeat …?* The elders understood that their defeat was more an indication of God's displeasure than it was of Philistine military might. Israel's pagan

asked, "Why[s] did the LORD bring defeat
upon us today before the Philistines? Let
us bring the ark[t] of the LORD's covenant
from Shiloh,[u] so that it[a] may go with us[v]
and save us from the hand of our enemies."
4So the people sent men to Shiloh, and
they brought back the ark of the covenant
of the LORD Almighty, who is enthroned
between the cherubim.[w] And Eli's two
sons, Hophni and Phinehas, were there
with the ark of the covenant of God.
5When the ark of the LORD's covenant
came into the camp, all Israel raised such
a great shout[x] that the ground shook.
6Hearing the uproar, the Philistines asked,
"What's all this shouting in the Hebrew[y]
camp?"
When they learned that the ark of the
LORD had come into the camp, 7the Philistines were afraid.[z] "A god has come into
the camp," they said. "We're in trouble!
Nothing like this has happened before.
8Woe to us! Who will deliver us from the
hand of these mighty gods? They are the
gods who struck[a] the Egyptians with all
kinds of plagues[b] in the desert. 9Be strong,
Philistines! Be men, or you will be subject
to the Hebrews, as they[c] have been to you.
Be men, and fight!"
10So the Philistines fought, and the Israelites were defeated[d] and every man fled
to his tent. The slaughter was very great;
Israel lost thirty thousand foot soldiers.

4:3 [s]Jos 7:7 [t]S Jos 6:7 [u]S Jos 18:1; S 1Sa 2:32 [v]2Ch 13:8 **4:4** [w]S Ge 3:24; S Ex 25:22 **4:5** [x]S Jos 6:5, 10 **4:6** [y]S Ge 14:13 **4:7** [z]S Ex 15:14 **4:8** [a]Ex 12:30; 1Sa 5:12 [b]Rev 11:6 **4:9** [c]S Jdg 13:1 **4:10** [d]S Dt 28:25

11The ark of God was captured, and Eli's
two sons, Hophni and Phinehas, died.[e]

Death of Eli

12That same day a Benjamite[f] ran
from the battle line and went to Shiloh,
his clothes torn and dust[g] on his head.
13When he arrived, there was Eli[h] sitting
on his chair by the side of the road, watching, because his heart feared for the ark of
God. When the man entered the town and
told what had happened, the whole town
sent up a cry.
14Eli heard the outcry and asked, "What
is the meaning of this uproar?"
The man hurried over to Eli, 15who was
ninety-eight years old and whose eyes[i]
were set so that he could not see. 16He told
Eli, "I have just come from the battle line;
I fled from it this very day."
Eli asked, "What happened, my son?"
17The man who brought the news replied, "Israel fled before the Philistines,
and the army has suffered heavy losses.
Also your two sons, Hophni and Phinehas,
are dead,[j] and the ark of God has been
captured."[k]
18When he mentioned the ark of God,
Eli fell backward off his chair by the side
of the gate. His neck was broken and he
died, for he was an old man and heavy. He
had led[b][l] Israel forty years.[m]

4:11 [e]Ps 78:64; Jer 7:12 **4:12** [f]Eze 24:26; 33:21 [g]S Jos 7:6; S 2Sa 1:2 **4:13** [h]ver 18 **4:15** [i]S 1Sa 3:2 **4:17** [j]1Sa 22:18; Ps 78:64 [k]Ps 78:61 **4:18** [l]S Jdg 2:16; S 16:31 [m]1Sa 2:31

[a] 3 Or *he* [b] 18 Traditionally *judged*

neighbors also believed that the outcome of battle was decided by the gods. *so that it may go with us and save us.* See NIV text note. In an attempt to secure the Lord's presence with them in the struggle against the Philistines, the elders sent for the ark of the covenant. They were correct in thinking there was a connection between God's presence with his people and the ark (cf. v. 4), and no doubt they remembered the presence of the ark at notable victories in Israel's past history (see Nu 10:33–36; Jos 3:3,11,14–17 and note on 3:3; 6:6,12–20). But they incorrectly believed that the Lord's presence with the ark was guaranteed, rather than being subject to his free decision. They reflect the pagan notion that the deity is identified with the symbol of his presence, and that God's favor could automatically be gained by manipulating the symbol.

4:4 *enthroned between the cherubim.* On each end of the atonement cover of the ark of the covenant were cherubim of gold with their wings spread upward over the ark (see Ex 25:17–22). In the space between these cherubim God's presence with his people was localized in a special way, so that the atonement cover of the ark came to be viewed as the throne of Israel's divine King (see 2Sa 6:2 and note; Ps 80:1; 99:1; see also note on Ex 25:18). *Hophni and Phinehas.* These wicked priests (see 2:12 and note) did not restrain the army from its improper use of the ark but actually accompanied the ark to the battlefield.

4:6 *Hebrew.* See note on Ge 14:13.

4:7 *A god has come into the camp.* The Philistines also identified the God of Israel with the symbol of his presence (see note on v. 3).

4:8 *mighty gods.* The Philistines could think only in polytheistic terms. *Egyptians ... plagues.* See note on 6:6.

4:11 *The ark of God was captured.* This phrase or a variation of it occurs five times in the chapter (here, vv. 17,19,21–22) and is the focal point of the narrative. In this disastrous event, God's word in 3:11 finds a swift fulfillment. *Hophni and Phinehas, died.* The fulfillment of 2:34; 3:12.

4:12 *his clothes torn and dust on his head.* A sign of grief and sorrow, here marking the messenger as a bearer of bad news (see 2Sa 1:2; 13:19; 15:32).

4:13 *his heart feared for the ark of God.* Eli had sufficient spiritual sensitivity to be aware of the danger inherent in the sinful and presumptuous act of taking the ark of God into the battle. And he seems to have been even more concerned for the ark than for his sons (see v. 18).

4:18 *he died.* The death of Eli marked the end of an era that had begun with the death of Joshua and the elders who served with him (see Jos 24:29,31). Incapable of restraining Israel or his sons from their wicked ways, and weakened and blinded by age, the old priest is an apt symbol of the flawed age now coming to its tragic close. He is also a striking contrast to the reign of David, which is a major focus of 1,2 Samuel. *heavy.* A bit of information that not only helps explain why Eli's fall was fatal but also links his death with the judgment announced earlier: "Why do you honor your sons more than me by fattening yourselves ...?" (2:29). *He had led Israel forty years.* See NIV text note. Eli is here included among the judges (see 2Sa 7:11; Jdg 2:16–19; Ru 1:1), who served as leaders of Israel in the period between the deaths of Joshua and of the elders who outlived him and the establishment of kingship (see Introduction to Judges: Theme and Theology). Eli's leadership of 40 years may have overlapped that of some of the judges, such as Jephthah and Samson.

19His daughter-in-law, the wife of Phinehas, was pregnant and near the time of
delivery. When she heard the news that
the ark of God had been captured and that
her father-in-law and her husband were
dead, she went into labor and gave birth,
but was overcome by her labor pains. 20As
she was dying, the women attending her
said, "Don't despair; you have given birth
to a son." But she did not respond or pay
any attention.
21She named the boy Ichabod,[a][n] saying, "The glory[o] has departed from Israel"—because of the capture of the ark of
God and the deaths of her father-in-law
and her husband. 22She said, "The glory[p]
has departed from Israel, for the ark of
God has been captured."[q]

The Ark in Ashdod and Ekron

5 After the Philistines had captured the
ark of God, they took it from Ebenezer[r]
to Ashdod.[s] 2Then they carried the ark into
Dagon's temple and set it beside Dagon.[t]
3When the people of Ashdod rose early the
next day, there was Dagon, fallen[u] on his
face on the ground before the ark of the
LORD! They took Dagon and put him back
in his place. 4But the following morning
when they rose, there was Dagon, fallen
on his face on the ground before the ark
of the LORD! His head and hands had been
broken[v] off and were lying on the threshold; only his body remained. 5That is why
to this day neither the priests of Dagon nor
any others who enter Dagon's temple at
Ashdod step on the threshold.[w]
6The LORD's hand[x] was heavy upon
the people of Ashdod and its vicinity; he
brought devastation[y] upon them and afflicted them with tumors.[b][z] 7When the men
of Ashdod saw what was happening, they
said, "The ark of the god of Israel must
not stay here with us, because his hand is
heavy upon us and upon Dagon our god."
8So they called together all the rulers[a] of the
Philistines and asked them, "What shall we
do with the ark of the god of Israel?"
They answered, "Have the ark of the
god of Israel moved to Gath.[b]" So they
moved the ark of the God of Israel.
9But after they had moved it, the LORD's
hand was against that city, throwing it into
a great panic.[c] He afflicted the people of
the city, both young and old, with an outbreak of tumors.[c] 10So they sent the ark of
God to Ekron.[d]

4:21 [n]S Ge 35:18 [o]S Ex 24:16; Ps 106:20; Jer 2:11; Eze 1:28; 9:3; 10:18
4:22 [p]S Ex 24:16; Ps 78:61 [q]Jer 7:12
5:1 [r]S 1Sa 4:1 [s]S Jos 11:22; S 13:3
5:2 [t]S Jdg 16:23; Isa 2:18; 19:1; 46:1
5:3 [u]Isa 40:20; 41:7; 46:7; Jer 10:4
5:4 [v]Eze 6:6; Mic 1:7
5:5 [w]Zep 1:9
5:6 [x]S Ex 9:3; Ac 13:11 [y]2Sa 6:7; Ps 78:66 [z]S Ex 15:26; 1Sa 6:5
5:8 [a]S Jdg 16:18 [b]S Jos 11:22
5:9 [c]S Ex 14:24

[a] 21 *Ichabod* means *no glory.* [b] 6 Hebrew; Septuagint and Vulgate *tumors. And rats appeared in their land, and death and destruction were throughout the city* [c] 9 Or *with tumors in the groin* (see Septuagint)

4:21 *The glory has departed.* The glory of Israel was Israel's God, not the ark (see 15:29; Heb 9:5 and notes), and loss of the ark did not mean that God had abandoned his people—God was not inseparably bound to the ark (see Jer 3:16–17 and notes). Yet the removal of the ark from Israel did signal estrangement in the relationship between God and his people, and it demonstrated the gravity of their error in thinking that in spite of their wickedness they had the power to coerce God into doing their will simply because they possessed the ark.

5:1 *Ashdod.* One of the five major cities of the Philistines (see Jos 13:3 and note), it was located near the Mediterranean coast about 35 miles west of Jerusalem. See note on Isa 20:1; see also map, p. 331.

5:2 *Dagon.* In Canaanite mythology the son (or brother) of El and the father of Baal. He was the principal god of the Philistines and was worshiped in temples at Gaza (Jdg 16:21,23,26), Ashdod (here) and Beth Shan (31:10–12; 1Ch 10:10). Veneration of this deity was widespread in the ancient world, extending from Mesopotamia to Aram and Canaan and attested in non-Biblical sources dating from the late third millennium B.C. until Maccabean times (second century B.C.; in the Apocrypha see 1 Maccabees 10:83–84). The precise nature of the worship of Dagon is obscure. Some have considered Dagon to be a fish god, but more recent evidence suggests either a storm or grain god. His name is related to a Hebrew word for "grain" (see note on Jdg 10:6).

5:3 *Dagon, fallen on his face.* The ark was placed next to the idol of Dagon by the Philistines in order to demonstrate Dagon's superiority over the God of Israel, but the symbolism was reversed when Dagon was toppled to a position of homage before the ark of the Lord.

5:4 *head and hands had been broken off.* Proving that the Lord had defeated Dagon. In the ancient Near East, the heads and/or right hands of slain enemy soldiers were often brought back to the victors' camp as trophies of war (see 17:51,54; 31:9; 1Ch 10:10) and to establish a body count (cf. 18:27 and note on 18:25).

5:5 *this day.* The time of the writing of 1,2 Samuel (see Introduction: Literary Features, Authorship and Date). *step on the threshold.* Apparently the threshold was considered to possess supernatural power because of its contact with parts of the fallen image of Dagon. Zep 1:9 (see note there) appears to be a reference to a more general and rather widespread pagan idea that the threshold was the dwelling place of spirits.

5:6 *The LORD's hand.* A pervasive motif in the ark narratives; it or its equivalent occurs eight times (here and in vv. 7,9,11; 6:3,5,9; 7:13; cf. also 4:8). *was heavy.* Dagon's broken hands lay on the threshold (v. 4), but the Lord showed the reality and strength of his own hand by bringing a plague (see note on 6:4) on the people of Ashdod and the surrounding area (see vv. 9,11). God would not be manipulated by his own people (see note on 4:3), nor would he permit the Philistines to think that their victory over the Israelites and the capture of the ark demonstrated the superiority of their god over the God of Israel. *tumors.* One of the many covenant curses that would be inflicted on the Israelites if they disobeyed God (Dt 28:58–60). Here the affliction fell on the Philistines. See also NIV text note on v. 9.

5:8 *rulers.* Of the five major cities of the Philistines (see 6:16; Jos 13:3; Jdg 3:3; see also map and accompanying text, p. 331). *Have the ark of the god of Israel moved to Gath.* Evidently the leaders of the Philistines did not share the opinion of the Ashdodites that there was a direct connection between what had happened in Ashdod and the presence of the ark; they seem to have suspected that the sequence of events was merely coincidental (see 6:9). The removal of the ark to Gath (12 miles southeast of Ashdod) put the matter to a test.

5:10 *Ekron.* The northernmost of the five major Philistine cities (see Jos 13:3), located 11 miles northeast of Ashdod and close to Israelite territory (see map, p. 331).

As the ark of God was entering Ekron, the people of Ekron cried out, "They
have brought the ark of the god of Israel
around to us to kill us and our people."
11 So they called together all the rulers[e] of
the Philistines and said, "Send the ark of
the god of Israel away; let it go back to
its own place, or it[a] will kill us and our
people." For death had filled the city with
panic; God's hand was very heavy upon
it. 12 Those who did not die[f] were afflicted with tumors, and the outcry of the city
went up to heaven.

The Ark Returned to Israel

6 When the ark of the LORD had been in
Philistine territory seven months, 2 the
Philistines called for the priests and the diviners[g] and said, "What shall we do with
the ark of the LORD? Tell us how we should
send it back to its place."

3 They answered, "If you return the ark
of the god of Israel, do not send it away
empty,[h] but by all means send a guilt offering[i] to him. Then you will be healed,
and you will know why his hand[j] has not
been lifted from you."

4 The Philistines asked, "What guilt offering should we send to him?"

They replied, "Five gold tumors and
five gold rats, according to the number[k]
of the Philistine rulers, because the same
plague[l] has struck both you and your rulers. 5 Make models of the tumors[m] and of
the rats that are destroying the country,
and pay honor[n] to Israel's god. Perhaps he
will lift his hand from you and your gods
and your land. 6 Why do you harden[o] your
hearts as the Egyptians and Pharaoh did?
When he[b] treated them harshly,[p] did they[q]
not send the Israelites out so they could go
on their way?

7 "Now then, get a new cart[r] ready, with
two cows that have calved and have never
been yoked.[s] Hitch the cows to the cart,
but take their calves away and pen them
up. 8 Take the ark of the LORD and put it on
the cart, and in a chest beside it put the
gold objects you are sending back to him
as a guilt offering. Send it on its way, 9 but
keep watching it. If it goes up to its own
territory, toward Beth Shemesh,[t] then the
LORD has brought this great disaster on us.
But if it does not, then we will know that
it was not his hand that struck us and that
it happened to us by chance."

10 So they did this. They took two such
cows and hitched them to the cart and
penned up their calves. 11 They placed the
ark of the LORD on the cart and along with
it the chest containing the gold rats and the
models of the tumors. 12 Then the cows went
straight up toward Beth Shemesh, keeping
on the road and lowing all the way; they
did not turn to the right or to the left. The
rulers of the Philistines followed them as
far as the border of Beth Shemesh.

13 Now the people of Beth Shemesh were
harvesting their wheat[u] in the valley, and
when they looked up and saw the ark,
they rejoiced at the sight. 14 The cart came
to the field of Joshua of Beth Shemesh,
and there it stopped beside a large rock.
The people chopped up the wood of the
cart and sacrificed the cows as a burnt
offering[v] to the LORD. 15 The Levites[w] took
down the ark of the LORD, together with
the chest containing the gold objects, and
placed them on the large rock.[x] On that
day the people of Beth Shemesh[y] offered
burnt offerings and made sacrifices to the
LORD. 16 The five rulers of the Philistines
saw all this and then returned that same
day to Ekron.

17 These are the gold tumors the Phi-

5:10 [d] S Jos 13:3 **5:11** [e] ver 8 **5:12** [f] S 1Sa 4:8 **6:2** [g] S Ex 7:11; S Isa 44:25 **6:3** [h] S Ex 22:29; S 34:20 [i] S Lev 5:15 [j] ver 9 **6:4** [k] S Jos 13:3 [l] 2Sa 24:25 **6:5** [m] S 1Sa 5:6-11 [n] S Jos 7:19; Rev 14:7 **6:6** [o] S Ex 4:21 [p] Ex 10:2 [q] S Ex 12:33 **6:7** [r] 2Sa 6:3; 1Ch 13:7 [s] S Nu 19:2 **6:9** [t] S Jos 15:10; 21:16 **6:13** [u] S Ge 30:14; Ru 2:23; 1Sa 12:17 **6:14** [v] 1Sa 11:7; 2Sa 24:22; 1Ki 19:21 **6:15** [w] Jos 3:3 [x] ver 18 [y] Jos 21:16

[a] *11* Or *he* [b] *6* That is, God

5:11 *Send the ark of the god of Israel away.* After three successive towns had been struck by disease upon the arrival of the ark, there was little doubt in the people's minds that the power of the God of Israel was the cause of their distress.
6:2 *priests and ... diviners.* The experts on religious matters (priests) and the discerners of hidden knowledge by interpretation of omens (diviners) were consulted (see Dt 18:10 and note on 18:9; Isa 2:6; Eze 21:21 and note).
6:3 *guilt offering.* The priests and diviners suggest returning the ark with a gift, signifying recognition of guilt in taking the ark from Israel and compensation for this violation of the Lord's honor (see v. 5). For the guilt offering in Israel see Lev 5:14—6:7 and note on 5:15.
6:4 *Five gold tumors.* Corresponding to the symptoms of the plague (see 5:6). *five gold rats.* The disease was accompanied by an infestation of rats (v. 5). The pre-Christian Greek translation of the OT (the Septuagint) includes this information earlier in the narrative (see NIV text note on 5:6). It is likely that the rats were the hosts of fleas, which in turn were carriers of the disease.
6:5 *Make models ... and pay honor to Israel's god.* The gold models were an acknowledgment that the disease and the rats were a judgment from the hand of the God of Israel (see note on v. 3).
6:6 *harden your hearts.* See notes on Ex 4:21; Dt 2:3; Jos 11:20. *the Egyptians and Pharaoh.* The plagues that God inflicted on the Egyptians at the time of the exodus made a lasting impression on the surrounding nations (see 4:8; Jos 2:10 and note on 2:9–11).
6:7 *have never been yoked.* Have not been trained to pull a cart. *take their calves away.* Normally cows do not willingly leave their suckling calves.
6:9 *Beth Shemesh.* A town near the Philistine border, belonging to Judah (see Jos 15:10). *by chance.* See note on 5:8.
6:12 *the cows went ... keeping on the road.* Further indication that the Lord was directing them (see v. 7 and note).
6:13 *harvesting their wheat.* The time of wheat harvest is from mid-April until mid-June.
6:14–15 The arrival of the ark at Beth Shemesh is just as much a revelation of the hand of God as the journey itself, because it was one of the priestly towns (see Jos 21:13–16).
6:17 *guilt offering.* See note on v. 3.

listines sent as a guilt offering to the
LORD — one each[z] for Ashdod, Gaza, Ashkelon, Gath and Ekron. 18And the number of the gold rats was according to the
number of Philistine towns belonging to
the five rulers — the fortified towns with
their country villages. The large rock, on
which[a] they set the ark of the LORD, is a
witness to this day in the field of Joshua
of Beth Shemesh.

19But God struck down[a] some of the
men of Beth Shemesh, putting seventy[b]
of them to death because they had looked[b]
into the ark of the LORD. The people
mourned because of the heavy blow the
LORD had dealt them, 20and the men of
Beth Shemesh asked, "Who can stand[c] in
the presence of the LORD, this holy[d] God?
To whom will the ark go up from here?"

21Then they sent messengers to the people of Kiriath Jearim,[e] saying, "The Philistines have returned the ark of the LORD.
Come down and take it up to your place."

7 1So the men of Kiriath Jearim came and
took up the ark[f] of the LORD. They took
it to Abinadab's[g] house on the hill and
consecrated Eleazar his son to guard the
ark of the LORD.

Samuel Subdues the Philistines at Mizpah

2It was a long time, twenty years in all,
that the ark remained at Kiriath Jearim,[h]
and all the people of Israel mourned and
sought after the LORD.[i] 3And Samuel said
to the whole house of Israel, "If you are
returning[j] to the LORD with all your hearts,
then rid[k] yourselves of the foreign gods
and the Ashtoreths[l] and commit[m] yourselves to the LORD and serve him only,[n]
and he will deliver[o] you out of the hand of
the Philistines." 4So the Israelites put away
their Baals and Ashtoreths, and served the
LORD only.

5Then Samuel[p] said, "Assemble all Israel at Mizpah[q] and I will intercede[r] with the
LORD for you." 6When they had assembled
at Mizpah,[s] they drew water and poured[t]
it out before the LORD. On that day they
fasted and there they confessed, "We have
sinned against the LORD." And Samuel was
leader[c][u] of Israel at Mizpah.

7When the Philistines heard that Israel
had assembled at Mizpah, the rulers of the
Philistines came up to attack them. And
when the Israelites heard of it, they were
afraid[v] because of the Philistines. 8They
said to Samuel, "Do not stop crying[w] out to
the LORD our God for us, that he may rescue us from the hand of the Philistines."

6:17 [z] S Jos 13:3 **6:19** [a] 2Sa 6:7 [b] S Ex 19:21 **6:20** [c] 2Sa 6:9; Ps 130:3; Mal 3:2; Rev 6:17 [d] S Lev 11:45 **6:21** [e] S Jos 9:17 **7:1** [f] S Jos 6:7 [g] 2Sa 6:3; 1Ch 13:7 **7:2** [h] 1Ch 13:5; Ps 132:6 [i] 1Ch 13:3 **7:3** [j] Dt 30:10; 2Ki 18:5; 23:25; Jer 24:7 [k] S Ge 31:19; S Jos 24:14 [l] S Jdg 2:12-13; 1Sa 12:10; 31:10 [m] Joel 2:12 [n] S Dt 6:13; Mt 4:10; Lk 4:8 [o] S Jdg 2:18 **7:5** [p] S 1Sa 1:20; Ps 99:6; Jer 15:1 [q] S Jos 11:3; Jdg 21:5; 1Sa 10:17 [r] S ver 8; S Ge 20:7; S Dt 9:19 **7:6** [s] S Jos 11:3 [t] La 2:19 [u] S Jdg 2:16; S 16:31 **7:7** [v] 1Sa 17:11 **7:8** [w] ver 5; S Ex 32:30; S Nu 21:7; 1Sa 12:19,23; 1Ki 18:24; Isa 37:4; Jer 15:1; 27:18

[a] *18* A few Hebrew manuscripts (see also Septuagint); most Hebrew manuscripts *villages as far as Greater Abel, where* [b] *19* A few Hebrew manuscripts; most Hebrew manuscripts and Septuagint *50,070* [c] *6* Traditionally *judge*

6:18 *witness.* A kind of monument to the event. *this day.* The time of the writing of 1,2 Samuel (see Introduction: Literary Features, Authorship and Date).

6:19 *seventy.* The additional 50,000 in most Hebrew manuscripts (see NIV text note) is apparently a copyist's mistake because it is added in an ungrammatical way (no conjunction). Furthermore, this small town could not have contained that many inhabitants. *looked into the ark.* The men of Beth Shemesh (Levites and priests among them) were judged by God for their irreverent curiosity. Because God had so closely linked the manifestation of his own presence among his people with the ark, it was to be treated with great honor (see 2Sa 6:7 and note; Nu 4:15,17–20). This attitude of respect, however, is quite different from the superstitious attitude that led the elders to take the ark into battle against the Philistines, thus treating it as an object with magical power (see note on 4:3).

6:20 *this holy God.* See 2:2 and note. *To whom will the ark go up from here?* The inhabitants of Beth Shemesh respond to God's judgment in much the same way as the inhabitants of Ashdod, Gath and Ekron (see 5:8–10).

6:21 *Kiriath Jearim.* Located nine miles west of Jerusalem.

7:1 *Abinadab's house.* The ark remained in relative obscurity at Abinadab's house until David brought it to Jerusalem (see 2Sa 6:2–3 and notes). Somehow the Tent of Meeting (and the altar of burnt offering) escaped the destruction of Shiloh (see Jer 7:12,14 and note on 7:12; 26:6). It apparently was first moved to Nob (see 21:1–9 and note on 21:1). In David's and Solomon's days it was located at Gibeon, five miles northwest of Jerusalem (see 1Ki 3:4; 1Ch 16:39 and notes; 21:29; 2Ch 1:3,13 and note on 1:2–13). The Gibeonites had been condemned to be menial laborers at the Lord's sanctuary (see Jos 9:23,27 and notes). After Solomon completed the construction of the temple, he brought both the ark and the Tent of Meeting to it (see 1Ki 8:3–6 and note on 8:4).

7:2–17 Samuel's leadership as prophet and judge characterized.

7:2 *twenty years in all.* Probably the 20-year interval between the return of the ark to Israel and the assembly called by Samuel at Mizpah (see v. 5).

7:3 *Ashtoreths.* A general term for foreign goddesses, as elsewhere in the ancient Near East. More specifically, however, Ashtoreth herself was a goddess of love, fertility and war, worshiped in various forms by many peoples including the Canaanites (see note on Jdg 2:13). The worship of Ashtoreth is frequently combined with the worship of Baal (see v. 4; 12:10; Jdg 2:13; 10:6), in accordance with the common practice in fertility religions to associate male and female deities.

7:5 *Mizpah.* See note on 2Ki 25:23; a town in the territory of Benjamin (Jos 18:26), located about seven and a half miles north of Jerusalem. It was here that the Israelites had previously gathered to undertake disciplinary action against Benjamin (Jdg 20:1; 21:1) after the abuse and murder of the concubine of a traveling Levite in Gibeah of Benjamin. Several other places bore the same name (see 22:3; Ge 31:49; Jos 11:3,8; 15:38). *I will intercede.* See 7:8–9; 8:6; 12:17–19,23; 15:11. Samuel, like Moses, was later remembered as a great intercessor (see Ps 99:6; Jer 15:1 and notes). Both were appointed by God to mediate his rule over his people, representing God to Israel and speaking on Israel's behalf to God.

7:6 *they drew water and poured it out before the LORD.* There is no other reference to this type of ceremony in the OT. It appears to symbolize the pouring out of one's heart in repentance and humility before the Lord. For related expressions see 1:15; Ps 62:8; La 2:19 and note. *Samuel was leader.* See NIV text note and v. 15; see also note on 4:18.

7:8 *Do not stop crying out to the LORD our God for us.* As persons who were called out from among the people

9Then Samuel[x] took a suckling lamb and
offered it up as a whole burnt offering to
the LORD. He cried out to the LORD on Israel's behalf, and the LORD answered him.[y]
10While Samuel was sacrificing the
burnt offering, the Philistines drew near
to engage Israel in battle. But that day
the LORD thundered[z] with loud thunder
against the Philistines and threw them
into such a panic[a] that they were routed
before the Israelites. 11The men of Israel
rushed out of Mizpah and pursued the
Philistines, slaughtering them along the
way to a point below Beth Car.
12Then Samuel took a stone[b] and set it
up between Mizpah and Shen. He named
it Ebenezer,[a][c] saying, "Thus far has the
LORD helped us." 13So the Philistines were
subdued[d] and did not invade Israelite territory again.
Throughout Samuel's lifetime, the hand
of the LORD was against the Philistines.
14The towns from Ekron[e] to Gath that the
Philistines had captured from Israel were
restored to her, and Israel delivered the
neighboring territory from the power of
the Philistines. And there was peace between Israel and the Amorites.[f]
15Samuel[g] continued as judge[h] over Israel all[i] the days of his life. 16From year
to year he went on a circuit from Bethel[j]
to Gilgal[k] to Mizpah, judging[l] Israel in all
those places. 17But he always went back to
Ramah,[m] where his home was, and there
he also judged[n] Israel. And he built an altar[o] there to the LORD.

Israel Asks for a King

8 When Samuel grew old, he appointed[p]
his sons as judges for Israel. 2The name
of his firstborn was Joel and the name of
his second was Abijah,[q] and they served
at Beersheba.[r] 3But his sons[s] did not walk
in his ways. They turned aside[t] after dishonest gain and accepted bribes[u] and perverted[v] justice.
4So all the elders[w] of Israel gathered together and came to Samuel at Ramah.[x]
5They said to him, "You are old, and your
sons do not walk in your ways; now appoint a king[y] to lead[b][z] us, such as all the
other nations[a] have."
6But when they said, "Give us a king[b]
to lead us," this displeased[c] Samuel; so
he prayed to the LORD. 7And the LORD told
him: "Listen[d] to all that the people are

[a] 12 *Ebenezer* means *stone of help.* [b] 5 Traditionally *judge*; also in verses 6 and 20

7:9 [x]Ps 99:6 [y]S Ex 32:11; S Dt 9:19 **7:10** [z]S Ex 9:23; S 1Sa 2:10 [a]S Ge 35:5; S Ex 14:24 **7:12** [b]S Ge 28:22; S Dt 27:2; Jos 4:9 [c]S 1Sa 4:1 **7:13** [d]Jdg 13:1,5 **7:14** [e]S Jos 13:3 [f]S Jdg 1:34 **7:15** [g]ver 6; 1Sa 12:11 [h]S Jdg 2:16 [i]Jdg 2:18 **7:16** [j]S Ge 12:8 [k]S Jos 10:43; S 1Sa 10:8; Am 5:5 [l]ver 6; Ac 13:20 **7:17** [m]S Jos 18:25; 1Sa 8:4; 15:34; 19:18; 25:1; 28:3 [n]ver 6 [o]1Sa 9:12; 14:35; 20:6; 2Sa 24:25 **8:1** [p]Dt 16:18-19 **8:2** [q]1Ch 6:28 [r]Ge 22:19; 1Ki 19:3; Am 5:4-5 **8:3** [s]1Sa 2:12 [t]Ne 9:29; Job 34:27; Ps 14:3; 58:3; Isa 53:6 [u]Ex 23:8; 1Sa 12:3; Job 8:22; Pr 17:23 [v]S Ex 23:2 **8:4** [w]S Jdg 11:11; 1Sa 11:3 [x]S 1Sa 7:17 **8:5** [y]ver 19; S Dt 17:14-20; 1Sa 10:19; 12:12,13; Hos 13:11 [z]1Sa 3:20; 12:2 [a]ver 20 **8:6** [b]Hos 13:10 [c]1Sa 12:17; 15:11; 16:1 **8:7** [d]ver 22; 1Sa 12:1

to mediate God's word to them, prophets were given unique access to God's council chamber (see 1Ki 22:19 and note). This privilege of having such access to God as to be mediators of God's rule over his people brought with it the special responsibility to be intercessors for God's people—as Moses was (Ex 32:11–14; 34:8–9; Nu 14:13–19), and as were Isaiah (2Ki 19:1–4), Jeremiah (see Jer 7:16; 15:1 and notes) and Amos (Am 7:2–3,5–6).

7:10 *the LORD thundered with loud thunder.* The Lord had promised to be the protector of his people when they were obedient to their covenant obligations (see Ex 23:22; Dt 20:1–4; see also 2Sa 5:19–25; Jos 10:11–14; Jdg 5:20–21; 2Ki 7:6; 19:35; 2Ch 20:17,22).

7:12 *Ebenezer.* See NIV text note and note on 4:1.

7:13 *did not invade Israelite territory again.* Some interpreters see a contradiction between this statement and subsequent references to the Philistines in 9:16; 10:5; 13:3,5; 17:1; 23:27. This statement, however, only indicates that the Philistines did not immediately counterattack. See 2Ki 6:23–24 for a similar situation.

7:14 *Amorites.* See note on Ge 10:16.

7:15 A summary statement marking the end of the author's account of Samuel's ministry as Israel's leader (see v. 6).

7:16 *from Bethel to Gilgal to Mizpah.* A relatively small area (see map No. 4 at the end of this study Bible). *judging Israel.* See note on 4:18.

7:17 *Ramah.* See note on 1:1.

8:1—12:25 Transition from Samuel's leadership to the establishment of the monarchy as the political form of the nation of Israel, through which God would reestablish (under David) his theocratic order over his people—as in the days of Moses and Joshua (see note on Jdg 17:1—21:25).

8:1 *When Samuel grew old.* Probably about 20 years after the victory at Mizpah (see 7:11), when Samuel was approximately 65 years old (see Introduction: Chronology).

8:2 *Joel.* Means "The LORD is God." *Abijah.* Means "The LORD is my Father." Despite their names, Samuel's two sons "did not walk in his ways" (v. 3). *Beersheba.* Located 45 miles southwest of Jerusalem (see also note on Ge 21:31).

8:3 *did not walk in his ways.* See v. 5; cf. 2:12–17; 3:13; 4:4 and note. *accepted bribes.* Contrast 12:3. Perversion of justice through bribery was explicitly forbidden in Pentateuchal law (see Ex 23:8; Dt 16:19).

8:5 *appoint a king to lead us.* The elders cite Samuel's age and the misconduct of his sons as justifications for their request for a king. It soon becomes apparent, however, that the more basic reason for their request was a desire to be like the surrounding nations—to have a human king as a symbol of national power and unity who would lead them in battle and guarantee their security (see v. 20; 10:19; 12:12 and note; see also Introduction: Contents and Theme).

8:7 *Listen to all that the people are saying to you.* Anticipations of kingship in Israel are present already in the Pentateuch (see Ge 49:10; Nu 24:7,17; Dt 17:14–20 and notes); Samuel is therefore instructed to listen to the people's request (see vv. 9,22). *it is not you they have rejected, but they have rejected me as their king.* Cf. Jdg 8:23 and note. The sin of Israel in requesting a king (see 10:19; 12:12,17,19–20 and note on 12:12) did not rest in any evil inherent in kingship itself, but in the kind of kingship the people envisioned and their reasons for requesting it (see Introduction: Contents and Theme). Their desire was for a form of kingship that denied their covenant relationship with the Lord, who himself was pledged to be their savior and deliverer. In requesting a king "like all the other nations" (v. 20) they broke the covenant, rejected the Lord who was their King (see 12:12; Nu 23:21; Dt 33:5 and note) and forgot his constant provision for their protection in the past (see 10:18; 12:8–11 and notes on 12:9–11).

saying to you; it is not you they have rejected,[e] but they have rejected me as their
king.[f] 8As they have done from the day I
brought them up out of Egypt until this
day, forsaking[g] me and serving other gods,
so they are doing to you. 9Now listen to
them; but warn them solemnly and let
them know[h] what the king who will reign
over them will do."
10Samuel told[i] all the words of the LORD
to the people who were asking him for a
king. 11He said, "This is what the king who
will reign over you will do: He will take[j]
your sons and make them serve[k] with his
chariots and horses, and they will run in
front of his chariots.[l] 12Some he will assign to be commanders[m] of thousands and
commanders of fifties, and others to plow
his ground and reap his harvest, and still
others to make weapons of war and equipment for his chariots. 13He will take your
daughters to be perfumers and cooks and
bakers. 14He will take the best of your[n]
fields and vineyards[o] and olive groves and
give them to his attendants.[p] 15He will take
a tenth[q] of your grain and of your vintage
and give it to his officials and attendants.
16Your menservants and maidservants and
the best of your cattle[a] and donkeys he
will take for his own use. 17He will take a
tenth of your flocks, and you yourselves
will become his slaves. 18When that day
comes, you will cry out for relief from the
king you have chosen, and the LORD will
not answer[r] you in that day.[s]"
19But the people refused[t] to listen to
Samuel. "No!" they said. "We want[u] a
king[v] over us. 20Then we will be like all
the other nations,[w] with a king to lead
us and to go out before us and fight our
battles."
21When Samuel heard all that the people
said, he repeated[x] it before the LORD. 22The

8:7 [e]S Nu 11:20 [f]S Ex 16:8 **8:8** [g]1Sa 12:10; 2Ki 21:22; Jer 2:17 **8:9** [h]ver 11-18; S Dt 17:14-20; 1Sa 10:25 **8:10** [i]S Ex 19:7 **8:11** [j]1Sa 14:52 [k]S Ge 41:46 [l]S Dt 17:16; 2Sa 15:1; 1Ki 1:5; 2Ch 1:14; 9:25; SS 3:7 **8:12** [m]S Dt 1:15 **8:14** [n]Eze 46:18 [o]1Ki 21:7,15; Mic 2:2 [p]2Ki 22:12 **8:15** [q]S Ge 41:34; 1Sa 17:25 **8:18** [r]1Sa 28:6; Job 27:9; 35:12,13; Ps 18:41; 66:18; Pr 1:28; Isa 1:15; 58:4; 59:2; Jer 14:12; Eze 8:18; Mic 3:4 [s]1Sa 10:25; 1Ki 12:4 **8:19** [t]Pr 1:24; Isa 50:2; 66:4; Jer 7:13; 8:12; 13:10; 44:16 [u]Ac 13:21 [v]S ver 5 **8:20** [w]S ver 5 **8:21** [x]S Jdg 11:11 **8:22** [y]S ver 7 **9:1** [z]Jos 18:11-20 [a]S Ru 2:1 [b]1Sa 14:51; 1Ch 8:33; 9:39; Est 2:5; Ac 13:21 **9:2** [c]S Ge 39:6 [d]1Sa 10:24 [e]1Sa 10:23 **9:3** [f]ver 20; 1Sa 10:14,16 **9:4** [g]S Jos 24:33 [h]2Ki 4:42 [i]1Sa 10:2 **9:5** [j]1Sa 1:1 [k]1Sa 10:2

LORD answered, "Listen[y] to them and give
them a king."
Then Samuel said to the men of Israel,
"Everyone go back to his town."

Samuel Anoints Saul

9 There was a Benjamite,[z] a man of
standing,[a] whose name was Kish[b] son
of Abiel, the son of Zeror, the son of Be-
corath, the son of Aphiah of Benjamin.
2He had a son named Saul, an impressive[c]
young man without equal[d] among the Israelites—a head taller[e] than any of the
others.
3Now the donkeys[f] belonging to Saul's
father Kish were lost, and Kish said to his
son Saul, "Take one of the servants with
you and go and look for the donkeys."
4So he passed through the hill[g] country
of Ephraim and through the area around
Shalisha,[h] but they did not find them.
They went on into the district of Shaalim,
but the donkeys[i] were not there. Then he
passed through the territory of Benjamin,
but they did not find them.
5When they reached the district of
Zuph,[j] Saul said to the servant who was
with him, "Come, let's go back, or my father will stop thinking about the donkeys
and start worrying[k] about us."
6But the servant replied, "Look, in this
town there is a man of God;[l] he is highly
respected, and everything[m] he says comes
true. Let's go there now. Perhaps he will
tell us what way to take."
7Saul said to his servant, "If we go,
what can we give the man? The food in
our sacks is gone. We have no gift[n] to take
to the man of God. What do we have?"

[a] *16* Septuagint; Hebrew *young men*

9:6 [l]S Dt 33:1; S Jdg 13:6 [m]1Sa 3:19 **9:7** [n]S Ge 32:20; 1Ki 13:7; 14:3; 2Ki 4:42; 5:5,15; Jer 40:5

8:9,11 *what the king ... will do.* Using a description of the policies of contemporary Canaanite kings (vv. 11–17), Samuel warns the people of the burdens associated with the type of kingship they long for.
8:11 *chariots.* See note on Jos 11:6; see also Dt 17:16 and note on 17:16–17.
8:15 *tenth.* This king's portion would be over and above the tenth Israel was to devote to the Lord (Lev 27:30–32; Nu 18:26; Dt 14:22,28; 26:12). In fact, the demands of the king would parallel all that Israel was to consecrate to the Lord as her Great King (persons, lands, crops, livestock)—even the whole population (v. 17).
8:18 *cry out for relief from the king.* See 1Ki 12:4 and note; Jer 22:13–17.
8:20 *like all the other nations.* See notes on vv. 5,7.
9:1—11:15 God's establishment of Saul as king over Israel took place in three distinct stages; He was (1) anointed by Samuel (9:1—10:16), (2) chosen by lot (10:17–27) and (3) confirmed by public acclamation (11:1–15).
9:1 *man of standing.* Saul (v. 2) and David are each depicted as descending from an ancestor who was a noteworthy member of his community (see Ru 2:1; 4:21–22).
9:2 *a head taller than any of the others.* Physically of kingly stature (see 10:23).
9:3 *donkeys ... were lost.* Saul is introduced as a donkey wrangler sent in search of donkeys that had strayed from home—perhaps symbolizing Saul and the rebellious people who had asked for a king (cf. Isa 1:3). David would be introduced as a shepherd caring for his father's flock (16:11–13) and later pictured as the shepherd over the Lord's flock (see 2Sa 5:2 and note; 7:7–8; Ps 78:70–72 and note on 78:72).
9:5 *Zuph.* Perhaps the region in which Ramah was located (see notes on v. 6; 1:1).
9:6 *But the servant replied.* Saul's ignorance of Samuel is an early hint of his character. *this town.* Probably Ramah (see 7:17), the hometown of Samuel, to which he had just returned from a journey (see v. 12). *man of God.* See note on 2:27; here a reference to Samuel. *everything he says comes true.* See 3:19 and note.
9:7 *what can we give the man?* Other examples of gifts offered to prophets are found in 1Ki 14:3; 2Ki 4:42; 5:15–16; 8:8–9. Whether Samuel accepted the gift and whether he was dependent on such gifts for a livelihood are not clear. Elisha refused Naaman's gift (see 2Ki 5:16 and note). False prophets

8The servant answered him again.
"Look," he said, "I have a quarter of a
shekel[a] of silver. I will give it to the man
of God so that he will tell us what way to
take." 9(Formerly in Israel, if a man went
to inquire[o] of God, he would say, "Come,
let us go to the seer," because the prophet
of today used to be called a seer.)[p]
10"Good," Saul said to his servant.
"Come, let's go." So they set out for the
town where the man of God was.
11As they were going up the hill to the
town, they met some girls coming out to
draw[q] water, and they asked them, "Is the
seer here?"
12"He is," they answered. "He's ahead
of you. Hurry now; he has just come to
our town today, for the people have a sacrifice[r] at the high place.[s] 13As soon as you
enter the town, you will find him before he
goes up to the high place to eat. The people will not begin eating until he comes,
because he must bless[t] the sacrifice; afterward, those who are invited will eat.
Go up now; you should find him about
this time."
14They went up to the town, and as they
were entering it, there was Samuel, coming toward them on his way up to the high
place.
15Now the day before Saul came, the
LORD had revealed this to Samuel: 16"About
this time tomorrow I will send you a man
from the land of Benjamin. Anoint[u] him
leader[v] over my people Israel; he will deliver[w] my people from the hand of the Philistines.[x] I have looked upon my people,
for their cry[y] has reached me."
17When Samuel caught sight of Saul,
the LORD said to him, "This[z] is the man
I spoke to you about; he will govern my
people."
18Saul approached Samuel in the gateway and asked, "Would you please tell me
where the seer's house is?"
19"I am the seer," Samuel replied. "Go
up ahead of me to the high place, for today you are to eat with me, and in the
morning I will let you go and will tell you
all that is in your heart. 20As for the donkeys[a] you lost three days ago, do not worry
about them; they have been found. And to
whom is all the desire[b] of Israel turned, if
not to you and all your father's family?"
21Saul answered, "But am I not a Benjamite, from the smallest tribe[c] of Israel, and
is not my clan the least[d] of all the clans of
the tribe of Benjamin?[e] Why do you say
such a thing to me?"
22Then Samuel brought Saul and his servant into the hall and seated them at the
head of those who were invited—about
thirty in number. 23Samuel said to the
cook, "Bring the piece of meat I gave you,
the one I told you to lay aside."
24So the cook took up the leg[f] with what
was on it and set it in front of Saul. Samuel said, "Here is what has been kept for
you. Eat, because it was set aside for you
for this occasion, from the time I said, 'I

9:9 [o]S Ge 25:22 [p]2Sa 15:27; 24:11; 2Ki 17:13; 1Ch 9:22; 21:9; 26:28; 29:29; 2Ch 19:2; Isa 29:10; 30:10; Am 7:12 **9:11** [q]S Ge 24:11, 13 **9:12** [r]Nu 28:11-15; S 1Sa 7:17 [s]S Lev 26:30 **9:13** [t]S Mt 14:19; 1Co 10:16; 1Ti 4:3-5 **9:16** [u]Ex 30:25; S 1Sa 2:35; 12:3; 15:1; 26:9; 2Ki 11:12; Ps 2:2 [v]2Sa 7:8; 1Ki 8:16; 1Ch 5:2 [w]Ex 3:7-9 [x]1Sa 23:4; 2Sa 3:18 [y]S Ge 16:11; Ps 102:1 **9:17** [z]1Sa 16:12 **9:20** [a]S ver 3 [b]1Sa 12:13; Ezr 6:8; Isa 60:4-9; Da 2:44; Hag 2:7; Mal 3:1 **9:21** [c]Ps 68:27 [d]S Ex 3:11; Mt 2:6; 1Co 15:9 [e]Jdg 6:15; 20:35, 46; 1Sa 18:18 **9:24** [f]S Lev 7:32-34

[a] 8 That is, about 1/10 ounce (about 3 grams)

usually adjusted their message to the desires of those who supported them (see Nu 22:4–7; 23:8 and note; 1Ki 22:6,8,18; Jer 28; Mic 3:5,11).

9:8 *a quarter of a shekel of silver.* See NIV text note. Before the use of coins, gold or silver was weighed out for each monetary transaction (see 13:21; Job 28:15).

9:9 *the prophet of today used to be called a seer.* There was no essential difference between a seer and a prophet. The person popularly designated as a prophet at the time of the writing of 1,2 Samuel was termed a seer in the time of Saul. This need not mean that the term "prophet" was unknown in the time of Saul or that the term "seer" was unknown in later times (see Isa 30:10). The reference is to popular usage.

9:11 *girls coming out to draw water.* In the cool of the evening (see Ge 24:11 and note).

9:12 *high place.* After entrance into the promised land, the Israelites often followed the custom of the Canaanites in building local altars on hills. (At this time the central sanctuary was not functioning because the ark of God was separated from the tabernacle; Shiloh had been destroyed, and the priestly family, after the death of Eli's sons, was apparently still inactive.) Worship at these high places often led Israelites to combine Baal worship with their worship of the Lord and, for this reason, it was condemned (see note on 1Ki 3:2).

9:13 *he must bless the sacrifice.* Samuel presided over the sacrificial meal (see 1:4; 2:13–16), at which he gave a prayer, probably similar to those referred to in the NT (see Mt 26:26–27; Jn 6:11,23; 1Ti 4:3–5).

9:16 *Anoint him.* Priests were also anointed (see Ex 29:7; 40:12–15; Lev 4:3; 8:12), but from this point in the OT it is usually the king who is referred to as "the LORD's anointed" (see note on 2:10; see also 24:6; 26:9,11,16; 2Sa 1:14,16; 19:21; cf. Ps 2:2; but see also Zec 4:14). Anointing signifies separation to the Lord for a particular task and divine equipping for the task (see 10:1,6; 16:13; Isa 61:1). *leader.* The Hebrew for this word (see 10:1; 13:14; 25:30) indicates one designated by the Lord to be the ruler of his people (the same Hebrew word is translated "ruler" in 2Sa 5:2; 7:8; 1Ch 11:2; 17:7). It served as a useful term to ease the transition between the leadership of the judges and that of the kings. *Philistines.* See note on 7:13.

9:20 *all the desire of Israel.* A reference to Israel's desire for a king.

9:21 *smallest tribe … least of all the clans.* Saul's origins were among the humblest in Israel (Benjamin was the youngest of Jacob's sons, and the tribe had been greatly reduced in the time of the judges; see Jdg 20:46–48). His elevation to king shows that God "exalts" whomever he will (2:7), which is one of the central themes running throughout Samuel. God's use of the powerless to promote his kingdom on earth is a common feature in the Biblical testimony and underscores the truth that his kingdom is not of this world (cf. 1Co 1:26–31).

9:24 *leg.* The Hebrew for this word specifies the thigh, which was normally reserved for the Lord's consecrated priest (see Ex 29:22,27; Lev 7:32–33,35; Nu 6:20; 18:18). The presentation of this choice piece of the sacrificial animal to Saul was a distinct honor and anticipated his being designated the Lord's anointed.

have invited guests.' " And Saul dined with
Samuel that day.
25After they came down from the high
place to the town, Samuel talked with Saul
on the roof[g] of his house. 26They rose about
daybreak and Samuel called to Saul on the
roof, "Get ready, and I will send you on
your way." When Saul got ready, he and
Samuel went outside together. 27As they
were going down to the edge of the town,
Samuel said to Saul, "Tell the servant to
go on ahead of us"—and the servant did
so—"but you stay here awhile, so that I
may give you a message from God."

10 Then Samuel took a flask[h] of oil and
poured it on Saul's head and kissed
him, saying, "Has not the LORD anointed[i]
you leader over his inheritance?[a] [j] 2When
you leave me today, you will meet two
men near Rachel's tomb,[k] at Zelzah on
the border of Benjamin. They will say to
you, 'The donkeys[l] you set out to look for
have been found. And now your father
has stopped thinking about them and is
worried[m] about you. He is asking, "What
shall I do about my son?" '
3"Then you will go on from there until
you reach the great tree of Tabor. Three
men going up to God at Bethel[n] will meet
you there. One will be carrying three young
goats, another three loaves of bread, and
another a skin of wine. 4They will greet
you and offer you two loaves of bread,[o]
which you will accept from them.
5"After that you will go to Gibeah[p] of
God, where there is a Philistine outpost.[q]
As you approach the town, you will meet
a procession of prophets[r] coming down
from the high place[s] with lyres, tambourines,[t] flutes[u] and harps[v] being played before them, and they will be prophesying.[w]
6The Spirit[x] of the LORD will come upon
you in power, and you will prophesy with
them; and you will be changed[y] into a different person. 7Once these signs are fulfilled, do whatever[z] your hand[a] finds to
do, for God is with[b] you.
8"Go down ahead of me to Gilgal.[c] I will
surely come down to you to sacrifice burnt
offerings and fellowship offerings,[b] but
you must wait seven[d] days until I come to
you and tell you what you are to do."

Saul Made King

9As Saul turned to leave Samuel, God
changed[e] Saul's heart, and all these signs[f]
were fulfilled[g] that day. 10When they arrived at Gibeah, a procession of prophets
met him; the Spirit[h] of God came upon him
in power, and he joined in their prophesying.[i] 11When all those who had formerly
known him saw him prophesying with the
prophets, they asked each other, "What is
this[j] that has happened to the son of Kish?
Is Saul also among the prophets?"[k]
12A man who lived there answered,
"And who is their father?" So it became

9:25 [g] S Dt 22:8; S Jos 2:8; S Mt 24:17; Lk 5:19 **10:1** [h] 1Sa 16:1; 2Ki 9:1,3,6 [i] S Ex 29:7; S 1Sa 9:16; S 1Ki 1:39 [j] S Ex 34:9; 2Sa 20:19; Ps 78:62,71 **10:2** [k] Ge 35:20 [l] 1Sa 9:4 [m] 1Sa 9:5 **10:3** [n] S Ge 35:7-8 **10:4** [o] ver 27; 1Sa 16:20; Pr 18:16 **10:5** [p] ver 26; 1Sa 11:4; 15:34 [q] 1Sa 13:3 [r] S Nu 11:29; 1Ki 20:35; 2Ki 2:3,15; 4:1; 6:1; 9:1; Am 7:14 [s] S Lev 26:30 [t] S Ge 31:27; Jer 31:4 [u] 1Ki 1:40; Isa 30:29 [v] 1Sa 16:16; 18:10; 19:9; 2Ki 3:15; Ps 92:3 [w] ver 10; 1Sa 19:20; 1Ch 25:1; 1Co 14:1 **10:6** [x] S Nu 11:25 [y] ver 9 **10:7** [z] 2Sa 7:3; 1Ki 8:17; 1Ch 22:7; 28:2; 2Ch 6:7; Ecc 9:10 [a] Jdg 9:33 [b] S Jos 1:5; Lk 1:28; Heb 13:5 **10:8** [c] Jos 4:20; S 10:43; 1Sa 7:16; 11:14-15 [d] 1Sa 13:8

[a] *1* Hebrew; Septuagint and Vulgate *over his people Israel? You will reign over the LORD's people and save them from the power of their enemies round about. And this will be a sign to you that the LORD has anointed you leader over his inheritance:* [b] *8* Traditionally *peace offerings*

10:9 [e] ver 6 [f] S Dt 13:2 [g] ver 7 **10:10** [h] S Nu 11:25; 1Sa 11:6 [i] S ver 5-6 **10:11** [j] Mt 13:54; Jn 7:15 [k] ver 12; 1Sa 19:24; 2Ki 9:11; Jer 29:26; Hos 9:7

9:25 *on the roof.* Where they could catch the cool evening breeze (see v. 11; 2Sa 11:2 and notes) and where Saul would sleep that night (see v. 26).

10:1 *oil.* Olive oil, no doubt spiced in some manner (see Ex 30:22–33). *Has not the LORD anointed you ...?* See note on 9:16. *leader.* See 9:16 and note. *his inheritance.* "My people Israel" (9:16). The Lord's inheritance includes both the people (see Ex 34:9) and the land (see Ex 15:17). After departing from Samuel, Saul is to receive three signs (see vv. 2–7) to authenticate Samuel's words and to assure him that the Lord has indeed chosen him to be king.

10:2 *Rachel's tomb.* Rachel, Jacob's favorite wife, had died on the road to Bethlehem while giving birth to Benjamin. Her tomb had become a notable landmark (see Ge 35:20 and note).

10:3 *great tree.* A large tree was often a conspicuous point of reference for pilgrims and other travelers (see Ge 12:6 and note). *Bethel.* Located ten miles north of Jerusalem (see note on Ge 12:8).

10:5 *Gibeah of God.* Gibeah was Saul's hometown (see v. 26; 11:4), located in the tribal area of Benjamin (Jos 18:28; Jdg 19:12–14). It was usually called "Gibeah" or "Gibeah in Benjamin" (as in 13:2,15), but three times "Gibeah of Saul" (11:4; 15:34; 2Sa 21:6). The present designation (used only here) may have been Samuel's way of reminding Saul that the land of Canaan belonged to God and not to the Philistines (see Dt 32:43; Isa 14:2; Hos 9:3 and note). *prophets.* The bands of prophets with which Samuel was associated (as also the "sons of the prophets" with whom Elijah and Elisha were associated; see note on 1Ki 20:35) appear to have been small communities of men who banded together in spiritually decadent times for mutual cultivation of their religious zeal. *lyres ... harps.* The actions of individual prophets or groups of prophets were sometimes accompanied by musical instruments (see 2Ki 3:15; 1Ch 25:1). *prophesying.* Here (and in vv. 6,10–11,13) appears to designate an ecstatic praising of God inspired by the Spirit of the Lord (see Nu 11:24–30 for similar use of the term).

10:6 *changed into a different person.* God's Spirit would enable Saul to be Israel's king.

10:7 *do whatever your hand finds to do.* Saul is to take whatever action is appropriate when the situation presents itself to manifest publicly his royal leadership (see 11:4–11).

10:8 *Go down ahead of me to Gilgal.* At some unspecified future time, perhaps previously discussed (see 9:25), Saul is to go to Gilgal and wait seven days for Samuel's arrival (see 13:7–14). *Gilgal.* See note on Jos 4:19.

10:11 *Is Saul also among the prophets?* See 19:24 and note; an expression of surprise at Saul's behavior by those who had known him previously—another subtle indication of his character (see notes on 9:3,6).

10:12 *who is their father?* Some understand the question as an expression of contempt for prophets generally, others as implying the recognition that prophetic inspiration comes from God and therefore could be imparted to whomever God chose. However, since leading prophets were sometimes called

a saying: "Is Saul also among the prophets?"[l] 13After Saul stopped prophesying,[m]
he went to the high place.
14Now Saul's uncle[n] asked him and his
servant, "Where have you been?"
"Looking for the donkeys,[o]" he said.
"But when we saw they were not to be
found, we went to Samuel."
15Saul's uncle said, "Tell me what Samuel said to you."
16Saul replied, "He assured us that the
donkeys[p] had been found." But he did not
tell his uncle what Samuel had said about
the kingship.
17Samuel summoned the people of Israel
to the LORD at Mizpah[q] 18and said to them,
"This is what the LORD, the God of Israel,
says: 'I brought Israel up out of Egypt, and
I delivered you from the power of Egypt
and all the kingdoms that oppressed[r] you.'
19But you have now rejected[s] your God,
who saves[t] you out of all your calamities
and distresses. And you have said, 'No, set
a king[u] over us.'[v] So now present[w] yourselves before the LORD by your tribes and
clans."
20When Samuel brought all the tribes of
Israel near, the tribe of Benjamin was chosen. 21Then he brought forward the tribe
of Benjamin, clan by clan, and Matri's clan
was chosen.[x] Finally Saul son of Kish was
chosen. But when they looked for him, he
was not to be found. 22So they inquired[y]
further of the LORD, "Has the man come
here yet?"
And the LORD said, "Yes, he has hidden
himself among the baggage."
23They ran and brought him out, and
as he stood among the people he was a
head taller[z] than any of the others. 24Sam-
uel said to all the people, "Do you see the
man the LORD has chosen?[a] There is no
one like[b] him among all the people."
Then the people shouted, "Long live[c]
the king!"
25Samuel explained[d] to the people the
regulations[e] of the kingship.[f] He wrote
them down on a scroll and deposited it
before the LORD. Then Samuel dismissed
the people, each to his own home.
26Saul also went to his home in Gibeah,[g] accompanied by valiant men[h] whose
hearts God had touched. 27But some troublemakers[i] said, "How can this fellow save
us?" They despised him and brought him
no gifts.[j] But Saul kept silent.

Saul Rescues the City of Jabesh

11 Nahash[k] the Ammonite went up and
besieged Jabesh Gilead.[l] And all the
men of Jabesh said to him, "Make a treaty[m]
with us, and we will be subject to you."
2But Nahash the Ammonite replied, "I
will make a treaty with you only on the
condition[n] that I gouge[o] out the right eye
of every one of you and so bring disgrace[p]
on all Israel."
3The elders[q] of Jabesh said to him, "Give
us seven days so we can send messengers
throughout Israel; if no one comes to rescue[r] us, we will surrender[s] to you."
4When the messengers came to Gibeah[t]
of Saul and reported these terms to the

10:12 [l]S ver 11
10:13 [m]1Sa 19:23
10:14 [n]1Sa 14:50 [o]S 1Sa 9:3
10:16 [p]S 1Sa 9:3
10:17 [q]S 1Sa 7:5
10:18 [r]S Ex 1:14; S Nu 10:9
10:19 [s]S Nu 11:20; S Dt 33:5 [t]Ps 7:10; 18:48; 68:20; 145:19 [u]S 1Sa 8:5-7 [v]S Dt 17:14 [w]Jos 7:14
10:21 [x]Est 3:7; Pr 16:33
10:22 [y]S Ge 25:22; S Jdg 18:5
10:23 [z]1Sa 9:2
10:24 [a]Dt 17:15; 2Sa 21:6 [b]1Sa 9:2 [c]1Ki 1:25,34,39; 2Ki 11:12
10:25 [d]S 1Sa 8:9 [e]S Dt 17:14-20; S 1Sa 8:11-18; 2Ki 11:12 [f]1Sa 11:14
10:26 [g]S ver 5; S Jdg 19:14 [h]S Jdg 20:44
10:27 [i]S Dt 13:13; S 1Sa 20:7 [j]S ver 4; 1Ki 10:25; 2Ch 17:5; 32:23; Ps 68:29
11:1 [k]S Ge 19:38; 1Sa 12:12; 2Sa 10:2; 17:27; 1Ch 19:1 [l]Jdg 21:8; 1Sa 31:11; 2Sa 2:4,5; 21:12 [m]S Ex 23:32; S Jer 37:1
11:2 [n]Ge 34:15 [o]S Nu 16:14 [p]1Sa 17:26
11:3 [q]S 1Sa 8:4 [r]S Jdg 2:16 [s]ver 10
11:4 [t]S 1Sa 10:5,26

"father" (2Ki 2:12; 6:21; 13:14), the speaker may have intended a disdainful reference to Samuel or an ironical gibe at Saul.

10:17 *Samuel summoned the people.* After the private designation and anointing of Saul to be king (9:15–17,20–21,27; 10:1), an assembly is called by Samuel to make the Lord's choice known to the people (v. 21) and to define the king's task (v. 25). *Mizpah.* See note on 7:5.

10:18 *I delivered you.* Speaking through Samuel, the Lord emphasizes to the people that he has been their deliverer throughout their history. He brought them out of Egypt and delivered them from all their enemies during the time of the judges. Although the judges themselves are sometimes referred to as Israel's deliverers (see Jdg 3:9,15,31; 6:14; 10:1; 13:5), this was true only in a secondary sense, for they were instruments of the Lord's deliverance (see Jdg 2:18). It was the Lord who sent them (see 12:11 and note; Jdg 6:14).

10:19 *rejected your God.* See note on 8:7.

10:20 *tribe of Benjamin was chosen.* By casting lots (see 14:41–42; Jos 7:16–18). The Urim and Thummim were used for this purpose (see notes on 2:28; Ex 28:30).

10:23 *a head taller.* See 9:2 and note.

10:24 *Long live the king!* See note on Ps 62:4.

10:25 *regulations of the kingship.* Samuel here takes the first step toward resolving the tension that existed between Israel's misdirected desire for a king (and their misconceived notion of what the king's role and function should be) and the Lord's intent to give them one (see Introduction: Contents and Theme). This description of the duties and prerogatives of the Israelite king was given for the benefit of both the people and the king-designate. It was intended to clearly distinguish Israelite kingship from that of the surrounding nations and to ensure that the king's role in Israel was compatible with the continued rule of the Lord over Israel as her Great King (see Dt 17:14–20). *scroll.* See note on Ex 17:14. *deposited it before the LORD.* Cf. note on Ex 31:18. The legal document defining the role of the king in governing God's covenant people was preserved at the sanctuary (the tabernacle, later the temple).

10:27 *troublemakers.* See 2:12; see also note on Dt 13:13. *How can this fellow save us?* Reflects the people's continued apostate idea that national security was to be sought in the person of the human king (see note on v. 18; see also 8:20).

11:1 *Ammonite.* The Ammonites were descended from Lot (see Ge 19:36–38 and note; Dt 2:19) and lived east of the Jordan River and south of the Jabbok (see Dt 2:37; Jos 12:2). Previous attempts by the Ammonites to occupy Israelite territory are referred to in Jdg 3:13; 11:4–33. The Philistine threat to Israel in the west presented the Ammonites with an opportunity to move against Israel from the east with supposed impunity. *Jabesh Gilead.* A town east of the Jordan (see map No. 4 at the end of this study Bible).

11:2 *gouge out the right eye.* Besides causing humiliation (see note on Jdg 16:21), the loss of the right eye would destroy the military capability of archers.

11:4 *Gibeah of Saul.* See 10:26 and note on 10:5. Close family ties undoubtedly prompted the inhabitants of Jabesh to seek help from the tribe of Benjamin (see Jdg 21:12–14).

people, they all wept[u] aloud. 5Just then
Saul was returning from the fields, behind
his oxen, and he asked, "What is wrong
with the people? Why are they weeping?"
Then they repeated to him what the men
of Jabesh had said.
6When Saul heard their words, the Spirit[v] of God came upon him in power, and
he burned with anger. 7He took a pair of
oxen,[w] cut them into pieces, and sent the
pieces by messengers throughout Israel,[x]
proclaiming, "This is what will be done to
the oxen of anyone[y] who does not follow
Saul and Samuel." Then the terror of the
LORD fell on the people, and they turned
out as one man.[z] 8When Saul mustered[a]
them at Bezek,[b] the men of Israel numbered three hundred thousand and the
men of Judah thirty thousand.
9They told the messengers who had
come, "Say to the men of Jabesh Gilead,
'By the time the sun is hot tomorrow, you
will be delivered.'" When the messengers
went and reported this to the men of Jabesh, they were elated. 10They said to the
Ammonites, "Tomorrow we will surrender[c] to you, and you can do to us whatever seems good to you."
11The next day Saul separated his men
into three divisions;[d] during the last watch
of the night they broke into the camp of
the Ammonites[e] and slaughtered them until the heat of the day. Those who survived
were scattered, so that no two of them
were left together.

Saul Confirmed as King

12The people then said to Samuel,
"Who[f] was it that asked, 'Shall Saul reign
over us?' Bring these men to us and we
will put them to death."
13But Saul said, "No one shall be put
to death today,[g] for this day the LORD has
rescued[h] Israel."
14Then Samuel said to the people,
"Come, let us go to Gilgal[i] and there reaffirm the kingship.[j]" 15So all the people
went to Gilgal[k] and confirmed Saul as
king[l] in the presence of the LORD. There
they sacrificed fellowship offerings[a] before
the LORD, and Saul and all the Israelites
held a great celebration.

Samuel's Farewell Speech

12 Samuel said to all Israel, "I have listened[m] to everything you said to me
and have set a king[n] over you. 2Now you
have a king as your leader.[o] As for me, I
am old and gray, and my sons[p] are here
with you. I have been your leader from my
youth until this day. 3Here I stand. Testify against me in the presence of the LORD
and his anointed.[q] Whose ox have I taken?
Whose donkey[r] have I taken? Whom have
I cheated? Whom have I oppressed? From
whose hand have I accepted a bribe[s] to
make me shut my eyes? If I have done[t] any
of these, I will make it right."[u]
4"You have not cheated or oppressed

[a] 15 Traditionally *peace offerings*

11:4 [u]S Ge 27:38; S Nu 25:6 **11:6** [v]S Jdg 3:10 **11:7** [w]S 1Sa 6:14 [x]S Jdg 19:29 [y]Jdg 21:5 [z]S Jdg 20:1 **11:8** [a]Jdg 20:2 [b]Jdg 1:4 **11:10** [c]ver 3 **11:11** [d]S Jdg 7:16 [e]S Ge 19:38 **11:12** [f]S Dt 13:13; Lk 19:27 **11:13** [g]2Sa 19:22 [h]1Sa 19:5; 1Ch 11:14 **11:14** [i]S Jos 10:43; S 1Sa 10:8 [j]1Sa 10:25 **11:15** [k]S Jos 5:9; 2Sa 19:15 [l]1Sa 12:1 **12:1** [m]S 1Sa 8:7 [n]1Sa 11:15 **12:2** [o]S 1Sa 8:5 [p]1Sa 8:3 **12:3** [q]S 1Sa 9:16; 24:6; 26:9,11; 2Sa 1:14; 19:21; Ps 105:15 [r]Nu 16:15 [s]S Ex 18:21; S 1Sa 8:3 [t]Ex 20:17; Ac 20:33 [u]S Lev 25:14

11:5 *Saul was returning from the fields.* After Saul's public selection as the king-designate at Mizpah (10:17–25), he returned home (10:26) to resume his normal activities and to wait for the Lord's leading for the next step in his elevation to the throne (see notes on v. 15; 10:7).
11:6 *the Spirit of God came upon him in power.* See 10:6,10. For similar endowment of Israel's deliverers with extraordinary vigor by God's Spirit see Jdg 11:29 and note; 14:6,19; 15:14.
11:7 *sent the pieces by messengers throughout Israel.* For a similar case see Jdg 19:29 and note.
11:8 *Bezek.* Located north of Shechem, west of the Jordan River but within striking distance of Jabesh Gilead.
11:11 *last watch of the night.* The third watch (2:00–6:00 A.M.; see note on Mt 14:25).
11:13 *the LORD has rescued Israel.* Saul recognizes Israel's true deliverer (see note on 10:18). The victory, in combination with Saul's confession, places yet another seal of divine approval on Saul as the man the Lord has chosen to be king.
11:14 *let us go to Gilgal and there reaffirm the kingship.* Samuel perceives that it is now the appropriate time for the people to renew their allegiance to the Lord. The kingship he speaks of is the Lord's, not Saul's. Samuel calls for an assembly to restore the covenant relationship between the Lord and his people. He wants to inaugurate Saul's rule in a manner demonstrating that the continued rule of the Lord as Israel's Great King is in no way diminished or violated in the new era of the monarchy (see Introduction: Contents and Theme). Verses 14–15 are a brief synopsis of the Gilgal assembly and are prefaced to the more detailed account of the same assembly in ch. 12. *Gilgal.* Located east of Jericho near the Jordan River. It was a particularly appropriate place for Israel to renew her allegiance to the Lord (see Jos 4:19—5:10; 10:7–15).
11:15 *confirmed Saul as king in the presence of the LORD.* Saul had previously been anointed in private by Samuel at Ramah (see 10:1 and note) and publicly selected as the king-designate at Mizpah (10:17–27). In the subsequent Ammonite crisis (vv. 1–13) his leadership did not rest on public recognition of his royal authority but on the military victory. Now at Gilgal Saul is inaugurated as God's chosen king and formally assumes the privileges and responsibilities of this office. *fellowship offerings.* This type of offering was an important element in the original ceremony of covenant ratification at Sinai (see Ex 24:5,11 and note on 24:11). It represented the communion or peace between the Lord and his people when the people lived in conformity with their covenant obligations (see Lev 7:11–21; 22:21–23). *held a great celebration.* Rejoicing is the expression of people who have renewed their commitment to the Lord, confessed their sin (see 12:19 and note) and been given a king.
12:2 *your leader.* Lit. "one who goes before you." The Hebrew imagery is probably that of a king or leader as shepherd of his people (see 2Sa 5:2 and note; Eze 34:23 and notes on 34:1–31 and 34:2; cf. note on Ps 23:1; Mic 2:12–13—and ultimately Jesus in Jn 10:3–4,11,14–15,27 [cf. note on 10:1–30]).
12:3 *Testify against me.* Legal language. When Samuel presents the newly inaugurated king to the people, he seeks to establish publicly his own past faithfulness to the covenant as leader of the nation. His purpose is to exonerate himself and provide an example for Saul in his new responsibilities. *Whose ox have I taken? Whose donkey have I taken?*

us," they replied. "You have not taken anything from anyone's hand."

5Samuel said to them, "The LORD is witness[v] against you, and also his anointed is witness this day, that you have not found anything[w] in my hand.[x]"

"He is witness," they said.

6Then Samuel said to the people, "It is the LORD who appointed Moses and Aaron and brought[y] your forefathers up out of Egypt. 7Now then, stand[z] here, because I am going to confront[a] you with evidence before the LORD as to all the righteous acts[b] performed by the LORD for you and your fathers.

8"After Jacob[c] entered Egypt, they cried[d] to the LORD for help, and the LORD sent[e] Moses and Aaron, who brought your forefathers out of Egypt and settled them in this place.

9"But they forgot[f] the LORD their God; so he sold them[g] into the hand of Sisera,[h] the commander of the army of Hazor,[i] and into the hands of the Philistines[j] and the king of Moab,[k] who fought against them. 10They cried[l] out to the LORD and said, 'We have sinned; we have forsaken[m] the LORD and served the Baals and the Ashtoreths.[n] But now deliver us from the hands of our enemies, and we will serve you.' 11Then the LORD sent Jerub-Baal,[a][o] Barak,[b][p] Jephthah[q] and Samuel,[c][r] and he delivered you from the hands of your enemies on every side, so that you lived securely.

12"But when you saw that Nahash[s] king[t] of the Ammonites was moving against you, you said to me, 'No, we want a king to rule[u] over us'—even though the LORD your God was your king. 13Now here is the king[v] you have chosen, the one you asked[w] for; see, the LORD has set a king over you. 14If you fear[x] the LORD and serve and obey him and do not rebel[y] against his commands, and if both you and the king who reigns over you follow the LORD your God—good! 15But if you do not obey the LORD, and if you rebel against[z] his commands, his hand will be against you, as it was against your fathers.

16"Now then, stand still[a] and see[b] this great thing the LORD is about to do before your eyes! 17Is it not wheat harvest[c] now? I will call[d] upon the LORD to send thunder[e] and rain.[f] And you will realize what an evil[g] thing you did in the eyes of the LORD when you asked for a king."

18Then Samuel called upon the LORD,[h] and that same day the LORD sent thunder

12:5 [v]S Ge 31:50 [w]Ac 23:9; 24:20 [x]Ex 22:4 **12:6** [y]S Ex 3:10; Mic 6:4 **12:7** [z]S Jos 24:1 [a]Isa 1:18; 3:14; Jer 2:9; 25:31; Eze 17:20; 20:35; Mic 6:1-5 [b]S Jdg 5:11 **12:8** [c]S Ge 46:6 [d]S Ex 2:23 [e]S Ex 3:10; 4:16 **12:9** [f]S Dt 32:18; S Jdg 3:7 [g]S Dt 32:30 [h]Jdg 4:2 [i]S Jos 11:1 [j]Jdg 10:7 [k]Jdg 3:12 **12:10** [l]S Jdg 3:9 [m]S 1Sa 8:8 [n]S 1Sa 7:3 **12:11** [o]Jdg 6:32 [p]S Jdg 4:6 [q]S Jdg 11:1 [r]S 1Sa 7:15 **12:12** [s]S 1Sa 11:1 [t]S 1Sa 8:5 [u]1Sa 25:30; 2Sa 5:2; 1Ch 5:2 **12:13** [v]S 1Sa 8:5 [w]S 1Sa 9:20 **12:14** [x]S Jos 24:14 [y]Jer 4:17; La 1:18 **12:15** [z]Lev 26:16; Jos 24:20; Isa 1:20; Jer 4:17; 26:4

[a] *11* Also called *Gideon* [b] *11* Some Septuagint manuscripts and Syriac; Hebrew *Bedan* [c] *11* Hebrew; some Septuagint manuscripts and Syriac *Samson*

12:16 [a]S Ex 14:14 [b]S Ex 14:13 **12:17** [c]S Ge 30:14; S 1Sa 6:13 [d]1Ki 18:42; Jas 5:18 [e]S Ex 9:23; S 1Sa 2:10 [f]Ge 7:12; Ex 9:18; Job 37:13; Pr 26:1 [g]S 1Sa 8:6-7 **12:18** [h]Ps 99:6

See Ex 20:17; 22:1,4,9. Unlike his sons, Samuel has not used his position for personal gain (see 8:3 and note; cf. Nu 16:15). *Whom have I cheated? Whom have I oppressed?* See Lev 19:13; Dt 24:14. *From whose hand have I accepted a bribe ... ?* Contrast 8:3. See Ex 23:8; Dt 16:19.

12:6 *Samuel said to the people.* Samuel now turns to the matter of the people's request for a king, which he views as a covenant-breaking act and a serious apostasy. *It is the LORD.* Samuel emphasizes that in the past the Lord had provided the necessary leadership for the nation.

12:7 *confront you with evidence.* The terminology is that of a legal proceeding, as in vv. 2–5, but now the relationship of the parties is reversed. This time Samuel is the accuser, the people are the defendants, and the Lord is the Judge. *righteous acts performed by the LORD.* These acts (see vv. 8–11) not only demonstrate the constancy of the Lord's covenant faithfulness toward his people in the past but also serve to expose their present apostasy.

12:9–11 A summary of the dreary cycle of apostasy, divine chastening, urgent appeals to God, and divine restoration that characterized the period of the judges (see, e.g., note on Jdg 2:6—3:6; see also Introduction to Judges: Themes and Theology; Literary Features).

12:9 *forgot the LORD.* This would become Israel's persistent failure (see Hos 2:13 and note).

12:10 *the Baals and the Ashtoreths.* See notes on 7:3; Jdg 2:13.

12:11 *he delivered you.* The Lord repeatedly rescued Israel from her enemies right up to Samuel's own lifetime (see 7:3,8,10,12), demonstrating again the people's apostasy in desiring a king.

12:12 *when you saw that Nahash ... was moving against you.* In the face of the combined threat from the Philistines in the west (9:16) and the Ammonites in the east (11:1–13), the Israelites sought to find security in the person of a human king. *No, we want a king ... the LORD your God was your king.* The Israelite desire for and trust in a human leader constituted a rejection of the kingship of the Lord and betrayed a loss of confidence in his care, in spite of his faithfulness during the time of the exodus, conquest and judges (see 8:7 and note).

12:13 *the LORD has set a king over you.* In spite of the sinfulness of the people's request, the Lord had chosen to incorporate kingship into the structure of the theocracy (his kingdom). Kingship was given by the Lord to his people and was to function as an instrument of his rule over them (see Introduction: Contents and Theme).

12:14 *If you ...* Samuel relates the covenant conditions (see Ex 19:5–6 and note on 19:5; Dt 8:19; 11:13–15,22–23; 28:1,15; 30:17–18; Jos 24:20) to the new era Israel is entering with the establishment of the monarchy. *if both you and the king ... follow the LORD your God—good!* Israel and her king are to demonstrate that although human kingship has been established, they will continue to recognize the Lord as their true King. In this new era where potential for divided loyalty between the Lord and the human king arises, Israel's loyalty to the Lord must remain inviolate.

12:15 *But if you do not obey.* Samuel confronts Israel with the same alternatives Moses had expressed centuries earlier (see Dt 28:1,15; 30:15–20). The introduction of kingship into Israel's social and political structures has not changed the fundamental nature of her relationship to the Lord.

12:16 *see this great thing.* See v. 24 and note. Samuel calls the people to observe as the Lord himself demonstrates his existence and power and authenticates the truthfulness and seriousness of Samuel's words.

12:17 *wheat harvest.* See note on 6:13.

12:18 *stood in awe of the LORD and of Samuel.* See Ex 14:31 and note.

and rain. So all the people stood in awe[i] of
the LORD and of Samuel.
19The people all said to Samuel, "Pray[j]
to the LORD your God for your servants so
that we will not die,[k] for we have added
to all our other sins the evil of asking for
a king."
20"Do not be afraid," Samuel replied.
"You have done all this evil;[l] yet do not
turn away from the LORD, but serve the
LORD with all your heart. 21Do not turn
away after useless[m] idols.[n] They can do
you no good, nor can they rescue you, because they are useless. 22For the sake[o] of
his great name[p] the LORD will not reject[q]
his people, because the LORD was pleased
to make[r] you his own. 23As for me, far be
it from me that I should sin against the
LORD by failing to pray[s] for you. And I will
teach[t] you the way that is good and right.
24But be sure to fear[u] the LORD and serve
him faithfully with all your heart;[v] consider[w] what great[x] things he has done for
you. 25Yet if you persist[y] in doing evil, both
you and your king[z] will be swept[a] away."

Samuel Rebukes Saul

13 Saul was ⌞thirty⌟[a] years old when he
became king, and he reigned over Israel ⌞forty-⌟[b] two years.
2Saul[c] chose three thousand men from
Israel; two thousand[b] were with him at
Micmash[c] and in the hill country of Bethel, and a thousand were with Jonathan at
Gibeah[d] in Benjamin. The rest of the men
he sent back to their homes.
3Jonathan attacked the Philistine outpost[e] at Geba,[f] and the Philistines heard
about it. Then Saul had the trumpet[g]
blown throughout the land and said, "Let
the Hebrews hear!" 4So all Israel heard
the news: "Saul has attacked the Philistine outpost, and now Israel has become a
stench[h] to the Philistines." And the people
were summoned to join Saul at Gilgal.
5The Philistines assembled[i] to fight Israel, with three thousand[d] chariots, six
thousand charioteers, and soldiers as numerous as the sand[j] on the seashore. They
went up and camped at Micmash,[k] east of
Beth Aven.[l] 6When the men of Israel saw
that their situation was critical and that
their army was hard pressed, they hid[m] in
caves and thickets, among the rocks, and
in pits and cisterns.[n] 7Some Hebrews even
crossed the Jordan to the land of Gad[o] and
Gilead.
Saul remained at Gilgal, and all the
troops with him were quaking[p] with fear.
8He waited seven[q] days, the time set by
Samuel; but Samuel did not come to Gilgal, and Saul's men began to scatter. 9So
he said, "Bring me the burnt offering and
the fellowship offerings.[e]" And Saul offered[r] up the burnt offering. 10Just as he
finished making the offering, Samuel[s] arrived, and Saul went out to greet[t] him.
11"What have you done?" asked Samuel.
Saul replied, "When I saw that the men
were scattering, and that you did not

12:18 [i]S Ge 3:10; S Ex 14:31 **12:19** [j]S Ex 8:8; S 1Sa 7:8; S Jer 37:3; Jas 5:18; 1Jn 5:16 [k]S Dt 9:19 **12:20** [l]S Ex 32:30 **12:21** [m]Isa 40:20; 41:24, 29; 44:9; Jer 2:5, 11; 14:22; 16:19; Jnh 2:8; Hab 2:18; Ac 14:15 [n]Dt 11:16 **12:22** [o]Ps 25:11; 106:8; Isa 48:9, 11; Jer 14:7; Da 9:19 [p]S Jos 7:9; 2Sa 7:23; Jn 17:12 [q]S Lev 26:11; S Dt 31:6 [r]Dt 7:7; 1Pe 2:9 **12:23** [s]S Nu 11:2; S 1Sa 1:20; S 7:8; Ro 1:9-10 [t]1Ki 8:36; Ps 25:4; 34:11; 86:11; 94:12; Pr 4:11 **12:24** [u]Dt 6:2; Ecc 12:13 [v]Dt 6:5; S Jos 24:14 [w]Job 34:27; Isa 5:12; 22:11; 26:10 [x]S Dt 10:21 **12:25** [y]1Sa 31:1-5 [z]Dt 28:36 [a]S Jos 24:20; S 1Ki 14:10 **13:2** [b]ver 15 [c]ver 5, 11, 23; Ne 11:31; Isa 10:28 [d]S Jdg 19:14 **13:3** [e]S 1Sa 10:5 [f]S Jos 18:24 [g]S Lev 25:9; S Jdg 3:27

[a] *1* A few late manuscripts of the Septuagint; Hebrew does not have *thirty.* [b] *1* See the round number in Acts 13:21; Hebrew does not have *forty-.* [c] *1,2* Or *and when he had reigned over Israel two years, ²he* [d] *5* Some Septuagint manuscripts and Syriac; Hebrew *thirty thousand* [e] *9* Traditionally *peace offerings*

13:4 [h]S Ge 34:30 **13:5** [i]1Sa 17:1 [j]S Jos 11:4; Rev 20:8 [k]S ver 2 [l]S Jos 7:2 **13:6** [m]1Sa 14:11, 22 [n]S Jdg 6:2; Eze 33:27 **3:7** [o]S Nu 32:33 [p]S Ge 35:5; S Ex 19:16 **13:8** [q]1Sa 10:8 **13:9** [r]Dt 12:5-14; 2Sa 24:25; 1Ki 3:4 **13:10** [s]1Sa 15:13 [t]1Sa 25:14

12:19 *Pray to the LORD your God.* Samuel's indictment (vv. 6–15) combined with the awesome sign of thunder and rain in the dry season (vv. 16–18) prompted the people to confess their sin and request Samuel's intercession for them.

12:20 *yet do not turn away from the LORD.* Samuel again brings into focus the central issue in the controversy surrounding the establishment of kingship in Israel.

12:21 *useless idols.* No rivals to the Lord can deliver or guarantee security (see Ex 20:3 and note).

12:23 *by failing to pray for you.* See 7:8 and note. *I will teach you the way that is good and right.* Samuel is not retiring from his prophetic role when he presents the people with their king. He will continue to intercede for the people (see v. 19; 7:8–9) and will instruct them in their covenant obligations (see Dt 6:18; 12:28). Saul and all future kings are to be subject to instruction and correction by the Lord's prophets.

12:24 *fear the LORD.* See notes on Ge 20:11; Ps 15:4; 111:10; Pr 1:7. Samuel summarizes Israel's obligation of loyalty to the Lord as an expression of gratitude for the great things he has done for them.

12:25 *you and your king will be swept away.* Should the nation persist in covenant-breaking conduct, it will bring upon itself its own destruction.

13:1—14:52 Saul's reign characterized: his disobedience, folly and failure.

13:1 *⌞thirty⌟ years old . . . ⌞forty-⌟two years.* See NIV text notes. The wording of the verse follows the regularly used formula that introduces the reigns of later kings (see, e.g., 2Sa 2:10; 5:4; 1Ki 14:21; 2Ki 8:26).

13:2 *Micmash.* Located southeast of Bethel and northeast of Gibeah near a pass (see v. 23). *Jonathan.* Saul's oldest son (see 14:49; 31:2), mentioned here for the first time.

13:3,7 *Hebrews.* See note on Ge 14:13.

13:3 *Geba.* Located across a ravine and south of Micmash.

13:4 *stench.* A metaphor depicting an object of strong hostility, as in 2Sa 10:6; 16:21; Ge 34:30; Ex 5:21. *Gilgal.* See note on 11:14. By prearrangement Saul had been instructed to wait for Samuel there (see notes on v. 8; 10:8).

13:5 *three thousand chariots.* The Israelites did not acquire chariots until the time of Solomon (see 1Ki 4:26 and note). *six thousand charioteers.* See note on 1Ki 22:34.

13:8 *time set by Samuel.* See note on 10:8. Saul is fully aware that Samuel's previous instructions had reference to this gathering at Gilgal. *Saul's men began to scatter.* The seven-day delay heightened the fear of the Israelite soldiers.

13:9 *Saul offered up the burnt offering.* Samuel had promised to make these offerings himself (see 10:8) before Israel went to battle (see 7:9), and he had directed Saul to await his arrival and instructions.

come at the set time, and that the Philistines were assembling at Micmash,[u] 12I
thought, 'Now the Philistines will come
down against me at Gilgal,[v] and I have not
sought the LORD's favor.[w]' So I felt compelled to offer the burnt offering."
13"You acted foolishly,[x]" Samuel said.
"You have not kept[y] the command the LORD
your God gave you; if you had, he would
have established your kingdom over Israel
for all time.[z] 14But now your kingdom[a] will
not endure; the LORD has sought out a man
after his own heart[b] and appointed[c] him
leader[d] of his people, because you have
not kept[e] the LORD's command."
15Then Samuel left Gilgal[a] and went up
to Gibeah[f] in Benjamin, and Saul counted
the men who were with him. They numbered about six hundred.[g]

Israel Without Weapons

16Saul and his son Jonathan and the
men with them were staying in Gibeah[b][h]
in Benjamin, while the Philistines camped
at Micmash. 17Raiding[i] parties went out
from the Philistine camp in three detach-
ments. One turned toward Ophrah[j] in the
vicinity of Shual, 18another toward Beth
Horon,[k] and the third toward the border-
land overlooking the Valley of Zeboim[l]
facing the desert.
19Not a blacksmith[m] could be found in
the whole land of Israel, because the Philistines had said, "Otherwise the Hebrews
will make swords or spears![n]" 20So all Israel went down to the Philistines to have
their plowshares, mattocks, axes and sickles[c] sharpened. 21The price was two thirds
of a shekel[d] for sharpening plowshares
and mattocks, and a third of a shekel[e] for
sharpening forks and axes and for repoint-
ing goads.
22So on the day of the battle not a soldier with Saul and Jonathan[o] had a sword
or spear[p] in his hand; only Saul and his
son Jonathan had them.

Jonathan Attacks the Philistines

23Now a detachment of Philistines
had gone out to the pass[q] at Micmash.[r]
14 1One day Jonathan son of Saul said
to the young man bearing his armor,
"Come, let's go over to the Philistine outpost on the other side." But he did not tell
his father.
2Saul was staying[s] on the outskirts of
Gibeah[t] under a pomegranate tree[u] in Migron.[v] With him were about six hundred
men, 3among whom was Ahijah, who was
wearing an ephod. He was a son of Ichabod's[w] brother Ahitub[x] son of Phinehas,
the son of Eli,[y] the LORD's priest in Shiloh.[z]
No one was aware that Jonathan had left.
4On each side of the pass[a] that Jonathan
intended to cross to reach the Philistine
outpost was a cliff; one was called Bozez,
and the other Seneh. 5One cliff stood to
the north toward Micmash, the other to
the south toward Geba.[b]
6Jonathan said to his young armor-bearer, "Come, let's go over to the outpost of
those uncircumcised[c] fellows. Perhaps the

13:11 [u]S ver 2 **13:12** [v]S Jos 10:43 [w]S Dt 4:29; Ps 119:58; Jer 26:19 **13:13** [x]2Ch 16:9 [y]ver 14; S Jos 22:16; 1Sa 15:23,24; 2Sa 7:15; 1Ch 10:13 [z]Ps 72:5 **13:14** [a]1Sa 15:28; 18:8; 24:20; 1Ch 10:14 [b]Ac 7:46; 13:22 [c]2Sa 6:21 [d]1Sa 25:30; 2Sa 5:2; Ps 18:43; Isa 16:5; 55:4; Jer 30:9; Eze 34:23-24; 37:24; Da 9:25; Hos 3:5; Mic 5:2 [e]1Sa 15:26; 16:1; 2Sa 12:9; 1Ki 13:21; Hos 13:11 **13:15** [f]1Sa 14:2 [g]ver 2 **13:16** [h]S Jos 18:24 **13:17** [i]1Sa 14:15 [j]S Jos 18:23 **13:18** [k]S Jos 10:10 [l]Ne 11:34 **13:19** [m]S Ge 4:22 [n]S Nu 25:7 **13:22** [o]1Ch 9:39 [p]S Nu 25:7; 1Sa 14:6; 17:47; Zec 4:6 **13:23** [q]1Sa 14:4 [r]S ver 2 **14:2** [s]S Jdg 4:5 [t]1Sa 13:15 [u]S Ex 28:33 [v]Isa 10:28 **14:3** [w]S Ge 35:18 [x]1Sa 22:11,20 [y]S 1Sa 1:3 [z]Ps 78:60 **14:4** [a]1Sa 13:23 **14:5** [b]S Jos 18:24 **14:6** [c]Jdg 14:3; 1Sa 17:26,36; 31:4; Jer 9:26; Eze 28:10

[a] *15* Hebrew; Septuagint *Gilgal and went his way; the rest of the people went after Saul to meet the army, and they went out of Gilgal* [b] *16* Two Hebrew manuscripts; most Hebrew manuscripts *Geba,* a variant of *Gibeah* [c] *20* Septuagint; Hebrew *plowshares* [d] *21* Hebrew *pim*; that is, about 1/4 ounce (about 8 grams) [e] *21* That is, about 1/8 ounce (about 4 grams)

13:13 *You acted foolishly.* The foolish and sinful aspect (see 26:21 and note; 2Sa 24:10; 2Ch 16:9; Isa 32:6 and note) of Saul's act was that he thought he could strengthen Israel's chances against the Philistines while disregarding the instruction of the Lord's prophet Samuel. *You have not kept the command the LORD your God gave you.* Saul was to recognize the word of the prophet Samuel as the word of the Lord (see 3:20; 15:1; Ex 20:18–19; see also note on Ex 7:1–2). In disobeying Samuel's instructions, Saul violated a fundamental requirement of his theocratic office. His kingship was not to function independently of the law and the prophets (see notes on 12:14,23; 15:11).

13:14 *your kingdom will not endure.* Saul will not be followed by his sons; there will be no dynasty bearing his name (contrast the Lord's word to David, 2Sa 7:11–16). There is a striking parallel in the word of the Lord to Eli (see 2:30,35 and notes). *the LORD has sought out a man after his own heart and appointed him.* Paul quotes from this passage (Ac 13:22). *leader.* See note on 9:16.

13:15 *six hundred.* The seven-day delay had greatly depleted Saul's forces (see vv. 2,4,6–8,11).

13:17 *Raiding parties.* The purpose of these Philistine contingents was not to engage the Israelites in battle, but to plunder the land and demoralize its inhabitants.

13:18 *Valley of Zeboim.* Located to the east toward the Jordan Valley.

13:19 *Not a blacksmith.* A Philistine monopoly on the technology of iron production placed the Israelites at a great disadvantage in the fashioning and maintenance of agricultural implements and military weapons.

13:20 *plowshares.* See note on Isa 2:4.

13:21 *price.* Probably exorbitant. *two thirds of a shekel.* The Hebrew word (*pim*) for this phrase, which occurs only here in the OT, has now been found on weights that have turned up in various excavations.

13:22 *not ... a sword or spear.* The Israelites were armed only with the long-range weapons of slingshot and bow and arrow.

14:1 *on the other side.* The Philistines were encamped to the north of the pass and the Israelites to the south.

14:2 *Gibeah.* Saul had retreated farther south from Geba (13:3) to Gibeah. *under a pomegranate tree.* It appears to have been customary for leaders in early Israel to hold court under well-known trees that served as landmarks in an otherwise unmapped countryside (see 22:6; Jdg 4:5).

14:3 *Ahijah.* Either the brother and predecessor of Ahimelech son of Ahitub (referred to in 21:1; 22:9,11) or an alternative name for Ahimelech. *wearing an ephod.* See note on 2:28. *Ichabod's brother.* See 4:21.

14:6 *uncircumcised fellows.* A term of contempt (see 17:26,36; 31:4; 2Sa 1:20; Jdg 14:3 and note; 15:18), which draws attention to Israel's covenant relationship to the Lord (see Ge 17:10

LORD will act in our behalf. Nothing[d] can
hinder the LORD from saving, whether by
many[e] or by few.[f]”
7“Do all that you have in mind,” his armor-bearer said. “Go ahead; I am with you
heart and soul.”
8Jonathan said, “Come, then; we will
cross over toward the men and let them
see us. 9If they say to us, ‘Wait there until
we come to you,’ we will stay where we
are and not go up to them. 10But if they
say, ‘Come up to us,’ we will climb up, because that will be our sign[g] that the LORD
has given them into our hands.[h]”
11So both of them showed themselves
to the Philistine outpost. “Look!” said
the Philistines. “The Hebrews[i] are crawling out of the holes they were hiding[j] in.”
12The men of the outpost shouted to Jonathan and his armor-bearer, “Come up to
us and we’ll teach you a lesson.[k]”
So Jonathan said to his armor-bearer,
“Climb up after me; the LORD has given
them into the hand[l] of Israel.”
13Jonathan climbed up, using his hands
and feet, with his armor-bearer right behind him. The Philistines fell before Jonathan, and his armor-bearer followed
and killed behind him. 14In that first attack Jonathan and his armor-bearer killed
some twenty men in an area of about half
an acre.[a]

Israel Routs the Philistines

15Then panic[m] struck the whole
army—those in the camp and field, and
those in the outposts and raiding[n] parties—and the ground shook. It was a panic sent by God.[b]

14:6 [d]S 1Sa 13:22; S 1Ki 19:12; S Mt 19:26; Heb 11:34 [e]Jdg 7:4 [f]Ps 33:16 **14:10** [g]S Ge 24:14 [h]S Jos 2:24 **14:11** [i]S Ge 14:13 [j]S 1Sa 13:6 **14:12** [k]Jdg 8:16 [l]1Sa 17:46; 2Sa 5:24 **14:15** [m]S Ge 35:5; S Ex 14:24; S 19:16; 2Ki 7:5-7 [n]1Sa 13:17 **14:16** [o]2Sa 18:24; 2Ki 9:17; Isa 52:8; Eze 33:2 **14:18** [p]1Sa 30:7 [q]S Jdg 18:5 **14:19** [r]Nu 27:21 **14:20** [s]S Jdg 7:22; Eze 38:21; Zec 14:13 **14:21** [t]1Sa 29:4 **14:22** [u]S 1Sa 13:6 **14:23** [v]S Ex 14:30 [w]S Jos 7:2 **14:24** [x]Jos 6:26

16Saul’s lookouts[o] at Gibeah in Benjamin saw the army melting away in all directions. 17Then Saul said to the men who
were with him, “Muster the forces and see
who has left us.” When they did, it was
Jonathan and his armor-bearer who were
not there.
18Saul said to Ahijah, “Bring[p] the ark[q]
of God.” (At that time it was with the Israelites.)[c] 19While Saul was talking to the
priest, the tumult in the Philistine camp
increased more and more. So Saul said to
the priest,[r] “Withdraw your hand.”
20Then Saul and all his men assembled and went to the battle. They found
the Philistines in total confusion, striking[s]
each other with their swords. 21Those Hebrews who had previously been with the
Philistines and had gone up with them to
their camp went[t] over to the Israelites who
were with Saul and Jonathan. 22When all
the Israelites who had hidden[u] in the hill
country of Ephraim heard that the Philistines were on the run, they joined the battle in hot pursuit. 23So the LORD rescued[v]
Israel that day, and the battle moved on
beyond Beth Aven.[w]

Jonathan Eats Honey

24Now the men of Israel were in distress
that day, because Saul had bound the people under an oath,[x] saying, “Cursed be any
man who eats food before evening comes,
before I have avenged myself on my enemies!” So none of the troops tasted food.

[a] 14 Hebrew *half a yoke*; a “yoke” was the land plowed by a yoke of oxen in one day. [b] 15 Or *a terrible panic* [c] 18 Hebrew; Septuagint *“Bring the ephod.” (At that time he wore the ephod before the Israelites.)*

and note) and, by implication, to the illegitimacy of the Philistine presence in the land. *by many or by few.* See note on 17:47. Jonathan’s bold plan is undertaken as an act of faith (cf. Heb 11:32–34) founded on God’s promise (9:16).

14:10 *our sign.* See Jdg 6:36–40; Isa 7:11 and note; see also note on Ex 3:12.

14:11 *Hebrews.* See v. 21; 4:6; 13:3,7 and note on Ge 14:13.

14:15 *ground shook.* See 7:10; 2Sa 22:12–16; Jos 10:11–14 and note on 10:11; Ps 77:18 for other instances of divine intervention in nature to bring deliverance to Israel.

14:18 *Bring the ark of God.* Saul decides to seek God’s will before entering into battle with the Philistines (see Nu 27:21; Dt 20:2–4). Here the Septuagint (the pre-Christian Greek translation of the OT) may preserve the original text (see NIV text note) for the following reasons: (1) In 7:1 the ark was located at Kiriath Jearim, where it remained until David brought it to Jerusalem (2Sa 6), but the ephod was present in Saul’s camp at Gibeah (see v. 3). (2) Nowhere else in the OT is the ark used to determine God’s will, but the ephod (with the Urim and Thummim) was given for this purpose (see 23:9; 30:7 and notes on 2:18,28). (3) The command to the priest to withdraw his hand (v. 19) is more appropriate with the ephod than with the ark.

14:19 *Withdraw your hand.* Stop the priestly action I asked you to perform. Due to the urgency of the moment, Saul decides that to wait for the word of the Lord might jeopardize his military advantage. As in 13:8–12, his decision rests on his own insight rather than on dependence upon the Lord and a commitment to obey him.

14:23 *So the LORD rescued Israel that day.* The writer attributes the victory to the Lord, not to either Saul or Jonathan (see vv. 6,10,12,15; 11:13).

14:24–46 Following the account of the great victory the Lord had given, the author relates Saul’s actions that strikingly illustrated his lack of fitness to be king. His foolish curse before the battle (see v. 24 and note) brought “distress” to the army and, as Jonathan tellingly observed, “made trouble for the country” (v. 29) rather than contributing to the victory (cf. Jos 7:25; 1Ki 18:17–18 and note on 18:18). And later, when hindered from taking advantage of the battle’s outcome by the Lord’s refusal to answer (v. 37), Saul was ready to execute Jonathan as the cause, though Jonathan had contributed most to the victory, as everyone else recognized (v. 45). Saul’s growing egocentrism was turning into an all-consuming passion that threatened the very welfare of the nation. Rather than serving the cause of the Lord and his people, he was in fact becoming a king “such as all the other nations have” (8:5).

14:24 *in distress.* Saul’s rash action in requiring his troops to fast placed them at an unnecessary disadvantage in the battle (see vv. 29–30). *Cursed.* Thus Saul as king “bound the army under a strict oath” (v. 28), a most serious matter because an oath directly invoked God’s involvement, whether it concerned giving testimony (Ex 20:7; Lev 19:12),

25The entire army[a] entered the woods,
and there was honey on the ground.
26When they went into the woods, they
saw the honey oozing out, yet no one
put his hand to his mouth, because they
feared the oath. 27But Jonathan had not
heard that his father had bound the people with the oath, so he reached out the
end of the staff that was in his hand
and dipped it into the honeycomb.[y] He
raised his hand to his mouth, and his
eyes brightened.[b] 28Then one of the soldiers told him, "Your father bound the
army under a strict oath, saying, 'Cursed
be any man who eats food today!' That is
why the men are faint."
29Jonathan said, "My father has made
trouble[z] for the country. See how my eyes
brightened[c] when I tasted a little of this
honey. 30How much better it would have
been if the men had eaten today some of
the plunder they took from their enemies.
Would not the slaughter of the Philistines
have been even greater?"
31That day, after the Israelites had
struck down the Philistines from Micmash[a] to Aijalon,[b] they were exhausted.
32They pounced on the plunder[c] and, taking sheep, cattle and calves, they butchered them on the ground and ate them,
together with the blood.[d] 33Then someone
said to Saul, "Look, the men are sinning
against the LORD by eating meat that has
blood[e] in it."
"You have broken faith," he said. "Roll
a large stone over here at once." 34Then
he said, "Go out among the men and tell
them, 'Each of you bring me your cattle
and sheep, and slaughter them here and
eat them. Do not sin against the LORD by
eating meat with blood still[f] in it.'"
So everyone brought his ox that night
and slaughtered it there. 35Then Saul built
an altar[g] to the LORD; it was the first time
he had done this.
36Saul said, "Let us go down after the
Philistines by night and plunder them till
dawn, and let us not leave one of them
alive."
"Do whatever seems best to you," they
replied.
But the priest said, "Let us inquire[h] of
God here."
37So Saul asked God, "Shall I go down
after the Philistines? Will you give them
into Israel's hand?" But God did not answer[i] him that day.
38Saul therefore said, "Come here, all
you who are leaders of the army, and let
us find out what sin has been committed[j]
today. 39As surely as the LORD who rescues
Israel lives,[k] even if it lies with my son
Jonathan,[l] he must die."[m] But not one of
the men said a word.
40Saul then said to all the Israelites, "You
stand over there; I and Jonathan my son
will stand over here."
"Do what seems best to you," the men
replied.
41Then Saul prayed to the LORD, the God
of Israel, "Give[n] me the right[o] answer."[d]
And Jonathan and Saul were taken by lot,
and the men were cleared. 42Saul said,
"Cast the lot[p] between me and Jonathan
my son." And Jonathan was taken.
43Then Saul said to Jonathan, "Tell me
what you have done."[q]
So Jonathan told him, "I merely tasted a
little honey[r] with the end of my staff. And
now must I die?"
44Saul said, "May God deal with me, be
it ever so severely,[s] if you do not die, Jonathan.[t]"
45But the men said to Saul, "Should Jonathan die—he who has brought about this
great deliverance in Israel? Never! As surely as the LORD lives, not a hair[u] of his head
will fall to the ground, for he did this today with God's help." So the men rescued[v]
Jonathan, and he was not put to death.
46Then Saul stopped pursuing the Philistines, and they withdrew to their own
land.

14:27 [y] ver 43; Ps 19:10; Pr 16:24; 24:13 **14:29** [z] Jos 7:25; 1Ki 18:18 **14:31** [a] ver 5 [b] S Jos 10:12 **14:32** [c] 1Sa 15:19; Est 9:10 [d] S Ge 9:4 **14:33** [e] S Ge 9:4 **14:34** [f] Lev 19:26 **14:35** [g] S 1Sa 7:17

14:36 [h] S Ge 25:22; S Jdg 18:5 **14:37** [i] 1Sa 28:6, 15; 2Sa 22:42; Ps 18:41 **14:38** [j] Jos 7:11 **14:39** [k] S Nu 14:21; 2Sa 12:5; Job 19:25; Ps 18:46; 42:2 [l] ver 44 [m] Jos 7:15 **14:41** [n] Ac 1:24 [o] Pr 16:33 **14:42** [p] Jnh 1:7 **14:43** [q] S Jos 7:19 [r] S ver 27 **14:44** [s] S Ru 1:17 [t] ver 39 **14:45** [u] 1Ki 1:52; S Mt 10:30 [v] 2Sa 14:11

[a] 25 Or *Now all the people of the land* [b] 27 Or *his strength was renewed* [c] 29 Or *my strength was renewed* [d] 41 Hebrew; Septuagint *"Why have you not answered your servant today? If the fault is in me or my son Jonathan, respond with Urim, but if the men of Israel are at fault, respond with Thummim."*

making commitments (Ge 21:23–24; 24:3–4) or prohibiting action (here). It appealed to God as the supreme enforcement power and the all-knowing Judge of human actions. *I have avenged myself on my enemies.* Saul perceives the conflict with the Philistines more as a personal vendetta (see note on 15:12) than as a battle for the honor of the Lord and the security of the Lord's people (note the contrast between his attitude and that of Jonathan in vv. 6,10,12).

14:31 *Aijalon.* Located to the west near the Philistines' own territory (see Jos 10:12).

14:33 *eating meat that has blood in it.* The Israelites were not permitted to eat blood (see Ge 9:4; Lev 17:10–11; 19:26; Dt 12:16,24; Eze 33:25; Ac 15:20 and notes). *broken faith.* See Mal 2:10–11 and notes. The same Hebrew term is translated "faithless" (Ps 78:57), "unfaithful" (Jer 3:7–8,10–11) and "treacherous" (Isa 48:8).

14:35 *first time he had done this.* Another indication of Saul's personal lack of interest in religious matters (see notes on 9:3,6; 10:11).

14:36 *priest.* Ahijah (see v. 3).

14:37 *Saul asked God.* The means of ascertaining God's will appears to have been the ephod with its Urim and Thummim (see v. 3 and note on v. 18). *God did not answer.* Because an oath had been broken in the battle, God refused to answer Saul's inquiry concerning further military action.

14:39,45 *As surely as the LORD ... lives.* An oath formula (see note on v. 24; 19:6; see also Ge 42:15; Hos 4:15 and notes).

14:41 *taken by lot.* See 10:20–21; Jos 7:14–18 and note on 7:14; Pr 16:33 and note.

14:44 A curse formula (see note on v. 24; see also 3:17 and note).

14:45 *he did this today with God's help.* The men of Saul's army

47After Saul had assumed rule over Israel, he fought against their enemies on every side: Moab,[w] the Ammonites,[x] Edom,[y] the kings[a] of Zobah,[z] and the Philistines. Wherever he turned, he inflicted punishment on them.[b] 48He fought valiantly and defeated the Amalekites,[a] delivering Israel from the hands of those who had plundered them.

Saul's Family

49Saul's sons were Jonathan, Ishvi and Malki-Shua.[b] The name of his older daughter was Merab, and that of the younger was Michal.[c] 50His wife's name was Ahinoam daughter of Ahimaaz. The name of the commander of Saul's army was Abner[d] son of Ner, and Ner was Saul's uncle.[e] 51Saul's father Kish[f] and Abner's father Ner were sons of Abiel.

52All the days of Saul there was bitter war with the Philistines, and whenever Saul saw a mighty or brave man, he took[g] him into his service.

The LORD Rejects Saul as King

15 Samuel said to Saul, "I am the one the LORD sent to anoint[h] you king over his people Israel; so listen now to the message from the LORD. 2This is what the LORD Almighty says: 'I will punish the Amalekites[i] for what they did to Israel when they waylaid them as they came up from Egypt. 3Now go, attack the Amalekites and totally[j] destroy[c] everything that belongs to them. Do not spare them; put to death men and women, children and infants, cattle and sheep, camels and donkeys.'"

4So Saul summoned the men and mustered them at Telaim—two hundred thousand foot soldiers and ten thousand men from Judah. 5Saul went to the city of Amalek and set an ambush in the ravine. 6Then he said to the Kenites,[k] "Go away, leave the Amalekites so that I do not destroy you along with them; for you showed kindness to all the Israelites when they came up out of Egypt." So the Kenites moved away from the Amalekites.

7Then Saul attacked the Amalekites[l] all the way from Havilah to Shur,[m] to the east of Egypt. 8He took Agag[n] king of the Amalekites alive,[o] and all his people he totally destroyed with the sword. 9But Saul and the army spared[p] Agag and the best of the sheep and cattle, the fat calves[d] and lambs—everything that was good. These they were unwilling to destroy completely, but everything that was despised and weak they totally destroyed.

10Then the word of the LORD came to Samuel: 11"I am grieved[q] that I have made Saul king, because he has turned[r] away from me and has not carried out my in-

14:47 [w]S Ge 19:37 [x]S Ge 19:38; 2Sa 12:31 [y]1Sa 21:7 [z]2Sa 8:3; 10:6; 23:36 **14:48** [a]S Ge 36:12; Nu 13:29; Jdg 3:13; 1Sa 15:2,7; 27:8; 28:18; 30:13; 2Sa 1:13; 1Ch 4:43 **14:49** [b]1Sa 31:2; 1Ch 8:33 [c]S Ge 29:26 **14:50** [d]2Sa 2:8; 3:6; 1Ki 2:5 [e]1Sa 10:14 **14:51** [f]S 1Sa 9:1 **14:52** [g]1Sa 8:11 **15:1** [h]S 1Sa 9:16 **15:2** [i]S Ge 14:7; S 1Sa 14:48; S 2Sa 1:8 **15:3** [j]ver 9,19; S Ge 14:23; Jos 6:17; 1Sa 22:19; 27:9; 28:18; Est 3:13; 9:5 **15:6** [k]S Ge 15:19; Nu 24:22; Jdg 1:16; 1Sa 30:29 **15:7** [l]S 1Sa 14:48 [m]S Ge 16:7 **15:8** [n]Ex 17:8-16; S Nu 24:7 [o]S Jos 8:23 **15:9** [p]S ver 3 **15:11** [q]S Ge 6:6; S Ex 32:14 [r]S Jos 22:16

[a] *47* Masoretic Text; Dead Sea Scrolls and Septuagint *king* [b] *47* Hebrew; Septuagint *he was victorious*
[c] *3* The Hebrew term refers to the irrevocable giving over of things or persons to the LORD, often by totally destroying them; also in verses 8, 9, 15, 18, 20 and 21.
[d] *9* Or *the grown bulls*; the meaning of the Hebrew for this phrase is uncertain.

recognize the inappropriateness of taking the life of the one through whom God has delivered his people.

14:47–48 A summary of Saul's military victories to the east (Moab and the Ammonites), south (Edom), north (Zobah) and west (Philistines).

14:47 *Ammonites.* See note on 11:1; see also Dt 2:19–21,37.

14:48 *Amalekites.* See note on 15:2.

14:49 *Saul's sons.* See 31:2; 1Ch 9:39 and notes. *Merab … Michal.* See 18:17,20; 19:11–17; 25:44; 2Sa 6:16–23.

14:50 *Ahinoam.* The only reference to a wife of Saul. His concubine Rizpah is mentioned in 2Sa 3:7; 21:8–11.

14:52 *All the days of Saul.* Closes the main account of Saul's reign. *he took him into his service.* Saul developed a special cadre of professional soldiers bound to himself, much as David was to do later (see 22:2; 23:13; 25:13; 27:2–3; 29:2; 30:1,9–10; 2Sa 2:3; 5:6; 8:18; 15:18; 23:8–39).

15:1—2Sa 5:5 Thematically, this large segment of 1,2 Samuel relates in significant detail the events that brought about the transition from the reign of Saul to that of David.

15:1–35 The event that occasioned Saul's rejection. Although no time designation is given, it evidently occurred after the conflicts of 14:47, in a time of relative peace and security. It is likely that David was anointed (16:1–13) shortly after the rejection of Saul (vv. 23,26,28), thus c. 1025 B.C.

15:2 *Amalekites.* See note on Ge 14:7. *what they did to Israel.* See 14:48; Ex 17:8–15; Nu 14:43, 45; Dt 25:17–19; cf. Jdg 3:13; 6:3–5,33; 7:12; 10:12.

15:3 *totally destroy.* See NIV text note; Dt 13:12–18; see also notes on Lev 27:28–29; Jos 6:17–18. Saul is given an opportunity as king to demonstrate his allegiance to the Lord by obedience in this assigned task.

15:4 *Telaim.* Probably the same as Telem in Jos 15:24, located in the southern part of Judah. *foot soldiers.* From the northern tribes (see 11:8).

15:5 *city of Amalek.* A settlement of Amalekites, most likely located between Telaim and Kadesh Barnea, possibly the residence of their king.

15:6 *Kenites.* A nomadic people of the Sinai, closely related to the Midianites. Moses had married a Kenite woman (see Ex 2:16,21–22; Nu 10:29; Jdg 1:16; 4:11), and some of the Kenites had accompanied the Israelites when they settled in the land of Canaan (see 27:10; Jdg 1:16; 4:17–23; 5:24; 1Ch 2:55).

15:7 *Havilah to Shur.* Ishmael's descendants occupied this area (see Ge 25:18). The location of Havilah is uncertain. Shur was on the eastern frontier of Egypt (see 27:8; Ge 16:7; 20:1).

15:8 *Agag king of the Amalekites.* His descendants would later oppress Israel (see note on Est 3:1). *all his people.* All the Amalekites they encountered. Some Amalekites survived (see 27:8; 30:1,18; 2Sa 1:8,13; 8:12; 1Ch 4:43).

15:9 When Israel refused to obey the Lord's command (v. 3), their holy war against the Amalekites degenerated into personal aggrandizement, much like that of Achan at the time of the conquest of Canaan (see Jos 7:1). Giving to the Lord by destruction only what was despised and weak was a contemptible act (see Mal 1:7–12 and notes), not to be excused (see v. 19) by the protestation that the best had been preserved for sacrifice to the Lord (vv. 15,21).

15:11 *grieved.* See note on v. 29. *he has turned away from me.* A violation of the fundamental requirement of his office as king (see notes on 12:14–15).

structions."[s] Samuel was troubled,[t] and he
cried out to the LORD all that night.
12 Early in the morning Samuel got up
and went to meet Saul, but he was told,
"Saul has gone to Carmel.[u] There he has
set up a monument[v] in his own honor and
has turned and gone on down to Gilgal."
13 When Samuel reached him, Saul said,
"The LORD bless you! I have carried out
the LORD's instructions."
14 But Samuel said, "What then is this
bleating of sheep in my ears? What is this
lowing of cattle that I hear?"
15 Saul answered, "The soldiers brought
them from the Amalekites; they spared
the best of the sheep and cattle to sacrifice to the LORD your God, but we totally
destroyed the rest."
16 "Stop!" Samuel said to Saul. "Let me
tell you what the LORD said to me last
night."
"Tell me," Saul replied.
17 Samuel said, "Although you were once
small[w] in your own eyes, did you not become the head of the tribes of Israel? The
LORD anointed you king over Israel. 18 And
he sent you on a mission, saying, 'Go and
completely destroy those wicked people,
the Amalekites; make war on them until
you have wiped them out.' 19 Why did you
not obey the LORD? Why did you pounce
on the plunder[x] and do evil in the eyes of
the LORD?"
20 "But I did obey[y] the LORD," Saul said.
"I went on the mission the LORD assigned
me. I completely destroyed the Amalekites
and brought back Agag their king. 21 The
soldiers took sheep and cattle from the
plunder, the best of what was devoted to
God, in order to sacrifice them to the LORD
your God at Gilgal."
22 But Samuel replied:

"Does the LORD delight in burnt
offerings and sacrifices
as much as in obeying the voice of
the LORD?
To obey is better than sacrifice,[z]
and to heed is better than the fat of
rams.
23 For rebellion is like the sin of
divination,[a]
and arrogance like the evil of
idolatry.
Because you have rejected[b] the word of
the LORD,
he has rejected you as king."

24 Then Saul said to Samuel, "I have
sinned.[c] I violated[d] the LORD's command
and your instructions. I was afraid[e] of the
people and so I gave in to them. 25 Now
I beg you, forgive[f] my sin and come
back with me, so that I may worship the
LORD."
26 But Samuel said to him, "I will not
go back with you. You have rejected[g] the
word of the LORD, and the LORD has rejected you as king over Israel!"
27 As Samuel turned to leave, Saul caught
hold of the hem of his robe,[h] and it tore.[i]
28 Samuel said to him, "The LORD has torn[j]
the kingdom[k] of Israel from you today and

15:11 [s] Job 21:14; 34:27; Ps 28:5; Isa 5:12; 53:6; Jer 48:10; Eze 18:24 [t] S ver 35; S 1Sa 8:6
15:12 [u] Jos 15:55 [v] S Nu 32:42
15:17 [w] S Ex 3:11
15:19 [x] S Ge 14:23; S 1Sa 14:32
15:20 [y] 1Sa 28:18
15:22 [z] Ps 40:6-8; 51:16; Pr 21:3; Isa 1:11-15; Jer 7:22; Hos 6:6; Am 5:25; Mic 6:6-8; S Mk 12:33
15:23 [a] Dt 18:10 [b] S 1Sa 13:13
15:24 [c] S Ex 9:27; S Nu 22:34; Ps 51:4 [d] S 1Sa 13:13 [e] Pr 29:25; Isa 51:12-13; Jer 42:11
15:25 [f] Ex 10:17
15:26 [g] S Nu 15:31; S 1Sa 13:14; S 1Ki 14:10
15:27 [h] 1Sa 28:14 [i] 1Ki 11:11,31; 14:8; 2Ki 17:21
15:28 [j] 1Sa 28:17 [k] S 1Sa 13:14

15:12 *Carmel.* Located about seven miles south of Hebron (see 25:2; Jos 15:55). *monument in his own honor.* Saul's self-glorification here contrasts sharply with his self-abasement after the victory over the Ammonites (see note on 11:13; cf. v. 17; 2Sa 18:18). *Gilgal.* Saul returns to the place where he was inaugurated and instructed in the responsibilities of his office (see 11:14–15). This was also the place where he had been told that he would not have a continuing dynasty because of his disobedience (see 13:13–14 and notes).

15:13 *I have carried out the LORD's instructions.* Here and in v. 20 Saul is clearly less than honest in his statements to Samuel.

15:15 *The soldiers … spared the best … to sacrifice.* Saul attempts to shift responsibility from himself to the army and to excuse their action by claiming pious intentions. *the LORD your God.* Saul's use of the pronoun "your" instead of "my" here and in vv. 21,30 indicates an awareness of his own alienation from the Lord (see 12:19 for a similar case), even though he speaks of obedience and the intent to honor God by sacrifice.

15:17 *you were once small in your own eyes.* See 9:21 and note; 10:22.

15:22 Samuel does not suggest that sacrifice is unimportant but that it is acceptable only when brought with an attitude of obedience and devotion to the Lord (see Ps 51:16–17; Isa 1:11–15; Jer 7:22–23; Hos 6:6; Am 5:21–23; Mic 6:6–8 and notes). *fat of rams.* The fat of sacrificed animals belonged to the Lord (see 2:15 and note; Ex 23:18; Lev 3:14–16; 7:30).

15:23 *rebellion.* Samuel charges Saul with violating the central requirement of the covenant condition given to him when he became king (see 12:14–15 and notes). *sin of divination.* A serious offense against the Lord (see Lev 19:26; Dt 18:9–12 and note on 18:9), which Saul himself condemned (28:3,9). *you have rejected the word of the LORD.* A king who sets his own will above the command of the Lord ceases to be an instrument of the Lord's rule over his people, violating the very nature of his theocratic office. *he has rejected you as king.* The judgment here goes beyond the one given earlier (see note on 13:14). Now Saul himself is to be set aside as king. Although this did not happen immediately, as chs. 16–31 show, the process began that led to his death. It included in its relentless course the removal of God's Spirit and favor from him (see 16:14 and note), the defection of his son Jonathan and daughter Michal to David (18:1–4,20; 19:11–17) and the insubordination of his own officials (22:17).

15:24 Saul's confession retains an element of self-justification and a shift of blame (contrast David's confession; see 2Sa 12:13; Ps 51:4 and notes). Previously (vv. 15,21) he had attempted to justify his soldiers' actions.

15:25 *come back with me.* Saul's greatest concern was not to worship God but to avoid an open break with the prophet Samuel, a break that would undermine his authority as king (see v. 30).

15:28 *one of your neighbors.* David (see 28:17 and note on 13:14).

has given it to one of your neighbors—to
one better than you.[l] 29He who is the Glory of Israel does not lie[m] or change[n] his
mind; for he is not a man, that he should
change his mind."
30Saul replied, "I have sinned.[o] But
please honor[p] me before the elders of my
people and before Israel; come back with
me, so that I may worship the LORD your
God." 31So Samuel went back with Saul,
and Saul worshiped the LORD.
32Then Samuel said, "Bring me Agag
king of the Amalekites."
Agag came to him confidently,[a] thinking, "Surely the bitterness of death is
past."
33But Samuel said,

"As your sword has made women
childless,
so will your mother be childless
among women."[q]

And Samuel put Agag to death before the
LORD at Gilgal.
34Then Samuel left for Ramah,[r] but
Saul went up to his home in Gibeah[s] of
Saul. 35Until the day Samuel[t] died, he did
not go to see Saul again, though Samuel
mourned[u] for him. And the LORD was
grieved[v] that he had made Saul king over
Israel.

Samuel Anoints David

16 The LORD said to Samuel, "How long
will you mourn[w] for Saul, since I
have rejected[x] him as king over Israel? Fill
your horn with oil[y] and be on your way; I
am sending you to Jesse[z] of Bethlehem. I
have chosen[a] one of his sons to be king."
2But Samuel said, "How can I go? Saul
will hear about it and kill me."
The LORD said, "Take a heifer with you
and say, 'I have come to sacrifice to the
LORD.' 3Invite Jesse to the sacrifice, and
I will show[b] you what to do. You are to
anoint[c] for me the one I indicate."
4Samuel did what the LORD said. When
he arrived at Bethlehem,[d] the elders of the
town trembled[e] when they met him. They
asked, "Do you come in peace?[f]"
5Samuel replied, "Yes, in peace; I have
come to sacrifice to the LORD. Consecrate[g]
yourselves and come to the sacrifice with
me." Then he consecrated Jesse and his
sons and invited them to the sacrifice.
6When they arrived, Samuel saw Eliab[h]
and thought, "Surely the LORD's anointed
stands here before the LORD."
7But the LORD said to Samuel, "Do not
consider his appearance or his height, for
I have rejected him. The LORD does not
look at the things man looks at. Man looks
at the outward appearance,[i] but the LORD
looks at the heart."[j]
8Then Jesse called Abinadab[k] and had
him pass in front of Samuel. But Samuel
said, "The LORD has not chosen this one
either." 9Jesse then had Shammah[l] pass
by, but Samuel said, "Nor has the LORD
chosen this one." 10Jesse had seven of his
sons pass before Samuel, but Samuel said
to him, "The LORD has not chosen these."
11So he asked Jesse, "Are these all[m] the
sons you have?"
"There is still the youngest," Jesse answered, "but he is tending the sheep."[n]
Samuel said, "Send for him; we will not
sit down[b] until he arrives."
12So he[o] sent and had him brought in.

[a] 32 Or *him trembling, yet* [b] 11 Some Septuagint manuscripts; Hebrew *not gather around*

15:28 [l] 2Sa 6:21; 7:15
15:29 [m] Tit 1:2 [n] S Nu 23:19; Heb 7:21
15:30 [o] S Nu 22:34 [p] Isa 29:13; Jn 12:43
15:33 [q] Est 9:7-10; Jer 18:21
15:34 [r] S 1Sa 7:17 [s] S Jdg 19:14; S 1Sa 10:5
15:35 [t] 1Sa 19:24 [u] ver 11; 1Sa 16:1 [v] S Ge 6:6
16:1 [w] S 1Sa 8:6; S 15:35 [x] S 1Sa 13:14 [y] S 1Sa 10:1 [z] S Ru 4:17 [a] 2Sa 5:2; 7:8; 1Ki 8:16; 1Ch 12:23; Ps 78:70; Ac 13:22
16:3 [b] Ex 4:15 [c] S Dt 17:15
16:4 [d] S Ge 48:7; Lk 2:4 [e] 1Sa 21:1 [f] 1Ki 2:13; 2Ki 9:17
16:5 [g] S Ex 19:10,22
16:6 [h] 1Sa 17:13; 1Ch 2:13
16:7 [i] Ps 147:10 [j] S 1Sa 2:3; 2Sa 7:20; S Ps 44:21; S 139:23; S Rev 2:23
16:8 [k] 1Sa 17:13
16:9 [l] 1Sa 17:13; 2Sa 13:3; 21:21
16:11 [m] 1Sa 17:12 [n] S Ge 37:2; 2Sa 7:8
16:12 [o] 1Sa 9:17

15:29 *Glory of Israel.* In Ps 106:20; Jer 2:11; Hos 4:7 God is called "Glory" (see 4:21; Heb 9:5 and notes). Cf. 2Sa 1:19 and note; Ps 89:17; Isa 13:19. *does not lie or change his mind.* See Nu 23:19; Mal 3:6 and notes; see also Ps 110:4; Jer 4:28. There is no conflict between this statement and vv. 11,35, where the Lord is said to "grieve" that he had made Saul king.

15:31 *So Samuel went back with Saul.* Samuel's purpose in agreeing to Saul's request is not to honor Saul, but to carry out the divine sentence on Agag and in so doing to reemphasize Saul's neglect of duty.

15:34 *Ramah.* Samuel's home (see 7:17; see also note on 1:1). *Gibeah of Saul.* See note on 10:5.

15:35 *Samuel mourned.* Samuel regarded Saul as if dead (see the use of "mourned" in 6:19). Even though his love for him remained (see v. 11; 16:1), he sought no further contact with him because God had rejected him as king. Saul did come to Samuel on one other occasion (see 19:24).

16:1 *The LORD said to Samuel.* Probably c. 1025 B.C. (see note on 15:1–35). *Jesse.* For Jesse's genealogy see Ru 4:18–22; Mt 1:3–6. *Bethlehem.* A town five miles south of Jerusalem, formerly known as Ephrath (see Ge 35:16 and note). It was later to become renowned as the "town of David" (Lk 2:4) and the birthplace of the Messiah (see Mic 5:2; Mt 2:1 and notes; Lk 2:4–7 and note on 2:4). *I have chosen one of his sons to be king.* See notes on 13:14; 15:28.

16:2 *Saul will … kill me.* The road from Ramah (where Samuel was, 15:34) to Bethlehem passed through Gibeah of Saul. Saul already knew that the Lord had chosen someone to replace him as king (see 15:28). Samuel fears that jealousy will incite Saul to violence. Later incidents (18:10–11; 19:10; 20:33) demonstrate that Samuel's fears were well-founded. *say, 'I have come to sacrifice to the LORD.'* This response is true but incomplete, and it was intended to deceive Saul.

16:3 *anoint.* See vv. 1,13 and note on 9:16.

16:5 *Consecrate yourselves.* Involves preparing oneself spiritually as well as making oneself ceremonially clean by washing and putting on clean clothes (see Ex 19:10,14; Lev 15; Nu 19:11–22).

16:6 *Eliab.* Jesse's oldest son (17:13); see chart, p. 402.

16:7 *his appearance or his height.* Samuel is not to focus on these outward features, which had characterized Saul (see 9:2; 10:23–24). *heart.* The Lord is concerned with a person's inner disposition and character (see 1Ki 8:39; 1Ch 28:9; Lk 16:15; Jn 2:25; Ac 1:24).

16:8 *Abinadab.* Jesse's second son (17:13).

16:9 *Shammah.* Jesse's third son (17:13).

16:11 *he is tending the sheep.* The Lord's chosen one is a shepherd (see note on 9:3; see also 2Sa 7:7–8 and note on 7:7; Ps 78:71–72 and note on 78:72).

He was ruddy, with a fine appearance and handsome[p] features.

Then the LORD said, "Rise and anoint him; he is the one."

13So Samuel took the horn of oil and anointed[q] him in the presence of his brothers, and from that day on the Spirit of the LORD[r] came upon David in power.[s] Samuel then went to Ramah.

16:12 [p]S Ge 39:6
16:13 [q]S 1Sa 2:35; S 2Sa 22:51 [r]1Sa 18:12 [s]S 1Sa 11:6
16:14 [t]S Jdg 16:20 [u]ver 23; S Jdg 9:23; [v]1Sa 18:10 [w]2Sa 7:15

David in Saul's Service

14Now the Spirit of the LORD had departed[t] from Saul, and an evil[a] spirit[u] from the LORD tormented him.[v]

15Saul's attendants said to him, "See, an evil spirit from God is tormenting you.

[a] 14 Or *injurious*; also in verses 15, 16 and 23

16:13–14 These two verses, taken together, relate the transfer of God's enabling Spirit from Saul to David and mark the beginning of God's displacement of Saul by David as Israel's king. This transition constitutes the literary, historical and theological crux of the first half of 1,2 Samuel (see Introduction: Outline). Cf. Ps 51:11 and note.

16:13 *horn of oil.* See 1Ki 1:39 and note. *in the presence of his brothers.* The small circle of witnesses to David's anointing assured its confidentiality, but also provided ample testimony for the future that David had been anointed by Samuel and that he was not merely a usurper of Saul's office. *the Spirit of the LORD came upon David in power.* See v. 14 and note; 10:5–6,10; 11:6 and note; Jdg 15:14 and note. This is the first mention of David by name in 1 Samuel. See chart below.

16:14—17:58 In the next two episodes, David is introduced to Saul's court and to Israel as a gifted musician and warrior. With these two gifts he would become famous in Israel and would lead the nation to spiritual and political vigor (see 2Sa 22; 23:1–7). Also through these two gifts Saul would become dependent upon David.

16:14 *the Spirit of the LORD had departed from Saul.* Cf. Jdg 16:20 and note. The removal of the Spirit from Saul and the giving of the Spirit to David (v. 13) determined the contrasting courses of their lives. *evil spirit from the LORD.* This statement and similar ones in Scripture indicate that evil spirits are subject to God's control and operate only within divinely determined boundaries (see 1Ki 22:19,23; Job 1:12; 2:6 and notes; see also 2Sa 24:1 and note). Saul's disobedience continued to be punished by the assaults of an evil spirit (vv. 15–16,23; 18:10; 19:9). *tormented him.* Saul's increasing tendencies to despondency, jealousy and violence were no doubt occasioned by his knowledge of his rejection as king (see 13:13–14 and notes; 15:22–26; 18:9; 20:30–33;

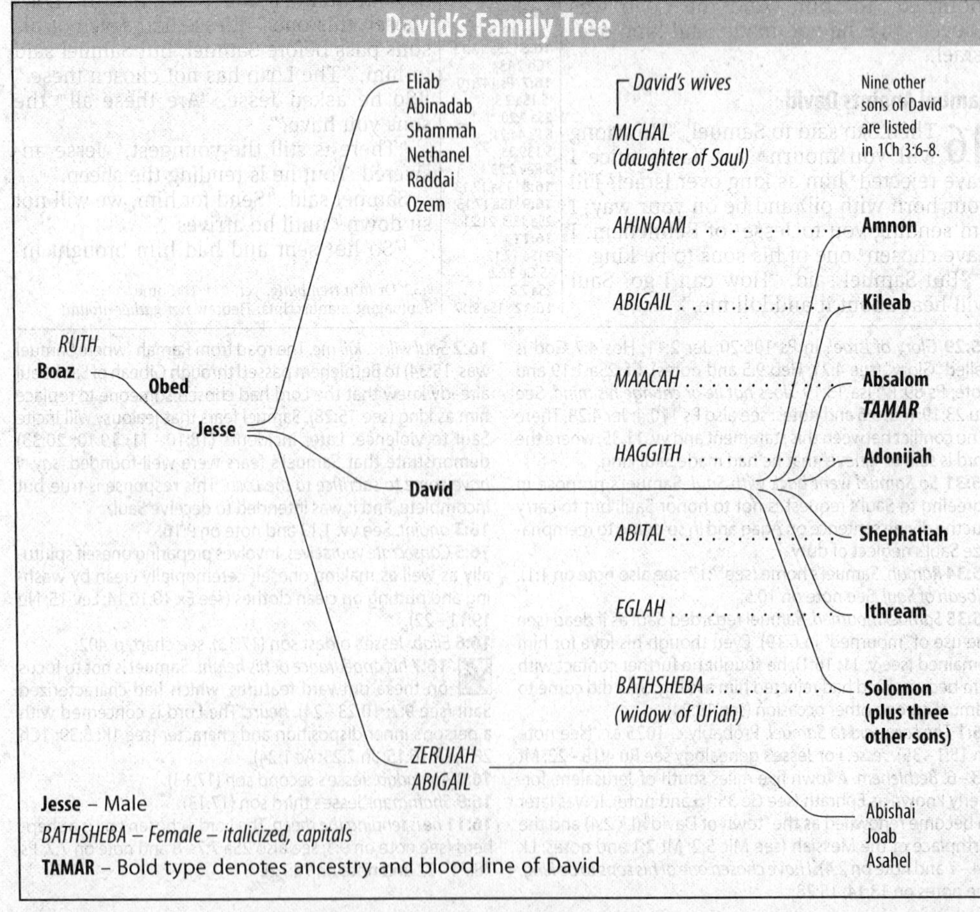

16Let our lord command his servants here
to search for someone who can play the
harp.[w] He will play when the evil spirit
from God comes upon you, and you will
feel better."
17So Saul said to his attendants, "Find
someone who plays well and bring him
to me."
18One of the servants answered, "I have
seen a son of Jesse[x] of Bethlehem who
knows how to play the harp. He is a brave
man and a warrior.[y] He speaks well and is
a fine-looking man. And the LORD is with[z]
him."
19Then Saul sent messengers to Jesse
and said, "Send me your son David, who
is with the sheep.[a]" 20So Jesse took a donkey loaded with bread,[b] a skin of wine and
a young goat and sent them with his son
David to Saul.
21David came to Saul and entered his
service.[c] Saul liked him very much, and
David became one of his armor-bearers.
22Then Saul sent word to Jesse, saying,
"Allow David to remain in my service, for
I am pleased with him."
23Whenever the spirit from God came
upon Saul, David would take his harp
and play. Then relief would come to Saul;
he would feel better, and the evil spirit[d]
would leave him.

David and Goliath

17 Now the Philistines gathered their
forces for war and assembled[e] at Socoh in Judah. They pitched camp at Ephes
Dammim, between Socoh[f] and Azekah.[g]
2Saul and the Israelites assembled and
camped in the Valley of Elah[h] and drew
up their battle line to meet the Philistines.
3The Philistines occupied one hill and the
Israelites another, with the valley between
them.
4A champion named Goliath,[i] who was
from Gath, came out of the Philistine
camp. He was over nine feet[a] tall. 5He had
a bronze helmet on his head and wore a
coat of scale armor of bronze weighing
five thousand shekels[b]; 6on his legs he
wore bronze greaves, and a bronze javelin[j] was slung on his back. 7His spear shaft
was like a weaver's rod,[k] and its iron point
weighed six hundred shekels.[c] His shield
bearer[l] went ahead of him.
8Goliath stood and shouted to the ranks
of Israel, "Why do you come out and line
up for battle? Am I not a Philistine, and
are you not the servants of Saul? Choose[m]
a man and have him come down to me. 9If
he is able to fight and kill me, we will become your subjects; but if I overcome him
and kill him, you will become our subjects
and serve us." 10Then the Philistine said,
"This day I defy[n] the ranks of Israel! Give
me a man and let us fight each other.[o]"
11On hearing the Philistine's words, Saul
and all the Israelites were dismayed and
terrified.
12Now David was the son of an Ephrathite[p] named Jesse,[q] who was from Bethlehem[r] in Judah. Jesse had eight[s] sons, and
in Saul's time he was old and well advanced in years. 13Jesse's three oldest sons
had followed Saul to the war: The firstborn was Eliab;[t] the second, Abinadab;[u]
and the third, Shammah.[v] 14David was the
youngest. The three oldest followed Saul,
15but David went back and forth from Saul
to tend[w] his father's sheep[x] at Bethlehem.

16:16 [w] ver 23; S 1Sa 10:5,6; 2Ch 29:26-27; Ps 49:4 **16:18** [x] S Ru 4:17 [y] 2Sa 17:8 [z] S Ge 39:2; 1Sa 17:32-37; 20:13; 1Ch 22:11; Mt 1:23 **16:19** [a] 1Sa 17:15 **16:20** [b] S Ge 32:13; S 1Sa 10:4 **16:21** [c] S Ge 41:46 **16:23** [d] S ver 14; S Jdg 9:23 **17:1** [e] 1Sa 13:5 [f] Jos 15:35; 2Ch 28:18 [g] S Jos 10:10,11 **17:2** [h] 1Sa 21:9 **17:4** [i] 1Sa 21:9; 2Sa 21:19 **17:6** [j] ver 45; 1Sa 18:10 **17:7** [k] 2Sa 21:19; 1Ch 11:23; 20:5 [l] ver 41 **17:8** [m] 2Sa 2:12-17 **17:10** [n] ver 26,45; 2Sa 21:21 [o] ver 23 **17:12** [p] S Ge 35:16; S 48:7; Ps 132:6 [q] S Ru 4:17 [r] S Ge 35:19 [s] 1Sa 16:11 **17:13** [t] S 1Sa 16:6 [u] 1Sa 16:8 [v] S 1Sa 16:9 **17:15** [w] S Ge 37:2 [x] 1Sa 16:19

[a] 4 Hebrew *was six cubits and a span* (about 3 meters)
[b] 5 That is, about 125 pounds (about 57 kilograms)
[c] 7 That is, about 15 pounds (about 7 kilograms)

22:16–18) and his awareness of David's growing popularity, but an evil spirit was also involved in these psychological aberrations (see 18:10–12; 19:9–10).

16:16 *you will feel better.* The soothing effect of certain types of music on a troubled spirit is a generally recognized phenomenon (see 2Ki 3:15). Beyond this natural effect of music, however, it would appear that in this instance the Spirit of the Lord was active in David's music to suppress the evil spirit temporarily (see v. 23).

16:18 *the LORD is with him.* Said also of Samuel (see 3:19 and note). The fact that God was with David (see also 17:37; 18:12,14,28; 2Sa 5:10) outweighs everything David was.

16:19 *Send me your son David.* Saul unknowingly invites to the court the person God chose to be his replacement. In this way David is brought into contact with Saul, and his introduction to Israel begins.

16:21 *David became one of his armor-bearers.* May refer to a later time after David's victory over Goliath (see 18:2).

17:1 *Socoh.* Located about 15 miles west of Bethlehem (see 2Ch 28:18) near the Philistine border. *Azekah.* Located a little over a mile northwest of Socoh.

17:2 *Valley of Elah.* Located between Azekah and Socoh.

17:4 *champion.* The ancient Greeks, to whom the Philistines were apparently related, sometimes decided issues of war through chosen champions who met in combat between the armies. Through this economy of warriors the judgment of the gods on the matter at stake was determined (trial by battle ordeal). Israel too may have known this practice (see 2Sa 2:14–16 and note on 2:17). *Gath.* See 5:8 and note.

17:11 *Saul and all the Israelites were ... terrified.* Israel's giant warrior (see 9:2; 10:23) quakes before the Philistine champion. The fear of Saul and the Israelite army (see vv. 24,32) betrays a loss of faith in the covenant promises of the Lord (see Ex 23:22; Dt 3:22 and note; 20:1–4). Their fear also demonstrates that the Israelite search for security in a human king (apart from trust in the Lord; see notes on 8:5,7) had failed. On the basis of God's covenant promises, Israel was never to fear her enemies but to trust in the Lord (see 2Sa 10:12; Ex 14:13–14 and note on 14:14; Nu 14:9 and note; Jos 10:8; 2Ch 20:17 and note on 20:20).

17:12 *Ephrathite.* See note on Ru 1:2.

17:15 *David went back and forth from Saul.* David's position at the court (see 16:21–23) was not permanent, but was performed on an intermittent basis. For the relationship between chs. 16 and 17 see note on v. 55.

16For forty days the Philistine came forward every morning and evening and took
his stand.
17Now Jesse said to his son David, "Take
this ephah[a][y] of roasted grain[z] and these
ten loaves of bread for your brothers and
hurry to their camp. 18Take along these ten
cheeses to the commander of their unit.[b]
See how your brothers[a] are and bring back
some assurance[c] from them. 19They are
with Saul and all the men of Israel in the
Valley of Elah, fighting against the Philistines."
20Early in the morning David left the
flock with a shepherd, loaded up and set
out, as Jesse had directed. He reached the
camp as the army was going out to its battle positions, shouting the war cry. 21Israel
and the Philistines were drawing up their
lines facing each other. 22David left his
things with the keeper of supplies,[b] ran
to the battle lines and greeted his brothers. 23As he was talking with them, Goliath, the Philistine champion from Gath,
stepped out from his lines and shouted
his usual[c] defiance, and David heard it.
24When the Israelites saw the man, they
all ran from him in great fear.
25Now the Israelites had been saying,
"Do you see how this man keeps coming
out? He comes out to defy Israel. The king
will give great wealth to the man who kills
him. He will also give him his daughter[d]
in marriage and will exempt his father's
family from taxes[e] in Israel."
26David asked the men standing near
him, "What will be done for the man who
kills this Philistine and removes this disgrace[f] from Israel? Who is this uncircumcised[g] Philistine that he should defy[h] the
armies of the living[i] God?"
27They repeated to him what they had
been saying and told him, "This is what
will be done for the man who kills him."
28When Eliab, David's oldest brother, heard him speaking with the men,
he burned with anger[j] at him and asked,
"Why have you come down here? And
with whom did you leave those few sheep
in the desert? I know how conceited you
are and how wicked your heart is; you
came down only to watch the battle."
29"Now what have I done?" said David.
"Can't I even speak?" 30He then turned
away to someone else and brought up the
same matter, and the men answered him
as before. 31What David said was overheard and reported to Saul, and Saul sent
for him.
32David said to Saul, "Let no one lose
heart[k] on account of this Philistine; your
servant will go and fight him."
33Saul replied,[l] "You are not able to go
out against this Philistine and fight him;
you are only a boy, and he has been a
fighting man from his youth."
34But David said to Saul, "Your servant has been keeping his father's sheep.
When a lion[m] or a bear came and carried
off a sheep from the flock, 35I went after
it, struck it and rescued the sheep from its
mouth. When it turned on me, I seized[n]
it by its hair, struck it and killed it. 36Your
servant has killed both the lion[o] and the
bear; this uncircumcised Philistine will be
like one of them, because he has defied
the armies of the living God. 37The LORD
who delivered[p] me from the paw of the
lion[q] and the paw of the bear will deliver
me from the hand of this Philistine."
Saul said to David, "Go, and the LORD
be with[r] you."
38Then Saul dressed David in his own[s]
tunic. He put a coat of armor on him and
a bronze helmet on his head. 39David fastened on his sword over the tunic and
tried walking around, because he was not
used to them.
"I cannot go in these," he said to Saul,

[a] *17* That is, probably about 3/5 bushel (about 22 liters)
[b] *18* Hebrew *thousand* [c] *18* Or *some token*; or *some pledge of spoils*

17:17 [y]S Lev 19:36 [z]S Lev 23:14; 1Sa 25:18 **17:18** [a]Ge 37:14 **17:22** [b]S Jos 1:11 **17:23** [c]ver 8-10 **17:25** [d]1Sa 18:17 [e]S 1Sa 8:15 **17:26** [f]1Sa 11:2 [g]S 1Sa 14:6 [h]S ver 10 [i]Dt 5:26; S Jos 3:10; 2Ki 18:35 **17:28** [j]S Ge 27:41; Pr 18:19 **17:32** [k]S Dt 20:3; Ps 18:45; Isa 7:4; Jer 4:9; 38:4; Da 11:30 **17:33** [l]Nu 13:31 **17:34** [m]Job 10:16; Isa 31:4; Jer 49:19; Hos 13:8; Am 3:12 **17:35** [n]Jdg 14:6 **17:36** [o]1Ch 11:22 **17:37** [p]2Co 1:10 [q]2Ti 4:17 [r]S 1Sa 16:18; S 18:12 **17:38** [s]S Ge 41:42

17:24 *great fear.* See note on v. 11.
17:25 *The king will give great wealth.* See 8:14; 22:7 and note. *give him his daughter in marriage.* See 18:17–27 and note on 18:17; cf. Jos 15:16.
17:26,36 *uncircumcised.* See note on 14:6.
17:26 *Who is this ...?* David sees the issues clearly—which sets him apart from Saul and all the other Israelites on that battlefield. Because of the Philistine threat and the cowering of Saul and his army in the face of it, the coming of the kingdom of God into the world through God's ways with Israel was at stake. David seems to have been aware of this. It marked him as one more worthy than Saul—or any other man there—to wear the crown in Israel.
17:28 *he burned with anger.* Eliab's anger may arise from jealousy toward his brother and a sense of guilt for the defeatist attitude of the Israelites. His evaluation of David stands in sharp contrast to that of Saul's attendant (see 16:18). Eliab does not comprehend David's indomitable spirit (see 16:13 and note).
17:32 *Let no one lose heart on account of this Philistine.* David's confidence does not rest in his own prowess (see vv. 37,47 and note) but in the power of the living God, whose honor has been violated by the Philistines and whose covenant promises have been scorned by the Israelites.
17:33 *You are not able.* Saul does not take into account the power of God (see vv. 37,47).
17:34 *lion ... bear.* For the presence of lions and bears in Canaan at that time see 2Sa 17:8; 23:20; Jdg 14:5–11 and note on 14:6; 1Ki 13:24–26; 2Ki 2:24; Am 3:12; 5:19.
17:37 *The LORD ... will deliver me.* Reliance on the Lord was essential for the true theocratic king (see notes on 10:18; 11:13). Here David's faith contrasts sharply with Saul's loss of faith (see 11:6–7 for Saul's earlier fearlessness). *Saul said to David, "Go."* Saul is now dependent on David not only for his sanity (see note on 16:16) but also for the security of his realm. *the LORD be with you.* See note on 16:18.

"because I am not used to them." So he
took them off. 40 Then he took his staff in
his hand, chose five smooth stones from
the stream, put them in the pouch of his
shepherd's bag and, with his sling in his
hand, approached the Philistine.
41 Meanwhile, the Philistine, with his
shield bearer[t] in front of him, kept coming closer to David. 42 He looked David
over and saw that he was only a boy, ruddy and handsome,[u] and he despised[v] him.
43 He said to David, "Am I a dog,[w] that you
come at me with sticks?" And the Philistine
cursed David by his gods. 44 "Come here,"
he said, "and I'll give your flesh to the birds
of the air[x] and the beasts of the field![y]"
45 David said to the Philistine, "You come
against me with sword and spear and javelin,[z] but I come against you in the name[a]
of the LORD Almighty, the God of the armies of Israel, whom you have defied.[b]
46 This day the LORD will hand[c] you over
to me, and I'll strike you down and cut
off your head. Today I will give the carcasses[d] of the Philistine army to the birds
of the air and the beasts of the earth, and
the whole world[e] will know that there is
a God in Israel.[f] 47 All those gathered here
will know that it is not by sword[g] or spear
that the LORD saves;[h] for the battle[i] is the
LORD's, and he will give all of you into our
hands."
48 As the Philistine moved closer to attack him, David ran quickly toward the
battle line to meet him. 49 Reaching into
his bag and taking out a stone, he slung it
and struck the Philistine on the forehead.
The stone sank into his forehead, and he
fell facedown on the ground.
50 So David triumphed over the Philistine
with a sling[j] and a stone; without a sword
in his hand he struck down the Philistine
and killed him.
51 David ran and stood over him. He took
hold of the Philistine's sword and drew it
from the scabbard. After he killed him, he
cut[k] off his head with the sword.[l]
When the Philistines saw that their hero
was dead, they turned and ran. 52 Then the
men of Israel and Judah surged forward
with a shout and pursued the Philistines
to the entrance of Gath[a] and to the gates
of Ekron.[m] Their dead were strewn along
the Shaaraim[n] road to Gath and Ekron.
53 When the Israelites returned from chasing the Philistines, they plundered their
camp. 54 David took the Philistine's head
and brought it to Jerusalem, and he put
the Philistine's weapons in his own tent.
55 As Saul watched David[o] going out to
meet the Philistine, he said to Abner, commander of the army, "Abner,[p] whose son is
that young man?"
Abner replied, "As surely as you live,
O king, I don't know."
56 The king said, "Find out whose son
this young man is."
57 As soon as David returned from killing
the Philistine, Abner took him and brought
him before Saul, with David still holding
the Philistine's head.
58 "Whose son are you, young man?"
Saul asked him.
David said, "I am the son of your servant Jesse[q] of Bethlehem."

Saul's Jealousy of David

18 After David had finished talking with
Saul, Jonathan[r] became one in spirit
with David, and he loved[s] him as himself.[t]

17:41 [t] ver 7 **17:42** [u] 1Sa 16:12 [v] Ps 123:3-4; Pr 16:18 **17:43** [w] 1Sa 24:14; 2Sa 3:8; 9:8; 2Ki 8:13 **17:44** [x] S Ge 40:19; Rev 19:17 [y] 2Sa 21:10; Jer 34:20 **17:45** [z] S ver 6 [a] Dt 20:1; 2Ch 13:12; 14:11; 32:8; Ps 20:7-8; 124:8; Heb 11:32-34 [b] S ver 10 **17:46** [c] S 1Sa 14:12 [d] S Dt 28:26 [e] S Jos 4:24; S Isa 11:9 [f] 1Ki 18:36; 2Ki 5:8; 19:19; Isa 37:20 **17:47** [g] Hos 1:7 [h] 1Sa 14:6; 2Ch 14:11; Jer 39:18 [i] S Ex 14:14; S Nu 21:14; S 1Sa 2:9; 2Ch 20:15; Ps 44:6-7 **17:50** [j] 1Sa 25:29 **17:51** [k] Heb 11:34 [l] 1Sa 21:9; 22:10 **17:52** [m] Jos 15:11 [n] S Jos 15:36 **17:55** [o] 1Sa 16:21 [p] 1Sa 26:5 **17:58** [q] S Ru 4:17 **18:1** [r] 1Sa 19:1; 20:16; 31:2; 2Sa 4:4 [s] 2Sa 1:26 [t] S Ge 44:30

[a] 52 Some Septuagint manuscripts; Hebrew *a valley*

17:40 *his staff.* God's newly appointed shepherd of his people (see 2Sa 5:2; 7:7; Ps 78:72 and notes) goes to defend the Lord's threatened and frightened flock. *stones.* See Jdg 20:16 and note. Usually the stones chosen were round and smooth and somewhat larger than a baseball. *his sling.* For the skill with a sling achieved by many Benjamites see Jdg 20:16 and note.

17:43 *Am I a dog ...?* See 2Sa 9:8 and note.

17:45 *in the name of the LORD Almighty.* David's strength was his reliance on the Lord (see Ps 9:10). *name of the LORD.* See notes on Ex 3:13–14; Dt 12:5. *LORD Almighty.* See note on 1:3.

17:46 *the whole world will know.* The victory that David anticipates will demonstrate to the world around the existence and power of Israel's God (see Ex 7:17; 9:14,16,29; Dt 4:34–35; Jos 2:10–11; 4:23–24; 1Ki 8:59–60; 18:36–39; 2Ki 5:15; 19:19; cf. Eze 6:7 and note).

17:47 *the battle is the LORD's.* Both the Israelite and the Philistine armies will be shown the error of placing trust in human devices for personal or national security (see 2:10; 14:6; 2Ch 14:11; 20:15; Ps 33:16–22; 44:6–7; Ecc 9:11; Hos 1:7; Zec 4:6).

17:51 *cut off his head.* See 5:4; 31:9 and notes. *they turned and ran.* Most likely the Philistines saw the fall of their champion as the judgment of the gods, but they did not honor Goliath's original proposal (see v. 9).

17:54 *brought it to Jerusalem.* Jerusalem had not at this time been conquered by the Israelites. David may have kept Goliath's head as a trophy of victory and brought the skull with him to Jerusalem when he took that city and made it his capital (see 2Sa 5:6–9). Or, having grown up almost under the shadow of the Jebusite city, he may have displayed Goliath's head to its defiant inhabitants as a warning of what the God of Israel was able to do and eventually would do. *put the Philistine's weapons in his own tent.* As his personal spoils of the battle. Since Goliath's sword is later in the custody of the priest at Nob (see 21:9), David must have dedicated it to the Lord, the true victor in the fight (cf. 31:10).

17:55 *whose son is that young man?* The seeming contradiction between vv. 55–58 and 16:16–23 may be resolved by noting that prior to this time David was not a permanent resident at Saul's court (see v. 15; 18:2; see also note on 16:21), so that Saul's knowledge of David and his family may have been minimal. Further, Saul may have been so incredulous at David's courage that he was wondering if his family background and social standing might explain his extraordinary conduct.

18:1—20:42 Saul's alienation from David, even while members of his family protect David.

18:1 It appears that David spoke with Saul at length, and he may have explained his actions as an expression of his faith

2From that day Saul kept David with him
and did not let him return to his father's
house. 3And Jonathan made a covenant[u]
with David because he loved him as himself. 4Jonathan took off the robe[v] he was
wearing and gave it to David, along with
his tunic, and even his sword, his bow and
his belt.[w]
5Whatever Saul sent him to do, David
did it so successfully[a x] that Saul gave him
a high rank in the army.[y] This pleased all
the people, and Saul's officers as well.
6When the men were returning home
after David had killed the Philistine, the
women came out from all the towns of Israel to meet King Saul with singing and
dancing,[z] with joyful songs and with tambourines[a] and lutes. 7As they danced, they
sang:[b]

> "Saul has slain his thousands,
> and David his tens[c] of thousands."

8Saul was very angry; this refrain galled
him. "They have credited David with tens
of thousands," he thought, "but me with
only thousands. What more can he get but
the kingdom?[d]" 9And from that time on
Saul kept a jealous[e] eye on David.
10The next day an evil[b] spirit[f] from God
came forcefully upon Saul. He was prophesying in his house, while David was playing the harp,[g] as he usually[h] did. Saul had
a spear[i] in his hand 11and he hurled it, saying to himself,[j] "I'll pin David to the wall."
But David eluded[k] him twice.[l]
12Saul was afraid[m] of David, because
the LORD[n] was with[o] David but had left[p]
Saul. 13So he sent David away from him
and gave him command over a thousand
men, and David led[q] the troops in their
campaigns.[r] 14In everything he did he had
great success,[c s] because the LORD was
with[t] him. 15When Saul saw how successful[d] he was, he was afraid of him. 16But all
Israel and Judah loved David, because he
led them in their campaigns.[u]
17Saul said to David, "Here is my older
daughter[v] Merab. I will give her to you in
marriage;[w] only serve me bravely and fight
the battles[x] of the LORD." For Saul said to
himself,[y] "I will not raise a hand against
him. Let the Philistines do that!"
18But David said to Saul, "Who am I,[z]
and what is my family or my father's clan
in Israel, that I should become the king's
son-in-law?[a]" 19So[e] when the time came
for Merab,[b] Saul's daughter, to be given to
David, she was given in marriage to Adriel
of Meholah.[c]
20Now Saul's daughter Michal[d] was in
love with David, and when they told Saul
about it, he was pleased.[e] 21"I will give her
to him," he thought, "so that she may be a
snare[f] to him and so that the hand of the
Philistines may be against him." So Saul
said to David, "Now you have a second
opportunity to become my son-in-law."
22Then Saul ordered his attendants:
"Speak to David privately and say, 'Look,
the king is pleased with you, and his attendants all like you; now become his son-
in-law.' "
23They repeated these words to David.

18:3 [u] 1Sa 20:8,16,17,42; 22:8; 23:18; 24:21; 2Sa 21:7 **18:4** [v] S Ge 41:42 [w] 2Sa 18:11 **18:5** [x] ver 30 [y] 2Sa 5:2 **18:6** [z] S Ex 15:20; 2Sa 1:20 [a] Ps 68:25 **18:7** [b] Ex 15:21 [c] 1Sa 21:11; 29:5; 2Sa 18:3 **18:8** [d] S 1Sa 13:14; 1Sa 15:8 **18:9** [e] 1Sa 19:1 **18:10** [f] S Jdg 9:23; S 1Sa 16:14 [g] S 1Sa 10:5 [h] 1Sa 16:21; 19:7 [i] S 1Sa 17:6 **18:11** [j] ver 25; 1Sa 20:7,33 [k] 1Sa 19:10 [l] Ps 132:1 **18:12** [m] ver 29 [n] 1Sa 16:13 [o] Jos 1:5; 1Sa 17:37; 20:13; 1Ch 22:11 [p] S Jdg 16:20 **18:13** [q] Nu 27:17 [r] 2Sa 5:2 **18:14** [s] S Ge 39:3 [t] S Ge 39:2; S Nu 14:43; 2Sa 7:9 **18:16** [u] 2Sa 5:2 **18:17** [v] 1Sa 17:25 [w] S Ge 29:26 [x] S Nu 21:14 [y] ver 25; 1Sa 20:33 **18:18** [z] S Ex 3:11; S 1Sa 9:21 [a] ver 23 **18:19** [b] 2Sa 21:8 [c] S Jdg 7:22 **18:20** [d] ver 28; S Ge 29:26 [e] ver 29 **18:21** [f] S Ex 10:7; S Dt 7:16

[a] 5 Or *wisely* [b] 10 Or *injurious* [c] 14 Or *he was very wise* [d] 15 Or *wise* [e] 19 Or *However,*

in the Lord, thus attracting the love and loyalty of Jonathan (see v. 3 and note; 14:6; 19:5). Their friendship endured even when it became clear that David was to replace him as the successor to his father's throne.

18:2 *Saul kept David with him.* See note on 17:15.

18:3 *Jonathan made a covenant with David.* The initiative comes from Jonathan. The terms of the agreement are not here specified (see further 19:1; 20:8,12–16,41–42; 23:18) but would appear to involve a pledge of mutual loyalty and friendship. At the very least, Jonathan accepts David as his equal.

18:4 *took off the robe ... and gave it to David.* Jonathan ratifies the covenant in an act that symbolizes giving himself to David. His act may even signify his recognition that David was to assume his place as successor to Saul (see 20:14–15,31; 23:17 and note)—a possibility that seems the more likely in that he also gave David "even his sword, his bow and his belt" (cf. 13:22).

18:5 *Whatever Saul sent him to do.* During the rest of the campaign.

18:6 *women came out ... with tambourines.* See Ex 15:20 and note.

18:7 *David his tens of thousands.* See 21:11; 29:5. In accordance with the normal conventions of Hebrew poetry, this was the women's way of saying "Saul and David have slain thousands" (10,000 was normally used as the parallel of 1,000—see Dt 32:30; Ps 91:7 and note; Da 7:10; Mic 6:7; also in Canaanite poetry found at Ugarit). It is a measure of Saul's insecurity and jealousy that he read their intentions incorrectly and took offense (see v. 8). His resentment may have been initially triggered by the mention of David's name alongside his own. See note on 21:11 for how the Philistines interpreted the song.

18:10 *evil spirit from God.* See note on 16:14. *prophesying.* The Hebrew for this word is sometimes used to indicate uncontrolled ecstatic behavior (see note on 1Ki 18:29) and is best understood in that sense in this context (see also note on 10:5). *as he usually did.* See 16:23.

18:12 *the LORD was with David.* See 16:18 and note. *but had left Saul.* See 16:14 and note.

18:13 *he sent David away.* His apparent motive was the hope that David would be killed in battle (see vv. 17,21,25; 19:1), but the result was greater acclaim for David (see vv. 14,16,30).

18:14 *the LORD was with him.* See note on 16:18.

18:17 *Here is my older daughter.* David was entitled to have Saul's daughter as his wife because of his victory over Goliath (see 17:25). This promise had not been kept and is now made conditional on further military service, in which Saul hoped David would be killed. *battles of the LORD.* See 25:28 and note.

18:20 *Michal was in love with David.* See v. 28 and note.

18:21 *second opportunity to become my son-in-law.* For the first see 17:25.

But David said, "Do you think it is a small
matter to become the king's son-in-law?[g]
I'm only a poor man and little known."
24When Saul's servants told him what
David had said, 25Saul replied, "Say to David, 'The king wants no other price[h] for
the bride than a hundred Philistine foreskins, to take revenge[i] on his enemies.'"
Saul's plan[j] was to have David fall by the
hands of the Philistines.
26When the attendants told David these
things, he was pleased to become the
king's son-in-law. So before the allotted
time elapsed, 27David and his men went
out and killed two hundred Philistines. He
brought their foreskins and presented the
full number to the king so that he might
become the king's son-in-law. Then Saul
gave him his daughter Michal[k] in marriage.
28When Saul realized that the LORD was
with David and that his daughter Michal[l]
loved David, 29Saul became still more
afraid[m] of him, and he remained his enemy the rest of his days.
30The Philistine commanders continued
to go out to battle, and as often as they
did, David met with more success[a n] than
the rest of Saul's officers, and his name
became well known.

Saul Tries to Kill David

19 Saul told his son Jonathan[o] and all
the attendants to kill[p] David. But
Jonathan was very fond of David 2and
warned him, "My father Saul is looking
for a chance to kill you. Be on your guard
tomorrow morning; go into hiding[q] and
stay there. 3I will go out and stand with
my father in the field where you are. I'll
speak[r] to him about you and will tell you
what I find out."
4Jonathan spoke[s] well of David to Saul
his father and said to him, "Let not the
king do wrong[t] to his servant David; he
has not wronged you, and what he has
done has benefited you greatly. 5He took
his life[u] in his hands when he killed the
Philistine. The LORD won a great victory[v] for all Israel, and you saw it and were
glad. Why then would you do wrong to an
innocent[w] man like David by killing him
for no reason?"
6Saul listened to Jonathan and took this
oath: "As surely as the LORD lives, David
will not be put to death."
7So Jonathan called David and told him
the whole conversation. He brought him
to Saul, and David was with Saul as before.[x]
8Once more war broke out, and David
went out and fought the Philistines. He
struck them with such force that they fled
before him.
9But an evil[b] spirit[y] from the LORD came
upon Saul as he was sitting in his house
with his spear in his hand. While David
was playing the harp,[z] 10Saul tried to pin
him to the wall with his spear, but David
eluded[a] him as Saul drove the spear into
the wall. That night David made good his
escape.
11Saul sent men to David's house to
watch[b] it and to kill him in the morning.[c]
But Michal, David's wife, warned him, "If
you don't run for your life tonight, tomorrow you'll be killed." 12So Michal let David down through a window,[d] and he fled
and escaped. 13Then Michal took an idol[c e]
and laid it on the bed, covering it with a
garment and putting some goats' hair at
the head.
14When Saul sent the men to capture
David, Michal said,[f] "He is ill."
15Then Saul sent the men back to see
David and told them, "Bring him up to me
in his bed so that I may kill him." 16But
when the men entered, there was the idol
in the bed, and at the head was some
goats' hair.
17Saul said to Michal, "Why did you
deceive me like this and send my enemy
away so that he escaped?"

18:23 [g]ver 18 **18:25** [h]S Ge 34:12 [i]Ps 8:2; 44:16; Jer 20:10 [j]S ver 11, S 17; ver 17 **18:27** [k]2Sa 3:14; 6:16 **18:28** [l]S ver 20 **18:29** [m]ver 12 **18:30** [n]ver 5 **19:1** [o]S 1Sa 18:1 [p]1Sa 18:9 **19:2** [q]1Sa 20:5,19 **19:3** [r]1Sa 20:12 **19:4** [s]1Sa 20:32; 22:14; Pr 31:8,9; Jer 18:20 [t]1Sa 25:21; Pr 17:13 **19:5** [u]S Jdg 9:17; S 12:3 [v]S 1Sa 11:13 [w]S Ge 31:36; Dt 19:10-13 **19:7** [x]S 1Sa 18:2,13 **19:9** [y]S Jdg 9:23 [z]S 1Sa 10:5 **19:10** [a]1Sa 18:11 **19:11** [b]Ps 59 Title [c]Jdg 16:2 **19:12** [d]S Jos 2:15; Ac 9:25; 2Co 11:33 **19:13** [e]S Ge 31:19 **19:14** [f]S Ex 1:19; Jos 2:4

[a] 30 Or *David acted more wisely* [b] 9 Or *injurious* [c] 13 Hebrew *teraphim*; also in verse 16

18:25 *no other price.* Normally a bride-price was paid by the bridegroom to the father of the bride (see Ge 34:12; Ex 22:16 and note) as compensation for the loss of his daughter and insurance for her support if widowed. Saul requires David instead to pass a test appropriate for a great warrior, hoping that he will "fall" (see vv. 17,21).

18:28 *the LORD was with David.* See note on 16:18. *Michal loved David.* God's favor on David is revealed not only in his military accomplishments, but also in Michal's love for him—now added to that of Jonathan. Everything Saul seeks to use against David turns to David's advantage.

18:29 *Saul became still more afraid of him.* Saul's perception that God's hand was on David did not lead him to repentance and acceptance of his own lot (see 15:26) but to greater fear and jealousy toward David.

19:1 *Saul told his son ... to kill David.* Saul now abandons his indirect attempts on David's life (see 18:13,17,21,25) and adopts a more direct approach, leading to David's departure from the court and from service to Saul (see vv. 12,18; 20:42).

19:4 *Jonathan spoke well of David.* Jonathan does not let his own personal ambition distort his perception of David's true theocratic spirit (see v. 5 and notes on 14:6; 17:11; 18:1).

19:5 *The LORD won a great victory.* See notes on 10:18; 12:11; 14:23.

19:6 *Saul listened to Jonathan and took this oath.* See 14:24,44 for previous oaths that Saul did not keep (see notes on 14:24 and 14:39,45).

19:9 *evil spirit from the LORD.* See note on 16:14; cf. 18:10–11.

19:10 *with his spear.* See 18:10–11; 20:33.

19:12 *through a window.* For similar escapes see Jos 2:15; Ac 9:25.

19:13,16 *idol.* See NIV text note and note on Ge 31:19.

Michal told him, "He said to me, 'Let
me get away. Why should I kill you?' "
18When David had fled and made his escape, he went to Samuel at Ramah[g] and told
him all that Saul had done to him. Then he
and Samuel went to Naioth and stayed there.
19Word came to Saul: "David is in Naioth at
Ramah"; 20so he sent men to capture him.
But when they saw a group of prophets[h]
prophesying, with Samuel standing there
as their leader, the Spirit of God came upon[i]
Saul's men and they also prophesied.[j] 21Saul
was told about it, and he sent more men,
and they prophesied too. Saul sent men a
third time, and they also prophesied. 22Fi-
nally, he himself left for Ramah and went
to the great cistern at Secu. And he asked,
"Where are Samuel and David?"
"Over in Naioth at Ramah," they said.
23So Saul went to Naioth at Ramah. But
the Spirit of God came even upon him,
and he walked along prophesying[k] until
he came to Naioth. 24He stripped[l] off his
robes and also prophesied in Samuel's[m]
presence. He lay that way all that day and
night. This is why people say, "Is Saul also
among the prophets?"[n]

19:18 [g]S 1Sa 7:17
19:20 [h]S Nu 11:29 [i]S Nu 11:25 [j]S 1Sa 10:5
19:23 [k]1Sa 10:13
19:24 [l]2Sa 6:20; Isa 20:2 [m]1Sa 15:35 [n]S 1Sa 10:11

David and Jonathan

20 Then David fled from Naioth at Ramah and went to Jonathan and
asked, "What have I done? What is my
crime? How have I wronged[o] your father,
that he is trying to take my life?"[p]
2"Never!" Jonathan replied. "You are
not going to die! Look, my father doesn't
do anything, great or small, without con-
fiding in me. Why would he hide this from
me? It's not so!"
3But David took an oath[q] and said,
"Your father knows very well that I have
found favor in your eyes, and he has said
to himself, 'Jonathan must not know this
or he will be grieved.' Yet as surely as the
LORD lives and as you live, there is only a
step between me and death."
4Jonathan said to David, "Whatever you
want me to do, I'll do for you."
5So David said, "Look, tomorrow is the
New Moon festival,[r] and I am supposed to
dine with the king; but let me go and hide[s]
in the field until the evening of the day
after tomorrow. 6If your father misses me
at all, tell him, 'David earnestly asked my
permission[t] to hurry to Bethlehem,[u] his
hometown, because an annual[v] sacrifice
is being made there for his whole clan.' 7If
he says, 'Very well,' then your servant is
safe. But if he loses his temper,[w] you can
be sure that he is determined[x] to harm me.
8As for you, show kindness to your servant, for you have brought him into a covenant[y] with you before the LORD. If I am
guilty, then kill[z] me yourself! Why hand
me over to your father?"
9"Never!" Jonathan said. "If I had the
least inkling that my father was determined to harm you, wouldn't I tell you?"
10David asked, "Who will tell me if your
father answers you harshly?"
11"Come," Jonathan said, "let's go out
into the field." So they went there together.
12Then Jonathan said to David: "By
the LORD, the God of Israel, I will surely
sound[a] out my father by this time the day
after tomorrow! If he is favorably disposed
toward you, will I not send you word and
let you know? 13But if my father is inclined
to harm you, may the LORD deal with me,
be it ever so severely,[b] if I do not let you
know and send you away safely. May the
LORD be with[c] you as he has been with my
father. 14But show me unfailing kindness[d]
like that of the LORD as long as I live, so
that I may not be killed, 15and do not ever
cut off your kindness from my family[e]—
not even when the LORD has cut off every

20:1 [o]1Sa 24:9 [p]1Sa 22:23; 23:15; 24:11; 25:29; Ps 40:14; 54:3; 63:9; 70:2
20:3 [q]Dt 6:13
20:5 [r]S Nu 10:10 [s]S 1Sa 19:2
20:6 [t]ver 28 [u]1Sa 17:58 [v]S 1Sa 1:3
20:7 [w]1Sa 10:27; 25:17 [x]S 1Sa 18:11
20:8 [y]S 1Sa 18:3 [z]2Sa 14:32
20:12 [a]1Sa 19:3
20:13 [b]S Ru 1:17 [c]S 1Sa 16:18; S 18:12
20:14 [d]S Ge 40:14
20:15 [e]1Sa 24:21; 2Sa 9:7

19:18 *Ramah.* Samuel's home (see 7:17 and note on 1:1). *Naioth.* Means "habitations" or "dwellings." The term appears to designate a complex of houses in a certain section of Ramah where a company of prophets resided (see vv. 19–20,22–23).

19:20 *group of prophets.* See 10:5 and note. *prophesying.* See notes on 10:5; 18:10.

19:24 *He lay that way all that day and night.* Saul was so overwhelmed by the power of the Spirit of God that he was prevented from carrying out his intention to take David's life. His frustrated attempts to kill David—his own inability to harm David and the thwarting of his plans by Jonathan's loyalty, by Michal's deception and by David's own cleverness—all reach their climax here. *Is Saul also among the prophets?* This second occasion reinforced the first (see 10:11 and note). Its repetition underscores how alien Saul's spirit was from that of these zealous servants of the Lord.

20:1 *Naioth at Ramah.* See note on 19:18.

20:3 *as surely as the LORD lives.* See note on 14:39,45.

20:5 *New Moon festival.* Each month of the year was consecrated to the Lord by bringing special sacrifices (Nu 28:11–15) and blowing trumpets (Nu 10:10; Ps 81:3). This observance also involved cessation from normal work, especially at the beginning of the seventh month (Lev 23:24–25; Nu 29:1–6; 2Ki 4:23; Isa 1:13; Am 8:5).

20:6 *annual sacrifice.* David's statement indicates that it was customary for families to observe the New Moon festival together once in the year. There is no other reference in the OT to this practice.

20:8 *covenant.* See note on 18:3.

20:11 *let's go out into the field.* Jonathan acted to save David. Cain had said the same to Abel, but in order to kill him (Ge 4:8; but see NIV text note there).

20:13 *may the LORD deal with me, be it ever so severely.* A common curse formula (see note on 3:17). *May the LORD be with you as he has been with my father.* A clear indication that Jonathan expects David to become king.

20:14 *that I may not be killed.* It was quite common in the ancient world for the first ruler of a new dynasty to secure his position by murdering all potential claimants to the throne from the preceding dynasty (see 1Ki 15:29; 16:11; 2Ki 10:7; 11:1).

20:15 *do not ever cut off your kindness from my family.* This

one of David's enemies from the face of
the earth."
16 So Jonathan[f] made a covenant[g] with
the house of David, saying, "May the LORD
call David's enemies to account.[h]" 17 And
Jonathan had David reaffirm his oath[i] out
of love for him, because he loved him as
he loved himself.
18 Then Jonathan said to David: "Tomorrow is the New Moon festival. You will be
missed, because your seat will be empty.[j]
19 The day after tomorrow, toward evening,
go to the place where you hid[k] when this
trouble began, and wait by the stone Ezel.
20 I will shoot three arrows[l] to the side of
it, as though I were shooting at a target.
21 Then I will send a boy and say, 'Go, find
the arrows.' If I say to him, 'Look, the arrows are on this side of you; bring them
here,' then come, because, as surely as the
LORD lives, you are safe; there is no danger.
22 But if I say to the boy, 'Look, the arrows
are beyond[m] you,' then you must go, because the LORD has sent you away. 23 And
about the matter you and I discussed — remember, the LORD is witness[n] between you
and me forever."

20:16 [f] S 1Sa 18:1 [g] S 1Sa 18:3 [h] S Jos 22:23
20:17 [i] S Jos 9:18; S 1Sa 18:3
20:18 [j] ver 25
20:19 [k] S 1Sa 19:2
20:20 [l] 2Ki 13:15
20:22 [m] ver 37
20:23 [n] S Ge 31:50
20:24 [o] S Nu 10:10
20:25 [p] ver 18
20:26 [q] Lev 7:20-21
20:28 [r] ver 6
20:29 [s] S Ge 8:20

24 So David hid in the field, and when
the New Moon festival[o] came, the king
sat down to eat. 25 He sat in his customary
place by the wall, opposite Jonathan,[a] and
Abner sat next to Saul, but David's place
was empty.[p] 26 Saul said nothing that day,
for he thought, "Something must have
happened to David to make him ceremonially unclean — surely he is unclean.[q]"
27 But the next day, the second day of the
month, David's place was empty again.
Then Saul said to his son Jonathan, "Why
hasn't the son of Jesse come to the meal,
either yesterday or today?"
28 Jonathan answered, "David earnestly
asked me for permission[r] to go to Bethlehem. 29 He said, 'Let me go, because our
family is observing a sacrifice[s] in the town
and my brother has ordered me to be there.
If I have found favor in your eyes, let me
get away to see my brothers.' That is why
he has not come to the king's table."
30 Saul's anger flared up at Jonathan and
he said to him, "You son of a perverse and
rebellious woman! Don't I know that you

[a] 25 Septuagint; Hebrew *wall. Jonathan arose*

request was based on the covenant previously concluded between Jonathan and David (see note on 18:3) and was subsequently honored in David's dealings with Jonathan's son Mephibosheth (see 2Sa 9:3,7 and note on 9:1; 21:7).
20:16 *May the LORD call David's enemies to account.* Jonathan aligns himself completely with David, calling for destruction of his enemies, even if that should include his father Saul.
20:17 *reaffirm his oath.* See vv. 14–15,42; 18:3. *he loved him as he loved himself.* See 18:3; 2Sa 1:26 and note.
20:18 *New Moon festival.* See note on v. 5.
20:19 *the place where you hid.* Perhaps the place referred to in 19:2.
20:21 *as surely as the LORD lives.* See note on 14:39,45.
20:23 *the matter you and I discussed.* See vv. 14–17. *the LORD is witness.* Invoking God to act as witness and judge between them ensures that their agreement will be kept.
20:25 *Abner.* Saul's cousin and the commander of his army (see 14:50–51; 26:5).
20:26 *ceremonially unclean.* See note on 16:5; cf. Lev 7:19–21; 15:16; Dt 23:10.
20:27,30–31 *son of Jesse.* A contemptuous way of referring to David (see 22:7–9,13; 25:10; cf. 2Sa 16:10; Isa 7:4).
20:30 *son of a perverse and rebellious woman.* The Hebrew idiom intends to characterize Jonathan, not his mother.

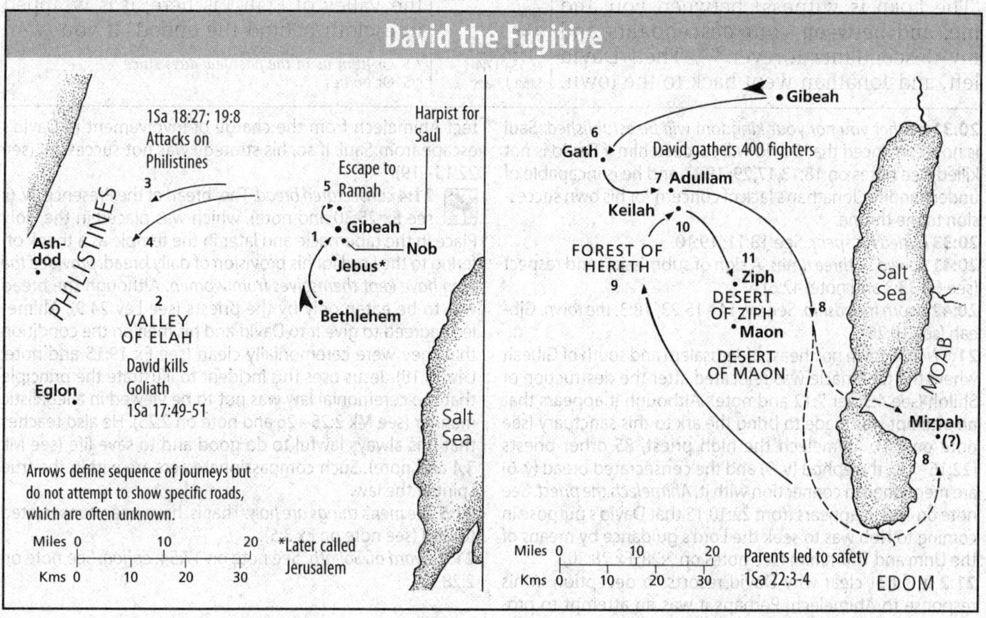

have sided with the son of Jesse to your own shame and to the shame of the mother who bore you? [31]As long as the son of Jesse lives on this earth, neither you nor your kingdom[t] will be established. Now send and bring him to me, for he must die!"

[32]"Why[u] should he be put to death? What[v] has he done?" Jonathan asked his father. [33]But Saul hurled his spear at him to kill him. Then Jonathan knew that his father intended[w] to kill David.

[34]Jonathan got up from the table in fierce anger; on that second day of the month he did not eat, because he was grieved at his father's shameful treatment of David.

[35]In the morning Jonathan went out to the field for his meeting with David. He had a small boy with him, [36]and he said to the boy, "Run and find the arrows I shoot." As the boy ran, he shot an arrow beyond him. [37]When the boy came to the place where Jonathan's arrow had fallen, Jonathan called out after him, "Isn't the arrow beyond[x] you?" [38]Then he shouted, "Hurry! Go quickly! Don't stop!" The boy picked up the arrow and returned to his master. [39](The boy knew nothing of all this; only Jonathan and David knew.) [40]Then Jonathan gave his weapons to the boy and said, "Go, carry them back to town."

[41]After the boy had gone, David got up from the south side ⌊of the stone⌋ and bowed down before Jonathan three times, with his face to the ground.[y] Then they kissed each other and wept together—but David wept the most.

[42]Jonathan said to David, "Go in peace,[z] for we have sworn friendship[a] with each other in the name of the LORD,[b] saying, 'The LORD is witness[c] between you and me, and between your descendants and my descendants forever.[d]' " Then David left, and Jonathan went back to the town.

20:31 [t]1Sa 23:17; 24:20
20:32 [u]S 1Sa 19:4; Mt 27:23 [v]S Ge 31:36
20:33 [w]S 1Sa 18:11,17
20:37 [x]ver 22
20:41 [y]S Ge 33:3; Ru 2:10; 1Sa 24:8; 25:23; 2Sa 1:2
20:42 [z]S 1Sa 1:17; S Ac 15:33 [a]S Ge 40:14; 2Sa 1:26; Pr 18:24 [b]Isa 48:1 [c]S Ge 31:50; S 1Sa 18:3 [d]2Sa 9:1
21:1 [e]1Sa 22:9, 19; Ne 11:32; Isa 10:32 [f]1Sa 16:4
21:4 [g]Lev 24:8-9 [h]Mt 12:4 [i]S Ex 19:15; S Lev 15:18
21:5 [j]Dt 23:9-11; Jos 3:5; 2Sa 11:11 [k]1Th 4:4
21:6 [l]S Ex 25:30; 1Sa 22:10; Mt 12:3-4; Mk 2:25-28; Lk 6:1-5
21:7 [m]1Sa 22:9,22 [n]1Sa 14:47; Ps 52 Title
21:9 [o]S 1Sa 17:51 [p]S 1Sa 17:4 [q]1Sa 17:2

David at Nob

21 David went to Nob,[e] to Ahimelech the priest. Ahimelech trembled[f] when he met him, and asked, "Why are you alone? Why is no one with you?"

[2]David answered Ahimelech the priest, "The king charged me with a certain matter and said to me, 'No one is to know anything about your mission and your instructions.' As for my men, I have told them to meet me at a certain place. [3]Now then, what do you have on hand? Give me five loaves of bread, or whatever you can find."

[4]But the priest answered David, "I don't have any ordinary bread[g] on hand; however, there is some consecrated[h] bread here—provided the men have kept[i] themselves from women."

[5]David replied, "Indeed women have been kept from us, as usual[j] whenever[a] I set out. The men's things[b] are holy[k] even on missions that are not holy. How much more so today!" [6]So the priest gave him the consecrated bread,[l] since there was no bread there except the bread of the Presence that had been removed from before the LORD and replaced by hot bread on the day it was taken away.

[7]Now one of Saul's servants was there that day, detained before the LORD; he was Doeg[m] the Edomite,[n] Saul's head shepherd.

[8]David asked Ahimelech, "Don't you have a spear or a sword here? I haven't brought my sword or any other weapon, because the king's business was urgent."

[9]The priest replied, "The sword[o] of Goliath[p] the Philistine, whom you killed in the Valley of Elah,[q] is here; it is wrapped in a cloth behind the ephod. If you want

[a] 5 Or *from us in the past few days since*
[b] 5 Or *bodies*

20:31 *neither you nor your kingdom will be established.* Saul is now convinced that David will succeed him if David is not killed (see notes on 18:13,17,29; 19:1), and he is incapable of understanding Jonathan's lack of concern for his own succession to the throne.

20:33 *hurled his spear.* See 18:11; 19:10.

20:41 *bowed ... three times.* A sign of submission and respect (see Ge 33:3 and note; 42:6).

20:42 *sworn friendship.* See vv. 14–15,23; 18:3. *the town.* Gibeah (see 10:26).

21:1 *Nob.* A town northeast of Jerusalem and south of Gibeah where the tabernacle was relocated after the destruction of Shiloh (see 4:3; Jer 7:12 and note). Although it appears that no attempt was made to bring the ark to this sanctuary (see note on 7:1), Ahimelech the high priest, 85 other priests (22:16–18), the ephod (v. 9) and the consecrated bread (v. 6) are mentioned in connection with it. *Ahimelech the priest.* See note on 14:3. It appears from 22:10,15 that David's purpose in coming to Nob was to seek the Lord's guidance by means of the Urim and Thummim (see notes on 2:28; Ex 28:30).

21:2 It is not clear why David resorts to deception in his response to Ahimelech. Perhaps it was an attempt to protect Ahimelech from the charge of involvement in David's escape from Saul. If so, his strategy was not successful (see 22:13–19).

21:4 *consecrated bread.* The "bread of the Presence" (v. 6; see Ex 25:30 and note), which was placed in the Holy Place in the tabernacle and later in the temple as a thank offering to the Lord for his provision of daily bread. *provided the men have kept themselves from women.* Although the bread was to be eaten only by the priests (see Lev 24:9), Ahimelech agreed to give it to David and his men on the condition that they were ceremonially clean (see Ex 19:15 and note; Lev 15:18). Jesus uses this incident to illustrate the principle that the ceremonial law was not to be viewed in a legalistic manner (see Mk 2:25–26 and note on 2:25). He also teaches that it is always lawful to do good and to save life (see Mk 3:4 and note). Such compassionate acts are within the true spirit of the law.

21:5 *The men's things are holy.* That is, have been consecrated to God (see note on Ex 3:5).

21:9 *sword of Goliath.* See note on 17:54. *ephod.* See note on 2:28.

it, take it; there is no sword here but that
one."
David said, "There is none like it; give
it to me."

David at Gath

10 That day David fled from Saul and
went[r] to Achish king of Gath. 11 But the
servants of Achish said to him, "Isn't this
David, the king of the land? Isn't he the
one they sing about in their dances:

"'Saul has slain his thousands,
and David his tens of thousands'?"[s]

12 David took these words to heart and
was very much afraid of Achish king of
Gath. 13 So he pretended to be insane[t] in
their presence; and while he was in their
hands he acted like a madman, making
marks on the doors of the gate and letting
saliva run down his beard.
14 Achish said to his servants, "Look at
the man! He is insane! Why bring him to
me? 15 Am I so short of madmen that you
have to bring this fellow here to carry on
like this in front of me? Must this man
come into my house?"

David at Adullam and Mizpah

22 David left Gath and escaped to the
cave[u] of Adullam.[v] When his brothers and his father's household heard about
it, they went down to him there. 2 All those
who were in distress or in debt or discontented gathered[w] around him, and he became their leader. About four hundred
men were with him.
3 From there David went to Mizpah
in Moab and said to the king of Moab,
"Would you let my father and mother
come and stay with you until I learn what
God will do for me?" 4 So he left them with
the king of Moab,[x] and they stayed with
him as long as David was in the stronghold.
5 But the prophet Gad[y] said to David,
"Do not stay in the stronghold. Go into
the land of Judah." So David left and went
to the forest of Hereth.[z]

Saul Kills the Priests of Nob

6 Now Saul heard that David and his
men had been discovered. And Saul, spear
in hand, was seated[a] under the tamarisk[b]
tree on the hill at Gibeah, with all his officials standing around him. 7 Saul said
to them, "Listen, men of Benjamin! Will
the son of Jesse give all of you fields and
vineyards? Will he make all of you commanders[c] of thousands and commanders
of hundreds? 8 Is that why you have all
conspired[d] against me? No one tells me
when my son makes a covenant[e] with the
son of Jesse.[f] None of you is concerned[g]
about me or tells me that my son has incited my servant to lie in wait for me, as
he does today."
9 But Doeg[h] the Edomite, who was
standing with Saul's officials, said, "I saw
the son of Jesse come to Ahimelech son of
Ahitub[i] at Nob.[j] 10 Ahimelech inquired[k] of
the LORD for him; he also gave him provisions[l] and the sword[m] of Goliath the Philistine."
11 Then the king sent for the priest Ahimelech son of Ahitub and his father's whole
family, who were the priests at Nob, and
they all came to the king. 12 Saul said, "Listen now, son of Ahitub."
"Yes, my lord," he answered.
13 Saul said to him, "Why have you conspired[n] against me, you and the son of

21:10 [r] 1Sa 25:13; 27:2 **21:11** [s] S 1Sa 18:7 **21:13** [t] Ps 34 Title **22:1** [u] Ps 57 Title; 142 Title [v] S Ge 38:1 **22:2** [w] 1Sa 23:13; 25:13; 2Sa 15:20

22:4 [x] S Ge 19:37 **22:5** [y] 2Sa 24:11; 1Ch 21:9; 29:29; 2Ch 29:25 [z] 2Sa 23:14 **22:6** [a] S Jdg 4:5 [b] S Ge 21:33 **22:7** [c] S Dt 1:15 **22:8** [d] ver 13 [e] S 1Sa 18:3 [f] 2Sa 20:1 [g] 1Sa 23:21 **22:9** [h] S 1Sa 21:7 [i] 1Sa 14:3 [j] S 1Sa 21:1 **22:10** [k] S Ge 25:22; S 1Sa 23:2 [l] S 1Sa 21:6 [m] S 1Sa 17:51 **22:13** [n] ver 8

21:10 *Achish.* See note on Ps 34 title. The name may have been a traditional title used by Philistine rulers (see note on 1Ki 2:39). It appears as the title of a king of Ekron several centuries later (as attested in the annals of the Assyrian kings Esarhaddon and Ashurbanipal as well as in an inscription found at Ekron in 1996). *Gath.* See 5:8 and note.
21:11 See 29:5 and note on 18:7. *king of the land.* The designation of David as "king" by the Philistines may be understood as a popular exaggeration expressing an awareness of the enormous success and popularity of David among the Israelite people.
22:1 *cave of Adullam.* See 2Sa 23:13; Ge 38:1 and note; Jos 12:15; 15:35.
22:2 *four hundred men were with him.* David, officially an outlaw, was joined by others in similar circumstances, so that he began to develop a military power base that would sustain him throughout his later years as king (see note on 14:52).
22:3 *let my father and mother come and stay with you.* The king of Moab was a natural ally for David because Saul had warred against Moab (see 14:47) and David's own great-grandmother was a Moabite (see Ru 4:5,13,22).
22:4 *stronghold.* Perhaps a specific fortress, but more likely a reference to a geographical area in which it was easy to hide (see 23:14; 2Sa 5:17 and notes; 23:14).
22:5 *prophet Gad.* The king-designate is now served also by a prophet. Later a priest would come to him (v. 20) and complete the basic elements of a royal entourage—and they were all refugees from Saul's administration. This is the first appearance of the prophet who later assisted David in musical arrangements for the temple services (see 2Ch 29:25), wrote a history of David's reign (see 1Ch 29:29) and confronted David with the Lord's rebuke for his sin of numbering the Israelites (see 2Sa 24:11–25). *forest of Hereth.* Located in the tribal area of Judah (see map, p. 409).
22:6 *tamarisk tree.* See note on Ge 21:33. *Gibeah.* See note on 10:5.
22:7–9,13 *son of Jesse.* See note on 20:27,30–31.
22:7 *men of Benjamin.* Saul, a Benjamite (9:1–2; 10:21), seeks to strengthen his position with his own officials by emphasizing tribal loyalty. David was from the tribe of Judah (see notes on 16:1; 2Sa 2:4). *give all of you fields and vineyards?* Saul does exactly what Samuel had warned him that he would do—become like the kings of other nations (see 8:14 and note on 8:5). His actions are contrary to the covenantal ideal for kingship (see notes on 8:7; 10:25). *commanders of thousands ... hundreds.* See 8:12.
22:10 *Ahimelech inquired of the LORD for him.* See note on 21:1.

Jesse, giving him bread and a sword and inquiring of God for him, so that he has rebelled against me and lies in wait for me, as he does today?"

14Ahimelech answered the king, "Who[o] of all your servants is as loyal as David, the king's son-in-law, captain of your bodyguard and highly respected in your household? 15Was that day the first time I inquired of God for him? Of course not! Let not the king accuse your servant or any of his father's family, for your servant knows nothing at all about this whole affair."

16But the king said, "You will surely die, Ahimelech, you and your father's whole family.[p]"

17Then the king ordered the guards at his side: "Turn and kill the priests of the LORD, because they too have sided with David. They knew he was fleeing, yet they did not tell me."

But the king's officials were not willing[q] to raise a hand to strike the priests of the LORD.

18The king then ordered Doeg, "You turn and strike down the priests."[r] So Doeg the Edomite turned and struck them down. That day he killed eighty-five men who wore the linen ephod.[s] 19He also put to the sword[t] Nob,[u] the town of the priests, with its men and women, its children and infants, and its cattle, donkeys and sheep.

20But Abiathar,[v] a son of Ahimelech son of Ahitub,[w] escaped and fled to join David.[x] 21He told David that Saul had killed the priests of the LORD. 22Then David said to Abiathar: "That day, when Doeg[y] the Edomite was there, I knew he would be sure to tell Saul. I am responsible for the death of your father's whole family. 23Stay with me; don't be afraid; the man who is seeking your life[z] is seeking mine also. You will be safe with me."

David Saves Keilah

23 When David was told, "Look, the Philistines are fighting against Keilah[a] and are looting the threshing floors,"[b] 2he inquired[c] of the LORD, saying, "Shall I go and attack these Philistines?"

The LORD answered him, "Go, attack the Philistines and save Keilah."

3But David's men said to him, "Here in Judah we are afraid. How much more, then, if we go to Keilah against the Philistine forces!"

4Once again David inquired[d] of the LORD, and the LORD answered him, "Go down to Keilah, for I am going to give the Philistines[e] into your hand.[f]" 5So David and his men went to Keilah, fought the Philistines and carried off their livestock. He inflicted heavy losses on the Philistines and saved the people of Keilah. 6(Now Abiathar[g] son of Ahimelech had brought the ephod[h] down with him when he fled to David at Keilah.)

Saul Pursues David

7Saul was told that David had gone to Keilah, and he said, "God has handed him over[i] to me, for David has imprisoned himself by entering a town with gates and bars."[j] 8And Saul called up all his forces for battle, to go down to Keilah to besiege David and his men.

9When David learned that Saul was plotting against him, he said to Abiathar[k] the priest, "Bring the ephod.[l]" 10David said, "O LORD, God of Israel, your servant has heard definitely that Saul plans to come to Keilah and destroy the town on account of me. 11Will the citizens of Keilah surrender me to him? Will Saul come down, as your servant has heard? O LORD, God of Israel, tell your servant."

And the LORD said, "He will."

12Again David asked, "Will the citizens of Keilah surrender[m] me and my men to Saul?"

And the LORD said, "They will."

13So David and his men,[n] about six hundred in number, left Keilah and kept moving from place to place. When Saul was told that David had escaped from Keilah, he did not go there.

22:14 [o]S 1Sa 19:4
22:16 [p]S 1Sa 2:31
22:17 [q]S Ex 1:17
22:18 [r]S 1Sa 4:17 [s]S 1Sa 2:18, 31
22:19 [t]S 1Sa 15:3 [u]S 1Sa 21:1
22:20 [v]1Sa 23:6, 9; 30:7; 2Sa 15:24; 20:25; 1Ki 1:7; 2:22, 26, 27; 4:4; 1Ch 15:11; 27:34 [w]S 1Sa 14:3 [x]S 1Sa 2:32
22:22 [y]S 1Sa 21:7
22:23 [z]S 1Sa 20:1
23:1 [a]S Jos 15:44 [b]S Nu 18:27; S Jdg 6:11
23:2 [c]ver 4, 12; 1Sa 22:10; 30:8; 2Sa 2:1; 5:19, 23; Ps 50:15
23:4 [d]S ver 2 [e]S 1Sa 9:16 [f]S Jos 8:7
23:6 [g]S 1Sa 22:20 [h]S 1Sa 2:28
23:7 [i]S Dt 32:30 [j]Ps 31:21
23:9 [k]S 1Sa 22:20 [l]S 1Sa 2:18
23:12 [m]ver 20
23:13 [n]S 1Sa 22:2

22:17 *They knew he was fleeing.* How much the priests really knew is not clear. David himself had not told them (see 21:2–3,8).

22:18 *linen ephod.* See note on 2:18.

22:19 *put to the sword Nob.* Thus the prophecy of judgment against the house of Eli is fulfilled (see 2:31 and note).

22:20 *Abiathar ... escaped and fled to join David.* See note on v. 5. Abiathar brought the high-priestly ephod with him (see 23:6) and subsequently "inquired of the LORD" for David (see 23:2,4 and note; see also 23:4,9; 30:7–8; 2Sa 2:1 and note; 5:19,23). Abiathar served as high priest until removed from office by Solomon for participating in the rebellion of Adonijah (see 1Ki 2:26–27).

23:1—26:25 Four tests of David's use of his growing power: (1) Will he use that power to defend Israel or only to promote his personal ambitions? (23:1–6). (2) Will he use the power in his hand to kill the king who is trying to kill him? (23:7—24:22). (3) Will he use his power to avenge the disdain of a commoner in the realm? (ch. 25). (4) Will he use the power in his hand to kill the king who is out to destroy him? (ch. 26).

23:1 *Keilah.* Located about three miles southeast of Adullam.

23:2,4 *inquired of the LORD.* By means of the Urim and Thummim through the high priest Abiathar (see vv. 6,9 and notes on 2:28; 22:20).

23:5 *saved the people of Keilah.* God uses David rather than Saul to be Israel's protective "shepherd"—so again David protects Saul's "flock."

23:9 *Bring the ephod.* See notes on vv. 2,4; 2:28.

23:13 *about six hundred.* The number of David's men has grown significantly (cf. 22:2).

14David stayed in the desert[o] strongholds
and in the hills of the Desert of Ziph.[p] Day
after day Saul searched[q] for him, but God
did not[r] give David into his hands.
15While David was at Horesh in the Desert of Ziph, he learned that Saul had come
out to take his life.[s] 16And Saul's son Jonathan went to David at Horesh and helped
him find strength[t] in God. 17"Don't be
afraid," he said. "My father Saul will not
lay a hand on you. You will be king[u] over
Israel, and I will be second to you. Even
my father Saul knows this." 18The two of
them made a covenant[v] before the LORD.
Then Jonathan went home, but David remained at Horesh.
19The Ziphites[w] went up to Saul at Gibeah and said, "Is not David hiding among
us[x] in the strongholds at Horesh, on the
hill of Hakilah,[y] south of Jeshimon? 20Now,
O king, come down whenever it pleases
you to do so, and we will be responsible
for handing[z] him over to the king."
21Saul replied, "The LORD bless[a] you for
your concern[b] for me. 22Go and make further preparation. Find out where David
usually goes and who has seen him there.
They tell me he is very crafty. 23Find out
about all the hiding places he uses and
come back to me with definite information.[a] Then I will go with you; if he is in
the area, I will track[c] him down among all
the clans of Judah."
24So they set out and went to Ziph
ahead of Saul. Now David and his men
were in the Desert of Maon,[d] in the Arabah south of Jeshimon.[e] 25Saul and his
men began the search, and when David
was told about it, he went down to the
rock and stayed in the Desert of Maon.
When Saul heard this, he went into the
Desert of Maon in pursuit of David.
26Saul[f] was going along one side of the
mountain, and David and his men were on
the other side, hurrying to get away from
Saul. As Saul and his forces were closing in on David and his men to capture
them, 27a messenger came to Saul, saying,
"Come quickly! The Philistines are raiding
the land." 28Then Saul broke off his pursuit of David and went to meet the Philistines. That is why they call this place Sela
Hammahlekoth.[b] 29And David went up
from there and lived in the strongholds[g]
of En Gedi.[h]

David Spares Saul's Life

24 After Saul returned from pursuing
the Philistines, he was told, "David
is in the Desert of En Gedi.[i]" 2So Saul took
three thousand chosen men from all Israel
and set out to look[j] for David and his men
near the Crags of the Wild Goats.
3He came to the sheep pens along the
way; a cave[k] was there, and Saul went
in to relieve[l] himself. David and his men
were far back in the cave. 4The men said,
"This is the day the LORD spoke[m] of when
he said[c] to you, 'I will give your enemy
into your hands for you to deal with as
you wish.'"[n] Then David crept up unnoticed and cut[o] off a corner of Saul's robe.
5Afterward, David was conscience-
stricken[p] for having cut off a corner of his

23:14 [o] Ps 55:7 [p] S Jos 15:24, 55 [q] Ps 54:3-4 [r] Ps 32:7 **23:15** [s] S 1Sa 20:1 **23:16** [t] 1Sa 30:6; Ps 18:2; 27:14 **23:17** [u] S 1Sa 20:31 **23:18** [v] S 1Sa 18:3; 2Sa 9:1 **23:19** [w] 1Sa 26:1 [x] Ps 54 Title [y] 1Sa 26:3 **23:20** [z] ver 12 **23:21** [a] Ru 2:20; 2Sa 2:5 [b] 1Sa 22:8 **23:23** [c] S Ge 31:36 **23:24** [d] S Jos 15:55 [e] 1Sa 26:1 **23:26** [f] Ps 17:9 **23:29** [g] 1Sa 24:22 [h] S Jos 15:62; 2Ch 20:2; SS 1:14 **24:1** [i] S Jos 15:62 **24:2** [j] 1Sa 26:2 **24:3** [k] Ps 57 Title; 142 Title [l] Jdg 3:24 **24:4** [m] 1Sa 25:28-30 [n] 2Sa 4:8 [o] ver 10, 11 **24:5** [p] 1Sa 26:9; 2Sa 24:10

[a] 23 Or *me at Nacon* [b] 28 *Sela Hammahlekoth* means *rock of parting.* [c] 4 Or *"Today the LORD is saying*

23:14 *desert strongholds.* Inaccessible places (see v. 19 and note on 22:4). *Desert of Ziph.* Located south of Hebron. *God did not give David into his hands.* The reality of God's protection over David portrayed here contrasts sharply with the wishful thinking of Saul in v. 7.

23:17 *You will be king over Israel.* See notes on 18:4; 20:13,16,31. *I will be second to you.* Jonathan's love and respect for David enable him to accept a role subordinate to David without any sign of resentment or jealousy (see notes on 18:3; 19:4). This is the last recorded meeting between Jonathan and David. *Saul knows this.* See 18:8 and note on 20:31.

23:18 *covenant.* See notes on 18:3; 20:14–15.

23:19 *strongholds.* (see v. 14 and note on 22:4).

23:29 *En Gedi.* See note on SS 1:14.

24:1—26:25 In each of the three episodes in these chapters, David is put to a severe test in the desert as the Lord's anointed (16:1–13; cf. Dt 8, the testing of Israel in the desert; Mt 4:1–11, the testing of Jesus in the desert). In all three events, circumstances place David in a position of power with opportunity to use that power for purely personal ends (avenging wrongs done to him) rather than in the service of the Lord and Israel. To have failed this test would have disqualified David—as it had disqualified Saul—from serving as the Lord's appointed king over Israel.

Within these three chapters the final two confrontations between Saul and David take place. In both, the tables are turned and Saul is at the mercy of David. These two episodes (chs. 24; 26) bracket another (ch. 25) in which David has dealings with Nabal, a wealthy Judahite whose flocks David and his men have protected—as they have protected Saul's "flock" from Philistine aggression. In this center episode, Nabal serves as a literary picture of Saul, who is thus exposed as a fool whom the Lord will soon strike down (see 25:38; cf. 26:10; 28:19; 31:4).

24:1–22 Saul at the mercy of David while seeking privacy in a cave.

24:4 *This is the day the LORD spoke of when he said.* There is no previous record of the divine revelation here alluded to by David's men. Perhaps this was their own interpretation of the anointing of David to replace Saul (see 16:13–14), or of assurances given to David that he would survive Saul's vendetta against him and ultimately become king (see 20:14–15; 23:17). If the alternative given in the NIV text note is taken, the reference would not be to a verbal communication from the Lord but to the providential nature of the incident itself, which David's men understood as a revelation from God that David should not ignore. *I will give your enemy into your hands.* So it seemed to David's men (see also 26:8). Cf. what David says to Saul in v. 10 and contrast what the author has stated in 23:14 (see note there). *cut off a corner of Saul's robe.* Perhaps David was symbolically depriving Saul of his royal authority and transferring it to himself (see v. 11; cf. also 15:27–28; 18:4 and note).

robe. 6He said to his men, "The LORD forbid that I should do such a thing to my master, the LORD's anointed,[q] or lift my hand against him; for he is the anointed of the LORD." 7With these words David rebuked his men and did not allow them to attack Saul. And Saul left the cave and went his way.

8Then David went out of the cave and called out to Saul, "My lord the king!" When Saul looked behind him, David bowed down and prostrated himself with his face to the ground.[r] 9He said to Saul, "Why do you listen[s] when men say, 'David is bent on harming[t] you'? 10This day you have seen with your own eyes how the LORD delivered you into my hands in the cave. Some urged me to kill you, but I spared[u] you; I said, 'I will not lift my hand against my master, because he is the LORD's anointed.' 11See, my father, look at this piece of your robe in my hand! I cut[v] off the corner of your robe but did not kill you. Now understand and recognize that I am not guilty[w] of wrongdoing[x] or rebellion. I have not wronged[y] you, but you are hunting[z] me down to take my life.[a] 12May the LORD judge[b] between you and me. And may the LORD avenge[c] the wrongs you have done to me, but my hand will not touch you. 13As the old saying goes, 'From evildoers come evil deeds,[d]' so my hand will not touch you.

14"Against whom has the king of Israel come out? Whom are you pursuing? A dead dog?[e] A flea?[f] 15May the LORD be our judge[g] and decide[h] between us. May he consider my cause and uphold[i] it; may he vindicate[j] me by delivering[k] me from your hand."

16When David finished saying this, Saul asked, "Is that your voice,[l] David my son?" And he wept aloud. 17"You are more righteous than I,"[m] he said. "You have treated me well,[n] but I have treated you badly.[o] 18You have just now told me of the good you did to me; the LORD delivered[p] me into your hands, but you did not kill me. 19When a man finds his enemy, does he let him get away unharmed? May the LORD reward[q] you well for the way you treated me today. 20I know that you will surely be king[r] and that the kingdom[s] of Israel will be established in your hands. 21Now swear[t] to me by the LORD that you will not cut off my descendants or wipe out my name from my father's family.[u]"

22So David gave his oath to Saul. Then Saul returned home, but David and his men went up to the stronghold.[v]

David, Nabal and Abigail

25 Now Samuel died,[w] and all Israel assembled and mourned[x] for him; and they buried him at his home in Ramah.[y]

24:6 [q] S Ge 26:11; S 1Sa 12:3 **24:8** [r] S 1Sa 20:41 **24:9** [s] 1Sa 26:19 [t] 1Sa 20:1 **24:10** [u] S ver 4 **24:11** [v] S ver 4 [w] Ps 7:3 [x] 1Sa 25:28 [y] Ps 35:7 [z] S Ge 31:36; 1Sa 26:20 [a] S 1Sa 20:1 **24:12** [b] S Ge 16:5; S 1Sa 25:38; S Job 9:15 [c] S Nu 31:3 **24:13** [d] Mt 7:20 **24:14** [e] S 1Sa 17:43 [f] 1Sa 26:20 **24:15** [g] ver 12 [h] S Ge 16:5 [i] Ps 35:1,23; Isa 49:25 [j] Ps 26:1; 35:24; 43:1; 50:4; 54:1; 135:14 [k] Ps 119:134,154 **24:16** [l] 1Sa 26:17 **24:17** [m] Ge 38:26 [n] Mt 5:44 [o] S Ex 9:27 **24:18** [p] 1Sa 26:23 **24:19** [q] S Ru 2:12; S 2Ch 15:7 **24:20** [r] S 1Sa 20:31 [s] S 1Sa 13:14

24:21 [t] Ge 21:23; S 47:31; S 1Sa 18:3; 2Sa 21:1-9 [u] S 1Sa 20:14-15 **24:22** [v] 1Sa 23:29 **25:1** [w] 1Sa 28:3 [x] S Lev 10:6; Dt 34:8 [y] S 1Sa 7:17

24:6 *for he is the anointed of the LORD.* See v. 10; 26:9,11,16,23; 2Sa 1:14,16. Because Saul's royal office carried divine sanction by virtue of his anointing (see note on 9:16), David refuses to wrest the kingship from Saul by his own hand but leaves its disposition to the Lord who gave it (see vv. 12,15; 26:10).

24:11 *my father.* See also Saul's address to David as "my son" (v. 16). David uses this form of address either because (1) Saul was David's father-in-law (see 18:27) or because (2) the special relationship between father and son was at times used as a metaphor for an intimate relationship between king and subject (see notes on 2Sa 7:14; Ps 2:7; see also chart, p. 19).

24:14 *dead dog.* See note on 2Sa 9:8. *flea.* See note on 26:20.

24:16 *he wept aloud.* Saul experiences temporary remorse (see 26:21 and note) for his actions against David but quickly reverts to his former determination to kill him (see 26:2).

24:21 *not cut off my descendants.* See notes on 20:14–15.

24:22 *stronghold.* An inaccessible place (see note on 22:4). From previous experience David did not place any confidence in Saul's words of repentance.

25:1–44 David's dealings with Nabal (see notes on 23:1—26:25; 24:1—26:25). Nabal, the "fool" (see v. 25 and note), lived near Carmel, where Saul had erected a monument in his own honor (see 15:12 and note). The account of Nabal effectively serves the author's purpose in a number of ways: (1) Nabal's general character, his disdainful attitude toward David though David had guarded his flocks, and his sudden death at the Lord's hand all parallel Saul (whose "flock" David had also protected). Thus the author indirectly characterizes Saul as a fool (see 13:13; 26:21 and notes) and foreshadows his end. (2) David's vengeful attitude toward Nabal displays his natural tendency and highlights his restraint toward Saul, the Lord's anointed (this event is sandwiched between the two instances in which David spared Saul in spite of the urging of his men). (3) Abigail's prudent action prevents David from using his power as leader for personal vengeance (the very thing Saul was doing). In this way the Lord (who avenged his servant) keeps David's sword clean, teaching him a lesson he does not forget. (4) Abigail's confident acknowledgment of David's future accession to the throne foreshadows that event and even anticipates the Lord's commitment to establish David's house as a "lasting dynasty" (v. 28 [see note there]; cf. 2Sa 7:11–16). (5) Abigail's marriage to David provides him a wise and worthy wife, while Saul gives away David's wife Michal to another, illustrating how the Lord counters every move Saul makes against David.

25:1 The author begins the David-Nabal episode by noting David's loss of his chief protector in Israel (see 19:18–24) and ends it with a notation that David also loses his wife Michal, one of his protectors in the royal family itself (see 19:11–17). Meanwhile he obtains a wife whose wisdom rivals that of Ahithophel (see 2Sa 16:23). She is one of two wives who link him with the aristocracy of Judah. This account of how David obtained Nabal's wife serves as a foil to the later account of how David obtained the wife of Uriah the Hittite (2Sa 11). There it is David who misuses his royal power and acts the fool. *all Israel … mourned for him.* Samuel was recognized as a leader of national prominence who played a key role in the restructuring of the theocracy with the establishment of the monarchy (see chs. 8–12). The loss of his leadership was mourned much like that of other prominent figures in Israel's past history, including Jacob (Ge 50:10), Aaron (see Nu 20:29 and note) and Moses (Dt 34:8). *Ramah.* See 7:17 and note on 1:1.

Then David moved down into the Desert of Maon.[a] 2A certain man in Maon,[z] who had property there at Carmel, was very wealthy.[a] He had a thousand goats and three thousand sheep, which he was shearing[b] in Carmel. 3His name was Nabal and his wife's name was Abigail.[c] She was an intelligent and beautiful woman, but her husband, a Calebite,[d] was surly and mean in his dealings.

4While David was in the desert, he heard that Nabal was shearing sheep. 5So he sent ten young men and said to them, "Go up to Nabal at Carmel and greet him in my name. 6Say to him: 'Long life to you! Good health[e] to you and your household! And good health to all that is yours![f]

7" 'Now I hear that it is sheep-shearing time. When your shepherds were with us, we did not mistreat[g] them, and the whole time they were at Carmel nothing of theirs was missing. 8Ask your own servants and they will tell you. Therefore be favorable toward my young men, since we come at a festive time. Please give your servants and your son David whatever[h] you can find for them.' "

9When David's men arrived, they gave Nabal this message in David's name. Then they waited.

10Nabal answered David's servants, "Who[i] is this David? Who is this son of Jesse? Many servants are breaking away from their masters these days. 11Why should I take my bread[j] and water, and the meat I have slaughtered for my shearers, and give it to men coming from who knows where?"

12David's men turned around and went back. When they arrived, they reported every word. 13David said to his men[k], "Put on your swords!" So they put on their swords, and David put on his. About four hundred men went[l] up with David, while two hundred stayed with the supplies.[m]

14One of the servants told Nabal's wife Abigail: "David sent messengers from the desert to give our master his greetings,[n] but he hurled insults at them. 15Yet these men were very good to us. They did not mistreat[o] us, and the whole time we were out in the fields near them nothing was missing.[p] 16Night and day they were a wall[q] around us all the time we were herding our sheep near them. 17Now think it over and see what you can do, because disaster is hanging over our master and his whole household. He is such a wicked[r] man that no one can talk to him."

18Abigail lost no time. She took two hundred loaves of bread, two skins of wine, five dressed sheep, five seahs[b] of roasted grain,[s] a hundred cakes of raisins[t] and two hundred cakes of pressed figs, and loaded them on donkeys.[u] 19Then she told her servants, "Go on ahead;[v] I'll follow you." But she did not tell[w] her husband Nabal.

20As she came riding her donkey into a mountain ravine, there were David and his men descending toward her, and she met them. 21David had just said, "It's been useless—all my watching over this fellow's property in the desert so that nothing of his was missing.[x] He has paid[y] me back evil[z] for good. 22May God deal with David,[c] be it ever so severely,[a] if by morning I leave alive one male[b] of all who belong to him!"

23When Abigail saw David, she quickly got off her donkey and bowed down before David with her face to the ground.[c] 24She fell at his feet and said: "My lord, let the blame[d] be on me alone. Please let your servant speak to you; hear what your

25:2 [z]S Jos 15:55 [a]2Sa 19:32 [b]S Ge 31:19 **25:3** [c]Pr 31:10 [d]S Jos 14:13; S 15:13 **25:6** [e]Ps 122:7; Mt 10:12 [f]1Ch 12:18 **25:7** [g]ver 15 **25:8** [h]Ne 8:10 **25:10** [i]Jdg 9:28 **25:11** [j]Jdg 8:6 **25:13** [k]S 1Sa 22:2 [l]S 1Sa 21:10 [m]S Nu 31:27 **25:14** [n]1Sa 13:10 **25:15** [o]ver 7 [p]ver 21 **25:16** [q]Ex 14:22; Job 1:10; Ps 139:5 **25:17** [r]S Dt 13:13; S 1Sa 20:7 **25:18** [s]S Lev 23:14; S 1Sa 17:17 [t]1Ch 12:40 [u]S Ge 42:26; 2Sa 16:1; Isa 30:6 **25:19** [v]Ge 32:20 [w]ver 36 **25:21** [x]ver 15 [y]Ps 109:5 [z]S 1Sa 19:4 **25:22** [a]S Ru 1:17 [b]1Ki 14:10; 21:21; 2Ki 9:8 **25:23** [c]S Ge 19:1; S 1Sa 20:41 **25:24** [d]2Sa 14:9

[a] *1* Some Septuagint manuscripts; Hebrew *Paran*
[b] *18* That is, probably about a bushel (about 37 liters)
[c] *22* Some Septuagint manuscripts; Hebrew *with David's enemies*

25:2 In ancient times wealth often consisted primarily of livestock (see Ge 12:16; 13:2 and notes).

25:3 *intelligent and beautiful ... surly and mean.* The stark contrast between the foolish Nabal and the wise Abigail is played out through the rest of the chapter. *Calebite.* A descendant of Caleb (see Nu 14:24 and note), who settled at Hebron (see Jos 14:13) after the conquest of Canaan. Since Caleb's name can mean "dog," Nabal is subtly depicted as a dog as well as a fool. He would soon be a dead dog (see note on 2Sa 9:8), when the LORD would avenge his acts of contempt toward David. The hint is strong that, when the LORD avenges Saul's sins against David (see 24:12,15), the king will no longer pursue a dead dog (see 24:14) but will himself become one—a case of biting irony.

25:4 *shearing sheep.* A festive occasion (see v. 8; 2Sa 13:23–24 and note on 13:23).

25:8 *give ... whatever you can find for them.* David and his men ask for some consideration for their protection of Nabal's shepherds and flocks against pillage (see vv. 15–16,21).

25:10 *son of Jesse.* See note on 20:27,30–31.

25:17 *wicked man.* See note on Dt 13:13. *no one can talk to him.* In this way, too, Nabal is like Saul (cf., e.g., 20:27–33).

25:18 *She took ... bread ... wine ... sheep ... grain ... raisins ... figs.* A feast for a king. Cf. what Nabal had mentioned in v. 11, and cf. v. 36.

25:19 *did not tell her husband.* Cf. Michal's treatment of Saul (19:11–17).

25:22 *May God deal with David, be it ever so severely.* See note on 3:17. David invokes a curse on himself if he should fail to kill every male in Nabal's household and so obliterate Nabal's family. *one male.* Lit. "one who urinates against a wall," a not-so-subtle reference to Nabal's (the "dog"; see v. 3 and note) sons and servants as his pups.

25:24 *let the blame be on me alone.* That is, whatever blame may follow from David's granting her plea (see 2Sa 14:9 and note). Abigail begins her appeal to David on an apologetic note (she is not taking on herself the blame for Nabal's action) as she does again when she begins the second half of her appeal (v. 28). Contrast Nabal's high-handed treatment of David.

servant has to say. 25May my lord pay no
attention to that wicked man Nabal. He
is just like his name—his name is Fool[e], [f]
and folly goes with him. But as for me,
your servant, I did not see the men my
master sent.
26"Now since the LORD has kept you, my
master, from bloodshed[g] and from avenging[h] yourself with your own hands, as
surely as the LORD lives and as you live,
may your enemies and all who intend to
harm my master be like Nabal.[i] 27And let
this gift,[j] which your servant has brought
to my master, be given to the men who
follow you. 28Please forgive[k] your servant's offense, for the LORD will certainly make a lasting[l] dynasty for my master, because he fights the LORD's battles.[m]
Let no wrongdoing[n] be found in you as
long as you live. 29Even though someone
is pursuing you to take your life,[o] the life
of my master will be bound securely in
the bundle of the living by the LORD your
God. But the lives of your enemies he will
hurl[p] away as from the pocket of a sling.[q]
30When the LORD has done for my master
every good thing he promised concerning him and has appointed him leader[r]
over Israel, 31my master will not have on
his conscience the staggering burden of
needless bloodshed or of having avenged
himself. And when the LORD has brought
my master success, remember[s] your servant."[t]
32David said to Abigail, "Praise[u] be
to the LORD, the God of Israel, who has
sent you today to meet me. 33May you
be blessed for your good judgment and
for keeping me from bloodshed[v] this day
and from avenging myself with my own
hands. 34Otherwise, as surely as the LORD,
the God of Israel, lives, who has kept me
from harming you, if you had not come
quickly to meet me, not one male belonging to Nabal[w] would have been left alive
by daybreak."
35Then David accepted from her hand
what she had brought him and said, "Go
home in peace. I have heard your words
and granted[x] your request."
36When Abigail went to Nabal, he was
in the house holding a banquet like that
of a king. He was in high[y] spirits and
very drunk.[z] So she told[a] him nothing
until daybreak. 37Then in the morning,
when Nabal was sober, his wife told him
all these things, and his heart failed him
and he became like a stone.[b] 38About ten
days later, the LORD struck[c] Nabal and he
died.
39When David heard that Nabal was
dead, he said, "Praise be to the LORD, who
has upheld my cause against Nabal for
treating me with contempt. He has kept
his servant from doing wrong and has
brought Nabal's wrongdoing down on his
own head."
Then David sent word to Abigail, asking her to become his wife. 40His servants
went to Carmel and said to Abigail, "David has sent us to you to take you to become his wife."
41She bowed down with her face to the
ground and said, "Here is your maidservant, ready to serve you and wash the feet
of my master's servants." 42Abigail[d] quickly got on a donkey and, attended by her
five maids, went with David's messengers
and became his wife. 43David had also
married Ahinoam[e] of Jezreel, and they

25:25 [e] Pr 17:12 [f] Pr 12:16; 14:16; 20:3; Isa 32:5 **25:26** [g] ver 33 [h] Heb 10:30 [i] ver 34; 2Sa 18:32 **25:27** [j] S Ge 33:11 **25:28** [k] ver 24; 2Sa 14:9 [l] 2Sa 7:11,26 [m] 1Sa 18:17 [n] 1Sa 24:11 **25:29** [o] S 1Sa 20:1 [p] Jer 10:18; 22:26 [q] 1Sa 17:50; 2Sa 4:8 **25:30** [r] S 1Sa 12:12; S 13:14 **25:31** [s] S Ge 40:14 [t] 2Sa 3:10 **25:32** [u] S Ge 24:27 **25:33** [v] ver 26 **25:34** [w] S ver 26 **25:35** [x] S Ge 19:21 **25:36** [y] S Ru 3:7 [z] Pr 20:1; Ecc 10:17; Isa 5:11,22; 22:13; 28:7; 56:12; Hos 4:11 [a] ver 19 **25:37** [b] Ex 15:16 **25:38** [c] Dt 32:35; 1Sa 24:12; 26:10; 2Sa 6:7; 12:15 **25:42** [d] 2Sa 2:2; 3:3; 1Ch 3:1 **25:43** [e] 2Sa 3:2; 1Ch 3:1

25:25 *wicked man.* See v. 17 and note on Dt 13:13. *He is just like his name.* In ancient times one's name was believed to reflect one's nature and character.
25:26 *as surely as the LORD lives.* See note on 14:39,45.
25:28 *the LORD will certainly make a lasting dynasty.* While the idea that David was destined to become king in place of Saul may have spread among the general populace, Abigail's assessment of David contrasts sharply with that of her husband (see v. 10). *he fights the LORD's battles.* Abigail is familiar with David's victories over the Philistines, in which he sought to glorify the Lord rather than advance his own honor (see 17:26,45–47; 18:17). *Let no wrongdoing be found in you.* See v. 39. Abigail shows concern for the preservation of David's integrity in view of the office he was later to assume (see vv. 30–31).
25:29 *bound securely in the bundle of the living.* Using the figure of placing a valuable possession in a carefully wrapped package for safekeeping, Abigail assures David that the Lord will preserve his life in the midst of danger. *hurl away as from the pocket of a sling.* A word that soon comes true for Nabal after he becomes "like a stone" (v. 37).
25:30 *leader.* See note on 9:16.
25:31 *needless bloodshed.* See note on v. 28.
25:32–34 Cf. David's words in vv. 21–22 and note on v. 22. His words there and here bracket the account of his meeting with Abigail and highlight the crucial role of wise Abigail's actions.
25:32 *who has sent you.* David recognizes the providential leading of the Lord in his encounter with Abigail (see v. 39).
25:33 *your good judgment.* See v. 3 and note.
25:36 *holding a banquet.* See Pr 30:21–22. *like that of a king.* Another clue that the author is using Nabal as a subtle portrayal of Saul.
25:37 *when Nabal was sober.* Lit. "when the wine had gone out of Nabal"—containing a clever wordplay on Nabal's name: *Nabal* becomes an empty *nebel* (wineskin, as in v. 18). *became like a stone.* Perhaps he suffered a stroke—he who was without moral sensitivity (was a *nabal;* see v. 25 and note) became as senseless as a stone (see v. 29 and note).
25:42 *became his wife.* She who acknowledged the Lord's anointed came to share in his kingdom while her fool of a husband ended up a dead dog, a dead fool, an empty wineskin, a stone flung from a sling. He typifies Saul and all who reject the Lord's anointed.
25:43 *Ahinoam.* The mother of David's first son, Amnon (see 2Sa 3:2). *Jezreel.* Located near Carmel (see v. 2; Jos 15:55–56) and not to be confused with the northern town of the same name, where Israel camped against the Philistines (see 29:1,11) and where Ahab resided in later times (see 1Ki 18:45–46; 21:1).

both were his wives.[f] 44But Saul had given
his daughter Michal, David's wife, to Paltiel[a][g] son of Laish, who was from Gallim.[h]

David Again Spares Saul's Life

26 The Ziphites[i] went to Saul at Gibeah
and said, "Is not David hiding[j] on the
hill of Hakilah, which faces Jeshimon?[k]"
2So Saul went down to the Desert of
Ziph, with his three thousand chosen men
of Israel, to search[l] there for David. 3Saul
made his camp beside the road on the hill
of Hakilah[m] facing Jeshimon, but David
stayed in the desert. When he saw that
Saul had followed him there, 4he sent out
scouts and learned that Saul had definitely
arrived.[b]
5Then David set out and went to the
place where Saul had camped. He saw
where Saul and Abner[n] son of Ner, the
commander of the army, had lain down.
Saul was lying inside the camp, with the
army encamped around him.
6David then asked Ahimelech the Hittite[o] and Abishai[p] son of Zeruiah,[q] Joab's
brother, "Who will go down into the camp
with me to Saul?"
"I'll go with you," said Abishai.
7So David and Abishai went to the army
by night, and there was Saul, lying asleep
inside the camp with his spear stuck in
the ground near his head. Abner and the
soldiers were lying around him.
8Abishai said to David, "Today God has
delivered your enemy into your hands.
Now let me pin him to the ground with
one thrust of my spear; I won't strike him
twice."
9But David said to Abishai, "Don't destroy him! Who can lay a hand on the
LORD's anointed[r] and be guiltless?[s] 10As
surely as the LORD lives," he said, "the

25:43 [f]1Sa 27:3; 30:5; 2Sa 2:2
25:44 [g]2Sa 3:15 [h]Isa 10:30
26:1 [i]1Sa 23:19 [j]Ps 54 Title [k]1Sa 23:24
26:2 [l]1Sa 24:2
26:3 [m]1Sa 23:19
26:5 [n]1Sa 17:55
26:6 [o]S Ge 10:15 [p]2Sa 2:18; 10:10; 16:9; 18:2; 19:21; 23:18; 1Ch 11:20; 19:11 [q]1Ch 2:16
26:9 [r]ver 16; S Ge 26:11; S 1Sa 9:16; 2Sa 1:14; 19:21; La 4:20 [s]S 1Sa 24:5
26:10 [t]S Ge 16:5; S 1Sa 25:38; S Ro 12:19 [u]Dt 31:14; Ps 37:13 [v]1Sa 31:6; 2Sa 1:1
26:12 [w]S Jdg 4:21
26:17 [x]1Sa 24:16
26:18 [y]Job 13:23; Jer 37:18
26:19 [z]1Sa 24:9 [a]2Sa 16:11

LORD himself will strike[t] him; either his
time[u] will come and he will die,[v] or he
will go into battle and perish. 11But the
LORD forbid that I should lay a hand on
the LORD's anointed. Now get the spear
and water jug that are near his head, and
let's go."
12So David took the spear and water jug
near Saul's head, and they left. No one saw
or knew about it, nor did anyone wake up.
They were all sleeping, because the LORD
had put them into a deep sleep.[w]
13Then David crossed over to the other side and stood on top of the hill some
distance away; there was a wide space between them. 14He called out to the army
and to Abner son of Ner, "Aren't you going
to answer me, Abner?"
Abner replied, "Who are you who calls
to the king?"
15David said, "You're a man, aren't you?
And who is like you in Israel? Why didn't
you guard your lord the king? Someone
came to destroy your lord the king. 16What
you have done is not good. As surely as
the LORD lives, you and your men deserve
to die, because you did not guard your
master, the LORD's anointed. Look around
you. Where are the king's spear and water
jug that were near his head?"
17Saul recognized David's voice and
said, "Is that your voice,[x] David my son?"
David replied, "Yes it is, my lord the
king." 18And he added, "Why is my lord
pursuing his servant? What have I done,
and what wrong[y] am I guilty of? 19Now
let my lord the king listen[z] to his servant's
words. If the LORD has incited you against
me, then may he accept an offering.[a] If,

[a] 44 Hebrew *Palti,* a variant of *Paltiel* [b] 4 Or *had come to Nacon*

25:44 *Michal, David's wife.* See 18:27.
26:1–25 Saul is at the mercy of David while sleeping in the midst of his army encampment (see notes on 23:1—26:25; 24:1—26:25; 24:1-22).
26:1 *Ziphites.* See 23:19; see also note on 23:14. *Gibeah.* The site of Saul's royal residence (see 10:26 and note on 10:5).
26:2 *Desert of Ziph.* See 23:19; see also note on 23:14. *three thousand.* Apparently Saul's standing army (see 24:2).
26:5 *Abner.* Saul's cousin (see 20:25 and note). *lain down.* David arrived at Saul's camp during the night when the men were sleeping.
26:6 *Ahimelech the Hittite.* Not referred to elsewhere. Hittites had long resided in Canaan (see note on Ge 10:15; see also Ge 15:20; 23:3-20; Dt 7:1; 20:17). Another Hittite in David's service was Uriah (see 2Sa 11:6-7; 23:39). *Abishai son of Zeruiah, Joab's brother.* Zeruiah was David's sister (1Ch 2:16), so Abishai and Joab (and their brother Asahel, 2Sa 2:18) were David's nephews as well as trusted military leaders. Joab would serve as the commander of his army a long time.
26:8 *delivered your enemy into your hands.* See 24:4 and note. *pin him to the ground with ... my spear.* Just as Saul had tried to pin David to the wall with his spear (see 18:11; 19:10).
26:9,11 See note on 24:6.
26:10,16 *As surely as the LORD lives.* See note on 14:39,45.
26:12 *David took the spear and water jug.* In this way he sought to prove again to Saul that he did not seek his life. But he also showed Saul that God had given him the power to take away the spear with which Saul had often tried to kill him and the water jug on which Saul's very life depended in the hot and dry Desert of Ziph.
26:19 *may he accept an offering.* David knows no reason why God should be angry with him; but if for some reason God is behind Saul's determined effort to kill him, David appeals for God to accept an offering of appeasement (cf. 16:5)—in any event, to let the matter be settled between David and God without Saul's involvement. *may they be cursed before the LORD!* David commits any such men to the judgment of God. *the LORD's inheritance.* See note on 10:1. David appeals to Saul's conscience by describing his present exclusion from the fellowship of God's people and from living at peace in the Lord's land. *Go, serve other gods.* In their view, to be expelled from the Lord's land was to be separated from the Lord's sanctuary (an OT form of excommunication) and left to serve the gods of whatever land one may settle in (see Jos 22:24-27 and note on 1Ki 5:7).

however, men have done it, may they be
cursed before the LORD! They have now
driven me from my share in the LORD's inheritance[b] and have said, 'Go, serve other
gods.'[c] 20Now do not let my blood[d] fall to
the ground far from the presence of the
LORD. The king of Israel has come out to
look for a flea[e]—as one hunts a partridge
in the mountains.[f]"
21Then Saul said, "I have sinned.[g] Come
back, David my son. Because you considered my life precious[h] today, I will not try
to harm you again. Surely I have acted like
a fool and have erred greatly."
22"Here is the king's spear," David answered. "Let one of your young men come
over and get it. 23The LORD rewards[i] every man for his righteousness[j] and faithfulness. The LORD delivered[k] you into my
hands today, but I would not lay a hand
on the LORD's anointed. 24As surely as I
valued your life today, so may the LORD
value my life and deliver[l] me from all
trouble."

26:19 [b] Dt 20:16; 32:9; 2Sa 14:16; 20:19; 21:3 [c] S Dt 4:28; S 11:28
26:20 [d] S 1Sa 24:11 [e] 1Sa 24:14 [f] Jer 4:29; 16:16; Am 9:3
26:21 [g] S Ex 9:27 [h] Ps 72:14
26:23 [i] S Ge 16:5; S Ru 2:12; Ps 62:12 [j] 2Sa 22:21,25; Ps 7:8; 18:20,24 [k] 1Sa 24:18
26:24 [l] Ps 54:7
26:25 [m] S Ru 2:12
27:2 [n] 1Sa 30:9; 2Sa 2:3 [o] S 1Sa 21:10 [p] 1Ki 2:39
27:3 [q] S 1Sa 25:43

25Then Saul said to David, "May you be
blessed,[m] my son David; you will do great
things and surely triumph."
So David went on his way, and Saul returned home.

David Among the Philistines

27 But David thought to himself, "One
of these days I will be destroyed by
the hand of Saul. The best thing I can do
is to escape to the land of the Philistines.
Then Saul will give up searching for me
anywhere in Israel, and I will slip out of
his hand."
2So David and the six hundred men[n]
with him left and went[o] over to Achish[p]
son of Maoch king of Gath. 3David and
his men settled in Gath with Achish. Each
man had his family with him, and David
had his two wives:[q] Ahinoam of Jezreel
and Abigail of Carmel, the widow of Nabal. 4When Saul was told that David had
fled to Gath, he no longer searched for
him.

26:20 *look for a flea.* See 24:14. David suggests that Saul is making a fool of himself in his fanatical pursuit of an innocent and undesigning man.

26:21 *I have sinned.* See 24:17 and note on 24:16. *I have acted like a fool.* Saul confesses that his behavior has been not only unwise but also ungodly (see notes on 13:13; 25:1–44).

26:23 *I would not lay a hand on the LORD's anointed.* See v. 9 and note on 24:6.

26:25 *you will … triumph.* Saul makes a veiled reference to his own conviction that David will replace him as king (see 24:20).

27:1—31:13 David's flight to Philistia and Saul's final defeat by the Philistines—while David is engaged in a campaign against the Amalekites.

27:1 *I will be destroyed by the hand of Saul.* Under the pressure of Saul's superior forces David feels compelled to seek security outside Israel's borders. *land of the Philistines.* For the second time David seeks refuge in Philistia (see 21:10–15).

27:2 *Achish … king of Gath.* See 21:10 and note. In contrast to David's previous excursion into Philistia, Achish is now ready to receive him because he has become known as a formidable adversary of Saul. Moreover, to offer sanctuary under the circumstances would obligate David and his men to serve at his call in any military venture (see 28:1 and note).

27:3 *Ahinoam.* See note on 25:43. *Abigail.* See 25:39–42 and note on 25:1–44.

27:4 *he no longer searched for him.* Saul did not have sufficient military strength to make incursions into Philistine territory,

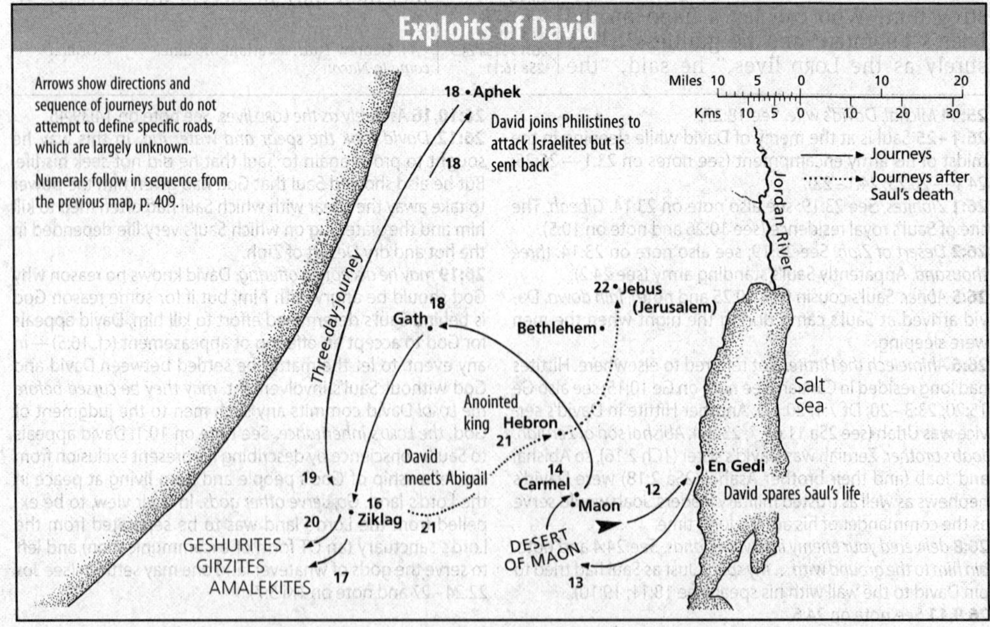

5Then David said to Achish, "If I have
found favor in your eyes, let a place be assigned to me in one of the country towns,
that I may live there. Why should your servant live in the royal city with you?"
6So on that day Achish gave him Ziklag,[r]
and it has belonged to the kings of Judah
ever since. 7David lived[s] in Philistine territory a year and four months.
8Now David and his men went up and
raided the Geshurites,[t] the Girzites and the
Amalekites.[u] (From ancient times these
peoples had lived in the land extending
to Shur[v] and Egypt.) 9Whenever David attacked an area, he did not leave a man or
woman alive,[w] but took sheep and cattle,
donkeys and camels, and clothes. Then he
returned to Achish.
10When Achish asked, "Where did
you go raiding today?" David would say,
"Against the Negev of Judah" or "Against
the Negev of Jerahmeel[x]" or "Against the
Negev of the Kenites.[y]" 11He did not leave
a man or woman alive to be brought to
Gath, for he thought, "They might inform
on us and say, 'This is what David did.'"
And such was his practice as long as he
lived in Philistine territory. 12Achish trusted David and said to himself, "He has become so odious[z] to his people, the Israelites, that he will be my servant forever.[a]"

Saul and the Witch of Endor

28 In those days the Philistines gathered[b] their forces to fight against
Israel. Achish said to David, "You must
understand that you and your men will
accompany me in the army."
2David said, "Then you will see for
yourself what your servant can do."
Achish replied, "Very well, I will make
you my bodyguard[c] for life."
3Now Samuel was dead,[d] and all Israel had mourned for him and buried him
in his own town of Ramah.[e] Saul had expelled[f] the mediums and spiritists[g] from
the land.
4The Philistines assembled and came
and set up camp at Shunem,[h] while Saul
gathered all the Israelites and set up camp
at Gilboa.[i] 5When Saul saw the Philistine
army, he was afraid; terror[j] filled his heart.
6He inquired[k] of the LORD, but the LORD
did not answer him by dreams[l] or Urim[m]
or prophets.[n] 7Saul then said to his attendants, "Find me a woman who is a medium,[o] so I may go and inquire of her."
"There is one in Endor,[p]" they said.

27:6 [r]Jos 15:31; 19:5; 1Sa 30:1; 1Ch 12:20; Ne 11:28 **27:7** [s]1Sa 29:3 **27:8** [t]S Jos 12:5 [u]S Ex 17:14; S 1Sa 14:48; 30:1; 2Sa 1:8; 8:12 [v]S Ge 16:7 **27:9** [w]S 1Sa 15:3 **27:10** [x]1Sa 30:29 [y]Jdg 1:16 **27:12** [z]S Ge 34:30 [a]1Sa 29:6 **28:1** [b]1Sa 29:1 **28:2** [c]1Sa 29:2 **28:3** [d]1Sa 25:1 [e]S 1Sa 7:17 [f]ver 9 [g]S Ex 22:18 **28:4** [h]S Jos 19:18 [i]1Sa 31:1,3; 2Sa 1:6,21; 21:12 **28:5** [j]S Ex 19:16 **28:6** [k]S 1Sa 8:18; 14:37 [l]S Dt 13:3 [m]S Ex 28:30; S Lev 8:8 [n]Eze 20:3; Am 8:11; Mic 3:7 **28:7** [o]1Ch 10:13; Ac 16:16 [p]Jos 17:11; Ps 83:10

and with David out of the country he no longer faced an internal threat to his throne.

27:5 *in one of the country towns.* David desired more independence and freedom of movement than was possible while residing under the very eyes of the king of Gath. *Why should your servant live in the royal city with you?* David implies that he is not worthy of this honor.

27:6 *Ziklag.* Location unknown, but it is included in a list of towns in southern Judah (see Jos 15:31 and map, p. 418). It was given to the tribe of Simeon (see Jos 19:1–5) and was presumably occupied by them (cf. Jdg 1:17–18), only to be lost to the Philistines at a later, undisclosed time. *it has belonged to the kings of Judah ever since.* As royal property.

27:7 *David lived in Philistine territory a year and four months.* It was not until after the death of Saul that David moved his residence from Ziklag (see 2Sa 1:1; 2:1–3 and note on 2:1) to Hebron.

27:8 *Geshurites.* A people residing in the area south of Philistia who were not defeated by the Israelites at the time of the conquest (see Jos 13:1–3) and who are to be distinguished from the Geshurites residing in the north near the upper Jordan in Aram (see 2Sa 3:3 and note; 13:37–38; Dt 3:14 and note; Jos 12:5). *Girzites.* Not mentioned elsewhere in the OT. *Amalekites.* See note on 15:2. *Shur.* See note on 15:7.

27:9 *he did not leave a man or woman alive.* David's reason for this is given in v. 11; his action conformed to that of Joshua in the conquest of Canaan (see, e.g., Jos 6:21 and note on 6:17).

27:10 *Negev of Judah.* Negev in Hebrew means "dry" and designates a large area from Beersheba to the highlands of the Sinai peninsula. *Jerahmeel.* The Jerahmeelites were descendants of Judah through Hezron (see 1Ch 2:9,25 and note on 2:25–33). *Kenites.* See note on 15:6.

27:12 *Achish trusted David.* David led Achish to believe that he was raiding outposts of Israelite territory when in actuality he was attacking the Geshurites, Girzites and Amalekites (see v. 8 and map, p. 418).

28:1 *accompany me in the army.* In the ancient Near East, to accept sanctuary in a country involved obligations of military service (see note on 27:2).

28:2 *you will see for yourself what your servant can do.* Perhaps an ambiguous answer. *I will make you my bodyguard.* Very likely this was conditional on David's proof of his loyalty and effectiveness in the projected campaign. Later, David would have a personal guard made up largely of Philistines (see 2Sa 15:18 and note).

28:3 *Now Samuel was dead.* See 25:1 and note. Saul could not turn to him, even in desperation. *expelled ... from the land.* Possibly a euphemism for "put to death," in agreement with Pentateuchal law (see vv. 9,21). *mediums and spiritists.* See Lev 19:31; 20:6,27 and note on 20:6; Dt 18:11 and note on 18:9.

28:4 *Shunem.* The Philistines assembled their forces far to the north, along the plain of Jezreel in the territory of Issachar (see Jos 19:18). *Gilboa.* A range of mountains east of the plain of Jezreel (see map, p. 342).

28:5 *terror filled his heart.* Because he was estranged from the Lord and was not performing his role as the true theocratic king (see note on 17:11).

28:6 *He inquired of the LORD.* Presumably through the agency of a priest. Saul seems to sense disaster in the approaching battle and seeks divine revelation concerning its outcome. *dreams.* Direct personal revelation (see Nu 12:6 and note on 12:6–8). *Urim.* Revelation through the priest (see note on 2:28). Since the authentic ephod and its Urim were with Abiathar, who was aligned with David (see 23:2,6,9), either Saul had fabricated another ephod for his use or the author used a conventional statement including the three visual forms of revelation to underscore his point. *prophets.* David had a prophet (Gad, 22:5), but after Samuel's alienation from Saul (15:35) no prophet served Saul.

28:7 *Find me a woman who is a medium.* In his desperation Saul turns to a pagan practice that he himself had previously outlawed (v. 3; see note there) in accordance with the Mosaic law. *Endor.* Located about six miles northwest of Shunem (see v. 4; Jos 17:11).

[8]So Saul disguised[q] himself, putting on other clothes, and at night he and two men went to the woman. "Consult[r] a spirit for me," he said, "and bring up for me the one I name."

[9]But the woman said to him, "Surely you know what Saul has done. He has cut off[s] the mediums and spiritists from the land. Why have you set a trap[t] for my life to bring about my death?"

[10]Saul swore to her by the LORD, "As surely as the LORD lives, you will not be punished for this."

[11]Then the woman asked, "Whom shall I bring up for you?"

"Bring up Samuel," he said.

[12]When the woman saw Samuel, she cried out at the top of her voice and said to Saul, "Why have you deceived me?[u] You are Saul!"

[13]The king said to her, "Don't be afraid. What do you see?"

The woman said, "I see a spirit[a] coming up out of the ground."[v]

[14]"What does he look like?" he asked.

"An old man wearing a robe[w] is coming up," she said.

Then Saul knew it was Samuel, and he bowed down and prostrated himself with his face to the ground.

[15]Samuel said to Saul, "Why have you disturbed me by bringing me up?"

"I am in great distress," Saul said. "The Philistines are fighting against me, and God has turned[x] away from me. He no longer answers[y] me, either by prophets or by dreams.[z] So I have called on you to tell me what to do."

[16]Samuel said, "Why do you consult me, now that the LORD has turned away from you and become your enemy? [17]The LORD has done what he predicted through me. The LORD has torn[a] the kingdom out of your hands and given it to one of your neighbors—to David. [18]Because you did not obey[b] the LORD or carry out his fierce wrath[c] against the Amalekites,[d] the LORD has done this to you today. [19]The LORD will hand over both Israel and you to the Philistines, and tomorrow you and your sons[e] will be with me. The LORD will also hand over the army of Israel to the Philistines."

[20]Immediately Saul fell full length on the ground, filled with fear because of Samuel's words. His strength was gone, for he had eaten nothing all that day and night.

[21]When the woman came to Saul and saw that he was greatly shaken, she said, "Look, your maidservant has obeyed you. I took my life[f] in my hands and did what you told me to do. [22]Now please listen to your servant and let me give you some food so you may eat and have the strength to go on your way."

[23]He refused[g] and said, "I will not eat."

But his men joined the woman in urging him, and he listened to them. He got up from the ground and sat on the couch.

[24]The woman had a fattened calf[h] at the house, which she butchered at once. She took some flour, kneaded it and baked bread without yeast. [25]Then she set it before Saul and his men, and they ate. That same night they got up and left.

Achish Sends David Back to Ziklag

29 The Philistines gathered[i] all their forces at Aphek,[j] and Israel camped by the spring in Jezreel.[k] [2]As the Philistine rulers marched with their units of hundreds and thousands, David and his men were marching at the rear[l] with Achish. [3]The commanders of the Philistines asked, "What about these Hebrews?"

[a] *13* Or *see spirits*; or *see gods*

28:8 [q] 1Ki 22:30; 2Ch 18:29; 35:22 [r] 2Ki 1:3; Isa 8:19
28:9 [s] ver 3 [t] Job 18:10; Ps 31:4; 69:22; Isa 8:14
28:12 [u] S Ge 27:36; 1Ki 14:6
28:13 [v] ver 15; S Lev 19:31; 2Ch 33:6
28:14 [w] 1Sa 15:27
28:15 [x] S Jdg 16:20 [y] S 1Sa 14:37 [z] S Dt 13:3
28:17 [a] 1Sa 15:28
28:18 [b] 1Sa 15:20 [c] S Dt 9:8; S 1Sa 15:3 [d] S Ge 14:7; S 1Sa 14:48
28:19 [e] 1Sa 31:2; 1Ch 8:33
28:21 [f] S Jdg 9:17; S 12:3
28:23 [g] 1Ki 21:4
28:24 [h] S Ge 18:7
29:1 [i] 1Sa 28:1 [j] S 1Sa 4:1 [k] Jos 17:16; 1Ki 18:45; 21:1,23; 2Ki 9:30; Jer 50:5; Hos 1:4,5,11; 2:22
29:2 [l] 1Sa 28:2

28:9 *Why have you set a trap for my life...?* The woman is very cautious about practicing her trade with strangers lest she be betrayed to Saul (see note on v. 3).

28:10 *As surely as the LORD lives.* See note on 14:39,45.

28:12 *When the woman saw Samuel.* The episode has been understood in many different ways, among them the following: (1) God permitted the spirit of Samuel to appear to the woman. (2) The woman had contact with an evil spirit in the form of Samuel by whom she was deceived and controlled. (3) By using parapsychological powers such as telepathy or clairvoyance, the woman was able to discern Saul's thoughts and picture Samuel in her own mind. Whatever the explanation of this mysterious affair, the medium was used in some way to convey to Saul that the impending battle would bring death, would dash his hopes for a dynasty and would conclude his reign with a devastating defeat of Israel that would leave the nation at the mercy of the Philistines, the very people against whom he had struggled all his years as king. And this would come, as Samuel had previously announced (15:26,28), because of his unfaithfulness to the Lord. *she cried out... You are Saul!* By whatever means, the medium suddenly becomes aware that she is dealing with Saul.

28:14 *An old man wearing a robe.* Saul remembers Samuel as customarily dressed in this apparel (see 15:27).

28:17 *torn the kingdom out of your hands and given it ... to David.* See 15:28 and note. In an act of desperation Saul had torn Samuel's robe, an act symbolizing the Lord's snatching the kingdom away from Saul (see 15:27–28). David had cut off a corner of Saul's robe, with similar symbolic meaning (see 24:4 and note).

28:18 See 15:17–26.

28:19 *tomorrow you and your sons will be with me.* In the realm of the dead—Saul's doom is sealed (see 31:6).

28:21 *When the woman came to Saul.* This statement suggests that the woman removed herself from the direct view of Saul while she gave her oracles.

29:1 *The Philistines gathered all their forces.* The narrative flow broken at 28:2 is resumed. *Aphek.* A place in the vicinity of Shunem (28:4), to be distinguished from another place of the same name referred to in 4:1 (see note there; see also 1Ki 20:26,30 and note on 20:26; 2Ki 13:17).

29:2 *Philistine rulers.* See note on 5:8.

29:3 *I have found no fault in him.* David's tactics described in 27:10–12 (see note on 27:12) were highly successful.

Achish replied, "Is this not David,[m] who
was an officer of Saul king of Israel? He
has already been with me for over a year,[n]
and from the day he left Saul until now, I
have found no fault in him."
4But the Philistine commanders were
angry with him and said, "Send[o] the man
back, that he may return to the place you
assigned him. He must not go with us into
battle, or he will turn[p] against us during
the fighting. How better could he regain
his master's favor than by taking the heads
of our own men? 5Isn't this the David they
sang about in their dances:

" 'Saul has slain his thousands,
and David his tens of thousands'?"[q]

6So Achish called David and said to
him, "As surely as the LORD lives, you
have been reliable, and I would be pleased
to have you serve with me in the army.
From the day[r] you came to me until now,
I have found no fault in you, but the rulers[s] don't approve of you. 7Turn back and
go in peace; do nothing to displease the
Philistine rulers."
8"But what have I done?" asked David. "What have you found against your
servant from the day I came to you until
now? Why can't I go and fight against the
enemies of my lord the king?"
9Achish answered, "I know that you
have been as pleasing in my eyes as an
angel[t] of God; nevertheless, the Philistine
commanders[u] have said, 'He must not go
up with us into battle.' 10Now get up early, along with your master's servants who
have come with you, and leave[v] in the
morning as soon as it is light."
11So David and his men got up early in
the morning to go back to the land of the
Philistines, and the Philistines went up to
Jezreel.

David Destroys the Amalekites

30 David and his men reached Ziklag[w]
on the third day. Now the Amalekites[x] had raided the Negev and Ziklag.
They had attacked Ziklag and burned[y] it,
2and had taken captive the women and all
who were in it, both young and old. They
killed none of them, but carried them off
as they went on their way.
3When David and his men came to Ziklag, they found it destroyed by fire and
their wives and sons and daughters tak-
en captive.[z] 4So David and his men wept[a]
aloud until they had no strength left to
weep. 5David's two wives[b] had been captured—Ahinoam of Jezreel and Abigail,
the widow of Nabal of Carmel. 6David was
greatly distressed because the men were
talking of stoning[c] him; each one was
bitter[d] in spirit because of his sons and
daughters. But David found strength[e] in
the LORD his God.
7Then David said to Abiathar[f] the
priest, the son of Ahimelech, "Bring me
the ephod.[g]" Abiathar brought it to him,
8and David inquired[h] of the LORD, "Shall I
pursue this raiding party? Will I overtake
them?"
"Pursue them," he answered. "You will
certainly overtake them and succeed[i] in
the rescue.[j]"
9David and the six hundred men[k] with
him came to the Besor Ravine, where
some stayed behind, 10for two hundred
men were too exhausted[l] to cross the ravine. But David and four hundred men
continued the pursuit.
11They found an Egyptian in a field and
brought him to David. They gave him water to drink and food to eat— 12part of a
cake of pressed figs and two cakes of raisins. He ate and was revived,[m] for he had
not eaten any food or drunk any water for
three days and three nights.
13David asked him, "To whom do you
belong, and where do you come from?"
He said, "I am an Egyptian, the slave of
an Amalekite.[n] My master abandoned me
when I became ill three days ago. 14We
raided the Negev of the Kerethites[o] and the

29:3 [m] 1Ch 12:19 [n] 1Sa 27:7
29:4 [o] 1Ch 12:19 [p] 1Sa 14:21
29:5 [q] S 1Sa 18:7
29:6 [r] 1Sa 27:8-12 [s] ver 3
29:9 [t] 2Sa 14:17,20; 19:27 [u] ver 4
29:10 [v] 1Ch 12:19
30:1 [w] S 1Sa 27:6 [x] S 1Sa 27:8 [y] ver 14
30:3 [z] S Ge 31:26
30:4 [a] S Ge 27:38
30:5 [b] S 1Sa 25:43
30:6 [c] S Ex 17:4; Jn 8:59 [d] S Ru 1:13 [e] S 1Sa 23:16; Ro 4:20
30:7 [f] S 1Sa 22:20 [g] S 1Sa 2:28
30:8 [h] S 1Sa 23:2 [i] S Ge 14:16 [j] S Ex 2:17
30:9 [k] S 1Sa 27:2
30:10 [l] ver 21
30:12 [m] S Jdg 15:19
30:13 [n] S 1Sa 14:48
30:14 [o] 2Sa 8:18; 15:18; 20:7,23; 1Ki 1:38,44; 1Ch 18:17; Eze 25:16; Zep 2:5

29:4 *the place you assigned him.* Ziklag (see 27:6 and note). *or he will turn against us during the fighting.* The Philistines had experienced just such a reversal on a previous occasion (see 14:21). *taking the heads.* As trophies of victory (see 17:51; see also 5:4; 31:9 and notes).
29:5 See 21:11 and note on 18:7.
29:6 *As surely as the LORD lives.* See note on 14:39,45. Achish swears by the God of Israel apparently as a means of proving his sincerity to David.
29:8 *But what have I done?* David pretends disappointment in order to keep intact his strategy of deception. In reality this turn of events rescued David from a serious dilemma. *Why can't I go and fight against the enemies of my lord the king?* David again uses an ambiguous statement (see 28:2). To whom was he referring as "my lord the king"—Achish or Saul or the Lord?
29:9 *as an angel of God.* A common simile (see 2Sa 14:17 and note).
29:11 *Jezreel.* The place of Israel's camp (see v. 1).
30:1—31:13 While Saul goes to his death at the hands of the Philistines, David is drawn into and pursues the Lord's continuing war with the Amalekites (see 15:2–3 and notes).
30:1 *Ziklag.* See note on 27:6. *Amalekites.* See 27:8 and note on 15:2; see also note on Ge 14:7. The absence of David and his warriors gave the Amalekites opportunity for revenge. *Negev.* See note on 27:10.
30:5 *Ahinoam.* See note on 25:43. *Abigail.* See 25:42.
30:6 *David found strength in the LORD.* As he had throughout his life (see 17:37 and note).
30:7 *Abiathar the priest.* See note on 22:20. *ephod.* See note on 2:28.
30:14 *Negev.* See note on 27:10. *Kerethites.* Along with the Pelethites, they later contributed contingents of professional warriors to David's private army (see 2Sa 8:18 and note; 15:18; 20:7; 1Ki 1:38). The name may indicate that they originally came from the island of Crete (see Jer 47:4 and note).

territory belonging to Judah and the Negev of Caleb.[p] And we burned[q] Ziklag."

15David asked him, "Can you lead me down to this raiding party?"

He answered, "Swear to me before God that you will not kill me or hand me over to my master,[r] and I will take you down to them."

16He led David down, and there they were, scattered over the countryside, eating, drinking and reveling[s] because of the great amount of plunder[t] they had taken from the land of the Philistines and from Judah. 17David fought[u] them from dusk until the evening of the next day, and none of them got away, except four hundred young men who rode off on camels and fled.[v] 18David recovered[w] everything the Amalekites had taken, including his two wives. 19Nothing was missing: young or old, boy or girl, plunder or anything else they had taken. David brought everything back. 20He took all the flocks and herds, and his men drove them ahead of the other livestock, saying, "This is David's plunder."

21Then David came to the two hundred men who had been too exhausted[x] to follow him and who were left behind at the Besor Ravine. They came out to meet David and the people with him. As David and his men approached, he greeted them. 22But all the evil men and troublemakers among David's followers said, "Because they did not go out with us, we will not share with them the plunder we recovered. However, each man may take his wife and children and go."

23David replied, "No, my brothers, you must not do that with what the LORD has given us. He has protected us and handed over to us the forces that came against us. 24Who will listen to what you say? The share of the man who stayed with the supplies is to be the same as that of him who went down to the battle. All will share alike.[y]" 25David made this a statute and ordinance for Israel from that day to this.

26When David arrived in Ziklag, he sent some of the plunder to the elders of Judah, who were his friends, saying, "Here is a present[z] for you from the plunder of the LORD's enemies."

27He sent it to those who were in Bethel,[a] Ramoth[b] Negev and Jattir;[c] 28to those in Aroer,[d] Siphmoth,[e] Eshtemoa[f] 29and Racal; to those in the towns of the Jerahmeelites[g] and the Kenites;[h] 30to those in Hormah,[i] Bor Ashan,[j] Athach 31and Hebron;[k] and to those in all the other places where David and his men had roamed.

30:14 [p] S Jos 14:13; S 15:13 [q] ver 1 **30:15** [r] Dt 23:15 **30:16** [s] Lk 12:19 [t] S ver 17; S Jos 22:8 **30:17** [u] ver 16; 1Sa 11:11; 2Sa 1:1 [v] 2Sa 1:8 **30:18** [w] S Ge 14:16 **30:21** [x] ver 10 **30:24** [y] S Nu 31:27; S Jdg 5:30 **30:26** [z] S Ge 33:11 **30:27** [a] S Jos 7:2 [b] S Jos 10:40 [c] S Jos 15:48 **30:28** [d] S Nu 32:34; S Jos 13:16 [e] 1Ch 27:27 [f] S Jos 15:50 **30:29** [g] 1Sa 27:10 [h] S 1Sa 15:6 **30:30** [i] S Nu 14:45; S 21:3 [j] S Jos 15:42 **30:31** [k] Nu 13:22; S Jos 10:36; 2Sa 2:1,4 **31:1** [l] S 1Sa 28:4 **31:2** [m] S 1Sa 28:19 [n] S 1Sa 18:1 [o] S 1Sa 14:49 **31:3** [p] S 1Sa 28:4 **31:4** [q] S Jdg 9:54 [r] S Ge 34:14; S 1Sa 14:6 **31:6** [s] S 1Sa 26:10

Saul Takes His Life

31:1-13pp — 2Sa 1:4-12; 1Ch 10:1-12

31 Now the Philistines fought against Israel; the Israelites fled before them, and many fell slain on Mount Gilboa.[l] 2The Philistines pressed hard after Saul and his sons,[m] and they killed his sons Jonathan,[n] Abinadab and Malki-Shua.[o] 3The fighting grew fierce around Saul, and when the archers overtook him, they wounded[p] him critically.

4Saul said to his armor-bearer, "Draw your sword and run me through,[q] or these uncircumcised[r] fellows will come and run me through and abuse me."

But his armor-bearer was terrified and would not do it; so Saul took his own sword and fell on it. 5When the armor-bearer saw that Saul was dead, he too fell on his sword and died with him. 6So Saul and his three sons and his armor-bearer and all his men died[s] together that same day.

7When the Israelites along the valley and those across the Jordan saw that the Israelite army had fled and that Saul and his sons had died, they abandoned their towns and fled. And the Philistines came and occupied them.

30:14 *Negev of Caleb.* The area south of Hebron (see Jos 14:13).
30:17 *camels.* The mount of choice for the Amalekites and other eastern peoples (see Jdg 6:3,5 and note on 6:5).
30:22 *troublemakers.* See note on Dt 13:13.
30:23 *what the LORD has given us.* See 25:28 and note. David gently but firmly rejects the idea that their victory is to be attributed to their own prowess. Because the Lord gave the victory, no segment of David's men could claim any greater right to the spoils than any other.
30:24 *All will share alike.* Cf. Ex 16:18 and note.
30:26 *elders of Judah, who were his friends.* David sent the plunder as an expression of gratitude to those who had assisted him during his flight from Saul (see v. 31), thus preparing the way for his later elevation to kingship in Judah (see 2Sa 2:1–7 and notes).
30:29 *Jerahmeelites.* See note on 27:10. *Kenites.* See note on 15:6.
30:31 *Hebron.* The most important city in the central part of Judah. The other locations mentioned are to the southwest and southeast of Hebron.
31:1,8 *Mount Gilboa.* A range of hills (see 2Sa 1:21) at the southeast end of the Plain of Jezreel and at the head of the valley that leads down to Beth Shan (see map, p. 342). It is referred to elsewhere in the OT only as the place where Saul died (see 2Sa 1:6,21; 21:12).
31:2 *Jonathan, Abinadab and Malki-Shua.* See note on 14:49. The surviving son, Ish-Bosheth or Esh-Baal (see 1Ch 8:33 and note; 9:39), was afterward promoted by Abner, who somehow survived the battle, to succeed his father as king (see 2Sa 2:8–9 and notes).
31:4 *uncircumcised fellows.* See 14:6 and note. *abuse me.* A practice that was not uncommon; previously the Philistines had mutilated and humiliated Samson after his capture (see Jdg 16:21–25). *took his own sword and fell on it.* The culmination of a long process of self-destruction.
31:6 *all his men.* Those who had served around him in his administration (but see note on v. 2).

[8]The next day, when the Philistines[t]
came to strip the dead, they found Saul
and his three sons fallen on Mount Gilboa.
[9]They cut off his head and stripped off his
armor, and they sent messengers throughout the land of the Philistines to proclaim
the news[u] in the temple of their idols and
among their people.[v] [10]They put his armor
in the temple of the Ashtoreths[w] and fastened his body to the wall of Beth Shan.[x]
[11]When the people of Jabesh Gilead[y]
heard of what the Philistines had done
to Saul, [12]all their valiant men[z] journeyed
through the night to Beth Shan. They took
down the bodies of Saul and his sons from
the wall of Beth Shan and went to Jabesh,
where they burned[a] them. [13]Then they
took their bones[b] and buried them under
a tamarisk[c] tree at Jabesh, and they fasted[d] seven days.[e]

31:8 [t]2Sa 1:20 **31:9** [u]2Sa 1:20; 4:4 [v]S Jdg 16:24 **31:10** [w]S Jdg 2:12-13; S 1Sa 7:3 [x]S Jos 17:11 **31:11** [y]S Jdg 21:8; S 1Sa 11:1 **31:12** [z]Ps 76:5 [a]S Ge 38:24; Am 6:10 **31:13** [b]2Sa 21:12-14 [c]S Ge 21:33 [d]2Sa 3:35; 12:19-23 [e]S Ge 50:10

31:9 *They cut off his head.* David had done the same to Goliath (see 17:51). *sent messengers throughout the land.* Probably bearing Saul's head and armor as proof and trophies of their victory (see 5:4 and note).
31:10 *They put his armor in the temple.* Symbolic of ascribing the victory to the Philistine gods. *Ashtoreths.* See note on 7:3. *Beth Shan.* See note on Jos 17:11.
31:11 *Jabesh Gilead.* See note on 11:1.
31:12 *They took down the bodies of Saul and his sons.* The men of Jabesh Gilead had not forgotten how Saul had come to their defense when they were threatened by the Ammonites (see 11:1–11). *burned them.* Cremation was not customary in ancient Israel and here appears to have been done to prevent any further abuse of the bodies of Saul and his sons by the Philistines.
31:13 *took their bones and buried them.* David later had their remains removed from Jabesh and placed in the family burial grounds of Zela in Benjamin (see 2Sa 21:12–14 and note). *fasted seven days.* As an indication of their mourning for Saul (cf. 2Sa 1:12 and note; 3:35; 12:16,21–23).

2 Samuel

I N T R O D U C T I O N

Title

1 and 2 Samuel were originally one book (see Introduction to 1 Samuel: Title).

Literary Features, Authorship and Date

See Introduction to 1 Samuel: Literary Features, Authorship and Date.

Contents and Theme: Kingship and Covenant

2 Samuel depicts David as a true (though imperfect) representative of the ideal theocratic king. David was initially acclaimed king at Hebron by the tribe of Judah (chs. 1 – 4), and subsequently was accepted by the remaining tribes after the murder of Ish-Bosheth, one of Saul's surviving sons (5:1 – 5). David's leadership was decisive and effective. He captured Jerusalem from the Jebusites and made it his royal city and residence (5:6 – 13). Shortly afterward he brought the ark of the Lord from the house of Abinadab to Jerusalem, publicly acknowledging the Lord's kingship and rule over himself and the nation (ch. 6; Ps 132:3 – 5).

Under David's rule the Lord caused the nation to prosper, to defeat its enemies and, in fulfillment of his promise (see Ge 15:18 and note), to extend its borders from Egypt to the Euphrates (ch. 8). David wanted to build a temple for the Lord — as his royal house, as a place for his throne (the ark) and as a place for Israel to worship him. But the prophet Nathan told David that he was not to build the Lord a house (temple); rather, the Lord would build David a house (dynasty). Ch. 7 announces the Lord's promise that this Davidic dynasty would endure forever. This climactic chapter also describes the establishment of the Davidic covenant (see notes on 7:1 – 29; Ps 89:30 – 37). Later the prophets make clear that a descendant of David who sits on David's throne will perfectly fulfill the role of the theocratic king. He will complete the redemption of God's people (see Isa

> **A Quick Look**
>
> **Author:**
> Unknown
>
> **Audience:**
> God's chosen people, the Israelites
>
> **Date:**
> Sometime after Israel was divided into the northern and southern kingdoms in about 930 B.C.
>
> **Theme:**
> 2 Samuel presents the story of David's 40-year reign, beginning with his rise to become Israel's model king and ending with his subsequent decline caused by sin.

9:6–7; 11:1–16; Jer 23:5–6; 30:8–9; 33:14–16; Eze 34:23–24; 37:24–25 and relevant notes), thus enabling them to achieve the promised victory with him (cf. Ro 16:20 and note).

After the description of David's rule in its glory and success, chs. 10–20 depict the darker side of his reign and describe David's weaknesses and failures. Even though David was a king after God's own heart because he was willing to acknowledge his sin and repent (see 12:13 and note), he nevertheless fell far short of the theocratic ideal and suffered the disciplinary results of his disobedience (12:10–12; see notes on 12:10–11). His sin with Bathsheba (chs. 11–12) and his leniency both with the wickedness of his sons (13:12–39; see note on 13:21; 14:1,33; 19:4–6) and with the insubordination of Joab (3:28–39; 20:10,23) led to intrigue, violence and bloodshed within his own family and the nation. It eventually drove him from Jerusalem at the time of Absalom's rebellion. Nonetheless the Lord was gracious to David, and his reign became a standard by which the reigns of later kings were measured (see 2Ki 18:3; 22:2 and notes).

David was a king after God's own heart because he was willing to acknowledge his sin and repent.

The book ends with David's own words of praise to God, who had delivered him from all his enemies (22:31–51), and with words of expectation for the fulfillment of God's promise that a king will come from the house of David and rule "over men in righteousness" (23:3; see notes on 23:3–5). These songs echo many of the themes of Hannah's song (1Sa 2:1–10), and together they frame (and interpret) the basic narrative.

Chronology

See Introduction to 1 Samuel: Chronology.

Outline

Below is an outline for 2 Samuel. For an outline of both 1 and 2 Samuel see Introduction to 1 Samuel: Outline.

7. David's reaction to and lament over Saul's death (2Sa 1)

C. David Becomes King over Judah (2:1—3:5)

D. David Becomes King over All Israel (3:6—5:5)

VII. David's Reign Characterized Illustratively (5:6—8:18)

A. David's Conquest of Jerusalem and His Recognition by the King of Tyre (5:6–16)

B. David's Crushing of the Philistine Threat (5:17–25)

C. David's Bringing the Ark (God's Throne) into His Royal City (ch. 6)

D. God's Covenant with David (ch. 7)

E. David's Victories that Secure the Boundaries of His Kingdom (ch. 8)

VIII. Threats to David's Reign Overcome (chs. 9–20)

A. David's Kindness to Saul's Remaining Heir (ch. 9)

B. Defeat of the Ammonite-Aramean Challenge to David's Reign (10:1–19; 12:26–31)

C. David's Shameful Abuse of His Royal Power in the Matter of Bathsheba and Uriah (11:1—12:25)

D. Absalom's Challenge to David's Rule (chs. 13–20)

1. Amnon's abuse of power and Absalom's revenge (ch. 13)
2. Absalom's revolt crushed (chs. 14–19)
3. Absalom's attempt sparks another unsuccessful revolt (ch. 20)

IX. Sidebars to the David Story (Chiastically Arranged) (chs. 21–24)

A. God's Wrath against Israel because of Something Saul Had Done (21:1–14)

B. Exploits of David's Mighty Men in Wars against Philistines (21:15–22)

C. David's Song in Praise of the Lord for Victories Granted (ch. 22)

C'. David's "Last Song" that Speaks of God's Ways with Him and His House (23:1–7)

B'. David's Mighty Men and Their Exploits, Especially against Philistines (23:8–39)

A'. God's Wrath against Israel because of Something David Did (ch. 24)

David Hears of Saul's Death

1:4-12pp — 1Sa 31:1-13; 1Ch 10:1-12

1 After the death[a] of Saul, David returned
from defeating[b] the Amalekites[c] and
stayed in Ziklag two days. 2On the third
day a man[d] arrived from Saul's camp,
with his clothes torn and with dust on his
head.[e] When he came to David, he fell[f] to
the ground to pay him honor.[g]
3"Where have you come from?" David
asked him.
He answered, "I have escaped from the
Israelite camp."
4"What happened?" David asked.
"Tell me."
He said, "The men fled from the battle.
Many of them fell and died. And Saul and
his son Jonathan are dead."
5Then David said to the young man
who brought him the report, "How do you
know that Saul and his son Jonathan are
dead?"
6"I happened to be on Mount Gilboa,[h]"
the young man said, "and there was Saul,
leaning on his spear, with the chariots and
riders almost upon him. 7When he turned
around and saw me, he called out to me,
and I said, 'What can I do?'
8"He asked me, 'Who are you?'
"'An Amalekite,[i]' I answered.
9"Then he said to me, 'Stand over me
and kill me![j] I am in the throes of death,
but I'm still alive.'
10"So I stood over him and killed him,
because I knew that after he had fallen he
could not survive. And I took the crown[k]
that was on his head and the band on his
arm and have brought them here to my
lord."
11Then David and all the men with him
took hold of their clothes and tore[l] them.
12They mourned and wept and fasted till
evening for Saul and his son Jonathan,
and for the army of the LORD and the
house of Israel, because they had fallen
by the sword.
13David said to the young man who
brought him the report, "Where are you
from?"
"I am the son of an alien, an Amalekite,[m]" he answered.
14David asked him, "Why were you
not afraid to lift your hand to destroy the
LORD's anointed?[n]"
15Then David called one of his men and
said, "Go, strike him down!"[o] So he struck
him down, and he died.[p] 16For David had
said to him, "Your blood be on your own
head.[q] Your own mouth testified against
you when you said, 'I killed the LORD's
anointed.'"

David's Lament for Saul and Jonathan

17David took up this lament[r] concerning
Saul and his son Jonathan,[s] 18and ordered
that the men of Judah be taught this lament of the bow (it is written in the Book
of Jashar):[t]

19"Your glory, O Israel, lies slain on your
heights.
How the mighty[u] have fallen![v]

1:1 [a]S 1Sa 26:10; 1Ch 10:13 [b]S Jos 22:8; S 1Sa 30:17 [c]S Ge 14:7; Nu 13:29 **1:2** [d]2Sa 4:10 [e]S 1Sa 4:12; Job 2:12; Eze 27:30 [f]S 1Sa 20:41 [g]S Ge 37:7 **1:6** [h]ver 21; S 1Sa 28:4 **1:8** [i]ver 13; S 1Sa 15:2; S 27:8; 30:13,17 **1:9** [j]S Jdg 9:54 **1:10** [k]2Ki 11:12 **1:11** [l]S Ge 37:29; S Nu 14:6 **1:13** [m]S ver 8; S 1Sa 14:48 **1:14** [n]S 1Sa 12:3; S 26:9 **1:15** [o]2Sa 4:12 [p]2Sa 4:10 **1:16** [q]S Lev 20:9; Mt 27:24-25; Ac 18:6 **1:17** [r]S Ge 50:10; S Eze 32:2 [s]ver 26 **1:18** [t]Jos 10:13 **1:19** [u]2Sa 23:8; Ps 29:1; 45:3 [v]2Sa 3:38

1:1–27 David's reaction to and lament over Saul's death. This opening segment of 2 Samuel is actually the narrative hinge of the full book of Samuel (see notes on 22:1–51; 1Sa 2:1).
1:1 *After the death of.* See Jos 1:1; Jdg 1:1; 2Ki 1:1. The narrative thread of 1 Samuel is continued. 1 and 2 Samuel were originally one book (see Introduction to 1 Samuel: Title). *David returned from defeating the Amalekites.* See 1Sa 30:1; Ge 14:7 and notes. *Ziklag.* See note on 1Sa 27:6.
1:2 *his clothes torn … dust on his head.* See note on 1Sa 4:12; see also Jos 7:6; Ac 14:14 and notes.
1:8 *Amalekite.* It is not necessary to conclude from v. 3 that this Amalekite was a member of Saul's army. His statement that he "happened to be on Mount Gilboa" (v. 6) is probably not as innocent as it appears. He may have been there as a scavenger to rob the fallen soldiers of their valuables and weapons. It is ironic that Saul's death is reported by an Amalekite (see 1Sa 15).
1:10 *I stood over him and killed him.* The Amalekite's story conflicts with 1Sa 31:3–6, where Saul is depicted as taking his own life. It appears that the Amalekite fabricated this version of Saul's death, expecting David to reward him (see 4:10). His miscalculation of David's response cost him his life (see v. 15 and note). *I took the crown.* Apparently he got to Saul before the Philistines did (see 1Sa 31:8–9).
1:11 *took hold of their clothes and tore them.* See note on v. 2.
1:12 *mourned and wept.* David and his men expressed their grief in typical Near Eastern fashion (see Ge 23:2; 1Ki 13:30; Jer 22:18). *fasted.* See note on 1Sa 31:13.
1:13 *Amalekite.* The man was probably unaware of David's recent hostile encounters with the Amalekites (see v. 1; 1Sa 30; see also note on 1Sa 15:2).
1:14 The Amalekite understood nothing of the deep significance that David attached to the sanctity of the royal office in Israel (see 1Sa 24:6 and note). *the LORD's anointed.* See note on 1Sa 9:16.
1:15 *strike him down!* David displays no personal satisfaction over Saul's death and condemns to death the one he believes to be his murderer (see note on v. 10; see also 4:10).
1:16 *Your blood be on your own head.* The Amalekite's own testimony brought about his execution (see Jos 2:19 and note; 1Ki 2:37).
1:17 *lament.* It was a common practice in the ancient Near East to compose laments for fallen leaders, heroes and royal cities (see 2Ch 35:25 and note; Lamentations, particularly its Introduction: Themes and Theology).
1:18 *lament of the bow.* Perhaps David taught his men to sing this lament while they practiced with the bow (Israel's most common weapon; see, e.g., 22:35) as a motivation to master the weapon thoroughly so they would not experience a similar defeat (see note on Eze 21:9). *Book of Jashar.* See note on Jos 10:13.
1:19 *Your glory.* A reference to Saul and Jonathan as divinely designated leaders of God's covenant people, who had achieved many significant victories over Israel's enemies (see 1Sa 14:47–48 and note; cf. 1Sa 4:21 and note). *heights.* Of Gilboa (see v. 25; 1Sa 31:1,8 and note; see also note on 1Sa 28:4). *How the mighty have fallen!* The theme of David's lament (see vv. 25,27). David's words contain no suggestion

20 "Tell it not in Gath,[w]
proclaim it not in the streets of Ashkelon,[x]
lest the daughters of the Philistines[y] be glad,
lest the daughters of the uncircumcised rejoice.[z]

21 "O mountains of Gilboa,[a]
may you have neither dew[b] nor rain,[c]
nor fields that yield offerings[d] ⌞of grain⌟.
For there the shield of the mighty was defiled,
the shield of Saul—no longer rubbed with oil.[e]
22 From the blood[f] of the slain,
from the flesh of the mighty,
the bow[g] of Jonathan did not turn back,
the sword of Saul did not return unsatisfied.
23 "Saul and Jonathan—
in life they were loved and gracious,
and in death they were not parted.
They were swifter than eagles,[h]
they were stronger than lions.[i]

24 "O daughters of Israel,
weep for Saul,
who clothed you in scarlet and finery,
who adorned your garments with ornaments of gold.[j]

25 "How the mighty have fallen in battle!
Jonathan lies slain on your heights.
26 I grieve[k] for you, Jonathan[l] my brother;[m]
you were very dear to me.
Your love for me was wonderful,[n]
more wonderful than that of women.

27 "How the mighty have fallen!
The weapons of war have perished!"[o]

1:20 [w] Mic 1:10 [x] S Jos 13:3 [y] 1Sa 31:8 [z] S 1Sa 18:6 1:21 [a] S ver 6 [b] S Ge 27:28; S Isa 18:4 [c] Dt 11:17; 1Ki 8:35; 17:1; 18:1; 2Ch 6:26; Job 36:27; 38:28; Ps 65:10; 147:8; Isa 5:6; Jer 5:24; 14:4; Am 1:2 [d] Jer 12:4; Eze 31:15 [e] Isa 21:5 1:22 [f] Isa 34:3,7; 49:26 [g] Dt 32:42 1:23 [h] S Dt 28:49 [i] Jdg 14:18 1:24 [j] S Jdg 5:30 1:26 [k] Jer 22:18; 34:5 [l] ver 17 [m] S 1Sa 20:42 [n] S 1Sa 18:1 1:27 [o] S 1Sa 2:4 2:1 [p] S 1Sa 23:2, 11-12 [q] S Ge 13:18; S 23:19 2:2 [r] S 1Sa 25:43 [s] S 1Sa 25:42 2:3 [t] S 1Sa 27:2; 1Ch 12:22 [u] S Ge 13:18; 23:2; 37:14 2:4 [v] S 1Sa 30:31 [w] S 1Sa 2:35; 2Sa 5:3-5; 1Ch 12:23-40 [x] S Jdg 21:8; S 1Sa 11:1 2:5 [y] S Jdg 17:2; S 1Sa 23:21; 2Ti 1:16 2:6 [z] Ex 34:6

David Anointed King Over Judah

2 In the course of time, David inquired[p]
of the LORD. "Shall I go up to one of the
towns of Judah?" he asked.
The LORD said, "Go up."
David asked, "Where shall I go?"
"To Hebron,"[q] the LORD answered.
2 So David went up there with his two
wives,[r] Ahinoam of Jezreel and Abigail,[s]
the widow of Nabal of Carmel. 3 David
also took the men who were with him,[t]
each with his family, and they settled in
Hebron[u] and its towns. 4 Then the men
of Judah came to Hebron[v] and there they
anointed[w] David king over the house of
Judah.
When David was told that it was the
men of Jabesh Gilead[x] who had buried
Saul, 5 he sent messengers to the men of
Jabesh Gilead to say to them, "The LORD
bless[y] you for showing this kindness to
Saul your master by burying him. 6 May
the LORD now show you kindness and
faithfulness,[z] and I too will show you the
same favor because you have done this.

of bitterness toward Saul but rather recall the good qualities and accomplishments of Saul and Jonathan. However, David's lament over "fallen" Saul is Saul's epitaph and stands in significant contrast to Hannah's song in 1Sa 2:1–10 and David's song in 2Sa 22.

1:20 *Tell it not in Gath … Ashkelon.* As the major Philistine cities located the closest and farthest from Israel's borders, Gath and Ashkelon represent the entire Philistine nation. David does not want the enemies of God's covenant people to take pleasure in Israel's defeat (as he knew they would; see 1Sa 31:9–10) and thus bring reproach on the name of the Lord (see Ex 32:12; Nu 14:13–19; Dt 9:28; see also Jos 7:9; Mic 1:10 and notes). *uncircumcised.* See note on 1Sa 14:6.

1:21 *O mountains of Gilboa.* As an expression of profound grief, David rhetorically pronounces a curse on the place where Israel was defeated and Saul and Jonathan were killed (for other such rhetorical curses see Job 3:3–26; Jer 20:14–18). *no longer rubbed with oil.* Leather shields were rubbed with oil to preserve their toughness (see Isa 21:5).

1:23 *in death they were not parted.* Even though Jonathan opposed his father's treatment of David, he gave his life beside his father in Israel's defense.

1:26 *more wonderful than that of women.* David is not suggesting that marital love is inferior to that of friendship, nor do his remarks have any sexual implications. He is simply calling attention to Jonathan's nearly inexplicable self-denying commitment to David, whom he had long recognized as the Lord's choice to succeed his father rather than himself (see notes on 1Sa 20:13–17).

1:27 *weapons of war.* Probably a metaphor for Saul and Jonathan.

2:1—3:5 David's elevation to kingship over Judah, and Abner's response.

2:1 *In the course of time.* This phrase introduces significant episodes in David's life: his anointing as king over Judah (here), his most notable military victories (8:1), his adultery with Bathsheba and murder of Uriah (10:1), the death of his firstborn son Amnon (13:1) and the conspiracy of his son Absalom (15:1). *David inquired of the LORD.* By means of the ephod through the priest Abiathar (see notes on Ex 28:30; 1Sa 2:28; 23:2). *one of the towns of Judah.* Even though Saul was dead and David had many friends and contacts among the people of his own tribe (see 1Sa 30:26–31), David did not presume to return from Philistine territory to assume the kingship promised to him without first seeking the Lord's guidance. *Hebron.* An old and important city (see Ge 13:18; 23:2 and note; Jos 15:13–14; Jdg 16:3 and note; see also note on 1Sa 30:31) centrally located in the tribe of Judah.

2:2 *Ahinoam of Jezreel.* See note on 1Sa 25:43. *Abigail.* See note on 1Sa 25:1–44.

2:3 *men who were with him.* See note on v. 13.

2:4 *anointed David king.* See notes on 1Sa 2:10; 9:16. David had previously been anointed privately by Samuel in the presence of his own family (see note on 1Sa 16:13). Here the anointing ceremony is repeated as a public recognition by his own tribe of his divine calling to be king. *over the house of Judah.* Very likely the tribe of Simeon was also involved (see Jos 19:1; Jdg 1:3 and notes), but the Judahites in every way

7Now then, be strong[a] and brave, for Saul
your master is dead, and the house of Judah has anointed me king over them."

War Between the Houses of David and Saul

3:2-5pp — 1Ch 3:1-4

8Meanwhile, Abner[b] son of Ner, the
commander of Saul's army, had taken Ish-
Bosheth[c] son of Saul and brought him over
to Mahanaim.[d] 9He made him king over
Gilead,[e] Ashuri[a][f] and Jezreel, and also
over Ephraim, Benjamin and all Israel.[g]
10Ish-Bosheth son of Saul was forty
years old when he became king over Israel, and he reigned two years. The house
of Judah, however, followed David. 11The
length of time David was king in Hebron
over the house of Judah was seven years
and six months.[h]

12Abner son of Ner, together with the
men of Ish-Bosheth son of Saul, left Mahanaim and went to Gibeon.[i] 13Joab[j] son
of Zeruiah and David's men went out and
met them at the pool of Gibeon. One group
sat down on one side of the pool and one
group on the other side.

14Then Abner said to Joab, "Let's have
some of the young men get up and fight
hand to hand in front of us."

"All right, let them do it," Joab said.

15So they stood up and were counted
off — twelve men for Benjamin and Ish-
Bosheth son of Saul, and twelve for David.
16Then each man grabbed his opponent by
the head and thrust his dagger[k] into his
opponent's side, and they fell down together. So that place in Gibeon was called
Helkath Hazzurim.[b]

17The battle that day was very fierce,
and Abner and the men of Israel were defeated[l] by David's men.[m]

18The three sons of Zeruiah[n] were there:
Joab,[o] Abishai[p] and Asahel.[q] Now Asahel
was as fleet-footed as a wild gazelle.[r] 19He
chased Abner, turning neither to the right
nor to the left as he pursued him. 20Ab-
ner looked behind him and asked, "Is that
you, Asahel?"

"It is," he answered.

21Then Abner said to him, "Turn aside
to the right or to the left; take on one of
the young men and strip him of his weapons." But Asahel would not stop chasing
him.

22Again Abner warned Asahel, "Stop
chasing me! Why should I strike you

2:7 [a]S Jos 1:6; S Jdg 5:21 **2:8** [b]S 1Sa 14:50; S 2Sa 3:27 [c]2Sa 4:5; 1Ch 8:33; 9:39 [d]S Ge 32:2 **2:9** [e]S Nu 32:26 [f]S Jos 19:24-31 [g]1Ch 12:29 **2:11** [h]2Sa 5:5 **2:12** [i]S Jos 9:3 **2:13** [j]2Sa 8:16; 19:13; 1Ki 1:7; 1Ch 2:16; 11:6; 27:34 **2:16** [k]S Jdg 3:21 **2:17** [l]2Sa 3:1 [m]S 1Sa 17:8 **2:18** [n]2Sa 3:39; 16:10; 19:22 [o]2Sa 3:30; 10:7; 11:1; 14:1; 18:14; 20:8; 24:3; 1Ki 1:7; 2:5,34 [p]S 1Sa 26:6 [q]2Sa 23:24; 1Ch 2:16; 11:26; 27:7 [r]1Ch 12:8; Pr 6:5; SS 2:9

[a] 9 Or *Asher* [b] 16 *Helkath Hazzurim* means *field of daggers* or *field of hostilities.*

dominated the area. *men of Jabesh Gilead.* See notes on 1Sa 11:1; 31:12. *buried Saul.* See note on 1Sa 31:13.

2:7 *your master is dead, and the house of Judah has anointed me king over them.* David's concluding statement to the men of Jabesh Gilead is a veiled invitation to them to recognize him as their king just as the tribe of Judah had done. This appeal for their support, however, was ignored.

2:8 *Abner son of Ner.* See 1Sa 14:50–51; 20:25 and note. *Saul's army.* His small standing army of professionals loyal to him and his family (see 1Sa 13:2,15 and note on 13:15; 14:2,52 and note on 14:52). *Ish-Bosheth.* The name was originally Ish-(or Esh-)Baal (1Ch 8:33) but was changed by the author of Samuel to Ish-Bosheth, meaning "man of the shameful thing" (see notes on 4:4; Jdg 6:32; Jer 2:26; 3:24–25; 11:13). Evidently Baal (meaning "lord" or "master") was at this time still used to refer to the Lord. Later this was discontinued because of confusion with the Canaanite god Baal (see, e.g., Hos 2:16–17 and note), and the author of Samuel reflects the later sensitivity. *son of Saul.* See note on 1Sa 31:2. *brought him.* Abner takes the initiative in the power vacuum created by Saul's death, using the unassertive Ish-Bosheth as a pawn for his own ambitions (see 3:11 and note on 4:1). There is no evidence that Ish-Bosheth had strong support among the Israelites generally. *Mahanaim.* A Gileadite town east of the Jordan River and thus beyond the sphere of Philistine domination — a kind of refugee capital.

2:9 *He made him king.* As a relative of Saul (see 1Sa 14:50–51), Abner had both a family and a career interest in ensuring dynastic succession for Saul's house. *Gilead ... all Israel.* This delineation of Ish-Bosheth's realm suggests that his actual rule, while involving territory both east and west of the Jordan, was quite limited and that "all Israel" was more claim than reality. David ruled over Judah and Simeon, and the Philistines controlled large sections of the northern tribal regions.

2:11 *seven years and six months.* Cf. Ish-Bosheth's two-year reign in Mahanaim (v. 10). Because it appears that David was made king over all Israel shortly after Ish-Bosheth's death (5:1–5) and moved his capital to Jerusalem not long afterward (5:6–12), reconciling the lengths of David's and Ish-Bosheth's reigns is difficult. The difficulty is best resolved by assuming that it took Ish-Bosheth a number of years to be recognized as his father's successor, and that the two years of his reign roughly correspond to the last two or three years of David's reign in Hebron.

2:12 Abner initiates an action to prevent David's sphere of influence from spreading northward out of Judah. Gibeon was located in the tribal area of Benjamin (see Jos 18:21,25), to which Saul and his family belonged, and which the Philistines had not occupied.

2:13 *Joab son of Zeruiah.* See note on 1Sa 26:6. Joab became a figure of major importance during David's reign as a competent but ruthless military leader (see 10:7–14; 11:1; 12:26; 1Ki 11:15–16). At times David was unable to control him (see 3:39; 18:5,14; 1Ki 2:5–6 and note on 2:5), and he was eventually executed for his wanton assassinations and his part in the conspiracy to place Adonijah rather than Solomon on David's throne (see 1Ki 2:28–34 and note on 2:29). *David's men.* Some, at least, of David's small force of loyal supporters who had gathered around him (see 1Sa 22:2 and note; 23:13; 27:2; 30:3,9). *pool of Gibeon.* See Jer 41:12. In 1956 archaeologists uncovered a large, cylindrical pool at el-Jib (ancient Gibeon), probably the one near where the battle recorded in vv. 15–16 took place.

2:15 *Benjamin.* At this time Ish-Bosheth seems to have been supported mainly by his own tribesmen.

2:17 *The battle that day was very fierce.* Because the representative combat (see note on 1Sa 17:4) by 12 men from each side was indecisive, a full-scale battle ensued in which David's forces were victorious. The attempt to use representative combat to avoid the destructiveness of civil war failed (see 3:1).

2:21 *Turn aside.* Abner tried unsuccessfully to avoid the necessity of killing Asahel.

2:22 *How could I look your brother Joab in the face?* Abner did

down? How could I look your brother Joab
in the face?"[s]
23 But Asahel refused to give up the pursuit; so Abner thrust the butt of his spear
into Asahel's stomach,[t] and the spear
came out through his back. He fell there
and died on the spot. And every man
stopped when he came to the place where
Asahel had fallen and died.[u]
24 But Joab and Abishai pursued Abner,
and as the sun was setting, they came to
the hill of Ammah, near Giah on the way
to the wasteland of Gibeon. 25 Then the
men of Benjamin rallied behind Abner.
They formed themselves into a group and
took their stand on top of a hill.
26 Abner called out to Joab, "Must the
sword devour[v] forever? Don't you realize
that this will end in bitterness? How long
before you order your men to stop pursuing their brothers?"
27 Joab answered, "As surely as God
lives, if you had not spoken, the men
would have continued the pursuit of their
brothers until morning.[a]"
28 So Joab[w] blew the trumpet,[x] and all the
men came to a halt; they no longer pursued Israel, nor did they fight anymore.
29 All that night Abner and his men
marched through the Arabah.[y] They
crossed the Jordan, continued through the
whole Bithron[b] and came to Mahanaim.[z]
30 Then Joab returned from pursuing Abner and assembled all his men. Besides Asahel, nineteen of David's men were found
missing. 31 But David's men had killed
three hundred and sixty Benjamites who
were with Abner. 32 They took Asahel and
buried him in his father's tomb[a] at Bethlehem. Then Joab and his men marched all
night and arrived at Hebron by daybreak.
3 The war between the house of Saul
and the house of David lasted a long
time.[b] David grew stronger and stronger,[c]
while the house of Saul grew weaker and
weaker.[d]
2 Sons were born to David in Hebron:
His firstborn was Amnon[e] the son
of Ahinoam[f] of Jezreel;
3 his second, Kileab the son of Abigail[g] the widow of Nabal of Carmel;
the third, Absalom[h] the son of Maacah daughter of Talmai king of Geshur;[i]
4 the fourth, Adonijah[j] the son of
Haggith;
the fifth, Shephatiah the son of Abi-
tal;
5 and the sixth, Ithream the son of
David's wife Eglah.
These were born to David in Hebron.

Abner Goes Over to David

6 During the war between the house of
Saul and the house of David, Abner[k] had
been strengthening his own position in the
house of Saul. 7 Now Saul had had a concubine[l] named Rizpah[m] daughter of Aiah.
And Ish-Bosheth said to Abner, "Why did
you sleep with my father's concubine?"
8 Abner was very angry because of what
Ish-Bosheth said and he answered, "Am I
a dog's head[n] — on Judah's side? This very
day I am loyal to the house of your father Saul and to his family and friends.
I haven't handed you over to David. Yet
now you accuse me of an offense involving this woman! 9 May God deal with Abner, be it ever so severely, if I do not do

2:22 [s] 2Sa 3:27 **2:23** [t] 2Sa 3:27; 4:6 [u] 2Sa 20:12 **2:26** [v] S Dt 32:42; Jer 46:10,14; Na 2:13; 3:15 **2:28** [w] 2Sa 18:16; 20:23 [x] S Jdg 3:27 **2:29** [y] S Dt 3:17 [z] S Ge 32:2 **2:32** [a] S Ge 49:29

3:1 [b] 1Ki 14:30 [c] 2Sa 5:10 [d] 2Sa 2:17; 22:44; Est 9:4 **3:2** [e] 2Sa 13:1 [f] S 1Sa 25:43 **3:3** [g] S 1Sa 25:42 [h] 2Sa 13:1,28 [i] 2Sa 13:37; 14:32; 15:8 **3:4** [j] 1Ki 1:5,11; 2:13,22 **3:6** [k] S 1Sa 14:50 **3:7** [l] S Ge 22:24; 2Sa 16:21-22; S 1Ki 1:3 [m] 2Sa 21:8-11 **3:8** [n] S 1Sa 17:43; 2Sa 9:8; 16:9; 2Ki 8:13

[a] 27 Or *spoken this morning, the men would not have taken up the pursuit of their brothers*; or *spoken, the men would have given up the pursuit of their brothers by morning* [b] 29 Or *morning*; or *ravine*; the meaning of the Hebrew for this word is uncertain.

not want the hostility between himself and Joab to be intensified by the practice of blood revenge (see note on 3:27).
2:23 Stabbing an enemy in the stomach was the method of execution noted also in 3:27; 4:6 (cf. Jdg 3:21).
2:26 *Must the sword devour forever?* Abner proposes an armistice as a means of avoiding the awful consequences of civil war.
2:27 *As surely as God lives.* An oath formula (see note on 1Sa 14:39,45).
2:28 *nor did they fight anymore.* For the present the open conflict ceased, but the hostility remained (see 3:1).
2:29 *Arabah.* See note on Dt 1:1.
3:1 *house of David.* See 1Ki 12:19 and note.
3:2–5 See chart, p. 402. The list of six sons born to David in Hebron is given as an evidence of the strengthening of David's house in contrast to that of Saul (v. 1). That these six sons were each born of a different mother indirectly informs us that David married four additional wives (see 2:2) during his time in Hebron.
3:2 *Amnon.* Later raped his sister Tamar and was killed by his brother Absalom (see ch. 13). *Ahinoam of Jezreel.* See note on 1Sa 25:43.
3:3 *Kileab.* Called Daniel in 1Ch 3:1. *Abigail.* See note on 2:2. *Absalom.* Later avenged the rape of Tamar by killing Amnon, and conspired against his father David in an attempt to make himself king (see chs. 13–18). *Maacah daughter of Talmai.* David's marriage to Maacah undoubtedly had political implications. With Talmai as an ally on Ish-Bosheth's northern border, David flanked the northern kingdom both south and north. *Geshur.* A small Aramean city kingdom (see 15:8) located northeast of the Sea of Galilee (see Jos 12:5; 13:11–13; see also map, p. 444).
3:4 *Adonijah.* Was put to death for attempting to take over the throne before Solomon could be crowned (see 1Ki 1–2).
3:6—5:5 David's elevation to kingship over the rest of Israel.
3:7 *Rizpah.* See 21:8–11. *Why did you sleep with my father's concubine?* Ish-Bosheth suspects that Abner's act was part of a conspiracy to seize the kingship (cf. v. 6). Great significance was attached to taking the concubine of a former king (see notes on 12:8; 16:21; 1Ki 2:22).
3:8 *dog's head.* Cf. note on 9:8.
3:9 *May God deal with Abner, be it ever so severely.* A curse formula (see note on 1Sa 3:17).

for David what the LORD promised[o] him on
oath 10and transfer the kingdom from the
house of Saul and establish David's throne
over Israel and Judah from Dan to Beersheba."[p] 11Ish-Bosheth did not dare to say
another word to Abner, because he was
afraid of him.
12Then Abner sent messengers on his
behalf to say to David, "Whose land is it?
Make an agreement with me, and I will
help you bring all Israel over to you."
13"Good," said David. "I will make an
agreement with you. But I demand one
thing of you: Do not come into my presence unless you bring Michal daughter of
Saul when you come to see me."[q] 14Then
David sent messengers to Ish-Bosheth son
of Saul, demanding, "Give me my wife Michal,[r] whom I betrothed to myself for the
price of a hundred Philistine foreskins."
15So Ish-Bosheth gave orders and had
her taken away from her husband[s] Paltiel[t] son of Laish. 16Her husband, however,
went with her, weeping behind her all the
way to Bahurim.[u] Then Abner said to him,
"Go back home!" So he went back.
17Abner conferred with the elders[v] of Israel and said, "For some time you have
wanted to make David your king. 18Now
do it! For the LORD promised David, 'By
my servant David I will rescue my people
Israel from the hand of the Philistines[w] and
from the hand of all their enemies.[x]'"
19Abner also spoke to the Benjamites in
person. Then he went to Hebron to tell David everything that Israel and the whole
house of Benjamin[y] wanted to do. 20When
Abner, who had twenty men with him,
came to David at Hebron, David prepared
a feast[z] for him and his men. 21Then Abner said to David, "Let me go at once and
assemble all Israel for my lord the king, so
that they may make a compact[a] with you,
and that you may rule over all that your
heart desires."[b] So David sent Abner away,
and he went in peace.

Joab Murders Abner

22Just then David's men and Joab returned from a raid and brought with them
a great deal of plunder. But Abner was no
longer with David in Hebron, because David had sent him away, and he had gone
in peace. 23When Joab and all the soldiers
with him arrived, he was told that Abner
son of Ner had come to the king and that
the king had sent him away and that he
had gone in peace.
24So Joab went to the king and said,
"What have you done? Look, Abner came
to you. Why did you let him go? Now he
is gone! 25You know Abner son of Ner;
he came to deceive you and observe your
movements and find out everything you
are doing."
26Joab then left David and sent messengers after Abner, and they brought him
back from the well of Sirah. But David did
not know it. 27Now when Abner[c] returned
to Hebron, Joab took him aside into the
gateway, as though to speak with him privately. And there, to avenge the blood of
his brother Asahel, Joab stabbed him[d] in
the stomach, and he died.[e]

3:9 [o] S 1Sa 15:28 **3:10** [p] S Jdg 20:1; 1Sa 25:28-31; 2Sa 24:2 **3:13** [q] S Ge 43:5 **3:14** [r] S 1Sa 18:27 **3:15** [s] Dt 24:1-4 [t] 1Sa 25:44 **3:16** [u] 2Sa 16:5; 17:18 **3:17** [v] S Jdg 11:11 **3:18** [w] S 1Sa 9:16 [x] 2Sa 8:6 **3:19** [y] 1Ch 12:2,16,29 **3:20** [z] 1Ch 12:39 **3:21** [a] 2Sa 5:3 [b] 1Ki 11:37 **3:27** [c] 2Sa 2:8; 4:1; 1Ki 2:5,32 [d] S Ex 21:14; S Jdg 3:21; S 2Sa 2:23 [e] 2Sa 2:22

3:9 *what the LORD promised him on oath.* The knowledge of David's divine designation as successor to Saul had spread widely (see notes on 2:4; 1Sa 16:13; 25:28).

3:10 *transfer the kingdom.* Abner was the real power behind the throne. *Dan to Beersheba.* See note on 1Sa 3:20.

3:12 *Whose land is it?* Possibly a rhetorical question that presumed that the land belonged either to Abner or to David. The former seems more likely from the following sentence. *Make an agreement with me.* Abner wants assurance that he will face no reprisals for his past loyalty to the house of Saul.

3:13 *Michal daughter of Saul.* Although Saul had given Michal to David (1Sa 18:27), he later gave her to another man after David fled from his court (1Sa 25:44). David probably sensed that in the minds of the northern elders, his reunion with Michal would strengthen his claim to the throne as a legitimate son-in-law of Saul.

3:14 *David sent messengers to Ish-Bosheth.* David wanted Michal returned as an open and official act of Ish-Bosheth himself, rather than as part of a subterfuge planned by Abner. David knew that Ish-Bosheth would not dare to defy Abner's wishes (see v. 11). *a hundred Philistine foreskins.* See 1Sa 18:25. Saul had required 100 Philistine foreskins; David presented him with 200 (1Sa 18:27).

3:16 *Bahurim.* Near the Mount of Olives.

3:17 *elders of Israel.* The collective leadership of the various tribes comprised an informal national ruling body (see notes on Ex 3:16; Joel 1:2; see also 1Sa 8:4; 2Sa 5:3; 1Ki 8:1,3; 20:7; 2Ki 10:1; 23:1). *you have wanted to make David your king.* Apparently Ish-Bosheth's support came mainly from the tribe of Benjamin (see 2:15 and note) and from Gilead east of the Jordan River (see 2:8; 1Sa 11:9–11; 31:11–13).

3:18 *the LORD promised David.* By this time Samuel's anointing of David must have become common knowledge (see 5:2). Abner probably interpreted the anointing as a promise from the Lord, since Samuel was the Lord's much-revered prophet.

3:19 *Abner also spoke to the Benjamites in person.* Because Saul and his family were from the tribe of Benjamin, Abner was careful to consult the Benjamites concerning the transfer of kingship to the tribe of Judah. Apparently they consented, but Abner was not above representing matters in a way that was favorable to his purpose.

3:21 *make a compact with you.* See 5:3 and note.

3:25 *he came to deceive you.* Joab despised Abner for killing his brother (2:18,23; 3:27) and sought to discredit him in David's eyes as a mere opportunist. Perhaps he also sensed that his own position of leadership would be threatened if Abner joined forces with David, since Abner was obviously a power among the northern tribes.

3:27 *gateway ... privately.* City gateways usually had small side chambers. *Joab stabbed him in the stomach, and he died.* Joab's murder of Abner is not to be excused either as an act of war or as justifiable blood revenge (cf. Nu 35:12; Dt 19:11–13). Asahel had been killed by Abner in the course of battle (see v. 30; see also 2:21,23 and notes).

28 Later, when David heard about this, he
said, "I and my kingdom are forever innocent[f] before the LORD concerning the blood
of Abner son of Ner. 29 May his blood[g] fall
upon the head of Joab and upon all his
father's house![h] May Joab's house never
be without someone who has a running
sore[i] or leprosy[a] or who leans on a crutch
or who falls by the sword or who lacks
food."
30 (Joab and his brother Abishai murdered Abner because he had killed their
brother Asahel in the battle at Gibeon.)
31 Then David said to Joab and all the
people with him, "Tear your clothes and
put on sackcloth[j] and walk in mourning[k]
in front of Abner." King David himself
walked behind the bier. 32 They buried Abner in Hebron, and the king wept[l] aloud at
Abner's tomb. All the people wept also.
33 The king sang this lament[m] for Abner:

"Should Abner have died as the
lawless die?
34 Your hands were not bound,
your feet were not fettered.[n]
You fell as one falls before wicked
men."

And all the people wept over him
again.
35 Then they all came and urged David
to eat something while it was still day;
but David took an oath, saying, "May God
deal with me, be it ever so severely,[o] if
I taste bread[p] or anything else before the
sun sets!"
36 All the people took note and were
pleased; indeed, everything the king did
pleased them. 37 So on that day all the
people and all Israel knew that the king
had no part[q] in the murder of Abner son
of Ner.

3:28 [f] ver 37; Dt 21:9
3:29 [g] S Lev 20:9 [h] 1Ki 2:31-33 [i] S Lev 15:2
3:31 [j] Ps 30:11; 35:13; 69:11; Isa 20:2 [k] S Ge 37:34
3:32 [l] S Nu 14:1; Pr 24:17
3:33 [m] S Ge 50:10
3:34 [n] Job 36:8; Ps 2:3; 149:8; Isa 45:14; Na 3:10
3:35 [o] S Ru 1:17 [p] S 1Sa 31:13; 2Sa 12:17; Jer 16:7
3:37 [q] S ver 28
3:38 [r] 2Sa 1:19
3:39 [s] S 2Sa 2:18 [t] 2Sa 16:9; 18:11 [u] S Jdg 18:26 [v] 1Ki 2:32; Ps 41:10; 101:8
4:1 [w] S 2Sa 3:27
4:2 [x] S Jos 9:17
4:3 [y] Ne 11:33
4:4 [z] S 1Sa 18:1 [a] S 1Sa 31:9 [b] S Lev 21:18 [c] 2Sa 9:8,12; 16:1-4; 19:24; 21:7-8; 1Ch 8:34; 9:40
4:5 [d] S 2Sa 2:8 [e] Ru 2:7
4:6 [f] S 2Sa 2:23

38 Then the king said to his men, "Do
you not realize that a prince and a great
man has fallen[r] in Israel this day? 39 And
today, though I am the anointed king, I am
weak, and these sons of Zeruiah[s] are too
strong[t] for me.[u] May the LORD repay[v] the
evildoer according to his evil deeds!"

Ish-Bosheth Murdered

4 When Ish-Bosheth son of Saul heard
that Abner[w] had died in Hebron, he lost
courage, and all Israel became alarmed.
2 Now Saul's son had two men who were
leaders of raiding bands. One was named
Baanah and the other Recab; they were
sons of Rimmon the Beerothite from the
tribe of Benjamin—Beeroth[x] is considered
part of Benjamin, 3 because the people of
Beeroth fled to Gittaim[y] and have lived
there as aliens to this day.
4 (Jonathan[z] son of Saul had a son who
was lame in both feet. He was five years
old when the news[a] about Saul and Jonathan came from Jezreel. His nurse picked
him up and fled, but as she hurried to
leave, he fell and became crippled.[b] His
name was Mephibosheth.)[c]
5 Now Recab and Baanah, the sons of
Rimmon the Beerothite, set out for the
house of Ish-Bosheth,[d] and they arrived
there in the heat of the day while he was
taking his noonday rest.[e] 6 They went into
the inner part of the house as if to get
some wheat, and they stabbed[f] him in the
stomach. Then Recab and his brother Baanah slipped away.
7 They had gone into the house while he
was lying on the bed in his bedroom. After they stabbed and killed him, they cut
off his head. Taking it with them, they

[a] *29* The Hebrew word was used for various diseases affecting the skin—not necessarily leprosy.

3:29 *May his blood fall upon the head of Joab and upon all his father's house!* After disclaiming any personal or official involvement in the plot to assassinate Abner (v. 28), David cursed Joab and thereby called on God to judge his wicked act. In this crucial hour when David's relationship to the northern tribes hung in the balance, he appears not to have felt sufficiently secure in his own position to bring Joab publicly to justice (see v. 39). The crime went unpunished until early in the reign of Solomon (see 1Ki 2:5–6,29–34 and note on 2:29).

3:31 *Joab.* He too was compelled to join the mourners. It may be that Joab's involvement was not widely known and that David hoped to keep the matter secret for the time being.

3:32 *Hebron.* David's royal city at the time. *the king wept aloud at Abner's tomb.* Because Abner's murder had the potential of destroying the union of the nation under David's rule, David did everything possible to demonstrate his innocence to the people. In this he was successful (see vv. 36–37).

3:33–34 For another lament sung by David over fallen leaders, see 1:19–27.

3:35 *urged David to eat … but.* See 1:12; see also 1Sa 31:13 and note. *May God deal with me, be it ever so severely.* A curse formula (see note on 1Sa 3:17).

3:39 *May the LORD repay the evildoer.* See note on v. 29.

4:1 *he lost courage.* Ish-Bosheth was very much aware of his dependence on Abner (see note on 2:8). *all Israel became alarmed.* Civil strife threatened, and the northern tribes were now without a strong leader.

4:2 *Beeroth.* One of the Gibeonite cities (Jos 9:17) assigned to Benjamin (Jos 18:21,25).

4:4 *Jonathan son of Saul had a son who was lame in both feet.* The writer emphasizes that with the death of Ish-Bosheth (see v. 6) there was no other viable claimant to the throne from the house of Saul. *news about Saul and Jonathan.* See 1:4; 1Sa 31:2–6. *Mephibosheth.* See 9:1–13; 16:1–4; 19:24–30; 21:7. The name was originally Merib-Baal (apparently meaning "opponent of Baal"; see 1Ch 8:34), perhaps to be spelled "Meri-Baal" (meaning "loved by Baal"), but was changed by the author of Samuel to Mephibosheth (meaning "from the mouth of the shameful thing"). See note on 2:8.

4:6 *stabbed him in the stomach.* See 2:23 and note.

4:7 *cut off his head.* See 1Sa 5:4 and note.

traveled all night by way of the Arabah.[g]
8They brought the head[h] of Ish-Bosheth
to David at Hebron and said to the king,
"Here is the head of Ish-Bosheth son of
Saul,[i] your enemy, who tried to take your
life. This day the LORD has avenged[j] my
lord the king against Saul and his offspring."
9David answered Recab and his brother
Baanah, the sons of Rimmon the Beerothite, "As surely as the LORD lives, who has
delivered[k] me out of all trouble, 10when a
man told me, 'Saul is dead,' and thought
he was bringing good news, I seized him
and put him to death in Ziklag.[l] That was
the reward I gave him for his news! 11How
much more—when wicked men have
killed an innocent man in his own house
and on his own bed—should I not now
demand his blood[m] from your hand and
rid the earth of you!"
12So David gave an order to his men,
and they killed them.[n] They cut off their
hands and feet and hung the bodies by the
pool in Hebron. But they took the head of
Ish-Bosheth and buried it in Abner's tomb
at Hebron.

David Becomes King Over Israel

5:1-3pp — 1Ch 11:1-3

5 All the tribes of Israel[o] came to David
at Hebron and said, "We are your own
flesh and blood.[p] 2In the past, while Saul
was king over us, you were the one who
led Israel on their military campaigns.[q]
And the LORD said[r] to you, 'You will shepherd[s] my people Israel, and you will become their ruler.[t]'"

4:7 [g] S Dt 3:17
4:8 [h] 2Sa 20:21; 2Ki 10:7
[i] 1Sa 24:4; 25:29
[j] S Nu 31:3
4:9 [k] S Ge 48:16; 1Ki 1:29
4:10 [l] 2Sa 1:2-16
4:11 [m] S Ge 4:10; 9:5; Ps 9:12; 72:14
4:12 [n] 2Sa 1:15
5:1 [o] 2Sa 19:43
[p] S Ge 29:14; 35:26
5:2 [q] 1Sa 18:5,13,16
[r] S 1Sa 11:6
[s] S Ge 48:15; S 1Sa 16:1; 2Sa 7:7; Mt 2:6; Jn 21:16
[t] S 1Sa 12:12; S 13:14; S 2Sa 6:21

4:7 *Arabah.* See note on Dt 1:1.
4:8 *This day the LORD has avenged my lord the king against Saul.* Recab and Baanah depict their assassination of Ish-Bosheth in pious terms, expecting David to commend them for their act—a serious miscalculation.
4:9 *As surely as the LORD lives.* An oath formula (see note on 1Sa 14:39,45).
4:11 *demand his blood from your hand.* A call for the death penalty (see Ge 9:5–6 and notes). David here does what he was unable to do with Joab (see note on 3:29).
4:12 *their hands and feet.* The hands that had assassinated Ish-Bosheth and the feet that had run with the news (cf. note on 1Sa 5:4).
5:1—24:25 Beginning with ch. 5 there are sections of 2 Samuel (see also 3:2–5) that have parallel passages in 1 Chronicles (they are listed at the sectional headings). In some instances these parallel accounts are nearly identical; in others there are variations.
5:1 *All the tribes of Israel.* Representatives of each tribe, including elders and armed soldiers (see 1Ch 12:23–40). *your own flesh and blood.* The representatives of the various tribes cite three reasons for recognizing David as their king. The first of these is the acknowledgment that David is an Israelite. Even though national unity had been destroyed in the civil strife following Saul's death (2:8—3:1), this blood relationship had not been forgotten.
5:2 *the one who led Israel on their military campaigns.* The second reason (see note on v. 1) for recognizing David as king (see 1Sa 18:5,13–14,16,30). *the LORD said to you.* The third and most important reason (see 1Sa 13:13–14; 16:1,13–14; 23:17; 25:26–31 and notes). *shepherd ... ruler.* "Shepherd" was often used as a metaphor for political rule in the OT (see Ps

The City of the Jebusites/ David's Jerusalem

Substantial historical evidence, both Biblical and extra-Biblical, places the temple of Solomon on the holy spot where King David built an altar to the Lord. David had purchased the land from Araunah the Jebusite, who was using the exposed bedrock as a threshing floor (2Sa 24:18-25). Tradition claims a much older sanctity for the site, associating it with the altar of Abraham on Mount Moriah (Ge 22:1-19; see 1 Ch 3:1 and note). The writer of Genesis equates Moriah with "the mountain of the LORD" (see Ge 22:14 and note; see also 1Ch 3:1 and note).

c. 1000 B.C.

Less than 11 acres in size, Jebus, a Canaanite city, could well defend itself against attack, with walls atop steep canyons and shafts reaching an underground water source. David captured the stronghold c. 1000 B.C. and made it his capital.

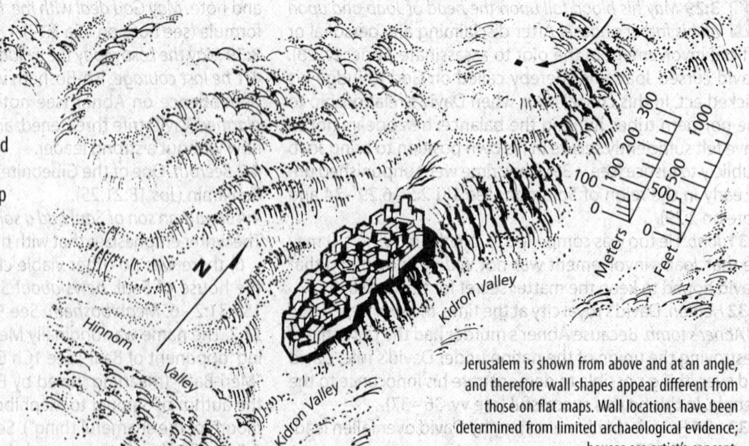

Jerusalem is shown from above and at an angle, and therefore wall shapes appear different from those on flat maps. Wall locations have been determined from limited archaeological evidence; houses are artist's concept.

3When all the elders of Israel had come
to King David at Hebron, the king made
a compact[u] with them at Hebron before
the LORD, and they anointed[v] David king
over Israel.
4David was thirty years old[w] when he
became king, and he reigned[x] forty[y] years.
5In Hebron he reigned over Judah seven
years and six months,[z] and in Jerusalem
he reigned over all Israel and Judah thirty-three years.

David Conquers Jerusalem

5:6-10pp — 1Ch 11:4-9
5:11-16pp — 1Ch 3:5-9; 14:1-7

6The king and his men marched to Jerusalem[a] to attack the Jebusites,[b] who lived
there. The Jebusites said to David, "You
will not get in here; even the blind and
the lame can ward you off." They thought,
"David cannot get in here." 7Nevertheless,
David captured the fortress of Zion,[c] the
City of David.[d][e]
8On that day, David said, "Anyone who
conquers the Jebusites will have to use
the water shaft[a][f] to reach those 'lame and
blind'[g] who are David's enemies.[b]" That is
why they say, "The 'blind and lame' will
not enter the palace."
9David then took up residence in the
fortress and called it the City of David.
He built up the area around it, from the
supporting terraces[c][h] inward. 10And he became more and more powerful,[i] because
the LORD God Almighty[j] was with him.[k]
11Now Hiram[l] king of Tyre sent messengers to David, along with cedar logs and
carpenters and stonemasons, and they

5:3 [u] 2Sa 3:21 [v] S Dt 17:15; 2Sa 2:4 **5:4** [w] S Ge 37:2; Lk 3:23 [x] 1Ki 2:11; 1Ch 3:4 [y] 1Ch 26:31 **5:5** [z] 2Sa 2:11; 1Ki 2:11; 1Ch 3:4 **5:6** [a] S Jdg 1:8 [b] S Jos 15:8 **5:7** [c] Ps 76:2 [d] Jer 21:13 [e] 2Sa 6:12, 16; 1Ki 2:10; 8:1; Isa 29:1; Jer 25:29 **5:8** [f] 2Ki 20:20; 2Ch 32:30 [g] Mt 21:14 **5:9** [h] 1Ki 9:15, 24 **5:10** [i] 2Sa 3:1 [j] Ps 24:10 [k] 2Sa 7:9 **5:11** [l] 1Ki 5:1, 18; 2Ch 2:3

[a] 8 *Or use scaling hooks* [b] 8 *Or are hated by David* [c] 9 *Or the Millo*

23:1; Jer 2:8; Eze 34:2 and notes) and elsewhere in the ancient Near East (see, e.g., the prologue to Hammurapi's Code — see chart, p. xxii). See also note on 1Sa 12:2 ("your leader"); cf. note on 1Sa 9:16 ("leader").

5:3 *the king made a compact with them ... before the LORD.* David and Israel entered into a covenant in which both the king and the people obligated themselves before the Lord to carry out their mutual responsibilities (see 2Ki 11:17 and note). Thus, while David was king over Judah as the one elevated to that position by his tribe and later became king over Jerusalem by conquest (vv. 6 – 10), his rule over the northern tribes was by virtue of a treaty (covenant) of submission. That treaty was not renewed with David's grandson Rehoboam because he refused to negotiate its terms at the time of his accession to the throne (1Ki 12:1 – 16). *they anointed David king over Israel.* The third time David was anointed (see note on 2:4).

5:5 *In Hebron he reigned ... seven years and six months.* See 2:11 and note. *Israel and Judah.* The specific relationship of David to these two segments of his realm appears to have remained distinct (see note on v. 3).

5:6 — 8:18 David's reign characterized: his victories over Israel's enemies, his devotion to the Lord, and the Lord's covenant with him to give him an enduring dynasty (cf. the corresponding segment of Saul's story in which his reign is characterized; see note on 1Sa 13:1 — 14:52).

5:6 – 25 Accounts of David's initial victories (over the Jebusites in Jerusalem and over the Philistines) and his later victories by which he secured all of Israel's borders (ch. 8) frame the accounts of David's devotion to the Lord (ch. 6) and the Lord's covenant with him (ch. 7).

5:6 *Jerusalem.* One of the most significant accomplishments of David's reign was the establishment of Jerusalem as his royal city and the nation's capital (see Introduction: Contents and Theme). The site was first occupied in the third millennium B.C. and was a royal city in the time of Abraham (see note on Ge 14:18). It was located on the border between Judah and Benjamin but was controlled by neither tribe. At the time of the conquest both Judah and Benjamin had attacked the city (see notes on Jdg 1:8,21), but it was quickly lost again to the Jebusites (see Jos 15:63 and note) and was sometimes referred to by the name Jebus (see Jdg 19:10; 1Ch 11:4). The city David conquered covered somewhat less than 11 acres and could have housed not many more than 3,500 inhabitants. By locating his royal city in a newly conquered town on the border between the two segments of his realm, David united the kingdom under his rule without seeming to subordinate one part to the other. *Jebusites.* A Canaanite people (see Ge 10:15 – 16 and note on 10:16) inhabiting Jerusalem (Jos 15:8; 18:16). *the blind and the lame can ward you off.* Jerusalem was a natural fortress because of its location on a rise surrounded on three sides by deep valleys; so the Jebusites were confident that their walls could easily be defended.

5:7 *fortress.* Probably the fortified city itself. *Zion.* The first occurrence of the name in the OT. Originally the name appears to have been given to the southernmost hill of the city on which the Jebusite fortress was located. As the city expanded (from the days of Solomon onward), the name continued to be applied to the entire city (see Isa 1:8 and note; 2:3). *City of David.* As Jerusalem's conqueror, David becomes its owner and gives it his name. Jerusalem's southeast hill (Ophel; see note on Ne 3:26) continued to bear the name long after David's time (see Isa 22:9; cf. also Isa 29:1).

5:8 *On that day, David said.* 1Ch 11:6 may be combined with this verse for a more complete account. Joab's part in the conquest of the city demonstrated again his military prowess and reconfirmed him in the position of commander of David's armies. *water shaft.* Although the Hebrew for this term is obscure (see NIV text note), it appears that David knew of a secret tunnel — perhaps running from the Gihon spring outside the city into the fortress — that gave access to water when the city was under siege (see 2Ch 32:30). *lame and blind.* An ironic reference to the Jebusites (cf. v. 6 and note). *The 'blind and lame' will not enter the palace.* The proverb may mean that the Jebusites did not have access to the royal palace, though they were allowed to remain in the city and its environs.

5:9 *supporting terraces.* Stone terraces on the steep slopes of the hill, creating additional space for buildings (but see NIV text note; see also note on Jdg 9:6).

5:10 *the LORD ... was with him.* See note on 1Sa 16:18.

5:11 *Hiram king of Tyre.* This Phoenician king was the first to accord the newly established King David international recognition. It was vital to him that he have good relations with the king of Israel since Israel dominated the inland trade routes to Tyre, and Tyre was dependent on Israelite agriculture for much of its food (also true in the first century A.D.; see Ac 12:20 and note). A close relationship existed between these two realms until the Babylonian invasions. *Tyre.* An important Phoenician seaport on the Mediterranean coast north of Israel (see Eze 26 – 27). *cedar.* A strong, durable wood used by the powerful and wealthy throughout the ancient

built a palace for David. 12And David knew
that the LORD had established him as king
over Israel and had exalted his kingdom[m]
for the sake of his people Israel.

13After he left Hebron, David took more
concubines and wives[n] in Jerusalem, and
more sons and daughters were born to
him. 14These are the names of the children born to him there:[o] Shammua, Shobab, Nathan,[p] Solomon, 15Ibhar, Elishua,
Nepheg, Japhia, 16Elishama, Eliada and
Eliphelet.

David Defeats the Philistines

5:17-25pp — 1Ch 14:8-17

17When the Philistines heard that David
had been anointed king over Israel, they
went up in full force to search for him, but
David heard about it and went down to
the stronghold.[q] 18Now the Philistines had
come and spread out in the Valley of Rephaim;[r] 19so David inquired[s] of the LORD,
"Shall I go and attack the Philistines? Will
you hand them over to me?"

The LORD answered him, "Go, for I will
surely hand the Philistines over to you."

20So David went to Baal Perazim, and
there he defeated them. He said, "As waters break out, the LORD has broken out
against my enemies before me." So that
place was called Baal Perazim.[a t] 21The
Philistines abandoned their idols there,
and David and his men carried them
off.[u]

22Once more the Philistines came up
and spread out in the Valley of Rephaim;
23so David inquired of the LORD, and he
answered, "Do not go straight up, but circle around behind them and attack them
in front of the balsam trees. 24As soon as
you hear the sound[v] of marching in the
tops of the balsam trees, move quickly,
because that will mean the LORD has gone
out in front[w] of you to strike the Philistine army." 25So David did as the LORD
commanded him, and he struck down the
Philistines[x] all the way from Gibeon[b y] to
Gezer.[z]

The Ark Brought to Jerusalem

6:1-11pp — 1Ch 13:1-14
6:12-19pp — 1Ch 15:25–16:3

6 David again brought together out of Israel chosen men, thirty thousand in all.
2He and all his men set out from Baalah[a]
of Judah[c] to bring up from there the ark[b]
of God, which is called by the Name,[d c] the
name of the LORD Almighty, who is enthroned[d] between the cherubim[e] that are

5:12 [m]S Nu 24:7 **5:13** [n]S Dt 17:17 **5:14** [o]1Ch 3:5 [p]Lk 3:31 **5:17** [q]2Sa 23:14; 1Ch 11:16 **5:18** [r]S Jos 15:8; S 17:15 **5:19** [s]S Jdg 18:5; S 1Sa 23:2 **5:20** [t]S Ge 38:29 **5:21** [u]Dt 7:5; Isa 46:2 **5:24** [v]S Ex 14:24 [w]Jdg 4:14 **5:25** [x]2Sa 8:12; 21:15 [y]Isa 28:21 [z]S Jos 10:33 **6:2** [a]S Jos 15:9 [b]1Sa 4:4; 7:1 [c]Lev 24:16; Dt 28:10; Isa 63:14 [d]Ps 99:1; 132:14 [e]S Ge 3:24; S Ex 25:22

[a] 20 *Baal Perazim* means *the lord who breaks out.*
[b] 25 Septuagint (see also 1 Chron. 14:16); Hebrew *Geba*
[c] 2 That is, Kiriath Jearim; Hebrew *Baale Judah*, a variant of *Baalah of Judah*
[d] 2 Hebrew; Septuagint and Vulgate do not have *the Name.*

Near East for building and decorating temples and palaces (see 1Ki 5:6 and note; 6:9; SS 5:15 and note; 8:9; Jer 22:14–15; Hag 1:4 and note).

5:12 *David knew that the LORD had established him as king.* In the ideology of the ancient Near East the king's possession of a palace was the chief symbolic indication of his status. *for the sake of his people Israel.* David acknowledged that his elevation to kingship over all Israel was the Lord's doing and that it was an integral part of his continuing redemptive program for Israel—just as the ministries of Moses, Joshua, the judges and Samuel had been.

5:13 *David took more concubines and wives.* See notes on 3:2–5; Ge 25:6.

5:14 *Shammua, Shobab, Nathan, Solomon.* 1Ch 3:5 designates Bathsheba as their mother.

5:17 *When the Philistines heard that David had been anointed king.* Chronologically it is likely that the Philistine attack followed immediately after the events of v. 3 and before the capture of Jerusalem (vv. 6–10). (The author arranged his narrative by topics; see note on 7:1.) The Philistines had not been disturbed by David's reign over Judah, but now they acted to protect their interests in the north, much of which they dominated after the defeat of Saul (1Sa 31). *stronghold.* Probably a reference to the desert area in southern Judah where David had hidden from Saul (see notes on 1Sa 22:4; 23:14). This action of David suggests that he had not yet taken Jerusalem.

5:18,22 *Valley of Rephaim.* Bordering ancient Jerusalem on the west and southwest (see Jos 15:8; 18:16; see also note on Isa 17:5).

5:19 *David inquired of the LORD.* See notes on 2:1; 1Sa 2:28; 22:20; 23:2,4.

5:20 *the LORD has broken out … Baal Perazim.* See NIV text note. As a true theocratic king, David attributes the victory to the Lord and does not claim the glory for himself (see notes on 1Sa 10:18,27; 11:13; 12:11; 14:23; 17:11,45–47).

5:21 *abandoned their idols there.* As the Israelites had taken the ark into battle (see note on 1Sa 4:3), so the Philistines carried images of their deities into battle in the hope that this would ensure victory. *carried them off.* In compliance with the instruction of Dt 7:5, the Israelites also burned them (see 1Ch 14:12 and note).

5:23 *he answered.* As had been true in the case of the conquest under Joshua, the Lord ordered the battle and he himself marched against the enemy with his heavenly host (see Jos 6:2–5 and note on 6:2; 8:1–2; 10:8,14; 11:6). David's wars were a continuation and completion of the wars fought by Joshua.

5:24 *sound of marching.* The heavenly host of the Lord going into battle (see Jos 5:14 and note).

5:25 *Gibeon.* See notes on 2:12–13; Jos 9:3. *Gezer.* Fifteen miles west of Gibeon, overlooking the Philistine plain (see note on Jos 10:33).

6:1–23 The supreme expression of David's devotion to the Lord.

6:2 *Baalah of Judah.* See NIV text note; see also Jos 15:60; 18:14; 1Sa 6:21 and note; 7:1. *ark of God.* See Ex 25:10–22 and note on 25:10; see also notes on 1Sa 4:3–4,21. The ark had remained at Kiriath Jearim during the reign of Saul. *called by the Name.* Used elsewhere to designate ownership (see 12:28; Dt 28:10; Isa 4:1; 43:7 and note; 63:19). *LORD Almighty.* See note on 1Sa 1:3. *enthroned between the cherubim.* See note on 1Sa 4:4; see also 1Ch 28:2 ("footstool of our God"). David recognized the great significance of the ark as the earthly throne of Israel's God. As a true theocratic king, he wished to acknowledge the Lord's kingship and rule over both himself and the people by restoring the ark to the center of the nation's life.

on the ark. 3They set the ark of God on a
new cart[f] and brought it from the house of
Abinadab, which was on the hill.[g] Uzzah
and Ahio, sons of Abinadab, were guiding the new cart 4with the ark of God on
it,[a] and Ahio was walking in front of it.
5David and the whole house of Israel were
celebrating[h] with all their might before the
LORD, with songs[b] and with harps, lyres,
tambourines, sistrums and cymbals.[i]
6When they came to the threshing
floor of Nacon, Uzzah reached out and
took hold of[j] the ark of God, because the
oxen stumbled. 7The LORD's anger burned
against Uzzah because of his irreverent
act;[k] therefore God struck him down[l] and
he died there beside the ark of God.
8Then David was angry because the
LORD's wrath[m] had broken out against Uzzah, and to this day that place is called
Perez Uzzah.[c][n]
9David was afraid of the LORD that day
and said, "How[o] can the ark of the LORD
ever come to me?" 10He was not willing
to take the ark of the LORD to be with him
in the City of David. Instead, he took it
aside to the house of Obed-Edom[p] the Gittite. 11The ark of the LORD remained in the
house of Obed-Edom the Gittite for three
months, and the LORD blessed him and his
entire household.[q]
12Now King David[r] was told, "The LORD
has blessed the household of Obed-Edom
and everything he has, because of the ark
of God." So David went down and brought
up the ark of God from the house of Obed-
Edom to the City of David with rejoicing.
13When those who were carrying the ark
of the LORD had taken six steps, he sacrificed[s] a bull and a fattened calf. 14David,
wearing a linen ephod,[t] danced[u] before
the LORD with all his might, 15while he
and the entire house of Israel brought up
the ark of the LORD with shouts[v] and the
sound of trumpets.[w]
16As the ark of the LORD was entering the
City of David,[x] Michal[y] daughter of Saul
watched from a window. And when she
saw King David leaping and dancing before
the LORD, she despised him in her heart.
17They brought the ark of the LORD and
set it in its place inside the tent that David
had pitched for it,[z] and David sacrificed
burnt offerings[a] and fellowship offerings[d]
before the LORD. 18After he had finished
sacrificing[b] the burnt offerings and fellowship offerings, he blessed[c] the people in
the name of the LORD Almighty. 19Then he
gave a loaf of bread, a cake of dates and a
cake of raisins[d] to each person in the whole
crowd of Israelites, both men and women.[e]
And all the people went to their homes.
20When David returned home to bless
his household, Michal daughter of Saul
came out to meet him and said, "How the
king of Israel has distinguished himself
today, disrobing[f] in the sight of the slave
girls of his servants as any vulgar fellow
would!"
21David said to Michal, "It was before
the LORD, who chose me rather than your

6:3 [f] ver 7; Nu 7:4-9; S 1Sa 6:7 [g] 2Sa 7:1
6:5 [h] S Ex 15:20 [i] Ezr 3:10; Ne 12:27; Ps 150:5
6:6 [j] S Nu 4:15, 19-20
6:7 [k] 1Ch 15:13-15 [l] S Ex 19:22; S 1Sa 5:6; 6:19; S 25:38
6:8 [m] Ps 7:11 [n] S Ge 38:29
6:9 [o] S 1Sa 6:20
6:10 [p] 1Ch 15:18; 26:4-5
6:11 [q] S Ge 30:27; 39:5
6:12 [r] 1Ki 8:1
6:13 [s] 1Ki 8:5,62; Ezr 6:17
6:14 [t] Ex 19:6; S 1Sa 2:18 [u] S Ex 15:20
6:15 [v] S Jos 6:5 [w] Ps 47:5; 98:6
6:16 [x] S 2Sa 5:7 [y] S 1Sa 18:27
6:17 [z] 1Ki 8:6; 1Ch 15:1; 2Ch 1:4 [a] Lev 1:1-17; 1Ki 8:62-64
6:18 [b] 1Ki 8:22 [c] S Ex 39:43
6:19 [d] Hos 3:1 [e] Dt 26:13; Ne 8:10
6:20 [f] S 1Sa 19:24

[a] 3,4 Dead Sea Scrolls and some Septuagint manuscripts; Masoretic Text *cart* 4*and they brought it with the ark of God from the house of Abinadab, which was on the hill* [b] 5 See Dead Sea Scrolls, Septuagint and 1 Chron. 13:8; Masoretic Text *celebrating before the LORD with all kinds of instruments made of pine.* [c] 8 *Perez Uzzah* means *outbreak against Uzzah.* [d] 17 Traditionally *peace offerings*; also in verse 18

6:3 *new cart.* David follows the example of the Philistines (see 1Sa 6:7) rather than the instructions of Ex 25:12–15; Nu 4:5–6,15, which require that the ark be carried on the shoulders of the Levites (see 1Ch 15:13–15 and note). *from the house of Abinadab.* See 1Sa 7:1 and note. *Uzzah and Ahio, sons of Abinadab.* 1Sa 7:1 speaks of Eleazar as the son of Abinadab. The Hebrew word for "son" can have the broader meaning of "descendant."

6:5 *sistrums.* Percussion instruments played by shaking with the hand; mentioned only here in the Bible.

6:7 *his irreverent act.* Although Uzzah's intent may have been good, he violated the clear instructions the Lord had given for handling the ark (see notes on v. 3; 1Sa 6:19). At this important new beginning in Israel's life with the Lord, the Lord gives a shocking and vivid reminder to David and Israel that those who claim to serve him must acknowledge his rule with absolute seriousness (see Lev 10:1–3; Jos 7:24–25 and notes; Ac 5:1–11—all instances of stern divine judgments at the beginnings of new eras in the history of redemption).

6:8 *David was angry.* David's initial reaction was resentment that his attempt to honor the Lord had resulted in a display of God's wrath. *to this day.* Until the time of the writing of 2 Samuel. *Perez Uzzah.* See NIV text note. The place-name memorialized a divine warning that was not soon forgotten (see Jos 7:26 and NIV text note). Evenhanded in his judgment against sinners, the Lord plays no favorites as he "breaks out" against friend and foe alike (see 5:20 and note).

6:9 *David was afraid of the LORD.* David's anger was accompanied by fear—not the wholesome fear of proper honor and respect for the Lord (see 1Sa 12:24; Jos 24:14 and note; see also notes on Ge 20:11; Pr 1:7) but an anxiety arising from an acute sense of his own guilt (Ge 3:10; Dt 5:5).

6:10 *Gittite.* He appears to have been a Levite (see note on 1Ch 13:13; cf. 1Ch 15:18,24; 16:5; 26:4–8,15; 2Ch 25:24), though many think the term "Gittite" fixes his place of birth at the Philistine city of Gath (see 15:18 and note). However, Gittite may be a reference to the Levitical city Gath Rimmon in Dan or Manasseh (Jos 21:20–25).

6:12 *David ... brought up the ark.* God's blessing on the household of Obed-Edom showed David that God's anger had been appeased.

6:13 *those ... carrying the ark.* David had become aware of his previous error (see 1Ch 15:13–15 and note).

6:14 *linen ephod.* See note on 1Sa 2:18.

6:16 *she despised him.* Michal had no appreciation for the significance of the event and deeply resented David's public display as unworthy of the dignity of a king (see vv. 20–23).

6:17 *burnt offerings.* See note on Lev 1:3. *fellowship offerings.* See notes on Lev 3:1; 1Sa 11:15.

6:18 *he blessed the people.* As Solomon would later do at the dedication of the temple (1Ki 8:55–61). *LORD Almighty.* See note on 1Sa 1:3.

6:21 *ruler.* See note on 1Sa 9:16 ("leader").

father or anyone from his house when
he appointed[g] me ruler[h] over the LORD's
people Israel—I will celebrate before the
LORD. 22I will become even more undigni-
fied than this, and I will be humiliated in
my own eyes. But by these slave girls you
spoke of, I will be held in honor."
23And Michal daughter of Saul had no
children to the day of her death.

God's Promise to David

7:1-17pp — 1Ch 17:1-15

7 After the king was settled in his palace[i]
and the LORD had given him rest from
all his enemies[j] around him,[k] 2he said to
Nathan[l] the prophet, "Here I am, living in
a palace[m] of cedar, while the ark of God
remains in a tent."[n]
3Nathan replied to the king, "Whatever
you have in mind,[o] go ahead and do it, for
the LORD is with you."
4That night the word of the LORD came
to Nathan, saying:
5"Go and tell my servant David,
'This is what the LORD says: Are you[p]
the one to build me a house to dwell
in?[q] 6I have not dwelt in a house from
the day I brought the Israelites up out
of Egypt to this day.[r] I have been moving from place to place with a tent[s]
as my dwelling.[t] 7Wherever I have
moved with all the Israelites,[u] did I
ever say to any of their rulers whom I
commanded to shepherd[v] my people
Israel, "Why have you not built me a
house[w] of cedar?[x]"'
8"Now then, tell my servant David,
'This is what the LORD Almighty says:
I took you from the pasture and from
following the flock[y] to be ruler[z] over
my people Israel.[a] 9I have been with
you wherever you have gone,[b] and I
have cut off all your enemies from before you.[c] Now I will make your name
great, like the names of the greatest
men of the earth.[d] 10And I will provide a place for my people Israel and
will plant[e] them so that they can have
a home of their own and no longer be
disturbed.[f] Wicked[g] people will not
oppress them anymore,[h] as they did
at the beginning 11and have done ever
since the time I appointed leaders[a][i]
over my people Israel. I will also give
you rest from all your enemies.[j]
"'The LORD declares[k] to you that
the LORD himself will establish[l] a
house[m] for you: 12When your days
are over and you rest[n] with your fathers, I will raise up your offspring

[a] *11* Traditionally *judges*

6:21 [g] 1Sa 13:14; S 15:28 [h] 2Sa 5:2; 7:8; 1Ch 5:2; 17:7; Mic 5:2 **7:1** [i] 2Sa 6:3 [j] ver 11 [k] 1Ch 22:18 **7:2** [l] 2Sa 12:1; 1Ki 1:8, 22; 1Ch 29:29; 2Ch 9:29 [m] 2Sa 5:11; 1Ki 3:1; 7:1, 2, 7; 9:1; 2Ch 8:1; Jer 22:14; Hag 1:4 [n] S Ex 26:1; Ps 132:3; Ac 7:45-46 **7:3** [o] S 1Sa 10:7; Ps 132:1-5 **7:5** [p] 1Ki 8:19; 1Ch 22:8 [q] 1Ki 5:3-5; 1Ch 28:3 **7:6** [r] Ac 7:45 [s] Ex 40:18, 34; Jos 18:1 [t] 1Ki 8:16 **7:7** [u] Dt 23:14 [v] S 2Sa 5:2 [w] 1Ki 8:27; Isa 66:1 [x] Lev 26:11-12 **7:8** [y] S 1Sa 16:11; 1Ch 21:17; Ps 74:1; Am 7:15 [z] S 1Sa 2:7-8; S 9:16; S 16:1; S 2Sa 6:21 [a] Ps 78:70-72; 2Co 6:18* **7:9** [b] S 1Sa 18:14; 2Sa 5:10 [c] Ps 18:37-42 [d] S Ex 11:3 **7:10** [e] S Ex 15:17; Isa 5:1-7 [f] 2Ki 21:8; 2Ch 33:8 [g] Ps 89:22-23 [h] Ps 147:14; Isa 54:14; 60:18 **7:11** [i] S Jdg 2:16; 1Sa 12:9-11 [j] ver 1 [k] 1Ki 2:24 [l] 1Sa 25:28; Ps 89:35-37; S Mt 1:1; Lk 1:32-33; Ac 13:22-23; 2Ti 2:8 [m] S Ex 1:21; Isa 7:2 **7:12** [n] S Ge 15:15; 1Ki 2:1; Ac 13:36

6:23 *Michal ... had no children.* Probably a punishment for her pride and at the same time another manifestation of God's judgment on the house of Saul.

7:1–29 God's great promise to David (see Introduction: Contents and Theme). Although it is not expressly called a covenant here, it is elsewhere (see 23:5 and note; Ps 89:3,28,34,39 and note on 89:30–37; cf. Ps 132:11 and note), and David responds with language suggesting his recognition that a covenant had been made (see also notes on vv. 11,16,20,28).

7:1 *After the king was settled in his palace.* See 5:11–12 and notes. *the LORD had given him rest from all his enemies.* Cf. 1Ki 5:4 and note. Chronologically the victories noted in 8:1–14 probably preceded the events of this chapter. The arrangement of material is topical (see notes on 5:17; 8:1)—ch. 6 records the bringing of the ark to Jerusalem; ch. 7 tells of David's desire to build a temple in Jerusalem in which to house the ark.

7:2 *Nathan.* The first reference to this prophet. *cedar.* See note on 5:11. *tent.* See v. 6; 6:17. Now that he himself had a royal palace (symbolic of his established kingship), a tent did not seem to David to be an appropriate place for the throne of Israel's divine King (see note on 6:2; see also Ps 132:1–5 and notes; Ac 7:46). He wanted to build Israel's heavenly King a royal house in the capital city of his kingdom.

7:3 *Nathan replied.* In consulting a prophet, David sought God's will, but Nathan boldly voiced approval of David's plans in the Lord's name before he had received a revelation from the Lord. *the LORD is with you.* See v. 9; see also note on 1Sa 16:18.

7:5–16 The Davidic covenant (see note on v. 11).

7:5 *Are you the one ... ?* David's desire was commendable (1Ki 8:17–19), but his gift and mission were to fight the Lord's battles until Israel was securely at rest in the promised land (see v. 10; 1Ki 5:3–4; 1Ch 22:8–9 and notes).

7:7 *did I ever say ..., "Why have you not built me a house ... ?"* David misunderstood the Lord's priorities. He reflected the pagan notion that the gods were interested in human beings only as builders and maintainers of their temples and as practitioners of their religion. Instead, the Lord had raised up rulers in Israel only to shepherd his people (that is also why he had brought David "from the pasture," v. 8).

7:9 *I have cut off all your enemies.* See note on v. 1.

7:10 *I will provide a place for my people Israel.* It is for this purpose that the Lord has made David king, and through David he will do it. *at the beginning.* In Egypt.

7:11 *leaders.* During the period of the judges (see NIV text note). *I will also give you rest from all your enemies.* See vv. 1,9. David's victories over threatening powers will be complete, so that the rest already enjoyed will be assured for the future. *the LORD himself will establish a house for you.* Compare this statement with the rhetorical question of v. 5. In a beautiful play on words God says that David is not to build him a house (temple); rather, God will build David a house (royal dynasty) that will last forever (v. 16). God has been building Israel ever since the days of Abraham, and now he commits himself to build David's royal house so that the promise to Israel may be fulfilled—rest in the promised land. It is God's building that effects his kingdom. This covenant with David is unconditional, like those with Noah, Abram and Phinehas (see note on Ge 9:9; see also chart, p. 19), grounded only in God's firm and gracious purpose. It finds its ultimate fulfillment in the kingship of Christ, who was born of the tribe of Judah and the house of David (see 23:5; Ps 89:3–4,30–37; 132:11–18; Isa 9:1–7; 55:3; Mt 1:1; Lk 1:32–33,69; Ac 2:29–30; 13:22–23; Ro 1:2–3; 2Ti 2:8; Rev 3:7; 5:5; 22:16 and relevant notes).

7:12 *raise up your offspring to succeed you.* The royal line of

to succeed you, who will come from
your own body,[o] and I will establish
his kingdom.[p] 13He is the one who
will build a house[q] for my Name,[r]
and I will establish the throne of his
kingdom forever.[s] 14I will be his father, and he will be my son.[t] When
he does wrong, I will punish him[u]
with the rod[v] of men, with floggings
inflicted by men. 15But my love will
never be taken away from him,[w] as I
took it away from Saul,[x] whom I removed from before you. 16Your house
and your kingdom will endure forever
before me[a]; your throne[y] will be established[z] forever.[a]'"

17Nathan reported to David all the words
of this entire revelation.

David's Prayer

7:18-29pp — 1Ch 17:16-27

18Then King David went in and sat before the LORD, and he said:

"Who am I,[b] O Sovereign LORD,
and what is my family, that you have
brought me this far? 19And as if this
were not enough in your sight, O Sovereign LORD, you have also spoken
about the future of the house of your
servant. Is this your usual way of dealing with man,[c] O Sovereign LORD?
20"What more can David say[d] to
you? For you know[e] your servant,[f]
O Sovereign LORD. 21For the sake of
your word and according to your will,
you have done this great thing and
made it known to your servant.
22"How great[g] you are,[h] O Sovereign
LORD! There is no one like[i] you, and
there is no God[j] but you, as we have
heard with our own ears.[k] 23And who
is like your people Israel[l]—the one
nation on earth that God went out to
redeem as a people for himself, and
to make a name[m] for himself, and to
perform great and awesome wonders[n]
by driving out nations and their gods
from before your people, whom you
redeemed[o] from Egypt?[b] 24You have
established your people Israel as your
very own[p] forever, and you, O LORD,
have become their God.[q]
25"And now, LORD God, keep forever the promise[r] you have made concerning your servant and his house.
Do as you promised, 26so that your
name[s] will be great forever. Then men
will say, 'The LORD Almighty is God
over Israel!' And the house of your

7:12 [o] 1Ki 8:20; Ps 132:11-12; Jer 30:21; 33:15 [p] 2Ch 23:3 **7:13** [q] S Dt 12:5; 1Ki 6:12 [r] Dt 16:11; 1Ki 5:5; 8:19, 29; 2Ki 21:4, 7 [s] ver 16; S Ge 9:16; 2Sa 22:51; 1Ki 2:4, 45; 1Ch 22:10; 28:6; 2Ch 6:16; 7:18; 13:5; 21:7; Ps 89:3-4, 29, 35-37; Pr 25:5; Isa 9:7; 16:5; Jer 17:25; 33:17, 21; Da 7:27 **7:14** [t] Ps 2:7; 89:26; Jer 3:19; S Mt 3:17; Jn 1:49; 2Co 6:18*; Heb 1:5*; Rev 21:7 [u] S Dt 8:5; 1Ki 11:34; 1Ch 22:10; Heb 12:7 [v] Ps 89:30-33; Pr 13:24 **7:15** [w] ver 25; 1Ki 2:4; 6:12; 8:25; 9:5; 11:13, 32; 2Ki 19:34; 2Ch 6:16; 7:18; 21:7; Ps 89:24, 33; Jer 33:17 [x] S 1Sa 13:13; S 15:28; 16:14 **7:16** [y] Ps 89:36-37; S Lk 1:33 [z] Ps 9:7; 93:2; 103:19 [a] S ver 13

[a] *16* Some Hebrew manuscripts and Septuagint; most Hebrew manuscripts *you* [b] *23* See Septuagint and 1 Chron. 17:21; Hebrew *wonders for your land and before your people, whom you redeemed from Egypt, from the nations and their gods.*

7:18 [b] S Ex 3:11 **7:19** [c] Isa 55:8-9 **7:20** [d] Isa 38:15 [e] Jn 21:17 [f] S 1Sa 16:7 **7:22** [g] Ps 48:1; 77:13; 86:10; Jer 10:6 [h] Dt 3:24 [i] S Ex 9:14 [j] S Ex 8:10; S 20:4 [k] Ex 10:2; S Jdg 6:13; Ps 44:1 **7:23** [l] Dt 4:32-38; S 33:29; S 1Sa 12:22 [m] S Nu 6:27 [n] Dt 10:21 [o] Dt 7:7-8; S 9:26 **7:24** [p] Dt 26:18 [q] Ex 6:6-7; Ps 48:14 **7:25** [r] S ver 15; S Nu 23:19; 2Ch 1:9 **7:26** [s] S Ex 6:3; Ne 9:5; Ps 72:19; 96:8; Mt 6:9

David, in contrast to that of Saul, would continue after David's death by dynastic succession.

7:13 *He is the one who will build a house for my Name.* God's priorities are that his own royal house, where his throne (the ark) can finally come to rest (1Ch 6:31; 28:2), will wait until Israel is at rest and David's dynasty (in the person of his son Solomon) is secure. "Name" is equivalent to "me" in v. 5 (see note on 1Sa 25:25).

7:14 *his father ... my son.* This familial language expresses the special relationship God promises to maintain with the descendant(s) of David whom he will establish on David's throne. It marks him as the one whom God has chosen and enthroned to rule in his name as the official representative of God's rule over his people (see notes on Ps 2:7; 45:6; 89:27; see also 89:26). In Jesus Christ this promise comes to ultimate fulfillment (see Mk 1:11; Heb 1:5 and notes).

7:15 *my love.* God's special and unfailing favor (see note on Ps 6:4).

7:16 *your throne will be established forever.* See note on v. 11; see also Introduction: Contents and Theme. The promise of an everlasting kingdom for the house of David became the focal point for many later prophecies and powerfully influenced the development of the Messianic hope in Israel.

7:18–29 David's prayer expresses wonder that God would make such commitments to him and his descendants. But he also acknowledges that what God had pledged to him is for Israel's sake, that its purpose is the fulfillment of God's covenanted promises to his people, and that its ultimate effect will be the honor and praise of God throughout the world.

7:18 *went in.* Presumably into the tent (6:17) in which the ark was kept. *sat before the LORD.* The ark was the symbol of God's presence with his people (see Ex 25:22; see also notes on 1Sa 4:3–4,21).

7:19 *Is this your usual way of dealing with man, O Sovereign LORD?* The meaning of this clause is uncertain (cf. 1Ch 17:17). It has also been taken as an exclamation ("This is your law for man, O Sovereign LORD!") and understood as a summation of the divine decree concerning David and his house.

7:20 *know.* Or "especially acknowledge" (see Hos 2:20; 6:6 and notes) or "choose" (see Ge 18:19; Am 3:2). David recognizes God's promise as a covenant (see 23:5 and note).

7:21 *your word.* Probably God's covenant word of promise to his people.

7:22 *no God but you.* See 22:32; 1Sa 2:2; cf. Ex 20:3; Dt 4:35; 6:4 and notes.

7:23 *the one nation on earth that God went out to redeem as a people for himself.* Israel's uniqueness did not consist in her national achievements but in God's choice of her to be his own people (see Dt 7:6,8 and notes; 33:26–29). *to make a name for himself.* The basis for God's electing love, revealed in his dealings with Israel, did not lie in any meritorious characteristic of the Israelite people but in his own sovereign purposes (see 1Sa 12:22; Dt 7:6–8; 9:4–6; Ne 9:10; Isa 63:12; Jer 32:20–21; Eze 36:22–38).

7:24 *your people ... their God.* David recalls the essence of God's covenant relationship with his people (see Jer 7:23 and note). *you, O LORD, have become their God.* What God has pledged to David, he has pledged as the God of Israel (see Zec 8:8 and note).

servant David will be established[t] before you.
27“O LORD Almighty, God of Israel,
you have revealed this to your servant, saying, ‘I will build a house
for you.’ So your servant has found
courage to offer you this prayer. 28O
Sovereign LORD, you are God! Your
words are trustworthy,[u] and you have
promised these good things to your
servant. 29Now be pleased to bless
the house of your servant, that it may
continue forever in your sight; for
you, O Sovereign LORD, have spoken,
and with your blessing[v] the house of
your servant will be blessed forever.”

David's Victories

8:1-14pp — 1Ch 18:1-13

8 In the course of time, David defeated
the Philistines[w] and subdued[x] them,
and he took Metheg Ammah from the control of the Philistines.
2David also defeated the Moabites.[y] He
made them lie down on the ground and
measured them off with a length of cord.
Every two lengths of them were put to
death, and the third length was allowed
to live. So the Moabites became subject to
David and brought tribute.[z]
3Moreover, David fought Hadadezer[a]
son of Rehob, king of Zobah,[b] when he
went to restore his control along the Euphrates[c] River. 4David captured a thousand of his chariots, seven thousand charioteers[a] and twenty thousand foot soldiers.
He hamstrung[d] all but a hundred of the
chariot horses.
5When the Arameans of Damascus[e]
came to help Hadadezer king of Zobah,
David struck down twenty-two thousand
of them. 6He put garrisons[f] in the Aramean kingdom of Damascus, and the Arameans became subject[g] to him and brought
tribute. The LORD gave David victory wherever he went.[h]
7David took the gold shields[i] that belonged to the officers of Hadadezer and
brought them to Jerusalem. 8From Tebah[b]
and Berothai,[j] towns that belonged to
Hadadezer, King David took a great quantity of bronze.
9When Tou[c] king of Hamath[k] heard
that David had defeated the entire army
of Hadadezer,[l] 10he sent his son Joram[d] to
King David to greet him and congratulate
him on his victory in battle over Hadadezer, who had been at war with Tou. Joram brought with him articles of silver and
gold and bronze.
11King David dedicated[m] these articles to
the LORD, as he had done with the silver
and gold from all the nations he had subdued: 12Edom[e][n] and Moab,[o] the Ammonites[p] and the Philistines,[q] and Amalek.[r]
He also dedicated the plunder taken from
Hadadezer son of Rehob, king of Zobah.
13And David became famous[s] after he
returned from striking down eighteen
thousand Edomites[f] in the Valley of Salt.[t]

7:26 [t]S 1Sa 25:28 **7:28** [u]Ex 34:6; Jn 17:17 **7:29** [v]Nu 6:23-27 **8:1** [w]Ps 60:8; 87:4; 108:9 [x]Heb 11:32-33 **8:2** [y]S Ge 19:37; S Nu 21:29 [z]S Jdg 3:15; S Isa 45:14 **8:3** [a]2Sa 10:16,19; 1Ki 11:23 [b]S 1Sa 14:47 [c]S Ge 2:14 **8:4** [d]S Ge 49:6; Jos 11:9 **8:5** [e]S Ge 14:15; 2Sa 10:6; 1Ki 11:24; 2Ki 8:7; 14:28
8:6 [f]1Ki 20:34 [g]2Sa 10:19 [h]2Sa 3:18 **8:7** [i]1Ki 10:16; 14:26; 2Ki 11:10 **8:8** [j]Eze 47:16 **8:9** [k]1Ki 8:65; 2Ki 14:28; 2Ch 8:4 [l]Lk 14:31-32 **8:11** [m]ver 12; 1Ki 7:51; 15:15; 1Ch 26:26; 2Ch 5:1 **8:12** [n]S Nu 24:18 [o]ver 2 [p]2Sa 10:14 [q]S 2Sa 5:25 [r]S Nu 24:20; S 1Sa 27:8 **8:13** [s]2Sa 7:9 [t]2Ki 14:7; 1Ch 18:12; Ps 60 Title

[a] *4* Septuagint (see also Dead Sea Scrolls and 1 Chron. 18:4); Masoretic Text *captured seventeen hundred of his charioteers* [b] *8* See some Septuagint manuscripts (see also 1 Chron. 18:8); Hebrew *Betah.* [c] *9* Hebrew *Toi,* a variant of *Tou*; also in verse 10 [d] *10* A variant of *Hadoram* [e] *12* Some Hebrew manuscripts, Septuagint and Syriac (see also 1 Chron. 18:11); most Hebrew manuscripts *Aram* [f] *13* A few Hebrew manuscripts, Septuagint and Syriac (see also 1 Chron. 18:12); most Hebrew manuscripts *Aram* (that is, Arameans)

7:27 *your servant has found courage to offer you this prayer.* David's prayer lays claim to God's promise.

7:28 *good things.* A common summary expression for covenant benefits from God (see, e.g., 1Sa 2:32, "good"; Nu 10:29,32; Dt 26:11; Jos 21:45; 23:14, "good promises"; Isa 63:7; Jer 29:32; 32:40 – 41, "good"; 33:9).

8:1 – 18 See note on 5:6 – 25.

8:1 *In the course of time.* See note on 2:1. Chronologically the events of this chapter, or many of them, are probably to be placed between chs. 5 and 6 (see 7:1 and note). *Metheg Ammah.* Perhaps a way of referring to Gath and its environs (see 1Ch 18:1).

8:2 *Moabites.* Descendants of Lot (see Ge 19:36 – 38 and note), occupying territory east of the Dead Sea. Saul fought against the Moabites (1Sa 14:47), and David sought refuge in Moab for his parents during his exile from Israel (see 1Sa 22:3 – 4 and note on 22:3). David's great-grandmother Ruth was from Moab (see Ru 1:4; 4:13,21 – 22).

8:3 *Hadadezer.* Means "Hadad is (my) help." Hadad was an Aramean deity equivalent to the Canaanite Baal. *Zobah.* Saul had previously fought against the kings of Zobah (1Sa 14:47), whose territory was apparently located in the Beqaa Valley between the Lebanon and Anti-Lebanon mountains, thus on Israel's northern border. *restore.* Saul's earlier victories over the kings of Zobah had extended Israelite control, if only briefly, as far as the fringes of the Euphrates Valley. *Euphrates River.* The land promised to Abraham had included borders from Egypt to the Euphrates (see Ge 15:18; Dt 1:7 and notes; 11:24; Jos 1:4 and note). Here is at least another provisional fulfillment of this promise (see 1Ki 4:21,24 and notes; see also Ge 17:8; Jos 21:43 – 45 and note). See map No. 5 at the end of this study Bible.

8:4 See NIV text note. *hamstrung all but a hundred of the chariot horses.* See Jos 11:6 and note. David's action is often attributed to his supposed ignorance of the value of the chariot as a military weapon. It is more likely, however, that he was acting in obedience to the ancient divine command not to "acquire great numbers of horses for himself" (Dt 17:16; cf. 1Sa 8:11 and note).

8:5 *Arameans.* See notes on Dt 26:5; 1Ch 18:5. *came to help Hadadezer.* They feared Israelite expansion to the north.

8:6,14 *The LORD … wherever he went.* The sentence summarizes David's victories at two critical points in this section (vv. 1 – 14) and reminds the reader that God, not David, is the true Savior of his people.

8:7 *gold shields.* Shields adorned with gold — the phrase is similar to "iron chariots" (see Jos 17:16 and note).

8:8 *bronze.* Later used by Solomon in the construction of the temple (see 1Ch 18:8 and note).

8:9 *Hamath.* A kingdom centered on the Orontes River, north of Zobah (see v. 3 and note).

8:13 *eighteen thousand.* As king, David receives the credit for

14 He put garrisons throughout Edom,
and all the Edomites[u] became subject to
David.[v] The LORD gave David victory[w]
wherever he went.[x]

David's Officials

8:15-18pp — 1Ch 18:14-17

15 David reigned over all Israel, doing
what was just and right[y] for all his people.
16 Joab[z] son of Zeruiah was over the army;
Jehoshaphat[a] son of Ahilud was recorder;[b] 17 Zadok[c] son of Ahitub and Ahimelech
son of Abiathar[d] were priests; Seraiah was
secretary;[e] 18 Benaiah[f] son of Jehoiada was
over the Kerethites[g] and Pelethites; and
David's sons were royal advisers.[a]

David and Mephibosheth

9 David asked, "Is there anyone still left
of the house of Saul to whom I can
show kindness for Jonathan's sake?"[h]
2 Now there was a servant of Saul's
household named Ziba.[i] They called him
to appear before David, and the king said
to him, "Are you Ziba?"
"Your servant," he replied.
3 The king asked, "Is there no one still
left of the house of Saul to whom I can
show God's kindness?"
Ziba answered the king, "There is still
a son of Jonathan;[j] he is crippled[k] in both
feet."
4 "Where is he?" the king asked.
Ziba answered, "He is at the house of
Makir[l] son of Ammiel in Lo Debar."
5 So King David had him brought from
Lo Debar, from the house of Makir son of
Ammiel.
6 When Mephibosheth son of Jonathan,
the son of Saul, came to David, he bowed
down to pay him honor.[m]
David said, "Mephibosheth!"
"Your servant," he replied.
7 "Don't be afraid," David said to him,
"for I will surely show you kindness for
the sake of your father Jonathan.[n] I will
restore to you all the land that belonged

[a] 18 Or *were priests*

8:14 [u] Nu 24:17-18; Ps 108:9; Isa 34:5; 63:1; Jer 49:7; Eze 25:12 [v] S Ge 27:29, 37-40 [w] Ps 144:10 [x] 2Sa 22:44; Ps 18:43 **8:15** [y] S Ge 18:19; 1Ki 11:38; 14:8; 15:11; 22:43; 2Ki 12:2; Job 29:14; Ps 5:12; 119:121; Heb 11:33 **8:16** [z] S 2Sa 2:13 [a] 2Sa 20:24; 1Ki 4:3 [b] Isa 36:3, 22 **8:17** [c] S 1Sa 2:35; 2Sa 15:24, 29; 20:25; 1Ki 1:8; 4:4; 1Ch 6:8, 53; 16:39; 24:3; 27:17; 2Ch 31:10; Eze 40:46; 43:19; 44:15; 48:11 [d] Mk 2:26 [e] 1Ki 4:3; 2Ki 12:10; 19:2; 22:3; Isa 36:3; Jer 36:12 **8:18** [f] 2Sa 20:23; 23:20; 1Ki 1:8, 38; 2:25, 35, 46; 4:4 [g] S 1Sa 30:14 **9:1** [h] S 1Sa 20:14-17, 42; S 23:18 **9:2** [i] 2Sa 16:1-4; 19:17, 26, 29 **9:3** [j] 1Ch 8:34; 1Sa 20:14 [k] S Lev 21:18 **9:4** [l] 2Sa 17:27-29 **9:6** [m] S Ge 37:7 **9:7** [n] S 1Sa 20:14-15

striking down 18,000 Edomites. Abishai, however, was one of David's army commanders in this battle (see 1Ch 18:12 and note). The 12,000 Edomites struck down under Joab's leadership according to the title of Ps 60 were probably part of the 18,000. *Valley of Salt.* See 2Ki 14:7 and note; see also Ps 60 title.

8:15 *just and right.* As a true theocratic king, David's reign was characterized by adherence to God's standards of right rule (see notes on 1Sa 8:3; 12:3; Ps 119:121), as no doubt laid down in Samuel's "regulations of the kingship" (see 1Sa 10:25; 1Ki 2:3-4 and notes).

8:16 *Joab son of Zeruiah was over the army.* See notes on 2:13; 5:8. *recorder.* The precise duties of this official are not indicated, though the position was an important one in the court and was maintained throughout the period of the monarchy (see 2Ki 18:18,37; 2Ch 34:8). He may have been a kind of chancellor or chief administrator of royal affairs, responsible among other things for the royal chronicles and annals.

8:17 *Zadok son of Ahitub.* First mentioned here, Zadok was a descendant of Eleazar son of Aaron (see 1Ch 6:4-8,50-52; 24:1-3). His father, Ahitub, is not to be identified with Ichabod's brother of the same name (1Sa 14:3). Zadok remained loyal to David throughout his reign (15:24-29; 17:15-16; 19:11). Zadok and the prophet Nathan eventually anointed Solomon as David's successor (1Ki 1:43-45). *Ahimelech son of Abiathar.* A copyist's error may have occurred here (see also 1Ch 24:6) in which these two names have been transposed. Abiathar is referred to as son of Ahimelech in 1Sa 22:20. While it is true that the Abiathar of 1Sa 22:20 could have had a son named Ahimelech (after his grandfather), such a person does not appear elsewhere in the narratives of Samuel and Kings as a colleague of Zadok, but Abiathar consistently does (15:29,35; 17:15; 19:11; 20:25; 1Ki 1:7-8; 2:35; 4:4). *Seraiah.* Perhaps the same person elsewhere called Sheva (20:25), Shisha (1Ki 4:3) and Shavsha (1Ch 18:16). *secretary.* His duties presumably included domestic and foreign correspondence, perhaps keeping records of important political events, and various administrative functions (2Ki 12:10-12).

8:18 *Kerethites.* See note on 1Sa 30:14. *Pelethites.* Probably an alternate form of "Philistines." *royal advisers.* Translates the Hebrew word commonly used to refer to "priests" (see NIV text note; see also 20:26) — but that sense appears unlikely here. Several early translations render the term by some word other than "priests." Chronicles calls these men "chief officials at the king's side" (see 1Ch 18:17 and note), which supports the meaning "royal advisers."

9:1 — 20:26 An account of threats to David's reign being overcome. These chapters, together with 1Ki 1:1 — 2:46, are one of the finest examples of historical narrative to have been produced in the ancient world.

9:1-13 The events of this chapter occurred a number of years after David's capture of Jerusalem. Mephibosheth was five years old at the time of his father's death (4:4); now he has a son of his own (v. 12). Mephibosheth's condition and David's gracious treatment of him make clear that all potential threats from the old royal house of Saul have been neutralized.

9:1 *I can show kindness for Jonathan's sake.* David has not forgotten his promise to Jonathan (cf. 1Sa 20:14-17,42).

9:2 *Ziba.* The chief steward of Saul's estate, which had been inherited by Mephibosheth son of Jonathan, Saul's firstborn (see 16:1-4; 19:17).

9:3 *There is still a son of Jonathan.* Saul had other descendants (see 21:8), but Ziba mentions only the one in whom David would be chiefly interested.

9:3,13 *crippled in both feet.* And thus disqualified from contesting David's position as king (see 4:4 and note).

9:4 *Makir.* Apparently a wealthy benefactor of Mephibosheth who later also came to David's aid (17:27). *Lo Debar.* A town deep in Gileadite territory in Transjordan.

9:6 *Mephibosheth.* See 4:4 and note.

9:7 *restore to you.* Either the property Saul had acquired as king had been taken over by David, or Ziba as steward had virtually taken possession of it and was profiting from its income (see 16:1-4; 19:26-30). *you will always eat at my table.* A matter of honor — but probably also so that David could keep a watchful eye on him (cf. 1Sa 20:24-27; 2Ki 25:29). In any event, Mephibosheth's general financial needs were to be cared for by the produce of Saul's estate (v. 10).

to your grandfather Saul, and you will always eat at my table.[o]"
8Mephibosheth[p] bowed down and said,
"What is your servant, that you should notice a dead dog[q] like me?"
9Then the king summoned Ziba, Saul's
servant, and said to him, "I have given
your master's grandson everything that
belonged to Saul and his family. 10You and
your sons and your servants are to farm
the land for him and bring in the crops, so
that your master's grandson[r] may be provided for. And Mephibosheth, grandson of
your master, will always eat at my table."
(Now Ziba had fifteen sons and twenty
servants.)
11Then Ziba said to the king, "Your servant will do whatever my lord the king
commands his servant to do." So Mephibosheth ate at David's[a] table like one of the
king's sons.[s]
12Mephibosheth had a young son named
Mica, and all the members of Ziba's household were servants of Mephibosheth.[t]
13And Mephibosheth lived in Jerusalem,
because he always ate at the king's table,
and he was crippled in both feet.

David Defeats the Ammonites

10:1-19pp — 1Ch 19:1-19

10 In the course of time, the king of the
Ammonites died, and his son Hanun
succeeded him as king. 2David thought, "I
will show kindness to Hanun son of Nahash,[u] just as his father showed kindness
to me." So David sent a delegation to express his sympathy to Hanun concerning
his father.
When David's men came to the land of
the Ammonites, 3the Ammonite nobles
said to Hanun their lord, "Do you think
David is honoring your father by sending
men to you to express sympathy? Hasn't
David sent them to you to explore the city
and spy it out[v] and overthrow it?" 4So Hanun seized David's men, shaved off half of
each man's beard,[w] cut off their garments
in the middle at the buttocks,[x] and sent
them away.
5When David was told about this, he
sent messengers to meet the men, for
they were greatly humiliated. The king
said, "Stay at Jericho till your beards have
grown, and then come back."
6When the Ammonites realized that they
had become a stench[y] in David's nostrils,
they hired twenty thousand Aramean[z] foot
soldiers from Beth Rehob[a] and Zobah,[b] as
well as the king of Maacah[c] with a thousand men, and also twelve thousand men
from Tob.[d]
7On hearing this, David sent Joab[e] out
with the entire army of fighting men. 8The
Ammonites came out and drew up in battle formation at the entrance to their city
gate, while the Arameans of Zobah and
Rehob and the men of Tob and Maacah
were by themselves in the open country.
9Joab saw that there were battle lines in
front of him and behind him; so he selected some of the best troops in Israel and
deployed them against the Arameans. 10He
put the rest of the men under the command of Abishai[f] his brother and deployed
them against the Ammonites. 11Joab said,
"If the Arameans are too strong for me,
then you are to come to my rescue; but if
the Ammonites are too strong for you, then
I will come to rescue you. 12Be strong[g] and
let us fight bravely for our people and the
cities of our God. The LORD will do what is
good in his sight."[h]
13Then Joab and the troops with him advanced to fight the Arameans, and they
fled before him. 14When the Ammonites[i]
saw that the Arameans were fleeing, they
fled before Abishai and went inside the

[a] 11 Septuagint; Hebrew *my*

9:7 [o] ver 13; 2Sa 19:28; 21:7; 1Ki 2:7; 2Ki 25:29; Jer 52:33
9:8 [p] S 2Sa 4:4 [q] S 2Sa 3:8
9:10 [r] 2Sa 16:3
9:11 [s] Job 36:7; Ps 113:8
9:12 [t] S 2Sa 4:4
10:2 [u] S 1Sa 11:1
10:3 [v] S Nu 21:32
10:4 [w] S Lev 19:27; Isa 7:20; 15:2; 50:6; 52:14; Jer 48:37; Eze 5:1 [x] Isa 20:4
10:6 [y] S Ge 34:30 [z] S 2Sa 8:5 [a] S Nu 13:21 [b] S 1Sa 14:47 [c] S Dt 3:14 [d] Jdg 11:3-5
10:7 [e] S 2Sa 2:18
10:10 [f] S 1Sa 26:6
10:12 [g] S Dt 1:21; 31:6; S Eph 6:10 [h] S Jdg 10:15; Ne 4:14
10:14 [i] 2Sa 8:12

9:8 *dead dog like me.* An expression of deep self-abasement. The author has used the "(dead) dog" motif with great effect. First Goliath, scornfully disdaining the young warrior David, asks, "Am I a dog ...?" (1Sa 17:43) — and unwittingly foreshadows his own end. Then David, in a self-deprecating manner, describes himself as a "dead dog" (1Sa 24:14) to suggest to Saul that the king of Israel should not consider him worth so much attention. In the Nabal episode, that "dog" (a "Calebite") and his sudden death characterize Saul and foreshadow his unhappy end (see note on 1Sa 25:3). Here a grandson of Saul and in 16:9 a relative of Saul who curses David are similarly described. For the author, "dead dog" fittingly characterizes those who foolishly scorn or oppose the Lord's anointed, while David's own self-deprecation (see 7:18; 1Sa 18:18) is conducive to his exaltation.
9:12 *had a young son named Mica.* Who also had descendants (1Ch 8:35 – 39).
10:1 – 19 This account of the threat to David's kingdom from the Ammonite-Aramean coalition is interrupted by the story of David's abuse of his royal power (11:1 — 12:25) and is concluded in 12:26 – 31.
10:1 *In the course of time.* See note on 2:1. *king.* Nahash (see v. 2; 1Sa 11). *Ammonites.* See note on 1Sa 11:1.
10:2 *show kindness.* The Hebrew for this expression suggests that a formal treaty existed between the Israelites and the Ammonites (cf. 1Sa 20:8).
10:3,14 *city.* Rabbah, the capital (11:1; 12:26). See note on Dt 3:11.
10:4 *shaved off half of each man's beard.* In the world of that time this was considered an insult of the most serious kind (cf. Isa 7:20). *cut off their garments in the middle at the buttocks.* A customary way of degrading prisoners of war (cf. Isa 20:4).
10:5 *Jericho.* See notes on Jos 6:1; 1Ki 16:34. Jericho remained unrestored during the centuries between Joshua's conquest and the time of Ahab.
10:6 *stench.* See note on 1Sa 13:4. *Beth Rehob.* See Nu 13:21; Jdg 18:28 and notes. *Zobah.* See note on 8:3. *Maacah.* See Dt 3:14 and note; Jos 12:5; 13:13. *Tob.* See Jdg 11:3 – 6 and note on 11:3.
10:10 *Abishai.* See note on 1Sa 26:6.

city. So Joab returned from fighting the
Ammonites and came to Jerusalem.
15 After the Arameans saw that they had
been routed by Israel, they regrouped.
16 Hadadezer had Arameans brought from
beyond the River[a]; they went to Helam,
with Shobach the commander of Hadadezer's army leading them.
17 When David was told of this, he gathered all Israel, crossed the Jordan and went
to Helam. The Arameans formed their battle lines to meet David and fought against
him. 18 But they fled before Israel, and David killed seven hundred of their charioteers and forty thousand of their foot soldiers.[b] He also struck down Shobach the
commander of their army, and he died
there. 19 When all the kings who were vassals of Hadadezer saw that they had been
defeated by Israel, they made peace with
the Israelites and became subject[j] to them.
So the Arameans[k] were afraid to help
the Ammonites anymore.

David and Bathsheba

11 In the spring,[l] at the time when kings
go off to war, David sent Joab[m] out
with the king's men and the whole Israelite army.[n] They destroyed the Ammonites and besieged Rabbah.[o] But David remained in Jerusalem.
2 One evening David got up from his bed
and walked around on the roof[p] of the palace. From the roof he saw[q] a woman bathing. The woman was very beautiful, 3 and
David sent someone to find out about her.
The man said, "Isn't this Bathsheba,[r] the
daughter of Eliam[s] and the wife of Uriah[t]
the Hittite?" 4 Then David sent messengers
to get her.[u] She came to him, and he slept[v]
with her. (She had purified herself from
her uncleanness.)[w] Then[c] she went back
home. 5 The woman conceived and sent
word to David, saying, "I am pregnant."
6 So David sent this word to Joab: "Send
me Uriah[x] the Hittite." And Joab sent him
to David. 7 When Uriah came to him, David
asked him how Joab was, how the soldiers
were and how the war was going. 8 Then
David said to Uriah, "Go down to your
house and wash your feet."[y] So Uriah left
the palace, and a gift from the king was sent
after him. 9 But Uriah slept at the entrance
to the palace with all his master's servants
and did not go down to his house.
10 When David was told, "Uriah did not
go home," he asked him, "Haven't you
just come from a distance? Why didn't
you go home?"
11 Uriah said to David, "The ark[z] and Israel and Judah are staying in tents, and

10:19 [j] 2Sa 8:6 [k] 1Ki 11:25; 22:31; 2Ki 5:1 **11:1** [l] 1Ki 20:22,26 [m] S 2Sa 2:18 [n] 1Ch 20:1 [o] S Dt 3:11 **11:2** [p] S Dt 22:8; S Jos 2:8 [q] Mt 5:28 **11:3** [r] 1Ch 3:5 [s] 2Sa 23:34 [t] 2Sa 23:39 **11:4** [u] S Lev 20:10; Ps 51 Title; Jas 1:14-15 [v] Dt 22:22 [w] S Lev 15:25-30 **11:6** [x] 1Ch 11:41 **11:8** [y] S Ge 18:4 **11:11** [z] 2Sa 7:2

[a] *16* That is, the Euphrates [b] *18* Some Septuagint manuscripts (see also 1 Chron. 19:18); Hebrew *horsemen* [c] *4* Or *with her. When she purified herself from her uncleanness,*

10:16 *Hadadezer.* See note on 8:3.

10:18 *seven hundred.* Perhaps a copyist's mistake; in 1Ch 19:18 the figure is 7,000.

10:19 *they made peace with the Israelites.* There is no indication that Hadadezer himself made peace with Israel as his vassals did in the aftermath of this defeat. These events represent David's last major campaign against combined foreign powers.

11:1 — 12:25 David's shameful abuse of his royal power and how the Lord dealt with it.

11:1 - 27 This detailed account of David's sin has as its foil the story of how David came to receive Nabal's wife Abigail as his wife (1Sa 25). There the Lord removes the husband because of his disdain for the Lord's anointed, and Abigail comes to David as the one who has prevented him from using his incipient royal power for personal ends. Here David abuses his royal power to obtain the wife of another whom he callously removes by royal manipulation of events. David commits the great sin of those entrusted by God with power — using it for personal ends. David's abuse of royal power and the consequences that flowed from it (see chs. 11 - 20) constitute the greatest threat to his reign and to the continuance of his dynasty (cf. Jer 22:1 - 5,13 - 19). Contrast what David's greatest Son said about his own ministry (see Mk 10:45 and note).

11:1 *the spring.* Of the year following the events reported in ch. 10. *the time when kings go off to war.* When the rains have ended. At that time the roads became passable and the spring harvest provided food for armies on the march as well as fodder for their animals. *Rabbah.* See note on 10:3,14. Though now alone (see 10:19), the Ammonites had not yet been subjugated.

11:2 *walked around on the roof.* Where he could enjoy the cool evening air (see note on 1Sa 9:25).

11:3 *Eliam.* Perhaps the same Eliam who was a member of David's personal bodyguard (23:34) and a son of his counselor Ahithophel (see 15:12 and note). *Uriah.* Also listed among those comprising David's royal guard (23:39). His name suggests that even though he was a Hittite, he had adopted the Israelite faith (Uriah means "The LORD is my light"). *Hittite.* See note on 1Sa 26:6.

11:4 *David sent messengers to get her.* See notes on v. 27; 1Sa 25:1; cf. 1Sa 25:39 and note on Ps 51:4. *She came to him, and he slept with her.* Bathsheba appears to have been an unprotesting partner in this adulterous relationship with David. (*She had purified herself from her uncleanness.*) The purpose of this statement is to indicate Bathsheba's condition at the time of her sexual relations with David. She had just become ceremonially clean (Lev 15:28 - 30) after the seven-day period of monthly impurity due to menstruation (Lev 15:19). It is thus clear that she was not already pregnant by her own husband when David took her.

11:5 *I am pregnant.* Bathsheba leaves the next step up to David. The law prescribed the death penalty for both David and Bathsheba (Lev 20:10), as they well knew.

11:6 *Send me Uriah.* Under the pretense of seeking information about the course of the war, David brings Uriah back to Jerusalem.

11:8 *Go down to your house and wash your feet.* In essence, David tells Uriah to go home and relax. What he does not say specifically is what is most important, and well understood by Uriah (v. 11). *a gift from the king was sent after him.* The Hebrew word for "gift" has the meaning of "food" in Ge 43:34 ("portions" from the king's table). David wanted Uriah and Bathsheba to enjoy their evening together.

11:11 *ark.* Uriah's statement suggests that the ark was in the field camp with the army rather than in the tent that David had set up for it in Jerusalem (6:17). If so, it was prob-

my master Joab and my lord's men are
camped in the open fields. How could I go
to my house to eat and drink and lie[a] with
my wife? As surely as you live, I will not
do such a thing!"
12Then David said to him, "Stay here
one more day, and tomorrow I will send
you back." So Uriah remained in Jerusalem that day and the next. 13At David's
invitation, he ate and drank with him, and
David made him drunk. But in the evening Uriah went out to sleep on his mat
among his master's servants; he did not
go home.
14In the morning David wrote a letter[b]
to Joab and sent it with Uriah. 15In it he
wrote, "Put Uriah in the front line where
the fighting is fiercest. Then withdraw
from him so he will be struck down[c] and
die.[d]"
16So while Joab had the city under siege,
he put Uriah at a place where he knew the
strongest defenders were. 17When the men
of the city came out and fought against
Joab, some of the men in David's army
fell; moreover, Uriah the Hittite died.
18Joab sent David a full account of the
battle. 19He instructed the messenger:
"When you have finished giving the king
this account of the battle, 20the king's anger may flare up, and he may ask you,
'Why did you get so close to the city to
fight? Didn't you know they would shoot
arrows from the wall? 21Who killed Abimelech[e] son of Jerub-Besheth[a]? Didn't
a woman throw an upper millstone on
him from the wall,[f] so that he died in
Thebez? Why did you get so close to the
wall?' If he asks you this, then say to
him, 'Also, your servant Uriah the Hittite
is dead.' "
22The messenger set out, and when he
arrived he told David everything Joab had
sent him to say. 23The messenger said to
David, "The men overpowered us and
came out against us in the open, but we
drove them back to the entrance to the
city gate. 24Then the archers shot arrows
at your servants from the wall, and some
of the king's men died. Moreover, your
servant Uriah the Hittite is dead."
25David told the messenger, "Say this to
Joab: 'Don't let this upset you; the sword
devours one as well as another. Press the
attack against the city and destroy it.' Say
this to encourage Joab."
26When Uriah's wife heard that her
husband was dead, she mourned for him.
27After the time of mourning[g] was over,
David had her brought to his house, and
she became his wife and bore him a son.
But the thing David had done displeased[h]
the LORD.

11:11 [a]S 1Sa 21:5 **11:14** [b]1Ki 21:8 **11:15** [c]ver 14-17; 2Sa 12:9 [d]2Sa 12:12 **11:21** [e]S Jdg 8:31 [f]Jdg 9:50-54

Nathan Rebukes David

11:1; 12:29-31pp — 1Ch 20:1-3

12 The LORD sent Nathan[i] to David.[j]
When he came to him,[k] he said,
"There were two men in a certain town,
one rich and the other poor. 2The rich man
had a very large number of sheep and cattle, 3but the poor man had nothing except
one little ewe lamb he had bought. He
raised it, and it grew up with him and his
children. It shared his food, drank from
his cup and even slept in his arms. It was
like a daughter to him.
4"Now a traveler came to the rich man,
but the rich man refrained from taking
one of his own sheep or cattle to prepare
a meal for the traveler who had come to
him. Instead, he took the ewe lamb that
belonged to the poor man and prepared it
for the one who had come to him."

11:27 [g]Dt 34:8 [h]2Sa 12:9; Ps 51:4-5 **12:1** [i]S 2Sa 7:2 [j]Ps 51 Title [k]2Sa 14:4

[a] *21* Also known as *Jerub-Baal* (that is, Gideon)

ably there for purposes of worship and to seek guidance for the war. But then the circumstances are even more damning for David—the Lord is in the field with his army while David stays at home in leisure. *How could I go to my house to eat …?* See note on v. 8 ("gift"). Uriah's devotion to duty exposes by sharp contrast David's dalliance at home while his men are in the field. *As surely as you live.* See note on 1Sa 14:39,45.

11:13 *David made him drunk.* In the hope that in this condition he would relent and go to Bathsheba.

11:14 Uriah is unaware that he is carrying his own death warrant to Joab.

11:15 *so he will be struck down and die.* Unsuccessful in making it appear that Uriah was the father of Bathsheba's child, David plotted Uriah's death so he could marry Bathsheba himself as quickly as possible.

11:16 *city.* Rabbah (see note on 10:3,14).

11:17 *Uriah the Hittite died.* This phrase or its equivalent echoes like a death knell throughout the rest of the chapter (vv. 21,24; cf. also vv. 15,26).

11:21 *Jerub-Besheth.* Another possible spelling is "Jerub-Bosheth." In Judges he is called Jerub-Baal (see note on Jdg 6:32; see also NIV text note there). For similar name changes elsewhere in 2 Samuel see notes on 2:8; 4:4. *millstone.* See Jdg 9:53 and note. *Uriah … is dead.* Joab knows that this news is of great importance to David, and he uses it to squelch any criticism David might otherwise have had of the battle tactics.

11:24 *some of the king's men died.* Other brave soldiers were sacrificed along with Uriah, a fact that exposes David's callousness as well as the enormity of his sinful cover-up.

11:25 *David told the messenger.* David hid his satisfaction over the news with a hypocritical statement that war is war and the death of Uriah should not be a discouragement.

11:27 *time of mourning was over.* Presumably a period of seven days (see 1Sa 31:13 and note; Ge 50:10). *she became his wife.* See note on 5:14. *the thing David had done displeased the LORD.* Not only had David brazenly violated God's laws (see Ex 20:13–14,17) but, even worse, he had shamelessly abused his royal power, which the Lord had entrusted to him to shepherd the Lord's people (see 5:2; 7:7 and notes).

12:1 *The LORD sent.* Prophets were messengers from the Lord. Here the Great King sends his emissary to rebuke and announce judgment on the king he had enthroned over his people. *Nathan.* See note on 7:2.

5David[l] burned with anger[m] against the
man[n] and said to Nathan, "As surely as the
LORD lives,[o] the man who did this deserves
to die! 6He must pay for that lamb four
times over,[p] because he did such a thing
and had no pity."
7Then Nathan said to David, "You are
the man![q] This is what the LORD, the God
of Israel, says: 'I anointed[r] you[s] king over
Israel, and I delivered you from the hand
of Saul. 8I gave your master's house to
you,[t] and your master's wives into your
arms. I gave you the house of Israel and
Judah. And if all this had been too little,
I would have given you even more. 9Why
did you despise[u] the word of the LORD by
doing what is evil in his eyes? You struck
down[v] Uriah[w] the Hittite with the sword
and took his wife to be your own. You
killed[x] him with the sword of the Ammonites. 10Now, therefore, the sword[y] will never depart from your house, because you
despised me and took the wife of Uriah
the Hittite to be your own.'
11"This is what the LORD says: 'Out of
your own household[z] I am going to bring
calamity upon you.[a] Before your very eyes
I will take your wives and give them to
one who is close to you, and he will lie
with your wives in broad daylight.[b] 12You
did it in secret,[c] but I will do this thing in
broad daylight[d] before all Israel.' "
13Then David said to Nathan, "I have
sinned[e] against the LORD."
Nathan replied, "The LORD has tak-
en away[f] your sin.[g] You are not going to
die.[h] 14But because by doing this you have
made the enemies of the LORD show utter contempt,[a][i] the son born to you will
die."
15After Nathan had gone home, the
LORD struck[j] the child that Uriah's wife
had borne to David, and he became ill.
16David pleaded with God for the child. He
fasted and went into his house and spent
the nights lying[k] on the ground. 17The elders of his household stood beside him
to get him up from the ground, but he
refused,[l] and he would not eat any food
with them.[m]
18On the seventh day the child died.
David's servants were afraid to tell him
that the child was dead, for they thought,
"While the child was still living, we spoke
to David but he would not listen to us.
How can we tell him the child is dead? He
may do something desperate."
19David noticed that his servants were
whispering among themselves and he realized the child was dead. "Is the child
dead?" he asked.
"Yes," they replied, "he is dead."
20Then David got up from the ground.
After he had washed,[n] put on lotions and
changed his clothes,[o] he went into the
house of the LORD and worshiped. Then he
went to his own house, and at his request
they served him food, and he ate.
21His servants asked him, "Why are you
acting this way? While the child was alive,
you fasted and wept,[p] but now that the
child is dead, you get up and eat!"

[a] 14 Masoretic Text; an ancient Hebrew scribal tradition *this you have shown utter contempt for the LORD*

12:5 [l] 1Ki 20:40 [m] S Ge 34:7 [n] Ro 2:1 [o] S 1Sa 14:39 **12:6** [p] Ex 22:1 **12:7** [q] 2Sa 14:13; Da 4:22 [r] S 1Sa 2:35 [s] 1Ki 20:42 **12:8** [t] S 2Sa 9:7 **12:9** [u] S Nu 15:31; S 1Sa 13:14 [v] S 2Sa 11:15 [w] 1Ki 15:5 [x] Ps 26:9; 51:14 **12:10** [y] 2Sa 13:28; 18:14-15; 1Ki 2:25 **12:11** [z] 2Sa 16:11 [a] Dt 28:30; 2Sa 16:21-22 [b] S Dt 17:17 **12:12** [c] 2Sa 11:4-15 [d] 2Sa 16:22 **12:13** [e] S Ge 13:13; S 20:6; S Nu 22:34 [f] Ps 32:1-5; 51:1,9; 103:12; Isa 43:25; 44:22; Zec 3:4,9 [g] Pr 28:13; Jer 2:35; Mic 7:18-19 [h] Lev 20:10; 24:17 **12:14** [i] Isa 52:5; Ro 2:24 **12:15** [j] S 1Sa 25:38 **12:16** [k] Ps 5:7; 95:6 **12:17** [l] S Ge 37:35; S 1Sa 1:7 [m] S 2Sa 3:35; Da 6:18 **12:20** [n] Mt 6:17 [o] S Ge 41:14 **12:21** [p] Jdg 20:26

12:5 *As surely as the LORD lives.* See note on 1Sa 14:39,45.

12:6 *four times over.* In agreement with the requirements of Ex 22:1.

12:7 *You are the man!* Nathan identifies David as the rich man in the parable of vv. 1–4. David's sentence of fourfold retribution against that man (v. 6) came true in his own experience: As a result of his engineering Uriah's death, David lost four of his sons (see vv. 10,18 and note on v. 10). Indeed, his sin against Uriah became a permanent stain on his otherwise godly life (see 1Ki 15:5).

12:8 *your master's wives.* Earlier narratives refer to only one wife of Saul (Ahinoam, 1Sa 14:50) and one concubine (Rizpah, 2Sa 3:7; 21:8–11). This statement suggests that there were others. But since it was customary for new kings to assume the harem of their predecessors (see note on 3:7), it may be that Nathan merely uses conventional language to emphasize that the Lord had placed David on Saul's throne. *I gave you the house of Israel and Judah.* See 2:1,4; 5:2–3.

12:9 *despise the word of the LORD.* See notes on 11:4,27. *You killed him.* David is held directly responsible for Uriah's death even though Uriah fell in battle (see 11:15 and note).

12:10 *the sword will never depart from your house.* Three of David's sons died violently: Amnon (13:28–29), Absalom (18:14–15) and Adonijah (1Ki 2:25). See note on v. 7.

12:11 *Out of your own household I am going to bring calamity upon you.* David was driven from Jerusalem by Absalom's conspiracy to seize the kingship from his own father (15:1–17). *he will lie with your wives in broad daylight.* Fulfilled at the time of Absalom's rebellion (see note on 16:22).

12:13 *I have sinned against the LORD.* David recognizes his guilt and confesses his sin in response to Nathan's rebuke (see Ps 51:4 and note). There is a clear contrast between David's confession and Saul's (see note on 1Sa 15:24). *The LORD has taken away your sin.* David experienced the joy of knowing his sin was forgiven (see Ps 32:1,5; cf. Ps 51:8,12). *You are not going to die.* The Lord, in his grace, released David from the customary death penalty for adultery and murder (Lev 20:10; 24:17,21).

12:14 *you have made the enemies of the LORD show utter contempt.* David is required to suffer the disciplinary results of his sin in a manner open to public view. But see NIV text note.

12:16 *pleaded ... fasted.* See note on Ezr 8:23.

12:18 *seventh day.* If reference is to the child's age, his life was so short that he remained uncircumcised and unnamed (see Lk 1:59 and note; 2:21; cf. Ge 21:3–4)—and therefore was not counted among the Israelites.

12:20 *put on lotions.* A practice associated with the cessation of mourning (see 14:2). *changed his clothes.* Took off his mourning garments and put on his normal clothing. *went into the house of the LORD and worshiped.* In this way David openly demonstrated his humble acceptance of the disciplinary results of his sin. Again (see note on v. 13) there is a contrast between David's attitude and Saul's (see note on 1Sa 15:25).

David's Conquests

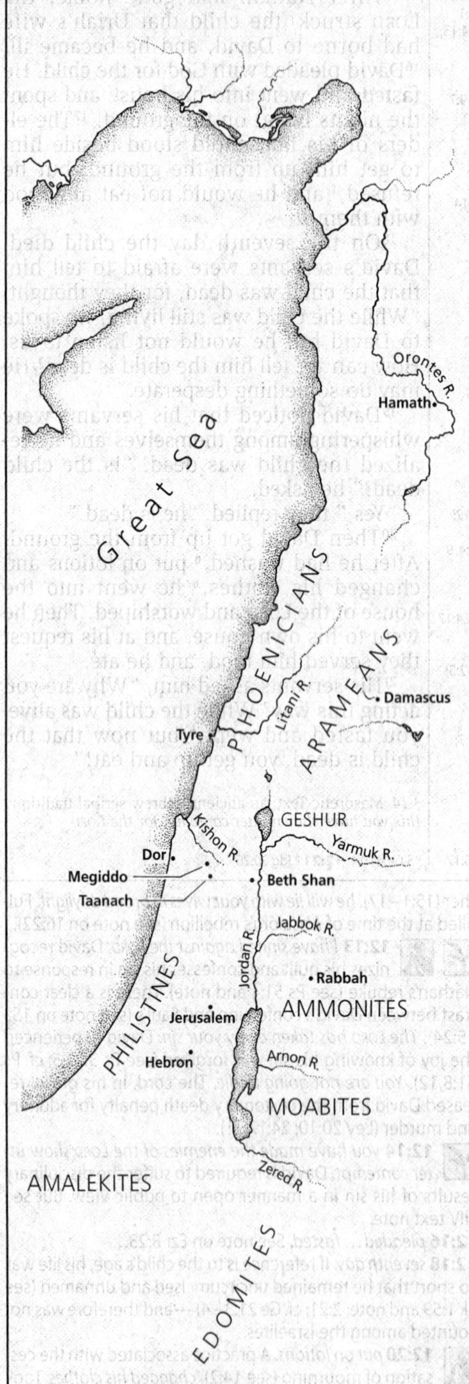

Once he had become king over all Israel (2Sa 5:1-5), David:

1. Conquered the Jebusite fortress of Zion/Jerusalem and made it his royal city (5:6-10);

2. Received the recognition of and assurance of friendship from Hiram of Tyre, king of the Phoenicians (5:11-12);

3. Decisively defeated the Philistines so that their hold on Israelite territory was broken and their threat to Israel eliminated (5:17-25; 8:1);

4. Defeated the Moabites and imposed his authority over them (8:2);

5. Crushed the Aramean kingdoms of Hadadezer (king of Zobah), Damascus and Maacah and put them under tribute (8:3-8; 10:6-19). Talmai, the Aramean king of Geshur, apparently had made peace with David while he was still reigning in Hebron and sealed the alliance by giving his daughter Maacah in marriage to David (3:3; cf. 1Ch 2:23);

6. Subdued Edom and incorporated it into his empire (8:13-14);

7. Defeated the Ammonites and brought them into subjection (12:26-31);

8. Subjugated the remaining Canaanite cities that had previously maintained their independence from Israel, such as Beth Shan, Megiddo, Taanach and Dor.

Since David had earlier crushed the Amalekites (1Sa 30:17-18), his wars thus completed the conquest begun by Joshua and secured all the borders of Israel. His empire (united Israel plus the subjugated kingdoms) reached from Ezion Geber on the eastern arm of the Red Sea to the Euphrates River.

22He answered, "While the child was still alive, I fasted and wept. I thought, 'Who knows?[q] The LORD may be gracious to me and let the child live.'[r] 23But now that he is dead, why should I fast? Can I bring him back again? I will go to him,[s] but he will not return to me."[t]

24Then David comforted his wife Bathsheba,[u] and he went to her and lay with her. She gave birth to a son, and they named him Solomon.[v] The LORD loved him; 25and because the LORD loved him, he sent word through Nathan the prophet to name him Jedidiah.[a][w]

26Meanwhile Joab fought against Rabbah[x] of the Ammonites and captured the royal citadel. 27Joab then sent messengers to David, saying, "I have fought against Rabbah and taken its water supply. 28Now muster the rest of the troops and besiege the city and capture it. Otherwise I will take the city, and it will be named after me."

29So David mustered the entire army and went to Rabbah, and attacked and captured it. 30He took the crown[y] from the head of their king[b]—its weight was a talent[c] of gold, and it was set with precious stones—and it was placed on David's head. He took a great quantity of plunder from the city 31and brought out the people who were there, consigning them to labor with saws and with iron picks and axes, and he made them work at brickmaking.[d] He did this to all the Ammonite[z] towns. Then David and his entire army returned to Jerusalem.

Amnon and Tamar

13 In the course of time, Amnon[a] son of David fell in love with Tamar,[b] the beautiful sister of Absalom[c] son of David.

2Amnon became frustrated to the point of illness on account of his sister Tamar, for she was a virgin, and it seemed impossible for him to do anything to her.

3Now Amnon had a friend named Jonadab son of Shimeah,[d] David's brother. Jonadab was a very shrewd man. 4He asked Amnon, "Why do you, the king's son, look so haggard morning after morning? Won't you tell me?"

Amnon said to him, "I'm in love with Tamar, my brother Absalom's sister."

5"Go to bed and pretend to be ill," Jonadab said. "When your father comes to see you, say to him, 'I would like my sister Tamar to come and give me something to eat. Let her prepare the food in my sight so I may watch her and then eat it from her hand.'"

6So Amnon lay down and pretended to be ill. When the king came to see him, Amnon said to him, "I would like my sister Tamar to come and make some special bread in my sight, so I may eat from her hand."

7David sent word to Tamar at the palace: "Go to the house of your brother Amnon and prepare some food for him." 8So Tamar went to the house of her brother Amnon, who was lying down. She took some dough, kneaded it, made the bread in his sight and baked it. 9Then she took the pan and served him the bread, but he refused to eat.

"Send everyone out of here,"[e] Amnon said. So everyone left him. 10Then Amnon said to Tamar, "Bring the food here into my bedroom so I may eat from your hand." And Tamar took the bread she had prepared and brought it to her brother Amnon in his bedroom. 11But when she took it to him to eat, he grabbed[f] her and said, "Come to bed with me, my sister."[g]

12"Don't, my brother!" she said to him. "Don't force me. Such a thing should not be done in Israel![h] Don't do this wicked thing.[i] 13What about me?[j] Where could I get rid of my disgrace? And what about

12:22 [q]Jnh 3:9 [r]Isa 38:1-5 **12:23** [s]Ge 37:35 [t]S 1Sa 31:13; 2Sa 13:39; Job 7:10; 10:21 **12:24** [u]1Ki 1:11 [v]1Ki 1:10; 1Ch 22:9; 28:5; Mt 1:6 **12:25** [w]Ne 13:26 **12:26** [x]S Dt 3:11 **12:30** [y]Est 8:15; Ps 21:3; 132:18 **12:31** [z]S 1Sa 14:47 **13:1** [a]2Sa 3:2 [b]2Sa 14:27; 1Ch 3:9 [c]S 2Sa 3:3

13:3 [d]S 1Sa 16:9 **13:9** [e]Ge 45:1 **13:11** [f]S Ge 39:12 [g]S Ge 38:16 **13:12** [h]Lev 20:17 [i]S Ge 34:7 **13:13** [j]S Lev 18:9; S Dt 22:21,23-24

[a] 25 *Jedidiah* means *loved by the LORD.* [b] 30 Or *of Milcom* (that is, Molech) [c] 30 That is, about 75 pounds (about 34 kilograms) [d] 31 The meaning of the Hebrew for this clause is uncertain.

12:23 *I will go to him.* Like the child, David will die and join him in the grave (see note on Ge 37:35). *he will not return to me.* See Job 7:9 and note.

12:24 *Solomon.* See 1Ch 22:9 and NIV text note.

12:25 *Jedidiah.* See NIV text note. The giving of this name suggests that the Lord's special favor rested on Solomon from his birth. And since the name also contained an echo of David's name, it provided assurance to David that the Lord also loved him and would continue his dynasty.

12:26–31 The conclusion of the Ammonite war (see note on 10:1–19).

12:26 *Joab fought against Rabbah.* The writer now returns to the outcome of the attack against the Ammonites (11:1,25), which provided the background for the story of David and Bathsheba. Even while the Lord was displeased with David (11:27), he gave the Israelites victory over a people who had abused them.

12:30 *the crown … was placed on David's head.* A crown of such weight (see NIV text note) would have been worn only briefly and on very special occasions. Perhaps it was worn only once in a symbolic act of transferring to David sovereignty over Ammon.

12:31 *consigning them to labor.* Victorious kings often used prisoners of war as menial laborers in royal building projects (see 1Ki 9:20–21 and note on 9:15; cf. also Ex 1:11).

13:1–39 Amnon's abuse of power and Absalom's personal revenge. The trouble within David's family begins (see notes on 12:7,10–11).

13:1 *In the course of time.* See note on 2:1. *Amnon.* David's firstborn son (3:2). *Tamar.* David's daughter by Maacah of Geshur (cf. 3:3 and note), and Absalom's full sister.

13:3 *Shimeah.* Called Shammah in 1Sa 16:9.

13:6 *When the king came to see him.* Amnon used his father David to obtain his illicit purpose, just as David had used Joab (see 11:14–17).

13:12 *wicked thing.* Hebrew *nebalah,* from the same root word as the name Nabal (see 1Sa 25:25).

13:13 *what about you?* This act would jeopardize Amnon's

you? You would be like one of the wicked
fools in Israel. Please speak to the king;
he will not keep me from being married to
you." 14But he refused to listen to her, and
since he was stronger than she, he raped
her.[k]
15Then Amnon hated her with intense
hatred. In fact, he hated her more than he
had loved her. Amnon said to her, "Get up
and get out!"
16"No!" she said to him. "Sending me
away would be a greater wrong than what
you have already done to me."
But he refused to listen to her. 17He
called his personal servant and said, "Get
this woman out of here and bolt the door
after her." 18So his servant put her out and
bolted the door after her. She was wearing
a richly ornamented[a] robe,[l] for this was
the kind of garment the virgin daughters
of the king wore. 19Tamar put ashes[m] on
her head and tore the ornamented[b] robe
she was wearing. She put her hand on her
head and went away, weeping aloud as
she went.
20Her brother Absalom said to her, "Has
that Amnon, your brother, been with you?
Be quiet now, my sister; he is your brother. Don't take this thing to heart." And Tamar lived in her brother Absalom's house,
a desolate woman.
21When King David heard all this, he
was furious.[n] 22Absalom never said a word
to Amnon, either good or bad;[o] he hated[p]
Amnon because he had disgraced his sister Tamar.

13:14 [k]S Ge 34:2; Eze 22:11 **13:18** [l]S Ge 37:23 **13:19** [m]S Jos 7:6; Est 4:1; Da 9:3 **13:21** [n]S Ge 34:7 **13:22** [o]Ge 31:24 [p]Lev 19:17-18; 1Jn 2:9-11

13:23 [q]1Sa 25:7 **13:28** [r]S 2Sa 3:3 [s]S Ru 3:7 [t]S 2Sa 12:10 **13:31** [u]S Nu 14:6

Absalom Kills Amnon

23Two years later, when Absalom's
sheepshearers[q] were at Baal Hazor near
the border of Ephraim, he invited all the
king's sons to come there. 24Absalom went
to the king and said, "Your servant has
had shearers come. Will the king and his
officials please join me?"
25"No, my son," the king replied. "All
of us should not go; we would only be a
burden to you." Although Absalom urged
him, he still refused to go, but gave him
his blessing.
26Then Absalom said, "If not, please let
my brother Amnon come with us."
The king asked him, "Why should he
go with you?" 27But Absalom urged him,
so he sent with him Amnon and the rest
of the king's sons.
28Absalom[r] ordered his men, "Listen!
When Amnon is in high[s] spirits from
drinking wine and I say to you, 'Strike
Amnon down,' then kill him. Don't be
afraid. Have not I given you this order? Be
strong and brave.[t]" 29So Absalom's men
did to Amnon what Absalom had ordered.
Then all the king's sons got up, mounted
their mules and fled.
30While they were on their way, the report came to David: "Absalom has struck
down all the king's sons; not one of them
is left." 31The king stood up, tore[u] his
clothes and lay down on the ground; and

[a] *18* The meaning of the Hebrew for this phrase is uncertain. [b] *19* The meaning of the Hebrew for this word is uncertain.

position as crown prince and heir to the throne. *one of the wicked fools.* That is, a *nabal* (see note on v. 12; see also NIV text note on Pr 1:7). David's wicked folly in his dealings with Bathsheba yields the bitter fruit of imitation by his oldest son, who by his act becomes another Nabal.

13:15 *Amnon hated her.* The reversal in Amnon's feelings toward Tamar demonstrates that his former "love" (v. 1) was nothing but sensual desire.

13:16 *Sending me away would be a greater wrong.* No longer a virgin, she could not be offered by her father to any other potential husband (see v. 21 and note).

13:18 *richly ornamented robe.* See Ge 37:3 and note.

13:19 *put ashes on her head and tore the . . . robe she was wearing.* Signs of grief (see 1Sa 4:12 and note), expressing her anguish and announcing that her virginity had been violated.

13:20 *Be quiet now, my sister . . . Don't take this thing to heart.* Absalom urges his sister not to make the matter a public scandal. Meanwhile, he formulates his own secret plans for revenge (see vv. 22,28,32).

13:21 *he was furious.* Although David was incensed by Amnon's rape of Tamar, there is no record that he took any punitive action against him. Most likely the memory of his own sin with Bathsheba adversely affected his judicious handling of the matter. Whatever the reason, David abdicated his responsibility both as king and as father. This disciplinary leniency toward his sons (see notes on 14:33; 1Ki 1:6) eventually led to the death of Amnon and the revolts of Absalom and Adonijah.

13:22 *Absalom never said a word to Amnon . . . he hated Amnon.* He quietly bided his time.

13:23 *Two years later.* After two years it was clear to Absalom that King David was not going to do anything to Amnon for raping Tamar. *Baal Hazor.* Located about five miles north-northeast of Bethel. *he invited all the king's sons.* The time of sheepshearing was a festive occasion (see 1Sa 25:4,8).

13:26 *let my brother Amnon come.* Upon David's refusal of the invitation, Absalom diplomatically requested that Amnon, the crown prince and oldest son, be his representative. *Why should he go with you?* David's question suggests some misgivings because of the strained relationship between the two half brothers (see v. 22).

13:28 *kill him.* Absalom arranged for the murder of his half brother, usurping his father's royal authority and acting in violation of long-established rules of hospitality. In the wicked acts of Amnon and Absalom, David's oldest sons became guilty of sexual immorality and murder, as their father had before them. With the murder of Amnon, Absalom not only avenged the rape of his sister but also secured for himself the position of successor to the throne (see 3:3; 15:1–6). Kileab, David's second son (3:3), may have died in his youth since there is no reference to him beyond the announcement of his birth.

13:29 *mules.* Apparently the normal mount for royalty in David's kingdom (see 18:9; 1Ki 1:33,38,44; see also note on 1Ki 1:33).

13:31 *tore his clothes and lay down on the ground.* Common ways of expressing grief (see v. 19; Jos 7:6 and notes; 1Ki 21:27; Est 4:1,3; Job 1:20; 2:8).

all his servants stood by with their clothes
torn.
32 But Jonadab son of Shimeah, David's
brother, said, "My lord should not think
that they killed all the princes; only Amnon is dead. This has been Absalom's expressed intention ever since the day Amnon raped his sister Tamar. 33 My lord the
king should not be concerned about the
report that all the king's sons are dead.
Only Amnon is dead."
34 Meanwhile, Absalom had fled.
Now the man standing watch looked up
and saw many people on the road west of
him, coming down the side of the hill. The
watchman went and told the king, "I see
men in the direction of Horonaim, on the
side of the hill."[a]
35 Jonadab said to the king, "See, the
king's sons are here; it has happened just
as your servant said."
36 As he finished speaking, the king's sons
came in, wailing loudly. The king, too, and
all his servants wept very bitterly.
37 Absalom fled and went to Talmai[v] son
of Ammihud, the king of Geshur. But King
David mourned for his son every day.
38 After Absalom fled and went to Geshur, he stayed there three years. 39 And
the spirit of the king[b] longed to go to Absalom,[w] for he was consoled[x] concerning
Amnon's death.

Absalom Returns to Jerusalem

14 Joab[y] son of Zeruiah knew that the
king's heart longed for Absalom. 2 So
Joab sent someone to Tekoa[z] and had a
wise woman[a] brought from there. He
said to her, "Pretend you are in mourning. Dress in mourning clothes, and don't
use any cosmetic lotions.[b] Act like a woman who has spent many days grieving for
the dead. 3 Then go to the king and speak
these words to him." And Joab[c] put the
words in her mouth.
4 When the woman from Tekoa went[c]
to the king, she fell with her face to the
ground to pay him honor, and she said,
"Help me, O king!"
5 The king asked her, "What is troubling
you?"
She said, "I am indeed a widow; my
husband is dead. 6 I your servant had two
sons. They got into a fight with each other in the field, and no one was there to
separate them. One struck the other and
killed him. 7 Now the whole clan has risen
up against your servant; they say, 'Hand
over the one who struck his brother down,
so that we may put him to death[d] for the
life of his brother whom he killed; then
we will get rid of the heir[e] as well.' They
would put out the only burning coal I have
left,[f] leaving my husband neither name
nor descendant on the face of the earth."
8 The king said to the woman, "Go
home,[g] and I will issue an order in your
behalf."
9 But the woman from Tekoa said to him,
"My lord the king, let the blame[h] rest on
me and on my father's family,[i] and let the
king and his throne be without guilt.[j]"
10 The king replied, "If anyone says anything to you, bring him to me, and he will
not bother you again."
11 She said, "Then let the king invoke the
LORD his God to prevent the avenger[k] of

13:37 [v] S 2Sa 3:3 **13:39** [w] 2Sa 14:13 [x] S 2Sa 12:19-23 **14:1** [y] S 2Sa 2:18 **14:2** [z] Ne 3:5; Jer 6:1; Am 1:1 [a] 2Sa 20:16 [b] S Ru 3:3; S Isa 1:6

14:3 [c] ver 19 **14:7** [d] Nu 35:19 [e] Mt 21:38 [f] Dt 19:10-13 **14:8** [g] 1Sa 25:35 **14:9** [h] 1Sa 25:24 [i] Mt 27:25 [j] 1Sa 25:28 **14:11** [k] S Nu 35:12,21

[a] *34* Septuagint; Hebrew does not have this sentence.
[b] *39* Dead Sea Scrolls and some Septuagint manuscripts; Masoretic Text *But* ⌞*the spirit of*⌟ *David the king*
[c] *4* Many Hebrew manuscripts, Septuagint, Vulgate and Syriac; most Hebrew manuscripts *spoke*

13:34 *Horonaim.* The Levitical cities of Upper and Lower Beth Horon located in Ephraim (see Jos 21:20,22; 1Ch 7:24) two miles apart and about 11 miles northwest of Jerusalem (see note on Ne 2:10, "Horonite"; see also map, p. 309).

13:37 *Talmai son of Ammihud, the king of Geshur.* Absalom's grandfather (see 3:3 and note).

13:39 *longed to go to Absalom.* With Absalom a refugee, David had lost both of his oldest living sons. Moreover, he could not bring Absalom to account for what he did to Amnon since he had blood on his own hands.

14:1—19:43 The threat to David's reign that emerged after Absalom's restoration from exile, and how that threat was crushed.

14:1 *Joab son of Zeruiah.* See notes on 2:13; 1Sa 26:6. *the king's heart longed for Absalom.* Torn between anger and love (and perhaps remorse), David again leaves the initiative to others.

14:2 *So Joab sent.* Joab appears to have been motivated by a concern for the political implications of the unresolved dispute between David and the son in line for the throne. He attempts to move David to action by means of a story designed to elicit a response clearly applicable, by analogy, to David's own predicament. A similar technique was used by Nathan the prophet (12:1–7; see also 1Ki 20:38–43). *Tekoa.* A town a few miles south of Bethlehem, from which the prophet Amos also came (see Introduction to Amos: Author).

14:7 *the whole clan has risen up against your servant.* It was customary in Israel for a murder victim's next of kin to avenge the blood of his relative by putting the murderer to death (see note on 3:27; see also map and accompanying text, p. 239). In the case presented, however, blood revenge would wipe out the family line, which was something Israelite law and custom tried to avoid if at all possible (see notes on Dt 25:5–6; Ru 2:20). *we will get rid of the heir as well.* The woman suggests that the motivation for blood revenge was more a selfish desire to acquire the family inheritance than a desire for justice (see Nu 27:11). *leaving my husband neither name nor descendant.* The implication is that it would be a more serious offense to terminate a man's family line than to permit a murder to go unpunished by blood revenge. Apparently Joab hoped subtly to suggest to David that if he did not restore Absalom, a struggle for the throne would eventually ensue.

14:8 *I will issue an order in your behalf.* David's judicial action may have rested on the legal ground that the murder was not premeditated (see Dt 19:4–6).

14:9 *blame.* That is, whatever blame may follow from the king's granting her request.

14:11 *let the king invoke the LORD his God.* The woman wants David to confirm his promise by an oath in the Lord's name.

blood from adding to the destruction, so
that my son will not be destroyed."
"As surely as the LORD lives," he said,
"not one hair[l] of your son's head will fall
to the ground.[m]"
12Then the woman said, "Let your servant speak a word to my lord the king."
"Speak," he replied.
13The woman said, "Why then have
you devised a thing like this against the
people of God? When the king says this,
does he not convict himself,[n] for the king
has not brought back his banished son?[o]
14Like water[p] spilled on the ground, which
cannot be recovered, so we must die.[q] But
God does not take away life; instead, he
devises ways so that a banished person[r]
may not remain estranged from him.
15"And now I have come to say this to
my lord the king because the people have
made me afraid. Your servant thought, 'I
will speak to the king; perhaps he will do
what his servant asks. 16Perhaps the king
will agree to deliver his servant from the
hand of the man who is trying to cut off
both me and my son from the inheritance[s]
God gave us.'
17"And now your servant says, 'May the
word of my lord the king bring me rest, for
my lord the king is like an angel[t] of God
in discerning[u] good and evil. May the LORD
your God be with you.' "
18Then the king said to the woman, "Do
not keep from me the answer to what I am
going to ask you."
"Let my lord the king speak," the woman said.
19The king asked, "Isn't the hand of
Joab[v] with you in all this?"
The woman answered, "As surely as you
live, my lord the king, no one can turn to
the right or to the left from anything my
lord the king says. Yes, it was your servant
Joab who instructed me to do this and
who put all these words into the mouth
of your servant. 20Your servant Joab did
this to change the present situation. My
lord has wisdom[w] like that of an angel of
God—he knows everything that happens
in the land.[x]"
21The king said to Joab, "Very well, I
will do it. Go, bring back the young man
Absalom."
22Joab fell with his face to the ground to
pay him honor, and he blessed the king.[y]
Joab said, "Today your servant knows that
he has found favor in your eyes, my lord
the king, because the king has granted his
servant's request."
23Then Joab went to Geshur and brought
Absalom back to Jerusalem. 24But the king
said, "He must go to his own house; he
must not see my face." So Absalom went
to his own house and did not see the face
of the king.
25In all Israel there was not a man so
highly praised for his handsome appearance as Absalom. From the top of his head
to the sole of his foot there was no blemish in him. 26Whenever he cut the hair of
his head[z]—he used to cut his hair from
time to time when it became too heavy for
him—he would weigh it, and its weight
was two hundred shekels[a] by the royal
standard.
27Three sons[a] and a daughter were
born to Absalom. The daughter's name
was Tamar,[b] and she became a beautiful
woman.
28Absalom lived two years in Jerusalem

14:11 [l]S Mt 10:30 [m]S 1Sa 14:45 **14:13** [n]S 2Sa 12:7; 1Ki 20:40 [o]2Sa 13:38-39 **14:14** [p]Job 14:11; Ps 58:7; Isa 19:5 [q]Job 10:8; 17:13; 30:23; Ps 22:15; Heb 9:27 [r]Nu 35:15,25-28 **14:16** [s]S Ex 34:9; S 1Sa 26:19 **14:17** [t]S 1Sa 29:9 [u]1Ki 3:9; Da 2:21 **14:19** [v]ver 3 **14:20** [w]1Ki 3:12,28; 10:23-24; Isa 28:6 [x]2Sa 18:13 **14:22** [y]S Ge 47:7 **14:26** [z]2Sa 18:9 **14:27** [a]2Sa 18:18 [b]S 2Sa 13:1

[a] *26* That is, about 5 pounds (about 2.3 kilograms)

As surely as the LORD lives. An oath formula (see notes on Ge 42:15; 1Sa 14:39,45) that solemnly binds David to his commitment.
14:13 *against the people of God.* The woman's suggestion is that David has done the same thing to Israel that her family members have done to her. The people of Israel want their crown prince returned safely to them. *does he not convict himself . . . ?* The argument is that when David exempted the fictitious murderer from blood revenge, he in effect rendered himself guilty for not doing the same in the case of Absalom. The analogy places David in the position of the blood avenger.
14:14 *Like water spilled on the ground.* Blood revenge will not return the victim of murder to life, just as water spilled on the ground cannot be recovered. *God does not take away life.* In the suggestion that the avenging of blood is contrary to God's ways of dealing with people, the woman apparently distorts Biblical teaching of God's justice (see note on Ge 9:6). But she dwells on the mercy of God, who would rather preserve life than take it (see Eze 18:32; 33:11 and notes). David's own guilt and subsequent experience of God's mercy appear to give added weight to the woman's argument (see notes on 12:13; 13:21).
14:15 *the people have made me afraid.* The woman reverts to her own fabricated story. "The people" are evidently those of her own family who are seeking blood revenge.
14:17 *like an angel of God in discerning good and evil.* Possessing superhuman powers of discernment—as a king ideally should (see v. 20; 19:27).
14:21 *Joab.* He appears to have been present the whole time.
14:23 *Joab went to Geshur.* See 13:37.
14:24 *he must not see my face.* David still vacillates (see note on v. 1); he does not offer forgiveness and restoration.
14:25 *not a man so highly praised.* Absalom's handsomeness brought him attention and popular favor—which he was soon to cultivate.
14:26 *hair of his head.* For the people of that time, hair was a sign of vigor. Kings and heroic figures were usually portrayed with abundant locks, while baldness was a disgrace (see 2Ki 2:23 and note). In this, too, Absalom seemed destined for the throne. *royal standard.* The royal shekel was perhaps heavier than the sanctuary shekel (see Ex 30:13 and note).
14:27 *Three sons.* Their names are unknown; 18:18 suggests that they died in their youth. *Tamar.* Absalom named his daughter after his sister (see 13:1 and note). Maacah (see 1Ki 15:2 and note) was probably a daughter of Tamar, and Absalom's granddaughter (see note on 2Ch 11:20).

without seeing the king's face. 29 Then Absalom sent for Joab in order to send him
to the king, but Joab refused to come to
him. So he sent a second time, but he refused to come. 30 Then he said to his servants, "Look, Joab's field is next to mine,
and he has barley[c] there. Go and set it on
fire." So Absalom's servants set the field
on fire.
31 Then Joab did go to Absalom's house
and he said to him, "Why have your servants set my field on fire?[d]"
32 Absalom said to Joab, "Look, I sent
word to you and said, 'Come here so I can
send you to the king to ask, "Why have I
come from Geshur?[e] It would be better for
me if I were still there!"' Now then, I want
to see the king's face, and if I am guilty of
anything, let him put me to death."[f]
33 So Joab went to the king and told him
this. Then the king summoned Absalom,
and he came in and bowed down with his
face to the ground before the king. And
the king kissed[g] Absalom.

Absalom's Conspiracy

15 In the course of time,[h] Absalom provided himself with a chariot[i] and
horses and with fifty men to run ahead
of him. 2 He would get up early and stand
by the side of the road leading to the city
gate.[j] Whenever anyone came with a complaint to be placed before the king for a
decision, Absalom would call out to him,
"What town are you from?" He would
answer, "Your servant is from one of the
tribes of Israel." 3 Then Absalom would
say to him, "Look, your claims are valid
and proper, but there is no representative of the king to hear you."[k] 4 And Absalom would add, "If only I were appointed
judge in the land![l] Then everyone who has
a complaint or case could come to me and
I would see that he gets justice."
5 Also, whenever anyone approached
him to bow down before him, Absalom
would reach out his hand, take hold of
him and kiss him. 6 Absalom behaved
in this way toward all the Israelites who
came to the king asking for justice, and so
he stole the hearts[m] of the men of Israel.
7 At the end of four[a] years, Absalom said
to the king, "Let me go to Hebron and fulfill a vow I made to the LORD. 8 While your
servant was living at Geshur[n] in Aram,
I made this vow:[o] 'If the LORD takes me
back to Jerusalem, I will worship the LORD
in Hebron.[b]'"
9 The king said to him, "Go in peace." So
he went to Hebron.
10 Then Absalom sent secret messengers
throughout the tribes of Israel to say, "As
soon as you hear the sound of the trumpets,[p] then say, 'Absalom is king in Hebron.'" 11 Two hundred men from Jerusalem had accompanied Absalom. They had
been invited as guests and went quite
innocently, knowing nothing about the
matter. 12 While Absalom was offering sacrifices, he also sent for Ahithophel[q] the
Gilonite, David's counselor,[r] to come from
Giloh,[s] his hometown. And so the conspiracy gained strength, and Absalom's
following kept on increasing.[t]

David Flees

13 A messenger came and told David,
"The hearts of the men of Israel are with
Absalom."

[a] 7 Some Septuagint manuscripts, Syriac and Josephus; Hebrew *forty* [b] 8 Some Septuagint manuscripts; Hebrew does not have *in Hebron.*

14:30 [c] S Ex 9:31
14:31 [d] S Jdg 15:5
14:32 [e] S 2Sa 3:3 [f] 1Sa 20:8
14:33 [g] Lk 15:20
15:1 [h] S 2Sa 12:11 [i] S 1Sa 8:11
15:2 [j] S Ge 23:10; 2Sa 19:8
15:3 [k] Pr 12:2
15:4 [l] Jdg 9:29
15:6 [m] Ro 16:18
15:8 [n] S 2Sa 3:3 [o] S Ge 28:20
15:10 [p] 1Ki 1:34,39; 2Ki 9:13
15:12 [q] ver 31,34; 2Sa 16:15,23; 17:14; 23:34; 1Ch 27:33 [r] Job 19:14; Ps 41:9; 55:13; Jer 9:4 [s] Jos 15:51 [t] Ps 3:1

14:32 *if I am guilty of anything, let him put me to death.* Absalom demands either full pardon and restoration or death, but he still gives no sign of repentance.

14:33 *the king kissed Absalom.* Signifying his forgiveness and Absalom's reconciliation with the royal family. David sidesteps repentance and justice, and in this way he probably contributes to the fulfillment of the prophecy of Nathan (see 12:10 – 11 and notes).

15:1 *In the course of time.* See note on 2:1. *chariot and horses.* As far as is known, Absalom was the first Israelite leader to acquire a chariot and horses (cf. Dt 17:16 and note on 17:16 – 17). *fifty men.* They probably functioned as bodyguards and provided a display of royal pomp that appealed to the masses. Absalom and his brother Adonijah (see 1Ki 1:5 and note) are parade examples of precisely what Samuel had warned against (see 1Sa 8:11 and note; see also note on 8:9,11).

15:2 The main gateway of a city was the primary site where legal cases were settled (see notes on Ge 19:1; Ru 4:1).

15:3 *your claims are valid.* Absalom seeks to ingratiate himself with the people by endorsing their grievances apart from any investigation into their merit.

15:4 *If only I were appointed judge in the land!* Absalom presents himself as the solution to the people's legal grievances. In the case of Amnon, he had taken matters into his own hands because of his father's laxity. Absalom has found, he believes, the weakness in his father's reign, and he capitalizes on it with political astuteness.

15:7 *four years.* After Absalom's return to the court (14:33). By this time he must have been about 30 years old, so his revolt must be dated early in the last decade of David's reign. *Hebron.* Where David was first proclaimed king (see notes on 2:1,4; 5:3,5) and where Absalom was born (see 3:2 – 3 and note on 3:3). Absalom may have had reason to believe that he could count on some local resentment over David's transfer of the capital to Jerusalem. Hebron was also the site of an important sanctuary. *fulfill a vow I made to the LORD.* Absalom piously lies to his father in order to mask his true intentions; cf. David's masking his intentions in the matter of Uriah (11:7 – 15).

15:8 *Geshur.* See 13:37 and note on 3:3.

15:12 *Ahithophel.* Bathsheba's grandfather (see 11:3; 23:34 and notes) and a wise and respected counselor (16:23). He appears to have secretly aligned himself with Absalom's rebellion in its planning stage, perhaps in retaliation against David for his treatment of Bathsheba and Uriah. This unsuspected betrayal by a trusted friend may have prompted David's statements in Ps 41:9 (see note there); 55:12 – 14. *Giloh.* Near Hebron (see Jos 15:51,54).

14Then David said to all his officials who
were with him in Jerusalem, "Come! We
must flee,[u] or none of us will escape from
Absalom.[v] We must leave immediately, or
he will move quickly to overtake us and
bring ruin upon us and put the city to the
sword."
15The king's officials answered him,
"Your servants are ready to do whatever
our lord the king chooses."
16The king set out, with his entire household following him; but he left ten concubines[w] to take care of the palace. 17So the
king set out, with all the people following
him, and they halted at a place some distance away. 18All his men marched past
him, along with all the Kerethites[x] and
Pelethites; and all the six hundred Gittites
who had accompanied him from Gath
marched before the king.
19The king said to Ittai[y] the Gittite,
"Why should you come along with us? Go
back and stay with King Absalom. You are
a foreigner,[z] an exile from your homeland.
20You came only yesterday. And today shall
I make you wander[a] about with us, when I
do not know where I am going? Go back,
and take your countrymen. May kindness
and faithfulness[b] be with you."
21But Ittai replied to the king, "As surely
as the LORD lives, and as my lord the king
lives, wherever my lord the king may be,
whether it means life or death, there will
your servant be."[c]
22David said to Ittai, "Go ahead, march
on." So Ittai the Gittite marched on with
all his men and the families that were with
him.
23The whole countryside wept aloud[d]
as all the people passed by. The king also
crossed the Kidron Valley,[e][f] and all the
people moved on toward the desert.
24Zadok[g] was there, too, and all the Levites who were with him were carrying
the ark[h] of the covenant of God. They set
down the ark of God, and Abiathar[i] offered sacrifices[a] until all the people had
finished leaving the city.
25Then the king said to Zadok, "Take the
ark of God back into the city. If I find favor
in the LORD's eyes, he will bring me back
and let me see it and his dwelling place[j]
again. 26But if he says, 'I am not pleased
with you,' then I am ready; let him do to
me whatever seems good to him.[k]"
27The king also said to Zadok the priest,
"Aren't you a seer?[l] Go back to the city in
peace, with your son Ahimaaz and Jonathan[m] son of Abiathar. You and Abiathar take your two sons with you. 28I will
wait at the fords[n] in the desert until word
comes from you to inform me." 29So Zadok and Abiathar took the ark of God back
to Jerusalem and stayed there.
30But David continued up the Mount of
Olives, weeping[o] as he went; his head[p]
was covered and he was barefoot. All
the people with him covered their heads
too and were weeping as they went up.
31Now David had been told, "Ahithophel[q]
is among the conspirators with Absalom."
So David prayed, "O LORD, turn Ahithophel's counsel into foolishness."
32When David arrived at the summit,
where people used to worship God, Hushai[r] the Arkite[s] was there to meet him,
his robe torn and dust[t] on his head. 33Da-
vid said to him, "If you go with me, you

15:14 [u] 1Ki 2:26; Ps 3 Title; 132:1 [v] 2Sa 19:9 **15:16** [w] 2Sa 16:21-22; 20:3 **15:18** [x] S 1Sa 30:14; 2Sa 20:7, 23; 1Ki 1:38, 44; 1Ch 18:17 **15:19** [y] 2Sa 18:2 [z] S Ge 31:15 **15:20** [a] S 1Sa 22:2 [b] 2Sa 2:6 **15:21** [c] Ru 1:16-17; Pr 17:17 **15:23** [d] 1Sa 11:4; Job 2:12 [e] 1Ki 2:37; 2Ki 23:12; 2Ch 15:16; 29:16; 30:14; Jer 31:40 [f] Jn 18:1 **15:24** [g] S 2Sa 8:17; 19:11 [h] Nu 4:15; S 10:33; 1Ki 2:26 [i] S 1Sa 22:20 **15:25** [j] Ex 15:13; S Lev 15:31; Ps 43:3; 46:4; 84:1; 132:7 **15:26** [k] S Jdg 10:15; 2Sa 22:20 **15:27** [l] S 1Sa 9:9 [m] ver 36; 2Sa 17:17; 1Ki 1:42 **15:28** [n] 2Sa 17:16 **15:30** [o] S Nu 25:6; S Ps 30:5 [p] Est 6:12 **15:31** [q] S ver 12 **15:32** [r] ver 37; 2Sa 16:16; 17:5; 1Ki 4:16 [s] Jos 16:2 [t] S Jos 7:6

[a] 24 Or *Abiathar went up*

15:14 *none of us will escape from Absalom.* Uncertain of the extent of Absalom's support (see v. 13), David fears being trapped in Jerusalem, and he wants to spare the city a bloodbath.
15:16 *he left ten concubines to take care of the palace.* See 5:13; see also note on 3:2–5. David unknowingly arranges for the fulfillment of one of Nathan's prophecies (see notes on 12:11; 16:22; see also 20:3).
15:18 *Kerethites and Pelethites.* See notes on 8:18; Jer 47:4. *six hundred Gittites.* Philistine soldiers who had joined David's personal military force. Their commander was Ittai (v. 19; 18:2).
15:19 *Go back and stay with King Absalom.* David releases the Philistine contingent from further obligations to him.
15:21 *As surely as the LORD lives.* An oath of loyalty taken in the name of Israel's God (see note on 1Sa 14:39,45). *wherever my lord ... may be, ... there will your servant be.* For a similar declaration of commitment see Ru 1:16–17.
15:23 *Kidron Valley.* Just east of Jerusalem (see note on Isa 22:7). *desert.* The northern part of the Desert of Judah that lies between Jerusalem and the Dead Sea.
15:24 *Zadok.* See note on 8:17. *Abiathar.* See note on 8:17; see also 1Sa 22:20–23 and note on 22:20.
15:25 *Take the ark of God back into the city.* David reveals a true understanding of the connection between the ark and God's presence with his people. He knows that possession of the ark does not guarantee God's blessing (see notes on 1Sa 4:3,21). He also recognizes that the ark belongs in the capital city as a symbol of the Lord's rule over the nation (see note on 6:2), no matter who the king might be.
15:26 *let him do to me whatever seems good to him.* David confesses that he has no exclusive claim to the throne and that Israel's divine King is free to confer the kingship on whomever he chooses.
15:27 *Aren't you a seer?* Perhaps an allusion to the high priest's custody of the Urim and Thummim as a means of divine revelation (see notes on Ex 28:30; 1Sa 2:28). See also note on 1Sa 9:9.
15:28 *fords in the desert.* Fords across the Jordan in the vicinity of Gilgal.
15:30 *Mount of Olives.* See notes on Zec 14:4; Mk 11:1. *his head was covered.* A sign of sorrow (see Est 6:12; Jer 14:3–4; cf. 2Sa 19:4 and note). *he was barefoot.* A sign of mourning (see Eze 24:17; Mic 1:8 and notes) and shame (see Isa 20:4).
15:31 *Ahithophel.* See note on v. 12.
15:32 *Hushai the Arkite.* The Arkites were a clan (some think non-Israelite) that inhabited an area southwest of Bethel (Jos 16:2). Since Hushai was a trusted member of David's court (see note on v. 37), his appearance was the beginning of an answer to David's prayer (v. 31).

will be a burden[u] to me. 34But if you return to the city and say to Absalom, 'I will be your servant, O king; I was your father's servant in the past, but now I will be your servant,'[v] then you can help me by frustrating[w] Ahithophel's advice. 35Won't the priests Zadok and Abiathar be there with you? Tell them anything you hear in the king's palace.[x] 36Their two sons, Ahimaaz[y] son of Zadok and Jonathan[z] son of Abiathar, are there with them. Send them to me with anything you hear."

37So David's friend Hushai[a] arrived at Jerusalem as Absalom[b] was entering the city.

David and Ziba

16 When David had gone a short distance beyond the summit, there was Ziba,[c] the steward of Mephibosheth, waiting to meet him. He had a string of donkeys saddled and loaded with two hundred loaves of bread, a hundred cakes of raisins, a hundred cakes of figs and a skin of wine.[d]

2The king asked Ziba, "Why have you brought these?"

Ziba answered, "The donkeys are for the king's household to ride on, the bread and fruit are for the men to eat, and the wine is to refresh[e] those who become exhausted in the desert."

3The king then asked, "Where is your master's grandson?"[f]

Ziba[g] said to him, "He is staying in Jerusalem, because he thinks, 'Today the house of Israel will give me back my grandfather's kingdom.'"

4Then the king said to Ziba, "All that belonged to Mephibosheth[h] is now yours."

"I humbly bow," Ziba said. "May I find favor in your eyes, my lord the king."

Shimei Curses David

5As King David approached Bahurim,[i] a man from the same clan as Saul's family came out from there. His name was Shimei[j] son of Gera, and he cursed[k] as he came out. 6He pelted David and all the king's officials with stones, though all the troops and the special guard were on David's right and left. 7As he cursed, Shimei said, "Get out, get out, you man of blood, you scoundrel! 8The LORD has repaid you for all the blood you shed in the household of Saul, in whose place you have reigned.[l] The LORD has handed the kingdom over to your son Absalom. You have come to ruin because you are a man of blood!"[m]

9Then Abishai[n] son of Zeruiah said to the king, "Why should this dead dog[o] curse my lord the king? Let me go over and cut off his head."[p]

10But the king said, "What do you and I have in common, you sons of Zeruiah?[q] If he is cursing because the LORD said to him, 'Curse David,' who can ask, 'Why do you do this?'"[r]

11David then said to Abishai and all his officials, "My son,[s] who is of my own flesh, is trying to take my life. How much more, then, this Benjamite! Leave him alone; let him curse, for the LORD has told him to.[t] 12It may be that the LORD will see my distress[u] and repay me with good[v] for the cursing I am receiving today.[w]"

13So David and his men continued along the road while Shimei was going along the hillside opposite him, cursing as he went and throwing stones at him and showering him with dirt. 14The king and all the people with him arrived at their destination exhausted.[x] And there he refreshed himself.

The Advice of Ahithophel and Hushai

15Meanwhile, Absalom[y] and all the men of Israel came to Jerusalem, and Ahithophel[z] was with him. 16Then Hushai[a] the Arkite, David's friend, went to Absalom and said to him, "Long live the king! Long live the king!"

17Absalom asked Hushai, "Is this the love you show your friend? Why didn't you go with your friend?"[b]

15:33 [u]2Sa 19:35 **15:34** [v]2Sa 16:19 [w]2Sa 17:14; Pr 11:14 **15:35** [x]2Sa 17:15-16 **15:36** [y]2Sa 18:19 [z]S ver 27; 2Sa 17:17; 1Ki 1:42 **15:37** [a]1Ch 27:33 [b]2Sa 16:15 **16:1** [c]2Sa 9:1-13 [d]S 1Sa 25:18; 1Ch 12:40 **16:2** [e]2Sa 17:27-29 **16:3** [f]2Sa 9:9-10 [g]S 2Sa 9:2 **16:4** [h]S 2Sa 4:4 **16:5** [i]S 2Sa 3:16 [j]2Sa 19:16-23; 1Ki 2:8-9,36,44 [k]S Ex 22:28 **16:8** [l]2Sa 19:28; 21:9 [m]2Sa 19:19; Ps 55:3 **16:9** [n]S 1Sa 26:6 [o]S 2Sa 3:8 [p]S 2Sa 3:39; Lk 9:54 **16:10** [q]S 2Sa 2:18; 19:22 [r]Ro 9:20 **16:11** [s]2Sa 12:11 [t]S Ge 45:5; 1Sa 26:19 **16:12** [u]Ps 4:1; 25:18 [v]Dt 23:5; Ro 8:28 [w]Ps 109:28 **16:14** [x]2Sa 17:2 **16:15** [y]S 2Sa 15:37 [z]S 2Sa 15:12 **16:16** [a]S 2Sa 15:32 **16:17** [b]2Sa 19:25

15:37 *David's friend Hushai.* See 16:16. 1Ch 27:33 calls him the "king's friend," which seems to be an official title for the king's most trusted adviser (see 1Ki 4:5, where the Hebrew for "king's friend" is translated "personal adviser to the king").

16:1 *Ziba.* See ch. 9 and note on 9:2. *Mephibosheth.* See note on 4:4.

16:2 *Ziba answered.* Since David assumed control of Saul's estate (9:7 – 10, but see note on 9:7), Ziba, always the opportunist, seeks to profit from the political crisis.

16:3 *your master's grandson.* Mephibosheth (see 9:2 – 3,9).

16:4 *All that belonged to Mephibosheth is now yours.* Because the revolt was so widespread and loyalties so uncertain, David was quick to assume the worst — and judged badly.

16:5 *Bahurim.* Near the Mount of Olives. *same clan as Saul's family.* The clan of Matri (see 1Sa 10:21). *Gera.* See note on 1Ki 2:8.

16:6 *the troops and the special guard.* The Kerethites, Pelethites and 600 Gittites (see 15:18 and note).

16:7 *scoundrel.* See note on Dt 13:13.

16:8 *blood you shed in the household of Saul.* Shimei may be referring to the executions reported in 21:1 – 14, but the time of that event is uncertain (see note on 21:1).

16:9 *Abishai.* See note on 1Sa 26:6. *this dead dog.* An expression of absolute contempt (see note on 9:8).

16:10 *sons of Zeruiah.* Intended as an insult (cf. note on 1Sa 20:27,30 – 31). *If … because the LORD said to him, 'Curse David.'* David leaves open the possibility that God has seen fit to terminate his rule — the verdict is not yet in (see 15:26 and note). For David's later actions regarding Shimei see 19:18 – 23; 1Ki 2:8 – 9.

16:15 *Ahithophel.* See note on 15:12.

16:16 *Hushai the Arkite, David's friend.* See notes on 15:32,37. *Long live the king!* See note on Ps 62:4.

18Hushai said to Absalom, "No, the one
chosen by the LORD, by these people, and
by all the men of Israel—his I will be, and
I will remain with him. 19Furthermore,
whom should I serve? Should I not serve
the son? Just as I served your father, so I
will serve you."[c]
20Absalom said to Ahithophel, "Give us
your advice. What should we do?"
21Ahithophel answered, "Lie with your
father's concubines whom he left to take
care of the palace. Then all Israel will hear
that you have made yourself a stench in
your father's nostrils, and the hands of
everyone with you will be strengthened."
22So they pitched a tent for Absalom on
the roof, and he lay with his father's concubines in the sight of all Israel.[d]
23Now in those days the advice[e] Ahithophel gave was like that of one who inquires of God. That was how both David[f]
and Absalom regarded all of Ahithophel's
advice.

17 Ahithophel said to Absalom, "I
would[a] choose twelve thousand men
and set out tonight in pursuit of David. 2I
would[b] attack him while he is weary and
weak.[g] I would[b] strike him with terror,
and then all the people with him will flee.
I would[b] strike down only the king[h] 3and
bring all the people back to you. The death
of the man you seek will mean the return
of all; all the people will be unharmed."
4This plan seemed good to Absalom and
to all the elders of Israel.
5But Absalom said, "Summon also Hushai[i] the Arkite, so we can hear what he
has to say." 6When Hushai came to him,
Absalom said, "Ahithophel has given this
advice. Should we do what he says? If not,
give us your opinion."
7Hushai replied to Absalom, "The advice Ahithophel has given is not good this
time. 8You know your father and his men;
they are fighters, and as fierce as a wild
bear robbed of her cubs.[j] Besides, your
father is an experienced fighter;[k] he will
not spend the night with the troops. 9Even
now, he is hidden in a cave or some other place.[l] If he should attack your troops
first,[c] whoever hears about it will say,
'There has been a slaughter among the
troops who follow Absalom.' 10Then even
the bravest soldier, whose heart is like the
heart of a lion,[m] will melt[n] with fear, for all
Israel knows that your father is a fighter
and that those with him are brave.[o]
11"So I advise you: Let all Israel, from
Dan to Beersheba[p]—as numerous as the
sand[q] on the seashore—be gathered to
you, with you yourself leading them into
battle. 12Then we will attack him wherever
he may be found, and we will fall on him
as dew settles on the ground. Neither he
nor any of his men will be left alive. 13If he
withdraws into a city, then all Israel will
bring ropes to that city, and we will drag it
down to the valley[r] until not even a piece
of it can be found."
14Absalom and all the men of Israel said,
"The advice[s] of Hushai the Arkite is better than that of Ahithophel."[t] For the LORD
had determined to frustrate[u] the good advice of Ahithophel in order to bring disaster[v] on Absalom.[w]
15Hushai told Zadok and Abiathar, the
priests, "Ahithophel has advised Absalom
and the elders of Israel to do such and
such, but I have advised them to do so
and so. 16Now send a message immediately and tell David, 'Do not spend the night
at the fords in the desert;[x] cross over without fail, or the king and all the people with
him will be swallowed up.[y]' "
17Jonathan[z] and Ahimaaz were staying
at En Rogel.[a] A servant girl was to go and
inform them, and they were to go and tell
King David, for they could not risk being
seen entering the city. 18But a young man
saw them and told Absalom. So the two of

16:19 [c]2Sa 15:34 **16:22** [d]S 2Sa 3:7; 12:11-12; S 15:16 **16:23** [e]2Sa 17:14,23 [f]S 2Sa 15:12 **17:2** [g]2Sa 16:14 [h]1Ki 22:31; Zec 13:7 **17:5** [i]S 2Sa 15:32 **17:8** [j]Hos 13:8 [k]1Sa 16:18 **17:9** [l]Jer 41:9 **17:10** [m]1Ch 12:8 [n]Jos 2:9,11; Eze 21:15 [o]2Sa 23:8; 1Ch 11:11 **17:11** [p]S Jdg 20:1 [q]S Ge 12:2; S Jos 11:4 **17:13** [r]Mic 1:6 **17:14** [s]S 2Sa 16:23 [t]S 2Sa 15:12 [u]S 2Sa 15:34; Ne 4:15 [v]Ps 9:16 [w]2Ch 10:8 **17:16** [x]2Sa 15:28 [y]2Sa 15:35 **17:17** [z]S 2Sa 15:27, 36 [a]Jos 15:7; 18:16; 1Ki 1:9

[a] 1 Or *Let me* [b] 2 Or *will* [c] 9 Or *When some of the men fall at the first attack*

16:18 Hushai's statement is deliberately ambiguous. Nowhere is Absalom referred to as God's "chosen" one, but David is often called the Lord's "chosen" one or its equivalent (see 6:21; 1Sa 16:8–13; 1Ki 8:16; 11:34; 1Ch 28:4; Ps 78:70).
16:21 *Lie with your father's concubines.* This would signify Absalom's assumption of royal power; it would also be a definitive and irreversible declaration of the break between father and son (see notes on 3:7; 12:8; 1Ki 2:22). *stench.* See note on 1Sa 13:4.
16:22 *he lay with his father's concubines.* A fulfillment of Nathan's prophecy (see 12:11–12 and note on 12:11). For additional significance see note on v. 21.
17:1–3 Ahithophel's advice to Absalom envisioned a cheap and easy victory that would not leave the nation weakened.
17:4 *all the elders of Israel.* See note on 3:17. Absalom's rebellion appears to have gained extensive backing from prominent tribal leaders.
17:5 *Hushai the Arkite.* See 16:16–19; see also notes on 15:32, 37.
17:7–13 Hushai's advice subtly capitalizes on Absalom's uncertainty, his fear and his egotism.
17:11 *from Dan to Beersheba.* See note on 1Sa 3:20.
17:12–13 *we ... we ... we.* Hushai carefully links himself with the revolt.
17:14 *the LORD had determined to frustrate the good advice of Ahithophel.* An answer to David's prayer (see 15:31; cf. Ps 33:10; Pr 21:30 and note).
17:15 *Zadok and Abiathar.* See 15:24–29,35–36 and note on 15:24.
17:16 *fords in the desert.* See 15:28 and note. *cross over.* Hushai advises David to cross the Jordan River, knowing that Absalom might change his mind and immediately set out after him.
17:17 *Jonathan and Ahimaaz.* See 15:36. *En Rogel.* A spring in the Kidron Valley just outside the walls of Jerusalem. *A servant girl.* A servant going to the spring for water would attract no attention.
17:18 *Bahurim.* See note on 16:5.

them left quickly and went to the house of
a man in Bahurim.[b] He had a well in his
courtyard, and they climbed down into it.
19His wife took a covering and spread it
out over the opening of the well and scattered grain over it. No one knew anything
about it.[c]
20When Absalom's men came to the
woman[d] at the house, they asked, "Where
are Ahimaaz and Jonathan?"
The woman answered them, "They
crossed over the brook."[a] The men
searched but found no one, so they returned to Jerusalem.
21After the men had gone, the two
climbed out of the well and went to inform King David. They said to him, "Set
out and cross the river at once; Ahithophel
has advised such and such against you."
22So David and all the people with him set
out and crossed the Jordan. By daybreak,
no one was left who had not crossed the
Jordan.
23When Ahithophel saw that his advice[e] had not been followed, he saddled
his donkey and set out for his house in his
hometown. He put his house in order[f] and
then hanged himself. So he died and was
buried in his father's tomb.
24David went to Mahanaim,[g] and Absalom crossed the Jordan with all the men
of Israel. 25Absalom had appointed Amasa[h] over the army in place of Joab. Amasa
was the son of a man named Jether,[b][i] an
Israelite[c] who had married Abigail,[d] the
daughter of Nahash and sister of Zeruiah
the mother of Joab. 26The Israelites and
Absalom camped in the land of Gilead.
27When David came to Mahanaim, Shobi son of Nahash[j] from Rabbah[k] of the
Ammonites, and Makir[l] son of Ammiel
from Lo Debar, and Barzillai[m] the Gileadite[n] from Rogelim 28brought bedding and
bowls and articles of pottery. They also
brought wheat and barley, flour and roasted grain, beans and lentils,[e] 29honey and
curds, sheep, and cheese from cows' milk
for David and his people to eat.[o] For they
said, "The people have become hungry
and tired and thirsty in the desert.[p]"

Absalom's Death

18 David mustered the men who were
with him and appointed over them
commanders of thousands and commanders of hundreds. 2David sent the troops
out[q]—a third under the command of
Joab, a third under Joab's brother Abishai[r]
son of Zeruiah, and a third under Ittai[s] the
Gittite. The king told the troops, "I myself
will surely march out with you."
3But the men said, "You must not go
out; if we are forced to flee, they won't
care about us. Even if half of us die, they
won't care; but you are worth ten[t] thousand of us.[f] It would be better now for you
to give us support from the city."[u]
4The king answered, "I will do whatever
seems best to you."
So the king stood beside the gate while
all the men marched out in units of hundreds and of thousands. 5The king commanded Joab, Abishai and Ittai, "Be gentle with the young man Absalom for my
sake." And all the troops heard the king
giving orders concerning Absalom to each
of the commanders.
6The army marched into the field to
fight Israel, and the battle took place in
the forest[v] of Ephraim. 7There the army of
Israel was defeated by David's men, and
the casualties that day were great—twenty thousand men. 8The battle spread out
over the whole countryside, and the forest claimed more lives that day than the
sword.

17:18 [b]S 2Sa 3:16 **17:19** [c]S Jos 2:6 **17:20** [d]S Ex 1:19 **17:23** [e]2Sa S 2Sa 16:23 [f]2Ki 20:1 **17:24** [g]S Ge 32:2 **17:25** [h]2Sa 19:13; 20:4,9-12; 1Ki 2:5,32; 1Ch 12:18 [i]1Ch 2:13-17 **17:27** [j]S 1Sa 11:1 [k]S Dt 3:11 [l]2Sa 9:4 [m]2Sa 19:31-39; 1Ki 2:7 [n]2Sa 19:31; Ezr 2:61 **17:29** [o]1Ch 12:40 [p]2Sa 16:2; S Ro 12:13 **18:2** [q]S Jdg 7:16; 1Sa 11:11 [r]S 1Sa 26:6 [s]2Sa 15:19 **18:3** [t]S 1Sa 18:7 [u]2Sa 21:17 **18:6** [v]S Jos 17:15

[a] 20 Or *"They passed by the sheep pen toward the water."* [b] 25 Hebrew *Ithra,* a variant of *Jether* [c] 25 Hebrew and some Septuagint manuscripts; other Septuagint manuscripts (see also 1 Chron. 2:17) *Ishmaelite* or *Jezreelite* [d] 25 Hebrew *Abigal,* a variant of *Abigail* [e] 28 Most Septuagint manuscripts and Syriac; Hebrew *lentils, and roasted grain* [f] 3 Two Hebrew manuscripts, some Septuagint manuscripts and Vulgate; most Hebrew manuscripts *care; for now there are ten thousand like us*

17:23 *his hometown.* Giloh (see 15:12 and note). *hanged himself.* Ahithophel was convinced that the rebellion would fail and that he would be found guilty of treason as a co-conspirator.

17:24 *Mahanaim.* Ironically the same place where Ish-Bosheth had sought refuge after Saul's death (see 2:8 and note).

17:25 *Amasa.* Nephew of David and cousin of both Absalom and Joab son of Zeruiah. *Abigail, the daughter of Nahash and sister of Zeruiah.* Zeruiah was David's sister (see 1Ch 2:16 and note on 2:10–17). Since the father of Abigail and Zeruiah is Nahash rather than Jesse, their unnamed mother may have married Jesse after the death of Nahash.

17:27 *Shobi son of Nahash.* Apparently the brother of Hanun (see 10:2–4), whom David had defeated earlier in his reign (11:1; 12:26–31). *Rabbah of the Ammonites.* See note on 10:3,14. *Makir.* See note on 9:4. *Barzillai.* A wealthy benefactor of David during his flight to Mahanaim (see 19:32; 1Ki 2:7). After the Babylonian exile, there were claimants to the priesthood among his descendants (Ezr 2:61–63).

18:2 *Ittai the Gittite.* See 15:18–22.

18:3 *You must not go out.* In addition to the reason given, David was growing old and was no longer the warrior he had been. This is essentially the same idea that Ahithophel had expressed to Absalom (see 17:2).

18:5 *Be gentle with … Absalom for my sake.* David's love for his (now) oldest son was undying—and almost his undoing (see 19:5–7 and note on 19:5).

18:6 *Israel.* Absalom's army (see 15:13; 16:15; 17:4,11,24–26). *forest of Ephraim.* The battle was apparently fought in Gilead, east of the Jordan (see 17:24,26). The name "forest of Ephraim" may have derived from an Ephraimite claim on the area (see Jdg 12:1–4).

18:8 *The battle spread out.* The armies apparently became dispersed, and many of the men got lost in the forest.

9Now Absalom happened to meet David's men. He was riding his mule, and as
the mule went under the thick branches of
a large oak, Absalom's head[w] got caught
in the tree. He was left hanging in midair, while the mule he was riding kept on
going.
10When one of the men saw this, he told
Joab, "I just saw Absalom hanging in an
oak tree."
11Joab said to the man who had told him
this, "What! You saw him? Why didn't you
strike[x] him to the ground right there? Then
I would have had to give you ten shekels[a]
of silver and a warrior's belt.[y]"
12But the man replied, "Even if a thousand shekels[b] were weighed out into my
hands, I would not lift my hand against
the king's son. In our hearing the king
commanded you and Abishai and Ittai,
'Protect the young man Absalom for my
sake.[c]' 13And if I had put my life in jeopardy[d]—and nothing is hidden from the
king[z]—you would have kept your distance from me."
14Joab[a] said, "I'm not going to wait like
this for you." So he took three javelins in
his hand and plunged them into Absalom's heart while Absalom was still alive
in the oak tree. 15And ten of Joab's armor-
bearers surrounded Absalom, struck him
and killed him.[b]
16Then Joab[c] sounded the trumpet, and
the troops stopped pursuing Israel, for
Joab halted them. 17They took Absalom,
threw him into a big pit in the forest and
piled up[d] a large heap of rocks[e] over him.
Meanwhile, all the Israelites fled to their
homes.
18During his lifetime Absalom had taken
a pillar and erected it in the King's Valley[f] as a monument[g] to himself, for he
thought, "I have no son[h] to carry on the
memory of my name." He named the pillar after himself, and it is called Absalom's
Monument to this day.

David Mourns

19Now Ahimaaz[i] son of Zadok said, "Let
me run and take the news to the king that
the LORD has delivered him from the hand
of his enemies.[j]"
20"You are not the one to take the news
today," Joab told him. "You may take the
news another time, but you must not do
so today, because the king's son is dead."
21Then Joab said to a Cushite, "Go, tell
the king what you have seen." The Cushite bowed down before Joab and ran off.
22Ahimaaz son of Zadok again said to
Joab, "Come what may, please let me run
behind the Cushite."
But Joab replied, "My son, why do you
want to go? You don't have any news that
will bring you a reward."
23He said, "Come what may, I want to
run."
So Joab said, "Run!" Then Ahimaaz ran
by way of the plain[e] and outran the Cushite.
24While David was sitting between the
inner and outer gates, the watchman[k]
went up to the roof of the gateway by the
wall. As he looked out, he saw a man running alone. 25The watchman called out to
the king and reported it.
The king said, "If he is alone, he must
have good news." And the man came closer and closer.
26Then the watchman saw another
man running, and he called down to the
gatekeeper, "Look, another man running
alone!"
The king said, "He must be bringing
good news,[l] too."
27The watchman said, "It seems to me
that the first one runs like[m] Ahimaaz son
of Zadok."
"He's a good man," the king said. "He
comes with good news."
28Then Ahimaaz called out to the king,
"All is well!" He bowed down before the

18:9 [w] 2Sa 14:26 **18:11** [x] S 2Sa 3:39 [y] 1Sa 18:4 **18:13** [z] 2Sa 14:19-20 **18:14** [a] S 2Sa 2:18 **18:15** [b] S 2Sa 12:10 **18:16** [c] S 2Sa 2:28 **18:17** [d] Jos 7:26 [e] Jos 8:29 **18:18** [f] Ge 14:17 [g] S Ge 50:5; S Nu 32:42 [h] 2Sa 14:27 **18:19** [i] S 2Sa 15:36 [j] Jdg 11:36 **18:24** [k] S 1Sa 14:16; S Jer 51:12 **18:26** [l] 1Ki 1:42; Isa 52:7; 61:1 **18:27** [m] 2Ki 9:20

[a] *11* That is, about 4 ounces (about 115 grams)
[b] *12* That is, about 25 pounds (about 11 kilograms)
[c] *12* A few Hebrew manuscripts, Septuagint, Vulgate and Syriac; most Hebrew manuscripts may be translated *Absalom, whoever you may be.*
[d] *13* Or *Otherwise, if I had acted treacherously toward him*
[e] *23* That is, the plain of the Jordan

18:9 *his mule.* See note on 13:29. *Absalom's head got caught in the tree.* Whether by the entanglement of his abundant hair (14:26) or by some other means is not stated, but his handsome head (see 14:25) was in the end—ironically—his undoing.

18:11 *I would have had to give you.* Joab must be referring to an announced intent on his part to reward anyone killing Absalom. His actions and interests did not always coincide with David's wishes (see note on 2:13).

18:15 *killed him.* The easiest and most certain way of ending the rebellion—but the brutal overkill is indicative of the deep animosity felt by David's men toward Absalom.

18:17 *large heap of rocks.* A mound of rocks that mocked the monument Absalom himself had erected (v. 18). *all the Israelites.* See note on v. 6.

18:18 *erected it . . . as a monument to himself.* As Saul had done (see 1Sa 15:12 and note). *King's Valley.* Near Jerusalem (see Ge 14:17; Josephus, *Antiquities*, 7.10.3). *I have no son.* See 14:27 and note. *Absalom's Monument.* Not to be confused with the much later monument of the same name that is still visible today in the valley east of Jerusalem.

18:19 *Ahimaaz son of Zadok.* See 15:27; 17:17–21.

18:20 *not the one to take the news.* The choice of a messenger depended on the content of the message (see v. 27 and note).

18:21 *Cushite.* A foreigner (see note on Nu 12:1).

18:27 *He comes with good news.* David presumed that Joab would not have sent someone like Ahimaaz to carry bad news (see v. 20 and note).

king with his face to the ground and said,
"Praise be to the LORD your God! He has
delivered up the men who lifted their
hands against my lord the king."
29 The king asked, "Is the young man
Absalom safe?"
Ahimaaz answered, "I saw great confusion just as Joab was about to send the
king's servant and me, your servant, but I
don't know what it was."
30 The king said, "Stand aside and wait
here." So he stepped aside and stood
there.
31 Then the Cushite arrived and said,
"My lord the king, hear the good news!
The LORD has delivered you today from all
who rose up against you."
32 The king asked the Cushite, "Is the
young man Absalom safe?"
The Cushite replied, "May the enemies
of my lord the king and all who rise up to
harm you be like that young man."[n]
33 The king was shaken. He went up to
the room over the gateway and wept. As
he went, he said: "O my son Absalom! My
son, my son Absalom! If only I had died[o]
instead of you—O Absalom, my son, my
son!"[p]

19 Joab was told, "The king is weeping
and mourning for Absalom." 2 And
for the whole army the victory that day
was turned into mourning, because on
that day the troops heard it said, "The
king is grieving for his son." 3 The men
stole into the city that day as men steal in
who are ashamed when they flee from battle. 4 The king covered his face and cried
aloud, "O my son Absalom! O Absalom,
my son, my son!"
5 Then Joab went into the house to the
king and said, "Today you have humiliated all your men, who have just saved your
life and the lives of your sons and daughters and the lives of your wives and concubines. 6 You love those who hate you and
hate those who love you. You have made it
clear today that the commanders and their
men mean nothing to you. I see that you
would be pleased if Absalom were alive
today and all of us were dead. 7 Now go
out and encourage your men. I swear by
the LORD that if you don't go out, not a
man will be left with you by nightfall. This
will be worse for you than all the calamities that have come upon you from your
youth till now."[q]
8 So the king got up and took his seat
in the gateway. When the men were told,
"The king is sitting in the gateway,[r]" they
all came before him.

David Returns to Jerusalem

Meanwhile, the Israelites had fled to
their homes. 9 Throughout the tribes of
Israel, the people were all arguing with
each other, saying, "The king delivered
us from the hand of our enemies; he is
the one who rescued us from the hand
of the Philistines.[s] But now he has fled
the country because of Absalom;[t] 10 and
Absalom, whom we anointed to rule over
us, has died in battle. So why do you say
nothing about bringing the king back?"
11 King David sent this message to Zadok[u] and Abiathar, the priests: "Ask the
elders of Judah, 'Why should you be the
last to bring the king back to his palace,
since what is being said throughout Israel has reached the king at his quarters?
12 You are my brothers, my own flesh
and blood. So why should you be the
last to bring back the king?' 13 And say
to Amasa,[v] 'Are you not my own flesh
and blood?[w] May God deal with me, be it
ever so severely,[x] if from now on you are
not the commander of my army in place
of Joab.[y]'"
14 He won over the hearts of all the men
of Judah as though they were one man.
They sent word to the king, "Return, you

18:32 [n] Jdg 5:31; S 1Sa 25:26 **18:33** [o] Ex 32:32 [p] S Ge 43:14; 2Sa 19:4
19:7 [q] Pr 14:28 **19:8** [r] S 2Sa 15:2 **19:9** [s] 2Sa 8:1-14 [t] 2Sa 15:14 **19:11** [u] S 2Sa 15:24 **19:13** [v] S 2Sa 17:25 [w] S Ge 29:14 [x] S Ru 1:17 [y] S 2Sa 2:13

18:29 *I saw great confusion.* Ahimaaz avoids a direct answer to David's question, though he knew Absalom was dead.

18:33 *O my son Absalom!* One of the most moving expressions in all literature of a father's grief over his son's death—in spite of all that Absalom had done. *If only I had died instead of you.* The intensity of David's grief springs in no small part from his recognition that he himself bore large responsibility for the course of events that led to Absalom's death. His own actions had set a negative example for his children and at the same time had rendered him incapable of acting judicially as a king ought—all of which led up to Absalom's rebellion. In Absalom's violent death at the hands of Joab, David's sinful abuse of royal power had finally produced its most bitter fruit.

19:4 *covered his face.* Cf. note on 15:30.

19:5 *Joab went ... to the king.* Apparently confident that the king was unaware of Joab's part in Absalom's death. David never indicates that he learned of it (see 1Ki 2:5 and note). *you have humiliated all your men.* Joab boldly rebukes David for allowing his personal grief to keep him from expressing his appreciation for the loyalty of those who risked their lives to preserve his throne. Joab warns David that his love for Absalom can still undo him.

19:9 *The king delivered us.* With Absalom dead, the northern tribes remember what David had done for them (see 3:17–18; 5:2 and notes).

19:11 *Ask the elders of Judah.* Even though the rebellion had begun in Hebron in Judah (see 15:9–12), David appeals to the elders of his own tribe to take the initiative in restoring him to the throne in Jerusalem (see 2:4; 1Sa 30:26 and notes). This appeal produced the desired result, but it also led to the arousal of tribal jealousies (see vv. 41–43).

19:13 *Amasa ... my own flesh and blood.* See 17:25 and note. Although Amasa deserved death for treason, David appointed him commander of his army in place of Joab, hoping to secure the allegiance of those who had followed Amasa, especially the Judahites (see 20:4 and note). *May God deal with me, be it ever so severely.* A curse formula (see note on 1Sa 3:17).

and all your men." 15Then the king returned and went as far as the Jordan.
Now the men of Judah had come to Gilgal[z] to go out and meet the king and bring
him across the Jordan. 16Shimei[a] son of
Gera, the Benjamite from Bahurim, hurried down with the men of Judah to meet
King David. 17With him were a thousand
Benjamites, along with Ziba,[b] the steward
of Saul's household,[c] and his fifteen sons
and twenty servants. They rushed to the
Jordan, where the king was. 18They crossed
at the ford to take the king's household
over and to do whatever he wished.
When Shimei son of Gera crossed the
Jordan, he fell prostrate before the king
19and said to him, "May my lord not hold
me guilty. Do not remember how your servant did wrong on the day my lord the
king left Jerusalem.[d] May the king put it
out of his mind. 20For I your servant know
that I have sinned, but today I have come
here as the first of the whole house of Joseph to come down and meet my lord the
king."
21Then Abishai[e] son of Zeruiah said,
"Shouldn't Shimei be put to death for this?
He cursed[f] the LORD's anointed."[g]
22David replied, "What do you and I
have in common, you sons of Zeruiah?[h]
This day you have become my adversaries! Should anyone be put to death in Israel today?[i] Do I not know that today I
am king over Israel?" 23So the king said to
Shimei, "You shall not die." And the king
promised him on oath.[j]
24Mephibosheth,[k] Saul's grandson, also
went down to meet the king. He had not
taken care of his feet or trimmed his mus-
tache or washed his clothes from the day
the king left until the day he returned
safely. 25When he came from Jerusalem to
meet the king, the king asked him, "Why
didn't you go with me,[l] Mephibosheth?"
26He said, "My lord the king, since I
your servant am lame,[m] I said, 'I will have
my donkey saddled and will ride on it, so
I can go with the king.' But Ziba[n] my servant betrayed me. 27And he has slandered
your servant to my lord the king. My lord
the king is like an angel[o] of God; so do
whatever pleases you. 28All my grandfather's descendants deserved nothing but
death[p] from my lord the king, but you gave
your servant a place among those who eat
at your table.[q] So what right do I have to
make any more appeals to the king?"
29The king said to him, "Why say more?
I order you and Ziba to divide the fields."
30Mephibosheth said to the king, "Let
him take everything, now that my lord the
king has arrived home safely."
31Barzillai[r] the Gileadite also came down
from Rogelim to cross the Jordan with the
king and to send him on his way from
there. 32Now Barzillai was a very old man,
eighty years of age. He had provided for
the king during his stay in Mahanaim, for
he was a very wealthy[s] man. 33The king
said to Barzillai, "Cross over with me and
stay with me in Jerusalem, and I will provide for you."
34But Barzillai answered the king, "How
many more years will I live, that I should
go up to Jerusalem with the king? 35I am
now eighty[t] years old. Can I tell the difference between what is good and what is
not? Can your servant taste what he eats
and drinks? Can I still hear the voices of
men and women singers?[u] Why should
your servant be an added[v] burden to my
lord the king? 36Your servant will cross
over the Jordan with the king for a short
distance, but why should the king reward
me in this way? 37Let your servant return,
that I may die in my own town near the
tomb of my father[w] and mother. But here
is your servant Kimham.[x] Let him cross
over with my lord the king. Do for him
whatever pleases you."

19:15 [z]S 1Sa 11:15 **19:16** [a]2Sa 16:5-13 **19:17** [b]S 2Sa 9:2 [c]S Ge 43:16 **19:19** [d]S 2Sa 16:6-8 **19:21** [e]S 1Sa 26:6 [f]S Ex 22:28 [g]S 1Sa 12:3; S 26:9 **19:22** [h]S 2Sa 2:18; S 16:10 [i]1Sa 11:13 **19:23** [j]1Ki 2:8,42 **19:24** [k]S 2Sa 4:4 **19:25** [l]2Sa 16:17 **19:26** [m]S Lev 21:18 [n]S 2Sa 9:2 **19:27** [o]S 1Sa 29:9 **19:28** [p]S 2Sa 16:8 [q]S 2Sa 9:7,13 **19:31** [r]S 2Sa 17:27-29; 1Ki 2:7 **19:32** [s]1Sa 25:2 **19:35** [t]Ps 90:10 [u]2Ch 35:25; Ezr 2:65; Ecc 2:8; 12:1 [v]2Sa 15:33 **19:37** [w]S Ge 49:29 [x]Jer 41:17

19:15 *Gilgal.* See note on Jos 4:19.
19:17 *a thousand Benjamites.* No doubt they feared they would be suspected by the king of being implicated in Shimei's deed.
19:19 *your servant did wrong.* See 16:5–13.
19:20 *I your servant know that I have sinned.* Shimei's guilt was common knowledge; he could only seize the most appropriate time to plead for mercy. *house of Joseph.* A common way of referring to the northern tribes (see Jos 18:5; see also Jdg 1:22; 1Ki 11:28; Am 5:6; Zec 10:6 and notes)—of which Ephraim and Manasseh (sons of Joseph) were the most prominent (see Nu 26:28).
19:21 *Abishai.* See 16:9; see also note on 1Sa 26:6. *the LORD's anointed.* See note on 1Sa 9:16; see also 1Sa 24:6; 26:9,11; Ex 22:28; 1Ki 21:10.
19:22 *sons of Zeruiah.* See 16:10 and note on 1Sa 26:6. *Should anyone be put to death in Israel today?* It was a day for general amnesty (see 1Sa 11:13).
19:23 *You shall not die.* David kept his pledge; he would not himself avenge the wrong committed against him (see note on 1Sa 25:1–44). But on his deathbed he instructed Solomon to take Shimei's case in hand (see 1Ki 2:8–9,36–46 and note on 2:46).
19:24 *Mephibosheth.* See 9:6–13 and note on 4:4.
19:25 *Why didn't you go with me . . . ?* David remembers Ziba's previous allegations (see 16:3).
19:26 *lame.* See 4:4; 9:3.
19:27 *he has slandered your servant.* See 16:3. *like an angel of God.* See 14:17 and note. *do whatever pleases you.* Mephibosheth discreetly requests David to reconsider the grant of his property to Ziba (see 16:4).
19:29 *divide the fields.* Faced with conflicting testimony that could not be corroborated, David withholds judgment and orders the division of Saul's estate (cf. 1Ki 3:25 and note).
19:31 *Barzillai.* See note on 17:27.
19:35 Cf. Ecc 12:2–5 and note. *difference between what is good and what is not.* At his age, he would be indifferent to all the pleasures of the court.
19:37 *Kimham.* Likely a son of Barzillai (see 1Ki 2:7).

38The king said, "Kimham shall cross over with me, and I will do for him whatever pleases you. And anything you desire from me I will do for you."

39So all the people crossed the Jordan, and then the king crossed over. The king kissed Barzillai and gave him his blessing,[y] and Barzillai returned to his home.

40When the king crossed over to Gilgal, Kimham crossed with him. All the troops of Judah and half the troops of Israel had taken the king over.

41Soon all the men of Israel were coming to the king and saying to him, "Why did our brothers, the men of Judah, steal the king away and bring him and his household across the Jordan, together with all his men?"[z]

42All the men of Judah answered the men of Israel, "We did this because the king is closely related to us. Why are you angry about it? Have we eaten any of the king's provisions? Have we taken anything for ourselves?"

43Then the men of Israel[a] answered the men of Judah, "We have ten shares in the king; and besides, we have a greater claim on David than you have. So why do you treat us with contempt? Were we not the first to speak of bringing back our king?"

But the men of Judah responded even more harshly than the men of Israel.

Sheba Rebels Against David

20 Now a troublemaker named Sheba son of Bicri, a Benjamite, happened to be there. He sounded the trumpet and shouted,

"We have no share[b] in David,[c]
no part in Jesse's son![d]
Every man to his tent, O Israel!"

2So all the men of Israel deserted David to follow Sheba son of Bicri. But the men of Judah stayed by their king all the way from the Jordan to Jerusalem.

3When David returned to his palace in Jerusalem, he took the ten concubines[e] he had left to take care of the palace and put them in a house under guard. He provided for them, but did not lie with them. They were kept in confinement till the day of their death, living as widows.

4Then the king said to Amasa,[f] "Summon the men of Judah to come to me within three days, and be here yourself." 5But when Amasa went to summon Judah, he took longer than the time the king had set for him.

6David said to Abishai,[g] "Now Sheba son of Bicri will do us more harm than Absalom did. Take your master's men and pursue him, or he will find fortified cities and escape from us." 7So Joab's men and the Kerethites[h] and Pelethites and all the mighty warriors went out under the command of Abishai. They marched out from Jerusalem to pursue Sheba son of Bicri.

8While they were at the great rock in Gibeon,[i] Amasa came to meet them. Joab[j] was wearing his military tunic, and strapped over it at his waist was a belt with a dagger in its sheath. As he stepped forward, it dropped out of its sheath.

9Joab said to Amasa, "How are you, my brother?" Then Joab took Amasa by the beard with his right hand to kiss him. 10Amasa was not on his guard against the dagger[k] in Joab's[l] hand, and Joab plunged it into his belly, and his intestines spilled out on the ground. Without being stabbed again, Amasa died. Then Joab and his brother Abishai pursued Sheba son of Bicri.

11One of Joab's men stood beside Amasa and said, "Whoever favors Joab, and whoever is for David, let him follow Joab!" 12Amasa lay wallowing in his blood in the middle of the road, and the man saw that all the troops came to a halt[m] there. When he realized that everyone who came up to Amasa stopped, he dragged him from the road into a field and threw a garment over

19:39 [y] S Ge 47:7
19:41 [z] Jdg 8:1; 12:1
19:43 [a] S 2Sa 5:1
20:1 [b] S Ge 31:14 [c] S Ge 29:14; 1Ki 12:16 [d] 1Sa 22:7-8
20:3 [e] S 2Sa 15:16
20:4 [f] S 2Sa 17:25
20:6 [g] 2Sa 21:17
20:7 [h] S 1Sa 30:14; S 2Sa 15:18
20:8 [i] S Jos 9:3 [j] S 2Sa 2:18
20:10 [k] S Jdg 3:21 [l] 1Ki 2:5
20:12 [m] S 2Sa 2:23

19:40 *Gilgal.* See v. 15 and note.
19:43 *ten shares.* The ten tribes, excluding Judah and Simeon (see note on 2:4). *we have a greater claim on David.* The grounds for this assertion may be that the Lord had chosen David to reign in the place of Saul (see 3:17–18; 5:2 and notes).
20:1–25 The last threat to David's reign overcome.
20:1 *troublemaker.* See note on Dt 13:13. *Benjamite.* Tribal jealousy still simmered over the transfer of the royal house from Benjamin (Saul's tribe) to Judah. *there.* In Gilgal (19:40). *We have no share in David.* Sheba appeals to the Israelite suspicion that David favored his own tribe (Judah) over the other tribes (see 1Ki 12:16 and note). *Jesse's son.* See note on 1Sa 20:27,30–31.
20:2 *all the men of Israel.* Those referred to in 19:41–43.
20:3 *ten concubines.* See notes on 15:16; 16:22; Ge 25:6.
20:4 *Amasa.* See notes on 17:25; 19:13. David bypasses Joab.
20:6 *Abishai.* See note on 1Sa 26:6. David bypasses Joab a second time (see v. 7). *your master's men.* "Joab's men" (v. 7).
20:7 *Joab's men.* See 18:2. It becomes clear that Joab also accompanied the soldiers and, though not in command (by the king's order), he was obviously the leader recognized by the soldiers (see vv. 7,11,15). *Kerethites and Pelethites.* See note on 8:18. *mighty warriors.* See 23:8–39 and note. Once more in a time of crisis David depended mainly on the small force of professionals (many of them non-Israelite) who made up his private army.
20:8 *Gibeon.* See note on 2:12. *Amasa came.* Apparently with some troops (see v. 11 and note).
20:10 *into his belly.* See 2:23; 3:27 and notes. For the second time Joab commits murder to secure his position as commander of David's army (see 1Ki 2:5–6 and note on 2:5). *Joab and his brother Abishai.* In defiance of David's order, Joab reassumes command on his own initiative (see v. 23 and note).
20:11 *Whoever favors Joab, and whoever is for David.* To dispel any idea that Joab was aligned with Sheba's conspiracy, an appeal is made to Amasa's troops to support Joab if they are truly loyal to David.

him. 13After Amasa had been removed
from the road, all the men went on with
Joab to pursue Sheba son of Bicri.
14Sheba passed through all the tribes of
Israel to Abel Beth Maacah[a] and through
the entire region of the Berites,[n] who gathered together and followed him. 15All the
troops with Joab came and besieged Sheba in Abel Beth Maacah.[o] They built a
siege ramp[p] up to the city, and it stood
against the outer fortifications. While they
were battering the wall to bring it down,
16a wise woman[q] called from the city, "Listen! Listen! Tell Joab to come here so I can
speak to him." 17He went toward her, and
she asked, "Are you Joab?"
"I am," he answered.
She said, "Listen to what your servant
has to say."
"I'm listening," he said.
18She continued, "Long ago they used to
say, 'Get your answer at Abel,' and that
settled it. 19We are the peaceful[r] and faithful in Israel. You are trying to destroy a city
that is a mother in Israel. Why do you want
to swallow up the LORD's inheritance?"[s]
20"Far be it from me!" Joab replied, "Far
be it from me to swallow up or destroy!
21That is not the case. A man named Sheba
son of Bicri, from the hill country of Ephraim, has lifted up his hand against the king,
against David. Hand over this one man,
and I'll withdraw from the city."
The woman said to Joab, "His head[t] will
be thrown to you from the wall."
22Then the woman went to all the people with her wise advice,[u] and they cut off
the head of Sheba son of Bicri and threw
it to Joab. So he sounded the trumpet, and
his men dispersed from the city, each returning to his home. And Joab went back
to the king in Jerusalem.
23Joab[v] was over Israel's entire army; Benaiah son of Jehoiada was over the Kerethites and Pelethites; 24Adoniram[b][w] was in
charge of forced labor; Jehoshaphat[x] son
of Ahilud was recorder; 25Sheva was secretary; Zadok[y] and Abiathar were priests;
26and Ira the Jairite was David's priest.

The Gibeonites Avenged

21 During the reign of David, there was
a famine[z] for three successive years;
so David sought[a] the face of the LORD. The
LORD said, "It is on account of Saul and his

20:14 [n]Nu 21:16
20:15 [o]1Ki 15:20; 2Ki 15:29 [p]Isa 37:33; Jer 6:6; 32:24
20:16 [q]2Sa 14:2
20:19 [r]S Dt 2:26 [s]S 1Sa 26:19
20:21 [t]S 2Sa 4:8
20:22 [u]Ecc 9:13
20:23 [v]S 2Sa 2:28; 8:16-18; 24:2
20:24 [w]1Ki 4:6; 5:14; 12:18; 2Ch 10:18 [x]S 2Sa 8:16
20:25 [y]S 1Sa 2:35; S 2Sa 8:17
21:1 [z]S Ge 12:10; S Dt 32:24 [a]S Ex 32:11

[a] 14 Or *Abel, even Beth Maacah*; also in verse 15
[b] 24 Some Septuagint manuscripts (see also 1 Kings 4:6 and 5:14); Hebrew *Adoram*

20:14 *Abel Beth Maacah.* See NIV text note; located to the north of Dan (see 1Ki 15:20; 2Ch 16:4 and NIV text note). Sheba's strategy was to gather as many volunteers for his revolt as possible, but he was obviously afraid to assemble his ragtag army anywhere within close reach of David's men.
20:18 *Get your answer at Abel.* The city was famous for the wisdom of its inhabitants.
20:19 *a mother in Israel.* A town that produced faithful Israelites — cities were commonly personified as women (see Jer 50:12 and note; Gal 4:26). *the LORD's inheritance.* See note on 1Sa 10:1.
20:21 *hill country of Ephraim.* Either Sheba, a Benjamite (see v. 1), lived in the tribal territory of Ephraim or this was the designation of a geographical, rather than a strictly tribal, region.
20:22 *Joab went back to the king in Jerusalem.* See notes on vv. 7,10.
20:23 – 26 These royal officials apparently served David during most of his reign (see 8:15 – 18 and notes).
20:23 *Joab was over Israel's entire army.* Though in some disfavor, he held this position until he participated in Adonijah's conspiracy (see 1Ki 1:7 and note; 2:28 – 35). *Kerethites and Pelethites.* See note on 8:18.
20:24 *Adoniram was in charge of forced labor.* A position not established in the early years of David's reign (see 8:15 – 18 and notes). Adoniram must have been a late appointee of David since he continued to serve under Solomon (see 1Ki 4:6 and note; 5:14) and was eventually killed in the early days of the reign of Rehoboam (1Ki 12:18). *forced labor.* Labor usually performed by prisoners of war from defeated nations (see 12:31 and note; 1Ki 9:15, 20 – 21). *recorder.* See note on 8:16.
20:25 *Sheva.* See note on 8:17 ("Seraiah"). *secretary.* See note on 8:17. *Zadok and Abiathar.* See note on 8:17.
20:26 *Jairite.* A reference either to Jair of the tribe of Manasseh or to an inhabitant of one of the settlements known as Havvoth Jair (Nu 32:41; 1Ki 4:13). *priest.* See note on 8:18.
21:1 — 24:25 This concluding section forms an appendix to 1,2 Samuel and contains additional materials (without concern for chronology) relating to David's reign. Its topical arrangement is striking in that it employs the literary pattern *a-b-c/c'-b'-a',* frequently found elsewhere in OT literature (cf., e.g., Ps 25 and its introduction; cf. also Isa 6:10 and note). The first and last units (21:1 – 14; 24:1 – 25) are narratives of two events in which David had to deal with God's wrath against Israel (the first occasioned by an act of Saul, the second by his own). The second and fifth units (21:15 – 22; 23:8 – 39) are accounts of David's warriors (the second much longer than the first). At the center (22:1 — 23:7) are two songs of David (the first much longer than the second), one of which celebrates David's victories as warrior-king while the other recalls his role as psalmist (see note on 1Sa 16:14 — 17:58). It is unknown whether motivation for this *a-b-c/c'-b'-a'* arrangement went beyond aesthetic considerations. Its unusual placement of David's lengthy song of praise for the Lord's deliverance suggests that the motivation was thematic — it could have been expected that this song would follow immediately upon the accounts of the successful suppression of the Absalom and Sheba revolts (cf. the Song of Moses, Ex 15; the Song of Deborah, Jdg 5; the Song of Hannah, 1Sa 2; David's Lament for Saul, 2Sa 1; see also Isa 12). It is possible that the author appended these materials and did so in this way to recall to mind the triumph song of the women who came to meet King Saul and David after their victories over the Philistines ("Saul has slain his thousands, and David his tens of thousands," 1Sa 18:7). If so, he suggests that what the women said of Saul and David in their victories over foreign enemies came true (bitterly) also as a result of their royal sins, but now those "slain" were Israelites. However that may be, King David's triumph song in ch. 22 and Hannah's song in 1Sa 2:1 – 10 form a literary frame around the main body of the book (see note on 1Sa 2:1) and poetically highlight its central themes.
21:1 – 14 This event appears to have occurred after David's kindness was extended to Mephibosheth (ch. 9) and before Absalom's rebellion (16:7 – 8; 18:28; see note on 16:8).
21:1 *he put the Gibeonites to death.* Saul's action against the

blood-stained house; it is because he put the Gibeonites to death."

2The king summoned the Gibeonites[b] and spoke to them. (Now the Gibeonites were not a part of Israel but were survivors of the Amorites; the Israelites had sworn to ⌞spare⌟ them, but Saul in his zeal for Israel and Judah had tried to annihilate them.) 3David asked the Gibeonites, "What shall I do for you? How shall I make amends so that you will bless the LORD's inheritance?"[c]

4The Gibeonites answered him, "We have no right to demand silver or gold from Saul or his family, nor do we have the right to put anyone in Israel to death."[d]

"What do you want me to do for you?" David asked.

5They answered the king, "As for the man who destroyed us and plotted against us so that we have been decimated and have no place anywhere in Israel, 6let seven of his male descendants be given to us to be killed and exposed[e] before the LORD at Gibeah of Saul—the LORD's chosen[f] one."

So the king said, "I will give them to you."

7The king spared Mephibosheth[g] son of Jonathan, the son of Saul, because of the oath[h] before the LORD between David and Jonathan son of Saul. 8But the king took Armoni and Mephibosheth, the two sons of Aiah's daughter Rizpah,[i] whom she had borne to Saul, together with the five sons of Saul's daughter Merab,[a] whom she had borne to Adriel son of Barzillai the Meholathite.[j] 9He handed them over to the Gibeonites, who killed and exposed them on a hill before the LORD. All seven of them fell together; they were put to death[k] during the first days of the harvest, just as the barley harvest was beginning.[l]

10Rizpah daughter of Aiah took sackcloth and spread it out for herself on a rock. From the beginning of the harvest till the rain poured down from the heavens on the bodies, she did not let the birds of the air touch them by day or the wild animals by night.[m] 11When David was told what Aiah's daughter Rizpah, Saul's concubine, had done, 12he went and took the bones of Saul[n] and his son Jonathan from the citizens of Jabesh Gilead.[o] (They had taken them secretly from the public square at Beth Shan,[p] where the Philistines had hung[q] them after they struck Saul down on Gilboa.)[r] 13David brought the bones of Saul and his son Jonathan from there, and the bones of those who had been killed and exposed were gathered up.

14They buried the bones of Saul and his son Jonathan in the tomb of Saul's father Kish, at Zela[s] in Benjamin, and did everything the king commanded. After that,[t] God answered prayer[u] in behalf of the land.[v]

Wars Against the Philistines

21:15-22pp — 1Ch 20:4-8

15Once again there was a battle between the Philistines[w] and Israel. David went down with his men to fight against the Philistines, and he became exhausted.

21:2 [b]S Jos 9:15 **21:3** [c]S 1Sa 26:19 **21:4** [d]Nu 35:33-34 **21:6** [e]Nu 25:4 [f]S 1Sa 10:24 **21:7** [g]2Sa 4:4 [h]S 1Sa 18:3; S 2Sa 9:7 **21:8** [i]2Sa 3:7 [j]1Sa 18:19 **21:9** [k]S 2Sa 16:8 [l]S Ru 1:22 **21:10** [m]S Ge 40:19; S 1Sa 17:44 **21:12** [n]1Sa 31:11-13 [o]S Jdg 21:8; S 1Sa 11:1 [p]S Jos 17:11 [q]1Sa 31:10 [r]S 1Sa 28:4 **21:14** [s]Jos 18:28 [t]Jos 7:26 [u]2Sa 24:25 [v]1Ch 8:34 **21:15** [w]S 2Sa 5:25

[a] *8* Two Hebrew manuscripts, some Septuagint manuscripts and Syriac (see also 1 Samuel 18:19); most Hebrew and Septuagint manuscripts *Michal*

Gibeonites is not related elsewhere but appears to have been instituted early in his reign, motivated by an excessive nationalism. Perhaps tribalism was also involved, since the Gibeonites occupied territory partly assigned to Benjamin, and Saul's great-grandfather was known as the "father of Gibeon" (1Ch 8:29; 9:35).

21:2 *Amorites.* A comprehensive name sometimes used to designate all the pre-Israelite inhabitants of Canaan (see Ge 15:16 and note; Jos 24:18; Jdg 6:10 and note; Am 2:10). More precisely, the Gibeonites were called Hivites (see Jos 9:7 and note; 11:19). *the Israelites had sworn to ⌞spare⌟ them.* A pledge sworn in the name of the Lord (see Jos 9:15,18–21 and note on 9:15). *tried to annihilate them.* The reason Saul was unsuccessful is not known.

21:3 *bless.* Since the oath sworn to them in the Lord's name had been violated, they could rightly call down his curse on the land. *the LORD's inheritance.* See note on 1Sa 10:1.

21:5 *the man.* Saul. *no place anywhere in Israel.* Those who escaped Saul's attack had been driven from their towns and lands (see 4:2–3).

21:6 *seven.* Because it would represent a full number (seven symbolized completeness)—though many more Gibeonites had been slain. *Gibeah.* The place of Saul's residence (see 1Sa 10:26 and note on 10:5).

21:7 *oath before the LORD between David and Jonathan.* See 9:1–13; 1Sa 18:3; 20:15 and note.

21:8 *Rizpah.* See 3:7. *Merab.* See 1Sa 18:19. *Barzillai the Meholathite.* Not to be confused with Barzillai the Gileadite (see 17:27 and note; 19:31; Ezr 2:61).

21:9 *All seven of them fell together.* This nearly extinguished the house of Saul, which God had rejected (see 1Sa 13:13–14 and notes; 15:23–26 and note on 15:23). In 1Ch 8:29–39; 9:35–44 no descendants of Saul are listed other than from the line of Jonathan. *barley harvest was beginning.* About the middle of April (see note on Ru 1:22).

21:10 *sackcloth.* See note on Ge 37:34. *rain poured down.* An indication that the famine was caused by drought and evidence that the judgment on Israel for breaking the oath sworn to the Gibeonites (see v. 1) was now over.

21:12–14 *bones of Saul and his son Jonathan.* See 1Sa 31:11–13 and notes. David's final act toward Saul and Jonathan was a deed of deep respect for the king he had honored and the friend he had loved.

21:14 *God answered prayer in behalf of the land.* Concludes the first unit of the *a-b-c/c'-b'-a'* literary structure that characterizes the last four chapters of 2 Samuel, just as its echo in 24:25 concludes the last unit (see note on 21:1—24:25).

21:15–21 These four Philistine episodes (vv. 15–17,18,19, 20–21) cannot be chronologically located with any certainty (see note on 21:1—24:25). Each involves a heroic accomplishment by one of David's mighty men, resulting in the death of a descendant of Rapha (see v. 22).

16And Ishbi-Benob, one of the descendants
of Rapha, whose bronze spearhead weighed
three hundred shekels[a] and who was armed
with a new ⌞sword⌟, said he would kill David. 17But Abishai[x] son of Zeruiah came
to David's rescue; he struck the Philistine
down and killed him. Then David's men
swore to him, saying, "Never again will you
go out with us to battle, so that the lamp[y] of
Israel will not be extinguished.[z]"
18In the course of time, there was another battle with the Philistines, at Gob. At
that time Sibbecai[a] the Hushathite killed
Saph, one of the descendants of Rapha.
19In another battle with the Philistines
at Gob, Elhanan son of Jaare-Oregim[b] the
Bethlehemite killed Goliath[c] the Gittite,[b]
who had a spear with a shaft like a weaver's rod.[c]
20In still another battle, which took
place at Gath, there was a huge man with
six fingers on each hand and six toes on
each foot—twenty-four in all. He also was
descended from Rapha. 21When he taunted[d] Israel, Jonathan son of Shimeah,[e] David's brother, killed him.
22These four were descendants of Rapha
in Gath, and they fell at the hands of David and his men.

David's Song of Praise

22:1-51pp — Ps 18:1-50

22 David sang[f] to the LORD the words
of this song when the LORD delivered
him from the hand of all his enemies and
from the hand of Saul. 2He said:

"The LORD is my rock,[g] my fortress[h]
and my deliverer;[i]
3 my God is my rock, in whom I take
refuge,[j]
my shield[k] and the horn[d][l] of my
salvation.
He is my stronghold,[m] my refuge
and my savior—
from violent men you save me.
4I call to the LORD, who is worthy[n]
of praise,
and I am saved from my enemies.

5"The waves[o] of death swirled about
me;
the torrents of destruction
overwhelmed me.
6The cords of the grave[e][p] coiled
around me;
the snares of death confronted
me.
7In my distress[q] I called[r] to the
LORD;
I called out to my God.
From his temple he heard my
voice;
my cry came to his ears.

21:17 [x]2Sa 20:6 [y]1Ki 11:36; 15:4; 2Ki 8:19; 2Ch 21:7; Ps 132:17 [z]2Sa 18:3 **21:18** [a]1Ch 11:29; 27:11 **21:19** [b]S 1Sa 17:4 [c]S 1Sa 17:7 **21:21** [d]S 1Sa 17:10 [e]S 1Sa 16:9 **22:1** [f]S Ex 15:1 **22:2** [g]S 1Sa 2:2 [h]Ps 31:3; 91:2 [i]Ps 144:2 **22:3** [j]S Dt 23:15; S 32:37; Ps 14:6; 31:2; 59:16; 71:7; 91:2; 94:22; Pr 10:29; Isa 25:4; Jer 16:19; Joel 3:16 [k]S Ge 15:1 [l]S Dt 33:17; S Lk 1:69 [m]Ps 9:9; 52:7 **22:4** [n]Ps 48:1; 96:4; 145:3 **22:5** [o]Ps 69:14-15; Jnh 2:3 **22:6** [p]Ps 116:3; Ac 2:24 **22:7** [q]Ge 35:3; S Jdg 2:15; 2Ch 15:4; Ps 4:1; 77:2; 120:1; Isa 26:16 [r]Ps 34:6, 15; 116:4

[a] *16* That is, about 7 1/2 pounds (about 3.5 kilograms) [b] *19* Or *son of Jair the weaver* [c] *19* Hebrew and Septuagint; 1 Chron. 20:5 *son of Jair killed Lahmi the brother of Goliath* [d] *3 Horn* here symbolizes strength. [e] *6* Hebrew *Sheol*

21:16,18,20,22 *Rapha.* The ancestor of at least one group of Rephaites (see 1Ch 20:4,8 and note on 20:4). In calling the four formidable enemy warriors referred to in this series "descendants of Rapha" (v. 22), the writer most likely identifies them as giants (see v. 20; Dt 2:10–11,20–21). In that case, they may have been related to the Anakites (see Nu 13:28,32–33; Jos 11:21–22). The list of the ten peoples of Canaan in Ge 15:19–21 mentions Rephaites but not Anakites, though the Anakites (but not Rephaites) figure significantly in the accounts of the conquest (Dt 9:2; Jos 14:12,15; Jdg 1:20).
21:17 *Abishai.* See note on 1Sa 26:6. *so that the lamp of Israel will not be extinguished.* A striking metaphor depicting Israel's dependence on David for its security and continuing existence as a nation—its national hope (see 22:29; 23:3–4; 1Ki 11:36 and note; cf. 2Sa 22:29 and note; 23:3–4).
21:18–19 *Gob.* Mentioned nowhere else in the OT, it may have been in the near vicinity of Gezer, where 1Ch 20:4 locates this same battle. On the other hand, many Hebrew manuscripts read "Nob," a well-known town northeast of Jerusalem (see 1Sa 21:1 and note). In that case, the text nicely echoes the proper name Ishbi-Benob (v. 16), which apparently means "inhabitant of Nob."
21:19 *Elhanan ... killed Goliath.* See second NIV text note. Since it is clear from 1Sa 17 that David killed Goliath, an early copyist probably misread the Hebrew for "Lahmi the brother of" (see 1Ch 20:5) as "the Bethlehemite" (in Hebrew the word for "killed" stands first in the clause). *Jaare-Oregim.* See first NIV text note. The Hebrew for "Oregim" occurs also at the end of the verse, where it is translated "weaver's." An early copyist probably inserted it in the name by mistake, since 1Ch 20:5 reads "Jair" (apparently correctly) instead of "Jaare-Oregim."
21:21 *taunted Israel.* As Goliath had done (see 1Sa 17:10,25). *Shimeah.* Also called Shammah (1Sa 16:9; 17:13).
22:1–51 For the relationship of this song to Hannah's song in the overall literary structure of 1 and 2 Samuel, see notes on 1Sa 2:1–10, especially on 2:1. David's song is preserved also as Ps 18 (see notes on that psalm). Besides an introduction (vv. 2–4) and conclusion (vv. 47–51), the song consists of three major sections: The first describes David's deliverance from mortal danger at the hands of his enemies (vv. 5–20); the second sets forth the moral grounds for God's saving help (vv. 21–30); the third recounts the help that the Lord gave him (vv. 31–46). The song was probably composed shortly after David's victories over foreign enemies (8:1–14) and before his sins against Bathsheba and Uriah (11:2–4,14–17; compare vv. 21–25 with 1Ki 15:5).
22:1 *from ... all his enemies.* See 8:1–14. *from ... Saul.* See 1Sa 18–27.
22:2 *rock.* A figure particularly appropriate to David's experience (see vv. 3,32,47; 23:3; cf. Dt 32:4,15,18,31; Ps 28:1; 31:2; 61:2; 78:35; 89:26; 94:22; 95:1). He had often taken refuge among the rocks of the desert (1Sa 23:25; 24:2), but he realized that true security was found only in the Lord. *fortress.* The Hebrew for this word occurs in 5:17 ("stronghold"); 23:14; 1Sa 22:4–5; 24:22, referring to one or more strongholds where David sought refuge.
22:3 *my shield.* See v. 31; Ge 15:1 and note. *horn.* See NIV text note; 1Sa 2:1 and note; Dt 33:17; Jer 48:25.
22:5 *waves of death.* In vv. 5–6 David depicts his experiences in poetic figures of mortal danger.
22:6 *grave.* See note on Jnh 2:2.
22:7 *his temple.* Heaven, where the Lord is enthroned as King (see Ps 11:4; Isa 6:1 and notes; see also Jnh 2:7 and note on 2:4).

[8]"The earth[s] trembled and quaked,[t]
the foundations[u] of the heavens[a]
shook;
they trembled because he was angry.
[9]Smoke rose from his nostrils;
consuming fire[v] came from his
mouth,
burning coals[w] blazed out of it.
[10]He parted the heavens and came
down;
dark clouds[x] were under his feet.
[11]He mounted the cherubim[y] and flew;
he soared[b] on the wings of the wind.[z]
[12]He made darkness[a] his canopy around
him —
the dark[c] rain clouds of the sky.
[13]Out of the brightness of his presence
bolts of lightning[b] blazed forth.
[14]The LORD thundered[c] from heaven;
the voice of the Most High
resounded.
[15]He shot arrows[d] and scattered ⌞the
enemies⌟,
bolts of lightning and routed them.
[16]The valleys of the sea were exposed
and the foundations of the earth laid
bare
at the rebuke[e] of the LORD,
at the blast[f] of breath from his
nostrils.
[17]"He reached down from on high[g] and
took hold of me;
he drew[h] me out of deep waters.
[18]He rescued[i] me from my powerful
enemy,
from my foes, who were too strong
for me.
[19]They confronted me in the day of my
disaster,
but the LORD was my support.[j]
[20]He brought me out into a spacious[k]
place;
he rescued[l] me because he
delighted[m] in me.[n]
[21]"The LORD has dealt with me according
to my righteousness;[o]
according to the cleanness[p] of my
hands[q] he has rewarded me.
[22]For I have kept[r] the ways of the LORD;
I have not done evil by turning from
my God.
[23]All his laws are before me;[s]
I have not turned[t] away from his
decrees.
[24]I have been blameless[u] before him
and have kept myself from sin.
[25]The LORD has rewarded me according
to my righteousness,[v]
according to my cleanness[d] in his
sight.

[26]"To the faithful you show yourself
faithful,
to the blameless you show yourself
blameless,
[27]to the pure[w] you show yourself pure,
but to the crooked you show yourself
shrewd.[x]
[28]You save the humble,[y]
but your eyes are on the haughty[z] to
bring them low.[a]
[29]You are my lamp,[b] O LORD;
the LORD turns my darkness into light.
[30]With your help I can advance against a
troop[e];
with my God I can scale a wall.

[31]"As for God, his way is perfect;[c]
the word of the LORD is flawless.[d]
He is a shield[e]
for all who take refuge in him.
[32]For who is God besides the LORD?
And who is the Rock[f] except our
God?[g]

22:8 [s]Jdg 5:4; Ps 97:4 [t]S Ex 19:18; S Jdg 5:4; Ps 68:8; 77:18; Jer 10:10 [u]Job 9:6; 26:11; Ps 75:3 **22:9** [v]Ps 50:3; 97:3; Heb 12:29; S Rev 11:5 [w]Isa 6:6; Eze 1:13; 10:2 **22:10** [x]S Ex 19:9; Lev 16:2; S Dt 33:26; 1Ki 8:12; Job 26:9; Ps 104:3; Isa 19:1; Jer 4:13; Na 1:3 **22:11** [y]S Ge 3:24; S Ex 25:22 [z]Ps 104:3 **22:12** [a]S Ex 19:9 **22:13** [b]Job 37:3; Ps 77:18 **22:14** [c]S 1Sa 2:10 **22:15** [d]S Dt 32:23 **22:16** [e]Ps 6:1; 50:8, 21; 106:9; Na 1:4 [f]S Ex 14:21; Isa 30:33; 40:24 **22:17** [g]Ps 144:7 [h]Ex 2:10 **22:18** [i]Lk 1:71 **22:19** [j]Ps 23:4 **22:20** [k]Job 36:16; Ps 31:8 [l]Ps 118:5 [m]Ps 22:8; Isa 42:1; Mt 12:18 [n]S 2Sa 15:26 **22:21** [o]S 1Sa 26:23 [p]Ps 26:6 [q]Job 17:9; 22:30; 42:7-8; Ps 24:4 **22:22** [r]Ge 18:19; Ps 128:1; Pr 8:32 **22:23** [s]Dt 6:4-9; Ps 119:30-32 [t]Ps 119:102 **22:24** [u]S Ge 6:9; Eph 1:4 **22:25** [v]S 1Sa 26:23 **22:27** [w]Mt 5:8 [x]Lev 26:23-24 **22:28** [y]S Ex 3:8; 1Sa 2:8-9; Ps 72:12-13 [z]Ps 131:1; Pr 30:13; Da 4:31; Zep 3:11 [a]Isa 2:12, 17; 5:15; S Lk 1:51 **22:29** [b]Ps 27:1; Isa 2:5; Mic 7:8; Rev 21:23; 22:5 **22:31** [c]S Dt 32:4; Mt 5:48 [d]Ps 12:6; 119:140; Pr 30:5-6 [e]S Ge 15:1 **22:32** [f]S 1Sa 2:2 [g]S 2Sa 7:22

[a] *8* Hebrew; Vulgate and Syriac (see also Psalm 18:7) *mountains* [b] *11* Many Hebrew manuscripts (see also Psalm 18:10); most Hebrew manuscripts *appeared* [c] *12* Septuagint and Vulgate (see also Psalm 18:11); Hebrew *massed* [d] *25* Hebrew; Septuagint and Vulgate (see also Psalm 18:24) *to the cleanness of my hands* [e] *30* Or *can run through a barricade*

22:8 – 16 See note on Ps 18:7 – 15.
22:9 *Smoke rose from his nostrils.* See note on Ps 18:8.
22:10 *parted the heavens and came down.* See Isa 64:1 and note.
22:11 *mounted the cherubim and flew.* See notes on 1Sa 4:4; Ge 3:24; Ps 18:10; Eze 1:5.
22:14 *The LORD thundered.* The reference to thunder as the voice of God is common in the OT (see introduction to Ps 29; Job 37:2 – 5 and note on 37:2). Thunder is particularly suited to expressing God's power and majesty.
22:17 *He reached down from on high.* In vv. 17 – 20 David describes his deliverance, initially in figurative terms (v. 17; cf. v. 5) and subsequently in more literal language (vv. 18 – 20).
22:20 *spacious place.* See note on Ps 18:19. *delighted in.* The Hebrew underlying this expression is used in 15:26 ("pleased with"); Ps 22:8 (cf. Mt 3:17, "well pleased with") and expresses the idea of the sovereign good pleasure and favor of God toward his anointed one (v. 51).
22:21,25 *according to my righteousness.* See 1Ki 15:5. In vv. 21 – 25 David refers to the Lord's deliverances as a reward for his own righteousness. While these statements may give the impression of self-righteous boasting and a meritorious basis for divine favor, they should be understood in their context as: (1) David's desire to please the Lord in his service as the Lord's anointed (see note on v. 51); (2) his recognition that the Lord rewards those who faithfully seek to serve him.
22:26 – 30 See notes on Ps 18:25 – 29.
22:29 *You are my lamp.* The Lord causes David's life and undertakings to flourish (see Job 18:5 – 6; 21:17; see also note on Ps 27:1).
22:31 *his way is perfect.* The remainder of the song (vv. 31 – 51) accentuates David's praise to God for his deliverances.
22:32,47 *Rock.* See note on v. 2.

33 It is God who arms me with strength[a]
and makes my way perfect.
34 He makes my feet like the feet of a deer;[h]
he enables me to stand on the heights.[i]
35 He trains my hands[j] for battle;
my arms can bend a bow[k] of bronze.
36 You give me your shield[l] of victory;
you stoop down to make me great.
37 You broaden the path[m] beneath me,
so that my ankles do not turn.

38 "I pursued my enemies and crushed them;
I did not turn back till they were destroyed.
39 I crushed[n] them completely, and they could not rise;
they fell beneath my feet.
40 You armed me with strength for battle;
you made my adversaries bow at my feet.[o]
41 You made my enemies turn their backs[p] in flight,
and I destroyed my foes.
42 They cried for help,[q] but there was no one to save them—[r]
to the LORD, but he did not answer.[s]
43 I beat them as fine as the dust[t] of the earth;
I pounded and trampled[u] them like mud[v] in the streets.

44 "You have delivered[w] me from the attacks of my people;
you have preserved[x] me as the head of nations.
People[y] I did not know are subject to me,
45 and foreigners come cringing[z] to me;
as soon as they hear me, they obey me.[a]
46 They all lose heart;
they come trembling[b][b] from their strongholds.

47 "The LORD lives! Praise be to my Rock!
Exalted[c] be God, the Rock, my Savior![d]
48 He is the God who avenges[e] me,[f]
who puts the nations under me,
49 who sets me free from my enemies.[g]
You exalted me[h] above my foes;
from violent men you rescued me.
50 Therefore I will praise you, O LORD,
among the nations;
I will sing praises[i] to your name.[j]
51 He gives his king great victories;[k]
he shows unfailing kindness to his anointed,[l]
to David[m] and his descendants forever."[n]

22:34 [h]Isa 35:6; Hab 3:19 [i]S Dt 32:13 22:35 [j]Ps 144:1 [k]Ps 7:12; 11:2; Zec 9:13 22:36 [l]Eph 6:16 22:37 [m]Pr 4:11 22:39 [n]Ps 44:5; 110:6; Mal 4:3 22:40 [o]S Jos 10:24; S 1Ki 5:3 22:41 [p]S Ex 23:27 22:42 [q]Isa 1:15 [r]Ps 50:22 [s]S 1Sa 14:37 22:43 [t]1Ki 20:10; 2Ki 13:7; Isa 41:2; Am 1:3 [u]Ps 7:5; Isa 41:25; Mic 7:10; Zec 10:5 [v]Isa 5:25; 10:6; 22:5; Mic 7:10 22:44 [w]S Ex 11:3; S 2Sa 3:1 [x]Dt 28:13 [y]S 2Sa 8:1-14; Isa 55:3-5 22:45 [z]Ps 66:3; 81:15 [a]S Dt 33:29 22:46 [b]Mic 7:17 22:47 [c]S Ex 15:2 [d]Dt 32:15; Ps 18:31; 89:26; 95:1 22:48 [e]S Nu 31:3 [f]Ps 144:2 22:49 [g]Ps 140:1,4 [h]Ps 27:6 22:50 [i]Ps 9:11; 47:6; 68:4 [j]Ro 15:9* 22:51 [k]Ps 21:1; 144:9-10 [l]1Sa 16:13; Ps 89:20; Ac 13:23 [m]S 2Sa 7:13 [n]Ps 89:24,29 23:1 [o]S Ex 11:3; Ps 78:70-71; 89:27 [p]1Sa 2:10,35; Ps 18:50; 20:6; 84:9; Isa 45:1; Hab 3:13 23:2 [q]Mt 22:43; Mk 12:36; 2Pe 1:21 23:3 [r]Dt 32:4; S 1Sa 2:2; Ps 18:31 [s]Ps 72:2 [t]S Ge 42:18

The Last Words of David

23 These are the last words of David:

"The oracle of David son of Jesse,
the oracle of the man exalted[o] by the Most High,
the man anointed[p] by the God of Jacob,
Israel's singer of songs[c]:

2 "The Spirit[q] of the LORD spoke through me;
his word was on my tongue.
3 The God of Israel spoke,
the Rock[r] of Israel said to me:
'When one rules over men in righteousness,[s]
when he rules in the fear[t] of God,[u]
4 he is like the light[v] of morning[w] at sunrise[x]
on a cloudless morning,
like the brightness after rain[y]
that brings the grass from the earth.'

5 "Is not my house right with God?
Has he not made with me an everlasting covenant,[z]
arranged and secured in every part?
Will he not bring to fruition my salvation
and grant me my every desire?

[a] *33* Dead Sea Scrolls, some Septuagint manuscripts, Vulgate and Syriac (see also Psalm 18:32); Masoretic Text *who is my strong refuge* [b] *46* Some Septuagint manuscripts and Vulgate (see also Psalm 18:45); Masoretic Text *they arm themselves.* [c] *1* Or *Israel's beloved singer*

[u]Isa 11:1-5 23:4 [v]Jn 1:5 [w]Ps 119:147; 130:6; Pr 4:18 [x]S Jdg 5:31; Mt 13:43 [y]S Dt 32:2 23:5 [z]S Ge 9:16; Ps 89:29

22:34 See Hab 3:19 and note.
22:47 *The LORD lives!* See note on Ps 18:46.
22:50 *I will praise you, O LORD, among the nations.* For Paul's reference to this vow see Ro 15:9 and note.
22:51 *his king ... his anointed.* See notes on 1Sa 2:10; 10:25; 12:14–15. David refers to himself in the third person in a way that acknowledges the covenantal character of his kingship. It is in the context of David's official capacity as the Lord's anointed that the entire song is to be read and understood (see note on vv. 21,25). *his descendants forever.* David speaks of God's promise through Nathan (see 7:12–16 and note on 7:16).
23:1 *last words of David.* Probably to be understood as David's last poetic testimony (in the manner of his psalms), perhaps composed at the time of his final instructions and warnings to his son Solomon (see 1Ki 2:1–10).
23:2 See notes on 2Ti 3:16; 2Pe 1:20.
23:3 *Rock.* See note on 22:2; see also 1Sa 2:2 and note; Dt 32:4,15,18,30–31. *When one rules over men in righteousness.* In brief and vivid strokes David portrays the ideal theocratic king—to be fully realized only in the rule of great David's greater Son, Jesus Christ. This prophetic utterance complements that of 7:12–16 and anticipates those of Isa 9:7; 11:1–5; Jer 23:5–6; 33:15–16; Zec 9:9 (see relevant notes on these passages).
23:4 *like the light of morning.* See notes on Ps 27:1; 36:9.
23:5 *Is not my house right with God?* A rhetorical question recalling God's covenant with David and his dynasty (see

6 But evil men are all to be cast aside
like thorns,[a]
which are not gathered with the
hand.
7 Whoever touches thorns
uses a tool of iron or the shaft of a
spear;
they are burned up where they lie."

David's Mighty Men

23:8-39pp — 1Ch 11:10-41

8 These are the names of David's mighty
men:[b]
Josheb-Basshebeth,[a][c] a Tahkemonite,[b]
was chief of the Three; he raised his spear
against eight hundred men, whom he
killed[c] in one encounter.
9 Next to him was Eleazar son of Dodai[d]
the Ahohite.[e] As one of the three mighty
men, he was with David when they taunted the Philistines gathered ⌞at Pas Dam-
mim⌟[d] for battle. Then the men of Israel
retreated, 10 but he stood his ground and
struck down the Philistines till his hand
grew tired and froze to the sword. The
LORD brought about a great victory that
day. The troops returned to Eleazar, but
only to strip the dead.
11 Next to him was Shammah son of Agee
the Hararite. When the Philistines banded together at a place where there was a
field full of lentils, Israel's troops fled from
them. 12 But Shammah took his stand in
the middle of the field. He defended it and
struck the Philistines down, and the LORD
brought about a great victory.
13 During harvest time, three of the thirty
chief men came down to David at the cave
of Adullam,[f] while a band of Philistines
was encamped in the Valley of Rephaim.[g]
14 At that time David was in the stronghold,[h] and the Philistine garrison was at
Bethlehem.[i] 15 David longed for water and
said, "Oh, that someone would get me a
drink of water from the well near the gate
of Bethlehem!" 16 So the three mighty men
broke through the Philistine lines, drew
water from the well near the gate of Bethlehem and carried it back to David. But he
refused to drink it; instead, he poured[j] it
out before the LORD. 17 "Far be it from me,
O LORD, to do this!" he said. "Is it not the
blood[k] of men who went at the risk of their
lives?" And David would not drink it.
Such were the exploits of the three
mighty men.
18 Abishai[l] the brother of Joab son of
Zeruiah was chief of the Three.[e] He raised
his spear against three hundred men,
whom he killed, and so he became as famous as the Three. 19 Was he not held in
greater honor than the Three? He became
their commander, even though he was not
included among them.
20 Benaiah[m] son of Jehoiada was a valiant fighter from Kabzeel,[n] who performed
great exploits. He struck down two of Moab's best men. He also went down into a
pit on a snowy day and killed a lion. 21 And
he struck down a huge Egyptian. Although
the Egyptian had a spear in his hand, Benaiah went against him with a club. He
snatched the spear from the Egyptian's
hand and killed him with his own spear.
22 Such were the exploits of Benaiah son
of Jehoiada; he too was as famous as the
three mighty men. 23 He was held in greater
honor than any of the Thirty, but he was
not included among the Three. And David
put him in charge of his bodyguard.

24 Among the Thirty were:
Asahel[o] the brother of Joab,
Elhanan son of Dodo from Bethle-
hem,

23:6 [a] Isa 5:6; 9:18; 10:17; 27:4; 33:12; Mic 7:4; Na 1:10; Mt 13:40-41
23:8 [b] S 2Sa 17:10 [c] 1Ch 27:2
23:9 [d] 1Ch 27:4 [e] 1Ch 8:4
23:13 [f] S Ge 38:1; S Jos 12:15 [g] S Jos 17:15
23:14 [h] 1Sa 22:4-5; S 2Sa 5:17 [i] Ru 1:19
23:16 [j] S Ge 35:14
23:17 [k] Lev 17:10-12
23:18 [l] S 1Sa 26:6
23:20 [m] S 2Sa 8:18; 1Ch 27:5 [n] Jos 15:21
23:24 [o] S 2Sa 2:18

[a] 8 Hebrew; some Septuagint manuscripts suggest *Ish-Bosheth,* that is, *Esh-Baal* (see also 1 Chron. 11:11 *Jashobeam*). [b] 8 Probably a variant of *Hacmonite* (see 1 Chron. 11:11) [c] 8 Some Septuagint manuscripts (see also 1 Chron. 11:11); Hebrew and other Septuagint manuscripts *Three; it was Adino the Eznite who killed eight hundred men* [d] 9 See 1 Chron. 11:13; Hebrew *gathered there.* [e] 18 Most Hebrew manuscripts (see also 1 Chron. 11:20); two Hebrew manuscripts and Syriac *Thirty*

7:12–16). *everlasting covenant.* David expressly calls God's promise to him a covenant that will not be abrogated (see notes on 7:20,28; Isa 55:3; see also Ps 89:3–4,28–29,34–37; 132:11–12). *bring to fruition.* Through David's promised descendants.

23:6 *evil men ... cast aside.* Godless people who have no interest in the righteous king will be destroyed (see Ps 2:8–9 and note on 2:9; 110:5–6 and notes).

23:8–39 See note on 21:1—24:25. This list of 37 (see v. 39) of David's most valiant warriors and the description of some of their exploits are paralleled in 1Ch 11:11–41. There the list is expanded by 16 names (1Ch 11:41–47).

23:8 *Three.* Two groups of three warriors (vv. 8–12 and 13–23) and one group of 30 warriors (vv. 24–39) are mentioned (see v. 39 for the total number of warriors).

23:13 *harvest time.* See 11:1 and note. The circumstances of this event suggest that it happened shortly after David had fled from Saul, when men first began to gather to his cause (see 1Sa 22:1–4 and notes), or shortly after his conquest of Jerusalem (see 2Sa 5:17–18 and note on 5:17). *three.* Probably not the same as the three mighty men of v. 9. *thirty chief men.* See vv. 23–24,39. *cave of Adullam.* See 1Sa 22:1. *Rephaim.* See 5:18; Isa 17:5 and note.

23:14 *stronghold.* See note on 1Sa 22:4.

23:15–17 See note on 1Ch 11:15–19.

23:15 *Bethlehem.* David's hometown (1Sa 17:58; see note on 1Sa 16:1).

23:18 *Abishai.* See 10:10,14; 18:2; see also note on 1Sa 26:6. *Three.* Presumably those referred to in vv. 13–17.

23:20 *Benaiah son of Jehoiada.* Commander of the Kerethites and Pelethites (see 8:18 and note; 20:23; see also v. 23) and of the division of troops for the third month of the year (1Ch 27:5). He supported Solomon's succession to the throne (1Ki 1–2) and eventually replaced Joab as commander of the army (1Ki 2:35).

23:24 *Thirty.* At least 30 names are listed in vv. 24–39. Since the three of vv. 13–17 are also included in the Thirty (see v. 13), the total number of warriors mentioned is at least 33.

[25]Shammah the Harodite,[p]
Elika the Harodite,
[26]Helez[q] the Paltite,
Ira[r] son of Ikkesh from Tekoa,
[27]Abiezer[s] from Anathoth,[t]
Mebunnai[a] the Hushathite,
[28]Zalmon the Ahohite,
Maharai[u] the Netophathite,[v]
[29]Heled[b][w] son of Baanah the Netophathite,
Ithai son of Ribai from Gibeah[x] in Benjamin,
[30]Benaiah the Pirathonite,[y]
Hiddai[c] from the ravines of Gaash,[z]
[31]Abi-Albon the Arbathite,
Azmaveth the Barhumite,[a]
[32]Eliahba the Shaalbonite,
the sons of Jashen,
Jonathan [33]son of[d] Shammah the Hararite,
Ahiam son of Sharar[e] the Hararite,
[34]Eliphelet son of Ahasbai the Maacathite,[b]
Eliam[c] son of Ahithophel[d] the Gilonite,
[35]Hezro the Carmelite,[e]
Paarai the Arbite,
[36]Igal son of Nathan from Zobah,[f]
the son of Hagri,[f]
[37]Zelek the Ammonite,
Naharai the Beerothite,[g] the armor-bearer of Joab son of Zeruiah,
[38]Ira the Ithrite,[h]
Gareb the Ithrite
[39]and Uriah[i] the Hittite.
There were thirty-seven in all.

David Counts the Fighting Men

24:1-17pp — 1Ch 21:1-17

24 Again[j] the anger of the LORD burned against Israel,[k] and he incited David against them, saying, "Go and take a census of[l] Israel and Judah."

[2]So the king said to Joab[m] and the army commanders[g] with him, "Go throughout the tribes of Israel from Dan to Beersheba[n] and enroll[o] the fighting men, so that I may know how many there are."

[3]But Joab[p] replied to the king, "May the LORD your God multiply the troops a hundred times over,[q] and may the eyes of my lord the king see it. But why does my lord the king want to do such a thing?"

[4]The king's word, however, overruled Joab and the army commanders; so they left the presence of the king to enroll the fighting men of Israel.

[5]After crossing the Jordan, they camped near Aroer,[r] south of the town in the gorge, and then went through Gad and on to Jazer.[s] [6]They went to Gilead and the region of Tahtim Hodshi, and on to Dan Jaan and around toward Sidon.[t] [7]Then they went toward the fortress of Tyre[u] and all the towns of the Hivites[v] and Canaanites. Finally, they went on to Beersheba[w] in the Negev[x] of Judah.

[8]After they had gone through the entire land, they came back to Jerusalem at the end of nine months and twenty days.

[9]Joab reported the number of the fighting men to the king: In Israel there were

23:25 [p]Jdg 7:1 **23:26** [q]1Ch 27:10 [r]1Ch 27:9 **23:27** [s]1Ch 27:12 [t]S Jos 21:18 **23:28** [u]1Ch 27:13 [v]2Ki 25:23; Ezr 2:22; Ne 7:26; Jer 40:8 **23:29** [w]1Ch 27:15 [x]S Jos 15:57 **23:30** [y]S Jdg 12:13 [z]Jos 24:30 **23:31** [a]2Sa 3:16 **23:34** [b]S Dt 3:14 [c]S 2Sa 11:3 [d]S 2Sa 15:12 **23:35** [e]S Jos 12:22 **23:36** [f]S 1Sa 14:47 **23:37** [g]S Jos 9:17 **23:38** [h]1Ch 2:53 **23:39** [i]2Sa 11:3 **24:1** [j]S Jos 9:15 [k]Job 1:6; Zec 3:1 [l]S Ex 30:12; 1Ch 27:23 **24:2** [m]S 2Sa 20:23 [n]S 2Sa 3:10 [o]2Ch 2:17; 17:14; 25:5 **24:3** [p]S 2Sa 2:18 [q]S Dt 1:11 **24:5** [r]S Jos 13:9 [s]S Nu 21:32 **24:6** [t]S Ge 10:19; Jdg 1:31 **24:7** [u]S Jos 19:29 [v]S Ex 3:8 [w]Ge 21:31 [x]S Dt 1:7

[a] *27* Hebrew; some Septuagint manuscripts (see also 1 Chron. 11:29) *Sibbecai* [b] *29* Some Hebrew manuscripts and Vulgate (see also 1 Chron. 11:30); most Hebrew manuscripts *Heleb* [c] *30* Hebrew; some Septuagint manuscripts (see also 1 Chron. 11:32) *Hurai* [d] *33* Some Septuagint manuscripts (see also 1 Chron. 11:34); Hebrew does not have *son of.* [e] *33* Hebrew; some Septuagint manuscripts (see also 1 Chron. 11:35) *Sacar* [f] *36* Some Septuagint manuscripts (see also 1 Chron. 11:38); Hebrew *Haggadi* [g] *2* Septuagint (see also verse 4 and 1 Chron. 21:2); Hebrew *Joab the army commander*

1Ch 11:41–47 lists 16 additional names for this group and apparently includes the names of replacements for vacancies when a warrior either dropped out or died. *Asahel.* See 2:18–23.

23:34 *Eliam.* Father of Bathsheba (see 11:3 and note) and son of David's counselor Ahithophel, who joined in Absalom's conspiracy (see 15:12 and note; 16:20–23; 17:1–23).

23:39 *Uriah.* Husband of Bathsheba (see 11:3–27 and notes on 11:3,17; 12:7).

24:1 *Again.* The previous occasion may have been the famine of 21:1. *the anger of the LORD burned against Israel.* The specific reason for the Lord's displeasure is not stated. Because the anger is said to be directed against Israel rather than David, some have concluded that it was occasioned by the widespread support among the people for the rebellions of Absalom and Sheba against David (see 15:12; 17:11,24–26; 18:7; 20:1–2), the divinely chosen and anointed theocratic king. This would mean that the events of this chapter are to be placed chronologically shortly after those of chs. 15–20 and so after 980 B.C. (see note on 15:7). *the LORD ... incited David against them.* 1Ch 21:1 says that Satan inspired David to take the census. Although Scripture is clear that God does not cause anyone to sin (Jas 1:13–14), it is also clear that the evil acts of people and Satan are under God's sovereign control (see Ex 4:21; 7:3; 9:12; 10:1,20,27; 11:10; 14:4,8; Jos 11:20; 1Ki 22:22–23; Job 1:12; 2:6; Eze 3:20; 14:9; Ac 4:28). *take a census of Israel and Judah.* David's military census (see vv. 2–3) does not appear to have been prompted by any immediate external threat. Since he wanted to "know how many there are" (v. 2), it is evident that his action was motivated either by pride in the size of the empire he had acquired or by reliance for his security on the size of the reserve of manpower he could muster in an emergency or, more likely, both. The mere taking of a census was hardly sinful (see Nu 1:2–3; 26:2–4), but in this instance it represented an unwarranted glorying in and dependence on human power rather than the Lord (not much different from Israel's initial desire to have a king for their security; see 1Sa 8–12). The act was uncharacteristic of David (see 22:2–4,47–51; 1Sa 17:26,37,45–47).

24:2,15 *from Dan to Beersheba.* See note on 1Sa 3:20.

24:3 *But why ... ?* David's directive does not go unchallenged. The fact that he does not answer suggests that he knew his reasons were highly questionable. In any event, Joab's challenge renders David the more guilty.

24:5–8 The military census was begun in southern Transjordan and moved northward, then west across the Jordan, moving from north to south.

24:9 *eight hundred thousand ... five hundred thousand.* These

eight hundred thousand able-bodied men
who could handle a sword, and in Judah
five hundred thousand.[y]
10David was conscience-stricken[z] after
he had counted the fighting men, and he
said to the LORD, "I have sinned[a] greatly in
what I have done. Now, O LORD, I beg you,
take away the guilt of your servant. I have
done a very foolish thing.[b]"
11Before David got up the next morning,
the word of the LORD had come to Gad[c]
the prophet, David's seer:[d] 12"Go and tell
David, 'This is what the LORD says: I am
giving you three options. Choose one of
them for me to carry out against you.' "
13So Gad went to David and said to him,
"Shall there come upon you three[a] years
of famine[e] in your land? Or three months
of fleeing from your enemies while they
pursue you? Or three days of plague[f] in
your land? Now then, think it over and
decide how I should answer the one who
sent me."
14David said to Gad, "I am in deep distress. Let us fall into the hands of the LORD,
for his mercy[g] is great; but do not let me
fall into the hands of men."
15So the LORD sent a plague on Israel
from that morning until the end of the
time designated, and seventy thousand
of the people from Dan to Beersheba
died.[h] 16When the angel stretched out his
hand to destroy Jerusalem, the LORD was
grieved[i] because of the calamity and said
to the angel who was afflicting the people,
"Enough! Withdraw your hand." The angel of the LORD[j] was then at the threshing
floor of Araunah the Jebusite.
17When David saw the angel who was
striking down the people, he said to the
LORD, "I am the one who has sinned and
done wrong. These are but sheep.[k] What
have they done?[l] Let your hand fall upon
me and my family."[m]

David Builds an Altar

24:18-25pp — 1Ch 21:18-26

18On that day Gad went to David and
said to him, "Go up and build an altar to
the LORD on the threshing floor of Araunah[n] the Jebusite." 19So David went up, as
the LORD had commanded through Gad.
20When Araunah looked and saw the king
and his men coming toward him, he went
out and bowed down before the king with
his face to the ground.
21Araunah said, "Why has my lord the
king come to his servant?"
"To buy your threshing floor," David
answered, "so I can build an altar to the
LORD, that the plague on the people may
be stopped."[o]
22Araunah said to David, "Let my lord
the king take whatever pleases him and
offer it up. Here are oxen[p] for the burnt offering, and here are threshing sledges and
ox yokes for the wood. 23O king, Araunah
gives[q] all this to the king." Araunah also
said to him, "May the LORD your God accept you."
24But the king replied to Araunah, "No,
I insist on paying you for it. I will not sacrifice to the LORD my God burnt offerings
that cost me nothing."[r]
So David bought the threshing floor and
the oxen and paid fifty shekels[b][s] of silver
for them. 25David built an altar[t] to the
LORD there and sacrificed burnt offerings
and fellowship offerings.[c] Then the LORD
answered prayer[u] in behalf of the land,
and the plague on Israel was stopped.

[a] 13 Septuagint (see also 1 Chron. 21:12); Hebrew *seven*
[b] 24 That is, about 1 1/4 pounds (about 0.6 kilogram)
[c] 25 Traditionally *peace offerings*

24:9 [y] S Nu 1:44-46
24:10 [z] S 1Sa 24:5 [a] S Nu 22:34 [b] S Nu 12:11
24:11 [c] S 1Sa 22:5 [d] 1Sa 9:9
24:13 [e] Dt 28:38-42, 48; S 32:24; Eze 14:21 [f] S Ex 5:3; S 30:12; S Lev 26:25; Dt 28:21-22, 27-28, 35
24:14 [g] Ne 9:28; Ps 4:1; 51:1; 86:5; 103:8, 13; 119:132; 130:4; Isa 54:7; 55:7; Jer 33:8; 42:12; Da 9:9
24:15 [h] 1Ch 27:24
24:16 [i] S Ge 6:6 [j] S Ge 16:7; S 19:13; S Ex 12:23; Ac 12:23
24:17 [k] Ps 74:1; 100:3; Jer 49:20 [l] S Ge 18:23 [m] Jnh 1:12
24:18 [n] Ge 22:2; 2Ch 3:1
24:21 [o] Nu 16:44-50
24:22 [p] S 1Sa 6:14
24:23 [q] Ge 23:11
24:24 [r] Mal 1:13-14 [s] S Ge 23:16
24:25 [t] S 1Sa 7:17 [u] 2Sa 21:14

figures differ from those of 1Ch 21:5 (see notes on 1Ch 21:5–6).

24:10 *I have sinned greatly.* See note on v. 1.

24:11 *Gad the prophet, David's seer.* See notes on 1Sa 9:9; 22:5.

24:12 *Go and tell David.* See 12:1 and note. *three options.* The three alternative judgments (v. 13) were all included in the curses that Moses said would come on God's people when they failed to adhere to their covenant obligations (see Dt 28:15–25).

24:14 *not … into the hands of men.* David, who knew both God and war, knew that even in his anger God is more merciful than human beings let loose in the rampages of war (see Ps 30:5).

24:16 *angel.* Angels appear elsewhere in Scripture as instruments of God's judgment (see Ex 33:2; 2Ki 19:35; Ps 35:5–6; 78:49; Mt 13:41; Ac 12:23). *the LORD was grieved.* See note on 1Sa 15:29. *threshing floor of Araunah.* Located on Mount Moriah, immediately north of David's city and overlooking it. Later it would become the site of the temple (see 1Ch 21:28—22:1; 2Ch 3:1). *Jebusite.* See note on 5:6.

24:17 *Let your hand fall upon me and my family.* Although the people of Israel were not without guilt (see v. 1 and note), David assumes full blame for his own act and acknowledges his responsibility as king for the well-being of the Lord's people (see 5:2 and note; 7:7–8).

24:19 *as the LORD had commanded.* The Lord himself appointed the atoning sacrifice in answer to David's prayer.

24:21 *To buy your threshing floor.* David does not simply expropriate the property for his royal purposes (see v. 24; cf. 1Sa 8:14).

24:22 *threshing sledges.* See Am 1:3 and note.

24:24 *burnt offerings.* See Lev 1:1–17 and note on 1:3. *David bought the threshing floor.* Thus the later site of the temple (see note on v. 16) became the royal property of the house of David. *and the oxen.* David's haste could not wait for oxen to be brought some distance from his own herds. *fifty shekels.* See note on 1Ch 21:25.

24:25 *fellowship offerings.* See notes on 1Sa 11:15; Lev 3:1; see also note on Lev 7:11–36. Reconciliation and restoration of covenant fellowship were obtained by the king's repentance, intercessory prayer and the offering of sacrifices. *the LORD answered prayer in behalf of the land.* See note on 21:14.

1 Kings

INTRODUCTION

Title

1 and 2 Kings (like 1 and 2 Samuel and 1 and 2 Chronicles) are actually one literary work, called in Hebrew tradition simply "Kings." The division of this work into two books was introduced by the translators of the Septuagint (the pre-Christian Greek translation of the OT) and was subsequently followed in the Latin Vulgate (C. A.D. 400) and most modern versions. In 1448 the division into two sections also appeared in a Hebrew manuscript and was perpetuated in later printed editions of the Hebrew text. Both the Septuagint and the Latin Vulgate further designated Samuel and Kings in a way that emphasized the relationship of these two works (Septuagint: First, Second, Third and Fourth Book of Kingdoms; Latin Vulgate: First, Second, Third and Fourth Kings). Together 1 and 2 Samuel and 1 and 2 Kings relate the whole history of the monarchy, from its rise under the ministry of the prophet Samuel to its fall at the hands of the Babylonians.

The division between 1 and 2 Kings has been made at a somewhat arbitrary and yet appropriate place, shortly after the deaths of Ahab of the northern kingdom (22:37) and Jehoshaphat of the southern kingdom (22:50). Placing the division at this point causes the account of the reign of Ahaziah of Israel to overlap the end of 1 Kings (22:51 – 53) and the beginning of 2 Kings (ch. 1). The same is true of the narration of the ministry of Elijah, which for the most part appears in 1 Kings (chs. 17 – 19). However, his final act of judgment and the passing of his cloak to Elisha at the moment of his ascension to heaven in a whirlwind are contained in 2 Kings (1:1 — 2:17).

Author, Sources and Date

There is little conclusive evidence as to the identity of the author of 1,2 Kings. Although Jewish tradition credits Jeremiah, few today accept this as likely. Whoever the author was, it is clear that he was familiar with the book of Deuteronomy — as were many of Israel's prophets. It is also clear that he used a variety of sources in compiling his history of the monarchy. Three such sources are named: "the book of the annals of Solomon" (11:41), "the book of the annals of the kings of Israel" (14:19), "the book of the annals of the kings of Judah" (14:29). It is likely that other written sources were also employed (such as those mentioned in Chronicles; see below).

Although some scholars have concluded that the three sources specifically cited in 1,2 Kings are to be viewed as official court annals from the royal archives in Jerusalem and Samaria, this is by no means certain. It seems at least questionable whether such annals would have included details of conspiracies such as those referred to in 16:20; 2Ki 15:15. It is also questionable whether such annals would have been readily accessible for public scrutiny, as the author clearly implies in his references to them. Such considerations have led some scholars to conclude that these sources were probably records of the reigns of the kings of Israel and Judah compiled by the succession of Israel's prophets spanning the kingdom period. 1,2 Chronicles makes reference to a number of such writings: "the records of Samuel the seer, the records of Nathan the prophet and the records of Gad the seer" (1Ch 29:29), "the prophecy of Ahijah the Shilonite" and "the visions of Iddo the seer" (2Ch 9:29), "the records of Shemaiah the prophet" (2Ch 12:15), "the annals of Jehu son of Hanani" (2Ch 20:34), "the annotations on the book of the kings" (2Ch 24:27), the "events of Uzziah's reign ... recorded by the prophet Isaiah son of Amoz" (2Ch 26:22; see also 2Ch 32:32) — and there may have been others. It is most likely, for example, that for the ministries of Elijah and Elisha the author depended on a prophetic source (perhaps from the eighth century) that had drawn up an account of those two prophets in which they were already compared with Moses and Joshua.

Some scholars place the date of composition of 1,2 Kings in the time subsequent to Jehoiachin's release from prison (562 B.C.; 2Ki 25:27–30) and prior to the end of the Babylonian exile in 538. This position is challenged by others on the basis of statements in 1,2 Kings that speak of certain things in the preexilic period that are said to have continued in existence "to this day" (see, e.g., 8:8, the poles used to carry the ark; 9:20–21, conscripted labor; 12:19, Israel in rebellion against the house of David; 2Ki 8:22, Edom in rebellion against the kingdom of Judah). From such statements it is argued that the writer must have been a person living in Judah in the preexilic period rather than in Babylon in postexilic times. If this argument is accepted, one must conclude that the original book was composed about the time of the death of Josiah and that the material pertaining to the time subsequent to his reign was added during the exile c. 550. While this "two-edition" viewpoint is possible, it rests largely on the "to this day" statements.

An alternative is to understand these statements as those of the original source used by the author rather than statements of the author himself. A comparison of 2Ch 5:9 with 1Ki 8:8 suggests that this is a legitimate conclusion. Chronicles is clearly a postexilic writing, yet the wording of the statement concerning the poles used to carry the ark ("they are still there today") is the same in Chronicles as it is in Kings. Probably the Chronicler was simply quoting his source, namely, 1Ki 8:8. There is no reason that the author of 1,2 Kings could not have done the same thing in quoting from his earlier sources. This explanation allows for positing a single author living in exile and using the source materials at his disposal.

A Quick Look

Author:
Unknown

Audience:
God's chosen people, the Israelites

Date:
Probably about 550 B.C., during the Babylonian exile

Theme:
After Solomon's death, the nation is divided into the northern kingdom (Israel) and the southern kingdom (Judah).

Theme: Kingship and Covenant

1,2 Kings contains no explicit statement of purpose or theme. Reflection on its content, however, reveals that the author has selected and arranged his material in a manner that provides a sequel to the history found in 1,2 Samuel — a history of kingship regulated by covenant. In general, 1,2 Kings describes the history of the kings of Israel and Judah in the light of God's covenants. The guiding thesis of the book is that the welfare of Israel and her kings depended on their submission to and reliance on Israel's covenant God — their obedience to the Sinaitic covenant regulations and their faithful response to God's prophets.

It is clearly not the author's intention to present a social, political and economic history of Israel's monarchy in accordance with the principles of modern historiography. The author repeatedly refers the reader to other sources for more detailed information about the reigns of the various kings (see, e.g., 11:41; 14:19,29; 15:7,31; 16:5,14,20,27), and he gives a covenantal rather than a social or political or economic assessment of their reigns. From the standpoint of a political historian, Omri would be considered one of the more important rulers in the northern kingdom. He established a powerful dynasty and made Samaria the capital city. According to the Moabite Stone (see chart, p. xxiii), Omri was the ruler who subjugated the Moabites to the northern kingdom. Long after Omri's death, Assyrian rulers referred to Jehu as the "son of Omri" (either mistakenly or merely in accordance with their literary conventions when speaking of a later king of a realm). Yet in spite of Omri's political importance, his reign is dismissed in six verses (16:23–28) with the statement that he "did evil in the eyes of the LORD and sinned more than all those before him" (16:25). Similarly, the reign of Jeroboam II, who presided over the northern kingdom during the time of its greatest political and economic power, is treated only briefly (2Ki 14:23–29).

Together 1 and 2 Samuel and 1 and 2 Kings relate the whole history of the monarchy, from its rise under the ministry of the prophet Samuel to its fall at the hands of the Babylonians.

Another example of the writer's covenantal rather than merely political or economic interest can be seen in the description of the reign of Josiah of Judah. Nothing is said about the early years of his reign, but a detailed description is given of the reformation and renewal of the covenant that he promoted in his 18th year as king (2Ki 22:3—23:28). Nor is anything said of the motives leading Josiah to oppose Pharaoh Neco of Egypt at Megiddo, or of the major shift in geopolitical power from Assyria to Babylon that was connected with this incident (see notes on 2Ki 23:29–30).

It becomes apparent, then, that the kings who receive the most attention in 1,2 Kings are those during whose reigns there was either notable deviation from or affirmation of the covenant (or significant interaction between a king and God's prophet; see below). Ahab son of Omri is an example of the former (16:29—22:39). His reign is given extensive treatment, not so much because of its extraordinary political importance, but because of the serious threat to covenant fidelity and continuity that arose in the northern kingdom during his reign. Ultimately the pagan influence of Ahab's wife Jezebel through Ahab's daughter Athaliah (whether she was Jezebel's daughter is unknown) nearly led to the extermination of the house of David in Judah (see 2Ki 11:1–3 and note on 11:1).

Manasseh (2Ki 21:1–18) is an example of a similar sort. Here again it is deviation from the covenant that is emphasized in the account of his reign rather than political features, such as involvement in the Assyrian-Egyptian conflict (mentioned in Assyrian records but not in 2 Kings). The extreme apostasy characterizing Manasseh's reign made exile for Judah inevitable (2Ki 21:10–15; 23:26–27).

On the positive side, Hezekiah (2Ki 18:1—20:21) and Josiah (2Ki 22:1—23:29) are given extensive treatment because of their involvement in covenant renewal. These are the only two kings given unqualified approval by the writer for their loyalty to the Lord (see 2Ki 18:3–5; 22:2 and notes). It is noteworthy that all the kings of the northern kingdom are said to have done evil in the eyes of the Lord and walked in the ways of Jeroboam, who caused Israel to sin (see, e.g., 16:26,31; 22:52; 2Ki 3:3; 10:29). It was Jeroboam who established the golden calf worship at Bethel and Dan shortly after the division of the kingdom (see 12:26–33; 13:1–6).

While the writer depicts Israel's obedience or disobedience to the Sinai covenant as decisive for her historical destiny, he also recognizes the far-reaching historical significance of the Davidic covenant, which promised that David's dynasty would endure forever. This is particularly noticeable in references to the "lamp" that the Lord had promised David (see 11:36 and note; 15:4; 2Ki 8:19; see also note on 2Sa 21:17). It also appears in more general references to the promise to David (8:20,25) and its consequences for specific historical developments in Judah's later history (11:12–13,32; 2Ki 19:34; 20:6). In addition, the writer uses the life and reign of David as a standard by which the lives of later kings are measured (see, e.g., 9:4; 11:4,6,33,38; 14:8; 15:3,5,11; 2Ki 16:2; 18:3; 22:2).

Another prominent feature of the narratives of 1,2 Kings is the emphasis on the relationship between prophecy and fulfillment in the historical developments of the monarchy. On at least 11 occasions a prophecy is recorded that is later said to have been fulfilled (see, e.g., 2Sa 7:13 and 1Ki

8:20; 1Ki 11:29–39 and 1Ki 12:15; 1Ki 13 and 2Ki 23:16–18). The result of this emphasis is that the history of the kingdom is not presented as a chain of chance occurrences or the mere interplay of human actions but as the unfolding of Israel's historical destiny under the guidance of an omniscient and omnipotent God—Israel's covenant Lord, who rules all history in accordance with his sovereign purposes (see 8:56; 2Ki 10:10).

The author also stresses the importance of the prophets themselves in their role as official emissaries from the court of Israel's covenant Lord, the Great King to whom Israel and her king were bound in service through the covenant. The Lord sent a long succession of such prophets to call king and people back to covenant loyalty (see 2Ki 17:13 and note). For the most part their warnings and exhortations fell on deaf ears. Many of these prophets are mentioned in the narratives of 1,2 Kings (see, e.g., Ahijah, 11:29–40; 14:5–18; Shemaiah, 12:22–24; Micaiah, 22:8–28; Jonah, 2Ki 14:25; Isaiah, 2Ki 19:1–7,20–34; Huldah, 2Ki 22:14–20), but particular attention is given to the ministries of Elijah and Elisha (1Ki 17–19; 2Ki 1–13).

Reflection on these features of 1,2 Kings suggests that it was written to explain to a people in exile that the reason for their condition of humiliation was their stubborn persistence in breaking the covenant. In bringing the exile upon his people, God, after much patience, imposed the curses of the covenant, which had stood as a warning to them from the beginning (see Lev 26:27–45; Dt 28:64–68). This is made explicit with respect to the captivity of the northern kingdom in 2Ki 17:7–23; 18:9–12, and with respect to the southern kingdom in 2Ki 21:12–15. The reformation under Josiah in the southern kingdom is viewed as too little, too late (see 2Ki 23:26–27; 24:3).

The book, then, provides a retrospective analysis of Israel's history. It explains the reasons both for the destruction of Samaria and Jerusalem and their respective kingdoms and for the bitter experience of being forced into exile. This does not mean, however, that there is no hope for the future. The writer consistently keeps the promise to David in view as a basis on which Israel in exile may look to the future with hope rather than with despair. In this connection the final four verses of the book, reporting Jehoiachin's release from prison in Babylon and his elevation to a place of honor in the court there (see 2Ki 25:27–30 and note on 25:28), take on added significance (see also Jer 52:31–34 and note). The future remains open for a new work of the Lord in faithfulness to his promise to the house of David.

It is important to note that, although the author was undoubtedly a Judahite exile, and although the northern kingdom had been dispersed for well over a century and a half at the time of his writing, the scope of his concern was all Israel—the whole covenant people. Neither he nor the prophets (see Isa 10:20–21; 11:11–13; Jer 31; Eze 48:1–29; Hos 11:8–11; Am 9:11–15; Zec 9:10–13) viewed the division of the Israelite kingdom as a divine rejection of the ten tribes, nor did they see the earlier exile of the northern kingdom as a final exclusion of the northern tribes from Israel's future. As a matter of fact, many from the north had fled south during the Assyrian invasions so that a significant remnant of the northern tribes lived on in the kingdom of Judah and shared in its continuing history.

Chronology

1,2 Kings presents the reader with abundant chronological data. Not only is the length of the reign of each king given, but during the period of the divided kingdom the beginning of the reign of each king is synchronized with the regnal year of the ruling king in the opposite kingdom. Often additional data, such as the age of the ruler at the time of his accession, are also provided.

By integrating Biblical data with those derived from Assyrian chronological records, the year 853 B.C. can be fixed as the year of Ahab's death and 841 as the year Jehu began to reign. The years in which Ahab and Jehu had contacts with Shalmaneser III of Assyria can also be given definite dates (by means of astronomical calculations based on an Assyrian reference to a solar eclipse). With these fixed points, it is then possible to work both forward and backward in the lines of the kings of Israel and Judah to give dates for each king. By the same means it can be determined that the division of the kingdom occurred in 930, that Samaria fell to the Assyrians in 722–721 and that Jerusalem fell to the Babylonians in 586.

The synchronistic data correlating the reigns of the kings of Israel and Judah present some knotty problems, which have long been considered nearly insoluble. In more recent times, most of these problems have been resolved in a satisfactory way through recognizing such possibilities as overlapping reigns, coregencies of sons with their fathers, differences in the time of the year in which the reign of a king officially began, and differences in the way a king's first year was reckoned (e.g., see notes on 15:33; 2Ki 8:25; see also chart, pp. 504–505).

Content

1,2 Kings narrates the history of Israel during the period of the monarchy from the closing days of David's rule until the time of the Babylonian exile. After an extensive account of Solomon's reign, the narrative relates the division of the kingdom and then presents an interrelated account of developments within the two kingdoms. In this account, special attention is given to the ministries of Elijah and Elisha in the northern kingdom, with almost a third of the book (nearly equal to the amount of narrative given to Solomon's reign) devoted to God's efforts through his prophets to turn that kingdom away from its apostasies back to covenant faithfulness (see note on 1Ki 12:25—2Ki 17:41).

Kingship in the northern kingdom was plagued with instability and violence. Twenty rulers represented nine different dynasties during the approximately 210 years from the division of the kingdom in 930 B.C. to the fall of Samaria in 722–721. In the southern kingdom there were also 20 rulers, but these were all descendants of David (except Athaliah, whose usurping of the throne interrupted the sequence for a few years) and spanned a period of about 345 years from the division of the kingdom until the fall of Jerusalem in 586.

Outline

1,2 Kings can be broadly outlined by relating its contents to the major historical periods it describes and to the ministries of Elijah and Elisha.

- I. The Solomonic Era (1:1—12:24)
  - A. Solomon's Succession to the Throne (1:1—2:12)
  - B. Solomon's Throne Established (2:13–46)
  - C. Solomon's Wisdom (ch. 3)
  - D. Solomon's Reign Characterized (ch. 4)
  - E. Solomon's Building Projects (5:1—9:9)
    1. Preparation for building the temple (ch. 5)
    2. Building the temple (ch. 6)
    3. Building the palace (7:1–12)
    4. The temple furnishings (7:13–51)
    5. Dedication of the temple (ch. 8)
    6. The Lord's response and warning (9:1–9)
  - F. Solomon's Reign Characterized (9:10—10:29)
  - G. Solomon's Folly (11:1–13)
  - H. Solomon's Throne Threatened (11:14–43)
  - I. Rehoboam's Succession to the Throne (12:1–24)
- II. Israel and Judah from Jeroboam I/Rehoboam to Ahab/Asa (12:25—16:34)
  - A. Jeroboam I of Israel (12:25—14:20)
  - B. Rehoboam of Judah (14:21–31)
  - C. Abijah of Judah (15:1–8)
  - D. Asa of Judah (15:9–24)
  - E. Nadab of Israel (15:25–32)
  - F. Baasha of Israel (15:33—16:7)
  - G. Elah of Israel (16:8–14)
  - H. Zimri of Israel (16:15–20)

- I. Omri of Israel (16:21 – 28)
- J. Ahab of Israel (16:29 – 34)

III. The Ministries of Elijah and Other Prophets from Ahab/Asa to Ahaziah/Jehoshaphat (chs. 17 – 22)

- A. Elijah (and Other Prophets) in the Reign of Ahab (17:1 — 22:40)
  1. Elijah and the drought (ch. 17)
  2. Elijah on Mount Carmel (ch. 18)
  3. Elijah's flight to Horeb (ch. 19)
  4. A prophet condemns Ahab for sparing Ben-Hadad (ch. 20)
  5. Elijah condemns Ahab for seizing Naboth's vineyard (ch. 21)
  6. Micaiah prophesies Ahab's death; its fulfillment (22:1 – 40)
- B. Jehoshaphat of Judah (22:41 – 50)
- C. Ahaziah of Israel (22:51 – 53)

IV. The Ministries of Elijah and Elisha during the Reigns of Ahaziah and Joram (2Ki 1:1 — 8:15)

- A. Elijah in the Reign of Ahaziah (ch. 1)
- B. Elijah's Translation; Elisha's Inauguration (2:1 – 18)
- C. Elisha in the Reign of Joram (2:19 — 8:15)
  1. Elisha's initial miraculous signs (2:19 – 25)
  2. Elisha during the campaign against Moab (ch. 3)
  3. Elisha's ministry to needy ones in Israel (ch. 4)
  4. Elisha heals Naaman (ch. 5)
  5. Elisha's deliverance of one of the prophets (6:1 – 7)
  6. Elisha's deliverance of Joram from Aramean raiders (6:8 – 23)
  7. Aramean siege of Samaria lifted, as Elisha prophesied (6:24 — 7:20)
  8. The Shunammite's land restored (8:1 – 6)
  9. Elisha prophesies Hazael's oppression of Israel (8:7 – 15)

V. Israel and Judah from Joram/Jehoram to the Exile of Israel (8:16 — 17:41)

- A. Jehoram of Judah (8:16 – 24)
- B. Ahaziah of Judah (8:25 – 29)
- C. Jehu's Revolt and Reign in Israel (chs. 9 – 10)
  1. Elisha orders Jehu's anointing (9:1 – 13)
  2. Jehu's assassination of Joram and Ahaziah (9:14 – 29)
  3. Jehu's execution of Jezebel (9:30 – 37)
  4. Jehu's slaughter of Ahab's family (10:1 – 17)
  5. Jehu's eradication of Baal worship (10:18 – 36)
- D. Athaliah and Joash of Judah; Repair of the Temple (chs. 11 – 12)
- E. Jehoahaz of Israel (13:1 – 9)
- F. Jehoash of Israel; Elisha's Last Prophecy (13:10 – 25)
- G. Amaziah of Judah (14:1 – 22)
- H. Jeroboam II of Israel (14:23 – 29)
- I. Azariah of Judah (15:1 – 7)
- J. Zechariah of Israel (15:8 – 12)
- K. Shallum of Israel (15:13 – 16)
- L. Menahem of Israel (15:17 – 22)
- M. Pekahiah of Israel (15:23 – 26)
- N. Pekah of Israel (15:27 – 31)
- O. Jotham of Judah (15:32 – 38)
- P. Ahaz of Judah (ch. 16)
- Q. Hoshea of Israel (17:1 – 6)
- R. Exile of Israel; Resettlement of the Land (17:7 – 41)

- VI. Judah from Hezekiah to the Babylonian Exile (chs. 18–25)
  - A. Hezekiah (chs. 18–20)
    - 1. Hezekiah's good reign (18:1–8)
    - 2. The Assyrian threat and deliverance (18:9—19:37)
    - 3. Hezekiah's illness and alliance with Babylon (ch. 20)
  - B. Manasseh (21:1–18)
  - C. Amon (21:19–26)
  - D. Josiah (22:1—23:30)
    - 1. Repair of the temple; discovery of the Book of the Law (ch. 22)
    - 2. Renewal of the covenant; end of Josiah's reign (23:1–30)
  - E. Jehoahaz Exiled to Egypt (23:31–35)
  - F. Jehoiakim: First Babylonian Deportation (23:36—24:7)
  - G. Jehoiachin: Second Babylonian Deportation (24:8–17)
  - H. Zedekiah: Third Babylonian Deportation (24:18—25:21)
  - I. Removal of the Remnant to Egypt (25:22–26)
  - J. Elevation of Jehoiachin in Babylon (25:27–30)

The narrative of the Solomonic era in 1Ki 1:1—12:24 is an exquisite example of literary inversion (a-b-c-d-e/d′-c′-b′-a′ pattern), in this case consisting of nine sections:

a Solomon's succession to the throne (1:1—2:12)
b Solomon's throne established (2:13–46)
c Solomon's wisdom (3:1–28)
d Solomon's reign characterized (4:1–34)
e Solomon's building projects (5:1—9:9)
d′ Solomon's reign characterized (9:10—10:29)
c′ Solomon's folly (11:1–13)
b′ Solomon's throne threatened (11:14–43)
a′ Rehoboam's succession to the throne (12:1–24)

Significant are the contrasts thus highlighted and the length of the centered section, which notably focuses on Solomon's building projects (see Outline above).

Chronology of Foreign Kings

This is a chronology of selected foreign kings mentioned in this study Bible.

ASSYRIA	Tiglath-Pileser III		745–727*
	Shalmaneser V		727–722
	Sargon II		721–705
	Sennacherib		705–681
	Esarhaddon		681–669
	Ashurbanipal		669–627
BABYLONIA	Nebuchadnezzar II		605–562
	Nabonidus		556–539
	Belshazzar	*Coregency with Nabonidus*	553(?)–539
PERSIA	Cyrus the Great		559–530
	Cambyses		530–522
	Darius I the Great		522–486
	Xerxes (Ahasuerus)		486–465
	Artaxerxes I		465–424
	Darius II		423–404

*All dates are B.C. and are those of the kings' reigns.

Adonijah Sets Himself Up as King

1 When King David was old and well
advanced in years, he could not keep
warm even when they put covers over
him. 2So his servants said to him, "Let us
look for a young virgin to attend the king
and take care of him. She can lie beside
him so that our lord the king may keep
warm."
3Then they searched throughout Israel
for a beautiful girl and found Abishag,[a] a
Shunammite,[b] and brought her to the king.
4The girl was very beautiful; she took care
of the king and waited on him, but the
king had no intimate relations with her.
5Now Adonijah,[c] whose mother was
Haggith, put himself forward and said,
"I will be king." So he got chariots[d] and
horses[a] ready, with fifty men to run ahead
of him. 6(His father had never interfered[e]
with him by asking, "Why do you behave
as you do?" He was also very handsome
and was born next after Absalom.)
7Adonijah conferred with Joab[f] son of
Zeruiah and with Abiathar[g] the priest, and
they gave him their support. 8But Zadok[h]
the priest, Benaiah[i] son of Jehoiada, Nathan[j] the prophet, Shimei[k] and Rei[b] and
David's special guard[l] did not join Adonijah.

9Adonijah then sacrificed sheep, cattle
and fattened calves at the Stone of Zo-
heleth near En Rogel.[m] He invited all his
brothers, the king's sons,[n] and all the men
of Judah who were royal officials, 10but he
did not invite[o] Nathan the prophet or Benaiah or the special guard or his brother
Solomon.[p]
11Then Nathan asked Bathsheba,[q] Solomon's mother, "Have you not heard that
Adonijah,[r] the son of Haggith, has become
king without our lord David's knowing it?
12Now then, let me advise[s] you how you
can save your own life and the life of your
son Solomon. 13Go in to King David and
say to him, 'My lord the king, did you not
swear[t] to me your servant: "Surely Solomon your son shall be king after me, and
he will sit on my throne"? Why then has
Adonijah become king?' 14While you are
still there talking to the king, I will come
in and confirm what you have said."
15So Bathsheba went to see the aged
king in his room, where Abishag[u] the Shunammite was attending him. 16Bathsheba
bowed low and knelt before the king.
"What is it you want?" the king asked.
17She said to him, "My lord, you yourself
swore[v] to me your servant by the LORD your

[a] 5 Or *charioteers* [b] 8 Or possibly *and his friends*

1:3 [a] ver 15; S 2Sa 3:7; 1Ki 2:17,22 [b] S Jos 19:18
1:5 [c] S 2Sa 3:4 [d] S 1Sa 8:11
1:6 [e] 1Sa 3:13
1:7 [f] S 2Sa 2:13,18 [g] S 1Sa 22:20
1:8 [h] S 1Sa 2:35; S 2Sa 8:17 [i] S 2Sa 8:18 [j] S 2Sa 7:2 [k] 1Ki 4:18 [l] 2Sa 23:8
1:9 [m] S 2Sa 17:17 [n] 1Ch 29:24
1:10 [o] ver 26 [p] S 2Sa 12:24
1:11 [q] 2Sa 12:24 [r] S 2Sa 3:4
1:12 [s] Pr 15:22
1:13 [t] ver 17,30
1:15 [u] S ver 3
1:17 [v] S ver 13

1:1—12:24 The narrative of the Solomonic era is an exquisite example of literary inversion, in this case consisting of nine sections (see diagram, p. 472).

1:1—2:12 Solomon's succession to the throne (see note on 1:1—12:24).

1:1 *advanced in years.* 2Sa 5:4 indicates that David died at about 70 years of age (cf. 1Ki 2:11).

1:2 *may keep warm.* The Jewish historian Josephus (first century A.D.) and the Greek physician Galen (second century A.D.) both refer to the ancient medical practice of using a healthy person's body to provide warmth for one who is ill.

1:3 *Shunammite.* Abishag came from Shunem (2Ki 4:8; Jos 19:18; 1Sa 28:4), located near the plain of Jezreel in the tribal territory of Issachar (see map, p. 518).

1:4 *had no intimate relations with her.* Significant in connection with Adonijah's request to be given Abishag as his wife after the death of David (see notes on 2:17,22).

1:5 *Adonijah.* The fourth son of David (see 2Sa 3:4), who was at this time approximately 35 years of age. It is likely that he was the oldest surviving son of David (see note on 2Sa 13:28; see also 2Sa 18:14). *put himself forward.* A unilateral attempt to usurp the throne, bypassing King David's right to designate his own successor (Adonijah must at least have known that his father favored Solomon; see v. 10). If successful, it would have thwarted God's and David's choice of Solomon (see vv. 13,17,30 and note on v. 13; 1Ch 22:9–10; see also note on 2Sa 12:25). *fifty men to run ahead of him.* Adonijah here follows the example of Absalom before him (see note on 2Sa 15:1).

1:6 *never interfered.* David appears to have been consistently negligent in disciplining his sons (see notes on 2Sa 13:21; 14:33). *very handsome.* Attractive physical appearance was an important asset to an aspirant to the throne (see 1Sa 9:2 and note; 16:12; 2Sa 14:25).

1:7 *Joab son of Zeruiah.* See notes on 1Sa 26:6; 2Sa 2:13; 19:13; 20:10,23. Joab's alignment with Adonijah may have been motivated by a struggle for power with Benaiah (see v. 8; 2Sa 8:18; 20:23; 23:20–23 and note on 23:20). Joab held his position more by his standing with the army than by the favor and confidence of David (see 2:5–6). *Abiathar the priest.* See note on 2Sa 8:17.

1:8 *Zadok the priest.* See note on 2Sa 8:17. *Benaiah son of Jehoiada.* See note on 2Sa 23:20. *Nathan the prophet.* See 2Sa 12:1–25. *Shimei.* Not the Shimei of 2:8,46; 2Sa 16:5–8; perhaps the same as Shimei son of Ela (4:18). *Rei.* See NIV text note. There is no other OT reference to Rei if taken as a proper name. *David's special guard.* See 2Sa 23:8–39.

1:9 *Adonijah then sacrificed.* Here also (see note on v. 5) Adonijah followed the example of Absalom (see 2Sa 15:7–12). *En Rogel.* Means "the spring of Rogel"; located just south of Jerusalem in the Kidron Valley. Apparently the site of a spring had some kind of symbolic significance for the business at hand (see v. 33 and note).

1:11 *Bathsheba, Solomon's mother.* The queen mother held an important and influential position in the royal court (see 2:19; 15:13; 2Ki 10:13; 2Ch 15:16). *has become king.* Although the preceding narrative does not relate the actual proclamation of Adonijah's kingship, it can be assumed (see v. 25 and note; 2:15; cf. 2Sa 15:10).

1:12 *save your own life and the life of your son Solomon.* It was common in the ancient Near East for a usurper to liquidate all potential claimants to the throne in an attempt to secure his own position (see 15:29; 2Ki 10:11; 11:1 and note).

1:13 *did you not swear to me . . . ?* Although 2 Samuel does not record David's oath concerning the succession of Solomon, it does suggest that Solomon was the son through whom the Lord's promise to David for an eternal dynasty would be carried forward (see note on v. 5).

1:15 *Shunammite.* See note on v. 3.

1:17 *you yourself swore to me . . . by the LORD your God.* An oath taken in the Lord's name was inviolable (see Ex 20:7; Lev 19:12; Jos 9:15,18,20; Jdg 11:30,35 and notes; Ecc 5:4–7 and note on 5:6).

God: 'Solomon your son shall be king after me, and he will sit on my throne.' 18But
now Adonijah has become king, and you,
my lord the king, do not know about it.
19He has sacrificed[w] great numbers of cattle, fattened calves, and sheep, and has invited all the king's sons, Abiathar the priest
and Joab the commander of the army, but
he has not invited Solomon your servant.
20My lord the king, the eyes of all Israel are
on you, to learn from you who will sit on
the throne of my lord the king after him.
21Otherwise, as soon as my lord the king is
laid to rest[x] with his fathers, I and my son
Solomon will be treated as criminals."

22While she was still speaking with the
king, Nathan the prophet arrived. 23And
they told the king, "Nathan the prophet
is here." So he went before the king and
bowed with his face to the ground.

24Nathan said, "Have you, my lord the
king, declared that Adonijah shall be king
after you, and that he will sit on your
throne? 25Today he has gone down and
sacrificed great numbers of cattle, fattened
calves, and sheep. He has invited all the
king's sons, the commanders of the army
and Abiathar the priest. Right now they are
eating and drinking with him and saying,
'Long live King Adonijah!' 26But me your
servant, and Zadok the priest, and Benaiah son of Jehoiada, and your servant Solomon he did not invite.[y] 27Is this something
my lord the king has done without letting
his servants know who should sit on the
throne of my lord the king after him?"

David Makes Solomon King

1:28-53pp — 1Ch 29:21-25

28Then King David said, "Call in Bathsheba." So she came into the king's presence and stood before him.

1:19 [w]ver 9
1:21 [x]S Ge 15:15; 1Ki 2:10
1:26 [y]ver 10
1:29 [z]S 2Sa 4:9
1:30 [a]S ver 13; 1Ch 23:1
1:32 [b]S 1Sa 2:35
1:33 [c]Jdg 10:4; Zec 9:9 [d]ver 38; 2Ch 32:30; 33:14
1:34 [e]S 1Sa 2:35; 10:1 [f]S 2Sa 15:10
1:37 [g]Jos 1:5,17 [h]ver 47
1:38 [i]ver 8 [j]S 1Sa 30:14; S 2Sa 15:18 [k]S ver 33
1:39 [l]S Ex 29:7; S 1Sa 10:1; 2Ki 11:12; Ps 89:20 [m]S Ex 26:1; S 27:21 [n]S 2Sa 15:10; 2Ki 11:14 [o]ver 34; Nu 23:21; Ps 47:5; Zec 9:9
1:40 [p]S 1Sa 10:5

29The king then took an oath: "As surely
as the LORD lives, who has delivered me
out of every trouble,[z] 30I will surely carry out today what I swore[a] to you by the
LORD, the God of Israel: Solomon your son
shall be king after me, and he will sit on
my throne in my place."

31Then Bathsheba bowed low with her
face to the ground and, kneeling before
the king, said, "May my lord King David
live forever!"

32King David said, "Call in Zadok[b] the
priest, Nathan the prophet and Benaiah
son of Jehoiada." When they came before
the king, 33he said to them: "Take your
lord's servants with you and set Solomon
my son on my own mule[c] and take him
down to Gihon.[d] 34There have Zadok the
priest and Nathan the prophet anoint[e] him
king over Israel. Blow the trumpet[f] and
shout, 'Long live King Solomon!' 35Then
you are to go up with him, and he is to
come and sit on my throne and reign in
my place. I have appointed him ruler over
Israel and Judah."

36Benaiah son of Jehoiada answered the
king, "Amen! May the LORD, the God of
my lord the king, so declare it. 37As the
LORD was with my lord the king, so may
he be with[g] Solomon to make his throne
even greater[h] than the throne of my lord
King David!"

38So Zadok[i] the priest, Nathan the
prophet, Benaiah son of Jehoiada, the Kerethites[j] and the Pelethites went down and
put Solomon on King David's mule and
escorted him to Gihon.[k] 39Zadok the priest
took the horn of oil[l] from the sacred tent[m]
and anointed Solomon. Then they sounded
the trumpet[n] and all the people shouted,[o]
"Long live King Solomon!" 40And all the
people went up after him, playing flutes[p]

1:21 *laid to rest with his fathers.* A conventional expression for death (see Ge 25:8 and note; 47:30; 49:29; Dt 31:16).

1:24 Nathan approached David diplomatically by raising a question that revealed the dilemma. Either David had secretly encouraged Adonijah to claim the throne and thereby had broken his oath to Bathsheba and Solomon (see v. 27), or he had been betrayed by Adonijah.

1:25 *Long live King Adonijah!* An expression of recognition and acclamation of the new king (see 1Sa 10:24; 2Sa 16:16; 2Ki 11:12; see also note on Ps 62:4).

1:31 *May my lord King David live forever!* An expression of Bathsheba's thanks in the stereotyped hyperbolic language of the court (see Ne 2:3; Da 2:4; 3:9; 5:10; 6:21).

1:33 *your lord's servants.* Presumably including the Kerethites and Pelethites (see v. 38). *my own mule.* Although crossbreeding was forbidden in the Mosaic law (Lev 19:19), mules (perhaps imported; see Eze 27:14) were used in the time of David, at least as mounts for royalty (see 2Sa 13:29 and note; 18:9). To ride on David's own mule was a public proclamation that Solomon's succession to the throne was sanctioned by David (see Ge 41:43 and first NIV text note; Est 6:7–9). *Gihon.* The site of a spring on the eastern slope of Mount Zion (see notes on v. 9; 2Sa 5:8).

1:34 *anoint him.* See notes on 1Sa 2:10; 9:16. *Blow the trumpet.* See 2Ki 9:13; 2Sa 15:10; 20:1; see also notes on Nu 10:3; Joel 2:1,15. *Long live King Solomon!* See note on v. 25.

1:35 *Israel and Judah.* The distinction between Israel and Judah was rooted in the separate arrangements by which David became king over these two tribal units (see 2Sa 2:4; 5:3 and notes).

1:36 *Amen! May the LORD … so declare it.* See Jer 28:6.

1:37 *even greater.* Not a deprecation of David's accomplishments, but an expression of total loyalty to David and Solomon. Benaiah shared David's own desire for his chosen successor (see vv. 47–48).

1:38 *the Kerethites and the Pelethites.* See note on 2Sa 8:18.

1:39 *Zadok … anointed Solomon.* Kings chosen by God to rule over his people who were not in a line of dynastic succession were anointed by prophets (Saul, 1Sa 9:16; David, 1Sa 16:12; Jehu, 2Ki 9). Kings who assumed office in the line of dynastic succession were anointed by priests (Solomon, here; Joash, 2Ki 11:12). The distinction seems to be that the priest worked within the established order while the prophets introduced new divine initiatives. *horn of oil.* Perhaps containing the anointing oil described in Ex 30:22–33. *sacred tent.* The tent David had erected in Jerusalem to house the ark (see

and rejoicing greatly, so that the ground
shook with the sound.
41Adonijah and all the guests who were
with him heard it as they were finishing
their feast. On hearing the sound of the
trumpet, Joab asked, “What’s the meaning
of all the noise in the city?”[q]
42Even as he was speaking, Jonathan[r]
son of Abiathar the priest arrived. Adonijah said, “Come in. A worthy man like you
must be bringing good news.”[s]
43“Not at all!” Jonathan answered. “Our
lord King David has made Solomon king.
44The king has sent with him Zadok the
priest, Nathan the prophet, Benaiah son
of Jehoiada, the Kerethites and the Pelethites, and they have put him on the king’s
mule, 45and Zadok the priest and Nathan
the prophet have anointed him king at Gihon. From there they have gone up cheering, and the city resounds[t] with it. That’s
the noise you hear. 46Moreover, Solomon
has taken his seat[u] on the royal throne.
47Also, the royal officials have come to
congratulate our lord King David, saying,
‘May your God make Solomon’s name
more famous than yours and his throne
greater[v] than yours!’ And the king bowed
in worship on his bed 48and said, ‘Praise
be to the LORD, the God of Israel, who has
allowed my eyes to see a successor[w] on
my throne today.’ ”
49At this, all Adonijah’s guests rose in
alarm and dispersed. 50But Adonijah, in
fear of Solomon, went and took hold of
the horns[x] of the altar. 51Then Solomon
was told, “Adonijah is afraid of King Solomon and is clinging to the horns of the
altar. He says, ‘Let King Solomon swear to
me today that he will not put his servant
to death with the sword.’ ”
52Solomon replied, “If he shows himself to be a worthy man, not a hair[y] of his
head will fall to the ground; but if evil is
found in him, he will die.” 53Then King
Solomon sent men, and they brought him
down from the altar. And Adonijah came
and bowed down to King Solomon, and
Solomon said, “Go to your home.”

David’s Charge to Solomon

2:10-12pp — 1Ch 29:26-28

2 When the time drew near for David to
die,[z] he gave a charge to Solomon his
son.
2“I am about to go the way of all the
earth,”[a] he said. “So be strong,[b] show
yourself a man, 3and observe[c] what the
LORD your God requires: Walk in his ways,
and keep his decrees and commands, his
laws and requirements, as written in the
Law of Moses, so that you may prosper[d] in
all you do and wherever you go, 4and that
the LORD may keep his promise[e] to me: ‘If
your descendants watch how they live,
and if they walk faithfully[f] before me with
all their heart and soul, you will never fail
to have a man on the throne of Israel.’
5“Now you yourself know what Joab[g]
son of Zeruiah did to me — what he did

1:41 [q]2Ch 23:12-13 **1:42** [r]S 2Sa 15:27,36 [s]S 2Sa 18:26 **1:45** [t]ver 40 **1:46** [u]S Dt 17:18 **1:47** [v]ver 37 **1:48** [w]1Ki 3:6 **1:50** [x]S Ex 27:2 **1:52** [y]S 1Sa 14:45 **2:1** [z]S Ge 27:2; S Nu 27:13 **2:2** [a]Jos 23:14 [b]S Jos 1:6 **2:3** [c]S Dt 4:6; S 10:12; S 17:14-20; S Jos 1:7 [d]1Ch 22:13 **2:4** [e]S 2Sa 7:13,25; 2Ch 23:3 [f]2Ki 18:3-6; 20:3; Ps 26:1-3; 132:12 **2:5** [g]S 2Sa 2:18

2Sa 6:17) rather than the tabernacle at Gibeon (see 3:4 and note; 2Ch 1:3).

1:41 *heard it.* Although Gihon may not have been visible from En Rogel, the distance was not great and the sound would carry down the Kidron Valley.

1:42 *Jonathan son of Abiathar.* See 2Sa 17:17 – 21.

1:47 *more famous.* See note on v. 37.

1:48 *successor.* In Solomon’s succession to the throne David sees a fulfillment of the promise in 2Sa 7:12,16 (see notes there).

1:49 *dispersed.* No one wanted to be identified with Adonijah’s abortive coup now that it appeared certain to fail.

1:50 *took hold of the horns of the altar.* The horns of the altar were vertical projections at each corner. The idea of seeking asylum at the altar was rooted in the Pentateuch (see Ex 21:13 – 14 and note on 21:14). The priest smeared the blood of the sacrifice on the horns of the altar (see Ex 29:12; Lev 4:7,18,25,30,34) during the sacrificial ritual. Adonijah thus seeks to place his own destiny under the protection of God.

1:52 *worthy man.* Who recognizes and submits to Solomon’s office and authority. *if evil is found in him.* If he shows evidence of continuing opposition to Solomon’s succession to the throne.

2:1 *he gave a charge.* Moses (Dt 31:1 – 8), Joshua (Jos 23:1 – 16) and Samuel (1Sa 12:1 – 25), as representatives of the Lord’s rule, had all given final instructions and admonitions shortly before their deaths.

2:2 *the way of all the earth.* To the grave (see Jos 23:14). *be strong.* See Dt 31:7,23; Jos 1:6 – 7,9,18.

2:3 *observe what the LORD your God requires.* See Ge 26:5; Lev 18:30; Dt 11:1. *Walk in his ways.* A characteristic expression of Deuteronomy for obedience to covenant obligations (Dt 5:33; 8:6; 10:12; 11:22; 19:9; 26:17; 28:9; 30:16). *his decrees and commands, his laws and requirements.* Four generally synonymous terms for covenant obligations (see 6:12; 8:58; 2Ki 17:37; Dt 8:11; 11:1; 26:17; 28:15,45; 30:10,16). *that you may prosper.* See Dt 29:9.

2:4 *that the LORD may keep his promise to me.* David here alludes to the covenanted promise of an everlasting dynasty given to him by God through Nathan the prophet (see notes on 2Sa 7:11 – 16). Although the covenant promise to David was unconditional, individual participation in its blessing on the part of David’s royal descendants was conditioned on obedience to the obligations of the Sinaitic covenant (see 2Ch 7:17 – 22). *with all their heart and soul.* See Dt 4:29; 6:5 and notes; 10:12; 30:6. *you will never fail to have a man on the throne of Israel.* Both Solomon and his descendants fell short of their covenant obligations. This led to the division of the kingdom and eventually to the exile of both the northern and southern kingdoms. It was only in the coming of Christ that the fallen tent of David would be restored (see notes on Am 9:11 – 15; Ac 15:16) and the promise of David’s eternal dynasty ultimately fulfilled. When the nation and its king turned away from the requirements of the Sinai covenant, they experienced the covenant curses rather than blessings; but in all this God remained faithful to his covenant promises to Abraham and to David (see Lev 26:42 – 45; Isa 9:6 – 7; 11:1 – 16; 16:5; 55:3; Jer 23:5 – 6; 30:9; 31:36 – 37; 33:17,20 – 22,25 – 26; Eze 34:23 – 24; 37:24 – 28).

2:5 *Joab son of Zeruiah.* See note on 1:7. *Abner son of Ner.* See notes on 1Sa 20:25; 26:5; 2Sa 3:25 – 32. *Amasa son of Jether.* See 2Sa 17:25 and note; 20:10. *shedding their*

to the two commanders of Israel's armies,
Abner[h] son of Ner and Amasa[i] son of Jether. He killed them, shedding their blood
in peacetime as if in battle, and with that
blood stained the belt around his waist
and the sandals on his feet. 6 Deal with
him according to your wisdom,[j] but do not
let his gray head go down to the grave[d]
in peace.
7 "But show kindness[k] to the sons of
Barzillai[l] of Gilead and let them be among
those who eat at your table.[m] They stood
by me when I fled from your brother Absalom.
8 "And remember, you have with you
Shimei[n] son of Gera, the Benjamite from
Bahurim, who called down bitter curses on me the day I went to Mahanaim.[o]
When he came down to meet me at the
Jordan, I swore[p] to him by the LORD: 'I
will not put you to death by the sword.'
9 But now, do not consider him innocent.
You are a man of wisdom;[q] you will know
what to do to him. Bring his gray head
down to the grave in blood."
10 Then David rested with his fathers and
was buried[r] in the City of David.[s] 11 He had
reigned[t] forty years over Israel — seven
years in Hebron and thirty-three in Jerusalem. 12 So Solomon sat on the throne[u] of
his father David, and his rule was firmly
established.[v]

Solomon's Throne Established

13 Now Adonijah,[w] the son of Haggith,
went to Bathsheba, Solomon's mother. Bathsheba asked him, "Do you come
peacefully?"[x]
He answered, "Yes, peacefully." 14 Then he
added, "I have something to say to you."
"You may say it," she replied.
15 "As you know," he said, "the kingdom
was mine. All Israel looked to me as their
king. But things changed, and the kingdom has gone to my brother; for it has
come to him from the LORD. 16 Now I have
one request to make of you. Do not refuse me."
"You may make it," she said.
17 So he continued, "Please ask King
Solomon — he will not refuse you — to
give me Abishag[y] the Shunammite as my
wife."
18 "Very well," Bathsheba replied, "I will
speak to the king for you."
19 When Bathsheba went to King Solomon to speak to him for Adonijah, the
king stood up to meet her, bowed down to
her and sat down on his throne. He had a
throne brought for the king's mother,[z] and
she sat down at his right hand.[a]
20 "I have one small request to make of
you," she said. "Do not refuse me."
The king replied, "Make it, my mother;
I will not refuse you."
21 So she said, "Let Abishag[b] the Shunammite be given in marriage to your
brother Adonijah."
22 King Solomon answered his mother,
"Why do you request Abishag[c] the Shunammite for Adonijah? You might as well
request the kingdom for him — after all,
he is my older brother[d] — yes, for him and
for Abiathar[e] the priest and Joab son of
Zeruiah!"
23 Then King Solomon swore by the LORD:
"May God deal with me, be it ever so severely,[f] if Adonijah does not pay with his

2:5 [h] S 1Sa 14:50; S 2Sa 3:27 [i] S 2Sa 17:25 **2:6** [j] ver 9 **2:7** [k] S Ge 40:14 [l] S 2Sa 17:27; 19:31-39 [m] S 2Sa 9:7 **2:8** [n] ver 36-46; 2Sa 16:5-13 [o] S Ge 32:2 [p] 2Sa 19:18-23 **2:9** [q] ver 6 **2:10** [r] Ac 2:29 [s] S 2Sa 5:7 **2:11** [t] S 2Sa 5:4,5 **2:12** [u] 1Ch 17:14; 29:23; 2Ch 9:8 [v] ver 46; 2Ch 1:1; 12:13; 17:1; 21:4 **2:13** [w] S 2Sa 3:4 [x] S 1Sa 16:4
2:17 [y] S 1Ki 1:3 **2:19** [z] 1Ki 15:13; 2Ki 10:13; 24:15; 2Ch 15:16; Jer 13:18; 22:26; 29:2 [a] Ps 45:9 **2:21** [b] 1Ki 1:3 **2:22** [c] S Ge 22:24; S 1Ki 1:3 [d] 1Ch 3:2 [e] S 1Sa 22:20 **2:23** [f] S Ru 1:17

[d] 6 Hebrew *Sheol*; also in verse 9

blood in peacetime. Joab's actions were unlawful assassinations (see Dt 19:1 – 13; 21:1 – 9) and only served his own self-interest. In addition, he murdered David's son Absalom (see 2Sa 18:14 – 15) and participated in Adonijah's conspiracy to usurp the throne (see 1:7,19).

2:7 *sons of Barzillai.* See note on 2Sa 17:27. *eat at your table.* A position of honor that brought with it other benefits (see 18:19; 2Ki 25:29; 2Sa 9:7; 19:28; Ne 5:17). See also, however, note on 2Sa 9:7.

2:8 See 2Sa 16:5 – 13. *Shimei son of Gera, the Benjamite.* Gera was probably the ancestor of Shimei's particular line of descent rather than his immediate father (see Ge 46:21; Jdg 3:15). See NIV text notes on Ge 10:2; Da 5:22.

2:9 *do not consider him innocent.* The Mosaic law prohibited cursing a ruler (see 21:10; Ex 22:28 and notes).

2:10 *rested with his fathers.* See note on 1:21. *City of David.* See 2Sa 5:7 and note. Peter implies that David's tomb was still known in his day (Ac 2:29).

2:11 *forty years.* See 2Sa 5:4 – 5. David ruled c. 1010 – 970 B.C. (see Introduction to 1 Samuel: Chronology).

2:13 – 46 Solomon's throne established (see note on 1:1 — 12:24).

2:13 *Adonijah, the son of Haggith.* See note on 1:5. *Do you come peacefully?* The question (see 1Sa 16:4; 2Ki 9:22) reveals Bathsheba's apprehension concerning Adonijah's intention (see 1:5).

2:15 *the kingdom was mine.* See 1:11. *All Israel looked to me as their king.* A gross exaggeration (see 1:7 – 8). *it has come to him from the LORD.* Adonijah professes to view Solomon's kingship as God's will and to have no further intentions of seeking the position for himself.

2:17 *give me Abishag the Shunammite as my wife.* Adonijah's request has the appearance of being innocent (but see note on v. 22) since Abishag had remained a virgin throughout the period of her care for David (see 1:1 – 4; Dt 22:30).

2:19 *right hand.* The position of honor (see Ps 110:1; Mt 20:21).

2:20 *one small request.* Bathsheba does not seem to have attached any great significance to Adonijah's request.

2:22 *You might as well request the kingdom for him.* Solomon immediately understood Adonijah's request as another attempt to gain the throne. Possession of the royal harem was widely regarded as signifying the right of succession to the throne (see notes on 2Sa 3:7; 12:8; 16:21). Although Abishag was a virgin, she would be regarded by the people as belonging to David's harem; so marriage to Abishag would greatly strengthen Adonijah's claim to the throne. *for Abiathar the priest and Joab son of Zeruiah.* See note on 1:7. Solomon assumes that Abiathar and Joab continue to be involved in Adonijah's treacherous schemes.

2:23 *May God deal with me, be it ever so severely.* A curse formula (see note on 1Sa 3:17).

life for this request! [24]And now, as surely
as the LORD lives—he who has established
me securely on the throne of my father
David and has founded a dynasty for me
as he promised[g]—Adonijah shall be put
to death today!" [25]So King Solomon gave
orders to Benaiah[h] son of Jehoiada, and he
struck down Adonijah and he died.[i]

[26]To Abiathar[j] the priest the king said,
"Go back to your fields in Anathoth.[k] You
deserve to die, but I will not put you to
death now, because you carried the ark[l] of
the Sovereign LORD before my father David
and shared all my father's hardships."[m]
[27]So Solomon removed Abiathar from the
priesthood of the LORD, fulfilling[n] the word
the LORD had spoken at Shiloh about the
house of Eli.

[28]When the news reached Joab, who
had conspired with Adonijah though not
with Absalom, he fled to the tent of the
LORD and took hold of the horns[o] of the
altar. [29]King Solomon was told that Joab
had fled to the tent of the LORD and was
beside the altar.[p] Then Solomon ordered
Benaiah[q] son of Jehoiada, "Go, strike him
down!"

[30]So Benaiah entered the tent[r] of the
LORD and said to Joab, "The king says,
'Come out![s]'"

But he answered, "No, I will die here."

Benaiah reported to the king, "This is
how Joab answered me."

[31]Then the king commanded Benaiah,
"Do as he says. Strike him down and bury
him, and so clear me and my father's
house of the guilt of the innocent blood[t]
that Joab shed. [32]The LORD will repay[u] him
for the blood he shed,[v] because without
the knowledge of my father David he attacked two men and killed them with the
sword. Both of them—Abner son of Ner,
commander of Israel's army, and Amasa[w] son of Jether, commander of Judah's
army—were better[x] men and more upright
than he. [33]May the guilt of their blood rest
on the head of Joab and his descendants
forever. But on David and his descendants,
his house and his throne, may there be the
LORD's peace forever."

2:24 [g] 2Sa 7:11
2:25 [h] S 2Sa 8:18 [i] S 2Sa 12:10
2:26 [j] S 1Sa 22:20 [k] S Jos 21:18 [l] S 2Sa 15:24 [m] S 2Sa 15:14
2:27 [n] S 1Sa 2:27-36
2:28 [o] S Ex 27:2
2:29 [p] Ex 21:14 [q] ver 25
2:30 [r] 2Ki 11:15 [s] Ex 21:14
2:31 [t] S Dt 19:13
2:32 [u] Jdg 9:57 [v] S Ge 4:14; S Jdg 9:24 [w] S 2Sa 17:25 [x] 2Ch 21:13

2:24 *has founded a dynasty for me.* Solomon's son and successor, Rehoboam, was born shortly before Solomon became king (cf. 11:42; 14:21). *as he promised.* See 1Ch 22:9–10.
2:25 *Benaiah son of Jehoiada.* See notes on 1:7; 2Sa 23:20.
2:26 *you carried the ark.* See 2Sa 15:24–25,29; 1Ch 15:11–12. *shared all my father's hardships.* See 1Sa 22:20–23; 23:6–9; 30:7; 2Sa 17:15; 19:11.
2:27 *fulfilling the word the LORD had spoken at Shiloh about the house of Eli.* See notes on 1Sa 2:30–35.
2:28 *news.* Of Adonijah's death and Abiathar's banishment. *conspired with Adonijah.* See 1:7. *tent of the LORD.* See note on 1:39. *took hold of the horns of the altar.* See note on 1:50.
2:29 *strike him down!* The right of asylum was extended only to those who accidentally caused someone's death (see Ex 21:14). Solomon was completely justified in denying this right to Joab, not only for his complicity in Adonijah's conspiracy, but also for his murder of Abner and Amasa (see vv. 31–33). In this incident Solomon finds a suitable occasion for carrying out his father's instruction (see vv. 5–6).
2:32 *he attacked two men and killed them.* See 2Sa 3:27; 20:9–10. *Israel's army.* See 2Sa 2:8–9 and notes. *Judah's army.* See 2Sa 20:4.

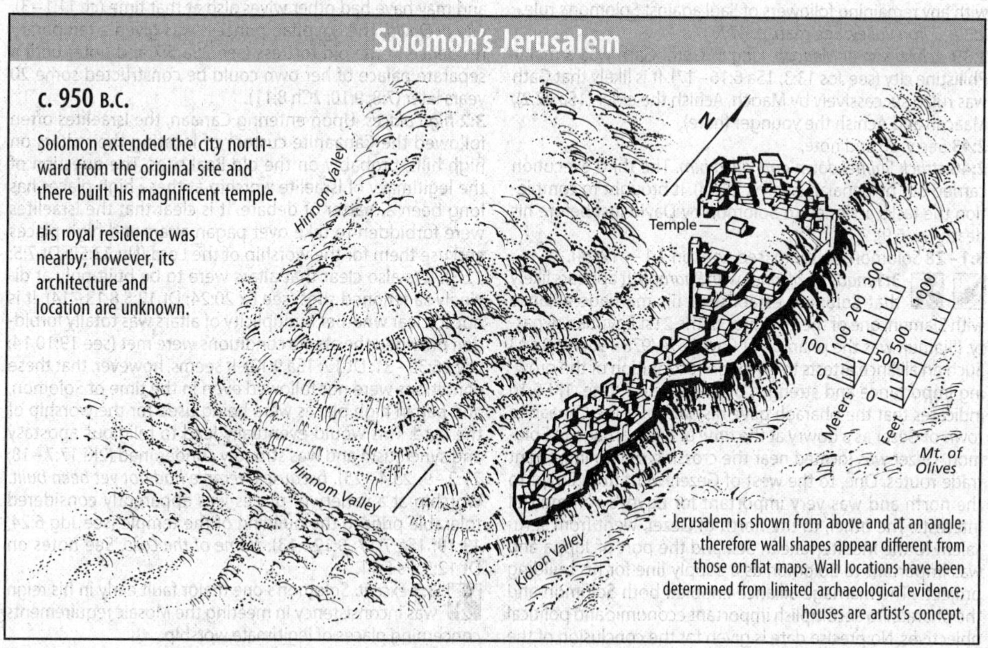

Solomon's Jerusalem
c. 950 B.C.
Solomon extended the city northward from the original site and there built his magnificent temple.
His royal residence was nearby; however, its architecture and location are unknown.
Hinnom Valley
N
Temple
Hinnom Valley
Kidron Valley
Mt. of Olives
Meters
Feet
0 100 200 300
0 500 1000
Jerusalem is shown from above and at an angle; therefore wall shapes appear different from those on flat maps. Wall locations have been determined from limited archaeological evidence; houses are artist's concept.

34So Benaiah[y] son of Jehoiada went up
and struck down Joab[z] and killed him, and
he was buried on his own land[a] in the desert. 35The king put Benaiah[a] son of Jehoiada over the army in Joab's position and
replaced Abiathar with Zadok[b] the priest.
36Then the king sent for Shimei[c] and
said to him, "Build yourself a house in
Jerusalem and live there, but do not go
anywhere else. 37The day you leave and
cross the Kidron Valley,[d] you can be sure
you will die; your blood will be on your
own head."[e]
38Shimei answered the king, "What you
say is good. Your servant will do as my
lord the king has said." And Shimei stayed
in Jerusalem for a long time.
39But three years later, two of Shimei's
slaves ran off to Achish[f] son of Maacah,
king of Gath, and Shimei was told, "Your
slaves are in Gath." 40At this, he saddled
his donkey and went to Achish at Gath in
search of his slaves. So Shimei went away
and brought the slaves back from Gath.
41When Solomon was told that Shimei had gone from Jerusalem to Gath and
had returned, 42the king summoned Shimei and said to him, "Did I not make you
swear by the LORD and warn[g] you, 'On the
day you leave to go anywhere else, you
can be sure you will die'? At that time you
said to me, 'What you say is good. I will
obey.' 43Why then did you not keep your
oath to the LORD and obey the command
I gave you?"
44The king also said to Shimei, "You
know in your heart all the wrong[h] you did
to my father David. Now the LORD will repay you for your wrongdoing. 45But King
Solomon will be blessed, and David's
throne will remain secure[i] before the LORD
forever."
46Then the king gave the order to Benaiah[j] son of Jehoiada, and he went out and
struck Shimei[k] down and killed him.
The kingdom was now firmly established[l] in Solomon's hands.

Solomon Asks for Wisdom

3:4-15pp — 2Ch 1:2-13

3 Solomon made an alliance with Pharaoh king of Egypt and married[m] his
daughter.[n] He brought her to the City of
David[o] until he finished building his palace[p] and the temple of the LORD, and the
wall around Jerusalem. 2The people, however, were still sacrificing at the high places,[q] because a temple had not yet been
built for the Name[r] of the LORD. 3Solomon
showed his love[s] for the LORD by walking[t]

2:34 [y] ver 25 [z] S 2Sa 2:18 **2:35** [a] S 2Sa 8:18 [b] S 1Sa 2:35 **2:36** [c] S 2Sa 16:5 **2:37** [d] S 2Sa 15:23; Jn 18:1 [e] S Lev 20:9 **2:39** [f] 1Sa 27:2 **2:42** [g] S 2Sa 19:23 **2:44** [h] 2Sa 16:5-13 **2:45** [i] S 2Sa 7:13 **2:46** [j] S 2Sa 8:18 [k] S ver 8 [l] S ver 12 **3:1** [m] 1Ki 7:8; 11:1-13 [n] 1Ki 9:24; 2Ch 8:11 [o] 2Sa 5:7; 1Ki 2:10 [p] S 2Sa 7:2; 1Ki 9:10 **3:2** [q] Lev 17:3-5; S 26:30; Dt 12:14; 1Ki 15:14; 22:43 [r] S Dt 14:23 **3:3** [s] Dt 6:5; Ps 31:23; 145:20 [t] S Dt 10:12; S Jos 1:7

[a] 34 Or *buried in his tomb*

2:34 *on his own land.* See NIV text note. The tomb of Joab's father was located near Bethlehem (see 2Sa 2:32). *desert.* Of Judah, east of Bethlehem.
2:35 *Benaiah son of Jehoiada.* See note on 2Sa 23:20. *Zadok the priest.* See notes on 1Sa 2:35; 2Sa 8:17.
2:36 *do not go anywhere else.* Confinement to Jerusalem would greatly reduce the possibility of Shimei's (see v. 8) conspiring with any remaining followers of Saul against Solomon's rule.
2:37 *Kidron Valley.* See map, p. 477.
2:39 *Achish son of Maacah, king of Gath.* Gath was a major Philistine city (see Jos 13:3; 1Sa 6:16–17). It is likely that Gath was ruled successively by Maoch, Achish the elder (1Sa 27:2), Maacah and Achish the younger (here).
2:43 See v. 36 and note.
2:46 *struck Shimei down and killed him.* The third execution carried out by Benaiah (see vv. 25,34). It brought to completion the tasks assigned to Solomon by David just before his death (vv. 6,9).
3:1–28 Solomon's wisdom (see note on 1:1—12:24).
3:1 *made an alliance with Pharaoh.* It appears likely that Solomon established his marriage alliance with Siamun, one of the last kings of the 21st Egyptian dynasty. (Siamun was the pharaoh of Egypt 979/978–960/959 B.C.) Such an alliance attests to Egyptian recognition of the growing importance and strength of the Israelite state. 1Ki 9:16 indicates that the pharaoh gave his daughter the Canaanite town of Gezer as a dowry at the time of her marriage to Solomon. Gezer was located near the crossing of two important trade routes. One, to the west of Gezer, went from Egypt to the north and was very important for Egypt's commercial interests. The other, to the north of Gezer, went from Jerusalem to the Mediterranean Sea and the port of Joppa and was important to Solomon as a supply line for his building projects. The marriage alliance enabled both Solomon and the pharaoh to accomplish important economic and political objectives. No precise date is given for the conclusion of the marriage alliance, though it appears to have occurred in the third or fourth year of Solomon's reign (see 2:39). Solomon began construction of the temple in his fourth year (6:1), and control of the Gezer area was important to him for the beginning of this project (see map No. 5 at the end of this study Bible). *married his daughter.* See 7:8; 9:16,24. Solomon had already married Rehoboam's mother Naamah (see 14:21,31) and may have had other wives also at that time (cf. 11:1–3). *City of David.* The Egyptian princess was given a temporary residence in the old fortress (see 2Sa 5:7 and note) until a separate palace of her own could be constructed some 20 years later (7:8; 9:10; 2Ch 8:11).
3:2 *high places.* Upon entering Canaan, the Israelites often followed the Canaanite custom of locating their altars on high hills, probably on the old Baal sites. The question of the legitimacy of Israelite worship at these high places has long been a matter of debate. It is clear that the Israelites were forbidden to take over pagan altars and high places and use them for the worship of the Lord (Nu 33:52; Dt 7:5; 12:3). It is also clear that altars were to be built only at divinely sanctioned sites (see Ex 20:24; Dt 12:5,8,13–14). It is not so clear whether multiplicity of altars was totally forbidden provided the above conditions were met (see 19:10,14; Lev 26:30–31; Dt 12; 1Sa 9:12). It seems, however, that these conditions were not followed even in the time of Solomon, and pagan high places were being used for the worship of the Lord. This would eventually lead to religious apostasy and syncretism and was strongly condemned (2Ki 17:7–18; 21:2–9; 23:4–25). *because a temple had not yet been built.* Worship at a variety of places was apparently considered tolerable prior to the building of the temple (see Jdg 6:24; 13:19; 1Sa 7:17; 9:12–13). *Name of the LORD.* See notes on Dt 12:5; Ps 5:11.
3:3 *except.* Solomon's one major fault early in his reign was inconsistency in meeting the Mosaic requirements concerning places of legitimate worship.

according to the statutes[u] of his father David, except that he offered sacrifices and
burned incense on the high places.[v]
4The king went to Gibeon[w] to offer sacrifices, for that was the most important
high place, and Solomon offered a thousand burnt offerings on that altar. 5At Gibeon the LORD appeared[x] to Solomon during
the night in a dream,[y] and God said, "Ask[z]
for whatever you want me to give you."
6Solomon answered, "You have shown
great kindness to your servant, my father
David, because he was faithful[a] to you and
righteous and upright in heart. You have
continued this great kindness to him and
have given him a son[b] to sit on his throne
this very day.
7"Now, O LORD my God, you have made
your servant king in place of my father
David. But I am only a little child[c] and
do not know how to carry out my duties.
8Your servant is here among the people
you have chosen,[d] a great people, too numerous to count or number.[e] 9So give your
servant a discerning[f] heart to govern your
people and to distinguish[g] between right
and wrong. For who is able[h] to govern this
great people of yours?"
10The Lord was pleased that Solomon
had asked for this. 11So God said to him,
"Since you have asked[i] for this and not for
long life or wealth for yourself, nor have
asked for the death of your enemies but
for discernment[j] in administering justice,
12I will do what you have asked.[k] I will
give you a wise[l] and discerning heart, so
that there will never have been anyone like
you, nor will there ever be. 13Moreover, I
will give you what you have not[m] asked
for—both riches and honor[n]—so that
in your lifetime you will have no equal[o]
among kings. 14And if you walk[p] in my
ways and obey my statutes and commands
as David your father did, I will give you a
long life."[q] 15Then Solomon awoke[r]—and
he realized it had been a dream.[s]
He returned to Jerusalem, stood before
the ark of the Lord's covenant and sacrificed burnt offerings[t] and fellowship offerings.[a][u] Then he gave a feast[v] for all his
court.

3:3 [u]S Dt 17:19; S 1Ki 14:8 [v]S ver 2; Lev 17:3-5; 2Ki 12:3; 15:4,35; 16:4; 21:3 **3:4** [w]S Jos 9:3 **3:5** [x]1Ki 9:2; 11:9 [y]S Mt 27:19 [z]S Mt 7:7 **3:6** [a]S Ge 17:1 [b]1Ki 1:48 **3:7** [c]Nu 27:17; 1Ch 22:5; 29:1; Jer 1:6 **3:8** [d]S Dt 7:6 [e]S Ge 12:2; 15:5; S 1Ch 27:23 **3:9** [f]S 2Sa 14:17; Jas 1:5 [g]S Dt 1:16 [h]2Co 2:16 **3:11** [i]Jas 4:3 [j]1Ch 22:12 **3:12** [k]1Jn 5:14-15 [l]S 2Sa 14:20; 1Ki 4:29,30,31; 5:12; 10:23; Ecc 1:16 **3:13** [m]Mt 6:33; Eph 3:20 [n]Pr 3:1-2,16; 8:18 [o]1Ki 10:23; 2Ch 9:22; Ne 13:26 **3:14** [p]1Ki 9:4; Ps 25:13; 101:2; 128:1; Pr 3:1-2,16 [q]Ps 61:6 **3:15** [r]S Ge 28:16 [s]ver 5 [t]Lev 6:8-13 [u]Lev 7:11-21 [v]Est 1:3,9; 2:18; 5:8; 6:14; 9:17; Da 5:1

A Wise Ruling

16Now two prostitutes came to the king
and stood before him. 17One of them said,
"My lord, this woman and I live in the
same house. I had a baby while she was
there with me. 18The third day after my
child was born, this woman also had a
baby. We were alone; there was no one in
the house but the two of us.
19"During the night this woman's son
died because she lay on him. 20So she got
up in the middle of the night and took
my son from my side while I your servant
was asleep. She put him by her breast and
put her dead son by my breast. 21The next
morning, I got up to nurse my son—and
he was dead! But when I looked at him
closely in the morning light, I saw that it
wasn't the son I had borne."
22The other woman said, "No! The living
one is my son; the dead one is yours."
But the first one insisted, "No! The dead
one is yours; the living one is mine." And
so they argued before the king.

[a] 15 Traditionally *peace offerings*

3:4 *Gibeon.* The Gibeonites tricked Joshua and Israel into a peace treaty at the time of the conquest of Canaan (see Jos 9:3–27). The city was subsequently given to the tribe of Benjamin and set apart for the Levites (Jos 18:25; 21:17). David avenged Saul's violation of the Gibeonite treaty by the execution of seven of Saul's descendants (see 2Sa 21:1–9). *most important high place.* The reason for Gibeon's importance was the presence there of the tabernacle and the ancient bronze altar (see 1Ch 21:29; 2Ch 1:2–6). These must have been salvaged after the destruction of Shiloh by the Philistines (see note on 1Sa 7:1).
3:5 *dream.* Revelation through dreams is found elsewhere in the OT (see Ge 28:12; 31:11; 46:2; Nu 12:6; Jdg 7:13; Da 2:4; 7:1), as well as in the NT (see, e.g., Mt 1:20; 2:12,22).
3:6 *kindness.* The Hebrew for this word often refers to God's covenant favors (see notes on 2Sa 7:15; Ps 6:4). Solomon is praising the Lord for faithfulness to his promises to David (2Sa 7:8–16). *because.* See note on 2Sa 22:21,25.
3:7 *I am only a little child.* The birth of Solomon is generally placed in approximately the middle of David's 40-year reign, meaning that Solomon was about 20 years old at the beginning of his own reign (see 2:11–12) and lacked experience in assuming the responsibilities of his office (cf. Jer 1:6).
3:8 *great people, too numerous to count.* From the small beginnings of a single family living in Egypt (see Ge 46:26–27; Dt 7:7), the Israelites had increased to an extent approaching that anticipated in the promise given to Abraham (Ge 13:16; 22:17–18) and Jacob (Ge 32:12). See 4:20 and note.
3:9 *a discerning heart.* Lit. "a hearing heart." The phrase indicates the ability to listen patiently to all sides of an issue in order to come to true and wise decisions—a characteristic traditionally associated with a good king in the ancient Near East (cf. Isa 11:2–5).
3:11 *long life ... wealth ... death of your enemies.* Typical desires of ancient Near Eastern monarchs.
3:12 *never ... anyone like you.* See 4:29–34; 10:1–13.
3:13 *I will give you what you have not asked for.* Cf. Jesus' promise in Lk 12:31 (see note there).
3:14 *if you walk in my ways ... I will give you a long life.* Echoes Dt 6:2; 17:20; 22:7. Unfortunately Solomon did not remain obedient to the covenant as his father David had (11:6), and he did not live to be much more than 60 years of age (see note on v. 7; cf. 11:42).
3:15 *ark of the Lord's covenant.* See notes on 6:19; 2Sa 6:2. *fellowship offerings.* See notes on Lev 3:1; 1Sa 11:15.
3:16 *two prostitutes came to the king.* It was possible for Israelites (and others within the realm) to bypass lower judicial officials (Dt 16:18) and appeal directly to the king (see 2Ki 8:3; 2Sa 15:2).
3:17 *live in the same house.* Brothels were common in ancient Near Eastern cities.

23The king said, "This one says, 'My son
is alive and your son is dead,' while that
one says, 'No! Your son is dead and mine
is alive.'"
24Then the king said, "Bring me a
sword." So they brought a sword for the
king. 25He then gave an order: "Cut the
living child in two and give half to one and
half to the other."
26The woman whose son was alive was
filled with compassion[w] for her son and
said to the king, "Please, my lord, give her
the living baby! Don't kill him!"

But the other said, "Neither I nor you shall have him. Cut him in two!"

27Then the king gave his ruling: "Give the living baby to the first woman. Do not kill him; she is his mother."

28When all Israel heard the verdict the king had given, they held the king in awe, because they saw that he had wisdom[x] from God to administer justice.

Solomon's Officials and Governors

4 So King Solomon ruled over all Israel.
2And these were his chief officials:[y]

Azariah[z] son of Zadok—the priest;
3Elihoreph and Ahijah, sons of Shisha—secretaries;[a]
Jehoshaphat[b] son of Ahilud—recorder;
4Benaiah[c] son of Jehoiada—commander in chief;
Zadok[d] and Abiathar—priests;
5Azariah son of Nathan—in charge of the district officers;
Zabud son of Nathan—a priest and personal adviser to the king;
6Ahishar—in charge of the palace;[e]
Adoniram[f] son of Abda—in charge of forced labor.[g]

7Solomon also had twelve district governors[h] over all Israel, who supplied provisions for the king and the royal household. Each one had to provide supplies for
one month in the year. 8These are their
names:

Ben-Hur—in the hill country[i] of Ephraim;
9Ben-Deker—in Makaz, Shaalbim,[j] Beth Shemesh[k] and Elon Bethhanan;
10Ben-Hesed—in Arubboth (Socoh[l] and all the land of Hepher[m] were his);
11Ben-Abinadab—in Naphoth Dor[a][n] (he was married to Taphath daughter of Solomon);
12Baana son of Ahilud—in Taanach and Megiddo, and in all of Beth Shan[o] next to Zarethan[p] below Jezreel, from Beth Shan to Abel Meholah[q] across to Jokmeam;[r]
13Ben-Geber—in Ramoth Gilead (the settlements of Jair[s] son of Manasseh in Gilead[t] were his, as well as the district of Argob in Bashan and its sixty large walled cities[u] with bronze gate bars);
14Ahinadab son of Iddo—in Mahanaim;[v]
15Ahimaaz[w]—in Naphtali (he had married Basemath daughter of Solomon);

3:26 [w] Ps 102:13; Isa 49:15; 63:15; Jer 3:12; 31:20; Hos 11:8 **3:28** [x] S 2Sa 14:20; Col 2:3 **4:2** [y] 1Ki 12:6; Job 12:12 [z] 1Ch 6:10; 2Ch 26:17 **4:3** [a] S 2Sa 8:17 [b] S 2Sa 8:16 **4:4** [c] S 2Sa 8:18 [d] S 2Sa 8:17 **4:6** [e] S Ge 41:40 [f] S 2Sa 20:24 [g] S Ge 49:15 **4:7** [h] ver 27 **4:8** [i] S Jos 24:33 **4:9** [j] Jdg 1:35 [k] S Jos 15:10 **4:10** [l] S Jos 15:35 [m] S Jos 12:17 **4:11** [n] S Jos 11:2 **4:12** [o] S Jos 17:11 [p] S Jos 3:16 [q] S Jdg 7:22 [r] 1Ch 6:68 **4:13** [s] S Nu 32:41 [t] Nu 32:40 [u] Dt 3:4 **4:14** [v] Jos 13:26 **4:15** [w] 2Sa 15:27

[a] *11* Or *in the heights of Dor*

3:25 *Cut the living child in two.* This royal command, issued in Solomon's wisdom whereby he resolved a judicial enigma and restored a violated relationship, served the author as a narrative foil to expose more effectively the folly Solomon later displayed, which led to God's judicial cutting of the kingdom in two, giving one part to Solomon's son and one part to Jeroboam (see 11:9–13). In the prophetic literature, these two kingdoms are often compared to prostitutes (see v. 16; see also Jer. 3:6–12; Eze 16:15–46; 23:3–5; Hos 1:2 and notes).

3:28 *they saw that he had wisdom from God.* This episode strikingly demonstrated that the Lord had answered Solomon's prayer for a discerning heart (see vv. 9,12 and note on v. 9).

4:1–34 Solomon's reign characterized (see note on 1:1—12:24).

4:1 *ruled over all Israel.* Solomon ruled over an undivided kingdom, as his father had before him (see 2Sa 8:15).

4:2 *son.* According to 2Sa 15:27,36 and 1Ch 6:8–9, Azariah was the son of Ahimaaz and the grandson of Zadok (see note on 2:8). Apparently Zadok's son Ahimaaz had died, so that Zadok was succeeded by his grandson Azariah. *Zadok.* See 2:27,35; see also notes on 1Sa 2:35; 2Sa 8:17.

4:3 *Shisha.* See note on 2Sa 8:17. *secretaries.* See note on 2Sa 8:17. *Jehoshaphat son of Ahilud.* The same person who served in David's court (see 2Sa 8:16). *recorder.* See note on 2Sa 8:16.

4:4 *Benaiah.* Replaced Joab as commander of the army (see 2:35; 2Sa 8:18; see also note on 2Sa 23:20). *Zadok and Abiathar.* Abiathar was banished at the beginning of Solomon's reign (2:27,35), and Zadok was succeeded by his grandson Azariah (v. 2).

4:5 *Nathan.* Either the prophet (1:11) or the son of David (2Sa 5:14). *district officers.* See vv. 7–19. *priest.* See note on 2Sa 8:18 ("royal advisers"). *personal adviser to the king.* See note on 2Sa 15:37.

4:6 *in charge of the palace.* The first OT reference to an office mentioned frequently in 1,2 Kings (1Ki 16:9; 18:3; 2Ki 18:18,37; 19:2). It is likely that this official was administrator of the palace and steward of the king's properties. *Adoniram.* Served not only under Solomon, but also under David before him (see 2Sa 20:24 and note) and Rehoboam after him (1Ki 12:18). *forced labor.* See notes on 9:15; 2Sa 20:24.

4:7 *Solomon ... had twelve district governors.* The 12 districts were not identical to tribal territories, possibly because the tribes varied greatly in agricultural productivity.

4:8 *Ben-Hur.* The Hebrew *Ben* means "son of."

4:11 *Ben-Abinadab.* Most likely the "son of" David's brother Abinadab (see 1Sa 16:8 and note; 17:13), making him Solomon's first cousin (he was also his son-in-law).

4:12 *Baana son of Ahilud.* Probably a brother of Jehoshaphat the recorder (v. 3).

16 Baana son of Hushai[x] — in Asher and
in Aloth;
17 Jehoshaphat son of Paruah — in Issachar;
18 Shimei[y] son of Ela — in Benjamin;
19 Geber son of Uri — in Gilead (the
country of Sihon[z] king of the Amorites and the country of Og[a] king of
Bashan). He was the only governor
over the district.

Solomon's Daily Provisions

20 The people of Judah and Israel were
as numerous as the sand[b] on the seashore;
they ate, they drank and they were happy.[c]
21 And Solomon ruled[d] over all the kingdoms from the River[a][e] to the land of the
Philistines, as far as the border of Egypt.[f]
These countries brought tribute[g] and were
Solomon's subjects all his life.
22 Solomon's daily provisions[h] were thirty cors[b] of fine flour and sixty cors[c] of
meal, 23 ten head of stall-fed cattle, twenty
of pasture-fed cattle and a hundred sheep
and goats, as well as deer, gazelles, roe-
bucks and choice fowl.[i] 24 For he ruled over
all the kingdoms west of the River, from
Tiphsah[j] to Gaza, and had peace[k] on all
sides. 25 During Solomon's lifetime Judah
and Israel, from Dan to Beersheba,[l] lived
in safety,[m] each man under his own vine
and fig tree.[n]
26 Solomon had four[d] thousand stalls
for chariot horses,[o] and twelve thousand
horses.[e]

4:16 [x] S 2Sa 15:32 **4:18** [y] 1Ki 1:8 **4:19** [z] S Jos 12:2 [a] Dt 3:8-10; S Jos 12:4 **4:20** [b] S Ge 12:2; S 32:12 [c] 1Ch 22:9 **4:21** [d] 2Ch 9:26; Ezr 4:20; Ps 72:11; La 1:1 [e] S Ge 2:14; Ps 72:8 [f] S Ex 23:31 [g] S Jdg 3:15; Eze 16:13 **4:22** [h] 1Ki 10:5 **4:23** [i] Ne 5:18 **4:24** [j] 2Ki 15:16 [k] S Jos 14:15 **4:25** [l] S Jdg 20:1 [m] 1Ch 22:9; Jer 23:6; Eze 28:26; 39:26 [n] Dt 8:8; 2Ki 18:31; Ps 105:33; Isa 36:16; Jer 5:17; Joel 2:22; Mic 4:4; Zec 3:10 **4:26** [o] S Dt 17:16

4:27 [p] ver 7 **4:29** [q] S 1Ki 3:12 [r] S Ge 32:12 **4:30** [s] S Ge 25:6; S Jdg 6:3; Da 1:20; Mt 2:1 [t] Isa 19:11; Ac 7:22 **4:31** [u] S 1Ki 3:12 **4:32** [v] Pr 1:1; 10:1; 25:1; Ecc 12:9 [w] Ps 78:63; SS 1:1; Eze 33:32

27 The district officers,[p] each in his
month, supplied provisions for King Solomon and all who came to the king's table.
They saw to it that nothing was lacking.
28 They also brought to the proper place
their quotas of barley and straw for the
chariot horses and the other horses.

Solomon's Wisdom

29 God gave Solomon wisdom[q] and very
great insight, and a breadth of understanding as measureless as the sand[r] on
the seashore. 30 Solomon's wisdom was
greater than the wisdom of all the men of
the East,[s] and greater than all the wisdom
of Egypt.[t] 31 He was wiser[u] than any other
man, including Ethan the Ezrahite — wiser
than Heman, Calcol and Darda, the sons
of Mahol. And his fame spread to all the
surrounding nations. 32 He spoke three
thousand proverbs[v] and his songs[w] numbered a thousand and five. 33 He described
plant life, from the cedar of Lebanon to
the hyssop[x] that grows out of walls. He
also taught about animals and birds, reptiles and fish. 34 Men of all nations came
to listen to Solomon's wisdom, sent by all
the kings[y] of the world, who had heard of
his wisdom.

[a] *21* That is, the Euphrates; also in verse 24 [b] *22* That is, probably about 185 bushels (about 6.6 kiloliters) [c] *22* That is, probably about 375 bushels (about 13.2 kiloliters) [d] *26* Some Septuagint manuscripts (see also 2 Chron. 9:25); Hebrew *forty* [e] *26* Or *charioteers*

4:33 [x] S Lev 14:49 **4:34** [y] 2Ch 9:23

4:16 *Baana son of Hushai.* Perhaps the son of David's trusted adviser (see notes on 2Sa 15:32,37).

4:18 *Shimei son of Ela.* Perhaps the same Shimei mentioned in 1:8 (see note there).

4:20 *as numerous as the sand on the seashore.* See 3:8 and note; see also v. 29; Ge 22:17; 2Sa 17:11; Isa 10:22; Jer 33:22; Hos 1:10; cf. Ge 41:49; Jos 11:4; Jdg 7:12; Ps 78:27. *they ate, they drank and they were happy.* Judah and Israel prospered (see 5:4).

4:21 *from the River to the land of the Philistines, as far as the border of Egypt.* The borders of Solomon's empire extended to the limits originally promised to Abraham (see Ge 15:18; 2Sa 8:3 and notes). However, rebellion was brewing in Edom (11:14–21) and Damascus (11:23–25). *brought tribute.* From the outset of his reign, Solomon enjoyed the submission of the peoples David had conquered (cf. note on Ps 2:1–3).

4:22 *Solomon's daily provisions.* For all his household, his palace servants and his court officials and their families.

4:24 *Tiphsah.* A city on the west bank of the Euphrates River. *Gaza.* The southernmost city of the Philistines on the Mediterranean coast.

4:25 *from Dan to Beersheba.* See note on 1Sa 3:20.

4:26 *four thousand.* See NIV text note. 1Ki 10:26 and 2Ch 1:14 indicate that Solomon had 1,400 chariots, meaning he maintained stalls for two horses for each chariot, with places for about 1,200 reserve horses. By way of comparison, an Assyrian account of the battle of Qarqar in 853 B.C. (about a century after Solomon) speaks of 1,200 chariots from Damascus, 700 chariots from Hamath and 2,000 chariots from Israel (the northern kingdom). *chariot horses.* See 2Sa 15:1 and note.

4:27 *district officers.* See v. 7 and note.

4:29 *as measureless as the sand on the seashore.* See note on v. 20.

4:30 *men of the East.* See Job 1:3. The phrase is general and appears to refer to the peoples of Mesopotamia (see Ge 29:1) and Arabia (see Jer 49:28; Eze 25:4,10 and note on 25:4) — those associated with Israel's northeastern and eastern horizons, just as Egypt was the main region on her southwestern horizon. Many examples of Mesopotamian wisdom literature have been recovered. *wisdom of Egypt.* See Ge 41:8; Ex 7:11; Ac 7:22. Examples of Egyptian wisdom literature are to be found in the proverbs of Ptahhotep (c. 2450 B.C.) and Amenemope (see Introduction to Proverbs: Date; see also chart, p. xxii).

4:31 *He was wiser than any other man.* That is, of his time (cf. Lk 11:31–32 and note). *Ethan the Ezrahite.* See note on Ps 89 title. *Heman, Calcol and Darda.* See note on 1Ch 2:6. *his fame spread.* See, e.g., 10:1,6–7 and note on 10:1.

4:32 *three thousand proverbs.* Only some of these are preserved in the book of Proverbs.

4:33 *cedar of Lebanon.* See notes on 5:6; Jdg 9:15; Isa 9:10. *hyssop.* See note on Ex 12:22. *animals and birds, reptiles and fish.* Examples of Solomon's knowledge of these creatures are found in Pr 6:6–8; 26:2–3,11; 27:8; 28:1,15.

4:34 *all nations ... all the kings of the world.* A general statement referring to the Near Eastern world (cf. Ge 41:57 and note).

Preparations for Building the Temple

5:1-16pp — 2Ch 2:1-18

5 When Hiram[z] king of Tyre heard that
Solomon had been anointed king to
succeed his father David, he sent his envoys to Solomon, because he had always
been on friendly terms with David. 2Solo-
mon sent back this message to Hiram:

3"You know that because of the
wars[a] waged against my father David
from all sides, he could not build[b] a
temple for the Name of the LORD his
God until the LORD put his enemies
under his feet.[c] 4But now the LORD my
God has given me rest[d] on every side,
and there is no adversary[e] or disaster.
5I intend, therefore, to build a temple[f]
for the Name of the LORD my God, as
the LORD told my father David, when
he said, 'Your son whom I will put on
the throne in your place will build the
temple for my Name.'[g]

6"So give orders that cedars[h] of
Lebanon be cut for me. My men will
work with yours, and I will pay you
for your men whatever wages you
set. You know that we have no one
so skilled in felling timber as the Sidonians."

7When Hiram heard Solomon's message, he was greatly pleased and said,
"Praise be to the LORD[i] today, for he has
given David a wise son to rule over this
great nation."

8So Hiram sent word to Solomon:

"I have received the message you
sent me and will do all you want in
providing the cedar and pine logs.
9My men will haul them down from
Lebanon to the sea[j], and I will float
them in rafts by sea to the place you
specify. There I will separate them
and you can take them away. And
you are to grant my wish by providing food[k] for my royal household."

10In this way Hiram kept Solomon supplied with all the cedar and pine logs he
wanted, 11and Solomon gave Hiram twenty
thousand cors[a] of wheat as food[l] for his
household, in addition to twenty thousand
baths[b,c] of pressed olive oil. Solomon continued to do this for Hiram year after year.
12The LORD gave Solomon wisdom,[m] just as
he had promised him. There were peaceful relations between Hiram and Solomon,
and the two of them made a treaty.[n]

13King Solomon conscripted laborers[o]
from all Israel—thirty thousand men.
14He sent them off to Lebanon in shifts of
ten thousand a month, so that they spent
one month in Lebanon and two months
at home. Adoniram[p] was in charge of the
forced labor. 15Solomon had seventy thousand carriers and eighty thousand stonecutters in the hills, 16as well as thirty-three

5:1 [z] S 2Sa 5:11 **5:3** [a] 1Ch 22:8; 28:3 [b] S 2Sa 7:5 [c] 2Sa 22:40; Ps 8:6; 110:1; S Mt 22:44; 1Co 15:25 **5:4** [d] S Jos 14:15; 1Ch 22:9; Lk 2:14 [e] 1Ki 11:14, 23 **5:5** [f] S Dt 12:5; 1Ch 17:12; 1Co 3:16; Rev 21:22 [g] Dt 12:5; 2Sa 7:13 **5:6** [h] 1Ch 14:1; 22:4 **5:7** [i] 1Ki 10:9; Isa 60:6 **5:9** [j] Ezr 3:7 [k] ver 11; Eze 27:17; Ac 12:20 **5:11** [l] S ver 9 **5:12** [m] S 1Ki 3:12 [n] Jos 9:7; 1Ki 15:19; Am 1:9 **5:13** [o] S Ge 49:15; S Lev 25:39; 1Ki 9:15 **5:14** [p] S 2Sa 20:24; 1Ki 4:6; 2Ch 10:18

[a] *11* That is, probably about 125,000 bushels (about 4,400 kiloliters) [b] *11* Septuagint (see also 2 Chron. 2:10); Hebrew *twenty cors* [c] *11* That is, about 115,000 gallons (about 440 kiloliters)

5:1—9:9 Solomon's building projects (see note on 1:1—12:24).

5:1 *Hiram king of Tyre.* Hiram ruled over Tyre c. 978–944 B.C. He may have also served as coregent with his father Abibaal as early as 993. Before Solomon was born, Hiram provided timber and workmen for the building of David's palace (see 2Sa 5:11 and note).

5:3 *he could not build a temple.* Although David was denied the privilege of building the temple, he did make plans and provisions for its construction (see 1Ch 22:2–5; 28:2; cf. also note on Ps 30 title).

5:4 *rest.* Described here as "no adversary or disaster." God's promises to his people (see Ex 33:14; Dt 25:19; Jos 1:13,15) and to David (2Sa 7:11) have now been fulfilled (see 8:56 and note), so that the Israelites are free to concentrate their strength and resources on building their Great King's royal house (see note on 2Sa 7:11).

5:5 *Name of the LORD.* See 3:2 and note. *as the LORD told my father David.* See 2Sa 7:12–13; 1Ch 22:8–10.

5:6 *So give orders.* A more detailed account of Solomon's request is found in 2Ch 2:3–10. *cedars of Lebanon.* Widely used in the ancient Near East in the construction of royal houses and temples.

5:7 *Praise be to the LORD.* In polytheistic cultures it was common practice for the people of one nation to recognize the deities of another nation (see 10:9; 11:5) and even to ascribe certain powers to them (see 2Ki 18:25; see also 2Ch 2:12).

5:9 *place you specify.* Joppa (2Ch 2:16; see note on 1Ki 3:1). *providing food for my royal household.* Provision of food for Hiram's court personnel appears to cover only the cost of the wood itself. In addition, Solomon would have to provide for the wages of the Phoenician laborers (v. 6). Comparison of v. 11 with 2Ch 2:10 indicates that besides wheat and olive oil for Hiram's court, Solomon also sent barley and wine for labor costs. Hiram may have sold some of these provisions in order to pay the laborers. See also note on 9:11.

5:11 *twenty thousand cors of wheat.* See NIV text note. By way of comparison, Solomon's court received 10,950 cors of flour and 21,900 cors of meal on an annual basis (see 4:22). Solomon's whole grain payment to Hiram of 20,000 cors of wheat and 20,000 cors of barley (2Ch 2:10) would probably yield about 26,666 cors of refined flour and meal, or about 20 percent less than the requirements of Solomon's own court.

5:13 *conscripted laborers.* See notes on 9:15; 2Sa 20:24. Resentment among the people toward this sort of forced labor eventually led to a civil uprising and the division of Solomon's kingdom immediately after his death (12:1–18).

5:15 *seventy thousand carriers and eighty thousand stonecutters.* Conscripted from the non-Israelite population that David had subdued and incorporated into his kingdom (see 2Ch 2:17–18 and note). *hills.* The limestone hills of the surrounding area where the stone was quarried.

5:16 *thirty-three hundred foremen.* 1Ki 9:23 refers to 550 supervisors. If these are two different categories of supervisory personnel, the total is 3,850 men. 2Ch 2:2 refers to 3,600 foremen, and 2Ch 8:10 speaks of 250 supervisors, which again yields a total of 3,850 men in a supervisory capacity.

hundred[a] foremen[q] who supervised the
project and directed the workmen. 17At
the king's command they removed from
the quarry[r] large blocks of quality stone[s]
to provide a foundation of dressed stone
for the temple. 18The craftsmen of Solomon and Hiram[t] and the men of Gebal[e][u]
cut and prepared the timber and stone for
the building of the temple.

Solomon Builds the Temple

6:1-29pp — 2Ch 3:1-14

6 In the four hundred and eightieth[b]
year after the Israelites had come out
of Egypt, in the fourth year of Solomon's
reign over Israel, in the month of Ziv, the
second month,[v] he began to build the temple of the LORD.[w]
2The temple[x] that King Solomon built
for the LORD was sixty cubits long, twenty wide and thirty high.[c] 3The portico[y] at
the front of the main hall of the temple
extended the width of the temple, that is
twenty cubits,[d] and projected ten cubits[e]
from the front of the temple. 4He made
narrow clerestory windows[z] in the temple. 5Against the walls of the main hall
and inner sanctuary he built a structure
around the building, in which there were
side rooms.[a] 6The lowest floor was five
cubits[f] wide, the middle floor six cubits[g]
and the third floor seven.[h] He made offset
ledges around the outside of the temple
so that nothing would be inserted into the
temple walls.
7In building the temple, only blocks
dressed[b] at the quarry were used, and no
hammer, chisel or any other iron tool[c] was
heard at the temple site while it was being built.
8The entrance to the lowest[i] floor was
on the south side of the temple; a stairway led up to the middle level and from
there to the third. 9So he built the temple
and completed it, roofing it with beams
and cedar[d] planks. 10And he built the side
rooms all along the temple. The height of
each was five cubits, and they were attached to the temple by beams of cedar.
11The word of the LORD came[e] to Solomon: 12"As for this temple you are building, if you follow my decrees, carry out my
regulations and keep all my commands[f]
and obey them, I will fulfill through you
the promise[g] I gave to David your father.
13And I will live among the Israelites and
will not abandon[h] my people Israel."
14So Solomon[i] built the temple and
completed[j] it. 15He lined its interior walls
with cedar boards, paneling them from the
floor of the temple to the ceiling,[k] and covered the floor of the temple with planks of
pine.[l] 16He partitioned off twenty cubits[j]

5:16 [q] 1Ki 9:23 **5:17** [r] 1Ki 6:7 [s] 1Ch 22:2 **5:18** [t] S 2Sa 5:11 [u] S Jos 13:5 **6:1** [v] Ezr 3:8 [w] Ezr 5:11 **6:2** [x] Ex 26:1 **6:3** [y] Eze 40:49 **6:4** [z] Eze 41:16 **6:5** [a] Jer 35:2; Eze 41:5-6 **6:7** [b] S Ex 20:25 [c] S Dt 27:5 **6:9** [d] SS 1:17 **6:11** [e] 1Ki 12:22; 13:20; 16:1,7; 17:2; 21:17; Jer 40:1 **6:12** [f] 1Ki 11:10 [g] 2Sa 7:12-16; 1Ki 9:5 **6:13** [h] S Lev 26:11; S Dt 31:6; Jn 14:18; Heb 13:5 **6:14** [i] Ac 7:47 [j] 1Ch 28:20; 2Ch 5:1 **6:15** [k] 1Ki 7:7 [l] Eze 41:15-16

[a] *16* Hebrew; some Septuagint manuscripts (see also 2 Chron. 2:2,18) *thirty-six hundred* [e] *18* That is, Byblos [b] *1* Hebrew; Septuagint *four hundred and fortieth* [c] *2* That is, about 90 feet (about 27 meters) long and 30 feet (about 9 meters) wide and 45 feet (about 13.5 meters) high [d] *3* That is, about 30 feet (about 9 meters) [e] *3* That is, about 15 feet (about 4.5 meters) [f] *6* That is, about 7 1/2 feet (about 2.3 meters); also in verses 10 and 24 [g] *6* That is, about 9 feet (about 2.7 meters) [h] *6* That is, about 10 1/2 feet (about 3.1 meters) [i] *8* Septuagint; Hebrew *middle* [j] *16* That is, about 30 feet (about 9 meters)

5:17 *large blocks of quality stone.* For the size of these stones see 7:10. Transportation of such stones to Jerusalem would require enormous manpower.

5:18 *men of Gebal.* See NIV text note; see also Eze 27:9 and note.

6:1–38 See diagram, p. 484.

6:1 *four hundred and eightieth year … fourth year.* Synchronizations between certain events in the reigns of later Israelite kings and Assyrian chronological records fix the fourth year of Solomon's reign at c. 966 B.C. (see Introduction: Chronology). If Israel's exodus is placed 480 years prior to 966, it would have occurred c. 1446 (the chronology followed in this study Bible) during the rule of the 18th-dynasty Egyptian pharaoh, Amunhotep II. On the basis of Ex 1:11 and certain other historical considerations, however, some have concluded that the exodus could not have occurred prior to the rule of the 19th-dynasty pharaoh, Rameses II—thus not until c. 1290 (see note on Ge 47:11). This would mean that the 480 years of this verse would be understood as either a schematic (perhaps representative of 12 generations multiplied by the conventional, but not always actual, 40-year length of a generation) or aggregate figure (the combined total of a number of subsidiary time periods, which in reality were partly concurrent, examples of which are to be found in Egyptian and Mesopotamian records). See Introductions to Exodus: Chronology; Joshua: Historical Setting.

6:2 *temple that King Solomon built.* The temple was patterned after the tabernacle (and, in general, other temples of the time) and was divided into three major areas: the Most Holy Place, the Holy Place and the outer courtyard. The Most Holy Place in the temple was cubical, as it probably was in the tabernacle. The dimensions of the temple in most instances seem to be double those of the tabernacle (see Ex 26:15–30; 36:20–34).

6:6 *offset ledges.* To avoid making holes in the temple wall, it was built with a series of ledges on which the beams for the three floors of side chambers rested. This accounts for the different widths of the rooms on each floor.

6:8 *entrance to the lowest floor.* Of the side chambers.

6:11 *The word of the LORD came to Solomon.* As the temple neared completion the Lord spoke to Solomon, perhaps through an unnamed prophet (but see 3:5,11–14; 9:2–9).

6:12 *if you follow my decrees … , I will fulfill through you the promise.* In words similar to those spoken by David (see 2:1–4 and notes), the Lord assures Solomon of a continuing dynasty (see 2Sa 7:12–16 and notes), but Solomon must remain faithful to the Sinaitic covenant if he is to experience the fulfillment of the Davidic covenant promise (see "through you"; see also chart, p. 19).

6:13 *I will live among the Israelites.* In the temple being built (see 9:3). To avoid any apprehension among the Israelites concerning his presence with them (cf. Ps 78:60; Jer 26:6,9; see note on 1Sa 7:1), the Lord gives assurance that he will dwell in their midst (see 8:10–13 and note on 8:10; Lev 26:11).

6:16 *Most Holy Place.* The same terminology was used for the inner sanctuary housing the ark in the tabernacle (see Ex 26:33–34; Lev 16:2,16–17,20,23).

at the rear of the temple with cedar boards
from floor to ceiling to form within the
temple an inner sanctuary, the Most Holy
Place.[m] 17The main hall in front of this
room was forty cubits[a] long. 18The inside of the temple was cedar,[n] carved with
gourds and open flowers. Everything was
cedar; no stone was to be seen.
19He prepared the inner sanctuary[o]
within the temple to set the ark of the
covenant[p] of the LORD there. 20The inner
sanctuary[q] was twenty cubits long, twenty wide and twenty high.[b] He overlaid the
inside with pure gold, and he also overlaid
the altar of cedar.[r] 21Solomon covered the
inside of the temple with pure gold, and
he extended gold chains across the front
of the inner sanctuary, which was overlaid with gold. 22So he overlaid the whole
interior with gold. He also overlaid with
gold the altar that belonged to the inner
sanctuary.
23In the inner sanctuary he made a pair
of cherubim[s] of olive wood, each ten cubits[c] high. 24One wing of the first cherub
was five cubits long, and the other wing

6:16 [m] S Ex 26:33
6:18 [n] ver 29; Ps 74:6; Eze 41:18
6:19 [o] 1Ki 8:6 [p] S Ex 25:10; S 1Sa 3:3
6:20 [q] Eze 41:3-4 [r] S Ex 30:1
6:23 [s] S Ex 37:1-9

[a] *17* That is, about 60 feet (about 18 meters)
[b] *20* That is, about 30 feet (about 9 meters) long, wide and high
[c] *23* That is, about 15 feet (about 4.5 meters)

6:19 *ark of the covenant of the LORD.* The Ten Commandments are called the "words of the covenant" in Ex 34:28. The stone tablets on which the Ten Commandments were inscribed are called the "tablets of the covenant" in Dt 9:9. The ark in which the tablets were kept (see Ex 25:16,21; 40:20; Dt 10:1–5) is thus sometimes called the "ark of the covenant of the LORD" (see Dt 10:8; 31:9,25; Jos 3:11). Elsewhere the ark is variously designated as the "ark of the LORD" (Jos 3:13; 4:11), the "ark of the Testimony" (Ex 30:6 [see note there]; 31:7) and the "ark of God" (1Sa 3:3; 4:11,17,21; 5:1–2).
6:20 *pure gold.* The extensive use of gleaming gold probably symbolized the glory of God and his heavenly temple (cf. Rev 21:10–11,18,21).
6:21 *gold chains.* The curtain covering the entrance to the Most Holy Place was probably hung on these chains (see 2Ch 3:14; Mt 27:51 and note; Heb 6:19).
6:22 *altar that belonged to the inner sanctuary.* The incense altar (see 7:48; Ex 30:1,6; 37:25–28; Heb 9:3–4 and note on 9:4).
6:23 *cherubim.* See note on Ex 25:18. They were to stand on either side of the ark (8:6–7; 2Ch 3:10–13). Two additional cherubim stood on the ark—one on each end of its atone-

Solomon's Temple

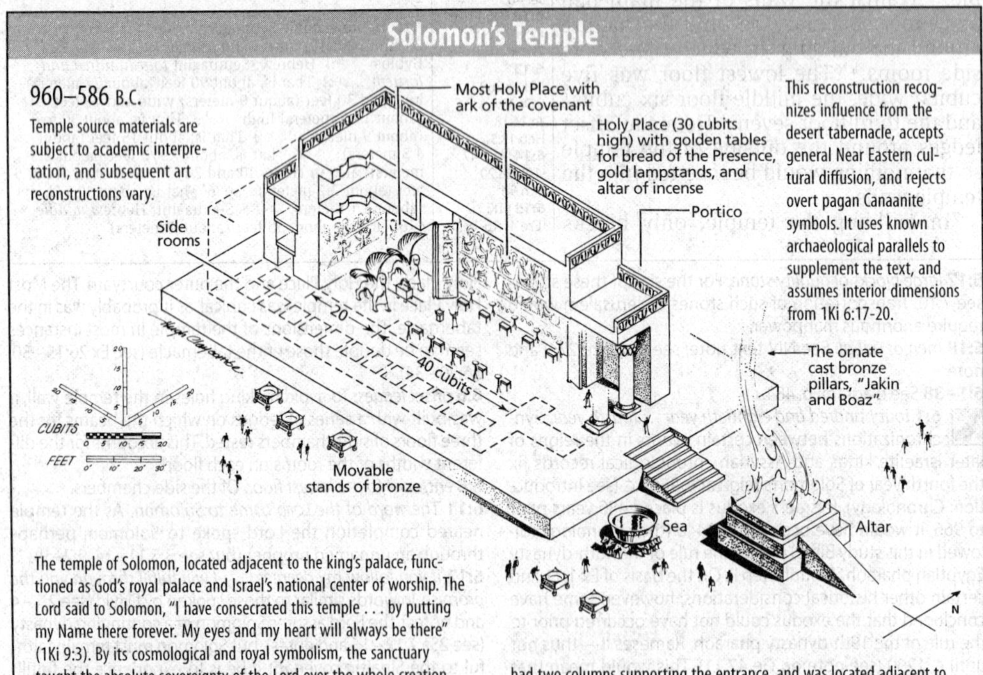
960–586 B.C.
Temple source materials are subject to academic interpretation, and subsequent art reconstructions vary.
Most Holy Place with ark of the covenant
Holy Place (30 cubits high) with golden tables for bread of the Presence, gold lampstands, and altar of incense
Portico
This reconstruction recognizes influence from the desert tabernacle, accepts general Near Eastern cultural diffusion, and rejects overt pagan Canaanite symbols. It uses known archaeological parallels to supplement the text, and assumes interior dimensions from 1Ki 6:17-20.
Side rooms
20
40 cubits
The ornate cast bronze pillars, "Jakin and Boaz"
CUBITS
FEET
Movable stands of bronze
Sea
Altar
N

The temple of Solomon, located adjacent to the king's palace, functioned as God's royal palace and Israel's national center of worship. The Lord said to Solomon, "I have consecrated this temple . . . by putting my Name there forever. My eyes and my heart will always be there" (1Ki 9:3). By its cosmological and royal symbolism, the sanctuary taught the absolute sovereignty of the Lord over the whole creation and his special headship over Israel.

The floor plan is a type that has a long history in Semitic religion, particularly among the West Semites. An early example of the tripartite division into portico, main hall and inner sanctuary has been found at Syrian Ebla (c. 2300 B.C.) and, much later but more contemporaneous with Solomon, at Tell Tainat in the Orontes basin (c. 900 B.C.). Like Solomon's, the temple at Tell Tainat had three divisions, had two columns supporting the entrance, and was located adjacent to the royal palace.

Many archaeological parallels can be drawn to the methods of construction used in the temple, e.g., the "stone and cedar beam" technique described in 1Ki 6:36. Interestingly, evidence for the largest bronze-casting industry ever found in the Holy Land comes from the same locale and period as that indicated in Scripture: Zarethan in the Jordan Valley c. 1000 B.C.

five cubits—ten cubits from wing tip to
wing tip. 25The second cherub also measured ten cubits, for the two cherubim
were identical in size and shape. 26The
height of each cherub was ten cubits.
27He placed the cherubim[t] inside the innermost room of the temple, with their
wings spread out. The wing of one cherub touched one wall, while the wing of
the other touched the other wall, and their
wings touched each other in the middle
of the room. 28He overlaid the cherubim
with gold.

29On the walls[u] all around the temple, in
both the inner and outer rooms, he carved
cherubim,[v] palm trees and open flowers.
30He also covered the floors of both the
inner and outer rooms of the temple with
gold.

31For the entrance of the inner sanctuary he made doors of olive wood with five-
sided jambs. 32And on the two olive wood
doors[w] he carved cherubim, palm trees and
open flowers, and overlaid the cherubim
and palm trees with beaten gold. 33In the
same way he made four-sided jambs of olive wood for the entrance to the main hall.
34He also made two pine doors, each having two leaves that turned in sockets. 35He
carved cherubim, palm trees and open
flowers on them and overlaid them with
gold hammered evenly over the carvings.

36And he built the inner courtyard[x] of
three courses[y] of dressed stone and one
course of trimmed cedar beams.

37The foundation of the temple of the
LORD was laid in the fourth year, in the
month of Ziv. 38In the eleventh year in
the month of Bul, the eighth month, the
temple was finished in all its details[z] according to its specifications.[a] He had spent
seven years building it.

6:27 [t]S Ge 3:24; S Ex 25:18 **6:29** [u]S ver 18 [v]ver 32, 35; Eze 41:18, 25 **6:32** [w]Eze 41:23 **6:36** [x]2Ch 4:9 [y]1Ki 7:12; Ezr 6:4 **6:38** [z]1Ch 28:19 [a]Ex 25:9; Heb 8:5

Solomon Builds His Palace

7 It took Solomon thirteen years, however, to complete the construction of his
palace.[b] 2He built the Palace[c] of the Forest
of Lebanon[d] a hundred cubits long, fifty
wide and thirty high,[a] with four rows of
cedar columns supporting trimmed cedar
beams. 3It was roofed with cedar above the
beams that rested on the columns—forty-
five beams, fifteen to a row. 4Its windows
were placed high in sets of three, facing
each other. 5All the doorways had rectangular frames; they were in the front part in
sets of three, facing each other.[b]

6He made a colonnade fifty cubits long
and thirty wide.[c] In front of it was a portico, and in front of that were pillars and an
overhanging roof.

7He built the throne hall, the Hall of Justice, where he was to judge,[e] and he covered
it with cedar from floor to ceiling.[d][f] 8And
the palace in which he was to live, set farther back, was similar in design. Solomon
also made a palace like this hall for Pharaoh's daughter, whom he had married.[g]

9All these structures, from the outside
to the great courtyard and from foundation to eaves, were made of blocks of high-
grade stone cut to size and trimmed with
a saw on their inner and outer faces. 10The
foundations were laid with large stones of
good quality, some measuring ten cubits[e]
and some eight.[f] 11Above were high-grade
stones, cut to size, and cedar beams. 12The
great courtyard was surrounded by a wall

7:1 [b]S 2Sa 7:2 **7:2** [c]S 2Sa 7:2 [d]1Ki 10:17; 2Ch 9:16; Isa 22:8; 37:24; Jer 22:6, 23 **7:7** [e]1Sa 7:15; Ps 122:5; Pr 20:8 [f]1Ki 6:15 **7:8** [g]S 1Ki 3:1

[a] *2* That is, about 150 feet (about 46 meters) long, 75 feet (about 23 meters) wide and 45 feet (about 13.5 meters) high [b] *5* The meaning of the Hebrew for this verse is uncertain. [c] *6* That is, about 75 feet (about 23 meters) long and 45 feet (about 13.5 meters) wide [d] *7* Vulgate and Syriac; Hebrew *floor* [e] *10* That is, about 15 feet (about 4.5 meters) [f] *10* That is, about 12 feet (about 3.6 meters)

ment cover (Ex 25:17–22). *ten cubits high.* The Most Holy Place, where the cherubim stood, was 20 cubits high (v. 16).

6:29 *he carved cherubim.* Not a violation of the second commandment, which prohibited making anything to serve as a representation of God and worshiping it (see note on Ex 20:4). *palm trees and open flowers.* The depiction of cherubim and beautiful trees and flowers is reminiscent of the Garden of Eden, from which Adam and Eve had been driven as a result of sin (Ge 3:24). In a symbolic sense, readmission to the paradise of God is now to be had only by means of atonement for sin at the sanctuary (see note on Ex 26:1, "tabernacle"). Early Jewish synagogues were adorned with similar motifs.

6:36 *inner courtyard.* Suggests that there was an outer courtyard (see 8:64). 2Ch 4:9 refers to the "courtyard of the priests" (inner) and the "large court" (outer). The inner courtyard is also called the upper courtyard (Jer 36:10) because of its higher position on the temple mount.

6:37 *fourth year.* Of Solomon's reign (see v. 1 and note). *Ziv.* See chart, p. 104.

6:38 *eleventh year.* Of Solomon's reign (959 B.C.). *Bul.* See chart, p. 104.

7:1 *thirteen years.* Solomon spent almost twice as long building his own house as he did the Lord's house (see 6:38; see also Hag 1:2–4).

7:2 *Palace of the Forest of Lebanon.* Four rows of cedar pillars in the palace created the impression of a great forest. *a hundred cubits long, fifty wide and thirty high.* See NIV text note. Compare these measurements with those of the temple in 6:2.

7:3 *forty-five beams, fifteen to a row.* Suggests that there were three floors in the building above the main hall on the ground level. The building included storage space for weaponry (see 10:16–17).

7:6 *colonnade.* Apparently an entrance hall to the Palace of the Forest of Lebanon. Its length (50 cubits) corresponds to the width of the palace.

7:7 *throne hall.* It is not clear whether the throne hall (the Hall of Justice), Solomon's own living quarters (v. 8) and the palace for the pharaoh's daughter (v. 8) were separate buildings or locations within the Palace of the Forest of Lebanon.

7:9 *trimmed with a saw.* The pinkish white limestone of the Holy Land is easily cut when originally quarried, but gradually hardens with exposure.

7:12 *great courtyard.* Constructed in the same way as the inner courtyard of the temple (6:36).

of three courses[h] of dressed stone and one
course of trimmed cedar beams, as was
the inner courtyard of the temple of the
LORD with its portico.

The Temple's Furnishings

7:23-26pp — 2Ch 4:2-5
7:38-51pp — 2Ch 4:6,10–5:1

13King Solomon sent to Tyre and brought
Huram,[a][i] 14whose mother was a widow
from the tribe of Naphtali and whose father was a man of Tyre and a craftsman
in bronze. Huram was highly skilled[j] and
experienced in all kinds of bronze work.
He came to King Solomon and did all[k] the
work assigned to him.
15He cast two bronze pillars,[l] each
eighteen cubits high and twelve cubits
around,[b] by line. 16He also made two capitals[m] of cast bronze to set on the tops of
the pillars; each capital was five cubits[c]
high. 17A network of interwoven chains
festooned the capitals on top of the pillars,
seven for each capital. 18He made pomegranates in two rows[d] encircling each network to decorate the capitals on top of the
pillars.[e] He did the same for each capital.
19The capitals on top of the pillars in the
portico were in the shape of lilies, four cubits[f] high. 20On the capitals of both pillars, above the bowl-shaped part next to
the network, were the two hundred pomegranates[n] in rows all around. 21He erected
the pillars at the portico of the temple. The
pillar to the south he named Jakin[g] and
the one to the north Boaz.[h][o] 22The capitals
on top were in the shape of lilies. And so
the work on the pillars[p] was completed.
23He made the Sea[q] of cast metal, circular in shape, measuring ten cubits[i] from
rim to rim and five cubits high. It took a
line[r] of thirty cubits[j] to measure around it.
24Below the rim, gourds encircled it — ten
to a cubit. The gourds were cast in two
rows in one piece with the Sea.
25The Sea stood on twelve bulls,[s] three
facing north, three facing west, three facing south and three facing east. The Sea
rested on top of them, and their hind-
quarters were toward the center. 26It was
a handbreadth[k] in thickness, and its rim
was like the rim of a cup, like a lily blossom. It held two thousand baths.[l]
27He also made ten movable stands[t] of
bronze; each was four cubits long, four
wide and three high.[m] 28This is how the
stands were made: They had side panels
attached to uprights. 29On the panels between the uprights were lions, bulls and
cherubim — and on the uprights as well.
Above and below the lions and bulls were
wreaths of hammered work. 30Each stand[u]
had four bronze wheels with bronze axles, and each had a basin resting on four
supports, cast with wreaths on each side.
31On the inside of the stand there was an
opening that had a circular frame one cubit[n] deep. This opening was round, and
with its basework it measured a cubit and
a half.[o] Around its opening there was engraving. The panels of the stands were
square, not round. 32The four wheels were
under the panels, and the axles of the
wheels were attached to the stand. The
diameter of each wheel was a cubit and a
half. 33The wheels were made like chariot

7:12 [h]S 1Ki 6:36
7:13 [i]ver 45; 2Ch 2:13; 4:16
7:14 [j]Ex 31:2-5; S 35:31 [k]2Ch 4:11,16
7:15 [l]2Ki 11:14; 23:3; 25:17; 2Ch 3:15; 23:13; 34:31; Jer 27:19; 52:17,21; Eze 40:49
7:16 [m]ver 20,42; 2Ki 25:17; Jer 52:22
7:20 [n]ver 18; 2Ch 3:16; 4:13
7:21 [o]2Ch 3:17
7:22 [p]2Ki 25:17
7:23 [q]ver 47; 2Ki 25:13; 1Ch 18:8; 2Ch 4:18; Jer 52:17; Rev 4:6 [r]Jer 31:39; Zec 2:1
7:25 [s]Jer 52:20
7:27 [t]2Ki 16:17
7:30 [u]2Ki 16:17

[a] *13* Hebrew *Hiram,* a variant of *Huram*; also in verses 40 and 45 [b] *15* That is, about 27 feet (about 8.1 meters) high and 18 feet (about 5.4 meters) around [c] *16* That is, about 7 1/2 feet (about 2.3 meters); also in verse 23 [d] *18* Two Hebrew manuscripts and Septuagint; most Hebrew manuscripts *made the pillars, and there were two rows* [e] *18* Many Hebrew manuscripts and Syriac; most Hebrew manuscripts *pomegranates* [f] *19* That is, about 6 feet (about 1.8 meters); also in verse 38 [g] *21* *Jakin* probably means *he establishes.* [h] *21* *Boaz* probably means *in him is strength.* [i] *23* That is, about 15 feet (about 4.5 meters) [j] *23* That is, about 45 feet (about 13.5 meters) [k] *26* That is, about 3 inches (about 8 centimeters) [l] *26* That is, probably about 11,500 gallons (about 44 kiloliters); the Septuagint does not have this sentence. [m] *27* That is, about 6 feet (about 1.8 meters) long and wide and about 4 1/2 feet (about 1.3 meters) high [n] *31* That is, about 1 1/2 feet (about 0.5 meter) [o] *31* That is, about 2 1/4 feet (about 0.7 meter); also in verse 32

7:13 *King Solomon sent.* Prior to the completion of the temple and the construction of Solomon's palace (see 2Ch 2:7,13–14). *Huram.* See NIV text note. His full name is Huram-Abi (see 2Ch 2:13 and note).

7:14 *widow from the tribe of Naphtali.* 2Ch 2:14 indicates that Huram-Abi's mother was from Dan. Apparently she was born in the city of Dan in northern Israel close to the tribe of Naphtali, from which her first husband came. After he died, she married a man from Tyre. *all kinds of bronze work.* Huram-Abi had a much wider range of skills as well (see 2Ch 2:7,14 and note on 2:7).

7:15 *two bronze pillars.* One was placed on each side of the main entrance to the temple (v. 21). Surely decorative, they may also have embodied a symbolism not known to us. Some believe that the pillars were freestanding, like those found at certain excavations in the Near East. Others think that they supported a roof (forming a portico to the temple) and an architrave.

7:16 *five cubits.* See 2Ki 25:17 and note.

7:21 *pillar to the south.* The temple, like the tabernacle before it, faced east (see Eze 8:16 and note).

7:23 *Sea of cast metal.* This enormous reservoir of water corresponded to the bronze basin made for the tabernacle (see Ex 30:17–21; 38:8). Its water was used by the priests for ritual cleansing (2Ch 4:6). *thirty cubits.* Technically speaking, this should be 31.416 cubits because of the ten-cubit diameter of the circular top. Thirty may be a round number here.

7:24 *ten to a cubit.* With ten gourds to a cubit it took 300 gourds to span the entire reservoir, or 600 gourds counting both rows.

7:26 *two thousand baths.* See 2Ch 4:5 and note.

7:27 *ten movable stands.* These movable bronze stands were designed to hold water basins (see v. 38) of much smaller dimensions than the bronze Sea. The water from the basins was used to wash certain prescribed parts of the animals that were slaughtered for burnt offerings (see Lev 1:9,13; 2Ch 4:6).

wheels; the axles, rims, spokes and hubs
were all of cast metal.
34Each stand had four handles, one on
each corner, projecting from the stand.
35At the top of the stand there was a circular band half a cubit[a] deep. The supports and panels were attached to the top
of the stand. 36He engraved cherubim, lions and palm trees on the surfaces of the
supports and on the panels, in every available space, with wreaths all around. 37This
is the way he made the ten stands. They
were all cast in the same molds and were
identical in size and shape.
38He then made ten bronze basins,[v]
each holding forty baths[b] and measuring
four cubits across, one basin to go on each
of the ten stands. 39He placed five of the
stands on the south side of the temple and
five on the north. He placed the Sea on
the south side, at the southeast corner of
the temple. 40He also made the basins and
shovels and sprinkling bowls.[w]

So Huram finished all the work he had
undertaken for King Solomon in the temple of the LORD:

41 the two pillars;
the two bowl-shaped capitals on top of the pillars;
the two sets of network decorating the two bowl-shaped capitals on top of the pillars;
42 the four hundred pomegranates for the two sets of network (two rows of pomegranates for each network, decorating the bowl-shaped capitals[x] on top of the pillars);
43 the ten stands with their ten basins;
44 the Sea and the twelve bulls under it;
45 the pots, shovels and sprinkling bowls.[y]

7:38 [v] S Ex 30:18
7:40 [w] S Ex 27:3; Jer 52:18
7:42 [x] S ver 16
7:45 [y] S Ex 27:3; Jer 52:18

[a] *35* That is, about 3/4 foot (about 0.2 meter)
[b] *38* That is, about 230 gallons (about 880 liters)

7:36 *He engraved cherubim, lions and palm trees.* See note on 6:29.
7:40 *basins.* Perhaps used for cooking meat to be eaten in connection with the fellowship offerings (see Lev 7:11–17; 22:21–23). *shovels.* Used for removing ashes from the altar. *sprinkling bowls.* For use by the priests in various rites involving the sprinkling of blood or water (see Ex 27:3 and note).
7:41 *two sets of network.* See v. 17.
7:42 *four hundred pomegranates.* See vv. 18,20.
7:43 *ten stands with their ten basins.* See vv. 27–37 and note on v. 27.
7:44 *the Sea and the twelve bulls.* See vv. 23–26 and note on v. 23.
7:45 *pots, shovels and sprinkling bowls.* See v. 40 and note.

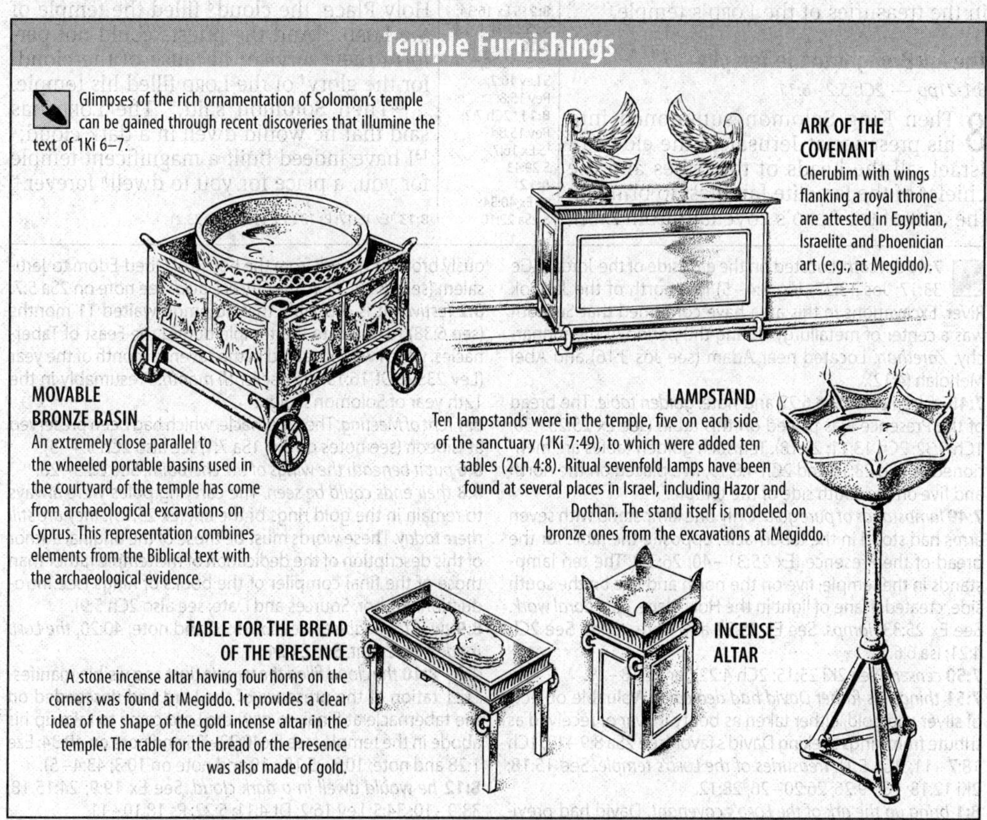

Temple Furnishings
Glimpses of the rich ornamentation of Solomon's temple can be gained through recent discoveries that illumine the text of 1Ki 6–7.
ARK OF THE COVENANT
Cherubim with wings flanking a royal throne are attested in Egyptian, Israelite and Phoenician art (e.g., at Megiddo).
MOVABLE BRONZE BASIN
An extremely close parallel to the wheeled portable basins used in the courtyard of the temple has come from archaeological excavations on Cyprus. This representation combines elements from the Biblical text with the archaeological evidence.
LAMPSTAND
Ten lampstands were in the temple, five on each side of the sanctuary (1Ki 7:49), to which were added ten tables (2Ch 4:8). Ritual sevenfold lamps have been found at several places in Israel, including Hazor and Dothan. The stand itself is modeled on bronze ones from the excavations at Megiddo.
TABLE FOR THE BREAD OF THE PRESENCE
INCENSE ALTAR
A stone incense altar having four horns on the corners was found at Megiddo. It provides a clear idea of the shape of the gold incense altar in the temple. The table for the bread of the Presence was also made of gold.

All these objects that Huram[z] made for
King Solomon for the temple of the LORD
were of burnished bronze. 46The king had
them cast in clay molds in the plain[a] of the
Jordan between Succoth[b] and Zarethan.[c]
47Solomon left all these things unweighed,[d]
because there were so many;[e] the weight
of the bronze[f] was not determined.

48Solomon also made all[g] the furnishings that were in the LORD's temple:

the golden altar;
the golden table[h] on which was the
bread of the Presence;[i]
49the lampstands[j] of pure gold (five
on the right and five on the left, in
front of the inner sanctuary);
the gold floral work and lamps and
tongs;
50the pure gold basins, wick trimmers,
sprinkling bowls, dishes[k] and censers;[l]
and the gold sockets for the doors of
the innermost room, the Most Holy
Place, and also for the doors of the
main hall of the temple.

51When all the work King Solomon had
done for the temple of the LORD was finished, he brought in the things his father
David had dedicated[m]—the silver and gold
and the furnishings[n]—and he placed them
in the treasuries of the LORD's temple.

The Ark Brought to the Temple

8:1-21pp — 2Ch 5:2-6:11

8 Then King Solomon summoned into
his presence at Jerusalem the elders of
Israel, all the heads of the tribes and the
chiefs[o] of the Israelite families, to bring up
the ark[p] of the LORD's covenant from Zion,
the City of David.[q] 2All the men of Israel
came together to King Solomon at the time
of the festival[r] in the month of Ethanim,
the seventh month.[s]

3When all the elders of Israel had arrived, the priests[t] took up the ark, 4and
they brought up the ark of the LORD and
the Tent of Meeting[u] and all the sacred furnishings in it. The priests and Levites[v] carried them up, 5and King Solomon and the
entire assembly of Israel that had gathered
about him were before the ark, sacrificing[w] so many sheep and cattle that they
could not be recorded or counted.

6The priests then brought the ark of
the LORD's covenant[x] to its place in the
inner sanctuary of the temple, the Most
Holy Place,[y] and put it beneath the wings
of the cherubim.[z] 7The cherubim spread
their wings over the place of the ark and
overshadowed[a] the ark and its carrying
poles. 8These poles were so long that their
ends could be seen from the Holy Place in
front of the inner sanctuary, but not from
outside the Holy Place; and they are still
there today.[b] 9There was nothing in the
ark except the two stone tablets[c] that Moses had placed in it at Horeb, where the
LORD made a covenant with the Israelites
after they came out of Egypt.

10When the priests withdrew from the
Holy Place, the cloud[d] filled the temple of
the LORD. 11And the priests could not perform their service[e] because of the cloud,
for the glory[f] of the LORD filled his temple.

12Then Solomon said, "The LORD has
said that he would dwell in a dark cloud;[g]
13I have indeed built a magnificent temple
for you, a place for you to dwell[h] forever."

[z] S ver 13 **7:46** [a] S Ge 13:10 [b] S Ge 33:17 [c] Jos 3:16 **7:47** [d] 1Ch 22:3; Jer 52:20 [e] Ex 36:5-7 [f] S ver 23 **7:48** [g] Ex 39:32-43 [h] S Ex 25:23 [i] S Ex 25:30 **7:49** [j] S Ex 25:31-38 **7:50** [k] S Nu 7:14 [l] 2Ki 25:13; Jer 52:19 **7:51** [m] S 2Sa 8:11 [n] 2Ki 12:13; 24:13; Jer 27:19 **8:1** [o] Nu 7:2 [p] S 1Sa 3:3; Rev 11:19 [q] S 2Sa 5:7 **8:2** [r] ver 65; S Lev 23:36; Ne 8:17 [s] S Lev 23:34; S Nu 29:12 **8:3** [t] S Jos 3:3 **8:4** [u] S Lev 17:4 [v] 1Ch 15:13 **8:5** [w] S 2Sa 6:13; S 2Ch 30:24 **8:6** [x] S Ex 26:33; S 2Sa 6:17; Rev 11:19 [y] S Ex 26:33 [z] S Ge 3:24; S Ex 25:18 **8:7** [a] S Ex 25:20 **8:8** [b] Ex 25:13-15 **8:9** [c] S Ex 16:34; S 25:16; Heb 9:4 **8:10** [d] S Ex 16:10; S Lev 16:2; Rev 15:8 **8:11** [e] 2Ch 7:2; Rev 15:8 [f] S Ex 16:7; S 29:43 **8:12** [g] S Ex 40:34; S 2Sa 22:10 **8:13** [h] Ex 15:17; Ps 132:13; 135:21; Mt 23:21

7:46 *Succoth.* Located on the east side of the Jordan (Ge 33:17; Jos 13:27; Jdg 8:4–5) just north of the Jabbok River. Excavations in this area have confirmed that Succoth was a center of metallurgy during the period of the monarchy. *Zarethan.* Located near Adam (see Jos 3:16) and Abel Meholah (4:12).

7:48 *golden altar.* See 6:22 and note. *golden table.* The bread of the Presence was placed on this table (see Ex 25:23–30; 1Ch 9:32; 2Ch 13:11; 29:18). Ten such golden tables are mentioned in 1Ch 28:16 and 2Ch 4:8,19, five placed on the north and five on the south side of the temple.

7:49 *lampstands of pure gold.* Only one lampstand with seven arms had stood in the tabernacle, opposite the table for the bread of the Presence (Ex 25:31–40; 26:35). The ten lampstands in the temple, five on the north and five on the south side, created a lane of light in the Holy Place. *gold floral work.* See Ex 25:33. *lamps.* See Ex 25:37 and note. *tongs.* See 2Ch 4:21; Isa 6:6.

7:50 *censers.* See 2Ki 25:15; 2Ch 4:22; Jer 52:18–19.

7:51 *things his father David had dedicated.* Valuable objects of silver and gold, either taken as booty in war or received as tribute from kings seeking David's favor (see 2Sa 8:9–12; 1Ch 18:7–11; 2Ch 5:1). *treasuries of the LORD's temple.* See 15:18; 2Ki 12:18; 1Ch 9:26; 26:20–26; 28:12.

8:1 *bring up the ark of the LORD's covenant.* David had previously brought the ark from the house of Obed-Edom to Jerusalem (see 2Sa 6). *Zion, the City of David.* See note on 2Sa 5:7.

8:2 *festival.* It is probable that Solomon waited 11 months (see 6:38) to dedicate the temple during the Feast of Tabernacles, which was observed in the seventh month of the year (Lev 23:34; Dt 16:13–15). *seventh month.* Presumably in the 12th year of Solomon's reign.

8:4 *Tent of Meeting.* The tabernacle, which had been preserved at Gibeon (see notes on 3:4; 1Sa 7:1; see also 2Ch 5:4–5).

8:6 *put it beneath the wings of the cherubim.* See 6:23–28.

8:8 *their ends could be seen.* The carrying poles were always to remain in the gold rings of the ark (Ex 25:15). *they are still there today.* These words must be those of the original author of this description of the dedication of the temple rather than those of the final compiler of the books of Kings (see Introduction: Author, Sources and Date; see also 2Ch 5:9).

8:9 *two stone tablets.* See Ex 25:16 and note; 40:20. *the LORD made a covenant.* See Ex 24.

8:10 *the cloud filled the temple.* Just as a visible manifestation of the presence of the Lord had descended on the tabernacle at Sinai, so now the Lord came to take up his abode in the temple (see Ex 40:33–35 and note on 40:34; Eze 1:28 and note; 10:3–5,18–19 and note on 10:3; 43:4–5).

8:12 *he would dwell in a dark cloud.* See Ex 19:9; 24:15,18; 33:9–10; 34:5; Lev 16:2; Dt 4:11; 5:22; Ps 18:10–11.

14While the whole assembly of Israel
was standing there, the king turned around
and blessed[i] them. 15Then he said:

"Praise be to the LORD,[j] the God of
Israel, who with his own hand has
fulfilled what he promised with his
own mouth to my father David. For
he said, 16'Since the day I brought my
people Israel out of Egypt,[k] I have not
chosen a city in any tribe of Israel to
have a temple built for my Name[l] to
be there, but I have chosen[m] David[n]
to rule my people Israel.'

17"My father David had it in his
heart[o] to build a temple[p] for the
Name of the LORD, the God of Israel.
18But the LORD said to my father David, 'Because it was in your heart to
build a temple for my Name, you did
well to have this in your heart. 19Nev-
ertheless, you[q] are not the one to
build the temple, but your son, who
is your own flesh and blood — he is
the one who will build the temple for
my Name.'[r]

20"The LORD has kept the promise
he made: I have succeeded[s] David my
father and now I sit on the throne of
Israel, just as the LORD promised, and
I have built[t] the temple for the Name
of the LORD, the God of Israel. 21I have
provided a place there for the ark, in
which is the covenant of the LORD
that he made with our fathers when
he brought them out of Egypt."

Solomon's Prayer of Dedication

8:22-53pp — 2Ch 6:12-40

22Then Solomon stood before the altar
of the LORD in front of the whole assembly of Israel, spread out his hands[u] toward
heaven 23and said:

8:14 [i]S Ex 39:43 **8:15** [j]1Ch 16:36; Lk 1:68 **8:16** [k]S Ex 3:10 [l]S Dt 12:5 [m]S 1Sa 9:16; S 16:1 [n]Ps 89:3-4 **8:17** [o]S 1Sa 10:7; Ac 7:46 [p]2Sa 7:27; 1Ch 22:7; Ps 26:8; 132:5 **8:19** [q]S 2Sa 7:5 [r]S 2Sa 7:13 **8:20** [s]S 2Sa 7:12 [t]1Ch 28:6 **8:22** [u]S Ex 9:29 **8:23** [v]S Ex 9:14 [w]S Dt 7:9,12; Ne 1:5; 9:32; Da 9:4 **8:25** [x]S 2Sa 7:15; 1Ch 17:23; 2Ch 1:9 **8:26** [y]S 2Sa 7:25 **8:27** [z]Ac 7:48; 17:24 [a]S Dt 10:14 [b]2Ch 2:6; Ps 139:7-16; Isa 66:1; Jer 23:24 **8:29** [c]ver 52; 2Ki 19:16; 2Ch 7:15; Ne 1:6; Ps 5:1; 31:2; 102:17; 130:2; Isa 37:17 [d]Ps 28:2; 138:2; Da 6:10 [e]S Dt 11:12; 12:11; S 2Sa 7:13 **8:30** [f]ver 47; Lev 26:40; Ne 1:6; Jer 29:12; Da 9:4 [g]ver 39; Ps 34:6 [h]S Ex 34:7,9; Lev 26:40-42; Ps 85:2 **8:31** [i]S Ex 22:11

"O LORD, God of Israel, there is no
God like[v] you in heaven above or on
earth below — you who keep your
covenant of love[w] with your servants
who continue wholeheartedly in your
way. 24You have kept your promise to
your servant David my father; with
your mouth you have promised and
with your hand you have fulfilled
it — as it is today.

25"Now LORD, God of Israel, keep
for your servant David my father the
promises[x] you made to him when you
said, 'You shall never fail to have a
man to sit before me on the throne of
Israel, if only your sons are careful in
all they do to walk before me as you
have done.' 26And now, O God of Israel, let your word that you promised[y]
your servant David my father come
true.

27"But will God really dwell[z] on
earth? The heavens, even the highest
heaven,[a] cannot contain[b] you. How
much less this temple I have built!
28Yet give attention to your servant's
prayer and his plea for mercy, O LORD
my God. Hear the cry and the prayer
that your servant is praying in your
presence this day. 29May your eyes be
open[c] toward[d] this temple night and
day, this place of which you said, 'My
Name[e] shall be there,' so that you will
hear the prayer your servant prays
toward this place. 30Hear the supplication of your servant and of your
people Israel when they pray[f] toward
this place. Hear[g] from heaven, your
dwelling place, and when you hear,
forgive.[h]

31"When a man wrongs his neighbor and is required to take an oath
and he comes and swears the oath[i]

8:15 *what he promised.* See 2Sa 7:5–16.
8:16 *have not chosen a city.* See Dt 12:5 and note. *my Name.* See 3:2 and note.
8:21 *covenant of the LORD.* The two tablets containing the Ten Commandments (see Ex 25:16 and note; Heb 9:4).
8:22 *spread out his hands.* In prayer (see Ex 9:29 and note).
8:23 *no God like you.* No other god has acted in history as has the God of Israel, performing great miracles and directing the course of events so that his long-range covenant promises are fulfilled (see Ex 15:11 and note; Dt 4:39; 7:9; Ps 86:8–10). *who keep your covenant of love.* See Dt 7:9,12 and note. *who continue … in your way.* Cf. Ex 20:6 and note.
8:24 *your promise.* See v. 15; 2Sa 7:5–16.
8:25 *if only your sons … walk before me.* See 9:4–9; 2Ch 7:17–22; see also note on 1Ki 2:4.
8:27 *How much less this temple I have built!* With the construction of the temple and the appearance of a visible manifestation of the presence of God within its courts, the erroneous notion that God was irreversibly and exclusively bound to the temple in a way that guaranteed his assistance to Israel no matter how the people lived could very easily arise (see Jer 7:4–14 and note on 7:4; Mic 3:11). Solomon confessed that even though God had chosen to dwell among his people in a special and localized way, he far transcended containment by anything in all creation.
8:29 *My Name.* See note on 3:2.
8:30 *pray toward this place.* When an Israelite was unable to pray in the temple itself, he was to direct his prayers toward the place where God had pledged to be present among his people (see Da 6:10 and note). *heaven, your dwelling place.* See note on v. 27.
8:31 *required to take an oath.* In cases such as default in pledges (Ex 22:10–12) or alleged adultery (Nu 5:11–31), when there was insufficient evidence to establish the legitimacy of the charge, the supposed offender was required to take an oath of innocence at the sanctuary. Such an oath, with its attendant blessings and curses, was considered a divinely given means of determining innocence or guilt since the consequences of the oath became apparent in the life of the individual either by his experiencing the blessing or the curse or by direct divine revelation through the Urim and Thummim (see Ex 28:29–30 and note on 28:30; Lev 8:8; Nu 27:21).

before your altar in this temple, 32then
hear from heaven and act. Judge between your servants, condemning the
guilty and bringing down on his own
head what he has done. Declare the
innocent not guilty, and so establish
his innocence.[j]
33"When your people Israel have
been defeated[k] by an enemy because
they have sinned[l] against you, and
when they turn back to you and confess your name, praying and making
supplication to you in this temple,[m]
34then hear from heaven and forgive
the sin of your people Israel and bring
them back to the land you gave to
their fathers.
35"When the heavens are shut up
and there is no rain[n] because your
people have sinned[o] against you, and
when they pray toward this place and
confess your name and turn from
their sin because you have afflicted
them, 36then hear from heaven and
forgive the sin of your servants, your
people Israel. Teach[p] them the right
way[q] to live, and send rain[r] on the
land you gave your people for an inheritance.
37"When famine[s] or plague[t] comes
to the land, or blight[u] or mildew, locusts or grasshoppers,[v] or when an
enemy besieges them in any of their
cities, whatever disaster or disease
may come, 38and when a prayer or
plea is made by any of your people
Israel—each one aware of the afflictions of his own heart, and spreading
out his hands[w] toward this temple—
39then hear[x] from heaven, your dwelling place. Forgive[y] and act; deal with
each man according to all he does,
since you know[z] his heart (for you
alone know the hearts of all men),
40so that they will fear[a] you all the
time they live in the land[b] you gave
our fathers.
41"As for the foreigner[c] who does
not belong to your people Israel but
has come from a distant land because of your name— 42for men will
hear[d] of your great name and your
mighty hand[e] and your outstretched
arm—when he comes and prays toward this temple, 43then hear from
heaven, your dwelling place, and do
whatever the foreigner asks of you, so
that all the peoples of the earth may
know[f] your name and fear[g] you, as
do your own people Israel, and may
know that this house I have built
bears your Name.[h]
44"When your people go to war
against their enemies, wherever you
send them, and when they pray[i] to
the LORD toward the city you have
chosen and the temple I have built for
your Name, 45then hear from heaven
their prayer and their plea, and uphold their cause.[j]
46"When they sin against you—for
there is no one who does not sin[k]—
and you become angry with them and
give them over to the enemy, who
takes them captive[l] to his own land,
far away or near; 47and if they have
a change of heart in the land where

8:32 [j] Dt 25:1; Eze 18:20 **8:33** [k] S Lev 26:17 [l] Lev 26:39 [m] Isa 37:1, 14, 38 **8:35** [n] S Dt 28:24; S 2Sa 1:21 [o] Jer 5:25 **8:36** [p] S Dt 8:3; S 1Sa 12:23 [q] Ps 5:8; 27:11; 107:7; Pr 11:5; Isa 45:13; Jer 6:16; 7:23; 31:21 [r] ver 35; 1Ki 17:1; 18:1, 45; Jer 5:24; 10:3; 14:22; Zec 10:1 **8:37** [s] S Lev 26:26 [t] S Ex 30:12; S Lev 26:25 [u] S Dt 28:22 [v] S Ex 10:13; Ps 105:34 **8:38** [w] S Ex 9:29 **8:39** [x] S ver 30 [y] Ps 130:4 [z] S Jos 22:22; S Ps 44:21; Jn 2:24; S Rev 2:23 **8:40** [a] ver 39-40; Dt 6:13; Ps 103:11; 130:4 [b] S Dt 12:1 **8:41** [c] S Ge 31:15; Isa 56:3, 6; 61:5 **8:42** [d] 1Ki 10:1; Isa 60:3; Ac 8:27 [e] Dt 3:24 **8:43** [f] S Jos 4:24; S 1Sa 17:46 [g] Ps 102:15 [h] S Dt 28:10 **8:44** [i] 1Ch 5:20; 2Ch 14:11 **8:45** [j] Ps 9:4; 140:12 **8:46** [k] Ps 130:3; 143:2; Pr 20:9; S Ro 3:9 [l] Lev 26:33-39; S Dt 4:27; S 21:10; S 28:64; 2Ki 25:21

8:32 *hear from heaven.* It is clear that Solomon viewed the oath as an appeal to God to act and not as an automatic power that worked in a magical way.

8:33 *defeated by an enemy because they have sinned against you.* Defeat by enemies was listed in Dt 28:25 as one of the curses that would come on Israel if she disobeyed the covenant. Solomon's prayer reflects an awareness of the covenant obligations the Lord had placed on his people and a knowledge of the consequences that disobedience would entail.

8:34 *bring them back to the land.* A reference to prisoners taken in battle.

8:35 *no rain.* Drought was another of the covenant curses listed in Dt 28:22–24.

8:36 *right way to live.* In accordance with covenant obligations (see Dt 6:18; 12:25; 13:18; 1Sa 12:23 and note).

8:37 *famine.* See Dt 32:24. *plague.* See Dt 28:21–22; 32:24. *locusts or grasshoppers.* See Dt 28:38,42. *an enemy besieges them in any of their cities.* See Dt 28:52. *disaster.* See Dt 28:61; 31:29; 32:23–25.

8:38 *aware of the afflictions of his own heart.* Conscious of one's guilt before God, with an attitude of repentance and the desire for God's forgiveness and grace (see 2Ch 6:29; Ps 38:17–18; Jer 17:9 and note).

8:39 *deal with each man according to all he does.* Not to be viewed as a request for retribution for the wrong committed (forgiveness and retribution are mutually exclusive), but as a desire for whatever discipline God in his wisdom may use to correct his people and to instruct them in the way of the covenant (see v. 40; Pr 3:11–12; Heb 12:5–15 and notes).

8:40 *fear you.* Honor and obediently serve you (see notes on Ge 20:11; Pr 1:7; see also Dt 5:29; 6:1–2; 8:6; 31:13; 2Ch 6:31; Ps 130:4).

8:41 *foreigner who does not belong to your people Israel.* One who comes from a foreign land to pray to Israel's God at the temple, as distinguished from a resident alien.

8:42 *men will hear.* See 9:9 (foreign nations generally); 10:1 (queen of Sheba); Jos 2:9–11 (Rahab); 1Sa 4:6–8 (Philistines). *your great name and your mighty hand and your outstretched arm.* God's great power, demonstrated by his interventions in the history of his people (see Dt 4:34; 5:15; 7:19; 11:2; 26:8).

8:44 *go to war ... wherever you send them.* Military initiatives undertaken with divine sanction (see, e.g., Lev 26:7; Dt 20; 21:10; 1Sa 15:3; 23:2,4 and note; 30:8; 2Sa 5:19,24 and note on 5:24). *toward the city you have chosen.* See note on v. 30.

8:46 *no one who does not sin.* A striking acknowledgment that sin is universal (see Ps 14:1 and note; see also Ge 6:5; 8:21; Ro 3:10–23). *the enemy, who takes them captive.* On the basis of Lev 26:33–45; Dt 28:64–68; 30:1–5 Solomon knew that stubborn disobedience would lead to exile from the promised land.

they are held captive, and repent and
plead[m] with you in the land of their
conquerors and say, 'We have sinned,
we have done wrong, we have acted
wickedly';[n] 48and if they turn back[o]
to you with all their heart[p] and soul
in the land of their enemies who took
them captive, and pray[q] to you toward the land you gave their fathers,
toward the city you have chosen
and the temple[r] I have built for your
Name;[s] 49then from heaven, your
dwelling place, hear their prayer and
their plea, and uphold their cause.
50And forgive your people, who have
sinned against you; forgive all the offenses they have committed against
you, and cause their conquerors to
show them mercy;[t] 51for they are your
people and your inheritance,[u] whom
you brought out of Egypt, out of that
iron-smelting furnace.[v]

52"May your eyes be open[w] to your
servant's plea and to the plea of your
people Israel, and may you listen to
them whenever they cry out to you.[x]
53For you singled them out from all
the nations of the world to be your
own inheritance,[y] just as you declared
through your servant Moses when
you, O Sovereign LORD, brought our
fathers out of Egypt."

54When Solomon had finished all these
prayers and supplications to the LORD, he
rose from before the altar of the LORD,
where he had been kneeling with his
hands spread out toward heaven. 55He
stood and blessed[z] the whole assembly of
Israel in a loud voice, saying:

56"Praise be to the LORD, who has
given rest[a] to his people Israel just as
he promised. Not one word has failed
of all the good promises[b] he gave
through his servant Moses. 57May the
LORD our God be with us as he was
with our fathers; may he never leave
us nor forsake[c] us. 58May he turn our
hearts[d] to him, to walk in all his ways
and to keep the commands, decrees
and regulations he gave our fathers.
59And may these words of mine,
which I have prayed before the LORD,
be near to the LORD our God day and
night, that he may uphold the cause
of his servant and the cause of his
people Israel according to each day's
need, 60so that all the peoples[e] of the
earth may know that the LORD is God
and that there is no other.[f] 61But your
hearts[g] must be fully committed[h] to
the LORD our God, to live by his decrees and obey his commands, as at
this time."

The Dedication of the Temple

8:62-66pp — 2Ch 7:1-10

62Then the king and all Israel with him
offered sacrifices[i] before the LORD. 63Solomon offered a sacrifice of fellowship offerings[a] to the LORD: twenty-two thousand
cattle and a hundred and twenty thousand
sheep and goats. So the king and all the Israelites dedicated[j] the temple of the LORD.
64On that same day the king consecrated
the middle part of the courtyard in front
of the temple of the LORD, and there he
offered burnt offerings, grain offerings
and the fat[k] of the fellowship offerings,
because the bronze altar[l] before the LORD
was too small to hold the burnt offerings,
the grain offerings and the fat of the fellowship offerings.[m]
65So Solomon observed the festival[n] at
that time, and all Israel with him—a vast
assembly, people from Lebo[b] Hamath[o]

[a] 63 Traditionally *peace offerings*; also in verse 64
[b] 65 Or *from the entrance to*

8:47 [m]S ver 30; S Lev 5:5; Ezr 9:15; Ne 1:6; Jer 14:20 [n]Ezr 9:7; Ps 106:6; Jer 3:25 **8:48** [o]S Dt 4:30 [p]S Dt 4:29 [q]1Jn 1:8-10 [r]Ps 5:7; 11:4; Jnh 2:4 [s]Dt 12:11-14; Ne 1:9; Jer 23:3; 31:8 **8:50** [t]2Ki 25:28; 2Ch 30:9; Ps 106:46; Da 1:9 **8:51** [u]S Ex 34:9; S Dt 9:29 [v]S Ex 1:13; Isa 48:10; Jer 11:4 **8:52** [w]S ver 29 [x]Job 30:20; Ps 3:4; 22:2; 77:1; 142:1 **8:53** [y]Ex 19:5; S 34:9 **8:55** [z]S Ex 39:43; Nu 6:23 **8:56** [a]S Ex 33:14; Dt 12:10; Heb 4:8 [b]S Jos 23:15; S Jer 29:10 **8:57** [c]S Dt 4:31; S 31:6; S Mt 28:20; Heb 13:5 **8:58** [d]S Jos 24:23 **8:60** [e]S Jos 4:24 [f]S Dt 4:35 **8:61** [g]Dt 6:5 [h]1Ki 9:4; 11:4; 15:3,14; 22:43; 2Ki 20:3; 1Ch 28:9; 29:19; 2Ch 16:9; 17:6; 25:2; Ps 119:80; Isa 38:3 **8:62** [i]S 2Sa 6:13; 1Ch 29:21; Eze 45:17 **8:63** [j]Ezr 6:16 **8:64** [k]S Ex 29:13 [l]S Ex 27:1; 2Ki 16:14; 2Ch 4:1; 8:12; 15:8; Eze 43:13-17 [m]S 2Sa 6:17 **8:65** [n]S ver 2 [o]S Nu 13:21

8:51 *iron-smelting furnace.* See Dt 4:20 and note.
8:53 *you singled them out ... to be your own inheritance.* Solomon began his prayer with an appeal to the Davidic covenant (vv. 23–30), and he closes with an appeal to the Sinaitic covenant (see Ex 19:5 and note; Lev 20:24,26; Dt 7:6 and note; 32:9).
8:54 *he had been kneeling.* Cf. v. 22; see 2Ch 6:13; see also 2Sa 7:18; Lk 22:41; Eph 3:14.
8:56 *Praise be to the LORD.* Solomon understood this historic day to be a testimony to God's covenant faithfulness. *rest to his people.* After the conquest of Canaan under the leadership of Joshua, the Lord gave the Israelites a period of rest from their enemies (Jos 11:23; 21:44; 22:4), even though there remained much land to be possessed (Jos 13:1; Jdg 1). It was only with David's victories that the rest was made durable and complete (see 2Sa 7:1; see also note on 1Ki 5:4). *as he promised.* See Dt 12:9–10. *good promises.* See Jos 21:44–45 and note on 21:45.
8:58 *turn our hearts to him.* Solomon asks for a divine work of grace within his people that will enable them to be faithful to the covenant (see Dt 30:6; Ps 51:10–12 and note; Php 2:13).
8:59 *his servant.* The king, who, as the Lord's anointed, serves as the earthly representative of God's rule over his people (see notes on Ps 2:2,7).
8:60 *so that all ... may know.* See note on Ps 46:10.
8:63 *fellowship offerings.* Involved a communion meal (see note on 1Sa 11:15). *twenty-two thousand cattle and a hundred and twenty thousand sheep and goats.* Although these numbers may seem large, there were vast numbers of people who participated in the dedication ceremony, which lasted 14 days (see vv. 1–2; see also v. 65).
8:65 *Lebo Hamath.* See note on Eze 47:15. *Wadi of Egypt.* Probably Wadi el-Arish (see note on Ge 15:18). People came to Jerusalem for the dedication of the temple from nearly the entire area of Solomon's dominion (see note on 4:21). *seven days and seven days more, fourteen days in all.* It appears that the seven-day celebration for the dedication of the temple was followed by the seven-day Feast of Tabernacles (see note on v. 2), which was observed from the 15th to the 21st of the

to the Wadi of Egypt.[p] They celebrated it
before the LORD our God for seven days
and seven days more, fourteen days in all.
66On the following day he sent the people away. They blessed the king and then
went home, joyful and glad in heart for all
the good[q] things the LORD had done for his
servant David and his people Israel.

The LORD Appears to Solomon

9:1-9pp — 2Ch 7:11-22

9 When Solomon had finished[r] building
the temple of the LORD and the royal
palace, and had achieved all he had desired to do, 2the LORD appeared[s] to him a
second time, as he had appeared to him at
Gibeon. 3The LORD said to him:

"I have heard[t] the prayer and plea
you have made before me; I have consecrated this temple, which you have
built, by putting my Name[u] there forever. My eyes[v] and my heart will always be there.
4"As for you, if you walk before me
in integrity of heart[w] and uprightness,
as David[x] your father did, and do all
I command and observe my decrees
and laws,[y] 5I will establish[z] your royal
throne over Israel forever, as I promised David your father when I said,
'You shall never fail[a] to have a man
on the throne of Israel.'
6"But if you[a] or your sons turn
away[b] from me and do not observe
the commands and decrees I have
given you[a] and go off to serve other
gods[c] and worship them, 7then I will
cut off Israel from the land[d] I have
given them and will reject this temple I have consecrated for my Name.[e]

8:65 [p]S Ge 15:18
8:66 [q]S Ex 18:9
9:1 [r]S 2Sa 7:2
9:2 [s]S 1Ki 3:5
9:3 [t]S 1Sa 9:16; 2Ki 19:20; 20:5; Ps 10:17; 34:17 [u]S Ex 20:24; S Dt 12:5 [v]S Dt 11:12
9:4 [w]S Ge 17:1 [x]Dt 17:20; 1Ki 14:8; 15:5 [y]S 1Ki 3:14; 1Ch 28:9; Pr 4:4
9:5 [z]1Ch 22:10 [a]S 2Sa 7:15
9:6 [b]Dt 28:15; 2Sa 7:14; 2Ki 18:12; Jer 17:27; 26:4; 32:23; 44:23 [c]1Ki 11:10
9:7 [d]Lev 18:24-28; Dt 4:26; S Jos 23:13; 2Ki 17:23; Jer 24:10 [e]Dt 12:5; Jer 7:14 [f]Job 17:6; Ps 44:14; Jer 24:9; Joel 2:17 [g]S Dt 28:37; Eze 5:15
9:8 [h]S Lev 26:32 [i]S Dt 29:24; Jer 7:4-15; Mt 23:38
9:9 [j]Dt 29:25; 2Ki 22:17; Jer 5:19; 13:22; 16:11,13; 22:9 [k]S Nu 25:3; Jer 40:3; 44:23; La 4:12 [l]S Dt 31:29
9:11 [m]ver 14
9:13 [n]Jos 19:27
9:14 [o]ver 11
9:15 [p]1Ki 5:13 [q]S 2Sa 5:9 [r]Jos 11:10-11 [s]S Jos 10:33

Israel will then become a byword[f]
and an object of ridicule[g] among all
peoples. 8And though this temple is
now imposing, all who pass by will
be appalled[h] and will scoff and say,
'Why has the LORD done such a thing
to this land and to this temple?'[i] 9Peo-
ple will answer,[j] 'Because they have
forsaken[k] the LORD their God, who
brought their fathers out of Egypt,
and have embraced other gods, worshiping and serving them — that is
why the LORD brought all this disaster[l] on them.'"

Solomon's Other Activities

9:10-28pp — 2Ch 8:1-18

10At the end of twenty years, during
which Solomon built these two buildings — the temple of the LORD and the royal palace — 11King Solomon gave twenty
towns in Galilee to Hiram king of Tyre,
because Hiram had supplied him with all
the cedar and pine and gold[m] he wanted.
12But when Hiram went from Tyre to see
the towns that Solomon had given him, he
was not pleased with them. 13"What kind
of towns are these you have given me, my
brother?" he asked. And he called them
the Land of Cabul,[b][n] a name they have to
this day. 14Now Hiram had sent to the king
120 talents[c] of gold.[o]
15Here is the account of the forced labor King Solomon conscripted[p] to build
the LORD's temple, his own palace, the
supporting terraces,[c][q] the wall of Jerusalem, and Hazor,[r] Megiddo and Gezer.[s]

[a] 6 The Hebrew is plural. [b] 13 *Cabul* sounds like the Hebrew for *good-for-nothing.* [c] 14 That is, about 4 1/2 tons (about 4 metric tons) [d] 15 Or *the Millo;* also in verse 24

seventh month. According to Chronicles, this was followed by a final assembly on the next day, in accordance with Lev 23:33 – 36; then on the 23rd of the month the people were sent to their homes (see 2Ch 7:8 – 10).

9:1 *When Solomon had finished.* At the earliest this would be in the 24th year (4 + 7 + 13 = 24) of Solomon's reign — 946 B.C. (see 6:1,37 – 38; 7:1; 9:10).

9:2 *he had appeared to him at Gibeon.* See 3:4 – 15.

9:3 *putting my Name there forever.* See notes on 3:2; 8:16. *My eyes and my heart will always be there.* See 8:29.

9:4 – 5 *if you walk before me in integrity of heart ... I will establish your royal throne over Israel forever.* See 8:25 and note on 2:4. The Lord reemphasizes to Solomon the importance of obedience to the covenant in order to experience its blessings rather than its curses. This was particularly necessary as Solomon's kingdom grew in influence and wealth, with all the potential for covenant-breaking that prosperity brought (see Dt 8:12 – 14,17; 31:20; 32:15).

9:6 *serve other gods and worship them.* See 11:1 – 13 and notes.

9:7 *a byword and an object of ridicule among all peoples.* See the covenant curse in Dt 28:37.

9:9 *that is why the LORD brought all this disaster on them.* See Dt 29:22 – 28; Jer 22:8 – 30.

9:10 — 10:29 Solomon's reign characterized (see note on 1:1 — 12:24).

9:10 – 28 See map No. 5 at the end of this study Bible.

9:11 *Solomon gave twenty towns in Galilee to Hiram king of Tyre.* Comparison of vv. 10 – 14 with 5:1 – 12 suggests that during Solomon's 20 years of building activity he became more indebted to Hiram than anticipated in their original agreement (see note on 5:9), which had provided for payment for labor (5:6) and wood (5:10 – 11). From vv. 11,14 it is evident that in addition to wood and labor Solomon had also acquired great quantities of gold from Hiram. It appears that Solomon gave Hiram the 20 towns in the Phoenician-Galilee border area as a surety for repayment of the gold. 2Ch 8:1 – 2 indicates that at some later date when Solomon's gold reserves were increased, perhaps after the return of the expedition to Ophir (1Ki 9:26 – 28; 10:11) or the visit of the queen of Sheba (10:1 – 13), he settled his debt with Hiram and recovered the 20 towns held as collateral.

9:13 *my brother.* A term used in international diplomacy indicating a relationship of alliance between equals (see 20:32 and note; see also chart, p. 19).

9:15 *forced labor.* Non-Israelite slave labor of a permanent nature (in contrast to the temporary conscription of Israelite workmen described in 5:13 – 16). *supporting ter-*

16(Pharaoh king of Egypt had attacked and
captured Gezer. He had set it on fire. He
killed its Canaanite inhabitants and then
gave it as a wedding gift to his daughter,[t]
Solomon's wife. 17And Solomon rebuilt Gezer.) He built up Lower Beth Horon,[u] 18Ba-
alath,[v] and Tadmor[a] in the desert, within
his land, 19as well as all his store cities[w]
and the towns for his chariots[x] and for his
horses[b]—whatever he desired to build in
Jerusalem, in Lebanon and throughout all
the territory he ruled.
20All the people left from the Amorites,
Hittites,[y] Perizzites, Hivites and Jebusites[z] (these peoples were not Israelites),
21that is, their descendants[a] remaining
in the land, whom the Israelites could
not exterminate[c][b]—these Solomon conscripted for his slave labor force,[c] as it is
to this day. 22But Solomon did not make
slaves[d] of any of the Israelites; they were
his fighting men, his government officials, his officers, his captains, and the
commanders of his chariots and charioteers. 23They were also the chief officials[e]
in charge of Solomon's projects—550 officials supervising the men who did the
work.
24After Pharaoh's daughter[f] had come
up from the City of David to the palace
Solomon had built for her, he constructed
the supporting terraces.[g]
25Three[h] times a year Solomon sacrificed burnt offerings and fellowship offerings[d] on the altar he had built for the
LORD, burning incense before the LORD
along with them, and so fulfilled the temple obligations.
26King Solomon also built ships[i] at Ezion Geber,[j] which is near Elath[k] in Edom,
on the shore of the Red Sea.[e] 27And Hiram sent his men—sailors[l] who knew the
sea—to serve in the fleet with Solomon's
men. 28They sailed to Ophir[m] and brought
back 420 talents[f] of gold,[n] which they delivered to King Solomon.

9:16 [t] 1Ki 3:1; Ps 45:12; 68:29; 72:10 **9:17** [u] S Jos 10:10 **9:18** [v] S Jos 19:44 **9:19** [w] S Ex 1:11 [x] S Dt 17:16; 1Ki 4:26; 2Ch 1:14; 9:25 **9:20** [y] S Nu 13:29 [z] S Jos 11:3 **9:21** [a] S Ge 9:25-26 [b] S Jos 15:63 [c] S Ge 49:15; S Ex 1:11; S Dt 20:11 **9:22** [d] S Lev 25:39 **9:23** [e] 1Ki 5:16 **9:24** [f] S 1Ki 3:1 [g] 2Sa 5:9; 1Ki 11:27 **9:25** [h] S Ex 23:14 **9:26** [i] 1Ki 10:22; 22:48; 2Ch 20:37; Isa 2:16 [j] S Nu 33:35 [k] 2Ki 14:22; 16:6 **9:27** [l] Eze 27:8 **9:28** [m] S Ge 10:29 [n] ver 14; 1Ki 10:10, 11, 14, 21; 2Ch 1:15; Ecc 2:8 **10:1** [o] S Ge 10:7, 28; S 25:3; Mt 12:42; Lk 11:31 [p] Eze 16:14

The Queen of Sheba Visits Solomon

10:1-13pp — 2Ch 9:1-12

10 When the queen of Sheba[o] heard
about the fame[p] of Solomon and
his relation to the name of the LORD, she

[a] *18* The Hebrew may also be read *Tamar.* [b] *19* Or *charioteers* [c] *21* The Hebrew term refers to the irrevocable giving over of things or persons to the LORD, often by totally destroying them. [d] *25* Traditionally *peace offerings* [e] *26* Hebrew *Yam Suph*; that is, Sea of Reeds [f] *28* That is, about 16 tons (about 14.5 metric tons)

races. Probably for Solomon's expansion of Jerusalem on the ridge north from David's city (see note on 2Sa 5:9). *Hazor.* Solomon's building activity at Hazor, Megiddo and Gezer was intended to strengthen the fortifications of these ancient, strategically located towns (Solomonic gates, probably built by the same masons, have been found at all three sites). Hazor was the most important fortress in the northern Galilee area, controlling the trade route running from the Euphrates River to Egypt. *Megiddo.* Another fortress along the great north-south trade route; it commanded the pass through the Carmel range from the plain of Jezreel to the coastal plain of Sharon. *Gezer.* See note on 3:1.

9:16 *Pharaoh.* See note on 3:1. *killed its Canaanite inhabitants.* Although Joshua had killed the king of Gezer at the time of the conquest (Jos 10:33; 12:12), the tribe of Ephraim had been unable to drive out its inhabitants (Jos 16:10; Jdg 1:29).

9:17 *Lower Beth Horon.* Located about nine miles northwest of Jerusalem at a pass giving entrance to the Judahite highlands and Jerusalem from the coastal plain.

9:18 *Baalath.* To be identified with either the Bealoth of Jos 15:24 located to the south of Hebron in the tribe of Judah or the Baalath southwest of Beth Horon in the tribe of Dan (Jos 19:44). *Tadmor.* See NIV text note; see also 2Ch 8:4; Eze 47:18–19 and note on 47:18.

9:19 *towns for his chariots and ... horses.* These towns are not mentioned by name but must have been strategically located throughout the land. Although Solomon was a man of peace, he was fully prepared for war (cf. Dt 17:16–17 and note).

9:20 *Amorites ... Jebusites.* See Dt 7:1; 20:17; see also notes on Ge 10:15–18; 13:7; 15:16; 23:9; Jos 5:1; Jdg 3:3; 6:10; 2Sa 21:2.

9:22 *Solomon did not make slaves of any of the Israelites.* See note on v. 15.

9:23 *550 officials.* See note on 5:16.

9:25 *Three times a year.* On the occasion of the three important annual festivals: the Feast of Unleavened Bread, the Feast of Weeks, and the Feast of Tabernacles (see Ex 23:14–17; 2Ch 8:13).

9:26 *ships.* Used in a large trading business that brought great wealth to Solomon's court (see v. 28; 10:11 and note). *Ezion Geber.* Located at the northern tip of the Gulf of Aqaba (see 22:48; Nu 33:35; Dt 2:8). *Red Sea.* The Hebrew for this term, normally read as *Yam Suph* ("sea of reeds"; see NIV text note), refers to the body of water through which the Israelites passed at the time of the exodus (see notes on Ex 13:18; 14:2). It can also be read, however, as *Yam Soph* ("sea of ⌞land's⌟ end"), a more likely reading when referring to the Red Sea, and especially (as here) to its eastern arm (the Gulf of Aqaba).

9:28 *Ophir.* A source for gold (see Ge 10:29 and note; 2Ch 8:18; Job 28:16; Ps 45:9; Isa 13:12), almugwood and precious stones (10:11), and silver, ivory, apes and baboons (10:22). Such a place is attested on a Hebrew ostracon (see note on Jer 34:7) dating perhaps to the eighth century B.C. It contains this note: "Gold of Ophir for Beth Horon—30 shekels." However, its location is disputed: Southeastern Arabia, southwestern Arabia, the northeastern African coast (in the area of Somalia), India and Zimbabwe have all been suggested. If Ophir was located in Arabia, it was probably a trading center for goods from farther east as well as from east Africa. But the three-year voyages of Solomon's merchant vessels (10:22) suggest a more distant location than the Arabian coast.

10:1 *Sheba.* Archaeological evidence suggests that Sheba is to be identified with a mercantile kingdom (Saba) that flourished in southwest Arabia (see notes on Ge 10:28; Joel 3:8) c. 900–450 B.C. It profited from the sea trade of India and east Africa by transporting luxury commodities north to Damascus and Gaza on caravan routes through the Arabian Desert. It is possible that Solomon's fleet of ships threatened Sheba's continued dominance of this trading business. *fame of Solomon.* See 4:31 and note. *his relation to the name of the LORD.* The queen of Sheba recognized a connection between the wisdom of Solomon and the God he served. Jesus used

came to test him with hard questions.[q]
2 Arriving at Jerusalem with a very great
caravan[r]—with camels carrying spices, large quantities of gold, and precious
stones—she came to Solomon and talked
with him about all that she had on her
mind. 3 Solomon answered all her questions; nothing was too hard for the king
to explain to her. 4 When the queen of Sheba saw all the wisdom of Solomon and
the palace he had built, 5 the food on his
table,[s] the seating of his officials, the attending servants in their robes, his cup-
bearers, and the burnt offerings he made
at[a] the temple of the LORD, she was overwhelmed.
6 She said to the king, "The report I
heard in my own country about your
achievements and your wisdom is true.
7 But I did not believe[t] these things until I
came and saw with my own eyes. Indeed,
not even half was told me; in wisdom and
wealth[u] you have far exceeded the report
I heard. 8 How happy your men must be!
How happy your officials, who continually
stand before you and hear[v] your wisdom!
9 Praise[w] be to the LORD your God, who
has delighted in you and placed you on
the throne of Israel. Because of the LORD's
eternal love[x] for Israel, he has made you
king, to maintain justice[y] and righteousness."
10 And she gave the king 120 talents[b] of
gold,[z] large quantities of spices, and precious stones. Never again were so many
spices brought in as those the queen of
Sheba gave to King Solomon.
11 (Hiram's ships brought gold from
Ophir;[a] and from there they brought
great cargoes of almugwood[c] and precious stones. 12 The king used the almugwood to make supports for the temple of
the LORD and for the royal palace, and to
make harps and lyres for the musicians.
So much almugwood has never been imported or seen since that day.)
13 King Solomon gave the queen of Sheba all she desired and asked for, besides
what he had given her out of his royal
bounty. Then she left and returned with
her retinue to her own country.

Solomon's Splendor

10:14-29pp — 2Ch 1:14-17; 9:13-28

14 The weight of the gold[b] that Solomon
received yearly was 666 talents,[d] 15 not including the revenues from merchants and
traders and from all the Arabian kings and
the governors of the land.
16 King Solomon made two hundred large
shields[c] of hammered gold; six hundred
bekas[e] of gold went into each shield. 17 He
also made three hundred small shields of
hammered gold, with three minas[f] of gold
in each shield. The king put them in the
Palace of the Forest of Lebanon.[d]
18 Then the king made a great throne inlaid with ivory and overlaid with fine gold.
19 The throne had six steps, and its back had
a rounded top. On both sides of the seat
were armrests, with a lion standing beside
each of them. 20 Twelve lions stood on the
six steps, one at either end of each step.
Nothing like it had ever been made for
any other kingdom. 21 All King Solomon's
goblets were gold, and all the household
articles in the Palace of the Forest of Lebanon were pure gold.[e] Nothing was made
of silver, because silver was considered of
little value in Solomon's days. 22 The king
had a fleet of trading ships[g][f] at sea along
with the ships[g] of Hiram. Once every three
years it returned, carrying gold, silver and
ivory, and apes and baboons.
23 King Solomon was greater in riches[h]

10:1 [q] S Nu 12:8; S Jdg 14:12 **10:2** [r] S Ge 24:10 **10:5** [s] 1Ki 4:22 **10:7** [t] S Ge 45:26 [u] 1Ch 29:25 **10:8** [v] Pr 8:34 **10:9** [w] S 1Ki 5:7; S Isa 42:10 [x] S Dt 7:8 [y] Ps 11:7; 33:5; 72:2; 99:4; 103:6 **10:10** [z] S 1Ki 9:28; Isa 60:6 **10:11** [a] S Ge 10:29

10:14 [b] S 1Ki 9:28 **10:16** [c] S 2Sa 8:7 **10:17** [d] S 1Ki 7:2 **10:21** [e] Isa 60:17 **10:22** [f] S 1Ki 9:26 [g] 1Ki 9:27; Ps 48:7; Isa 2:16; 23:1, 14; 60:6, 9 **10:23** [h] 1Ki 3:13; Mt 6:29

[a] *5* Or *the ascent by which he went up to* [b] *10* That is, about 4 1/2 tons (about 4 metric tons) [c] *11* Probably a variant of *algumwood*; also in verse 12 [d] *14* That is, about 25 tons (about 23 metric tons) [e] *16* That is, about 7 1/2 pounds (about 3.5 kilograms) [f] *17* That is, about 3 3/4 pounds (about 1.7 kilograms) [g] *22* Hebrew *of ships of Tarshish*

her example to condemn the people of his own day who had not recognized that "one greater than Solomon" was in their midst (Mt 12:42; Lk 11:31).

10:9 *Praise be to the LORD your God.* The queen of Sheba's confession is beautifully worded and reflects a profound understanding of Israel's covenant relationship with the Lord. However, it does not necessarily imply anything more than her recognition of the Lord as Israel's national God in conformity with the ideas of polytheistic paganism (see note on 5:7; see also 2Ch 2:12; Da 3:28–29). There is no confession that Solomon's God has become her God to the exclusion of all others.

10:10 *120 talents of gold.* See notes on 9:11,28.

10:11 *Hiram's ships.* See 9:26–28 and note on 9:26. Hiram had supplied the wood, the sailors and the expertise in construction that Israel lacked. *almugwood.* Perhaps juniper; see NIV text note and 2Ch 9:10–11. It was apparently available from Lebanon as well as Ophir (2Ch 2:8).

10:13 *all she desired and asked for.* The exchange of gifts between Solomon and the queen may have signified the effecting of a trade agreement (see note on v. 1). There is no basis for the idea sometimes suggested that she desired offspring fathered by Solomon and left Jerusalem carrying his child.

10:15 *revenues from … Arabian kings.* Tribute for passage of their caravans through Israelite territory. *governors of the land.* Perhaps those of 4:7–19.

10:16 *large shields.* Rectangular shields that afforded maximum protection (in distinction from the smaller round shields). These gold shields were probably not intended for battle but for ceremonial use, symbolizing Israel's wealth and glory. They were probably made of wood overlaid with gold. Shishak of Egypt carried them off as plunder in the fifth regnal year of Solomon's son Rehoboam (see 14:25–26). Ancient Greek sources also refer to gold shields.

10:17 *Palace of the Forest of Lebanon.* See 7:2 and note.

10:22 *fleet of trading ships.* See NIV text note; 2Ch 9:21. The same fleet is referred to in v. 11; 9:26–28. "Ships of Tarshish" are not necessarily ships that sail to Tarshish (see note on Jnh 1:3) but can designate large trading vessels.

and wisdom[i] than all the other kings of
the earth. 24The whole world sought audience with Solomon to hear the wisdom[j]
God had put in his heart. 25Year after year,
everyone who came brought a gift[k]—articles of silver and gold, robes, weapons
and spices, and horses and mules.
26Solomon accumulated chariots and
horses;[l] he had fourteen hundred chariots and twelve thousand horses,[a] which
he kept in the chariot cities and also with
him in Jerusalem. 27The king made silver
as common[m] in Jerusalem as stones,[n] and
cedar as plentiful as sycamore-fig[o] trees in
the foothills. 28Solomon's horses were imported from Egypt[b] and from Kue[c]—the
royal merchants purchased them from
Kue. 29They imported a chariot from Egypt
for six hundred shekels[d] of silver, and a
horse for a hundred and fifty.[e] They also
exported them to all the kings of the Hittites[p] and of the Arameans.

Solomon's Wives

11 King Solomon, however, loved many
foreign women[q] besides Pharaoh's
daughter—Moabites, Ammonites,[r] Edomites, Sidonians and Hittites. 2They were
from nations about which the LORD had
told the Israelites, "You must not intermarry[s] with them, because they will
surely turn your hearts after their gods."
Nevertheless, Solomon held fast to them
in love. 3He had seven hundred wives
of royal birth and three hundred concubines,[t] and his wives led him astray.[u] 4As
Solomon grew old, his wives turned his
heart after other gods,[v] and his heart was
not fully devoted[w] to the LORD his God, as
the heart of David his father had been. 5He
followed Ashtoreth[x] the goddess of the Sidonians, and Molech[f][y] the detestable god
of the Ammonites. 6So Solomon did evil[z]
in the eyes of the LORD; he did not follow
the LORD completely, as David his father
had done.
7On a hill east[a] of Jerusalem, Solomon
built a high place for Chemosh[b] the detestable god of Moab, and for Molech[c] the
detestable god of the Ammonites. 8He did
the same for all his foreign wives, who
burned incense and offered sacrifices to
their gods.
9The LORD became angry with Solomon
because his heart had turned away from
the LORD, the God of Israel, who had appeared[d] to him twice. 10Although he had
forbidden Solomon to follow other gods,[e]
Solomon did not keep the LORD's command.[f] 11So the LORD said to Solomon,
"Since this is your attitude and you have
not kept my covenant and my decrees,[g]
which I commanded you, I will most certainly tear[h] the kingdom away from you
and give it to one of your subordinates.
12Nevertheless, for the sake of David[i] your
father, I will not do it during your lifetime.
I will tear it out of the hand of your son.

10:23 [i] S 1Ki 3:12; Mt 12:42
10:24 [j] S 2Sa 14:20
10:25 [k] S 1Sa 10:27
10:26 [l] S Dt 17:16
10:27 [m] Dt 17:17 [n] Job 27:16; Isa 60:17 [o] 1Ch 27:28; Am 7:14
10:29 [p] S Nu 13:29
11:1 [q] S ver 3; S Ex 34:16 [r] 1Ki 14:21,31
11:2 [s] S Ex 34:16; 1Ki 16:31
11:3 [t] S Ge 22:24; S Est 2:14 [u] ver 1; Dt 17:17; Ne 13:26; Pr 31:3
11:4 [v] S Ex 34:16 [w] S 1Ki 8:61; S 1Ch 29:19
11:5 [x] S Jdg 2:13 [y] ver 7; S Lev 18:21; Isa 57:9; Zep 1:5
11:6 [z] S Dt 4:25
11:7 [a] 2Ki 23:13 [b] S Nu 21:29 [c] S Lev 18:21; 20:2-5; Ac 7:43
11:9 [d] S 1Ki 3:5
11:10 [e] S 1Ki 9:6 [f] 1Ki 6:12
11:11 [g] S Lev 18:4 [h] ver 31; S 1Sa 15:27; 2Ki 17:21; Mt 21:43
11:12 [i] Ps 89:33

[a] 26 Or *charioteers* [b] 28 Or possibly *Muzur,* a region in Cilicia; also in verse 29 [c] 28 Probably *Cilicia*
[d] 29 That is, about 15 pounds (about 7 kilograms)
[e] 29 That is, about 3 3/4 pounds (about 1.7 kilograms)
[f] 5 Hebrew *Milcom*; also in verse 33

10:26 *chariots and horses.* See note on 4:26. Accumulation of horses by the king was forbidden in the Mosaic law (Dt 17:16).
10:27 *sycamore-fig trees.* See note on Am 7:14.
10:29 *imported ... exported.* Through his agents (v. 28) Solomon was the middleman in a lucrative trading business. *Hittites.* See note on Ge 10:15. *Arameans.* An ancient people who occupied a large area north and east of the Sea of Galilee (cf. notes on Ge 10:22; Dt 26:5; 1Ch 18:15).

11:1–13 Solomon's folly—counterpoint to his wisdom (see ch. 3 and note on 1:1—12:24).

11:1 *loved many foreign women.* Many of Solomon's marriages were no doubt for the purpose of sealing international relationships with various kingdoms, large and small—a common practice in the ancient Near East. But this violated not only Dt 17:17 with respect to the multiplicity of wives, but also the prohibition against taking wives from the pagan peoples among whom Israel settled (see Ex 34:16; Dt 7:1–6 and note; Jos 23:12–13; Ezr 9:2; 10:2–3; Ne 13:23–27). *Moabites.* See note on Ge 19:36–38. *Ammonites.* See note on Ge 19:36–38; see also 14:21; Dt 23:3. *Edomites.* See notes on Ge 25:26; 36:1; Am 1:11; 9:12; see also Dt 23:7–8. *Sidonians.* See 16:31. *Hittites.* See note on Ge 10:15.

11:2 *they will surely turn your hearts after their gods.* As indeed they did (v. 4). An example in Israel's earlier history is found in Nu 25:1–15.
11:3 *seven hundred ... three hundred.* Cf. SS 6:8, but see note there. *concubines.* See note on Ge 25:6.

11:4 *his wives turned his heart after other gods.* As the Lord had warned (v. 2; cf. note on Dt 7:1–6). *his heart was not fully devoted to the LORD.* See 8:61. The atmosphere of paganism and idolatry introduced into Solomon's court by his foreign wives gradually led Solomon into syncretistic religious practices.
11:5 *Ashtoreth.* See v. 33; 14:15; 2Ki 23:13; see also notes on Jdg 2:13; 1Sa 7:3. *Molech.* See 2Sa 12:30 and NIV text note. Molech and Milcom (see NIV text note) are alternative names for the same pagan deity (see note on Jdg 10:6). Worship of this god not only severely jeopardized the continued recognition of the absolute kingship of the Lord over his people, but also involved (on rare occasions) the abomination of child sacrifice (see 2Ki 16:3; 17:17; 21:6; Lev 18:21 and note; 20:2–5). The names Ashtoreth and Molech have been given the vowel pattern of Hebrew *bosheth* ("shameful thing"). *Bosheth* is often substituted as a degrading name for Baal (see notes on Jdg 6:32; Jer 7:31).

11:6 *as David his father had done.* Although David committed grievous sins, he was repentant, and he was never involved in idolatrous worship.
11:7 *high place.* See note on 3:2. *Chemosh.* See note on 2Ki 3:27.
11:9 *appeared to him twice.* See 3:4–5; 9:1–9.

11:11 *not kept my covenant.* Solomon had broken the most basic demands of the covenant (see Ex 20:2–5) and thereby severely undermined the entire covenant relationship between God and his people.
11:12 *for the sake of David your father.* Because of David's unwavering loyalty to the Lord and God's covenant with him (see 2Sa 7:11–16 and notes).

[13]Yet I will not tear the whole kingdom from him, but will give him one tribe[j] for the sake[k] of David my servant and for the sake of Jerusalem, which I have chosen."[l]

Solomon's Adversaries

[14]Then the LORD raised up against Solomon an adversary,[m] Hadad the Edomite, from the royal line of Edom. [15]Earlier when David was fighting with Edom, Joab the commander of the army, who had gone up to bury the dead, had struck down all the men in Edom.[n] [16]Joab and all the Israelites stayed there for six months, until they had destroyed all the men in Edom. [17]But Hadad, still only a boy, fled to Egypt with some Edomite officials who had served his father. [18]They set out from Midian and went to Paran.[o] Then taking men from Paran with them, they went to Egypt, to Pharaoh king of Egypt, who gave Hadad a house and land and provided him with food.

[19]Pharaoh was so pleased with Hadad that he gave him a sister of his own wife, Queen Tahpenes, in marriage. [20]The sister of Tahpenes bore him a son named Genubath, whom Tahpenes brought up in the royal palace. There Genubath lived with Pharaoh's own children.

[21]While he was in Egypt, Hadad heard that David rested with his fathers and that Joab the commander of the army was also dead. Then Hadad said to Pharaoh, "Let me go, that I may return to my own country."

[22]"What have you lacked here that you want to go back to your own country?" Pharaoh asked.

"Nothing," Hadad replied, "but do let me go!"

[23]And God raised up against Solomon another adversary,[p] Rezon son of Eliada, who had fled from his master, Hadadezer[q] king of Zobah. [24]He gathered men around him and became the leader of a band of rebels when David destroyed the forces[a] ⌞of Zobah⌟; the rebels went to Damascus,[r] where they settled and took control. [25]Rezon was Israel's adversary as long as Solomon lived, adding to the trouble caused by Hadad. So Rezon ruled in Aram[s] and was hostile toward Israel.

Jeroboam Rebels Against Solomon

[26]Also, Jeroboam son of Nebat rebelled[t] against the king. He was one of Solomon's officials, an Ephraimite from Zeredah, and his mother was a widow named Zeruah.

[27]Here is the account of how he rebelled against the king: Solomon had built the supporting terraces[b][u] and had filled in the gap in the wall of the city of David his father. [28]Now Jeroboam was a man of standing,[v] and when Solomon saw how well[w] the young man did his work, he put him in charge of the whole labor force of the house of Joseph.

[29]About that time Jeroboam was going out of Jerusalem, and Ahijah[x] the prophet of Shiloh met him on the way, wearing a new cloak. The two of them were alone out in the country, [30]and Ahijah took hold of the new cloak he was wearing and tore[y]

11:13 [j] 1Ki 12:20 [k] S 2Sa 7:15 [l] Dt 12:11
11:14 [m] S 1Ki 5:4
11:15 [n] 1Ch 18:12
11:18 [o] Nu 10:12
11:23 [p] S 1Ki 5:4 [q] S 2Sa 8:3
11:24 [r] S 2Sa 8:5
11:25 [s] S Ge 10:22; S 2Sa 10:19
11:26 [t] 2Ch 13:6
11:27 [u] S 1Ki 9:24
11:28 [v] S Ru 2:1 [w] S Ge 39:4; Pr 22:29
11:29 [x] 1Ki 12:15; 14:2; 2Ch 9:29; 10:15
11:30 [y] 1Sa 15:27

[a] 24 Hebrew *destroyed them* [b] 27 Or *the Millo*

11:13 *one tribe.* Judah (see note on vv. 31–32; see also 12:20). *for the sake of Jerusalem, which I have chosen.* Now that Jerusalem contained the temple built by David's son in accordance with 2Sa 7:13, the destiny of Jerusalem and the Davidic dynasty were closely linked (see 2Ki 19:34; 21:7–8; Ps 132). The temple represented God's royal palace, where his earthly throne (the ark) was situated and where he had pledged to be present as Israel's Great King (9:3).

11:14–43 Solomon's throne threatened (see note on 1:1—12:24).

11:14 *Hadad.* The name of a Semitic storm god (see notes on Jdg 2:13; Zec 12:11) that was also taken by many Aramean (see 15:18; 20:1 and note) and Edomite kings (see Ge 36:35,39) as their royal name.

11:15 *David was fighting with Edom.* See 2Sa 8:13–14; see also map, p. 497.

11:16 *all the Israelites ... all the men in Edom.* All those, on both sides, who took part in the campaign.

11:17 *only a boy.* Probably in his early teens.

11:18 *Midian.* At this time Midianites inhabited a region on the eastern borders of Moab and Edom. *Paran.* A desert area southeast of Kadesh in the central area of the Sinai peninsula (see Nu 10:12; 12:16; 13:3). *Pharaoh king of Egypt.* See note on 3:1. *gave Hadad a house and land and ... food.* In a time of Israel's growing strength it was in Egypt's interest to befriend those who would harass Israel and keep her power in check.

11:21 *Let me go.* It appears that Hadad returned to Edom during the early days of Solomon's reign.

11:22 *What have you lacked here ... ?* Because Egypt had by this time established relatively good relations with Israel (see note on 3:1), the pharaoh was reluctant to see Hadad return to Edom and provoke trouble with Solomon.

11:23 *Zobah.* See note on 2Sa 8:3; cf. 1Ch 18:3.

11:24 *gathered men around him and became the leader.* As David had done (1Sa 22:1–2), and Jephthah before him (Jdg 11:3). *went to Damascus, where they settled and took control.* Presumably this took place in the early part of Solomon's reign (see 2Sa 8:6 for the situation in Damascus during the time of David). It is likely that Solomon's expedition (2Ch 8:3) against Hamath Zobah (the kingdom formerly ruled by Hadadezer, 2Sa 8:3–6) was provoked by opposition led by Rezon. Even though Solomon was able to retain control of the territory north of Damascus to the Euphrates (4:21,24), he was not able to drive Rezon from Damascus itself.

11:26 *rebelled against the king.* See note on v. 40.

11:27 *supporting terraces.* See 9:15 and note.

11:28 *whole labor force of the house of Joseph.* See 5:13–18. Jeroboam's supervision of the conscripted laborers from the tribes of Ephraim and Manasseh made him aware of the smoldering discontent among the people over Solomon's policies (see 12:4 and note).

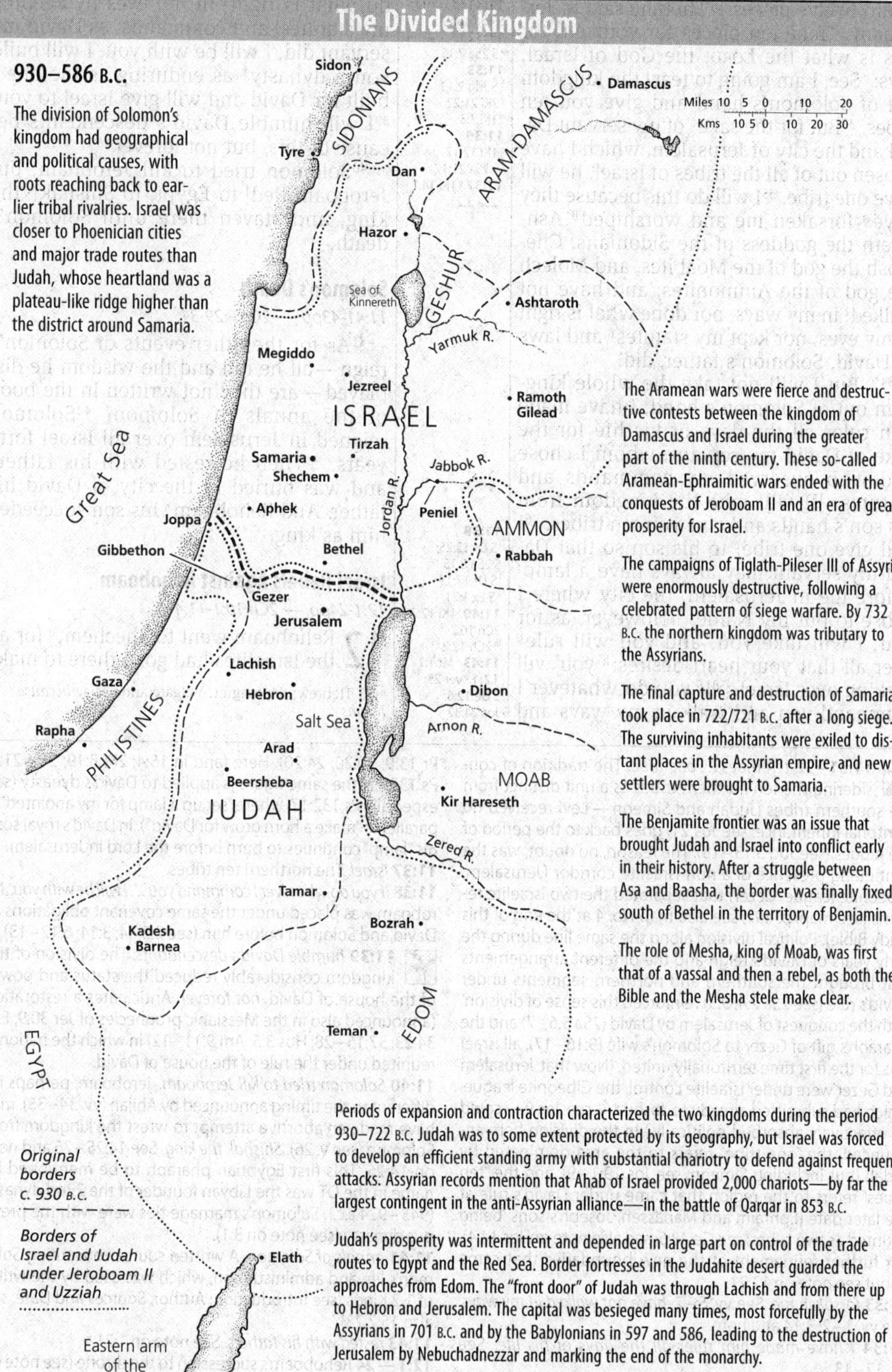
The Divided Kingdom
930–586 B.C.
The division of Solomon's kingdom had geographical and political causes, with roots reaching back to earlier tribal rivalries. Israel was closer to Phoenician cities and major trade routes than Judah, whose heartland was a plateau-like ridge higher than the district around Samaria.
Sidon
SIDONIANS
Tyre
Damascus
ARAM-DAMASCUS
Miles 10 5 0 10 20
Kms 10 5 0 10 20 30
Dan
Hazor
GESHUR
Sea of Kinnereth
Ashtaroth
Yarmuk R.
Megiddo
Jezreel
Ramoth Gilead
ISRAEL
Great Sea
Samaria
Tirzah
Shechem
Jabbok R.
Jordan R.
Aphek
Peniel
Joppa
AMMON
Gibbethon
Bethel
Rabbah
Gezer
Jerusalem
Lachish
Gaza
Hebron
Dibon
Salt Sea
Arnon R.
Rapha
PHILISTINES
Arad
Beersheba
MOAB
JUDAH
Kir Hareseth
Zered R.
Tamar
Bozrah
Kadesh Barnea
EDOM
Teman
EGYPT
Elath
Eastern arm of the Red Sea
Original borders c. 930 B.C.
Borders of Israel and Judah under Jeroboam II and Uzziah
The Aramean wars were fierce and destructive contests between the kingdom of Damascus and Israel during the greater part of the ninth century. These so-called Aramean-Ephraimitic wars ended with the conquests of Jeroboam II and an era of great prosperity for Israel.
The campaigns of Tiglath-Pileser III of Assyria were enormously destructive, following a celebrated pattern of siege warfare. By 732 B.C. the northern kingdom was tributary to the Assyrians.
The final capture and destruction of Samaria took place in 722/721 B.C. after a long siege. The surviving inhabitants were exiled to distant places in the Assyrian empire, and new settlers were brought to Samaria.
The Benjamite frontier was an issue that brought Judah and Israel into conflict early in their history. After a struggle between Asa and Baasha, the border was finally fixed south of Bethel in the territory of Benjamin.
The role of Mesha, king of Moab, was first that of a vassal and then a rebel, as both the Bible and the Mesha stele make clear.
Periods of expansion and contraction characterized the two kingdoms during the period 930–722 B.C. Judah was to some extent protected by its geography, but Israel was forced to develop an efficient standing army with substantial chariotry to defend against frequent attacks. Assyrian records mention that Ahab of Israel provided 2,000 chariots—by far the largest contingent in the anti-Assyrian alliance—in the battle of Qarqar in 853 B.C.
Judah's prosperity was intermittent and depended in large part on control of the trade routes to Egypt and the Red Sea. Border fortresses in the Judahite desert guarded the approaches from Edom. The "front door" of Judah was through Lachish and from there up to Hebron and Jerusalem. The capital was besieged many times, most forcefully by the Assyrians in 701 B.C. and by the Babylonians in 597 and 586, leading to the destruction of Jerusalem by Nebuchadnezzar and marking the end of the monarchy.
An impressive devotion to the Davidic dynastic line characterized the southern kingdom and helped to maintain stability, in contrast to the more mercurial northern kingdom.

it into twelve pieces. 31Then he said to Jeroboam, "Take ten pieces for yourself, for
this is what the LORD, the God of Israel,
says: 'See, I am going to tear[z] the kingdom
out of Solomon's hand and give you ten
tribes. 32But for the sake[a] of my servant David and the city of Jerusalem, which I have
chosen out of all the tribes of Israel, he will
have one tribe. 33I will do this because they
have[a] forsaken me and worshiped[b] Ashtoreth the goddess of the Sidonians, Chemosh the god of the Moabites, and Molech
the god of the Ammonites, and have not
walked[c] in my ways, nor done what is right
in my eyes, nor kept my statutes[d] and laws
as David, Solomon's father, did.
34" 'But I will not take the whole kingdom out of Solomon's hand; I have made
him ruler all the days of his life for the
sake of David my servant, whom I chose
and who observed my commands and
statutes. 35I will take the kingdom from
his son's hands and give you ten tribes. 36I
will give one tribe[e] to his son so that David my servant may always have a lamp[f]
before me in Jerusalem, the city where I
chose to put my Name. 37However, as for
you, I will take you, and you will rule[g]
over all that your heart desires;[h] you will
be king over Israel. 38If you do whatever I
command you and walk in my ways and

11:31 [z] S ver 11; S 1Sa 15:27
11:32 [a] S 2Sa 7:15
11:33 [b] S Jdg 2:13 [c] 2Ki 21:22 [d] 1Ki 3:3
11:36 [e] 1Ki 12:17 [f] S 2Sa 21:17
11:37 [g] 1Ki 14:7 [h] 2Sa 3:21
11:38 [i] S Dt 12:25; S 2Sa 8:15 [j] S Dt 17:19 [k] S Ex 1:21
11:40 [l] 1Ki 12:2; 2Ch 10:2 [m] 2Ch 12:2
11:43 [n] Mt 1:7
12:1 [o] ver 25; S Ge 12:6; Jos 24:32

do what is right[i] in my eyes by keeping
my statutes[j] and commands, as David my
servant did, I will be with you. I will build
you a dynasty[k] as enduring as the one I
built for David and will give Israel to you.
39I will humble David's descendants because of this, but not forever.' "
40Solomon tried to kill Jeroboam, but
Jeroboam fled[l] to Egypt, to Shishak[m] the
king, and stayed there until Solomon's
death.

Solomon's Death

11:41-43pp — 2Ch 9:29-31

41As for the other events of Solomon's
reign—all he did and the wisdom he displayed—are they not written in the book
of the annals of Solomon? 42Solomon
reigned in Jerusalem over all Israel forty
years. 43Then he rested with his fathers
and was buried in the city of David his
father. And Rehoboam[n] his son succeeded
him as king.

Israel Rebels Against Rehoboam

12:1-24pp — 2Ch 10:1-11:4

12 Rehoboam went to Shechem,[o] for all
the Israelites had gone there to make

[a] 33 Hebrew; Septuagint, Vulgate and Syriac *because he has*

11:31–32 *ten tribes ... one tribe.* The tradition of considering the ten northern tribes as a unit distinct from the southern tribes (Judah and Simeon—Levi received no territorial inheritance; see Jos 21) goes back to the period of the judges (see Jdg 5:13–18). The reason, no doubt, was the continuing presence of a non-Israelite corridor (Jerusalem, Gibeonite league, Gezer) that separated the two Israelite regions (see map, p. 497; see also map No. 4 at the end of this study Bible). Political division along the same line during the early years of David's reign and the different arrangements that brought the southern and northern segments under David's rule (see 2Sa 2:4; 5:3) reinforced this sense of division. With the conquest of Jerusalem by David (2Sa 5:6–7) and the pharaoh's gift of Gezer to Solomon's wife (9:16–17), all Israel was for the first time territorially united. (Now that Jerusalem and Gezer were under Israelite control, the Gibeonite league, which had submitted already to Joshua—see Jos 9—could be effectively absorbed politically.) In the division here announced, the "one tribe" refers to the area dominated by Judah (but including Simeon; see Jos 19:1–9), and the "ten tribes" refers to the region that came under David's rule at the later date (Ephraim and Manasseh, Joseph's sons, being counted as two tribes; see Ge 48:5; see also note on Jos 14:4). For further refinement of the new boundaries that came about see note on 12:21.

11:33 *forsaken me.* See vv. 5–7. *have not walked in my ways.* See vv. 1–2; 3:14 and note.

11:34 *I have made him ruler all the days of his life.* See vv. 12–13.

11:35 *from his son's hands.* From Rehoboam (see 12:1–24).

11:36 *a lamp before me in Jerusalem.* Symbolizes the continuance of the Davidic dynasty in the city where God had chosen to cause his Name to dwell (see v. 13 and note). In a number of passages, the burning or snuffing out of one's lamp signifies the flourishing or ceasing of one's life (Job 18:6; 21:17; Pr 13:9; 20:20; 24:20). Here (and in 15:4; 2Ki 8:19; 2Ch 21:7; Ps 132:17) the same figure is applied to David's dynasty (see especially Ps 132:17, where "set up a lamp for my anointed" is parallel to "make a horn grow for David"). In David's royal sons his "lamp" continues to burn before the Lord in Jerusalem.

11:37 *Israel.* The northern ten tribes.

11:38 *If you do whatever I command you ... I will be with you.* Jeroboam was placed under the same covenant obligations as David and Solomon before him (see 2:3–4; 3:14; 6:12–13).

11:39 *humble David's descendants.* The division of the kingdom considerably reduced the status and power of the house of David. *not forever.* Anticipates a restoration (announced also in the Messianic prophecies of Jer 30:9; Eze 34:23; 37:15–28; Hos 3:5; Am 9:11–12) in which the nation is reunited under the rule of the house of David.

11:40 *Solomon tried to kill Jeroboam.* Jeroboam, perhaps indifferent to the timing announced by Ahijah (vv. 34–35), may have made an abortive attempt to wrest the kingdom from Solomon (see v. 26). *Shishak the king.* See 14:25–26 and note on 14:25. This first Egyptian pharaoh to be mentioned by name in the OT was the Libyan founder of the 22nd dynasty (945–924 B.C.). Solomon's marriage ties were with the previous dynasty (see note on 3:1).

11:41 *annals of Solomon.* A written source concerning Solomon's life and administration, which was used by the writer of 1,2 Kings (see Introduction: Author, Sources and Date; see also 15:7,23).

11:43 *rested with his fathers.* See note on 1:21.

12:1—24 Rehoboam's succession to the throne (see note on 1:1—12:24).

12:1 *Shechem.* A city of great historical significance located in the hill country of northern Ephraim (see Ge 12:6; 33:18–20; Jos 8:30–35 and note on 8:30; see also Jos 20:7; 21:21; 24:1–33). *all the Israelites.* That is, representatives of the northern tribes (see v. 16). The fact that David became king

him king. 2When Jeroboam son of Nebat
heard this (he was still in Egypt, where he
had fled[p] from King Solomon), he returned
from[a] Egypt. 3So they sent for Jeroboam,
and he and the whole assembly of Israel
went to Rehoboam and said to him: 4"Your
father put a heavy yoke[q] on us, but now
lighten the harsh labor and the heavy yoke
he put on us, and we will serve you."
5Rehoboam answered, "Go away for
three days and then come back to me." So
the people went away.
6Then King Rehoboam consulted the
elders[r] who had served his father Solomon during his lifetime. "How would you
advise me to answer these people?" he
asked.
7They replied, "If today you will be a
servant to these people and serve them
and give them a favorable answer,[s] they
will always be your servants."
8But Rehoboam rejected[t] the advice the
elders gave him and consulted the young
men who had grown up with him and
were serving him. 9He asked them, "What
is your advice? How should we answer
these people who say to me, 'Lighten the
yoke your father put on us'?"
10The young men who had grown up
with him replied, "Tell these people who
have said to you, 'Your father put a heavy
yoke on us, but make our yoke lighter'—tell them, 'My little finger is thicker than my father's waist. 11My father
laid on you a heavy yoke; I will make
it even heavier. My father scourged you
with whips; I will scourge you with scorpions.'"

12:2 [p]S 1Ki 11:40
12:4 [q]S 1Sa 8:11-18; 1Ki 4:20-28
12:6 [r]S 1Ki 4:2
12:7 [s]Pr 15:1
12:8 [t]Lev 19:32
12:14 [u]Ex 1:14
12:15 [v]S Dt 2:30; 2Ch 25:20 [w]S 1Ki 11:29
12:16 [x]S Ge 31:14 [y]S 2Sa 20:1 [z]Isa 7:17
12:17 [a]1Ki 11:13,36
12:18 [b]S 2Sa 20:24 [c]S Jos 7:25
12:19 [d]2Ki 17:21

12Three days later Jeroboam and all
the people returned to Rehoboam, as the
king had said, "Come back to me in three
days." 13The king answered the people
harshly. Rejecting the advice given him
by the elders, 14he followed the advice of
the young men and said, "My father made
your yoke heavy; I will make it even heavier. My father scourged[u] you with whips; I
will scourge you with scorpions." 15So the
king did not listen to the people, for this
turn of events was from the LORD,[v] to fulfill the word the LORD had spoken to Jeroboam son of Nebat through Ahijah[w] the
Shilonite.
16When all Israel saw that the king refused to listen to them, they answered the
king:

"What share[x] do we have in David,
what part in Jesse's son?
To your tents, O Israel![y]
Look after your own house,
O David!"

So the Israelites went home.[z] 17But as
for the Israelites who were living in the
towns of Judah,[a] Rehoboam still ruled
over them.
18King Rehoboam sent out Adoniram,[bb]
who was in charge of forced labor, but all
Israel stoned him to death.[c] King Rehoboam, however, managed to get into his
chariot and escape to Jerusalem. 19So Israel has been in rebellion against the house
of David[d] to this day.

[a] 2 Or *he remained in* [b] 18 Some Septuagint manuscripts and Syriac (see also 1 Kings 4:6 and 5:14); Hebrew *Adoram*

over the northern tribes on the basis of a covenant (see 2Sa 5:3) suggests that their act of submission was to be renewed with each new king and that it was subject to negotiation.
12:2 *heard this.* Heard about the death of Solomon (11:43). *returned from Egypt.* See 2Ch 10:2.
12:4 *put a heavy yoke on us.* Smoldering discontent with Solomon's heavy taxation and conscription of labor and military forces flared up into strong expression (see 4:7, 22–23,27–28; 5:13–14; 9:22; see also notes on 9:15; 11:28). Conditions had progressively worsened since the early days of Solomon's rule (see 4:20).
12:6 *elders who had served his father Solomon.* Officials of Solomon's government such as Adoniram (4:6) and the district governors (4:7–19).
12:7 Authority in the kingdom of God is for service, not for personal aggrandizement.
12:8 *young men.* Young in comparison to the officials who had served Solomon. Rehoboam was 41 years old when he became king (14:21). *serving him.* Apparently Rehoboam had quickly established new administrative positions for friends and associates of his own generation.
12:10 *My little finger is thicker than my father's waist.* A proverb claiming that Rehoboam's weakest measures will be far stronger than his father's strongest measures.
12:11 *scorpions.* Metal-spiked leather lashes. Not only will governmental burdens on the people be increased, but the punishment for not complying with the government's directives will also be intensified.
12:14 *followed the advice of the young men.* Rehoboam's answer reflects a despotic spirit completely contrary to the covenantal character of Israelite kingship (see Dt 17:14–20 and notes; see also note on 1Sa 10:25).
12:15 *this turn of events was from the LORD.* By this statement the writer of Kings does not condone either the foolish act of Rehoboam or the revolutionary spirit of the northern tribes, but he reminds the reader that all these things occurred to bring about the divinely announced punishment on the house of David for Solomon's idolatry and breach of the covenant (11:9–13). For the relationship between divine sovereignty over all things and human responsibility for evil acts see note on 2Sa 24:1. *the word the LORD had spoken to Jeroboam ... through Ahijah.* See 11:29–39.
12:16 *all Israel.* The northern tribes (see note on v. 1). *David.* The Davidic dynasty (see 2Sa 20:1 for an earlier expression of the same sentiment).
12:17 *Israelites who were living in the towns of Judah.* People originally from the northern tribes who had settled in Judah. They were later to be joined by others from the north who desired to serve the Lord and worship at the temple (see 2Ch 11:16–17).
12:18 *Adoniram, who was in charge of forced labor.* He had served in the same capacity under both David (2Sa 20:24 and note) and Solomon (see 1Ki 4:6 and note; 5:14).
12:19 *house of David.* An early non-Biblical reference to the "house of David" was found in 1993 on a fragment of a stele at Tell Dan. The reading "house of David" is clear, but

[20]When all the Israelites heard that Jeroboam had returned, they sent and called
him to the assembly and made him king
over all Israel. Only the tribe of Judah remained loyal to the house of David.[e]
[21]When Rehoboam arrived in Jerusalem,
he mustered the whole house of Judah
and the tribe of Benjamin — a hundred
and eighty thousand fighting men — to
make war[f] against the house of Israel and
to regain the kingdom for Rehoboam son
of Solomon.
[22]But this word of God came to Shemaiah[g] the man of God:[h] [23]"Say to Rehoboam son of Solomon king of Judah, to the
whole house of Judah and Benjamin, and
to the rest of the people, [24]'This is what the
LORD says: Do not go up to fight against
your brothers, the Israelites. Go home, every one of you, for this is my doing.'" So
they obeyed the word of the LORD and went
home again, as the LORD had ordered.

12:20 [e]1Ki 11:13,32; Eze 37:16 **12:21** [f]1Ki 14:30; 15:6,16; 2Ch 11:1 **12:22** [g]2Ch 12:5-7 [h]S Dt 33:1; 2Ki 4:7

12:25 [i]S ver 1 [j]S Jdg 8:8,17 **12:27** [k]Dt 12:5-6 **12:28** [l]S Ex 32:4; S 2Ch 11:15 [m]S Ex 32:8 **12:29** [n]S Ge 12:8; S Jos 7:2 [o]Jdg 18:27-31; Am 8:14

Golden Calves at Bethel and Dan

[25]Then Jeroboam fortified Shechem[i]
in the hill country of Ephraim and lived
there. From there he went out and built
up Peniel.[a][j]
[26]Jeroboam thought to himself, "The
kingdom will now likely revert to the
house of David. [27]If these people go up to
offer sacrifices at the temple of the LORD
in Jerusalem,[k] they will again give their
allegiance to their lord, Rehoboam king
of Judah. They will kill me and return to
King Rehoboam."
[28]After seeking advice, the king made
two golden calves.[l] He said to the people,
"It is too much for you to go up to Jerusalem. Here are your gods, O Israel, who
brought you up out of Egypt."[m] [29]One he
set up in Bethel,[n] and the other in Dan.[o]

[a] 25 Hebrew *Penuel*, a variant of *Peniel*

two other names had to be partially restored. If the restorations are correct, the king of Damascus (probably Hazael) is boasting of victories over "Joram son of Ahab, king of Israel" and "Ahaziah son of Jehoram, king of the house of David." Since Joram ruled over Israel 852–841 B.C. and Ahaziah over Judah in 841, this would date the inscription to 841 or shortly after — less than a century and a half after David's reign (1010–970). *this day.* The time of the writing of the source from which the author of 1 Kings derived this account (see Introduction: Author, Sources and Date).

12:20–24 The kingdom is divided (see map, p. 497; see also chart, pp. 504–505, and note on 12:25 — 2Ki 17:41).

12:21 *tribe of Benjamin.* Although the bulk of Benjamin was aligned with the northern tribes (see note on 11:31–32), the area around Jerusalem remained under Rehoboam's control (as did the Gibeonite cities and Gezer). The northern boundary of Judah must have reached almost to Bethel (12 miles north of Jerusalem) — which Abijah, Rehoboam's son, even held for a short while (see 2Ch 13:19). *a hundred and eighty thousand fighting men.* Probably includes all support personnel together with those who would actually be committed to battle.

12:22 *Shemaiah.* Wrote a history of Rehoboam's reign (2Ch 12:15). Another of his prophecies is recorded in 2Ch 12:5–8. *man of God.* A common way of referring to a prophet (see, e.g., 13:1; Dt 18:18; 33:1; 1Sa 2:27; 9:9–10).

12:23 *rest of the people.* See note on v. 17.

12:24 *went home again.* Although full-scale civil war was averted, intermittent skirmishes and battles between Israel and Judah continued throughout the reigns of Rehoboam, Abijah and Asa, until political instability in Israel after the death of Baasha finally brought the conflict to a halt. Asa's son Jehoshaphat entered into an alliance with Ahab and sealed the relationship by the marriage of his son Jehoram to Ahab's daughter Athaliah (see 14:30; 15:6,16 and note on 15:16; 22:2,44 and note on 22:44; 2Ki 8:18 and note). However, Jeroboam's use of a pagan fertility-god symbol to signify the Lord's presence in Israel (vv. 28–30) involved a radical departure from the representation of the Lord seated enthroned on the ark of the covenant that held the tablets of the covenant law that spelled out the basic law for the Lord's kingdom people. In this way he prepared the way for the thoroughly paganized view of Israel's God against which the prophets powerfully protested. This is the great sin that led to the downfall of Jeroboam's dynasty (see v. 30; 13:34 and notes), and ultimately to the downfall of the northern kingdom (see 14:16; 2Ki 17:21,23 and notes).

12:25 — 2Ki 17:41 The period of the two kingdoms. In this large central section of 1,2 Kings major attention is given to the northern kingdom (of 839 verses only 157 are devoted to the Davidic kings of Judah) — to the acts of its kings and the prophetic activities related to them. It was in the north that the emerging kingdom of God was most at risk, the movement toward apostasy more powerful, and the Lord's struggle for the hearts of his people the more intense. In the face of apostatizing kings, with their puppet priests and prophets, the only faithful representatives of God's rule were the prophets he raised up, especially Elijah and Elisha (see Introduction: Content). Through their ministries the Lord was uniquely present among his people, not through the unfaithful kings and their paid religious functionaries. In the southern kingdom he was uniquely present among his people primarily through his own presence and his priests at the temple in Jerusalem.

12:25 *Peniel.* A town in Transjordan (see Ge 32:31; Jdg 8:9,17) of strategic importance for defense against the Arameans of Damascus (see 11:23–25) and the Ammonites.

12:26 *revert to the house of David.* Jeroboam did not have confidence in the divine promise given to him through Ahijah (see 11:38) and thus took action that forfeited the theocratic basis for his kingship.

12:28 *two golden calves.* Pagan gods of the Arameans and Canaanites were often represented as standing on calves or bulls as symbols of their strength and fertility (see note on Jdg 2:13). *Here are your gods, O Israel, who brought you up out of Egypt.* Like Aaron (Ex 32:4–5), Jeroboam attempted to combine the pagan calf symbol with the worship of the Lord, though he attempted no physical representation of the Lord — no "god" stood on the backs of his bulls.

12:29 *Bethel.* Located about 12 miles north of Jerusalem close to the border of Ephraim but within the territory of Benjamin (Jos 18:11–13,22). Bethel held a prominent place in the history of Israel's worship of the Lord (see Ge 12:8; 28:11–19; 35:6–7; Jdg 20:26–28; 1Sa 7:16). After Jerusalem, Bethel is the city most often mentioned by name in the OT. *Dan.* Located in the far north of the land near Mount Hermon. A similarly paganized worship was practiced there from the days of the judges (Jdg 18:30–31). A raised platform ("high place") and shrine found at Dan may be the ones built by Jeroboam I and used by his successors (see vv. 30–31).

30 And this thing became a sin;[p] the people went even as far as Dan to worship the one there.

31 Jeroboam built shrines[q] on high places and appointed priests[r] from all sorts of people, even though they were not Levites. 32 He instituted a festival on the fifteenth day of the eighth[s] month, like the festival held in Judah, and offered sacrifices on the altar. This he did in Bethel,[t] sacrificing to the calves he had made. And at Bethel he also installed priests at the high places he had made. 33 On the fifteenth day of the eighth month, a month of his own choosing, he offered sacrifices on the altar he had built at Bethel.[u] So he instituted the festival for the Israelites and went up to the altar to make offerings.

The Man of God From Judah

13 By the word of the LORD a man of God[v] came from Judah to Bethel,[w] as Jeroboam was standing by the altar to make an offering. 2 He cried out against the altar by the word of the LORD: "O altar, altar! This is what the LORD says: 'A son named Josiah[x] will be born to the house of David. On you he will sacrifice the priests of the high places[y] who now make offerings here, and human bones will be burned on you.' " 3 That same day the man of God gave a sign:[z] "This is the sign the LORD has declared: The altar will be split apart and the ashes on it will be poured out."

4 When King Jeroboam heard what the man of God cried out against the altar at Bethel, he stretched out his hand from the altar and said, "Seize him!" But the hand he stretched out toward the man shriveled up, so that he could not pull it back. 5 Also, the altar was split apart and its ashes poured out according to the sign given by the man of God by the word of the LORD.

6 Then the king said to the man of God, "Intercede[a] with the LORD your God and pray for me that my hand may be restored." So the man of God interceded with the LORD, and the king's hand was restored and became as it was before.

7 The king said to the man of God, "Come home with me and have something to eat, and I will give you a gift."[b]

8 But the man of God answered the king, "Even if you were to give me half your possessions,[c] I would not go with you, nor would I eat bread[d] or drink water here. 9 For I was commanded by the word of the LORD: 'You must not eat bread or drink water or return by the way you came.' " 10 So he took another road and did not return by the way he had come to Bethel.

11 Now there was a certain old prophet living in Bethel, whose sons came and told him all that the man of God had done there that day. They also told their father what he had said to the king. 12 Their father asked them, "Which way did he go?" And his sons showed him which road the man of God from Judah had taken. 13 So he said to his sons, "Saddle the donkey for me." And when they had saddled the donkey for him, he mounted it 14 and rode after the man of God. He found him sitting under an oak tree and asked, "Are

12:30 [p] 1Ki 13:34; 14:16; 15:26,30; 16:2; 2Ki 3:3; 10:29; 13:2; 17:21
12:31 [q] S Lev 26:30; 1Ki 13:32; 2Ki 17:29 [r] S Ex 29:9; 1Ki 13:33; 2Ki 17:32; 2Ch 11:14-15; 13:9
12:32 [s] S Nu 29:12 [t] 2Ki 10:29
12:33 [u] 2Ki 23:15; Am 7:13
13:1 [v] S Dt 33:1; S Jdg 13:6 [w] Am 7:13
13:2 [x] 2Ki 23:15-16, 20; 2Ch 34:5 [y] S Lev 26:30
13:3 [z] S Ge 24:14; S Ex 4:8; S Jn 2:11
13:6 [a] S Ge 20:7; S Nu 11:2; S Jer 37:3; Ac 8:24
13:7 [b] S 1Sa 9:7
13:8 [c] Nu 22:18 [d] ver 16

12:30 *this thing became a sin.* Jeroboam's royal policy promoted violation of the second commandment (Ex 20:4–6). It inevitably led to Israel's violation of the first commandment also (Ex 20:3) and opened the door for the entrance of fully pagan practices into Israel's religious rites (especially in the time of Ahab; see 16:29–34). Jeroboam foolishly abandoned religious principle for political expediency and in so doing forfeited the promise given him by the prophet Ahijah (see 11:38).
12:31 *Jeroboam built shrines on high places.* See note on 3:2. *not Levites.* Many of the priests and Levites of the northern kingdom migrated to Judah because Jeroboam bypassed them when appointing priests in the north (see 2Ch 11:13–16).
12:32 *festival held in Judah.* Apparently the Feast of Tabernacles, observed in Judah on the 15th to the 21st of the seventh month (see 8:2; Lev 23:34).
13:1 *man of God.* See note on 12:22. *from Judah to Bethel.* God sent a prophet from the southern kingdom to Bethel in the northern kingdom. Possibly he did this to emphasize that the divinely appointed political division (11:11,29–39; 12:15,24) was not intended to establish rival religious systems in the two kingdoms. Two centuries later the prophet Amos from Tekoa in Judah also went to Bethel in the northern kingdom to pronounce God's judgment on Jeroboam II (Am 7:10–17).
13:2 *Josiah.* A prophetic announcement of the rule of King Josiah, who came to the throne in Judah nearly 300 years after the division of the kingdom. *will sacrifice the priests of the high places.* Fulfilled in 2Ki 23:15–20.
13:3 *sign.* The immediate fulfillment of a short-term prediction would serve to authenticate the reliability of the longer-term prediction (see Dt 18:21–22 and note on Dt 13:1–5).
13:5 *its ashes poured out.* Visibly demonstrating God's power to fulfill the words of the prophet (see note on v. 3) and providing a clear sign to Jeroboam that his offering was unacceptable to the Lord (see Lev 6:10–11).
13:6 *your God.* Should not be taken as implying that Jeroboam no longer considered the Lord as his own God (cf. 2:3; Ge 27:20), but as suggesting he recognized that the prophet had a privileged access to God. *king's hand was restored.* The Lord's gracious response to Jeroboam's request is to be seen as an additional sign (see v. 3) given to confirm the word of the prophet and to move Jeroboam to repentance.
13:7 *Come home with me.* Jeroboam attempted to renew his prestige in the eyes of the people by creating the impression that there was no fundamental break between himself and the prophetic order (see 1Sa 15:30 for a similar situation).
13:9 *You must not.* The prophet's refusal of Jeroboam's invitation rested on a previously given divine command. It underscored God's extreme displeasure with the apostate worship at Bethel.

you the man of God who came from Judah?"
"I am," he replied.
15 So the prophet said to him, "Come
home with me and eat."
16 The man of God said, "I cannot turn
back and go with you, nor can I eat bread[e]
or drink water with you in this place. 17 I
have been told by the word of the LORD:
'You must not eat bread or drink water
there or return by the way you came.'"
18 The old prophet answered, "I too am a
prophet, as you are. And an angel said to
me by the word of the LORD:[f] 'Bring him
back with you to your house so that he
may eat bread and drink water.'" (But he
was lying[g] to him.) 19 So the man of God
returned with him and ate and drank in
his house.
20 While they were sitting at the table, the
word of the LORD came to the old prophet
who had brought him back. 21 He cried out
to the man of God who had come from
Judah, "This is what the LORD says: 'You
have defied[h] the word of the LORD and
have not kept the command the LORD your
God gave you. 22 You came back and ate
bread and drank water in the place where
he told you not to eat or drink. Therefore
your body will not be buried in the tomb
of your fathers.'"
23 When the man of God had finished
eating and drinking, the prophet who had
brought him back saddled his donkey for
him. 24 As he went on his way, a lion[i] met
him on the road and killed him, and his
body was thrown down on the road, with
both the donkey and the lion standing beside it. 25 Some people who passed by saw
the body thrown down there, with the lion
standing beside the body, and they went
and reported it in the city where the old
prophet lived.
26 When the prophet who had brought
him back from his journey heard of it, he
said, "It is the man of God who defied[j] the
word of the LORD. The LORD has given him
over to the lion, which has mauled him
and killed him, as the word of the LORD
had warned him."
27 The prophet said to his sons, "Saddle the donkey for me," and they did so.
28 Then he went out and found the body
thrown down on the road, with the donkey
and the lion standing beside it. The lion
had neither eaten the body nor mauled
the donkey. 29 So the prophet picked up the
body of the man of God, laid it on the donkey, and brought it back to his own city
to mourn for him and bury him. 30 Then
he laid the body in his own tomb,[k] and
they mourned over him and said, "Oh, my
brother!"[l]
31 After burying him, he said to his sons,
"When I die, bury me in the grave where
the man of God is buried; lay my bones[m]
beside his bones. 32 For the message he declared by the word of the LORD against the
altar in Bethel and against all the shrines
on the high places[n] in the towns of Samaria[o] will certainly come true."[p]
33 Even after this, Jeroboam did not
change his evil ways,[q] but once more appointed priests for the high places from
all sorts[r] of people. Anyone who wanted to become a priest he consecrated for
the high places. 34 This was the sin[s] of the
house of Jeroboam that led to its downfall and to its destruction[t] from the face
of the earth.

13:16 [e] ver 8 **13:18** [f] 1Ki 22:6, 12; 2Ch 35:21; Isa 36:10 [g] S Ge 19:14; S Dt 13:3 **13:21** [h] ver 26; S 1Sa 13:14; 1Ki 20:35 **13:24** [i] 1Ki 20:36 **13:26** [j] S ver 21 **13:30** [k] 2Ki 23:17 [l] Jer 22:18 **13:31** [m] 2Ki 23:18 **13:32** [n] S Lev 26:30; S 1Ki 12:31 [o] 1Ki 16:24, 28; 20:1; 2Ki 10:1; 15:13 [p] 2Ki 23:16 **13:33** [q] 1Ki 15:26 [r] S 1Ki 12:31 **13:34** [s] S 1Ki 12:30 [t] 1Ki 14:10; 15:29; 2Ki 9:9; Jer 35:17; Am 7:9

13:18 *I too am a prophet, as you are.* A half-truth. It is likely that the old prophet in Bethel had faithfully proclaimed the word of the Lord in former days, but those days had long since passed.

13:19 *the man of God returned with him.* Neither the old prophet's lie nor his own need justified disobedience to the direct and explicit command of the Lord. His public action in this matter undermined respect for the divine authority of all he had said at Bethel.

13:20 *the word of the LORD came to the old prophet.* The fundamental distinction between a true and a false prophecy here becomes apparent. The false prophecy arises from one's own imagination (Jer 23:16; Eze 13:2,7) while the true prophecy is from God (Ex 4:16; Dt 18:18; Jer 1:9; 2Pe 1:21). For a classic exposition of this truth see Jer 28 and notes.

13:22 *your body will not be buried in the tomb of your fathers.* The man of God from Judah will die far from his own home and family burial plot.

13:24 *killed him.* A stern warning to Jeroboam that God takes his word very seriously. *the donkey and the lion standing beside it.* The remarkable fact that the donkey did not run and the lion did not attack the donkey or disturb the man's body (v. 28) clearly stamped the incident as a divine judgment. This additional miracle was reported in Bethel (v. 25) and provided yet another sign authenticating the message that the man of God from Judah had delivered at Jeroboam's altar. But Jeroboam was still not moved to repentance (v. 33).

13:30 *laid the body in his own tomb.* See v. 22 and note. The old prophet did the only thing left for him to do in order to make amends for his deliberate and fatal deception.

13:31 *grave where the man of God is buried.* The old prophet chose in this way to identify himself with the message that the man of God from Judah had given at Bethel.

13:32 *Samaria.* As the capital of the northern kingdom, Samaria is used to designate the entire territory of the northern ten tribes (see note on 16:24). However, Samaria was not established until about 50 years after this (16:23–24). The use of the name here reflects the perspective of the author of Kings (see note on Ge 14:14 for a similar instance of the use of a place-name — Dan — of later origin than the historical incident with which it is connected).

13:33 *appointed priests ... from all sorts of people.* See 12:31 and note.

13:34 *sin.* The sin in 12:30 was the establishment of a paganized worship; here it is persistence in this worship with all its attendant evils.

Ahijah's Prophecy Against Jeroboam

14 At that time Abijah son of Jeroboam
became ill, 2and Jeroboam said to his
wife, "Go, disguise yourself, so you won't
be recognized as the wife of Jeroboam.
Then go to Shiloh. Ahijah[u] the prophet
is there — the one who told me I would
be king over this people. 3Take ten loaves
of bread[v] with you, some cakes and a jar
of honey, and go to him. He will tell you
what will happen to the boy." 4So Jeroboam's wife did what he said and went to
Ahijah's house in Shiloh.
Now Ahijah could not see; his sight was
gone because of his age. 5But the LORD had
told Ahijah, "Jeroboam's wife is coming
to ask you about her son, for he is ill, and
you are to give her such and such an answer. When she arrives, she will pretend
to be someone else."
6So when Ahijah heard the sound of her
footsteps at the door, he said, "Come in,
wife of Jeroboam. Why this pretense?[w] I
have been sent to you with bad news. 7Go,
tell Jeroboam that this is what the LORD,
the God of Israel, says:[x] 'I raised you up
from among the people and made you a
leader[y] over my people Israel. 8I tore[z] the
kingdom away from the house of David
and gave it to you, but you have not been
like my servant David, who kept my commands and followed me with all his heart,
doing only what was right[a] in my eyes.
9You have done more evil[b] than all who
lived before you.[c] You have made for yourself other gods, idols[d] made of metal; you
have provoked[e] me to anger and thrust me
behind your back.[f]
10" 'Because of this, I am going to bring
disaster[g] on the house of Jeroboam. I will
cut off from Jeroboam every last male in
Israel — slave or free.[h] I will burn up the
house of Jeroboam as one burns dung,
until it is all gone.[i] 11Dogs[j] will eat those
belonging to Jeroboam who die in the city,
and the birds of the air[k] will feed on those
who die in the country. The LORD has spoken!'
12"As for you, go back home. When you
set foot in your city, the boy will die. 13All
Israel will mourn for him and bury him.
He is the only one belonging to Jeroboam
who will be buried, because he is the only
one in the house of Jeroboam in whom
the LORD, the God of Israel, has found anything good.[l]
14"The LORD will raise up for himself a
king over Israel who will cut off the family
of Jeroboam. This is the day! What? Yes,
even now.[a] 15And the LORD will strike Israel, so that it will be like a reed swaying
in the water. He will uproot[m] Israel from
this good land that he gave to their forefathers and scatter them beyond the River,[b]

14:2 [u]S 1Ki 11:29
14:3 [v]S 1Sa 9:7
14:6 [w]S 1Sa 28:12
14:7 [x]1Ki 15:29 [y]1Ki 11:37
14:8 [z]S 1Sa 15:27 [a]S 2Sa 8:15; 1Ki 3:3; 15:5; 2Ki 14:3; 15:3,34; 16:2; 18:3; 20:3; 22:2
14:9 [b]1Ki 16:30,33; 21:25; 2Ki 21:9,11; 24:3 [c]1Ki 16:2 [d]S Ex 20:4; S 32:4; 2Ch 11:15 [e]Dt 32:16; 1Ki 16:2; Ps 78:58; Jer 7:18; 8:19; 32:32; 44:3; Eze 8:17; 16:26 [f]Ne 9:26; Ps 50:17; Jer 2:27; 32:33; Eze 23:35
14:10 [g]S Jos 23:15; S 1Ki 13:34 [h]S Dt 32:36; 2Ki 9:8-9 [i]1Sa 12:25; 15:26; 1Ki 15:29; Hos 13:11
14:11 [j]1Ki 16:4; 21:24 [k]S Ge 40:19; S Dt 28:26
14:13 [l]2Ch 12:12; 19:3
14:15 [m]S Dt 29:28; S 2Ch 7:20 [n]Jer 44:3 [o]S Dt 12:3

[a] *14* The meaning of the Hebrew for this sentence is uncertain. [b] *15* That is, the Euphrates

14:1 *At that time.* Probably indicating a time not far removed from the event narrated in ch. 13. *Abijah.* Means "My (divine) Father is the LORD," suggesting that Jeroboam, at least to some degree, desired to be regarded as a worshiper of the Lord.

14:2 *disguise yourself.* Jeroboam's attempt to mislead the prophet Ahijah into giving a favorable prophecy concerning the sick boy indicates (1) his consciousness of his own guilt, (2) his superstition that prophecy worked in a magical way and (3) his confused but real respect for the power of the Lord's prophet. *Shiloh.* See note on 1Sa 1:3. *who told me I would be king over this people.* See 11:29–39.

14:5 *the LORD had told Ahijah.* See 1Sa 9:15–17; 2Ki 6:32 for other examples of divine revelation concerning an imminent visit.

14:6 *Come in, wife of Jeroboam.* Ahijah's recognition of the woman and his knowledge of the purpose of her visit served to authenticate his message as truly being the word of the Lord.

14:7–8 *raised you up ... made you a leader ... tore the kingdom away.* Jeroboam is first reminded of the gracious acts of the Lord in his behalf (see 11:26,30–38).

14:8 *you have not been like my servant David.* Jeroboam had not responded to God's gracious acts and had ignored the requirements given when Ahijah told him he would become king (see 11:38 and note).

14:9 *all who lived before you.* Jeroboam's wickedness surpassed that of Saul, David and Solomon in that he implemented a paganized system of worship for the entire populace of the northern kingdom. *other gods.* See notes on 12:28,30.

14:10 *slave or free.* Without exception (see 21:21; 2Ki 9:8; 14:26).

14:11 *birds ... will feed on those who die in the country.* See note on 16:4. The covenant curse of Dt 28:26 is applied to Jeroboam's male descendants, none of whom will receive an honorable burial.

14:12 *boy.* The Hebrew for this word allows for wide latitude in age (the same term is used for the young advisers of Rehoboam; see 12:8 and note). *will die.* Although the death of Abijah was a severe disappointment to Jeroboam and his wife, it was an act of God's mercy to the prince, sparing him the disgrace and suffering that were to come on his father's house (see Isa 57:1–2).

14:13 *All Israel will mourn for him and bury him.* Perhaps an indication that Abijah was the crown prince, and was well known and loved by the people. *buried.* He alone of Jeroboam's descendants would receive an honorable burial.

14:14 *a king ... who will cut off the family of Jeroboam.* Ahijah looked beyond the brief reign of Nadab, Jeroboam's son (15:25–26), to the revolt of Baasha (15:27—16:7).

14:15 *like a reed swaying in the water.* Descriptive of the instability of the royal house in the northern kingdom, which was to be characterized by assassinations and revolts (see 15:27–28; 16:16; 2Ki 9:24; 15:10,14,25,30; see also Introduction: Content). *He will uproot Israel.* See 2Ki 17:22–23 for the fulfillment of this prophecy; see also the list of curses for covenant breaking found in Dt 28:63–64; 29:25–28. *Asherah poles.* See NIV text note. Ahijah perceived that Jeroboam's use of golden bulls in worship would inevitably lead to the adoption of other elements of Canaanite nature religion. The goddess Asherah was the consort of El, and the Asherah poles were probably wooden representations of the goddess (see notes on Ex 34:13; Jdg 2:13).

Rulers of the Divided Kingdom of Israel and Judah

DATA AND DATES IN ORDER OF SEQUENCE

	SCRIPTURE	KINGS	SYNCHRONISM OR CORRELATION	LENGTH OF REIGN	HISTORICAL DATA	DATES
1.	*1Ki 12:1-24* *1Ki 14:21-31*	***Rehoboam** (Judah)*		*17 years*		*930-913*
2.	1Ki 12:25–14:20	**Jeroboam I** (Israel)		22 years		930-909
3.	*1Ki 15:1-8*	***Abijah** (Judah)*	*18th of Jeroboam*	*3 years*		*913-910*
4.	*1Ki 15:9-24*	***Asa** (Judah)*	*20th of Jeroboam*	*41 years*		*910-869*
5.	1Ki 15:25-31	**Nadab** (Israel)	2nd of Asa	2 years		909-908
6.	1Ki 15:32–16:7	**Baasha** (Israel)	3rd of Asa	24 years		908-886
7.	1Ki 16:8-14	**Elah** (Israel)	26th of Asa	2 years		886-885
8.	1Ki 16:15-20	**Zimri** (Israel)	27th of Asa	7days		885
9.	1Ki 16:21-22	**Tibni** (Israel)			Overlap with Omri	885-880
10.	1Ki 16:23-28	**Omri** (Israel)	27th of Asa 31st of Asa	12 years	Made king by the people Overlap with Tibni Official reign = 11 actual years Sole reign	885 885-880 885-874 880-874
11.	1Ki 16:29–22:40	**Ahab** (Israel)	38th of Asa	22 years	Official reign = 21 actual years	874-853
12.	*1Ki 22:41-50*	***Jehoshaphat** (Judah)*	*4th of Ahab*	*25 years*	*Coregency with Asa* *Official reign* *Sole reign* *Has Jehoram as regent*	*872-869* *872-848* *869-853* *853-848*
13.	1Ki 22:51– 2Ki 1:18	**Ahaziah** (Israel)	17th of Jehoshaphat	2 years	Official reign = 1 yr. actual reign	853-852
14.	2Ki 1:17 2Ki 3:1–8:15	**Joram** (Israel)	2nd of Jehoram 18th of Jehoshaphat	12 years	Official reign = 11 actual years	852 852-841
15.	*2Ki 8:16-24*	***Jehoram** (Judah)*	*5th of Joram*	*8 years*	*Coregency with Jehoshaphat* *Sole reign* *Official reign = 7 actual years*	*853-848* *848-841* *848-841*
16.	*2Ki 8:25-29* *2Ki 9:29*	***Ahaziah** (Judah)*	*12th of Joram* *11th of Joram*	*1 year*	*Nonaccession-year reckoning* *Accession-year reckoning*	*841* *841*
17.	2Ki 9:30–10:36	**Jehu** (Israel)		28 years		841-814
18.	*2Ki 11*	***Athaliah** (Judah)*		*7 years*		*841-835*
19.	*2Ki 12*	***Joash** (Judah)*	*7th of Jehu*	*40 years*		*835-796*
20.	2Ki 13:1-9	**Jehoahaz** (Israel)	23rd of Joash	17 years		814-798
21.	2Ki 13:10-25	**Jehoash** (Israel)	37th of Joash	16 years		798-782

SCRIPTURE	KINGS	SYNCHRONISM OR CORRELATION	LENGTH OF REIGN	HISTORICAL DATA	DATES
22. *2Ki 14:1-22*	***Amaziah*** *(Judah)*	*2nd of Jehoash*	*29 years*	 *Overlap with Azariah*	*796-767* *792-767*
23. 2Ki 14:23-29	**Jeroboam II** (Israel)	 15th of Amaziah	41 years	Coregency with Jehoash Total reign Sole reign	793-782 793-753 782-753
24. *2Ki 15:1-7*	***Azariah*** *(Judah)* *(= Uzziah)*	*27th of Jeroboam*	*52 years*	*Overlap with Amaziah* *Total reign* *Sole reign*	*792-767* *792-740* *767-750*
25. 2Ki 15:8-12	**Zechariah** (Israel)	38th of Azariah	6 months		753
26. 2Ki 15:13-15	**Shallum** (Israel)	39th of Azariah	1 month		752
27. 2Ki 15:16-22	**Menahem** (Israel)	39th of Azariah	10 years	Ruled in Samaria	752-742
28. 2Ki 15:23-26	**Pekahiah** (Israel)	50th of Azariah	2 years		742-740
29. 2Ki 15:27-31	**Pekah** (Israel)	 52nd of Azariah	20 years	In Gilead; overlapping years Total reign Sole reign	752-740 752-732 740-732
30. *2Ki 15:32-38* *2Ki 15:30*	***Jotham*** *(Judah)*	*2nd of Pekah*	*16 years*	*Coregency with Azariah* *Official reign* *Reign to his 20th year*	*750-740* *750-735* *750-732*
31. *2Ki 16*	***Ahaz*** *(Judah)*	*17th of Pekah*	*16 years*	*Total reign* *From 20th of Jotham*	*735-715* *735* *732-715*
32. 2Ki 15:30 2Ki 17	**Hoshea** (Israel)	12th of Ahaz	9 years	20th of Jotham	732 732-722
33. *2Ki 18:1–20:21*	***Hezekiah*** *(Judah)*	*3rd of Hoshea*	*29 years*	 *Coregency with Ahaz*	*715-686* *729-715*
34. *2Ki 21:1-18*	***Manasseh*** *(Judah)*		*55 years*	*Coregency with Hezekiah* *Total reign*	*697-686* *697-642*
35. *2Ki 21:19-26*	***Amon*** *(Judah)*		*2 years*		*642-640*
36. *2Ki 22:1–23:30*	***Josiah*** *(Judah)*		*31 years*		*640-609*
37. *2Ki 23:31-33*	***Jehoahaz*** *(Judah)*		*3 months*		*609*
38. *2Ki 23:34–24:7*	***Jehoiakim*** *(Judah)*		*11 years*		*609-598*
39. *2Ki 24:8-17*	***Jehoiachin*** *(Judah)*		*3 months*		*598-597*
40. *2Ki 24:18–25:26*	***Zedekiah*** *(Judah)*		*11 years*		*597-586*

*Italics denote kings of **Judah**.*
Non-italic type denotes kings of **Israel**.

because they provoked[n] the LORD to anger by making Asherah[o] poles.[a] 16And he will give Israel up because of the sins[p] Jeroboam has committed and has caused Israel to commit."

17Then Jeroboam's wife got up and left and went to Tirzah.[q] As soon as she stepped over the threshold of the house, the boy died. 18They buried him, and all Israel mourned for him, as the LORD had said through his servant the prophet Ahijah.

19The other events of Jeroboam's reign, his wars and how he ruled, are written in the book of the annals of the kings of Israel. 20He reigned for twenty-two years and then rested with his fathers. And Nadab his son succeeded him as king.

Rehoboam King of Judah

14:21,25-31pp — 2Ch 12:9-16

21Rehoboam son of Solomon was king in Judah. He was forty-one years old when he became king, and he reigned seventeen years in Jerusalem, the city the LORD had chosen out of all the tribes of Israel in which to put his Name. His mother's name was Naamah; she was an Ammonite.[r]

22Judah[s] did evil in the eyes of the LORD. By the sins they committed they stirred up his jealous anger[t] more than their fathers had done. 23They also set up for themselves high places, sacred stones[u] and Asherah poles[v] on every high hill and under every spreading tree.[w] 24There were even male shrine prostitutes[x] in the land; the people engaged in all the detestable[y] practices of the nations the LORD had driven out before the Israelites.

25In the fifth year of King Rehoboam, Shishak king of Egypt attacked[z] Jerusalem. 26He carried off the treasures of the temple[a] of the LORD and the treasures of the royal palace. He took everything, including all the gold shields[b] Solomon had made. 27So King Rehoboam made bronze shields to replace them and assigned these to the commanders of the guard on duty at the entrance to the royal palace.[c] 28Whenever the king went to the LORD's temple, the guards bore the shields, and afterward they returned them to the guardroom.

29As for the other events of Rehoboam's reign, and all he did, are they not written in the book of the annals of the kings of Judah? 30There was continual warfare[d] between Rehoboam and Jeroboam. 31And Rehoboam rested with his fathers and was buried with them in the City of David. His mother's name was Naamah; she was an Ammonite.[e] And Abijah[b] his son succeeded him as king.

Abijah King of Judah

15:1-2,6-8pp — 2Ch 13:1-2,22–14:1

15 In the eighteenth year of the reign of Jeroboam son of Nebat, Abijah[c] be-

[a] *15* That is, symbols of the goddess Asherah; here and elsewhere in 1 Kings [b] *31* Some Hebrew manuscripts and Septuagint (see also 2 Chron. 12:16); most Hebrew manuscripts *Abijam* [c] *1* Some Hebrew manuscripts and Septuagint (see also 2 Chron. 12:16); most Hebrew manuscripts *Abijam*; also in verses 7 and 8

14:16 [p]S 1Ki 12:30; S 15:26
14:17 [q]S Jos 12:24; S 1Ki 15:33
14:21 [r]S 1Ki 11:1
14:22 [s]2Ki 17:19; 2Ch 12:1 [t]Dt 32:21; Ps 78:58; Jer 44:3; S 1Co 10:22
14:23 [u]S Ex 23:24; Dt 16:22; Hos 10:1 [v]S Dt 12:3 [w]S Dt 12:2; Eze 6:13
14:24 [x]S Dt 23:17 [y]1Ki 11:5-7; 2Ki 21:2; Ezr 9:11; Pr 21:27; Isa 1:13; Jer 16:18; 32:35; 44:4
14:25 [z]2Ch 12:2
14:26 [a]1Ki 15:15,18 [b]S 2Sa 8:7
14:27 [c]2Ki 11:5
14:30 [d]2Sa 3:1; S 1Ki 12:21
14:31 [e]S 1Ki 11:1

14:16 *sins Jeroboam has committed.* See 12:26–33; 13:33–34. *caused Israel to commit.* A phrase repeated often in 1,2 Kings (e.g., 15:26; 16:2,13,19,26).

14:17 *Tirzah.* Used by the kings of Israel as the royal city until Omri purchased and built up Samaria to serve that purpose (see 16:24 and note). It is probably modern Tell el-Far'ah, about seven miles north of Shechem (see note on SS 6:4).

14:19 *his wars.* See v. 30; 15:6; 2Ch 13:2–20. *annals of the kings of Israel.* A record of the reigns of the kings of the northern kingdom used by the author of 1,2 Kings and apparently accessible to those interested in further details of the history of the reigns of Israelite kings. It is not to be confused with the canonical book of 1,2 Chronicles, which was written later than 1,2 Kings and contains the history of the reigns of the kings of Judah only (see Introduction: Author, Sources and Date).

14:20 *twenty-two years.* 930–909 B.C. *rested with his fathers.* See note on 1:21. *Nadab.* See 15:25–32.

14:21 *seventeen years.* 930–913 B.C. *city the LORD had chosen ... to put his Name.* See 9:3; Ps 132:13.

14:22 *Judah did evil in the eyes of the LORD.* The reign of Rehoboam is described in greater detail in 2Ch 11–12. The priests and Levites who immigrated to Judah from the north led the country to follow the way of David and Solomon for the first three years of Rehoboam's reign (see 12:24; 2Ch 11:17). In later years Rehoboam and the people of Judah turned away from the Lord (2Ch 12:1).

14:23 *high places.* See note on 3:2. *sacred stones.* Stone pillars, bearing a religious significance, that were placed next to the altars. The use of such pillars was common among the Canaanites and was explicitly forbidden to the Israelites in the Mosaic law (see Ex 23:24; Lev 26:1 and note; Dt 7:5 and note; 16:21–22). It is likely that the pillars were intended to be representations of the deity (see 2Ki 3:2 and note). For legitimate uses of stone pillars see Ge 28:18 and note; 31:45; Ex 24:4. *Asherah poles.* See note on v. 15.

14:24 *male shrine prostitutes.* Ritual prostitution was an important feature of Canaanite fertility religion. The Israelites had been warned by Moses not to engage in this abominable practice (see Dt 23:17–18; see also 1Ki 15:12; 2Ki 23:7; Hos 4:14 and note).

14:25 *fifth year of King Rehoboam.* 926 B.C. *Shishak.* See note on 11:40. *attacked Jerusalem.* Shishak's invasion is described in more detail in 2Ch 12:2–4 (see note on 2Ch 12:2) and is also attested in a victory inscription found on the walls of the temple of Amun in Thebes, where more than 150 towns that Shishak plundered in Judah and Israel are listed (see chart, p. xxiii). 2Ch 12:5–8 indicates that fear of the impending invasion led to a temporary reformation in Judah.

14:26 *gold shields Solomon had made.* See note on 10:16.

14:27 *bronze shields.* The reduced realm could not match the great wealth Solomon had accumulated in Jerusalem (see 10:21,23,27).

14:29 *annals of the kings of Judah.* A record of the reigns of the kings of Judah similar to the one for the kings of the northern kingdom (see note on v. 19; see also Introduction: Author, Sources and Date).

14:30 *continual warfare.* See notes on v. 19; 12:24.

14:31 *rested with his fathers.* See note on 1:21.

15:1 *eighteenth year of the reign of Jeroboam.* The first of nu-

came king of Judah, 2and he reigned in
Jerusalem three years. His mother's name
was Maacah[f] daughter of Abishalom.[a]
3He committed all the sins his father had
done before him; his heart was not fully
devoted[g] to the LORD his God, as the heart
of David his forefather had been. 4Never-
theless, for David's sake the LORD his God
gave him a lamp[h] in Jerusalem by raising
up a son to succeed him and by making
Jerusalem strong. 5For David had done
what was right in the eyes of the LORD and
had not failed to keep[i] any of the LORD's
commands all the days of his life — except
in the case of Uriah[j] the Hittite.
6There was war[k] between Rehoboam[b]
and Jeroboam throughout ⌞Abijah's⌟ lifetime. 7As for the other events of Abijah's
reign, and all he did, are they not written
in the book of the annals of the kings of
Judah? There was war between Abijah and
Jeroboam. 8And Abijah rested with his fathers and was buried in the City of David.
And Asa his son succeeded him as king.

Asa King of Judah

15:9-22pp — 2Ch 14:2-3; 15:16–16:6
15:23-24pp — 2Ch 16:11–17:1

9In the twentieth year of Jeroboam king
of Israel, Asa became king of Judah, 10and
he reigned in Jerusalem forty-one years.
His grandmother's name was Maacah[l]
daughter of Abishalom.
11Asa did what was right in the eyes of
the LORD, as his father David[m] had done.
12He expelled the male shrine prostitutes[n]
from the land and got rid of all the idols[o]
his fathers had made. 13He even deposed
his grandmother Maacah[p] from her position as queen mother,[q] because she had
made a repulsive Asherah pole. Asa cut
the pole down[r] and burned it in the Kidron
Valley. 14Although he did not remove[s] the
high places, Asa's heart was fully committed[t] to the LORD all his life. 15He brought
into the temple of the LORD the silver and
gold and the articles that he and his father
had dedicated.[u]
16There was war[v] between Asa and Baasha king of Israel throughout their reigns.
17Baasha king of Israel went up against Judah and fortified Ramah[w] to prevent anyone from leaving or entering the territory
of Asa king of Judah.
18Asa then took all the silver and gold
that was left in the treasuries of the LORD's
temple[x] and of his own palace. He en-

15:2 [f] ver 10,13; 2Ch 11:20
15:3 [g] S 1Ki 8:61
15:4 [h] S 2Sa 21:17
15:5 [i] S Dt 5:32; S 1Ki 9:4 [j] 2Sa 11:2-27; 12:9
15:6 [k] ver 16,32; S 1Ki 12:21; 2Ch 16:9
15:10 [l] S ver 2
15:11 [m] 1Ki 9:4
15:12 [n] 1Ki 14:24 [o] 2Ch 15:8
15:13 [p] S ver 2 [q] S 1Ki 2:19 [r] S Ex 34:13
15:14 [s] 2Ch 14:5; 17:6 [t] S 1Ki 8:61
15:15 [u] S 2Sa 8:11
15:16 [v] S ver 6; S 1Ki 12:21
15:17 [w] S Jos 18:25
15:18 [x] S 1Ki 14:26

[a] 2 A variant of *Absalom*; also in verse 10 [b] 6 Most Hebrew manuscripts; some Hebrew manuscripts and Syriac *Abijam* (that is, Abijah)

merous synchronisms in 1,2 Kings between the reigns of the kings in the north and those in Judah (see, e.g., vv. 9,25,33; 16:8,15,29; see also chart, pp. 504–505, and Introduction: Chronology). *Abijah.* See note on 14:1. Both Rehoboam and Jeroboam had sons by this name.

15:2 *three years.* 913–910 B.C. *Maacah daughter of Abishalom.* See NIV text note. Abijah's mother is said to be a daughter of Uriel of Gibeah in 2Ch 13:2. It is likely that Maacah was the granddaughter of Absalom and the daughter of a marriage between Tamar (Absalom's daughter; see 2Sa 14:27) and Uriel. Absalom's mother was also named Maacah (2Sa 3:3).

15:3 *sins his father had done.* See 14:22–24. *not fully devoted to the LORD his God, as ... David his forefather had been.* Although David fell into grievous sin, his heart was never divided between serving the Lord and serving the nature deities of the Canaanites.

15:4 *lamp in Jerusalem.* See note on 11:36.

15:5 *Uriah the Hittite.* See 2Sa 11 and notes on 11:3,17; 12:7.

15:6 *Rehoboam.* See NIV text note; see also note on 12:24.

15:7 *other events of Abijah's reign.* See 2Ch 13. *annals of the kings of Judah.* See note on 14:29. *war between Abijah and Jeroboam.* Cf. v. 6; 14:30. From 2Ch 13 it is clear that the chronic hostile relations of preceding years flared into serious combat in which Abijah defeated Jeroboam and took several towns from him, including Bethel (2Ch 13:19).

15:8 *rested with his fathers.* See note on 1:21.

15:9 *twentieth year of Jeroboam.* 910 B.C. (see note on 14:20).

15:10 *forty-one years.* 910–869 B.C. *Maacah daughter of Abishalom.* See note on v. 2.

15:12 *male shrine prostitutes.* See note on 14:24. *got rid of all the idols his fathers had made.* See 14:23 and note. *idols.* See note on Lev 26:30.

15:13 *deposed his grandmother Maacah.* 2Ch 14:1—15:16 indicates a progression in Asa's reform over a period of years. Although Asa had destroyed pagan idols and altars early in his reign (2Ch 14:2–3), it was not until after a victory over Zerah the Cushite (2Ch 14:8–15) that Asa responded to the message of the prophet Azariah son of Oded by calling for a covenant renewal assembly in Jerusalem in the 15th year of his reign (see 2Ch 15:10 and note). After this assembly Asa deposed his grandmother Maacah because of her idolatry (2Ch 15:16). *made a repulsive Asherah pole.* See note on 14:15. It appears that Maacah's action was a deliberate attempt to counter Asa's reform. *Kidron Valley.* See note on Isa 22:7 and map, p. 477. For similar use of the Kidron Valley during reform efforts by kings of Judah, see 2Ki 23:4,6,12 (Josiah) and 2Ch 29:16; 30:14 (Hezekiah).

15:14 *did not remove the high places.* The reference here and in 2Ch 15:17 is to those high places where the Lord was worshiped (for the question of legitimacy of worship of the Lord at high places see note on 3:2). When 2Ch 14:3 indicates that Asa removed the high places, it is to be taken as a reference to the high places that were centers of pagan Canaanite worship (see 2Ch 17:6; 20:33 for the same distinction). This same statement of qualified approval that is made of Asa is made of five other kings of Judah prior to the time of Hezekiah (Jehoshaphat, 22:43; Joash, 2Ki 12:3; Amaziah, 2Ki 14:4; Azariah, 2Ki 15:4; Jotham, 2Ki 15:35). *fully committed to the LORD.* See note on v. 3.

15:15 *silver and gold and the articles.* Most likely consisting of war booty that Abijah had taken from Jeroboam (2Ch 13) and that Asa acquired from Zerah the Cushite (2Ch 14:8–15).

15:16 *war between Asa and Baasha ... throughout their reigns.* A reference to the chronic hostile relations that had existed ever since the division of the kingdom, rather than to full-scale combat (see notes on v. 7; 12:24; see also 2Ch 15:19).

15:17 *fortified Ramah.* Baasha had recaptured the territory previously taken from Jeroboam by Abijah (see note on v. 7; see also 2Ch 13:19) since Ramah was located south of Bethel and only about five miles north of Jerusalem. *prevent anyone from leaving or entering the territory of Asa.* See 2Ch 15:9–10.

15:18 *silver and gold that was left.* That which remained after

trusted it to his officials and sent[y] them to
Ben-Hadad[z] son of Tabrimmon, the son of
Hezion, the king of Aram, who was ruling
in Damascus. 19“Let there be a treaty[a] between me and you,” he said, “as there was
between my father and your father. See, I
am sending you a gift of silver and gold.
Now break your treaty with Baasha king
of Israel so he will withdraw from me.”
20Ben-Hadad agreed with King Asa and
sent the commanders of his forces against
the towns of Israel. He conquered[b] Ijon,
Dan, Abel Beth Maacah and all Kinnereth
in addition to Naphtali. 21When Baasha
heard this, he stopped building Ramah[c]
and withdrew to Tirzah.[d] 22Then King Asa
issued an order to all Judah—no one was
exempt—and they carried away from Ramah[e] the stones and timber Baasha had
been using there. With them King Asa[f] built
up Geba[g] in Benjamin, and also Mizpah.[h]
23As for all the other events of Asa's
reign, all his achievements, all he did and
the cities he built, are they not written in
the book of the annals of the kings of Judah? In his old age, however, his feet became diseased. 24Then Asa rested with his
fathers and was buried with them in the
city of his father David. And Jehoshaphat[i]
his son succeeded him as king.

Nadab King of Israel

25Nadab son of Jeroboam became king
of Israel in the second year of Asa king
of Judah, and he reigned over Israel two
years. 26He did evil[j] in the eyes of the
LORD, walking in the ways of his father[k]
and in his sin, which he had caused Israel
to commit.
27Baasha son of Ahijah of the house
of Issachar plotted against him, and he
struck him down[l] at Gibbethon,[m] a Philistine town, while Nadab and all Israel were
besieging it. 28Baasha killed Nadab in the
third year of Asa king of Judah and succeeded him as king.
29As soon as he began to reign, he killed
Jeroboam's whole family.[n] He did not
leave Jeroboam anyone that breathed, but
destroyed them all, according to the word
of the LORD given through his servant Ahijah the Shilonite— 30because of the sins[o]
Jeroboam had committed and had caused[p]
Israel to commit, and because he provoked
the LORD, the God of Israel, to anger.
31As for the other events of Nadab's
reign, and all he did, are they not written in the book of the annals[q] of the kings
of Israel? 32There was war[r] between Asa
and Baasha king of Israel throughout their
reigns.

Baasha King of Israel

33In the third year of Asa king of Judah,
Baasha son of Ahijah became king of all
Israel in Tirzah,[s] and he reigned twenty-

15:18 [y] 2Ki 12:18; 16:8; 18:14-16, 15; Joel 3:5 [z] ver 18-20; 1Ki 20:1; 2Ki 6:24; 13:3; Jer 49:27
15:19 [a] S Ex 23:32; S 1Ki 5:12
15:20 [b] 1Ki 20:34
15:21 [c] S Jos 18:25 [d] 1Ki 16:15-17
15:22 [e] ver 17 [f] ver 9-24; Jer 41:9 [g] S Jos 18:24; 2Ki 23:8 [h] S Jos 11:3
15:24 [i] Mt 1:8
15:26 [j] S Dt 4:25 [k] S 1Ki 12:30
15:27 [l] 1Ki 14:14 [m] S Jos 19:44
15:29 [n] S 1Ki 13:34
15:30 [o] S 1Ki 12:30 [p] 1Ki 16:26; 2Ki 3:3; 14:24; 15:28; 21:16
15:31 [q] 1Ki 11:41
15:32 [r] S ver 6
15:33 [s] 1Ki 14:17; 16:6, 23; 2Ki 15:14; SS 6:4

the plundering of Jerusalem by Shishak of Egypt (see 14:25 and note). *Hezion.* It is not clear whether Hezion is to be identified with Rezon of Damascus (see 11:23–25) or regarded as the founder of a new dynasty.

15:19 *treaty ... between my father and your father.* A reference to a previously unmentioned treaty between Abijah and Tabrimmon of Aram. When Tabrimmon died, Baasha succeeded in establishing a treaty with his successor Ben-Hadad. Asa saw no hope for success against Baasha without the assistance provided by a renewal of the old treaty with Aram. Although his plan seemed to be successful, it was condemned by Hanani the prophet as a foolish act and a denial of reliance on the Lord (see 2Ch 16:7–10). The true theocratic king was never to fear his enemies but to trust in the God of the covenant for security and protection (see note on 1Sa 17:11). Ahaz was later to follow Asa's bad example and seek Assyria's help when he was attacked by Israel and Aram (see 2Ki 16:5–9 and note on 16:7; Isa 7).

15:20 *Naphtali.* The cities that Ben-Hadad conquered in Naphtali were of particular importance because the major trade routes from Damascus going west to Tyre and southwest through the plain of Jezreel to the coastal plain and Egypt transversed this area. This same territory was later seized by the Assyrian ruler Tiglath-Pileser III (2Ki 15:29).

15:21 *Tirzah.* See note on 14:17.

15:22 *order to all Judah.* Asa's action is reminiscent of the labor force conscripted by Solomon (5:13–14; 11:28). *Geba ... Mizpah.* Asa established two border fortresses to check Baasha's desire to expand his territory southward. Geba was east of Ramah, and Mizpah was southwest of Ramah.

15:23 *other events of Asa's reign.* See 2Ch 14:2—16:14. *annals of the kings of Judah.* See note on 14:29. *feet became diseased.* See 2Ch 16:12.

15:24 *rested with his fathers.* See note on 1:21. *Jehoshaphat his son succeeded him.* For the reign of Jehoshaphat see 22:41–50; 2Ch 17:1—21:1.

15:25 *second year of Asa.* See note on v. 1. The second year of Asa of Judah corresponded to the 22nd and last year of Jeroboam of Israel (see v. 9; 14:20). *two years.* 909–908 B.C.

15:26 *his sin, which he had caused Israel to commit.* Jeroboam's sin (see note on 14:16). Although Abijah of Judah occupied Bethel during the reign of Jeroboam (see note on v. 7), it is probable that the paganized worship Jeroboam initiated was continued elsewhere until control of Bethel was regained by Baasha.

15:27 *Gibbethon.* A town located between Jerusalem and Joppa (probably a few miles west of Gezer) in the territory originally assigned to Dan (Jos 19:43–45). This Levitical city (Jos 21:23) probably fell into Philistine hands at the time of the Philistine expansion in the period of the judges (see map, p. 497).

15:28 *third year of Asa.* 908 B.C. (see note on v. 10). It is likely that Baasha was a commander in Nadab's army and was able to secure the support of the military for his revolt.

15:29 *the word ... given through ... Ahijah.* See 14:10–11.

15:30 *sins Jeroboam had committed and had caused Israel to commit.* See note on 14:16.

15:31 *annals of the kings of Israel.* See note on 14:19.

15:32 *war ... throughout their reigns.* See note on v. 16. The demise of Jeroboam's dynasty did not improve relations between the two kingdoms.

15:33 *third year of Asa.* 908 B.C. (see note on v. 10). *Tirzah.* See note on 14:17. *twenty-four years.* 908–886 B.C. His official years were counted as 24, though his actual years were 23 (see 16:8; see also Introduction: Chronology).

four years. 34He did evil[t] in the eyes of the LORD, walking in the ways of Jeroboam and in his sin, which he had caused Israel to commit.

16 Then the word of the LORD came to Jehu[u] son of Hanani[v] against Baasha: 2"I lifted you up from the dust[w] and made you leader[x] of my people Israel, but you walked in the ways of Jeroboam and caused[y] my people Israel to sin and to provoke me to anger by their sins. 3So I am about to consume Baasha[z] and his house,[a] and I will make your house like that of Jeroboam son of Nebat. 4Dogs[b] will eat those belonging to Baasha who die in the city, and the birds of the air[c] will feed on those who die in the country."

5As for the other events of Baasha's reign, what he did and his achievements, are they not written in the book of the annals[d] of the kings of Israel? 6Baasha rested with his fathers and was buried in Tirzah.[e] And Elah his son succeeded him as king.

7Moreover, the word of the LORD came[f] through the prophet Jehu[g] son of Hanani to Baasha and his house, because of all the evil he had done in the eyes of the LORD, provoking him to anger by the things he did, and becoming like the house of Jeroboam—and also because he destroyed it.

Elah King of Israel

8In the twenty-sixth year of Asa king of Judah, Elah son of Baasha became king of Israel, and he reigned in Tirzah two years.

9Zimri, one of his officials, who had command of half his chariots, plotted against him. Elah was in Tirzah at the time, getting drunk[h] in the home of Arza, the man in charge[i] of the palace at Tirzah. 10Zimri came in, struck him down and killed him in the twenty-seventh year of Asa king of Judah. Then he succeeded him as king.[j]

11As soon as he began to reign and was seated on the throne, he killed off Baasha's whole family.[k] He did not spare a single male, whether relative or friend. 12So Zimri destroyed the whole family of Baasha, in accordance with the word of the LORD spoken against Baasha through the prophet Jehu— 13because of all the sins Baasha and his son Elah had committed and had caused Israel to commit, so that they provoked the LORD, the God of Israel, to anger by their worthless idols.[l]

14As for the other events of Elah's reign, and all he did, are they not written in the book of the annals of the kings of Israel?

Zimri King of Israel

15In the twenty-seventh year of Asa king of Judah, Zimri reigned in Tirzah seven days. The army was encamped near Gibbethon,[m] a Philistine town. 16When the Israelites in the camp heard that Zimri had plotted against the king and murdered him, they proclaimed Omri, the commander of the army, king over Israel that very day there in the camp. 17Then Omri and all the Israelites with him withdrew from Gibbethon and laid siege to Tirzah. 18When Zimri saw that the city was taken,

15:34 [t]ver 26
16:1 [u]ver 7; 2Ch 19:2; 20:34 [v]2Ch 16:7
16:2 [w]1Sa 2:8 [x]S 1Ki 14:7-9 [y]S 1Ki 12:30
16:3 [z]2Ki 9:9 [a]ver 11; 1Ki 21:22
16:4 [b]S 1Ki 14:11 [c]S Ge 40:19
16:5 [d]1Ki 15:31
16:6 [e]S 1Ki 15:33
16:7 [f]S 1Ki 6:11 [g]S ver 1
16:9 [h]1Ki 20:12, 16; Pr 31:4-5 [i]1Ki 18:3
16:10 [j]2Ki 9:31
16:11 [k]S ver 3
16:13 [l]S Dt 32:21
16:15 [m]S Jos 19:44

15:34 *his sin, which he had caused Israel to commit.* See note on 14:16. The assessment of Baasha's reign indicates no improvement over the reign of Nadab, whom he replaced (see v. 26).
16:1 *Jehu.* Not to be confused with the later Israelite king having the same name (see 2Ki 9:1–3). Like his father before him (see 2Ch 16:7–10), Jehu brought God's word of condemnation to a king. Much as the man of God from Judah (see note on 13:1) and later the prophet Amos, he was sent from the south to a northern king. His period of prophetic activity lasted until the reign of Jehoshaphat of Judah (2Ch 19:2; 20:34)—a period of about 50 years.
16:2 *I lifted you up from the dust.* Cf. 14:7. *walked in the ways of Jeroboam.* See note on 14:16.
16:3 *consume Baasha and his house.* Cf. 14:10 (the house of Jeroboam); 21:21–22 (the house of Ahab).
16:4 Identical to the prophecy against Jeroboam's dynasty in 14:11.
16:5 *his achievements.* For the purposes of the writer of Kings (see Introduction: Theme), it was not necessary to list any of Baasha's achievements. He may have been a very successful ruler from a military-political point of view. *annals of the kings of Israel.* See note on 14:19.
16:6 *rested with his fathers.* See note on 1:21.
16:7 *evil he had done ... like the house of Jeroboam.* See v. 2; 15:34. *he destroyed it.* Although Baasha fulfilled God's purpose (14:10,14) in destroying the house of Jeroboam, he remained responsible for this violent and unlawful act (cf. Ge 50:20 and note; Isa 10:5–7,12).
16:8 *twenty-sixth year of Asa.* 886 B.C. (see note on 15:10; see also Introduction: Chronology). *two years.* 886–885 B.C.
16:9 *getting drunk.* The fact that Elah was carousing at Tirzah while the army was laying siege to Gibbethon (v. 15) indicates he had little perception of his responsibilities as king.
16:10 *twenty-seventh year of Asa.* 885 B.C.
16:11 *killed off Baasha's whole family.* See 15:29; 2Ki 10:1–7; 11:1; see also note on 1Sa 20:14. *friend.* Probably the chief adviser to the king (see note on 2Sa 15:37).
16:12 *word of the LORD ... through the prophet Jehu.* See vv. 1–4. Zimri did not consciously decide to fulfill Jehu's prophecy, but unwittingly he became the instrument by which Jehu's prediction was fulfilled (see note on v. 7) when he conspired against Elah and destroyed the dynasty of Baasha.
16:13 *sins Baasha and his son Elah had committed.* See 15:34 and note. *worthless idols.* A reference to all the paganism in Israel's religious observances, including the use of the golden calves in worship (see 12:28; 14:9 and notes).
16:14 *annals of the kings of Israel.* See note on 14:19.
16:15 *twenty-seventh year of Asa.* 885 B.C. (see notes on 15:1,10). *Gibbethon.* See notes on v. 9; 15:27.
16:16 *plotted against the king and murdered him.* See vv. 9–12. *Omri, the commander of the army.* He held a higher rank than Zimri did under Elah (v. 9).
16:17 *Tirzah.* The royal residence (see vv. 8–10; see also note on 14:17).

he went into the citadel of the royal palace and set the palace on fire around him.
So he died, 19because of the sins he had
committed, doing evil in the eyes of the
LORD and walking in the ways of Jeroboam
and in the sin he had committed and had
caused Israel to commit.
20As for the other events of Zimri's
reign, and the rebellion he carried out, are
they not written in the book of the annals
of the kings of Israel?

Omri King of Israel

21Then the people of Israel were split
into two factions; half supported Tibni son
of Ginath for king, and the other half supported Omri. 22But Omri's followers proved
stronger than those of Tibni son of Ginath.
So Tibni died and Omri became king.
23In the thirty-first year of Asa king of
Judah, Omri became king of Israel, and
he reigned twelve years, six of them in Tirzah.[n] 24He bought the hill of Samaria from
Shemer for two talents[a] of silver and built
a city on the hill, calling it Samaria,[o] after
Shemer, the name of the former owner of
the hill.
25But Omri did evil[p] in the eyes of the
LORD and sinned more than all those before him. 26He walked in all the ways of
Jeroboam son of Nebat and in his sin,
which he had caused[q] Israel to commit,
so that they provoked the LORD, the God of
Israel, to anger by their worthless idols.[r]
27As for the other events of Omri's reign,
what he did and the things he achieved,
are they not written in the book of the annals of the kings of Israel? 28Omri rested
with his fathers and was buried in Samaria.[s] And Ahab his son succeeded him as
king.

Ahab Becomes King of Israel

29In the thirty-eighth year of Asa king of
Judah, Ahab son of Omri became king of
Israel, and he reigned in Samaria over Israel twenty-two years. 30Ahab son of Omri
did more[t] evil in the eyes of the LORD than
any of those before him. 31He not only
considered it trivial to commit the sins of
Jeroboam son of Nebat, but he also married[u] Jezebel daughter[v] of Ethbaal king of
the Sidonians, and began to serve Baal[w]

16:23 [n]S Jos 12:24; S 1Ki 15:33
16:24 [o]S 1Ki 13:32; S Mt 10:5
16:25 [p]ver 25-26; S Dt 4:25; Mic 6:16
16:26 [q]S 1Ki 15:30 [r]S Dt 32:21
16:28 [s]S 1Ki 13:32
16:30 [t]S 1Ki 14:9
16:31 [u]S 1Ki 11:2 [v]S Jdg 3:6; 2Ki 9:34 [w]S Jdg 2:11

[a] *24* That is, about 150 pounds (about 70 kilograms)

16:19 *ways of Jeroboam.* See note on 14:16.
16:20 *annals of the kings of Israel.* See note on 14:19.
16:22 *Tibni died.* It is not clear whether Tibni's death was due to natural causes or the result of the military struggle for control of the land.
16:23 *thirty-first year of Asa.* 880 B.C. (see note on 15:10; see also Introduction: Chronology). *became king.* Became sole king. The struggle for control of the northern kingdom between Omri and Tibni lasted four years (compare this verse with v. 15). *twelve years.* 885–874. The 12 years of Omri's reign include the four years of struggle between Omri and Tibni (cf. vv. 15,29). *Tirzah.* See note on 14:17. Omri had been able to capture Tirzah in a matter of days (vv. 15–19).
16:24 *Samaria.* Seven miles northwest of Shechem, Samaria rose about 300 feet above the surrounding fertile valleys (referred to as a "wreath" in Isa 28:1; see note there). The original owner may have been persuaded to sell his property (see 21:3) on the condition that the city be named after him (cf. Ru 4:5 and note). The site provided an ideal location for a nearly impregnable capital city for the northern kingdom (see 20:1–21; 2Ki 6:25; 18:9–10). With the establishment of this royal city, the kings of the north came to possess a royal citadel-city like that of the Davidic dynasty (see 2Sa 5:6–12). Archaeologists have discovered that Omri and Ahab also adorned it with magnificent structures to rival those Solomon had erected in Jerusalem. From this time on, the northern kingdom could be designated by the name of the royal city, just as the southern kingdom could be designated by its capital, Jerusalem (see, e.g., 21:1 and note; Isa 10:10; Am 6:1).
16:25 *sinned more than all.* Omri's alliance with Ethbaal of Tyre and Sidon (Omri's son Ahab married Ethbaal's daughter Jezebel to seal the alliance) led to widespread Baal worship in the northern kingdom (vv. 31–33) and eventually to the near extinction of the Davidic line in the southern kingdom (see 2Ki 11 and note on 11:1; see also note on 2Ki 8:18). This marriage alliance must have been established in the early years of Omri's reign (see note on v. 23), perhaps to strengthen his hand against Tibni (see vv. 21–22).
16:26 *sin, which he had caused Israel to commit.* See 12:26–33; see also note on 14:16. *worthless idols.* See note on v. 13.
16:27 *things he achieved.* Omri's military and political accomplishments were not of importance for the purposes of the writer of Kings (see Introduction: Theme). Apart from establishing Samaria as the capital of the northern kingdom, about all that is known of him from the Biblical account is that he organized a governmental structure in the northern kingdom that was in place during the rule of his son, Ahab (see 20:14–15). Omri's dynasty, however, endured for over 40 years. A century and a half later (732 B.C.) Tiglath-Pileser III of Assyria referred to Israel as the "house of Omri" in his annals. Omri is also mentioned in the Mesha Stele (see chart, p. xxiii), and a later Assyrian king (Sargon II) referred to the kingdom of Israel as "Omri-land." *annals of the kings of Israel.* See note on 14:19.
16:28 *rested with his fathers.* See note on 1:21.
16:29 *thirty-eighth year of Asa.* 874 B.C. (see notes on 15:9–10). *twenty-two years.* 874–853 B.C.
16:30 *more evil ... than any.* Omri sinned more than those before him (see v. 25 and note), and Ahab sinned more than his father had. Evil became progressively worse in the royal house of the northern kingdom. Nearly a third of the narrative material in 1,2 Kings concerns the 34-year period of the reigns of Ahab and his two sons, Ahaziah and Joram. In this period the struggle against pagan religious influences and for faithfulness to the Lord (championed especially by Elijah and Elisha) was especially intense.
16:31 *married Jezebel daughter of Ethbaal.* The first-century Jewish historian Josephus refers to Ethbaal as a king-priest who ruled over Tyre and Sidon for 32 years. Ahab had already married Jezebel during the reign of his father (see note on v. 25). *Baal.* Perhaps Melqart, the local manifestation of Baal in Tyre, whose worship was brought to Israel by Jezebel. It is probable that Ahab participated in the worship of this deity at the time of his marriage. The names of Ahab's sons (Ahaziah, "The LORD grasps"; Joram, "The LORD is exalted") suggest that Ahab did not intend to replace the worship of the Lord with the worship of Baal but to worship both deities in a syncretistic way.

and worship him. 32He set up an altar[x] for
Baal in the temple[y] of Baal that he built
in Samaria. 33Ahab also made an Asherah
pole[z] and did more[a] to provoke the LORD,
the God of Israel, to anger than did all the
kings of Israel before him.
34In Ahab's time, Hiel of Bethel rebuilt
Jericho. He laid its foundations at the cost
of his firstborn son Abiram, and he set up
its gates at the cost of his youngest son
Segub, in accordance with the word of the
LORD spoken by Joshua son of Nun.[b]

Elijah Fed by Ravens

17 Now Elijah[c] the Tishbite, from Tishbe[a] in Gilead,[d] said to Ahab, "As
the LORD, the God of Israel, lives, whom I
serve, there will be neither dew nor rain[e]
in the next few years except at my word."
2Then the word of the LORD came to Elijah: 3"Leave here, turn eastward and hide[f]
in the Kerith Ravine, east of the Jordan.
4You will drink from the brook, and I have
ordered the ravens[g] to feed you there."
5So he did what the LORD had told him.
He went to the Kerith Ravine, east of the
Jordan, and stayed there. 6The ravens
brought him bread and meat in the morning[h] and bread and meat in the evening,
and he drank from the brook.

The Widow at Zarephath

7Some time later the brook dried up because there had been no rain in the land.
8Then the word of the LORD came to him:
9"Go at once to Zarephath[i] of Sidon and
stay there. I have commanded a widow[j]
in that place to supply you with food."

16:32 [x] S Jdg 6:28 [y] 2Ki 10:21,27; 11:18; Jer 43:12 **16:33** [z] S Jdg 3:7; 2Ki 13:6 [a] S 1Ki 14:9; 21:25 **16:34** [b] Jos 6:26 **17:1** [c] Mal 4:5; Mt 11:14; 17:3 [d] Jdg 12:4 [e] S Dt 11:17; S 28:24; S 2Sa 1:21; S 1Ki 8:36; Job 12:15; S Lk 4:25 **17:3** [f] 1Ki 18:4,10; Jer 36:19,26 **17:4** [g] S Ge 8:7 **17:6** [h] Ex 16:8 **17:9** [i] Ob 1:20 [j] Lk 4:26

[a] *1* Or *Tishbite, of the settlers*

16:32 *temple of Baal that he built in Samaria.* Ahab imported the Phoenician Baal worship of his wife Jezebel into the northern kingdom by constructing a temple of Baal in Samaria, just as Solomon had erected the temple of the Lord in Jerusalem. This pagan temple and its sacred stone (see note on 14:23) were later destroyed by Jehu (2Ki 10:21–27).
16:33 *Asherah pole.* See note on 14:15. *than did all the kings of Israel.* See note on v. 30. Ahab elevated the worship of Baal to an official status in the northern kingdom at the beginning of his reign.
16:34 *rebuilt Jericho.* Does not mean that Jericho had remained uninhabited since its destruction by Joshua (see Jos 18:21; Jdg 1:16; 3:13; 2Sa 10:5 and note), but that it had remained an unwalled town or village. During the rule of Ahab, Hiel fortified the city by reconstructing its walls and gates (see 9:17 for a similar use of "rebuild"). This violated God's intention that the ruins of Jericho be a perpetual reminder that Israel had received the land of Canaan from God's hand as a gift of grace. Accordingly, Hiel suffered the curse Joshua had pronounced (see Jos 6:26 and note).
17:1—2Ki 8:15 The ministries of Elijah and Elisha and other prophets from Ahab/Asa to Joram/Jehoshaphat—during the great religious crisis in the history of the kingdom of Israel.
17:1 *Elijah.* Elijah's name (meaning "The LORD is my God") was the essence of his message (18:21,39; cf. 2Ki 2:14). He was sent to oppose vigorously, by word and action, both Baal worship and those who engaged in it. *from Tishbe in Gilead.* See NIV text note. Gilead was in the northern Transjordan area. The precise location of Tishbe is unknown, but see map No. 7 at the end of this study Bible. *whom I serve.* Lit. "before whom I stand," a technical expression indicating one who stands in the service of a king. Kings and priests in Israel were anointed to serve as official representatives of the Lord, Israel's Great King, leading Israel in the way of faithfulness to the Lord and channeling his covenantal care and blessings to them. Since the days of Jeroboam the northern kingdom had not had such a priest (see 12:31 and note), and its kings had all been unfaithful. Now, in the great crisis brought on by Ahab's promotion of Baal worship, the Lord sent Elijah (and after him Elisha) to serve as his representative (instead of king and priest), much as he had sent Moses long ago. The author of Kings highlights many parallels between the ministries of Elijah and Moses. *neither dew nor rain.* The drought was not only a divine judgment on a nation that had turned to idolatry, but also a demonstration that even though Baal was considered the god of fertility and lord of the rain clouds, he was powerless to give rain (cf. Lev 26:3–4; Hos 2:5,8 and notes).
17:3 *Leave here.* With this command God withdrew his prophet from his land and people to leave them isolated from his word and blessings. The absence of the prophet confirmed and intensified the judgment (cf. Am 8:11 and note). *Kerith Ravine, east of the Jordan.* Perhaps a gorge leading into the Jordan Valley (see map, p. 518, and map No. 7 at the end of this study Bible).
17:4 *ravens to feed you there.* The Lord's faithful servant Elijah was miraculously sustained beyond the Jordan (like Israel in the desert in the time of Moses) while Israel in the promised land was going hungry—a clear testimony against Israel's reliance on Baal. The fact that Elijah was sustained in a miraculous way while not living among his own people demonstrated that the word of God was not dependent on the people, but the people were dependent on the word of God. *ravens.* Lived mainly on the carcasses of birds and animals they found in the fields and on the leftovers of wild kills. Since they normally fed on these where they found them, a flock of circling ravens would suggest to an observer only the presence of a dead body, thus keeping Elijah's hiding place secure. And the fact that birds of such habit here served as carriers of food heightens the miraculous element.
17:6 *meat.* Since the ravens themselves were not to be eaten (Lev 11:15; Dt 14:14) and the meat they normally ate was also forbidden food (see Lev 7:24; Dt 14:21 and note; Eze 4:14), the kind of "meat" referred to and its source remain mysterious. *in the morning … in the evening.* To eat meat every day, to say nothing of twice a day, was not common fare for common people. Among them meat was reserved for special occasions. Kings, on the other hand, seem to have had meat daily on their table (see 1Ki 4:23). It appears, then, that Yahweh's servant Elijah is here depicted as eating at King Yahweh's table (see Ex 29:38–41; Nu 28:4–8; cf. 2Ki 4:42 and note; see also 1Ki 18:19, where Elijah speaks of the "prophets … who eat at Jezebel's table") while apostate Israel goes hungry.
17:9 *Zarephath of Sidon.* A coastal town located between Tyre and Sidon in the territory ruled by Jezebel's father Ethbaal (16:31). Elijah is commanded to go and reside in the heart of the very land from which the Baal worship now being promoted in Israel had come. *I have commanded a widow in that place to supply you with food.* Elijah, as the bearer of God's word, was now to be sustained by human hands, but they were the hands of a poor widow facing starvation (v. 12). She was, moreover, from outside the circle of God's own people (cf. Lk 4:25–26)—in fact, she was from the pagan nation that at that time (much like Egypt earlier and Babylon later) represented the forces arrayed against God's kingdom.

Ancient Near Eastern Deities

Palestinian Deities in Scripture:

DEITY	COUNTRY	POSITION	REFERENCE
Baal	Canaan	Young storm god	1Ki 16:31; 18:18 – 46
Ashtoreth (Astarte)	Canaan	Mother-goddess; love; fertility	Jdg 2:13; 10:6; 1Sa 12:10; 1Ki 11:5
Chemosh	Moab	National god of war	Nu 21:29; Jdg 11:24; 1Ki 11:7,33; Jer 48:7
Molech (Malcam, Milcom)	Ammon	National god	Jer 49:1; Zep 1:5
Dagon	Philistia	National god of grain	Jdg 16:23;1Sa 5:2 – 7
Queen of Heaven	Canaan	Same as Ashtoreth (similar to Anath and Ishtar)	Jer 7:18; 44:17 – 25

Mesopotamian Deities in Scripture:

DEITY	COUNTRY	POSITION	REFERENCE
Marduk	Babylon	Young storm god; chief god	Jer 50:2
Bel	Babylon	Another name for Marduk	Isa 46:1; Jer 50:2; 51:44
Nebo (Nabu)	Babylon	Son of Marduk	Isa 46:1
Tammuz (Dumuzi)	Sumerian	Young storm god	Eze 8:14

Major Deities not in Scripture:

EGYPT	MESOPOTAMIA	CANAAN-SYRIA
Osiris — death	**Anu** — head of pantheon (officially recognized gods)	**El** — head of Canaanite pantheon
Isis — life	**Enlil** — storm	**Anath** — war
Horus — sun	**Ea/Enki** — fresh water and subterranean water	**Mot** — death, sterility
Hathor — mother-goddess	**Sin (Nanna)** — moon	**Adad** — Syrian storm god
Ra (Re) — sun	**Ishtar** — sex, fertility	**Teshub** — Hittite storm god
Seth — evil storm	**Ninurta** — war	**Hannahanna** — Hittite mother-goddess
Ptah — artists; Memphite creator	**Tiamat** — salt water	**Arinna** — Hittite sun goddess

Deities of these civilizations, particularly Egypt, vary as to attributes and rank, depending upon the time period and the areas of the country. The ones listed are basic.

Chronological and Background Charts of the Old Testament, p. 83

10 So he went to Zarephath. When he came to the town gate, a widow was there gathering sticks. He called to her and asked, "Would you bring me a little water in a jar so I may have a drink?"[k] 11 As she was going to get it, he called, "And bring me, please, a piece of bread."

12 "As surely as the LORD your God lives," she replied, "I don't have any bread—only a handful of flour in a jar and a little oil[l] in a jug. I am gathering a few sticks to take home and make a meal for myself and my son, that we may eat it—and die."

13 Elijah said to her, "Don't be afraid. Go home and do as you have said. But first make a small cake of bread for me from what you have and bring it to me, and then make something for yourself and your son. 14 For this is what the LORD, the God of Israel, says: 'The jar of flour will not be used up and the jug of oil will not run dry until the day the LORD gives rain[m] on the land.' "

15 She went away and did as Elijah had told her. So there was food every day for Elijah and for the woman and her family. 16 For the jar of flour was not used up and the jug of oil did not run dry, in keeping with the word of the LORD spoken by Elijah.

17 Some time later the son of the woman who owned the house became ill. He grew worse and worse, and finally stopped breathing. 18 She said to Elijah, "What do you have against me, man of God? Did you come to remind me of my sin[n] and kill my son?"

19 "Give me your son," Elijah replied. He took him from her arms, carried him to the upper room where he was staying, and laid him on his bed. 20 Then he cried[o] out to the LORD, "O LORD my God, have you brought tragedy also upon this widow I am staying with, by causing her son to die?" 21 Then he stretched[p] himself out on the boy three times and cried to the LORD, "O LORD my God, let this boy's life return to him!"

22 The LORD heard Elijah's cry, and the boy's life returned to him, and he lived. 23 Elijah picked up the child and carried him down from the room into the house. He gave him to his mother[q] and said, "Look, your son is alive!"

24 Then the woman said to Elijah, "Now I know[r] that you are a man of God[s] and that the word of the LORD from your mouth is the truth."[t]

Elijah and Obadiah

18 After a long time, in the third[u] year, the word of the LORD came to Elijah: "Go and present[v] yourself to Ahab, and I will send rain[w] on the land." 2 So Elijah went to present himself to Ahab.

17:10 [k] S Ge 24:17; Jn 4:7 **17:12** [l] 2Ki 4:2 **17:14** [m] ver 1 **17:18** [n] Lk 5:8 **17:20** [o] 2Ki 4:33 **17:21** [p] 2Ki 4:34; Ac 20:10 **17:23** [q] Heb 11:35 **17:24** [r] Jn 16:30 [s] ver 18 [t] 1Ki 22:16; Ps 119:43; Jn 17:17 **18:1** [u] 1Ki 17:1; Lk 4:25 [v] ver 15 [w] S Dt 28:12 **18:2** [x] S Lev 26:26

17:10 *So he went.* Elijah's reliance on the Lord demonstrated the faith in the Lord that Israel should have been living by.

17:12 *As surely as the LORD your God lives.* Her oath in the name of the Lord was no doubt an accommodation to Elijah, whom she recognized as an Israelite (see notes on 5:7; 10:9).

17:13 *first make a small cake of bread for me ... then make something for yourself and your son.* As a prophet, Elijah's words are the command of the Lord. The widow is asked to give all she has to sustain the bearer of the word of God. The demand to give her all is in essence equal to the demands of the covenant that Israel had broken.

17:14 *will not be used up ... will not run dry until.* The Lord does not ask more than he promises to give.

17:15 *did as Elijah had told her.* By an act of faith the woman received the promised blessing. Israel had forsaken the covenant and followed Baal and Asherah in search of prosperity. Now in the midst of a pagan kingdom a widow realized that trustful obedience to the word of God is the way that leads to life.

17:16 *jar of flour was not used up.* God miraculously provided for this non-Israelite who, in an act of faith in the Lord's word, had laid her life on the line. He gave her "manna" from heaven even while he was withholding food from his unfaithful people in the promised land. The warning of Dt 32:21 was being fulfilled (cf. Ro 10:19 and note; 11:11,14).

17:18 *Did you come to remind me of my sin and kill my son?* The widow concluded that Elijah's presence in her house had called God's attention to her sin, and that the death of her son was a divine punishment for this sin. Although her sense of guilt seems to have been influenced by pagan ideas, both she and Elijah are confronted with the question: Why did the God who promised life bring death instead?

17:21 *stretched himself out on the boy three times.* The apparent intent of this physical contact was to transfer the bodily warmth and vitality of the prophet to the child (cf. 2Ki 4:33–34 and notes). Elijah's prayer, however, makes it clear that he expected the life of the child to return as an answer to prayer, not as a result of bodily contact. *let this boy's life return to him.* Moved by a faith like that of Abraham (see Ro 4:17 and note; Heb 11:19), Elijah prayed for the child's return to life so that the veracity and trustworthiness of God's word might be demonstrated.

17:22 *the boy's life returned to him.* The first instance of raising the dead recorded in Scripture. This non-Israelite widow was granted the supreme covenant blessing, the gift of life rescued from the power of death. This blessing came in the person of her son, the only hope for a widow in ancient society (see 2Ki 4:14; Ru 1:11–12 and notes; 4:15–17 and note on 4:17; Lk 7:12).

17:24 *you are a man of God.* See note on 1Sa 2:27. The widow had addressed Elijah as a man of God previously (v. 18), but now she knew in a much more experiential way that he truly was a prophet of the Lord (see note on 12:22). *the word of the LORD from your mouth is the truth.* God used this experience to convince the Phoenician widow that his word was completely reliable. Her confession was one that the Lord's own people in Israel had failed to make.

18:1 *third year.* Apparently of the drought. Later Jewish tradition indicates that the drought lasted three and a half years (cf. Lk 4:25; Jas 5:17 and note), but that probably represents a symbolic number for a drought cut short (half of seven years; see Ge 41:27; 2Ki 8:1). *present yourself to Ahab, and I will send rain on the land.* Elijah's return is not occasioned by repentance in Israel but by the command of the Lord, who in his sovereign grace determined to reveal himself anew to his people.

Now the famine was severe[x] in Samaria, 3and Ahab had summoned Obadiah,
who was in charge[y] of his palace. (Obadiah was a devout believer[z] in the LORD.
4While Jezebel[a] was killing off the LORD's
prophets, Obadiah had taken a hundred
prophets and hidden[b] them in two caves,
fifty in each, and had supplied[c] them
with food and water.) 5Ahab had said to
Obadiah, "Go through the land to all the
springs[d] and valleys. Maybe we can find
some grass to keep the horses and mules
alive so we will not have to kill any of our
animals."[e] 6So they divided the land they
were to cover, Ahab going in one direction
and Obadiah in another.
7As Obadiah was walking along, Elijah
met him. Obadiah recognized[f] him, bowed
down to the ground, and said, "Is it really
you, my lord Elijah?"
8"Yes," he replied. "Go tell your master,
'Elijah is here.' "
9"What have I done wrong," asked Obadiah, "that you are handing your servant
over to Ahab to be put to death? 10As surely as the LORD your God lives, there is not
a nation or kingdom where my master has
not sent someone to look[g] for you. And
whenever a nation or kingdom claimed
you were not there, he made them swear
they could not find you. 11But now you
tell me to go to my master and say, 'Elijah
is here.' 12I don't know where the Spirit[h]
of the LORD may carry you when I leave
you. If I go and tell Ahab and he doesn't
find you, he will kill me. Yet I your servant
have worshiped the LORD since my youth.
13Haven't you heard, my lord, what I did
while Jezebel was killing the prophets of
the LORD? I hid a hundred of the LORD's
prophets in two caves, fifty in each, and
supplied them with food and water. 14And
now you tell me to go to my master and
say, 'Elijah is here.' He will kill me!"
15Elijah said, "As the LORD Almighty
lives, whom I serve, I will surely present[i]
myself to Ahab today."

Elijah on Mount Carmel

16So Obadiah went to meet Ahab and
told him, and Ahab went to meet Elijah.
17When he saw Elijah, he said to him, "Is
that you, you troubler[j] of Israel?"
18"I have not made trouble for Israel,"
Elijah replied. "But you[k] and your father's
family have. You have abandoned[l] the
LORD's commands and have followed the
Baals. 19Now summon[m] the people from
all over Israel to meet me on Mount Carmel.[n] And bring the four hundred and fifty prophets of Baal and the four hundred
prophets of Asherah, who eat at Jezebel's
table."[o]
20So Ahab sent word throughout all Israel
and assembled the prophets on Mount Carmel.[p] 21Elijah went before the people and
said, "How long will you waver[q] between
two opinions? If the LORD[r] is God, follow
him; but if Baal is God, follow him."
But the people said nothing.
22Then Elijah said to them, "I am the
only one of the LORD's prophets left,[s] but
Baal has four hundred and fifty prophets.[t]
23Get two bulls for us. Let them choose
one for themselves, and let them cut it
into pieces and put it on the wood but not
set fire to it. I will prepare the other bull
and put it on the wood but not set fire to
it. 24Then you call[u] on the name of your
god, and I will call on the name of the

18:3 [y] 1Ki 16:9 [z] Ne 7:2 **18:4** [a] 1Ki 21:23; 2Ki 9:7 [b] S 1Ki 17:3; Isa 16:3; 25:4; 32:2; Ob 1:14 [c] Jer 26:24 **18:5** [d] Jer 14:3 [e] S Ge 47:4 **18:7** [f] 2Ki 1:8; Zec 13:4 **18:10** [g] S 1Ki 17:3 **18:12** [h] 2Ki 2:16; Eze 3:14; Ac 8:39 **18:15** [i] ver 1 **18:17** [j] Jos 7:25; 1Sa 14:29; 1Ki 21:20; Jer 38:4 **18:18** [k] 1Ki 16:31,33; 21:25 [l] S Dt 31:16 **18:19** [m] 2Ki 10:19 [n] S Jos 19:26 [o] 2Ki 9:22 **18:20** [p] 2Ki 2:25; 4:25 **18:21** [q] Jos 24:15; 2Ki 17:41; Ps 119:113; Mt 6:24 [r] ver 39; Ps 100:3; 118:27 **18:22** [s] 1Ki 19:10 [t] Jer 2:8; 23:13 **18:24** [u] S 1Sa 7:8

18:3 *Obadiah.* A common OT name, meaning "servant of the LORD." *in charge of his palace.* See note on 4:6.

18:5 The famine did not move Ahab to repentance (contrast Ahab's response to the famine with that of David, 2Sa 21:1). But when his military strength seemed to be jeopardized, he scoured the land for food and water (see 10:26; according to the annals of the Assyrian ruler Shalmaneser III, Ahab could bring 2,000 chariots against him).

18:8 *tell your master, 'Elijah is here.'* This action would publicly identify Obadiah with Elijah in contrast to his previous clandestine support of the prophets sought by Jezebel (see vv. 4,13).

18:12 *I don't know where the Spirit of the LORD may carry you.* Elijah's disappearance earlier and now his sudden reappearance suggested to Obadiah that God's Spirit was miraculously transporting the prophet about (see 2Ki 2:16 and note).

18:13 *Jezebel was killing the prophets.* Possibly in an attempt to please Baal so he would send rain. *prophets of the LORD.* Probably members of the communities of "prophets" that had sprung up in Israel during this time of apostasy (see note on 20:35).

18:17 *you troubler of Israel.* Ahab holds Elijah responsible for the drought and charges him with a crime against the state worthy of death (he calls him a "trouble bringer"; see Jos 7:25).

18:18 *You have abandoned the LORD's commands and have followed the Baals.* The source of Israel's trouble was not Elijah or even the drought, but Ahab's breach of covenantal loyalty.

18:19 *Mount Carmel.* A high ridge next to the Mediterranean Sea, where the effects of the drought would be least apparent (see Am 1:2 and note) and the power of Baal to nurture life would seem to be strongest. *prophets of Baal ... prophets of Asherah.* See v. 29 and note. *Asherah.* See note on 14:15. *eat at Jezebel's table.* See notes on 2:7; 17:6.

18:21 *waver.* The Hebrew for this word is the same as that used for "danced" in v. 26 (see note there). Elijah speaks with biting irony: In her religious ambivalence Israel is but engaging in a wild and futile religious "dance." *If the LORD is God, follow him; but if Baal is God, follow him.* Elijah placed a clear choice before the people. He drew a sharp contrast between the worship of the Lord and that of Baal to eliminate the apostate idea that people could worship both deities.

18:22 *only one ... left.* At least the only one to stand boldly and publicly against the king and the prophets of Baal (but see v. 4; 19:10,14; 20:13,28,35; 22:6,8; cf. 19:18 and note; Ro 11:4 and note on 11:5).

18:24 *I will call ... who answers.* See note on Ps 118:5. *The god who answers by fire—he is God.* Both the Lord and Baal were said to ride the thunderstorm as their divine chariot (see Ps

LORD.[v] The god who answers by fire[w]—he
is God."
Then all the people said, "What you say
is good."
25Elijah said to the prophets of Baal,
"Choose one of the bulls and prepare it
first, since there are so many of you. Call
on the name of your god, but do not light
the fire." 26So they took the bull given
them and prepared it.
Then they called[x] on the name of Baal
from morning till noon. "O Baal, answer
us!" they shouted. But there was no response;[y] no one answered. And they
danced around the altar they had made.
27At noon Elijah began to taunt them.
"Shout louder!" he said. "Surely he is a
god! Perhaps he is deep in thought, or
busy, or traveling. Maybe he is sleeping
and must be awakened."[z] 28So they shouted louder and slashed[a] themselves with
swords and spears, as was their custom,
until their blood flowed. 29Midday passed,
and they continued their frantic prophesying until the time for the evening sacrifice.[b] But there was no response, no one
answered, no one paid attention.[c]
30Then Elijah said to all the people,
"Come here to me." They came to him,
and he repaired the altar[d] of the LORD,
which was in ruins. 31Elijah took twelve
stones, one for each of the tribes descended from Jacob, to whom the word of the
LORD had come, saying, "Your name shall
be Israel."[e] 32With the stones he built an
altar in the name[f] of the LORD, and he dug
a trench around it large enough to hold
two seahs[a] of seed. 33He arranged[g] the
wood, cut the bull into pieces and laid it
on the wood. Then he said to them, "Fill

18:24 [v]S Ge 4:26 [w]S ver 38; S Ex 19:18; S Lev 9:24 **18:26** [x]Isa 44:17; 45:20 [y]Ps 115:4-5; 135:16; Isa 41:26, 28; 46:7; Jer 10:5; 1Co 8:4; 12:2 **18:27** [z]Hab 2:19 **18:28** [a]S Lev 19:28 **18:29** [b]S Ex 29:41 [c]2Ki 19:12; Isa 16:12; Jer 10:5 **18:30** [d]1Ki 19:10 **18:31** [e]S Ge 17:5; 2Ki 17:34 **18:32** [f]S Dt 18:7; Col 3:17 **18:33** [g]S Ge 22:9 **18:36** [h]S Ex 29:39, 41 [i]S Ge 24:12; S Ex 4:5; Mt 22:32 [j]S Jos 4:24; S 1Sa 17:46; S Ps 46:10 [k]Nu 16:28 **18:37** [l]S Jos 4:24 **18:38** [m]ver 24; S Ex 19:18; S Lev 9:24; 2Ki 1:10; 1Ch 21:26; 2Ch 7:1; Job 1:16 **18:39** [n]S Lev 9:24 [o]S ver 24; S Ps 46:10 **18:40** [p]S Jdg 4:7 [q]S Ex 22:20; S Dt 17:12; S 2Ki 11:18 **18:42** [r]S 1Sa 12:17; Jas 5:18

four large jars with water and pour it on
the offering and on the wood."
34"Do it again," he said, and they did
it again.
"Do it a third time," he ordered, and
they did it the third time. 35The water ran
down around the altar and even filled the
trench.
36At the time[h] of sacrifice, the prophet Elijah stepped forward and prayed:
"O LORD, God of Abraham,[i] Isaac and Israel, let it be known[j] today that you are
God in Israel and that I am your servant
and have done all these things at your
command.[k] 37Answer me, O LORD, answer
me, so these people will know[l] that you,
O LORD, are God, and that you are turning
their hearts back again."
38Then the fire[m] of the LORD fell and
burned up the sacrifice, the wood, the
stones and the soil, and also licked up the
water in the trench.
39When all the people saw this, they fell
prostrate[n] and cried, "The LORD—he is
God! The LORD—he is God!"[o]
40Then Elijah commanded them, "Seize
the prophets of Baal. Don't let anyone get
away!" They seized them, and Elijah had
them brought down to the Kishon Valley[p]
and slaughtered[q] there.
41And Elijah said to Ahab, "Go, eat and
drink, for there is the sound of a heavy
rain." 42So Ahab went off to eat and drink,
but Elijah climbed to the top of Carmel,
bent down to the ground and put his face
between his knees.[r]

[a] *32* That is, probably about 13 quarts (about 15 liters)

104:3 and note); thunder was their voice (see Ps 29:3–9 and note) and lightning ("fire") their weapon (see Ps 18:14 and note). Elijah's challenge is direct. Cf. Lev 9:24 and note.

18:26 *danced around the altar.* The ecstatic dance was part of the pagan ritual intended to arouse the deity to perform some desired action (see note on v. 21).

18:27 *deep in thought ... sleeping.* Elijah ridicules, but as he does he shows knowledge of the Baal myths that depict the gods as having very human characteristics.

18:28 *until their blood flowed.* Self-inflicted wounds (causing blood to flow) were symbolic of self-sacrifice as an extreme method of arousing the deity to action. Such mutilation of the body was strictly forbidden in the Mosaic law (see Lev 19:28; Dt 14:1 and notes).

18:29 *frantic prophesying.* Indicative of ecstatic raving, in which the ritual reached its climax (see notes on 1Sa 10:5; 18:10). *time for the evening sacrifice.* See Ex 29:38–41; Nu 28:3–8. *no response.* Dramatic demonstration of Baal's impotence (see Ps 115:4–8; 135:15–18; Jer 10:5 and notes).

18:30 *altar of the LORD, which was in ruins.* It is possible that the altar had been built by people of the northern ten tribes after the division of the kingdom (see note on 3:2) and that it had been destroyed by the agents of Jezebel (vv. 4,13; 19:10,14).

18:31 *twelve stones, one for each of the tribes.* In this way Elijah called attention to the covenant unity of Israel as the people of God in spite of her political division. What was about to happen concerned the entire nation, not just the northern ten tribes.

18:33 *water.* By drenching the whole installation Elijah showed to all that he was using no tricks.

18:36 *prayed.* Elijah's simple but earnest prayer stands in sharp contrast to the frantic shouts and "dancing" and self-mutilation of the Baal prophets. *God of Abraham, Isaac and Israel.* An appeal to the Lord to remember his ancient covenant with the patriarchs, and to Israel to remember all that the Lord has done for her since the days of her ancestors.

18:38 *fire of the LORD fell.* See note on v. 24.

18:40 *Kishon Valley.* The Kishon River flows below Mount Carmel (see map, p. 518). *slaughtered there.* Elijah, acting on the authority of the Lord, who sent him, carried out the sentence pronounced in the Mosaic law for prophets of pagan deities (Dt 13:13–18; 17:2–5).

18:41 *sound of a heavy rain.* Now that Baal worship has been struck a devastating blow, there is the promise of rain (see 17:1 and note). Significantly, Ahab takes no action—either to carry out the Mosaic sentence or to halt Elijah. He still wavers between two opinions (see v. 21 and note).

18:42 *Elijah ... bent down to the ground and put his face between his knees.* Now that the people had confessed that the Lord alone is God, Elijah prayed for the covenant curse to be lifted (see note on 17:1) by the coming of rain (see 8:35 and note; 2Ch 7:13–14).

43 "Go and look toward the sea," he told
his servant. And he went up and looked.
"There is nothing there," he said.
Seven times Elijah said, "Go back."
44 The seventh time[s] the servant reported, "A cloud[t] as small as a man's hand is
rising from the sea."
So Elijah said, "Go and tell Ahab, 'Hitch
up your chariot and go down before the
rain stops you.'"
45 Meanwhile, the sky grew black with
clouds, the wind rose, a heavy rain[u] came
on and Ahab rode off to Jezreel.[v] 46 The
power[w] of the LORD came upon Elijah and,
tucking his cloak into his belt,[x] he ran
ahead of Ahab all the way to Jezreel.

Elijah Flees to Horeb

19 Now Ahab told Jezebel[y] everything
Elijah had done and how he had
killed[z] all the prophets with the sword. 2 So
Jezebel sent a messenger to Elijah to say,
"May the gods deal with me, be it ever so
severely,[a] if by this time tomorrow I do not
make your life like that of one of them."[b]
3 Elijah was afraid[a] and ran[c] for his life.[d]
When he came to Beersheba[e] in Judah, he
left his servant there, 4 while he himself
went a day's journey into the desert. He
came to a broom tree,[f] sat down under it
and prayed that he might die. "I have had
enough, LORD," he said. "Take my life;[g] I
am no better than my ancestors." 5 Then he
lay down under the tree and fell asleep.[h]
All at once an angel[i] touched him and
said, "Get up and eat." 6 He looked around,
and there by his head was a cake of bread
baked over hot coals, and a jar of water. He
ate and drank and then lay down again.
7 The angel of the LORD came back a second time and touched him and said, "Get
up and eat, for the journey is too much
for you." 8 So he got up and ate and drank.
Strengthened by that food, he traveled forty[j] days and forty nights until he reached
Horeb,[k] the mountain of God. 9 There he
went into a cave[l] and spent the night.

The LORD Appears to Elijah

And the word of the LORD came to him:
"What are you doing here, Elijah?"[m]
10 He replied, "I have been very zealous[n]
for the LORD God Almighty. The Israelites have rejected your covenant,[o] broken
down your altars,[p] and put your prophets
to death with the sword. I am the only
one left,[q] and now they are trying to kill
me too."
11 The LORD said, "Go out and stand on
the mountain[r] in the presence of the LORD,
for the LORD is about to pass by."[s]
Then a great and powerful wind[t] tore
the mountains apart and shattered[u] the
rocks before the LORD, but the LORD was
not in the wind. After the wind there was
an earthquake, but the LORD was not in the
earthquake. 12 After the earthquake came
a fire,[v] but the LORD was not in the fire.
And after the fire came a gentle whisper.[w]

[a] 3 Or *Elijah saw*

18:44 [s] S Jos 6:15 [t] Lk 12:54 **18:45** [u] S 1Ki 8:36; Job 37:13 [v] S 1Sa 29:1; S Hos 1:4 **18:46** [w] S Jdg 3:10; S 1Sa 11:6; Lk 1:35; 4:14 [x] 2Ki 4:29; 9:1 **19:1** [y] 1Ki 16:31 [z] S Ex 22:20 **19:2** [a] S Ru 1:17 [b] Ps 13:4; Jer 20:10; 26:21; 36:26 **19:3** [c] S Ge 31:21 [d] S Ge 19:17 [e] S Jos 19:2 **19:4** [f] Job 30:4 [g] S Nu 11:15; Job 6:9; 7:16; 10:1; Ps 69:19; Jer 20:18; Jnh 4:8 **19:5** [h] Ge 28:11 [i] S Ge 16:7 **19:8** [j] Ex 24:18; Mt 4:2 [k] S Ex 3:1 **19:9** [l] S Ex 33:22 [m] S Ge 3:9 **19:10** [n] S Nu 25:13; Ac 22:3; Gal 4:18 [o] S Dt 31:16 [p] 1Ki 18:30 [q] 1Ki 18:4,22; Jer 5:11; 9:2; Ro 11:3* **19:11** [r] Ex 34:2; Mt 17:1-3 [s] Ex 33:19 [t] S Ex 14:21; S 2Ki 2:1 [u] Na 1:6 **19:12** [v] S Ex 3:2 [w] ver 11; S 1Sa 14:6; Job 4:16; Zec 4:6; 2Co 12:9

18:43 *Seven times.* The number symbolic of completeness.
18:44 *rising from the sea.* Appearing on the western horizon above the Mediterranean.
18:46 *ran ahead of Ahab all the way to Jezreel.* Divinely energized by extraordinary strength, Elijah ran before Ahab's chariot to Jezreel (a distance of c. 16 miles). This dramatic scene, with the Lord's prophet running before the king and the Lord himself racing behind him riding his mighty thundercloud chariot (see note on v. 24), served as a powerful appeal to Ahab to break once for all with Baal and henceforth to rule as the servant of the Lord.
19:1 *Jezebel.* Ahab's wife and a worshiper of Baal-Melqart, the god of Phoenicia (see notes on 16:25, 31 – 32; 18:13).
19:2 *May the gods deal with me, be it ever so severely.* A curse formula (see note on 1Sa 3:17). *one of them.* The dead prophets of Baal (v. 1).
19:3 *Elijah was afraid and ran for his life.* In spite of Elijah's great triumph in the trial on Mount Carmel and the dramatic demonstration that his God is the Lord of heaven and earth and the source of Israel's blessings, Jezebel is undaunted. Hers is no empty threat, and Ahab has shown that he is either unwilling or unable to restrain her. So Elijah knows that one of the main sources of Israel's present apostasy is still spewing out its poison and that his own life is in danger. *Beersheba.* The southernmost city in Judah (see notes on Ge 21:31; Am 5:5; see also Jdg 20:1 and note).
19:4 *broom tree.* A desert shrub, sometimes large enough to offer some shade. *prayed that he might die.* Cf. Jnh 4:3,8 and note on 4:3. Elijah concluded that his work was fruitless and consequently that life was not worth living. He had lost his confidence in the triumph of the kingdom of God and was withdrawing from the arena of conflict.
19:7 *angel of the LORD.* See note on Ge 16:7. God in his mercy provided sustenance and rest for his discouraged servant. *the journey is too much for you.* Evidently Elijah had already determined to go to Mount Horeb, where God had established his covenant with his people. There is no indication that the Lord had instructed him to do this as he had previously directed him to go to Kerith (17:2 – 3) and to Zarephath (17:8 – 9) and to meet Ahab (18:1).
19:8 *forty days and forty nights.* Sustained by the Lord as Moses had been for the same length of time on Mount Sinai (Ex 24:18; 34:28) and as Jesus would be in the desert (Mt 4:2,11). *Horeb, the mountain of God.* Probably an alternative name for Mount Sinai (see Ex 3:1 and note; 19:1 – 3; Dt 1:2), located in the desert about 250 miles south of Beersheba.
19:9 *What are you doing here, Elijah?* The question implies that Elijah had come to Sinai for his own misguided reasons and not because the Lord had sent him.
19:10 Elijah did not give a direct answer to the Lord's question but implied that the work the Lord had begun centuries earlier with the establishment of the Sinai covenant had now come to nothing. Whereas Moses had interceded for Israel when they sinned with the golden calf (Ex 32:11 – 13), Elijah condemned the Israelites for breaking the covenant, and bitterly complained over the fruitlessness of his own work. *only one left.* See note on 18:22.
19:12 *gentle whisper.* In the symbolism of these occurrences (vv. 11 – 12) the Lord appears to be telling Elijah that although his servant's indictment of Israel was a call for

13When Elijah heard it, he pulled his cloak
over his face[x] and went out and stood at
the mouth of the cave.
Then a voice said to him, "What are you
doing here, Elijah?"
14He replied, "I have been very zealous
for the LORD God Almighty. The Israelites
have rejected your covenant, broken down
your altars, and put your prophets to death
with the sword. I am the only one left,[y]
and now they are trying to kill me too."
15The LORD said to him, "Go back the
way you came, and go to the Desert of Damascus. When you get there, anoint Hazael[z] king over Aram. 16Also, anoint[a] Jehu
son of Nimshi king over Israel, and anoint
Elisha[b] son of Shaphat from Abel Meholah[c] to succeed you as prophet. 17Jehu will
put to death any who escape the sword of
Hazael,[d] and Elisha will put to death any
who escape the sword of Jehu.[e] 18Yet I reserve[f] seven thousand in Israel—all whose
knees have not bowed down to Baal and
all whose mouths have not kissed[g] him."

The Call of Elisha

19So Elijah went from there and found
Elisha son of Shaphat. He was plowing
with twelve yoke of oxen, and he himself
was driving the twelfth pair. Elijah went
up to him and threw his cloak[h] around
him. 20Elisha then left his oxen and ran
after Elijah. "Let me kiss my father and
mother good-by,"[i] he said, "and then I will
come with you."
"Go back," Elijah replied. "What have I
done to you?"
21So Elisha left him and went back. He
took his yoke of oxen[j] and slaughtered
them. He burned the plowing equipment
to cook the meat and gave it to the people,
and they ate. Then he set out to follow Elijah and became his attendant.[k]

Ben-Hadad Attacks Samaria

20 Now Ben-Hadad[l] king of Aram mustered his entire army. Accompanied
by thirty-two kings with their horses and
chariots, he went up and besieged Samaria[m] and attacked it. 2He sent messengers
into the city to Ahab king of Israel, saying, "This is what Ben-Hadad says: 3'Your
silver and gold are mine, and the best of
your wives and children are mine.'"

19:13 [x]Ex 3:6
19:14 [y]1Ki 18:22; Ro 11:3*
19:15 [z]2Ki 8:7-15
19:16 [a]2Ki 9:1-3,6 [b]ver 21; 2Ki 2:1; 3:11 [c]S Jdg 7:22
19:17 [d]2Ki 8:12,29; 10:32; 12:17; 13:3,7,22; Am 1:4 [e]Jer 48:44
19:18 [f]Ro 11:4* [g]Hos 13:2
19:19 [h]S Ge 41:42; 2Ki 2:8,14
19:20 [i]Lk 9:61
19:21 [j]S 1Sa 6:14 [k]S ver 16
20:1 [l]S 1Ki 15:18 [m]S 1Ki 13:32

God to judge his people with windstorm, earthquake and fire, it was not God's will to do so now. Elijah must return to continue God's mission to his people, and Elisha is to carry it on for another generation (see v. 16 and note).

19:13 *What are you doing here, Elijah?* After demonstrating his presence in the gentle whisper rather than in the wind, earthquake or fire, the Lord gave Elijah an opportunity to revise the answer he had previously given to the same question (vv. 9–10).

19:14 Elijah's unrevised answer demonstrated that he did not understand the significance of the divine revelation he had just witnessed.

19:15 *The LORD said to him.* Giving instructions to Elijah that revealed his sovereign power over people and nations. Even though Israel would experience divine judgment through Hazael, Jehu and Elisha, God would continue to preserve a remnant faithful to himself among the people. *go to the Desert of Damascus.* Apparently Elijah is to go back by way of the road east of the Dead Sea and the Jordan. As it turns out, all three anointings take place east of the Jordan, though it is Elisha who effects the anointing of the two kings. *anoint.* Appears to mean here no more than "designate as divinely appointed." This anointing was actually done by Elijah's successor Elisha (see 2Ki 8:7–15). *Hazael.* Subsequently became a serious threat to Israel during the reigns of Joram, Jehu and Jehoahaz (see 2Ki 8:28–29; 10:32–33; 12:17–18; 13:3,22). There are references to Hazael on ivory fragments from Arslan Tash (north Syria) and Nimrud (Assyria). Tiglath-Pileser III, king of Assyria (see chart, p. 472), called Damascus (Aram) the "House of Hazael."

19:16 *anoint Jehu.* Jehu was a military commander under Ahab and Joram, Ahab's son (2Ki 9:5–6). He was anointed king over Israel by a "man from the company of the prophets" at the instruction of Elisha (2Ki 9:1–16), with the mandate to destroy the house of Ahab. *Elisha.* As with Elijah (see note on 17:1), Elisha's name (meaning "God is salvation" or "God saves") was the essence of his ministry. His name evokes memory of Joshua ("The LORD saves"). Elijah is given someone to finish his work just as Moses was, and Elisha channels the covenant blessings to the faithful in Israel just as Joshua brought Israel into the promised land (see the account of Elisha's ministry in 2Ki 2:19—8:15; 9:1–3; 13:14–20). In the NT John the Baptist ("Elijah," Mt 11:14; 17:12–13) was followed by Jesus ("Joshua"; see NIV text note on Mt 1:21) to complete God's saving work. *son of Shaphat.* Shaphat means "He judges," which is also in accordance with Elisha's ministry. *Abel Meholah.* See map, p. 518.

19:17 *Jehu will put to death any who escape the sword of Hazael.* See 2Ki 9:24. *Elisha will put to death any who escape the sword of Jehu.* How this may have been fulfilled we are not told, but see 2Ki 2:24; 8:1 and notes (see also Hos 6:5 and note).

19:18 *seven thousand.* A round number, no doubt symbolic of the fullness or completeness of the divinely preserved godly remnant (see Ro 11:2–4 and note on 11:5). In any case Elijah had been mistaken in his conclusion that he alone had remained faithful (see vv. 10,14; 18:22 and note). *not kissed him.* See Hos 13:2 and note.

19:19 *threw his cloak around him.* Thus designating Elisha as his successor (see note on v. 16).

19:21 *slaughtered them ... burned the plowing equipment.* Elisha's break with his past vocation was complete, though he obviously came from a wealthy family. *attendant.* In Hebrew the same designation as used for Joshua's relationship to Moses ("aide," Ex 24:13; 33:11).

20:1 *Ben-Hadad king of Aram.* Chronological considerations suggest that this was Ben-Hadad II (see note on 2Ki 8:7), either a son or a grandson of Ben-Hadad I, who had ruled Aram as early as 900–895 B.C. (see notes on 15:9–10,18–20,33). The events of this chapter span parts of two years (see vv. 22–26) followed by three years of peace between Israel and Aram (see 22:1). Ahab died at the conclusion of the three years of peace in a battle against the Arameans (22:37) in 853. This means that the events of this chapter are to be dated c. 857. *Aram.* See notes on Ge 10:22; Dt 26:5. *thirty-two kings.* Tribal chieftains or city-state kings who were vassals of Ben-Hadad II. *Samaria.* See note on 16:24.

[4]The king of Israel answered, "Just as you say, my lord the king. I and all I have are yours."

[5]The messengers came again and said, "This is what Ben-Hadad says: 'I sent to demand your silver and gold, your wives and your children. [6]But about this time tomorrow I am going to send my officials to search your palace and the houses of your officials. They will seize everything you value and carry it away.' "

[7]The king of Israel summoned all the elders[n] of the land and said to them, "See how this man is looking for trouble![o] When he sent for my wives and my children, my silver and my gold, I did not refuse him."

[8]The elders and the people all answered, "Don't listen to him or agree to his demands."

[9]So he replied to Ben-Hadad's messengers, "Tell my lord the king, 'Your servant will do all you demanded the first time, but this demand I cannot meet.' " They left and took the answer back to Ben-Hadad.

[10]Then Ben-Hadad sent another message to Ahab: "May the gods deal with me, be it ever so severely, if enough dust[p] remains in Samaria to give each of my men a handful."

[11]The king of Israel answered, "Tell him: 'One who puts on his armor should not boast[q] like one who takes it off.' "

[12]Ben-Hadad heard this message while he and the kings were drinking[r] in their tents,[a] and he ordered his men: "Prepare to attack." So they prepared to attack the city.

20:7 [n] 1Sa 11:3 [o] 2Ki 5:7
20:10 [p] S 2Sa 22:43
20:11 [q] Pr 27:1; Jer 9:23; Am 2:14
20:12 [r] S 1Ki 16:9

[a] 12 Or *in Succoth*; also in verse 16

20:4 *I and all I have are yours.* Ahab's submission to Ben-Hadad's demand suggests that Israel saw little hope for the possibility of a military victory over the Aramean forces. The negotiated settlement would end the siege on Samaria, spare Ahab's life and avoid the plundering of the city.

20:6 *I am going to send my officials to search your palace and the houses of your officials.* Ben-Hadad's new demand required the surrender of the city to his forces.

20:9 *this demand I cannot meet.* Ahab replied in language conceding Ben-Hadad's superiority ("my lord the king, 'Your servant ...' ") but was adamant in refusing to surrender the city.

20:10 *May the gods deal with me, be it ever so severely.* A curse formula (see note on 1Sa 3:17).

20:11 *One who puts on his armor should not boast like one who takes it off.* A saying similar to the familiar "Don't count your chickens before they hatch."

Lives of Elijah and Elisha

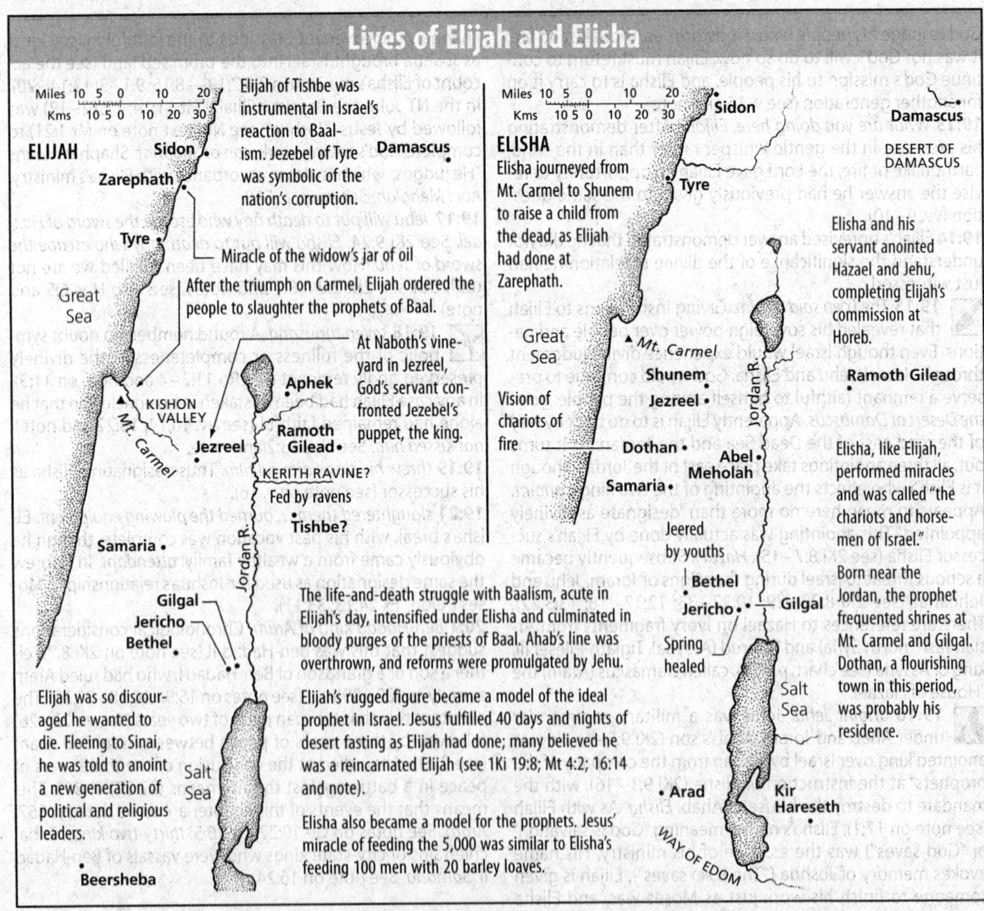

Miles 10 5 0 10 20
Kms 10 5 0 10 20 30
ELIJAH
Elijah of Tishbe was instrumental in Israel's reaction to Baalism. Jezebel of Tyre was symbolic of the nation's corruption.
Sidon
Damascus
Zarephath
Tyre
Miracle of the widow's jar of oil
After the triumph on Carmel, Elijah ordered the people to slaughter the prophets of Baal.
Great Sea
At Naboth's vineyard in Jezreel, God's servant confronted Jezebel's puppet, the king.
Aphek
KISHON VALLEY
Mt. Carmel
Jezreel
Ramoth Gilead
KERITH RAVINE?
Fed by ravens
Tishbe?
Samaria
Jordan R.
Gilgal
Jericho
Bethel
Elijah was so discouraged he wanted to die. Fleeing to Sinai, he was told to anoint a new generation of political and religious leaders.
Salt Sea
Beersheba
The life-and-death struggle with Baalism, acute in Elijah's day, intensified under Elisha and culminated in bloody purges of the priests of Baal. Ahab's line was overthrown, and reforms were promulgated by Jehu.
Elijah's rugged figure became a model of the ideal prophet in Israel. Jesus fulfilled 40 days and nights of desert fasting as Elijah had done; many believed he was a reincarnated Elijah (see 1Ki 19:8; Mt 4:2; 16:14 and note).
Elisha also became a model for the prophets. Jesus' miracle of feeding the 5,000 was similar to Elisha's feeding 100 men with 20 barley loaves.
Miles 10 5 0 10 20
Kms 10 5 0 10 20 30
ELISHA
Elisha journeyed from Mt. Carmel to Shunem to raise a child from the dead, as Elijah had done at Zarephath.
Sidon
Damascus
DESERT OF DAMASCUS
Tyre
Elisha and his servant anointed Hazael and Jehu, completing Elijah's commission at Horeb.
Great Sea
Mt. Carmel
Shunem
Ramoth Gilead
Jordan R.
Vision of chariots of fire
Jezreel
Dothan
Abel Meholah
Samaria
Elisha, like Elijah, performed miracles and was called "the chariots and horsemen of Israel."
Jeered by youths
Bethel
Jericho
Gilgal
Born near the Jordan, the prophet frequented shrines at Mt. Carmel and Gilgal. Dothan, a flourishing town in this period, was probably his residence.
Spring healed
Salt Sea
Arad
Kir Hareseth
WAY OF EDOM

Ahab Defeats Ben-Hadad

13Meanwhile a prophet[s] came to Ahab
king of Israel and announced, "This is
what the LORD says: 'Do you see this vast
army? I will give it into your hand today,
and then you will know[t] that I am the
LORD.' "
14"But who will do this?" asked Ahab.
The prophet replied, "This is what the
LORD says: 'The young officers of the provincial commanders will do it.' "
"And who will start[u] the battle?" he
asked.
The prophet answered, "You will."
15So Ahab summoned the young officers of the provincial commanders, 232
men. Then he assembled the rest of the
Israelites, 7,000 in all. 16They set out at
noon while Ben-Hadad and the 32 kings
allied with him were in their tents getting
drunk.[v] 17The young officers of the provincial commanders went out first.
Now Ben-Hadad had dispatched scouts,
who reported, "Men are advancing from
Samaria."
18He said, "If they have come out for
peace, take them alive; if they have come
out for war, take them alive."
19The young officers of the provincial
commanders marched out of the city with
the army behind them 20and each one
struck down his opponent. At that, the
Arameans fled, with the Israelites in pursuit. But Ben-Hadad king of Aram escaped
on horseback with some of his horsemen.
21The king of Israel advanced and overpowered the horses and chariots and inflicted heavy losses on the Arameans.
22Afterward, the prophet[w] came to the
king of Israel and said, "Strengthen your
position and see what must be done, because next spring[x] the king of Aram will
attack you again."
23Meanwhile, the officials of the king
of Aram advised him, "Their gods are
gods[y] of the hills. That is why they were
too strong for us. But if we fight them
on the plains, surely we will be stronger
than they. 24Do this: Remove all the kings
from their commands and replace them
with other officers. 25You must also raise
an army like the one you lost—horse for
horse and chariot for chariot—so we can
fight Israel on the plains. Then surely we
will be stronger than they." He agreed
with them and acted accordingly.
26The next spring[z] Ben-Hadad mustered
the Arameans and went up to Aphek[a] to
fight against Israel. 27When the Israelites
were also mustered and given provisions,
they marched out to meet them. The Israelites camped opposite them like two
small flocks of goats, while the Arameans
covered the countryside.[b]
28The man of God came up and told the
king of Israel, "This is what the LORD says:
'Because the Arameans think the LORD is
a god of the hills and not a god[c] of the
valleys, I will deliver this vast army into
your hands, and you will know[d] that I am
the LORD.' "
29For seven days they camped opposite
each other, and on the seventh day the
battle was joined. The Israelites inflicted a hundred thousand casualties on the
Aramean foot soldiers in one day. 30The
rest of them escaped to the city of Aphek,[e]
where the wall collapsed[f] on twenty-seven

20:13 [s]S Jdg 6:8 [t]S Ex 6:7 **20:14** [u]S Jdg 1:1 **20:16** [v]S 1Ki 16:9 **20:22** [w]S Jdg 6:8 [x]S 2Sa 11:1 **20:23** [y]ver 28; Isa 36:20; Ro 1:21-23 **20:26** [z]S 2Sa 11:1 [a]ver 30; S 1Sa 4:1; 2Ki 13:17 **20:27** [b]Jdg 6:6; S 1Sa 13:6 **20:28** [c]S ver 23 [d]S Ex 6:7; Jer 16:19-21 **20:30** [e]S ver 26 [f]Ps 62:4; Isa 26:21; 30:13

20:13 *you will know that I am the LORD.* Although Ahab had not sought God's help in the crisis confronting the city, the Lord graciously chose to reveal himself yet another time (see 18:36–37) to the king and people, this time through a deliverance.

20:14 *young officers of the provincial commanders.* See note on 16:27. Organizational details of the provincial government of the northern kingdom are unknown.

20:15 *232 men ... 7,000 in all.* Not a large military force (though a significant number for a city under siege) but one of fitting size for demonstrating that the imminent victory was from the Lord rather than from Israel's own military superiority (cf. Jdg 7:2).

20:20 *each one struck down his opponent.* Apparently they were met by a small advance force like their own (see 2Sa 2:15–16). *escaped on horseback with some of his horsemen.* Since fighting on horseback did not come until later, reference must be to chariot horses and charioteers. After their defeat, the Arameans seem to have withdrawn to Damascus.

20:22 *the king of Aram will attack you again.* The anonymous prophet (see v. 13) warned Ahab against undue self-confidence. The prophet's announcement of an impending renewed attack by Ben-Hadad should have driven Ahab to more complete reliance on the God who had revealed himself on Mount Carmel and in the recent military victory.

20:23 *gods of the hills.* An expression of the pagan idea that a deity's power extended only over the limited area of his particular jurisdiction. *That is why they were too strong for us.* The Arameans believed that the outcome of military conflicts depended on the relative strength of the gods of the opposing forces rather than on the inherent strength of the two armies. For this reason, their strategy was to fight the next battle in a way that advantageously maximized the supposed strengths and weaknesses of the deities involved.

20:26 *Aphek.* Presumably the Aphek located a few miles east of the Sea of Galilee (see map, p. 518). The battle apparently took place in the Jordan Valley near the juncture of the Yarmuk and Jordan rivers.

20:28 *man of God.* Apparently the same prophet mentioned in vv. 13,22. *you will know that I am the LORD.* See note on v. 13. God will again demonstrate that he is the sovereign ruler over all nature and history and that the pagan nature deities are powerless before him.

20:29 *a hundred thousand casualties.* For the problem of apparently excessively large numbers of people in Biblical narrative, see Introduction to Numbers: Special Problem.

20:30 *wall collapsed.* The God of Israel not only gave Israel's army a victory in battle but also caused an additional disaster to fall on the Aramean army. *twenty-seven thousand.* See note on v. 29.

thousand of them. And Ben-Hadad fled to
the city and hid[g] in an inner room.
31His officials said to him, "Look, we
have heard that the kings of the house of
Israel are merciful.[h] Let us go to the king
of Israel with sackcloth[i] around our waists
and ropes around our heads. Perhaps he
will spare your life."
32Wearing sackcloth around their waists
and ropes around their heads, they went to
the king of Israel and said, "Your servant
Ben-Hadad says: 'Please let me live.' "
The king answered, "Is he still alive? He
is my brother."
33The men took this as a good sign and
were quick to pick up his word. "Yes, your
brother Ben-Hadad!" they said.
"Go and get him," the king said. When
Ben-Hadad came out, Ahab had him come
up into his chariot.
34"I will return the cities[j] my father
took from your father," Ben-Hadad[k] offered.
"You may set up your own market
areas[l] in Damascus,[m] as my father did in
Samaria."
⌞Ahab said,⌟ "On the basis of a treaty[n]
I will set you free." So he made a treaty
with him, and let him go.

A Prophet Condemns Ahab

35By the word of the LORD one of the
sons of the prophets[o] said to his companion,
"Strike me with your weapon," but
the man refused.[p]
36So the prophet said, "Because you
have not obeyed the LORD, as soon as you
leave me a lion[q] will kill you." And after
the man went away, a lion found him and
killed him.
37The prophet found another man and
said, "Strike me, please." So the man
struck him and wounded him.
38Then the
prophet went and stood by the road waiting
for the king. He disguised himself with
his headband down over his eyes.
39As the
king passed by, the prophet called out to
him, "Your servant went into the thick of
the battle, and someone came to me with
a captive and said, 'Guard this man. If he
is missing, it will be your life for his life,[r]
or you must pay a talent[a] of silver.'
40While
your servant was busy here and there, the
man disappeared."
"That is your sentence,"[s] the king of Israel
said. "You have pronounced it yourself."
41Then the prophet quickly removed the
headband from his eyes, and the king of
Israel recognized him as one of the prophets.
42He said to the king, "This is what
the LORD says: 'You[t] have set free a man I
had determined should die.[b][u] Therefore it
is your life for his life,[v] your people for his
people.' "
43Sullen and angry,[w] the king of
Israel went to his palace in Samaria.

20:30 [g] 1Ki 22:25
20:31 [h] Job 41:3 [i] S Ge 37:34
20:34 [j] 1Ki 15:20 [k] S Ge 10:22 [l] 2Sa 8:6 [m] S Ge 14:15; Jer 49:23-27 [n] S Ex 23:32
20:35 [o] S 1Sa 10:5; Am 7:14 [p] S 1Ki 13:21
20:36 [q] 1Ki 13:24
20:39 [r] S Jos 2:14
20:40 [s] 2Sa 12:5; S 14:13
20:42 [t] S 2Sa 12:7 [u] Jer 48:10 [v] S Jos 2:14
20:43 [w] 1Ki 21:4

[a] *39* That is, about 75 pounds (about 34 kilograms)
[b] *42* The Hebrew term refers to the irrevocable giving over of things or persons to the LORD, often by totally destroying them.

20:31 *kings of the house of Israel are merciful.* The Arameans recognized that Israel's kings were different from, e.g., the ruthless Assyrian kings. *sackcloth ... ropes.* Perhaps here symbolic of humility and submission.
20:32 *Your servant.* In the diplomatic language of the time, Ben-Hadad acknowledged his inferiority and subordination to Ahab by designating himself Ahab's servant (see note on v. 9). *my brother.* Ahab disregarded Ben-Hadad's concession and responded in terminology used by rulers who considered themselves equals (see 9:13 and note). In doing this, Ahab gave much more than Ben-Hadad had asked or expected.
20:33 *come up into his chariot.* Not the treatment normally accorded a defeated military opponent.
20:34 *cities my father took from your father.* Perhaps Ramoth Gilead (see 22:3 and note) along with some of the cities Ben-Hadad I had taken from Baasha (15:20) at an even earlier time. *your own market areas.* Outlets for engaging in the lucrative international trade—a distinct economic advantage; usually such privileges were a jealously guarded local monopoly. *made a treaty with him, and let him go.* A parity treaty (a peace treaty between equals) that included among its provisions the political and trade agreements proposed by Ben-Hadad. In all this, the Lord was not consulted.
20:35 *sons of the prophets.* An expression designating members of prophetic companies (see 2Ki 2:3,5,7,15 and note on 2:3; 4:1,38; 5:22; 6:1; 9:1). "Son" is not to be understood here as "male child" or "descendant" but as the member of a group. These companies of prophets were apparently religious communities that sprang up in the face of general indifference and apostasy for the purpose of mutual edification and the cultivation of the experience of God. It seems likely that they were known as prophets because their religious practices (sometimes ecstatic) were called prophesying (see 18:29 and note; Nu 11:25–27; 1Sa 10:5–6, 10–11; 18:10; 19:20–24)—to be distinguished from "prophet" in the sense of one bringing ("prophesying") a word from the Lord. The relationship of the Lord's great prophets (such as Samuel, Elijah and Elisha) to these communities was understandably a close one, the Lord's prophets probably being viewed as their spiritual mentors.
20:36 *as soon as you leave me a lion will kill you.* A penalty reminiscent of what happened to the man of God from Judah (13:23–24).
20:39 *talent.* See NIV text note. Because few soldiers could have paid such a large sum, it would appear to Ahab that the man's life was at stake.
20:40 *That is your sentence.* Ahab refused to grant clemency. Little did he know that he was pronouncing his own death sentence (cf. the similar technique used by Nathan the prophet, 2Sa 12:1–12).
20:42 *a man I had determined should die.* See NIV text note and notes on Lev 27:28; Jos 6:17. It is not clear whether Ahab violated a previous revelation or erred by simply neglecting to inquire of the Lord before releasing Ben-Hadad. In any case, the Lord had given Ben-Hadad into Ahab's hand (see v. 28), and Ahab was responsible to the Lord for his custody. *your life for his life, your people for his people.* Because Ahab sinned in his official capacity as king, the sentence fell not only on Ahab personally but also on the people of the northern kingdom. Ahab died in battle against the Arameans (22:29–39), and Israel was severely humiliated by them during the reigns of Jehu and Jehoahaz (2Ki 10:32; 13:3).

Naboth's Vineyard

21 Some time later there was an incident involving a vineyard belonging
to Naboth[x] the Jezreelite. The vineyard
was in Jezreel,[y] close to the palace of
Ahab king of Samaria. 2 Ahab said to Naboth, "Let me have your vineyard to use
for a vegetable garden, since it is close to
my palace. In exchange I will give you a
better vineyard or, if you prefer, I will pay
you whatever it is worth."
3 But Naboth replied, "The LORD forbid
that I should give you the inheritance[z] of
my fathers."
4 So Ahab went home, sullen and angry[a]
because Naboth the Jezreelite had said,
"I will not give you the inheritance of my
fathers." He lay on his bed sulking and
refused[b] to eat.
5 His wife Jezebel came in and asked
him, "Why are you so sullen? Why won't
you eat?"
6 He answered her, "Because I said to
Naboth the Jezreelite, 'Sell me your vineyard; or if you prefer, I will give you another vineyard in its place.' But he said, 'I
will not give you my vineyard.'"
7 Jezebel his wife said, "Is this how you
act as king over Israel? Get up and eat!
Cheer up. I'll get you the vineyard[c] of Naboth the Jezreelite."
8 So she wrote letters[d] in Ahab's name,
placed his seal[e] on them, and sent them
to the elders and nobles who lived in Naboth's city with him. 9 In those letters she
wrote:

> "Proclaim a day of fasting and seat
> Naboth in a prominent place among
> the people. 10 But seat two scoundrels[f]
> opposite him and have them testify
> that he has cursed[g] both God and the
> king. Then take him out and stone
> him to death."

11 So the elders and nobles who lived in
Naboth's city did as Jezebel directed in
the letters she had written to them. 12 They
proclaimed a fast[h] and seated Naboth in a
prominent place among the people. 13 Then
two scoundrels came and sat opposite him
and brought charges against Naboth before
the people, saying, "Naboth has cursed
both God and the king." So they took him
outside the city and stoned him to death.[i]
14 Then they sent word to Jezebel: "Naboth
has been stoned and is dead."
15 As soon as Jezebel heard that Naboth
had been stoned to death, she said to
Ahab, "Get up and take possession of the
vineyard[j] of Naboth the Jezreelite that he
refused to sell you. He is no longer alive,
but dead." 16 When Ahab heard that Naboth was dead, he got up and went down
to take possession of Naboth's vineyard.
17 Then the word of the LORD came to
Elijah the Tishbite: 18 "Go down to meet
Ahab king of Israel, who rules in Samaria.
He is now in Naboth's vineyard, where he
has gone to take possession of it. 19 Say to
him, 'This is what the LORD says: Have you
not murdered a man and seized his property?'[k] Then say to him, 'This is what the
LORD says: In the place where dogs licked
up Naboth's blood,[l] dogs[m] will lick up
your blood—yes, yours!'"
20 Ahab said to Elijah, "So you have
found me, my enemy!"[n]
"I have found you," he answered, "because you have sold[o] yourself to do evil
in the eyes of the LORD. 21 'I am going to
bring disaster on you. I will consume your
descendants and cut off from Ahab every

21:1 [x]2Ki 9:21 [y]S 1Sa 29:1; 2Ki 10:1 **21:3** [z]S Lev 25:23 **21:4** [a]1Ki 20:43 [b]1Sa 28:23 **21:7** [c]S 1Sa 8:14 **21:8** [d]2Sa 11:14 [e]S Ge 38:18 **21:10** [f]S Dt 13:13; Ac 6:11 [g]S Ex 22:28; Lev 24:15-16 **21:12** [h]Isa 58:4 **21:13** [i]S Lev 24:16 **21:15** [j]S 1Sa 8:14 **21:19** [k]Job 24:6; 31:39 [l]2Ki 9:26; Ps 9:12; Isa 14:20 [m]1Ki 22:38; Ps 68:23; Jer 15:3 **21:20** [n]S 1Ki 18:17 [o]2Ki 17:17; Ro 7:14

21:1 *close to the palace of Ahab.* Ahab maintained a residence in Jezreel in addition to his official palace in Samaria (see 18:45; 2Ki 9:30). *Samaria.* The entire northern kingdom is here represented by its capital city (see note on 16:24).
21:2 *Let me have your vineyard.* Because royal power in Israel was limited by covenantal law (see Dt 17:14–20; 1Sa 10:25), Ahab was unable simply to confiscate privately held land, as was customary with Canaanite kings (see note on v. 7; see also 1Sa 8:9–17).
21:3 Naboth's refusal to dispose of his land was based on the conviction that the land was the Lord's, that he had granted a perpetual lease to each Israelite family and that this lease was to be jealously preserved as the family's permanent inheritance in the promised land.
21:7 *Is this how you act as king over Israel?* A sarcastic remark of incredulity spoken by one accustomed to the despotic practices of the Phoenician and Canaanite kings, who would not hesitate a moment to use their power to satisfy personal interests (contrast the attitude and practice of Samuel in the exercise of his civil power, 1Sa 12:3–4).
21:9 *Proclaim a day of fasting.* Jezebel attempted to create the impression that a disaster threatened the people that could be averted only if they would humble themselves before the Lord and remove any person whose sin had brought God's judgment on them (cf. Jdg 20:26; 1Sa 7:5–6; 2Ch 20:2–4).
21:10 *two.* Mosaic law required two witnesses for capital offenses (Nu 35:30; Dt 17:6; 19:15). *scoundrels.* See note on Dt 13:13 ("wicked"). *have them testify.* The entire scenario was designed to give an appearance of legitimate judicial procedure (see Ex 20:16; 23:7; Lev 19:16). *he has cursed both God and the king.* For this the Mosaic law prescribed death by stoning (Lev 24:15–16).
21:13 *outside the city.* In accordance with Mosaic law (Lev 24:14; Nu 15:35–36). Naboth was stoned on his own field (compare v. 19 with 2Ki 9:21,26), and his sons were stoned with him (see 2Ki 9:26; cf. the case of Achan, Jos 7: 24–25), thus also eliminating his heirs.
21:19 *Have you not murdered a man and seized his property?* Ahab's willing compliance with Jezebel's scheme made him guilty of murder and theft. *In the place where dogs licked up Naboth's blood, dogs will lick up your blood.* Ahab's subsequent repentance (v. 29) occasioned the postponement of certain aspects of this prophecy until the time of his son Joram, whose body was thrown on the field of Naboth (2Ki 9:25–26). Ahab himself was killed in battle at Ramoth Gilead (22:29–37) and his body brought to Samaria, where the dogs licked the blood being washed from his chariot (22:38).
21:21 *slave or free.* See note on 14:10.

last male[p] in Israel—slave or free.[q] 22I will
make your house[r] like that of Jeroboam
son of Nebat and that of Baasha son of
Ahijah, because you have provoked me to
anger and have caused Israel to sin.'[s]
23"And also concerning Jezebel the LORD
says: 'Dogs[t] will devour Jezebel by the
wall of[a] Jezreel.'
24"Dogs[u] will eat those belonging to
Ahab who die in the city, and the birds of
the air[v] will feed on those who die in the
country."
25(There was never[w] a man like Ahab,
who sold himself to do evil in the eyes of
the LORD, urged on by Jezebel his wife.
26He behaved in the vilest manner by going after idols, like the Amorites[x] the LORD
drove out before Israel.)
27When Ahab heard these words, he tore
his clothes, put on sackcloth[y] and fasted. He
lay in sackcloth and went around meekly.[z]
28Then the word of the LORD came to
Elijah the Tishbite: 29"Have you noticed
how Ahab has humbled himself before
me? Because he has humbled[a] himself, I
will not bring this disaster in his day,[b] but
I will bring it on his house in the days of
his son."[c]

Micaiah Prophesies Against Ahab

22:1-28pp — 2Ch 18:1-27

22 For three years there was no war between Aram and Israel. 2But in the
third year Jehoshaphat king of Judah went
down to see the king of Israel. 3The king of
Israel had said to his officials, "Don't you
know that Ramoth Gilead[d] belongs to us
and yet we are doing nothing to retake it
from the king of Aram?"
4So he asked Jehoshaphat, "Will you
go with me to fight[e] against Ramoth Gilead?"
Jehoshaphat replied to the king of Israel, "I am as you are, my people as your
people, my horses as your horses." 5But
Jehoshaphat also said to the king of Israel,
"First seek the counsel[f] of the LORD."
6So the king of Israel brought together the prophets—about four hundred
men—and asked them, "Shall I go to
war against Ramoth Gilead, or shall I refrain?"
"Go,"[g] they answered, "for the Lord will
give it into the king's hand."[h]
7But Jehoshaphat asked, "Is there not a
prophet[i] of the LORD here whom we can
inquire[j] of?"
8The king of Israel answered Jehoshaphat, "There is still one man through
whom we can inquire of the LORD, but I
hate[k] him because he never prophesies
anything good[l] about me, but always bad.
He is Micaiah son of Imlah."

21:21 [p] Jdg 9:5; 2Ki 10:7 [q] S Dt 32:36 **21:22** [r] 1Ki 16:3 [s] S 1Ki 12:30 **21:23** [t] 2Ki 9:10, 34-36 **21:24** [u] 1Ki 14:11 [v] S Ge 40:19; S Dt 28:26 **21:25** [w] S 1Ki 14:9; S 16:33 **21:26** [x] S Ge 15:16 **21:27** [y] S Ge 37:34; S Jer 4:8 [z] Isa 38:15 **21:29** [a] S Ex 10:3 [b] S Ex 32:14; 2Ki 22:20 [c] Ex 20:5; 2Ki 9:26; 10:6-10 **22:3** [d] S Dt 4:43 **22:4** [e] 2Ki 3:7 **22:5** [f] Ex 33:7; 2Ki 3:11; Job 38:2; Ps 32:8; 73:24; 107:11 **22:6** [g] S Jdg 18:6 [h] S 1Ki 13:18 **22:7** [i] Dt 18:15; 2Ki 3:11; 5:8 [j] S Nu 27:21; 2Ki 3:11 **22:8** [k] Am 5:10 [l] ver 13; Isa 5:20; 30:10; Jer 23:17

[a] *23* Most Hebrew manuscripts; a few Hebrew manuscripts, Vulgate and Syriac (see also 2 Kings 9:26) *the plot of ground at*

21:22 *like that of Jeroboam.* See 14:10; 15:28–30. *that of Baasha.* See 16:3–4,11–13.
21:24 See notes on 14:11; 16:4.
21:25 *urged on by Jezebel.* See 16:31; 18:4; 19:1–2; 21:7.
21:26 *idols.* See note on Lev 26:30. *Amorites.* Here a designation for the entire pre-Israelite population of Canaan (see Ge 15:16; Dt 1:7 and notes).
21:27 *sackcloth.* See note on Ge 37:34.
21:29 *Because . . . , I will not bring this disaster.* See Jnh 3:10 and note. *in the days of his son.* The judgment was postponed but not rescinded (see note on v. 19).
22:1 *three years.* See note on 20:1. *no war between Aram and Israel.* The annals of the Assyrian ruler Shalmaneser III (859–824 B.C.) record the participation of both "Ahab the Israelite" and Hadadezer (Ben-Hadad) of Damascus in a coalition of 12 rulers that fought against Assyrian forces at Qarqar on the Orontes River in 853. According to the Assyrian records, Ahab contributed 2,000 chariots and 10,000 foot soldiers to the allied forces. Assyrian claims of victory appear exaggerated since they withdrew and did not venture westward again for four or five years.
22:2 *Jehoshaphat king of Judah went down to see the king of Israel.* Perhaps to congratulate him on the success of the western alliance against the Assyrian threat (see notes on v. 1; 2Ch 18:2).
22:3 *Ramoth Gilead.* Located near the Yarmuk River in Transjordan; an Israelite city since the days of Moses (see 4:13; Dt 4:43; Jos 20:8). *belongs to us.* Israel could lay claim to Ramoth Gilead also by virtue of the treaty concluded with Ben-Hadad a few years earlier (see 20:34 and note), the provisions of which he had apparently failed to honor.
22:4 *he asked Jehoshaphat.* Ironically, the king whom Ahab asked to go with him in battle to secure his victory bore the name Jehoshaphat, which means "The LORD judges/rules." Little did he realize—and he would not believe—that the judging Lord would "go with" him into the battle to guide a certain arrow. Significantly, in this episode the king of Israel is named only once, and that by the Lord in the heavenly court scene (v. 20). But the narrator bombards the reader with the fateful name Jehoshaphat 12 times. And then there is Zedekiah ("The LORD is righteous"), and there is Micaiah ("Who is like the LORD?"). Even though Ahab had just been allied with the Arameans against the Assyrians, now that the Assyrian threat was over he did not hesitate to seize an opportunity to free Ramoth Gilead from Aramean control. *I am as you are, my people as your people, my horses as your horses.* In this alliance, Jehoshaphat completely reversed the policy of his father Asa, who had entered into an alliance with the Arameans against Baasha of the northern kingdom (see 15:17–23). Of the two allies, only Jehosphaphat realized that the two Israelite kings had actually to do with two other kings: the king of Aram and the King sitting on the heavenly throne (see v. 19 and note). Jehoshaphat was later to be condemned by the prophet Jehu (see 2Ch 19:2 and note) for violating the Lord's will by joining forces with Ahab.
22:5 *First seek the counsel of the LORD.* Jehoshaphat hesitated to proceed with the planned action without the assurance of the Lord's favor (see 1Sa 23:1–4; 2Sa 2:1).
22:6 *prophets.* No doubt associated with the paganized worship at Bethel (see notes on 12:28–29), they exercised their "office" by proclaiming messages designed to please the king (see Am 7:10–13).
22:7 *Is there not a prophet of the LORD here . . . ?* Jehoshaphat recognized that the 400 prophets were not to be relied on (see Eze 13:2–3) and asked for consultation with a true prophet of the Lord.
22:8 *never prophesies anything good.* Ahab's assessment of a

"The king should not say that," Jehoshaphat replied.
9 So the king of Israel called one of his
officials and said, "Bring Micaiah son of
Imlah at once."
10 Dressed in their royal robes, the king
of Israel and Jehoshaphat king of Judah
were sitting on their thrones at the threshing floor[m] by the entrance of the gate of
Samaria, with all the prophets prophesying before them. 11 Now Zedekiah[n] son of
Kenaanah had made iron horns[o] and he
declared, "This is what the LORD says:
'With these you will gore the Arameans
until they are destroyed.'"
12 All the other prophets were prophesying the same thing. "Attack Ramoth Gilead and be victorious," they said, "for the
LORD will give it into the king's hand."
13 The messenger who had gone to summon Micaiah said to him, "Look, as one
man the other prophets are predicting success for the king. Let your word agree with
theirs, and speak favorably."[p]
14 But Micaiah said, "As surely as the
LORD lives, I can tell him only what the
LORD tells me."[q]
15 When he arrived, the king asked him,
"Micaiah, shall we go to war against Ramoth Gilead, or shall I refrain?"
"Attack and be victorious," he answered, "for the LORD will give it into the
king's hand."
16 The king said to him, "How many
times must I make you swear to tell me
nothing but the truth in the name of the
LORD?"
17 Then Micaiah answered, "I saw all Israel scattered[r] on the hills like sheep without a shepherd,[s] and the LORD said, 'These
people have no master. Let each one go
home in peace.'"
18 The king of Israel said to Jehoshaphat,
"Didn't I tell you that he never prophesies
anything good about me, but only bad?"
19 Micaiah continued, "Therefore hear
the word of the LORD: I saw the LORD sitting on his throne[t] with all the host[u] of
heaven standing around him on his right
and on his left. 20 And the LORD said, 'Who
will entice Ahab into attacking Ramoth
Gilead and going to his death there?'
"One suggested this, and another that.
21 Finally, a spirit came forward, stood before the LORD and said, 'I will entice him.'
22 "'By what means?' the LORD asked.
"'I will go out and be a lying[v] spirit in
the mouths of all his prophets,' he said.
"'You will succeed in enticing him,' said
the LORD. 'Go and do it.'
23 "So now the LORD has put a lying[w]
spirit in the mouths of all these prophets[x]
of yours. The LORD has decreed disaster[y]
for you."
24 Then Zedekiah[z] son of Kenaanah
went up and slapped[a] Micaiah in the face.
"Which way did the spirit from[a] the LORD
go when he went from me to speak[b] to
you?" he asked.
25 Micaiah replied, "You will find out
on the day you go to hide[c] in an inner
room."

22:10 [m] S Jdg 6:37
22:11 [n] ver 24 [o] Dt 33:17; Jer 27:2; 28:10; Zec 1:18-21
22:13 [p] S ver 8
22:14 [q] S Nu 22:18; S 1Sa 3:17
22:17 [r] S Ge 11:4; Na 3:18 [s] Nu 27:17; Isa 13:14; S Mt 9:36
22:19 [t] Ps 47:8; Isa 6:1; 63:15; Eze 1:26; Da 7:9 [u] Job 1:6; 15:8; 38:7; Ps 103:20-21; 148:2; Jer 23:18,22; Lk 2:13
22:22 [v] S Jdg 9:23; 2Th 2:11
22:23 [w] S Dt 13:3 [x] Eze 14:9 [y] S Dt 31:29
22:24 [z] ver 11 [a] Ac 23:2 [b] Job 26:4
22:25 [c] 1Ki 20:30

[a] 24 Or *Spirit of*

prophet depended on whether his message was favorable to him (see 18:17; 21:20).

22:10 A pause in the action to describe a scene on earth (kings in royal splendor on their thrones surrounded by Ahab's minions and confidently planning a campaign of conquest), a scene that will shortly be outmatched by the description of a scene in heaven (Israel's Great King on his throne surrounded by his heavenly host and planning his campaign against King Ahab [vv. 19–23]). By reporting that Ahab and Jehoshaphat were sitting "at the threshing floor [where sheaves are crushed (Mic 4:12) and grain is winnowed (Jer 15:7)] by the entrance of the gate [where courts sit in judgment (Dt 21:19; Ru 4:1,11)] of Samaria," the author hints with biting irony at the outcome of Ahab's grand design.

22:11 *Zedekiah.* Evidently the spokesman for the 400 prophets. *iron horns.* A symbol of power (see Dt 33:17).

22:13 *Let your word agree with theirs.* A bit of advice reflecting the view that all prophets were merely self-serving.

22:15 *we.* A subtle shift (see v. 6) that seeks a favorable response by including Jehoshaphat as a cosponsor of the enterprise. *Attack ... for the LORD will give it into the king's hand.* Micaiah sarcastically mimics the 400 false prophets (see v. 12).

22:16 *tell me nothing but the truth.* Micaiah apparently betrayed his lack of seriousness, and Ahab immediately recognized this.

22:17 *like sheep without a shepherd ... These people have no master.* Using the imagery of shepherd and sheep (see Nu 27:16–17; Zec 13:7; Mt 9:36; 26:31), Micaiah depicts Ahab's death in the upcoming battle.

22:19 *I saw the LORD sitting on his throne.* A true prophet was one who had, as it were, been made privy to what had transpired in God's heavenly throne room and so could truthfully declare what God intended to do (see Isa 6:1; Jer 23:16–22). Micaiah's description of the heavenly scene puts the earthly scene into which he had been brought (see v. 10 and note) in its true light—a powerful portrayal of where the true power lies and of the folly of human pretensions.

22:23 *the LORD has put a lying spirit in the mouths of all these prophets.* Some view the lying spirit as Satan or one of his agents. Others have suggested a spirit of God who undertakes the task of a lying spirit (but see 1Sa 15:29 and note). Still others understand the lying spirit as a symbolic picture of the power of the lie. The Lord had given the 400 prophets over to the power of the lie because they did not love the truth and had chosen to speak out of their own hearts (see Jer 14:14; 23:16,26; Eze 13:2–3,17; see also note on 2Sa 24:1; cf. 2Th 2:9–12 and note on 2:11). King Ahab, who was content to live by a lie and hated the prophet who spoke the truth, was fittingly lured by God to his execution through a lie he wanted to believe (see also Nu 11:18–20; Ps 18:25–26; Eze 14:9 and note).

22:24 *Which way did the spirit from the LORD go when he went from me to speak to you?* By this sarcastic question Zedekiah suggests that one prophet can be a liar just as well as another.

22:25 *hide in an inner room.* Where Zedekiah will seek refuge (cf. 20:30). This will vindicate Micaiah's prophetic authority.

26The king of Israel then ordered, "Take
Micaiah and send him back to Amon the
ruler of the city and to Joash the king's
son 27and say, 'This is what the king says:
Put this fellow in prison[d] and give him
nothing but bread and water until I return
safely.' "
28Micaiah declared, "If you ever return
safely, the LORD has not spoken[e] through
me." Then he added, "Mark my words, all
you people!"

Ahab Killed at Ramoth Gilead

22:29-36pp — 2Ch 18:28-34

29So the king of Israel and Jehoshaphat
king of Judah went up to Ramoth Gilead.
30The king of Israel said to Jehoshaphat, "I
will enter the battle in disguise,[f] but you
wear your royal robes." So the king of Israel disguised himself and went into battle.
31Now the king of Aram[g] had ordered
his thirty-two chariot commanders, "Do
not fight with anyone, small or great, except the king[h] of Israel." 32When the chariot commanders saw Jehoshaphat, they
thought, "Surely this is the king of Israel."
So they turned to attack him, but when
Jehoshaphat cried out, 33the chariot commanders saw that he was not the king of
Israel and stopped pursuing him.
34But someone drew his bow[i] at random
and hit the king of Israel between the sections of his armor. The king told his chariot driver, "Wheel around and get me out
of the fighting. I've been wounded." 35All
day long the battle raged, and the king
was propped up in his chariot facing the
Arameans. The blood from his wound ran
onto the floor of the chariot, and that evening he died. 36As the sun was setting, a
cry spread through the army: "Every man
to his town; everyone to his land!"[j]
37So the king died and was brought
to Samaria, and they buried him there.
38They washed the chariot at a pool in
Samaria (where the prostitutes bathed),[a]
and the dogs[k] licked up his blood, as the
word of the LORD had declared.
39As for the other events of Ahab's reign,
including all he did, the palace he built
and inlaid with ivory,[l] and the cities he
fortified, are they not written in the book
of the annals of the kings of Israel? 40Ahab
rested with his fathers. And Ahaziah his
son succeeded him as king.

Jehoshaphat King of Judah

22:41-50pp — 2Ch 20:31 – 21:1

41Jehoshaphat son of Asa became king
of Judah in the fourth year of Ahab king of
Israel. 42Jehoshaphat was thirty-five years
old when he became king, and he reigned
in Jerusalem twenty-five years. His mother's name was Azubah daughter of Shilhi. 43In everything he walked in the ways
of his father Asa[m] and did not stray from
them; he did what was right in the eyes of
the LORD. The high places,[n] however, were
not removed, and the people continued
to offer sacrifices and burn incense there.
44Jehoshaphat was also at peace with the
king of Israel.
45As for the other events of Jehoshaphat's reign, the things he achieved and
his military exploits, are they not written
in the book of the annals of the kings of
Judah? 46He rid the land of the rest of the
male shrine prostitutes[o] who remained

22:27 [d] 2Ch 16:10; Jer 20:2; 26:21; 37:15; Heb 11:36 **22:28** [e] S Dt 18:22 **22:30** [f] S 1Sa 28:8 **22:31** [g] S Ge 10:22; S 2Sa 10:19 [h] S 2Sa 17:2 **22:34** [i] 2Ki 9:24; 2Ch 35:23 **22:36** [j] 2Ki 14:12 **22:38** [k] S 1Ki 21:19 **22:39** [l] 2Ch 9:17; Ps 45:8; Am 3:15 **22:43** [m] S 1Ki 8:61; 2Ch 17:3 [n] S 1Ki 3:2 **22:46** [o] S Dt 23:17

[a] 38 Or *Samaria and cleaned the weapons*

22:26 *king's son.* Probably a royal official (see note on Jer 36:26).
22:27 *This is what the king says.* Ahab speaks his royal word against the Lord's prophet because he trusts the (false) divine word proclaimed by his paid prophet (see v. 11).
22:30 *The king of Israel said.* Ahab still thought he was in control. *disguise.* By this strategy he thought he could direct attention away from himself and so minimize any chance for fulfillment of Micaiah's prediction. The king who loved the lie thought he could escape the truth by living a lie.
22:31 *except the king of Israel.* If the leader was killed or captured, ancient armies usually fell apart (cf. vv. 35 – 36).
22:34 *drew his bow at random.* The heavenly King aimed the arrow. *chariot driver.* A war chariot normally carried two men — a fighter and a driver. Sometimes, it appears, there were three men, but the third seems to have been an officer who commanded a chariot unit (see 9:22; 2Ki 9:25; Ex 14:7 and note; 15:4, where these officers are called lit. "the third").
22:35 *that evening he died.* Fulfilling Micaiah's prophecy (vv. 17,28).
22:38 *as the word of the LORD had declared.* A partial fulfillment of Elijah's prophecy concerning Ahab's death (see note on 21:19).
22:39 *the palace he built and inlaid with ivory.* Excavators of Samaria have found ivory inlays in the ruins of some of the buildings dating from this period of Israel's history. Ahab's use of ivory is indicative of the realm's economic prosperity during his reign. *cities he fortified.* Excavators have found evidence that Ahab strengthened the fortifications of Megiddo and Hazor. *annals of the kings of Israel.* See note on 14:19.
22:40 *rested with his fathers.* See note on 1:21. *Ahaziah his son succeeded him.* For the reign of Ahaziah see vv. 51 – 53; 2Ki 1.
22:41 *Jehoshaphat . . . became king of Judah in the fourth year of Ahab.* Appears to refer to the beginning of Jehoshaphat's reign as sole king in 869 B.C. (see notes on v. 42; 16:29; see also Introduction: Chronology).
22:42 *twenty-five years.* 872 – 848 B.C. The full span of Jehoshaphat's reign dates from the 39th year of King Asa, when he became coregent with his father (see note on 15:10; see also 2Ch 16:12).
22:43 *The high places, however, were not removed.* See notes on 3:2; 15:14.
22:44 *king.* Probably to be understood in the collective sense and as including Ahab, Ahaziah and Joram, all of whom ruled in the north during the reign of Jehoshaphat in the south (see note on v. 4).
22:45 *military exploits.* See 2Ki 3; 2Ch 17:11; 20. *annals of the kings of Judah.* See note on 14:29.
22:46 *male shrine prostitutes.* See note on 14:24.

there even after the reign of his father Asa.
[47]There was then no king[p] in Edom; a deputy ruled.

[48]Now Jehoshaphat built a fleet of trading ships[a][q] to go to Ophir for gold, but they never set sail—they were wrecked at Ezion Geber.[r] [49]At that time Ahaziah son of Ahab said to Jehoshaphat, "Let my men sail with your men," but Jehoshaphat refused.

[50]Then Jehoshaphat rested with his fathers and was buried with them in the city of David his father. And Jehoram his son succeeded him.

22:47 [p] 1Ki 11:14-18; 2Ki 3:9; 8:20
22:48 [q] S 1Ki 9:26 [r] S Nu 33:35
22:52 [s] 1Ki 15:26
22:53 [t] S Jdg 2:11 [u] 1Ki 21:25

Ahaziah King of Israel

[51]Ahaziah son of Ahab became king of Israel in Samaria in the seventeenth year of Jehoshaphat king of Judah, and he reigned over Israel two years. [52]He did evil[s] in the eyes of the LORD, because he walked in the ways of his father and mother and in the ways of Jeroboam son of Nebat, who caused Israel to sin. [53]He served and worshiped Baal[t] and provoked the LORD, the God of Israel, to anger, just as his father[u] had done.

[a] 48 Hebrew *of ships of Tarshish*

22:47 *no king in Edom.* Suggests that Edom was subject to Judah (see 2Sa 8:14; 2Ki 8:20 and note).
22:48 *Ophir.* See note on 9:28. *wrecked at Ezion Geber.* The destruction of the trading ships was a judgment of God on Jehoshaphat for entering into an alliance with Ahaziah of the northern kingdom (see 2Ch 20:35–37).
22:50 *rested with his fathers.* See note on 1:21. *Jehoram his son succeeded him.* For the reign of Jehoram see 2Ki 8:16–24; 2Ch 21.
22:51 *seventeenth year of Jehoshaphat.* 853 B.C. (see notes on vv. 41–42). *two years.* 853–852 (see note on 2Ki 1:17).
22:52 *ways of his father and mother.* See 16:30–33 and notes. *ways of Jeroboam.* See 12:28–33.

2 Kings

I N T R O D U C T I O N

See Introduction to 1 Kings.

Outline

Below is an outline for 2 Kings. For an outline of both 1 and 2 Kings see Introduction to 1 Kings: Outline.

- IV. The Ministries of Elijah and Elisha during the Reigns of Ahaziah and Joram (1:1 — 8:15)
  - A. Elijah in the Reign of Ahaziah (ch. 1)
  - B. Elijah's Translation; Elisha's Inauguration (2:1 – 18)
  - C. Elisha in the Reign of Joram (2:19 — 8:15)
    1. Elisha's initial miraculous signs (2:19 – 25)
    2. Elisha during the campaign against Moab (ch. 3)
    3. Elisha's ministry to needy ones in Israel (ch. 4)
    4. Elisha heals Naaman (ch. 5)
    5. Elisha's deliverance of one of the prophets (6:1 – 7)
    6. Elisha's deliverance of Joram from Aramean raiders (6:8 – 23)
    7. Aramean siege of Samaria lifted, as Elisha prophesied (6:24 — 7:20)
    8. The Shunammite's land restored (8:1 – 6)
    9. Elisha prophesies Hazael's oppression of Israel (8:7 – 15)
- V. Israel and Judah from Joram/Jehoram to the Exile of Israel (8:16 — 17:41)
  - A. Jehoram of Judah (8:16 – 24)
  - B. Ahaziah of Judah (8:25 – 29)
  - C. Jehu's Revolt and Reign in Israel (chs. 9 – 10)
    1. Elisha orders Jehu's anointing (9:1 – 13)
    2. Jehu's assassination of Joram and Ahaziah (9:14 – 29)
    3. Jehu's execution of Jezebel (9:30 – 37)
    4. Jehu's slaughter of Ahab's family (10:1 – 17)
    5. Jehu's eradication of Baal worship (10:18 – 36)
  - D. Athaliah and Joash of Judah; Repair of the Temple (chs. 11 – 12)
  - E. Jehoahaz of Israel (13:1 – 9)
  - F. Jehoash of Israel; Elisha's Last Prophecy (13:10 – 25)

G. Amaziah of Judah (14:1 – 22)
H. Jeroboam II of Israel (14:23 – 29)
I. Azariah of Judah (15:1 – 7)
J. Zechariah of Israel (15:8 – 12)
K. Shallum of Israel (15:13 – 16)
L. Menahem of Israel (15:17 – 22)
M. Pekahiah of Israel (15:23 – 26)
N. Pekah of Israel (15:27 – 31)
O. Jotham of Judah (15:32 – 38)
P. Ahaz of Judah (ch. 16)
Q. Hoshea of Israel (17:1 – 6)
R. Exile of Israel; Resettlement of the Land (17:7 – 41)

VI. Judah from Hezekiah to the Babylonian Exile (chs. 18 – 25)
A. Hezekiah (chs. 18 – 20)
1. Hezekiah's good reign (18:1 – 8)
2. The Assyrian threat and deliverance (18:9 — 19:37)
3. Hezekiah's illness and alliance with Babylon (ch. 20)
B. Manasseh (21:1 – 18)
C. Amon (21:19 – 26)
D. Josiah (22:1 — 23:30)
1. Repair of the temple; discovery of the Book of the Law (ch. 22)
2. Renewal of the covenant; end of Josiah's reign (23:1 – 30)
E. Jehoahaz Exiled to Egypt (23:31 – 35)
F. Jehoiakim: First Babylonian Deportation (23:36 — 24:7)
G. Jehoiachin: Second Babylonian Deportation (24:8 – 17)
H. Zedekiah : Third Babylonian Deportation (24:18 — 25:21)
I. Removal of the Remnant to Egypt (25:22 – 26)
J. Elevation of Jehoiachin in Babylon (25:27 – 30)

The LORD's Judgment on Ahaziah

1 After Ahab's death, Moab[a] rebelled
against Israel. 2Now Ahaziah had fall-
en through the lattice of his upper room
in Samaria and injured himself. So he
sent messengers,[b] saying to them, "Go
and consult Baal-Zebub,[c] the god of Ekron,[d] to see if I will recover[e] from this
injury."
3But the angel[f] of the LORD said to Elijah[g] the Tishbite, "Go up and meet the
messengers of the king of Samaria and
ask them, 'Is it because there is no God
in Israel[h] that you are going off to consult
Baal-Zebub, the god of Ekron?' 4Therefore
this is what the LORD says: 'You will not
leave[i] the bed you are lying on. You will
certainly die!' " So Elijah went.
5When the messengers returned to the
king, he asked them, "Why have you
come back?"
6"A man came to meet us," they replied.
"And he said to us, 'Go back to the king
who sent you and tell him, "This is what
the LORD says: Is it because there is no God
in Israel that you are sending men to consult Baal-Zebub, the god of Ekron? Therefore you will not leave[j] the bed you are
lying on. You will certainly die!" ' "
7The king asked them, "What kind of
man was it who came to meet you and
told you this?"
8They replied, "He was a man with a
garment of hair[k] and with a leather belt
around his waist."
The king said, "That was Elijah the
Tishbite."
9Then he sent[l] to Elijah a captain[m] with
his company of fifty men. The captain
went up to Elijah, who was sitting on the
top of a hill, and said to him, "Man of
God, the king says, 'Come down!' "
10Elijah answered the captain, "If I am
a man of God, may fire come down from
heaven and consume you and your fifty
men!" Then fire[n] fell from heaven and
consumed the captain and his men.
11At this the king sent to Elijah another captain with his fifty men. The captain
said to him, "Man of God, this is what the
king says, 'Come down at once!' "
12"If I am a man of God," Elijah replied,
"may fire come down from heaven and
consume you and your fifty men!" Then
the fire of God fell from heaven and consumed him and his fifty men.
13So the king sent a third captain with
his fifty men. This third captain went up
and fell on his knees before Elijah. "Man
of God," he begged, "please have respect
for my life[o] and the lives of these fifty
men, your servants! 14See, fire has fallen
from heaven and consumed the first two
captains and all their men. But now have
respect for my life!"

1:1 [a] S Ge 19:37; 2Ki 3:5
1:2 [b] ver 16 [c] S Mk 3:22 [d] 1Sa 6:2; Isa 2:6; 14:29 [e] S Jdg 18:5
1:3 [f] ver 15 [g] 1Ki 17:1 [h] S 1Sa 28:8
1:4 [i] ver 6, 16; Ps 41:8
1:6 [j] S ver 4
1:8 [k] S 1Ki 18:7; Mt 3:4; Mk 1:6
1:9 [l] 2Ki 6:14 [m] Ex 18:25; Isa 3:3
1:10 [n] S 1Ki 18:38; S Rev 11:5; S 13:13
1:13 [o] Ps 72:14

1:1 *After Ahab's death.* See 1Ki 22:37. *Moab rebelled.* Moab had been brought into subjection by David (see 2Sa 8:2), but when the northern and Transjordan tribes rebelled and made Jeroboam their king, political domination of Moab probably also shifted to the northern kingdom. An inscription of Mesha king of Moab (see chart, p. xxiii) indicates that during the reign of Omri's "son" (probably a reference to his grandson Joram, not to Ahab) the Moabites were able to free the area of Medeba from Israelite control (see map No. 5 at the end of this study Bible).
1:2 *Baal-Zebub.* See note on Jdg 10:6. *Ekron.* The northernmost of the five major Philistine cities (see Jos 13:3; 1Sa 5:10 and note). *if I will recover.* Ahaziah appears to have feared that his injury would be fatal. He turned to the pagan deity for a revelatory oracle, not for healing.
1:3 *angel of the LORD.* See 1Ki 19:7; see also note on Ge 16:7. The Lord usually spoke directly to the consciousness of the prophet (1Ki 17:2,8; 18:1; 19:9; 21:17). Perhaps the means of revelation was changed in this instance to heighten the contrast between the messengers of Ahaziah (vv. 2–3,5) and the angel (which means "messenger") of the Lord. *Elijah the Tishbite.* See note on 1Ki 17:1. *king of Samaria.* See note on 1Ki 21:1.
1:4 *You will certainly die!* Ahaziah will receive the oracle he sought, but it will come from the Lord through Elijah, not from Baal-Zebub.
1:5 *Why have you come back?* Ahaziah realized the messengers could not have traveled so quickly to Ekron and back.
1:8 *garment of hair.* Elijah's cloak (1Ki 19:19) was probably of sheepskin or camel's hair, tied with a simple leather thong (cf. Mt 3:4 and note). His dress contrasted sharply with the fine linen clothing (see Jer 13:1) of his wealthy contemporaries and constituted a protest against the materialistic attitudes of the king and the upper classes (cf. Mt 11:7–8; Lk 7:24–25). *That was Elijah the Tishbite.* Ahaziah was familiar with Elijah's appearance because of the prophet's many encounters with Ahab, his father.
1:9 *he sent to Elijah a captain with his company of fifty men.* The pagan people of that time thought that the magical power of curses could be nullified either by forcing the pronouncer of the curse to retract his statement or by killing him so that his curse would go with him to the netherworld. It appears that Ahaziah shared this view and desired to take Elijah prisoner in order to counteract the pronouncement of his death. *Man of God, the king says, 'Come down!'* Ahaziah attempted to place the prophet under the authority of the king. This constituted a violation of the covenant nature of Israelite kingship, in which the king's actions were always to be placed under the scrutiny and authority of the word of the Lord spoken by his prophets (see notes on 1Sa 10:25; 12:23).
1:10 *fire fell from heaven and consumed the captain and his men.* Another link between the ministries of Elijah and Moses (see Lev 10:2; Nu 16:35). At stake in this incident was the question of who was sovereign in Israel. Would Ahaziah recognize that the king in Israel was only a vice-regent under the authority and kingship of the Lord, or would he exercise despotic power, like pagan kings (see notes on 1Sa 12:14–15)? At Mount Carmel the Lord had revealed himself and authenticated his prophet by fire from heaven (see 1Ki 18:38–39). Now this previous revelation is confirmed to Ahaziah.
1:11 *the king sent to Elijah another captain.* Ahaziah refused to submit to the word of the Lord in spite of the dramatic revelation of God's power.
1:13 *fell on his knees before Elijah.* The third captain, recognizing that Elijah was the bearer of the word of the Lord, feared for his life and bowed before him with a humble request.

15 The angel[p] of the LORD said to Elijah,
"Go down with him; do not be afraid[q] of
him." So Elijah got up and went down
with him to the king.
16 He told the king, "This is what the
LORD says: Is it because there is no God
in Israel for you to consult that you have
sent messengers[r] to consult Baal-Zebub,
the god of Ekron? Because you have done
this, you will never leave[s] the bed you are
lying on. You will certainly die!" 17 So he
died,[t] according to the word of the LORD
that Elijah had spoken.
Because Ahaziah had no son, Joram[a][u]
succeeded him as king in the second year
of Jehoram son of Jehoshaphat king of Judah. 18 As for all the other events of Ahaziah's reign, and what he did, are they not
written in the book of the annals of the
kings of Israel?

Elijah Taken Up to Heaven

2 When the LORD was about to take[v] Elijah up to heaven in a whirlwind,[w] Elijah and Elisha[x] were on their way from
Gilgal.[y] 2 Elijah said to Elisha, "Stay here;[z]
the LORD has sent me to Bethel."
But Elisha said, "As surely as the LORD
lives and as you live, I will not leave you."[a]
So they went down to Bethel.
3 The company[b] of the prophets at Bethel came out to Elisha and asked, "Do you
know that the LORD is going to take your
master from you today?"
"Yes, I know," Elisha replied, "but do
not speak of it."
4 Then Elijah said to him, "Stay here, Elisha; the LORD has sent me to Jericho.[c]"
And he replied, "As surely as the LORD
lives and as you live, I will not leave you."
So they went to Jericho.
5 The company[d] of the prophets at Jericho went up to Elisha and asked him, "Do
you know that the LORD is going to take
your master from you today?"
"Yes, I know," he replied, "but do not
speak of it."
6 Then Elijah said to him, "Stay here;[e]
the LORD has sent me to the Jordan."[f]
And he replied, "As surely as the LORD
lives and as you live, I will not leave you."[g]
So the two of them walked on.
7 Fifty men of the company of the prophets went and stood at a distance, facing
the place where Elijah and Elisha had
stopped at the Jordan. 8 Elijah took his
cloak,[h] rolled it up and struck[i] the water
with it. The water divided[j] to the right and
to the left, and the two of them crossed
over on dry[k] ground.
9 When they had crossed, Elijah said to
Elisha, "Tell me, what can I do for you before I am taken from you?"
"Let me inherit a double[l] portion of
your spirit,"[m] Elisha replied.
10 "You have asked a difficult thing," Elijah said, "yet if you see me when I am
taken from you, it will be yours—otherwise not."
11 As they were walking along and talking together, suddenly a chariot of fire[n]
and horses of fire appeared and separated
the two of them, and Elijah went up to
heaven[o] in a whirlwind.[p] 12 Elisha saw this
and cried out, "My father! My father! The

1:15 [p] ver 3 [q] Isa 51:12; 57:11; Jer 1:17; Eze 2:6 **1:16** [r] S ver 2 [s] ver 4 **1:17** [t] 2Ki 8:15; Jer 20:6; 28:17 [u] 2Ki 3:1; 8:16 **2:1** [v] S Ge 5:24 [w] ver 11; 1Ki 19:11; Isa 5:28; 66:15; Jer 4:13; Na 1:3 [x] S 1Ki 19:16,21 [y] S Dt 11:30; 2Ki 4:38 **2:2** [z] ver 6 [a] Ru 1:16 **2:3** [b] S 1Sa 10:5 **2:4** [c] Jos 3:16 **2:5** [d] ver 3 **2:6** [e] ver 2 [f] Jos 3:15 [g] Ru 1:16 **2:8** [h] S 1Ki 19:19 [i] ver 14 [j] S Ex 14:21 [k] Ex 14:22,29 **2:9** [l] S Dt 21:17 [m] S Nu 11:17 **2:11** [n] 2Ki 6:17; Ps 68:17; 104:3,4; Isa 66:15; Hab 3:8; Zec 6:1 [o] S Ge 5:24 [p] S ver 1

[a] 17 Hebrew *Jehoram*, a variant of *Joram*

1:15 *The angel of the LORD said to Elijah.* See note on v. 3.
1:17 *died, according to the word of the LORD.* In the end Ahaziah was punished for turning away from the God of Israel to a pagan deity, and the word of the Lord was shown to be both reliable and beyond the power of the king to annul. *Joram.* Ahaziah's younger brother (see 3:1; 1Ki 22:51). *second year of Jehoram son of Jehoshaphat.* Jehoram's reign overlapped that of his father Jehoshaphat from 853 to 848 B.C. (see note on 8:16). The reference here is to the second year of that coregency. The 18th year of Jehoshaphat (3:1) is therefore the same as the second year of Jehoram's coregency (852).
1:18 *annals of the kings of Israel.* See note on 1Ki 14:19.
2:1 *Gilgal.* Probably not the well-known town in the Jordan Valley, since they "went down" from it to Bethel (v. 2; see also 4:38); rather, it is more likely the Gilgal located some eight miles north of Bethel (see Jdg 3:19 and note).
2:2 *I will not leave you.* Elisha was aware that Elijah's ministry was almost finished and that his departure was near (v. 5). He was determined to accompany him until the moment the Lord took him. His commitment to Elijah and to Elijah's ministry was unfailing (see v. 9; 1Ki 19:21).
2:3 *company of.* Lit. "sons of" (see note on 1Ki 20:35). During the days of Elijah and Elisha, companies of prophets were located at Bethel (here), Jericho (v. 5) and Gilgal (4:38). It appears that Elijah journeyed by divine instruction to Gilgal (v. 1), Bethel (v. 2) and Jericho (v. 4) for a last meeting with each of these companies.
2:7 *Fifty men.* Israel's heavenly King could also muster 50 companies of 50 men (see 1:9,11,13; 2:16–17; 1Ki 18:4). The present company of 50 men were to witness the miracle by which Elijah and Elisha crossed the river.
2:8 *Elijah took his cloak ... and struck the water with it.* Elijah used his cloak much as Moses had used his staff at the time of Israel's passage through the "Red Sea" (see Ex 14:16,21,26).
2:9 *Let me inherit a double portion.* Elisha was not expressing a desire for a ministry twice as great as Elijah's, but he was using terms derived from inheritance law to express his desire to carry on Elijah's ministry. Inheritance law assigned a double portion of a father's possessions to the firstborn son (see Dt 21:17 and note).
2:10 *difficult thing.* Although Elijah had previously been told to anoint Elisha as his successor (1Ki 19:16,19–21), Elijah's response clearly showed that the issue rested solely with the Lord's sovereign good pleasure. *if you see me ... it will be yours—otherwise not.* Elijah left the answer to Elisha's request in the Lord's hands.
2:11 *chariot of fire and horses of fire.* The Lord's heavenly host has accompanied and supported Elijah's ministry (as it had that of Moses; see Ex 15:1–10), and now at his departure Elisha is allowed to see it (cf. 6:17). *Elijah went up to heaven in a whirlwind.* Elijah, like Enoch before him (see Ge 5:24 and note), was taken up to heaven bodily without experiencing death; like Moses (Dt 34:4–6), Elijah was outside the promised land when he was taken away.
2:12 *father.* See note on 1Sa 10:12. *chariots and horsemen of Israel!* Elisha depicted Elijah as em-

chariots[q] and horsemen of Israel!" And Elisha saw him no more. Then he took hold
of his own clothes and tore[r] them apart.
13He picked up the cloak that had fall-
en from Elijah and went back and stood
on the bank of the Jordan. 14Then he took
the cloak[s] that had fallen from him and
struck[t] the water with it. "Where now is
the LORD, the God of Elijah?" he asked.
When he struck the water, it divided to the
right and to the left, and he crossed over.
15The company[u] of the prophets from
Jericho, who were watching, said, "The
spirit[v] of Elijah is resting on Elisha." And
they went to meet him and bowed to the
ground before him. 16"Look," they said,
"we your servants have fifty able men. Let
them go and look for your master. Perhaps
the Spirit[w] of the LORD has picked him up[x]
and set him down on some mountain or
in some valley."
"No," Elisha replied, "do not send
them."
17But they persisted until he was too
ashamed[y] to refuse. So he said, "Send
them." And they sent fifty men, who
searched for three days but did not find
him. 18When they returned to Elisha, who
was staying in Jericho, he said to them,
"Didn't I tell you not to go?"

Healing of the Water

19The men of the city said to Elisha,
"Look, our lord, this town is well situated,
as you can see, but the water is bad and
the land is unproductive."
20"Bring me a new bowl," he said, "and
put salt in it." So they brought it to him.
21Then he went out to the spring and
threw[z] the salt into it, saying, "This is
what the LORD says: 'I have healed this
water. Never again will it cause death or
make the land unproductive.'" 22And the
water has remained wholesome[a] to this
day, according to the word Elisha had
spoken.

Elisha Is Jeered

23From there Elisha went up to Bethel.
As he was walking along the road, some
youths came out of the town and jeered[b] at
him. "Go on up, you baldhead!" they said.
"Go on up, you baldhead!" 24He turned
around, looked at them and called down a
curse[c] on them in the name[d] of the LORD.
Then two bears came out of the woods
and mauled forty-two of the youths. 25And
he went on to Mount Carmel[e] and from
there returned to Samaria.

Moab Revolts

3 Joram[a][f] son of Ahab became king of
Israel in Samaria in the eighteenth year
of Jehoshaphat king of Judah, and he

2:12 [q] 2Ki 6:17; 13:14 [r] S Ge 37:29 **2:14** [s] S 1Ki 19:19 [t] ver 8 **2:15** [u] S 1Sa 10:5 [v] S Nu 11:17 **2:16** [w] S 1Ki 18:12 [x] Ac 8:39 **2:17** [y] S Jdg 3:25 **2:21** [z] S Ex 15:25; 2Ki 4:41; 6:6 **2:22** [a] Ex 15:25 **2:23** [b] S Ex 22:28; 2Ch 30:10; 36:16; Job 19:18; Ps 31:18 **2:24** [c] S Ge 4:11 [d] S Dt 18:19 **2:25** [e] S 1Ki 18:20 **3:1** [f] S 2Ki 1:17

[a] *1* Hebrew *Jehoram,* a variant of *Joram*; also in verse 6

bodying the true strength of the nation. He, rather than the apostate king, is the Lord's representative. The same description was later used of Elisha (see 13:14 and note). *tore them.* See Ge 44:13 and note.

2:13 *He picked up the cloak.* See note on v. 8. Possession of Elijah's cloak symbolized Elisha's succession to Elijah's ministry (see 1Ki 19:19).

2:14 *When he struck the water, it divided.* See v. 8. The Lord authenticated Elisha's succession to Elijah's ministry and demonstrated that the same divine power that had accompanied Elijah's ministry was now operative in the ministry of Elisha. In crossing the Jordan as Joshua had before him, Elisha is shown to be Elijah's "Joshua" (Elisha and Joshua are very similar names, Elisha meaning "God saves" and Joshua "The LORD saves").

2:15 *bowed to the ground before him.* Indicated their recognition of Elisha's succession to Elijah's position. Elisha was now the Lord's official representative in this time of royal apostasy.

2:16 *Perhaps the Spirit of the LORD has picked him up and set him down.* Obadiah expressed the same idea years earlier (see 1Ki 18:12). *do not send them.* Elisha knew their search would be fruitless.

2:17 *too ashamed.* The same Hebrew word is used in Jdg 3:25 ("to the point of embarrassment"). Under pressure to allow the prophets to send men to look for Elijah, Elisha no longer had the heart to say no. *Send them.* When the company of prophets refused to be satisfied with Elisha's answer, he permitted them to go so that the authority and truth of his words would be confirmed to them.

2:19 *city.* Evidently Jericho (see v. 18). *the water is bad and the land is unproductive.* The inhabitants of Jericho were experiencing the effects of the covenant curse (contrast Dt 28:15–18 with Ex 23:25–26; Lev 26:9; Dt 28:1–4). See 1Ki 16:34; Jos 6:26.

2:20 *new bowl.* That which was to be used in the service of the Lord was to be undefiled by profane use (see Lev 1:3,10; Nu 19:2; Dt 21:3; 1Sa 6:7). *put salt in it.* Elisha may have used salt because of its known preservative qualities, but it is more likely that he used it to symbolize the covenant faithfulness of the Lord (see note on Nu 18:19; see also 2Ch 13:5).

2:21 *I have healed this water.* Any idea of a magical effect of the salt in the purification of the water is excluded by the explicit statement that the Lord himself healed (purified) the water. In this symbolic way Elisha was able, as the first act of his ministry, to proclaim to the people that in spite of their disobedience the Lord was merciful and was still reaching out to them in his grace (see 13:23).

2:23 *Go on up.* Since Bethel was the royal religious center of the northern kings (1Ki 12:29; Am 7:13) and Elijah and Elisha were known to frequent Samaria (perhaps even as their main residence; see note on 5:3), the youths from Bethel no doubt assumed that Elisha was going up to Samaria to continue Elijah's struggle against royal apostasy. *you baldhead!* Baldness was uncommon among the ancient Jews, and luxuriant hair seems to have been viewed as a sign of strength and vigor (see note on 2Sa 14:26). By calling Elisha "baldhead," the youths from Bethel expressed that city's utter disdain for the Lord's representative, who, they felt, had no power.

2:24 *called down a curse on them in the name of the LORD.* Elisha pronounced a curse similar to the covenant curse of Lev 26:21–22. The result gave warning of the judgment that would come on the entire nation should it persist in disobedience and apostasy (see 2Ch 36:16). Thus Elisha's first acts were indicative of his ministry that would follow: God's covenant blessings would come to those who looked to him (vv. 19–22), but God's covenant curses would fall on those who turned away from him (cf. 1Ki 19:17 and note).

3:1 *Joram son of Ahab became king ... in the eighteenth year of Jehoshaphat.* See note on 1:17. *twelve years.* 852–841 B.C.

reigned twelve years. 2He did evil[g] in the
eyes of the LORD, but not as his father[h]
and mother had done. He got rid of the
sacred stone[i] of Baal that his father had
made. 3Nevertheless he clung to the sins[j]
of Jeroboam son of Nebat, which he had
caused Israel to commit; he did not turn
away from them.
4Now Mesha king of Moab[k] raised
sheep, and he had to supply the king of
Israel with a hundred thousand lambs[l]
and with the wool of a hundred thousand
rams. 5But after Ahab died, the king of
Moab rebelled[m] against the king of Israel.
6So at that time King Joram set out from
Samaria and mobilized all Israel. 7He also
sent this message to Jehoshaphat king of
Judah: "The king of Moab has rebelled
against me. Will you go with me to fight[n]
against Moab?"
"I will go with you," he replied. "I am
as you are, my people as your people, my
horses as your horses."
8"By what route shall we attack?" he
asked.
"Through the Desert of Edom," he answered.
9So the king of Israel set out with the
king of Judah and the king of Edom.[o] After a roundabout march of seven days, the
army had no more water for themselves or
for the animals with them.
10"What!" exclaimed the king of Israel.
"Has the LORD called us three kings together only to hand us over to Moab?"

3:2 [g]1Ki 15:26 [h]1Ki 16:30-32 [i]S Ex 23:24
3:3 [j]S 1Ki 12:28-32
3:4 [k]S Ge 19:37; 2Ki 1:1 [l]Ezr 7:17; Isa 16:1
3:5 [m]S 2Ki 1:1
3:7 [n]1Ki 22:4
3:9 [o]S 1Ki 22:47
3:11 [p]S Ge 25:22; S 1Ki 22:5 [q]S Ge 20:7 [r]S 1Ki 19:16
3:12 [s]S Nu 11:17
3:15 [t]S 1Sa 10:5 [u]Jer 15:17; Eze 1:3
3:17 [v]Ps 107:35; Isa 12:3; 32:2; 35:6; 41:18; 65:13
3:18 [w]S Ge 18:14; 2Ki 20:10; Isa 49:6; Jer 32:17,27; Mk 10:27

11But Jehoshaphat asked, "Is there no
prophet of the LORD here, that we may inquire[p] of the LORD through him?"
An officer of the king of Israel answered, "Elisha[q] son of Shaphat is here.
He used to pour water on the hands of
Elijah."[a][r]
12Jehoshaphat said, "The word[s] of the
LORD is with him." So the king of Israel
and Jehoshaphat and the king of Edom
went down to him.
13Elisha said to the king of Israel, "What
do we have to do with each other? Go to
the prophets of your father and the prophets of your mother."
"No," the king of Israel answered, "because it was the LORD who called us three
kings together to hand us over to Moab."
14Elisha said, "As surely as the LORD Almighty lives, whom I serve, if I did not
have respect for the presence of Jehoshaphat king of Judah, I would not look at
you or even notice you. 15But now bring
me a harpist."[t]
While the harpist was playing, the
hand[u] of the LORD came upon Elisha 16and
he said, "This is what the LORD says: Make
this valley full of ditches. 17For this is what
the LORD says: You will see neither wind
nor rain, yet this valley will be filled with
water,[v] and you, your cattle and your other animals will drink. 18This is an easy[w]
thing in the eyes of the LORD; he will also

[a] *11* That is, he was Elijah's personal servant.

3:2 *not as his father and mother had done.* Not as Ahab (see notes on 1Ki 16:30–34) and Jezebel (see 1Ki 18:4; 19:1–2; 21:7–15). *sacred stone of Baal that his father had made.* Apparently a reference to the stone representation of the male deity (see note on 1Ki 14:23) that Ahab placed in the temple he had constructed for Jezebel in Samaria (see 1Ki 16:32–33). From 10:27 it appears that this stone was later reinstated, perhaps by Jezebel, then destroyed again by Jehu.

3:3 *sins of Jeroboam … he had caused Israel to commit.* See note on 1Ki 14:16.

3:4 *Mesha king of Moab.* See note on 1:1. *a hundred thousand lambs and … the wool of a hundred thousand rams.* The heavy annual tribute (see Isa 16:1) that Israel required from the Moabites as a vassal state.

3:5 *king of Moab rebelled.* See note on 1:1.

3:7 *Will you go with me to fight against Moab?* Joram wished to attack Moab from the rear (v. 8), but to do that his army had to pass through Judah. *I am as you are, my people as your people, my horses as your horses.* See 1Ki 22:4. Jehoshaphat had already been condemned by prophets of the Lord for his alliance with the northern kings Ahab (see 2Ch 18:1; 19:1–2) and Ahaziah (2Ch 20:35–37), yet he agreed to join with Joram against Moab. Perhaps he was disturbed by the potential danger to Judah posed by the growing strength of Moab (see 2Ch 20), and he may have considered Joram less evil than his predecessors (see v. 2).

3:8 *Through the Desert of Edom.* This route of attack took the armies of Israel and Judah south of the Dead Sea, enabling them to circumvent the fortifications of Moab's northern frontier and to avoid the possibility of a rearguard action against them by the Arameans of Damascus. The Edomites, who were subject to Judah, were in no position to resist the movement of Israel's army through their territory.

3:9 *king of Edom.* Although here designated a king, he was in reality a governor appointed by Jehoshaphat (see 8:20; 1Ki 22:47).

3:11 *Is there no prophet of the LORD here … ?* See 1Ki 22:7. Only after the apparent failure of their own strategies did the three rulers seek the word of the Lord (v. 12). *Elisha son of Shaphat is here.* Since Elijah is reported to have sent a letter to Jehoshaphat's son Jehoram after his father's death (2Ch 21:12–15), it seems that Elisha accompanied the armies on this campaign as the representative of the aged Elijah. The event is narrated here after the account of Elisha's initiation as Elijah's successor and the two events that foreshadowed the character of his ministry. Following this introduction to Elisha's ministry, the present episode is topically associated with the series of Elisha's acts that now occupies the narrative.

3:13 *Go to the prophets of your father and … mother.* See 1Ki 22:6.

3:14 *if I did not have respect for … Jehoshaphat … I would not look at you.* Joram will share in the blessing of the word of God only because of his association with Jehoshaphat.

3:15 *bring me a harpist.* To create a disposition conducive to receiving the word of the Lord. *hand of the LORD.* See note on Eze 1:3.

3:16 *this valley.* The Israelite armies were encamped in the broad valley (the Arabah) between the highlands of Moab on the east and those of Judah on the west, just south of the Dead Sea.

3:17 *will be filled with water.* The word of the Lord contained a promise and a directive. The Lord will graciously provide for his people, but they must respond to his word in faith and obedience (v. 16).

hand Moab over to you. 19You will overthrow every fortified city and every major town. You will cut down every good
tree, stop up all the springs, and ruin every
good field with stones."
20The next morning, about the time[x] for
offering the sacrifice, there it was — water
flowing from the direction of Edom! And
the land was filled with water.[y]
21Now all the Moabites had heard that
the kings had come to fight against them;
so every man, young and old, who could
bear arms was called up and stationed on
the border. 22When they got up early in
the morning, the sun was shining on the
water. To the Moabites across the way, the
water looked red — like blood. 23"That's
blood!" they said. "Those kings must have
fought and slaughtered each other. Now to
the plunder, Moab!"
24But when the Moabites came to the
camp of Israel, the Israelites rose up and
fought them until they fled. And the Israelites invaded the land and slaughtered the Moabites. 25They destroyed the
towns, and each man threw a stone on
every good field until it was covered.
They stopped up all the springs and cut
down every good tree. Only Kir Hareseth[z]
was left with its stones in place, but men
armed with slings surrounded it and attacked it as well.
26When the king of Moab saw that
the battle had gone against him, he took
with him seven hundred swordsmen to
break through to the king of Edom, but
they failed. 27Then he took his firstborn[a]
son, who was to succeed him as king,
and offered him as a sacrifice on the city
wall. The fury against Israel was great;
they withdrew and returned to their own
land.

The Widow's Oil

4 The wife of a man from the company[b] of the prophets cried out to Elisha,
"Your servant my husband is dead, and
you know that he revered the LORD. But
now his creditor[c] is coming to take my two
boys as his slaves."
2Elisha replied to her, "How can I help
you? Tell me, what do you have in your
house?"
"Your servant has nothing there at all,"
she said, "except a little oil."[d]
3Elisha said, "Go around and ask all
your neighbors for empty jars. Don't ask
for just a few. 4Then go inside and shut
the door behind you and your sons. Pour
oil into all the jars, and as each is filled,
put it to one side."
5She left him and afterward shut the
door behind her and her sons. They
brought the jars to her and she kept pouring. 6When all the jars were full, she said
to her son, "Bring me another one."
But he replied, "There is not a jar left."
Then the oil stopped flowing.
7She went and told the man of God,[e]
and he said, "Go, sell the oil and pay your
debts. You and your sons can live on what
is left."

The Shunammite's Son Restored to Life

8One day Elisha went to Shunem.[f] And
a well-to-do woman was there, who urged
him to stay for a meal. So whenever he
came by, he stopped there to eat. 9She said
to her husband, "I know that this man
who often comes our way is a holy man
of God. 10Let's make a small room on the
roof and put in it a bed and a table, a chair
and a lamp for him. Then he can stay[g]
there whenever he comes to us."

3:20 [x]S Ex 29:41 [y]S Ex 17:6
3:25 [z]Isa 15:1; 16:7; Jer 48:31,36
3:27 [a]S Dt 12:31; 2Ki 16:3; 21:6; 2Ch 28:3; Ps 106:38; Jer 19:4-5; Mic 6:7
4:1 [b]S 1Sa 10:5 [c]S Ex 22:26; Lev 25:39-43; Ne 5:3-5; Job 22:6; 24:9
4:2 [d]S 1Ki 17:12
4:7 [e]S 1Ki 12:22
4:8 [f]S Jos 19:18
4:10 [g]Mt 10:41; S Ro 12:13

3:19 The two armies will devastate the rebellious country.
3:20 *time for offering.* See Ex 29:38–39; Nu 28:3–4. *water flowing from the direction of Edom.* Flash floods in the distant mountains of Edom caused water to flow north through the broad, usually dry, valley that sloped toward the Dead Sea (see note on v. 16).
3:23 *Those kings must have ... slaughtered each other.* The Moabites would have good reason to suspect that an internal conflict had arisen between the parties of an alliance whose members had previously been mutually hostile.
3:25 *Kir Hareseth.* The capital city of Moab (see Isa 16:7,11; Jer 48:31,36), usually identified with present-day Kerak, located about 11 miles east of the Dead Sea and 15 miles south of the Arnon River (see map, p. 518).
3:26 *break through to the king of Edom.* A desperate attempt by the king of Moab to induce Edom to turn against Israel and Judah.
3:27 *offered him as a sacrifice on the city wall.* King Mesha offered his oldest son, the crown prince, as a burnt offering (see 16:3; Jer 7:31) to the Moabite god Chemosh (see 1Ki 11:7; Nu 21:29; Jer 48:46) in an attempt to induce the deity to come to his aid. *The fury against Israel was great.* It seems that just when total victory appeared to be in Israel's grasp, God's displeasure with the Ahab dynasty showed itself in some way that caused the Israelite kings to give up the campaign.
4:1 *company of the prophets.* See notes on 2:3; 1Ki 20:35. *take my two boys as his slaves.* Servitude as a means of debt payment by labor was permitted in the Mosaic law (Ex 21:1–2; Lev 25:39–41; Dt 15:1–11). It appears that the practice was much abused (see Ne 5:5,8; Am 2:6; 8:6), even though the law limited the term of such bondage and required that those so held be treated as hired workers.
4:4 *shut the door behind you and your sons.* The impending miracle was not intended to be a public sensation but to demonstrate privately God's mercy and grace to this widow (cf. Ps 68:5). She did not hesitate to respond to the instructions of the Lord's prophet in faith and obedience.
4:8 *Shunem.* See note on 1Ki 1:3.
4:9 *holy man of God.* The woman recognized that Elisha was a person set apart to the Lord's work in a very special sense (see note on Ex 3:5). Nowhere else in the OT is the term "holy" applied to a prophet.
4:10 *he can stay there whenever he comes to us.* By her hospitality the woman was able to assist in sustaining the proclamation of God's word through Elisha.

11One day when Elisha came, he went
up to his room and lay down there. 12He
said to his servant Gehazi, "Call the Shunammite."[h] So he called her, and she stood
before him. 13Elisha said to him, "Tell her,
'You have gone to all this trouble for us.
Now what can be done for you? Can we
speak on your behalf to the king or the
commander of the army?'"
She replied, "I have a home among my
own people."
14"What can be done for her?" Elisha
asked.
Gehazi said, "Well, she has no son and
her husband is old."
15Then Elisha said, "Call her." So he
called her, and she stood in the doorway.
16"About this time[i] next year," Elisha said,
"you will hold a son in your arms."
"No, my lord," she objected. "Don't
mislead your servant, O man of God!"
17But the woman became pregnant, and
the next year about that same time she
gave birth to a son, just as Elisha had told
her.
18The child grew, and one day he went
out to his father, who was with the reapers.[j] 19"My head! My head!" he said to his
father.
His father told a servant, "Carry him to
his mother." 20After the servant had lifted
him up and carried him to his mother, the
boy sat on her lap until noon, and then
he died. 21She went up and laid him on
the bed[k] of the man of God, then shut the
door and went out.
22She called her husband and said,
"Please send me one of the servants and
a donkey so I can go to the man of God
quickly and return."

4:12 [h] 2Ki 8:1
4:16 [i] S Ge 18:10
4:18 [j] S Ru 2:3
4:21 [k] ver 32
4:23 [l] S Nu 10:10; 1Ch 23:31; Ps 81:3
4:25 [m] S 1Ki 18:20
4:27 [n] 1Sa 1:15
4:29 [o] S 1Ki 18:46 [p] S Ex 4:2

23"Why go to him today?" he asked. "It's
not the New Moon[l] or the Sabbath."
"It's all right," she said.
24She saddled the donkey and said to
her servant, "Lead on; don't slow down
for me unless I tell you." 25So she set out
and came to the man of God at Mount Carmel.[m]
When he saw her in the distance, the
man of God said to his servant Gehazi,
"Look! There's the Shunammite! 26Run to
meet her and ask her, 'Are you all right?
Is your husband all right? Is your child all
right?'"
"Everything is all right," she said.
27When she reached the man of God at
the mountain, she took hold of his feet.
Gehazi came over to push her away, but
the man of God said, "Leave her alone!
She is in bitter distress,[n] but the LORD has
hidden it from me and has not told me
why."
28"Did I ask you for a son, my lord?"
she said. "Didn't I tell you, 'Don't raise
my hopes'?"
29Elisha said to Gehazi, "Tuck your cloak
into your belt,[o] take my staff[p] in your hand
and run. If you meet anyone, do not greet
him, and if anyone greets you, do not answer. Lay my staff on the boy's face."
30But the child's mother said, "As surely as the LORD lives and as you live, I will
not leave you." So he got up and followed
her.
31Gehazi went on ahead and laid the
staff on the boy's face, but there was no
sound or response. So Gehazi went back
to meet Elisha and told him, "The boy has
not awakened."

4:12 *Gehazi.* Referred to here for the first time; he appears to have served Elisha in some of the same ways as Elisha had served Elijah, though the two men were of drastically different character (see 5:19–27; 6:15).
4:13 *I have a home among my own people.* The Shunammite woman felt secure and content in the community of her own family and tribe, and she had no need or desire for favors from high government officials.
4:14 *she has no son and her husband is old.* A great disappointment because it meant that the family's name would cease and its land and possessions would pass on to others. It was also a great threat to this young wife's future in that she faced the likelihood of many years as a widow with no provider or protector — children were a widow's only social security in old age (see 8:1–6; see also note on 1Ki 17:22).
4:16 *About this time next year.* See Ge 17:21; 18:14. *Don't mislead your servant, O man of God!* The woman's response revealed the depths of her desire for a son and her fear of disappointment more than it showed a lack of confidence in the word of Elisha.
4:17 *just as Elisha had told her.* The trustworthiness of Elisha's word was confirmed, and the birth of the son was shown to be the result of God's gracious intervention in her behalf.
4:20 *he died.* The child, given as an evidence of God's grace and the reliability of his word, was suddenly taken from the woman in a severe test of her faith. Her subsequent actions demonstrate the strength of her faith in the face of great calamity.
4:21 *laid him on the bed of the man of God.* In this way the woman concealed the child's death from the rest of the household while she went to seek the prophet at whose word the child had been born.
4:23 *Why go to him today?* The question suggests that it was not uncommon for the woman to go to Elisha, but that on this occasion the timing of her visit was unusual.
4:26 *Everything is all right.* The woman was determined to share her distress with no one but the prophet from whom she had received the promise of the birth of her son.
4:28 *Didn't I tell you, 'Don't raise my hopes'?* The woman struggled with the question of why the Lord would take from her that which she had been given as a special demonstration of his grace and the trustworthiness of his word.
4:29 *Lay my staff on the boy's face.* It appears that Elisha expected the Lord to restore the boy's life when the staff was placed on him. This does not suggest that Elisha attributed magical power to the staff, but that he viewed it as a representation of his own presence and a symbol of divine power (see note on 2:8; cf. Ex 14:16; Ac 19:12).
4:30 *I will not leave you.* The woman was not convinced that Gehazi's mission would be successful and insisted that Elisha himself accompany her to Shunem.

[32]When Elisha reached the house, there
was the boy lying dead on his couch.[q]
[33]He went in, shut the door on the two
of them and prayed[r] to the LORD. [34]Then
he got on the bed and lay upon the boy,
mouth to mouth, eyes to eyes, hands to
hands. As he stretched[s] himself out upon
him, the boy's body grew warm. [35]Elisha
turned away and walked back and forth
in the room and then got on the bed and
stretched out upon him once more. The
boy sneezed seven times[t] and opened his
eyes.[u]
[36]Elisha summoned Gehazi and said,
"Call the Shunammite." And he did. When
she came, he said, "Take your son."[v] [37]She
came in, fell at his feet and bowed to the
ground. Then she took her son and went
out.

Death in the Pot

[38]Elisha returned to Gilgal[w] and there
was a famine[x] in that region. While the
company of the prophets was meeting
with him, he said to his servant, "Put on
the large pot and cook some stew for these
men."
[39]One of them went out into the fields
to gather herbs and found a wild vine. He
gathered some of its gourds and filled the
fold of his cloak. When he returned, he
cut them up into the pot of stew, though
no one knew what they were. [40]The stew
was poured out for the men, but as they
began to eat it, they cried out, "O man of
God, there is death in the pot!" And they
could not eat it.

4:32 [q]ver 21 **4:33** [r]1Ki 17:20; Mt 6:6 **4:34** [s]1Ki 17:21; Ac 20:10 **4:35** [t]S Jos 6:15 [u]2Ki 8:5 **4:36** [v]Heb 11:35 **4:38** [w]S 2Ki 2:1 [x]S Lev 26:26; 2Ki 8:1

[41]Elisha said, "Get some flour." He put it
into the pot and said, "Serve it to the people to eat." And there was nothing harmful in the pot.[y]

Feeding of a Hundred

[42]A man came from Baal Shalishah,[z]
bringing the man of God twenty loaves[a]
of barley bread[b] baked from the first ripe
grain, along with some heads of new grain.
"Give it to the people to eat," Elisha said.
[43]"How can I set this before a hundred
men?" his servant asked.
But Elisha answered, "Give it to the people to eat.[c] For this is what the LORD says:
'They will eat and have some left over.[d]' "
[44]Then he set it before them, and they ate
and had some left over, according to the
word of the LORD.

Naaman Healed of Leprosy

5 Now Naaman was commander of the
army of the king of Aram.[e] He was a
great man in the sight of his master and
highly regarded, because through him the
LORD had given victory to Aram. He was a
valiant soldier, but he had leprosy.[a][f]
[2]Now bands[g] from Aram had gone out
and had taken captive a young girl from Israel, and she served Naaman's wife. [3]She
said to her mistress, "If only my master
would see the prophet[h] who is in Samaria!
He would cure him of his leprosy."

[a] *1* The Hebrew word was used for various diseases affecting the skin — not necessarily leprosy; also in verses 3, 6, 7, 11 and 27.

4:41 [y]S Ex 15:25; S 2Ki 2:21 **4:42** [z]1Sa 9:4 [a]Mt 14:17; 15:36 [b]S 1Sa 9:7 **4:43** [c]Lk 9:13 [d]Mt 14:20; Jn 6:12 **5:1** [e]S Ge 10:22; S 2Sa 10:19 [f]S Ex 4:6; S Nu 12:10; Lk 4:27 **5:2** [g]2Ki 6:23; 13:20; 24:2 **5:3** [h]S Ge 20:7

4:33 *shut the door on the two of them and prayed.* Just as Elijah had done in a similar situation years before (see 1Ki 17:20–22), Elisha first turned to the Lord in earnest prayer for restoration of life to the dead child. His prayer is clear evidence that his subsequent actions were not intended as a magical means of restoring life.
4:34 *lay upon the boy.* See note on 1Ki 17:21. Perhaps Elisha was familiar with the earlier similar action of Elijah.
4:37 *fell at his feet and bowed to the ground.* The woman gratefully acknowledged the special favor granted to her by the Lord through Elisha, and silently reaffirmed the verbal confession of the widow of Zarephath (see 1Ki 17:24).
4:38 *Gilgal.* See note on 2:1. *famine in that region.* Perhaps the same famine mentioned in 8:1. Famine was a covenant curse (see Lev 26:19–20,26; Dt 28:18,23–24; 1Ki 8:36–37) and evidence of God's anger with his people's disobedience to their covenant obligations. *company of the prophets.* See note on 2:3.
4:39 *wild vine ... gourds.* The precise type of plant is not specified.
4:41 *flour.* The flour itself did not make the stew edible (see 2:21 and note). It was simply a means by which the Lord provided for those who were faithful to the covenant, at a time when others suffered under the covenant curse.
4:42 *first ripe grain.* Instead of bringing the firstfruits of the new harvest (see Lev 2:14; 23:15–17; Dt 18:3–5) to the apostate priests at Bethel and Dan (see 1Ki 12:28–31), godly people in the northern kingdom may have contributed their offerings for the sustenance of Elisha and those associated with him (see note on v. 23). Thus they looked upon Elisha rather than the apostate king and priests as the true representative of their covenant Lord.
4:43 *the LORD says.* The bread was multiplied at the word of the Lord through Elisha apart from any intermediate means (contrast v. 41; 2:20; cf. Mk 6:35–43 and note on 6:43).
5:1 *king of Aram.* Probably Ben-Hadad II (see notes on 8:7; 13:3; 1Ki 20:1). *the LORD had given victory to Aram.* Probably a reference to an otherwise undocumented Aramean victory over the Assyrians in the aftermath of the battle of Qarqar in 853 B.C. (see note on 1Ki 22:1). In the narrator's theological perspective, this victory is attributable to the sovereignty of the God of Israel, who is seen as the ruler and controller of the destinies of all nations, not just that of Israel (see Eze 30:24; Am 2:1–3; 9:7). *leprosy.* See NIV text note; see also note on Lev 13:2.
5:2 *bands from Aram.* Although Israel had concluded a peace treaty with the Arameans during the reign of Ahab (see 1Ki 20:34), minor border skirmishes continued between the two states in the aftermath of the battle for control of Ramoth Gilead, in which Ahab had been killed (see note on 1Ki 22:4; see also 1Ki 22:35). *young girl from Israel.* In sharp contrast to the Israelite king in Samaria, this young girl held captive in Damascus was very much aware of God's saving presence with his people through his servant Elisha, and she selflessly shared that knowledge with her Aramean captors.
5:3 *prophet who is in Samaria.* Elisha, who maintained a residence in Samaria (see v. 9; 2:25; 6:19).

4Naaman went to his master and told
him what the girl from Israel had said.
5"By all means, go," the king of Aram replied. "I will send a letter to the king of Israel." So Naaman left, taking with him ten
talents[a] of silver, six thousand shekels[b] of
gold and ten sets of clothing.[i] 6The letter that he took to the king of Israel read:
"With this letter I am sending my servant
Naaman to you so that you may cure him
of his leprosy."
7As soon as the king of Israel read the
letter,[j] he tore his robes and said, "Am I
God?[k] Can I kill and bring back to life?[l]
Why does this fellow send someone to me
to be cured of his leprosy? See how he is
trying to pick a quarrel[m] with me!"
8When Elisha the man of God heard that
the king of Israel had torn his robes, he
sent him this message: "Why have you
torn your robes? Have the man come to me
and he will know that there is a prophet[n]
in Israel." 9So Naaman went with his horses and chariots and stopped at the door of
Elisha's house. 10Elisha sent a messenger
to say to him, "Go, wash[o] yourself seven
times[p] in the Jordan, and your flesh will
be restored and you will be cleansed."
11But Naaman went away angry and
said, "I thought that he would surely come
out to me and stand and call on the name
of the LORD his God, wave his hand[q] over
the spot and cure me of my leprosy. 12Are
not Abana and Pharpar, the rivers of Damascus, better than any of the waters[r] of
Israel? Couldn't I wash in them and be
cleansed?" So he turned and went off in
a rage.[s]
13Naaman's servants went to him and
said, "My father,[t] if the prophet had told
you to do some great thing, would you not
have done it? How much more, then, when
he tells you, 'Wash and be cleansed'!" 14So
he went down and dipped himself in the
Jordan seven times,[u] as the man of God
had told him, and his flesh was restored[v]
and became clean like that of a young
boy.[w]
15Then Naaman and all his attendants
went back to the man of God[x]. He stood
before him and said, "Now I know[y] that
there is no God in all the world except in
Israel. Please accept now a gift[z] from your
servant."
16The prophet answered, "As surely as
the LORD lives, whom I serve, I will not accept a thing." And even though Naaman
urged him, he refused.[a]
17"If you will not," said Naaman,
"please let me, your servant, be given as
much earth[b] as a pair of mules can carry, for your servant will never again make

5:5 [i]ver 22; S Ge 24:53; Jdg 14:12; S 1Sa 9:7
5:7 [j]2Ki 19:14 [k]S Ge 30:2 [l]S Dt 32:39 [m]1Ki 20:7
5:8 [n]S 1Ki 22:7
5:10 [o]Jn 9:7 [p]S Ge 33:3; S Lev 14:7
5:11 [q]S Ex 7:19
5:12 [r]Isa 8:6 [s]Pr 14:17,29; 19:11; 29:11
5:13 [t]2Ki 6:21; 13:14
5:14 [u]S Ge 33:3; S Lev 14:7; S Jos 6:15 [v]S Ex 4:7 [w]Job 33:25
5:15 [x]S Jos 2:11 [y]S Jos 4:24; S 1Sa 17:46 [z]S 1Sa 9:7
5:16 [a]ver 20,26; Ge 14:23; Da 5:17
5:17 [b]Ex 20:24

[a] 5 That is, about 750 pounds (about 340 kilograms)
[b] 5 That is, about 150 pounds (about 70 kilograms)

5:5 *I will send a letter to the king of Israel.* The border skirmishes had not nullified the official peace between the two nations as established by treaty. The king of Israel was Joram (see 1:17; 3:1; 9:24). *ten talents of silver.* See NIV text note. An idea of the relative value of this amount of silver can be seen by comparing it with the price Omri paid for the hill of Samaria (see 1Ki 16:24).

5:6 *so that you may cure him of his leprosy.* Ben-Hadad (king of Aram [see note on v. 1]) assumed that the prophet described by the Israelite slave girl was subject to the authority of the king and that his services could be bought with a sufficiently large gift. He thought he could buy with worldly wealth one of the chief blessings of God's saving presence among his people.

5:7 *he is trying to pick a quarrel with me!* Joram concluded that the entire incident was an attempt by Ben-Hadad to create a pretext for a declaration of war. So blind was the king to God's saving presence through Elisha that he could think only of international intrigue.

5:8 *Why have you torn your robes?* Elisha chided Joram for his fear (see note on 1Sa 17:11) and for his failure to consult the Lord's prophet (see 3:13–14 for evidence of the tension that existed between Joram and Elisha).

5:9 *with his horses and chariots.* This proud pagan would command the healing by his lordly presence.

5:10 *wash yourself seven times in the Jordan.* The instruction is designed to demonstrate to Naaman that healing would come by the power of the God of Israel, but only if he obeyed the word of the Lord's prophet. The prophet himself was not a healer. Ritual washings were practiced among Eastern religions as a purification rite, and the number seven was generally known as a symbol of completeness. Naaman was to wash in the muddy waters of the Jordan River, demonstrating that there was no natural connection between the washing and the desired healing. Perhaps it also suggested that one needed to pass through the Jordan, as Israel had done, in order to obtain healing from the God of Israel (see notes on Jos 3:1—4:24; 3:10).

5:11 *wave his hand over the spot and cure me of my leprosy.* Naaman expected to be healed by the magical technique of the prophet rather than by the power of God operative in connection with his own obedient response to God's word.

5:12 *Abana and Pharpar.* The Abana was termed the Golden River by the Greeks. It is usually identified with the Barada River of today, rising in the Anti-Lebanon mountains and flowing through the city of Damascus. The Pharpar River flows east from Mount Hermon just to the south of Damascus (see map, p. 1570).

5:14 *his flesh was restored and became clean like that of a young boy.* Physically he was reborn (see also v. 15 and note). As he obeyed God's word, Naaman received the gift of God's grace. Naaman is here a sign to disobedient Israel that God's blessing is found only in the path of trustful obedience. When his own people turn away from covenant faithfulness, God will raise up those who will follow his word from outside the covenant nation (see notes on 1Ki 17:9–24; see also Mt 8:10–12; Lk 4:27).

5:15 *no God in all the world except in Israel.* Naaman's confession put to shame the Israelites who continued to waver in their opinion on whether Baal and the Lord (Yahweh) were both gods, or whether Yahweh alone was God (see note on 1Ki 18:21).

5:16 *I will not accept a thing.* Elisha did not seek monetary gain for proclaiming the word of the Lord (see Mt 10:8). Naaman was healed solely by divine grace, not by the power of Elisha.

5:17 *let me ... be given as much earth as a pair of mules can carry.* In the ancient world it was commonly thought that a deity

burnt offerings and sacrifices to any other god but the LORD. 18But may the LORD forgive your servant for this one thing: When my master enters the temple of Rimmon to bow down and he is leaning[c] on my arm and I bow there also — when I bow down in the temple of Rimmon, may the LORD forgive your servant for this."

19"Go in peace,"[d] Elisha said.

After Naaman had traveled some distance, 20Gehazi, the servant of Elisha the man of God, said to himself, "My master was too easy on Naaman, this Aramean, by not accepting from him what he brought. As surely as the LORD[e] lives, I will run after him and get something from him."

21So Gehazi hurried after Naaman. When Naaman saw him running toward him, he got down from the chariot to meet him. "Is everything all right?" he asked.

22"Everything is all right," Gehazi answered. "My master sent me to say, 'Two young men from the company of the prophets have just come to me from the hill country of Ephraim. Please give them a talent[a] of silver and two sets of clothing.'"[f]

23"By all means, take two talents," said Naaman. He urged Gehazi to accept them, and then tied up the two talents of silver in two bags, with two sets of clothing. He gave them to two of his servants, and they carried them ahead of Gehazi. 24When Gehazi came to the hill, he took the things from the servants and put them away in the house. He sent the men away and they left. 25Then he went in and stood before his master Elisha.

"Where have you been, Gehazi?" Elisha asked.

"Your servant didn't go anywhere," Gehazi answered.

26But Elisha said to him, "Was not my spirit with you when the man got down from his chariot to meet you? Is this the time[g] to take money, or to accept clothes, olive groves, vineyards, flocks, herds, or menservants and maidservants?[h] 27Naaman's leprosy[i] will cling to you and to your descendants forever." Then Gehazi[j] went from Elisha's presence and he was leprous, as white as snow.[k]

5:18 [c] 2Ki 7:2 **5:19** [d] 1Sa 1:17; S Ac 15:33 **5:20** [e] Ex 20:7 **5:22** [f] S ver 5; S Ge 45:22

5:26 [g] S ver 16 [h] Jer 45:5 **5:27** [i] S Nu 12:10 [j] Col 3:5 [k] S Ex 4:6 **6:1** [l] S 1Sa 10:5 **6:6** [m] S Ex 15:25; S 2Ki 2:21

An Axhead Floats

6 The company[l] of the prophets said to Elisha, "Look, the place where we meet with you is too small for us. 2Let us go to the Jordan, where each of us can get a pole; and let us build a place there for us to live."

And he said, "Go."

3Then one of them said, "Won't you please come with your servants?"

"I will," Elisha replied. 4And he went with them.

They went to the Jordan and began to cut down trees. 5As one of them was cutting down a tree, the iron axhead fell into the water. "Oh, my lord," he cried out, "it was borrowed!"

6The man of God asked, "Where did it fall?" When he showed him the place, Elisha cut a stick and threw[m] it there, and made the iron float. 7"Lift it out," he said. Then the man reached out his hand and took it.

[a] *22* That is, about 75 pounds (about 34 kilograms)

could be worshiped only on the soil of the nation to which he was bound (see v. 15). For this reason Naaman wanted to take Israelite soil with him in order to have a place in Damascus for the worship of the Lord.

5:18 *my master.* Ben-Hadad, king of Aram. *Rimmon.* Also known as Hadad (and in Canaan and Phoenicia as Baal), this Aramean deity was the god of storm ("Rimmon" means "thunderer") and war. The two names, Hadad and Rimmon, were sometimes combined (see note on Zec 12:11).

5:19 *Go in peace.* Elisha did not directly address Naaman's problem of conscience (v. 18), but commended him to the leading and grace of God as he returned to his pagan environment and official responsibilities.

5:20 *As surely as the LORD lives.* An oath formula (see note on 1Sa 14:39,45).

5:22 *company of the prophets.* See note on 2:3. *Please give them a talent of silver and two sets of clothing.* Gehazi deceived Naaman in order to satisfy his desire for material gain. The evil of his lie was compounded in that it obscured the gracious character of the Lord's work in Naaman's healing and blurred the distinction between Elisha's function as a true prophet of the Lord and the self-serving actions of false prophets and pagan soothsayers.

5:24 *house.* Of Elisha (see v. 9).

5:26 *Is this the time to take money ...?* Gehazi sought to use the grace of God granted to another individual for his own material advantage. This was equivalent to making merchandise of God's grace (see note on 2Co 2:17). "Money" here and elsewhere in 2 Kings refers to gold or silver in various weights, not to coins, which were a later invention. *clothes ... maidservants.* Evidently what Gehazi secretly hoped to acquire with the two talents of silver (see note on v. 5).

5:27 *leprosy.* See NIV text note on v. 1. *to you and to your descendants forever.* For the extension of punishment to the children of an offender of God's law see Ex 20:5 and note; see also note on Jos 7:24. *white as snow.* See Ex 4:6; Nu 12:10. Along with some of Naaman's wealth, which he coveted, Gehazi also received Naaman's dreaded disease.

6:1 *company of the prophets.* See note on 2:3.

6:2 *a place there for us to live.* The Hebrew for this phrase could be translated "a place there for us to sit," referring to some type of assembly hall. It is implied in 4:1–7 that there were separate dwellings for the members of the prophetic companies to live in (see note on 1Sa 19:18).

6:5 *it was borrowed.* At that time an iron axhead was a costly tool, too expensive for the members of the prophetic company to purchase. Having lost it, the borrower faced the prospect of having to work off the value as a slave.

6:6 *Elisha cut a stick and threw it there, and made the iron float.* The Lord demonstrated here his concern for the welfare of his faithful ones.

Elisha Traps Blinded Arameans

8Now the king of Aram was at war with
Israel. After conferring with his officers,
he said, "I will set up my camp in such
and such a place."
9The man of God sent word to the king[n]
of Israel: "Beware of passing that place, because the Arameans are going down there."
10So the king of Israel checked on the place
indicated by the man of God. Time and
again Elisha warned[o] the king, so that he
was on his guard in such places.
11This enraged the king of Aram. He
summoned his officers and demanded of
them, "Will you not tell me which of us is
on the side of the king of Israel?"
12"None of us, my lord the king[p]," said
one of his officers, "but Elisha, the prophet
who is in Israel, tells the king of Israel the
very words you speak in your bedroom."
13"Go, find out where he is," the king
ordered, "so I can send men and capture
him." The report came back: "He is in Dothan."[q] 14Then he sent[r] horses and chariots and a strong force there. They went by
night and surrounded the city.
15When the servant of the man of God
got up and went out early the next morning, an army with horses and chariots had
surrounded the city. "Oh, my lord, what
shall we do?" the servant asked.
16"Don't be afraid,"[s] the prophet answered. "Those who are with us are more[t]
than those who are with them."
17And Elisha prayed, "O LORD, open
his eyes so he may see." Then the LORD
opened the servant's eyes, and he looked
and saw the hills full of horses and chariots[u] of fire all around Elisha.
18As the enemy came down toward him,
Elisha prayed to the LORD, "Strike these
people with blindness."[v] So he struck them
with blindness, as Elisha had asked.
19Elisha told them, "This is not the road
and this is not the city. Follow me, and I
will lead you to the man you are looking
for." And he led them to Samaria.
20After they entered the city, Elisha said,
"LORD, open the eyes of these men so they
can see." Then the LORD opened their eyes
and they looked, and there they were, inside Samaria.
21When the king of Israel saw them, he
asked Elisha, "Shall I kill them, my father?[w] Shall I kill them?"
22"Do not kill them," he answered.
"Would you kill men you have captured[x]
with your own sword or bow? Set food and
water before them so that they may eat and
drink and then go back to their master."
23So he prepared a great feast for them, and
after they had finished eating and drinking, he sent them away, and they returned
to their master. So the bands[y] from Aram
stopped raiding Israel's territory.

Famine in Besieged Samaria

24Some time later, Ben-Hadad[z] king
of Aram mobilized his entire army and
marched up and laid siege[a] to Samaria.
25There was a great famine[b] in the city;
the siege lasted so long that a donkey's

6:9 [n] ver 12 **6:10** [o] Jer 11:18 **6:12** [p] ver 9 **6:13** [q] Ge 37:17 **6:14** [r] 2Ki 1:9 **6:16** [s] S Ge 15:1 [t] 2Ch 32:7; Ps 55:18; Ro 8:31; 1Jn 4:4
6:17 [u] S 2Ki 2:11,12 **6:18** [v] Ge 19:11; Ac 13:11 **6:21** [w] S 2Ki 5:13 **6:22** [x] S Dt 20:11; 2Ch 28:8-15 **6:23** [y] S 2Ki 5:2 **6:24** [z] S 1Ki 15:18; 2Ki 8:7 [a] Dt 28:52 **6:25** [b] S Lev 26:26; S Ru 1:1

6:8 *king of Aram.* Probably Ben-Hadad II (see note on 5:1). *war with Israel.* A reference to border clashes rather than full-scale hostility (see v. 23; see also note on 5:2). Some indication of Israelite weakness and Aramean strength is seen in the ability of the Arameans to send forces to Dothan (only about 11 miles north of Samaria) without apparent difficulty (see vv. 13–14).
6:9 *man of God.* Elisha (see v. 10). *king of Israel.* Probably Joram (see 1:17; 3:1; 9:24).
6:11 *which of us is on the side of the king of Israel?* Repeated evidence that Israel possessed advance knowledge of Aramean military plans led the king of Aram to suspect that there was a traitor among his top officials.
6:12 *king of Israel.* Joram (see 3:1).
6:13 *capture him.* The king of Aram thought he could eliminate Elisha's influence by denying him contact with Israel's king. *Dothan.* Located on a hill about halfway between Jezreel and Samaria, where the main royal residences were (see 1:2; 3:1; 8:29; 9:15; 10:1; 1Ki 21:1).
6:16 *Those who are with us are more than those who are with them.* Elisha knew that there was greater strength in the unseen reality of the hosts of heaven than in the visible reality of the Aramean forces (see 2Ch 32:7–8; Ps 34:7; 1Jn 4:4).
6:17 *saw the hills full of horses and chariots.* In response to Elisha's prayer, his servant was able to see the protecting might of the heavenly hosts gathered about Elisha (see Ge 32:1–2; Ps 34:7; 91:11–12; Mt 18:10; 26:53; see also note on 2Ki 2:11).
6:18 *Strike these people with blindness.* Elisha had prayed for the eyes of his servant to be opened to the unseen reality of the heavenly hosts; now he prays for the eyes of the Aramean soldiers to be closed to earthly reality (see Ge 19:11).
6:19 *This is not the road and this is not the city.* Elisha's statement led the Aramean soldiers to believe that they were being directed to the city where Elisha could be found. Technically this statement was not an untruth, since Elisha accompanied them to Samaria, but it was a means of deceiving the Aramean soldiers into a trap inside Samaria, the fortress-like capital city of the northern kingdom (see Ex 1:19–20; Jos 2:6; 1Sa 16:1–2 for other instances of deception recorded in the OT).
6:20 *there they were, inside Samaria.* The power of the Lord operative through Elisha turned the intended captors into captives.
6:21 *king of Israel.* Joram (see note on v. 9).
6:22 *Do not kill them.* In reality the Aramean soldiers had been taken captive by the power of the Lord, not by Joram's military prowess. The Lord's purpose was to demonstrate to them and their king and to the Israelites and their king that Israel's national security ultimately was grounded in the Lord, not in military forces or strategies.
6:23 *bands from Aram stopped raiding Israel's territory.* See notes on v. 8; 5:2. Temporarily the Arameans recognized the futility of opposition to the power of the God of Israel.
6:24 *Ben-Hadad.* The same Ben-Hadad who had besieged Samaria on a previous occasion (see notes on 13:3; 1Ki 20:1). This siege is probably to be dated c. 850 B.C.
6:25 *donkey's head.* According to Pentateuchal law the donkey was unclean and not to be eaten (see Lev 11:2–7; Dt 14:4–8). The severity of the famine caused the inhabitants

head sold for eighty shekels[a] of silver, and
a quarter of a cab[b] of seed pods[c] [c] for five
shekels.[d]
26As the king of Israel was passing by on
the wall, a woman cried to him, "Help me,
my lord the king!"
27The king replied, "If the LORD does not
help you, where can I get help for you?
From the threshing floor? From the winepress?" 28Then he asked her, "What's the
matter?"
She answered, "This woman said to me,
'Give up your son so we may eat him today, and tomorrow we'll eat my son.' 29So
we cooked my son and ate[d] him. The next
day I said to her, 'Give up your son so we
may eat him,' but she had hidden him."
30When the king heard the woman's
words, he tore[e] his robes. As he went along
the wall, the people looked, and there, underneath, he had sackcloth[f] on his body.
31He said, "May God deal with me, be it
ever so severely, if the head of Elisha son
of Shaphat remains on his shoulders today!"
32Now Elisha was sitting in his house,
and the elders[g] were sitting with him. The
king sent a messenger ahead, but before
he arrived, Elisha said to the elders, "Don't
you see how this murderer[h] is sending
someone to cut off my head?[i] Look, when
the messenger comes, shut the door and
hold it shut against him. Is not the sound
of his master's footsteps behind him?"
33While he was still talking to them, the
messenger came down to him. And ⌞the
king⌟ said, "This disaster is from the LORD.
Why should I wait[j] for the LORD any longer?"
7 Elisha said, "Hear the word of the LORD.
This is what the LORD says: About this
time tomorrow, a seah[e] of flour will sell
for a shekel[f] and two seahs[g] of barley for
a shekel[k] at the gate of Samaria."
2The officer on whose arm the king was
leaning[l] said to the man of God, "Look,
even if the LORD should open the floodgates[m] of the heavens, could this happen?"
"You will see it with your own eyes,"
answered Elisha, "but you will not eat[n]
any of it!"

The Siege Lifted

3Now there were four men with lepro-
sy[h] [o] at the entrance of the city gate. They
said to each other, "Why stay here until we die? 4If we say, 'We'll go into the
city'—the famine is there, and we will
die. And if we stay here, we will die. So
let's go over to the camp of the Arameans
and surrender. If they spare us, we live; if
they kill us, then we die."
5At dusk they got up and went to the
camp of the Arameans. When they reached
the edge of the camp, not a man was there,
6for the Lord had caused the Arameans to
hear the sound[p] of chariots and horses and
a great army, so that they said to one another, "Look, the king of Israel has hired[q]
the Hittite[r] and Egyptian kings to attack
us!" 7So they got up and fled[s] in the dusk
and abandoned their tents and their horses and donkeys. They left the camp as it
was and ran for their lives.
8The men who had leprosy[t] reached
the edge of the camp and entered one of
the tents. They ate and drank, and carried
away silver, gold and clothes, and went off
and hid them. They returned and entered
another tent and took some things from it
and hid them also.

6:25 [c] Isa 36:12 **6:29** [d] S Lev 26:29; Dt 28:53-55 **6:30** [e] 2Ki 18:37; Isa 22:15 [f] S Ge 37:34 **6:32** [g] Eze 8:1; 14:1; 20:1 [h] 1Ki 18:4 [i] ver 31 **6:33** [j] Lev 24:11; Job 2:9; 14:14; Isa 40:31 **7:1** [k] ver 16 **7:2** [l] 2Ki 5:18 [m] ver 19; Ge 7:11; Ps 78:23; Mal 3:10 [n] ver 17 **7:3** [o] Lev 13:45-46; Nu 5:1-4 **7:6** [p] S Ex 14:24; Eze 1:24 [q] 2Sa 10:6; Jer 46:21 [r] S Nu 13:29 **7:7** [s] Jdg 7:21; Ps 48:4-6; Pr 28:1; Isa 30:17 **7:8** [t] Isa 33:23; 35:6

[a] *25* That is, about 2 pounds (about 1 kilogram) [b] *25* That is, probably about 1/2 pint (about 0.3 liter) [c] *25* Or *of doves' dung* [d] *25* That is, about 2 ounces (about 55 grams) [e] *1* That is, probably about 7 quarts (about 7.3 liters); also in verses 16 and 18 [f] *1* That is, about 2/5 ounce (about 11 grams); also in verses 16 and 18 [g] *1* That is, probably about 13 quarts (about 15 liters); also in verses 16 and 18 [h] *3* The Hebrew word is used for various diseases affecting the skin—not necessarily leprosy; also in verse 8.

of Samaria not only to disregard the laws of uncleanness, but also to place a high value on the least edible part of the donkey. *eighty shekels of silver.* See NIV text note; see also note on 5:5.

6:27 *If the LORD does not help you, where can I get help for you?* Joram correctly recognized his own inability to assist the woman if the Lord himself did not act in Israel's behalf, but he wrongly implied that the Lord was to be blamed for a situation brought on by Israel's own disobedience and idolatry.

6:28 *tomorrow we'll eat my son.* The sins of the king and people were so great that the covenant curses of Lev 26:29 and Dt 28:53,57 were being inflicted (cf. La 4:10).

6:30 *tore his robes.* More an expression of anger toward Elisha and the Lord (see v. 31) than one of repentance and sorrow for the sins that had provoked the covenant curse. *sackcloth.* A coarse cloth usually worn as a sign of mourning (see notes on Ge 37:34; Rev 11:3).

6:31 *May God deal with me, be it ever so severely.* A curse formula (see note on 1Sa 3:17). *if the head of Elisha … remains on his shoulders today!* Joram considered Elisha in some way responsible for the conditions in the city. Cf. Ahab's attitude toward Elijah (1Ki 18:10,16–17; 21:20).

6:32 *elders.* Leaders of the city (see notes on Ex 3:16; 2Sa 3:17). They sit with Elisha rather than with the king.

6:33 *Why should I wait for the LORD any longer?* Joram felt himself deceived by Elisha and abandoned by the Lord, whom he blamed for the disastrous conditions in the city.

7:1 *a seah of flour will sell for a shekel.* See NIV text notes. This was about double the normal cost of flour, but a phenomenal improvement over the highly inflated prices the famine had caused.

7:2 *floodgates of the heavens.* See v. 19; Ge 8:2; Isa 24:18.

7:3 *entrance of the city gate.* Pentateuchal law excluded persons with skin diseases from residence in the community (Lev 13:46; Nu 5:2–3).

7:6 *the Lord had caused the Arameans to hear the sound.* See 2Sa 5:24 and note. *Hittite … kings.* Kings of small city-states ruled by dynasties of Hittite origin, which had arisen in northern Aram after the fall of the Hittite empire c. 1200 B.C.

9Then they said to each other, "We're
not doing right. This is a day of good news
and we are keeping it to ourselves. If we
wait until daylight, punishment will overtake us. Let's go at once and report this to
the royal palace."
10So they went and called out to the
city gatekeepers and told them, "We went
into the Aramean camp and not a man
was there — not a sound of anyone — only
tethered horses and donkeys, and the tents
left just as they were." 11The gatekeepers
shouted the news, and it was reported
within the palace.
12The king got up in the night and said
to his officers, "I will tell you what the Arameans have done to us. They know we
are starving; so they have left the camp to
hide[u] in the countryside, thinking, 'They
will surely come out, and then we will
take them alive and get into the city.' "
13One of his officers answered, "Have
some men take five of the horses that are
left in the city. Their plight will be like that
of all the Israelites left here — yes, they
will only be like all these Israelites who
are doomed. So let us send them to find
out what happened."
14So they selected two chariots with
their horses, and the king sent them after the Aramean army. He commanded
the drivers, "Go and find out what has
happened." 15They followed them as far
as the Jordan, and they found the whole
road strewn with the clothing and equipment the Arameans had thrown away in
their headlong flight.[v] So the messengers
returned and reported to the king. 16Then
the people went out and plundered[w] the
camp of the Arameans. So a seah of flour
sold for a shekel, and two seahs of barley
sold for a shekel,[x] as the LORD had said.
17Now the king had put the officer on
whose arm he leaned in charge of the gate,
and the people trampled him in the gateway, and he died,[y] just as the man of God
had foretold when the king came down
to his house. 18It happened as the man of
God had said to the king: "About this time
tomorrow, a seah of flour will sell for a
shekel and two seahs of barley for a shekel
at the gate of Samaria."
19The officer had said to the man of
God, "Look, even if the LORD should open
the floodgates[z] of the heavens, could this
happen?" The man of God had replied,
"You will see it with your own eyes, but
you will not eat any of it!" 20And that is
exactly what happened to him, for the
people trampled him in the gateway, and
he died.

The Shunammite's Land Restored

8 Now Elisha had said to the woman[a]
whose son he had restored to life, "Go
away with your family and stay for a while
wherever you can, because the LORD has
decreed a famine[b] in the land that will last
seven years."[c] 2The woman proceeded to
do as the man of God said. She and her
family went away and stayed in the land
of the Philistines seven years.
3At the end of the seven years she came
back from the land of the Philistines and
went to the king to beg for her house and
land. 4The king was talking to Gehazi, the
servant of the man of God, and had said,
"Tell me about all the great things Elisha
has done." 5Just as Gehazi was telling the
king how Elisha had restored[d] the dead
to life, the woman whose son Elisha had
brought back to life came to beg the king
for her house and land.
Gehazi said, "This is the woman, my
lord the king, and this is her son whom
Elisha restored to life." 6The king asked
the woman about it, and she told him.
Then he assigned an official to her case
and said to him, "Give back everything
that belonged to her, including all the income from her land from the day she left
the country until now."

7:12 [u] Jos 8:4
7:15 [v] Job 27:22
7:16 [w] Isa 33:4,23 [x] ver 1
7:17 [y] S ver 2
7:19 [z] S ver 2
8:1 [a] 2Ki 4:8-37 [b] S Lev 26:26; S Dt 28:22; S Ru 1:1 [c] S Ge 12:10
8:5 [d] 2Ki 4:35

7:9 Fear of punishment can be a valid motive for changing one's behavior.
7:12 *what the Arameans have done to us.* Joram's unbelief caused him to conclude that the report of the four leprous men was part of an Aramean war strategy rather than an evidence of the fulfillment of Elisha's prophecy (see v. 1).
7:16 – 20 *as the LORD had said ... as the man of God had foretold ... as the man of God had said ... that is exactly what happened to him.* Emphasizing the trustworthiness of the prophetic word spoken by Elisha. In the fulfillment of Elisha's prophecy Israel was reminded that deliverance from her enemies was a gift of God's grace and that rejection of God's word provoked the wrath of divine judgment.
8:1 *the LORD has decreed a famine.* The famine should have been perceived by the people of the northern kingdom as a covenant curse sent on them because of their sin (see note on 4:38). *seven years.* It is not clear whether this famine began before or after the Aramean siege of Samaria (see 4:38; 6:24 — 7:20).
8:2 *She and her family went away.* Elisha's instruction enabled this godly woman and her family to escape the privations of the famine.
8:3 *went to the king.* See note on 1Ki 3:16. *beg for her house and land.* Either someone had illegally occupied the woman's property during her absence, or it had fallen to the domain of the king by virtue of its abandonment.
8:4 *Tell me about all the great things Elisha has done.* The king's lack of familiarity with Elisha's ministry is perhaps an indication that this incident occurred in the early days of the reign of Jehu rather than in the time of Joram, who had had numerous contacts with Elisha (see 3:13 – 14; 5:7 – 10; 6:10 – 23; 6:24 — 7:20). But see note on 5:7.
8:6 *Give back everything that belonged to her.* The widow and her son were living examples of the Lord's provision and blessing for those who were obedient to the word of the Lord through his prophets.

Hazael Murders Ben-Hadad

7Elisha went to Damascus,[e] and Ben-
Hadad[f] king of Aram was ill. When the
king was told, "The man of God has come
all the way up here," 8he said to Hazael,[g]
"Take a gift[h] with you and go to meet the
man of God. Consult[i] the LORD through
him; ask him, 'Will I recover from this illness?'"
9Hazael went to meet Elisha, taking
with him as a gift forty camel-loads of all
the finest wares of Damascus. He went in
and stood before him, and said, "Your son
Ben-Hadad king of Aram has sent me to
ask, 'Will I recover from this illness?'"
10Elisha answered, "Go and say to him,
'You will certainly recover';[j] but[a] the LORD
has revealed to me that he will in fact die."
11He stared at him with a fixed gaze until Hazael felt ashamed.[k] Then the man of
God began to weep.[l]
12"Why is my lord weeping?" asked
Hazael.

"Because I know the harm[m] you will do
to the Israelites," he answered. "You will
set fire to their fortified places, kill their
young men with the sword, dash[n] their little children[o] to the ground, and rip open[p]
their pregnant women."
13Hazael said, "How could your servant,
a mere dog,[q] accomplish such a feat?"

"The LORD has shown me that you will
become king[r] of Aram," answered Elisha.
14Then Hazael left Elisha and returned
to his master. When Ben-Hadad asked,
"What did Elisha say to you?" Hazael replied, "He told me that you would certainly recover." 15But the next day he took a
thick cloth, soaked it in water and spread
it over the king's face, so that he died.[s]
Then Hazael succeeded him as king.

Jehoram King of Judah

8:16-24pp — 2Ch 21:5-10,20

16In the fifth year of Joram[t] son of Ahab
king of Israel, when Jehoshaphat was king
of Judah, Jehoram[u] son of Jehoshaphat
began his reign as king of Judah. 17He was
thirty-two years old when he became king,
and he reigned in Jerusalem eight years.
18He walked in the ways of the kings of
Israel, as the house of Ahab had done, for
he married a daughter[v] of Ahab. He did
evil in the eyes of the LORD. 19Neverthe-
less, for the sake of his servant David, the
LORD was not willing to destroy[w] Judah.
He had promised to maintain a lamp[x] for
David and his descendants forever.
20In the time of Jehoram, Edom rebelled
against Judah and set up its own king.[y]
21So Jehoram[b] went to Zair with all his
chariots. The Edomites surrounded him
and his chariot commanders, but he rose

8:7 [e] S 2Sa 8:5 [f] S 2Ki 6:24 **8:8** [g] 1Ki 19:15 [h] S Ge 32:20; S 1Sa 9:7 [i] S Jdg 18:5 **8:10** [j] Isa 38:1 **8:11** [k] S Jdg 3:25 [l] Lk 19:41 **8:12** [m] S 1Ki 19:17 [n] Ps 137:9; Isa 13:16; Hos 13:16; Na 3:10; Lk 19:44 [o] S Ge 34:29 [p] 2Ki 15:16; Am 1:13 **8:13** [q] S 1Sa 17:43; S 2Sa 3:8 [r] 1Ki 19:15 **8:15** [s] S 2Ki 1:17 **8:16** [t] S 2Ki 1:17 [u] 2Ch 21:1-4 **8:18** [v] ver 26; 2Ki 11:1 **8:19** [w] S Ge 6:13 [x] S 2Sa 21:17; Rev 21:23 **8:20** [y] S 1Ki 22:47

[a] *10* The Hebrew may also be read *Go and say, 'You will certainly not recover,' for.* [b] *21* Hebrew *Joram,* a variant of *Jehoram*; also in verses 23 and 24

8:7 *Elisha went to Damascus.* The time had come for Elisha to carry out one of the three tasks originally given to Elijah at Mount Horeb (see notes on 1Ki 19:15–16). The annals of the Assyrian ruler Shalmaneser III record Assyrian victories over Ben-Hadad (Hadadezer) of Damascus in 846 B.C. and Hazael of Damascus in 842. Elisha's visit to Damascus is to be dated c. 843.
8:8 *Consult the LORD through him.* In a reversal of the situation described in 1:1–4, a pagan king seeks an oracle from Israel's God. *Will I recover . . . ?* The question is the same as that of Ahaziah in 1:2.
8:9 *forty camel-loads of all the finest wares of Damascus.* Damascus was the center for trade between Egypt, Asia Minor and Mesopotamia. Ben-Hadad evidently thought a generous gift would favorably influence Elisha's oracle (cf. Naaman's gift in 5:5). *Your son Ben-Hadad.* Use of father-son terminology is a tacit acknowledgment by Ben-Hadad of Elisha's superiority (see 6:21; 1Sa 25:8).
8:10 *You will certainly recover.* An assertion that Ben-Hadad's illness was not terminal. *in fact die.* By the hand of Hazael (vv. 14–15).
8:12 *harm you will do to the Israelites.* The Lord gave Elisha a clear picture of the severity of the judgment he was about to send on Israel by the hand of Hazael (see 9:14–16; 10:32; 12:17–18; 13:3,22). *rip open their pregnant women.* This vicious act was often carried out by victorious armies at that time (see 15:16; Hos 13:16; Am 1:13). Such an atrocity likely was intended to make sure that no male children would be born to provide a remnant of the conquered people, which could rise up again and reclaim the land. Elisha's words do not sanction such acts but simply describe Hazael's future attacks on Israel.
8:13 *How could your servant, a mere dog, accomplish such a feat?* See 2Sa 9:8 and note. Hazael did not show repulsion at these violent acts but saw no possibility to gain the power necessary to accomplish them. *you will become king of Aram.* Elisha's prophecy suggests that Hazael was not a legitimate successor to Ben-Hadad. In an Assyrian inscription Hazael is designated "the son of a nobody" (i.e., a commoner) who usurped the throne.
8:15 *died.* Elisha's prophecy of Hazael's kingship did not legitimize the assassination. Hazael's murder of Ben-Hadad as well as his future acts of violence against Israel were wicked acts arising out of his own sinful heart (see Isa 10:5–19). He was followed by a son he named Ben-Hadad (13:24).
8:16 *fifth year of Joram.* 848 B.C. Jehoram had been coregent with his father since 853 (see note on 1:17), but he now began his reign as sole king.
8:17 *reigned in Jerusalem eight years.* Jehoram's sole reign is to be dated 848–841 B.C.
8:18 *as the house of Ahab had done.* Jehoram introduced Baal worship in Judah, as Ahab had done in the northern kingdom (see 11:18). Baal worship now spread to the southern kingdom at the same time it was being restricted in the northern kingdom by Ahab's son Joram (see 3:1–2). *married a daughter of Ahab.* Jehoram's wife was Athaliah, a daughter of Ahab but probably not of Jezebel (see v. 26; 2Ch 18:1). Athaliah's influence on Jehoram paralleled that of Jezebel on Ahab (see 1Ki 16:31; 18:4; 19:1–2; 2Ch 21:6).
8:19 *lamp for David.* See note on 1Ki 11:36; see also Ps 132:17. The Lord spared Judah and its royal house the judgment he brought on the house of Ahab because of the covenant he had made with David (see 2Sa 7:16,29; 2Ch 21:7).
8:20 *set up its own king.* Previously Edom had been subject to Judah and had been ruled by a deputy (see note on 3:9; see also 1Ki 22:47).

up and broke through by night; his army, however, fled back home. 22To this day Edom has been in rebellion[z] against Judah. Libnah[a] revolted at the same time.

23As for the other events of Jehoram's reign, and all he did, are they not written in the book of the annals of the kings of Judah? 24Jehoram rested with his fathers and was buried with them in the City of David. And Ahaziah his son succeeded him as king.

Ahaziah King of Judah

8:25-29pp — 2Ch 22:1-6

25In the twelfth[b] year of Joram son of Ahab king of Israel, Ahaziah son of Jehoram king of Judah began to reign. 26Ahaziah was twenty-two years old when he became king, and he reigned in Jerusalem one year. His mother's name was Athaliah,[c] a granddaughter of Omri[d] king of Israel. 27He walked in the ways of the house of Ahab[e] and did evil[f] in the eyes of the LORD, as the house of Ahab had done, for he was related by marriage to Ahab's family.

28Ahaziah went with Joram son of Ahab to war against Hazael king of Aram at Ramoth Gilead.[g] The Arameans wounded Joram; 29so King Joram returned to Jezreel[h] to recover from the wounds the Arameans had inflicted on him at Ramoth[a] in his battle with Hazael[i] king of Aram.

Then Ahaziah[j] son of Jehoram king of Judah went down to Jezreel to see Joram son of Ahab, because he had been wounded.

Jehu Anointed King of Israel

9 The prophet Elisha summoned a man from the company[k] of the prophets and said to him, "Tuck your cloak into your belt,[l] take this flask of oil[m] with you and go to Ramoth Gilead.[n] 2When you get there, look for Jehu son of Jehoshaphat, the son of Nimshi. Go to him, get him away from his companions and take him into an inner room. 3Then take the flask and pour the oil[o] on his head and declare, 'This is what the LORD says: I anoint you king over Israel.' Then open the door and run; don't delay!"

4So the young man, the prophet, went to Ramoth Gilead. 5When he arrived, he found the army officers sitting together. "I have a message for you, commander," he said.

"For which of us?" asked Jehu.

"For you, commander," he replied.

6Jehu got up and went into the house. Then the prophet poured the oil[p] on Jehu's head and declared, "This is what the LORD, the God of Israel, says: 'I anoint you king over the LORD's people Israel. 7You are to destroy the house of Ahab your master, and I will avenge[q] the blood of my servants[r] the prophets and the blood of all the LORD's servants shed by Jezebel.[s] 8The whole house[t] of Ahab will perish. I will cut off from Ahab every last male[u] in Israel — slave or free. 9I will make the house of Ahab like the house of Jeroboam[v] son of Nebat and like the house of Baasha[w] son of Ahijah. 10As for Jezebel, dogs[x] will devour her on the plot of ground at Jezreel, and no one will bury her.'" Then he opened the door and ran.

11When Jehu went out to his fellow officers, one of them asked him, "Is everything all right? Why did this madman[y] come to you?"

"You know the man and the sort of things he says," Jehu replied.

12"That's not true!" they said. "Tell us."

8:22 [z]Ge 27:40 [a]S Nu 33:20; Jos 21:13; 2Ki 19:8 **8:25** [b]2Ki 9:29 **8:26** [c]S ver 18 [d]1Ki 16:23 **8:27** [e]1Ki 16:30 [f]1Ki 15:26 **8:28** [g]S Dt 4:43; 2Ki 9:1, 14 **8:29** [h]1Ki 21:29; 2Ki 9:21 [i]1Ki 19:15, 17 [j]2Ki 10:13 **9:1** [k]S 1Sa 10:5 [l]S 1Ki 18:46 [m]S 1Sa 10:1 [n]S 2Ki 8:28 **9:3** [o]1Ki 19:16 **9:6** [p]1Ki 19:16 **9:7** [q]S Ge 4:24; S Rev 6:10 [r]S Dt 32:43 [s]S 1Ki 18:4 **9:8** [t]2Ki 10:17 [u]S 1Sa 25:22 **9:9** [v]S 1Ki 13:34; S 14:10 [w]1Ki 16:3 **9:10** [x]S 1Ki 21:23 **9:11** [y]S 1Sa 10:11; S Jn 10:20

[a] 29 Hebrew *Ramah,* a variant of *Ramoth*

8:22 *To this day.* Until the time of the writing of the account of Jehoram's reign used by the author of 1,2 Kings (see Introduction to 1 Kings: Author, Sources and Date; see also note on 1Ki 8:8). Later, Amaziah of Judah was able to inflict a serious defeat on Edom (14:7), and his successor Azariah regained control of the trade route to Elath through Edomite territory (14:22; 2Ch 26:2). *Libnah revolted at the same time.* Libnah appears to have been located close to the Philistine border near Lachish (see 19:8). It is likely that the revolt of Libnah was connected with that of the Philistines and Arabs described in 2Ch 21:16–17.
8:23 *other events of Jehoram's reign.* See 2Ch 21:4–20. *annals of the kings of Judah.* See note on 1Ki 14:29.
8:24 *rested with his fathers.* See notes on 1Ki 1:21; 2Ch 21:20.
8:25 *twelfth year of Joram.* 841 B.C. In 9:29 the first year of Joram's reign was counted as his accession year and his second year as the first year of his reign, whereas here his accession year was counted as the first year of his reign (see Introduction to 1 Kings: Chronology).
8:26 *twenty-two years old when he became king.* See note on 2Ch 22:2. *Athaliah.* See note on v. 18.
8:27 *ways of the house of Ahab.* See 2Ch 22:3–5.
8:28 *Ahaziah went with Joram … to war against Hazael … at Ramoth Gilead.* As Jehoshaphat had joined Ahab in battle against the Arameans at Ramoth Gilead (1Ki 22), so now Ahaziah joined his uncle Joram in a similar venture. On the previous occasion Ahab met his death (1Ki 22:37). On this occasion Joram was wounded and, while recuperating in Jezreel (see note on 1Ki 21:1), both he and his nephew Ahaziah were assassinated by Jehu (see 9:14–28). *Hazael.* See note on 1Ki 19:15.
9:1 *company of the prophets.* See note on 2:3.
9:3 *I anoint you king.* See notes on 1Sa 2:10; 9:16; 1Ki 19:16.
9:7 *destroy the house of Ahab.* Jehu learned that he was the divinely appointed agent to inflict the judgment Elijah had pronounced many years earlier in his own hearing against the house of Ahab (see vv. 25–26; 1Ki 21:21–24). *blood of all the LORD's servants shed by Jezebel.* See 1Ki 18:4; 21:13.
9:8 *slave or free.* See note on 1Ki 14:10.
9:9 *like the house of Jeroboam.* See 1Ki 14:7–11; 15:27–30. *like the house of Baasha.* See 1Ki 16:1–4,8–12. Elijah had spoken the same words to Ahab years before (see 1Ki 21:21–24).
9:11 *this madman.* The epithet betrays a scornful attitude on the part of the military officers of the northern kingdom toward members of the prophetic companies. Cf. 1Sa 21:13–15.

Jehu said, "Here is what he told me:
'This is what the LORD says: I anoint you
king over Israel.'"
13They hurried and took their cloaks
and spread[z] them under him on the bare
steps. Then they blew the trumpet[a] and
shouted, "Jehu is king!"

Jehu Kills Joram and Ahaziah

9:21-29pp — 2Ch 22:7-9

14So Jehu son of Jehoshaphat, the son
of Nimshi, conspired against Joram. (Now
Joram and all Israel had been defending
Ramoth Gilead[b] against Hazael king of
Aram, 15but King Joram[a] had returned to
Jezreel to recover[c] from the wounds the
Arameans had inflicted on him in the battle with Hazael king of Aram.) Jehu said,
"If this is the way you feel, don't let anyone slip out of the city to go and tell the
news in Jezreel." 16Then he got into his
chariot and rode to Jezreel, because Joram
was resting there and Ahaziah[d] king of Judah had gone down to see him.
17When the lookout[e] standing on the
tower in Jezreel saw Jehu's troops approaching, he called out, "I see some
troops coming."
"Get a horseman," Joram ordered.
"Send him to meet them and ask, 'Do you
come in peace?[f]'"
18The horseman rode off to meet Jehu
and said, "This is what the king says: 'Do
you come in peace?'"
"What do you have to do with peace?"
Jehu replied. "Fall in behind me."
The lookout reported, "The messenger
has reached them, but he isn't coming
back."
19So the king sent out a second horseman. When he came to them he said,
"This is what the king says: 'Do you come
in peace?'"
Jehu replied, "What do you have to do
with peace? Fall in behind me."
20The lookout reported, "He has reached
them, but he isn't coming back either. The
driving is like[g] that of Jehu son of Nimshi—he drives like a madman."
21"Hitch up my chariot," Joram ordered.
And when it was hitched up, Joram king
of Israel and Ahaziah king of Judah rode
out, each in his own chariot, to meet Jehu.
They met him at the plot of ground that
had belonged to Naboth[h] the Jezreelite.
22When Joram saw Jehu he asked, "Have
you come in peace, Jehu?"
"How can there be peace," Jehu replied,
"as long as all the idolatry and witchcraft
of your mother Jezebel[i] abound?"
23Joram turned about and fled, calling
out to Ahaziah, "Treachery,[j] Ahaziah!"
24Then Jehu drew his bow[k] and shot
Joram between the shoulders. The arrow
pierced his heart and he slumped down
in his chariot. 25Jehu said to Bidkar, his
chariot officer, "Pick him up and throw
him on the field that belonged to Naboth
the Jezreelite. Remember how you and I
were riding together in chariots behind
Ahab his father when the LORD made this
prophecy[l] about him: 26'Yesterday I saw
the blood of Naboth[m] and the blood of his
sons, declares the LORD, and I will surely
make you pay for it on this plot of ground,
declares the LORD.'[b] Now then, pick him
up and throw him on that plot, in accordance with the word of the LORD."[n]
27When Ahaziah king of Judah saw
what had happened, he fled up the road
to Beth Haggan.[c] Jehu chased him, shouting, "Kill him too!" They wounded him in
his chariot on the way up to Gur near Ibleam,[o] but he escaped to Megiddo[p] and died
there. 28His servants took him by chariot[q]
to Jerusalem and buried him with his fathers in his tomb in the City of David. 29(In
the eleventh[r] year of Joram son of Ahab,
Ahaziah had become king of Judah.)

Jezebel Killed

30Then Jehu went to Jezreel. When
Jezebel heard about it, she painted[s] her
eyes, arranged her hair and looked out of
a window. 31As Jehu entered the gate, she
asked, "Have you come in peace, Zimri,[t]
you murderer of your master?"[d]

9:13 [z] Mt 21:8; Lk 19:36 [a] S 2Sa 15:10 **9:14** [b] S Dt 4:43; S 2Ki 8:28 **9:15** [c] S 2Ki 8:29 **9:16** [d] 2Ch 22:7 **9:17** [e] S 1Sa 14:16; Isa 21:6 [f] S 1Sa 16:4 **9:20** [g] 2Sa 18:27 **9:21** [h] 1Ki 21:1-7, 15-19 **9:22** [i] 1Ki 18:19; Rev 2:20 **9:23** [j] 2Ki 11:14 **9:24** [k] S 1Ki 22:34 **9:25** [l] 1Ki 21:19-22, 24-29 **9:26** [m] S 1Ki 21:19 [n] S 1Ki 21:29 **9:27** [o] S Jdg 1:27 [p] 2Ki 23:29 **9:28** [q] 2Ki 14:20; 23:30 **9:29** [r] 2Ki 8:25 **9:30** [s] Jer 4:30; Eze 23:40 **9:31** [t] 1Ki 16:9-10

[a] 15 Hebrew *Jehoram,* a variant of *Joram;* also in verses 17 and 21-24 [b] 26 See 1 Kings 21:19. [c] 27 Or *fled by way of the garden house* [d] 31 Or *"Did Zimri have peace, who murdered his master?"*

9:15 *Jezreel.* About 45 miles from Ramoth Gilead. Joram apparently had a summer palace there (see 1Ki 21:1 and note). *don't let anyone ... go and tell the news in Jezreel.* For the success of Jehu's revolt and to avoid a civil conflict it was important to take Joram totally by surprise.
9:16 *Ahaziah ... had gone down to see him.* See 8:29.
9:21 *plot of ground that had belonged to Naboth.* See notes on 1Ki 21:2–3,13,19.
9:22 *idolatry and witchcraft.* Both punishable by death (see Dt 13; 18:10–12).
9:25 *chariot officer.* See note on 1Ki 22:34.
9:26 *in accordance with the word of the LORD.* Jehu saw himself providentially placed in the position of fulfilling the prophecy of Elijah given years before (see 1Ki 21:18–24). Even though Ahab's own blood was not shed on Naboth's field (see 1Ki 21:29 and note), Jehu saw in Joram's death the fulfillment of Elijah's prophecy (see note on 1Ki 21:19).
9:27 *escaped to Megiddo and died there.* It may be questioned whether Jehu was justified in extending the purge of Ahab's house (see Hos 1:4) to the descendants of the house of David through Ahab's daughter Athaliah (see 8:18,26).
9:31 *Zimri, you murderer of your master.* In bitter sarcasm Jezebel called Jehu by the name Zimri. About 45 years earlier Zimri had seized the throne from Elah by assassination and then had destroyed the whole house of Baasha. He ruled, however, for only seven days before Omri seized power (see 1Ki 16:8–20).

32He looked up at the window and
called out, "Who is on my side? Who?"
Two or three eunuchs looked down at
him. 33"Throw her down!" Jehu said. So
they threw her down, and some of her
blood spattered the wall and the horses as
they trampled her underfoot.[u]
34Jehu went in and ate and drank. "Take
care of that cursed woman," he said, "and
bury her, for she was a king's daughter."[v]
35But when they went out to bury her, they
found nothing except her skull, her feet
and her hands. 36They went back and told
Jehu, who said, "This is the word of the
LORD that he spoke through his servant Elijah the Tishbite: On the plot of ground at
Jezreel dogs[w] will devour Jezebel's flesh.[a][x]
37Jezebel's body will be like refuse[y] on the
ground in the plot at Jezreel, so that no
one will be able to say, 'This is Jezebel.'"

Ahab's Family Killed

10 Now there were in Samaria[z] seventy
sons[a] of the house of Ahab. So Jehu
wrote letters and sent them to Samaria: to
the officials of Jezreel,[b][b] to the elders and
to the guardians[c] of Ahab's children. He
said, 2"As soon as this letter reaches you,
since your master's sons are with you and
you have chariots and horses, a fortified
city and weapons, 3choose the best and
most worthy of your master's sons and set
him on his father's throne. Then fight for
your master's house."
4But they were terrified and said, "If two
kings could not resist him, how can we?"
5So the palace administrator, the city
governor, the elders and the guardians
sent this message to Jehu: "We are your
servants[d] and we will do anything you say.
We will not appoint anyone as king; you
do whatever you think best."
6Then Jehu wrote them a second letter,
saying, "If you are on my side and will
obey me, take the heads of your master's
sons and come to me in Jezreel by this
time tomorrow."
Now the royal princes, seventy of them,
were with the leading men of the city,
who were rearing them. 7When the letter
arrived, these men took the princes and
slaughtered all seventy[e] of them. They put
their heads[f] in baskets and sent them to
Jehu in Jezreel. 8When the messenger arrived, he told Jehu, "They have brought
the heads of the princes."
Then Jehu ordered, "Put them in two
piles at the entrance of the city gate until
morning."
9The next morning Jehu went out.
He stood before all the people and said,
"You are innocent. It was I who conspired
against my master and killed him, but
who killed all these? 10Know then, that not
a word the LORD has spoken against the
house of Ahab will fail. The LORD has done
what he promised[g] through his servant Elijah."[h] 11So Jehu[i] killed everyone in Jezreel
who remained of the house of Ahab, as

9:33 [u]Ps 7:5
9:34 [v]S 1Ki 16:31
9:36 [w]Ps 68:23; Jer 15:3 [x]S 1Ki 21:23
9:37 [y]Ps 83:10; Isa 5:25; Jer 8:2; 9:22; 16:4; 25:33; Zep 1:17
10:1 [z]S 1Ki 13:32 [a]S Jdg 8:30 [b]S 1Ki 21:1 [c]ver 5
10:5 [d]Jos 9:8
10:7 [e]S 1Ki 21:21 [f]S 2Sa 4:8
10:10 [g]2Ki 9:7-10 [h]S 1Ki 21:29
10:11 [i]Hos 1:4

[a] *36* See 1 Kings 21:23. [b] *1* Hebrew; some Septuagint manuscripts and Vulgate *of the city*

9:36 *the word of the LORD that he spoke through his servant Elijah.* In the manner of Jezebel's death the word of the Lord was confirmed—the word she had defied during her life (see 1Ki 21:23).

10:1 *Samaria.* In order to consolidate his coup and establish control of the northern kingdom, Jehu still faced the formidable problems of taking the nearly impregnable fortress of Samaria (see note on 1Ki 16:24) and then of completing the destruction of Ahab's house. *seventy sons of the house of Ahab.* The 70 could include both sons and grandsons. *officials.* Officers appointed by the king (see 1Ki 4:1–6). *elders.* Local leaders by virtue of their position in the tribal and family structure (see notes on Ex 3:16; 2Sa 3:17). *guardians of Ahab's children.* Those entrusted with the care and upbringing of the princes in the royal family.

10:3 *fight for your master's house.* Jehu's strategy was to induce the leaders of Samaria into submission to his rule by bluffing a military confrontation.

10:4 *terrified.* The leaders of Samaria were completely intimidated by Jehu's challenge. *two kings.* Joram and Ahaziah (see 9:24,27).

10:5 *palace administrator.* See note on 1Ki 4:6. *city governor.* Probably an official appointed by the king who served as commander of the militia of the capital city. *the elders and the guardians.* See notes on these in v. 1.

10:6 *take the heads of your master's sons and come to me.* The wording of Jehu's command contains what appears to be a deliberate ambiguity. The "heads of your master's sons" could be understood as a reference to the leading figures among the 70 descendants of Ahab, such as the crown prince and several other sons of special ability and standing. On the other hand, the expression could be taken as a reference to the literal heads of all 70 princes.

10:7 *slaughtered all seventy.* The leaders of the city understood the communique in the literal sense, as Jehu most certainly had hoped they would. *put their heads in baskets and sent them to Jehu.* The leaders of Samaria did not carry the heads of the princes to Jezreel themselves as they had been ordered to do by Jehu (see v. 6). It is likely that they feared for their lives.

10:8 *Put them in two piles at the entrance of the city gate.* This gruesome procedure imitated the barbaric practice of the Assyrian rulers Ashurnasirpal and Shalmaneser III, whose reigns were characterized by acts of terror.

10:9 *It was I who ... killed him.* Jehu openly confessed his own part in the overthrow of the government of Joram. *who killed all these?* Because of the ambiguous communique Jehu sent to the leaders of Samaria (see note on v. 6), he can now deny any personal responsibility for the slaughter of the 70 sons of Ahab and can lay the blame for it on the leaders of Samaria.

10:10 *what he promised through his servant Elijah.* See 1Ki 21:20–24,29. Jehu implies a divine sanction not only for what had already been done but also for his intent to continue the purge of Ahab's house and associates.

10:11 *all his chief men, his close friends and his priests.* Jehu went beyond the responsibility given to him (see 9:7; Hos 1:4) and acted solely on grounds of political self-interest. Jehu himself had been in the service of Ahab (see 9:25).

well as all his chief men, his close friends
and his priests, leaving him no survivor.[j]
12 Jehu then set out and went toward Samaria. At Beth Eked of the Shepherds, 13 he
met some relatives of Ahaziah king of Judah and asked, "Who are you?"

They said, "We are relatives of Ahaziah,[k] and we have come down to greet
the families of the king and of the queen
mother.[l]"

14 "Take them alive!" he ordered. So they
took them alive and slaughtered them by
the well of Beth Eked — forty-two men. He
left no survivor.[m]

15 After he left there, he came upon Jehonadab[n] son of Recab,[o] who was on his
way to meet him. Jehu greeted him and
said, "Are you in accord with me, as I am
with you?"

"I am," Jehonadab answered.

"If so," said Jehu, "give me your hand."[p]
So he did, and Jehu helped him up into
the chariot. 16 Jehu said, "Come with me
and see my zeal[q] for the LORD." Then he
had him ride along in his chariot.

17 When Jehu came to Samaria, he killed
all who were left there of Ahab's family;[r]
he destroyed them, according to the word
of the LORD spoken to Elijah.

Ministers of Baal Killed

18 Then Jehu brought all the people together and said to them, "Ahab served[s]
Baal a little; Jehu will serve him much.
19 Now summon[t] all the prophets of Baal,
all his ministers and all his priests. See
that no one is missing, because I am going
to hold a great sacrifice for Baal. Anyone
who fails to come will no longer live." But
Jehu was acting deceptively in order to destroy the ministers of Baal.

20 Jehu said, "Call an assembly[u] in honor
of Baal." So they proclaimed it. 21 Then he
sent word throughout Israel, and all the
ministers of Baal came; not one stayed
away. They crowded into the temple of
Baal until it was full from one end to the
other. 22 And Jehu said to the keeper of the
wardrobe, "Bring robes for all the ministers of Baal." So he brought out robes for
them.

23 Then Jehu and Jehonadab son of Recab went into the temple of Baal. Jehu said
to the ministers of Baal, "Look around and
see that no servants of the LORD are here
with you — only ministers of Baal." 24 So
they went in to make sacrifices and burnt
offerings. Now Jehu had posted eighty
men outside with this warning: "If one of
you lets any of the men I am placing in
your hands escape, it will be your life for
his life."[v]

25 As soon as Jehu had finished making
the burnt offering, he ordered the guards
and officers: "Go in and kill[w] them; let no
one escape."[x] So they cut them down with
the sword. The guards and officers threw
the bodies out and then entered the inner shrine of the temple of Baal. 26 They
brought the sacred stone[y] out of the temple of Baal and burned it. 27 They demolished the sacred stone of Baal and tore
down the temple[z] of Baal, and people have
used it for a latrine to this day.

28 So Jehu[a] destroyed Baal worship in Israel. 29 However, he did not turn away from
the sins[b] of Jeroboam son of Nebat, which
he had caused Israel to commit — the worship of the golden calves[c] at Bethel[d] and
Dan.

30 The LORD said to Jehu, "Because you
have done well in accomplishing what
is right in my eyes and have done to the
house of Ahab all I had in mind to do,
your descendants will sit on the throne
of Israel to the fourth generation."[e] 31 Yet
Jehu was not careful[f] to keep the law of
the LORD, the God of Israel, with all his

10:11 [j] ver 14; Job 18:19; Mal 4:1 **10:13** [k] 2Ki 8:24, 29; 2Ch 22:8 [l] S 1Ki 2:19 **10:14** [m] S ver 11 **10:15** [n] Jer 35:6, 14-19 [o] 1Ch 2:55; Jer 35:2 [p] Ezr 10:19; Eze 17:18 **10:16** [q] S Nu 25:13 **10:17** [r] 2Ki 9:8 **10:18** [s] S Jdg 2:11 **10:19** [t] 1Ki 18:19 **10:20** [u] S Ex 32:5 **10:24** [v] S Jos 2:14 **10:25** [w] S Ex 22:20; S 2Ki 11:18 [x] S 1Ki 18:40 **10:26** [y] S Ex 23:24 **10:27** [z] S 1Ki 16:32 **10:28** [a] 1Ki 19:17 **10:29** [b] S 1Ki 12:30 [c] S Ex 32:4 [d] 1Ki 12:32 **10:30** [e] 2Ki 15:12 **10:31** [f] Dt 4:9; Pr 4:23

10:13 *relatives of Ahaziah.* See 2Ch 21:17. *families of the king and of the queen mother.* Members of the royal family from Judah who had not yet heard of the deaths of Joram and Jezebel.

10:15 *Jehonadab son of Recab.* Jehonadab was the leader of a conservative movement among the Israelites that was characterized by strong opposition to Baalism as well as to various practices of a settled agricultural society, including the building of houses, the sowing of crops and the use of wine. His followers still adhered to these principles over 200 years later and were known as Recabites (see Jer 35:6 – 10).

10:16 *had him ride along.* Public association with Jehonadab gave Jehu added credentials among the rural populace as a follower of the Lord.

10:18 *Ahab served Baal a little; Jehu will serve him much.* After settling in Samaria, Jehu gave the appearance of having previously appealed to the word of the Lord as a mere political maneuver.

10:19 *will no longer live.* Jehu's reputation made this no idle threat.

10:26 *burned it.* May refer to the Asherah pole (see note on 1Ki 14:15) that usually accompanied a sacred stone (see 1Ki 16:32 – 33).

10:27 *sacred stone of Baal.* See note on 1Ki 14:23. *to this day.* See note on 8:22.

10:29 *sins of Jeroboam ... he had caused Israel to commit.* See 1Ki 12:26 – 32; 13:33 – 34; 14:16.

10:30 *Because you have done ... to the house of Ahab all I had in mind.* Jehu was the Lord's instrument to bring judgment on the house of Ahab, for which he was commended. But he was later condemned by the prophet Hosea for the killing of all Ahab's associates, as well as Ahaziah of Judah and the 42 Judahite princes — the "massacre at Jezreel" (Hos 1:4). *fourth generation.* The restriction of this blessing to four generations is reflective of the qualified approval given to Jehu's reign. Nevertheless, his dynasty survived longer than any other dynasty of the northern kingdom, lasting nearly 100 years. It included the reigns of Jehoahaz, Jehoash, Jeroboam II and Zechariah (see note on 15:12).

10:31 *was not careful to keep the law of the LORD ... with all his heart.* Jehu seems to have been driven more by a political desire to secure his own position on the throne of

heart. He did not turn away from the sins[g]
of Jeroboam, which he had caused Israel
to commit.
32In those days the LORD began to reduce[h] the size of Israel. Hazael[i] overpowered the Israelites throughout their territory 33east of the Jordan in all the land of
Gilead (the region of Gad, Reuben and Manasseh), from Aroer[j] by the Arnon[k] Gorge
through Gilead to Bashan.
34As for the other events of Jehu's reign,
all he did, and all his achievements, are
they not written in the book of the annals[l]
of the kings of Israel?
35Jehu rested with his fathers and was
buried in Samaria. And Jehoahaz his son
succeeded him as king. 36The time that
Jehu reigned over Israel in Samaria was
twenty-eight years.

Athaliah and Joash

11:1-21pp — 2Ch 22:10-23:21

11 When Athaliah[m] the mother of Ahaziah saw that her son was dead, she
proceeded to destroy the whole royal family. 2But Jehosheba, the daughter of King
Jehoram[a] and sister of Ahaziah, took Joash[n] son of Ahaziah and stole him away
from among the royal princes, who were
about to be murdered. She put him and
his nurse in a bedroom to hide him from
Athaliah; so he was not killed.[o] 3He remained hidden with his nurse at the temple of the LORD for six years while Athaliah
ruled the land.
4In the seventh year Jehoiada sent for
the commanders of units of a hundred,
the Carites[p] and the guards and had them
brought to him at the temple of the LORD.
He made a covenant with them and put
them under oath at the temple of the LORD.
Then he showed them the king's son. 5He
commanded them, saying, "This is what
you are to do: You who are in the three
companies that are going on duty on the
Sabbath[q]—a third of you guarding the
royal palace,[r] 6a third at the Sur Gate, and
a third at the gate behind the guard, who
take turns guarding the temple— 7and
you who are in the other two companies
that normally go off Sabbath duty are all
to guard the temple for the king. 8Station
yourselves around the king, each man
with his weapon in his hand. Anyone
who approaches your ranks[b] must be put
to death. Stay close to the king wherever
he goes."
9The commanders of units of a hundred
did just as Jehoiada the priest ordered.
Each one took his men—those who were
going on duty on the Sabbath and those
who were going off duty—and came to
Jehoiada the priest. 10Then he gave the
commanders the spears and shields[s] that
had belonged to King David and that were
in the temple of the LORD. 11The guards,
each with his weapon in his hand, stationed themselves around the king—near
the altar and the temple, from the south
side to the north side of the temple.

10:31 [g] 1Ki 12:30 **10:32** [h] 2Ki 13:25; Ps 107:39 [i] S 1Ki 19:17 **10:33** [j] S Nu 32:34; Dt 2:36; Jdg 11:26; Isa 17:2 [k] S Nu 21:13 **10:34** [l] 1Ki 15:31 **11:1** [m] S 2Ki 8:18 **11:2** [n] 2Ki 12:1 [o] S Jdg 9:5 **11:4** [p] ver 19 **11:5** [q] 1Ch 9:25 [r] 1Ki 14:27 **11:10** [s] S 2Sa 8:7

[a] 2 Hebrew *Joram*, a variant of *Jehoram*
[b] 8 Or *approaches the precincts*

the northern kingdom than by a desire to serve the Lord. In this he was guilty of using God's judgment on the house of Ahab to serve his self-interest.

10:32 *the LORD began to reduce the size of Israel.* The climax of the covenant curses enumerated in Lev 26 and Dt 28 was Israel's expulsion from Canaan. During the rule of Jehu the northern kingdom experienced the beginnings of this curse (see 17:7–18 for its full realization).

10:33 All of Transjordan was lost to Hazael and the Arameans of Damascus.

10:34 *other events of Jehu's reign.* The Black Obelisk of the Assyrian ruler Shalmaneser III informs us that Jehu paid tribute to the Assyrians shortly after coming to the throne of the northern kingdom in 841 B.C. In the Assyrian inscription Jehu is incorrectly called the "son of Omri," but this may simply be Shalmaneser's way of identifying Jehu with Samaria (or Israel). There is no reference to this payment of tribute in the Biblical narratives of Jehu's reign. *annals of the kings of Israel.* See note on 1Ki 14:19.

10:35 *rested with his fathers.* See note on 1Ki 1:21. *Jehoahaz his son succeeded him.* For the reign of Jehoahaz see 13:1–9.

10:36 *twenty-eight years.* 841–814 B.C.

11:1 *Athaliah.* See note on 8:18. *her son was dead.* See 9:27. *destroy the whole royal family.* To secure the throne in Judah for herself (see note on 1Sa 20:14). By this time the royal family in Judah had already been reduced to a mere remnant. Jehoram, the late husband of Athaliah and the father of Ahaziah, had killed all his brothers when he succeeded his father Jehoshaphat on the throne (see 2Ch 21:4). Jehu had slain another 42 members of the royal house of Judah, perhaps including many of the sons of Jehoram's brothers (10:12–14; 2Ch 22:8–9), and the brothers of Ahaziah had been killed by marauding Arabs (2Ch 22:1). It is likely that Athaliah's purge focused primarily on the children of Ahaziah, i.e., her own grandchildren. Ahaziah had died at the young age of 22 (see 8:26). This attempt to completely destroy the house of David was an attack on God's redemptive plan—a plan that centered in the Messiah, which the Davidic covenant promised (see notes on 2Sa 7:11,16; 1Ki 8:25).

11:2 *daughter of King Jehoram and sister of Ahaziah.* It is likely that Jehosheba was the daughter of Jehoram by a wife other than Athaliah, and thus she was a half sister of Ahaziah. She was married to the high priest Jehoiada (see 2Ch 22:11). *him and his nurse.* The child was not more than a year old and had not yet been weaned (see vv. 3,21).

11:4 *seventh year.* Of Athaliah's rule. *commanders of units of a hundred.* 2Ch 23:1 lists the names of five commanders, all native Israelites. *Carites.* Mercenary soldiers from Caria in southwest Asia Minor who served as royal bodyguards. *had them brought to him at the temple.* 2Ch 23:2 includes the Levites and family leaders of Judah in the conspiracy.

11:10 *shields that had belonged to King David and that were in the temple.* David had taken gold shields as plunder in his battle with Hadadezer and then dedicated them to the Lord (see 2Sa 8:7–11). The temple and palace were plundered by Shishak king of Egypt during Rehoboam's reign (see 1Ki 14:26). Apparently David's shields had been hidden and were not taken.

12 Jehoiada brought out the king's son
and put the crown on him; he presented
him with a copy of the covenant[t] and proclaimed him king. They anointed[u] him,
and the people clapped their hands[v] and
shouted, "Long live the king!"[w]
13 When Athaliah heard the noise made
by the guards and the people, she went to
the people at the temple of the LORD. 14 She
looked and there was the king, standing by
the pillar,[x] as the custom was. The officers
and the trumpeters were beside the king,
and all the people of the land were rejoicing and blowing trumpets.[y] Then Athaliah
tore[z] her robes and called out, "Treason!
Treason!"[a]
15 Jehoiada the priest ordered the commanders of units of a hundred, who were
in charge of the troops: "Bring her out
between the ranks[a] and put to the sword
anyone who follows her." For the priest
had said, "She must not be put to death
in the temple[b] of the LORD." 16 So they
seized her as she reached the place where
the horses enter[c] the palace grounds, and
there she was put to death.[d]
17 Jehoiada then made a covenant[e] between the LORD and the king and people
that they would be the LORD's people. He
also made a covenant between the king
and the people.[f] 18 All the people of the
land went to the temple[g] of Baal and tore it
down. They smashed[h] the altars and idols
to pieces and killed Mattan the priest[i] of
Baal in front of the altars.
Then Jehoiada the priest posted guards
at the temple of the LORD. 19 He took with
him the commanders of hundreds, the
Carites,[j] the guards and all the people of
the land, and together they brought the
king down from the temple of the LORD
and went into the palace, entering by way
of the gate of the guards. The king then
took his place on the royal throne, 20 and
all the people of the land rejoiced.[k] And
the city was quiet, because Athaliah had
been slain with the sword at the palace.
21 Joash[b] was seven years old when he
began to reign.

Joash Repairs the Temple

12:1-21pp — 2Ch 24:1-14; 24:23-27

12 In the seventh year of Jehu, Joash[c][l]
became king, and he reigned in Jerusalem forty years. His mother's name
was Zibiah; she was from Beersheba. 2 Joash did what was right[m] in the eyes of the
LORD all the years Jehoiada the priest instructed him. 3 The high places,[n] however,
were not removed; the people continued
to offer sacrifices and burn incense there.
4 Joash said to the priests, "Collect[o] all
the money that is brought as sacred offerings[p] to the temple of the LORD—the
money collected in the census,[q] the money received from personal vows and the
money brought voluntarily[r] to the temple.
5 Let every priest receive the money from

11:12 [t] Ex 25:16; 2Ki 23:3 [u] S 1Sa 9:16; S 1Ki 1:39 [v] Ps 47:1; 98:8; Isa 55:12 [w] S 1Sa 10:24
11:14 [x] S 1Ki 7:15 [y] S 1Ki 1:39 [z] S Ge 37:29 [a] 2Ki 9:23
11:15 [b] 1Ki 2:30
11:16 [c] Ne 3:28; Jer 31:40 [d] S Ge 4:14
11:17 [e] S Ex 24:8; 2Sa 5:3; 2Ch 15:12; 23:3; 29:10; 34:31; Ezr 10:3 [f] 2Ki 23:3; Jer 34:8
11:18 [g] S 1Ki 16:32 [h] S Dt 12:3 [i] 1Ki 18:40; 2Ki 10:25; 23:20
11:19 [j] ver 4
11:20 [k] Pr 11:10; 28:12; 29:2
12:1 [l] 2Ki 11:2
12:2 [m] S Dt 12:25; S 2Sa 8:15
12:3 [n] S 1Ki 3:3; S 2Ki 18:4
12:4 [o] 2Ki 22:4 [p] Nu 18:19 [q] S Ex 30:12 [r] S Ex 25:2; S 35:29

[a] 15 Or *out from the precincts* [b] 21 Hebrew *Jehoash,* a variant of *Joash* [c] 1 Hebrew *Jehoash,* a variant of *Joash;* also in verses 2, 4, 6, 7 and 18

11:12 *covenant.* Probably (1) the Ten Commandments, (2) the entire Sinaitic covenant or (3) a document dealing more specifically with the covenant responsibilities of the king (see Dt 17:14–20; see also note on 1Sa 10:25). The third option is most likely. *anointed him.* See notes on 1Sa 2:10; 9:16; 1Ki 1:39. *Long live the king!* See note on Ps 62:4.
11:14 *pillar.* Apparently one of the two bronze pillars of the portico of the temple, named Jakin and Boaz (see 23:3; 1Ki 7:15–22; 2Ch 23:13). *all the people of the land.* It is likely that Jehoiada had chosen to stage his coup on a Sabbath during one of the major religious festivals, when many from the realm who were loyal to the Lord would be in Jerusalem.
11:15 *not be put to death in the temple.* So as not to defile God's holy house (see Ex 21:14 and note).
11:17 *covenant between the LORD and the king and people that they would be the LORD's people.* A renewal of the Sinaitic covenant, by which Israel had been constituted as the Lord's people (see Ex 19:5–6; Dt 4:20). The years of apostasy, involving both the royal house and the people of Judah, necessitated a renewal of allegiance to the Lord at the time of an important new beginning for the southern kingdom (see notes on 1Sa 11:14–15; 12:14–15,24–25). *covenant between the king and the people.* Defined responsibilities and mutual obligations of king and people that were compatible with Israel's covenant relationship with the Lord (see notes on 1Sa 10:25; 2Sa 5:3).
11:18 *idols.* Stone pillars (see note on 1Ki 14:23) and Asherah poles (see note on 1Ki 14:15).
11:19 *commanders of hundreds, the Carites, the guards.* See note on v. 4.
11:21 See v. 3. The Lord had preserved a lamp for David in Jerusalem (see 1Ki 11:36).
12:1 *seventh year of Jehu.* 835 B.C. (see note on 10:36). *forty years.* 835–796.
12:2 *all the years Jehoiada the priest instructed him.* After Jehoiada died, Joash turned away from the Lord (see 2Ch 24:17–27).
12:3 *high places ... were not removed.* These were high places where the Lord was worshiped rather than pagan deities (see note on 1Ki 15:14). They were nevertheless potential sources for the entrance of pagan practices into Israel's worship (see note on 1Ki 3:2).
12:4 *money ... brought as sacred offerings to the temple.* The money was derived from three different sources: (1) *money collected in the census.* At the age of 20, Israelite youths were required to register for military service and to make an offering of half a shekel (see note on 5:26) for use in the service of the central sanctuary (see Ex 30:11–16; 38:25–26). (2) *money received from personal vows.* Various types of vows and their equivalence in monetary assessments are described in Lev 27:1–25. (3) *money brought voluntarily to the temple.* For voluntary offerings see Lev 22:18–23; Dt 16:10.
12:5 *treasurers.* Temple functionaries who handled financial matters for the priests relative to the people's sacrifices and offerings. *whatever damage is found in the temple.* Construction of the temple had been completed 124 years before the beginning of the reign of Joash (see notes on v. 1; 1Ki 6:38). In addition to deterioration due to age, it had fallen into disrepair and abuse during the rule of Athaliah (see 2Ch 24:7).

one of the treasurers, and let it be used to
repair[s] whatever damage is found in the
temple."
6But by the twenty-third year of King Joash the priests still had not repaired the
temple. 7Therefore King Joash summoned
Jehoiada the priest and the other priests
and asked them, "Why aren't you repairing the damage done to the temple? Take
no more money from your treasurers, but
hand it over for repairing the temple."
8The priests agreed that they would not
collect any more money from the people
and that they would not repair the temple
themselves.
9Jehoiada the priest took a chest and
bored a hole in its lid. He placed it beside
the altar, on the right side as one enters the
temple of the LORD. The priests who guarded the entrance[t] put into the chest all the
money[u] that was brought to the temple of
the LORD. 10Whenever they saw that there
was a large amount of money in the chest,
the royal secretary[v] and the high priest
came, counted the money that had been
brought into the temple of the LORD and
put it into bags. 11When the amount had
been determined, they gave the money to
the men appointed to supervise the work
on the temple. With it they paid those who
worked on the temple of the LORD—the
carpenters and builders, 12the masons and
stonecutters.[w] They purchased timber and
dressed stone for the repair of the temple
of the LORD, and met all the other expenses of restoring the temple.
13The money brought into the temple
was not spent for making silver basins,
wick trimmers, sprinkling bowls, trumpets
or any other articles of gold[x] or silver for
the temple of the LORD; 14it was paid to the
workmen, who used it to repair the temple. 15They did not require an accounting
from those to whom they gave the money to pay the workers, because they acted
with complete honesty.[y] 16The money from
the guilt offerings[z] and sin offerings[a] was
not brought into the temple of the LORD; it
belonged[b] to the priests.
17About this time Hazael[c] king of Aram
went up and attacked Gath and captured
it. Then he turned to attack Jerusalem.
18But Joash king of Judah took all the sacred objects dedicated by his fathers—Jehoshaphat, Jehoram and Ahaziah, the
kings of Judah—and the gifts he himself
had dedicated and all the gold found in
the treasuries of the temple of the LORD
and of the royal palace, and he sent[d] them
to Hazael king of Aram, who then withdrew[e] from Jerusalem.
19As for the other events of the reign of
Joash, and all he did, are they not written in the book of the annals of the kings
of Judah? 20His officials[f] conspired against
him and assassinated[g] him at Beth Millo,[h]
on the road down to Silla. 21The officials
who murdered him were Jozabad son of

12:5 [s] 2Ki 22:5 **12:9** [t] 2Ki 25:18; Jer 35:4; 52:24 [u] Mk 12:41; Lk 21:1 **12:10** [v] S 2Sa 8:17 **12:12** [w] 2Ki 22:5-6 **12:13** [x] S 1Ki 7:48-51 **12:15** [y] 2Ki 22:7; 1Co 4:2 **12:16** [z] Lev 5:14-19 [a] Lev 4:1-35 [b] S Lev 7:7 **12:17** [c] 2Ki 8:12 **12:18** [d] S 1Ki 15:18; S 2Ch 21:16-17 [e] 1Ki 15:21; 2Ki 15:20; 19:36 **12:20** [f] 2Ki 14:5 [g] 2Ki 14:19; 15:10,14,25,30; 21:23; 25:25 [h] Jdg 9:6

12:6 *twenty-third year of King Joash.* Joash may have instituted his plan for restoration of the temple a few years before the 23rd year of his reign. Now at age 30 he asserts his royal authority and takes charge of the temple repairs.
12:7 *Take no more money from your treasurers.* The proceeds from the sources of revenue mentioned in v. 4 were no longer to be given to the priests.
12:8 *priests agreed.* Apparently a compromise was reached: The priests would no longer take the money received from the people, but neither would they pay for the temple repairs from the money they had already received.
12:9 *priests who guarded the entrance.* Three high-ranking priests charged with protecting the temple from unlawful (profane) entry (see 25:18; Jer 52:24). *put into the chest all the money.* When the people were assured that all their offerings would be used for the temple restoration, they responded with greater generosity. See 22:3–7 for continuation (or renewal) of this practice in the reign of Josiah.
12:10 *royal secretary.* See note on 2Sa 8:17. Joash arranges for direct royal supervision of the temple's monetary affairs.
12:11 *men appointed.* The whole matter is taken out of the hands of the priests.
12:13 *articles of gold or silver for the temple.* All the money was initially designated for the restoration of the temple. When the restoration was completed, additional funds were used for the acquisition of silver and gold articles for use in the temple service (see 2Ch 24:14).
12:16 *money from the guilt offerings.* See Lev 5:16; 6:5; Nu 5:7–10 for references to priestly income in connection with the bringing of a guilt offering.
12:17 *About this time.* These events must have taken place toward the end of Joash's reign. From 2Ch 24:17–24 it is clear that the Aramean attack was occasioned by Joash's turning away from the Lord after Jehoiada's death. Joash's apostasy reached its climax in the stoning of Jehoiada's son Zechariah (2Ch 24:22). Probably because of Joash's earlier zeal for the temple, the author of Kings did not choose to relate these matters. *Hazael.* See 8:7–15; 10:32–33; 13:3,22; see also note on 1Ki 19:15. *Gath.* One of the major Philistine cities (see Jos 13:3) that David had conquered (1Ch 18:1) and that continued to be subject to Judah during the reign of Rehoboam (2Ch 11:8). In the latter years of the reign of Joash of Judah (835–796 B.C.) and during the reign of Jehoahaz of Israel (814–798; see 13:3,7), the Arameans had virtually overrun the northern kingdom, enabling them to advance against the Philistines and the kingdom of Judah with little resistance. *he turned to attack Jerusalem.* See 2Ch 24:23–24.
12:18 *sacred objects ... gold ... he sent them to Hazael.* Years earlier, Asa had sought to secure assistance from the Arameans with a similar gift (see 1Ki 15:18).
12:19 *annals of the kings of Judah.* See note on 1Ki 14:29. A fuller account of the reign of Joash is also found in 2Ch 22:10—24:27.
12:20 *conspired against him.* The conspiracy was aroused in response to Joash's murder of Zechariah son of Jehoiada (see 2Ch 24:25). *Beth Millo.* Beth means "house"; for the meaning of Millo see note on Jdg 9:6. Here the reference may be to a building (perhaps a kind of barracks) built on the "Millo" in the old City of David (see 2Sa 5:9 and note; 1Ki 11:27). Perhaps the king was staying there temporarily with his troops at the time of his assassination; Chronicles says he was killed "in his bed" (2Ch 24:25).
12:21 *officials.* Sons of Ammonite and Moabite mothers (2Ch 24:26), suggesting that they may have been mercenary mili-

Shimeath and Jehozabad son of Shomer.
He died and was buried with his fathers
in the City of David. And Amaziah his son
succeeded him as king.

Jehoahaz King of Israel

13 In the twenty-third year of Joash son
of Ahaziah king of Judah, Jehoahaz
son of Jehu became king of Israel in Samaria, and he reigned seventeen years.
2He did evil[i] in the eyes of the LORD by
following the sins of Jeroboam son of Nebat, which he had caused Israel to commit, and he did not turn away from them.
3So the LORD's anger[j] burned against Israel, and for a long time he kept them under
the power[k] of Hazael king of Aram and
Ben-Hadad[l] his son.
4Then Jehoahaz sought[m] the LORD's favor, and the LORD listened to him, for he
saw[n] how severely the king of Aram was
oppressing[o] Israel. 5The LORD provided
a deliverer[p] for Israel, and they escaped
from the power of Aram. So the Israelites
lived in their own homes as they had before. 6But they did not turn away from the
sins[q] of the house of Jeroboam, which he
had caused Israel to commit; they continued in them. Also, the Asherah pole[a][r] remained standing in Samaria.
7Nothing had been left[s] of the army of
Jehoahaz except fifty horsemen, ten chariots and ten thousand foot soldiers, for
the king of Aram had destroyed the rest
and made them like the dust[t] at threshing time.
8As for the other events of the reign of
Jehoahaz, all he did and his achievements,
are they not written in the book of the annals of the kings of Israel? 9Jehoahaz rested with his fathers and was buried in Samaria. And Jehoash[b] his son succeeded
him as king.

Jehoash King of Israel

10In the thirty-seventh year of Joash
king of Judah, Jehoash son of Jehoahaz
became king of Israel in Samaria, and he
reigned sixteen years. 11He did evil in the
eyes of the LORD and did not turn away
from any of the sins of Jeroboam son of
Nebat, which he had caused Israel to commit; he continued in them.
12As for the other events of the reign of
Jehoash, all he did and his achievements,
including his war against Amaziah[u] king
of Judah, are they not written in the book
of the annals[v] of the kings of Israel? 13Je-
hoash rested with his fathers, and Jeroboam[w] succeeded him on the throne. Jehoash was buried in Samaria with the kings
of Israel.
14Now Elisha was suffering from the illness from which he died. Jehoash king of
Israel went down to see him and wept over
him. "My father! My father!" he cried.
"The chariots[x] and horsemen of Israel!"
15Elisha said, "Get a bow and some arrows," [y] and he did so. 16"Take the bow in

13:2 [i] 1Ki 12:26-33 **13:3** [j] S Dt 31:17 [k] S 1Ki 19:17 [l] ver 24 **13:4** [m] S Dt 4:29 [n] S Dt 26:7 [o] S Nu 10:9; 2Sa 7:10 **13:5** [p] S Ge 45:7; S Dt 28:29; S Jdg 2:18 **13:6** [q] 1Ki 12:30 [r] S 1Ki 16:33 **13:7** [s] 2Ki 10:32-33 [t] S 2Sa 22:43 **13:12** [u] 2Ki 14:15 [v] 1Ki 15:31 **13:13** [w] 2Ki 14:23; Hos 1:1 **13:14** [x] S 2Ki 2:12 **13:15** [y] 1Sa 20:20

[a] 6 That is, a symbol of the goddess Asherah; here and elsewhere in 2 Kings [b] 9 Hebrew *Joash*, a variant of *Jehoash*; also in verses 12-14 and 25

tary officers whose services could have been bought by others. *buried with his fathers.* But see 2Ch 24:25. *Amaziah his son succeeded him.* For the reign of Amaziah see 14:1–22.

13:1 *twenty-third year of Joash.* 814 B.C. (see note on 12:1; see also Introduction to 1 Kings: Chronology). *seventeen years.* 814–798.

13:2 *sins of Jeroboam.* See 1Ki 12:26–32; 13:33–34; 14:16.

13:3 *Hazael.* See notes on 8:12,13,15; 10:33; 1Ki 19:15. *Ben-Hadad.* See v. 24. His reign began in either 806 or 796 B.C.

13:4 *the LORD listened to him.* Although deliverance did not come during the lifetime of Jehoahaz (see v. 22), the Lord was merciful to his people in spite of their sin, because of his covenant with Abraham, Isaac and Jacob (v. 23).

13:5 *deliverer for Israel.* Probably (1) the Assyrian ruler Adad-nirari III (810–783 B.C.), whose attacks on the Arameans of Damascus in 806 and 804 enabled the Israelites to break Aramean control over Israelite territory (see v. 25; 14:25), or (2) Jehoash son of Jehoahaz (vv. 17,19,25), or (3) Jeroboam II, who was able to extend Israel's boundaries far to the north (see 14:25,27) after the Assyrians had broken the military power of the Arameans.

13:6 *Asherah pole remained standing.* This idol had been set up by Ahab (see 1Ki 16:33) and had either escaped destruction by Jehu when he purged Baal worship from Samaria (see 10:27–28) or had been reintroduced during the reign of Jehoahaz.

13:7 *ten chariots.* In effect, a very small police force. Cf. the 2,000 chariots that Ahab was able to deploy against the Assyrians at the battle of Qarqar in 853 B.C. (see note on 1Ki 22:1). *ten thousand foot soldiers.* At the battle of Qarqar Ahab had supplied 10,000 foot soldiers to the coalition of forces opposing the Assyrians. At that time this would have represented only a contingent of Israel's army, while now it represented the entire Israelite infantry. In 857 Ahab had inflicted 100,000 casualties on the Aramean foot soldiers in one day (see 1Ki 20:29 and note).

13:8 *annals of the kings of Israel.* See note on 1Ki 14:19.

13:9 *rested with his fathers.* See note on 1Ki 1:21.

13:10 *thirty-seventh year of Joash.* 798 B.C. (see note on 12:1). *sixteen years.* 798–782.

13:11 *sins of Jeroboam.* See 1Ki 12:26–32; 13:33–34; 14:16.

13:12 *war against Amaziah.* See 14:8–14; 2Ch 25:17–24. *annals of the kings of Israel.* See note on 1Ki 14:19.

13:13 *rested with his fathers.* See note on 1Ki 1:21. *Jeroboam succeeded him.* For the reign of Jeroboam II see 14:23–29.

13:14 *Elisha was suffering.* Ch. 9 contains the last previous reference to Elisha. Since Jehu had been anointed in 841 B.C. (see note on 10:36) and Jehoash began to reign in 798 (see note on v. 10), there is at least a 43-year period in which we are told nothing of Elisha's activities. Based on Elisha's relationship with Elijah, he must have been born prior to 880 and he must have lived to be more than 80 years of age. *The chariots and horsemen of Israel!* An expression of recognition by Jehoash that Elisha was of greater significance for Israel's military success than Israel's military forces were (see notes on 2:12; 6:13,16–23).

13:16 *put his hands on the king's hands.* By this symbolic act Elisha indicated that Jehoash was to engage the Arameans in battle with the Lord's blessing on him.

your hands,” he said to the king of Israel. When he had taken it, Elisha put his
hands on the king’s hands.
17“Open the east window,” he said, and
he opened it. “Shoot!”[z] Elisha said, and
he shot. “The LORD’s arrow of victory, the
arrow of victory over Aram!” Elisha declared. “You will completely destroy the
Arameans at Aphek.”[a]
18Then he said, “Take the arrows,”
and the king took them. Elisha told him,
“Strike the ground.” He struck it three
times and stopped. 19The man of God was
angry with him and said, “You should
have struck the ground five or six times;
then you would have defeated Aram and
completely destroyed it. But now you will
defeat it only three times.”[b]
20Elisha died and was buried.
Now Moabite raiders[c] used to enter the
country every spring. 21Once while some
Israelites were burying a man, suddenly
they saw a band of raiders; so they threw
the man’s body into Elisha’s tomb. When
the body touched Elisha’s bones, the man
came to life[d] and stood up on his feet.
22Hazael king of Aram oppressed[e] Israel throughout the reign of Jehoahaz. 23But
the LORD was gracious to them and had
compassion and showed concern for them
because of his covenant[f] with Abraham,
Isaac and Jacob. To this day he has been
unwilling to destroy[g] them or banish them
from his presence.[h]
24Hazael king of Aram died, and Ben-
Hadad[i] his son succeeded him as king.
25Then Jehoash son of Jehoahaz recaptured from Ben-Hadad son of Hazael the
towns he had taken in battle from his father Jehoahaz. Three times[j] Jehoash defeated him, and so he recovered[k] the Israelite towns.

Amaziah King of Judah

14:1-7pp — 2Ch 25:1-4,11-12
14:8-22pp — 2Ch 25:17–26:2

14 In the second year of Jehoash[a] son
of Jehoahaz king of Israel, Amaziah
son of Joash king of Judah began to reign.
2He was twenty-five years old when he became king, and he reigned in Jerusalem
twenty-nine years. His mother’s name was
Jehoaddin; she was from Jerusalem. 3He
did what was right in the eyes of the LORD,
but not as his father David had done. In
everything he followed the example of his
father Joash. 4The high places,[l] however,
were not removed; the people continued
to offer sacrifices and burn incense there.
5After the kingdom was firmly in his
grasp, he executed[m] the officials[n] who had
murdered his father the king. 6Yet he did
not put the sons of the assassins to death,
in accordance with what is written in the
Book of the Law[o] of Moses where the LORD
commanded: “Fathers shall not be put to
death for their children, nor children put
to death for their fathers; each is to die for
his own sins.”[b][p]
7He was the one who defeated ten thousand Edomites in the Valley of Salt[q] and
captured Sela[r] in battle, calling it Joktheel,
the name it has to this day.

13:17 [z]Jos 8:18 [a]S 1Ki 20:26 **13:19** [b]ver 25 **13:20** [c]S 2Ki 5:2 **13:21** [d]Mt 27:52 **13:22** [e]S 1Ki 19:17 **13:23** [f]S Ex 2:24 [g]S Dt 29:20 [h]S Ex 33:15; 2Ki 17:18; 24:3,20 **13:24** [i]ver 3 **13:25** [j]ver 18,19 [k]S 2Ki 10:32 **14:4** [l]2Ki 12:3 **14:5** [m]2Ki 21:24 [n]2Ki 12:20 **14:6** [o]S Dt 28:61 [p]S Nu 26:11; Job 21:20; Jer 31:30; 44:3; Eze 18:4,20 **14:7** [q]S 2Sa 8:13 [r]S Jdg 1:36

[a] *1* Hebrew *Joash*, a variant of *Jehoash*; also in verses 13, 23 and 27 [b] *6* Deut. 24:16

13:17 *east window.* Faced Transjordan, which was controlled by the Arameans (see 10:32–33). *Aphek.* About 60 years earlier Ahab had won a decisive victory at Aphek over the Arameans and Ben-Hadad II (see 1Ki 20:26–30 and note on 20:26).

13:18 *struck it three times and stopped.* The moderately enthusiastic response to Elisha's directive reflected insufficient zeal for accomplishing the announced task.

13:19 *defeat it only three times.* Jehoash's moderate enthusiasm in striking the ground with arrows symbolized the moderate success he would have against the Arameans. It would be left for Jeroboam II son of Jehoash to gain complete victory over them (see 14:25,28).

13:21 *When the body touched Elisha's bones, the man came to life.* The life-giving power of God that Elisha represented is demonstrated once again in this last OT reference to Elisha (for previous demonstrations of this power see 4:32–37 and 1Ki 17:17–24; for Elijah's translation to heaven without dying see 2:11–12).

13:23 *To this day.* Until the time of the writing of the source from which the author derived this account (see note on 1Ki 8:8; see also Introduction to 1 Kings: Author, Sources and Date). *unwilling to destroy them or banish them.* In his mercy and grace the Lord was long-suffering toward his people and refrained from full implementation of the covenant curse of exile from Canaan (see note on 10:32). This postponement of judgment provided Israel with the opportunity to repent and return to covenant faithfulness.

13:24 *Ben-Hadad.* See note on v. 3.

13:25 *towns he had taken … from … Jehoahaz.* Probably towns west of the Jordan, since the area east of the Jordan had been lost already in the time of Jehu (see 10:32–33). It was not until the time of Jeroboam II that the area east of the Jordan was fully recovered for Israel (see 14:25). *Three times.* In fulfillment of Elisha's prophecy (v. 19).

14:1 *second year of Jehoash.* 796 B.C. (see note on 13:10).

14:2 *twenty-nine years.* 796–767. Amaziah's 29-year reign included a 24-year coregency with his son Azariah (see notes on v. 21; 15:1–2).

14:3 *not as his father David.* Amaziah did not remain completely free from involvement with the worship of pagan deities (see 2Ch 25:14–16). His loyalty to the Lord fell short of that of Asa and Jehoshaphat before him (see 1Ki 15:11,14; 22:43; see also 1Ki 9:4; 11:4).

14:4 *high places, however, were not removed.* See note on 1Ki 15:14.

14:7 *defeated ten thousand Edomites.* Amaziah was able to regain temporarily (see 2Ch 28:17) some of Judah's control over the Edomites, which had been lost during the reign of Jehoram (see 8:20–22). *Valley of Salt.* The same battlefield on which David had defeated the Edomites (see 2Sa 8:13; 1Ch 18:12; Ps 60 title), generally identified with the Arabah directly south of the Dead Sea. *Sela.* See notes on Isa 16:1; Ob 3). *to this day.* Until the time of the writing of the account of Amaziah's reign used by the author (see note on 1Ki 8:8; see also Introduction to 1 Kings: Author, Sources and Date).

8 Then Amaziah sent messengers to Jehoash son of Jehoahaz, the son of Jehu,
king of Israel, with the challenge: "Come,
meet me face to face."
9 But Jehoash king of Israel replied to
Amaziah king of Judah: "A thistle[s] in Lebanon sent a message to a cedar in Lebanon, 'Give your daughter to my son in
marriage.' Then a wild beast in Lebanon
came along and trampled the thistle underfoot. 10 You have indeed defeated Edom
and now you are arrogant.[t] Glory in your
victory, but stay at home! Why ask for
trouble and cause your own downfall and
that of Judah also?"
11 Amaziah, however, would not listen,
so Jehoash king of Israel attacked. He and
Amaziah king of Judah faced each other
at Beth Shemesh[u] in Judah. 12 Judah was
routed by Israel, and every man fled to his
home.[v] 13 Jehoash king of Israel captured
Amaziah king of Judah, the son of Joash,
the son of Ahaziah, at Beth Shemesh.
Then Jehoash went to Jerusalem and
broke down the wall[w] of Jerusalem from
the Ephraim Gate[x] to the Corner Gate[y] — a
section about six hundred feet long.[a] 14 He
took all the gold and silver and all the articles found in the temple of the LORD and in
the treasuries of the royal palace. He also
took hostages and returned to Samaria.
15 As for the other events of the reign
of Jehoash, what he did and his achievements, including his war[z] against Amaziah king of Judah, are they not written in
the book of the annals of the kings of Israel? 16 Jehoash rested with his fathers and
was buried in Samaria with the kings of
Israel. And Jeroboam his son succeeded
him as king.
17 Amaziah son of Joash king of Judah
lived for fifteen years after the death of Jehoash son of Jehoahaz king of Israel. 18 As
for the other events of Amaziah's reign,
are they not written in the book of the annals of the kings of Judah?
19 They conspired[a] against him in Jerusalem, and he fled to Lachish,[b] but they sent
men after him to Lachish and killed him
there. 20 He was brought back by horse[c]
and was buried in Jerusalem with his fathers, in the City of David.
21 Then all the people of Judah took Azariah,[b][d] who was sixteen years old, and
made him king in place of his father Amaziah. 22 He was the one who rebuilt Elath[e]
and restored it to Judah after Amaziah
rested with his fathers.

Jeroboam II King of Israel

23 In the fifteenth year of Amaziah son
of Joash king of Judah, Jeroboam[f] son
of Jehoash king of Israel became king in
Samaria, and he reigned forty-one years.
24 He did evil in the eyes of the LORD and
did not turn away from any of the sins
of Jeroboam son of Nebat, which he had

14:9 [s] Jdg 9:8-15 **14:10** [t] 2Ch 26:16; 32:25 **14:11** [u] S Jos 15:10 **14:12** [v] 1Ki 22:36 **14:13** [w] 1Ki 3:1; 2Ch 33:14; 36:19; Jer 39:2 [x] Ne 8:16; 12:39 [y] 2Ch 26:9; Jer 31:38; Zec 14:10 **14:15** [z] 2Ki 13:12

14:19 [a] S 2Ki 12:20 [b] S Jos 10:3 **14:20** [c] S 2Ki 9:28 **14:21** [d] 2Ki 15:1; 2Ch 26:23; Isa 1:1; Hos 1:1; Am 1:1 **14:22** [e] S 1Ki 9:26 **14:23** [f] S 2Ki 13:13; 1Ch 5:17; Am 1:1; 7:10

[a] 13 Hebrew *four hundred cubits* (about 180 meters)
[b] 21 Also called *Uzziah*

14:8 *meet me face to face.* A challenge amounting to a declaration of war. Perhaps it was provoked by the hostile actions of mercenary troops from the northern kingdom after their dismissal from the Judahite army (see 2Ch 25:10,13) and by the refusal of Jehoash to establish a marriage alliance with Amaziah (see v. 9).
14:9 *Jehoash ... replied.* For his reply Jehoash used a fable (see Jdg 9:8–15) in which he represented himself as a strong cedar and Amaziah as an insignificant thistle that could easily be trampled underfoot.
14:11 *would not listen.* See 2Ch 25:20. *Beth Shemesh.* A town about 15 miles west of Jerusalem (see Jos 15:10; 1Sa 6:9 and note).
14:13 *Jehoash ... captured Amaziah.* It is likely that Amaziah was taken back to the northern kingdom as a prisoner, where he remained until being released to return to Judah after the death of Jehoash (see vv. 15–16; see also note on v. 21). *Ephraim Gate to the Corner Gate.* The Corner Gate (see Jer 31:38; Zec 14:10) was at the northwest corner of the wall around Jerusalem. The Ephraim Gate was on the north side of Jerusalem (see Ne 12:39), 600 feet east of the Corner Gate. This northwestern section of the wall of Jerusalem was the point at which the city was most vulnerable to attack.
14:14 *gold and silver and all the articles found in the temple ... and ... the royal palace.* The value of the plundered articles was probably not great, because Joash had previously stripped the temple and palace to pay tribute to Hazael of Damascus (see 12:17–18). *took hostages.* The hostages were probably intended to secure additional payments of tribute in view of the meager war booty.
14:15 *annals of the kings of Israel.* See note on 1Ki 14:19.
14:16 *rested with his fathers.* See 13:12–13; see also note on 1Ki 1:21.
14:17 *lived for fifteen years after the death of Jehoash.* Jehoash died in 782 B.C. and Amaziah in 767.
14:18 *annals of the kings of Judah.* See note on 1Ki 14:29.
14:19 *conspired against him.* 2Ch 25:27 connects the conspiracy against Amaziah with his turning away from the Lord, but it did not serve the purpose of the author of Kings to note this. *Lachish.* A fortress city in southern Judah 15 miles west of Hebron, presently known as Tell ed-Duweir (see 18:14; 2Ch 11:9).
14:21 *Then all the people of Judah took Azariah, who was.* Or "Now all the people of Judah had taken Azariah, when he was." See NIV text note and 15:13. *made him king in place of his father Amaziah.* It is likely that this occurred after Amaziah had been taken prisoner by Jehoash (see v. 13). Thus Azariah's reign substantially overlapped that of his father Amaziah (see notes on v. 2; 15:2).
14:22 *rebuilt Elath and restored it to Judah.* Azariah extended the subjugation of the Edomites begun by his father (see v. 7) and reestablished Israelite control over the important port city on the Gulf of Aqaba (see 1Ki 9:26). A royal seal inscribed "belonging to Jotham" (see 15:32) found near the site of ancient Elath attests Judahite presence there during this period. *rested with his fathers.* See note on 1Ki 1:21.
14:23 *fifteenth year of Amaziah.* 782 B.C. (see note on v. 2). This was the beginning of Jeroboam's sole reign. He had previously served as coregent with his father Jehoash. *forty-one years.* 793–753 (including the coregency with his father).
14:24 *sins of Jeroboam.* See 1Ki 12:26–32; 13:33–34; 14:16; Am 3:13–14; 4:4–5; 5:4–6; 7:10–17.

caused Israel to commit.[g] 25He was the one
who restored the boundaries of Israel from
Lebo[a] Hamath[h] to the Sea of the Arabah,[b i]
in accordance with the word of the LORD,
the God of Israel, spoken through his servant Jonah[j] son of Amittai, the prophet
from Gath Hepher.
26The LORD had seen how bitterly everyone in Israel, whether slave or free,[k]
was suffering;[l] there was no one to help
them.[m] 27And since the LORD had not said
he would blot out[n] the name of Israel from
under heaven, he saved[o] them by the hand
of Jeroboam son of Jehoash.
28As for the other events of Jeroboam's
reign, all he did, and his military achievements, including how he recovered for Israel both Damascus[p] and Hamath,[q] which
had belonged to Yaudi,[c] are they not written in the book of the annals[r] of the kings
of Israel? 29Jeroboam rested with his fathers, the kings of Israel. And Zechariah
his son succeeded him as king.

Azariah King of Judah

15:1-7pp — 2Ch 26:3-4,21-23

15 In the twenty-seventh year of Jeroboam king of Israel, Azariah[s] son
of Amaziah king of Judah began to reign.
2He was sixteen years old when he became king, and he reigned in Jerusalem
fifty-two years. His mother's name was
Jecoliah; she was from Jerusalem. 3He did
what was right[t] in the eyes of the LORD,
just as his father Amaziah had done. 4The
high places, however, were not removed;
the people continued to offer sacrifices
and burn incense there.
5The LORD afflicted[u] the king with leprosy[d] until the day he died, and he lived in a
separate house.[e v] Jotham[w] the king's son
had charge of the palace[x] and governed
the people of the land.
6As for the other events of Azariah's
reign, and all he did, are they not written
in the book of the annals of the kings of
Judah? 7Azariah rested[y] with his fathers
and was buried near them in the City of
David. And Jotham[z] his son succeeded
him as king.

Zechariah King of Israel

8In the thirty-eighth year of Azariah
king of Judah, Zechariah son of Jeroboam
became king of Israel in Samaria, and he
reigned six months. 9He did evil[a] in the
eyes of the LORD, as his fathers had done.
He did not turn away from the sins of Jeroboam son of Nebat, which he had caused
Israel to commit.
10Shallum son of Jabesh conspired
against Zechariah. He attacked him in

14:24 [g] S 1Ki 15:30 **14:25** [h] S Nu 13:21 [i] Dt 3:17 [j] Jnh 1:1; Mt 12:39 **14:26** [k] Dt 32:36 [l] 2Ki 13:4 [m] Ps 18:41; 22:11; 72:12; 107:12; Isa 63:5; La 1:7 **14:27** [n] S Dt 29:20 [o] S Jdg 6:14 **14:28** [p] S 2Sa 8:5 [q] S 2Sa 8:9 [r] 1Ki 15:31 **15:1** [s] S ver 32; S 2Ki 14:21 **15:3** [t] S 1Ki 14:8 **15:5** [u] S Ge 12:17 [v] Lev 13:46 [w] ver 7,32; 2Ch 27:1; Mic 1:1 [x] S Ge 41:40 **15:7** [y] Isa 6:1; 14:28 [z] S ver 5 **15:9** [a] 1Ki 15:26

[a] 25 Or *from the entrance to* [b] 25 That is, the Dead Sea [c] 28 Or *Judah* [d] 5 The Hebrew word was used for various diseases affecting the skin—not necessarily leprosy. [e] 5 Or *in a house where he was relieved of responsibility*

14:25 *from Lebo Hamath.* Jeroboam II was able to free the northern kingdom from the oppression it had suffered at the hands of Hazael and Ben-Hadad (see 10:32; 12:17; 13:3,22,25). He also extended Israelite political control over the Arameans of Damascus, an undertaking that had been begun by his father Jehoash (see 13:25). Assyrian pressure on the Arameans, including attacks on Damascus by Shalmaneser IV in 773 B.C. and Ashur-Dan III in 772, had weakened the Arameans enough to enable Jeroboam II to gain the upper hand over them. Meanwhile, Assyria also became too weak to suppress Jeroboam's expansion. *Sea of the Arabah.* See NIV text note. According to Am 6:14 the southern limit of Jeroboam's kingdom in Transjordan was the "valley of the Arabah"—probably to be connected with the Valley of Salt (see note on v. 7). If so, Jeroboam had also subdued Moab and the Ammonites. *word of the LORD ... spoken through ... Jonah.* Not found in the book of Jonah. However, mention of the prophet here helps to date his ministry. *Gath Hepher.* Located in the tribe of Zebulun, northeast of Nazareth (see Jos 19:13).

14:26 *slave or free.* See note on 1Ki 14:10. *suffering.* At the hands of the Arameans (see 10:32–33; 13:3–7), the Moabites (13:20) and the Ammonites (Am 1:13).

14:27 *had not said.* The sin of the Israelites had not yet reached its full measure, and the Lord mercifully extended to the nation an additional period of grace in which there was opportunity to repent (see note on 13:23; cf. Ge 15:16 and note). Persistence in apostasy, however, would bring certain judgment (see Am 4:2–3; 6:14). *saved them by the hand of Jeroboam.* See note on 13:5.

14:28 *all he did.* During Jeroboam's reign the northern kingdom enjoyed greater material prosperity than at any time since the rule of David and Solomon. Unfortunately, it was also a time of religious formalism and apostasy as well as social injustice (see the books of Amos and Hosea, who prophesied during Jeroboam's reign). *Damascus and Hamath.* See note on v. 25. *annals of the kings of Israel.* See note on 1Ki 14:19.

14:29 *rested with his fathers.* See note on 1Ki 1:21. *Zechariah his son succeeded him.* For the reign of Zechariah see 15:8–12.

15:1 *twenty-seventh year of Jeroboam.* 767 B.C., based on dating the beginning of Jeroboam's coregency with Jehoash in 793 (see note on 14:23). *Azariah ... began to reign.* He began his sole reign, after a 24-year coregency with his father Amaziah (see notes on v. 2; 14:2,21). (His actual years were one less than his official years.)

15:2 *fifty-two years.* 792–740 B.C. (but he was coregent with his father Amaziah 792–767). See note on v. 1.

15:3 *as his father Amaziah had done.* See note on 14:3.

15:4 *high places, however, were not removed.* See 14:4; see also note on 1Ki 15:14.

15:5 *afflicted the king with leprosy.* A punishment for usurping the priestly function of burning incense on the altar in the temple (see 2Ch 26:16–21; cf. Lev 13:46). *had charge of the palace and governed the people of the land.* Jotham ruled for his father for the remainder of Azariah's life (750–740 B.C.; see note on v. 33).

15:6 *all he did.* A more detailed account of Azariah's accomplishments is found in 2Ch 26:1–15. *annals of the kings of Judah.* See note on 1Ki 14:29.

15:7 *rested with his fathers.* See note on 1Ki 1:21. *Jotham his son succeeded him.* For the reign of Jotham see vv. 32–38.

15:8 *thirty-eighth year of Azariah.* 753 B.C. (see note on v. 2).

15:9 *sins of Jeroboam.* See 1Ki 12:26–32; 13:33–34; 14:16.

Assyrian Campaigns against Israel and Judah

The Assyrian invasions of the eighth century B.C. were the most traumatic political events in the entire history of Israel.

The brutal Assyrian style of warfare relied on massive armies, superbly equipped with the world's first great siege machines manipulated by an efficient corps of engineers.

Psychological terror, however, was Assyria's most effective weapon. It was ruthlessly applied, with corpses impaled on stakes, severed heads stacked in heaps, and captives skinned alive.

The shock of bloody military sieges on both Israel and Judah was profound. The prophets did not fail to speak out against their horror, while at the same time pleading with the people to see God's hand in history, to recognize spiritual causes in the present punishment.

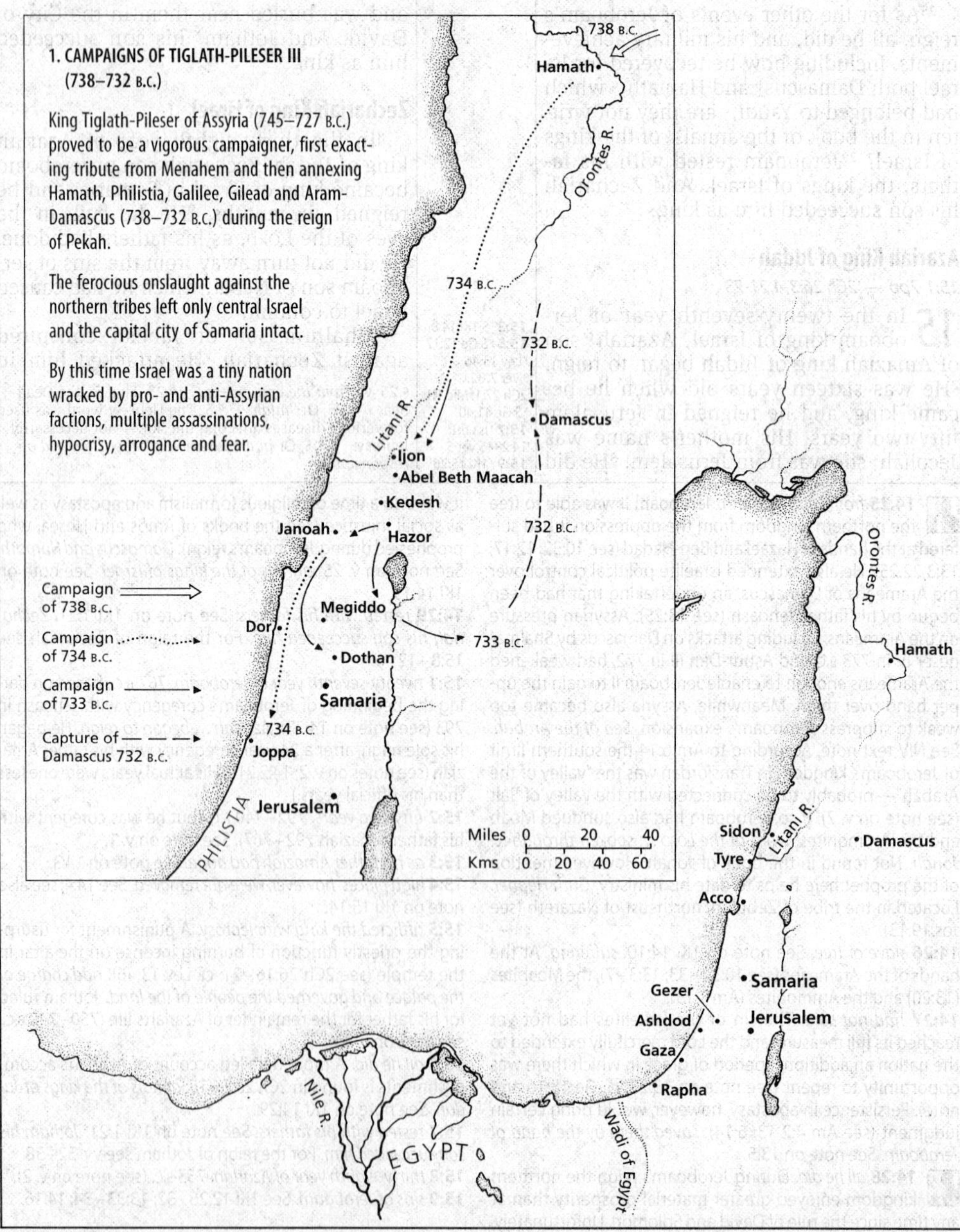

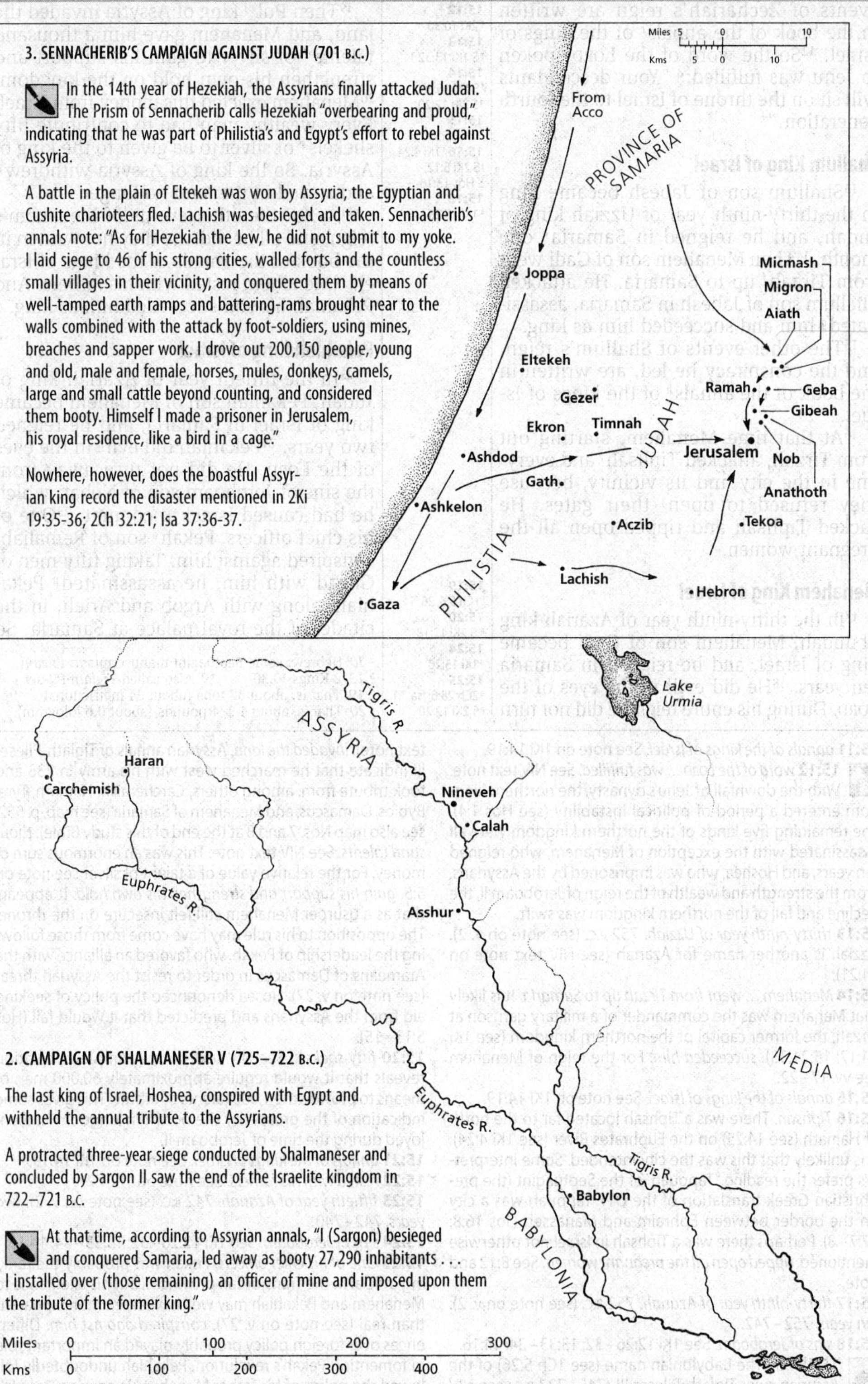

3. SENNACHERIB'S CAMPAIGN AGAINST JUDAH (701 B.C.)

In the 14th year of Hezekiah, the Assyrians finally attacked Judah. The Prism of Sennacherib calls Hezekiah "overbearing and proud," indicating that he was part of Philistia's and Egypt's effort to rebel against Assyria.

A battle in the plain of Eltekeh was won by Assyria; the Egyptian and Cushite charioteers fled. Lachish was besieged and taken. Sennacherib's annals note: "As for Hezekiah the Jew, he did not submit to my yoke. I laid siege to 46 of his strong cities, walled forts and the countless small villages in their vicinity, and conquered them by means of well-tamped earth ramps and battering-rams brought near to the walls combined with the attack by foot-soldiers, using mines, breaches and sapper work. I drove out 200,150 people, young and old, male and female, horses, mules, donkeys, camels, large and small cattle beyond counting, and considered them booty. Himself I made a prisoner in Jerusalem, his royal residence, like a bird in a cage."

Nowhere, however, does the boastful Assyrian king record the disaster mentioned in 2Ki 19:35-36; 2Ch 32:21; Isa 37:36-37.

2. CAMPAIGN OF SHALMANESER V (725–722 B.C.)

The last king of Israel, Hoshea, conspired with Egypt and withheld the annual tribute to the Assyrians.

A protracted three-year siege conducted by Shalmaneser and concluded by Sargon II saw the end of the Israelite kingdom in 722–721 B.C.

At that time, according to Assyrian annals, "I (Sargon) besieged and conquered Samaria, led away as booty 27,290 inhabitants . . . I installed over (those remaining) an officer of mine and imposed upon them the tribute of the former king."

front of the people,[a] assassinated[b] him and succeeded him as king. 11 The other events of Zechariah's reign are written in the book of the annals[c] of the kings of Israel. 12 So the word of the LORD spoken to Jehu was fulfilled:[d] "Your descendants will sit on the throne of Israel to the fourth generation."[b]

Shallum King of Israel

13 Shallum son of Jabesh became king in the thirty-ninth year of Uzziah king of Judah, and he reigned in Samaria[e] one month. 14 Then Menahem son of Gadi went from Tirzah[f] up to Samaria. He attacked Shallum son of Jabesh in Samaria, assassinated[g] him and succeeded him as king.

15 The other events of Shallum's reign, and the conspiracy he led, are written in the book of the annals[h] of the kings of Israel.

16 At that time Menahem, starting out from Tirzah, attacked Tiphsah[i] and everyone in the city and its vicinity, because they refused to open[j] their gates. He sacked Tiphsah and ripped open all the pregnant women.

Menahem King of Israel

17 In the thirty-ninth year of Azariah king of Judah, Menahem son of Gadi became king of Israel, and he reigned in Samaria ten years. 18 He did evil[k] in the eyes of the LORD. During his entire reign he did not turn away from the sins of Jeroboam son of Nebat, which he had caused Israel to commit.

19 Then Pul[c][l] king of Assyria invaded the land, and Menahem gave him a thousand talents[d] of silver to gain his support and strengthen his own hold on the kingdom. 20 Menahem exacted this money from Israel. Every wealthy man had to contribute fifty shekels[e] of silver to be given to the king of Assyria. So the king of Assyria withdrew[m] and stayed in the land no longer.

21 As for the other events of Menahem's reign, and all he did, are they not written in the book of the annals of the kings of Israel? 22 Menahem rested with his fathers. And Pekahiah his son succeeded him as king.

Pekahiah King of Israel

23 In the fiftieth year of Azariah king of Judah, Pekahiah son of Menahem became king of Israel in Samaria, and he reigned two years. 24 Pekahiah did evil[n] in the eyes of the LORD. He did not turn away from the sins of Jeroboam son of Nebat, which he had caused Israel to commit. 25 One of his chief officers, Pekah[o] son of Remaliah, conspired against him. Taking fifty men of Gilead with him, he assassinated[p] Pekahiah, along with Argob and Arieh, in the citadel of the royal palace at Samaria. So

15:10 [b]S 2Ki 12:20
15:11 [c]1Ki 15:31
15:12 [d]2Ki 10:30
15:13 [e]S 1Ki 13:32
15:14 [f]S 1Ki 15:33 [g]S 2Ki 12:20
15:15 [h]1Ki 15:31
15:16 [i]1Ki 4:24 [j]S 2Ki 8:12; S Hos 13:16
15:18 [k]1Ki 15:26
15:19 [l]1Ch 5:6, 26
15:20 [m]S 2Ki 12:18
15:24 [n]1Ki 15:26
15:25 [o]2Ch 28:6; Isa 7:1 [p]S 2Ki 12:20

[a] *10* Hebrew; some Septuagint manuscripts *in Ibleam*
[b] *12* 2 Kings 10:30
[c] *19* Also called *Tiglath-Pileser*
[d] *19* That is, about 37 tons (about 34 metric tons)
[e] *20* That is, about 1 1/4 pounds (about 0.6 kilogram)

15:11 *annals of the kings of Israel.* See note on 1Ki 14:19.

15:12 *word of the LORD ... was fulfilled.* See NIV text note. With the downfall of Jehu's dynasty, the northern kingdom entered a period of political instability (see Hos 1:4). The remaining five kings of the northern kingdom were all assassinated with the exception of Menahem, who reigned ten years, and Hoshea, who was imprisoned by the Assyrians. From the strength and wealth of the reign of Jeroboam II, the decline and fall of the northern kingdom was swift.

15:13 *thirty-ninth year of Uzziah.* 752 B.C. (see note on v. 2). Uzziah is another name for Azariah (see NIV text note on 14:21).

15:14 *Menahem ... went from Tirzah up to Samaria.* It is likely that Menahem was the commander of a military garrison at Tirzah, the former capital of the northern kingdom (see 1Ki 14:17; 15:21,33). *succeeded him.* For the reign of Menahem see vv. 17–22.

15:15 *annals of the kings of Israel.* See note on 1Ki 14:19.

15:16 *Tiphsah.* There was a Tiphsah located far to the north of Hamath (see 14:25) on the Euphrates River (see 1Ki 4:24). It is unlikely that this was the city intended. Some interpreters prefer the reading "Tappuah" of the Septuagint (the pre-Christian Greek translation of the OT). Tappuah was a city on the border between Ephraim and Manasseh (Jos 16:8; 17:7–8). Perhaps there was a Tiphsah in Israel not otherwise mentioned. *ripped open all the pregnant women.* See 8:12 and note.

15:17 *thirty-ninth year of Azariah.* 752 B.C. (see note on v. 2). *ten years.* 752–742.

15:18 *sins of Jeroboam.* See 1Ki 12:26–32; 13:33–34; 14:16.

15:19 *Pul.* The Babylonian name (see 1Ch 5:26) of the Assyrian ruler Tiglath-Pileser III (745–727 B.C.; see NIV text note). *invaded the land.* Assyrian annals of Tiglath-Pileser III indicate that he marched west with his army in 738 and took tribute from, among others, Carchemish, Hamath, Tyre, Byblos, Damascus, and Menahem of Samaria (see map, p. 552; see also map Nos. 7 and 8 at the end of this study Bible). *thousand talents.* See NIV text note. This was an enormous sum of money. For the relative value of a talent of silver see note on 5:5. *gain his support and strengthen his own hold.* It appears that as a usurper Menahem still felt insecure on the throne. The opposition to his rule may have come from those following the leadership of Pekah, who favored an alliance with the Arameans of Damascus in order to resist the Assyrian threat (see note on v. 27). Hosea denounced the policy of seeking aid from the Assyrians and predicted that it would fail (Hos 5:13–15).

15:20 *fifty shekels.* See NIV text note. A simple calculation reveals that it would require approximately 60,000 men of means to provide the 1,000 talents of tribute. This gives some indication of the prosperity the northern kingdom had enjoyed during the time of Jeroboam II.

15:21 *annals of the kings of Israel.* See note on 1Ki 14:19.

15:22 *rested with his fathers.* See note on 1Ki 1:21.

15:23 *fiftieth year of Azariah.* 742 B.C. (see note on v. 2). *two years.* 742–740.

15:24 *sins of Jeroboam.* See 1Ki 12:26–32; 13:33–34; 14:16.

15:25 *One of his chief officers.* Pekah was probably the ranking official in the Transjordan provinces, but his allegiance to Menahem and Pekahiah may well have been more apparent than real (see note on v. 27). *conspired against him.* Differences over foreign policy probably played an important role in fomenting Pekah's revolution. Pekahiah undoubtedly followed the policy of his father Menahem in seeking Assyria's

Pekah killed Pekahiah and succeeded him
as king.
26 The other events of Pekahiah's reign,
and all he did, are written in the book of
the annals of the kings of Israel.

Pekah King of Israel

27 In the fifty-second year of Azariah
king of Judah, Pekah[q] son of Remaliah[r]
became king of Israel in Samaria, and he
reigned twenty years. 28 He did evil in the
eyes of the LORD. He did not turn away
from the sins of Jeroboam son of Nebat,
which he had caused Israel to commit.
29 In the time of Pekah king of Israel,
Tiglath-Pileser[s] king of Assyria came and
took Ijon,[t] Abel Beth Maacah, Janoah,
Kedesh and Hazor. He took Gilead and
Galilee, including all the land of Naphtali,[u] and deported[v] the people to Assyria. 30 Then Hoshea[w] son of Elah conspired
against Pekah son of Remaliah. He attacked and assassinated[x] him, and then
succeeded him as king in the twentieth
year of Jotham son of Uzziah.
31 As for the other events of Pekah's reign,
and all he did, are they not written in the
book of the annals[y] of the kings of Israel?

Jotham King of Judah

15:33-38pp — 2Ch 27:1-4,7-9

32 In the second year of Pekah son of
Remaliah king of Israel, Jotham[z] son of
Uzziah king of Judah began to reign.
33 He was twenty-five years old when he
became king, and he reigned in Jerusalem sixteen years. His mother's name
was Jerusha daughter of Zadok. 34 He
did what was right[a] in the eyes of the
LORD, just as his father Uzziah had done.
35 The high places,[b] however, were not
removed; the people continued to offer
sacrifices and burn incense there. Jotham rebuilt the Upper Gate[c] of the temple of the LORD.
36 As for the other events of Jotham's
reign, and what he did, are they not
written in the book of the annals of the
kings of Judah? 37 (In those days the LORD
began to send Rezin[d] king of Aram and
Pekah son of Remaliah against Judah.)
38 Jotham rested with his fathers and was
buried with them in the City of David,
the city of his father. And Ahaz his son
succeeded him as king.

Ahaz King of Judah

16:1-20pp — 2Ch 28:1-27

16 In the seventeenth year of Pekah son
of Remaliah, Ahaz[e] son of Jotham
king of Judah began to reign. 2 Ahaz was
twenty years old when he became king,
and he reigned in Jerusalem sixteen years.
Unlike David his father, he did not do
what was right[f] in the eyes of the LORD his

15:27 [q] 2Ch 28:6; Isa 7:1 [r] Isa 7:4 **15:29** [s] 2Ki 16:7; 17:6; 1Ch 5:26; 2Ch 28:20; Jer 50:17 [t] 1Ki 15:20 [u] 2Ki 16:9; 17:24; 2Ch 16:4; Isa 7:9; 9:1; 10:9, 10; 28:1; 36:19; 37:18 [v] 2Ki 24:14-16; 1Ch 5:22; Isa 14:6, 17; 36:17; 45:13 **15:30** [w] 2Ki 17:1 [x] S 2Ki 12:20 **15:31** [y] 1Ki 15:31 **15:32** [z] ver 1, S 5; 1Ch 5:17; Isa 1:1; Hos 1:1 **15:34** [a] S 1Ki 14:8 **15:35** [b] 2Ki 12:3 [c] S Ge 23:10; 2Ch 23:20 **15:37** [d] 2Ki 16:5; Isa 7:1; 8:6; 9:11 **16:1** [e] Isa 1:1; 7:1; 14:28; Hos 1:1; Mic 1:1 **16:2** [f] S 1Ki 14:8

friendship (see v. 20). Pekah advocated friendly relations with the Arameans of Damascus in order to counter potential Assyrian aggression (see 16:1–9; Isa 7:1–2,4–6).

15:26 *annals of the kings of Israel.* See note on 1Ki 14:19.

15:27 *fifty-second year of Azariah.* 740 B.C. (see note on v. 2). *twenty years.* 752–732, based on the assumptions (which the data seem to require) that Pekah had established in Transjordan virtually a rival government to that of Menahem when Menahem assassinated Shallum (see notes on vv. 17,19,25), and that the number of regnal years given here includes this period of rival rule.

15:28 *sins of Jeroboam.* See 1Ki 12:26–32; 13:33–34; 14:16.

15:29 *Tiglath-Pileser king of Assyria came.* See note on v. 19; see also map, p. 552. The historical background for this attack is found in 16:5–9; 2Ch 28:16–21; Isa 7:1–17. *Ijon ... Naphtali.* Over 150 years earlier Ben-Hadad I of Damascus had taken this same territory from the northern kingdom in response to an appeal by a king of Judah (see notes on 1Ki 15:19–20). *deported the people to Assyria.* See 1Ch 5:26. The forced exile of Israelites from their homeland was a fulfillment of the covenant curse (see note on 10:32).

15:30 *Hoshea ... conspired against Pekah.* Hoshea probably represented the faction in the northern kingdom that favored cooperation with Assyria rather than resistance. In one of his annals Tiglath-Pileser III claims to have placed Hoshea on the throne of the northern kingdom and to have taken ten talents of gold and 1,000 talents of silver as tribute from him. *twentieth year of Jotham.* 732 B.C. (see notes on vv. 32–33). Reference is to his 20th official year, which was his 19th actual year.

15:31 *annals of the kings of Israel.* See note on 1Ki 14:19.

15:32 *second year of Pekah.* 750 B.C. (see note on v. 27).

15:33 *sixteen years.* 750–735 B.C. Jotham was coregent with his father 750–740 (see note on v. 5). Jotham's reign was in some sense terminated in 735, and his son Ahaz took over. However, Jotham continued to live until at least 732 (see notes on vv. 30,37).

15:34 *as his father Uzziah had done.* See note on v. 3; see also 2Ch 27:2.

15:35 *high places, however, were not removed.* See v. 4; see also note on 1Ki 15:14. *Upper Gate of the temple.* See 2Ch 23:20; Jer 20:2; Eze 9:2. Additional information on Jotham's building activities is given in 2Ch 27:3–4.

15:36 *other events of Jotham's reign.* See 2Ch 27:1–6. *annals of the kings of Judah.* See note on 1Ki 14:29.

15:37 This parenthetical statement concerning Jotham's reign supports the idea of an overlap between the reigns of Jotham and Ahaz (see note on v. 33), since 16:5–12; 2Ch 28:5–21; Isa 7:1–17 all place the major effort of Rezin and Pekah in the time of Ahaz.

15:38 *rested with his fathers.* See note on 1Ki 1:21.

16:1 *seventeenth year of Pekah.* 735 B.C. (see note on 15:27). The reign of Ahaz apparently overlapped that of Jotham, with Ahaz serving as a senior partner beginning his 735 (see notes on 15:33,37; see also notes on v. 2; 17:1 and chart, p. 505). *Ahaz son of Jotham king of Judah.* In 1996 a clay seal impression reading "Belonging to Ahaz (son of) Jotham king of Judah" came to light. Written in the ancient Hebrew script used during the divided monarchy, it is the first authentic seal inscription that can be attributed to a king of Judah.

16:2 *twenty years old when he became king.* Perhaps the age at which Ahaz became a senior coregent with his father Jotham in 735 B.C. (see note on v. 1). Otherwise, according to the ages and dates provided, Ahaz would have been 11 or 12 instead of 14 or 15 years old when his son Hezekiah was born (cf. 18:1–2). *sixteen years.* The synchronizations of the reigns of Ahaz and

God. 3He walked in the ways of the kings
of Israel[g] and even sacrificed his son[h] in[a]
the fire, following the detestable[i] ways of
the nations the LORD had driven out before
the Israelites. 4He offered sacrifices and
burned incense[j] at the high places, on the
hilltops and under every spreading tree.[k]
5Then Rezin[l] king of Aram and Pekah
son of Remaliah king of Israel marched up
to fight against Jerusalem and besieged
Ahaz, but they could not overpower him.
6At that time, Rezin[m] king of Aram recovered Elath[n] for Aram by driving out the
men of Judah. Edomites then moved into
Elath and have lived there to this day.
7Ahaz sent messengers to say to Tiglath-Pileser[o] king of Assyria, "I am your
servant and vassal. Come up and save[p] me
out of the hand of the king of Aram and of
the king of Israel, who are attacking me."
8And Ahaz took the silver and gold found
in the temple of the LORD and in the treasuries of the royal palace and sent it as a
gift[q] to the king of Assyria. 9The king of
Assyria complied by attacking Damascus[r]
and capturing it. He deported its inhabitants to Kir[s] and put Rezin to death.

16:3 [g] 2Ki 17:19 [h] S Lev 18:21; S 2Ki 3:27 [i] S Lev 18:3; S Dt 9:4
16:4 [j] 2Ki 22:17; 23:5 [k] Dt 12:2; Eze 6:13
16:5 [l] S 2Ki 15:37
16:6 [m] Isa 9:12 [n] S 1Ki 9:26
16:7 [o] S 2Ki 15:29 [p] Isa 2:6; 10:20; Jer 2:18; 3:1; Eze 16:28; 23:5; Hos 10:6
16:8 [q] S 1Ki 15:18; 2Ki 12:18
16:9 [r] S Ge 14:15; S 2Ki 15:29 [s] Isa 22:6; Am 1:5; 9:7
16:10 [t] ver 11,15,16; Isa 8:2
16:12 [u] 2Ch 26:16
16:13 [v] Lev 6:8-13 [w] Lev 6:14-23 [x] S Ex 29:40 [y] Lev 7:11-21

10Then King Ahaz went to Damascus to
meet Tiglath-Pileser king of Assyria. He
saw an altar in Damascus and sent to Uriah[t] the priest a sketch of the altar, with
detailed plans for its construction. 11So
Uriah the priest built an altar in accordance with all the plans that King Ahaz
had sent from Damascus and finished it
before King Ahaz returned. 12When the
king came back from Damascus and saw
the altar, he approached it and presented offerings[b] [u] on it. 13He offered up his
burnt offering[v] and grain offering,[w] poured
out his drink offering,[x] and sprinkled the
blood of his fellowship offerings[c] [y] on the
altar. 14The bronze altar[z] that stood before
the LORD he brought from the front of the
temple—from between the new altar and
the temple of the LORD—and put it on the
north side of the new altar.
15King Ahaz then gave these orders to
Uriah the priest: "On the large new altar,
offer the morning[a] burnt offering and the

[a] 3 Or *even made his son pass through* [b] 12 Or *and went up* [c] 13 Traditionally *peace offerings*

16:14 [z] S Ex 20:24; S 40:6; S 1Ki 8:64 **16:15** [a] Ex 29:38-41

Hezekiah of Judah with those of Pekah and Hoshea of the northern kingdom present some apparent chronological difficulties (see notes on v. 1; 17:1; 18:1,9–10). It seems best to take the 16 years specified here as the number of years Ahaz reigned after the death of Jotham, thus 732–715 (see notes on 15:30,33). The beginning of his reign appears to be dated in a variety of ways in the Biblical text: (1) in 744/743, which presupposes a coregency with his grandfather Azariah at the tender age of 11 or 12 (see 17:1); (2) in 735, when he became senior coregent with Jotham (see v. 1); and (3) in 732, when he began his sole reign after the death of Jotham. *Unlike David his father.* Ahaz does not even receive the qualified approval given to Amaziah (14:3), Azariah (15:3) and Jotham (15:34).

16:3 *ways of the kings of Israel.* It is unlikely that Ahaz adhered to the calf worship introduced by Jeroboam I at Bethel and Dan (see 1Ki 12:26–32; 13:33–34; 14:16). The reference here is probably to Baal worship in the spirit of Ahab (see notes on 1Ki 16:31–33; see also 2Ch 28:2). *sacrificed his son.* Israel had been warned by Moses not to engage in this pagan rite (see Lev 18:21; Dt 18:10). In Israel the firstborn son in each household was to be consecrated to the Lord and redeemed by a payment of five shekels to the priests (see Ex 13:1,11–13; Nu 18:16). See also 3:27; 17:17; 21:6; 23:10; 2Ch 28:3; Jer 7:31; 32:35.

16:4 *high places.* See 15:4,35; see also note on 1Ki 15:14. These high places appear to be those assimilated from pagan Baal worship and used by those who worshiped Baal even while also worshiping the Lord. *under every spreading tree.* Large trees were viewed as symbols of fertility by the pre-Israelite inhabitants of Canaan. Immoral pagan rites were performed at shrines located under such trees. Contrary to the explicit prohibition of the Mosaic covenant, the Israelites adopted this pagan custom (see 17:10; 1Ki 14:23; Dt 12:2; Jer 2:20; 3:6; 17:2; Eze 6:13; 20:28; Hos 4:13–14).

16:5 *Rezin ... and Pekah ... marched up to fight against Jerusalem.* See notes on 15:25,37. *could not overpower.* See Isa 7:1–17; 2Ch 28:5–21. Rezin and Pekah desired to replace Ahaz on the throne of the southern kingdom with the son of Tabeel in order to gain another ally in their anti-Assyrian political policy (see notes on 15:19,25). The Lord delivered Judah and Ahaz from this threat in spite of their wickedness because of the promises of the Davidic covenant (see 1Ki 11:36; 2Sa 7:13; Isa 7:3–7,14).

16:6 *Rezin king of Aram recovered Elath.* See note on 14:22. *Edomites then moved into Elath.* See 2Ch 28:17. The Philistines also took this opportunity to avenge previous defeats (compare 2Ch 26:5–7 with 2Ch 28:18). *to this day.* See note on 1Ki 8:8.

16:7 *Tiglath-Pileser.* See notes on 15:19,29. *your servant and vassal.* Ahaz preferred to seek security for Judah by means of a treaty with Assyria rather than by obedience to the Lord and trust in his promises (see Ex 23:22; Isa 7:10–16).

16:8 *silver and gold found in the temple.* The temple treasure must have been restored to some degree by Jotham (see 12:18; 14:14). The name "Jehoahaz of Judah" (Ahaz) appears on an inscription of Tiglath-Pileser that contains a list of rulers (including those of the Philistines, Ammonites, Moabites and Edomites) who brought tribute to him in 734 B.C.

16:9 *attacking Damascus and capturing it.* In 732 B.C. Tiglath-Pileser III moved against Damascus and destroyed it (see the prophecies of Isa 7:16; Am 1:3–5). *deported its inhabitants to Kir.* The Arameans were sent back to the place from which they had come (Am 9:7) in fulfillment of the prophecy of Amos (Am 1:5). The location of Kir is unknown, though it is mentioned in connection with Elam in Isa 22:6.

16:10 *Ahaz went to Damascus to meet Tiglath-Pileser.* As a vassal king to express his gratitude and loyalty to the victorious Assyrian ruler. *altar in Damascus.* Perhaps that of the god Rimmon (see 5:18; 2Ch 28:23), but more likely a royal altar of Tiglath-Pileser. Ahaz's reproduction of such an altar would have been a further sign of submission to the Assyrians.

16:13 *burnt offering ... grain offering ... drink offering ... fellowship offerings.* See chart, p. 153. With the exception of the drink offering, these same sacrifices were offered at the dedication of the temple (1Ki 8:64).

16:14 *north side of the new altar.* Ahaz removed the bronze altar from its prominent place in front of the temple and gave it a place alongside the new stone altar.

16:15 *large new altar.* Even though fire from heaven had inaugurated and sanctioned the use of the bronze altar

evening grain offering, the king's burnt offering and his grain offering, and the burnt offering of all the people of the land, and their grain offering and their drink offering. Sprinkle on the altar all the blood of the burnt offerings and sacrifices. But I will use the bronze altar for seeking guidance."[b] 16And Uriah the priest did just as King Ahaz had ordered.

17King Ahaz took away the side panels and removed the basins from the movable stands. He removed the Sea from the bronze bulls that supported it and set it on a stone base.[c] 18He took away the Sabbath canopy[a] that had been built at the temple and removed the royal entryway outside the temple of the LORD, in deference to the king of Assyria.[d]

19As for the other events of the reign of Ahaz, and what he did, are they not written in the book of the annals of the kings of Judah? 20Ahaz rested[e] with his fathers and was buried with them in the City of David. And Hezekiah his son succeeded him as king.

Hoshea Last King of Israel

17:3-7pp — 2Ki 18:9-12

17 In the twelfth year of Ahaz king of Judah, Hoshea[f] son of Elah became king of Israel in Samaria, and he reigned nine years. 2He did evil[g] in the eyes of the LORD, but not like the kings of Israel who preceded him.

3Shalmaneser[h] king of Assyria came up to attack Hoshea, who had been Shalmaneser's vassal and had paid him tribute.[i] 4But the king of Assyria discovered that Hoshea was a traitor, for he had sent envoys to So[b] king of Egypt,[j] and he no longer paid tribute to the king of Assyria, as he had done year by year. Therefore Shalmaneser seized him and put him in prison.[k] 5The king of Assyria invaded the entire land, marched against Samaria and laid siege[l] to it for three years. 6In the ninth year of Hoshea, the king of Assyria[m] captured Samaria[n] and deported[o] the Israelites to Assyria. He settled them in Halah, in Gozan[p] on the Habor River and in the towns of the Medes.

Israel Exiled Because of Sin

7All this took place because the Israelites had sinned[q] against the LORD their God, who had brought them up out of Egypt[r] from under the power of Pharaoh king of Egypt. They worshiped other gods

16:15 [b] 1Sa 9:9
16:17 [c] 1Ki 7:27
16:18 [d] Eze 16:28
16:20 [e] Isa 14:28
17:1 [f] 2Ki 15:30
17:2 [g] S Dt 4:25
17:3 [h] Hos 10:14 [i] S Jdg 3:15
17:4 [j] Ps 146:3; Isa 30:1,7; 36:6; Jer 2:36; Hos 12:1 [k] Hos 13:10
17:5 [l] Hos 13:16
17:6 [m] ver 20; S 2Ki 15:29; Isa 42:24 [n] Isa 10:9 [o] S Dt 4:27; S 24:1; S 2Ki 15:29; Am 7:17 [p] 1Ch 5:26
17:7 [q] S Jos 7:11 [r] Ex 14:15-31

[a] 18 Or *the dais of his throne* (see Septuagint)
[b] 4 Or *to Sais, to the*; *So* is possibly an abbreviation for *Osorkon.*

for the worship of the Lord (see 2Ch 7:1), Ahaz now replaced it with an altar built on the pattern of the pagan altar from Damascus. Although the bronze altar was quite large (see 2Ch 4:1), the new altar was larger. *morning burnt offering.* See 3:20; Ex 29:38–39; Nu 28:3–4. *evening grain offering.* See note on 1Ki 18:29. *king's burnt offering and his grain offering.* There is no other reference to these special offerings of the king in the OT, with the possible exception of Ezekiel's depiction of the offerings of a future prince (Eze 46:12). *I will use the bronze altar for seeking guidance.* Seeking omens by the examination of the entrails of sacrificed animals is well attested in ancient Near Eastern texts. Here Ahaz states his intention to follow an Assyrian divination technique in an attempt to secure the Lord's guidance.

16:17 *side panels and … basins from the movable stands.* See 1Ki 7:27–39. *removed the Sea from the bronze bulls.* See 1Ki 7:23–26. Perhaps the bronze was needed for tribute required by Tiglath-Pileser III.

16:18 *in deference to the king of Assyria.* As a vassal of Tiglath-Pileser, Ahaz was forced to relinquish some of the symbols of his own royal power.

16:19 *other events of the reign of Ahaz.* See 2Ch 28, where, among other things, it is said that Ahaz went so far as to "shut the doors of the temple" (2Ch 28:24). *annals of the kings of Judah.* See note on 1Ki 14:29.

16:20 *rested with his fathers.* See note on 1Ki 1:21; see also 2Ch 28:27. *Hezekiah his son succeeded him.* For the reign of Hezekiah see 18:1—20:21.

17:1 *twelfth year of Ahaz.* 732 B.C. (see note on 15:30), on the assumption that Ahaz began a coregency with Azariah in 744/743 (see notes on 16:1–2). *nine years.* 732–722 (see Introduction to 1 Kings: Chronology); cf. note on 15:30.

17:3 *Shalmaneser.* Hoshea had become a vassal to Assyria under the rule of Tiglath-Pileser III (see note on 15:30). The latter was succeeded on the Assyrian throne by Shalmaneser V, who ruled 727–722 B.C. (see chart, p. 472).

17:5 *three years.* 725–722 B.C. Samaria was a strongly fortified city and extremely difficult to subdue (see note on 1Ki 16:24).

17:6 *ninth year of Hoshea.* 722 B.C. (see note on v. 1). *king of Assyria captured Samaria.* In the winter (December) of 722–721 Shalmaneser V died (possibly by assassination), and the Assyrian throne was seized by Sargon II (721–705). In his annals Sargon lays claim to the capture of Samaria at the beginning of his reign, but it was hardly more than a mopping-up operation. *deported the Israelites.* Because the northern kingdom refused to be obedient to their covenant obligations, the Lord brought on them the judgment pronounced already by Ahijah during the reign of the northern kingdom's first king, Jeroboam I (see note on 1Ki 14:15). In his annals Sargon II claims to have deported 27,290 Israelites. He then settled other captured people in the vacated towns of the northern kingdom (see v. 24). *Gozan on the Habor River.* Gozan was an Assyrian provincial capital located on a tributary (the Habor) of the Euphrates River. *towns of the Medes.* Towns located in the area south of the Caspian Sea and northeast of the Tigris River.

17:7–23 A theological explanation for the downfall of the northern kingdom (see map and accompanying text, p. 558). Israel had repeatedly spurned the Lord's gracious acts, had refused to heed the prophets' warnings of impending judgment (vv. 13–14,23) and had failed to keep her covenant obligations (v. 15). The result was the implementation of the covenant curse precisely as it had been presented to the Israelites by Moses before they entered Canaan (Dt 28:49–68; 32:1–47).

17:7 *brought them up out of Egypt.* The deliverance from Egypt was the fundamental redemptive event in Israel's history. She owed her very existence as a nation to this gracious and mighty act of the Lord (see Ex 20:2; Dt 5:15; 26:8; Jos 24:5–7,17; Jdg 10:11; 1Sa 12:6; Ne 9:9–13; Mic 6:4).

Exile of the Northern Kingdom

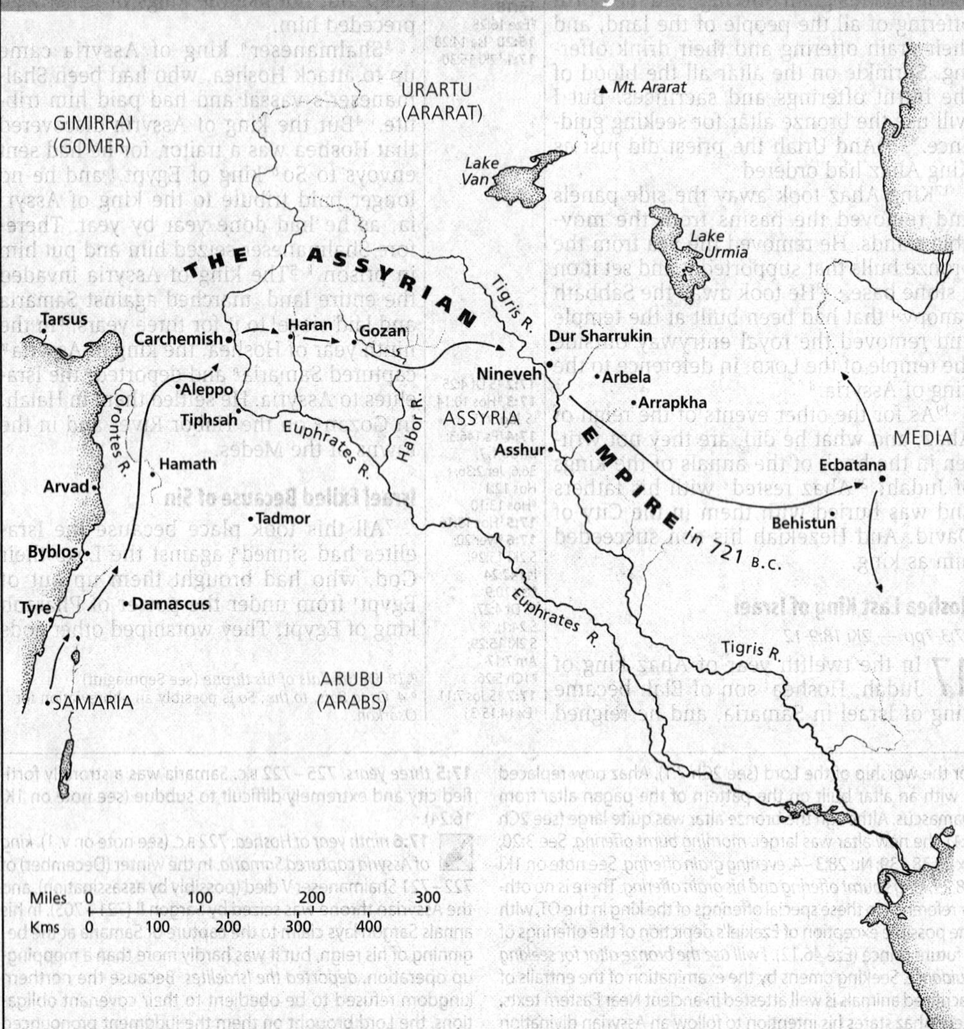

The mass deportation policy of the Assyrians was a companion piece to the brutal and calculated terror initiated by Ashurnasirpal and followed by all his successors. It was intended to forestall revolts but, like all Draconian measures, it merely spread misery and engendered hatred. In the end, it hastened the disintegration of the Assyrian empire.

There is some evidence that Israel experienced its first deportations under Tiglath-Pileser III (745–727 B.C.), a cruelty repeated by Sargon II (721–705 B.C.) at the time of the fall of Samaria. The latter king's inscriptions boast of carrying away 27,290 inhabitants of the city "as booty." According to 2Ki 17:6, they were sent to Assyria, to Halah, to Gozan on the Habor River, and apparently to the eastern frontiers of the empire (to the towns of the Medes, most probably somewhere in the vicinity of Ecbatana, the modern Hamadan).

The sequel is provided by the inscriptions of Sargon: "The Arabs who live far away in the desert, who know neither overseers nor officials, and who had not yet brought their tribute to any king, I deported and settled them in Samaria."

Much mythology has developed around the theme of the so-called ten lost tribes of Israel. A close examination of Assyrian records reveals that the deportations approximated only a limited percentage of the population, usually consisting of noble families. Agricultural workers, no doubt the majority, were deliberately left to care for the crops (cf. the Babylonian practice, 2Ki 24:14; 25:12).

8and followed the practices of the nations[s]
the LORD had driven out before them, as
well as the practices that the kings of Israel had introduced. 9The Israelites secretly did things against the LORD their God
that were not right. From watchtower to
fortified city[t] they built themselves high
places in all their towns. 10They set up sacred stones[u] and Asherah poles[v] on every
high hill and under every spreading tree.[w]
11At every high place they burned incense,
as the nations whom the LORD had driven
out before them had done. They did wicked things that provoked the LORD to anger.
12They worshiped idols,[x] though the LORD
had said, "You shall not do this."[a] 13The
LORD warned[y] Israel and Judah through
all his prophets and seers:[z] "Turn from
your evil ways.[a] Observe my commands
and decrees, in accordance with the entire Law that I commanded your fathers to
obey and that I delivered to you through
my servants the prophets."[b]
14But they would not listen and were as
stiff-necked[c] as their fathers, who did not
trust in the LORD their God. 15They rejected
his decrees and the covenant[d] he had made
with their fathers and the warnings he
had given them. They followed worthless
idols[e] and themselves became worthless.[f]
They imitated the nations[g] around them
although the LORD had ordered them, "Do
not do as they do," and they did the things
the LORD had forbidden them to do.
16They forsook all the commands of the
LORD their God and made for themselves
two idols cast in the shape of calves,[h] and
an Asherah[i] pole. They bowed down to
all the starry hosts,[j] and they worshiped
Baal.[k] 17They sacrificed[l] their sons and
daughters in[b] the fire. They practiced divination and sorcery[m] and sold[n] themselves
to do evil in the eyes of the LORD, provoking him to anger.
18So the LORD was very angry with Israel and removed them from his presence.[o]
Only the tribe of Judah was left, 19and
even Judah did not keep the commands
of the LORD their God. They followed the
practices Israel had introduced.[p] 20There-
fore the LORD rejected all the people of Israel; he afflicted them and gave them into
the hands of plunderers,[q] until he thrust
them from his presence.[r]
21When he tore[s] Israel away from the
house of David, they made Jeroboam son
of Nebat their king.[t] Jeroboam enticed
Israel away from following the LORD and
caused them to commit a great sin.[u] 22The
Israelites persisted in all the sins of Jeroboam and did not turn away from them 23un-
til the LORD removed them from his presence,[v] as he had warned[w] through all his
servants the prophets. So the people of Israel were taken from their homeland[x] into
exile in Assyria, and they are still there.

[a] *12* Exodus 20:4,5 [b] *17* Or *They made their sons and daughters pass through*

17:8 [s]S Ex 34:15; S Lev 18:3; S Dt 9:4 **17:9** [t]2Ki 18:8 **17:10** [u]S Ex 23:24 [v]Ex 34:13; Isa 17:8; Mic 5:14 [w]S Dt 12:2 **17:12** [x]S Ex 20:4 **17:13** [y]S Jdg 6:8; S 2Ch 7:14; S Job 34:33; Eze 3:17-19 [z]S 1Sa 9:9 [a]Jer 4:1; 18:11; 23:22; 25:5; 35:15; 36:3; Zec 1:4 [b]Mt 23:34 **17:14** [c]S Ex 32:9; Ac 7:51 **17:15** [d]S Lev 26:11; Dt 29:25; Jdg 2:20; 1Ki 11:11; 2Ki 18:12; Ps 78:10; Eze 5:6; Mal 2:10 [e]S Dt 32:21; Hos 11:2; Ro 1:21-23 [f]Jer 2:5 [g]S Dt 12:4 **17:16** [h]S Ex 32:4 [i]S Dt 16:21 [j]S Ge 2:1; Isa 40:26; Jer 19:13 [k]S Jdg 2:11 **17:17** [l]S Dt 12:31; 18:10-12; 2Ki 16:3; Eze 16:21 [m]S Lev 19:26 [n]S 1Ki 21:20; Ro 7:14 **17:18** [o]S Ge 4:14; S Ex 33:15; S 2Ki 13:23; 2Th 1:9 **17:19** [p]2Ki 16:3; Jer 3:6-10; Eze 23:13 **17:20** [q]S ver 6 [r]Jer 7:15; 15:1 **17:21** [s]S 1Sa 15:27; S 1Ki 11:11 [t]1Ki 12:20 [u]S 1Ki 12:30 **17:23** [v]Eze 39:23-24 [w]S Jdg 6:8 [x]S 1Ki 9:7

worshiped other gods. A violation of the most basic obligation of Israel's covenant with the Lord (see v. 35; Dt 5:7; 6:14; Jos 24:14–16,20; Jer 1:16; 2:5–6; 25:6; 35:15).

17:8 *practices of the nations.* See Dt 18:9; Jdg 2:12–13. *practices that the kings of Israel had introduced.* See, e.g., 10:31 (Jehu); 14:24 (Jeroboam II); 1Ki 12:28–33 (Jeroboam I); 16:25–26 (Omri); 16:30–34 (Ahab).

17:9 *high places in all their towns.* See 14:4; 15:4,35; see also notes on 16:4; 1Ki 3:2; 15:14.

17:10 *sacred stones.* See note on 1Ki 14:23. *Asherah poles.* See note on 1Ki 14:15. *on every high hill and under every spreading tree.* See 16:4; 1Ki 14:23; Jer 2:20; 3:6,13; 17:2.

17:11 *wicked things.* Perhaps a reference to ritual prostitution (see note on 1Ki 14:24; see also Hos 4:13–14).

17:12 *idols.* See note on Lev 26:30. *You shall not do this.* See NIV text note; see also Ex 23:13; Lev 26:1; Dt 5:6–10.

17:13 *warned Israel and Judah through all his prophets.* Israel not only violated the requirements of the Sinai covenant, but she also spurned the words of prophets the Lord had graciously sent to call his people back to the covenant (see, e.g., 1Ki 13:1–3; 14:6–16; Jdg 6:8–10; 1Sa 3:19–21 as well as the ministries of Elijah, Elisha, Amos and Hosea). *seers.* See note on 1Sa 9:9.

17:14 *stiff-necked.* A figure derived from the obstinate resistance of an ox to being placed under a yoke (see Dt 10:16; Jer 2:20; 7:26; 17:23; 19:15; Hos 4:16).

17:15 *followed worthless idols.* See Dt 32:21; Jer 2:5; 8:19; 10:8; 14:22; 51:18.

17:16 *two idols cast in the shape of calves.* The golden calves of Bethel and Dan (see 1Ki 12:28–30). *Asherah pole.* See note on 1Ki 14:15. *all the starry hosts.* Israel had been commanded not to worship the stars like her pagan neighbors (see Dt 4:19; 17:3). Although this form of idolatry is not mentioned previously in 1,2 Kings, the prophet Amos apparently alludes to its practice in the northern kingdom during the reign of Jeroboam II (see note on Am 5:26). It was later introduced in the southern kingdom during the reign of Manasseh (see 21:3,5) and abolished during the reformation of Josiah (see 23:4–5,12; see also Eze 8:16).

17:17 *sacrificed their sons and daughters.* See note on 16:3. *practiced divination and sorcery.* Such practices were forbidden in the Mosaic covenant (see note on 16:15; see also Lev 19:26; Dt 18:10 and note on 18:9).

17:18 *removed them from his presence.* The exile of the northern kingdom (see v. 6; 23:27; see also map, p. 558). *Only the tribe of Judah was left.* The southern kingdom included elements of the tribes of Simeon and Benjamin, but Judah was the only tribe in the south to retain its complete integrity (see notes on 1Ki 11:31–32; see also note on 2Ki 19:4).

17:20 *afflicted them and gave them into the hands of plunderers.* See 10:32–33; 13:3,20; 24:2; 2Ch 21:16; 28:18; Am 1:13; cf. also Jdg 2:14–15.

17:21 *tore Israel away from the house of David.* See 1Ki 11:11,31; 12:24. The division of the kingdom was of the Lord, but it came to the nation as a punishment for their sins. *Jeroboam . . . caused them to commit a great sin.* See 1Ki 12:26–32; 13:33–34; see also note on Ge 20:9.

17:23 *warned through all his servants the prophets.* See 1Ki 14:15–16; Hos 10:1–7; 11:5; Am 5:27.

Samaria Resettled

24The king of Assyria[y] brought people
from Babylon, Cuthah, Avva, Hamath and
Sepharvaim[z] and settled them in the towns
of Samaria to replace the Israelites. They
took over Samaria and lived in its towns.
25When they first lived there, they did not
worship the LORD; so he sent lions[a] among
them and they killed some of the people.
26It was reported to the king of Assyria:
“The people you deported and resettled in
the towns of Samaria do not know what
the god of that country requires. He has
sent lions among them, which are killing
them off, because the people do not know
what he requires.”

27Then the king of Assyria gave this
order: “Have one of the priests you took
captive from Samaria go back to live there
and teach the people what the god of the
land requires.” 28So one of the priests
who had been exiled from Samaria came
to live in Bethel and taught them how to
worship the LORD.

29Nevertheless, each national group
made its own gods in the several towns[b]
where they settled, and set them up in
the shrines[c] the people of Samaria had
made at the high places.[d] 30The men from
Babylon made Succoth Benoth, the men
from Cuthah made Nergal, and the men
from Hamath made Ashima; 31the Avvites
made Nibhaz and Tartak, and the Sephar-
vites burned their children in the fire as
sacrifices to Adrammelech[e] and Anammelech, the gods of Sepharvaim.[f] 32They worshiped the LORD, but they also appointed
all sorts[g] of their own people to officiate
for them as priests in the shrines at the
high places. 33They worshiped the LORD,
but they also served their own gods in accordance with the customs of the nations
from which they had been brought.

34To this day they persist in their former practices. They neither worship the
LORD nor adhere to the decrees and ordinances, the laws and commands that
the LORD gave the descendants of Jacob,
whom he named Israel.[h] 35When the LORD
made a covenant with the Israelites, he
commanded them: “Do not worship[i] any
other gods or bow down to them, serve
them or sacrifice to them.[j] 36But the LORD,
who brought you up out of Egypt with
mighty power and outstretched arm,[k] is
the one you must worship. To him you
shall bow down and to him offer sacrifices. 37You must always be careful[l] to keep
the decrees[m] and ordinances, the laws
and commands he wrote for you. Do not
worship other gods. 38Do not forget[n] the
covenant I have made with you, and do
not worship other gods. 39Rather, worship
the LORD your God; it is he who will deliver you from the hand of all your enemies.”

40They would not listen, however, but
persisted in their former practices. 41Even
while these people were worshiping the
LORD,[o] they were serving their idols. To
this day their children and grandchildren
continue to do as their fathers did.

17:24 [y] 2Ki 19:37; Ezr 4:2,10; Isa 37:38 [z] ver 31; S 2Ki 15:29; 18:34; Isa 36:19; 37:13; Am 6:2
17:25 [a] S Ge 37:20; Isa 5:29; 15:9; Jer 50:17
17:29 [b] Jer 2:28; 11:13 [c] S Lev 26:30; S 1Ki 12:31 [d] Mic 4:5
17:31 [e] 2Ki 19:37 [f] S ver 24
17:32 [g] S 1Ki 12:31
17:34 [h] S Ge 17:5; S 1Ki 18:31
17:35 [i] S Ex 20:5 [j] S Ex 20:3
17:36 [k] S Ex 3:20; Ps 136:12
17:37 [l] Dt 5:32 [m] S Lev 19:37
17:38 [n] S Dt 6:12
17:41 [o] S 1Ki 18:21; Ezr 4:2; Mt 6:24

17:24 *king of Assyria.* Primarily Sargon II (721–705 B.C.), though later Assyrian rulers, including Esarhaddon (681–669) and Ashurbanipal (669–627), settled additional non-Israelites in Samaria (see Ezr 4:2,9–10). *Babylon, Cuthah.* Babylon and Cuthah (located about eight miles northeast of Babylon) were forced to submit to Assyrian rule by Sargon II in 709. *Avva.* Probably the same as Ivvah (see 18:34; 19:13). Its association with Hamath and Arpad suggests a location somewhere in Aram (Syria). *Hamath.* Located on the Orontes River (see 14:25; 18:34; see also note on Eze 47:15). In 720 Sargon II made the kingdom of Hamath into an Assyrian province. *Sepharvaim.* See note on Isa 36:19. *Samaria.* Here a designation for the entire northern kingdom (see note on 1Ki 13:32). **17:25** *did not worship the LORD.* They worshiped their own national deities. *sent lions among them.* Lions had always been present in Canaan (see 1Ki 13:24; 20:36; Jdg 14:5; 1Sa 17:34; Am 3:12). In the aftermath of the disruption and depopulation caused by the conflict with the Assyrians, the lions greatly increased in number (see Ex 23:29). This was viewed by the inhabitants of the land and the writer of Kings as a punishment from the Lord (see Lev 26:21–22).
17:26 *king of Assyria.* Sargon II. *what the god of that country requires.* According to the religious ideas of that time, each regional deity required special ritual observances, which, if ignored or violated, would bring disaster on the land.
17:27 *one of the priests.* Probably a priest of the religion Jeroboam I established in the northern kingdom (see 1Ki 12:31 and note).
17:28 *came to live in Bethel.* Bethel continued to be the center for the apostate form of Yahweh worship that had been promoted in the northern kingdom since the time of Jeroboam I (see notes on 1Ki 12:28–30).
17:29 *people of Samaria.* The mixed population of the former territory of the northern kingdom. These people of mixed ancestry eventually came to be known as Samaritans. In later times the Samaritans rejected the idolatry of their polytheistic origins and followed the teachings of Moses, including monotheism. In NT times Jesus testified to a Samaritan woman (Jn 4:4–26), and many Samaritans were converted under the ministry of Philip (Ac 8:4–25).
17:32 *officiate for them as priests.* See note on 1Ki 12:31.
17:33 *They worshiped the LORD, but they also served their own gods.* A classic statement of a mixed religion.
17:34 *To this day.* Until the time of the writing of 1,2 Kings. *worship the LORD.* Here used in the sense of faithful worship. In vv. 32–33 "worship the LORD" refers to a paganized worship.
17:35 *Do not worship any other gods.* The Mosaic covenant demanded exclusive worship of the Lord (see Ex 20:3 and note; Dt 5:9). This was the "first and greatest commandment" (Mt 22:38), and it was to distinguish Israel from all other peoples.
17:36 *the LORD, who brought you up out of Egypt ... you must worship.* Here, as in v. 7, the deliverance from Egypt is cited as the gracious act of the Lord par excellence that entitled him to exclusive claim on Israel's loyalty.
17:39 *will deliver you from ... all your enemies.* See Ex 23:22; Dt 20:1–4; 23:14.
17:41 *To this day.* See note on v. 34.

Hezekiah King of Judah

18:2-4pp — 2Ch 29:1-2; 31:1
18:5-7pp — 2Ch 31:20-21
18:9-12pp — 2Ki 17:3-7

18 In the third year of Hoshea son of Elah king of Israel, Hezekiah[p] son of Ahaz king of Judah began to reign. 2 He was twenty-five years old when he became king, and he reigned in Jerusalem twenty-nine years.[q] His mother's name was Abijah[a] daughter of Zechariah. 3 He did what was right[r] in the eyes of the LORD, just as his father David[s] had done. 4 He removed[t] the high places,[u] smashed the sacred stones[v] and cut down the Asherah poles. He broke into pieces the bronze snake[w] Moses had made, for up to that time the Israelites had been burning incense to it. (It was called[b] Nehushtan.[c])

5 Hezekiah trusted[x] in the LORD, the God of Israel. There was no one like him among all the kings of Judah, either before him or after him. 6 He held fast[y] to the LORD and did not cease to follow him; he kept the commands the LORD had given Moses. 7 And the LORD was with him; he was successful[z] in whatever he undertook. He rebelled[a] against the king of Assyria and did not serve him. 8 From watchtower to fortified city,[b] he defeated the Philistines, as far as Gaza and its territory.

9 In King Hezekiah's fourth year,[c] which was the seventh year of Hoshea son of Elah king of Israel, Shalmaneser king of Assyria marched against Samaria and laid siege to it. 10 At the end of three years the Assyrians took it. So Samaria was captured in Hezekiah's sixth year, which was the ninth year of Hoshea king of Israel. 11 The king[d] of Assyria deported Israel to Assyria and settled them in Halah, in Gozan on the Habor River and in towns of the Medes.[e] 12 This happened because they had not obeyed the LORD their God, but had violated his covenant[f]—all that Moses the servant of the LORD commanded.[g] They neither listened to the commands[h] nor carried them out.

13 In the fourteenth year[i] of King Hezekiah's reign, Sennacherib king of Assyria attacked all the fortified cities of Judah[j] and captured them. 14 So Hezekiah king of Judah sent this message to the king of

18:1 [p]Isa 1:1; Hos 1:1; Mic 1:1
18:2 [q]ver 13; Isa 38:5
18:3 [r]S 1Ki 14:8 [s]Isa 38:5
18:4 [t]2Ch 31:1; Isa 36:7 [u]2Ki 12:3; 21:3 [v]S Ex 23:24 [w]Nu 21:9
18:5 [x]ver 19; S 1Sa 7:3; 2Ki 19:10; Ps 21:7; 125:1; Pr 3:26
18:6 [y]Dt 10:20; S Dt 6:18
18:7 [z]S Ge 39:3; S Job 22:25 [a]2Ki 24:1; Ezr 4:19; Isa 36:5
18:8 [b]2Ki 17:9
18:9 [c]Isa 1:1; 36:1
18:11 [d]Isa 37:12 [e]Eze 16:39; 23:9
18:12 [f]S 2Ki 17:15 [g]2Ki 21:8; Da 9:6,10 [h]S 1Ki 9:6
18:13 [i]S ver 2 [j]Isa 1:7; Mic 1:9

[a] 2 Hebrew *Abi,* a variant of *Abijah* [b] 4 Or *He called it* [c] 4 *Nehushtan* sounds like the Hebrew for *bronze* and *snake* and *unclean thing.*

18:1 *third year of Hoshea ... Hezekiah ... began to reign.* 729 B.C. (see 17:1). Hezekiah was coregent with his father Ahaz from 729 to 715 (see notes on 16:2; Isa 36:1). *Hezekiah son of Ahaz king of Judah.* In 1998 a clay impression of a royal stamp seal came to light that reads "Belonging to Hezekiah (son of) Ahaz king of Judah." It is one of only two such royal Judahite seals known (see note on 14:22).

18:2 *became king.* Became sole king of Judah. *twenty-nine years.* 715–686 B.C. See also 2Ch 29–32 and Isa 36–39 for a description of the events of his reign, including a more detailed account of the reformation he led (2Ch 29–31). One of his first acts was to reopen the temple, which had been closed by his father Ahaz (see note on 16:19; see also 2Ch 29:3).

18:3 *right ... as his father David.* Hezekiah is one of the few kings who is compared favorably with David. The others are Asa (1Ki 15:11), Jehoshaphat (1Ki 22:43) and Josiah (2Ki 22:2). A qualification is introduced, however, with both Asa and Jehoshaphat: They did not remove the high places (see 1Ki 15:14; 22:43).

18:4 *removed the high places.* Hezekiah was not the first king to destroy high places (see notes on 1Ki 3:2; 15:14), but he was the first to destroy high places dedicated to the worship of the Lord (see 12:3; 14:4; 15:4,35; 17:9; 1Ki 22:43). This became known even to the Assyrian king, Sennacherib (see v. 22). *sacred stones.* See 3:2; 10:26–27; 17:10; see also note on 1Ki 14:23. *Asherah poles.* See 13:6; 17:10,16; 1Ki 16:23; see also note on 1Ki 14:15. *Israelites had been burning incense to it.* It is unlikely that the bronze snake had been an object of worship all through the centuries of Israel's existence as a nation. Perhaps the idolatrous significance attached to it occurred during the reign of Hezekiah's father Ahaz (see ch. 16). Snake worship of various types was common among ancient Near Eastern peoples. See note on Nu 21:8–9.

18:5 *no one like him ... either before him or after him.* A difference of emphasis is to be seen in this statement when compared to that of 23:25. Hezekiah's uniqueness is to be found in his trust in the Lord, while Josiah's uniqueness is to be found in his scrupulous observance of the Mosaic law.

18:7 *rebelled against the king of Assyria.* Judah had become a vassal to Assyria under Ahaz (see 16:7)—which required at least formal recognition of Assyrian deities. Hezekiah reversed the policy of his father Ahaz and sought independence from Assyrian dominance. It is likely that sometime shortly after 705 B.C., when Sennacherib replaced Sargon II on the Assyrian throne, Hezekiah refused to pay the annual tribute due the Assyrians.

18:8 *defeated the Philistines.* In a reversal of the conditions existing during the time of Ahaz, in which the Philistines captured Judahite cities in the hill country and Negev (see 2Ch 28:18), Hezekiah was able once again to subdue the Philistines. Probably Hezekiah tried to coerce the Philistines into joining his anti-Assyrian policy. In one of his annals Sennacherib tells of forcing Hezekiah to release Padi, king of the Philistine city of Ekron, whom Hezekiah held prisoner in Jerusalem. This occurred in connection with Sennacherib's military campaign in 701 B.C.

18:9 *Hezekiah's fourth year.* 725 B.C., the fourth year of Hezekiah's coregency with Ahaz (see notes on v. 1; 17:1). *Shalmaneser.* See note on 17:3.

18:10 *three years.* See note on 17:5. *ninth year of Hoshea.* See note on 17:6.

18:11 *king of Assyria deported Israel.* See note on 17:6.

18:12 *violated his covenant.* See 17:7–23.

18:13 *fourteenth year.* Of Hezekiah's sole reign: 701 B.C. (see note on v. 2). *Sennacherib ... attacked.* See chart, p. 472. Verses 13–16 correspond very closely with Sennacherib's own account of his 701 campaign against Phoenicia, Judah and Egypt. *captured them.* In his annals, Sennacherib claims to have captured 46 of Hezekiah's fortified cities, as well as numerous open villages, and to have taken 200,150 of the people captive. He says he made Hezekiah "a prisoner in Jerusalem, his royal residence, like a bird in a cage," but he does not say he took Jerusalem (see 19:35–36).

18:14 *Lachish.* See notes on 14:19; Isa 36:2. *three hundred talents of silver and thirty talents of gold.* See NIV text notes. The Assyrian and Biblical reports of the amount of tribute paid by Hezekiah to Sennacherib agree with respect

Assyria at Lachish:[k] "I have done wrong.[l]
Withdraw from me, and I will pay whatever you demand of me." The king of Assyria exacted from Hezekiah king of Judah
three hundred talents[a] of silver and thirty
talents[b] of gold. 15So Hezekiah gave[m] him
all the silver that was found in the temple
of the LORD and in the treasuries of the
royal palace.
16At this time Hezekiah king of Judah
stripped off the gold with which he had
covered the doors[n] and doorposts of the
temple of the LORD, and gave it to the king
of Assyria.

Sennacherib Threatens Jerusalem

18:13,17-37pp — Isa 36:1-22
18:17-35pp — 2Ch 32:9-19

17The king of Assyria sent his supreme
commander,[o] his chief officer and his field
commander with a large army, from Lachish to King Hezekiah at Jerusalem. They
came up to Jerusalem and stopped at the
aqueduct of the Upper Pool,[p] on the road
to the Washerman's Field. 18They called
for the king; and Eliakim[q] son of Hilkiah
the palace administrator, Shebna[r] the secretary, and Joah son of Asaph the recorder
went out to them.
19The field commander said to them,
"Tell Hezekiah:

"'This is what the great king, the
king of Assyria, says: On what are
you basing this confidence[s] of yours?
20You say you have strategy and military strength — but you speak only
empty words. On whom are you depending, that you rebel against me?
21Look now, you are depending on
Egypt,[t] that splintered reed of a staff,[u]
which pierces a man's hand and
wounds him if he leans on it! Such is
Pharaoh king of Egypt to all who depend on him. 22And if you say to me,
"We are depending on the LORD our
God" — isn't he the one whose high
places and altars Hezekiah removed,
saying to Judah and Jerusalem, "You
must worship before this altar in Jerusalem"?
23"'Come now, make a bargain
with my master, the king of Assyria:
I will give you two thousand horses — if you can put riders on them!
24How can you repulse one officer[v] of
the least of my master's officials, even
though you are depending on Egypt
for chariots and horsemen[c]? 25Fur-
thermore, have I come to attack and
destroy this place without word from
the LORD?[w] The LORD himself told me
to march against this country and destroy it.'"

26Then Eliakim son of Hilkiah, and
Shebna and Joah said to the field commander, "Please speak to your servants in
Aramaic,[x] since we understand it. Don't
speak to us in Hebrew in the hearing of
the people on the wall."
27But the commander replied, "Was it
only to your master and you that my master sent me to say these things, and not
to the men sitting on the wall — who, like
you, will have to eat their own filth and
drink their own urine?"
28Then the commander stood and called
out in Hebrew: "Hear the word of the great
king, the king of Assyria! 29This is what
the king says: Do not let Hezekiah de-

18:14 [k] 2Ki 19:8 [l] Isa 24:5; 33:8
18:15 [m] S 1Ki 15:18; Isa 39:2
18:16 [n] 2Ch 29:3
18:17 [o] Isa 20:1 [p] 2Ki 20:20; 2Ch 32:4,30; Ne 2:14; Isa 22:9
18:18 [q] 2Ki 19:2; Isa 22:20; 36:3,11,22; 37:2 [r] ver 26,37; Isa 22:15
18:19 [s] S ver 5; S Job 4:6
18:21 [t] Isa 20:5; 31:1; Eze 29:6 [u] 2Ki 24:7; Isa 20:6; 30:5,7; Jer 25:19; 37:7; 46:2
18:24 [v] Isa 10:8
18:25 [w] 2Ki 19:6,22; 24:3; 2Ch 35:21
18:26 [x] Ezr 4:7

[a] 14 That is, about 11 tons (about 10 metric tons)
[b] 14 That is, about 1 ton (about 1 metric ton)
[c] 24 Or *charioteers*

to the 30 talents of gold, but Sennacherib claims to have received 800 talents of silver rather than the 300 specified in the Biblical text.

18:15 *silver … in the temple … and in the treasuries of the royal palace.* See 12:10,18; 14:14; 16:8; 1Ki 7:51; 14:26; 15:18.

18:17—19:37 See Isa 36–37; cf. 2Ch 32.

18:17 *aqueduct … Field.* See note on Isa 7:3. It is ironic that the Assyrian officials demand Judah's surrender on the very spot where Isaiah had warned Ahaz to trust in the Lord rather than in an alliance with Assyria for deliverance from the threat against him from Aram and the northern kingdom of Israel (see 16:5–10; Isa 7:1–17).

18:18 *palace administrator.* See note on 1Ki 4:6. *secretary.* See note on 2Sa 8:17. *recorder.* See note on 2Sa 8:16.

18:19 *great king.* A frequently used title of the Assyrian rulers — and occasionally of the Lord (Ps 47:2; 48:2; 95:3; Mal 1:14; Mt 5:35). *says.* The following address is a masterpiece of calculated intimidation and psychological warfare designed to destroy the morale of the inhabitants of Jerusalem (see vv. 26–27; cf. note on Jos 6:5).

18:21 *depending on Egypt.* See 19:9; Isa 30:1–5; 31:1–3.

18:22 *isn't he the one whose high places and altars Hezekiah removed … ?* The Assyrians cleverly attempted to drive a wedge between Hezekiah and the people. They attempted to exploit any resentment that may have existed among those who opposed Hezekiah's reformation and his destruction of the high places (see note on v. 4).

18:23 *if you can put riders on them!* With this sarcastic taunt, the Assyrians undoubtedly accurately suggest that the Judahites were so weak in military personnel that they could not even take advantage of such a generous offer. In contrast with the Assyrians, the army of Judah at the time consisted largely of foot soldiers. The city under siege would have contained few chariots, and it is not known whether the Israelites ever employed mounted men in combat.

18:26 *Aramaic.* Had become the international language of the Near East, known and used by those engaged in diplomacy and commerce. It is surprising that the Assyrian officials were able to speak the Hebrew dialect of the common people of Judah (see 2Ch 32:18).

18:27 *men sitting on the wall.* The Assyrian strategy was to negotiate in the hearing of the people in order to demoralize them and turn them against Hezekiah. *eat their own filth and drink their own urine.* A vivid portrayal of the potential hardship of a prolonged siege.

18:29 *the king says.* The Assyrian officials now address their remarks directly to the populace rather than to the officials of Hezekiah, as in vv. 19–27. *Do not let Hezekiah deceive you.*

ceive[y] you. He cannot deliver you from my
hand. 30Do not let Hezekiah persuade you
to trust in the LORD when he says, 'The
LORD will surely deliver us; this city will
not be given into the hand of the king of
Assyria.'
31"Do not listen to Hezekiah. This is
what the king of Assyria says: Make peace
with me and come out to me. Then every one of you will eat from his own vine
and fig tree[z] and drink water from his own
cistern,[a] 32until I come and take you to a
land like your own, a land of grain and
new wine, a land of bread and vineyards,
a land of olive trees and honey. Choose
life[b] and not death!

"Do not listen to Hezekiah, for he is
misleading you when he says, 'The LORD
will deliver us.' 33Has the god[c] of any nation ever delivered his land from the hand
of the king of Assyria? 34Where are the
gods of Hamath[d] and Arpad?[e] Where are
the gods of Sepharvaim, Hena and Ivvah?
Have they rescued Samaria from my hand?
35Who of all the gods of these countries
has been able to save his land from me?
How then can the LORD deliver Jerusalem
from my hand?"[f]
36But the people remained silent and
said nothing in reply, because the king
had commanded, "Do not answer him."
37Then Eliakim[g] son of Hilkiah the palace administrator, Shebna the secretary
and Joah son of Asaph the recorder went
to Hezekiah, with their clothes torn,[h] and
told him what the field commander had
said.

Jerusalem's Deliverance Foretold

19:1-13pp — Isa 37:1-13

19 When King Hezekiah heard this, he
tore[i] his clothes and put on sackcloth
and went into the temple of the LORD.
2He sent Eliakim[j] the palace administrator, Shebna the secretary and the leading priests,[k] all wearing sackcloth,[l] to the
prophet Isaiah[m] son of Amoz. 3They told
him, "This is what Hezekiah says: This
day is a day of distress and rebuke and
disgrace, as when children come to the
point[n] of birth and there is no strength to
deliver them. 4It may be that the LORD your
God will hear all the words of the field
commander, whom his master, the king
of Assyria, has sent to ridicule[o] the living God, and that he will rebuke[p] him for
the words the LORD your God has heard.
Therefore pray for the remnant[q] that still
survives."
5When King Hezekiah's officials came
to Isaiah, 6Isaiah said to them, "Tell your
master, 'This is what the LORD says: Do not
be afraid[r] of what you have heard—those
words with which the underlings of the
king of Assyria have blasphemed[s] me.
7Listen! I am going to put such a spirit
in him that when he hears a certain report,[t] he will return to his own country,
and there I will have him cut down with
the sword.[u]' "

18:29 [y] 2Ki 19:10
18:31 [z] S Nu 13:23; S 1Ki 4:25 [a] Jer 14:3; La 4:4
18:32 [b] Dt 30:19
18:33 [c] 2Ki 19:12
18:34 [d] S 2Ki 17:24; S Jer 49:23 [e] Isa 10:9
18:35 [f] Ps 2:1-2
18:37 [g] S ver 18; Isa 33:7; 36:3,22 [h] S 2Ki 6:30
19:1 [i] S Ge 37:34; S Nu 14:6
19:2 [j] S 2Ki 18:18 [k] Jer 19:1 [l] S Ge 37:34 [m] Isa 1:1
19:3 [n] Hos 13:13
19:4 [o] S 1Sa 17:26 [p] 2Sa 16:12 [q] S Ge 45:7; S Jer 37:3
19:6 [r] S Dt 3:2; S Jos 1:9 [s] S 2Ki 18:25
19:7 [t] S Ex 14:24; Jer 51:46 [u] ver 37; 2Ch 32:21; Isa 10:12

Here and in vv. 30–31 the people are urged three times to turn against Hezekiah.

18:30 *this city will not be given into the hand of the king of Assyria.* Hezekiah could say this on the basis of God's promise to him (see 20:6; see also note on Isa 38:6).

18:31 *eat from his own vine and fig tree and drink water from his own cistern.* Depicting peaceful and prosperous times (see 1Ki 4:25; Mic 4:4; Zec 3:10).

18:32 *until I come and take you to a land like your own.* Ultimately surrender meant deportation, but Sennacherib pictured it as something desirable. *Choose life and not death!* The alternatives depicted for the people are: (1) Trust in the Lord and Hezekiah and die, or (2) trust in the Assyrians and enjoy prosperity and peace. These words directly contradict the alternatives placed before Israel by Moses in Dt 30:15–20.

18:33–35 *Has the god of any nation ever delivered his land from the hand of the king of Assyria?... How then can the LORD deliver Jerusalem from my hand?* The flaw in the Assyrian reasoning was to equate the one true and living God with the no-gods (Dt 32:21) of the pagan peoples the Assyrians had defeated (see 19:4,6; 2Ch 32:13–19; Isa 10:9–11).

18:34 *Hamath.* See notes on 14:25; 17:24. *Arpad.* A city located near Hamath and taken by the Assyrians in 740 B.C. (see 19:13; Isa 10:9; Jer 49:23). *Ivvah.* See note on 17:24.

18:36 *because the king had commanded, "Do not answer him."* The Assyrian attempt to stir up a popular revolt against the leadership and authority of Hezekiah had failed.

18:37 *clothes torn.* An expression of great emotion (see 6:30; 1Ki 21:27). Perhaps in this instance it was motivated by the Assyrian blasphemy against the true God (see 19:4,6; Mt 26:65; Mk 14:63–64).

19:1 *sackcloth.* See note on 6:30.

19:2 *palace administrator.* See note on 1Ki 4:6. *secretary.* See note on 2Sa 8:17. *leading priests.* Probably the oldest members of various priestly families (see Jer 19:1). The crisis involved not only the city of Jerusalem, but also the temple. *prophet Isaiah.* The first reference to Isaiah in the book of Kings, though he had been active in the reigns of Uzziah, Jotham and Ahaz (see Isa 1:1).

19:3 *as when children come to the point of birth and there is no strength to deliver them.* Depicts the critical nature of the threat facing the city.

19:4 *living God.* In contrast to the no-gods of 18:33–35. See 1Sa 17:26,36,45 for another example of ridiculing the living and true God. *pray.* Intercessory prayer was an important aspect of the ministry of the prophets (see, e.g., the intercession of Moses and Samuel: Ex 32:31–32; 33:12–17; Nu 14:13–19; 1Sa 7:8–9; 12:19,23; Ps 99:6; Jer 15:1). *remnant.* Those left in Judah after Sennacherib's capture of many towns and numerous people (see note on 18:13; cf. Isa 10:28–32). Archaeological evidence reveals that many Israelites fled the northern kingdom during the Assyrian assaults and settled in Judah, so that the nation of Judah became the remnant of all Israel.

19:7 *spirit.* Of insecurity and fear. *report.* Some interpreters link this report with the challenge to Sennacherib from Tirhakah of Egypt (v. 9). Others regard it as disturbing information from Sennacherib's homeland. *cut down with the sword.* See v. 37. Here the eventual murder of Sennacherib is connected with his blasphemy against the living God.

[8]When the field commander heard that
the king of Assyria had left Lachish,[v] he
withdrew and found the king fighting
against Libnah.[w]
[9]Now Sennacherib received a report that
Tirhakah, the Cushite[a] king ⌊of Egypt⌋,
was marching out to fight against him.
So he again sent messengers to Hezekiah
with this word: [10]"Say to Hezekiah king
of Judah: Do not let the god you depend[x]
on deceive[y] you when he says, 'Jerusalem will not be handed over to the king
of Assyria.' [11]Surely you have heard what
the kings of Assyria have done to all the
countries, destroying them completely.
And will you be delivered? [12]Did the gods
of the nations that were destroyed by my
forefathers deliver[z] them: the gods of Gozan,[a] Haran,[b] Rezeph and the people of
Eden who were in Tel Assar? [13]Where is
the king of Hamath, the king of Arpad, the
king of the city of Sepharvaim, or of Hena
or Ivvah?"[c]

Hezekiah's Prayer

19:14-19pp — Isa 37:14-20

[14]Hezekiah received the letter[d] from the
messengers and read it. Then he went
up to the temple of the LORD and spread
it out before the LORD. [15]And Hezekiah
prayed to the LORD: "O LORD, God of Israel, enthroned between the cherubim,[e]
you alone[f] are God over all the kingdoms
of the earth. You have made heaven and
earth. [16]Give ear,[g] O LORD, and hear;[h] open
your eyes,[i] O LORD, and see; listen to the
words Sennacherib has sent to insult the
living God.
[17]"It is true, O LORD, that the Assyrian
kings have laid waste these nations and
their lands. [18]They have thrown their gods
into the fire and destroyed them, for they
were not gods[j] but only wood and stone,
fashioned by men's hands.[k] [19]Now, O LORD
our God, deliver[l] us from his hand, so that
all kingdoms[m] on earth may know[n] that
you alone, O LORD, are God."

Isaiah Prophesies Sennacherib's Fall

19:20-37pp — Isa 37:21-38
19:35-37pp — 2Ch 32:20-21

[20]Then Isaiah son of Amoz sent a message to Hezekiah: "This is what the LORD,
the God of Israel, says: I have heard[o] your
prayer concerning Sennacherib king of Assyria. [21]This is the word that the LORD has
spoken against[p] him:

"'The Virgin Daughter[q] of Zion
despises[r] you and mocks[s] you.
The Daughter of Jerusalem
tosses her head[t] as you flee.
[22]Who is it you have insulted and
blasphemed?[u]
Against whom have you raised
your voice
and lifted your eyes in pride?
Against the Holy One[v] of Israel!
[23]By your messengers
you have heaped insults on the
Lord.
And you have said,[w]
"With my many chariots[x]
I have ascended the heights of the
mountains,
the utmost heights of Lebanon.
I have cut down[y] its tallest cedars,
the choicest of its pines.
I have reached its remotest parts,
the finest of its forests.
[24]I have dug wells in foreign lands
and drunk the water there.
With the soles of my feet
I have dried up all the streams of
Egypt."

[a] 9 That is, from the upper Nile region

19:8 [v]2Ki 18:14 [w]S Nu 33:20; S 2Ki 8:22 **19:10** [x]S 2Ki 18:5 [y]2Ki 18:29 **19:12** [z]2Ki 18:33; 2Ch 32:17 [a]2Ki 17:6 [b]S Ge 11:31 **19:13** [c]Isa 10:9-11; Jer 49:23 **19:14** [d]2Ki 5:7 **19:15** [e]S Ge 3:24; S Ex 25:22 [f]S Ge 1:1; S Jos 2:11 **19:16** [g]Ps 31:2; 71:2; 88:2; 102:2 [h]S 1Ki 8:29 [i]S Ex 3:16 **19:18** [j]Isa 44:9-11; Jer 10:3-10 [k]Dt 4:28; Ps 115:4; Ac 17:29 **19:19** [l]1Sa 12:10; Job 6:23; Ps 3:7; 71:4 [m]S 1Ki 8:43; 1Ch 16:8 [n]S Jos 4:24; S 1Sa 17:46 **19:20** [o]S 1Ki 9:3 **19:21** [p]Isa 10:5; 33:1 [q]Isa 47:1; Jer 14:17; 18:13; 31:4; 46:11; La 2:13; Am 5:2 [r]Ps 53:5 [s]Pr 1:26; 3:34 [t]Job 16:4; Ps 44:14; 64:8; 109:25; Jer 18:16 **19:22** [u]S 2Ki 18:25 [v]Lev 19:2; 1Sa 2:2; Job 6:10; Ps 16:10; 22:3; 71:22; 78:41; 89:18; Isa 1:4; 6:3; 57:15; Hos 11:9 **19:23** [w]Isa 10:18; Jer 21:14; Eze 20:47 [x]Ps 20:7; Jer 50:37 [y]Isa 10:34; 14:8; 33:9; Eze 31:3

19:8 *Libnah.* See note on 8:22.
19:9 *Tirhakah.* See note on Isa 37:9. *Cushite.* See NIV text note.
19:12 *Gozan.* See note on 17:6. *Haran.* See note on Ge 11:31. It is not known just when Haran was taken by the Assyrians. *Rezeph.* Located south of the Euphrates River and northeast of Hamath. *Eden.* A district along the Euphrates River south of Haran (see Eze 27:23; Am 1:5), not to be confused with the Garden of Eden. It was incorporated into the Assyrian empire by Shalmaneser III in 855 B.C.
19:13 *Hamath ... Ivvah.* See note on 17:24.
19:14 *letter.* See 2Ch 32:17.
19:15 *enthroned between the cherubim.* See notes on Ex 25:18; 1Sa 4:4. *you alone are God.* See v. 19; Dt 4:35,39; see also 2Ki 18:33–35; Isa 43:11 and notes.
19:18 *fashioned by men's hands.* For the foolishness and futility of idolatry see Ps 115:3–8; 135:15–18; Isa 2:20; 40:19–20; 41:7; 44:9–20.
19:19 *that all kingdoms on earth may know.* Hezekiah recognizes that the Lord's reputation is at stake in the welfare of his covenant people (see 1Sa 12:22; see also Jos 7:9; 2Sa 7:23; Ps 23:3; Eze 5:13; 6:7 and notes).
19:20 *heard your prayer.* On this occasion Isaiah's message to Hezekiah was unsolicited by the king (contrast v. 2).
19:21–28 The arrogance of the Assyrians and their ridicule of the Israelites and their God are countered with a derisive pronouncement of judgment (cf. Ps 2) on the misconceived Assyrian pride (see Isa 10:5–34).
19:21 *Virgin Daughter of Zion ... Daughter of Jerusalem.* Better: "Virgin Daughter Zion ... Daughter Jerusalem"; in Hebrew poetry (mainly) a conventional way of referring to a royal city, a nation or a people when these are personified as a woman, found often in the prophetic literature, with special concentration in Lamentations.
19:22 *Holy One of Israel.* A designation of the God of Israel characteristic of Isaiah (see Lev 11:44; Isa 1:4 and notes).
19:23 *Lebanon ... its tallest cedars.* See note on 1Ki 5:6.
19:24 *dried up all the streams of Egypt.* A presumptuous boast for one who had not even conquered Egypt.

25 " 'Have you not heard?[z]
  Long ago I ordained it.
In days of old I planned[a] it;
  now I have brought it to pass,
that you have turned fortified cities
  into piles of stone.[b]
26 Their people, drained of power,[c]
  are dismayed[d] and put to shame.
They are like plants in the field,
  like tender green shoots,[e]
like grass sprouting on the roof,
  scorched[f] before it grows up.

27 " 'But I know[g] where you stay
  and when you come and go
  and how you rage against me.
28 Because you rage against me
  and your insolence has reached my
    ears,
I will put my hook[h] in your nose
  and my bit[i] in your mouth,
and I will make you return[j]
  by the way you came.'

29 "This will be the sign[k] for you, O Hezekiah:

"This year you will eat what grows by
    itself,[l]
  and the second year what springs
    from that.
But in the third year sow and reap,
  plant vineyards[m] and eat their fruit.
30 Once more a remnant[n] of the house of
    Judah
  will take root[o] below and bear fruit
    above.
31 For out of Jerusalem will come a
    remnant,[p]
  and out of Mount Zion a band of
    survivors.[q]
The zeal[r] of the LORD Almighty will accomplish this.

32 "Therefore this is what the LORD says
concerning the king of Assyria:

"He will not enter this city
  or shoot an arrow here.
He will not come before it with shield
  or build a siege ramp against it.
33 By the way that he came he will
    return;[s]
  he will not enter this city,
        declares the LORD.
34 I will defend[t] this city and save it,
  for my sake and for the sake of
    David[u] my servant."

35 That night the angel of the LORD[v] went
out and put to death a hundred and
eighty-five thousand men in the Assyrian
camp. When the people got up the next
morning—there were all the dead bodies![w] 36 So Sennacherib king of Assyria
broke camp and withdrew.[x] He returned
to Nineveh[y] and stayed there.

37 One day, while he was worshiping in
the temple of his god Nisroch, his sons
Adrammelech[z] and Sharezer cut him down
with the sword,[a] and they escaped to the
land of Ararat.[b] And Esarhaddon[c] his son
succeeded him as king.

19:25 [z]Isa 40:21,28 [a]Isa 22:11 [b]Mic 1:6 **19:26** [c]Isa 13:7; Eze 7:17; Zep 3:16 [d]Ps 6:10; 71:24; 83:17; Isa 41:23; Jer 8:9 [e]Isa 4:2; 11:1; 53:2; Jer 23:5 [f]Job 8:12; Ps 37:2; 129:6 **19:27** [g]Ps 139:1-4 **19:28** [h]2Ch 33:11; Eze 19:9; 29:4; 38:4; Am 4:2 [i]Isa 30:28 [j]ver 33 **19:29** [k]S Ex 7:9; S Dt 13:2; Lk 2:12 [l]Lev 25:5 [m]Ps 107:37; Isa 65:21; Am 9:14 **19:30** [n]S Ge 45:7 [o]Isa 5:24; 11:1; 27:6; Eze 17:22; Am 2:9 **19:31** [p]S Ge 45:7 [q]Isa 66:19; Zep 2:9; Zec 14:16 [r]Isa 9:7 **19:33** [s]ver 28 **19:34** [t]2Ki 20:6 [u]S 2Sa 7:15 **19:35** [v]S Ge 19:13; S Ex 12:23 [w]Job 24:24; Isa 17:14; 41:12; Na 3:3 **19:36** [x]S 2Ki 12:18 [y]S Ge 10:11 **19:37** [z]2Ki 17:31 [a]S ver 7 [b]S Ge 8:4 [c]S 2Ki 17:24

Hezekiah's Illness

20:1-11pp — 2Ch 32:24-26; Isa 38:1-8

20 In those days Hezekiah became ill
and was at the point of death. The
prophet Isaiah son of Amoz went to him
and said, "This is what the LORD says: Put
your house in order, because you are going to die; you will not recover."

19:25 *I ordained it . . . now I have brought it to pass.* The God of Israel is the ruler of all nations and history. The Assyrians attributed their victories to their own military superiority. However, Isaiah said that God alone ordained these victories (see Isa 10:5–19; cf. Eze 30:24–26).

19:28 *hook in your nose.* At the top of an Assyrian obelisk an Assyrian king (probably Esarhaddon, 681–669 B.C.) is pictured holding ropes attached to rings in the noses of four of his enemies. Here Isaiah portrays the same thing happening to Sennacherib (see note on Isa 37:29; cf. Eze 38:4; Am 4:2).

19:29 *This year you will eat what grows by itself.* Sennacherib had apparently either destroyed or confiscated the entire harvest that had been sown the previous fall. The people would only have use of the later, second growth that came from seeds dropped from the previous year's harvest (see Lev 25:5). This suggests that Sennacherib came to Judah in March or April about the time of harvest. *the second year what springs from that.* Sennacherib's departure would be too late in the fall (October) for new crops to be planted for the coming year. In the Holy Land, crops are normally sown in September and October. *in the third year sow and reap.* The routine times for sowing and harvesting could be observed in the following year. The third year is likely a reference to the third year of harvests detrimentally affected by the Assyrian presence.

19:30–31 *remnant.* See note on v. 4. For use of the term "remnant" as a designation for those who will participate in the future unfolding of God's redemptive program see Isa 11:11,16; 28:5; Mic 4:7; Ro 11:5.

19:32 *not enter this city.* Sennacherib, who was presently at Libnah (see v. 8; see also note on 8:22), would not be able to carry out his threats against Jerusalem (see note on 18:13).

19:34 *for the sake of David my servant.* See note on 1Ki 11:13.

19:35 *angel of the LORD.* See note on Ge 16:7. *a hundred and eighty-five thousand.* See Isa 37:36 and note.

19:36 *Nineveh.* The capital of the Assyrian empire.

19:37 *Adrammelech.* Ancient records refer to the murder of Sennacherib by his son Arad-Millissu who then escaped to the land of Urartu. *Ararat;* see note on Ge 8:4. *Esarhaddon his son succeeded him.* And reigned 681–669 B.C. (see chart, p. 472). Assyrian inscriptions speak of a struggle among Sennacherib's sons for the right of succession to the Assyrian throne. Sennacherib's designation of Esarhaddon as heir apparent, even though he was younger than several of his brothers, may have sparked the abortive attempt at a coup by Adrammelech and Sharezer.

20:1 *In those days.* Hezekiah's illness (vv. 1–11) as well as his reception of envoys from Babylon (vv. 12–19) must have preceded the Assyrian campaign in 701 B.C. (see v. 6; see also notes on vv. 12–13). Babylonian records indicate that Merodach-Baladan (v. 12) died in Elam after being expelled

2Hezekiah turned his face to the wall
and prayed to the LORD, 3"Remember,[d]
O LORD, how I have walked[e] before you
faithfully[f] and with wholehearted devotion and have done what is good in your
eyes." And Hezekiah wept bitterly.
4Before Isaiah had left the middle court,
the word of the LORD came to him: 5"Go
back and tell Hezekiah, the leader of my
people, 'This is what the LORD, the God
of your father David, says: I have heard[g]
your prayer and seen your tears;[h] I will
heal you. On the third day from now you
will go up to the temple of the LORD. 6I will
add fifteen years to your life. And I will
deliver you and this city from the hand of
the king of Assyria. I will defend[i] this city
for my sake and for the sake of my servant
David.' "
7Then Isaiah said, "Prepare a poultice
of figs." They did so and applied it to the
boil,[j] and he recovered.
8Hezekiah had asked Isaiah, "What will
be the sign that the LORD will heal me and
that I will go up to the temple of the LORD
on the third day from now?"
9Isaiah answered, "This is the LORD's
sign[k] to you that the LORD will do what
he has promised: Shall the shadow go
forward ten steps, or shall it go back ten
steps?"
10"It is a simple[l] matter for the shadow
to go forward ten steps," said Hezekiah.
"Rather, have it go back ten steps."
11Then the prophet Isaiah called upon
the LORD, and the LORD made the shadow
go back[m] the ten steps it had gone down
on the stairway of Ahaz.

Envoys From Babylon

20:12-19pp — Isa 39:1-8
20:20-21pp — 2Ch 32:32-33

12At that time Merodach-Baladan son
of Baladan king of Babylon sent Hezekiah
letters and a gift, because he had heard
of Hezekiah's illness. 13Hezekiah received
the messengers and showed them all that
was in his storehouses—the silver, the
gold, the spices and the fine oil—his armory and everything found among his
treasures. There was nothing in his palace
or in all his kingdom that Hezekiah did
not show them.
14Then Isaiah the prophet went to King
Hezekiah and asked, "What did those men
say, and where did they come from?"
"From a distant land," Hezekiah replied.
"They came from Babylon."
15The prophet asked, "What did they
see in your palace?"
"They saw everything in my palace,"
Hezekiah said. "There is nothing among
my treasures that I did not show them."
16Then Isaiah said to Hezekiah, "Hear
the word of the LORD: 17The time will surely come when everything in your palace,
and all that your fathers have stored up
until this day, will be carried off to Babylon.[n] Nothing will be left, says the LORD.

20:3 [d]S Ge 8:1; Ne 1:8; 5:19; 13:14 [e]S Ge 5:22 [f]S 1Ki 2:4; 2Ch 31:20 **20:5** [g]S 1Ki 9:3 [h]Ps 6:6, 8; 39:12; 56:8 **20:6** [i]S 2Ki 19:34; S 1Ch 17:19 **20:7** [j]S Ex 9:9 **20:9** [k]S Dt 13:2; Jer 44:29 **20:10** [l]S 2Ki 3:18 **20:11** [m]Jos 10:13; 2Ch 32:31 **20:17** [n]2Ki 24:13; 2Ch 36:10; Jer 20:5; 27:22; 52:17-23

from Babylon in 703. *Put your house in order.* Arrangements of a testamentary nature needed to be made, especially with respect to throne succession. *you are going to die.* Assuming that Hezekiah was 25 years old in 715 when he began his sole reign (see 18:2) and that his illness occurred a little more than 15 years prior to his death (see note on v. 6), he would have been about 37 or 38 years old at this time.

20:3 *walked before you faithfully … and have done what is good.* Hezekiah's prayer is not an appeal for divine favor that is based on good works, but it expresses the realization that the Lord graciously favors those who earnestly serve him (see note on 2Sa 22:21).

20:5 *I will heal you.* God is the one who sovereignly ordains all that comes to pass (Ps 139:16; Eph 1:11). Hezekiah's petition and God's response demonstrate that (1) divine sovereignty does not make prayer inappropriate but, on the contrary, establishes it, and (2) both prayer and the divine response to prayer are to be included in one's conception of God's sovereign plan (see 1Ki 21:29; Eze 33:13–16).

20:6 *add fifteen years to your life.* Hezekiah died in 686 B.C. The beginning of the extension of his life is thus to be placed no later than 702. *for my sake and for the sake of my servant David.* See 19:34; see also note on 1Ki 11:13.

20:7 *poultice.* The Lord healed Hezekiah (see v. 5), but divine healing does not necessarily exclude the use of known remedies.

20:9 *steps.* See v. 11 (see also note on Isa 38:8).

20:10 *simple matter … go forward.* Because that was the natural direction of the shadow's movement. Hezekiah chose the more difficult movement to make sure the sign was from the Lord.

20:11 *stairway of Ahaz.* Possibly refers to one leading to his house or to some kind of instrument used to measure time.

20:12 *Merodach-Baladan.* Means "(The god) Marduk has given me a son." He ruled in Babylon 721–710 B.C. before being forced to submit to Assyrian domination by Sargon II of Assyria. Sometime after Sargon's death in 705, Merodach-Baladan briefly reestablished Babylonian independence and ruled in Babylon until Sennacherib forced him to flee in 703 (see note on v. 1). *sent Hezekiah letters and a gift.* It is likely that Merodach-Baladan was attempting to draw Hezekiah into an alliance against Assyria. Although Hezekiah rejected the pro-Assyrian policies of his father Ahaz (see 16:7) and rebelled against Assyria (see 18:7), he erred in seeking to strengthen Israel's security by friendship with Babylon and Egypt (see 2Ch 32:31; Isa 30–31; see also notes on 1Sa 17:11; 1Ki 15:19).

20:13 *received the messengers and showed them all.* Hezekiah's reception of the delegation from Babylon was overly hospitable. Perhaps it was an attempt to bolster Judah's security by impressing the Babylonians with the wealth and power of his kingdom as a basis for mutual cooperation against the Assyrians. In principle this was a denial of the covenantal nature of the royal office in Israel (see note on 2Sa 24:1). *silver … oil.* The presence of these treasures in Jerusalem is evidence that this incident occurred before the payment of tribute to Sennacherib in 701 B.C. (see 18:15–16).

20:14 *What did those men say …?* Hezekiah gave no response to Isaiah's question concerning the diplomatic purpose of the Babylonian envoys.

20:17 *carried off to Babylon.* Hezekiah's reception of the Babylonians would bring the exact opposite of what he desired and expected. Isaiah's prediction of Babylonian exile

18 And some of your descendants,[o] your
own flesh and blood, that will be born to
you, will be taken away, and they will become eunuchs in the palace of the king of
Babylon."[p]
19 "The word of the LORD you have spoken is good," Hezekiah replied. For he
thought, "Will there not be peace and security in my lifetime?"
20 As for the other events of Hezekiah's
reign, all his achievements and how he
made the pool[q] and the tunnel[r] by which
he brought water into the city, are they not
written in the book of the annals of the
kings of Judah? 21 Hezekiah rested with his
fathers. And Manasseh his son succeeded
him as king.

Manasseh King of Judah

21:1-10pp — 2Ch 33:1-10
21:17-18pp — 2Ch 33:18-20

21 Manasseh was twelve years old when
he became king, and he reigned in
Jerusalem fifty-five years. His mother's
name was Hephzibah.[s] 2 He did evil[t] in
the eyes of the LORD, following the detestable practices[u] of the nations the LORD had
driven out before the Israelites. 3 He rebuilt
the high places[v] his father Hezekiah had
destroyed; he also erected altars to Baal[w]
and made an Asherah pole,[x] as Ahab king
of Israel had done. He bowed down to all
the starry hosts[y] and worshiped them. 4 He
built altars[z] in the temple of the LORD, of
which the LORD had said, "In Jerusalem I
will put my Name."[a] 5 In both courts[b] of
the temple of the LORD, he built altars to
all the starry hosts. 6 He sacrificed his own
son[c] in[a] the fire, practiced sorcery and divination,[d] and consulted mediums and spiritists.[e] He did much evil in the eyes of the
LORD, provoking[f] him to anger.
7 He took the carved Asherah pole[g] he
had made and put it in the temple,[h] of
which the LORD had said to David and to
his son Solomon, "In this temple and in
Jerusalem, which I have chosen out of all
the tribes of Israel, I will put my Name[i]
forever. 8 I will not again[j] make the feet of
the Israelites wander from the land I gave
their forefathers, if only they will be careful to do everything I commanded them
and will keep the whole Law that my servant Moses[k] gave them." 9 But the people
did not listen. Manasseh led them astray,
so that they did more evil[l] than the nations[m] the LORD had destroyed before the
Israelites.
10 The LORD said through his servants the
prophets: 11 "Manasseh king of Judah has
committed these detestable sins. He has
done more evil[n] than the Amorites[o] who
preceded him and has led Judah into sin
with his idols.[p] 12 Therefore this is what the
LORD, the God of Israel, says: I am going
to bring such disaster[q] on Jerusalem and
Judah that the ears of everyone who hears
of it will tingle.[r] 13 I will stretch out over
Jerusalem the measuring line used against

[a] 6 Or *He made his own son pass through*

20:18 [o] 2Ki 24:15; Da 1:3 [p] Mic 4:10 **20:20** [q] S 2Ki 18:17 [r] S 2Sa 5:8 **21:1** [s] Isa 62:4 **21:2** [t] ver 16; S Dt 4:25; Jer 15:4 [u] Dt 9:4; S 18:9; S 1Ki 14:24; 2Ki 16:3 **21:3** [v] S 1Ki 3:3; S 2Ki 18:4 [w] S Jdg 6:28 [x] S Dt 16:21 [y] S Ge 2:1; Dt 17:3; Jer 19:13 **21:4** [z] Isa 66:4; Jer 4:1; 7:30; 23:11; 32:34; Eze 23:39 [a] S Ex 20:24; S 2Sa 7:13 **21:5** [b] 1Ki 7:12; 2Ki 23:12 **21:6** [c] S Lev 18:21; S Dt 18:10; S 2Ki 3:27 [d] Dt 18:14 [e] S Lev 19:31 [f] 2Ki 23:26 **21:7** [g] Dt 16:21; 2Ki 23:4 [h] S Lev 15:31 [i] S Ex 20:24; S 2Sa 7:13 **21:8** [j] S 2Sa 7:10 [k] S 2Ki 18:12 **21:9** [l] S 1Ki 14:9; Eze 5:7 [m] Dt 9:4 **21:11** [n] S 1Ki 14:9 [o] S Ge 15:16 [p] Eze 18:12 **21:12** [q] 2Ki 23:26; 24:3; Jer 15:4; Eze 7:5 [r] S 1Sa 3:11

at least 115 years before it happened is all the more remarkable because, when he spoke, it appeared that Assyria rather than Babylon was the world power from whom Judah had the most to fear.

20:18 *some of your descendants ... will be taken away.* Hezekiah's own son Manasseh was taken by the Assyrians and held prisoner for a while in Babylon (see 2Ch 33:11); later, many more from the house of David were to follow (see 24:15; 25:7; Da 1:3).

20:19 *word ... is good.* Although it is possible to understand Hezekiah's statement as a selfish expression of relief that he himself would not experience the announced adversity, it seems better to take it as a humble acceptance of the Lord's judgment (see 2Ch 32:26) and as gratefulness for the intervening time of peace that the Lord in his mercy was granting to his people.

20:20 *the pool and the tunnel.* Hezekiah built a tunnel from the Gihon spring (see 1Ki 1:33,38) to a cistern (2Ch 32:30) inside the city's walls (see map No. 10 at the end of this study Bible). This greatly reduced Jerusalem's vulnerability to siege by guaranteeing a continuing water supply. In 1880 an inscription (the Siloam inscription; see chart, p. xxiii) was found in the rock wall at the southern exit of this tunnel, describing the method of its construction. The tunnel, cut through solid rock, is c. 1,750 feet long; its height varies from 4 feet to 12 feet and it averages 2 feet in width. *annals of the kings of Judah.* See note on 1Ki 14:29.

20:21 *rested with his fathers.* See note on 1Ki 1:21.

21:1 *twelve years old.* Thus Manasseh was born c. 709 B.C. *fifty-five years.* 697–642 B.C., including a ten-year coregency (697–686) with his father Hezekiah. This was the longest reign of any king in either Israel or Judah.

21:2 *detestable practices.* Manasseh reversed the religious policies of his father Hezekiah (see 18:3–5) and reverted to those of Ahaz (see 16:3).

21:3 *high places ... Hezekiah had destroyed.* See note on 18:4; see also 2Ch 31:1. *Asherah pole.* See 1Ki 14:15, 23; 15:13; 16:33. *as Ahab.* Manasseh was the Ahab of Judah (see 1Ki 16:30–33). *bowed down to all the starry hosts.* See note on 17:16.

21:4 *In Jerusalem I will put my Name.* See 1Ki 8:16; 9:3 and notes.

21:6 *sacrificed his own son.* See note on 16:3; see also 17:17; cf. 3:27 and note. *practiced sorcery and divination.* See notes on 16:15; 17:17. *consulted mediums and spiritists.* See Lev 19:31; Dt 18:11; 1Sa 28:3,7–9 and notes.

21:7 *carved Asherah pole.* See note on 1Ki 14:15. *David.* See 2Sa 7:13. *Solomon.* See 1Ki 9:3. *chosen out of all the tribes.* See 1Ki 11:13,32,36.

21:9 *nations the LORD had destroyed.* See 1Ki 14:24; Dt 12:29–31; 31:3.

21:10 *his servants the prophets.* See 2Ch 33:10,18.

21:11 *more evil than the Amorites.* See note on 1Ki 21:26. *idols.* See note on Lev 26:30.

21:12 *disaster on Jerusalem.* Fulfilled in the final destruction of the city by the Babylonians in 586 B.C. (see ch. 25). *ears of everyone ... will tingle.* See Jer 19:3 and note.

21:13 *measuring line ... plumb line.* Instruments normally associated with construction are used here as symbols of destruction (see Isa 34:11; Am 7:7–9,17).

Samaria and the plumb line[s] used against
the house of Ahab. I will wipe[t] out Jerusalem as one wipes a dish, wiping it and
turning it upside down. 14I will forsake[u]
the remnant[v] of my inheritance and hand
them over to their enemies. They will be
looted and plundered by all their foes,
15because they have done evil[w] in my eyes
and have provoked[x] me to anger from the
day their forefathers came out of Egypt until this day."
16Moreover, Manasseh also shed so
much innocent blood[y] that he filled Jerusalem from end to end—besides the sin
that he had caused Judah[z] to commit, so
that they did evil in the eyes of the LORD.
17As for the other events of Manasseh's
reign, and all he did, including the sin he
committed, are they not written in the
book of the annals of the kings of Judah?
18Manasseh rested with his fathers and
was buried in his palace garden,[a] the garden of Uzza. And Amon his son succeeded
him as king.

Amon King of Judah

21:19-24pp — 2Ch 33:21-25

19Amon was twenty-two years old when
he became king, and he reigned in Jerusalem two years. His mother's name was
Meshullemeth daughter of Haruz; she was
from Jotbah. 20He did evil[b] in the eyes of
the LORD, as his father Manasseh had
done. 21He walked in all the ways of his
father; he worshiped the idols his father
had worshiped, and bowed down to them.
22He forsook[c] the LORD, the God of his fathers, and did not walk[d] in the way of the
LORD.
23Amon's officials conspired against
him and assassinated[e] the king in his palace. 24Then the people of the land killed[f]
all who had plotted against King Amon,
and they made Josiah[g] his son king in his
place.
25As for the other events of Amon's
reign, and what he did, are they not written in the book of the annals of the kings
of Judah? 26He was buried in his grave in
the garden[h] of Uzza. And Josiah his son
succeeded him as king.

The Book of the Law Found

22:1-20pp — 2Ch 34:1-2,8-28

22 Josiah[i] was eight years old when he
became king, and he reigned in Jerusalem thirty-one years. His mother's name
was Jedidah daughter of Adaiah; she was
from Bozkath.[j] 2He did what was right[k] in
the eyes of the LORD and walked in all the
ways of his father David, not turning aside
to the right[l] or to the left.
3In the eighteenth year of his reign, King
Josiah sent the secretary, Shaphan[m] son of
Azaliah, the son of Meshullam, to the temple of the LORD. He said: 4"Go up to Hilkiah[n]

21:13 [s]Isa 28:17; 34:11; La 2:8; Am 7:7-9 [t]2Ki 23:27
21:14 [u]Ps 78:58-60; Jer 12:7; 23:33 [v]2Ki 19:4; Ezr 9:8; Ne 1:2; Isa 1:9; 10:21; Jer 6:9; 40:15; 42:2; 44:7,28; 50:20; Mic 2:12
21:15 [w]S Ex 32:22 [x]Jer 25:7
21:16 [y]2Ki 24:4; Job 22:14; Ps 10:11; 94:7; 106:38; Isa 29:15; 47:10; 59:3,7; Jer 2:34; 7:6; 19:4; 22:17; La 4:13; Eze 7:23; 8:12; 9:9; 22:3-4; Hos 4:2; Zep 1:12 [z]S ver 2,11
21:18 [a]ver 26; Est 1:5; 7:7
21:20 [b]1Ki 15:26
21:22 [c]S 1Sa 8:8 [d]1Ki 11:33
21:23 [e]S 2Ki 12:20
21:24 [f]2Ki 14:5 [g]2Ch 33:21; Zep 1:1
21:26 [h]S ver 18
22:1 [i]Jer 1:2; 25:3 [j]Jos 15:39
22:2 [k]S Dt 17:19; S 1Ki 14:8 [l]S Dt 5:32
22:3 [m]2Ch 34:20; Jer 39:14
22:4 [n]Ezr 7:1

21:14 *I will forsake.* In the sense of giving over to judgment (see Jer 12:7), not in the sense of abrogation of the covenant (see 1Sa 12:22; Isa 43:1–7). *remnant of my inheritance.* Upon the destruction of the northern kingdom, Judah had become the remnant of the Lord's inheritance (see 1Ki 8:51; Dt 4:20; 1Sa 10:1; Ps 28:9; see also note on 2Ki 19:4).

21:15 The history of Israel was a history of covenant breaking. With the reign of Manasseh the cup of God's wrath overflowed, and the judgment of exile from the land of promise (see note on 17:7–23) became inevitable (see 24:1–4).

21:16 *innocent blood.* A reference to godly people and perhaps even prophets who were martyred for opposition to Manasseh's evil practices (see vv. 10–11). According to a Jewish tradition (not otherwise substantiated) Isaiah was sawed in two during Manasseh's reign (cf. Heb 11:37).

21:17 *other events of Manasseh's reign.* See 2Ch 33:12–19. *annals of the kings of Judah.* See note on 1Ki 14:29.

21:18 *rested with his fathers.* See note on 1Ki 1:21. *Uzza.* Probably a shortened form of Uzziah (see NIV text note on 14:21; see also 2Ch 26:1 and note).

21:19 *two years.* 642–640 B.C. *Jotbah.* Some identify it with the Jotbathah of Nu 33:33–34 and Dt 10:7, near Ezion Geber. Others, including the church father Jerome, have located it in Judah.

21:20 *did evil.* Amon did not share in the change of heart that characterized his father Manasseh in the last days of his life (see 2Ch 33:12–19). He must have restored the idolatrous practices that Manasseh abolished because these were again in existence in the time of Josiah (see 23:5–7,12).

21:23 *conspired against him.* Whether this palace revolt was motivated by religious or political considerations is not known.

21:24 *people of the land.* The citizenry in general (see 11:14,18; 14:21; 23:30).

21:25 *annals of the kings of Judah.* See note on 1Ki 14:29.

21:26 *Uzza.* See note on v. 18.

22:1 *thirty-one years.* 640–609 B.C. (see note on 21:19). *Bozkath.* Located in Judah in the vicinity of Lachish (see Jos 15:39).

22:2 *ways of his father David.* See note on 18:3. Josiah was the last godly king of the Davidic line prior to the exile. Jeremiah, who prophesied during the time of Josiah (see Jer 1:2), spoke highly of him (Jer 22:15–16). Zephaniah also prophesied in the early days of his reign (Zep 1:1).

22:3 *eighteenth year.* 622 B.C. Josiah was then 26 years old (see v. 1). He had begun to serve the Lord faithfully at the age of 16 (the 8th year of his reign, 2Ch 34:3). When he was 20 years old (the 12th year of his reign, 2Ch 34:3), he had already begun to purge the land of its idolatrous practices. *secretary, Shaphan.* See note on 2Sa 8:17. Two additional individuals are mentioned as accompanying Shaphan in 2Ch 34:8. *Azaliah, the son of Meshullam.* This name has been found on a seal impression dating to Jeremiah's time.

22:4 *Hilkiah.* Father of Azariah and grandfather of Seraiah, the high priest executed at the time of the destruction of Jerusalem by the Babylonians (see 25:18–21). It is unlikely that this Hilkiah was also the father of Jeremiah (see Jer 1:1). *money ... the doorkeepers have collected.* Josiah used the method devised by Joash for collecting funds for the restoration of the temple (see 12:1–16; 2Ch 34:9).

the high priest and have him get ready
the money that has been brought into the
temple of the LORD, which the doorkeepers have collected[o] from the people. 5Have
them entrust it to the men appointed to supervise the work on the temple. And have
these men pay the workers who repair[p]
the temple of the LORD— 6the carpenters,
the builders and the masons. Also have
them purchase timber and dressed stone
to repair the temple.[q] 7But they need not
account for the money entrusted to them,
because they are acting faithfully."[r]
8Hilkiah the high priest said to Shaphan
the secretary, "I have found the Book of
the Law[s] in the temple of the LORD." He
gave it to Shaphan, who read it. 9Then
Shaphan the secretary went to the king
and reported to him: "Your officials have
paid out the money that was in the temple
of the LORD and have entrusted it to the
workers and supervisors at the temple."
10Then Shaphan the secretary informed
the king, "Hilkiah the priest has given me
a book." And Shaphan read from it in the
presence of the king.[t]
11When the king heard the words of the
Book of the Law,[u] he tore his robes. 12He
gave these orders to Hilkiah the priest,
Ahikam[v] son of Shaphan, Acbor son of Micaiah, Shaphan the secretary and Asaiah
the king's attendant:[w] 13"Go and inquire[x]
of the LORD for me and for the people
and for all Judah about what is written
in this book that has been found. Great
is the LORD's anger[y] that burns against us
because our fathers have not obeyed the
words of this book; they have not acted in
accordance with all that is written there
concerning us."
14Hilkiah the priest, Ahikam, Acbor,
Shaphan and Asaiah went to speak to the
prophetess[z] Huldah, who was the wife of
Shallum son of Tikvah, the son of Harhas,
keeper of the wardrobe. She lived in Jerusalem, in the Second District.
15She said to them, "This is what the
LORD, the God of Israel, says: Tell the man
who sent you to me, 16'This is what the
LORD says: I am going to bring disaster[a]
on this place and its people, according to
everything written in the book[b] the king
of Judah has read. 17Because they have
forsaken[c] me and burned incense to other gods and provoked me to anger by all
the idols their hands have made,[a] my anger will burn against this place and will
not be quenched.' 18Tell the king of Judah,
who sent you to inquire[d] of the LORD, 'This
is what the LORD, the God of Israel, says
concerning the words you heard: 19Be-
cause your heart was responsive and you
humbled[e] yourself before the LORD when
you heard what I have spoken against this
place and its people, that they would become accursed[f] and laid waste,[g] and because you tore your robes and wept in my
presence, I have heard you, declares the
LORD. 20Therefore I will gather you to your
fathers, and you will be buried in peace.[h]
Your eyes[i] will not see all the disaster I am
going to bring on this place.'"
So they took her answer back to the
king.

Josiah Renews the Covenant

23:1-3pp — 2Ch 34:29-32
23:4-20Ref — 2Ch 34:3-7,33
23:21-23pp — 2Ch 35:1,18-19
23:28-30pp — 2Ch 35:20-36:1

23 Then the king called together all the
elders of Judah and Jerusalem. 2He
went up to the temple of the LORD with the
men of Judah, the people of Jerusalem,

22:4 [o]2Ki 12:4-5 **22:5** [p]2Ki 12:5,11-14 **22:6** [q]2Ki 12:11-12 **22:7** [r]S 2Ki 12:15 **22:8** [s]S Dt 28:61; S 31:24; Gal 3:10 **22:10** [t]Jer 36:21 **22:11** [u]ver 8 **22:12** [v]2Ki 25:22; Jer 26:24; 39:14 [w]1Sa 8:14 **22:13** [x]S Ge 25:22; S 1Sa 9:9 [y]Dt 29:24-28; S 31:17; Isa 5:25; 42:25; Am 2:4 **22:14** [z]S Ex 15:20 **22:16** [a]S Dt 31:29; S Jos 23:15; Jer 6:19; 11:11; 18:11; 35:17 [b]Da 9:11 **22:17** [c]S 1Ki 9:9 **22:18** [d]Jer 21:2; 37:3,7 **22:19** [e]S Ex 10:3; Isa 57:15; 61:1; Mic 6:8 [f]Jer 24:9; 25:18; 26:6 [g]Lev 26:31 **22:20** [h]Isa 47:11; 57:1; Jer 18:11 [i]S 1Ki 21:29

[a] *17 Or by everything they have done*

22:5 *men appointed to supervise.* See 2Ch 34:12–13.
22:8 *Book of the Law.* Some interpreters hold that this refers to a copy of the entire Pentateuch, but more likely it is a reference to a copy of part or all of Deuteronomy alone (see Dt 31:24,26; 2Ch 34:14).
22:11 *tore his robes.* See notes on 18:37; Jos 7:6; contrast Josiah's reaction with that of Jehoiakim to the words of the scroll written by Jeremiah (see Jer 36:24). Perhaps the covenant curses of Dt 28, climaxing with the threat of exile, were the statements that especially disturbed Josiah.
22:12 *Ahikam son of Shaphan.* This official's name has been found on a seal impression dating to the time of Jeremiah. Ahikam was the father of Gedaliah, who was later to be appointed governor of Judah by Nebuchadnezzar (see 25:22; Jer 39:14). Ahikam was also the protector of Jeremiah when his life was threatened during the reign of Jehoiakim (see Jer 26:24 and note). *Acbor.* His son Elnathan is mentioned in 24:8; Jer 26:22; 36:12. *Shaphan the secretary.* See note on v. 3.
22:14 *prophetess Huldah.* For other OT prophetesses see notes on Ex 15:20; Jdg 4:4. *Shallum ... keeper of the wardrobe.* Perhaps the same Shallum who was the uncle of Jeremiah (see Jer 32:7). *Second District.* A section of the city (the Hebrew for this phrase is translated "New Quarter" in Zep 1:10) probably located in a newly developed area between the first and second walls in the northwest part of Jerusalem (see 2Ch 33:14; 34:22; Ne 11:9 and note).
22:16 *this place.* Jerusalem.
22:19 *your heart was responsive.* See v. 11.
22:20 *gather you to your fathers.* See note on 1Ki 1:21. *you will be buried in peace.* This prediction refers to Josiah's death before God's judgment on Jerusalem through Nebuchadnezzar and so is not contradicted by his death in battle with Pharaoh Neco of Egypt (see 23:29–30). Josiah was assured that the final judgment on Judah and Jerusalem would not come in his own days.
23:1 *elders.* See note on 10:1.
23:2 *prophets.* Here possibly the Levites (cf. 2Ch 34:30 and note) appointed to serve in the temple liturgy (cf. also note on 1Ch 25:1). *Book of the Covenant.* Although this designation is used in Ex 24:7 with reference to the contents of Ex 20–23, it is here applied to either all or part of the book of Deuteronomy. Whatever else the scroll contained, it clearly included the covenant curses of Dt 28 (see notes on v. 21; 22:8,11).

the priests and the prophets—all the people from the least to the greatest. He read[j]
in their hearing all the words of the Book
of the Covenant,[k] which had been found
in the temple of the LORD. 3The king stood
by the pillar[l] and renewed the covenant[m]
in the presence of the LORD—to follow[n]
the LORD and keep his commands, regulations and decrees with all his heart and
all his soul, thus confirming the words of
the covenant written in this book. Then
all the people pledged themselves to the
covenant.

4The king ordered Hilkiah the high
priest, the priests next in rank and the
doorkeepers[o] to remove[p] from the temple of the LORD all the articles made for
Baal and Asherah and all the starry hosts.
He burned them outside Jerusalem in the
fields of the Kidron Valley and took the
ashes to Bethel. 5He did away with the pagan priests appointed by the kings of Judah to burn incense on the high places of
the towns of Judah and on those around
Jerusalem—those who burned incense[q] to
Baal, to the sun and moon, to the constellations and to all the starry hosts.[r][s] 6He
took the Asherah pole from the temple of
the LORD to the Kidron Valley[t] outside Jerusalem and burned it there. He ground it
to powder[u] and scattered the dust over the
graves[v] of the common people.[w] 7He also
tore down the quarters of the male shrine
prostitutes,[x] which were in the temple of
the LORD and where women did weaving
for Asherah.

8Josiah brought all the priests from the
towns of Judah and desecrated the high
places, from Geba[y] to Beersheba, where
the priests had burned incense. He broke
down the shrines[a] at the gates—at the entrance to the Gate of Joshua, the city governor, which is on the left of the city gate.
9Although the priests of the high places
did not serve[z] at the altar of the LORD in Jerusalem, they ate unleavened bread with
their fellow priests.

10He desecrated Topheth,[a] which was
in the Valley of Ben Hinnom,[b] so no one
could use it to sacrifice his son[c] or daughter in[b] the fire to Molech. 11He removed
from the entrance to the temple of the
LORD the horses that the kings of Judah[d]
had dedicated to the sun. They were in the
court near the room of an official named
Nathan-Melech. Josiah then burned the
chariots dedicated to the sun.[e]

12He pulled down[f] the altars the kings
of Judah had erected on the roof[g] near
the upper room of Ahaz, and the altars
Manasseh had built in the two courts[h] of
the temple of the LORD. He removed them
from there, smashed them to pieces and
threw the rubble into the Kidron Valley.[i]
13The king also desecrated the high places
that were east of Jerusalem on the south of
the Hill of Corruption—the ones Solomon[j]
king of Israel had built for Ashtoreth the
vile goddess of the Sidonians, for Chemosh
the vile god of Moab, and for Molech[c] the
detestable[k] god of the people of Ammon.[l]

[a] 8 Or *high places* [b] 10 Or *to make his son or daughter pass through* [c] 13 Hebrew *Milcom*

23:2 [j] S Dt 31:11 [k] S Ex 24:7
23:3 [l] S 1Ki 7:15 [m] S 2Ki 11:12 [n] S Dt 13:4
23:4 [o] 2Ki 25:18; Jer 35:4 [p] S 2Ki 21:7
23:5 [q] S 2Ki 16:4 [r] Jer 8:2 [s] Jer 43:13
23:6 [t] Jer 31:40 [u] S Ex 32:20 [v] S Nu 19:16 [w] Jer 26:23
23:7 [x] S Ge 38:21; 1Ki 14:24; Eze 16:16
23:8 [y] S Jos 18:24; S 1Ki 15:22
23:9 [z] Eze 44:10-14
23:10 [a] Isa 30:33; Jer 7:31,32; 19:6 [b] S Jos 15:8 [c] S Lev 18:21; S Dt 18:10
23:11 [d] ver 5,19; Ne 9:34; Jer 44:9 [e] S Dt 4:19
23:12 [f] 2Ch 33:15 [g] Jer 19:13; Zep 1:5 [h] S 2Ki 21:5 [i] S 2Sa 15:23
23:13 [j] 1Ki 11:7 [k] S Dt 27:15 [l] Jer 11:13

23:3 *pillar.* See note on 11:14. *renewed the covenant.* Josiah carries out the function of covenant mediator; cf. Moses (Ex 24:3–8; Deuteronomy), Joshua (Jos 24), Samuel (1Sa 11:14—12:25) and Jehoiada (2Ki 11:17). *follow the LORD.* See notes on 1Sa 12:14,20. *pledged themselves to the covenant.* It is likely that some sort of ratification rite was performed, in which the people participated and pledged by oath to be loyal to the covenant. Whether this was done symbolically (see Jer 34:18) or verbally (see Dt 27:11–26) is not clear.

23:4 *doorkeepers.* See 12:9. *Baal and Asherah.* See note on 1Ki 14:15. *starry hosts.* See note on 17:16. *Kidron Valley.* See note on Isa 22:7 and map, p. 477; see also 1Ki 15:13 and note. *took the ashes to Bethel.* See vv. 15–16. Bethel was located just over the border between Judah and the former northern kingdom in territory nominally under Assyrian control. With a decline in Assyrian power, Josiah was able to exert his own influence in the north. He apparently deposited the ashes at Bethel in order to desecrate (see note on v. 14) the very place where golden calf worship had originally polluted the land (see notes on 1Ki 12:28–30).

23:5 *pagan priests.* See Hos 10:5; Zep 1:4. *kings of Judah.* A reference to Manasseh and Amon, and perhaps to Ahaz before them. *high places.* See note on 18:4.

23:6 *Asherah pole.* See note on 1Ki 14:15. The Asherah poles destroyed by Hezekiah (18:4) were reintroduced by Manasseh (21:7). When Manasseh turned to the Lord, it is likely that he too got rid of the Asherah poles (see 2Ch 33:15) and that they were then again reintroduced by Amon (2Ki 21:21; 2Ch 33:22). *scattered the dust over the graves of the common people.* Intended as a defilement of the goddess, not as a desecration of the graves of the poor (see Jer 26:23).

23:7 *male shrine prostitutes.* See note on 1Ki 14:24.

23:8 *desecrated the high places.* See note on 18:4. *Geba to Beersheba.* Geba was on the northern border of the southern kingdom (see 1Ki 15:22), and Beersheba was on its southern border (see note on 1Sa 3:20).

23:9 *ate unleavened bread with their fellow priests.* Although not permitted to serve at the temple altar, these priests were to be sustained by a share of the priestly provisions (see Lev 2:10; 6:16–18). They occupied a status similar to that of priests with physical defects (see Lev 21:16–23).

23:10 *Topheth ... Molech.* See note on 1Ki 11:5. Topheth was an area in the Valley of Hinnom where altars used for child sacrifice were located (see Isa 30:33; Jer 7:31; 19:5–6 and notes). *sacrifice his son or daughter.* See 17:17; 21:6; see also note on 16:3.

23:11 *horses ... dedicated to the sun.* If live, the horses may have been used to pull chariots bearing images of a sun-god in religious processions. Small images of horses have recently been found in a pagan shrine just outside one of the ancient walls of Jerusalem. *Nathan-Melech.* Perhaps the official in charge of the chariots. His name has been found on a seal impression dating to the late seventh century B.C.

23:12 *altars ... on the roof.* Altars dedicated to the worship of all the starry hosts (see Jer 19:13; Zep 1:5)—erected by Ahaz (2Ki 16:3–4,10–16), Manasseh (21:3) and Amon (21:21–22).

23:13 *high places ... Solomon ... had built.* See note on 1Ki 11:5.

14Josiah smashed[m] the sacred stones and
cut down the Asherah poles and covered
the sites with human bones.[n]
15Even the altar[o] at Bethel, the high
place made by Jeroboam[p] son of Nebat, who had caused Israel to sin—even
that altar and high place he demolished.
He burned the high place and ground it
to powder, and burned the Asherah pole
also. 16Then Josiah[q] looked around, and
when he saw the tombs that were there
on the hillside, he had the bones removed
from them and burned on the altar to defile it, in accordance[r] with the word of the
LORD proclaimed by the man of God who
foretold these things.
17The king asked, "What is that tombstone I see?"
The men of the city said, "It marks the
tomb of the man of God who came from
Judah and pronounced against the altar
of Bethel the very things you have done
to it."
18"Leave it alone," he said. "Don't let
anyone disturb his bones[s]." So they spared
his bones and those of the prophet[t] who
had come from Samaria.
19Just as he had done at Bethel, Josiah removed and defiled all the shrines at
the high places that the kings of Israel had
built in the towns of Samaria that had provoked the LORD to anger. 20Josiah slaughtered[u] all the priests of those high places
on the altars and burned human bones[v] on
them. Then he went back to Jerusalem.
21The king gave this order to all the people: "Celebrate the Passover[w] to the LORD
your God, as it is written in this Book of
the Covenant."[x] 22Not since the days of the
judges who led Israel, nor throughout the
days of the kings of Israel and the kings
of Judah, had any such Passover been
observed. 23But in the eighteenth year of
King Josiah, this Passover was celebrated
to the LORD in Jerusalem.[y]
24Furthermore, Josiah got rid of the mediums and spiritists,[z] the household gods,[a]
the idols and all the other detestable[b]
things seen in Judah and Jerusalem. This
he did to fulfill the requirements of the law
written in the book that Hilkiah the priest
had discovered in the temple of the LORD.
25Neither before nor after Josiah was there
a king like him who turned[c] to the LORD
as he did—with all his heart and with all
his soul and with all his strength, in accordance with all the Law of Moses.[d]
26Nevertheless, the LORD did not turn
away from the heat of his fierce anger,[e]
which burned against Judah because of
all that Manasseh[f] had done to provoke
him to anger. 27So the LORD said, "I will
remove[g] Judah also from my presence[h]
as I removed Israel, and I will reject[i] Jerusalem, the city I chose, and this temple, about which I said, 'There shall my
Name be.'[a]"
28As for the other events of Josiah's
reign, and all he did, are they not written
in the book of the annals of the kings of
Judah?
29While Josiah was king, Pharaoh Neco[j]
king of Egypt went up to the Euphrates
River to help the king of Assyria. King Josiah marched out to meet him in battle, but
Neco faced him and killed him at Megiddo.[k]

[a] 27 1 Kings 8:29

23:14 [m]S Ex 23:24 [n]S Nu 19:16; S Ps 53:5
23:15 [o]S Jos 7:2; 1Ki 13:1-3 [p]S 1Ki 12:33
23:16 [q]S 1Ki 13:2 [r]1Ki 13:32
23:18 [s]1Ki 13:31 [t]1Ki 13:29
23:20 [u]S Ex 22:20; S 2Ki 11:18 [v]S 1Ki 13:2
23:21 [w]S Ex 12:11; Dt 16:1-8 [x]S Ex 24:7
23:23 [y]S Ex 12:11; S Nu 28:16
23:24 [z]S Lev 19:31; S Dt 18:11 [a]S Ge 31:19 [b]Dt 7:26; 2Ki 16:3
23:25 [c]S 1Sa 7:3 [d]Jer 22:15
23:26 [e]2Ki 21:6; Jer 23:20; 30:24 [f]S 2Ki 21:12
23:27 [g]2Ki 21:13 [h]S Ex 33:15; 2Ki 24:3 [i]Jer 27:10; 32:31
23:29 [j]ver 33-35; Jer 46:2 [k]2Ki 9:27

23:14 *covered the sites with human bones.* The bones would defile these sites and make them unsuitable for pagan use in the future (see Nu 19:16).
23:15 *altar at Bethel.* See 1Ki 12:32–33. Nothing is said of the golden calf, which undoubtedly had been sent to Assyria as tribute at the time of the captivity of the northern kingdom (see Hos 10:5–6).
23:16 *tombs.* Of the priests of the Bethel sanctuary (see 1Ki 13:2). *burned on the altar to defile it.* See notes on vv. 6,14. *the man of God who foretold these things.* See 1Ki 13:1–2,32.
23:18 *prophet who had come from Samaria.* See 1Ki 13:31–32. Samaria is here not to be understood as the city by that name since the prophet came from Bethel (see 1Ki 13:11), and the city Samaria did not yet exist (see 1Ki 16:24). Rather, it is to be taken as a designation for the entire area of the former northern kingdom (see notes on 17:24,29; 1Ki 13:32).
23:20 *slaughtered all the priests of those high places.* These were non-Levitical priests of the apostate worship practiced in the area of the former northern kingdom (see notes on 17:27–28,33–34). They were treated like the pagan priests of Judah (see v. 5) in contrast to Josiah's treatment of the priests at the high places in Judah (see vv. 8–9). Josiah's actions in this matter conformed to the requirements of Dt 13; 17:2–7.
23:21 *Celebrate the Passover.* A more complete description of this observance is found in 2Ch 35:1–19. *as it is written in this Book of the Covenant.* See note on v. 2. This appears to refer to Dt 16:1–8, where the Passover is described in a communal setting at a sanctuary (see Ex 23:15–17; 34:23–24; Lev 23:4–14) rather than in the family setting of Ex 12:1–14,43–49.
23:22 The uniqueness of Josiah's Passover celebration seems to be in the fact that all the Passover lambs were slaughtered exclusively by the Levites (see 2Ch 35:1–19; cf. 2Ch 30:2–3,17–20 for the Passover observed in the time of Hezekiah).
23:23 *eighteenth year.* See note on 22:3.
23:24 *household gods.* See note on Ge 31:19. *idols.* See Lev 26:30. *requirements of the law.* See notes on v. 2; 22:8.
23:25 *was there a king like him.* See note on 18:5. *with all his heart… soul and… strength.* See Dt 6:5.
23:26 *Nevertheless, the LORD did not turn away from the heat of his fierce anger.* The judgment against Judah and Jerusalem was postponed but not rescinded because of Josiah's reformation (see notes on 21:15; 22:20).
23:27 *as I removed Israel.* See 17:18–23. *Jerusalem, the city I chose.* See 21:4,7,13. *this temple, about which I said, 'There shall my Name be.'* See note on 1Ki 8:16.
23:28 *annals of the kings of Judah.* See note on 1Ki 14:29.
23:29 *Pharaoh Neco king of Egypt.* Ruled 610–595 B.C. *help the king of Assyria.* Pharaoh Neco intended to help Ashur-Uballit II, the last Assyrian king, in his struggle against the rising power of Babylon under Nabopolassar. The Assyrian capital, Nineveh, had already fallen to the Babylonians and Medes in

Nebuchadnezzar's Campaigns Against Judah

605–586 B.C.

Events in Judah moved swiftly following the death of Josiah. Pharaoh Neco pressed his advantage by deporting Jehoahaz, the new ruler, and appointing a second son of Josiah, Jehoiakim, as king.

LYDIA

Haran

Tiphsah

Hamath

Riblah

Great Sea

The prophet Jeremiah was taken to Egypt by Judahite refugees fleeing from Babylonian-controlled territory. They brought him to Tahpanhes, where he continued his prophecies.

Sidon

Tyre

Tahpanhes

Migdol

AMMON

JUDAH

Jerusalem

KEDAR

EDOM

On

Memphis

Wadi of Egypt

EGYPT

CONQUEST OF JERUSALEM c. 597 B.C.

Route of main Babylonian army

Captives deported

Raids by Babylonian allies 602 B.C.

Sea of Galilee

Megiddo

Samaria

Shechem

Shiloh

Great Sea

Mizpah

Gibeon

Ramah

Jerusalem

Azekah

Lachish

Hebron

Dead Sea

Miles 10 5 0 10 20

Kms 10 5 0 10 20 30

Soon a stronger power appeared in the north in the person of Nebuchadnezzar, king of the Chaldeans (Neo-Babylonians), who determined to follow the fierce policies of his Assyrian predecessors.

The tribute of Jehoiakim was paid at a distance when he heard of Nebuchadnezzar's approach. After three years as a Babylonian vassal, he rebelled, bringing a rapid response in the form of small-scale raids from Babylonians, Arameans, Moabites and Ammonites (c. 602 B.C.). Finally, Nebuchadnezzar's forces controlled all of the coastal territory north of the Wadi of Egypt.

When 18-year-old Jehoiachin had ruled just three months (597 B.C.), the main Babylonian army struck, capturing Jerusalem and exiling the king as a captive in Babylon. Ten thousand persons were deported.

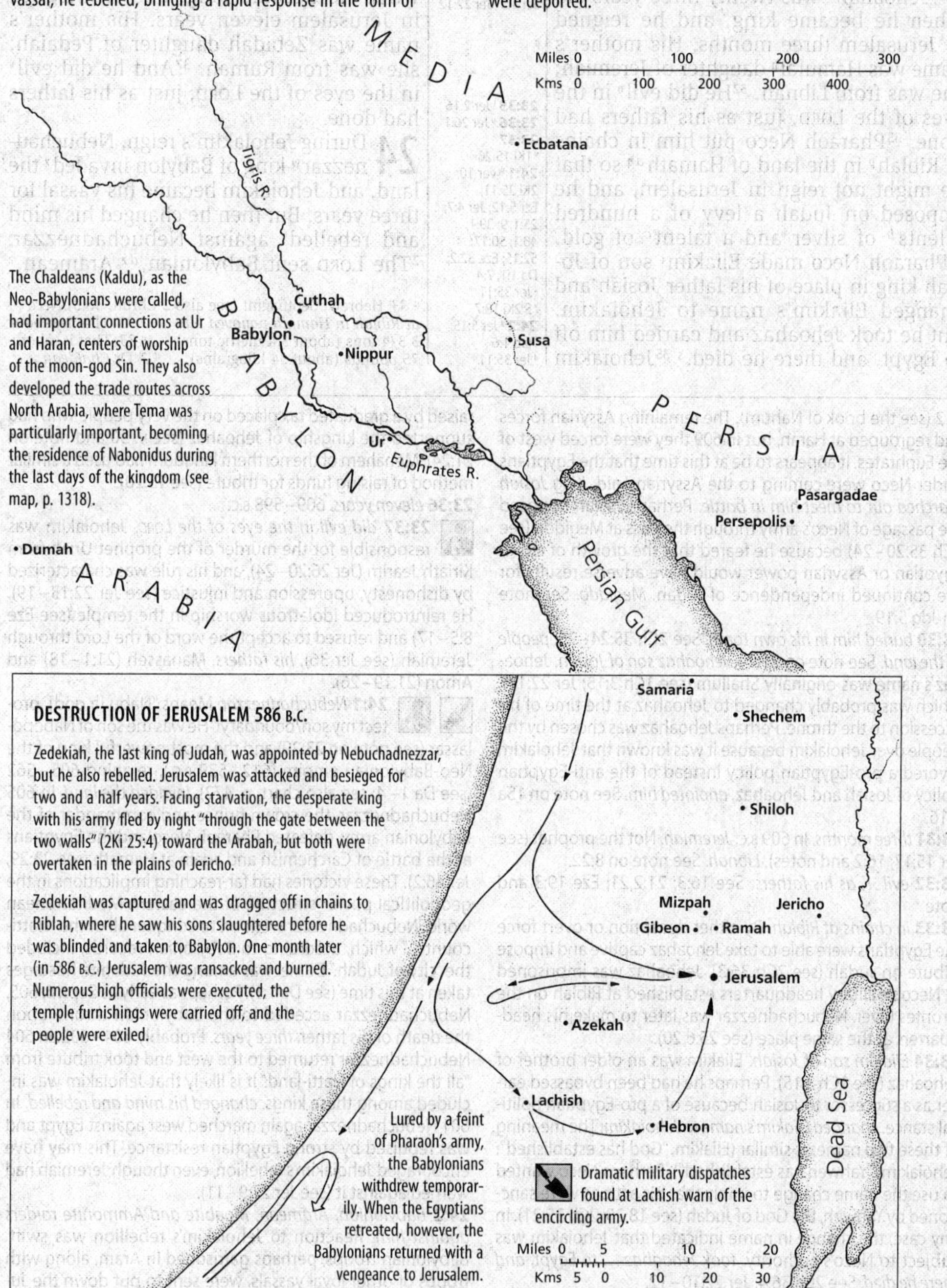

The Chaldeans (Kaldu), as the Neo-Babylonians were called, had important connections at Ur and Haran, centers of worship of the moon-god Sin. They also developed the trade routes across North Arabia, where Tema was particularly important, becoming the residence of Nabonidus during the last days of the kingdom (see map, p. 1318).

DESTRUCTION OF JERUSALEM 586 B.C.

Zedekiah, the last king of Judah, was appointed by Nebuchadnezzar, but he also rebelled. Jerusalem was attacked and besieged for two and a half years. Facing starvation, the desperate king with his army fled by night "through the gate between the two walls" (2Ki 25:4) toward the Arabah, but both were overtaken in the plains of Jericho.

Zedekiah was captured and was dragged off in chains to Riblah, where he saw his sons slaughtered before he was blinded and taken to Babylon. One month later (in 586 B.C.) Jerusalem was ransacked and burned. Numerous high officials were executed, the temple furnishings were carried off, and the people were exiled.

Lured by a feint of Pharaoh's army, the Babylonians withdrew temporarily. When the Egyptians retreated, however, the Babylonians returned with a vengeance to Jerusalem.

Dramatic military dispatches found at Lachish warn of the encircling army.

30 Josiah's servants brought his body in a
chariot[l] from Megiddo to Jerusalem and
buried him in his own tomb. And the people of the land took Jehoahaz son of Josiah and anointed him and made him king
in place of his father.

Jehoahaz King of Judah

23:31-34pp — 2Ch 36:2-4

31 Jehoahaz[m] was twenty-three years old
when he became king, and he reigned
in Jerusalem three months. His mother's
name was Hamutal[n] daughter of Jeremiah;
she was from Libnah. 32 He did evil[o] in the
eyes of the LORD, just as his fathers had
done. 33 Pharaoh Neco put him in chains
at Riblah[p] in the land of Hamath[a][q] so that
he might not reign in Jerusalem, and he
imposed on Judah a levy of a hundred
talents[b] of silver and a talent[c] of gold.
34 Pharaoh Neco made Eliakim[r] son of Josiah king in place of his father Josiah and
changed Eliakim's name to Jehoiakim.
But he took Jehoahaz and carried him off
to Egypt, and there he died.[s] 35 Jehoiakim
paid Pharaoh Neco the silver and gold he
demanded. In order to do so, he taxed the
land and exacted the silver and gold from
the people of the land according to their
assessments.[t]

Jehoiakim King of Judah

23:36 – 24:6pp — 2Ch 36:5-8

36 Jehoiakim[u] was twenty-five years old
when he became king, and he reigned
in Jerusalem eleven years. His mother's
name was Zebidah daughter of Pedaiah;
she was from Rumah. 37 And he did evil[v]
in the eyes of the LORD, just as his fathers
had done.

24 During Jehoiakim's reign, Nebuchadnezzar[w] king of Babylon invaded[x] the
land, and Jehoiakim became his vassal for
three years. But then he changed his mind
and rebelled[y] against Nebuchadnezzar.
2 The LORD sent Babylonian,[d][z] Aramean,[a]

23:30 [l] S 2Ki 9:28 **23:31** [m] 1Ch 3:15; Jer 22:11 [n] 2Ki 24:18 **23:32** [o] 1Ki 15:26 **23:33** [p] S Nu 34:11 [q] 1Ki 8:65 **23:34** [r] 2Ki 24:6; 1Ch 3:15; 2Ch 36:5-8; Jer 1:3 [s] Jer 22:12 **23:35** [t] Jer 2:16 **23:36** [u] Jer 26:1 **23:37** [v] 1Ki 15:26 **24:1** [w] ver 10; 2Ki 25:11; Ezr 5:12; Jer 4:7; 25:1,9; 39:1; 40:1; 50:17; 52:15; Eze 32:2; Da 1:1; 7:4 [x] Jer 35:11 [y] S 2Ki 18:7 **24:2** [z] Jer 5:15; Hab 1:6 [a] Jer 35:11

[a] 33 Hebrew; Septuagint (see also 2 Chron. 36:3) *Neco at Riblah in Hamath removed him* [b] 33 That is, about 3 3/4 tons (about 3.4 metric tons) [c] 33 That is, about 75 pounds (about 34 kilograms) [d] 2 Or *Chaldean*

---

612 (see the book of Nahum). The remaining Assyrian forces had regrouped at Haran, but in 609 they were forced west of the Euphrates. It appears to be at this time that the Egyptians under Neco were coming to the Assyrians' aid. *King Josiah marched out to meet him in battle.* Perhaps Josiah opposed the passage of Neco's army through the pass at Megiddo (see 2Ch 35:20 – 24) because he feared that the growth of either Egyptian or Assyrian power would have adverse results for the continued independence of Judah. *Megiddo.* See note on Jdg 5:19.

23:30 *buried him in his own tomb.* See 2Ch 35:24 – 25. *people of the land.* See note on 21:24. *Jehoahaz son of Josiah.* Jehoahaz's name was originally Shallum (see 1Ch 3:15; Jer 22:11), which was probably changed to Jehoahaz at the time of his accession to the throne. Perhaps Jehoahaz was chosen by the people over Jehoiakim because it was known that Jehoiakim favored a pro-Egyptian policy instead of the anti-Egyptian policy of Josiah and Jehoahaz. *anointed him.* See note on 1Sa 9:16.

23:31 *three months.* In 609 B.C. *Jeremiah.* Not the prophet (see Jer 15:17; 16:2 and notes). *Libnah.* See note on 8:22.

23:32 *evil … as his fathers.* See 16:3; 21:2,21; Eze 19:3 and note.

23:33 *in chains at Riblah.* By either deception or overt force the Egyptians were able to take Jehoahaz captive and impose tribute on Judah (see 2Ch 36:3). Jehoahaz was imprisoned at Neco's military headquarters established at Riblah on the Orontes River. Nebuchadnezzar was later to make his headquarters at the same place (see 25:6,20).

23:34 *Eliakim son of Josiah.* Eliakim was an older brother of Jehoahaz (see 1Ch 3:15). Perhaps he had been bypassed earlier as a successor to Josiah because of a pro-Egyptian political stance. *changed Eliakim's name to Jehoiakim.* The meaning of these two names is similar (Eliakim, "God has established"; Jehoiakim, "Yahweh has established"). Perhaps Neco wanted to use the name change to imply that his actions were sanctioned by Yahweh, the God of Judah (see 18:25; 2Ch 35:21). In any case, the change in name indicated that Jehoiakim was subject to Neco's authority. *took Jehoahaz … to Egypt, and there he died.* See 2Ch 36:4; Jer 22:10 – 12.

23:35 *from the people of the land.* The tribute for Neco was raised by a graduated tax placed on the very people who had supported the kingship of Jehoahaz (see v. 30 and note on 21:24). Menahem of the northern kingdom had used a similar method of raising funds for tribute (see 15:20).

23:36 *eleven years.* 609 – 598 B.C.

23:37 *did evil in the eyes of the LORD.* Jehoiakim was responsible for the murder of the prophet Uriah from Kiriath Jearim (Jer 26:20 – 24), and his rule was characterized by dishonesty, oppression and injustice (see Jer 22:13 – 19). He reintroduced idolatrous worship in the temple (see Eze 8:5 – 17) and refused to accept the word of the Lord through Jeremiah (see Jer 36). *his fathers.* Manasseh (21:1 – 18) and Amon (21:19 – 26).

24:1 *Nebuchadnezzar.* Means "Nabu [a god], protect my son/boundary!" He was the son of Nabopolassar (see note on 23:29) and the most powerful king of the Neo-Babylonian empire (612 – 539 B.C.), reigning 605 – 562 (see Da 1 – 4; see also chart, p. 472). *invaded the land.* In 605 Nebuchadnezzar, the crown prince and commander of the Babylonian army, defeated Pharaoh Neco and the Egyptians at the battle of Carchemish and again at Hamath (see 23:29; Jer 46:2). These victories had far-reaching implications in the geopolitical power structure of the eastern Mediterranean world. Nebuchadnezzar went on to conquer all of the "Hatti-country," which, according to Babylonian records, included the "city of Judah." Daniel was among the Judahite hostages taken at this time (see Da 1:1). Perhaps as early as Sept. 6, 605, Nebuchadnezzar acceded to the Babylonian throne upon the death of his father. *three years.* Probably 604 – 602. In 604 Nebuchadnezzar returned to the west and took tribute from "all the kings of Hatti-land." It is likely that Jehoiakim was included among these kings. *changed his mind and rebelled.* In 601 Nebuchadnezzar again marched west against Egypt and was repulsed by strong Egyptian resistance. This may have encouraged Jehoiakim's rebellion, even though Jeremiah had warned against it (see Jer 27:9 – 11).

24:2 *Babylonian, Aramean, Moabite and Ammonite raiders against him.* Reaction to Jehoiakim's rebellion was swift. Babylonian troops, perhaps garrisoned in Aram, along with troops of other loyal vassals, were sent to put down the Judahite rebellion.

Moabite and Ammonite raiders[b] against
him. He sent them to destroy[c] Judah, in
accordance with the word of the LORD
proclaimed by his servants the prophets.[d]
3Surely these things happened to Judah
according to the LORD's command,[e] in order to remove them from his presence[f] because of the sins of Manasseh[g] and all he
had done, 4including the shedding of innocent blood.[h] For he had filled Jerusalem
with innocent blood, and the LORD was
not willing to forgive.[i]

5As for the other events of Jehoiakim's
reign,[j] and all he did, are they not written in the book of the annals of the kings
of Judah? 6Jehoiakim rested[k] with his fathers. And Jehoiachin[l] his son succeeded
him as king.

7The king of Egypt[m] did not march out
from his own country again, because the
king of Babylon[n] had taken all his territory, from the Wadi of Egypt to the Euphrates River.

Jehoiachin King of Judah

24:8-17pp — 2Ch 36:9-10

8Jehoiachin[o] was eighteen years old
when he became king, and he reigned
in Jerusalem three months. His mother's
name was Nehushta[p] daughter of Elnathan; she was from Jerusalem. 9He did
evil[q] in the eyes of the LORD, just as his
father had done.

10At that time the officers of Nebuchadnezzar[r] king of Babylon advanced on Jerusalem and laid siege to it, 11and Nebuchadnezzar himself came up to the city while
his officers were besieging it. 12Jehoiachin
king of Judah, his mother, his attendants,
his nobles and his officials all surrendered[s]
to him.

In the eighth year of the reign of the king
of Babylon, he took Jehoiachin prisoner.
13As the LORD had declared,[t] Nebuchadnezzar removed all the treasures[u] from
the temple of the LORD and from the royal
palace, and took away all the gold articles[v]
that Solomon[w] king of Israel had made for
the temple of the LORD. 14He carried into
exile[x] all Jerusalem: all the officers and
fighting men,[y] and all the craftsmen and
artisans — a total of ten thousand. Only
the poorest[z] people of the land were left.

15Nebuchadnezzar took Jehoiachin[a]
captive to Babylon. He also took from Jerusalem to Babylon the king's mother,[b] his
wives, his officials and the leading men[c]
of the land. 16The king of Babylon also deported to Babylon the entire force of seven
thousand fighting men, strong and fit for
war, and a thousand craftsmen and artisans.[d] 17He made Mattaniah, Jehoiachin's
uncle, king in his place and changed his
name to Zedekiah.[e]

Zedekiah King of Judah

24:18-20pp — 2Ch 36:11-16; Jer 52:1-3

18Zedekiah[f] was twenty-one years old
when he became king, and he reigned
in Jerusalem eleven years. His mother's
name was Hamutal[g] daughter of Jeremiah; she was from Libnah. 19He did evil[h]
in the eyes of the LORD, just as Jehoiakim
had done. 20It was because of the LORD's
anger that all this happened to Jerusalem
and Judah, and in the end he thrust[i] them
from his presence.[j]

24:2 [b]S 2Ki 5:2 [c]Isa 28:18-19 [d]Jer 12:7-9; 25:1; 26:1; 36:1; Eze 23:23; Da 1:2 **24:3** [e]S 2Ki 18:25 [f]2Ki 13:23 [g]S 1Ki 14:9; S 2Ki 21:12; Jer 15:4 **24:4** [h]S 2Ki 21:16; Jer 22:3 [i]S Ex 23:21; La 3:42 **24:5** [j]Jer 22:18-19 **24:6** [k]Jer 22:19; 36:30 [l]1Ch 3:16; Jer 22:24,28; Eze 19:1 **24:7** [m]S Ge 15:18; S 2Ki 18:21; S Jer 46:25 [n]Jer 1:14; 25:9; 46:24 **24:8** [o]1Ch 3:16; Jer 22:24; 37:1 [p]ver 15; Jer 13:18; 22:26; 29:2 **24:9** [q]1Ki 15:26 **24:10** [r]S ver 1 **24:12** [s]2Ki 25:27; Jer 13:18; 22:24-30; 24:1; 29:2 **24:13** [t]2Ki 20:17 [u]2Ki 25:15; Isa 39:6; 42:22 [v]2Ki 25:14; Ezr 1:7; Isa 39:6; Jer 15:13; 17:3; 20:5; 27:16; 28:3; Eze 7:21; Da 1:2; 5:2,23; Zep 1:13 [w]S 1Ki 7:51 **24:14** [x]S Dt 28:36; S 2Ch 36:20; S Mt 1:11 [y]Isa 3:1-3 [z]Dt 15:11; 2Ki 25:12; Job 5:16; Ps 9:18; Jer 40:7; 52:16 **24:15** [a]S 2Ki 20:18; Eze 19:9 [b]S ver 8; S 1Ki 2:19 [c]Est 2:6; Isa 39:7; La 2:9; Eze 1:2; 17:12-14; Da 1:3 **24:16** [d]Ezr 2:1; Jer 24:1 **24:17** [e]1Ch 3:15; 2Ch 36:11; Jer 1:3; 37:1; 52:1; Eze 17:13 **24:18** [f]1Ch 3:16; Jer 39:1 [g]2Ki 23:31 **24:19** [h]1Ki 15:26; Jer 37:2 **24:20** [i]Dt 4:26; 29:27 [j]S Ex 33:15; S 2Ki 13:23

24:3 *sins of Manasseh.* See 21:11–12; 23:26–27; Jer 15:3–4.
24:4 *innocent blood.* See note on 21:16. *not willing to forgive.* See 22:17.
24:5 *annals of the kings of Judah.* See note on 1Ki 14:29.
24:6 *rested with his fathers.* See note on 1Ki 1:21. Jehoiakim died shortly before Jerusalem fell to the Babylonian siege (see vv. 8–12). Whether his death was due to natural causes or political intrigue is not indicated.
24:7 *The king of Egypt did not march out from his own country again.* This was due to the Egyptian defeat at Carchemish (see Jer 46:2) in 605 B.C., and it explains why Jehoiakim received no help from Egypt in his rebellion against the Babylonians. *Wadi of Egypt.* See note on 1Ki 8:65.
24:8 *three months.* Babylonian records place this capture of Jerusalem by Nebuchadnezzar on Mar. 16, 597 B.C. This means that the three-month and ten-day reign (see 2Ch 36:9–10) of Jehoiachin began in December, 598.
24:9 *as his father.* See 23:37; Jer 22:20–30.
24:12 *eighth year.* April, 597 B.C. (see 2Ch 36:10; see also note on Jer 52:28, where a different system of dating is reflected).
24:13 *As the LORD had declared.* See 20:13,17.
24:14 *ten thousand.* This figure may include the 7,000 fighting men and 1,000 craftsmen mentioned in v. 16 (see note on Jer 52:28, where a different number of captives is mentioned).
24:15 *Jehoiachin captive to Babylon.* Fulfilling Jeremiah's prophecy (Jer 22:24–27; see 2Ki 25:27–30).
24:17 *Mattaniah, Jehoiachin's uncle.* Mattaniah was a son of Josiah (see 1Ch 3:15; Jer 1:3) and brother of Jehoiachin's father, Jehoiakim. *changed his name to Zedekiah.* Mattaniah's name (meaning "gift of Yahweh") was changed to Zedekiah ("righteousness of Yahweh"). Perhaps Nebuchadnezzar wanted to imply that his actions against Jerusalem and Jehoiachin were just. In any case, the name change signified subjection to Nebuchadnezzar (see note on 23:34).
24:18 *eleven years.* 597–586 B.C. *Jeremiah.* See note on 23:31. *Libnah.* See note on 8:22.
24:19 *did evil ... as Jehoiakim.* See note on 23:37. During Zedekiah's reign idolatrous practices continued to increase in Jerusalem (see 2Ch 36:14; Eze 8–11). He was a weak and indecisive ruler (see Jer 38:5,19), who refused to heed the word of the Lord given through Jeremiah (2Ch 36:12).
24:20 *Zedekiah rebelled.* Most interpreters link Zedekiah's revolt with the succession to the Egyptian throne in 589 B.C. of the ambitious pharaoh Hophra (see Jer 44:30 and note). Zedekiah had sworn allegiance to Nebuchadnezzar (Eze 17:13), he had sent envoys to Babylon (see Jer 29:3), and he had made a personal visit (see Jer 51:59). However, he seems to have capitulated to the seductive propaganda of the anti-

The Fall of Jerusalem

25:1-12pp — Jer 39:1-10
25:1-21pp — 2Ch 36:17-20; Jer 52:4-27
25:22-26pp — Jer 40:7-9; 41:1-3, 16-18

Now Zedekiah rebelled against the king
of Babylon.

25 So in the ninth[k] year of Zedekiah's
reign, on the tenth day of the tenth
month, Nebuchadnezzar[l] king of Babylon
marched against Jerusalem with his whole
army. He encamped outside the city and
built siege works[m] all around it. 2 The city
was kept under siege until the eleventh
year of King Zedekiah. 3 By the ninth day
of the ⌞fourth⌟[a] month the famine[n] in the
city had become so severe that there was
no food for the people to eat. 4 Then the
city wall was broken through,[o] and the
whole army fled at night through the gate
between the two walls near the king's garden, though the Babylonians[b] were surrounding[p] the city. They fled toward the
Arabah,[c] 5 but the Babylonian[d] army pursued the king and overtook him in the
plains of Jericho. All his soldiers were separated from him and scattered,[q] 6 and he
was captured.[r] He was taken to the king
of Babylon at Riblah,[s] where sentence was

25:1 [k] Jer 32:1 [l] Jer 21:2; 34:1-7 [m] Isa 23:13; 29:3; Jer 4:16-17; 32:2; 33:4; Eze 21:22; 24:2 **25:3** [n] S Lev 26:26; Isa 22:2; Jer 14:18; 37:21; La 2:20; 4:9 **25:4** [o] Job 30:14; Ps 144:14; Jer 50:15; 51:44,58; Eze 33:21 [p] Jer 4:17; 6:3 **25:5** [q] S Lev 26:36; Eze 12:14; 17:21; **25:6** [r] Isa 22:3; Jer 38:23 [s] S Nu 34:11

[a] 3 See Jer. 52:6. [b] 4 Or *Chaldeans*; also in verses 13, 25 and 26 [c] 4 Or *the Jordan Valley* [d] 5 Or *Chaldean*; also in verses 10 and 24

Babylonian and pro-Egyptian faction in Jerusalem (see Jer 37:5; Eze 17:15–16) in a tragically miscalculated effort to gain independence from Babylon.

25:1 *ninth year ... tenth day ... tenth month.* Jan. 15, 588 B.C. (see Jer 39:1; 52:4; Eze 24:1–2). *Nebuchadnezzar ... marched against Jerusalem.* Earlier, Nebuchadnezzar had subdued all the fortified cities in Judah except Lachish and Azekah (see Jer 34:7). A number of Hebrew inscriptions on potsherds were found at Lachish in 1935 and 1938. These Lachish ostraca (or letters; see chart, p. xxii) describe conditions at Lachish and Azekah during the Babylonian siege.

25:2–3 *eleventh year ... ninth day ... ⌞fourth⌟ month.* July 18, 586 B.C. (see Jer 39:2; 52:5–7). Some scholars follow a different dating system and place the fall of Jerusalem in the summer of 587.

25:3 *famine in the city had become so severe.* See Jer 38:2–9.

25:6 *king of Babylon at Riblah.* See note on 23:33; see also Jer 39:5; 52:9.

Exile of the Southern Kingdom

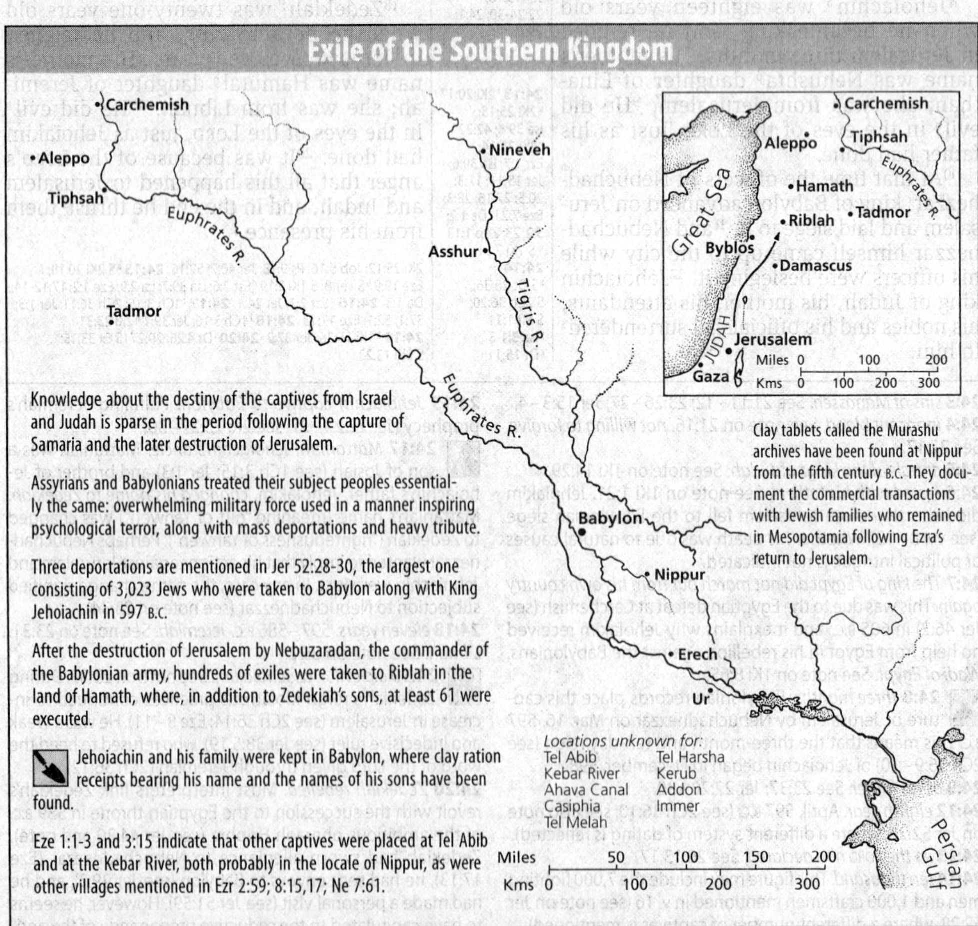

Knowledge about the destiny of the captives from Israel and Judah is sparse in the period following the capture of Samaria and the later destruction of Jerusalem.

Assyrians and Babylonians treated their subject peoples essentially the same: overwhelming military force used in a manner inspiring psychological terror, along with mass deportations and heavy tribute.

Three deportations are mentioned in Jer 52:28-30, the largest one consisting of 3,023 Jews who were taken to Babylon along with King Jehoiachin in 597 B.C.

After the destruction of Jerusalem by Nebuzaradan, the commander of the Babylonian army, hundreds of exiles were taken to Riblah in the land of Hamath, where, in addition to Zedekiah's sons, at least 61 were executed.

Jehoiachin and his family were kept in Babylon, where clay ration receipts bearing his name and the names of his sons have been found.

Eze 1:1-3 and 3:15 indicate that other captives were placed at Tel Abib and at the Kebar River, both probably in the locale of Nippur, as were other villages mentioned in Ezr 2:59; 8:15,17; Ne 7:61.

Clay tablets called the Murashu archives have been found at Nippur from the fifth century B.C. They document the commercial transactions with Jewish families who remained in Mesopotamia following Ezra's return to Jerusalem.

Locations unknown for:
Tel Abib, Kebar River, Ahava Canal, Casiphia, Tel Melah, Tel Harsha, Kerub, Addon, Immer

pronounced on him. 7They killed the sons
of Zedekiah before his eyes. Then they
put out his eyes, bound him with bronze
shackles and took him to Babylon.[t]
8On the seventh day of the fifth month,
in the nineteenth year of Nebuchadnezzar king of Babylon, Nebuzaradan commander of the imperial guard, an official
of the king of Babylon, came to Jerusalem. 9He set fire[u] to the temple of the
LORD, the royal palace and all the houses
of Jerusalem. Every important building he
burned down.[v] 10The whole Babylonian
army, under the commander of the imperial guard, broke down the walls[w] around
Jerusalem. 11Nebuzaradan the commander
of the guard carried into exile[x] the people
who remained in the city, along with the
rest of the populace and those who had
gone over to the king of Babylon.[y] 12But
the commander left behind some of the
poorest people[z] of the land to work the
vineyards and fields.
13The Babylonians broke[a] up the bronze
pillars, the movable stands and the bronze
Sea that were at the temple of the LORD
and they carried the bronze to Babylon.
14They also took away the pots, shovels, wick trimmers, dishes[b] and all the
bronze articles[c] used in the temple service. 15The commander of the imperial
guard took away the censers and sprinkling bowls — all that were made of pure
gold or silver.[d]
16The bronze from the two pillars, the
Sea and the movable stands, which Solomon had made for the temple of the LORD,
was more than could be weighed. 17Each
pillar[e] was twenty-seven feet[a] high. The
bronze capital on top of one pillar was
four and a half feet[b] high and was decorated with a network and pomegranates
of bronze all around. The other pillar, with
its network, was similar.
18The commander of the guard took as
prisoners Seraiah[f] the chief priest, Zephaniah[g] the priest next in rank and the three
doorkeepers.[h] 19Of those still in the city,
he took the officer in charge of the fighting men and five royal advisers. He also
took the secretary who was chief officer
in charge of conscripting the people of the
land and sixty of his men who were found
in the city. 20Nebuzaradan the commander took them all and brought them to the
king of Babylon at Riblah. 21There at Riblah,[i] in the land of Hamath, the king had
them executed.[j]
So Judah went into captivity,[k] away
from her land.[l]
22Nebuchadnezzar king of Babylon appointed Gedaliah[m] son of Ahikam,[n] the
son of Shaphan, to be over the people he
had left behind in Judah. 23When all the
army officers and their men heard that the
king of Babylon had appointed Gedaliah
as governor, they came to Gedaliah at Mizpah — Ishmael son of Nethaniah, Johanan
son of Kareah, Seraiah son of Tanhumeth
the Netophathite, Jaazaniah the son of
the Maacathite, and their men. 24Gedaliah
took an oath to reassure them and their
men. "Do not be afraid of the Babylonian
officials," he said. "Settle down in the land
and serve the king of Babylon, and it will
go well with you."

25:7 [t] S Dt 28:36; Jer 21:7; 32:4-5; 34:3,21; Eze 12:11; 19:9; 40:1
25:9 [u] Isa 60:7; 63:15,18; 64:11 [v] S Dt 13:16; Ne 1:3; Ps 74:3-8; 79:1; Jer 2:15; 17:27; 21:10; 26:6,18; La 4:11; Am 2:5; Mic 3:12
25:10 [w] Ne 1:3; Jer 50:15
25:11 [x] S Lev 26:44; 2Ki 24:14 [y] S Dt 28:36; S 2Ki 24:1
25:12 [z] S 2Ki 24:14
25:13 [a] S 1Ki 7:50
25:14 [b] S Nu 7:14 [c] S 2Ki 24:13; Ezr 1:7
25:15 [d] S 2Ki 24:13; Jer 15:13; 20:5; 27:16-22
25:17 [e] 1Ki 7:15-22
25:18 [f] ver 18-21; 1Ch 6:14; Ezr 7:1; Ne 11:11 [g] Jer 21:1; 29:25; 37:3 [h] S 2Ki 12:9; S 23:4
25:21 [i] S Nu 34:11 [j] Jer 34:21 [k] S 1Ki 8:46 [l] S Ge 12:7; S Jos 23:13
25:22 [m] Jer 39:14; 40:5,7; 41:18 [n] S 2Ki 22:12

[a] 17 Hebrew *eighteen cubits* (about 8.1 meters)
[b] 17 Hebrew *three cubits* (about 1.3 meters)

25:7 *killed the sons of Zedekiah ... put out his eyes ... took him to Babylon.* See Jer 32:4–5; 34:2–3; 38:18; 39:6–7; 52:10–11. Ezekiel (12:13) had predicted that Zedekiah would be brought to Babylon, but that he would not see it. Zedekiah could have spared his own life and prevented the destruction of Jerusalem if he had listened to Jeremiah (see Jer 38:14–28).
25:8–21 See map and accompanying text, p. 576.
25:8 *seventh day ... fifth month ... nineteenth year.* Aug. 14, 586 B.C. (see Jer 52:12 and note).
25:9 *set fire to the temple.* See 2Ch 36:19; Jer 39:8; 52:13.
25:13 *bronze pillars.* See 1Ki 7:15–22. *movable stands.* See 1Ki 7:27–39. *bronze Sea.* See 1Ki 7:23–26.
25:14 *all the bronze articles used in the temple service.* See 1Ki 7:40,45.
25:17 *bronze capital ... was four and a half feet high.* See NIV text note. In 1Ki 7:16 and Jer 52:22 the height of the capital is given as seven and a half feet (five cubits). The two-cubit difference may be due to a copyist's error.
25:18 *Seraiah the chief priest.* Seraiah was the grandson of Hilkiah (see note on 22:4; see also 22:8; 1Ch 6:13–14). His son Jehozadak was taken captive to Babylon. Ezra was one of Jehozadak's descendants (see Ezr 7:1).
25:19 *people of the land.* See note on 21:24.
25:20 *brought them to the king of Babylon at Riblah.* See v. 6 and note.
25:21 *Judah went into captivity, away from her land.* Judah's exile from Canaan fulfilled the prediction of judgment given during the reign of Manasseh (see 23:27). Exile was the most dire of the covenant curses (see Lev 26:33; Dt 28:36; see also Jer 25:8–11).
25:22 *Gedaliah.* See note on 22:12. Gedaliah shared Jeremiah's nonresistance approach to the Babylonians (see v. 24) and won their confidence as a trustworthy governor of Judah (see Jer 41:10).
25:23 *Mizpah.* Had been a town of important political significance in the time just before the establishment of the monarchy (see note on 1Sa 7:5). Jeremiah found Gedaliah there (see Jer 40:1–6). *Ishmael son of Nethaniah.* Verse 25 gives a fuller genealogy. Elishama, Ishmael's grandfather, was the royal secretary under Jehoiakim (Jer 36:12). *Jaazaniah.* In 1932 an agate seal was found at Tell en-Nasbeh (Mizpah) bearing the name of Jaazaniah (perhaps the man mentioned here) with the inscription: "Belonging to Jaazaniah the servant of the king."
25:24 Gedaliah urged submission to the Babylonians as the judgment of God. He advocated the restoration of the normal pursuits of a peacetime society (see Jer 27). A similar message had been given by Jeremiah to the captives taken to Babylon in 597 B.C. (see Jer 29:4–7).

[25]In the seventh month, however, Ishmael son of Nethaniah, the son of Elishama, who was of royal blood, came with
ten men and assassinated[o] Gedaliah and
also the men of Judah and the Babylonians who were with him at Mizpah.[p] [26]At
this, all the people from the least to the
greatest, together with the army officers,
fled to Egypt[q] for fear of the Babylonians.

Jehoiachin Released

25:27-30pp — Jer 52:31-34

[27]In the thirty-seventh year of the exile
of Jehoiachin king of Judah, in the year
Evil-Merodach[a] became king of Babylon,
he released Jehoiachin[r] from prison on the
twenty-seventh day of the twelfth month.
[28]He spoke kindly[s] to him and gave him
a seat of honor[t] higher than those of the
other kings who were with him in Babylon. [29]So Jehoiachin put aside his prison
clothes and for the rest of his life ate regularly at the king's table.[u] [30]Day by day the
king gave Jehoiachin a regular allowance
as long as he lived.[v]

25:25 [o]S 2Ki 12:20 [p]Zec 7:5 **25:26** [q]Isa 30:2; Jer 43:7 **25:27** [r]S 2Ki 24:12 **25:28** [s]S 1Ki 8:50 [t]Ezr 5:5; 7:6,28; 9:9; Ne 2:1; Da 2:48 **25:29** [u]S 2Sa 9:7 **25:30** [v]Ge 43:34; Est 2:9; 9:22; Jer 28:4

[a] 27 Also called *Amel-Marduk*

25:25 *seventh month.* October, 586 B.C. *assassinated Gedaliah.* A more complete account of the assassination of Gedaliah is given in Jer 40:13—41:15. Ishmael appears to have had personal designs on the throne, to have resented Gedaliah's ready submission to the Babylonians, and to have been manipulated by the Ammonites, who also chafed under Babylonian domination (see Jer 40:14; 41:10,15).

25:26 *fled to Egypt.* Pharaoh Hophra was then ruler in Egypt (see note on 24:20).

25:27 *thirty-seventh year...twenty-seventh day...twelfth month.* Mar. 22, 561 B.C. *in the year Evil-Merodach became king of Babylon.* 561 B.C. (some scholars place Evil-Merodach's succession to the throne in October, 562 B.C.; see note on 24:1). His name means "man of (the god) Marduk." *released Jehoiachin from prison.* Babylonian administrative tablets (see chart, p. xxii), recording the payment of rations in oil and barley to prisoners held in Babylon, mention Jehoiachin king of Judah and five of his sons (cf. 24:15). No reason is given for Jehoiachin's release. Perhaps it was part of a general amnesty proclaimed at the beginning of Evil-Merodach's reign.

25:28 *spoke kindly to him and gave him a seat of honor.* The book of Kings ends on a hopeful note. The judgment of exile will not destroy the people of Israel or the line of David. God's promise concerning David's house remains (see 2Sa 7:14–16).

1 Chronicles

I N T R O D U C T I O N

Title

The Hebrew title (*dibre hayyamim*) can be translated "the events (or annals) of the days (or years)." The same phrase occurs in references to sources used by the author or compiler of Kings (translated "annals" in, e.g., 1Ki 14:19,29; 15:7,23,31; 16:5,14,20,27; 22:45). The Septuagint (the pre-Christian Greek translation of the OT) refers to the book as "the things omitted," indicating that its translators regarded it as a supplement to Samuel and Kings. Jerome (A.D. 347–420), translator of the Latin Vulgate, suggested that a more appropriate title would be "chronicle of the whole sacred history." Luther took over this suggestion in his German version, and others have followed him. Chronicles was first divided into two books by the Septuagint translators.

Author, Date and Sources

According to ancient Jewish tradition, Ezra wrote Chronicles, Ezra and Nehemiah (see Introduction to Ezra: Literary Form and Authorship), but this cannot be established with certainty. A growing consensus dates Chronicles in the latter half of the fifth century B.C., thus possibly within Ezra's lifetime. And it must be acknowledged that the author, if not Ezra himself, at least shared many basic concerns with that reforming priest—though Chronicles is not so narrowly "priestly" in its perspective as was long affirmed.

Some believe the text contains evidence here and there of later expansions after the basic work had been composed. While editorial revisions are not unlikely, all specific proposals regarding them remain tentative.

In his recounting of history long past, the Chronicler relied on many written sources. About half his work was taken from Samuel and Kings; he also drew on the Pentateuch, Judges, Ruth, Psalms, Isaiah, Jeremiah, Lamentations and Zechariah (though he used texts of these books that varied somewhat from those that have been preserved in the later standardized Hebrew texts). And there are frequent references to still other sources: "the book of

A Quick Look

Author:
Unknown; possibly Ezra

Audience:
The people of Judah who had returned from exile in Babylon

Date:
Between 450 and 400 B.C.

Theme:
1 Chronicles begins with Israel's genealogical records from Adam to King Saul, then focuses more extensively on an idealized portrait of King David's reign.

the kings of Israel" (9:1; 2Ch 20:34; cf. 2Ch 33:18), "the book of the annals of King David" (27:24), "the book of the kings of Judah and Israel" or " . . . of Israel and Judah" (2Ch 16:11; 25:26; 27:7; 28:26; 32:32; 35:27; 36:8), "the annotations on the book of the kings" (2Ch 24:27). It is unclear whether these all refer to the same source or to different sources, and what their relationship is to Samuel and Kings or to the royal annals referred to in Kings. In addition, the author cites a number of prophetic writings: those of "Samuel the seer" (29:29), "Nathan the prophet" (29:29; 2Ch 9:29), "Gad the seer" (29:29), "Ahijah the Shilonite" (2Ch 9:29), "Iddo the seer" (2Ch 9:29; 12:15; 13:22), "Shemaiah the prophet" (2Ch 12:15), "the prophet Isaiah" (2Ch 26:22), "the seers" (2Ch 33:19). All these he used, often with only minor changes, to tell his own story of the past. He did not invent, but he did select, arrange and integrate his sources to compose a narrative "sermon" for postexilic Israel as she struggled to reorient herself as the people of God in a new situation.

Purpose and Themes

Just as the author of Kings had organized and interpreted the data of Israel's history to address the needs of the exiled community, so the author of 1 and 2 Chronicles wrote for the restored community. The burning issue was the question of continuity with the past: Is God still interested in us? Are his covenants still in force? Now that we have no Davidic king and are subject to Persia, do God's promises to David still have meaning for us? After the great judgment (the dethroning of the house of David, the destruction of the nation, of Jerusalem and of the temple, and the exile to Babylon), what is our relationship to Israel of old? Several elements go into the Chronicler's answer:

1. Continuity with the past is signified by the temple in Jerusalem, rebuilt by the Lord's sovereign influence over a Persian imperial edict (2Ch 36:22–23). For a generation that had no independent political status and no Davidic king the author takes great pains to show that the temple of the Lord and its service (including its book of prayer and praise, an early edition of the Psalms) are supreme gifts of God given to Israel through the Davidic dynasty. For that reason his account of the reigns of David and Solomon is largely devoted to David's preparation for and Solomon's building of the temple and to David's instructions for the temple service (with the counsel of Gad the seer and Nathan the prophet, 2Ch 29:25, and also of the Levites Asaph, Heman and Jeduthun, 2Ch 35:15). See also the Chronicler's accounts of the reigns of Asa, Jehoshaphat, Joash, Hezekiah and Josiah. The temple of the Lord in the ancient holy city and its service (including the Psalms) were the chief legacy left to the restored community by the house of David.

2. The value of this legacy is highlighted by the author's emphasis on God's furtherance of his gracious purposes toward Israel through his sovereign acts of election: (1) of the tribe of Levi to serve before the ark of the covenant (15:2; see 23:24–32), (2) of David to be king over Israel (28:4; 2Ch 6:6), (3) of Solomon his son to be king and to build the temple (28:5–6,10; 29:1), (4) of Jerusalem (2Ch 6:6,34,38; 12:13; 33:7) and (5) of the temple (2Ch 7:12,16; 33:7) to be the place where God's Name would be present among his people. These divine acts give assurance to postexilic Israel that her rebuilt temple in Jerusalem and its continuing service mark her as God's people whose election has not been annulled.

3. In addition to the temple, Israel has the law and the prophets as a major focus of her covenant life under the leadership of the house of David. Neither the Davidic kings nor the temple had in themselves assured Israel's security and blessing. All had been conditional on Israel's and the king's faithfulness to the law (28:7; 2Ch 6:16; 7:17; 12:1; 33:8). In the Chronicler's account, a primary feature of the reign of every faithful Davidic king was his attempt to bring about compliance with the law: David (6:49; 15:13,15; 16:40; 22:11–13; 29:19), Asa (2Ch 14:4; 15:12–14), Jehoshaphat (2Ch 17:3–9; 19:8–10), Joash (2Ch 24:6,9), Hezekiah (2Ch 29:10,31; 30:15–16; 31:3–4,21), Josiah (2Ch 34:19–21,29–33; 35:6,12,26). And to heed God's prophetic word was no less crucial. The faithful kings, such as David, Asa, Jehoshaphat, Hezekiah and Josiah—and even Rehoboam (2Ch 11:4; 12:6) and Amaziah (2Ch 25:7–10)—honored it; the unfaithful kings disregarded it to their destruction (Jehoram, 2Ch 21:12–19; Joash, 2Ch 24:19–25; Amaziah, 2Ch 25:15–16,20; Manasseh, 2Ch 33:10–11; see 36:15–16). Chronicles, in fact, notes the ministries of more prophets than do

Samuel and Kings. Jehoshaphat's word to Israel expresses the Chronicler's view succinctly: "Have faith in the LORD your God and you will be upheld; have faith in his prophets and you will be successful" (2Ch 20:20). In the Chronicler's account of Israel's years under the kings, Israel's response to the law and the prophets was more decisive for her destiny than the reigns of kings.

Thus the law and the prophets, like the temple, are more crucial to Israel's continuing relationship with the Lord than the presence or absence of a king, the reigns of the Davidic kings themselves being testimony.

4. The Chronicler further underscores the importance of obedience to the law and the prophets by emphasizing the theme of immediate retribution. See the express statements of David (28:9), of the Lord (2Ch 7:14) and of the prophets (2Ch 12:5; 15:2,7; 16:7,9; 19:2–3; 21:14–15; 24:20; 25:15–16; 28:9; 34:24–28). In writing his accounts of individual reigns, he never tires of demonstrating how sin always brings judgment in the form of disaster (usually either illness or defeat in war), whereas repentance, obedience and trust yield peace, victory and prosperity.

The author of 1 and 2 Chronicles wrote for the restored community. The burning issue was the question of continuity with the past: Is God still interested in us?

5. Clearly the author of Chronicles wished to sustain Israel's hope for the promised Messiah, son of David, in accordance with the Davidic covenant (2Sa 7) and the assurances of the prophets, including those near to him (Haggai, Zechariah and Malachi). He was careful to recall the Lord's pledge to David (1Ch 17) and to follow this with many references back to it (see especially his account of Solomon's reign and also 2Ch 13:5; 21:7; 23:3). But perhaps even more indicative are his idealized depictions of David, Solomon, Asa, Jehoshaphat, Hezekiah and Josiah. While not portrayed as flawless, these Davidic kings are presented as prime examples of the Messianic ideal, i.e., as royal servants of the Lord whose reigns promoted godliness and covenant faithfulness in Israel. They were crowned with God's favor toward his people in the concrete forms of victories, deliverances and prosperity. They sat, moreover, on the "throne of the LORD" (29:23; see 28:5; 2Ch 9:8) and ruled over the Lord's kingdom (17:14; 2Ch 13:8). Thus they served as types, foreshadowing the "David" to come of whom the prophets had spoken, and their remembrance nurtured hope in the face of much discouragement (see the book of Malachi). See further the next section on "Portrait of David and Solomon."

6. Yet another major theme of the Chronicler's history is his concern with "all Israel" (see, e.g., 9:1; 11:1–4; 12:38–40; 16:1–3; 18:14; 21:1–5; 28:1–8; 29:21–26; 2Ch 1:1–3; 7:8–10; 9:30; 10:1–3,16; 12:1; 18:16; 28:23; 29:24; 30:1–13,23–27; 34:6–9,33). As a matter of fact, he viewed the restored community as the remnant of all Israel, both north and south (9:2–3). This was more than a theological conceit. His narrative makes frequent note of movements of godly people from Israel to Judah for specifically religious reasons. The first were Levites in the time of Rehoboam (2Ch 11:14). In the reign of Asa others followed from Ephraim and Manasseh (2Ch 15:9). Shortly after the Assyrian destruction of the northern kingdom, many from that devastated land resettled in Judah at Hezekiah's invitation (2Ch 30). Presumably not all who came for Hezekiah's great Passover remained, but archaeology has shown a sudden large increase in population in the region around Jerusalem at this time, and the Chronicler specifically mentions "men of Israel ... who lived in the towns of Judah" (2Ch 31:6). He also speaks of "the people of Manasseh, Ephraim and the entire remnant of Israel" who joined with "the people of Judah and Benjamin and the inhabitants of Jerusalem" in restoring the temple in the days of Josiah (2Ch 34:9). These were also present at Josiah's Passover (2Ch 35:17–18). So the kingdom of "Judah" had absorbed many from the northern kingdom through the years, and the Chronicler viewed it as the remnant of all Israel from the time of Samaria's fall.

7. The genealogies also demonstrate continuity with the past. To the question "Is God still interested in us?" the Chronicler answers, "He has always been." God's grace and love for the restored community did not begin with David or the conquest or the exodus—but with creation (1:1). For the genealogies, see p. 583.

8. The Chronicler often introduces speeches not found in Samuel and Kings, using them to convey some of his main emphases. Of the 165 speeches in Chronicles of varying lengths, only 95 are found in the parallel texts of Samuel and Kings. Cf., e.g., the speeches of Abijah (2Ch 13:4–12), Asa (2Ch 14:11) and Jehoshaphat (2Ch 20:5–12).

Portrait of David and Solomon

The bulk of the Chronicler's history is devoted to the reigns of David (chs. 11–29) and Solomon (2Ch 1–9). His portraits of these two kings are quite distinctive and provide a key to his concerns:

1. The Chronicler has idealized David and Solomon. Anything in his source material (mainly Samuel and Kings) that might tarnish his picture of them is omitted. He makes no reference to the wars between Saul's house and David, the negotiations with Abner, or the murders of Abner and Ish-Bosheth (2Sa 1–4). The Chronicler presents David as being immediately anointed king over all Israel after the death of Saul (ch. 11) and enjoying the total support of the people (11:10—12:40; see note on 3:1–9). Subsequent difficulties for David are also not recounted. No mention is made of David's sin with Bathsheba, the crime and death of Amnon, the fratricide by Absalom and his plot against his father, the flight of David from Jerusalem, the rebellions of Sheba and Shimei, and other incidents that might diminish the glory of David's reign (2Sa 11–20). David is presented without blemish, apart from the incident of the census (the Chronicler had a special purpose for including it; see ch. 21 and notes).

The Chronicler handles Solomon similarly. Solomon is specifically named in a divine oracle as David's successor (22:7–10; 28:6). His accession to the throne is announced publicly by David and is greeted with the unanimous support of all Israel (chs. 28–29). No mention is made of the bedridden David, who must overturn the attempted coup by Adonijah at the last moment to secure the throne for Solomon. Nor is there mention that the military commander Joab and the high priest Abiathar supported Adonijah's attempt (1Ki 1). Solomon's execution of those who had wronged David (1Ki 2) is also omitted. The accession of Solomon is without competition or detracting incident. The account of his reign is devoted almost wholly to the building of the temple (2Ch 2–8), and no reference to his failures is included. No mention is made of his idolatry, his foreign wives or the rebellions against his rule (1Ki 11). Even the blame for the schism is removed from Solomon (1Ki 11:26–40; 12:1–4) and placed on the scheming of Jeroboam. Solomon's image in Chronicles is such that he can be paired with David in the most favorable light (2Ch 11:17).

The David and Solomon of the Chronicler, then, must be seen not only as the David and Solomon of history, but also as typifying the Messianic king of the Chronicler's expectation.

2. Not only is there idealization of David and Solomon, but the author also appears to consciously adopt the account of the succession of Moses and Joshua as a model for the succession of David and Solomon:

a. Both David and Moses fail to attain their goals—one to build the temple and the other to enter the promised land. In both cases the divine prohibition is related to the appointment of a successor (22:5–13; 28:2–8; Dt 1:37–38; 31:2–8).

b. Both Solomon and Joshua bring the people of God into rest (22:8–9; Jos 11:23; 21:44).

c. There are a number of verbal parallels in the appointments of Solomon and Joshua (compare 22:11–13,16; 28:7–10,20; 2Ch 1:1 with Dt 31:5–8,23; Jos 1:5,7–9).

d. There are both private and public announcements of the appointment of the successors: private (22:6; Dt 31:23); public (28:8; Dt 31:7—both "in the presence/sight of all Israel").

e. Both enjoy the immediate and wholehearted support of the people (29:23–24; Dt 34:9; Jos 1:16–18).

f. It is twice reported that God "exalted" or "made great" Solomon and Joshua (29:25; 2Ch 1:1; Jos 3:7; 4:14).

The Chronicler also uses other models from Pentateuchal history in his portrayal of David and Solomon. Like Moses, David received the plans for the temple from God (28:11–19; Ex 25:9) and called on the people to bring voluntary offerings for its construction (29:1–9; Ex 25:1–7). Solomon's relationship to Huram-Abi, the craftsman from Tyre (2Ch 2:13–14), echoes the role of Bezalel and Oholiab in the building of the tabernacle (Ex 35:30—36:7). See note on 2Ch 1:5.

Genealogies

Analysis of genealogies, both inside and outside the Bible, has disclosed that they serve a variety of functions (with different principles governing the lists), that they vary in form (some being segmented, others linear) and depth (number of generations listed), and that they are often fluid (subject to change).

There are three general areas in which genealogies function: the familial or domestic, the legal-political, and the religious. In the domestic area an individual's social status, privileges and obligations may be reflected in his placement in the lineage (see 7:14–19); the rights of the firstborn son and the secondary status of the children of concubines are examples from the Bible. In the political sphere genealogies substantiate claims to hereditary office or settle competing claims when the office is contested. Land organization and territorial groupings of social units may also be determined by genealogical reckoning—e.g., the division of the land among the 12 tribes. In Israel military levies also proceeded along genealogical lines; several of the genealogies in Chronicles reflect military conscription (5:1–26; 7:1–12,30–40; 8:1–40). Genealogies function in the religious sphere primarily by establishing membership among the priests and Levites (6:1–30; 9:10–34; Ne 7:61–65).

As to form, some genealogical lists trace several lines of descent (segmented genealogies) while others are devoted to a single line (linear genealogies).

Comparison of genealogical lists of the same tribal or family line often brings to light surprising differences. This fluidity of the lists may reflect variation in function. But sometimes changes in the status or relations of social structures are reflected in genealogies by changes in the relationships of names in the genealogy (see notes on 1:35–42; 6:22,27) or by the addition of names or segments to a lineage (see notes on 5:11–22; 6:27; 7:6–12). The most common type of fluidity in Biblical materials is telescoping, the omission of names from the list. Unimportant names are left out in order to relate an individual to a prominent ancestor, or possibly to achieve the desired number of names in the genealogy. Some Biblical genealogies, for example, omit names to achieve multiples of 7: For the period from David to the exile, Matthew gives 14 generations (2 times 7), while Luke gives 21 (3 times 7), and the same authors give similar multiples of 7 for the period from the exile to Jesus (Mt 1:1–17; Lk 3:23–38).

The genealogies of Chronicles show variation in all these properties; the arrangements often reflect the purpose for which the genealogies were composed prior to their being adopted by the Chronicler as part of his record.

Outline

I. Genealogies: From Creation to Israel's Restoration from Exile (1Ch 1–9)
   A. The Patriarchs (ch. 1)
   B. The 12 Sons of Jacob/Israel (2:1–2)
   C. The Family of Judah (2:3—4:23)
   D. The Sons of Simeon (4:24–43)
   E. Reuben, Gad and the Half-Tribe of Manasseh (ch. 5)
   F. Levi and Families (ch. 6)
   G. Issachar, Benjamin, Naphtali, Manasseh, Ephraim and Asher (chs. 7–9)
II. The Reign of David (1Ch 10–29)
   A. Death of Saul (ch. 10)
   B. Capture of Jerusalem; David's Power Base (chs. 11–12)
   C. Return of the Ark; Establishment of David's Kingdom (chs. 13–16)
   D. Dynastic Promise (ch. 17)
   E. David's Conquests (chs. 18–20)
   F. The Census (ch. 21)

- G. Preparations for the Temple (ch. 22)
- H. Organization of the Temple Service (chs. 23 – 26)
- I. Administrative Structures of the Kingdom (ch. 27)
- J. David's Final Preparations for Succession and the Temple (28:1 — 29:20)
- K. Succession of Solomon; Death of David (29:21 – 30)

III. The Reign of Solomon (2Ch 1 – 9)

- A. The Gift of Wisdom (ch. 1)
- B. Building the Temple (2:1 — 5:1)
- C. Dedication of the Temple (5:2 — 7:22)
- D. Solomon's Other Activities (ch. 8)
- E. Solomon's Wisdom, Splendor and Death (ch. 9)

IV. The Schism, and the History of the Kings of Judah (2Ch 10 – 36)

- A. Rehoboam (chs. 10 – 12)
- B. Abijah (13:1 — 14:1)
- C. Asa (14:2 — 16:14)
- D. Jehoshaphat (17:1 — 21:3)
- E. Jehoram and Ahaziah (21:4 — 22:9)
- F. Joash (22:10 — 24:27)
- G. Amaziah (ch. 25)
- H. Uzziah (ch. 26)
- I. Jotham (ch. 27)
- J. Ahaz (ch. 28)
- K. Hezekiah (chs. 29 – 32)
- L. Manasseh (33:1 – 20)
- M. Amon (33:21 – 25)
- N. Josiah (34:1 — 36:1)
- O. Josiah's Successors (36:2 – 14)
- P. Exile and Restoration (36:15 – 23)

Historical Records From Adam to Abraham

To Noah's Sons

1 Adam,[a] Seth, Enosh, 2 Kenan,[b] Mahalalel,[c] Jared,[d] 3 Enoch,[e] Methuselah,[f] Lamech,[g] Noah.[h]

4 The sons of Noah:[a i]
Shem, Ham and Japheth.[j]

The Japhethites

1:5-7pp — Ge 10:2-5

5 The sons[b] of Japheth:
Gomer, Magog, Madai, Javan, Tubal, Meshech and Tiras.
6 The sons of Gomer:
Ashkenaz, Riphath[c] and Togarmah.
7 The sons of Javan:
Elishah, Tarshish, the Kittim and
the Rodanim.

The Hamites

1:8-16pp — Ge 10:6-20

8 The sons of Ham:
Cush, Mizraim,[d] Put and Canaan.
9 The sons of Cush:
Seba, Havilah, Sabta, Raamah and
Sabteca.
The sons of Raamah:
Sheba and Dedan.
10 Cush was the father[e] of
Nimrod, who grew to be a mighty
warrior on earth.
11 Mizraim was the father of
the Ludites, Anamites, Lehabites,
Naphtuhites, 12 Pathrusites, Caslu-
hites (from whom the Philistines
came) and Caphtorites.
13 Canaan was the father of
Sidon his firstborn,[f] and of the Hittites, 14 Jebusites, Amorites, Girgashites, 15 Hivites, Arkites, Sinites,
16 Arvadites, Zemarites and Hamathites.

The Semites

1:17-23pp — Ge 10:21-31; 11:10-27

17 The sons of Shem:
Elam, Asshur, Arphaxad, Lud and
Aram.
The sons of Aram:[g]
Uz, Hul, Gether and Meshech.
18 Arphaxad was the father of Shelah,
and Shelah the father of Eber.
19 Two sons were born to Eber:
One was named Peleg,[h] because in
his time the earth was divided; his
brother was named Joktan.
20 Joktan was the father of
Almodad, Sheleph, Hazarmaveth,
Jerah, 21 Hadoram, Uzal, Diklah,
22 Obal,[i] Abimael, Sheba, 23 Ophir,

1:1 [a] Ge 5:1-32; Lk 3:36-38 **1:2** [b] S Ge 5:9 [c] S Ge 5:12 [d] S Ge 5:15 **1:3** [e] S Ge 5:18; Jude 1:14 [f] S Ge 5:21 [g] S Ge 5:25 [h] S Ge 5:29 **1:4** [i] Ge 6:10; 10:1 [j] S Ge 5:32

[a] *4* Septuagint; Hebrew does not have this line. [b] *5 Sons* may mean *descendants* or *successors* or *nations*; also in verses 6-10, 17 and 20. [c] *6* Many Hebrew manuscripts and Vulgate (see also Septuagint and Gen. 10:3); most Hebrew manuscripts *Diphath* [d] *8* That is, Egypt; also in verse 11 [e] *10 Father* may mean *ancestor* or *predecessor* or *founder*; also in verses 11, 13, 18 and 20. [f] *13* Or *of the Sidonians, the foremost* [g] *17* One Hebrew manuscript and some Septuagint manuscripts (see also Gen. 10:23); most Hebrew manuscripts do not have this line. [h] *19 Peleg* means *division*. [i] *22* Some Hebrew manuscripts and Syriac (see also Gen. 10:28); most Hebrew manuscripts *Ebal*

1:1—9:44 The genealogies succinctly show the restored community's continuity with the past. The great deeds of God on Israel's behalf prior to the rise of David are passed over in silence, but the genealogies serve as a skeleton of history to show that the Israel of the restoration stands at the center of the divine purpose from the beginning (from Adam, v. 1). And the genealogies also serve the very practical purpose of legitimizing the present. They provide the framework by which the ethnic and religious purity of the people can be maintained. They also establish the continuing line of royal succession and the legitimacy of the priests for the postexilic temple service. See Introduction: Genealogies.

1:1—2:1 The Chronicler here covers the period from Adam to Jacob, and the materials are drawn almost entirely from Genesis. The subsidiary lines of descent are presented first: Japheth and Ham (vv. 5–16) are given before Shem (vv. 17–27), the sons of Shem other than those in Abraham's ancestry (vv. 17–23) before that line (vv. 24–27), the sons of Abraham's concubines (vv. 28–33) before Isaac's line (v. 34), the descendants of Esau and the Edomite ruling houses (vv. 35–54) before the sons of Israel (2:1). In each case the elect lineage is given last. Several features of this genealogy are striking when compared with non-Biblical materials. The genealogy begins without an introduction. Two sections of the genealogy have no kinship terms and are only lists of names: the first 13 names (vv. 1–4; see note on v. 4) and vv. 24–27. In vv. 5–16 (and following v. 27) kinship terms are used. Both segmented (those tracing several lines of descent) and linear (those tracing a single line) genealogies are included. This identical structure is found in a copy of the Assyrian King List: There is no introduction, and the scribe has drawn lines across the tablet dividing it into four sections, two of which are lists of names without kinship terms, alternating with two lists in which relations are specified; both segmented and linear genealogies are used. This suggests that the Chronicler was following a known literary pattern for his composition.

1:1–4 From creation to the flood. This list is taken from Ge 5:1–32 (see notes there). The omission of Cain and Abel demonstrates the Chronicler's interest in the chosen line (see Ge 4:17–25).

1:4 *The sons of Noah.* Not found in the Hebrew text (see NIV text note); this omission parallels the Assyrian King List (see note on 1:1—2:1). The Chronicler's readers would have known that these were the sons of Noah and would not have needed the kinship notice; the Septuagint (the pre-Christian Greek translation of the OT) and most modern translations insert the phrase to clarify the relationship.

1:5–23 This genealogy is drawn from the table of nations in Ge 10:2–29 (see notes there). The arrangement is primarily geographical and cultural rather than biological. Omitting the Philistines (v. 12) as a parenthesis, a total of 70 nations is achieved: Japheth, 14; Ham, 30; Shem, 26 (see note on Ge 10:2)—an example of a genealogy telescoped to attain multiples of 7 (see Introduction: Genealogies).

Havilah and Jobab. All these were
sons of Joktan.

24 Shem,[k] Arphaxad,[a] Shelah,
25 Eber, Peleg, Reu,
26 Serug, Nahor, Terah
27 and Abram (that is, Abraham).

The Family of Abraham

28 The sons of Abraham:
Isaac and Ishmael.

Descendants of Hagar

1:29-31pp — Ge 25:12-16

29 These were their descendants:
Nebaioth the firstborn of Ishmael,
Kedar, Adbeel, Mibsam, 30 Mishma,
Dumah, Massa, Hadad, Tema, 31 Je-
tur, Naphish and Kedemah. These
were the sons of Ishmael.

Descendants of Keturah

1:32-33pp — Ge 25:1-4

32 The sons born to Keturah, Abraham's
concubine:[l]
Zimran, Jokshan, Medan, Midian,
Ishbak and Shuah.
The sons of Jokshan:
Sheba and Dedan.[m]
33 The sons of Midian:
Ephah, Epher, Hanoch, Abida and
Eldaah.
All these were descendants of Ketu-
rah.

Descendants of Sarah

1:35-37pp — Ge 36:10-14

34 Abraham[n] was the father of Isaac.[o]
The sons of Isaac:
Esau and Israel.[p]

Esau's Sons

35 The sons of Esau:[q]
Eliphaz, Reuel,[r] Jeush, Jalam and
Korah.
36 The sons of Eliphaz:
Teman, Omar, Zepho,[b] Gatam and
Kenaz;
by Timna: Amalek.[c s]
37 The sons of Reuel:[t]
Nahath, Zerah, Shammah and Miz-
zah.

1:24 [k]S Ge 10:21-25; Lk 3:34-36
1:32 [l]S Ge 22:24 [m]S Ge 10:7
1:34 [n]Lk 3:34 [o]Mt 1:2; Ac 7:8 [p]S Ge 17:5
1:35 [q]Ge 36:19 [r]S Ge 36:4
1:36 [s]S Ex 17:14
1:37 [t]Ge 36:17
1:40 [u]S Ge 36:2
1:45 [v]S Ge 36:11

The People of Seir in Edom

1:38-42pp — Ge 36:20-28

38 The sons of Seir:
Lotan, Shobal, Zibeon, Anah, Di-
shon, Ezer and Dishan.
39 The sons of Lotan:
Hori and Homam. Timna was Lo-
tan's sister.
40 The sons of Shobal:
Alvan,[d] Manahath, Ebal, Shepho
and Onam.
The sons of Zibeon:
Aiah and Anah.[u]
41 The son of Anah:
Dishon.
The sons of Dishon:
Hemdan,[e] Eshban, Ithran and Ke-
ran.
42 The sons of Ezer:
Bilhan, Zaavan and Akan.[f]
The sons of Dishan[g]:
Uz and Aran.

The Rulers of Edom

1:43-54pp — Ge 36:31-43

43 These were the kings who reigned
in Edom before any Israelite king
reigned[h]:
Bela son of Beor, whose city was
named Dinhabah.
44 When Bela died, Jobab son of Zerah from Bozrah succeeded him as
king.
45 When Jobab died, Husham from the
land of the Temanites[v] succeeded
him as king.
46 When Husham died, Hadad son of
Bedad, who defeated Midian in the
country of Moab, succeeded him as
king. His city was named Avith.

[a] *24* Hebrew; some Septuagint manuscripts *Arphaxad, Cainan* (see also note at Gen. 11:10) [b] *36* Many Hebrew manuscripts, some Septuagint manuscripts and Syriac (see also Gen. 36:11); most Hebrew manuscripts *Zephi* [c] *36* Some Septuagint manuscripts (see also Gen. 36:12); Hebrew *Gatam, Kenaz, Timna and Amalek* [d] *40* Many Hebrew manuscripts and some Septuagint manuscripts (see also Gen. 36:23); most Hebrew manuscripts *Alian* [e] *41* Many Hebrew manuscripts and some Septuagint manuscripts (see also Gen. 36:26); most Hebrew manuscripts *Hamran* [f] *42* Many Hebrew and Septuagint manuscripts (see also Gen. 36:27); most Hebrew manuscripts *Zaavan, Jaakan* [g] *42* Hebrew *Dishon,* a variant of *Dishan* [h] *43* Or *before an Israelite king reigned over them*

1:24–27 See notes on 1:1—2:1; Ge 11:10–26.
1:28–34 See notes on Ge 25:1–18.
1:35–42 See Ge 36:10–28 and notes.
1:36 *sons of Eliphaz.* These correspond to Ge 36:11–12, but with one difficulty: The Hebrew text of Chronicles (see second NIV text note on this verse) lists Timna as a son of Eliphaz, while Ge 36:12 designates Timna as the concubine of Eliphaz and mother of Amalek. The NIV follows the Septuagint (the pre-Christian Greek translation of the OT), which regarded Timna as the mother of Amalek, not as the son of Eliphaz. According to this solution, the Hebrew text is here in error, or perhaps the Chronicler has once again omitted kinship terminology (see notes on 1:1—2:1; v. 4). Alternatively, some regard this as an example of genealogical fluidity (see Introduction: Genealogies): Since the name Timna also became the name of a chiefdom in Edom (v. 51; Ge 36:40), during the course of time Timna was moved in the Edomite genealogies to the position of a son of Eliphaz and brother of Amalek.
1:43–54 See Ge 36:31–43. The Chronicler continues with extensive coverage of Edom. This is striking in contrast to his omission of the line of Cain and the brief treatment of the line of Ishmael. It probably reflects the fact that the Edomites were important in the Chronicler's own day (see 18:11–13; 2Ch 8:17; 21:8; 25:20; 28:17).

[47]When Hadad died, Samlah from Masrekah succeeded him as king.
[48]When Samlah died, Shaul from Rehoboth on the river[a] succeeded him
as king.
[49]When Shaul died, Baal-Hanan son of
Acbor succeeded him as king.
[50]When Baal-Hanan died, Hadad succeeded him as king. His city was
named Pau,[b] and his wife's name
was Mehetabel daughter of Matred,
the daughter of Me-Zahab. [51]Hadad
also died.

The chiefs of Edom were:
Timna, Alvah, Jetheth, [52]Oholiba-
mah, Elah, Pinon, [53]Kenaz, Teman,
Mibzar, [54]Magdiel and Iram. These
were the chiefs of Edom.

Israel's Sons

2:1-2pp — Ge 35:23-26

2 These were the sons of Israel:
Reuben, Simeon, Levi, Judah, Issachar, Zebulun, [2]Dan, Joseph, Benjamin, Naphtali, Gad and Asher.

Judah

2:5-15pp — Ru 4:18-22; Mt 1:3-6

To Hezron's Sons

[3]The sons of Judah:[w]
Er, Onan and Shelah.[x] These three
were born to him by a Canaanite
woman, the daughter of Shua.[y] Er,
Judah's firstborn, was wicked in
the LORD's sight; so the LORD put
him to death.[z] [4]Tamar,[a] Judah's
daughter-in-law,[b] bore him Perez[c]
and Zerah. Judah had five sons in
all.
[5]The sons of Perez:[d]
Hezron[e] and Hamul.
[6]The sons of Zerah:
Zimri, Ethan, Heman, Calcol and
Darda[c]—five in all.
[7]The son of Carmi:
Achar,[d f] who brought trouble on Israel by violating the ban on taking
devoted things.[e g]
[8]The son of Ethan:
Azariah.
[9]The sons born to Hezron[h] were:
Jerahmeel, Ram and Caleb.[f]

From Ram Son of Hezron

[10]Ram[i] was the father of
Amminadab[j], and Amminadab the
father of Nahshon,[k] the leader of

2:3 [w] S Ge 29:35; 38:2-10 [x] S Ge 38:5 [y] S Ge 38:2 [z] S Nu 26:19 **2:4** [a] Ge 38:11-30 [b] S Ge 11:31 [c] S Ge 38:29 **2:5** [d] S Ge 46:12 [e] Nu 26:21 **2:7** [f] S Jos 7:1 [g] S Jos 6:18 **2:9** [h] S Nu 26:21 **2:10** [i] Lk 3:32-33 [j] S Ex 6:23 [k] S Nu 1:7

[a] 48 Possibly the Euphrates [b] 50 Many Hebrew manuscripts, some Septuagint manuscripts, Vulgate and Syriac (see also Gen. 36:39); most Hebrew manuscripts *Pai* [c] 6 Many Hebrew manuscripts, some Septuagint manuscripts and Syriac (see also 1 Kings 4:31); most Hebrew manuscripts *Dara* [d] 7 *Achar* means *trouble*; *Achar* is called *Achan* in Joshua. [e] 7 The Hebrew term refers to the irrevocable giving over of things or persons to the LORD, often by totally destroying them. [f] 9 Hebrew *Kelubai*, a variant of *Caleb*

2:1–2 Although there are numerous lists of the 12 tribes in the OT, only four are given in genealogical form: (1) Ge 29:31—30:24; 35:16–20; (2) Ge 35:22–26; (3) Ge 46:8–27; (4) here. Other lists of the tribes are found in 12:24–37; 27:16–22; Ex 1:2–5; Dt 27:12–13; 33; Eze 48:31–34. In other lists the tribe of Levi is omitted, and the number 12 is achieved by dividing Joseph into the tribes of Ephraim and Manasseh (Nu 1:5–15; 1:20–43; 2:3–31; 7:12–83; 10:14–28; 13:4–15; 26:5–51). In this passage the Chronicler appears to follow Ge 35:22–26 except for the position of the tribe of Dan, which is found in seventh instead of ninth place. The list here does not set the order in which the Chronicler will take up the tribes; rather, he moves immediately to his major concern with the house of David and the tribe of Judah (2:3—4:23), even though Judah is fourth in the genealogy. In the lists of these chapters the Chronicler maintains the number 12, but with the following names: Judah, Simeon, Reuben, Gad, half of Manasseh, Levi, Issachar, Benjamin, Naphtali, Ephraim, Manasseh and Asher. Zebulun and Dan are omitted. For a similar omission of Dan see Rev 7:6 and note.

2:3–9 The lineage of Judah is traced to Hezron's sons (v. 9), whose descendants are given in 2:10—3:24. Of Judah's five sons, the first two (Er and Onan) died as the result of sin recorded in Ge 38. The lineage of the third son, Shelah, is taken up in 4:21; this section focuses on the remaining two (see Ge 46:12; Nu 26:19–22).

2:6 *Ethan, Heman, Calcol and Darda.* Not immediate descendants of Zerah; rather, they are from the later period of the reign of Solomon (1Ki 4:31). A Heman and an Ethan were David's musicians (see 15:19; Ps 88–89 titles), but whether these are the same individuals is uncertain. If they are the same, the fact that in 6:33–42 and 15:19 Heman and Ethan are assigned to the tribe of Levi may be another example of genealogical fluidity, where these men's musical skills brought them into the Levitical lineage. Or the reverse may have occurred: As Levites associated with Judah, they were brought into that lineage.

2:7 *Achar.* The change from Achan to Achar (meaning "trouble"; see NIV text note) is probably a play on words reflecting the trouble he brought to Israel (Jos 7).

2:10—3:24 That the Chronicler's primary concern in the genealogy of Judah is with the line of David is seen in his arrangement of this section's material as an inversion:

Descendants of Ram (David's ancestry), 2:10–17
Descendants of Caleb, 2:18–24
Descendants of Jerahmeel, 2:25–33
Supplementary material on Jerahmeel, 2:34–41
Supplementary material on Caleb, 2:42–55
Supplementary material on Ram (David's descendants), ch. 3

The Chronicler has structured this central portion of the Judah genealogy to highlight the Davidic ancestry and descent, which frame this section and emphasize the position of David—in line with the Chronicler's interests in the historical portions that follow (see note on 4:1–23).

2:10–17 Verses 10–12 are a linear genealogy from Ram to Jesse; then Jesse's lineage is segmented, reminiscent of 1Sa 16:1–13. The source for most of the material is Ru 4:19–22. In 1Sa 16:10–13 David was the eighth of Jesse's sons to appear before Samuel; in this passage only seven are named, enabling David to occupy the favored place of the seventh son (v. 15; see Introduction: Genealogies). David was the half-uncle of his famous warriors Abishai, Joab, Asahel and Amasa (11:6,20,26; 2Sa 2:13,18; 17:25; 19:13).

the people of Judah. 11Nahshon
was the father of Salmon,[a] Salmon
the father of Boaz, 12Boaz[l] the father of Obed and Obed the father
of Jesse.[m]
13Jesse[n] was the father of
Eliab[o] his firstborn; the second
son was Abinadab, the third Shimea, 14the fourth Nethanel, the fifth
Raddai, 15the sixth Ozem and the
seventh David. 16Their sisters were
Zeruiah[p] and Abigail. Zeruiah's[q]
three sons were Abishai, Joab[r] and
Asahel. 17Abigail was the mother of
Amasa,[s] whose father was Jether
the Ishmaelite.

Caleb Son of Hezron

18Caleb son of Hezron had children by
his wife Azubah (and by Jerioth).
These were her sons: Jesher, Shobab and Ardon. 19When Azubah
died, Caleb[t] married Ephrath, who
bore him Hur. 20Hur was the father
of Uri, and Uri the father of Bezalel.[u]
21Later, Hezron lay with the daughter
of Makir the father of Gilead[v] (he
had married her when he was sixty years old), and she bore him Segub. 22Segub was the father of Jair,
who controlled twenty-three towns
in Gilead. 23(But Geshur and Aram
captured Havvoth Jair,[b w] as well as
Kenath[x] with its surrounding settlements — sixty towns.) All these
were descendants of Makir the father of Gilead.

24After Hezron died in Caleb Ephrathah,
Abijah the wife of Hezron bore him
Ashhur[y] the father[c] of Tekoa.

Jerahmeel Son of Hezron

25The sons of Jerahmeel the firstborn of
Hezron:
Ram his firstborn, Bunah, Oren,
Ozem and[d] Ahijah. 26Jerahme-
el had another wife, whose name
was Atarah; she was the mother of
Onam.

2:12 [l] S Ru 2:1 [m] S Ru 4:17 **2:13** [n] S Ru 4:17 [o] S 1Sa 16:6 **2:16** [p] 1Sa 26:6 [q] 2Sa 2:18 [r] S 2Sa 2:13 **2:17** [s] 2Sa 17:25 **2:19** [t] ver 42,50 **2:20** [u] S Ex 31:2 **2:21** [v] S Nu 27:1 **2:23** [w] S Nu 32:41; Dt 3:14 [x] Nu 32:42 **2:24** [y] 1Ch 4:5

27The sons of Ram the firstborn of Jerahmeel:
Maaz, Jamin and Eker.
28The sons of Onam:
Shammai and Jada.
The sons of Shammai:
Nadab and Abishur.
29Abishur's wife was named Abihail,
who bore him Ahban and Molid.
30The sons of Nadab:
Seled and Appaim. Seled died without children.
31The son of Appaim:
Ishi, who was the father of Sheshan.
Sheshan was the father of Ahlai.
32The sons of Jada, Shammai's brother:
Jether and Jonathan. Jether died
without children.
33The sons of Jonathan:
Peleth and Zaza.
These were the descendants of Jerahmeel.
34Sheshan had no sons — only daughters.
He had an Egyptian servant named
Jarha. 35Sheshan gave his daughter
in marriage to his servant Jarha,
and she bore him Attai.
36Attai was the father of Nathan,
Nathan the father of Zabad,[z]
37Zabad the father of Ephlal,
Ephlal the father of Obed,
38Obed the father of Jehu,
Jehu the father of Azariah,
39Azariah the father of Helez,
Helez the father of Eleasah,
40Eleasah the father of Sismai,
Sismai the father of Shallum,
41Shallum the father of Jekamiah,
and Jekamiah the father of Elishama.

The Clans of Caleb

42The sons of Caleb[a] the brother of Jerahmeel:
Mesha his firstborn, who was the fa-

[a] 11 Septuagint (see also Ruth 4:21); Hebrew *Salma* [b] 23 Or *captured the settlements of Jair* [c] 24 *Father* may mean *civic leader* or *military leader*; also in verses 42, 45, 49-52 and possibly elsewhere. [d] 25 Or *Oren and Ozem, by*

2:36 [z] 1Ch 11:41 **2:42** [a] S ver 19

2:18–24 For the Chronicler the important name in this genealogy of the Calebites is Bezalel (v. 20), the wise master craftsman who supervised the building of the tabernacle (Ex 31:1–5). He is mentioned in the Bible only in Exodus and Chronicles. The Chronicler uses Bezalel and Oholiab (Ex 31:6) as a model for his portrait of Solomon and Huram-Abi in the building of the temple (see note on 2Ch 1:5). By inserting a reference to the builder of the tabernacle next to the genealogy of David in vv. 10–17, the Chronicler characteristically juxtaposes the themes of king and temple — so important to his historical narrative.
2:25–33 This section is identified as a separate entity from the supplementary material by its opening and closing formulas: "The sons of Jerahmeel" (v. 25) and "These were the descendants of Jerahmeel" (v. 33). Verses 25–41 are the only genealogical materials on the Jerahmeelites in the Bible. 1Sa 27:10 and 30:27–29 place their settlements in the Negev.
2:34–41 Supplementary material on the line of Sheshan (v. 31); it is a linear genealogy to a depth of 13 generations. The generation of Elishama (v. 41) would be the 23rd since Judah, if there has been no telescoping in this lineage. If no names are omitted, Elishama would likely be contemporary with David, though we know nothing of him.
2:42–55 The same opening and closing formulas noted in vv. 25,33 occur in vv. 42,50a: "The sons of Caleb ... These were the descendants of Caleb." The list in this section is a mixture

ther of Ziph, and his son Mareshah,[a]
who was the father of Hebron.
43 The sons of Hebron:
Korah, Tappuah, Rekem and Shema. 44 Shema was the father of
Raham, and Raham the father of
Jorkeam. Rekem was the father of
Shammai. 45 The son of Shammai
was Maon[b], and Maon was the father of Beth Zur.[c]
46 Caleb's concubine Ephah was the
mother of Haran, Moza and Gazez.
Haran was the father of Gazez.
47 The sons of Jahdai:
Regem, Jotham, Geshan, Pelet,
Ephah and Shaaph.
48 Caleb's concubine Maacah was the
mother of Sheber and Tirhanah.
49 She also gave birth to Shaaph
the father of Madmannah[d] and to
Sheva the father of Macbenah and
Gibea. Caleb's daughter was Acsah.[e] 50 These were the descendants
of Caleb.

The sons of Hur[f] the firstborn of Ephrathah:
Shobal the father of Kiriath Jearim,[g] 51 Salma the father of Bethlehem, and Hareph the father of Beth
Gader.
52 The descendants of Shobal the father
of Kiriath Jearim were:
Haroeh, half the Manahathites,
53 and the clans of Kiriath Jearim:
the Ithrites,[h] Puthites, Shumath-
ites and Mishraites. From these descended the Zorathites and Eshtao-
lites.
54 The descendants of Salma:
Bethlehem, the Netophathites,[i] Atroth Beth Joab, half the Manahathites, the Zorites, 55 and the clans of
scribes[b] who lived at Jabez: the Tirathites, Shimeathites and Sucathites. These are the Kenites[j] who
came from Hammath,[k] the father
of the house of Recab.[c][l]

2:45 [b] S Jos 15:55 [c] S Jos 15:58 **2:49** [d] Jos 15:31 [e] Jos 15:16 **2:50** [f] 1Ch 4:4 [g] S ver 19 **2:53** [h] 2Sa 23:38 **2:54** [i] Ezr 2:22; Ne 7:26; 12:28 **2:55** [j] S Ge 15:19; S Jdg 4:11 [k] Jos 19:35 [l] 2Ki 10:15, 23; Jer 35:2-19

The Sons of David

3:1-4pp — 2Sa 3:2-5
3:5-8pp — 2Sa 5:14-16; 1Ch 14:4-7

3 These were the sons of David[m] born to
him in Hebron:
The firstborn was Amnon the son
of Ahinoam[n] of Jezreel;[o]
the second, Daniel the son of Abigail[p] of Carmel;
2 the third, Absalom the son of Maacah daughter of Talmai king of Geshur;
the fourth, Adonijah[q] the son of
Haggith;
3 the fifth, Shephatiah the son of Abi-
tal;
and the sixth, Ithream, by his wife
Eglah.
4 These six were born to David in
Hebron,[r] where he reigned seven
years and six months.[s]
David reigned in Jerusalem thirty-three
years, 5 and these were the children born
to him there:
Shammua,[d] Shobab, Nathan and
Solomon. These four were by
Bathsheba[e][t] daughter of Ammiel.
6 There were also Ibhar, Elishua,[f]
Eliphelet, 7 Nogah, Nepheg, Japhia, 8 Elishama, Eliada and Eliphelet — nine in all. 9 All these were
the sons of David, besides his sons
by his concubines. And Tamar[u]
was their sister.[v]

The Kings of Judah

10 Solomon's son was Rehoboam,[w]
Abijah[x] his son,
Asa[y] his son,
Jehoshaphat[z] his son,

3:1 [m] 1Ch 14:3; 28:5 [n] S 1Sa 25:43 [o] S Jos 15:56 [p] S 1Sa 25:42 **3:2** [q] 1Ki 2:22 **3:4** [r] S 2Sa 5:4; 1Ch 29:27 [s] S 2Sa 5:5 **3:5** [t] 2Sa 11:3 **3:9** [u] S 2Sa 13:1 [v] 1Ch 14:4 **3:10** [w] 1Ki 14:21-31; 2Ch 12:16 [x] 1Ki 15:1-8; 2Ch 13:1 [y] 1Ki 15:9-24 [z] 2Ch 17:1-21:3

[a] *42* The meaning of the Hebrew for this phrase is uncertain. [b] *55* Or *of the Sopherites* [c] *55* Or *father of Beth Recab* [d] *5* Hebrew *Shimea,* a variant of *Shammua* [e] *5* One Hebrew manuscript and Vulgate (see also Septuagint and 2 Samuel 11:3); most Hebrew manuscripts *Bathshua* [f] *6* Two Hebrew manuscripts (see also 2 Samuel 5:15 and 1 Chron. 14:5); most Hebrew manuscripts *Elishama*

of personal and place-names; the phrase "father of" must often be understood as "founder of" or "leader of" a city (see NIV text notes on 1:10; 4:4).

2:50b – 55 Resumes the genealogy of Hur (v. 20). The same formulas for identifying the genealogical sections in vv. 25,33 and in vv. 42,50a are used in v. 50b and 4:4: "The sons of Hur ... These were the descendants of Hur." The presence of these formulas suggests that this section and 4:1 – 4 were once a unit; the Chronicler has inserted his record of the Davidic descent (ch. 3) into the middle of this other genealogy, apparently to balance the sections of his material (see notes on 2:10 — 3:24; 4:1 – 23). Otherwise the disruption of the genealogy of Hur may have already occurred in the Chronicler's sources.

2:55 *Tirathites, Shimeathites and Sucathites.* May refer to three families, as translated here, or possibly to three different classes of scribes, perhaps those who (1) read, (2) copied and (3) checked the work. *Kenites.* Originally a foreign people, many of the Kenites were incorporated into Judah (see Nu 10:29 – 32; Jdg 1:16; 4:11).

3:1 – 24 See note on 2:10 — 3:24.

3:1 – 9 This list of David's children is largely drawn from 2Sa 3:2 – 5; 5:13 – 16; 13:1 (see notes there; see also chart, p. 402). The sons born in Jerusalem are repeated in 1Ch 14:3 – 7. The name Eliphelet occurs twice (vv. 6,8); in 14:5,7 two spellings of the name are given (only one son having this name is mentioned in 2Sa 5:14 – 16). The reference to David's seven-year rule in Hebron (v. 4) is repeated in 29:27, though the Chronicler does not deal with this period in his narrative. The references to Absalom, Tamar, Adonijah, Amnon and Bathsheba all recall unhappy incidents in the life of David, incidents the Chronicler has omitted from his later narrative (see 2Sa 11 – 15; 17 – 18; 1Ki 1).

3:10 *Rehoboam.* See 2Ch 10 – 12 and note on 11:1 – 23. *Abijah.* See note on 2Ch 13:1 — 14:1. *Asa.* See note on 2Ch 14:2 — 16:14. *Jehoshaphat.* See note on 2Ch 17:1 — 21:3.

11 Jehoram[a][a] his son,
Ahaziah[b] his son,
Joash[c] his son,
12 Amaziah[d] his son,
Azariah[e] his son,
Jotham[f] his son,
13 Ahaz[g] his son,
Hezekiah[h] his son,
Manasseh[i] his son,
14 Amon[j] his son,
Josiah[k] his son.
15 The sons of Josiah:
Johanan the firstborn,
Jehoiakim[l] the second son,
Zedekiah[m] the third,
Shallum[n] the fourth.
16 The successors of Jehoiakim:
Jehoiachin[b][o] his son,
and Zedekiah.[p]

The Royal Line After the Exile

17 The descendants of Jehoiachin the captive:
Shealtiel[q] his son, 18 Malkiram, Pedaiah, Shenazzar,[r] Jekamiah, Hoshama and Nedabiah.[s]
19 The sons of Pedaiah:
Zerubbabel[t] and Shimei.
The sons of Zerubbabel:
Meshullam and Hananiah.
Shelomith was their sister.
20 There were also five others:
Hashubah, Ohel, Berekiah, Hasadiah and Jushab-Hesed.
21 The descendants of Hananiah:
Pelatiah and Jeshaiah, and the sons of Rephaiah, of Arnan, of Obadiah and of Shecaniah.
22 The descendants of Shecaniah:
Shemaiah and his sons:
Hattush,[u] Igal, Bariah, Neariah and Shaphat — six in all.
23 The sons of Neariah:
Elioenai, Hizkiah and Azrikam — three in all.
24 The sons of Elioenai:
Hodaviah, Eliashib, Pelaiah, Akkub, Johanan, Delaiah and Anani — seven in all.

Other Clans of Judah

4 The descendants of Judah:[v]
Perez, Hezron,[w] Carmi, Hur and Shobal.

3:11 [a] 2Ki 8:16-24; 2Ch 21:1 [b] 2Ki 8:25-10:14; 2Ch 22:1-10 [c] 2Ki 11:1-12:21; 2Ch 22:11-24:27 **3:12** [d] 2Ki 14:1-22; 2Ch 25:1-28 [e] 2Ki 15:1-7; 2Ch 26:1-23 [f] 2Ki 15:32-38; 2Ch 27:1; Isa 1:1; Hos 1:1; Mic 1:1 **3:13** [g] 2Ki 16:1-20; 2Ch 28:1; Isa 7:1 [h] 2Ki 18:1-20:21; 2Ch 29:1; Isa 1:1; Jer 26:19; Hos 1:1; Mic 1:1 [i] 2Ki 21:1-18; 2Ch 33:1 **3:14** [j] 2Ki 21:19-26; 2Ch 33:21; Zep 1:1 [k] 2Ki 22:1; 2Ch 34:1; Jer 1:2; 3:6; 25:3 **3:15** [l] S 2Ki 23:34 [m] Jer 37:1 [n] S 2Ki 23:31 **3:16** [o] S 2Ki 24:6,8 [p] S 2Ki 24:18 **3:17** [q] Ezr 3:2 **3:18** [r] Ezr 1:8; 5:14 [s] Jer 22:30 **3:19** [t] Ezr 2:2; 3:2; 5:2; Ne 7:7; 12:1; Hag 1:1; 2:2; Zec 4:6 **3:22** [u] Ezr 8:2-3 **4:1** [v] S Ge 29:35; S 1Ch 2:3 [w] Nu 26:21

[a] *11* Hebrew *Joram,* a variant of *Jehoram*
[b] *16* Hebrew *Jeconiah,* a variant of *Jehoiachin*; also in verse 17

3:11 *Jehoram.* See 2Ch 21. *Ahaziah.* See note on 2Ch 22:1 – 9. *Joash.* See note on 2Ch 23:1 — 24:27.
3:12 *Amaziah.* See note on 2Ch 25:1 – 28. *Azariah.* Also called Uzziah (see note on 2Ch 26:1 – 23). *Jotham.* See 2Ch 27; see also 2Ki 15:32 – 38 and notes.
3:13 *Ahaz.* See 2Ch 28:1 – 27 and notes. *Hezekiah.* See note on 2Ch 29:1 — 32:13. *Manasseh.* See note on 2Ch 33:1 – 20.
3:14 *Amon.* See note on 2Ch 33:21 – 25. *Josiah.* See note on 2Ch 34:1 — 36:1.
3:15 *Johanan the firstborn.* Not mentioned elsewhere and may have died before Josiah. The genealogy is segmented at this point, instead of linear as in vv. 10 – 14. Since Josiah's other three sons would all occupy the throne, the succession was not uniformly father to son. Shallum/Jehoahaz (2Ch 36:2 – 4; 2Ki 23:30 – 35) was replaced by Jehoiakim (2Ch 36:5 – 8; 2Ki 23:34 — 24:6); Jehoiakim was succeeded by his son Jehoiachin (2Ch 36:9 – 10; 2Ki 24:8 – 16). After Jehoiachin was taken captive to Babylon by Nebuchadnezzar, Josiah's son Zedekiah became the last king of Judah (2Ch 36:11 – 14; 2Ki 24:17 — 25:7).
3:17 – 20 Seven sons are attributed to Jehoiachin, but not one succeeded him (see notes on v. 15; Jer 22:30). Tablets found in Babylon dating from the 10th to the 35th year of Nebuchadnezzar (595 – 570 B.C.) and listing deliveries of rations mention Jehoiachin and five sons as well as other Judahites held in Babylon. Jehoiachin received similar largess from Nebuchadnezzar's successor Evil-Merodach (562 – 560 B.C.; see 2Ki 25:27 – 30).
3:18 *Shenazzar.* May be another spelling of the name Sheshbazzar. If so, the treasures of the temple were consigned to his care for return to Judah (Ezr 1:11). He also served for a short time as the first governor of the returnees and made an initial attempt at rebuilding the temple (Ezr 5:14 – 16). Little is known of him; he soon disappeared from the scene and was overshadowed by his nephew Zerubbabel, who assumes such importance in Ezra, Haggai and Zechariah. But see note on Ezr 1:8.
3:19 *Pedaiah.* Other texts name Shealtiel (v. 17) as Zerubbabel's father (Ezr 3:2,8; Ne 12:1; Hag 1:1,12,14; 2:2,23). Suggestions offered to resolve this difficulty are: (1) Shealtiel may have died early, and Pedaiah became the head of the family. (2) Pedaiah may have married the childless widow of Shealtiel; Zerubbabel would then be regarded as the son of Shealtiel according to the law of levirate marriage (Dt 25:5 – 6). In Lk 3:27 Neri instead of Jehoiachin (v. 17) is identified as the father of Shealtiel. Suggestions similar to those above could be made in this instance as well. It is also interesting to note that the genealogies of Jesus in Mt 1 and Lk 3 both trace his descent to Zerubbabel, but that none of the names subsequent to Zerubbabel (vv. 19 – 24) is found in the NT genealogies.
3:20 *five others.* May have been sons of Zerubbabel, but no kinship terms are provided. Since the sons of Hananiah (v. 19) are specified in v. 21, they could also be the sons of Meshullam (v. 19).
3:21 *sons of Rephaiah ... Shecaniah.* Probably other Davidic families at the time of Zerubbabel (v. 19) or Pelatiah and Jeshaiah. If they are understood as contemporary with Zerubbabel, his genealogy was carried only two generations (his sons and grandsons) and a date for Chronicles as early as 450 B.C. is possible (see Introduction: Author, Date and Sources).
3:22 *six.* Shemaiah appears to have five sons, but the total is given as six. Either one of the six names is missing, or Shemaiah is to be understood as the brother of the five persons named (in which case there should be a semicolon after "sons" instead of a colon) — all six then being sons of Shecaniah.
4:1 – 23 None of the genealogies of Judah in this section appears elsewhere in Scripture. Although the section may have the appearance of miscellaneous notes, the careful shaping of the Chronicler is evident in light of the overall inverted structure of the genealogies of Judah:

2Reaiah son of Shobal was the father
of Jahath, and Jahath the father of
Ahumai and Lahad. These were the
clans of the Zorathites.
3These were the sons[a] of Etam:
Jezreel, Ishma and Idbash. Their
sister was named Hazzelelponi.
4Penuel was the father of Gedor,
and Ezer the father of Hushah.
These were the descendants of Hur,[x]
the firstborn of Ephrathah and father[b] of Bethlehem.[y]
5Ashhur[z] the father of Tekoa had two
wives, Helah and Naarah.
6Naarah bore him Ahuzzam, Hepher,
Temeni and Haahashtari. These
were the descendants of Naarah.
7The sons of Helah:
Zereth, Zohar, Ethnan, 8and Koz,
who was the father of Anub and
Hazzobebah and of the clans of
Aharhel son of Harum.

9Jabez was more honorable than his
brothers. His mother had named him Jabez,[c] saying, "I gave birth to him in pain."
10Jabez cried out to the God of Israel, "Oh,
that you would bless me and enlarge my
territory! Let your hand be with me, and
keep me from harm so that I will be free
from pain." And God granted his request.

11Kelub, Shuhah's brother, was the father of Mehir, who was the father
of Eshton. 12Eshton was the father
of Beth Rapha, Paseah and Tehin-
nah the father of Ir Nahash.[d] These
were the men of Recah.

13The sons of Kenaz:
Othniel[a] and Seraiah.
The sons of Othniel:
Hathath and Meonothai.[e] 14Meono-
thai was the father of Ophrah.
Seraiah was the father of Joab,
the father of Ge Harashim.[f] It was
called this because its people were
craftsmen.
15The sons of Caleb son of Jephunneh:
Iru, Elah and Naam.
The son of Elah:
Kenaz.
16The sons of Jehallelel:
Ziph, Ziphah, Tiria and Asarel.
17The sons of Ezrah:
Jether, Mered, Epher and Jalon.
One of Mered's wives gave birth to
Miriam,[b] Shammai and Ishbah the
father of Eshtemoa. 18(His Judean
wife gave birth to Jered the father
of Gedor, Heber the father of Soco,
and Jekuthiel the father of Zanoah.[c]) These were the children of
Pharaoh's daughter Bithiah, whom
Mered had married.
19The sons of Hodiah's wife, the sister
of Naham:
the father of Keilah[d] the Garmite,
and Eshtemoa the Maacathite.[e]
20The sons of Shimon:
Amnon, Rinnah, Ben-Hanan and
Tilon.
The descendants of Ishi:
Zoheth and Ben-Zoheth.
21The sons of Shelah[f] son of Judah:
Er the father of Lecah, Laadah the
father of Mareshah and the clans of
the linen workers at Beth Ashbea,
22Jokim, the men of Cozeba, and
Joash and Saraph, who ruled in
Moab and Jashubi Lehem. (These
records are from ancient times.)
23They were the potters who lived
at Netaim and Gederah; they stayed
there and worked for the king.

4:4 [x] 1Ch 2:50 [y] Ru 1:19 **4:5** [z] 1Ch 2:24 **4:13** [a] S Jos 15:17 **4:17** [b] S Ex 15:20 **4:18** [c] S Jos 15:34 **4:19** [d] S Jos 15:44 [e] S Dt 3:14 **4:21** [f] S Ge 38:5

[a] *3* Some Septuagint manuscripts (see also Vulgate); Hebrew *father* [b] *4* *Father* may mean *civic leader* or *military leader*; also in verses 12, 14, 17, 18 and possibly elsewhere. [c] *9* *Jabez* sounds like the Hebrew for *pain.* [d] *12* Or *of the city of Nahash* [e] *13* Some Septuagint manuscripts and Vulgate; Hebrew does not have *and Meonothai.* [f] *14* *Ge Harashim* means *valley of craftsmen.*

2:3 Shelah
2:4–8 Perez
2:9—3:24 Hezron
4:1–20 Perez
4:21–23 Shelah

This balancing of the material in inverse order shows the centrality of the section of the lineage of Hezron and the house of David; the same balancing in inverse order is observed within the Hezron section (see note on 2:10—3:24). The record of Judah's oldest surviving son, Shelah, frames the entire genealogy of Judah. There are 15 fragmentary genealogies in this section, with two to six generations in each.

4:1–2 The descendants of Judah here are not brothers; rather, the genealogy is linear.

4:1 *Carmi.* Either a scribal confusion or an alternative name for Caleb (2:9); the confusion may have been induced by 2:7.

4:2 *Reaiah.* A variant of Haroeh (2:52).

4:5–8 Supplementary to 2:24.

4:9–10 The practice of inserting short historical notes into genealogical records is amply attested in non-Biblical genealogical texts from the ancient Near East as well as in other Biblical genealogies (Ge 4:19–24; 10:8–12).

4:13 *Othniel.* The first of Israel's judges (Jos 15:17; Jdg 1:13; 3:9–11).

4:16–20 This portion of the genealogy is from preexilic times; several of the places named were not included in the province of Judah in the restoration period (e.g., Ziph and Eshtemoa).

4:17 *One of Mered's wives.* The pharaoh's daughter (v. 18). Mered is otherwise unknown; the fact that he married a daughter of a pharaoh suggests his prominence. The event may be associated with the fortunes of Israel in Egypt under Joseph.

4:21,23 This section accurately reflects a feature of ancient Near Eastern society. Clans were often associated not only with particular localities but also with special trades or guilds, such as linen workers (v. 21), potters (v. 23), royal patronage (v. 23) and scribes (2:55).

Simeon

4:28-33pp — Jos 19:2-10

24 The descendants of Simeon:[g]
Nemuel, Jamin, Jarib,[h] Zerah and
Shaul;
25 Shallum was Shaul's son, Mibsam
his son and Mishma his son.
26 The descendants of Mishma:
Hammuel his son, Zaccur his son
and Shimei his son.
27 Shimei had sixteen sons and six
daughters, but his brothers did not have
many children; so their entire clan did
not become as numerous as the people of
Judah. 28 They lived in Beersheba,[i] Moladah,[j] Hazar Shual, 29 Bilhah, Ezem,[k] To-
lad, 30 Bethuel, Hormah,[l] Ziklag,[m] 31 Beth
Marcaboth, Hazar Susim, Beth Biri and
Shaaraim.[n] These were their towns until
the reign of David. 32 Their surrounding
villages were Etam, Ain,[o] Rimmon, Token
and Ashan[p]—five towns— 33 and all the
villages around these towns as far as Baalath.[a] These were their settlements. And
they kept a genealogical record.

34 Meshobab, Jamlech, Joshah son of
Amaziah, 35 Joel, Jehu son of Joshi-
biah, the son of Seraiah, the son of
Asiel, 36 also Elioenai, Jaakobah, Jesh-
ohaiah, Asaiah, Adiel, Jesimiel, Benaiah, 37 and Ziza son of Shiphi, the son
of Allon, the son of Jedaiah, the son
of Shimri, the son of Shemaiah.

38 The men listed above by name were
leaders of their clans. Their families increased greatly, 39 and they went to the outskirts of Gedor[q] to the east of the valley in
search of pasture for their flocks. 40 They
found rich, good pasture, and the land
was spacious, peaceful and quiet.[r] Some
Hamites had lived there formerly.
41 The men whose names were listed
came in the days of Hezekiah king of Judah. They attacked the Hamites in their
dwellings and also the Meunites[s] who
were there and completely destroyed[b]
them, as is evident to this day. Then they
settled in their place, because there was
pasture for their flocks. 42 And five hundred of these Simeonites, led by Pelatiah,
Neariah, Rephaiah and Uzziel, the sons
of Ishi, invaded the hill country of Seir.[t]
43 They killed the remaining Amalekites[u]
who had escaped, and they have lived
there to this day.

Reuben

5 The sons of Reuben[v] the firstborn of
Israel (he was the firstborn, but when
he defiled his father's marriage bed,[w] his
rights as firstborn were given to the sons
of Joseph[x] son of Israel;[y] so he could not
be listed in the genealogical record in accordance with his birthright,[z] 2 and though
Judah[a] was the strongest of his brothers
and a ruler[b] came from him, the rights of
the firstborn[c] belonged to Joseph)— 3 the
sons of Reuben[d] the firstborn of Israel:
Hanoch, Pallu,[e] Hezron[f] and Carmi.
4 The descendants of Joel:
Shemaiah his son, Gog his son,
Shimei his son, 5 Micah his son,
Reaiah his son, Baal his son,
6 and Beerah his son, whom Tiglath-
Pileser[c][g] king of Assyria took into
exile. Beerah was a leader of the
Reubenites.
7 Their relatives by clans,[h] listed according to their genealogical records:
Jeiel the chief, Zechariah, 8 and
Bela son of Azaz, the son of She-
ma, the son of Joel. They settled in

4:24 [g] S Ge 29:33 [h] Nu 26:12 **4:28** [i] S Ge 21:14 [j] S Jos 15:26 **4:29** [k] S Jos 15:29 **4:30** [l] S Nu 14:45 [m] S Jos 15:31 **4:31** [n] S Jos 15:36 **4:32** [o] S Nu 34:11 [p] S Jos 15:42 **4:39** [q] S Jos 15:58 **4:40** [r] Jdg 18:7-10 **4:41** [s] 2Ch 20:1; 26:7 **4:42** [t] S Ge 14:6 **4:43** [u] S Ge 14:7; Est 3:1; 9:16 **5:1** [v] S Ge 29:32 [w] Ge 35:22; 49:4 [x] S Ge 48:16,22; S 49:26 [y] Ge 48:5 [z] 1Ch 26:10 **5:2** [a] S Ge 49:10,12 [b] S 1Sa 9:16; S 12:12; S 2Sa 6:21; 1Ch 11:2; S 2Ch 7:18; Mt 2:6 [c] S Ge 25:31 **5:3** [d] S Ge 29:32; 46:9; Ex 6:14; Nu 26:5-11 [e] S Nu 26:5 [f] S Nu 26:6 **5:6** [g] ver 26; S 2Ki 15:19; 16:10; 2Ch 28:20 **5:7** [h] Jos 13:15-23

[a] *33* Some Septuagint manuscripts (see also Joshua 19:8); Hebrew *Baal* [b] *41* The Hebrew term refers to the irrevocable giving over of things or persons to the LORD, often by totally destroying them. [c] *6* Hebrew *Tilgath-Pilneser,* a variant of *Tiglath-Pileser*; also in verse 26

4:24–43 The genealogy of Simeon is also found in Ge 46:10; Ex 6:15; Nu 26:12–13. Simeon settled in part of the territory of Judah; the list of occupied towns should be compared with Jos 15:26–32,42; 19:2–7. Since Simeon occupied areas allotted to Judah, this tribe was politically incorporated into Judah and appears to have lost much of its own identity in history (see Ge 34:24–31; 49:5–7; see also notes on Ge 34:25; 49:7). Geographical and historical notes are inserted in the genealogy (see note on vv. 9–10). Apparently two genealogies are included here: vv. 24–33—ending with the formula, "they kept a genealogical record"—and vv. 34–43. Overpopulation (v. 38) caused them to expand toward Gedor and east toward Edom at the time of Hezekiah (vv. 39–43). The long hostility between Israel and Amalek surfaced once again (v. 43; cf. Ex 17:8–16; Dt 25:17–19; 1Sa 15; see Introduction to Esther: Purpose, Themes and Literary Features).

5:1–26 The genealogical records of the tribes east of the Jordan: Reuben, Gad and half of Manasseh (see Nu 32:33–42). The Chronicler's concern with "all Israel" includes incorporating the genealogical records of these tribes that were no longer significant entities in Israel's life in the restoration period, having been swept away in the Assyrian conquests.

5:1–10 The necessity to explain why the birthright of the firstborn did not remain with Reuben (see Ge 35:22; 49:4 for Reuben's sin) interrupts the initial statement (v. 1), which is then repeated after the explanation (v. 3). The parenthetical material (vv. 1–2) shows the writer's partiality for Judah, even though Joseph received the double portion (Ephraim and Manasseh) of the firstborn. The Hebrew term translated "ruler" (v. 2) is used of David in 11:2; 17:7; 2Sa 5:2; 6:21; 7:8. The use of military titles (vv. 6–7) and a battle account (v. 10) suggest that this genealogy may have functioned in military organization (see Introduction: Genealogies). The source for some of this material on Reuben is Nu 26:5–11. The Chronicler has omitted reference to Eliab and his three sons who perished in the rebellion of Korah (see Nu 26:8–10) and so were not relevant to his purpose.

5:6 *Tiglath-Pileser.* This Assyrian king (745–727 B.C.; see chart, p. 472) attacked Israel (v. 26; 2Ki 15:29) and also imposed tribute on Ahaz of Judah (2Ch 28:19–20; 2Ki 16:7–10).

the area from Aroer[i] to Nebo[j] and
Baal Meon.[k] 9To the east they occupied the land up to the edge of the
desert that extends to the Euphrates[l] River, because their livestock
had increased in Gilead.[m]
10During Saul's reign they waged
war against the Hagrites[n], who were
defeated at their hands; they occupied
the dwellings of the Hagrites throughout the entire region east of Gilead.

Gad

11The Gadites[o] lived next to them in Bashan, as far as Salecah:[p]
12Joel was the chief, Shapham the
second, then Janai and Shaphat, in
Bashan.
13Their relatives, by families, were:
Michael, Meshullam, Sheba, Jorai,
Jacan, Zia and Eber—seven in all.
14These were the sons of Abihail son
of Huri, the son of Jaroah, the son
of Gilead, the son of Michael, the
son of Jeshishai, the son of Jahdo,
the son of Buz.
15Ahi son of Abdiel, the son of Guni,
was head of their family.
16The Gadites lived in Gilead, in Bashan and its outlying villages, and
on all the pasturelands of Sharon as
far as they extended.
17All these were entered in the genealogical records during the reigns of Jotham[q] king of Judah and Jeroboam[r] king
of Israel.

18The Reubenites, the Gadites and the
half-tribe of Manasseh had 44,760 men
ready for military service[s]—able-bodied men who could handle shield and
sword, who could use a bow, and who
were trained for battle. 19They waged war
against the Hagrites, Jetur,[t] Naphish and
Nodab. 20They were helped[u] in fighting
them, and God handed the Hagrites and
all their allies over to them, because they
cried[v] out to him during the battle. He answered their prayers, because they trusted[w] in him. 21They seized the livestock of
the Hagrites—fifty thousand camels, two
hundred fifty thousand sheep and two
thousand donkeys. They also took one
hundred thousand people captive, 22and
many others fell slain, because the battle[x]
was God's. And they occupied the land
until the exile.[y]

The Half-Tribe of Manasseh

23The people of the half-tribe of Manasseh[z] were numerous; they settled in the
land from Bashan to Baal Hermon, that is,
to Senir (Mount Hermon).[a]
24These were the heads of their families: Epher, Ishi, Eliel, Azriel, Jeremiah,
Hodaviah and Jahdiel. They were brave
warriors, famous men, and heads of their
families. 25But they were unfaithful[b] to
the God of their fathers and prostituted[c]
themselves to the gods of the peoples of
the land, whom God had destroyed before
them. 26So the God of Israel stirred up the
spirit[d] of Pul[e] king of Assyria (that is, Tiglath-Pileser[f] king of Assyria), who took the
Reubenites, the Gadites and the half-tribe
of Manasseh into exile. He took them to
Halah,[g] Habor, Hara and the river of Gozan, where they are to this day.

Levi

6 The sons of Levi:[h]
Gershon, Kohath and Merari.
2The sons of Kohath:
Amram, Izhar, Hebron and Uzziel.[i]

5:8 [i]S Nu 32:34; Jdg 11:26 [j]S Nu 32:3 [k]S Jos 13:17 **5:9** [l]S Ge 2:14 [m]S Nu 32:26 **5:10** [n]ver 22; 1Ch 27:31 **5:11** [o]S Ge 30:11; S Nu 1:25; S Jos 13:24-28 [p]S Dt 3:10 **5:17** [q]S 2Ki 15:32 [r]S 2Ki 14:23 **5:18** [s]S Nu 1:3 **5:19** [t]Ge 25:15 **5:20** [u]Ps 37:40; 46:5; 54:4 [v]1Ki 8:44; 2Ch 6:34; 13:14; 14:11; Ps 20:7-9; 22:5; 107:6 [w]Ps 26:1; Isa 26:3; Da 6:23 **5:22** [x]S Dt 20:4; 2Ch 32:8 [y]S ver 10; S 2Ki 15:29 **5:23** [z]1Ch 7:14 [a]S Dt 3:8,9; SS 4:8 **5:25** [b]Dt 32:15-18; 1Ch 9:1; 10:13; 2Ch 12:2; 26:16; 28:19; 29:6; 30:7; 36:14 [c]S Ex 34:15; S Lev 18:3 **5:26** [d]Isa 37:7 [e]S 2Ki 15:19 [f]S ver 6; S 2Ki 15:29 [g]2Ki 17:6 **6:1** [h]S Ge 29:34; S Nu 3:17 **6:2** [i]S Ex 6:18

5:10 *Hagrites.* See vv. 19–22. Named among the enemies of Israel (Ps 83:6), this tribe is apparently associated with Hagar, the mother of Ishmael (Ge 16), but see note on Ps 83:6.

5:11–22 The materials in this list for the tribe of Gad have no parallels in the Bible. The other genealogies of Gad are organized around his seven sons (Ge 46:16; Nu 26:15–18); here four names are given, none found in the other lists. The Chronicler states (v. 17) that these records came from the period of Jotham of Judah (750–732 B.C.) and Jeroboam II of Israel (793–753). The presence of military titles and narratives (vv. 12,18–22) suggests that this genealogy originated as part of a military census. The territory of Gad is delineated in Dt 3:12.

5:18–22 The first example of the Chronicler's theme of immediate retribution (see Introduction: Purpose and Themes). Success in warfare is attributed to their crying out to God (v. 20; cf. 2Ch 6:24–25,34–39; 12:7–12; 13:13–16; 14:9–15; 18:31; 20:1–30; 32:1–23).

5:23–26 Manasseh is treated further in 7:14–19; the half-tribe that settled east of the Jordan River is dealt with here since it shared the same fate as Reuben and Gad, and possibly also so that the Chronicler could keep the total of 12 for his tribal genealogies (see note on 2:1–2). Again immediate retribution is apparent: Just as trust in God can bring victory (vv. 18–22), so also defeat comes to the unfaithful (vv. 25–26). The use of the retributive theme in these two accounts argues for the unity of the genealogies with the historical portions of Chronicles. The list of names given here is not properly a genealogy but a list of clans. Since they are described as brave warriors in connection with a battle report (vv. 24–26), this section too is likely derived from records of military conscription (see note on vv. 1–10; see also 2Ki 15:19,29; 17:6; 18:11).

5:25 *were unfaithful ... prostituted themselves.* See Ex 34:15 and note.

5:26 *Pul.* Tiglath-Pileser's throne name in Babylon.

6:1–81 This chapter is devoted to a series of lists, all pertaining to the tribe of Levi. The first section (vv. 1–15) records the line of the high priests down to the exile; the clans of Levi follow (vv. 16–30). David's appointees as temple musicians came from the three clans of Levi: Gershon, Kohath and Merari (vv. 31–47). The generations between Aaron and Ahimaaz are given a separate listing (vv. 49–53), reinforcing the separate duties of priests and Levites (see note on Ex 32:26). The listing of the Levitical possessions among the tribes concludes the chapter (vv. 54–81).

6:1–3 A short segmented genealogy narrows the descendants of Levi to the lineage of Eleazar, in whose line the high

3 The children of Amram:
Aaron, Moses and Miriam.[j]
The sons of Aaron:
Nadab, Abihu,[k] Eleazar[l] and Ithamar.[m]
4 Eleazar was the father of Phinehas,[n]
Phinehas the father of Abishua,
5 Abishua the father of Bukki,
Bukki the father of Uzzi,
6 Uzzi the father of Zerahiah,
Zerahiah the father of Meraioth,
7 Meraioth the father of Amariah,
Amariah the father of Ahitub,
8 Ahitub the father of Zadok,[o]
Zadok the father of Ahimaaz,
9 Ahimaaz the father of Azariah,
Azariah the father of Johanan,
10 Johanan the father of Azariah[p] (it
was he who served as priest in the
temple Solomon built in Jerusalem),
11 Azariah the father of Amariah,
Amariah the father of Ahitub,
12 Ahitub the father of Zadok,
Zadok the father of Shallum,
13 Shallum the father of Hilkiah,[q]
Hilkiah the father of Azariah,
14 Azariah the father of Seraiah,[r]
and Seraiah the father of Jehozadak.
15 Jehozadak[s] was deported when the
LORD sent Judah and Jerusalem into
exile by the hand of Nebuchadnezzar.

16 The sons of Levi:[t]
Gershon,[a] Kohath and Merari.[u]
17 These are the names of the sons of
Gershon:
Libni and Shimei.[v]
18 The sons of Kohath:
Amram, Izhar, Hebron and Uz-
ziel.[w]
19 The sons of Merari:[x]
Mahli and Mushi.[y]
These are the clans of the Levites list-
ed according to their fathers:
20 Of Gershon:
Libni his son, Jehath his son,
Zimmah his son, 21 Joah his son,
Iddo his son, Zerah his son
and Jeatherai his son.
22 The descendants of Kohath:
Amminadab his son, Korah[z] his
son,
Assir his son, 23 Elkanah his son,
Ebiasaph his son, Assir his son,
24 Tahath his son, Uriel[a] his son,
Uzziah his son and Shaul his son.
25 The descendants of Elkanah:
Amasai, Ahimoth,
26 Elkanah his son,[b] Zophai his son,
Nahath his son, 27 Eliab his son,
Jeroham his son, Elkanah[b] his son
and Samuel[c] his son.[c]

6:3 [j] S Ex 15:20 [k] S Lev 10:1; S 10:1-20:2 [l] Lev 10:6 [m] S Ex 6:23 **6:4** [n] Ezr 7:5 **6:8** [o] S 2Sa 8:17; S 1Ch 12:28; S Ezr 7:2 **6:10** [p] S 1Ki 4:2 **6:13** [q] 2Ki 22:1-20; 2Ch 34:9; 35:8 **6:14** [r] S 2Ki 25:18; S Ezr 2:2 **6:15** [s] Ne 12:1; Hag 1:1,14; 2:2,4; Zec 6:11 **6:16** [t] S Ge 29:34; S Nu 3:17-20 [u] S Nu 26:57 **6:17** [v] S Ex 6:17 **6:18** [w] S Ex 6:18 **6:19** [x] S Ge 46:11; 1Ch 23:21; 24:26 [y] S Ex 6:19 **6:22** [z] S Ex 6:24 **6:24** [a] 1Ch 15:5 **6:27** [b] S 1Sa 1:1 [c] S 1Sa 1:20

[a] *16* Hebrew *Gershom,* a variant of *Gershon*; also in verses 17, 20, 43, 62 and 71 [b] *26* Some Hebrew manuscripts, Septuagint and Syriac; most Hebrew manuscripts *Ahimoth* [26]*and Elkanah. The sons of Elkanah:* [c] *27* Some Septuagint manuscripts (see also 1 Samuel 1:19,20 and 1 Chron. 6:33,34); Hebrew does not have *and Samuel his son.*

priests are presented in linear form (vv. 4–15). The sons of Levi (v. 1) always appear in this order, based on age (v. 16; Ge 46:11; Ex 6:16; Nu 3:17; 26:57). Of Aaron's four sons (v. 3), the first two died as a result of sacrilege (Lev 10:1–2; Nu 26:61); succeeding generations of priests would trace their lineage to either Eleazar or Ithamar.

6:4–15 This list of high priests from the time of Eleazar to the exile has been sharply telescoped. The following high priests known from the OT are not mentioned: Jehoiada (2Ki 12:2), Uriah (2Ki 16:10–16), possibly two other Azariahs (2Ch 26:17, 20; 31:10–13), Eli (1Sa 1:9; 14:3) and Abiathar (see 2Sa 8:17 and note). The list is repeated with some variation in Ezr 7:1–5 (see notes there).

6:8 *Ahitub the father of Zadok.* This Zadok was one of David's two priests (18:16; 2Sa 8:17). When David's other priest, Abiathar (see note on vv. 4–15), supported the rebellion of Adonijah, Zadok supported Solomon (1Ki 1). After the expulsion of Abiathar (1Ki 2:26–27), Zadok alone held the office (1Ch 29:22), which continued in his line (1Ki 4:2). The Ahitub mentioned here should not be confused with the priest who was the grandson of Eli (1Sa 14:3) and grandfather of Abiathar (1Sa 22:20); the line of Zadok replaced the line of Eli (1Sa 2:27–36; 1Ki 2:26–27). For the importance of the line of Zadok see Eze 40:46; 43:19; 44:15; 48:11. Ezra was concerned to trace his own priestly lineage to this house (Ezr 7:1–5).

6:13 *Hilkiah.* Discovered the Book of the Law in the temple at the time of Josiah (2Ki 22; 2Ch 34).

6:14 *Seraiah.* Executed by the Babylonians after the conquest of Jerusalem in 586 B.C. (2Ki 25:18–21). *Jehozadak.* Father of Joshua (see note on Ezr 2:2), the high priest in the first generation of the restoration period (see Hag 1:1; 2:2; Zec 3:1 and note; 6:11); his name is also spelled "Jozadak" (Ezr 3:2; 5:2; 10:18).

6:16–19a Repeated from Ex 6:16–19; Nu 3:17–20; 26:57–61.

6:22–23 *Assir ... Elkanah ... Ebiasaph.* Ex 6:24 names these men as sons of Korah, but here they are presented in the form ordinarily used for a linear genealogy of successive generations (see vv. 20–21,25–26,29–30). Either this is another example of genealogical fluidity, or one must understand "his son" as referring to Kohath and not to the immediately preceding name.

6:22 *Amminadab.* The almost parallel genealogy later in this chapter lists Izhar in the place of Amminadab—who is nowhere else listed as a son of Kohath, while every other list includes Izhar (vv. 2,37–38; Ex 6:18,21). Either Amminadab is an otherwise unattested alternative name of Izhar, or he is an otherwise unknown son. Or this may be another example of genealogical fluidity in which the Levites are linked with the tribe of Judah and the lineage of David (see Ru 4:18–22; see also Mt 1:4; Lk 3:33) in view of Aaron's marriage to the daughter of Amminadab of Judah (Ex 6:23; see 1Ch 2:10).

6:24 *Uriel.* Possibly the one who led the Kohathites in David's day (15:5).

6:26–27 *Zophai ... Nahath ... Eliab.* Apparently variant names for Zuph, Toah and Eliel (vv. 34–35).

6:27 *Samuel.* His lineage is also given in 1Sa 1:1, where his family is identified as Ephraimite (see note there). Either this is an example of genealogical fluidity, in which Samuel's involvement in the tabernacle (1Sa 3) and performance of

[28]The sons of Samuel:
Joel[a][d] the firstborn
and Abijah the second son.
[29]The descendants of Merari:
Mahli, Libni his son,
Shimei his son, Uzzah his son,
[30]Shimea his son, Haggiah his son
and Asaiah his son.

The Temple Musicians

6:54-80pp — Jos 21:4-39

[31]These are the men[e] David put in charge of the music[f] in the house of the LORD after the ark came to rest there. [32]They ministered with music before the tabernacle, the Tent of Meeting, until Solomon built the temple of the LORD in Jerusalem. They performed their duties according to the regulations laid down for them.

[33]Here are the men who served, together with their sons:
From the Kohathites:
Heman,[g] the musician,
the son of Joel,[h] the son of Samuel,
[34]the son of Elkanah,[i] the son of Jeroham,
the son of Eliel, the son of Toah,
[35]the son of Zuph, the son of Elkanah,
the son of Mahath, the son of Amasai,
[36]the son of Elkanah, the son of Joel,
the son of Azariah, the son of Zephaniah,
[37]the son of Tahath, the son of Assir,
the son of Ebiasaph, the son of Korah,[j]
[38]the son of Izhar,[k] the son of Kohath,
the son of Levi, the son of Israel;
[39]and Heman's associate Asaph,[l] who served at his right hand:
Asaph son of Berekiah, the son of Shimea,[m]
[40]the son of Michael, the son of Baaseiah,[b]
the son of Malkijah, [41]the son of Ethni,
the son of Zerah, the son of Adaiah,
[42]the son of Ethan, the son of Zimmah,
the son of Shimei, [43]the son of Jahath,
the son of Gershon, the son of Levi;
[44]and from their associates, the Merarites,[n] at his left hand:
Ethan son of Kishi, the son of Abdi,
the son of Malluch, [45]the son of Hashabiah,
the son of Amaziah, the son of Hilkiah,
[46]the son of Amzi, the son of Bani,
the son of Shemer, [47]the son of Mahli,
the son of Mushi, the son of Merari,
the son of Levi.

[48]Their fellow Levites[o] were assigned to all the other duties of the tabernacle, the house of God. [49]But Aaron and his descendants were the ones who presented offerings on the altar[p] of burnt offering and on the altar of incense[q] in connection with all that was done in the Most Holy Place, making atonement for Israel, in accordance with all that Moses the servant of God had commanded.

[50]These were the descendants of Aaron:
Eleazar his son, Phinehas his son,
Abishua his son, [51]Bukki his son,
Uzzi his son, Zerahiah his son,
[52]Meraioth his son, Amariah his son,
Ahitub his son, [53]Zadok[r] his son
and Ahimaaz his son.

[54]These were the locations of their settlements[s] allotted as their territory (they were assigned to the descendants of Aaron who were from the Kohathite clan, because the first lot was for them):
[55]They were given Hebron in Judah
with its surrounding pasturelands.

6:28 [d] ver 33; 1Sa 8:2 **6:31** [e] 1Ch 25:1; 2Ch 29:25-26; Ne 12:45 [f] 1Ch 9:33; 15:19; Ezr 3:10; Ps 68:25 **6:33** [g] 1Ki 4:31; 1Ch 15:17; 25:1 [h] S ver 28 **6:34** [i] S 1Sa 1:1 **6:37** [j] S Ex 6:24 **6:38** [k] Ex 6:21 **6:39** [l] 1Ch 25:1, 9; 2Ch 29:13; Ne 11:17 [m] 1Ch 15:17

6:44 [n] 1Ch 15:17 **6:48** [o] 1Ch 23:32 **6:49** [p] Ex 27:1-8 [q] S Ex 30:1-7, 10; 2Ch 26:18 **6:53** [r] S 2Sa 8:17 **6:54** [s] S Nu 31:10

[a] *28* Some Septuagint manuscripts and Syriac (see also 1 Samuel 8:2 and 1 Chron. 6:33); Hebrew does not have *Joel.* [b] *40* Most Hebrew manuscripts; some Hebrew manuscripts, one Septuagint manuscript and Syriac *Maaseiah*

priestly duties (9:22; 1Sa 2:18; 3:1) resulted in his incorporation into the Levites, or the term "Ephraimite" is to be understood as a place of residence, not as a statement of lineage.

6:31–48 Each of the three Levitical clans contributed musicians for the temple: Heman from the family of Kohath, Asaph from Gershon, and Ethan (also called Jeduthun) from Merari. The Chronicler makes frequent reference to the appointment of the musical guilds by David (15:16,27; 25:1–31; 2Ch 29:25–26; see Ne 12:45–47). The frequent mention of the role of the Levites has led many to assume that the author was a member of the musicians. Non-Biblical literature also attests to guilds of singers and musicians in Canaanite temples. This genealogy appears to function as a means of legitimizing the Levites of the restoration period (Ezr 2:40–41; Ne 7:43–44; 10:9–13,28–29; 11:15–18; 12:24–47).

6:49–53 Repeats vv. 4–8 but presumably serves a different function: to legitimize the line of Zadok, which is traced down to Solomon's time, as the only Levitical division authorized to offer sacrifices.

6:54–81 This list of Levitical possessions is taken from Jos 21 with only minor differences (see notes there). The Levites, who were given no block of territory of their own, were distributed throughout Israel.

56But the fields and villages around
the city were given to Caleb son of
Jephunneh.[t]
57So the descendants of Aaron were
given Hebron (a city of refuge), and
Libnah,[a u] Jattir,[v] Eshtemoa, 58Hilen,
Debir,[w] 59Ashan,[x] Juttah[b] and Beth
Shemesh, together with their pasturelands. 60And from the tribe of Benjamin they were given Gibeon,[c] Geba,
Alemeth and Anathoth,[y] together
with their pasturelands.
These towns, which were distributed among the Kohathite clans, were
thirteen in all.
61The rest of Kohath's descendants were
allotted ten towns from the clans of half
the tribe of Manasseh.
62The descendants of Gershon, clan by
clan, were allotted thirteen towns from the
tribes of Issachar, Asher and Naphtali, and
from the part of the tribe of Manasseh that
is in Bashan.
63The descendants of Merari, clan by
clan, were allotted twelve towns from the
tribes of Reuben, Gad and Zebulun.
64So the Israelites gave the Levites these
towns[z] and their pasturelands. 65From the
tribes of Judah, Simeon and Benjamin they
allotted the previously named towns.
66Some of the Kohathite clans were giv-
en as their territory towns from the tribe
of Ephraim.
67In the hill country of Ephraim
they were given Shechem (a city of
refuge), and Gezer,[d a] 68Jokmeam,[b]
Beth Horon,[c] 69Aijalon[d] and Gath
Rimmon,[e] together with their pasturelands.
70And from half the tribe of Manasseh the Israelites gave Aner and Bile-
am, together with their pasturelands,
to the rest of the Kohathite clans.
71The Gershonites[f] received the following:
From the clan of the half-tribe of Manasseh
they received Golan in Bashan[g] and
also Ashtaroth, together with their
pasturelands;
72from the tribe of Issachar
they received Kedesh, Daberath,[h]
73Ramoth and Anem, together with
their pasturelands;
74from the tribe of Asher
they received Mashal, Abdon,[i]
75Hukok[j] and Rehob,[k] together with
their pasturelands;

6:56 [t] S Jos 14:13; S 15:13
6:57 [u] S Nu 33:20 [v] S Jos 15:48
6:58 [w] S Jos 10:3
6:59 [x] S Jos 15:42
6:60 [y] Jer 1:1
6:64 [z] Nu 35:1-8
6:67 [a] S Jos 10:33
6:68 [b] 1Ki 4:12 [c] S Jos 10:10
6:69 [d] S Jos 10:12 [e] S Jos 19:45
6:71 [f] 1Ch 23:7 [g] S Jos 20:8
6:72 [h] S Jos 19:12
6:74 [i] S Jos 19:28
6:75 [j] Jos 19:34 [k] S Nu 13:21

76and from the tribe of Naphtali
they received Kedesh in Galilee,
Hammon[l] and Kiriathaim,[m] together with their pasturelands.
77The Merarites (the rest of the Levites)
received the following:
From the tribe of Zebulun
they received Jokneam, Kartah,[e]
Rimmono and Tabor, together with
their pasturelands;
78from the tribe of Reuben across the
Jordan east of Jericho
they received Bezer[n] in the desert,
Jahzah, 79Kedemoth[o] and Mephaath, together with their pasturelands;
80and from the tribe of Gad
they received Ramoth in Gilead,[p]
Mahanaim,[q] 81Heshbon and Jazer,[r]
together with their pasturelands.[s]

Issachar

7 The sons of Issachar:[t]
Tola, Puah,[u] Jashub and Shimron—four in all.
2The sons of Tola:
Uzzi, Rephaiah, Jeriel, Jahmai, Ib-
sam and Samuel—heads of their
families. During the reign of David, the descendants of Tola listed
as fighting men in their genealogy
numbered 22,600.
3The son of Uzzi:
Izrahiah.
The sons of Izrahiah:
Michael, Obadiah, Joel and Isshiah.
All five of them were chiefs. 4Ac-
cording to their family genealogy,
they had 36,000 men ready for battle, for they had many wives and
children.
5The relatives who were fighting men
belonging to all the clans of Issachar, as listed in their genealogy,
were 87,000 in all.

Benjamin

6Three sons of Benjamin:[v]
Bela, Beker and Jediael.
7The sons of Bela:
Ezbon, Uzzi, Uzziel, Jerimoth and

6:76 [l] Jos 19:28 [m] S Nu 32:37
6:78 [n] S Jos 20:8
6:79 [o] S Dt 2:26
6:80 [p] Jos 20:8 [q] S Ge 32:2
6:81 [r] S Nu 21:32 [s] 2Ch 11:14
7:1 [t] S Ge 30:18 [u] S Ge 46:13
7:6 [v] S Nu 26:38

[a] 57 See Joshua 21:13; Hebrew *given the cities of refuge: Hebron, Libnah.* [b] 59 Syriac (see also Septuagint and Joshua 21:16); Hebrew does not have *Juttah.* [c] 60 See Joshua 21:17; Hebrew does not have *Gibeon.* [d] 67 See Joshua 21:21; Hebrew *given the cities of refuge: Shechem, Gezer.* [e] 77 See Septuagint and Joshua 21:34; Hebrew does not have *Jokneam, Kartah.*

7:1–5 Parts of the genealogy of Issachar are taken from Ge 46:13; Nu 1:28; 26:23–25, though many of the names are otherwise unattested. This list of the clans appears to come from a military muster (vv. 2,4–5) from the time of David (v. 2), perhaps reflecting the census of ch. 21 and 2Sa 24.

7:6–12 There is considerable fluidity among the Biblical sources listing the sons of Benjamin. This list gives three sons; Ge 46:21 records ten; Nu 26:38–39 and 1Ch 8:1–2 both list five (the only name appearing in all these sources is Bela, the firstborn). The variations reflect different origins and functions for these genealogies. The list here appears to function in the military sphere (vv. 7,9,11).

Iri, heads of families — five in all.
Their genealogical record listed
22,034 fighting men.
8 The sons of Beker:
Zemirah, Joash, Eliezer, Elioenai,
Omri, Jeremoth, Abijah, Anathoth
and Alemeth. All these were the
sons of Beker. 9 Their genealogical
record listed the heads of families
and 20,200 fighting men.
10 The son of Jediael:
Bilhan.
The sons of Bilhan:
Jeush, Benjamin, Ehud, Kenaanah, Zethan, Tarshish and Ahish-
ahar. 11 All these sons of Jediael
were heads of families. There were
17,200 fighting men ready to go out
to war.
12 The Shuppites and Huppites were the
descendants of Ir, and the Hushites
the descendants of Aher.

Naphtali

13 The sons of Naphtali:[w]
Jahziel, Guni, Jezer and Shillem[a] — the descendants of Bilhah.

Manasseh

14 The descendants of Manasseh:[x]
Asriel was his descendant through
his Aramean concubine. She gave
birth to Makir the father of Gilead.[y]
15 Makir took a wife from among the
Huppites and Shuppites. His sister's
name was Maacah.
Another descendant was named
Zelophehad,[z] who had only daughters.
16 Makir's wife Maacah gave birth
to a son and named him Peresh. His
brother was named Sheresh, and his
sons were Ulam and Rakem.
17 The son of Ulam:
Bedan.
These were the sons of Gilead[a] son of
Makir, the son of Manasseh. 18 His
sister Hammoleketh gave birth to
Ishhod, Abiezer[b] and Mahlah.
19 The sons of Shemida[c] were:
Ahian, Shechem, Likhi and Aniam.

Ephraim

20 The descendants of Ephraim:[d]
Shuthelah, Bered his son,
Tahath his son, Eleadah his son,
Tahath his son, 21 Zabad his son
and Shuthelah his son.
Ezer and Elead were killed by the
native-born men of Gath, when they
went down to seize their livestock.
22 Their father Ephraim mourned for
them many days, and his relatives
came to comfort him. 23 Then he lay
with his wife again, and she became
pregnant and gave birth to a son. He
named him Beriah,[b] because there
had been misfortune in his family.
24 His daughter was Sheerah, who
built Lower and Upper Beth Horon[e]
as well as Uzzen Sheerah.
25 Rephah was his son, Resheph his
son,[c]
Telah his son, Tahan his son,
26 Ladan his son, Ammihud his son,
Elishama his son, 27 Nun his son
and Joshua his son.
28 Their lands and settlements included
Bethel and its surrounding villages, Naa-
ran to the east, Gezer[f] and its villages to
the west, and Shechem and its villages all
the way to Ayyah and its villages. 29 Along
the borders of Manasseh were Beth Shan,[g]
Taanach, Megiddo and Dor,[h] together with
their villages. The descendants of Joseph
son of Israel lived in these towns.

Asher

30 The sons of Asher:[i]
Imnah, Ishvah, Ishvi and Beriah.
Their sister was Serah.
31 The sons of Beriah:
Heber and Malkiel, who was the fa-
ther of Birzaith.

7:13 [w] S Ge 30:8 **7:14** [x] S Ge 41:51; S Jos 17:1; 1Ch 5:23 [y] S Nu 26:30 **7:15** [z] S Nu 26:33; 36:1-12 **7:17** [a] S Nu 26:30 **7:18** [b] S Jos 17:2 **7:19** [c] Jos 17:2 **7:20** [d] S Ge 41:52; S Nu 1:33 **7:24** [e] S Jos 10:10 **7:28** [f] Jos 10:33 **7:29** [g] S Jos 17:11 [h] S Jos 11:2 **7:30** [i] S Nu 1:40

[a] *13* Some Hebrew and Septuagint manuscripts (see also Gen. 46:24 and Num. 26:49); most Hebrew manuscripts *Shallum* [b] *23 Beriah* sounds like the Hebrew for *misfortune.* [c] *25* Some Septuagint manuscripts; Hebrew does not have *his son.*

7:13 Repeats Ge 46:24; Nu 26:48 – 50. *descendants of Bilhah.* Dan and Naphtali were the actual "sons" of Jacob's concubine Bilhah (Ge 30:3 – 8), so Naphtali's sons are Bilhah's "descendants."

7:14 – 19 See note on 5:23 – 26. The sources for this genealogy are Nu 26:29 – 34; Jos 17:1 – 18. The daughters of Zelophehad (v. 15) prompted the rulings on the inheritance rights of women (Nu 26:29 – 34; 27:1 – 11; 36:1 – 12; Jos 17:3 – 4). Of the 13 different clans of the tribe of Manasseh known from these genealogies, seven are mentioned in the Samaria ostraca (about 65 inscribed potsherds containing records of deliveries of wine, oil, barley and other commodities in the eighth century B.C.). The prominence of women in this genealogy is unusual; this suggests that it may have functioned in the domestic sphere, perhaps as a statement of the social status of the various clans of Manasseh (see Introduction: Genealogies).

7:20 – 29 The source for part of the genealogy of Ephraim is Nu 26:35. If Rephah (v. 25) is the grandson of Ephraim, ten generations are recorded from Ephraim to Joshua, a number that fits very well the 400-year interval when Israel was in Egypt. Joshua's Ephraimite ancestry is also mentioned in Nu 13:8 (where he is called "Hoshea"; see Nu 13:16). The raid against Gath (vv. 21 – 22) must have taken place well before the conquest of Canaan and must have originated in Egypt. The list of settlements (vv. 28 – 29) summarizes Jos 16 – 17.

7:30 – 40 The genealogy of Asher follows Ge 46:17 for the first three generations; it is also parallel to Nu 26:44 – 46, except that the name Ishvah (v. 30) is missing there. This genealogy too reflects a military function (v. 40).

32 Heber was the father of Japhlet, Shomer and Hotham and of their sister Shua.
33 The sons of Japhlet:
Pasach, Bimhal and Ashvath.
These were Japhlet's sons.
34 The sons of Shomer:
Ahi, Rohgah,[a] Hubbah and Aram.
35 The sons of his brother Helem:
Zophah, Imna, Shelesh and Amal.
36 The sons of Zophah:
Suah, Harnepher, Shual, Beri, Imrah, 37 Bezer, Hod, Shamma, Shil-
shah, Ithran[b] and Beera.
38 The sons of Jether:
Jephunneh, Pispah and Ara.
39 The sons of Ulla:
Arah, Hanniel and Rizia.
40 All these were descendants of Asher—heads of families, choice men, brave
warriors and outstanding leaders. The
number of men ready for battle, as listed
in their genealogy, was 26,000.

The Genealogy of Saul the Benjamite

8:28-38pp — 1Ch 9:34-44

8 Benjamin[j] was the father of Bela his
firstborn,
Ashbel the second son, Aharah the
third,
2 Nohah the fourth and Rapha the
fifth.
3 The sons of Bela were:
Addar,[k] Gera, Abihud,[c] 4 Abishua,
Naaman, Ahoah,[l] 5 Gera, Shephu-
phan and Huram.
6 These were the descendants of
Ehud,[m] who were heads of families
of those living in Geba and were
deported to Manahath:
7 Naaman, Ahijah, and Gera, who
deported them and who was the father of Uzza and Ahihud.
8 Sons were born to Shaharaim in Moab
after he had divorced his wives Hushim and Baara. 9 By his wife Ho-
desh he had Jobab, Zibia, Mesha,
Malcam, 10 Jeuz, Sakia and Mirmah.
These were his sons, heads of families. 11 By Hushim he had Abitub
and Elpaal.

8:1 [j] S Ge 46:21 **8:3** [k] S Ge 46:21 **8:4** [l] 2Sa 23:9 **8:6** [m] Jdg 3:12-30

8:12 [n] Ezr 2:33; Ne 6:2; 7:37; 11:35 **8:13** [o] S Jos 10:12 [p] S Jos 11:22 **8:29** [q] S Jos 9:3 **8:33** [r] S 1Sa 28:19 [s] S 1Sa 9:1 [t] 1Sa 14:49 [u] S 2Sa 2:8 **8:34** [v] S 2Sa 9:12 [w] S 2Sa 4:4; S 21:7-14

12 The sons of Elpaal:
Eber, Misham, Shemed (who built
Ono[n] and Lod with its surrounding
villages), 13 and Beriah and Shema, who were heads of families of
those living in Aijalon[o] and who
drove out the inhabitants of Gath.[p]
14 Ahio, Shashak, Jeremoth, 15 Zebadiah,
Arad, Eder, 16 Michael, Ishpah and
Joha were the sons of Beriah.
17 Zebadiah, Meshullam, Hizki, Heber,
18 Ishmerai, Izliah and Jobab were
the sons of Elpaal.
19 Jakim, Zicri, Zabdi, 20 Elienai, Zillethai, Eliel, 21 Adaiah, Beraiah and
Shimrath were the sons of Shimei.
22 Ishpan, Eber, Eliel, 23 Abdon, Zicri,
Hanan, 24 Hananiah, Elam, Antho-
thijah, 25 Iphdeiah and Penuel were
the sons of Shashak.
26 Shamsherai, Shehariah, Athaliah,
27 Jaareshiah, Elijah and Zicri were
the sons of Jeroham.
28 All these were heads of families, chiefs
as listed in their genealogy, and they lived
in Jerusalem.

29 Jeiel[d] the father[e] of Gibeon lived in
Gibeon.[q]
His wife's name was Maacah, 30 and
his firstborn son was Abdon, followed by Zur, Kish, Baal, Ner,[f]
Nadab, 31 Gedor, Ahio, Zeker 32 and
Mikloth, who was the father of
Shimeah. They too lived near their
relatives in Jerusalem.
33 Ner[r] was the father of Kish,[s] Kish the
father of Saul[t], and Saul the father
of Jonathan, Malki-Shua, Abinadab
and Esh-Baal.[g][u]
34 The son of Jonathan:[v]
Merib-Baal,[h][w] who was the father
of Micah.
35 The sons of Micah:
Pithon, Melech, Tarea and Ahaz.

[a] 34 Or *of his brother Shomer: Rohgah* [b] 37 Possibly a variant of *Jether* [c] 3 Or *Gera the father of Ehud* [d] 29 Some Septuagint manuscripts (see also 1 Chron. 9:35); Hebrew does not have *Jeiel.* [e] 29 *Father* may mean *civic leader* or *military leader.* [f] 30 Some Septuagint manuscripts (see also 1 Chron. 9:36); Hebrew does not have *Ner.* [g] 33 Also known as *Ish-Bosheth* [h] 34 Also known as *Mephibosheth*

8:1–40 The inclusion of a second and even more extensive genealogy of Benjamin (see note on 7:6–12) reflects both the importance of this tribe and the Chronicler's interest in Saul. Judah, Simeon and part of Benjamin had composed the southern kingdom (1Ki 12:1–21), and their territory largely comprised the restoration province of Judah in the Chronicler's own time. The genealogy of Benjamin is more extensive than that of all the other tribes except Judah and Levi. The Chronicler is also concerned with the genealogy of Saul (vv. 29–38) in order to set the stage for the historical narrative that begins with the end of his reign (ch. 10); Saul's genealogy is repeated in 9:35–44. Several references suggest that this genealogy also originated in the military sphere (vv. 6,10,13,28,40).

8:1–5 Cf. the lists in 7:6–12; Ge 46:21–22; Nu 26:38–41.

8:6–27 Unique to Chronicles.

8:29–38 Essentially the same as the list in 9:35–44.

8:33 For the sons of Saul see 1Sa 14:49; 31:2. *Jonathan.* The firstborn and the best known of the sons of Saul, both for his military prowess and for his friendship with David (1Sa 13–14; 18:1–4; 19:1–7; 20:1–42; 23:16–18; 2Sa 21:13–14). *Esh-Baal.* See NIV text note; see also note on 2Sa 2:8.

8:34 *Merib-Baal.* See NIV text note; see also note on 2Sa 4:4.

36Ahaz was the father of Jehoaddah, Jehoaddah was the father of
Alemeth, Azmaveth and Zimri,
and Zimri was the father of Moza.
37Moza was the father of Binea; Ra-
phah was his son, Eleasah his son
and Azel his son.
38Azel had six sons, and these were
their names:
Azrikam, Bokeru, Ishmael, Sheari-
ah, Obadiah and Hanan. All these
were the sons of Azel.
39The sons of his brother Eshek:
Ulam his firstborn, Jeush the second son and Eliphelet the third.
40The sons of Ulam were brave
warriors who could handle the
bow. They had many sons and
grandsons—150 in all.
All these were the descendants of
Benjamin.[x]

9 All Israel[y] was listed in the genealogies
recorded in the book of the kings of Israel.

The People in Jerusalem

9:1-17pp — Ne 11:3-19

The people of Judah were taken captive
to Babylon[z] because of their unfaithfulness.[a] 2Now the first to resettle on their
own property in their own towns[b] were
some Israelites, priests, Levites and temple servants.[c]
3Those from Judah, from Benjamin, and
from Ephraim and Manasseh who lived in
Jerusalem were:
4Uthai son of Ammihud, the son of
Omri, the son of Imri, the son of
Bani, a descendant of Perez son of
Judah.[d]
5Of the Shilonites:
Asaiah the firstborn and his sons.
6Of the Zerahites:
Jeuel.
The people from Judah numbered
690.

7Of the Benjamites:
Sallu son of Meshullam, the son of
Hodaviah, the son of Hassenuah;
8Ibneiah son of Jeroham; Elah son
of Uzzi, the son of Micri; and Meshullam son of Shephatiah, the son
of Reuel, the son of Ibnijah.
9The people from Benjamin, as listed in their genealogy, numbered
956. All these men were heads of
their families.
10Of the priests:
Jedaiah; Jehoiarib; Jakin;
11Azariah son of Hilkiah, the son of
Meshullam, the son of Zadok, the
son of Meraioth, the son of Ahitub,
the official in charge of the house
of God;
12Adaiah son of Jeroham, the son of
Pashhur,[e] the son of Malkijah; and
Maasai son of Adiel, the son of Jah-
zerah, the son of Meshullam, the
son of Meshillemith, the son of Immer.
13The priests, who were heads of
families, numbered 1,760. They
were able men, responsible for
ministering in the house of God.
14Of the Levites:
Shemaiah son of Hasshub, the son
of Azrikam, the son of Hashabiah,
a Merarite; 15Bakbakkar, Heresh,
Galal and Mattaniah[f] son of Mica,
the son of Zicri, the son of Asaph;
16Obadiah son of Shemaiah, the
son of Galal, the son of Jeduthun;
and Berekiah son of Asa, the son of
Elkanah, who lived in the villages
of the Netophathites.[g]
17The gatekeepers:[h]
Shallum, Akkub, Talmon, Ahiman
and their brothers, Shallum their
chief 18being stationed at the King's
Gate[i] on the east, up to the present
time. These were the gatekeepers
belonging to the camp of the Levites. 19Shallum[j] son of Kore, the

8:40 [x]S Nu 26:38 **9:1** [y]1Ch 11:1,10; 12:38; 14:8; 15:3,28; 18:14; 19:17; 21:5; 28:4,8; 29:21,23; 2Ch 1:2; 5:3; 7:8; 10:3,16; 12:1; 13:4,15; 18:16; 24:5; 28:23; 29:24; 30:1 [z]S Dt 21:10 [a]S 1Ch 5:25 **9:2** [b]Jos 9:27; Ezr 2:70 [c]Ezr 2:43,58; 8:20; Ne 7:60 **9:4** [d]S Ge 38:29; 46:12 **9:12** [e]Ezr 2:38; 10:22; Ne 10:3; Jer 21:1; 38:1 **9:15** [f]2Ch 20:14; Ne 11:22 **9:16** [g]Ne 12:28 **9:17** [h]ver 22; 1Ch 26:1; 2Ch 8:14; 31:14; Ezr 2:42; Ne 7:45 **9:18** [i]1Ch 26:14; Eze 43:1; 46:1 **9:19** [j]Jer 35:4

9:1 *All Israel.* The Chronicler's concern with "all Israel" is one key to why he included the genealogies (see Introduction: Purpose and Themes). *book of the kings of Israel.* See Introduction: Author, Date and Sources.

9:2–34 This list of the members of the restored community reflects the Chronicler's concern with the institutions of his own day, especially the legitimacy of officeholders. He lists laity ("Israelites," v. 2) in vv. 3–9, priests in vv. 10–13 and Levites in vv. 14–34. He mentions a fourth class of returnees—the temple servants (v. 2)—but does not give them separate listing in the material that follows. They may have been originally foreigners who were incorporated into the Levites (Jos 9:23; Ezr 8:20) and so are not listed apart from that tribe. A similar office is known in the temple at ancient Ugarit. The list here is related to the one in Ne 11, but less than half the names are the same in the two lists.

9:3 *Ephraim and Manasseh.* Again reflecting his concern with "all Israel," the Chronicler shows that the returnees were not only from Judah and Benjamin but also from the northern tribes.

9:4–6 See 2:3–6; 4:21. The returnees of Judah are traced to Judah's sons Perez, Zerah and Shelah (see Nu 26:20).

9:10–13 The list of priests is essentially the same as that in Ne 11:10–14. Since it is tied to the list of priests earlier in the genealogies (6:1–15,50–53), contemporary Israel's continuity with her past is shown.

9:15–16 *Asaph ... Jeduthun.* Leaders of musical groups (6:39; 16:41). Later the Chronicler also lists the musicians (ch. 25) before the gatekeepers (ch. 26).

9:16 *Netophathites.* See note on Ne 12:28.

9:17–21 The Chronicler gives the names of four gatekeepers, while Ne 11:19 mentions only two. The chief of the gatekeepers had the honor of responsibility for the gate used by the king (Eze 46:1–2). The gatekeepers are also listed in ch. 26; Ezr 2:42. These officers traced their origin to Phinehas (v. 20; 6:4; Nu 3:32; 25:6–13).

son of Ebiasaph, the son of Korah,
and his fellow gatekeepers from his
family (the Korahites) were responsible for guarding the thresholds of
the Tent[a] just as their fathers had
been responsible for guarding the
entrance to the dwelling of the
LORD. 20In earlier times Phinehas[k]
son of Eleazar was in charge of the
gatekeepers, and the LORD was with
him. 21Zechariah[l] son of Meshelemiah was the gatekeeper at the entrance to the Tent of Meeting.
22Altogether, those chosen to be gatekeepers[m] at the thresholds numbered 212.
They were registered by genealogy in
their villages. The gatekeepers had been
assigned to their positions of trust by David and Samuel the seer.[n] 23They and their
descendants were in charge of guarding
the gates of the house of the LORD—the
house called the Tent. 24The gatekeepers
were on the four sides: east, west, north
and south. 25Their brothers in their villages had to come from time to time and
share their duties for seven-day[o] periods.
26But the four principal gatekeepers, who
were Levites, were entrusted with the responsibility for the rooms and treasuries[p]
in the house of God. 27They would spend
the night stationed around the house of
God,[q] because they had to guard it; and
they had charge of the key[r] for opening it
each morning.
28Some of them were in charge of the
articles used in the temple service; they
counted them when they were brought in
and when they were taken out. 29Others
were assigned to take care of the furnishings and all the other articles of the sanctuary,[s] as well as the flour and wine, and
the oil, incense and spices. 30But some[t] of
the priests took care of mixing the spices.
31A Levite named Mattithiah, the firstborn
son of Shallum the Korahite, was entrusted with the responsibility for baking the
offering bread. 32Some of their Kohathite
brothers were in charge of preparing for
every Sabbath the bread set out on the table.[u]
33Those who were musicians,[v] heads of
Levite families, stayed in the rooms of the
temple and were exempt from other duties because they were responsible for the
work day and night.[w]
34All these were heads of Levite families, chiefs as listed in their genealogy, and
they lived in Jerusalem.

The Genealogy of Saul

9:34-44pp — 1Ch 8:28-38

35Jeiel[x] the father[b] of Gibeon lived in
Gibeon.
His wife's name was Maacah, 36and
his firstborn son was Abdon, followed by Zur, Kish, Baal, Ner, Nadab, 37Gedor, Ahio, Zechariah and
Mikloth. 38Mikloth was the father
of Shimeam. They too lived near
their relatives in Jerusalem.
39Ner[y] was the father of Kish,[z] Kish the
father of Saul, and Saul the father
of Jonathan,[a] Malki-Shua, Abinadab and Esh-Baal.[c b]
40The son of Jonathan:
Merib-Baal,[d c] who was the father
of Micah.
41The sons of Micah:
Pithon, Melech, Tahrea and Ahaz.[e]
42Ahaz was the father of Jadah, Jadah[f] was the father of Alemeth, Azmaveth and Zimri, and Zimri was
the father of Moza. 43Moza was the
father of Binea; Rephaiah was his
son, Eleasah his son and Azel his
son.
44Azel had six sons, and these were
their names:
Azrikam, Bokeru, Ishmael, Shea-
riah, Obadiah and Hanan. These
were the sons of Azel.

Saul Takes His Life

10:1-12pp — 1Sa 31:1-13; 2Sa 1:4-12

10 Now the Philistines fought against
Israel; the Israelites fled before
them, and many fell slain on Mount Gilboa. 2The Philistines pressed hard after

9:20 [k]Nu 25:7-13
9:21 [l]1Ch 26:2, 14
9:22 [m]S ver 17 [n]S 1Sa 9:9
9:25 [o]2Ki 11:5
9:26 [p]1Ch 26:22
9:27 [q]S Nu 3:38 [r]Isa 22:22
9:29 [s]S Nu 3:28; 1Ch 23:29
9:30 [t]S Ex 30:23-25
9:32 [u]Lev 24:5-8; 1Ch 23:29; 2Ch 13:11
9:33 [v]S 1Ch 6:31; 25:1-31; S 2Ch 5:12
[w]Ps 134:1
9:35 [x]1Ch 8:29
9:39 [y]S 1Ch 8:33 [z]S 1Sa 9:1 [a]1Sa 13:22 [b]S 2Sa 2:8
9:40 [c]S 2Sa 4:4

[a] 19 That is, the temple; also in verses 21 and 23 [b] 35 *Father* may mean *civic leader* or *military leader.* [c] 39 Also known as *Ish-Bosheth* [d] 40 Also known as *Mephibosheth* [e] 41 Vulgate and Syriac (see also Septuagint and 1 Chron. 8:35); Hebrew does not have *and Ahaz.* [f] 42 Some Hebrew manuscripts and Septuagint (see also 1 Chron. 8:36); most Hebrew manuscripts *Jarah, Jarah*

9:22–27 Twenty-four guard stations were manned in three shifts around the clock; 72 men would be needed for each week. With a total of 212 men, each would have a tour of duty approximately every three weeks (26:12–18).
9:28–34 The Levites not only were responsible for the temple precincts and for opening the gates in the morning, but they also had charge of the chambers and supply rooms (23:28; 26:20–29) as well as the implements, supplies and furnishings (28:13–18; Ezr 1:9–11). In addition they were responsible for the preparation of baked goods (Ex 25:30; Lev 2:5–7; 7:9). The priests alone prepared the perfumed anointing oil and spices (Ex 30:23–33).
9:35–44 The genealogy of Saul is duplicated here (see 8:29–38) as a transition to the short account of his reign that begins the Chronicler's narration (ch. 10).
10:1–14 This brief account of Saul's death introduces the reign of David, one of the Chronicler's major interests (see Introduction: Purpose and Themes; Portrait of David and Solomon).
10:2 For the strategy of pursuing the king in battle see note on 1Ki 22:31.

Saul and his sons, and they killed his sons Jonathan, Abinadab and Malki-Shua. 3The fighting grew fierce around Saul, and when the archers overtook him, they wounded him.

4Saul said to his armor-bearer, "Draw your sword and run me through, or these uncircumcised fellows will come and abuse me."

But his armor-bearer was terrified and would not do it; so Saul took his own sword and fell on it. 5When the armor-bearer saw that Saul was dead, he too fell on his sword and died. 6So Saul and his three sons died, and all his house died together.

7When all the Israelites in the valley saw that the army had fled and that Saul and his sons had died, they abandoned their towns and fled. And the Philistines came and occupied them.

8The next day, when the Philistines came to strip the dead, they found Saul and his sons fallen on Mount Gilboa. 9They stripped him and took his head and his armor, and sent messengers throughout the land of the Philistines to proclaim the news among their idols and their people. 10They put his armor in the temple of their gods and hung up his head in the temple of Dagon.[d]

11When all the inhabitants of Jabesh Gilead[e] heard of everything the Philistines had done to Saul, 12all their valiant men went and took the bodies of Saul and his sons and brought them to Jabesh. Then they buried their bones under the great tree in Jabesh, and they fasted seven days.

13Saul died[f] because he was unfaithful[g] to the LORD; he did not keep[h] the word of the LORD and even consulted a medium[i] for guidance, 14and did not inquire of the LORD. So the LORD put him to death and turned[j] the kingdom[k] over to David son of Jesse.

10:10 [d]S Jdg 16:23
10:11 [e]S Jdg 21:8
10:13 [f]S 2Sa 1:1 [g]S 1Ch 5:25 [h]S 1Sa 13:13 [i]S Lev 19:31; S 20:6; Dt 18:9-14
10:14 [j]1Ch 12:23 [k]S 1Sa 13:14

David Becomes King Over Israel

11:1-3pp — 2Sa 5:1-3

11 All Israel[l] came together to David at Hebron[m] and said, "We are your own flesh and blood. 2In the past, even while Saul was king, you were the one who led Israel on their military campaigns.[n] And the LORD your God said to you, 'You will shepherd[o] my people Israel, and you will become their ruler.[p]' "

3When all the elders of Israel had come to King David at Hebron, he made a compact with them at Hebron before the LORD, and they anointed[q] David king over Israel, as the LORD had promised through Samuel.

David Conquers Jerusalem

11:4-9pp — 2Sa 5:6-10

4David and all the Israelites marched to Jerusalem (that is, Jebus). The Jebusites[r] who lived there 5said to David, "You will not get in here." Nevertheless, David captured the fortress of Zion, the City of David.

6David had said, "Whoever leads the attack on the Jebusites will become commander-in-chief." Joab[s] son of Zeruiah went up first, and so he received the command.

7David then took up residence in the fortress, and so it was called the City of David. 8He built up the city around it, from the supporting terraces[a][t] to the surrounding wall, while Joab restored the rest of the city. 9And David became more and more powerful,[u] because the LORD Almighty was with him.

David's Mighty Men

11:10-41pp — 2Sa 23:8-39

10These were the chiefs of David's mighty men—they, together with all Israel,[v] gave his kingship strong support to extend it over the whole land, as the LORD had promised[w]— 11this is the list of David's mighty men:[x]

11:1 [l]S 1Ch 9:1 [m]S Ge 13:18; S 23:19
11:2 [n]S 1Sa 18:5, 16 [o]Ps 78:71; Mt 2:6 [p]S 1Ch 5:2
11:3 [q]1Sa 16:1-13
11:4 [r]S Ge 10:16; S 15:18-21; S Jos 3:10; S 15:8
11:6 [s]S 2Sa 2:13
11:8 [t]S 2Sa 5:9; 2Ch 32:5
11:9 [u]Est 9:4
11:10 [v]ver 1 [w]ver 3; 1Ch 12:23
11:11 [x]S 2Sa 17:10

[a] 8 Or *the Millo*

10:6 *his three sons.* See v. 2 (Ish-Bosheth survived; see note on 1Sa 31:2). *all his house.* His three sons and his chief officials (his official "house"), not all his descendants (see 8:33–34 and notes; 1Sa 31:6).

10:13–14 These verses are not paralleled in the Samuel account; they were put here by the Chronicler in line with his concern with immediate retribution (see Introduction: Purpose and Themes). Seeking mediums was forbidden (Dt 18:9–14) and brought death to Saul. The Chronicler is obviously writing to an audience already familiar with Samuel and Kings, and he frequently assumes that knowledge. Here the consultation with the medium at Endor is alluded to (see 1Sa 28), but the Chronicler does not recount the incident.

11:1—2Ch 9:31 See Introduction: Portrait of David and Solomon.

11:1–3 The material here parallels that in 2Sa 5:1–3, but is recast by the Chronicler in accordance with his emphasis on the popular support given David by "all Israel" (v. 1). While the Chronicler twice mentions the seven-year reign at Hebron before the death of Ish-Bosheth and the covenant with the northern tribes (3:4; 29:27), these incidents are bypassed in the narrative portion of the book. Most striking is the elimination at this point of the information in 2Sa 5:4–5. Rather, the Chronicler paints a picture of immediate accession over "all Israel," followed by the immediate conquest of Jerusalem (see Introduction: Portrait of David and Solomon). The author once again assumes the reader's knowledge of the parallel account.

11:4–9 See 2Sa 5:6–10 and notes. The "all Israel" theme appears in v. 4 as a substitute for "the king and his men" (2Sa 5:6).

11:10–41a See 2Sa 23:8–39 and notes. In the Samuel account this list of David's mighty men is given near the end of his reign. The Chronicler has moved the list to the beginning of his reign and has greatly expanded it (11:41b—12:40), again as part of his emphasis on the broad support of "all Israel" for the kingship of David (v. 10).

11:11 *three hundred.* Actually 800 (see 2Sa 23:8), 300 here apparently being a copyist's mistake, perhaps influenced by the same number in v. 20.

Jashobeam,[a] a Hacmonite, was chief of
the officers[b]; he raised his spear against
three hundred men, whom he killed in
one encounter.
12 Next to him was Eleazar son of Dodai the Ahohite, one of the three mighty
men. 13 He was with David at Pas Dammim when the Philistines gathered there
for battle. At a place where there was a
field full of barley, the troops fled from the
Philistines. 14 But they took their stand in
the middle of the field. They defended it
and struck the Philistines down, and the
LORD brought about a great victory.[y]
15 Three of the thirty chiefs came down
to David to the rock at the cave of Adullam, while a band of Philistines was encamped in the Valley[z] of Rephaim. 16 At
that time David was in the stronghold,[a]
and the Philistine garrison was at Bethlehem. 17 David longed for water and
said, "Oh, that someone would get me
a drink of water from the well near the
gate of Bethlehem!" 18 So the Three broke
through the Philistine lines, drew water
from the well near the gate of Bethlehem
and carried it back to David. But he refused to drink it; instead, he poured[b] it
out before the LORD. 19 "God forbid that I
should do this!" he said. "Should I drink
the blood of these men who went at the
risk of their lives?" Because they risked
their lives to bring it back, David would
not drink it.

Such were the exploits of the three
mighty men.
20 Abishai[c] the brother of Joab was chief
of the Three. He raised his spear against
three hundred men, whom he killed, and
so he became as famous as the Three. 21 He
was doubly honored above the Three and
became their commander, even though he
was not included among them.
22 Benaiah son of Jehoiada was a valiant
fighter from Kabzeel,[d] who performed
great exploits. He struck down two of Moab's best men. He also went down into
a pit on a snowy day and killed a lion.[e]
23 And he struck down an Egyptian who
was seven and a half feet[c] tall. Although
the Egyptian had a spear like a weaver's
rod[f] in his hand, Benaiah went against
him with a club. He snatched the spear
from the Egyptian's hand and killed him
with his own spear. 24 Such were the exploits of Benaiah son of Jehoiada; he too
was as famous as the three mighty men.
25 He was held in greater honor than any of
the Thirty, but he was not included among
the Three. And David put him in charge of
his bodyguard.

26 The mighty men were:
Asahel[g] the brother of Joab,
Elhanan son of Dodo from Bethlehem,
27 Shammoth[h] the Harorite,
Helez the Pelonite,
28 Ira son of Ikkesh from Tekoa,
Abiezer[i] from Anathoth,
29 Sibbecai[j] the Hushathite,
Ilai the Ahohite,
30 Maharai the Netophathite,
Heled son of Baanah the Netophathite,
31 Ithai son of Ribai from Gibeah in
Benjamin,
Benaiah[k] the Pirathonite,[l]
32 Hurai from the ravines of Gaash,
Abiel the Arbathite,
33 Azmaveth the Baharumite,
Eliahba the Shaalbonite,
34 the sons of Hashem the Gizonite,
Jonathan son of Shagee the Hararite,
35 Ahiam son of Sacar the Hararite,
Eliphal son of Ur,
36 Hepher the Mekerathite,
Ahijah the Pelonite,
37 Hezro the Carmelite,
Naarai son of Ezbai,
38 Joel the brother of Nathan,
Mibhar son of Hagri,
39 Zelek the Ammonite,
Naharai the Berothite, the armor-
bearer of Joab son of Zeruiah,
40 Ira the Ithrite,
Gareb the Ithrite,
41 Uriah[m] the Hittite,
Zabad[n] son of Ahlai,
42 Adina son of Shiza the Reubenite,
who was chief of the Reubenites,
and the thirty with him,
43 Hanan son of Maacah,
Joshaphat the Mithnite,
44 Uzzia the Ashterathite,[o]
Shama and Jeiel the sons of Hotham the Aroerite,
45 Jediael son of Shimri,
his brother Joha the Tizite,
46 Eliel the Mahavite,
Jeribai and Joshaviah the sons of
Elnaam,
Ithmah the Moabite,
47 Eliel, Obed and Jaasiel the Mezoba-
ite.

11:14 [y] S Ex 14:30; S 1Sa 11:13 **11:15** [z] 1Ch 14:9; Isa 17:5 **11:16** [a] S 2Sa 5:17 **11:18** [b] S Dt 12:16 **11:20** [c] S 1Sa 26:6 **11:22** [d] S Jos 15:21 [e] 1Sa 17:36 **11:23** [f] S 1Sa 17:7 **11:26** [g] S 2Sa 2:18 **11:27** [h] 1Ch 27:8 **11:28** [i] 1Ch 27:12 **11:29** [j] S 2Sa 21:18 **11:31** [k] 1Ch 27:14 [l] S Jdg 12:13 **11:41** [m] 2Sa 11:6 [n] 1Ch 2:36 **11:44** [o] S Dt 1:4

[a] *11* Possibly a variant of *Jashob-Baal* [b] *11* Or *Thirty*; some Septuagint manuscripts *Three* (see also 2 Samuel 23:8) [c] *23* Hebrew *five cubits* (about 2.3 meters)

11:15–19 David recognizes that he is not worthy of such devotion and makes the water a drink offering to the Lord (see Ge 35:14; 2Ki 16:13; Jer 7:18; Hos 9:4).

11:41b—12:40 See note on vv. 10–41a. The list in 2Sa 23 ends with Uriah the Hittite (2Sa 11); the source for the additional names is not known. The emphasis continues to be on the support of "all Israel"—even Saul's own kinsmen recognized the legitimacy of David's kingship before Saul's death (12:1–7,16–18,23,29).

Warriors Join David

12 These were the men who came to
David at Ziklag,[p] while he was banished from the presence of Saul son of
Kish (they were among the warriors who
helped him in battle; 2they were armed
with bows and were able to shoot arrows
or to sling stones right-handed or left-
handed;[q] they were kinsmen of Saul[r] from
the tribe of Benjamin):

3Ahiezer their chief and Joash the
sons of Shemaah the Gibeathite; Je-
ziel and Pelet the sons of Azmaveth;
Beracah, Jehu the Anathothite, 4and
Ishmaiah the Gibeonite, a mighty
man among the Thirty, who was a
leader of the Thirty; Jeremiah, Jahaziel, Johanan, Jozabad the Gede-
rathite,[s] 5Eluzai, Jerimoth, Bealiah,
Shemariah and Shephatiah the Ha-
ruphite; 6Elkanah, Isshiah, Azarel,
Joezer and Jashobeam the Korahites;
7and Joelah and Zebadiah the sons of
Jeroham from Gedor.[t]

8Some Gaditesu[u] defected to David at his
stronghold in the desert. They were brave
warriors, ready for battle and able to handle the shield and spear. Their faces were
the faces of lions,[v] and they were as swift
as gazelles[w] in the mountains.

9Ezer was the chief,
Obadiah the second in command, Eliab the third,
10Mishmannah the fourth, Jeremiah the
fifth,
11Attai the sixth, Eliel the seventh,
12Johanan the eighth, Elzabad the
ninth,
13Jeremiah the tenth and Macbannai
the eleventh.

14These Gadites were army commanders; the least was a match for a hundred,[x]
and the greatest for a thousand.[y] 15It was
they who crossed the Jordan in the first
month when it was overflowing all its
banks,[z] and they put to flight everyone
living in the valleys, to the east and to the
west.

16Other Benjamites[a] and some men from
Judah also came to David in his stronghold. 17David went out to meet them and
said to them, "If you have come to me in
peace, to help me, I am ready to have you
unite with me. But if you have come to
betray me to my enemies when my hands
are free from violence, may the God of our
fathers see it and judge you."

18Then the Spirit[b] came upon Amasai,[c]
chief of the Thirty, and he said:

"We are yours, O David!
We are with you, O son of Jesse!
Success,[d] success to you,
and success to those who help you,
for your God will help you."

So David received them and made them
leaders of his raiding bands.

19Some of the men of Manasseh defected to David when he went with the Philistines to fight against Saul. (He and his
men did not help the Philistines because,
after consultation, their rulers sent him
away. They said, "It will cost us our heads
if he deserts to his master Saul.")[e] 20When
David went to Ziklag,[f] these were the men
of Manasseh who defected to him: Adnah,
Jozabad, Jediael, Michael, Jozabad, Elihu
and Zillethai, leaders of units of a thousand in Manasseh. 21They helped David
against raiding bands, for all of them were
brave warriors, and they were commanders in his army. 22Day after day men came
to help David, until he had a great army,
like the army of God.[a]

Others Join David at Hebron

23These are the numbers of the men
armed for battle who came to David at
Hebron[g] to turn[h] Saul's kingdom over to
him, as the LORD had said:[i]

12:1 [p] S Jos 15:31 **12:2** [q] S Jdg 3:15 [r] S 2Sa 3:19 **12:4** [s] Jos 15:36 **12:7** [t] S Jos 15:58 **12:8** [u] S Ge 30:11 [v] 2Sa 17:10 [w] S 2Sa 2:18 **12:14** [x] S Lev 26:8 [y] S Dt 32:30 **12:15** [z] S Jos 3:15 **12:16** [a] S 2Sa 3:19 **12:18** [b] S Jdg 3:10; 1Ch 28:12; 2Ch 15:1; 20:14; 24:20 [c] S 2Sa 17:25 [d] 1Sa 25:5-6 **12:19** [e] 1Sa 29:2-11 **12:20** [f] S 1Sa 27:6 **12:23** [g] 2Sa 2:3-4 [h] 1Ch 10:14 [i] S 1Sa 16:1; 1Ch 11:10

[a] 22 Or *a great and mighty army*

12:1 The Chronicler assumes the reader's knowledge of the events at Ziklag (1Sa 27); see vv. 19 – 20.
12:8 – 15 The men of Gad were from Transjordan. Melting snows to the north would have brought the Jordan to flood stage in the first month (March-April) at the time of their crossing (v. 15). The most appropriate time for this incident would have been in the period of David's wandering in the region of the Dead Sea (1Sa 23:14; 24:1; 25:1; 26:1).
12:23 – 37 The emphasis remains on "all Israel" (v. 38). Though 13 tribes are named, they are grouped in order to maintain the traditional number of 12 (see note on 2:1 – 2). The northernmost tribes and those east of the Jordan River send the largest number of men (vv. 33 – 37), reinforcing the degree of support that David enjoyed not only in Judah and Benjamin but throughout the other tribes as well. The numbers in this section seem quite high. Essentially two approaches are followed on this question: (1) It is possible to explain the numbers so that a lower figure is actually attained. The Hebrew word for "thousand" may represent a unit of a tribe, each having its own commander (13:1; see Nu 31:14,48,52,54). In this case the numbers would be read not as a total figure, but as representative commanders. For example, the 6,800 from Judah (v. 24) would be read either as six commanders of 1,000 and eight commanders of 100 (see 13:1), or possibly as six commanders of thousands and 800 men (see Introduction to Numbers: Special Problem). Reducing the numbers in this fashion fits well with 13:1 and with the list of commanders alone found for Zadok's family (v. 28) and the tribe of Issachar (v. 32). Taking the numbers as straight totals would require the presence of 340,800 persons in Hebron for a feast at the same time. (2) Another approach is to allow the numbers to stand and to view them as hyperbole on the part of the Chronicler to achieve a number "like the army of God" (v. 22). This approach would fit well with the Chronicler's glorification of David and with the banquet scene that follows.

24 men of Judah, carrying shield and spear—6,800 armed for battle;
25 men of Simeon, warriors ready for battle—7,100;
26 men of Levi—4,600, 27 including Jehoiada, leader of the family of Aaron, with 3,700 men, 28 and Zadok,[j] a brave young warrior, with 22 officers from his family;
29 men of Benjamin,[k] Saul's kinsmen—3,000, most[l] of whom had remained loyal to Saul's house until then;
30 men of Ephraim, brave warriors, famous in their own clans—20,800;
31 men of half the tribe of Manasseh, designated by name to come and make David king—18,000;
32 men of Issachar, who understood the times and knew what Israel should do[m]—200 chiefs, with all their relatives under their command;
33 men of Zebulun, experienced soldiers prepared for battle with every type of weapon, to help David with undivided loyalty—50,000;
34 men of Naphtali—1,000 officers, together with 37,000 men carrying shields and spears;
35 men of Dan, ready for battle—28,600;
36 men of Asher, experienced soldiers prepared for battle—40,000;
37 and from east of the Jordan, men of Reuben, Gad and the half-tribe of Manasseh, armed with every type of weapon—120,000.
38 All these were fighting men who volunteered to serve in the ranks. They came
to Hebron fully determined to make David king over all Israel.[n] All the rest of the
Israelites were also of one mind to make
David king. 39 The men spent three days
there with David, eating and drinking,[o]
for their families had supplied provisions
for them. 40 Also, their neighbors from as
far away as Issachar, Zebulun and Naphtali came bringing food on donkeys, camels, mules and oxen. There were plentiful supplies[p] of flour, fig cakes, raisin[q] cakes, wine, oil, cattle and sheep, for there was joy[r] in Israel.

12:28 [j] 1Ch 6:8; 15:11; 16:39; 27:17 **12:29** [k] S 2Sa 3:19 [l] 2Sa 2:8-9 **12:32** [m] Est 1:13 **12:38** [n] S 1Ch 9:1 **12:39** [o] 2Sa 3:20; Isa 25:6-8 **12:40** [p] S 2Sa 16:1; 17:29 [q] 1Sa 25:18 [r] 1Ch 29:22 **13:3** [s] 1Sa 7:1-2 [t] 2Ch 1:5 **13:5** [u] 1Ch 11:1; 15:3 [v] S Jos 13:3 [w] S Nu 13:21 [x] S 1Sa 7:2 **13:6** [y] S Jos 15:9 [z] S Ex 25:22; 2Ki 19:15 **13:7** [a] S 1Sa 7:1 **13:8** [b] 1Ch 15:16, 19, 24; 2Ch 5:12; Ps 92:3

Bringing Back the Ark

13:1-14pp — 2Sa 6:1-11

13 David conferred with each of his officers, the commanders of thousands
and commanders of hundreds. 2 He then
said to the whole assembly of Israel, "If it seems good to you and if it is the will of the LORD our God, let us send word far and wide to the rest of our brothers throughout the territories of Israel, and also to the priests and Levites who are with them in their towns and pasturelands, to come and
join us. 3 Let us bring the ark of our God
back to us,[s] for we did not inquire[t] of[a] it[b] during the reign of Saul." 4 The whole
assembly agreed to do this, because it seemed right to all the people.
5 So David assembled all the Israelites,[u] from the Shihor River[v] in Egypt to Lebo[c] Hamath,[w] to bring the ark of God from Kiriath Jearim.[x] 6 David and all the Israelites
with him went to Baalah[y] of Judah (Kiriath Jearim) to bring up from there the ark of God the LORD, who is enthroned between the cherubim[z]—the ark that is called by the Name.
7 They moved the ark of God from Abinadab's[a] house on a new cart, with Uzzah
and Ahio guiding it. 8 David and all the
Israelites were celebrating with all their might before God, with songs and with harps, lyres, tambourines, cymbals and trumpets.[b]

[a] 3 Or *we neglected* [b] 3 Or *him* [c] 5 Or *to the entrance to*

12:38–40 The Chronicler's portrait of David is influenced by his Messianic expectations (see Introduction: Purpose and Themes). In the presence of a third of a million people (see note on vv. 23–37) David's coronation banquet typifies the future Messianic feast (Isa 25:6–8). The imagery of the Messianic banquet became prominent in the intertestamental literature (*Apocalypse of Baruch* 29:4–8; *Enoch* 62:14) and in the NT (see Mt 8:11–12 and Lk 13:28–30; Mt 22:1–10 and Lk 14:16–24; see also Mt 25:1–13; Lk 22:28–30; Rev 19:7–9). The Lord's Supper anticipates that coming banquet (Mt 26:29; Mk 14:25; Lk 22:15–18; 1Co 11:23–26).

13:1–14 See 2Sa 6:1–11 and notes. The author abandons the chronological order as given in 2Sa 5–6 and puts the transfer of the ark first, delaying his account of the palace building and the Philistine campaign until later (ch. 14). This is in accordance with his portrayal of David; David's concern with the ark was expressed immediately upon his accession—his consultation with the leaders appears to be set in the context of the coronation banquet (12:38–40).

13:1–4 These verses are not found in Samuel and reflect the Chronicler's own concerns with "all Israel." The semi-military expedition to retrieve the ark in 2Sa 6:1 is here broadened by consultation with and support from the whole assembly of Israel, "throughout the territories" (v. 2), including the priests and Levites—an important point for the Chronicler since only they are allowed to move the ark (15:2,13; 23:25–27; Dt 10:8).

13:3 *we did not inquire of it during the reign of Saul.* 1Sa 14:18 may be an exception (but see NIV text note there).

13:5–6 The emphasis remains on the united action of "all Israel." Israelites came to participate in this venture all the way from Lebo Hamath in the north and from the Shihor River in the south.

13:5 *Shihor.* An Egyptian term meaning "the pool of Horus." It appears to be a part of the Nile or one of the major canals of the Nile (see Jos 13:3; Isa 23:3; Jer 2:18 and notes).

13:6 *Baalah.* The Canaanite name for Kiriath Jearim, also known as Kiriath Baal (Jos 18:14). The Chronicler assumes that his readers are familiar with the account of how the ark came to be at Kiriath Jearim (1Sa 6:1—7:1). *the Name.* See Ex 23:21 and note.

13:7 *Uzzah and Ahio.* Sons or descendants of Abinadab (2Sa 6:3).

[9]When they came to the threshing floor
of Kidon, Uzzah reached out his hand to
steady the ark, because the oxen stumbled. [10]The LORD's anger[c] burned against
Uzzah, and he struck him down[d] because
he had put his hand on the ark. So he died
there before God.
[11]Then David was angry because the
LORD's wrath had broken out against Uzzah, and to this day that place is called
Perez Uzzah.[a][e]
[12]David was afraid of God that day and
asked, "How can I ever bring the ark of
God to me?" [13]He did not take the ark to be
with him in the City of David. Instead, he
took it aside to the house of Obed-Edom[f]
the Gittite. [14]The ark of God remained with
the family of Obed-Edom in his house for
three months, and the LORD blessed his
household[g] and everything he had.

David's House and Family

14:1-7pp — 2Sa 5:11-16; 1Ch 3:5-8

14 Now Hiram king of Tyre sent messengers to David, along with cedar
logs,[h] stonemasons and carpenters to
build a palace for him. [2]And David knew
that the LORD had established him as king
over Israel and that his kingdom had been
highly exalted[i] for the sake of his people
Israel.
[3]In Jerusalem David took more wives
and became the father of more sons[j] and
daughters. [4]These are the names of the
children born to him there:[k] Shammua,
Shobab, Nathan, Solomon, [5]Ibhar, Elishua,
Elpelet, [6]Nogah, Nepheg, Japhia, [7]Elisha-
ma, Beeliada[b] and Eliphelet.

David Defeats the Philistines

14:8-17pp — 2Sa 5:17-25

[8]When the Philistines heard that David
had been anointed king over all Israel,[l]
they went up in full force to search for
him, but David heard about it and went
out to meet them. [9]Now the Philistines
had come and raided the Valley[m] of Rephaim; [10]so David inquired of God: "Shall I go
and attack the Philistines? Will you hand
them over to me?"
The LORD answered him, "Go, I will
hand them over to you."
[11]So David and his men went up to Baal
Perazim,[n] and there he defeated them. He
said, "As waters break out, God has broken out against my enemies by my hand."
So that place was called Baal Perazim.[c]
[12]The Philistines had abandoned their
gods there, and David gave orders to burn[o]
them in the fire.[p]
[13]Once more the Philistines raided the
valley;[q] [14]so David inquired of God again,
and God answered him, "Do not go straight
up, but circle around them and attack them
in front of the balsam trees. [15]As soon as
you hear the sound of marching in the tops
of the balsam trees, move out to battle, because that will mean God has gone out in
front of you to strike the Philistine army."
[16]So David did as God commanded him,
and they struck down the Philistine army,
all the way from Gibeon[r] to Gezer.[s]
[17]So David's fame[t] spread throughout
every land, and the LORD made all the nations fear[u] him.

[a] *11 Perez Uzzah* means *outbreak against Uzzah.*
[b] *7* A variant of *Eliada* [c] *11 Baal Perazim* means *the lord who breaks out.*

13:10 [c]1Ch 15:13,15 [d]S Lev 10:2 **13:11** [e]1Ch 15:13; Ps 7:11 **13:13** [f]1Ch 15:18,24; 16:38; 26:4-5,15 **13:14** [g]S 2Sa 6:11 **14:1** [h]S 1Ki 5:6; 1Ch 17:6; 22:4; 2Ch 2:3; Ezr 3:7; Hag 1:8 **14:2** [i]S Nu 24:7; S Dt 26:19 **14:3** [j]S 1Ch 3:1 **14:4** [k]S 1Ch 3:9 **14:8** [l]1Ch 11:1 **14:9** [m]ver 13; S Jos 15:8; S 1Ch 11:15 **14:11** [n]Ps 94:16; Isa 28:21 **14:12** [o]S Ex 32:20 [p]S Jos 7:15 **14:13** [q]S ver 9 **14:16** [r]S Jos 9:3 [s]Jos 10:33 **14:17** [t]S Jos 6:27 [u]Ex 15:14-16; S Dt 2:25; Ps 2:1-12

13:10 *because he had put his hand on the ark.* The ark was to be moved only by Levites, who carried it with poles inserted through rings in the sides of the ark (Ex 25:12–15). None of the holy things was to be touched, on penalty of death (Nu 4:15). These strictures were observed in the second and successful attempt to move the ark to Jerusalem (15:1–15). It cannot be known whether Uzzah and Ahio were Levites—the Samuel account does not mention the presence of Levites, but the Chronicler's careful inclusion of Levites in this expedition suggests that they were present (see note on vv. 1–4). In any case, the ark should not have been moved on a cart (as done by the Philistines, 1Sa 6) or touched.
13:13 *Obed-Edom.* Perhaps the same man mentioned in 15:18,21,24. In 26:4 God's blessing on Obed-Edom included numerous sons. This reference also establishes that Obed-Edom was a Levite and that the ark was properly left in his care.
14:1–17 The Chronicler backtracks to pick up material from 2Sa 5 deferred to this point (see note on 13:1–14). The three-month period that the ark remained with Obed-Edom (13:14) was filled with incidents showing God's blessing on David: the building of his royal house (vv. 1–2), his large family (vv. 3–7) and his success in warfare (vv. 8–16)—all because of the Lord's blessing (vv. 2,17).
14:1–2 See 2Sa 5:11–12 and notes.
14:1 *Hiram.* Later provided materials and labor for building the temple (2Ch 2). His mention here implies international recognition of David as king over Israel and a treaty between David and Hiram.
14:3–7 See 3:1–9 and note; 2Sa 5:13–16. David's children born in Hebron are omitted (3:1–4; 2Sa 3:2–5; see note on 11:1–3).
14:7 *Beeliada.* Eliada (see NIV text note) in 3:8; 2Sa 5:16.
14:8–12 See 2Sa 5:17–21 and notes.
14:11 *break out... Perazim.* The Hebrew underlying the name of this place where the Lord broke out against the Philistines is the same as that underlying the word used in 13:11 when the Lord broke out against Uzzah (see NIV text notes there and here).
14:12 *gave orders to burn them.* 2Sa 5:21 does not mention burning but says that David and his men carried the idols away. Many have seen here an intentional change on the part of the Chronicler in order to bring David's actions into strict conformity with the law, which required that pagan idols be burned (Dt 7:5,25). However, some Septuagint (the pre-Christian Greek translation of the OT) manuscripts of Samuel agree with Chronicles that David burned the idols. This would indicate that the Chronicler was not innovating for theological reasons but was carefully reproducing the Hebrew text he had before him, which differed from the Masoretic (later Hebrew) text of Samuel.
14:13–16 See 2Sa 5:22–25 and notes.
14:17 *the LORD made all the nations fear him.* Here and elsewhere the Chronicler uses an expression that refers to an

The Ark Brought to Jerusalem

15:25–16:3pp — 2Sa 6:12-19

15 After David had constructed buildings for himself in the City of David, he prepared[v] a place for the ark of God and pitched[w] a tent for it. 2Then David said, "No one but the Levites[x] may carry[y] the ark of God, because the LORD chose them to carry the ark of the LORD and to minister[z] before him forever."

3David assembled all Israel[a] in Jerusalem to bring up the ark of the LORD to the place he had prepared for it. 4He called together the descendants of Aaron and the Levites:[b]

5From the descendants of Kohath,
Uriel[c] the leader and 120 relatives;
6from the descendants of Merari,
Asaiah the leader and 220 relatives;
7from the descendants of Gershon,[a]
Joel the leader and 130 relatives;
8from the descendants of Elizaphan,[d]
Shemaiah the leader and 200 relatives;
9from the descendants of Hebron,[e]
Eliel the leader and 80 relatives;
10from the descendants of Uzziel,
Amminadab the leader and 112 relatives.

11Then David summoned Zadok[f] and Abiathar[g] the priests, and Uriel, Asaiah, Joel, Shemaiah, Eliel and Amminadab the Levites. 12He said to them, "You are the heads of the Levitical families; you and your fellow Levites are to consecrate[h] yourselves and bring up the ark of the LORD, the God of Israel, to the place I have prepared for it. 13It was because you, the Levites,[i] did not bring it up the first time that the LORD our God broke out in anger against us.[j] We did not inquire of him about how to do it in the prescribed way.[k]" 14So the priests and Levites consecrated themselves in order to bring up the ark of the LORD, the God of Israel. 15And the Levites carried the ark of God with the poles on their shoulders, as Moses had commanded[l] in accordance with the word of the LORD.[m]

16David[n] told the leaders of the Levites[o] to appoint their brothers as singers[p] to sing joyful songs, accompanied by musical instruments: lyres, harps and cymbals.[q]

17So the Levites appointed Heman[r] son of Joel; from his brothers, Asaph[s] son of Berekiah; and from their brothers the Merarites,[t] Ethan son of Kushaiah; 18and with them their brothers next in rank: Zechariah,[b] Jaaziel, Shemiramoth, Jehiel, Unni, Eliab, Benaiah, Maaseiah, Mattithiah, Eliphelehu, Mikneiah, Obed-Edom[u] and Jeiel,[c] the gatekeepers.

19The musicians Heman,[v] Asaph and Ethan were to sound the bronze cymbals; 20Zechariah, Aziel, Shemiramoth, Jehiel, Unni, Eliab, Maaseiah and Benaiah were to play the lyres according to *alamoth,*[d] 21and Mattithiah, Eliphelehu, Mikneiah, Obed-Edom, Jeiel and Azaziah were to play the harps, directing according to *sheminith.*[d] 22Kenaniah the head Levite was in charge of the singing; that was his responsibility because he was skillful at it.

23Berekiah and Elkanah were to be doorkeepers for the ark. 24Shebaniah, Joshaphat, Nethanel, Amasai, Zechariah, Benaiah and Eliezer the priests were to blow trumpets[w] before the ark of God. Obed-Edom and Jehiah were also to be doorkeepers for the ark.

25So David and the elders of Israel and the commanders of units of a thousand went to bring up the ark[x] of the covenant of the LORD from the house of Obed-Edom, with rejoicing. 26Because God had helped the Levites who were carrying the ark of the covenant of the LORD, seven bulls and seven rams[y] were sacrificed. 27Now David was clothed in a robe of fine linen, as were

[a] 7 Hebrew *Gershom,* a variant of *Gershon* [b] 18 Three Hebrew manuscripts and most Septuagint manuscripts (see also verse 20 and 1 Chron. 16:5); most Hebrew manuscripts *Zechariah son and* or *Zechariah, Ben and* [c] 18 Hebrew; Septuagint (see also verse 21) *Jeiel and Azaziah* [d] 20,21 Probably a musical term

15:1 [v]Ps 132:1-18 [w]S 2Sa 6:17; 1Ch 16:1; 17:1
15:2 [x]S Nu 3:6; 4:15; Dt 10:8; 31:25; 2Ch 5:5 [y]S Dt 31:9 [z]1Ch 16:4; 23:13; 2Ch 29:11; 31:2; Ps 134:1; 135:2
15:3 [a]S 1Ch 13:5
15:4 [b]S Nu 3:17-20
15:5 [c]1Ch 6:24
15:8 [d]S Ex 6:22
15:9 [e]Ex 6:18
15:11 [f]S 1Ch 12:28 [g]S 1Sa 22:20
15:12 [h]S Ex 29:1; 30:19-21,30; 40:31-32; S Lev 11:44
15:13 [i]1Ki 8:4 [j]S 1Ch 13:7-10 [k]S Lev 5:10
15:15 [l]S Ex 25:14 [m]2Sa 6:7
15:16 [n]1Ch 6:31 [o]2Ch 7:6 [p]Ezr 2:41; Ne 11:23; Ps 68:25 [q]S 1Ch 13:8; 23:5; 2Ch 29:26; Ne 12:27,36; Job 21:12; Ps 150:5; Am 6:5
15:17 [r]S 1Ch 6:33 [s]1Ch 6:39 [t]1Ch 6:44
15:18 [u]S 2Sa 6:10; 1Ch 26:4-5
15:19 [v]1Ch 16:41; 25:6
15:24 [w]2Ch 5:12; 7:6; 29:26
15:25 [x]2Ch 1:4; 5:2; Jer 3:16
15:26 [y]Nu 23:1-4,29

incapacitating terror brought on by the sense that the awesome power of God is present in behalf of his people (see Ex 15:16). Thus David is seen by the nations as the very representative of God (similarly Asa, 2Ch 14:14; Jehoshaphat, 2Ch 17:10; 20:29).

15:1—16:3 This account of the successful attempt to move the ark to Jerusalem is greatly expanded over the material in 2 Samuel. Only 15:25—16:3 has a parallel (2Sa 6:12–19); the rest of the material is unique to the Chronicler and reflects his own interests, especially in the Levites and worship musicians (vv. 3–24; see Introduction: Purpose and Themes). Ps 132 should also be read in connection with this account.

15:1 *constructed buildings for himself.* See 14:1–2 and note on 13:1–14.

15:2–3 See note on 13:10.

15:4–10 The three clans of Levi are represented (Kohath, Merari and Gershon), as well as three distinct subgroups within Kohath (Elizaphan, Hebron and Uzziel)—862 in all.

15:12 *consecrate yourselves.* Through ritual washings and avoidance of ceremonial defilement (Ex 29:1–37; 30:19–21; 40:31–32; Lev 8:5–35).

15:13–15 The Chronicler provides the explanation for the failure in the first attempt to move the ark, an explanation not found in the Samuel account (see note on 13:10).

15:18,21,24 *Obed-Edom.* See note on 13:13.

15:24 *priests were to blow trumpets.* See 16:6; Nu 10:1–10.

15:27 Both 2Sa 6:14 and the Chronicler mention David's wearing a linen ephod, a garment worn by priests (1Sa 2:18; 22:18). The Chronicler adds, however, that David (as well as the rest of the Levites in the procession) was wearing a robe of fine linen, further associating him with the dress of the priestly functionaries. Apparently the Chronicler viewed David as a priest-king, a kind of Messianic figure (see Ps 110; Zec 6:9–15).

all the Levites who were carrying the ark,
and as were the singers, and Kenaniah,
who was in charge of the singing of the
choirs. David also wore a linen ephod.[z]
28 So all Israel[a] brought up the ark of the
covenant of the LORD with shouts,[b] with
the sounding of rams' horns[c] and trumpets, and of cymbals, and the playing of
lyres and harps.
29 As the ark of the covenant of the LORD
was entering the City of David, Michal
daughter of Saul watched from a window.
And when she saw King David dancing and
celebrating, she despised him in her heart.

16 They brought the ark of God and
set it inside the tent that David had
pitched[d] for it, and they presented burnt
offerings and fellowship offerings[a] before
God. 2 After David had finished sacrificing
the burnt offerings and fellowship offerings, he blessed[e] the people in the name of
the LORD. 3 Then he gave a loaf of bread, a
cake of dates and a cake of raisins[f] to each
Israelite man and woman.
4 He appointed some of the Levites
to minister[g] before the ark of the LORD,
to make petition, to give thanks, and to
praise the LORD, the God of Israel: 5 Asaph
was the chief, Zechariah second, then Jeiel, Shemiramoth, Jehiel, Mattithiah, Eliab, Benaiah, Obed-Edom and Jeiel. They
were to play the lyres and harps, Asaph
was to sound the cymbals, 6 and Benaiah
and Jahaziel the priests were to blow the
trumpets regularly before the ark of the
covenant of God.

David's Psalm of Thanks

16:8-22pp — Ps 105:1-15
16:23-33pp — Ps 96:1-13
16:34-36pp — Ps 106:1,47-48

7 That day David first committed to Asaph
and his associates this psalm[h] of thanks
to the LORD:

8 Give thanks[i] to the LORD, call on his
name;
make known among the nations[j]
what he has done.
9 Sing to him, sing praise[k] to him;
tell of all his wonderful acts.

15:27 [z]S 1Sa 2:18
15:28 [a]S 1Ch 9:1 [b]S 1Ki 1:39; Zec 4:7 [c]S Ex 19:13
16:1 [d]S 1Ch 15:1
16:2 [e]S Ex 39:43; Nu 6:23-27
16:3 [f]Isa 16:7
16:4 [g]S 1Ch 15:2
16:7 [h]Ps 47:7
16:8 [i]ver 34; Ps 107:1; 118:1; 136:1 [j]S 2Ki 19:19
16:9 [k]S Ex 15:1; Ps 7:17
16:10 [l]Ps 8:1; 29:2; 66:2
16:11 [m]ver 10; 1Ch 28:9; 2Ch 7:14; 14:4; 15:2, 12; 16:12; 18:4; 20:4; 34:3; Ps 24:6; 27:8; 105:4; 119:2, 58; Pr 8:17
16:12 [n]Ps 77:11 [o]S Dt 4:34 [p]Ps 78:43
16:14 [q]Isa 4:4; 26:9
16:15 [r]S Ge 8:1; Ps 98:3; 111:5; 115:12; 136:23
16:16 [s]S Ge 12:7; S 15:18; 22:16-18
16:17 [t]Ge 35:9-12
16:18 [u]Ge 13:14-17
16:19 [v]Dt 7:7
16:20 [w]S Ge 20:13
16:21 [x]Ge 12:17; S 20:3; Ex 7:15-18; Ps 9:5
16:22 [y]S Ge 20:7
16:24 [z]Isa 42:12; 66:19
16:25 [a]Ps 18:3; 48:1 [b]Ps 76:7; 89:7 [c]Ex 18:11; Dt 32:39; 2Ch 2:5; Ps 135:5; Isa 40:25
16:26 [d]Ps 8:3; 102:25

10 Glory in his holy name;[l]
let the hearts of those who seek the
LORD rejoice.
11 Look to the LORD and his strength;
seek[m] his face always.
12 Remember[n] the wonders[o] he has done,
his miracles,[p] and the judgments he
pronounced,
13 O descendants of Israel his servant,
O sons of Jacob, his chosen ones.

14 He is the LORD our God;
his judgments[q] are in all the earth.
15 He remembers[b][r] his covenant forever,
the word he commanded, for a
thousand generations,
16 the covenant[s] he made with Abraham,
the oath he swore to Isaac.
17 He confirmed it to Jacob[t] as a decree,
to Israel as an everlasting covenant:
18 "To you I will give the land of Canaan[u]
as the portion you will inherit."

19 When they were but few in number,[v]
few indeed, and strangers in it,
20 they[c] wandered[w] from nation to nation,
from one kingdom to another.
21 He allowed no man to oppress them;
for their sake he rebuked kings:[x]
22 "Do not touch my anointed ones;
do my prophets[y] no harm."

23 Sing to the LORD, all the earth;
proclaim his salvation day after day.
24 Declare his glory[z] among the nations,
his marvelous deeds among all
peoples.
25 For great is the LORD and most worthy
of praise;[a]
he is to be feared[b] above all gods.[c]
26 For all the gods of the nations are
idols,
but the LORD made the heavens.[d]
27 Splendor and majesty are before him;
strength and joy in his dwelling
place.

[a] *1* Traditionally *peace offerings*; also in verse 2
[b] *15* Some Septuagint manuscripts (see also Psalm 105:8); Hebrew *Remember*
[c] *18-20* One Hebrew manuscript, Septuagint and Vulgate (see also Psalm 105:12); most Hebrew manuscripts *inherit, / [19]though you are but few in number, / few indeed, and strangers in it." / [20]They*

15:29 Parallel to 2Sa 6:16, but the Chronicler omits the remainder of this incident recorded there (2Sa 6:20–23). Some interpreters regard this omission as part of the Chronicler's positive view of David, so that a possibly unseemly account is omitted. On the other hand, it is equally plausible that the Chronicler here simply assumes the reader's knowledge of the other account (see notes on 10:13–14; 11:1–3; 12:1; 13:6).
16:1–3 David is further associated with the priests in his supervision of the sacrifices and his exercising the priestly prerogative of blessing the people (Nu 6:22–27; see note on 15:27). The baked goods provided by David were for the sacrificial meal following the fellowship offerings (Lev 3:1–17; 7:11–21,28–36).
16:4 *to make petition, to give thanks, and to praise the LORD.* The three main types of psalms: (1) lament and/or petition, (2) thanksgiving and (3) praise (see Introduction to Psalms: Psalm Types; see also note on Col 3:16).
16:8–36 Similar to various parts of the book of Psalms (for vv. 8–22 see Ps 105:1–15; for vv. 23–33, Ps 96; for vv. 34–36, Ps 106:1,47–48). This psalm is not found in the Samuel account. The use of the lengthy historical portion from Ps 105 emphasizing the promises to Abraham would be particularly relevant to the Chronicler's postexilic audience, for whom the faithfulness of God was a fresh reality in their return to the land. The citation from Ps 106 would also be of immediate relevance to the Chronicler's audience as those who had been gathered and delivered from the nations (v. 35).

[28]Ascribe to the LORD, O families of
nations,
ascribe to the LORD glory and
strength,[e]
29 ascribe to the LORD the glory due his
name.[f]
Bring an offering and come before him;
worship the LORD in the splendor of
his[a] holiness.[g]
[30]Tremble[h] before him, all the earth!
The world is firmly established; it
cannot be moved.[i]
[31]Let the heavens rejoice, let the earth be
glad;[j]
let them say among the nations,
"The LORD reigns![k]"
[32]Let the sea resound, and all that is in
it;[l]
let the fields be jubilant, and
everything in them!
[33]Then the trees[m] of the forest will sing,
they will sing for joy before the
LORD,
for he comes to judge[n] the earth.
[34]Give thanks[o] to the LORD, for he is
good;[p]
his love endures forever.[q]
[35]Cry out, "Save us, O God our Savior;[r]
gather us and deliver us from the
nations,
that we may give thanks to your holy
name,
that we may glory in your praise."
[36]Praise be to the LORD, the God of
Israel,[s]
from everlasting to everlasting.

Then all the people said "Amen" and
"Praise the LORD."

[37]David left Asaph and his associates
before the ark of the covenant of the LORD
to minister there regularly, according to
each day's requirements.[t] [38]He also left
Obed-Edom[u] and his sixty-eight associates to minister with them. Obed-Edom
son of Jeduthun, and also Hosah,[v] were
gatekeepers.
[39]David left Zadok[w] the priest and his
fellow priests before the tabernacle of the
LORD at the high place in Gibeon[x] [40]to present burnt offerings to the LORD on the
altar of burnt offering regularly, morning and evening, in accordance with everything written in the Law[y] of the LORD,
which he had given Israel. [41]With them
were Heman[z] and Jeduthun and the rest
of those chosen and designated by name
to give thanks to the LORD, "for his love
endures forever." [42]Heman and Jeduthun
were responsible for the sounding of the
trumpets and cymbals and for the playing
of the other instruments for sacred song.[a]
The sons of Jeduthun[b] were stationed at
the gate.
[43]Then all the people left, each for his
own home, and David returned home to
bless his family.

God's Promise to David

17:1-15pp — 2Sa 7:1-17

17 After David was settled in his palace,
he said to Nathan the prophet, "Here
I am, living in a palace of cedar, while the
ark of the covenant of the LORD is under
a tent.[c]"
[2]Nathan replied to David, "Whatever
you have in mind,[d] do it, for God is with
you."
[3]That night the word of God came to
Nathan, saying:
[4]"Go and tell my servant David,
'This is what the LORD says: You[e] are
not the one to build me a house to
dwell in. [5]I have not dwelt in a house
from the day I brought Israel up out of
Egypt to this day. I have moved from
one tent site to another, from one
dwelling place to another. [6]Wherever
I have moved with all the Israelites,
did I ever say to any of their leaders[b]
whom I commanded to shepherd my
people, "Why have you not built me
a house of cedar?[f]" '
[7]"Now then, tell my servant David,
'This is what the LORD Almighty says:
I took you from the pasture and from
following the flock, to be ruler[g] over
my people Israel. [8]I have been with
you wherever you have gone, and I

16:28 [e]Ps 29:1-2 **16:29** [f]Ps 8:1 [g]2Ch 20:21; Ps 29:1-2 **16:30** [h]Ps 2:11; 33:8; 76:8; 99:1; 114:7 [i]Ps 93:1 **16:31** [j]Isa 44:23; 49:13 [k]Ps 9:7; 47:8; 93:1; 97:1; 99:1; 146:10; Isa 52:7; La 5:19 **16:32** [l]Ex 20:11; Isa 42:10 **16:33** [m]Isa 14:8; 55:12 [n]1Sa 2:10; Ps 7:8; 96:10; 98:9; 110:6; Isa 2:4 **16:34** [o]S ver 8; Ps 105:1; Isa 12:4 [p]Ps 25:7; 34:8; 100:5; 135:3; 145:9; Na 1:7 [q]2Ch 5:13; 7:3; Ezr 3:11; Ps 136:1-26; Jer 33:11 **16:35** [r]Dt 32:15; Ps 18:46; 38:22; Mic 7:7 **16:36** [s]S 1Ki 8:15; Ps 72:18-19 **16:37** [t]2Ch 8:14 **16:38** [u]S 1Ch 13:13; 26:4-5 [v]1Ch 26:10 **16:39** [w]S 1Sa 2:35; S 2Sa 8:17; S 1Ch 12:28 [x]S Jos 9:3; 2Ch 1:3 **16:40** [y]S Ex 29:38; Nu 28:1-8 **16:41** [z]S 1Ch 15:19 **16:42** [a]2Ch 7:6 [b]1Ch 25:3 **17:1** [c]S 1Ch 15:1 **17:2** [d]1Ch 22:7; 28:2; 2Ch 6:7 **17:4** [e]1Ch 22:10; 28:3 **17:6** [f]S 1Ch 14:1 **17:7** [g]S 2Sa 6:21

[a] 29 Or *LORD with the splendor of* [b] 6 Traditionally *judges*; also in verse 10

16:29 *splendor of his holiness.* See 2Ch 20:21; see also Ps 29:2 and note; 96:9; 110:3.
16:39 *tabernacle ... in Gibeon.* The tabernacle remained at Gibeon until Solomon's construction of the temple in Jerusalem (2Ch 1:13; 5:5), when it was stored within the temple. The existence of these two shrines — the tabernacle and the temporary structure for the ark in Jerusalem (v. 1) — accounts for the two high priests: Zadok serving in Gibeon and Abiathar in Jerusalem (18:16; 27:34; see note on 6:8).
16:42 *sounding of the trumpets.* See Nu 10:1 – 10.
17:1 – 27 See 2Sa 7 and notes.
17:1,10 In these verses the Chronicler omits the statement that David had rest from his enemies (2Sa 7:1,11). Several factors may be at work in this omission: (1) The account of David's major wars is yet to come (chs. 18 – 20). Chronologically, this passage should follow the account of the wars (v. 8), but the author has placed it here to continue his concern with the ark and the building of the temple (vv. 4 – 6,12). (2) The Chronicler also views David as a man of war through most of his life (22:6 – 8), in contrast to Solomon, who is the man of "peace and rest" (22:9) and who will build the temple (22:10). For the Chronicler, David has rest from enemies only late in his life (22:18). (3) As part of his concern to parallel David and Solomon to Moses and Joshua, Solomon (like Joshua) brings the people to rest from enemies (see Introduction: Portrait of David and Solomon).

have cut off all your enemies from before you. Now I will make your name
like the names of the greatest men of
the earth. 9And I will provide a place
for my people Israel and will plant
them so that they can have a home of
their own and no longer be disturbed.
Wicked people will not oppress them
anymore, as they did at the beginning
10and have done ever since the time
I appointed leaders[h] over my people
Israel. I will also subdue all your enemies.

"'I declare to you that the LORD will
build a house for you: 11When your
days are over and you go to be with
your fathers, I will raise up your offspring to succeed you, one of your
own sons, and I will establish his
kingdom. 12He is the one who will
build[i] a house for me, and I will establish his throne forever.[j] 13I will be his
father,[k] and he will be my son.[l] I will
never take my love away from him, as
I took it away from your predecessor.
14I will set him over my house and my
kingdom forever; his throne[m] will be
established forever.[n]'"

15Nathan reported to David all the words
of this entire revelation.

David's Prayer

17:16-27pp — 2Sa 7:18-29

16Then King David went in and sat before the LORD, and he said:

"Who am I, O LORD God, and what
is my family, that you have brought
me this far? 17And as if this were not
enough in your sight, O God, you have
spoken about the future of the house
of your servant. You have looked on
me as though I were the most exalted
of men, O LORD God.

18"What more can David say to you
for honoring your servant? For you
know your servant, 19O LORD. For the
sake[o] of your servant and according
to your will, you have done this great
thing and made known all these great
promises.[p]

20"There is no one like you, O LORD,
and there is no God but you,[q] as we
have heard with our own ears. 21And
who is like your people Israel—the
one nation on earth whose God went
out to redeem[r] a people for himself,
and to make a name for yourself,
and to perform great and awesome
wonders by driving out nations from
before your people, whom you redeemed from Egypt? 22You made your
people Israel your very own forever,[s]
and you, O LORD, have become their
God.

23"And now, LORD, let the promise[t] you have made concerning your
servant and his house be established
forever. Do as you promised, 24so that
it will be established and that your
name will be great forever. Then men
will say, 'The LORD Almighty, the God
over Israel, is Israel's God!' And the
house of your servant David will be
established before you.

25"You, my God, have revealed
to your servant that you will build
a house for him. So your servant
has found courage to pray to you.
26O LORD, you are God! You have
promised these good things to your
servant. 27Now you have been pleased
to bless the house of your servant,
that it may continue forever in your
sight;[u] for you, O LORD, have blessed
it, and it will be blessed forever."

David's Victories

18:1-13pp — 2Sa 8:1-14

18 In the course of time, David defeated the Philistines and subdued them,
and he took Gath and its surrounding villages from the control of the Philistines.

17:10 [h]S Jdg 2:16 **17:12** [i]S 1Ki 5:5 [j]1Ch 22:10; 2Ch 7:18; 13:5 **17:13** [k]2Co 6:18 [l]1Ch 28:6; Lk 1:32; Heb 1:5* **17:14** [m]S 1Ki 2:12; 1Ch 28:5; 29:23; 2Ch 9:8 [n]Ps 132:11; Jer 33:17 **17:19** [o]2Sa 7:16-17; 2Ki 20:6; Isa 9:7; 37:35; 55:3 [p]S 2Sa 7:25 **17:20** [q]S Ex 8:10; S 9:14; S 15:11; Isa 44:6; 46:9 **17:21** [r]S Ex 6:6 **17:22** [s]Ex 19:5-6 **17:23** [t]S 1Ki 8:25 **17:27** [u]Ps 16:11; 21:6

17:12–14 Though in this context these words refer to Solomon, the NT applies them to Jesus (Mk 1:11; Lk 1:32–33; Heb 1:5).

17:13 The Chronicler omits from his source (2Sa 7:14) any reference to "punishment with the rod" or "flogging" as discipline for Solomon. This omission reflects his idealization of Solomon as a Messianic figure, for whom such punishment would not be appropriate (see Introduction: Portrait of David and Solomon).

17:14 The Chronicler introduces his own concerns by the changes in the pronouns found in his source (2Sa 7:16); instead of "your house and your kingdom," the Chronicler reads "my house and my kingdom." This same emphasis on theocracy (God's rule) is found in several other passages unique to Chronicles (28:5–6; 29:23; 2Ch 1:11; 9:8; 13:4–8).

17:16 *sat.* Aside from its parallel in 2Sa 7:18, the only other reference in the OT to sitting as a posture for prayer is 1Ki 19:4. Three other postures for prayer are mentioned in Scripture: (1) lying prostrate (Dt 9:25–26; Mt 26:39); (2) standing (1Sa 1:26; Mt 6:5; Mk 11:25; Lk 18:11); (3) kneeling (Da 6:10; Lk 22:41; Ac 9:40; 20:36; 21:5).

17:21–22 The references to the exodus from Egypt would remind the Chronicler's audience of the second great exodus, the release of the restoration community from the period of Babylonian exile.

18:1—20:8 The accounts of David's wars serve to show the blessing of God on his reign; God keeps his promise to subdue David's enemies (17:10). These accounts are also particularly relevant to a theme developed in the postexilic prophets: that the silver and gold of the nations would flow to Jerusalem; the tribute of enemy peoples builds the temple of God (18:7–8,11; 22:2–5,14–15; cf. Hag 2:1–9,20–23; Zec 2:7–13; 6:9–15; 14:12–14). While this passage of Chronicles portrays God's blessing on David, it simultaneously explains

2 David also defeated the Moabites,[v] and
they became subject to him and brought
tribute.
3 Moreover, David fought Hadadezer
king of Zobah,[w] as far as Hamath, when
he went to establish his control along the
Euphrates River.[x] 4 David captured a thousand of his chariots, seven thousand charioteers and twenty thousand foot soldiers.
He hamstrung[y] all but a hundred of the
chariot horses.
5 When the Arameans of Damascus[z]
came to help Hadadezer king of Zobah,
David struck down twenty-two thousand
of them. 6 He put garrisons in the Aramean
kingdom of Damascus, and the Arameans
became subject to him and brought tribute. The LORD gave David victory everywhere he went.
7 David took the gold shields carried
by the officers of Hadadezer and brought
them to Jerusalem. 8 From Tebah[a] and Cun,
towns that belonged to Hadadezer, David
took a great quantity of bronze, which Solomon used to make the bronze Sea,[a] the
pillars and various bronze articles.
9 When Tou king of Hamath heard that
David had defeated the entire army of
Hadadezer king of Zobah, 10 he sent his
son Hadoram to King David to greet him
and congratulate him on his victory in battle over Hadadezer, who had been at war
with Tou. Hadoram brought all kinds of
articles of gold and silver and bronze.
11 King David dedicated these articles to
the LORD, as he had done with the silver
and gold he had taken from all these nations: Edom[b] and Moab, the Ammonites
and the Philistines, and Amalek.[c]
12 Abishai son of Zeruiah struck down
eighteen thousand Edomites[d] in the Valley
of Salt. 13 He put garrisons in Edom, and
all the Edomites became subject to David.
The LORD gave David victory everywhere
he went.

David's Officials

18:14-17pp — 2Sa 8:15-18

14 David reigned[e] over all Israel,[f] doing
what was just and right for all his people.
15 Joab[g] son of Zeruiah was over the army;
Jehoshaphat son of Ahilud was recorder;
16 Zadok[h] son of Ahitub and Ahimelech[b][i]
son of Abiathar were priests; Shavsha was
secretary; 17 Benaiah son of Jehoiada was
over the Kerethites and Pelethites;[j] and
David's sons were chief officials at the
king's side.

The Battle Against the Ammonites

19:1-19pp — 2Sa 10:1-19

19 In the course of time, Nahash king
of the Ammonites[k] died, and his son
succeeded him as king. 2 David thought, "I
will show kindness to Hanun son of Nahash, because his father showed kindness
to me." So David sent a delegation to express his sympathy to Hanun concerning
his father.
When David's men came to Hanun in the

18:2 [v] S Nu 21:29 **18:3** [w] 1Ch 19:6 [x] S Ge 2:14 **18:4** [y] S Ge 49:6 **18:5** [z] 2Ki 16:9 **18:8** [a] S 1Ki 7:23; 2Ch 4:2-5
18:11 [b] S Nu 24:18 [c] Nu 24:20 **18:12** [d] 1Ki 11:15 **18:14** [e] 1Ch 29:26 [f] 1Ch 11:1 **18:15** [g] 2Sa 5:6-8 **18:16** [h] 1Ch 6:8 [i] 1Ch 24:6 **18:17** [j] S 1Sa 30:14; S 2Sa 15:18 **19:1** [k] S Ge 19:38; Jdg 10:17-11:33; 2Ch 20:1-2; Zep 2:8-11

a 8 Hebrew *Tibhath,* a variant of *Tebah* *b* 16 Some Hebrew manuscripts, Vulgate and Syriac (see also 2 Samuel 8:17); most Hebrew manuscripts *Abimelech*

the Chronicler's report later (22:6–8; 28:3) that David could not build the temple because he was a man of war. The material in these chapters essentially follows the Chronicler's source in 2 Samuel. The major differences are not changes the Chronicler introduces into the text, but items he chooses not to deal with — in particular 2Sa 9; 11:2 — 12:25, where accounts not compatible with his portrait of David occur.

18:1 – 13 See 2Sa 8:1 – 14 and notes.

18:2 The Chronicler omits the harsh treatment of the Moabites recorded in 2Sa 8:2, perhaps so that no unnecessary cruelty or brutality would tarnish his portrait of David.

18:5 *Arameans.* Mentioned also among the enemies of Saul (1Sa 14:47, "Zobah"). By the time of David they were united north (Zobah) and south (Beth Rehob, 2Sa 10:6) under Hadadezer. They persisted as a foe of Israel for two centuries until they fell to Assyria shortly before the northern kingdom likewise fell (2Ki 16:7 – 9). See note on Dt 26:5.

18:8 *Tebah and Cun.* Located in the valley between the Lebanon and Anti-Lebanon mountain ranges. *which Solomon used to make ... various bronze articles.* See 2Ch 4:2 – 5,18.

18:12 *Abishai.* 2Sa 8:13 speaks only of David (see 1Ki 11:15 – 16; Ps 60 title).

18:15 – 17 The titles and duties of these officers at David's court appear to be modeled on the organization of Egyptian functionaries serving the pharaoh.

18:15 For the account of how Joab attained his position over the army see 11:4 – 6; 2Sa 5:6 – 8.

18:16 *Zadok ... Ahimelech son of Abiathar.* See notes on 6:8; 16:39; 2Sa 8:17.

18:17 *Kerethites and Pelethites.* A group of foreign mercenaries who constituted part of the royal bodyguard (2Sa 8:18; 20:23; see note on 1Sa 30:14). They remained loyal to David at the time of the rebellions of Absalom (2Sa 15:18) and Sheba (2Sa 20:7) and supported the succession of Solomon against his rival Adonijah (1Ki 1:38,44). *chief officials.* The earlier narrative at this point uses the Hebrew term ordinarily translated "priests" (see note on 2Sa 8:18). The Chronicler has used a term for civil service instead of sacral service. Two approaches to this passage are usually followed: (1) Some interpreters see here an attempt by the Chronicler to keep the priesthood restricted to the Levitical line as part of his larger concern with legitimacy of religious institutions in his own day. (2) Others argue that the Hebrew term used in 2Sa 8:18 could earlier have had a broader meaning than "priest" and could be used of some other types of officials (cf. 2Sa 20:26; 1Ki 4:5). The Chronicler used an equivalent term, since by his day the Hebrew term for "priest" was restricted to priestly functionaries.

19:1 — 20:3 The Chronicler follows 2Sa 10 – 12 closely (see notes there), apart from his omission of the account of David's sin with Bathsheba (11:2 — 12:25). The Ammonites were a traditional enemy of Israel (2Ch 20:1 – 2,23; 27:5; Jdg 3:13; 10:7 – 9; 10:17 — 11:33; 1Sa 11:1 – 13; 14:47; 2Ki 10:32 – 33; Jer 49:1 – 6; Zep 2:8 – 11). Even during the postexilic period Tobiah the Ammonite troubled Jerusalem (Ne 2:19; 4:3,7; 6:1,12,14; 13:4 – 9).

19:1 *Nahash.* Possibly the same as Saul's foe (1Sa 11:1), or perhaps his descendant.

land of the Ammonites to express sympathy to him, 3the Ammonite nobles said to Hanun, "Do you think David is honoring your father by sending men to you to express sympathy? Haven't his men come to you to explore and spy out[l] the country and overthrow it?" 4So Hanun seized David's men, shaved them, cut off their garments in the middle at the buttocks, and sent them away.

5When someone came and told David about the men, he sent messengers to meet them, for they were greatly humiliated. The king said, "Stay at Jericho till your beards have grown, and then come back."

6When the Ammonites realized that they had become a stench[m] in David's nostrils, Hanun and the Ammonites sent a thousand talents[a] of silver to hire chariots and charioteers from Aram Naharaim,[b] Aram Maacah and Zobah.[n] 7They hired thirty-two thousand chariots and charioteers, as well as the king of Maacah with his troops, who came and camped near Medeba,[o] while the Ammonites were mustered from their towns and moved out for battle.

8On hearing this, David sent Joab out with the entire army of fighting men. 9The Ammonites came out and drew up in battle formation at the entrance to their city, while the kings who had come were by themselves in the open country.

10Joab saw that there were battle lines in front of him and behind him; so he selected some of the best troops in Israel and deployed them against the Arameans. 11He put the rest of the men under the command of Abishai[p] his brother, and they were deployed against the Ammonites. 12Joab said, "If the Arameans are too strong for me, then you are to rescue me; but if the Ammonites are too strong for you, then I will rescue you. 13Be strong and let us fight bravely for our people and the cities of our God. The LORD will do what is good in his sight."

14Then Joab and the troops with him advanced to fight the Arameans, and they fled before him. 15When the Ammonites saw that the Arameans were fleeing, they too fled before his brother Abishai and went inside the city. So Joab went back to Jerusalem.

16After the Arameans saw that they had been routed by Israel, they sent messengers and had Arameans brought from beyond the River,[c] with Shophach the commander of Hadadezer's army leading them.

17When David was told of this, he gathered all Israel[q] and crossed the Jordan; he advanced against them and formed his battle lines opposite them. David formed his lines to meet the Arameans in battle, and they fought against him. 18But they fled before Israel, and David killed seven thousand of their charioteers and forty thousand of their foot soldiers. He also killed Shophach the commander of their army.

19When the vassals of Hadadezer saw that they had been defeated by Israel, they made peace with David and became subject to him.

So the Arameans were not willing to help the Ammonites anymore.

The Capture of Rabbah

20:1-3pp — 2Sa 11:1; 12:29-31

20 In the spring, at the time when kings go off to war, Joab led out the armed forces. He laid waste the land of the Ammonites and went to Rabbah[r] and besieged it, but David remained in Jerusalem. Joab attacked Rabbah and left it in ruins.[s] 2David took the crown from the head of their king[d]—its weight was found to be a talent[e] of gold, and it was set with precious stones—and it was placed on David's head. He took a great quantity of plunder from the city 3and brought out the people who were there, consigning them to labor with saws and with iron picks and axes.[t] David did this to all the Ammonite towns. Then David and his entire army returned to Jerusalem.

War With the Philistines

20:4-8pp — 2Sa 21:15-22

4In the course of time, war broke out with the Philistines, at Gezer.[u] At that time Sibbecai the Hushathite killed Sippai, one

19:3 [l] S Nu 21:32
19:6 [m] S Ge 34:30 [n] S 1Ch 18:3
19:7 [o] S Nu 21:30
19:11 [p] S 1Sa 26:6
19:17 [q] S 1Ch 9:1
20:1 [r] S Dt 3:11 [s] Am 1:13-15
20:3 [t] S Dt 29:11
20:4 [u] Jos 10:33

[a] *6* That is, about 37 tons (about 34 metric tons)
[b] *6* That is, Northwest Mesopotamia
[c] *16* That is, the Euphrates
[d] *2* Or *of Milcom,* that is, Molech
[e] *2* That is, about 75 pounds (about 34 kilograms)

19:6 *Aram Naharaim, Aram Maacah and Zobah.* 2Sa 10:6 also mentions Beth Rehob and Tob. All these states were north and northeast of Israel and formed a solid block from the region of Lake Huleh through the Anti-Lebanon mountains to beyond the Euphrates.

19:7 *Medeba.* A town in Moab apparently in the hands of the Ammonites.

19:9 *their city.* The capital city, Rabbah, to which Joab would lay siege the following year (20:1 – 3).

19:18 *seven thousand.* 2Sa 10:18 has 700, which may be a copyist's mistake.

20:1 *when kings go off to war.* Immediately following the spring harvest when there was some relaxation of agricultural labors and armies on the move could live off the land. *Rabbah.* See note on 19:9. Rabbah is the site of modern Amman, Jordan.

20:2 – 3 The Chronicler assumes that the reader is familiar with 2Sa 12:26 – 29; he does not offer an explanation of how David, who had remained in Jerusalem (v. 1), came to be at Rabbah.

20:4 *Sibbecai.* See 11:29; 27:11. *Rephaites.* Ancient people known for their large size (see Ge 14:5; Dt 2:10 – 11; see also note on 2Sa 21:16).

of the descendants of the Rephaites,[v] and
the Philistines were subjugated.
5In another battle with the Philistines,
Elhanan son of Jair killed Lahmi the brother of Goliath the Gittite, who had a spear
with a shaft like a weaver's rod.[w]
6In still another battle, which took place
at Gath, there was a huge man with six
fingers on each hand and six toes on each
foot—twenty-four in all. He also was descended from Rapha. 7When he taunted
Israel, Jonathan son of Shimea, David's
brother, killed him.
8These were descendants of Rapha in
Gath, and they fell at the hands of David
and his men.

David Numbers the Fighting Men

21:1-26pp — 2Sa 24:1-25

21 Satan[x] rose up against Israel and incited David to take a census[y] of Israel. 2So David said to Joab and the commanders of the troops, "Go and count[z] the
Israelites from Beersheba to Dan. Then report back to me so that I may know how
many there are."
3But Joab replied, "May the LORD multiply his troops a hundred times over.[a] My
lord the king, are they not all my lord's subjects? Why does my lord want to do this?
Why should he bring guilt on Israel?"
4The king's word, however, overruled
Joab; so Joab left and went throughout
Israel and then came back to Jerusalem.
5Joab reported the number of the fighting
men to David: In all Israel[b] there were one
million one hundred thousand men who
could handle a sword, including four hundred and seventy thousand in Judah.
6But Joab did not include Levi and
Benjamin in the numbering, because the
king's command was repulsive to him.
7This command was also evil in the sight
of God; so he punished Israel.

20:4 [v]S Ge 14:5
20:5 [w]S 1Sa 17:7
21:1 [x]S 2Ch 18:21; S Ps 109:6 [y]2Ch 14:8; 25:5
21:2 [z]1Ch 27:23-24
21:3 [a]S Dt 1:11
21:5 [b]S 1Ch 9:1
21:9 [c]S 1Sa 22:5 [d]S 1Sa 9:9
21:12 [e]S Dt 32:24 [f]Eze 30:25 [g]S Ge 19:13
21:13 [h]Ps 6:4; 86:15; 130:4,7
21:14 [i]1Ch 27:24
21:15 [j]S Ge 32:1 [k]Ps 125:2 [l]S Ge 6:6; S Ex 32:14 [m]S Ge 19:13
21:16 [n]S Nu 14:5; S Jos 7:6

8Then David said to God, "I have sinned
greatly by doing this. Now, I beg you, take
away the guilt of your servant. I have done
a very foolish thing."
9The LORD said to Gad,[c] David's seer,[d]
10"Go and tell David, 'This is what the
LORD says: I am giving you three options.
Choose one of them for me to carry out
against you.'"
11So Gad went to David and said to him,
"This is what the LORD says: 'Take your
choice: 12three years of famine,[e] three
months of being swept away[a] before your
enemies, with their swords overtaking
you, or three days of the sword[f] of the
LORD[g]—days of plague in the land, with
the angel of the LORD ravaging every part
of Israel.' Now then, decide how I should
answer the one who sent me."
13David said to God, "I am in deep distress. Let me fall into the hands of the
LORD, for his mercy[h] is very great; but do
not let me fall into the hands of men."
14So the LORD sent a plague on Israel,
and seventy thousand men of Israel fell
dead.[i] 15And God sent an angel[j] to destroy
Jerusalem.[k] But as the angel was doing so,
the LORD saw it and was grieved[l] because
of the calamity and said to the angel who
was destroying[m] the people, "Enough!
Withdraw your hand." The angel of the
LORD was then standing at the threshing
floor of Araunah[b] the Jebusite.
16David looked up and saw the angel
of the LORD standing between heaven and
earth, with a drawn sword in his hand extended over Jerusalem. Then David and
the elders, clothed in sackcloth, fell facedown.[n]
17David said to God, "Was it not I who
ordered the fighting men to be counted?

[a] 12 Hebrew; Septuagint and Vulgate (see also 2 Samuel 24:13) *of fleeing* [b] 15 Hebrew *Ornan*, a variant of *Araunah*; also in verses 18-28

20:5 See note on 2Sa 21:19. *weaver's rod.* See 11:23; 1Sa 17:7.

20:6 *Rapha.* See note on 2Sa 21:16.

21:1—22:1 See 2Sa 24 and notes. Although the story of David's census is quite similar in both narratives, the two accounts function differently. In Samuel the account belongs to the appendix (2Sa 21–24), which begins and ends with accounts of the Lord's anger against Israel during the reign of David because of actions by her kings (in ch. 21, an act of Saul; in ch. 24, an act of David). See note on 2Sa 21:1—24:25. The Chronicler appears to include it in order to account for the purchase of the ground on which the temple would be built. The additional material in Chronicles that is not found in Samuel (21:28—22:1) makes this interest clear. The census is the preface to David's preparations for the temple (chs. 22–29).

21:1 See note on 2Sa 24:1. *Satan.* See NIV text notes on Job 1:6; Zec 3:1; see also notes on Mt 16:23; 2Co 4:4; 1Th 3:5; 1Jn 3:8.

21:4 The Chronicler abridges the more extensive account of Joab's itinerary found in 2Sa 24:4–8; he does not mention that the census required nine months and 20 days (2Sa 24:8).

21:5 *In all Israel … one million one hundred thousand men … including four hundred and seventy thousand in Judah.* 2Sa 24:9 has 800,000 in Israel and 500,000 (which could be a round number for 470,000) in Judah. The reason for the difference is unclear. Perhaps it is to be related to the unofficial and incomplete nature of the census (see 27:23–24), with the differing figures representing the inclusion or exclusion of certain unspecified groupings among the people (see v. 6). Or perhaps it is simply due to a copyist's mistake. The NIV relieves the problem somewhat by translating the conjunction here as "including" instead of "and." See note on 12:23–37; see also Introduction to Numbers: Special Problem.

21:6 The Chronicler adds the note that Joab exempted Levi and Benjamin from the counting. This additional note reflects the Chronicler's concern with the Levites and with the worship of Israel. The tabernacle in Gibeon and the ark in Jerusalem both fell within the borders of Benjamin.

21:9 *Gad.* A longtime friend of David, having been with him when he was a fugitive from Saul (1Sa 22:3–5; cf. 1Ch 29:29; 2Ch 29:25).

21:12 *three years of famine.* See NIV text note on 2Sa 24:13.

I am the one who has sinned and done wrong. These are but sheep.[o] What have they done? O LORD my God, let your hand fall upon me and my family,[p] but do not let this plague remain on your people."

18 Then the angel of the LORD ordered Gad to tell David to go up and build an altar to the LORD on the threshing floor[q] of Araunah the Jebusite. 19 So David went up in obedience to the word that Gad had spoken in the name of the LORD.

20 While Araunah was threshing wheat,[r] he turned and saw the angel; his four sons who were with him hid themselves. 21 Then David approached, and when Araunah looked and saw him, he left the threshing floor and bowed down before David with his face to the ground.

22 David said to him, "Let me have the site of your threshing floor so I can build an altar to the LORD, that the plague on the people may be stopped. Sell it to me at the full price."

23 Araunah said to David, "Take it! Let my lord the king do whatever pleases him. Look, I will give the oxen for the burnt offerings, the threshing sledges for the wood, and the wheat for the grain offering. I will give all this."

24 But King David replied to Araunah, "No, I insist on paying the full price. I will not take for the LORD what is yours, or sacrifice a burnt offering that costs me nothing."

25 So David paid Araunah six hundred shekels[a] of gold for the site. 26 David built an altar to the LORD there and sacrificed burnt offerings and fellowship offerings.[b] He called on the LORD, and the LORD answered him with fire[s] from heaven on the altar of burnt offering.

27 Then the LORD spoke to the angel, and he put his sword back into its sheath. 28 At that time, when David saw that the LORD had answered him on the threshing floor of Araunah the Jebusite, he offered sacrifices there. 29 The tabernacle of the LORD, which Moses had made in the desert, and the altar of burnt offering were at that time on the high place at Gibeon.[t] 30 But David could not go before it to inquire of God, because he was afraid of the sword of the angel of the LORD.

22 Then David said, "The house of the LORD God[u] is to be here, and also the altar of burnt offering for Israel."

Preparations for the Temple

2 So David gave orders to assemble the aliens[v] living in Israel, and from among them he appointed stonecutters[w] to prepare dressed stone for building the house of God. 3 He provided a large amount of iron to make nails for the doors of the gateways and for the fittings, and more bronze than could be weighed.[x] 4 He also provided more cedar logs[y] than could be counted, for the Sidonians and Tyrians had brought large numbers of them to David.

5 David said, "My son Solomon is young[z] and inexperienced, and the house to be built for the LORD should be of great magnificence and fame and splendor[a] in the sight of all the nations. Therefore I will make preparations for it." So David made extensive preparations before his death.

6 Then he called for his son Solomon and charged him to build[b] a house for the LORD, the God of Israel. 7 David said to Solomon: "My son, I had it in my heart[c] to build[d] a house for the Name[e] of the LORD my

21:17 [o] S 2Sa 7:8 [p] Jnh 1:12 **21:18** [q] 2Ch 3:1 **21:20** [r] S Jdg 6:11 **21:26** [s] S Ex 19:18; S Jdg 6:21 **21:29** [t] S Jos 9:3 **22:1** [u] S Ge 28:17 **22:2** [v] S Ex 1:11; S Dt 20:11; 2Ch 8:10; S Isa 56:6 [w] 1Ki 5:17-18; Ezr 3:7 **22:3** [x] S 1Ki 7:47; 1Ch 29:2-5 **22:4** [y] S 1Ki 5:6 **22:5** [z] S 1Ki 3:7; 1Ch 29:1 [a] 2Ch 2:5 **22:6** [b] Ac 7:47 **22:7** [c] S 1Ch 17:2 [d] S 1Ki 8:17 [e] Dt 12:5, 11

[a] 25 That is, about 15 pounds (about 7 kilograms)
[b] 26 Traditionally *peace offerings*

21:20–21 The Chronicler reports that Araunah was threshing wheat as the king approached—information not found in 2Sa 24:20. However, Josephus and a fragmentary text of Samuel from Qumran both mention this information.

21:25 *six hundred shekels of gold.* 2Sa 24:24 says 50 shekels of silver were paid for the threshing floor and oxen. The difference has been explained by some as the Chronicler's attempt to glorify David and the temple by inflating the price. However, the difference is more likely explained by the Chronicler's statement that this was the price for the "site," i.e., for a much larger area than the threshing floor alone.

21:26 *fire from heaven.* Underscores the divine approval and the sanctity of the site (see 2Ch 7:1; Lev 9:24; 1Ki 18:37–38).

21:28—22:1 This material is not found in 2Sa 24. It reflects the Chronicler's main concern in reporting this narrative (see note on 21:1—22:1).

21:30 *it.* The tabernacle.

22:1—29:30 This material is unique to Chronicles and displays some of the Chronicler's most characteristic interests: the preparations for the building of the temple, the legitimacy of the priests and Levites, and the royal succession. The chapters portray a theocratic "Messianic" kingdom as it existed under David and Solomon.

22:1 David dedicates this property (21:18–30) as the site for the temple (see vv. 2–6; see also note on Ps 30 title).

22:2–19 Solomon's appointment to succeed David was twofold: (1) a private audience, with David and some leaders in attendance (vv. 17–19), and (2) a public announcement to the people (ch. 28), similar to when Joshua succeeded Moses (see Introduction: Portrait of David and Solomon).

22:2 *aliens … stonecutters.* 2Sa 20:24 confirms the use of forced labor by David, but does not specify that these laborers were aliens, not Israelites. Solomon used Israelites in conscripted labor (1Ki 5:13–18; 9:15–23; 11:28), but the Chronicler mentions only his use of aliens (2Ch 8:7–10). Though they were personally free, aliens were without political rights and could be easily exploited. The OT frequently warns that they were not to be oppressed (Ex 22:21; 23:9; Lev 19:33; Dt 24:14; Jer 7:6; Zec 7:10). Isaiah prophesies the participation of foreigners in the building of Jerusalem's walls in the future (Isa 60:10–12).

22:3 *bronze.* See note on 18:8.

22:5 *young.* Solomon's age at the time of his accession is not known with certainty. He came to the throne in 970 B.C. and was likely born c. 991.

22:7 *house for the Name.* See 1Ki 3:2 and note.

God. 8But this word of the LORD came to
me: 'You have shed much blood and have
fought many wars.[f] You are not to build
a house for my Name,[g] because you have
shed much blood on the earth in my sight.
9But you will have a son who will be a man
of peace[h] and rest,[i] and I will give him rest
from all his enemies on every side. His
name will be Solomon,[a][j] and I will grant Israel peace and quiet[k] during his reign. 10He
is the one who will build a house for my
Name.[l] He will be my son,[m] and I will be
his father. And I will establish[n] the throne
of his kingdom over Israel forever.'[o]
11"Now, my son, the LORD be with[p] you,
and may you have success and build the
house of the LORD your God, as he said
you would. 12May the LORD give you discretion and understanding[q] when he puts
you in command over Israel, so that you
may keep the law of the LORD your God.
13Then you will have success[r] if you are
careful to observe the decrees and laws[s]
that the LORD gave Moses for Israel. Be
strong and courageous.[t] Do not be afraid
or discouraged.
14"I have taken great pains to provide for
the temple of the LORD a hundred thousand
talents[b] of gold, a million talents[c] of silver,
quantities of bronze and iron too great to
be weighed, and wood and stone. And you
may add to them.[u] 15You have many workmen: stonecutters, masons and carpenters,[v] as well as men skilled in every kind
of work 16in gold and silver, bronze and
iron—craftsmen[w] beyond number. Now begin the work, and the LORD be with you."
17Then David ordered[x] all the leaders of
Israel to help his son Solomon. 18He said
to them, "Is not the LORD your God with
you? And has he not granted you rest[y] on
every side?[z] For he has handed the inhabitants of the land over to me, and the land
is subject to the LORD and to his people.
19Now devote your heart and soul to seeking the LORD your God.[a] Begin to build the
sanctuary of the LORD God, so that you
may bring the ark of the covenant of the
LORD and the sacred articles belonging to
God into the temple that will be built for
the Name of the LORD."

22:8 [f] S 1Ki 5:3 [g] 1Ch 28:3 **22:9** [h] S Jos 14:15; S 1Ki 5:4 [i] ver 18; 1Ch 23:25; 2Ch 14:6,7; 15:15; 20:30; 36:21 [j] S 2Sa 12:24; S 1Ch 23:1 [k] 1Ki 4:20 **22:10** [l] S 1Ch 17:12 [m] S 2Sa 7:13 [n] 1Ki 9:5 [o] S 2Sa 7:14; S 1Ch 17:4; 2Ch 6:15 **22:11** [p] S 1Sa 16:18; S 18:12 **22:12** [q] 1Ki 3:9-12 **22:13** [r] 1Ki 2:3 [s] 1Ch 28:7 [t] S Dt 31:6 **22:14** [u] 1Ch 29:2-5,19 **22:15** [v] Ezr 3:7 **22:16** [w] 2Ch 2:7 **22:17** [x] 1Ch 28:1-6 **22:18** [y] S ver 9 [z] 2Sa 7:1 **22:19** [a] 2Ch 7:14

The Levites

23 When David was old and full of
years, he made his son Solomon[b]
king over Israel.[c]
2He also gathered together all the leaders
of Israel, as well as the priests and Levites.
3The Levites thirty years old or more[d] were
counted,[e] and the total number of men
was thirty-eight thousand.[f] 4David said,
"Of these, twenty-four thousand are to
supervise[g] the work[h] of the temple of the
LORD and six thousand are to be officials
and judges.[i] 5Four thousand are to be gatekeepers and four thousand are to praise
the LORD with the musical instruments[j] I
have provided for that purpose."[k]
6David divided[l] the Levites into groups
corresponding to the sons of Levi:[m] Gershon, Kohath and Merari.

Gershonites

7Belonging to the Gershonites:[n]
Ladan and Shimei.
8The sons of Ladan:
Jehiel the first, Zetham and Joel—
three in all.
9The sons of Shimei:
Shelomoth, Haziel and Haran—
three in all.
These were the heads of the families of Ladan.
10And the sons of Shimei:
Jahath, Ziza,[d] Jeush and Beriah.
These were the sons of Shimei—
four in all.

23:1 [b] 1Ch 22:9; 28:5; 2Ch 1:8 [c] S 1Ki 1:30; 1Ch 29:28 **23:3** [d] Nu 8:24 [e] 1Ch 21:7 [f] Nu 4:3-49 **23:4** [g] Ezr 3:8 [h] 2Ch 34:13; Ne 4:10 [i] 1Ch 26:29; 2Ch 19:8; Eze 44:24 **23:5** [j] S 1Ch 15:16; Ps 92:3 [k] Ne 12:45 **23:6** [l] 2Ch 8:14; 23:18; 29:25 [m] S Nu 3:17; 1Ch 24:20 **23:7** [n] 1Ch 6:71

[a] *9 Solomon* sounds like and may be derived from the Hebrew for *peace.* [b] *14* That is, about 3,750 tons (about 3,450 metric tons) [c] *14* That is, about 37,500 tons (about 34,500 metric tons) [d] *10* One Hebrew manuscript, Septuagint and Vulgate (see also verse 11); most Hebrew manuscripts *Zina*

22:8–9 See note on 17:1. In 1Ki 5:3 Solomon explains that David could not build the temple because he was too busy with wars. The Chronicler's nuance is slightly different—not just that wars took so much of his time, but that David was in some sense defiled by them because of the bloodshed. A pun on Solomon's name is woven into the divine oracle (see NIV text note on v. 9).

22:10 See note on 17:12–14.

22:12–13 See Introduction: Portrait of David and Solomon.

22:19 *bring the ark ... into the temple.* See 2Ch 5:2–7.

23:1—27:34 David's preparations for the temple were not restricted to amassing materials for the building; he also arranged for its administration and worship. Unique to Chronicles (see note on 22:1—29:30), these details of the organization of the theocracy (God's kingdom) were of vital concern in the Chronicler's own day. Characteristically for the Chronicler, details about religious and sacred matters (chs. 23–26) take precedence over those that are civil and secular (ch. 27). David's arrangements provided the basis and authority for the practices of the restored community.

23:1 *made his son Solomon king.* The account of Solomon's succession is resumed in chs. 28–29. The Chronicler omits the accounts of disputed succession and bloody consolidation recorded in 1Ki 1–2 (see note on 28:1—29:30) since these would not be in accord with his overall portrait of David and Solomon (see Introduction: Portrait of David and Solomon).

23:2–5 The Levites were not counted in the census that had provoked the wrath of God (21:6–7).

23:3 *Levites thirty years old or more.* The census of Levites was made first in accordance with the Mosaic prescription (Nu 4:1–3). Apparently soon after this count, David instructed that the age be lowered to 20 years (vv. 24,27); a similar adjustment to age 25 had been made under Moses (Nu 8:23–24, but see note on 8:24).

23:6 *Gershon, Kohath and Merari.* The Levites were organized by their three clans (ch. 6; Ex 6:16–19; Nu 3). This list parallels those in 6:16–30; 24:20–30.

11 Jahath was the first and Ziza the
second, but Jeush and Beriah did
not have many sons; so they were
counted as one family with one assignment.

Kohathites

12 The sons of Kohath:[o]
Amram, Izhar, Hebron and Uzziel—
four in all.
13 The sons of Amram:[p]
Aaron and Moses.
Aaron was set apart,[q] he and his descendants forever, to consecrate the
most holy things, to offer sacrifices
before the LORD, to minister[r] before
him and to pronounce blessings[s] in
his name forever. 14 The sons of Moses the man[t] of God were counted
as part of the tribe of Levi.
15 The sons of Moses:
Gershom and Eliezer.[u]
16 The descendants of Gershom:[v]
Shubael was the first.
17 The descendants of Eliezer:
Rehabiah[w] was the first.
Eliezer had no other sons, but the
sons of Rehabiah were very numerous.
18 The sons of Izhar:
Shelomith[x] was the first.
19 The sons of Hebron:[y]
Jeriah the first, Amariah the second, Jahaziel the third and Jekameam the fourth.
20 The sons of Uzziel:
Micah the first and Isshiah the second.

Merarites

21 The sons of Merari:[z]
Mahli and Mushi.[a]
The sons of Mahli:
Eleazar and Kish.
22 Eleazar died without having sons:
he had only daughters. Their cousins, the sons of Kish, married
them.[b]
23 The sons of Mushi:
Mahli, Eder and Jerimoth—three
in all.

23:12 [o]S Ge 46:11; S Ex 6:18 **23:13** [p]Ex 6:20 [q]Ex 30:7-10 [r]S 1Ch 15:2 [s]S Nu 6:23 **23:14** [t]Dt 33:1 **23:15** [u]Ex 18:4 **23:16** [v]1Ch 26:24-28 **23:17** [w]1Ch 24:21 **23:18** [x]1Ch 26:25 **23:19** [y]1Ch 24:23; 26:31 **23:21** [z]S 1Ch 6:19 [a]S Ex 6:19 **23:22** [b]Nu 36:8
23:24 [c]S Nu 4:3 **23:25** [d]S 1Ch 22:9 **23:26** [e]Nu 4:5,15; 7:9; Dt 10:8 **23:28** [f]2Ch 29:15; Ne 13:9; Mal 3:3 **23:29** [g]S Ex 25:30 [h]Lev 2:4-7; 6:20-23 [i]Lev 19:35-36; S 1Ch 9:29,32 **23:30** [j]S 1Ch 9:33; Ps 134:1 **23:31** [k]S 2Ki 4:23 [l]Nu 28:9-29:39; Isa 1:13-14; Col 2:16 **23:32** [m]1Ch 6:48 [n]Nu 3:6-8,38 [o]2Ch 23:18; 31:2; Eze 44:14 **24:1** [p]1Ch 23:6; 28:13; 2Ch 5:11; 8:14; 23:8; 31:2; 35:4,5; Ezr 6:18 [q]Nu 3:2-4 [r]S Ex 6:23 **24:2** [s]Lev 10:1-2 **24:3** [t]S 2Sa 8:17

24 These were the descendants of Levi
by their families—the heads of families
as they were registered under their names
and counted individually, that is, the
workers twenty years old or more[c] who
served in the temple of the LORD. 25 For David had said, "Since the LORD, the God of
Israel, has granted rest[d] to his people and
has come to dwell in Jerusalem forever,
26 the Levites no longer need to carry the
tabernacle or any of the articles used in its
service."[e] 27 According to the last instructions of David, the Levites were counted
from those twenty years old or more.
28 The duty of the Levites was to help
Aaron's descendants in the service of the
temple of the LORD: to be in charge of the
courtyards, the side rooms, the purification[f] of all sacred things and the performance of other duties at the house of God.
29 They were in charge of the bread set out
on the table,[g] the flour for the grain offerings,[h] the unleavened wafers, the baking and the mixing, and all measurements
of quantity and size.[i] 30 They were also to
stand every morning to thank and praise
the LORD. They were to do the same in the
evening[j] 31 and whenever burnt offerings
were presented to the LORD on Sabbaths
and at New Moon[k] festivals and at appointed feasts.[l] They were to serve before
the LORD regularly in the proper number
and in the way prescribed for them.
32 And so the Levites[m] carried out their
responsibilities for the Tent of Meeting,[n]
for the Holy Place and, under their brothers the descendants of Aaron, for the service of the temple of the LORD.[o]

The Divisions of Priests

24 These were the divisions[p] of the sons
of Aaron:[q]
The sons of Aaron were Nadab, Abihu, Eleazar and Ithamar.[r] 2 But Nadab and
Abihu died before their father did,[s] and
they had no sons; so Eleazar and Ithamar served as the priests. 3 With the help
of Zadok[t] a descendant of Eleazar and
Ahimelech a descendant of Ithamar, David separated them into divisions for their
appointed order of ministering. 4 A larger number of leaders were found among

23:24,27 *twenty years old or more.* See note on v. 3.
23:28 – 32 See note on 9:28 – 34. The function of the Levites was to assist the priests. In addition to the care of the precincts and implements, baked goods and music (mentioned as Levitical duties in 9:22 – 34), the Chronicler adds details on the role of the Levites assisting in sacrifices.
23:30 *morning ... evening.* See Ex 29:38 – 41; Nu 28:3 – 8.
24:1 – 19 There are several lists of priests from the postexilic period (see 6:3 – 15; 9:10 – 13; Ezr 2:36 – 39; Ne 10:1 – 8; 11:10 – 12; 12:1 – 7,12 – 21).
24:2 *Nadab and Abihu died.* The Chronicler alludes to the events recorded in Lev 10:1 – 3 (see note on 6:1 – 3).
24:3 *Zadok ... Ahimelech.* Zadok and Abiathar had served as David's high priests. Here, late in David's life, Abiathar's son Ahimelech appears to have taken over some of his father's duties (see note on 6:8), but see note on 2Sa 8:17.
24:4 *sixteen ... eight.* A total of 24 divisions were selected by lot. This would allow either for service in monthly shifts, as was done by priests in Egyptian mortuary temples, or for two-week shifts once each year. For the names of these divisions see vv. 7 – 18. The names of the first, second, fourth, ninth and 24th divisions also occur in a Dead Sea scroll, and the name of the eighth appears in Lk 1:5. See essay, p. 1452; see also note on Ne 12:7.

Eleazar's descendants than among Ithamar's, and they were divided accordingly:
sixteen heads of families from Eleazar's
descendants and eight heads of families
from Ithamar's descendants. 5They divided them impartially by drawing lots,[u] for
there were officials of the sanctuary and
officials of God among the descendants of
both Eleazar and Ithamar.

6The scribe Shemaiah son of Nethanel, a Levite, recorded their names in the presence of the king and of the officials: Zadok the priest, Ahimelech[v] son of Abiathar and the heads of families of the priests and of the Levites—one family being taken from Eleazar and then one from Ithamar.

7The first lot fell to Jehoiarib,
the second to Jedaiah,[w]
8the third to Harim,[x]
the fourth to Seorim,
9the fifth to Malkijah,
the sixth to Mijamin,
10the seventh to Hakkoz,
the eighth to Abijah,[y]
11the ninth to Jeshua,
the tenth to Shecaniah,
12the eleventh to Eliashib,
the twelfth to Jakim,
13the thirteenth to Huppah,
the fourteenth to Jeshebeab,
14the fifteenth to Bilgah,
the sixteenth to Immer,[z]
15the seventeenth to Hezir,[a]
the eighteenth to Happizzez,
16the nineteenth to Pethahiah,
the twentieth to Jehezkel,
17the twenty-first to Jakin,
the twenty-second to Gamul,
18the twenty-third to Delaiah
and the twenty-fourth to Maaziah.

19This was their appointed order of ministering when they entered the temple of the LORD, according to the regulations prescribed for them by their forefather Aaron, as the LORD, the God of Israel, had commanded him.

The Rest of the Levites

20As for the rest of the descendants of Levi:[b]
from the sons of Amram: Shubael;
from the sons of Shubael: Jehdeiah.
21As for Rehabiah,[c] from his sons:
Isshiah was the first.
22From the Izharites: Shelomoth;
from the sons of Shelomoth: Jahath.
23The sons of Hebron:[d] Jeriah the first,[a]
Amariah the second, Jahaziel the third and Jekameam the fourth.
24The son of Uzziel: Micah;
from the sons of Micah: Shamir.
25The brother of Micah: Isshiah;
from the sons of Isshiah: Zechariah.
26The sons of Merari:[e] Mahli and Mushi.
The son of Jaaziah: Beno.
27The sons of Merari:
from Jaaziah: Beno, Shoham, Zaccur and Ibri.
28From Mahli: Eleazar, who had no sons.
29From Kish: the son of Kish:
Jerahmeel.
30And the sons of Mushi: Mahli, Eder and Jerimoth.

These were the Levites, according to
their families. 31They also cast lots,[f] just
as their brothers the descendants of Aaron
did, in the presence of King David and of
Zadok, Ahimelech, and the heads of families of the priests and of the Levites. The
families of the oldest brother were treated
the same as those of the youngest.

The Singers

25 David, together with the commanders of the army, set apart some of the sons of Asaph,[g] Heman[h] and Jeduthun[i] for the ministry of prophesying,[j] accompanied by harps, lyres and cymbals.[k] Here is the list of the men[l] who performed this service:[m]

2From the sons of Asaph:
Zaccur, Joseph, Nethaniah and Asa-

a 23 Two Hebrew manuscripts and some Septuagint manuscripts (see also 1 Chron. 23:19); most Hebrew manuscripts *The sons of Jeriah:*

24:5 [u] ver 31; 1Ch 25:8; 26:13 **24:6** [v] 1Ch 18:16 **24:7** [w] Ezr 2:36; Ne 12:6 **24:8** [x] Ezr 2:39; 10:21; Ne 10:5 **24:10** [y] Ne 12:4, 17; Lk 1:5 **24:14** [z] Ezr 2:37; 10:20; Jer 20:1 **24:15** [a] Ne 10:20 **24:20** [b] S 1Ch 23:6 **24:21** [c] 1Ch 23:17 **24:23** [d] S 1Ch 23:19 **24:26** [e] S 1Ch 6:19 **24:31** [f] S ver 5 **25:1** [g] S 1Ch 6:39 [h] S 1Ch 6:33 [i] 1Ch 16:41, 42; Ne 11:17 [j] S 1Sa 10:5; 2Ki 3:15 [k] S 1Ch 15:16 [l] S 1Ch 6:31 [m] 2Ch 5:12; 8:14; 34:12; 35:15; Ezr 3:10

24:5 *drawing lots.* See notes on Ex 28:30; Jos 7:14; Ne 11:1; Pr 16:33; Jnh 1:7; Ac 1:26.

24:7 *Jehoiarib.* Mattathias, father of the Maccabees, was a member of the Jehoiarib division (in the Apocrypha see 1 Maccabees 2:1).

24:10 *Abijah.* The father of John the Baptist "belonged to the priestly division of Abijah" (Lk 1:5).

24:15 *Hezir.* The division from the family of Hezir was prominent in intertestamental times; the name appears on one of the large tombs in the Kidron Valley, east of Jerusalem.

24:20–31 This list supplements 23:7–23 by extending some of the family lines mentioned there.

25:1 *commanders of the army.* David often sought the counsel of military leaders (11:10; 12:32; 28:1), even in religious matters (13:1; 15:25). *set apart.* David's organizing of the temple musicians may reflect his overall interest in music (1Sa 16:23; 18:10; 19:9; 2Sa 1:17–27; 6:5,14). *Asaph, Heman and Jeduthun.* See notes on 6:31–48; Ps 39 title. *ministry of prophesying.* While there are several passages in Chronicles, largely in portions unique to these books, where temple personnel are said to have issued prophetic messages (Jahaziel, a Levite descended from Asaph, 2Ch 20:14–17; Zechariah, a priest, 2Ch 24:19–20), and while three of the leading Levites are referred to as David's seer (Heman, 1Ch 25:5; Asaph, 2Ch 29:30; Jeduthun/Ethan, 35:15), reference

relah. The sons of Asaph were under
the supervision of Asaph, who proph-
esied under the king's supervision.
3 As for Jeduthun, from his sons:[n]
Gedaliah, Zeri, Jeshaiah, Shimei,[a]
Hashabiah and Mattithiah, six in all,
under the supervision of their father
Jeduthun, who prophesied, using the
harp[o] in thanking and praising the
LORD.
4 As for Heman, from his sons:
Bukkiah, Mattaniah, Uzziel, Shubael and Jerimoth; Hananiah, Hanani,
Eliathah, Giddalti and Romamti-Ezer;
Joshbekashah, Mallothi, Hothir and
Mahazioth.
5 All these were sons of
Heman the king's seer. They were giv-
en him through the promises of God
to exalt him.[b] God gave Heman fourteen sons and three daughters.

6 All these men were under the supervision of their fathers[p] for the music of the
temple of the LORD, with cymbals, lyres and
harps, for the ministry at the house of God.
Asaph, Jeduthun and Heman[q] were under
the supervision of the king.[r]
7 Along with
their relatives—all of them trained and
skilled in music for the LORD—they numbered 288.
8 Young and old alike, teacher as
well as student, cast lots[s] for their duties.

9 The first lot, which was for
Asaph,[t] fell to Joseph,
his sons and relatives,[c] 12[d]
the second to Gedaliah,
he and his relatives and sons, 12
10 the third to Zaccur,
his sons and relatives, 12
11 the fourth to Izri,[e]
his sons and relatives, 12
12 the fifth to Nethaniah,
his sons and relatives, 12
13 the sixth to Bukkiah,
his sons and relatives, 12
14 the seventh to Jesarelah,[f]
his sons and relatives, 12
15 the eighth to Jeshaiah,
his sons and relatives, 12
16 the ninth to Mattaniah,
his sons and relatives, 12
17 the tenth to Shimei,
his sons and relatives, 12
18 the eleventh to Azarel,[g]
his sons and relatives, 12
19 the twelfth to Hashabiah,
his sons and relatives, 12
20 the thirteenth to Shubael,
his sons and relatives, 12
21 the fourteenth to Mattithiah,
his sons and relatives, 12
22 the fifteenth to Jerimoth,
his sons and relatives, 12
23 the sixteenth to Hananiah,
his sons and relatives, 12
24 the seventeenth to
Joshbekashah,
his sons and relatives, 12
25 the eighteenth to Hanani,
his sons and relatives, 12
26 the nineteenth to Mallothi,
his sons and relatives, 12
27 the twentieth to Eliathah,
his sons and relatives, 12
28 the twenty-first to Hothir,
his sons and relatives, 12
29 the twenty-second to Giddalti,
his sons and relatives, 12
30 the twenty-third to Mahazioth,
his sons and relatives, 12
31 the twenty-fourth to Romamti-
Ezer,
his sons and relatives, 12[u]

The Gatekeepers

26 The divisions of the gatekeepers:[v]
From the Korahites: Meshelemiah son
of Kore, one of the sons of Asaph.
2 Meshelemiah had sons:
Zechariah[w] the firstborn,
Jediael the second,
Zebadiah the third,
Jathniel the fourth,

25:3 [n] 1Ch 16:41-42 [o] S Ge 4:21; Ps 33:2 **25:6** [p] S 1Ch 15:16 [q] S 1Ch 15:19 [r] 2Ch 23:18; 29:25 **25:8** [s] 1Ch 26:13 **25:9** [t] S 1Ch 6:39 **25:31** [u] S 1Ch 9:33 **26:1** [v] S 1Ch 9:17 **26:2** [w] S 1Ch 9:21

[a] *3* One Hebrew manuscript and some Septuagint manuscripts (see also verse 17); most Hebrew manuscripts do not have *Shimei.* [b] *5* Hebrew *exalt the horn* [c] *9* See Septuagint; Hebrew does not have *his sons and relatives.* [d] *9* See the total in verse 7; Hebrew does not have *twelve.* [e] *11* A variant of *Zeri* [f] *14* A variant of *Asarelah* [g] *18* A variant of *Uzziel*

to "prophesying" here appears clearly to refer to the musical contribution of the Levites, with instruments and song, to the liturgy of temple worship (as initially appointed by David; see 1Ch 6:31–46; 15:16–22; 16:7–38; cf. 2Ch 29:30; 35:15). The Chronicler associates this ministry on the part of the Levites with the "prophesying" stirred up by the Spirit of God in the elders appointed by Moses in the wilderness (Nu 11:25–27; see note on v. 25) and in the band of prophets with which Samuel was associated (1Sa 10:5–11; see note on v. 5; 19:20–24). For a similar use of the term "prophesying," but now by "the prophets of Baal," see 1Ki 18:29 and note. The Chronicler's association of priests and Levites with prophesying may reflect postexilic interest in the prophet-priest-king figure of Messianic expectation: In Chronicles not only do priests and Levites prophesy, but kings also function as priests (see notes on 15:27; 16:1–3).

25:5 *king's seer.* Heman, as well as Asaph and Jeduthun/Ethan (see note on v. 1), may be called "seers" because David consulted them for guidance when he organized the temple liturgy (see 1Ch 15:16–22; 2Ch 35:15). *fourteen sons and three daughters.* Numerous progeny are a sign of divine blessing (see Job 1:2; 42:13). This is specifically stated for Heman as the result of the promises of God to exalt him. See 3:1–9; 14:2–7; 26:4–5; 2Ch 11:18–21; 13:21; 21:2; 24:3.

26:1–19 The most extensive of the Chronicler's lists of gatekeepers (see 9:17–27; 16:37–38). A list of gatekeepers in the postexilic period is found in Ezr 2:42 (Ne 7:45).

26:1 *Asaph.* This name appears to be an abbreviation of Ebiasaph (6:23; 9:19); he should not be confused with the temple musician (25:1–2,6).

3Elam the fifth,
Jehohanan the sixth
and Eliehoenai the seventh.
4Obed-Edom also had sons:
Shemaiah the firstborn,
Jehozabad the second,
Joah the third,
Sacar the fourth,
Nethanel the fifth,
5Ammiel the sixth,
Issachar the seventh
and Peullethai the eighth.
(For God had blessed Obed-Edom.[x])

6His son Shemaiah also had sons, who
were leaders in their father's family because they were very capable
men. 7The sons of Shemaiah: Oth-
ni, Rephael, Obed and Elzabad; his
relatives Elihu and Semakiah were
also able men. 8All these were descendants of Obed-Edom; they and
their sons and their relatives were
capable men with the strength
to do the work — descendants of
Obed-Edom, 62 in all.
9Meshelemiah had sons and relatives,
who were able men — 18 in all.

10Hosah the Merarite had sons: Shimri
the first (although he was not the
firstborn, his father had appointed
him the first),[y] 11Hilkiah the second, Tabaliah the third and Zechariah the fourth. The sons and relatives of Hosah were 13 in all.
12These divisions of the gatekeepers,
through their chief men, had duties for
ministering[z] in the temple of the LORD, just
as their relatives had. 13Lots[a] were cast
for each gate, according to their families,
young and old alike.
14The lot for the East Gate[b] fell to Shelemiah.[a] Then lots were cast for his son
Zechariah,[c] a wise counselor, and the lot
for the North Gate fell to him. 15The lot for
the South Gate fell to Obed-Edom,[d] and
the lot for the storehouse fell to his sons.
16The lots for the West Gate and the Shalleketh Gate on the upper road fell to Shup-
pim and Hosah.
Guard was alongside of guard: 17There
were six Levites a day on the east, four a
day on the north, four a day on the south
and two at a time at the storehouse. 18As
for the court to the west, there were four
at the road and two at the court itself.
19These were the divisions of the gatekeepers who were descendants of Korah
and Merari.[e]

The Treasurers and Other Officials

20Their fellow Levites[f] were[b] in charge
of the treasuries of the house of God and
the treasuries for the dedicated things.[g]
21The descendants of Ladan, who were
Gershonites through Ladan and who were
heads of families belonging to Ladan the
Gershonite,[h] were Jehieli, 22the sons of Jehieli, Zetham and his brother Joel. They
were in charge of the treasuries[i] of the
temple of the LORD.
23From the Amramites, the Izharites, the
Hebronites and the Uzzielites:[j]

24Shubael,[k] a descendant of Gershom
son of Moses, was the officer in
charge of the treasuries. 25His relatives through Eliezer: Rehabiah
his son, Jeshaiah his son, Joram
his son, Zicri his son and Shelomith[l] his son. 26Shelomith and his
relatives were in charge of all the
treasuries for the things dedicated[m] by King David, by the heads of
families who were the commanders of thousands and commanders of hundreds, and by the other
army commanders. 27Some of the
plunder taken in battle they dedicated for the repair of the temple
of the LORD. 28And everything dedicated by Samuel the seer[n] and by
Saul son of Kish, Abner son of Ner
and Joab son of Zeruiah, and all
the other dedicated things were in

[a] 14 A variant of *Meshelemiah* [b] 20 Septuagint; Hebrew *As for the Levites, Ahijah was*

26:5 [x] S 2Sa 6:10; S 1Ch 13:13; S 16:38 **26:10** [y] Dt 21:16; 1Ch 5:1 **26:12** [z] 1Ch 9:22 **26:13** [a] S 1Ch 24:5,31; 25:8 **26:14** [b] S 1Ch 9:18 [c] S 1Ch 9:21 **26:15** [d] S 1Ch 13:13; 2Ch 25:24 **26:19** [e] 2Ch 35:15; Ne 7:1; Eze 44:11 **26:20** [f] 2Ch 24:5 [g] 1Ch 28:12 **26:21** [h] 1Ch 23:7; 29:8 **26:22** [i] 1Ch 9:26 **26:23** [j] S Nu 3:27 **26:24** [k] 1Ch 23:16 **26:25** [l] 1Ch 23:18 **26:26** [m] S 2Sa 8:11 **26:28** [n] S 1Sa 9:9

26:4–5 Numerous sons are again a sign of divine blessing (see note on 25:5).
26:4 *Obed-Edom.* Had cared for the ark when it was left at his house (see note on 13:13).
26:12 *duties.* Elaborated in 9:22–29.
26:14 *East Gate.* The main entrance; it had six guard posts, as opposed to four at the other gates (v. 17).
26:15 *South Gate.* The palaces of David and Solomon were south of the temple hill. The southern gate would be the main one used by the king, and this assignment probably reflects a particular honor for Obed-Edom (see notes on 26:4–5; see also Eze 46:1–10).
26:16 *Shalleketh Gate.* The only reference to a gate by this name; presumably it was on the western side. The Chronicler writes to an audience familiar with these topographical details.
26:20 *treasuries of the house of God.* The Levites in charge of these treasuries received the offerings of the people and cared for the valuable temple equipment (9:28–29). *treasuries for the dedicated things.* Contained the plunder from warfare (vv. 27–28). Texts from Mesopotamian temples confirm the presence of temple officers who served as assayers to handle and refine the precious metals received as revenue and offerings. The procedure with reference to the offerings of the people may be seen in the reign of Joash (2Ch 24:4–14; 2Ki 12:4–16). Numerous passages reflect on the wealth collected in the temple (see, e.g., 29:1–9; 2Ch 4:1–22; 34:9–11; 36:7,10,18–19; 1Ki 14:25–28; 15:15,18; 2Ki 12:4–18; 14:14; 16:8; 25:13–17).
26:26 *things dedicated by King David.* See note on 18:1—20:8; see also 2Ch 5:1.
26:27 *plunder taken in battle they dedicated.* Cf. Ge 14:17–20.

the care of Shelomith and his relatives.
29 From the Izharites: Kenaniah and his
sons were assigned duties away
from the temple, as officials and
judges[o] over Israel.
30 From the Hebronites: Hashabiah[p]
and his relatives—seventeen hundred able men—were responsible
in Israel west of the Jordan for all
the work of the LORD and for the
king's service. 31 As for the Hebronites,[q] Jeriah was their chief according to the genealogical records of
their families. In the fortieth[r] year
of David's reign a search was made
in the records, and capable men
among the Hebronites were found
at Jazer in Gilead. 32 Jeriah had
twenty-seven hundred relatives,
who were able men and heads of
families, and King David put them
in charge of the Reubenites, the
Gadites and the half-tribe of Manasseh for every matter pertaining
to God and for the affairs of the
king.

Army Divisions

27 This is the list of the Israelites—heads
of families, commanders of thousands and commanders of hundreds, and
their officers, who served the king in all
that concerned the army divisions that
were on duty month by month throughout the year. Each division consisted of
24,000 men.

2 In charge of the first division, for the
first month, was Jashobeam[s] son of
Zabdiel. There were 24,000 men in
his division. 3 He was a descendant of
Perez and chief of all the army officers for the first month.
4 In charge of the division for the second
month was Dodai[t] the Ahohite; Mikloth was the leader of his division.
There were 24,000 men in his division.
5 The third army commander, for the
third month, was Benaiah[u] son of Jehoiada the priest. He was chief and
there were 24,000 men in his division. 6 This was the Benaiah who was
a mighty man among the Thirty and
was over the Thirty. His son Ammiz-
abad was in charge of his division.
7 The fourth, for the fourth month, was
Asahel[v] the brother of Joab; his son
Zebadiah was his successor. There
were 24,000 men in his division.
8 The fifth, for the fifth month, was the
commander Shamhuth[w] the Izrahite.
There were 24,000 men in his division.
9 The sixth, for the sixth month, was Ira[x]
the son of Ikkesh the Tekoite. There
were 24,000 men in his division.
10 The seventh, for the seventh month,
was Helez[y] the Pelonite, an Ephraimite. There were 24,000 men in his division.
11 The eighth, for the eighth month, was
Sibbecai[z] the Hushathite, a Zerahite.
There were 24,000 men in his division.
12 The ninth, for the ninth month, was
Abiezer[a] the Anathothite, a Benjamite. There were 24,000 men in his
division.
13 The tenth, for the tenth month, was Maharai[b] the Netophathite, a Zerahite.
There were 24,000 men in his division.
14 The eleventh, for the eleventh month,
was Benaiah[c] the Pirathonite, an
Ephraimite. There were 24,000 men
in his division.
15 The twelfth, for the twelfth month, was
Heldai[d] the Netophathite, from the
family of Othniel.[e] There were 24,000
men in his division.

26:29 [o]Dt 17:8-13; S 1Ch 23:4
26:30 [p]1Ch 27:17
26:31 [q]S 1Ch 23:19 [r]S 2Sa 5:4
27:2 [s]2Sa 23:8
27:4 [t]S 2Sa 23:9
27:5 [u]S 2Sa 23:20
27:7 [v]S 2Sa 2:18
27:8 [w]1Ch 11:27
27:9 [x]2Sa 23:26
27:10 [y]2Sa 23:26
27:11 [z]S 2Sa 21:18
27:12 [a]2Sa 23:27
27:13 [b]2Sa 23:28
27:14 [c]S 1Ch 11:31
27:15 [d]2Sa 23:29 [e]S Jos 15:17

26:29–32 These verses designate the 6,000 officials and judges (23:4) who would work outside Jerusalem; they are drawn from two sub-clans of Kohath (6:18). Dt 17:8–13 envisages a judicial function for the priests and Levites (see 2Ch 19:4–11).

26:30,32 *for all the work of the LORD and for the king's service ... for every matter pertaining to God and for the affairs of the king.* In the theocracy (kingdom of God) there is no division between secular and sacred, no tension in serving God and the king (cf. Mt 22:15–22; Lk 16:10–13; Ro 13:1–7; 1Ti 2:1–4; 1Pe 2:13–17).

26:31 *fortieth year.* The last year of David's reign.

27:1–15 The names of the commanders of David's army are the same as those found in the list of his mighty men (see 11:11–47; see also 2Sa 23:8–39 and notes). Those who had served David while he fled from Saul became commanders in the regular army.

27:1 *24,000.* See note on 12:23–37. Although a national militia consisting of 12 units of 24,000 each (a total of 288,000) is not unreasonable, the stress in this passage on unit commanders and divisions suggests that here too the Hebrew word for "1,000" should perhaps be taken as the designation of a military unit. To designate a division as "1,000" would be to give the upper limit of the number of men in such a unit, though such units would ordinarily not have a full complement of men. If this approach is followed, the figures in the following verses would be read as "24 units" instead of 24,000.

27:2 *Jashobeam.* See 11:11.

27:4 *Dodai.* See 11:12.

27:5 *Benaiah.* See 11:22–25; 18:17.

27:7 *Asahel.* See 11:26; 2Sa 2:18–23.

27:9–15 The remainder of the commanders were selected from among the Thirty (see 11:25 and the names listed in 11:27–31).

Officers of the Tribes

16 The officers over the tribes of Israel:

over the Reubenites: Eliezer son of Zicri;
over the Simeonites: Shephatiah son of Maacah;
17 over Levi: Hashabiah[f] son of Kemuel;
over Aaron: Zadok;[g]
18 over Judah: Elihu, a brother of David;
over Issachar: Omri son of Michael;
19 over Zebulun: Ishmaiah son of Obadiah;
over Naphtali: Jerimoth son of Azriel;
20 over the Ephraimites: Hoshea son of Azaziah;
over half the tribe of Manasseh: Joel son of Pedaiah;
21 over the half-tribe of Manasseh in Gilead: Iddo son of Zechariah;
over Benjamin: Jaasiel son of Abner;
22 over Dan: Azarel son of Jeroham.

These were the officers over the tribes of Israel.

23 David did not take the number of the
men twenty years old or less,[h] because the
LORD had promised to make Israel as numerous as the stars[i] in the sky. 24 Joab son
of Zeruiah began to count the men but did
not finish. Wrath came on Israel on account of this numbering,[j] and the number
was not entered in the book[a] of the annals
of King David.

The King's Overseers

25 Azmaveth son of Adiel was in charge of the royal storehouses.

Jonathan son of Uzziah was in charge of the storehouses in the outlying districts, in the towns, the villages and the watchtowers.

26 Ezri son of Kelub was in charge of the field workers who farmed the land.

27 Shimei the Ramathite was in charge of the vineyards.

Zabdi the Shiphmite was in charge of the produce of the vineyards for the wine vats.

28 Baal-Hanan the Gederite was in charge of the olive and sycamore-fig[k] trees in the western foothills.

Joash was in charge of the supplies of olive oil.

29 Shitrai the Sharonite was in charge of the herds grazing in Sharon.[l]

Shaphat son of Adlai was in charge of the herds in the valleys.

30 Obil the Ishmaelite was in charge of the camels.

Jehdeiah the Meronothite was in charge of the donkeys.

31 Jaziz the Hagrite[m] was in charge of the flocks.

All these were the officials in charge of King David's property.

32 Jonathan, David's uncle, was a counselor, a man of insight and a scribe. Jehiel son of Hacmoni took care of the king's sons.

33 Ahithophel[n] was the king's counselor.

Hushai[o] the Arkite was the king's friend.
34 Ahithophel was succeeded by Jehoiada son of Benaiah and by Abiathar.[p]

Joab[q] was the commander of the royal army.

David's Plans for the Temple

28 David summoned[r] all the officials[s] of Israel to assemble at Jerusalem: the officers over the tribes, the commanders of the divisions in the service of the king, the commanders of thousands and commanders of hundreds, and the officials in charge

[a] 24 Septuagint; Hebrew *number*

27:17 [f] 1Ch 26:30 [g] S 2Sa 8:17; S 1Ch 12:28 **27:23** [h] S 2Sa 24:1; 1Ch 21:2-5 [i] S Ge 12:2 **27:24** [j] S 2Sa 24:15; 1Ch 21:14 **27:28** [k] S 1Ki 10:27 **27:29** [l] SS 2:1; Isa 33:9; 35:2; 65:10 **27:31** [m] S 1Ch 5:10 **27:33** [n] S 2Sa 15:12 [o] S 2Sa 15:37 **27:34** [p] S 1Sa 22:20 [q] S 2Sa 2:13 **28:1** [r] 1Ch 22:17 [s] 1Ch 27:1-31; 29:6

27:16–22 The Chronicler's interest in "all Israel" appears in this list of officers who were over the 12 tribes (see Introduction: Purpose and Themes). The number is kept at 12 by omitting Gad and Asher (see note on 2:1–2).
27:17 *Zadok.* See note on 6:8; see also 12:28; 16:39.
27:18 *Elihu.* Not named elsewhere among the brothers of David. Perhaps he is the unnamed son from the list in 2:10–17 (see note there). Elihu could also be a variant of the name of Jesse's oldest son, Eliab, or the term "brother" could be taken in the sense of "relative," in which case Elihu would be a more distant kinsman.
27:21 *Abner.* A relative of King Saul (see 26:28; 1Sa 14:50–51; 17:55–58; 26:5–16; 2Sa 2:8—4:1).
27:23–24 *number.* Refers to the census narrative in ch. 21 (2Sa 24).
27:23 *twenty years old or less.* The figures reported in ch. 21 and 2Sa 24 were the numbers of those older than 20 years. *promised to make Israel as numerous as the stars.* The patriarchal promises of numerous descendants (Ge 12:2; 13:16; 15:5; 22:17) appear to have been the basis for the objections of Joab (v. 24) to the taking of a census (21:3; 2Sa 24:3).
27:24 *did not finish.* Joab did not count those under age 20, nor did he include the tribes of Levi and Benjamin (21:6). *book of the annals of King David.* See Introduction: Author, Date and Sources.
27:25–31 A list of the administrators of David's property (v. 31). The large cities of the ancient Near East had three basic economic sectors: (1) royal, (2) temple and (3) private. There is no evidence of direct taxation during the reign of David; his court appears to have been financed by extensive landholdings, commerce, plunder from his many wars, and tribute from subjugated kingdoms.
27:27 *wine vats.* See note on Hag 2:16.
27:32–34 A list of David's cabinet members, supplementary to that in 18:14–17.
27:33 *Ahithophel.* Was replaced after he committed suicide, following his support of Absalom's rebellion (2Sa 15:12,31–37; 16:20—17:23).
27:34 *Benaiah.* See v. 5.
28:1—29:30 The account of the transition from the reign of David to that of Solomon is one of the clearest demonstrations of the Chronicler's idealization of their

of all the property and livestock belonging
to the king and his sons, together with the
palace officials, the mighty men and all
the brave warriors.
2King David rose to his feet and said:
"Listen to me, my brothers and my people.
I had it in my heart[t] to build a house as a
place of rest[u] for the ark of the covenant
of the LORD, for the footstool[v] of our God,
and I made plans to build it.[w] 3But God
said to me,[x] 'You are not to build a house
for my Name,[y] because you are a warrior
and have shed blood.'[z]
4"Yet the LORD, the God of Israel, chose
me[a] from my whole family[b] to be king over
Israel forever. He chose Judah[c] as leader,
and from the house of Judah he chose my
family, and from my father's sons he was
pleased to make me king over all Israel.[d]
5Of all my sons—and the LORD has given
me many[e]—he has chosen my son Solomon[f] to sit on the throne[g] of the kingdom
of the LORD over Israel. 6He said to me: 'Solomon your son is the one who will build[h]
my house and my courts, for I have chosen
him to be my son,[i] and I will be his father.
7I will establish his kingdom forever if he is
unswerving in carrying out my commands
and laws,[j] as is being done at this time.'
8"So now I charge you in the sight of all
Israel[k] and of the assembly of the LORD,
and in the hearing of our God: Be careful
to follow all the commands[l] of the LORD
your God, that you may possess this good
land and pass it on as an inheritance to
your descendants forever.[m]
9"And you, my son Solomon, acknowledge the God of your father, and serve him
with wholehearted devotion[n] and with a
willing mind, for the LORD searches every
heart[o] and understands every motive behind the thoughts. If you seek him,[p] he
will be found by you; but if you forsake[q]
him, he will reject[r] you forever. 10Consider
now, for the LORD has chosen you to build
a temple as a sanctuary. Be strong and do
the work."
11Then David gave his son Solomon the
plans[s] for the portico of the temple, its
buildings, its storerooms, its upper parts,
its inner rooms and the place of atonement. 12He gave him the plans of all that
the Spirit[t] had put in his mind for the
courts of the temple of the LORD and all
the surrounding rooms, for the treasuries
of the temple of God and for the treasuries for the dedicated things.[u] 13He gave
him instructions for the divisions[v] of the
priests and Levites, and for all the work
of serving in the temple of the LORD, as
well as for all the articles to be used in
its service. 14He designated the weight of
gold for all the gold articles to be used in
various kinds of service, and the weight of
silver for all the silver articles to be used
in various kinds of service: 15the weight
of gold for the gold lampstands[w] and their
lamps, with the weight for each lampstand
and its lamps; and the weight of silver for
each silver lampstand and its lamps, according to the use of each lampstand; 16the
weight of gold for each table[x] for consecrated bread; the weight of silver for the
silver tables; 17the weight of pure gold for
the forks, sprinkling bowls[y] and pitchers;
the weight of gold for each gold dish; the
weight of silver for each silver dish; 18and
the weight of the refined gold for the altar
of incense.[z] He also gave him the plan for
the chariot,[a] that is, the cherubim of gold
that spread their wings and shelter[b] the
ark of the covenant of the LORD.
19"All this," David said, "I have in writing from the hand of the LORD upon me,
and he gave me understanding in all the
details[c] of the plan.[d]"
20David also said to Solomon his son,
"Be strong and courageous,[e] and do the

28:2 [t]S 1Sa 10:7; S 1Ch 17:2 [u]2Ch 6:41 [v]Ps 99:5; 132:7; Isa 60:13 [w]Ps 132:1-5 **28:3** [x]S 2Sa 7:5 [y]1Ch 22:8 [z]S 1Ki 5:3; S 1Ch 17:4 **28:4** [a]2Ch 6:6 [b]1Sa 16:1-13 [c]S Ge 49:10; Nu 24:17-19 [d]1Ch 11:1 **28:5** [e]S 1Ch 3:1 [f]S 2Sa 12:24; S 1Ch 23:1 [g]S 1Ch 17:14 **28:6** [h]1Ki 8:20 [i]S 2Sa 7:13; S 1Ch 17:13 **28:7** [j]1Ch 22:13 **28:8** [k]S 1Ch 9:1 [l]Dt 6:1 [m]Dt 4:1; S 17:14-20 **28:9** [n]S 1Ch 29:19 [o]S 1Sa 2:3; 2Ch 6:30; Ps 7:9 [p]S 1Ch 16:11; S Ps 40:16 [q]S Dt 4:31; S Jos 24:20; S 2Ch 7:19; 15:2 [r]1Ki 9:7; Ps 44:23; 74:1; 77:7 **28:11** [s]S Ex 25:9; Ac 7:44; Heb 8:5 **28:12** [t]S 1Ch 12:18 [u]1Ch 26:20 **28:13** [v]S 1Ch 24:1 **28:15** [w]Ex 25:31 **28:16** [x]S Ex 25:23 **28:17** [y]S Ex 27:3 **28:18** [z]Ex 30:1-10 [a]S Ex 25:22 [b]S Ex 25:20 **28:19** [c]1Ki 6:38 [d]S Ex 25:9 **28:20** [e]S Dt 31:6; 1Ch 22:13; 2Ch 19:11; Hag 2:4

reigns when it is compared with the succession narrative in 1Ki 1–2. The Chronicler makes no mention of the infirmities of the aged David (1Ki 1:1–4), the rebellion of Adonijah and the king's sons (1Ki 1:5–10), the court intrigue to secure Solomon's succession (1Ki 1:11–31) or David's charge to Solomon to punish his enemies after his death (1Ki 2:1–9). His selection of material presents a transition of power that is smooth and peaceful and receives the support of "all Israel" (29:25), the officials and the people (28:1–2; 29:6–9,21–25). Instead of the bedridden David who sends others to anoint Solomon (1Ki 1:32–35), David himself is present and in charge of the ceremonies (see 23:1 and note).

28:1 The assembly is composed largely of the groups named in ch. 27. This public announcement (v. 5) follows the private announcement of Solomon's succession in ch. 22 (see note on 22:2–19).

28:3 *you are a warrior and have shed blood.* See note on 22:8–9.

28:5 *chosen my son Solomon.* See vv. 6,10; 29:1. These are the only uses in the OT of the Hebrew verb for "chosen" with reference to any king after David (see Introduction: Purpose and Themes). The Chronicler's application of this term to Solomon is consistent with his depiction of that king. *kingdom of the LORD.* See note on 17:14.

28:6 *my son.* See 17:12–14 and note; see also 22:10.

28:8–9 See Introduction: Portrait of David and Solomon.

28:11 *portico.* See diagram, p. 484.

28:12 David provides Solomon with the plans for the temple. This reflects the Chronicler's modeling David after Moses: Just as Moses received the plans for the tabernacle from God (Ex 25–30), so also David received the plans for the temple.

28:18 *chariot.* Probably God's mobile throne (see note on Ps 18:10).

28:19 *I have in writing from the hand of the LORD upon me.* The Chronicler may intend no more than the ordinary process of inspiration whereby David wrote under divine influence. On the other hand, he may imply a parallel with Moses, who also received documents from the hand of the Lord (Ex 25:40; 27:8; 31:18; 32:16).

28:20 See Introduction: Portrait of David and Solomon.

work. Do not be afraid or discouraged,
for the LORD God, my God, is with you.
He will not fail you or forsake[f] you until
all the work for the service of the temple
of the LORD is finished.[g] 21The divisions
of the priests and Levites are ready for all
the work on the temple of God, and every willing man skilled[h] in any craft will
help you in all the work. The officials and
all the people will obey your every command."

Gifts for Building the Temple

29 Then King David said to the whole
assembly: "My son Solomon, the one
whom God has chosen, is young and inexperienced.[i] The task is great, because
this palatial structure is not for man but
for the LORD God. 2With all my resources I have provided for the temple of my
God—gold[j] for the gold work, silver for
the silver, bronze for the bronze, iron
for the iron and wood for the wood, as
well as onyx for the settings, turquoise,[a][k]
stones of various colors, and all kinds of
fine stone and marble—all of these in
large quantities.[l] 3Besides, in my devotion to the temple of my God I now give
my personal treasures of gold and silver
for the temple of my God, over and above
everything I have provided[m] for this holy
temple: 4three thousand talents[b] of gold
(gold of Ophir)[n] and seven thousand talents[c] of refined silver,[o] for the overlaying
of the walls of the buildings, 5for the gold
work and the silver work, and for all the
work to be done by the craftsmen. Now,
who is willing to consecrate himself today
to the LORD?"

6Then the leaders of families, the officers of the tribes of Israel, the commanders of thousands and commanders of hundreds, and the officials[p] in charge of the
king's work gave willingly.[q] 7They[r] gave
toward the work on the temple of God five
thousand talents[d] and ten thousand darics[e] of gold, ten thousand talents[f] of silver, eighteen thousand talents[g] of bronze
and a hundred thousand talents[h] of iron.
8Any who had precious stones[s] gave them
to the treasury of the temple of the LORD in
the custody of Jehiel the Gershonite.[t] 9The
people rejoiced at the willing response of
their leaders, for they had given freely and
wholeheartedly[u] to the LORD. David the
king also rejoiced greatly.

28:20 [f]S Dt 4:31; S Jos 24:20 [g]S 1Ki 6:14; 2Ch 7:11 **28:21** [h]Ex 35:25-36:5 **29:1** [i]1Ki 3:7; 1Ch 22:5; 2Ch 13:7 **29:2** [j]ver 7, 14, 16; Ezr 1:4; 6:5; Hag 2:8 [k]Isa 54:11 [l]1Ch 22:2-5 **29:3** [m]2Ch 24:10; 31:3; 35:8 **29:4** [n]S Ge 10:29 [o]1Ch 22:14 **29:6** [p]1Ch 27:1; S 28:1 [q]ver 9; Ex 25:1-8; 35:20-29; 36:2; 2Ch 24:10; Ezr 7:15 **29:7** [r]S Ex 25:2; Ne 7:70-71 **29:8** [s]Ex 35:27 [t]S 1Ch 26:21 **29:9** [u]1Ki 8:61

29:11 [v]Ps 24:8; 59:17; 62:11 [w]Ps 89:11 [x]Rev 5:12-13 **29:12** [y]2Ch 1:12; 32:27; Ezr 7:27; Ecc 5:19 [z]2Ch 20:6 **29:14** [a]Ps 8:4; 144:3 [b]S ver 2 **29:15** [c]S Ge 17:8; S 23:4; Ps 39:12; S Heb 11:13 [d]Job 7:6; 8:9; 14:2; 32:7; Ps 102:11; 144:4; Ecc 6:12 **29:17** [e]Ps 139:23; Pr 15:11; 17:3; Jer 11:20; 17:10 [f]1Ch 28:9; Ps 15:1-5; Pr 11:20 **29:19** [g]S 1Ki 8:61; 11:4; 1Ch 28:9; Isa 38:3 [h]Ps 72:1 [i]S 1Ch 22:14

David's Prayer

10David praised the LORD in the presence
of the whole assembly, saying,

"Praise be to you, O LORD,
God of our father Israel,
from everlasting to everlasting.
11Yours, O LORD, is the greatness and
the power[v]
and the glory and the majesty and
the splendor,
for everything in heaven and earth
is yours.[w]
Yours, O LORD, is the kingdom;
you are exalted as head over all.[x]
12Wealth and honor[y] come from you;
you are the ruler[z] of all things.
In your hands are strength and
power
to exalt and give strength to all.
13Now, our God, we give you thanks,
and praise your glorious name.

14"But who am I, and who are my people, that we should be able to give as generously as this?[a] Everything comes from
you, and we have given you only what
comes from your hand.[b] 15We are aliens
and strangers[c] in your sight, as were all
our forefathers. Our days on earth are
like a shadow,[d] without hope. 16O LORD
our God, as for all this abundance that
we have provided for building you a temple for your Holy Name, it comes from
your hand, and all of it belongs to you.
17I know, my God, that you test the heart[e]
and are pleased with integrity. All these
things have I given willingly and with
honest intent. And now I have seen with
joy how willingly your people who are
here have given to you.[f] 18O LORD, God
of our fathers Abraham, Isaac and Israel, keep this desire in the hearts of your
people forever, and keep their hearts loyal
to you. 19And give my son Solomon the
wholehearted devotion[g] to keep your commands, requirements and decrees[h] and to
do everything to build the palatial structure for which I have provided."[i]

[a] 2 The meaning of the Hebrew for this word is uncertain. [b] 4 That is, about 110 tons (about 100 metric tons) [c] 4 That is, about 260 tons (about 240 metric tons) [d] 7 That is, about 190 tons (about 170 metric tons) [e] 7 That is, about 185 pounds (about 84 kilograms) [f] 7 That is, about 375 tons (about 345 metric tons) [g] 7 That is, about 675 tons (about 610 metric tons) [h] 7 That is, about 3,750 tons (about 3,450 metric tons)

29:1 *chosen.* See note on 28:5. *young.* See note on 22:5.

29:2–9 After donating his personal fortune to the construction of the temple, David appeals to the people for their voluntary gifts. The Chronicler again appears to be modeling his account of David on events from the life of Moses (Ex 25:1–8; 35:4–9,20–29). The willing response of the people aided the building of both tabernacle and temple.

29:7 *darics.* See NIV text note. The daric was a Persian gold coin, apparently named for Darius I (522–486 B.C.) in whose reign it first appears (see Ezr 8:27). Since the Chronicler's readers were familiar with it, he could use it as an up-to-date standard of value for an earlier treasure of gold.

29:10–11 See note on Mt 6:13.

[20]Then David said to the whole assembly, "Praise the LORD your God." So they all praised the LORD, the God of their fathers; they bowed low and fell prostrate before the LORD and the king.

Solomon Acknowledged as King

29:21-25pp — 1Ki 1:28-53

[21]The next day they made sacrifices to the LORD and presented burnt offerings to him:[j] a thousand bulls, a thousand rams and a thousand male lambs, together with their drink offerings, and other sacrifices in abundance for all Israel.[k] [22]They ate and drank with great joy[l] in the presence of the LORD that day.

Then they acknowledged Solomon son of David as king a second time, anointing him before the LORD to be ruler and Zadok[m] to be priest. [23]So Solomon sat[n] on the throne[o] of the LORD as king in place of his father David. He prospered and all Israel obeyed him. [24]All the officers and mighty men, as well as all of King David's sons,[p] pledged their submission to King Solomon.

[25]The LORD highly exalted[q] Solomon in the sight of all Israel and bestowed on him royal splendor[r] such as no king over Israel ever had before.[s]

The Death of David

29:26-28pp — 1Ki 2:10-12

[26]David son of Jesse was king[t] over all Israel.[u] [27]He ruled over Israel forty years — seven in Hebron[v] and thirty-three in Jerusalem.[w] [28]He died[x] at a good old age, having enjoyed long life, wealth and honor. His son Solomon succeeded him as king.[y]

[29]As for the events of King David's reign, from beginning to end, they are written in the records of Samuel the seer,[z] the records of Nathan[a] the prophet and the records of Gad[b] the seer, [30]together with the details of his reign and power, and the circumstances that surrounded him and Israel and the kingdoms of all the other lands.

29:21 [j]S 1Ki 8:62 [k]1Ch 11:1 **29:22** [l]1Ch 12:40 [m]S 1Sa 2:35 **29:23** [n]S Dt 17:18 [o]S 1Ki 2:12; S 1Ch 17:14 **29:24** [p]1Ki 1:9 **29:25** [q]S Jos 3:7 [r]1Ki 10:7; 2Ch 1:1,12 [s]Ecc 2:9 **29:26** [t]1Ch 18:14 [u]1Ch 11:1 **29:27** [v]S Ge 23:19 [w]2Sa 5:4-5; S 1Ch 3:4 **29:28** [x]S Ge 15:15; Ac 13:36 [y]S 1Ch 23:1 **29:29** [z]S 1Sa 9:9 [a]S 2Sa 7:2 [b]S 1Sa 22:5

29:22 *ate and drank.* See 12:38–40 and note. The anointing of both Solomon and Zadok portrays the harmony between them (see Zec 4:14; 6:13 and notes). *second time.* Perhaps the first time was Solomon's anointing recorded in 1Ki 1:32–36, but omitted by the Chronicler (see note on 28:1—29:30). However, the phrase "second time" is missing in the Septuagint (the pre-Christian Greek translation of the OT), suggesting that it may have been an addition to the Hebrew text of this passage by an ancient scribe after the Septuagint had already been translated, in order to harmonize the Chronicles account with Kings. Multiple anointings are found in the cases of both Saul (1Sa 10:1,24; 11:14–15) and David (1Sa 16:13; 2Sa 2:4; 5:3).
29:24 *all ... pledged their submission.* But compare the rebellion of Adonijah, in which the officers and sons of the king had assisted the attempted coup (1Ki 1:9,19,25). Again the Chronicler has bypassed a negative event that would tarnish his image of David and Solomon.
29:25 *all Israel.* See 11:1,10; 12:38–40; see also Introduction: Purpose and Themes.
29:27 See note on 3:1–9.
29:28 *long life, wealth and honor.* As a feature of the Chronicler's theme of immediate retribution (see Introduction: Purpose and Themes), the righteous enjoy these blessings (cf. Ps 128; Pr 3:2,4,9–10,16,22,33–35).
29:29 See Introduction: Author, Date and Sources.
29:30 *kingdoms of all the other lands.* Those immediately surrounding David's kingdom.

2 Chronicles

INTRODUCTION

See Introduction to 1 Chronicles.

The Building of the Temple in Chronicles

The author of 1 and 2 Chronicles has used the Pentateuchal history as a model for his account of the reigns of David and Solomon. Similarly, the Pentateuchal record of the building of the tabernacle affects his account of the building of the temple:

1. The building of the tabernacle was entrusted to Bezalel and Oholiab (Ex 35:30 — 36:7), and they provide the Chronicler's model for the relationship of Solomon and Huram-Abi (2Ch 2:13). It is significant that the only references to Bezalel outside the book of Exodus are in Chronicles (1Ch 2:20; 2Ch 1:5).

Solomon is the new Bezalel: (1) Both Solomon and Bezalel are designated by name for their tasks by God; they are the only workers on their projects to be chosen by name (Ex 31:2; 35:30 — 36:2; 38:22 – 23; 1Ch 28:6). (2) Both are from the tribe of Judah (Ex 31:2; 35:30; 1Ch 2:20; 3:10). (3) Both receive the Spirit to endow them with wisdom (Ex 31:3; 35:30 – 31; 2Ch 1:1 – 13), and Solomon's vision at Gibeon (2Ch 1:3 – 13) dominates the preface to the account of the temple construction (2Ch 2 – 7). (4) Both build a bronze altar for the sanctuary (2Ch 1:5; 4:1; 7:7) — significantly, the bronze altar is not mentioned in the summary list of Huram-Abi's work (4:12 – 16). (5) Both make the sanctuary furnishings (Ex 31:1 – 10; 37:10 – 29; 2Ch 4:19 – 22).

Similarly, Huram-Abi becomes the new Oholiab: (1) In the account of the temple building in Kings, Huram-Abi is not mentioned until after the story of the main construction of temple and palace has been told (1Ki 7:13 – 45); in Chronicles he is introduced as being involved in the building work from the beginning, just as Oholiab worked on the tabernacle from the beginning (Ex 31:6; 2Ch 2:13). (2) Kings speaks only of Huram-Abi's skill in casting bronze (1Ki 7:14); in Chronicles, however, his

> **A Quick Look**
>
> **Author:**
> Unknown; possibly Ezra
>
> **Audience:**
> The people of Judah who had returned from exile in Babylonia
>
> **Date:**
> Sometime after 440 B.C.
>
> **Theme:**
> 2 Chronicles covers the period from Solomon's reign (970 B.C.) to the Babylonian exile (586 B.C.), presenting an idealized history of the southern kingdom of Judah.

list of skills is the same as Oholiab's (Ex 31:1 – 6; 35:30 — 36:2; 38:22 – 23; 2Ch 2:14). (3) Kings reports that the mother of Huram-Abi was a widow from the tribe of Naphtali (1Ki 7:14); Chronicles, however, states that she was a widow from the tribe of Dan (2Ch 2:14), thus giving Huram-Abi the same ancestry as Oholiab (Ex 31:6; 35:34; 38:23). See note on 2Ch 2:13.

2. The plans for both tabernacle and temple are given by God (Ex 25:1 — 30:37; see Ex 25:9,40; 27:8; see also 1Ch 28:11 – 19 — not mentioned in Samuel and Kings).

3. The spoils of war are used as building materials for both tabernacle and temple (Ex 3:21 – 22; 12:35 – 36; see 1Ch 18:6 – 11 — not mentioned in Samuel and Kings).

The author of 1 and 2 Chronicles has used the Pentateuchal history as a model for his account of the reigns of David and Solomon.

4. The people contribute willingly and generously for both structures (Ex 25:1 – 7; 36:3 – 7; see 1Ch 29:1 – 9 — not mentioned in Samuel and Kings).

5. The glory cloud appears at the dedication of both structures (Ex 40:34 – 35; 2Ch 7:1 – 3).

Outline

- III. The Reign of Solomon (2Ch 1 – 9)
  - A. The Gift of Wisdom (ch. 1)
  - B. Building the Temple (2:1 — 5:1)
  - C. Dedication of the Temple (5:2 — 7:22)
  - D. Solomon's Other Activities (ch. 8)
  - E. Solomon's Wisdom, Splendor and Death (ch. 9)
- IV. The Schism, and the History of the Kings of Judah (2Ch 10 – 36)
  - A. Rehoboam (chs. 10 – 12)
  - B. Abijah (13:1 — 14:1)
  - C. Asa (14:2 — 16:14)
  - D. Jehoshaphat (17:1 — 21:3)
  - E. Jehoram and Ahaziah (21:4 — 22:9)
  - F. Joash (22:10 — 24:27)
  - G. Amaziah (ch. 25)
  - H. Uzziah (ch. 26)
  - I. Jotham (ch. 27)
  - J. Ahaz (ch. 28)
  - K. Hezekiah (chs. 29 – 32)
  - L. Manasseh (33:1 – 20)
  - M. Amon (33:21 – 25)
  - N. Josiah (34:1 — 36:1)
  - O. Josiah's Successors (36:2 – 14)
  - P. Exile and Restoration (36:15 – 23)

Solomon Asks for Wisdom

1:2-13pp — 1Ki 3:4-15
1:14-17pp — 1Ki 10:26-29; 2Ch 9:25-28

1 Solomon son of David established[a]
himself firmly over his kingdom, for
the LORD his God was with[b] him and made
him exceedingly great.[c]
2Then Solomon spoke to all Israel[d]—to
the commanders of thousands and commanders of hundreds, to the judges and
to all the leaders in Israel, the heads of
families— 3and Solomon and the whole
assembly went to the high place at Gibeon,[e] for God's Tent of Meeting[f] was
there, which Moses[g] the LORD's servant
had made in the desert. 4Now David had
brought up the ark[h] of God from Kiriath
Jearim to the place he had prepared for
it, because he had pitched a tent[i] for it in
Jerusalem. 5But the bronze altar[j] that Bezalel[k] son of Uri, the son of Hur, had made
was in Gibeon in front of the tabernacle of
the LORD; so Solomon and the assembly
inquired[l] of him there. 6Solomon went up
to the bronze altar before the LORD in the
Tent of Meeting and offered a thousand
burnt offerings on it.
7That night God appeared[m] to Solomon
and said to him, "Ask for whatever you
want me to give you."
8Solomon answered God, "You have
shown great kindness to David my father and have made me[n] king in his place.
9Now, LORD God, let your promise[o] to my
father David be confirmed, for you have
made me king over a people who are as
numerous as the dust of the earth.[p] 10Give
me wisdom and knowledge, that I may
lead[q] this people, for who is able to govern
this great people of yours?"
11God said to Solomon, "Since this is
your heart's desire and you have not asked
for wealth,[r] riches or honor, nor for the
death of your enemies, and since you have
not asked for a long life but for wisdom
and knowledge to govern my people over
whom I have made you king, 12therefore
wisdom and knowledge will be given you.
And I will also give you wealth, riches
and honor,[s] such as no king who was before you ever had and none after you will
have.[t]"
13Then Solomon went to Jerusalem from
the high place at Gibeon, from before the
Tent of Meeting. And he reigned over Israel.
14Solomon accumulated chariots[u] and
horses; he had fourteen hundred chariots and twelve thousand horses,[a] which
he kept in the chariot cities and also with
him in Jerusalem. 15The king made silver and gold[v] as common in Jerusalem as
stones, and cedar as plentiful as sycamore-
fig trees in the foothills. 16Solomon's horses were imported from Egypt[b] and from
Kue[c]—the royal merchants purchased
them from Kue. 17They imported a chariot[w] from Egypt for six hundred shekels[d] of
silver, and a horse for a hundred and fifty.[e]
They also exported them to all the kings of
the Hittites and of the Arameans.

Preparations for Building the Temple

2:1-18pp — 1Ki 5:1-16

2 Solomon gave orders to build a temple[x] for the Name of the LORD and a
royal palace for himself.[y] 2He conscripted seventy thousand men as carriers and
eighty thousand as stonecutters in the hills
and thirty-six hundred as foremen over
them.[z]

[a] 14 Or *charioteers* [b] 16 Or possibly *Muzur,* a region in Cilicia; also in verse 17 [c] 16 Probably Cilicia
[d] 17 That is, about 15 pounds (about 7 kilograms)
[e] 17 That is, about 3 3/4 pounds (about 1.7 kilograms)

1:1 [a]S 1Ki 2:12,26; S 2Ch 12:1 [b]S Ge 21:22; S 39:2; S Nu 14:43 [c]S 1Ch 29:25 **1:2** [d]S 1Ch 9:1 **1:3** [e]S Jos 9:3 [f]S Lev 17:4 [g]Ex 40:18 **1:4** [h]S 1Ch 15:25 [i]2Sa 6:17 **1:5** [j]Ex 38:2 [k]S Ex 31:2 [l]1Ch 13:3 **1:7** [m]2Ch 7:12 **1:8** [n]S 1Ch 23:1 **1:9** [o]S 2Sa 7:25; S 1Ki 8:25 [p]S Ge 12:2 **1:10** [q]Nu 27:17; 2Sa 5:2; Pr 8:15-16 **1:11** [r]S Dt 17:17 **1:12** [s]S 1Ch 29:12 [t]S 1Ch 29:25; 2Ch 9:22; Ne 13:26 **1:14** [u]S 1Sa 8:11; S 1Ki 9:19 **1:15** [v]S 1Ki 9:28; Isa 60:5 **1:17** [w]SS 1:9 **2:1** [x]S Dt 12:5 [y]Ecc 2:4 **2:2** [z]2Ch 10:4

1:1—9:31 The account of the reign of Solomon is primarily devoted to his building of the temple (chs. 2–7); his endowment with wisdom is mainly to facilitate the building work. Much of the material in Kings that does not bear on building the temple is omitted by the Chronicler; e.g., he does not mention the judgment between the prostitutes (1Ki 3:16–28) or the building of the royal palace (1Ki 7:1–12).

1:1 *established himself.* This expression, or a variation of it, is common in Chronicles (12:13; 13:7–8,21; 15:8; 16:9; 17:1; 21:4; 23:1; 25:11; 27:6; 32:5; 1Ch 11:10; 19:13). Here and in 21:4 it includes the elimination of enemies and rivals to the throne (see 1Ki 2, especially v. 46).

1:2–13 See 1Ki 3:4–15 and notes. Verses 2–6 are largely unique to Chronicles and show some of the writer's concerns: (1) The support of "all Israel" (v. 2) is emphasized (see Introduction to 1 Chronicles: Purpose and Themes). (2) While the writer of Kings is somewhat apologetic about Solomon's visit to a high place (1Ki 3:3), the Chronicler adds the note that this was the location of the tabernacle made by Moses in the desert (v. 3), bringing Solomon's action into line with the provisions of the law (Lev 17:8–9).

1:5 *Bezalel.* See Introduction: The Building of the Temple in Chronicles. It is specifically in connection with his offering on the altar built by Bezalel (Ex 31:1–11; 38:1–2) that Solomon receives the wisdom from God to reign. In the account that follows, Solomon devotes his gift of wisdom primarily to building the temple, just as Bezalel had been gifted by God to serve as the master craftsman of the tabernacle.

1:9 *numerous as the dust.* In provisional fulfillment of the promise to Abraham (Ge 13:16; 22:17; see note on 1Ch 27:23; cf. Ge 28:14).

1:14–17 The Chronicler does not include the material in 1Ki 3:16—4:34. He moves rather to the account of Solomon's wealth in 1Ki 10:26–29; part of this material is repeated in 2Ch 9:25–28. Recounting Solomon's wealth at this point shows the fulfillment of God's promise (v. 12).

1:15 *sycamore-fig trees.* See note on Am 7:14.

1:17 *imported ... exported.* See note on 1Ki 10:29. *Hittites.* See note on Ge 10:15. *Arameans.* See notes on 1Ch 18:5; Dt 26:5.

2:1 *palace.* Although the Chronicler frequently mentions the palace Solomon built (7:11; 8:1; 9:11), he gives no details of its construction (see 1Ki 7:1–12).

2:2 See vv. 17–18 and note.

[3]Solomon sent this message to Hiram[a][a]
king of Tyre:

"Send me cedar logs[b] as you did
for my father David when you sent
him cedar to build a palace to live in.
[4]Now I am about to build a temple[c]
for the Name of the LORD my God and
to dedicate it to him for burning fragrant incense[d] before him, for setting
out the consecrated bread[e] regularly,
and for making burnt offerings[f] every
morning and evening and on Sabbaths[g] and New Moons[h] and at the
appointed feasts of the LORD our God.
This is a lasting ordinance for Israel.
[5]"The temple I am going to build
will be great,[i] because our God is
greater than all other gods.[j] [6]But who
is able to build a temple for him, since
the heavens, even the highest heavens,
cannot contain him?[k] Who then am I[l]
to build a temple for him, except as a
place to burn sacrifices before him?
[7]"Send me, therefore, a man skilled
to work in gold and silver, bronze and
iron, and in purple, crimson and blue
yarn, and experienced in the art of
engraving, to work in Judah and Jerusalem with my skilled craftsmen,[m]
whom my father David provided.
[8]"Send me also cedar, pine and algum[b] logs from Lebanon, for I know
that your men are skilled in cutting
timber there. My men will work with
yours [9]to provide me with plenty of
lumber, because the temple I build
must be large and magnificent. [10]I will
give your servants, the woodsmen
who cut the timber, twenty thousand
cors[c] of ground wheat, twenty thousand cors of barley, twenty thousand
baths[d] of wine and twenty thousand
baths of olive oil.[n]"

2:3 [a]S 2Sa 5:11 [b]S 1Ch 14:1 **2:4** [c]S Dt 12:5 [d]S Ex 30:7 [e]Ex 25:30 [f]Ex 29:42; 2Ch 13:11; 29:28 [g]S Lev 23:38 [h]S Nu 28:14 **2:5** [i]1Ch 22:5 [j]S Ex 12:12; S 1Ch 16:25 **2:6** [k]S 1Ki 8:27; Jer 23:24 [l]S Ex 3:11 **2:7** [m]S Ex 35:31; 1Ch 22:16 **2:10** [n]Ezr 3:7

2:11 [o]1Ki 10:9; 2Ch 9:8 **2:12** [p]Ne 9:6; Ps 8:3; 33:6; 96:5; 102:25; 146:6 **2:13** [q]S 1Ki 7:13 **2:14** [r]S Ex 31:6 [s]S Ex 35:31 [t]Ex 35:35 **2:15** [u]Ezr 3:7 **2:16** [v]S Jos 19:46; Jnh 1:3 **2:17** [w]1Ch 22:2 [x]S 2Sa 24:2 **2:18** [y]1Ch 22:2; 2Ch 8:8

[11]Hiram king of Tyre replied by letter to
Solomon:

"Because the LORD loves[o] his people, he has made you their king."

[12]And Hiram added:

"Praise be to the LORD, the God of
Israel, who made heaven and earth![p]
He has given King David a wise son,
endowed with intelligence and discernment, who will build a temple for
the LORD and a palace for himself.
[13]"I am sending you Huram-Abi,[q]
a man of great skill, [14]whose mother was from Dan[r] and whose father
was from Tyre. He is trained[s] to work
in gold and silver, bronze and iron,
stone and wood, and with purple and
blue[t] and crimson yarn and fine lin-
en. He is experienced in all kinds of
engraving and can execute any design
given to him. He will work with your
craftsmen and with those of my lord,
David your father.
[15]"Now let my lord send his servants the wheat and barley and the
olive oil[u] and wine he promised, [16]and
we will cut all the logs from Lebanon
that you need and will float them in
rafts by sea down to Joppa.[v] You can
then take them up to Jerusalem."

[17]Solomon took a census of all the aliens[w]
who were in Israel, after the census[x] his father David had taken; and they were found
to be 153,600. [18]He assigned[y] 70,000 of
them to be carriers and 80,000 to be stonecutters in the hills, with 3,600 foremen over
them to keep the people working.

[a] *3* Hebrew *Huram,* a variant of *Hiram*; also in verses 11 and 12 [b] *8* Probably a variant of *almug*; possibly juniper [c] *10* That is, probably about 125,000 bushels (about 4,400 kiloliters) [d] *10* That is, probably about 115,000 gallons (about 440 kiloliters)

2:3–10 The Chronicler's theological interests appear in his handling of Solomon's correspondence with Hiram of Tyre. In the Kings account the correspondence was initiated by Hiram (1Ki 5:1). The Chronicler omits this (and also the material in 1Ki 5:3–5) but adds his own material, reflecting his concerns with the temple worship in vv. 3–7.
2:4 See 1Ch 23:28–32 and note.
2:7 See Introduction: The Building of the Temple in Chronicles. In the Kings account Solomon's request for a master craftsman is found late in the narrative (1Ki 7:13); to carry out his parallel between Oholiab and Huram-Abi, the Chronicler includes it in the initial correspondence. Furthermore, here and in vv. 13–14 the list of Huram-Abi's skills is expanded and matches that of Bezalel and Oholiab (Kings is concerned only with casting bronze).
2:10 The payment here differs from that reported in 1Ki 5:11, but the texts speak of two different payments: In Kings the payment is an annual sum delivered to the royal household of Hiram, while Chronicles speaks of one payment to those "who cut the timber." The goods paid are also not identical; the oil specified in Kings is of a finer quality.
2:11–16 See 1Ki 5:7–9; 7:13–14 and notes.

2:13 *Huram-Abi.* See note on v. 7. Kings reports that the ancestry of Huram-Abi was through a widow of Naphtali (1Ki 7:14); Chronicles strengthens the parallel between Huram-Abi and Oholiab by assigning him Danite ancestry. These statements are not necessarily contradictory: (1) The mother's ancestry may have been Danite, though she lived in the territory of Naphtali; or (2) her parents may have been from Dan and Naphtali, allowing her descent to be reckoned to either. The Danites had been previously associated with the Phoenicians (Jdg 18:7).
2:17–18 See 1Ki 5:13–18 and notes. The Chronicler specifies that this levy of forced laborers was from aliens resident in the land, not from Israelites. This is not stated in the parallel passage in Kings, though 1Ki 9:20–22 confirms that alien labor was used (see 8:8).
2:18 *3,600 foremen.* See v. 2. The number given in 1Ki 5:16 is 3,300; however, some manuscripts of the Septuagint (the pre-Christian Greek translation of the OT) also have 3,600. The Chronicler may have been following a different text of Kings from the traditional Hebrew text at this point (but see note on 1Ki 5:16).

Solomon Builds the Temple

3:1-14pp — 1Ki 6:1-29

3 Then Solomon began to build[z] the temple of the LORD[a] in Jerusalem on Mount
Moriah, where the LORD had appeared to
his father David. It was on the threshing
floor of Araunah[a][b] the Jebusite, the place
provided by David. 2He began building on
the second day of the second month in the
fourth year of his reign.[c]
3The foundation Solomon laid for building the temple of God was sixty cubits
long and twenty cubits wide[b][d] (using the
cubit of the old standard). 4The portico at
the front of the temple was twenty cubits[c]
long across the width of the building and
twenty cubits[d] high.
He overlaid the inside with pure gold.
5He paneled the main hall with pine and
covered it with fine gold and decorated it with palm tree[e] and chain designs.
6He adorned the temple with precious
stones. And the gold he used was gold of
Parvaim. 7He overlaid the ceiling beams,
doorframes, walls and doors of the temple with gold, and he carved cherubim[f]
on the walls.
8He built the Most Holy Place,[g] its
length corresponding to the width of the
temple—twenty cubits long and twenty
cubits wide. He overlaid the inside with
six hundred talents[e] of fine gold. 9The
gold nails[h] weighed fifty shekels.[f] He also
overlaid the upper parts with gold.
10In the Most Holy Place he made a pair[i]
of sculptured cherubim and overlaid them
with gold. 11The total wingspan of the
cherubim was twenty cubits. One wing of
the first cherub was five cubits[g] long and
touched the temple wall, while its other
wing, also five cubits long, touched the
wing of the other cherub. 12Similarly one
wing of the second cherub was five cubits
long and touched the other temple wall,
and its other wing, also five cubits long,
touched the wing of the first cherub. 13The
wings of these cherubim[j] extended twenty
cubits. They stood on their feet, facing the
main hall.[h]
14He made the curtain[k] of blue, purple
and crimson yarn and fine linen, with
cherubim[l] worked into it.
15In the front of the temple he made two
pillars,[m] which ⌞together⌟ were thirty-five
cubits[i] long, each with a capital[n] on top
measuring five cubits. 16He made interwoven chains[j][o] and put them on top of the
pillars. He also made a hundred pomegranates[p] and attached them to the chains.
17He erected the pillars in the front of the
temple, one to the south and one to the
north. The one to the south he named Jakin[k] and the one to the north Boaz.[l]

3:1 [z] Ac 7:47 [a] S Ge 28:17 [b] S 2Sa 24:18 **3:2** [c] Ezr 5:11 **3:3** [d] Eze 41:2 **3:5** [e] Eze 40:16 **3:7** [f] Ge 3:24; Eze 41:18 **3:8** [g] S Ex 26:33 **3:9** [h] Ex 26:32 **3:10** [i] Ex 25:18 **3:13** [j] S Ex 25:18 **3:14** [k] S Ex 26:31,33 [l] Ge 3:24 **3:15** [m] S 1Ki 7:15; Rev 3:12 [n] 1Ki 7:22 **3:16** [o] 1Ki 7:17 [p] S 1Ki 7:20

[a] *1* Hebrew *Ornan,* a variant of *Araunah* [b] *3* That is, about 90 feet (about 27 meters) long and 30 feet (about 9 meters) wide [c] *4* That is, about 30 feet (about 9 meters); also in verses 8, 11 and 13 [d] *4* Some Septuagint and Syriac manuscripts; Hebrew *and a hundred and twenty* [e] *8* That is, about 23 tons (about 21 metric tons) [f] *9* That is, about 1 1/4 pounds (about 0.6 kilogram) [g] *11* That is, about 7 1/2 feet (about 2.3 meters); also in verse 15 [h] *13* Or *facing inward* [i] *15* That is, about 52 feet (about 16 meters) [j] *16* Or possibly *made chains in the inner sanctuary*; the meaning of the Hebrew for this phrase is uncertain. [k] *17* *Jakin* probably means *he establishes.* [l] *17* *Boaz* probably means *in him is strength.*

3:1–17 The Chronicler has considerably curtailed the description of the temple's construction found in Kings, omitting completely 1Ki 6:4–20. This abridgment probably indicates that the Chronicler's audience was familiar with the details of the earlier history and that the temple of the restoration period was less elaborate than the original Solomonic structure (Hag 2:3). On the other hand, the Chronicler goes into more detail on the furnishings and implements (3:6–9; 4:1,6–9).

3:1 *Mount Moriah.* The only passage in the OT where Mount Zion is identified with Mount Moriah, the place where Abraham was commanded to offer Isaac (Ge 22:2,14). *place provided by David.* See 1Ch 21:18—22:1.

3:2 *second month in the fourth year.* In the spring of 966 B.C. (see note on 1Ki 6:1).

3:3 *cubit of the old standard.* About three inches longer than the common cubit, which was c. 18 inches (see Eze 40:5 and note).

3:4 *portico.* See diagram, p. 484. *overlaid.* Or "inlaid," which perhaps gives a more correct picture: not that the entire interior was covered with gold leaf, but that designs (palm trees, chains) were inlaid with gold leaf (v. 5).

3:6 *Parvaim.* Designates either the source of the gold (perhaps southeast Arabia) or a particular quality of fine gold.

3:7 *cherubim.* See vv. 10–14; see also notes on Ge 3:24; Eze 1:5.

3:8 *twenty cubits long and twenty cubits wide.* It was also 20 cubits high (1Ki 6:20), making the dimensions of the Most Holy Place a perfect cube, as probably also in the tabernacle. In the new Jerusalem there is no temple (Rev 21:22); rather, the whole city is in the shape of a cube (Rev 21:16), for the whole city becomes "the Most Holy Place."

3:9 *gold nails.* The fact that gold is a soft metal would make it unlikely that nails were made of this substance. It is probable that this small amount (only 1 1/4 pounds; see NIV text note) represents gold leaf or sheeting used to gild the nail heads.

3:10–13 See 1Ki 6:23–27 and notes.

3:14 *curtain.* Also separated the two rooms of the tabernacle (Ex 26:31). Wooden doors could also be closed across the opening (4:22; 1Ki 6:31–32; cf. Mt 27:51; Heb 9:8).

3:15 *⌞together⌟ were thirty-five cubits long.* The NIV supplies the word "together" in an attempt to harmonize this measurement with the 18 cubits (each) in 1Ki 7:15; 2Ki 25:17 (see NIV text note there); Jer 52:21 (though the Septuagint at Jer 52:21 has 35). Alternatively, 35 may be the result of a copyist's mistake.

3:17 *pillars.* Remains of such pillars have been found in the excavations of numerous temples in the Holy Land. Cf. Rev 3:12. *Jakin ... Boaz.* See NIV text notes.

4:1 *bronze altar.* The parallel text in Kings does not mention the main altar of the temple described here (1Ki 7:22–23), though several other passages in Kings do refer to it (1Ki 8:64; 9:25; 2Ki 16:14). The main altar of Solomon's temple was similar to the altar with steps that is described in Eze 43:13–17.

The Temple's Furnishings

4:2-6,10–5:1pp — 1Ki 7:23-26,38-51

4 He made a bronze altar[q] twenty cubits
long, twenty cubits wide and ten cubits
high.[a] 2He made the Sea[r] of cast metal, circular in shape, measuring ten cubits from
rim to rim and five cubits[b] high. It took a
line of thirty cubits[c] to measure around it.
3Below the rim, figures of bulls encircled
it—ten to a cubit.[d] The bulls were cast in
two rows in one piece with the Sea.
4The Sea stood on twelve bulls, three
facing north, three facing west, three facing south and three facing east.[s] The Sea
rested on top of them, and their hind-
quarters were toward the center. 5It was
a handbreadth[e] in thickness, and its rim
was like the rim of a cup, like a lily blossom. It held three thousand baths.[f]
6He then made ten basins[t] for washing
and placed five on the south side and five
on the north. In them the things to be used
for the burnt offerings[u] were rinsed, but
the Sea was to be used by the priests for
washing.
7He made ten gold lampstands[v] according to the specifications[w] for them and
placed them in the temple, five on the
south side and five on the north.
8He made ten tables[x] and placed them
in the temple, five on the south side and
five on the north. He also made a hundred
gold sprinkling bowls.[y]
9He made the courtyard[z] of the priests,
and the large court and the doors for the
court, and overlaid the doors with bronze.
10He placed the Sea on the south side, at
the southeast corner.
11He also made the pots and shovels and
sprinkling bowls.
So Huram finished[a] the work he had undertaken for King Solomon in the temple
of God:

12the two pillars;
the two bowl-shaped capitals on top
of the pillars;
the two sets of network decorating
the two bowl-shaped capitals on
top of the pillars;
13the four hundred pomegranates for
the two sets of network (two rows
of pomegranates for each network,
decorating the bowl-shaped capitals on top of the pillars);
14the stands[b] with their basins;
15the Sea and the twelve bulls under it;
16the pots, shovels, meat forks and all
related articles.

All the objects that Huram-Abi[c] made for
King Solomon for the temple of the LORD
were of polished bronze. 17The king had
them cast in clay molds in the plain of the
Jordan between Succoth[d] and Zarethan.[g]
18All these things that Solomon made
amounted to so much that the weight of
the bronze[e] was not determined.
19Solomon also made all the furnishings
that were in God's temple:

the golden altar;
the tables[f] on which was the bread of
the Presence;
20the lampstands[g] of pure gold with
their lamps, to burn in front of the
inner sanctuary as prescribed;
21the gold floral work and lamps and
tongs (they were solid gold);
22the pure gold wick trimmers, sprinkling bowls, dishes[h] and censers;[i]
and the gold doors of the temple:
the inner doors to the Most Holy
Place and the doors of the main
hall.

5 When all the work Solomon had done
for the temple of the LORD was finished,[j]
he brought in the things his father David

4:1 [q] S Ex 20:24; S 40:6; S 1Ki 8:64
4:2 [r] Rev 4:6; 15:2
4:4 [s] Nu 2:3-25; Eze 48:30-34; Rev 21:13
4:6 [t] S Ex 30:18 [u] Ne 13:5,9; Eze 40:38
4:7 [v] S Ex 25:31 [w] Ex 25:40
4:8 [x] S Ex 25:23 [y] S Nu 4:14
4:9 [z] 1Ki 6:36; 2Ch 33:5
4:11 [a] 1Ki 7:14
4:14 [b] 1Ki 7:27-30
4:16 [c] S 1Ki 7:13
4:17 [d] S Ge 33:17
4:18 [e] S 1Ki 7:23
4:19 [f] S Ex 25:23,30
4:20 [g] Ex 25:31
4:22 [h] S Nu 7:14 [i] S Lev 10:1
5:1 [j] S 1Ki 6:14

[a] *1* That is, about 30 feet (about 9 meters) long and wide, and about 15 feet (about 4.5 meters) high [b] *2* That is, about 7 1/2 feet (about 2.3 meters) [c] *2* That is, about 45 feet (about 13.5 meters) [d] *3* That is, about 1 1/2 feet (about 0.5 meter) [e] *5* That is, about 3 inches (about 8 centimeters) [f] *5* That is, about 17,500 gallons (about 66 kiloliters) [g] *17* Hebrew *Zeredatha,* a variant of *Zarethan*

4:2 *Sea of cast metal.* A larger reservoir of water that replaced the bronze basin of the tabernacle (Ex 30:18); it was used by the priests for their ceremonial washing (v. 6; Ex 30:21). The NT views these rituals as foreshadowing the cleansing provided by Christ (Tit 3:5; Heb 9:11–14). In the temple of Ezekiel, the Sea, which was on the south side in front of the temple (v. 10), has been replaced by a life-giving river that flows from the south side of the temple (Eze 47:1–12; cf. Joel 3:18; Zec 14:8; Jn 4:9–15; Rev 22:1–2).
4:3 *bulls.* 1Ki 7:24 has "gourds." The Hebrew for the two words is very similar, so the difference may be due to a copyist's mistake.
4:4 *twelve bulls.* Possibly symbolic of the 12 tribes, which also encamped three on each side of the tabernacle during the desert journeys (Nu 2; cf. Eze 48:30–35).
4:5 *three thousand baths.* 1Ki 7:26 has 2,000 baths. The Hebrew for these figures could easily have been misread by the ancient scribes.
4:6 *ten basins.* See 1Ki 7:38–39.
4:7 *ten gold lampstands.* Instead of one, as in the tabernacle (Ex 25:31–40). *specifications.* See 1Ch 28:15. These lamps were not necessarily of the same shape as described in Ex 25:31–40, but could have resembled the style of lamp depicted in Zec 4:2–6.
4:8 *ten tables.* Instead of one, as in the tabernacle (Ex 25:23–30; 40:4; Lev 24:5–9; 1Sa 21:1–6; Eze 41:22; Heb 9:2; cf. 2Ch 13:11; 29:18).
4:11–16 See 1Ki 7:40–45.
4:11 *sprinkling bowls.* See notes on Ex 27:3; 1Ki 7:40.
4:17–22 See 1Ki 7:46–50 and notes.
4:17 *clay molds.* The clay of the Jordan plain was used to make molds for these bronze castings. *Succoth and Zarethan.* See note on 1Ki 7:46.
5:1 *things his father David had dedicated.* See notes on 1Ch 18:1—20:8; 22:2–16; 29:2–5; see also 1Ch 26:26 and note.

had dedicated[k]—the silver and gold and
all the furnishings—and he placed them
in the treasuries of God's temple.

The Ark Brought to the Temple

5:2–6:11pp — 1Ki 8:1-21

2Then Solomon summoned to Jerusalem the elders of Israel, all the heads of
the tribes and the chiefs of the Israelite
families, to bring up the ark[l] of the LORD's
covenant from Zion, the City of David.
3And all the men of Israel[m] came together
to the king at the time of the festival in the
seventh month.
4When all the elders of Israel had arrived, the Levites took up the ark, 5and
they brought up the ark and the Tent of
Meeting and all the sacred furnishings in
it. The priests, who were Levites,[n] carried
them up; 6and King Solomon and the entire assembly of Israel that had gathered
about him were before the ark, sacrificing
so many sheep and cattle that they could
not be recorded or counted.
7The priests then brought the ark[o] of the
LORD's covenant to its place in the inner
sanctuary of the temple, the Most Holy
Place, and put it beneath the wings of the
cherubim. 8The cherubim[p] spread their
wings over the place of the ark and covered the ark and its carrying poles. 9These
poles were so long that their ends, extending from the ark, could be seen from in
front of the inner sanctuary, but not from
outside the Holy Place; and they are still
there today. 10There was nothing in the
ark except[q] the two tablets[r] that Moses
had placed in it at Horeb, where the LORD
made a covenant with the Israelites after
they came out of Egypt.
11The priests then withdrew from the
Holy Place. All the priests who were there
had consecrated themselves, regardless
of their divisions.[s] 12All the Levites who
were musicians[t]—Asaph, Heman, Jeduthun and their sons and relatives—stood
on the east side of the altar, dressed in
fine linen and playing cymbals, harps and
lyres. They were accompanied by 120
priests sounding trumpets.[u] 13The trumpeters and singers joined in unison, as
with one voice, to give praise and thanks
to the LORD. Accompanied by trumpets,
cymbals and other instruments, they
raised their voices in praise to the LORD
and sang:

"He is good;
his love endures forever."[v]

Then the temple of the LORD was filled
with a cloud,[w] 14and the priests could
not perform[x] their service because of the
cloud,[y] for the glory[z] of the LORD filled the
temple of God.

6 Then Solomon said, "The LORD has said
that he would dwell in a dark cloud;[a] 2I
have built a magnificent temple for you, a
place for you to dwell forever.[b]"
3While the whole assembly of Israel was
standing there, the king turned around
and blessed them. 4Then he said:

"Praise be to the LORD, the God of Israel, who with his hands has fulfilled
what he promised with his mouth to
my father David. For he said, 5'Since
the day I brought my people out of
Egypt, I have not chosen a city in any
tribe of Israel to have a temple built
for my Name to be there, nor have I
chosen anyone to be the leader over
my people Israel. 6But now I have
chosen Jerusalem[c] for my Name[d] to
be there, and I have chosen David[e] to
rule my people Israel.'
7"My father David had it in his
heart[f] to build a temple for the Name
of the LORD, the God of Israel. 8But
the LORD said to my father David, 'Because it was in your heart to build a
temple for my Name, you did well to
have this in your heart. 9Nevertheless,
you are not the one to build the temple, but your son, who is your own
flesh and blood—he is the one who
will build the temple for my Name.'
10"The LORD has kept the promise
he made. I have succeeded David my
father and now I sit on the throne of

5:1 [k]S 2Sa 8:11 **5:2** [l]S Nu 3:31; S 1Ch 15:25 **5:3** [m]S 1Ch 9:1 **5:5** [n]S Nu 3:31; S 1Ch 15:2 **5:7** [o]Rev 11:19 **5:8** [p]S Ge 3:24 **5:10** [q]Heb 9:4 [r]S Ex 16:34; S Dt 10:2 **5:11** [s]S 1Ch 24:1 **5:12** [t]1Ki 10:12; 1Ch 9:33; S 25:1; Ps 68:25

[u]S 1Ch 13:8 **5:13** [v]S 1Ch 16:34,41; 2Ch 7:3; 20:21; Ezr 3:11; Ps 100:5; 106:1; 107:1; 118:1; 136:1; Jer 33:11 [w]S Ex 40:34 **5:14** [x]Ex 40:35; Rev 15:8 [y]Ex 19:16 [z]S Ex 29:43; S 40:35 **6:1** [a]S Ex 19:9 **6:2** [b]Ezr 6:12; 7:15; Ps 135:21 **6:6** [c]S Dt 12:5; S Isa 14:1 [d]S Ex 20:24 [e]S 1Ch 28:4 **6:7** [f]S 1Sa 10:7; S 1Ch 17:2; Ac 7:46

5:2–14 See 1Ki 8:1–11 and notes.
5:2 *ark.* Had been in a tent provided for it 40 years earlier when David brought it to Jerusalem (1Ch 15:1—16:6).
5:3 *festival in the seventh month.* The Feast of Tabernacles. The month is designated by its Canaanite name Ethanim in 1Ki 8:2; the Hebrew name is Tishri. According to 1Ki 6:38 the temple was completed in the eighth month of Solomon's 11th year, i.e., September-October, 959 B.C. This celebration of dedication probably took place 11 months after the completion of the work (see note on 1Ki 8:2).
5:5 *brought up ... the Tent of Meeting.* The tabernacle had been at Gibeon (see 1:13; see also note on 1Ch 16:39).
5:6 Cf. David's bringing of the ark to Jerusalem (1Ch 15:26; 16:1–3).
5:9 *still there today.* See note on 1Ki 8:8; see also 8:8; 10:19; 20:26; 21:10; 35:25; 1Ch 4:41,43; 5:26; 13:11; 17:5.
5:10 *two tablets.* See Ex 31:18 and note; see also Ex 32:15–16. The ark had earlier contained also the gold jar of manna (Ex 16:32–34) and Aaron's staff (Nu 17:10–11; Heb 9:4). These items were presumably lost, perhaps while the ark was in Philistine hands.
5:12 *fine linen.* See 1Ch 15:27 and note.
5:14 *cloud ... glory of the LORD.* Cf. 7:1–3. The glory cloud represented the presence of God. It had guided Israel out of Egypt and through the desert, and was present above the tabernacle (Ex 13:21–22; 40:34–38; cf. Eze 43:1–5; Hag 2:9; Zec 1:16; 2:10; 8:3).
6:1–11 See notes on 1Ki 8:12–21.
6:8–9 Cf. David's speech in 1Ch 28:2–3.

Israel, just as the LORD promised, and
I have built the temple for the Name
of the LORD, the God of Israel. 11There
I have placed the ark, in which is the
covenant[g] of the LORD that he made
with the people of Israel."

Solomon's Prayer of Dedication

6:12-40pp — 1Ki 8:22-53
6:41-42pp — Ps 132:8-10

12Then Solomon stood before the altar of
the LORD in front of the whole assembly of
Israel and spread out his hands. 13Now he
had made a bronze platform,[h] five cubits[a]
long, five cubits wide and three cubits[b]
high, and had placed it in the center of
the outer court. He stood on the platform
and then knelt down[i] before the whole assembly of Israel and spread out his hands
toward heaven. 14He said:

"O LORD, God of Israel, there is
no God like you[j] in heaven or on
earth—you who keep your covenant
of love[k] with your servants who continue wholeheartedly in your way.
15You have kept your promise to your
servant David my father; with your
mouth you have promised[l] and with
your hand you have fulfilled it—as it
is today.

16"Now LORD, God of Israel, keep
for your servant David my father the
promises you made to him when you
said, 'You shall never fail[m] to have a
man to sit before me on the throne
of Israel, if only your sons are careful in all they do to walk before me
according to my law,[n] as you have
done.' 17And now, O LORD, God of Israel, let your word that you promised
your servant David come true.

18"But will God really dwell[o] on
earth with men? The heavens,[p] even
the highest heavens, cannot contain you. How much less this temple I have built! 19Yet give attention
to your servant's prayer and his plea
for mercy, O LORD my God. Hear the
cry and the prayer that your servant is
praying in your presence. 20May your
eyes[q] be open toward this temple day
and night, this place of which you
said you would put your Name[r] there.
May you hear[s] the prayer your servant prays toward this place. 21Hear
the supplications of your servant and
of your people Israel when they pray
toward this place. Hear from heaven,
your dwelling place; and when you
hear, forgive.[t]

22"When a man wrongs his neighbor and is required to take an oath[u]
and he comes and swears the oath before your altar in this temple, 23then
hear from heaven and act. Judge between your servants, repaying[v] the
guilty by bringing down on his own
head what he has done. Declare the
innocent not guilty and so establish
his innocence.

24"When your people Israel have
been defeated[w] by an enemy because
they have sinned against you and
when they turn back and confess your
name, praying and making supplication before you in this temple, 25then
hear from heaven and forgive the sin
of your people Israel and bring them
back to the land you gave to them
and their fathers.

26"When the heavens are shut up
and there is no rain[x] because your
people have sinned against you, and
when they pray toward this place and
confess your name and turn from
their sin because you have afflicted
them, 27then hear from heaven and
forgive[y] the sin of your servants, your
people Israel. Teach them the right
way to live, and send rain on the land
you gave your people for an inheritance.

28"When famine[z] or plague comes
to the land, or blight or mildew, locusts or grasshoppers, or when enemies besiege them in any of their
cities, whatever disaster or disease
may come, 29and when a prayer or
plea is made by any of your people
Israel—each one aware of his afflictions and pains, and spreading out his
hands toward this temple— 30then
hear from heaven, your dwelling
place. Forgive,[a] and deal with each
man according to all he does, since
you know his heart (for you alone
know the hearts of men),[b] 31so that
they will fear you[c] and walk in your
ways all the time they live in the land
you gave our fathers.

6:11 [g] S Dt 10:2; Ps 25:10; 50:5 **6:13** [h] Ne 8:4 [i] Ps 95:6 **6:14** [j] S Ex 8:10; 15:11 [k] S Dt 7:9 **6:15** [l] S 1Ch 22:10 **6:16** [m] S 2Sa 7:13, 15; 2Ch 23:3 [n] Ps 132:12 **6:18** [o] S Rev 21:3 [p] Ps 11:4; Isa 40:22; 66:1 **6:20** [q] S Ex 3:16; Ps 34:15 [r] Dt 12:11 [s] 2Ch 7:14; 30:20 **6:21** [t] Ps 51:1; Isa 33:24; 40:2; 43:25; 44:22; 55:7; Mic 7:18 **6:22** [u] S Ex 22:11 **6:23** [v] Isa 3:11; 65:6; S Mt 16:27 **6:24** [w] S Lev 26:17 **6:26** [x] Lev 26:19; S Dt 11:17; 28:24; S 2Sa 1:21 **6:27** [y] ver 30, 39; 2Ch 7:14 **6:28** [z] 2Ch 20:9 **6:30** [a] S ver 27 [b] S 1Sa 2:3; Ps 7:9; 44:21; Pr 16:2; 17:3 **6:31** [c] S Dt 6:13; Ps 34:7, 9; 103:11, 13; Pr 8:13

[a] *13* That is, about 7 1/2 feet (about 2.3 meters)
[b] *13* That is, about 4 1/2 feet (about 1.3 meters)

6:12–21 See notes on 1Ki 8:22–30.
6:13 Not in 1Ki 8. Some think that the Chronicler may have wished to clarify the fact that Solomon was not "before the altar" (v. 12) exercising priestly duties. On the other hand, the verse may have been dropped from Kings by a copying error.
6:14 *who keep your covenant of love.* See 1Ki 8:23 and note.
6:18 Cf. 2:6.
6:22–39 See notes on 1Ki 8:31–46.
6:22–23 See Ex 22:10–11; Lev 6:3–5.
6:24–25 See Lev 26:17,23; Dt 28:25,36–37,48–57,64; Jos 7:11–12.
6:26–27 See Lev 26:19; Dt 11:10–15; 28:18,22–24.
6:28–31 See Lev 26:16,20,25–26; Dt 28:20–22,27–28, 35,42.

32"As for the foreigner who does
not belong to your people Israel but
has come[d] from a distant land because of your great name and your
mighty hand[e] and your outstretched
arm—when he comes and prays toward this temple, 33then hear from
heaven, your dwelling place, and do
whatever the foreigner[f] asks of you,
so that all the peoples of the earth
may know your name and fear you,
as do your own people Israel, and
may know that this house I have built
bears your Name.
34"When your people go to war
against their enemies,[g] wherever you
send them, and when they pray[h] to
you toward this city you have chosen
and the temple I have built for your
Name, 35then hear from heaven their
prayer and their plea, and uphold
their cause.
36"When they sin against you—for
there is no one who does not sin[i]—
and you become angry with them and
give them over to the enemy, who
takes them captive[j] to a land far away
or near; 37and if they have a change of
heart[k] in the land where they are held
captive, and repent and plead with
you in the land of their captivity and
say, 'We have sinned, we have done
wrong and acted wickedly'; 38and if
they turn back to you with all their
heart and soul in the land of their
captivity where they were taken, and
pray toward the land you gave their
fathers, toward the city you have chosen and toward the temple I have built
for your Name; 39then from heaven,
your dwelling place, hear their prayer
and their pleas, and uphold their
cause. And forgive[l] your people, who
have sinned against you.
40"Now, my God, may your eyes be
open and your ears attentive[m] to the
prayers offered in this place.

6:32 [d] 2Ch 9:6 [e] S Ex 3:19,20 **6:33** [f] S Ex 12:43 **6:34** [g] Dt 28:7 [h] S 1Ch 5:20 **6:36** [i] S 1Ki 8:46; Job 11:12; 15:14; Ps 143:2; Ecc 7:20; Jer 9:5; 13:23; 17:9; S Ro 3:9; Eph 2:3 [j] S Lev 26:44 **6:37** [k] 1Ki 8:48; 2Ch 7:14; 12:6,12; 30:11; 33:12,19,23; 34:27; 36:12; Isa 58:3; Jer 24:7; 29:13 **6:39** [l] S ver 27; 2Ch 30:9 **6:40** [m] S 1Ki 8:29,52; 2Ch 7:15; Ne 1:6,11; Ps 17:1,6; 116:1; 130:2; Isa 37:17

6:41 [n] Ps 3:7; 7:6; 59:4; Isa 33:10 [o] 1Ch 28:2 [p] Ps 132:16 [q] Ps 13:6; 27:13; 116:12; 142:7 **6:42** [r] Ps 2:2 [s] Ps 89:24,28 **7:1** [t] S Ex 19:18; S Lev 9:24; S 1Ki 18:38 [u] S Ex 16:10 [v] Ps 26:8 **7:2** [w] S 1Ki 8:11 [x] S Ex 29:43; S 40:35 **7:3** [y] S 1Ch 16:34; 2Ch 5:13; Ezr 3:11 **7:6** [z] 1Ch 15:16 [a] S 1Ch 15:24

41"Now arise,[n] O LORD God, and
come to your resting place,[o]
you and the ark of your might.
May your priests,[p] O LORD God, be
clothed with salvation,
may your saints rejoice in your
goodness.[q]
42O LORD God, do not reject your
anointed one.[r]
Remember the great love[s]
promised to David your
servant."

The Dedication of the Temple

7:1-10pp — 1Ki 8:62-66

7 When Solomon finished praying, fire[t]
came down from heaven and consumed
the burnt offering and the sacrifices, and
the glory of the LORD filled[u] the temple.[v]
2The priests could not enter[w] the temple
of the LORD because the glory[x] of the LORD
filled it. 3When all the Israelites saw the
fire coming down and the glory of the
LORD above the temple, they knelt on the
pavement with their faces to the ground,
and they worshiped and gave thanks to
the LORD, saying,

"He is good;
his love endures forever."[y]

4Then the king and all the people offered
sacrifices before the LORD. 5And King Solomon offered a sacrifice of twenty-two
thousand head of cattle and a hundred
and twenty thousand sheep and goats. So
the king and all the people dedicated the
temple of God. 6The priests took their positions, as did the Levites[z] with the LORD's
musical instruments,[a] which King David
had made for praising the LORD and which
were used when he gave thanks, saying,
"His love endures forever." Opposite the
Levites, the priests blew their trumpets,
and all the Israelites were standing.
7Solomon consecrated the middle part of
the courtyard in front of the temple of the
LORD, and there he offered burnt offerings

6:32–33 The prophets also envisaged the Gentiles coming to Jerusalem to worship the Lord (Isa 2:3; 56:6–8; Mic 4:2; Zec 8:20–23; 14:16–21), and so did the psalmists (Ps 22:27–31; 65:2; 66:4; 86:9; 102:21–22; cf. Ps 87; 96; 98; 100; 117).

6:34–35 See Lev 26:7–8; Dt 28:6–7. The Chronicler repeatedly demonstrates God's answer to prayer in time of battle (ch. 13; 14:9–15; 18:31; 20:1–29; 25:5–13; 32:20–22).

6:36 *no one who does not sin.* See note on 1Ki 8:46. *captive to a land far away.* See 36:15–20; Lev 26:33,44–45; Dt 28:49–52; 2Ki 17:7–20; 25:1–21.

6:40–42 The Chronicler replaces the ending of Solomon's prayer in Kings (1Ki 8:50–53) with Ps 132:8–10, a psalm that deals with bringing the ark to the temple, the theme of this section in Chronicles (5:2–14). The prayer in Kings ends with an appeal to the exodus deliverance under Moses, while in Chronicles the appeal is on the basis of the eternal promises to David.

7:1–22 See 1Ki 8:54—9:9 and notes.

7:1–3 Not found in 1Ki 8. The addition of the fire descending from heaven to consume the sacrifices provides the same sign of divine acceptance given at the dedication of the tabernacle (Lev 9:23–24) and at David's offering on the threshing floor of Araunah the Jebusite (1Ch 21:26; cf. 1Ki 18:38). While vv. 1–3 are unique to Chronicles, the Chronicler has omitted Solomon's blessing of the congregation (1Ki 8:55–61).

7:1 *glory of the LORD.* See 5:14 and note.

7:3 *He is good … forever.* See v. 6; 5:13; Ps 136:1.

7:6 The verse is unique to Chronicles and reflects the author's overall interest in the Levites, especially the musicians (cf. 29:26–27; see note on 1Ch 6:31–48). *all the Israelites.* See Introduction to 1 Chronicles: Purpose and Themes.

and the fat[b] of the fellowship offerings,[a]
because the bronze altar he had made
could not hold the burnt offerings, the
grain offerings and the fat portions.
8 So Solomon observed the festival[c] at
that time for seven days, and all Israel[d]
with him — a vast assembly, people from
Lebo[b] Hamath[e] to the Wadi of Egypt.[f]
9 On the eighth day they held an assembly,
for they had celebrated[g] the dedication
of the altar for seven days and the festival[h] for seven days more. 10 On the twenty-third day of the seventh month he sent
the people to their homes, joyful and glad
in heart for the good things the LORD had
done for David and Solomon and for his
people Israel.

The LORD Appears to Solomon

7:11-22pp — 1Ki 9:1-9

11 When Solomon had finished[i] the temple of the LORD and the royal palace, and
had succeeded in carrying out all he had in
mind to do in the temple of the LORD and
in his own palace, 12 the LORD appeared[j] to
him at night and said:

"I have heard your prayer and have
chosen[k] this place for myself[l] as a
temple for sacrifices.
13 "When I shut up the heavens so
that there is no rain,[m] or command
locusts to devour the land or send a
plague among my people, 14 if my people, who are called by my name,[n] will
humble[o] themselves and pray and
seek my face[p] and turn[q] from their
wicked ways, then will I hear[r] from
heaven and will forgive[s] their sin and
will heal[t] their land. 15 Now my eyes
will be open and my ears attentive to
the prayers offered in this place.[u] 16 I
have chosen[v] and consecrated this
temple so that my Name may be there

7:7 [b]S Ex 29:13 **7:8** [c]2Ch 30:26; Ne 8:17 [d]S 1Ch 9:1 [e]S Nu 13:21 [f]S Ge 15:18 **7:9** [g]2Ch 30:23 [h]S Lev 23:36 **7:11** [i]S 1Ch 28:20 **7:12** [j]2Ch 1:7 [k]Dt 12:11 [l]S Dt 12:5 **7:13** [m]S Dt 11:17; Am 4:7 **7:14** [n]S Nu 6:27 [o]S Ex 10:3; S Lev 26:41; S 2Ch 6:37 [p]S 1Ch 16:11 [q]S 2Ki 17:13; Isa 55:7; Eze 18:32; Zec 1:4 [r]S 2Ch 6:20 [s]S 2Ch 6:27 [t]S Ex 15:26; 2Ch 30:20; Ps 60:2; Isa 30:26; 53:5; 57:18; Jer 33:6; Mal 4:2 **7:15** [u]S 1Ki 8:29; S 2Ch 6:40; Ne 1:6 **7:16** [v]S Dt 12:5; 2Ch 33:7

7:17 [w]S 1Ki 9:4 [x]S Lev 19:37 **7:18** [y]Isa 9:7; Jer 33:17,21 [z]S 1Ch 5:2; Isa 55:4; Mic 5:2 [a]S 2Sa 7:13; S 1Ch 17:12; 2Ch 13:5; 23:3 **7:19** [b]S Dt 28:15 [c]S 1Ch 28:9; 2Ch 12:1; 24:18; Jer 9:13; 11:8 **7:20** [d]S Dt 29:28 [e]1Ki 14:15; Jer 12:14; 16:13; 50:11 [f]S Dt 28:37 **7:21** [g]Jer 19:8 [h]Dt 29:24 **7:22** [i]Jer 16:11 **8:1** [j]S 2Sa 7:2

forever. My eyes and my heart will always be there.
17 "As for you, if you walk before
me[w] as David your father did, and
do all I command, and observe my
decrees[x] and laws, 18 I will establish
your royal throne, as I covenanted[y]
with David your father when I said,
'You shall never fail to have a man[z]
to rule over Israel.'[a]
19 "But if you[c] turn away[b] and forsake[c] the decrees and commands I
have given you[c] and go off to serve
other gods and worship them, 20 then
I will uproot[d] Israel from my land,[e]
which I have given them, and will
reject this temple I have consecrated
for my Name. I will make it a byword
and an object of ridicule[f] among all
peoples. 21 And though this temple is
now so imposing, all who pass by will
be appalled[g] and say,[h] 'Why has the
LORD done such a thing to this land
and to this temple?' 22 People will answer, 'Because they have forsaken the
LORD, the God of their fathers, who
brought them out of Egypt, and have
embraced other gods, worshiping
and serving them[i] — that is why he
brought all this disaster on them.' "

Solomon's Other Activities

8:1-18pp — 1Ki 9:10-28

8 At the end of twenty years, during
which Solomon built the temple of the
LORD and his own palace,[j] 2 Solomon rebuilt the villages that Hiram[d] had given
him, and settled Israelites in them. 3 Solomon then went to Hamath Zobah and
captured it. 4 He also built up Tadmor in
the desert and all the store cities he had

[a] *7* Traditionally *peace offerings* [b] *8* Or *from the entrance to* [c] *19* The Hebrew is plural. [d] *2* Hebrew *Huram*, a variant of *Hiram*; also in verse 18

7:8 *from Lebo Hamath to the Wadi of Egypt.* Not only were the patriarchal promises of descendants provisionally fulfilled under David and Solomon (see 1:9; 1Ch 27:23 – 24 and notes), but also the promises of land (Ge 15:18 – 21).

7:9 *eighth day.* The final day of the Feast of Tabernacles (see 5:3 and note; Lev 23:36; Nu 29:35). *seven days ... seven days.* The dedication had run from the 8th to the 14th day of the month, and the Feast of Tabernacles from the 15th to the 22nd day. The Day of Atonement was on the 10th day of the 7th month (Lev 16; cf. 1Ki 8:65 – 66).

7:12 *appeared to him.* The second time God appeared to Solomon; the first was at Gibeon (1:3 – 13; 1Ki 9:2). *your prayer.* See 6:14 – 42.

7:13 – 15 Unique to Chronicles. These verses illustrate the writer's emphasis on immediate retribution (see Introduction to 1 Chronicles: Purpose and Themes). The Chronicler subsequently portrays the kings in a way that demonstrates this principle (see v. 22).

7:14 See, e.g., 12:6 – 7,12.

7:17 – 18 See 1Ki 9:4 – 5. Such words as these reinforced ancient Israel's Messianic hopes.

7:19 – 22 See 1Ki 9:6 – 9.

8:1 – 18 See 1Ki 9:10 – 18 and notes. Verses 13 – 16 are unique to Chronicles and underscore the Chronicler's concern to show continuity with the past and his association of David with Moses (see Introduction to 1 Chronicles: Purpose and Themes).

8:1 – 2 In 1 Ki 9:10 – 14 the cities were given to Hiram by Solomon, whereas in Chronicles the reverse is true. Perhaps as part of his effort to idealize Solomon, the Chronicler does not record the fact that Hiram found these cities unacceptable payment (1Ki 9:11 – 13); he mentions only the sequel to the story, the return of the cities to Solomon and their subsequent improvement. They may also have served as a kind of collateral against the monies owed Hiram, who returned them when the debt was satisfied (see note on 1Ki 9:11). The Chronicler also says nothing about the pharaoh's gift of Gezer to Solomon (1Ki 9:16).

8:3 – 4 The Chronicler records an additional military campaign to the north, not mentioned in Kings. David had also campaigned in the north against Zobah (1Ch 18:3 – 9; 19:6; 2Sa 8:3 – 12; 10:6 – 8; cf. 1Ki 11:23 – 24).

built in Hamath.[k] 5He rebuilt Upper Beth
Horon[l] and Lower Beth Horon as fortified
cities, with walls and with gates and bars,
6as well as Baalath[m] and all his store cities,
and all the cities for his chariots and for
his horses[a]—whatever he desired to build
in Jerusalem, in Lebanon and throughout
all the territory he ruled.
7All the people left from the Hittites,
Amorites, Perizzites, Hivites and Jebusites[n] (these peoples were not Israelites),
8that is, their descendants remaining in
the land, whom the Israelites had not destroyed—these Solomon conscripted[o] for
his slave labor force, as it is to this day.
9But Solomon did not make slaves of the
Israelites for his work; they were his fighting men, commanders of his captains,
and commanders of his chariots and charioteers. 10They were also King Solomon's
chief officials—two hundred and fifty officials supervising the men.
11Solomon brought Pharaoh's daughter[p]
up from the City of David to the palace
he had built for her, for he said, "My wife
must not live in the palace of David king
of Israel, because the places the ark of the
LORD has entered are holy."
12On the altar[q] of the LORD that he had
built in front of the portico, Solomon sacrificed burnt offerings to the LORD, 13accord-
ing to the daily requirement[r] for offerings
commanded by Moses for Sabbaths,[s] New
Moons[t] and the three[u] annual feasts—the
Feast of Unleavened Bread,[v] the Feast of
Weeks[w] and the Feast of Tabernacles.[x] 14In
keeping with the ordinance of his father
David, he appointed the divisions[y] of the
priests for their duties, and the Levites[z]
to lead the praise and to assist the priests
according to each day's requirement. He
also appointed the gatekeepers[a] by divisions for the various gates, because this
was what David the man of God[b] had ordered.[c] 15They did not deviate from the
king's commands to the priests or to the
Levites in any matter, including that of the
treasuries.

16All Solomon's work was carried out,
from the day the foundation of the temple
of the LORD was laid until its completion.
So the temple of the LORD was finished.
17Then Solomon went to Ezion Geber
and Elath on the coast of Edom. 18And
Hiram sent him ships commanded by
his own officers, men who knew the sea.
These, with Solomon's men, sailed to
Ophir and brought back four hundred and
fifty talents[b] of gold,[d] which they delivered to King Solomon.

The Queen of Sheba Visits Solomon

9:1-12pp — 1Ki 10:1-13

9 When the queen of Sheba[e] heard of
Solomon's fame, she came to Jerusalem to test him with hard questions. Arriving with a very great caravan—with
camels carrying spices, large quantities
of gold, and precious stones—she came
to Solomon and talked with him about all
she had on her mind. 2Solomon answered
all her questions; nothing was too hard for
him to explain to her. 3When the queen
of Sheba saw the wisdom of Solomon,[f] as
well as the palace he had built, 4the food
on his table, the seating of his officials, the
attending servants in their robes, the cup-
bearers in their robes and the burnt offerings he made at[c] the temple of the LORD,
she was overwhelmed.
5She said to the king, "The report I heard
in my own country about your achievements and your wisdom is true. 6But I did
not believe what they said until I came[g]
and saw with my own eyes. Indeed, not
even half the greatness of your wisdom
was told me; you have far exceeded the report I heard. 7How happy your men must
be! How happy your officials, who continually stand before you and hear your
wisdom! 8Praise be to the LORD your God,
who has delighted in you and placed you

[a] 6 Or *charioteers* [b] 18 That is, about 17 tons (about 16 metric tons) [c] 4 Or *the ascent by which he went up to*

8:4 [k]S 2Sa 8:9 **8:5** [l]S Jos 10:10 **8:6** [m]S Jos 19:44 **8:7** [n]S Ge 10:16; S 15:18-21; Ezr 9:1 **8:8** [o]S 2Ch 2:18 **8:11** [p]S 1Ki 3:1 **8:12** [q]S 1Ki 8:64; 2Ch 15:8 **8:13** [r]S Ex 29:38 [s]Nu 28:9 [t]S Nu 10:10 [u]S Ex 23:14 [v]S Ex 12:17; Nu 28:16-25 [w]S Ex 23:16 [x]Nu 29:12-38; Ne 8:17 **8:14** [y]S 1Ch 24:1 [z]S 1Ch 25:1 [a]S 1Ch 9:17 [b]Ne 12:24,36 [c]S 1Ch 23:6; Ne 12:45 **8:18** [d]2Ch 9:9 **9:1** [e]S Ge 10:7; Eze 23:42; Mt 12:42; Lk 11:31 **9:3** [f]1Ki 5:12 **9:6** [g]2Ch 6:32

8:5 The two Beth Horons were situated on a strategic road from the coastal plain to the area just north of Jerusalem.
8:7 *not Israelites.* See 2:17; 1Ch 22:2; 1Ki 9:21.
8:8 *to this day.* See note on 5:9.
8:11 *holy.* Both 1Ki 9:24 and Chronicles record the transfer of the pharaoh's daughter to special quarters, but only Chronicles adds the reason: Not only the temple but also David's palace was regarded as holy, because of the presence of the ark (see note on Lev 11:44).
8:12–16 In line with his overall interests, the Chronicler elaborates on the sacrificial and temple provisions made by Solomon. While 1Ki 9:25 mentions only the sacrifices at the three annual feasts, the Chronicler adds the offerings on Sabbaths and New Moons to conform these provisions fully to Mosaic prescription (Lev 23:1–37; Nu 28–29).
8:17–18 See 1Ki 9:26–28. This joint venture between Solomon and Hiram secured for these kings the lucrative trade routes through the Mediterranean to the south Arabian peninsula; Solomon became the middleman between these economic spheres.
8:17 *Ezion Geber and Elath.* See note on Dt 2:8.
8:18 *Hiram sent him ships.* Presumably ships crafted in Phoenicia and assembled at the port of Ezion Geber after being shipped overland (see 9:21).
9:1–12 See 1Ki 10:1–13 and notes. The visit of the queen of Sheba portrays the fulfillment of God's promise to give Solomon wisdom and wealth (1:12). Although the themes of Solomon's wisdom and wealth are here put to the fore, a major motive for the queen's visit may have been commercial, perhaps prompted by Solomon's naval operations toward south Arabia (8:17–18).
9:1 *Sheba.* See note on 1Ki 10:1; see also Job 1:15; 6:19; Ps 72:10,15; Isa 60:6; Jer 6:20; Eze 27:22; 38:13; Joel 3:8.
9:8 *his throne.* The most significant variation from the account

on his throne[h] as king to rule for the LORD your God. Because of the love of your God for Israel and his desire to uphold them forever, he has made you king[i] over them, to maintain justice and righteousness."

9 Then she gave the king 120 talents[a] of gold,[j] large quantities of spices, and precious stones. There had never been such spices as those the queen of Sheba gave to King Solomon.

10 (The men of Hiram and the men of Solomon brought gold from Ophir;[k] they also brought algumwood[b] and precious stones. 11 The king used the algumwood to make steps for the temple of the LORD and for the royal palace, and to make harps and lyres for the musicians. Nothing like them had ever been seen in Judah.)

12 King Solomon gave the queen of Sheba all she desired and asked for; he gave her more than she had brought to him. Then she left and returned with her retinue to her own country.

Solomon's Splendor

9:13-28pp — 1Ki 10:14-29; 2Ch 1:14-17

13 The weight of the gold that Solomon received yearly was 666 talents,[c] 14 not including the revenues brought in by merchants and traders. Also all the kings of Arabia[l] and the governors of the land brought gold and silver to Solomon.

15 King Solomon made two hundred large shields of hammered gold; six hundred bekas[d] of hammered gold went into each shield. 16 He also made three hundred small shields[m] of hammered gold, with three hundred bekas[e] of gold in each shield. The king put them in the Palace of the Forest of Lebanon.[n]

17 Then the king made a great throne inlaid with ivory[o] and overlaid with pure gold. 18 The throne had six steps, and a footstool of gold was attached to it. On both sides of the seat were armrests, with a lion standing beside each of them. 19 Twelve lions stood on the six steps, one at either end of each step. Nothing like it had ever been made for any other kingdom. 20 All King Solomon's goblets were gold, and all the household articles in the Palace of the Forest of Lebanon were pure gold. Nothing was made of silver, because silver was considered of little value in Solomon's day. 21 The king had a fleet of trading ships[f] manned by Hiram's[g] men. Once every three years it returned, carrying gold, silver and ivory, and apes and baboons.

22 King Solomon was greater in riches and wisdom than all the other kings of the earth.[p] 23 All the kings[q] of the earth sought audience with Solomon to hear the wisdom God had put in his heart. 24 Year after year, everyone who came brought a gift[r]—articles of silver and gold, and robes, weapons and spices, and horses and mules.

25 Solomon had four thousand stalls for horses and chariots,[s] and twelve thousand horses,[h] which he kept in the chariot cities and also with him in Jerusalem. 26 He ruled[t] over all the kings from the River[i][u] to the land of the Philistines, as far as the border of Egypt.[v] 27 The king made silver as common in Jerusalem as stones, and cedar as plentiful as sycamore-fig trees in the foothills. 28 Solomon's horses were imported from Egypt[j] and from all other countries.

Solomon's Death

9:29-31pp — 1Ki 11:41-43

29 As for the other events of Solomon's reign, from beginning to end, are they not written in the records of Nathan[w] the prophet, in the prophecy of Ahijah[x] the Shilonite and in the visions of Iddo the seer concerning Jeroboam[y] son of Nebat? 30 Solomon reigned in Jerusalem over all Israel forty years. 31 Then he rested with his fathers and was buried in the city of David[z] his father. And Rehoboam his son succeeded him as king.

Israel Rebels Against Rehoboam

10:1-11:4pp — 1Ki 12:1-24

10 Rehoboam went to Shechem, for all the Israelites had gone there to make

9:8 [h] S 1Ki 2:12; S 1Ch 17:14; 2Ch 13:8 [i] 2Ch 2:11 **9:9** [j] 2Ch 8:18 **9:10** [k] 2Ch 8:18 **9:14** [l] 2Ch 17:11; Isa 21:13; Jer 25:24; Eze 27:21; 30:5 **9:16** [m] 2Ch 12:9 [n] S 1Ki 7:2 **9:17** [o] S 1Ki 22:39 **9:22** [p] S 1Ki 3:13; S 2Ch 1:12 **9:23** [q] 1Ki 4:34 **9:24** [r] 2Ch 32:23; Ps 45:12; 68:29; 72:10; Isa 18:7 **9:25** [s] S 1Sa 8:11 **9:26** [t] S 1Ki 4:21 [u] Ps 72:8-9 [v] Ge 15:18-21 **9:29** [w] S 2Sa 7:2 [x] S 1Ki 11:29 [y] 2Ch 10:2 **9:31** [z] 1Ki 2:10

[a] *9* That is, about 4 1/2 tons (about 4 metric tons) [b] *10* Probably a variant of *almugwood* [c] *13* That is, about 25 tons (about 23 metric tons) [d] *15* That is, about 7 1/2 pounds (about 3.5 kilograms) [e] *16* That is, about 3 3/4 pounds (about 1.7 kilograms) [f] *21* Hebrew *of ships that could go to Tarshish* [g] *21* Hebrew *Huram,* a variant of *Hiram* [h] *25* Or *charioteers* [i] *26* That is, the Euphrates [j] *28* Or possibly *Muzur,* a region in Cilicia

of the queen's visit in 1 Kings (10:9) is found here. The queen's speech becomes the vehicle for the Chronicler's conviction that the throne of Israel is the throne of God, for whom the king ruled (see 13:18; see also note on 1Ch 17:14).

9:16,20 *Palace of the Forest of Lebanon.* The royal palace in Jerusalem (cf. note on 1Ki 7:2).

9:26 See 7:8 and note.

9:27 See 1:15.

9:28 The Chronicler omits the accounts of Solomon's wives and the rebellions at the end of his reign (1Ki 11:1-40), both of which would detract from his uniformly positive portrayal of Solomon. *horses ... Egypt.* See note on 1:17.

9:29-31 See 1Ki 11:41-43.

10:1—36:23 The material covering the divided monarchy in Chronicles is considerably shorter than that in Kings: 27 chapters compared to 36 (1Ki 12-2Ki 25). Moreover, about half of this material is unique to Chronicles and shows no dependence on Kings. The most obvious reason for this is that the Chronicler has written a history of the Davidic dynasty in Judah; the history of the northern kingdom is passed over in

him king. 2When Jeroboam[a] son of Nebat
heard this (he was in Egypt, where he had
fled[b] from King Solomon), he returned
from Egypt. 3So they sent for Jeroboam,
and he and all Israel[c] went to Rehoboam
and said to him: 4"Your father put a heavy
yoke on us,[d] but now lighten the harsh labor and the heavy yoke he put on us, and
we will serve you."
5Rehoboam answered, "Come back to
me in three days." So the people went
away.
6Then King Rehoboam consulted the
elders[e] who had served his father Solomon during his lifetime. "How would you
advise me to answer these people?" he
asked.
7They replied, "If you will be kind to
these people and please them and give
them a favorable answer,[f] they will always
be your servants."
8But Rehoboam rejected[g] the advice the
elders[h] gave him and consulted the young
men who had grown up with him and
were serving him. 9He asked them, "What
is your advice? How should we answer
these people who say to me, 'Lighten the
yoke your father put on us'?"
10The young men who had grown up
with him replied, "Tell the people who have
said to you, 'Your father put a heavy yoke
on us, but make our yoke lighter'—tell
them, 'My little finger is thicker than my
father's waist. 11My father laid on you a
heavy yoke; I will make it even heavier.
My father scourged you with whips; I will
scourge you with scorpions.'"
12Three days later Jeroboam and all the
people returned to Rehoboam, as the king
had said, "Come back to me in three days."
13The king answered them harshly. Rejecting the advice of the elders, 14he followed
the advice of the young men and said,
"My father made your yoke heavy; I will
make it even heavier. My father scourged
you with whips; I will scourge you with
scorpions." 15So the king did not listen
to the people, for this turn of events was
from God,[i] to fulfill the word the LORD had
spoken to Jeroboam son of Nebat through
Ahijah the Shilonite.[j]
16When all Israel[k] saw that the king refused to listen to them, they answered the
king:

"What share do we have in David,[l]
what part in Jesse's son?
To your tents, O Israel!
Look after your own house,
O David!"

So all the Israelites went home. 17But as
for the Israelites who were living in the
towns of Judah, Rehoboam still ruled over
them.
18King Rehoboam sent out Adoniram,[a][m]
who was in charge of forced labor, but the
Israelites stoned him to death. King Rehoboam, however, managed to get into his
chariot and escape to Jerusalem. 19So Israel has been in rebellion against the house
of David to this day.

11 When Rehoboam arrived in Jerusalem,[n] he mustered the house of Judah and Benjamin—a hundred and eighty
thousand fighting men—to make war
against Israel and to regain the kingdom
for Rehoboam.
2But this word of the LORD came to Shemaiah[o] the man of God: 3"Say to Rehoboam son of Solomon king of Judah and to
all the Israelites in Judah and Benjamin,
4'This is what the LORD says: Do not go up
to fight against your brothers.[p] Go home,
every one of you, for this is my doing.'"
So they obeyed the words of the LORD and
turned back from marching against Jeroboam.

[a] 18 Hebrew *Hadoram,* a variant of *Adoniram*

10:2 [a] S 2Ch 9:29 [b] S 1Ki 11:40 **10:3** [c] S 1Ch 9:1 **10:4** [d] 2Ch 2:2 **10:6** [e] Job 8:8-9; 12:12; 15:10; 32:7 **10:7** [f] Pr 15:1 **10:8** [g] S 2Sa 17:14 [h] Pr 13:20
10:15 [i] 2Ch 11:4; 25:16-20 [j] S 1Ki 11:29 **10:16** [k] S 1Ch 9:1 [l] S 2Sa 20:1 **10:18** [m] S 2Sa 20:24; S 1Ki 5:14 **11:1** [n] S 1Ki 12:21 **11:2** [o] S 1Ki 12:22; 2Ch 12:5-7,15 **11:4** [p] 2Ch 28:8-11

silence except where it impinges on that of Judah. At least two considerations prompt this treatment of the divided kingdom: (1) The Chronicler is concerned to trace God's faithfulness to his promise to give David an unbroken line of descent on the throne of Israel. (2) At the time of the Chronicler the restored community was confined to the returnees of the kingdom of Judah, who were actually the remnant of all Israel (see Introduction to 1 Chronicles: Purpose and Themes).

10:1–19 See 1Ki 12:1–20 and notes. Somewhat in line with his idealization of Solomon, the Chronicler places most of the blame for the schism on the rebellious Jeroboam (cf. 13:6–7).

10:1 *Rehoboam.* Reigned 930–913 B.C.

10:2 *Jeroboam.* Reigned 930–909 B.C.; his second mention in Chronicles (see 9:29). The Chronicler assumes the reader's familiarity with 1Ki 11:26–40.

10:15 *Ahijah.* The Chronicler assumes the reader's familiarity with 1Ki 11:29–33.

10:18 *Adoniram ... in charge of forced labor.* Had held the same office under Solomon (1Ki 4:6; 5:14).

10:19 *to this day.* See note on 5:9.

11:1–23 Verses 1–4 are parallel to 1Ki 12:21–24; vv. 5–23 are largely unique to Chronicles. The Chronicler's account of Rehoboam is a good example of his emphasis on immediate retribution (see Introduction to 1 Chronicles: Purpose and Themes). Ch. 11 traces the rewards for obedience to the command of God (vv. 1–4): Rehoboam enjoys prosperity and power (vv. 5–12), popular support (vv. 13–17) and progeny (vv. 18–23). Ch. 12 demonstrates the reverse: Disobedience brings judgment.

11:2 *Shemaiah.* The function of the prophets as guardians of the theocracy (God's kingdom) is prominent in Chronicles; most of Judah's kings are portrayed as receiving advice from prophets (see Introduction to 1 Chronicles: Purpose and Themes).

11:3 *all the Israelites in Judah and Benjamin.* A variation from the wording found in 1Ki 12:23, in accordance with the Chronicler's interest in "all Israel."

11:4 *my doing.* See 10:15.

Rehoboam Fortifies Judah

5 Rehoboam lived in Jerusalem and built up towns for defense in Judah: 6 Bethlehem, Etam, Tekoa, 7 Beth Zur, Soco, Adullam, 8 Gath, Mareshah, Ziph, 9 Adoraim, Lachish, Azekah, 10 Zorah, Aijalon and Hebron. These were fortified cities[q] in Judah and Benjamin. 11 He strengthened their defenses and put commanders in them, with supplies of food, olive oil and wine. 12 He put shields and spears in all the cities, and made them very strong. So Judah and Benjamin were his.

13 The priests and Levites from all their districts throughout Israel sided with him. 14 The Levites[r] even abandoned their pasturelands and property,[s] and came to Judah and Jerusalem because Jeroboam and his sons had rejected them as priests of the LORD. 15 And he appointed[t] his own priests[u] for the high places and for the goat[v] and calf[w] idols he had made. 16 Those from every tribe of Israel[x] who set their hearts on seeking the LORD, the God of Israel, followed the Levites to Jerusalem to offer sacrifices to the LORD, the God of their fathers. 17 They strengthened[y] the kingdom of Judah and supported Rehoboam son of Solomon three years, walking in the ways of David and Solomon during this time.

Rehoboam's Family

18 Rehoboam married Mahalath, who was the daughter of David's son Jerimoth and of Abihail, the daughter of Jesse's son Eliab. 19 She bore him sons: Jeush, Shemariah and Zaham. 20 Then he married Maacah[z] daughter of Absalom, who bore him Abijah,[a] Attai, Ziza and Shelomith. 21 Rehoboam loved Maacah daughter of Absalom more than any of his other wives and concubines. In all, he had eighteen wives[b] and sixty concubines, twenty-eight sons and sixty daughters.

22 Rehoboam appointed Abijah[c] son of Maacah to be the chief prince among his brothers, in order to make him king. 23 He acted wisely, dispersing some of his sons throughout the districts of Judah and Benjamin, and to all the fortified cities. He gave them abundant provisions[d] and took many wives for them.

Shishak Attacks Jerusalem

12:9-16pp — 1Ki 14:21, 25-31

12 After Rehoboam's position as king was established[e] and he had become strong,[f] he and all Israel[a][g] with him abandoned[h] the law of the LORD. 2 Because they had been unfaithful[i] to the LORD, Shishak[j] king of Egypt attacked Jerusalem in the fifth year of King Rehoboam. 3 With twelve hundred chariots and sixty thousand horsemen and the innumerable troops of Libyans,[k] Sukkites and Cushites[b][l] that

11:10 [q] S Jos 10:20; 2Ch 12:4; 17:2,19; 21:3 **11:14** [r] S Nu 35:2-5 [s] 1Ch 6:81 **11:15** [t] S 1Ki 13:33 [u] S 1Ki 12:31 [v] Lev 17:7 [w] 1Ki 12:28; 2Ch 13:8 **11:16** [x] 2Ch 15:9 **11:17** [y] 2Ch 12:1 **11:20** [z] S 1Ki 15:2 [a] 2Ch 12:16; 13:2 **11:21** [b] S Dt 17:17 **11:22** [c] Dt 21:15-17 **11:23** [d] 2Ch 21:3 **12:1** [e] ver 13; 2Ch 1:1 [f] 2Ch 11:17 [g] S 1Ch 9:1 [h] S 2Ch 7:19 **12:2** [i] 1Ki 14:22-24; S 1Ch 5:25 [j] 1Ki 11:40 **12:3** [k] Da 11:43 [l] S Ge 10:6; 2Ch 14:9; 16:8; Isa 18:2; Am 9:7; Na 3:9

[a] *1* That is, Judah, as frequently in 2 Chronicles
[b] *3* That is, people from the upper Nile region

11:5–10 This list of cities is not found in Kings. Rehoboam fortified his eastern, western and southern borders, but not the north, perhaps demonstrating his hope of reunification of the kingdoms, as well as the threat of invasion from Egypt.
11:13–17 The Chronicler assumes the reader's familiarity with 1Ki 12:26–33. This material is unique to Chronicles and reflects the author's concern both with the temple and its personnel and with showing that the kingdom of Judah was the remnant of all Israel.
11:14 *pasturelands and property.* See 1Ch 6:54–80; Lev 25:32–34; Nu 35:1–5; see also Introduction to 1 Chronicles: Purpose and Themes.
11:15 *goat and calf idols.* The account in Kings mentions only the golden calves. For the worship of goat idols see Lev 17:7.
11:17 *three years.* See note on 12:2. *ways of David and Solomon.* Characteristic of the Chronicler's idealization of Solomon; contrast the portrait of Solomon in 1Ki 11:1–13.
11:18–22 The report on the size of Rehoboam's family is placed here as part of the Chronicler's effort to show God's blessing on his obedience (see note on 11:1–23). The material is not in chronological sequence with the surrounding context but summarizes events throughout his reign. The Chronicler uses numerous progeny as a sign of divine blessing (see 13:21; see also notes on 21:2; 1Ch 25:5).
11:20 *Maacah daughter of Absalom.* See note on 1Ki 15:2. She was likely the granddaughter of Absalom, through his daughter Tamar (2Sa 14:27; 18:18), who was married to Uriel (2Ch 13:2).
11:21–22 These verses explain why the eldest son was not appointed Rehoboam's successor.
11:23 *dispersing some of his sons.* Rehoboam may have sought to secure the succession of Abijah by assigning other sons to outlying posts, perhaps to avoid the difficulties faced by David, whose sons at court (Absalom and Adonijah) had attempted to seize power.
12:1–14 See note on 11:1–23. Whereas obedience to the prophetic word (11:1–4) had brought blessing (11:5–23), now the prophet comes to announce judgment for disobedience (see 1Ki 14:25–28). While the writer of Kings also reports the attack of Shishak, the Chronicler alone adds the rationale that the invasion was because of forsaking the commands of God (vv. 1–2,5).
12:1 *all Israel.* Used in a variety of ways in 2 Chronicles: (1) of both kingdoms (9:30), (2) of the northern kingdom (10:16; 11:13) or (3) of the southern kingdom alone (as here; 11:3). See also Introduction to 1 Chronicles: Purpose and Themes: 6. *abandoned.* The opposite of "seeking the LORD" (v. 14); see v. 5; see also note on 24:18,20,24.
12:2 *Shishak.* Founder of the 22nd dynasty of Egypt, he ruled c. 945–924 B.C. The Bible mentions this invasion only as it affected Jerusalem, but Shishak's own inscription on the wall of the temple of Amun at Karnak (Thebes) indicates that his armies also swept as far north as Megiddo. *fifth year.* 925 B.C. The Chronicler often introduces chronological notes not found in Kings (e.g., 11:17; 15:10,19; 16:1,12–13; 17:7; 21:20; 24:15,17,23; 26:16; 27:5,8; 29:3; 34:3; 36:21). These become a vehicle for his emphasis on immediate retribution by dividing the reigns of individual kings into cycles of obedience-blessing and disobedience-punishment. This sequence is clear for Rehoboam: Three years of obedience and blessing (11:17) are followed by rebellion, presumably in the fourth year (12:1), and punishment in the fifth (here).
12:3 *Sukkites.* Probably a group of mercenary soldiers of Libyan origin who are known from Egyptian texts.
12:5 See notes on vv. 1–14; v. 1.

came with him from Egypt, 4he captured
the fortified cities[m] of Judah and came as
far as Jerusalem.
5Then the prophet Shemaiah[n] came to
Rehoboam and to the leaders of Judah
who had assembled in Jerusalem for fear
of Shishak, and he said to them, "This is
what the LORD says, 'You have abandoned
me; therefore, I now abandon[o] you to Shishak.' "
6The leaders of Israel and the king humbled[p] themselves and said, "The LORD is
just."[q]
7When the LORD saw that they humbled themselves, this word of the LORD
came to Shemaiah: "Since they have humbled themselves, I will not destroy them
but will soon give them deliverance.[r] My
wrath[s] will not be poured out on Jerusalem through Shishak. 8They will, however,
become subject[t] to him, so that they may
learn the difference between serving me
and serving the kings of other lands."
9When Shishak king of Egypt attacked
Jerusalem, he carried off the treasures of
the temple of the LORD and the treasures
of the royal palace. He took everything,
including the gold shields[u] Solomon had
made. 10So King Rehoboam made bronze
shields to replace them and assigned these
to the commanders of the guard on duty at
the entrance to the royal palace. 11When-
ever the king went to the LORD's temple,
the guards went with him, bearing the
shields, and afterward they returned them
to the guardroom.
12Because Rehoboam humbled[v] himself,
the LORD's anger turned from him, and he
was not totally destroyed. Indeed, there
was some good[w] in Judah.
13King Rehoboam established[x] himself
firmly in Jerusalem and continued as king.
He was forty-one years old when he became king, and he reigned seventeen years
in Jerusalem, the city the LORD had chosen out of all the tribes of Israel in which
to put his Name.[y] His mother's name was
Naamah; she was an Ammonite. 14He did
evil because he had not set his heart on
seeking the LORD.
15As for the events of Rehoboam's reign,
from beginning to end, are they not written in the records of Shemaiah[z] the prophet and of Iddo the seer that deal with genealogies? There was continual warfare
between Rehoboam and Jeroboam. 16Re-
hoboam[a] rested with his fathers and was
buried in the City of David. And Abijah[b]
his son succeeded him as king.

Abijah King of Judah

13:1-2,22 – 14:1pp — 1Ki 15:1-2,6-8

13 In the eighteenth year of the reign of
Jeroboam, Abijah became king of Judah, 2and he reigned in Jerusalem three
years. His mother's name was Maacah,[a][c]
a daughter[b] of Uriel of Gibeah.
There was war between Abijah[d] and
Jeroboam.[e] 3Abijah went into battle with a
force of four hundred thousand able fighting men, and Jeroboam drew up a battle
line against him with eight hundred thousand able troops.
4Abijah stood on Mount Zemaraim,[f]
in the hill country of Ephraim, and said,
"Jeroboam and all Israel,[g] listen to me!
5Don't you know that the LORD, the God
of Israel, has given the kingship of Israel
to David and his descendants forever[h] by
a covenant of salt?[i] 6Yet Jeroboam son of
Nebat, an official of Solomon son of David, rebelled[j] against his master. 7Some
worthless scoundrels[k] gathered around
him and opposed Rehoboam son of Solomon when he was young and indecisive[l]
and not strong enough to resist them.
8"And now you plan to resist the kingdom of the LORD, which is in the hands
of David's descendants.[m] You are indeed
a vast army and have with you[n] the gold-
en calves[o] that Jeroboam made to be your
gods. 9But didn't you drive out the priests[p]
of the LORD,[q] the sons of Aaron, and the

12:4 [m]S 2Ch 11:10 **12:5** [n]2Ch 11:2 [o]S Dt 28:15 **12:6** [p]S Lev 26:41; S 2Ch 6:37 [q]Ex 9:27; Ezr 9:15; Ps 11:7; 116:5; Da 9:14 **12:7** [r]Ps 78:38 [s]Dt 9:19; Ps 69:24; Jer 7:20; 42:18; Eze 5:13 **12:8** [t]Dt 28:48 **12:9** [u]2Ch 9:16 **12:12** [v]S 2Ch 6:37 [w]S 1Ki 14:13; 2Ch 19:3 **12:13** [x]S ver 1; S 1Ki 2:12 [y]S Ex 20:24; Dt 12:5

12:15 [z]S 2Ch 11:2 **12:16** [a]S 1Ch 3:10 [b]S 2Ch 11:20 **13:2** [c]2Ch 15:16 [d]S 2Ch 11:20 [e]1Ki 15:6 **13:4** [f]Jos 18:22 [g]1Ch 11:1 **13:5** [h]S 2Sa 7:13; S 1Ch 17:12 [i]S Lev 2:13 **13:6** [j]1Ki 11:26 **13:7** [k]S Jdg 9:4 [l]S 1Ch 29:1 **13:8** [m]S 2Ch 9:8 [n]1Sa 4:3 [o]S Ex 32:4; S 2Ch 11:15 **13:9** [p]S 1Ki 12:31 [q]2Ch 11:14-15

[a] 2 Most Septuagint manuscripts and Syriac (see also 2 Chron. 11:20 and 1 Kings 15:2); Hebrew *Micaiah*
[b] 2 Or *granddaughter*

12:6 – 7 See v. 12. The Chronicler has in mind God's promise in 7:14.

12:13 *seventeen years.* See note on 10:1.

12:15 – 16 See 1Ki 14:29 – 31.

13:1 — 14:1 The Chronicler's account of Abijah's reign is about three times longer than that in 1Ki 15:1 – 8, largely due to Abijah's lengthy speech (13:4 – 12; see note on 28:1 – 27). The most striking difference in the accounts of Abijah's reign in Kings and in Chronicles is the evaluation given in each: Kings offers a negative evaluation (1Ki 15:3), for which there was no doubt warrant, while the assessment in Chronicles is positive, in view of what the Chronicler is able to report of him. The kings' reigns, like the lives of common people, were often a mixture of good and evil.

13:2 *three years.* 913 – 910 B.C. *Maacah.* See note on 11:20.

13:3 *four hundred thousand ... eight hundred thousand.* Surprisingly large figures but in line with those in 1Ch 21:5 (see note there; see also Introduction to Numbers: Special Problem).

13:4 *Mount Zemaraim.* The town Zemaraim was in the territory of Benjamin (Jos 18:22); presumably the battle was along the common border of Benjamin and Israel. *all Israel.* See note on 12:1; here and in v. 15 the reference is to the northern kingdom.

13:5 See 7:17 – 18; 1Ch 17:13 – 14. *covenant of salt.* See notes on Nu 18:19; 2Ki 2:20.

13:6 See note on 10:1 – 19.

13:7 Not all in the northern kingdom are rebuked, only the leadership — a subtle appeal to those in the north who had been led into rebellion. *scoundrels.* See note on Dt 13:13. *young and indecisive.* Cf. 1Ch 22:5; 29:1. Rehoboam was 41 years old at the time of the schism (12:13).

13:8 *kingdom of the LORD.* The house of David represents the kingdom of God (see 9:8 and note).

13:9 See 1Ki 12:25 – 33. *consecrate himself.* Cf. Ex 29:1.

Levites, and make priests of your own as
the peoples of other lands do? Whoever
comes to consecrate himself with a young
bull[r] and seven rams[s] may become a priest
of what are not gods.[t]
10"As for us, the LORD is our God, and
we have not forsaken him. The priests
who serve the LORD are sons of Aaron, and
the Levites assist them. 11Every morning
and evening[u] they present burnt offerings
and fragrant incense[v] to the LORD. They set
out the bread on the ceremonially clean
table[w] and light the lamps[x] on the gold
lampstand every evening. We are observing the requirements of the LORD our God.
But you have forsaken him. 12God is with
us; he is our leader. His priests with their
trumpets will sound the battle cry against
you.[y] Men of Israel, do not fight against
the LORD,[z] the God of your fathers, for you
will not succeed."[a]
13Now Jeroboam had sent troops around
to the rear, so that while he was in front
of Judah the ambush[b] was behind them.
14Judah turned and saw that they were being attacked at both front and rear. Then
they cried out[c] to the LORD. The priests
blew their trumpets 15and the men of Judah raised the battle cry. At the sound of
their battle cry, God routed Jeroboam and
all Israel[d] before Abijah and Judah. 16The
Israelites fled before Judah, and God delivered[e] them into their hands. 17Abijah and
his men inflicted heavy losses on them,
so that there were five hundred thousand
casualties among Israel's able men. 18The
men of Israel were subdued on that occasion, and the men of Judah were victorious because they relied[f] on the LORD, the
God of their fathers.
19Abijah pursued Jeroboam and took
from him the towns of Bethel, Jeshanah

13:9 [r]Ex 29:35-36 [s]S Ex 29:31 [t]Jer 2:11; Gal 4:8 **13:11** [u]S Ex 29:39; S 2Ch 2:4 [v]S Ex 25:6 [w]S 1Ch 9:32 [x]S Ex 25:37 **13:12** [y]S Nu 10:8-9 [z]S Jdg 2:15; Ac 5:39 [a]Job 9:4; Pr 21:30; 29:1 **13:13** [b]Jos 8:9; 2Ch 20:22 **13:14** [c]S 1Ch 5:20; 2Ch 14:11; 18:31 **13:15** [d]S 1Ch 9:1 **13:16** [e]2Ch 16:8 **13:18** [f]2Ch 14:11; 16:7; Ps 22:5

and Ephron, with their surrounding villages. 20Jeroboam did not regain power
during the time of Abijah. And the LORD
struck him down and he died.
21But Abijah grew in strength. He married fourteen wives and had twenty-two
sons and sixteen daughters.
22The other events of Abijah's reign,
what he did and what he said, are written
in the annotations of the prophet Iddo.
14 And Abijah rested with his fathers
and was buried in the City of David.
Asa his son succeeded him as king, and
in his days the country was at peace for
ten years.

Asa King of Judah

14:2-3pp — 1Ki 15:11-12

2Asa did what was good and right in the
eyes of the LORD his God.[g] 3He removed
the foreign altars[h] and the high places,
smashed the sacred stones[i] and cut down
the Asherah poles.[a][j] 4He commanded Judah to seek the LORD,[k] the God of their
fathers, and to obey his laws and commands. 5He removed the high places[l] and
incense altars[m] in every town in Judah,
and the kingdom was at peace under him.
6He built up the fortified cities of Judah,
since the land was at peace. No one was
at war with him during those years, for the
LORD gave him rest.[n]
7"Let us build up these towns," he said
to Judah, "and put walls around them,
with towers, gates and bars. The land is
still ours, because we have sought the
LORD our God; we sought him and he has
given us rest[o] on every side." So they built
and prospered.

14:2 [g]2Ch 21:12 **14:3** [h]S Jdg 2:2 [i]S Ex 23:24 [j]S Ex 34:13 **14:4** [k]S 1Ch 16:11 **14:5** [l]S 1Ki 15:14 [m]Isa 27:9; Eze 6:4 **14:6** [n]S 1Ch 22:9 **14:7** [o]S 1Ch 22:9

[a] 3 That is, wooden symbols of the goddess Asherah; here and elsewhere in 2 Chronicles

13:10–12 The Chronicler's concern with acceptable worship focuses on the legitimate priests and the observance of prescribed worship (cf. 1Ch 23:28–31).

13:21 See note on 11:18–22.

14:1 *peace for ten years.* For the Chronicler peace and prosperity go hand in hand with righteous rule. This first decade of Asa's reign (910–900 B.C.) preceded the invasion by Zerah (14:9–15) and was followed by 20 more years of peace, from the 15th (15:10) to the 35th years (15:19). Contrast this account with the statement that there was war between Asa and Baasha throughout their reigns (see 1Ki 15:16 and note). The tensions between the two kingdoms may have accounted for Asa's fortifications (14:7–8), though actual combat was likely confined to raids until the major campaign was launched in Asa's 36th year (16:1). See 15:8 and note.

14:2—16:14 The account of Asa's reign (910–869 B.C.) here is greatly expanded over the one in 1Ki 15:9–24. The expansions characteristically express the Chronicler's view concerning the relationship between obedience and blessing, disobedience and punishment. The author introduces chronological notes into his account to divide Asa's reign into these periods (see note on 12:2): For ten years Asa did what was right and prospered (14:1–7), and an invasion by a powerful Cushite force was repulsed because he called on the Lord (14:8–15). There followed further reforms (15:1–9) and a covenant renewal in Asa's 15th year (15:10–18), and so he enjoyed peace until his 35th year (15:19). But then came a change: When confronted by an invasion from the northern kingdom in his 36th year (16:1), he hired Aramean reinforcements rather than trusting in the Lord (16:2–6), and imprisoned the prophet who rebuked him (16:7–10). In his 39th year he was afflicted with a disease (16:12), but still steadfastly refused to seek the Lord. In his 41st year he died (16:13).

14:3 *sacred stones.* See note on 1Ki 14:23. *Asherah poles.* See note on Ex 34:13.

14:5 *removed the high places.* 1Ki 15:14 states that Asa did not remove the high places. This difficulty is best resolved by the Chronicler's own statement in 15:17, which is properly parallel to 1Ki 15:14: Early in his reign Asa did attempt to remove the high places, but pagan worship was extremely resilient, and ultimately his efforts were unsuccessful (15:17). Statements that the high places both were and were not removed are also found in the reign of Jehoshaphat (17:6; 20:33). Cf. Dt 12:2–3.

14:7 *rest on every side.* See note on 20:30.

8 Asa had an army of three hundred
thousand[p] men from Judah, equipped
with large shields and with spears, and
two hundred and eighty thousand from
Benjamin, armed with small shields and
with bows. All these were brave fighting
men.
9 Zerah the Cushite[q] marched out against
them with a vast army[a] and three hundred
chariots, and came as far as Mareshah.[r]
10 Asa went out to meet him, and they took
up battle positions in the Valley of Zephathah near Mareshah.
11 Then Asa called[s] to the LORD his God
and said, "LORD, there is no one like you
to help the powerless against the mighty.
Help us,[t] O LORD our God, for we rely[u] on
you, and in your name[v] we have come
against this vast army. O LORD, you are
our God; do not let man prevail[w] against
you."
12 The LORD struck down[x] the Cushites
before Asa and Judah. The Cushites fled,
13 and Asa and his army pursued them
as far as Gerar.[y] Such a great number of
Cushites fell that they could not recover;
they were crushed[z] before the LORD and
his forces. The men of Judah carried off
a large amount of plunder.[a] 14 They destroyed all the villages around Gerar, for
the terror[b] of the LORD had fallen upon
them. They plundered all these villages,
since there was much booty there. 15 They
also attacked the camps of the herdsmen
and carried off droves of sheep and goats
and camels. Then they returned to Jerusalem.

Asa's Reform

15:16-19pp — 1Ki 15:13-16

15 The Spirit of God came upon[c] Azariah son of Oded. 2 He went out to
meet Asa and said to him, "Listen to me,
Asa and all Judah and Benjamin. The LORD
is with you[d] when you are with him.[e] If
you seek[f] him, he will be found by you,
but if you forsake him, he will forsake
you.[g] 3 For a long time Israel was without
the true God, without a priest to teach[h]
and without the law.[i] 4 But in their distress
they turned to the LORD, the God of Israel, and sought him,[j] and he was found
by them. 5 In those days it was not safe to
travel about,[k] for all the inhabitants of the
lands were in great turmoil. 6 One nation
was being crushed by another and one city
by another,[l] because God was troubling
them with every kind of distress. 7 But as
for you, be strong[m] and do not give up, for
your work will be rewarded."[n]
8 When Asa heard these words and the
prophecy of Azariah son of[b] Oded the
prophet, he took courage. He removed the
detestable idols[o] from the whole land of
Judah and Benjamin and from the towns
he had captured[p] in the hills of Ephraim. He repaired the altar[q] of the LORD that
was in front of the portico of the LORD's
temple.
9 Then he assembled all Judah and
Benjamin and the people from Ephraim, Manasseh and Simeon who had settled among them, for large numbers[r] had
come over to him from Israel when they
saw that the LORD his God was with him.
10 They assembled at Jerusalem in the
third month[s] of the fifteenth year of Asa's
reign. 11 At that time they sacrificed to the
LORD seven hundred head of cattle and
seven thousand sheep and goats from the
plunder[t] they had brought back. 12 They
entered into a covenant[u] to seek the LORD,[v]
the God of their fathers, with all their heart
and soul. 13 All who would not seek the
LORD, the God of Israel, were to be put to
death,[w] whether small or great, man or

[a] 9 Hebrew *with an army of a thousand thousands* or *with an army of thousands upon thousands*
[b] 8 Vulgate and Syriac (see also Septuagint and verse 1); Hebrew does not have *Azariah son of.*

14:8 [p] S 1Ch 21:1
14:9 [q] S 2Ch 12:3 [r] S Ge 10:8-9; 2Ch 11:8; 24:24
14:11 [s] S 1Ki 8:44; S 2Ch 13:14; 25:8 [t] Ps 60:11-12; 79:9 [u] S 2Ch 13:18 [v] S 1Sa 17:45 [w] Ps 9:19
14:12 [x] 1Ki 8:45
14:13 [y] Ge 10:19 [z] 2Sa 22:38; Ne 9:24; Ps 44:2, 19; 135:10 [a] 2Ch 15:11, 18
14:14 [b] S Ge 35:5; S Dt 2:25; 11:25
15:1 [c] S Nu 11:25, 26
15:2 [d] 2Ch 20:17 [e] Jas 4:8 [f] 2Ch 7:14; Ps 78:34; Isa 45:19; 55:6; Jer 29:13; Hos 3:5 [g] S Dt 31:17; S 1Ch 28:9
15:3 [h] S Lev 10:11 [i] La 2:9; Am 8:11
15:4 [j] S Dt 4:29
15:5 [k] S Jdg 5:6; 19:20; Zec 8:10
15:6 [l] Isa 19:2; Mt 24:7; Mk 13:8; Lk 21:10
15:7 [m] Jos 1:7, 9 [n] 1Sa 24:19; Ps 18:20; 58:11; Pr 14:14; Jer 31:16
15:8 [o] 1Ki 15:12 [p] 2Ch 17:2 [q] S 1Ki 8:64; S 2Ch 8:12
15:9 [r] 2Ch 11:16-17
15:10 [s] S Lev 23:15-21
15:11 [t] S 2Ch 14:13
15:12 [u] S 2Ki 11:17 [v] S 1Ch 16:11
15:13 [w] S Ex 22:20; Dt 13:9-16

14:9 *Zerah.* Probably a general leading Egyptian forces in the service of Pharaoh Osorkon I. The invasion appears to have been an attempt to duplicate the attack of Shishak 30 years earlier (12:1 – 12), but the results against Asa were quite different. *Cushite.* See vv. 12 – 13. The Cushites were natives of Nubia, the region that borders Egypt on the south — not to be confused with modern Ethiopia (Abyssinia). See also note on Isa 18:1.

14:10 *Valley of Zephathah.* Marked the entrance to a road leading to the hills of Judah and Jerusalem. *Mareshah.* Earlier fortified by Rehoboam (11:8) to protect the route mentioned here.

14:13 *Gerar.* See note on Ge 20:1. *plunder.* Much of this booty (v. 14) made its way to the storehouses of the temple (15:18; see note on 1Ch 18:1 — 20:8).

14:14 *terror of the LORD.* See note on 1Ch 14:17.

15:1 – 19 This chapter appears to recount a second stage in the reforms introduced by Asa, beginning with the victory over Zerah and encouraged by the preaching of Azariah (v. 1).

15:3 *priest to teach.* The duties of the priests were not only to officiate at the altar, but also to teach the law (see 17:7 – 9; Lev 10:11; Dt 17:9 – 11).

15:8 *towns he had captured in … Ephraim.* A tacit admission that there had been some fighting between Baasha and Asa prior to Asa's 36th year (16:1); see 17:1.

15:9 *large numbers had come over to him.* Cf. the defection from the northern kingdom that also occurred under Rehoboam (11:13 – 17).

15:10 *third month of the fifteenth year.* Spring, 895 B.C., the year after Zerah's invasion (v. 19). The Feast of Weeks (or Pentecost) was held in the third month (Lev 23:15 – 21) and may have been the occasion for this assembly.

15:12 *covenant.* A renewal of the covenant made at Sinai, similar to the covenant renewals on the plain of Moab (Dt 29:1), at Mount Ebal (Jos 8:30 – 35), at Shechem (Jos 24:25) and at Gilgal (1Sa 11:14; see note there). Later the priest Jehoiada (23:16), as well as Hezekiah (29:10) and Josiah (34:31), would also lead in renewals of the covenant — events of primary significance in the view of the Chronicler.

15:13 *would not seek the LORD.* Would turn to other gods. *were*

woman. 14They took an oath to the LORD
with loud acclamation, with shouting and
with trumpets and horns. 15All Judah rejoiced about the oath because they had
sworn it wholeheartedly. They sought God[x]
eagerly, and he was found by them. So the
LORD gave them rest[y] on every side.
16King Asa also deposed his grandmother Maacah[z] from her position as queen
mother,[a] because she had made a repulsive Asherah pole.[b] Asa cut the pole down,
broke it up and burned it in the Kidron
Valley.[c] 17Although he did not remove the
high places from Israel, Asa's heart was
fully committed ⌊to the LORD⌋ all his life.
18He brought into the temple of God the
silver and gold and the articles that he and
his father had dedicated.[d]
19There was no more war until the thir-
ty-fifth year of Asa's reign.

Asa's Last Years

16:1-6pp — 1Ki 15:17-22
16:11–17:1pp — 1Ki 15:23-24

16 In the thirty-sixth year of Asa's
reign Baasha[e] king of Israel went up
against Judah and fortified Ramah to prevent anyone from leaving or entering the
territory of Asa king of Judah.
2Asa then took the silver and gold out of
the treasuries of the LORD's temple and of
his own palace and sent it to Ben-Hadad
king of Aram, who was ruling in Damascus.[f] 3"Let there be a treaty[g] between me
and you," he said, "as there was between
my father and your father. See, I am sending you silver and gold. Now break your
treaty with Baasha king of Israel so he will
withdraw from me."
4Ben-Hadad agreed with King Asa and
sent the commanders of his forces against
the towns of Israel. They conquered Ijon,
Dan, Abel Maim[a] and all the store cities
of Naphtali.[h] 5When Baasha heard this, he
stopped building Ramah and abandoned
his work. 6Then King Asa brought all the
men of Judah, and they carried away from
Ramah the stones and timber Baasha had
been using. With them he built up Geba
and Mizpah.[i]
7At that time Hanani[j] the seer came to
Asa king of Judah and said to him: "Because you relied[k] on the king of Aram and
not on the LORD your God, the army of
the king of Aram has escaped from your
hand. 8Were not the Cushites[b][l] and Libyans a mighty army with great numbers[m]
of chariots and horsemen[c]? Yet when you
relied on the LORD, he delivered[n] them
into your hand. 9For the eyes[o] of the LORD
range throughout the earth to strengthen
those whose hearts are fully committed to
him. You have done a foolish[p] thing, and
from now on you will be at war.[q]"
10Asa was angry with the seer because
of this; he was so enraged that he put him
in prison.[r] At the same time Asa brutally
oppressed some of the people.
11The events of Asa's reign, from beginning to end, are written in the book of the
kings of Judah and Israel. 12In the thirty-
ninth year of his reign Asa was afflicted[s]
with a disease in his feet. Though his disease was severe, even in his illness he did
not seek[t] help from the LORD,[u] but only
from the physicians. 13Then in the forty-
first year of his reign Asa died and rested
with his fathers. 14They buried him in the
tomb that he had cut out for himself[v] in
the City of David. They laid him on a bier
covered with spices and various blended
perfumes,[w] and they made a huge fire[x] in
his honor.

Jehoshaphat King of Judah

17 Jehoshaphat his son succeeded him
as king and strengthened[y] himself

[a] 4 Also known as *Abel Beth Maacah* [b] 8 That is, people from the upper Nile region [c] 8 Or *charioteers*

15:15 [x]Dt 4:29 [y]S 1Ch 22:9
15:16 [z]2Ch 13:2 [a]S 1Ki 2:19 [b]S Ex 34:13 [c]S 2Sa 15:23
15:18 [d]S 2Ch 14:13
16:1 [e]2Ki 9:9; Jer 41:9
16:2 [f]2Ch 19:1-20:37; 22:1-9
16:3 [g]2Ch 20:35; 25:7
16:4 [h]S 2Ki 15:29
16:6 [i]Jer 41:9
16:7 [j]1Ki 16:1 [k]S 2Ch 13:18
16:8 [l]S Ge 10:6, 8-9; S 2Ch 12:3 [m]2Ch 24:24 [n]2Ch 13:16
16:9 [o]Job 24:23; Ps 33:13-15; Pr 15:3; Jer 16:17; Zec 3:9; 4:10 [p]1Sa 13:13 [q]S 1Ki 15:6; 2Ch 19:2; 25:7; 28:16-21
16:10 [r]S 1Ki 22:27
16:12 [s]2Ch 21:18; 26:19; Ps 103:3 [t]2Ch 7:14 [u]Jer 17:5-6
16:14 [v]S Ge 50:5 [w]S Ge 50:2 [x]2Ch 21:19; Jer 34:5
17:1 [y]S 1Ki 2:12

to be put to death. In accordance with basic covenant law (Ex 22:20; Dt 13:6–9).

15:15 *rest.* See note on 20:30.

15:16 *Asherah pole.* See NIV text note on 14:3. *Kidron Valley.* Just east of Jerusalem (see note on Isa 22:7 and map, p. 477; see also 1Ki 15:13 and note).

15:17 *did not remove the high places.* See 14:5 and note.

16:1 *thirty-sixth year of Asa's reign Baasha.* According to Kings, Baasha ruled for 24 years and was succeeded by Elah in the 26th year of Asa (1Ki 15:33; 16:8). Obviously Baasha could not have been alive in the 36th year of Asa, where this passage places him—he had been dead for a decade. The action described here is not dated in 1Ki 15:17. Perhaps the Chronicler's dates here and in 15:19 are the result of a copyist's error (possibly for an original 25th and 26th).

16:2–9 Hiring foreign troops brought Asa into a foreign alliance, which showed lack of trust in the Lord. Other examples of condemned foreign alliances are found in the reigns of Jehoshaphat (20:35–37), Ahaziah (22:1–9) and Ahaz (28:16–21). By hiring Ben-Hadad to the north, Asa opened a two-front war for Baasha and forced his withdrawal.

16:3 *treaty ... between my father and your father.* See note on 1Ki 15:19.

16:9 *eyes of the LORD range throughout the earth.* Asserted also in Zec 4:10.

16:11 *book of the kings of Judah and Israel.* See Introduction to 1 Chronicles: Author, Date and Sources.

16:12 *disease in his feet.* For other examples of disease as punishment for sin see 21:16–20; 26:16–23; Ac 12:23. Cf. 2Ki 15:5. *did not seek help from the LORD, but only from the physicians.* Contrast King Hezekiah (Isa 38); cf. Jer 17:5–8; Jas 5:14–16.

17:1—21:3 The Chronicler's account of Jehoshaphat's reign is more than twice as long as that in Kings, where the interest in Ahab and Elijah overshadows the space allotted to Jehoshaphat (1Ki 22:1–46). The Chronicler has also used Jehoshaphat's reign to emphasize immediate retribution. This theme is specifically announced in 19:10 and is illustrated in the blessing of Jehoshaphat's obedient faith and in the reproof for his wrongdoing (19:2–3; 20:35–37). Jehoshaphat reigned 872–848 B.C., from 872 to 869 likely as

against Israel. 2He stationed troops in all
the fortified cities[z] of Judah and put garrisons in Judah and in the towns of Ephraim
that his father Asa had captured.[a]
3The LORD was with Jehoshaphat because in his early years he walked in the
ways his father David[b] had followed. He
did not consult the Baals 4but sought[c] the
God of his father and followed his commands rather than the practices of Israel.
5The LORD established the kingdom under
his control; and all Judah brought gifts[d] to
Jehoshaphat, so that he had great wealth
and honor.[e] 6His heart was devoted[f] to
the ways of the LORD; furthermore, he removed the high places[g] and the Asherah
poles[h] from Judah.[i]
7In the third year of his reign he sent
his officials Ben-Hail, Obadiah, Zechariah, Nethanel and Micaiah to teach[j] in the
towns of Judah. 8With them were certain
Levites[k]—Shemaiah, Nethaniah, Zebadiah, Asahel, Shemiramoth, Jehonathan,
Adonijah, Tobijah and Tob-Adonijah—and
the priests Elishama and Jehoram. 9They
taught throughout Judah, taking with
them the Book of the Law[l] of the LORD;
they went around to all the towns of Judah and taught the people.
10The fear[m] of the LORD fell on all the
kingdoms of the lands surrounding Judah, so that they did not make war with
Jehoshaphat. 11Some Philistines brought
Jehoshaphat gifts and silver as tribute,
and the Arabs[n] brought him flocks:[o] seven
thousand seven hundred rams and seven
thousand seven hundred goats.
12Jehoshaphat became more and more
powerful; he built forts and store cities
in Judah 13and had large supplies in the
towns of Judah. He also kept experienced
fighting men in Jerusalem. 14Their enroll-
ment[p] by families was as follows:

From Judah, commanders of units of 1,000:
Adnah the commander, with 300,000 fighting men;
15next, Jehohanan the commander, with 280,000;
16next, Amasiah son of Zicri, who volunteered[q] himself for the service of the LORD, with 200,000.
17From Benjamin:[r]
Eliada, a valiant soldier, with 200,000 men armed with bows and shields;
18next, Jehozabad, with 180,000 men armed for battle.

19These were the men who served the
king, besides those he stationed in the fortified cities[s] throughout Judah.[t]

17:2 [z]S 2Ch 11:10 [a]2Ch 15:8 **17:3** [b]S 1Ki 22:43 **17:4** [c]2Ch 22:9 **17:5** [d]S 1Sa 10:27 [e]2Ch 18:1 **17:6** [f]S 1Ki 8:61 [g]S 1Ki 15:14; 2Ch 19:3; 20:33 [h]S Ex 34:13 [i]2Ch 21:12 **17:7** [j]S Lev 10:11; Dt 6:4-9; 2Ch 19:4-11; 35:3; Ne 8:7; Mal 2:7 **17:8** [k]2Ch 19:8; Ne 8:7-8; Hos 4:6 **17:9** [l]S Dt 28:61 **17:10** [m]S Ge 35:5; S Dt 2:25 **17:11** [n]S 2Ch 9:14 [o]2Ch 21:16 **17:14** [p]S 2Sa 24:2 **17:16** [q]S Jdg 5:9 **17:17** [r]S Nu 1:36 **17:19** [s]S 2Ch 11:10 [t]2Ch 25:5 **18:1** [u]2Ch 17:5 [v]2Ch 19:1-3; 22:3 [w]2Ch 21:6

Micaiah Prophesies Against Ahab

18:1-27pp — 1Ki 22:1-28

18 Now Jehoshaphat had great wealth
and honor,[u] and he allied[v] himself
with Ahab[w] by marriage. 2Some years later he went down to visit Ahab in Samaria.
Ahab slaughtered many sheep and cattle for him and the people with him and
urged him to attack Ramoth Gilead. 3Ahab
king of Israel asked Jehoshaphat king of
Judah, "Will you go with me against Ramoth Gilead?"
Jehoshaphat replied, "I am as you are,
and my people as your people; we will join
you in the war." 4But Jehoshaphat also

coregent with his father Asa (see 20:31 and note). The details of his reign may not be in chronological order; the teaching mission of 17:7–9 may have been part of the reforms noted in 19:4–11.

17:2 *cities of Judah ... towns of Ephraim.* See note on 15:8. Abijah (13:19), Asa (15:8) and now Jehoshaphat had managed to hold these cities; they would be lost under Amaziah (25:17–24).

17:6 *removed the high places.* Just as his father Asa had attempted to remove the high places, only to have them be restored (14:5; 15:17), so also Jehoshaphat removed them initially, only to have them revive and persist (20:33; cf. 1Ki 22:43). But see notes on 1Ki 3:2; 15:14. *Asherah poles.* See NIV text note on 14:3.

17:7–9 This incident may be part of the reform more fully detailed in 19:4–11. In the theocracy, the law of the Lord was supposed to be an integral part of the law of the land; the king and his officials, as well as the priests and prophets, were representatives of the Lord's kingship over his people.

17:7 *third year.* Perhaps the first year of his sole reign after a coregency of three years with his father Asa (see 20:31 and note).

17:9 *Book of the Law of the LORD.* See 34:14–15; Jos 8:31,34; 23:6; see also notes on Jos 1:8; 2Ki 22:8; Ne 8:1.

17:10–11 See note on 1Ch 18:1—20:8.

17:10 *fear of the LORD.* See note on 1Ch 14:17.

17:14–18 *300,000 ... 280,000 ... 200,000 ... 200,000 ... 180,000.* See notes on 1Ch 12:23–37; 27:1.

18:1—19:3 See 1Ki 22:1–40 and notes. In conformity with his interest in the southern kingdom and Jehoshaphat, the Chronicler omits elaboration on the death of Ahab and his succession (1Ki 22:36–40) and adds the material on the prophetic condemnation of Jehoshaphat's involvement (19:1–3).

18:1 Not found in 1Ki 22. The verse enhances the status of Jehoshaphat by mentioning the blessing of wealth for his fidelity, and also sets the stage for an entangling foreign alliance condemned by the prophet in 19:2–3. *allied himself with Ahab by marriage.* This marriage alliance to Athaliah, daughter of Ahab, resulted later in an attempt to exterminate the Davidic line (22:10—23:21).

18:2 The Chronicler further enhances the status of Jehoshaphat by noting the large number of animals Ahab slaughtered in his honor, a note not found in 1Ki 22. *urged him.* Also not found in the parallel text. The Hebrew for this verb is often used in the sense of "inciting to evil" (e.g., 1Ch 21:1) and may express the Chronicler's attitude toward Jehoshaphat's involvement. *Ramoth Gilead.* See notes on 22:5; 1Ki 22:3; see also map No. 7 at the end of this study Bible.

18:4 *seek the counsel of the LORD.* This request fits the Chronicler's overall positive portrait of Jehoshaphat.

said to the king of Israel, "First seek the
counsel of the LORD."
5 So the king of Israel brought together
the prophets—four hundred men—and
asked them, "Shall we go to war against
Ramoth Gilead, or shall I refrain?"
"Go," they answered, "for God will give
it into the king's hand."
6 But Jehoshaphat asked, "Is there not
a prophet of the LORD here whom we can
inquire of?"
7 The king of Israel answered Jehoshaphat, "There is still one man through
whom we can inquire of the LORD, but
I hate him because he never prophesies
anything good about me, but always bad.
He is Micaiah son of Imlah."
"The king should not say that," Jehoshaphat replied.
8 So the king of Israel called one of his
officials and said, "Bring Micaiah son of
Imlah at once."
9 Dressed in their royal robes, the king
of Israel and Jehoshaphat king of Judah
were sitting on their thrones at the threshing floor by the entrance to the gate of Samaria, with all the prophets prophesying
before them. 10 Now Zedekiah son of Kenaanah had made iron horns, and he declared, "This is what the LORD says: 'With
these you will gore the Arameans until
they are destroyed.'"
11 All the other prophets were prophesying the same thing. "Attack Ramoth Gilead[x] and be victorious," they said, "for the
LORD will give it into the king's hand."
12 The messenger who had gone to summon Micaiah said to him, "Look, as one
man the other prophets are predicting success for the king. Let your word agree with
theirs, and speak favorably."
13 But Micaiah said, "As surely as the
LORD lives, I can tell him only what my
God says."[y]
14 When he arrived, the king asked him,
"Micaiah, shall we go to war against Ramoth Gilead, or shall I refrain?"
"Attack and be victorious," he answered,
"for they will be given into your hand."
15 The king said to him, "How many
times must I make you swear to tell me
nothing but the truth in the name of the
LORD?"
16 Then Micaiah answered, "I saw all Israel[z] scattered on the hills like sheep without a shepherd,[a] and the LORD said, 'These
people have no master. Let each one go
home in peace.'"
17 The king of Israel said to Jehoshaphat,
"Didn't I tell you that he never prophesies
anything good about me, but only bad?"

18:11 [x] 2Ch 22:5
18:13 [y] Nu 22:18, 20, 35
18:16 [z] S 1Ch 9:1 [a] S Nu 27:17
18:18 [b] Da 7:9
18:21 [c] 1Ch 21:1; Job 1:6; Zec 3:1; Jn 8:44
18:22 [d] Job 12:16; Eze 14:9
18:23 [e] Ac 23:2
18:26 [f] Heb 11:36
18:29 [g] S 1Sa 28:8
18:31 [h] S 2Ch 13:14

18 Micaiah continued, "Therefore hear
the word of the LORD: I saw the LORD sitting on his throne[b] with all the host of
heaven standing on his right and on his
left. 19 And the LORD said, 'Who will entice
Ahab king of Israel into attacking Ramoth
Gilead and going to his death there?'
"One suggested this, and another that.
20 Finally, a spirit came forward, stood before the LORD and said, 'I will entice him.'
"'By what means?' the LORD asked.
21 "'I will go and be a lying spirit[c] in the
mouths of all his prophets,' he said.
"'You will succeed in enticing him,' said
the LORD. 'Go and do it.'
22 "So now the LORD has put a lying spirit
in the mouths of these prophets of yours.[d]
The LORD has decreed disaster for you."
23 Then Zedekiah son of Kenaanah went
up and slapped[e] Micaiah in the face.
"Which way did the spirit from[a] the LORD
go when he went from me to speak to
you?" he asked.
24 Micaiah replied, "You will find out on
the day you go to hide in an inner room."
25 The king of Israel then ordered, "Take
Micaiah and send him back to Amon the
ruler of the city and to Joash the king's
son, 26 and say, 'This is what the king
says: Put this fellow in prison[f] and give
him nothing but bread and water until I
return safely.'"
27 Micaiah declared, "If you ever return
safely, the LORD has not spoken through
me." Then he added, "Mark my words, all
you people!"

Ahab Killed at Ramoth Gilead

18:28-34pp — 1Ki 22:29-36

28 So the king of Israel and Jehoshaphat
king of Judah went up to Ramoth Gilead.
29 The king of Israel said to Jehoshaphat,
"I will enter the battle in disguise, but
you wear your royal robes." So the king
of Israel disguised[g] himself and went into
battle.
30 Now the king of Aram had ordered his
chariot commanders, "Do not fight with
anyone, small or great, except the king
of Israel." 31 When the chariot commanders saw Jehoshaphat, they thought, "This
is the king of Israel." So they turned to
attack him, but Jehoshaphat cried out,[h]
and the LORD helped him. God drew them
away from him, 32 for when the chariot
commanders saw that he was not the king
of Israel, they stopped pursuing him.
33 But someone drew his bow at random and hit the king of Israel between the

[a] 23 Or *Spirit of*

18:10 *Arameans.* See notes on 1Ch 18:5; Dt 26:5.
18:22 *lying spirit.* See note on 1Ki 22:23.
18:29 The fact that Ahab directs Jehoshaphat into battle in royal regalia, thus making Jehoshaphat the logical target for attack, is consistent with Israel's dominant position at this time.

sections of his armor. The king told the
chariot driver, "Wheel around and get me
out of the fighting. I've been wounded."
34All day long the battle raged, and the
king of Israel propped himself up in his
chariot facing the Arameans until evening.
Then at sunset he died.[i]

19 When Jehoshaphat king of Judah
returned safely to his palace in Jerusalem, 2Jehu[j] the seer, the son of Hanani, went out to meet him and said to
the king, "Should you help the wicked[k]
and love[a] those who hate the LORD?[l] Because of this, the wrath[m] of the LORD is
upon you. 3There is, however, some good[n]
in you, for you have rid the land of the
Asherah poles[o] and have set your heart on
seeking God.[p]"

Jehoshaphat Appoints Judges

4Jehoshaphat lived in Jerusalem, and he
went out again among the people from Beersheba to the hill country of Ephraim and
turned them back to the LORD, the God of
their fathers. 5He appointed judges[q] in the
land, in each of the fortified cities of Judah. 6He told them, "Consider carefully
what you do,[r] because you are not judging
for man[s] but for the LORD, who is with you
whenever you give a verdict. 7Now let the
fear of the LORD be upon you. Judge carefully, for with the LORD our God there is no
injustice[t] or partiality[u] or bribery."
8In Jerusalem also, Jehoshaphat appointed some of the Levites,[v] priests[w] and
heads of Israelite families to administer[x]
the law of the LORD and to settle disputes.

18:34 [i]2Ch 22:5 **19:2** [j]S 1Ki 16:1 [k]S 2Ch 16:2-9 [l]Ps 139:21-22 [m]2Ch 24:18; 32:25; Ps 7:11 **19:3** [n]S 1Ki 14:13 [o]S 2Ch 17:6 [p]S 2Ch 18:1; 20:35; 25:7 **19:5** [q]S Ge 47:6; S Ex 18:26 **19:6** [r]S Lev 19:15 [s]Dt 16:18-20; 17:8-13 **19:7** [t]S Ge 18:25; S Job 8:3 [u]S Ex 18:16; Dt 10:17; Job 13:10; 32:21; 34:19 **19:8** [v]S 1Ch 23:4 [w]Eze 44:24 [x]2Ch 17:8-9

19:10 [y]Dt 17:8-13 **19:11** [z]S 1Ch 28:20 **20:1** [a]Ps 83:6 [b]S 1Ch 4:41 **20:2** [c]2Ch 24:24 [d]S Ge 14:7 [e]S 1Sa 23:29; SS 1:14 **20:3** [f]1Sa 7:6; Ezr 8:23; Ne 1:4; Est 4:16; Isa 58:6; Jer 36:9; Da 9:3; Joel 1:14; 2:15; Jnh 3:5,7 **20:4** [g]Jer 36:6

And they lived in Jerusalem. 9He gave
them these orders: "You must serve faithfully and wholeheartedly in the fear of the
LORD. 10In every case that comes before
you from your fellow countrymen who
live in the cities—whether bloodshed or
other concerns of the law, commands,
decrees or ordinances—you are to warn
them not to sin against the LORD;[y] otherwise his wrath will come on you and your
brothers. Do this, and you will not sin.
11"Amariah the chief priest will be over
you in any matter concerning the LORD,
and Zebadiah son of Ishmael, the leader
of the tribe of Judah, will be over you in
any matter concerning the king, and the
Levites will serve as officials before you.
Act with courage,[z] and may the LORD be
with those who do well."

Jehoshaphat Defeats Moab and Ammon

20 After this, the Moabites[a] and Ammonites with some of the Meunites[b][b]
came to make war on Jehoshaphat.
2Some men came and told Jehoshaphat,
"A vast army[c] is coming against you from
Edom,[c] from the other side of the Sea.[d] It
is already in Hazazon Tamar[d]" (that is, En
Gedi).[e] 3Alarmed, Jehoshaphat resolved to
inquire of the LORD, and he proclaimed a
fast[f] for all Judah. 4The people of Judah[g]
came together to seek help from the LORD;
indeed, they came from every town in Judah to seek him.

[a] 2 Or *and make alliances with* [b] *1* Some Septuagint manuscripts; Hebrew *Ammonites* [c] *2* One Hebrew manuscript; most Hebrew manuscripts, Septuagint and Vulgate *Aram* [d] *2* That is, the Dead Sea

19:1–3 Not found in 1Ki 22.

19:2 *Should you help the wicked...?* Jehu's father Hanani had earlier given Jehoshaphat's father Asa the same warning (see 16:7–9). Jehoshaphat later committed the same sin again and suffered for it (20:35–37).

19:3 *Asherah poles.* See NIV text note on 14:3.

19:4 *Jehoshaphat... went... among the people.* The king traveled throughout the realm personally to promote religious reformation.

19:5 *appointed judges.* The name Jehoshaphat (meaning "The LORD judges") is appropriate for the king who instituted this judicial reform. The arrangement of the courts under Jehoshaphat (vv. 5–11) would be of particular interest to the Chronicler's audience in the postexilic period, when the courts of the restored community would have their own existence and structure legitimized by this precedent.

19:6 Cf. Dt 16:18–20; 17:8–13.

19:7 *let the fear of the LORD be upon you.* Let a terrifying sense of God's presence restrain you from any injustice (see note on 1Ch 14:17).

19:8 *Levites, priests... to administer the law.* See note on 1Ch 26:29–32. One effect of this judicial reform appears to be the bringing of the traditional system of justice administered by the elders of the city under closer royal and priestly supervision.

19:11 *any matter concerning the LORD... any matter concerning the king.* This division into the affairs of religion and the affairs of the king reflects the postexilic structure of the Chronicler's day. Cf. the anointing of Solomon and Zadok (1Ch 29:22) and the administration of the postexilic community by Zerubbabel, a Davidic descendant, and Joshua, the high priest (Zec 4:14; 6:9–15).

20:1–30 This episode held special interest for the Chronicler since the restored community was being harassed by the descendants of these same peoples (see Ne 2:19; 4:1–3,7–9; 6:1–4; 13). He uses it to encourage his contemporaries to trust in the Lord and his prophets, as Jehoshaphat son of David had exhorted (v. 20). The account is significantly structured. Apart from the outer frame, which highlights the reversal of circumstances (vv. 1–4,28–30), it falls into three divisions: (1) Jehoshaphat's prayer (vv. 5–13), (2) the Lord's response (vv. 14–19), (3) the great victory (vv. 20–27). At the center of each is its crucial statement, and these are all linked by a key word: v. 9, "we will stand in your presence before this temple"; v. 17, "stand firm and see the deliverance the LORD will give you"; v. 23, "The men of Ammon and Moab rose up (lit. 'stood up') against the men from Mount Seir to destroy ... them."

20:1 *Meunites.* A people from the region of Mount Seir in Edom (26:7; 1Ch 4:41; cf. 2Ch 20:10,22–23).

20:2 *Edom.* See NIV text note. Since the Arameans are well to the north and not mentioned among the attackers named in v. 1, the NIV has followed the reading "Edom." The difference between "Aram" and "Edom" in Hebrew is only one letter, which is very similar in shape and was often confused in the process of copying manuscripts.

5Then Jehoshaphat stood up in the assembly of Judah and Jerusalem at the temple of the LORD in the front of the new courtyard 6and said:

"O LORD, God of our fathers,[h] are you not the God who is in heaven?[i] You rule over all the kingdoms[j] of the nations. Power and might are in your hand, and no one can withstand you.[k] 7O our God, did you not drive out the inhabitants of this land[l] before your people Israel and give it forever to the descendants of Abraham your friend?[m] 8They have lived in it and have built in it a sanctuary[n] for your Name, saying, 9'If calamity comes upon us, whether the sword of judgment, or plague or famine,[o] we will stand in your presence before this temple that bears your Name and will cry out to you in our distress, and you will hear us and save us.'

10"But now here are men from Ammon, Moab and Mount Seir, whose territory you would not allow Israel to invade when they came from Egypt;[p] so they turned away from them and did not destroy them. 11See how they are repaying us by coming to drive us out of the possession[q] you gave us as an inheritance. 12O our God, will you not judge them?[r] For we have no power to face this vast army that is attacking us. We do not know what to do, but our eyes are upon you.[s]"

13All the men of Judah, with their wives and children and little ones, stood there before the LORD.

14Then the Spirit[t] of the LORD came upon Jahaziel son of Zechariah, the son of Benaiah, the son of Jeiel, the son of Mattaniah,[u] a Levite and descendant of Asaph, as he stood in the assembly.

15He said: "Listen, King Jehoshaphat and all who live in Judah and Jerusalem! This is what the LORD says to you: 'Do not be afraid or discouraged[v] because of this vast army. For the battle[w] is not yours, but God's. 16Tomorrow march down against them. They will be climbing up by the Pass of Ziz, and you will find them at the end of the gorge in the Desert of Jeruel. 17You will not have to fight this battle. Take up your positions; stand firm and see[x] the deliverance the LORD will give you, O Judah and Jerusalem. Do not be afraid; do not be discouraged. Go out to face them tomorrow, and the LORD will be with you.'"

18Jehoshaphat bowed[y] with his face to the ground, and all the people of Judah and Jerusalem fell down in worship before the LORD. 19Then some Levites from the Kohathites and Korahites stood up and praised the LORD, the God of Israel, with a very loud voice.

20Early in the morning they left for the Desert of Tekoa. As they set out, Jehoshaphat stood and said, "Listen to me, Judah and people of Jerusalem! Have faith[z] in the LORD your God and you will be upheld; have faith in his prophets and you will be successful.[a]" 21After consulting the people, Jehoshaphat appointed men to sing to the LORD and to praise him for the splendor of his[a] holiness[b] as they went out at the head of the army, saying:

"Give thanks to the LORD,
for his love endures forever."[c]

22As they began to sing and praise, the LORD set ambushes[d] against the men of Ammon and Moab and Mount Seir who were invading Judah, and they were defeated. 23The men of Ammon[e] and Moab rose up against the men from Mount Seir[f] to destroy and annihilate them. After they finished slaughtering the men from Seir, they helped to destroy one another.[g]

24When the men of Judah came to the place that overlooks the desert and looked toward the vast army, they saw only dead bodies lying on the ground; no one had escaped. 25So Jehoshaphat and his men went to carry off their plunder, and they found among them a great amount of equipment and clothing[b] and also articles of value—more than they could take away. There was so much plunder that it took three days to collect it. 26On the fourth day they assembled in the Valley

20:6 [h]Mt 6:9 [i]Dt 4:39 [j]1Ch 29:11-12 [k]2Ch 25:8; Job 25:2; 41:10; 42:2; Isa 14:27; Jer 32:27; 49:19 **20:7** [l]S Ge 12:7 [m]Isa 41:8; Jas 2:23 **20:8** [n]2Ch 6:20 **20:9** [o]S 2Ch 6:28 **20:10** [p]Nu 20:14-21; Dt 2:4-6, 9, 18-19 **20:11** [q]Ps 83:1-12 **20:12** [r]Jdg 11:27 [s]Ps 25:15; Isa 30:15; 45:22; Mic 7:7 **20:14** [t]S 1Ch 12:18 [u]S 1Ch 9:15 **20:15** [v]2Ch 32:7 [w]S 1Sa 17:47; Ps 91:8 **20:17** [x]S Ex 14:13 **20:18** [y]S Ge 24:26; 2Ch 29:29 **20:20** [z]Isa 7:9 [a]S Ge 39:3; Pr 16:3 **20:21** [b]S 1Ch 16:29 [c]S 2Ch 5:13; Ps 136:1 **20:22** [d]S 2Ch 13:13 **20:23** [e]S Ge 19:38 [f]2Ch 21:8 [g]S Jdg 7:22; 1Sa 14:20; Eze 38:21

[a] 21 Or *him with the splendor of* [b] 25 Some Hebrew manuscripts and Vulgate; most Hebrew manuscripts *corpses*

20:5–12 Jehoshaphat's prayer shows him to be a true theocratic king, a worthy son of David and type (foreshadowing) of the awaited Messiah (see Introduction to 1 Chronicles: Purpose and Themes).
20:7 *Abraham your friend.* See Isa 41:8; Jas 2:23 and note.
20:9 An apparent reference to Solomon's prayer and the divine promise of response (6:14–42; 7:12–22).
20:15 See Ex 14:13–14 and note on 14:14.
20:16 *Pass of Ziz.* Began seven miles north of En Gedi and wound inland, emerging west of Tekoa. *Jeruel.* Southeast of Tekoa.
20:19 *Levites.* The Chronicler's interest in the priests and Levites is apparent throughout the account (vv. 14,21–22,28).
20:20 *Have faith in the LORD your God and ... in his prophets.* A particularly apt word for the Chronicler's contemporaries to hear from this son of David—at a time when their only hope for the future lay with the Lord and the reassuring words he had given through his prophets.
20:21 *splendor of his holiness.* See note on 1Ch 16:29.
20:22 *ambushes.* The nature of this "ambush" is indicated in v. 23: Israel's foes destroyed each other in the confusion of battle, similar to the victory under Gideon (Jdg 7:22).
20:26 *to this day.* See note on 5:9.

of Beracah, where they praised the LORD.
This is why it is called the Valley of Beracah[a] to this day.
27 Then, led by Jehoshaphat, all the men
of Judah and Jerusalem returned joyfully to Jerusalem, for the LORD had given
them cause to rejoice over their enemies.
28 They entered Jerusalem and went to the
temple of the LORD with harps and lutes
and trumpets.
29 The fear[h] of God came upon all the
kingdoms of the countries when they
heard how the LORD had fought[i] against
the enemies of Israel. 30 And the kingdom
of Jehoshaphat was at peace, for his God
had given him rest[j] on every side.

The End of Jehoshaphat's Reign

20:31–21:1pp — 1Ki 22:41-50

31 So Jehoshaphat reigned over Judah.
He was thirty-five years old when he became king of Judah, and he reigned in Jerusalem twenty-five years. His mother's
name was Azubah daughter of Shilhi. 32 He
walked in the ways of his father Asa and
did not stray from them; he did what was
right in the eyes of the LORD. 33 The high
places,[k] however, were not removed, and
the people still had not set their hearts on
the God of their fathers.
34 The other events of Jehoshaphat's
reign, from beginning to end, are written in
the annals of Jehu[l] son of Hanani, which
are recorded in the book of the kings of
Israel.
35 Later, Jehoshaphat king of Judah
made an alliance[m] with Ahaziah king of
Israel, who was guilty of wickedness.[n]
36 He agreed with him to construct a fleet
of trading ships.[b] After these were built
at Ezion Geber, 37 Eliezer son of Dodavahu
of Mareshah prophesied against Jehoshaphat, saying, "Because you have made an
alliance with Ahaziah, the LORD will destroy what you have made." The ships[o]
were wrecked and were not able to set
sail to trade.[c]

21 Then Jehoshaphat rested with his fathers and was buried with them in
the City of David. And Jehoram[p] his son
succeeded him as king. 2 Jehoram's brothers, the sons of Jehoshaphat, were Azariah, Jehiel, Zechariah, Azariahu, Michael
and Shephatiah. All these were sons of
Jehoshaphat king of Israel.[d] 3 Their father
had given them many gifts[q] of silver and
gold and articles of value, as well as fortified cities[r] in Judah, but he had given the
kingdom to Jehoram because he was his
firstborn son.

Jehoram King of Judah

21:5-10,20pp — 2Ki 8:16-24

4 When Jehoram established[s] himself
firmly over his father's kingdom, he
put all his brothers[t] to the sword along
with some of the princes of Israel. 5 Jehoram was thirty-two years old when he
became king, and he reigned in Jerusalem eight years. 6 He walked in the ways
of the kings of Israel,[u] as the house of
Ahab had done, for he married a daughter of Ahab.[v] He did evil in the eyes of
the LORD. 7 Nevertheless, because of the
covenant the LORD had made with David,[w] the LORD was not willing to destroy
the house of David.[x] He had promised to
maintain a lamp[y] for him and his descendants forever.

20:29 [h]S Ge 35:5; S Dt 2:25 [i]S Ex 14:14 **20:30** [j]S 1Ch 22:9 **20:33** [k]S 2Ch 17:6 **20:34** [l]S 1Ki 16:1 **20:35** [m]S 2Ch 16:3 [n]S 2Ch 19:1-3 **20:37** [o]S 1Ki 9:26 **21:1** [p]S 1Ch 3:11 **21:3** [q]2Ch 11:23 [r]S 2Ch 11:10 **21:4** [s]S 1Ki 2:12 [t]Jdg 9:5 **21:6** [u]1Ki 12:28-30 [v]2Ch 18:1; 22:3 **21:7** [w]S 2Sa 7:13 [x]S 2Sa 7:15; 2Ch 23:3 [y]S 2Sa 21:17

[a] 26 *Beracah* means *praise.* [b] 36 Hebrew *of ships that could go to Tarshish* [c] 37 Hebrew *sail for Tarshish* [d] 2 That is, Judah, as frequently in 2 Chronicles

20:29 *The fear of God.* See note on 1Ch 14:17.

20:30 *rest on every side.* Rest from enemies is part of God's blessing for obedience in Chronicles (14:5–7; 15:15; 1Ch 22:8–9,18). Righteous kings have victory in warfare (Abijah, Asa, Jehoshaphat, Uzziah, Hezekiah), while wicked rulers experience defeat (Jehoram, Ahaz, Joash, Zedekiah).

20:31 *twenty-five years.* The book of Kings reports 22 (18 in 2Ki 3:1, and 4 more in 8:16). These figures are reconciled by suggesting a coregency with his father Asa for three years, probably due to the severity of his father's illness and the need to arrange for a secure succession (16:10–14). The book of Kings speaks only of his years of sole reign after his father's death.

20:33 *high places … were not removed.* See note on 17:6.

20:34 *Jehu son of Hanani.* See note on 19:2.

20:35–37 See 1Ki 22:48–49. The lucrative maritime trade through the Gulf of Aqaba no doubt tempted Jehoshaphat to enter into this improper alliance (see 19:2 and note). Solomon's earlier alliance for the same purpose had been with a non-Israelite king (8:17–18).

20:35 *Ahaziah.* Reigned 853–852 B.C. (see 1Ki 22:51—2Ki 1:18 for the account of his reign).

21:2 *sons of Jehoshaphat.* The Chronicler shows the blessing of God on Jehoshaphat by mentioning his large family, particularly his seven sons (see 11:18–22; 1Ch 25:5 and notes). Jehoshaphat's large number of sons is in striking contrast to the wicked Jehoram who, after murdering his brothers (v. 4), is left with but one son (v. 17). Jehoram's wife Athaliah would later perform a similar slaughter (22:10).

21:3 Cf. the similar actions of Rehoboam (11:23).

21:4–20 See 2Ki 8:16–24 and notes.

21:4 This bloody assassination of all potential rivals is not reported in Kings, but it fits the pattern of the northern kings (see v. 6). The princes of Israel were probably leading men in the southern kingdom who opposed having a king married to a daughter of Ahab. For this use of "Israel" see note on 12:1.

21:5 *eight years.* 848–841 B.C. The period 853–848 was probably a coregency of Jehoram with his father Jehoshaphat—Jehoshaphat's 18th year was also Jehoram's second year (cf. 2Ki 1:17; 3:1).

21:6 *married a daughter of Ahab.* Probably the marriage referred to in 18:1, used to cement the alliance between Jehoshaphat and Ahab. Such political marriages were common. Many of Solomon's marriages sealed international relationships, as did Ahab's marriage to Jezebel.

8 In the time of Jehoram, Edom[z] rebelled
against Judah and set up its own king. 9 So
Jehoram went there with his officers and
all his chariots. The Edomites surrounded him and his chariot commanders, but
he rose up and broke through by night.
10 To this day Edom has been in rebellion
against Judah.
Libnah[a] revolted at the same time, because Jehoram had forsaken the LORD,
the God of his fathers. 11 He had also built
high places on the hills of Judah and had
caused the people of Jerusalem to prostitute themselves and had led Judah astray.
12 Jehoram received a letter from Elijah[b]
the prophet, which said:

"This is what the LORD, the God of
your father[c] David, says: 'You have
not walked in the ways of your father
Jehoshaphat or of Asa[d] king of Judah.
13 But you have walked in the ways of
the kings of Israel, and you have led
Judah and the people of Jerusalem
to prostitute themselves, just as the
house of Ahab did.[e] You have also
murdered your own brothers, members of your father's house, men who
were better[f] than you. 14 So now the
LORD is about to strike your people,
your sons, your wives and everything
that is yours, with a heavy blow.
15 You yourself will be very ill with a
lingering disease[g] of the bowels, until the disease causes your bowels to
come out.'"

16 The LORD aroused against Jehoram the
hostility of the Philistines and of the
Arabs[h] who lived near the Cushites. 17 They
attacked Judah, invaded it and carried off
all the goods found in the king's palace,
together with his sons and wives. Not a
son was left to him except Ahaziah,[a] the
youngest.[i]
18 After all this, the LORD afflicted Jehoram with an incurable disease of the bowels. 19 In the course of time, at the end of
the second year, his bowels came out because of the disease, and he died in great
pain. His people made no fire in his hon-
or,[j] as they had for his fathers.
20 Jehoram was thirty-two years old
when he became king, and he reigned in
Jerusalem eight years. He passed away,
to no one's regret, and was buried[k] in the
City of David, but not in the tombs of the
kings.

21:8 [z] 2Ch 20:22-23
21:10 [a] S Nu 33:20
21:12 [b] 2Ki 1:16-17 [c] 2Ch 17:3-6 [d] 2Ch 14:2
21:13 [e] 1Ki 16:29-33 [f] 1Ki 2:32
21:15 [g] S Nu 12:10
21:16 [h] 2Ch 17:10-11; 22:1; 26:7
21:17 [i] 2Ki 12:18; 2Ch 22:1; Joel 3:5
21:19 [j] S 2Ch 16:14
21:20 [k] 2Ch 24:25; 28:27; 33:20
22:1 [l] 2Ch 33:25; 36:1 [m] 2Ch 23:20-21; 26:1 [n] S 2Ch 21:16-17
22:3 [o] S 2Ch 18:1 [p] S 2Ch 21:6

Ahaziah King of Judah

22:1-6pp — 2Ki 8:25-29
22:7-9pp — 2Ki 9:21-29

22 The people[l] of Jerusalem[m] made Ahaziah, Jehoram's youngest son, king
in his place, since the raiders,[n] who came
with the Arabs into the camp, had killed
all the older sons. So Ahaziah son of Jehoram king of Judah began to reign.
2 Ahaziah was twenty-two[b] years old
when he became king, and he reigned in
Jerusalem one year. His mother's name
was Athaliah, a granddaughter of Omri.
3 He too walked[o] in the ways of the house
of Ahab,[p] for his mother encouraged him
in doing wrong. 4 He did evil in the eyes of
the LORD, as the house of Ahab had done,

[a] 17 Hebrew *Jehoahaz,* a variant of *Ahaziah*
[b] 2 Some Septuagint manuscripts and Syriac (see also 2 Kings 8:26); Hebrew *forty-two*

21:8 – 10 The pious Jehoshaphat had enjoyed victory over Edom (20:1 – 30), while the wicked Jehoram is defeated in his attempt to keep Edom in subjection to Judah (see note on 20:30).
21:10 *To this day.* See note on 5:9. *Libnah.* Located between Judah and Philistia. *because Jehoram had forsaken the LORD.* Not found in 2Ki 8:22. The Chronicler introduces this judgment as an indication of immediate retribution (see notes on 12:1 – 14; 12:2; see also Introduction to 1 Chronicles: Purpose and Themes).
21:11 *prostitute themselves.* See Ex 34:15 and note.
21:12 – 20a Not found in the parallel text in 2Ki 8.
21:12 – 15 This reference to a letter from Elijah is the only mention in Chronicles of that prophet, to whom the books of Kings give so much attention (1Ki 17 – 2Ki 2). Elijah's letter specifically announces the immediate consequences of Jehoram's disobedience — further defeat in war, which will cost Jehoram his wives and sons; and disease, which will lead to his death (see note on 16:12). Cf. also the foot disease of Asa (16:12 – 14) and the leprosy of Uzziah (26:16 – 23). The book of Kings does not mention the nature of Jehoram's death. Some have argued that this letter could not be authentic because, they claim, Elijah was taken to heaven before Jehoram became king. But this is not a necessary conclusion (see 2Ki 1:17; see also note on 2Ki 3:11). Elijah's translation may well have taken place as late as 848 B.C.
21:16 *Cushites.* See note on 14:9; see also NIV text note on 16:8.
21:20 *eight years.* See note on v. 5. *not in the tombs of the kings.* Only the Chronicler mentions the refusal of the people to accord Jehoram the customary burial honors of a tomb with the other kings of Judah (cf. 24:25).
22:1 – 9 The Chronicler's account of Ahaziah's reign is much shorter than the parallel in 2Ki 8:24 — 9:29, probably due to the fact that the Kings account focuses on the rebellion of Jehu and the downfall of the dynasty of Omri (see 2Ki 8:26; see also 1Ki 16:21 – 28) — events in the northern kingdom, in which the Chronicler is not interested. The Chronicler's account again shows his interest in immediate retribution: Ahaziah's personal wickedness and his involvement in a foreign alliance result in immediate judgment and a reign of only one year (see note on 16:2 – 9; see also Introduction to 1 Chronicles: Purpose and Themes).
22:1 *had killed all the older sons.* Emphasizes divine retribution: Jehoram, who murdered all his brothers, had to watch the death of his own sons (21:4,13,16 – 17).
22:2 *twenty-two.* See NIV text note. The Hebrew reading of "42" would make Ahaziah older than his father (21:20). *one year.* 841 B.C.
22:3 – 4 The great influence of the dynasty of Omri in Judah is indicated by the power of Athaliah and the presence of advisers from the northern kingdom (see note on 18:29).

for after his father's death they became his
advisers, to his undoing. 5He also followed
their counsel when he went with Joram[a]
son of Ahab king of Israel to war against
Hazael king of Aram at Ramoth Gilead.[q] The
Arameans wounded Joram; 6so he returned
to Jezreel to recover from the wounds they
had inflicted on him at Ramoth[b] in his battle with Hazael[r] king of Aram.

Then Ahaziah[c] son of Jehoram king
of Judah went down to Jezreel to see Joram son of Ahab because he had been
wounded.

7Through Ahaziah's[s] visit to Joram,
God brought about Ahaziah's downfall.
When Ahaziah arrived, he went out with
Joram to meet Jehu son of Nimshi, whom
the LORD had anointed to destroy the
house of Ahab. 8While Jehu was executing judgment on the house of Ahab,[t] he
found the princes of Judah and the sons
of Ahaziah's relatives, who had been attending Ahaziah, and he killed them. 9He
then went in search of Ahaziah, and his
men captured him while he was hiding[u]
in Samaria. He was brought to Jehu and
put to death. They buried him, for they
said, "He was a son of Jehoshaphat, who
sought[v] the LORD with all his heart." So
there was no one in the house of Ahaziah
powerful enough to retain the kingdom.

22:5 [q] 2Ch 18:11,34 **22:6** [r] 1Ki 19:15; 2Ki 8:13-15 **22:7** [s] 2Ki 9:16 **22:8** [t] S 2Ki 10:13 **22:9** [u] S Jdg 9:5 [v] 2Ch 17:4

Athaliah and Joash

22:10–23:21pp — 2Ki 11:1-21

10When Athaliah the mother of Ahaziah saw that her son was dead, she proceeded to destroy the whole royal family
of the house of Judah. 11But Jehosheba,[d]
the daughter of King Jehoram, took Joash
son of Ahaziah and stole him away from
among the royal princes who were about
to be murdered and put him and his nurse
in a bedroom. Because Jehosheba,[d] the
daughter of King Jehoram and wife of the
priest Jehoiada, was Ahaziah's sister, she
hid the child from Athaliah so she could
not kill him. 12He remained hidden with
them at the temple of God for six years
while Athaliah ruled the land.

23 In the seventh year Jehoiada showed
his strength. He made a covenant
with the commanders of units of a hundred: Azariah son of Jeroham, Ishmael
son of Jehohanan, Azariah son of Obed,
Maaseiah son of Adaiah, and Elishaphat
son of Zicri. 2They went throughout Judah
and gathered the Levites[w] and the heads
of Israelite families from all the towns.

23:2 [w] S Nu 35:2-5

[a] 5 Hebrew *Jehoram,* a variant of *Joram*; also in verses 6 and 7 [b] 6 Hebrew *Ramah,* a variant of *Ramoth* [c] 6 Some Hebrew manuscripts, Septuagint, Vulgate and Syriac (see also 2 Kings 8:29); most Hebrew manuscripts *Azariah* [d] 11 Hebrew *Jehoshabeath,* a variant of *Jehosheba*

22:5 *went with Joram ... to war.* An action similar to that for which Jehoshaphat had been rebuked (see 19:2 and note). *Hazael.* Had been anointed by Elisha; he later killed his master in a coup to seize the throne (2Ki 8:13–15; cf. 1Ki 19:15 and note). *Ramoth Gilead.* Located in the Transjordan border area between Israel and Aram. More than ten years earlier Jehoshaphat had participated with Ahab in a battle there that cost Ahab his life (ch. 18; 1Ki 22).

22:6 *returned to Jezreel.* Joram apparently recovered Ramoth Gilead and left Jehu in charge (2Ki 8:28—9:28).

22:7 *God brought about Ahaziah's downfall.* The Chronicler assumes that the reader is familiar with the account of Jehu's anointing and the additional details of the coup, which resulted in the deaths of Joram and Ahaziah (2Ki 8:28—9:28). While the writer of Kings primarily portrays the end of the dynasty of Omri as a result of the judgment of God (1Ki 21:20–29; 2Ki 9:24—10:17), the Chronicler notes that the assassination of Ahaziah was also brought about by God.

22:9 The account of Ahaziah's death appears to be somewhat different in the two histories (cf. 2Ki 9:21–27; 10:12–14). Since the writer of Chronicles presumes the reader's familiarity with the other account (see note on v. 7), it is best to take the details of Chronicles as supplementary to Kings, not contradictory, though it is difficult to know the precise sequence and location of events. Apart from the Chronicler's statement that Ahaziah received a decent burial because of his father's piety rather than his own, the apparent differences in the two accounts do not appear to be theologically motivated.

22:10–12 See 2Ki 11:1–3. In the history of Judah, Athaliah represents the only break in the continuity of the Davidic dynasty; she is the only queen of Judah to rule in her own name (841–835 B.C.). Her attempt to wipe out the royal family repeated the action of her husband Jehoram (21:4). It threatened the continuity of the Davidic dynasty, and if she had succeeded, Judah may have been claimed by the dynasty of Omri in the north since Athaliah was from that dynasty and had no living son and heir.

22:11 *wife of the priest Jehoiada.* Not noted in Kings.

23:1—24:27 See 2Ki 11:4—12:21 and notes. The Chronicler divides the reign of Joash (835–796 B.C.) into three parts: (1) the recovery of the throne for the house of David (ch. 23); (2) Joash and Jehoiada—the good years (24:1–16); (3) Joash alone—the bad years (24:17–27). The last section is largely unique to Chronicles and further develops the theme of immediate retribution: Once again chronological notes provide the framework for cycles of obedience and disobedience (24:15–17,23); see notes on 12:2; 14:2—16:14.

23:1–21 See 2Ki 11:4–20. The Chronicler has followed his source rather closely but has introduced material reflecting his own concerns in three areas: (1) The account in Kings has more to say about the participation of the military in the coup; the Chronicler adds material emphasizing the presence of temple officials and their role (vv. 2,6,8,13,18–19). (2) The Chronicler stresses the widespread popular support for the coup by mentioning the presence of large groups of people, such as "all the people" or "the whole assembly" (vv. 3,5–6, 8,10,16–17). (3) The Chronicler shows additional concern for the sanctity of the temple area by inserting notes showing the steps taken to ensure that only qualified personnel enter the temple precincts (vv. 5–6,19).

23:1 *Azariah ... Elishaphat.* The Chronicler names the commanders, which was not done in Kings, but he does not mention the Carites, mercenaries who served as a royal guard (see note on 2Ki 11:4). Verse 20 exhibits the same omission (cf. 2Ki 11:19). The Chronicler's motive may have been his concern that only authorized persons enter the temple precincts.

23:2 *the Levites and the heads of Israelite families.* Reflects both the Chronicler's concerns with the temple personnel and the widespread support for the coup against Athaliah.

When they came to Jerusalem, 3the whole
assembly made a covenant[x] with the king
at the temple of God.
Jehoiada said to them, "The king's son
shall reign, as the LORD promised concerning the descendants of David.[y] 4Now this is
what you are to do: A third of you priests
and Levites who are going on duty on the
Sabbath are to keep watch at the doors, 5a
third of you at the royal palace and a third
at the Foundation Gate, and all the other men are to be in the courtyards of the
temple of the LORD. 6No one is to enter the
temple of the LORD except the priests and
Levites on duty; they may enter because
they are consecrated, but all the other men
are to guard[z] what the LORD has assigned
to them.[a] 7The Levites are to station themselves around the king, each man with his
weapons in his hand. Anyone who enters
the temple must be put to death. Stay close
to the king wherever he goes."
8The Levites and all the men of Judah
did just as Jehoiada the priest ordered.[a]
Each one took his men—those who were
going on duty on the Sabbath and those
who were going off duty—for Jehoiada
the priest had not released any of the divisions.[b] 9Then he gave the commanders
of units of a hundred the spears and the
large and small shields that had belonged
to King David and that were in the temple
of God. 10He stationed all the men, each
with his weapon in his hand, around
the king—near the altar and the temple,
from the south side to the north side of
the temple.
11Jehoiada and his sons brought out the
king's son and put the crown on him; they
presented him with a copy[c] of the covenant
and proclaimed him king. They anointed
him and shouted, "Long live the king!"
12When Athaliah heard the noise of the
people running and cheering the king, she
went to them at the temple of the LORD.
13She looked, and there was the king,[d]
standing by his pillar[e] at the entrance. The
officers and the trumpeters were beside the
king, and all the people of the land were
rejoicing and blowing trumpets, and singers with musical instruments were leading
the praises. Then Athaliah tore her robes
and shouted, "Treason! Treason!"

23:3 [x] S 2Ki 11:17 [y] S 2Sa 7:12; S 1Ki 2:4; S 2Ch 6:16; S 7:18; S 21:7 **23:6** [z] Zec 3:7 **23:8** [a] 2Ki 11:9 [b] S 1Ch 24:1 **23:11** [c] Dt 17:18 **23:13** [d] 1Ki 1:41 [e] S 1Ki 7:15 **23:15** [f] Jer 31:40 **23:16** [g] 2Ch 29:10; 34:31; Ne 9:38 **23:17** [h] Dt 13:6-9 **23:18** [i] S 1Ch 23:28-32 [j] S 1Ch 23:6; S 25:6 **23:19** [k] 1Ch 9:22 **23:20** [l] S 2Ki 15:35 **23:21** [m] S 2Ch 22:1 **24:2** [n] 2Ch 25:2; 26:5

14Jehoiada the priest sent out the commanders of units of a hundred, who were
in charge of the troops, and said to them:
"Bring her out between the ranks[b] and put
to the sword anyone who follows her."
For the priest had said, "Do not put her to
death at the temple of the LORD." 15So they
seized her as she reached the entrance of
the Horse Gate[f] on the palace grounds,
and there they put her to death.
16Jehoiada then made a covenant[g] that
he and the people and the king[c] would be
the LORD's people. 17All the people went to
the temple of Baal and tore it down. They
smashed the altars and idols and killed[h]
Mattan the priest of Baal in front of the
altars.
18Then Jehoiada placed the oversight of
the temple of the LORD in the hands of the
priests, who were Levites,[i] to whom David had made assignments in the temple,[j]
to present the burnt offerings of the LORD
as written in the Law of Moses, with rejoicing and singing, as David had ordered.
19He also stationed doorkeepers[k] at the
gates of the LORD's temple so that no one
who was in any way unclean might enter.
20He took with him the commanders
of hundreds, the nobles, the rulers of the
people and all the people of the land and
brought the king down from the temple
of the LORD. They went into the palace
through the Upper Gate[l] and seated the
king on the royal throne, 21and all the people of the land rejoiced. And the city was
quiet, because Athaliah had been slain
with the sword.[m]

Joash Repairs the Temple

24:1-14pp — 2Ki 12:1-16
24:23-27pp — 2Ki 12:17-21

24 Joash was seven years old when he
became king, and he reigned in Jerusalem forty years. His mother's name
was Zibiah; she was from Beersheba. 2Jo-
ash did what was right in the eyes of the
LORD[n] all the years of Jehoiada the priest.
3Jehoiada chose two wives for him, and he
had sons and daughters.

[a] 6 Or *to observe the LORD's command ⌞not to enter⌟*
[b] 14 Or *out from the precincts* [c] 16 Or *covenant between ⌞the LORD,⌟ and the people and the king that they* (see 2 Kings 11:17)

23:3 *as the LORD promised.* See 2Sa 7:11–16.
23:11 *copy of the covenant.* May refer to the covenant sworn by the assembly (vv. 1,3; cf. v. 16) or to the law of God, by which the king was to rule (see Dt 17:18–20). See note on 2Ki 11:12. *Long live the king!* See note on Ps 62:4.
23:13 *singers with musical instruments.* The Chronicler adds a word (not found in 2Ki 11:14) about the presence of Levitical musicians, who were leading the praises (see note on 1Ch 6:31–48).
23:18–19 The Chronicler adds information on the temple ritual and the guards at the gates (see note on vv. 1–21).
23:20 See note on v. 1.
24:1–14 See 2Ki 12:1–17 and notes.
24:1 *forty years.* 835–796 B.C.
24:2 Provides the outline for the Chronicler's treatment of Joash—the good years while Jehoiada was alive (vv. 1–16), and the turn to evil after his death (vv. 17–27). See note on 25:2.
24:3 Another expression of the Chronicler's conviction that large families represent the blessing of God (see v. 27; see also note on 1Ch 25:5).

[4]Some time later Joash decided to restore the temple of the LORD. [5]He called together the priests and Levites and said to them, "Go to the towns of Judah and collect the money[o] due annually from all Israel,[p] to repair the temple of your God. Do it now." But the Levites[q] did not act at once.

[6]Therefore the king summoned Jehoiada the chief priest and said to him, "Why haven't you required the Levites to bring in from Judah and Jerusalem the tax imposed by Moses the servant of the LORD and by the assembly of Israel for the Tent of the Testimony?"[r]

[7]Now the sons of that wicked woman Athaliah had broken into the temple of God and had used even its sacred objects for the Baals.

[8]At the king's command, a chest was made and placed outside, at the gate of the temple of the LORD. [9]A proclamation was then issued in Judah and Jerusalem that they should bring to the LORD the tax that Moses the servant of God had required of Israel in the desert. [10]All the officials and all the people brought their contributions gladly,[s] dropping them into the chest until it was full. [11]Whenever the chest was brought in by the Levites to the king's officials and they saw that there was a large amount of money, the royal secretary and the officer of the chief priest would come and empty the chest and carry it back to its place. They did this regularly and collected a great amount of money. [12]The king and Jehoiada gave it to the men who carried out the work required for the temple of the LORD. They hired[t] masons and carpenters to restore the LORD's temple, and also workers in iron and bronze to repair the temple.

[13]The men in charge of the work were diligent, and the repairs progressed under them. They rebuilt the temple of God according to its original design and reinforced it. [14]When they had finished, they brought the rest of the money to the king and Jehoiada, and with it were made articles for the LORD's temple: articles for the service and for the burnt offerings, and also dishes and other objects of gold and silver. As long as Jehoiada lived, burnt offerings were presented continually in the temple of the LORD.

[15]Now Jehoiada was old and full of years, and he died at the age of a hundred and thirty. [16]He was buried with the kings in the City of David, because of the good he had done in Israel for God and his temple.

The Wickedness of Joash

[17]After the death of Jehoiada, the officials of Judah came and paid homage to the king, and he listened to them. [18]They abandoned[u] the temple of the LORD, the God of their fathers, and worshiped Asherah poles and idols.[v] Because of their guilt, God's anger[w] came upon Judah and Jerusalem. [19]Although the LORD sent prophets to the people to bring them back to him, and though they testified against them, they would not listen.[x]

[20]Then the Spirit[y] of God came upon Zechariah[z] son of Jehoiada the priest. He stood before the people and said, "This is what God says: 'Why do you disobey the LORD's commands? You will not prosper.[a] Because you have forsaken the LORD, he has forsaken[b] you.' "

[21]But they plotted against him, and by order of the king they stoned[c] him to death[d] in the courtyard of the LORD's temple.[e] [22]King Joash did not remember the kindness Zechariah's father Jehoiada had shown him but killed his son, who said as he lay dying, "May the LORD see this and call you to account."[f]

[23]At the turn of the year,[a] the army of

[a] 23 Probably in the spring

24:5 [o] S Ex 30:16; Ne 10:32-33; Mt 17:24 [p] 1Ch 11:1 [q] S 1Ch 26:20
24:6 [r] S Ex 38:21
24:10 [s] S Ex 25:2; S 1Ch 29:3,6,9
24:12 [t] 2Ch 34:11
24:18 [u] S Jos 24:20; S 2Ch 7:19 [v] S Ex 34:13; 2Ch 33:3; Jer 17:2 [w] S 2Ch 19:2
24:19 [x] S Nu 11:29; Jer 7:25; Zec 1:4
24:20 [y] S Jdg 3:10; S 1Ch 12:18 [z] Mt 23:35; Lk 11:51 [a] Nu 14:41 [b] S Dt 31:17
24:21 [c] S Jos 7:25 [d] Jer 26:21 [e] Jer 20:2
24:22 [f] S Ge 9:5

24:4 *restore the temple.* The vandalism and atrocities of Athaliah (v. 7) required the refurbishing of the temple.

24:5 The writer of 2 Kings speaks of three different sources of revenue (2Ki 12:4–5), whereas the Chronicler mentions only the census tax (see Ex 30:14; 38:26; Mt 17:24). The reason for the tardiness of the priests is not stated (see 2Ki 12:6–8). The writer of Kings notes that the audience with the priests takes place in the 23rd year of Joash's reign, when he is presumably no longer the ward of Jehoiada. Resistance on the part of the priests to the reassignment of the temple revenues for repair work may be the underlying cause.

24:8 *chest.* Mesopotamian texts speak of a similar offering box placed in temples. Representatives of both the king and the temple officials administered temple revenues (see note on 1Ch 26:20).

24:14 See 2Ki 12:13–14. *As long as Jehoiada lived.* An additional note on the part of the Chronicler to introduce the turn to the worse in the reign of Joash upon Jehoiada's death (vv. 15–16).

24:15–22 This section is unique to the Chronicler and shows his emphasis on immediate retribution (see note on 23:1—24:27). After a period of righteous rule until the death of Jehoiada, Joash turns to idolatry and murders Jehoiada's son. In the following year he is invaded and defeated by Aram because Judah, under his leadership, "had forsaken the LORD" (v. 24).

24:18,20,24 *abandoned … forsaken … forsaken … forsaken.* The Hebrew word is the same in these verses; it is a verb frequently used by the Chronicler to denote the reason for divine punishment (see note on 12:1; see also 7:19,22; 12:5; 13:10–11; 15:2; 21:10; 24:18,20,24; 28:6; 29:6; 34:25; 1Ch 28:9,20).

24:19 *Although the LORD sent prophets.* Israel's failure to heed the Lord's prophets ultimately led to her destruction (see 36:16; cf. 20:20; see also Introduction to 1 Chronicles: Purpose and Themes).

24:20 *Zechariah.* See note on Mt 23:35.

Aram marched against Joash; it invaded
Judah and Jerusalem and killed all the
leaders of the people.[g] They sent all the
plunder to their king in Damascus. 24Al-
though the Aramean army had come with
only a few men,[h] the LORD delivered into
their hands a much larger army.[i] Because
Judah had forsaken the LORD, the God of
their fathers, judgment was executed on
Joash. 25When the Arameans withdrew,
they left Joash severely wounded. His officials conspired against him for murdering
the son of Jehoiada the priest, and they
killed him in his bed. So he died and was
buried[j] in the City of David, but not in the
tombs of the kings.
26Those who conspired against him were
Zabad,[a] son of Shimeath an Ammonite
woman, and Jehozabad, son of Shimrith[b][k]
a Moabite woman.[l] 27The account of his
sons, the many prophecies about him, and
the record of the restoration of the temple
of God are written in the annotations on
the book of the kings. And Amaziah his
son succeeded him as king.

Amaziah King of Judah

25:1-4pp — 2Ki 14:1-6
25:11-12pp — 2Ki 14:7
25:17-28pp — 2Ki 14:8-20

25 Amaziah was twenty-five years old
when he became king, and he reigned
in Jerusalem twenty-nine years. His mother's name was Jehoaddin[c]; she was from
Jerusalem. 2He did what was right in the
eyes of the LORD, but not wholeheartedly.[m] 3After the kingdom was firmly in his
control, he executed the officials who had
murdered his father the king. 4Yet he did
not put their sons to death, but acted in accordance with what is written in the Law,
in the Book of Moses,[n] where the LORD
commanded: "Fathers shall not be put to
death for their children, nor children put
to death for their fathers; each is to die for
his own sins."[d][o]
5Amaziah called the people of Judah
together and assigned them according to
their families to commanders of thousands
and commanders of hundreds for all Judah
and Benjamin. He then mustered[p] those
twenty years old[q] or more and found that
there were three hundred thousand men
ready for military service,[r] able to handle
the spear and shield. 6He also hired a hundred thousand fighting men from Israel for
a hundred talents[e] of silver.
7But a man of God came to him and
said, "O king, these troops from Israel[s]
must not march with you, for the LORD is
not with Israel—not with any of the people of Ephraim. 8Even if you go and fight
courageously in battle, God will overthrow
you before the enemy, for God has the
power to help or to overthrow."[t]
9Amaziah asked the man of God, "But
what about the hundred talents I paid for
these Israelite troops?"
The man of God replied, "The LORD can
give you much more than that."[u]
10So Amaziah dismissed the troops who
had come to him from Ephraim and sent
them home. They were furious with Judah
and left for home in a great rage.[v]
11Amaziah then marshaled his strength
and led his army to the Valley of Salt,
where he killed ten thousand men of Seir.
12The army of Judah also captured ten
thousand men alive, took them to the top
of a cliff and threw them down so that all
were dashed to pieces.[w]

24:23 [g]2Ki 12:17-18
24:24 [h]S 2Ch 14:9; 16:8; 20:2, 12 [i]Lev 26:23-25; Dt 28:25
24:25 [j]S 2Ch 21:20
24:26 [k]2Ki 12:21 [l]S Ru 1:4
25:2 [m]S 1Ki 8:61; S 2Ch 24:2
25:4 [n]S Dt 28:61 [o]S Nu 26:11
25:5 [p]S 2Sa 24:2 [q]S Ex 30:14 [r]S 1Ch 21:1; 2Ch 17:14-19
25:7 [s]S 2Ch 16:2-9; S 19:1-3
25:8 [t]S 2Ch 14:11; S 20:6
25:9 [u]Dt 8:18; Pr 10:22
25:10 [v]ver 13
25:12 [w]Ps 141:6; Ob 1:3

[a] *26* A variant of *Jozabad* [b] *26* A variant of *Shomer* [c] *1* Hebrew *Jehoaddan,* a variant of *Jehoaddin* [d] *4* Deut. 24:16 [e] *6* That is, about 3 3/4 tons (about 3.4 metric tons); also in verse 9

24:24 *only a few men.* Just as God had helped the small army of Judah against overwhelming odds when the king and people were faithful to him (14:8–9; 20:2,12), so now in their unfaithfulness they are defeated by a much smaller force of invaders (see note on 20:30).
24:25 *for murdering ... they killed him.* Only the Chronicler mentions that this assassination was revenge for the murder of Zechariah. *not in the tombs of the kings.* Burial in the tombs of the kings was an honor accorded to Jehoiada (v. 16), but withheld from his rebellious ward Joash (see note on 21:20).
24:26 *an Ammonite ... a Moabite.* Information not given in Kings but important to the Chronicler (see note on 20:1–30).
24:27 *annotations on the book of the kings.* See Introduction to 1 Chronicles: Author, Date and Sources.
25:1–28 Typically, the Chronicler divides the reign of Amaziah into two parts: (1) the good years, marked by obedience, divine blessing and victory (vv. 1–13), and (2) the bad years of idolatry, defeat and regicide (vv. 14–28). See 2Ki 14:1–20 and notes.
25:1 *twenty-nine years.* 796–767 B.C.
25:2 The Chronicler does not indicate that Amaziah failed to remove the high places, which continued to be used as places for sacrifice by the people (see 2Ki 14:4). Also compare 24:2 with 2Ki 12:2–4, and 26:4 with 2Ki 15:3–4. The writer appears to be motivated by his outline, which covered the good years first and then the reversion to evil. Negative comments about these kings are held to the second half of the account of their reigns, whereas in Kings the summary judgment about their reigns and the high places is given immediately.
25:5–16 An expansion of 2Ki 14:7. The book of Kings mentions the successful war with Edom only as a prelude to Amaziah's challenge to Jehoash, but the Chronicler sets it in the framework of his emphasis on immediate retribution: Obedience brings victory over Edom, while the subsequent idolatry (vv. 14–16) brings defeat in the campaign against Israel. By expanding his account the Chronicler gives the theological reason for both the victory over Edom and the defeat before Israel.
25:7 *troops from Israel must not march with you.* Another instance of the Chronicler's condemnation of alliances that imply lack of trust in the Lord (see notes on 16:2–9; 22:5). Cf. other prophetic speeches that call on the people to trust in God (20:15–17,20; 32:7–8).

13 Meanwhile the troops that Amaziah
had sent back and had not allowed to take
part in the war raided Judean towns from
Samaria to Beth Horon. They killed three
thousand people and carried off great
quantities of plunder.
14 When Amaziah returned from slaughtering the Edomites, he brought back the
gods of the people of Seir. He set them up
as his own gods,[x] bowed down to them
and burned sacrifices to them. 15 The anger of the LORD burned against Amaziah,
and he sent a prophet to him, who said,
"Why do you consult this people's gods,
which could not save[y] their own people
from your hand?"
16 While he was still speaking, the king
said to him, "Have we appointed you an
adviser to the king? Stop! Why be struck
down?"
So the prophet stopped but said, "I
know that God has determined to destroy
you, because you have done this and have
not listened to my counsel."
17 After Amaziah king of Judah consulted his advisers, he sent this challenge
to Jehoash[a] son of Jehoahaz, the son of
Jehu, king of Israel: "Come, meet me face
to face."
18 But Jehoash king of Israel replied to
Amaziah king of Judah: "A thistle[z] in Lebanon sent a message to a cedar in Lebanon, 'Give your daughter to my son in
marriage.' Then a wild beast in Lebanon
came along and trampled the thistle underfoot. 19 You say to yourself that you have
defeated Edom, and now you are arrogant
and proud. But stay at home! Why ask for
trouble and cause your own downfall and
that of Judah also?"
20 Amaziah, however, would not listen,
for God so worked that he might hand
them over to ⌞Jehoash⌟, because they
sought the gods of Edom.[a] 21 So Jehoash
king of Israel attacked. He and Amaziah
king of Judah faced each other at Beth
Shemesh in Judah. 22 Judah was routed by
Israel, and every man fled to his home.
23 Jehoash king of Israel captured Amaziah king of Judah, the son of Joash, the
son of Ahaziah,[b] at Beth Shemesh. Then
Jehoash brought him to Jerusalem and
broke down the wall of Jerusalem from
the Ephraim Gate[b] to the Corner Gate[c]—a
section about six hundred feet[c] long. 24 He
took all the gold and silver and all the articles found in the temple of God that had
been in the care of Obed-Edom,[d] together
with the palace treasures and the hostages, and returned to Samaria.
25 Amaziah son of Joash king of Judah
lived for fifteen years after the death of
Jehoash son of Jehoahaz king of Israel.
26 As for the other events of Amaziah's
reign, from beginning to end, are they not
written in the book of the kings of Judah
and Israel? 27 From the time that Amaziah
turned away from following the LORD, they
conspired against him in Jerusalem and he
fled to Lachish[e], but they sent men after
him to Lachish and killed him there. 28 He
was brought back by horse and was buried with his fathers in the City of Judah.

25:14 [x] Ex 20:3; 2Ch 28:23; Isa 44:15
25:15 [y] Isa 36:20
25:18 [z] Jdg 9:8-15
25:20 [a] S 2Ch 10:15
25:23 [b] 2Ki 14:13; Ne 8:16; 12:39 [c] 2Ch 26:9; Jer 31:38
25:24 [d] S 1Ch 26:15
25:27 [e] S Jos 10:3
26:1 [f] S 2Ch 22:1

Uzziah King of Judah

26:1-4pp — 2Ki 14:21-22; 15:1-3
26:21-23pp — 2Ki 15:5-7

26 Then all the people of Judah[f] took
Uzziah,[d] who was sixteen years old,
and made him king in place of his father
Amaziah. 2 He was the one who rebuilt
Elath and restored it to Judah after Ama-
ziah rested with his fathers.

[a] 17 Hebrew *Joash,* a variant of *Jehoash*; also in verses 18, 21, 23 and 25 [b] 23 Hebrew *Jehoahaz,* a variant of *Ahaziah* [c] 23 Hebrew *four hundred cubits* (about 180 meters) [d] 1 Also called *Azariah*

25:13 This may be the inciting incident for the later war with the north. *Samaria.* A town by this name in the southern kingdom is not otherwise known. The reference may be a copyist's error.

25:14 – 25 The Chronicler's account of the war with the north is close to the parallel in 2Ki 14:8 – 14, except for some additions in line with his theme of immediate retribution. The Chronicler mentions Amaziah's foolish idolatry and the prophetic speech of judgment, neither of which is found in Kings. He also adds notes in vv. 20,27 to emphasize that the idolatry of Amaziah was being punished.

25:18 Cf. the parable in Jdg 9:7 – 15.

25:23 *Ephraim Gate to the Corner Gate.* Both gates were located in the northern wall of the city, the Ephraim Gate at the northwest and the Corner Gate at the northeast.

25:24 The family of Obed-Edom was the Levitical family into whose care the temple storehouse had been entrusted (1Ch 26:15; cf. 2Sa 6:10 and note).

25:27 See note on vv. 14 – 25.

25:28 *City of Judah.* A later name for the City of David (2Ki 14:20).

26:1 – 23 See 2Ki 15:1 – 7 and notes. The Chronicler characteristically divides his account of Uzziah's reign into two parts: the good years, then the bad; cf. his treatment of Uzziah's father Amaziah and his grandfather Joash (see notes on 24:2; 25:1 – 28). The Chronicler elaborates on the blessings and divine help that flowed from Uzziah's obedience and fidelity (vv. 4 – 15), whereas the author of Kings only alludes to his fidelity (2Ki 15:3). Where Kings only mentions Uzziah's leprosy (2Ki 15:5), the Chronicler gives additional details to show that the disease was a result of unfaithfulness (vv. 16 – 21). Under Uzziah and his contemporary in the north, Jeroboam II, the borders of Israel and Judah briefly reached the extent they had attained under David and Solomon (vv. 6 – 8; 2Ki 14:25). In part, this flourishing of the two kingdoms was facilitated by the removal of the Aramean threat by Assyria under Adadnirari III (802 B.C.), following which Assyria herself went into a period of weakness.

26:1 *Uzziah.* See NIV text note (see also, e.g., 2Ki 15:6 – 7; 1Ch 3:12). It is likely that Uzziah was a throne name, while Azariah was his personal name.

3Uzziah was sixteen years old when he
became king, and he reigned in Jerusalem
fifty-two years. His mother's name was
Jecoliah; she was from Jerusalem. 4He did
what was right in the eyes of the LORD,
just as his father Amaziah had done. 5He
sought God during the days of Zechariah,
who instructed him in the fear[a] of God.[g]
As long as he sought the LORD, God gave
him success.[h]
6He went to war against the Philistines[i]
and broke down the walls of Gath, Jabneh
and Ashdod.[j] He then rebuilt towns near
Ashdod and elsewhere among the Philistines. 7God helped him against the Philistines and against the Arabs[k] who lived in
Gur Baal and against the Meunites.[l] 8The
Ammonites[m] brought tribute to Uzziah,
and his fame spread as far as the border
of Egypt, because he had become very
powerful.
9Uzziah built towers in Jerusalem at
the Corner Gate,[n] at the Valley Gate[o] and
at the angle of the wall, and he fortified
them. 10He also built towers in the desert
and dug many cisterns, because he had
much livestock in the foothills and in the
plain. He had people working his fields
and vineyards in the hills and in the fertile
lands, for he loved the soil.
11Uzziah had a well-trained army, ready
to go out by divisions according to their
numbers as mustered by Jeiel the secretary
and Maaseiah the officer under the direction of Hananiah, one of the royal officials.
12The total number of family leaders over
the fighting men was 2,600. 13Under their
command was an army of 307,500 men
trained for war, a powerful force to support the king against his enemies. 14Uz-
ziah provided shields, spears, helmets,
coats of armor, bows and slingstones for
the entire army.[p] 15In Jerusalem he made
machines designed by skillful men for use
on the towers and on the corner defenses to shoot arrows and hurl large stones.
His fame spread far and wide, for he was
greatly helped until he became powerful.
16But after Uzziah became powerful, his
pride[q] led to his downfall.[r] He was unfaithful[s] to the LORD his God, and entered
the temple of the LORD to burn incense[t] on
the altar of incense. 17Azariah[u] the priest
with eighty other courageous priests of the
LORD followed him in. 18They confronted
him and said, "It is not right for you, Uzziah, to burn incense to the LORD. That is for
the priests,[v] the descendants[w] of Aaron,[x]
who have been consecrated to burn incense.[y] Leave the sanctuary, for you have
been unfaithful; and you will not be honored by the LORD God."
19Uzziah, who had a censer in his hand
ready to burn incense, became angry.
While he was raging at the priests in their
presence before the incense altar in the
LORD's temple, leprosy[b][z] broke out on his
forehead. 20When Azariah the chief priest
and all the other priests looked at him,
they saw that he had leprosy on his forehead, so they hurried him out. Indeed, he
himself was eager to leave, because the
LORD had afflicted him.
21King Uzziah had leprosy until the
day he died. He lived in a separate
house[c][a]—leprous, and excluded from the
temple of the LORD. Jotham his son had
charge of the palace and governed the
people of the land.
22The other events of Uzziah's reign,
from beginning to end, are recorded by

26:5 [g]S 2Ch 24:2 [h]2Ch 27:6 **26:6** [i]Isa 2:6; 11:14; 14:29; Jer 25:20 [j]Am 1:8; 3:9 **26:7** [k]S 2Ch 21:16 [l]2Ch 20:1 **26:8** [m]S Ge 19:38 **26:9** [n]S 2Ki 14:13; S 2Ch 25:23 [o]Ne 2:13; 3:13 **26:14** [p]Jer 46:4 **26:16** [q]S 2Ki 14:10 [r]Dt 32:15 [s]S 1Ch 5:25 [t]2Ki 16:12 **26:17** [u]S 1Ki 4:2 **26:18** [v]Nu 16:39 [w]Nu 18:1-7 [x]S Ex 30:7 [y]S 1Ch 6:49 **26:19** [z]S Nu 12:10 **26:21** [a]S Ex 4:6; Lev 13:46; S 14:8; Nu 5:2; S 19:12

[a] 5 Many Hebrew manuscripts, Septuagint and Syriac; other Hebrew manuscripts *vision* [b] 19 The Hebrew word was used for various diseases affecting the skin—not necessarily leprosy; also in verses 20, 21 and 23. [c] 21 Or *in a house where he was relieved of responsibilities*

26:3 *fifty-two years.* 792–740 B.C., including a coregency with Amaziah from 792 to 767.

26:4 The Chronicler constructs his account of Uzziah's reign to give it the same outline as that for Amaziah and Joash (see note on vv. 1–23). He also once again bypasses the statement in the parallel account that the king did not remove the high places (2Ki 15:4), just as he does in the accounts of the other two kings (see note on 25:2).

26:5 *days of Zechariah.* The author again uses chronological notes to portray the cycles of blessing and judgment associated with the individual king's response to God's commands (see note on 12:2).

26:6–8 Uzziah's conquests were toward the southeast and the southwest; Israel's powerful Jeroboam II was in control to the north of Judah.

26:7 *Meunites.* See note on 20:1.

26:9 *Corner Gate … Valley Gate.* Found at the northeast and southwest portions of the walls. *fortified.* This construction along the wall of Jerusalem may reflect, in part, repair of the damage done by Jehoash during the reign of Amaziah (25:23).

26:10 *towers … cisterns.* Towers and cisterns have been found in several excavations (Qumran, Gibeah, Beersheba). A seal bearing Uzziah's name has been found in a cistern at Tell Beit Mirsim.

26:11 *Uzziah had a well-trained army.* Tiglath-Pileser III of Assyria states that he was opposed in his advance toward the west (743 B.C.) by a coalition headed by "Azriau of Yaudi," perhaps Azariah (Uzziah) of Judah.

26:15 *machines … shoot arrows and hurl large stones.* Since the catapult was not known in the military technology of the period, and since torsion-operated devices for shooting arrows did not appear for approximately another three centuries, the devices mentioned here may refer to defensive constructions to protect those shooting arrows and hurling stones from the tops of the walls.

26:16 *after Uzziah became powerful.* See note on v. 5.

26:19 *leprosy.* See note on Lev 13:2; for disease as a punishment for sin see notes on 16:12; 21:12–15.

26:21 *Uzziah … died.* See Isa 6:1 and note. *separate house.* See NIV text note; the same phrase in the Canaanite texts from Ugarit suggests a kind of quarantine or separation.

26:22 *recorded by … Isaiah.* Not a reference to the canonical book but to some other work no longer in existence.

the prophet Isaiah[b] son of Amoz. [23]Uzziah[c] rested with his fathers and was buried near them in a field for burial that belonged to the kings, for people said, "He had leprosy." And Jotham his son succeeded him as king.[d]

Jotham King of Judah

27:1-4,7-9pp — 2Ki 15:33-38

27 Jotham[e] was twenty-five years old when he became king, and he reigned in Jerusalem sixteen years. His mother's name was Jerusha daughter of Zadok. [2]He did what was right in the eyes of the LORD, just as his father Uzziah had done, but unlike him he did not enter the temple of the LORD. The people, however, continued their corrupt practices. [3]Jotham rebuilt the Upper Gate of the temple of the LORD and did extensive work on the wall at the hill of Ophel.[f] [4]He built towns in the Judean hills and forts and towers in the wooded areas.

[5]Jotham made war on the king of the Ammonites[g] and conquered them. That year the Ammonites paid him a hundred talents[a] of silver, ten thousand cors[b] of wheat and ten thousand cors of barley. The Ammonites brought him the same amount also in the second and third years.

[6]Jotham grew powerful[h] because he walked steadfastly before the LORD his God.

[7]The other events in Jotham's reign, including all his wars and the other things he did, are written in the book of the kings of Israel and Judah. [8]He was twenty-five years old when he became king, and he reigned in Jerusalem sixteen years. [9]Jotham rested with his fathers and was buried in the City of David. And Ahaz his son succeeded him as king.

26:22 [b] 2Ki 15:1; Isa 1:1; 6:1
26:23 [c] Isa 1:1; 6:1 [d] S 2Ki 14:21; Am 1:1
27:1 [e] S 2Ki 15:5,32; S 1Ch 3:12
27:3 [f] 2Ch 33:14; Ne 3:26
27:5 [g] S Ge 19:38
27:6 [h] 2Ch 26:5
28:1 [i] S 1Ch 3:13; Isa 1:1
28:2 [j] Ex 34:17
28:3 [k] S Jos 15:8 [l] S Lev 18:21; S 2Ki 3:27; Eze 20:26 [m] S Dt 18:9; 2Ch 33:2
28:5 [n] Isa 7:1
28:6 [o] S 2Ki 15:25,27 [p] ver 8; Isa 9:21; 11:13

Ahaz King of Judah

28:1-27pp — 2Ki 16:1-20

28 Ahaz[i] was twenty years old when he became king, and he reigned in Jerusalem sixteen years. Unlike David his father, he did not do what was right in the eyes of the LORD. [2]He walked in the ways of the kings of Israel and also made cast idols[j] for worshiping the Baals. [3]He burned sacrifices in the Valley of Ben Hinnom[k] and sacrificed his sons[l] in the fire, following the detestable[m] ways of the nations the LORD had driven out before the Israelites. [4]He offered sacrifices and burned incense at the high places, on the hilltops and under every spreading tree.

[5]Therefore the LORD his God handed him over to the king of Aram.[n] The Arameans defeated him and took many of his people as prisoners and brought them to Damascus.

He was also given into the hands of the king of Israel, who inflicted heavy casualties on him. [6]In one day Pekah[o] son of Remaliah killed a hundred and twenty thousand soldiers in Judah[p]—because Judah had forsaken the LORD, the God of their fathers. [7]Zicri, an Ephraimite warrior, killed Maaseiah the king's son, Azrikam the officer in charge of the palace, and El-

[a] 5 That is, about 3 3/4 tons (about 3.4 metric tons)
[b] 5 That is, probably about 62,000 bushels (about 2,200 kiloliters)

26:23 *buried ... in a field ... that belonged to the kings.* Cf. 2Ki 15:7. Apparently due to his leprosy, Uzziah was buried in a cemetery belonging to the kings, though not in the tombs of the kings.

27:1-9 See 2Ki 15:32-38 and notes.

27:1 *sixteen years.* 750-735 B.C., including a coregency with Uzziah (750-740). His reign also overlapped that of his successor Ahaz from 735 to 732.

27:2 *did not enter the temple.* The Chronicler commends Jotham for not making the same error Uzziah did (26:16). *corrupt practices.* Appears to refer to the flourishing high places (2Ki 15:35).

27:3-6 Unique to the Chronicler and an elaboration of his thesis that fidelity to God's commands brings blessing: in construction, military victory and prosperity—all "because he walked steadfastly before the LORD" (v. 6). Judah's relationship with the Ammonites held particular interest for the Chronicler (see notes on 20:1-30; 24:26).

27:7 *all his wars.* See, e.g., 2Ki 15:37.

28:1-27 See 2Ki 16:1-20 and notes, though only the introduction and conclusion in the two accounts are strictly parallel. The reign of Ahaz is the only one for which the Chronicler does not mention a single redeeming feature. In his account the Chronicler appears to adopt explicit parallels from the speech of Abijah condemning the northern kingdom (ch. 13) in order to show that under Ahaz the southern kingdom had sunk to the same depths of apostasy. Judah's religious fidelity, of which Abijah had boasted, was completely overthrown under Ahaz.

28:1 *sixteen years.* 732-715 B.C., not including the coregency with Jotham (735-732).

28:2 *made cast idols.* Cf. 13:8. *Baals.* See notes on Jdg 2:11,13.

28:3 *Valley of Ben Hinnom.* See 33:6; see also notes on Ne 11:30; Jer 7:31. Josiah put an end to the pagan practices observed there (2Ki 23:10). *sacrificed his sons.* See Lev 20:1-5; Jer 7:31-32. 2Ki 16:3 has the singular "son." Some have regarded the plural as a deliberate inflation on the part of the Chronicler to heighten the wickedness of Ahaz. However, some manuscripts of the Septuagint (the pre-Christian Greek translation of the OT) also have a plural in 2Ki 16:3, suggesting that the Chronicler faithfully copied the text before him.

28:5 Cf. 13:16-17. *God handed him over.* According to the Chronicler's view on immediate retribution, defeat in war is one of the results of disobedience (see note on 20:30). *also given into the hands of the king of Israel.* 2Ki 16:5-6 and Isa 7 make it clear that Rezin (king of Aram) and Pekah acted together against Judah. The Chronicler has chosen either to treat them separately or to report on two different episodes of the Aram-Israel coalition.

28:6 *Pekah.* Reigned over the northern kingdom 752-732 B.C. (see 2Ki 15:27-31). *had forsaken the LORD.* The same charge Abijah made against the northern kingdom (13:11).

kanah, second to the king. 8The Israelites took captive from their kinsmen[q] two hundred thousand wives, sons and daughters. They also took a great deal of plunder, which they carried back to Samaria.[r]

9But a prophet of the LORD named Oded was there, and he went out to meet the army when it returned to Samaria. He said to them, "Because the LORD, the God of your fathers, was angry[s] with Judah, he gave them into your hand. But you have slaughtered them in a rage that reaches to heaven.[t] 10And now you intend to make the men and women of Judah and Jerusalem your slaves.[u] But aren't you also guilty of sins against the LORD your God? 11Now listen to me! Send back your fellow countrymen you have taken as prisoners, for the LORD's fierce anger rests on you.[v]"

12Then some of the leaders in Ephraim — Azariah son of Jehohanan, Berekiah son of Meshillemoth, Jehizkiah son of Shallum, and Amasa son of Hadlai — confronted those who were arriving from the war. 13"You must not bring those prisoners here," they said, "or we will be guilty before the LORD. Do you intend to add to our sin and guilt? For our guilt is already great, and his fierce anger rests on Israel."

14So the soldiers gave up the prisoners and plunder in the presence of the officials and all the assembly. 15The men designated by name took the prisoners, and from the plunder they clothed all who were naked. They provided them with clothes and sandals, food and drink,[w] and healing balm. All those who were weak they put on donkeys. So they took them back to their fellow countrymen at Jericho, the City of Palms,[x] and returned to Samaria.[y]

16At that time King Ahaz sent to the king[a] of Assyria[z] for help. 17The Edomites[a] had again come and attacked Judah and carried away prisoners,[b] 18while the Philistines[c] had raided towns in the foothills and in the Negev of Judah. They captured and occupied Beth Shemesh, Aijalon[d] and Gederoth,[e] as well as Soco,[f] Timnah[g] and Gimzo, with their surrounding villages. 19The LORD had humbled Judah because of Ahaz king of Israel,[b] for he had promoted wickedness in Judah and had been most unfaithful[h] to the LORD. 20Tiglath-Pileser[c][i] king of Assyria[j] came to him, but he gave him trouble[k] instead of help.[l] 21Ahaz[m] took some of the things from the temple of the LORD and from the royal palace and from the princes and presented them to the king of Assyria, but that did not help him.[n]

22In his time of trouble King Ahaz became even more unfaithful[o] to the LORD. 23He offered sacrifices to the gods[p] of Damascus, who had defeated him; for he thought, "Since the gods of the kings of Aram have helped them, I will sacrifice to them so they will help me."[q] But they were his downfall and the downfall of all Israel.[r]

24Ahaz gathered together the furnishings[s] from the temple of God[t] and took them away.[d] He shut the doors[u] of the LORD's temple and set up altars[v] at every street corner in Jerusalem. 25In every town in Judah he built high places to burn sacrifices to other gods and provoked the LORD, the God of his fathers, to anger.

26The other events of his reign and all his ways, from beginning to end, are written in the book of the kings of Judah and Israel. 27Ahaz rested[w] with his fathers and was buried[x] in the city of Jerusalem, but

[a] *16* One Hebrew manuscript, Septuagint and Vulgate (see also 2 Kings 16:7); most Hebrew manuscripts *kings*
[b] *19* That is, Judah, as frequently in 2 Chronicles
[c] *20* Hebrew *Tilgath-Pilneser,* a variant of *Tiglath-Pileser*
[d] *24* Or *and cut them up*

28:8 [q] Dt 28:25-41 [r] 2Ch 29:9
28:9 [s] Isa 10:6; 47:6; Zec 1:15 [t] Ezr 9:6; Rev 18:5
28:10 [u] Lev 25:39-46
28:11 [v] 2Ch 11:4
28:15 [w] 2Ki 6:22; Pr 25:21-22 [x] S Dt 34:3; S Jdg 1:16 [y] Lk 10:25-37
28:16 [z] S 2Ki 16:7; Eze 23:12
28:17 [a] Ps 137:7; Isa 34:5; 63:1; Jer 25:21; Eze 16:57; 25:12; Am 1:11 [b] 2Ch 29:9
28:18 [c] Isa 9:12; 11:14; Jer 25:20; Eze 16:27,57; 25:15 [d] S Jos 10:12 [e] Jos 15:41 [f] S 1Sa 17:1 [g] S Ge 38:12
28:19 [h] S 1Ch 5:25
28:20 [i] S 2Ki 15:29; S 1Ch 5:6 [j] Isa 7:17; 8:7; 10:5-6; 36:1 [k] Isa 10:20 [l] S 2Ki 16:7
28:21 [m] S 2Ch 16:2-9 [n] Jer 2:36
28:22 [o] Jer 5:3; 15:7; 17:23
28:23 [p] S 2Ch 25:14 [q] Isa 10:20; Jer 44:17-18 [r] 1Ch 11:1; Jer 18:15
28:24 [s] 2Ch 29:19 [t] S 2Ki 16:18 [u] Mal 1:10 [v] 2Ch 30:14
28:27 [w] Isa 14:28-32 [x] S 2Ch 21:20

28:9–15 The kindness of the northern captors to their captives from Judah, especially as recorded in vv. 14–15, may be the background for Jesus' parable of the Good Samaritan (Lk 10:25–37). Oded's attitude to the north is shown by his willingness to call them "fellow countrymen" (v. 11). In this case, too, the record of ch. 13 has been reversed: The northern tribes are more righteous than the south.
28:17–18 *Edomites … attacked Judah … Philistines had raided.* Foreign alliances (v. 16) led to further defeats for Ahaz (see note on 16:2–9).
28:19 *The LORD had humbled Judah because of Ahaz.* The same formula used to describe the defeat of the northern tribes in 13:18, though under Ahaz it is Judah that is subdued.
28:20 *Tiglath-Pileser.* King of Assyria 745–727 B.C. (see 1Ch 5:26 and note). *trouble instead of help.* Appears on the surface to contradict the statement in 2Ki 16:9 that Tiglath-Pileser III responded to Ahaz's request by attacking and capturing Damascus, exiling its population and killing Rezin. The Chronicler assumes the reader's familiarity with the other account and knows of the temporary respite for Judah gained by Assyrian intervention against Damascus and the northern kingdom of Israel. But he focuses on the long-range results, in which Judah herself was reduced to vassalage to Assyria.
28:22–23 The Chronicler presumes the reader's familiarity with Ahaz's trip to Damascus and his copying of the altar and practices there (2Ki 16:10–16).
28:24–25 Additional details on Ahaz's alterations are found in 2Ki 16:17–18. The Chronicler also adds details in his description of Hezekiah's reforming activities to correct some of the abuses under Ahaz: Not only had the doors been shut, but also the lamps were put out and offerings were not made at the sanctuary (29:7); the altar and utensils were desecrated, and the table for the consecrated bread was neglected (29:18–19). It is precisely these accoutrements of proper temple service about which Abijah had boasted when he proclaimed the faithfulness of Judah in contrast to that of the northern kingdom (13:11). Now these orthodox furnishings are lacking under Ahaz and make the southern kingdom just like the north (see note on vv. 1–27).
28:27 *not placed in the tombs of the kings.* The third king whose wickedness resulted in the loss of this honor at death. The others were Jehoram (21:20) and Joash (24:25). Uzziah's sin and leprosy brought the same result, though it is not reported in exactly the same terms (26:23). Cf. also Manasseh (33:20).

he was not placed in the tombs of the
kings of Israel. And Hezekiah his son succeeded him as king.

Hezekiah Purifies the Temple

29:1-2pp — 2Ki 18:2-3

29 Hezekiah[y] was twenty-five years
old when he became king, and he
reigned in Jerusalem twenty-nine years.
His mother's name was Abijah daughter
of Zechariah. 2 He did what was right in
the eyes of the LORD, just as his father David[z] had done.
3 In the first month of the first year of his
reign, he opened the doors of the temple of
the LORD and repaired[a] them. 4 He brought
in the priests and the Levites, assembled
them in the square on the east side 5 and
said: "Listen to me, Levites! Consecrate[b]
yourselves now and consecrate the temple of the LORD, the God of your fathers.
Remove all defilement from the sanctuary.
6 Our fathers[c] were unfaithful;[d] they did
evil in the eyes of the LORD our God and
forsook him. They turned their faces away
from the LORD's dwelling place and turned
their backs on him. 7 They also shut the
doors of the portico and put out the lamps.
They did not burn incense[e] or present any
burnt offerings at the sanctuary to the God
of Israel. 8 Therefore, the anger of the LORD
has fallen on Judah and Jerusalem; he has
made them an object of dread and horror[f]
and scorn,[g] as you can see with your own
eyes. 9 This is why our fathers have fall-
en by the sword and why our sons and
daughters and our wives are in captivity.[h] 10 Now I intend to make a covenant[i]
with the LORD, the God of Israel, so that
his fierce anger[j] will turn away from us.
11 My sons, do not be negligent now, for the
LORD has chosen you to stand before him
and serve him,[k] to minister[l] before him
and to burn incense."
12 Then these Levites[m] set to work:
from the Kohathites,
Mahath son of Amasai and Joel son
of Azariah;
from the Merarites,
Kish son of Abdi and Azariah son
of Jehallelel;
from the Gershonites,
Joah son of Zimmah and Eden[n] son
of Joah;
13 from the descendants of Elizaphan,[o]
Shimri and Jeiel;
from the descendants of Asaph,[p]
Zechariah and Mattaniah;
14 from the descendants of Heman,
Jehiel and Shimei;
from the descendants of Jeduthun,
Shemaiah and Uzziel.
15 When they had assembled their brothers and consecrated themselves, they went
in to purify[q] the temple of the LORD, as the
king had ordered, following the word of
the LORD. 16 The priests went into the sanctuary of the LORD to purify it. They brought
out to the courtyard of the LORD's temple
everything unclean that they found in the
temple of the LORD. The Levites took it and
carried it out to the Kidron Valley.[r] 17 They
began the consecration on the first day of
the first month, and by the eighth day of
the month they reached the portico of the
LORD. For eight more days they consecrated the temple of the LORD itself, finishing
on the sixteenth day of the first month.
18 Then they went in to King Hezekiah
and reported: "We have purified the en-

29:1 [y] S 1Ch 3:13
29:2 [z] 2Ch 34:2
29:3 [a] 2Ki 18:16
29:5 [b] S Lev 11:44; Ne 13:9
29:6 [c] Ezr 9:7; Ps 106:6-47; Jer 2:27; 18:17; Eze 23:35; Da 9:5-6 [d] S 1Ch 5:25
29:7 [e] S Ex 30:7
29:8 [f] S Dt 28:25 [g] S Lev 26:32; Jer 18:16; 19:8; 25:9,18
29:9 [h] 2Ch 28:5-8,17
29:10 [i] S 2Ki 11:17; S 2Ch 23:16 [j] S Nu 25:4; 2Ch 30:8; Ezr 10:14
29:11 [k] S Nu 3:6; 8:6,14 [l] S 1Ch 15:2
29:12 [m] S Nu 3:17-20 [n] 2Ch 31:15
29:13 [o] S Ex 6:22 [p] S 1Ch 6:39
29:15 [q] S 1Ch 23:28; S Isa 1:25
29:16 [r] S 2Sa 15:23

29:1 — 32:33 The Chronicler devotes more attention to Hezekiah than to any other post-Solomonic king. Although the parallel text (2Ki 18 – 20) has about the same amount of material, only about a fourth of the total relates the same or similar material; only a few verses are strict literary parallels (29:1 – 2; 32:32 – 33). In Kings preeminence among the post-Solomonic kings is given to Josiah (2Ki 22 – 23; cf. 1Ki 13:2), and the record of Hezekiah is primarily devoted to his confrontation with Sennacherib of Assyria. By contrast, the Chronicler highlights almost exclusively Hezekiah's religious reform and his devotion to matters of ceremony and ritual. The parallel passage (2Ki 18:1 – 6) touches the religious reform only briefly. The numerous parallels in these chapters with the account of Solomon's reign suggest that the Chronicler viewed Hezekiah as a second Solomon in his celebration of the Passover (30:2,5,23,25 – 26), his arrangements for worship (29:7,18,35; 31:2 – 3), his wealth (32:27 – 29), the honor accorded him by the Gentiles (32:23) and the extent of his dominion (30:25).

29:1 *twenty-nine years.* 715 – 686 B.C. (but see note on Isa 36:1), including a 15-year extension of life granted by God (2Ki 20:6) but not mentioned by the Chronicler.

29:3 — 30:27 Not found in Kings.

29:3 *first year.* 715 B.C., another example of the Chronicler's practice of introducing chronological materials into his narrative (see note on 12:2). *opened the doors of the temple.* Necessary after the actions of Ahaz (28:24). *repaired them.* The repairs to the doors included new gold overlay (2Ki 18:16).

29:5 – 11 Hezekiah's speech demonstrates again the Chronicler's convictions about the coherence of action and effect: The sins of the past bring difficulty and judgment, but renewed fidelity brings relief.

29:7 Hezekiah reinstitutes these temple arrangements — following the pattern of Solomon (2:4; 4:7).

29:8 *object of dread and horror and scorn.* Echoes the language of the prophets, especially Jeremiah (see Jer 19:8; 25:9,18; 29:18; 51:37). Reference is to the Assyrian devastation of the northern kingdom and much of Judah.

29:12 *Kohathites … Merarites … Gershonites.* The three clans of Levi (1Ch 6:1).

29:13 – 14 *Asaph … Heman … Jeduthun.* Founders of the three families of Levitical musicians (1Ch 6:31 – 48; 25:1 – 31).

29:13 *Elizaphan.* A leader of the Kohathites (Nu 3:30), whose family had achieved status almost as a sub-clan (see 1Ch 15:8 and note on 15:4 – 10).

29:16 *Kidron Valley.* See note on Isa 22:7 and map, p. 477; see also 1Ki 15:13 and note.

29:18 These actions under Hezekiah mirror those of Solomon (2:4).

tire temple of the LORD, the altar of burnt offering with all its utensils, and the table for setting out the consecrated bread, with all its articles. 19We have prepared and consecrated all the articles[s] that King Ahaz removed in his unfaithfulness while he was king. They are now in front of the LORD's altar."

20Early the next morning King Hezekiah gathered the city officials together and went up to the temple of the LORD. 21They brought seven bulls, seven rams, seven male lambs and seven male goats[t] as a sin offering[u] for the kingdom, for the sanctuary and for Judah. The king commanded the priests, the descendants of Aaron, to offer these on the altar of the LORD. 22So they slaughtered the bulls, and the priests took the blood and sprinkled it on the altar; next they slaughtered the rams and sprinkled their blood on the altar; then they slaughtered the lambs and sprinkled their blood[v] on the altar. 23The goats[w] for the sin offering were brought before the king and the assembly, and they laid their hands[x] on them. 24The priests then slaughtered the goats and presented their blood on the altar for a sin offering to atone[y] for all Israel, because the king had ordered the burnt offering and the sin offering for all Israel.[z]

25He stationed the Levites in the temple of the LORD with cymbals, harps and lyres in the way prescribed by David[a] and Gad[b] the king's seer and Nathan the prophet; this was commanded by the LORD through his prophets. 26So the Levites stood ready with David's instruments,[c] and the priests with their trumpets.[d]

27Hezekiah gave the order to sacrifice the burnt offering on the altar. As the offering began, singing to the LORD began also, accompanied by trumpets and the instruments[e] of David king of Israel. 28The whole assembly bowed in worship, while the singers sang and the trumpeters played. All this continued until the sacrifice of the burnt offering[f] was completed.

29When the offerings were finished, the king and everyone present with him knelt down and worshiped.[g] 30King Hezekiah and his officials ordered the Levites to praise the LORD with the words of David and of Asaph the seer. So they sang praises with gladness and bowed their heads and worshiped.

31Then Hezekiah said, "You have now dedicated yourselves to the LORD. Come and bring sacrifices[h] and thank offerings to the temple of the LORD." So the assembly brought sacrifices and thank offerings, and all whose hearts were willing[i] brought burnt offerings.

32The number of burnt offerings[j] the assembly brought was seventy bulls, a hundred rams and two hundred male lambs—all of them for burnt offerings to the LORD. 33The animals consecrated as sacrifices amounted to six hundred bulls and three thousand sheep and goats. 34The priests, however, were too few to skin all the burnt offerings;[k] so their kinsmen the Levites helped them until the task was finished and until other priests had been consecrated,[l] for the Levites had been more conscientious in consecrating themselves than the priests had been. 35There were burnt offerings in abundance, together with the fat[m] of the fellowship offerings[a n] and the drink offerings[o] that accompanied the burnt offerings.

So the service of the temple of the LORD was reestablished. 36Hezekiah and all the people rejoiced at what God had brought about for his people, because it was done so quickly.[p]

Hezekiah Celebrates the Passover

30 Hezekiah sent word to all Israel[q] and Judah and also wrote letters to Ephraim and Manasseh,[r] inviting them to come to the temple of the LORD in Jerusalem and celebrate the Passover[s] to the LORD, the God of Israel. 2The king and his officials and the whole assembly in Jerusalem decided to celebrate[t] the Passover in the second month. 3They had not been able to celebrate it at the regular time be-

[a] 35 Traditionally *peace offerings*

29:19 [s] 2Ch 28:24
29:21 [t] Ezr 6:17; 8:35 [u] S Lev 4:13-14
29:22 [v] S Lev 4:18; Nu 18:17
29:23 [w] S Lev 16:5 [x] Lev 4:15
29:24 [y] S Ex 29:36; Lev 4:26 [z] 1Ch 11:1; Ezr 8:35
29:25 [a] S 1Ch 25:6; 28:19 [b] S 1Sa 22:5
29:26 [c] S 1Ch 15:16 [d] S 1Ch 15:24
29:27 [e] S 1Sa 16:16
29:28 [f] S 2Ch 2:4
29:29 [g] S 2Ch 20:18
29:31 [h] Heb 13:15-16 [i] S Ex 25:2; 35:22
29:32 [j] Lev 1:1-17
29:34 [k] Eze 44:11 [l] 2Ch 30:3, 15
29:35 [m] S Ge 4:4; S Ex 29:13 [n] Lev 7:11-21 [o] S Ge 35:14
29:36 [p] 2Ch 35:8
30:1 [q] S 1Ch 9:1 [r] S Ge 41:52 [s] S Ex 12:11; S Nu 28:16
30:2 [t] Nu 9:10

29:21 *sin offering.* See Lev 4:1—5:13 and chart, p. 153.
29:22 *sprinkled their blood.* See Lev 17:6; Nu 18:17.
29:23 *laid their hands on them.* See Lev 4:13–15; 8:14–15; Nu 8:12.
29:25 *Gad ... Nathan.* See 1Sa 22:5 and note; 2Sa 7; 12.
29:26 *David's instruments.* See 1Ch 23:5.
29:30 *seer.* See note on 1Ch 25:5. *sang praises with gladness.* See v. 36; 30:21,23,25–26.
29:35 *burnt offerings in abundance ... fellowship offerings ... drink offerings.* Reminiscent of the dedication of the temple under Solomon (7:4–6). For the laws regarding the fellowship offerings see Lev 3; 7:11–21; for the drink offerings see Nu 15:1–12. *service of the temple of the LORD was reestablished.* Similar to the formula used in 8:16 with reference to Solomon's work.

30:1–27 Unique to the Chronicler; cf. the famous Passover under Josiah (35:1–19; 2Ki 23:21–23). Hezekiah allowed two deviations from the law (Ex 12; Dt 16:1–8) in this observance: (1) the date in the second month (v. 2) and (2) exemption from some ritual requirements (vv. 18–19).
30:1 *all Israel and Judah.* See Introduction to 1 Chronicles: Purpose and Themes. With the northern kingdom now ended as the result of the Assyrian invasion and deportation (which surprisingly is not mentioned), the Chronicler shows "all Israel" once again united around the Davidic king and the temple (see vv. 5,18–19,25).
30:2 *second month.* After the division of the kingdom, Jeroboam deferred the sacral calendar of the northern kingdom by one month (1Ki 12:32), possibly to further wean the subjects in the north away from devotion to Jerusalem. By

cause not enough priests had consecrated[u] themselves and the people had not assembled in Jerusalem. 4The plan seemed
right both to the king and to the whole
assembly. 5They decided to send a proclamation throughout Israel, from Beersheba
to Dan,[v] calling the people to come to Jerusalem and celebrate the Passover to the
LORD, the God of Israel. It had not been
celebrated in large numbers according to
what was written.

6At the king's command, couriers went
throughout Israel and Judah with letters
from the king and from his officials, which
read:

"People of Israel, return to the
LORD, the God of Abraham, Isaac and
Israel, that he may return to you who
are left, who have escaped from the
hand of the kings of Assyria. 7Do not
be like your fathers[w] and brothers,
who were unfaithful[x] to the LORD, the
God of their fathers, so that he made
them an object of horror,[y] as you see.
8Do not be stiff-necked,[z] as your fathers were; submit to the LORD. Come
to the sanctuary, which he has consecrated forever. Serve the LORD your
God, so that his fierce anger[a] will turn
away from you. 9If you return[b] to the
LORD, then your brothers and your
children will be shown compassion[c]
by their captors and will come back
to this land, for the LORD your God is
gracious and compassionate.[d] He will
not turn his face from you if you return to him."

10The couriers went from town to town
in Ephraim and Manasseh, as far as Zebulun, but the people scorned and ridiculed[e]
them. 11Nevertheless, some men of Asher,
Manasseh and Zebulun humbled[f] themselves and went to Jerusalem.[g] 12Also in

30:3 [u]Nu 9:6-13; S 2Ch 29:34 30:5 [v]S Jdg 20:1 30:7 [w]Ps 78:8,57; 106:6; Jer 11:10; Eze 20:18 [x]S 1Ch 5:25 [y]S Dt 28:25 30:8 [z]S Ex 32:9 [a]S Nu 25:4; S 2Ch 29:10 30:9 [b]Dt 30:2-5; Isa 1:16; 55:7; Jer 25:5; Eze 33:11 [c]S Ex 3:21; S 1Ki 8:50 [d]S Ex 22:27; S Dt 4:31; S 2Ch 6:39; Mic 7:18 30:10 [e]2Ch 36:16 30:11 [f]S 2Ch 6:37 [g]ver 25
30:12 [h]Jer 32:39; Eze 11:19 30:13 [i]S Nu 28:16 30:14 [j]2Ch 28:24 [k]S 2Sa 15:23 30:15 [l]S 2Ch 29:34 30:16 [m]2Ch 35:10 30:17 [n]2Ch 35:11; Ezr 6:20 30:18 [o]Ex 12:43-49; Nu 9:6-10 30:20 [p]S 2Ch 6:20 [q]S 2Ch 7:14; Mal 4:2 [r]Jas 5:16 30:21 [s]Ex 12:15,17; 13:6

Judah the hand of God was on the people to give them unity[h] of mind to carry
out what the king and his officials had ordered, following the word of the LORD.

13A very large crowd of people assembled in Jerusalem to celebrate the Feast of
Unleavened Bread[i] in the second month.
14They removed the altars[j] in Jerusalem
and cleared away the incense altars and
threw them into the Kidron Valley.[k]

15They slaughtered the Passover lamb
on the fourteenth day of the second
month. The priests and the Levites were
ashamed and consecrated[l] themselves and
brought burnt offerings to the temple of
the LORD. 16Then they took up their regular positions[m] as prescribed in the Law of
Moses the man of God. The priests sprinkled the blood handed to them by the Levites. 17Since many in the crowd had not
consecrated themselves, the Levites had to
kill[n] the Passover lambs for all those who
were not ceremonially clean and could
not consecrate ⌞their lambs⌟ to the LORD.
18Although most of the many people who
came from Ephraim, Manasseh, Issachar
and Zebulun had not purified themselves,[o]
yet they ate the Passover, contrary to what
was written. But Hezekiah prayed for
them, saying, "May the LORD, who is good,
pardon everyone 19who sets his heart on
seeking God—the LORD, the God of his fathers—even if he is not clean according to
the rules of the sanctuary." 20And the LORD
heard[p] Hezekiah and healed[q] the people.[r]

21The Israelites who were present in Jerusalem celebrated the Feast of Unleavened Bread[s] for seven days with great rejoicing, while the Levites and priests sang
to the LORD every day, accompanied by the
LORD's instruments of praise.[a]

[a] 21 Or *priests praised the LORD every day with resounding instruments belonging to the LORD*

delaying the celebration of Passover one month, Hezekiah not only allows time for the priests to consecrate themselves (v. 3) and for the people to gather (vv. 3,13), but also achieves unity between the kingdoms on the date of the Passover for the first time since the schism more than two centuries earlier. Delaying the date reflects Hezekiah's concern to involve "all Israel." For the first time since Solomon the entire nation observes Passover together, reflecting the Chronicler's view that Hezekiah is a second Solomon. Passover was prescribed for the 14th day of the first month (Ex 12:2,6; Dt 16:1–8), but could not be celebrated at that time due to the defilement of the temple and the purification rites under way (29:3,17). For celebration of Passover by the restored community shortly after the dedication of the rebuilt temple see Ezr 6:16–22.

30:5 *large numbers.* Another comparison with the time of Solomon (see v. 26). At the time of its inception, Passover was primarily a family observance (Ex 12). It later became a national celebration at the temple (v. 8; see Dt 16:1–8).

30:8 *Come to the sanctuary.* Passover was one of three annual pilgrim feasts requiring attendance at the temple (see Nu 28:9—29:39).

30:9 *shown compassion by their captors.* In Solomon's prayer in 6:39 the Chronicler omitted the phrase found in the parallel account (1Ki 8:50) that their conquerors would "show them mercy." Here the phrase is found in the speech of Hezekiah, again portraying him as a second Solomon (see Lev 26:40–42). *will come back to this land.* Those who repent will have hope of return, even those from the Assyrian captivity.

30:14 *Kidron Valley.* See 29:16 and note.

30:15 *The priests and the Levites ... consecrated themselves.* The reproach previously directed against the priests (v. 3; 29:34) is here broadened to include also the Levites—an exhortation to the priests and Levites of the restored community to be faithful.

30:17 *Levites had to kill the Passover lambs.* See Ex 12:6; Dt 16:6. According to the law the heads of families were to slay the Passover sacrifice. The Levites perhaps acted for the recent arrivals from the northern kingdom who were not ceremonially clean. Cf. Jn 11:55.

30:18–19 Faith and obedience take precedence over ritual (see Mk 7:1–23; Jn 7:22–23; 9:14–16).

30:20 The response to Hezekiah's prayer recalls the prayer of Solomon (7:14).

22Hezekiah spoke encouragingly to all
the Levites, who showed good understanding of the service of the LORD. For
the seven days they ate their assigned portion and offered fellowship offerings[a] and
praised the LORD, the God of their fathers.
23The whole assembly then agreed to
celebrate[t] the festival seven more days; so
for another seven days they celebrated joyfully. 24Hezekiah king of Judah provided[u] a
thousand bulls and seven thousand sheep
and goats for the assembly, and the officials provided them with a thousand bulls
and ten thousand sheep and goats. A great
number of priests consecrated themselves.
25The entire assembly of Judah rejoiced,
along with the priests and Levites and all
who had assembled from Israel[v], including the aliens who had come from Israel
and those who lived in Judah. 26There was
great joy in Jerusalem, for since the days
of Solomon[w] son of David king of Israel
there had been nothing like this in Jerusalem. 27The priests and the Levites stood
to bless[x] the people, and God heard them,
for their prayer reached heaven, his holy
dwelling place.

31 When all this had ended, the Israelites who were there went out to
the towns of Judah, smashed the sacred
stones and cut down[y] the Asherah poles.
They destroyed the high places and the
altars throughout Judah and Benjamin
and in Ephraim and Manasseh. After they
had destroyed all of them, the Israelites
returned to their own towns and to their
own property.

Contributions for Worship

31:20-21pp — 2Ki 18:5-7

2Hezekiah[z] assigned the priests and Levites to divisions[a]—each of them according to their duties as priests or Levites—
to offer burnt offerings and fellowship offerings,[a] to minister,[b] to give thanks and
to sing praises[c] at the gates of the LORD's
dwelling.[d] 3The king contributed[e] from his
own possessions for the morning and evening burnt offerings and for the burnt offerings on the Sabbaths, New Moons and
appointed feasts as written in the Law of
the LORD.[f] 4He ordered the people living
in Jerusalem to give the portion[g] due the
priests and Levites so they could devote
themselves to the Law of the LORD. 5As
soon as the order went out, the Israelites
generously gave the firstfruits[h] of their
grain, new wine,[i] oil and honey and all
that the fields produced. They brought a
great amount, a tithe of everything. 6The
men of Israel and Judah who lived in the
towns of Judah also brought a tithe[j] of
their herds and flocks and a tithe of the
holy things dedicated to the LORD their
God, and they piled them in heaps.[k] 7They
began doing this in the third month and
finished in the seventh month.[l] 8When
Hezekiah and his officials came and saw
the heaps, they praised the LORD and
blessed[m] his people Israel.

9Hezekiah asked the priests and Levites about the heaps; 10and Azariah the
chief priest, from the family of Zadok,[n]
answered, "Since the people began to
bring their contributions to the temple
of the LORD, we have had enough to eat
and plenty to spare, because the LORD has
blessed his people, and this great amount
is left over."[o]

11Hezekiah gave orders to prepare storerooms in the temple of the LORD, and this
was done. 12Then they faithfully brought
in the contributions, tithes and dedicated
gifts. Conaniah,[p] a Levite, was in charge of
these things, and his brother Shimei was
next in rank. 13Jehiel, Azaziah, Nahath,
Asahel, Jerimoth, Jozabad,[q] Eliel, Ismaki-
ah, Mahath and Benaiah were supervisors
under Conaniah and Shimei his brother,
by appointment of King Hezekiah and Azariah the official in charge of the temple
of God.

[a] 22,2 Traditionally *peace offerings*

30:23 [t] 2Ch 7:9 **30:24** [u] 1Ki 8:5; 2Ch 35:7; Ezr 6:17; 8:35 **30:25** [v] ver 11 **30:26** [w] S 2Ch 7:8 **30:27** [x] S Ex 39:43 **31:1** [y] S 2Ki 18:4; 2Ch 32:12; Isa 36:7 **31:2** [z] S 2Ch 29:9 [a] S 1Ch 24:1 [b] S 1Ch 15:2 [c] Ps 7:17; 9:2; 47:6; 71:22 [d] S 1Ch 23:28-32 **31:3** [e] S 1Ch 29:3; 2Ch 35:7; Eze 45:17 [f] Nu 28:1-29:40 **31:4** [g] S Nu 18:8; S Dt 18:8; Ne 13:10 **31:5** [h] S Nu 18:12, 24; Ne 13:12; Eze 44:30 [i] Dt 12:17 **31:6** [j] S Lev 27:30; Ne 13:10-12 [k] S Ru 3:7 **31:7** [l] Ex 23:16 **31:8** [m] Ps 144:13-15 **31:10** [n] S 2Sa 8:17 [o] S Ex 36:5; Eze 44:30; Mal 3:10-12 **31:12** [p] 2Ch 35:9 **31:13** [q] 2Ch 35:9

30:23 *another seven days.* The festival was observed for two weeks, just as the observance of the dedication of Solomon's temple had been (7:8–9).
30:26 *since the days of Solomon.* An explicit indication of the Chronicler's modeling of the reign of Hezekiah after that of Solomon (see note on 29:1—32:33).
30:27 *prayer reached heaven, his holy dwelling place.* Another echo of Solomon's dedication prayer (6:21,30,33,39).
31:1–21 Apart from the first verse, which parallels 2Ki 18:4, the material of this chapter is unique to the Chronicler, whose interest in the Levites and the temple predominates. Hezekiah's efforts to ensure the material support of the Levites (v. 4) probably had relevance to the postexilic audience for whom the Chronicler wrote.
31:1 *the Israelites ... the Israelites.* Lit. "all Israel ... all the Israelites." The Chronicler's interest in "all Israel" as united under Hezekiah is again apparent. *sacred stones.* See note on 1Ki 14:23. *Asherah poles.* See NIV text note on 14:3.
31:2 Echoes 8:14. The Chronicler continues to model Hezekiah as a second Solomon (see notes on 29:7,18).
31:3 *king contributed.* The king's giving from his own wealth prompted a generous response from the people, as it had also under David (1Ch 29:3–9).
31:5–6 See Dt 12:5–19; 14:22–27. The grain, new wine and olive oil had to be brought to the temple (Dt 12:17). Those coming from a distance, however, could bring the value of their offerings and purchase them on arrival (Dt 14:24). Only those who actually lived in Judah brought the tithe of their herds and flocks, a difficult procedure for those who lived farther away. For the restored community's commitment to bring their firstfruits, tithes and offerings see Ne 10:35–39. For their failure to do so see Ne 13:10–13; Mal 3:8–10.
31:7 *third month.* May-June, the time of the Feast of Pentecost and the grain harvest. *seventh month.* September-October, the time of the Feast of Tabernacles and the fruit and vine harvest (see Ex 23:16).

14Kore son of Imnah the Levite, keeper
of the East Gate, was in charge of the freewill offerings given to God, distributing
the contributions made to the LORD and
also the consecrated gifts. 15Eden,[r] Miniamin, Jeshua, Shemaiah, Amariah and
Shecaniah assisted him faithfully in the
towns[s] of the priests, distributing to their
fellow priests according to their divisions,
old and young alike.

16In addition, they distributed to the
males three years old or more whose
names were in the genealogical records[t]—all who would enter the temple
of the LORD to perform the daily duties
of their various tasks, according to their
responsibilities and their divisions. 17And
they distributed to the priests enrolled by
their families in the genealogical records
and likewise to the Levites twenty years
old or more, according to their responsibilities and their divisions. 18They included
all the little ones, the wives, and the sons
and daughters of the whole community
listed in these genealogical records. For
they were faithful in consecrating themselves.

19As for the priests, the descendants
of Aaron, who lived on the farm lands
around their towns or in any other towns,[u]
men were designated by name to distribute portions to every male among them
and to all who were recorded in the genealogies of the Levites.

20This is what Hezekiah did throughout Judah, doing what was good and right
and faithful[v] before the LORD his God. 21In
everything that he undertook in the service of God's temple and in obedience to
the law and the commands, he sought his
God and worked wholeheartedly. And so
he prospered.[w]

Sennacherib Threatens Jerusalem

32:9-19pp — 2Ki 18:17-35; Isa 36:2-20
32:20-21pp — 2Ki 19:35-37; Isa 37:36-38

32 After all that Hezekiah had so faithfully done, Sennacherib[x] king of Assyria came and invaded Judah. He laid
siege to the fortified cities, thinking to
conquer them for himself. 2When Hezekiah saw that Sennacherib had come and
that he intended to make war on Jerusalem,[y] 3he consulted with his officials and
military staff about blocking off the water
from the springs outside the city, and they
helped him. 4A large force of men assembled, and they blocked all the springs[z] and
the stream that flowed through the land.
"Why should the kings[a] of Assyria come
and find plenty of water?" they said. 5Then
he worked hard repairing all the broken
sections of the wall[a] and building towers
on it. He built another wall outside that
one and reinforced the supporting terraces[b][b] of the City of David. He also made
large numbers of weapons[c] and shields.

6He appointed military officers over the
people and assembled them before him
in the square at the city gate and encouraged them with these words: 7"Be strong
and courageous.[d] Do not be afraid or discouraged[e] because of the king of Assyria
and the vast army with him, for there is
a greater power with us than with him.[f]
8With him is only the arm of flesh,[g] but
with us[h] is the LORD our God to help us
and to fight our battles."[i] And the people
gained confidence from what Hezekiah
the king of Judah said.

9Later, when Sennacherib king of Assyria and all his forces were laying siege to
Lachish,[j] he sent his officers to Jerusalem
with this message for Hezekiah king of Judah and for all the people of Judah who
were there:

10"This is what Sennacherib king of
Assyria says: On what are you basing
your confidence,[k] that you remain in
Jerusalem under siege? 11When Hezekiah says, 'The LORD our God will
save us from the hand of the king of
Assyria,' he is misleading[l] you, to let
you die of hunger and thirst. 12Did
not Hezekiah himself remove this
god's high places and altars, saying

31:15 [r]2Ch 29:12 [s]Jos 21:9-19
31:16 [t]1Ch 23:3
31:19 [u]S Nu 35:2-5
31:20 [v]S 2Ki 20:3
31:21 [w]S Dt 29:9
32:1 [x]Isa 36:1; 37:9,17,37
32:2 [y]Isa 22:7; Jer 1:15
32:4 [z]S 2Ki 18:17; Isa 22:9,11; Na 3:14
32:5 [a]Isa 22:10 [b]S 1Ch 11:8 [c]Isa 22:8
32:7 [d]S Dt 31:6 [e]2Ch 20:15 [f]S Nu 14:9; 2Ki 6:16
32:8 [g]Job 40:9; Isa 52:10; Jer 17:5; 32:21 [h]S Dt 3:22; S 1Sa 17:45 [i]S 1Ch 5:22; Ps 20:7; Isa 28:6
32:9 [j]S Jos 10:3,31
32:10 [k]Eze 29:16
32:11 [l]Isa 37:10

[a] 4 Hebrew; Septuagint and Syriac *king* [b] 5 Or *the Millo*

31:16 *three years.* Although no ancient versions or manuscripts disagree with this figure, it may represent a copyist's mistake for "30 years," the age at which duties were assigned in the temple (1Ch 23:3).

31:20–21 Another brief indication of the Chronicler's emphasis on immediate retribution: Not only does disobedience bring immediate chastening, but obedience and seeking God bring prosperity.

32:1–23 The record of Sennacherib's invasion is much more detailed in 2 Kings and Isaiah (see note on 29:1—32:33).

32:1 The Chronicler omits the date of the invasion (701 B.C., Hezekiah's 14th year; see 2Ki 18:13; Isa 36:1; see also chart, p. 472).

32:2–8 Normal preparations for invasion.

32:3–4 See v. 30.

32:9 The Chronicler omits 2Ki 18:14–16, which records Hezekiah's suit for peace with its accompanying bribe stripped from the temple treasures. These acts were apparently out of accord with the Chronicler's portrait of Hezekiah. He also omits 2Ki 18:17b–18.

32:10 The Chronicler omits 2Ki 18:20–21 (and Isa 36:5–6), containing a portion of the Assyrian commander's speech ridiculing Hezekiah and the citizens of Jerusalem for trusting in Egypt and the pharaoh. This, too, may be theologically motivated, in the light of the Chronicler's attitude toward foreign alliances (see note on 16:2–9). The same concern with foreign alliances is also likely the reason for the omission of the material in 2Ki 18:23–27 (and Isa 36:8–12), where mention is again made of the hope of Egyptian intervention (see 2Ki 19:9 for the incursion of Tirhakah).

to Judah and Jerusalem, 'You must worship before one altar[m] and burn sacrifices on it'?

13"Do you not know what I and my fathers have done to all the peoples of the other lands? Were the gods of those nations ever able to deliver their land from my hand?[n] 14Who of all the gods of these nations that my fathers destroyed has been able to save his people from me? How then can your god deliver you from my hand? 15Now do not let Hezekiah deceive[o] you and mislead you like this. Do not believe him, for no god of any nation or kingdom has been able to deliver[p] his people from my hand or the hand of my fathers.[q] How much less will your god deliver you from my hand!"

16Sennacherib's officers spoke further against the LORD God and against his servant Hezekiah. 17The king also wrote letters[r] insulting[s] the LORD, the God of Israel, and saying this against him: "Just as the gods[t] of the peoples of the other lands did not rescue their people from my hand, so the god of Hezekiah will not rescue his people from my hand." 18Then they called out in Hebrew to the people of Jerusalem who were on the wall, to terrify them and make them afraid in order to capture the city. 19They spoke about the God of Jerusalem as they did about the gods of the other peoples of the world—the work of men's hands.[u]

20King Hezekiah and the prophet Isaiah son of Amoz cried out in prayer[v] to heaven about this. 21And the LORD sent an angel,[w] who annihilated all the fighting men and the leaders and officers in the camp of the Assyrian king. So he withdrew to his own land in disgrace. And when he went into the temple of his god, some of his sons cut him down with the sword.[x]

22So the LORD saved Hezekiah and the people of Jerusalem from the hand of Sennacherib king of Assyria and from the hand of all others. He took care of them[a] on every side. 23Many brought offerings to Jerusalem for the LORD and valuable gifts[y] for Hezekiah king of Judah. From then on he was highly regarded by all the nations.

Hezekiah's Pride, Success and Death

32:24-33pp — 2Ki 20:1-21; Isa 37:21-38; 38:1-8

24In those days Hezekiah became ill and was at the point of death. He prayed to the LORD, who answered him and gave him a miraculous sign.[z] 25But Hezekiah's heart was proud[a] and he did not respond to the kindness shown him; therefore the LORD's wrath[b] was on him and on Judah and Jerusalem. 26Then Hezekiah repented[c] of the pride of his heart, as did the people of Jerusalem; therefore the LORD's wrath did not come upon them during the days of Hezekiah.[d]

27Hezekiah had very great riches and honor,[e] and he made treasuries for his silver and gold and for his precious stones, spices, shields and all kinds of valuables. 28He also made buildings to store the harvest of grain, new wine and oil; and he made stalls for various kinds of cattle, and pens for the flocks. 29He built villages and acquired great numbers of flocks and herds, for God had given him very great riches.[f]

30It was Hezekiah who blocked[g] the upper outlet of the Gihon[h] spring and channeled[i] the water down to the west side of the City of David. He succeeded in everything he undertook. 31But when envoys were sent by the rulers of Babylon[j] to ask him about the miraculous sign[k] that had occurred in the land, God left him to test[l] him and to know everything that was in his heart.

32The other events of Hezekiah's reign and his acts of devotion are written in the vision of the prophet Isaiah son of Amoz in the book of the kings of Judah and Israel. 33Hezekiah rested with his fathers and was buried on the hill where the tombs

a 22 Hebrew; Septuagint and Vulgate *He gave them rest*

32:12 [m]S 2Ch 31:1 **32:13** [n]ver 15 **32:15** [o]Isa 37:10 [p]Da 3:15 [q]Ex 5:2 **32:17** [r]Isa 37:14 [s]Ps 74:22; Isa 37:4,17 [t]S 2Ki 19:12 **32:19** [u]Ps 115:4-8; Isa 2:8; 17:8; 37:19; Jer 1:16 **32:20** [v]Isa 1:15; 37:15 **32:21** [w]S Ge 19:13 [x]S 2Ki 19:7; Isa 37:7,38; Jer 41:2 **32:23** [y]S 1Sa 10:27; S 2Ch 9:24; Ps 68:18,29; 76:11; Isa 16:1; 18:7; 45:14; Zep 3:10; Zec 14:16-17 **32:24** [z]ver 31 **32:25** [a]S 2Ki 14:10 [b]S 2Ch 19:2 **32:26** [c]Jer 26:18-19 [d]2Ch 34:27,28; Isa 39:8 **32:27** [e]S 1Ch 29:12; S 2Ch 9:24 **32:29** [f]Isa 39:2 **32:30** [g]S 2Ki 18:17 [h]S 1Ki 1:33 [i]S 2Sa 5:8 **32:31** [j]Isa 13:1; 39:1 [k]S ver 24; Isa 38:7 [l]S Ge 22:1; Dt 8:16

32:16 *spoke further.* The Chronicler appears to assume his reader's familiarity with the longer account of the Assyrian taunts found in Kings and Isaiah.
32:18 *called out in Hebrew.* Assumes knowledge of the fuller story (2Ki 18:26–28; Isa 36:11–13).
32:20 This brief reference to the prayers of Hezekiah and Isaiah abridges the much longer narrative in 2Ki 19:1–34 (and Isa 37:1–35).
32:21 See 2Ki 19:35–37; Isa 37:36–38. The Chronicler and the parallel accounts telescope events somewhat: Sennacherib's invasion of Judah was in 701 B.C., while his death at the hand of his sons was in 681.
32:23 *highly regarded by all the nations.* Another effort to compare Hezekiah with Solomon (see 9:23–24).
32:24 The Chronicler again abridges the narrative in 2Ki 20:1–11 (and Isa 38:1–8), assuming the reader's familiarity with the role of Isaiah and the miraculous sign of the shadow reversing ten steps.
32:25–30 Not found in the parallel texts.
32:25–26 *proud ... pride.* The Chronicler does not specify the nature of Hezekiah's pride (however, see v. 31; 2Ki 20:12–13; Isa 39:1–2). Even for a second Solomon like Hezekiah, disobedience brings anger from the Lord.
32:27–29 The Chronicler likens Hezekiah to Solomon also by recounting his wealth (9:13–14).
32:30 See vv. 2–4; 2Ki 20:20 and note.
32:31 See v. 25. The Chronicler assumes the reader's knowledge of the fuller account in 2Ki 20:12–19 (and Isa 39:1–8). The envoys from Babylon were apparently interested in joint efforts against the Assyrians, hoping to open two fronts against them simultaneously.

of David's descendants are. All Judah and the people of Jerusalem honored him when he died. And Manasseh his son succeeded him as king.

Manasseh King of Judah

33:1-10pp — 2Ki 21:1-10
33:18-20pp — 2Ki 21:17-18

33 Manasseh[m] was twelve years old when he became king, and he reigned in Jerusalem fifty-five years. 2He did evil in the eyes of the LORD,[n] following the detestable[o] practices of the nations the LORD had driven out before the Israelites. 3He rebuilt the high places his father Hezekiah had demolished; he also erected altars to the Baals and made Asherah poles.[p] He bowed down[q] to all the starry hosts and worshiped them. 4He built altars in the temple of the LORD, of which the LORD had said, "My Name[r] will remain in Jerusalem forever." 5In both courts of the temple of the LORD,[s] he built altars to all the starry hosts. 6He sacrificed his sons[t] in[a] the fire in the Valley of Ben Hinnom, practiced sorcery, divination and witchcraft, and consulted mediums[u] and spiritists.[v] He did much evil in the eyes of the LORD, provoking him to anger.

7He took the carved image he had made and put it in God's temple,[w] of which God had said to David and to his son Solomon, "In this temple and in Jerusalem, which I have chosen out of all the tribes of Israel, I will put my Name forever. 8I will not again make the feet of the Israelites leave the land[x] I assigned to your forefathers, if only they will be careful to do everything I commanded them concerning all the laws, decrees and ordinances given through Moses." 9But Manasseh led Judah and the people of Jerusalem astray, so that they did more evil than the nations the LORD had destroyed before the Israelites.[y]

10The LORD spoke to Manasseh and his people, but they paid no attention. 11So the LORD brought against them the army commanders of the king of Assyria, who took Manasseh prisoner,[z] put a hook[a] in his nose, bound him with bronze shackles[b] and took him to Babylon. 12In his distress he sought the favor of the LORD his God and humbled[c] himself greatly before the God of his fathers. 13And when he prayed to him, the LORD was moved by his entreaty and listened to his plea; so he brought him back to Jerusalem and to his kingdom. Then Manasseh knew that the LORD is God.

14Afterward he rebuilt the outer wall of the City of David, west of the Gihon[d] spring in the valley, as far as the entrance of the Fish Gate[e] and encircling the hill of Ophel;[f] he also made it much higher. He stationed military commanders in all the fortified cities in Judah.

15He got rid of the foreign gods and removed[g] the image from the temple of the LORD, as well as all the altars he had built on the temple hill and in Jerusalem; and he threw them out of the city. 16Then he

[a] 6 Or *He made his sons pass through*

33:1 [m]S 1Ch 3:13 **33:2** [n]Jer 15:4 [o]S Dt 18:9 **33:3** [p]Dt 16:21-22; S 2Ch 24:18 [q]Dt 17:3 **33:4** [r]2Ch 7:16 **33:5** [s]S 2Ch 4:9 **33:6** [t]S Lev 18:21; S Dt 18:10 [u]S Ex 22:18; S Lev 19:31 [v]S 1Sa 28:13 **33:7** [w]S 2Ch 7:16 **33:8** [x]S 2Sa 7:10 **33:9** [y]Jer 15:4; Eze 5:7 **33:11** [z]S Dt 28:36 [a]S 2Ki 19:28; Isa 37:29; Eze 29:4; 38:4; Am 4:2 [b]Ps 149:8 **33:12** [c]S 2Ch 6:37 **33:14** [d]S 1Ki 1:33 [e]Ne 3:3; 12:39; Zep 1:10 [f]2Ch 27:3; Ne 3:26 **33:15** [g]2Ki 23:12

33:1 – 20 See 2Ki 21:1 – 18 and notes. Manasseh had the longest reign of any of the kings of Judah, a total of 55 years (v. 1). The emphasis in the two accounts differs: While both histories report at length the evil done in Manasseh's reign, only the Chronicler mentions his journey to Babylon and his repentance and restoration to rule. For the writer of Kings, the picture is only a bad one in which Manasseh could be considered almost single-handedly the cause of the exile (2Ki 21:10 – 15; 23:26). Some interpreters regard the record of Manasseh's repentance in Chronicles as motivated by the author's emphasis on immediate retribution: Length of reign is viewed as a blessing for obedience, so that the Chronicler deliberately records some good in Manasseh as a ground for his long reign. However, it must be noted that length of reign is not elsewhere used by the Chronicler as an indication of divine blessing. The usual indicators for such blessing in his account are peace and prosperity, building projects, success in warfare and large families.

33:1 *fifty-five years.* 697 – 642 B.C.

33:3,19 *Asherah poles.* See note on Ex 34:13.

33:4 *My Name will remain in Jerusalem forever.* See 1Ki 3:2 and note; 9:3; Ps 132:13 – 14.

33:6 *sacrificed his sons ... Valley of Ben Hinnom.* See 28:3 and note.

33:10 See note on vv. 1 – 20. The Chronicler abridges what the Lord said to Manasseh and the people through the prophets; the fuller record is found in 2Ki 21:10 – 15.

33:11 – 17 Unique to the Chronicler, showing his stress on immediate retribution: Manasseh's evil brings invasion and defeat, while his repentance brings restoration to rule.

33:11 *took him to Babylon.* In extant non-Biblical records there is no reference as yet to Manasseh being taken to Babylon by an Assyrian king. Esarhaddon (681 – 669 B.C.) lists him among 22 kings required to forward materials for his building projects, and Ashurbanipal (669 – 627) names him as one of a number of vassals supporting his campaign against Egypt. The fact that an Assyrian king would have him taken to Babylon suggests that this incident may have taken place during the rebellion of Shamash-Shum-Ukin against his brother and overlord Ashurbanipal. This rebellion lasted from 652 to 648, and Manasseh may have joined or at least have been suspected of assisting in the Babylonian defection from Assyria. Manasseh may have been found innocent, or he may have been pardoned on the basis of a renewed pledge of loyalty. Egypt had also bolted from the Assyrian yoke under the new 26th dynasty, and the return of Manasseh to rule may reflect the Assyrian need of a vassal near the border of Egypt.

33:12 The language is reminiscent of Solomon's prayer (7:14).

33:14 *rebuilt the outer wall.* For the Chronicler such building programs are a sign of divine blessing (8:1 – 6; 11:5 – 12; 14:6 – 7; 26:9 – 10,14 – 15; 32:1 – 5,27 – 30; 1Ch 11:7 – 9; 15:1).

33:15 – 16 Whatever the precise nature of Manasseh's reforms, Josiah would later still need to remove "the altars Manasseh had built in the two courts of the temple" (2Ki 23:12).

restored the altar of the LORD and sacrificed fellowship offerings[a] and thank offerings[h] on it, and told Judah to serve the LORD, the God of Israel. 17 The people, however, continued to sacrifice at the high places, but only to the LORD their God.

18 The other events of Manasseh's reign, including his prayer to his God and the words the seers spoke to him in the name of the LORD, the God of Israel, are written in the annals of the kings of Israel.[b] 19 His prayer and how God was moved by his entreaty, as well as all his sins and unfaithfulness, and the sites where he built high places and set up Asherah poles and idols before he humbled[i] himself—all are written in the records of the seers.[c][j] 20 Manasseh rested with his fathers and was buried[k] in his palace. And Amon his son succeeded him as king.

Amon King of Judah

33:21-25pp — 2Ki 21:19-24

21 Amon[l] was twenty-two years old when he became king, and he reigned in Jerusalem two years. 22 He did evil in the eyes of the LORD, as his father Manasseh had done. Amon worshiped and offered sacrifices to all the idols Manasseh had made. 23 But unlike his father Manasseh, he did not humble[m] himself before the LORD; Amon increased his guilt.

24 Amon's officials conspired against him and assassinated him in his palace. 25 Then the people[n] of the land killed all who had plotted against King Amon, and they made Josiah his son king in his place.

Josiah's Reforms

34:1-2pp — 2Ki 22:1-2
34:3-7Ref — 2Ki 23:4-20
34:8-13pp — 2Ki 22:3-7

34 Josiah[o] was eight years old when he became king,[p] and he reigned in Jerusalem thirty-one years. 2 He did what was right in the eyes of the LORD and walked in the ways of his father David,[q] not turning aside to the right or to the left.

3 In the eighth year of his reign, while he was still young, he began to seek the God[r] of his father David. In his twelfth year he began to purge Judah and Jerusalem of high places, Asherah poles, carved idols and cast images. 4 Under his direction the altars of the Baals were torn down; he cut to pieces the incense altars that were above them, and smashed the Asherah poles,[s] the idols and the images. These he broke to pieces and scattered over the graves of those who had sacrificed to them.[t] 5 He burned[u] the bones of the priests on their altars, and so he purged Judah and Jerusalem. 6 In the towns of Manasseh, Ephraim and Simeon, as far as Naphtali, and in the ruins around them, 7 he tore down the altars and the Asherah poles and crushed

33:16 [h] Lev 7:11-18
33:19 [i] S 2Ch 6:37 [j] 2Ki 21:17
33:20 [k] 2Ki 21:18; S 2Ch 21:20
33:21 [l] S 1Ch 3:14
33:23 [m] S Ex 10:3; 2Ch 7:14; Ps 18:27; 147:6; Pr 3:34
33:25 [n] S 2Ch 22:1
34:1 [o] S 1Ch 3:14 [p] Zep 1:1
34:2 [q] 2Ch 29:2
34:3 [r] S 1Ch 16:11
34:4 [s] S Ex 34:13 [t] Ex 32:20; S Lev 26:30; 2Ki 23:11; Mic 1:5
34:5 [u] S 1Ki 13:2

[a] *16* Traditionally *peace offerings* [b] *18* That is, Judah, as frequently in 2 Chronicles [c] *19* One Hebrew manuscript and Septuagint; most Hebrew manuscripts *of Hozai*

33:20 *buried in his palace.* Cf. 2Ki 21:18. His burial in the palace garden makes Manasseh the fifth king the Chronicler names who was not buried in the tombs of the kings (see note on 28:27).

33:21–25 See 2Ki 21:19–26. The Chronicler's account of the reign of Amon (642–640 B.C.) is quite similar to that in Kings, apart from (1) the additional note that Amon was not repentant like his father Manasseh, a note based on a passage unique to the Chronicler (vv. 12–13), and (2) the absence of the death formula.

34:1—36:1 See 2Ki 22:1—23:30 and notes. Both accounts of Josiah's reign are about the same length and treat the same subjects, but with considerable variation in emphasis. Both deal with three different aspects of Josiah's reform: (1) the removal of foreign religions, (2) the finding of the Book of the Law and the covenant renewal that followed and (3) the celebration of Passover. On the second item the two histories are quite similar. On the first item the writer of Kings goes to great lengths (2Ki 23:4–20), while the Chronicler summarizes it only briefly (34:3–7,33). The account of the Passover is greatly expanded in Chronicles (35:1–19), while only alluded to in 2 Kings (23:21–23). Not only are these items treated at different lengths, but the order is also changed. In Kings the finding of the Book of the Law in the temple in Josiah's 18th year is the first incident mentioned. The writer appears to have organized his material geographically, i.e., beginning with the temple and spreading through the city, then into the rest of the nation. The Chronicler, on the other hand, has arranged the incidents in order of their occurrence and has characteristically introduced a number of chronological notes into the text: 34:3 (two notes without parallel in Kings); 34:8 (see 2Ki 22:3); 35:19 (see 2Ki 23:23; see also note on 2Ch 12:2). Chronicles makes it clear that the reform began in Josiah's 12th year (34:3), six years before the discovery of the Book of the Law.

34:1–2 See 2Ki 22:1–2.

34:1 *thirty-one years.* 640–609 B.C.

34:3–7 The writer of Kings covers this aspect of Josiah's reform in much greater detail (2Ki 23:4–20). He also delays his account of the removal of pagan religions until after the discovery of the Book of the Law, while the Chronicler places it before.

34:3 Some interpreters have sought to tie the events of Josiah's 8th (v. 3), 12th (v. 3) and 18th (v. 8) years to stages in the progressive decline and fall of the Assyrian empire, which had dominated the area for about two centuries. The demise of Assyrian control over Aram and Israel undoubtedly facilitated and encouraged Josiah's reassertion of Davidic authority over former Assyrian provinces (vv. 6–7). However, one must not undercut religious motives in Josiah's reforms. If one does, the reform is reduced to a mere political rebellion. *Asherah poles.* See note on Ex 34:13.

34:6 *Manasseh, Ephraim and Simeon, as far as Naphtali.* The Chronicler's concern for "all Israel" (see Introduction to 1 Chronicles: Purpose and Themes) is apparent in his recording the involvement of the northern tribes in Josiah's reform (see also vv. 9,21,33). The Chronicler again shows all Israel united under a Davidic king, just as he did under Hezekiah (see note on 30:1). *Simeon.* Some Simeonites must have migrated from Judah to the north.

34:7 *throughout Israel.* Defined by the list of tribes in v. 6.

the idols to powder[v] and cut to pieces all
the incense altars throughout Israel. Then
he went back to Jerusalem.
8In the eighteenth year of Josiah's reign,
to purify the land and the temple, he sent
Shaphan son of Azaliah and Maaseiah the
ruler of the city, with Joah son of Joahaz,
the recorder, to repair the temple of the
LORD his God.
9They went to Hilkiah[w] the high priest
and gave him the money that had been
brought into the temple of God, which the
Levites who were the doorkeepers had
collected from the people of Manasseh,
Ephraim and the entire remnant of Israel and from all the people of Judah and
Benjamin and the inhabitants of Jerusalem. 10Then they entrusted it to the men
appointed to supervise the work on the
LORD's temple. These men paid the workers who repaired and restored the temple.
11They also gave money[x] to the carpenters
and builders to purchase dressed stone,
and timber for joists and beams for the
buildings that the kings of Judah had allowed to fall into ruin.[y]
12The men did the work faithfully.[z] Over
them to direct them were Jahath and Obadiah, Levites descended from Merari, and
Zechariah and Meshullam, descended
from Kohath. The Levites—all who were
skilled in playing musical instruments—[a]
13had charge of the laborers[b] and supervised all the workers from job to job. Some
of the Levites were secretaries, scribes and
doorkeepers.

The Book of the Law Found

34:14-28pp — 2Ki 22:8-20
34:29-32pp — 2Ki 23:1-3

14While they were bringing out the
money that had been taken into the temple of the LORD, Hilkiah the priest found
the Book of the Law of the LORD that had
been given through Moses. 15Hilkiah said
to Shaphan the secretary, "I have found
the Book of the Law[c] in the temple of the
LORD." He gave it to Shaphan.
16Then Shaphan took the book to the
king and reported to him: "Your officials
are doing everything that has been committed to them. 17They have paid out the
money that was in the temple of the LORD
and have entrusted it to the supervisors
and workers." 18Then Shaphan the secretary informed the king, "Hilkiah the priest
has given me a book." And Shaphan read
from it in the presence of the king.
19When the king heard the words of the
Law,[d] he tore[e] his robes. 20He gave these
orders to Hilkiah, Ahikam son of Shaphan[f], Abdon son of Micah,[a] Shaphan
the secretary and Asaiah the king's attendant: 21"Go and inquire of the LORD for me
and for the remnant in Israel and Judah
about what is written in this book that has
been found. Great is the LORD's anger that
is poured out[g] on us because our fathers
have not kept the word of the LORD; they
have not acted in accordance with all that
is written in this book."
22Hilkiah and those the king had sent
with him[b] went to speak to the prophetess[h] Huldah, who was the wife of Shallum
son of Tokhath,[c] the son of Hasrah,[d] keeper of the wardrobe. She lived in Jerusalem,
in the Second District.
23She said to them, "This is what the
LORD, the God of Israel, says: Tell the man
who sent you to me, 24'This is what the
LORD says: I am going to bring disaster[i] on
this place and its people[j]—all the curses[k]
written in the book that has been read in
the presence of the king of Judah. 25Be-
cause they have forsaken me[l] and burned
incense to other gods and provoked me to
anger by all that their hands have made,[e]
my anger will be poured out on this place
and will not be quenched.' 26Tell the king
of Judah, who sent you to inquire of the
LORD, 'This is what the LORD, the God of Israel, says concerning the words you heard:
27Because your heart was responsive[m] and
you humbled[n] yourself before God when
you heard what he spoke against this
place and its people, and because you
humbled yourself before me and tore your
robes and wept in my presence, I have
heard you, declares the LORD. 28Now I will
gather you to your fathers,[o] and you will
be buried in peace. Your eyes will not see
all the disaster I am going to bring on this
place and on those who live here.'"[p]
So they took her answer back to the
king.
29Then the king called together all the
elders of Judah and Jerusalem. 30He went
up to the temple of the LORD[q] with the

34:7 [v] S Ex 32:20
34:9 [w] S 1Ch 6:13
34:11 [x] 2Ch 24:12 [y] 2Ch 33:4-7
34:12 [z] 2Ki 12:15 [a] S 1Ch 25:1
34:13 [b] S 1Ch 23:4
34:15 [c] S 2Ki 22:8; Ezr 7:6; Ne 8:1
34:19 [d] Dt 28:3-68 [e] Isa 36:22; 37:1
34:20 [f] S 2Ki 22:3
34:21 [g] La 2:4; 4:11; Eze 36:18
34:22 [h] S Ex 15:20; Ne 6:14
34:24 [i] Pr 16:4; Isa 3:9; Jer 40:2; 42:10; 44:2,11 [j] 2Ch 36:14-20 [k] Dt 28:15-68
34:25 [l] 2Ch 33:3-6; Jer 22:9
34:27 [m] S 2Ch 32:26 [n] S Ex 10:3; S 2Ch 6:37
34:28 [o] 2Ch 35:20-25 [p] S 2Ch 32:26
34:30 [q] S 2Ki 23:2

[a] 20 Also called *Acbor son of Micaiah* [b] 22 One Hebrew manuscript, Vulgate and Syriac; most Hebrew manuscripts do not have *had sent with him.* [c] 22 Also called *Tikvah* [d] 22 Also called *Harhas* [e] 25 Or *by everything they have done*

34:8–21 See 2Ki 22:3–13 and notes.
34:9 *Manasseh, Ephraim and the entire remnant of Israel.* Again as part of his concern with "all Israel," the Chronicler notes that worshipers from the north also brought gifts to the temple (not explicitly indicated in 2Ki 22:4).
34:10–13 Cf. 24:8–12.
34:14 *Book of the Law of the LORD.* See note on 17:9.
34:22–28 See 2Ki 22:14–20 and notes.
34:22 *prophetess Huldah.* See note on 2Ki 22:14.
34:28 *will be buried in peace.* See the death and burial account (35:20–25).
34:29–31 See 2Ki 23:1–3 and notes.
34:30 *the priests and the Levites.* Cf. 2Ki 23:2, which has "the priests and the prophets."

men of Judah, the people of Jerusalem,
the priests and the Levites — all the people from the least to the greatest. He read
in their hearing all the words of the Book
of the Covenant, which had been found in
the temple of the LORD. 31The king stood
by his pillar[r] and renewed the covenant[s]
in the presence of the LORD — to follow[t]
the LORD and keep his commands, regulations and decrees with all his heart and
all his soul, and to obey the words of the
covenant written in this book.
32Then he had everyone in Jerusalem
and Benjamin pledge themselves to it; the
people of Jerusalem did this in accordance
with the covenant of God, the God of their
fathers.
33Josiah removed all the detestable[u]
idols from all the territory belonging to the
Israelites, and he had all who were present
in Israel serve the LORD their God. As long
as he lived, they did not fail to follow the
LORD, the God of their fathers.

Josiah Celebrates the Passover

35:1,18-19pp — 2Ki 23:21-23

35 Josiah celebrated the Passover[v] to the
LORD in Jerusalem, and the Passover
lamb was slaughtered on the fourteenth
day of the first month. 2He appointed the
priests to their duties and encouraged
them in the service of the LORD's temple.
3He said to the Levites, who instructed[w]
all Israel and who had been consecrated to
the LORD: "Put the sacred ark in the temple
that Solomon son of David king of Israel
built. It is not to be carried about on your
shoulders. Now serve the LORD your God
and his people Israel. 4Prepare yourselves
by families in your divisions,[x] according
to the directions written by David king of
Israel and by his son Solomon.
5"Stand in the holy place with a group of
Levites for each subdivision of the families
of your fellow countrymen, the lay people.
6Slaughter the Passover lambs, consecrate
yourselves[y] and prepare ⌞the lambs⌟ for
your fellow countrymen, doing what the
LORD commanded through Moses."
7Josiah provided for all the lay people
who were there a total of thirty thousand
sheep and goats for the Passover offerings,[z] and also three thousand cattle — all
from the king's own possessions.[a]
8His officials also contributed[b] voluntarily to the people and the priests and Levites. Hilkiah,[c] Zechariah and Jehiel, the
administrators of God's temple, gave the
priests twenty-six hundred Passover offerings and three hundred cattle. 9Also Conaniah[d] along with Shemaiah and Nethanel,
his brothers, and Hashabiah, Jeiel and Jozabad,[e] the leaders of the Levites, provided
five thousand Passover offerings and five
hundred head of cattle for the Levites.
10The service was arranged and the
priests stood in their places with the Levites in their divisions[f] as the king had ordered.[g] 11The Passover lambs were slaughtered,[h] and the priests sprinkled the blood
handed to them, while the Levites skinned
the animals. 12They set aside the burnt offerings to give them to the subdivisions of
the families of the people to offer to the
LORD, as is written in the Book of Moses.
They did the same with the cattle. 13They
roasted the Passover animals over the fire
as prescribed,[i] and boiled the holy offerings in pots, caldrons and pans and served
them quickly to all the people. 14After this,
they made preparations for themselves
and for the priests, because the priests,
the descendants of Aaron, were sacrificing
the burnt offerings and the fat portions[j]
until nightfall. So the Levites made preparations for themselves and for the Aaronic
priests.
15The musicians,[k] the descendants of
Asaph, were in the places prescribed by
David, Asaph, Heman and Jeduthun the
king's seer. The gatekeepers at each gate
did not need to leave their posts, because
their fellow Levites made the preparations
for them.
16So at that time the entire service of the
LORD was carried out for the celebration
of the Passover and the offering of burnt
offerings on the altar of the LORD, as King
Josiah had ordered. 17The Israelites who
were present celebrated the Passover at
that time and observed the Feast of Unleavened Bread for seven days. 18The Passover had not been observed like this in Israel since the days of the prophet Samuel;

34:31 [r]S 1Ki 7:15 [s]S 2Ki 11:17; S 2Ch 23:16 [t]S Dt 13:4
34:33 [u]S Dt 18:9
35:1 [v]Ex 12:1-30; S Nu 28:16
35:3 [w]S 2Ch 17:7
35:4 [x]ver 10; S 1Ch 24:1; Ezr 6:18
35:6 [y]S Lev 11:44
35:7 [z]S 2Ch 30:24 [a]S 2Ch 31:3
35:8 [b]S 1Ch 29:3; 2Ch 29:31-36 [c]S 1Ch 6:13
35:9 [d]2Ch 31:12 [e]2Ch 31:13
35:10 [f]S ver 4 [g]2Ch 30:16
35:11 [h]S 2Ch 30:17
35:13 [i]Ex 12:2-11
35:14 [j]S Ex 29:13
35:15 [k]S 1Ch 25:1; S 26:12-19; 2Ch 29:30; Ne 12:46; Ps 68:25

34:33 *all the territory belonging to the Israelites … all who were present in Israel.* See note on v. 6.

35:1 – 19 The Chronicler gives much more extensive coverage to Josiah's Passover celebration than is found in the brief allusion in Kings (2Ki 23:21 – 23).

35:1 *first month.* The traditional month; contrast the Passover of Hezekiah (see note on 30:2).

35:3 *Put the sacred ark in the temple.* Implies that it had been removed, perhaps for protection during the evil reigns of Manasseh and Amon, who preceded Josiah.

35:4 *David … Solomon.* The Chronicler specifically parallels David and Solomon in three cases: 7:10 (contrast 1Ki 8:66, where only David is mentioned); 11:17; and here. This tendency reflects his glorification and idealization of both (see Introduction to 1 Chronicles: Portrait of David and Solomon).

35:7 – 9 The emphasis in Chronicles on voluntary and joyful giving (24:8 – 14; 29:31 – 36; 31:3 – 21; 1Ch 29:3 – 9) presumably had direct relevance to the postexilic readers for whom the Chronicler wrote.

35:15 *seer.* See note on 1Ch 25:5.

35:18 *since the days of the prophet Samuel.* Instead of "since the days of the judges" (2Ki 23:22). This is the Chronicler's way of highlighting the importance of the prophets (see Introduction to 1 Chronicles: Purpose and Themes: 3).

and none of the kings of Israel had ever celebrated such a Passover as did Josiah, with the priests, the Levites and all Judah and Israel who were there with the people of Jerusalem. 19 This Passover was celebrated in the eighteenth year of Josiah's reign.

The Death of Josiah

35:20–36:1pp — 2Ki 23:28-30

20 After all this, when Josiah had set the temple in order, Neco king of Egypt went up to fight at Carchemish[l] on the Euphrates,[m] and Josiah marched out to meet him in battle. 21 But Neco sent messengers to him, saying, "What quarrel is there between you and me, O king of Judah? It is not you I am attacking at this time, but the house with which I am at war. God has told[n] me to hurry; so stop opposing God, who is with me, or he will destroy you."

22 Josiah, however, would not turn away from him, but disguised[o] himself to engage him in battle. He would not listen to what Neco had said at God's command but went to fight him on the plain of Megiddo.

23 Archers[p] shot King Josiah, and he told his officers, "Take me away; I am badly wounded." 24 So they took him out of his chariot, put him in the other chariot he had and brought him to Jerusalem, where he died. He was buried in the tombs of his fathers, and all Judah and Jerusalem mourned for him.

25 Jeremiah composed laments for Josiah, and to this day all the men and women singers commemorate Josiah in the laments.[q] These became a tradition in Israel and are written in the Laments.[r]

35:20 [l] Isa 10:9; Jer 46:2 [m] S Ge 2:14 **35:21** [n] S 1Ki 13:18; S 2Ki 18:25 **35:22** [o] S 1Sa 28:8 **35:23** [p] S 1Ki 22:34 **35:25** [q] S Ge 50:10; Jer 22:10, 15-16 [r] 2Ch 34:28

26 The other events of Josiah's reign and his acts of devotion, according to what is written in the Law of the LORD— 27 all the events, from beginning to end, are written in the book of the kings of Israel and

36 Judah. 1 And the people[s] of the land took Jehoahaz son of Josiah and made him king in Jerusalem in place of his father.

Jehoahaz King of Judah

36:2-4pp — 2Ki 23:31-34

2 Jehoahaz[a] was twenty-three years old when he became king, and he reigned in Jerusalem three months. 3 The king of Egypt dethroned him in Jerusalem and imposed on Judah a levy of a hundred talents[b] of silver and a talent[c] of gold. 4 The king of Egypt made Eliakim, a brother of Jehoahaz, king over Judah and Jerusalem and changed Eliakim's name to Jehoiakim. But Neco[t] took Eliakim's brother Jehoahaz and carried him off to Egypt.[u]

Jehoiakim King of Judah

36:5-8pp — 2Ki 23:36–24:6

5 Jehoiakim[v] was twenty-five years old when he became king, and he reigned in Jerusalem eleven years. He did evil in the eyes of the LORD his God. 6 Nebuchadnezzar[w] king of Babylon attacked him and bound him with bronze shackles to take him to Babylon.[x] 7 Nebuchadnezzar also took to Babylon articles from the temple of the LORD and put them in his temple[d] there.[y]

36:1 [s] S 2Ch 22:1 **36:4** [t] Jer 22:10-12 [u] Eze 19:4 **36:5** [v] Jer 22:18; 25:1; 26:1; 35:1; 36:1; 45:1; 46:2 **36:6** [w] Jer 25:9; 27:6; Eze 29:18 [x] Eze 19:9; Da 1:1 **36:7** [y] ver 18; Ezr 1:7; Jer 27:16; Da 1:2

[a] 2 Hebrew *Joahaz,* a variant of *Jehoahaz*; also in verse 4 [b] 3 That is, about 3 3/4 tons (about 3.4 metric tons) [c] 3 That is, about 75 pounds (about 34 kilograms) [d] 7 Or *palace*

35:19 *eighteenth year.* The same year as the discovery of the Book of the Law (34:8,14).

35:20–27 See 2Ki 23:28–30. In 609 B.C. Pharaoh Neco "went up to the Euphrates River to help the king of Assyria" (2Ki 23:29) against the Babylonians.

35:21–22 Unique to the Chronicler, showing his view on retribution once again: Josiah's death in battle comes as a result of his disobedience to the word of God as heard even in the mouth of the pagan pharaoh.

35:21 *house with which I am at war.* A reference to the Babylonians; Nabopolassar was on the throne of Babylon, while his son Nebuchadnezzar was commanding the armies in the field. Nebuchadnezzar would succeed his father after another battle at Carchemish against Egypt in 605 B.C. Josiah may have been an ally of Babylon (see 32:31; 33:11 and notes).

35:22 *disguised himself.* Cf. Ahab and Jehoshaphat (see 18:29 and note). *plain of Megiddo.* See note on Jdg 5:19.

35:24b–25 Unique to Chronicles.

35:25 *Jeremiah composed laments for Josiah.* Jeremiah held Josiah in high esteem (Jer 22:15–16). The statement that he composed laments is one of the reasons the book of Lamentations has been traditionally associated with him. *to this day.* See note on 5:9.

36:2–14 Josiah is the only king of Judah to be succeeded by three of his sons (Jehoahaz, Jehoiakim and Zedekiah). The Chronicler's account of the reigns of the remaining kings of Judah is quite brief.

36:2 See 2Ki 23:31–35. With the death of Josiah at the hands of Pharaoh Neco, Judah slipped into a period of Egyptian domination (vv. 3–4). *three months.* In 609 B.C. Neco's assertion of authority over Judah ended the brief 20 years of Judahite independence under Josiah. The Chronicler makes no moral judgment on this brief reign, though the author of Kings does (2Ki 23:32).

36:4 Just as Neco took Jehoahaz into captivity and replaced him with Eliakim, whose name he changed to Jehoiakim, so also Nebuchadnezzar would later take Jehoiachin to Babylon, replacing him with Mattaniah, whose name he changed to Zedekiah (2Ki 24:15–17). Each conqueror wanted to place his own man on the throne; the change of name implied authority over him.

36:5–8 See 2Ki 23:36—24:7. Jehoiakim persecuted the prophets and is the object of scathing denunciation by Jeremiah (Jer 25–26; 36). After the Egyptian defeat at Carchemish (Jer 46:2) in 605 B.C., Jehoiakim transferred allegiance to Nebuchadnezzar of Babylon. When he later rebelled and again allied himself with Egypt, Nebuchadnezzar sent a punitive army against him. But Jehoiakim died before the army arrived, and Nebuchadnezzar took his son Jehoiachin into captivity.

36:5 *eleven years.* 609–598 B.C.

36:6 *Nebuchadnezzar . . . attacked him.* See chart, p. 472.

8The other events of Jehoiakim's reign,
the detestable things he did and all that
was found against him, are written in the
book of the kings of Israel and Judah. And
Jehoiachin his son succeeded him as king.

Jehoiachin King of Judah

36:9-10pp — 2Ki 24:8-17

9Jehoiachin[z] was eighteen[a] years old
when he became king, and he reigned
in Jerusalem three months and ten days.
He did evil in the eyes of the LORD. 10In
the spring, King Nebuchadnezzar sent for
him and brought him to Babylon,[a] together with articles of value from the temple
of the LORD, and he made Jehoiachin's uncle,[b] Zedekiah, king over Judah and Jerusalem.

Zedekiah King of Judah

36:11-16pp — 2Ki 24:18-20; Jer 52:1-3

11Zedekiah[b] was twenty-one years old
when he became king, and he reigned
in Jerusalem eleven years. 12He did evil
in the eyes of the LORD[c] his God and did
not humble[d] himself before Jeremiah the
prophet, who spoke the word of the LORD.
13He also rebelled against King Nebuchadnezzar, who had made him take an oath[e]
in God's name. He became stiff-necked[f]
and hardened his heart and would not
turn to the LORD, the God of Israel. 14Fur-
thermore, all the leaders of the priests and
the people became more and more unfaithful,[g] following all the detestable practices of the nations and defiling the temple
of the LORD, which he had consecrated in
Jerusalem.

The Fall of Jerusalem

36:17-20pp — 2Ki 25:1-21; Jer 52:4-27
36:22-23pp — Ezr 1:1-3

15The LORD, the God of their fathers, sent
word to them through his messengers[h]
again and again,[i] because he had pity on
his people and on his dwelling place. 16But
they mocked God's messengers, despised
his words and scoffed[j] at his prophets until
the wrath[k] of the LORD was aroused against
his people and there was no remedy.[l] 17He
brought up against them the king of the
Babylonians,[c][m] who killed their young
men with the sword in the sanctuary, and
spared neither young man[n] nor young
woman, old man or aged.[o] God handed
all of them over to Nebuchadnezzar.[p] 18He
carried to Babylon all the articles[q] from
the temple of God, both large and small,
and the treasures of the LORD's temple and
the treasures of the king and his officials.
19They set fire[r] to God's temple[s] and broke
down the wall[t] of Jerusalem; they burned
all the palaces and destroyed[u] everything
of value there.[v]

20He carried into exile[w] to Babylon the
remnant, who escaped from the sword,
and they became servants[x] to him and
his sons until the kingdom of Persia came
to power. 21The land enjoyed its sabbath
rests;[y] all the time of its desolation it rested,[z] until the seventy years[a] were completed in fulfillment of the word of the LORD
spoken by Jeremiah.

22In the first year of Cyrus[b] king of Persia, in order to fulfill the word of the LORD
spoken by Jeremiah, the LORD moved the
heart of Cyrus king of Persia to make a
proclamation throughout his realm and to
put it in writing:

[a] *9* One Hebrew manuscript, some Septuagint manuscripts and Syriac (see also 2 Kings 24:8); most Hebrew manuscripts *eight* [b] *10* Hebrew *brother,* that is, relative (see 2 Kings 24:17) [c] *17* Or *Chaldeans*

36:9 [z] Jer 22:24-28; 24:1; 27:20; 29:21; 52:31 **36:10** [a] ver 18; S 2Ki 20:17; Ezr 1:7; Isa 52:11; Jer 14:18; 21:7; 22:25; 24:1; 27:16, 20, 22; 29:1; 34:21; 40:1; Eze 17:12; Da 5:2 **36:11** [b] S 2Ki 24:17; Jer 27:1; 28:1; 34:2; 37:1; 39:1 **36:12** [c] Jer 37:1-39:18 [d] S Dt 8:3; 7:14; Jer 44:10 **36:13** [e] Eze 17:13 [f] S Ex 32:9; S Dt 9:27 **36:14** [g] S 1Ch 5:25 **36:15** [h] Isa 5:4; 44:26; Jer 7:25; Hag 1:13; Zec 1:4; Mal 2:7; 3:1; S Mt 5:12 [i] Jer 7:13, 25; 11:7; 25:3-4; 35:14, 15; 44:4-6 **36:16** [j] S 2Ki 2:23; Job 8:2; Isa 28:14, 22; 29:20; 57:4; Jer 5:13; 43:2; Mic 2:11 [k] Ezr 5:12; Pr 1:30-31; Jer 44:3 [l] Ne 9:30; Pr 29:1; Jer 7:26; 20:8; 25:4; 30:12; Da 9:6; Zec 1:2 **36:17** [m] S Ge 10:10 [n] Jer 6:11; 9:21; 18:21; 44:7 [o] S Dt 32:25; Jer 51:22 [p] Ezr 5:12; Jer 32:28; La 2:21; Eze 9:6; 23:47 **36:18** [q] S ver 7; S ver 10; Jer 27:20

36:19 [r] Jer 11:16; 17:27; 21:10, 14; 22:7; 32:29; 39:8; La 4:11; Eze 20:47; Am 2:5; Zec 11:1 [s] 1Ki 9:8-9 [t] S 2Ki 14:13 [u] La 2:6 [v] Ps 79:1-3 **36:20** [w] S Lev 26:44; S 2Ki 24:14; Ezr 2:1; Ne 7:6 [x] Jer 27:7 **36:21** [y] S Lev 25:4 [z] S 1Ch 22:9 [a] Jer 1:1; 25:11; 27:22; 29:10; 40:1; Da 9:2; Zec 1:12; 7:5 **36:22** [b] Isa 44:28; 45:1, 13; Da 1:21; 6:28; 10:1

36:9 – 10 See 2Ki 24:8 – 17; see also Jer 22:24 – 28; 24:1; 29:2; 52:31. Although Jehoiachin was taken into captivity (597 B.C.) with a large retinue, including the queen mother and high officials, and was succeeded by Zedekiah, the exiles continued to date in terms of his reign (Jer 52:31; Eze 1:2; cf. Est 2:5 – 6).

36:9 *three months and ten days.* 598 – 597 B.C.

36:11 – 14 See 2Ki 24:18 – 20; Jer 52:1 – 3. Verses 13b – 14 are unique to the Chronicler (cf. Jer 1:3; 21:1 – 7; 24:8; 27:1 – 15; 32:1 – 5; 34:1 – 7,21; 37:1 — 39:7). Zedekiah succumbed to the temptation to look to Egypt for help and rebelled against Nebuchadnezzar. Babylonian reaction was swift. Jerusalem was besieged (Jer 21:3 – 7) in 588 B.C. and held out for over two years before being destroyed in the summer of 586.

36:11 *eleven years.* 597 – 586 B.C.

36:15 – 16 See 24:19 and note.

36:20 – 21 The conclusions of the two Biblical histories are interestingly different: (1) The author(s) of Kings had sought to show why the exile occurred and had traced the sad history of Israel's disobedience to the exile. With the state at an end, the author(s) could still show God's faithfulness to his promises to David (2Ki 25:27 – 30) by reporting the favor bestowed on his descendants. (2) The Chronicler, whose vantage point was after the exile, was able to look back on the exile not only as judgment, but also as containing hope for the future. For him the purified remnant had returned to a purified land (vv. 22 – 23), and a new era of hope was beginning. The exile was not judgment alone, but also blessing, for it allowed the land to catch up on its sabbath rests (Lev 26:40 – 45). And God had remembered his covenant (Lev 26:45) and restored his people to the land (see note on vv. 22 – 23).

36:22 – 23 Not found in Kings. It is repeated at the beginning of Ezra (1:1 – 3), which resumes the history at the point where Chronicles ends — indicating that Chronicles and Ezra may have been written by the same author. See the prophecy of Jeremiah (Jer 25:1 – 14; cf. Da 9). Cyrus also issued decrees for other captive peoples, allowing them to return to their lands. Under God's sovereignty, this effort by a Persian king to win the favor of peoples treated harshly by the Babylonians also inaugurated the restoration period. See notes on Ezr 1:1 – 4.

36:22 *Cyrus king of Persia.* See note on Ezr 1:1.

23 "This is what Cyrus king of Persia says:
" 'The LORD, the God of heaven,
has given me all the kingdoms of the
earth and he has appointed[c] me to
build a temple for him at Jerusalem in
Judah. Anyone of his people among
you — may the LORD his God be with
him, and let him go up.' "

36:23 [c] S Jdg 4:10

36:23 *God of heaven.* See note on Ezr 1:2.

Ezra

INTRODUCTION

Ezra and Nehemiah

Although the caption to Ne 1:1, "The words of Nehemiah son of Hacaliah," indicates that Ezra and Nehemiah were originally two separate compositions, they were combined as one very early. Josephus (c. A.D. 37 – 100) and the Jewish Talmud refer to the book of Ezra but not to a separate book of Nehemiah. The oldest manuscripts of the Septuagint (the pre-Christian Greek translation of the OT) also treat Ezra and Nehemiah as one book.

Origen (c. A.D. 185 – 253) is the first writer known to distinguish between two books, which he called 1 Ezra and 2 Ezra. In translating the Latin Vulgate (c. A.D. 390 – 405), Jerome called Nehemiah the second book of Esdrae (Ezra). The English translations by Wycliffe (1382) and Coverdale (1535) also called Ezra "I Esdras" and Nehemiah "II Esdras." The oldest extant Hebrew manuscript to contain this separation dates from 1448.

A Quick Look

Author:
Unknown; possibly Ezra

Audience:
The people of Judah who had returned from exile in Babylon

Date:
Sometime after 440 B.C.

Theme:
A remnant of the Israelites, who had been exiled to Babylonia, return to Judah and Jerusalem to rebuild the temple under God's direction.

Literary Form and Authorship

As in the closely related books of 1,2 Chronicles, one notes the prominence of various lists in Ezra and Nehemiah. These evidently reflect official sources. Included are lists of (1) temple articles (Ezr 1:9 – 11), (2) the returned exiles (Ezr 2, which is virtually the same as Ne 7:6 – 73), (3) the genealogy of Ezra (Ezr 7:1 – 5), (4) the heads of the clans (Ezr 8:1 – 14), (5) those involved in mixed marriages (Ezr 10:18 – 43), (6) those who helped rebuild the wall (Ne 3), (7) those who sealed the covenant (Ne 10:1 – 27), (8) residents of Jerusalem and other towns (Ne 11:3 – 36) and (9) priests and Levites (Ne 12:1 – 26).

Also included in Ezra are seven official documents or letters (all in Aramaic except the first, which is in Hebrew): (1) the decree of Cyrus (1:2 – 4), (2) the accusation of Rehum and others against the Jews (4:11 – 16), (3) the reply of Artaxerxes I (4:17 – 22), (4) the report from Tattenai (5:7 – 17), (5) the memorandum of Cyrus's decree (6:2b – 5), (6) Darius's reply to Tattenai (6:6 – 12) and (7) the authorization given by Artaxerxes I to Ezra (7:12 – 26). The documents are similar to contemporary non-Biblical documents of the Persian period.

Certain materials in Ezra are first-person extracts from his memoirs: 7:27 – 28; 8:1 – 34; 9. Other sections are written in the third person: 7:1 – 26; 10; see also Ne 8. Linguistic analysis has shown that the first-person and third-person extracts resemble each other, making it likely that the same author wrote both.

Most scholars conclude that the author/compiler of Ezra and Nehemiah was also the author of 1,2 Chronicles. This viewpoint is based on certain characteristics common to both Chronicles and Ezra-Nehemiah. The verses at the end of Chronicles and at the beginning of Ezra are virtually identical. Both Chronicles and Ezra-Nehemiah exhibit a fondness for lists, for the description of religious festivals and for such phrases as "heads of families" and "the house of God." Especially striking in these books is the prominence of Levites and temple personnel. The words for "singer," "gatekeeper" and "temple servants" are used almost exclusively in Chronicles and Ezra-Nehemiah. See Introduction to 1 Chronicles: Author, Date and Sources.

Ezra and Nehemiah relate how God's covenant people were restored from Babylonian exile to the covenant land as a people under God's rule.

Date

The Ezra memoirs (see note on 7:28) may be dated c. 440 B.C. and the Nehemiah memoirs c. 430. These were then combined with other materials somewhat later. See Introduction to 1 Chronicles: Author, Date and Sources.

The Order of Ezra and Nehemiah

According to the traditional view, Ezra arrived in Jerusalem in the seventh year (Ezr 7:8) of Artaxerxes I (458 B.C.), followed by Nehemiah, who arrived in the king's 20th year (444 B.C.; Ne 2:1,11).

Some have proposed a reverse order in which Nehemiah arrived in 444 B.C., while Ezra arrived in the seventh year of Artaxerxes II (398 B.C.). By amending "seventh" (Ezr 7:8) to either "27th" or "37th," others place Ezra's arrival after Nehemiah's but still maintain that they were contemporaries.

These alternative views, however, present more problems than the traditional position. As the text stands, Ezra arrived before Nehemiah and they are found together in Ne 8:9 (at the reading of the Law) and Ne 12:26,36 (at the dedication of the wall). See chart, p. 675; see also notes on Ne 1:1; 2:1.

Languages

Ezra and Nehemiah were written in a form of late Hebrew with the exception of Ezr 4:8 — 6:18; 7:12 – 26, which were written in Aramaic, the language of international diplomacy during the Persian period. Of these 67 Aramaic verses, 52 are in records or letters. Ezra evidently found these documents in Aramaic and copied them, inserting connecting verses in Aramaic.

Major Theological Themes

The books of Ezra and Nehemiah relate how God's covenant people were restored from Babylonian exile to the covenant land as a people under God's rule. The major theological themes of this account are:

1. The restoration of Israel from exile was God's doing. He moved the hearts of Persian emperors; he moved the hearts of the repatriates and those who supported them; he raised up prophets to prod and support the repatriates; he protected them on the way and delivered them from their opponents; he stirred up Ezra and Nehemiah to perform their separate ministries; he prospered the rebuilding of the temple and Jerusalem.

2. The restoration of the covenant community was complete — even though political independence was not attained. "All Israel" was repatriated through a representative remnant; the temple was rebuilt and its services (daily sacrifices, priestly ministries, Levitical praise, annual feasts) revived in accordance with the Law of Moses and the regulations instituted by David; the Law was reestablished as regulative for the life of the community; the "holy city" (Jerusalem) was rebuilt and inhabited; the people were purged; the covenant was renewed.

3. Just as God used the world powers to judge his people, so he used them to restore his people; imperial action and authority directly and indirectly initiated, protected and sustained every aspect of the restoration.

4. Israel's restoration evoked fierce opposition, but that opposition was thwarted at every turn.

5. The restored community was a chastened people, yet they were also in need of frequent rebuke and reformation. Israel remained a wayward people. They still awaited the "new covenant" of which Jeremiah had spoken (ch. 31) and the renewal to be effected by God's Spirit as announced by Joel (ch. 1) and Ezekiel (ch. 36).

Outline

- I. Initial Return from Exile and the Rebuilding of the Temple (chs. 1–6)
  - A. First Return of the Exiles (ch. 1)
    1. The edict of Cyrus (1:1–4)
    2. The return under Sheshbazzar (1:5–11)
  - B. List of Returning Exiles (ch. 2)
  - C. Revival of Temple Worship (ch. 3)
    1. The rebuilding of the altar (3:1–3)
    2. The Feast of Tabernacles (3:4–6)
    3. The beginning of temple reconstruction (3:7–13)
  - D. Opposition to Rebuilding (4:1–23)
    1. Opposition during the reign of Cyrus (4:1–5)
    2. Opposition during the reign of Xerxes (4:6)
    3. Opposition during the reign of Artaxerxes (4:7–23)
  - E. Completion of the Temple (4:24—6:22)
    1. Resumption of work under Darius (4:24)
    2. A new beginning inspired by Haggai and Zechariah (5:1–2)
    3. Intervention of the governor, Tattenai (5:3–5)
    4. Report to Darius (5:6–17)
    5. Search for the decree of Cyrus (6:1–5)
    6. Darius's order for the rebuilding of the temple (6:6–12)
    7. Completion of the temple (6:13–15)
    8. Dedication of the temple (6:16–18)
    9. Celebration of Passover (6:19–22)
- II. Ezra's Return and Reforms (chs. 7–10)
  - A. Ezra's Return to Jerusalem (chs. 7–8)
    1. Introduction (7:1–10)
    2. The authorization by Artaxerxes (7:11–26)
    3. Ezra's doxology (7:27–28)
    4. List of those returning with Ezra (8:1–14)
    5. The search for Levites (8:15–20)
    6. Prayer and fasting (8:21–23)
    7. Assignment of the sacred articles (8:24–30)
    8. The journey and arrival in Jerusalem (8:31–36)
  - B. Ezra's Reforms (chs. 9–10)
    1. The offense of mixed marriages (9:1–5)
    2. Ezra's confession and prayer (9:6–15)
    3. The people's response (10:1–4)
    4. The calling of a public assembly (10:5–15)
    5. Investigation of the offenders (10:16–17)
    6. The list of offenders (10:18–43)
    7. The dissolution of mixed marriages (10:44)

Cyrus Helps the Exiles to Return

1:1-3pp — 2Ch 36:22-23

1 In the first year of Cyrus king of Persia,
in order to fulfill the word of the LORD
spoken by Jeremiah,[a] the LORD moved the
heart[b] of Cyrus king of Persia to make a
proclamation throughout his realm and to
put it in writing:

2"This is what Cyrus king of Persia
says:
" 'The LORD, the God of heaven,
has given me all the kingdoms of
the earth and he has appointed[c] me
to build[d] a temple for him at Jerusalem in Judah. 3Anyone of his people
among you—may his God be with
him, and let him go up to Jerusalem
in Judah and build the temple of the
LORD, the God of Israel, the God who
is in Jerusalem. 4And the people of
any place where survivors[e] may now
be living are to provide him with silver and gold,[f] with goods and livestock, and with freewill offerings[g] for
the temple of God[h] in Jerusalem.' "[i]

5Then the family heads of Judah and
Benjamin,[j] and the priests and Levites—
everyone whose heart God had moved[k]—
prepared to go up and build the house[l] of
the LORD in Jerusalem. 6All their neighbors
assisted them with articles of silver and
gold,[m] with goods and livestock, and with

1:1 [a]Jer 25:11-12; 29:10-14; Zec 1:12-16 [b]Ezr 6:22; 7:27 **1:2** [c]S Jdg 4:10; Ps 72:11; Isa 41:2, 25; 44:28; 45:13; 46:11; 49:7, 23; 60:3, 10 [d]Hag 1:2 **1:4** [e]Isa 10:20-22 [f]S Ex 3:22 [g]Nu 15:3; Ps 50:14; 54:6; 116:17 [h]Ps 72:8-11; Rev 21:24 [i]Ezr 3:7; 4:3; 5:13; 6:3, 14 **1:5** [j]2Ch 11:1, 3, 10, 12, 23; 15:2, 8-9; 25:5; 31:1; 34:9; Ezr 4:1; 10:9; Ne 11:4; 12:34 [k]ver 1; Ex 35:20-22; 2Ch 36:22; Hag 1:14; S Php 2:13 [l]Ps 127:1 **1:6** [m]S Ex 3:22

1:1–3a Virtually identical with the last two verses of 2 Chronicles. This fact has been used to argue that Chronicles and Ezra-Nehemiah were written and/or edited by the same person, the so-called Chronicler (see Introduction: Literary Form and Authorship; see also note on 2Ch 36:22–23).

1:1 *first year.* Of the reign of Cyrus over Babylon, beginning in March, 538 B.C., after he captured Babylon in October, 539. Cyrus, the founder of the Persian empire, reigned over the Persians from 559 until 530 (see chart, p. 472). Isa 44:28; 45:1 speak of him as the Lord's "shepherd" and his "anointed." *to fulfill the word of the LORD spoken by Jeremiah.* Jeremiah prophesied a 70-year Babylonian exile (Jer 25:11–12; 29:10). The first deportation began in 605, the third year of Jehoiakim (see Da 1:1 and note); in 538, approximately 70 years later, the people began to return.

1:2–4 This oral proclamation of Cyrus's decree was written in Hebrew, the language of the Israelite captives, in contrast to the copy of the decree in 6:3–5, which was an Aramaic memorandum for the archives.

1:2 *God of heaven.* A Persian title for God. Of the 22 OT occurrences of the phrase, 17 occur in Ezra, Nehemiah and Daniel. *temple ... at Jerusalem.* Jerusalem and the house of God are prominent subjects in Ezra and Nehemiah.

1:3 Cyrus instituted the policy of placating the gods of his subject peoples instead of carrying off their idols as the Assyrians and the Babylonians had done earlier. His generosity to the Jews was paralleled by his benevolence to the Babylonians.

1:4 *people of any place.* Probably designates the many Jews who did not wish to leave Mesopotamia. *freewill offerings.* A key to the restoration of God's temple and its services (see 2:68; 3:5; 8:28).

1:5 *family heads.* In ancient times families were extended families—more like clans than modern nuclear families. The authority figure was the patriarch, who was the "family head." See 10:16; see also 2:59; Ne 7:61; 10:34. *Judah and Benjamin.* The two main tribes of the kingdom of Judah, which the Babylonians had exiled. *Levites.* See Introduction to Leviticus: Title; see also Nu 3:5–38 and notes.

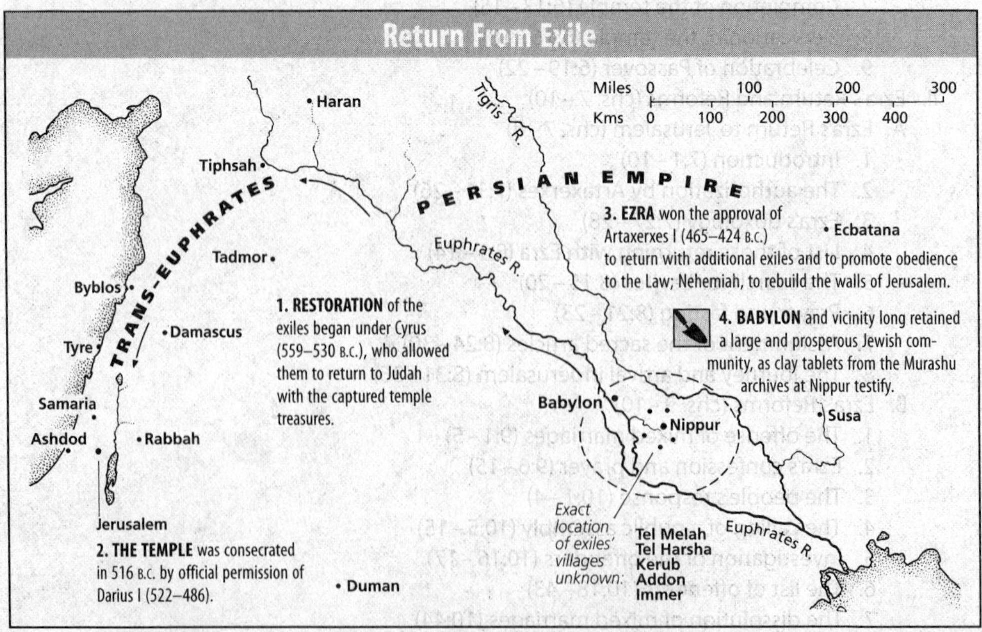
Return From Exile
Miles 0 100 200 300
Kms 0 100 200 300 400
Haran
Tigris R.
Tiphsah
TRANS-EUPHRATES
PERSIAN EMPIRE
Tadmor
Euphrates R.
Byblos
Damascus
Tyre
Samaria
Ashdod
Rabbah
Jerusalem
Duman
Babylon
Nippur
Susa
Ecbatana
1. RESTORATION of the exiles began under Cyrus (559–530 B.C.), who allowed them to return to Judah with the captured temple treasures.
2. THE TEMPLE was consecrated in 516 B.C. by official permission of Darius I (522–486).
3. EZRA won the approval of Artaxerxes I (465–424 B.C.) to return with additional exiles and to promote obedience to the Law; Nehemiah, to rebuild the walls of Jerusalem.
4. BABYLON and vicinity long retained a large and prosperous Jewish community, as clay tablets from the Murashu archives at Nippur testify.
Exact location of exiles' villages unknown:
Tel Melah
Tel Harsha
Kerub
Addon
Immer

valuable gifts, in addition to all the freewill
offerings. 7Moreover, King Cyrus brought
out the articles belonging to the temple of
the LORD, which Nebuchadnezzar had carried away from Jerusalem and had placed
in the temple of his god.[a n] 8Cyrus king of
Persia had them brought by Mithredath
the treasurer, who counted them out to
Sheshbazzar[o] the prince of Judah.

9This was the inventory:

gold dishes	30
silver dishes	1,000
silver pans[b]	29
10gold bowls	30
matching silver bowls	410
other articles	1,000

11In all, there were 5,400 articles of gold and of silver. Sheshbazzar brought all these along when the exiles came up from Babylon to Jerusalem.

1:7 [n] S 2Ki 24:13; S 2Ch 36:7, 10; Ezr 5:14; 6:5; Jer 52:17-19 1:8 [o] S 1Ch 3:18

The List of the Exiles Who Returned

2:1-70pp — Ne 7:6-73

2 Now these are the people of the province who came up from the captivity of
the exiles,[p] whom Nebuchadnezzar king
of Babylon[q] had taken captive to Babylon
(they returned to Jerusalem and Judah,
each to his own town,[r] 2in company with
Zerubbabel,[s] Jeshua,[t] Nehemiah, Seraiah,[u] Reelaiah, Mordecai, Bilshan, Mispar,
Bigvai, Rehum and Baanah):

The list of the men of the people of Israel:

3the descendants of Parosh[v]	2,172
4of Shephatiah	372
5of Arah	775
6of Pahath-Moab (through the line of Jeshua and Joab)	2,812
7of Elam	1,254
8of Zattu	945
9of Zaccai	760
10of Bani	642
11of Bebai	623
12of Azgad	1,222
13of Adonikam[w]	666
14of Bigvai	2,056

2:1 [p] S 2Ch 36:20 [q] S 2Ki 24:16; 25:12 [r] ver 70; 1Ch 9:2; Ne 7:73; 11:3 2:2 [s] S 1Ch 3:19; Mt 1:12; Lk 3:27 [t] Ezr 3:2; 5:2; 10:18; Ne 12:1, 8; Hag 1:1, 12; 2:4; Zec 3:1-10; 6:9-15 [u] 1Ch 6:14; Ne 10:2; 11:11; 12:1 2:3 [v] Ezr 8:3; 10:25; Ne 3:25 2:13 [w] Ezr 8:13

[a] 7 Or *gods* [b] 9 The meaning of the Hebrew for this word is uncertain.

1:7 It was the custom for conquerors to carry off the images of the gods of conquered cities. Since the Jews did not have an image of the Lord (see note on Ex 20:4), Nebuchadnezzar (see chart, p. 472) carried away only the temple articles.

1:8 *Mithredath.* A Persian name meaning "given by/to Mithra" (a Persian god). Mithra became popular among Roman soldiers in the second century A.D. *Sheshbazzar.* A Babylonian name meaning either "Sin, protect the father" or "Shamash/Shashu, protect the father." Sin was the moon-god, and Shamash (Shashu is a variant) was the sun-god. In spite of his Babylonian name, Sheshbazzar was probably a Jewish official who served as a deputy governor of Judah under the satrap in Samaria (see 5:14). Some believe that Sheshbazzar and Zerubbabel were the same person and give the following reasons: (1) Both were governors (5:14; Hag 1:1; 2:2). (2) Both are said to have laid the foundation of the temple (3:2–8; 5:16; Hag 1:14–15; Zec 4:6–10). (3) Jews in Babylon were often given "official" Babylonian names (cf. Da 1:7). (4) Josephus (*Antiquities*, 11.1.3) seems to identify Sheshbazzar with Zerubbabel.

Others point out, however, that the Apocrypha distinguishes between the two men (1 Esdras 6:18). Furthermore, it is likely that Sheshbazzar was an elderly man at the time of the return, while Zerubbabel was probably a younger contemporary. Sheshbazzar also may have been viewed as the official governor, while Zerubbabel served as the popular leader (3:8–11). Whereas the high priest Jeshua is associated with Zerubbabel, no priest is associated with Sheshbazzar. Although Sheshbazzar presided over the foundation of the temple in 536 B.C., so little was accomplished that Zerubbabel had to preside over a second foundation some 16 years later (see Hag 1:14–15; Zec 4:6–10).

Still others hold that Sheshbazzar is to be identified with Shenazzar (1Ch 3:18), the fourth son of King Jehoiachin. Zerubbabel would then have been Sheshbazzar's nephew (compare 3:2 with 1Ch 3:17–18).

1:9–11 When Assyrian and Babylonian conquerors carried off plunder, their scribes made a careful inventory of all the goods seized. The total of the figures in vv. 9–10 adds up to 2,499 rather than the 5,400 of v. 11. It may be that only the larger and more valuable vessels were specified.

1:11 We are not told anything about the details of Sheshbazzar's journey, which probably took place in 537 B.C. Judging from Ezra's later journey (7:8–9), the trip took about four months. See map No. 8b at the end of this study Bible; see also map, p. 672.

2:1–70 The list of returning exiles in ch. 2 almost exactly parallels the list in Ne 7:6–73 (see also 1 Esdras 5:4–46 in the Apocrypha). The list of localities indicates that people retained the memories of their homes and that exiles from a wide background of tribes, villages and towns returned. In comparing the list here with that in Ne 7, one notes many differences in the names and numbers listed. About 20 percent of the numbers, e.g., are not the same in Ezra and Nehemiah. Many of these differences may be explained, however, by assuming that a cipher notation was used with vertical strokes for units and horizontal strokes for tens, which led to copying errors.

2:1 *province.* Probably Judah (cf. 5:8, where the Aramaic word for "province" is translated "district"; see also Ne 1:3).

2:2 *Zerubbabel.* See notes on 3:2; 5:2. *Jeshua.* Means "The LORD saves" and is an Aramaic variant of Hebrew "Joshua." The Greek form is "Jesus" (see NIV text note on Mt 1:21). This Jeshua is the same as the Joshua of Hag 1:1, the son of the high priest Jehozadak (Jozadak, Ezr 3:2), who was taken into exile (1Ch 6:15). *Nehemiah.* Not the Nehemiah of the book by that name. *Mordecai.* A Babylonian name based on that of Marduk the god of Babylon (cf. Jer 50:2). Esther's cousin had the same name (see Est 2:5 and note).

2:3 *Parosh.* Means "flea" (Israelites were often named after insects and animals). Other members of this family, as well as of several other families named in vv. 6–14, returned with Ezra (8:3–14).

2:5 *Arah.* Probably means "wild ox." Since the name is rare in the OT and has been found in documents from Mesopotamia, it may have been adopted during the exile.

2:6 *Pahath-Moab.* Means "governor of Moab" and may have once designated an official title.

2:12 *Azgad.* Cf. 8:12; means "Gad is strong." It is a reference either to Gad (the god of fortune, referred to in Isa 65:11) or to the Transjordanian tribe of Gad.

[15]of Adin 454
[16]of Ater (through Hezekiah) 98
[17]of Bezai 323
[18]of Jorah 112
[19]of Hashum 223
[20]of Gibbar 95

[21]the men of Bethlehem[x] 123
[22]of Netophah 56
[23]of Anathoth 128
[24]of Azmaveth 42
[25]of Kiriath Jearim,[a] Kephirah and Beeroth 743
[26]of Ramah[y] and Geba 621
[27]of Micmash 122
[28]of Bethel and Ai[z] 223
[29]of Nebo 52
[30]of Magbish 156
[31]of the other Elam 1,254
[32]of Harim 320
[33]of Lod, Hadid and Ono 725
[34]of Jericho[a] 345
[35]of Senaah 3,630

[36]The priests:

the descendants of Jedaiah[b] (through the family of Jeshua) 973
[37]of Immer[c] 1,052
[38]of Pashhur[d] 1,247
[39]of Harim[e] 1,017

[40]The Levites:[f]

the descendants of Jeshua[g] and Kadmiel (through the line of Hodaviah) 74

[41]The singers:[h]

the descendants of Asaph 128

[42]The gatekeepers[i] of the temple:

the descendants of
Shallum, Ater, Talmon,
Akkub, Hatita and Shobai 139

[43]The temple servants:[j]

the descendants of
Ziha, Hasupha, Tabbaoth,
[44]Keros, Siaha, Padon,
[45]Lebanah, Hagabah, Akkub,
[46]Hagab, Shalmai, Hanan,
[47]Giddel, Gahar, Reaiah,
[48]Rezin, Nekoda, Gazzam,
[49]Uzza, Paseah, Besai,
[50]Asnah, Meunim, Nephusim,
[51]Bakbuk, Hakupha, Harhur,
[52]Bazluth, Mehida, Harsha,
[53]Barkos, Sisera, Temah,
[54]Neziah and Hatipha

[55]The descendants of the servants of Solomon:

the descendants of
Sotai, Hassophereth, Peruda,
[56]Jaala, Darkon, Giddel,
[57]Shephatiah, Hattil,
Pokereth-Hazzebaim and Ami

[58]The temple servants[k] and the descendants of the servants of Solomon 392

[59]The following came up from the towns of Tel Melah, Tel Harsha, Kerub, Addon and Immer, but they could not show that their families were descended[l] from Israel:

2:21 [x]Mic 5:2 **2:26** [y]S Jos 18:25 **2:28** [z]S Ge 12:8 **2:34** [a]1Ki 16:34; 2Ch 28:15 **2:36** [b]S 1Ch 24:7 **2:37** [c]S 1Ch 24:14 **2:38** [d]S 1Ch 9:12 **2:39** [e]S 1Ch 24:8 **2:40** [f]Ge 29:34; Nu 3:9; Dt 18:6-7; 1Ch 16:4; Ezr 7:7; 8:15; Ne 12:24 [g]Ezr 3:9 **2:41** [h]S 1Ch 15:16 **2:42** [i]1Sa 3:15; S 1Ch 9:17 **2:43** [j]S 1Ch 9:2; Ne 11:21 **2:58** [k]S 1Ch 9:2 **2:59** [l]S Nu 1:18

[a] 25 See Septuagint (see also Neh. 7:29); Hebrew *Kiriath Arim.*

2:16 *Ater.* Means "left-handed," as in Jdg 3:15; 20:16.

2:21–35 Whereas the names in vv. 3–20 are of families, vv. 21–35 present a series of villages and towns, many of which were in Benjamite territory north of Jerusalem. It is significant that there are no references to towns in the Negev, south of Judah. When Nebuchadnezzar overran Judah in 597 B.C. (Jer 13:19), the Edomites (see the book of Obadiah) took advantage of the situation and occupied that area.

2:23 *Anathoth.* See note on Jer 1:1.

2:28 *Bethel.* See note on Ge 12:8. Towns such as Bethel, Mizpah, Gibeon and Gibeah seem to have escaped the Babylonian assault. Bethel, however, was destroyed in the transition between the Babylonian and Persian periods. Archaeological excavations reveal that there was a small town on the site in Ezra's day. *Ai.* See note on Jos 7:2.

2:31 See v. 7.

2:33 *Lod.* Modern Lydda.

2:35 *Senaah.* The largest number of returnees—3,630 (3,930 in Ne 7:38)—is associated with Senaah. It has therefore been suggested that they did not come from a specific locality or family, but represented the poorer and lower classes of people, as inferred from the meaning of the name ("the hated one").

2:36–39 Four clans of priests numbering 4,289, about a tenth of the total.

2:40 *Levites.* See note on 1:5. *74.* The number of Levites who returned was relatively small (cf. 8:15).

2:41 *Asaph.* One of the three Levites appointed by David over the temple singers (1Ch 25:1; 2Ch 5:12; 35:15), whose duties are detailed in 1Ch 15:16–24.

2:42 *gatekeepers.* Usually Levites (1Ch 9:26; 2Ch 23:4; 35:15; Ne 7:45; 12:25; 13:22). They are mentioned 16 times in Ezra-Nehemiah and 19 times in Chronicles. Their primary function was to tend the doors and gates of the temple (1Ch 9:17–27) and to perform other menial tasks (1Ch 9:28–32; 2Ch 31:14).

2:43–58 The temple servants and the descendants of Solomon's servants together numbered 392 (v. 58), which was more than the total of the Levites, singers and gatekeepers together (vv. 40–42).

2:46 *Hanan.* Means "(God) is gracious." The verb "to be gracious" and its derivatives are the components of numerous personal names in the OT—e.g., Johanan ("The LORD is gracious"; see 8:12), which has given us the English name John (see note on Mk 1:4).

2:55,58 *descendants of the servants of Solomon.* The phrase occurs only here and in Ne 7:57,60; 11:3. These may be the descendants of the Canaanites whom Solomon enslaved (1Ki 9:20–21).

2:59–63 Individuals who lacked evidence of their ancestry.

2:59 *towns.* Places in Mesopotamia where the Jews were settled by their Babylonian captors. *Tel Melah.* Means "mound of salt," possibly a mound on which salt had been scattered (see Jdg 9:45 and note). The Hebrew word *tel* designates a hill-like mound (see note on Jos 11:13) formed by the

Chronology: Ezra–Nehemiah

Dates below are given according to a Nisan-to-Nisan Jewish calendar (see chart, p. 104).
Roman numerals represent months;
Arabic numerals represent days.

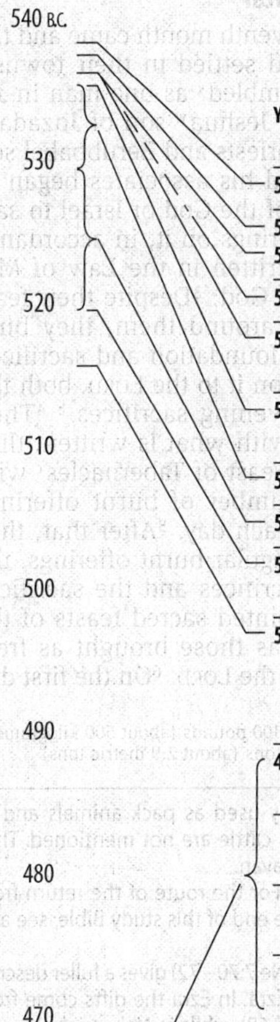

540 B.C. · 530 · 520 · 510 · 500 · 490 · 480 · 470 · 460 · 450 · 440 · 430

YEAR	MONTH	DAY	EVENT	REFERENCE
539 B.C.	Oct.	12	Capture of Babylon	Da 5:30
538 **537**	Mar. to Mar.	24 11	Cyrus's first year	Ezr 1:1-4
537(?)			Return under Sheshbazzar	Ezr 1:11
537	VII		Building of altar	Ezr 3:1
536	II		Work on temple begun	Ezr 3:8
536–530			Opposition during Cyrus's reign	Ezr 4:1-5
530–520			Work on temple ceased	Ezr 4:24
520	VI =Sept.	24 21	Work on temple renewed under Darius	Ezr 5:2; Hag 1:14
516	XII =Mar.	3 12	Temple completed	Ezr 6:15
458	I =Apr.	1 8	Ezra departs from Babylon	Ezr 7:6-9
	V =Aug.	1 4	Ezra arrives in Jerusalem	Ezr 7:8-9
	IX =Dec.	20 19	People assemble	Ezr 10:9
	X =Dec.	1 29	Committee begins investigation	Ezr 10:16
457	I =Mar.	1 27	Committee ends investigation	Ezr 10:17
445 **444**	Apr to Apr.	13 2	20th year of Artaxerxes I	Ne 1:1
444	I =Mar.–Apr.		Nehemiah approaches the king	Ne 2:1
	Aug.(?)		Nehemiah arrives in Jerusalem	Ne 2:11
	VI =Oct.	25 2	Completion of wall	Ne 6:15
	VII=Oct. to Nov.	8 5	Public assembly	Ne 7:73–8:1
	VII =Oct.	15-22 22-28	Feast of Tabernacles	Ne 8:14
	VII =Oct.	24 30	Fast	Ne 9:1
433 **432**	Apr. to Apr.	1 19	32nd year of Artaxerxes; Nehemiah's recall and return	Ne 5:14; 13:6

60The descendants of
Delaiah, Tobiah and Nekoda 652

61And from among the priests:

The descendants of
Hobaiah, Hakkoz and Barzillai
(a man who had married
a daughter of Barzillai the
Gileadite[m] and was called by
that name).

62These searched for their family records, but they could not find them and so were excluded from the priesthood[n] as unclean. 63The governor ordered them not to eat any of the most sacred food[o] until there was a priest ministering with the Urim and Thummim.[p]

64The whole company numbered 42,360, 65besides their 7,337 menservants and maidservants; and they also had 200 men and women singers.[q] 66They had 736 horses,[r] 245 mules, 67435 camels and 6,720 donkeys.

68When they arrived at the house of the LORD in Jerusalem, some of the heads of the families[s] gave freewill offerings toward the rebuilding of the house of God on its site. 69According to their ability they gave to the treasury for this work 61,000 drachmas[a] of gold, 5,000 minas[b] of silver and 100 priestly garments.

70The priests, the Levites, the singers, the gatekeepers and the temple servants settled in their own towns, along with some of the other people, and the rest of the Israelites settled in their towns.[t]

Rebuilding the Altar

3 When the seventh month came and the Israelites had settled in their towns,[u] the people assembled[v] as one man in Jerusalem. 2Then Jeshua[w] son of Jozadak[x] and his fellow priests and Zerubbabel son of Shealtiel[y] and his associates began to build the altar of the God of Israel to sacrifice burnt offerings on it, in accordance with what is written in the Law of Moses[z] the man of God. 3Despite their fear[a] of the peoples around them, they built the altar on its foundation and sacrificed burnt offerings on it to the LORD, both the morning and evening sacrifices.[b] 4Then in accordance with what is written, they celebrated the Feast of Tabernacles[c] with the required number of burnt offerings prescribed for each day. 5After that, they presented the regular burnt offerings, the New Moon[d] sacrifices and the sacrifices for all the appointed sacred feasts of the LORD,[e] as well as those brought as freewill offerings to the LORD. 6On the first day

2:61 [m]S 2Sa 17:27 **2:62** [n]Nu 3:10; 16:39-40 **2:63** [o]Lev 2:3,10 [p]S Ex 28:30 **2:65** [q]S 2Sa 19:35 **2:66** [r]Isa 66:20 **2:68** [s]S Ex 25:2 **2:70** [t]S ver 1; S 1Ch 9:2; Ne 11:3-4 **3:1** [u]Ne 7:73 [v]S Lev 23:24 **3:2** [w]S Ezr 2:2 [x]Hag 1:1; Zec 6:11 [y]1Ch 3:17 [z]S Ex 20:24; Dt 12:5-6 **3:3** [a]Ezr 4:4; Da 9:25 [b]S Ex 29:39; Nu 28:1-8 **3:4** [c]S Ex 23:16; Nu 29:12-38; Ne 8:14-18; Zec 14:16-19 **3:5** [d]S Nu 28:3,11,14; Col 2:16 [e]Lev 23:1-44; S Nu 29:39

[a] *69* That is, about 1,100 pounds (about 500 kilograms)
[b] *69* That is, about 3 tons (about 2.9 metric tons)

remains of a ruined city. The Jewish exiles had been settled along the Kebar River (Eze 1:1), perhaps near Nippur, a city in southern Mesopotamia that was the stronghold of rebels. The Jews had probably been settled on the mounds of ruined cities that had been depopulated by the Babylonians.
2:63 *governor.* Probably either Sheshbazzar or Zerubbabel (see note on 1:8). *Urim and Thummim.* See note on Ex 28:30.
2:64 *42,360.* Considerably more than the sum of the other figures given:

Categories	*Ezra*	*Nehemiah*	*1 Esdras*
Men of Israel	24,144	25,406	25,947
Priests	4,289	4,289	5,288
Levites, singers, gatekeepers	341	360	341
Temple servants, descendants of Solomon's servants	392	392	372
Men of unproven origin	652	642	652
Totals	29,818	31,089	32,600

It is difficult to account for the difference of about 10,000–12,000. The figure may refer to an unspecified 10,000–12,000 women and/or children, and it doubtless includes the priests of unproven origin referred to in vv. 61–63. Some suggest that the groups explicitly counted were returnees from Judah and Benjamin, while the remainder were from other tribes.
2:65 *menservants and maidservants.* The ratio of servants to others (one to six) is relatively high. The fact that so many returned with their masters speaks highly of the benevolent treatment of servants by the Jews. *singers.* The male and female singers listed here may be secular singers who sang at social events such as weddings and funerals (2Ch 35:25), as distinct from the temple singers of v. 41, who were all male.
2:66 *horses.* Perhaps a donation from Cyrus for the nobility. *mules.* See 1Ki 1:33 and note.
2:67 *donkeys.* Were widely used as pack animals and as mounts. Sheep, goats and cattle are not mentioned. They would have slowed the caravan.
2:68 *arrived ... Jerusalem.* For the route of the return from exile see map No. 8b at the end of this study Bible; see also map, p. 672.
2:69 The parallel passage (Ne 7:70–72) gives a fuller description than the account in Ezra. In Ezra the gifts come from the heads of the families (v. 68), while in Nehemiah the gifts are credited to three sources: the governor, the heads of the families, and the rest of the people. *drachmas.* The drachma was a Greek silver coin. Some believe that the coin intended here was the Persian *daric,* a gold coin (see note on 1Ch 29:7). *minas.* In the sexagesimal system (based on the number 60) that originated in Mesopotamia, there were 60 shekels in a mina and 60 minas in a talent. A shekel, which was about two-fifths of an ounce of silver, was the average wage for a month's work. Thus a mina would be the equivalent of five years' wages, and a talent would be 300 years' wages.
2:70 Later, Nehemiah (11:1–2) would be compelled to move people by lot to reinforce the population of Jerusalem.
3:1 *seventh month.* Tishri (September-October), about three months after the arrival of the exiles in Judah (in 537 B.C.). Tishri was one of the most sacred months of the Jewish year (see Lev 23:23–43 and notes).
3:2 *Jeshua ... Zerubbabel.* The priest takes precedence over the civil leader in view of the nature of the occasion (contrast 3:8; 4:3; 5:2; Hag 1:1).
3:4 *Feast of Tabernacles.* See Lev 23:33–43 and notes.
3:5 *New Moon.* See note on 1Sa 20:5. *appointed sacred feasts.* See note on Lev 23:2. *freewill offerings.* See note on 1:4. It is noteworthy that the restoration of the sacrifices preceded the erection of the temple itself.

of the seventh month they began to offer burnt offerings to the LORD, though the foundation of the LORD's temple had not yet been laid.

Rebuilding the Temple

[7]Then they gave money to the masons and carpenters,[f] and gave food and drink and oil to the people of Sidon and Tyre, so that they would bring cedar logs[g] by sea from Lebanon[h] to Joppa, as authorized by Cyrus[i] king of Persia.

[8]In the second month[j] of the second year after their arrival at the house of God in Jerusalem, Zerubbabel[k] son of Shealtiel, Jeshua son of Jozadak and the rest of their brothers (the priests and the Levites and all who had returned from the captivity to Jerusalem) began the work, appointing Levites twenty[l] years of age and older to supervise the building of the house of the LORD. [9]Jeshua[m] and his sons and brothers and Kadmiel and his sons (descendants of Hodaviah[a]) and the sons of Henadad and their sons and brothers—all Levites—joined together in supervising those working on the house of God.

[10]When the builders laid[n] the foundation of the temple of the LORD, the priests

3:7 [f]1Ch 22:15 [g]S 1Ch 14:1 [h]Isa 35:2; 60:13 [i]S Ezr 1:2-4
3:8 [j]1Ki 6:1 [k]Zec 4:9 [l]S Nu 4:3
3:9 [m]Ezr 2:40
3:10 [n]Ezr 5:16; 6:3; Hag 2:15

[a] 9 Hebrew *Yehudah,* probably a variant of *Hodaviah*

3:7 *cedar logs.* As in the case of the first temple, the Phoenicians cooperated by sending timber and workers (1Ki 5:6–12).

3:8 *second month.* The same month (April-May) in which Solomon had begun his temple (1Ki 6:1). *second year.* Since the Jews probably returned to Judah in the spring of 537 B.C., the second year would be the spring of 536. *twenty years.* In earlier times the lower age limit for Levites was 30 (Nu 4:3) or 25 years (Nu 8:24). It was later reduced to 20 (1Ch 23:24,27; 2Ch 31:17), probably because there were so few Levites.

3:10 *trumpets.* Made of hammered silver (see Nu 10:2 and note). According to Josephus (*Antiquities,* 3.12.6), the trumpet was "in length a little short of a cubit; it is a narrow tube, slightly thicker than a flute." With the possible exception of their use at the coronation of Joash (2Ki 11:14; 2Ch 23:13), the trumpets were always blown by priests. They were most often used on joyous occasions, such as here and at the dedication of the rebuilt walls of Jerusalem (Ne 12:35; cf. 2Ch 5:13; Ps 98:6). *cymbals.* The Hebrew for this word occurs 13 times in the OT, all in Chronicles except here and Ne 12:27.

Zerubbabel's Temple

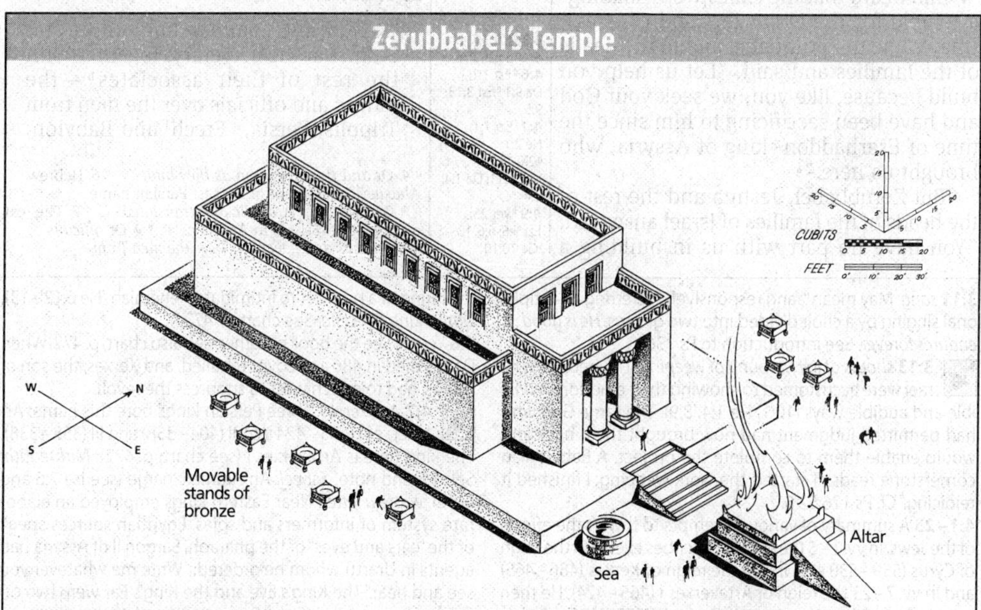

Construction of the second temple was started in 536 B.C. on the Solomonic foundations leveled a half-century earlier by the Babylonians. People who remembered the earlier temple wept at the comparison (Ezr 3:12). Not until 516 B.C., the 6th year of the Persian emperor Darius I (522–486), was the temple finally completed at the urging of Haggai and Zechariah (Ezr 6:13–15).

Archaeological evidence confirms that the Persian period in the Holy Land was a comparatively impoverished one in terms of material culture. Later Aramaic documents from Elephantine in Upper Egypt illustrate the official process of gaining permission to construct a Jewish place of worship and the opposition engendered by such a project.

Of the temple and its construction, little is known. Consequently, all art reconstructions of it are tentative. Among the few contemporary buildings, the Persian palace at Lachish and the Tobiad monument at Iraq el-Amir may be compared in terms of technique.

Unlike the more famous structures razed in 586 B.C. and A.D. 70, the temple begun by Zerubbabel suffered no major hostile destruction, but was gradually repaired and reconstructed over a long period. Eventually it was replaced entirely by Herod's magnificent edifice.

in their vestments and with trumpets,[o]
and the Levites (the sons of Asaph) with
cymbals, took their places to praise[p] the
LORD, as prescribed by David[q] king of Israel.[r] 11With praise and thanksgiving they
sang to the LORD:

"He is good;
his love to Israel endures forever."[s]

And all the people gave a great shout[t] of
praise to the LORD, because the foundation[u] of the house of the LORD was laid.
12But many of the older priests and Levites and family heads, who had seen the
former temple,[v] wept[w] aloud when they
saw the foundation of this temple being
laid, while many others shouted for joy.
13No one could distinguish the sound
of the shouts of joy[x] from the sound of
weeping, because the people made so
much noise. And the sound was heard
far away.

Opposition to the Rebuilding

4 When the enemies of Judah and Benjamin heard that the exiles were building[y]
a temple for the LORD, the God of Israel,
2they came to Zerubbabel and to the heads
of the families and said, "Let us help you
build because, like you, we seek your God
and have been sacrificing to him since the
time of Esarhaddon[z] king of Assyria, who
brought us here."[a]
3But Zerubbabel, Jeshua and the rest of
the heads of the families of Israel answered,
"You have no part with us in building a
temple to our God. We alone will build it
for the LORD, the God of Israel, as King Cyrus, the king of Persia, commanded us."[b]
4Then the peoples around them set out to
discourage the people of Judah and make
them afraid to go on building.[a c] 5They
hired counselors to work against them and
frustrate their plans during the entire reign
of Cyrus king of Persia and down to the
reign of Darius king of Persia.

Later Opposition Under Xerxes and Artaxerxes

6At the beginning of the reign of Xerxes,[b d] they lodged an accusation against
the people of Judah and Jerusalem.[e]
7And in the days of Artaxerxes[f] king of
Persia, Bishlam, Mithredath, Tabeel and
the rest of his associates wrote a letter
to Artaxerxes. The letter was written in
Aramaic script and in the Aramaic[g] language.[c,d]
8Rehum the commanding officer and
Shimshai the secretary wrote a letter
against Jerusalem to Artaxerxes the king
as follows:

9Rehum the commanding officer and
Shimshai the secretary, together with
the rest of their associates[h]—the
judges and officials over the men from
Tripolis, Persia,[e] Erech[i] and Babylon,

3:10 [o]S Nu 10:2; S 2Sa 6:5; 1Ch 16:6; 2Ch 5:13; Ne 12:35 [p]S 1Ch 25:1 [q]S 1Ch 6:31 [r]Zec 6:12 **3:11** [s]1Ch 16:34, 41; S 2Ch 7:3; Ps 30:5; 107:1; 118:1; 138:8 [t]S Jos 6:5, 10 [u]Hag 2:18; Zec 4:9; 8:9 **3:12** [v]Hag 2:3, 9 [w]Jer 31:9; 50:4 **3:13** [x]Job 8:21; 33:26; Ps 27:6; 42:4; Isa 16:9; Jer 48:33 **4:1** [y]Ne 2:20 **4:2** [z]S 2Ki 17:24 [a]S 2Ki 17:41 **4:3** [b]Ezr 1:1-4 **4:4** [c]S Ezr 3:3 **4:6** [d]Est 1:1; Da 9:1 [e]Est 3:13; 9:5 **4:7** [f]Ezr 7:1; Ne 2:1 [g]2Ki 18:26; Isa 36:11; Da 1:4; 2:4 **4:9** [h]ver 23; Ezr 5:6; 6:6, 13 [i]Ge 10:10

[a] 4 Or *and troubled them as they built* [b] 6 Hebrew *Ahasuerus,* a variant of Xerxes' Persian name [c] 7 Or *written in Aramaic and translated* [d] 7 The text of Ezra 4:8—6:18 is in Aramaic. [e] 9 Or *officials, magistrates and governors over the men from*

3:11 *sang.* May mean "sang responsively," referring to antiphonal singing by a choir divided into two groups. *He is good . . . endures forever.* See introduction to Ps 136.

3:13 *shouts of joy . . . sound of weeping.* The people of Israel were accustomed to showing their emotions in visible and audible ways (10:1; Ne 1:4; 8:9). The same God who had permitted judgment had now brought them back and would enable them to complete the project. A Babylonian cornerstone reads: "I started the work weeping, I finished it rejoicing." Cf. Ps 126:5–6.

4:1–23 A summary of various attempts to thwart the efforts of the Jews. In vv. 1–5 the author describes events in the reign of Cyrus (559–530 B.C.), in v. 6 the reign of Xerxes (486–465) and in vv. 7–23 the reign of Artaxerxes I (465–424). He then reverts in v. 24 to the time of Darius I (522–486), during whose reign the temple was completed (see 5:1–2; 6:13–15; Haggai; Zec 1:1–17; 4:9).

4:1 *enemies.* The people who offered their "help" (v. 2) were from Samaria. *Judah and Benjamin.* See notes on 1:5; 1Ki 12:21.

4:2 After the fall of Samaria in 722–721 B.C., the Assyrian kings brought in people from Mesopotamia and Aram (modern Syria). These people served their own gods but also took up the worship of the Lord as the god of the land (2Ki 17:24–41). *Esarhaddon.* See note on 2Ki 19:37; see also chart, p. 472.

4:4 *make them afraid.* The Hebrew for this verb often describes the fear aroused in a battle situation (Jdg 20:41; 2Sa 4:1; 2Ch 32:18).

4:5 *hired.* Cf. the hiring of Balaam (Dt 23:4–5; Ne 13:2) and the hiring of a prophet to intimidate Nehemiah (Ne 6:12–13). *Darius king of Persia.* See chart, p. 472.

4:6 *Xerxes.* See the book of Esther; see also chart, p. 472. When Darius died in 486 B.C., Egypt rebelled, and Xerxes, the son of Darius, had to march west to suppress the revolt.

4:7 *Artaxerxes.* Three Persian kings bore this name: Artaxerxes I (465–424 B.C.), II (404–358) and III (358–338). The king here is Artaxerxes I (see chart, p. 472). *Mithredath.* See 1:8 and note. *Tabeel.* An Aramaic name (see Isa 7:6 and note). *wrote a letter.* Near Eastern kings employed an elaborate system of informers and spies. Egyptian sources speak of the "ears and eyes" of the pharaoh. Sargon II of Assyria had agents in Urartu whom he ordered: "Write me whatever you see and hear." The King's Eye and the King's Ear were two officials who reported to the Persian monarch.

4:8—6:18 For this passage the author draws upon Aramaic documents; a further Aramaic section is 7:12–26.

4:8 *commanding officer.* An official who had the role of a chancellor or commissioner. Perhaps Rehum dictated, and Shimshai wrote, the letter in Aramaic. (Alternatively, Shimshai may have been a high official rather than a scribe.) The letter would then be read in a Persian translation before the king (v. 18). According to Herodotus (3.128), royal scribes were attached to each governor to report directly to the Persian king.

4:9 *associates.* See vv. 17,23; 5:3,6; 6:6 ("fellow officials"); 6:13. One of the striking characteristics of Persian bureaucracy was that each responsibility was shared among colleagues. *Erech.* See note on Ge 10:10. *Babylon.* During the reign of the As-

the Elamites of Susa,[j] 10and the other
people whom the great and honorable
Ashurbanipal[a k] deported and settled
in the city of Samaria and elsewhere
in Trans-Euphrates.[l]

11(This is a copy of the letter they sent
him.)

To King Artaxerxes,

From your servants, the men of Trans-Euphrates:

12The king should know that the
Jews who came up to us from you
have gone to Jerusalem and are rebuilding that rebellious and wicked
city. They are restoring the walls and
repairing the foundations.[m]
13Furthermore, the king should
know that if this city is built and
its walls are restored, no more taxes, tribute or duty[n] will be paid, and
the royal revenues will suffer. 14Now
since we are under obligation to the
palace and it is not proper for us to
see the king dishonored, we are sending this message to inform the king,
15so that a search may be made in
the archives[o] of your predecessors.
In these records you will find that
this city is a rebellious city, troublesome to kings and provinces, a place
of rebellion from ancient times. That
is why this city was destroyed.[p] 16We
inform the king that if this city is built
and its walls are restored, you will be
left with nothing in Trans-Euphrates.

17The king sent this reply:

To Rehum the commanding officer, Shimshai the secretary and the rest of their associates living in Samaria and elsewhere in Trans-Euphrates:[q]

Greetings.

18The letter you sent us has been
read and translated in my presence.
19I issued an order and a search was
made, and it was found that this city
has a long history of revolt[r] against
kings and has been a place of rebellion and sedition. 20Jerusalem has
had powerful kings ruling over the
whole of Trans-Euphrates,[s] and taxes,
tribute and duty were paid to them.
21Now issue an order to these men to
stop work, so that this city will not
be rebuilt until I so order. 22Be careful not to neglect this matter. Why let
this threat grow, to the detriment of
the royal interests?[t]

23As soon as the copy of the letter of
King Artaxerxes was read to Rehum and
Shimshai the secretary and their associates,[u] they went immediately to the Jews
in Jerusalem and compelled them by force
to stop.

4:9 [j] Ne 1:1; Est 1:2; Da 8:2 **4:10** [k] S 2Ki 17:24 [l] ver 17; Ne 4:2 **4:12** [m] Ezr 5:3,9 **4:13** [n] Ezr 7:24; Ne 5:4 **4:15** [o] Ezr 5:17; 6:1 [p] Est 3:8 **4:17** [q] S ver 10 **4:19** [r] S 2Ki 18:7 **4:20** [s] Ge 15:18-21; S Ex 23:31; S Jos 1:4; S 1Ki 4:21; 1Ch 18:3; Ps 72:8-11 **4:22** [t] Da 6:2 **4:23** [u] S ver 9

[a] *10* Aramaic *Osnappar,* a variant of *Ashurbanipal*

syrian king Ashurbanipal (669 – 627 B.C.), a major revolt had taken place (652 – 648), involving Shamash-Shum-Ukin, the brother of the king and the ruler over Babylonia. After a long siege Shamash-Shum-Ukin hurled himself into the flames. Doubtless these men of Babylon and the other cities mentioned were the descendants of the rebels, whom the Assyrians deported to the west. *Susa.* See note on Est 1:2; the major city of Elam (in southwest Iran). Because of Susa's part in the revolt, Ashurbanipal brutally destroyed it in 640 (two centuries before Rehum's letter).

4:10 *Ashurbanipal.* The last great Assyrian king (see chart, p. 472), famed for his library at Nineveh. He is not named elsewhere in the OT, but he is probably the king who freed Manasseh from exile (2Ch 33:11 – 13). *deported.* Ashurbanipal may be the unnamed Assyrian king who brought people to Samaria according to 2Ki 17:24. It is characteristic of such deportations that the descendants of populations that had been removed from their homelands nearly two centuries earlier should still stress their origins. *Samaria.* The murder of Amon king of Judah (642 – 640 B.C.; see 2Ki 21:23; 2Ch 33:24) was probably the result of an anti-Assyrian movement inspired by the revolt in Elam and Babylonia. The Assyrians may then have deported the rebellious Samaritans and replaced them with the rebellious Elamites and Babylonians. *Trans-Euphrates.* Lit. "beyond the River," i.e., the Euphrates River. From Israel's point of view the land "beyond the River" was Mesopotamia (Jos 24:2 – 3,14 – 15; 2Sa 10:16). From the Mesopotamian point of view the land "beyond the River" extended from the Euphrates to Gaza (1Ki 4:24).

4:12 *Jews.* See note on Jer 34:9. *restoring the walls and repairing the foundations.* As Isaiah had foretold (see Isa 58:12 and note).

4:13 Most of the gold and silver coins that came into Persia's treasury were melted down to be stored as bullion. Very little of the taxes returned to benefit the provinces.

4:14 *we are under obligation to the palace.* Lit. "we eat the salt of the palace." Salt was made a royal monopoly by the Ptolemies in Egypt, and perhaps by the Persians as well.

4:15 *archives.* See 5:17; 6:1 and note; Est 2:23; 6:1 – 2. There were several repositories of such documents at the major capitals. These royal archives preserved documents for centuries. In the third century B.C. the Babylonian priest Berossus made use of the Babylonian Chronicles in his history of Babylon, which covered events from the Assyrian to the Hellenistic (which began with Alexander's conquest of Babylon in 330 B.C.) eras.

4:18 *read.* Since the king probably could not read Aramaic, he would have had the document read to him. *translated.* From Aramaic into Persian (see NIV text notes on v. 7; Ne 8:8).

4:19 *rebellion.* There is some truth in the accusation. Jerusalem had rebelled against the Assyrians in 701 B.C. (2Ki 18:7) and against the Babylonians in 600 and 589 (2Ki 24:1,20).

4:21 – 23 As a result of the intervention of the provincial authorities, Artaxerxes I (see v. 11 and note on v. 7) ordered that the Jews stop rebuilding the walls of Jerusalem (see note on Ne 1:3). The events of vv. 7 – 23 probably occurred prior to 444 B.C. The forcible destruction of these recently rebuilt walls rather than the destruction by Nebuchadnezzar would then be the basis of the report made to Nehemiah (Ne 1:3).

24Thus the work on the house of God
in Jerusalem came to a standstill until the
second year of the reign of Darius[v] king
of Persia.

Tattenai's Letter to Darius

5 Now Haggai[w] the prophet and Zechariah[x] the prophet, a descendant of Iddo,
prophesied[y] to the Jews in Judah and Jerusalem in the name of the God of Israel,
who was over them. 2Then Zerubbabel[z]
son of Shealtiel and Jeshua[a] son of Jozadak set to work[b] to rebuild the house of
God in Jerusalem. And the prophets of
God were with them, helping them.
3At that time Tattenai,[c] governor of
Trans-Euphrates, and Shethar-Bozenai[d]
and their associates went to them and
asked, "Who authorized you to rebuild
this temple and restore this structure?"[e]
4They also asked, "What are the names of
the men constructing this building?"[a] 5But
the eye of their God[f] was watching over
the elders of the Jews, and they were not
stopped until a report could go to Darius
and his written reply be received.
6This is a copy of the letter that Tattenai, governor of Trans-Euphrates, and
Shethar-Bozenai and their associates, the
officials of Trans-Euphrates, sent to King
Darius. 7The report they sent him read as
follows:

To King Darius:

Cordial greetings.

8The king should know that we
went to the district of Judah, to the
temple of the great God. The people
are building it with large stones and
placing the timbers in the walls. The
work[g] is being carried on with diligence and is making rapid progress
under their direction.
9We questioned the elders and
asked them, "Who authorized you to
rebuild this temple and restore this
structure?"[h] 10We also asked them
their names, so that we could write
down the names of their leaders for
your information.
11This is the answer they gave us:

"We are the servants of the God
of heaven and earth, and we are rebuilding the temple[i] that was built
many years ago, one that a great king
of Israel built and finished. 12But because our fathers angered[j] the God
of heaven, he handed them over to
Nebuchadnezzar the Chaldean, king
of Babylon, who destroyed this temple and deported the people to Babylon.[k]
13"However, in the first year of Cyrus king of Babylon, King Cyrus issued a decree[l] to rebuild this house
of God. 14He even removed from the
temple[b] of Babylon the gold and silver
articles of the house of God, which
Nebuchadnezzar had taken from the
temple in Jerusalem and brought to
the temple[b] in Babylon.[m]
"Then King Cyrus gave them to a
man named Sheshbazzar,[n] whom he
had appointed governor, 15and he told
him, 'Take these articles and go and
deposit them in the temple in Jerusalem. And rebuild the house of God on
its site.' 16So this Sheshbazzar came

4:24 [v] Ne 2:1-8; Da 9:25; Hag 1:1,15; Zec 1:1
5:1 [w] Ezr 6:14; Hag 1:1,3,12; 2:1,10,20 [x] Zec 1:1; 7:1 [y] Hag 1:14-2:9; Zec 4:9-10; 8:9
5:2 [z] S 1Ch 3:19; Hag 1:14; 2:21; Zec 4:6-10 [a] S Ezr 2:2 [b] ver 8; Hag 2:2-5
5:3 [c] Ezr 6:6 [d] Ezr 6:6 [e] S Ezr 4:12
5:5 [f] S 2Ki 25:28; Ezr 7:6,9,28; 8:18,22,31; Ne 2:8,18; Ps 33:18; Isa 66:14
5:8 [g] S ver 2
5:9 [h] S Ezr 4:12
5:11 [i] 1Ki 6:1; 2Ch 3:1-2
5:12 [j] S 2Ch 36:16 [k] S Dt 21:10; S 28:36; S 2Ki 24:1; S Jer 1:3
5:13 [l] S Ezr 1:2-4
5:14 [m] Ezr 1:7 [n] S 1Ch 3:18

[a] 4 See Septuagint; Aramaic *4We told them the names of the men constructing this building.* [b] 14 Or *palace*

4:24 After this long digression describing the opposition to Jewish efforts, the writer returns to his original subject of the rebuilding of the temple (vv. 1 – 5). *second year of the reign of Darius.* According to Persian reckoning, the second regnal year of Darius I began on Nisan 1 (Apr. 3), 520 B.C., and lasted until Feb. 21, 519. In that year the prophet Haggai (Hag 1:1 – 5) exhorted Zerubbabel to begin rebuilding the temple on the first day of the sixth month (Aug. 29). Work began on the temple on the 24th day of the month, Sept. 21 (Hag 1:15). During his first two years, Darius had to establish his right to the throne by fighting numerous rebels, as recounted in his famous Behistun (Bisitun) inscription (see note on Hag 1:1). It was only after the stabilization of the Persian empire that efforts to rebuild the temple could be permitted.

5:1 *Haggai … Zechariah.* Beginning on Aug. 29, 520 B.C. (see Hag 1:1 and note), and continuing until Dec. 18 (see Hag 2:1,10,20 and notes), the prophet Haggai delivered a series of messages to stir up the people to resume work on the temple. Two months after Haggai's first speech, Zechariah began to prophesy (see Zec 1:1 and note; see also Introduction to Zechariah: Dates).

5:2 *Zerubbabel.* A Babylonian name meaning "offspring of Babylon," referring to his birth in exile. He was the son of Shealtiel and the grandson of Jehoiachin (1Ch 3:17), the next-to-last king of Judah. Zerubbabel was the last of the Davidic line to be entrusted with political authority by the occupying powers. He was also an ancestor of Jesus (Mt 1:12 – 13; Lk 3:27). *Jeshua.* See note on 2:2.

5:3 *Tattenai.* Probably a Babylonian name. *Shethar-Bozenai.* Perhaps a Persian official.

5:5 *not stopped.* The Persian governor gave the Jews the benefit of the doubt by not stopping the work while the inquiry was proceeding.

5:6 – 7 *sent to King Darius … sent him.* Texts found in the royal city of Persepolis vividly confirm that such inquiries were sent directly to the king himself, revealing the close attention he paid to minute details.

5:8 *timbers.* The Hebrew word may refer to interior paneling (1Ki 6:15 – 18) or to logs alternating with the brick or stone layers in the walls (see note on 6:4).

5:11 *great king of Israel.* According to 1Ki 6:1 Solomon began building the temple in the fourth year of his reign (966 B.C.). The project lasted seven years (1Ki 6:38).

5:12 *Chaldean.* The Akkadian word means "conqueror." The origin of the Chaldeans is obscure. Led by Nebuchadnezzar's father Nabopolassar, they overthrew the Assyrians and established the Neo-Babylonian empire (612 – 539 B.C.).

5:14 *Sheshbazzar … governor.* See note on 1:8.

and laid the foundations of the house of God[o] in Jerusalem. From that day to the present it has been under construction but is not yet finished."

17Now if it pleases the king, let a search be made in the royal archives[p] of Babylon to see if King Cyrus did in fact issue a decree to rebuild this house of God in Jerusalem. Then let the king send us his decision in this matter.

The Decree of Darius

6 King Darius then issued an order, and they searched in the archives[q] stored in the treasury at Babylon. 2A scroll was found in the citadel of Ecbatana in the province of Media, and this was written on it:

Memorandum:

3In the first year of King Cyrus, the king issued a decree concerning the temple of God in Jerusalem:

Let the temple be rebuilt as a place to present sacrifices, and let its foundations be laid.[r] It is to be ninety feet[a] high and ninety feet wide, 4with three courses[s] of large stones and one of timbers. The costs are to be paid by the royal treasury.[t] 5Also, the gold[u] and silver articles of the house of God, which Nebuchadnezzar took from the temple in Jerusalem and brought to Babylon, are to be returned to their places in the temple in Jerusalem; they are to be deposited in the house of God.[v]

6Now then, Tattenai,[w] governor of Trans-Euphrates, and Shethar-Bozenai[x] and you, their fellow officials of that province, stay away from there. 7Do not interfere with the work on this temple of God. Let the governor of the Jews and the Jewish elders rebuild this house of God on its site.

8Moreover, I hereby decree what you are to do for these elders of the Jews in the construction of this house of God:

The expenses of these men are to be fully paid out of the royal treasury,[y] from the revenues[z] of Trans-Euphrates, so that the work will not stop. 9Whatever is needed—young bulls, rams, male lambs for burnt offerings[a] to the God of heaven, and wheat, salt, wine and oil, as requested by the priests in Jerusalem—must be given them daily without fail, 10so that they may offer sacrifices pleasing to the God of heaven and pray for the well-being of the king and his sons.[b]

11Furthermore, I decree that if anyone changes this edict, a beam is to be pulled from his house and he is to

5:16 [o]S Ezr 3:10
5:17 [p]S Ezr 4:15
6:1 [q]S Ezr 4:15
6:3 [r]S Ezr 3:10; Hag 2:3
6:4 [s]S 1Ki 6:36 [t]ver 8; Ezr 7:20
6:5 [u]S 1Ch 29:2 [v]S Ezr 1:7
6:6 [w]Ezr 5:3 [x]Ezr 5:3
6:8 [y]S ver 4 [z]S 1Sa 9:20
6:9 [a]Lev 1:3,10
6:10 [b]Ezr 7:23; 1Ti 2:1-2

[a] 3 Aramaic *sixty cubits* (about 27 meters)

6:1 *archives ... in the treasury at Babylon.* Many documents have also been found in the so-called "treasury" area of Persepolis (see map, p. 573).

6:2 *Ecbatana.* One of the four capitals (along with Babylon, Persepolis and Susa) of the Persian empire. Located in what is today the Iranian city of Hamadan, its remains have not yet been excavated. This is the only reference to the site in the OT, though there are numerous references in the Apocryphal books (Judith 1:1–4; Tobit 3:7; 7:1; 14:12–14; 2 Maccabees 9:3). *Media.* The homeland of the Medes in northwestern Iran. The Medes were an Indo-European tribe related to the Persians. After the rise of Cyrus in 550 B.C., they became subordinate to the Persians. The name of the area was retained as late as the NT era (cf. Ac 2:9).

6:3–5 Compare this Aramaic memorandum of the decree of Cyrus with the Hebrew version in 1:2–4. The Aramaic is written in a more sober administrative style without any reference to the Lord (Yahweh). A similar memorandum dealing with permission to rebuild the Jewish temple at Elephantine in Upper Egypt was found among fifth-century B.C. Aramaic papyri recovered at that site.

6:3 *ninety feet high and ninety feet wide.* These dimensions, which differ from those of Solomon's temple (see NIV text note on 1Ki 6:2), are probably not specifications of the temple as built but of the outer limits of a building the Persians were willing to subsidize. The second temple was not as grandiose as the first (3:12; Hag 2:3).

6:4 *large stones ... timbers.* See 5:8. The same kind of construction is mentioned in 1Ki 6:36; 7:12. Such a design was possibly intended to cushion the building against earthquake shocks. *costs are to be paid by the royal treasury.* In 1973 archaeologists discovered at Xanthos in southwest Turkey a temple foundation charter from the late Persian period that provides some striking parallels with this decree of Cyrus. As in Ezra, amounts of sacrifices, names of priests and the responsibility for the upkeep of the temple are specified. The Persian king seems to have known details of the temple. See also notes on v. 8; 7:20.

6:8 *paid out of the royal treasury.* It was a consistent policy of Persian kings to help restore sanctuaries in their empire. For example, a memorandum concerning the rebuilding of the Jewish temple at Elephantine was written by the Persian governors of Judah and Samaria. Also from non-Biblical sources we learn that Cyrus repaired temples at Uruk (Erech) and Ur. Cambyses, successor to Cyrus, gave funds for the temple at Sais in Egypt. The temple of Amun in the Khargah Oasis was rebuilt by order of Darius.

6:9 That the Persian monarchs were interested in the details of foreign religions is shown clearly by the ordinances of Cambyses and Darius I, regulating the temples and priests in Egypt. On the authority of Darius II (423–404 B.C.) a letter was written to the Jews at Elephantine concerning the keeping of the Feast of Unleavened Bread.

6:10 *pray for the well-being of the king and his sons.* In the inscription on the Cyrus Cylinder (made of baked clay; see chart, p. xxii), the king asks: "May all the gods whom I have resettled in their sacred cities ask Bel and Nebo daily for a long life for me." The Jews of Elephantine offered to pray for the Persian governor of Judah. The daily synagogue services included a prayer for the royal family (cf. 1Ti 2:1–2).

6:11 *if anyone changes this edict.* It was customary at the end of decrees and treaties to append a long list of curses against

be lifted up and impaled[c] on it. And
for this crime his house is to be made
a pile of rubble.[d] 12May God, who
has caused his Name to dwell there,[e]
overthrow any king or people who
lifts a hand to change this decree or
to destroy this temple in Jerusalem.
I Darius[f] have decreed it. Let it be
carried out with diligence.

Completion and Dedication of the Temple

13Then, because of the decree King
Darius had sent, Tattenai, governor of
Trans-Euphrates, and Shethar-Bozenai and
their associates[g] carried it out with diligence. 14So the elders of the Jews continued to build and prosper under the preaching[h] of Haggai the prophet and Zechariah,
a descendant of Iddo. They finished building the temple according to the command
of the God of Israel and the decrees of
Cyrus,[i] Darius[j] and Artaxerxes,[k] kings of
Persia. 15The temple was completed on the
third day of the month Adar, in the sixth
year of the reign of King Darius.[l]
16Then the people of Israel — the priests,
the Levites and the rest of the exiles — celebrated the dedication[m] of the house of
God with joy. 17For the dedication of this
house of God they offered[n] a hundred
bulls, two hundred rams, four hundred
male lambs and, as a sin offering for all
Israel, twelve male goats, one for each of
the tribes of Israel. 18And they installed the
priests in their divisions[o] and the Levites
in their groups[p] for the service of God at
Jerusalem, according to what is written in
the Book of Moses.[q]

The Passover

19On the fourteenth day of the first
month, the exiles celebrated the Passover.[r] 20The priests and Levites had purified themselves and were all ceremonially
clean. The Levites slaughtered[s] the Passover lamb for all the exiles, for their brothers the priests and for themselves. 21So the
Israelites who had returned from the exile
ate it, together with all who had separated
themselves[t] from the unclean practices[u]
of their Gentile neighbors in order to seek
the LORD,[v] the God of Israel. 22For seven
days they celebrated with joy the Feast of
Unleavened Bread,[w] because the LORD had
filled them with joy by changing the attitude[x] of the king of Assyria, so that he
assisted them in the work on the house of
God, the God of Israel.

6:11 [c]S Dt 21:22-23; Est 2:23; 5:14; 9:14 [d]Ezr 7:26; Da 2:5; 3:29 **6:12** [e]S Ex 20:24; S Dt 12:5; S 2Ch 6:2 [f]ver 14 **6:13** [g]S Ezr 4:9 **6:14** [h]S Ezr 5:1 [i]S Ezr 1:1-4 [j]ver 12 [k]Ezr 7:1; Ne 2:1 **6:15** [l]Zec 1:1; 4:9 **6:16** [m]S 1Ki 8:63 **6:17** [n]S 2Sa 6:13; S 2Ch 29:21; S 30:24 **6:18** [o]S 2Ch 35:4; Lk 1:5 [p]S 1Ch 24:1 [q]Nu 3:6-9; 8:9-11; 18:1-32 **6:19** [r]S Ex 12:11; S Nu 28:16 **6:20** [s]S 2Ch 30:15, 17; 35:11 **6:21** [t]Ezr 9:1; Ne 9:2 [u]S Dt 18:9; Eze 36:25 [v]1Ch 22:19; Ps 14:2 **6:22** [w]S Ex 12:17 [x]S Ezr 1:1

anyone who might disregard them. *impaled.* According to Herodotus (3.159), Darius I impaled 3,000 Babylonians when he took the city of Babylon. See note on Est 2:23.

6:12 *May God … overthrow any king or people.* At the end of his famous Behistun (Bisitun) inscription Darius I warned: "If you see this inscription or these sculptures, and destroy them and do not protect them as long as you have strength, may Ahuramazda strike you, and may you not have a family, and what you do … may Ahuramazda utterly destroy." *caused his Name to dwell.* See note on Dt 12:5.

6:13 – 14 Work on the temple had made little progress not only because of opposition but also because of the preoccupation of the returnees with their own homes (Hag 1:2 – 9). Because they had placed their own interests first (cf. Mt 6:33), God sent them famine as a judgment (Hag 1:5 – 6,10 – 11). Spurred by the preaching of Haggai and Zechariah, and under the leadership of Zerubbabel and Jeshua, a new effort was begun (Hag 1:12 – 15).

6:14 *Artaxerxes.* The reference to him seems out of place, because he did not contribute to rebuilding the temple. He may have been inserted here since he contributed to the work of the temple at a later date under Ezra (7:21 – 24).

6:15 *temple was completed.* On Mar. 12, 516 B.C., almost 70 years after its destruction. The renewed work on the temple had begun on Sept. 21, 520 (Hag 1:15), and sustained effort had continued for almost three and a half years. According to Hag 2:3, the older members who could remember the splendor of Solomon's temple were disappointed when they saw the smaller size of Zerubbabel's temple (cf. Ezr 3:12). Yet in the long run the second temple, though not as grand as the first, enjoyed a much longer life. The general plan of the second temple was similar to that of Solomon's, but the Most Holy Place was left empty because the ark of the covenant had been lost through the Babylonian conquest. According to Josephus, on the Day of Atonement the high priest placed his censer on the slab of stone that marked the former location of the ark. The Holy Place was furnished with a table for the bread of the Presence, the incense altar, and one lampstand (in the Apocrypha cf. 1 Maccabees 1:21 – 22; 4:49 – 51) instead of Solomon's ten (1Ki 7:49).

6:16 *exiles … dedication.* Cf. the dedication of Solomon's temple (1Ki 8). The leaders of those who returned from exile were responsible for the completion of the temple. "Dedication" translates the Aramaic word *ḥanukkah.* The Jewish holiday in December that celebrates the recapture of the temple from the Seleucids and its rededication (165 B.C.) is also known as Hanukkah (see Jn 10:22 and note).

6:17 *hundred … two hundred … four hundred.* The number of animals sacrificed was small in comparison with similar services in the reigns of Solomon (1Ki 8:5,63), Hezekiah (2Ch 30:24) and Josiah (2Ch 35:7), when thousands rather than hundreds were offered.

6:18 *divisions.* The priests were separated into 24 divisions (1Ch 24:1 – 19), each of which served at the temple for a week at a time (cf. Lk 1:5,8). In 1962 fragments of a synagogue inscription listing the 24 divisions were found at Caesarea. *written in the Book of Moses.* Perhaps referring to such passages as Ex 29; Lev 8; Nu 3; 8:5 – 26; 18.

6:19 *fourteenth day … first month … Passover.* The date would have been about Apr. 21, 516 B.C. For the origin and meaning of the Passover and the Feast of Unleavened Bread (v. 22) see Ex 12:1 – 30 and notes.

6:20 *purified themselves … ceremonially clean.* See note on Lev 4:12. Priests and Levites had to be ceremonially clean to fulfill their ritual functions.

6:21 *with all who had separated themselves.* The returning exiles were willing to accept those who separated themselves from the paganism of the foreigners who had been introduced into the area by the Assyrians.

6:22 *king of Assyria.* A surprising title for Darius, the Persian king. But even after the fall of Nineveh in 612 B.C., the term "Assyria" continued to be used for former territories the Assyrians had occupied. Persian kings adopted a variety of titles, including "king of Babylon" (cf. 5:13; Ne 13:6).

Ezra Comes to Jerusalem

7 After these things, during the reign
of Artaxerxes[y] king of Persia, Ezra son of
Seraiah,[z] the son of Azariah, the son
of Hilkiah,[a] 2the son of Shallum, the son
of Zadok,[b] the son of Ahitub,[c] 3the son of
Amariah, the son of Azariah, the son
of Meraioth, 4the son of Zerahiah, the
son of Uzzi, the son of Bukki, 5the son
of Abishua, the son of Phinehas,[d] the
son of Eleazar, the son of Aaron the chief
priest— 6this Ezra[e] came up from Babylon. He was a teacher well versed in the
Law of Moses, which the LORD, the God
of Israel, had given. The king had granted[f] him everything he asked, for the hand
of the LORD his God was on him.[g] 7Some
of the Israelites, including priests, Levites,
singers, gatekeepers and temple servants,
also came up to Jerusalem in the seventh
year of King Artaxerxes.[h]
8Ezra arrived in Jerusalem in the fifth
month of the seventh year of the king. 9He
had begun his journey from Babylon on
the first day of the first month, and he arrived in Jerusalem on the first day of the
fifth month, for the gracious hand of his
God was on him.[i] 10For Ezra had devoted
himself to the study and observance of the
Law of the LORD, and to teaching[j] its decrees and laws in Israel.

King Artaxerxes' Letter to Ezra

11This is a copy of the letter King Artaxerxes had given to Ezra the priest and
teacher, a man learned in matters concerning the commands and decrees of the LORD
for Israel:

12 [a]Artaxerxes, king of kings,[k]

To Ezra the priest, a teacher of the
Law of the God of heaven:

Greetings.

13Now I decree that any of the Israelites in my kingdom, including
priests and Levites, who wish to go
to Jerusalem with you, may go. 14You
are sent by the king and his seven
advisers[l] to inquire about Judah and
Jerusalem with regard to the Law of
your God, which is in your hand.

7:1 [y] S Ezr 4:7; S 6:14 [z] S 2Ki 25:18 [a] 2Ki 22:4 **7:2** [b] 1Ki 1:8; 2:35; 1Ch 6:8; Eze 40:46; 43:19; 44:15 [c] Ne 11:11 **7:5** [d] 1Ch 6:4 **7:6** [e] Ne 12:36 [f] S 2Ki 25:28 [g] S Ezr 5:5; S Isa 41:20 **7:7** [h] Ezr 8:1 **7:9** [i] ver 6 **7:10** [j] S Dt 33:10 **7:12** [k] Eze 26:7; Da 2:37 **7:14** [l] Est 1:14

[a] 12 The text of Ezra 7:12-26 is in Aramaic.

7:1–5 The genealogy of Ezra given here lists 16 ancestors back to Aaron, the brother of Moses.

7:1 *After these things.* The events of the preceding chapter concluded with the completion of the temple in 516 B.C. *Artaxerxes.* The identity of the king mentioned in this chapter has been disputed. If this was Artaxerxes I, which seems likely, Ezra would have arrived in Judah in 458, and there would be a gap of almost 60 years between the events of ch. 6 and those of ch. 7. The only recorded event during this interval is the opposition to the rebuilding of Jerusalem in the reign of Xerxes (486–465) in 4:6. *Ezra.* Perhaps a shortened form of Azariah ("The LORD helps"), a name that occurs twice in the list of his ancestors. The Greek form is Esdras, as in the Apocrypha. *Seraiah.* Means "The LORD is prince." He was the high priest under Zedekiah who was killed in 586 by Nebuchadnezzar (2Ki 25:18–21) some 128 years before Ezra's arrival. He was therefore the ancestor rather than the father of Ezra; "son" often means "descendant" (see 1Ch 6:14–15). *Hilkiah.* Means "My portion is the LORD." He was the high priest under Josiah (2Ki 22:4).

7:2 *Zadok.* Means "righteous." He was a priest under David (2Sa 8:17). Solomon appointed Zadok as high priest in place of Abiathar, who supported the rebel Adonijah (1Ki 1:7–8; 2:35). Ezekiel regarded the Zadokites as free from idolatry (Eze 44:15). They held the office of high priest until 171 B.C. The Sadducees may have been named after Zadok, and the Qumran community (see essay, p. 1453) looked for the restoration of the Zadokite priesthood. *Ahitub.* Probably means "My (divine) brother is good." He was actually the grandfather of Zadok (Ne 11:11).

7:3 *Azariah … Meraioth.* See note on Ge 4:17–18.

7:5 *Eleazar.* Means "God helps."

7:6 *teacher.* Lit. "scribe" (see Ne 8:1,4,9,13; 12:26,36). Earlier, scribes served kings as secretaries, such as Shaphan under Josiah (2Ki 22:3, where the Hebrew word for "scribe" is translated "secretary"). Other scribes took dictation—such as Baruch, who wrote down what Jeremiah spoke (Jer 36:32). From the exilic period on, the "scribes" were scholars who studied and taught the Scriptures ("scribes" is rendered "teachers of the law" in the NT; see notes on Mt 2:4; Lk 5:17). In the NT period they, among others, were addressed as "rabbis" (cf. Mt 23:7). *well versed.* The Hebrew for this phrase is translated "skillful" in Ps 45:1 and "skilled" in Pr 22:29. *Law of Moses.* Perhaps the complete Pentateuch (the five books of Moses). *hand of the LORD.* For this striking description of God's power and favor cf. also vv. 9,28; 8:18,22,31; Ne 2:8,18.

7:7–9 *seventh year … first day of the first month … first day of the fifth month.* Ezra began his journey on the first of Nisan (Apr. 8, 458 B.C.) and arrived in Jerusalem on the first of Ab (Aug. 4, 458). The journey took four months, including an 11-day delay indicated by the comparison of v. 9 with 8:31. The spring was the most auspicious time for such journeys; most armies went on campaigns at this time of the year (see 2Sa 11:1 and note). Although the actual distance between Babylon and Jerusalem is about 500 miles, the travelers had to cover a total of about 900 miles, going northwest along the Euphrates River and then south. The relatively slow pace was caused by the presence of the elderly and the children. See map No. 8b at the end of this study Bible; see also map, p. 672.

7:10 *study … observance … teaching.* See Ne 8.

7:11 *letter.* Many regard the letter of Artaxerxes I as the beginning point of Daniel's first 69 "sevens" (Da 9:24–27). Others regard the commission of Nehemiah by the same king as the starting point of this prophecy (Ne 1:1,11; 2:1–8). By using either a solar calendar with the former date (458 B.C.) or a lunar calendar with the latter date (444), one can arrive remarkably close to the date of Jesus' public ministry.

7:12 See NIV text note. *king of kings.* The phrase was originally used by Assyrian kings, since their empires incorporated many kingdoms. It was then used by the later Babylonian (Eze 26:7; Da 2:37) and Persian kings. Cf. 1Ti 6:15; Rev 17:14; 19:16.

7:13 *Israelites.* The markedly Jewish coloring of this decree may have resulted from the king's use of Jewish officials, quite possibly Ezra himself, to help him compose it.

7:14 *seven advisers.* Cf. Est 1:14, which refers to the seven nobles who "had special access to the king." This corresponds with Persian practice as reported by the early Greek historians Herodotus and Xenophon. *Law of your God.* Perhaps the complete Pentateuch (see v. 6 and note).

15Moreover, you are to take with you
the silver and gold that the king and
his advisers have freely given[m] to the
God of Israel, whose dwelling[n] is in
Jerusalem, 16together with all the silver and gold[o] you may obtain from
the province of Babylon, as well as
the freewill offerings of the people
and priests for the temple of their
God in Jerusalem.[p] 17With this money
be sure to buy bulls, rams and male
lambs,[q] together with their grain offerings and drink offerings,[r] and sacrifice[s] them on the altar of the temple
of your God in Jerusalem.
18You and your brother Jews may
then do whatever seems best with
the rest of the silver and gold, in accordance with the will of your God.
19Deliver[t] to the God of Jerusalem all
the articles entrusted to you for worship in the temple of your God. 20And
anything else needed for the temple
of your God that you may have occasion to supply, you may provide from
the royal treasury.[u]
21Now I, King Artaxerxes, order
all the treasurers of Trans-Euphrates
to provide with diligence whatever Ezra the priest, a teacher of the
Law of the God of heaven, may ask
of you— 22up to a hundred talents[a]
of silver, a hundred cors[b] of wheat,
a hundred baths[c] of wine, a hundred
baths[c] of olive oil, and salt without
limit. 23Whatever the God of heaven
has prescribed, let it be done with diligence for the temple of the God of
heaven. Why should there be wrath
against the realm of the king and
of his sons?[v] 24You are also to know
that you have no authority to impose
taxes, tribute or duty[w] on any of the
priests, Levites, singers, gatekeepers,
temple servants or other workers at
this house of God.[x]
25And you, Ezra, in accordance
with the wisdom of your God, which
you possess, appoint[y] magistrates and
judges to administer justice to all the
people of Trans-Euphrates—all who
know the laws of your God. And you
are to teach[z] any who do not know
them. 26Whoever does not obey the
law of your God and the law of the
king must surely be punished by
death, banishment, confiscation of
property, or imprisonment.[a]

27Praise be to the LORD, the God of our
fathers, who has put it into the king's
heart[b] to bring honor[c] to the house of the
LORD in Jerusalem in this way 28and who
has extended his good favor[d] to me before
the king and his advisers and all the king's
powerful officials. Because the hand of the
LORD my God was on me,[e] I took courage
and gathered leading men from Israel to
go up with me.

7:15 [m]S 1Ch 29:6 [n]S Dt 12:5; S 2Ch 6:2 **7:16** [o]S Ex 3:22 [p]Zec 6:10 **7:17** [q]S 2Ki 3:4 [r]Nu 15:5-12 [s]Dt 12:5-11 **7:19** [t]Ezr 5:14; Jer 27:22 **7:20** [u]S Ezr 6:4 **7:23** [v]S Ezr 6:10 **7:24** [w]S Ezr 4:13 [x]Ezr 8:36 **7:25** [y]S Ex 18:21,26 [z]S Lev 10:11 **7:26** [a]S Ezr 6:11 **7:27** [b]S Ezr 1:1 [c]S 1Ch 29:12 **7:28** [d]S 2Ki 25:28 [e]S Ezr 5:5

[a] *22* That is, about 3 3/4 tons (about 3.4 metric tons) [b] *22* That is, probably about 600 bushels (about 22 kiloliters) [c] *22* That is, probably about 600 gallons (about 2.2 kiloliters)

7:15 *silver and gold.* Cf. Hag 2:8. *freely given.* The Persian treasury had ample funds, and financial support for the worship of the various peoples' gods was a well-attested policy of Persian kings.

7:16 *offerings of the people.* The custom of sending gifts to Jerusalem from the Jews who lived outside the Holy Land continued until the Jewish-Roman War (A.D. 66–73), when the Romans forced the Jews to send such contributions to the temple of Jupiter instead (Josephus, *Antiquities*, 18.9.1; *Wars*, 7.6.6). There are close parallels to such directives in the contemporary letters from the Jewish garrison at Elephantine in Egypt, including a papyrus in which Darius II ordered: "Let grain offering, incense and burnt offering be offered" on Yahweh's altar "in your name."

7:20 *provide from the royal treasury.* Texts from the treasury at Persepolis also record the disbursement of supplies and funds from the royal purse.

7:22 *hundred talents.* An enormous amount (see NIV text note). *hundred cors.* The total was relatively small (see NIV text note). The wheat would be used in grain offerings. *salt without limit.* See note on 4:14. A close parallel is the benefaction of Antiochus III as recorded by Josephus (*Antiquities*, 12.3.3): "In the first place we have decided, on account of their piety, to furnish for their sacrifices an allowance of sacrificial animals, wine, oil and frankincense to the value of 20,000 pieces of silver, and sacred artabae of fine flour in accordance with their native law, and 1,460 medimni of wheat and 375 medimni of salt."

7:23 *wrath against the realm of the king.* Egypt had revolted against the Persians in 460 B.C. and had expelled the Persians with the help of the Athenians in 459. In 458, when Ezra traveled to Jerusalem, the Persians were involved in suppressing this revolt. *his sons.* We do not know how many sons the king had at this time, but he ultimately had 18, according to Ctesias (a Greek physician who wrote an extensive history of Persia).

7:24 *no ... taxes ... or duty on any of the priests ... temple servants.* Priests and other temple personnel were often given exemptions from enforced labor or taxes. A close parallel is found in the Gadates Inscription of Darius I to a governor in western Turkey, granting exemptions to the priests of Apollo. Antiochus III granted similar exemptions to the Jews: "The priests, the scribes of the temple and the temple singers shall be relieved from the poll tax, the crown tax and the salt tax that they pay" (Josephus, *Antiquities*, 12.3.3).

7:26 *Whoever does not obey ... must surely be punished.* The extensive powers given to Ezra are striking and extend to secular fields. Perhaps the implementation of these provisions involved Ezra in a great deal of traveling, which would explain the silence about his activities between his arrival and the arrival of Nehemiah 13 years later. A close parallel to the king's commission of Ezra may be found in an earlier commission by Darius I, who sent Udjahorresenet, a priest and scholar, back to Egypt. He ordered the codification of the Egyptian laws by the chief men of Egypt—a task that took from 518 to 503 B.C.

7:28 *me.* The first occurrence of the first person for Ezra—a trait that characterizes the Ezra memoirs, which begin in v. 27 and continue to the end of ch. 9.

List of the Family Heads Returning With Ezra

8 These are the family heads and those
registered with them who came up
with me from Babylon during the reign of
King Artaxerxes:[f]
2 of the descendants of Phinehas, Gershom;
of the descendants of Ithamar, Daniel;
of the descendants of David, Hattush
3 of the descendants of Shecaniah;[g]
of the descendants of Parosh,[h] Zechariah, and with him were registered 150 men;
4 of the descendants of Pahath-Moab,[i] Eliehoenai son of Zerahiah, and with him 200 men;
5 of the descendants of Zattu,[a] Shecaniah son of Jahaziel, and with him 300 men;
6 of the descendants of Adin,[j] Ebed son of Jonathan, and with him 50 men;
7 of the descendants of Elam, Jeshaiah son of Athaliah, and with him 70 men;
8 of the descendants of Shephatiah, Zebadiah son of Michael, and with him 80 men;
9 of the descendants of Joab, Obadiah son of Jehiel, and with him 218 men;
10 of the descendants of Bani,[b] Shelomith son of Josiphiah, and with him 160 men;
11 of the descendants of Bebai, Zechariah son of Bebai, and with him 28 men;
12 of the descendants of Azgad, Johanan son of Hakkatan, and with him 110 men;
13 of the descendants of Adonikam,[k] the last ones, whose names were Eliphelet, Jeuel and Shemaiah, and with them 60 men;
14 of the descendants of Bigvai, Uthai and Zaccur, and with them 70 men.

The Return to Jerusalem

15 I assembled them at the canal that
flows toward Ahava,[l] and we camped
there three days. When I checked among
the people and the priests, I found no Levites[m] there. 16 So I summoned Eliezer, Ariel, Shemaiah, Elnathan, Jarib, Elnathan,
Nathan, Zechariah and Meshullam, who
were leaders, and Joiarib and Elnathan,
who were men of learning, 17 and I sent
them to Iddo, the leader in Casiphia. I told
them what to say to Iddo and his kinsmen,
the temple servants[n] in Casiphia, so that
they might bring attendants to us for the
house of our God. 18 Because the gracious
hand of our God was on us,[o] they brought
us Sherebiah,[p] a capable man, from the
descendants of Mahli son of Levi, the son
of Israel, and Sherebiah's sons and brothers, 18 men; 19 and Hashabiah, together
with Jeshaiah from the descendants of
Merari, and his brothers and nephews, 20
men. 20 They also brought 220 of the temple servants[q]—a body that David and the

8:1 [f]Ezr 7:7
8:3 [g]1Ch 3:22 [h]S Ezr 2:3
8:4 [i]Ezr 2:6
8:6 [j]Ezr 2:15; Ne 7:20; 10:16
8:13 [k]Ezr 2:13
8:15 [l]ver 21,31 [m]S Ezr 2:40
8:17 [n]Ezr 2:43
8:18 [o]S Ezr 5:5 [p]ver 24
8:20 [q]S 1Ch 9:2

[a] *5* Some Septuagint manuscripts (also 1 Esdras 8:32); Hebrew does not have *Zattu.* [b] *10* Some Septuagint manuscripts (also 1 Esdras 8:36); Hebrew does not have *Bani.*

8:1–21 In vv. 1–14 Ezra lists those who accompanied him in his return from Mesopotamia, including the descendants of 15 individuals. The figures of the men given total 1,496 in addition to the individuals named. There were also women and children (see note on v. 21). About 40 Levites (vv. 18–19) are also included, as are 220 "temple servants" (v. 20).
8:2 *Gershom.* For the meaning of the name see NIV text note on Ex 2:22. *Ithamar.* Also the name of the fourth son of Aaron (Ex 6:23).
8:3 *Zechariah.* Cf. v. 11. The name means "The LORD remembers"; it was the name of about 30 individuals mentioned in the Bible, including both the OT prophet and the father of John the Baptist (Lk 1:5–67).
8:4 *Eliehoenai.* Means "On the LORD are my eyes"; the name occurs only here and in 1Ch 26:3. Cf. Ps 25:15.
8:6 *Ebed.* May be a shortened form of Obadiah (cf. v. 9), meaning "servant of the LORD." *Jonathan.* Means "The LORD gives"; it was the name of 15 OT individuals.
8:7 *Athaliah.* The father of Jeshaiah. Athaliah was also the name of a famous queen, daughter of Ahab (2Ki 11).
8:8 *Michael.* Means "Who is like God?" It was the name of ten other Biblical personages, including the archangel (Da 10:13; Jude 9; Rev 12:7).
8:10 *Shelomith.* Although it is a feminine form (see also note on SS 6:13), it is often a man's name, as here. The Greek equivalent is Salome.
8:12 *Azgad.* See note on 2:12. *Johanan.* See note on 2:46.
8:15 *canal that flows toward Ahava.* Probably flows into either the Euphrates or the Tigris at a place not far from Babylon (the Kebar "River" in Eze 1:1 was also a canal; see note there). *three days.* Perhaps from the 9th to the 12th day of Nisan; the journey began on the 12th (see v. 31). *no Levites.* A Rabbinic midrash (comment) on Ps 137 relates the legend that Levites were in the caravan but that they were not qualified to officiate because when Nebuchadnezzar had ordered them to sing for him the songs of Zion, "they refused and bit off the ends of their fingers, so that they could not play on the harps." In the Hellenistic era (following Alexander's conquest of the Holy Land in 333 B.C.) the role of the Levites declined sharply, though the Temple Scroll among the Dead Sea Scrolls from Qumran (see essay, pp. 1453–1454) assigns important roles to them.
8:16 *Ariel.* Means "lion of God" or "altar hearth" or possibly "city of God" (see note on Isa 29:1–2,7). It occurs only here as a personal name. *Meshullam.* Some assume that he is the same as the Meshullam who opposed the marriage reforms (10:15).
8:17 *Casiphia.* Some have located it at the site that was later to become the Parthian capital of Ctesiphon on the Tigris River, north of Babylon.
8:18–19 *18 men … 20 men.* Only about 40 Levites from two families were found who were willing to join Ezra's caravan.
8:20 *temple servants.* See note on 2:43–57.

officials had established to assist the Levites. All were registered by name.
21 There, by the Ahava Canal,[r] I proclaimed a fast, so that we might humble
ourselves before our God and ask him for
a safe journey[s] for us and our children,
with all our possessions. 22 I was ashamed
to ask the king for soldiers[t] and horsemen
to protect us from enemies on the road,
because we had told the king, "The gracious hand of our God is on everyone[u]
who looks to him, but his great anger is
against all who forsake him.[v]" 23 So we
fasted[w] and petitioned our God about this,
and he answered our prayer.
24 Then I set apart twelve of the leading
priests, together with Sherebiah,[x] Hashabiah and ten of their brothers, 25 and I
weighed out[y] to them the offering of silver
and gold and the articles that the king, his
advisers, his officials and all Israel present there had donated for the house of our
God. 26 I weighed out to them 650 talents[a]
of silver, silver articles weighing 100 talents,[b] 100 talents[b] of gold, 27 20 bowls of
gold valued at 1,000 darics,[c] and two fine
articles of polished bronze, as precious as
gold.
28 I said to them, "You as well as these
articles are consecrated to the LORD.[z] The
silver and gold are a freewill offering to
the LORD, the God of your fathers. 29 Guard
them carefully until you weigh them out
in the chambers of the house of the LORD
in Jerusalem before the leading priests and
the Levites and the family heads of Israel."
30 Then the priests and Levites received the
silver and gold and sacred articles that had
been weighed out to be taken to the house
of our God in Jerusalem.

8:21 [r] S ver 15 [s] Ps 5:8; 27:11; 107:7
8:22 [t] Ne 2:9; Jer 41:16 [u] S Ezr 5:5 [v] S Dt 31:17
8:23 [w] S 2Ch 20:3; Ac 14:23
8:24 [x] ver 18
8:25 [y] ver 33
8:28 [z] S Lev 21:6; 22:2-3

31 On the twelfth day of the first month
we set out from the Ahava Canal[a] to go to
Jerusalem. The hand of our God was on
us,[b] and he protected us from enemies and
bandits along the way. 32 So we arrived in
Jerusalem, where we rested three days.[c]
33 On the fourth day, in the house of our
God, we weighed out[d] the silver and gold
and the sacred articles into the hands of
Meremoth[e] son of Uriah, the priest. Eleazar son of Phinehas was with him, and so
were the Levites Jozabad[f] son of Jeshua
and Noadiah son of Binnui.[g] 34 Everything
was accounted for by number and weight,
and the entire weight was recorded at that
time.
35 Then the exiles who had returned
from captivity sacrificed burnt offerings to
the God of Israel: twelve bulls[h] for all Israel,[i] ninety-six rams, seventy-seven male
lambs and, as a sin offering, twelve male
goats.[j] All this was a burnt offering to the
LORD. 36 They also delivered the king's orders[k] to the royal satraps and to the governors of Trans-Euphrates,[l] who then gave
assistance to the people and to the house
of God.[m]

Ezra's Prayer About Intermarriage

9 After these things had been done, the
leaders came to me and said, "The people of Israel, including the priests and the
Levites, have not kept themselves separate[n] from the neighboring peoples with
their detestable practices, like those of
the Canaanites, Hittites, Perizzites, Jebusites,[o] Ammonites,[p] Moabites,[q] Egyptians

8:31 [a] S ver 15 [b] S Ezr 5:5
8:32 [c] S Ge 40:13
8:33 [d] ver 25 [e] Ne 3:4,21 [f] Ne 11:16 [g] Ne 3:24
8:35 [h] S Lev 1:3 [i] S 2Ch 29:24 [j] S 2Ch 29:21; S 30:24
8:36 [k] Ezr 7:21-24 [l] Ne 2:7 [m] Est 9:3
9:1 [n] S Ezr 6:21 [o] S Ge 10:16; S Jos 15:8 [p] Ge 19:38 [q] S Ge 19:37

[a] *26* That is, about 25 tons (about 22 metric tons)
[b] *26* That is, about 3 3/4 tons (about 3.4 metric tons)
[c] *27* That is, about 19 pounds (about 8.5 kilograms)

8:21 *safe journey.* Lit. "straight way"—unimpeded by obstacles and dangers (see v. 31; cf. Pr 3:6). *possessions.* The vast treasures they were carrying with them offered a great temptation for robbers.

8:22 *I was ashamed.* Scripture speaks often of unholy shame (Jer 48:13; 49:23; Mic 3:7) and on occasion, as here, of holy shame. Ezra was quick to blush with such shame (see also 9:6). Having proclaimed his faith in God's ability to protect the caravan, he was embarrassed to ask for human protection. Grave dangers faced travelers going the great distance between Mesopotamia and the Holy Land. Some 13 years later Nehemiah was accompanied by an armed escort. The difference, however, does not mean that Nehemiah was a man of lesser faith (see note on Ne 2:9).

8:23 *fasted and petitioned.* For the association of fasting and prayer see 2Sa 12:16; Ne 1:4; Da 9:3; Mt 17:21 (NIV text note); Ac 14:23.

8:26 *650 talents ... 100 talents.* Enormous sums, worth millions of dollars today. See also note on 7:22.

8:27 *darics.* See NIV text note. The word occurs only here and in 1Ch 29:7 (but see note on 2:69). *polished.* This kind of bronze may have been orichalc, a bright yellow (the Hebrew for "yellow" in Lev 13:30,32,36 is related to the Hebrew for "polished" here) alloy of copper, which resembles gold and was highly prized in ancient times.

8:31 *twelfth day.* See notes on v. 15; 7:7–9.

8:32 *rested three days.* Nehemiah also took a similar rest period after his arrival in Jerusalem (Ne 2:11).

8:33 *Meremoth son of Uriah.* Probably the same as the man who repaired two sections of the wall (Ne 3:4,21).

8:34 *recorded.* According to Babylonian practice (e.g., in the Code of Hammurapi; see chart, p. xxii) almost every transaction, including sales and marriages, had to be recorded in writing. Ezra may have had to send back to Artaxerxes a signed certification of the delivery of the treasures.

8:35 *sacrificed.* Except for the identical number of male goats, the offerings here were far fewer than those presented by the returnees under Zerubbabel (6:17), who brought with him a far greater number of families.

9:1 *After these things had been done ... have not kept themselves separate.* Ezra had reached Jerusalem in the fifth month (7:9). The measures dealing with the problem of intermarriage were announced in the ninth month (10:9), or four months after his arrival. Those who brought Ezra's attention to the problem were probably the ordinary members of the community rather than the leaders, who were themselves guilty (v. 2). Malachi, who prophesied about the same time as Ezra's mission, indicates that some Jews had divorced their wives to marry "the daughter of a foreign god" (Mal 2:11; see Mal 2:10–16 and notes). One of the reasons for such inter-

and Amorites.[r] 2They have taken some of
their daughters[s] as wives for themselves
and their sons, and have mingled[t] the holy
race[u] with the peoples around them. And
the leaders and officials have led the way
in this unfaithfulness."[v]
3When I heard this, I tore[w] my tunic and
cloak, pulled hair from my head and beard
and sat down appalled.[x] 4Then everyone
who trembled[y] at the words of the God of
Israel gathered around me because of this
unfaithfulness of the exiles. And I sat there
appalled[z] until the evening sacrifice.
5Then, at the evening sacrifice,[a] I rose
from my self-abasement, with my tunic
and cloak torn, and fell on my knees with
my hands[b] spread out to the LORD my God
6and prayed:

"O my God, I am too ashamed[c] and
disgraced to lift up my face to you,
my God, because our sins are higher than our heads and our guilt has
reached to the heavens.[d] 7From the
days of our forefathers[e] until now,
our guilt has been great. Because of
our sins, we and our kings and our
priests have been subjected to the
sword[f] and captivity,[g] to pillage and
humiliation[h] at the hand of foreign
kings, as it is today.
8"But now, for a brief moment, the
LORD our God has been gracious[i] in
leaving us a remnant[j] and giving us
a firm place[k] in his sanctuary, and so
our God gives light to our eyes[l] and
a little relief in our bondage. 9Though
we are slaves,[m] our God has not deserted us in our bondage. He has
shown us kindness[n] in the sight of
the kings of Persia: He has granted us
new life to rebuild the house of our
God and repair its ruins,[o] and he has
given us a wall of protection in Judah
and Jerusalem.
10"But now, O our God, what can
we say after this? For we have disregarded the commands[p] 11you gave
through your servants the prophets
when you said: 'The land you are entering[q] to possess is a land polluted[r]
by the corruption of its peoples. By

9:1 [r]Ex 13:5; 23:28; Dt 20:17; S Jos 3:10; S Jdg 3:5; 1Ki 9:20; S 2Ch 8:7; Ne 9:8 **9:2** [s]S Ex 34:16; S Ru 1:4 [t]Ps 106:35 [u]S Ex 22:31; S Lev 27:30; S Dt 14:2 [v]Ezr 10:2 **9:3** [w]S Nu 14:6 [x]S Ex 32:19; S 33:4 **9:4** [y]Ezr 10:3; Ps 119:120; Isa 66:2, 5 [z]Ne 1:4; Ps 119:136; Da 10:2 **9:5** [a]S Ex 29:41 [b]Ne 8:6; Ps 28:2; 134:2 **9:6** [c]Jer 31:19 [d]S 2Ch 28:9; Job 42:6; Ps 38:4; Isa 59:12; Jer 3:25; 14:20; Rev 18:5 **9:7** [e]S 2Ch 29:6 [f]Eze 21:1-32 [g]S Dt 28:64 [h]S Dt 28:37 **9:8** [i]Ps 25:16; 67:1; 119:58; Isa 33:2 [j]S Ge 45:7 [k]Ecc 12:11; Isa 22:23 [l]Ps 13:3; 19:8 **9:9** [m]S Ex 1:14; Ne 9:36 [n]S 2Ki 25:28; Ps 106:46 [o]Ps 69:35; Isa 43:1; 44:26; 48:20; 52:9; 63:9; Jer 32:44; Zec 1:16-17 **9:10** [p]Dt 11:8; Isa 1:19-20 **9:11** [q]Dt 4:5 [r]S Lev 18:25-28

marriages may have been the shortage of returning Jewish women who were available. What happened to a Jewish community that was lax concerning intermarriage can be seen in the example of the Elephantine settlement in Egypt, which was contemporary with Ezra and Nehemiah. There the Jews who married pagan spouses expressed their devotion to pagan gods in addition to the Lord. The Elephantine community was gradually assimilated and disappeared. *neighboring peoples.* The eight groups mentioned are representative of the original inhabitants of Canaan before the Israelite conquest (see note on Ex 3:8). Only the Ammonites, Moabites and Egyptians were still living there in the postexilic period (cf. 2Ch 8:7 – 8). *Canaanites.* See note on Ge 10:6. *Hittites.* See note on Ge 10:15. *Perizzites.* See note on Ge 13:7. *Jebusites.* See note on Ge 10:16. *Ammonites, Moabites.* See note on Ge 19:36 – 38. *Amorites.* See note on Ge 10:16.

9:2 *holy race.* The Hebrew for this phrase is translated "holy seed" in Isa 6:13 (see note there). *led the way.* In the wrong direction (see 10:18). *unfaithfulness.* See 10:6; Jos 22:16; Da 9:7. Marrying those who were not worshipers of the Lord was an act of infidelity for the people of Israel (cf. Dt 7:1 – 6; 1Co 7:39 and notes).

9:3 *tore my tunic and cloak.* A common way to express grief or distress (see v. 5; Ge 37:29,34; Jos 7:6; Jdg 11:35; 2Sa 13:19; 2Ch 34:27; Est 4:1; Job 1:20; Isa 36:22; Jer 41:5; Mt 26:65). *pulled hair from my head and beard.* Unique in the Bible. Elsewhere we read about the shaving of one's head and/or beard (Job 1:20; Jer 41:5; 47:5; Eze 7:18; Am 8:10). When Nehemiah was confronted with the same problem of intermarriage, instead of pulling out his own hair he pulled out the hair of the offending parties (Ne 13:25).

9:4 *everyone who trembled.* Cf. Ex 19:16; Isa 66:2; Heb 12:21. *appalled.* See v. 3; cf. Da 4:19; 8:27. *evening sacrifice.* See Ex 12:6. The informants had probably visited Ezra in the morning, so that he must have sat appalled for many hours. The time of the evening sacrifice, usually about 3:00 P.M., was also the appointed time for prayer and confession (Ac 3:1).

9:5 – 15 See similar prayers in Ne 9:5 – 37; Da 9:3 – 19 (see also notes there).

9:5 *fell on my knees.* Cf. 1Ki 8:54; Ps 95:6; Da 6:10. *with my hands spread out.* See note on Ex 9:29.

9:6 *ashamed and disgraced.* See 8:22 and note; Lk 18:13. Ezra felt both an inner shame before God and an outward humiliation before people for his own sins and the sins of his people. The two Hebrew verbs often occur together; see Ps 35:4; Isa 45:16; Jer 31:19 ("ashamed and humiliated"). *our sins . . . our guilt.* Cf. also vv. 7,13,15; 10:10,19; 1Ch 21:3; 2Ch 24:18; Ps 38:4. *has reached to the heavens.* See Rev 18:1. But God's love is more than a match for our guilt (Ps 103:11 – 12).

9:7 *From the days of our forefathers.* The Israelites were always conscious of their corporate solidarity with their ancestors. *sword.* Cf. Ne 4:13. In Eze 21 "the sword of the king of Babylon" (21:19) is described as an instrument of divine judgment. *humiliation.* Cf. Da 9:7 – 8; 2Ch 32:21.

9:8 *remnant.* See Ge 45:7; Isa 1:9; 10:20 – 22; Ro 11:5 and notes. *firm place.* Lit. "nail" or "peg" — hence, like a nail driven into a wall (see Isa 22:23 and note) or a tent peg driven into the ground (Isa 33:20; 54:2). *gives light to our eyes.* Gives new vitality, hope and joy (Ps 13:3; 19:8; see note on Ps 6:7; cf. also note on Ps 27:1).

9:9 *kings of Persia.* The Achaemenid Persian kings (see chart, p. 472) were favorably disposed to the Jews: Cyrus the Great (559 – 530 B.C.) gave them permission to return (see 1:1 and note); his son Cambyses (530 – 522), though not named in the Bible, also favored the Jews, as we learn from the Elephantine papyri (see chart, p. xxii); Darius I (522 – 486) renewed the decree of Cyrus (ch. 6); his son Xerxes (486 – 465) granted privileges and protection to Jews (Est 8 – 10); his son Artaxerxes I (465 – 424) gave authorizations to Ezra (ch. 7) and to Nehemiah (Ne 2). *repair its ruins.* Isaiah had prophesied that the Lord would restore Jerusalem's ruins (Isa 44:26), which would burst into singing (Isa 52:9; cf. 58:12; 61:4). *wall of protection.* Used of a city wall only in Mic 7:11. The use here is metaphorical (cf. Zec 2:4 – 5).

9:11 – 12 The references are not to a single OT passage but to several passages, such as Dt 11:8 – 9; Isa 1:19; Eze 37:25.

9:11 *your servants the prophets.* See Ex 14:31; Dt 34:5; Jer 7:25 and notes. *corruption.* Canaanite idolatry and

their detestable practices[s] they have
filled it with their impurity from one
end to the other. 12Therefore, do not
give your daughters in marriage to
their sons or take their daughters
for your sons. Do not seek a treaty
of friendship with them[t] at any time,
that you may be strong[u] and eat the
good things[v] of the land and leave it
to your children as an everlasting inheritance.'[w]
13"What has happened to us is a result of our evil[x] deeds and our great
guilt, and yet, our God, you have
punished us less than our sins have
deserved[y] and have given us a remnant like this. 14Shall we again break
your commands and intermarry[z] with
the peoples who commit such detestable practices? Would you not be angry enough with us to destroy us,[a]
leaving us no remnant[b] or survivor?
15O LORD, God of Israel, you are righteous![c] We are left this day as a remnant. Here we are before you in our
guilt, though because of it not one of
us can stand[d] in your presence.[e]"

The People's Confession of Sin

10 While Ezra was praying and confessing,[f] weeping[g] and throwing
himself down before the house of God,
a large crowd of Israelites—men, wom-
en and children—gathered around him.
They too wept bitterly. 2Then Shecaniah
son of Jehiel, one of the descendants of
Elam,[h] said to Ezra, "We have been unfaithful[i] to our God by marrying foreign
women from the peoples around us. But
in spite of this, there is still hope for Israel.[j] 3Now let us make a covenant[k] before
our God to send away[l] all these women
and their children, in accordance with the
counsel of my lord and of those who fear
the commands of our God. Let it be done
according to the Law. 4Rise up; this matter
is in your hands. We will support you, so
take courage and do it."
5So Ezra rose up and put the leading
priests and Levites and all Israel under
oath[m] to do what had been suggested.
And they took the oath. 6Then Ezra withdrew from before the house of God and
went to the room of Jehohanan son of Eliashib. While he was there, he ate no food
and drank no water,[n] because he continued to mourn over the unfaithfulness of
the exiles.
7A proclamation was then issued
throughout Judah and Jerusalem for all
the exiles to assemble in Jerusalem. 8Any-
one who failed to appear within three
days would forfeit all his property, in accordance with the decision of the officials
and elders, and would himself be expelled
from the assembly of the exiles.

9Within the three days, all the men of
Judah and Benjamin[o] had gathered in Jerusalem. And on the twentieth day of the
ninth month, all the people were sitting in
the square before the house of God, great-

9:11 [s]S Dt 9:4; S 18:9; S 1Ki 14:24 **9:12** [t]S Ex 34:15 [u]Dt 11:8 [v]S Ge 45:18 [w]Ps 103:17; Eze 37:25; Joel 3:20 **9:13** [x]S Ex 32:22 [y]Job 11:6; 15:5; 22:5; 33:27; Ps 103:10 **9:14** [z]Ne 13:27 [a]S Dt 9:8 [b]Dt 9:14 **9:15** [c]S Ge 18:25; S 2Ch 12:6; Ne 9:8; Ps 51:4; 129:4; 145:17; Isa 24:16; Jer 12:1; 23:6; 33:16; La 1:18; Da 9:7; Zep 3:5 [d]Ps 76:7; 130:3; Mal 3:2 [e]S 1Ki 8:47 **10:1** [f]2Ch 20:9; Da 9:20 [g]S Nu 25:6

10:2 [h]ver 26 [i]S Ezr 9:2 [j]Dt 30:8-10 **10:3** [k]S 2Ki 11:17 [l]S Ex 34:16 **10:5** [m]Ne 5:12; 13:25 **10:6** [n]S Ex 34:28; Dt 9:18; Ps 102:4; Jnh 3:7 **10:9** [o]S Ezr 1:5

the immoral practices associated with it (Lev 18:3; 2Ch 29:5; La 1:17; Eze 7:20; 36:17). The degrading practices and beliefs of the Canaanites are described in texts from ancient Ugarit (see chart, p. xxiii).

9:14 *be angry.* God's anger came upon the Israelites because they had violated his covenant with them (Dt 7:4; 11:16–17; 29:26–28; Jos 23:16; Jdg 2:20).

9:15 *you are righteous.* See note on Ps 4:1. *our guilt.* Awareness of God's righteousness made Ezra more conscious of Israel's guilt. See Isa 6:1–5; Lk 5:8. For comparable passages of national lament see Ps 44; 60; 74; 79–80; 83; 85; 90; 108; 126; 129; 137.

10:1 *weeping.* Not silently but out loud (see 3:13 and note; Ne 1:4; Joel 2:12). *throwing himself down.* The prophets and other leaders used object lessons, even bizarre actions, to attract people's attention (Isa 7:3; 8:1–4,18; Jer 13:1–11; 19; 27:2–12; Eze 4:1—5:4).

10:2 Ezra, as a wise teacher, waited for his audience to draw their own conclusions about what should be done. *Shecaniah.* Perhaps his father Jehiel is the Jehiel mentioned in v. 26 since he was also of the family of Elam. If so, Shecaniah was doubtless grieved that his father had married a non-Jewish woman. Six members of the clan of Elam were involved in intermarriage (v. 26).

10:3 *women and their children.* Mothers were given custody of their children when marriages were dissolved. When Hagar was dismissed, Ishmael was sent with her (Ge 21:14). In Babylonia divorced women were granted their children and had to wait for them to grow up before remarrying, according to the Code of Hammurapi (see chart, p. xxii). In Greece, however, children from broken homes remained with their fathers.

10:4 *Rise up.* Cf. David's exhortation (1Ch 22:16).

10:6 *room.* Such temple chambers were used as storerooms (8:29; Ne 13:4–5). *ate no food and drank no water.* Complete fasting from both food and drink was rare. Moses did it twice (Ex 34:28; Dt 9:18), and the Ninevites also did it (Jnh 3:7). Ordinarily, fasting involved abstaining only from eating (1Sa 1:7; 2Sa 3:35). *mourn.* The Hebrew for this word often describes the reaction of those aware of the threat of deserved judgment (Ex 33:4; Nu 14:39).

10:7–8 While Ezra continued to fast and pray, the officials and elders ordered all the exiles to assemble in Jerusalem. Although Ezra had been invested with great authority (7:25–26), he used it sparingly and influenced the people by his example.

10:8 *within three days.* Since the territory of Judah had been much reduced, the most distant people would not be more than 50 miles from Jerusalem. The borders were Bethel in the north, Beersheba in the south, Jericho in the east and Ono in the west (cf. Ne 7:26–38; 11:25–35). *forfeit.* The Hebrew for this word means "to ban from profane use and to devote to the Lord," either by destruction (see Ex 22:20; Dt 13:12–18 and NIV text notes) or by giving it to the Lord's treasury (cf. Lev 27:28; Jos 6:19; 7:1–15).

10:9,16–17 See chart, p. 675.

10:9 *Judah and Benjamin.* See note on 1:5. *square.* Either the outer court of the temple or the open space before the Water Gate (Ne 8:1). *rain.* The Hebrew for this word is a plural of intensity, indicating heavy torrential rains. The ninth month,

ly distressed by the occasion and because
of the rain. 10 Then Ezra[p] the priest stood
up and said to them, "You have been unfaithful; you have married foreign wom-
en, adding to Israel's guilt.[q] 11 Now make
confession to the LORD, the God of your
fathers, and do his will. Separate yourselves from the peoples around you and
from your foreign wives."[r]
12 The whole assembly responded with a
loud voice:[s] "You are right! We must do as
you say. 13 But there are many people here
and it is the rainy season; so we cannot
stand outside. Besides, this matter cannot
be taken care of in a day or two, because
we have sinned greatly in this thing. 14 Let
our officials act for the whole assembly.
Then let everyone in our towns who has
married a foreign woman come at a set
time, along with the elders and judges[t] of
each town, until the fierce anger[u] of our
God in this matter is turned away from
us." 15 Only Jonathan son of Asahel and
Jahzeiah son of Tikvah, supported by Meshullam and Shabbethai[v] the Levite, opposed this.
16 So the exiles did as was proposed. Ezra
the priest selected men who were family
heads, one from each family division, and
all of them designated by name. On the
first day of the tenth month they sat down
to investigate the cases, 17 and by the first
day of the first month they finished dealing with all the men who had married foreign women.

Those Guilty of Intermarriage

18 Among the descendants of the priests,
the following had married foreign
women:[w]

From the descendants of Jeshua[x] son
of Jozadak, and his brothers: Maaseiah, Eliezer, Jarib and Gedaliah.
19 (They all gave their hands[y] in
pledge to put away their wives, and
for their guilt they each presented a
ram from the flock as a guilt offering.)[z]
20 From the descendants of Immer:[a]
Hanani and Zebadiah.
21 From the descendants of Harim:[b]
Maaseiah, Elijah, Shemaiah, Jehiel
and Uzziah.
22 From the descendants of Pashhur:[c]
Elioenai, Maaseiah, Ishmael, Nethanel, Jozabad and Elasah.
23 Among the Levites:[d]

Jozabad, Shimei, Kelaiah (that is,
Kelita), Pethahiah, Judah and Eli-
ezer.
24 From the singers:
Eliashib.[e]
From the gatekeepers:
Shallum, Telem and Uri.

25 And among the other Israelites:

From the descendants of Parosh:[f]
Ramiah, Izziah, Malkijah, Mijamin,
Eleazar, Malkijah and Benaiah.
26 From the descendants of Elam:[g]
Mattaniah, Zechariah, Jehiel, Abdi,
Jeremoth and Elijah.
27 From the descendants of Zattu:
Elioenai, Eliashib, Mattaniah, Jere-
moth, Zabad and Aziza.
28 From the descendants of Bebai:
Jehohanan, Hananiah, Zabbai and
Athlai.
29 From the descendants of Bani:
Meshullam, Malluch, Adaiah, Ja-
shub, Sheal and Jeremoth.
30 From the descendants of Pahath-
Moab:
Adna, Kelal, Benaiah, Maaseiah,
Mattaniah, Bezalel, Binnui and Manasseh.
31 From the descendants of Harim:
Eliezer, Ishijah, Malkijah, Shemaiah, Shimeon, 32 Benjamin, Malluch
and Shemariah.

10:10 [p] Ezr 7:21 [q] 2Ch 28:13
10:11 [r] S Dt 24:1; Mal 2:10-16
10:12 [s] S Jos 6:5
10:14 [t] Dt 16:18 [u] S Nu 25:4; S 2Ch 29:10
10:15 [v] Ne 11:16
10:18 [w] S Jdg 3:6 [x] S Ezr 2:2
10:19 [y] S 2Ki 10:15 [z] S Lev 5:15; 6:6
10:20 [a] S 1Ch 24:14
10:21 [b] S 1Ch 24:8
10:22 [c] S 1Ch 9:12
10:23 [d] Ne 8:7; 9:4
10:24 [e] Ne 3:1; 12:10; 13:7,28
10:25 [f] S Ezr 2:3
10:26 [g] S ver 2

Kislev (November-December), is in the middle of the "rainy season" (v. 13), which begins with light showers in October and lasts to mid-April. December and January are also cold months, with temperatures in the 50s and even 40s in Jerusalem. The people shivered not only because they were drenched, but perhaps also because they sensed divine displeasure in the heavy rains (see 1Sa 12:17–18; Eze 13:11,13).

10:10 *adding to Israel's guilt.* See Ex 9:34; Jdg 3:12; 4:1; 2Ch 28:13. The sins and failures of the exiles were great enough, but they added insult to injury by marrying pagan women.

10:11 *Separate yourselves.* See Nu 16:21; 2Co 6:14.

10:12 *with a loud voice.* See Ne 9:4.

10:14 *elders and judges of each town.* See Dt 16:18; 19:12; 21:3,19; Ru 4:2.

10:15 Perhaps these four men opposed the measure because they wanted to protect themselves or their relatives, or they may have viewed it as being too harsh. *Tikvah.* Means "hope" (found elsewhere only in 2Ki 22:14). *Meshullam.* See note on 8:16. If he is the Meshullam of v. 29, he himself had married a pagan wife.

10:16–17 The committee completed its work in three months, discovering that about 110 men were guilty of marrying pagan wives.

10:18–22 See 2:36–39.

10:19 *gave their hands.* For the symbolic use of the hands in making commitments or pledges, cf. notes on Ge 14:22; Pr 6:1. *ram.* Guilt offerings were to be made for sins committed unintentionally against the Lord (Lev 5:14–19), and also for sins committed intentionally against a neighbor (Lev 6:1–7), and a ram was the appropriate offering in either case (Lev 5:15; 6:6).

10:24 It is striking that only one singer and three gatekeepers were involved. No temple servants (2:43–54) or descendants of Solomon's servants (2:55–57) sinned through intermarriage.

10:25–43 See 2:3–20.

10:30 *Bezalel.* Cf. Ex 31:2.

10:31 *Shimeon.* The Hebrew for this name is the same as

[33]From the descendants of Hashum:
Mattenai, Mattattah, Zabad, Eliphelet, Jeremai, Manasseh and
Shimei.
[34]From the descendants of Bani:
Maadai, Amram, Uel, [35]Benaiah,
Bedeiah, Keluhi, [36]Vaniah, Meremoth, Eliashib, [37]Mattaniah, Mattenai and Jaasu.
[38]From the descendants of Binnui:[a]
Shimei, [39]Shelemiah, Nathan, Adaiah, [40]Macnadebai, Shashai, Sharai,
[41]Azarel, Shelemiah, Shemariah,
[42]Shallum, Amariah and Joseph.
[43]From the descendants of Nebo:
Jeiel, Mattithiah, Zabad, Zebina,
Jaddai, Joel and Benaiah.

[44]All these had married foreign women,
and some of them had children by these
wives.[b]

[a] *37,38* See Septuagint (also 1 Esdras 9:34); Hebrew *Jaasu [38]and Bani and Binnui,* [b] *44* Or *and they sent them away with their children*

that for Simeon, Jacob's second son (see NIV text note on Ge 29:33). In Greek the name became Simon (e.g., Mt 4:18).

10:43 *Nebo.* The Hebrew equivalent of the name of the Babylonian god Nabu (see Isa 46:1); found only here as a personal name.

10:44 Some of the marriages had produced children, but this was not accepted as a reason for halting the divorce proceedings. See NIV text note.

Nehemiah

INTRODUCTION

See Introduction to Ezra.

Outline

- I. Nehemiah's First Administration (chs. 1 – 12)
  - A. Nehemiah's Response to the Situation in Jerusalem (ch. 1)
    1. News of the plight of Jerusalem (1:1 – 4)
    2. Nehemiah's prayer (1:5 – 11)
  - B. Nehemiah's Journey to Jerusalem (2:1 – 10)
    1. The king's permission (2:1 – 8)
    2. The journey itself (2:9 – 10)
  - C. Nehemiah's First Actions upon Arrival (2:11 – 20)
    1. His nocturnal inspection of the walls (2:11 – 16)
    2. His exhortation to rebuild (2:17 – 18)
    3. His response to opposition (2:19 – 20)
  - D. List of the Builders of the Wall (ch. 3)
    1. The northern section (3:1 – 7)
    2. The western section (3:8 – 13)
    3. The southern section (3:14)
    4. The eastern section (3:15 – 32)
  - E. Opposition to Rebuilding the Wall (ch. 4)
    1. The derision of Sanballat and Tobiah (4:1 – 5)
    2. The threat of attack (4:6 – 15)
    3. Rebuilding the wall (4:16 – 23)
  - F. Social and Economic Problems (ch. 5)
    1. The complaints of the poor (5:1 – 5)
    2. The cancellation of debts (5:6 – 13)
    3. Nehemiah's unselfish example (5:14 – 19)
  - G. The Wall Rebuilt Despite Opposition (ch. 6)
    1. Attempts to snare Nehemiah (6:1 – 9)
    2. The hiring of false prophets (6:10 – 14)
    3. The completion of the wall (6:15 – 19)

A Quick Look

Author:

Unknown; possibly Ezra or Nehemiah

Audience:

The people of Judah who had returned from exile in Babylonia

Date:

Sometime after 430 B.C.

Theme:

Nehemiah travels from Susa in Elam to Jerusalem in Judah to lead the Jews in rebuilding the city walls.

- H. List of Exiles (7:1 – 73a)
  1. Provisions for the protection of Jerusalem (7:1 – 3)
  2. Nehemiah's discovery of the list of returnees (7:4 – 5)
  3. The returnees delineated (7:6 – 72)
  4. Settlement of the exiles (7:73a)
- I. Ezra's Preaching and the Outbreak of Revival (7:73b — 10:39)
  1. The public exposition of the Scriptures (7:73b — 8:12)
  2. The Feast of Tabernacles (8:13 – 18)
  3. A day of fasting, confession and prayer (9:1 – 37)
  4. A binding agreement (9:38)
  5. A list of those who sealed it (10:1 – 29)
  6. Provisions of the agreement (10:30 – 39)
- J. New Residents of Judah and Jerusalem (ch. 11)
  1. New residents for Jerusalem (11:1 – 24)
  2. New residents for Judah (11:25 – 36)
- K. Lists of Priests and the Dedication of the Wall (ch. 12)
  1. Priests and Levites from the first return (12:1 – 9)
  2. High priests and Levites since Joiakim (12:10 – 26)
  3. Dedication of the wall of Jerusalem (12:27 – 43)
  4. Regulation of the temple offerings and services (12:44 – 47)

II. Nehemiah's Second Administration (ch. 13)

- A. Abuses during His Absence (13:1 – 5)
  1. Mixed marriages (13:1 – 3)
  2. Tobiah's occupation of the temple quarters (13:4 – 5)
- B. Nehemiah's Return (13:6 – 9)
  1. His arrival (13:6 – 7)
  2. His expulsion of Tobiah (13:8 – 9)
- C. Reorganization and Reforms (13:10 – 31)
  1. Offerings for the temple staff (13:10 – 14)
  2. Abuse of the Sabbath (13:15 – 22)
  3. Mixed marriages (13:23 – 29)
  4. Provisions of wood and firstfruits (13:30 – 31)

Nehemiah's Prayer

1 The words of Nehemiah son of Hacaliah:

In the month of Kislev[a] in the twentieth
year, while I was in the citadel of Susa,[b]
2Hanani,[c] one of my brothers, came from
Judah with some other men, and I questioned them about the Jewish remnant[d]
that survived the exile, and also about Jerusalem.

3They said to me, "Those who survived
the exile and are back in the province are
in great trouble and disgrace. The wall of
Jerusalem is broken down, and its gates
have been burned with fire.[e]"

4When I heard these things, I sat down
and wept.[f] For some days I mourned and
fasted[g] and prayed before the God of heav-
en. 5Then I said:

"O LORD, God of heaven, the great
and awesome God,[h] who keeps his
covenant of love[i] with those who
love him and obey his commands,
6let your ear be attentive and your
eyes open to hear[j] the prayer[k] your
servant is praying before you day and
night for your servants, the people of
Israel. I confess[l] the sins we Israelites, including myself and my father's
house, have committed against you.
7We have acted very wickedly[m] toward you. We have not obeyed the
commands, decrees and laws you
gave your servant Moses.

8"Remember[n] the instruction you
gave your servant Moses, saying, 'If
you are unfaithful, I will scatter[o] you
among the nations, 9but if you return
to me and obey my commands, then
even if your exiled people are at the
farthest horizon, I will gather[p] them
from there and bring them to the
place I have chosen as a dwelling for
my Name.'[q]

10"They are your servants and your
people, whom you redeemed by your
great strength and your mighty hand.[r]
11O Lord, let your ear be attentive[s] to
the prayer of this your servant and to
the prayer of your servants who de-

1:1 [a]Zec 7:1 [b]S Ezr 4:9; S Est 2:8 **1:2** [c]Ne 7:2 [d]S 2Ki 21:14; Ne 7:6; Jer 52:28 **1:3** [e]S Lev 26:31; 2Ki 25:10; Ne 2:3,13,17; Isa 22:9; Jer 39:8; 52:14; La 2:9 **1:4** [f]Ps 137:1 [g]S 2Ch 20:3; S Ezr 9:4; Da 9:3 **1:5** [h]S Dt 7:21; Ne 4:14 [i]S Dt 7:9; S 1Ki 8:23; Da 9:4 **1:6** [j]S 1Ki 8:29; S 2Ch 7:15 [k]S 1Ki 8:30 [l]S 1Ki 8:47 **1:7** [m]Ps 106:6 **1:8** [n]S Ge 8:1; S 2Ki 20:3; Ne 4:14; 5:19; 6:14; 13:22,29,31 [o]S Lev 26:33 **1:9** [p]S Dt 30:4; Ps 106:47; 107:3; Isa 11:12; 56:8; Jer 42:12; Eze 11:17 [q]S 1Ki 8:48; Jer 29:14; Eze 11:17; 20:34-38; 36:24-38; Mic 2:12 **1:10** [r]S Ex 32:11; Isa 51:9-11 **1:11** [s]S 2Ch 6:40

1:1 *The words of.* Originally an introduction to the title of a separate composition (see Jer 1:1; Am 1:1), though the books of Ezra and Nehemiah appear as a single work from earliest times (see Introduction to Ezra: Ezra and Nehemiah). *Nehemiah.* Means "The LORD comforts." *Kislev ... twentieth year.* November-December, 445 B.C. See chart, p. 675. *Susa.* See note on Ezr 4:9.

1:2 *Hanani.* Probably a shortened form of Hananiah, which means "The LORD is gracious." *one of my brothers.* See 7:2. The Elephantine papyri (see chart, p. xxii) mention a Hananiah who was the head of Jewish affairs in Jerusalem. Many believe that he is to be identified with Nehemiah's brother, and that he may have governed between Nehemiah's first and second terms (see NIV text note on 7:2). *Jewish remnant.* See Ezr 9:8 and notes on Ge 45:7; 2Ki 19:30–31; Isa 1:9; 10:20–22; Zec 8:23.

1:3 *province.* See note on Ezr 2:1. *wall of Jerusalem is broken down.* The lack of a city wall meant that the people were defenseless against their enemies. Thucydides (1.89) describes the comparable condition of Athens after its devastation by the Persians in 480–479 B.C. Excavations at Jerusalem during A.D. 1961–67 revealed that the lack of a wall on the eastern slopes also meant the disintegration of the terraces there. When Nebuchadnezzar assaulted Jerusalem in 586 B.C., he battered and broke down the walls around it (2Ki 25:10). But most interpreters do not believe that Nehemiah's distress was caused by Nebuchadnezzar's destruction but by the episode of Ezr 4:7–23. The Jews had attempted to rebuild the walls earlier in the reign of Artaxerxes I; but after the protest of Rehum and Shimshai, the king ordered the Jews to desist. See note on Ezr 4:21–23.

1:4 *sat down.* Cf. Ezr 9:3; Job 2:13. *wept.* See 8:9; Ezr 3:13 and note; 10:1; Est 8:3. *mourned.* See Ezr 10:6; Da 10:2. *fasted and prayed.* See note on Ezr 8:23. During the exile, fasting became a common practice, including solemn fasts to commemorate the fall of Jerusalem and the murder of Gedaliah (see note on Zec 8:19; see also Est 4:16; Da 9:3; 10:3; Zec 7:3–7). *God of heaven.* See note on Ezr 1:2.

1:5 *who keeps his covenant of love.* See 9:32; see also Dt 7:9,12 and note. *who love him and obey his commands.* See Da 9:4; Ex 20:6 and note.

1:6 *praying before you day and night.* Cf. Ps 42:3; 88:1; Jer 9:1; 14:17; La 2:18; Lk 2:37; 1Th 3:10; 1Ti 5:5; 2Ti 1:3. *sins ... myself and my father's house.* Nehemiah does not exclude himself or members of his own family in his confession of sins. A true sense of the awesome holiness of God reveals the depths of our own sinfulness (Isa 6:1–5; Lk 5:8).

1:7 *commands, decrees and laws.* See note on Ge 26:5. *laws you gave ... Moses.* For the prominence of the Law of Moses in Ezra and Nehemiah see Ezr 3:2; 6:18; 7:6; Ne 1:8; 8:1,14; 9:14; 10:29; 13:1.

1:8 *Remember.* A key word in the book (see 4:14; 5:19; 6:14; 13:14,22,29,31 and note on 13:31). *unfaithful ... scatter.* Dispersion was the forewarned judgment of God on Israel's unfaithfulness (see Lev 26:33; Dt 28:64 and note). By the NT period there were still more Jews in the Diaspora (dispersion) than in the Holy Land.

1:9 *I will gather them.* See Dt 30:1–5; a frequent promise, especially in the prophets (e.g., Isa 11:12; Jer 23:3; 31:8–10; Eze 20:34,41; 36:24; Mic 2:12). *chosen as a dwelling for my Name.* See Dt 12:5 and note; Ps 132:13.

1:10 *your people ... you redeemed.* Although they had sinned and failed, they were still God's people, whom he had redeemed from Egyptian bondage (see Dt 4:34; 9:29) and with whom he had made the covenant at Sinai (see Ex 19:5–6 and notes).

1:11 *Give your servant success today.* Cf. Ge 24:12. *cupbearer.* Lit. "one who gives (someone) something to drink." The Hebrew for this word occurs 11 other times in the OT in the sense of "cupbearer" (Ge 40:1–2,5,9,13,20–21,23; 41:9; 1Ki 10:5; 2Ch 9:4). According to the Greek historian Xenophon (*Cyropaedia*, 1.3.9), one of the cupbearer's duties was to choose and taste the king's wine to make certain that it was not poisoned (see 2:1). Thus Nehemiah had to be a man who enjoyed the unreserved confidence of the king. The need for trustworthy court attendants is underscored by the intrigues that characterized the Achaemenid court of Persia. Xerxes, the father of Artaxerxes I, was killed in his own bedchamber by a courtier.

light in revering your name. Give your
servant success today by granting him
favor[t] in the presence of this man."

I was cupbearer[u] to the king.

Artaxerxes Sends Nehemiah to Jerusalem

2 In the month of Nisan in the twentieth
year of King Artaxerxes,[v] when wine
was brought for him, I took the wine and
gave it to the king. I had not been sad in
his presence before; 2so the king asked me,
"Why does your face look so sad when
you are not ill? This can be nothing but
sadness of heart."

I was very much afraid, 3but I said to
the king, "May the king live forever![w]
Why should my face not look sad when
the city[x] where my fathers are buried lies
in ruins, and its gates have been destroyed
by fire?[y]"

4The king said to me, "What is it you
want?"

Then I prayed to the God of heaven,
5and I answered the king, "If it pleases the
king and if your servant has found favor
in his sight, let him send me to the city in
Judah where my fathers are buried so that
I can rebuild it."

6Then the king[z], with the queen sitting
beside him, asked me, "How long will
your journey take, and when will you get
back?" It pleased the king to send me; so
I set a time.

7I also said to him, "If it pleases the
king, may I have letters to the governors
of Trans-Euphrates,[a] so that they will provide me safe-conduct until I arrive in Judah? 8And may I have a letter to Asaph,
keeper of the king's forest, so he will give
me timber to make beams for the gates
of the citadel[b] by the temple and for the
city wall and for the residence I will occupy?" And because the gracious hand of my
God was upon me,[c] the king granted my
requests.[d] 9So I went to the governors of
Trans-Euphrates and gave them the king's
letters. The king had also sent army officers and cavalry[e] with me.

10When Sanballat[f] the Horonite and Tobiah[g] the Ammonite official heard about
this, they were very much disturbed that
someone had come to promote the welfare
of the Israelites.[h]

1:11 [t] S Ex 3:21 [u] S Ge 40:1
2:1 [v] S Ezr 4:7; S 6:14
2:3 [w] 1Ki 1:31; Da 2:4; 3:9; 5:10; 6:6,21 [x] Ps 137:6 [y] S Ne 1:3
2:6 [z] Ne 5:14; 13:6
2:7 [a] S Ezr 8:36
2:8 [b] Ne 7:2 [c] S Ezr 5:5 [d] S Ezr 4:24
2:9 [e] S Ezr 8:22
2:10 [f] ver 19; Ne 4:1,7; 6:1-2,5,12,14; 13:28 [g] Ne 4:3; 13:4-7 [h] Est 10:3

2:1 *Nisan ... twentieth year.* March-April, 444 B.C. (see chart, p. 675). *King Artaxerxes.* See chart, p. 472. *sad in his presence.* No matter what one's personal problems were, the king's servants were expected to keep their feelings to themselves and to display a cheerful disposition before him.

2:3 *May the king live forever!* A common form of address to kings (cf. note on Ps 62:4).

2:4 *prayed.* Before turning to answer the king, Nehemiah utters a brief, spontaneous prayer to God. One of Nehemiah's striking characteristics is his frequent recourse to prayer (1:4; 4:4,9; 5:19; 6:9,14; 13:14,22,29,31).

2:6 *queen.* The Hebrew for this word is used only here and in Ps 45:9 ("royal bride"). The Aramaic equivalent is found only in Da 5:2–3,23, where it is translated "wives." Ctesias, a Greek who lived at the Achaemenid court, informs us that the name of Artaxerxes's queen was Damaspia and that he had at least three concubines. Like Esther (Est 5), Damaspia may have used her influence with the king. The Achaemenid court was notorious for the great influence exercised by the royal women. *How long will your journey take ...?* Nehemiah probably asked for a brief leave of absence, which he then had extended. We can infer from 5:14 that he spent 12 years on his first term as governor of Judah. In the 32nd year of Artaxerxes, Nehemiah returned to report to the king and then came back to Judah for a second term (13:6–7).

2:7 *letters ... provide me safe-conduct.* A contemporary document from Arsames, the satrap of Egypt who was at the Persian court, to one of his officers who was returning to Egypt, orders Persian officials to provide this officer with food and drink on the stages of his journey. *Trans-Euphrates.* See note on Ezr 4:10.

2:8 *forest.* The Hebrew for this word is *pardes*, a loanword from Old Persian meaning "enclosure," a pleasant retreat or park. The word occurs elsewhere in the OT only in Ecc 2:5 ("parks") and SS 4:13 ("orchard"). In the Septuagint (the pre-Christian Greek translation of the OT) the Greek transliteration *paradeisos* is used here. In the period between the OT and the NT, the word acquired the sense of the abode of the blessed dead, i.e., "paradise." It appears three times in the NT (Lk 23:43; 2Co 12:4; Rev 2:7). As to the location of the "king's forest," some believe that it was in Lebanon, which was famed for its forests of cedars and other coniferous trees (see notes on Jdg 9:15; Ezr 3:7). But a more plausible suggestion is that it should be identified with Solomon's gardens at Etham, about six miles south of Jerusalem (see Josephus, *Antiquities*, 8.7.3). For city gates, costly imported cedars from Lebanon would not be used but rather indigenous oak, poplar or terebinth (Hos 4:13). *citadel.* Probably refers to the fortress north of the temple, the forerunner of the Antonia fortress built by Herod the Great (Josephus, *Antiquities*, 15.11.4; see Ac 21:34,37; 22:24).

2:9 *army officers and cavalry.* In striking contrast to Ezra (see note on Ezr 8:22), Nehemiah was accompanied by an armed escort since he was officially Judah's governor.

2:10 *Sanballat.* A Babylonian name, meaning "Sin (the moon-god) has given life." *Horonite.* Identifies him as coming from (1) Hauran (Eze 47:16,18), east of the Sea of Galilee, (2) Horonaim, in Moab (Jer 48:34), or, most probably, (3) either Upper or Lower Beth Horon, two key cities about 11 miles northwest of Jerusalem, which guarded the main road to Jerusalem (Jos 10:10; 16:3,5; 1 Maccabees 3:16; 7:39). Sanballat was the chief political opponent of Nehemiah (v. 19; 4:1,7; 6:1–2,5,12,14; 13:28). He held the position of governor over Samaria (cf. 4:1–2). An Elephantine papyrus letter of the late fifth century B.C. to Bagohi (Bigvai), governor of Judah, refers to "Delaiah and Shelemiah, the sons of Sanballat, governor of Samaria." In 1962 a fourth-century B.C. papyrus was found in a cave north of Jericho, listing the name Sanballat, probably a descendant of Nehemiah's contemporary. *Tobiah.* Means "The LORD is good." He was probably a worshiper of the Lord (Yahweh), as indicated not only by his name but also by that of his son Jehohanan (6:17–18), meaning "The LORD is gracious." Jehohanan was married to the daughter of Meshullam son of Berekiah, the leader of one of the groups repairing the wall (3:4,30; 6:18). Tobiah also had a close relationship with Eliashib the priest (13:4–7). *Ammonite.* See Ezr 9:1; see also note on Ge 19:36–38. Tobiah was probably governor of Transjordan under the Persians. In later generations a

Nehemiah Inspects Jerusalem's Walls

11I went to Jerusalem, and after staying there three days[i] 12I set out during the
night with a few men. I had not told anyone what my God had put in my heart to
do for Jerusalem. There were no mounts
with me except the one I was riding on.
13By night I went out through the Valley Gate[j] toward the Jackal[a] Well and the
Dung Gate,[k] examining the walls[l] of Jerusalem, which had been broken down, and
its gates, which had been destroyed by
fire. 14Then I moved on toward the Fountain Gate[m] and the King's Pool,[n] but there
was not enough room for my mount to get
through; 15so I went up the valley by night,
examining the wall. Finally, I turned back
and reentered through the Valley Gate.
16The officials did not know where I had
gone or what I was doing, because as yet I
had said nothing to the Jews or the priests
or nobles or officials or any others who
would be doing the work.
17Then I said to them, "You see the
trouble we are in: Jerusalem lies in ruins,
and its gates have been burned with fire.[o]
Come, let us rebuild the wall[p] of Jerusalem,
and we will no longer be in disgrace.[q]" 18I
also told them about the gracious hand of

2:11 [i] S Ge 40:13 **2:13** [j] S 2Ch 26:9 [k] Ne 3:13; 12:31 [l] S Ne 1:3 **2:14** [m] Ne 3:15; 12:37 [n] S 2Ki 18:17
2:17 [o] S Ne 1:3 [p] Ps 102:16; Isa 30:13; 58:12 [q] Eze 5:14

[a] *13* Or *Serpent* or *Fig*

prominent family bearing the name of Tobiah was sometimes associated with the region of Ammon in non-Biblical texts. *very much disturbed.* The reasons for the opposition of Sanballat and Tobiah were not basically religious but political. The authority of the Samaritan governor in particular was threatened by Nehemiah's arrival.

2:11 *three days.* See note on Ezr 8:32.

2:12 Nehemiah was cautious and discreet as he inspected the city's fortifications. *one I was riding on.* Probably a mule or donkey.

2:13 Nehemiah did not make a complete circuit of the walls, but only of the southern area (see map below). Jerusalem was always attacked from the north because it was most vulnerable there, so the walls had probably been completely destroyed in that part of the city. *Valley Gate.* See 3:13. According to 2Ch 26:9 Uzziah fortified towers in the west wall, which overlooked the central valley between the Hinnom and Kidron valleys. Excavations in 1927–28 uncovered the remains of a gate from the Persian period, which has been identified as the Valley Gate. *Jackal Well.* Many interpreters suggest that this was En Rogel (Jos 15:7–8; 18:16; 2Sa 17:17; 1Ki 1:9), a well situated at the junction of the Hinnom and Kidron valleys, 250 yards south of the southeast ridge of Jerusalem (see map below). Others suggest that it was the Pool of Siloam. *Dung Gate.* Perhaps the gate leading to the rubbish dump in the Hinnom Valley (cf. 3:13–14; 12:31; 2Ki 23:10). It was situated about 500 yards south of the Valley Gate (3:13).

2:14 *Fountain Gate.* Possibly in the southeast wall facing toward En Rogel (see 3:15; 12:37). *King's Pool.* Hezekiah may have diverted the overflow from his Siloam tunnel (cf. 2Ki 20:20; 2Ch 32:30) to irrigate the royal gardens (2Ki 25:4) located outside the city walls at the junction of the Kidron and Hinnom valleys. The King's Pool was probably therefore the Pool of Siloam (3:15) or the adjacent Birket el-Hamra. *not enough room.* Possibly because of the collapse of the supporting terraces (cf. 2Sa 5:9; 1Ki 9:15,24) on the east side of the city.

2:15 *valley.* The Kidron.

2:17 *ruins.* The condition of the walls and gates of the city since their destruction by Nebuchadnezzar in 586 B.C., in spite of abortive attempts to rebuild them. The leaders and people had evidently become reconciled to this sad state of affairs. It took an outsider to assess the situation and to rally them to renewed efforts.

2:18 *my God … and … the king.* Nehemiah could personally attest that God was alive and active in his behalf and that he (Nehemiah) had come with royal sanction and authority.

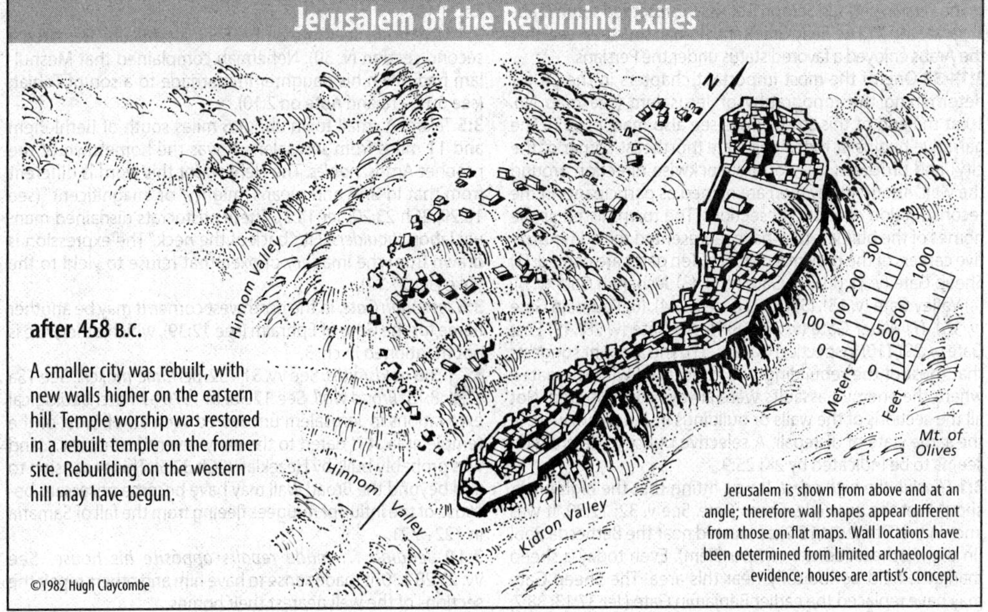

after 458 B.C.

A smaller city was rebuilt, with new walls higher on the eastern hill. Temple worship was restored in a rebuilt temple on the former site. Rebuilding on the western hill may have begun.

Jerusalem is shown from above and at an angle; therefore wall shapes appear different from those on flat maps. Wall locations have been determined from limited archaeological evidence; houses are artist's concept.

my God upon me[r] and what the king had
said to me.
They replied, "Let us start rebuilding."
So they began this good work.
19But when Sanballat[s] the Horonite, Tobiah the Ammonite official and Geshem[t]
the Arab heard about it, they mocked
and ridiculed us.[u] "What is this you are
doing?" they asked. "Are you rebelling
against the king?"
20I answered them by saying, "The God
of heaven will give us success. We his servants will start rebuilding,[v] but as for you,
you have no share[w] in Jerusalem or any
claim or historic right to it."

Builders of the Wall

3 Eliashib[x] the high priest and his fellow
priests went to work and rebuilt[y] the
Sheep Gate.[z] They dedicated it and set its
doors in place, building as far as the Tower
of the Hundred, which they dedicated, and
as far as the Tower of Hananel.[a] 2The men
of Jericho[b] built the adjoining section, and
Zaccur son of Imri built next to them.
3The Fish Gate[c] was rebuilt by the sons
of Hassenaah. They laid its beams and put
its doors and bolts and bars in place. 4Mer-
emoth[d] son of Uriah, the son of Hakkoz,
repaired the next section. Next to him Meshullam son of Berekiah, the son of Meshezabel, made repairs, and next to him
Zadok son of Baana also made repairs.
5The next section was repaired by the men
of Tekoa,[e] but their nobles would not put
their shoulders to the work under their supervisors.[a]
6The Jeshanah[b] Gate[f] was repaired by
Joiada son of Paseah and Meshullam son
of Besodeiah. They laid its beams and
put its doors and bolts and bars in place.
7Next to them, repairs were made by men
from Gibeon[g] and Mizpah—Melatiah of
Gibeon and Jadon of Meronoth—places under the authority of the governor of
Trans-Euphrates. 8Uzziel son of Harhaiah,
one of the goldsmiths, repaired the next
section; and Hananiah, one of the perfume-makers, made repairs next to that.
They restored[c] Jerusalem as far as the
Broad Wall.[h] 9Rephaiah son of Hur, ruler of a half-district of Jerusalem, repaired
the next section. 10Adjoining this, Jedaiah
son of Harumaph made repairs opposite

2:18 [r]S Ezr 5:5 **2:19** [s]S ver 10 [t]Ne 6:1,2,6 [u]Ps 44:13-16 **2:20** [v]Ezr 4:1 [w]Ezr 4:3; Ac 8:21 **3:1** [x]S Ezr 10:24 [y]Isa 58:12 [z]ver 32; Ne 12:39; Jn 5:2 [a]Ne 12:39; Ps 48:12; Jer 31:38; Zec 14:10 **3:2** [b]Ne 7:36 **3:3** [c]S 2Ch 33:14 **3:4** [d]S Ezr 8:33 **3:5** [e]ver 27; S 2Sa 14:2 **3:6** [f]Ne 12:39 **3:7** [g]S Jos 9:3 **3:8** [h]Ne 12:38

[a] 5 Or *their Lord* or *the governor* [b] 6 Or *Old*
[c] 8 Or *They left out part of*

2:19 *Sanballat ... Tobiah.* See note on v. 10. *Geshem.* Inscriptions from Dedan in northwest Arabia and from Tell el-Maskhutah near Ismailia in Egypt bear the name Geshem, who may have been in charge of a north Arabian confederacy that controlled vast areas from northeast Egypt to northern Arabia, including the southern part of the Holy Land. Geshem may have been opposed to Nehemiah's development of an independent kingdom because he feared that it might interfere with his lucrative spice trade. *Arab.* See 2Ch 9:14; Isa 21:13; Jer 25:24. Arabs became dominant in Transjordan from the Assyrian to the Persian periods. Sargon II of Assyria resettled some Arabs in Samaria in 715 B.C. Early Greek and Roman sources reveal that the Arabs enjoyed a favored status under the Persians.

3:1–32 One of the most important chapters in the OT for determining the topography of Jerusalem (see map No. 10 at the end of this study Bible; see also map, p. 695). The narrative begins at the Sheep Gate (northeast corner of the city) and proceeds in a counterclockwise direction around the wall. About 40 key men are named as participants in the reconstruction of about 45 sections. The towns listed as the homes of the builders may have represented the administrative centers of the province of Judah. Ten gates are named: (1) Sheep Gate (v. 1), (2) Fish Gate (v. 3), (3) Jeshanah Gate (v. 6), (4) Valley Gate (v. 13), (5) Dung Gate (v. 14), (6) Fountain Gate (v. 15), (7) Water Gate (v. 26), (8) Horse Gate (v. 28), (9) East Gate (v. 29), (10) Inspection Gate (v. 31). The account suggests that most of the rebuilding was concerned with the gates, where the enemy's assaults were always concentrated. Not all the sections of the walls or buildings in Jerusalem were in the same state of disrepair. A selective policy of destruction seems to be indicated by 2Ki 25:9.

3:1 *Eliashib the high priest.* It was fitting that the high priest should set the example. *Sheep Gate.* See v. 32; 12:39. It was known in NT times (Jn 5:2) as located near the Bethesda Pool (in the northeast corner of Jerusalem). Even today a sheep market is held periodically near this area. The Sheep Gate may have replaced the earlier Benjamin Gate (Jer 37:13; 38:7; Zec 14:10). *Tower of the Hundred.* See 12:39. "Hundred" may refer to (1) its height (100 cubits), (2) the number of its steps or (3) a military unit (cf. Dt 1:15). *Tower of Hananel.* The towers were associated with the "citadel by the temple" (2:8) in protecting the vulnerable northern approaches to the city.

3:3 *Fish Gate.* See 12:39. During the days of Solomon's temple, it was one of Jerusalem's main entrances (2Ch 33:14; Zep 1:10). Merchants brought fish from either Tyre or the Sea of Galilee to the fish market (13:16) through this entrance, which was located in the north wall of the city (see note on Zep 1:10).

3:4 *Meremoth.* See note on Ezr 8:33. *Meshullam.* Repaired a second section (v. 30). Nehemiah complained that Meshullam had given his daughter in marriage to a son of Tobiah (see 6:17–18 and note on 2:10).

3:5 *Tekoa.* A small town about 6 miles south of Bethlehem and 11 miles from Jerusalem. It was the hometown of the prophet Amos. *nobles.* The Hebrew for this word is different from that in 2:16 and means "mighty" or "magnificent" (see 10:29; 2Ch 23:20; Jer 14:3). These aristocrats disdained manual labor. *shoulders.* Lit. "back of the neck." The expression is drawn from the imagery of oxen that refuse to yield to the yoke (Jer 27:12).

3:6 *Jeshanah Gate.* In the northwest corner. It may be another name for the Gate of Ephraim (see 12:39), which otherwise is not mentioned in ch. 3.

3:8 *goldsmiths.* See vv. 31–32. *perfume-makers.* See 1Sa 8:13. *Broad Wall.* See 12:38. In 1970–71 archaeological excavations in Jerusalem uncovered such a wall west of the temple area. It is dated to the early seventh century B.C. and was probably built by Hezekiah (2Ch 32:5). This expansion to and beyond the Broad Wall may have become necessary because of the influx of refugees fleeing from the fall of Samaria in 722–721.

3:10 *Jedaiah ... made repairs opposite his house.* See vv. 23,28–30. It made sense to have him and others repair the sections of the wall nearest their homes.

his house, and Hattush son of Hashabneiah made repairs next to him. 11Malkijah
son of Harim and Hasshub son of Pahath-Moab repaired another section and
the Tower of the Ovens.[i] 12Shallum son of
Hallohesh, ruler of a half-district of Jerusalem, repaired the next section with the
help of his daughters.

13The Valley Gate[j] was repaired by Hanun and the residents of Zanoah.[k] They
rebuilt it and put its doors and bolts and
bars in place. They also repaired five hundred yards[a] of the wall as far as the Dung
Gate.[l]

14The Dung Gate was repaired by Malkijah son of Recab, ruler of the district of
Beth Hakkerem.[m] He rebuilt it and put its
doors and bolts and bars in place.

15The Fountain Gate was repaired by
Shallun son of Col-Hozeh, ruler of the district of Mizpah. He rebuilt it, roofing it over
and putting its doors and bolts and bars
in place. He also repaired the wall of the
Pool of Siloam,[b][n] by the King's Garden, as
far as the steps going down from the City
of David. 16Beyond him, Nehemiah son of
Azbuk, ruler of a half-district of Beth Zur,[o]
made repairs up to a point opposite the
tombs[c][p] of David, as far as the artificial
pool and the House of the Heroes.

17Next to him, the repairs were made
by the Levites under Rehum son of Bani.
Beside him, Hashabiah, ruler of half the
district of Keilah,[q] carried out repairs for
his district. 18Next to him, the repairs were

3:11 [i]Ne 12:38
3:13 [j]S 2Ch 26:9 [k]S Jos 15:34 [l]S Ne 2:13
3:14 [m]Jer 6:1
3:15 [n]Isa 8:6; Jn 9:7
3:16 [o]S Jos 15:58 [p]Ac 2:29
3:17 [q]S Jos 15:44
3:21 [r]S Ezr 8:33
3:24 [s]S Ezr 8:33
3:25 [t]Jer 32:2; 37:21; 39:14 [u]S Ezr 2:3
3:26 [v]Ne 7:46; 11:21 [w]S 2Ch 33:14 [x]Ne 8:1,3,16; 12:37
3:27 [y]S ver 5

made by their countrymen under Binnui[d]
son of Henadad, ruler of the other half-district of Keilah. 19Next to him, Ezer son of
Jeshua, ruler of Mizpah, repaired another
section, from a point facing the ascent to
the armory as far as the angle. 20Next to
him, Baruch son of Zabbai zealously repaired another section, from the angle to
the entrance of the house of Eliashib the
high priest. 21Next to him, Meremoth[r] son
of Uriah, the son of Hakkoz, repaired another section, from the entrance of Eliashib's house to the end of it.

22The repairs next to him were made by
the priests from the surrounding region.
23Beyond them, Benjamin and Hasshub
made repairs in front of their house; and
next to them, Azariah son of Maaseiah,
the son of Ananiah, made repairs beside
his house. 24Next to him, Binnui[s] son of
Henadad repaired another section, from
Azariah's house to the angle and the corner, 25and Palal son of Uzai worked opposite the angle and the tower projecting
from the upper palace near the court of
the guard.[t] Next to him, Pedaiah son of
Parosh[u] 26and the temple servants[v] living
on the hill of Ophel[w] made repairs up to
a point opposite the Water Gate[x] toward
the east and the projecting tower. 27Next to
them, the men of Tekoa[y] repaired another

[a] *13* Hebrew *a thousand cubits* (about 450 meters)
[b] *15* Hebrew *Shelah,* a variant of *Shiloah,* that is, Siloam
[c] *16* Hebrew; Septuagint, some Vulgate manuscripts and Syriac *tomb*
[d] *18* Two Hebrew manuscripts and Syriac (see also Septuagint and verse 24); most Hebrew manuscripts *Bavvai*

3:11 *Tower of the Ovens.* It was on the western wall, perhaps in the same location as one built by Uzziah (2Ch 26:9). The ovens may have been those situated in the "street of the bakers" (Jer 37:21).
3:12 *daughters.* A unique reference to women working on the wall. When the Athenians attempted to rebuild their walls after the Persians had destroyed them (in 480 B.C.), it was decreed that "the whole population of the city—men, women and children—should take part in the wall-building" (Thucydides, 1.90.3).
3:13 *Valley Gate.* See note on 2:13. *five hundred yards.* An extraordinary length; probably most of the section was relatively intact. *Dung Gate.* See note on 2:13.
3:14 *Beth Hakkerem.* Means "house of the vineyard." It was a fire-signal point (Jer 6:1) and is identified with Ramat Rahel, two miles south of Jerusalem. It may have been the residence of a district governor in the Persian period.
3:15 *Fountain Gate.* See note on 2:14. *Pool of Siloam.* Perhaps the Lower Pool of Isa 22:9 (see NIV text note; see also note on Isa 8:6). *King's Garden.* See note on 2:14. *City of David.* See 12:37; see also 2Sa 5:7 and note.
3:16 *Beth Zur.* A district capital, 13 miles south of Jerusalem. Excavations in 1931 and 1957 revealed that occupation was sparse during the early Persian period but was resumed in the fifth century B.C. *tombs of David.* Cf. 2:5. David was buried in the city area (1Ki 2:10; 2Ch 21:20; 32:33; Ac 2:29). The so-called Tomb of David on Mount Zion venerated today by Jewish pilgrims is in the Coenaculum building, erected in the 14th century A.D. Such a site for David's tomb is mentioned no earlier than the ninth century A.D. *House of the Heroes.* May have been the house of David's mighty men (see 2Sa 23:8–39), which perhaps served later as the barracks or armory.
3:17–18 *Keilah.* Located about 15 miles southwest of Jerusalem, it played an important role in David's early history (1Sa 23:1–13).
3:19 *armory.* See note on v. 16. *angle.* See 2Ch 26:9.
3:20–21 The residences of the high priest and his fellow priests were located inside the city along the eastern wall.
3:25 *upper palace.* Perhaps the old palace of David (see 12:37). Like Solomon's palace, it would have had a guardhouse (Jer 32:2).
3:26 *Ophel.* See v. 27. The word means "swelling" or "bulge," hence a (fortified) "hill" (as in Mic 4:8; see NIV text note there), specifically the northern part of the southeastern hill of Jerusalem, which formed the original City of David, just south of the temple area (2Ch 27:3). *Water Gate.* So called because it led to the main source of Jerusalem's water, the Gihon spring. It must have opened onto a large area, for the reading of the Law took place there (8:1,3,16; 12:37). *projecting tower.* Perhaps the large tower whose ruins were discovered by archaeologists on the crest of the Ophel hill in 1923–25. Excavations at the base of the tower in 1978 revealed a level dating to the Persian era.
3:27 *men of Tekoa.* The common people of Tekoa did double duty, whereas the nobles of Tekoa shirked their responsibility (see note on v. 5).

section, from the great projecting tower[z] to the wall of Ophel.

28Above the Horse Gate,[a] the priests made repairs, each in front of his own house. 29Next to them, Zadok son of Immer made repairs opposite his house. Next to him, Shemaiah son of Shecaniah, the guard at the East Gate, made repairs. 30Next to him, Hananiah son of Shelemiah, and Hanun, the sixth son of Zalaph, repaired another section. Next to them, Meshullam son of Berekiah made repairs opposite his living quarters. 31Next to him, Malkijah, one of the goldsmiths, made repairs as far as the house of the temple servants and the merchants, opposite the Inspection Gate, and as far as the room above the corner; 32and between the room above the corner and the Sheep Gate[b] the goldsmiths and merchants made repairs.

Opposition to the Rebuilding

4 When Sanballat[c] heard that we were rebuilding the wall, he became angry and was greatly incensed. He ridiculed the Jews, 2and in the presence of his associates[d] and the army of Samaria, he said, "What are those feeble Jews doing? Will they restore their wall? Will they offer sacrifices? Will they finish in a day? Can they bring the stones back to life from those heaps of rubble[e]—burned as they are?"

3Tobiah[f] the Ammonite, who was at his side, said, "What they are building—if even a fox climbed up on it, he would break down their wall of stones!"[g]

4Hear us, O our God, for we are despised.[h] Turn their insults back on their own heads. Give them over as plunder in a land of captivity. 5Do not cover up their guilt[i] or blot out their sins from your sight,[j] for they have thrown insults in the face of[a] the builders.

6So we rebuilt the wall till all of it reached half its height, for the people worked with all their heart.

7But when Sanballat, Tobiah,[k] the Arabs, the Ammonites and the men of Ashdod heard that the repairs to Jerusalem's walls had gone ahead and that the gaps were being closed, they were very angry. 8They all plotted together[l] to come and fight against Jerusalem and stir up trouble against it. 9But we prayed to our God and posted a guard day and night to meet this threat.

10Meanwhile, the people in Judah said, "The strength of the laborers[m] is giving out, and there is so much rubble that we cannot rebuild the wall."

11Also our enemies said, "Before they know it or see us, we will be right there among them and will kill them and put an end to the work."

12Then the Jews who lived near them came and told us ten times over, "Wherever you turn, they will attack us."

13Therefore I stationed some of the people behind the lowest points of the wall at the exposed places, posting them by families, with their swords, spears and bows. 14After I looked things over, I stood up and said to the nobles, the officials and the rest of the people, "Don't be afraid[n] of them. Remember[o] the Lord, who is great and awesome,[p] and fight[q] for your brothers, your sons and your daughters, your wives and your homes."

15When our enemies heard that we were aware of their plot and that God had frustrated it,[r] we all returned to the wall, each to his own work.

16From that day on, half of my men did the work, while the other half were equipped with spears, shields, bows and armor. The officers posted themselves behind all the people of Judah 17who were building the wall. Those who carried materials did their work with one hand and

3:27 [z]Ps 48:12 **3:28** [a]S 2Ki 11:16 **3:32** [b]S ver 1; Jn 5:2 **4:1** [c]S Ne 2:10 **4:2** [d]S Ezr 4:9-10 [e]Ps 79:1; Jer 26:18 **4:3** [f]S Ne 2:10 [g]Job 13:12; 15:3 **4:4** [h]Ps 44:13; 123:3-4; Jer 33:24 **4:5** [i]Isa 2:9; La 1:22 [j]2Ki 14:27; Ps 51:1; 69:27-28; 109:14; Jer 18:23 **4:7** [k]S Ne 2:10 **4:8** [l]Ps 2:2; 83:1-18 **4:10** [m]S 1Ch 23:4 **4:14** [n]S Ge 28:15; S Dt 1:29 [o]S Ne 1:8 [p]S Ne 1:5 [q]S 2Sa 10:12 **4:15** [r]S 2Sa 17:14; Job 5:12

[a] 5 Or *have provoked you to anger before*

3:28 *Horse Gate.* Where Athaliah was slain (2Ch 23:15). It may have been the easternmost point in the city wall—a gate through which one could reach the Kidron Valley (Jer 31:40).
3:29 *East Gate.* May have been the predecessor of the present Golden Gate (see note on Eze 44:2).
3:31 *goldsmiths.* See v. 8. *Inspection Gate.* In the northern part of the eastern wall.
3:32 *Sheep Gate.* Back to the point of departure (see v. 1).
4:1 *Jews.* See note on Jer 34:9.
4:2 *he said.* Disputes between rival Persian governors were frequent. Sanballat asked several derisive questions to taunt the Jews and to discourage them in their efforts. *burned.* Fire had damaged the stones, which were probably limestone, and had caused many of them to crack and crumble.
4:4–5 As in the so-called imprecatory psalms (see note on Ps 5:10), Nehemiah does not himself take action against his opponents but calls down on them redress from God. In v. 5 Nehemiah's prayer echoes the language of Jer 18:23.
4:7 *Ashdod.* See note on Isa 20:1. It became a district capital under Persian rule.
4:9 *prayed … posted a guard.* Prayer and watchfulness blend faith and action, and also emphasize both the divine side and the human side (cf. notes on Jas 2:14–26).
4:10 *giving out.* The picture is of workers staggering under the weight of their load and ready to fall at any step.
4:11 *our enemies said.* Either Nehemiah had friendly informants, or the enemy was spreading unsettling rumors.
4:12 *ten times over.* Many times.
4:13 *lowest points … exposed places.* Nehemiah posted men conspicuously in the areas that were the most vulnerable along the wall. *spears.* Used as thrusting weapons (Nu 25:7–8; 1Ki 18:28).
4:14 *Don't be afraid of them. Remember the Lord.* See note on 1:8. The best way to dispel fear is to remember the Lord, who alone is to be feared (see Dt 3:22; 20:3; 31:6; Ps 56:3–4).
4:16 *shields.* Made primarily of wood or wickerwork and covered with ox hides rubbed with oil (see 2Sa 1:21 and note) and therefore combustible (Eze 39:9). *armor.* The Hebrew for this word designated primarily a breastplate of metal or a coat of mail (see 2Ch 18:33).

held a weapon[s] in the other, 18and each of
the builders wore his sword at his side as
he worked. But the man who sounded the
trumpet[t] stayed with me.
19Then I said to the nobles, the officials
and the rest of the people, "The work
is extensive and spread out, and we are
widely separated from each other along
the wall. 20Wherever you hear the sound
of the trumpet,[u] join us there. Our God
will fight[v] for us!"
21So we continued the work with half
the men holding spears, from the first light
of dawn till the stars came out. 22At that
time I also said to the people, "Have every
man and his helper stay inside Jerusalem
at night, so they can serve us as guards by
night and workmen by day." 23Neither I nor
my brothers nor my men nor the guards
with me took off our clothes; each had his
weapon, even when he went for water.[a]

Nehemiah Helps the Poor

5 Now the men and their wives raised a
great outcry against their Jewish brothers. 2Some were saying, "We and our sons
and daughters are numerous; in order
for us to eat and stay alive, we must get
grain."
3Others were saying, "We are mortgaging our fields,[w] our vineyards and our
homes to get grain during the famine."[x]
4Still others were saying, "We have had
to borrow money to pay the king's tax[y]
on our fields and vineyards. 5Although we
are of the same flesh and blood[z] as our
countrymen and though our sons are as
good as theirs, yet we have to subject our
sons and daughters to slavery.[a] Some of
our daughters have already been enslaved,
but we are powerless, because our fields
and our vineyards belong to others."[b]
6When I heard their outcry and these
charges, I was very angry. 7I pondered
them in my mind and then accused the nobles and officials. I told them, "You are exacting usury[c] from your own countrymen!"
So I called together a large meeting to deal

4:17 [s] Ps 149:6 **4:18** [t] S Nu 10:2 **4:20** [u] Eze 33:3 [v] S Ex 14:14; S Dt 20:4; Jos 10:14 **5:3** [w] Ps 109:11 [x] Ge 47:23 **5:4** [y] S Ezr 4:13 **5:5** [z] S Ge 29:14 [a] Lev 25:39-43, 47; S 2Ki 4:1; Isa 50:1 [b] Dt 15:7-11; S 2Ki 4:1 **5:7** [c] Ex 22:25-27; S Lev 25:35-37; Dt 23:19-20; 24:10-13

[a] *23* The meaning of the Hebrew for this clause is uncertain.

4:18 *trumpet.* See note on Isa 18:3; see also Jos 6:4,6,8,13.

4:20 *Our God will fight for us!* See Jos 5:13–15 and notes; 10:14,42; Jdg 4:14; 20:35; 2Sa 5:24; see also essay, p. 286.

4:21 *till the stars came out.* Indicates the earnestness of their efforts, since the usual time to stop working was at sunset (Dt 24:15; Mt 20:8).

4:22 *guards by night.* Even men from outside Jerusalem stayed in the city at night so that some of them could serve as sentries.

4:23 See NIV text note. Although the precise meaning of the end of the verse is not clear, the implication is that constant preparedness was the rule.

5:1–19 During his major effort to rebuild the walls of Jerusalem, Nehemiah confronted a socioeconomic crisis that had deep moral implications. Since the building of the wall took only 52 days (6:15), it is surprising that Nehemiah called a "large meeting" (v. 7) in the midst of such a project. Perhaps the pressures created by the rebuilding program brought to light problems that had long been simmering and that had to be dealt with before work could proceed. Among the classes affected by the crisis were (1) the landless, who were short of food (v. 2); (2) the landowners, who were compelled to mortgage their properties (v. 3); (3) those forced to borrow money at exorbitant interest rates and sell their children into slavery (vv. 4–5).

5:1 *wives.* The situation was so serious that the wives joined in the protest as they ran short of funds and supplies to feed their families. They complained not against the foreign authorities but against their own countrymen who were taking advantage of their poorer neighbors at a time when all were needed for the defense of the country.

5:2 *grain.* About six to seven bushels would be needed for a man to feed his family for a month.

5:3 *mortgaging.* Even those who had property were forced to mortgage it, benefiting the wealthy few (cf. Isa 5:8). In times of economic stress the rich got richer, and the poor got poorer. *famine.* The economic situation was aggravated by the natural conditions that had produced a famine. Some 75 years earlier the prophet Haggai had referred to a time of drought, when food was insufficient (Hag 1:5–11). Such times of distress were considered to be expressions of God's judgment (Isa 51:19; Jer 14:13–18; Am 4:6). Famines were not uncommon in Canaan. They occurred in the time of Abraham (Ge 12:10), Isaac (Ge 26:1), Joseph (Ge 41:27,54), Ruth (Ru 1:1), David (2Sa 21:1), Elijah (1Ki 18:2), Elisha (2Ki 4:38) and Claudius (Ac 11:28).

5:4 *tax.* It is estimated that the Persian king collected the equivalent of 20 million darics (see NIV text note on Ezr 8:27) a year in taxes. Little was ever returned to benefit the provinces, because most of it was melted down and stored as bullion. Alexander the Great found at Susa alone 9,000 talents (about 340 tons) of coined gold and 40,000 talents (about 1,500 tons) of silver stored as bullion. As coined money was increasingly taken out of circulation by taxes, poverty increased dramatically. The acquisition of land by the Persians and its removal from production also helped produce a 50 percent rise in prices during the Persian period.

5:5 *slavery.* In times of economic distress families would borrow funds, using family members as collateral. If a man could not repay the loan and its interest, his children, his wife, or even the man himself might be sold into bondage. An Israelite who fell into debt, however, would serve his creditor as a "hired worker" (Lev 25:39–40). He was to be released in the seventh year (Dt 15:12–18), unless he chose to stay voluntarily. During the seven-year famine in Egypt, Joseph was approached by people who asked him to accept their land and their bodies in exchange for food (Ge 47:18–19). The irony for the Israelites was that at least as exiles in Mesopotamia their families were together, but now, because of dire economic necessity, their children were being sold into slavery.

5:6 *I was very angry.* Sometimes it becomes necessary to express righteous indignation against social injustice (cf. Mk 11:15–18; Eph 4:26).

5:7 *usury.* See notes on Ex 22:25–27; Lev 25:36; Dt 23:20. Josephus (*Antiquities*, 4.8.25) explains: "Let it not be permitted to lend upon usury to any Hebrew either meat or drink; for it is not just to draw a revenue from the misfortunes of a fellow countryman. Rather, in consoling him in his distress, you should reckon as gain the gratitude of such persons and the recompense that God has in store for an act of generosity."

with them 8and said: "As far as possible,
we have bought[d] back our Jewish brothers
who were sold to the Gentiles. Now you
are selling your brothers, only for them to
be sold back to us!" They kept quiet, because they could find nothing to say.[e]
9So I continued, "What you are doing
is not right. Shouldn't you walk in the
fear of our God to avoid the reproach[f] of
our Gentile enemies? 10I and my brothers
and my men are also lending the people
money and grain. But let the exacting of
usury stop![g] 11Give back to them immediately their fields, vineyards, olive groves
and houses, and also the usury[h] you are
charging them—the hundredth part of the
money, grain, new wine and oil."
12"We will give it back," they said. "And
we will not demand anything more from
them. We will do as you say."
Then I summoned the priests and made
the nobles and officials take an oath[i] to do
what they had promised. 13I also shook[j]
out the folds of my robe and said, "In this
way may God shake out of his house and
possessions every man who does not keep
this promise. So may such a man be shak-
en out and emptied!"
At this the whole assembly said,
"Amen,"[k] and praised the LORD. And the
people did as they had promised.

14Moreover, from the twentieth year of
King Artaxerxes,[l] when I was appointed
to be their governor[m] in the land of Judah, until his thirty-second year—twelve
years—neither I nor my brothers ate
the food allotted to the governor. 15But
the earlier governors—those preceding
me—placed a heavy burden on the people and took forty shekels[a] of silver from
them in addition to food and wine. Their
assistants also lorded it over the people.
But out of reverence for God[n] I did not act
like that. 16Instead,[o] I devoted myself to
the work on this wall. All my men were
assembled there for the work; we[b] did not
acquire any land.
17Furthermore, a hundred and fifty Jews
and officials ate at my table, as well as
those who came to us from the surrounding nations. 18Each day one ox, six choice
sheep and some poultry[p] were prepared
for me, and every ten days an abundant
supply of wine of all kinds. In spite of all
this, I never demanded the food allotted to
the governor, because the demands were
heavy on these people.
19Remember[q] me with favor, O my God,
for all I have done for these people.

5:8 [d] Lev 25:47 [e] Jer 34:8 **5:9** [f] Isa 52:5 **5:10** [g] S Ex 22:25 **5:11** [h] Isa 58:6 **5:12** [i] S Ezr 10:5 **5:13** [j] S Mt 10:14 [k] Dt 27:15-26 **5:14** [l] S Ne 2:6 [m] Ge 42:6; Ezr 6:7; Jer 40:7; Hag 1:1 **5:15** [n] S Ge 20:11 **5:16** [o] 2Th 3:7-10 **5:18** [p] 1Ki 4:23 **5:19** [q] S Ge 8:1; S 2Ki 20:3; S Ne 1:8

[a] *15* That is, about 1 pound (about 0.5 kilogram)
[b] *16* Most Hebrew manuscripts; some Hebrew manuscripts, Septuagint, Vulgate and Syriac *I*

5:8 *Jewish brothers who were sold.* Impoverished fellow Jews could be forced to pay off their debt by service as hired servants, but they were not to be sold as slaves (Lev 25:39–42). *to the Gentiles.* The sale of fellow Hebrews as slaves to foreigners was forbidden (Ex 21:8). *kept quiet.* Their guilt was so obvious that they had no rebuttal or excuse (cf. Jn 8:7–10).

5:10 *let the exacting of usury stop!* The OT condemns the greed that seeks to profit from the poverty of others (Ps 119:36; Isa 56:9–12; 57:17; Jer 6:13; 8:10; 22:13–17; Eze 22:12–13; 33:31). In view of the economic crisis facing his people, Nehemiah urges the creditors to give up all demands for repayment with interest.

5:11 *hundredth part.* Perhaps one percent per month, an annual interest rate of 12 percent. *grain, new wine and oil.* See notes on 10:37; Dt 7:13.

5:13 *shook out the folds of my robe.* Symbolizing the solemnity of an oath and reinforcing the attendant curses for its nonfulfillment. *Amen.* See 8:6; Nu 5:22; see also note on Dt 27:15.

5:14 *thirty-second year.* From Apr. 1, 433 B.C., to Apr. 19, 432. Nehemiah served his first term as governor for 12 years before being recalled to court (13:6), after which he returned to Jerusalem (13:7) for a second term whose length cannot be determined. *food allotted to the governor.* See v. 18. Provincial governors normally assessed the people in their provinces for their support. But Nehemiah, like Paul (1Co 9; 2Th 3:8–9), sacrificed even what was normally his in order to serve as an example to the people.

5:15 *governors.* The Hebrew for this word is used of Sheshbazzar (Ezr 5:14) and Zerubbabel (Hag 1:1,14; 2:2) as well as of various Persian officials (Ezr 5:3,6; 6:6–7,13; 8:36; Ne 2:7,9; 3:7). Nehemiah was not referring here to men of the caliber of Zerubbabel. Some believe that Judah did not have governors before Nehemiah and that the reference here is to governors of Samaria. But new archaeological evidence, in the form of seals and seal impressions, confirms the reference to the previous governors of Judah. *heavy burden.* It was customary Persian practice to exempt temple personnel from taxation, which increased the burden on lay people. *assistants.* If the governors themselves used extortion, their underlings often proved even more oppressive (cf. Mt 18:21–35; 20:25–28). *reverence for God.* Those in high positions are in danger of abusing their authority over their subordinates if they forget that they themselves are servants of a superior "Master in heaven" (Col 4:1; cf. Ge 39:9; 2Co 5:11).

5:16 *did not acquire any land.* Nehemiah's behavior as governor was guided by principles of service rather than by opportunism.

5:17 *ate at my table.* As part of his social responsibility, a ruler or governor was expected to entertain lavishly. A text found at Nimrud has Ashurnasirpal II feeding 69,574 guests at a banquet for ten days. When Solomon dedicated the temple, he sacrificed 22,000 cattle and 120,000 sheep and goats, and held a great festival for the assembly for 14 days (1Ki 8:62–65). We are not told how many he fed (cf. 1Ki 4:27).

5:18 *Each day.* The meat listed here would provide one meal for 600–800 persons, including the 150 Jews and officials of v. 17. Cf. Solomon's provisions for one day (1Ki 4:22–23). *choice sheep.* Cf. Mal 1:8. *poultry.* Chickens were domesticated in the Indus River Valley by 2000 B.C. and were brought to Egypt by the time of Thutmose III (15th century B.C.). They were known in Mesopotamia and in Greece by the eighth century. The earliest inscriptional evidence of poultry in the land of Canaan is the seal of Jaazaniah (dated c. 600 B.C.), which depicts a fighting rooster (see note on 2Ki 25:23).

5:19 *Remember me.* See note on 1:8; cf. Heb 6:10. Perhaps Nehemiah's memoirs (see Introduction to Ezra: Literary Form and Authorship) were inscribed as a memorial that was set up in the temple. A striking parallel to Nehemiah's

Further Opposition to the Rebuilding

6 When word came to Sanballat, Tobiah,[r] Geshem[s] the Arab and the rest of our enemies that I had rebuilt the wall and not a gap was left in it—though up to that time I had not set the doors in the gates— 2Sanballat and Geshem sent me this message: "Come, let us meet together in one of the villages[a] on the plain of Ono.[t]"

But they were scheming to harm me; 3so I sent messengers to them with this reply: "I am carrying on a great project and cannot go down. Why should the work stop while I leave it and go down to you?" 4Four times they sent me the same message, and each time I gave them the same answer.

5Then, the fifth time, Sanballat[u] sent his aide to me with the same message, and in his hand was an unsealed letter 6in which was written:

"It is reported among the nations—and Geshem[b v] says it is true—that you and the Jews are plotting to revolt, and therefore you are building the wall. Moreover, according to these reports you are about to become their king 7and have even appointed prophets to make this proclamation about you in Jerusalem: 'There is a king in Judah!' Now this report will get back to the king; so come, let us confer together."

8I sent him this reply: "Nothing like what you are saying is happening; you are just making it up out of your head."

9They were all trying to frighten us, thinking, "Their hands will get too weak for the work, and it will not be completed."

⌞But I prayed,⌟ "Now strengthen my hands."

10One day I went to the house of Shemaiah son of Delaiah, the son of Mehetabel, who was shut in at his home. He said, "Let us meet in the house of God, inside the temple[w], and let us close the temple doors, because men are coming to kill you—by night they are coming to kill you."

11But I said, "Should a man like me run away? Or should one like me go into the temple to save his life? I will not go!" 12I realized that God had not sent him, but that he had prophesied against me[x] because Tobiah and Sanballat[y] had hired him. 13He had been hired to intimidate me so that I would commit a sin by doing this, and then they would give me a bad name to discredit me.[z]

14Remember[a] Tobiah and Sanballat,[b] O my God, because of what they have done; remember also the prophetess[c] Noadiah and the rest of the prophets[d] who have been trying to intimidate me.

6:1 [r]Ne 2:10 [s]S Ne 2:19
6:2 [t]S 1Ch 8:12
6:5 [u]S Ne 2:10
6:6 [v]S Ne 2:19
6:10 [w]Nu 18:7
6:12 [x]Eze 13:22-23 [y]S Ne 2:10
6:13 [z]Jer 20:10
6:14 [a]S Ne 1:8 [b]S Ne 2:10 [c]S Ex 15:20; Eze 13:17-23; S Ac 21:9; Rev 2:20 [d]Jer 23:9-40; Zec 13:2-3

[a] 2 Or *in Kephirim* [b] 6 Hebrew *Gashmu*, a variant of *Geshem*

prayer is found in a prayer of Nebuchadnezzar: "O Marduk, my lord, do remember my deeds favorably as good [deeds]; may (these) my good deeds be always before your mind."

6:1 *Sanballat, Tobiah, Geshem.* See notes on 2:10,19.

6:2 *Ono.* Located about seven miles southeast of Joppa near Lod (Lydda; see note on Ezr 2:33), in the westernmost area settled by the returning Jews (Ne 7:37; 11:35). It may have been proposed as neutral territory, but Nehemiah recognized the invitation as a trap (cf. Ge 4:8; Jer 41:1–3).

6:3 Nehemiah's sharp reply may seem like a haughty response to a reasonable invitation, but he correctly discerned the insincerity of his enemies. He refused to be distracted by matters that would divert his energies from rebuilding Jerusalem's wall.

6:4 *Four times.* Nehemiah's foes were persistent, but he was equally persistent in resisting them.

6:5 *unsealed letter.* During this period a letter was ordinarily written on a papyrus or leather sheet, which was rolled up, tied with a string and sealed with a clay bulla (seal impression) to guarantee the letter's authenticity. Sanballat apparently wanted the contents of his letter to be made known to the public at large.

6:6 *their king.* The Persian kings did not tolerate the claims of pretenders to kingship, as can be seen from the Behistun (Bisitun) inscription of Darius I (see note on Hag 1:1). In NT times the Roman emperor was likewise suspicious of any unauthorized claims to royalty (Jn 19:12; cf. Mt 2:1–13).

6:8 *Nothing.* Nehemiah does not mince words. He calls the report a lie. He may have sent his own messenger to the Persian king to assure him of his loyalty.

6:9 *hands will get … weak.* Figurative language to express the idea of discouragement. The Hebrew for this phrase is used also in Ezr 4:4; Jer 38:4, as well as on an ostracon from Lachish dated c. 588 B.C. (see chart, p. xxii; see also note on Jer 34:7).

6:10 *Shemaiah … was shut in.* Perhaps as a symbolic action to indicate that his own life was in danger and to suggest that both Nehemiah and he must flee to the temple (for other symbolic actions see 1Ki 22:11; Isa 20:2–4; Jer 27:2–7; 28:10–11; Eze 4:1–17; 12:3–11; Ac 21:11). Since Shemaiah had access to the temple, he may have been a priest. He was clearly a friend of Tobiah (cf. v. 12), and therefore Nehemiah's enemy. It was at least credible for Shemaiah to propose that Nehemiah take refuge in the temple area at the altar of asylum (see Ex 21:13–14 and notes), but not in the "house of God," the temple building itself.

6:11 Even if the threat against his life was real, Nehemiah was not a coward who would run into hiding. Nor would he transgress the law to save his life. As a layman, he was not permitted to enter the sanctuary (Nu 18:7). When King Uzziah entered the temple to burn incense, he was punished by being afflicted with leprosy (2Ch 26:16–21).

6:12 The fact that Shemaiah proposed a course of action contrary to God's law exposed him as a false prophet (cf. Dt 18:20; Isa 8:19–20; see note on Dt 13:1–5).

6:13 If Nehemiah had wavered in the face of the threat against him, his leadership would have been discredited and morale among the people would have plummeted.

6:14 *Remember.* See note on 1:8. *prophetess.* See note on Ex 15:20.

The Completion of the Wall

15 So the wall was completed on the
twenty-fifth of Elul, in fifty-two days.
16 When all our enemies heard about this,
all the surrounding nations were afraid
and lost their self-confidence, because
they realized that this work had been done
with the help of our God.

17 Also, in those days the nobles of Judah
were sending many letters to Tobiah, and
replies from Tobiah kept coming to them.
18 For many in Judah were under oath to
him, since he was son-in-law to Shecaniah
son of Arah, and his son Jehohanan had
married the daughter of Meshullam son of
Berekiah. 19 Moreover, they kept reporting
to me his good deeds and then telling him
what I said. And Tobiah sent letters to intimidate me.

7 After the wall had been rebuilt and I
had set the doors in place, the gatekeepers[e] and the singers[f] and the Levites[g]
were appointed. 2 I put in charge of Jerusalem my brother Hanani,[h] along with[a]
Hananiah[i] the commander of the citadel,[j] because he was a man of integrity
and feared[k] God more than most men do.
3 I said to them, "The gates of Jerusalem
are not to be opened until the sun is hot.
While the gatekeepers are still on duty,
have them shut the doors and bar them.
Also appoint residents of Jerusalem as
guards, some at their posts and some near
their own houses."

The List of the Exiles Who Returned

7:6-73pp — Ezr 2:1-70

4 Now the city was large and spacious,
but there were few people in it,[l] and the
houses had not yet been rebuilt. 5 So my
God put it into my heart to assemble the
nobles, the officials and the common people for registration by families. I found the
genealogical record of those who had been
the first to return. This is what I found
written there:

6 These are the people of the province who came up from the captivity
of the exiles[m] whom Nebuchadnezzar king of Babylon had taken captive (they returned to Jerusalem and
Judah, each to his own town, 7 in
company with Zerubbabel,[n] Jeshua,
Nehemiah, Azariah, Raamiah, Naha-
mani, Mordecai, Bilshan, Mispereth,
Bigvai, Nehum and Baanah):

The list of the men of Israel:

8 the descendants of Parosh 2,172
9 of Shephatiah 372
10 of Arah 652
11 of Pahath-Moab (through the line of Jeshua and Joab) 2,818
12 of Elam 1,254
13 of Zattu 845
14 of Zaccai 760
15 of Binnui 648
16 of Bebai 628
17 of Azgad 2,322
18 of Adonikam 667
19 of Bigvai 2,067
20 of Adin[o] 655
21 of Ater (through Hezekiah) 98
22 of Hashum 328
23 of Bezai 324
24 of Hariph 112
25 of Gibeon 95

26 the men of Bethlehem and Netophah[p] 188
27 of Anathoth[q] 128
28 of Beth Azmaveth 42
29 of Kiriath Jearim, Kephirah[r] and Beeroth[s] 743
30 of Ramah and Geba 621
31 of Micmash 122
32 of Bethel and Ai[t] 123
33 of the other Nebo 52
34 of the other Elam 1,254
35 of Harim 320
36 of Jericho[u] 345
37 of Lod, Hadid and Ono[v] 721
38 of Senaah 3,930

39 The priests:

the descendants of Jedaiah (through the family of Jeshua) 973
40 of Immer 1,052
41 of Pashhur 1,247
42 of Harim 1,017

7:1 [e] 1Ch 9:27; S 26:12-19 [f] Ps 68:25 [g] Ne 8:9 **7:2** [h] Ne 1:2 [i] Ne 10:23 [j] Ne 2:8 [k] 1Ki 18:3 **7:4** [l] Ne 11:1 **7:6** [m] S 2Ch 36:20; S Ne 1:2 **7:7** [n] S 1Ch 3:19 **7:20** [o] S Ezr 8:6 **7:26** [p] S 2Sa 23:28; S 1Ch 2:54 **7:27** [q] S Jos 21:18 **7:29** [r] S Jos 18:26 [s] S Jos 18:25 **7:32** [t] S Ge 12:8 **7:36** [u] Ne 3:2 **7:37** [v] S 1Ch 8:12

[a] 2 Or *Hanani, that is,*

6:15 *twenty-fifth of Elul.* Oct. 2, 444 B.C. *fifty-two days.* The walls that lay in ruins for nearly a century and a half were rebuilt in less than two months once the people were galvanized into action by Nehemiah's leadership. Archaeological investigations have shown that the circumference of the wall in Nehemiah's day was much reduced. Josephus states (*Antiquities*, 11.5.8) that the rebuilding of the wall took two years and four months, but he is doubtless including such additional tasks as further strengthening of various sections, embellishing and beautifying, and the like. The dedication of the wall is described in 12:27–47.

6:17–18 Tobiah was related to an influential family in Judah, since his son Jehohanan was married to the daughter of Meshullam, who had helped repair the wall of Jerusalem (3:4,30).

7:2 *in charge of Jerusalem.* Over Rephaiah and Shallum, who were over sections of the city (3:9,12). *Hanani.* See note on 1:2. *citadel.* See notes on 2:8; 3:1.

7:3 *until the sun is hot.* Normally the gates would be opened at dawn, but their opening was to be delayed until the sun was high in the heavens to prevent the enemy from making a surprise attack before most of the people were up.

7:6–73 Essentially the same as Ezr 2. See notes there for the nature of the list and the reasons for the numerous variations in names and numbers between the two lists.

43The Levites:

the descendants of Jeshua
(through Kadmiel through
the line of Hodaviah) 74

44The singers:[w]

the descendants of Asaph 148

45The gatekeepers:[x]

the descendants of
Shallum, Ater, Talmon,
Akkub, Hatita and Shobai 138

46The temple servants:[y]

the descendants of
Ziha, Hasupha, Tabbaoth,
47Keros, Sia, Padon,
48Lebana, Hagaba, Shalmai,
49Hanan, Giddel, Gahar,
50Reaiah, Rezin, Nekoda,
51Gazzam, Uzza, Paseah,
52Besai, Meunim, Nephusim,
53Bakbuk, Hakupha, Harhur,
54Bazluth, Mehida, Harsha,
55Barkos, Sisera, Temah,
56Neziah and Hatipha

57The descendants of the servants of
Solomon:

the descendants of
Sotai, Sophereth, Perida,
58Jaala, Darkon, Giddel,
59Shephatiah, Hattil,
Pokereth-Hazzebaim and Amon

60The temple servants and the
descendants of the servants
of Solomon[z] 392

61The following came up from the
towns of Tel Melah, Tel Harsha, Kerub, Addon and Immer, but they
could not show that their families
were descended from Israel:

62the descendants of
Delaiah, Tobiah and
Nekoda 642

63And from among the priests:

the descendants of
Hobaiah, Hakkoz and Barzillai
(a man who had married
a daughter of Barzillai the
Gileadite and was called by that
name).

64These searched for their family records, but they could not find
them and so were excluded from the
priesthood as unclean. 65The governor, therefore, ordered them not to
eat any of the most sacred food until
there should be a priest ministering
with the Urim and Thummim.[a]

66The whole company numbered
42,360, 67besides their 7,337 menservants and maidservants; and they
also had 245 men and women singers.
68There were 736 horses, 245 mules,[a]
69435 camels and 6,720 donkeys.

70Some of the heads of the families
contributed to the work. The governor gave to the treasury 1,000 drachmas[b] of gold, 50 bowls and 530 garments for priests. 71Some of the heads
of the families[b] gave to the treasury
for the work 20,000 drachmas[c] of
gold and 2,200 minas[d] of silver. 72The
total given by the rest of the people
was 20,000 drachmas of gold, 2,000
minas[e] of silver and 67 garments for
priests.[c]

73The priests, the Levites, the gatekeepers, the singers and the temple
servants,[d] along with certain of the
people and the rest of the Israelites,
settled in their own towns.[e]

Ezra Reads the Law

When the seventh month came and the
8 Israelites had settled in their towns,[f]
1all the people assembled as one man
in the square before the Water Gate.[g] They
told Ezra the scribe to bring out the Book
of the Law of Moses,[h] which the LORD had
commanded for Israel.

2So on the first day of the seventh
month[i] Ezra the priest brought the Law[j]

7:44 [w]Ne 11:23
7:45 [x]S 1Ch 9:17
7:46 [y]S Ne 3:26
7:60 [z]S 1Ch 9:2
7:65 [a]S Ex 28:30
7:71 [b]S 1Ch 29:7
7:72 [c]S Ex 25:2
7:73 [d]Ne 1:10; Ps 34:22; 103:21; 113:1; 135:1 [e]S Ezr 3:1; Ne 11:1 [f]Ezr 3:1
8:1 [g]S Ne 3:26 [h]S Dt 28:61; S 2Ch 34:15
8:2 [i]Lev 23:23-25; Nu 29:1-6 [j]S Dt 31:11

[a] 68 Some Hebrew manuscripts (see also Ezra 2:66); most Hebrew manuscripts do not have this verse.
[b] 70 That is, about 19 pounds (about 8.5 kilograms)
[c] 71 That is, about 375 pounds (about 170 kilograms); also in verse 72
[d] 71 That is, about 1 1/3 tons (about 1.2 metric tons)
[e] 72 That is, about 1 1/4 tons (about 1.1 metric tons)

7:43 *74.* See note on Ezr 2:40.
7:57,60 *descendants of the servants of Solomon.* See note on Ezr 2:55,58.
7:70 *drachmas.* See note on Ezr 2:69.
7:73 *settled in their own towns.* See note on Ezr 2:70. *seventh month.* October-November, 444 B.C.
8:1–18 The reading of the Law of Moses by Ezra is the first reference to Ezra in almost 13 years since his arrival in 458 B.C.
8:1 *all the people assembled.* See Ezr 3:1, which also refers to an assembly called in the seventh month (Tishri), the beginning of the civil year (see chart, p. 104). *square before the Water Gate.* See vv. 3,16; see also notes on 3:26; Ezr 10:9. Such open spaces were normally located near a city gate (2Ch 32:6). *scribe.* See note on Ezr 7:6. *Book of the Law of Moses.* Cf. vv. 2–3,5,8–9,13–15,18. Several views have been proposed concerning the extent of this Book: (1) the laws of Exodus and Leviticus, (2) the laws of Deuteronomy, (3) the Pentateuch. See notes on Jos 1:8; 2Ki 22:8.
8:2 *first day of the seventh month.* Oct. 8, 444 B.C.; the New Year's Day of the civil calendar (see note on Lev 23:24), celebrated as the Feast of Trumpets (Nu 29:1–6), with cessation of labor and a sacred assembly. *women.* See 10:28. Women did not usually participate in assemblies (see note on Ex 10:11), but were brought, together with children, on such solemn occasions (Dt 31:12; Jos 8:35; 2Ki 23:2).

before the assembly, which was made up
of men and women and all who were able
to understand. 3He read it aloud from daybreak till noon as he faced the square before the Water Gate[k] in the presence of the
men, women and others who could understand. And all the people listened attentively to the Book of the Law.

4Ezra the scribe stood on a high wood-
en platform[l] built for the occasion. Beside
him on his right stood Mattithiah, Shema,
Anaiah, Uriah, Hilkiah and Maaseiah; and
on his left were Pedaiah, Mishael, Malkijah, Hashum, Hashbaddanah, Zechariah
and Meshullam.

5Ezra opened the book. All the people
could see him because he was standing[m]
above them; and as he opened it, the people all stood up. 6Ezra praised the LORD, the
great God; and all the people lifted their
hands[n] and responded, "Amen! Amen!"
Then they bowed down and worshiped the
LORD with their faces to the ground.

7The Levites[o]—Jeshua, Bani, Sherebiah, Jamin, Akkub, Shabbethai, Hodiah,
Maaseiah, Kelita, Azariah, Jozabad, Hanan and Pelaiah—instructed[p] the people
in the Law while the people were standing there. 8They read from the Book of the
Law of God, making it clear[a] and giving
the meaning so that the people could understand what was being read.

9Then Nehemiah the governor, Ezra the
priest and scribe, and the Levites[q] who
were instructing the people said to them
all, "This day is sacred to the LORD your
God. Do not mourn or weep."[r] For all the
people had been weeping as they listened
to the words of the Law.

10Nehemiah said, "Go and enjoy choice
food and sweet drinks, and send some to
those who have nothing[s] prepared. This
day is sacred to our Lord. Do not grieve,
for the joy[t] of the LORD is your strength."

11The Levites calmed all the people, saying, "Be still, for this is a sacred day. Do
not grieve."

12Then all the people went away to eat
and drink, to send portions of food and
to celebrate with great joy,[u] because they
now understood the words that had been
made known to them.

13On the second day of the month, the
heads of all the families, along with the
priests and the Levites, gathered around
Ezra the scribe to give attention to the
words of the Law. 14They found written in
the Law, which the LORD had commanded through Moses, that the Israelites were
to live in booths[v] during the feast of the
seventh month 15and that they should proclaim this word and spread it throughout
their towns and in Jerusalem: "Go out into
the hill country and bring back branches
from olive and wild olive trees, and from
myrtles, palms and shade trees, to make
booths"—as it is written.[b]

16So the people went out and brought
back branches and built themselves booths
on their own roofs, in their courtyards, in
the courts of the house of God and in the
square by the Water Gate[w] and the one by

[a] 8 Or *God, translating it* [b] 15 See Lev. 23:37-40.

8:3 [k]S Ne 3:26 **8:4** [l]2Ch 6:13 **8:5** [m]Jdg 3:20 **8:6** [n]S Ezr 9:5; 1Ti 2:8 **8:7** [o]S Ezr 10:23 [p]S Lev 10:11; S 2Ch 17:7 **8:9** [q]Ne 7:1,65,70 [r]Dt 12:7,12; 16:14-15 **8:10** [s]1Sa 25:8; S 2Sa 6:19; Est 9:22; Lk 14:12-14 [t]S Lev 23:40; S Dt 12:18; 16:11,14-15 **8:12** [u]Est 9:22 **8:14** [v]S Ex 23:16 **8:16** [w]S Ne 3:26

8:3 *read it aloud.* See Ex 24:7; Ac 8:30 and note; 1Ti 4:13; Rev 1:3. *from daybreak till noon.* The people evidently stood (vv. 5,7) for five or six hours, listening attentively to the reading and exposition (vv. 7–8,12) of the Scriptures.
8:5 *book.* Scroll (see note on Ex 17:14). *people all stood up.* The rabbis deduced from this verse that the congregation should stand for the reading of the Torah.
8:6 *lifted their hands.* See Ex 9:29 and note; Ps 28:2; 134:2; 1Ti 2:8. *Amen! Amen!* See notes on Dt 27:15; Ro 1:25. The repetition conveys the intensity of feeling behind the affirmation (for other repetitions see Ge 22:11 and note; cf. 2Ki 11:14; Lk 23:21). *worshiped.* In its original sense the Hebrew for this verb meant "to prostrate oneself on the ground," as the frequently accompanying phrase "to the ground" indicates. Private acts of worship often involved prostration "to the ground," as in the case of Abraham's servant (Ge 24:52), Moses (Ex 34:8), Joshua (Jos 5:14) and Job (Job 1:20). There are three cases of spontaneous communal worship in Exodus (4:31; 12:27; 33:10). In 2Ch 20:18 Jehoshaphat and the people "fell down in worship before the LORD" when they heard his promise of victory.
8:7 *instructed.* See v. 8; Ezr 7:6,10 and note on 7:6.
8:8 *read.* See note on v. 3. *making it clear.* Rabbinic tradition understands the Hebrew for this expression as referring to translation from Hebrew into an Aramaic Targum (see NIV text note). But there is no evidence of such Targums (free Aramaic translations of OT books or passages) from such an early date. The earliest known extensive Targum is one on Job dated c. 150–100 B.C. (from Qumran).Targums exist for every book of the OT except Daniel and Ezra-Nehemiah. *understand.* See v. 12.
8:9 *Nehemiah … Ezra.* An explicit reference showing that they were contemporaries (see 12:26,36). *Do not mourn.* See Ezr 10:6 and note; Est 9:22; Isa 57:18–19; Jer 31:13. *weep.* See 1:4; Ezr 3:13 and note; 10:1. *weeping as they listened.* Out of remorse for their own failures and those of their ancestors.
8:10 *choice food.* Delicious festive food prepared with much fat. The fat of sacrificial animals was offered to God as the choicest element of the burnt offering (Lev 1:8,12), the fellowship offering (Lev 3:9–10), the sin offering (Lev 4:8–10) and the guilt offering (Lev 7:3–4). The fat was not to be eaten in these cases. *send some to those who have nothing.* See Est 9:22; cf. Lk 14:12–14.
8:14 *booths.* See notes on Ex 23:16; Lev 23:34,42; Jn 7:37.
8:15 *myrtles.* Evergreen bushes with a pleasing odor (Isa 41:19; 55:13; Zec 1:8,10–11). *palms.* The date palm was common around Jericho (Dt 34:3; 2Ch 28:15). *shade trees.* Cf. Eze 6:13; 20:28. Later Jewish celebrations of the Feast of Tabernacles include waving the *lulav* (made of branches of palms, myrtles and willows) with the right hand and holding branches of the *ethrog* (a citrus native to Canaan) in the left.
8:16 *courts of the house of God.* See note on 13:7. The temple that Ezekiel saw in his visions had an outer and an inner court (see diagram, p. 1297). Ezekiel's temple was to some extent patterned after Solomon's, which had an inner court for the priests and an outer court (1Ki 6:36; 7:12; 2Ki 21:5; 23:12; 2Ch 4:9; 33:5). The temple of the NT era had a court for the Gentiles and an inner court, which was

the Gate of Ephraim.[x] 17The whole company that had returned from exile built
booths and lived in them.[y] From the days
of Joshua son of Nun until that day, the
Israelites had not celebrated[z] it like this.
And their joy was very great.
18Day after day, from the first day to the
last, Ezra read[a] from the Book of the Law[b]
of God. They celebrated the feast for sev-
en days, and on the eighth day, in accordance with the regulation,[c] there was an
assembly.[d]

The Israelites Confess Their Sins

9 On the twenty-fourth day of the same
month, the Israelites gathered together,
fasting and wearing sackcloth and having
dust on their heads.[e] 2Those of Israelite
descent had separated themselves from
all foreigners.[f] They stood in their places
and confessed their sins and the wickedness of their fathers.[g] 3They stood where
they were and read from the Book of the
Law of the LORD their God for a quarter
of the day, and spent another quarter in
confession and in worshiping the LORD
their God. 4Standing on the stairs were the
Levites[h]—Jeshua, Bani, Kadmiel, Shebaniah, Bunni, Sherebiah, Bani and Kena-
ni—who called with loud voices to the
LORD their God. 5And the Levites—Jeshua, Kadmiel, Bani, Hashabneiah, Sherebiah, Hodiah, Shebaniah and Pethahiah—said: "Stand up and praise the LORD
your God,[i] who is from everlasting to
everlasting.[a]"

"Blessed be your glorious name,[j]
and may it be exalted above all blessing and praise. 6You alone are the
LORD.[k] You made the heavens,[l] even
the highest heavens, and all their
starry host,[m] the earth[n] and all that
is on it, the seas[o] and all that is in
them.[p] You give life to everything,
and the multitudes of heaven[q] worship you.
7"You are the LORD God, who chose
Abram[r] and brought him out of Ur of
the Chaldeans[s] and named him Abraham.[t] 8You found his heart faithful to
you, and you made a covenant with
him to give to his descendants the
land of the Canaanites, Hittites, Amorites, Perizzites, Jebusites and Girgashites.[u] You have kept your promise[v]
because you are righteous.[w]
9"You saw the suffering of our forefathers in Egypt;[x] you heard their cry
at the Red Sea.[b][y] 10You sent miraculous signs[z] and wonders[a] against
Pharaoh, against all his officials and
all the people of his land, for you
knew how arrogantly the Egyptians
treated them. You made a name[b] for
yourself,[c] which remains to this day.
11You divided the sea before them,[d]
so that they passed through it on dry
ground, but you hurled their pursuers into the depths,[e] like a stone into
mighty waters.[f] 12By day[g] you led[h]
them with a pillar of cloud,[i] and by
night with a pillar of fire to give them
light on the way they were to take.
13"You came down on Mount Si-
nai;[j] you spoke[k] to them from heav-
en.[l] You gave them regulations and
laws that are just[m] and right, and decrees and commands that are good.[n]

[a] 5 Or *God for ever and ever* [b] 9 Hebrew *Yam Suph*; that is, Sea of Reeds

8:16 [x]S 2Ch 25:23 **8:17** [y]Hos 12:9 [z]S 1Ki 8:2; S 2Ch 7:8; S 8:13 **8:18** [a]Dt 31:11; S 33:10 [b]S Dt 28:61 [c]S Lev 23:36,40; S Ezr 3:4 [d]S Lev 23:36 **9:1** [e]Lev 26:40-45; S Jos 7:6; 2Ch 7:14-16 **9:2** [f]S Ezr 6:21; Ne 10:28; 13:3,30 [g]S Lev 26:40; S Ezr 10:11; Ps 106:6 **9:4** [h]S Ezr 10:23 **9:5** [i]Ps 78:4 [j]S 2Sa 7:26 **9:6** [k]S Dt 6:4 [l]S Ex 8:19 [m]Isa 40:26; 45:12 [n]S Ge 1:1; Isa 37:16 [o]Ps 95:5; 146:6; Jnh 1:9 [p]Dt 10:14; Ac 4:24; Rev 10:6 [q]Ps 103:20; 148:2 **9:7** [r]S Ge 16:11 [s]S Ge 11:28 [t]S Ge 17:5 **9:8** [u]S Ge 15:18-21; S Ezr 9:1 [v]S Jos 21:45 [w]Ge 15:6; S Ezr 9:15 **9:9** [x]Ex 2:23-25; 3:7 [y]Ex 14:10-30 **9:10** [z]S Ex 10:1; Ps 74:9 [a]S Ex 3:20; S 6:6 [b]Jer 32:20; Da 9:15 [c]S Nu 6:27 **9:11** [d]Ps 78:13 [e]S Ex 14:28 [f]Ex 15:4-5,10; Heb 11:29 **9:12** [g]S Dt 1:33 [h]S Ex 15:13 [i]S Ex 13:21 **9:13** [j]S Ex 19:11 [k]S Ex 19:19 [l]S Ex 20:22 [m]Ps 119:137 [n]S Ex 20:1; Dt 4:7-8

subdivided into courts for the women, for Israel and for the priests. The Temple Scroll from Qumran has God setting forth in detail an ideal temple. Columns 40–46 describe the outer court as follows: "On the roof of the third story are columns for the constructing of booths for the Feast of Tabernacles, to be occupied by the elders, tribal chieftains and commanders of thousands and hundreds." *Gate of Ephraim.* A gate of the oldest rampart of Jerusalem (see note on 3:6; see also 2Ki 14:13). It was restored by Nehemiah (12:39).

8:17 *From the days of Joshua ... until that day.* The phrase does not mean that the Feast of Tabernacles had not been celebrated since Joshua's time, because such celebrations took place after the dedication of Solomon's temple (2Ch 7:8–10) and after the return of the exiles (Ezr 3:4). What apparently is meant is that the feast had not been celebrated before with such great joy (cf. 2Ch 30:26; 35:18).

8:18 *assembly.* See Nu 29:35.

9:1–37 The ninth chapters of Ezra, Nehemiah and Daniel (after these books were divided into "chapters") are all similar in that they are devoted to confessions of national sin and to prayers for God's grace.

9:1 *twenty-fourth day.* Oct. 30, 444 B.C.; a day of penance in the spirit of the Day of Atonement, which was held on the tenth day (Lev 16:29–30). *fasting ... sackcloth ... dust.* See notes on Ge 37:34; Ezr 8:23; 10:6; Joel 1:13–14.

9:3 *quarter of the day.* About three hours.

9:5–37 One of the most beautiful prayers outside the Psalms, it reviews God's grace and power (1) in creation (v. 6), (2) in the Abrahamic covenant (vv. 7–8), (3) in Egypt and at the Red Sea (vv. 9–11), (4) in the desert and at Sinai (vv. 12–21), (5) during the conquest of Canaan (vv. 22–25), (6) through the judges (vv. 26–28), (7) through the prophets (vv. 29–31) and (8) in the present situation (vv. 32–37). Cf. Ps 78; 105–106. See similar prayers in Ezr 9:5–15; Da 9:3–19 (see also note there).

9:6 *You alone are the LORD.* Though not in the words of Dt 6:4, which expresses the central monotheistic conviction of Israel's faith, the prayer begins with a similar affirmation (cf. 2Ki 19:15; Ps 86:10). *highest heavens.* See Dt 10:14; 1Ki 8:27; 2Ch 2:6; Ps 148:4. *multitudes of heaven worship you.* See Ps 89:5–7.

9:7 *Ur of the Chaldeans.* See note on Ge 11:28. *named him Abraham.* See note on Ge 17:5.

9:8 *faithful.* Compare Ro 4:16–22 with Jas 2:21–23. *made a covenant with him.* See note on Ge 15:18. *Canaanites ... Girgashites.* See notes on Ge 10:6,15–18; 13:7; Ex 3:8; Ezr 9:1.

9:9 *Red Sea.* See notes on Ex 13:18; 14:2.

9:11 *divided the sea.* See Ex 14:21–22; 1Co 10:1.

14 You made known to them your holy
Sabbath[o] and gave them commands,
decrees and laws through your servant Moses. 15 In their hunger you
gave them bread from heaven[p] and in
their thirst you brought them water
from the rock;[q] you told them to go in
and take possession of the land you
had sworn with uplifted hand[r] to give
them.[s]
16 "But they, our forefathers, became arrogant and stiff-necked,[t]
and did not obey your commands.[u]
17 They refused to listen and failed to
remember[v] the miracles[w] you performed among them. They became
stiff-necked[x] and in their rebellion
appointed a leader in order to return
to their slavery.[y] But you are a forgiving God,[z] gracious and compassionate,[a] slow to anger[b] and abounding
in love.[c] Therefore you did not desert them,[d] 18 even when they cast for
themselves an image of a calf[e] and
said, 'This is your god, who brought
you up out of Egypt,' or when they
committed awful blasphemies.[f]
19 "Because of your great compassion you did not abandon[g] them in
the desert. By day the pillar of cloud[h]
did not cease to guide them on their
path, nor the pillar of fire by night to
shine on the way they were to take.
20 You gave your good Spirit[i] to instruct[j] them. You did not withhold
your manna[k] from their mouths, and
you gave them water[l] for their thirst.
21 For forty years[m] you sustained them
in the desert; they lacked nothing,[n]
their clothes did not wear out nor did
their feet become swollen.[o]
22 "You gave them kingdoms and
nations, allotting to them even the remotest frontiers. They took over the
country of Sihon[a][p] king of Heshbon
and the country of Og king of Bashan.[q]
23 You made their sons as numerous as
the stars in the sky,[r] and you brought
them into the land that you told their
fathers to enter and possess. 24 Their
sons went in and took possession of
the land.[s] You subdued[t] before them
the Canaanites, who lived in the land;
you handed the Canaanites over to
them, along with their kings and the
peoples of the land, to deal with them
as they pleased. 25 They captured fortified cities and fertile land;[u] they took
possession of houses filled with all
kinds of good things,[v] wells already
dug, vineyards, olive groves and fruit
trees in abundance. They ate to the
full and were well-nourished;[w] they
reveled in your great goodness.[x]
26 "But they were disobedient and
rebelled against you; they put your
law behind their backs.[y] They killed[z]
your prophets,[a] who had admonished
them in order to turn them back to
you; they committed awful blasphemies.[b] 27 So you handed them over to
their enemies,[c] who oppressed them.
But when they were oppressed they
cried out to you. From heaven you
heard them, and in your great compassion[d] you gave them deliverers,[e]
who rescued them from the hand of
their enemies.
28 "But as soon as they were at rest,
they again did what was evil in your
sight.[f] Then you abandoned them to
the hand of their enemies so that they
ruled over them. And when they cried
out to you again, you heard from

9:14 [o]S Ge 2:3; Ex 20:8-11 **9:15** [p]S Ex 16:4; Ps 78:24-25; Jn 6:31 [q]Ex 17:6; Nu 20:7-13 [r]S Ge 14:22 [s]Dt 1:8,21 **9:16** [t]S Ex 32:9; Jer 7:26; 17:23; 19:15 [u]Dt 1:26-33; 31:29 **9:17** [v]Jdg 8:34; Ps 78:42 [w]Ps 77:11; 78:12; 105:5; 106:7 [x]Jer 7:26; 19:15 [y]Nu 14:1-4 [z]Ps 130:4; Da 9:9 [a]S Dt 4:31 [b]S Ex 34:6; Ps 103:8; Na 1:3 [c]S Ex 22:27; Nu 14:17-19; Ps 86:15 [d]Ps 78:11; Eze 5:6 **9:18** [e]S Ex 32:4 [f]S Ex 20:23 **9:19** [g]Ex 13:22 [h]S Ex 13:21 **9:20** [i]Nu 9:17; 11:17; Isa 63:11,14; Hag 2:5; Zec 4:6 [j]Ps 23:3; 143:10 [k]S Ex 16:15 [l]Ex 17:6 **9:21** [m]S Ex 16:35 [n]S Dt 2:7 [o]S Dt 8:4 **9:22** [p]S Nu 21:21 [q]S Nu 21:33; Dt 2:26-3:11 **9:23** [r]S Ge 12:2; S Lev 26:9; S Nu 10:36 **9:24** [s]S Jos 11:23 [t]S Jdg 4:23; S 2Ch 14:13 **9:25** [u]S Dt 11:11 [v]S Ex 18:9 [w]Dt 6:10-12 [x]8:8-11; 32:12-15; Ps 23:6; 25:7; 69:16 **9:26** [y]S 1Ki 14:9; Jer 44:10 [z]S Jos 7:25 [a]Jer 2:30; 26:8; Mt 21:35-36; 23:29-36; Ac 7:52 [b]S Jdg 2:12-13 **9:27** [c]S Nu 25:17; S Jdg 2:14 [d]Ps 51:1; 103:8; 106:45; 119:156 [e]S Jdg 3:9 **9:28** [f]S Ex 32:22; S Jdg 2:17

[a] *22* One Hebrew manuscript and Septuagint; most Hebrew manuscripts *Sihon, that is, the country of the*

9:14 *holy Sabbath.* According to the rabbis, "the Sabbath outweighs all the commandments of the Torah." See 10:31–33; 13:15–22.

9:15 *bread from heaven.* See note on Ex 16:4. *water from the rock.* See note on Ex 17:6. *sworn with uplifted hand.* See Ge 14:22 and note; 22:15–17; Ex 6:8; Eze 20:6; 47:14.

9:16 *stiff-necked.* See vv. 17,29; see also notes on 3:5; Ex 32:9.

9:17 *appointed a leader.* Their intention to do so is recorded in Nu 14:4. *gracious ... abounding in love.* See note on Ex 34:6–7.

9:18 *blasphemies.* See v. 26; Ex 32:4; Eze 35:12.

9:19 *compassion.* See vv. 27–28.

9:20 *Spirit to instruct.* See Ex 31:3.

9:21 *clothes did not wear out.* Evidence of the special providence of God (see Dt 8:4; 29:5; contrast Jos 9:13). *swollen.* Or "blistered"; the Hebrew for this word occurs only here and in Dt 8:4.

9:22 *Sihon ... Og.* See Nu 21:21–35.

9:23 *numerous as the stars.* See notes on Ge 13:16; 15:5; 22:17.

9:25 See Dt 6:10–12 and note; Jos 24:13. *fertile.* See v. 35; cf. Nu 14:7; Dt 8:7; Jos 23:13. *wells already dug.* Because of the lack of rainfall during much of the year, almost every house had its own well or a cistern in which to store water from the rainy seasons (2Ki 18:31; Pr 5:15). By 1200 B.C. the technique of waterproofing cisterns was developed, permitting greater occupation of the central hills of Judah. *vineyards, olive groves and fruit trees.* Cf. Dt 8:8. The Egyptian story of Sinuhe (c. 2000 B.C.; see chart, p. xxiii) describes Canaan as follows: "Figs were in it, and grapes. It had more wine than water. Plentiful was its honey, abundant its olives. Every (kind of) fruit was on its trees." *well-nourished.* Elsewhere the Hebrew for this word always implies physical fullness and spiritual insensitivity.

9:26–28 See note on Jdg 2:6—3:6.

9:26 *put your law behind their backs.* Totally disregarded God's law (cf. Ps 50:17; Jer 2:27; 32:33; Eze 23:35). *killed your prophets.* See 1Ki 18:4,13; 19:10,14; 2Ch 24:20–21; Jer 2:30; 26:20–23; cf. Lk 11:50–51; Heb 11:32,36–38.

9:27 *deliverers.* See Introduction to Judges: Title.

heaven, and in your compassion[g] you
delivered them[h] time after time.
29“You warned[i] them to return to
your law, but they became arrogant[j]
and disobeyed your commands. They
sinned against your ordinances, by
which a man will live if he obeys
them.[k] Stubbornly they turned their
backs[l] on you, became stiff-necked[m]
and refused to listen.[n] 30For many
years you were patient with them.
By your Spirit you admonished them
through your prophets.[o] Yet they paid
no attention, so you handed them over
to the neighboring peoples.[p] 31But in
your great mercy you did not put an
end[q] to them or abandon them, for
you are a gracious and merciful[r] God.
32“Now therefore, O our God, the
great, mighty[s] and awesome God,[t]
who keeps his covenant of love,[u] do
not let all this hardship seem trifling
in your eyes—the hardship[v] that has
come upon us, upon our kings and
leaders, upon our priests and prophets, upon our fathers and all your
people, from the days of the kings of
Assyria until today. 33In all that has
happened to us, you have been just;[w]
you have acted faithfully, while we
did wrong.[x] 34Our kings,[y] our leaders, our priests and our fathers[z] did
not follow your law; they did not
pay attention to your commands or
the warnings you gave them. 35Even
while they were in their kingdom, enjoying your great goodness[a] to them
in the spacious and fertile land you
gave them, they did not serve you[b] or
turn from their evil ways.
36“But see, we are slaves[c] today,
slaves in the land you gave our forefathers so they could eat its fruit and
the other good things it produces.
37Because of our sins, its abundant
harvest goes to the kings you have
placed over us. They rule over our
bodies and our cattle as they please.
We are in great distress.[d]

The Agreement of the People

38“In view of all this, we are making a
binding agreement,[e] putting it in writing,[f]
and our leaders, our Levites and our
priests are affixing their seals to it.”

10 Those who sealed it were:

Nehemiah the governor, the son of Hacaliah.

Zedekiah, 2Seraiah,[g] Azariah, Jeremiah,
3Pashhur,[h] Amariah, Malkijah,
4Hattush, Shebaniah, Malluch,
5Harim,[i] Meremoth, Obadiah,
6Daniel, Ginnethon, Baruch,
7Meshullam, Abijah, Mijamin,
8Maaziah, Bilgai and Shemaiah.
These were the priests.[j]

9The Levites:[k]

Jeshua son of Azaniah, Binnui of the sons of Henadad, Kadmiel,
10and their associates: Shebaniah,
Hodiah, Kelita, Pelaiah, Hanan,
11Mica, Rehob, Hashabiah,
12Zaccur, Sherebiah, Shebaniah,
13Hodiah, Bani and Beninu.

14The leaders of the people:

Parosh, Pahath-Moab, Elam, Zattu, Bani,
15Bunni, Azgad, Bebai,
16Adonijah, Bigvai, Adin,[l]
17Ater, Hezekiah, Azzur,
18Hodiah, Hashum, Bezai,
19Hariph, Anathoth, Nebai,
20Magpiash, Meshullam, Hezir,[m]
21Meshezabel, Zadok, Jaddua,
22Pelatiah, Hanan, Anaiah,
23Hoshea, Hananiah,[n] Hasshub,
24Hallohesh, Pilha, Shobek,
25Rehum, Hashabnah, Maaseiah,
26Ahiah, Hanan, Anan,
27Malluch, Harim and Baanah.

28“The rest of the people—priests,
Levites, gatekeepers, singers, temple servants[o] and all who separated themselves from the neighboring
peoples[p] for the sake of the Law of
God, together with their wives and
all their sons and daughters who are
able to understand— 29all these now
join their brothers the nobles, and
bind themselves with a curse and an

9:28 [g]S 2Sa 24:14 [h]Ps 22:4; 106:43; 136:24 **9:29** [i]S Jdg 6:8 [j]ver 16-17; Ps 5:5; Isa 2:11; Jer 43:2 [k]S Dt 30:16 [l]S 1Sa 8:3 [m]Jer 19:15 [n]Zec 7:11-12 **9:30** [o]2Ki 17:13-18; S 2Ch 36:16 [p]Jer 16:11; Zec 7:12 **9:31** [q]Isa 48:9; 65:9 [r]S Dt 4:31 **9:32** [s]Job 9:19; Ps 24:8; 89:8; 93:4 [t]S Dt 7:21 [u]S Dt 7:9; S 1Ki 8:23; Da 9:4 [v]S Ex 18:8 **9:33** [w]S Ge 18:25 [x]Jer 44:3; Da 9:7-8, 14 **9:34** [y]S 2Ki 23:11 [z]Jer 44:17 **9:35** [a]Isa 63:7 [b]Dt 28:45-48 **9:36** [c]S Ezr 9:9 **9:37** [d]Dt 28:33; La 5:5 **9:38** [e]S 2Ch 23:16 [f]Isa 44:5

10:2 [g]S Ezr 2:2 **10:3** [h]S 1Ch 9:12 **10:5** [i]S 1Ch 24:8 **10:8** [j]Ne 12:1 **10:9** [k]Ne 12:1 **10:16** [l]S Ezr 8:6 **10:20** [m]1Ch 24:15 **10:23** [n]S Ne 7:2 **10:28** [o]Ps 135:1 [p]2Ch 6:26; S Ne 9:2

9:29 *will live if he obeys.* See note on Lev 18:5. *Stubbornly they turned their backs.* See Zec 7:11; cf. the similar expressions in v. 16; 3:5; Hos 4:16.
9:32 *who keeps his covenant of love.* See 1:5; see also Dt 7:9,12 and note. *kings of Assyria.* Including Tiglath-Pileser III, also known as Pul (1Ch 5:26); Shalmaneser V (2Ki 18:9); Sargon II (Isa 20:1); Sennacherib (2Ki 18:13); Esarhaddon (Ezr 4:2); and Ashurbanipal (Ezr 4:10).
9:37 *rule over our bodies.* See 1Sa 8:11–13. The Persian rulers drafted their subjects into military service. Some Jews may have accompanied Xerxes on his invasion of Greece in 480 B.C.
10:1–27 A legal list, bearing the official seal and containing a roster of 84 names.
10:2–8 About half of these names occur again in 12:1–7.
10:9–13 Most of these names appear also in the lists of Levites in 8:7; 9:4–5.
10:14–27 Almost half of the names in this category are also found in the lists of 7:6–63; Ezr 2:1–61.
10:28 *The rest of the people.* Those who did not affix their seals to the agreement (cf. 9:38—10:1). *Levites.* See note on Ezr 1:5. *gatekeepers.* See note on Ezr 2:42. *wives ... sons and daughters.* See note on 8:2.

oath[q] to follow the Law of God given
through Moses the servant of God and
to obey carefully all the commands,
regulations and decrees of the LORD
our Lord.
30“We promise not to give our
daughters in marriage to the peoples
around us or take their daughters for
our sons.[r]
31“When the neighboring peoples
bring merchandise or grain to sell on
the Sabbath,[s] we will not buy from
them on the Sabbath or on any holy
day. Every seventh year we will forgo
working the land[t] and will cancel all
debts.[u]
32“We assume the responsibility for
carrying out the commands to give a
third of a shekel[a] each year for the
service of the house of our God: 33for
the bread set out on the table;[v] for
the regular grain offerings and burnt
offerings; for the offerings on the Sabbaths, New Moon[w] festivals and appointed feasts; for the holy offerings;
for sin offerings to make atonement
for Israel; and for all the duties of the
house of our God.[x]
34“We—the priests, the Levites and
the people—have cast lots[y] to determine when each of our families is
to bring to the house of our God at
set times each year a contribution of
wood[z] to burn on the altar of the LORD
our God, as it is written in the Law.
35“We also assume responsibility
for bringing to the house of the LORD
each year the firstfruits[a] of our crops
and of every fruit tree.[b]
36“As it is also written in the Law,
we will bring the firstborn[c] of our sons
and of our cattle, of our herds and of
our flocks to the house of our God, to
the priests ministering there.[d]
37“Moreover, we will bring to the
storerooms of the house of our God,
to the priests, the first of our ground
meal, of our ⌞grain⌟ offerings, of the
fruit of all our trees and of our new
wine and oil.[e] And we will bring a
tithe[f] of our crops to the Levites,[g] for
it is the Levites who collect the tithes
in all the towns where we work.[h] 38A
priest descended from Aaron is to accompany the Levites when they receive the tithes, and the Levites are
to bring a tenth of the tithes[i] up to the
house of our God, to the storerooms
of the treasury. 39The people of Israel, including the Levites, are to bring
their contributions of grain, new wine
and oil to the storerooms where the
articles for the sanctuary are kept
and where the ministering priests, the
gatekeepers and the singers stay.
“We will not neglect the house of
our God.”[j]

The New Residents of Jerusalem

11:3-19pp — 1Ch 9:1-17

11 Now the leaders of the people settled in Jerusalem, and the rest of the
people cast lots to bring one out of every
ten to live in Jerusalem,[k] the holy city,[l]
while the remaining nine were to stay in

10:29 [q]S Nu 5:21; Ps 119:106
10:30 [r]S Ex 34:16; Ne 13:23
10:31 [s]Ne 13:16,18; Jer 17:27; Eze 23:38; Am 8:5 [t]S Ex 23:11; Lev 25:1-7 [u]S Dt 15:1
10:33 [v]Lev 24:6 [w]Nu 10:10; Ps 81:3; Isa 1:14 [x]S 2Ch 24:5
10:34 [y]S Lev 16:8 [z]Ne 13:31
10:35 [a]S Ex 22:29; S Nu 18:12 [b]Dt 26:1-11
10:36 [c]S Ex 13:2; S Nu 18:14-16 [d]Ne 13:31
10:37 [e]S Nu 18:12 [f]S Lev 27:30; S Nu 18:21 [g]Dt 14:22-29 [h]Eze 44:30
10:38 [i]Nu 18:26
10:39 [j]Ne 13:11,12
11:1 [k]Ne 7:4 [l]Isa 48:2; 52:1; 64:10; Zec 14:20-21

[a] *32* That is, about 1/8 ounce (about 4 grams)

10:31–33 Perhaps a code drawn up by Nehemiah to correct the abuses listed in 13:15–22.

10:31 *sell on the Sabbath.* See Jer 17:19–27; Am 8:5 and note. *seventh year … forgo working the land … cancel all debts.* See note on Lev 25:4. The Romans misrepresented the Sabbath and the sabbath year as caused by laziness. According to Tacitus, the Jews "were led by the charms of indolence to give over the seventh year as well to inactivity."

10:32 *third of a shekel.* Ex 30:13–14 speaks of a "half shekel" as "an offering to the LORD" from each man who was 20 years old or more as a symbolic ransom. Later Joash used the annual contributions for the repair of the temple (2Ch 24:4–14). In the NT period Jewish men from everywhere sent an offering of a half shekel (actually two drachmas, its equivalent; see Josephus, *Antiquities,* 3.8.2) for the temple in Jerusalem (Mt 17:24). The pledge of a third of a shekel in Nehemiah's time may have been due to economic circumstances.

10:33 *bread.* See note on Lev 24:8.

10:34 *cast lots.* See notes on Pr 13:23; Eze 21:21; Jnh 1:7. *contribution of wood.* Though there is no specific reference to a wood offering in the Pentateuch, the perpetual burning of fire on the sanctuary altar (Lev 6:12–13) would have required a continual supply of wood. Josephus mentions "the festival of wood offering" on the 14th day of the fifth month (Ab). The Jewish Mishnah (Rabbinic interpretations and applications of Pentateuchal laws) lists nine times when certain families brought wood, and stipulates that all kinds of wood were suitable except the vine and the olive. The Temple Scroll from Qumran describes the celebration of a wood offering festival for six days following a new oil festival.

10:35 *firstfruits.* Brought to the sanctuary to support the priests and Levites (see Ex 23:19 and note; Nu 18:13; Dt 26:1–11; Eze 44:30).

10:36 *firstborn.* See note on Ex 13:13.

10:37 *storerooms.* Chambers in the courts of the temple were used as storage rooms for silver, gold and sacred articles (cf. vv. 38–39; 12:44; 13:4–5,9; Ezr 8:28–30). *new wine.* See note on Dt 7:13. Though the Hebrew for this term can refer to freshly pressed grape juice (Isa 65:8; Mic 6:15), it can also be used of intoxicating wine (Hos 4:11). *tithe.* See notes on Ge 14:20; 28:22; Lev 27:30; Am 4:4. *Levites.* Tithes were meant for their support (13:12–13; Nu 18:21–32).

10:39 See 13:11. *We will not neglect.* Haggai (Hag 1:4–9) had accused the people of neglecting the temple.

11:1 *cast lots.* See note on 10:34. *one out of every ten to live in Jerusalem.* The practice of redistributing populations was also used about that same time to establish Greek and Hellenistic cities. It involved the forcible transfer from rural settlements to urban centers. Later, Tiberias on the Sea of Galilee was populated with Gentiles by such a process by Herod Antipas in A.D. 18. *holy city.* See Isa 48:2 and note; Da 9:24; Mt 4:5; 27:53; Rev 11:2; cf. Joel 3:17.

their own towns.[m] 2The people commended all the men who volunteered to live in
Jerusalem.

3These are the provincial leaders who
settled in Jerusalem (now some Israelites,
priests, Levites, temple servants and descendants of Solomon's servants lived in
the towns of Judah, each on his own property in the various towns,[n] 4while other
people from both Judah and Benjamin[o]
lived in Jerusalem):[p]

From the descendants of Judah:

Athaiah son of Uzziah, the son of
Zechariah, the son of Amariah, the
son of Shephatiah, the son of Mahalalel, a descendant of Perez; 5and Maaseiah son of Baruch, the son of Col-
Hozeh, the son of Hazaiah, the son
of Adaiah, the son of Joiarib, the son
of Zechariah, a descendant of Shelah.
6The descendants of Perez who lived
in Jerusalem totaled 468 able men.

7From the descendants of Benjamin:

Sallu son of Meshullam, the son of
Joed, the son of Pedaiah, the son of
Kolaiah, the son of Maaseiah, the son
of Ithiel, the son of Jeshaiah, 8and his
followers, Gabbai and Sallai—928
men. 9Joel son of Zicri was their chief
officer, and Judah son of Hassenuah
was over the Second District of the
city.

10From the priests:

Jedaiah; the son of Joiarib; Jakin;
11Seraiah[q] son of Hilkiah, the son of
Meshullam, the son of Zadok, the son
of Meraioth, the son of Ahitub,[r] su-
pervisor in the house of God, 12and
their associates, who carried on work
for the temple—822 men; Adaiah son
of Jeroham, the son of Pelaliah, the
son of Amzi, the son of Zechariah, the
son of Pashhur, the son of Malkijah,
13and his associates, who were heads
of families—242 men; Amashsai son
of Azarel, the son of Ahzai, the son
of Meshillemoth, the son of Immer,
14and his[a] associates, who were able
men—128. Their chief officer was
Zabdiel son of Haggedolim.

15From the Levites:

Shemaiah son of Hasshub, the son
of Azrikam, the son of Hashabiah,
the son of Bunni; 16Shabbethai[s] and
Jozabad,[t] two of the heads of the Levites, who had charge of the outside
work of the house of God; 17Matta-
niah[u] son of Mica, the son of Zabdi,
the son of Asaph,[v] the director who
led in thanksgiving and prayer; Bakbukiah, second among his associates;
and Abda son of Shammua, the son
of Galal, the son of Jeduthun.[w] 18The
Levites in the holy city[x] totaled 284.

19The gatekeepers:

Akkub, Talmon and their associates,
who kept watch at the gates—172
men.

20The rest of the Israelites, with the
priests and Levites, were in all the towns
of Judah, each on his ancestral property.
21The temple servants[y] lived on the hill
of Ophel, and Ziha and Gishpa were in
charge of them.
22The chief officer of the Levites in Jerusalem was Uzzi son of Bani, the son of
Hashabiah, the son of Mattaniah,[z] the son
of Mica. Uzzi was one of Asaph's descendants, who were the singers responsible
for the service of the house of God. 23The
singers[a] were under the king's orders,
which regulated their daily activity.
24Pethahiah son of Meshezabel, one of
the descendants of Zerah[b] son of Judah,
was the king's agent in all affairs relating
to the people.

11:1 [m]S Ne 7:73 **11:3** [n]S Ezr 2:1 **11:4** [o]S Ezr 1:5 [p]S Ezr 2:70 **11:11** [q]S 2Ki 25:18; S Ezr 2:2 [r]S Ezr 7:2 **11:16** [s]Ezr 10:15 [t]S Ezr 8:33 **11:17** [u]S 1Ch 9:15; Ne 12:8 [v]2Ch 5:12 [w]S 1Ch 25:1 **11:18** [x]S Rev 21:2 **11:21** [y]S Ezr 2:43; S Ne 3:26 **11:22** [z]S 1Ch 9:15 **11:23** [a]S 1Ch 15:16; Ne 7:44 **11:24** [b]S Ge 38:30

[a] *14* Most Septuagint manuscripts; Hebrew *their*

11:2 In addition to those chosen by lot (v. 1), some volunteered out of a sense of duty. But evidently most preferred to stay in their hometowns.
11:3–19 A census roster that parallels 1Ch 9:2–21, a list of the first residents in Jerusalem after the return from Babylonia. About half the names in the two lists are the same.
11:8 *928.* The men of Benjamin provided twice as many men as Judah (v. 6) to live in and protect the city of Jerusalem.
11:9 *Second District.* See 2Ki 22:14 and note; 2Ch 34:22 (in Zep 1:10 the Hebrew for this phrase is translated "New Quarter"). Like the "market district" (Zep 1:11), which was probably the Tyropoeon Valley area, the Second District was a new suburb (see map No. 10 at the end of this study Bible). Excavations indicate that the city had spread outside the walls in this direction by the late eighth century B.C. before the so-called Broad Wall was built c. 700 by Hezekiah (see note on 3:8).
11:16 *outside work.* Duties outside the temple (cf. 1Ch 26:29) but connected with it.
11:17 *Asaph.* See note on Ezr 2:41; see also titles of Ps 50; 73–83. *Jeduthun.* See 1Ch 16:42; 25:1,3; 2Ch 5:12; titles of Ps 39; 62; 77.
11:18 *284.* The relatively small number of Levites, compared with 1,192 priests (the total of 822, 242 and 128 in vv. 12–13), is striking (see note on Ezr 2:40).
11:20 *ancestral property.* Inalienable hereditary possessions—including land, buildings and movable goods—acquired by either conquest or inheritance (Ge 31:14; Nu 18:21; 27:7; 34:2; 36:3; 1Ki 21:1–4).
11:21 *Ophel.* See note on 3:26.
11:23 *king's orders ... regulated.* David had regulated the services of the Levites, including the singers (1Ch 25). The Persian king, Darius I, gave a royal stipend so that the Jewish elders might "pray for the well-being of the king and his sons" (Ezr 6:10). Artaxerxes I may have done much the same for the Levite choir.

25 As for the villages with their fields,
some of the people of Judah lived in Kiriath Arba[c] and its surrounding settlements,
in Dibon[d] and its settlements, in Jekabzeel
and its villages, 26 in Jeshua, in Moladah,[e]
in Beth Pelet,[f] 27 in Hazar Shual,[g] in Beersheba[h] and its settlements, 28 in Ziklag,[i] in
Meconah and its settlements, 29 in En Rimmon, in Zorah,[j] in Jarmuth,[k] 30 Zanoah,[l]
Adullam[m] and their villages, in Lachish[n]
and its fields, and in Azekah[o] and its settlements. So they were living all the way
from Beersheba[p] to the Valley of Hinnom.
31 The descendants of the Benjamites
from Geba[q] lived in Micmash,[r] Aija, Bethel[s] and its settlements, 32 in Anathoth,[t]
Nob[u] and Ananiah, 33 in Hazor,[v] Ramah[w]
and Gittaim,[x] 34 in Hadid, Zeboim[y] and Ne-
ballat, 35 in Lod and Ono,[z] and in the Valley
of the Craftsmen.
36 Some of the divisions of the Levites of
Judah settled in Benjamin.

Priests and Levites

12 These were the priests[a] and Levites[b]
who returned with Zerubbabel[c] son
of Shealtiel[d] and with Jeshua:[e]

11:25 [c] S Ge 35:27 [d] S Nu 21:30
11:26 [e] Jos 15:26 [f] Jos 15:27
11:27 [g] Jos 15:28 [h] S Ge 21:14
11:28 [i] S 1Sa 27:6
11:29 [j] Jos 15:33 [k] S Jos 10:3; S 15:35
11:30 [l] Jos 15:34 [m] Jos 15:35 [n] S Jos 10:3; 15:39 [o] S Jos 10:10 [p] Jos 15:28
11:31 [q] Jos 21:17; Isa 10:29 [r] S 1Sa 13:2 [s] S Jos 12:9
11:32 [t] Jos 21:18; Isa 10:30; Jer 1:1 [u] S 1Sa 21:1
11:33 [v] S Jos 11:1 [w] S Jos 18:25 [x] 2Sa 4:3
11:34 [y] 1Sa 13:18
11:35 [z] S 1Ch 8:12
12:1 [a] Ne 10:1-8

Seraiah,[f] Jeremiah, Ezra,
2 Amariah, Malluch, Hattush,
3 Shecaniah, Rehum, Meremoth,
4 Iddo,[g] Ginnethon,[a] Abijah,[h]
5 Mijamin,[b] Moadiah, Bilgah,
6 Shemaiah, Joiarib, Jedaiah,[i]
7 Sallu, Amok, Hilkiah and Jedaiah.
These were the leaders of the priests and
their associates in the days of Jeshua.
8 The Levites were Jeshua,[j] Binnui, Kadmiel, Sherebiah, Judah, and also Mattaniah,[k] who, together with his associates,
was in charge of the songs of thanksgiving. 9 Bakbukiah and Unni, their associates, stood opposite them in the services.
10 Jeshua was the father of Joiakim, Joiakim the father of Eliashib,[l] Eliashib the
father of Joiada, 11 Joiada the father of
Jonathan, and Jonathan the father of Jaddua.

[a] 4 Many Hebrew manuscripts and Vulgate (see also Neh. 12:16); most Hebrew manuscripts *Ginnethoi*
[b] 5 A variant of *Miniamin*

[b] Ne 10:9 [c] S 1Ch 3:19; Ezr 3:2; Zec 4:6-10 [d] Ezr 3:2 [e] S Ezr 2:2 [f] S Ezr 2:2 **12:4** [g] ver 16; Zec 1:1 [h] S 1Ch 24:10; Lk 1:5 **12:6** [i] S 1Ch 24:7 **12:8** [j] S Ezr 2:2 [k] S Ne 11:17 **12:10** [l] S Ezr 10:24; Ne 3:20

11:25–30 An important list, corresponding to earlier lists of towns in Judah. All these names also appear in Jos 15 with the exception of Dibon, Jekabzeel (but see Kabzeel in Jos 15:21), Jeshua, Meconah and En Rimmon (but see Ain and Rimmon in Jos 15:32). The list, however, is not comprehensive, since a number of towns listed in ch. 3; Ezr 2:21–22 are lacking. No Judean coins have been found outside the area designated by vv. 25–30.

11:25 *Kiriath Arba.* See note on Ge 23:2. In the Hellenistic era it fell to the Idumeans, together with other Judean towns.

11:26 *Moladah.* Near Beersheba; later occupied by the Idumeans. *Beth Pelet.* Means "house of refuge," a site near Beersheba.

11:27 *Beersheba.* See note and NIV text note on Ge 21:31. Archaeological excavations reveal that the city was destroyed by Sennacherib in 701 B.C. and only resettled in the Persian period.

11:28 *Ziklag.* See Jos 15:31; given to David by Achish, king of Gath (1Sa 27:6).

11:29 *En Rimmon.* Means "spring of the pomegranate," probably Khirbet Umm er-Ramamin, nine miles north-northeast of Beersheba (see Jos 15:32). *Zorah.* See note on Jdg 13:2. *Jarmuth.* One of five Canaanite cities in the south that attempted to halt Joshua's invasion (see Jos 10:3–5 and note on 10:5; see also map No. 3 at the end of this study Bible).

11:30 *Zanoah.* A village in the Shephelah district of low hills between Judah and Philistia. The men of Zanoah repaired the Valley Gate (3:13). The site has been identified with Khirbet Zanu, three miles south-southeast of Beth Shemesh. *Adullam.* See note on Ge 38:1. *Lachish.* See Jos 10:3; see also notes on Isa 36:2; Mic 1:13. *Azekah.* See note on Jer 34:7. *the Valley of Hinnom.* Hebrew *Ge Hinnom* (Gehenna in the NT); the valley west and south of Jerusalem.

11:31–35 Most of the Benjamite towns listed here appear also in 7:26–38; Ezr 2:23–35.

11:31 *Geba.* See 12:29; see also note on 1Sa 13:3. *Micmash.* See note on 1Sa 13:2. *Aija.* An alternative name for Ai (see note on Jos 7:2). *Bethel.* See notes on Ge 12:8; Jos 7:2; Ezr 2:28; Am 4:4.

11:32 *Anathoth.* See note on Jer 1:1. *Nob.* See note on 1Sa 21:1. *Ananiah.* Probably Bethany, meaning "house of Ananiah" (see note on Mt 21:17).

11:33 *Gittaim.* Its location is not known.

11:34 *Hadid.* Three to four miles northeast of Lod (see 7:37; Ezr 2:33).

11:35 *Lod.* See note on Ezr 2:33. *Ono.* See note on 6:2. *Valley of the Craftsmen.* See 1Ch 4:14 and NIV text note; the broad valley between Lod and Ono. The name may preserve the ancient memory that the Philistines in that area were blacksmiths (1Sa 13:19–20).

12:1 *Zerubbabel son of Shealtiel.* See Ezr 3:2,8; 5:2; see also note on Hag 1:1. *Jeshua.* Returned from Babylonian exile in 538/537 B.C. (see vv. 10,26; 7:7; Ezr 2:2 and note; Hag 1:1; Zec 3:1 and note). *Ezra.* Not the Ezra of the book, who was the leader of the exiles who returned 80 years later.

12:7 *leaders of the priests.* The rotation of 24 priestly divisions was established at the time of David (see 1Ch 24:3,7–19 and note on 24:4). Twenty-two heads of priestly houses are mentioned in vv. 1–7. Inscriptions listing the 24 divisions of the priests probably hung in many synagogues in the Holy Land in later times. So far, only fragments of two such inscriptions have been recovered—from Ashkelon in the 1920s and from Caesarea in the 1960s (dated to the third and fourth centuries A.D.).

12:9 *opposite them.* See v. 24; Ezr 3:11 and note; cf. 2Ch 7:6. The singing was antiphonal, with two sections of the choir standing opposite each other. *services.* The Hebrew for this word (*Mishmarot*) is the title of a work from Qumran, which discusses in detail the rotation of the priestly families' service in the temple according to the sect's solar calendar and synchronized with the conventional lunar calendar.

12:10 *Jeshua.* See note on v. 1. *Joiakim.* See vv. 12,26. *Eliashib.* See vv. 22–23; the high priest who assisted in rebuilding the wall (3:1,20–21; 13:28). A priest named Eliashib was guilty of defiling the temple by assigning rooms to Tobiah the Ammonite (13:4,7). It is not known whether this Eliashib was the same as the high priest.

12:11 *Jonathan.* Since v. 22 mentions a Johanan after Joiada and before Jaddua, and v. 23 identifies Johanan

12 In the days of Joiakim, these were the
heads of the priestly families:
of Seraiah's family, Meraiah;
of Jeremiah's, Hananiah;
13 of Ezra's, Meshullam;
of Amariah's, Jehohanan;
14 of Malluch's, Jonathan;
of Shecaniah's,[a] Joseph;
15 of Harim's, Adna;
of Meremoth's,[b] Helkai;
16 of Iddo's,[m] Zechariah;
of Ginnethon's, Meshullam;
17 of Abijah's,[n] Zicri;
of Miniamin's and of Moadiah's, Piltai;
18 of Bilgah's, Shammua;
of Shemaiah's, Jehonathan;
19 of Joiarib's, Mattenai;
of Jedaiah's, Uzzi;
20 of Sallu's, Kallai;
of Amok's, Eber;
21 of Hilkiah's, Hashabiah;
of Jedaiah's, Nethanel.
22 The family heads of the Levites in the
days of Eliashib, Joiada, Johanan and Jaddua, as well as those of the priests, were
recorded in the reign of Darius the Persian.
23 The family heads among the descendants of Levi up to the time of Johanan
son of Eliashib were recorded in the book
of the annals. 24 And the leaders of the Levites[o] were Hashabiah, Sherebiah, Jeshua
son of Kadmiel, and their associates, who
stood opposite them to give praise and
thanksgiving, one section responding to
the other, as prescribed by David the man
of God.[p]
25 Mattaniah, Bakbukiah, Obadiah, Meshullam, Talmon and Akkub were gatekeepers who guarded the storerooms at
the gates. 26 They served in the days of Joiakim son of Jeshua, the son of Jozadak,
and in the days of Nehemiah the governor
and of Ezra the priest and scribe.

Dedication of the Wall of Jerusalem

27 At the dedication[q] of the wall of Jerusalem, the Levites were sought out from
where they lived and were brought to Jerusalem to celebrate joyfully the dedication with songs of thanksgiving and with
the music of cymbals,[r] harps and lyres.[s]
28 The singers also were brought together
from the region around Jerusalem—from
the villages of the Netophathites,[t] 29 from
Beth Gilgal, and from the area of Geba
and Azmaveth, for the singers had built
villages for themselves around Jerusalem.
30 When the priests and Levites had purified themselves ceremonially, they purified the people,[u] the gates and the wall.
31 I had the leaders of Judah go up on
top[c] of the wall. I also assigned two large
choirs to give thanks. One was to proceed
on top[d] of the wall to the right, toward
the Dung Gate.[v] 32 Hoshaiah and half the
leaders of Judah followed them, 33 along
with Azariah, Ezra, Meshullam, 34 Judah,
Benjamin,[w] Shemaiah, Jeremiah, 35 as well
as some priests with trumpets,[x] and also
Zechariah son of Jonathan, the son of
Shemaiah, the son of Mattaniah, the son

12:16 [m] S ver 4 12:17 [n] S 1Ch 24:10 12:24 [o] S Ezr 2:40 [p] S 2Ch 8:14 12:27 [q] Dt 20:5 [r] S 2Sa 6:5 [s] S 1Ch 15:16,28; 25:6; Ps 92:3 12:28 [t] S 1Ch 2:54; 9:16 12:30 [u] Ex 19:10; Job 1:5 12:31 [v] Ne 2:13 12:34 [w] S Ezr 1:5 12:35 [x] S Ezr 3:10

[a] *14* Very many Hebrew manuscripts, some Septuagint manuscripts and Syriac (see also Neh. 12:3); most Hebrew manuscripts *Shebaniah's* [b] *15* Some Septuagint manuscripts (see also Neh. 12:3); Hebrew *Meraioth's* [c] *31* Or *go alongside* [d] *31* Or *proceed alongside*

as "son" of Eliashib, some believe that "Jonathan" is an error for "Johanan." Further complicating the identification are attempts to identify this high priest with a "Johanan" mentioned in the Elephantine papyri (see chart, p. xxii) and in Josephus (*Antiquities*, 11.7.1). Such an identification, however, is disputable.

12:12–21 All but one (Hattush, v. 2) of the 22 priestly families listed in vv. 1–7 are repeated (Rehum, v. 3, is a variant of Harim, v. 15; Mijamin, v. 5, is a variant of Miniamin, v. 17) in this later list, which dates to the time of Joiakim (v. 12), high priest in the late sixth and/or early fifth centuries B.C.

12:22 *Darius the Persian.* Either Darius II Nothus (423–404 B.C.) or Darius III Codomannus (336–331).

12:23 *book of the annals.* Cf. 7:5. This may have been the official temple chronicle, containing various lists and records. Cf. the annals of the Persian kings (Ezr 4:15; Est 2:23; 6:1; 10:2); cf. also the "book of the annals of the kings," mentioned frequently in 1, 2 Kings.

12:26 *Nehemiah ... Ezra.* See note on 8:9.

12:27 *dedication.* See note on Ezr 6:16. *cymbals.* See note on Ezr 3:10. Cymbals were used in religious ceremonies (1Ch 16:42; 25:1; 2Ch 5:12; 29:25). Ancient examples have been found at Beth Shemesh and Tell Abu Hawam. *harps.* See note on Ge 31:27; used mainly in religious ceremonies (1Sa 10:5; 2Sa 6:5; Ps 150:3). Ancient harps have been reconstructed from information derived from the remains of harps at Ur, pictures of harps, and cuneiform texts describing in detail the tuning of harps. *lyres.* Had strings of the same length but of different diameters and tensions (see 1Ch 15:16; Da 3:5).

12:28 *Netophathites.* From Netophah, a town near Bethlehem (7:26).

12:29 *Beth Gilgal.* Perhaps the Gilgal near Jericho (see note on Jos 4:19), or the Gilgal of Elijah (2Ki 2:1), about seven miles north of Bethel.

12:30 *purified.* See note on Lev 4:12. The Levites are said to have purified all that was sacred in the temple (1Ch 23:28) and the temple itself (2Ch 29:15) during times of revival. Ritual purity was intended to teach God's holiness and moral purity (Lev 16:30).

12:31 *two large choirs.* See note on v. 38. The two great processions probably started from the area of the Valley Gate (2:13,15; 3:13) near the center of the western section of the wall. The first procession, led by Ezra (v. 36), moved in a counterclockwise direction upon the wall; the second, with Nehemiah (v. 38), moved in a clockwise direction. Both met between the Water Gate (v. 37) and the Gate of the Guard (v. 39), then entered the temple area. Cf. Ps 48:12–13. *to the right.* Or "to the south." Semites oriented themselves facing east, so the right hand represented the south (see Jos 17:7; 1Sa 23:24; Job 23:9). *Dung Gate.* See note on 2:13.

12:35 *trumpets.* See note on Ezr 3:10. Each choir had priests blowing trumpets, as well as Levites playing other musical instruments.

of Micaiah, the son of Zaccur, the son of
Asaph, 36and his associates—Shemaiah,
Azarel, Milalai, Gilalai, Maai, Nethanel,
Judah and Hanani—with musical instruments[y] ⌊prescribed by⌋ David the man of
God.[z] Ezra[a] the scribe led the procession.
37At the Fountain Gate[b] they continued directly up the steps of the City of David on
the ascent to the wall and passed above
the house of David to the Water Gate[c] on
the east.

38The second choir proceeded in the opposite direction. I followed them on top[a]
of the wall, together with half the people—past the Tower of the Ovens[d] to the
Broad Wall,[e] 39over the Gate of Ephraim,[f]
the Jeshanah[b] Gate,[g] the Fish Gate,[h] the
Tower of Hananel[i] and the Tower of the
Hundred,[j] as far as the Sheep Gate.[k] At the
Gate of the Guard they stopped.

40The two choirs that gave thanks then
took their places in the house of God; so
did I, together with half the officials, 41as
well as the priests—Eliakim, Maaseiah,
Miniamin, Micaiah, Elioenai, Zechariah
and Hananiah with their trumpets— 42and
also Maaseiah, Shemaiah, Eleazar, Uzzi,
Jehohanan, Malkijah, Elam and Ezer. The
choirs sang under the direction of Jezra-
hiah. 43And on that day they offered great
sacrifices, rejoicing because God had giv-
en them great joy. The women and children also rejoiced. The sound of rejoicing
in Jerusalem could be heard far away.

44At that time men were appointed to be
in charge of the storerooms[l] for the contributions, firstfruits and tithes.[m] From the
fields around the towns they were to bring
into the storerooms the portions required
by the Law for the priests and the Levites,
for Judah was pleased with the ministering priests and Levites.[n] 45They performed
the service of their God and the service
of purification, as did also the singers and
gatekeepers, according to the commands
of David[o] and his son Solomon.[p] 46For long
ago, in the days of David and Asaph,[q] there
had been directors for the singers and for
the songs of praise[r] and thanksgiving to
God. 47So in the days of Zerubbabel and of
Nehemiah, all Israel contributed the daily
portions for the singers and gatekeepers.
They also set aside the portion for the other Levites, and the Levites set aside the
portion for the descendants of Aaron.[s]

Nehemiah's Final Reforms

13 On that day the Book of Moses was
read aloud in the hearing of the people
and there it was found written that no Ammonite or Moabite should ever be admitted
into the assembly of God,[t] 2because they
had not met the Israelites with food and
water but had hired Balaam[u] to call a curse
down on them.[v] (Our God, however, turned
the curse into a blessing.)[w] 3When the people heard this law, they excluded from Israel all who were of foreign descent.[x]

4Before this, Eliashib the priest had
been put in charge of the storerooms[y] of
the house of our God. He was closely associated with Tobiah,[z] 5and he had provided him with a large room formerly used
to store the grain offerings and incense
and temple articles, and also the tithes[a] of
grain, new wine and oil prescribed for the
Levites, singers and gatekeepers, as well
as the contributions for the priests.

6But while all this was going on, I was
not in Jerusalem, for in the thirty-second
year of Artaxerxes[b] king of Babylon I had
returned to the king. Some time later I
asked his permission 7and came back to Jerusalem. Here I learned about the evil thing
Eliashib[c] had done in providing Tobiah[d]
a room in the courts of the house of God.

[a] 38 Or *them alongside* [b] 39 Or *Old*

12:36 [y] S 1Ch 15:16 [z] S 2Ch 8:14 [a] Ezr 7:6 **12:37** [b] S Ne 2:14 [c] S Ne 3:26 **12:38** [d] Ne 3:11 [e] Ne 3:8 **12:39** [f] S 2Ki 14:13 [g] Ne 3:6 [h] S 2Ch 33:14 [i] S Ne 3:1 [j] Ne 3:1 [k] S Ne 3:1 **12:44** [l] Ne 13:4,13 [m] S Lev 27:30 [n] S Dt 18:8 **12:45** [o] S 2Ch 8:14 [p] S 1Ch 6:31; 23:5 **12:46** [q] S 2Ch 35:15 [r] 2Ch 29:27; Ps 137:4 **12:47** [s] S Dt 18:8 **13:1** [t] ver 23; Dt 23:3 **13:2** [u] Nu 22:3-11 [v] S Nu 23:7; S Dt 23:3 [w] S Nu 23:11; Dt 23:4-5 **13:3** [x] ver 23; S Ne 9:2 **13:4** [y] S Ne 12:44 [z] Ne 2:10 **13:5** [a] S Lev 27:30; S Nu 18:21 **13:6** [b] S Ne 2:6 **13:7** [c] S Ezr 10:24 [d] S Ne 2:10

12:35 *Asaph.* See note on 11:17.
12:36 *Ezra the scribe.* See notes on Ezr 7:1,6.
12:37 *Fountain Gate.* See note on 2:14. *City of David.* See 3:15; see also note on 2Sa 5:7. *house of David.* Probably the ancient site of David's or Solomon's palace (see 3:25 and note). *Water Gate.* See note on 3:26.
12:38 *choir.* Lit. "thanks," i.e., "thanksgiving choir" (see v. 40). *Tower of the Ovens.* See note on 3:11. *Broad Wall.* See note on 3:8.
12:39 *Gate of Ephraim.* See notes on 3:6; 8:16. *Jeshanah Gate.* See note on 3:6. *Fish Gate.* See note on 3:3. *Tower of Hananel ... Tower of the Hundred ... Sheep Gate.* See note on 3:1. *Gate of the Guard.* Cf. Jer 32:2.
12:43 *God had given them great joy.* See 1Ch 29:9. *women.* See 8:2; Ex 15:20 and notes. *heard far away.* See note on Ezr 3:13; cf. 1Ki 1:40; 2Ki 11:13.
12:44 *Judah was pleased.* The people cheerfully contributed their offerings to support the priests and Levites (cf. 2Co 9:7). *ministering.* See Dt 10:8.
12:46 *Asaph.* See note on 11:17.
12:47 *Zerubbabel.* See Ezr 1:2 and note. *contributed.* The Hebrew for this verb implies continued giving.
13:1–2 See Dt 23:3–6.
13:2 *Balaam.* See notes on Nu 22:5,8.
13:4 *Eliashib.* See note on 12:10. *Tobiah.* See note on 2:10.
13:5 *provided him with a large room.* During Nehemiah's absence from the city to return to the Persian king's court, Tobiah, one of his archenemies, had used his influence with Eliashib to gain entrance into a chamber ordinarily set aside for the storage of tithes and other offerings (see 10:37 and note; cf. Nu 18:21–32; Dt 14:28–29; 26:12–15). Elsewhere we read of the chamber of Meshullam (3:30) and of Jehohanan (Ezr 10:6).
13:6 *thirty-second year of Artaxerxes.* See note on 5:14. *king of Babylon.* The title was assumed by Cyrus after his conquest of Babylon (see Ezr 5:13) and was adopted by subsequent Achaemenid (Persian) kings.
13:7 *came back to Jerusalem.* Nehemiah's second term must have ended before 407 B.C., when Bagohi (Bigvai) was governor of Judah according to the Elephantine papyri. Some have suggested that after Nehemiah's first term he was succeeded by his brother Hanani (see note on 1:2). *courts.* See note on 8:16. Zerubbabel's temple had two courtyards (Zec 3:7; cf. Isa 62:9).

8 I was greatly displeased and threw all Tobiah's household goods out of the room.[e]
9 I gave orders to purify the rooms,[f] and
then I put back into them the equipment
of the house of God, with the grain offerings and the incense.[g]
10 I also learned that the portions assigned to the Levites had not been given to
them,[h] and that all the Levites and singers
responsible for the service had gone back
to their own fields.[i] 11 So I rebuked the officials and asked them, "Why is the house
of God neglected?"[j] Then I called them together and stationed them at their posts.
12 All Judah brought the tithes[k] of grain,
new wine and oil into the storerooms.[l]
13 I put Shelemiah the priest, Zadok the
scribe, and a Levite named Pedaiah in
charge of the storerooms and made Hanan son of Zaccur, the son of Mattaniah,
their assistant, because these men were
considered trustworthy. They were made
responsible for distributing the supplies to
their brothers.[m]

14 Remember[n] me for this, O my God, and
do not blot out what I have so faithfully
done for the house of my God and its services.

15 In those days I saw men in Judah treading winepresses on the Sabbath and bringing in grain and loading it on donkeys, together with wine, grapes, figs and all other
kinds of loads. And they were bringing all
this into Jerusalem on the Sabbath.[o] Therefore I warned them against selling food
on that day. 16 Men from Tyre who lived
in Jerusalem were bringing in fish and all
kinds of merchandise and selling them in
Jerusalem on the Sabbath[p] to the people of
Judah. 17 I rebuked the nobles of Judah and
said to them, "What is this wicked thing
you are doing—desecrating the Sabbath
day? 18 Didn't your forefathers do the same
things, so that our God brought all this calamity upon us and upon this city?[q] Now
you are stirring up more wrath against Israel by desecrating the Sabbath."[r]
19 When evening shadows fell on the gates
of Jerusalem before the Sabbath,[s] I ordered
the doors to be shut and not opened until
the Sabbath was over. I stationed some of
my own men at the gates so that no load
could be brought in on the Sabbath day.
20 Once or twice the merchants and sellers
of all kinds of goods spent the night outside Jerusalem. 21 But I warned them and
said, "Why do you spend the night by the
wall? If you do this again, I will lay hands
on you." From that time on they no longer
came on the Sabbath. 22 Then I commanded the Levites to purify themselves and go
and guard the gates in order to keep the
Sabbath day holy.

Remember[t] me for this also, O my God,
and show mercy to me according to your
great love.

13:8 [e] Mt 21:12-13; Mk 11:15-17; Lk 19:45-46; Jn 2:13-16 **13:9** [f] S 1Ch 23:28; S 2Ch 29:5 [g] S Lev 2:1 **13:10** [h] S Dt 12:19 [i] S 2Ch 31:4 **13:11** [j] S Ne 10:37-39; Hag 1:1-9; Mal 3:8-9 **13:12** [k] S 2Ch 31:6 [l] S Dt 18:8; 1Ki 7:51; S 2Ch 31:5; S Ne 10:37-39; Mal 3:10 **13:13** [m] S Ne 12:44; Ac 6:1-5 **13:14** [n] S Ge 8:1; S 2Ki 20:3 **13:15** [o] Ex 20:8-11; S 34:21; Dt 5:12-15 **13:16** [p] S Ne 10:31 **13:18** [q] Jer 44:23 [r] S Ne 10:31 **13:19** [s] Lev 23:32 **13:22** [t] S Ge 8:1; S Ne 1:8

13:8 *displeased ... threw.* Nehemiah expressed his indignation by taking action (cf. vv. 24–25; 5:6–7). Contrast the reaction of Ezra, who "sat down appalled" (Ezr 9:3). Nehemiah's action reminds us of Christ's expulsion of the money changers from the temple area (Mt 21:12–13).

13:9 *rooms.* Though only a single chamber was mentioned in vv. 5–8, additional rooms were involved. A parallel to the occupation and desecration of the temple by Tobiah comes from a century earlier in Egypt, where Greek mercenaries had occupied the temple of Neith at Sais. Upon the appeal of the Egyptian priest, Udjahorresnet, the Persian king had the squatters driven out and the temple's ceremonies, processions and revenues restored: "And His Majesty commanded that all the foreigners who had settled in the temple of Neith should be driven out and that all their houses and all their superfluities that were in this temple should be thrown down, and that all their own baggage should be carried for them outside the wall of this temple."

13:10 Nehemiah was apparently correcting an abuse of long standing.

13:11 *neglected.* See note on 10:39.

13:12 *tithes.* See 12:44. Temples in Mesopotamia also levied temple taxes for the support of their personnel.

13:13 Of the four treasurers, one was a priest, one a Levite, one a scribe and one a layman of rank. *trustworthy.* Nehemiah appointed honest men to make sure that supplies were distributed equitably—just as later the church appointed deacons for this purpose (Ac 6:1–5).

13:15 *treading winepresses.* See notes on Isa 5:2; 16:10. *Sabbath.* The temptation to violate the Sabbath rest was especially characteristic of non-Jewish merchants (see 10:31; Isa 56:1–8). On the other hand, the high regard that some Jews had for the Sabbath was expressed by parents who called their children Shabbethai (see 8:7; 11:16; Ezr 10:15).

13:16 *Tyre.* See note on Isa 23:1. *fish.* Fish imported from Tyre (see Eze 26:4–5,14) would have been dried and salted. Fish was an important part of the Israelite diet, but much of it came from the Sea of Galilee (Lev 11:9; Nu 11:5; Mt 15:34; Lk 24:42; Jn 21:5–13). It was sold at the market near the Fish Gate (see note on 3:3).

13:17–18 *desecrating the Sabbath.* Cf. Ex 16:28–29; Nu 15:32–36; Isa 58:13–14; Jer 17:19–27; Am 8:5,7–8. "Desecrating" means turning what is sacred into common use and so profaning it (see Mal 2:10–11).

13:17 *rebuked the nobles.* Because they were the leaders in desecrating the Sabbath.

13:19 *When evening shadows fell on the gates.* Before sunset, when the Sabbath began. The Israelites, like the Babylonians, counted their days from sunset to sunset (the Egyptians reckoned theirs from dawn to dawn). The precise moment when the Sabbath began was heralded by the blowing of a trumpet by a priest. According to a later tradition preserved in the Jewish Mishnah, "On the eve of Sabbath they used to blow six more blasts, three to cause the people to cease from work and three to mark the break between the sacred and the profane." And Josephus (*Wars*, 4.9.12) speaks of the location on the parapet of the temple where the priests "gave a signal beforehand, with a trumpet, at the beginning of every seventh day, in the evening twilight, and also at the evening when that day was finished, announcing to the people the respective hours for ceasing work and for resuming their labors." Excavators at the temple mount recovered a stone from the southwest corner of the parapet, which had fallen to the ground in Titus's siege, with the inscription "for the place of the blowing (of the trumpet)."

13:22 *Remember me.* See note on 1:8.

23Moreover, in those days I saw men
of Judah who had married[u] women from
Ashdod, Ammon and Moab.[v] 24Half of
their children spoke the language of Ashdod or the language of one of the other
peoples, and did not know how to speak
the language[w] of Judah. 25I rebuked them
and called curses down on them. I beat
some of the men and pulled out their
hair. I made them take an oath[x] in God's
name and said: "You are not to give your
daughters in marriage to their sons, nor
are you to take their daughters in marriage
for your sons or for yourselves.[y] 26Was it
not because of marriages like these that
Solomon king of Israel sinned? Among the
many nations there was no king like him.[z]
He was loved by his God,[a] and God made
him king over all Israel, but even he was
led into sin by foreign women.[b] 27Must
we hear now that you too are doing all
this terrible wickedness and are being unfaithful to our God by marrying[c] foreign
women?"

28One of the sons of Joiada son of Eliashib[d] the high priest was son-in-law to
Sanballat[e] the Horonite. And I drove him
away from me.

29Remember[f] them, O my God, because
they defiled the priestly office and the
covenant of the priesthood and of the Levites.[g]

30So I purified the priests and the Levites
of everything foreign,[h] and assigned them
duties, each to his own task. 31I also made
provision for contributions of wood[i] at
designated times, and for the firstfruits.[j]

Remember[k] me with favor, O my God.

13:23 [u] Ezr 9:1-2; Mal 2:11 [v] ver 1; S ver 1, S 3; Ex 34:16; S Ru 1:4; S Ne 10:30
13:24 [w] Est 1:22; 3:12; 8:9
13:25 [x] S Ezr 10:5 [y] S Ex 34:16
13:26 [z] S 1Ki 3:13; S 2Ch 1:12 [a] 2Sa 12:25 [b] S Ex 34:16; S 1Ki 11:3
13:27 [c] Ezr 9:14
13:28 [d] S Ezr 10:24 [e] S Ne 2:10
13:29 [f] S Ne 1:8 [g] S Nu 3:12
13:30 [h] S Ne 9:2
13:31 [i] Ne 10:34 [j] Ne 10:35-36 [k] S Ge 8:1; S Ne 1:8

13:23 Ezra had dealt with the same problem of intermarriage some 25 years before (see note on Ezr 9:1). *Ashdod.* See 4:7; Isa 20:1 and notes. *Ammon and Moab.* See note on Ge 19:36–38.

13:25 *pulled out their hair.* See Ezr 9:3; Isa 50:6 and notes. *You are not to give.* Nehemiah's action was designed to prevent future intermarriages, whereas Ezra dissolved the existing unions.

13:26 *Solomon.* Israel's outstanding king in terms of wealth and political achievements (1Ki 3:13; 2Ch 1:12). Solomon began his reign by humbly asking for wisdom from the LORD (1Ki 3:5–9). *he was led into sin.* In later years his foreign wives led him to worship other gods (1Ki 11:4). And he also built high places for the false gods his foreign wives worshiped (1Ki 11:7–8).

13:28 *son-in-law to Sanballat.* According to Lev 21:14 the high priest was not to marry a foreigner. The expulsion of Joiada's son followed either this special ban or the general prohibition against intermarriage. The union described in this verse was especially rankling to Nehemiah in the light of Sanballat's enmity (see 2:10). Josephus (*Antiquities*, 11.7.2) records that an almost identical episode, involving a marriage between the daughter of a Sanballat of Samaria and the brother of the Jewish high priest, took place a little over a century later in the time of Alexander the Great.

13:30 *duties.* Or "divisions," referring to the assignment of particular duties to groups of priests and Levites, possibly on a rotating basis (see note on 12:9).

13:31 *wood.* See 10:34 and note. *Remember me with favor.* The last recorded words of Nehemiah recapitulate a theme running through the final chapter (vv. 14,22; see note on 1:8). His motive throughout his ministry was to please and to serve his divine Sovereign.

Esther

INTRODUCTION

Author and Date

Although we do not know who wrote the book of Esther, from internal evidence it is possible to make some inferences about the author and the date of composition. It is clear that the author was a Jew, both from his emphasis on the origin of a Jewish festival and from the Jewish nationalism that permeates the story. The author's knowledge of Persian customs, the setting of the story in the city of Susa and the absence of any reference to conditions or circumstances in the land of Judah suggest that he was a resident of a Persian city. The earliest date for the book would be shortly after the events narrated, i.e., c. 460 B.C. (before Ezra's return to Jerusalem; see note on 8:12). Internal evidence also suggests that the festival of Purim had been observed for some time prior to the actual writing of the book (9:19) and that Xerxes had already died (see 10:2 and note). Several scholars have dated the book later than 330 B.C.; the absence of Greek words and the style of the author's Hebrew dialect, however, suggest that the book must have been written before the Persian empire fell to Greece in 331.

A Quick Look

Author:
Unknown

Audience:
The Jewish people

Date:
Sometime after 460 B.C.

Theme:
The book of Esther describes how the Jews of Persia are saved from certain destruction through divine providence.

Purpose, Themes and Literary Features

The author's central purpose was to record the institution of the annual festival of Purim and to keep alive for later generations the memory of the great deliverance of the Jewish people during the reign of Xerxes. The book accounts for both the initiation of that observance and the obligation for its perpetual commemoration (see 3:7; 9:26 – 32; see also chart, pp. 178 – 179).

Throughout much of the story the author calls to mind the ongoing conflict between Israel and the Amalekites (see notes on 2:5; 3:1 – 6; 9:5 – 10), a conflict that began during the exodus (Ex 17:8 – 16; Dt 25:17 – 19) and continued through Israel's history (1Sa 15; 1Ch 4:43; and, of course, Esther). As the first to attack Israel after their deliverance from Egypt, the Amalekites were viewed — and the author of Esther views them — as the epitome of all the powers of the world arrayed against God's people (see Nu 24:20; 1Sa 15:2 – 3; 28:18). Now that Israel has been released from captivity, Haman's edict is the final major effort in the OT period to destroy them.

Closely associated with the conflict with the Amalekites is the rest that is promised to the people of God (see Dt 25:19). With Haman's defeat the Jews enjoy rest from their enemies (9:16,22).

The author also draws upon the remnant motif that recurs throughout the Bible (natural disasters, disease, warfare or other calamities threaten God's people; those who survive constitute a remnant). Events in the Persian city of Susa threatened the continuity of God's purposes in redemptive history. The future existence of God's chosen people, and ultimately the appearance of the Redeemer-Messiah, are jeopardized by Haman's edict to destroy the Jews. The author of Esther patterned much of his material on the events of the Joseph story (see notes on 2:3–4,9,21–23; 3:4; 4:14; 6:1,8,14; 8:6), in which the remnant motif is also central to the narrative (see Ge 45:7 and note).

The future existence of God's chosen people, and ultimately the appearance of the Redeemer-Messiah, are jeopardized by Haman's edict to destroy the Jews.

Feasting is another prominent theme in Esther, as shown in the outline below. Banquets provide the setting for important plot developments. There are ten banquets: (1) 1:3–4, (2) 1:5–8, (3) 1:9, (4) 2:18, (5) 3:15, (6) 5:5–6, (7) 7:1–10, (8) 8:17, (9) 9:17, (10) 9:18. The three pairs of banquets that mark the beginning, middle and end of the story are particularly prominent: the two banquets given by Xerxes, the two prepared by Esther and the double celebration of Purim.

Recording duplications appears to be one of the favorite compositional techniques of the writer. In addition to the three groups of banquets that come in pairs there are two lists of the king's servants (1:10,14), two reports that Esther concealed her identity (2:10,20), two gatherings of women (2:8,19), two fasts (4:3,16), two consultations of Haman with his wife and friends (5:14; 6:13), two unscheduled appearances of Esther before the king (5:2; 8:3), two investitures for Mordecai (6:10–11; 8:15), two coverings of Haman's face (6:12; 7:8), two royal edicts (3:12–15; 8:1–14), two references to the subsiding of the king's anger (2:1; 7:10), two references to the irrevocability of the Persian laws (1:19; 8:8), two days for the Jews to take vengeance (9:5–12,13–15) and two letters instituting the commemoration of Purim (9:20–28,29–32).

An outstanding feature of this book—one that has given rise to considerable discussion—is the complete absence of any explicit reference to God, worship, prayer, or sacrifice. This "secularity" has produced many detractors who have judged the book to be of little religious value. However, it appears that the author has deliberately refrained from mentioning God or any religious activity as a literary device to heighten the fact that it is God who controls and directs all the seemingly insignificant coincidences (see, e.g., note on 6:1) that make up the plot and issue in deliverance for the Jews. God's sovereign rule is assumed at every point (see notes on 4:12–16; 6:1), an assumption made all the more effective by the total absence of reference to him. It becomes clear to the careful reader that Israel's Great King exercises his providential and sovereign control over all the vicissitudes of his beleaguered covenant people.

Outline

I. The Feasts of Xerxes (1:1—2:18)
  A. Vashti Deposed (ch. 1)
  B. Esther Made Queen (2:1–18)
II. The Feasts of Esther (2:19—7:10)
  A. Mordecai Uncovers a Plot (2:19–23)
  B. Haman's Plot (ch. 3)
  C. Mordecai Persuades Esther to Help (ch. 4)
  D. Esther's Request to the King: Her First Banquet (5:1–8)
  E. A Sleepless Night (5:9—6:14)
  F. Haman Hanged: Esther's Second Banquet (ch. 7)
III. The Feasts of Purim (chs. 8–10)
  A. The King's Edict in Behalf of the Jews (ch. 8)
  B. The Institution of Purim (ch. 9)
  C. The Promotion of Mordecai (ch. 10)

Queen Vashti Deposed

1 This is what happened during the time
of Xerxes,[a][a] the Xerxes who ruled over
127 provinces[b] stretching from India to
Cush[b]:[c] 2At that time King Xerxes reigned
from his royal throne in the citadel of
Susa,[d] 3and in the third year of his reign
he gave a banquet[e] for all his nobles and
officials. The military leaders of Persia and
Media, the princes, and the nobles of the
provinces were present.
4For a full 180 days he displayed the
vast wealth of his kingdom and the splendor and glory of his majesty. 5When these
days were over, the king gave a banquet,
lasting seven days,[f] in the enclosed garden[g] of the king's palace, for all the people
from the least to the greatest, who were in
the citadel of Susa. 6The garden had hang-
ings of white and blue linen, fastened with
cords of white linen and purple material to
silver rings on marble pillars. There were
couches[h] of gold and silver on a mosaic
pavement of porphyry, marble, mother-of-
pearl and other costly stones. 7Wine was
served in goblets of gold, each one different from the other, and the royal wine was
abundant, in keeping with the king's liberality.[i] 8By the king's command each guest
was allowed to drink in his own way, for
the king instructed all the wine stewards
to serve each man what he wished.
9Queen Vashti also gave a banquet[j] for
the women in the royal palace of King
Xerxes.
10On the seventh day, when King Xerxes
was in high spirits[k] from wine,[l] he commanded the seven eunuchs who served
him — Mehuman, Biztha, Harbona,[m]
Bigtha, Abagtha, Zethar and Carcas —
11to bring[n] before him Queen Vashti,
wearing her royal crown, in order to
display her beauty[o] to the people and
nobles, for she was lovely to look at.
12But when the attendants delivered the
king's command, Queen Vashti refused
to come. Then the king became furious
and burned with anger.[p]
13Since it was customary for the king
to consult experts in matters of law and
justice, he spoke with the wise men who
understood the times[q] 14and were closest
to the king — Carshena, Shethar, Admatha,
Tarshish, Meres, Marsena and Memucan,
the seven nobles[r] of Persia and Media who
had special access to the king and were
highest in the kingdom.
15"According to law, what must be done
to Queen Vashti?" he asked. "She has not
obeyed the command of King Xerxes that
the eunuchs have taken to her."
16Then Memucan replied in the presence of the king and the nobles, "Queen
Vashti has done wrong, not only against
the king but also against all the nobles and
the peoples of all the provinces of King
Xerxes. 17For the queen's conduct will become known to all the women, and so
they will despise their husbands and say,
'King Xerxes commanded Queen Vashti
to be brought before him, but she would
not come.' 18This very day the Persian and
Median women of the nobility who have
heard about the queen's conduct will respond to all the king's nobles in the same
way. There will be no end of disrespect
and discord.[s]

1:1 [a]S Ezr 4:6 [b]Est 9:30; Da 3:2; 6:1 [c]Est 8:9 **1:2** [d]S Ezr 4:9; S Est 2:8 **1:3** [e]S 1Ki 3:15 **1:5** [f]Jdg 14:17 [g]S 2Ki 21:18 **1:6** [h]Est 7:8; Eze 23:41; Am 3:12; 6:4 **1:7** [i]Est 2:18; Da 5:2 **1:9** [j]S 1Ki 3:15 **1:10** [k]S Jdg 16:25; S Ru 3:7 [l]S Ge 14:18; Est 3:15; 5:6; 7:2; Pr 31:4-7; Da 5:1-4 [m]Est 7:9 **1:11** [n]SS 2:4 [o]Ps 45:11; Eze 16:14 **1:12** [p]Ge 39:19; Est 2:21; 7:7; Pr 19:12 **1:13** [q]1Ch 12:32 **1:14** [r]Ezr 7:14 **1:18** [s]Pr 19:13; 27:15

[a] *1* Hebrew *Ahasuerus,* a variant of Xerxes' Persian name; here and throughout Esther [b] *1* That is, the upper Nile region

1:1 *Xerxes.* A transliteration of the Greek form of the Persian name Khshayarshan (see NIV text note). Xerxes succeeded his father Darius and ruled 486 – 465 B.C. (see chart, p. 472). *127 provinces.* See 8:9. The Greek historian Herodotus (3.89) records that Xerxes's father Darius had organized the empire into 20 satrapies. (Satraps, the rulers of the satrapies, are mentioned in 3:12; 8:9; 9:3.) The provinces were smaller administrative units.

1:2 *citadel of Susa.* The fortified acropolis and palace complex; it is distinguished from the surrounding city in 3:15; 8:14 – 15. Several archaeological investigations have been made at the site since the mid – 19th century. Xerxes had made extensive renovations in the palace structures. *Susa.* The winter residence of the Persian kings (see note on Ezr 4:9). The three other capitals were Ecbatana (see Ezr 6:2 and note), Babylon and Persepolis. One of Daniel's visions was set in Susa (Da 8:2); Nehemiah also served there (Ne 1:1).

1:3 – 4 The year (483 – 482 B.C.), the persons in attendance and the length of the meeting suggest that the purpose of the gathering may have been to plan for the disastrous campaigns of 482 – 479 against Greece. Herodotus (7.8) possibly describes this assembly.

1:3 *banquet.* Feasting is a prominent theme in Esther (see Introduction: Purpose, Themes and Literary Features).

1:5 – 6 The excavations at Susa have unearthed a text in which Xerxes's father Darius describes in some detail the building of his palace. Xerxes continued the work his father had begun.

1:9 *Queen Vashti.* Deposed in 484/483 B.C.; Esther became queen in 479/478 (2:16 – 17). The Greek historians call Xerxes's queen Amestris; they record her influence during the early part of his reign and as queen mother during the following reign of her son Artaxerxes (Ezr 7:1,7,11 – 12,21; 8:1; Ne 2:1; 5:14; 13:6) until the time of her own death c. 424. Artaxerxes came to the throne when he was 18 years old; therefore he was born c. 484/483, approximately at the time when Vashti was deposed. Since he was the third son of Amestris, the name Amestris cannot be identified with Esther and must be viewed as a Greek version of the name Vashti. Comparatively little is known of the late portions of Xerxes's reign, nor is it possible to determine the subsequent events of the life of Esther. Apparently after Esther's death or her fall from favor, Vashti was able to reassert her power and to exercise a controlling influence over her son.

1:12 *refused to come.* We are not told why.

1:13 – 14 Ezr 7:14 and the Greek historian Herodotus indicate that seven men functioned as the immediate advisers to the king.

19“Therefore, if it pleases the king,[t] let
him issue a royal decree and let it be written in the laws of Persia and Media, which
cannot be repealed,[u] that Vashti is never
again to enter the presence of King Xerxes.
Also let the king give her royal position
to someone else who is better than she.
20Then when the king's edict is proclaimed
throughout all his vast realm, all the wom-
en will respect their husbands, from the
least to the greatest.”
21The king and his nobles were pleased
with this advice, so the king did as Memucan proposed. 22He sent dispatches to
all parts of the kingdom, to each province
in its own script and to each people in its
own language,[v] proclaiming in each people's tongue that every man should be
ruler over his own household.

Esther Made Queen

2 Later when the anger of King Xerxes
had subsided,[w] he remembered Vashti
and what she had done and what he had
decreed about her. 2Then the king's personal attendants proposed, “Let a search
be made for beautiful young virgins for the
king. 3Let the king appoint commissioners
in every province of his realm to bring all
these beautiful girls into the harem at the
citadel of Susa. Let them be placed under
the care of Hegai, the king's eunuch, who
is in charge of the women; and let beauty treatments be given to them. 4Then let
the girl who pleases the king be queen instead of Vashti.” This advice appealed to
the king, and he followed it.
5Now there was in the citadel of Susa a
Jew of the tribe of Benjamin, named Mordecai son of Jair, the son of Shimei, the
son of Kish,[x] 6who had been carried into
exile from Jerusalem by Nebuchadnezzar king of Babylon, among those taken
captive with Jehoiachin[a][y] king of Judah.[z]
7Mordecai had a cousin named Hadassah,
whom he had brought up because she had
neither father nor mother. This girl, who
was also known as Esther,[a] was lovely[b] in
form and features, and Mordecai had tak-
en her as his own daughter when her father and mother died.
8When the king's order and edict had
been proclaimed, many girls were brought
to the citadel of Susa[c] and put under the
care of Hegai. Esther also was taken to the
king's palace and entrusted to Hegai, who

1:19 [t] Ecc 8:4 [u] Est 8:8; Da 6:8, 12
1:22 [v] S Ne 13:24
2:1 [w] Est 7:10
2:5 [x] S 1Sa 9:1
2:6 [y] S 2Ki 24:6, 15 [z] Da 1:1-5; 5:13
2:7 [a] Ge 41:45 [b] S Ge 39:6
2:8 [c] Ne 1:1; Est 1:2; Da 8:2

[a] 6 Hebrew *Jeconiah,* a variant of *Jehoiachin*

1:19 *cannot be repealed.* The irrevocability of Persian laws is mentioned in 8:8 and Da 6:8,12. *never again to enter.* The punishment corresponds to the crime: Since Vashti refused to appear before the king, it is decreed that she never appear before him again. Furthermore, from this point on she is no longer given the title “Queen” in the book of Esther.

1:22 *proclaiming ... household.* Or “that every man should be ruler over his own household and that his native language should be used in the home,” thus referring to the practice in ethnically mixed marriages of using the husband's native language as a sign of his rule in the home (see Ne 13:23–25).

2:1 *Later.* Esther was taken to Xerxes “in the seventh year of his reign” (v. 16), i.e., in December, 479 B.C., or January, 478. The Greek wars intervened before a new queen was sought (see note on 1:3–4).

2:2 *virgins for the king.* To add to his harem.

2:3–4 The phraseology here is similar to that in Ge 41:34–37. This and numerous other parallels suggest that the author of Esther modeled his work after the Joseph story (see Introduction: Purpose, Themes and Literary Features). Both accounts are set in the courts of foreign monarchs and portray Israelite heroes who rise to prominence and provide the means by which their people are saved (see notes on vv. 9,21–23; 3:4; 4:14; 6:1,8,14; 8:6).

2:5 *in the citadel of Susa a Jew.* As far back as the fall of the northern kingdom in 722–721 B.C. Israelites had been exiled among the cities of the Medes (2Ki 17:6). After the conquest of Babylon by King Cyrus of Persia in 539, some of the Jewish population taken there by the Babylonians (605–586) probably moved eastward into the cities of Medo-Persia. Only 50,000 returned to Israel in the restoration of 538/537 (Ezr 2:64–65). The presence of a large Jewish population in Medo-Persia is confirmed by the discovery of an archive of texts in Nippur (southern Mesopotamia) from the period of Artaxerxes I (465–424) and Darius II (424–405). This archive contains the names of about 100 Jews who lived in that city. Some had attained positions of importance and wealth (see map, p. 672, item 4, and chart, p. xxiii). Similar Jewish populations are probable in many other Medo-Persian cities. *Mordecai.* The name is derived from that of the Babylonian deity Marduk. There are numerous examples in the Bible of Israelites having double names—a Hebrew name and a “Gentile” name. Mordecai likely had a Hebrew name, as did Esther (v. 7), Daniel and his friends (Da 1:6–7), Joseph (Ge 41:45) and others, but the text does not mention Mordecai's Hebrew name. A cuneiform tablet from Borsippa near Babylon mentions a scribe by the name of Mardukaya; he was an accountant or minister at the court of Susa in the early years of Xerxes. Many interpreters identify him with Mordecai. *son of Jair, the son of Shimei, the son of Kish.* The persons named could be immediate ancestors, in which case Mordecai would be the great-grandson of a Kish who was among the exiles with Jehoiachin in 597 B.C. It is more likely, however, that the names refer to remote ancestors in the tribe of Benjamin (see 2Sa 16:5 for Shimei, 1Sa 9:1 for Kish). This association with the tribe and family of King Saul sets the stage for the ongoing conflict between Israel and the Amalekites (see notes on 3:1–6). If the names are those of remote ancestors, the clause “who had been carried into exile” (v. 6) would not apply to Mordecai, who would have been over 100 years old in that case; rather, it would have to be taken as an elliptical construction in the sense “whose family had been carried into exile.”

2:6 *carried into exile.* In 597 B.C. *Jehoiachin king of Judah.* See 2Ki 24:8–17; 2Ch 36:9–10.

2:7 *Hadassah.* Esther's Hebrew name, meaning “myrtle.” The name Esther is likely derived from the Persian word for “star,” though some derive it from the name of the Babylonian goddess Ishtar (see note on Jer 7:18). If the latter, it would parallel the derivation of her cousin Mordecai's name from that of the Babylonian god Marduk (see note on v. 5).

2:8 *Esther also was taken.* Neither she nor Mordecai would have had any choice in the matter (cf. 2Sa 11:4).

had charge of the harem. 9 The girl pleased
him and won his favor.[d] Immediately he
provided her with her beauty treatments
and special food.[e] He assigned to her sev-
en maids selected from the king's palace
and moved her and her maids into the
best place in the harem.
10 Esther had not revealed her nationality
and family background, because Mordecai
had forbidden her to do so.[f] 11 Every day he
walked back and forth near the courtyard
of the harem to find out how Esther was
and what was happening to her.
12 Before a girl's turn came to go in to
King Xerxes, she had to complete twelve
months of beauty treatments prescribed
for the women, six months with oil of
myrrh and six with perfumes[g] and cosmetics. 13 And this is how she would go
to the king: Anything she wanted was
given her to take with her from the harem to the king's palace. 14 In the evening
she would go there and in the morning
return to another part of the harem to
the care of Shaashgaz, the king's eunuch
who was in charge of the concubines.[h]
She would not return to the king unless
he was pleased with her and summoned
her by name.[i]
15 When the turn came for Esther (the
girl Mordecai had adopted, the daughter of
his uncle Abihail[j]) to go to the king,[k] she
asked for nothing other than what Hegai,
the king's eunuch who was in charge of
the harem, suggested. And Esther won the
favor[l] of everyone who saw her. 16 She was
taken to King Xerxes in the royal residence
in the tenth month, the month of Tebeth,
in the seventh year of his reign.
17 Now the king was attracted to Esther
more than to any of the other women, and
she won his favor and approval more than
any of the other virgins. So he set a royal
crown on her head and made her queen[m]
instead of Vashti. 18 And the king gave a
great banquet,[n] Esther's banquet, for all
his nobles and officials.[o] He proclaimed a
holiday throughout the provinces and distributed gifts with royal liberality.[p]

Mordecai Uncovers a Conspiracy

19 When the virgins were assembled a
second time, Mordecai was sitting at the
king's gate.[q] 20 But Esther had kept secret
her family background and nationality just
as Mordecai had told her to do, for she
continued to follow Mordecai's instructions as she had done when he was bringing her up.[r]
21 During the time Mordecai was sitting
at the king's gate, Bigthana[a] and Teresh,
two of the king's officers[s] who guarded the
doorway, became angry[t] and conspired to
assassinate King Xerxes. 22 But Mordecai
found out about the plot and told Queen
Esther, who in turn reported it to the king,
giving credit to Mordecai. 23 And when the
report was investigated and found to be
true, the two officials were hanged[u] on a
gallows.[b] All this was recorded in the book
of the annals[v] in the presence of the king.[w]

2:9 [d] S Ge 39:21 [e] S Ge 37:3; 1Sa 9:22-24; S 2Ki 25:30; Est 9:19; Eze 16:9-13; Da 1:5 **2:10** [f] ver 20 **2:12** [g] Pr 27:9; SS 1:3; Isa 3:24 **2:14** [h] 1Ki 11:3; SS 6:8; Da 5:2 [i] Est 4:11 **2:15** [j] Est 9:29 [k] Ps 45:14 [l] S Ge 18:3; S 30:27; Est 5:8; 7:3; 8:5

2:17 [m] Eze 16:9-13 **2:18** [n] S 1Ki 3:15 [o] S Ge 40:20 [p] S Est 1:7 **2:19** [q] Est 4:2; 5:13 **2:20** [r] ver 10 **2:21** [s] S Ge 40:2 [t] S Est 1:12; 3:5; 5:9; 7:7 **2:23** [u] S Ge 40:19; S Dt 21:22-23; Ps 7:14-16; Pr 26:27; Ecc 10:8 [v] Est 6:1; 10:2 [w] Est 6:2

[a] 21 Hebrew *Bigthan,* a variant of *Bigthana*
[b] 23 Or *were hung* (or *impaled*) *on poles*; similarly elsewhere in Esther

2:9 *special food.* Unlike Daniel and his friends (Da 1:5–10), Esther does not observe the dietary laws, perhaps in part to conceal her Jewish identity (vv. 10,20). Giving such portions is a sign of special favor (1Sa 9:22–24; 2Ki 25:29–30; Da 1:5–10; negatively, Jer 13:25); in the Joseph narrative cf. Ge 43:34 and note. The motif of giving portions appears later as a practice in observing Purim (9:19,22).
2:10 The fact that Esther concealed her identity is reported twice—here and in v. 20 (for the author's use of duplications see Introduction: Purpose, Themes and Literary Features).
2:14 *to another part of the harem.* To the chambers of the concubines.
2:16 *tenth month ... seventh year.* December, 479 B.C., or January, 478 (see notes on 1:3–4; 2:1). Esther's tenure as queen continued through the events of the book, i.e., through 473 (see 3:7 and note; see also 8:9–13; 9:1). She may have died or fallen from favor shortly thereafter (see note on 1:9).
2:18 *holiday.* The Hebrew for this word, unique to this verse, may imply a remission of taxes, an emancipation of slaves, a cancellation of debts or a remission of obligatory military service.
2:19 See Introduction: Purpose, Themes and Literary Features. The enlargement of the harem apparently continued unabated. Perhaps there is a causal connection between the second gathering of women and the assassination plot (vv. 21–23); some have suggested that it reflects palace intrigue in support of the deposed Vashti. *king's gate.* The gateway of an ancient city was its major commercial and legal center. Markets were held in the gateway; the court sat there to transact its business (see Dt 21:18–20; Jos 20:4; Ru 4:1–11; Ps 69:12). A king might hold an audience at the gate (see 2Sa 19:8; 1Ki 22:10). Daniel was at the king's gate (NIV "royal court") as ruler over all Babylon (Da 2:48–49). Mordecai's sitting at the king's gate confirms his holding a high position in the civil service of the empire (see note on v. 5). From this vantage point he might overhear plans for the murder of the king.
2:21–23 Another point of comparison with the Joseph narrative is the involvement of two chamberlains (Ge 40:1–3; see note on vv. 3–4).
2:23 *hanged.* See NIV text note. Among the Persians this form of execution was impalement, as is confirmed in pictures and statues from the ancient Near East and in the comments of the Greek historian Herodotus (3.125,129; 4.43). According to Herodotus (3.159) Darius I impaled 3,000 Babylonians when he took Babylon, an act that Darius himself recorded in his Behistun (Bisitun) inscription (see note on Hag 1:1). In Israelite and Canaanite practice, hanging was an exhibition of the corpse and not the means of execution itself (Dt 21:22–23; Jos 8:29; 10:26; 1Sa 31:8–10; 2Sa 4:12). The sons of Haman were killed by the sword, and then their corpses were displayed on poles (9:5–14). The execution of the pharaoh's chief baker in the Joseph narrative was similar (Ge 40:19). *annals.* The concern of the author of Esther with rhetorical symmetry is seen in the fact that the annals are mentioned in the

Haman's Plot to Destroy the Jews

3 After these events, King Xerxes honored Haman son of Hammedatha, the
Agagite,[x] elevating him and giving him a
seat of honor higher than that of all the
other nobles. 2All the royal officials at the
king's gate knelt down and paid honor to
Haman, for the king had commanded this
concerning him. But Mordecai would not
kneel down or pay him honor.
3Then the royal officials at the king's
gate asked Mordecai, "Why do you disobey
the king's command?"[y] 4Day after day they
spoke to him but he refused to comply.[z]
Therefore they told Haman about it to see
whether Mordecai's behavior would be tolerated, for he had told them he was a Jew.
5When Haman saw that Mordecai would
not kneel down or pay him honor, he was
enraged.[a] 6Yet having learned who Mordecai's people were, he scorned the idea
of killing only Mordecai. Instead Haman
looked for a way[b] to destroy[c] all Mordecai's people, the Jews,[d] throughout the
whole kingdom of Xerxes.
7In the twelfth year of King Xerxes, in
the first month, the month of Nisan, they
cast the *pur*[e] (that is, the lot[f]) in the presence of Haman to select a day and month.
And the lot fell on[a] the twelfth month, the
month of Adar.[g]
8Then Haman said to King Xerxes,
"There is a certain people dispersed and
scattered among the peoples in all the
provinces of your kingdom whose customs[h] are different from those of all other
people and who do not obey[i] the king's
laws; it is not in the king's best interest to
tolerate them.[j] 9If it pleases the king, let
a decree be issued to destroy them, and
I will put ten thousand talents[b] of silver
into the royal treasury for the men who
carry out this business."[k]
10So the king took his signet ring[l] from
his finger and gave it to Haman son of
Hammedatha, the Agagite, the enemy of
the Jews. 11"Keep the money," the king
said to Haman, "and do with the people
as you please."
12Then on the thirteenth day of the first
month the royal secretaries were summoned. They wrote out in the script of
each province and in the language[m] of
each people all Haman's orders to the

3:1 [x]S Ex 17:8-16; S Nu 24:7; Dt 25:17-19; 1Sa 14:48
3:3 [y]Est 5:9; Da 3:12
3:4 [z]Ge 39:10
3:5 [a]S Est 2:21
3:6 [b]Pr 16:25 [c]Ps 74:8; 83:4 [d]Est 9:24
3:7 [e]Est 9:24,26 [f]S Lev 16:8; S 1Sa 10:21 [g]ver 13; Est 9:19
3:8 [h]Ac 16:20-21 [i]Jer 29:7; Da 6:13 [j]Ezr 4:15
3:9 [k]Est 7:4
3:10 [l]S Ge 41:42
3:12 [m]S Ne 13:24

[a] 7 Septuagint; Hebrew does not have *And the lot fell on.*
[b] 9 That is, about 375 tons (about 345 metric tons)

beginning (here), middle (6:1) and end (10:2) of the narrative. The episode dealing with the plot of Bigthana and Teresh is a good example of the many "coincidences" in the book that later take on crucial significance for the story, showing God's providence at work.

3:1 *After these events.* Four years have elapsed since Esther's selection as queen (v. 7; 2:16–17). *son of Hammedatha, the Agagite.* There is some debate about the ancestry of Haman. The name Hammedatha appears to be Persian and probably refers to an immediate ancestor. The title "Agagite" could refer to some other immediate ancestor or to an unknown place; however, it is far more likely that it refers to Agag, king of Amalek (1Sa 15:20). The Amalekites had attacked Israel after she fled from Egypt (Ex 17:8–16; 1Sa 15:2); for this reason the Lord would "be at war against the Amalekites from generation to generation" (Ex 17:16). Israel was not to forget, but must "blot out the memory of Amalek from under heaven" (Dt 25:19). Saul's attack on Amalek (1Sa 15) resulted in the death of most, though not all (1Ch 4:42–43), of King Agag's people and later in the death of the king himself. Centuries after the battle led by the Benjamite Saul, the Benjamite Mordecai (see note on 2:5) continues the war with the Amalekites. *elevating him.* The fact that no reason is given for the promotion of Haman provides an ironic contrast between the unrewarded merit of Mordecai (2:21–23; see 6:3) and the unmerited reward of Haman.
3:2–6 Obedience to the second commandment (Ex 20:4–5) is not the issue in Mordecai's refusal to bow down to Haman, for Israelites were willing to bow down to kings (see 1Sa 24:8; 2Sa 14:4; 1Ki 1:16) and to other persons (see Ge 23:7; 33:3; 44:14). Only the long-standing enmity between Israel and Amalek accounts both for Mordecai's refusal and for Haman's intent to destroy all the Jews (vv. 5–6). The threat against the Jews "throughout the whole kingdom" (v. 6) is a threat against the ultimate issue of redemptive history (see Introduction: Purpose, Themes and Literary Features).
3:4 Compare the phraseology with that in the Joseph story (Ge 39:10).

3:7 *twelfth year ... first month.* April or May, 474 B.C., the fifth year of Esther's reign. *they.* Either indefinite or the men who assisted Haman (5:10,14; 6:12–13). *pur.* See 9:24,26. This word is found in Akkadian texts with the meaning "lot" (as here). The celebration known as Purim takes its name from the plural of this noun (see 9:26). There is irony in the fact that the month of the Jews' celebration of the Passover deliverance from Egypt is also the month that Haman begins plotting their destruction (Ex 12:2–11). *twelfth month.* An 11-month delay is contemplated between the securing of the decree and the execution of it in the month Adar (February-March).
3:8 *a certain people.* The name of the people Haman wishes to destroy is slyly omitted in this blend of the true and the false: The Jews did have their own customs and laws, but they were not disobedient to the king (Jer 29:7). *dispersed.* See 8:11,17; 9:2,12,16,19–20,28.
3:9 *ten thousand talents.* Herodotus (3.95) records that the annual income of the Persian empire was 15,000 talents. If this figure is correct, Haman offers two-thirds of that amount — a huge sum. Presumably the money would have come from the plundered wealth of the victims of the decree. Verse 13 implies that those who would take part in the massacre were to be allowed to keep the plunder, perhaps adding financial incentive to the execution of the decree since Xerxes disavows taking the money (v. 11). On the other hand, 4:7 may imply that the king had planned on collecting some of the money (see also 7:4 and note). *men who carry out this business.* This clause may represent the title of revenue officers who would bring the money to the treasury, or it could refer to those who carry out the decree. The Amalekites had once before plundered Israel (1Sa 14:48); Haman plans a recurrence.
3:10 *took his signet ring ... and gave it to Haman.* Authorizing Haman to put the king's seal on the royal decree (v. 12). *enemy of the Jews.* An epithet also applied to Haman later in the book (8:1; 9:10; cf. also 7:6; 9:24).
3:12 *thirteenth day ... first month.* In the 12th year of Xerxes's reign (v. 7), i.e., Apr. 17, 474 B.C.

king's satraps, the governors of the various provinces and the nobles of the various peoples. These were written in the
name of King Xerxes himself and sealed[n]
with his own ring. 13Dispatches were sent
by couriers to all the king's provinces
with the order to destroy, kill and annihilate all the Jews[o]—young and old, wom-
en and little children—on a single day,
the thirteenth day of the twelfth month,
the month of Adar,[p] and to plunder[q] their
goods. 14A copy of the text of the edict
was to be issued as law in every province and made known to the people of
every nationality so they would be ready
for that day.[r]
15Spurred on by the king's command,
the couriers went out, and the edict was
issued in the citadel of Susa.[s] The king
and Haman sat down to drink,[t] but the
city of Susa was bewildered.[u]

Mordecai Persuades Esther to Help

4 When Mordecai learned of all that had
been done, he tore his clothes,[v] put on
sackcloth and ashes,[w] and went out into
the city, wailing[x] loudly and bitterly. 2But
he went only as far as the king's gate,[y]
because no one clothed in sackcloth was
allowed to enter it. 3In every province
to which the edict and order of the king
came, there was great mourning among
the Jews, with fasting, weeping and wailing. Many lay in sackcloth and ashes.
4When Esther's maids and eunuchs
came and told her about Mordecai, she
was in great distress. She sent clothes for
him to put on instead of his sackcloth, but
he would not accept them. 5Then Esther
summoned Hathach, one of the king's eunuchs assigned to attend her, and ordered
him to find out what was troubling Mordecai and why.
6So Hathach went out to Mordecai in
the open square of the city in front of the
king's gate. 7Mordecai told him everything
that had happened to him, including the
exact amount of money Haman had promised to pay into the royal treasury for the
destruction of the Jews.[z] 8He also gave
him a copy of the text of the edict for their
annihilation, which had been published in
Susa, to show to Esther and explain it to
her, and he told him to urge her to go into
the king's presence to beg for mercy and
plead with him for her people.
9Hathach went back and reported to Esther what Mordecai had said. 10Then she
instructed him to say to Mordecai, 11"All
the king's officials and the people of the
royal provinces know that for any man or
woman who approaches the king in the
inner court without being summoned[a] the
king has but one law:[b] that he be put to
death. The only exception to this is for the
king to extend the gold scepter[c] to him and
spare his life. But thirty days have passed
since I was called to go to the king."
12When Esther's words were reported
to Mordecai, 13he sent back this answer:
"Do not think that because you are in the
king's house you alone of all the Jews will
escape. 14For if you remain silent[d] at this
time, relief[e] and deliverance[f] for the Jews
will arise from another place, but you and
your father's family will perish. And who
knows but that you have come to royal
position for such a time as this?"[g]
15Then Esther sent this reply to Mordecai: 16"Go, gather together all the Jews
who are in Susa, and fast[h] for me. Do not
eat or drink for three days, night or day. I
and my maids will fast as you do. When

3:12 [n]S Ge 38:18 **3:13** [o]S 1Sa 15:3; S Ezr 4:6 [p]S ver 7 [q]Est 8:11; 9:10 **3:14** [r]Est 8:8; 9:1 **3:15** [s]Est 8:14 [t]S Est 1:10 [u]Est 8:15 **4:1** [v]S Nu 14:6 [w]S 2Sa 13:19; Eze 27:30-31 [x]S Ex 11:6; Ps 30:11 **4:2** [y]S Est 2:19

4:7 [z]Est 7:4 **4:11** [a]Est 2:14 [b]Da 2:9 [c]Est 5:1,2; 8:4; Ps 125:3 **4:14** [d]Job 34:29; Ps 28:1; 35:22; Ecc 3:7; Isa 42:14; 57:11; 62:1; 64:12; Am 5:13 [e]Est 9:16,22 [f]S Ge 45:7; S Dt 28:29 [g]S Ge 50:20 **4:16** [h]S 2Ch 20:3; Est 9:31

3:13 Haman's decree against Israel mandates virtually the same destruction that had earlier been decreed against Amalek (1Sa 15:3). *thirteenth day ... twelfth month.* Mar. 7, 473 B.C. (see 8:12).
3:15 Haman and the king will drink together again in the story when the fate of the Jews is once again being decided (7:1–2), but then it will be at the dissolution of their relationship and the reversal of the decree here celebrated. The celebration here is in sharp contrast to the fasting and mourning of the Jews (4:1–3,16).
4:2 *king's gate.* See note on 2:19.
4:3 See note on 3:15. The prominence of feasting throughout the book of Esther sets the fasts of vv. 3,16 in sharp relief; a pair of fasts matches the prominent pairs of banquets (see Introduction: Purpose, Themes and Literary Features; see also note on 9:31).
4:5–15 The fact that the dialogue of Esther and Mordecai is mediated by Hathach reflects the prohibition against Mordecai's entering the royal citadel dressed in mourning (v. 2).
4:7 See note on 3:9. That Mordecai is aware of the amount Haman promised to the king is a reminder of his high position in the bureaucracy at Susa (2:21–23; see also note on 2:5).
4:11 Herodotus (3.118,140) also notes that anyone approaching the Persian king unsummoned would be killed unless the king gave immediate pardon.
4:12–16 The themes of the book of Esther are most clearly expressed in this passage. Mordecai's confidence that the Jews would be delivered is based on God's sovereignty in working out his purposes and fulfilling his promises. Their deliverance will come, even if through some means other than Esther. Yet that sovereignty is not fatalistic: Unless Esther exercises her individual responsibility, she and her family will perish. Cf. Mt 26:24; Ac 2:23 for similar treatments of the relationship between divine sovereignty and human responsibility.
4:14 *from another place.* As close as the book comes to an explicit reference to God (see Introduction: Purpose, Themes and Literary Features). In Jewish tradition, "the Place" is one of the surrogates used for God's name. *such a time as this.* Cf. Ge 45:5–7 in the Joseph narrative.
4:16 *fast.* See note on v. 3. Prayer, which usually accompanied such fasting, was presumably a part of this fast as well (see Jdg 20:26–27; 1Sa 7:6; 2Sa 12:16; Ezr 8:21–23; Ne 9:1–3; Isa 58:3–4; Jer 14:12; Joel 1:14; 2:12–17; Jnh 3:7–8). The omission of any reference to prayer or to God is consistent with the author's intention; absence of any distinctively religious concepts or vocabulary is a rhetorical device used to heighten the fact that it is indeed God who has been active in the whole narrative (see Introduction: Purpose, Themes

this is done, I will go to the king, even though it is against the law. And if I perish, I perish."[i]

17So Mordecai went away and carried out all of Esther's instructions.

Esther's Request to the King

5 On the third day Esther put on her royal robes[j] and stood in the inner court of the palace, in front of the king's[k] hall. The king was sitting on his royal throne in the hall, facing the entrance. 2When he saw Queen Esther standing in the court, he was pleased with her and held out to her the gold scepter that was in his hand. So Esther approached and touched the tip of the scepter.[l]

3Then the king asked, "What is it, Queen Esther? What is your request? Even up to half the kingdom,[m] it will be given you."

4"If it pleases the king," replied Esther, "let the king, together with Haman, come today to a banquet I have prepared for him."

5"Bring Haman at once," the king said, "so that we may do what Esther asks."

So the king and Haman went to the banquet Esther had prepared. 6As they were drinking wine,[n] the king again asked Esther, "Now what is your petition? It will be given you. And what is your request? Even up to half the kingdom,[o] it will be granted."[p]

7Esther replied, "My petition and my request is this: 8If the king regards me with favor[q] and if it pleases the king to grant my petition and fulfill my request, let the king and Haman come tomorrow to the banquet[r] I will prepare for them. Then I will answer the king's question."

Haman's Rage Against Mordecai

9Haman went out that day happy and in high spirits. But when he saw Mordecai at the king's gate and observed that he neither rose nor showed fear in his presence, he was filled with rage[s] against Mordecai.[t] 10Nevertheless, Haman restrained himself and went home.

Calling together his friends and Zeresh,[u] his wife, 11Haman boasted[v] to them about his vast wealth, his many sons,[w] and all the ways the king had honored him and how he had elevated him above the other nobles and officials. 12"And that's not all," Haman added. "I'm the only person[x] Queen Esther invited to accompany the king to the banquet she gave. And she has invited me along with the king tomorrow. 13But all this gives me no satisfaction as long as I see that Jew Mordecai sitting at the king's gate.[y]"

14His wife Zeresh and all his friends said to him, "Have a gallows built, seventy-five feet[a] high,[z] and ask the king in the morning to have Mordecai hanged[a] on it. Then go with the king to the dinner and be happy." This suggestion delighted Haman, and he had the gallows built.

Mordecai Honored

6 That night the king could not sleep;[b] so he ordered the book of the chronicles,[c] the record of his reign, to be brought in and read to him. 2It was found recorded there that Mordecai had exposed Bigthana and Teresh, two of the king's officers who guarded the doorway, who had conspired to assassinate King Xerxes.[d]

3"What honor and recognition has Mordecai received for this?" the king asked.

"Nothing has been done for him,"[e] his attendants answered.

4The king said, "Who is in the court?" Now Haman had just entered the outer

4:16 [i]S Ge 43:14 **5:1** [j]Eze 16:13 [k]Pr 21:1 **5:2** [l]S Est 4:11 **5:3** [m]Est 7:2; Da 5:16; Mk 6:23 **5:6** [n]S Est 1:10 [o]Da 5:16; Mk 6:23 [p]Est 9:12 **5:8** [q]S Est 2:15 [r]S 1Ki 3:15 **5:9** [s]S Est 2:21; Pr 14:17 [t]S Est 3:3, 5 **5:10** [u]Est 6:13 **5:11** [v]Pr 13:16 [w]Est 9:7-10, 13 **5:12** [x]Job 22:29; Pr 16:18; 29:23 **5:13** [y]S Est 2:19 **5:14** [z]Est 7:9 [a]S Ezr 6:11 **6:1** [b]Da 2:1; 6:18 [c]S Est 2:23 **6:2** [d]Est 2:21-23 **6:3** [e]Ecc 9:13-16

[a] 14 Hebrew *fifty cubits* (about 23 meters)

and Literary Features). *if I perish, I perish.* Esther's defining moment. Cf. the similar formulation in the Joseph narrative (Ge 43:14).

5:2 An example of divine providence influencing a king, as in Pr 21:1 (see note there).

5:6 – 7 One can only speculate regarding Esther's reasons for delaying her answer to the king's question until he had asked it a third time (vv. 3,6; 7:2). The author uses these delays as plot retardation devices that sustain the tension and permit the introduction of new material on Haman's self-aggrandizement (vv. 11 – 12) and Mordecai's reward (6:6 – 11).

5:9 Haman's rage is kindled when Mordecai does not rise in his presence — an ironic contrast to his earlier refusal to bow (3:2 – 5).

5:11 *many sons.* Haman had ten sons (9:7 – 10). Herodotus (1.136) reports that the Persians prized a large number of sons second only to valor in battle; the Persian king sent gifts to the subject with the most sons (cf. Ps 127:3 – 5).

5:12 – 13 See Pr 16:18; 29:23.

5:13 *that Jew Mordecai.* See notes on 6:10; 7:6.

5:14 *seventy-five feet high.* Perhaps hyperbolic. Some, however, suggest that the pole (see note and NIV text note on 2:23) was set up atop another structure to achieve this height, e.g., the city wall (see 1Sa 31:10). *hanged.* See note on 2:23.

6:1 This verse marks the literary center of the narrative. When things could not look worse, a series of seemingly trivial coincidences marks a critical turn that brings resolution to the story. The king's inability to sleep, his requesting the reading of the annals, the reading of the passage reporting Mordecai's past kindness (v. 2), Haman's preparations in the early hours of the morning (5:14), his sudden entry into the outer court (6:5) and his assumption that he was the man the king wished to honor (v. 6) — all are events testifying to the sovereignty of God over the events of the narrative. Circumstances that seemed incidental earlier in the narrative take on crucial significance later. Just as in the Joseph story (Ge 41:1 – 45), the hero's personal fortunes are reversed because of the monarch's disturbed sleep (cf. Da 2:1; 6:18).

6:2 The scribe was reading from the annals that recorded events five years earlier (compare 3:7 with 2:16).

6:4 – 6 Again, the irony is evident: Just as Haman had withheld from the king the identity of the "certain people" (see 3:8 and note), so now the king unintentionally keeps from Haman the identity of the "man the king delights to honor" (v. 6).

court of the palace to speak to the king
about hanging Mordecai on the gallows he
had erected for him.
5His attendants answered, "Haman is
standing in the court."
"Bring him in," the king ordered.
6When Haman entered, the king asked
him, "What should be done for the man
the king delights to honor?"
Now Haman thought to himself, "Who is
there that the king would rather honor than
me?" 7So he answered the king, "For the
man the king delights to honor, 8have them
bring a royal robe[f] the king has worn and a
horse[g] the king has ridden, one with a royal
crest placed on its head. 9Then let the robe
and horse be entrusted to one of the king's
most noble princes. Let them robe the man
the king delights to honor, and lead him on
the horse through the city streets, proclaiming before him, 'This is what is done for the
man the king delights to honor![h]' "
10"Go at once," the king commanded Haman. "Get the robe and the horse and do
just as you have suggested for Mordecai the
Jew, who sits at the king's gate. Do not neglect anything you have recommended."
11So Haman got[i] the robe and the horse.
He robed Mordecai, and led him on horseback through the city streets, proclaiming
before him, "This is what is done for the
man the king delights to honor!"
12Afterward Mordecai returned to the
king's gate. But Haman rushed home,
with his head covered[j] in grief, 13and told
Zeresh[k] his wife and all his friends everything that had happened to him.
His advisers and his wife Zeresh said to
him, "Since Mordecai, before whom your
downfall[l] has started, is of Jewish origin,
you cannot stand against him — you will
surely come to ruin!"[m] 14While they were
still talking with him, the king's eunuchs
arrived and hurried Haman away to the
banquet[n] Esther had prepared.

6:8 [f] S Ge 41:42; S Isa 52:1 [g] 1Ki 1:33 **6:9** [h] Ge 41:43 **6:11** [i] S Ge 41:42 **6:12** [j] 2Sa 15:30; Est 7:8; Jer 14:3,4; Mic 3:7 **6:13** [k] Est 5:10 [l] Ps 57:6; Pr 26:27; 28:18 [m] Est 7:7 **6:14** [n] S 1Ki 3:15

Haman Hanged

7 So the king and Haman went to dine[o]
with Queen Esther, 2and as they were
drinking wine[p] on that second day, the
king again asked, "Queen Esther, what is
your petition? It will be given you. What
is your request? Even up to half the kingdom,[q] it will be granted.[r]"
3Then Queen Esther answered, "If I
have found favor[s] with you, O king, and
if it pleases your majesty, grant me my
life — this is my petition. And spare my
people — this is my request. 4For I and
my people have been sold for destruction and slaughter and annihilation.[t] If we
had merely been sold as male and female
slaves, I would have kept quiet, because
no such distress would justify disturbing
the king.[a]"
5King Xerxes asked Queen Esther, "Who
is he? Where is the man who has dared to
do such a thing?"
6Esther said, "The adversary and enemy
is this vile Haman."
Then Haman was terrified before the
king and queen. 7The king got up in a rage,[u]
left his wine and went out into the palace
garden.[v] But Haman, realizing that the king
had already decided his fate,[w] stayed behind to beg Queen Esther for his life.
8Just as the king returned from the palace garden to the banquet hall, Haman
was falling on the couch[x] where Esther
was reclining.[y]
The king exclaimed, "Will he even molest the queen while she is with me in the
house?"[z]
As soon as the word left the king's
mouth, they covered Haman's face.[a] 9Then
Harbona,[b] one of the eunuchs attending
the king, said, "A gallows seventy-five
feet[b] high[c] stands by Haman's house. He

[a] 4 Or *quiet, but the compensation our adversary offers cannot be compared with the loss the king would suffer*
[b] 9 Hebrew *fifty cubits* (about 23 meters)

7:1 [o] Ge 40:20-22; Mt 22:1-14 **7:2** [p] S Est 1:10 [q] S Est 5:3 [r] Est 9:12 **7:3** [s] S Est 2:15 **7:4** [t] Est 3:9; S 4:7 **7:7** [u] S Ge 34:7; S Est 1:12; Pr 19:12; 20:1-2 [v] S 2Ki 21:18 [w] Est 6:13 **7:8** [x] S Est 1:6 [y] Ge 39:14; Jn 13:23 [z] S Ge 34:7 [a] S Est 6:12 **7:9** [b] Est 1:10 [c] Est 5:14

6:8 *royal robe the king has worn.* See 8:15; see also Introduction: Purpose, Themes and Literary Features. Cf. in the Joseph story Ge 41:41 – 43. Great significance was attached to the king's garment in ancient times; wearing his garments was a sign of unique favor (1Sa 18:4). To wear another's garments was to partake of his power, stature, honor or sanctity (2Ki 2:13 – 14; Isa 61:3,10; Zec 3:3 – 7; cf. Mk 5:27 – 28). Haman's suggestion is not only a great honor to the recipient, but it is also considerably flattering to the king: Wearing his garment was chosen instead of wealth.
6:10 *Mordecai the Jew.* An ironic echo of Haman's sarcastic epithet "that Jew Mordecai" (5:13; see also note on 7:6).
6:13 *his wife and all his friends.* See 5:14; see also Introduction: Purpose, Themes and Literary Features.
6:14 Guests were usually escorted to feasts (see in the Joseph narrative Ge 43:15 – 26; cf. Mt 22:1 – 14).
7:2 See 5:3,6; see also note on 5:6 – 7.
7:3 *found favor with you.* See 2:15,17.
7:4 *sold . . . annihilation.* Esther refers to the bribe Haman offered to the king (3:9; 4:7); she also paraphrases Haman's edict (3:13). *because no such distress . . . king.* See NIV text note. The statement probably means either (1) that the affliction of the Jews would be less injurious to the king if slavery was all that was involved, or (2) that Esther would not trouble the king if slavery was the only issue.
7:6 *this vile Haman.* Esther's biting words are a rhetorical counterpoint to Haman's sneering characterization of Mordecai as "that Jew Mordecai" (5:13; see also note on 6:10).
7:7 *went out.* The king's leaving the room sets the stage for the final twist that would seal Haman's fate.
7:8 *falling on the couch where Esther was reclining.* Meals were customarily taken reclining on a couch (see Am 6:4,7; Jn 13:23 and note). It is ironic that Haman, who became angry when the Jew Mordecai would not bow down (which set the whole story in motion), now falls before the Jewess Esther (see 6:13). *covered Haman's face.* See 6:12; see also Introduction: Purpose, Themes and Literary Features.
7:9 Before this moment there is no evidence that Esther had known of Mordecai's triumph earlier in the day (6:1 – 11); she has pleaded for the life of her people. Harbona's reference

had it made for Mordecai, who spoke up
to help the king."
The king said, "Hang him on it!"[d] 10 So
they hanged[e] Haman[f] on the gallows[g] he
had prepared for Mordecai.[h] Then the
king's fury subsided.[i]

The King's Edict in Behalf of the Jews

8 That same day King Xerxes gave Queen
Esther the estate of Haman,[j] the enemy of the Jews. And Mordecai came into
the presence of the king, for Esther had
told how he was related to her. 2 The king
took off his signet ring,[k] which he had reclaimed from Haman, and presented it to
Mordecai. And Esther appointed him over
Haman's estate.[l]
3 Esther again pleaded with the king,
falling at his feet and weeping. She begged
him to put an end to the evil plan of Haman the Agagite,[m] which he had devised
against the Jews. 4 Then the king extended
the gold scepter[n] to Esther and she arose
and stood before him.
5 "If it pleases the king," she said, "and
if he regards me with favor[o] and thinks it
the right thing to do, and if he is pleased
with me, let an order be written overruling
the dispatches that Haman son of Hammedatha, the Agagite, devised and wrote to
destroy the Jews in all the king's provinces. 6 For how can I bear to see disaster fall
on my people? How can I bear to see the
destruction of my family?"[p]
7 King Xerxes replied to Queen Esther
and to Mordecai the Jew, "Because Haman
attacked the Jews, I have given his estate
to Esther, and they have hanged[q] him on
the gallows. 8 Now write another decree[r]
in the king's name in behalf of the Jews
as seems best to you, and seal[s] it with the
king's signet ring[t]—for no document written in the king's name and sealed with his
ring can be revoked."[u]
9 At once the royal secretaries were
summoned—on the twenty-third day
of the third month, the month of Sivan.
They wrote out all Mordecai's orders to
the Jews, and to the satraps, governors
and nobles of the 127 provinces stretch-

7:9 [d]S Dt 21:22-23; Ps 7:14-16; 9:16; Pr 11:5-6; S 26:27; S Mt 7:2 **7:10** [e]Ge 40:22 [f]Pr 10:28 [g]Est 9:25 [h]Da 6:24 [i]Est 2:1 **8:1** [j]Pr 22:22-23 **8:2** [k]S Ge 24:22; S 41:42 [l]S Ge 41:41; Pr 13:22; 14:35; Da 2:48 **8:3** [m]S Ex 17:8-16 **8:4** [n]S Est 4:11 **8:5** [o]S Est 2:15 **8:6** [p]Ge 44:34 **8:7** [q]S Dt 21:22-23 **8:8** [r]S Est 3:12-14 [s]S Ge 38:18 [t]S Ge 41:42 [u]S Est 1:19; Da 6:15

to the pole (see NIV text note on 2:23) in effect introduces a second charge against Haman—his attempt to kill the king's benefactor.

7:10 *hanged Haman on the gallows he had prepared for Mordecai.* John Calvin said, "Man falls as God's providence ordains, but he falls by his own fault." Cf. Jer 50:15,29; Eze 9:10; 16:43; Ob 15 and note. *subsided.* See 2:1; see also Introduction: Purpose, Themes and Literary Features.

8:1–17 By echoing much of the phraseology of 3:1—4:3, the author emphasizes how the tables were turned (see chart below).

8:1 *gave Queen Esther the estate of Haman.* Herodotus (3.128–129) and Josephus (*Antiquities*, 11.17) confirm that the property of a traitor reverted to the crown; Xerxes presents Haman's wealth (5:11) to Esther.

8:2 Cf. 3:10–11, where the king's offer of his ring includes Haman's keeping the money; here Mordecai receives the office and the estate of Haman.

8:3–6 Esther and Mordecai are secure (7:4—8:2), but the irrevocable decree is still a threat to the rest of the Jews.

8:3 *Agagite.* See note on 3:1.

8:5 *favor.* See 4:11; 5:2.

8:6 Cf. the Joseph story (Ge 44:34).

8:8 *write another decree.* See 1:19 and note; see also Introduction: Purpose, Themes and Literary Features. The dilemma is the same as the one that confronted Darius the Mede in Daniel (Da 6:8,12,15). The solution is to issue another decree (cf. Da 6:25–27) that in effect counters the original decree of Haman (3:12; cf. Da 6:7–9) without formally revoking it (see note on 9:2–3).

8:9–13 The phraseology is taken from the parallel in 3:12–14. The extent of the destruction mandated is virtually

Chiastic Structure of Reversals in Esther

3:10–	the king gives Haman his ring	8:2–	the king gives Mordecai the same ring
3:12–	Haman summons the king's scribes	8:9–	Mordecai summons the king's scribes
3:12–	letters written, sealed with ring	8:10–	letters written, sealed with same ring
3:13–	the Jews, even women and children, to be killed on one day	8:11–	in self defense, the Jews can kill their enemies in one day
3:14–	Haman's decree publicly displayed as law	8:13–	Mordecai's decree publicly displayed as law
3:15–	couriers go out in haste	8:14–	couriers go out in haste
3:15–	the city of Susa is bewildered	8:15–	the city of Susa rejoices
4:1–	Mordecai wears sackcloth and ashes	8:15–	Mordecai wears royal robes
4:1–	Mordecai goes through city crying	6:11–	Mordecai led through the city in honor
5:14–	Zeresh advises Mordecai's death	6:13–	Zeresh predicts Haman's ruin

ing from India to Cush.[a][v] These orders
were written in the script of each province and the language of each people and
also to the Jews in their own script and
language.[w] 10Mordecai wrote in the name
of King Xerxes, sealed the dispatches with
the king's signet ring, and sent them by
mounted couriers, who rode fast horses
especially bred for the king.
11The king's edict granted the Jews in
every city the right to assemble and protect themselves; to destroy, kill and annihilate any armed force of any nationality
or province that might attack them and
their women and children; and to plunder[x] the property of their enemies. 12The
day appointed for the Jews to do this in
all the provinces of King Xerxes was the
thirteenth day of the twelfth month, the
month of Adar.[y] 13A copy of the text of
the edict was to be issued as law in every province and made known to the people of every nationality so that the Jews
would be ready on that day[z] to avenge
themselves on their enemies.
14The couriers, riding the royal horses,
raced out, spurred on by the king's command. And the edict was also issued in the
citadel of Susa.[a]
15Mordecai[b] left the king's presence
wearing royal garments of blue and white,
a large crown of gold[c] and a purple robe
of fine linen.[d] And the city of Susa held a
joyous celebration.[e] 16For the Jews it was
a time of happiness and joy,[f] gladness and
honor.[g] 17In every province and in every
city, wherever the edict of the king went,
there was joy[h] and gladness among the
Jews, with feasting and celebrating. And
many people of other nationalities became
Jews because fear[i] of the Jews had seized
them.[j]

Triumph of the Jews

9 On the thirteenth day of the twelfth
month, the month of Adar,[k] the edict
commanded by the king was to be carried out. On this day the enemies of the
Jews had hoped to overpower them, but
now the tables were turned and the Jews
got the upper hand[l] over those who hated
them.[m] 2The Jews assembled in their cities[n] in all the provinces of King Xerxes to
attack those seeking their destruction. No
one could stand against them,[o] because
the people of all the other nationalities
were afraid of them. 3And all the nobles
of the provinces, the satraps, the governors and the king's administrators helped
the Jews,[p] because fear of Mordecai had
seized them.[q] 4Mordecai[r] was prominent[s] in the palace; his reputation spread
throughout the provinces, and he became
more and more powerful.[t]
5The Jews struck down all their enemies with the sword, killing and destroying them,[u] and they did what they pleased
to those who hated them. 6In the citadel
of Susa, the Jews killed and destroyed five
hundred men. 7They also killed Parshan-
datha, Dalphon, Aspatha, 8Poratha, Ada-
lia, Aridatha, 9Parmashta, Arisai, Aridai
and Vaizatha, 10the ten sons[v] of Haman
son of Hammedatha, the enemy of the
Jews.[w] But they did not lay their hands on
the plunder.[x]
11The number of those slain in the citadel of Susa was reported to the king that
same day. 12The king said to Queen Esther,
"The Jews have killed and destroyed five
hundred men and the ten sons of Haman
in the citadel of Susa. What have they
done in the rest of the king's provinces?
Now what is your petition? It will be giv-
en you. What is your request? It will also
be granted."[y]
13"If it pleases the king," Esther answered, "give the Jews in Susa permission
to carry out this day's edict tomorrow also,
and let Haman's ten sons[z] be hanged[a] on
gallows."

8:9 [v] Est 1:1 [w] S Ne 13:24 **8:11** [x] S Ge 14:23; S Est 3:13; 9:10,15,16 **8:12** [y] Est 3:13; 9:1 **8:13** [z] Est 3:14 **8:14** [a] Est 3:15 **8:15** [b] Est 9:4; 10:2 [c] S 2Sa 12:30 [d] S Ge 41:42 [e] Est 3:15 **8:16** [f] Ps 97:10-12 [g] Est 4:1-3; Ps 112:4; Jer 29:4-7 **8:17** [h] Ps 35:27; 45:15; 51:8; Pr 11:10 [i] S Ex 15:14,16; Dt 11:25; Da 6:26 [j] Est 9:3 **9:1** [k] S Est 8:12 [l] Jer 29:4-7 [m] S Est 3:12-14; Pr 22:22-23 **9:2** [n] S Ge 22:17 [o] Ps 35:26; 40:14; 70:2; 71:13,24 **9:3** [p] S Ezr 8:36 [q] Est 8:17 **9:4** [r] S Est 8:15 [s] S Ex 11:3 [t] S 2Sa 3:1; 1Ch 11:9 **9:5** [u] Dt 25:17-19; S 1Sa 15:3; S Ezr 4:6 **9:10** [v] S Est 5:11; Ps 127:3-5 [w] S 1Sa 15:33 [x] S Ge 14:23; S 1Sa 14:32; S Est 3:13 **9:12** [y] Est 5:6; 7:2 **9:13** [z] S Est 5:11 [a] S Dt 21:22-23

[a] *9* That is, the upper Nile region

the same as that earlier decreed against Amalek (see note on 3:13).

8:9 *twenty-third day ... third month.* In Xerxes's 12th year, i.e., June 25, 474 B.C., two months and ten days after the proclamation of Haman's edict (see note on 3:12).

8:12 *thirteenth day ... twelfth month.* Mar. 7, 473 B.C. (see 3:13 and note). Some 15 years after this first Purim, Ezra would lead his expedition to Jerusalem in 458 B.C. (Ezr 7:9).

8:14 – 17 The phraseology is taken from 3:15 — 4:3.

8:15 *royal garments.* See note on 6:8; Mordecai's second investiture (see 6:7 – 11; see also Introduction: Purpose, Themes and Literary Features).

9:1 The Jews carry out the edict of Mordecai eight months and 20 days later (see 8:9). *tables were turned.* The statement that the opposite happened points to the author's concern with literary symmetry: He balances most of the details from the first half of the story with their explicit reversal in the second half (see chart, p. 724).

9:2 – 3 An illustration of Ge 12:3. Confronted with two conflicting edicts issued in the king's name — the edict of Haman (see 3:12) and the edict of Mordecai (see 8:7 – 14) — the governors follow the edict of the current regime.

9:3 Just as "people of other nationalities" were seized by "fear of the Jews" (8:17), so also the government officials of Persia were seized by "fear of Mordecai."

9:5 – 10 The Jews attend to the unfinished business of blotting out the memory of the Amalekites (Ex 17:14 – 16; Dt 25:17 – 19; see notes on 3:1 – 6). This incident is presented as the antithesis of 1Sa 15: The narrator is emphatic that the Jews did not take plunder, in spite of the king's permission to do so (8:11). Seizing the plunder centuries earlier in the battle against Amalek had cost Saul his kingship (1Sa 15:17 – 19,23); here, not taking the plunder brings royal power to Mordecai as well as grateful recognition by his people (vv. 20 – 23). See vv. 15 – 16; cf. Ge 14:22 — 15:1.

9:12 See 5:3,6; 7:2.

9:13 – 14 The reference to hanging in this case is to the display of the corpses, not to the means of the execution (see vv. 7 – 10 and note on 2:23).

9:13 *Susa.* The city, not the citadel (vv. 11 – 12; see note on 1:2).

14So the king commanded that this be
done. An edict was issued in Susa, and
they hanged[b] the ten sons of Haman.
15The Jews in Susa came together on the
fourteenth day of the month of Adar, and
they put to death in Susa three hundred
men, but they did not lay their hands on
the plunder.[c]
16Meanwhile, the remainder of the Jews
who were in the king's provinces also assembled to protect themselves and get relief[d] from their enemies.[e] They killed seventy-five thousand of them[f] but did not lay
their hands on the plunder.[g] 17This happened on the thirteenth day of the month
of Adar, and on the fourteenth they rested
and made it a day of feasting[h] and joy.

Purim Celebrated

18The Jews in Susa, however, had assembled on the thirteenth and fourteenth,
and then on the fifteenth they rested and
made it a day of feasting and joy.
19That is why rural Jews—those living
in villages—observe the fourteenth of the
month of Adar[i] as a day of joy and feasting,
a day for giving presents to each other.[j]
20Mordecai recorded these events, and
he sent letters to all the Jews throughout
the provinces of King Xerxes, near and far,
21to have them celebrate annually the fourteenth and fifteenth days of the month of
Adar 22as the time when the Jews got relief[k] from their enemies, and as the month
when their sorrow was turned into joy and
their mourning into a day of celebration.[l]
He wrote them to observe the days as
days of feasting and joy and giving presents of food[m] to one another and gifts to
the poor.[n]
23So the Jews agreed to continue the celebration they had begun, doing what Mordecai had written to them. 24For Haman
son of Hammedatha, the Agagite,[o] the enemy of all the Jews, had plotted against
the Jews to destroy them and had cast the
pur[p] (that is, the lot[q]) for their ruin and
destruction.[r] 25But when the plot came to
the king's attention,[a] he issued written orders that the evil scheme Haman had devised against the Jews should come back
onto his own head,[s] and that he and his
sons should be hanged[t] on the gallows.[u]
26(Therefore these days were called Purim,
from the word *pur*.[v]) Because of everything
written in this letter and because of what
they had seen and what had happened to
them, 27the Jews took it upon themselves
to establish the custom that they and their
descendants and all who join them should
without fail observe these two days every
year, in the way prescribed and at the time
appointed. 28These days should be remembered and observed in every generation by
every family, and in every province and in
every city. And these days of Purim should
never cease to be celebrated by the Jews,
nor should the memory of them die out
among their descendants.
29So Queen Esther, daughter of Abihail,[w]
along with Mordecai the Jew, wrote with
full authority to confirm this second letter
concerning Purim. 30And Mordecai sent
letters to all the Jews in the 127 provinces[x]
of the kingdom of Xerxes—words of goodwill and assurance— 31to establish these
days of Purim at their designated times, as
Mordecai the Jew and Queen Esther had
decreed for them, and as they had established for themselves and their descendants in regard to their times of fasting[y]
and lamentation.[z] 32Esther's decree confirmed these regulations about Purim, and
it was written down in the records.

The Greatness of Mordecai

10 King Xerxes imposed tribute throughout the empire, to its distant shores.[a]
2And all his acts of power and might, together with a full account of the greatness
of Mordecai[b] to which the king had raised
him,[c] are they not written in the book of
the annals[d] of the kings of Media and Persia? 3Mordecai the Jew was second[e] in
rank[f] to King Xerxes,[g] preeminent among
the Jews, and held in high esteem by his
many fellow Jews, because he worked for
the good of his people and spoke up for
the welfare of all the Jews.[h]

9:14 [b] S Ezr 6:11 **9:15** [c] S Ge 14:23; S Est 8:11 **9:16** [d] S Est 4:14 [e] Dt 25:19 [f] S 1Ch 4:43 [g] S Est 8:11 **9:17** [h] S 1Ki 3:15 **9:19** [i] S Est 3:7 [j] Dt 16:11,14; S Est 2:9; Rev 11:10 **9:22** [k] S Est 4:14 [l] Ne 8:12; Ps 30:11-12 [m] S 2Ki 25:30 [n] S Ne 8:10 **9:24** [o] S Ex 17:8-16 [p] S Est 3:7 [q] S Lev 16:8 [r] Est 3:6

9:25 [s] Ps 7:16 [t] S Dt 21:22-23 [u] Est 7:10 **9:26** [v] S Est 3:7 **9:29** [w] Est 2:15 **9:30** [x] S Est 1:1 **9:31** [y] S Est 4:16 [z] Est 4:1-3 **10:1** [a] Ps 72:10; 97:1 **10:2** [b] S Est 8:15 [c] S Ge 41:44 [d] S Est 2:23 **10:3** [e] Da 5:7 [f] Ge 41:43 [g] Ge 41:40 [h] Ne 2:10; Jer 29:4-7; Da 6:3

[a] 25 Or *when Esther came before the king*

9:15–16 See note on vv. 5–10.
9:16,22 *relief from their enemies.* Closely associated with the vengeance on their enemies is the rest promised to Israel (Dt 25:19). The defeat of Haman brings rest to the Jews (see Introduction: Purpose, Themes and Literary Features; cf. 1Ch 22:6–10; Ps 95:7–11; Isa 32:18; Heb 3:7—4:11).
9:18–19 The author accounts for the tradition of observing Purim on two different days: It is observed on the 14th in most towns, but the Jews of Susa observed it on the 15th. Today it is observed on the 14th except in Jerusalem, where it is observed on the 15th.
9:20 *Mordecai recorded these events.* Some take this as indicating that Mordecai wrote the book of Esther; however, the more natural understanding is that he recorded the events in the letters he sent.
9:22 *presents of food.* See note on 2:9; cf. Ne 8:10,12.
9:24,26 *pur.* See note on 3:7.
9:25 *come back onto his own head.* See notes on v. 1; Ob 15.
9:31 *fasting.* See notes on 4:3,16. No date is assigned for this fast. Jews traditionally observe the 13th of Adar, Haman's propitious day (see 3:7,13), as a fast ("the fast of Esther") before the celebration of Purim. These three days of victory celebration on the 13th–15th days of Adar rhetorically balance the three days of Esther's fasting prior to interceding with the king (4:16).
10:1–2 The reference to this taxation may represent material in the author's source, to which he directs the reader for additional information and confirmation (see note on 2:23).
10:2 This verse indicates that the book of Esther was written after the death of Xerxes (cf. 1Ki 11:41; 14:19,29 and often in 1,2 Kings).

Wisdom Literature

An ancient tradition among the Jews divided the collection of their holy books into three major divisions: the Law (Pentateuch), the Prophets (Former and Latter) and the Writings. Included within the third division are Psalms and wisdom materials such as Job, Proverbs and Ecclesiastes (also some psalms and probably the Song of Songs — see introduction to that book: Interpretation).

This wisdom literature is usually associated with the sages who are mentioned along with priests and prophets as an important force in Israelite society (see, e.g., Jer 18:18 and note). These gifted persons were recognized as possessing wide knowledge of the created world (see 1Ki 4:29 – 34), special insight into human affairs (as exemplified by proverbs) and exceptionally good judgment regarding courses of action to be followed to attain success in various enterprises (see 2Sa 16:15 – 23). In general, priests and prophets dealt with religious and moral concerns (proclaiming, teaching, interpreting and applying God's word to his people), whereas the sages generally focused more on the practical aspects of how life should be guided in the created order of things (Proverbs) and on the intellectual challenges that arise from the ambiguities of human experience (Job, Ecclesiastes).

Israel's sages reflected on life in light of God's special revelations to his people, but for their unique contribution to understanding how people ought to live in God's world they drew heavily on human experience of the created order. In this they learned much from the sages and wisdom traditions of other peoples. Comparison of their writings with those of their neighbors discloses their acquaintance with the larger intellectual world of the ancient Near East but also the distinctive perspective they brought to their reflections on the human condition.

Job

INTRODUCTION

Author

Although most of the book consists of the words of Job and his friends, Job himself was not the author. We may be sure that the author was an Israelite, since he (not Job or his friends) frequently uses the Israelite covenant name for God (Yahweh; NIV "the LORD"). In the prologue (chs. 1 – 2), divine discourses (38:1 — 42:6) and epilogue (42:7 – 17) "LORD" occurs a total of 25 times, while in the rest of the book (chs. 3 – 37) it appears only once (12:9).

This unknown author probably had access to a tradition (oral or written) about an ancient righteous man who endured great suffering with remarkable "perseverance" (Jas 5:11; see note there) and without turning against God (see Eze 14:14,20), a tradition he put to use for his own purposes. While the author preserves much of the archaic and non-Israelite flavor in the language of Job and his friends, he also reveals his own style as a writer of wisdom literature. The book's profound insights, its literary structures and the quality of its rhetoric display the author's genius.

Date

Two dates are involved: (1) that of Job himself and (2) that of the composition of the book. The latter could be dated anytime from the reign of Solomon to the time of Israel's exile in Babylonia. Although the author was an Israelite, he mentions nothing of Israel's history. He had an account of a non-Israelite sage Job (1:1) who probably lived in the second millennium B.C. (2000 – 1000). Like the Hebrew patriarchs, Job lived more than 100 years (42:16). Like them, his wealth was measured in livestock and servants (1:3), and like them he acted as priest for his family (1:5). The raiding of Sabean (1:15) and Chaldean (1:17) tribes fits the second millennium, as does the mention of the *keśiṭah*, "a piece of silver," in 42:11 (see Ge 33:19; Jos 24:32). The discovery of a Targum (Aramaic paraphrase) on Job dating to the first or second century B.C. (the earliest written Targum yet discovered) makes a very late date for composition highly unlikely.

Language and Text

In many places Job is difficult to translate because of its many unusual words and its style. For that reason, modern translations frequently differ widely. Even the pre-Christian translator(s) of Job into Greek (the Septuagint) seem(s) often to have been perplexed. The Septuagint of Job is about 400 lines shorter than the accepted Hebrew text, and it may be that the translator(s) simply omitted lines he (they) did not understand. The early Syriac (Peshitta), Aramaic (Targum) and Latin (Vulgate) translators had similar difficulties.

Setting and Perspective

While it may be that the author intended his book to be a contribution to an ongoing high-level discussion of major theological issues in an exclusive company of learned men, it seems more likely that he intended his story to be told to godly sufferers who like Job were struggling with the crisis of faith brought on by prolonged bitter suffering. He seems to sit too close to the suffering — to be more the sympathetic and compassionate pastor than the detached theologian or philosopher. He has heard what the learned theologians of his day have been saying about the ways of God and what brings on suffering, and he lets their voices be heard. And he knows that the godly sufferers of his day have also heard the "wisdom" of the learned and have internalized it as the wisdom of the ages. But he also knows what miserable comfort (see 16:2) that so-called wisdom gives — that it only rubs salt in the wounds and creates a stumbling-block for faith. Against that wisdom he has no rational arguments to marshal. But he has a story to tell that challenges it at its very roots and speaks to the struggling faith of the sufferer. In effect he says to the godly sufferer, "Forget the logical arguments spun out by those who sit together at their ease and discuss the ways of God, and forget those voices in your own heart that are little more than echoes of their pronouncements. Let me tell you a story."

Theological Theme and Message

When good people (those who fear God and shun evil, see 1:1) suffer, the human spirit struggles to understand. Throughout recorded history people have asked: How can this be? If God is almighty and "holds the whole world in his hands" and if he is truly good, how can he allow such an outrage? The way this question has often been put leaves open three possibilities: (1) God is not almighty after all; (2) God is not just (is not wholly good but has a demonic streak in him); (3) humans may be innocent. In ancient Israel, however, it was indisputable that God is almighty, that he is perfectly just and that no human is pure in his sight. These three assumptions were also fundamental to the theology of Job and his friends. Simple logic then dictated the conclusion: Every person's suffering is indicative of the measure of their guilt in the eyes of God. In the abstract, this conclusion appeared inescapable, logically imperative and theologically satisfying.

But what thus appeared to be theologically self-evident and unassailable in the abstract was often in radical tension with actual human experience. There were those whose godliness was genuine, whose moral character was upright and who had kept themselves from great transgression, but who nonetheless were made to suffer bitterly (see, e.g., Ps 73). For these the apparently self-evident theology brought no consolation and offered no guidance. It only gave rise to a great enigma. And the God to whom the sufferer was accustomed to turn in moments of need became himself the overwhelming enigma. This theology left innocent sufferers imprisoned in windowless cells to agonize over their crisis of faith. In the speeches of chs. 3 – 37, we hear on the one hand the flawless logic but wounding thrusts of those who insisted on the traditional theology, and on the other hand the writhing of soul of the righteous sufferer struggling with the great enigma even while being wounded by his well-intended, theologically orthodox friends (see note on 5:27). Their learned theology had no helpful, encouraging or comforting word for a truly godly sufferer.

A Quick Look

Author:
Unknown

Audience:
God's people

Date:
Unknown, though Job himself probably lived during the patriarchal period

Theme:
This wisdom book deals with the question of whether God is a God of justice in the light of all of life's perplexities, such as human suffering.

The author of the book of Job broke out of the tight, logical mold of the traditional orthodox theology of his day. He saw that it led to a dead end, that it had no way to cope with the suffering of godly people. It could only deny the reality of the experienced anomaly and add to the pain and inner turmoil of the sufferer. Instead of offering logical arguments, he tells a story. And in his story he shifts the angle of perspective. All around him, among theologians and common people alike, were those who attempted to solve the "God problem" in the face of human suffering (are the ways of God just?) at the expense of humans (they must all deserve what they get). Even those who were suffering were told they must see matters in that light. The author of Job, on the other hand, gave encouragement to godly sufferers by showing them that their suffering provided an occasion like no other for exemplifying what true godliness is for human beings.

He begins by introducing a third party into the equation. The relationship between God and humans is not exclusive and closed. Among God's creatures there is the great adversary (see chs. 1–2). Incapable of contending with God hand to hand, power pitted against power, he is bent on frustrating God's creation enterprise centered on God's relationship with the creature that bears his image. As tempter he seeks to alienate humans from God (see Ge 3; Mt 4:1); as accuser (one of the names by which he is called, *śāṭan*, means "accuser") he seeks to alienate God from humans (see Zec 3:1; Rev 12:9–10). His all-consuming purpose is to drive an irremovable wedge between God and humans to effect an alienation that cannot be reconciled.

In his story, the author portrays this adversary in his boldest and most radical assault on God and godly people in the special and intimate relationship that is dearest to them both. When God calls up the name of Job before the accuser and testifies to his righteousness—this creature in whom God takes special delight—Satan attempts with one crafty thrust both to assail God's beloved and to show up God as a fool. True to one of his modes of operation, he accuses Job before God. He charges that Job's godliness is evil. The very godliness in which God takes such delight lacks all integrity; it is a terrible sin. Job's godliness is mere self-serving; he is righteous only because it pays. If God will only let Satan tempt Job by breaking the link between righteousness and blessing, he will expose this man and all righteous people as the frauds they are.

It is the adversary's ultimate challenge. He is sure he has found in the very structure of creation an opening to accomplish his purpose. Humans are totally dependent on God for their very lives and well-being. That fact can occasion one of humankind's greatest temptations: to love the gifts rather than the Giver, to try to please God merely for the sake of his benefits, to be "religious" and "good" only because it pays. Satan's accusation of Job is that this is the deep truth concerning his apparently godly and upright conduct—that this is, in fact, the deep truth about the godliness of all righteous people. If he is right, if the godliness of the righteous in whom God delights can be shown to be evil, then a chasm of alienation stands between God and human beings that cannot be bridged. Then even the redemption of human beings is unthinkable, for the godliest among them would be shown to be the most ungodly. God's whole enterprise in creation and redemption would be shown to be radically flawed, and God can only sweep it all away in awful judgment.

When good people suffer, the human spirit struggles to understand. Throughout recorded history people have asked: How can this be? If God is almighty and "holds the whole world in his hands" and if he is truly good, how can he allow such an outrage?

The accusation, once raised, cannot be ignored, and it cannot be silenced—not even by destroying the accuser; it strikes too deeply into the very structure of creation and is rooted too deeply in the human condition within that structure. So God lets the adversary have his way with Job (within specified limits) so that God and righteous Job may be vindicated and the great accuser silenced. From this comes Job's profound anguish, robbed as he is of every sign of God's favor so that God becomes for him the great enigma. And his righteousness is also assailed on earth through the logic of the orthodox theology of his friends. Alone he agonizes. But he knows in the depths of his heart that his godliness has been authentic and that someday he will be vindicated (see 13:18; 14:13–17;

16:19; 19:25 – 27). And in spite of all, though he may curse the day of his birth (ch. 3) and chide God for treating him unjustly (9:28 – 35) — the uncalculated outcry of a distraught spirit — he will not curse God (as his wife, the human nearest his heart, proposed; see 2:9; see also notes on 1:12; 2:10; 3:3; 9:2 – 3). In fact, what pains him most is God's apparent alienation from him.

So the adversary is silenced, and God's delight in the godly is vindicated. Robbed of every sign of God's favor, Job refuses to repudiate his Maker. He faces toward God with anguish, puzzlement, anger and bitter complaints, but never turns his back on him to march off — godless — into the dark night. His whole being yearns, not for God's gifts as such, but for a sign of God's favor (cf. Ps 42). Godly Job, dependent creature that he is, passes the supreme test occasioned by the adversary's accusation.

This first test of Job's godliness inescapably involves a second that challenges his godliness at a level no less deep than the first. For the test that sprang from Satan's accusation to be real, Job has to be kept in the dark about the goings-on in God's council chamber. But Job belongs to a race of creatures endowed with wisdom, understanding and insight (something of their godlikeness) that cannot rest until it knows and understands all it can about the creation and the ways of God. For that reason, Job's sudden loss of all that makes life good — every good gift from God — cries out for explanation and puts human wisdom to a supreme test. Job's friends confidently assume that the logic of their theology can account for all God's ways. However, Job's experience makes bitterly clear to him that their "wisdom" cannot fathom the truth of his situation. Yet Job's wisdom is also at a loss to understand. Still, he demands of God an explanation; he wants to reason matters out with God as his equal. When the dialogue between Job and his three wise friends finally stalemates, and before Job's last defense (chs. 29 – 31), before the vain attempt of a brash younger voice to explain Job's plight (chs. 32 – 37), and before Yahweh's own breaking-in on the scene (chs. 38 – 41), the author introduces a poetic essay on wisdom (ch. 28) that exposes the limits of all human wisdom. The wisdom God has given human beings can indeed understand creaturely things, but from these creaturely things humans cannot learn all of God's ways. For them the supreme wisdom is to "fear . . . the Lord . . . and to shun evil" (see v. 28) — the very wisdom that had marked Job's life all the while (see 1:8). Standing as it does at a major juncture between the dialogue and the final major speeches, this authorial commentary on what has been going on in the stalemated dialogue anticipates God's final word to Job, which silences his arguments and defenses. In the end Job passes the second supreme test of his godliness — of all true godliness — namely, to live by the wisdom God gave him (28:28) even while acknowledging the limits of human wisdom. But that insight and Job's acceptance of it came only after the long night of suffering and a new hearing of the voice of the Creator speaking from behind the glory curtain of the creation (cf. Ps 104). See note on 28:1 – 28.

In the end the adversary is silenced. Job's friends are silenced. And Job is silenced. But God is not. And when he speaks, it is to the godly Job that he speaks, bringing the silence of regret for hasty words in days of suffering and the silence of repose in the ways of the Almighty (see 38:1 — 42:6). Furthermore, as his heavenly friend, God hears Job's intercessions for his associates (42:8 – 10), and he restores Job's blessed state (42:10 – 17).

In summary, the author's pastoral word to godly sufferers is that God treasures their righteousness above all else. And Satan knows that if he is to thwart the all-encompassing purpose of God, he must assail the godly righteousness of human beings (see 1:21 – 22; 2:9 – 10; 23:8,10; cf. Ge 15:6). At stake in the suffering of the truly godly is the outcome of the titanic struggle between the great adversary and God. At the same time the author gently reminds the godly sufferer that true godly wisdom is to reverently love God more than all his gifts and to trust the wise goodness of God even though his ways are at times past the power of human wisdom to fathom. So here is presented a profound, but painfully practical, drama that wrestles with the wisdom and justice of the Great King's rule (a "theodicy"; see chart, p. xxii ["Babylonian Theodicy"]). Righteous sufferers must trust in, acknowledge, serve and submit to the omniscient and omnipotent Sovereign, realizing that some suffering is the result of unseen, spiritual conflicts between the kingdom of God and the kingdom of Satan — between the kingdom of light and the kingdom of darkness (cf. Eph 6:10 – 18; Col 1:12 – 13 and notes).

Literary Form and Structure

Like some other ancient compositions, the book of Job has a sandwich literary structure: prologue (prose), main body (poetry), and epilogue (prose), revealing a creative composition, not an arbitrary compilation. Some of Job's words are lament (cf. ch. 3 and many shorter poems in his speeches), but the form of lament is unique to Job and often unlike the regular format of most lament psalms (except Ps 88). Much of the book takes the form of legal disputation. Although the friends come to console him, they end up arguing over the reason for Job's suffering. The argument breaks down in ch. 27, and Job then proceeds to make his final appeal to God for vindication (chs. 29–31). The wisdom poem in ch. 28 appears to be the words of the author, who sees the failure of the dispute as evidence of a lack of wisdom. So in praise of true wisdom he centers his structural apex between the three cycles of dialogue-dispute (chs. 3–27) and the three monologues: Job's (chs. 29–31), Elihu's (chs. 32–37) and God's (38:1—42:6). Job's monologue turns directly to God for a legal decision: that he is innocent of the charges his counselors have leveled against him. Elihu's monologue—another human perspective on why people suffer—rebukes Job but moves beyond the punishment theme to the value of divine chastening and God's redemptive purpose in it. God's monologue gives the divine perspective: Job is not condemned, but neither is a logical or legal answer given to why Job has suffered. That remains a mystery to Job, though the readers are ready for Job's restoration in the epilogue because they have had the heavenly vantage point of the prologue all along. So the literary structure and the theological significance of the book are beautifully tied together.

Outline

- I. Prologue (chs. 1–2)
  - A. Job's Happiness (1:1–5)
  - B. Job's Testing (1:6—2:13)
    1. Satan's first accusation (1:6–12)
    2. Job's faith despite loss of family and property (1:13–22)
    3. Satan's second accusation (2:1–6)
    4. Job's faith during personal suffering (2:7–10)
    5. The coming of the three friends (2:11–13)
- II. Dialogue/Dispute (chs. 3–27)
  - A. Job's Opening Lament (ch. 3)
  - B. First Cycle of Speeches (chs. 4–14)
    1. Eliphaz (chs. 4–5)
    2. Job's reply (chs. 6–7)
    3. Bildad (ch. 8)
    4. Job's reply (chs. 9–10)
    5. Zophar (ch. 11)
    6. Job's reply (chs. 12–14)
  - C. Second Cycle of Speeches (chs. 15–21)
    1. Eliphaz (ch. 15)
    2. Job's reply (chs. 16–17)
    3. Bildad (ch. 18)
    4. Job's reply (ch. 19)
    5. Zophar (ch. 20)
    6. Job's reply (ch. 21)
  - D. Third Cycle of Speeches (chs. 22–26)
    1. Eliphaz (ch. 22)
    2. Job's reply (chs. 23–24)
    3. Bildad (ch. 25)
    4. Job's reply (ch. 26)
  - E. Job's Closing Discourse (ch. 27)

- III. Interlude on Wisdom (ch. 28)
- IV. Monologues (29:1 — 42:6)
  - A. Job's Call for Vindication (chs. 29 – 31)
    - 1. His past honor and blessing (ch. 29)
    - 2. His present dishonor and suffering (ch. 30)
    - 3. His protestations of innocence and his final oath (ch. 31)
  - B. Elihu's Speeches (chs. 32 – 37)
    - 1. Introduction (32:1 – 5)
    - 2. The speeches themselves (32:6 — 37:24)
      - a. First speech (32:6 — 33:33)
      - b. Second speech (ch. 34)
      - c. Third speech (ch. 35)
      - d. Fourth speech (chs. 36 – 37)
  - C. Divine Discourses (38:1 — 42:6)
    - 1. God's first discourse (38:1 — 40:2)
    - 2. Job's response (40:3 – 5)
    - 3. God's second discourse (40:6 — 41:34)
    - 4. Job's repentance (42:1 – 6)
- V. Epilogue (42:7 – 17)
  - A. God's Verdict (42:7 – 9)
  - B. Job's Restoration (42:10 – 17)

Prologue

1 In the land of Uz[a] there lived a man
whose name was Job.[b] This man was
blameless[c] and upright;[d] he feared God[e]
and shunned evil.[f] 2He had seven sons[g]
and three daughters,[h] 3and he owned sev-
en thousand sheep, three thousand camels, five hundred yoke of oxen and five
hundred donkeys,[i] and had a large number of servants.[j] He was the greatest man[k]
among all the people of the East.[l]
4His sons used to take turns holding
feasts[m] in their homes, and they would
invite their three sisters to eat and drink
with them. 5When a period of feasting had
run its course, Job would send and have
them purified.[n] Early in the morning he
would sacrifice a burnt offering[o] for each
of them, thinking, "Perhaps my children
have sinned[p] and cursed God[q] in their
hearts." This was Job's regular custom.

Job's First Test

6One day the angels[a][r] came to present
themselves before the LORD, and Satan[b][s]
also came with them.[t] 7The LORD said to
Satan, "Where have you come from?"
Satan answered the LORD, "From roaming through the earth and going back and
forth in it."[u]
8Then the LORD said to Satan, "Have you
considered my servant Job?[v] There is no
one on earth like him; he is blameless and
upright, a man who fears God[w] and shuns
evil."[x]
9"Does Job fear God for nothing?"[y] Satan replied. 10"Have you not put a hedge[z]
around him and his household and everything he has?[a] You have blessed the work
of his hands, so that his flocks and herds
are spread throughout the land.[b] 11But
stretch out your hand and strike everything he has,[c] and he will surely curse you
to your face."[d]
12The LORD said to Satan, "Very well,
then, everything he has[e] is in your hands,
but on the man himself do not lay a finger."[f]
Then Satan went out from the presence
of the LORD.
13One day when Job's sons and daughters[g] were feasting[h] and drinking wine at
the oldest brother's house, 14a messenger
came to Job and said, "The oxen were
plowing and the donkeys were grazing[i]
nearby, 15and the Sabeans[j] attacked and
carried them off. They put the servants to
the sword, and I am the only one who has
escaped to tell you!"

1:1 [a]S Ge 10:23 [b]Eze 14:14, 20; Jas 5:11 [c]S Ge 6:9; S Job 23:10 [d]Job 23:7; Ps 11:7; 107:42; Pr 21:29; Mic 7:2 [e]S Ge 22:12 [f]ver 8; S Dt 4:6; Job 2:3; 1Th 5:22 **1:2** [g]S Ru 4:15 [h]ver 13, 18; Job 42:13; Ps 127:3; 144:12 **1:3** [i]S Ge 13:2 [j]S Ge 12:16 [k]ver 8; Job 29:25 [l]S Ge 25:6; Job 42:10; Ps 103:10 **1:4** [m]ver 13, 18 **1:5** [n]S Ne 12:30 [o]S Ge 8:20 [p]Job 8:4 [q]1Ki 21:10, 13; Ps 10:3; 74:10 **1:6** [r]S 1Ki 22:19; *fn* Ge 6:2 [s]S 2Sa 24:1; S 2Ch 18:21; S Ps 109:6; Lk 22:31 [t]Job 2:1 **1:7** [u]S Ge 3:1; 1Pe 5:8 **1:8** [v]S Jos 1:7 [w]Ps 25:12; 112:1; 128:4 [x]S ver 1; S Ex 20:20 **1:9** [y]1Ti 6:5 **1:10** [z]S 1Sa 25:16 [a]ver 12; Job 2:4; Ps 34:7 [b]ver 3; Job 8:7; 29:6; 42:12, 17 **1:11** [c]Job 19:21; Lk 22:31 [d]Lev 24:11; Job 2:5; Isa 3:8; 65:3; Rev 12:9-10 **1:12** [e]S ver 10 [f]Job 2:6; 1Co 10:13 **1:13** [g]S ver 2 [h]S ver 4 **1:14** [i]Ge 36:24 **1:15** [j]S Ge 10:7; S Job 9:24

[a] 6 Hebrew *the sons of God* [b] 6 *Satan* means *accuser.*

1:1 *land of Uz.* A large territory east of the Jordan Valley (see v. 3), which included Edom in the south (see Ge 36:28; La 4:21) and Aram in the north (see Ge 10:23; 22:21; see also note on 1Ch 18:5). The story of Job takes place, then, outside Israel, set by the author in a land far away toward the sunrise—and in a time long ago (see Introduction: Author). *blameless and upright.* Spiritually and morally upright (see note on Ps 26:1). This does not mean that Job was sinless. He later defends his moral integrity but also admits he is a sinner (see 6:24; 7:21 and note). *feared God.* See 28:28; Pr 3:7 and note; see also note on Ge 20:11.
1:2 *seven sons.* An ideal number, signifying completeness (see notes on 42:13; Ru 4:15).
1:3 *seven thousand sheep.* See note on 42:12. Job's enormous wealth was in livestock, not land (see Ge 12:16 and note; 13:2; 26:14). *camels.* See note on Ge 12:16. *donkeys.* The Hebrew for this word is feminine in form. Donkeys that produced offspring were very valuable. *people of the East.* The Hebrew for this phrase is translated "eastern peoples" in Ge 29:1; Jdg 6:3 (see note there).
1:5 *period of feasting.* On special occasions, feasts might last a week (see Ge 29:27; Jdg 14:12). *purified.* Made ceremonially clean in preparation for the sacrifices he offered for his children (see Ex 19:10,14, where the Hebrew for this verb is translated "consecrate"). *he would sacrifice.* In early times the patriarchal head of the household acted as priest for the household (see Ge 15:9–10).
1:6 *angels came to present themselves.* See NIV text note here and on 2:1; 38:7. They came as members of the heavenly council who stand in the presence of God (see 1Ki 22:19 and note; Ps 89:5–7; Jer 23:18,22 and note on 23:18). *Satan.* Lit. "the accuser" (see NIV text note; see also Rev 12:10 and note). In Job the Hebrew for this word is always preceded by the definite article. In the Hebrew of 1Ch 21:1 the article is not used, indicating that "Satan" had become a proper name.
1:7 *The LORD.* That is, Yahweh, the Israelite covenant name for God (see Introduction: Author; see also note on Ge 2:4).
1:8 *Have you considered … Job?* The Lord, not Satan, initiates the dialogue that leads to the testing of Job. He holds up Job as one against whom "the accuser" can lodge no accusation. *my servant.* God's acknowledgment that Job had been faithful and loyal to him. See Isa 42:1 and note.
1:9 "The accuser" boldly accuses the man God commends: He charges that the righteousness of Job in which God expresses such delight is actually self-serving. This is the heart of Satan's attack on both God and on his faithful servant.
1:10 *hedge.* Symbolizes protection (see Isa 5:5; contrast Job 3:23).
1:11 *stretch out your hand and strike.* See 4:5. *he will … curse you.* But Job never did curse God (see 2:9–10 and notes).
1:12 Satan, the accuser, is given power to afflict Job (v. 12a) but is kept on a leash (v. 12b). In all the evil he effects among human beings (vv. 15,17) or in nature (vv. 16,19), Satan is under God's power (compare 1Ch 21:1 with 2Sa 24:1; see 1Sa 16:14 and note; 2Sa 24:16; 1Co 5:5 and note; 2Co 12:7; Heb 2:14). The contest, however, is not a sham. Will Job curse God to his face? If Job does not, the accuser will be proven false and God's delight in Job vindicated.
1:15 *Sabeans.* Probably south Arabians from Sheba, whose descendants became wealthy traders in spices, gold and precious stones (see the account of the queen of Sheba in 1Ki 10:1–13; see also Ps 72:10,15; Isa 60:6; Jer 6:20; Eze 27:22; Joel 3:8). Job 6:19 calls the Sabeans "traveling merchants" and associates them with Tema (about 350 miles southeast of Jerusalem).

16While he was still speaking, another messenger came and said, "The fire of
God fell from the sky[k] and burned up the
sheep and the servants,[l] and I am the only
one who has escaped to tell you!"
17While he was still speaking, another messenger came and said, "The Chaldeans[m] formed three raiding parties and
swept down on your camels and carried
them off. They put the servants to the
sword, and I am the only one who has
escaped to tell you!"
18While he was still speaking, yet another messenger came and said, "Your sons
and daughters[n] were feasting[o] and drinking wine at the oldest brother's house,
19when suddenly a mighty wind[p] swept in
from the desert and struck the four corners of the house. It collapsed on them
and they are dead,[q] and I am the only one
who has escaped to tell you![r]"
20At this, Job got up and tore his robe[s]
and shaved his head.[t] Then he fell to the
ground in worship[u] 21and said:

"Naked I came from my mother's
womb,
and naked I will depart.[a][v]
The LORD gave and the LORD has taken
away;[w]
may the name of the LORD be
praised."[x]

22In all this, Job did not sin by charging
God with wrongdoing.[y]

Job's Second Test

2 On another day the angels[b][z] came to
present themselves before the LORD,
and Satan also came with them[a] to present
himself before him. 2And the LORD said to
Satan, "Where have you come from?"
Satan answered the LORD, "From roaming through the earth and going back and
forth in it."[b]
3Then the LORD said to Satan, "Have you
considered my servant Job? There is no
one on earth like him; he is blameless and
upright, a man who fears God and shuns
evil.[c] And he still maintains his integrity,[d]
though you incited me against him to ruin
him without any reason."[e]
4"Skin for skin!" Satan replied. "A man
will give all he has[f] for his own life. 5But
stretch out your hand and strike his flesh
and bones,[g] and he will surely curse you
to your face."[h]
6The LORD said to Satan, "Very well,
then, he is in your hands;[i] but you must
spare his life."[j]
7So Satan went out from the presence
of the LORD and afflicted Job with painful
sores from the soles of his feet to the top
of his head.[k] 8Then Job took a piece of
broken pottery and scraped himself with
it as he sat among the ashes.[l]
9His wife said to him, "Are you still
holding on to your integrity?[m] Curse God
and die!"[n]
10He replied, "You are talking like a foolish[c] woman. Shall we accept good from
God, and not trouble?"[o]
In all this, Job did not sin in what he
said.[p]

a 21 Or *will return there* *b* 1 Hebrew *the sons of God* *c* 10 The Hebrew word rendered *foolish* denotes moral deficiency.

1:16 [k]S 1Ki 18:38; 2Ki 1:12; Job 20:26 [l]S Ge 18:17; S Lev 10:2; S Nu 11:1-3 **1:17** [m]S Ge 11:28,31; S Job 9:24 **1:18** [n]S ver 2 [o]S ver 4 **1:19** [p]Ps 11:6; Isa 5:28; 21:1; Jer 4:11; 13:24; 18:17; Eze 17:10; Hos 13:15; Mt 7:25 [q]Job 16:7; 19:13-15 [r]Eze 24:26 **1:20** [s]S Ge 37:29; S Mk 14:63 [t]Isa 3:24; 15:2; 22:12; Jer 7:29; 16:6; Eze 27:31; 29:18; Mic 1:16 [u]1Pe 5:6 **1:21** [v]Ecc 5:15; 1Ti 6:7 [w]Ru 1:21; 1Sa 2:7 [x]S Jdg 10:15; Job 2:10; Ecc 7:14; Jer 40:2; S Eph 5:20; 1Th 5:18; Jas 5:11 **1:22** [y]Job 2:10; Ps 39:1; Pr 10:19; 13:3; Isa 53:7; Ro 9:20 **2:1** [z]*fn* Ge 6:2 [a]S Job 1:6 **2:2** [b]S Ge 3:1 **2:3** [c]S Ex 20:20; S Job 1:1,8 [d]Job 6:29; 13:18; 27:6; 31:6; 32:1; 40:8 [e]Job 9:17; Ps 44:17 **2:4** [f]S Job 1:10 **2:5** [g]Job 16:8; 19:20; 33:21; Ps 102:5; La 4:8 [h]S Ex 20:7; S Job 1:11 **2:6** [i]2Co 12:7 [j]S Job 1:12 **2:7** [k]S Dt 28:35; S Job 16:16 **2:8** [l]Ge 18:27; Est 4:3; Job 16:15; 19:9; 30:19; 42:6; Ps 7:5; Isa 58:5; 61:3; Jer 6:26; La 3:29; Eze 26:16; Jnh 3:5-8,6; Mt 11:21 **2:9** [m]Job 6:29; 13:15; 27:5; 33:9; 35:2; 1Th 5:8 [n]S Ex 20:7; S 2Ki 6:33 **2:10** [o]S Job 1:21; S Ecc 2:24; La 3:38 [p]S Job 1:22; S 6:24; Jas 1:12; 5:11

1:16 *fire of God.* Lightning (see Nu 11:1 and note; 1Ki 18:38; 2Ki 1:12).
1:17 *Chaldeans.* A people who were nomadic until c. 1000 B.C., when they settled in southern Mesopotamia and later became the nucleus of Nebuchadnezzar's Neo-Babylonian empire (see note on Ezr 5:12).
1:19 *mighty wind.* Tornado.
1:20 *At this, Job got up.* He is silent until his children are killed. *tore his robe and shaved his head.* In mourning (see notes on Ge 37:34; Isa 15:2).
1:21 *depart.* See NIV text note; see also Ge 2:7; 3:19 and note. *The LORD gave and the LORD has taken away.* Job's faith leads him to see the sovereign God's hand at work, and that gives him repose even in the face of calamity (see 2:10; cf. 40:3–5; 42:1–6).
2:1–3 Except for the final sentence, this passage is almost identical to 1:6–8. He who accused Job of having a deceitful motive is now shown to have a deceitful motive himself: to discredit the Lord through Job.
2:3 *you incited me.* God cannot be stirred up to do things against his will. Though it is not always clear how, everything that happens is part of his divine purpose (see 42:2 and note).
2:4 *Skin for skin!* Probably a proverbial statement equivalent to our "quid pro quo" (this for that).
2:5 *strike his flesh and bones.* See 1:11–12; cf. Ge 2:23; Lk 24:39.
2:6 *spare his life.* Satan is still limited by God. If Job should die, neither God nor Job could be vindicated.
2:7 The precise nature of Job's sickness is uncertain, but its symptoms were painful festering sores over the whole body (7:5), nightmares (7:14), scabs that peeled and became black (30:28,30), disfigurement and revolting appearance (2:12; 19:19), bad breath (19:17), excessive thinness (17:7; 19:20), fever (30:30) and pain day and night (30:17). *sores.* The Hebrew for this word is translated "boils" in Ex 9:9; Lev 13:18; 2Ki 20:7.
2:8 *ashes.* Symbolic of mourning (see 42:6; Est 4:3; cf. Jnh 3:6, which speaks of sitting in dust).
2:9 *Curse God.* The Hebrew for this expression here and in 1:5 employs a euphemism (lit. "Bless God"). Satan is using Job's wife to tempt Job as he used Eve to tempt Adam. *and die.* Since nothing but death is left for Job, his wife wants him to provoke God to administer the final stroke due to all who curse him (Lev 24:10–16).
2:10 *Shall we accept good from God, and not trouble?* A key theme of the book: Trouble and suffering are not always punishment for sin; for God's people they

Job's Three Friends

[11]When Job's three friends, Eliphaz the
Temanite,[q] Bildad the Shuhite[r] and Zophar the Naamathite,[s] heard about all the
troubles that had come upon him, they set
out from their homes and met together by
agreement to go and sympathize with him
and comfort him.[t] [12]When they saw him
from a distance, they could hardly recognize him;[u] they began to weep aloud,[v]
and they tore their robes[w] and sprinkled
dust on their heads.[x] [13]Then they sat on
the ground[y] with him for seven days and
seven nights.[z] No one said a word to him,[a]
because they saw how great his suffering
was.

Job Speaks

3 After this, Job opened his mouth and
cursed the day of his birth.[b] [2]He said:

[3]"May the day of my birth perish,
and the night it was said, 'A boy is
born!'[c]
[4]That day — may it turn to darkness;
may God above not care about it;
may no light shine upon it.
[5]May darkness and deep shadow[a][d]
claim it once more;
may a cloud settle over it;
may blackness overwhelm its light.
[6]That night — may thick darkness[e]
seize it;
may it not be included among the
days of the year
nor be entered in any of the
months.
[7]May that night be barren;
may no shout of joy[f] be heard in it.
[8]May those who curse days[b] curse that
day,[g]
those who are ready to rouse
Leviathan.[h]
[9]May its morning stars become dark;
may it wait for daylight in vain
and not see the first rays of dawn,[i]
[10]for it did not shut the doors of the
womb on me
to hide trouble from my eyes.
[11]"Why did I not perish at birth,
and die as I came from the womb?[j]
[12]Why were there knees to receive me[k]
and breasts that I might be nursed?
[13]For now I would be lying down[l] in
peace;
I would be asleep and at rest[m]
[14]with kings and counselors of the
earth,[n]
who built for themselves places now
lying in ruins,[o]
[15]with rulers[p] who had gold,
who filled their houses with silver.[q]
[16]Or why was I not hidden in the ground
like a stillborn child,[r]
like an infant who never saw the
light of day?[s]
[17]There the wicked cease from turmoil,[t]
and there the weary are at rest.[u]
[18]Captives[v] also enjoy their ease;
they no longer hear the slave
driver's[w] shout.[x]

[a] 5 Or *and the shadow of death* [b] 8 Or *the sea*

2:11 [q]S Ge 36:11 [r]S Ge 25:2 [s]Job 11:1; 20:1 [t]S Ge 37:35; S Job 6:10; Jn 11:19 **2:12** [u]Job 17:7; Isa 52:14 [v]S 2Sa 15:23 [w]S Ge 37:29; S Mk 14:63 [x]S Jos 7:6; S 2Sa 1:2 **2:13** [y]Isa 3:26; 47:1; Jer 48:18; La 2:10; Eze 26:16; Jnh 3:6; Hag 2:22 [z]S Ge 50:10 [a]Pr 17:28; Isa 23:2; 47:5 **3:1** [b]Jer 15:10; 20:14 **3:3** [c]ver 11, 16; Job 10:18-19; Ecc 4:2; 6:3; Jer 20:14-18; Mt 26:24 **3:5** [d]Job 10:21, 22; 34:22; 38:17; Ps 23:4; 44:19; 88:12; Jer 2:6; 13:16 **3:6** [e]Job 23:17; 30:26 **3:7** [f]Ps 20:5; 33:3; 65:13; Isa 26:19; Jer 51:48 **3:8** [g]Job 10:18; Jer 20:14 [h]S Ge 1:21; Job 41:1, 8, 10, 25; Ps 74:14; 104:26 **3:9** [i]Job 41:18; Hab 3:4 **3:11** [j]S ver 3 **3:12** [k]S Ge 48:12; Isa 66:12 **3:13** [l]Job 17:13; 30:23 [m]ver 17; Job 7:8-10, 21; 10:22; 13:19; 14:10-12; 19:27; 21:13, 23; 27:19; Ps 139:11; Isa 8:22 **3:14** [n]Job 9:24; 12:17; Isa 14:9; Eze 32:28-32 [o]Job 15:28; Jer 51:37; Na 3:7 **3:15** [p]Job 12:21; Isa 45:1 [q]Job 15:29; 20:10; 27:17; Ps 49:16-17; Pr 13:22; 28:8; Ecc 2:26; Isa 2:7; Zep 1:11 **3:16** [r]Ps 58:8; Ecc 4:3; 6:3 [s]S ver 3; Ps 71:6 **3:17** [t]ver 26; Job 30:26; Ecc 4:2; Isa 14:3 [u]S ver 13 **3:18** [v]Isa 51:14 [w]S Ge 15:13 [x]Job 39:7

may serve as a trial (as here) or as a discipline that culminates in spiritual gain (see note on 5:17–26; see also Dt 8:5; 2Sa 7:14; Ps 94:12; Pr 3:11–12; 1Co 11:32; Heb 12:5–11 and notes). Job's reply to his wife silences the accuser, who is not heard from again. The first test of Job's godliness is over (see Introduction: Theological Theme and Message). And true to his word here, Job refuses to turn his back on God throughout the long struggle that follows. He faces God with questions, complaints, accusations and appeals, but he continues to face him — and never curses him, as Satan said he would (v. 5; 1:11).

2:11 *three friends.* Older than Job (see 15:10). *Eliphaz.* An Edomite name (see note on Ge 36:11). *Temanite.* Teman was a village in Edom, south of the Dead Sea (see Ge 36:11; Jer 49:7; Eze 25:13; Am 1:12; Ob 9 and notes). *Shuhite.* Bildad may have been a descendant of Shuah, the youngest son of Abraham and Keturah (Ge 25:2).

2:12 *could hardly recognize him.* Cf. Isa 52:14; 53:3. *tore their robes and sprinkled dust on their heads.* Visible signs of mourning (see note on 1:20).

2:13 *sat on the ground with him.* See Eze 3:15; possibly an expression of sympathy or shock. *seven.* The number of completeness (see 1:2; Ge 50:10; 1Sa 31:13 and note; see also note on Ru 4:15). *No one said a word to him.* A wiser response than their later speeches would prove to be (see 16:2–3).

3:1–26 Job's first speech is addressed to no one in particular. In it he simply gives expression to the depths of his suffering.

3:3 *May the day of my birth perish.* Job's very existence, which has been a joy to him because of God's favor, is now his intolerable burden. He is as close as he will ever come to cursing God, but he does not do it (see Jer 20:14–18 and note).

3:4 *may it turn to darkness.* God had said in Ge 1:3, "Let there be light." Job, using similar language, would negate God's creative act.

3:8 *those who curse days.* Eastern soothsayers, like Balaam (see Nu 22–24), who pronounced curses on people, objects and days. *Leviathan.* Using vivid, figurative language, Job wishes that "those who curse days" would arouse the sea monster Leviathan (see note on Isa 27:1) to swallow the day and night of his birth (see v. 3).

3:11–12,16,20–23 A series of rhetorical questions.

3:16 Since in fact his birth had taken place, the next possibility would have been a stillbirth. He would then have lived only in the grave (or Sheol), which he envisions as a place of peace and rest (vv. 13–19; see note on Ge 37:35). Such a situation would be much better than his present intolerable condition, in which he can find neither peace nor rest (v. 26).

3:18 *slave driver's shout.* As in Egypt (see Ex 5:13–14).

19 The small and the great are there,[y]
and the slave is freed from his
master.
20 "Why is light given to those in misery,
and life to the bitter of soul,[z]
21 to those who long for death that does
not come,[a]
who search for it more than for
hidden treasure,[b]
22 who are filled with gladness
and rejoice when they reach the
grave?[c]
23 Why is life given to a man
whose way is hidden,[d]
whom God has hedged in?[e]
24 For sighing[f] comes to me instead of
food;[g]
my groans[h] pour out like water.[i]
25 What I feared has come upon me;
what I dreaded[j] has happened to me.[k]
26 I have no peace,[l] no quietness;
I have no rest,[m] but only turmoil."[n]

Eliphaz

4 Then Eliphaz the Temanite[o] replied:

2 "If someone ventures a word with you,
will you be impatient?
But who can keep from speaking?[p]
3 Think how you have instructed many,[q]
how you have strengthened feeble
hands.[r]
4 Your words have supported those who
stumbled;[s]
you have strengthened faltering
knees.[t]
5 But now trouble comes to you, and
you are discouraged;[u]
it strikes[v] you, and you are
dismayed.[w]
6 Should not your piety be your
confidence[x]
and your blameless[y] ways your
hope?

7 "Consider now: Who, being innocent,
has ever perished?[z]
Where were the upright ever
destroyed?[a]
8 As I have observed,[b] those who plow
evil[c]
and those who sow trouble reap it.[d]
9 At the breath of God[e] they are
destroyed;
at the blast of his anger they perish.[f]
10 The lions may roar[g] and growl,
yet the teeth of the great lions[h] are
broken.[i]
11 The lion perishes for lack of prey,[j]
and the cubs of the lioness are
scattered.[k]
12 "A word[l] was secretly brought to me,
my ears caught a whisper[m] of it.[n]
13 Amid disquieting dreams in the night,
when deep sleep falls on men,[o]
14 fear and trembling[p] seized me
and made all my bones shake.[q]
15 A spirit glided past my face,
and the hair on my body stood on
end.[r]
16 It stopped,
but I could not tell what it was.
A form stood before my eyes,
and I heard a hushed voice:[s]
17 'Can a mortal be more righteous than
God?[t]
Can a man be more pure than his
Maker?[u]

3:19 [y] Job 9:22; 17:16; 21:33; 24:24; 30:23; Ecc 12:5 **3:20** [z] S 1Sa 1:10; Eze 27:30-31 **3:21** [a] Rev 9:6 [b] Ps 119:127; Pr 2:4 **3:22** [c] Job 7:16; Ecc 4:3; Jer 8:3 **3:23** [d] Pr 4:19; Isa 59:10; Jer 13:16; 23:12 [e] Job 6:4; 16:13; 19:6, 8, 12; Ps 88:8; La 2:4; 3:7; Hos 2:6 **3:24** [f] Ps 5:1; 38:9; Isa 35:10 [g] Job 6:7; 33:20; Ps 107:18 [h] Ps 22:1; 32:3; 38:8 [i] 1Sa 1:15; Job 30:16; Ps 6:6; 22:14; 42:3, 4; 80:5; Isa 53:12; La 2:12 **3:25** [j] Job 7:9; 9:28; 30:15; Hos 13:3 [k] S Ge 42:36 **3:26** [l] Isa 48:22; Jn 14:27 [m] Job 7:4, 14; Ps 6:6; Da 4:5; Mt 11:28 [n] S ver 17; S Job 10:18; S 19:8 **4:1** [o] S Ge 36:11; Job 15:1; 22:1 **4:2** [p] Job 32:20; Jer 4:19; 20:9 **4:3** [q] Dt 32:2; Job 29:23; Hos 6:3 [r] Job 26:2; Ps 71:9; Isa 13:7; 35:3; Zep 3:16; Heb 12:12 **4:4** [s] Job 16:5; 29:16, 25; Isa 1:17 [t] Job 29:11, 15; Isa 35:3; Jer 31:8; Heb 12:12 **4:5** [u] S Jos 1:9 [v] Ru 1:13; Job 1:11; 19:21; 30:21; Ps 38:2; Isa 53:4 [w] Job 6:14; Pr 24:10

4:6 [x] 2Ki 18:19; Ps 27:3; 71:5; Pr 3:26 [y] S Ge 6:9 **4:7** [z] Job 5:11; 36:7; Ps 41:12; 2Pe 2:9 [a] Job 8:20; Ps 37:25; 91:9-10; Pr 12:21; 19:23 **4:8** [b] Job 5:3; 15:17 [c] Jdg 14:18; Job 5:6; 15:35; Ps 7:14; Isa 59:4 [d] Ps 7:15; 9:15; Pr 11:18; 22:8; Isa 17:11; Hos 8:7; 10:13; Gal 6:7-8 **4:9** [e] S Ex 15:10; S Job 41:21; 2Th 2:8 [f] S Lev 26:38; Job 40:13; Isa 25:7 **4:10** [g] Ps 22:13 [h] Ps 17:12; 22:21; Pr 28:15 [i] Job 5:15; 29:17; 36:6; 38:15; Ps 35:10; 58:6 **4:11** [j] Dt 28:41; Job 27:14; 29:17; Ps 34:10; 58:6; Pr 30:14 [k] Job 5:4 **4:12** [l] ver 17-21; Job 32:13; Jer 9:23 [m] Job 26:14 [n] Job 33:14 **4:13** [o] Job 33:15 **4:14** [p] Job 21:6; Ps 48:6; 55:5; 119:120, 161; Jer 5:22; Hab 3:16; S 2Co 7:15 [q] Jer 23:9; Da 10:8; Hab 3:16 **4:15** [r] Da 5:6; 7:15, 28; 10:8; Mt 14:26 **4:16** [s] S 1Ki 19:12 **4:17** [t] Job 9:2; 13:18; Ps 143:2 [u] Job 8:3; 10:3; 14:4; 15:14; 21:14; 25:4; 31:15; 32:22; 35:10; 36:3, 13; 37:23; 40:19; Ps 18:26; 51:5; 119:73; Pr 20:9; Ecc 7:20; Isa 51:13; Mal 2:10; Ac 17:24

3:23 *whom God has hedged in.* God, who had put a hedge of protection around him (see 1:10 and note), has now, he feels, hemmed him in with turmoil (see v. 26).

4:1 *Eliphaz the Temanite.* See note on 2:11. Teman was an Edomite town noted for wisdom (see Jer 49:7). The speeches of Job's three friends contain elements of truth, but they must be carefully interpreted in context. The problem is not so much with what the friends knew but with what they did not know: God's hidden purpose in allowing Satan to buffet Job.

4:2 *ventures a word.* Eliphaz seems to be genuinely concerned with Job's well-being and offers a complimentary word (vv. 3 – 4). *impatient.* See note on 9:2 – 3.

4:5 *strikes you.* See 1:11; 2:5; 19:21.

4:6 – 7 Eliphaz counsels Job to be confident that his piety will count with God, that though God is now chastening him for some sin, it is for a good purpose (see 5:17), and he can be assured that God will not destroy him along with the wicked.

4:6 *piety.* Lit. "fear (of God)" (see note on 1:1). The word is used only by Eliphaz (see 15:4; 22:4).

4:7 – 9 If Job is truly innocent, he will not be destroyed.

4:8 – 11 Just as the strongest lions eventually die (vv. 10 – 11), so the wicked are eventually destroyed (vv. 8 – 9); cf. Ps 34:10.

4:8 *those who sow trouble reap it.* Cf. Gal 6:7 – 8 and notes.

4:9 *blast of his anger.* See Ex 15:7 – 8. God's judgment is fearfully severe.

4:12 – 21 Eliphaz tells of a hair-raising (see v. 15), mystical experience mediated through a dream (see v. 13), through which he claims to have received divine revelation and on which he bases his advice to Job.

4:13 *Amid . . . dreams . . . when deep sleep falls on men.* Cf. Elihu's words in 33:15.

4:14 *all my bones shake.* A sign of great distress (see Ps 6:2 and note; 22:14; 31:10; 32:3; 38:3; 42:10; 102:3; Jer 23:9; Hab 3:16).

4:17 – 21 All mortals are sinful; therefore God has a right to punish them. Job should be thankful for the correction God is giving him (see 5:17 – 26 and note).

18 If God places no trust in his servants,[v]
if he charges his angels with
error,[w]
19 how much more those who live in
houses of clay,[x]
whose foundations[y] are in the
dust,[z]
who are crushed[a] more readily than
a moth![b]
20 Between dawn and dusk they are
broken to pieces;
unnoticed, they perish forever.[c]
21 Are not the cords of their tent pulled
up,[d]
so that they die[e] without wisdom?'[a][f]

5 "Call if you will, but who will answer
you?[g]
To which of the holy ones[h] will you
turn?
2 Resentment[i] kills a fool,
and envy slays the simple.[j]
3 I myself have seen[k] a fool taking
root,[l]
but suddenly[m] his house was
cursed.[n]
4 His children[o] are far from safety,[p]
crushed in court[q] without a
defender.[r]
5 The hungry consume his harvest,[s]
taking it even from among thorns,
and the thirsty pant after his
wealth.
6 For hardship does not spring from the
soil,
nor does trouble sprout from the
ground.[t]
7 Yet man is born to trouble[u]
as surely as sparks fly upward.
8 "But if it were I, I would appeal to
God;
I would lay my cause before him.[v]
9 He performs wonders[w] that cannot be
fathomed,[x]
miracles that cannot be counted.[y]
10 He bestows rain on the earth;[z]
he sends water upon the
countryside.[a]
11 The lowly he sets on high,[b]
and those who mourn[c] are lifted[d]
to safety.
12 He thwarts the plans[e] of the crafty,
so that their hands achieve no
success.[f]
13 He catches the wise[g] in their
craftiness,[h]
and the schemes of the wily are
swept away.[i]
14 Darkness[j] comes upon them in the
daytime;
at noon they grope as in the night.[k]
15 He saves the needy[l] from the sword
in their mouth;
he saves them from the clutches of
the powerful.[m]
16 So the poor[n] have hope,
and injustice shuts its mouth.[o]
17 "Blessed is the man whom God
corrects;[p]
so do not despise the discipline[q] of
the Almighty.[b][r]

[a] *21* Some interpreters end the quotation after verse 17.
[b] *17* Hebrew *Shaddai*; here and throughout Job

4:18 [v]Heb 1:14 [w]Job 15:15; 21:22; 25:5 **4:19** [x]Job 10:9; 33:6; Isa 64:8; Ro 9:21; 2Co 4:7; 5:1 [y]Job 22:16 [z]S Ge 2:7 [a]Job 5:4 [b]Job 7:17; 15:16; 17:14; 25:6; Ps 22:6; Isa 41:14 **4:20** [c]Job 14:2, 20; 15:33; 20:7; 24:24; Ps 89:47; 90:5-6; Jas 4:14 **4:21** [d]Job 8:22; Isa 38:12 [e]Jn 8:24 [f]Job 18:21; 36:12; Pr 5:23; Jer 9:3 **5:1** [g]Hab 1:2 [h]Job 15:15; Ps 89:5, 7 **5:2** [i]Job 21:15; 36:13 [j]Pr 12:16; Gal 5:26 **5:3** [k]S Job 4:8 [l]Ps 37:35; Isa 40:24; Jer 12:2; Eze 17:6 [m]Pr 6:15 [n]Job 24:18; Ps 37:22, 35-36; 109:9-10; Pr 3:33 **5:4** [o]Job 20:10; 27:14 [p]S Job 4:11 [q]Job 4:19; Am 5:12 [r]Ps 109:12; Isa 9:17; 1Jn 2:1 **5:5** [s]Lev 26:16; S Jdg 2:15; Job 20:18; 31:8; Mic 6:15 **5:6** [t]S Job 4:8 **5:7** [u]S Ge 3:17; Job 10:17; 15:35; Ps 51:5; 58:3; 90:10; Pr 22:8 **5:8** [v]Job 8:5; 11:13; 13:3, 15; 23:4; 40:1; Ps 35:23; 50:15; Jer 12:1; 1Co 4:4 **5:9** [w]Ps 78:4; 111:2 [x]Dt 29:29; Job 9:4, 10; 11:7; 25:2; 26:14; 33:12; 36:5, 22, 26; 37:5, 14, 16, 23; 42:3; Ps 40:5; 71:17; 72:18; 86:10; 131:1; 139:6, 17; 145:3; Isa 40:28; Ro 11:33 [y]Ps 71:15 **5:10** [z]Mt 5:45 [a]S Lev 26:4; Job 36:28; 37:6, 13; 38:28, 34; Ps 135:7; Jer 14:22 **5:11** [b]S 1Sa 2:7-8; S Job 4:7; Ps 75:7; 113:7-8 [c]Isa 61:2; Mt 5:4; Ro 12:15 [d]S Mt 23:12; Jas 4:10 **5:12** [e]Ne 4:15; Ps 33:10; Isa 8:10; 19:3; Jer 19:7 [f]Job 12:23; Ps 78:59; 140:8 **5:13** [g]Job 37:24; Isa 29:14; 44:25; Jer 8:8; 18:18; 51:57 [h]Job 15:5; Ps 36:3; Lk 20:23; 1Co 3:19*; 2Co 11:3; Eph 4:14 [i]Job 9:4; 18:7; Pr 21:30; 29:6; Jer 8:9 **5:14** [j]Job 15:22, 30; 18:6, 18; 20:26; 22:11; 27:20; Isa 8:22; Jn 12:35 [k]S Dt 28:29; S Job 18:5; Am 8:9 **5:15** [l]S Ex 22:23; Job 8:6; 22:27; 33:26; 36:15 [m]S Job 4:10; S 31:22 **5:16** [n]Job 20:19; 31:16; Pr 17:5; 22:22; Isa 11:4; 41:17; 61:1 [o]Ps 63:11; 107:42; Ro 3:19 **5:17** [p]Dt 8:5; Job 33:19; 36:10; Zep 3:7; Jas 1:12 [q]Ps 94:12; Pr 3:11; Jer 31:18 [r]S Ge 17:1; S Job 15:11; Heb 12:5-11

4:18–19 See 15:15–16.
4:18 *servants.* That is, his heavenly servants (see Ps 103:20–21).
4:19 *houses of clay.* Bodies made of dust (see 10:9; 33:6; see also note on Ge 2:7). *moth.* A symbol of fragility (cf. 27:18).
4:20 *Between dawn and dusk.* A vivid picture of the shortness of life.
4:21 *tent.* A temporary home, like the human body (see 2Co 5:1,4; 2Pe 1:13 and notes). *without wisdom.* Needlessly and senselessly (see v. 20).
5:1 *To which … will you turn?* To plead your case with God. The idea of a mediator, someone to arbitrate between God and Job, is an important motif in the book (see 9:33; 16:19–20 and notes; see also note and NIV text note on 19:25). *holy ones.* Holy angels, the "sons of God" in the prologue (see NIV text notes on 1:6; 2:1).
5:2 Without mentioning him, Eliphaz implies that Job is resentful against God and that harm will follow. *fool.* One who pays no attention to God (see NIV text notes on 2:10; Pr 1:7; see also note on Pr 1:7).
5:3 *A fool taking root.* A wicked man prospering like a tree taking root (see Ps 1:3).
5:6 Unlike a weed, trouble must be sown and cultivated.
5:7 *man is born to trouble.* Proof that no one is righteous in the eyes of God (see notes on 4:17–21; 13:28—14:1). Job should stop behaving like a fool (see vv. 1–7) and should humble himself. Then God would bless, and injustice would shut its mouth (see v. 16). *sparks.* Lit. "sons of Resheph." In Canaanite mythology, Resheph was a god of plague and destruction. "(Sons of) Resheph" is used as a poetic image for fire (SS 8:6), bolts of lightning (Ps 78:48) and pestilence (Dt 32:24; Hab 3:5).
5:9 Repeated in 9:10.
5:13 Quoted in part in 1Co 3:19 (the only clear quotation of Job in the NT).
5:17–26 While the preceding poem (vv. 8–16) spoke of God's goodness and justice, this poem celebrates the blessedness of the one whom God disciplines (see Pr 1:2,7; 3:12 and note; 5:12 and note; 23:13,23). Eliphaz believed that discipline is temporary and is followed by healing (v. 18), and that those who are good will always be rescued. But with Job's wealth gone and his children dead, these words about security (v. 24) and children (v. 25) must have seemed cruel and hollow to him.
5:17 *Almighty.* The first of 31 times that the Hebrew word *Shaddai* is used in Job (see note on Ge 17:1).

[18]For he wounds, but he also binds up;[s]
he injures, but his hands also
heal.[t]
[19]From six calamities he will rescue[u]
you;
in seven no harm will befall you.[v]
[20]In famine[w] he will ransom you from
death,
and in battle from the stroke of the
sword.[x]
[21]You will be protected from the lash of
the tongue,[y]
and need not fear[z] when destruction
comes.[a]
[22]You will laugh[b] at destruction and
famine,[c]
and need not fear the beasts of the
earth.[d]
[23]For you will have a covenant[e] with the
stones[f] of the field,
and the wild animals will be at
peace with you.[g]
[24]You will know that your tent is
secure;[h]
you will take stock of your property
and find nothing missing.[i]
[25]You will know that your children will
be many,[j]
and your descendants like the grass
of the earth.[k]
[26]You will come to the grave in full
vigor,[l]
like sheaves gathered in season.[m]

[27]"We have examined this, and it is true.
So hear it[n] and apply it to yourself."[o]

Job

6 Then Job replied:
[2]"If only my anguish could be weighed
and all my misery be placed on the
scales![p]
[3]It would surely outweigh the sand[q] of
the seas—
no wonder my words have been
impetuous.[r]

5:18 [s]Ps 147:3; Isa 57:15; 61:1; Hos 6:1 [t]S Dt 32:39 **5:19** [u]Da 3:17; 6:16 [v]Ps 34:19; 91:10; Pr 3:25-26; 24:15-16 **5:20** [w]ver 22; Ps 33:19; 37:19 [x]Ps 22:20; 91:7; 140:7; 144:10; Jer 39:18 **5:21** [y]Ps 12:2-4; 31:20 [z]Ps 23:4; 27:1; 91:5 [a]ver 15 **5:22** [b]Job 8:21; 39:7, 18, 22; 41:29 [c]S ver 20 [d]S Lev 25:18; Ps 91:13; Hos 2:18; Mk 1:13 **5:23** [e]Isa 28:15; Hos 2:18 [f]2Ki 3:19, 25; Ps 91:12; Mt 13:8 [g]Job 40:20; Isa 11:6-9; 65:25; Eze 34:25 **5:24** [h]Job 12:6; 21:9 [i]Job 8:6; 22:23 **5:25** [j]Dt 28:4; Ps 112:2 [k]Ps 72:16; Isa 44:3-4; 48:19 **5:26** [l]S Ge 15:15; S Dt 11:21; S Ecc 8:13 [m]Pr 3:21-26 **5:27** [n]Job 32:10, 17 [o]Job 8:5; 11:13; 22:27 **6:2** [p]Job 31:6; Pr 11:1; Da 5:27 **6:3** [q]1Ki 4:29; Pr 27:3 [r]ver 11, 26; Job 7:11; 16:6; 21:4; 23:2

6:4 [s]S Dt 32:23; Ps 38:2 [t]S Ge 17:1 [u]Job 7:20; 16:12, 13; 19:12; La 3:12 [v]Job 21:20 [w]S Dt 32:32; Job 30:21; 34:6; Jer 15:18;

[4]The arrows[s] of the Almighty[t] are in me,[u]
my spirit drinks[v] in their poison;[w]
God's terrors[x] are marshaled against
me.[y]
[5]Does a wild donkey[z] bray[a] when it has
grass,
or an ox bellow when it has fodder?[b]
[6]Is tasteless food eaten without salt,
or is there flavor in the white of an
egg[a]?[c]
[7]I refuse to touch it;
such food makes me ill.[d]

[8]"Oh, that I might have my request,
that God would grant what I hope
for,[e]
[9]that God would be willing to crush[f]
me,
to let loose his hand and cut me off![g]
[10]Then I would still have this
consolation[h]—
my joy in unrelenting pain[i]—
that I had not denied the words[j] of
the Holy One.[k]

[11]"What strength do I have, that I should
still hope?
What prospects, that I should be
patient?[l]
[12]Do I have the strength of stone?
Is my flesh bronze?[m]
[13]Do I have any power to help myself,[n]
now that success has been driven
from me?

[14]"A despairing man[o] should have the
devotion[p] of his friends,[q]
even though he forsakes the fear of
the Almighty.[r]

[a] *6* The meaning of the Hebrew for this phrase is uncertain.

30:12 [x]Job 9:34; 13:21; 18:11; 23:6; 27:20; 30:15; 33:16 [y]S Job 3:23; Ps 88:15-18 **6:5** [z]S Ge 16:12 [a]Job 30:7 [b]Job 24:6; Isa 30:24 **6:6** [c]Job 33:20; Ps 107:18 **6:7** [d]S Job 3:24 **6:8** [e]Job 14:13 **6:9** [f]Job 19:2 [g]S Nu 11:15; S Ps 31:22 **6:10** [h]S Job 2:11; 15:11; Ps 94:19 [i]Ps 38:17; Jer 4:19; 45:3 [j]Job 22:22; 23:12; Ps 119:102; Mk 8:38 [k]S Lev 11:44; S 2Ki 19:22; S Isa 31:1 **6:11** [l]S ver 3 **6:12** [m]Job 26:2 **6:13** [n]Job 26:2 **6:14** [o]S Job 4:5 [p]1Sa 20:42; Job 15:4 [q]Job 12:4; 17:2, 6; 19:19, 21; 21:3; 30:1, 10; Ps 38:11; 69:20; 1Jn 3:17 [r]S Ge 17:1

5:18–19 See Hos 6:1–2.
5:19 *six ... seven.* See 33:29; 40:5; Pr 6:16 and note; 30:15,18,21,29; Ecc 11:2; Am 1:3,6,9,11,13 and note on 1:3; 2:1,4,6; Mic 5:5 and note.
5:23 *covenant with the stones.* A figurative way of saying that stones will "be at peace with you" and will not ruin the crops (see 2Ki 3:19; Isa 5:2; Mt 13:5).
5:25 *like the grass of the earth.* As numerous as blades of grass (see note on Ge 13:16).
5:26 Eliphaz's prediction was more accurate than he realized (see 42:16–17).
5:27 *apply it to yourself.* Eliphaz's conclusion: Job must turn from unrighteousness (4:7) and resentment against God (v. 2) to humility (v. 11) and the acceptance of God's righteous discipline (v. 17). Eliphaz's purpose is to offer theological comfort and counsel to Job (2:11), but instead he wounds him with false accusation.
6:2–3 Job appeals for a sympathetic understanding of the harsh words he spoke in ch. 3.
6:4 *arrows of the Almighty.* Job shares Eliphaz's "orthodox" theology and believes that God is aiming his arrows of judgment at him—though he does not know why (see 7:20 and note; 16:12–13; see also La 3:12; cf. Dt 32:23; Ps 7:13; 38:2).
6:5–6 Job claims the right to bray and bellow, since he has been wounded by God and offered tasteless food (words) by his friends.
6:5 *wild donkey.* Properly the wild ass (onager). See 39:5–8 and notes on Ge 16:12; Jer 2:24.
6:10 *Then.* In the afterlife, Job would have the joy of knowing that he had remained true to God.
6:11–13 With no human resources left, Job considers his condition hopeless.
6:11 *patient.* See note on 9:2–3.
6:14–17 Job needs spiritual help, but his friends are proving to be undependable (cf. Gal 6:1).

15 But my brothers are as undependable
as intermittent streams,[s]
as the streams that overflow
16 when darkened by thawing ice
and swollen with melting snow,[t]
17 but that cease to flow in the dry
season,
and in the heat[u] vanish from their
channels.
18 Caravans turn aside from their routes;
they go up into the wasteland and
perish.
19 The caravans of Tema[v] look for water,
the traveling merchants of Sheba[w]
look in hope.
20 They are distressed, because they had
been confident;
they arrive there, only to be
disappointed.[x]
21 Now you too have proved to be of no
help;
you see something dreadful and are
afraid.[y]
22 Have I ever said, 'Give something on
my behalf,
pay a ransom[z] for me from your
wealth,[a]
23 deliver me from the hand of the
enemy,
ransom me from the clutches of the
ruthless'?[b]
24 "Teach me, and I will be quiet;[c]
show me where I have been wrong.[d]
25 How painful are honest words![e]
But what do your arguments prove?
26 Do you mean to correct what I say,
and treat the words of a despairing
man as wind?[f]
27 You would even cast lots[g] for the
fatherless[h]
and barter away your friend.
28 "But now be so kind as to look at me.
Would I lie to your face?[i]
29 Relent, do not be unjust;[j]
reconsider, for my integrity[k] is at
stake.[a][l]
30 Is there any wickedness on my lips?[m]
Can my mouth not discern[n] malice?

6:15 [s] Job 13:4; 16:2; 21:34; Ps 22:1; 38:11; Jer 15:18 **6:16** [t] Ps 147:18 **6:17** [u] Job 24:19 **6:19** [v] S Ge 25:15 [w] S Ge 10:7, 28 **6:20** [x] Jer 14:3; Joel 1:11 **6:21** [y] Ps 38:11 **6:22** [z] S Nu 35:31; Job 33:24; Ps 49:7 [a] Jer 15:10 **6:23** [b] S 2Ki 19:19 **6:24** [c] S Job 2:10; 33:33; Ps 39:1; 141:3; Pr 10:19; 11:12; 17:27; Ecc 5:2 [d] Job 19:4 **6:25** [e] Ecc 12:11; Isa 22:23 **6:26** [f] S ver 3; S Ge 41:6; Job 8:2; 15:3; 16:3; Jer 5:13 **6:27** [g] Eze 24:6; Joel 3:3; Ob 1:11; Na 3:10 [h] S Ex 22:22, 24; Job 31:17, 21; Isa 10:2 **6:28** [i] Job 9:15; 24:25; 27:4; 32:10; 33:1, 3; 34:6; 36:3, 4 **6:29** [j] Job 19:6; 27:2; 40:8; Isa 40:27 [k] S Job 2:3 [l] Job 9:21; 10:7; 11:2; 12:4; 23:7, 10; 33:9, 32; 34:5, 36; 35:2; 42:6; Ps 66:10; Zec 13:9 **6:30** [m] Job 27:4 [n] Job 12:11

7:1 [o] Job 14:14; Isa 40:2 [p] S Job 5:7 [q] S Lev 25:50 **7:2** [r] Job 14:1; Ecc 2:23 [s] S Lev 19:13; S Job 14:6 **7:3** [t] Job 16:7; Ps 6:6; 42:3; 56:8; Ecc 4:1; Isa 16:9; Jer 9:1; La 1:2, 16 **7:4** [u] Dt 28:67 [v] ver 13-14 **7:5** [w] Job 17:14; 21:26; 24:20; 25:6; Isa 14:11 [x] S Dt 28:35

7 "Does not man have hard service[o] on
earth?[p]
Are not his days like those of a hired
man?[q]
2 Like a slave longing for the evening
shadows,[r]
or a hired man waiting eagerly for
his wages,[s]
3 so I have been allotted months of
futility,
and nights of misery have been
assigned to me.[t]
4 When I lie down I think, 'How long
before I get up?'[u]
The night drags on, and I toss till
dawn.[v]
5 My body is clothed with worms[w] and
scabs,
my skin is broken and festering.[x]
6 "My days are swifter than a weaver's
shuttle,[y]
and they come to an end without
hope.[z]
7 Remember, O God, that my life is but a
breath;[a]
my eyes will never see happiness
again.[b]
8 The eye that now sees me will see me
no longer;
you will look for me, but I will be no
more.[c]
9 As a cloud vanishes[d] and is gone,
so he who goes down to the grave[b][e]
does not return.[f]
10 He will never come to his house again;
his place[g] will know him no more.[h]
11 "Therefore I will not keep silent;[i]
I will speak out in the anguish[j] of
my spirit,
I will complain[k] in the bitterness of
my soul.[l]

[a] 29 Or *my righteousness still stands* [b] 9 Hebrew *Sheol*

7:6 [y] Job 9:25; Ps 39:5; Isa 38:12 [z] Job 13:15; 14:19; 17:11, 15; 19:10; Ps 37:4; 52:9 **7:7** [a] ver 16; Ge 27:46; Ps 39:4, 5, 11; 62:9; 78:39; 89:47; 144:4; Ecc 7:15; S Jas 4:14 [b] Job 10:20 **7:8** [c] S Job 3:13; 8:18; 15:29; 20:7, 9, 21; 27:17; Ps 37:36; 103:16; Isa 41:12; Jn 16:16; Ac 20:25 **7:9** [d] S Job 3:25 [e] S Job 3:13; 11:8; 14:13; 17:16; 26:6; 38:17; Am 9:2 [f] 2Sa 12:23 **7:10** [g] Job 18:21; 21:18; 27:21, 23; Ps 58:9; Jer 18:17; 19:8 [h] S ver 8; Ps 37:10; 104:35 **7:11** [i] Job 9:35; 13:13; Ps 22:2; 40:9 [j] Job 10:1; Ps 6:3; Isa 38:15, 17 [k] ver 13; Job 9:27; 21:4; 23:2 [l] S 1Sa 1:10; S Job 6:3

6:15 *brothers.* By calling his friends his "brothers," Job makes their callousness stand out more sharply.
6:19 *Tema.* See note on Isa 21:14. *Sheba.* See note on 1:15.
6:22–23 Job has not asked them for anything except what will cost them nothing: their friendship and counsel.
6:25 *honest words.* Job is referring to his own words.
6:26 *wind.* See 8:2.
6:27 In addition to dishonesty, Job accuses his friends of heartless cruelty.
6:29 Job softens his tone, pleading that his friends take back their false accusations.
7:1–21 Having replied to Eliphaz, Job now addresses his complaint toward God.
7:1 *hard service.* See 14:14; cf. Isa 40:2 and note.
7:2 *evening shadows.* End of the workday.
7:5 See note on 2:7.
7:7 *my life is but a breath.* As a chronic sufferer he has lost all sense of purpose in life (see v. 3; see also Ps 144:3–4). He does not anticipate healing and sees death as his only escape.
7:8 *you will look … no more.* See v. 21.
7:9 *he who goes down to the grave does not return.* Such statements are based on common observation and are not meant to dogmatize about what happens after death. Mesopotamian descriptions of the netherworld refer to it similarly as the "land of no return" (see note on v. 21). For the OT perspective on life after death, see Ps 6:5 and note.
7:11 *not keep silent.* Job is determined to cry out against the apparent injustice of God who, it seems, will not leave him alone (vv. 17–20). *speak out in … anguish.* See Jer 4:19. *bitterness of … soul.* See 10:1 and note; 21:25; 27:2.

12 Am I the sea,[m] or the monster of the deep,[n]
that you put me under guard?[o]
13 When I think my bed will comfort me
and my couch will ease my complaint,[p]
14 even then you frighten me with dreams
and terrify[q] me with visions,[r]
15 so that I prefer strangling and death,[s]
rather than this body of mine.[t]
16 I despise my life;[u] I would not live forever.[v]
Let me alone;[w] my days have no meaning.[x]

17 "What is man that you make so much of him,
that you give him so much attention,[y]
18 that you examine him every morning[z]
and test him[a] every moment?[b]
19 Will you never look away from me,[c]
or let me alone even for an instant?[d]
20 If I have sinned, what have I done to you,[e]
O watcher of men?
Why have you made me your target?[f]
Have I become a burden to you?[a][g]
21 Why do you not pardon my offenses
and forgive my sins?[h]
For I will soon lie down in the dust;[i]
you will search for me, but I will be no more."[j]

Bildad

8 Then Bildad the Shuhite[k] replied:

2 "How long will you say such things?[l]
Your words are a blustering wind.[m]
3 Does God pervert justice?[n]
Does the Almighty pervert what is right?[o]
4 When your children sinned against him,
he gave them over to the penalty of their sin.[p]
5 But if you will look to God
and plead[q] with the Almighty,[r]
6 if you are pure and upright,
even now he will rouse himself on your behalf[s]
and restore you to your rightful place.[t]
7 Your beginnings will seem humble,
so prosperous[u] will your future be.[v]

8 "Ask the former generations[w]
and find out what their fathers learned,
9 for we were born only yesterday and know nothing,[x]
and our days on earth are but a shadow.[y]
10 Will they not instruct[z] you and tell you?
Will they not bring forth words from their understanding?[a]
11 Can papyrus grow tall where there is no marsh?[b]
Can reeds[c] thrive without water?

[a] 20 A few manuscripts of the Masoretic Text, an ancient Hebrew scribal tradition and Septuagint; most manuscripts of the Masoretic Text *I have become a burden to myself.*

7:12 [m] Job 38:8-11 [n] S Ge 1:21 [o] ver 20; Isa 1:14 **7:13** [p] S ver 11 **7:14** [q] Job 9:34 [r] S Ge 41:8; S Job 3:26 **7:15** [s] 1Ki 19:4; Jnh 4:3 [t] Job 6:9; Rev 9:6 **7:16** [u] S 1Ki 19:4; Job 9:21 [v] S Job 3:22 [w] ver 19; Job 10:20; Ps 39:13 [x] S ver 7 **7:17** [y] S Job 4:19; 22:2; Ps 8:4; 144:3; Heb 2:6 **7:18** [z] Ps 73:14 [a] Job 23:10; Ps 139:23 [b] Job 14:3; Ps 17:3; 26:2; 66:10; 139:1-6; 143:2 **7:19** [c] S ver 16 [d] Job 9:18; 13:26; 14:6; 27:2; Ps 139:7 **7:20** [e] Job 35:6; Jer 7:19 [f] S Job 6:4 [g] S ver 12 **7:21** [h] Job 9:28; 10:14; 16:6; Ps 119:120; Isa 43:25; Jer 31:34; Heb 1:3 [i] S Ge 3:19; Job 10:9; 34:15; Ps 7:5; 22:15; 90:3; 104:29 [j] S ver 8; S Job 3:13 **8:1** [k] S Ge 25:2; Job 18:1; 25:1 **8:2** [l] Job 11:2; 18:2 [m] S 2Ch 36:16; S Job 6:26 **8:3** [n] S Job 4:17; 34:12; Isa 29:15; Ro 3:5 [o] S Ge 18:25; S Jer 12:1 **8:4** [p] Job 1:19 **8:5** [q] Job 9:15 [r] S Job 5:8, 27 **8:6** [s] S Job 5:15; 22:27; 33:26; 34:28; Isa 58:9; 65:24 [t] S Job 5:24 **8:7** [u] Job 21:13; 22:21; 36:11; Ps 25:13 [v] S Job 1:10; Jer 29:11; 31:17 **8:8** [w] S Dt 32:7; S Ps 71:18 **8:9** [x] S Ge 47:9 [y] S 1Ch 29:15; S 2Ch 10:6; S Ps 39:6 **8:10** [z] Pr 1:8 [a] Pr 2:1-2; 4:1 **8:11** [b] Job 40:21 [c] S Ex 2:3; Isa 19:6; 35:7

7:12 *the sea, or the monster of the deep.* See 3:8 and NIV text note. The boisterous sea monster was a symbol of chaos (see Ps 74:13–14 and note; Isa 27:1 and note; 51:9), and Job objects to being treated like it.

7:13–15 Job thinks that even the nightmares that disturb his sleep are from God.

7:16 *I despise my life.* See note on 9:21.

7:17 *What is man that you make so much of him ...?* See Ps 144:3; cf. Ps 8:4–8, where the answer is given that humanity is created in God's image to have dominion over the world (see notes on Ge 1:26–28; Ps 8:6–8). Job's words (vv. 18–21) are a parody on this theme—as if God's only interest in people is to scrutinize them unmercifully and take quick offense at their slightest fault.

7:19 *even for an instant.* Lit. "long enough for me to swallow my saliva."

7:20 *If I have sinned, what have I done to you ...?* I have not been perfect, but what terrible sin have I committed that deserves this kind of suffering? *watcher.* The Hebrew for this word is used in a favorable sense in Isa 27:3, but here Job complains that God is too critical (cf. v. 12). *made me your target.* See note on 6:4. *burden to you.* See NIV text note. Ancient Hebrew scribes report that a change in the text had been made from "you" to "myself" because the reading "you" involved too presumptuous a questioning of God's justice.

7:21 *offenses ... sins.* Job confesses that he is a sinner, but he cannot understand why God refuses to forgive him. *lie down in the dust.* Of the netherworld, as in Mesopotamian descriptions of it (see note on v. 9).

8:2 *How long ...?* See 18:2. In contrast to the older Eliphaz, Bildad is impatient.

8:3 *Does God pervert justice?* But Job has not yet blatantly accused God of injustice.

8:5–6 Bildad reasons as follows: God cannot be unjust, so Job and his family must be suffering as a result of sinfulness. Job should plead for mercy, and if he has been upright, God will restore him.

8:6 *if you are pure and upright.* We know God's verdict about Job (see 1:8; 2:3), but Bildad is confident that Job is a hypocrite (see v. 13).

8:7 See v. 21. Bildad spoke more accurately than he realized (see 42:10–17).

8:8 *Ask the former generations.* Eliphaz appealed to revelation from the spirit world (see 4:12–21), while Bildad appeals to the accumulated wisdom of tradition.

8:9 *our days ... are but a shadow.* A common motif in wisdom literature (see 14:2 and note; 1Ch 29:15; Ps 102:11; 144:4; Ecc 6:12; 8:13).

8:11–19 A practical wisdom poem, giving words of instruction learned from "the former generations" and "their fathers" (v. 8). It is introduced in v. 10 and applied to Job in vv. 20–22.

12 While still growing and uncut,
they wither more quickly than
grass.[d]
13 Such is the destiny[e] of all who forget
God;[f]
so perishes the hope of the godless.[g]
14 What he trusts in is fragile[a];
what he relies on is a spider's web.[h]
15 He leans on his web,[i] but it gives way;
he clings to it, but it does not hold.[j]
16 He is like a well-watered plant in the
sunshine,
spreading its shoots[k] over the
garden;[l]
17 it entwines its roots around a pile of
rocks
and looks for a place among the
stones.
18 But when it is torn from its spot,
that place disowns[m] it and says, 'I
never saw you.'[n]
19 Surely its life withers[o] away,
and[b] from the soil other plants
grow.[p]

20 "Surely God does not reject a
blameless[q] man
or strengthen the hands of
evildoers.[r]
21 He will yet fill your mouth with
laughter[s]
and your lips with shouts of joy.[t]
22 Your enemies will be clothed in
shame,[u]
and the tents[v] of the wicked will be
no more."[w]

Job

9 Then Job replied:

2 "Indeed, I know that this is true.
But how can a mortal be righteous
before God?[x]
3 Though one wished to dispute with
him,[y]
he could not answer him one time
out of a thousand.[z]
4 His wisdom[a] is profound, his power is
vast.[b]
Who has resisted[c] him and come out
unscathed?[d]
5 He moves mountains[e] without their
knowing it
and overturns them in his anger.[f]
6 He shakes the earth[g] from its place
and makes its pillars tremble.[h]
7 He speaks to the sun and it does not
shine;[i]
he seals off the light of the stars.[j]
8 He alone stretches out the heavens[k]
and treads on the waves of the sea.[l]
9 He is the Maker[m] of the Bear and Orion,
the Pleiades and the constellations of
the south.[n]
10 He performs wonders[o] that cannot be
fathomed,
miracles that cannot be counted.[p]
11 When he passes me, I cannot see him;
when he goes by, I cannot perceive
him.[q]
12 If he snatches away, who can stop
him?[r]
Who can say to him, 'What are you
doing?'[s]

[a] *14* The meaning of the Hebrew for this word is uncertain. [b] *19* Or *Surely all the joy it has / is that*

8:12 [d] ver 19; S 2Ki 19:26; Job 18:16; 20:5; Ps 90:5-6; 102:11; Isa 34:4; 40:7,24 **8:13** [e] Ps 37:38; 73:17 [f] Ps 9:17; 50:22; Isa 51:13; Jer 17:6 [g] Job 6:9; 11:20; 13:16; 15:34; 20:5; 27:8; 34:30; Ps 37:1-2; 112:10; Pr 10:28; 11:7; Jer 15:9 **8:14** [h] ver 15; Job 27:18; Isa 59:5 **8:15** [i] S ver 14 [j] Ps 49:11; Mt 7:26-27 **8:16** [k] Ps 80:11; Isa 16:8 [l] Ps 37:35; Jer 11:16 **8:18** [m] Job 20:9; Ps 103:16 [n] S Job 7:8; S 14:20 **8:19** [o] S ver 12; S Job 15:30 [p] Ps 119:90; Ecc 1:4 **8:20** [q] Job 1:1 [r] S Ge 18:25 **8:21** [s] S Job 5:22 [t] S Ezr 3:13; Job 35:10; Ps 47:5; 107:22; 118:15; 126:2; 132:16; Isa 35:6 **8:22** [u] Job 27:7; Ps 6:10; 35:26; 44:7; 53:5; 71:13; 86:17; 109:29; 132:18; Eze 7:27; 26:16 [v] S Job 4:21 [w] S 1Sa 8:3; Job 18:6,14,21; 21:28; 27:8,18; 34:26; 36:6; 38:13; Ps 52:5; Pr 14:11 **9:2** [x] S Job 4:17; Ro 3:20 **9:3** [y] ver 32; Job 40:5 [z] ver 12,14,29, 32; Job 10:2; 12:14; 13:9,14; 22:4; 23:7,13; 37:19; 40:2; Ps 44:21; Isa 14:24 **9:4** [a] Job 11:6; 28:12,20,23; 38:36; Ps 51:6; Pr 2:6; Ecc 2:26 [b] ver 19; S Job 5:9; 12:13,16; 23:6; 24:22; 26:12; 30:18; Ps 93:4; 95:3; Pr 8:14; Isa 40:26; 63:1; Da 2:20; 4:35 [c] Jer 50:24 [d] S 2Ch 13:12; S Job 5:13 **9:5** [e] Mt 17:20 [f] Ps 18:7; 46:2-3; Isa 13:13; Mic 1:4 **9:6** [g] S Ex 19:18; Isa 2:21; 13:13; 24:18-20; Am 8:8; Heb 12:26 [h] S 2Sa 22:8; Job 26:14; 36:29; 37:4-5; Ps 75:3; Hab 3:4 **9:7** [i] Isa 34:4; Jer 4:28; Joel 2:2,10,31; 3:15; Zep 1:15; Zec 14:6 [j] Isa 13:10; Jer 4:23; Eze 32:8 **9:8** [k] S Ge 1:1,8; S Isa 48:13 [l] Job 38:16; Ps 77:19; Pr 8:28; Hab 3:15; Mt 14:25; Mk 6:48; Jn 6:19 **9:9** [m] Job 32:22; 40:15,19 [n] S Ge 1:16 **9:10** [o] Dt 6:22; Ps 72:18; 136:4; Jer 32:20 [p] S Job 5:9 **9:11** [q] Job 23:8-9; 35:14 **9:12** [r] Nu 23:20; Job 11:10; Isa 14:27; 43:13 [s] S ver 3; S Dt 32:39; Isa 29:16; 45:9; Da 2:21; 4:32; Ro 9:20

8:20 Bildad is blunt about Job's being an evildoer, whereas Eliphaz had resorted to insinuation (see 4:7–9).
8:21 See note on v. 7.
8:22 *clothed in.* See note on Ps 109:29.
9:2–3 Job does not believe he is sinless (see note on 1:1), but he wishes to have his day in court so he can prove he is innocent of the kind of sin that deserves the suffering he endures. In his despair he voices awful complaints against God (see vv. 16–20,22–24,29–35; 10:1–7,13–17). Yet he does not abandon God; he does not curse him (see 10:2,8–12; see also Introduction: Theological Theme and Message), as Satan said he would (see 1:11; 2:5; cf. 2:9). Ch. 42 implies that Job persevered, but chs. 9–10 show that he did so with impatience (see 4:2; 6:11; 21:4). Cf. Jas 5:11, which speaks of Job's perseverance, not (as traditionally) his patience.
9:3 *dispute.* See v. 14. Job's speech is filled with the imagery of the courtroom: "answer him" (vv. 3,15,32), "argue with him" (v. 14), "innocent ... plead ... Judge" (v. 15), "summon(ed)" (vv. 16,19), "pronounce me guilty" (v. 20), "judges" (v. 24), "court" (v. 32), "charges ... against me" (10:2), "witnesses" (10:17). Job argues his innocence, but he feels that because God is so great there is no use in contending with him (v. 14). Job's innocence does him no good (v. 15).
9:5–10 A beautiful hymn about God's greatness. But Job is not blessed by it, for he does not see that God's power is controlled by goodness and justice.
9:6 For the metaphor of the earth resting on a foundation see 38:6; 1Sa 2:8 and note; Ps 24:2 and note; 75:3; 104:5.
9:8 *stretches out the heavens.* Either (1) creates the heavens (see Isa 44:24), or perhaps (2) causes the dawn to spread, like someone stretching out a tent (see Ps 104:2). *treads on the waves.* Canaanite texts describe the goddess Asherah as walking on the sea (or sea-god) to subdue it. Similarly, God "treads on the waves" to control the boisterous sea.
9:9 *Bear ... Orion ... Pleiades.* These three constellations are mentioned again in 38:31–32, and the last two are mentioned in Am 5:8 (see note there). Despite their limited knowledge of astronomy, the ancient Israelites were awed by the fact that God had created the constellations.
9:10 The same words are spoken by Eliphaz in 5:9.
9:12 *who can stop him?* Job argues that God has an unchallengeable, sovereign freedom that works to accomplish everything he pleases.

13 God does not restrain his anger;[t]
even the cohorts of Rahab[u] cowered
at his feet.

14 "How then can I dispute with him?
How can I find words to argue with
him?[v]
15 Though I were innocent, I could not
answer him;[w]
I could only plead[x] with my Judge[y]
for mercy.[z]
16 Even if I summoned him and he
responded,
I do not believe he would give me a
hearing.[a]
17 He would crush me[b] with a storm[c]
and multiply[d] my wounds for no
reason.[e]
18 He would not let me regain my breath
but would overwhelm me with
misery.[f]
19 If it is a matter of strength, he is
mighty![g]
And if it is a matter of justice, who
will summon him[a]?[h]
20 Even if I were innocent, my mouth
would condemn me;
if I were blameless, it would
pronounce me guilty.[i]

21 "Although I am blameless,[j]
I have no concern for myself;[k]
I despise my own life.[l]
22 It is all the same; that is why I say,
'He destroys both the blameless and
the wicked.'[m]
23 When a scourge[n] brings sudden death,
he mocks the despair of the
innocent.[o]
24 When a land falls into the hands of the
wicked,[p]
he blindfolds its judges.[q]
If it is not he, then who is it?[r]

25 "My days are swifter than a runner;[s]
they fly away without a glimpse of
joy.[t]
26 They skim past[u] like boats of papyrus,[v]
like eagles swooping down on their
prey.[w]
27 If I say, 'I will forget my complaint,[x]
I will change my expression, and
smile,'
28 I still dread[y] all my sufferings,
for I know you will not hold me
innocent.[z]
29 Since I am already found guilty,
why should I struggle in vain?[a]
30 Even if I washed myself with soap[b][b]
and my hands[c] with washing soda,[d]
31 you would plunge me into a slime pit[e]
so that even my clothes would detest
me.[f]

32 "He is not a man[g] like me that I might
answer him,[h]
that we might confront each other in
court.[i]
33 If only there were someone to arbitrate
between us,[j]
to lay his hand upon us both,[k]
34 someone to remove God's rod from
me,[l]
so that his terror would frighten me
no more.[m]
35 Then I would speak up without fear of
him,[n]
but as it now stands with me, I
cannot.[o]

10 "I loathe my very life;[p]
therefore I will give free rein to my
complaint
and speak out in the bitterness of
my soul.[q]

[a] 19 See Septuagint; Hebrew *me.* [b] 30 Or *snow*

9:13 [t]Nu 14:18; Job 10:15; Ps 78:38; Isa 3:11; 6:5; 48:9 [u]Job 26:12; Ps 87:4; 89:10; Isa 30:7; 51:9 **9:14** [v]S ver 3 **9:15** [w]Job 10:15; 13:19; 34:5-6; 40:5; 42:7 [x]Job 8:5 [y]S Ge 18:25; 1Sa 24:12; Ps 50:6; 96:13 [z]ver 20, 29; Job 15:6; 23:4; 40:2 **9:16** [a]Job 13:22; Ro 9:20-21 **9:17** [b]Job 16:12; 30:16; Ps 10:10; Isa 38:13 [c]Job 30:22; Ps 83:15; Jnh 1:4 [d]Job 16:14 [e]S Job 2:3 **9:18** [f]S Job 7:19; S 10:1 **9:19** [g]S ver 4; S Ne 9:32 [h]ver 33; Jer 49:19 **9:20** [i]S ver 15 **9:21** [j]S Ge 6:9; Job 34:6, 7 [k]ver 14; S Job 6:29; 10:1; 13:13 [l]S Nu 11:15; S Job 7:16 **9:22** [m]S Job 3:19; 10:8; Ecc 9:2, 3; Eze 21:3 **9:23** [n]Heb 11:36 [o]Job 24:1, 12; Ps 64:4; Hab 1:3; 1Pe 1:7 **9:24** [p]Job 1:15, 17; 10:3; 16:11; 21:16; 22:18; 27:2; 40:8; Ps 73:3 [q]S Job 3:14; 12:6; 19:7; 21:7; 24:23; 31:35; 35:15; Ps 73:12; Ecc 8:11; Jer 12:1; La 3:9 [r]Job 12:9; 13:1; 24:12; Isa 41:20 **9:25** [s]S Job 7:6 [t]Job 7:7; 10:20 **9:26** [u]Job 24:18; Ps 46:3 [v]Isa 18:2 [w]Job 39:29; Hab 1:8 **9:27** [x]S Job 7:11 **9:28** [y]S Job 3:25 [z]S Ex 34:7; S Job 7:21 **9:29** [a]S ver 3, S 15; Ps 37:33 **9:30** [b]Mal 3:2 [c]Job 17:9; 31:7; Isa 1:15 [d]Job 14:4, 17; 33:9; Isa 1:18; Jer 2:22; Hos 13:12 **9:31** [e]Ps 35:7; 40:2; 51:9; Jer 2:22; Na 3:6; Mal 2:3 [f]S Job 7:20; 34:9; 35:3; Ps 73:13 **9:32** [g]S Nu 23:19 [h]S ver 3; Ro 9:20 [i]Ps 143:2; Ecc 6:10 **9:33** [j]S 1Sa 2:25 [k]S ver 19 **9:34** [l]Job 21:9; Ps 39:10; 73:5 [m]S Job 6:4; 7:14; 33:7; Ps 32:4 **9:35** [n]S Job 7:11 [o]Job 7:15; 13:21 **10:1** [p]S Nu 11:15; S 1Ki 19:4 [q]S 1Sa 1:10; S Job 7:11; 9:18, 21

9:13 *Rahab.* A mythical sea monster (see 26:12), elsewhere used as symbolic of Egypt (see Isa 30:7 and note). See 3:8; 7:12 and notes. The name Rahab in Jos 2 is from a different Hebrew root.
9:15 Job believes that his only recourse before the lofty majesty of God is to throw himself on God's mercy.
9:17 Job does not know that God has allowed Satan to crush him for a high purpose.
9:20 *my mouth would condemn me.* See 15:6.
9:21 *I despise my own life.* See 7:16; words of despairing resignation that would be partially echoed in Job's final outpouring of repentance (see 42:6 and note).
9:22–24 God has become Job's great enigma. Job describes a phantom God—one who does not exist, except in Job's mind. The God of the Bible is not morally indifferent (cf. God's words in 38:2; 40:2 and Job's response in 42:3).
9:24 *blindfolds its judges.* Statues of Lady Justice are blindfolded, implying that she will judge impartially. But Job's accusation against God is that he has blindfolded the judges so that they see neither crimes nor innocence.
9:26 *boats of papyrus.* See note on Ex 2:3.
9:28 *you will not hold me innocent.* Job wants to stand before God as an innocent man—not sinless, but innocent of any sin commensurate with his suffering.
9:29 *already found guilty.* As appears from the bitter suffering he is enduring.
9:30 *soda.* A vegetable alkali used as a cleansing agent. The Hebrew underlying this word is translated "soap" in Jer 2:22; Mal 3:2.
9:33 *someone to arbitrate between us.* See note on 5:1. God is so mighty that Job feels he needs someone who can help him, someone who can argue his case in court. Job's call is not directly predicting the mediatorship of Christ, for Job is not looking for one to forgive him but for one who can testify to his innocence (see 16:18–21; 19:25–26 and notes).
9:34 See 13:21. *God's rod.* Symbolic of divine judgment and wrath (see, e.g., Ps 89:30–37; La 3:1 and notes).
10:1 *I loathe my very life.* See note on 9:21. *bitterness of my soul.* Because Job is so bitter, his mind has conjured up a false picture of God.

[2]I will say to God:[r] Do not condemn me,
but tell me what charges[s] you have
against me.[t]
[3]Does it please you to oppress me,[u]
to spurn the work of your hands,[v]
while you smile on the schemes of
the wicked?[w]
[4]Do you have eyes of flesh?
Do you see as a mortal sees?[x]
[5]Are your days like those of a mortal
or your years like those of a man,[y]
[6]that you must search out my faults
and probe after my sin[z]—
[7]though you know that I am not
guilty[a]
and that no one can rescue me
from your hand?[b]

[8]"Your hands shaped[c] me and made
me.
Will you now turn and destroy me?[d]
[9]Remember that you molded me like
clay.[e]
Will you now turn me to dust
again?[f]
[10]Did you not pour me out like milk
and curdle me like cheese,
[11]clothe me with skin and flesh
and knit me together[g] with bones
and sinews?
[12]You gave me life[h] and showed me
kindness,[i]
and in your providence[j] watched
over[k] my spirit.

[13]"But this is what you concealed in
your heart,
and I know that this was in your
mind:[l]
[14]If I sinned, you would be watching
me[m]
and would not let my offense go
unpunished.[n]
[15]If I am guilty[o]—woe to me![p]
Even if I am innocent, I cannot lift
my head,[q]
for I am full of shame
and drowned in[a] my affliction.[r]

10:2 [r]Job 13:3; 40:1 [s]Isa 3:13; Hos 4:1; 5:1; 12:2; Mic 6:2; Ro 8:33 [t]S Job 9:3
10:3 [u]S Job 9:22; 16:9, 14; 19:6, 21; 22:10; 30:13, 21; 31:23; 34:6 [v]ver 8; Ge 1:26; S Job 4:17; 14:15; 34:19; Ps 8:6; 95:6; 100:3; 138:8; 149:2; Isa 60:21; 64:8 [w]S Job 9:24
10:4 [x]1Sa 16:7; Job 11:11; 14:16; 24:23; 28:24; 31:4; 34:21; 41:11; Ps 11:4; 33:15; 119:168; 139:12; Pr 5:21; 15:3; Jer 11:20-23; 16:17
10:5 [y]Job 36:26; Ps 39:5; 90:2, 4; 102:24; 2Pe 3:8
10:6 [z]Job 14:16
10:7 [a]ver 15; S Job 6:29; 11:4; 16:17; 27:5, 6; 31:6; 32:1 [b]S Dt 32:39
10:8 [c]Ge 2:7 [d]S ver 3; S 2Sa 14:14; S Job 30:15
10:9 [e]S Job 4:19; Isa 29:16 [f]S Ge 2:7; S Job 7:21
10:11 [g]Ps 139:13, 15
10:12 [h]S Ge 2:7 [i]S Ge 24:12 [j]S Ge 45:5 [k]1Pe 2:25
10:13 [l]Job 23:13; Ps 115:3
10:14 [m]Job 13:27 [n]S Ex 34:7; S Job 7:21
10:15 [o]S ver 7 [p]S Job 9:13 [q]S Job 9:15 [r]Ps 25:16
10:16 [s]S 1Sa 17:34; Ps 7:2; Isa 38:13;

[16]If I hold my head high, you stalk me
like a lion[s]
and again display your awesome
power against me.[t]
[17]You bring new witnesses against me[u]
and increase your anger toward me;[v]
your forces come against me wave
upon wave.[w]

[18]"Why then did you bring me out of the
womb?[x]
I wish I had died before any eye saw
me.[y]
[19]If only I had never come into being,
or had been carried straight from the
womb to the grave![z]
[20]Are not my few days[a] almost over?[b]
Turn away from me[c] so I can have a
moment's joy[d]
[21]before I go to the place of no return,[e]
to the land of gloom and deep
shadow,[b][f]
[22]to the land of deepest night,
of deep shadow[g] and disorder,
where even the light is like
darkness."[h]

Zophar

11

Then Zophar the Naamathite[i] replied:

[2]"Are all these words to go
unanswered?[j]
Is this talker to be vindicated?[k]
[3]Will your idle talk[l] reduce men to
silence?
Will no one rebuke you when you
mock?[m]

[a] *15* Or *and aware of* [b] *21* Or *and the shadow of death*; also in verse 22

Jer 5:6; 25:38; La 3:10; Hos 5:14; 13:7 [t]Job 5:9; Isa 28:21; 29:14; 65:7 **10:17** [u]1Ki 21:10; Job 16:8 [v]Ru 1:21 [w]S Job 5:7 **10:18** [x]S Job 3:8; S Ps 22:9 [y]Job 3:26; Ecc 4:2; 7:1 **10:19** [z]S Job 3:3; Jer 15:10 **10:20** [a]Job 14:1; Ecc 6:12 [b]S Job 7:7 [c]S Job 7:16 [d]S Job 9:25 **10:21** [e]S 2Sa 12:23; S Job 3:13; 16:22; Ps 39:13; Ecc 12:5 [f]S Job 3:5 **10:22** [g]S Job 3:5 [h]S 1Sa 2:9; S Job 3:13 **11:1** [i]S Job 2:11 **11:2** [j]S Job 8:2; S 16:3 [k]S Ge 41:6; S Job 6:29 **11:3** [l]Eph 4:29; 5:4 [m]Job 12:4; 16:10; 17:2; 21:3; 30:1; Ps 1:1

10:3 Job imagines that God is angry with him, an innocent man (see 9:28 and note), and that he takes delight in the wicked. Such words are a reminder that the sickroom is not the place to argue theology (cf. 2:13 and note); in times of severe suffering, people may say things that require a response of love and understanding. Job himself will eventually repent, and God will forgive (42:1–6).
10:8–17 Job continues to question God as if he were his adversary in court. He wants to know how God, who so wonderfully formed him in the womb, could all the while have planned (see v. 13) to punish him—even though he may be innocent.
10:8–11 A poetic description of God making a baby in the womb (see Ps 139:13–16 and notes).
10:8 See Ps 119:73.
10:9 *molded me like clay.* See note on 4:19. *turn me to dust.* See note on Ge 3:19.
10:10 *like milk … like cheese.* As semen poured into the womb produces an embryo.
10:15–16 Job says that whether he is guilty or innocent, the all-powerful God will not treat him justly.
10:17 *witnesses against me.* See note on 9:3.
10:18–22 See notes on ch. 3.
10:21 *place of no return.* See note on 7:9. *land of gloom and deep shadow.* See 38:17. Ancient Mesopotamian documents refer to the netherworld as the "house of darkness" (see note on Ecc 12:5).
11:1–20 Like Eliphaz (see 4:7–11) and Bildad (see 8:3–6), Zophar claims that Job's sins have caused his troubles.
11:2–3 Zophar's failure to put himself in Job's place before condemning him shows a lack of compassion. Job has sincerely challenged what he perceives to be God's unjust actions (see 9:14–24), but he has not mocked God, as Zophar accuses him of having done.

4 You say to God, 'My beliefs are
flawless[n]
and I am pure[o] in your sight.'
5 Oh, how I wish that God would
speak,[p]
that he would open his lips against
you
6 and disclose to you the secrets of
wisdom,[q]
for true wisdom has two sides.
Know this: God has even forgotten
some of your sin.[r]

7 "Can you fathom[s] the mysteries of
God?
Can you probe the limits of the
Almighty?
8 They are higher[t] than the
heavens[u] — what can you do?
They are deeper than the depths
of the grave[a][v] — what can you
know?[w]
9 Their measure[x] is longer than the
earth
and wider than the sea.[y]

10 "If he comes along and confines you
in prison
and convenes a court, who can
oppose him?[z]
11 Surely he recognizes deceitful men;
and when he sees evil, does he not
take note?[a]
12 But a witless man can no more become
wise
than a wild donkey's colt[b] can be
born a man.[b][c]

13 "Yet if you devote your heart[d] to him
and stretch out your hands[e] to him,[f]
14 if you put away[g] the sin that is in your
hand
and allow no evil[h] to dwell in your
tent,[i]
15 then you will lift up your face[j] without
shame;
you will stand firm[k] and without
fear.[l]
16 You will surely forget your trouble,[m]
recalling it only as waters gone by.[n]
17 Life will be brighter than noonday,[o]
and darkness will become like
morning.[p]
18 You will be secure, because there is
hope;
you will look about you and take
your rest[q] in safety.[r]
19 You will lie down, with no one to make
you afraid,[s]
and many will court your favor.[t]
20 But the eyes of the wicked will fail,[u]
and escape will elude them;[v]
their hope will become a dying
gasp."[w]

Job

12 Then Job replied:

2 "Doubtless you are the people,
and wisdom will die with you![x]
3 But I have a mind as well as you;
I am not inferior to you.
Who does not know all these
things?[y]

[a] 8 Hebrew *than Sheol* [b] 12 Or *wild donkey can be born tame*

11:4 [n]Job 9:21 [o]S Job 10:7 **11:5** [p]Ex 20:19; Job 23:5; 32:13; 38:1 **11:6** [q]S Job 9:4; 1Co 2:10 [r]S Ezr 9:13; S Job 15:5 **11:7** [s]S Job 5:9; Ecc 3:11 **11:8** [t]Eph 3:18 [u]S Ge 15:5; Job 22:12; 25:2; Ps 57:10; Isa 55:9 [v]S Job 7:9 [w]Job 15:13,25; 33:13; 40:2; Ps 139:8 **11:9** [x]Eph 3:19-20 [y]Job 22:12; 35:5; 36:26; 37:5,23; Isa 40:26 **11:10** [z]S Job 9:12; Rev 3:7 **11:11** [a]S Job 10:4; 31:37; 34:11,25; 36:7; Ps 10:14 **11:12** [b]S Ge 16:12 [c]S 2Ch 6:36 **11:13** [d]1Sa 7:3; Ps 78:8 [e]S Ex 9:29 [f]S Job 5:8,27 **11:14** [g]S Jos 24:14 [h]Ps 101:4 [i]Job 22:23 **11:15** [j]Job 22:26 [k]S 1Sa 2:9; Ps 20:8; 37:23; 40:2; 119:5; Eph 6:14 [l]S Ge 4:7; S Ps 3:6 **11:16** [m]Isa 26:16; 37:3; 65:16 [n]Jos 7:5; Job 22:11; Ps 58:7; 112:10; Eze 21:7 **11:17** [o]Job 22:28; Ps 37:6; Isa 58:8,10; 62:1 [p]Job 17:12; 18:6; 29:3; Ps 18:28; 112:4; 119:105; Isa 5:20; Jn 8:12 **11:18** [q]Ps 3:5; 4:8; 127:2; Ecc 5:12 [r]S Lev 26:6; Pr 3:24; Isa 11:10; 14:3; 28:12; 30:15; 32:18; Zec 3:10 **11:19** [s]S Lev 26:6 [t]Isa 45:14 **11:20** [u]Dt 28:65; Job 17:5 [v]Job 12:10; 18:18; 27:22; 34:22; 36:6; Ps 139:11-12; Jer 11:11; 23:24; 25:35; Am 2:14; 9:2-3 [w]S Job 8:13 **12:2** [x]Job 15:8; 17:10 **12:3** [y]Job 13:2; 15:9

11:4 *I am pure.* In 10:7,15 Job had disclaimed being guilty, and in 9:21 he said he was "blameless," the word God used to describe him in 1:8; 2:3. Zophar, however, implies that Job was claiming purity, but Job nowhere makes such a claim.
11:5 Zophar thought God should speak against Job, but eventually God spoke against Zophar himself (see 42:7 – 9 and notes).
11:6 *true wisdom has two sides.* OT wisdom literature (especially Proverbs) makes abundant use of the term *mashal* ("proverb," "riddle," "parable"), which often had a hidden as well as an obvious meaning. Zophar thinks Job is shallow and lacks an understanding of the true nature of God (see vv. 7 – 9).
11:7 Unwittingly, Zophar anticipates the Lord's discourses in 38:1 — 42:6.
11:8 – 9 In the same way that Zophar speaks of the height, depth, length and width of God's knowledge, Paul speaks of Christ's love (see Eph 3:18).
11:8 *what can you do?* Can you climb into the heavens and explore God's knowledge? (Cf. ch. 28.)
11:11 – 12 *deceitful ... witless.* Zophar claims that it would take a miracle to change Job.
11:12 *wild donkey's colt.* See 6:5 and note. The NIV text note contrasts two related but different animals — the wild ass and the domestic donkey. Then the point would be that a witless man can no more become wise than a wild ass can be born as a domestic donkey.
11:13 – 20 Zophar assumes that Job's problems are rooted in his sin; all Job has to do is to repent, and then his life will become blessed and happy. But God nowhere guarantees a life "brighter than noonday" (v. 17) simply because we are his children. He has higher purposes for us than our physical prosperity, or people courting our favor (v. 19). Zophar's philosophy is in conflict with Ps 73.
11:13 *stretch out your hands to him.* To pray for help (see Ex 9:29; 17:11 and notes; Ps 28:2; 44:20; 77:2; 88:9; 141:2; 143:6; Isa 1:15; 1Ti 2:8).
11:15 *lift up your face without shame.* Zophar echoes Job's thought in 10:15.
11:20 Bildad ended his speech in a similar way (see 8:22).
12:1 — 14:22 As before, Job's reply is divided into two parts: He speaks to his three friends (12:2 — 13:19), then to God (13:20 — 14:22).
12:2 For the first time, Job reacts with sarcasm to the harshness of his counselors (see v. 20).
12:3 *Who does not know ...?* See v. 9. The advice of Job's friends is trivial and commonplace.

[4] "I have become a laughingstock[z] to my
friends,[a]
though I called upon God and he
answered[b]—
a mere laughingstock, though
righteous and blameless![c]
[5] Men at ease have contempt[d] for
misfortune
as the fate of those whose feet are
slipping.[e]
[6] The tents of marauders are
undisturbed,[f]
and those who provoke God are
secure[g]—
those who carry their god in their
hands.[a]

[7] "But ask the animals, and they will
teach you,[h]
or the birds of the air,[i] and they will
tell you;[j]
[8] or speak to the earth, and it will teach
you,
or let the fish of the sea inform you.
[9] Which of all these does not know[k]
that the hand of the LORD has done
this?[l]
[10] In his hand is the life[m] of every
creature
and the breath of all mankind.[n]
[11] Does not the ear test words
as the tongue tastes food?[o]
[12] Is not wisdom found among the
aged?[p]
Does not long life bring
understanding?[q]

[13] "To God belong wisdom[r] and power;[s]
counsel and understanding are his.[t]
[14] What he tears down[u] cannot be
rebuilt;[v]
the man he imprisons cannot be
released.[w]
[15] If he holds back the waters,[x] there is
drought;[y]
if he lets them loose, they devastate
the land.[z]
[16] To him belong strength and victory;[a]
both deceived and deceiver are his.[b]
[17] He leads counselors away stripped[c]
and makes fools of judges.[d]
[18] He takes off the shackles[e] put on by
kings
and ties a loincloth[b] around their
waist.[f]
[19] He leads priests away stripped[g]
and overthrows men long
established.[h]
[20] He silences the lips of trusted advisers
and takes away the discernment of
elders.[i]
[21] He pours contempt on nobles[j]
and disarms the mighty.[k]
[22] He reveals the deep things of darkness[l]
and brings deep shadows[m] into the
light.[n]
[23] He makes nations great, and destroys
them;[o]
he enlarges nations,[p] and disperses
them.[q]
[24] He deprives the leaders of the earth of
their reason;[r]
he sends them wandering through a
trackless waste.[s]
[25] They grope in darkness with no light;[t]
he makes them stagger like
drunkards.[u]

13

[1] "My eyes have seen all this,[v]
my ears have heard and understood
it.
[2] What you know, I also know;
I am not inferior to you.[w]

[a] 6 Or *secure / in what God's hand brings them*
[b] 18 Or *shackles of kings / and ties a belt*

12:4 [z] S Ge 38:23 [a] S Job 6:14; S 11:3; S 16:10; S 19:14 [b] Ps 91:15 [c] S Ge 6:9; S Job 6:29; S 15:16 **12:5** [d] Ps 123:4 [e] Ps 17:5; 37:31; 38:16; 66:9; 73:2; 94:18 **12:6** [f] S Job 5:24 [g] S Job 9:24 **12:7** [h] Job 35:11 *fn* [i] Mt 6:26 [j] Job 18:3; Ro 1:20 **12:9** [k] Isa 1:3 [l] S Job 9:24 **12:10** [m] Da 5:23 [n] S Ge 2:7; S Nu 16:22; S Job 11:20; Ac 17:28 **12:11** [o] Job 34:3 **12:12** [p] S 1Ki 4:2; Job 15:10 [q] ver 20; Job 17:4; 32:7,9; 34:4,10 **12:13** [r] Pr 21:30; Isa 45:9 [s] S Job 9:4; S Jer 32:19; 1Co 1:24 [t] S Nu 23:19; 1Ki 3:12; Job 32:8; 38:36; Pr 2:6; Isa 40:13-14; Da 1:17 **12:14** [u] Job 16:9; 19:10 [v] Dt 13:16; Ps 127:1; Isa 24:20; 25:2; Eze 26:14 [w] S Job 9:3; Isa 22:22; Rev 3:7 **12:15** [x] Job 28:25; Isa 40:12 [y] S Dt 28:22; S 1Ki 17:1 [z] S Ge 7:24 **12:16** [a] S Job 9:4 [b] 2Ch 18:22; Job 13:7,9; 27:4; Ro 2:11 **12:17** [c] ver 19; Job 19:9; Isa 20:4 [d] S Job 3:14; 1Co 1:20

12:18 [e] Ps 107:14; 116:16; Na 1:13 [f] ver 21; Job 34:18; Ps 107:40; Isa 5:27; 40:23 **12:19** [g] S ver 17 [h] S Dt 24:15; S Job 9:24; 14:20; 22:8; 24:12,22; 34:20,28; 35:9; Isa 2:22; 31:8; 40:17,23; Jer 25:18; Da 2:21,34; Lk 1:52 **12:20** [i] S ver 12,24; Da 4:33-34 **12:21** [j] S ver 18; S Isa 34:12 [k] S Job 3:15 **12:22** [l] 1Co 4:5 [m] Job 3:5 [n] Ps 139:12; Da 2:22 **12:23** [o] Ps 2:1; 46:6; Isa 13:4; Jer 25:9 [p] S Ex 34:24; Ps 107:38; Isa 9:3; 26:15; 54:3 [q] S Job 5:12; Ac 17:26 **12:24** [r] S ver 20 [s] Ps 107:40 **12:25** [t] S Dt 28:29; Job 18:6; 21:17; 29:3 [u] Ps 107:27; Isa 24:20 **13:1** [v] S Job 9:24 **13:2** [w] S Job 12:3

12:4 *God ... answered.* In the days before his suffering began (contrast 9:16).
12:6 Such statements (see 9:21 – 24) irked the counselors and made them brand Job as a man whose feet were slipping (see v. 5).
12:7 – 12 Job appeals to all creation to testify that God does what he pleases.
12:9 *LORD.* The only place in Job's and his friends' speeches (chs. 3 – 37) where the divine name "LORD" (Hebrew *Yahweh*) is used (see Introduction: Author).
12:11 Echoed by Elihu in 34:3. Cf. 6:6, where Job says that Eliphaz's words are like "tasteless food."
12:12 Job sarcastically chides his counselors for being elders and yet lacking in true wisdom.
12:13 – 25 The theme of this section is stated in v. 13: God is sovereign in the created world, and especially in history. The rest of the poem dwells on the negative aspects of God's power and wisdom — e.g., the destructive forces of nature (vv. 14 – 15), how judges become fools (v. 17), how priests become humiliated (v. 19), how trusted advisers are silenced and elders deprived of good sense (v. 20). Contrast the claim of Eliphaz that God always uses his power in ways that make sense (5:10 – 16).
12:20 See note on v. 2.
12:21a,24b The Hebrew text of these lines is repeated verbatim in Ps 107:40 (see note there).
12:22 God knows even plans conceived and held in secret.
12:25 *grope in darkness.* Job concludes this section with a parody of Eliphaz's confident assertion in 5:14.
13:1 – 12 Job feels that his counselors have become completely untrustworthy (see v. 12). He calls them quacks (see v. 4; see also 16:2 and note) and accuses them of showing partiality to God through their false accusations (see vv. 7 – 8). Someday God will examine them and punish them (see vv. 9 – 11).
13:1 *all this.* God's sovereign actions as described in ch. 12.
13:2 See 15:9. *I am not inferior to you.* See 12:3 and note.

3 But I desire to speak to the Almighty[x]
and to argue my case with God.[y]
4 You, however, smear me with lies;[z]
you are worthless physicians,[a] all of you![b]
5 If only you would be altogether silent![c]
For you, that would be wisdom.[d]
6 Hear now my argument;
listen to the plea of my lips.[e]
7 Will you speak wickedly on God's behalf?
Will you speak deceitfully for him?[f]
8 Will you show him partiality?[g]
Will you argue the case for God?
9 Would it turn out well if he examined you?[h]
Could you deceive him as you might deceive men?[i]
10 He would surely rebuke you
if you secretly showed partiality.[j]
11 Would not his splendor[k] terrify you?
Would not the dread of him fall on you?[l]
12 Your maxims are proverbs of ashes;
your defenses are defenses of clay.[m]

13 "Keep silent[n] and let me speak;[o]
then let come to me what may.[p]
14 Why do I put myself in jeopardy
and take my life in my hands?[q]
15 Though he slay me, yet will I hope[r] in him;[s]
I will surely[a] defend my ways to his face.[t]
16 Indeed, this will turn out for my deliverance,[u]
for no godless[v] man would dare come before him![w]
17 Listen carefully to my words;[x]
let your ears take in what I say.
18 Now that I have prepared my case,[y]
I know I will be vindicated.[z]
19 Can anyone bring charges against me?[a]
If so, I will be silent[b] and die.[c]

20 "Only grant me these two things, O God,
and then I will not hide from you:
21 Withdraw your hand[d] far from me,
and stop frightening me with your terrors.[e]
22 Then summon me and I will answer,[f]
or let me speak, and you reply.[g]
23 How many wrongs and sins have I committed?[h]
Show me my offense and my sin.[i]
24 Why do you hide your face[j]
and consider me your enemy?[k]
25 Will you torment[l] a windblown leaf?[m]
Will you chase[n] after dry chaff?[o]
26 For you write down bitter things against me
and make me inherit the sins of my youth.[p]
27 You fasten my feet in shackles;[q]
you keep close watch on all my paths[r]
by putting marks on the soles of my feet.

28 "So man wastes away like something rotten,
like a garment[s] eaten by moths.[t]

14 "Man born of woman[u]
is of few days[v] and full of trouble.[w]
2 He springs up like a flower[x] and withers away;[y]

[a] 15 Or *He will surely slay me; I have no hope — / yet I will*

13:3 [x] Job 5:17; 40:2 [y] S Job 5:8; 9:14-20; S 10:2 **13:4** [z] Ps 119:69; Isa 9:15; Jer 23:32 [a] Jer 8:22 [b] S Job 6:15 **13:5** [c] ver 13; S Jdg 18:19 [d] Pr 17:28 **13:6** [e] Job 33:1; 36:4 **13:7** [f] S Job 12:16; S 16:17 **13:8** [g] S Lev 19:15 **13:9** [h] S Job 9:3 [i] S Job 12:16; Gal 6:7 **13:10** [j] S Lev 19:15; S 2Ch 19:7 **13:11** [k] Job 31:23 [l] S Ex 3:6 **13:12** [m] S Ne 4:2-3 **13:13** [n] S ver 5 [o] S Job 7:11 [p] S Job 9:21 **13:14** [q] S Jdg 9:17 **13:15** [r] S Job 7:6 [s] Ps 23:4; 27:1; Pr 14:32; Isa 12:2; Da 3:28 [t] S Job 5:8; 27:5 **13:16** [u] Ps 30:5; Isa 12:1; 54:7-8; Hos 14:4; Php 1:19 [v] S Job 8:13 [w] S Ge 3:8 **13:17** [x] Job 21:2 **13:18** [y] S ver 3; Job 23:4; 37:19 [z] S Job 2:3; S 9:21 **13:19** [a] Job 40:4; Isa 50:8; Ro 8:33 [b] S Job 9:15 [c] S Job 3:13; 10:8 **13:21** [d] S Ex 9:3; Heb 10:31 [e] S Job 6:4 **13:22** [f] Job 9:35; 14:15 [g] S Job 9:16 **13:23** [h] S 1Sa 26:18 [i] Job 7:21; 9:21; 14:17; 33:9 **13:24** [j] S Dt 32:20 [k] Job 16:9; 19:11; 33:10; Ps 88:14-15; Jer 30:14; La 2:5 **13:25** [l] Job 19:2 [m] Lev 26:36 [n] Job 19:22, 28 [o] Job 21:18; Ps 1:4; 35:5; 83:13; Isa 17:13; 42:3; 43:17; Hos 13:3 **13:26** [p] Job 18:7; 20:11; 21:23; Ps 25:7 **13:27** [q] S Ge 40:15; Job 33:11; Jer 20:2; Ac 16:24 [r] Job 10:14 **13:28** [s] Ps 102:26; Mk 2:21 [t] S Dt 28:35; Ps 39:11; Isa 50:9; 51:8; Hos 5:12; Jas 5:2 **14:1** [u] Job 15:14; Mt 11:11 [v] S Job 10:20 [w] S Ge 3:17; S Job 7:2 **14:2** [x] Ps 103:15; S Jas 1:10 [y] Ps 37:2; 90:5-6; Isa 40:6-8

13:5 See v. 13. The friends' earlier silence may have ministered to Job (see 2:13 and note); his current retort is intended as sarcasm (cf. Pr 17:28).

13:12 *defenses.* Arguments in their defense of God's judgment.

13:15 See NIV text note. Both readings state that no matter what happens, Job intends to seek vindication from God and believes that he will receive it (see v. 18).

13:16 *turn out for my deliverance.* See Php 1:19 (perhaps Paul was reflecting on Job's experience).

13:17 Job asks his friends to listen to what he is going to say to God in 13:20—14:22.

13:20 *two things.* Job wants God (1) to withdraw his hand of punishment (v. 21), and (2) to start communicating with him (v. 22).

13:21 See 9:34.

13:23 Job's words are based on the counselors' point that suffering always implies sinfulness. He does not yet understand that God has a higher purpose in his suffering. *wrongs ... sins ... offense.* The three most important Hebrew terms for sin lie behind these translations (see Ex 34:7; see also notes on Ps 32:5; 51:1–2; Isa 59:12).

13:24 *hide your face.* Withhold your blessing (see note on Ps 13:1).

13:25 *windblown leaf ... dry chaff.* See note on Ps 1:4.

13:26 *write down ... things against me.* See Ps 130:3; Hos 13:12; contrast 1Co 13:5. *sins of my youth.* Since Job feels that he is not presently guilty of a sinful life, God must still be holding the sins of his youth against him.

13:27 *You fasten ... my paths.* Elihu later quotes Job's words (see 33:11). *marks on the soles of my feet.* The Babylonian Code of Hammurapi (see chart, p. xxii) attests to the practice of putting marks on slaves. Job feels that he is being harassed by a God who has taken him captive and is tormenting him (see v. 25).

13:28—14:1 The introduction to ch. 14, expressing the pessimistic theme that the legacy of human beings is trouble and their destiny is death.

13:28 *garment eaten by moths.* See Mt 6:19–20 and notes; Lk 12:33.

14:1 See 5:7 and note.

14:2–6 A symmetrical poem centered around v. 4 (v. 2 corresponds to v. 5, and v. 3 to v. 6). Job complains to God: Given the insignificance of humans and their inherent impurity, why do you take them so seriously (see 13:25)?

14:2 *He ... withers away.* Life at best is brief and fragile (see 8:9; Ps 37:2; Isa 40:7,24; cf. Jas 1:10). *like a fleeting shadow.* See note on 8:9.

like a fleeting shadow,[z] he does not
endure.[a]
3 Do you fix your eye on such a one?[b]
Will you bring him[a] before you for
judgment?[c]
4 Who can bring what is pure[d] from the
impure?[e]
No one![f]
5 Man's days are determined;[g]
you have decreed the number of his
months[h]
and have set limits he cannot exceed.[i]
6 So look away from him and let him
alone,[j]
till he has put in his time like a hired
man.[k]

7 "At least there is hope for a tree:[l]
If it is cut down, it will sprout again,
and its new shoots[m] will not fail.[n]
8 Its roots may grow old in the ground
and its stump[o] die in the soil,
9 yet at the scent of water[p] it will bud
and put forth shoots like a plant.[q]
10 But man dies and is laid low;[r]
he breathes his last and is no more.[s]
11 As water disappears from the sea
or a riverbed becomes parched and
dry,[t]
12 so man lies down and does not rise;[u]
till the heavens are no more,[v] men
will not awake
or be roused from their sleep.[w]

13 "If only you would hide me in the
grave[b][x]
and conceal me till your anger has
passed![y]
If only you would set me a time
and then remember[z] me![a]
14 If a man dies, will he live again?
All the days of my hard service[b]
I will wait for my renewal[c][c] to come.
15 You will call and I will answer you;[d]
you will long for the creature your
hands have made.[e]
16 Surely then you will count my steps[f]
but not keep track of my sin.[g]
17 My offenses will be sealed[h] up in a bag;[i]
you will cover over my sin.[j]

14:2 [z] Job 8:9; Ps 39:4; 102:11; 109:23; 144:4; Ecc 6:12 [a] S Job 4:20; Ps 49:12 **14:3** [b] Ps 8:4; 144:3 [c] S Job 7:18 **14:4** [d] Ps 51:10 [e] S Job 4:17; Eph 2:1-3 [f] S Job 9:30; Jn 3:6; Ro 5:12; 7:14 **14:5** [g] Job 24:1; Ps 31:15; 139:16 [h] Job 21:21; Ps 39:4; 90:12 [i] Ac 17:26 **14:6** [j] S Job 7:19 [k] Job 7:1, 2; Ps 39:13; Isa 16:14; 21:16 **14:7** [l] Job 19:10; 24:20; Ps 52:5 [m] Isa 11:1; 53:2; 60:21 [n] Isa 6:13 **14:8** [o] Isa 6:13; 11:1; 53:2 **14:9** [p] Job 29:19; Ps 1:3; Jer 17:8; Eze 31:7 [q] Lev 26:4; Eze 34:27; Zec 10:1 **14:10** [r] ver 12 [s] S Job 10:21; 13:19 **14:11** [t] S 2Sa 14:14 **14:12** [u] ver 10 [v] Ps 102:26; Rev 20:11; 21:1 [w] Ac 3:21 **14:13** [x] S Job 7:9 [y] Ps 30:5; Isa 26:20; 54:7 [z] S Ge 8:1 [a] Job 6:8 **14:14** [b] S Job 7:1 [c] S 2Ki 6:33 **14:15** [d] S Job 13:22 [e] S Job 10:3 **14:16** [f] S Job 10:4; Ps 139:1-3; Pr 5:21; Jer 16:17; 32:19 [g] Job 10:6; 1Co 13:5 **14:17** [h] Jer 32:10 [i] S Dt 32:34 [j] S Job 9:30; S 13:23 **14:18** [k] Eze 38:20 [l] Job 18:4

18 "But as a mountain erodes and
crumbles[k]
and as a rock is moved from its
place,[l]
19 as water wears away stones
and torrents[m] wash away the soil,[n]
so you destroy man's hope.[o]
20 You overpower him once for all, and
he is gone;[p]
you change his countenance and
send him away.[q]
21 If his sons are honored, he does not
know it;
if they are brought low, he does not
see it.[r]
22 He feels but the pain of his own body[s]
and mourns only for himself.[t]"

Eliphaz

15 Then Eliphaz the Temanite[u] replied:

2 "Would a wise man answer with
empty notions
or fill his belly with the hot east
wind?[v]
3 Would he argue with useless words,
with speeches that have no value?[w]
4 But you even undermine piety
and hinder devotion to God.[x]
5 Your sin[y] prompts your mouth;[z]
you adopt the tongue of the crafty.[a]
6 Your own mouth condemns you, not
mine;
your own lips testify against you.[b]

7 "Are you the first man ever born?[c]
Were you brought forth before the
hills?[d]
8 Do you listen in on God's council?[e]
Do you limit wisdom to yourself?[f]

[a] *3* Septuagint, Vulgate and Syriac; Hebrew *me*
[b] *13* Hebrew *Sheol* [c] *14* Or *release*

14:19 [m] Eze 13:13 [n] S Ge 7:23 [o] S Job 7:6 **14:20** [p] S Job 4:20 [q] S Job 7:10; 8:18; S 12:19; 27:19; Jas 1:10 **14:21** [r] Job 21:21; Ecc 9:5; Isa 63:16 **14:22** [s] Ps 38:7; Isa 21:3; Jer 4:19 [t] Job 21:21 **15:1** [u] S Job 4:1 **15:2** [v] S Ge 41:6 **15:3** [w] S Ne 4:2-3; S Job 6:26 **15:4** [x] Job 25:6 **15:5** [y] Job 11:6; 22:5 [z] Pr 16:23 [a] S Job 5:13 **15:6** [b] S Job 9:15; 18:7; Ps 10:2; S Mt 12:37; Lk 19:22 **15:7** [c] Job 38:21 [d] S 1Sa 2:8; Ps 90:2; Pr 8:25 **15:8** [e] Job 29:4; Isa 9:6; 40:13; 41:28; Jer 23:18; Ro 11:34; 1Co 2:11 [f] S Job 12:2

14:7–12 People are like a flower that lives its short life and is gone (v. 2), not like a tree that revives even after it has been cut down.

14:7 *sprout.* The Hebrew root underlying this word is translated "renewal" in v. 14.

14:13–17 Job's spirit now appears to rise above the despair engendered by his rotting body. Although resurrection in the fullest sense is not taught here, Job is saying that if God so desires he is able to hide Job in the grave, then raise him back to life at a time when the divine anger is past.

14:14 *hard service.* See note on 7:1.

14:18–22 Job's pessimism arises not from skepticism about the possibility of resurrection from the dead but rather from God's apparent unwillingness to do something immediately for a person like him, whose life has become a nightmare of pain and mourning.

15:1–6 Up to this point Eliphaz has been the most sympathetic of the three counselors, but now he has run out of patience with Job and denounces him more severely than before.

15:2 *empty.* The Hebrew for this word is translated "long-winded" in 16:3, where Job hurls Eliphaz's charges back at him. *hot east wind.* The sirocco that blows in from the desert (see 27:21; 38:24; see also notes on Ge 41:6; Jer 4:11).

15:4 *piety.* See note on 4:6.

15:5 See Mt 15:11,17–18.

15:6 *mouth condemns you.* See 9:20.

15:7–10 Job, says Eliphaz, presumes to be wise enough to sit among the members of God's council in heaven (see note on 1:6) when in reality he is no wiser than ordinary elders and sages on earth.

[9]What do you know that we do not know?
What insights do you have that we do not have?[g]
[10]The gray-haired and the aged[h] are on our side,
men even older than your father.[i]
[11]Are God's consolations[j] not enough for you,
words[k] spoken gently to you?[l]
[12]Why has your heart[m] carried you away,
and why do your eyes flash,
[13]so that you vent your rage[n] against God
and pour out such words[o] from your mouth?[p]

[14]"What is man, that he could be pure,
or one born of woman,[q] that he could be righteous?[r]
[15]If God places no trust in his holy ones,[s]
if even the heavens are not pure in his eyes,[t]
[16]how much less man, who is vile and corrupt,[u]
who drinks up evil[v] like water![w]

[17]"Listen to me and I will explain to you;
let me tell you what I have seen,[x]
[18]what wise men have declared,
hiding nothing received from their fathers[y]
[19](to whom alone the land[z] was given
when no alien passed among them):
[20]All his days the wicked man suffers torment,[a]
the ruthless through all the years stored up for him.[b]
[21]Terrifying sounds fill his ears;[c]
when all seems well, marauders attack him.[d]
[22]He despairs of escaping the darkness;[e]
he is marked for the sword.[f]
[23]He wanders about[g]—food for vultures[a];[h]
he knows the day of darkness[i] is at hand.[j]
[24]Distress and anguish[k] fill him with terror;[l]
they overwhelm him, like a king[m] poised to attack,
[25]because he shakes his fist[n] at God
and vaunts himself against the Almighty,[o]
[26]defiantly charging against him
with a thick, strong shield.[p]

[27]"Though his face is covered with fat
and his waist bulges with flesh,[q]
[28]he will inhabit ruined towns
and houses where no one lives,[r]
houses crumbling to rubble.[s]
[29]He will no longer be rich and his wealth will not endure,[t]
nor will his possessions spread over the land.[u]
[30]He will not escape the darkness;[v]
a flame[w] will wither his shoots,[x]
and the breath of God's mouth[y] will carry him away.[z]
[31]Let him not deceive[a] himself by trusting what is worthless,[b]
for he will get nothing in return.[c]
[32]Before his time[d] he will be paid in full,[e]
and his branches will not flourish.[f]
[33]He will be like a vine stripped of its unripe grapes,[g]
like an olive tree shedding its blossoms.[h]
[34]For the company of the godless[i] will be barren,
and fire will consume[j] the tents of those who love bribes.[k]

[a] 23 Or *about, looking for food*

15:9 [g] S Job 12:3 **15:10** [h] S Job 12:12 [i] S 2Ch 10:6 **15:11** [j] S Ge 37:35; S Job 6:10; 2Co 1:3-4 [k] Zec 1:13 [l] S Dt 8:3; S 32:39; S Job 5:17; 22:22; 23:12; 36:16; Ps 119:11,72; Jer 15:16 **15:12** [m] Job 11:13; 36:13 **15:13** [n] Pr 29:11; Da 11:30 [o] Ps 94:4 [p] S Job 11:8; 22:5; 32:3 **15:14** [q] S Job 14:1 [r] S 2Ch 6:36; S Job 4:17 **15:15** [s] S Job 5:1 [t] S Job 4:18 **15:16** [u] S Lev 5:2; S Job 4:19; Ps 14:1 [v] Job 20:12 [w] Job 12:4; 34:7; Pr 19:28 **15:17** [x] S Job 4:8 **15:18** [y] S Dt 32:7 **15:19** [z] Ge 12:1; Job 22:8 **15:20** [a] ver 24; Isa 8:22; 50:11; 66:24 [b] Job 24:1; 27:13-23; Isa 2:12; Jer 46:10; Ob 1:15; Zep 1:7 **15:21** [c] ver 24; S 1Sa 3:11; Job 18:11; 20:25; Jer 6:25; 20:3 [d] Job 22:10; 27:20; Isa 13:3; Jer 51:25,53,56; 1Th 5:3 **15:22** [e] ver 23; S Job 5:14; 24:17; 38:15; Ps 91:5; SS 3:8 [f] Job 16:13; 18:19; 19:29; 20:24; 27:14; 33:18; 36:12; Pr 7:23; Isa 1:20; Jer 44:27; Hos 9:13; Am 5:19 **15:23** [g] Ps 109:10 [h] Pr 30:17; Eze 39:17; Mt 24:28; Lk 17:37 [i] S ver 22 [j] Job 18:12 **15:24** [k] Isa 8:22; 9:1 [l] S ver 20 [m] Job 18:14 **15:25** [n] Ps 44:16; Isa 10:32; 37:23 [o] S Job 11:8; 35:12; 36:9; 40:8; Ps 2:2-3; 73:9; 75:5; Pr 21:30; Isa 3:16; 45:9 **15:26** [p] Jer 44:16 **15:27** [q] S Jdg 3:17 **15:28** [r] Isa 5:9 [s] S Job 3:14 **15:29** [t] S Job 3:15; S 7:8 [u] Isa 5:8 **15:30** [v] S Job 5:14 [w] ver 34; Job 16:7; 20:26; 22:20; 31:12 [x] ver 32; Job 8:19; 18:16; 29:19; Hos 9:1-16; Mal 4:1 [y] S Ex 15:10 [z] Isa 40:23-24 **15:31** [a] Job 31:5; Pr 1:16; 6:18; Isa 44:20; 59:7; Mic 2:11; S Mk 13:5; Jas 1:16 [b] Isa 30:12; 47:10; 59:4; Jer 7:4,8; S Mt 6:19 [c] Job 20:7; 22:13; 27:9; 35:13; Pr 15:29; Isa 1:15; Jer 11:11; Mic 3:4 **15:32** [d] Ecc 7:17 [e] Job 22:16; 36:14; Ps 55:23; 109:8; Pr 10:27 [f] S ver 30 **15:33** [g] Hab 3:17 [h] S Job 4:20 **15:34** [i] S Job 8:13 [j] S ver 30; Heb 10:27 [k] S Ex 23:8; S 1Sa 8:3

15:10 In ancient times, wisdom was associated with advanced age (cf. 32:6–9).

15:11–13 Eliphaz chides Job for replying in rage to his friends' attempts to console him with gentle words, which Eliphaz believes come from God himself (v. 11). But Eliphaz has been guilty of cruel insinuation (ch. 5), and the other two counselors have been even more malicious. Genuine words of comfort for Job have been few indeed (see 4:2–6).

15:14–16 See 25:4–6. Eliphaz repeats what he had already said in 4:17–19, perhaps because he thought the earlier words had come to him through divine revelation (see note on 4:12–21).

15:14 *born of woman.* An echo of Job's words in 14:1.

15:15 *holy ones.* Angels (see note on 5:1).

15:16 *drinks up evil like water.* See Elihu's description of Job in 34:7.

15:17–26 Eliphaz now bolsters his earlier advice with traditional wisdom: The wicked can never escape the suffering they deserve.

15:19 *no alien passed among them.* Corrupting the community's traditions.

15:20–35 A poem on the fate of the wicked (see 8:11–19). Eliphaz continues with a variety of figures: belligerent sinners who attack God (vv. 24–26); fat, rich wicked people who finally get what they deserve (vv. 27–32); grapevines stripped before the fruit is ripe (v. 33a); olive trees shedding their blossoms (v. 33b). As long as Eliphaz rejects Job's insistence that the wicked go on prospering, he does not have to wrestle with the disturbing corollary: the mystery of why the innocent sometimes suffer.

15:23,30 *darkness.* Death, characterized by the journey to the netherworld (see note on 10:21).

35“They conceive trouble[l] and give birth
to evil;[m]
their womb fashions deceit.”

Job

16

1 Then Job replied:

2“I have heard many things like these;
miserable comforters[n] are you all![o]
3 Will your long-winded speeches never
end?[p]
What ails you that you keep on
arguing?[q]
4 I also could speak like you,
if you were in my place;
I could make fine speeches against you
and shake my head[r] at you.
5 But my mouth would encourage you;
comfort[s] from my lips would bring
you relief.[t]

6“Yet if I speak, my pain is not relieved;
and if I refrain, it does not go away.[u]
7 Surely, O God, you have worn me out;[v]
you have devastated my entire
household.[w]
8 You have bound me—and it has
become a witness;
my gauntness[x] rises up and testifies
against me.[y]
9 God assails me and tears[z] me in his
anger[a]
and gnashes his teeth at me;[b]
my opponent fastens on me his
piercing eyes.[c]
10 Men open their mouths[d] to jeer at me;[e]
they strike my cheek[f] in scorn
and unite together against me.[g]
11 God has turned me over to evil men
and thrown me into the clutches of
the wicked.[h]
12 All was well with me, but he shattered
me;
he seized me by the neck and
crushed me.[i]
He has made me his target;[j]
13 his archers surround me.[k]
Without pity, he pierces[l] my kidneys
and spills my gall on the ground.
14 Again and again[m] he bursts upon me;
he rushes at me like a warrior.[n]

15“I have sewed sackcloth[o] over my
skin
and buried my brow in the dust.[p]
16 My face is red with weeping,[q]
deep shadows ring my eyes;[r]
17 yet my hands have been free of
violence[s]
and my prayer is pure.[t]

18“O earth, do not cover my blood;[u]
may my cry[v] never be laid to
rest![w]
19 Even now my witness[x] is in heaven;[y]
my advocate is on high.[z]
20 My intercessor[a] is my friend[a][b]
as my eyes pour out[c] tears[d] to God;
21 on behalf of a man he pleads[e] with
God
as a man pleads for his friend.

22“Only a few years will pass
before I go on the journey of no
return.[f]

17

1 My spirit[g] is broken,
my days are cut short,[h]
the grave awaits me.[i]
2 Surely mockers[j] surround me;[k]
my eyes must dwell on their
hostility.

3“Give me, O God, the pledge you
demand.[l]
Who else will put up security[m] for
me?[n]

[a] 20 Or *My friends treat me with scorn*

15:35 [l] S Job 5:7 [m] S Job 4:8; S Isa 29:20; Gal 6:7; Jas 1:15 **16:2** [n] Ps 69:20 [o] S Job 6:15 **16:3** [p] Job 11:2; 18:2 [q] S Job 6:26 **16:4** [r] S 2Ki 19:21; Ps 22:7; Isa 37:22; Jer 48:27; La 2:15; Zep 2:15; S Mt 27:39 **16:5** [s] Job 29:25 [t] S Ge 37:35 **16:6** [u] S Job 6:3; S 7:21 **16:7** [v] S Jdg 8:5; S Job 7:3 [w] S Job 1:19 **16:8** [x] Job 17:7; 19:20; 33:21; Ps 6:7; 22:17; 88:9; 102:5; 109:24; La 5:17 [y] S Job 10:17 **16:9** [z] S Job 12:14; Hos 6:1 [a] S Job 9:5; 18:4; 19:11 [b] Job 30:21; Ps 35:16; 37:12; 112:10; La 2:16; Ac 7:54 [c] S Job 13:24 **16:10** [d] Ps 22:13; 35:21 [e] Job 12:4; 19:18; 21:3; 30:1, 9; Ps 22:13; 69:12; 119:51 [f] Isa 50:6; La 3:30; Mic 5:1; Ac 23:2 [g] ver 7; S Job 11:3; 19:12; 30:12; Ps 27:3; 35:15; Ac 7:57 **16:11** [h] S Job 9:24 **16:12** [i] S Job 9:17 [j] S Job 6:4; La 3:12 **16:13** [k] S Job 3:23 [l] Job 20:24; Pr 7:23; La 3:13 **16:14** [m] Job 9:17 [n] S Job 10:3; Joel 2:7 **16:15** [o] S Ge 37:34 [p] S Job 2:8 **16:16** [q] ver 20; Ps 6:6 [r] Job 2:7; 17:7; 30:17, 30; 33:19; Isa 52:14 **16:17** [s] Isa 55:7; 59:6; Jer 18:11; Jnh 3:8 [t] S Job 6:28; S 10:7; 13:7; Isa 53:9; Zep 3:13 **16:18** [u] S Ge 4:10; Isa 26:21 [v] Ps 5:2; 18:6; 102:1; 119:169 [w] Job 19:24; Ps 66:18-19; Heb 11:4 **16:19** [x] S Ge 31:50; S Ro 1:9; 1Th 2:5 [y] Job 22:12; 42:2 [z] Job 19:27; 21:17; 25:2; 27:13; 31:2; Ps 113:5; Isa 33:5; 57:15; 58:4; 66:1; Mk 11:10 **16:20** [a] S Ro 8:34 [b] Jn 15:15 [c] La 2:19 [d] S ver 16 **16:21** [e] 1Ki 8:45; Ps 9:4; 140:12 **16:22** [f] S Job 10:21 **17:1** [g] Ps 143:4 [h] Isa 38:12 [i] Ps 88:3-4; Ecc 12:1-7 **17:2** [j] S Job 11:3 [k] S Job 6:14; Ps 22:7; 119:51; Jer 20:7; La 3:14 **17:3** [l] Ps 35:27; 119:122 [m] Pr 6:1 [n] Ps 35:2; 40:17; Isa 38:14

15:35 *They conceive trouble and give birth to evil.* See Isa 59:4 and note. Once initiated, sinful thoughts develop quickly into evil acts (cf. Jas 1:15 and note).

16:2–5 Helpful advice is usually brief and encouraging, not lengthy and judgmental.

16:2 *miserable comforters.* See note on 13:1–12. Job would eventually be comforted, but not by his three friends (see 42:11).

16:3 *long-winded.* See note on 15:2.

16:4 *shake … head.* A gesture of insult and scorn (see Ps 22:7; Jer 48:27; Mt 27:39).

16:9 The figure here is graphic and disturbing: God, like a ferocious lion (see 10:16), attacks and tears at Job's flesh.

16:10–14 Job sees himself as God's target and views his situation as the reverse of Eliphaz's description in 15:25–26.

16:12 *All was well … but he shattered me.* See 2:3 and note. *made me his target.* See note on 6:4.

16:15–17 Job summarizes his misery: Though innocent, he continues to suffer.

16:15 *sackcloth … dust.* Signs of mourning (see notes on Ge 37:34; Jnh 3:5–6).

16:18–21 Verse 18 (see v. 22; 17:1) indicates that Job does not think he will live long enough to be vindicated before his peers. His only hope is that in heaven he has a friend (v. 20), a holy one (see 5:1), who will be his “witness,” his “advocate,” his “intercessor,” one who will plead with God on his behalf (v. 21; see 5:1; 9:33 and notes).

16:18 *blood … cry.* Job felt that his blood, like Abel's (see Ge 4:10 and note), was innocent and would therefore cry out from the ground after his death.

16:20 *intercessor.* The Hebrew for this word is translated “mediator” in 33:23 (see note on 33:23–28).

16:22 *Only a few years will pass.* Job does not expect his death immediately. *journey of no return.* To the netherworld (see notes on 7:9; 10:21).

17:1 *the grave awaits me.* See note on vv. 10–16.

17:3 *Give me … the pledge you demand.* Job is asking God for

[4]You have closed their minds to
understanding;[o]
therefore you will not let them
triumph.
[5]If a man denounces his friends for
reward,[p]
the eyes of his children will fail.[q]

[6]"God has made me a byword[r] to
everyone,[s]
a man in whose face people spit.[t]
[7]My eyes have grown dim with grief;[u]
my whole frame is but a shadow.[v]
[8]Upright men are appalled at this;
the innocent are aroused[w] against
the ungodly.
[9]Nevertheless, the righteous[x] will hold
to their ways,
and those with clean hands[y] will
grow stronger.[z]

[10]"But come on, all of you, try again!
I will not find a wise man among
you.[a]
[11]My days have passed,[b] my plans are
shattered,
and so are the desires of my heart.[c]
[12]These men turn night into day;[d]
in the face of darkness they say,
'Light is near.'[e]
[13]If the only home I hope for is the grave,[a][f]
if I spread out my bed[g] in darkness,[h]
[14]if I say to corruption,[i] 'You are my
father,'
and to the worm,[j] 'My mother' or
'My sister,'
[15]where then is my hope?[k]
Who can see any hope for me?[l]
[16]Will it go down to the gates of death[a]?[m]
Will we descend together into the
dust?"[n]

Bildad

18 Then Bildad the Shuhite[o] replied:

[2]"When will you end these speeches?[p]
Be sensible, and then we can talk.
[3]Why are we regarded as cattle[q]
and considered stupid in your
sight?[r]
[4]You who tear yourself[s] to pieces in
your anger,[t]
is the earth to be abandoned for
your sake?
Or must the rocks be moved from
their place?[u]

[5]"The lamp of the wicked is snuffed
out;[v]
the flame of his fire stops burning.[w]
[6]The light in his tent[x] becomes dark;[y]
the lamp beside him goes out.[z]
[7]The vigor[a] of his step is weakened;[b]
his own schemes[c] throw him
down.[d]
[8]His feet thrust him into a net[e]
and he wanders into its mesh.
[9]A trap seizes him by the heel;
a snare[f] holds him fast.[g]
[10]A noose[h] is hidden for him on the
ground;
a trap[i] lies in his path.[j]
[11]Terrors[k] startle him on every side[l]
and dog[m] his every step.
[12]Calamity[n] is hungry[o] for him;
disaster[p] is ready for him when he
falls.[q]
[13]It eats away parts of his skin;[r]
death's firstborn devours his limbs.[s]
[14]He is torn from the security of his
tent[t]
and marched off to the king[u] of
terrors.[v]

[a] 13,16 Hebrew *Sheol*

17:4 [o]S Job 12:12 **17:5** [p]S Ex 22:15 [q]S Job 11:20 **17:6** [r]S 1Ki 9:7; Job 30:9; Jer 15:4 [s]S ver 2 [t]S Nu 12:14 **17:7** [u]S Job 16:8 [v]S Job 2:12; S 16:16 **17:8** [w]S Ex 4:14 **17:9** [x]Pr 4:18 [y]S 2Sa 22:21; S Job 9:30 [z]S 1Sa 2:4; Ps 84:7 **17:10** [a]S Job 12:2 **17:11** [b]ver 15; Isa 38:10 [c]S Job 7:6 **17:12** [d]Isa 50:11 [e]Job 5:17-26; S 11:17 **17:13** [f]S 2Sa 14:14; S Job 3:13 [g]Ps 139:8 [h]Ps 88:18 **17:14** [i]Job 13:28; 30:28,30; Ps 16:10; 49:9 [j]S Job 4:19; S 7:5 **17:15** [k]S Job 7:6 [l]Ps 31:22; La 3:18; Eze 37:11 **17:16** [m]S Job 7:9; 33:28; Ps 9:13; 30:3; 107:18; Isa 38:10,17; Jnh 2:6 [n]S Ge 2:7; S Job 3:19; 20:11; 21:26 **18:1** [o]S Job 8:1 **18:2** [p]S Job 8:2; S 16:3 **18:3** [q]S Job 12:7 [r]Ps 73:22 **18:4** [s]Job 13:14 [t]S Job 16:9 [u]Job 14:18 **18:5** [v]Job 21:17; 35:15; Pr 13:9; 20:20; 24:20; Jer 25:10; Mt 25:8; Jn 8:12 [w]S Job 5:14; 12:25; 24:17; 38:15 **18:6** [x]S Job 8:22 [y]S Job 5:14 [z]S Job 11:17; S 12:25 **18:7** [a]S Job 13:26 [b]Ps 18:36; Pr 4:12 [c]S Job 5:13 [d]S Job 15:6 **18:8** [e]Job 19:6; Ps 9:15; 10:9; 35:7; 57:6; 66:11; 140:5; La 1:13; Mic 7:2; Hab 1:15 **18:9** [f]Job 22:10; 30:12; Isa 24:18; Jer 48:44; Am 5:19 [g]Pr 5:22 **18:10** [h]Pr 7:22; Isa 51:20 [i]S 1Sa 28:9 [j]Ps 140:5 **18:11** [k]ver 14; S Job 6:4; 20:25; 24:17; Ps 55:4; 88:15; Isa 28:19; Jer 15:8; La 2:22 [l]S Job 15:21; Ps 31:13 [m]ver 18; Job 20:8; Isa 22:18 **18:12** [n]Job 21:17 [o]Isa 8:21; 9:20; 65:13 [p]Job 31:3 [q]Job 15:23 **18:13** [r]Nu 12:12 [s]Zec 14:12 **18:14** [t]S Job 8:22 [u]Job 15:24 [v]S ver 11

a guarantee that he is right, that he is not guilty of sins that deserve punishment (as his counselors have said).

17:4 *their minds.* Those of his three friends.

17:5 Job quotes a proverb to counter the false accusations of his friends.

17:6–9 The guarantee Job asked for (v. 3) is not provided, so he feels that God is responsible for making him an object of scorn. If the tone of vv. 8–9 is intended as sarcastic (as v. 10 would seem to indicate), the so-called "upright" and "innocent" (v. 8) are the three counselors.

17:6 *byword.* See 30:9; an object of scorn and ridicule (see the covenant curse in Dt 28:37). *in whose face people spit.* See 30:10; see also Isa 50:6 and note; Mt 27:30.

17:7 *frame is but a shadow.* See note on 2:7.

17:10–16 Zophar had promised that Job's repentance would turn his darkness into light (11:17). Job now makes a parody on such advice (vv. 12–16). His only hope is the grave (see v. 1), which will not be as his home had been (vv. 13–15).

17:13 *home.* See Ecc 12:5 and note. *darkness.* The netherworld (see 10:21; 18:18 and notes).

17:14 In the grave, one's family consists only of decomposition and maggots.

17:15 *where ... is my hope?* See 14:19.

17:16 *gates of death.* See 38:17; Mt 16:18. In Mesopotamian literature, all who entered the netherworld passed through a series of seven gates. *dust.* See note on 7:21.

18:1–4 Bildad resents what he perceives to be a belittling attitude. He considers Job's emotional reaction as self-centered and irrational.

18:5–21 Another poem on the fate of the wicked (see 8:11–19; 15:20–35). Bildad wants to convince Job that he is wrong when he claims that the righteous suffer and the wicked prosper. Bildad is absolutely certain that every wicked person gets paid in full, in this life, for their wicked deeds.

18:5 *The lamp of the wicked is snuffed out.* See 21:17; Pr 13:9 and note. Life, symbolized by light, is extinguished.

18:13 *death's firstborn.* Probably a deadly disease (cf. 5:7 and note).

18:14 *king of terrors.* A vivid figure of speech referring to death, which is personified in v. 13. Canaanite literature

15 Fire resides[a] in his tent;[w]
burning sulfur[x] is scattered over his dwelling.
16 His roots dry up below[y]
and his branches wither above.[z]
17 The memory of him perishes from the earth;[a]
he has no name[b] in the land.[c]
18 He is driven from light into darkness[d]
and is banished[e] from the world.[f]
19 He has no offspring[g] or descendants[h]
among his people,
no survivor[i] where once he lived.[j]
20 Men of the west are appalled[k] at his fate;[l]
men of the east are seized with horror.
21 Surely such is the dwelling[m] of an evil man;[n]
such is the place[o] of one who knows not God."[p]

Job

19

Then Job replied:

2 "How long will you torment[q] me
and crush[r] me with words?
3 Ten times[s] now you have reproached[t] me;
shamelessly you attack me.
4 If it is true that I have gone astray,
my error[u] remains my concern alone.
5 If indeed you would exalt yourselves above me[v]
and use my humiliation against me,
6 then know that God has wronged me[w]
and drawn his net[x] around me.[y]

7 "Though I cry, 'I've been wronged!' I get no response;[z]
though I call for help,[a] there is no justice.[b]
8 He has blocked my way so I cannot pass;[c]
he has shrouded my paths in darkness.[d]
9 He has stripped[e] me of my honor[f]
and removed the crown from my head.[g]
10 He tears me down[h] on every side till I am gone;
he uproots my hope[i] like a tree.[j]
11 His anger[k] burns against me;
he counts me among his enemies.[l]
12 His troops advance in force;[m]
they build a siege ramp[n] against me
and encamp around my tent.[o]

13 "He has alienated my brothers[p] from me;
my acquaintances are completely estranged from me.[q]
14 My kinsmen have gone away;
my friends[r] have forgotten me.
15 My guests[s] and my maidservants[t]
count me a stranger;
they look upon me as an alien.
16 I summon my servant, but he does not answer,
though I beg him with my own mouth.
17 My breath is offensive to my wife;
I am loathsome[u] to my own brothers.
18 Even the little boys[v] scorn me;
when I appear, they ridicule me.[w]
19 All my intimate friends[x] detest me;[y]
those I love have turned against me.[z]

[a] 15 Or *Nothing he had remains*

18:15 [w] ver 18; Job 20:26 [x] S Ge 19:24 **18:16** [y] Isa 5:24; Hos 5:12; Am 2:9 [z] S Ge 27:28; S Job 8:12; S 15:30 **18:17** [a] S Dt 32:26 [b] Dt 9:14; Ps 9:5; 69:28; Pr 10:7; Isa 14:22 [c] Job 24:20; Ps 34:16; Pr 2:22; 10:7; Isa 49:15 **18:18** [d] S Job 5:14 [e] S ver 11 [f] S Job 11:20; 30:8 **18:19** [g] Ps 37:28; Isa 1:4; 14:20; Jer 22:30 [h] Ps 21:10; 109:13; Isa 14:22 [i] S 2Ki 10:11; S Eze 17:8 [j] Job 27:14-15 **18:20** [k] Ps 22:6-7; Isa 52:14; 53:2-3; Eze 27:35 [l] Ps 37:13; Jer 46:21; 50:27,31; Eze 7:7 **18:21** [m] Job 21:28 [n] Isa 57:20 [o] S Job 7:10 [p] S Job 4:21; 1Th 4:5 **19:2** [q] Job 13:25 [r] Job 6:9 **19:3** [s] S Ge 31:7 [t] Job 20:3 **19:4** [u] Job 6:24 **19:5** [v] Ps 35:26; 38:16; 55:12 **19:6** [w] S Job 6:29 [x] S Job 18:8 [y] S Job 10:3 **19:7** [z] Job 30:20; Ps 22:2 [a] Job 30:24,28; 31:35; Ps 5:2 [b] S Job 9:24; Hab 1:2-4 **19:8** [c] La 3:7; Hos 2:6 [d] Job 3:26; 23:17; 30:26; Ecc 6:4; Isa 59:9; Jer 8:15; 14:19; La 3:2 **19:9** [e] S Job 12:17 [f] Ge 43:28; Ex 12:42; Ps 15:4; 50:23; Pr 14:31 [g] S Job 2:8; 29:14; Ps 89:39,44; La 5:16 **19:10** [h] S Job 12:14 [i] S Job 7:6 [j] S Job 14:7 **19:11** [k] Job 16:9 [l] S Job 13:24 **19:12** [m] S Job 16:13 [n] S Job 16:10 [o] S Job 3:23 **19:13** [p] Ps 69:8 [q] ver 19; Job 16:7; 42:11; Ps 31:11; 38:11; 88:8 **19:14** [r] ver 19; S 2Sa 15:12; Job 12:4; 16:20; Ps 88:18; Jer 20:10; 38:22 **19:15** [s] Ge 14:14 [t] Ecc 2:7 **19:17** [u] Ps 38:5 **19:18** [v] S 2Ki 2:23 [w] S Job 16:10 **19:19** [x] S ver 14; S Job 6:14; Ps 55:12-13 [y] Job 30:10 [z] S ver 13; Jn 13:18

---

pictured death as the devouring god Mot. Isaiah reverses the figure and envisions the Lord as swallowing up death forever (see Isa 25:8 and note; see also 1Co 15:54).

18:15 *burning sulfur.* Reminiscent of the destruction of Sodom and Gomorrah (see Ge 19:24 and note).

18:16 *roots ... and ... branches.* Figurative for descendants (see, e.g., Isa 11:1,10) and/or ancestors (see, e.g., Jdg 5:14; Isa 14:29). See also Am 2:9 and note.

18:17 *memory of him perishes.* Apparently, for Bildad, the only retribution beyond death is having one's memory (name) cut off by not leaving any heirs (see v. 19).

18:18 *darkness.* The netherworld (see 10:21 and note; 17:13).

18:21 *evil man ... knows not God.* Having no intimate knowledge of God is synonymous with being wicked (see Hos 4:1–2,6).

19:3 *Ten times.* Several times. Ten is often used as a round number (see, e.g., Ge 31:41; 1Sa 1:8).

19:4 *my concern alone.* Job's friends have no right to interfere or to behave as if they were God (see v. 22).

19:6 *wronged.* Cf. 40:8 and note. The Hebrew for this verb is twice translated "pervert" in 8:3 (see note there), where Bildad denied that God perverts justice. But Job, struggling with the enigma of his suffering, can only conclude that God is his enemy, though in fact he is his friend who delights in him (see 1:8; 2:3). Job's true enemy, of course, is Satan the accuser (see notes on 1:6,12). *drawn his net.* The wicked may get themselves into trouble, as Bildad had pointed out (see 18:8–10), but Job here attributes his suffering to God.

19:7 *I cry, 'I've been wronged!'* Lit. "I cry, 'Violence!'" See Hab 1:2–4 and notes.

19:8–12 In Job's mind, God is at war with him (see 16:10–14 and note).

19:10 *uproots my hope like a tree.* Unlike 14:7–9, where Job had used as a symbol of hope a tree that is cut down but later sprouts again. See also 24:20.

19:12 *siege ramp.* See 30:12.

19:13–19 See Jer 12:6 and note. Very little in life hurts more than rejection by one's family and friends. Job's children are gone, and his wife, brothers, friends and servants find him repulsive.

19:17 *breath is offensive.* See note on 2:7.

19:18 *little boys scorn me.* An intolerable insult in a patriarchal society, where one's elders were to be honored and respected (see Ex 20:12 and note).

20 I am nothing but skin and bones;[a]
I have escaped with only the skin of my teeth.[a]

21 "Have pity on me, my friends,[b] have pity,
for the hand of God has struck[c] me.
22 Why do you pursue[d] me as God does?[e]
Will you never get enough of my flesh?[f]

23 "Oh, that my words were recorded,
that they were written on a scroll,[g]
24 that they were inscribed with an iron tool[h] on[b] lead,
or engraved in rock forever![i]
25 I know that my Redeemer[c][j] lives,[k]
and that in the end he will stand upon the earth.[d]
26 And after my skin has been destroyed,
yet[e] in[f] my flesh I will see God;[l]
27 I myself will see him
with my own eyes[m]—I, and not another.
How my heart yearns[n] within me!

28 "If you say, 'How we will hound[o] him,
since the root of the trouble lies in him,[g]'
29 you should fear the sword yourselves;
for wrath will bring punishment by the sword,[p]
and then you will know that there is judgment.[h]"[q]

Zophar

20 Then Zophar the Naamathite[r] replied:

2 "My troubled thoughts prompt me to answer
because I am greatly disturbed.[s]
3 I hear a rebuke[t] that dishonors me,
and my understanding inspires me to reply.

4 "Surely you know how it has been from of old,[u]
ever since man[i] was placed on the earth,
5 that the mirth of the wicked[v] is brief,
the joy of the godless[w] lasts but a moment.[x]
6 Though his pride[y] reaches to the heavens[z]
and his head touches the clouds,[a]
7 he will perish forever,[b] like his own dung;
those who have seen him will say, 'Where is he?'[c]
8 Like a dream[d] he flies away,[e] no more to be found,
banished[f] like a vision of the night.[g]
9 The eye that saw him will not see him again;
his place will look on him no more.[h]

[a] 20 Or *only my gums* [b] 24 Or *and* [c] 25 Or *defender* [d] 25 Or *upon my grave* [e] 26 Or *And after I awake, / though this ˻body˼ has been destroyed, / then* [f] 26 Or */ apart from* [g] 28 Many Hebrew manuscripts, Septuagint and Vulgate; most Hebrew manuscripts *me* [h] 29 Or */ that you may come to know the Almighty* [i] 4 Or *Adam*

19:20 [a]S Job 2:5 **19:21** [b]S Job 6:14 [c]S Jdg 2:15; S Job 4:5; S 10:3; La 3:1 **19:22** [d]S Job 13:25 [e]ver 6 [f]S 2Ch 28:9; Ps 14:4; 27:2; 69:26; Pr 30:14; Isa 53:4 **19:23** [g]S Ex 17:14; S Ps 40:7; S Isa 8:1 **19:24** [h]Jer 17:1 [i]S Job 16:18 **19:25** [j]S Ex 6:6; S Lev 25:25; Ps 68:5; 78:35; Pr 23:11; Isa 41:14; 43:14; 44:6, 24; 47:4; 48:17; 49:26; 54:5; 59:20; 60:16 [k]S 1Sa 14:39; Job 16:19 **19:26** [l]S Nu 12:8; S Mt 5:8; 1Co 13:12; 1Jn 3:2 **19:27** [m]Lk 2:30 [n]Ps 42:1; 63:1; 84:2 **19:28** [o]S Job 13:25 **19:29** [p]Job 15:22 [q]Job 27:13-23; Ps 1:5; 9:7; 58:11; Ecc 3:17; 11:9; 12:14 **20:1** [r]S Job 2:11 **20:2** [s]Ps 42:5; La 1:20 **20:3** [t]Job 19:3

20:4 [u]Dt 4:32; S 32:7 **20:5** [v]Ps 94:3 [w]S Job 8:13 [x]S Job 8:12; Ps 37:35-36; 73:19 **20:6** [y]Job 33:17; Isa 16:6 [z]S Ge 11:4 [a]Isa 14:13-14; Ob 1:3-4 **20:7** [b]S Job 4:20 [c]S Job 7:8; S 14:20 **20:8** [d]Ps 73:20; Ecc 5:3 [e]Ps 90:10; Ecc 6:12; 12:7 [f]S Job 18:11 [g]Job 27:20; 34:20; Ps 90:5; Isa 17:14; 29:7 **20:9** [h]S Job 7:8

19:20 *skin and bones.* See note on 2:7. *skin of my teeth.* The NIV text note understands the phrase to imply that even Job's teeth are gone.

19:21 *hand of God has struck me.* See note on v. 6; see also 1:11; 2:4–6.

19:23–27 Probably the best-known and most-loved passage in the book of Job, reaching a high point in Job's understanding of his own situation and of his relationship to God. Its position between two sections in which Job pleads with (vv. 21–22) and then warns (vv. 28–29) his friends causes it to stand out even more boldly.

19:23 *my words.* Job wishes that his complaint and defense were recorded, so that even after his death they would endure until he is finally vindicated. *scroll.* See note on Ex 17:14.

19:24 *iron.* See also 20:24; 28:2; 40:18; 41:27. Iron did not come into common use in the ancient Near East until the 12th century B.C., though limited use of iron in the region is attested at least as early as 2000 B.C.

19:25 *I know that my Redeemer lives.* This staunch confession of faith has been appropriated by generations of Christians, especially through the medium of Handel's *The Messiah.* But these celebrate redemption from guilt and judgment; Job had something else in mind. Although in other contexts he desires a defender (see NIV text note; see also Pr 23:11 and note) as an advocate in heaven who would plead with God on his behalf (see 9:33–34; 16:18–21 and notes; see also note on 5:1), here the Redeemer seems to be none other than God himself (see note on Ru 2:20). Job expresses confidence that ultimately God will vindicate his faithful servants in the face of all false accusations. *in the end.* Lit. "afterward" (after Job's life has ended). *he will stand.* To defend and vindicate me (see 42:7–10 and notes).

19:26 *my skin has been destroyed.* Job senses that the ravages of his disease will eventually bring about his death. *I will see God.* He is absolutely certain, however, that death is not the end of existence and that someday he will stand in the presence of his Redeemer and see him with his own eyes (see v. 27; see also Mt 5:8; 1Jn 3:2). See note on 42:5.

19:28 *hound.* The Hebrew for this verb is translated "pursue" in v. 22. It serves as a clue that Job's tirade against the counselors is being resumed after the intervening section (vv. 23–27).

20:1–29 Yet another poem on the fate of the wicked as held by the traditional theology of Job's friends (see 8:11–19; 15:20–35; 18:5–21).

20:2–3 Zophar takes Job's words, especially his closing words in 19:28–29, as a personal affront. Job has dared to assert that on Zophar's theory of retribution Zophar himself is due for punishment.

20:4–11 Zophar is proud that he is a healthy and prosperous man, for, in his view, that in itself is proof of his goodness and righteousness. But the joy and vigor of the wicked will always be brief and elusive (see Ps 73:18–20 and note).

20:6 *pride reaches to the heavens.* See Ge 11:4 and note.

20:7 *dung.* A symbol of what is temporary and worthless (see 1Ki 14:10).

10 His children[i] must make amends to the poor;
his own hands must give back his wealth.[j]
11 The youthful vigor[k] that fills his bones[l]
will lie with him in the dust.[m]

12 "Though evil[n] is sweet in his mouth
and he hides it under his tongue,[o]
13 though he cannot bear to let it go
and keeps it in his mouth,[p]
14 yet his food will turn sour in his stomach;[q]
it will become the venom of serpents[r] within him.
15 He will spit out the riches[s] he swallowed;
God will make his stomach vomit[t] them up.
16 He will suck the poison[u] of serpents;
the fangs of an adder will kill him.[v]
17 He will not enjoy the streams,
the rivers[w] flowing with honey[x] and cream.[y]
18 What he toiled for he must give back uneaten;[z]
he will not enjoy the profit from his trading.[a]
19 For he has oppressed the poor[b] and left them destitute;[c]
he has seized houses[d] he did not build.

20 "Surely he will have no respite from his craving;[e]
he cannot save himself by his treasure.[f]
21 Nothing is left for him to devour;
his prosperity will not endure.[g]
22 In the midst of his plenty, distress will overtake him;[h]
the full force of misery will come upon him.[i]
23 When he has filled his belly,[j]
God will vent his burning anger[k] against him
and rain down his blows upon him.[l]
24 Though he flees[m] from an iron weapon,
a bronze-tipped arrow pierces him.[n]
25 He pulls it out of his back,
the gleaming point out of his liver.
Terrors[o] will come over him;[p]
26 total darkness[q] lies in wait for his treasures.
A fire[r] unfanned will consume him[s]
and devour what is left in his tent.[t]
27 The heavens will expose his guilt;
the earth will rise up against him.[u]
28 A flood will carry off his house,[v]
rushing waters[a] on the day of God's wrath.[w]
29 Such is the fate God allots the wicked,
the heritage appointed for them by God."[x]

Job

21 Then Job replied:

2 "Listen carefully to my words;[y]
let this be the consolation you give me.[z]
3 Bear with me while I speak,
and after I have spoken, mock on.[a]

4 "Is my complaint[b] directed to man?
Why should I not be impatient?[c]
5 Look at me and be astonished;
clap your hand over your mouth.[d]
6 When I think about this, I am terrified;[e]
trembling seizes my body.[f]

20:10 [i] S Job 5:4 [j] ver 15, 18, 20; S Job 3:15; 31:8 **20:11** [k] S Job 13:26 [l] Job 21:24 [m] S Job 17:16 **20:12** [n] S Job 15:16 [o] Ps 10:7; 140:3 **20:13** [p] S Nu 11:18-20 **20:14** [q] Pr 20:17; Jer 2:19; 4:18; Rev 10:9 [r] S Nu 21:6 **20:15** [s] S ver 10 [t] S Lev 18:25 **20:16** [u] S Dt 32:32 [v] Dt 32:24 **20:17** [w] Ps 36:8 [x] Dt 32:13 [y] Dt 32:14; Job 29:6 **20:18** [z] S ver 10; S Job 5:5 [a] Ps 109:11 **20:19** [b] S Job 5:16; Ps 10:2; 94:6; 109:16 [c] S Dt 15:11; 24:14; Job 24:4, 14; 35:9; Pr 14:31; 28:28; Am 8:4 [d] Isa 5:8 **20:20** [e] Ecc 5:12-14 [f] S ver 10; Pr 11:4; Zep 1:18; Lk 12:15 **20:21** [g] S Job 7:8 **20:22** [h] S Jdg 2:15; Lk 12:16-20 [i] ver 29; Job 21:17, 30; 31:2-3 **20:23** [j] S Nu 11:18-20 [k] La 4:11; Eze 5:13; 6:12 [l] ver 14; Ps 78:30-31 **20:24** [m] Isa 24:18; Jer 46:21; 48:44 [n] S Job 15:22 **20:25** [o] S Job 18:11 [p] S Job 15:21; Ps 88:15-16

[a] 28 Or *The possessions in his house will be carried off, / washed away*

20:26 [q] S Job 5:14 [r] S Job 1:16 [s] Job 15:34; 26:6; 28:22; 31:12; Ps 21:9 [t] S Job 18:15 **20:27** [u] S Dt 31:28 **20:28** [v] Dt 28:31; Mt 7:26-27 [w] ver 29; Nu 14:28-32; Job 21:17, 20, 30; 40:11; Ps 60:3; 75:8; Pr 16:4; Isa 24:18; 51:17; Am 5:18; Jn 3:36; Ro 1:18; Eph 5:6 **20:29** [x] S ver 22; S Job 15:20; 22:5; 31:2; 36:17; Jer 13:25; Rev 21:8 **21:2** [y] S Job 13:17 [z] ver 34 **21:3** [a] S Job 6:14; S 11:3; S 16:10 **21:4** [b] S Job 7:11 [c] S Job 6:3 **21:5** [d] S Jdg 18:19; Job 29:9; 40:4 **21:6** [e] S Ge 45:3 [f] S Job 4:14

20:10,19 Oppression of the poor is the mark of the truly wicked (see, e.g., Am 2:6–8 and notes; 8:4–8). On this subject, Job had no quarrel with Zophar (see 31:16–23).
20:11 *dust.* See note on 7:21.
20:12–15 The wicked deeds of evil people are like tasty food that pleases their palates but turns sour in their stomachs.
20:15 *riches he swallowed.* After taking what belonged to the poor (see note on vv. 10,19).
20:17 *honey and cream.* See 29:6 and note; cf. Dt 6:3 and note.
20:18 *What he toiled for … he will not enjoy.* A common theme in wisdom literature (see, e.g., Ecc 2:18–23).
20:20–25 Although the wicked may fill their bellies, when God vents his anger against them there will be nothing for them to eat.
20:24 *iron.* See note on 19:24.
20:26 *darkness.* See note on 10:21.
20:27 See Dt 30:19 and note.
20:28 *flood … rushing waters.* Caused by intermittent streams that can overflow and cause extensive damage during the rainy season (see 6:15–16).
20:29 Like Bildad in 18:21 (see note there), Zophar concludes his speech with a summary statement in which he claims that all he has said is in accord with God's plans for judging sinners. *Such is the fate God allots the wicked.* Repeated almost verbatim by Job in 27:13.
21:2 *consolation you give me.* See v. 34 ("you console me"), which, with v. 2, frames Job's reply to Zophar.
21:4 *Is my complaint directed to man?* No, says Job, I am complaining to God, because he is responsible for my condition—at least Job so perceived it. *impatient.* See note on 9:2–3.
21:5 *Look at me.* Job addresses his three friends.
21:6 *this.* His complaint to God. *I am terrified.* To contemplate the morally upside-down situation in which the wicked flourish.

[7]Why do the wicked live on,
growing old and increasing in power?[g]
[8]They see their children established around them,
their offspring before their eyes.[h]
[9]Their homes are safe and free from fear;[i]
the rod of God is not upon them.[j]
[10]Their bulls never fail to breed;
their cows calve and do not miscarry.[k]
[11]They send forth their children as a flock;[l]
their little ones dance about.
[12]They sing to the music of tambourine and harp;[m]
they make merry to the sound of the flute.[n]
[13]They spend their years in prosperity[o]
and go down to the grave[a][p] in peace.[b][q]
[14]Yet they say to God, 'Leave us alone![r]
We have no desire to know your ways.[s]
[15]Who is the Almighty, that we should serve him?
What would we gain by praying to him?'[t]
[16]But their prosperity is not in their own hands,
so I stand aloof from the counsel of the wicked.[u]

[17]"Yet how often is the lamp of the wicked snuffed out?[v]
How often does calamity[w] come upon them,
the fate God allots in his anger?[x]
[18]How often are they like straw before the wind,
like chaff[y] swept away[z][a] by a gale?[b]
[19]⌊It is said,⌋ 'God stores up a man's punishment for his sons.'[c]
Let him repay the man himself, so that he will know it![d]
[20]Let his own eyes see his destruction;[e]
let him drink[f] of the wrath of the Almighty.[c][g]
[21]For what does he care about the family he leaves behind[h]
when his allotted months[i] come to an end?[j]

21:7 [g]ver 13; S Job 9:24; 12:19; Ps 37:1; 73:3; Ecc 7:15; 8:14; Hab 1:13; Mal 3:15 **21:8** [h]Ps 17:14; Mal 3:15 **21:9** [i]S Job 5:24 [j]S Job 9:34 **21:10** [k]Ex 23:26 **21:11** [l]Ps 78:52; 107:41 **21:12** [m]Ps 33:2 [n]S Ge 4:21; S 1Ch 15:16; Ps 71:22; 81:2; 108:2; Isa 5:12; Mt 11:17 **21:13** [o]S ver 7; S Job 8:7; Ps 10:1-12; 94:3 [p]Job 24:19; Ps 49:14; Isa 14:15 [q]S Job 3:13 **21:14** [r]S Job 4:17; 22:17; Isa 30:11 [s]S Dt 32:15; S 1Sa 15:11; Ps 95:10; Pr 1:29; Jer 2:20,31 **21:15** [t]S Job 5:2; 34:9; 35:3; Ps 73:13; 139:20; Isa 48:5; Jer 9:6; 44:17 **21:16** [u]Job 22:18; Ps 1:1; 26:5; 36:1 **21:17** [v]S Job 18:5 [w]Job 18:12 [x]S Job 20:22,28 **21:18** [y]S Job 13:25 [z]S Ge 19:15 [a]S Job 7:10; Pr 10:25 [b]S Ge 7:23 **21:19** [c]Ex 20:5; Jer 31:29; Eze 18:2; Jn 9:2 [d]Jer 25:14; 50:29; 51:6,24,56 **21:20** [e]S Ex 32:33; Nu 16:22; S 2Ki 14:6; Jer 42:16 [f]Job 6:4 [g]S Job 20:28; Jer 25:15; Rev 14:10 **21:21** [h]Job 14:22 [i]S Job 14:5 [j]S Job 14:21; Ecc 9:5-6 **21:22** [k]Job 35:11; 36:22; 39:17;

[22]"Can anyone teach knowledge to God,[k]
since he judges even the highest?[l]
[23]One man dies in full vigor,[m]
completely secure and at ease,[n]
[24]his body[d] well nourished,[o]
his bones[p] rich with marrow.[q]
[25]Another man dies in bitterness of soul,[r]
never having enjoyed anything good.
[26]Side by side they lie in the dust,[s]
and worms[t] cover them both.[u]

[27]"I know full well what you are thinking,
the schemes by which you would wrong me.
[28]You say, 'Where now is the great man's[v] house,
the tents where wicked men lived?'[w]
[29]Have you never questioned those who travel?
Have you paid no regard to their accounts—
[30]that the evil man is spared from the day of calamity,[x]
that he is delivered from[e] the day of wrath?[y]
[31]Who denounces his conduct to his face?
Who repays him for what he has done?[z]
[32]He is carried to the grave,
and watch is kept over his tomb.[a]
[33]The soil in the valley is sweet to him;[b]
all men follow after him,
and a countless throng goes[f] before him.[c]

[34]"So how can you console me[d] with your nonsense?
Nothing is left of your answers but falsehood!"[e]

[a] *13* Hebrew *Sheol* [b] *13* Or *in an instant* [c] *17-20* Verses 17 and 18 may be taken as exclamations and 19 and 20 as declarations. [d] *24* The meaning of the Hebrew for this word is uncertain. [e] *30* Or *man is reserved for the day of calamity, / that he is brought forth to* [f] *33* Or / *as a countless throng went*

Ps 94:12; Isa 40:13-14; Jer 32:33; Ro 11:34 [l]S Job 4:18; Ps 82:1; 86:8; 135:5 **21:23** [m]S Ge 15:15; S Job 13:26 [n]S Job 3:13 **21:24** [o]Ps 73:4 [p]Job 20:11 [q]Pr 3:8 **21:25** [r]S Job 10:1 **21:26** [s]S Job 17:16 [t]S Job 7:5 [u]Job 24:20; Ecc 9:2-3; Isa 14:11 **21:28** [v]Job 1:3; 12:21; 29:25; 31:37 [w]S Job 8:22 **21:30** [x]Job 31:3 [y]S Job 20:22,28; S Isa 5:30; Ro 2:5; 2Pe 2:9 **21:31** [z]Job 34:11; Ps 62:12; Pr 24:11-12; Isa 59:18 **21:32** [a]Isa 14:18 **21:33** [b]Job 3:22 [c]S Job 3:19 **21:34** [d]ver 2 [e]S Job 6:15; 8:20

21:7–15 Job's counselors have elaborated on the fate of the wicked (see 8:11–19; 15:20–35; 18:5–21; ch. 20), but Job insists that experience shows just the reverse of what his friends have said. The wicked, who want to know nothing of God's ways and who even consider prayer a useless exercise (vv. 14–15), flourish in all they do. Far from dying prematurely, as Zophar assumed concerning them (see 20:11), they live long and increase in power (v. 7). Bildad's claim that the wicked have no offspring or descendants (see 18:19) Job flatly denies (vv. 8,11).

21:9 *rod of God.* See note on 9:34.

21:13 *peace.* The Hebrew root underlying this word is translated "those who live quietly" in Ps 35:20.

21:16 See 22:18. Job disavows the unholy counsel of the wicked and knows that God is in control (see v. 17), but such knowledge makes God all the more of an enigma to him.

21:17 *lamp of the wicked snuffed out.* See 18:5 and note.

21:18 *straw . . . chaff.* See 13:25; see also note on Ps 1:4.

21:20 *drink . . . wrath of the Almighty.* See note on Isa 51:17.

21:22 *Can anyone teach . . . God . . . ?* See Isa 40:14. On the contrary, God is the one who does the teaching (see 35:11; 36:22; chs. 38–41).

21:26 *dust.* See note on 7:21.

21:34 *how can you console me . . . ?* See 16:2 and note.

Eliphaz

22 Then Eliphaz the Temanite[f] replied:

2 "Can a man be of benefit to God?[g]
Can even a wise man benefit him?[h]
3 What pleasure[i] would it give the Almighty if you were righteous?[j]
What would he gain if your ways were blameless?[k]
4 "Is it for your piety that he rebukes you
and brings charges against you?[l]
5 Is not your wickedness great?
Are not your sins[m] endless?[n]
6 You demanded security[o] from your brothers for no reason;[p]
you stripped men of their clothing, leaving them naked.[q]
7 You gave no water[r] to the weary
and you withheld food from the hungry,[s]
8 though you were a powerful man, owning land[t]—
an honored man,[u] living on it.[v]
9 And you sent widows[w] away empty-handed[x]
and broke the strength of the fatherless.[y]
10 That is why snares[z] are all around you,[a]
why sudden peril terrifies you,[b]
11 why it is so dark[c] you cannot see,
and why a flood of water covers you.[d]
12 "Is not God in the heights of heaven?[e]
And see how lofty are the highest stars!
13 Yet you say, 'What does God know?[f]
Does he judge through such darkness?[g]
14 Thick clouds[h] veil him, so he does not see us[i]
as he goes about in the vaulted heavens.'[j]
15 Will you keep to the old path
that evil men[k] have trod?[l]
16 They were carried off before their time,[m]
their foundations[n] washed away by a flood.[o]
17 They said to God, 'Leave us alone!
What can the Almighty do to us?'[p]
18 Yet it was he who filled their houses with good things,[q]
so I stand aloof from the counsel of the wicked.[r]
19 "The righteous see their ruin and rejoice;[s]
the innocent mock[t] them, saying,
20 'Surely our foes are destroyed,[u]
and fire[v] devours their wealth.'
21 "Submit to God and be at peace[w] with him;[x]
in this way prosperity will come to you.[y]
22 Accept instruction from his mouth[z]
and lay up his words[a] in your heart.[b]

22:1 [f] S Job 4:1 **22:2** [g] Lk 17:10 [h] S Job 7:17 **22:3** [i] Isa 1:11; Hag 1:8 [j] Ps 143:2 [k] Job 35:7; Pr 9:12 **22:4** [l] S Job 9:3; 19:29; Ps 143:2; Isa 3:14; Eze 20:35 **22:5** [m] S Ezr 9:13; S Job 15:5 [n] S Job 15:13; S 20:29; 29:17 **22:6** [o] S Ex 22:26 [p] S 2Ki 4:1 [q] S Ex 22:27; Dt 24:12-13 **22:7** [r] Mt 10:42 [s] ver 9; Job 29:12; 31:17,21,31; Isa 58:7,10; Eze 18:7; Mt 25:42 **22:8** [t] S Job 15:19 [u] Isa 3:3; 5:13; 9:15 [v] S Job 12:19 **22:9** [w] Job 29:13; 31:16; Ps 146:9 [x] Job 24:3,21; Isa 10:2; Lk 1:53 [y] S ver 7; S Job 6:27; S Isa 1:17 **22:10** [z] S Job 18:9 [a] S Job 10:3 [b] S Job 15:21 **22:11** [c] S Job 5:14 [d] S Ge 7:23; Job 36:28; 38:34,37; Ps 69:1-2; 124:4-5; Isa 58:10-11; La 3:54 **22:12** [e] S Job 11:8; S 16:19 **22:13** [f] ver 14; Ps 10:11; 59:7; 64:5; 73:11; 94:7; Isa 29:15; Eze 9:9; Zep 1:12 [g] Ps 139:11; Eze 8:12; Eph 6:12 **22:14** [h] Job 26:9; Ps 97:2; 105:39 [i] S ver 13; S 2Ki 21:16 [j] Job 37:18; Ps 18:11; Pr 8:27; Isa 40:22; Jer 23:23-24 **22:15** [k] Job 23:10; 34:36 [l] Job 34:8; Ps 1:1; 50:18 **22:16** [m] S Job 15:32 [n] S Job 4:19 [o] S Ge 7:23; Mt 7:26-27 **22:17** [p] Job 21:15 **22:18** [q] S Job 12:6 [r] S Job 21:16 **22:19** [s] Ps 5:11; 9:2; 32:11; 58:10; 64:10; 97:12; 107:42 [t] Job 21:3; Ps 52:6 **22:20** [u] Ps 18:39 [v] S Job 15:30 **22:21** [w] Isa 26:3,12; 27:5; Ro 5:1 [x] S Ge 17:1; Jer 9:24 [y] S Job 8:7; Ps 34:8-10; Pr 3:10; 1Pe 5:6 **22:22** [z] S Dt 8:3 [a] S Job 6:10 [b] S Job 15:11; 28:23; Ps 37:31; 40:8; Pr 2:6; Eze 3:10

22:1—26:14 This third cycle of speeches, unlike the first (chs. 4–14) and second (chs. 15–21), is truncated and abbreviated. Bildad's speech is very brief (25:1–6), and Zophar does not speak at all. The dialogue between Job and his friends comes to an end because the friends cannot convince Job of his guilt—Job cannot acknowledge what is not true.

22:2–4 Eliphaz's odd reasoning is as follows: All things have their origin in God. So when people give back what God has given them, that does not enhance God in any way. Indeed, God is indifferent to human goodness, because goodness is expected of them. It is when people become wicked that God is aroused (v. 4).

22:4 *piety.* See note on 4:6. *brings charges against.* See note on 9:3.

22:5–11 In his earlier speeches, Eliphaz was the least caustic and at first even offered consolation (4:6; 5:17). But despite what he said in 4:3–4, Eliphaz now reprimands Job for gross social sins against the needy, who are naked and hungry (vv. 6–7), and against widows and the fatherless (v. 9). The only proof Eliphaz has for Job's alleged wickedness is his present suffering (vv. 10–11). In ch. 29 Job emphatically denies the kind of behavior of which Eliphaz accuses him.

22:6 *demanded security … stripped men of their clothing.* Sins condemned by the prophets (see, e.g., Am 2:8 and note).

22:9 *widows … fatherless.* See 24:3; Isa 1:17 and note; Jas 1:27. *strength.* Lit. "arms" (as in 38:15).

22:10 *snares.* See 19:6 and note.

22:11 *dark … flood of water.* Two common figures of trouble and distress (see Ps 42:7 and note; Isa 8:7–8 and notes; 8:22; 43:2).

22:12–20 Eliphaz finally appears to support the argument of Bildad and Zophar, who were fully convinced that Job was a wicked man. Eliphaz makes a severe accusation: Job follows the path of the ungodly (v. 15), who defy God's power and say, "What can the Almighty do to us?" (v. 17; see vv. 13–14). They even have contempt for God's goodness (v. 18).

22:18 See 21:16 and note.

22:21–30 Eliphaz makes one last attempt to reach Job. In many ways it is a commendable call to repentance: Submit to God (v. 21), lay up God's words in your heart (v. 22), return to the Almighty and forsake wickedness (v. 23), find your delight in God rather than in gold (vv. 24–26), pray and obey (v. 27) and become concerned about sinners (vv. 29–30). But Eliphaz's advice assumes (1) that Job is a very wicked man and (2) that Job's major concern is the return of his prosperity (see v. 21). Job had already made it clear in 19:25–27 that he deeply yearned to see God and be his friend.

22:22 See Job's response in 23:12. *lay up his words in your heart.* The author of Ps 119 speaks similarly about the written word God gave to Israel (Ps 119:11; see Pr 2:1 and note).

23 If you return[c] to the Almighty, you will
be restored:[d]
If you remove wickedness far from
your tent[e]
24 and assign your nuggets[f] to the dust,
your gold[g] of Ophir[h] to the rocks in
the ravines,[i]
25 then the Almighty will be your gold,[j]
the choicest silver for you.[k]
26 Surely then you will find delight in the
Almighty[l]
and will lift up your face[m] to God.[n]
27 You will pray to him,[o] and he will hear
you,[p]
and you will fulfill your vows.[q]
28 What you decide on will be done,[r]
and light[s] will shine on your ways.[t]
29 When men are brought low[u] and you
say, 'Lift them up!'
then he will save the downcast.[v]
30 He will deliver even one who is not
innocent,[w]
who will be delivered through the
cleanness of your hands."[x]

Job

23

Then Job replied:

2 "Even today my complaint[y] is bitter;[z]
his hand[a] is heavy in spite of[b] my
groaning.[a]
3 If only I knew where to find him;
if only I could go to his dwelling![b]
4 I would state my case[c] before him
and fill my mouth with arguments.[d]
5 I would find out what he would
answer me,[e]
and consider what he would say.
6 Would he oppose me with great
power?[f]
No, he would not press charges
against me.[g]
7 There an upright man[h] could present
his case before him,[i]
and I would be delivered forever
from my judge.[j]

22:23 [c]Isa 31:6; 44:22; 55:7; 59:20; Jer 3:14,22; Eze 18:32; Zec 1:3; Mal 3:7 [d]S Job 5:24; Isa 19:22; Ac 20:32 [e]Job 11:14 **22:24** [f]Job 28:6 [g]Ps 19:10 [h]S Ge 10:29 [i]S Job 1:10; 31:25; Isa 2:20; 30:22; 31:7; 40:19-20; Mt 6:19 **22:25** [j]Job 31:24; Ps 49:6; 52:7; Pr 11:28 [k]2Ki 18:7; Isa 33:6; Mt 6:20-21 **22:26** [l]Job 27:10; Ps 2:8; 16:6; 37:4; Isa 58:14; 61:10 [m]Job 11:15 [n]Job 11:17; 33:26; Ps 27:6; 100:1 **22:27** [o]S Job 5:27 [p]S Job 5:15; S Ps 86:7; S Isa 30:19 [q]S Nu 30:2 **22:28** [r]Ps 103:11; 145:19 [s]Job 33:28; Ps 97:11; Pr 4:18 [t]S Job 11:17 **22:29** [u]S Est 5:12 [v]Ps 18:27; S Mt 23:12 **22:30** [w]Isa 1:18; Ro 4:5 [x]S 2Sa 22:21 **23:2** [y]S Job 7:11 [z]S 1Sa 1:10; S Job 6:3 [a]Ps 6:6; 32:4; Jer 45:3; Eze 21:7 **23:3** [b]Dt 4:29 **23:4** [c]S Job 13:18 [d]S Job 9:15 **23:5** [e]S Job 11:5 **23:6** [f]S Job 9:4 [g]S Job 6:4 **23:7** [h]S Job 1:1 [i]S Ge 3:8; S Job 9:3; 13:3 [j]S Job 6:29

8 "But if I go to the east, he is not
there;
if I go to the west, I do not find
him.
9 When he is at work in the north, I do
not see him;
when he turns to the south, I catch
no glimpse of him.[k]
10 But he knows the way that I take;[l]
when he has tested me,[m] I will come
forth as gold.[n]
11 My feet have closely followed his
steps;[o]
I have kept to his way without
turning aside.[p]
12 I have not departed from the
commands of his lips;[q]
I have treasured the words of his
mouth more than my daily
bread.[r]
13 "But he stands alone, and who can
oppose him?[s]
He does whatever he pleases.[t]
14 He carries out his decree against me,
and many such plans he still has
in store.[u]
15 That is why I am terrified before
him;[v]
when I think of all this, I fear
him.[w]
16 God has made my heart faint;[x]
the Almighty[y] has terrified me.[z]
17 Yet I am not silenced by the darkness,[a]
by the thick darkness that covers
my face.

[a] 2 Septuagint and Syriac; Hebrew / *the hand on me*
[b] 2 Or *heavy on me in*

23:9 [k]S Job 9:11 **23:10** [l]Job 1:1; 27:6; 31:6; 36:7; Ps 7:9; 11:5; 34:15; 37:18; 94:11; 119:168; 146:8 [m]S Job 7:18; Ps 139:1-3 [n]S Job 6:29; S 22:15; S Ps 12:6; 1Pe 1:7 **23:11** [o]Ps 17:5 [p]Job 31:7; Ps 40:4; 44:18; 119:51,59,157; 125:5; Jer 11:20 **23:12** [q]S Job 6:10 [r]S Job 15:11; Mt 4:4; Jn 4:32,34 **23:13** [s]S Job 9:3 [t]S Job 10:13; Isa 55:11 **23:14** [u]1Th 3:3; 1Pe 4:12 **23:15** [v]S Ge 45:3 [w]S Jos 24:14; Ps 34:9; 36:1; 111:10; Pr 1:7; Ecc 3:14; 12:13; 2Co 5:11 **23:16** [x]S Dt 20:3 [y]Job 27:2 [z]S Ex 3:6; Rev 6:16 **23:17** [a]S Job 3:6; S 19:8

22:24 *gold of Ophir.* The finest gold (see 28:16; see also notes on 1Ki 9:28; 10:11; Ps 45:9; Isa 13:12).

22:28 *light will shine on your ways.* Through obedience to the word of God (see vv. 22,27; 29:3; cf. Ps 119:105).

22:30 *cleanness of your hands.* See note on Ps 24:4.

23:2 *my complaint.* See 21:4 and note. *his hand is heavy.* See NIV text notes; 33:7 and note; see also note on 1Sa 5:6.

23:3 *where to find him.* See note on vv. 8–9.

23:6 *not press charges against me.* Job is seeking a fair trial. In 9:14–20 Job was fearful that he could not find words to argue with God. Now he is confident that if God would give him a hearing, he would be acquitted (see 13:13–19; see also Ps 17:1–3; 26:1–3 and notes).

23:8–9 *east … west … north … south.* Whatever direction Job went, he could not find God (contrast Ps 139:7–10).

23:8,10 *I do not find him … But he knows the way that I take.* Job is frustrated over his apparent inability to have an audience with God, who knows that he is an upright man. Job is here answering Eliphaz's admonition beginning in 22:21: "Submit to God and … prosperity will come." Job replies that this is what he has always done (vv. 11–12). He treasures God's words more than his daily food. He admits that God is testing him—not to purge away his sinful dross, but to show that Job is pure gold (see Ps 119:11,101,168; 1Pe 1:7 and note).

23:12 Job's response to the advice offered by Eliphaz in 22:22. *words … more than my daily bread.* See Dt 8:3; Mt 4:4 and notes.

23:13 *he stands alone.* Lit. "he is one (unique)." Though Job is not an Israelite, he worships the one true God—there is no other (see Dt 6:4 and note). *He does whatever he pleases.* He is sovereign (see Ps 115:3; 135:6 and notes; see also Lk 10:21).

23:15 *I am terrified.* See note on 21:6. A part of Job's faith is the recognition that God does what he pleases. By contrast, the counselors tried to make God predictable.

23:17 *I am not silenced by the darkness.* Job responds to Eliphaz's accusation in 22:11 (see note there).

24 "Why does the Almighty not set
times[b] for judgment?[c]
Why must those who know him look
in vain for such days?[d]
2 Men move boundary stones;[e]
they pasture flocks they have
stolen.[f]
3 They drive away the orphan's donkey
and take the widow's ox in pledge.[g]
4 They thrust the needy[h] from the path
and force all the poor[i] of the land
into hiding.[j]
5 Like wild donkeys[k] in the desert,
the poor go about their labor[l] of
foraging food;
the wasteland[m] provides food for
their children.
6 They gather fodder[n] in the fields
and glean in the vineyards[o] of the
wicked.[p]
7 Lacking clothes, they spend the night
naked;
they have nothing to cover
themselves in the cold.[q]
8 They are drenched[r] by mountain rains
and hug[s] the rocks for lack of
shelter.[t]
9 The fatherless[u] child is snatched[v] from
the breast;
the infant of the poor is seized[w] for
a debt.[x]
10 Lacking clothes, they go about naked;[y]
they carry the sheaves,[z] but still go
hungry.
11 They crush olives among the terraces[a];
they tread the winepresses,[a] yet
suffer thirst.[b]
12 The groans of the dying rise from the
city,
and the souls of the wounded cry
out for help.[c]
But God charges no one with
wrongdoing.[d]
13 "There are those who rebel against the
light,[e]
who do not know its ways
or stay in its paths.[f]
14 When daylight is gone, the murderer
rises up
and kills[g] the poor and needy;[h]
in the night he steals forth like a
thief.[i]
15 The eye of the adulterer[j] watches for
dusk;[k]
he thinks, 'No eye will see me,'[l]
and he keeps his face concealed.
16 In the dark, men break into houses,[m]
but by day they shut themselves in;
they want nothing to do with the
light.[n]
17 For all of them, deep darkness is their
morning[b];
they make friends with the terrors[o]
of darkness.[c][p]
18 "Yet they are foam[q] on the surface of
the water;[r]
their portion of the land is cursed,[s]
so that no one goes to the
vineyards.[t]
19 As heat and drought snatch away the
melted snow,[u]
so the grave[d][v] snatches away those
who have sinned.
20 The womb forgets them,
the worm[w] feasts on them;[x]
evil men are no longer remembered[y]
but are broken like a tree.[z]
21 They prey on the barren and childless
woman,
and to the widow show no
kindness.[a]

[a] 11 Or *olives between the millstones*; the meaning of the Hebrew for this word is uncertain. [b] 17 Or *them, their morning is like the shadow of death* [c] 17 Or *of the shadow of death* [d] 19 Hebrew *Sheol*

24:1 [b] S Job 14:5 [c] S Job 9:23; 2Pe 3:7 [d] S Job 15:20; Ac 1:7 **24:2** [e] S Dt 19:14 [f] Ex 20:15; Dt 28:31 **24:3** [g] S Job 6:27; S 22:9 **24:4** [h] Job 29:16; 31:19 [i] Job 29:12; 30:25; Ps 12:5; 41:1; 82:3,4; Isa 11:4 [j] S Job 20:19; S Pr 28:12 **24:5** [k] S Ge 16:12 [l] Ps 104:23 [m] Job 30:3 **24:6** [n] S Job 6:5 [o] ver 18 [p] Ru 2:22; S 1Ki 21:19 **24:7** [q] S Ex 22:27 **24:8** [r] Da 4:25,33 [s] La 4:5 [t] S Jdg 6:2 **24:9** [u] S Dt 24:17 [v] Job 29:17 [w] Ps 14:4; Pr 30:14; Isa 3:14; 10:1-2; Eze 18:12 [x] S Lev 25:47; S 2Ki 4:1 **24:10** [y] Dt 24:12-13 [z] S Lev 19:9 **24:11** [a] Isa 5:2; 16:10; Hag 2:16 [b] Mic 6:15 **24:12** [c] S Job 12:19; 30:28; Ps 5:2; 22:24; 39:12; 119:147; Isa 30:19; Jer 50:46; 51:52,54; Eze 26:15; Rev 6:10 [d] S Job 9:23 **24:13** [e] ver 16; Job 38:15; Jn 3:19-20; 1Th 5:4-5 [f] Job 17:12; 38:20; Ps 18:28; Isa 5:20; Eph 5:8-14 **24:14** [g] Isa 3:15; Mic 3:3 [h] S Job 20:19; Ps 37:32 [i] Ps 10:9 **24:15** [j] Job 31:9,27; Pr 1:10 [k] Pr 7:8-9 [l] Ps 10:11 **24:16** [m] S Ex 22:2; Mt 6:19 [n] S ver 13 **24:17** [o] S Job 18:11 [p] S Job 15:22; S 18:5 **24:18** [q] S Job 9:26; Jude 1:13 [r] Job 22:16; Isa 57:20 [s] S Job 5:3 [t] ver 6 **24:19** [u] Job 6:17 [v] S Job 21:13 **24:20** [w] S Job 7:5 [x] S Job 21:26 [y] S Job 18:17 [z] S Job 14:7; Ps 31:12; Da 4:14 **24:21** [a] S Job 22:9

24:1–12 Job describes the terrible injustice that often exists in the world. Robbery of both the haves (see v. 2) and the have-nots (see vv. 3–4) is equally obnoxious to him. But perhaps his suffering has enabled him to empathize with the poor, who must forage for food (v. 5) and "glean in the vineyards of the wicked" (v. 6). The scene he depicts is heart-rending: The naked shiver in the cold of night (vv. 7–8), fatherless infants are "snatched from the breast" (v. 9), field hands harvest food but go hungry (v. 10), vineyard workers make wine but suffer thirst (v. 11), groans rise from the dying and wounded (v. 12). Job cannot understand why God is silent and indifferent (vv. 1,12) in the face of such misery, but the fact that God waits disproves the counselors' theory of suffering. Job is no more out of God's favor as one of the victims than the criminal in vv. 13–17 is in God's favor because of God's inaction.

24:1 See note on vv. 21–24.

24:2 *move boundary stones.* A serious crime in ancient times (see note on Dt 19:14).

24:3 *orphan's … widow's.* See 22:9; Isa 1:17 and note; Jas 1:27.

24:5 *wild donkeys.* See 6:5 and note.

24:6 *glean.* See note on Ru 1:22.

24:7,10 Job implicitly denies the accusation of Eliphaz (see 22:6).

24:13–17 A description of those who cause the suffering depicted in vv. 2–12: the murderer (v. 14), the adulterer (v. 15), the robber (v. 16). Darkness is their element, the medium in which they thrive (see vv. 14–17; Jn 3:19; Ro 1:21).

24:18–20 Job seems to agree with the counselors here. But it is also legitimate to translate the verses as Job's call for redress against evildoers: "May their portion of the land be cursed … may the grave snatch away … May the womb forget them, may the worm feast on them; may evil men be no longer remembered but be broken like a tree."

24:20 *worm feasts on them.* See 21:26; Isa 14:11; 66:24 and note; Mk 9:48 and note. *broken like a tree.* See note on 19:10.

24:21–24 By way of summary, Job says that God judges the wicked, but he does so in his own good time. Job wishes, however, that God would give the righteous the satisfaction of seeing it happen (v. 1).

22 But God drags away the mighty by his
power;[b]
though they become established,[c]
they have no assurance of life.[d]
23 He may let them rest in a feeling of
security,[e]
but his eyes[f] are on their ways.[g]
24 For a little while they are exalted, and
then they are gone;[h]
they are brought low and gathered
up like all others;[i]
they are cut off like heads of grain.[j]

25 "If this is not so, who can prove me
false
and reduce my words to nothing?"[k]

Bildad

25 Then Bildad the Shuhite[l] replied:

2 "Dominion and awe belong to God;[m]
he establishes order in the heights of
heaven.[n]
3 Can his forces be numbered?
Upon whom does his light not rise?[o]
4 How then can a man be righteous
before God?
How can one born of woman be
pure?[p]
5 If even the moon[q] is not bright
and the stars are not pure in his
eyes,[r]
6 how much less man, who is but a
maggot—
a son of man,[s] who is only a
worm!"[t]

Job

26 Then Job replied:

2 "How you have helped the powerless![u]
How you have saved the arm that is
feeble![v]
3 What advice you have offered to one
without wisdom!
And what great insight[w] you have
displayed!
4 Who has helped you utter these words?
And whose spirit spoke from your
mouth?[x]

5 "The dead are in deep anguish,[y]
those beneath the waters and all that
live in them.
6 Death[a][z] is naked before God;
Destruction[b][a] lies uncovered.[b]
7 He spreads out the northern ⌞skies⌟[c]
over empty space;
he suspends the earth over nothing.[d]
8 He wraps up the waters[e] in his clouds,[f]
yet the clouds do not burst under
their weight.
9 He covers the face of the full moon,
spreading his clouds[g] over it.
10 He marks out the horizon on the face
of the waters[h]
for a boundary between light and
darkness.[i]
11 The pillars of the heavens quake,[j]
aghast at his rebuke.
12 By his power he churned up the sea;[k]
by his wisdom[l] he cut Rahab[m] to
pieces.
13 By his breath the skies[n] became fair;
his hand pierced the gliding serpent.[o]
14 And these are but the outer fringe of
his works;
how faint the whisper[p] we hear of
him![q]
Who then can understand the
thunder of his power?"[r]

[a] 6 Hebrew *Sheol* [b] 6 Hebrew *Abaddon*

24:22 [b] S Job 9:4 [c] S Job 12:19 [d] Dt 28:66; Mt 6:27; Jas 4:14 **24:23** [e] S Job 9:24; Am 6:1 [f] S 2Ch 16:9 [g] S Job 10:4 **24:24** [h] S 2Ki 19:35; S Job 4:20; Ps 37:10; 83:13; Isa 5:24; 17:13; 40:24; 41:2, 15 [i] S Job 3:19 [j] Isa 17:5 **24:25** [k] S Job 6:28; S 16:17 **25:1** [l] S Job 8:1 **25:2** [m] S Job 9:4; Ps 47:9; 89:18; Zec 9:7; Rev 1:6 [n] S 2Ch 20:6; S Job 11:8; S 16:19 **25:3** [o] Mt 5:45; Jas 1:17 **25:4** [p] S Job 4:17 **25:5** [q] Job 31:26 [r] S Job 4:18 **25:6** [s] Ps 80:17; 144:3; Eze 2:1 [t] S Job 4:19; S 7:5 **26:2** [u] Job 6:12 [v] S Job 4:3 **26:3** [w] Job 34:35 **26:4** [x] 1Ki 22:24 **26:5** [y] Ps 88:10; Isa 14:9; 26:14 **26:6** [z] Ps 139:8 [a] S Job 20:26; S Rev 9:11 [b] Job 10:22; 11:8; 38:17; 41:11; Ps 139:11-12; Pr 15:11; S Heb 4:13 **26:7** [c] Job 9:8 [d] Job 38:6; Ps 104:5; Pr 3:19-20; 8:27; Isa 40:22 **26:8** [e] Pr 30:4 [f] S Ge 1:2; Job 36:27; 37:11; Ps 147:8 **26:9** [g] S 2Sa 22:10; S Job 22:14 **26:10** [h] Pr 8:27, 29; Isa 40:22 [i] S Ge 1:4; S Job 28:3; 38:8-11 **26:11** [j] S 2Sa 22:8 **26:12** [k] S Ex 14:21 [l] Job 12:13 [m] S Job 9:13 **26:13** [n] Job 9:8 [o] Isa 27:1 **26:14** [p] Job 4:12 [q] Job 42:5; Hab 3:2; 1Co 13:12 [r] S Job 9:6

25:1–6 See note on 22:1—26:14. Bildad adds nothing new here, and Zophar, who has already admitted how disturbed he was (see 20:2), does not even comment.
25:2 *establishes order in the heights of heaven.* He who establishes order in heaven is sovereign over all creation.
25:3 *his forces.* Angels. *his light.* The sun.
25:4–6 Bildad echoes Eliphaz's earlier statements about human depravity (4:17–19; 15:14–16).
26:2–4 With biting sarcasm, Job responds to Bildad alone (the Hebrew for the words "you" and "your" in these verses is singular rather than plural), indicating that Eliphaz and Zophar have already been silenced.
26:2 *saved the arm that is feeble.* See 4:3–4; Isa 35:3; Heb 12:12.
26:5–14 Job's highly figurative description of the vast power of God—the theme also of Bildad's final speech (ch. 25).
26:5 *The dead.* The Hebrew for this expression is translated "spirits of the dead" in Pr 2:18, "spirits of the departed" in Isa 14:9 and "departed spirits" in Isa 26:14. The term is used figuratively of the deceased who inhabit the netherworld (see 3:13–15,17–19; see also note on 3:16). *waters.* Part of the world inhabited by living beings, and therefore above the netherworld.
26:6 *Death.* See NIV text note; personified elsewhere as the "king of terrors" (18:14; see note there). *Destruction.* See NIV text note; see also 28:22; 31:12; Pr 15:11 and NIV text notes. In Rev 9:11, Abaddon is the name of the "angel of the Abyss" (see NIV text note there).
26:7 See 37:18. *He.* God. *suspends the earth over nothing.* Perhaps Job's way of acknowledging that the landmasses are made secure only by God's sustaining power.
26:12 *churned up the sea.* See Isa 51:15; Jer 31:35. *Rahab.* See note on 9:13.
26:13 *gliding serpent.* A description of the sea monster Leviathan (see notes on 3:8; Isa 27:1).
26:14 *these are but the outer fringe of his works.* What God has revealed of his dominion over natural and supernatural forces amounts to no more than a whisper. Job is impressed with the severely limited character of human understanding. Zophar had chided Job about his inability to fathom the mysteries of God (11:7–9), but the knowledge possessed by Job's friends was not superior to that of Job himself (see 12:3; 13:2). *thunder of his power.* If it is difficult for us to comprehend the little that we know about God, how much more impossible it would be to understand the full extent of his might!

27 And Job continued his discourse:[s]

[2]"As surely as God lives, who has
denied me justice,[t]
the Almighty,[u] who has made me
taste bitterness of soul,[v]
[3]as long as I have life within me,
the breath of God[w] in my nostrils,
[4]my lips will not speak wickedness,
and my tongue will utter no deceit.[x]
[5]I will never admit you are in the right;
till I die, I will not deny my
integrity.[y]
[6]I will maintain my righteousness[z] and
never let go of it;
my conscience[a] will not reproach me
as long as I live.[b]

[7]"May my enemies be like the wicked,[c]
my adversaries[d] like the unjust!
[8]For what hope has the godless[e] when
he is cut off,
when God takes away his life?[f]
[9]Does God listen to his cry
when distress comes upon him?[g]
[10]Will he find delight in the Almighty?[h]
Will he call upon God at all times?

[11]"I will teach you about the power of
God;
the ways[i] of the Almighty I will not
conceal.[j]
[12]You have all seen this yourselves.
Why then this meaningless talk?

[13]"Here is the fate God allots to the
wicked,
the heritage a ruthless man receives
from the Almighty:[k]
[14]However many his children,[l] their fate
is the sword;[m]
his offspring will never have enough
to eat.[n]
[15]The plague will bury those who
survive him,
and their widows will not weep for
them.[o]
[16]Though he heaps up silver like dust[p]
and clothes like piles of clay,[q]
[17]what he lays up[r] the righteous will
wear,[s]
and the innocent will divide his
silver.[t]
[18]The house[u] he builds is like a moth's
cocoon,[v]
like a hut[w] made by a watchman.
[19]He lies down wealthy, but will do so
no more;[x]
when he opens his eyes, all is gone.[y]
[20]Terrors[z] overtake him like a flood;[a]
a tempest snatches him away in the
night.[b]
[21]The east wind[c] carries him off, and he
is gone;[d]
it sweeps him out of his place.[e]
[22]It hurls itself against him without
mercy[f]
as he flees headlong[g] from its
power.[h]
[23]It claps its hands[i] in derision
and hisses him out of his place.[j]

28 "There is a mine for silver
and a place where gold is refined.[k]
[2]Iron is taken from the earth,
and copper is smelted from ore.[l]

27:1 [s]Job 29:1 **27:2** [t]S Job 6:29; S 9:24; Isa 45:9; 49:4, 14 [u]Job 23:16 [v]S 1Sa 1:10; S Job 7:19; S 10:1 **27:3** [w]S Ge 2:7; Job 32:8; 33:4; 34:14; S Ps 144:4 **27:4** [x]S Job 6:28; S 12:16; S 16:17 **27:5** [y]S Job 2:9; S 10:7; S 32:2 **27:6** [z]Job 29:14; Ps 119:121; 132:9; Isa 59:17; 61:10 [a]S Ac 23:1; Ro 2:15 [b]S Job 2:3; S 10:7; S 23:10; S 34:17 **27:7** [c]S Job 8:22 [d]Job 31:35 **27:8** [e]S Job 8:13 [f]S Nu 16:22; S Job 8:22; S 11:20; Lk 12:20 **27:9** [g]S Dt 1:45; S 1Sa 8:18; S Job 15:31 **27:10** [h]S Job 22:26 **27:11** [i]Job 36:23 [j]ver 13 **27:13** [k]S Job 16:19; S 20:29 **27:14** [l]S Job 5:4 [m]S Job 15:22; S La 2:22 [n]S Job 4:11 **27:15** [o]Ps 78:64 **27:16** [p]S 1Ki 10:27 [q]Zec 9:3 **27:17** [r]Ps 39:6; 49:10; Ecc 2:26 [s]S Job 7:8; Pr 13:22; 28:8; Ecc 2:26 [t]Ex 3:22; S Job 3:15 **27:18** [u]S Job 8:22 [v]S Job 8:14 [w]Isa 1:8; 24:20 **27:19** [x]S Job 3:13; S 7:8 [y]S Job 14:20 **27:20** [z]S Job 6:4 [a]S Job 15:21 [b]S Job 20:8 **27:21** [c]Job 38:24; Jer 13:24; 22:22 [d]Job 30:22 [e]S Job 7:10 **27:22** [f]Jer 13:14; Eze 5:11; 24:14 [g]2Ki 7:15 [h]S Job 11:20 **27:23** [i]S Nu 24:10; Na 3:19 [j]S Job 7:10 **28:1** [k]Ps 12:6; 66:10; Jer 9:7; Da 11:35; Mal 3:3 **28:2** [l]Dt 8:9

27:1–23 The dialogue-dispute section of the book begins with Job's opening lament (ch. 3), continues with the three cycles of speeches (chs. 4–14; 15–21; 22–26) and concludes with Job's closing discourse (ch. 27), in which he reasserts his own innocence (vv. 2–6) and eloquently describes the ultimate fate of the wicked (vv. 13–23).

27:2 *As surely as God lives.* The most solemn of oaths (see note on Ge 42:15). Job's faith in God continued despite his perception of denied justice.

27:5 *you.* The Hebrew for this word is plural. In his summary statement, Job once again speaks to his three friends as a group.

27:6 *maintain my righteousness.* God had spoken similarly of Job (see 2:3).

27:7 *May my enemies be like the wicked.* Job calls for his friends, who had falsely accused him of being wicked, to be treated as though they themselves were wicked men (cf. Ps 109:6–15; 137:8–9).

27:11 *I will teach you.* Job is about to remind his counselors about an issue on which they all agree: that the truly wicked deserve God's wrath (vv. 13–23). The three friends had falsely put Job in that category.

27:12 *meaningless.* The theme word in Ecclesiastes (see Ecc 1:2 and note).

27:13–23 A poem that dramatizes the effect of Job's earlier call for redress (v. 7).

27:13 Job echoes the words of Zophar in 20:29 (see note there).

27:18 *cocoon … hut.* Symbols of fragility (see note on 4:19; Isa 1:8 and note; 24:20).

27:21 *east wind.* See note on 15:2.

28:1–28 Job's friends' application of traditional wisdom to human suffering has been even more unsatisfactory than Job's untraditional response. Both attempts to penetrate the mystery have failed, and the dialogue has come to a stalemate. Therefore the author of the book inserts a striking wisdom poem that answers the question, "Where can wisdom be found?" (v. 12; see v. 20). The poem consists of three parts: (1) humans find precious stones and metals by digging into the deep bowels of the earth (vv. 1–11); (2) but wisdom, the dearest treasure of all, is not found there, and it cannot be bought with precious stones or metals dug from the earth (vv. 12–19); (3) wisdom is found only in God (vv. 20–27). And God tells human beings that true wisdom for them is to "fear … the Lord … and to shun evil" (see v. 28). This chapter, then, anticipates the theme of God's speeches (38:1—42:6) and echoes the assessment of Job that God had given at the beginning (see Introduction: Theological Theme and Message).

28:1–11 A fascinating, lyrical description of ancient mining techniques.

28:2 *Iron.* See note on 19:24.

3 Man puts an end to the darkness;[m]
he searches the farthest recesses
for ore in the blackest darkness.[n]
4 Far from where people dwell he cuts a
shaft,[o]
in places forgotten by the foot of
man;
far from men he dangles and sways.
5 The earth, from which food comes,[p]
is transformed below as by fire;
6 sapphires[a q] come from its rocks,
and its dust contains nuggets of gold.[r]
7 No bird of prey knows that hidden path,
no falcon's eye has seen it.[s]
8 Proud beasts[t] do not set foot on it,
and no lion prowls there.[u]
9 Man's hand assaults the flinty rock[v]
and lays bare the roots of the
mountains.[w]
10 He tunnels through the rock;[x]
his eyes see all its treasures.[y]
11 He searches[b] the sources of the rivers[z]
and brings hidden things[a] to light.

12 "But where can wisdom be found?[b]
Where does understanding dwell?[c]
13 Man does not comprehend its worth;[d]
it cannot be found in the land of the
living.[e]
14 The deep[f] says, 'It is not in me';
the sea[g] says, 'It is not with me.'
15 It cannot be bought with the finest
gold,
nor can its price be weighed in
silver.[h]
16 It cannot be bought with the gold of
Ophir,[i]
with precious onyx or sapphires.[j]
17 Neither gold nor crystal can compare
with it,[k]
nor can it be had for jewels of gold.[l]
18 Coral[m] and jasper[n] are not worthy of
mention;
the price of wisdom is beyond
rubies.[o]

28:3 [m] Ecc 1:13; 7:25; 8:17 [n] S Job 26:10; 38:19 **28:4** [o] ver 10; 2Sa 5:8 **28:5** [p] Ge 1:29; Ps 104:14; 145:15 **28:6** [q] ver 16; SS 5:14; Isa 54:11 [r] S Job 22:24 **28:7** [s] ver 21 **28:8** [t] Job 41:34 [u] Isa 35:9 **28:9** [v] S Dt 8:15 [w] Jnh 2:6 **28:10** [x] S ver 4 [y] Pr 2:4 **28:11** [z] S Ge 7:11 [a] Isa 48:6; Jer 33:3 **28:12** [b] ver 28; Pr 1:20; 3:13-20; 8:1; 9:1-3; Ecc 7:24 [c] ver 20, 23 **28:13** [d] Pr 3:15; Mt 13:44-46 [e] Dt 29:29; Ps 27:13; 52:5; 116:9; 142:5; Isa 38:11; Jer 11:19; Eze 26:20; 32:24 **28:14** [f] Ps 42:7; Ro 10:7 [g] Dt 30:13 **28:15** [h] ver 17; Pr 3:13-14; 8:10-11; 16:16; Ac 8:20 **28:16** [i] S Ge 10:29 [j] S ver 6; S Ex 24:10 **28:17** [k] Ps 119:72; Pr 8:10 [l] S ver 15 **28:18** [m] Eze 27:16 [n] Rev 21:11 [o] Pr 3:15; 8:11

28:19 [p] Ex 28:17 [q] Isa 11:11 [r] Pr 3:14-15; 8:10-11, 19 **28:20** [s] S Job 9:4 **28:21** [t] ver 7 **28:22** [u] S Job 20:26;

19 The topaz[p] of Cush[q] cannot compare
with it;
it cannot be bought with pure gold.[r]
20 "Where then does wisdom come from?
Where does understanding dwell?[s]
21 It is hidden from the eyes of every
living thing,
concealed even from the birds of the
air.[t]
22 Destruction[c u] and Death[v] say,
'Only a rumor of it has reached our
ears.'
23 God understands the way to it
and he alone[w] knows where it
dwells,[x]
24 for he views the ends of the earth[y]
and sees everything under the
heavens.[z]
25 When he established the force of the
wind
and measured out the waters,[a]
26 when he made a decree for the rain[b]
and a path for the thunderstorm,[c]
27 then he looked at wisdom and
appraised it;
he confirmed it and tested it.[d]
28 And he said to man,
'The fear of the Lord—that is
wisdom,
and to shun evil[e] is understanding.[f]'"

29

Job continued his discourse:[g]
2 "How I long for the months gone by,[h]
for the days when God watched over
me,[i]

[a] *6* Or *lapis lazuli*; also in verse 16 [b] *11* Septuagint, Aquila and Vulgate; Hebrew *He dams up* [c] *22* Hebrew *Abaddon*

S Rev 9:11 [v] Pr 8:32-36 **28:23** [w] Ecc 3:11; 8:17 [x] S Job 9:4; S 22:22; Pr 8:22-31 **28:24** [y] Job 36:32; 37:3; 38:18, 24, 35; Ps 33:13-14; 66:7; Isa 11:12 [z] S Jos 3:11; S Job 10:4; S Heb 4:13 **28:25** [a] S Job 12:15; 38:8-11 **28:26** [b] Job 36:28; 37:6; Jer 51:16 [c] Job 36:33; 37:3, 8, 11; 38:25, 27; Ps 65:12; 104:14; 147:8; Isa 35:7 **28:27** [d] Pr 3:19; 8:22-31 **28:28** [e] Ps 11:5; 97:10; Pr 3:7; 8:13 [f] S Ex 20:20; S Dt 4:6; S Job 37:24 **29:1** [g] Job 27:1 **29:2** [h] S Ge 31:30 [i] Jer 1:12; 31:28; 44:27

28:3 *puts an end to the darkness.* By using an artificial source of light, such as a torch or lamp.

28:4 *dangles and sways.* Mining, then as now, is difficult and dangerous work. People will hazard everything to dig the earth's treasures.

28:6 *sapphires.* See v. 16; see also notes on SS 5:14; Isa 54:11.

28:9 *roots of the mountains.* A poetic expression emphasizing great depth (cf. Jnh 2:6).

28:10 *tunnels through the rock.* An eighth-century B.C. inscription found at the traditional site of Jerusalem's Pool of Siloam (see Jn 9:7 and note) testifies to the sophistication of ancient tunneling technology.

28:12 The questions, repeated almost verbatim in v. 20, are answered in v. 28.

28:16 *gold of Ophir.* See 22:24 and note.

28:18 *the price of wisdom is beyond rubies.* Cf. the value of a "wife of noble character" (Pr 31:10), who fears the Lord (Pr 31:30) and is therefore wise (see v. 28).

28:19 *Cush.* The upper Nile region, south of Egypt.

28:21 *hidden … from the birds.* As are precious stones and metals (see v. 7).

28:22 *Destruction and Death.* See note on 26:6.

28:25–27 Wisdom has been with God from the time of creation itself (see Pr 8:22–31 and notes).

28:28 *fear of the Lord … shun evil.* See the description of Job's character in 1:1,8; 2:3. *that is wisdom.* "The fear of the LORD is the beginning of wisdom" (Ps 111:10; Pr 9:10; see Pr 1:7).

29:1—31:40 Job submits his final defense in a three-part summation: Part one (ch. 29) is a nostalgic review of his former happiness, wealth and honor; part two (ch. 30) is a lament over the loss of everything, especially his honor; part three (ch. 31) is a final protestation of his innocence.

29:1–25 A classic example of Semitic rhetoric, using the symmetrical pattern *a-b-c/a-b*: blessing (vv. 2–6), honor (vv. 7–10), benevolence (vv. 11–17), blessing (vv. 18–20), honor (vv. 21–25).

29:2–6 Words charged with emotion. In earlier days, God had been Job's friend and companion.

[3]when his lamp shone upon my head
and by his light I walked through
darkness![j]
[4]Oh, for the days when I was in my
prime,
when God's intimate friendship[k]
blessed my house,[l]
[5]when the Almighty was still with me
and my children[m] were around me,[n]
[6]when my path was drenched with
cream[o]
and the rock[p] poured out for me
streams of olive oil.[q]

[7]"When I went to the gate[r] of the city
and took my seat in the public
square,
[8]the young men saw me and stepped
aside[s]
and the old men rose to their feet;[t]
[9]the chief men refrained from
speaking[u]
and covered their mouths with their
hands;[v]
[10]the voices of the nobles were hushed,[w]
and their tongues stuck to the roof of
their mouths.[x]
[11]Whoever heard me spoke well of me,
and those who saw me commended
me,[y]
[12]because I rescued the poor[z] who cried
for help,
and the fatherless[a] who had none to
assist him.[b]
[13]The man who was dying blessed me;[c]
I made the widow's[d] heart sing.
[14]I put on righteousness[e] as my clothing;
justice was my robe and my turban.[f]
[15]I was eyes[g] to the blind
and feet to the lame.[h]
[16]I was a father to the needy;[i]
I took up the case[j] of the stranger.[k]
[17]I broke the fangs of the wicked
and snatched the victims[l] from their
teeth.[m]

[18]"I thought, 'I will die in my own
house,
my days as numerous as the grains
of sand.[n]
[19]My roots will reach to the water,[o]
and the dew will lie all night on my
branches.[p]
[20]My glory will remain fresh[q] in me,
the bow[r] ever new in my hand.'[s]

[21]"Men listened to me expectantly,
waiting in silence for my counsel.[t]
[22]After I had spoken, they spoke no
more;[u]
my words fell gently on their ears.[v]
[23]They waited for me as for showers
and drank in my words as the
spring rain.[w]
[24]When I smiled at them, they scarcely
believed it;
the light of my face[x] was precious
to them.[a][y]
[25]I chose the way for them and sat as
their chief;[z]
I dwelt as a king[a] among his
troops;
I was like one who comforts
mourners.[b]

30 "But now they mock me,[c]
men younger than I,
whose fathers I would have disdained
to put with my sheep dogs.[d]
[2]Of what use was the strength of their
hands to me,
since their vigor had gone from
them?
[3]Haggard from want and hunger,
they roamed[b] the parched land[e]
in desolate wastelands[f] at night.[g]
[4]In the brush they gathered salt herbs,[h]
and their food[c] was the root of the
broom tree.[i]

[a] *24* The meaning of the Hebrew for this clause is uncertain. [b] *3* Or *gnawed* [c] *4* Or *fuel*

29:3 [j]S Job 11:17; S 12:25 **29:4** [k]S Job 15:8 [l]Ps 25:14; Pr 3:32 **29:5** [m]Ps 127:3-5; 128:3 [n]Ru 4:1 **29:6** [o]S Job 20:17 [p]Ps 81:16 [q]Ge 49:20; S Dt 32:13 **29:7** [r]ver 21; Job 5:4; 31:21; Jer 20:2; 38:7 **29:8** [s]1Ti 5:1 [t]S Lev 19:32 **29:9** [u]ver 21; Job 31:21 [v]S Jdg 18:19; Job 40:4; Pr 30:32 **29:10** [w]ver 22 [x]Ps 137:6 **29:11** [y]S Job 4:4; Heb 11:4 **29:12** [z]S Job 24:4 [a]S Dt 24:17; Job 31:17,21 [b]Ps 72:12; Pr 21:13 **29:13** [c]Job 31:20 [d]S Dt 10:18; S Job 22:9 **29:14** [e]S 2Sa 8:15; S Job 27:6; Eph 4:24; 6:14 [f]S Job 19:9 **29:15** [g]Nu 10:31 [h]S Job 4:4 **29:16** [i]S Job 24:4 [j]Ex 18:26 [k]S Job 4:4; Pr 22:22-23 **29:17** [l]Job 24:9 [m]S Job 4:10,11; S Ps 3:7 **29:18** [n]Ps 1:1-3; 15:5; 16:8; 30:6; 62:2; 139:18; Pr 3:1-2 **29:19** [o]S Nu 24:6; S Job 14:9 [p]S Ge 27:8; S Job 15:30; S Ps 133:3 **29:20** [q]Ps 92:14 [r]Job 30:11; Ps 18:34; Isa 38:12 [s]Ge 49:24 **29:21** [t]S ver 7, S 9 **29:22** [u]ver 10 [v]Dt 32:2 **29:23** [w]S Job 4:3 **29:24** [x]S Nu 6:25 [y]Pr 16:14,15 **29:25** [z]S Job 21:28 [a]S Job 1:3 [b]S Job 4:4 **30:1** [c]S Job 6:14; S 11:3; S Ps 119:21 [d]Isa 56:10 **30:3** [e]Isa 8:21 [f]Job 24:5 [g]Jer 17:6 **30:4** [h]Job 39:6 [i]S 1Ki 19:4

29:3 *by his light I walked.* See note on 22:28.
29:4 *when God's intimate friendship blessed my house.* Lit. "when God's council was by my tent," or "when God was an intimate in my tent." The clause evokes a situation similar to that in Ge 18, where God and two members of his heavenly council eat and drink at Abraham's tent—and there God discloses to his friend the imminent birth of the promised son and God's intentions concerning Sodom and Gomorrah.
29:5 *my children were around me.* See 1:2 and note.
29:6 *cream … olive oil.* Symbols of richness and luxury (see 20:17; Eze 16:19).
29:7 *gate of the city.* Where the most important business was conducted and the most significant legal cases were tried (see note on Ru 4:1). *took my seat.* As a city elder, a member of the ruling council (see note on Ge 19:1).
29:12–13 *I rescued … the fatherless … I made the widow's heart sing.* Implicitly responding to Eliphaz's accusation in 22:9 (see note on 22:5–11), Job expresses his concern for the helpless and unfortunate (see 24:9; 31:16–18,21).
29:14 *I put on righteousness … justice was my robe.* For similar imagery see Ps 132:9,16; Isa 59:17; 61:10; Ro 13:14; Eph 4:24; 6:14,17 and notes; see also note on Ps 109:29.
29:18 *I thought.* Job muses on what might have been the course of his life.
29:21–25 Job's counsel was valued (vv. 21–23), his approval sought (v. 24) and his civic leadership accepted with gratitude (v. 25).
30:1–31 In contrast to the positive notes of blessing and honor sounded in ch. 29, Job now bemoans the suffering and dishonor he has been forced to undergo. God has heaped overwhelming terrors on him (v. 15). His final, forlorn lament (see v. 31) over his condition shows that his rage has not yet subsided.
30:1,9 *now … mock me.* Earlier both young and old had deferred to him (see 29:8–11,21–25).
30:4 *salt herbs.* Probably saltwort, which grows in otherwise

[5]They were banished from their fellow men,
shouted at as if they were thieves.
[6]They were forced to live in the dry stream beds,
among the rocks and in holes in the ground.[j]
[7]They brayed[k] among the bushes[l]
and huddled in the undergrowth.
[8]A base and nameless brood,[m]
they were driven out of the land.[n]

[9]"And now their sons mock me[o] in song;[p]
I have become a byword[q] among them.
[10]They detest me[r] and keep their distance;
they do not hesitate to spit in my face.[s]
[11]Now that God has unstrung my bow[t]
and afflicted me,[u]
they throw off restraint[v] in my presence.
[12]On my right[w] the tribe[a] attacks;
they lay snares[x] for my feet,[y]
they build their siege ramps against me.[z]
[13]They break up my road;[a]
they succeed in destroying me[b]—
without anyone's helping them.[b]
[14]They advance as through a gaping breach;[c]
amid the ruins they come rolling in.
[15]Terrors[d] overwhelm me;[e]
my dignity is driven away as by the wind,
my safety vanishes like a cloud.[f]

[16]"And now my life ebbs away;[g]
days of suffering grip me.[h]
[17]Night pierces my bones;
my gnawing pains never rest.[i]
[18]In his great power[j] ⌊God⌋ becomes like clothing to me[c];
he binds me like the neck of my garment.
[19]He throws me into the mud,[k]
and I am reduced to dust and ashes.[l]

[20]"I cry out to you,[m] O God, but you do not answer;[n]
I stand up, but you merely look at me.
[21]You turn on me ruthlessly;[o]
with the might of your hand[p] you attack me.[q]
[22]You snatch me up and drive me before the wind;[r]
you toss me about in the storm.[s]
[23]I know you will bring me down to death,[t]
to the place appointed for all the living.[u]

[24]"Surely no one lays a hand on a broken man[v]
when he cries for help in his distress.[w]
[25]Have I not wept for those in trouble?[x]
Has not my soul grieved for the poor?[y]
[26]Yet when I hoped for good, evil came;
when I looked for light, then came darkness.[z]
[27]The churning inside me never stops;[a]
days of suffering confront me.[b]
[28]I go about blackened,[c] but not by the sun;
I stand up in the assembly and cry for help.[d]
[29]I have become a brother of jackals,[e]
a companion of owls.[f]
[30]My skin grows black[g] and peels;[h]
my body burns with fever.[i]
[31]My harp is tuned to mourning,[j]
and my flute[k] to the sound of wailing.

[a] *12* The meaning of the Hebrew for this word is uncertain. [b] *13* Or *me. / 'No one can help him,' ⌊they say⌋.* [c] *18* Hebrew; Septuagint *⌊God⌋ grasps my clothing*

30:6 [j] Isa 2:19; Hos 10:8 **30:7** [k] Job 6:5 [l] Job 39:5-6 **30:8** [m] S Jdg 9:4 [n] S Job 18:18 **30:9** [o] S Job 16:10; Ps 69:11 [p] Job 12:4; La 3:14,63 [q] S Job 17:6 **30:10** [r] Job 19:19 [s] S Dt 25:9; Mt 26:67 **30:11** [t] S Job 29:20 [u] S Ge 12:17; S Ru 1:21 [v] Job 41:13; Ps 32:9 **30:12** [w] Ps 109:6; Zec 3:1 [x] S Job 18:9 [y] Ps 140:4-5 [z] S Job 16:10 **30:13** [a] Isa 3:12 [b] S Job 10:3 **30:14** [c] S 2Ki 25:4 **30:15** [d] S Job 6:4 [e] S Ex 3:6; Job 10:8; 31:2-3,23; Ps 55:4-5 [f] S Job 3:25 **30:16** [g] S Job 3:24 [h] ver 27; S Job 9:17 **30:17** [i] S Dt 28:35; S Job 16:16 **30:18** [j] S Job 9:4 **30:19** [k] Ps 40:2; 69:2,14; 130:1; Jer 38:6,22 [l] S Ge 3:19; S Job 2:8 **30:20** [m] S 1Ki 8:52; Ps 34:17; Pr 2:3; Mic 4:9 [n] S Job 19:7; La 3:8 **30:21** [o] Jer 6:23; 30:14; 50:42 [p] Isa 9:12; 14:26; 31:3; Eze 6:14 [q] S Job 4:5; S 6:4; S 10:3 **30:22** [r] Job 27:21; Jude 1:12 [s] S Job 9:17 **30:23** [t] S 2Sa 14:14; S Job 3:13; S 10:3 [u] S Job 3:19

30:24 [v] Ps 145:14; Isa 42:3; 57:15 [w] S Job 19:7 **30:25** [x] Lk 19:41; Php 3:18 [y] S Job 24:4; Ps 35:13-14; Ro 12:15 **30:26** [z] S Job 3:6, 17; S 19:8; S Ps 82:5; S Jer 4:23 **30:27** [a] Ps 38:8; La 2:11 [b] S ver 16 **30:28** [c] S Job 17:14; La 4:8 [d] S Job 19:7; S 24:12 **30:29** [e] Ps 44:19; Isa 34:13; Jer 9:11 [f] Ps 102:6; Mic 1:8 **30:30** [g] S Job 17:14 [h] La 3:4; 4:8 [i] S Dt 28:35; S Job 16:16; Ps 102:3; La 1:13; 5:10 **30:31** [j] S Ge 8:8; Ps 137:2; Isa 16:11; 24:8; Eze 26:13 [k] S Ge 4:21

infertile areas, including the regions where Job and his friends lived. Cf. 39:6. *broom tree.* A large bush that grows in the deserts of the Middle East (see 1Ki 19:4; Ps 120:4 and notes).
30:9 *byword.* See note on 17:6.
30:11 *God has unstrung my bow.* In contrast to 29:20, where Job was confident that his bow would be new and strong.
30:12 *siege ramps.* See 19:12.
30:14 *breach.* In a city wall.
30:15 *driven ... as by the wind.* See v. 22.
30:17 *gnawing pains.* See note on 2:7.
30:18 *neck of my garment.* Tight-fitting collar.
30:19 *dust and ashes.* Symbolic of humiliation and insignificance (see note on Ge 18:27). Job would someday use "dust and ashes" to symbolize repentance (42:6).
30:20–23 Job now shifts his thoughts away from human beings and toward God. He accuses God of abusing his power by attacking him despite his pleas for mercy.
30:24 Job feels that he has been treated unjustly, whether by God or by humans.
30:26 Cf. Isa 5:2,7.
30:28 *blackened.* See v. 30; see also note on 2:7.
30:29 *brother of jackals ... companion of owls.* The prophet Micah uses similar imagery of himself in Mic 1:8.
30:30 *fever.* See note on 2:7.

31 "I made a covenant with my eyes[l]
not to look lustfully at a girl.[m]
2For what is man's lot[n] from God above,
his heritage from the Almighty on
high?[o]
3Is it not ruin[p] for the wicked,
disaster[q] for those who do wrong?[r]
4Does he not see my ways[s]
and count my every step?[t]

5"If I have walked in falsehood
or my foot has hurried after
deceit[u]—
6let God weigh me[v] in honest scales[w]
and he will know that I am
blameless[x]—
7if my steps have turned from the path,[y]
if my heart has been led by my eyes,
or if my hands[z] have been defiled,[a]
8then may others eat what I have
sown,[b]
and may my crops be uprooted.[c]

9"If my heart has been enticed[d] by a
woman,[e]
or if I have lurked at my neighbor's
door,
10then may my wife grind[f] another
man's grain,
and may other men sleep with her.[g]
11For that would have been shameful,[h]
a sin to be judged.[i]
12It is a fire[j] that burns to Destruction[a];[k]
it would have uprooted my harvest.[l]

13"If I have denied justice to my
menservants and maidservants[m]
when they had a grievance against
me,[n]
14what will I do when God confronts
me?[o]
What will I answer when called to
account?[p]
15Did not he who made me in the womb
make them?[q]
Did not the same one form us both
within our mothers?[r]

31:1 [l]Pr 4:25; 17:24; 2Pe 2:14 [m]Ex 20:14, 17; Dt 5:18; Mt 5:28 **31:2** [n]Nu 26:55; Ps 11:6; 16:5; 50:18; Ecc 3:22; 5:19; 9:9 [o]S Job 16:19; S 20:29 **31:3** [p]S Job 21:30 [q]Job 18:12 [r]Job 34:22; Ro 2:9 **31:4** [s]2Ch 16:9; Ps 139:3; Da 4:37; 5:23 [t]S ver 14; S Job 10:4 **31:5** [u]S Job 15:31 **31:6** [v]Ps 139:23 [w]S Lev 19:36; S Job 6:2 [x]S Ge 6:9; S Job 2:3; S 23:10 **31:7** [y]S Job 23:11 [z]S Job 9:30 [a]Ps 7:3 **31:8** [b]S Job 5:5; S 20:10; Jn 4:37 [c]ver 12; Mic 6:15 **31:9** [d]S Dt 11:16; S Job 24:15; Jas 1:14 [e]Pr 5:3; 7:5 **31:10** [f]S Jdg 16:21 [g]Dt 28:30 **31:11** [h]Pr 6:32-33 [i]S Ge 38:24; S Ex 21:12; Jn 8:4-5 **31:12** [j]S Job 15:30 [k]S Job 26:6 [l]S ver 8 **31:13** [m]S Dt 5:14 [n]Ex 21:2-11; Lev 25:39-46; Dt 24:14-15 **31:14** [o]Job 33:5 [p]ver 4, 37; Ps 10:13, 15; 94:7; Isa 10:3; Jer 5:31; Hos 9:7; Mic 7:4; Col 4:1 **31:15** [q]S Job 4:17; Pr 22:2

16"If I have denied the desires of the
poor[s]
or let the eyes of the widow[t] grow
weary,[u]
17if I have kept my bread to myself,
not sharing it with the fatherless[v]—
18but from my youth I reared him as
would a father,
and from my birth I guided the
widow[w]—
19if I have seen anyone perishing for lack
of clothing,[x]
or a needy[y] man without a garment,
20and his heart did not bless me[z]
for warming him with the fleece[a]
from my sheep,
21if I have raised my hand against the
fatherless,[b]
knowing that I had influence in
court,[c]
22then let my arm fall from the shoulder,
let it be broken off at the joint.[d]
23For I dreaded destruction from God,[e]
and for fear of his splendor[f] I could
not do such things.[g]

24"If I have put my trust in gold[h]
or said to pure gold, 'You are my
security,'[i]
25if I have rejoiced over my great wealth,[j]
the fortune my hands had gained,[k]
26if I have regarded the sun[l] in its
radiance
or the moon[m] moving in splendor,
27so that my heart was secretly enticed[n]
and my hand offered them a kiss of
homage,[o]

[a] 12 Hebrew *Abaddon*

[r]S Job 10:3; Eph 6:9 **31:16** [s]S Lev 25:17; S Job 5:16 [t]S Job 22:9; Jas 1:27 [u]Job 22:7 **31:17** [v]S Job 6:27; S 22:7 **31:18** [w]Isa 51:18 **31:19** [x]Job 22:6; Isa 58:7 [y]S Job 24:4 **31:20** [z]Job 29:13 [a]Jdg 6:37 **31:21** [b]S Job 22:7; Jas 1:27 [c]S Job 29:7, 9 **31:22** [d]Nu 15:30; Job 5:15; 38:15; Ps 10:15; 37:17; 137:5 **31:23** [e]S Job 10:3; S 30:15 [f]Job 13:11 [g]S Ge 20:11 **31:24** [h]S Job 22:25 [i]Mt 6:24; Lk 12:15 **31:25** [j]S Ge 12:16; Ps 49:6; 52:7; 62:10; Isa 10:14 [k]S Job 22:24; Eze 28:5; Lk 12:20-21 **31:26** [l]S Ge 1:16 [m]Job 25:5 **31:27** [n]S Dt 11:16; S Job 24:15; Jas 1:14 [o]Jer 8:2; 16:11

31:1–40 The climactic section of Job's three-part summation (see note on 29:1—31:40). It is negative in the sense that Job denies all the sins listed, but it has the positive purpose of attesting loyalty to God as his sovereign Lord. In the strongest legal terms, using a series of self-maledictory oaths, Job completes his defense. No more can be said (v. 40). He now affixes his signature to the document (v. 35), and the burden of proof that he is a wretched sinner rests with God. Job's call for vindication had reached a climax in 27:2–6. Now he amplifies that statement with the details of his godly life. Each of seven disavowals (vv. 5–7,9,13,16–21, 24–27,29–34,38–39) is accompanied by an oath that calls for the punishment the offense deserves (vv. 8,10–12,14–15,22–23,28,40). The principle at work is the so-called law of retaliation (see Ex 21:23–25; Lev 24:20 and notes).

31:1–12 Job begins with sins of the heart, especially sexual lust (vv. 1–4), cheating in business (vv. 5–8) and marital infidelity (vv. 9–12).

31:1 *look lustfully at a girl.* To do so is to sin (see Mt 5:28 and note).

31:4 Echoed by Elihu in 34:21.

31:6 *God weigh me in honest scales.* See 6:2; Pr 16:11 and note; 21:2; 24:12; Am 8:5; Mic 6:11. *blameless.* Does not imply sinless perfection (see note on 1:1).

31:12 *Destruction.* See note on 26:6.

31:13–23 Job reveals genuine understanding concerning matters of social justice: Human equality is based on creation (vv. 13–15), compassion toward those in need is essential (vv. 16–20), and power and influence must not be abused (vv. 21–23).

31:16–17 *widow ... fatherless.* See note on 29:12–13.

31:24–28 Covetous greed (vv. 24–25) and idolatry (vv. 26–27) are equally reprehensible in the eyes of God (v. 28; see Mt 6:19–21 and notes; Col 3:5).

31:25 *my great wealth.* See 1:3 and note; see also 1:10.

31:26–28 The sun and moon are not to be objects of worship (see note on Ge 1:16; see also Dt 4:19; 17:3; Eze 8:16–17).

31:27 *kiss.* An ancient gesture of worship (see 1Ki 19:18; Hos 13:2 and note).

28 then these also would be sins to be
judged,[p]
for I would have been unfaithful to
God on high.[q]

29 "If I have rejoiced at my enemy's
misfortune[r]
or gloated over the trouble that came
to him[s]—
30 I have not allowed my mouth to sin
by invoking a curse against his
life[t]—
31 if the men of my household have never
said,
'Who has not had his fill of Job's
meat?'[u]—
32 but no stranger had to spend the night
in the street,
for my door was always open to the
traveler[v]—
33 if I have concealed[w] my sin as men
do,[a]
by hiding[x] my guilt in my heart
34 because I so feared the crowd[y]
and so dreaded the contempt of the
clans
that I kept silent[z] and would not go
outside—
35 ("Oh, that I had someone to hear
me![a]
I sign now my defense—let the
Almighty answer me;
let my accuser[b] put his indictment
in writing.
36 Surely I would wear it on my
shoulder,[c]
I would put it on like a crown.[d]
37 I would give him an account of my
every step;[e]
like a prince[f] I would approach
him.)—

38 "if my land cries out against me[g]
and all its furrows are wet[h] with
tears,
39 if I have devoured its yield without
payment[i]
or broken the spirit of its tenants,[j]
40 then let briers[k] come up instead of
wheat
and weeds[l] instead of barley."

The words of Job are ended.[m]

Elihu

32 So these three men stopped answering Job,[n] because he was righteous
in his own eyes.[o] 2 But Elihu son of Barakel
the Buzite,[p] of the family of Ram, became
very angry with Job for justifying himself[q]
rather than God.[r] 3 He was also angry with
the three friends,[s] because they had found
no way to refute Job,[t] and yet had condemned him.[b u] 4 Now Elihu had waited
before speaking to Job because they were
older than he.[v] 5 But when he saw that the
three men had nothing more to say, his
anger was aroused.
6 So Elihu son of Barakel the Buzite
said:

"I am young in years,
and you are old;[w]
that is why I was fearful,
not daring to tell you what I
know.
7 I thought, 'Age should speak;
advanced years should teach
wisdom.'[x]

31:28 [p] S Ge 38:24; Dt 17:2-7 [q] S Nu 11:20; Eze 8:16 **31:29** [r] S Nu 14:1; Ps 35:15; Ob 1:12; Mt 5:44 [s] Pr 17:5; 24:17-18 **31:30** [t] Job 5:3; Ro 12:14 **31:31** [u] S Job 22:7 **31:32** [v] Ge 19:2-3; Jdg 19:20; Mt 25:35; S Ro 12:13 **31:33** [w] Ps 32:5; Pr 28:13 [x] S Ge 3:8 **31:34** [y] Ex 23:2 [z] Ps 32:3; 39:2 **31:35** [a] S Job 9:24; 30:28 [b] Job 27:7 **31:36** [c] S Ex 28:12 [d] Job 29:14 **31:37** [e] S ver 14; S Job 11:11 [f] S Job 21:28 **31:38** [g] S Ge 4:10 [h] Ps 65:10 **31:39** [i] S 1Ki 21:19 [j] S Lev 19:13; Jas 5:4 **31:40** [k] S Ge 3:18; Mt 13:7 [l] Zep 2:9; Mt 13:26 [m] Ps 72:20; Jer 51:64 **32:1** [n] ver 15 [o] S Job 2:3; S 10:7 **32:2** [p] S Ge 22:21 [q] ver 1 [r] S Job 13:19; 27:5; 30:21; 35:2 **32:3** [s] Job 42:7 [t] ver 12-13

[a] 33 Or *as Adam did* [b] 3 Masoretic Text; an ancient Hebrew scribal tradition *Job, and so had condemned God*

[u] S Job 15:13 **32:4** [v] S Lev 19:32 **32:6** [w] Job 15:10 **32:7** [x] S 1Ch 29:15; S 2Ch 10:6

31:29–32 The sin of gloating over one's enemy was condemned by Moses (see Ex 23:4–5 and note) and by Christ (see Mt 5:43–47).
31:33–34 A strong denial of hypocrisy.
31:33 *as men do.* See NIV text note and Ge 3:8–10; Hos 6:7.
31:35–37 Job's final call for justice. His signature endorses every word of the oaths he has just taken.
31:35 *someone to hear me.* See notes on 5:1; 9:33; 16:18–21; 19:25. *let the Almighty answer me.* See note on 38:1. *accuser.* The Hebrew for this word is not the same as that for "Satan" (see note on 1:6). Here Job's accuser is either (1) a human adversary (perhaps one of the three friends) or (2) God himself. In any event, Job assumes that accusations have been lodged against him before the court of heaven to which God has responded with judgments.
31:36 *shoulder.* Inscriptions were sometimes worn on the shoulder as a perpetual reminder of their importance (see Ex 28:12).
31:38–40 A climactic oath that completes an earlier theme and creates a unique emphasis. Job calls for a curse on his land if he has not been fully committed to social justice (see also vv. 13–15).
31:40 *The words of Job are ended.* His complaints and arguments are now over. He will only make brief statements of contrition (see 40:3–5; 42:1–6 and notes) following the divine discourses.
32:1—37:24 A fourth counselor, named Elihu and younger than the other three (32:4,6–7,9), has been standing on the sidelines, giving deference to age and listening to the dialogue-dispute. But now he declares himself ready to show that both Job and the three other counselors are in the wrong. The author introduces Elihu's four poetic speeches (32:6—33:33; ch. 34; ch. 35; chs. 36–37) with a short prose preface (32:1–5).
32:1 *righteous in his own eyes.* Job insisted on his innocence in spite of the terrible suffering he was experiencing.
32:2–3 *angry.* Elihu considers Job's emphasis on vindicating himself rather than God reprehensible, but he also believes that the friends' inability to refute Job was tantamount to condemning God (see NIV text note on v. 3).
32:2 *Elihu.* Means "He is my God." Elihu's speeches in some ways anticipate the divine word out of the storm (38:1—42:6). *Buzite.* An inhabitant of Buz, a desert region in the east (see Jer 25:23).
32:6,10,17 *tell … what I know.* Elihu is eager to share his knowledge and assumes that he can communicate it effectively (see note on 36:4).
32:6 *young … fearful.* See Jer 1:6–8; 1Ti 4:12; 2Ti 1:7 and notes.

8 But it is the spirit[a][y] in a man,
the breath of the Almighty,[z] that
gives him understanding.[a]
9 It is not only the old[b] who are wise,[b]
not only the aged[c] who understand
what is right.[d]

10 "Therefore I say: Listen to me;[e]
I too will tell you what I know.[f]
11 I waited while you spoke,
I listened to your reasoning;
while you were searching for words,
12 I gave you my full attention.
But not one of you has proved Job
wrong;
none of you has answered his
arguments.[g]
13 Do not say, 'We have found wisdom;[h]
let God refute[i] him, not man.'
14 But Job has not marshaled his words
against me,[j]
and I will not answer him with your
arguments.

15 "They are dismayed and have no more
to say;
words have failed them.[k]
16 Must I wait, now that they are silent,
now that they stand there with no
reply?
17 I too will have my say;
I too will tell what I know.[l]
18 For I am full of words,
and the spirit[m] within me compels
me;[n]
19 inside I am like bottled-up wine,
like new wineskins ready to burst.[o]
20 I must speak and find relief;
I must open my lips and reply.[p]
21 I will show partiality[q] to no one,[r]
nor will I flatter any man;[s]
22 for if I were skilled in flattery,
my Maker[t] would soon take me
away.[u]

32:8 [y]ver 18 [z]S Job 27:3 [a]S Job 12:13; S Ps 119:34; Jas 1:5 **32:9** [b]1Co 1:26 [c]Ps 119:100 [d]S Job 12:12,20; Lk 2:47; 1Ti 4:12 **32:10** [e]Job 33:1,31,33; 34:2,16; 37:2,14; Ps 34:11 [f]S Job 5:27 **32:12** [g]ver 3 **32:13** [h]S Job 4:12; S Ecc 9:11 [i]S Job 11:5 **32:14** [j]Job 23:4 **32:15** [k]ver 1 **32:17** [l]S Job 5:27; 33:3; 36:4 **32:18** [m]ver 8 [n]Ac 4:20; 1Co 9:16; 2Co 5:14 **32:19** [o]Jer 20:9; Am 3:8; Mt 9:17 **32:20** [p]S Job 4:2; S Jer 6:11 **32:21** [q]S Lev 19:15; S 2Ch 19:7; S Job 13:10 [r]Mt 22:16 [s]Pr 29:5; 1Th 2:5 **32:22** [t]S Job 4:17; S 9:9 [u]Ps 12:2-4

33:1 [v]Job 32:10 [w]S Job 6:28; S 13:6 **33:3** [x]1Ki 3:6; Ps 7:10; 11:2; 64:10 [y]S Job 6:28 **33:4** [z]S Ge 1:2 [a]Job 10:3 [b]S Job 27:3 [c]S Nu 16:22; S Job 12:10 **33:5** [d]ver 32 [e]Job 13:18 [f]S Job 31:14 **33:6** [g]Ac 14:15; Jas 5:17

33

"But now, Job, listen[v] to my words;
pay attention to everything I say.[w]
2 I am about to open my mouth;
my words are on the tip of my
tongue.
3 My words come from an upright
heart;[x]
my lips sincerely speak what I
know.[y]
4 The Spirit[z] of God has made me;[a]
the breath of the Almighty[b] gives
me life.[c]
5 Answer me[d] then, if you can;
prepare[e] yourself and confront me.[f]
6 I am just like you before God;[g]
I too have been taken from clay.[h]
7 No fear of me should alarm you,
nor should my hand be heavy upon
you.[i]

8 "But you have said in my hearing—
I heard the very words—
9 'I am pure[j] and without sin;[k]
I am clean and free from guilt.[l]
10 Yet God has found fault with me;
he considers me his enemy.[m]
11 He fastens my feet in shackles;[n]
he keeps close watch on all my
paths.'[o]

12 "But I tell you, in this you are not
right,
for God is greater than man.[p]
13 Why do you complain to him[q]
that he answers none of man's
words[c]?[r]

[a] *8* Or *Spirit*; also in verse 18 [b] *9* Or *many*; or *great*
[c] *13* Or *that he does not answer for any of his actions*

[h]S Job 4:19 **33:7** [i]S Job 9:34; 2Co 2:4 **33:9** [j]S Job 10:7 [k]S Job 9:30; S 13:23 [l]S Job 2:9 **33:10** [m]S Job 13:24 **33:11** [n]S Job 13:27 [o]Job 14:16; Pr 3:6; Isa 30:21 **33:12** [p]S Job 5:9; Ps 8:4; 50:21; Ecc 7:20; Isa 55:8-9 **33:13** [q]Job 40:2; Isa 45:9 [r]S Job 11:8

32:8 *breath of the Almighty.* See 33:4.

32:14 *I will not answer him with your arguments.* Elihu feels that something important has been left out and, where the wisdom of age has failed, he by the Spirit of God (see NIV text note on v. 8) has the understanding to supply the right answers.

32:15–22 Elihu delivers a soliloquy to himself, but it is also for the benefit of those who may be listening.

32:15–16 *words have failed them ... they stand there with no reply.* See v. 5. The breakdown of the third cycle in the dialogue-dispute cut short Bildad's last word and left Zophar without a third speech (see note on 22:1—26:14).

32:18 *I am full of words.* Elihu's speeches continue unabated through ch. 37. He has a genuine contribution to make, however, to the problems Job is facing. At the same time, he does not stoop to false accusation about Job's earlier life but usually confines his criticism of Job to quotations from Job himself. This is perhaps the reason that God, in the epilogue, does not condemn Elihu along with Job's three friends (see 42:7–9 and note).

32:19 *new wineskins ready to burst.* Old wineskins might be expected to crack or break (see Mt 9:17 and note), but not new ones. Elihu is obviously eager to speak.

33:1–33 Elihu turns to Job and speaks directly to him. Unlike the three friends, he addresses Job by name (vv. 1,31; 37:14).

33:1 *pay attention to everything I say.* He is thoroughly convinced of the importance and wisdom of the advice he is about to give (see vv. 31,33).

33:4 *Spirit of God has made me.* See Ge 1:2 and note. *breath of the Almighty.* See 32:8. *gives me life.* See 27:3; see also Ge 2:7 and note.

33:5 *Answer me.* He opens and closes his speech (see v. 32) with the same plea. *if you can.* His attitude of superiority shows through.

33:6 *I ... have been taken from clay.* See note on 4:19.

33:7 *hand ... heavy upon.* The idiom is elsewhere used only of God (see 23:2 and NIV text notes; see also note on 1Sa 5:6).

33:8 *But you have said.* Elihu's method is to quote Job (vv. 9–11; 34:5–6,9; 35:2–3) and then show him where and how he is wrong. The quotations are not always verbatim, which indicates that Elihu is content simply to repeat the substance of Job's arguments.

33:11 Elihu quotes Job's words almost verbatim here (see 13:27).

33:12 *you are not right.* Elihu feels that Job needs to be corrected. Certainly Job's perception of God as his

14 For God does speak[s]—now one way,
now another[t]—
though man may not perceive it.[u]
15 In a dream,[v] in a vision[w] of the night,[x]
when deep sleep[y] falls on men
as they slumber in their beds,
16 he may speak[z] in their ears
and terrify them[a] with warnings,[b]
17 to turn man from wrongdoing
and keep him from pride,[c]
18 to preserve his soul from the pit,[a][d]
his life from perishing by the
sword.[b][e]
19 Or a man may be chastened[f] on a bed
of pain[g]
with constant distress in his bones,[h]
20 so that his very being finds food[i]
repulsive
and his soul loathes the choicest
meal.[j]
21 His flesh wastes away to nothing,
and his bones,[k] once hidden, now
stick out.[l]
22 His soul draws near to the pit,[c][m]
and his life to the messengers of
death.[d][n]
23 "Yet if there is an angel on his side
as a mediator,[o] one out of a
thousand,
to tell a man what is right for him,[p]
24 to be gracious to him and say,
'Spare him from going down to the
pit[e];[q]
I have found a ransom for him'[r]—
25 then his flesh is renewed[s] like a
child's;
it is restored as in the days of his
youth.[t]
26 He prays to God and finds favor with
him,[u]
he sees God's face and shouts for
joy;[v]
he is restored by God to his
righteous state.[w]
27 Then he comes to men and says,
'I sinned,[x] and perverted what was
right,[y]
but I did not get what I deserved.[z]
28 He redeemed[a] my soul from going
down to the pit,[f][b]
and I will live to enjoy the light.'[c]
29 "God does all these things to a man[d]—
twice, even three times[e]—
30 to turn back[f] his soul from the pit,[g][g]
that the light of life[h] may shine on
him.[i]
31 "Pay attention, Job, and listen[j] to me;[k]
be silent,[l] and I will speak.
32 If you have anything to say, answer
me;[m]
speak up, for I want you to be
cleared.[n]
33 But if not, then listen to me;[o]
be silent,[p] and I will teach you
wisdom.[q]"

[a] 18 Or *preserve him from the grave* [b] 18 Or *from crossing the River* [c] 22 Or *He draws near to the grave* [d] 22 Or *to the dead* [e] 24 Or *grave* [f] 28 Or *redeemed me from going down to the grave* [g] 30 Or *turn him back from the grave*

33:14 [s]Ps 62:11 [t]ver 29 [u]Job 4:12 **33:15** [v]S Ge 20:3; Job 4:13; S Mt 27:19 [w]Ac 16:9 [x]S Ge 15:1; Da 2:19 [y]S Ge 2:21 **33:16** [z]Job 36:10,15 [a]S Job 6:4 [b]Ps 88:15-16 **33:17** [c]S Job 20:6 **33:18** [d]ver 22, 24,28,30; Ps 28:1; 30:9; 69:15; 88:6; 103:4; Pr 1:12; Isa 14:15; 38:17; Jnh 2:6; Zec 9:11 [e]S Job 15:22; Mt 26:52 **33:19** [f]S Job 5:17 [g]S Ge 17:1; S Dt 8:5; 2Co 12:7-10; Jas 1:3 [h]S Job 16:16; Ps 6:2; 38:3; Isa 38:13 **33:20** [i]Ps 102:4; 107:18 [j]S Job 3:24; S 6:6 **33:21** [k]S Job 2:5 [l]S Job 16:8 **33:22** [m]S ver 18 [n]Job 38:17; Ps 9:13; 88:3; 107:18; 116:3 **33:23** [o]Gal 3:19; Heb 8:6; 9:15 [p]Job 36:9-10; Mic 6:8 **33:24** [q]S ver 18 [r]S Job 6:22 **33:25** [s]Ps 103:5 [t]2Ki 5:14 **33:26** [u]S Job 5:15; Pr 8:35; 12:2; 18:22; Lk 2:52 [v]S Ezr 3:13; S Job 22:26 [w]Ps 13:5; 50:15; 51:12; 1Jn 1:9 **33:27** [x]S Nu 22:34 [y]Lk 15:21 [z]S Ezr 9:13; Ps 22:27; 51:13; Ro 6:21; Jas 2:13 **33:28** [a]S Ex 15:13; Ps 34:22; 107:20 [b]S ver 18; S Job 17:16 [c]S Job 22:28 **33:29** [d]Ps 139:16; Pr 16:9; 20:24; Jer 10:23; 1Co 12:6; Eph 1:11; Php 2:13 [e]ver 14 **33:30** [f]Jas 5:19 [g]S ver 18 [h]Ps 49:19; 56:13; 116:9; Isa 53:11 [i]Isa 60:1; Eph 5:14 **33:31** [j]Jer 23:18 [k]S Job 32:10 [l]ver 33 **33:32** [m]ver 5 [n]S Job 6:29; 35:2 **33:33** [o]S Job 32:10 [p]ver 31 [q]S Job 6:24; Pr 10:8,10,19

enemy (see v. 10; 13:24; 19:11) is wrong, but Elihu is also offended by what he considers Job's claim to purity (see v. 9). Job, however, had never claimed to be "pure and without sin," though some of his words were also understood that way by Eliphaz (see 15:14–16). Job admits being a sinner (7:21; 13:26) but disclaims the outrageous sins for which he thinks he is being punished. His complaints about God's silence (see v. 13) are also an offense to Elihu. But he imputes to Job the blanket statement that God never speaks to human beings, whereas Job's point is that God is silent in his present experience.

33:15 *In a dream ... when deep sleep falls on men.* Cf. Eliphaz's words in 4:13.

33:18 *pit.* A metaphor for the grave (see NIV text note; see also vv. 22,24,28,30), as often in the Psalms. *perishing by the sword.* See 36:12. The reading in the NIV text note in both verses refers to the figurative waterway between the land of the living and the realm of the dead. The Hebrew for "River" here is *shelaḥ* (from a root that means "to send") and sometimes means "water channel" (see Ne 3:15 and NIV text note), a conduit through which water is "sent" (see Jn 9:7 and note) by a spring. The "River" therefore is the figurative means of passage between this world and the next.

33:19 *a man may be chastened on a bed of pain.* Dreams and visions (see v. 15) are not the only ways in which God speaks. He can talk to us in ways that we do not perceive (see v. 14). Elihu rightly states that God speaks to humans in order to turn them from sin. But he overlooks Job's reason for wanting an audience with God: to find out what sins he is being accused of (see 13:22–23).

33:23–28 Having emphasized the importance of the chastening aspect of suffering, a point mentioned only briefly by Eliphaz (see 5:17; see also note on 5:17–26), Elihu now moves on to the possibility of deliverance and restoration based on a mediator (see note on 5:1). He further allows for God's gracious response of forgiveness where sincere repentance is present (vv. 27–28). But Elihu is still ignorant of the true nature of Job's relationship to God, known only in the divine council (chs. 1–2).

33:24 *Spare him from going down to the pit.* See Isa 38:17 and note. *ransom.* See Ps 49:7–9 and note.

33:25 *flesh is renewed like a child's ... restored.* Similar phrases are used in 2Ki 5:14 with reference to healing from leprosy.

33:26 *sees God's face.* Not literally (see note on Ge 16:13).

33:29 *twice ... three times.* See note on 5:19.

33:30 *to turn back his soul from the pit.* Elihu teaches that God's apparent harshness in chastening human beings is in reality an act of love, since they are never punished in this life in keeping with what they fully deserve (see v. 27). *light of life.* Spiritual well-being (see Ps 49:19; see also Ps 27:1 and note). In some contexts, the phrase refers to resurrection (see note on Isa 53:11).

33:32 *I want you to be cleared.* But this will happen, Elihu insists, only if Job repents.

34 Then Elihu said:

[2]"Hear my words, you wise men;
listen to me,[r] you men of learning.
[3]For the ear tests words
as the tongue tastes food.[s]
[4]Let us discern for ourselves what is right;[t]
let us learn together what is good.[u]

[5]"Job says, 'I am innocent,[v]
but God denies me justice.[w]
[6]Although I am right,
I am considered a liar;[x]
although I am guiltless,[y]
his arrow inflicts an incurable wound.'[z]
[7]What man is like Job,
who drinks scorn like water?[a]
[8]He keeps company with evildoers;
he associates with wicked men.[b]
[9]For he says, 'It profits a man nothing
when he tries to please God.'[c]

[10]"So listen to me,[d] you men of understanding.[e]
Far be it from God to do evil,[f]
from the Almighty to do wrong.[g]
[11]He repays a man for what he has done;[h]
he brings upon him what his conduct deserves.[i]
[12]It is unthinkable that God would do wrong,[j]
that the Almighty would pervert justice.[k]
[13]Who appointed[l] him over the earth?
Who put him in charge of the whole world?[m]
[14]If it were his intention
and he withdrew his spirit[a][n] and breath,[o]

34:2 [r]S Job 32:10 **34:3** [s]Job 12:11 **34:4** [t]S Job 12:12; Heb 5:14 [u]1Th 5:21 **34:5** [v]S Job 10:7 [w]S Job 6:29 **34:6** [x]S Job 6:28 [y]S Job 9:21 [z]S Job 6:4; S 10:3; S Jer 10:19 **34:7** [a]S Job 9:21; S 15:16 **34:8** [b]S Job 22:15 **34:9** [c]S Job 9:29-31; S 21:15 **34:10** [d]Job 32:10 [e]ver 16; S Job 12:12 [f]S Ge 18:25 [g]ver 12; Dt 32:4; Job 8:3; 36:23; Ps 92:15; Ro 3:5; 9:14 **34:11** [h]S Job 21:31; S Mt 16:27 [i]Jer 17:10; 32:19; Eze 33:20 **34:12** [j]S ver 10; Tit 1:2; Heb 6:18 [k]S Job 8:3; Ps 9:16; Col 3:25; 2Th 1:6 **34:13** [l]Heb 1:2 [m]Job 36:23; 38:4,6; Isa 40:14 **34:14** [n]S Ge 6:3 [o]S Nu 16:22; S Job 27:3

34:15 [p]S Ge 6:13; La 3:22; Mal 3:6; Jn 3:16 [q]S Ge 2:7; S Job 7:21; 9:22; Ps 90:10 **34:16** [r]S ver 10 [s]S Job 32:10

[15]all mankind would perish[p] together
and man would return to the dust.[q]

[16]"If you have understanding,[r] hear this;
listen to what I say.[s]
[17]Can he who hates justice govern?[t]
Will you condemn the just and mighty One?[u]
[18]Is he not the One who says to kings,
'You are worthless,'
and to nobles,[v] 'You are wicked,'[w]
[19]who shows no partiality[x] to princes
and does not favor the rich over the poor,[y]
for they are all the work of his hands?[z]
[20]They die in an instant, in the middle of the night;[a]
the people are shaken and they pass away;
the mighty are removed without human hand.[b]

[21]"His eyes are on the ways of men;[c]
he sees their every step.[d]
[22]There is no dark place,[e] no deep shadow,[f]
where evildoers can hide.[g]
[23]God has no need to examine men further,[h]
that they should come before him for judgment.[i]

[a] *14* Or *Spirit*

34:17 [t]ver 30; 2Sa 23:3-4; Pr 20:8,26; 24:23-25; 28:28 [u]ver 29; S Job 10:7; 40:8; Ro 3:5-6 **34:18** [v]S Job 12:18 [w]Ex 22:28; Isa 40:24 **34:19** [x]S Job 13:10; S Ac 10:34 [y]S Lev 19:15; Jas 2:5 [z]S Job 10:3 **34:20** [a]ver 25; S Ex 11:4; S Job 20:8 [b]S Job 12:19 **34:21** [c]Jer 32:19 [d]S Job 14:16; Pr 15:3; S Heb 4:13 **34:22** [e]Ps 74:20 [f]S Job 3:5 [g]S Ge 3:8; S Job 11:20 **34:23** [h]Ps 11:4 [i]Job 11:11

34:1 – 37 The second of Elihu's four speeches (see note on 32:1 — 37:24), divided into three sections: (1) addressed to a group of wise men (vv. 2 – 15), doubtless including the three friends; (2) addressed to Job (vv. 16 – 33); (3) addressed to himself (vv. 34 – 37), as in 32:15 – 22 (see note there).

34:2,10 *listen to me.* Although it is possible that Elihu is overly impressed with his own wisdom, it is more likely that he considered himself a messenger of God (see 32:8,18 and NIV text note), especially in the light of his humble attitude in v. 4.

34:2 *wise men ... men of learning.* Also referred to as "men of understanding" (vv. 10,34).

34:3 Elihu echoes the words of Job in 12:11 (see note there).

34:5,9 *Job says ... For he says.* Elihu again quotes Job and then goes on to defend God's justice against what he considers to be Job's false theology (e.g., 9:14 – 24; 16:11 – 17; 19:7; 21:17 – 18; 24:1 – 12; 27:2). The substance of the quotation in v. 5 is accurate (cf. 12:4; 13:18; 27:6), and much of v. 6 represents Job fairly (see 21:34; 27:5; see also 6:4 and note) — though Job had never claimed to be completely guiltless. Verse 9 is not a direct quotation from Job, who had only imagined the wicked saying something similar (see 21:15). But perhaps Elihu derives it from Job's repeated statement that God treats the righteous and the wicked in the same way (cf. 9:22; 21:17; 24:1 – 12), leading to the conclusion that it does not pay to please God.

34:7 *drinks scorn like water.* See Eliphaz's description of humans in 15:16.

34:10 *Far be it from God to do evil.* See Ge 18:25 and note. Elihu's concern that Job was making God the author of evil is commendable. Job, in his frustration, has come perilously close to charging God with wrongdoing (12:4 – 6; 24:1 – 12). He has suggested that this is the only conclusion he can reach on the basis of his knowledge and experience (9:24).

34:11 See Ecc 12:14; Ro 2:6 – 11; 2Co 5:10 and notes.

34:13 – 15 Elihu is zealous for God's glory as the sovereign Sustainer who demonstrates his grace every moment by granting life and breath to human beings.

34:15 *return to the dust.* See Ecc 12:7; see also Ge 3:19 and note.

34:16 *hear ... listen.* The Hebrew for these verbs is singular, addressed to Job. Elihu is concerned that Job's attitude about God's justice be corrected (see v. 17), so he stresses God's impartial rule as Lord of all, especially in meting out justice to the wicked in high places (see vv. 18 – 20).

34:18 *worthless.* See note on Dt 13:13.

34:21 – 28 God's omniscience guarantees that he will not make any mistakes when he punishes evildoers. It is not necessary for him to set times to examine people for judgment (see v. 23; contrast 24:1).

34:21 Elihu echoes the words of Job in 31:4.

24 Without inquiry he shatters[j] the
mighty[k]
and sets up others in their place.[l]
25 Because he takes note of their deeds,[m]
he overthrows them in the night[n]
and they are crushed.[o]
26 He punishes them for their
wickedness[p]
where everyone can see them,
27 because they turned from following
him[q]
and had no regard for any of his
ways.[r]
28 They caused the cry of the poor to
come before him,
so that he heard the cry of the
needy.[s]
29 But if he remains silent,[t] who can
condemn him?[u]
If he hides his face,[v] who can see
him?
Yet he is over man and nation alike,[w]
30 to keep a godless[x] man from ruling,[y]
from laying snares for the people.[z]

31 "Suppose a man says to God,
'I am guilty[a] but will offend no more.
32 Teach me what I cannot see;[b]
if I have done wrong, I will not do
so again.'[c]
33 Should God then reward you on your
terms,
when you refuse to repent?[d]
You must decide, not I;
so tell me what you know.

34 "Men of understanding declare,
wise men who hear me say to me,
35 'Job speaks without knowledge;[e]
his words lack insight.'[f]
36 Oh, that Job might be tested to the
utmost
for answering like a wicked man![g]
37 To his sin he adds rebellion;
scornfully he claps his hands[h]
among us
and multiplies his words[i] against
God."[j]

34:24 [j]Isa 8:9; 9:4; Jer 51:20; Da 2:34 [k]Job 12:19 [l]Da 2:21 **34:25** [m]S Job 11:11 [n]S ver 20 [o]Pr 5:21-23 **34:26** [p]S Ge 6:5; S Job 8:22; S 28:24; Ps 9:5; Jer 44:5 **34:27** [q]Ps 14:3 [r]S 1Sa 15:11 **34:28** [s]S Ex 22:23; S Job 5:15; S 12:19 **34:29** [t]Ps 28:1; 83:1; 109:1 [u]S ver 17; Ro 8:34 [v]Ps 13:1 [w]Ps 83:18; 97:9 **34:30** [x]S Job 8:13 [y]S ver 17 [z]Ps 25:15; 31:4; 91:3; 124:7; 140:5; Pr 29:2-12 **34:31** [a]Ps 51:5; Lk 15:21; Ro 7:24; 1Jn 1:8, 10 **34:32** [b]Ex 33:13; Job 35:11; 38:36; Ps 15:2; 25:4; 27:11; 51:6; 86:11; 139:23-24; 143:8 [c]Job 33:27; S Lk 19:8 **34:33** [d]S 2Ki 17:13; Job 33:23; 36:10, 15, 18, 21; 41:11; 42:6; Pr 17:23; Jnh 3:8 **34:35** [e]Job 35:16; 38:2; 42:3 [f]Job 26:3 **34:36** [g]S Job 6:29; S 22:15 **34:37** [h]S Job 27:23 [i]Job 35:16 [j]Job 23:2

35

Then Elihu said:

2 "Do you think this is just?
You say, 'I will be cleared[k] by God.'[a][l]
3 Yet you ask him, 'What profit is it to
me,[b]
and what do I gain by not
sinning?'[m]

4 "I would like to reply to you
and to your friends with you.
5 Look up at the heavens[n] and see;
gaze at the clouds so high above
you.[o]
6 If you sin, how does that affect him?
If your sins are many, what does
that do to him?[p]
7 If you are righteous, what do you give
to him,[q]
or what does he receive[r] from your
hand?[s]
8 Your wickedness affects only a man
like yourself,[t]
and your righteousness only the
sons of men.[u]

9 "Men cry out[v] under a load of
oppression;[w]
they plead for relief from the arm
of the powerful.[x]
10 But no one says, 'Where is God my
Maker,[y]
who gives songs[z] in the night,[a]
11 who teaches[b] more to[c] us than to[c] the
beasts of the earth
and makes us wiser than[d] the birds
of the air?'
12 He does not answer[d] when men cry
out
because of the arrogance[e] of the
wicked.[f]

[a] 2 Or *My righteousness is more than God's* [b] 3 Or *you* [c] 11 Or *teaches us by* [d] 11 Or *us wise by*

35:2 [k]S Job 33:32 [l]S Job 2:9; S 32:2 **35:3** [m]S Job 9:29-31; S 21:15 **35:5** [n]S Ge 15:5; S Dt 10:14 [o]S Job 11:7-9; Ps 19:1-4 **35:6** [p]S Job 7:20 **35:7** [q]Ro 11:35 [r]1Co 4:7 [s]S Job 22:2-3; Lk 17:10 **35:8** [t]Eze 18:24 [u]Eze 18:5-9; Zec 7:9-10 **35:9** [v]Ex 2:23 [w]S Job 20:19 [x]S Job 5:15; S 12:19 **35:10** [y]S Job 4:17 [z]S Job 8:21 [a]Ps 42:8; 77:6; 119:62; 149:5; Ac 16:25 **35:11** [b]S Job 21:22; Lk 12:24 [c]Job 12:7 **35:12** [d]S 1Sa 8:18 [e]S Job 15:25 [f]Ps 66:18

34:29 *if he remains silent, who can condemn him?* Elihu attempts to answer Job's complaint about God's silence (ch. 23). God watches over people and nations to see that right is done (vv. 29–30).

34:31–33 First indirectly (vv. 31–32) and then more directly (v. 33), Elihu condemns Job and calls for his repentance.

34:35 *Job speaks without knowledge.* A motif in the first discourse of the Lord (see 38:2 and note) and the final response of Job (see 42:3).

35:1–16 Elihu's third speech (see note on 32:1—37:24), addressed to Job.

35:2 *cleared.* The Hebrew for this word is translated "vindicated" in Job's statement in 13:18. Elihu thinks that it is unjust and inconsistent for Job to expect vindication from God and at the same time imply that God does not care whether we are righteous (see v. 3). But allowance must be made for Job to express his feelings. The psalmist who thirsted for God (Ps 42:1–2) also questioned why God had forgotten him (Ps 42:9) and rejected him (Ps 43:2).

35:5 *Look up at the heavens and see.* Elihu asserts that God is so far above human beings that there is really nothing they can do, good or bad, that will affect God's essential nature (see v. 6).

35:9 *Men cry out … they plead for relief.* Elihu states that those like Job who pray for help when suffering innocently never seem to get around to trusting the justice and goodness of their Maker, who is also the author of wisdom and joy (see vv. 10–11). Such failure is a sign of arrogance (see v. 12), so Job's complaint against God's justice and about God's silence is meaningless talk (see vv. 13–16).

35:10–11 *God … gives songs … teaches … makes us wiser.* God chooses to condescend, to reach out to people in love.

35:12 The verse is difficult. A comma after the first line would change the meaning and make more sense of the verse in context: Since the wicked are arrogant, God does not listen

[13]Indeed, God does not listen to their
empty plea;
the Almighty pays no attention to it.[g]
[14]How much less, then, will he listen
when you say that you do not see
him,[h]
that your case[i] is before him
and you must wait for him,[j]
[15]and further, that his anger never
punishes[k]
and he does not take the least notice
of wickedness.[a][l]
[16]So Job opens his mouth with empty
talk;[m]
without knowledge he multiplies
words."[n]

36 Elihu continued:

[2]"Bear with me a little longer and I will
show you
that there is more to be said in God's
behalf.
[3]I get my knowledge from afar;[o]
I will ascribe justice to my Maker.[p]
[4]Be assured that my words are not
false;[q]
one perfect in knowledge[r] is with
you.[s]

[5]"God is mighty,[t] but does not despise
men;[u]
he is mighty, and firm in his
purpose.[v]
[6]He does not keep the wicked alive[w]
but gives the afflicted their rights.[x]
[7]He does not take his eyes off the
righteous;[y]
he enthrones them with kings[z]
and exalts them forever.[a]
[8]But if men are bound in chains,[b]
held fast by cords of affliction,[c]
[9]he tells them what they have done—
that they have sinned arrogantly.[d]
[10]He makes them listen[e] to correction[f]
and commands them to repent of
their evil.[g]
[11]If they obey and serve him,[h]
they will spend the rest of their days
in prosperity[i]
and their years in contentment.[j]
[12]But if they do not listen,
they will perish by the sword[b][k]
and die without knowledge.[l]

[13]"The godless in heart[m] harbor
resentment;[n]
even when he fetters them, they do
not cry for help.[o]
[14]They die in their youth,[p]
among male prostitutes of the
shrines.[q]
[15]But those who suffer[r] he delivers in
their suffering;[s]
he speaks[t] to them in their
affliction.[u]

[16]"He is wooing[v] you from the jaws of
distress
to a spacious place[w] free from
restriction,[x]
to the comfort of your table[y] laden
with choice food.[z]
[17]But now you are laden with the
judgment due the wicked;[a]
judgment and justice have taken
hold of you.[b]
[18]Be careful that no one entices you by
riches;
do not let a large bribe[c] turn you
aside.[d]
[19]Would your wealth[e]
or even all your mighty efforts
sustain you so you would not be in
distress?

35:13 [g]S Dt 1:45; S 1Sa 8:18; S Job 15:31; S Pr 15:8 **35:14** [h]S Job 9:11 [i]Ps 37:6 [j]Job 31:35 **35:15** [k]S Job 9:24 [l]S Job 18:5; Ps 10:11; Hos 7:2; Am 8:7 **35:16** [m]Tit 1:10 [n]S Job 34:35, 37; 1Co 4:20; Jude 1:10 **36:3** [o]S Job 6:28 [p]S Job 4:17 **36:4** [q]S Job 6:28; S 13:6 [r]Job 37:5, 16, 23 [s]S Job 32:17 **36:5** [t]S Job 9:4 [u]Ps 5:2; 22:24; 31:22; 69:33; 102:17; 103:10 [v]S Nu 23:19; Ro 11:29 **36:6** [w]S Job 34:26 [x]S Job 4:10 **36:7** [y]S Job 11:11; Ps 11:5; 33:18; 34:15; Mt 6:18 [z]Ps 113:8; Isa 22:23 [a]S 1Sa 2:7-8; S Job 4:7 **36:8** [b]S 2Sa 3:34; 2Ki 23:33; Ps 107:10, 14 [c]ver 10, 15, 21; Ps 119:67, 71 **36:9** [d]S Job 15:25 **36:10** [e]S Job 33:16 [f]S Job 5:17 [g]S ver 8; S Jdg 6:8; S Job 34:33; 1Th 5:22 **36:11** [h]S Lev 26:33; Dt 28:1; Isa 1:19; Hag 1:12 [i]S Dt 30:15; S Job 8:7

[a] *15* Symmachus, Theodotion and Vulgate; the meaning of the Hebrew for this word is uncertain. [b] *12* Or *will cross the River*

[j]S Ex 8:22; S Dt 8:1; Jn 14:21; 1Ti 4:8 **36:12** [k]S Lev 26:38; S Job 15:22 [l]S Job 4:21; Eph 4:18 **36:13** [m]S Job 15:12; Ro 2:5 [n]S Job 5:2 [o]S Job 4:17; Am 4:11 **36:14** [p]S Job 15:32 [q]S Dt 23:17 **36:15** [r]S Job 5:15 [s]2Co 12:10 [t]S Job 33:16 [u]S ver 8; S Job 34:33 **36:16** [v]Hos 2:14 [w]S 2Sa 22:20; Ps 18:19 [x]Ps 118:5 [y]Ps 23:5; 78:19 [z]S Ge 17:1; S Job 15:11 **36:17** [a]S Job 20:29 [b]Job 22:11 **36:18** [c]S Ex 23:8; Am 5:12 [d]S Job 34:33 **36:19** [e]Ps 49:6; Jer 9:23

(see v. 13). Job himself shares their arrogance. He too receives no answer, because he does not ask rightly (see v. 14).

35:16 *without knowledge.* See 38:2 and note. *multiplies words.* "Against God" (34:37).

36:1—37:24 Elihu's fourth and final (see 36:2) speech (see note on 32:1—37:24), addressed for the most part to Job (but see note on 37:2).

36:2-4 Elihu desires to strengthen the case for God's goodness and justice.

36:4 *perfect in knowledge.* Here Elihu applies the phrase to himself, while in 37:16 he applies it to God—thus appearing to make himself equal to God. But the Hebrew for "knowledge" is not quite the same here as in 37:16. Elihu is probably referring to his ability as a communicator, i.e., he claims perfection in the knowledge of speech (see note on 32:6,10,17).

36:5 God's power assures the fulfillment of his purpose.

36:6-9 A classic statement of God's justice in rewarding the righteous and punishing sinners (in contrast to what Job has been claiming). In v. 7 Elihu perhaps has in mind Job's complaint that God will not leave him alone (see 7:17-19), and in v. 9 he may be thinking of Job's charge that God will not present his indictment against him (see 31:35-36).

36:10 *makes them listen to correction.* Elihu states that God uses trouble to gain people's attention.

36:12 See NIV text note (see also note on 33:18).

36:13-15 Elihu understands that the basic spiritual need of human beings stems from their hardness of heart—their refusal to yield to God, to cry out to God in their distress (see Ps 107:6 and note), or to hear the voice of God in their suffering.

36:14 *male prostitutes of the shrines.* See note on 1Ki 14:24.

36:16-21 Elihu warns Job to respond to God's discipline by turning away from evil (see v. 21). Verse 16 shows that he still views Job as a man for whom there is hope.

36:16 *He is wooing you.* With tender compassion, God brings his people back to himself (see Hos 2:14 and note).

[20]Do not long for the night,[f]
to drag people away from their
homes.[a]
[21]Beware of turning to evil,[g]
which you seem to prefer to
affliction.[h]

[22]"God is exalted in his power.[i]
Who is a teacher like him?[j]
[23]Who has prescribed his ways[k] for him,[l]
or said to him, 'You have done
wrong'?[m]
[24]Remember to extol his work,[n]
which men have praised in song.[o]
[25]All mankind has seen it;[p]
men gaze on it from afar.
[26]How great is God — beyond our
understanding![q]
The number of his years is past
finding out.[r]

[27]"He draws up the drops of water,[s]
which distill as rain to the streams[b];[t]
[28]the clouds pour down their moisture
and abundant showers[u] fall on
mankind.[v]
[29]Who can understand how he spreads
out the clouds,
how he thunders[w] from his
pavilion?[x]
[30]See how he scatters his lightning[y]
about him,
bathing the depths of the sea.[z]
[31]This is the way he governs[c] the
nations[a]
and provides food[b] in abundance.[c]
[32]He fills his hands with lightning
and commands it to strike its mark.[d]
[33]His thunder announces the coming
storm;[e]
even the cattle make known its
approach.[d][f]

37 "At this my heart pounds[g]
and leaps from its place.
[2]Listen![h] Listen to the roar of his
voice,[i]
to the rumbling that comes from
his mouth.[j]
[3]He unleashes his lightning[k] beneath
the whole heaven

36:20 [f]Job 34:20,25 **36:21** [g]S Job 34:33; Ps 66:18 [h]S ver 8; Heb 11:25 **36:22** [i]S Job 5:9; S 9:4 [j]S Job 21:22; S Ro 11:34 **36:23** [k]Job 27:11 [l]S Job 34:13; Ro 11:33 [m]S Ge 18:25; S Job 34:10 **36:24** [n]1Ch 16:24; Ps 35:27; 92:5; 111:2; 138:5; 145:10 [o]S Ex 15:1; Rev 15:3 **36:25** [p]Ro 1:20 **36:26** [q]S Job 5:9; 1Co 13:12 [r]S Ge 21:33; S Job 10:5; Heb 1:12 **36:27** [s]S Job 26:8 [t]S 2Sa 1:21; Job 28:26; 38:28; Isa 55:10 **36:28** [u]Ps 65:10; 72:6; Joel 2:23 [v]S Job 5:10; S 22:11; S 28:26; Mt 5:45 **36:29** [w]Ps 29:3; Jer 10:13 [x]S Job 9:6; 37:16; Ps 18:7-15; 19:4,5; 104:2; Pr 8:28; Isa 40:22 **36:30** [y]Ex 19:16; Job 37:11,15; Ps 18:12,14; 97:4; Jer 10:13; Hab 3:11 [z]Ps 68:22; Isa 51:10 **36:31** [a]Dt 28:23-24; 1Ki 17:1; Job 37:13; Am 4:7-8 [b]Ps 145:15 [c]Ps 104:14-15, 27-28; Isa 30:23; Ac 14:17 **36:32** [d]S Job 28:24; 37:12,15; Ps 18:14; 29:7-9 **36:33** [e]Job 37:5; 40:9 [f]S Job 28:26 **37:1** [g]Ps 38:10; Isa 15:5;

and sends it to the ends of the
earth.[l]
[4]After that comes the sound of his
roar;
he thunders[m] with his majestic
voice.[n]
When his voice resounds,
he holds nothing back.
[5]God's voice thunders[o] in marvelous
ways;[p]
he does great things beyond our
understanding.[q]
[6]He says to the snow,[r] 'Fall on the
earth,'
and to the rain shower, 'Be a mighty
downpour.'[s]
[7]So that all men he has made may
know his work,[t]
he stops every man from his labor.[e][u]
[8]The animals take cover;[v]
they remain in their dens.[w]
[9]The tempest comes out from its
chamber,[x]
the cold from the driving winds.[y]
[10]The breath of God produces ice,
and the broad waters become
frozen.[z]
[11]He loads the clouds with moisture;[a]
he scatters his lightning[b] through
them.[c]
[12]At his direction they swirl around
over the face of the whole earth
to do whatever he commands
them.[d]
[13]He brings the clouds to punish men,[e]
or to water his earth[f] and show his
love.[f]

[a] *20* The meaning of the Hebrew for verses 18-20 is uncertain. [b] *27* Or *distill from the mist as rain* [c] *31* Or *nourishes* [d] *33* Or *announces his coming— / the One zealous against evil* [e] *7* Or */ he fills all men with fear by his power* [f] *13* Or *to favor them*

Jer 4:19; Hab 3:16 **37:2** [h]S Job 32:10 [i]ver 5 [j]Ps 18:13; 29:3-9 **37:3** [k]S 2Sa 22:13; Ps 18:14 [l]S Job 36:32; Mt 24:27; Lk 17:24 **37:4** [m]S 1Sa 2:10 [n]S Ex 20:19 **37:5** [o]S 1Sa 2:10; Jn 12:29 [p]S Job 36:33 [q]S Job 5:9; S 11:7-9; S 36:4 **37:6** [r]Dt 28:12; Job 38:22 [s]S Ge 7:4; S Job 5:10; S 28:26 **37:7** [t]Ps 109:27 [u]Ps 104:19-23; 111:2 **37:8** [v]S Job 28:26 [w]Job 38:40; Ps 104:22 **37:9** [x]Ps 50:3 [y]Ps 147:17 **37:10** [z]Job 38:29-30; Ps 147:17 **37:11** [a]S Job 26:8 [b]S Job 36:30 [c]S Job 28:26 **37:12** [d]S ver 3; Ps 147:16; 148:8 **37:13** [e]S Ge 7:4; Ex 9:22-23; S 1Sa 12:17 [f]S 1Ki 18:45; S Job 5:10; S 36:31; 38:27

36:21 *Beware of turning to evil.* Elihu's evaluation of Job is the opposite of God's (see 1:8 and note; 2:3).
36:22 – 33 Elihu anticipates some of God's statements in the discourses of chs. 38 – 41.
36:24 *his work, which men have praised in song.* See, e.g., notes on Ex 15:1 – 18; Jdg 5:1 – 31.
36:26 *beyond our understanding.* See 37:5. That God's ways and thoughts are infinitely higher than ours is an important theme in chs. 38 – 41 (see also Isa 55:8 – 9; Ro 11:33 – 36).
36:30 *bathing.* That is, in light.
36:31 *governs.* The NIV text note understands the verse to mean that the Lord "nourishes" the nations with the showers mentioned in vv. 27 – 30.
37:1 – 13 A continuation of Elihu's hymnic description of God's marvels exhibited in the earth's atmosphere, beginning in 36:27. His heart pounds at the awesome display (see v. 1). The passage reveals a sophisticated observation of atmospheric conditions and their effects: the evaporation and distillation of water for rain (see 36:27 and NIV text note), the clouds as holders of moisture (see 36:28; 37:11) and the cyclonic behavior of clouds (see v. 12). Such forces originate from God's command and always perform his will for humankind, whether for good or for ill (v. 13).
37:2 *Listen.* The Hebrew for this verb is plural, indicating that others (including the three friends) besides Job are being addressed here (see note on 36:1 — 37:24). *roar of his voice … rumbling.* Thunder (see v. 4).
37:5 *beyond our understanding.* See note on 36:26.
37:10 *breath of God.* Here a metaphor for a chilling wind.

14 "Listen[g] to this, Job;
stop and consider God's wonders.[h]
15 Do you know how God controls the clouds
and makes his lightning[i] flash?[j]
16 Do you know how the clouds hang poised,[k]
those wonders of him who is perfect in knowledge?[l]
17 You who swelter in your clothes
when the land lies hushed under the south wind,[m]
18 can you join him in spreading out the skies,[n]
hard as a mirror of cast bronze?[o]

19 "Tell us what we should say to him;[p]
we cannot draw up our case[q]
because of our darkness.[r]
20 Should he be told that I want to speak?
Would any man ask to be swallowed up?
21 Now no one can look at the sun,[s]
bright as it is in the skies
after the wind has swept them clean.
22 Out of the north he comes in golden splendor;[t]
God comes in awesome majesty.[u]
23 The Almighty is beyond our reach and exalted in power;[v]
in his justice[w] and great righteousness, he does not oppress.[x]
24 Therefore, men revere him,[y]
for does he not have regard for all the wise[z] in heart?[a]"

37:14 [g]S Job 32:10 [h]S Job 5:9 **37:15** [i]S Job 36:30 [j]S Job 36:32 **37:16** [k]S Job 36:29 [l]S Job 5:9; S 36:4 **37:17** [m]Ac 27:13 **37:18** [n]S Ge 1:1,8; S Job 22:14 [o]Dt 28:23 **37:19** [p]Ro 8:26 [q]S Job 13:18 [r]S Job 9:3 **37:21** [s]S Jdg 5:31; Ac 22:11; 26:13 **37:22** [t]Ps 19:5 [u]Ex 24:17 **37:23** [v]S Job 5:9; S 36:4; Ro 11:33; 1Ti 6:16 [w]S Job 8:3 [x]S Job 4:17; Ps 44:1; Isa 63:9; Jer 25:5; La 3:33; Eze 18:23,32 **37:24** [y]S Ge 22:12; Job 28:28; Ecc 12:13; Mic 6:8; Mt 10:28 [z]S Job 5:13; Eph 5:15

The LORD Speaks

38 Then the LORD answered Job[a] out of the storm.[b] He said:

2 "Who is this that darkens my counsel[c]
with words without knowledge?[d]
3 Brace yourself like a man;
I will question you,
and you shall answer me.[e]

4 "Where were you when I laid the earth's foundation?[f]
Tell me, if you understand.[g]
5 Who marked off its dimensions?[h]
Surely you know!
Who stretched a measuring line[i] across it?
6 On what were its footings set,[j]
or who laid its cornerstone[k]—
7 while the morning stars[l] sang together[m]
and all the angels[b][n] shouted for joy?[o]

8 "Who shut up the sea behind doors[p]
when it burst forth from the womb,[q]
9 when I made the clouds its garment
and wrapped it in thick darkness,[r]
10 when I fixed limits for it[s]
and set its doors and bars in place,[t]

[a] 24 Or *for he does not have regard for any who think they are wise.* [b] 7 Hebrew *the sons of God*

38:1 [a]S Job 11:5 [b]S Ex 14:21; S 1Sa 2:10; Job 40:6; Isa 21:1; Eze 1:4 **38:2** [c]S 1Ki 22:5; Isa 40:13 [d]S Job 34:35; Mk 10:38; 1Ti 1:7 **38:3** [e]Job 40:7; 42:4; Mk 11:29 **38:4** [f]S ver 5; S Ge 1:1; S 1Sa 2:8 [g]ver 18; S Job 34:13; Pr 30:4 **38:5** [h]ver 4; Ps 102:25; Pr 8:29; Isa 40:12; 48:13; Jer 31:37 [i]Jer 31:39; Zec 1:16; 4:9-10 **38:6** [j]Pr 8:25 [k]S Job 26:7 **38:7** [l]S Ge 1:16 [m]Ps 19:1-4; 148:2-3 [n]S 1Ki 22:19 [o]S Dt 16:15 **38:8** [p]ver 11; Ps 33:7; Pr 8:29; Jer 5:22 [q]S Ge 1:9-10 **38:9** [r]S Ge 1:2 **38:10** [s]S Job 28:25; Ps 33:7; 104:9; Isa 40:12 [t]Ne 3:3; Job 7:12; 26:10

37:14–18 Elihu challenges Job to ponder God's power over the elements. The question format is also used in the divine discourses (chs. 38–41).
37:16 *perfect in knowledge.* See note on 36:4.
37:18 See 26:7.
37:19 *we cannot draw up our case.* Job had dared to sign his defense and call for an audience with God (see 31:35). For this, Elihu seeks to shame him. But he softens his tone by including himself as one equally vulnerable to God's majesty.
37:22 *Out of the north he comes.* See note on Ps 48:2. *God comes.* Elihu prepares Job for the appearance of God in the storm (chs. 38–41).
37:24 *revere.* Fear (see 28:28; Ge 20:11 and notes).
38:1—42:6 The theophany (appearance of God) to Job, consisting of two discourses by the Lord (38:1—40:2; 40:6—41:34), each of which receives a brief response from Job (40:3–5; 42:1–6).
38:1 *the LORD.* The Israelite covenant name for God (see Introduction: Author). *storm.* See 40:6. Elihu had imagined the appearance of the divine presence as a display of "golden splendor" and "awesome majesty" (37:22). He also had anticipated the storm or whirlwind (see note on 37:22), from which Job would hear the voice of God. Job had said, "Let the Almighty answer me" (31:35). Now God speaks to Job, but not to give Job the justification of his ways that Job had been demanding. Out of the awesome majesty of the thunderstorm, he reminds Job that the wisdom that directs the Creator's ways is beyond the reach of human understanding—that humanity's almost godlike wisdom should not presume to match God's wisdom or take its measure (cf. Isa 55:8–9).
38:2 See 35:16. In 42:3, Job echoes the Lord's words. God states that Job's complaining and raging against him are unjustified and proceed from limited understanding.
38:3 Repeated in 40:7 (see also 42:4). The format of God's response is to ply Job with rhetorical questions, to each of which Job must plead ignorance. God says nothing about Job's suffering, nor does he address Job's problem about divine justice. Job gets neither a bill of indictment nor a verdict of innocence. But, more important, God does not humiliate or condemn him—which surely would have been the case if the counselors had been right. So by implication Job is vindicated, and later his vindication is directly affirmed (see 42:7–9 and note). The divine discourses, then, succeed in bringing Job to complete faith in God's wisdom and goodness without his receiving a direct answer to his questions.
38:4–38 Inanimate creation testifies to God's sovereignty and power (the earth, vv. 4–7,18; the sea, vv. 8–11,16; the sun, vv. 12–15; the netherworld, v. 17; light and darkness, vv. 19–20; the weather, vv. 22–30,34–38; the constellations, vv. 31–33). See note on 38:39—39:30.
38:4–5 See the similar questions of Agur, and the similar irony in his demand for a response (see Pr 30:4; Isa 40:12 and note).
38:7 See Ps 148:2–3 and note on Ps 65:13. When the earth was created, the angels were there to sing the praises of the Creator, but Job was not (see vv. 4–5). He should therefore not expect to be able to understand even lesser aspects of God's plans for the world and for humankind. *angels.* See NIV text notes here and on 1:6; 2:1.
38:10–11 See Ps 33:7 and note; Jer 5:22.

11 when I said, 'This far you may come
and no farther;[u]
here is where your proud waves
halt'?[v]
12 "Have you ever given orders to the
morning,[w]
or shown the dawn its place,[x]
13 that it might take the earth by the
edges
and shake the wicked[y] out of it?[z]
14 The earth takes shape like clay under a
seal;[a]
its features stand out like those of a
garment.
15 The wicked are denied their light,[b]
and their upraised arm is broken.[c]

16 "Have you journeyed to the springs of
the sea
or walked in the recesses of the
deep?[d]
17 Have the gates of death[e] been shown
to you?
Have you seen the gates of the
shadow of death[a]?[f]
18 Have you comprehended the vast
expanses of the earth?[g]
Tell me, if you know all this.[h]

19 "What is the way to the abode of light?
And where does darkness reside?[i]
20 Can you take them to their places?
Do you know the paths[j] to their
dwellings?
21 Surely you know, for you were already
born![k]
You have lived so many years!

22 "Have you entered the storehouses of
the snow[l]
or seen the storehouses[m] of the hail,[n]
23 which I reserve for times of trouble,[o]
for days of war and battle?[p]
24 What is the way to the place where the
lightning is dispersed,[q]
or the place where the east winds[r]
are scattered over the earth?[s]
25 Who cuts a channel for the torrents of
rain,
and a path for the thunderstorm,[t]
26 to water[u] a land where no man lives,
a desert with no one in it,[v]
27 to satisfy a desolate wasteland
and make it sprout with grass?[w]
28 Does the rain have a father?[x]
Who fathers the drops of dew?
29 From whose womb comes the ice?
Who gives birth to the frost from the
heavens[y]
30 when the waters become hard as
stone,
when the surface of the deep is
frozen?[z]

31 "Can you bind the beautiful[b] Pleiades?
Can you loose the cords of Orion?[a]
32 Can you bring forth the constellations[b]
in their seasons[c]
or lead out the Bear[d] with its cubs?[c]
33 Do you know the laws[d] of the
heavens?[e]
Can you set up ⌞God's[e]⌟ dominion
over the earth?

34 "Can you raise your voice to the clouds
and cover yourself with a flood of
water?[f]
35 Do you send the lightning bolts on
their way?[g]
Do they report to you, 'Here we are'?
36 Who endowed the heart[f] with
wisdom[h]
or gave understanding[i] to the mind[f]?
37 Who has the wisdom to count the
clouds?
Who can tip over the water jars[j] of
the heavens[k]
38 when the dust becomes hard[l]
and the clods of earth stick
together?[m]

39 "Do you hunt the prey for the lioness
and satisfy the hunger of the lions[n]
40 when they crouch in their dens[o]
or lie in wait in a thicket?[p]

38:11 [u] S ver 8 [v] Ps 65:7; 89:9; 104:6-9 **38:12** [w] Ps 57:8 [x] Ps 74:16; Am 5:8 **38:13** [y] Ps 104:35 [z] S Job 8:22 **38:14** [a] Ex 28:11 **38:15** [b] S Dt 28:29; S Job 15:22; S 18:5 [c] S Ge 17:14; S Job 4:10; S 31:22 **38:16** [d] S Ge 1:7; S Job 9:8 **38:17** [e] S Job 33:22; Mt 16:18; Rev 1:18 [f] S Job 7:9 **38:18** [g] S Job 28:24; Isa 40:12 [h] S ver 4 **38:19** [i] S Ge 1:4; S Job 28:3; Ps 139:11-12 **38:20** [j] S Job 24:13 **38:21** [k] Job 15:7 **38:22** [l] S Job 37:6 [m] S Dt 28:12 [n] Ps 105:32; 147:17 **38:23** [o] Ps 27:5; Isa 28:17; 30:30; Eze 13:11 [p] Ex 9:26; Jos 10:11; Eze 13:13; Rev 16:21 **38:24** [q] S Job 28:24 [r] S Job 27:21 [s] Jer 10:13; 51:16 **38:25** [t] Job 28:26 **38:26** [u] Job 36:27 [v] Ps 84:6; 107:35; Isa 41:18 **38:27** [w] S Job 28:26; S 37:13; S Ps 104:14 **38:28** [x] S 2Sa 1:21; S Job 5:10 **38:29** [y] Ps 147:16-17 **38:30** [z] Job 37:10 **38:31** [a] Job 9:9; Am 5:8 **38:32** [b] 2Ki 23:5; Isa 13:10; 40:26; 45:12; Jer 19:13 [c] S Ge 1:16 **38:33** [d] Ps 148:6; Jer 31:36 [e] S Ge 1:16 **38:34** [f] S Job 5:10; S 22:11 **38:35** [g] S Job 36:32 **38:36** [h] S Job 9:4; S 34:32; Jas 1:5 [i] S Job 12:13 **38:37** [j] S Jos 3:16 [k] S Job 22:11 **38:38** [l] S Lev 26:19 [m] 1Ki 18:45 **38:39** [n] S Ge 49:9 **38:40** [o] S Job 37:8 [p] S Ge 49:9

[a] 17 Or *gates of deep shadows* [b] 31 Or *the twinkling*; or *the chains of the* [c] 32 Or *the morning star in its season* [d] 32 Or *out Leo* [e] 33 Or *his*; or *their* [f] 36 The meaning of the Hebrew for this word is uncertain.

38:11 *when I said.* God the Father controls the sea by speaking to it, as does God the Son (see Mk 4:41 and note; Lk 8:24–25).
38:12–13 The arrival of the dawn sends the wicked scurrying for cover.
38:14 *clay under a seal.* Either a cylinder seal (see note on Ge 38:18) or a stamp seal.
38:15 *their light.* The night is when the wicked are active (see Jn 3:19; for the imagery cf. Lk 11:35). *upraised arm is broken.* See 22:9 and note.
38:16 *springs of the sea.* See Ge 7:11; 8:2.
38:17 *gates of death.* See note on 17:16; see also 26:5–6.
38:22–23 *hail ... for days of war.* See, e.g., Jos 10:11; Isa 28:2 and notes.
38:24 *east winds.* See note on 15:2.
38:31–32 *Pleiades ... Orion ... Bear.* See note on 9:9.
38:36 *heart ... mind.* It is possible that the first word should be translated "ibis" and the second "rooster," two birds whose habits were sometimes observed by people who wished to forecast the weather. If so, the words would serve as a transition to the next major section of the first divine discourse.
38:39—39:30 Animate creation testifies to God's sovereignty, power and loving care (the lion, 38:39–40; the raven, 38:41; the mountain goat, 39:1–4; the wild donkey, vv. 5–8; the wild ox, vv. 9–12; the ostrich, vv. 13–18; the horse, vv. 19–25; the hawk, v. 26; the eagle, vv. 27–30). See note on 38:4–38.

41 Who provides food[q] for the raven[r]
when its young cry out to God
and wander about for lack of food?[s]

39 "Do you know when the mountain
goats[t] give birth?
Do you watch when the doe bears
her fawn?[u]
2 Do you count the months till they bear?
Do you know the time they give
birth?[v]
3 They crouch down and bring forth
their young;
their labor pains are ended.
4 Their young thrive and grow strong in
the wilds;
they leave and do not return.

5 "Who let the wild donkey[w] go free?
Who untied his ropes?
6 I gave him the wasteland[x] as his home,
the salt flats[y] as his habitat.[z]
7 He laughs[a] at the commotion in the
town;
he does not hear a driver's shout.[b]
8 He ranges the hills[c] for his pasture
and searches for any green thing.

9 "Will the wild ox[d] consent to serve
you?[e]
Will he stay by your manger[f] at
night?
10 Can you hold him to the furrow with a
harness?[g]
Will he till the valleys behind you?
11 Will you rely on him for his great
strength?[h]
Will you leave your heavy work to
him?
12 Can you trust him to bring in your
grain
and gather it to your threshing floor?

13 "The wings of the ostrich flap joyfully,
but they cannot compare with the
pinions and feathers of the
stork.[i]
14 She lays her eggs on the ground
and lets them warm in the sand,
15 unmindful that a foot may crush them,
that some wild animal may trample
them.[j]
16 She treats her young harshly,[k] as if
they were not hers;
she cares not that her labor was in
vain,
17 for God did not endow her with
wisdom
or give her a share of good sense.[l]
18 Yet when she spreads her feathers to
run,
she laughs[m] at horse and rider.

19 "Do you give the horse his strength[n]
or clothe his neck with a flowing
mane?
20 Do you make him leap like a locust,[o]
striking terror[p] with his proud
snorting?[q]
21 He paws fiercely, rejoicing in his
strength,[r]
and charges into the fray.[s]
22 He laughs[t] at fear, afraid of nothing;
he does not shy away from the
sword.
23 The quiver[u] rattles against his side,
along with the flashing spear[v] and
lance.
24 In frenzied excitement he eats up the
ground;
he cannot stand still when the
trumpet sounds.[w]
25 At the blast of the trumpet[x] he snorts,
'Aha!'
He catches the scent of battle from
afar,
the shout of commanders and the
battle cry.[y]

26 "Does the hawk take flight by your
wisdom
and spread his wings toward the
south?[z]
27 Does the eagle soar at your command
and build his nest on high?[a]
28 He dwells on a cliff and stays there at
night;
a rocky crag[b] is his stronghold.
29 From there he seeks out his food;[c]
his eyes detect it from afar.
30 His young ones feast on blood,
and where the slain are, there is
he."[d]

38:41 [q]S Ge 1:30 [r]S Ge 8:7; Lk 12:24 [s]Ps 147:9; S Mt 6:26 **39:1** [t]S Dt 14:5 [u]Ge 49:21 **39:2** [v]S Ge 31:7-9 **39:5** [w]S Ge 16:12 **39:6** [x]Job 24:5; Ps 107:34; Jer 2:24 [y]Job 30:4 [z]Job 30:7; Jer 14:6; 17:6 **39:7** [a]S Job 5:22 [b]Job 3:18 **39:8** [c]Isa 32:20 **39:9** [d]S Nu 23:22 [e]S Ex 21:6 [f]S Ge 42:27 **39:10** [g]Job 41:13; Ps 32:9 **39:11** [h]ver 19; Job 40:16; 41:12, 22; Ps 147:10 **39:13** [i]Zec 5:9 **39:15** [j]2Ki 14:9 **39:16** [k]ver 17; La 4:3 **39:17** [l]S ver 16; S Job 21:22 **39:18** [m]S Job 5:22 **39:19** [n]S ver 11 **39:20** [o]Joel 2:4-5; Rev 9:7 [p]Job 41:25 [q]Jer 8:16 **39:21** [r]ver 11 [s]Jer 8:6 **39:22** [t]S Job 5:22 **39:23** [u]Isa 5:28; Jer 5:16 [v]Na 3:3 **39:24** [w]Nu 10:9; Jer 4:5, 19; Eze 7:14; Am 3:6 **39:25** [x]Jos 6:5 [y]Jer 8:6; Am 1:14; 2:2 **39:26** [z]Jer 8:7 **39:27** [a]Jer 49:16; Ob 1:4; Hab 2:9 **39:28** [b]Jer 49:16; Ob 1:3 **39:29** [c]S Job 9:26 **39:30** [d]Mt 24:28; Lk 17:37

38:41 *provides food for the raven.* God cares for and feeds all the birds, of which the raven is representative (e.g., compare Lk 12:24 with Mt 6:26).
39:5 *wild donkey.* See 6:5 and note.
39:9–12 As 11:12 may have set up a contrast between the wild ass and the domestic donkey (see note there), so here there is a more explicit contrast between the wild ox and the domestic ox.
39:11 *great strength.* In the OT, the wild ox often symbolizes strength (see, e.g., Nu 23:22 and note; 24:8; Dt 33:17; Ps 22:21 and note; 29:6). Next to the elephant and rhinoceros, the wild ox was the largest and most powerful land animal of the OT world.
39:13–18 This stanza is unique in the discourses, because in it the Lord asks Job no questions.
39:13 *pinions and feathers of the stork.* A stork's wings were particularly impressive (see Zec 5:9).
39:18 *horse and rider.* Forms a transition to the next paragraph.
39:19–25 The horse is the only domestic animal in the discourses. This fact, though unexpected, serves the Lord's purpose, since it is specifically the war horse that is in view.
39:20 *like a locust.* Horses and locusts are compared also in Jer 51:27; Rev 9:7; cf. Joel 2:4 and note.
39:26 *hawk.* The sparrow hawk, though not resident to the Holy Land, stops there in its migration south for the winter.
39:27 *eagle.* Or possibly "vulture" (see v. 30).

40 The LORD said to Job:[e]

2 "Will the one who contends with the
Almighty[f] correct him?[g]
Let him who accuses God answer
him!"[h]

3 Then Job answered the LORD:

4 "I am unworthy[i]—how can I reply to
you?
I put my hand over my mouth.[j]
5 I spoke once, but I have no answer[k]—
twice, but I will say no more."[l]

6 Then the LORD spoke to Job out of the
storm:[m]

7 "Brace yourself like a man;
I will question you,
and you shall answer me.[n]
8 "Would you discredit my justice?[o]
Would you condemn me to justify
yourself?[p]
9 Do you have an arm like God's,[q]
and can your voice[r] thunder like his?[s]
10 Then adorn yourself with glory and
splendor,
and clothe yourself in honor and
majesty.[t]
11 Unleash the fury of your wrath,[u]
look at every proud man and bring
him low,[v]
12 look at every proud[w] man and humble
him,[x]
crush[y] the wicked where they stand.
13 Bury them all in the dust together;[z]
shroud their faces in the grave.[a]
14 Then I myself will admit to you
that your own right hand can save
you.[b]

40:1 [e]S Job 5:8; S 10:2 **40:2** [f]S Job 13:3 [g]S Job 9:15; S 11:8; S 33:13; Ro 9:20 [h]S Job 9:3 **40:4** [i]Job 42:6 [j]S Jdg 18:19; S Job 29:9 **40:5** [k]S Job 9:3 [l]S Job 9:15 **40:6** [m]S Ex 14:21; S Job 38:1 **40:7** [n]S Job 38:3 **40:8** [o]S Job 15:25; S 27:2; Ro 3:3 [p]S Job 2:3; S 34:17 **40:9** [q]S 2Ch 32:8; S Ps 98:1 [r]Isa 6:8; Eze 10:5 [s]S Ex 20:19; S Job 36:33 **40:10** [t]Ps 29:1-2; 45:3; 93:1; 96:6; 104:1; 145:5 **40:11** [u]S Job 20:28; Ps 7:11; Isa 5:25; 9:12, 19; 10:5; 13:3, 5; 30:27; 42:25; 51:20; Jer 7:20; Na 1:6; Zep 1:18 [v]Ps 18:27; Isa 2:11, 12, 17; 23:9; 24:10; 25:12; 26:5; 32:19 **40:12** [w]Ps 10:4; Isa 25:11; Jer 48:29; 49:16; Zep 2:10 [x]S 1Sa 2:7; S Ps 52:5; 1Pe 5:5 [y]Ps 60:12; Isa 22:5; 28:3; 63:2-3, 6; Da 5:20; Mic 5:8; 7:10; Zec 10:5; Mal 4:3

15 "Look at the behemoth,[a]
which I made[c] along with you
and which feeds on grass like an ox.[d]
16 What strength[e] he has in his loins,
what power in the muscles of his
belly![f]
17 His tail[b] sways like a cedar;
the sinews of his thighs are close-
knit.[g]
18 His bones are tubes of bronze,
his limbs[h] like rods of iron.[i]
19 He ranks first among the works of
God,[j]
yet his Maker[k] can approach him
with his sword.[l]
20 The hills bring him their produce,[m]
and all the wild animals play[n]
nearby.[o]
21 Under the lotus plants he lies,
hidden among the reeds[p] in the
marsh.[q]
22 The lotuses conceal him in their
shadow;
the poplars by the stream[r] surround
him.
23 When the river rages,[s] he is not
alarmed;
he is secure, though the Jordan[t]
should surge against his mouth.
24 Can anyone capture him by the eyes,[c]
or trap him and pierce his nose?[u]

[a] *15* Possibly the hippopotamus or the elephant
[b] *17* Possibly trunk [c] *24* Or *by a water hole*

40:13 [z]Nu 16:31-34 [a]S Job 4:9 **40:14** [b]Ex 15:6, 12; Ps 18:35; 20:6; 48:10; 60:5; 108:6; Isa 41:10; 63:5 **40:15** [c]S Job 9:9 [d]Isa 11:7; 65:25 **40:16** [e]S Job 39:11 [f]Job 41:9 **40:17** [g]Job 41:15 **40:18** [h]Job 41:12 [i]Isa 11:4; 49:2 **40:19** [j]Job 41:33; Ps 40:5; 139:14; Isa 27:1 [k]S Job 4:17; S 9:9 [l]S Ge 3:24 **40:20** [m]Ps 104:14 [n]Ps 104:26 [o]S Job 5:23 **40:21** [p]S Ge 41:2; Ps 68:30; Isa 35:7 [q]Job 8:11 **40:22** [r]Ps 1:3; Isa 44:4 **40:23** [s]Isa 8:7; 11:15 [t]S Jos 3:1 **40:24** [u]2Ki 19:28; Job 41:2, 7, 26; Isa 37:29

40:1–2 The conclusion of the first divine discourse. Once again, God challenges Job to answer him.
40:3–5 Job, duly chastened and no longer "like a prince" (31:37), is unwilling to speak another word of complaint.
40:4 *unworthy.* The Hebrew for this word can also mean "small" or "insignificant."
40:5 *once … twice.* See note on 5:19.
40:6 See 38:1 and note.
40:7 Repeated from 38:3 (see note there).
40:8–14 The prologue to the second divine discourse, which ends at 41:34. Unlike the first discourse, God here addresses the issues of his own justice and Job's futile attempt at self-justification. In chs. 21 and 24, Job had complained about God's indifference toward the evil actions of the wicked. Here the Lord asserts his ability and determination to administer justice—a matter over which Job has no control. Therefore by implication Job is admonished to leave all this, including his own vindication (see v. 14), under God's control (see v. 9).
40:8 *Would you condemn me to justify yourself?* In 19:6, Job had said, "God has wronged me."
40:10 *clothe yourself in honor and majesty.* The same Hebrew underlying this clause describes God in Ps 104:1: "you are clothed with splendor and majesty." The Lord here challenges Job to take on the appearance of deity—if he can. *clothe yourself in.* See note on Ps 109:29.
40:11–12 See Isa 13:11, where the Lord describes himself as doing these things.
40:13 *dust.* See note on 7:21.
40:14 *your own right hand can save you.* Contrast Ps 49:7–9 (see note there).
40:15–24 The first of two poems (ch. 41 constitutes the second) in this discourse, each describing a huge beast and resuming the animal theme of ch. 39.
40:15 *behemoth.* The word is Hebrew and means "beast par excellence," referring to a large land animal (for possible identifications see NIV text note). Much of the language used to describe him in vv. 16–24 is highly poetic and hyperbolic. *which I made.* He is one of God's creatures, not a mythical being.
40:18 *iron.* See note on 19:24.
40:19 *first among the works of God.* The Hebrew underlying this phrase is translated "first of his works" in Pr 8:22 with reference to the creation of wisdom (see Pr 8:12). Here the descriptive phrase stresses the importance of the behemoth as an example of a huge animal under the control of a sovereign God.
40:21–23 *reeds in the marsh … poplars … Jordan.* The area described is probably the Huleh region, north of the Sea of Galilee.
40:24 The proposal to capture the behemoth forms a transition to the similar proposal concerning the leviathan in 41:1.

41 "Can you pull in the leviathan[a][v]
with a fishhook[w]
or tie down his tongue with a rope?
2 Can you put a cord through his nose[x]
or pierce his jaw with a hook?[y]
3 Will he keep begging you for mercy?[z]
Will he speak to you with gentle
words?
4 Will he make an agreement with you
for you to take him as your slave for
life?[a]
5 Can you make a pet of him like a bird
or put him on a leash for your girls?
6 Will traders barter for him?
Will they divide him up among the
merchants?
7 Can you fill his hide with harpoons
or his head with fishing spears?[b]
8 If you lay a hand on him,
you will remember the struggle and
never do it again![c]
9 Any hope of subduing him is false;
the mere sight of him is
overpowering.[d]
10 No one is fierce enough to rouse him.[e]
Who then is able to stand against
me?[f]
11 Who has a claim against me that I
must pay?[g]
Everything under heaven belongs to
me.[h]

12 "I will not fail to speak of his limbs,[i]
his strength[j] and his graceful form.
13 Who can strip off his outer coat?
Who would approach him with a
bridle?[k]
14 Who dares open the doors of his
mouth,[l]
ringed about with his fearsome teeth?
15 His back has[b] rows of shields
tightly sealed together;[m]
16 each is so close to the next
that no air can pass between.
17 They are joined fast to one another;
they cling together and cannot be
parted.
18 His snorting throws out flashes of light;
his eyes are like the rays of dawn.[n]
19 Firebrands[o] stream from his mouth;
sparks of fire shoot out.
20 Smoke pours from his nostrils[p]
as from a boiling pot over a fire of
reeds.
21 His breath[q] sets coals ablaze,
and flames dart from his mouth.[r]
22 Strength[s] resides in his neck;
dismay goes before him.
23 The folds of his flesh are tightly joined;
they are firm and immovable.
24 His chest is hard as rock,
hard as a lower millstone.[t]
25 When he rises up, the mighty are
terrified;[u]
they retreat before his thrashing.[v]
26 The sword that reaches him has no
effect,
nor does the spear or the dart or the
javelin.[w][x]
27 Iron he treats like straw[y]
and bronze like rotten wood.
28 Arrows do not make him flee;[z]
slingstones are like chaff to him.
29 A club seems to him but a piece of
straw;[a]
he laughs[b] at the rattling of the
lance.
30 His undersides are jagged potsherds,
leaving a trail in the mud like a
threshing sledge.[c]
31 He makes the depths churn like a
boiling caldron[d]
and stirs up the sea like a pot of
ointment.[e]
32 Behind him he leaves a glistening
wake;
one would think the deep had white
hair.
33 Nothing on earth is his equal[f]—
a creature without fear.
34 He looks down on all that are
haughty;[g]
he is king over all that are proud.[h]"

Job

42 Then Job replied to the LORD:
2 "I know that you can do all things;[i]
no plan of yours can be thwarted.[j]
3 ⌞You asked,⌟ 'Who is this that
obscures my counsel without
knowledge?'[k]
Surely I spoke of things I did not
understand,
things too wonderful for me to
know.[l]

41:1 [v]S Job 3:8 [w]Am 4:2
41:2 [x]S Job 40:24 [y]Eze 19:4
41:3 [z]1Ki 20:31
41:4 [a]S Ex 21:6
41:7 [b]S Job 40:24
41:8 [c]S Job 3:8
41:9 [d]Job 40:16
41:10 [e]S Job 3:8 [f]S 2Ch 20:6; S Isa 46:5; Jer 50:44; Rev 6:17
41:11 [g]S Job 34:33; Ro 11:35 [h]Ps 24:1; 50:12; S Jos 3:11; S Job 10:4; Ac 4:24; 1Co 10:26
41:12 [i]Job 40:18 [j]S Job 39:11
41:13 [k]S Job 30:11; S 39:10
41:14 [l]Ps 22:13
41:15 [m]Job 40:17
41:18 [n]S Job 3:9
41:19 [o]Da 10:6
41:20 [p]Ps 18:8
41:21 [q]S Job 4:9; Isa 11:4; 40:7 [r]Ps 18:8; Isa 10:17; 30:27; 33:14; 66:14-16; Jer 4:4
41:22 [s]S Job 39:11
41:24 [t]Mt 18:6
41:25 [u]Job 39:20 [v]S Job 3:8
41:26 [w]S Jos 8:18 [x]S Job 40:24
41:27 [y]ver 29
41:28 [z]Ps 91:5
41:29 [a]ver 27 [b]S Job 5:22
41:30 [c]Isa 28:27; 41:15; Am 1:3
41:31 [d]1Sa 2:14 [e]Eze 32:2
41:33 [f]S Job 40:19
41:34 [g]Ps 18:27; 101:5; 131:1; Pr 6:17; 21:4; 30:13 [h]Job 28:8
42:2 [i]S Ge 18:14; S Mt 19:26 [j]S 2Ch 20:6; S Job 16:19; Ac 4:28; Eph 1:11
42:3 [k]S Job 34:35 [l]S Job 5:9

[a] 1 Possibly the crocodile [b] 15 Or *His pride is his*

41:1–34 The second of two poems in the Lord's final discourse (see note on 40:15–24).
41:1 *leviathan.* Its description in this chapter indicates that it is even more terrifying than the behemoth in ch. 40.
41:10 The leviathan is mighty, but God is infinitely more powerful.
41:11 Alluded to by Paul in Ro 11:35.
41:14–15 *doors of his mouth ... fearsome teeth ... back has rows of shields.* Characteristic of the crocodile (see NIV text note on v. 1).
41:18–21 Hyperbole (exaggerated poetic imagery).
41:27 *Iron.* See note on 19:24.
41:30 *jagged potsherds.* Broken pottery fragments.
41:34 *king over all that are proud.* The Lord alone can humble such creatures. Job cannot be expected to do so, though God challenges him to attempt it—if he so desires (see 40:11–12 and note).
42:1–6 Job's last words are his response to the Lord's second discourse.
42:2 Job finally sees that God and his purposes are supreme.
42:3 *You asked.* Job quotes the Lord's words in 38:2.

4 ⌞"You said,⌟ 'Listen now, and I will
speak;
I will question you,
and you shall answer me.'[m]
5 My ears had heard of you[n]
but now my eyes have seen you.[o]
6 Therefore I despise myself[p]
and repent[q] in dust and ashes."[r]

Epilogue

7 After the LORD had said these things
to Job[s], he said to Eliphaz the Temanite, "I am angry with you and your two
friends,[t] because you have not spoken of
me what is right, as my servant Job has.[u]
8 So now take seven bulls and seven rams[v]
and go to my servant Job[w] and sacrifice a
burnt offering[x] for yourselves. My servant
Job will pray for you, and I will accept his
prayer[y] and not deal with you according
to your folly.[z] You have not spoken of me
what is right, as my servant Job has."[a] 9 So
Eliphaz the Temanite, Bildad the Shuhite
and Zophar the Naamathite[b] did what the
LORD told them; and the LORD accepted
Job's prayer.[c]
10 After Job had prayed for his friends,
the LORD made him prosperous again[d] and
gave him twice as much as he had before.[e]
11 All his brothers and sisters and everyone
who had known him before[f] came and ate
with him in his house. They comforted
and consoled him over all the trouble the
LORD had brought upon him,[g] and each
one gave him a piece of silver[a] and a gold
ring.
12 The LORD blessed the latter part of
Job's life more than the first. He had fourteen thousand sheep, six thousand camels,
a thousand yoke of oxen and a thousand
donkeys. 13 And he also had seven sons
and three daughters. 14 The first daughter
he named Jemimah, the second Keziah
and the third Keren-Happuch. 15 Nowhere
in all the land were there found women
as beautiful as Job's daughters, and their
father granted them an inheritance along
with their brothers.
16 After this, Job lived a hundred and
forty years; he saw his children and their
children to the fourth generation. 17 And so
he died, old and full of years.[h]

42:4 [m] S Job 38:3 **42:5** [n] S Job 26:14; Ro 10:17 [o] Jdg 13:22; Isa 6:5; S Mt 5:8; Lk 2:30; Eph 1:17-18 **42:6** [p] Job 40:4; Eze 6:9; Ro 12:3 [q] S Job 34:33 [r] S Ex 10:3; S Ezr 9:6; S Job 2:8; S 6:29 **42:7** [s] S Jos 1:7 [t] Job 32:3 [u] ver 8; S Job 9:15 **42:8** [v] Nu 23:1,29; Eze 45:23 [w] Job 1:8 [x] S Ge 8:20 [y] Jas 5:15-16; 1Jn 5:16 [z] Ge 20:7; Job 22:30 [a] S ver 7 **42:9** [b] Job 2:11 [c] S Ge 19:21; S 20:17; Eze 14:14 **42:10** [d] Dt 30:3; Ps 14:7 [e] S Job 1:3; Ps 85:1-3; 126:5-6; Php 2:8-9; Jas 5:11

[a] *11* Hebrew *him a kesitah*; a kesitah was a unit of money of unknown weight and value.

42:11 [f] S Job 19:13 [g] S Ge 37:35 **42:17** [h] S Ge 15:15

42:4 *You said.* Job quotes the Lord's words in 38:3; 40:7.

42:5 Job—and his three friends, and Elihu—had only heard of God, but now Job has seen God (see Isa 6:5) with the eyes of faith and spiritual understanding. He can therefore accept God's ways with him (see v. 2)—which include suffering. *my eyes have seen you.* A down payment on the hope expressed in 19:26 (see note there).

42:6 *I despise myself.* See note on 9:21. To his humility (see 40:4–5) Job adds repentance for the presumptuous words he had spoken to God. *dust and ashes.* See 30:19 and note.

42:7–9 Despite Job's mistakes in word and attitude while he suffered, he is now commended and the counselors are rebuked. Why? Because even in his rage, even when he challenged God, he was determined to speak honestly before him. The counselors, on the other hand, mouthed many correct theological statements, but without living knowledge of the God they claimed to honor. Job spoke to God; they only spoke about God. Even worse, their spiritual arrogance caused them to claim knowledge they did not possess. They presumed to know why Job was suffering.

42:7–8 *my servant Job.* The phrase is used four times in these two verses (see note on 1:8).

42:10 Job's prayer for those who had abused him is a touching OT illustration of the high Christian virtue our Lord taught in Mt 5:44. Job's prayer marked the turning point back to prosperity for him. *made ... prosperous again.* The Hebrew for this expression is translated "restores the fortunes of" in Ps 14:7.

42:11 Contrast 16:2; 19:13. *piece of silver.* The Hebrew for this phrase (see NIV text note) is found elsewhere in the OT only in Ge 33:19 (see note there); Jos 24:32.

42:12–16 The cosmic contest with Satan, the accuser, is now over, and Job is restored. No longer is there a reason for Job to experience suffering—unless he was sinful and deserved it, which is not the case. God does not allow us to suffer for no reason, and even though the reason may be hidden in the mystery of his divine purpose (see Isa 55:8–9)—never for us to know in this life—we must trust in him as the God who does only what is right.

42:12 The number of animals is in each case twice as many (see v. 10) as Job had owned before (see 1:3).

42:13 *seven sons and three daughters.* To replace the children he had lost earlier (see 1:2,18–19).

42:14 Strikingly, only the names of the daughters are given. *Jemimah.* Means "dove." *Keziah.* Means "cinnamon." *Keren-Happuch.* Means "container of antimony," a highly prized eye shadow (see note on Jer 4:30).

42:15 *granted them an inheritance along with their brothers.* Cf. Zelophehad's daughters (Nu 27:1–11; 36).

42:16 *lived a hundred and forty years.* The longevity of a true patriarch (see note on Ex 6:16). *he saw ... to the fourth generation.* See Ge 50:23 and note.

42:17 *old and full of years.* See 5:26; Ge 25:8 and notes.

Psalms

INTRODUCTION

Title

The titles "Psalms" and "Psalter" come from the Septuagint (the pre-Christian Greek translation of the OT), where they originally referred to stringed instruments (such as harp, lyre and lute), then to songs sung with their accompaniment. The traditional Hebrew title is *tehillim* (meaning "praises"; see note on Ps 145 title), even though many of the psalms are *tephillot* (meaning "prayers"). In fact, one of the first collections included in the book was titled "the prayers of David son of Jesse" (72:20).

Collection, Arrangement and Date

The Psalter is a collection of collections and represents the final stage in a process that spanned centuries. It was put into its final form by postexilic temple personnel, who completed it probably in the fourth century B.C. It has often been called the prayer book of the second (Zerubbabel's and Herod's) temple and was used in synagogues as well. But it is more than a treasury of prayers and hymns for liturgical and private use on chosen occasions. Both the scope of its subject matter and the arrangement of the whole collection strongly suggest that this collection was viewed by its final editors as a book of instruction in the faith and in full-orbed godliness — thus a guide for the life of faith in accordance with the Law, the Prophets and the canonical wisdom literature (see chart, pp. 786 – 789). By the first century A.D. it was referred to as the "Book of Psalms" (Lk 20:42; Ac 1:20). At that time Psalms appears also to have been used as a title for the third and final section of the Hebrew OT canon more commonly known as the "Writings" (see Lk 24:44 and note), in which it is the first (and arguably the most important) book.

Many collections preceded this final compilation of the Psalms. In fact, the formation of psalters probably goes back to the early days of the "first" (Solomon's) temple (or even to the time of David), when the temple liturgy began to take shape. Reference has already been made to "the prayers of David." Additional collections expressly referred to in the present Psalter titles are: (1) the songs and/or psalms "of the Sons of Korah" (Ps 42 – 49; 84 – 85; 87 – 88), (2) the psalms and/or songs "of Asaph" (Ps 50; 73 – 83) and (3) the songs "of ascents" (Ps 120 – 134).

Other evidence points to further compilations. Ps 1 – 41 (Book I) make frequent use of the divine name Yahweh ("the LORD"), while Ps 42 – 72 (Book II) most commonly use the noun Elohim ("God"). (The reason for the Elohim collection in distinction from the Yahweh collection remains a matter of speculation.) Moreover, Ps 93 – 100 appear to be a traditional collection (see "The LORD reigns" in 93:1; 96:10; 97:1; 99:1). Other apparent groupings include Ps 111 – 118 (a series of Hallelujah psalms; see introduction to Ps 113), Ps 138 – 145 (all of which include "of David" in their titles) and Ps 146 – 150 (with their frequent "Praise the LORD"; see NIV text note on 111:1). Whether the "Great Hallel" (Ps 120 – 136) was already a recognized unit is not known.

In its final edition, the Psalter contains 150 psalms. On this the Septuagint and Hebrew texts agree, though they arrive at this number somewhat differently. The Septuagint unites Ps 9 – 10 (see NIV text note on Ps 9) and Ps 114 – 115 but divides Ps 116 and Ps 147 each into two psalms. It also attaches an extra psalm at the end, though it does not number it separately as Ps 151 (the extra psalm does, however, bear the notation "outside the number"). Strangely, both the Septuagint and Hebrew texts number Ps 42 – 43 as two psalms whereas they were evidently originally one (see NIV text note on Ps 42).

In its final form the Psalter was divided into five Books (Ps 1 – 41; 42 – 72; 73 – 89; 90 – 106; 107 – 150), each of which was provided with a concluding doxology (see 41:13; 72:18 – 19; 89:52; 106:48; 150). The first two of these Books, as already noted, were probably preexilic. The division of the remaining psalms into three Books, thus attaining the number five, was possibly in imitation of the five books of Moses (otherwise known simply as the Law). At least one of these divisions (between Ps 106 – 107) seems arbitrary (see introduction to Ps 107). In spite of this five-book division, the Psalter was clearly thought of as a whole, with an introduction (Ps 1 – 2) and a conclusion (Ps 146 – 150). Notes throughout the Psalms give additional indications of conscious arrangement (see also chart, pp. 786 – 789).

Authorship and Titles (or Superscriptions)

Of the 150 psalms, only 34 lack superscriptions of any kind (only 17 in the Septuagint). These so-called "orphan" psalms are found mainly in Books III – V, where they tend to occur in clusters: Ps 91; 93 – 97; 99; 104 – 107; 111 – 119; 135 – 137; 146 – 150. (In Books I – II, only Ps 1 – 2; 10; 33; 43; 71 lack titles, and Ps 10 and 43 are actually continuations of the preceding psalms.)

The contents of the superscriptions vary but fall into a few broad categories: (1) author, (2) name of collection, (3) type of psalm, (4) musical notations, (5) liturgical notations and (6) brief indications of occasion for composition. For details see notes on the titles of the various psalms.

Students of the Psalms are not agreed on the antiquity and reliability of these superscriptions. That many of them are at least preexilic appears evident from the fact that the Septuagint translators were sometimes unclear as to their meaning. Furthermore, the practice of attaching titles, including the name of the author, is ancient. On the other hand, comparison between the Septuagint and the Hebrew texts shows that the content of some titles was still subject to change well into the postexilic period. Most discussion centers on categories 1 and 6 above.

As for the superscriptions regarding occasion of composition, many of these brief notations of events read as if they had been taken from 1,2 Samuel. Moreover, they are sometimes not easily correlated with the content of the psalms they head. The suspicion therefore arises that they are later attempts to fit the psalms into the real-life events of history. But then why the limited number of such notations, and why the apparent mismatches? The arguments cut both ways.

> **A Quick Look**
>
> **Authors:**
> David, Asaph, the Sons of Korah, Solomon, Heman, Ethan, Moses and unknown authors
>
> **Audience:**
> God's people
>
> **Date:**
> Between the time of Moses (about 1440 B.C.) and the time following the Babylonian exile (after 538 B.C.)
>
> **Theme:**
> The book of Psalms contains ancient Israel's favorite hymns and prayers, which were used in their worship of the Lord, the Great King.

Regarding authorship, opinions are even more divided. The notations themselves are ambiguous since the Hebrew phraseology used, meaning in general "belonging to," can also be taken in the sense of "concerning" or "for the use of" or "dedicated to." The name may refer to the title of a collection of psalms that had been gathered under a certain name (as "Of Asaph" or "Of the Sons of Korah"). To complicate matters, there is evidence within the Psalter that at least some of the psalms were subjected to editorial revision in the course of their transmission. As for Davidic authorship, there can be little doubt that the Psalter contains psalms composed by that noted singer and musician and that there was at one time a "Davidic" psalter. This, however, may have also included psalms written concerning David, or concerning one of the later Davidic kings, or even psalms written in the manner of those he authored. It is also true that the tradition as to which psalms are "Davidic" remains somewhat indefinite, and some "Davidic" psalms seem clearly to reflect later situations (see, e.g., Ps 30 title — but see also note there; and see introduction to Ps 69 and note on Ps 122 title). Moreover, "David" is sometimes used elsewhere as a collective for the kings of his dynasty, and this could also be true in the psalm titles.

The word Selah is found in 39 psalms, all but two of which (Ps 140; 143, both "Davidic") are in Books I – III. It is also found in Hab 3, a psalm-like poem. Suggestions as to its meaning abound, but honesty must confess ignorance. Most likely, it is a liturgical notation. The common suggestions that it calls for a brief musical interlude or for a brief liturgical response by the congregation are plausible but unproven (the former may be supported by the Septuagint rendering). In some instances its present placement in the Hebrew text is highly questionable.

Psalm Types

Hebrew superscriptions to the Psalms acquaint us with an ancient system of classification: (1) *mizmor* ("psalm"); (2) *shiggaion* (see note on Ps 7 title); (3) *miktam* (see note on Ps 16 title); (4) *shir* ("song"); (5) *maśkil* (see note on Ps 32 title); (6) *tephillah* ("prayer"); (7) *tehillah* ("praise"); (8) *lehazkir* ("for being remembered" — i.e., before God, a petition); (9) *letodah* ("for praising" or "for giving thanks"); (10) *lelammed* ("for teaching"); and (11) *shir yedidot* ("song of loves" — i.e., a wedding song). The meaning of many of these terms, however, is uncertain. In addition, some titles contain two of these (especially *mizmor* and *shir*), indicating that the types are diversely based and overlapping.

Analysis of content has given rise to a different classification that has proven useful for study of the Psalms. The main types that can be identified are: (1) prayers of the individual (e.g., Ps 3 – 7); (2) praise from the individual for God's saving help (e.g., Ps 30; 34); (3) prayers of the community (e.g., Ps 12; 44; 79); (4) praise from the community for God's saving help (e.g., Ps 66; 75); (5) confessions of confidence in the Lord (e.g., Ps 11; 16; 52); (6) hymns in praise of God's majesty and virtues (e.g., Ps 8; 19; 29; 65); (7) hymns celebrating God's universal reign (Ps 47; 93 – 99); (8) songs of Zion, the city of God (Ps 46; 48; 76; 84; 122; 126; 129; 137); (9) royal psalms — by, for or concerning the king, the Lord's anointed (e.g., Ps 2; 18; 20; 45; 72; 89; 110); (10) pilgrimage songs (Ps 120 – 134); (11) liturgical songs (e.g., Ps 15; 24; 68); (12) didactic (instructional) songs (e.g., Ps 1; 34; 37; 73; 112; 119; 128; 133).

This classification also involves some overlapping. For example, "prayers of the individual" may include prayers of the king (in his special capacity as king) or even prayers of the community speaking in the collective first person singular. Nevertheless, it is helpful to study a psalm in conjunction with others of the same type. Attempts to fix specific liturgical settings for each type have not been convincing. For those psalms about which something can be said in this regard see introductions to the individual psalms.

Of all these psalm types, the prayers (both of the individual and of the community) are the most complex. Several speech functions are combined to form these appeals to God: (1) address to God: "O LORD," "my God," "my deliverer"; (2) initial appeal: "Arise," "Answer me," "Help," "Save me"; (3) description of distress: "Many are rising against me," "The wicked attack," "I am in distress"; (4) complaint against God: "Why have you forsaken me?" "How long will you hide your face from me?"; (5) petition: "Be not far from me," "Vindicate me"; (6) motivation for God to hear: "for I take refuge in you," "for your name's sake"; (7) accusation against the adversary: "There is no truth in their mouths," "Ruthless men seek my life" ("the wicked" are often quoted); (8) call for judicial redress: "Let them be put to shame," "Call him to account for his wickedness"; (9) claims of innocence:

"I have walked in my integrity," "They hate me without cause"; (10) confessions of sin: "I have sinned against you," "I confess my iniquity"; (11) professions of trust: "You are a shield about me," "You will answer me"; (12) vows to praise for deliverance: "I will sing your might," "My lips will praise you"; (13) calls to praise: "Magnify the LORD with me," "Sing praise to the LORD"; (14) motivations for praise: "for you have delivered me," "for the LORD hears the needy"; (15) words of praise: "you give us victory over our enemies," "Righteousness and justice are the foundation of your throne."

Though not all these appear in every prayer, they all belong to the conventions of prayer in the Psalter, with petition itself being but one (usually brief) element among the rest. On the whole they reflect the then-current conventions of a court trial, the psalmists presenting their cases before the heavenly King/Judge. When beset by wicked adversaries, the petitioners appeal to God for a hearing, describe their situation, plead their innocence ("righteousness"), lodge their accusations against their adversaries, and appeal for deliverance and judicial redress. When suffering at the hands of God (when God is their adversary), they confess their guilt and plead for mercy. Attention to these various speech functions and their role in the psalmists' judicial appeals to the heavenly Judge will significantly aid the reader's understanding of these psalms.

It should be noted that reference to "penitential" and "imprecatory" psalms as distinct psalm "types" has no basis in the Psalter collection itself. The former ("penitential") refers to an early Christian selection of seven psalms (6; 32; 38; 51; 102; 130; 143) for liturgical expressions of penitence; the latter ("imprecatory") is based on a misconstrual of one of the speech functions found in the prayers. What are actually appeals to the heavenly Judge for judicial redress (function 8 noted above) are taken to be curses ("imprecation" means "curse") pronounced by the psalmists on their adversaries. See note on 5:10.

Literary Features

The Psalter is poetry from first to last, even though it contains many prayers and not all OT prayers were poetic (see 1Ki 8:23 – 53; Ezr 9:6 – 15; Ne 9:5 – 37; Da 9:4 – 19) — nor, for that matter, was all praise poetic (see 1Ki 8:15 – 21). The Psalms are impassioned, vivid and concrete; they are rich in images, in simile and metaphor. Assonance, alliteration and wordplays abound in the Hebrew text. Effective use of repetition and the piling up of synonyms and complements to fill out the picture are characteristic. Key words frequently highlight major themes in prayer or song. Enclosure (repetition of a significant word or phrase at the end that occurs at the beginning) frequently wraps up a composition or a unit within it. The notes on the structure of the individual psalms often call attention to literary frames within which the psalm has been set.

Hebrew poetry lacks rhyme and regular meter. Its most distinctive and pervasive feature is parallelism. Most poetic lines are composed of two (sometimes three) balanced segments (the balance is often loose, with the second segment commonly somewhat shorter than the first). The second segment either echoes (synonymous parallelism), contrasts (antithetic parallelism) or syntactically completes (synthetic parallelism) the first. These three types are generalizations and are not wholly adequate to describe the rich variety that the creativity of the poets has achieved within the basic two-segment line structure. When the second or third segment of a poetic line repeats, echoes or overlaps the content of the preceding segment, it usually intensifies or more sharply focuses the thought or its expression. The three major types of parallelism can serve, however, as rough distinctions that will assist the reader. In the NIV the second and third segments of a line are slightly indented relative to the first.

Determining where the Hebrew poetic lines or line segments begin or end (scanning) is sometimes an uncertain matter. Even the Septuagint at times scans the lines differently from the way the Hebrew texts now available to us do. It is therefore not surprising that modern translations occasionally differ.

A related problem is the extremely concise, often elliptical writing style of the Hebrew poets. The syntactical connection of words must at times be inferred simply from context. Where more than one possibility presents itself, translators are confronted with ambiguity. They are not always sure with which line segment a border word or phrase is to be read.

The stanza structure of Hebrew poetry is also a matter of dispute. Occasionally, recurring refrains mark off stanzas, as in Ps 42–43; 46; 57. In Ps 110 two balanced stanzas are divided by their introductory oracles (see also introduction to Ps 132), while Ps 119 devotes eight lines to each letter of the Hebrew alphabet. For the most part, however, no such obvious indicators are present. The NIV has used spaces to mark off poetic paragraphs (called "stanzas" in the notes). Usually this could be done with some confidence, and the reader is advised to be guided by them. But there are a few places where these divisions are questionable—and are challenged in the notes.

Close study of the Psalms discloses that the authors commonly composed each psalm with a full structural design in view. This is clearly true of the alphabetic acrostics, in which the poet devoted to each letter of the Hebrew alphabet one line segment (as in Ps 111–112), or a single line (as in Ps 25; 34; 145), or two lines (as in Ps 37), or eight lines (as in Ps 119). In addition Ps 33; 38; 103 each have 22 lines, no doubt because this equaled the number of letters in the Hebrew alphabet (see Introduction to Lamentations: Literary Features). The oft-voiced notion that this device was used as a memory aid seems culturally prejudiced and quite unwarranted. Actually people of that time were conditioned by their (more oral) culture to memorize far more readily than most people today. It is more likely that the alphabet—which was relatively recently invented as a simple system of symbols capable of representing in writing the rich and complex patterns of human speech and therefore of inscribing all that can be put into words (one of the greatest intellectual achievements of all time)—commended itself as a framework on which to hang significant thoughts.

Other forms were also used. Ps 44 is a prayer fashioned after the design of a ziggurat (a Babylonian stepped pyramid; see note on Ge 11:4). A sense of symmetry is pervasive. There are psalms that devote the same number of lines to each stanza (as Ps 12; 41), or do so with variation only in the introductory or concluding stanza (as Ps 38; 83; 94). Others match the opening and closing stanzas and balance those between (as Ps 33; 86). A particularly interesting device is to place a key thematic line at the very center, sometimes constructing the whole or part of the poem around that center (see note on 6:6). Still other design features are pointed out in the notes. The authors of the psalms crafted their compositions very carefully. They were heirs of an ancient art (in many details showing that they had inherited a poetic tradition that goes back hundreds of years), and they developed it to a state of high sophistication. Their works are best appreciated when carefully studied and pondered.

Theology: Introduction

The Psalter is for the most part a book of prayer and praise. In it faith speaks to God in prayer and of God in praise. But there are also psalms that are explicitly didactic (instructional) in form and purpose (teaching the way of godliness). As noted above (Collection, Arrangement and Date), the manner in which the whole collection has been arranged suggests that one of its main purposes was instruction in the life of faith, a faith formed and nurtured by the Law, the Prophets and the Writings. Accordingly, the Psalter is theologically rich. Its theology is, however, not abstract or systematic but doxological, confessional and practical. So a summation of that "theology" impoverishes it by translating it into an objective mode.

Furthermore, any summation faces a still greater problem. The Psalter is a large collection of independent pieces of many kinds, serving different purposes and composed over the course of many centuries. Not only must a brief summary of its "theology" be selective and incomplete; it will also of necessity be somewhat artificial. It will suggest that each psalm reflects or at least presupposes the "theology" outlined, that there is no "theological" tension or progression within the Psalter. Manifestly this is not so.

Still, the final editors of the Psalter were obviously not eclectic in their selection. They knew that many voices from many times spoke here, but none that in their judgment was incompatible with the Law and the Prophets. No doubt they also assumed that each psalm was to be understood in the light of the collection as a whole. That assumption we may share. Hence something, after all, can be said concerning seven major theological themes that, while admittedly a bit artificial, need not seriously distort and can be helpful to the student of the Psalms.

Theology: Major Themes

1. At the core of the theology of the Psalter is the conviction that the gravitational center of life (of right human understanding, trust, hope, service, morality, adoration), but also of history and of the whole creation (heaven and earth), is *God* (Yahweh, "the LORD"; see Dt 6:4 and note). He is *the Great King* over all, the One to whom all things are subject. He created all things and preserves them; they are the robe of glory with which he has clothed himself. Because he ordered them, they have a well-defined and "true" identity. Because he maintains them, they are sustained and kept secure from disruption, confusion or annihilation. Because he alone is the sovereign God, they are governed by one hand and held in the service of one divine purpose. Under God creation is not chaos but a cosmos — an orderly and systematic whole. What we distinguish as "nature" and history had for the psalmists one Lord, under whose rule all things worked together. Through the creation the Great King's majestic glory is displayed. He is good (wise, righteous, faithful, amazingly benevolent and merciful — evoking trust), and he is great (his knowledge, thoughts and works are beyond human comprehension — evoking reverent awe). By his good and lordly rule he is shown to be the Holy One.

2. As the Great King by right of creation and enduring absolute sovereignty, *he ultimately will not tolerate any worldly power that opposes or denies or ignores him.* He will come to rule the nations so that all will be compelled to acknowledge him. This expectation is no doubt the root and broadest scope of the psalmists' long view of the future. Because the Lord is the Great King beyond all challenge, *his righteous and peaceable kingdom will come, overwhelming all opposition* and purging the creation of all rebellion against his rule — such will be the ultimate outcome of history.

3. As the Great King on whom all creatures depend, *he opposes the "proud," those who rely on their own resources (and/or the gods they have contrived) to work out their own destiny.* These are the ones who ruthlessly wield whatever power they possess to attain worldly wealth, status and security; who are a law to themselves and exploit others as they will. In the Psalter, this kind of "pride" is the root of all evil. Those who embrace it, though they may seem to prosper, will be brought down to death, their final end. The "humble," the "poor and needy," those who acknowledge their dependence on the Lord in all things — these are the ones in whom God delights. Hence the "fear of the LORD" — i.e., humble trust in and obedience to the Lord — is the "beginning" of all wisdom (111:10). Ultimately, those who embrace it will inherit the earth. Not even death can hinder their seeing the face of God.

> *The Psalter was put into its final form by postexilic temple personnel, who completed it probably in the fourth century B.C. It has often been called the prayer book of the second (Zerubbabel's and Herod's) temple and was used in synagogues as well.*

The psalmists' hope for the future — the future of God and his kingdom and the future of the godly — was firm, though somewhat generalized. None of the psalmists gives expression to a two-age vision of the future (the present evil age giving way to a new age of righteousness and peace on the other side of a great eschatological divide). Such a view began to appear in the intertestamental literature — a view that had been foreshadowed by Daniel (see especially 12:2 – 3) and by Isaiah (see chs. 24 – 27; 65:17 – 25; 66:22 – 24) — and it later received full expression in the teaching of Jesus and the apostles. But this revelation was only a fuller development consistent with the hopes the psalmists lived by.

4. Because God is the Great King, *he is the ultimate Executor of justice among humans (to avenge oneself is an act of the "proud").* God is the court of appeal when persons are threatened or wronged — especially when no earthly court that he has established has jurisdiction (as in the case of international conflicts) or is able to judge (as when one is wronged by public slander) or is willing to act (out of fear or corruption). *He is the mighty and faithful Defender of the defenseless and the wronged.* He knows every deed and the secrets of every heart. There is no escaping his scrutiny. No false testimony will mislead him in judgment. And he hears the pleas brought to him. As the good and faithful Judge, he delivers those who are oppressed or wrongfully attacked and

redresses the wrongs committed against them (see note on 5:10). This is the unwavering conviction that accounts for the psalmists' impatient complaints when they boldly, yet as "poor and needy," cry to him, "Why, O LORD, (have you not yet delivered me)?" "How long, O LORD (before you act)?"

5. As the Great King over all the earth, *the Lord has chosen Israel to be his servant people, his "inheritance" among the nations.* He has delivered them by mighty acts out of the hands of the world powers, he has given them a land of their own (territory that he took from other nations to be his own "inheritance" in the earth), *and he has united them with himself in covenant as the initial embodiment of his redeemed kingdom.* Thus both their destiny and his honor came to be bound up with this relationship. *To them he also gave his word of revelation*, which testified of him, made specific his promises and proclaimed his will. By God's covenant, Israel was to live among the nations, loyal only to her heavenly King. She was to trust solely in his protection, hope in his promises, live in accordance with his will and worship him exclusively. She was to sing his praises to the whole world—which in a special sense revealed Israel's anticipatory role in the evangelization of the nations.

6. As the Great King, Israel's covenant Lord, *God chose David to be his royal representative on earth.* In this capacity, David was the Lord's "servant"—i.e., a member of the Great King's administration. The Lord himself anointed him and adopted him as his royal "son" to rule in his name. Through him God made his people secure in the promised land and subdued all the powers that threatened them. What is more, *he covenanted to preserve the Davidic dynasty.* Henceforth the kingdom of God on earth, while not dependent on the house of David, was linked to it by God's decision and commitment. In its continuity and strength lay Israel's security and hope as she faced a hostile world. And since the Davidic kings were God's royal representatives on earth, in concept seated at God's right hand (110:1), the scope of their rule was potentially worldwide (see Ps 2).

The Lord's anointed, however, was more than a warrior king. He was to be endowed by God to govern his people with godlike righteousness: to deliver the oppressed, defend the defenseless, suppress the wicked, and thus bless the nation with internal peace and prosperity. He was also an intercessor with God in behalf of the nation, the builder and maintainer of the temple (as God's earthly palace and the nation's house of prayer) and the foremost voice calling the nation to worship the Lord. It is perhaps with a view to these last duties that he is declared to be not only king but also "priest" (see Ps 110 and notes).

7. As the Great King, Israel's covenant Lord, *God* (who had chosen David and his dynasty to be his royal representatives) *also chose Jerusalem (the City of David) as his own royal city, the earthly seat of his throne. Thus Jerusalem (Zion) became the earthly capital (and symbol) of the kingdom of God. There in his palace (the temple) he sat enthroned among his people.* There his people could meet with him to bring their prayers and praise, and to see his power and glory. From there he brought salvation, dispensed blessings and judged the nations. And with him as the city's great Defender, Jerusalem was the secure citadel of the kingdom of God, the hope and joy of God's people.

God's goodwill and faithfulness toward his people were most strikingly symbolized by his pledged presence among them at his temple in Jerusalem, the "city of the Great King" (48:2). But no manifestation of his benevolence was greater than his readiness to forgive the sins of those who humbly confessed them and whose hearts showed him that their repentance was genuine and that their professions of loyalty to him had integrity. As they anguished over their own sinfulness, the psalmists remembered the ancient testimony of their covenant Lord: I am Yahweh ("the LORD"), "the compassionate and gracious God, slow to anger, abounding in love and faithfulness, maintaining love to thousands, and forgiving wickedness, rebellion and sin" (Ex 34:6–7). Only so did they dare to submit to him as his people, to "fear" him (see 130:3–4).

Theology: Summary, Messianic Import and Conclusion

Unquestionably the supreme kingship of Yahweh (in which he displays his transcendent greatness and goodness) is the most basic metaphor and most pervasive theological concept in the Psalter—as in the OT generally. It provides the fundamental perspective in which people are to view themselves, the whole creation, events in "nature" and history, and the future. All creation is Yahweh's one kingdom. To be a creature in the world is to be a part of his kingdom and under his rule. To be a human being in the world is to be dependent on and responsible to him. To proudly deny that fact is the root of all wickedness — the wickedness that now pervades the world.

God's election of Israel and subsequently of David and Zion, together with the giving of his word, represent the renewed inbreaking of God's righteous kingdom into this world of rebellion and evil. It initiates the great divide between the righteous nation and the wicked nations, and on a deeper level between the righteous and the wicked, a more significant distinction that cuts even through Israel. In the end this divine enterprise will triumph. Human pride will be humbled, and wrongs will be redressed. The humble will be given the whole earth to possess, and the righteous and peaceable kingdom of God will come to full realization. These theological themes, of course, have profound religious and moral implications. Of these, too, the psalmists spoke.

One question that ought yet to be addressed is: Do the Psalms speak of the Christ? Yes, in a variety of ways — but not as the prophets do. The Psalter was never numbered among the "prophetic" books. On the other hand, when the Psalter was being given its final form, what the psalms said about the Lord and his ways with his people, about the Lord and his ways with the nations, about the Lord and his ways with the righteous and the wicked, and what the psalmists said about the Lord's anointed, his temple and his holy city — all this was understood in light of the prophetic literature (both Former and Latter Prophets). Relative to these matters, the Psalter and the Prophets were mutually reinforcing and interpretive.

When the Psalms speak of the king on David's throne, they speak of the king who is being crowned (as in Ps 2; 72; 110 — though some think 110 is an exception) or is reigning (as in Ps 45) at the time. They proclaim his status as the Lord's anointed and declare what the Lord will accomplish through him and his dynasty. Thus they also speak of the sons of David to come — and in the exile and the postexilic era, when there was no reigning king, they spoke to Israel only of the great Son of David whom the prophets had announced as the one in whom God's covenant with David would yet be fulfilled. So the NT quotes these psalms as testimonies to Christ, which in their unique way they are. In him they are truly fulfilled.

When in the Psalms righteous sufferers — who are "righteous" because they are innocent, not having provoked or wronged their adversaries, and because they are among the "humble" who trust in the Lord — cry out to God in their distress (as in Ps 22; 69), they give voice to the sufferings of God's servants in a hostile and evil world.

These cries became the prayers of God's oppressed "saints," and as such they were taken up into Israel's book of prayers. When Christ came in the flesh, he identified himself with God's "humble" people in the world. He became for them God's righteous servant par excellence, and he shared their sufferings at the hands of the wicked. Thus these prayers became his prayers also — uniquely his prayers. In him the suffering and deliverance of which these prayers speak are fulfilled (though they continue to be the prayers also of those who take up their cross and follow him).

Similarly, in speaking of God's covenant people, of the city of God, and of the temple in which God dwells, the Psalms ultimately speak of Christ's church. The Psalter is not only the prayer book of the second temple; it is also the enduring prayer book of the people of God. Now, however, it must be used in the light of the new era of redemption that dawned with the first coming of the Messiah, the Christ, the anointed King (see note on 2:2), and that will be consummated at his second coming.

Significant Arrangement of the Psalter

Instruction in the Godly Life under the Reign of God

BOOK I

Ps 1–2 Introduction, framed by two **'ashre** ("Blessed is/are") declarations

1 Evokes instructions of *Torah* [Law] and *Ḥokmah* [Wisdom]

2 Evokes Former and Latter Prophets (Yahweh and his anointed, Israel's only hope in the turmoil of history)

Thus 1. The Psalter must be read in the context of the rest of the OT canon.

2. As portal to the temple of the Psalter, these two psalms teach that those who would appropriate the prayers and praises of the Psalter must fit the profile of the framing declarations; their lives must be shaped by Law and godly Wisdom, and they must "take refuge" in Yahweh and his anointed—the two basic components of "the fear of Yahweh."

Ps 3–14

64 lines

3 Plea for deliverance from foes

4 Plea for relief in time of drought

5 Plea for deliverance from foes

6 Plea for healing

7 Plea for deliverance from foes

8 Praise of the Creator (the glory of God bestowed on humans)

64 lines

9 Plea for deliverance from hostile nations

10 Plea for deliverance from the wicked

11 Trust in Yahweh's righteous rule

12 Plea for help in an ungodly time

13 Plea for deliverance from serious illness and enemies

14 The folly of humankind ("The LORD looks down . . . to see . . . All have turned aside")

Ps 15–24

15 Who has access to the temple?

16 Confession of trust in Yahweh

17 Plea for deliverance from foes

18 Royal praise for deliverance

24 Who may ascend the holy hill?

23 Confession of trust in Yahweh

22 Plea for deliverance from foes

20–21 Prayer for king's victory; praise for victory

19 Yahweh's glory in Creation and Torah

(The summer sun moving across the face of the sky from east to west)

Ps 25–33

25 Alphabetic acrostic
Prayer for covenant mercies

26 Prayer of a "blameless" one

27 Appeal against false accusers
"Be strong and take heart,
and wait for the LORD."

28 Prayer of one "going down to the pit"
"strength . . . strength," vv. 7-8

33 Alphabetic acrostic (blank)
Praise for God's good rule

32 Blessedness of a penitent

31 Appeal against false accusers
"Be strong and take heart,
all you who hope in the LORD."

30 Praise of one spared from "going down
into the pit" / "stand firm" (strong), v. 7

29 Praise of the King of creation

(The winter thunderstorm moving across the face of the sky from west to east)

Ps 34–37

34 Alphabetic acrostic
Instruction in godly wisdom

35 Appeal against malicious slanderers

37 Alphabetic acrostic
Instruction in godly wisdom

36 Appeal against threats of godless wicked

Ps 38–41

38 Prayer for relief from serious illness and enemies: a confession of sin

39 Prayer for relief from serious illness and enemies: a confession of sin

40 Prayer for relief from troubles (serious illness?) and enemies: a confession of sin

41 Prayer for relief from serious illness and enemies: a confession of sin

40:4 'Ashre [Blessed is] the one who "makes the LORD his trust."

41:1 'Ashre [Blessed is] the one who "has regard for the weak."

BOOK II

Ps 42–45 Three prayers with a royal psalm attached (see Ps 69–72)

42 Prayer of individual ("Why have you forgotten me" in the face of the "oppression" of enemies?)

43 Continuation of Ps 42

44 Prayer of the community ("Why do you hide your face and forget our . . . oppression?")

45 Song in praise of the king on a day of his glory (wedding to a foreign princess)

("... ride forth . . . in behalf of truth, humility and righteousness")

("Your throne . . . will last for ever and ever")

Ps 46–48 In celebration of the security of Zion

46 Zion's security

47 Zion's Great King triumphant over all nations

48 Zion's security

Ps 49–53 The proper posture before God

49 The folly of those who "trust in their wealth" / "boast of their great riches"

50 God calls his people to account

51 Humble prayer for forgiveness and cleansing

52 The folly of the one who "trusted in his great wealth" / "boasted" in his evil ways

53 The folly of those who live as if there is no God (repeat of Ps 14)

Ps 54–60 Seven prayers at the center of Book II (Main weapon in Ps 54–59 is the mouth)

54 Prayer of individual for help against enemies (formally paradigmatic)

55 Prayer for help: a conspiracy in Jerusalem ("they prowl about on its walls")

("words...are drawn **swords**")

56 Prayer for help against enemies

57 Prayer for deliverance from enemies (May "God Most High" "be exalted")

("tongues are sharp **swords**")

58 Prayer for the heavenly Judge to set right what human rulers have not

59 Prayer for help: enemies surround Jerusalem ("they . . . prowl about the city")

("spew out **swords** from their lips")

60 Prayer of community for help after suffering devastating defeat (cf. Ps 44)

("you...have rejected us and no longer go out with our armies")

Ps 61–64 Four royal prayers with interweaving themes

61 Appeal for restoration to God's presence ("rock," "refuge," "strong tower," "in the shelter of your wings")

62 Appeal for deliverance from arrogant foes ("rock," "fortress," "mighty rock," "refuge"; "Surely you will reward each person according to what he has done")

63 Appeal for God's refreshing presence when threatened by enemies ("sing in the shadow of your wings"; "They who seek my life . . . will go down to the depths of the earth")

64 Appeal for God's protection against conspirators ("they shoot . . . suddenly . . . / God will shoot them . . . suddenly")

Ps 65–68 God's "awesome deeds" evoke the praise of "all...the earth"

65 God's blessing the earth into fruitfulness is highlighted ("the hope of all the ends of the earth")

66 God's saving acts on behalf of Israel are highlighted ("Shout with joy to God, all the earth!")

67 God's blessing the earth into fruitfulness is highlighted ("all the peoples praise . . . all the ends of the earth . . . fear")

68 God's saving acts in behalf of Israel are highlighted ("kings . . . bring you gifts . . . Sing to God, kingdoms of the earth")

Ps 69–72 Three prayers with a royal psalm attached (see Ps 42-45)

69 A king's prayer for deliverance when under vicious attack

70 A short prayer (repeat of Ps 40; see introduction to Ps 71)

71 A king's prayer for God's help in old age when under attack

72 A prayer that the king be specially gifted to rule justly

("... endure . . . through all generations")

("... all nations . . . be blessed through him")

BOOK III

Made up of three groups of six psalms (73–78), five psalms (79–83), six psalms (84–89)

Ps 73–78

73 Instruction based on individual experience

74 Communal prayer: God has "rejected" his people

75 Thanks to God: His "Name is near," and he "cuts off" the horns of the wicked but causes the "horns of the righteous" to be "lifted up."

76 Celebration: God's "name is great in Israel"; he "breaks the spirit of the [enemy] rulers."

77 Individual prayer: God has "rejected" him

78 Instruction based on communal experience

Ps 79–83

79 Communal prayer: when invaded by fierce enemies

80 Prayer for God to restore his people after they have been ravaged by enemies

81 Exhortation to Israel: "if Israel would follow my ways, how quickly would I subdue their enemies"

82 Prayer for God to judge the wicked rulers of the earth

83 Communal prayer: when attacked by coalition of enemies

Ps 84–89

84 Expression of yearning for "the courts of the LORD" and prayer for God to "look with favor" on "our shield," "your anointed"

85 Prayer for God to "restore" his people from some situation of distress

86 Individual prayer for God's help when under attack by enemies

87 Song celebrating God's special love for Zion and care for its citizens

88 Individual prayer for God to remove his wrath and deliver from death

89 Prayer for God to rescue his people, to remember his covenant with David

BOOKS IV AND V

Ps 90–100 Eleven psalms framed by "Adonai . . . our dwelling place throughout all generations" (90:1) and "Yahweh . . . his love . . . faithfulness continues through all generations" (100:5)

90 Plaintive prayer concerning the mortality of those who have long had the Lord as their "dwelling place"

91 Assurances for those who make the Most High their "dwelling" place (v. 9; cf. v. 1): "With long life will I satisfy" them (v. 16)

92 Celebration of Yahweh's righteous rule and its result (what the "senseless" do not know): "evildoers...will be forever destroyed" but "the righteous...will still bear fruit in old age"

93 Celebration of the invincible reign of Yahweh

94 Appeal to Yahweh to deal judicially with those who perpetrate injustices and oppression: "take heed, you senseless ones among the people"

95 Call for the delivered covenant community to joyfully worship Yahweh their God (and warning not to repeat earlier rebelliousness)

96 Call to all nations to worshipfully celebrate the universal reign of Yahweh—and its "coming"

97 Joyful celebration of Yahweh's universal reign—whose throne is founded on "righteousness and justice"

98 Call to all nations to worshipfully praise Yahweh for his saving acts in behalf of Israel—his reign is "coming"

99 Joyful celebration of Yahweh's universal reign, especially for what he has done for Israel

100 Concluding exhortation to worshipfully praise Yahweh, Israel's Maker and "good" Shepherd-King

BOOKS IV AND V, cont.

Ps 101–110 A "little psalter" framed by two royal psalms

101 A royal pledge to reign righteously — 110 Oracles concerning the Messianic King-Priest

102 Individual Lament — 109 Individual Lament

103 Praise of Yahweh for his "great love" — 108 Praise of Yahweh for his "great love"

104 Praise of Yahweh the Creator — 107 Call for praise of Yahweh who hears cries of distress

105 Recital of Israel's saving history — 106 Recital of Israel's history of rebellion

Ps 111–119 The "Egyptian Hallel" framed by 111/112 and 119

111/112 Formal and thematic twins: Righteous God (111:3) and God-fearing person, "who finds great delight in his (God's) commands" (112:1)

Egyptian Hallel

113

114 *Psalms used*

115 *in Israel's*

116 *great annual*

117 *festivals*

118

119 Prayer of one who "finds delight" in God's "commands" (v. 35)

Ps 120–137 Songs of Ascents plus two Appendices

120–134 The "Songs of Ascents"

135–136 Hymns traditionally associated by the Jews with the Songs of Ascents

137 Song of love for Zion by one returned from Babylonian exile (brings closure to the preceding collection)

Ps 138–145 Eight psalms assigned to David: prayers framed by praise

138 Praise of Yahweh: "When I called, you answered"; "May all the kings . . . praise you . . . for (your) glory"

139 Acknowledgment of total nakedness before the omniscient and omnipresent God

140–144 Five prayers for deliverance from:

140: evil men, men of violence, the wicked

141: evildoers

142: pursuers who "are too strong for me"

143: enemies

144: foreigners

145 (Acrostic) Praise of Yahweh, "the King": who "is near to all who call on him"; "All you have made will . . . tell of the glory of your kingdom . . . so that all . . . may know of . . . the glorious splendor of your kingdom."

Ps 146–150 Five Hallelujah psalms that conclude the Psalter

BOOK I

Psalms 1–41

Psalm 1

[1]Blessed is the man[a]
who does not walk[b] in the counsel
of the wicked[c]
or stand in the way[d] of sinners[e]
or sit[f] in the seat of mockers.[g]
[2]But his delight[h] is in the law of the
LORD,[i]
and on his law he meditates[j] day
and night.
[3]He is like a tree[k] planted by streams[l] of
water,[m]
which yields its fruit[n] in season
and whose leaf[o] does not wither.
Whatever he does prospers.[p]

[4]Not so the wicked!
They are like chaff[q]
that the wind blows away.
[5]Therefore the wicked will not stand[r] in
the judgment,[s]
nor sinners in the assembly[t] of the
righteous.

[6]For the LORD watches over[u] the way of
the righteous,
but the way of the wicked will
perish.[v]

Psalm 2

[1]Why do the nations conspire[a]
and the peoples plot[w] in vain?

[a] *1* Hebrew; Septuagint *rage*

1:1 [a]S Dt 33:29; Ps 40:4; 128:4 [b]Ps 89:15 [c]S Job 21:16; Ps 10:2-11 [d]S Ge 49:6 [e]Ps 26:9; 37:38; 51:13; 104:35 [f]Ps 26:4 [g]S Job 11:3; Pr 1:22; Isa 28:14; Hos 7:5 **1:2** [h]Ps 112:1; 119:16, 35; Ro 7:22 [i]Ps 19:7; 119:1; Eze 11:20; 18:17 [j]S Ge 24:63 **1:3** [k]Ps 52:8; 92:12; 128:3; Jer 11:16; Zec 4:3 [l]Ps 46:4; 65:9; Isa 33:21; Jer 31:9 [m]S Nu 24:6; S Job 14:9; S Eze 17:5 [n]Ps 92:14; Eze 47:12 [o]Isa 1:30; 64:6 [p]S Ge 39:3 **1:4** [q]S Job 13:25; Isa 40:24; Jer 13:24 **1:5** [r]Ps 5:5 [s]S Job 19:29 [t]Ps 26:12; 35:18; 82:1; 89:5; 107:32; 111:1; 149:1 **1:6** [u]Ps 37:18; 121:5; 145:20; Na 1:7 [v]S Lev 26:38; Ps 9:6 **2:1** [w]Ps 21:11; 83:5; Pr 24:2

Ps 1–2 These two "orphan" psalms (having no title) are bound together by framing clauses ("Blessed is the man ... [whose] delight is in the law of the LORD"; "Blessed are all who take refuge in him") that highlight their function as the introduction to the whole Psalter. Together they point on the one hand to God's law and to the instruction of the wisdom teachers (Ps 1) and on the other hand to a central theme in the Prophets, both Former and Latter, namely, what Yahweh has committed himself to accomplish for and through his anointed king from the house of David (Ps 2). In this way these two psalms link the Psalter with the rest of the OT literature and alert those who take it in hand that to hear the psalms aright they must be understood within that larger frame of reference. At the same time, as the port of entry into the Psalter, Ps 1–2 make clear that those who would find their own voice in the psalms and so would appropriate them as testimonies to their own faith must fit the profile of those called "blessed" here. See also note on Ps 40–41.

Ps 1 Author and date unknown. Godly wisdom here declares the final outcome of the two "ways": "the way of sinners" (v. 1) and "the way of the righteous" (v. 6). See 34:19–22; 37; see also essay, p. 727. The psalmist develops three contrasts that set the righteous apart from the wicked: (1) as to their "way" of life (vv.1–2); (2) as to the life conditions they experience ("like a tree," "like chaff," vv. 3–4); and, climactically, (3) as to God's judgment on their different "ways" (vv. 5–6). As part of the introduction to the Psalter, this psalm reminds the reader (1) that those of whom the Psalms speak (using various terms) as the people of God, those whom he receives in his presence and favors with his salvation and blessing, must be characterized by delight in God's revealed will—those who stubbornly choose the way of sinners have no place among them (v. 5; see Ps 15; 24)—and (2) that the godly piety that speaks in the Psalms is a faithful response to God's revealed (and written) directives for life—which is the path that leads to blessedness. For a prime indicator of the psalm's central theme cf. the first and last words, which frame the whole ("Blessed ... perish").

1:1 Speaks progressively of association with the ungodly and participation in their ungodly ways. *Blessed.* The happy condition of those who revere the Lord and do his will (see 94:12; 112:1; 119:1–2; 128:1; Pr 29:18; cf. Ps 41:1; 106:3; Pr 14:21; Isa 56:2) and who put their trust in him (see 40:4; 84:5,12; 144:15; 146:5; Pr 16:20; Isa 30:18; Jer 17:7; cf. Ps 2:12; 34:8). Reference is not first of all to health and wealth but to the assurance and experience that they live under the guardianship and faithful care of the gracious Lord of life. The Psalter begins by proclaiming the blessedness of the godly and ends by calling all living things to praise God in his earthly and heavenly sanctuaries (Ps 150). *walk in.* Order one's life according to. *counsel.* Plans and/or advice (see Pr 1:10–19). *stand.* Position oneself. *sinners.* Those for whom wickedness is habitual—a way of life (see v. 5). *sit.* Settle oneself. *mockers.* Those who ridicule God and defiantly reject his law (see Pr 1:22 and note).

1:2 *on his law he meditates.* Seeking guidance for life in God's law rather than in the deliberations of the wicked. *day and night.* See Jos 1:8.

1:3 *like a tree ... does not wither.* See Jer 17:8; a simile of the blessedness of the righteous. Such a tree withstands the buffeting of the winds and, flourishing, blesses people, animals and birds with its unfailing fruit and shade.

1:4 *like chaff ... blows away.* A simile of the wretchedness of the wicked. Chaff is carried away by the lightest wind, and its removal brings about cleansing by extracting what is utterly useless (see note on Ru 1:22).

1:5 *will not stand in the judgment.* Will not be able to withstand God's wrath when he judges (see 76:7; 130:3; Ezr 9:15; Na 1:6 and note; Mal 3:2; Mt 25:31–46; Rev 6:17). *assembly.* The worshiping assembly at God's sanctuary (as in 22:25; 26:12; 35:18; 40:9–10; 111:1; 149:1; see Ps 15; 24). *righteous.* One of several terms in the OT for God's people; it presents them as those who honor God and order their lives in all things according to his will. In every human relationship they faithfully fulfill the obligations that the relationship entails, remembering that power and authority (of whatever sort: domestic, social, political, economic, religious, intellectual) are to be used to bless, not to exploit.

1:6 *way ... way.* What is here said of the two "ways" applies by implication also to those who choose them (see 37:20; cf. Mt 7:13–14).

Ps 2 Author and date unknown (Peter and John ascribed it to David in Ac 4:25—possibly in accordance with the Jewish practice of honoring David as the primary author of the Psalter). A royal psalm, it was originally composed for the coronation of Davidic kings in light of the Lord's covenant with David (see 2Sa 7). Later, prophetic words of judgment against the house of David and announcements of God's future redemption of his people through an exalted royal son of David highlighted the Messianic import of this psalm. As the second half of a two-part introduction to the Psalms, it proclaims the blessedness of all who acknowledge the lordship

2 The kings[x] of the earth take their stand
and the rulers gather together
against the LORD
and against his Anointed[y] One.[a z]
3 "Let us break their chains,[a]" they say,
"and throw off their fetters."[b]

4 The One enthroned[c] in heaven laughs;[d]
the Lord scoffs at them.
5 Then he rebukes them in his anger[e]
and terrifies them in his wrath,[f]
saying,
6 "I have installed my King[b g]
on Zion,[h] my holy hill.[i]"

7 I will proclaim the decree of the LORD:

He said to me, "You are my Son[c];[j]
today I have become your Father.[d k]
8 Ask of me,
and I will make the nations[l] your
inheritance,[m]
the ends of the earth[n] your
possession.
9 You will rule them with an iron
scepter[e];[o]
you will dash them to pieces[p] like
pottery.[q]"

10 Therefore, you kings, be wise;[r]
be warned, you rulers[s] of the earth.
11 Serve the LORD with fear[t]
and rejoice[u] with trembling.[v]
12 Kiss the Son,[w] lest he be angry
and you be destroyed in your way,
for his wrath[x] can flare up in a
moment.
Blessed[y] are all who take refuge[z] in
him.

Psalm 3

A psalm of David. When he fled from
his son Absalom.[a]

1 O LORD, how many are my foes!
How many rise up against me!

[a] 2 Or *anointed one* [b] 6 Or *king* [c] 7 Or *son*; also in verse 12 [d] 7 Or *have begotten you* [e] 9 Or *will break them with a rod of iron*

2:2 [x] Ps 48:4 [y] S 1Sa 9:16; Jn 1:41 [z] Ac 4:25-26* **2:3** [a] S Job 36:8 [b] S 2Sa 3:34 **2:4** [c] Isa 37:16; 40:22; 66:1 [d] Ps 37:13; Pr 1:26 **2:5** [e] Ps 6:1; 27:9; 38:1 [f] Ps 21:9; 79:6; 90:7; 110:5 **2:6** [g] Ps 10:16; 24:10 [h] 2Ki 19:31; Ps 9:11; 48:2, 11; 78:68; 110:2; 133:3 [i] S Ex 15:17 **2:7** [j] S Mt 3:17; S 4:3 [k] S 2Sa 7:14; Ac 13:33*; Heb 1:5*; 5:5* **2:8** [l] Rev 2:26 [m] S Job 22:26; Mt 21:38 [n] Ps 22:27; 67:7 **2:9** [o] S Ge 49:10; Rev 12:5 [p] S Ex 15:6 [q] Isa 30:14; Jer 19:10; Rev 2:27*; 19:15 **2:10** [r] Pr 27:11 [s] Ps 141:6; Pr 8:15; Am 2:3 **2:11** [t] Ps 103:11 [u] Ps 9:2; 35:9; 104:34; Isa 61:10 [v] S 1Ch 16:30 **2:12** [w] ver 7 [x] S Dt 9:8; Rev 6:16 [y] Ps 84:12 [z] Ps 5:11; 34:8; 64:10 **3:Title** [a] 2Sa 15:14

of God and his anointed and "take refuge in him" (v. 12; see introductions to Ps 1 – 2 and Ps 1; see also note on 1:1) — as does the godly piety that speaks in the Psalms. This psalm is frequently quoted in the NT, where it is applied typologically to Christ as the great Son of David and God's Anointed.

Four balanced stanzas of three poetic lines each are divided at the center by a short prose line that serves as a thematic hinge. Stanzas two and three contain oracles from the heavenly King that warrant the warning to the "kings" (v. 10) whose rebellion (v. 2) is the focus of the first stanza.

2:1 – 3 The nations and their kings rebel. In the ancient Near East the coronation of a new king was often the occasion for the revolt of peoples and kings who had been subject to the crown. The newly anointed king is here pictured as ruler over an empire.

2:1 – 2 For a NT application see Ac 4:25 – 28.

2:1 *Why . . . ?* A rhetorical question that implies "How dare they!"

2:2 *LORD . . . his Anointed One.* To rebel against the Lord's Anointed is also to rebel against the One who anointed him. *Anointed One.* See NIV text notes here and on vv. 6 – 7. The psalm refers to the Davidic king and is ultimately fulfilled in Christ. The English word "Messiah" comes from the Hebrew word for "anointed one," and the English word "Christ" from the Greek word for "anointed one" (see NIV text note on Mt 1:17).

2:4 – 6 The Lord mocks the rebels. With derisive laughter the Lord meets the confederacy of rebellious world powers with the sovereign declaration that it is he who has established the Davidic king in his own royal city of Zion (Jerusalem).

2:4 See 59:8.

2:5 *anger . . . wrath.* God's anger is always an expression of his righteousness (see 7:11; see also note on 4:1).

2:6 *holy hill.* The site of the Jerusalem temple (see 2Ch 33:15); see also 3:4; 15:1; 43:3 ("holy mountain"); 99:9 ("holy mountain").

2:7 – 9 The Lord's Anointed proclaims the Lord's coronation decree. For NT application to Jesus' resurrection see Ac 13:33; to his superiority over angels see Heb 1:5; to his appointment as high priest see Heb 5:5.

2:7 *Son . . . Father.* In the ancient Near East the relationship between a great king and one of his subject kings, who ruled by his authority and owed him allegiance, was expressed not only by the words "lord" and "servant" but also by "father" and "son." The Davidic king was the Lord's "servant" and his "son" (2Sa 7:5,14).

2:8 *your inheritance.* Your domain — just as the promised land was the Lord's "inheritance" (Ex 15:17; see Jos 22:19; Ps 28:9; 79:1; 82:8). *ends of the earth.* Ultimately the rule of the Lord's Anointed will extend as far as the rule of God himself.

2:9 According to Rev 12:5; 19:15 – 16 this word will be fulfilled in the triumphant reign of Christ; in Rev 2:26 – 27 Christ declares that he will appoint those who remain faithful to him to share in his subjugating rule over the nations. *dash them to pieces like pottery.* See Jer 19:11.

2:10 – 12 The rebellious rulers are warned.

2:11 *rejoice.* Hail the Lord as King with joy. *trembling.* Awe and reverence.

2:12 *Kiss.* As a sign of submission (see 1Sa 10:1; 1Ki 19:18; Hos 13:2; see also note on Ge 41:40). Submission to an Assyrian king was expressed by kissing his feet. *he . . . his . . . him.* Most likely the reference is to "the LORD" (v. 11), who anointed "the Son." *destroyed in your way.* See 1:6 and note. *Blessed.* See 1:1 and note. *take refuge.* See 5:11; 34:8; 64:10; cf. 104:18.

Ps 3 – 14 A group of 12 psalms composed of ten prayers (but see introduction to Ps 11), divided into two groups of five (Ps 3 – 7; 9 – 13), each of which has appended to it a sixth that characterizes the human condition (Ps 8; 14). For the sharp contrast between these two characterizations and how their complementary depictions of humankind bear on the collection of prayers to which they have been attached, see introductions to Ps 8; 14.

Ps 3 Though threatened by many foes, the psalmist prays confidently to the Lord. Ps 3 and 4 are linked by references to glory (see v. 3; 4:2; see also NIV text notes on both verses) and to David's sleep at night (see v. 5; 4:8). In v. 5 David speaks of the assurance of his waking in the morning because the Lord will keep him while he sleeps; in 4:8 he speaks of the inner quietness with which he goes to sleep because of the Lord's care. This juxtaposition of prayers with references to waking (morning) and sleeping (evening) at the beginning of the Psalter suggests that God's faithful care sustains the godly day and night whatever the need or circumstances.

3 title *When he fled.* See 2Sa 15:13 — 17:22. References to

Types of Hebrew Parallelism

Type	Characteristic	Example
I. Synonymous	Repetition of same thought	
Identical	Each element is synonymous	Ps 24:1: The earth is the LORD's, and everything in it, the world, and all who live in it.
Similar	Each element is similar	Ps 19:2: Day after day they pour forth speech; night after night they display knowledge.
Incomplete	Second element of previous line is repeated	Jer 17:9: The heart is deceitful above all things and beyond cure. Who can understand it?
Continued	Second element is repeated and built upon	Ps 24:5: He will receive blessing from the LORD, and vindication from God his Savior.
II. Antithetic	Parallel by contrast (by use of the opposite)	Ps 1:6: For the LORD watches over the way of the righteous, but the way of the wicked will perish.
III. Synthetic	Building on a thought	
Completion	Completes a thought	Ps 2:6: I have installed my king on Zion, my holy hill.
Comparison	Draws an analogy	Pr 15:17: Better is a meal of vegetables where there is love than a fattened calf with turmoil.
Reason	Gives a reason	Pr 26:4: Do not answer a fool according to his folly, or you will be like him yourself.
Conceptual	Use of theme element	Ps 1:1: Blessed is the man who does not walk in the counsel of the wicked or stand in the way of sinners or sit in the seat of mockers.
IV. Climactic	Builds on same word	Ps 29:1: Ascribe to the LORD, O mighty ones, Ascribe to the LORD glory and strength.
V. Emblematic	Use of simile or metaphor	Ps 42:1: As the deer pants for streams of water, so my soul pants for you, O God. Pr 25:25: Like cold water to a weary soul is good news from a distant land.

[2]Many are saying of me,
"God will not deliver him.[b]" *Selah*[a]
[3]But you are a shield[c] around me,
O LORD;
you bestow glory on me and lift[b] up
my head.[d]
[4]To the LORD I cry aloud,[e]
and he answers me from his holy
hill.[f] *Selah*
[5]I lie down and sleep;[g]
I wake again,[h] because the LORD
sustains me.
[6]I will not fear[i] the tens of thousands
drawn up against me on every side.[j]
[7]Arise,[k] O LORD!
Deliver me,[l] O my God!
Strike[m] all my enemies on the jaw;
break the teeth[n] of the wicked.
[8]From the LORD comes deliverance.[o]
May your blessing[p] be on your
people. *Selah*

3:2 [b]Ps 22:8; 71:11; Isa 36:15; 37:20 **3:3** [c]S Ge 15:1 [d]Ps 27:6 **3:4** [e]S Job 30:20 [f]Ps 2:6 **3:5** [g]S Lev 26:6 [h]Ps 17:15; 139:18 **3:6** [i]Job 11:15; Ps 23:4; 27:3 [j]Ps 118:11 **3:7** [k]S 2Ch 6:41 [l]Ps 6:4; 7:1; 59:1; 109:21; 119:153; Isa 25:9; 33:22; 35:4; 36:15; 37:20; Jer 42:11; Mt 6:13 [m]Job 16:10 [n]Job 29:17; Ps 57:4; Pr 30:14; La 3:16 **3:8** [o]Ps 27:1; 37:39; 62:1; Isa 43:3,11; 44:6,8; 45:21; Hos 13:4; Jnh 2:9; Rev 7:10 [p]Nu 6:23; Ps 29:11; 129:8

Psalm 4

For the director of music.
With stringed instruments.
A psalm of David.

[1]Answer me[q] when I call to you,
O my righteous God.
Give me relief from my distress;[r]
be merciful[s] to me and hear my
prayer.[t]
[2]How long, O men, will you turn my
glory[u] into shame[c]?[v]
How long will you love delusions
and seek false gods[d]?[w] *Selah*

[a] 2 A word of uncertain meaning, occurring frequently in the Psalms; possibly a musical term [b] 3 Or *LORD, / my Glorious One, who lifts* [c] 2 Or *you dishonor my Glorious One* [d] 2 Or *seek lies*

4:1 [q]Ps 13:3; 27:7; 69:16; 86:7; 102:2 [r]S Ge 32:7; S Jdg 2:15 [s]Ps 30:10 [t]Ps 17:6; 54:2; 84:8; 88:2 **4:2** [u]Ex 16:7; 1Sa 4:21 [v]2Ki 19:26; Job 8:22; Ps 35:26 [w]Jdg 2:17; Ps 31:6; 40:4; Jer 13:25; 16:19; Am 2:4

events in David's life stand in the superscriptions of 13 psalms (3; 7; 18; 34; 51–52; 54; 56–57; 59–60; 63; 142), all but one (Ps 142) in Books I and II. See Introduction: Authorship and Titles (or Superscriptions).

3:1–2 David's need: threatened by many foes.

3:2 See 22:7–8; 71:10–11. The psalmists frequently quote their wicked oppressors in order to portray how they mock (see note on 1:1) God and his servants (see note on 10:11). *Selah.* See NIV text note; see also Introduction: Authorship and Titles (or Superscriptions).

3:3–4 David's confidence in God, who does not fail to answer his prayers.

3:3 Contains a strong thematic link with Ps 2. *shield.* That the king is a shield (protector) of his people was a common concept in ancient Israel (see NIV text notes on 7:10; 47:9; 59:11; 84:9; 89:18; Ge 15:1). That the Lord is the shield of his people is frequently asserted (see 84:11; 91:4; 115:9–11; Dt 33:29; Pr 30:5) or claimed (see 18:2,30; 28:7; 33:20; 119:114; 144:2). *you bestow glory on me.* David rejoices in the Lord as his provider and protector who has raised him to a position of honor. See NIV text note. *lift up my head.* In victory over his enemies (see 110:7).

3:4 *I cry ... he answers.* See note on 118:5. *holy hill.* The place of the Lord's sanctuary, the earthly counterpart of his heavenly throne room (see note on 2:6).

3:5–6 David's sense of security.

3:5 Even while David's own watchfulness is surrendered to sleep, the watchful Lord preserves him (see 4:8).

3:7–8 David's prayer.

3:7 *Arise ... Deliver.* Hebrew idiom frequently prefaces an imperative calling for immediate action with a call to "arise" (see Ex 12:31, "Up!"; Dt 2:13; Jdg 7:9, "Get up"). In poetry the two imperatives of the idiom are often distributed between the two halves of the Hebrew poetic line. Hence David's prayer is: "Arise (and) deliver me." *LORD ... my God.* That is, LORD my God; the two elements of a compound divine name are also frequently distributed between the two halves of a poetic line. *break the teeth.* Probably likening the enemies to wild animals (see note on 7:2).

3:8 *From the LORD comes deliverance.* A common feature in the prayers of the Psalter is a concluding expression of confidence that the prayer will be or has been heard (as in 6:8–10; 7:10–17; 10:16–18; 12:7; 13:5–6 and often elsewhere; see note on 12:5–6). Here David's confidence becomes a testimony to God's people. *May your blessing be on your people.* See 25:22; 28:8–9; 51:18. Those anointed by God to rule in Israel stood before the heavenly King as his servants responsible for the well-being of his people.

Ps 4 A prayer for relief from the threat of slanderers who falsely blame the king for some calamity (possibly a drought; see v. 7) that has stricken the nation, thereby undermining his public standing (his "glory," v. 2) and endangering the very security of his throne. Those spreading falsehoods (see v. 2 and note) appear to have looked to the king to preserve the nation from all disasters rather than to the Lord. See introductions to Ps 3 and 5 for links with those psalms.

4 title See Hab 3:19. *For the director of music.* Probably a liturgical notation, indicating either that the psalm was to be added to the collection of works to be used by the director of music in Israel's worship services, or that when the psalm was used in the temple worship it was to be spoken by the leader of the Levitical choir—or by the choir itself (see 1Ch 23:5,30; 25; Ne 11:17). In this liturgical activity the Levites functioned as representatives of the worshiping congregation. Following their lead the people probably responded with "Amen" and "Praise the LORD" (Hallelujah); see 1Ch 16:36; Ne 5:13; cf. 1Co 14:16; Rev 5:14; 7:12; 19:4. *With stringed instruments.* See Ps 6; 54; 55; 61; 67; 76 titles (cf. Hab 3:19 and note). This is a liturgical notation, indicating that the Levites were to accompany the psalm with harp and lyre (see 1Ch 23:5; 25:1,3,6; cf. Ps 33:2; 43:4; 71:22; see also notes on Ps 39; 42 titles).

4:1 Initial request to be heard. *Answer me when I call.* See note on 118:5. *righteous God.* Very often the "righteousness" of God in the Psalms (and frequently elsewhere in the OT) refers to the faithfulness with which he acts. This faithfulness is in full accordance with his commitments to his people and with his status as the divine King—to whom the powerless may look for protection, the oppressed for redress and the needy for help. *Give me relief.* Lit. "Make a spacious place for me" (see 18:19 and note). *my distress.* The threat of being publicly discredited by the slander of those who blame him for the nation's troubles.

4:2–3 David challenges those who have turned on him and warns them that the Lord will hear his prayer for deliverance from their attacks (see note on 5:9).

4:2 *How long ...?* See Introduction: Theology: Major Themes, 4; see also note on 6:3. *turn my glory into shame.* That is, through slander rob David of the public honor he had en-

[3]Know that the LORD has set apart the
godly[x] for himself;
the LORD will hear[y] when I call to him.
[4]In your anger do not sin;[z]
when you are on your beds,[a]
search your hearts and be silent.
Selah
[5]Offer right sacrifices
and trust in the LORD.[b]
[6]Many are asking, "Who can show us
any good?"
Let the light of your face shine upon
us,[c] O LORD.
[7]You have filled my heart[d] with greater
joy[e]
than when their grain and new wine[f]
abound.
[8]I will lie down and sleep[g] in peace,[h]
for you alone, O LORD,
make me dwell in safety.[i]

Psalm 5

For the director of music. For flutes.
A psalm of David.

[1]Give ear[j] to my words, O LORD,
consider my sighing.[k]
[2]Listen to my cry for help,[l]
my King and my God,[m]
for to you I pray.
[3]In the morning,[n] O LORD, you hear my
voice;
in the morning I lay my requests
before you
and wait in expectation.[o]
[4]You are not a God who takes pleasure
in evil;
with you the wicked[p] cannot
dwell.
[5]The arrogant[q] cannot stand[r] in your
presence;
you hate[s] all who do wrong.
[6]You destroy those who tell lies;[t]
bloodthirsty and deceitful men
the LORD abhors.
[7]But I, by your great mercy,
will come into your house;
in reverence[u] will I bow down[v]
toward your holy temple.[w]
[8]Lead me, O LORD, in your
righteousness[x]
because of my enemies—
make straight your way[y] before me.
[9]Not a word from their mouth can be
trusted;
their heart is filled with destruction.

4:3 [x]Ps 12:1; 30:4; 31:23; 79:2; Mic 7:2; 1Ti 4:7; 2Pe 3:11 [y]Ps 6:8; Mic 7:7 **4:4** [z]Eph 4:26* [a]Ps 63:6; Da 2:28 **4:5** [b]Ps 31:6; 115:9; Pr 3:5; 28:26; Isa 26:4; Jn 14:1 **4:6** [c]Nu 6:25 **4:7** [d]Ac 14:17 [e]Isa 9:3; 35:10; 65:14, 18 [f]S Ge 27:28; S Dt 28:51 **4:8** [g]S Lev 26:6 [h]S Nu 6:26; S Job 11:18 [i]S Dt 33:28; S Jer 32:37 **5:1** [j]S 1Ki 8:29; Ps 17:1; 40:1; 116:2; Da 9:18 [k]Ps 38:9; Isa 35:10; 51:11 **5:2** [l]S Job 19:7; S 24:12; S 36:5 [m]Ps 44:4; 68:24; 84:3 **5:3** [n]Isa 28:19; 50:4; Jer 21:12; Eze 46:13; Zep 3:5 [o]Ps 62:1; 119:81; 130:5; Hab 2:1; Ro 8:19 **5:4** [p]Ps 1:5; 11:5; 104:35; Pr 2:22 **5:5** [q]2Ki 19:32; Ps 73:3; 75:4; Isa 33:19; 37:33 [r]Ps 1:5 [s]Ps 45:7; 101:3; 119:104; Pr 8:13 **5:6** [t]Pr 19:22; S Jn 8:44; Ac 5:3; Rev 21:8 **5:7** [u]Dt 13:4; Jer 44:10; Da 6:26 [v]S 2Sa 12:16; Ps 138:2 [w]S 1Ki 8:48 **5:8** [x]Ps 23:3; 31:1; 71:2; 85:13; 89:16; Pr 8:20 [y]S 1Ki 8:36; Jn 1:23

joyed under the Lord's blessing and care (see 3:3 and note) and bring him into public disrepute (but see NIV text note). *delusions.* Rumors and accusations that were devoid of any truth. *false gods.* Or, more likely here, "lies," as indicated in the NIV text note (see 5:6 and note on 5:9).

4:3 *godly.* Hebrew *hasid,* which occurs 26 times in the Psalms (once of God: 145:17, "loving"; cf. 18:25) and is usually rendered (in the plural) in the NIV as "the godly" or "saints." It is one of several Hebrew words for God's people, referring to them as people who are or should be devoted to God and faithful to him (see note on 1Sa 2:9).

4:4–5 An exhortation not to give way to anger or fear and go looking for a scapegoat (the king) on whom to lay blame for their present troubles, but to search their own hearts and put their trust in the Lord.

4:4 *In your anger do not sin.* Paul uses these words in a different context (see Eph 4:26).

4:6 In the face of widespread uncertainty, David prays for the Lord to bless. *Who . . . ?* Because of the slanders being spread, many are looking for another leader to replace the king. *can show us any good.* See 34:10; 84:11; 85:12; 103:5; 107:9; cf. 16:2; Jas 1:17. *Let . . . your face shine upon.* David appeals to the Lord to restore the well-being of the nation—employing a common expression for favor (see note on 13:1), reminiscent of the Aaronic benediction (see Nu 6:24–26 and notes).

4:7–8 David's confidence (see note on 3:8).

4:7 *heart.* In Biblical language the center of the human spirit, from which spring emotions, thoughts, motivations, courage and action—"the wellspring of life" (Pr 4:23).

4:8 *I will lie down and sleep.* See 3:5 and note. *in peace.* Without anxiety.

Ps 5 This morning prayer, perhaps offered at the time of the morning sacrifice, is the psalmist's cry for help when his enemies spread malicious lies to destroy him. A stanza structure alternative to that reflected in the NIV and in the notes should be considered: vv. 1–2 (initial appeal to be heard); vv. 3–7 (seven lines in which the psalmist declares that he prays to God "in the morning" "toward your holy temple" because he can be confident of God's dealings toward the wicked); vv. 8–11 (seven lines in the Hebrew text in which he pleads his case against his enemies who seek to destroy him through slander); v. 12 (a concluding profession of confidence that God will surely protect the innocent).

5 title *For the director of music.* See note on Ps 4 title. *flutes.* The Hebrew for this word occurs only here; meaning uncertain.

5:1–3 Initial appeal to be heard.

5:2 *King.* See Introduction: Theology: Major Themes.

5:3 *In the morning.* See introduction to Ps 57; cf. Jer 21:12 and note.

5:4–6 An appeal to the righteousness of God's rule over humankind.

5:5 *The arrogant.* See note on 31:23.

5:6 *tell lies.* Destroy others by slander or false testimony (see v. 9 and note).

5:7–8 The psalmist presents his plea to the Lord in humble reverence (v. 7), trusting in the Lord's great mercy (v. 7) and righteousness (v. 8).

5:7 *great mercy.* See note on 6:4.

5:8 *Lead me.* Protectively, as a shepherd (see 23:3). *righteousness.* See note on 4:1. *make straight your way.* May the way down which you lead me be straight, level and smooth, free from obstacles and temptations. The psalmist prays that God will so direct him that his enemies will have no grounds for their malicious accusations (see 25:4; 27:11; 139:24; 143:8–10).

5:9–10 Accusation and call for judicial action (both are common elements in the prayers of the Psalter when the psalmist is under threat or attack from human adversaries).

5:9 *word from their mouth.* The most frequent weapon used against the psalmists is the tongue (for a striking

Their throat is an open grave;[z]
with their tongue they speak
deceit.[a]
10 Declare them guilty, O God!
Let their intrigues be their
downfall.
Banish them for their many sins,[b]
for they have rebelled[c] against
you.
11 But let all who take refuge in you be
glad;
let them ever sing for joy.[d]
Spread your protection over them,
that those who love your name[e]
may rejoice in you.[f]
12 For surely, O LORD, you bless the
righteous;[g]
you surround them[h] with your favor
as with a shield.[i]

5:9 [z]Jer 5:16; Lk 11:44 [a]Ps 12:2; 28:3; 36:3; Pr 15:4; Jer 9:8; Ro 3:13* **5:10** [b]La 1:5 [c]Ps 78:40; 106:7; 107:11; La 3:42 **5:11** [d]Ps 33:1; 81:1; 90:14; 92:4; 95:1; 145:7 [e]Ps 69:36; 119:132 [f]S Job 22:19 **5:12** [g]Ps 112:2 [h]Ps 32:7 [i]S Ge 15:1

6:1 [j]S Ps 2:5 **6:2** [k]Ps 4:1; 26:11; Jer 3:12; 12:15; 31:20 [l]Ps 61:2; 77:3; 142:3; Isa 40:31; Jer 8:18; Eze 21:7 [m]S Nu 12:13 [n]Ps 22:14; 31:10; 32:3; 38:3; 42:10; 102:3

Psalm 6

For the director of music. With stringed instruments. According to *sheminith.*[a] A psalm of David.

1 O LORD, do not rebuke me in your anger[j]
or discipline me in your wrath.
2 Be merciful to me,[k] LORD, for I am faint;[l]
O LORD, heal me,[m] for my bones are
in agony.[n]
3 My soul is in anguish.[o]
How long,[p] O LORD, how long?
4 Turn,[q] O LORD, and deliver me;
save me because of your unfailing
love.[r]

[a] Title: Probably a musical term

6:3 [o]S Job 7:11; Ps 31:7; 38:8; 55:4; S Jn 12:27; Ro 9:2; 2Co 2:4 [p]1Sa 1:14; 1Ki 18:21; Ps 4:2; 89:46; Isa 6:11; Jer 4:14; Hab 1:2; Zec 1:12 **6:4** [q]Ps 25:16; 31:2; 69:16; 71:2; 86:16; 88:2; 102:2; 119:132 [r]Ps 13:5; 31:16; 77:8; 85:7; 119:41; Isa 54:8,10

example see Ps 12; see also note on 10:7). The psalmists experienced that the tongue is as deadly as swords and arrows (see 55:21; 57:4; 59:7; 64:3–4; cf. Pr 12:18; 25:18). Perhaps appeals to God against those who maliciously wield the tongue are frequent in the Psalms because only in God's courtroom can a person experience redress for such attacks. *heart.* See note on 4:7. *throat ... grave.* See note on 49:14. *they speak deceit.* For the plots and intrigues of enemies, usually involving lies to discredit the king and bring him down, see Ps 17; 25; 27–28; 31; 35; 41; 52; 54–57; 59; 63–64; 71; 86; 109; 140–141—all ascribed to David. Frequently such attacks came when the king was "low" and seemingly abandoned by God (as in Ps 25; 35; 41; 71; 86; 109). In that case he was viewed as no longer fit to be king—God was no longer with him (and so he could no longer secure the safety of the nation; see 1Sa 8:20; 11:12; 12:12; 25:28; 2Sa 3:18; 7:9–11). In any event, he was an easy prey (see 3:2; 22:7–8; 71:11). See note on 86:17. See also Paul's use of this verse in Ro 3:13.

5:10 The presence of so-called imprecations (curses) in the Psalms has occasioned endless discussion and has caused many Christians to wince, in view of Jesus' instructions to turn the other cheek and to pray for one's enemies (see Mt 5:39,44), and his own example on the cross (see Lk 23:34). Actually, these "imprecations" are not that at all; rather, they are appeals to God to redress wrongs perpetrated against the psalmists by imposing penalties commensurate with the violence done (see 28:4)—in accordance also with God's norm for judicial action in human courts (see Dt 25:1–3; see also 2Th 1:6; Rev 6:10; 19:2). The psalmists knew that those who have been wronged are not to avenge that wrong by their own hand but are to leave redress to the Lord, who says, "It is mine to avenge; I will repay" (Dt 32:35; see Pr 20:22; Ro 12:19). Therefore they appeal their cases to the divine Judge (see Jer 15:15). *Banish them.* From God's presence, thus from the source of blessing and life (see Ge 3:23). *rebelled against you.* By their attacks on the psalmist.

5:11 The psalmist expands his prayer to include all the godly (see note on 3:8). *your name.* The name of the Lord is the manifestation of his character (see notes on Ex 3:14–15; 34:6–7). It has no separate existence apart from the Lord, but is synonymous with the Lord himself in his gracious manifestation and accessibility to his people. Hence the Jerusalem temple is the earthly residence of his name among his people (see 74:7; Dt 12:5,11 and note on 12:5; 2Sa 7:13), and his people can pray to him by calling on his name (see 79:6; 80:18; 99:6; 105:1; 116:4,13,17). The name of the Lord protects (see 20:1; Pr 18:10); the Lord saves by his name (see 54:1); and his saving acts testify that his name is near (see 52:9). Accordingly, the godly "trust in" his name (20:7; 33:21), hope in his name (see 52:9), "sing praise" to his name (7:17; 9:2; 18:49) and "rejoice in" his name (89:16). Both the "love" and the "fear" that belong alone to God are similarly directed toward his name (love: 69:36; 119:132; fear: 61:5; 86:11; 102:15).

5:12 See note on 3:8. *righteous.* Those not guilty of the crimes/sins alleged against them (see note on 1:5).

Ps 6 A prayer in time of severe illness, an occasion seized upon by David's enemies to vent their animosity. The stanza structure is symmetrical: three verses, two verses, two verses, three verses. In early Christian liturgical tradition Ps 6 was numbered with the seven penitential psalms (the others: Ps 32; 38; 51; 102; 130; 143).

6 title See note on Ps 4 title. *According to.* Represents a Hebrew preposition of varied usage (also found in the titles of Ps 8; 12; 46; 53; 81; 84; 88). *sheminith.* Occurs also in Ps 12 title and in 1Ch 15:21. It perhaps refers to an eight-stringed instrument (see NIV text note).

6:1–3 Initial appeal for mercy. Though the Lord has sent him illness to chasten him for his sin (see 32:3–5; 38:1–8,17–18), David asks that God would not in anger impose the full measure of the penalty for sin, for then death must come (see v. 5; see also 130:3).

6:1 Ps 38 begins similarly. *rebuke ... discipline.* That is, rebuke-and-discipline (see 39:11; see also note on 3:7). *anger ... wrath.* See note on 2:5.

6:2 *bones.* As the inner skeleton, they here represent the whole body.

6:3 *soul.* Not a spiritual aspect in distinction from the physical, nor the psalmist's "inner" being in distinction from his "outer" being, but his very self as a living, conscious, personal being. Its use in conjunction with "bones" (also in 35:9–10: "soul" and "whole being") did not for the Hebrew writer involve reference to two distinct entities but constituted for him two ways of referring to himself, as is the case also in the combination "soul" and "body" (31:9; 63:1). *How long ... how long?* See Introduction: Theology: Major Themes, 4. Such language of impatience and complaint is found frequently in the prayers of the Psalter (usually "how long?" or "when?" or "why?"). It expresses the anguish of relief not (yet) granted and exhibits the boldness with which the psalmists wrestled with God on the basis of their relationship with him and their conviction concerning his righteousness (see note on 4:1).

6:4–5 Earnest prayer for deliverance from death.

6:4 *unfailing love.* The Hebrew for this phrase denotes a strong sense of goodwill, especially such as can be

5 No one remembers you when he is dead.
Who praises you from the grave[a]?[s]

6 I am worn out[t] from groaning;[u]
all night long I flood my bed with weeping[v]
and drench my couch with tears.[w]
7 My eyes grow weak[x] with sorrow;
they fail because of all my foes.

8 Away from me,[y] all you who do evil,[z]
for the LORD has heard my weeping.
9 The LORD has heard my cry for mercy;[a]
the LORD accepts my prayer.
10 All my enemies will be ashamed and dismayed;[b]
they will turn back in sudden disgrace.[c]

Psalm 7

A *shiggaion*[b][d] of David, which he sang to the LORD concerning Cush, a Benjamite.

1 O LORD my God, I take refuge[e] in you;
save and deliver me[f] from all who pursue me,[g]
2 or they will tear me like a lion[h]
and rip me to pieces with no one to rescue[i] me.

3 O LORD my God, if I have done this
and there is guilt on my hands[j]—
4 if I have done evil to him who is at peace with me
or without cause[k] have robbed my foe—
5 then let my enemy pursue and overtake[l] me;
let him trample my life to the ground[m]
and make me sleep in the dust.[n] *Selah*

6 Arise,[o] O LORD, in your anger;
rise up against the rage of my enemies.[p]
Awake,[q] my God; decree justice.
7 Let the assembled peoples gather around you.
Rule over them from on high;[r]

[a] 5 Hebrew *Sheol* [b] Title: Probably a literary or musical term

6:5 [s] Ps 30:9; 88:10-12; 115:17; Ecc 9:10; Isa 38:18 **6:6** [t] S Jdg 8:5 [u] S Job 3:24; S 23:2; Ps 12:5; 77:3; 102:5; La 1:8,11,21,22 [v] S Job 16:16 [w] S Job 7:3; Lk 7:38; Ac 20:19 **6:7** [x] S Job 16:8; Ps 31:9; 69:3; 119:82; Isa 38:14 **6:8** [y] Ps 119:115; 139:19 [z] Ps 5:5; S Mt 7:23 **6:9** [a] Ps 28:6; 116:1 **6:10** [b] S 2Ki 19:26 [c] Ps 40:14 **7:Title** [d] Hab 3:1 **7:1** [e] Ps 2:12; 11:1; 31:1 [f] S Ps 3:7 [g] Ps 31:15; 119:86,157,161 **7:2** [h] S Ge 49:9; Rev 4:7 [i] Ps 3:2; 71:11 **7:3** [j] Isa 59:3 **7:4** [k] Ps 35:7,19; Pr 24:28 **7:5** [l] S Ex 15:9 [m] S 2Sa 22:43; 2Ki 9:33; Isa 10:6; La 3:16 [n] S Job 7:21 **7:6** [o] S 2Ch 6:41 [p] Ps 138:7 [q] Ps 35:23; 44:23 **7:7** [r] Ps 68:18

relied on in times of need. Appeal to God's "(unfailing) love" (sometimes rendered "kindness" or "mercy"; see note on Jos 2:12) is frequent in the OT since it summarizes all that the Lord covenanted to show to Israel (see Dt 7:9,12) as well as to David and his dynasty (see 89:24,28,33,49; 2Sa 7:15; Isa 55:3).

6:5 David urges that God's praise is at stake. It is the living, not the dead, who remember God's mercies and celebrate his deliverances. The Israelites usually viewed death as they saw it—the very opposite of life. And resurrection was not yet a part of their communal experience with God. The grave brought no escape from God (see 139:8), but just how they viewed the condition of the godly dead is not clear. (Non-Biblical documents from the ancient Near East indicate a general conception that immortality was reserved for the gods but that the dead continued to have some kind of shadowy existence in the dismal netherworld.) The OT writers knew that human beings were created for life, that God's will for his people was life and that he had power over death. They also knew that death was everyone's lot, and at its proper time the godly rested in God and accepted it with equanimity (see Ge 15:15; 25:8; 47:30; 49:33; 1Ki 2:2). Death could even be a blessing for the righteous, affording escape from the greater evil that would overtake the living (see 2Ki 22:20; Isa 57:1–2). Furthermore, the death of the righteous was reputedly better than that of the wicked (see Nu 23:10). It seems clear that there was even an awareness that death (as observed) was not the end of hope for the righteous, that God had more in store for them (see especially 16:9–11; 17:15; 49:14–15; 73:24; see also note on Ge 5:24). But when the psalmists wrestled with God for the preservation of life, it was death as they saw it, in its radical contradiction to life, that they prayed to be delivered from.

6:6–7 Anguish at night because of the prolongation of the illness and the barbs of the enemies.

6:6 *I am worn out from groaning.* The very center of the poem—thus underscoring the pathos of this prayer. This literary device—of placing a key thematic line at the very center of the psalm—was frequently used (see notes on 8:4; 14:4; 23:4; 34:8–14; 42:8; 47:5–6; 48:8; 54:4; 55:15; 63:6; 69; 71:14; 74:12; 82:5; 86:9; 97:7; 101; 106; 113:5; 138; 141:5; 147:10–11; see also Introduction: Literary Features).

6:7 *eyes grow weak ... fail.* In the vivid language of the OT the eyes are dimmed by failing strength (see 38:10; 1Sa 14:27,29 and NIV text notes; Jer 14:6), by grief (often associated with affliction: 31:9; 88:9; Job 17:7; La 2:11) and by longings unsatisfied or hope deferred (see 69:3; 119:82,123; Dt 28:32; Isa 38:14). *because of all my foes.* See note on 5:9.

6:8–10 Concluding expression of buoyant confidence (see note on 3:8).

6:10 At David's restoration, his enemies will be disgraced.

Ps 7 An appeal to the Lord's court of justice when enemies attack.

7 title *shiggaion.* See NIV text note. The word occurs only here (but see its plural in Hab 3:1). *Cush.* Not otherwise known, but as a Benjamite he was probably a supporter of Saul. Hence the title evokes Saul's determined attempts on David's life. See Introduction: Authorship and Titles (or Superscriptions).

7:1–2 Initial summation of David's appeal.

7:2 *like a lion.* As a young shepherd, David had been attacked by lions (see 1Sa 17:34–35). But it is also a convention in the Psalms to liken the attack of enemies to that of ferocious animals, especially the lion (see 10:9; 17:12; 22:12–13,16,20–21; 35:17; 57:4; 58:6; 124:6).

7:3–5 David pleads his own innocence; he has given his enemy no cause to attack him.

7:5 *me.* Lit. "my glory," a way of referring to the core of one's being (see 16:9; 30:12; 57:8; 108:1 and notes).

7:6–9 An appeal to the Judge of all the earth to execute his judgment over all peoples, and particularly to adjudicate David's case.

7:6 *Arise ... rise up.* See note on 3:7. *anger.* See v. 11 and note on 2:5. *Awake.* The Lord does not sleep (see 121:4) while evil triumphs and the oppressed cry to him in vain (as they do to Baal; see 1Ki 18:27). But the psalmists' language of urgent prayer vividly expresses their anguished impatience with God's inaction in the face of their great need (see 80:2; see also 78:65; Isa 51:9).

8 let the LORD judge[s] the peoples.
Judge me, O LORD, according to my righteousness,[t]
according to my integrity,[u] O Most High.[v]
9 O righteous God,[w]
who searches minds and hearts,[x]
bring to an end the violence of the wicked
and make the righteous secure.[y]

10 My shield[a z] is God Most High,
who saves the upright in heart.[a]
11 God is a righteous judge,[b]
a God who expresses his wrath[c] every day.
12 If he does not relent,[d]
he[b] will sharpen his sword;[e]
he will bend and string his bow.[f]
13 He has prepared his deadly weapons;
he makes ready his flaming arrows.[g]
14 He who is pregnant with evil
and conceives trouble gives birth[h] to disillusionment.
15 He who digs a hole and scoops it out
falls into the pit[i] he has made.[j]
16 The trouble he causes recoils on himself;
his violence comes down on his own head.

17 I will give thanks to the LORD because of his righteousness[k]
and will sing praise[l] to the name of the LORD Most High.[m]

Psalm 8

For the director of music. According to *gittith*.[c] A psalm of David.

1 O LORD, our Lord,
how majestic is your name[n] in all the earth!

You have set your glory[o]
above the heavens.[p]
2 From the lips of children and infants
you have ordained praise[d q]
because of your enemies,
to silence the foe[r] and the avenger.

3 When I consider your heavens,[s]
the work of your fingers,[t]
the moon and the stars,[u]
which you have set in place,

7:8 [s] S 1Ch 16:33 [t] S 1Sa 26:23; Ps 18:20 [u] S Ge 20:5 [v] S Ge 3:5; S Nu 24:16; S Mk 5:7 **7:9** [w] Jer 11:20 [x] S 1Ch 28:9; Ps 26:2; Rev 2:23 [y] Ps 37:23; 40:2 **7:10** [z] Ps 3:3 [a] S Job 33:3 **7:11** [b] S Ge 18:25; Ps 9:8; 67:4; 75:2; 96:13; 98:9; Isa 11:4; Jer 11:20 [c] S Dt 9:8 **7:12** [d] Eze 3:19; 33:9 [e] S Dt 32:41 [f] S 2Sa 22:35; Ps 21:12; Isa 5:28; 13:18 **7:13** [g] Ps 11:2; 18:14; 64:3 **7:14** [h] Isa 59:4; Jas 1:15 **7:15** [i] Ps 35:7,8; 40:2; 94:13; Pr 26:27 [j] S Job 4:8 **7:17** [k] Ps 5:8 [l] S 2Ch 31:2; Ro 15:11; Heb 2:12 [m] S Ge 14:18 **8:1** [n] S 1Ch 16:10 [o] S Ex 15:11; Lk 2:9 [p] Ps 57:5; 108:5; 113:4; 148:13; Hab 3:3 **8:2** [q] Mt 21:16* [r] Ps 143:12 **8:3** [s] S Ge 15:5; S Dt 10:14 [t] S Ex 8:19; S 1Ch 16:26; S 2Ch 2:12; Ps 102:25 [u] S Ge 1:16; 1Co 15:41

[a] *10* Or *sovereign* [b] *12* Or *If a man does not repent, / God* [c] Title: Probably a musical term [d] *2* Or *strength*

7:8 *my righteousness.* See vv. 3–5. *my integrity.* See note on 15:2.
7:9 *righteous God.* See note on 4:1. *minds and hearts.* Lit. "hearts and kidneys." The Israelites used the words as virtual synonyms (but "heart" most often) to refer to the innermost center of one's conscious life (see note on 4:7). To "search mind and heart" was a conventional expression for God's examination of one's hidden character and motives (see Jer 11:20; 17:10; 20:12). *the righteous.* See note on 1:5.
7:10–13 David's confidence that his prayer will be heard (see note on 3:8).
7:10 *shield.* See note on 3:3. *heart.* See note on 4:7.
7:11 *every day.* God's judgments are not all kept in store for some future day.
7:12–13 *sword … bow … flaming arrows.* The weapons of the heavenly Warrior King used in defense of his people (see Ex 15:3 and note) but also in judgment.
7:12 *his bow.* See note on Ge 9:13.
7:14–16 David comforts himself with the common wisdom that under God's rule "crime does not pay."
7:15 *digs a hole.* A metaphor from the hunt; pits were used to trap animals (see 9:15 and note).
7:16 *recoils on himself.* See note on Ob 15.
7:17 A vow to praise. Many prayers in the Psalter include such vows in anticipation of the expected answer to prayer. They reflect Israel's religious consciousness that praise must follow deliverance as surely as prayer springs from need—if God is to be truly honored. Such praise was usually offered with thank offerings and involved celebrating God's saving act in the presence of those assembled at the temple (see 50:14–15,23; see also note on 9:1). *name of the LORD.* See note on 5:11. *Most High.* See note on Ge 14:19.
Ps 8 In praise of the Creator (not of human beings—as is evident from the doxology that encloses it, vv. 1,9; see also note on 9:1) out of wonder over his sovereign ordering of the creation. Ge 1 (particularly vv. 26–28) clearly provides the lenses, but David speaks out of his present experience of reality (perhaps on a bright, clear night when the vast host of the heavenly lights, stretching from horizon to horizon, erased from his musings small everyday affairs and engaged his mind with deeper thoughts). Two matters especially impressed him: (1) the glory of God reflected in the starry heavens, and (2) the astonishing condescension of God to be mindful of puny mortals, to crown them with glory almost godlike and to grant them lordly power over his other creatures. At this juncture in the Psalter this psalm surprises. After five psalms (and 64 Hebrew poetic lines—following Ps 1–2, which introduce the Psalter; see introduction to Ps 1–2) in which the psalmists have called on Yahweh to deal with human perversity, this psalm's praise of Yahweh for his astounding endowment of the human race with royal "glory and honor" (v. 5) serves as a striking and unexpected counterpoint. Its placement here highlights the glory (God's gift) and disgrace (humanity's own doing) that characterize human beings and the corresponding range of differences in God's dealings with them. And after five more psalms (and 64 poetic lines), this psalm in turn receives a counterpoint (see introduction to Ps 14; see also chart, p. 786).
8 title *For the director of music.* See note on Ps 4 title. *According to.* See note on Ps 6 title. *gittith.* See Ps 81; 84 titles. The Hebrew word perhaps refers to either a winepress ("song of the winepress") or the Philistine city of Gath ("Gittite lyre or music"; see 2Sa 15:18).
8:1a *name.* See note on 5:11.
8:1b–2 The mighty God, whose glory is displayed across the face of the heavens, appoints (and evokes) the praise of little children to silence the dark powers arrayed against him (for a NT application see Mt 21:16).
8:2 *avenger.* See 44:16; one who strikes back in malicious revenge (not as in 9:12); cf. Dt 32:35 and note.
8:3–5 The vastness and majesty of the heavens as the handiwork of God (see 19:1–6; 104:19–23) evoke wonder for what their Maker has done for human beings, who are here today and gone tomorrow (see 144:3–4). (See Job 7:17–21 for Job's complaint that God takes humans too seriously.)
8:3 *fingers.* See note on Ex 8:19.

4 what is man that you are mindful of
him,
the son of man that you care for
him?[v]
5 You made him a little lower than the
heavenly beings[a w]
and crowned him with glory and
honor.[x]

6 You made him ruler[y] over the works
of your hands;[z]
you put everything under his
feet:[a b]
7 all flocks and herds,[c]
and the beasts of the field,[d]
8 the birds of the air,
and the fish of the sea,[e]
all that swim the paths of the seas.

9 O LORD, our Lord,
how majestic is your name in all the
earth![f]

Psalm 9[b]

For the director of music. To ⌊the tune of⌋ "The Death of the Son." A psalm of David.

1 I will praise you, O LORD, with all my
heart;[g]
I will tell of all your wonders.[h]
2 I will be glad and rejoice[i] in you;
I will sing praise[j] to your name,[k]
O Most High.

3 My enemies turn back;
they stumble and perish before you.
4 For you have upheld my right[l] and my
cause;[m]
you have sat on your throne,[n]
judging righteously.[o]

8:4 [v]S 1Ch 29:14 **8:5** [w]S Ge 1:26 [x]Ps 21:5; 103:4 **8:6** [y]S Ge 1:28 [z]S Job 10:3; Ps 19:1; 102:25; 145:10; Isa 26:12; 29:23; 45:11; Heb 1:10 [a]Heb 2:6-8* [b]S 1Ki 5:3; 1Co 15:25,27*; Eph 1:22 **8:7** [c]Ge 13:5; 26:14 [d]S Ge 2:19 **8:8** [e]Ge 1:26 **8:9** [f]ver 1

9:1 [g]Ps 86:12; 111:1; 119:2,10, 145; 138:1 [h]S Dt 4:34 **9:2** [i]S Job 22:19; Ps 14:7; 31:7; 70:4; 97:8; 126:3; Pr 23:15; Isa 25:9; Jer 30:19; Joel 2:21; Zep 3:14; S Mt 5:12; Rev 19:7 [j]S 2Ch 31:2 [k]Ps 92:1 **9:4** [l]S 1Ki 8:45 [m]S Job 16:21 [n]Ps 11:4; 47:8; Isa 6:1 [o]Ps 7:11; 67:4; 98:9; 1Pe 2:23

[a] 5 Or *than God* [b] Psalms 9 and 10 may have been originally a single acrostic poem, the stanzas of which begin with the successive letters of the Hebrew alphabet. In the Septuagint they constitute one psalm.

8:4–6 Heb 2:6–8, quoting the Septuagint (the pre-Christian Greek translation of the OT), applies these verses to Jesus, who as the incarnate Son of God is both the representative human being and the one in whom humanity's appointed destiny will be fully realized. The author of Hebrews thus makes use of the eschatological implications of these words in his testimony to Christ. Paul does the same with v. 6 in 1Co 15:27 (see also Eph 1:22).
8:4 *what.* The Hebrew for this word is translated "how" in vv. 1,9 and begins the line that serves as the center of the psalm (see note on 6:6). *are mindful of.* Lit. "remember" (see note on Ge 8:1). *son of man.* A literal translation of a Hebrew phrase commonly used to refer to a human being (see 80:17; 144:3; Da 8:17; see also note on Eze 2:1).
8:5 *heavenly beings.* The exalted angelic creatures that surround God in his heavenly realm (as, e.g., in Isa 6:2); but see NIV text note.
8:6–8 See Ge 1:26–27. The power to exercise rule over some of God's creatures is even now a part of humanity's "glory and honor" (v. 5). The full realization of that potential—and vocation—belongs to humanity's appointed destiny (the eschatological import drawn on by Paul and the author of Hebrews; see note on vv. 4–6). But this power—and vocation—to rule is not absolute or independent. It is participation, but not as an equal, in God's rule; and it is a gift, not a right.
8:9 Repeated verbatim from v. 1a (see note there).
Ps 9 That Ps 9 and 10 were sometimes viewed (or used) as one psalm is known from the Septuagint (the pre-Christian Greek translation of the OT; see NIV text note). Whether they were originally composed as one psalm is not known, though a number of indicators point in that direction. Ps 10 is the only psalm from Ps 3 to 32 that has no superscription, and the Hebrew text of the two psalms together appears to reflect an incomplete (or broken) acrostic structure. The first letter of each verse or pair of verses tends to follow the order of the Hebrew alphabet near the beginning of Ps 9 and again near the end of Ps 10. The thoughts also tend to be developed in two-verse units throughout. Ps 9 is predominantly praise (by the king) for God's deliverance from hostile nations (the specific occasion is unknown, but since there is no reference to victories on the part of Israel, God's destruction of the nations may have come by other means). It concludes with a short prayer for God's continuing righteous judgments (see v. 4) on the haughty nations. Ps 10 is predominantly prayer against the rapacity of unscrupulous people within the realm—as arrogant and wicked in their dealings with the "weak" (v. 2) as the nations were in their attacks on Israel (vv. 2–11 can serve equally as a description of both). The conjunction of these two within a single psalm is not unthinkable since the attacks of "the wicked" (9:5; 10:4), whether from within or from without, on the godly community are equally threatening to true Israel. Praise of God's past deliverances is often an integral part of prayer in the Psalter (see 3:3–4,8 and notes; 25:6; 40:1–5), as also in other ancient Near Eastern prayers. Such praise expressed the basis of the psalmist's hope that his present prayer would be heard, and it also functioned to motivate the Lord to act once more in his people's (or his servant's) behalf. For other lengthy prefaces to prayer see Ps 40; 44; 89. Probably Ps 9–10 came to be separated for the purpose of separate liturgical use, as did Ps 42–43 (see introduction there).
9 title *For the director of music.* See note on Ps 4 title. *To ⌊the tune of⌋.* See titles of Ps 22; 45; 56–60; 69; 75; 80; see also NIV text note on Ps 88 title. Nothing more is known of the apparent tune titles.
9:1–2 Initial announcement of praise.
9:1 *heart.* See note on 4:7. *tell of.* The Hebrew for this phrase is translated "declare" in v. 14. The praise of God in the Psalter is rarely a private matter between the psalmist and the Lord. It is usually a public (at the temple) celebration of God's holy virtues or of his saving acts or gracious bestowal of blessings. In his praise the psalmist proclaims to the assembled throng God's glorious attributes or his righteous (see note on 4:1) deeds (see, e.g., 22:22–31; 56:12–13; 61:8; 65:1; 69:30–33). To this is usually added a call to praise, summoning all who hear to take up the praise—to acknowledge and joyfully celebrate God's glory, his goodness and all his righteous acts. This aspect of praise in the Psalms has rightly been called the OT anticipation of NT evangelism. *wonders.* God's saving acts, sometimes involving miracles—as in the exodus from Egypt, the desert wanderings and the entrance into the promised land—and sometimes not, but always involving the manifestation of God's sovereign lordship over events. Here reference is to the destruction of the enemies celebrated in this psalm.
9:2,10 *your name.* See note on 5:11.
9:2 *Most High.* See note on Ge 14:19.
9:3–6 In destroying the enemies, God has redressed the wrongs committed by them against David (and Israel).
9:4 *throne.* See note on v. 7.

5 You have rebuked the nations[p] and
destroyed the wicked;
you have blotted out their name[q] for
ever and ever.
6 Endless ruin has overtaken the enemy,
you have uprooted their cities;[r]
even the memory of them[s] has
perished.

7 The LORD reigns forever;[t]
he has established his throne[u] for
judgment.
8 He will judge the world in
righteousness;[v]
he will govern the peoples with
justice.[w]
9 The LORD is a refuge[x] for the
oppressed,[y]
a stronghold in times of trouble.[z]
10 Those who know your name[a] will trust
in you,
for you, LORD, have never forsaken[b]
those who seek you.[c]

11 Sing praises[d] to the LORD, enthroned in
Zion;[e]
proclaim among the nations[f] what
he has done.[g]
12 For he who avenges blood[h] remembers;
he does not ignore the cry of the
afflicted.[i]

13 O LORD, see how my enemies[j]
persecute me!
Have mercy[k] and lift me up from the
gates of death,[l]
14 that I may declare your praises[m]
in the gates of the Daughter of
Zion[n]
and there rejoice in your salvation.[o]

15 The nations have fallen into the pit
they have dug;[p]
their feet are caught in the net they
have hidden.[q]
16 The LORD is known by his justice;
the wicked are ensnared by the
work of their hands.[r]
Higgaion.[a] *Selah*
17 The wicked return to the grave,[b][s]
all the nations that forget God.[t]
18 But the needy will not always be
forgotten,
nor the hope[u] of the afflicted[v] ever
perish.

19 Arise,[w] O LORD, let not man triumph;[x]
let the nations be judged[y] in your
presence.
20 Strike them with terror,[z] O LORD;
let the nations know they are
but men.[a] *Selah*

Psalm 10[c]

1 Why, O LORD, do you stand far off?[b]
Why do you hide yourself[c] in times
of trouble?

[a] 16 Or *Meditation*; possibly a musical notation
[b] 17 Hebrew *Sheol* [c] Psalms 9 and 10 may have been originally a single acrostic poem, the stanzas of which begin with the successive letters of the Hebrew alphabet. In the Septuagint they constitute one psalm.

9:5 [p] Ge 20:7; S 37:10; S 1Ch 16:21; Ps 59:5; 105:14; Isa 26:14; 66:15 [q] S Job 18:17 **9:6** [r] S Dt 29:28; Jer 2:3; 46:1-51:58; Zep 2:8-10 [s] Ps 34:16; 109:15; Ecc 9:5; Isa 14:22; 26:14 **9:7** [t] S 1Ch 16:31; Rev 19:6 [u] Ps 11:4; 47:8; 93:2; Isa 6:1; 66:1 **9:8** [v] S ver 4; Ps 7:11 [w] Ps 11:7; 45:6; 72:2 **9:9** [x] S Dt 33:27; S 2Sa 22:3 [y] Ps 10:18; 74:21 [z] Ps 32:7; 121:7 **9:10** [a] Ps 91:14 [b] S Ge 28:15; S Dt 4:31; Ps 22:1; 37:25; 71:11; Isa 49:14; Jer 15:18; Heb 13:5 [c] Ps 70:4 **9:11** [d] Ps 7:17 [e] S Ps 2:6 [f] Ps 18:49; 44:11; 57:9; 106:27; Isa 24:13; Eze 20:23; 1Ti 3:16 [g] Ps 105:1 **9:12** [h] S 2Sa 4:11 [i] ver 18; Ps 10:17; 22:24; 72:4; Isa 49:13 **9:13** [j] Nu 10:9; Ps 3:7; 18:3 [k] Ps 6:2; 41:4; 51:1; 86:3,16; 119:132 [l] S Job 17:16; Mt 16:18 **9:14** [m] Ps 51:15; 1Pe 2:9

[n] 2Ki 19:21; Isa 1:8; 10:32; 37:22; 62:11; Jer 4:31; 6:2; La 1:6; Mic 1:13; Zep 3:14; Zec 2:10; Mt 21:5; Jn 12:15 [o] Ps 13:5; 35:9; 50:23; 51:12 **9:15** [p] S Job 4:8; Ps 35:7 [q] Ps 35:8; 57:6 **9:16** [r] Pr 5:22 **9:17** [s] S Nu 16:30; Pr 5:5 [t] S Job 8:13 **9:18** [u] Ps 25:3; 39:7; 71:5; Pr 23:18; Jer 14:8 [v] ver 12; Ps 74:19 **9:19** [w] Ps 3:7 [x] 2Ch 14:11 [y] Ps 110:6; Isa 2:4; Joel 3:12 **9:20** [z] S Ge 35:5; Ps 31:13; Isa 13:8; Lk 21:26 [a] Ps 62:9; Isa 31:3; Eze 28:2 **10:1** [b] Ps 22:1,11; 35:22; 38:21; 71:12 [c] Ps 13:1

9:5 *blotted out their name.* As if from a register of all living persons written on a papyrus scroll (see Nu 5:23; see also Dt 9:14; 25:19; 29:20; 2Ki 14:27).
9:7–10 Celebration of the righteous rule of God (see note on 4:1; see also Ps 93; 96–99), which evokes trust in those who look to the Lord.
9:7 *his throne.* In heaven (see 11:4). See also v. 4.
9:8 See Ac 17:31.
9:10 *Those who know your name.* Those who acknowledge in their hearts who the Lord is and also live out that acknowledgment (see 91:14; see also note on 5:11).
9:11–12 A call to the assembly at the temple to take up the praise of God for his righteous judgments (see note on v. 1).
9:11 *enthroned in Zion.* God's heavenly throne (see v. 7) has its counterpart on earth in his temple at Jerusalem, from which center he rules the world (see 2:6; 3:4 and notes; 20:2). For God's election of Zion as the seat of his rule see 132:13.
9:12 *he who avenges blood.* See Dt 32:41,43.
9:13–14 Perhaps a recollection of David's prayer ("the cry of the afflicted," v. 12), which the Lord has now answered.
9:13 *gates of death.* See Job 17:16 and note.
9:14 *declare.* See notes on v. 1; 7:17. *gates.* Having been thrust down by the attacks of his enemies to "the gates of death" (v. 13), David prayed to be lifted up so he could celebrate his deliverance (see note on v. 1) in "the gates of ... Zion." *Daughter of Zion.* A personification of Jerusalem (see note on 2Ki 19:21).
9:15–18 Under the Lord's just rule, those who wickedly attack others bring destruction on themselves (see 7:14–16 and note) and their end will be the grave. But those who are attacked ("the needy," v. 18) will not trust in the Lord in vain.
9:15 *pit ... dug ... net ... hidden.* In the Psalter, imagery drawn from the hunt is frequently (in 14 psalms) employed to depict the cunning attacks of enemies who sought to destroy by hidden means or surprise attacks, the tongue being the most common weapon (see 5:9 and note). In ancient times hunters used snares, traps, nets and pits, often in combination, and always involving concealment. See note on Ob 15.
9:17 *forget.* Take no account of.
9:18 *needy ... afflicted.* In this psalm David and Israel are counted among them because of the threat from the enemies. *not ... forgotten.* Those who forget God will come to nothing, but the needy and afflicted will not be forgotten by God (see v. 12).
9:19–20 A prayer at the conclusion of praise, asking that the Lord may ever rule over the nations as he has done in the event here celebrated—that those who "forget God" (v. 17) may know that they are only weak mortals, not gods, and cannot withstand the God of Israel (see 10:18).
9:19 *Arise.* See note on 3:7.
Ps 10 A prayer for rescue from the attacks of unscrupulous people—containing a classic OT portrayal of "the wicked" (v. 4). See introduction to Ps 9.
10:1 See note on 6:3.

[2]In his arrogance the wicked man hunts
down the weak,[d]
who are caught in the schemes he
devises.
[3]He boasts[e] of the cravings of his heart;
he blesses the greedy and reviles the
LORD.[f]
[4]In his pride the wicked does not seek
him;
in all his thoughts there is no room
for God.[g]
[5]His ways are always prosperous;
he is haughty[h] and your laws are far
from him;
he sneers at all his enemies.
[6]He says to himself, "Nothing will
shake me;
I'll always be happy[i] and never have
trouble."
[7]His mouth is full of curses[j] and lies
and threats;[k]
trouble and evil are under his
tongue.[l]
[8]He lies in wait[m] near the villages;
from ambush he murders the
innocent,[n]
watching in secret for his victims.
[9]He lies in wait like a lion in cover;
he lies in wait to catch the helpless;[o]
he catches the helpless and drags
them off in his net.[p]
[10]His victims are crushed,[q] they collapse;
they fall under his strength.
[11]He says to himself, "God has
forgotten;[r]
he covers his face and never sees."[s]

[12]Arise,[t] LORD! Lift up your hand,[u]
O God.
Do not forget the helpless.[v]
[13]Why does the wicked man revile God?[w]
Why does he say to himself,
"He won't call me to account"?[x]
[14]But you, O God, do see trouble[y] and
grief;
you consider it to take it in hand.
The victim commits himself to you;[z]
you are the helper[a] of the fatherless.
[15]Break the arm of the wicked and evil
man;[b]
call him to account for his
wickedness
that would not be found out.

[16]The LORD is King for ever and ever;[c]
the nations[d] will perish from his
land.
[17]You hear, O LORD, the desire of the
afflicted;[e]
you encourage them, and you listen
to their cry,[f]
[18]defending the fatherless[g] and the
oppressed,[h]
in order that man, who is of the
earth, may terrify no more.

Psalm 11

For the director of music. Of David.

[1]In the LORD I take refuge.[i]
How then can you say to me:
"Flee[j] like a bird to your mountain.[k]

10:2 [d]ver 9; S Job 20:19 **10:3** [e]Ps 49:6; 94:4; Jer 48:30 [f]S Job 1:5 **10:4** [g]Ps 36:1 **10:5** [h]Ps 18:27; 101:5; Pr 6:17; Isa 13:11; Jer 48:29 **10:6** [i]Rev 18:7 **10:7** [j]Ro 3:14* [k]Ps 73:8; 119:134; Ecc 4:1; Isa 30:12 [l]S Job 20:12 **10:8** [m]Ps 37:32; 59:3; 71:10; Pr 1:11; Jer 5:26; Mic 7:2 [n]Hos 6:9 **10:9** [o]S ver 2 [p]S Job 18:8 **10:10** [q]S Job 9:17 **10:11** [r]Job 22:13; Ps 42:9; 77:9 [s]S Job 22:14 **10:12** [t]Ps 3:7 [u]Ps 17:7; 20:6; 106:26; Isa 26:11; Mic 5:9 [v]Ps 9:12 **10:13** [w]ver 3 [x]S Job 31:14 **10:14** [y]ver 7; Ps 22:11 [z]Ps 37:5 [a]S Dt 33:29 **10:15** [b]S Job 31:22 **10:16** [c]S Ex 15:18 [d]S Dt 8:20 **10:17** [e]S Ps 9:12 [f]S Ex 22:23 **10:18** [g]S Dt 24:17; Ps 146:9 [h]S Ps 9:9 **11:1** [i]S Ps 7:1 [j]S Ge 14:10 [k]Ps 50:11

10:2–11 Accusation lodged against the oppressors (see note on 5:9–10). Here the psalmist launches into a characterization of oppressors in general. Their deeds betray the arrogance (see vv. 2–5—so long as they prosper, v. 5) with which they defy God (see vv. 3–4,13; see especially their words in vv. 6,11,13). They greedily seek to glut their unrestrained appetites (see v. 3) by victimizing others, taking account of neither God (see v. 4) nor his law (see v. 5).

10:2 *hunts ... caught.* The psalmists often use imagery from the hunt (see vv. 8–9 and note on v. 9; see also 9:15 and note).

10:3 *heart.* See note on 4:7.

10:4 The wicked do not consider that they have God to contend with (see note on v. 11; see also 14:1; 36:1; 53:1).

10:6 See vv. 11,13 and note on 3:2. *to himself.* Lit. "in his heart" (also in vv. 11,13); see note on 4:7. *shake me.* Take away my well-being, destroy my security.

10:7 *curses and lies and threats.* The three most common weapons of the tongue in Israel's experience (see note on 5:9). *curses.* See note on Ge 12:3. *lies.* Slander and false testimony for malicious purposes (see, e.g., 1Ki 21:8–15).

10:9 See note on 7:2. *lies in wait.* The imagery shifts from the lion to the hunter (see note on 9:15).

10:11 See note on 3:2. The arrogance with which the wicked speak (see 17:10), especially their easy dismissal of God's knowledge of their evil acts and his unfailing prosecution of their malicious deeds, is frequently noted by the psalmists (see v. 13; 12:4; 42:3,10; 59:7; 64:5; 71:11; 73:11; 94:7; 115:2; see also Isa 29:15; Eze 8:12).

10:12–15 Prayer that God will call the wicked to account.

10:12 *Arise.* See note on 3:7. *forget.* See 9:18. *helpless.* Those at the mercy of the oppressors (see v. 9).

10:13 *Why ... ? Why ... ?* See note on 6:3.

10:14 Appeal to God's righteous rule (see 5:4–6).

10:15 *Break the arm.* Destroy the power to oppress. *call him to account.* Humble such arrogance (see v. 13) with your righteous judgment.

10:16–18 The psalmist's confidence in the righteous reign of the Lord (see note on 3:8). Reference to the nations (v. 16) and to the humbling of proud humans (see v. 18; see also 9:19–20) suggests links with Ps 9. As the conclusion to Ps 10, this stanza expands the vision of God's just rule to its universal scope and sets the purging of the Lord's land of all nations that do not acknowledge him (see v. 16) alongside God's judicial dealing with the wicked oppressors. Both belong to God's assertion of his righteous rule in the face of arrogant denial of it.

10:18 *who is of the earth.* Who is only a creature made from earth's dust and so constitutes no ultimate threat (see 49:12,20; 56:4,11; 62:9; 78:39; 103:14–16; 118:6,8–9; 144:4; Isa 31:3; Jer 17:5).

Ps 11 A confession of confident trust in the Lord's righteous rule, at a time when wicked adversaries seem to have the upper hand. Two four-line stanzas in the Hebrew text (vv. 1–3,4–6) are followed by a climactic profession of confident faith (v. 7).

11 title *For the director of music.* See note on Ps 4 title.

11:1–3 David testifies of his unshakable trust in the Lord (his refuge) to apprehensive people around him. These people, seeing the power and underhandedness of the enemy (they "shoot from the shadows," v. 2), fear that the foundations

2 For look, the wicked bend their
bows;[l]
they set their arrows[m] against the
strings
to shoot from the shadows[n]
at the upright in heart.[o]
3 When the foundations[p] are being
destroyed,
what can the righteous do[a]?"

4 The LORD is in his holy temple;[q]
the LORD is on his heavenly throne.[r]
He observes the sons of men;[s]
his eyes examine[t] them.
5 The LORD examines the righteous,[u]
but the wicked[b] and those who
love violence
his soul hates.[v]
6 On the wicked he will rain
fiery coals and burning sulfur;[w]
a scorching wind[x] will be their lot.

7 For the LORD is righteous,[y]
he loves justice;[z]
upright men[a] will see his face.[b]

Psalm 12

For the director of music. According to *sheminith.*[c] A psalm of David.

1 Help, LORD, for the godly are no more;[c]
the faithful have vanished from
among men.
2 Everyone lies[d] to his neighbor;
their flattering lips speak with
deception.[e]

3 May the LORD cut off all flattering lips[f]
and every boastful tongue[g]
4 that says, "We will triumph with our
tongues;[h]
we own our lips[d]—who is our
master?"

5 "Because of the oppression[i] of the
weak
and the groaning[j] of the needy,
I will now arise,[k]" says the LORD.
"I will protect them[l] from those who
malign them."
6 And the words of the LORD are
flawless,[m]
like silver refined[n] in a furnace[o] of
clay,
purified seven times.

11:2 [l]S 2Sa 22:35 [m]S Ps 7:13; S 58:7 [n]Ps 10:8 [o]S Job 33:3; Ps 7:10 **11:3** [p]Ps 18:15; 82:5; Isa 24:18 **11:4** [q]S 1Ki 8:48; Ps 18:6; 27:4; Jnh 2:7; Mic 1:2; Hab 2:20 [r]S 2Ch 6:18; S Ps 9:7; Mt 5:34; 23:22; S Rev 4:2 [s]Pr 15:3 [t]Ps 33:18; 66:7 **11:5** [u]S Dt 7:13; S Job 23:10 [v]S Job 28:28; Ps 5:5; 45:7; Isa 1:14 **11:6** [w]S Ge 19:24; S Rev 9:17 [x]S Ge 41:6; S Job 1:19 **11:7** [y]S 2Ch 12:6; S Ezr 9:15; 2Ti 4:8 [z]S Ps 9:8; 33:5; 99:4; Isa 28:17; 30:18; 56:1; 61:8; Jer 9:24 [a]S Job 1:1; Lk 23:50 [b]Ps 17:15; 140:13 **12:1** [c]Isa 57:1; Mic 7:2 **12:2** [d]Ps 5:6; 34:13; 141:3; Pr 6:19; 12:17; 13:3; Isa 32:7 [e]S Ps 5:9; Ro 16:18 **12:3** [f]Pr 26:28; 28:23 [g]Ps 73:9; Da 7:8; Jas 3:5; Rev 13:5 **12:4** [h]Pr 18:21; Jas 3:6 **12:5** [i]Ps 44:24; 62:10; 72:14; 73:8; Ecc 4:1; 5:8; Isa 3:15; 5:7; 30:12; 59:13; Ac 7:34 [j]S Ps 6:6 [k]Ps 3:7 [l]Ps 34:6; 35:10 **12:6** [m]S 2Sa 22:31; Ps 18:30 [n]S Job 23:10; S 28:1; Isa 48:10; Zec 13:9 [o]Ps 119:140

[a] 3 Or *what is the Righteous One doing* [b] 5 Or *The LORD, the Righteous One, examines the wicked, /* [c] Title: Probably a musical term [d] 4 Or */ our lips are our plowshares*

(v. 3) are crumbling and that flight to a mountain refuge is the only recourse. He dismisses their fearful advice with disdain.

11:2 It is not clear whether those who wield the bows and arrows are archers or false accusers (see 57:4; 64:3–4; see also note on 5:9). *heart.* See note on 4:7.

11:3 *foundations.* Of the world order (see 82:5). To those who counsel flight, the powerful upsurge of evil appears to indicate that the righteous can no longer count on a world order in which good triumphs over evil. *righteous.* See note on 1:5.

11:4–6 Reply to the fearful: The Lord is still securely on his heavenly throne. He discerns those who are righteous (v. 5), but "will rain" his judgment on the wicked (v. 6).

11:4 *The LORD is in his holy temple.* Repeated verbatim in Hab 2:20. Here reference is to his heavenly temple.

11:6 Perhaps recalling God's judgment on Sodom and Gomorrah (see Ge 19:24,28; see also Rev 14:10 and note; 20:10; 21:8). *their lot.* Lit. "the portion of their cup" (see 75:8 and note on 16:5).

11:7 The sure grounds for the psalmist's confidence. *righteous.* See note on 4:1. *upright men.* Those concerning whom the fearful despaired (see v. 2). *see his face.* The Hebrew for "see the king's face" was an expression denoting access to the king (see Ge 43:3,5; 44:23,26; 2Sa 3:13, "come into my presence"; 14:24,28,32). Sometimes it referred to those who served before the king (see 2Ki 25:19, "royal advisers"; Est 1:14, those "who had special access to the king"). Here David speaks of special freedom of access before the heavenly King. Reference is no doubt to his presence at the temple (God's earthly royal house), but that is still the presence of the One who sits on the heavenly throne. Ultimate access to the heavenly temple may also be implied (see 16:11; 17:15; see also 23:6; 140:13). Even the pagan peoples surrounding Israel believed that humans continued after death, though only in some kind of shadowy existence in the netherworld (see Isa 14:9–17).

Ps 12 A prayer for help when it seems that everyone is faithless and every tongue false (see Mic 7:1–7). The psalm is composed of four couplets (vv. 1–2,3–4,5–6,7–8), framed by references to the prevailing evil "among men" (vv. 1,8).

12 title *For the director of music.* See note on Ps 4 title. *According to sheminith.* See note on Ps 6 title.

12:1–2 Initial appeal, with description of the cause of distress.

12:1 *godly.* See note on 4:3. *the faithful.* Those who maintain moral integrity.

12:2 See 5:9 and note.

12:3–4 The prayer.

12:3 *cut off.* Put an end to (physical mutilation is not in view). *boastful.* See note on 10:2–11.

12:4 See notes on 3:2; 10:11.

12:5–6 A reassuring word from the Lord. Such words of assurance following prayer in the Psalms were perhaps spoken by a priest (see 1Sa 1:17) or a prophet (see 51:8 and note; 2Sa 12:13). It may be that abrupt transitions from prayer to confidence in the Psalms (see note on 3:8) presuppose such priestly or prophetic words, even when they are not contained in the psalm. Here it is possible that David merely recalls this appropriate word from the Lord; notice that it is a general reassurance concerning the righteous rule of God (see note on 4:1).

12:5 *I will now arise.* See Isa 33:10.

12:6 *words of the LORD.* Set in sharp contrast with the boastful words of the adversaries; they are as flawless as thoroughly refined silver. *furnace of clay.* In the metallurgy of the ancient Near East, heating in special furnaces was used to extract silver and gold from crushed ore and to remove the dross (base metals such as copper, tin, iron, bronze and lead). This process provided vivid metaphors for many of Israel's poets (see 66:10; Pr 17:3; 27:21; Isa 1:22a,25; 48:10; Jer 6:27–30; 9:7; Eze 22:17–22; Zec 13:9; Mal 3:3). *seven.* Signifies fullness or completeness—here thoroughness of refining.

7 O LORD, you will keep us safe[p]
and protect us from such people forever.[q]
8 The wicked freely strut[r] about
when what is vile is honored among men.

Psalm 13

For the director of music.
A psalm of David.

1 How long,[s] O LORD? Will you forget me[t] forever?
How long will you hide your face[u] from me?
2 How long must I wrestle with my thoughts[v]
and every day have sorrow in my heart?
How long will my enemy triumph over me?[w]

3 Look on me[x] and answer,[y] O LORD my God.
Give light to my eyes,[z] or I will sleep in death;[a]
4 my enemy will say, "I have overcome him,[b]"
and my foes will rejoice when I fall.[c]

5 But I trust in your unfailing love;[d]
my heart rejoices in your salvation.[e]
6 I will sing[f] to the LORD,
for he has been good to me.

Psalm 14

14:1-7pp — Ps 53:1-6

For the director of music. Of David.

1 The fool[a] says in his heart,
"There is no God."[g]
They are corrupt, their deeds are vile;
there is no one who does good.

2 The LORD looks down from heaven[h]
on the sons of men
to see if there are any who understand,[i]
any who seek God.[j]
3 All have turned aside,[k]
they have together become corrupt;[l]
there is no one who does good,[m]
not even one.[n]

[a] *1* The Hebrew words rendered *fool* in Psalms denote one who is morally deficient.

12:7 [p] Ps 16:1; 27:5 [q] Ps 37:28; Jn 17:12 **12:8** [r] Ps 55:10-11 **13:1** [s] Ps 6:3 [t] Ps 42:9; La 5:20 [u] S Dt 31:17; S Ps 22:24; S Isa 8:17; S 54:9 **13:2** [v] Ps 42:4; 55:2; 139:23; Isa 33:18; Da 7:28 [w] Ps 94:3 **13:3** [x] Ps 9:12; 25:18; 31:7; 35:23; 59:4; 80:14; 107:41; 119:50, 153 [y] S Ps 4:1 [z] S Ezr 9:8 [a] Ps 76:5; 90:5; Jer 51:39 **13:4** [b] S 1Ki 19:2; Ps 25:2 [c] Ps 38:16; 118:13 **13:5** [d] S Ps 6:4 [e] S Job 33:26; Ps 9:14; Isa 25:9; 33:2 **13:6** [f] S Ex 15:1; Ps 7:17 **14:1** [g] Ps 10:4 **14:2** [h] Job 41:34; Ps 85:11; 102:19; La 3:50 [i] Ps 92:6 [j] S Ezr 6:21 **14:3** [k] S 1Sa 8:3; 1Ti 5:15 [l] 2Pe 2:7 [m] 1Ki 8:46; Ps 143:2; Ecc 7:20 [n] Ro 3:10-12*

12:7–8 Concluding expression of confidence (see note on 3:8).
12:7 *such people.* The enemies of v. 5.
12:8 David is confident, even though at the present time the wicked think they have the upper hand (see vv. 1–4).
Ps 13 A cry to the Lord for deliverance from a serious illness that threatens to be fatal (see v. 3), which would give David's enemies just what they wanted. See introduction to Ps 6. The psalm is composed of three couplets of graduated diminishing length (in Hebrew) to form (probably deliberately) a rhetorical pyramid capped with a ringing profession of faith and vow to praise (vv. 5–6).
13 title *For the director of music.* See note on Ps 4 title.
13:1–2 An anguished complaint concerning a prolonged serious illness.
13:1 *How long ...?* See note on 6:3. *forget.* Ignore. *hide your face.* For use in combination with "forget" see 44:24. In moments of need the psalmists frequently ask God why he hides his face (see 30:7; 44:24; 88:14), or they plead with him not to do so (see 27:9; 69:17; 102:2; 143:7). When he does hide his face, those who depend on him can only despair (see 30:7; 104:29). When his face shines on a person, blessing and deliverance come (see 4:6 and note; 31:16; 44:3; 67:1; 80:3,7,19; 119:135; see also Nu 6:25 and note).
13:2 *heart.* See note on 4:7.
13:3–4 Appeal for deliverance from death.
13:3 *Give light to my eyes.* Restore me (see note on 6:7).
13:4 See notes on 3:2; 5:9. *fall.* Referring to death (as in 18:38; 82:7; 106:26; Jdg 5:27; 2Sa 1:19; Job 18:12).
13:5–6 Concluding expression of confidence (see note on 3:8).
13:5 *unfailing love.* See note on 6:4. *heart.* See note on 4:7. *rejoices.* It is David who will rejoice, not his enemies.
13:6 See note on 7:17.
Ps 14 A testimony concerning the moral folly of those who live as if there were no God and therefore feel free to cruelly prey on others who are at their mercy (Ps 53 is a somewhat revised duplicate). In its depiction of their godless arrogance, it has links with Ps 10; 12 (see also 28:3–5). And it shares with Ps 11 the conviction that the righteous Lord is on his heavenly throne. This psalm brings to closure the collection of prayers that began with Ps 3 (for the next grouping of psalms see introduction to Ps 15–24). Five psalms (and 64 Hebrew poetic lines) after Ps 8's surprising evocation of humanity's "glory and honor" (8:5), this psalm highlights their disgrace (see introduction to Ps 8). In this it serves as a counterpoint to that earlier recollection of humanity's high dignity and thereby exposes more sharply the depth of their disgrace—from which the petitioners in this and the preceding psalms have suffered.
14 title *For the director of music.* See note on Ps 4 title.
14:1–3 Characterization of the wicked. For Paul's use of these verses in a different context see Ro 3:10–12.
14:1 *fool.* See NIV text note. The Hebrew word is *nabal*; for its meaning see 1Sa 25:25; 2Sa 13:13; Isa 32:5–7 (in Proverbs "fool" renders two other Hebrew words; see NIV text notes on Pr 1:7,22). *says.* See note on 3:2. *heart.* See note on 4:7. *no God.* A practical atheism (see 10:4,6,11,13; 36:1; see also note on 10:4). *no one who does good.* Context limits the scope of this assertion—and the assertion in v. 3—to the "fools" who take no account of God and do not hesitate to show their malice toward "the company of the righteous" (see vv. 4–5)—as in 9:19–20; 10:2–11,13,18; 12:1–4,7–8 (this is also the situation that Ps 11 describes). In other psalms the psalmists do include themselves among those who are not righteous in God's eyes (see 130:3; 143:2; see also 1Ki 8:46; Job 9:2; Ecc 7:20).
14:2 *The LORD.* Emphatically contrasted with "the fool" (v. 1). *looks down from heaven.* See 33:13–14. *who seek God.* To "seek God" authentically is to "seek" what is morally "good" (Am 5:14–15); it is to "seek justice" in all human relationships (Isa 1:17). See also Ps 15.
14:3 *turned aside.* From God and goodness.

[4]Will evildoers never learn—[o]
those who devour my people[p] as
men eat bread
and who do not call on the LORD?[q]
[5]There they are, overwhelmed with
dread,
for God is present in the company of
the righteous.
[6]You evildoers frustrate the plans of the
poor,
but the LORD is their refuge.[r]
[7]Oh, that salvation for Israel would
come out of Zion![s]
When the LORD restores the fortunes[t]
of his people,
let Jacob rejoice and Israel be glad!

Psalm 15

A psalm of David.

[1]LORD, who may dwell[u] in your
sanctuary?[v]
Who may live on your holy hill?[w]

[2]He whose walk is blameless[x]
and who does what is righteous,
who speaks the truth[y] from his heart
[3]and has no slander[z] on his tongue,
who does his neighbor no wrong
and casts no slur on his fellowman,
[4]who despises a vile man
but honors[a] those who fear the LORD,
who keeps his oath[b]
even when it hurts,
[5]who lends his money without usury[c]
and does not accept a bribe[d] against
the innocent.

He who does these things
will never be shaken.[e]

Psalm 16

A *miktam*[a] of David.

[1]Keep me safe,[f] O God,
for in you I take refuge.[g]

[2]I said to the LORD, "You are my Lord;[h]
apart from you I have no good
thing."[i]

[a] Title: Probably a literary or musical term

14:4 [o]Ps 82:5; Jer 4:22 [p]Ps 27:2; Mic 3:3 [q]Ps 79:6; Isa 64:7; 65:1; Jer 10:25; Hos 7:7 **14:6** [r]S 2Sa 22:3 **14:7** [s]Ps 2:6 [t]S Dt 30:3; S Jer 48:47 **15:1** [u]Ex 29:46; Ps 23:6; 27:4; 61:4 [v]Ex 25:8; 1Ch 22:19; Ps 20:2; 78:69; 150:1 [w]S Ex 15:17 **15:2** [x]S Ge 6:9; S Ps 18:32; Eph 1:4; S 1Th 3:13; Tit 1:6 [y]Pr 16:13; Isa 45:19; Jer 7:28; 9:5; Zec 8:3,16; Ro 9:1; S Eph 4:25 **15:3** [z]S Lev 19:16 **15:4** [a]S Job 19:9; Ac 28:10 [b]S Dt 23:21; S Jos 9:18; Mt 5:33 **15:5** [c]S Ex 22:25 [d]S Ex 18:21; S 1Sa 8:3; Ac 24:26 [e]S Job 29:18; Ps 21:7; 112:6; Ac 2:25; Heb 12:28; 2Pe 1:10 **16:1** [f]S Ps 12:7 [g]Ps 2:12 **16:2** [h]Ps 31:14; 118:28; 140:6 [i]Ps 73:25

14:4–6 The folly of the wicked exposed.

14:4 *Will evildoers never learn ...?* In Hebrew the centered line of the psalm (see note on 6:6), containing the hinge on which the psalm's thematic development turns. *devour ... do not call on the LORD.* Renewed characterization of the wicked: They live by the violence of their own hands and do not rely on the Lord (see 10:2–4).

14:5 Even God's mighty defense of the righteous teaches them nothing. *righteous.* See note on 1:5.

14:6 *poor.* Those who lack the resources to defend themselves. The same Hebrew word is rendered "weak" in 10:2 and "helpless" in 10:9,12. *refuge.* See note on 2:12.

14:7 The psalmist longs for Israel's complete deliverance from her enemies—which will come when God deals with the wicked in defense of their victims. For a similar expansion of scope see 10:16–18 and note. *Zion.* See note on 9:11. *Jacob ... Israel.* Synonyms (see Ge 32:28).

Ps 15–24 Ps 15 and its distinctive counterpart, Ps 24, frame a cluster of psalms that have been arranged in a concentric pattern with Ps 19 serving as the hinge (for the thematic links between Ps 16 and 23, between Ps 17 and 22, and between Ps 18 and 20–21, see introductions to those psalms). The framing psalms (15; 24) are thematically linked by their evocation of the high majesty of God and their insistence on moral purity "without [which] no one will see the Lord" (Heb 12:14). At the center, Ps 19 uniquely combines a celebration of the divine majesty as displayed in the creation and an exposition of how moral purity is attained through God's law, forgiveness and shepherding care. Together, these three psalms (15; 19; 24) provide instructive words concerning the petitioners heard in the enclosed psalms, offer a counterpoint to Ps 14, and reinforce the instruction of Ps 1.

Ps 15 Instruction concerning those who wish to have access to God at his temple (see 24:3–6; Isa 33:14–16). See also introduction to Ps 15–24.

15:1 *dwell ... live on.* Not as a priest but as God's welcome guest in his holy, royal house, the temple (see 23:6; 27:4–6; 61:4; 84:10; 2Sa 12:20). *holy hill.* See note on 2:6.

15:2–5 Not sacrifices or ritual purity (as among the religions of the ancient Near East) but moral righteousness gives access to the Lord, the God of Israel (see the basic covenantal law: Ex 20:1–17; see also Isa 1:10–17; 33:14–16; 58:6–10; Jer 7:2–7; Eze 18:5–9; Hos 6:6; Am 5:14–15,21–24; Mic 6:6–8; Zec 7:9–10; 8:16–17).

15:2 *He ... righteous.* A summary introduction to the list that follows. *blameless.* That is, uniting loyalty to God and faithfulness to his covenant directives. See Ge 17:1 and note; see also how the Hebrew word is used in 18:23; 37:18; 84:1; 101:2,6; 119:1,80; Jos 24:14 ("all faithfulness"); Jdg 9:16,19 ("honorably"); and see how a closely related word is used in 7:8 ("integrity"); *righteous.* See note on 1:5. *heart.* See note on 4:7.

15:3 *tongue.* See note on 5:9.

15:4 *despises a vile man.* Or "despises those repudiated" by God—because they have become an offense to him. *those who fear the LORD.* Those who honor God and order their lives in accordance with his will (see note on Ge 20:11) because of their reverence for him.

15:5 *usury.* See note on Ex 22:25–27. *be shaken.* See note on 10:6.

Ps 16 A prayer for safekeeping (v. 1—the petition element in prayer psalms is often relatively short; see 3:7; 22:19–21; 44:23–26), pleading for the Lord's protection against the threat of death. In accordance with its dominant theme, it could also be called a psalm of trust. In this regard it has close thematic links with Ps 23 (compare 16:2 with 23:1; 16:5 with 23:5; 16:7–8 with 23:4; 16:11 with 23:6). Together these two psalms underscore faith/trust as the second essential characteristic (alongside conformity to God's law; see introduction to Ps 15–24) of those who bring their prayers to God (see introduction to Ps 1–2; see also note on 34:8–14).

16 title *miktam.* The term remains unexplained, though it always stands in the superscription of Davidic prayers occasioned by great danger (see Ps 56–60).

16:1 The petition and the basis for it. The rest of the psalm elaborates on the latter element.

16:2–4 The Lord is David's one and only good thing (see 73:25,28); David will have nothing to do with the counterfeit gods to whom others pour out their libations (see 4:2).

3 As for the saints[j] who are in the land,[k]
they are the glorious ones in whom
is all my delight.[a]
4 The sorrows[l] of those will increase
who run after other gods.[m]
I will not pour out their libations of
blood
or take up their names[n] on my lips.

5 LORD, you have assigned me my
portion[o] and my cup;[p]
you have made my lot[q] secure.
6 The boundary lines[r] have fallen for me
in pleasant places;
surely I have a delightful
inheritance.[s]

7 I will praise the LORD, who counsels
me;[t]
even at night[u] my heart instructs
me.
8 I have set the LORD always before me.
Because he is at my right hand,[v]
I will not be shaken.[w]

9 Therefore my heart is glad[x] and my
tongue rejoices;
my body also will rest secure,[y]
10 because you will not abandon me to
the grave,[b][z]
nor will you let your Holy One[c][a] see
decay.[b]
11 You have made[d] known to me the path
of life;[c]
you will fill me with joy in your
presence,[d]
with eternal pleasures[e] at your right
hand.[f]

Psalm 17

A prayer of David.

1 Hear,[g] O LORD, my righteous plea;
listen to my cry.[h]
Give ear[i] to my prayer—
it does not rise from deceitful lips.[j]
2 May my vindication[k] come from you;
may your eyes see what is right.[l]

3 Though you probe my heart[m] and
examine me at night,
though you test me,[n] you will find
nothing;[o]
I have resolved that my mouth will
not sin.[p]
4 As for the deeds of men—
by the word of your lips
I have kept myself
from the ways of the violent.

16:3 [j] Dt 33:3; Ps 30:4; 85:8; Da 7:18; Ac 9:13; Ro 1:7 [k] Ps 101:6 **16:4** [l] Ps 32:10; Pr 23:29 [m] Ex 18:11; 20:3; S Dt 8:19; S 31:20 [n] S Ex 23:13 **16:5** [o] S Lev 2:2 [p] Ps 23:5; 75:8; 116:13; Isa 51:17; La 4:21; Eze 23:32-34; Hab 2:16 [q] S Job 31:2 **16:6** [r] S Dt 19:14; Ps 104:9; Pr 8:29; Jer 5:22 [s] S Job 22:26 **16:7** [t] Ps 73:24; Pr 15:22; Isa 11:2 [u] Job 35:10; Ps 42:8; 77:6 **16:8** [v] 1Ki 2:19; 1Ch 6:39; Ps 73:23 [w] Ps 15:5 **16:9** [x] Ps 4:7; 13:5; 28:7; 30:11 [y] S Dt 33:28 **16:10** [z] S Nu 16:30; Ps 30:3; 31:17; 86:13; Hos 13:14 [a] S 2Ki 19:22 [b] S Job 17:14; Ac 2:31; 13:35* **16:11** [c] Ps 139:24; Mt 7:14 [d] Ac 2:25-28* [e] Ps 21:6 [f] Ps 80:17 **17:1** [g] Ps 30:10; 64:1; 80:1; 140:6 [h] Ps 5:2; 39:12; 142:6; 143:1 [i] S Ps 5:1 [j] Isa 29:13 **17:2** [k] Ps 24:5; 26:1; Isa 46:13; 50:8-9; 54:17 [l] Ps 99:4 **17:3** [m] Ps 139:1; Jer 12:3 [n] S Job 7:18 [o] Job 23:10; Jer 50:20 [p] Ps 39:1

[a] 3 Or *As for the pagan priests who are in the land / and the nobles in whom all delight, I said:* [b] 10 Hebrew *Sheol* [c] 10 Or *your faithful one* [d] 11 Or *You will make*

16:3 See Ps 101; see also NIV text note.
16:4 *sorrows … will increase.* In contrast with David's good "portion" (v. 5; see note on 11:6), which affords him much joy (see 73:18 – 26). *libations of blood.* Blood of sacrifices poured on altars. *take up their names.* Appeal to or worship them (see Jos 23:7).
16:5 – 6 Joy over the inheritance received from the Lord. David refers to what the Lord bestowed on his people in the promised land, either to the gift of fields there (see Nu 16:14) or to the Lord himself (as in 73:26; 119:57; 142:5; La 3:24), who was the inheritance of the priests (see Nu 18:20) and the Levites (see Dt 10:9).
16:5 *cup.* A metaphor referring to what the host offers his guests to drink. To the godly the Lord offers a cup of blessing (see 23:5) or salvation (see 116:13); he makes the wicked drink from a cup of wrath (see Jer 25:15; Rev 14:10; 16:19). *secure.* Just as each Israelite's family inheritance in the promised land was to be secure (see Lev 25; Nu 36:7).
16:7 – 8 Praise of the Lord who counsels and keeps.
16:7 *counsels.* Shows the way that leads to life (see v. 11). *heart.* Lit. "kidneys" (see note on 7:9). The reference here is probably to conscience.
16:8 *he is at my right hand.* As sustainer and protector (see 73:23; 109:31; 110:5; 121:5); complemented by the reference to the Lord's right hand in v. 11. *not be shaken.* See note on 10:6.
16:9 – 11 Describes the joy of the total security that God's faithful care provides. David speaks of himself and of the life he enjoys by the gracious provision and care of God. The Lord, in whom the psalmist takes refuge, wills life for him (hence he made known to him the path of life, v. 11) and will not abandon him to the grave, even though "flesh and … heart … fail" (73:26). But implicit in these words of assurance (if not actually explicit) is the confidence that, with the Lord as his refuge, even the grave cannot rob him of life (see 17:15; 73:24; see also note on 11:7). If this could be said of David — and of all those godly Israelites who made David's prayer their own — how much more of David's promised Son! So Peter quotes vv. 8 – 11 and declares that with these words David prophesied of Christ and his resurrection (Ac 2:25 – 28; see Paul's similar use of v. 10b in Ac 13:35). See also note on 6:5.
16:9 *heart.* See note on 4:7. *tongue.* Lit. "glory" (see note on 7:5).
16:10 *Holy One.* Hebrew *ḥasid* (see note on 4:3). Reference is first of all to David (hence the NIV text note; see also note on 2:2), but the psalm is ultimately fulfilled in Christ (see note on vv. 9 – 11).
16:11 *path of life.* See Pr 15:24. *your right hand.* See note on v. 8.
Ps 17 David appeals to the Lord as Judge when he is under attack by ungodly foes. The circumstances evoked and the petition to which they gave rise show considerable affinity with Ps 22 (see introduction to Ps 15 – 24). The psalm reflects many of the Hebrew conventions of lodging a judicial appeal before a king.
17 title *A prayer.* See titles of Ps 86; 90; 102; 142; see also 72:20.
17:1 – 2 The initial appeal for justice.
17:1 *my righteous plea.* For justice. His case is truly just, not a clever misrepresentation by deceitful lips (for a similar situation see 1Sa 24:15).
17:3 – 5 David's claim of innocence in support of the rightness of his case. He is not guilty of the ungodly ways of his attackers — let God examine him (cf. 139:23 – 24).
17:3 *heart.* See note on 4:7.
17:4 *word of your lips.* God's revealed will, by which he has made known the "paths" (v. 5) that people are to walk.

5 My steps have held to your paths;[q]
my feet have not slipped.[r]
6 I call on you, O God, for you will
answer me;[s]
give ear to me[t] and hear my prayer.[u]
7 Show the wonder of your great love,[v]
you who save by your right hand[w]
those who take refuge[x] in you from
their foes.
8 Keep me[y] as the apple of your eye;[z]
hide me[a] in the shadow of your
wings[b]
9 from the wicked who assail me,
from my mortal enemies who
surround me.[c]
10 They close up their callous hearts,[d]
and their mouths speak with
arrogance.[e]
11 They have tracked me down, they now
surround me,[f]
with eyes alert, to throw me to the
ground.
12 They are like a lion[g] hungry for prey,[h]
like a great lion crouching in cover.
13 Rise up,[i] O LORD, confront them, bring
them down;[j]
rescue me from the wicked by your
sword.
14 O LORD, by your hand save me from
such men,
from men of this world[k] whose
reward is in this life.[l]
You still the hunger of those you
cherish;
their sons have plenty,
and they store up wealth[m] for their
children.
15 And I—in righteousness I will see your
face;
when I awake,[n] I will be satisfied
with seeing your likeness.[o]

Psalm 18

18:Title–50pp — 2Sa 22:1-51

For the director of music. Of David the servant of the LORD. He sang to the LORD the words of this song when the LORD delivered him from the hand of all his enemies and from the hand of Saul. He said:

1 I love you, O LORD, my strength.[p]
2 The LORD is my rock,[q] my fortress[r] and
my deliverer;[s]
my God is my rock, in whom I take
refuge.[t]
He is my shield[u] and the horn[a] of
my salvation,[v] my stronghold.

[a] 2 *Horn* here symbolizes strength.

17:5 [q] Job 23:11; Ps 44:18; 119:133 [r] Dt 32:35; Ps 73:2; 121:3 **17:6** [s] Ps 86:7 [t] Ps 116:2 [u] S Ps 4:1 **17:7** [v] Ps 31:21; 69:13; 106:45; 107:43; 117:2 [w] S Ps 10:12 [x] Ps 2:12 **17:8** [y] S Nu 6:24 [z] S Dt 32:10; Pr 7:2 [a] Ps 27:5; 31:20; 32:7 [b] Ru 2:12; Ps 36:7; 63:7; Isa 34:15 **17:9** [c] Ps 109:3 **17:10** [d] Ps 73:7; 119:70; Isa 6:10 [e] S 1Sa 2:3 **17:11** [f] Ps 88:17 **17:12** [g] Ps 7:2; Jer 5:6; 12:8; La 3:10 [h] S Ge 49:9 **17:13** [i] S Nu 10:35 [j] Ps 35:8; 55:23; 73:18 **17:14** [k] Lk 16:8 [l] Ps 49:17; Lk 16:25 [m] Isa 2:7; 57:17 **17:15** [n] S Ps 3:5 [o] S Nu 12:8; S Mt 5:8; 1Jn 3:2 **18:1** [p] S Ex 15:2; S Dt 33:29; S 1Sa 2:10; Ps 22:19; 28:7; 59:9; 81:1; Isa 12:2; 49:5; Jer 16:19 **18:2** [q] S Ex 33:22 [r] Ps 28:8; 31:2,3; Isa 17:10; Jer 16:19 [s] Ps 40:17 [t] Ps 2:12; 9:9; 94:22 [u] S Ge 15:1; Ps 28:7; 84:9; 119:114; 144:2 [v] S 1Sa 2:1; S Lk 1:69

17:6–9 The petition: what David wants the Lord to do for him—motivated by David's trust in him ("for you will answer me," v. 6) and the Lord's unfailing righteousness (see v. 7).
17:6 *I call ... you will answer.* See note on 118:5.
17:7 *wonder.* See note on 9:1. *great love.* See note on 6:4.
17:8 *apple of your eye.* See note on Dt 32:10. *shadow.* A conventional Hebrew metaphor for protection against oppression—as shade protects from the oppressive heat of the hot desert sun. Kings were spoken of as the "shade" of those dependent on them for protection (as in Nu 14:9, "protection"—lit. "shade"; La 4:20; Eze 31:6,12,17). Similarly, the Lord is the protective "shade" of his people (see 91:1; 121:5; Isa 25:4; 49:2; 51:16). *wings.* Metaphor for the protective outreach of God's power (see 36:7; 57:1; 61:4; 63:7; 91:4; Ru 2:12; see also Mt 23:37).
17:10–12 The accusation lodged against the vicious adversaries (see note on 5:9–10).
17:10 *mouths.* See note on 5:9. *speak with arrogance.* See note on 10:11.
17:12 *lion.* See note on 7:2.
17:13–14a Petition: how David wants the Lord to deal with the two parties in the conflict.
17:13 *Rise up.* See note on 3:7. *bring them down.* See note on 5:10. *your sword.* See 7:12–13 and note.
17:14 *such men.* See 9:19–20; 10:18; 12:1–4,8; 14:1–3.
17:14b–15 Concluding confession of confidence (see note on 3:8).
17:15 *in righteousness.* The righteous Judge (see note on 4:1) will acknowledge and vindicate the innocence (righteousness) of the petitioner. *see your face.* See note on 11:7. *when I awake.* From the night of death (see note on 11:7)—in radical contrast to the destiny of the "men of this world" (v. 14; see notes on 6:5; 16:9–11). *seeing your likeness.* As Moses the servant of the Lord had seen it (see Nu 12:8).

Ps 18 This song of David occurs also (with minor variations) in 2Sa 22 (see notes there). In its structure, apart from the introduction (vv. 1–3) and the conclusion (vv. 46–50), the song is composed of three major divisions: (1) the Lord's deliverance of David from his mortal enemies in answer to his cry for help (vv. 4–19); (2) the moral grounds for the Lord's saving help (vv. 20–29); (3) the Lord's help recounted (vv. 30–45). David's celebration of God's saving help in answer to prayer when under threat from powerful enemies receives its counterpart in the two closely related psalms (Ps 20–21; see introductions to those psalms and introduction to Ps 15–24).
18 title *For the director of music.* See note on Ps 4 title. *servant of the LORD.* See 78:70; 89:3,20,39; 132:10; 144:10. The title designates David in his royal office as, in effect, an official in the Lord's own kingly rule over his people (see 2Sa 7:5)—as were Moses (see Ex 14:31 and note), Joshua (see Jos 24:29) and the prophets (Elijah, 2Ki 9:36; Jonah, 2Ki 14:25; Isaiah, Isa 20:3; Daniel, Da 6:20). *song.* See note on Ps 30 title. *when the LORD delivered him.* It is possible that David composed his song shortly after his victories over his foreign enemies (2Sa 8:1–14), but it may have been later in his life.
18:1–3 A prelude of praise.
18:1 Does not occur in 2Sa 22. *I love you.* From an unusual Hebrew expression that emphasizes the fervor of David's love.
18:2 *rock ... rock.* The translation of two different Hebrew words. "Rock" is a common poetic figure for God (or the gods: Dt 32:31,37; Isa 44:8), symbolizing his unfailing (see Isa 26:4) strength as a fortress refuge (see vv. 31,46; 31:2–3; 42:9; 62:7; 71:3; 94:22; Isa 17:10) or as deliverer (see 19:14; 62:2; 78:35; 89:26; 95:1; Dt 32:15). It is a figure particularly appropriate for David's experience (see 1Sa 23:14,25; 24:2,22; 26:20), for the Lord was his true security. *fortress.* See note on 2Sa 22:2. *shield.* See note on 3:3. *horn.* See NIV text note; Dt 33:17; Jer 48:25.

[3]I call to the LORD, who is worthy of
praise,[w]
and I am saved from my enemies.[x]
[4]The cords of death[y] entangled me;
the torrents[z] of destruction
overwhelmed me.
[5]The cords of the grave[a] coiled around
me;
the snares of death[a] confronted me.
[6]In my distress[b] I called to the LORD;[c]
I cried to my God for help.
From his temple he heard my voice;[d]
my cry came[e] before him, into his
ears.
[7]The earth trembled[f] and quaked,[g]
and the foundations of the
mountains shook;[h]
they trembled because he was
angry.[i]
[8]Smoke rose from his nostrils;[j]
consuming fire[k] came from his
mouth,
burning coals[l] blazed out of it.
[9]He parted the heavens and came
down;[m]
dark clouds[n] were under his feet.
[10]He mounted the cherubim[o] and flew;
he soared[p] on the wings of the
wind.[q]
[11]He made darkness his covering,[r] his
canopy[s] around him—
the dark rain clouds of the sky.
[12]Out of the brightness of his presence[t]
clouds advanced,
with hailstones[u] and bolts of
lightning.[v]
[13]The LORD thundered[w] from heaven;
the voice of the Most High
resounded.[b]
[14]He shot his arrows[x] and scattered ⌞the
enemies⌟,
great bolts of lightning[y] and routed
them.[z]
[15]The valleys of the sea were exposed
and the foundations[a] of the earth
laid bare
at your rebuke,[b] O LORD,
at the blast of breath from your
nostrils.[c]
[16]He reached down from on high and
took hold of me;
he drew me out of deep waters.[d]
[17]He rescued me from my powerful
enemy,[e]
from my foes, who were too strong
for me.[f]
[18]They confronted me in the day of my
disaster,[g]
but the LORD was my support.[h]
[19]He brought me out into a spacious
place;[i]
he rescued me because he delighted
in me.[j]
[20]The LORD has dealt with me according
to my righteousness;[k]
according to the cleanness of my
hands[l] he has rewarded me.[m]

18:3 [w]S 1Ch 16:25 [x]S Ps 9:13 **18:4** [y]Ps 116:3 [z]Ps 93:4; 124:4; Isa 5:30; 17:12; Jer 6:23; 51:42, 55; Eze 43:2 **18:5** [a]Pr 13:14 **18:6** [b]S Dt 4:30 [c]Ps 30:2; 99:6; 102:2; 120:1 [d]Ps 66:19; 116:1 [e]S Job 16:18 **18:7** [f]Ps 97:4; Isa 5:25; 64:3 [g]S Jdg 5:4 [h]S Jdg 5:5 [i]S Job 9:5; Jer 10:10 **18:8** [j]S Job 41:20 [k]S Ex 15:7; S 19:18; S Job 41:21; Ps 50:3; 97:3; Da 7:10 [l]Pr 25:22; Ro 12:20 **18:9** [m]S Ge 11:5; S Ps 57:3 [n]S Ex 20:21; S Dt 33:26; S Ps 104:3 **18:10** [o]S Ge 3:24; Eze 10:18 [p]S Dt 33:26 [q]Ps 104:3 **18:11** [r]S Ex 19:9; S Dt 4:11 [s]S Job 22:14; Isa 4:5; Jer 43:10 **18:12** [t]Ps 104:2 [u]S Jos 10:11 [v]S Job 36:30 **18:13** [w]S Ex 9:23; S 1Sa 2:10 **18:14** [x]S Dt 32:23 [y]S Job 36:30; Rev 4:5 [z]S Jdg 4:15 **18:15** [a]S Ps 11:3 [b]Ps 76:6; 104:7; 106:9; Isa 50:2 [c]S Ex 15:8 **18:16** [d]Ex 15:5; Ps 69:2; Pr 18:4; 20:5 **18:17** [e]ver 48; Ps 38:19; 59:1; 143:9 [f]S Jdg 18:26 **18:18** [g]Pr 1:27; 16:4; Jer 17:17; 40:2; Ob 1:13 [h]Ps 20:2; Isa 3:1 **18:19** [i]Ps 31:8 [j]S Nu 14:8 **18:20** [k]S 1Sa 26:23 [l]Job 22:30; Ps 24:4 [m]S Ru 2:12; S 2Ch 15:7; 1Co 3:8

[a] *5* Hebrew *Sheol* [b] *13* Some Hebrew manuscripts and Septuagint (see also 2 Samuel 22:14); most Hebrew manuscripts *resounded, / amid hailstones and bolts of lightning*

18:4–6 God heard his cry for help.
18:4–5 David depicts his experiences in poetic figures of mortal danger.
18:4 *cords.* 2Sa 22:5 has "waves." *torrents of destruction.* See note on 30:1.
18:5 *cords of the grave ... snares of death.* See 116:3. He had, as it were, been snared by death (personified) and bound as a prisoner of the grave (see Job 36:8). See also note on 30:3.
18:6 *temple.* God's heavenly abode, where he sits enthroned (see 11:4; 113:5; Isa 6:1; 40:22).
18:7–15 The Lord came to the aid of his servant—depicted as a fearful theophany (divine manifestation) of the heavenly Warrior descending in wrathful attack upon David's enemies (see 5:4–5; 68:1–8; 77:16–19; Mic 1:3–4; Na 1:2–6; Hab 3:3–15). He sweeps down upon them like a fierce thunderstorm (see Jos 10:11; Jdg 5:20–22; 1Sa 2:10; 7:10; 2Sa 5:24; Isa 29:6).
18:8 God's fierce majesty is portrayed in terms similar to those applied to the awesome leviathan (Job 41:19–21).
18:9 *parted the heavens and came down.* See Isa 64:1 and note.
18:10 *cherubim.* Symbols of royalty (see 80:1; 99:1; see also notes on Ge 3:24; Ex 25:18). In Eze 1 and 10, cherubim appear as the bearers of the throne-chariot of God.
18:13 *voice.* For thunder as the voice of God see Ps 29; Job 37:2–5. *Most High.* See note on Ge 14:19.
18:14 *arrows.* For shafts of lightning as the arrows of God see 77:17; 144:6; Hab 3:11; see also note on Ge 9:13.
18:15 Perhaps recalls the great deed of the heavenly Warrior when he defeated Israel's enemy at the Red Sea (see Ex 15:1–12).
18:16–19 The deliverance.
18:16 *deep waters.* See note on 32:6.
18:19 *spacious place.* See 4:1 and note; where he is free to roam unconfined by the threats and dangers that had hemmed him in (vv. 4–6,16–18). To be afflicted or oppressed is like being bound by fetters (Job 36:8,13). To be delivered is to be set free (Job 36:16). *delighted in me.* God was pleased with David as "a man after his own heart" (1Sa 13:14; see also 1Sa 15:28; 1Ki 14:8; 15:5), a man with whom he had made a covenant assuring him of an enduring dynasty (2Sa 7). The thought is further elaborated in vv. 20–29.
18:20–24 David's righteousness rewarded. David's assertion of his righteousness (like that of Samuel, 1Sa 12:3; Hezekiah, 2Ki 20:3; Job, Job 13:23; 27:6; 31; see also Ps 17:3–5; 26; 44:17–18; 101) is not a pretentious boast of sinless perfection (see 51:5). Rather, it is a claim that, in contrast to his enemies, he has devoted himself heart and life to the service of the Lord, that his has been a godliness with integrity—itself the fruit of God's gracious working in his heart (see 51:10–12).
18:20,24 *my righteousness.* See notes on 1:5; 2Sa 22:21,25. *rewarded me.* As a king benevolently rewards those who loyally serve him.

21 For I have kept the ways of the LORD;[n]
I have not done evil by turning[o] from my God.
22 All his laws are before me;[p]
I have not turned away from his decrees.
23 I have been blameless[q] before him
and have kept myself from sin.
24 The LORD has rewarded me according to my righteousness,[r]
according to the cleanness of my hands in his sight.

25 To the faithful[s] you show yourself faithful,[t]
to the blameless you show yourself blameless,
26 to the pure[u] you show yourself pure,
but to the crooked you show yourself shrewd.[v]
27 You save the humble[w]
but bring low those whose eyes are haughty.[x]
28 You, O LORD, keep my lamp[y] burning;
my God turns my darkness into light.[z]
29 With your help[a] I can advance against a troop[a];
with my God I can scale a wall.

30 As for God, his way is perfect;[b]
the word of the LORD is flawless.[c]
He is a shield[d]
for all who take refuge[e] in him.
31 For who is God besides the LORD?[f]
And who is the Rock[g] except our God?
32 It is God who arms me with strength[h]
and makes my way perfect.[i]
33 He makes my feet like the feet of a deer;[j]
he enables me to stand on the heights.[k]
34 He trains my hands for battle;[l]
my arms can bend a bow of bronze.
35 You give me your shield of victory,
and your right hand sustains[m] me;
you stoop down to make me great.

18:21 [n]2Ch 34:33; Ps 37:34; 119:2; Pr 8:32; 23:26 [o]Ps 119:102 **18:22** [p]Ps 119:30 **18:23** [q]S Ge 6:9 **18:24** [r]S 1Sa 26:23 **18:25** [s]Ps 31:23; 37:28; 50:5; Pr 2:8 [t]Ps 25:10; 40:11; 89:24; 146:6 **18:26** [u]Pr 15:26; Mt 5:8; Php 1:10; 1Ti 5:22; Tit 1:15; 1Jn 3:3 [v]Pr 3:34; Mt 10:16; Lk 16:8 **18:27** [w]S 2Ch 33:23; S Mt 23:12 [x]S Job 41:34; S Ps 10:5; Pr 3:33-34 **18:28** [y]1Ki 11:36; Ps 132:17 [z]Job 29:3; Ps 97:11; 112:4; Jn 1:5; S Ac 26:18; 2Co 4:6; 2Pe 1:19 **18:29** [a]ver 32, 39; Isa 45:5; Heb 11:34 **18:30** [b]S Dt 32:4 [c]S Ps 12:6; Pr 30:5 [d]Ps 3:3 [e]Ps 2:12 **18:31** [f]S Dt 4:35; 32:39; Ps 35:10; 86:8; 89:6; Isa 44:6, 8; 45:5, 6, 14, 18, 21; 46:9 [g]S Ge 49:24 **18:32** [h]S ver 29; 1Pe 5:10 [i]S Ps 15:2; 19:13; Heb 10:14; Jas 3:2 **18:33** [j]Ps 42:1; Pr 5:19; Isa 35:6; Hab 3:19 [k]S Dt 32:13 **18:34** [l]Ps 144:1 **18:35** [m]Ps 3:5; 37:5, 17; 41:3; 51:12; 54:4; 55:22; 119:116; Isa 41:4, 10, 13; 43:2; 46:4 **18:36** [n]Ps 31:8 [o]S Job 18:7; Ps 66:9

36 You broaden the path[n] beneath me,
so that my ankles do not turn.[o]

37 I pursued my enemies[p] and overtook them;
I did not turn back till they were destroyed.
38 I crushed them[q] so that they could not rise;[r]
they fell beneath my feet.[s]
39 You armed me with strength[t] for battle;
you made my adversaries bow[u] at my feet.
40 You made my enemies turn their backs[v] in flight,
and I destroyed[w] my foes.
41 They cried for help, but there was no one to save them[x]—
to the LORD, but he did not answer.[y]
42 I beat them as fine as dust[z] borne on the wind;
I poured them out like mud in the streets.
43 You have delivered me from the attacks of the people;
you have made me the head of nations;[a]
people I did not know[b] are subject to me.
44 As soon as they hear me, they obey me;
foreigners[c] cringe before me.
45 They all lose heart;[d]
they come trembling[e] from their strongholds.[f]

46 The LORD lives![g] Praise be to my Rock![h]
Exalted be God[i] my Savior![j]
47 He is the God who avenges[k] me,
who subdues nations[l] under me,

[a] 29 Or *can run through a barricade*

18:37 [p]S Lev 26:7 **18:38** [q]Ps 68:21; 110:6 [r]Ps 36:12; 140:10; Isa 26:14 [s]Ps 47:3 **18:39** [t]ver 32; Isa 45:5, 24 [u]ver 47; Ps 47:3; 144:2 **18:40** [v]S Jos 7:12 [w]ver 37 **18:41** [x]S 2Ki 14:26; Ps 50:22 [y]S 1Sa 8:18; S 14:37; Jer 11:11 **18:42** [z]S Dt 9:21; S Isa 2:22 **18:43** [a]2Sa 8:1-14 [b]Isa 55:5 **18:44** [c]Ps 54:3; 144:7, 11; Isa 25:5 **18:45** [d]S 1Sa 17:32; 2Co 4:1; Heb 12:3 [e]Isa 66:2; Hos 3:5; 11:10 [f]Ps 9:9; Mic 7:17 **18:46** [g]S Jos 3:10; S 1Sa 14:39; 2Co 13:4 [h]ver 31; Ex 33:22 [i]Ps 21:13; 35:27; 40:16; 108:5 [j]S 1Ch 16:35; S Lk 1:47 **18:47** [k]S Ge 4:24 [l]S ver 39; S Jdg 4:23

18:21 *ways of the LORD.* See 25:4 and note.
18:23 *blameless.* See note on 15:2.
18:25–29 Because God responds to people in accordance with their ways (see Job 34:11; Pr 3:34), David has experienced the Lord's favor.
18:26 *crooked.* Deviating from the straight path of truth and righteousness. *shrewd.* God responds to their perverse dealings thrust for thrust, like a wrestler countering his opponent (see 1Ki 22:23 and note; see also note on Jdg 11:35).
18:27 The thought of this verse fits well with David's and Saul's reversals of status. It also echoes the central theme of Hannah's song (1Sa 2:1–10), which the author of Samuel uses to highlight a major thesis of his account of the ways of God as he brings about his kingdom.
18:28 *keep my lamp burning.* God causes his life, his undertakings and his dynasty to flourish (see especially Job 18:5–6; 21:17). *light.* See note on 27:1.
18:30–36 By God's blessing David the king has thrived.
18:30 *is perfect.* Does not fail—and so, because of his blessing, David's way has not failed (see v. 32). *word of the LORD.* While the reference is general, it applies especially to God's promise to David (see 2Sa 7:8–16). *flawless.* See note on 12:6. *shield.* See note on 3:3.
18:37–42 With God's help David has crushed all his foes.
18:43–45 God has made David the head of nations (see 2Sa 5; 8; 10)—he who had been, it seemed, on the brink of death (see vv. 4–5 and note on v. 5), sinking into the depths (see v. 16).
18:43 *attacks of the people.* All the threats he had endured from his own people in the days of Saul, and perhaps also in the time of Absalom's rebellion. *people I did not know.* Those with whom he had had no previous relationship.
18:46–50 Concluding doxology.
18:46 *The LORD lives!* God's interventions and blessings in David's behalf have shown him to be the living God (see Dt 5:26).
18:47 *avenges me.* Redresses the wrongs committed against me (see Dt 32:41 and note on 32:35).

48 who saves[m] me from my enemies.[n]
You exalted me above my foes;
from violent men[o] you rescued me.
49 Therefore I will praise you among the
nations,[p] O LORD;
I will sing[q] praises to your name.[r]
50 He gives his king great victories;
he shows unfailing kindness to his
anointed,[s]
to David[t] and his descendants
forever.[u]

Psalm 19

For the director of music.
A psalm of David.

1 The heavens[v] declare[w] the glory of
God;[x]
the skies[y] proclaim the work of his
hands.[z]
2 Day after day they pour forth speech;
night after night they display
knowledge.[a]
3 There is no speech or language
where their voice is not heard.[a]
4 Their voice[b] goes out into all the earth,
their words to the ends of the
world.[b]

In the heavens he has pitched a tent[c]
for the sun,[d]
5 which is like a bridegroom[e] coming
forth from his pavilion,[f]
like a champion[g] rejoicing to run his
course.
6 It rises at one end of the heavens[h]
and makes its circuit to the other;[i]
nothing is hidden from its heat.

7 The law of the LORD[j] is perfect,[k]
reviving the soul.[l]
The statutes of the LORD are
trustworthy,[m]
making wise the simple.[n]
8 The precepts of the LORD are right,[o]
giving joy[p] to the heart.
The commands of the LORD are
radiant,
giving light to the eyes.[q]
9 The fear of the LORD[r] is pure,
enduring forever.
The ordinances of the LORD are sure
and altogether righteous.[s]
10 They are more precious than gold,[t]
than much pure gold;
they are sweeter than honey,[u]
than honey from the comb.[v]
11 By them is your servant warned;
in keeping them there is great
reward.

[a] 3 Or *They have no speech, there are no words; / no sound is heard from them* [b] 4 Septuagint, Jerome and Syriac; Hebrew *line*

18:48 [m] Ps 7:10; 37:40; Da 3:17 [n] S ver 17 [o] Ps 140:1 **18:49** [p] S Ps 9:11 [q] Ps 7:17; 9:2; 101:1; 108:1; 146:2 [r] Ro 15:9* **18:50** [s] S 2Sa 23:1 [t] Ps 144:10 [u] Ps 89:4 **19:1** [v] Ps 89:5; Isa 40:22 [w] Ps 50:6; 148:3; Ro 1:19 [x] Ps 4:2; 8:1; 97:6; Isa 6:3 [y] S Ge 1:8 [z] S Ps 8:6; S 103:22 **19:2** [a] Ps 74:16 **19:4** [b] Ro 10:18* [c] S Job 36:29; Ps 104:2 [d] S Jdg 5:31 **19:5** [e] Joel 2:16 [f] S Job 36:29 [g] 1Sa 17:4 **19:6** [h] Dt 30:4 [i] Ps 113:3; Ecc 1:5 **19:7** [j] S Ps 1:2 [k] Ps 119:142; Jas 1:25 [l] Ps 23:3 [m] Ps 93:5; 111:7; 119:138,144 [n] S Dt 4:6; Ps 119:130 **19:8** [o] Ps 33:4; 119:128 [p] Ps 119:14 [q] S Ezr 9:8; Ps 38:10 **19:9** [r] Ps 34:11; 111:10; Pr 1:7; Ecc 12:13; Isa 33:6 [s] Ps 119:138,142 **19:10** [t] S Job 22:24; Ps 119:72; Pr 8:10 [u] Ps 119:103; SS 4:11; Eze 3:3 [v] S 1Sa 14:27

18:49 David vows to praise the Lord among the nations (see note on 9:1). *name.* See note on 5:11.

18:50 *his king ... his anointed.* David views himself as the Lord's chosen and anointed king (see 1Sa 16:13; see also notes on 1Sa 10:25; 12:14–15). *shows unfailing kindness.* David's final words recall the Lord's covenant with him (see 2Sa 7:8–16). The whole song is to be understood in the context of David's official capacity and the Lord's covenant with him. What David claims in this grand conclusion—as, indeed, in the whole psalm—has been and is being fulfilled in Jesus Christ, David's great descendant.

Ps 19 A hymn extolling the majestic "glory of God" (v. 1) as displayed in the heavens, especially in the brilliant summer sun as it moves across a cloudless sky from east to west (see vv. 1–6; see also introduction to Ps 29), and "the law of the LORD" (v. 7), which blesses the lives of those who heed it (see vv. 7–13). An attached prayer (vv. 12–13) asks God to provide what his law cannot: forgiveness for "hidden faults" and a shepherd's care that preserves from "willful sins." Placed next to Ps 18, this psalm completes the cycle of praise—for the Lord's saving acts, for his glory reflected in creation and for his life-nurturing law. Placed at the center of Ps 15–24, it powerfully reinforces the themes of the two framing psalms (see introduction to Ps 15–24) and reminds all who would enter Yahweh's presence that they must come as those who have seen with their eyes his glory on display in the creation and who have in their hearts a deep devotion to his law.

19 title *For the director of music.* See note on Ps 4 title.

19:1–4a The silent heavens speak, declaring the glory of their Maker to all who are on the earth (cf. Ps 8; 148:3). The heavenly lights are not divine (see Ge 1:16 and note; Dt 4:19; 17:3), nor do they control or disclose anyone's destiny (see Isa 47:13; Jer 10:2; Da 4:7). Their glory testifies to the righteousness and faithfulness of the Lord who created them (see 50:6; 89:5–8; 97:6; see also Ro 1:19–20).

19:4 Interpreting this heavenly proclamation eschatologically in the light of Christ, Paul applies this verse to the proclamation of the gospel in his own day (see Ro 10:18). He thus associates these two universal proclamations.

19:4b–6 The heavens are the divinely pitched "tent" for the lordly sun—widely worshiped in the ancient Near East (cf. Dt 4:19; 17:3; 2Ki 23:5,11; Jer 8:2; Eze 8:16), but here, as in 136:7–8; Ge 1:16, a mere creature of God. Of the created realm, the sun is the supreme metaphor of the glory of God (see 84:11; Isa 60:19–20), as it makes its daily triumphant sweep across the whole extent of the heavens and pours out its warmth on every creature.

19:7–9 Stately, rhythmic celebration of the life-nurturing effects of the Lord's revealed law (see Ps 119).

19:7 *trustworthy.* God's laws are "trustworthy" (see also 111:7; 119:86) or "sure" (19:9) or "true" (119:142,151,160) in the sense that they faithfully represent God's righteous will (119:138,160), they endure generation after generation (they "stand firm," 93:5; see also 119:91,152,160), and they truly fulfill their purpose in the lives of those who honor them (see the effects noted here; see also 119:43,93,98–100,165)—they can be trusted. *the simple.* The childlike, those whose understanding and judgment have not yet matured (see 119:98–100; Pr 1:4; cf. also 2Ti 3:15; Heb 5:13–14).

19:8 *heart.* See note on 4:7.

19:9 *fear of the LORD.* The sum of what the law requires (see note on 15:4).

19:10–11 The matchless worth of God's law and its rich value for life (see Dt 5:33).

19:10 *sweeter than honey.* By contrast, those who abandon the law turn justice into bitterness (see Am 5:7; 6:12).

12 Who can discern his errors?
Forgive my hidden faults.[w]
13 Keep your servant also from willful sins;[x]
may they not rule over me.[y]
Then will I be blameless,[z]
innocent of great transgression.

14 May the words of my mouth and the meditation of my heart
be pleasing[a] in your sight,
O LORD, my Rock[b] and my Redeemer.[c]

Psalm 20

For the director of music.
A psalm of David.

1 May the LORD answer you when you are in distress;[d]
may the name of the God of Jacob[e] protect you.[f]
2 May he send you help[g] from the sanctuary[h]
and grant you support[i] from Zion.[j]
3 May he remember[k] all your sacrifices
and accept your burnt offerings.[l]
Selah

4 May he give you the desire of your heart[m]
and make all your plans succeed.[n]
5 We will shout for joy[o] when you are victorious
and will lift up our banners[p] in the name of our God.
May the LORD grant all your requests.[q]

6 Now I know that the LORD saves his anointed;[r]
he answers him from his holy heaven
with the saving power of his right hand.[s]
7 Some trust in chariots[t] and some in horses,[u]
but we trust in the name of the LORD our God.[v]
8 They are brought to their knees and fall,[w]
but we rise up[x] and stand firm.[y]

9 O LORD, save the king!
Answer[a] us[z] when we call!

Psalm 21

For the director of music.
A psalm of David.

1 O LORD, the king rejoices in your strength.[a]
How great is his joy in the victories you give![b]
2 You have granted him the desire of his heart[c]
and have not withheld the request of his lips.
Selah
3 You welcomed him with rich blessings
and placed a crown of pure gold[d] on his head.[e]
4 He asked you for life, and you gave it to him—
length of days, for ever and ever.[f]

[a] 9 Or *save! / O King, answer*

19:12 [w] Ps 51:2; 90:8; Ecc 12:14 **19:13** [x] S Nu 15:30 [y] Ps 119:133 [z] S Ge 6:9; S Ps 18:32 **19:14** [a] Ps 104:34 [b] Ps 18:31 [c] S Ex 6:6; S Job 19:25 **20:1** [d] Ps 4:1 [e] Ex 3:6; Ps 46:7,11 [f] Ps 59:1; 69:29; 91:14 **20:2** [g] Ps 30:10; 33:20; 37:40; 40:17; 54:4; 118:7 [h] S Nu 3:28 [i] S Ps 18:18 [j] Ps 2:6; 128:5; 134:3; 135:21 **20:3** [k] Ac 10:4 [l] S Dt 33:11 **20:4** [m] Ps 21:2; 37:4; 145:16,19; Isa 26:8; Eze 24:25; Ro 10:1 [n] Ps 140:8; Pr 16:3; Da 11:17 **20:5** [o] S Job 3:7 [p] S Nu 1:52; Ps 60:4; Isa 5:26; 11:10,12; 13:2; 30:17; 49:22; 62:10; Jer 50:2; 51:12,27 [q] 1Sa 1:17 **20:6** [r] S 2Sa 23:1; Ps 28:8 [s] S Job 40:14; Hab 3:13 **20:7** [t] S 2Ki 19:23 [u] S Dt 17:16; Ps 33:17; 147:10; Pr 21:31; Isa 31:1; 36:8,9 [v] S 2Ch 32:8 **20:8** [w] Ps 27:2; Isa 40:30; Jer 46:6; 50:32 [x] Mic 7:8 [y] S Job 11:15; Ps 37:23; Pr 10:25; Isa 7:9 **20:9** [z] Ps 17:6 **21:1** [a] S 1Sa 2:10 [b] S 2Sa 22:51 **21:2** [c] S Ps 20:4 **21:3** [d] S 2Sa 12:30; Rev 14:14 [e] Zec 6:11 **21:4** [f] Ps 10:16; 45:17; 48:14; 133:3

19:12–13 Humanity's moral consciousness remains flawed; hence people err without realizing it and have reason to seek pardon for hidden faults (v. 12; see Lev 5:2–4). Willful sins (v. 13), however, are open rebellion; they are the great transgression (v. 13) that leads to being cut off from God's people (see Nu 15:30–31).
19:14 The psalmist presents this hymn as a praise offering to the Lord. *heart.* See note on 4:7. *Rock ... Redeemer.* See 78:35. *Rock.* See notes on 18:2; Ge 49:24. *Redeemer.* See notes on Ex 6:6; Isa 41:14.
Ps 20 A liturgy of prayer for the king just before he goes out to battle against a threatening force (see 2Ch 20:1–30). Ps 20–21 serve as the counterpart of Ps 18 in the arrangement of Ps 15–24 (see introduction to Ps 15–24); in Ps 18 we hear the voice of the king, while in Ps 20–21 we hear the voices of the people.
20 title *For the director of music.* See note on Ps 4 title.
20:1–5 The people (perhaps his assembled army) address the king, adding their prayers to his prayer for victory.
20:1 *answer you.* Hear your prayers, offered in the present distress, accompanied by "sacrifices" (v. 3); see v. 9. *name.* See vv. 5,7; see also note on 5:11. *Jacob.* See note on 14:7. *protect you.* Lit. "raise you to a high, secure place."
20:2 *Zion.* See note on 9:11.
20:4 *heart.* See note on 4:7.
20:5 *We will shout ... name of our God.* See note on 5:11. *banners.* Probably the troop standards around which the units rallied.
20:6 A participant in the liturgy (perhaps a Levite; see 2Ch 20:14) announces assurance that the king's prayer will be heard. *his anointed.* The king appointed by the Lord to rule in his name (see 2:2 and note).
20:7–8 The army's confession of trust in the Lord rather than in a chariot corps (cf. 33:16–17)—the enemy perhaps came reinforced by such a prized corps. See David's similar confession of confidence when he faced Goliath (1Sa 17:45–47; see notes there).
20:9 The army's concluding petition. *Answer ... when.* See note on v. 1. The psalm ends as it began.
Ps 21 A psalm of praise for victories granted to the king. It is thus linked with Ps 20, but whether both were occasioned by the same events is unknown. Here the people's praise follows that of the king (see v. 1); there (Ps 20) the people's prayer was added to the king's. In its structure, the psalm is framed by vv. 1,13 ("O LORD, ... in your strength" is in both verses). See introduction to Ps 20; see also introduction to Ps 15–24.
21 title *For the director of music.* See note on Ps 4 title.
21:2–6 The people celebrate the Lord's many favors to the king: all "the desire of his heart" (v. 2). Verse 2 announces the theme; vv. 3–5 develop the theme; v. 6 climactically summarizes the theme.
21:2 *heart.* See note on 4:7.
21:3 *welcomed him.* Back from the battles. *placed a crown ... on his head.* Exchanged the warrior's helmet for the ceremonial emblem of royalty—possibly the captured crown of the defeated king (see 2Sa 12:30).
21:4 The king's life has been spared—to live "for ever

5 Through the victories[g] you gave, his
glory is great;
you have bestowed on him splendor
and majesty.[h]
6 Surely you have granted him eternal
blessings
and made him glad with the joy[i]
of your presence.[j]
7 For the king trusts in the LORD;[k]
through the unfailing love[l] of the
Most High[m]
he will not be shaken.[n]

8 Your hand will lay hold[o] on all your
enemies;
your right hand will seize your
foes.
9 At the time of your appearing
you will make them like a fiery
furnace.
In his wrath the LORD will swallow
them up,
and his fire will consume them.[p]
10 You will destroy their descendants
from the earth,
their posterity from mankind.[q]
11 Though they plot evil[r] against you
and devise wicked schemes,[s] they
cannot succeed;
12 for you will make them turn their
backs[t]
when you aim at them with drawn
bow.

13 Be exalted,[u] O LORD, in your
strength;[v]
we will sing and praise your
might.

21:5 [g] ver 1; Ps 18:50; 44:4 [h] S Ps 8:5; 45:3; 93:1; 96:6; 104:1 **21:6** [i] Ps 43:4; 126:3 [j] S 1Ch 17:27 **21:7** [k] S 2Ki 18:5 [l] Ps 6:4 [m] Ge 14:18 [n] S Ps 15:5; S 55:22 **21:8** [o] Isa 10:10 **21:9** [p] S Dt 32:22; Ps 50:3; Jer 15:14 **21:10** [q] Dt 28:18 **21:11** [r] Ps 2:1 [s] Job 10:3; Ps 10:2; 26:10; 37:7 **21:12** [t] S Ex 23:27 **21:13** [u] S Ps 18:46 [v] Ps 18:1

22:1 [w] S Job 6:15; S Ps 9:10; Mt 27:46*; Mk 15:34* [x] Ps 10:1 [y] S Job 3:24 **22:2** [z] S Job 19:7 [a] Ps 42:3; 88:1 **22:3** [b] S 2Ki 19:22; Ps 71:22; S Mk 1:24 [c] S Ex 15:2; Ps 148:14 **22:4** [d] Ps 78:53; 107:6 **22:5** [e] S 1Ch 5:20 [f] Isa 8:17; 25:9; 26:3; 30:18 [g] S 2Ch 13:18; Ps 25:3; 31:17; 71:1; Isa 49:23; Ro 9:33 **22:6** [h] S Job 4:19 [i] S 2Sa 12:14; Ps 31:11; 64:8; 69:19; 109:25 [j] Ps 119:141; Isa 49:7; 53:3; 60:14; Mal 2:9; Mt 16:21 **22:7** [k] S Job 17:2; Ps 35:16; 69:12; 74:18; Mt 27:41; Mk 15:31; Lk 23:36 [l] Mt 27:39, 44; Mk 15:32; Lk 23:39 [m] Mk 15:29 **22:8** [n] Ps 91:14

Psalm 22

For the director of music. To ⌊the tune of⌋ "The Doe of the Morning." A psalm of David.

1 My God, my God, why have you
forsaken me?[w]
Why are you so far[x] from saving me,
so far from the words of my
groaning?[y]
2 O my God, I cry out by day, but you do
not answer,[z]
by night,[a] and am not silent.

3 Yet you are enthroned as the Holy
One;[b]
you are the praise[c] of Israel.[a]
4 In you our fathers put their trust;
they trusted and you delivered
them.[d]
5 They cried to you[e] and were saved;
in you they trusted[f] and were not
disappointed.[g]

6 But I am a worm[h] and not a man,
scorned by men[i] and despised[j] by
the people.
7 All who see me mock me;[k]
they hurl insults,[l] shaking their
heads:[m]
8 "He trusts in the LORD;
let the LORD rescue him.[n]

[a] 3 Or *Yet you are holy, / enthroned on the praises of Israel*

and ever" (see 1Ki 1:31; Da 2:4; 3:9; see also 1Sa 10:24; 1Ki 1:25,34,39).

21:5 *glory ... splendor and majesty.* See 45:3; like that of his heavenly Overlord (see 96:3).

21:6 *eternal blessings.* Either (1) blessings of enduring value or (2) an unending flow of blessings. *your presence.* Your favor, which is the supreme cause of joy because it is the greatest blessing and the wellspring of all other blessings.

21:7 A participant in the liturgy (perhaps a priest or Levite) proclaims the reasons for the king's security. *LORD ... Most High.* That is, LORD Most High (see 7:17; see also note on 3:7). *unfailing love.* See note on 6:4. *Most High.* See note on Ge 14:19. *shaken.* See note on 10:6.

21:8–12 The people hail the future victories of their triumphant king. Verse 8 announces the theme; vv. 9–11 develop the theme; v. 12 summarizes the theme.

21:9 *In his wrath the LORD.* Credits the king's victories to the Lord's wrath (see note on 2:5).

21:10 The king's royal enemies will be left no descendants to rise up against him again.

21:12 *with drawn bow.* See note on Ge 9:13.

21:13 Conclusion—and return to the beginning: Lord, assert your strength, in which "the king rejoices" (v. 1; see also v. 7), and we will ever praise your might.

Ps 22 The anguished prayer of David as a godly sufferer victimized by the vicious and prolonged attacks of enemies whom he has not provoked and from whom the Lord has not (yet) delivered him. In the arrangement of Ps 15–24, this psalm serves as the counterpart of Ps 17 (see introduction to Ps 17; see also introduction to Ps 15–24). The prayer is in many ways similar to Ps 69, but it contains no calls for redress (see note on 5:10) such as are found in 69:22–28. No other psalm fitted quite so aptly the circumstances of Jesus at his crucifixion. Hence on the cross he took it on his lips (see Mt 27:46 and parallels), and the Gospel writers, especially Matthew and John, frequently alluded to it (as they did to Ps 69) in their accounts of Christ's passion (Mt 27:35,39,43; Jn 19:23–24,28). They saw in the passion of Jesus the fulfillment of this cry of the righteous sufferer. The author of Hebrews placed the words of v. 22 on Jesus' lips (see Heb 2:12 and note). No psalm is quoted more frequently in the NT.

22 title See notes on Ps 4; 9 titles.

22:1 *why ... ? Why ... ?* See note on 6:3.

22:1a Quoted by Jesus in Mt 27:46; Mk 15:34.

22:2 *I cry ... you do not answer.* See note on 118:5.

22:3–5 Recollection of what the Lord has been for Israel (see note on vv. 9–10).

22:3 *enthroned.* See note on 9:11. *Holy One.* See Lev 11:44 and note. *praise of Israel.* The one Israel praises for his saving acts in her behalf (see 148:14; Dt 10:21; Jer 17:14).

22:6 *a worm and not a man.* See Job 25:6; Isa 41:14.

22:7 *hurl insults, shaking their heads.* See Mt 27:39; Mk 15:29; see also note on 5:9.

22:8 Quoted in part in Mt 27:43; see note on 3:2.

Let him deliver him,[o]
since he delights[p] in him."

9 Yet you brought me out of the womb;[q]
you made me trust[r] in you
even at my mother's breast.
10 From birth[s] I was cast upon you;
from my mother's womb you have been my God.
11 Do not be far from me,[t]
for trouble is near[u]
and there is no one to help.[v]

12 Many bulls[w] surround me;[x]
strong bulls of Bashan[y] encircle me.
13 Roaring lions[z] tearing their prey[a]
open their mouths wide[b] against me.
14 I am poured out like water,
and all my bones are out of joint.[c]
My heart has turned to wax;[d]
it has melted away[e] within me.
15 My strength is dried up like a potsherd,[f]
and my tongue sticks to the roof of my mouth;[g]
you lay me[a] in the dust[h] of death.
16 Dogs[i] have surrounded me;
a band of evil men has encircled me,
they have pierced[b][j] my hands and my feet.
17 I can count all my bones;
people stare[k] and gloat over me.[l]
18 They divide my garments among them
and cast lots[m] for my clothing.[n]

19 But you, O LORD, be not far off;[o]
O my Strength,[p] come quickly[q] to help me.[r]
20 Deliver my life from the sword,[s]
my precious life[t] from the power of the dogs.[u]
21 Rescue me from the mouth of the lions;[v]
save[c] me from the horns of the wild oxen.[w]

22 I will declare your name to my brothers;
in the congregation[x] I will praise you.[y]
23 You who fear the LORD, praise him![z]
All you descendants of Jacob, honor him![a]
Revere him,[b] all you descendants of Israel!
24 For he has not despised[c] or disdained
the suffering of the afflicted one;[d]
he has not hidden his face[e] from him
but has listened to his cry for help.[f]

25 From you comes the theme of my praise in the great assembly;[g]
before those who fear you[d] will I fulfill my vows.[h]
26 The poor will eat[i] and be satisfied;
they who seek the LORD will praise him—[j]
may your hearts live forever!
27 All the ends of the earth[k]
will remember and turn to the LORD,
and all the families of the nations
will bow down before him,[l]

22:8 [o]S Ps 3:2 [p]S 2Sa 22:20; S Mt 3:17; 27:43 **22:9** [q]Job 10:18; Ps 71:6 [r]Ps 78:7; Na 1:7 **22:10** [s]Ps 71:6; Isa 46:3; 49:1 **22:11** [t]ver 19; S Ps 10:1 [u]S Ps 10:14 [v]S 2Ki 14:26; S Isa 41:28 **22:12** [w]Ps 68:30 [x]Ps 17:9; 27:6; 49:5; 109:3; 140:9 [y]Dt 32:14; Isa 2:13; Eze 27:6; 39:18; Am 4:1 **22:13** [z]ver 21; Eze 22:25; Zep 3:3 [a]S Ge 49:9 [b]La 3:46 **22:14** [c]S Ps 6:2 [d]Job 23:16; Ps 68:2; 97:5; Mic 1:4 [e]Jos 7:5; Ps 107:26; Da 5:6 **22:15** [f]Isa 45:9 [g]Ps 137:6; La 4:4; Eze 3:26; Jn 19:28 [h]S Job 7:21; Ps 104:29 **22:16** [i]Php 3:2 [j]Isa 51:9; 53:5; Zec 12:10; Jn 20:25 **22:17** [k]Lk 23:35 [l]Ps 25:2; 30:1; 35:19; 38:16; La 2:17; Mic 7:8 **22:18** [m]S Lev 16:8; Mt 27:35*; Mk 15:24; Lk 23:34; Jn 19:24* [n]Mk 9:12 **22:19** [o]S ver 11 [p]S Ps 18:1 [q]Ps 38:22; 70:5; 141:1 [r]Ps 40:13

[a] *15* Or / *I am laid* [b] *16* Some Hebrew manuscripts, Septuagint and Syriac; most Hebrew manuscripts / *like the lion,* [c] *21* Or / *you have heard* [d] *25* Hebrew *him*

22:20 [s]S Job 5:20; Ps 37:14 [t]Ps 35:17 [u]Php 3:2 **22:21** [v]S ver 13; S Job 4:10 [w]ver 12; S Nu 23:22 **22:22** [x]Ps 26:12; 40:9,10; 68:26 [y]Ps 35:18; Heb 2:12* **22:23** [z]Ps 33:2; 66:8; 86:12; 103:1; 106:1; 113:1; 117:1; 135:19 [a]Ps 50:15; Isa 24:15; 25:3; 49:23; 60:9; Jer 3:17 [b]S Dt 14:23; Ps 33:8 **22:24** [c]Ps 102:17 [d]S Ps 9:12 [e]Ps 13:1; 27:9; 69:17; 102:2; 143:7 [f]S Job 24:12; S 36:5; Heb 5:7 **22:25** [g]Ps 26:12; 35:18; 40:9; 82:1 [h]S Nu 30:2 **22:26** [i]Ps 107:9 [j]Ps 40:16 **22:27** [k]S Ps 2:8 [l]Ps 86:9; 102:22; Da 7:27; Mic 4:1

22:9–10 Recollection of what the Lord has been for him (see note on vv. 3–5).

22:12–18 The psalmist's deep distress. In vv. 12–13,16–18 he uses four figures to portray the attacks of his enemies; in vv. 14–15 he describes his inner sense of utter helplessness under their fierce attacks.

22:12–13,16 *bulls ... lions ... Dogs.* Metaphors for the enemies (see note on 7:2).

22:12 *Bashan.* Noted for its good pasturage, and hence for the size and vigor of its animals (see Dt 32:14, Eze 39:18 and note; Am 4:1).

22:14 *bones ... heart.* See note on 102:4. *heart.* See note on 4:7.

22:15 See Jn 19:28 and note. *dust of death.* See v. 29; see also Job 7:21 and note.

22:16 *pierced my hands and my feet.* The "dogs" wound his limbs as he seeks to ward off their attacks. But see also v. 20 and note on vv. 20–21; Isa 53:5; Zec 12:10; Jn 19:34,37.

22:17 *I can count all my bones.* Perhaps better, "I must display all my bones." The figure is probably that of one attacked by highway robbers or enemy soldiers, who strip him of his garments (see v. 18; see also note on vv. 20–21).

22:18 See introduction to this psalm; see also Jn 19:23–24.

22:20–21 The psalmist's prayer recalls in reverse order the four figures by which he portrayed his attackers in vv. 12–13,16–18: "sword," "dogs," "lions," "wild oxen." Here "sword" refers back to the scene described in vv. 16–18, and thus many interpret it as an attack by robbers or enemy soldiers, though "sword" is often used figuratively of any violent death.

22:21 *save me.* See NIV text note; see also note on 3:8. *wild oxen.* See note on Nu 23:22.

22:22–31 Vows to praise the Lord when the Lord's sure deliverance comes (see note on 7:17). The vows proper appear in vv. 22,25. Verses 23–24 anticipate the calls to praise that will accompany the psalmist's praise (see note on 9:1). Verses 26–31 describe the expanding company of those who will take up the praise—a worldwide company of persons from every station in life and continuing through the generations. No psalm or prophecy contains a grander vision of the scope of the throng of worshipers who will join in the praise of God's saving acts.

22:22 See Heb 2:12 and note. *name.* See note on 5:11.

22:23 *fear the LORD.* See v. 25; see also note on 15:4.

22:25 *assembly.* See note on 1:5.

22:26 *will eat and be satisfied.* As they share in the ceremonial festival of praise (see Lev 7:11–27).

22:27 *All the ends of the earth.* They too will be told of God's saving acts (see 18:49 and note on 9:1). The good news that the God of Israel hears the prayers of his people and saves them will move them to turn from their idols to the true God (cf. 1Th 1:9).

[28]for dominion belongs to the LORD[m]
and he rules over the nations.

[29]All the rich[n] of the earth will feast and
worship;[o]
all who go down to the dust[p] will
kneel before him—
those who cannot keep themselves
alive.[q]
[30]Posterity[r] will serve him;
future generations[s] will be told about
the Lord.
[31]They will proclaim his righteousness[t]
to a people yet unborn[u]—
for he has done it.[v]

Psalm 23

A psalm of David.

[1]The LORD is my shepherd,[w] I shall not
be in want.[x]
[2] He makes me lie down in green
pastures,
he leads me beside quiet waters,[y]
[3] he restores my soul.[z]
He guides me[a] in paths of
righteousness[b]
for his name's sake.[c]
[4]Even though I walk
through the valley of the shadow of
death,[a d]
I will fear no evil,[e]
for you are with me;[f]
your rod and your staff,
they comfort me.

[5]You prepare a table[g] before me
in the presence of my enemies.
You anoint my head with oil;[h]
my cup[i] overflows.
[6]Surely goodness and love[j] will follow
me
all the days of my life,
and I will dwell in the house of the
LORD
forever.

22:28 [m]Ps 47:7-8; Zec 14:9 **22:29** [n]Ps 45:12 [o]Ps 95:6; 96:9; 99:5; Isa 27:13; 49:7; 66:23; Zec 14:16 [p]Isa 26:19 [q]Ps 89:48 **22:30** [r]Isa 53:10; 54:3; 61:9; 66:22 [s]Ps 102:18 **22:31** [t]S Ps 5:8; 40:9 [u]Ps 71:18; 78:6; 102:18 [v]Lk 18:31; 24:44 **23:1** [w]S Ge 48:15; S Ps 28:9; S Jn 10:11 [x]Ps 34:9,10; 84:11; 107:9; Php 4:19 **23:2** [y]Ps 36:8; 46:4; Rev 7:17 **23:3** [z]S Ps 19:7 [a]Ps 25:9; 73:24; Isa 42:16 [b]S Ps 5:8 [c]Ps 25:11; 31:3; 79:9; 106:8; 109:21; 143:11 **23:4** [d]S Job 3:5; Ps 107:14 [e]Ps 3:6; 27:1 [f]Ps 16:8; Isa 43:2 **23:5** [g]S Job 36:16 [h]Ps 45:7; 92:10; Lk 7:46 [i]S Ps 16:5 **23:6** [j]S Ne 9:25

[a] 4 Or *through the darkest valley*

22:28 The rule of the God of Israel is universal, and the nations will come to recognize that fact through what he does in behalf of his people (see Ps 47; 117; Ge 12:2–3; see also Dt 32:21; Ro 10:19; 11:13–14).

22:29 *All the rich ... all who go down.* The most prosperous and those on the brink of death, and all those whose life situation falls in between these two extremes. *dust.* See v. 15; see also Job 7:21 and note.

22:31 *righteousness.* See note on 4:1.

Ps 23 A profession of joyful trust in the Lord as the good Shepherd-King. In the arrangement of Ps 15–24, it serves as the counterpart of Ps 16, with which it is thematically linked (see introduction to Ps 16; see also introduction to Ps 15–24). The psalm may have accompanied a festival of praise at "the house of the LORD" (v. 6) following a deliverance, such as is contemplated in 22:25–31 (see note on 7:17). The basic theme of the psalm is announced in v. 1a. Verses 1b–3 develop the theme by affirming the psalmist's total security under the Shepherd-King's care. Verse 4 elaborates on this theme by focusing on the Shepherd's protection in times of great danger and distress. Verse 5 describes the psalmist's privileged position as an honored guest at the Shepherd-King's table. In v. 6 the psalmist professes his full confidence for the future—a confidence grounded in the Shepherd-King's faithful covenant love. The psalm is framed by the first and last couplets, each of which refers to "the LORD."

23:1 *shepherd.* A widely used metaphor for kings in the ancient Near East, and also in Israel (see 78:70–72; 2Sa 5:2; Isa 44:28; Jer 3:15; 23:1–4; Mic 5:4; see also Jer 2:8 and note). For the Lord as the shepherd of Israel see 28:9; 79:13; 80:1; 95:7; 100:3; Ge 48:15; Isa 40:11; Jer 17:16; 31:10; 50:19; Eze 34:11–16. Here David the king acknowledges that the Lord is his Shepherd-King. For Jesus as the shepherd of his people see Jn 10:11,14; Heb 13:20; 1Pe 5:4; Rev 7:17. *not be in want.* On the contrary, he will enjoy "goodness" all his life (v. 6).

23:2 *lie down.* For flocks lying down in contented and secure rest see Isa 14:30; 17:2; Jer 33:12; Eze 34:14–15; Zep 2:7; 3:13. *green pastures.* Metaphor for all that makes life flourish (see Eze 34:14; Jn 10:9). *leads me.* Like a shepherd (see Isa 40:11). *quiet waters.* Lit. "waters of resting places," i.e., restful waters—waters that provide refreshment and well-being (see Isa 49:10).

23:3 *restores my soul.* Revives me, refreshes my spirit (see 19:7; Ru 4:15; Pr 25:13; La 1:16). *guides me in paths of righteousness.* As a shepherd leads his sheep (see 77:20; 78:72) in paths that offer safety and well-being, so David's Shepherd-King guides him in ways that cause him to be secure and prosperous. For this meaning of "righteousness" see Pr 8:18 ("prosperity"); 21:21 ("prosperity"); Isa 48:18; see also Pr 8:20–21. It is possible that "paths of righteousness" intentionally bears a double meaning, namely, that it also refers to paths that conform the psalmist's life to God's moral will (cf. Pr 4:11 and note). *for his name's sake.* The prosperity of the Lord's servant brings honor to the Lord's name (see 1Ki 8:41–42; Isa 48:9; Jer 14:21; Eze 20:9,14,22).

23:4 *with me.* See 16:8 and note; see also Dt 31:6,8; Mt 28:20 and note. *rod.* Instrument of authority (as in 2:9; 45:6; Ex 21:20; 2Sa 7:14; Job 9:34); used also by shepherds for counting, guiding, rescuing and protecting sheep (see Lev 27:32; Eze 20:37). *staff.* Instrument of support (as in Ex 21:19; Jdg 6:21; 2Ki 4:29; Zec 8:4). *comfort me.* Reassure me (as in 71:21; 86:17; Ru 2:13; Isa 12:1; 40:1; 49:13).

23:5 The heavenly Shepherd-King receives David at his table as his vassal king and takes him under his protection. In the ancient Near East, covenants were often concluded with a meal expressive of the bond of friendship (see 41:9; Ge 31:54; Ob 7); in the case of vassal treaties or covenants, the vassal was present as the guest of the overlord (see Ex 24:8–12). *anoint my head with oil.* Customary treatment of an honored guest at a banquet (see Lk 7:46; see also 2Sa 12:20; Ecc 9:8; Da 10:3). *cup.* Of the Lord's banquet (see note on 16:5).

23:6 *goodness and love.* Both frequently refer to covenant benefits (see note on 6:4); here they are personified (see 25:21; 43:3; 79:8; 89:14). *follow.* Lit. "pursue"—usually with hostile intent. Rather than having enemies ever in pursuit of him (see 1Sa 23:25; 24:14; 26:18,20), David will have the goodness and unfailing love of his Shepherd-King attending him. *dwell in the house of the LORD.* See note on 15:1. *forever.* The Hebrew for this word suggests "throughout the years," as in Pr 28:16 ("enjoy a long life"). But see also notes on 11:7; 16:9–11.

Psalm 24

Of David. A psalm.

[1] The earth is the LORD's,[k] and
everything in it,
the world, and all who live in it;[l]
[2] for he founded it upon the seas
and established it upon the waters.[m]

[3] Who may ascend the hill[n] of the LORD?
Who may stand in his holy place?[o]
[4] He who has clean hands[p] and a pure
heart,[q]
who does not lift up his soul to an
idol[r]
or swear by what is false.[a]
[5] He will receive blessing[s] from the LORD
and vindication[t] from God his
Savior.
[6] Such is the generation of those who
seek him,
who seek your face,[u] O God of
Jacob.[b] *Selah*

[7] Lift up your heads, O you gates;[v]
be lifted up, you ancient doors,
that the King[w] of glory[x] may come
in.[y]
[8] Who is this King of glory?
The LORD strong and mighty,[z]
the LORD mighty in battle.[a]
[9] Lift up your heads, O you gates;
lift them up, you ancient doors,
that the King of glory may come in.
[10] Who is he, this King of glory?
The LORD Almighty[b]—
he is the King of glory. *Selah*

24:1 [k]S Ex 9:29; Job 41:11 [l]1Co 10:26* **24:2** [m]S Ge 1:6; Ps 104:3; 2Pe 3:5 **24:3** [n]Ps 2:6 [o]Ps 15:1; 65:4 **24:4** [p]S 2Sa 22:21 [q]Ps 51:10; 73:1; Mt 5:8 [r]Eze 18:15 **24:5** [s]Dt 11:26 [t]Ps 17:2 **24:6** [u]Ps 27:8; 105:4; 119:58; Hos 5:15 **24:7** [v]Ps 118:19,20; Isa 26:2; 60:11,18; 62:10 [w]Ps 44:4; 74:12 [x]Ps 29:3; Ac 7:2; 1Co 2:8 [y]Zec 9:9; Mt 21:5 **24:8** [z]S 1Ch 29:11; Ps 89:13; Jer 50:34; Eph 6:10 [a]Ex 15:3,6; Dt 4:34

Psalm 25[c]

Of David.

[1] To you, O LORD, I lift up my soul;[c]

[a] 4 Or *swear falsely* [b] 6 Two Hebrew manuscripts and Syriac (see also Septuagint); most Hebrew manuscripts *face, Jacob* [c] This psalm is an acrostic poem, the verses of which begin with the successive letters of the Hebrew alphabet.

24:10 [b]S 1Sa 1:11 **25:1** [c]Ps 86:4; 143:8

Ps 24 A processional liturgy (see Ps 47; 68; 118; 132) celebrating the Lord's entrance into Zion—composed either for the occasion when David brought the ark to Jerusalem (see 2Sa 6) or for a festival commemorating the event. Together with Ps 15 it frames the intervening collection of psalms and with that psalm sharply delineates those who may approach God in prayer and "dwell in the house of the LORD" (23:6; see introduction to Ps 15–24). The church has long used this psalm in celebration of Christ's ascension into the heavenly Jerusalem—and into the sanctuary on high (see introduction to Ps 47).

24:1–2 The prelude (perhaps spoken by a Levite), proclaiming the Lord as the Creator, Sustainer and Possessor of the whole world (see 19:1–4), and therefore worthy of worship and reverent loyalty as "the King of glory" (vv. 7–10; see Ps 29; 33:6–11; 89:5–18; 93; 95:3–5; 96; 104).

24:1 *The earth … everything in it.* For Paul's use of this declaration see 1Co 10:25–26.

24:2 An echo of Ge 1:1–10. *founded … established.* A metaphor taken from the founding of a city (see Jos 6:26; 1Ki 16:24; Isa 14:32) or of a temple (see 1Ki 5:17; 6:37; Ezr 3:6–12; Isa 44:28; Hag 2:18; Zec 4:9; 8:9). Like a temple, the earth was depicted as having foundations (see 18:15; 82:5; 1Sa 2:8; Pr 8:29; Isa 24:18) and pillars (see 75:3; Job 9:6). In the ancient Near East, temples were thought of as microcosms of the created world, so language applicable to a temple could readily be applied to the earth (see note on Ex 26:1). *upon.* Or "above" (see 104:5–9; Ge 1:9; 7:11; 49:25; Ex 20:4; Dt 33:13).

24:3–6 Instruction concerning those who may enter the sanctuary (probably spoken by a priest).

24:3 *hill of the LORD.* See 2:6 and note.

24:4 *clean hands.* Guiltless actions. *pure heart.* Right attitudes and motives (see 51:10; 73:1). Jesus said that the "pure in heart … will see God" (Mt 5:8). *heart.* See note on 4:7. *lift up his soul to.* Worship or put his trust in (see 25:1–2; 86:4; 143:8). *soul.* See note on 6:3. *by what is false.* That is, by a false god (see Dt 6:13 and note; cf. Isa 19:18; Jer 7:9; Zep 1:5). But see NIV text note. If the latter is the sense, reference is probably to perjury (for the same concern see Ex 20:16 and note; Lev 19:12; Jer 5:2; 7:9; Zec 5:4; Mal 3:5).

24:5 *vindication.* That is, the fruits of vindication, such as righteous treatment from a faithful God; hence, here a synonym of "blessing" (see 23:3 and note).

24:6 *generation.* Or "company," as in 14:5 (those who share a common characteristic); see also 112:2; Pr 30:11–14 and notes on Ps 73:15; 78:8. *Jacob.* See note on 14:7.

24:7–10 Heralding the approach of the King of glory (perhaps spoken by the king at the head of the assembled Israelites, with responses by the keepers of the gates). The Lord's arrival at his sanctuary in Zion completes his march from Egypt. "The LORD Almighty" (v. 10), "the LORD mighty in battle" (v. 8; see Ex 15:1–18), has triumphed over all his enemies and comes now in victory to his own city (see Ps 46; 48; 76; 87), his "resting place" (132:8,14; see 68:7–8; Jdg 5:4–5; Hab 3:3–7). Henceforth Jerusalem is the royal city of the kingdom of God (see note on 9:11).

24:7 *Lift up your heads … be lifted up.* In jubilant reception of the victorious King of glory (see 3:3; 27:6; 110:7). *gates.* Reference could be to the gates of either the city or the sanctuary. *doors.* A synonym for "gates," not in this case the doors of the gates (as in Jdg 16:3; 1Sa 21:13). The gates are personified for dramatic effect, as in Isa 14:31.

24:10 *LORD Almighty.* See note on 1Sa 1:3. Here it stands in climactic position.

Ps 25–33 A group of nine psalms containing an unusual (even for the Psalter) concentration of pleas for "mercy" (25:16; 26:11; 27:7; 28:2; 30:8,10; 31:9) accompanied by professions of "trust" (25:2; 26:1; 27:3; 28:7; 31:6,14; 32:10; 33:21) and appeals to or celebrations of Yahweh's "(unfailing) love" (25:6–7,10; 26:3; 31:7,16,21; 32:10; 33:5,18,22). The series begins with an alphabetic acrostic prayer for God's saving help (Ps 25) and culminates in a 22-verse (the number of letters in the Hebrew alphabet) hymn of praise for Yahweh's sovereign rule and saving help (Ps 33). (For thematic links between these two psalms see note on 25:3). This prayer and hymn frame a concentrically arranged cluster that hinges on Ps 29 (for thematic links between Ps 26 and 32, between 27 and 31, and between 28 and 30, see introductions to those psalms). For the significance of Ps 29 as hinge see introduction to that psalm.

Ps 25 David prays for God's covenant mercies when suffering affliction for sins and when enemies seize the occasion to attack, perhaps by trying to discredit the king through false accusations (see note on 5:9). Appealing to God's covenant benevolence (his mercy, love, goodness, uprightness, faithfulness and grace; see vv. 6–8,10,16) and to

2 in you I trust,[d] O my God.
Do not let me be put to shame,
nor let my enemies triumph over me.
3 No one whose hope is in you
will ever be put to shame,[e]
but they will be put to shame
who are treacherous[f] without excuse.

4 Show me your ways, O LORD,
teach me your paths;[g]
5 guide me in your truth[h] and teach me,
for you are God my Savior,[i]
and my hope is in you[j] all day long.
6 Remember, O LORD, your great mercy
and love,[k]
for they are from of old.
7 Remember not the sins of my youth[l]
and my rebellious ways;[m]
according to your love[n] remember me,
for you are good,[o] O LORD.

8 Good and upright[p] is the LORD;
therefore he instructs[q] sinners in his ways.
9 He guides[r] the humble in what is right
and teaches them[s] his way.
10 All the ways of the LORD are loving and faithful[t]
for those who keep the demands of his covenant.[u]
11 For the sake of your name,[v] O LORD,
forgive[w] my iniquity,[x] though it is great.
12 Who, then, is the man that fears the LORD?[y]
He will instruct him in the way[z]
chosen for him.
13 He will spend his days in prosperity,[a]
and his descendants will inherit the land.[b]
14 The LORD confides[c] in those who fear him;
he makes his covenant known[d] to them.
15 My eyes are ever on the LORD,[e]
for only he will release my feet from the snare.[f]

16 Turn to me[g] and be gracious to me,[h]
for I am lonely[i] and afflicted.
17 The troubles[j] of my heart have multiplied;
free me from my anguish.[k]
18 Look upon my affliction[l] and my distress[m]
and take away all my sins.[n]
19 See how my enemies[o] have increased
and how fiercely they hate me![p]
20 Guard my life[q] and rescue me;[r]
let me not be put to shame,[s]
for I take refuge[t] in you.
21 May integrity[u] and uprightness[v] protect me,
because my hope is in you.[w]

25:2 [d] Ps 31:6; 143:8 **25:3** [e] S Ps 22:5; S Isa 29:22 [f] Isa 24:16; Hab 1:13; Zep 3:4; 2Ti 3:4 **25:4** [g] S Job 34:32 **25:5** [h] Ps 31:3; 43:3; Jn 16:13 [i] Ps 24:5 [j] ver 3; Ps 33:20; 39:7; 42:5; 71:5; 130:7; 131:3 **25:6** [k] Ps 5:7; 98:3; Isa 63:7,15; Jer 31:20; Hos 11:8 **25:7** [l] Job 13:26; Isa 54:4; Jer 3:25; 31:19; 32:30; Eze 16:22,60; 23:3; 2Ti 2:22 [m] S Ex 23:21; Ps 107:17 [n] Ps 6:4; 51:1; 69:16; 109:26; 119:124 [o] S 1Ch 16:34; Ps 34:8; 73:1 **25:8** [p] Ps 92:15; Isa 26:7 [q] Ps 32:8; Isa 28:26 **25:9** [r] S Ps 23:3 [s] ver 4; Ps 27:11 **25:10** [t] S Ps 18:25 [u] Ps 103:18; 132:12 **25:11** [v] S Ex 9:16; Ps 31:3; 79:9; Jer 14:7 [w] S Ex 34:9 [x] S Ex 32:30; S Ps 78:38 **25:12** [y] S Job 1:8 [z] ver 8

25:13 [a] S Dt 30:15; S 1Ki 3:14; S Job 8:7 [b] S Nu 14:24; Mt 5:5 **25:14** [c] Pr 3:32 [d] Ge 17:2; Jn 7:17 **25:15** [e] S 2Ch 20:12; Ps 123:2; Heb 12:2 [f] S Job 34:30; S Ps 119:110 **25:16** [g] S Ps 6:4 [h] S Nu 6:25 [i] Ps 68:6 **25:17** [j] 1Ki 1:29; Ps 34:6,17; 40:12; 54:7; 116:3 [k] Ps 6:3; 39:2 **25:18** [l] S Ps 13:3; Ro 12:12 [m] S 2Sa 16:12 [n] Ps 103:3 **25:19** [o] Ps 3:1; 9:13 [p] Ps 35:19; 38:19; 69:4 **25:20** [q] Ps 86:2 [r] Ps 17:13; 22:21; 43:1; 71:2; 116:4; 140:1; 142:6; 144:11 [s] ver 3 [t] Ps 2:12 **25:21** [u] S Ge 20:5; Pr 10:9 [v] 1Ki 9:4; Ps 85:10; 111:8; Isa 60:17; Mal 2:6 [w] ver 3

his own reliance on the Lord (see vv. 1,5,15,20–21), he prays for deliverance from his enemies (see vv. 2,19), for guidance in God's will (see vv. 4–5,21; see also vv. 8–10,12), for the forgiveness of his sins (see vv. 7,11,18) and for relief from his affliction (see vv. 2,16–18,20). These are related: God's forgiveness will express itself in removing his affliction, and then his enemies will no longer have occasion to slander him. And with God guiding him in "his way" (v. 9)—i.e., in "the demands of his covenant" (v. 10)—he will no longer wander into "rebellious ways" (v. 7). This psalm is linked with Ps 24 by its reference to "lifting up the soul" in reliance on God (see v. 1; 24:4). Structurally, the psalm is an alphabetic acrostic (somewhat irregular, with an additional, concluding verse that extends the lines beyond the alphabet).

25:1–3 Prayer for relief from distress or illness and the slander of his enemies that it occasions.

25:3 *hope.* The three references to "hope" in God occurring here (vv. 3,5,21) are echoed by three references to "hope" in 33:18,20,22 (by means of closely related Hebrew synonyms). *without excuse.* David has given no cause for the hostility of his adversaries.

25:4–7 Prayer for guidance and pardon.

25:4 *your ways ... your paths.* Metaphors for "the demands of his covenant" (v. 10; see Dt 8:6; 10:12–13; 26:17; 30:16; Jos 22:5; see also vv. 8–9; 18:21; 51:13; 81:13; 95:10; 119:3,15; 128:1 and note on 119:29).

25:5 *your truth.* Here synonymous with "your ways" and "your paths" (see note on v. 4; see also note on 19:7).

25:6–7 *Remember ... Remember not.* Remember your long-standing ("from of old") "mercy and love," but do not remember my long-standing sins (those "of my youth").

25:6 *love.* See v. 10 and note on 6:4.

25:8–15 Confidence in the Lord's covenant favors. In this context of prayer for pardon, David implicitly identifies himself with sinners (v. 8) as well as with the humble (v. 9)—those who keep God's covenant (see vv. 10,14) and those who fear the Lord (see vv. 12,14). As sinner he is in need of forgiveness; as humble servant of the Lord he hopefully awaits God's pardon and guidance in covenant faithfulness.

25:9 *humble.* Those who acknowledge that they are without resources.

25:10 *ways of the LORD.* The Lord's benevolent dealings (see 103:7; 138:5) with those who are true to his ways (see note on v. 4).

25:11 *For the sake of your name.* See note on 23:3; see also 1Jn 2:12. *name.* See note on 5:11.

25:12 *fears the LORD.* See notes on 15:4; 34:8–14; Ge 20:11; Pr 1:7; Lk 12:5. *the way chosen for him.* Or "the way he ought to choose."

25:13 *inherit the land.* Retain their family portion in the promised land (see 37:9,11,18,22,29,34; 69:36; Isa 60:21).

25:14 *confides.* Takes them into his confidence, as friends (see Ge 18:17–19; Job 29:4). *fear.* See note on 15:4.

25:15 *snare.* Set by the enemies (v. 2; see note on 9:15).

25:16–21 Prayer for relief from distress (probably illness) and the related attacks of his enemies (see note on 5:9).

25:17 *heart.* See note on 4:7.

25:21 *integrity and uprightness.* Personified virtues (see 23:6 and note). Pardon is not enough; David prays that God will enable him to live a life of unmarred moral rectitude—even as God is "good and upright" (v. 8; see 51:10–12). *integrity.* See note on 15:2.

22 Redeem Israel,[x] O God,
from all their troubles!

Psalm 26

Of David.

1 Vindicate me,[y] O LORD,
for I have led a blameless life;[z]
I have trusted[a] in the LORD
without wavering.[b]
2 Test me,[c] O LORD, and try me,
examine my heart and my mind;[d]
3 for your love[e] is ever before me,
and I walk continually[f] in your truth.[g]
4 I do not sit[h] with deceitful men,
nor do I consort with hypocrites;[i]
5 I abhor[j] the assembly of evildoers
and refuse to sit with the wicked.
6 I wash my hands in innocence,[k]
and go about your altar, O LORD,
7 proclaiming aloud your praise[l]
and telling of all your wonderful
deeds.[m]
8 I love[n] the house where you live,
O LORD,
the place where your glory dwells.[o]
9 Do not take away my soul along with
sinners,
my life with bloodthirsty men,[p]
10 in whose hands are wicked schemes,[q]
whose right hands are full of bribes.[r]
11 But I lead a blameless life;
redeem me[s] and be merciful to me.
12 My feet stand on level ground;[t]
in the great assembly[u] I will praise
the LORD.

Psalm 27

Of David.

1 The LORD is my light[v] and my
salvation[w] —
whom shall I fear?
The LORD is the stronghold[x] of my
life —
of whom shall I be afraid?[y]

25:22 [x] Ps 130:8; Lk 24:21 **26:1** [y] S 1Sa 24:15 [z] Ps 15:2; Pr 20:7 [a] Ps 22:4; 40:4; Isa 12:2; 25:9; Jer 17:7; Da 3:28 [b] 2Ki 20:3; Heb 10:23 **26:2** [c] Ps 66:10 [d] S Dt 6:6; S Ps 7:9; Jer 11:20; 20:12; Eze 11:5 **26:3** [e] Ps 6:4 [f] S 1Ki 2:4 [g] Ps 40:11; 43:3; 86:11; 119:30 **26:4** [h] Ps 1:1 [i] Ps 28:3; Mt 6:2 **26:5** [j] Ps 139:21 **26:6** [k] Ps 73:13; Mt 27:24 **26:7** [l] Isa 42:12; 60:6 [m] S Jos 3:5; Ps 9:1 **26:8** [n] Ps 122:6; Isa 66:10 [o] S Ex 29:43; 2Ch 7:1; Ps 96:6 **26:9** [p] Ps 5:6; 28:3; 55:23; 139:19; Pr 29:10 **26:10** [q] S Ps 21:11 [r] S Job 36:18; S Isa 1:23; S Eze 22:12 **26:11** [s] Ps 31:5; 69:18; 119:134; Tit 2:14 **26:12** [t] Ps 27:11; 40:2; 143:10; Isa 26:7; 40:3-4; 45:13; Zec 4:7; Lk 6:17 [u] S Ps 22:25 **27:1** [v] S 2Sa 22:29 [w] S Ex 15:2; S Ps 3:8 [x] Ps 9:9 [y] S Job 13:15; Ps 56:4, 11; 118:6

25:22 A concluding prayer in behalf of all God's people (see 3:8 and note). *Redeem.* Here, as often, a synonym for "deliver."

Ps 26 A prayer for God's discerning mercies — to spare his faithful and godly servant from the death that overtakes the wicked and ungodly. This prayer for vindication (v. 1) because the psalmist has led "a blameless life" (v. 11) and has refused "to sit with the wicked" (v. 5) has its counterpoint (in the concentric arrangement of Ps 25 – 33; see introduction to Ps 25 – 33) in Ps 32, which celebrates the blessedness of those who have confessed their sins and been forgiven. The king's prayer for vindication suggests that he is threatened by the "deceitful" (v. 4) and "bloodthirsty" (v. 9) to whom he refers (as in Ps 23; 25; 27 – 28). This psalm is linked with Ps 27 – 28 (see also Ps 23 – 24) by the theme of the Lord's house: Here David's "love" (v. 8) for the temple (or tabernacle) testifies to the authenticity of his piety; in Ps 27 the Lord's temple is David's sanctuary from his enemies; in Ps 28 David directs his cry for help to the Lord's throne room ("your Most Holy Place," 28:2) in the temple. Three thematically important verbs ("walk," v. 3; "sit," vv. 4 – 5; "stand," v. 12) recall the three thematic verbs of 1:1.

26:1 – 8 An appeal for God to take account of David's moral integrity, his unwavering trust and his genuine delight in the Lord — not a boast of self-righteousness, such as that of the Pharisee (Lk 18:9 – 14).

26:1 *blameless life.* A claim of moral integrity (see vv. 2 – 5; see also note on 15:2). *trusted.* Obedience and trust are the two sides of godliness, as the Abraham story exemplifies (see Ge 12:4 and note; 22:12; see also Ps 34:8 – 14 and note).

26:2 *heart … mind.* See note on 7:9.

26:3 *your love … your truth.* That is, your love-and-truth (see 40:10). David keeps his eye steadfastly on the Lord's love (see note on 6:4) and truth (faithfulness; see 25:10), which are pledged to those "who keep the demands of his covenant" (25:10). *walk continually.* In order to receive the covenant benefits.

26:4 – 5 *sit with.* David refuses to settle in or associate himself with that company he describes as "deceitful," "hypocrites," "evildoers," "wicked" (see 1:1 and note; see also Ps 101).

26:4 *hypocrites.* Context may suggest those who deal fraudulently — or people like those described in Pr 6:12 – 14.

26:6 *wash my hands in innocence.* Reference appears to be to a ritual claiming innocence. "Clean hands and a pure heart" are requisite for those who come to God (see 24:4 and note). *go about your altar.* To vocally celebrate God's saving acts beside his altar was a public act of devotion in which one also invited all the assembled worshipers to praise (see 43:4).

26:7 *your praise.* See note on 9:1.

26:8 *where your glory dwells.* Cf. notes on Eze 1:1 – 28; 1:28. The presence of God's glory signaled the presence of God himself (see Ex 24:16; 33:22). His glory dwelling in the tabernacle (see Ex 40:34 and note), and later the temple (see 1Ki 8:11), assured Israel of the Lord's holy, yet gracious, presence among them. Jn 1:14 announces that same presence in the Word who became flesh and who "made his dwelling among us."

26:9 – 11 An appeal that God will not bring on David the end (death) that awaits the wicked.

26:9 *soul.* See note on 6:3.

26:11 *lead a blameless life.* A return to the appeal with which David began (see v. 1). *redeem.* See note on 25:22.

26:12 A concluding confession of confidence (see note on 3:8) and a vow to praise (see note on 7:17). *level ground.* Where the going is smooth and free from the danger of falling (see 143:10; Isa 40:4; 42:16). *assembly.* See note on 1:5. *praise.* See note on 9:1.

Ps 27 David's triumphantly confident prayer to God to deliver him from all those who conspire to bring him down. The prayer very likely presupposes the Lord's covenant with David (see v. 13 and note). Faith's soliloquy (in two stanzas: vv. 1 – 3,4 – 6), which publicly testifies to the king's confident reliance on the Lord, introduces the prayer of vv. 7 – 12. The conclusion (vv. 13 – 14) echoes the confidence of vv. 1 – 6 and adds faith's dialogue with itself — faith exhorting faith to wait patiently for that which is sure, though not yet seen (see Ps 42 – 43; Heb 11:1). See further the introduction to Ps 26. In the concentric arrangement of Ps 25 – 33 (see introduction to Ps 25 – 33), Ps 27 stands in counterpoint with Ps 31,

[2]When evil men advance against me
to devour my flesh,[a]
when my enemies and my foes attack
me,
they will stumble and fall.[z]
[3]Though an army besiege me,
my heart will not fear;[a]
though war break out against me,
even then will I be confident.[b]

[4]One thing[c] I ask of the LORD,
this is what I seek:
that I may dwell in the house of the
LORD
all the days of my life,[d]
to gaze upon the beauty of the LORD
and to seek him in his temple.
[5]For in the day of trouble[e]
he will keep me safe[f] in his dwelling;
he will hide me[g] in the shelter of his
tabernacle
and set me high upon a rock.[h]
[6]Then my head will be exalted[i]
above the enemies who surround me;[j]
at his tabernacle will I sacrifice[k] with
shouts of joy;[l]
I will sing[m] and make music[n] to the
LORD.

[7]Hear my voice[o] when I call, O LORD;
be merciful to me and answer me.[p]
[8]My heart says of you, "Seek his[b] face!"[q]
Your face, LORD, I will seek.
[9]Do not hide your face[r] from me,
do not turn your servant away in
anger;[s]
you have been my helper.[t]
Do not reject me or forsake[u] me,
O God my Savior.[v]
[10]Though my father and mother forsake
me,
the LORD will receive me.
[11]Teach me your way,[w] O LORD;
lead me in a straight path[x]
because of my oppressors.[y]
[12]Do not turn me over to the desire of
my foes,
for false witnesses[z] rise up against
me,
breathing out violence.

[13]I am still confident of this:
I will see the goodness of the
LORD[a]
in the land of the living.[b]
[14]Wait[c] for the LORD;
be strong[d] and take heart
and wait for the LORD.

Psalm 28

Of David.

[1]To you I call, O LORD my Rock;
do not turn a deaf ear[e] to me.

27:2 [z]Ps 9:3; S 20:8; 37:24; Da 11:19; Ro 11:11 **27:3** [a]S Ge 4:7; S Ps 3:6 [b]S Job 4:6 **27:4** [c]Lk 10:42 [d]Ps 23:6; 61:4 **27:5** [e]S Job 38:23 [f]S Ps 12:7 [g]S Ps 17:8 [h]Ps 40:2 **27:6** [i]2Sa 22:49; Ps 3:3; 18:48 [j]S Ps 22:12 [k]Ps 50:14; 54:6; 107:22; 116:17 [l]S Ezr 3:13; S Job 22:26 [m]S Ex 15:1 [n]Ps 33:2; 92:1; 147:7; S Eph 5:19 **27:7** [o]Ps 5:3; 18:6; 55:17; 119:149; 130:2; Isa 28:23 [p]S Ps 4:1 **27:8** [q]S 1Ch 16:11 **27:9** [r]S Dt 31:17; S Ps 22:24 [s]S Ps 2:5 [t]S Ge 49:25; S Dt 33:29 [u]S Dt 4:31; Ps 37:28; 119:8; Isa 41:17; 62:12; Jer 14:9 [v]Ps 18:46 **27:11** [w]S Ex 33:13 [x]S Ezr 8:21; Ps 5:8 [y]Ps 72:4; 78:42; 106:10; Jer 21:12 **27:12** [z]S Dt 19:16; S Mt 26:60; Ac 6:13; 1Co 15:15 **27:13** [a]Ex 33:19; S 2Ch 6:41; Ps 23:6; 31:19; 145:7 [b]S Job 28:13 **27:14** [c]Ps 33:20; 130:5,6; Isa 8:17; 30:18; Hab 2:3; Zep 3:8; Ac 1:4 [d]S Dt 1:21; S Jdg 5:21; S Eph 6:10 **28:1** [e]S Dt 1:45

[a] *2* Or *to slander me* [b] *8* Or *To you, O my heart, he has said, "Seek my*

a similar confident prayer for Yahweh's saving help as the psalmist's refuge when under attack. In both, the adversaries try to destroy the psalmist by spreading lies. Both psalms speak of keeping "safe" in Yahweh's "dwelling" (27:5; 31:20) and of hiding in the "shelter" of Yahweh's "tabernacle" (27:5) or "presence" (31:20). Both conclude with an exhortation to "be strong and take heart" out of hope in the Lord. In addition, they share other significant vocabulary—e.g., reference to the "goodness" of Yahweh (27:13; 31:19).
27:1–3 The king's security in the Lord in the face of all that his enemies can do (see Ps 2).
27:1 *light.* Often symbolizes well-being (see 97:11; Job 18:5–6; 22:28; 29:3; Pr 13:9; La 3:2) or life and salvation (see 18:28; Isa 9:2; 49:6; 58:8; 59:9; Jer 13:16; Am 5:18–20). To say "The LORD is my light" is to confess confidence in him as the source of these benefits (see Isa 10:17; 60:1–2,19–20; Mic 7:8–9; cf. also note on Col 1:12). *my salvation.* My Savior (see v. 9).
27:2 *devour my flesh.* See 7:2 and note.
27:3 *heart.* See note on 4:7.
27:4–6 The Lord's temple (or tabernacle) is the king's stronghold—because the Lord himself is his stronghold (see v. 1; see notes on 9:11; 18:2).
27:4 *dwell in.* See note on 15:1. *beauty of the LORD.* His unfailing benevolence (see 90:17: "favor of the Lord").
27:5 *shelter of his tabernacle.* See 31:20; 32:7; 61:4; 91:1.
27:6 *will I sacrifice.* See note on 7:17. *I will sing.* See note on 9:1.
27:7–12 Prayer for deliverance from treacherous enemies. These remain unspecified, whether from inside or outside the kingdom or both. Their chief weapon is false charges intent on discrediting the king (see note on 5:9).
27:7 *I call … answer me.* See note on 118:5.
27:9 *hide your face.* See note on 13:1. *anger.* See note on 2:5. *you have been my helper.* Or "be my helper."
27:10 *the LORD will receive me.* Or "may the LORD receive me."
27:11 *Teach me your way.* Only those who know and do the Lord's will can expect to receive favorable response to their prayers (see Ps 24–26; see also 2Sa 7:14). *lead me in a straight path.* See 5:8 and note.
27:13–14 Concluding note of confidence (see note on 3:8).
27:13 *goodness of the LORD.* Possibly refers to the "good" things promised in the Lord's covenant with David (see 2Sa 7:28; see also 31:19 and note). *land of the living.* This life.
27:14 *Wait for the LORD.* Faith encouraging faith (see 42:5,11; 43:5; 62:5).
Ps 28 A prayer for deliverance from deadly peril at the hands of malicious and God-defying enemies. As with Ps 25, the prayer ends with intercession for all the people of the Lord (see 3:8 and note). Reference in the last verse to the Lord as the shepherd of his people connects this psalm with Ps 23. However, in the concentric arrangement of Ps 25–33 (see introduction to Ps 25–33) it is linked more closely with Ps 30. In Ps 28 the psalmist cries to Yahweh "for mercy" (vv. 2,6) when about to go "down to the pit" (v. 1); in Ps 30 the psalmist praises Yahweh for having heard his cry "for mercy" (vv. 8,11) and sparing him from going "down to the pit" (v. 3). These two psalms are also linked by other significant language: cf. 28:1 ("To you I call, O LORD") and 30:8 ("To you, O LORD, I called"); 28:2 and 30:2 ("call[ed] to you for help"); 28:7 ("I am helped") and 30:10 ("be my help").
28:1–2 Initial appeal to be heard.
28:1 *Rock.* See note on 18:2. *remain silent.* Do not act in my behalf. *pit.* Metaphor for the grave (see note on 30:1).

For if you remain silent,[f]
I will be like those who have gone
down to the pit.[g]
2 Hear my cry for mercy[h]
as I call to you for help,
as I lift up my hands[i]
toward your Most Holy Place.[j]

3 Do not drag me away with the wicked,
with those who do evil,
who speak cordially with their
neighbors
but harbor malice in their hearts.[k]
4 Repay them for their deeds
and for their evil work;
repay them for what their hands have
done[l]
and bring back upon them what they
deserve.[m]
5 Since they show no regard for the
works of the LORD
and what his hands have done,[n]
he will tear them down
and never build them up again.

6 Praise be to the LORD,[o]
for he has heard my cry for mercy.[p]
7 The LORD is my strength[q] and my
shield;
my heart trusts[r] in him, and I am
helped.
My heart leaps for joy[s]
and I will give thanks to him in
song.[t]

8 The LORD is the strength[u] of his people,
a fortress of salvation[v] for his
anointed one.[w]
9 Save your people[x] and bless your
inheritance;[y]
be their shepherd[z] and carry them[a]
forever.

Psalm 29

A psalm of David.

1 Ascribe to the LORD,[b] O mighty ones,[c]
ascribe to the LORD glory[d] and
strength.
2 Ascribe to the LORD the glory due his
name;
worship the LORD in the splendor of
his[a] holiness.[e]

[a] 2 Or *LORD with the splendor of*

28:1 [f]S Est 4:14 [g]S Job 33:18 **28:2** [h]Ps 17:1; 61:1; 116:1; 130:2; 142:1; 143:1 [i]S Ezr 9:5; Ps 63:4; 141:2; La 2:19; 1Ti 2:8 [j]Ps 5:7; 11:4 **28:3** [k]Ps 12:2; S 26:4; 55:21; Jer 9:8 **28:4** [l]Ps 62:12; 2Ti 4:14; Rev 22:12 [m]La 3:64; Rev 18:6 **28:5** [n]Isa 5:12 **28:6** [o]S Ge 24:27; 2Co 1:3; Eph 1:3; 1Pe 1:3 [p]ver 2 **28:7** [q]S Ps 18:1 [r]Ps 13:5; 112:7; Isa 26:3 [s]S Dt 16:15; S Ps 16:9 [t]Ps 33:3; 40:3; 69:30; 144:9; 149:1 **28:8** [u]Ps 18:1 [v]S Ex 15:2; Ps 27:1; Hab 3:13 [w]S Ps 20:6 **28:9** [x]1Ch 16:35; Ps 106:47; 118:25 [y]S Ex 34:9 [z]1Ch 11:2; S Ps 23:1; 78:52,71; 80:1; Isa 40:11; Jer 31:10; Eze 34:12-16,23,31; Mic 7:14 [a]S Dt 1:31; 32:11; Isa 46:3; 63:9 **29:1** [b]ver 2; 1Ch 16:28 [c]S 2Sa 1:19; Ps 103:20; Isa 10:13 [d]Ps 8:1 **29:2** [e]S 1Ch 16:29; Ps 96:7-9

28:2 *lift up my hands.* In worship and prayer (see 63:4; 134:2; 141:2). *Most Holy Place.* The inner sanctuary of the temple (see 1Ki 6:5), where the ark of the covenant stood (see 1Ki 8:6–8); it was God's throne room on earth.
28:3–5 Prayer for the Lord, enthroned in the temple, to deliver his servant and deal in judgment with those who harbor malice toward the king and God's people and defy God himself.
28:3 *harbor malice.* See note on 5:9. *hearts.* See note on 4:7.
28:4 *Repay them.* See note on 5:10; see also Mt 16:27; 2Ti 4:14; Rev 20:12–13; 22:12.
28:5 This expression of confidence climaxes the prayer and prepares for the shift to praise in vv. 6–7. *works of the LORD.* His redemption of Israel, the establishment of Israel as his kingdom (by covenant, Ex 19–24), and the appointment of the house of David (also by covenant, 2Sa 7) as his earthly regent over his people. *what his hands have done.* By "what their hands have done" (v. 4), "the wicked" (v. 3) show that they do not acknowledge Israel and David's regency as the work of God's hands. *he will tear.* Or "may he tear."
28:6–7 Joyful praise, in confidence of being heard (see note on 3:8).
28:7 *shield.* See note on 3:3. *heart.* See note on 4:7. *I will give thanks.* See notes on 7:16–17.
28:8–9 The Lord and his people (see note on 3:8).
28:8 *people ... anointed one.* These constitute a unity (see note on 2:2).
28:9 *Save ... bless.* God's two primary acts by which he effects his people's well-being: He saves from time to time as circumstances require; he blesses day by day to make their lives and labors fruitful. *your inheritance.* See Dt 9:29. *shepherd.* See introduction; see also 80:1; Isa 40:11; Jer 31:10; Eze 34; Mic 5:4 and note on Ps 23:1. The answer to this prayer—the last, full answer—has come in the ministry of the "good shepherd" (Jn 10:11,14).
Ps 29 A hymn in praise of the King of creation, whose glory is trumpeted by the thunderclaps that rumble through the cloudy mass of winter's rainstorms as they rise above the Mediterranean ("the mighty waters," v. 3), and move from west to east across the face of the sky, sweeping over the Lebanon range (see vv. 5–6) and reaching the wilds of (northern) Kadesh on the upper reaches of the Orontes River (v. 8). The glory of the Lord is not only visible in the creation (19:1–6; see introduction to that psalm; see also Ps 104); it is also audible in creation's most awesome voice. (The most powerful forces experienced by the ancients were earthquakes, the raging sea, and heavy thunderstorms.) This hymn to Yahweh ("the LORD") served also as a testimony and protest against the worship of the Canaanite god Baal, who was thought to be the divine power present in the thunderstorm (cf. 31:6). Its placement marks it as the hinge psalm in the concentric arrangement of Ps 25–33 (see introduction to Ps 25–33), a placement and function similar to that of Ps 19 (see introduction to Ps 19). In the midst of prayer and praise, it reminds those who meditate on the psalms and use them as their own that the One with whom they have to do is the mighty Lord over all that is. All creation displays his power and glory, evoking awe and praise (vv. 1–2), but his gracious ways with his people (v. 11) also invite confident prayer in every need.

In its structure, a two-verse introduction and a two-verse conclusion enclose a seven-verse stanza. In both the introduction and the conclusion the name Yahweh ("the LORD") is sounded four times; in the body of the psalm it is heard ten times. "The voice of the LORD" is repeated seven times—the seven thunders of God. (The numbers four, seven and ten often signified completeness in OT number symbolism.)
29:1–2 A summons to all beings in the divine realm (see note on v. 1) to worship the Lord—adapted from a conventional call to praise in the liturgy of the temple (see 96:7–9; 1Ch 16:28–29).
29:1 *mighty ones.* Lit. "sons of god(s)." Perhaps reference is to the angelic host (see 103:20; 148:2; Job 1:6 and NIV text note; 2:1 and NIV text note; Isa 6:2), or possibly to all those foolishly thought to be gods—as in Ps 97 (see 97:7), which has several thematic links with this psalm. The Lord alone must be acknowledged as the divine King.
29:2 *name.* See note on 5:11. *in the splendor of his holiness.* A rather literal translation of a difficult Hebrew phrase (see

3 The voice[f] of the LORD is over the
waters;
the God of glory[g] thunders,[h]
the LORD thunders over the mighty
waters.[i]
4 The voice of the LORD is powerful;[j]
the voice of the LORD is majestic.
5 The voice of the LORD breaks the
cedars;
the LORD breaks in pieces the cedars
of Lebanon.[k]
6 He makes Lebanon skip[l] like a calf,
Sirion[a][m] like a young wild ox.[n]
7 The voice of the LORD strikes
with flashes of lightning.[o]
8 The voice of the LORD shakes the
desert;
the LORD shakes the Desert of
Kadesh.[p]
9 The voice of the LORD twists the
oaks[b][q]
and strips the forests bare.
And in his temple all cry, "Glory!"[r]

10 The LORD sits[c] enthroned over the
flood;[s]
the LORD is enthroned as King
forever.[t]

29:3 [f]Job 37:5 [g]S Ps 24:7; Ac 7:2 [h]S 1Sa 2:10; Ps 18:13; 46:6; 68:33; 77:17; Jer 10:13; 25:30; Joel 2:11; Am 1:2 [i]S Ex 15:10 **29:4** [j]Ps 68:33 **29:5** [k]S Jdg 9:15 **29:6** [l]Ps 114:4 [m]Dt 3:9 [n]S Nu 23:22; Job 39:9; Ps 92:10 **29:7** [o]Eze 1:14; Rev 8:5 **29:8** [p]Nu 13:26; S 20:1 **29:9** [q]Isa 2:13; Eze 27:6; Am 2:9 [r]Ps 26:8 **29:10** [s]Ge 6:17 [t]S Ex 15:18 **29:11** [u]S Ps 18:1; 28:8; 68:35 [v]S Lev 26:6; S Nu 6:26 **30:1** [w]S Ex 15:2 [x]Job 11:8; Ps 63:9; 107:26; Pr 9:18; Isa 14:15 [y]S Ps 22:17 **30:2** [z]Ps 5:2; 88:13 [a]S Nu 12:13 **30:3** [b]S Ps 16:10; S 56:13 [c]Ps 28:1; 55:23; 69:15; 86:13; 143:7; Pr 1:12; Isa 38:17; Jnh 2:6 **30:4** [d]Ps 33:1; 47:7; 68:4 [e]S Ps 16:3 [f]Ex 3:15; Ps 33:21; 103:1; 145:21

11 The LORD gives strength to his people;[u]
the LORD blesses his people with
peace.[v]

Psalm 30

A psalm. A song. For the dedication
of the temple.[d] Of David.

1 I will exalt[w] you, O LORD,
for you lifted me out of the depths[x]
and did not let my enemies gloat
over me.[y]
2 O LORD my God, I called to you for
help[z]
and you healed me.[a]
3 O LORD, you brought me up from the
grave[e];[b]
you spared me from going down into
the pit.[c]

4 Sing[d] to the LORD, you saints[e] of his;
praise his holy name.[f]

[a] 6 That is, Mount Hermon [b] 9 Or *LORD makes the deer give birth* [c] 10 Or *sat* [d] Title: Or *palace* [e] 3 Hebrew *Sheol*

NIV text note; see also 96:9; 110:3; 1Ch 16:29; 2Ch 20:21). It is uncertain whether it describes God himself or the sanctuary or the (priestly) garb the worshipers are to wear when they approach God. The use of an almost identical Hebrew phrase in 110:3 (translated "in holy majesty") seems to support the last alternative, but the Hebrew text and the context of 2Ch 20:21 favor "in the splendor of his holiness."

29:3–9 Praise of the Lord, whose voice the crashing thunder is (see introduction; 68:4,33). The sound and fury of creation's awesome displays of power proclaim the glory of Israel's God.

29:5 *cedars of Lebanon.* The most majestic and highly prized trees of the Middle East (see SS 5:15 and note).

29:6 *skip.* See 114:4 and note.

29:9 *temple.* A primary thematic link with Ps 23–28. Reference may be to the temple in Jerusalem or to God's heavenly temple, where he sits enthroned (see 2:4; 11:4; 113:5; Isa 6:1; 40:22) as the Lord of all creation. But perhaps it is the creation itself that here is named God's temple (see note on 24:2). Then the "all" (those who cry "Glory!") is absolutely all—all creation shouts his praise (cf. 150:6). *Glory!* See note on 26:8.

29:10–11 The Lord's absolute and everlasting rule is committed to his people's complete salvation and unmixed blessedness—the crowning comfort in a world where threatening tides seem to make everything uncertain.

29:10 *enthroned over the flood.* As the One who by his word brought the ordered creation out of the formless "deep" (Ge 1:2,6–10).

Ps 30 A song of praise publicly celebrating the Lord's deliverance from the threat of death, probably brought on by illness ("you healed me," v. 2; see note on 7:17). For its relationship to Ps 28 see introduction to that psalm. The psalm is framed by commitments to praise (see vv. 1,12).

30 title *A song.* See titles of Ps 18; 45–46; 48; 65–68; 75–76; 83; 87–88; 92; 108—all psalms of praise except 83; 88. In addition there are the songs "of ascents" (Ps 120–134). *For the dedication of the temple. Of David.* If "Of David" indicates authorship, the most probable occasion for the psalm is recorded in 1Ch 21:1—22:6. In 1Ch 22:1–6 David dedicated both property and building materials for the temple, and he may well have intended that Ps 30 be used at the dedication of the temple itself. If this is the case, vv. 2–3 would refer to David's predicament in 1Ch 21:17–30. The "favor" of v. 5 would be an echo of the "mercy" of 1Ch 21:13, and v. 6 would refer to his sin of misplaced trust in a large, superior army (see 1Ch 21:1–8). Later, the psalm came to be applied to the exile experience of Israel. In Jewish liturgical practice dating from Talmudic times it is chanted in the winter (see Jn 10:22 and NIV text note) at Hanukkah, the feast that celebrates the rededication of the temple by Judas Maccabeus (165 B.C.) after its desecration by Antiochus Epiphanes (168). In such communal use, the "I" of the psalm becomes the collective "person" of Israel—a common mode of speaking in the OT.

30:1–3 Introductory announcement of the occasion for praise.

30:1 *lifted me out of the depths.* The vivid imagery that associates distress with "the depths"—so expressive of universal human experience—is common in OT poetry (see 69:2,15; 71:20; 88:6; 130:1; La 3:55; Jnh 2:2). The depths are often linked, as here, with Sheol ("the grave," v. 3) and "the pit" (v. 3), together with a cluster of related associations: silence (see 31:17; 94:17; 115:17; 1Sa 2:9), darkness (see 88:6,12; 143:3; Job 10:21–22; 17:13; Ecc 6:4; La 3:6), destruction (see v. 9; 18:4; 55:23, "corruption"; 88:11; Isa 38:17; Hos 13:14), dust (see v. 9; 7:5; 22:15,29; Job 17:16; 40:13; Isa 26:19; 29:4), mire (see 40:2; 69:2,14), slime (see 40:2) and mud (see 40:2; Job 30:19). See also note on 49:14. *my enemies gloat over me.* See introduction to Ps 6.

30:3 *grave.* Figurative of a "brink-of-death" experience, as in 18:5; Jnh 2:2. *pit.* See note on 28:1.

30:4–5 Call to the gathered worshipers to take up the praise of God (see note on 9:1).

30:4 *saints.* See note on 4:3. *name.* Lit. "name of renown" (see 97:12; 135:13; Isa 26:8; Hos 12:5). The Hebrew evokes Ex 3:15 and refers to the name around which clustered memories of all that God had done, especially in Israel's history.

[5]For his anger[g] lasts only a moment,[h]
but his favor lasts a lifetime;[i]
weeping[j] may remain for a night,
but rejoicing comes in the morning.[k]

[6]When I felt secure, I said,
"I will never be shaken."[l]
[7]O LORD, when you favored me,
you made my mountain[a] stand firm;
but when you hid your face,[m]
I was dismayed.

[8]To you, O LORD, I called;
to the Lord I cried for mercy:
[9]"What gain is there in my destruction,[b]
in my going down into the pit?[n]
Will the dust praise you?
Will it proclaim your faithfulness?[o]
[10]Hear,[p] O LORD, and be merciful to me;[q]
O LORD, be my help.[r]"

[11]You turned my wailing[s] into dancing;[t]
you removed my sackcloth[u] and
clothed me with joy,[v]
[12]that my heart may sing to you and not
be silent.
O LORD my God, I will give you
thanks[w] forever.[x]

Psalm 31

31:1-4pp — Ps 71:1-3

For the director of music. A psalm of David.

[1]In you, O LORD, I have taken refuge;[y]
let me never be put to shame;
deliver me in your righteousness.[z]
[2]Turn your ear to me,[a]
come quickly to my rescue;[b]
be my rock of refuge,[c]
a strong fortress to save me.
[3]Since you are my rock and my
fortress,[d]
for the sake of your name[e] lead
and guide me.
[4]Free me from the trap[f] that is set
for me,
for you are my refuge.[g]
[5]Into your hands I commit my spirit;[h]
redeem me, O LORD, the God of
truth.[i]

[6]I hate those who cling to worthless
idols;[j]
I trust in the LORD.[k]
[7]I will be glad and rejoice in your
love,
for you saw my affliction[l]
and knew the anguish[m] of my
soul.
[8]You have not handed me over[n] to the
enemy
but have set my feet in a spacious
place.[o]

[a] 7 Or *hill country* [b] 9 Or *there if I am silenced*

30:5 [g]Ps 103:9 [h]S Job 14:13 [i]S Ezr 3:11 [j]2Sa 15:30; Ps 6:6; 126:6; Jer 31:16 [k]2Co 4:17 **30:6** [l]S Job 29:18 **30:7** [m]S Dt 31:17 **30:9** [n]S Job 33:18; Isa 38:18 [o]S Ps 6:5; 88:11 **30:10** [p]S Ps 17:1 [q]Ps 4:1 [r]S Ps 20:2 **30:11** [s]S Est 4:1 [t]S Ex 15:20 [u]S 2Sa 3:31; S Ps 35:13 [v]S Dt 16:15; S Ps 16:9 **30:12** [w]Ps 35:18; 75:1; 118:21; Rev 11:17 [x]Ps 44:8; 52:9 **31:1** [y]S Ps 7:1 [z]Ps 5:8 **31:2** [a]S Ps 6:4 [b]S Ex 2:17 [c]S 2Sa 22:3; S Ps 18:2 **31:3** [d]S Ps 18:2 [e]S Ps 23:3 **31:4** [f]S 1Sa 28:9; S Job 18:10 [g]Ps 9:9 **31:5** [h]Lk 23:46; Ac 7:59 [i]Isa 45:19; 65:16 **31:6** [j]S Dt 32:21 [k]S Ps 4:5 **31:7** [l]S Ps 13:3 [m]S Ps 25:17; Lk 22:44 **31:8** [n]S Dt 32:30 [o]S 2Sa 22:20

30:5 *anger.* See note on 2:5. *lasts only a moment.* See Isa 54:7. *remain for a night.* Lit. "come in at evening to lodge." The figure is that of a guest staying for only one night.
30:6–10 Expanded recollection of the Lord's gracious deliverance.
30:6–7 In his security he had grown arrogant, forgetful of who had made his "mountain stand firm," but the Lord reminded him.
30:6 *never be shaken.* He spoke as do the wicked (see 10:6), and thus lost the blessing of the righteous (see 15:5). *shaken.* See note on 10:6.
30:7 *made my mountain stand firm.* Reference may be to David's security in his mountain fortress, Zion; or that mountain fortress may here serve as a metaphor for David's state as a vigorous and victorious king, the "mountain" on which he sat with such secure confidence in God. *hid your face.* See note on 13:1.
30:8–10 Shattered strength swept away all self-reliance; at the brink of death his cries for God's mercy rose.
30:9 See note on 6:5. *your faithfulness.* To your covenant.
30:11–12 God answered—and David vows to prolong his praise forever (see note on 7:17). Dancing and joy replace wailing and sackcloth so that songs of praise, not silence or lament, may attend the acts of God.
30:11 *sackcloth.* A coarse, black fabric (see Isa 50:3; Rev 11:3 and note) woven of goat hair and commonly used for making sacks. It was worn as a symbol of mourning (see 35:13; 69:11 and note on Ge 37:34).
30:12 *heart.* Lit. "glory" (see note on 7:5).
Ps 31 A prayer for deliverance when confronted by a conspiracy so powerful and open that all David's friends abandoned him. According to Lk 23:46, Jesus on the cross applied Ps 31:5 to his own circumstances; thus those who share in his sufferings at the hands of anti-Christian forces are encouraged to hear and use this psalm in a new light (see Ac 7:59; 1Pe 4:19). No psalm expresses a more sturdy trust in the Lord when powerful human forces threaten. The heart of the prayer itself is found in vv. 9–18, which is both preceded and followed by nine Hebrew poetic lines—stanzas that resound with the theme of trust (see v. 14). Verse 13, at the center of the psalm, expresses most clearly the prayer's occasion. For the linkage of this psalm with Ps 27 see introduction to that psalm.
31 title *For the director of music.* See note on Ps 4 title.
31:1–5 Initial appeal to the Lord, the faithful refuge.
31:1 *righteousness.* See note on 4:1.
31:2 *rock.* See note on 18:2.
31:3 *for the sake of your name.* God's honor is at stake in the safety of his servant now under attack (see note on 23:3). *name.* See note on 5:11. *lead and guide.* As a shepherd (see 23:2–3 and notes).
31:4 *trap that is set for me.* By his enemies (see v. 11; see also note on 9:15).
31:5 *Into your hands I commit my spirit.* The climactic expression of trust in the Lord—echoed by Jesus in Lk 23:46. *commit.* Lit. "deposit" (as in Jer 36:20, "put"), here in the very hands of God, thus entrusting to God's care (see Lev 6:4; 1Ki 14:27). *my spirit.* His very life. *redeem.* See note on 25:22. *God of truth.* The faithful, trustworthy God (see note on 30:9).
31:6–8 Confession of loyal trust in the Lord, whose past mercies to David when enemies threatened are joyfully recalled.
31:6 *hate.* Refuse to be associated with. *who cling to worthless idols.* See Jnh 2:8. *cling to.* Lit. "watch" (expectantly for the help of; see 59:9 and note).
31:7 *love.* See vv. 16,21; see also note on 6:4. *soul.* See note on 6:3.
31:8 *spacious place.* See note on 18:19.

[9]Be merciful to me, O LORD, for I am in
distress;[p]
my eyes grow weak with sorrow,[q]
my soul and my body[r] with grief.
[10]My life is consumed by anguish[s]
and my years by groaning;[t]
my strength fails[u] because of my
affliction,[a][v]
and my bones grow weak.[w]
[11]Because of all my enemies,[x]
I am the utter contempt[y] of my
neighbors;[z]
I am a dread to my friends—
those who see me on the street flee
from me.
[12]I am forgotten by them as though I
were dead;[a]
I have become like broken pottery.
[13]For I hear the slander[b] of many;
there is terror on every side;[c]
they conspire against me[d]
and plot to take my life.[e]
[14]But I trust[f] in you, O LORD;
I say, "You are my God."
[15]My times[g] are in your hands;
deliver me from my enemies
and from those who pursue me.
[16]Let your face shine[h] on your servant;
save me in your unfailing love.[i]
[17]Let me not be put to shame,[j] O LORD,
for I have cried out to you;
but let the wicked be put to shame
and lie silent[k] in the grave.[b]
[18]Let their lying lips[l] be silenced,
for with pride and contempt
they speak arrogantly[m] against the
righteous.

31:9 [p]Ps 4:1 [q]Ps 6:7 [r]Ps 63:1 **31:10** [s]ver 7 [t]Ps 6:6 [u]Ps 22:15; 32:4; 38:10; 73:26 [v]Ps 25:18 [w]S Ps 6:2 **31:11** [x]Dt 30:7; Ps 3:7; 25:19; 102:8 [y]S Ps 22:6 [z]Ps 38:11 **31:12** [a]Ps 28:1; 88:4 **31:13** [b]S Lev 19:16; Ps 50:20 [c]S Job 18:11; Isa 13:8; Jer 6:25; 20:3,10; 46:5; 49:5; La 2:22 [d]Ps 41:7; 56:6; 71:10; 83:3 [e]S Ge 37:18; S Mt 12:14 **31:14** [f]Ps 4:5 **31:15** [g]S Job 14:5 **31:16** [h]S Nu 6:25 [i]S Ps 6:4 **31:17** [j]S Ps 22:5 [k]1Sa 2:9; Ps 94:17; 115:17 **31:18** [l]Ps 120:2; Pr 10:18; 26:24 [m]S 1Sa 2:3; Jude 1:15

31:19 [n]S Ps 27:13; Ro 11:22 [o]Ps 23:5 [p]Ps 2:12 **31:20** [q]Ps 55:8 [r]S Ps 17:8 [s]S Ge 37:18 **31:21** [t]Ps 28:6 [u]S Ps 17:7 [v]1Sa 23:7 **31:22** [w]Ps 116:11 [x]Job 6:9; 17:1; Ps 37:9; 88:5; Isa 38:12 [y]Ps 6:9; 66:19; 116:1; 145:19 **31:23** [z]S Ps 4:3 [a]S Ps 18:25; Rev 2:10 [b]Dt 32:41; Ps 94:2 **31:24** [c]Ps 27:14 **32:1** [d]Ps 85:2; 103:3

[19]How great is your goodness,[n]
which you have stored up for those
who fear you,
which you bestow in the sight of
men[o]
on those who take refuge[p] in you.
[20]In the shelter[q] of your presence you
hide[r] them
from the intrigues of men;[s]
in your dwelling you keep them safe
from accusing tongues.
[21]Praise be to the LORD,[t]
for he showed his wonderful love[u]
to me
when I was in a besieged city.[v]
[22]In my alarm[w] I said,
"I am cut off[x] from your sight!"
Yet you heard my cry[y] for mercy
when I called to you for help.
[23]Love the LORD, all his saints![z]
The LORD preserves the faithful,[a]
but the proud he pays back[b] in full.
[24]Be strong and take heart,[c]
all you who hope in the LORD.

Psalm 32

Of David. A *maskil*.[c]

[1]Blessed is he
whose transgressions are forgiven,
whose sins are covered.[d]

[a] 10 Or *guilt* [b] 17 Hebrew *Sheol* [c] Title: Probably a literary or musical term

31:9–13 The distress described: He is utterly drained physically and emotionally (see vv. 9–10; see also 22:14–15); all his friends have abandoned him like a piece of broken pottery (see vv. 11–12); and all this because the conspiracy against him is so strong (v. 13).
31:9 *eyes grow weak.* See note on 13:3. *soul.* See note on 6:3.
31:10 *bones.* See note on 6:2.
31:11–12 Abandonment by friends was a common experience at a time when God seemed to have withdrawn his favor (see 38:11; 41:9; 69:8; 88:8,18; Job 19:13–19; Jer 12:6; 15:17).
31:13 *slander.* See note on 5:9. *terror on every side.* See notes on Jer 6:25; 20:3.
31:14–18 His trust in the Lord is unwavering; his defense against his powerful enemies is his reliance on God's faithfulness and discerning judgment.
31:14 Cf. v. 22.
31:15 *My times are in your hands.* All the events and circumstances of life are in the hands of the Lord, "my God" (v. 14).
31:16 *face shine.* See note on 13:1.
31:17–18 *but let the wicked ... be silenced.* See note on 5:10.
31:18 *lying lips.* See note on 5:9. *righteous.* See note on 1:5.
31:19–20 Confident anticipation of God's saving help (see note on 3:8).
31:19 *stored up.* David deposits his life in the hands of God to share in the covenant benefits that God has stored up for his faithful servants ("goodness"; see 27:13; Ex 18:9; Nu 10:29,32; Dt 26:11; Jos 21:45; 23:14–15; 2Ch 6:41; Ne 9:25,35; Isa 63:7; Jer 33:9; see also Jer 31:12,14, "bounty"). *fear.* See note on 15:4. *bestow in the sight of men.* Thus showing the Lord's approval of and his standing with his faithful servants in contrast to the accusations of their adversaries (see 86:17).
31:20 *shelter of your presence.* See note on 27:5. *accusing tongues.* See "slander" (v. 13) and "lying lips" (v. 18) and notes on those verses.
31:21–22 Praise anticipating deliverance (see note on 12:5–6).
31:21 *besieged city.* Metaphor for the threat he had experienced.
31:22 *cut off from your sight.* See note on 13:1.
31:23–24 Praise here culminates in words of encouragement addressed to those who put their trust in the Lord. Note how the imperatives "Love ... Be strong and take heart" frame the indicatives "preserves ... pays back"—which ground the imperatives.
31:23 *saints.* See note on 4:3. *the faithful.* Those who maintain moral integrity. *the proud.* Those who refuse to live in humble reliance on the Lord. They arrogantly try to make their way in the world either as a law to themselves (see, e.g., v. 18; 10:2–11; 73:6; 94:2–7; Dt 8:14; Isa 2:17; Eze 28:2,5; Hos 13:6) or by relying on false gods (see Jer 13:9–10). Hence "the proud" is often equivalent to "the wicked."

Ps 32 A grateful testimony of joy for God's gift of forgiveness toward those who with integrity confess their

2Blessed is the man
whose sin the LORD does not count
against him[e]
and in whose spirit is no deceit.[f]
3When I kept silent,[g]
my bones wasted away[h]
through my groaning[i] all day long.
4For day and night
your hand was heavy[j] upon me;
my strength was sapped[k]
as in the heat of summer. *Selah*
5Then I acknowledged my sin to
you
and did not cover up my iniquity.[l]
I said, "I will confess[m]
my transgressions[n] to the LORD"—
and you forgave
the guilt of my sin.[o] *Selah*

6Therefore let everyone who is godly
pray to you
while you may be found;[p]
surely when the mighty waters[q] rise,[r]
they will not reach him.[s]
7You are my hiding place;[t]
you will protect me from trouble[u]
and surround me with songs of
deliverance.[v] *Selah*

8I will instruct[w] you and teach you[x] in
the way you should go;
I will counsel you and watch over[y]
you.
9Do not be like the horse or the mule,
which have no understanding
but must be controlled by bit and
bridle[z]
or they will not come to you.
10Many are the woes of the wicked,[a]
but the LORD's unfailing love
surrounds the man who trusts[b] in
him.

32:2 [e]S Ro 4:7-8* [f]Jn 1:47; Rev 14:5 **32:3** [g]S Job 31:34 [h]Ps 31:10 [i]S Job 3:24; Ps 6:6 **32:4** [j]1Sa 5:6; S Job 9:34; Ps 38:2; 39:10 [k]Ps 22:15 **32:5** [l]Job 31:33 [m]Pr 28:13 [n]Ps 103:12 [o]S Lev 26:40; 1Jn 1:9 **32:6** [p]Ps 69:13; Isa 55:6 [q]S Ex 15:10 [r]Ps 69:1 [s]Isa 43:2 **32:7** [t]S Jdg 9:35 [u]S Ps 9:9 [v]S Jdg 5:1 **32:8** [w]S Ps 25:8 [x]Ps 34:11 [y]Ps 33:18 **32:9** [z]S Job 30:11; S 39:10; Jas 3:3 **32:10** [a]Ro 2:9 [b]Ps 4:5; Pr 16:20

sins and are receptive to God's rule in their lives. The psalm appears to be a liturgical dialogue between David and God in the presence of the worshipers at the sanctuary. In vv. 1–2 and again in v. 11 David speaks to the assembly; in vv. 3–7 he speaks to God (in their hearing); in vv. 8–10 he is addressed by one of the Lord's priests (but see note on vv. 8–10). In traditional Christian usage the psalm has been numbered among the penitential psalms (see introduction to Ps 6). Its placement in the concentric arrangement of Ps 25–33 (see introduction to Ps 25–33) suggests that the editors of the Psalter intended it to stand in counterpoint to Ps 26 (see introduction to that psalm).

32 title *maskil.* Occurs also in the titles of Ps 42; 44–45; 52–55; 74; 78; 88–89; 142. The Hebrew word perhaps indicates that these psalms contain instruction in godliness (see 14:2; 41:1, "he who has regard"; 53:2, "any who understand"; but see also 47:7 and NIV text note).

32:1–2 Exuberant proclamation of the happy state of those who experience God's forgiveness. *Blessed ... Blessed.* See note on 1:1. Repetition underscores (see Isa 6:3; 40:1 and notes). *are forgiven ... are covered ... does not count against him.* Repetition with variation emphasizes and illumines. For Paul's use of these verses see Ro 4:6–8.

32:2 *in whose spirit is no deceit.* Only those honest with God receive pardon.

32:3–5 Testimony to a personal experience of God's pardon. God's heavy hand, pressing down "day and night" on the stubborn silence of unacknowledged sin, filled life with groaning, but full confession brought blessed relief. Neither the sin nor the form of suffering is identified, other than that the latter was physically and psychologically devastating. But it would be uncharacteristic of the Psalms to speak of mere emotional disturbance brought on by suppressed guilt. Some affliction, perhaps illness, was most likely the instrument of God's discipline (see Ps 38).

32:4 *strength was sapped.* Under God's heavy hand he wilted like a plant in the heat of summer.

32:5 Again repetition is used (see note on vv. 1–2). *sin ... iniquity ... transgressions.* See 51:1–2; the three most common OT words for evil thoughts and actions (see Ex 34:7; Isa 59:12 and note). *confess.* See Ps 51; 2Sa 12:13.

32:6–7 A chastened confession that life is secure only with God.

32:6 Though addressed to God as confession, it is also intended for the ears of the fellow worshipers. He admonishes them to "seek the LORD while he may be found ... while he is near" (Isa 55:6) and not to foolishly provoke his withdrawal—and the coming near of his heavy hand—as David had done. A God who forgives is a God to whom one can entrust and devote his life (see 130:4). *godly.* See note on 4:3. *mighty waters.* Powerful imagery for threatening forces or circumstances. This and related imagery was borrowed from ancient Near Eastern creation myths. In many of these a primal mass of chaotic waters (their threatening and destructive forces were often depicted as a many-headed monster of the deep; see 74:13–14 and note) had to be subdued by the creator-god before he could fashion the world and/or rule as the divine king over the earth. Though in these myths the chaotic waters were subdued when the present world was created, they remained a constant threat to the security and well-being of the present order in the earth (the realm of dry land that is the normal habitat for people and animals). Hence by association they were linked with anything that in human experience endangered or troubled that order. They were also associated with the sea, whose angry waves seemed determined at times to engulf the land. Since in Canaanite mythology Sea and Death were the two great enemies of Baal ("lord" of earth), imagery drawn from both realms was used by OT poets, sometimes side by side, to depict threats and distress (see 18:4–5,16; 42:7; 65:7; 74:12–14; 77:16,19; 89:9–10; 93:3–4; 124:4–5; 144:7–8; Job 7:12; 26:12; 38:8–11; Isa 5:30; 8:7–8; 17:12–14; 51:9–10; Jer 5:22; 47:2; 51:55; Hab 3:8–10; see also note on SS 8:7). For imagery associated with the realm of death see notes on 30:1; 49:14.

32:7 *surround me with songs of deliverance.* Because of your help, I will be surrounded by people celebrating your acts of deliverance, as I bring my thank offerings to you (see notes on 7:17; 9:1; see also 35:27; 51:8).

32:8–10 A priestly word of godly instruction, either to David (do not be foolish toward God again) or to those who have just been exhorted to trust in the Lord (to trust add obedience). Some believe that the psalmist himself here turns to others to warn them against the ways into which he had fallen (see 51:13 and note).

32:9 God's servant must be wiser than beasts, more open to God's will than horses and mules are to the will of their masters (see Isa 1:3).

32:10 *unfailing love.* See note on 6:4.

[11] Rejoice in the LORD[c] and be glad, you
righteous;
sing, all you who are upright in
heart!

Psalm 33

[1] Sing joyfully[d] to the LORD, you
righteous;
it is fitting[e] for the upright[f] to praise
him.
[2] Praise the LORD with the harp;[g]
make music to him on the ten-
stringed lyre.[h]
[3] Sing to him a new song;[i]
play skillfully, and shout for joy.[j]

[4] For the word of the LORD is right[k] and
true;[l]
he is faithful[m] in all he does.
[5] The LORD loves righteousness and
justice;[n]
the earth is full of his unfailing love.[o]

[6] By the word[p] of the LORD were the
heavens made,[q]
their starry host[r] by the breath of his
mouth.
[7] He gathers the waters[s] of the sea into
jars[a];[t]
he puts the deep into storehouses.
[8] Let all the earth fear the LORD;[u]
let all the people of the world[v] revere
him.[w]
[9] For he spoke, and it came to be;
he commanded,[x] and it stood firm.
[10] The LORD foils[y] the plans[z] of the
nations;[a]
he thwarts the purposes of the
peoples.
[11] But the plans of the LORD stand firm[b]
forever,
the purposes[c] of his heart through all
generations.

[12] Blessed is the nation whose God is the
LORD,[d]
the people he chose[e] for his
inheritance.[f]
[13] From heaven the LORD looks down[g]
and sees all mankind;[h]
[14] from his dwelling place[i] he watches
all who live on earth—
[15] he who forms[j] the hearts of all,
who considers everything they do.[k]
[16] No king is saved by the size of his
army;[l]
no warrior escapes by his great
strength.
[17] A horse[m] is a vain hope for
deliverance;
despite all its great strength it cannot
save.

[a] 7 Or *sea as into a heap*

32:11 [c]Ps 64:10 **33:1** [d]S Ps 5:11; S 101:1 [e]Ps 147:1 [f]Ps 11:7 **33:2** [g]S Ge 4:21; 1Co 14:7; Rev 5:8 [h]Ps 92:3; 144:9 **33:3** [i]Ps 40:3; Isa 42:10; S Rev 5:9 [j]S Job 3:7; Ps 35:27; 47:1 **33:4** [k]S Ps 19:8 [l]Ps 119:142; Rev 19:9; 22:6 [m]Ps 18:25; 25:10 **33:5** [n]Ps 11:7 [o]Ps 6:4 **33:6** [p]S Ge 1:3; Heb 11:3 [q]S Ex 8:19; S 2Ch 2:12 [r]S Ge 1:16 **33:7** [s]S Ge 1:10 [t]S Jos 3:16 **33:8** [u]S Dt 6:13; Ps 2:11 [v]Ps 49:1; Isa 18:3; Mic 1:2 [w]S Dt 14:23 **33:9** [x]Ps 148:5 **33:10** [y]Isa 44:25 [z]S Job 5:12 [a]Ps 2:1 **33:11** [b]S Nu 23:19 [c]Jer 51:12,29 **33:12** [d]Ps 144:15 [e]S Ex 8:22; Dt 7:6; Ps 4:3; 65:4; 84:4 [f]S Ex 34:9 **33:13** [g]Ps 53:2; 102:19 [h]Job 28:24; Ps 11:4; 14:2; S Heb 4:13 **33:14** [i]S Lev 15:31; 1Ki 8:39 **33:15** [j]Job 10:8; Ps 119:73 [k]S Job 10:4; Jer 32:19 **33:16** [l]1Sa 14:6 **33:17** [m]S Ps 20:7

32:11 A final word to the assembled worshipers—let the praise of God resound (see note on 9:1). See also note on 1:5. *heart.* See note on 4:7.

Ps 33 A liturgy in praise of the Lord, the sovereign God of Israel—a counterpoint to the acrostic prayer of Ps 25. These two psalms frame the intervening psalms (see introduction to Ps 25–33). In the Psalms, calls to praise (as in vv. 1–3) and motivations for praise (as in vv. 4–19) belong to the language of praise (see note on 9:1). Most likely the voices of the Levitical choir (see 1Ch 16:7–36; 25:1) are heard in this psalm. Perhaps the choir leader spoke vv. 1–3, then the choir vv. 4–19, and the people responded with the words of vv. 20–22. The original occasion is unknown, but reference to a "new song" (see note on v. 3) suggests a national deliverance, such as Judah experienced in the time of Jehoshaphat (see 2Ch 20) or Hezekiah (see 2Ki 19); see vv. 10–11,16–17. Along with Ps 1–2; 10 (but see introduction to Ps 9), this is one of only four psalms in Book I without a superscription.

Although structurally not an alphabetic acrostic like the psalm that follows it, the length of the psalm (22 verses) has been determined by the length of the Hebrew alphabet (22 letters); see Ps 38; 103; La 5. The body of the psalm is framed by a three-verse introduction (call to praise) and a three-verse conclusion (response to praise). In vv. 4–19 are heard the praise of the Lord, developed in two parts of eight verses each (vv. 4–11,12–19). In the first of these, a four-verse stanza (vv. 6–9) has been inserted between the two halves of the main stanza (vv. 4–5,10–11) to reinforce its theme. A similar use of this poetic device can be found in Ps 77 (see introduction to that psalm and note on 77:16–19).

33:1–3 The call to praise. Cf. Eph 5:19.

33:1 *righteous.* The assembly of worshipers (see note on 1:5).

33:3 *new song.* Celebrating God's saving act, as in 40:3; 96:1; 98:1; 144:9; 149:1; see Isa 42:10; Rev 5:9; 14:3; see also note on 7:17.

33:4–19 The praise, in two eight-verse parts.

33:4–11 Under the Lord's rule by his sovereign "word" (v. 4) his "plans" for his people "stand firm" (v. 11), even as the creation order "stood firm" (v. 9) because ordered by his sovereign "word" (v. 6). Hence his chosen people are the blessed nation (see vv. 12–19).

33:4 *word.* God's royal word by which he governs all things (see 107:20; 147:15,18). *right and true.* Not chaotic, devious or erratic. Under the Lord's rule, order and goodness are present in the creation.

33:5 *loves.* Delights in doing. *righteousness and justice.* See note on 4:1. *his unfailing love.* Here, his goodness to all his creatures (see 36:5–9; 104:27–28; see also note on 6:4).

33:6 *word.* God's creating word (see v. 9; 104:7; 119:89; Ge 1; Job 38:8–11; Heb 11:3).

33:7 *into jars … storehouses.* Like a householder storing up olive oil and grain (see 104:9; Ge 1:9–10; Job 38:8–11; Pr 8:29; Jer 5:22).

33:8 *all the earth … all the people.* Not only Israel, but all humankind, for all experience the goodness of his sovereign rule (see note on 9:1)—but he foils all their contrary designs (vv. 10–11). *fear the LORD.* See v. 18; see also note on 15:4.

33:11 *heart.* See note on 4:7.

33:12–19 Israel is safe and secure under God's protective rule.

33:12 *Blessed.* See note on 1:1. *people he chose for his inheritance.* Israel (see Dt 9:29).

33:16 *king.* Nation (see v. 12) and king constitute an organic social unit (see 28:8 and note).

[18]But the eyes[n] of the LORD are on those
who fear him,
on those whose hope is in his
unfailing love,[o]
[19]to deliver them from death[p]
and keep them alive in famine.[q]

[20]We wait[r] in hope for the LORD;
he is our help and our shield.
[21]In him our hearts rejoice,[s]
for we trust in his holy name.[t]
[22]May your unfailing love[u] rest upon us,
O LORD,
even as we put our hope in you.

Psalm 34[a]

Of David. When he pretended to be insane before Abimelech, who drove him away, and he left.

[1]I will extol the LORD at all times;[v]
his praise will always be on my lips.
[2]My soul will boast[w] in the LORD;
let the afflicted hear and rejoice.[x]
[3]Glorify the LORD[y] with me;
let us exalt[z] his name together.

[4]I sought the LORD,[a] and he answered
me;
he delivered[b] me from all my fears.
[5]Those who look to him are radiant;[c]
their faces are never covered with
shame.[d]
[6]This poor man called, and the LORD
heard him;
he saved him out of all his troubles.[e]
[7]The angel of the LORD[f] encamps
around those who fear him,
and he delivers[g] them.

[8]Taste and see that the LORD is good;[h]
blessed is the man who takes refuge[i]
in him.
[9]Fear the LORD,[j] you his saints,
for those who fear him lack
nothing.[k]
[10]The lions may grow weak and hungry,
but those who seek the LORD lack no
good thing.[l]

33:18 [n]S Ex 3:16; S Ps 11:4; 1Pe 3:12 [o]S Ps 6:4 **33:19** [p]Ps 56:13; Ac 12:11 [q]S Job 5:20 **33:20** [r]S Ps 27:14 **33:21** [s]S 1Sa 2:1; S Joel 2:23 [t]S Ps 30:4; S 99:3 **33:22** [u]Ps 6:4 **34:1** [v]Ps 71:6; S Eph 5:20; 1Th 5:18 **34:2** [w]Ps 44:8; Jer 9:24; 1Co 1:31 [x]Ps 69:32; 107:42; 119:74 **34:3** [y]Ps 63:3; 86:12; Da 4:37; Jn 17:1; Ro 15:6 [z]S Ex 15:2 **34:4** [a]S Ex 32:11; Ps 77:2 [b]ver 17; Ps 18:43; 22:4; 56:13; 86:13 **34:5** [c]S Ex 34:29 [d]Ps 25:3; 44:15; 69:7; 83:16 **34:6** [e]S Ps 25:17

[a] This psalm is an acrostic poem, the verses of which begin with the successive letters of the Hebrew alphabet.

34:7 [f]S Ge 32:1; S Da 3:28; S Mt 18:10 [g]Ps 22:4; 37:40; 41:1; 97:10; Isa 31:5; Ac 12:11 **34:8** [h]Heb 6:5; 1Pe 2:3 [i]S Ps 2:12 **34:9** [j]S Dt 6:13; Rev 14:7 [k]S Ps 23:1 **34:10** [l]S Ps 23:1

33:18–19 This concluding couplet of the second eight-verse unit of praise contrasts with the concluding couplet of the first (vv. 10–11); both are climactic and together they voice the heart of the praise.
33:18,22 *unfailing love.* Here, his covenant favor toward Israel (see note on 6:4).
33:20–22 The people's response: faith's commitment expressed in confession (vv. 20–21) and petition (v. 22).
33:20 *shield.* See note on 3:3.
33:21 *hearts.* See note on 4:7. *name.* See note on 5:11.
Ps 34–37 This small grouping of four psalms is framed by two alphabetic acrostics that contain wisdom-like instruction (see essay, p. 727) in godliness and related warnings concerning the fate of the wicked—instruction and warnings that reinforce key themes in the two enclosed prayers (Ps 35–36).
Ps 34 An alphabetic acrostic that begins with praise of the Lord for deliverance in answer to prayer (vv. 1–7), then shifts to wisdom-like instruction. This shift is unusual in the Psalter (but see also Ps 92); more commonly, praise of the Lord leads to a call to praise, as in v. 3 (see note on 9:1). Together with Ps 37 it frames the two intervening psalms (see introduction to Ps 34–37). The structure of Ps 34 is somewhat complex, yet it is strikingly effective. Following an introduction of three verses, the poem's themes are developed in stanzas of four verses (4–7), seven verses (8–14), four verses (15–18) and four verses (19–22). For further details see following notes.
34 title The superscription assigns this psalm to the occasion in David's life (see note on Ps 3 title) narrated in 1Sa 21:10–15—but note "Abimelech" rather than "Achish" (perhaps Abimelech was a traditional dynastic name or title for Philistine kings; see Ge 20; 21:22–34; 26). Not all agree with this tradition, however; they feel that it is more likely that early Hebrew editors of the Psalms linked 1Sa 21 with Ps 34 on the basis of word association (the Hebrew for "pretended to be insane," 1Sa 21:13, comes from the same root as the Hebrew used here for "taste," v. 8).
34:1–7 Praise for the Lord's deliverance in answer to prayer.
34:1–3 Commitment to continual praise of the Lord—so that the godly who are afflicted may be encouraged (v. 2; see also the instruction that follows in vv. 8–22).
34:2 *soul.* See note on 6:3. *boast in the LORD.* That is, give the Lord all the praise.
34:3 *name.* See note on 5:11.
34:4–7 The occasion: God's saving answer to prayer. The theme is developed in alternating lines—an *a-b/a-b* pattern (note the shift from first-person singular references to third-person plural references—what Yahweh has done for the psalmist he will do for all those who "fear him," v. 7). For thematic links with vv. 15–18 see note on those verses.
34:5 *radiant.* With joy (see Isa 60:5).
34:6 *poor.* Here, as often in the Psalms, "poor" characterizes not necessarily one who has no possessions, but one who is (and recognizes that he is) without resources to effect his own deliverance (or secure his own life, safety or well-being)—and so is dependent on God.
34:7 *angel of the LORD.* God's heavenly representative, his "messenger," sent to effect his will on earth (see 35:5–6; see also note on Ge 16:7). *encamps around.* The line speaks of the security with which the Lord surrounds his people, individually and collectively; it does not teach a doctrine of individual "guardian angels." *those who fear him.* Those described in vv. 8–14 (see note on 25:12).
34:8–14 Instruction in "the fear of the LORD." These verses are thematically linked, with a title line (v. 11) at the center—Hebrew authors often centered key lines (see note on 6:6). Note the symmetrical pattern of the imperatives: "Taste and see" (v. 8), "Fear" (v. 9), "Come" (v. 11), "keep" (v. 13), "Turn … and do" (v. 14). And note also the symmetrical development of the theme "good" that dominates the stanza: Because the Lord is good (v. 8), those who trust in him will lack nothing good (v. 10); but in order to experience good days (v. 12), they must shun evil and do good (v. 14). To trust and obey—that is "the fear of the LORD." On the instruction of this stanza see Ps 37. For Peter's use of vv. 12–16 see 1Pe 3:8–12.
34:8 *blessed.* See note on 1:1.
34:9 *Fear the LORD.* See v. 11; see also note on 15:4. *saints.* See notes on Ex 3:5; Lev 11:44; Ro 1:7; 6:22; 1Co 1:2; 1Pe 1:16.
34:10 *those who seek the LORD lack no good thing.* See 84:11.

[11]Come, my children, listen[m] to me;
I will teach you[n] the fear of the LORD.[o]
[12]Whoever of you loves life[p]
and desires to see many good days,
[13]keep your tongue[q] from evil
and your lips from speaking lies.[r]
[14]Turn from evil and do good;[s]
seek peace[t] and pursue it.

[15]The eyes of the LORD[u] are on the righteous[v]
and his ears are attentive[w] to their cry;
[16]the face of the LORD is against[x] those who do evil,[y]
to cut off the memory[z] of them from the earth.

[17]The righteous cry out, and the LORD hears[a] them;
he delivers them from all their troubles.
[18]The LORD is close[b] to the brokenhearted[c]
and saves those who are crushed in spirit.

[19]A righteous man may have many troubles,[d]
but the LORD delivers him from them all;[e]
[20]he protects all his bones,
not one of them will be broken.[f]

[21]Evil will slay the wicked;[g]
the foes of the righteous will be condemned.
[22]The LORD redeems[h] his servants;
no one will be condemned who takes refuge[i] in him.

Psalm 35

Of David.

[1]Contend,[j] O LORD, with those who contend with me;
fight[k] against those who fight against me.
[2]Take up shield[l] and buckler;
arise[m] and come to my aid.[n]
[3]Brandish spear[o] and javelin[a][p]
against those who pursue me.
Say to my soul,
"I am your salvation.[q]"

[a] 3 Or *and block the way*

34:11 [m]Ps 66:16 [n]S Ps 32:8 [o]S Ps 19:9 **34:12** [p]Ecc 3:13 **34:13** [q]Ps 39:1; 141:3; Pr 13:3; 21:23; Jas 1:26 [r]S Ps 12:2; 1Pe 2:22 **34:14** [s]Ps 37:27; Isa 1:17; 3Jn 1:11 [t]S Ro 14:19 **34:15** [u]Ps 33:18 [v]S Job 23:10; S 36:7 [w]Mal 3:16; S Jn 9:31 **34:16** [x]Lev 17:10; Jer 23:30 [y]1Pe 3:10-12* [z]S Ex 17:14; Ps 9:6 **34:17** [a]Ps 145:19 **34:18** [b]Dt 4:7; Ps 119:151; 145:18; Isa 50:8 [c]Ps 51:17; 109:16; 147:3; Isa 61:1 **34:19** [d]ver 17; Ps 25:17 [e]S Job 5:19; 2Ti 3:11 **34:20** [f]Jn 19:36* **34:21** [g]Ps 7:9; 9:16; 11:5; 37:20; 73:27; 94:23; 106:43; 112:10; 140:11; Pr 14:32; 24:16 **34:22** [h]S Ex 6:6; S 15:13; Lk 1:68; Rev 14:3 [i]Ps 2:12 **35:1** [j]S 1Sa 24:15 [k]S Ex 14:14 **35:2** [l]Ps 3:3 [m]Ps 3:7 [n]S Ge 50:24; S Job 17:3 **35:3** [o]S Nu 25:7 [p]S Jos 8:18 [q]Ps 27:1

34:11 *Come, my children.* Conventional language of the wisdom teachers (see Introduction to Proverbs: Purpose and Teaching).
34:12–16 See 1Pe 3:10–12 and note.
34:13 See 15:2–3; Jas 3:5–10. For the tongue as a weapon see note on 5:9.
34:14 *Turn from evil and do good.* A key link with Ps 37 (see 37:27). *seek peace.* See 37:37; 120:7; Pr 12:20; Zec 8:19 (also Zec 8:16–17); Mt 5:9; Ro 12:18; 1Co 7:15; 2Co 13:11; 1Th 5:13; Heb 12:14; Jas 3:17–18.
34:15–18 Assurance that the Lord hears the prayers of the righteous. He so thoroughly thwarts those who do evil that they are forgotten (v. 16). As in vv. 4–7, which these verses structurally balance, the theme is developed in alternating lines (in an *a-b/a-b* pattern). Furthermore, the corresponding lines of these two balanced stanzas are thematically, and sometimes even verbally, linked (cf. vv. 4 and 15, vv. 5 and 16, vv. 6 and 17, vv. 7 and 18); godly instruction is patterned after the praise. And these two stanzas, each of which has four Hebrew poetic lines, frame the intervening seven-line stanza (vv. 8–14).
34:15 *righteous.* See vv. 8–14; see also note on 1:5.
34:16 *face of the LORD.* See note on 13:1.
34:17–18 See especially 51:17.
34:19–22 Assurance that the Lord is the unfailing deliverer of the righteous—and that he holds the wicked accountable for their hostility toward the righteous (see v. 21). Here, too, an *a-b/a-b* thematic pattern appears to be employed (note the contrast expressed in vv. 19,21 and the reinforcement of v. 20 found in v. 22).
34:20 *all his bones.* His whole being (see note on 6:2). *not one of them will be broken.* Perhaps John's Gospel applies this word to Jesus (see NIV text note on Jn 19:36)—as the one above all others who could be called a "righteous man" (v. 19).
34:21–22 *condemned.* Dealt with as guilty (cf. Jer 2:3; Hos 10:2).
34:22 *redeems.* See note on 25:22. *who takes refuge in him.* See 2:12.
Ps 35 An appeal to the heavenly King, as divine Warrior and Judge, to come to the defense of "his servant" (v. 27) who is being maliciously slandered by those toward whom he had shown only the most tender friendship. The attack seems to have been occasioned by some "distress" (v. 26) that had overtaken the king (see vv. 15,19,21,25), perhaps an illness (see v. 13; see also introduction to Ps 6). Ps 35 exemplifies such a "cry" to the Lord in expectation of vindication as that spoken of in 34:15–22—except that here the author does not expressly identify himself as one of the "righteous" (34:21); he appeals to the Lord rather as innocent victim of an unmotivated attack. This psalm has been paired with Ps 36 and placed between the two acrostic wisdom psalms (34 and 37; see introduction to Ps 34–37). Together they evoke the terrors of life in the midst of people who have no fear of God before their eyes (36:1) but also testify to the security of those who fear the Lord (cf. 34:7) and trust him (cf. 37:3,5), relying on his love (36:5,7,11) and righteousness (35:24,28; 36:6,10).
Regarding structure, two stanzas at the beginning, having four Hebrew poetic lines each (vv. 1–3,4–6), are balanced by two four-line stanzas at the end (vv. 22–25,26–27—for thematic links between the beginning and the end see notes on these stanzas). At the center a seven-line stanza (vv. 11–16)—flanked by two five-verse stanzas (vv. 7–10 and vv. 17–21; see following notes)—sets forth the psalmist's chief indictment against his adversaries. A final line (v. 28) brings the psalm to a close with a vow to praise (see note on 7:17).
35:1–3 Appeal for help to the Lord as Warrior-King (see Ex 15:1–18), David's Overlord. For links with vv. 22–25 see note on those verses.
35:2 *shield and buckler.* For defense. For the Lord himself as the psalmists' "shield" see 3:3; 7:10; 18:2,30; 28:7; 33:20; 59:11; 84:9,11; 89:18; 115:9–11; 119:114; 144:2. *arise.* See note on 3:7.
35:3 *spear and javelin.* For attack (but see NIV text note on

4 May those who seek my life[r]
be disgraced[s] and put to shame;[t]
may those who plot my ruin
be turned back[u] in dismay.
5 May they be like chaff[v] before the wind,
with the angel of the LORD[w] driving them away;
6 may their path be dark and slippery,
with the angel of the LORD pursuing them.
7 Since they hid their net[x] for me without cause[y]
and without cause dug a pit[z] for me,
8 may ruin overtake them by surprise —[a]
may the net they hid entangle them,
may they fall into the pit,[b] to their ruin.
9 Then my soul will rejoice[c] in the LORD
and delight in his salvation.[d]
10 My whole being will exclaim,
"Who is like you,[e] O LORD?
You rescue the poor from those too strong[f] for them,
the poor and needy[g] from those who rob them."
11 Ruthless witnesses[h] come forward;
they question me on things I know nothing about.
12 They repay me evil for good[i]
and leave my soul forlorn.
13 Yet when they were ill, I put on sackcloth[j]
and humbled myself with fasting.[k]
When my prayers returned to me unanswered,
14 I went about mourning[l]
as though for my friend or brother.
I bowed my head in grief
as though weeping for my mother.

35:4 [r]Ps 38:12; 40:14; Jer 4:30 [s]Ps 69:6, 19; 70:2; 83:17; Isa 45:16; Mal 2:9 [t]Ps 25:3 [u]Ps 129:5 **35:5** [v]S Job 13:25; Ps 1:4 [w]Ps 34:7 **35:7** [x]S Job 18:8 [y]S Ps 7:4 [z]S Job 9:31; S Ps 7:15; S 55:23 **35:8** [a]Isa 47:11; 1Th 5:3 [b]S Ps 7:15 **35:9** [c]S Ps 2:11; S Lk 1:47 [d]Ps 9:14; 13:5; 27:1 **35:10** [e]S Ex 9:14; S Ps 18:31; 113:5 [f]Ps 18:17 [g]Ps 12:5; 37:14; 74:21; 86:1; 109:16; 140:12; Isa 41:17 **35:11** [h]S Ex 23:1; S Mt 26:60 **35:12** [i]Ps 38:20; 109:5; Pr 17:13; Jer 18:20 **35:13** [j]S 2Sa 3:31; 1Ki 20:31; Ps 30:11; 69:11 [k]Job 30:25; Ps 69:10; 109:24 **35:14** [l]Ps 38:6; 42:9; 43:2 **35:15** [m]S Job 31:29 [n]S Job 16:10 **35:16** [o]S Ps 22:7; Mk 10:34 [p]S Job 16:9; Mk 9:18; Ac 7:54 **35:17** [q]Ps 6:3 [r]Ps 22:20 [s]Ps 22:21; 57:4; 58:6 **35:18** [t]S Ps 22:25 [u]Ps 42:4; 109:30 [v]S Ps 22:22

15 But when I stumbled, they gathered in glee;[m]
attackers gathered against me when I was unaware.
They slandered[n] me without ceasing.
16 Like the ungodly they maliciously mocked[a];[o]
they gnashed their teeth[p] at me.
17 O Lord, how long[q] will you look on?
Rescue my life from their ravages,
my precious life[r] from these lions.[s]
18 I will give you thanks in the great assembly;[t]
among throngs[u] of people I will praise you.[v]
19 Let not those gloat over me
who are my enemies[w] without cause;
let not those who hate me without reason[x]
maliciously wink the eye.[y]
20 They do not speak peaceably,
but devise false accusations[z]
against those who live quietly in the land.
21 They gape[a] at me and say, "Aha! Aha![b]
With our own eyes we have seen it."
22 O LORD, you have seen[c] this; be not silent.
Do not be far[d] from me, O Lord.
23 Awake,[e] and rise[f] to my defense!
Contend[g] for me, my God and Lord.
24 Vindicate me in your righteousness,
O LORD my God;
do not let them gloat[h] over me.

[a] *16* Septuagint; Hebrew may mean *ungodly circle of mockers.*

35:19 [w]Ps 9:13 [x]ver 7; Ps 38:19; 69:4; Jn 15:25* [y]Pr 6:13; 10:10 **35:20** [z]Ps 38:12; 55:21; Jer 9:8; Mic 6:12 **35:21** [a]S Job 16:10 [b]Ps 40:15; 70:3; Eze 25:3 **35:22** [c]Ex 3:7; Ps 10:14 [d]S Ps 10:1 **35:23** [e]S Ps 7:6; 80:2 [f]Ps 17:13 [g]S 1Sa 24:15 **35:24** [h]Ps 22:17

"javelin"). For the Lord wielding a spear see Hab 3:11. *soul.* See note on 6:3.
35:4–6 Appeal to the Lord to deal with the attackers by frustrating all their efforts and totally disabling them. For links with vv. 26–27 see note on those verses.
35:4 *plot my ruin.* See note on 5:9.
35:5–6 *angel of the LORD.* See 34:7 and note.
35:5 *like chaff.* See note on 1:4.
35:7–10 Appeal to the Lord to match the attackers' violent intent with his saving act (see note on 5:10)—which the psalmist will celebrate with praise (see note on 7:17).
35:7–8 *hid their net ... dug a pit ... net they hid ... fall into the pit.* See 9:15 and note.
35:9 *soul.* See note on 6:3.
35:10 *poor and needy.* See 34:6 and note.
35:11–16 The accusation: They repaid my friendship with malicious slander. This accusation stands at the center of the psalm (see note on 6:6).
35:12 *soul.* See note on 6:3.
35:13–14 The psalmist provides a living example of Jesus' later command to "pray for those who persecute you" (Mt 5:44)—as do Job (Job 42:7–10; see note on 42:10) and Jesus himself (Lk 23:34).
35:13 *sackcloth.* See note on 30:11. *fasting.* An act of mourning (see 69:10).
35:15 *stumbled.* Not morally. He was brought low by circumstances (see 9:3; 27:2; 37:24; 56:13; 119:165).
35:16 *gnashed their teeth.* In malice (see 37:12; La 2:16).
35:17–21 Renewed appeal for God's saving help, accompanied by a vow to praise (v. 18). This five-line stanza and the five-line stanza in vv. 7–10 frame the central accusation.
35:17 *how long ...?* See note on 6:3. *lions.* See note on 7:2.
35:18 *assembly.* See note on 1:5.
35:19 *enemies without cause.* See vv. 11–17; an experience frequently reflected also elsewhere in the Psalter (see 38:19; 69:4; 109:3; 119:78,86,161). See also La 3:52. *hate me without reason.* See 69:4. It is not known which of these passages is referred to in Jn 15:25. Both psalms reflect circumstances applicable also to Jesus' experience (but see introduction to Ps 69).
35:21 *Aha! Aha!* See v. 25; see also note on 3:2.
35:22–25 A return to the opening appeal (vv. 1–3) for God to arouse himself, take up the psalmist's cause and "contend" (v. 23) with those attacking him.
35:22 *be not silent.* Do not remain inactive (see 28:1 and note; 83:1; 109:1).
35:23 *Awake.* See note on 7:6. *rise.* See note on 3:7.
35:24 *righteousness.* See note on 4:1.

25 Do not let them think, "Aha,[i] just what
we wanted!"
or say, "We have swallowed him
up."[j]
26 May all who gloat[k] over my distress[l]
be put to shame[m] and confusion;
may all who exalt themselves over me[n]
be clothed with shame and disgrace.
27 May those who delight in my
vindication[o]
shout for joy[p] and gladness;
may they always say, "The LORD be
exalted,
who delights[q] in the well-being of
his servant."[r]
28 My tongue will speak of your
righteousness[s]
and of your praises all day long.[t]

Psalm 36

For the director of music. Of David the servant of the LORD.

1 An oracle is within my heart
concerning the sinfulness of the
wicked:[a][u]
There is no fear[v] of God
before his eyes.[w]
2 For in his own eyes he flatters himself
too much to detect or hate his sin.[x]
3 The words of his mouth[y] are wicked
and deceitful;[z]
he has ceased to be wise[a] and to do
good.[b]
4 Even on his bed he plots evil;[c]
he commits himself to a sinful
course[d]
and does not reject what is wrong.[e]
5 Your love, O LORD, reaches to the
heavens,
your faithfulness[f] to the skies.[g]
6 Your righteousness[h] is like the mighty
mountains,[i]
your justice like the great deep.[j]
O LORD, you preserve both man and
beast.[k]
7 How priceless is your unfailing love![l]
Both high and low among men
find[b] refuge in the shadow of your
wings.[m]
8 They feast on the abundance of your
house;[n]
you give them drink from your river[o]
of delights.[p]

35:25 [i] ver 21 [j] Ps 124:3; Pr 1:12; La 2:16 **35:26** [k] Ps 22:17 [l] Ps 4:1 [m] S Job 8:22; Ps 109:29; Mic 7:10 [n] Job 19:5; Ps 38:16 **35:27** [o] Ps 9:4 [p] Ps 20:5; S 33:3 [q] Ps 147:11; 149:4 [r] S Job 17:3 **35:28** [s] Ps 5:8; 51:14 [t] Ps 71:15,24; 72:15 **36:1** [u] S Job 21:16 [v] Jer 2:19; 36:16,24 [w] S Job 23:15; Ro 3:18* **36:2** [x] Dt 29:19 **36:3** [y] Ps 10:7 [z] S Job 5:13; Ps 5:6,9; 43:1; 144:8,11; Isa 44:20 [a] Ps 94:8 [b] Jer 4:22; 13:23; Am 3:10 **36:4** [c] Pr 4:16 [d] Isa 65:2 [e] Ps 52:3; Ro 12:9 **36:5** [f] Ps 89:1; 119:90 [g] Ps 57:10; 71:19; 89:2; 103:11; 108:4 **36:6** [h] Ps 5:8 [i] Ps 68:15 [j] S Ge 1:2; S 7:11 [k] Ne 9:6; Ps 104:14; 145:16 **36:7** [l] Ps 6:4 [m] S Ru 2:12; S Ps 17:8; 57:1; 91:4 **36:8** [n] Ps 65:4; Isa 25:6; Jer 31:12,14 [o] Job 20:17; Rev 22:1 [p] S Ps 23:2; 63:5

[a] *1* Or *heart: / Sin proceeds from the wicked.* [b] *7* Or *love, O God! / Men find*; or *love! / Both heavenly beings and men / find*

35:25 *swallowed.* See 124:3.

35:26–27 Again (see vv. 4–6) an appeal for God to bring "shame" and "disgrace" on the adversaries. For both form and substance cf. 40:14–16.

35:26 *who gloat over my distress.* In Hebrew a verbal echo of "who plot my ruin" (v. 4). *clothed with.* See note on 109:29.

35:27 May all who are faithful supporters of the Lord's "servant" (here no doubt equivalent to his "anointed"; see note on 2:2) have reason to rejoice and praise the Lord.

35:28 A concluding vow to praise (see note on 7:17). *righteousness.* See note on 4:1.

Ps 36 A prayer for God's unfailing protection, as the psalmist reflects on the godlessness of the wicked and the goodness of God. For this psalm's relationship with Ps 35 see introduction to Ps 34–37. Structurally, though different from the scansion in the NIV, a short couplet (v. 1) introduces a series of four stanzas of three Hebrew poetic lines each (vv. 2–4,5–7a, 7b–9,10–12). In later Jewish practice, vv. 7–10 became part of the morning prayer.

36 title *For the director of music.* See note on Ps 4 title. *servant of the LORD.* His royal servant (see notes on Ps 18 title; 35:27; see also 2Sa 7:20).

36:1 *oracle.* Usually reserved for words of revelation from God, such as those spoken by the prophets. Here reference is to an insight, perhaps coming like a flash, into the true character of the wicked. *heart.* See note on 4:7. *no fear of God.* Such as the psalmist calls for in Ps 34 and (implicitly) in Ps 37. See 55:19; Ge 20:11 and note. They take no account of his all-seeing eye, his righteous judgment and his power to deal with them (see note on 10:11). For Paul's use of this verse see Ro 3:18.

36:2–4 The wicked characterized (see also 10:2–11 and notes, and introduction to Ps 37).

36:2 *flatters himself.* Not in self-righteousness but out of the smug, conceited notion that he is accountable to no one.

36:3 *words of his mouth.* See note on 5:9. *are … deceitful.* See 35:20. *ceased to be wise.* See 94:8–11; Pr 2:9–11. *ceased … to do good.* In contrast to the wise and godly person (see 34:14; 37:3,27; see also note on 34:8–14).

36:4 *on his bed.* When one's thoughts are free to range, and to set the course for the activities of the day. The wicked do not meditate on God's law "day and night" (1:2; see 119:55). On the other hand, the heart of the godly instructs them at night (see 16:7); they commune at night with God (see 42:8), think of him (see 63:6) and reflect on his promises (see 119:148). *plots evil.* See 34:14; 37:27; cf. Mic 2:1.

36:5–7a The trustworthiness of the Lord.

36:5 *love … faithfulness.* That is, love-and-faithfulness (as in 57:3; 61:7; 85:10; 86:15; 89:14; 115:1; 138:2; Pr 3:3; 14:22; 16:6; 20:28; see note on 3:7). *reaches to the heavens … to the skies.* Encompasses all the realms of creaturely existence (see 57:10; 108:4).

36:6 *righteousness … justice.* That is, righteousness-and-justice (as in 33:5; 37:6; 89:14; 97:2; Hos 2:19; see also Isa 9:7; 33:5; Jer 9:24). *righteousness.* See note on 4:1. *like the mighty mountains … great deep.* As high as the mountains, as deep as the sea.

36:7a *unfailing love.* See v. 5; see also note on 6:4.

36:7b–9 The Lord's benevolence toward all his creatures (see 33:4–5).

36:7b *shadow of your wings.* See 17:8 and note.

36:8 *feast … drink.* Life-giving food and water. *house.* Here, God's whole estate or realm—i.e., the earth, from which springs the abundance of food for all living things (see note on 24:2). *river.* The "channel" (Job 38:25) by which God brings forth the rain out of his "storehouses" (33:7; see Job 38:8–11,22,37; Jer 10:13) in his "upper chambers" (104:13; see 65:9; Isa 30:25 and the references to "blessings" from heaven in Ge 49:25; Dt 33:23). This vivid imagery, depicting God's control over, and gift of, the waters from heaven, which

[9]For with you is the fountain of life;[q]
in your light[r] we see light.
[10]Continue your love[s] to those who
know you,[t]
your righteousness to the upright in
heart.[u]
[11]May the foot of the proud not come
against me,
nor the hand of the wicked[v] drive
me away.
[12]See how the evildoers lie fallen—
thrown down, not able to rise![w]

Psalm 37[a]

Of David.

[1]Do not fret because of evil men
or be envious[x] of those who do
wrong;[y]
[2]for like the grass they will soon
wither,[z]
like green plants they will soon die
away.[a]
[3]Trust in the LORD and do good;
dwell in the land[b] and enjoy safe
pasture.[c]

36:9 [q]Ps 87:7; Pr 10:11; 16:22; Jer 2:13 [r]Ps 4:6; 27:1; 76:4; 104:2; Isa 2:5; 9:2; 60:1,19; Jn 1:4; 1Pe 2:9 **36:10** [s]Jer 31:3 [t]Jer 9:24; 22:16 [u]Ps 7:10; 11:2; 94:15; 125:4 **36:11** [v]Ps 71:4; 140:4 **36:12** [w]S Ps 18:38 **37:1** [x]Pr 3:31; 23:17-18 [y]Ps 73:3; Pr 24:19 **37:2** [z]S 2Ki 19:26; Job 14:2; Ps 102:4; Isa 40:7 [a]ver 38; Ps 90:6; 92:7; Jas 1:10 **37:3** [b]Dt 30:20 [c]Eze 34:14; Jn 10:9 **37:4** [d]S Job 27:10 [e]S Job 7:6; Ps 21:2; 145:19; Mt 6:33 **37:5** [f]Ps 4:5 **37:6** [g]Ps 18:24; 103:17; 112:3 [h]S Job 11:17

[4]Delight[d] yourself in the LORD
and he will give you the desires of
your heart.[e]
[5]Commit your way to the LORD;
trust in him[f] and he will do this:
[6]He will make your righteousness[g]
shine like the dawn,[h]
the justice of your cause like the
noonday sun.
[7]Be still[i] before the LORD and wait
patiently[j] for him;
do not fret[k] when men succeed in
their ways,[l]
when they carry out their wicked
schemes.[m]
[8]Refrain from anger[n] and turn from
wrath;
do not fret[o]—it leads only to
evil.

[a] This psalm is an acrostic poem, the stanzas of which begin with the successive letters of the Hebrew alphabet.

37:7 [i]S Ex 14:14; S Isa 41:1 [j]S Ps 27:14; 40:1; 130:5; Isa 38:13; Hab 3:16; Ro 8:25 [k]ver 1 [l]Jer 12:1 [m]Ps 21:11; 26:10; 119:150 **37:8** [n]Eph 4:31; Col 3:8 [o]ver 1

feed the rivers and streams of earth to give life and health wherever they flow, is the source of the symbol of "the river of the water of life" that flows from the temple of God (Rev 22:1–2; see also Eze 47:1–12). *of delights.* Furnishing many sources of joy.

36:9 The climax and summation of vv. 5–9. *fountain of life.* See Jer 2:13; 17:13. Ultimately, for sinners, God provides the water of life through Jesus Christ (Jn 4:10,14). *your light.* See 27:1 and note. *see.* Experience, have, enjoy, as in 16:10; 27:13; 34:8,12; 49:9,19; 89:48; 90:15; 106:5 ("enjoy"); Job 9:25 ("glimpse"); 42:5; Ecc 1:16 ("experienced"); 3:13 ("find"); 6:6 ("enjoy"); 8:16; Isa 53:10; La 3:1. *light.* Life in its fullness as it was created to be. For the association of light with life see 49:19; 56:13; Job 3:20; 33:28,30; Isa 53:11.

36:10–12 The prayer: Your "love" (v. 5) and "righteousness" (v. 6), which you display in all creation—show these to all who know (acknowledge) you and are upright (the people of God). But keep the wicked, "foot" and "hand," from success against me (the king; see note on 33:16).

36:10 *love.* See note on 6:4. *those who know you.* See 9:10 and note. *righteousness.* See note on 4:1.

36:11 *proud.* See note on 31:23.

36:12 Confidence (see note on 3:8). *lie fallen.* Perhaps in death (see note on 13:4).

Ps 37 Instruction in godly wisdom. (For other "wisdom" psalms see 34:8–22; 49; 112; others closely related are Ps 1; 73; 91; 92:6–9,12–15; 111; 119; 127–128; 133; see also essay, p. 727.) This psalm's dominant theme is related to the contrast between the wicked and the righteous reflected in Ps 36. The central issue addressed is: Who will "inherit the land" (vv. 9,11,22,29), i.e., live to enjoy the blessings of the Lord in the promised land? Will the wicked, who plot (v. 12), scheme (vv. 7,32), default on debts (v. 21), use raw power to gain advantage (v. 14) and seem thereby to flourish (vv. 7,16,35)? Or will the righteous, who trust in the Lord (vv. 3,5,7,34) and are humble (v. 11), blameless (vv. 18,37), generous (vv. 21,26), upright (v. 37) and peaceable (v. 37), and from whose mouth is heard the moral wisdom that reflects meditation on God's law (vv. 30–31)? For a similar characterization of the wicked see 10:2–11; 73:4–12. For a similar characterization of the righteous see Ps 112. For a similar statement concerning the transitoriness of the wicked see Ps 49; 73:18–20.

Structurally, in this alphabetic acrostic, two verses are devoted to each letter of the alphabet, though with some irregularity. The main theme is developed in vv. 1–11, then further elaborated in the rest of the psalm. The whole is framed by statements contrasting the brief career of the wicked (vv. 1–2) and the Lord's sustaining help of the righteous (vv. 39–40). For this psalm's relationship to Ps 34–36 see introduction to Ps 34–37.

37:1–2 See v. 7; Ps 73.

37:1 Almost identical to Pr 24:19.

37:2 See note on v. 20.

37:3 See 34:8–14 and note.

37:4 *heart.* See note on 4:7.

37:5 *Commit.* See 1Pe 5:7.

37:6 *your righteousness.* That is, the prosperity and well-being that God will bestow in accordance with "your" faithful reliance on him (cf. v. 9; see Pr 8:18; 21:21 ["prosperity"] for this sense of the Hebrew word; see also Isa 48:18). *righteousness... justice.* That is, righteousness-and-justice (see note on 36:6). *the justice of your cause.* Or "your vindication" (as in 35:27; see note on that verse; see also Isa 54:17). The close Hebrew synonyms here rendered "righteousness" and "justice" both refer to manifestations of God's favor on those he pleases to bless or deliver, as in Isa 59:9 (where these terms are linked with "light") and 59:11 (where "justice" is linked with "deliverance"). Accordingly, "your righteousness" and "your justice/vindication" in this verse have direct links with "your (God's) righteousness" and "your (God's) justice" in 36:6. It is God's "righteousness" and "justice" that secure the "righteousness" and "justice" (in the sense here noted) of those who "trust in him" (v. 5).

37:8 *anger ... wrath.* Evidence of fretting over the wicked's prosperity that has been gained to the disadvantage of and even at the expense of the righteous.

9 For evil men will be cut off,[p]
but those who hope[q] in the LORD will
inherit the land.[r]

10 A little while, and the wicked will be
no more;[s]
though you look for them, they will
not be found.
11 But the meek will inherit the land[t]
and enjoy great peace.[u]

12 The wicked plot[v] against the righteous
and gnash their teeth[w] at them;
13 but the Lord laughs at the wicked,
for he knows their day is coming.[x]

14 The wicked draw the sword[y]
and bend the bow[z]
to bring down the poor and needy,[a]
to slay those whose ways are
upright.
15 But their swords will pierce their own
hearts,[b]
and their bows will be broken.[c]

16 Better the little that the righteous have
than the wealth[d] of many wicked;
17 for the power of the wicked will be
broken,[e]
but the LORD upholds[f] the righteous.

18 The days of the blameless are known
to the LORD,[g]
and their inheritance will endure
forever.[h]
19 In times of disaster they will not
wither;
in days of famine they will enjoy
plenty.

20 But the wicked will perish:[i]
The LORD's enemies will be like the
beauty of the fields,
they will vanish—vanish like
smoke.[j]

21 The wicked borrow and do not
repay,
but the righteous give generously;[k]
22 those the LORD blesses will inherit the
land,
but those he curses[l] will be cut off.[m]

23 If the LORD delights[n] in a man's way,
he makes his steps firm;[o]
24 though he stumble, he will not fall,[p]
for the LORD upholds[q] him with his
hand.

25 I was young and now I am old,
yet I have never seen the righteous
forsaken[r]
or their children begging[s] bread.
26 They are always generous and lend
freely;[t]
their children will be blessed.[u]

27 Turn from evil and do good;[v]
then you will dwell in the land
forever.[w]
28 For the LORD loves the just
and will not forsake his faithful
ones.[x]

They will be protected forever,
but the offspring of the wicked will
be cut off;[y]
29 the righteous will inherit the land[z]
and dwell in it forever.[a]

30 The mouth of the righteous man utters
wisdom,[b]
and his tongue speaks what is
just.

37:9 [p]S Ps 31:22; 101:8; 118:10; Pr 2:22 [q]Isa 25:9; 26:8; 40:31; 49:23; 51:5 [r]ver 22; Ps 25:13; Isa 49:8; 57:13; Mt 5:5 **37:10** [s]S Job 7:10; Eze 27:36 **37:11** [t]S Nu 14:24; Mt 5:5 [u]S Lev 26:6; S Nu 6:26 **37:12** [v]Ps 2:1; 31:13 [w]S Job 16:9; Ps 35:16; 112:10 **37:13** [x]1Sa 26:10; Eze 12:23 **37:14** [y]S Ps 22:20 [z]Ps 11:2 [a]S Ps 35:10 **37:15** [b]S Ps 9:16 [c]S 1Sa 2:4; Ps 46:9; Jer 49:35 **37:16** [d]Pr 15:16; 16:8 **37:17** [e]Job 38:15; Ps 10:15 [f]Ps 41:12; 140:12; 145:14; 146:7 **37:18** [g]S Job 23:10; Ps 44:21 [h]ver 27,29 **37:20** [i]S Ps 34:21 [j]Ps 68:2; 102:3; Isa 51:6 **37:21** [k]S Lev 25:35; Ps 112:5 **37:22** [l]S Job 5:3 [m]ver 9 **37:23** [n]S Nu 14:8; Ps 147:11 [o]S Job 11:15; S Ps 7:9; 66:9

37:24 [p]S Ps 13:4; 27:2; 38:17; 55:22; 119:165; Pr 3:23; 10:9 [q]2Ch 9:8; Ps 41:12; 145:14 **37:25** [r]ver 28; S Ge 15:1; Heb 13:5 [s]Ps 111:5; 145:15; Mk 10:46 **37:26** [t]S Lev 25:35 [u]Dt 28:4; Ps 112:2 **37:27** [v]Ps 34:14; 3Jn 1:11 [w]S Nu 24:21 **37:28** [x]S Dt 7:6; S Ps 18:25; S 97:10 [y]S Ge 17:14; S Dt 32:26; Pr 2:22 **37:29** [z]ver 9; Pr 2:21 [a]Isa 34:17 **37:30** [b]Ps 49:3; Pr 10:13

37:9 *hope in.* Or "wait for," as in v. 34. *inherit the land.* Receive from the Lord secure entitlement (for them and their children) to the promised land as the created and redeemed sphere and bountiful source of provision for the life of God's people. Those who hope in the Lord—i.e., trustfully look to him to bestow life and its blessings as a gift—will inherit the land, not those who apart from God and by evil means try to take possession of it and its wealth (see vv. 11,22,29; cf. Jos 7).

37:10 *A little while.* Shortness of time is here a figure for certainty of event (see 58:9; Job 20:5–11; Hag 2:6).

37:11 See Mt 5:5. *meek.* Those who humbly acknowledge their dependence on the goodness and grace of God and betray no arrogance toward others. *great peace.* Unmixed blessedness.

37:12 *righteous.* See note on 1:5. *gnash their teeth.* See 35:16 and note.

37:13 *Lord laughs.* See 2:4. *knows their day is coming.* Strikingly, the psalmist nowhere speaks of God's active involvement in bringing the wicked down—though he hints at it in v. 22. The certainty that the life of the wicked "will be cut off" is frequently asserted (vv. 9,22,28,34,38; cf. vv. 2,8,10,15,17, 20,36,38)—and the Lord also knows it—but God's positive action is here reserved for his care for and protection of the righteous. *their day.* The time when each will be "cut off," as in 1Sa 26:10 ("his time," lit. "his day"); Job 18:20 ("his fate").

37:14–15 *sword ... bow ... swords ... bows.* See 64:3–4,7–8; Pr 30:14 and note on Ps 5:9.

37:14 *poor and needy.* See 34:6 and note.

37:15 *pierce ... hearts.* See 45:5.

37:16–17 *righteous.* See note on 1:5.

37:18 *blameless.* See v. 37; see also 15:2 and note. *known to.* That is, "watched over by," as in 1:6.

37:20 *beauty.* The grass and flowers (cf. v. 2; 90:5–6; 92:7; 102:11; 103:15–16; Job 14:2 and note; Isa 40:6–7; see Jas 1:10–11).

37:21 Or "The wicked must borrow and cannot repay,/ but the righteous are able to give generously" (see Dt 15:6; 28:12,44).

37:24 See Pr 24:16.

37:26 See note on v. 21.

37:27 *Turn from evil and do good.* See 34:14 and note.

37:28 *faithful ones.* See note on 4:3.

37:29 *dwell in it forever.* They and their children and children's children, in contrast to the wicked (see v. 28).

37:30 *wisdom.* See 119:98,130; Dt 4:6.

31 The law of his God is in his heart;[c]
his feet do not slip.[d]
32 The wicked lie in wait[e] for the righteous,[f]
seeking their very lives;
33 but the LORD will not leave them in their power
or let them be condemned[g] when brought to trial.[h]

34 Wait for the LORD[i]
and keep his way.[j]
He will exalt you to inherit the land;
when the wicked are cut off,[k] you will see[l] it.

35 I have seen a wicked and ruthless man
flourishing[m] like a green tree in its native soil,
36 but he soon passed away and was no more;
though I looked for him, he could not be found.[n]

37 Consider the blameless,[o] observe the upright;[p]
there is a future[a] for the man of peace.[q]
38 But all sinners[r] will be destroyed;[s]
the future[b] of the wicked will be cut off.[t]

39 The salvation[u] of the righteous comes from the LORD;
he is their stronghold in time of trouble.[v]
40 The LORD helps[w] them and delivers[x] them;
he delivers them from the wicked and saves[y] them,
because they take refuge[z] in him.

37:31 [c]S Dt 6:6; S Job 22:22 [d]S Dt 32:35 **37:32** [e]S Ps 10:8 [f]Ps 11:5 **37:33** [g]Job 32:3; Ps 34:22; 79:11 [h]2Pe 2:9 **37:34** [i]Ps 27:14 [j]S Ps 18:21 [k]ver 9 [l]Ps 52:6 **37:35** [m]S Job 5:3 **37:36** [n]ver 10; Pr 12:7; Isa 41:12; Da 11:19 **37:37** [o]ver 18; S Ge 6:9; Ps 18:25 [p]Ps 11:7 [q]Isa 57:1-2 **37:38** [r]S Ps 1:1 [s]S ver 2; Ps 73:19 [t]ver 9 **37:39** [u]S Ps 3:8 [v]S Ps 9:9 **37:40** [w]S 1Ch 5:20; S Ps 20:2 [x]S Ps 34:7 [y]S Ps 18:48 [z]Ps 2:12

38:1 [a]Ps 6:1 **38:2** [b]S Job 6:4 **38:3** [c]Pr 3:8; 4:22 [d]S Job 33:19 **38:4** [e]Ps 40:12; 65:3 [f]S Nu 11:14; S Ezr 9:6; Lk 11:46 **38:5** [g]ver 11; Ps 147:3 [h]Job 19:17 [i]Ps 69:5; Pr 5:23; 12:23; 13:16; Ecc 10:3 **38:6** [j]Ps 57:6; 145:14; 146:8 [k]S Ps 35:14 **38:7** [l]S Job 14:22 [m]ver 3 **38:8** [n]Ps 34:18; Pr 17:22 [o]S Ps 6:6; 22:1; Pr 5:11 [p]S Ps 6:3

Psalm 38

A psalm of David. A petition.

1 O LORD, do not rebuke me in your anger
or discipline me in your wrath.[a]
2 For your arrows[b] have pierced me,
and your hand has come down upon me.
3 Because of your wrath there is no health[c] in my body;
my bones[d] have no soundness because of my sin.
4 My guilt has overwhelmed[e] me
like a burden too heavy to bear.[f]

5 My wounds[g] fester and are loathsome[h]
because of my sinful folly.[i]
6 I am bowed down[j] and brought very low;
all day long I go about mourning.[k]
7 My back is filled with searing pain;[l]
there is no health[m] in my body.
8 I am feeble and utterly crushed;[n]
I groan[o] in anguish of heart.[p]

9 All my longings[q] lie open before you, O Lord;
my sighing[r] is not hidden from you.
10 My heart pounds,[s] my strength fails[t] me;
even the light has gone from my eyes.[u]
11 My friends and companions avoid me
because of my wounds;[v]
my neighbors stay far away.
12 Those who seek my life set their traps,[w]

[a] *37* Or *there will be posterity* [b] *38* Or *posterity*

38:9 [q]Ps 119:20; 143:7 [r]S Job 3:24 **38:10** [s]S Job 37:1 [t]S Ps 31:10 [u]S Ps 6:7; S 19:8; 88:9 **38:11** [v]S ver 5 **38:12** [w]Ps 31:4; 140:5; 141:9

37:31 *heart.* See note on 4:7. *do not slip.* From the right path (see 17:5).
37:32 *lie in wait.* See 10:8 – 9; see also note on 7:2. *seeking their very lives.* Attempting to seize by false charges at court (see v. 33) the very livelihood of their intended victims.
37:34 See v. 9.
37:35 – 36 Cf. vv. 25 – 26.
37:37 – 38 The great contrast: hope for the "upright," no hope for the "wicked."
37:39 – 40 *the righteous ... them.* They are not at the mercy of the wicked: The Lord is their refuge, and in spite of all that the wicked do, the Lord makes secure their inheritance in the promised land.
Ps 38 – 41 The final four psalms of Book I are all linked by common central themes (see introductions to these psalms). One of these themes is confession of sin, which is found elsewhere in Book I only in Ps 25; 32 (see introductions to those psalms). Significantly, following a wisdom psalm (37), the first reference to sin here characterizes it as "folly" (38:5).
Ps 38 An urgent appeal for relief from a severe and painful illness, God's "rebuke" for a sin David has committed. Neither the specific occasion nor the illness can be identified. David's suffering is aggravated by the withdrawal of his friends (see v. 11) and the unwarranted efforts of his enemies to seize this opportunity to bring him down (vv. 12,16,19 – 20). In traditional Christian usage, this is one of seven penitential psalms (see introduction to Ps 6). Like Ps 33 (see introductory note on its structure), its length (22 verses) is based on the number of letters in the Hebrew alphabet. The psalm is composed of five stanzas of four verses each, with a two-verse conclusion.
38 title *A petition.* Occurs elsewhere only in the title of Ps 70.
38:1 – 4 Plea for relief from the Lord's rebuke.
38:1 *rebuke ... discipline.* That is, rebuke-and-discipline (see 39:11; see also note on 3:7). *anger ... wrath.* See note on 2:5.
38:2 *arrows.* A vivid metaphor for God's blows (see Job 6:4; 34:6; La 3:12; Eze 5:16; see also note on Ge 9:13). *your hand has come down upon me.* See 32:4 and note on 32:3 – 5.
38:3 *bones.* See note on 6:2.
38:4 *burden.* Not only a psychological "burden of guilt," but the heavy burden of suffering described in vv. 5 – 8.
38:5 – 8 The devastating physical and psychological effects of his illness.
38:8 *heart.* See note on 4:7.
38:9 – 12 Renewed appeal, with further elaboration of his troubles: his illness (v. 10), abandonment by his friends (v. 11) and the hostility of his enemies (v. 12).
38:10 *light has gone from my eyes.* See note on 13:3.
38:11 See note on 31:11 – 12.
38:12 See note on 5:9. *set their traps.* See note on 9:15.

those who would harm me talk of
my ruin;[x]
all day long they plot deception.[y]
13 I am like a deaf man, who cannot hear,[z]
like a mute, who cannot open his
mouth;
14 I have become like a man who does
not hear,
whose mouth can offer no reply.
15 I wait[a] for you, O LORD;
you will answer,[b] O Lord my God.
16 For I said, "Do not let them gloat[c]
or exalt themselves over me when
my foot slips."[d]

17 For I am about to fall,[e]
and my pain[f] is ever with me.
18 I confess my iniquity;[g]
I am troubled by my sin.
19 Many are those who are my vigorous
enemies;[h]
those who hate me[i] without reason[j]
are numerous.
20 Those who repay my good with evil[k]
slander[l] me when I pursue what is
good.

21 O LORD, do not forsake me;[m]
be not far[n] from me, O my God.
22 Come quickly[o] to help me,[p]
O Lord my Savior.[q]

Psalm 39

For the director of music. For Jeduthun.
A psalm of David.

1 I said, "I will watch my ways[r]
and keep my tongue from sin;[s]
I will put a muzzle on my mouth[t]
as long as the wicked are in my
presence."
2 But when I was silent[u] and still,
not even saying anything good,
my anguish[v] increased.
3 My heart grew hot[w] within me,
and as I meditated,[x] the fire[y] burned;
then I spoke with my tongue:

4 "Show me, O LORD, my life's end
and the number of my days;[z]
let me know how fleeting[a] is my
life.[b]
5 You have made my days[c] a mere
handbreadth;
the span of my years is as nothing
before you.
Each man's life is but a breath.[d]
Selah
6 Man is a mere phantom[e] as he goes to
and fro:[f]
He bustles about, but only in vain;[g]
he heaps up wealth,[h] not knowing
who will get it.[i]

7 "But now, Lord, what do I look for?
My hope is in you.[j]
8 Save me[k] from all my transgressions;[l]
do not make me the scorn[m] of fools.
9 I was silent;[n] I would not open my
mouth,[o]
for you are the one who has done
this.[p]

38:12 [x]Ps 35:4; 41:5 [y]S Ps 35:20 **38:13** [z]Ps 115:6; 135:17; Isa 43:8; Mk 7:37 **38:15** [a]Ps 27:14 [b]Ps 17:6 **38:16** [c]S Ps 22:17 [d]S Dt 32:35 **38:17** [e]S Ps 37:24 [f]ver 7; S Job 6:10 **38:18** [g]S Lev 26:40 **38:19** [h]S Ps 18:17 [i]S Ps 25:19 [j]S Ps 35:19 **38:20** [k]S Ge 44:4; 1Jn 3:12 [l]Ps 54:5; 59:10; 119:23 **38:21** [m]Ps 27:9; 71:18; 119:8 [n]S Ps 10:1; S 22:11; 35:22; 71:12 **38:22** [o]S Ps 22:19 [p]Ps 40:13 [q]S 1Ch 16:35 **39:1** [r]1Ki 2:4; Ps 119:9,59; Pr 20:11 [s]S Job 1:22; Ps 34:13; Jas 3:2 [t]S Job 6:24; Jas 1:26 **39:2** [u]ver 9; S Job 31:34; Ps 77:4 [v]Ps 6:3; S 25:17; 31:10 **39:3** [w]Lk 24:32 [x]Ps 1:2; 48:9; 77:12; 119:15 [y]Jer 5:14; 20:9; 23:29 **39:4** [z]S Job 14:5 [a]S Job 14:2 [b]S Ge 47:9; S Job 7:7 **39:5** [c]S Job 10:20; Ps 89:45; 102:23 [d]S Job 7:7; Ps 62:9 **39:6** [e]Job 8:9; Ps 102:11; Ecc 6:12; S Jas 4:14 [f]Jas 1:11 [g]Ps 127:2 [h]S Job 27:17 [i]Lk 12:20 **39:7** [j]S Ps 9:18; S 25:5 **39:8** [k]Ps 6:4; 51:14 [l]Ps 32:1; 51:1; Isa 53:5,8,10 [m]S Dt 28:37; Ps 69:7; 79:4; Isa 43:28; Da 9:16 **39:9** [n]S ver 2 [o]Ps 38:13 [p]Isa 38:15

38:13–16 Let the Lord answer (v. 15) my enemies. Like a deaf-mute, David will not reply to his enemies (vv. 13–14); he waits for the Lord to act in his behalf (vv. 15–16). See 1Sa 25:32–39; 2Sa 16:10,12.
38:16 *when my foot slips.* When he experiences a personal blow to health or circumstance—here referring to his illness (see 66:9; 94:18; 121:3).
38:17–20 As health declines, the vigor of his many enemies increases.
38:17 *about to fall.* Death seems near (see note on 13:4). *fall.* In Hebrew, a verbal link with 35:15 ("stumbled").
38:18 See vv. 3–4; Ps 32.
38:19–20 He has sinned against the Lord, but he is innocent of any wrong against those attacking him (see note on 35:19).
38:20 *repay my good.* See 35:12–14. *slander.* Accuse (falsely), as in 71:13; 109:4,20,29; Zec 3:1. *when.* Or "though." *good.* Morally good (see 34:14).
38:21–22 In conclusion, a renewed appeal.
Ps 39 David's poignant prayer when deeply troubled by the fragility of human life. He is reminded of this by the present illness through which God is rebuking him (vv. 10–11) for his "transgressions" (v. 8). Ps 38 speaks of silence before the enemy, Ps 39 of silence before God. Both are prayers in times of illness (God's "rebuke," v. 11; 38:1); both acknowledge sin, and both express deep trust in God. See introduction to Ps 40. In addition, this psalm has many links with Ps 90; see also Ps 49. The psalm's structure is symmetrical: The first two stanzas of five and three Hebrew poetic lines are balanced by the last two stanzas of five and three lines. At the center (v. 6; see note on 6:6) stands a wisdom observation that places David's situation in the broader context of a widespread human condition (see note on v. 6).
39 title *For the director of music.* See note on Ps 4 title. *Jeduthun.* One of David's three choir leaders (1Ch 16:41–42; 25:1,6; 2Ch 5:12; called his "seer" in 2Ch 35:15). Jeduthun is probably also the Ethan of 1Ch 6:44; 15:19; if so, he represented the family of Merari, even as Asaph did the family of Gershon and Heman the family of Kohath, the three sons of Levi (see 1Ch 6:16,33,39,43–44). See titles of Ps 62; 77; 89.
39:1–3 Introduction: Having determined to keep silent, he could finally no longer suppress his anguish.
39:1 He had kept a muzzle on his mouth for fear that rebellious words would escape in the hearing of the wicked (see Ps 73).
39:2–3 Suppressed anguish only intensified the agony (see Jer 20:9).
39:4–5 A prayer for understanding and patient acceptance of the brief span of human life.
39:4 *how fleeting is my life.* See 78:39 and note on 37:20.
39:5 *as nothing before you.* See 90:4. *but a breath.* See v. 11; 62:9; 144:4.
39:6 This wisdom observation (see introduction to this psalm) could almost serve as a summary of Ecclesiastes.
39:7–11 A modest prayer: Only grant me relief from your present rebuke.
39:8 *Save me.* As from an enemy. *scorn of fools.* If the Lord does not restore him, he will be mocked (see 22:7–8; 69:6–12) by godless fools (see 14:1).

10 Remove your scourge from me;
I am overcome by the blow[q] of your hand.[r]
11 You rebuke[s] and discipline[t] men for their sin;
you consume[u] their wealth like a moth[v]—
each man is but a breath.[w] *Selah*

12 "Hear my prayer, O LORD,
listen to my cry for help;[x]
be not deaf[y] to my weeping.[z]
For I dwell with you as an alien,[a]
a stranger,[b] as all my fathers were.[c]
13 Look away from me, that I may rejoice again
before I depart and am no more."[d]

Psalm 40

40:13-17pp — Ps 70:1-5

For the director of music.
Of David. A psalm.

1 I waited patiently[e] for the LORD;
he turned to me and heard my cry.[f]
2 He lifted me out of the slimy pit,[g]
out of the mud[h] and mire;[i]
he set my feet[j] on a rock[k]
and gave me a firm place to stand.
3 He put a new song[l] in my mouth,
a hymn of praise to our God.
Many will see and fear[m]
and put their trust[n] in the LORD.

4 Blessed is the man[o]
who makes the LORD his trust,[p]
who does not look to the proud,[q]
to those who turn aside to false gods.[a][r]
5 Many, O LORD my God,
are the wonders[s] you have done.
The things you planned for us
no one can recount[t] to you;
were I to speak and tell of them,
they would be too many[u] to declare.

6 Sacrifice and offering you did not desire,[v]
but my ears you have pierced[b,c];[w]
burnt offerings[x] and sin offerings
you did not require.
7 Then I said, "Here I am, I have come—
it is written about me in the scroll.[d][y]

39:10 [q]2Ch 21:14; Eze 7:9; 24:16 [r]S Ex 9:3 **39:11** [s]S Dt 28:20; Isa 66:15; Eze 5:15; 2Pe 2:16 [t]Ps 94:10; Isa 26:16 [u]Ps 90:7 [v]S Job 13:28; S Isa 51:8; Lk 12:33; S Jas 5:2 [w]S Job 7:7 **39:12** [x]S Ps 17:1 [y]S Dt 1:45 [z]S 2Ki 20:5 [a]Lev 25:23 [b]S Ge 23:4; S Heb 11:13 [c]S Ge 47:9; S 1Ch 29:15 **39:13** [d]S Job 10:21 **40:1** [e]S Ps 37:7 [f]Ps 6:9; S 31:22; 34:15; 116:1; 145:19 **40:2** [g]S Job 9:31; S Ps 7:15 [h]S Job 30:19 [i]Ps 69:14 [j]Ps 31:8 [k]Ps 27:5 **40:3** [l]S Ps 28:7; S 96:1; Rev 5:9 [m]Ps 52:6; 64:9 [n]S Ex 14:31

[a] 4 Or *to falsehood* [b] 6 Hebrew; Septuagint *but a body you have prepared for me* (see also Symmachus and Theodotion) [c] 6 Or *opened* [d] 7 Or *come / with the scroll written for me*

40:4 [o]Ps 34:8 [p]Ps 84:12 [q]Ps 101:5; 138:6; Pr 3:34; 16:5; Isa 65:5; 1Pe 5:5 [r]S Dt 31:20; S Ps 4:2; S 26:1 **40:5** [s]S Dt 4:34; Ps 75:1; 105:5; 136:4 [t]Ps 139:18 [u]Ps 71:15; 139:17 **40:6** [v]S 1Sa 15:22; Jer 6:20; Am 5:22 [w]Ex 21:6 [x]Ps 50:8; 51:16; Isa 1:11; Hos 6:6 **40:7** [y]Job 19:23; Jer 36:2; 45:1; Eze 2:9; Zec 5:1

39:10 *blow of your hand.* See 32:4; 38:2.
39:11 *rebuke and discipline.* See 6:1; 38:1. *but a breath.* See note on v. 5.
39:12 – 13 The modest prayer repeated even more modestly.
39:12 *an alien, a stranger.* He lives this life before God only as a pilgrim passing through.
39:13 *Look away from me.* See Job 7:17 – 19; 10:20 – 21; 14:6. *rejoice again.* See Job 9:27; 10:20. *am no more.* Here there is no glimpse of what lies beyond the horizon of death (see note on 6:5).
Ps 40 – 41 Book I of the Psalter closes with two psalms containing "Blessed is the man/he who" statements (40:4; 41:1), thus balancing the two psalms with which the Book begins (1:1; 2:12). In this way, the whole of Book I is framed by declarations of the blessedness of those who "delight in the law of the LORD" (1:2), who "take refuge in him" (2:12), who "do not look to the proud" but make the Lord their "trust" (40:4) and who have "regard for the weak" (41:1) — a concise instruction in godliness. See introduction to Ps 1 – 2.
Ps 40 A prayer for help when troubles abound. The causes of distress are not specified, but David acknowledges that they are occasioned by his sin (see v. 12), as in Ps 38 – 39; 41 (see introductions to Ps 39; 41). They are aggravated by the gloating of his enemies, a theme also present in Ps 38 – 39; 41 (see introduction to Ps 38). The prayer begins with praise of God for his past mercies (vv. 1 – 5: two stanzas of five Hebrew poetic lines each) and a testimony to the king's own faithfulness to the Lord (vv. 6 – 10: two three-line stanzas). These form the grounds for his present appeal for help (vv. 11 – 17: two five-line stanzas and a concluding couplet; note the structural centering of vv. 6 – 10). For other lengthy prefaces to prayer see Ps 44; 89. Ps 70 is a somewhat revised duplicate of vv. 13 – 17 of this psalm.
40 title *For the director of music.* See note on Ps 4 title.
40:1 – 5 Praise of the Lord for past mercies (see introduction to Ps 9).
40:1 – 3 David's experience of God's past help in time of trouble, which moved him to praise and others to faith (see notes on 7:17; 9:1).
40:2 See 30:1 and note.
40:3 *new song.* See note on 33:3. *Many will see.* As a result of David's praise (see 18:49; 22:22 – 31; see also note on 9:1). *fear.* See notes on 15:4; 34:8 – 14; Pr 1:7; Lk 12:5.
40:4 – 5 The Lord's benevolence to others: to all who trust in the Lord (v. 4), and to his people Israel (v. 5).
40:4 See Jer 17:7; praise of the Lord for the blessedness of those who trust in him (see 32:1 – 2; 146:5). *Blessed.* See note on 1:1. *proud.* See note on 31:23.
40:5 *wonders.* See note on 9:1. *planned.* God's actions in behalf of Israel are according to his predetermined purpose (see Isa 25:1; 46:10 – 11).
40:6 – 8 David's commitment to God's will. Heb 10:5 – 10 applies these verses to Christ (see notes there).
40:6 *did not desire ... not require.* More important is obedience (see 1Sa 15:22), especially to God's moral law (see Isa 1:10 – 17; Am 5:21 – 24; Mic 6:6 – 8) — i.e., the ten basic commandments of his covenant (see Ex 20:3 – 17; Dt 5:7 – 21). *pierced.* Lit. "dug." Translated "pierced," it probably refers to the sign by which a servant pledged lifelong service to his beloved master (see Ex 21:6; Dt 15:17). If, however, it is translated "opened" (see NIV text note), it refers to ears made able and eager to hear God's law (see Pr 28:9; Isa 48:8; 50:4 – 5).
40:7 *Here I am, I have come.* Probably refers to David's commitment to the Lord at the time of his enthronement. *it is written about me in the scroll.* Some take this to be a reference to a prophecy, perhaps Dt 17:14 – 15. The context, however, strongly suggests that the "scroll" refers to the personal copy of the law that the king is to take at the time of his enthronement to serve as the covenant charter of his

8 I desire to do your will,[z] O my God;[a]
your law is within my heart."[b]

9 I proclaim righteousness[c] in the great
assembly;[d]
I do not seal my lips,
as you know,[e] O LORD.
10 I do not hide your righteousness in my
heart;
I speak of your faithfulness[f] and
salvation.
I do not conceal your love and your
truth
from the great assembly.[g]

11 Do not withhold your mercy[h] from me,
O LORD;
may your love[i] and your truth[j]
always protect[k] me.
12 For troubles[l] without number surround
me;
my sins have overtaken me, and I
cannot see.[m]
They are more than the hairs of my
head,[n]
and my heart fails[o] within me.

13 Be pleased, O LORD, to save me;
O LORD, come quickly to help me.[p]
14 May all who seek to take my life[q]
be put to shame and confusion;[r]
may all who desire my ruin[s]
be turned back in disgrace.
15 May those who say to me, "Aha! Aha!"[t]
be appalled at their own shame.
16 But may all who seek you[u]
rejoice and be glad[v] in you;
may those who love your salvation
always say,
"The LORD be exalted!"[w]
17 Yet I am poor and needy;[x]
may the Lord think[y] of me.
You are my help[z] and my deliverer;[a]
O my God, do not delay.[b]

Psalm 41

For the director of music.
A psalm of David.

1 Blessed[c] is he who has regard for the
weak;[d]
the LORD delivers him in times of
trouble.[e]
2 The LORD will protect[f] him and
preserve his life;[g]
he will bless him in the land[h]
and not surrender him to the desire
of his foes.[i]
3 The LORD will sustain him on his
sickbed[j]
and restore him from his bed of
illness.[k]

4 I said, "O LORD, have mercy[l] on me;
heal[m] me, for I have sinned[n] against
you."
5 My enemies say of me in malice,
"When will he die and his name
perish?[o]"
6 Whenever one comes to see me,

40:8 [z]S Mt 26:39 [a]Heb 10:5-7* [b]S Dt 6:6; S Job 22:22; Ro 7:22 **40:9** [c]S Ps 22:31 [d]S Ps 22:25 [e]S Jos 22:22 **40:10** [f]Ps 89:1 [g]S Ps 22:22 **40:11** [h]Zec 1:12 [i]Pr 20:28 [j]S Ps 26:3 [k]Ps 61:7 **40:12** [l]S Ps 25:17 [m]Ps 38:4; 65:3 [n]Ps 69:4 [o]Ps 73:26 **40:13** [p]Ps 22:19; 38:22 **40:14** [q]S 1Sa 20:1 [r]S Est 9:2; Ps 35:26 [s]S Ps 35:4 **40:15** [t]S Ps 35:21 **40:16** [u]Dt 4:29; 1Ch 28:9; Ps 9:10; 119:2 [v]Ps 9:2 [w]Ps 35:27 **40:17** [x]Ps 86:1; 109:22 [y]Ps 144:3 [z]S Ps 20:2 [a]S Ps 18:2 [b]Ps 119:60 **41:1** [c]S Dt 14:29 [d]S Job 24:4 [e]Ps 25:17 **41:2** [f]Ps 12:5; 32:7 [g]Ezr 9:9; Ps 71:20; 119:88, 159; 138:7; 143:11 [h]Ps 37:22 [i]S Dt 6:24 **41:3** [j]Ps 6:6 [k]2Sa 13:5; 2Ki 1:4 **41:4** [l]Ps 6:2; S 9:13 [m]S Dt 32:39 [n]Ps 51:4 **41:5** [o]S Ps 38:12

administration (see Dt 17:18–20; 2Ki 11:12; cf. 1Ki 2:3; see also NIV text note).
40:8 *I desire.* Whatever is in full accord with God's "desire" (v. 6)—a claim that frames the stanza.
40:9–10 David's life is filled with praise, proclaiming God's faithful and loving acts in behalf of his people (cf. 85:10–11). This, too, God desires more than animal sacrifices (see 50:7–15,23).
40:9 *proclaim.* See 68:11; 96:2; as good tidings (see 1Ki 1:42; Isa 40:9; 41:27; 52:7; 61:1). *righteousness.* See note on 4:1. *in the great assembly.* See notes on 1:5; 9:1. *not seal my lips.* He is not silent about God's praise (see 38:13–16; 39:1 and notes).
40:10 *heart.* See note on 4:7. *your love and your truth.* See note on 26:3.
40:11–17 The prayer for help.
40:11–13 David's plea for deliverance from his troubles.
40:11 *your love and your truth.* Which he has been proclaiming to all at the temple (see v. 10 and note).
40:12 *sins have overtaken me.* In the form of the "troubles without number" that burden him (see Ps 38–39 and their introductions). *cannot see.* See note on 13:3. *more than the hairs of my head.* See Mt 10:30; Lk 12:7. *heart.* See note on 4:7.
40:14–16 Prayer for God's saving help to confound David's adversaries and move the godly to praise. For harassment by enemies in times of trouble see 38:12; 39:8; 41:5,7 and often in the Psalms (see note on 5:9). For both form and substance see 35:26–27.
40:14 *shame … confusion … disgrace.* David asks that those who have wished to put him to public shame be put to shame themselves (see note on 5:10).
40:15 *Aha! Aha!* See note on 3:2.
40:17 *poor and needy.* In need of God's help (see note on 34:6).
Ps 41 David's prayer for mercy when seriously ill. He acknowledges that his illness is related to his sin (v. 4). See introductions to Ps 38–40. His enemies greet the prospect of his death with malicious glee (see note on 5:9), and even his "close friend" (v. 9) betrays his friendship (see note on 31:11–12). This psalm concludes a collection of four psalms connected by common themes, and together with Ps 40 forms the conclusion to Book I (see introduction to Ps 40–41). (Book I begins and ends with a "Blessed" psalm.) In its structure, the psalm is very symmetrical, composed of four stanzas of three verses each. The first and fourth stanzas frame the prayer with expressions of confidence; stanzas two and three elaborate the prayer. Verse 13 is actually not part of the psalm but the doxology that closes Book I (see note on v. 13).
41 title *For the director of music.* See note on Ps 4 title.
41:1–3 Confidence that the Lord will restore.
41:1 *Blessed is he who has regard for the weak.* True of all, but especially of a king, whose duty it is to defend the powerless (see 72:2,4,12–14; 82:3–4; Pr 29:14; 31:8–9; Isa 11:4; Jer 22:16). *Blessed.* See note on 1:1.
41:4–6 Prayer for God to show mercy and to heal.
41:4 *sinned.* See note on 32:3–5.
41:5 *When will he die …?* See note on 3:2. *his name perish.* See note on 9:5.
41:6 *see me.* Visit him in his sickness. *speaks falsely.* Speaks as if he were a friend. *heart.* See note on 4:7.

he speaks falsely,[p] while his heart
gathers slander;[q]
then he goes out and spreads[r] it
abroad.
7 All my enemies whisper together[s]
against me;
they imagine the worst for me,
saying,
8 "A vile disease has beset him;
he will never get up[t] from the place
where he lies."
9 Even my close friend,[u] whom I trusted,
he who shared my bread,
has lifted up his heel against me.[v]
10 But you, O LORD, have mercy[w] on me;
raise me up,[x] that I may repay[y]
them.
11 I know that you are pleased with me,[z]
for my enemy does not triumph
over me.[a]
12 In my integrity[b] you uphold me[c]
and set me in your presence forever.[d]
13 Praise[e] be to the LORD, the God of
Israel,[f]
from everlasting to everlasting.
Amen and Amen.[g]

BOOK II

Psalms 42–72

Psalm 42[a]

For the director of music. A *maskil*[b]
of the Sons of Korah.

1 As the deer[h] pants for streams of
water,[i]
so my soul pants[j] for you, O God.

[a] In many Hebrew manuscripts Psalms 42 and 43 constitute one psalm. [b] Title: Probably a literary or musical term

41:6 [p] Ps 12:2; 101:7; Mt 5:11 [q] Pr 26:24 [r] S Lev 19:16 **41:7** [s] Ps 71:10 **41:8** [t] S 2Ki 1:4 **41:9** [u] S 2Sa 15:12; S Job 19:14 [v] Nu 30:2; Job 19:19; Ps 55:20; 89:34; Mt 26:23; Lk 22:21; Jn 13:18* **41:10** [w] ver 4 [x] Ps 3:3; 9:13 [y] S 2Sa 3:39 **41:11** [z] S Nu 14:8 [a] Ps 25:2 **41:12** [b] S Ps 25:21 [c] Ps 18:35; S 37:17; 63:8 [d] S Job 4:7; Ps 21:6; 61:7 **41:13** [e] S Ge 24:27 [f] Ps 72:18 [g] Ps 72:19; 89:52; 106:48 **42:1** [h] S Ps 18:33 [i] S Dt 10:7 [j] S Job 19:27; Ps 119:131; Joel 1:20

41:7–9 His enemies and his friend.

41:9 *close friend ... who shared my bread.* One who shared the king's table—i.e., was an honored, as well as trusted, friend (see note on 31:11–12). Reference may be to one who had sealed his friendship by a covenant (see note on 23:5). For Jesus' use of this verse in application to himself see Jn 13:18. In fulfilling the role of his royal ancestor as God's anointed king over Israel, the great Son of David also experienced the hostility of others and the betrayal of a trusted associate, and thus fulfilled his forefather's lament.

41:10–12 Prayer, with confidence.

41:10 *that I may repay them.* That I (as king) may call them to account.

41:12 *my integrity.* See note on 15:2. *set.* Establish. *in your presence.* As the royal servant of Israel's heavenly King. (For the idiom see 101:7; 1Sa 16:22, "in my service"; 1Ki 10:8, "before you"; 17:1, "whom I serve.") *forever.* Never to be rejected (see 2Sa 7:15–16).

41:13 The doxology with which the worshiping community is to respond to the contents of Book I (see 72:18–19; 89:52; 106:48; 150).

Ps 42–45 Book II of the Psalter begins with three prayers (but see introduction to Ps 42–43) and an attached royal psalm in perfect balance with the ending of Book II (see introduction to Ps 69–72). These prayers contain certain key words found elsewhere in Book II only in Ps 69–71—and in the cluster of seven psalms placed at the center of this Book (see introduction to Ps 54–60). Although Ps 42–43 is the prayer of an individual and Ps 44 a prayer of the community, the two have much in common. Central to both is the cry, "Why, God?" (42:9; 43:2; 44:23–24)—why have you forgotten me/us (42:9; 44:24) and rejected me/us (43:2; 44:23) in the face of the oppression of our enemies (42:9; 44:24)? But that "Why?" (see note on 6:3), so expressive of the tension faith experiences in the face of such circumstances as the psalmists describe, is not faith's last word. Just here—and that in the first of these two introductory psalms—faith responds with its own reassuring refrain, "Hope in God" (42:5,11; 43:5), because his "love" will not fail (42:8; 44:26).

Following the communal cry of anguish over God's apparently unprovoked abandonment of his people to the pillage and ridicule of foreign peoples (Ps 44), the editors of the Psalter have pointed its readers to the Lord's anointed as he is depicted in an honorific song on one of the high days of his reign. In this song two relevant themes loom large: (1) the king's responsibility to uphold justice within the realm and to protect the people from external enemies, and (2) the assurance of his enjoying God's favor so that his kingdom flourishes under his rule and his dynasty is stable and enduring—of which the glory of his wedding to a foreign princess is a token. This placement of Ps 45 hints at a Messianic reading of the psalm on the part of the Psalter's editors. See further the introduction to Ps 45 and the introduction to Ps 69–72.

Ps 42–43 A prayer for deliverance from being "oppressed by the enemy" (42:9; 43:2) and for restoration to the presence of God at his temple. That these two psalms form a single prayer (though they are counted as two psalms also in the Septuagint, the pre-Christian Greek translation of the OT) is evident from its unique structure (see below) and the development of common themes. Ps 43 (untitled) may have come to be separated from Ps 42 for a particular liturgical purpose (see introduction to Ps 9). The speaker may have been a leading member of the Korahites whose normal duties involved him in the liturgical activities of the temple (see especially 42:4 and note on Ps 42 title). It may be that the "ungodly nation" (43:1) referred to was the Arameans of Damascus and that the author had been taken captive by the Arameans during one of their incursions into Judah, such as that of Hazael (see 2Ki 12:17–18). (This attack by Hazael affected especially the area in which the Korahites, descendants of Kohath, had been assigned cities; see Jos 21:4,9–19.) See also notes below. This psalm begins Book II of the Psalter (see introduction to Ps 42–45), a collection that is distinguished from Book I primarily by the fact that the Hebrew word for "God" (*Elohim*) predominates, whereas in the first book the Hebrew word for "the LORD" (*Yahweh*) predominates.

Structurally, the three stanzas of this psalm are symmetrical (each contains four verses), and each is followed by the same refrain (42:5,11; 43:5). The middle stanza, however, has at its center (see note on 6:6) an additional verse (42:8) that interrupts the developing thought and injects a note of confidence, such as comes to expression also in the threefold refrain. Apart from the refrains, the prayer is framed by an expression of longing for God's presence (42:1) and a vow to praise God at his altar (43:4). For other psalms with recurring refrains see Ps 46; 49; 59; 80; 107.

42 title *For the director of music.* See note on Ps 4 title. *maskil.*

2 My soul thirsts[k] for God, for the living
God.[l]
When can I go[m] and meet with God?
3 My tears[n] have been my food
day and night,
while men say to me all day long,
"Where is your God?"[o]
4 These things I remember
as I pour out my soul:[p]
how I used to go with the multitude,
leading the procession to the house
of God,[q]
with shouts of joy[r] and thanksgiving[s]
among the festive throng.[t]

5 Why are you downcast,[u] O my soul?
Why so disturbed[v] within me?
Put your hope in God,[w]
for I will yet praise[x] him,
my Savior[y] and 6 my God.[z]

My[a] soul is downcast within me;
therefore I will remember[a] you
from the land of the Jordan,[b]
the heights of Hermon[c]—from
Mount Mizar.
7 Deep calls to deep[d]
in the roar of your waterfalls;
all your waves and breakers
have swept over me.[e]
8 By day the LORD directs his love,[f]
at night[g] his song[h] is with me—
a prayer to the God of my life.[i]

9 I say to God my Rock,[j]
"Why have you forgotten[k] me?
Why must I go about mourning,[l]
oppressed[m] by the enemy?"[n]
10 My bones suffer mortal agony[o]
as my foes taunt[p] me,
saying to me all day long,
"Where is your God?"[q]

11 Why are you downcast, O my soul?
Why so disturbed within me?
Put your hope in God,
for I will yet praise him,
my Savior and my God.[r]

42:2 [k]Ps 63:1; 143:6 [l]S Jos 3:10; S 1Sa 14:39; S Mt 16:16; Ro 9:26 [m]Ps 43:4; 84:7 **42:3** [n]S Job 3:24 [o]ver 10; Ps 79:10; 115:2; Joel 2:17; Mic 7:10 **42:4** [p]S 1Sa 1:15 [q]Ps 55:14; 122:1; Isa 2:2; 30:29 [r]S Ezr 3:13 [s]S Jos 6:5; Ps 95:2; 100:4; 147:7; Jnh 2:9 [t]Ps 35:18; 109:30 **42:5** [u]Ps 38:6; 77:3; La 3:20; Mt 26:38 [v]S Job 20:2 [w]S Ps 25:5; S 71:14 [x]Ps 9:1 [y]Ps 18:46 **42:6** [z]ver 11; Ps 43:5 [a]Ps 63:6; 77:11 [b]Ge 13:10; S Nu 13:29 [c]S Dt 3:8; S 4:48 **42:7** [d]S Ge 1:2; S 7:11 [e]Ps 69:2; Jnh 2:3 **42:8** [f]Ps 57:3 [g]S Ps 16:7 [h]Ps 77:6 [i]Ps 133:3; Ecc 5:18; 8:15 **42:9** [j]Ps 18:31 [k]S Ps 10:11 [l]S Ps 35:14 [m]Job 20:19; Ps 43:2; 106:42 [n]Ps 9:13; 43:2 **42:10** [o]S Ps 6:2 [p]Dt 32:27; Ps 44:16; 89:51; 102:8; 119:42 [q]S ver 3 **42:11** [r]ver 5; Ps 43:5

[a] 5,6 A few Hebrew manuscripts, Septuagint and Syriac; most Hebrew manuscripts *praise him for his saving help. / 6O my God, my*

See note on Ps 32 title. *of the Sons of Korah.* Or "for the Sons of Korah"; see "For Jeduthun" in Ps 39 title. "Sons of Korah" refers to the Levitical choir made up of the descendants of Korah appointed by David to serve in the temple liturgy. The Korahites represented the Levitical family of Kohath son of Levi. Their leader in the days of David was Heman (see Ps 88 title)—just as Asaph led the choir of the Gershonites and Jeduthun (Ethan) the choir of the Merarites (see 1Ch 6:31–47 and note on Ps 39 title). This is the first of a collection of seven psalms ascribed to the "Sons of Korah" (Ps 42–49); four more occur in Book III (Ps 84–85; 87–88).

42:1–4 Longing to be with God at the temple.

42:1 *deer pants for ... water.* Because its life depends on water—especially when being pressed by hunters, as the psalmist was by his oppressors. *soul.* See note on 6:3.

42:2 *living God.* See Dt 5:26. *When ...?* Circumstances (see v. 9; 43:1–2) now prevent him from being at the temple. *meet with God.* Enter his presence to commune with him (see Ex 19:17; 29:42–43; 30:6,36).

42:3 *day and night.* See vv. 8,10. *Where is your God?* See note on 10:11.

42:4 *soul.* See note on 6:3. *go with the multitude, leading the procession.* If this rendering is correct, the line suggests that the author normally had a leading role in the liturgy of the temple.

42:5 The refrain: faith encouraging faith (see 27:13–14 and introduction to Ps 27). *praise him.* For his saving help (see notes on 7:17; 9:1; see also 43:4).

42:6–10 The cause and depth of the trouble of his soul.

42:6 *soul is downcast.* See vv. 5,11; 43:5. *therefore I will remember you.* As he remembers (v. 4) in his exile the joy of his past intimacy with God, so now in his exile he remembers God and painfully wonders (vv. 7,9–10), yet not without hope (v. 8). (But some believe that the clause should be rendered "because I remember you.") *from the land ... from Mount Mizar.* Probably indicating that the author speaks from exile outside the contemporary boundaries of Israel and Judah. Some think the author locates himself at Mount Mizar (a small peak or village, not otherwise known) on the flanks of Mount Hermon somewhere near the headwaters of the Jordan. Others translate the Hebrew for "from" as "far from" and understand "the land of the Jordan" to refer to the promised land (which lies along the Jordan and from which the author was separated). The mention of "the heights of Hermon" may then be a reference to the high peak that marked the northern border of the land (see Dt 3:8; Jos 11:17; 13:11; 1Ch 5:23) and looked down upon it (see 133:3; SS 4:8). Some have suggested that "Mount Mizar" is an additional reference to "the heights of Hermon," calling that high peak the "little mountain" (literal translation) in comparison with Mount Zion (see 68:15–16).

42:7 *Deep calls ... your waterfalls.* Often taken to be an allusion to the cascading waters of the upper Jordan as they rush down from Mount Hermon. It is more likely, however, that this is a literary allusion to the "waterfalls" by which the waters from God's storehouse of water above (see note on 36:8)—the "deep" above—pour down into the streams and rivers that empty into the seas—the "deep" below. It pictures the great distress the author suffers, and the imagery is continued in the following reference to God's "waves and breakers" sweeping over him (see 69:1–2; 88:7; Jnh 2:3,5; see also note on 32:6). God's hand is involved in the psalmist's suffering, at least to the extent that God has allowed this catastrophe. He seems to the psalmist to have "forgotten" (v. 9)—to have "rejected" (43:2)—him. But he makes no link between this and any sin in his life (see Ps 44; 77).

42:8 The center: confession of hope in all the trouble. That is, "Day-and-night [cf. v. 3] the LORD directs his love, and his song is with me" (see note on 3:7). *the LORD.* Only here at the center in this psalm (see introduction). *directs his love.* Sends forth his love, like a messenger to do his will (see 43:3). *love.* See note on 6:4. *his song.* A song concerning him. *prayer.* Praise and prayer belong together in the thought of the psalmist.

42:9 Echoed in 43:2. *Rock.* See note on 18:2. *Why ...? Why ...?* See note on 6:3 and introduction to Ps 42–45.

42:10 See v. 3. *bones.* See note on 6:2.

Psalm 43[a]

[1]Vindicate me, O God,
and plead my cause[s] against an
ungodly nation;
rescue me[t] from deceitful and
wicked men.[u]
[2]You are God my stronghold.
Why have you rejected[v] me?
Why must I go about mourning,[w]
oppressed by the enemy?[x]
[3]Send forth your light[y] and your truth,[z]
let them guide me;[a]
let them bring me to your holy
mountain,[b]
to the place where you dwell.[c]
[4]Then will I go[d] to the altar[e] of God,
to God, my joy[f] and my delight.[g]
I will praise you with the harp,[h]
O God, my God.
[5]Why are you downcast, O my soul?
Why so disturbed within me?
Put your hope in God,
for I will yet praise him,
my Savior and my God.[i]

Psalm 44

For the director of music. Of the Sons of Korah. A *maskil.*[b]

[1]We have heard with our ears,[j] O God;
our fathers have told us[k]
what you did in their days,
in days long ago.[l]
[2]With your hand you drove out[m] the
nations
and planted[n] our fathers;
you crushed[o] the peoples
and made our fathers flourish.[p]
[3]It was not by their sword[q] that they
won the land,
nor did their arm bring them victory;
it was your right hand,[r] your arm,[s]
and the light[t] of your face, for you
loved[u] them.
[4]You are my King[v] and my God,[w]
who decrees[c] victories[x] for Jacob.
[5]Through you we push back[y] our
enemies;
through your name we trample[z] our
foes.
[6]I do not trust in my bow,[a]
my sword does not bring me victory;
[7]but you give us victory[b] over our
enemies,
you put our adversaries to shame.[c]
[8]In God we make our boast[d] all day
long,[e]
and we will praise your name
forever.[f] *Selah*
[9]But now you have rejected[g] and
humbled us;[h]
you no longer go out with our
armies.[i]
[10]You made us retreat[j] before the enemy,
and our adversaries have plundered[k]
us.
[11]You gave us up to be devoured like
sheep[l]
and have scattered us among the
nations.[m]

43:1 [s]S Jdg 6:31 [t]S Ps 25:20 [u]S Ps 36:3; 109:2 **43:2** [v]Ps 44:9; 74:1; 88:14; 89:38 [w]S Ps 35:14 [x]S Ps 42:9 **43:3** [y]Ps 27:1 [z]S Ps 26:3 [a]S Ps 25:5 [b]Ps 2:6 [c]S 2Sa 15:25 **43:4** [d]S Ps 42:2 [e]Ps 26:6; 84:3 [f]S Ps 21:6 [g]Ps 16:3 [h]S Ge 4:21 **43:5** [i]S Ps 42:6 **44:1** [j]2Sa 7:22; 1Ch 17:20; Jer 26:11 [k]S Jdg 6:13 [l]S Dt 32:7; S Job 37:23 **44:2** [m]S Jos 3:10; Ac 7:45 [n]S Ex 15:17; S Isa 60:21 [o]S Jdg 4:23; S 2Ch 14:13 [p]Ps 80:9; Jer 32:23 **44:3** [q]Jos 24:12 [r]Ps 78:54 [s]Ex 15:16; Ps 77:15; 79:11; 89:10; 98:1; Isa 40:10; 52:10; 63:5 [t]Ps 89:15 [u]S Dt 4:37 **44:4** [v]S Ps 24:7 [w]Ps 5:2 [x]S Ps 21:5 **44:5** [y]S Jos 23:5 [z]Ps 60:12; 108:13 **44:6** [a]Ge 48:22; Hos 1:7 **44:7** [b]S Dt 20:4 [c]S Job 8:22 **44:8** [d]S Ps 34:2; 1Co 1:31; 2Co 10:17 [e]Ps 52:1 [f]S Ps 30:12 **44:9** [g]S Ps 43:2 [h]S Dt 8:3; S 31:17; Ps 107:39; Isa 5:15 [i]S Jos 7:12; Ps 108:11 **44:10** [j]S Lev 26:17 [k]S Jdg 2:14 **44:11** [l]ver 22; Jer 12:3 [m]S Lev 26:33; S Ps 9:11; Eze 6:8; Zec 2:6

[a] In many Hebrew manuscripts Psalms 42 and 43 constitute one psalm. [b] Title: Probably a literary or musical term [c] *4* Septuagint, Aquila and Syriac; Hebrew *King, O God; / command*

43:1–4 Prayer for deliverance from the enemy and for restoration to God's presence.
43:1 A plea in the language of the court (see introduction to Ps 17).
43:2 Echoes 42:9.
43:3 *your light and your truth.* Personified as God's messengers who work out (1) his salvation (light; see note on 27:1) and (2) his faithful care in behalf of his own (truth; see 26:3; 30:9; 40:10). May these guide me back to your temple. *holy mountain.* See note on 2:6.
43:4 See note on 7:17. *to the altar.* See 26:6 and note.
Ps 44 Israel's cry for help after suffering a devastating defeat at the hand of an enemy. In the light of vv. 17–22, it is difficult to associate this psalm with any of those defeats announced by the prophets as judgments on Israel's covenant unfaithfulness. It probably relates to an experience of the kingdom of Judah, perhaps during the reign of Jehoshaphat or Hezekiah.
Structurally, three thematic developments rise one upon the other as the psalm advances to the prayer in the closing verses. Its structure is like the stages of a ziggurat (a stepped pyramidal structure that the Babylonians built as a mountain-like base for some of their temples; see Ge 11:4 and note) leading to the temple that crowns it. First there is praise of the Lord for past victories (vv. 1–8), second a description of the present defeat and its consequences (vv. 9–16), third a plea of innocence (vv. 17–22), then finally the prayer (vv. 23–26). Each of the themes (recalling of past mercies, description of the present distress, and claim of covenant loyalty) in its own way functions as a ground for the appeal for help (see Ps 40 and its introduction; see also the lengthy prefaces to prayer in Ps 40; 89). For the thematic links between Ps 44 and 42–43 and the function of these psalms in the arrangement of Book II, see introduction to Ps 42–45.
44 title See note on Ps 42 title.
44:1–8 Praise to God for past victories: (1) those by which Israel became established in the land (vv. 1–3); (2) those by which Israel has been kept secure in the land (vv. 4–8).
44:1 See 78:3.
44:3 *light of your face.* See notes on 4:6; 13:1.
44:4 *my.* Here and elsewhere in this psalm the first-person singular pronoun refers to the nation corporately (see note on Ps 30 title). *Jacob.* See note on 14:7.
44:5,8 *your name.* See v. 20; see also note on 5:11.
44:8 *In God we make our boast.* That is, we give God all the praise.
44:9–16 But now you have forsaken us: (1) You have caused us to suffer defeat (vv. 9–12); (2) you have shamed us before our enemies (vv. 13–16).
44:11 *gave us up to be devoured like sheep.* Have not protected us as our Shepherd-King (see v. 4 and note on 23:1).

12 You sold your people for a pittance,[n]
gaining nothing from their sale.
13 You have made us a reproach[o] to our
neighbors,[p]
the scorn[q] and derision[r] of those
around us.
14 You have made us a byword[s] among
the nations;
the peoples shake their heads[t] at us.
15 My disgrace[u] is before me all day long,
and my face is covered with shame[v]
16 at the taunts[w] of those who reproach
and revile[x] me,
because of the enemy, who is bent
on revenge.[y]

17 All this happened to us,
though we had not forgotten[z] you
or been false to your covenant.
18 Our hearts had not turned[a] back;
our feet had not strayed from your
path.
19 But you crushed[b] us and made us a
haunt for jackals[c]
and covered us over with deep
darkness.[d]

20 If we had forgotten[e] the name of our
God
or spread out our hands to a foreign
god,[f]
21 would not God have discovered it,
since he knows the secrets of the
heart?[g]
22 Yet for your sake we face death all day
long;
we are considered as sheep[h] to be
slaughtered.[i]

23 Awake,[j] O Lord! Why do you sleep?[k]
Rouse yourself![l] Do not reject us
forever.[m]
24 Why do you hide your face[n]
and forget[o] our misery and
oppression?[p]

25 We are brought down to the dust;[q]
our bodies cling to the ground.
26 Rise up[r] and help us;
redeem[s] us because of your unfailing
love.[t]

Psalm 45

For the director of music. To ⌞the tune of⌟ "Lilies." Of the Sons of Korah. A *maskil.*[a] A wedding song.[u]

1 My heart is stirred by a noble theme
as I recite my verses for the king;
my tongue is the pen of a skillful
writer.

[a] Title: Probably a literary or musical term

44:12 [n]S Dt 32:30; Isa 52:3; Jer 15:13; 50:1 **44:13** [o]S 2Ch 29:8; Isa 30:3; Jer 25:9; 42:18; 44:8 [p]Ps 79:4; 80:6; 89:41 [q]S Dt 28:37; S Mic 2:6 [r]Eze 23:32 **44:14** [s]S 1Ki 9:7 [t]S 2Ki 19:21 **44:15** [u]Ge 30:23; 2Ch 32:21; Ps 35:26 [v]S Ps 34:5 **44:16** [w]S Ps 42:10 [x]Ps 10:13; 55:3; 74:10 [y]S 1Sa 18:25; S Jer 11:19; Ro 12:19 **44:17** [z]S Dt 6:12; S 32:18; Ps 119:16,61, 153,176; Pr 3:1 **44:18** [a]Ps 119:51,157 **44:19** [b]S 2Ch 14:13; Ps 51:8 [c]S Job 30:29; S Isa 34:13 [d]S Job 3:5 **44:20** [e]S Dt 32:18; S Jdg 3:7 [f]S Ex 20:3; Isa 43:12; Jer 5:19 **44:21** [g]S 1Sa 16:7; 1Ki 8:39; Pr 15:11; Jer 12:3; 17:10 **44:22** [h]S ver 11 [i]Isa 53:7; Jer 11:19; 12:3; Ro 8:36* **44:23** [j]S Ps 7:6 [k]Ps 78:65 [l]Ps 59:5 [m]Ps 74:1; 77:7 **44:24** [n]S Dt 32:20; Ps 13:1 [o]La 5:20 [p]S Dt 26:7 **44:25** [q]Ps 119:25 **44:26** [r]S Nu 10:35; S Ps 12:5; 102:13 [s]Ps 26:11 [t]Ps 6:4 **45:Title** [u]SS 1:1

44:12 *sold your people.* Like chattel no longer valued (see Dt 32:30; Jdg 2:14). *for a pittance.* For nothing of value (see Isa 52:3; Jer 15:13; cf. Isa 43:3–4).
44:14 *shake their heads.* In scorn (see 64:8).
44:16 *bent on revenge.* See 8:2 and note.
44:17–22 Yet we have not been disloyal to you: (1) We have not been untrue to your covenant (vv. 17–19); (2) you are our witness that we have not turned to another god (vv. 20–22).
44:17 *your covenant.* See Ex 19–24.
44:18 *hearts.* See note on 4:7. *your path.* The way marked out in God's covenant (see note on 5:8).
44:19 *you crushed us.* But that cannot be used as evidence that we have been disloyal. *haunt for jackals.* A desolate place, uninhabited by people (see Isa 13:22; Jer 9:11). *deep darkness.* The absence of all that was associated with the metaphor "light" (see notes on 30:1; 36:9).
44:20 *spread out our hands.* Prayed (see Ex 9:29 and note).
44:22 *Yet.* Or "As a matter of fact" or "As you, O God, know." From the time of her stay in Egypt (see Ex 1), Israel has suffered the hostility of the nations because of her relationship with the Lord (see Mt 10:34). For Paul's application of this verse to the Christian community in the light of Christ's death and resurrection see Ro 8:36.
44:23–26 The appeal for help: (1) Awake to our need (vv. 23–24); (2) arise to our help (vv. 25–26; see introduction to Ps 16).
44:23 *Awake.* See note on 7:6. *Why …?* See note on 6:3 and introduction to Ps 42–45.
44:24 *hide your face.* See note on 13:1.
44:25 *We are brought down to the dust.* About to sink into death (see 22:29 and note; see also note on 30:1). In Hebrew there is a verbal link with the refrain, "Why are you downcast, O my soul?" in Ps 42–43.
44:26 *Rise up and help.* See 46:1,5; see also note on 3:7. *redeem.* See note on 25:22. *unfailing love.* See note on 6:4; see also 42:8 and note.
Ps 45 A song in praise of the king on his wedding day (see title; see also introduction to Ps 42–45). He undoubtedly belonged to David's dynasty, and the song may have been used at more than one royal wedding. Since the bride is a foreign princess (see vv. 10,12), the wedding reflects the king's standing as a figure of international significance (see note on v. 9). Accordingly he is addressed as one whose reign is to be characterized by victories over the nations (vv. 3–5; cf. Ps 2; 110). As a royal son of David, he is a type (foreshadowing) of Christ. After the exile this psalm was applied to the Messiah, the promised Son of David who would sit on David's throne (for the application of vv. 6–7 to Christ see Heb 1:8–9). The superscription implies that it was composed and sung by a member of the Levitical temple choir, a fact not surprising in view of the close link between the temple (housing the earthly throne room of Israel's heavenly King) and the Davidic dynasty (the Lord's appointed regents over his people, described throughout the books of Samuel, Kings and Chronicles). As a word from one of the temple personnel, the song was no doubt received as a word from the temple—and from the One who sat enthroned there.

In its structure, the song is framed by vv. 1,17 while vv. 2,16 constitute a secondary frame within them—all addressed to the king. The body of the song falls into two parts: (1) words addressed to the king (vv. 3–9) and (2) words addressed to the royal bride (vv. 10–15). These in turn each contain two parts, reflecting a similar pattern: (1) (a) exhortations to the king (vv. 3–5), (b) the glory of the king (vv. 6–9); (2) (a) exhortations to the bride (vv. 10–12), (b) the glory of the bride (vv. 13–15).
45 title *For the director of music.* See note on Ps 4 title. *To ⌞the*

2 You are the most excellent of men
and your lips have been anointed with grace,[v]
since God has blessed you forever.[w]
3 Gird your sword[x] upon your side,
O mighty one;[y]
clothe yourself with splendor and majesty.[z]
4 In your majesty ride forth victoriously[a]
in behalf of truth, humility and righteousness;[b]
let your right hand[c] display awesome deeds.[d]
5 Let your sharp arrows[e] pierce the hearts[f] of the king's enemies;[g]
let the nations fall beneath your feet.
6 Your throne, O God, will last for ever and ever;[h]
a scepter of justice will be the scepter of your kingdom.
7 You love righteousness[i] and hate wickedness;[j]
therefore God, your God, has set you above your companions
by anointing[k] you with the oil of joy.[l]
8 All your robes are fragrant[m] with myrrh[n] and aloes[o] and cassia;[p]
from palaces adorned with ivory[q]
the music of the strings[r] makes you glad.
9 Daughters of kings[s] are among your honored women;
at your right hand[t] is the royal bride[u] in gold of Ophir.[v]
10 Listen, O daughter,[w] consider[x] and give ear:
Forget your people[y] and your father's house.
11 The king is enthralled by your beauty;[z]
honor[a] him, for he is your lord.[b]
12 The Daughter of Tyre[c] will come with a gift,[a][d]
men of wealth will seek your favor.
13 All glorious[e] is the princess within ⌊her chamber⌋;
her gown is interwoven with gold.[f]
14 In embroidered garments[g] she is led to the king;[h]
her virgin companions[i] follow her
and are brought to you.
15 They are led in with joy and gladness;[j]
they enter the palace of the king.

[a] 12 Or *A Tyrian robe is among the gifts*

45:2 [v] Lk 4:22 [w] Ps 21:6 **45:3** [x] S Dt 32:41; Ps 149:6; Rev 1:16 [y] S 2Sa 1:19 [z] S Job 40:10; S Ps 21:5 **45:4** [a] Rev 6:2 [b] Zep 2:3 [c] Ps 21:8 [d] S Dt 4:34; Ps 65:5; 66:3 **45:5** [e] S Dt 32:23 [f] S Nu 24:8 [g] Ps 9:13; 92:9 **45:6** [h] S Ge 21:33; La 5:19 **45:7** [i] Ps 33:5 [j] S Ps 11:5 [k] Ps 2:2; Isa 45:1; 61:1; Zec 4:14 [l] S Ps 23:5; Heb 1:8-9* **45:8** [m] Pr 27:9; SS 1:3; 4:10 [n] S Ge 37:25 [o] S Nu 24:6; Jn 19:39 [p] S Ex 30:24 [q] S 1Ki 22:39 [r] Ps 144:9; 150:4; Isa 38:20 **45:9** [s] SS 6:8 [t] 1Ki 2:19 [u] Isa 62:5 [v] S Ge 10:29 **45:10** [w] Ru 1:11 [x] Jer 5:1 [y] Ru 1:16 **45:11** [z] S Est 1:11; S La 2:15 [a] Eph 5:33 [b] 1Pe 3:6 **45:12** [c] S Jos 19:29 [d] S 1Ki 9:16; S 2Ch 9:24 **45:13** [e] Isa 61:10 [f] Ex 39:3 **45:14** [g] S Jdg 5:30 [h] Est 2:15 [i] SS 1:3 **45:15** [j] S Est 8:17

tune of⌋. See note on Ps 9 title. *Lilies.* See Ps 69 title. "Lilies" may be an abbreviated form of "The Lily (Lilies) of the Covenant" found in the titles of Ps 60; 80. *Of the Sons of Korah.* See note on Ps 42 title. *maskil.* See note on Ps 32 title. *song.* See note on Ps 30 title.

45:1 See v. 17, where the speaker pledges (perhaps by means of this song) to perpetuate the king's memory throughout the generations and awaken the praise of the nations. *heart.* See note on 4:7.

45:2 *most excellent of men.* One who excels in manly traits and beauty, as a king should (see 1Sa 9:2; 16:18)—but he is so beyond ordinary men as to be almost Godlike (see note on v. 6). *lips ... anointed with grace.* See Pr 22:11; Ecc 10:12; cf. Isa 50:4; Lk 4:22; see also v. 16, where it is suggested that such a king will be perpetuated in his sons. *forever.* See note on v. 6.

45:3–5 Go forth with your sword victoriously in the service of all that is right, and clothe yourself thereby with glory—make your reign adorn you more truly than the wedding garb with which you are now arrayed (v. 8).

45:3 *clothe yourself with.* See note on 109:29. *splendor and majesty.* See 21:5 and note.

45:4 *righteousness.* See note on 1:5. *awesome deeds.* See 66:5; 106:22; 145:6.

45:5 *nations fall beneath your feet.* See 2:8–9; 110:1–2,5–6.

45:6–9 The glory of the king's reign: justice and righteousness (see Ps 72).

45:6 *O God.* Possibly the king's throne is called God's throne because he is God's appointed regent. But it is also possible that the king himself is addressed as "god." The Davidic king (the "LORD's anointed," 2Sa 19:21), because of his special relationship with God, was called at his enthronement the "son" of God (see 2:7; 2Sa 7:14; 1Ch 28:6; cf. 89:27). In this psalm, which praises the king and especially extols his "splendor and majesty" (v. 3), it is not unthinkable that he was called "god" as a title of honor (cf. Isa 9:6). Such a description of the Davidic king attains its fullest meaning when applied to Christ, as the author of Hebrews does (Heb 1:8–9). (The pharaohs of Egypt were sometimes addressed as "my god" by their vassal kings in Canaan, as evidenced by the Amarna letters; see chart, p. xxii.) *for ever and ever.* See vv. 2,17. Such was the language used with respect to kings (see note on 21:4). It here gains added significance in the light of God's covenant with David (see 89:4,29,36; 132:12; 2Sa 7:16). In Christ, the Son of David, it is fulfilled.

45:7 *companions.* The noble guests of the king, perhaps from other lands. *oil of joy.* God has anointed him with a more delightful oil than the aromatic oils with which his head and body were anointed on his wedding day—namely, with joy (see 23:5; Isa 61:3).

45:8–9 The glory of the king's wedding.

45:8 *myrrh.* See notes on Ge 37:25; SS 1:13. *aloes.* See note on SS 4:14. *cassia.* See note on Ex 25:6. *palaces adorned with ivory.* See 1Ki 22:39; Am 3:15; 6:4.

45:9 *Daughters of kings.* Whether members of his royal harem (see 1Ki 11:1–3) or guests at his wedding, they represent international recognition of the king. *in gold of Ophir.* Adorned with jewels of finest gold (see notes on Ge 10:29; 1Ki 9:28) and all the finery associated with it.

45:10–12 The word to the royal bride.

45:10–11 Be totally loyal to your adoring king.

45:12 *Daughter of Tyre.* A personification of the city of Tyre (see note on 2Ki 19:21). The king of Tyre was the first foreign ruler to recognize the Davidic dynasty (see 2Sa 5:11), and Solomon maintained close relations with that city-state (see 1Ki 5; 9:10–14,26–28). As a great trading center on the Mediterranean coast, Tyre was world-renowned for its wealth (see Isa 23; Eze 26:1—28:19). *men of wealth.* Such as those from your homeland. *seek your favor.* Desire to be in your good graces as the wife of this king. These honors will be yours if you faithfully honor your royal husband.

45:13–15 The royal bride's glory.

45:14 *virgin companions.* She too has "companions" (see v. 7), perhaps her permanent attendants. *to you.* To the king.

16 Your sons will take the place of your
fathers;
you will make them princes[k]
throughout the land.
17 I will perpetuate your memory through
all generations;[l]
therefore the nations will praise
you[m] for ever and ever.[n]

Psalm 46

For the director of music. Of the Sons of Korah. According to *alamoth*.[a] A song.

1 God is our refuge[o] and strength,[p]
an ever-present[q] help[r] in trouble.[s]
2 Therefore we will not fear,[t] though the
earth give way[u]
and the mountains fall[v] into the
heart of the sea,[w]
3 though its waters roar[x] and foam[y]
and the mountains quake[z] with their
surging. *Selah*

4 There is a river[a] whose streams[b] make
glad the city of God,[c]
the holy place where the Most High[d]
dwells.[e]
5 God is within her,[f] she will not
fall;[g]
God will help[h] her at break of day.
6 Nations[i] are in uproar,[j] kingdoms[k]
fall;
he lifts his voice,[l] the earth melts.[m]

7 The LORD Almighty[n] is with us;[o]
the God of Jacob[p] is our fortress.[q]
Selah

8 Come and see the works of the LORD,[r]
the desolations[s] he has brought on
the earth.
9 He makes wars[t] cease to the ends of
the earth;
he breaks the bow[u] and shatters the
spear,
he burns the shields[b] with fire.[v]

[a] Title: Probably a musical term [b] 9 Or *chariots*

45:16 [k] 1Sa 2:8; Ps 68:27; 113:8 **45:17** [l] S Ex 3:15; Ps 33:11; 119:90; 135:13 [m] Ps 138:4 [n] S Ps 21:4; Rev 22:5 **46:1** [o] Ps 9:9; 37:39; 61:3; 73:26; 91:2, 9; 142:5; Isa 33:16; Jer 16:19; 17:17; Joel 3:16; Na 1:7 [p] Ps 18:1 [q] Ps 34:18; La 3:57 [r] Ps 18:6; Lk 1:54 [s] S Dt 4:30; Ps 25:17 **46:2** [t] S Ge 4:7; Ps 3:6 [u] Ps 82:5; Isa 13:13; 24:1, 19, 20; Jer 4:23; Da 11:19; Am 8:14; S Rev 6:14 [v] ver 6; Ps 18:7; 97:5; Isa 54:10; Am 9:5; Mic 1:4; Na 1:5; Hab 3:6 [w] Ex 15:8 **46:3** [x] Ps 93:3; Isa 17:13; Jer 5:22; Eze 1:24; Rev 19:6 [y] S Job 9:26 [z] S Jdg 5:5 **46:4** [a] S Ge 2:10; Rev 22:1 [b] S Ps 1:3 [c] Ps 48:1, 8; 87:3; 101:8; Rev 3:12 [d] Ge 14:18 [e] S 2Sa 15:25 **46:5** [f] Dt 23:14; S Ps 26:8; Isa 12:6; Zec 2:5 [g] Ps 125:1 [h] S 1Ch 5:20 **46:6** [i] S Job 12:23 [j] Ps 74:23; Isa 5:30; 17:12 [k] Ps 68:32; 102:22; Isa 13:4, 13; 23:11; Eze 26:18; Mt 4:8 [l] S Ps 29:3; Isa 33:3 [m] S ver 2 **46:7** [n] S 1Sa 1:11 [o] S Ge 21:22 [p] S Ps 20:1 [q] ver 11; Ps 18:2 **46:8** [r] Ps 66:5 [s] Isa 17:9; 64:10; Da 9:26; Lk 21:20 **46:9** [t] Isa 2:4 [u] S Ps 37:15; S Isa 22:6 [v] Isa 9:5; Eze 39:9; Hos 2:18

45:16 *Your.* The king's. *take the place of your fathers.* As the family line continues (dynastic succession). Perhaps it is also hinted that they will surpass the fathers in honor (see note on v. 2). *land.* Or "earth."

45:17 See note on v. 1. *for ever and ever.* See note on v. 6.

Ps 46–48 Following the cluster of psalms that introduce Book II of the Psalter (see introduction to Ps 42–45), the next thematically related cluster of psalms expresses confidence in the security of God's people in the midst of a threatening world. Ps 46 and 48 focus on the security of Jerusalem, "the city of [our] God" (46:4; 48:1), and Ps 47 on the worldwide reign of "the great King" (47:2) whose royal city is Jerusalem (48:2).

Ps 46 A celebration of the security of Jerusalem as the city of God (the inspiration of Martin Luther's great hymn, "A Mighty Fortress Is Our God"; see vv. 7,11). Thematically this psalm is closely related to Ps 48 (see also Ps 76; 87), while Ps 47 celebrates God's victorious reign over the whole earth (see introduction to Ps 46–48). It probably predates the exile. However, as a song concerning the "city of God" (v. 4), the royal city of his kingdom on earth (see Ps 48), it remained for Israel a song of hope celebrating the certain triumph of God's kingdom. It was originally liturgical and sung at the temple: The citizens of Jerusalem (or the Levitical choir in their stead) apparently sang the opening stanza (vv. 1–3) and the responses (vv. 7,11), while the Levitical leader of the liturgy probably sang the second and third stanzas (vv. 4–6,8–10). In its structure, apart from the refrains (vv. 7,11), the psalm is composed of three symmetrical stanzas, each containing three verses. For other psalms with recurring refrains see introduction to Ps 42–43.

46 title *For the director of music.* See note on Ps 4 title. *Of the Sons of Korah.* See note on Ps 42 title. *According to.* See note on Ps 6 title. *alamoth.* See NIV text note. Since the Hebrew word appears to mean "maidens," the phrase "according to *alamoth*" may refer to the "maidens playing tambourines" who accompanied the singers as the liturgical procession made its way to the temple (68:25). *A song.* See note on Ps 30 title.

46:1–3 A triumphant confession of fearless trust in God, though the continents break up and sink beneath the surging waters of the seas—i.e., though the creation itself may seem to become uncreated (see 104:6–9; Ge 1:9–10) and all may appear to be going down before the onslaught of the primeval deep. The described upheaval is probably imagery for great threats to Israel's existence (see note on 32:6), especially from her enemies (see vv. 6,8–10; 65:5–8).

46:4–6 A description of blessed Zion—a comforting declaration of God's mighty, sustaining presence in his city.

46:4 *river.* Jerusalem had no river, unlike Thebes (Na 3:8), Damascus (2Ki 5:12), Nineveh (Na 2:6,8) or Babylon (137:1)—yet she had a "river." Here the "river" of 36:8 (see note there) serves as a metaphor for the continual outpouring of the sustaining and refreshing blessings of God, which make the city of God like the Garden of Eden (see v. 5; Ge 2:10; Isa 33:21; 51:3; cf. also Eze 31:4–9). *city of God.* See v. 5; see especially Ps 48. *God ... Most High.* That is, God Most High (see 57:2; see also note on 3:7). *Most High.* See note on Ge 14:19. *dwells.* See note on 9:11.

46:5 *at break of day.* Or "as dawn approaches"—i.e., when attacks against cities were likely to be launched. His help brings on the dawn of deliverance, dispelling the night of danger (see 44:19 and note; cf. Isa 37:36 for an example).

46:6 *Nations ... fall.* Because of God's victory (see vv. 8–9; 48:4–7). *in uproar.* See v. 3 and note on vv. 1–3; see also 2:1–3; Rev 11:18. *lifts his voice.* See 2:5; 9:5; Jer 25:30; Am 1:2; see also 104:7. God's thunder is evoked (see introduction to Ps 29), the thunder of his wrath (see 18:13; Isa 2:10). *earth melts.* As though struck by lightning (see 97:4–5).

46:7 The people's glad response (also v. 11). *LORD Almighty.* See note on 1Sa 1:3. *Jacob.* See note on 14:7.

46:8–10 A declaration of the blessed effects of God's triumph over the nations.

46:8 *Come and see.* An invitation to see God's victories in the world (see 48:8 and note). *the LORD.* Emphatic because of its rare use in Book II of the Psalter. *on the earth.* Among the hostile nations.

46:9 No more attacks against his city. The verse probably speaks of universal peace (see note on 65:6–7). *breaks ... shatters ... burns.* See 76:3; see also 1Sa 2:4. For

[10]"Be still, and know that I am God;[w]
I will be exalted[x] among the nations,
I will be exalted in the earth."

[11]The LORD Almighty is with us;
the God of Jacob[y] is our fortress.[z]
Selah

Psalm 47

For the director of music.
Of the Sons of Korah. A psalm.

[1]Clap your hands,[a] all you nations;
shout to God with cries of joy.[b]
[2]How awesome[c] is the LORD Most High,[d]
the great King[e] over all the earth!
[3]He subdued[f] nations under us,
peoples under our feet.
[4]He chose our inheritance[g] for us,
the pride of Jacob,[h] whom he loved.
Selah

[5]God has ascended[i] amid shouts of joy,[j]
the LORD amid the sounding of trumpets.[k]
[6]Sing praises[l] to God, sing praises;
sing praises to our King, sing praises.

[7]For God is the King of all the earth;[m]
sing to him a psalm[a][n] of praise.
[8]God reigns[o] over the nations;
God is seated on his holy throne.[p]
[9]The nobles of the nations assemble
as the people of the God of Abraham,
for the kings[b] of the earth belong to God;[q]
he is greatly exalted.[r]

Psalm 48

A song. A psalm of the Sons of Korah.

[1]Great is the LORD,[s] and most worthy of praise,[t]
in the city of our God,[u] his holy mountain.[v]

[a] 7 Or *a maskil* (probably a literary or musical term)
[b] 9 Or *shields*

46:10 [w]Dt 4:35; 1Ki 18:36,39; Ps 100:3; Isa 37:16,20; 43:11; 45:21; Eze 36:23 [x]Ps 18:46; Isa 2:11 **46:11** [y]S Ps 20:1 [z]S ver 7 **47:1** [a]S 2Ki 11:12 [b]S Ps 33:3 **47:2** [c]S Dt 7:21 [d]Ge 14:18 [e]Ps 2:6; 48:2; 95:3; Mt 5:35 **47:3** [f]Ps 18:39,47; Isa 14:6 **47:4** [g]Ps 2:8; 16:6; 78:55; 1Pe 1:4 [h]Am 6:8; 8:7 **47:5** [i]Ps 68:18; Eph 4:8 [j]S Job 8:21; S Ps 106:5 [k]S Nu 10:2; S 2Sa 6:15 **47:6** [l]S 2Sa 22:50 **47:7** [m]Zec 14:9 [n]1Ch 16:7; Col 3:16 **47:8** [o]S 1Ch 16:31 [p]S 1Ki 22:19; S Ps 9:4; Rev 4:9 **47:9** [q]S Job 25:2 [r]Ps 46:10; 97:9 **48:1** [s]Ps 86:10; 96:4; 99:2; 135:5; 147:5; Jer 10:6 [t]S 2Sa 22:4; S 1Ch 16:25; Ps 18:3 [u]S Ps 46:4 [v]S Dt 33:19; Ps 2:6; 87:1; Isa 11:9; 32:16; Jer 31:23; Da 9:16; Mic 4:1; Zec 8:3

the Messiah's universal victory over Israel's enemies see Isa 9:2–7.

46:10 God's voice breaks through, as he addresses the nations (see v. 6)—the climax. *Be still.* Here, the Hebrew for this phrase probably means "Enough!" as in 1Sa 15:16 ("Stop!"). *know.* Acknowledge. *I will be exalted ... in the earth.* God's mighty acts in behalf of his people will bring him universal recognition, a major theme in the Psalter (see 22:27; 47:9; 57:5,11; 64:9; 65:8; 66:1–7; 67:2–5,7; 77:14; 86:9; 98:2–3; 99:2–3; 102:15) and elsewhere in the OT (see Ex 7:5; 14:4,18; Lev 26:45; Nu 14:15; 1Sa 17:46; 1Ki 8:41–43; 2Ki 19:19; Isa 2:2–3; 11:10; 25:3; 49:6–7; 51:5; 52:10; 60:1–14; 62:1–2; Jer 16:19; Eze 20:41; 28:25; 36:23; Hab 2:14). This has proven to be supremely true of God's climactic saving act in the birth, life, death, resurrection and glorification of Jesus Christ—yet to be brought to complete fruition at his return.

46:11 See note on v. 7.

Ps 47 Celebration of the universal reign of Israel's God: a testimony to the nations. This psalm belongs to a group of hymns to the Great King found elsewhere clustered in Ps 92–100. Here it serves to link Ps 46 and 48, identifying the God who reigns in Zion as "the great King over all the earth" (v. 2; see v. 7; 48:2; see also introduction to Ps 46–48). It dates from the period of the monarchy and was composed for use in the temple liturgy on one of the high festival days. The specific setting is perhaps the Feast of Tabernacles (see Lev 23:34), which was also the festival for which Solomon waited to dedicate the temple (see 1Ki 8:2). A liturgical procession is presupposed (v. 5), similar to that indicated in Ps 24; 68. Later Jewish usage employed this psalm in the synagogue liturgy for *Rosh Hashanah* (the New Year festival). The Christian church has appropriately employed it in the celebration of Christ's ascension (see v. 5). Structurally, an introductory call to praise (v. 1) is followed by three stanzas of three Hebrew poetic lines each (vv. 2–4,5–7,8–9) devoted to the praise of which God is worthy as "the King of all the earth" (v. 7).

47 title See note on Ps 42 title.

47:1–4 The nations are called to rejoice in the God of Israel, the Lord over all the earth—OT anticipation of the evangelization of the nations (see notes on v. 9; 9:1).

47:1 *Clap your hands.* As at the enthronement of a king (see 2Ki 11:12; see also 98:8) or at other times of rejoicing (see Isa 55:12). *cries of joy.* See 1Ki 1:40; 2Ki 11:14.

47:2–3 The Lord of all the earth has shaped the destiny of his people Israel (see 105:6; 135:4; Ex 9:29; 15:1–18; 19:5–6; Dt 7:6; 14:2; Isa 41:8).

47:2 *How awesome ...!* See 68:35; 89:7; 99:3; 111:9; cf. note on 45:4. *Most High.* See note on Ge 14:19. *great King.* A title often used by the imperial rulers of Assyria (see note on 2Ki 18:19).

47:3 See 2Sa 5:17–25; 8:1–14; 10.

47:4 *inheritance.* The promised land (see Ge 12:7; 17:8; Ex 3:8; Dt 1:8; Jer 3:18). *pride.* That in which Jacob took supreme delight. *Jacob.* See note on 14:7.

47:5–6 The center of the poem (see note on 6:6). These verses portray the liturgical ascension of God to the temple—perhaps represented by the processional bearing of the ark into the temple. The ark is symbolic of God's throne; the temple is the earthly symbol of his heavenly palace (see Ps 24; 68).

47:5 *shouts of joy ... sounding of trumpets.* See note on v. 1. *trumpets.* The ram's horn, here announcing the presence of God as King (see 98:6; Ex 19:16,19; Jos 6:4).

47:7–9 The liturgical enthronement of God as world ruler.

47:7 *God is the King of all the earth.* See 2Sa 15:10; 2Ki 9:13; Isa 52:7. *psalm.* See NIV text note; see also note on Ps 32 title.

47:8 *seated on his holy throne.* In the Most Holy Place of the temple, where he takes the reins of world rule into his hands (see Jer 17:12). This verse is frequently echoed in Revelation (see Rev 4:9,10; 5:1,7,13; 6:16; 7:10,15; 19:4).

47:9 The nations acknowledge the God of Israel to be the Great King—anticipated as the final effect of God's rule (see note on 46:10). *as the people of the God of Abraham.* Thus the promises to Abraham will be fulfilled (see Ge 12:2–3 and note; 17:4–6; 22:17–18). *kings.* See NIV text note; see also note on 3:3; cf. Isa 2:2; 56:7.

Ps 48 A celebration of the security of Zion (as viewed with the eyes of faith) in that it is the city of the Great King (see introductions to Ps 46–47; see also introduction to Ps 46–48). It may have been sung by the Levitical choir on behalf of the assembled worshipers at the temple. Structure and theme are beautifully matched. The first and last verses combine to frame the whole with a comforting confession concern-

2 It is beautiful[w] in its loftiness,
the joy of the whole earth.
Like the utmost heights of Zaphon[a][x] is
Mount Zion,[y]
the[b] city of the Great King.[z]
3 God is in her citadels;[a]
he has shown himself to be her
fortress.[b]
4 When the kings joined forces,
when they advanced together,[c]
5 they saw ⌞her⌟ and were astounded;
they fled in terror.[d]
6 Trembling seized[e] them there,
pain like that of a woman in labor.[f]
7 You destroyed them like ships of
Tarshish[g]
shattered by an east wind.[h]

8 As we have heard,
so have we seen
in the city of the LORD Almighty,
in the city of our God:
God makes her secure forever.[i] *Selah*

9 Within your temple, O God,
we meditate[j] on your unfailing love.[k]
10 Like your name,[l] O God,
your praise reaches to the ends of
the earth;[m]
your right hand is filled with
righteousness.
11 Mount Zion rejoices,
the villages of Judah are glad
because of your judgments.[n]

12 Walk about Zion, go around her,
count her towers,[o]
13 consider well her ramparts,[p]
view her citadels,[q]
that you may tell of them to the next
generation.[r]
14 For this God is our God for ever and
ever;
he will be our guide[s] even to the
end.

Psalm 49

For the director of music.
Of the Sons of Korah. A psalm.

1 Hear[t] this, all you peoples;[u]
listen, all who live in this world,[v]

48:2 [w]Ps 50:2; La 2:15; Eze 16:14 [x]S Jos 13:27 [y]S Ps 2:6 [z]Mt 5:35 **48:3** [a]ver 13; Ps 122:7 [b]Ps 18:2 **48:4** [c]2Sa 10:1-19 **48:5** [d]Ex 15:16; Isa 13:8; Jer 46:5; Da 5:9 **48:6** [e]S Job 4:14 [f]S Ge 3:16 **48:7** [g]S Ge 10:4; S 1Ki 10:22; 22:48 [h]S Ge 41:6 **48:8** [i]Jer 23:6; Zec 8:13; 14:11 **48:9** [j]S Ps 39:3 [k]Ps 6:4 **48:10** [l]S Ex 6:3; S Jos 7:9 [m]1Sa 2:10; Ps 22:27; 65:5; 98:3; 100:1; Isa 11:12; 24:16; 42:10; 49:6 **48:11** [n]Ps 97:8 **48:12** [o]S Ne 3:1 **48:13** [p]2Sa 20:15; Isa 26:1; La 2:8; Hab 2:1 [q]S ver 3 [r]Ps 71:18; 78:6; 109:13 **48:14** [s]Ps 25:5; 73:24; Pr 6:22; Isa 49:10; 57:18; 58:11 **49:1** [t]Isa 1:2 [u]Ps 78:1 [v]S Ps 33:8

[a] 2 *Zaphon* can refer to a sacred mountain or the direction north. [b] 2 Or *earth, / Mount Zion, on the northern side / of the*

ing Zion's God. The center, v. 8 (see note on 6:6), summarizes the main theme of the body of the psalm. Four stanzas (having a symmetrical pattern in Hebrew: three lines, four lines, four lines, three lines) develop the theme: (1) the beauty of Zion as God's impregnable citadel (vv. 2–3); (2) the futility of all enemy attacks (vv. 4–7); (3) Zion's joy over God's saving acts (vv. 9–11)—related to the second stanza; (4) Zion as impregnable citadel (vv. 12–13)—related to the first stanza. Regularly distributed between the four main stanzas are allusions to the four primary directions (see notes on vv. 2,7,10,13)—suggesting that the city is secure from all points of attack.

48 title *song.* See note on Ps 30 title. *of the Sons of Korah.* See note on Ps 42 title.

48:1 *in the city of our God, his holy mountain.* See 46:4. *our God.* Occurs in this psalm only here, in the center (v. 8) and at the end (v. 14). *holy mountain.* See 43:3; see also note on 2:6.

48:2–3 Describes the lofty impregnability of Mount Zion.

48:2 *beautiful.* Its loftiness and secure position are its beauty (see note on 27:4). *loftiness.* Although not the highest ridge in its environment, in its significance as the mountain of God it is the "highest" mountain in the world (see 68:15–16 and note; Isa 2:2). *joy of the whole earth.* Perhaps referring to admiration from other nations, like that expressed by the queen of Sheba (see 1Ki 10:1–13). *Zaphon.* See NIV text note. Mount Zaphon in the far north was for the Phoenicians the sacred residence of El, the chief of their gods—as Mount Olympus was the mountain citadel of Zeus for the Greeks. *Great King.* See note on 47:2.

48:3 God himself, not her walls, was Zion's defense, a fact on which the next stanza elaborates (see note on vv. 12–13; see also Zec 2:5 and note). *her citadels.* See v. 13.

48:4–7 The futile attacks of hostile nations—they fled in panic when they saw that the Great King was in Zion. Such events as the destruction of the confederacy in the days of Jehoshaphat (see 2Ch 20) or the slaughter of the Assyrians in the time of Hezekiah (see 2Ki 19:35–36) may have been in the psalmist's mind.

48:7 *ships of Tarshish.* Great merchant ships of the Mediterranean (see 1Ki 10:22 and NIV text note). *shattered by an east wind.* See Ac 27:14; see also 1Ki 22:48. *east.* See introduction above.

48:8 The central verse and theme (see note on 6:6). *heard … seen.* "Seen" is climactic, as in Job 42:5. They had heard because "our fathers have told us what you did in their days" (44:1; see 78:3), but now in the liturgical experience of God at his temple they have "seen" how secure the city of God is. *LORD Almighty.* See note on 1Sa 1:3. *our God.* See note on v. 1.

48:9–11 The worshipers meditate at the temple with joy because of God's mighty acts in Zion's behalf.

48:9 *Within your temple.* In the temple courts. *unfailing love.* See note on 6:4. As is clear from vv. 10–11, reference here is to God's saving acts by which he has expressed his covenant love for his people (see 31:21; 40:9–10).

48:10 *name.* See note on 5:11. *reaches.* From the temple to the ends of the earth (see 9:11; 22:27). *right hand.* In Hebrew idiom a subtle reference to the south. *righteousness.* Righteous acts (see 40:9–10 and note; see also note on 4:1).

48:11 *judgments.* God's righteous judgments by which he has acted in defense of Zion.

48:12–13 The people contemplate Zion's defense, viewed from the perspective of what they have "seen" (v. 8) at the temple. The strength of Zion's "towers," "ramparts" and "citadels" is the presence of God.

48:13 *next generation.* Lit. "the generation behind"; in Hebrew idiom "behind" is a subtle reference to the west.

48:14 *our God.* See note on v. 1. *guide.* The great Shepherd-King (see notes on 23:1,3). *the end.* Lit. "death."

Ps 49–53 This cluster of psalms presents a striking contrast that brings the Psalter's call for godliness into sharp focus. On the one hand, we meet two psalms that face each other: (1) as God's summons to his people to come before him and hear his verdict concerning their lives (Ps 50), and (2) as a penitent's humble prayer for forgiveness and cleansing (Ps 51). On the other hand, these are bracketed by two psalms (49; 52) that denounce those who trust in their wealth (49:6;

[2]both low and high,[w]
rich and poor alike:
[3]My mouth will speak words of
wisdom;[x]
the utterance from my heart will give
understanding.[y]
[4]I will turn my ear to a proverb;[z]
with the harp[a] I will expound my
riddle:[b]

[5]Why should I fear[c] when evil days
come,
when wicked deceivers surround
me—
[6]those who trust in their wealth[d]
and boast[e] of their great riches?[f]
[7]No man can redeem the life of another
or give to God a ransom for him—
[8]the ransom[g] for a life is costly,
no payment is ever enough—[h]
[9]that he should live on[i] forever
and not see decay.[j]

[10]For all can see that wise men die;[k]
the foolish and the senseless[l] alike
perish
and leave their wealth[m] to others.[n]
[11]Their tombs[o] will remain their houses[a]
forever,
their dwellings for endless
generations,[p]
though they had[b] named[q] lands after
themselves.

[12]But man, despite his riches, does not
endure;[r]
he is[c] like the beasts that perish.[s]

[13]This is the fate of those who trust in
themselves,[t]
and of their followers, who approve
their sayings. *Selah*
[14]Like sheep they are destined[u] for the
grave,[d][v]
and death will feed on them.
The upright will rule[w] over them in the
morning;

49:2 [w]Ps 62:9 **49:3** [x]S Ps 37:30 [y]Ps 119:130 **49:4** [z]Ps 78:2; Pr 1:6; Eze 12:22; 16:44; 18:2-3; Lk 4:23 [a]S 1Sa 16:16; Ps 33:2 [b]S Nu 12:8 **49:5** [c]Ps 23:4; 27:1 **49:6** [d]S Job 22:25; Ps 73:12; Jer 48:7 [e]S Ps 10:3 [f]S Job 36:19 **49:8** [g]S Nu 35:31 [h]Mt 16:26 **49:9** [i]Ps 22:29; 89:48 [j]Ps 16:10 **49:10** [k]Ecc 2:16 [l]Ps 92:6; 94:8 [m]S Job 27:17 [n]Ecc 2:18,21; Lk 12:20 **49:11** [o]Mk 5:3; Lk 8:27 [p]Ps 106:31 [q]S Dt 3:14 **49:12** [r]S Job 14:2 [s]ver 20; 2Pe 2:12 **49:13** [t]Lk 12:20 **49:14** [u]Jer 43:11; Eze 31:14 [v]Nu 16:30; S Job 21:13; Ps 9:17; 55:15 [w]Isa 14:2; Da 7:18; 1Co 6:2

[a] *11* Septuagint and Syriac; Hebrew *In their thoughts their houses will remain* [b] *11* Or / *for they have* [c] *12* Hebrew; Septuagint and Syriac read verse 12 the same as verse 20. [d] *14* Hebrew *Sheol*; also in verse 15

52:7) and make their "boast" either in that wealth (49:6) or in the "evil" practices by which they obtained it (52:1). These descriptions of the ungodly are found nowhere else in the Psalter. In the first of these framing psalms, such people are characterized as "foolish" and "senseless" (49:10). So it is appropriate that this four-psalm segment of the Psalter has appended to it in climax Ps 53, a somewhat revised repetition of Ps 14 with its denunciation of the fools whose thoughts and ways are God-less. Placed immediately after Ps 46–48, these five psalms serve as a stern reminder that only those who put their trust in the Lord have reason to celebrate the security of "the city of our God" (48:1,8; see introduction to Ps 46–48).

Ps 49 A wisdom word concerning rich fools who proudly rely on their great wealth and on themselves to assure their welfare and security in the world (see Ps 52 and introduction to Ps 49–53). The Levitical author knows what it is to be without wealth (see Nu 18:21–24; Dt 14:27–29) and has observed the attitudes of many of the rich (see vv. 5–6). He has seen through their folly, however, and offers his wisdom for all to hear (vv. 1–2), so that those who are awed by the rich may be freed from their spell. Inescapable death is the destiny and undoing of such "foolish and … senseless" (49:10) people, and in the end the "upright will rule over them" (v. 14). As elsewhere (see note on structure in the introduction to Ps 33), the author has composed a poem of 22 Hebrew lines in accordance with the number of letters in the Hebrew alphabet. The thematic structure is symmetrical: Following a four-line introduction (vv. 1–4), the instruction proper is developed in two balanced stanzas of eight lines each (vv. 5–11,13–19) with appended refrains (vv. 12,20). For other psalms with recurring refrains see introduction to Ps 42–43. The date of this psalm may well be postexilic. See introduction to Ps 37.

49 title See note on Ps 42 title.

49:1–4 Introduction.

49:1–2 More like the address of the prophets (see 1Ki 22:28; Isa 34:1; Mic 1:2) than that of the wisdom teachers (see 34:11; Pr 1:8,10; 2:1).

49:3 See Mt 12:34. *wisdom.* See essay, p. 727. *heart.* See note on 4:7.

49:4 *turn my ear.* The wisdom he is about to speak first had to be "heard" by him—all true wisdom is from God (see Job 28). *proverb … riddle.* The two Hebrew words for these nouns were used to refer to insightful pieces of instruction that were artfully crafted (see 78:2 ["parables," "hidden things"]; Pr 1:6 ["proverbs," "riddles"]; Eze 17:2 ["parable," "allegory"]). *with the harp.* Another hint of the author's sense of inspiration (see 1Sa 10:5–6; 2Ki 3:15).

49:5–11 Those of little means or power need not be unsettled when surrounded by rich fools who threaten and strut; their destiny is death.

49:6 *who trust in their wealth.* See 52:7. *boast of.* Or "boast in," i.e., openly proclaim that they rely on their wealth to preserve them in a happy condition (see 52:1 and note).

49:7–9 Wealth cannot buy escape from death—not even one's family "redeemer" can accomplish it (cf. Ex 21:30; Lev 25:47–49). Only God himself can redeem a life from the grave (see v. 15 and note).

49:10 Any who have "eyes in their heads" (Ecc 2:14) can see that even the wise die (see Ecc 7:2; 9:5) and leave their wealth to others (see Ecc 2:18,21). How much more the fool (see 73:18–20; 92:6–7)! See also 52:5; 89:48; Job 30:23; Ecc 2:14–16. *wise … foolish … senseless.* Essentially the "righteous" and the "wicked" of Ps 37. *wealth.* Often gotten by devious means that their foolish "wisdom" had contrived (vv. 5,12; see also 52:1–4,7). *to others.* But not to their children (see note on 37:29; see also 39:6; Lk 12:20–21).

49:11 Though they lavish wealth on their tombs and try at least to perpetuate their memory by putting their names to their large landholdings (see Nu 32:41) as an enduring memorial, they only suffer the bitter irony of having their graves as their "eternal home" (Ecc 12:5). Cf. the psalmist's hope in v. 15.

49:12 Their epitaph (see note on 10:18; see also Ecc 3:19; 7:2) and the psalm's refrain (see NIV text note).

49:13–19 The final end of these rich fools and of the righteous—so why should any stand in awe of the rich?

49:13 *in themselves.* As those who have "succeeded" (see v. 6).

49:14 *Like sheep.* Death is already their shepherd, "guiding" them to the grave. *death will feed on them.* For the imagery of death (or the grave) as an insatiable monster feed-

their forms will decay in the grave,[a]
far from their princely mansions.
15 But God will redeem my life[b] from the grave;[x]
he will surely take me to himself.[y]
Selah

16 Do not be overawed when a man grows rich,
when the splendor of his house increases;
17 for he will take nothing[z] with him when he dies,
his splendor will not descend with him.[a]
18 Though while he lived he counted himself blessed—[b]
and men praise you when you prosper—
19 he will join the generation of his fathers,[c]
who will never see the light[d] ⌞of life⌟.
20 A man who has riches without understanding[e]
is like the beasts that perish.[f]

49:15 [x]Ps 56:13; Hos 13:14 [y]S Ge 5:24 **49:17** [z]1Ti 6:7 [a]S Ps 17:14 **49:18** [b]Ps 10:6; Lk 12:19 **49:19** [c]S Ge 15:15 [d]S Job 33:30 **49:20** [e]Pr 16:16 [f]S ver 12

Psalm 50

A psalm of Asaph.

1 The Mighty One, God, the LORD,[g]
speaks and summons the earth
from the rising of the sun to the place where it sets.[h]
2 From Zion,[i] perfect in beauty,[j]
God shines forth.[k]
3 Our God comes[l] and will not be silent;[m]
a fire devours[n] before him,[o]
and around him a tempest[p] rages.
4 He summons the heavens above,
and the earth,[q] that he may judge his people:[r]
5 "Gather to me my consecrated ones,[s]
who made a covenant[t] with me by sacrifice."

50:1 [g]Jos 22:22 [h]Ps 113:3 **50:2** [i]Ps 2:6 [j]S Ps 48:2; S La 2:15 [k]S Dt 33:2 **50:3** [l]Ps 96:13 [m]ver 21; Isa 42:14; 64:12; 65:6 [n]S Lev 10:2 [o]S Ps 18:8 [p]Job 37:9; Ps 83:15; 107:25; 147:18; Isa 29:6; 30:28; Jnh 1:4; Na 1:3 **50:4** [q]Dt 4:26; 31:28; Isa 1:2 [r]Heb 10:30 **50:5** [s]S Dt 7:6; S Ps 18:25 [t]Ex 24:7; S 2Ch 6:11

[a] *14* Hebrew *Sheol*; also in verse 15 [b] *15* Or *soul*

ing on its victims see 69:15; 141:7; Pr 1:12; 27:20; 30:15–16; Isa 5:14; Jnh 2:2 ("depths"; lit. "belly"); Hab 2:5. The imagery is borrowed from Canaanite mythology, which so depicts the god Mot (death). As one Canaanite document reads, "Do not approach divine Mot, or he will put you like a lamb into his mouth." *rule over.* See Lev 26:17; Isa 14:2; perhaps "prevail over" in contrast to the situation referred to in v. 5. *in the morning.* See vv. 15,19 and notes on 6:5; 11:7; 16:9–11; 17:15. But see also introduction to Ps 57.

49:15 See note on vv. 7–9. *redeem ... from the grave.* Cf. v. 11. While the psalmist may here refer to saving (for a while) from the universal prospect of death (as in Job 5:20; see 116:8), the context strongly suggests that he, as one of the upright, speaks of his final destiny. Perhaps the thought is of being conveyed into the presence of God in his heavenly temple, analogous to the later Jewish thought of being conveyed to "Abraham's side" (Lk 16:22; see notes on 6:5; 11:7; 16:9–11; 17:15). *my life.* Or "my soul" (see NIV text note; see also note on 6:3). *take me to himself.* See 73:24; Ge 5:24 and notes.

49:16 *his house.* His whole estate (see Ex 20:17).

49:17 *take nothing with him when he dies.* See 1Ti 6:7.

49:19 *light ⌞of life⌟.* See notes on 27:1; 36:9; see also Isa 53:11.

49:20 The last word. See note on v. 12.

Ps 50 The Lord calls his covenant people to account. For this psalm's place in the arrangement of the Psalter see introduction to Ps 49–53. The psalm appears to have been composed for a temple liturgy in which Israel reaffirms her commitment to God's covenant. A leader of the Levitical choir addresses Israel on behalf of the Lord (see Ps 15; 24, either of which may have been spoken earlier in the same liturgy). This liturgy was possibly related to the Feast of Tabernacles (see Dt 31:9–13; see also introduction to Ps 47). In its rebuke of a false understanding of sacrifice the psalm has affinity with the prophecies of Amos, Micah and Isaiah and so may date from the late eighth and/or early seventh centuries B.C. Others find a closer relationship with the reformation of Josiah (2Ki 22:1—23:25) and the ministry of Jeremiah. Structurally, the psalm has three parts: (1) the announcement of the "coming" of Israel's covenant Lord to call his people to account (vv. 1–6); (2) the Lord's words of correction for those of honest intent (vv. 7–15); (3) his sharp rebuke of "the wicked" among them (vv. 16–23).

50 title A traditional ascription of the psalm to Asaph; or it may mean "for Asaph" (see "For Jeduthun" in Ps 39 title) or for the descendants of Asaph who functioned in his place. This psalm may have been separated from the other psalms of Asaph (73–83) in order to be paired with Ps 51 in the cluster of Ps 49–53. Asaph was one of David's three choir leaders (see note on Ps 39 title).

50:1–6 The Lord comes (v. 3) in the temple worship to correct and rebuke his people: Israel must know that the God of Zion is the God of Sinai (see Ex 19:16–20).

50:1 *The Mighty One, God, the LORD.* A sequence found elsewhere only in Jos 22:22 (see note there). Ps 50 is noteworthy for its use of numerous names and titles for God (seven in all: three in v. 1, four in the rest of the psalm; see notes on vv. 6,14,21–22). *the earth.* See "the heavens ... the earth" (v. 4) and "the heavens" (v. 6). When Moses renewed the covenant between the Lord and Israel on the plains of Moab, he called upon heaven and earth to serve as third-party witnesses to the covenant (Dt 30:19; 31:28). The Lord now summons these (vv. 1–4) to testify that his present word to his people is in complete accord with that covenant (see Isa 1:2). God's relationship with his people has the whole creation as its context, and for that reason the whole creation is a party of interest to that relationship (see Ge 1–3; see also Jer 12:4; Ro 8:22 and notes).

50:2 *perfect in beauty.* Because God resides there (cf. Eze 27:3–4,11; 28:12). *shines forth.* Manifests his glory as he comes to act (see 80:1; 94:1; Dt 33:2; cf. Eze 28:7,17), now calling his people to account, but not yet announcing judgment as in Isa 1 or Mic 1.

50:3 *comes.* From his enthronement between the cherubim (see 80:1; 99:1; see also 1Sa 4:4; 2Sa 6:2; 2Ki 19:15) in the Most Holy Place of the temple (see note on 28:2; see also Isa 26:21; Mic 1:3). *will not be silent.* No longer (see v. 21) will he let their sins go unrebuked. *fire ... tempest.* See Ex 19:16,18.

50:4 *judge.* Call them to account in accordance with his covenant.

50:5 *consecrated ones.* See note on 4:3. *by sacrifice.* Sacrifices were a part of the ritual that sealed the covenant (see Ex 24:4–8 and note on 24:6) and continued to be an integral part of Israel's expression of covenant commitment to the Lord.

[6]And the heavens proclaim[u] his
righteousness,
for God himself is judge.[v] *Selah*

[7]"Hear, O my people, and I will speak,
O Israel, and I will testify[w] against
you:
I am God, your God.[x]
[8]I do not rebuke[y] you for your sacrifices
or your burnt offerings,[z] which are
ever before me.
[9]I have no need of a bull[a] from your stall
or of goats[b] from your pens,[c]
[10]for every animal of the forest[d] is mine,
and the cattle on a thousand hills.[e]
[11]I know every bird[f] in the mountains,
and the creatures of the field[g] are
mine.
[12]If I were hungry I would not tell you,
for the world[h] is mine, and all that is
in it.[i]
[13]Do I eat the flesh of bulls
or drink the blood of goats?
[14]Sacrifice thank offerings[j] to God,
fulfill your vows[k] to the Most High,[l]
[15]and call[m] upon me in the day of
trouble;[n]
I will deliver[o] you, and you will
honor[p] me."

[16]But to the wicked, God says:

"What right have you to recite my laws
or take my covenant[q] on your lips?[r]
[17]You hate[s] my instruction
and cast my words behind[t] you.
[18]When you see a thief, you join[u] with
him;
you throw in your lot with
adulterers.[v]
[19]You use your mouth for evil
and harness your tongue to deceit.[w]
[20]You speak continually against your
brother[x]
and slander your own mother's
son.
[21]These things you have done and I kept
silent;[y]
you thought I was altogether[a] like
you.
But I will rebuke[z] you
and accuse[a] you to your face.

[22]"Consider this, you who forget God,[b]
or I will tear you to pieces, with
none to rescue:[c]
[23]He who sacrifices thank offerings
honors me,
and he prepares the way[d]
so that I may show him[b] the
salvation of God.[e]"

Psalm 51

For the director of music. A psalm of
David. When the prophet Nathan came to
him after David had committed adultery
with Bathsheba.[f]

[1]Have mercy[g] on me, O God,
according to your unfailing love;[h]
according to your great compassion[i]
blot out[j] my transgressions.[k]

[a] 21 *Or thought the 'I AM' was* [b] 23 *Or and to him who considers his way / I will show*

50:6 [u]S Ps 19:1 [v]S Ge 16:5; S Job 9:15 **50:7** [w]Heb 2:4 [x]Ex 20:2; Ps 48:14 **50:8** [y]S 2Sa 22:16 [z]S Ps 40:6 **50:9** [a]S Lev 1:5 [b]S Lev 16:5 [c]S Nu 32:16 **50:10** [d]Ps 104:20; Isa 56:9; Mic 5:8 [e]Ps 104:24 **50:11** [f]Mt 6:26 [g]Ps 8:7; 80:13 **50:12** [h]Ex 19:5 [i]Dt 10:14; S Jos 3:11; Ps 24:1; 1Co 10:26 **50:14** [j]S Ezr 1:4; S Ps 27:6 [k]S Nu 30:2; S Ps 66:13; 76:11 [l]Ps 7:8 **50:15** [m]Ps 4:1; 81:7; Isa 55:6; 58:9; Zec 13:9 [n]Ps 69:17; 86:7; 107:6; 142:2; Jas 5:13 [o]Ps 3:7 [p]S Ps 22:23 **50:16** [q]Ps 25:10 [r]Isa 29:13 **50:17** [s]Pr 1:22 [t]S 1Ki 14:9 **50:18** [u]Ro 1:32; 1Ti 5:22 [v]S Job 22:15 **50:19** [w]Ps 10:7; 36:3; 52:2; 101:7 **50:20** [x]Mt 10:21 **50:21** [y]Isa 42:14; 57:11; 62:1; 64:12 [z]Ps 6:1; S 18:15; 76:6; 104:7; Isa 50:2 [a]Ps 85:5; Isa 57:16 **50:22** [b]S Job 8:13; S Isa 17:10 [c]S Dt 32:39; Mic 5:8 **50:23** [d]Ps 85:13 [e]S Ps 9:14; 91:16; 98:3; Isa 52:10 **51:Title** [f]2Sa 11:4; 12:1 **51:1** [g]S 2Sa 24:14; S Ps 9:13 [h]S Ps 25:7; S 119:88 [i]S Ne 9:27; Ps 86:15; Isa 63:7 [j]S 2Sa 12:13; S 2Ch 6:21; S Ne 4:5; Ac 3:19 [k]S Ps 39:8

50:6 *proclaim.* See note on v. 1. *righteousness.* See note on 4:1. *judge.* Lord over his people (the Hebrew for "judge" and that for "king" are sometimes used synonymously; see, e.g., Isa 33:22). "Judge" occurs as a title for God (see note on v. 1) in, e.g., 94:2; Ge 18:25 (see note there); Jdg 11:27 (see note there; see also Introduction to Amos: Theological Theme and Message).

50:7–15 The Lord corrects his people.

50:7 *my people.* "Our God" (v. 3) and "your God" (here) reflect the covenant bond. *I am God, your God.* See Ex 19:3–6; Lev 19:2–4,10,25,31,34,36; 20:7,24; 22:33; 23:22.

50:8–13 Israel had not failed to bring enough sacrifices (v. 8), but she was ever tempted to think that sacrifices were of first importance to God, as though he was dependent on them. This notion was widespread among Israel's pagan neighbors. See note on 40:6.

50:10 *thousand.* Used here figuratively for a very large number.

50:12 *the world … in it.* See 24:1 and note.

50:14–15 God wants Israel to acknowledge her dependence on him, by giving thank offerings for his mercies (v. 14) and by praying to him in times of need (v. 15; see 116:17–19). Those who do so may expect God's gracious answer to their prayers (stated more directly in v. 23). God also desires obedience to his moral law (see vv. 16–21 and note on 40:6).

50:14 *thank offerings.* See Lev 7:12–13. *God … Most High.* That is, God Most High (see 57:2 and note on 3:7). *fulfill.* See note on Ecc 5:6. *your vows.* Vows that accompanied prayer in times of need, usually involving thank offerings (see 66:13–15), always involving praise of the Lord for his answer to prayer (see note on 7:17). See also Heb 13:15. *Most High.* See note on v. 1; see also note on Ge 14:19.

50:15 *honor me.* With praise in the fulfillment of the vows (see v. 23) — and, implicitly, with obedience to his covenant law (see following verses).

50:16–23 The Lord's rebuke of the wicked.

50:16 *recite my laws.* Apparently a part of the liturgy of covenant commitment.

50:17 *You hate my instruction.* They formally participate in the holy ritual but reject God's law as the rule for life outside the ritual.

50:19 *use your mouth for evil.* See note on 5:9.

50:21 God's merciful and patient "silence" is distorted by the wicked into bad and self-serving theology (see Ecc 8:11; Isa 42:14; 57:11). *thought I was altogether.* See NIV text note; Ex 3:14 and note (see also note on v. 1). *accuse you to your face.* Confront you with the particulars of my indictment.

50:22 *God.* A relatively rare word for "God" (Hebrew *Eloah*), though common in Job. See note on v. 1.

50:23 See note on vv. 14–15.

Ps 51 David's humble prayer for forgiveness and cleansing. As the prayer of a contrite sinner, it represents a proper response to the Lord's confrontation of his people in Ps 50 (compare v. 16 with 50:8–15; see also introduction to Ps 49–53). This psalm has many points of contact with Ps 25.

[2]Wash away[l] all my iniquity
and cleanse[m] me from my sin.

[3]For I know my transgressions,
and my sin is always before me.[n]
[4]Against you, you only, have I sinned[o]
and done what is evil in your sight,[p]
so that you are proved right when you speak
and justified when you judge.[q]
[5]Surely I was sinful[r] at birth,[s]
sinful from the time my mother conceived me.
[6]Surely you desire truth in the inner parts[a];
you teach[b] me wisdom[t] in the inmost place.[u]

[7]Cleanse[v] me with hyssop,[w] and I will be clean;
wash me, and I will be whiter than snow.[x]
[8]Let me hear joy and gladness;[y]
let the bones[z] you have crushed rejoice.
[9]Hide your face from my sins[a]
and blot out[b] all my iniquity.

[10]Create in me a pure heart,[c] O God,
and renew a steadfast spirit within me.[d]
[11]Do not cast me[e] from your presence[f]
or take your Holy Spirit[g] from me.
[12]Restore to me the joy of your salvation[h]
and grant me a willing spirit,[i] to sustain me.[j]

[13]Then I will teach transgressors your ways,[k]
and sinners[l] will turn back to you.[m]

51:2 [l]S Ru 3:3; Jer 2:22; 13:27; Ac 22:16; 1Jn 1:9 [m]Pr 20:30; Isa 4:4; Eze 36:25; Zec 13:1; Mt 23:25-26; Heb 9:14 **51:3** [n]Isa 59:12 **51:4** [o]S 1Sa 15:24 [p]S Ge 20:6; Lk 15:21 [q]Ro 3:4* **51:5** [r]S Lev 5:2 [s]S Job 5:7 **51:6** [t]Ps 119:66; 143:10 [u]S Job 9:4; S 34:32 **51:7** [v]Isa 4:4; Eze 36:25; Zec 13:1 [w]S Ex 12:22; S Nu 19:6; Heb 9:19 [x]Isa 1:18; 43:25; 44:22 **51:8** [y]Isa 35:10; Jer 33:11; Joel 1:16 [z]S Ex 12:46

[a] 6 The meaning of the Hebrew for this phrase is uncertain. [b] 6 Or *you desired . . . ; / you taught*

51:9 [a]Jer 16:17; Zec 4:10 [b]S 2Sa 12:13 **51:10** [c]S Ps 24:4; 78:37; Mt 5:8; Ac 15:9 [d]Eze 18:31; 36:26 **51:11** [e]Ps 27:9; 71:9; 138:8 [f]S Ge 4:14; S Ex 33:15 [g]Ps 106:33; Isa 63:10; Eph 4:30 **51:12** [h]S Job 33:26 [i]Ps 110:3 [j]S Ps 18:35 **51:13** [k]S Ex 33:13; Ac 9:21-22 [l]S Ps 1:1 [m]S Job 33:27

In traditional Christian usage it is one of seven penitential psalms (see introduction to Ps 6). The psalm is constructed symmetrically: A two-verse introduction balances a two-verse conclusion, and the enclosed four stanzas in Hebrew consist of five lines, three lines and five lines respectively. The whole is framed by David's prayer for himself (vv. 1–2) and for Zion (vv. 18–19). The well-being of the king and the city stand and fall together (see 28:8 and note on 3:8).

51 title *For the director of music.* See note on Ps 4 title. *When.* For the event referred to see 2Sa 11:1—12:25; see also note on Ps 3 title.

51:1–2 Opening prayer for mercy and pardon (see Lk 18:13). Note the piling up of synonyms: mercy, unfailing love, great compassion; blot out, wash, cleanse; transgressions, iniquity, sin (for this last triad see note on 32:5).

51:1 *unfailing love.* See note on 6:4. *blot out.* See v. 9. The image is that of a papyrus scroll (see note on 9:5) on which God had recorded David's deeds. The "blotting out" of sins pictures forgiveness (Jer 18:23; see Isa 43:25). For the imagery of God's keeping records of the events in his realm in the way that earthly kings do, see 56:8 and note; 87:6; 130:3; 139:16 and note; Ne 13:14; Da 7:10; see also Ex 32:32–33.

51:2 See v. 7. *Wash.* As a filthy garment. *cleanse me.* Make me clean in your sight (see Lev 11:32).

51:3–6 Confession of sin (cf. Pr 28:13; 1Jn 1:9).

51:3 *before me.* On my mind.

51:4 *Against you … only.* David acknowledges that his sin was preeminently against God (see 2Sa 12:13; cf. Ge 20:6; 39:9; Lk 15:18). He had violated specific covenant stipulations (Ex 20:13–14,17). *when you speak … when you judge.* As the Lord did through Nathan the prophet (2Sa 12:7–12). For a NT application see Ro 3:4.

51:5 He cannot plead that this sin was a rare aberration in his life; it sprang from what he is and has been (in his "inner parts," v. 6) from birth (see 58:3; Ge 8:21; cf. Jn 9:34; Eph 2:3). The apparently similar statements in Job 14:4; 15:14; 25:4–6 rise from a different motivation.

51:6 The great contrast: He has acted absolutely contrary to what God desires and to what God has been teaching him "in the inmost place." But it is just this "desire" of God and this "teaching" of God that are his hope—what he pleads for in vv. 7,10. *truth.* Moral integrity. *inner parts.* See 139:13–16 and notes; Job 38:36. *wisdom.* Those who give themselves over to sin are fools; those who have God's law in their hearts are wise (see 37:30–31). *inmost place.* The most secret place within.

51:7–9 Renewed prayer for pardon (see note on vv. 1–2).

51:7 *Cleanse me.* Lit. "Un-sin me." *hyssop.* Used in ritual cleansing; see note on Ex 12:22. *be clean.* The Hebrew root for this phrase is the same as that for "cleanse" in v. 2. *whiter than snow.* Like a filthy garment, he needs washing (see note on v. 2); but if God washes him, he will be so pure that there is no figurative word that can describe him (see Isa 1:18; Da 7:9; Rev 7:14; 19:14).

51:8 *Let me hear joy.* Let me be surrounded by joy (see 32:7 and note; see also 35:27), or let me hear a prophetic oracle of forgiveness that will result in joy—from the assurance of sins forgiven (see 2Sa 12:13). *bones.* See note on 6:2.

51:9 *Hide your face.* From what is "always before me" (v. 3). *blot out.* See note on v. 1.

51:10–12 Prayer for purity—for a pure heart, a steadfast spirit of faithfulness and a willing spirit of service. These can be his only if God does not reject him and take his Holy Spirit from him. If granted, the joy of God's salvation will return to gladden his troubled soul.

51:10 *Create.* As something new, which cannot emerge from what now is (see v. 5), and which only God can fashion (see Ge 1:1 and note; Isa 65:17; Jer 31:22). *heart.* See note on 4:7.

51:11 The two requests are essentially one (see 139:7; Eze 39:29). David's prayer recalls the rejection of Saul (see 1Sa 16:1,14; 2Sa 7:15) and pleads for God not to take away his Spirit, by which he had equipped and qualified him for his royal office (see 1Sa 16:13; cf. 2Sa 23:1–2). *Holy Spirit.* The phrase is found elsewhere in the OT only in Isa 63:10–11. By his Spirit, God effected his purposes in creation (see 104:30; Ge 1:2; Job 33:4) and redemption (see Isa 32:15; 44:3; 63:11,14; Hag 2:5), equipped his servants for their appointed tasks (see Ex 31:3; Nu 11:29; Jdg 3:10; 1Sa 10:6; 16:13; Isa 11:2; 42:1), inspired his prophets (see Nu 24:2–3; 2Sa 23:2; Ne 9:30; Isa 59:21; 61:1; Eze 11:5; Mic 3:8; Zec 7:12) and directed their ministries (see 1Ki 18:12; 2Ki 2:16; Isa 48:16; Eze 2:2; 3:14). And it is by his Spirit that God gives his people a "new heart and … a new spirit" to live by his will (see Eze 36:26–27; see also Jer 24:7; 32:39; Eze 11:19; 18:31).

51:13–17 The vow to praise (see note on 7:17).

51:13 His praise for God's forgiveness and purification will be accompanied by instruction for "transgressors" and "sinners," whose waywardness he himself had been guilty of (see v. 3).

14 Save me[n] from bloodguilt,[o] O God,
the God who saves me,[p]
and my tongue will sing of your
righteousness.[q]
15 O Lord, open my lips,[r]
and my mouth will declare your
praise.
16 You do not delight in sacrifice,[s] or I
would bring it;
you do not take pleasure in burnt
offerings.
17 The sacrifices[t] of God are[a] a broken
spirit;
a broken and contrite heart,[u]
O God, you will not despise.
18 In your good pleasure make Zion[v]
prosper;
build up the walls of Jerusalem.[w]
19 Then there will be righteous
sacrifices,[x]
whole burnt offerings[y] to delight
you;
then bulls[z] will be offered on your
altar.

Psalm 52

For the director of music. A *maskil*[b]
of David. When Doeg the Edomite[a]
had gone to Saul and told him:
"David has gone to the house of
Ahimelech."

1 Why do you boast of evil, you mighty
man?
Why do you boast[b] all day long,[c]
you who are a disgrace in the eyes of
God?

2 Your tongue plots destruction;[d]
it is like a sharpened razor,[e]
you who practice deceit.[f]
3 You love evil[g] rather than good,
falsehood[h] rather than speaking the
truth. *Selah*
4 You love every harmful word,
O you deceitful tongue![i]

5 Surely God will bring you down to
everlasting ruin:
He will snatch you up and tear[j] you
from your tent;
he will uproot[k] you from the land of
the living.[l] *Selah*
6 The righteous will see and fear;
they will laugh[m] at him, saying,
7 "Here now is the man
who did not make God his
stronghold[n]
but trusted in his great wealth[o]
and grew strong by destroying
others!"

8 But I am like an olive tree[p]
flourishing in the house of God;
I trust[q] in God's unfailing love
for ever and ever.
9 I will praise you forever[r] for what you
have done;
in your name I will hope,[s] for your
name is good.[t]
I will praise you in the presence of
your saints.[u]

51:14 [n] S Ps 39:8 [o] S 2Sa 12:9 [p] Ps 25:5; 68:20; 88:1 [q] S Ps 5:8; 35:28; 71:15 **51:15** [r] Ex 4:15 **51:16** [s] S 1Sa 15:22 **51:17** [t] Pr 15:8; Hag 2:14 [u] Mt 11:29 **51:18** [v] Ps 102:16; 147:2; Isa 14:32; 51:3; Zec 1:16-17 [w] Ps 69:35; Isa 44:26 **51:19** [x] Dt 33:19 [y] Ps 66:13; 96:8; Jer 17:26 [z] Ps 66:15 **52:Title** [a] 1Sa 21:7; 22:9 **52:1** [b] Ps 10:3; 94:4 [c] Ps 44:8 **52:2** [d] Ps 5:9 [e] S Nu 6:5 [f] S Ps 50:19 **52:3** [g] Ex 10:10; 1Sa 12:25; Am 5:14-15; Jn 3:20 [h] Ps 58:3; Jer 9:5; Rev 21:8 **52:4** [i] Ps 5:9; 10:7; 109:2; 120:2, 3; Pr 10:31; 12:19 **52:5** [j] S Dt 29:28; S Job 40:12; Isa 22:19; Eze 17:24 [k] S Dt 28:63 [l] S Job 28:13 **52:6** [m] S Job 22:19 **52:7** [n] S 2Sa 22:3 [o] S Ps 49:6; S Pr 11:28; Mk 10:23 **52:8** [p] S Ps 1:3; S Rev 11:4 [q] Ps 6:4; 13:5 **52:9** [r] S Ps 30:12 [s] S Job 7:6; Ps 25:3 [t] Ps 54:6 [u] S Dt 7:6; Ps 16:3

[a] *17* Or *My sacrifice, O God, is* [b] Title: Probably a literary or musical term

He commits himself to go from praise of God to instruction of others, as did the author of Ps 34 (see also note on 32:8–10). *your ways.* See 25:4 and note.

51:14 If God will only forgive, praise will follow. *righteousness.* See note on 4:1.

51:15 *open my lips.* By granting the forgiveness and cleansing I seek.

51:16 See note on 40:6.

51:17 *broken spirit; a broken and contrite heart.* What pleases God more than sacrifices is a humble heart that looks to him when troubles crush and penitently pleads for mercy when sin has been committed (see 50:7–15 and notes; see also 34:17–18).

51:18–19 Prayer for Zion (see note on 3:8).

51:19 *righteous sacrifices.* Such as are pleasing to God; here, sacrifices accompanied by praise for God's mercies (see 50:14–15 and notes).

Ps 52 Fearless confidence in God when under attack by an arrogant and evil enemy. David stands in the presence of God and from the high tower of that refuge hurls his denunciation (much like the prophetic denunciation in Isa 22:15–19) into the face of his attacker. Though not a wisdom psalm, it has much in common with Ps 49 (see introduction to Ps 49–53; see also introduction to Ps 49). The extended depiction of David's enemy forms a sharp contrast with the spirit of Ps 51. See also David's denunciation of Goliath (1Sa 17:45–47).

52 title *For the director of music.* See note on Ps 4 title. *maskil.* See note on Ps 32 title. *When.* See note on Ps 3 title. For the event referred to see 1Sa 22:9–10.

52:1–4 The enemy castigated.

52:1 *Why ... ?* By what right? See 50:16; Isa 3:15. *boast.* By act as well as by word (see 75:4–5). *mighty man.* In his own estimation (see Isa 22:17).

52:2 *Your tongue.* See v. 4; see also note on 5:9.

52:3 Your whole moral sense is perverted. *love.* Prefer.

52:4 *tongue.* See note on v. 2.

52:5–7 The enemy's end announced (implicitly a prayer): God will slay you, and the righteous will mock you.

52:5 Note the triple imagery: "bring you down," "snatch you up," "uproot you." The arrogant enemy will meet the same end as the rich fools of Ps 49. *from your tent.* See Job 18:14. *uproot you.* Contrast v. 8.

52:6 *righteous.* See note on 1:5. *fear.* Learn from your downfall (see 40:3 and note).

52:7 See Ps 49.

52:8–9 David's security is God.

52:8 *like an olive tree.* Which lives for hundreds of years. *flourishing.* See 1:3. It will not be uprooted (see v. 5). *in the house of God.* Olive trees were not planted in the temple courts, but David had access to God's temple as his refuge (see 15:1; 23:6; 27:4; 61:4 and note), where he was kept safe (see 27:5 and note). *unfailing love.* See note on 6:4.

52:9 A vow to praise (see note on 7:17). *name.* See note on 5:11. *saints.* See note on 4:3.

Psalm 53

53:1-6pp — Ps 14:1-7

For the director of music. According to *mahalath.*[a] A *maskil*[b] of David.

1 The fool[v] says in his heart,
"There is no God."[w]
They are corrupt, and their ways are vile;
there is no one who does good.

2 God looks down from heaven[x]
on the sons of men
to see if there are any who understand,[y]
any who seek God.[z]
3 Everyone has turned away,
they have together become corrupt;
there is no one who does good,
not even one.[a]

4 Will the evildoers never learn—
those who devour my people as men eat bread
and who do not call on God?
5 There they were, overwhelmed with dread,
where there was nothing to dread.[b]
God scattered the bones[c] of those who attacked you;[d]
you put them to shame,[e] for God despised them.[f]

6 Oh, that salvation for Israel would come out of Zion!
When God restores the fortunes of his people,
let Jacob rejoice and Israel be glad!

Psalm 54

For the director of music. With stringed instruments. A *maskil*[b] of David. When the Ziphites[g] had gone to Saul and said, "Is not David hiding among us?"

1 Save me[h], O God, by your name;[i]
vindicate me by your might.[j]
2 Hear my prayer, O God;[k]
listen to the words of my mouth.

3 Strangers are attacking me;[l]
ruthless men[m] seek my life[n]—
men without regard for God.[o] *Selah*

4 Surely God is my help;[p]
the Lord is the one who sustains me.[q]

5 Let evil recoil[r] on those who slander me;
in your faithfulness[s] destroy them.

6 I will sacrifice a freewill offering[t] to you;
I will praise[u] your name, O LORD,
for it is good.[v]

[a] Title: Probably a musical term [b] Title: Probably a literary or musical term

53:1 [v] Ps 74:22; 107:17; Pr 10:23 [w] Ps 10:4 **53:2** [x] S Ps 33:13 [y] Ps 82:5; Jer 4:22; 8:8 [z] 2Ch 15:2 **53:3** [a] Ro 3:10-12* **53:5** [b] S Lev 26:17 [c] 2Ki 23:14; Ps 141:7; Jer 8:1; Eze 6:5 [d] 2Ki 17:20 [e] S Job 8:22 [f] Jer 6:30; 14:19; La 5:22 **54:Title** [g] 1Sa 23:19; 26:1 **54:1** [h] S 1Sa 24:15 [i] Ps 20:1 [j] 2Ch 20:6 **54:2** [k] S Ps 4:1; 5:1; 55:1 **54:3** [l] Ps 86:14 [m] Ps 18:48; 140:1,4,11 [n] S 1Sa 20:1 [o] Ps 36:1 **54:4** [p] S 1Ch 5:20; S Ps 20:2 [q] S Ps 18:35 **54:5** [r] S Dt 32:35; Ps 94:23; Pr 24:12 [s] Ps 89:49; Isa 42:3 **54:6** [t] S Lev 7:12,16; S Ezr 1:4; S Ps 27:6 [u] Ps 44:8; 69:30; 138:2; 142:7; 145:1 [v] Ps 52:9

Ps 53 A testimony concerning the folly of the wicked, a somewhat revised duplicate of Ps 14; see introduction there. (The main difference between the two psalms is that here the word "God" is used instead of "the LORD"; see also note on v. 5.) The original psalm may have been revised in the light of an event such as is narrated in 2Ch 20. Here it also serves as a further commentary on the kind of arrogant fool denounced in Ps 49; 52 (see introduction to Ps 49–53).

53 title *For the director of music.* See note on Ps 4 title. *According to.* See note on Ps 6 title. *mahalath.* Possibly the name of a tune (see note on Ps 9 title). The Hebrew appears to be the word for "suffering" or "sickness" (see Ps 88 title and NIV text note there). Perhaps the Hebrew phrase indicates here that the psalm is to be used in a time of affliction, when the godless mock (see Ps 102; see also note on 5:9). *maskil.* See note on Ps 32 title.

53:1–4 See notes on 14:1–4.

53:5 Differs considerably from 14:5–6, though the basic thought remains the same: God overwhelms the godless who attack his people. Here the verbs are in the past tense (perhaps to express the certainty of their downfall). *where there was nothing to dread.* They fell victim to fear when, humanly speaking, they were not even threatened. God's curse fell on them rather than on Israel (see Lev 26:36–37; see also Jdg 7:21; 2Ki 3:22–23; 7:6–7; Pr 28:1). *scattered the bones.* Over the battlefield of their defeat, their bodies left unburied like something loathsome (see Isa 14:18–20; Jer 8:2 and note). *God despised them.* As they had despised him.

53:6 See note on 14:7.

Ps 54–60 A cluster of seven prayers framed by a prayer of an individual (Ps 54) and a prayer of the community (Ps 60; see introduction to Ps 42–45). The psalm that introduces this cluster (Ps 54) is a seven-verse poem that is paradigmatic in its structure (see introduction to this psalm below). The psalm that concludes it echoes the key complaint of Ps 44, namely, that God has "rejected" his people and no longer goes out "with our armies" (44:9; 60:10). At the center is Ps 57, a prayer of 14 Hebrew lines (structurally a double seven), with a refrain that appeals to God to "be exalted" (vv. 5,11) above all creation through his saving acts. For the links between Ps 55 and 59 see introductions to those psalms; for the contrast between Ps 56 and 58 see introductions to those psalms.

Ps 54 A prayer for deliverance from enemies who want to have David killed. The prayer is short, like that of Ps 3; 4; 13; yet it is one of the most typical prayers of the Psalter, containing the main speech functions found in these prayers (see Introduction: Psalm Types). Completely symmetrical, the prayer is framed by David's cry for vindication (v. 1) and his statement of assurance that he will look in triumph on his foes (v. 7). A confession of confidence (v. 4) centers the prayer (see 42:8 and note on 6:6). The opening stanza has two verses, like the conclusion (and both refer to "your name"), while vv. 3,5 each form a separate element in the prayer. On the seven-verse structure see introduction to Ps 29.

54 title *For the director of music.* See note on Ps 4 title. *With stringed instruments.* See note on Ps 4 title. *maskil.* See note on Ps 32 title. *When.* For the event referred to see 1Sa 23:19; see also note on Ps 3 title.

54:1–2 Prayer for God to judge his case (see Ps 17).

54:1 *name.* See v. 6; see also note on 5:11.

54:3 The case against his enemies. *without regard for God.* Like those of Ps 53.

54:4 A confession of confidence at the center of the prayer (see 42:8 and note).

54:5 A call for judicial redress of the evil acts of his enemies (see note on 5:10).

54:6 The vow to praise (see note on 7:17). *name.* See v. 1 and note.

[7]For he has delivered me[w] from all my
troubles,
and my eyes have looked in triumph
on my foes.[x]

Psalm 55

For the director of music.
With stringed instruments. A *maskil*[a]
of David.

[1]Listen to my prayer, O God,
do not ignore my plea;[y]
[2] hear me and answer me.[z]
My thoughts trouble me and I am
distraught[a]
[3] at the voice of the enemy,
at the stares of the wicked;
for they bring down suffering upon
me[b]
and revile[c] me in their anger.[d]

[4]My heart is in anguish[e] within me;
the terrors[f] of death assail me.
[5]Fear and trembling[g] have beset me;
horror[h] has overwhelmed me.
[6]I said, "Oh, that I had the wings of a
dove!
I would fly away and be at rest—
[7]I would flee far away
and stay in the desert;[i] *Selah*
[8]I would hurry to my place of shelter,[j]
far from the tempest and storm.[k]"

[9]Confuse the wicked, O Lord, confound
their speech,[l]
for I see violence and strife[m] in the
city.[n]
[10]Day and night they prowl[o] about on its
walls;
malice and abuse are within it.
[11]Destructive forces[p] are at work in the
city;
threats and lies[q] never leave its
streets.

[12]If an enemy were insulting me,
I could endure it;
if a foe were raising himself against
me,
I could hide from him.
[13]But it is you, a man like myself,
my companion, my close friend,[r]
[14]with whom I once enjoyed sweet
fellowship[s]
as we walked with the throng at the
house of God.[t]

[15]Let death take my enemies by
surprise;[u]
let them go down alive to the
grave,[b][v]
for evil finds lodging among them.

[16]But I call to God,
and the LORD saves me.
[17]Evening,[w] morning[x] and noon[y]
I cry out in distress,
and he hears my voice.
[18]He ransoms me unharmed
from the battle waged against me,
even though many oppose me.

54:7 [w]Ps 34:6 [x]Ps 59:10; 92:11; 112:8; 118:7 **55:1** [y]Ps 27:9; La 3:56 **55:2** [z]Ps 4:1 [a]1Sa 1:15-16; Ps 77:3; 86:6-7; 142:2 **55:3** [b]S 2Sa 16:6-8; Ps 17:9; 143:3 [c]S Ps 44:16 [d]Ps 71:11 **55:4** [e]S Ps 6:3 [f]S Job 18:11 **55:5** [g]S Job 4:14; S 2Co 7:15 [h]Dt 28:67; Isa 21:4; Jer 46:5; 49:5; Eze 7:18 **55:7** [i]1Sa 23:14 **55:8** [j]Ps 31:20 [k]Ps 77:18; Isa 4:6; 25:4; 28:2; 29:6; 32:2 **55:9** [l]Ge 11:9; Ac 2:4 [m]Ps 11:5; Isa 59:6; Jer 6:7; Eze 7:11; Hab 1:3 [n]Ge 4:17 **55:10** [o]1Pe 5:8 **55:11** [p]Ps 5:9 [q]Ps 10:7 **55:13** [r]S 2Sa 15:12 **55:14** [s]Ac 1:16-17 [t]Ps 42:4 **55:15** [u]Ps 64:7; Pr 6:15; Isa 29:5; 47:9, 11; 1Th 5:3 [v]S Ps 49:14 **55:17** [w]Ps 141:2; Ac 3:1; 10:3, 30 [x]Ps 5:3; 88:13; 92:2 [y]Ac 10:9

[a] Title: Probably a literary or musical term
[b] *15* Hebrew *Sheol*

54:7 Assurance of being heard (see note on 3:8).

Ps 55 A prayer for God's help when threatened by a powerful conspiracy in Jerusalem under the leadership of a former friend. (Ps 59 is also a prayer for God's help against powerful foes who "prowl about" [55:10; 59:6,14] the city to achieve their evil ends and whose primary weapon is the mouth; see introduction to Ps 54–60.) The situation described is like that of Absalom's conspiracy against the king (see 2Sa 15–17): The city is in turmoil; danger is everywhere; there is uncertainty as to who can be trusted; rumors, false reports and slander are circulating freely. Under such circumstances David longs for a quiet retreat to escape it all (vv. 6–8). That being out of the question, he casts his cares on the Lord, whom he knows he can trust. In its structure, the prayer is framed by a plea for help (v. 1) and a simple confession of faith: "I trust in you" (v. 23); at the center (v. 15) stands the heart of the prayer. On either side of the center, 12 Hebrew lines link it with the introduction and conclusion, and each of these dozen lines is divided into a similar stanza pattern: five lines, three lines, four lines.

55 title *For the director of music.* See note on Ps 4 title. *With stringed instruments.* See note on Ps 4 title. *maskil.* See note on Ps 32 title.

55:1–3 Initial appeal for God to hear.

55:4–8 His heart's anguish.

55:4–5 Danger is everywhere (see 31:13), a danger so great that it is as if death itself were stalking him (see 18:4–5; 116:3).

55:4 *heart.* See note on 4:7. *terrors of death.* See 1Sa 5:11; 15:32; 28:5; Job 18:14.

55:6–8 He longs for a quiet retreat, away from treacherous and conniving people (see similarly Jer 9:2–6).

55:9–11 Prayer for God to foil the plots of his enemies.

55:9 *Confuse … confound their speech.* Paralyze the conspirators with conflicting designs, as at Babel (Ge 11:5–9; see 2Sa 17:1–14). *the city.* See v. 11; Jerusalem.

55:10 *malice and abuse.* Like watchmen on the walls (see 127:1; 130:6; SS 5:7).

55:11 *threats and lies.* Like watchmen who patrol the city streets (see SS 3:3).

55:12–14 The insults and plots of an enemy can be endured—but those of a treacherous friend?

55:13 *my companion, my close friend.* See v. 20; see also 41:9 and note.

55:14 *at the house of God.* Their ties of friendship had been a bond hallowed by common commitment to the Lord and sealed by its public display in the presence of God and the worshipers at the temple.

55:15 The centered (see note on 6:6) prayer for redress (see note on 5:10). *Let death take my enemies.* The conspirators were seeking his death. *alive to the grave.* May they go to the grave before life has run its normal course (see v. 23; Nu 16:29–33; Pr 1:12; Isa 5:14).

55:16–19 Assurance of being heard (see note on 3:8).

55:17 *Evening, morning and noon I cry out.* Cf. Da 6:10.

55:18 *ransoms.* Here a vivid synonym for "rescues" (see Isa 50:2; Jer 31:11 and note).

[19]God, who is enthroned forever,[z]
will hear[a] them and afflict them—
Selah
men who never change their ways
and have no fear of God.[b]

[20]My companion attacks his friends;[c]
he violates his covenant.[d]
[21]His speech is smooth as butter,[e]
yet war is in his heart;
his words are more soothing than oil,[f]
yet they are drawn swords.[g]

[22]Cast your cares on the LORD
and he will sustain you;[h]
he will never let the righteous fall.[i]
[23]But you, O God, will bring down the wicked
into the pit[j] of corruption;
bloodthirsty and deceitful men[k]
will not live out half their days.[l]

But as for me, I trust in you.[m]

Psalm 56

For the director of music. To ⌞the tune of⌟ "A Dove on Distant Oaks." Of David. A *miktam.*[a] When the Philistines had seized him in Gath.

[1]Be merciful to me,[n] O God, for men
hotly pursue me;[o]
all day long they press their attack.[p]
[2]My slanderers pursue me all day
long;[q]
many are attacking me in their
pride.[r]

[3]When I am afraid,[s]
I will trust in you.[t]
[4]In God, whose word I praise,[u]
in God I trust; I will not be afraid.[v]
What can mortal man do to me?[w]

[5]All day long they twist my words;[x]
they are always plotting to harm
me.
[6]They conspire,[y] they lurk,
they watch my steps,[z]
eager to take my life.[a]
[7]On no account let them escape;[b]
in your anger, O God, bring down
the nations.[c]

[8]Record my lament;
list my tears on your scroll[b][d]—
are they not in your record?[e]
[9]Then my enemies will turn back[f]
when I call for help.[g]
By this I will know that God is
for me.[h]

[10]In God, whose word I praise,
in the LORD, whose word I praise—
[11]in God I trust; I will not be afraid.
What can man do to me?

[12]I am under vows[i] to you, O God;
I will present my thank offerings to
you.

[a] Title: Probably a literary or musical term [b] 8 Or *put my tears in your wineskin*

55:19 [z]S Ex 15:18; Dt 33:27; Ps 29:10 [a]Ps 78:59 [b]Ps 36:1; 64:4 **55:20** [c]Ps 7:4 [d]S Ps 41:9 **55:21** [e]Ps 12:2 [f]Pr 5:3; 6:24 [g]Ps 28:3; 57:4; 59:7; 64:3; Pr 12:18; Rev 1:16 **55:22** [h]S Ps 18:35; Mt 6:25-34; 1Pe 5:7 [i]Ps 15:5; 21:7; 37:24; 112:6 **55:23** [j]Ps 9:15; S 30:3; 73:18; 94:13; Isa 14:15; Eze 28:8; S Lk 8:31 [k]Ps 5:6 [l]S Job 15:32 [m]Ps 11:1; 25:2; 56:3 **56:1** [n]Ps 6:2 [o]Ps 57:1-3 [p]Ps 17:9 **56:2** [q]Ps 35:25; 124:3 [r]Ps 35:1 **56:3** [s]Ps 55:4-5 [t]S Ps 55:23 **56:4** [u]ver 10 [v]S Ps 27:1 [w]Ps 118:6; Mt 10:28; Heb 13:6 **56:5** [x]Ps 41:7; 2Pe 3:16 **56:6** [y]Ps 59:3; 94:21; Mk 3:6 [z]Ps 17:11 [a]Ps 71:10 **56:7** [b]Pr 19:5; Eze 17:15; Ro 2:3; Heb 12:25 [c]Ps 36:12; 55:23 **56:8** [d]S 2Ki 20:5 [e]Isa 4:3; Da 7:10; 12:1; Mal 3:16 **56:9** [f]Ps 9:3 [g]Ps 102:2 [h]S Nu 14:8; S Dt 31:6; Ro 8:31 **56:12** [i]Ps 50:14

55:19 He who is the eternal King will deal with those who "never change their ways" and show "no fear of God" (see 36:1 and note; see also Ps 14; 53).
55:20–21 Further sorrowful (or angry) reflection over the treachery of his former friend.
55:20 *his friends.* Lit. "those at peace with him" (see 7:4).
55:21 See 28:3; Pr 5:3–4; see also note on 5:9. *heart.* See note on 4:7.
55:22–23 Once more, assurance of being heard.
55:22 A testimony to all who are assembled at the temple. 1Pe 5:7 echoes this assurance. *righteous.* See note on 1:5.
55:23 *pit of corruption.* The grave (see note on 30:1). *not live out half their days.* See note on v. 15.
Ps 56 A prayer for help when the psalmist is attacked by enemies and his very life is threatened. It is marked by consoling trust in the face of unsettling fear. Structurally, the prayer falls into two balanced halves of seven Hebrew lines each, as does Ps 57 (see introduction to that psalm). The structure of each half is the same (two lines, two lines, three lines) with a refrain at the center of each (on the use of refrains see introduction to Ps 42–43). The whole is framed by an urgent appeal to God (vv. 1–2) and a word of confident assurance (vv. 12–13). This confidence in God's defense and deliverance stands in sharp contrast to the failure of wicked earthly rulers referred to in Ps 58.
56 title *For the director of music.* See note on Ps 4 title. *To ⌞the tune of⌟.* See note on Ps 9 title. *miktam.* See note on Ps 16 title. *When.* See note on Ps 3 title. For the event referred to see 1Sa 21:10–15; see also Ps 34 title and note. *had seized.* Or "were about to seize."
56:1–2 Initial appeal for God's help.
56:2 *My slanderers.* The enemies' chief weapon is the tongue (see note on 5:9). *their pride.* Confident in their position of strength, they take no account of David's God (see notes on 3:2; 5:9; 10:11).
56:3–4 See vv. 10–11; confession of trust in the face of fear.
56:4 *word.* God's reassuring promise that he will be the God of his people and will come to their aid when they appeal to him (see 50:15; 91:15; see also 119:74,81; 130:5). *mortal man.* Lit. "flesh"—i.e., human feebleness compared with God's power (see note on 10:18).
56:5–7 Accusation and call for redress (see note on 5:9–10).
56:5 *twist my words.* See notes on v. 2; 3:2; 5:9; 10:11.
56:7 See note on 5:10. *anger.* See note on 2:5.
56:8–9 Appeal for God to take special note of the psalmist's troubles.
56:8 *Record ... list ... on your scroll.* Record my troubles in your heavenly royal records as matters calling for your action (see note on 51:1).
56:9 If God takes such note of his tears that he records them in his book, he will surely respond to David's call for help.
56:10–11 Renewed confession of trust in the face of fear (see vv. 3–4).
56:12–13 Assurance of being heard (see note on 3:8).
56:12 *I am under vows.* Speaking as if his prayer has already been heard, David acknowledges that now he must keep the vows he made to God when he was in trouble (see 66:14 and note on 7:17).

13 For you have delivered me[a] from
death[j]
and my feet from stumbling,
that I may walk before God
in the light of life.[b][k]

Psalm 57

57:7-11pp — Ps 108:1-5

For the director of music. ⌞To the tune of⌟ "Do Not Destroy." Of David. A *miktam.*[c] When he had fled from Saul into the cave.[l]

1 Have mercy on me, O God, have mercy
on me,
for in you my soul takes refuge.[m]
I will take refuge in the shadow of your
wings[n]
until the disaster has passed.[o]

2 I cry out to God Most High,
to God, who fulfills ⌞his purpose⌟ for
me.[p]
3 He sends from heaven and saves me,[q]
rebuking those who hotly pursue
me;[r] *Selah*
God sends his love and his
faithfulness.[s]

4 I am in the midst of lions;[t]
I lie among ravenous beasts—
men whose teeth are spears and
arrows,
whose tongues are sharp swords.[u]

5 Be exalted, O God, above the heavens;
let your glory be over all the earth.[v]

6 They spread a net for my feet[w]—
I was bowed down[x] in distress.
They dug a pit[y] in my path—
but they have fallen into it
themselves.[z] *Selah*

7 My heart is steadfast, O God,
my heart is steadfast;[a]
I will sing and make music.
8 Awake, my soul!
Awake, harp and lyre![b]
I will awaken the dawn.

9 I will praise you, O Lord, among the
nations;
I will sing of you among the peoples.
10 For great is your love, reaching to the
heavens;
your faithfulness reaches to the
skies.[c]

11 Be exalted, O God, above the heavens;[d]
let your glory be over all the earth.[e]

Psalm 58

For the director of music. ⌞To the tune of⌟ "Do Not Destroy." Of David. A *miktam.*[c]

1 Do you rulers indeed speak justly?[f]
Do you judge uprightly among men?

[a] 13 Or *my soul* [b] 13 Or *the land of the living*
[c] Title: Probably a literary or musical term

56:13 [j] Ps 30:3; 33:19; 49:15; 86:13; 107:20; 116:8 [k] S Job 33:30 **57:Title** [l] 1Sa 22:1; 24:3; Ps 142 Title **57:1** [m] Ps 2:12; 9:9; 34:22 [n] S Ru 2:12; S Mt 23:37 [o] Isa 26:20 **57:2** [p] Ps 138:8 **57:3** [q] Ps 18:9,16; 69:14; 142:6; 144:5,7 [r] Ps 56:1 [s] Ps 25:10; 40:11; 115:1 **57:4** [t] S Ps 35:17 [u] S Ps 55:21; Pr 30:14 **57:5** [v] ver 11; Ps 108:5 **57:6** [w] Ps 10:9; 31:4; 140:5 [x] S Ps 38:6; 145:14 [y] S Ps 9:15 [z] S Est 6:13; Ps 7:15; Pr 28:10; Ecc 10:8 **57:7** [a] Ps 112:7 **57:8** [b] Ps 33:2; 149:3; 150:3 **57:10** [c] S Ps 36:5 **57:11** [d] S Ps 8:1; 113:4 [e] S ver 5 **58:1** [f] Ps 82:2

56:13 *me.* See NIV text note; see also note on 6:3. *stumbling.* See note on 35:15. *before God.* See note on 11:7. *light of life.* The full blessedness of life (see note on 36:9).

Ps 57 A prayer for deliverance when threatened by fierce enemies (it has many links with Ps 56). The psalm appears to reflect the imagery of the night of danger (v. 4: "I lie [down]") followed by the morning of salvation (v. 8: "I will awaken the dawn"). For other instances of these associations see 30:5; 46:5; 59:6,14,16; 63:1,6; 90:14. Verses 7–11 are used again in 108:1–5. Structurally, the prayer is made up of two balanced halves, each having seven Hebrew lines and each composed of three couplets and a refrain (see introduction to Ps 56; see also introduction to Ps 54). For the placement of this psalm in the arrangement of Book II of the Psalter see introduction to Ps 42–45; see also introduction to Ps 54–60.

57 title See note on Ps 56 title. *Do Not Destroy.* See Ps 58; 59; 75 titles. *When.* For the event referred to see 1Sa 24:1–3; see also Ps 142 title.

57:1–5 The prayer.

57:1 Initial cry for God's merciful help. *my soul.* Or "I," as in v. 4, where the first "I" is lit. "My soul" (see note on 6:3). *shadow of your wings.* See note on 17:8.

57:2–3 Confidence of being heard.

57:2 *Most High.* See note on Ge 14:19. *who fulfills ⌞his purpose⌟ for me.* See 138:8. God will not let David's enemies thwart his divine purposes for anointing him king (see 1Sa 16:1,12; 2Sa 7). But the Hebrew can also be translated "who makes an end ⌞of troubles⌟ for me" (see 7:9).

57:3 *He sends.* God sends his love and faithfulness (here personified; see note on 23:6) as his messengers from heaven to save his servant (see note on 43:3). *his love and his faithfulness.* See note on 26:3. *love.* See note on 6:4.

57:4 The threatening situation. *I lie.* As a sheep among lions. *ravenous beasts.* The psalmists often compare their enemies to ferocious beasts (see note on 7:2). (The use of the metaphor here has no connection with the description of Saul and Jonathan in 2Sa 1:23.) *tongues.* See note on 5:9.

57:5 A prayer for God to show his exalted power and glory throughout his creation by coming to his servant's rescue (see 7:6–7; 21:13; 46:10; 59:5,8; 113:4–9; cf. Ex 14:4; Isa 26:15; 44:23; 59:19; see also note on Ps 46:10).

57:6–11 Praise for God's saving help—confidently anticipating the desired deliverance. For such a sudden transition from prayer to assurance see note on 3:8.

57:6 The threat and its outcome: The enemies suffer the calamity they plotted. *net ... pit.* They hunted him as if he were a wild beast, but the "lions" themselves were caught (see 7:15; 9:15 and notes).

57:7 All cause for fear has been removed. *heart.* See note on 4:7. *is steadfast.* Feels secure (see 112:7).

57:8 *Awake ... Awake.* Greet with joy the dawn of the day of deliverance (see Isa 51:9,17; 52:1). *soul.* Lit. "glory" (see note on 7:5). *harp and lyre.* Instruments (here personified) to accompany the praise of the Lord at his temple in celebration of deliverance (see 71:22; 81:2 and note on Ps 4 title). *awaken the dawn.* With joyful cries proclaiming God's saving act. (Dawn, too, is here personified—the Canaanites even deified it.)

57:9–10 The vow to praise (see notes on 7:17; 9:1).

57:10 *love.* See note on 6:4. *love ... faithfulness.* That is, love-and-faithfulness (see v. 3 and note on 36:5; see also note on 3:7). *reaching to the heavens ... to the skies.* See note on 36:5.

57:11 The refrain (see v. 5), but now as praise (see 18:46; 30:1; 34:3; 35:27; 40:16; 70:4; 92:8; 97:9; 99:2; 113:4; 148:13).

Ps 58 A prayer for God, the supreme Judge, to set human affairs right, judging those rulers who corrupt

2No, in your heart you devise injustice,[g]
and your hands mete out violence
on the earth.[h]
3Even from birth the wicked go astray;
from the womb they are wayward
and speak lies.
4Their venom is like the venom of a
snake,[i]
like that of a cobra that has stopped
its ears,
5that will not heed[j] the tune of the
charmer,[k]
however skillful the enchanter
may be.
6Break the teeth in their mouths,
O God;[l]
tear out, O LORD, the fangs of the
lions![m]
7Let them vanish like water that flows
away;[n]
when they draw the bow, let their
arrows be blunted.[o]
8Like a slug melting away as it moves
along,[p]
like a stillborn child,[q] may they
not see the sun.
9Before your pots can feel ˻the heat of˼
the thorns[r]—
whether they be green or dry—
the wicked will be swept
away.[a] [s]
10The righteous will be glad[t] when they
are avenged,[u]
when they bathe their feet in the
blood of the wicked.[v]
11Then men will say,
"Surely the righteous still are
rewarded;[w]
surely there is a God who judges
the earth."[x]

58:2 [g]Mt 15:19 [h]Ps 94:20; Isa 10:1; Lk 6:38 **58:4** [i]S Nu 21:6 **58:5** [j]Ps 81:11 [k]Ecc 10:11; Jer 8:17 **58:6** [l]Ps 3:7 [m]S Job 4:10 **58:7** [n]S Lev 26:36; S Job 11:16 [o]Ps 11:2; 57:4; 64:3 **58:8** [p]Isa 13:7 [q]S Job 3:16 **58:9** [r]Ps 118:12; Ecc 7:6 [s]S Job 7:10; S 21:18 **58:10** [t]S Job 22:19 [u]Dt 32:35; Ps 7:9; 91:8; Jer 11:20; Ro 12:17-21 [v]Ps 68:23 **58:11** [w]S Ge 15:1; S Ps 128:2; Lk 6:23 [x]S Ge 18:25

[a] *9* The meaning of the Hebrew for this verse is uncertain.

justice and championing the cause of the righteous. (The psalm was applied by the early church to Jesus' trial before the Sanhedrin; see Mt 26:57–68 and parallels.) Concern for the just use of judicial power is pervasive throughout the OT. This was the primary agency in the administrative structures of the ancient Near East for the protection of the innocent (usually the poor and powerless) against the assaults of unscrupulous people (usually the rich and powerful). Israelite society was troubled with the corruption of this judicial power from the days of Samuel to the end of the monarchy (see, e.g., 1Sa 8:3; Isa 1:23; 5:23; 10:1–2; Eze 22:6,12; Am 5:7,10–13; Mic 3:1–3,9–11; 7:2). Even in David's time all was not well (see 2Sa 15:1–4). For the central concern of this psalm see Ps 82. In the arrangement of the Psalter, Ps 58 stands in counterpoint to Ps 56 (see introduction to that psalm).

Structurally, the psalm is framed by a rhetorical address to the wicked judges (vv. 1–2) and by a reassuring word to "the righteous" (vv. 9–11). The frame emphasizes the fact that those who do not judge uprightly (v. 1) will be judged by God (v. 11). Between the framing verses, two three-verse stanzas flesh out the theme: Verses 3–5 elaborate on the ways of the wicked rulers, and vv. 6–8 call for their disablement and removal.

58 title *For the director of music.* See note on Ps 4 title. *˻To the tune of˼.* See note on Ps 9 title. *Do Not Destroy.* See Ps 57; 59; 75 titles. *miktam.* See note on Ps 16 title.

58:1–5 Accusation against the wicked judges.

58:1–2 Direct challenge to the wicked rulers: Their mouths, hearts and hands are united in the pursuit of injustice.

58:1 *rulers.* Lit. "gods" (see Ps 82:1 and note; see also introduction to Ps 82), a title applied to those whose administrative positions called upon them to act as earthly representatives of God's heavenly court (see NIV text notes on Ex 21:6; 22:8–9; see also Dt 1:17; 2Ch 19:6 and note on Ps 45:6). *speak justly.* Make just judicial pronouncements.

58:2 *heart.* See note on 4:7. *mete out violence.* Issue decisions that result in cruel injustice.

58:3–5 The depth and stubbornness of the rulers' wickedness.

58:3 *from birth ... from the womb.* Their corrupt ways are not sporadic; they act in accordance with their nature (see 51:5). Here reference is to "the wicked"; the author does not make a general statement about all people, as is the case in Ge 6:5; 8:21; Job 14:4; 15:14–16; 25:4–6. *the wicked.* Most probably a characterization of the rulers. For a description of the wicked in general see Ps 10. *speak lies.* They have never been concerned for the truth (see Jn 8:44).

58:4 *venom.* What issues from their mouths is as cruel and deadly as the venom of snakes (see 140:3; Mt 23:33; Jas 3:8). *stopped its ears.* They are incorrigible; nothing—neither appeals nor threats—will move them.

58:6–8 Appeal for God to defang the wicked rulers and purge the land of such perverse judges. The author uses imagery drawn from conventional curses of the ancient Near East (see note on 5:10).

58:6 Let the weapons of their mouths (see 57:4) be broken and torn out. *lions.* See note on 7:2.

58:7 *water that flows away.* And is absorbed by the ground. *arrows.* Malicious pronouncements (see 57:4—but the Hebrew of the whole clause is obscure).

58:8 *slug.* That appears to dry up to nothing as it moves over a stone in the hot sun.

58:9–11 Assurance that God will surely judge them (see note on 3:8).

58:9 See NIV text note. The verse may be speaking picturesquely of the speed of God's judgment—speed probably signifying here the inescapable certainty of his judgment (see note on 37:10; see also Lk 18:7–8). *thorns.* Twigs from wild thornbushes were used as fuel for quick heat (see 118:12; Ecc 7:6). *swept away.* As by a storm—God's storm (see Job 27:21).

58:10 *righteous.* Here a judicial term for those who are in the right but who have been wronged (see note on 1:5). *when they are avenged.* When the wrongs committed against them are redressed. *bathe their feet in the blood.* Vivid imagery borrowed from the literary conventions of the ancient Near East (see 68:23). Its origin is the exaggerated language of triumphant reports of victory on the battlefield.

58:11 The climax: When God has judged the unjust "gods" (see note on v. 1), all people will see that right ultimately triumphs under God's just rule (see note on 46:10; see also Ps 93; 96–99). No more will people despair, like those in Mal 3:15.

Psalm 59

For the director of music. ⌞To the tune of⌟ "Do Not Destroy." Of David. A *miktam*.[a] When Saul had sent men to watch David's house[y] in order to kill him.

[1]Deliver me from my enemies, O God;[z]
protect me from those who rise up against me.[a]
[2]Deliver me from evildoers[b]
and save me from bloodthirsty men.[c]
[3]See how they lie in wait for me!
Fierce men conspire[d] against me
for no offense or sin of mine,
O LORD.
[4]I have done no wrong,[e] yet they are ready to attack me.[f]
Arise to help me; look on my plight![g]
[5]O LORD God Almighty, the God of Israel,[h]
rouse yourself[i] to punish all the nations;[j]
show no mercy to wicked traitors.[k]
Selah

[6]They return at evening,
snarling like dogs,[l]
and prowl about the city.
[7]See what they spew from their mouths[m]—
they spew out swords[n] from their lips,
and they say, "Who can hear us?"[o]
[8]But you, O LORD, laugh at them;[p]
you scoff at all those nations.[q]
[9]O my Strength,[r] I watch for you;
you, O God, are my fortress,[s] [10]my loving God.

God will go before me
and will let me gloat over those who slander me.
[11]But do not kill them, O Lord our shield,[b][t]
or my people will forget.[u]
In your might make them wander about,
and bring them down.[v]
[12]For the sins of their mouths,[w]
for the words of their lips,[x]
let them be caught in their pride.[y]
For the curses and lies they utter,
[13]consume them in wrath,
consume them till they are no more.[z]
Then it will be known to the ends of the earth
that God rules over Jacob.[a]
Selah

59:Title [y]1Sa 19:11 **59:1** [z]Ps 143:9 [a]S Ps 20:1 **59:2** [b]Ps 14:4; 36:12; 53:4; 92:7; 94:16 [c]S Ps 26:9; 139:19; Pr 29:10 **59:3** [d]S Ps 56:6 **59:4** [e]Ps 119:3 [f]Mt 5:11 [g]S Ps 13:3 **59:5** [h]Ps 69:6; 80:4; 84:8 [i]S Ps 44:23 [j]S Ps 9:5; S Isa 10:3 [k]Jer 18:23 **59:6** [l]ver 14; Ps 22:16 **59:7** [m]Ps 94:4; Pr 10:32; 12:23; 15:2,28 [n]S Ps 55:21 [o]S Job 22:13 **59:8** [p]Ps 37:13; Pr 1:26 [q]Ps 2:4 **59:9** [r]S Ps 18:1 [s]Ps 9:9; 18:2; 62:2; 71:3 **59:11** [t]Ps 3:3; 84:9 [u]Dt 4:9; 6:12 [v]Ps 89:10; 106:27; 144:6; Isa 33:3 **59:12** [w]Ps 10:7 [x]Ps 64:8; Pr 10:14; 12:13 [y]Isa 2:12; 5:15; Zep 3:11 **59:13** [z]Ps 104:35 [a]Ps 83:18

[a] Title: Probably a literary or musical term
[b] 11 Or *sovereign*

Ps 59 A prayer for deliverance when endangered by enemy attacks (for links with Ps 55 see introduction to that psalm; see also introduction to Ps 54–60). If originally composed by David under the circumstances noted in the superscription, it must have been revised for use by one of David's royal sons when Jerusalem was under siege by a hostile force made up of troops from many nations—as when Hezekiah was besieged by the Assyrians (see 2Ki 18:19). (Some, however, ascribe it to Nehemiah; see Ne 4.) The enemy weapon most prominent is the tongue, attacking with slander and curses (see note on 5:9). In this psalm, too, the imagery of the night of danger (vv. 6,14), followed by the morning of deliverance (v. 16), is evoked (see introduction to Ps 57).

Regarding the structure, each of the two closely balanced halves of the psalm (vv. 1–9,10–17) concludes with an almost identical refrain (vv. 9,17), preceded by a stanza that begins with a like characterization of the enemies (vv. 6,14). The first half of the psalm is predominantly prayer, the second half predominantly assurance of deliverance. The whole is framed by a cry for protection (v. 1) and a joyful confession that God is the psalmist's "fortress" (v. 17, in Hebrew an echo of the word for "protect" in v. 1).

59 title See note on Ps 56 title. *Do Not Destroy.* See Ps 57; 58; 75 titles. *When.* For the event referred to see 1Sa 19:11.

59:1–2 The cry for deliverance.

59:1 *protect me.* Lit. "raise me to a high, secure place."

59:2 *evildoers … bloodthirsty men.* Common characterizations of those who attack the psalmists out of malice.

59:3–5 By slander (v. 10) and lies (v. 12) the enemies seek to justify their attacks, but the psalmist protests his innocence and pleads with God to judge those who wrong him (see 58:11).

59:3 *lie in wait.* See 10:8–9 and note on 7:2.

59:4 *Arise.* See note on 3:7.

59:5 *LORD God Almighty.* See note on 1Sa 1:3. *God of Israel.* This appeal to the Lord as the God of Israel to punish the nations makes clear that the attack on the psalmist involves an attack by the nations on Israel. *rouse yourself.* See note on 7:6. *punish … show no mercy.* See note on 5:10. *traitors.* Whether Israelites had joined in the attack is not clear; the Hebrew indicates only that the enemies were treacherous.

59:6–8 Confidence: Surely God mocks such a pack of dogs (see 22:16–17).

59:6 *about the city.* The enemies besiege the city like dogs at night on the prowl for food (see vv. 14–15).

59:7 *swords from their lips.* Their "curses and lies" (v. 12). For the imagery see 57:4; see also note on 5:9. *they say.* See note on 3:2.

59:9 *watch.* Hebrew *shamar* (see note on v. 17). This verb is used similarly in 31:6; Jnh 2:8 ("cling to"); the basic idea appears to be to "look to expectantly" for help. The psalmist watches as one who longingly waits for the morning (of salvation); see 130:6.

59:10–13 The prayer renewed. Confident that the Lord will hear his prayer (v. 10) and will punish the nations (v. 5), the psalmist prays that God will not sweep them away suddenly but will prolong their punishment so that Israel ("my people," v. 11) will not forget God's acts of salvation, as they had done so often before (see 78:11; 106:13). Nevertheless, the psalmist asks God not to allow the enemies to escape the full consequences of their malice (vv. 12–13).

59:10 *loving.* See note on 6:4. *slander.* See note on 5:9.

59:11 *shield.* See note on 3:3. *wander about.* Like vagabonds, with no place to settle (see Ge 4:12; 2Sa 15:20; La 4:15) and having to hunt for food (like dogs, v. 15; see 109:10; Am 4:8).

59:12 See note on v. 7. *caught in their pride.* Let the pride with which they treacherously attack the Lord's servant and his people be the trap that catches them. *curses and lies.* See 10:7; Ge 12:3 and notes.

59:13 *Then it will be known.* When God has thus dealt with Israel's enemies, all the world will acknowledge that the Judge

[14]They return at evening,
snarling like dogs,
and prowl about the city.
[15]They wander about for food[b]
and howl if not satisfied.
[16]But I will sing[c] of your strength,[d]
in the morning[e] I will sing of your
love;[f]
for you are my fortress,[g]
my refuge in times of trouble.[h]

[17]O my Strength, I sing praise to you;
you, O God, are my fortress, my
loving God.[i]

Psalm 60

60:5-12pp — Ps 108:6-13

For the director of music. To ⌊the tune of⌋ "The Lily of the Covenant." A *miktam*[a] of David. For teaching. When he fought Aram Naharaim[b] and Aram Zobah,[c] and when Joab returned and struck down twelve thousand Edomites in the Valley of Salt.[j]

[1]You have rejected us,[k] O God, and
burst forth upon us;
you have been angry[l]—now restore
us![m]
[2]You have shaken the land[n] and torn it
open;
mend its fractures,[o] for it is quaking.
[3]You have shown your people desperate
times;[p]
you have given us wine that makes
us stagger.[q]

[4]But for those who fear you, you have
raised a banner[r]
to be unfurled against the bow. *Selah*
[5]Save us and help us with your right
hand,[s]
that those you love[t] may be
delivered.
[6]God has spoken from his sanctuary:
"In triumph I will parcel out
Shechem[u]
and measure off the Valley of
Succoth.[v]
[7]Gilead[w] is mine, and Manasseh is
mine;
Ephraim[x] is my helmet,
Judah[y] my scepter.[z]

59:15 [b]Job 15:23 **59:16** [c]Ps 108:1 [d]S 1Sa 2:10 [e]Ps 5:3; 88:13 [f]Ps 101:1 [g]S 2Sa 22:3 [h]S Dt 4:30 **59:17** [i]ver 10 **60:Title** [j]2Sa 8:13 **60:1** [k]2Sa 5:20; Ps 44:9 [l]Ps 79:5 [m]Ps 80:3 **60:2** [n]Ps 18:7 [o]S 2Ch 7:14 **60:3** [p]Ps 71:20 [q]Ps 75:8; Isa 29:9; 51:17; 63:6; Jer 25:16; Zec 12:2; Rev 14:10 **60:4** [r]Isa 5:26; 11:10,12; 18:3 **60:5** [s]S Job 40:14 [t]S Dt 33:12 **60:6** [u]S Ge 12:6 [v]S Ge 33:17 **60:7** [w]Jos 13:31 [x]S Ge 41:52 [y]S Nu 34:19 [z]S Ge 49:10

[a] Title: Probably a literary or musical term [b] Title: That is, Arameans of Northwest Mesopotamia [c] Title: That is, Arameans of central Syria

of all the earth (see 58:11) is the God of Israel. *Jacob.* See note on 14:7.

59:14–16 Assurance of being heard (see note on 3:8). Just as God mocks the defiant pack of dogs (vv. 6–8), so the psalmist will sing for joy at God's triumph over them.

59:16 *strength ... love ... fortress.* See the refrain (vv. 9,17). *morning.* See introduction.

59:17 The vow to praise (see note on 7:17). *sing.* Hebrew *zamar* (see note on v. 9). The play on words in the refrain marks an advance from looking to God for help in the night of danger to singing in the morning of salvation (cf. 57:8 and note; cf. also 30:5).

Ps 60 A national prayer for God's help after suffering a severe blow by a foreign nation, presumably Edom (see v. 9). The prayer leader may have been the king (the "me" in v. 9), as in 2Ch 20. The lament that God has "rejected" (vv. 1,10) his people and no longer goes out "with our armies" (v. 10) links the psalm with Ps 44 (see 44:9; see also introduction to Ps 54–60). Verses 5–12 appear again in 108:6–13. As for its structure, the prayer is framed by three verses lamenting God's rejection of his people (vv. 1–3) and three verses expressing confidence that the God who has rejected them will yet give them victory (vv. 10–12). This transition from lament to confidence constitutes the overarching movement of the prayer.

60 title See note on Ps 56 title. *The Lily of the Covenant.* See Ps 80 title and note on Ps 45 title. *For teaching.* Only here in the psalm titles. For other songs that Israel was to learn see Dt 31:19,21; 2Sa 1:18. That it was intended for a variety of uses, especially to convey confidence in times of national threat, is illustrated by its use in Ps 108. *When.* For the events referred to see 2Sa 8; 1Ch 18 (perhaps also 2Sa 10). If the tradition that assigns the prayer to these events is correct, it must be supposed that our knowledge of the events is incomplete, since these accounts do not mention Edom. The Israelite war against Edom at this time of great northern battles may have been occasioned by an attack on the part of Edom trying to take advantage of Israel's preoccupation elsewhere, an attack in which Edom succeeded in overrunning the garrisons that guarded Judah's southern borders.

60:1–3 Lament over God's rejection of his people (see 44:9–16; 89:38–45) and prayer for restoration.

60:1 *rejected us.* At least momentarily (see 30:5). Defeat by the enemy is interpreted as a sign of God's anger (though no reason for that anger is noted, and the bond between Israel and God is not broken). *burst forth.* Like a flood (see 2Sa 5:20).

60:2 *shaken the land.* As by a devastating earthquake—such as was occasionally experienced in ancient Canaan.

60:3 *wine that makes us stagger.* God has made them drink from the cup of his wrath rather than from his cup of blessing and salvation (see note on 16:5).

60:4 *those who fear you.* Your people, in distinction from the nations (see 61:5; see also note on Ge 20:11). *banner.* Possibly the reassuring word from God recited in vv. 6–8 (see Ex 17:15). *bow.* The enemy armed with bows.

60:5–8 The petition (v. 5) followed by a reassuring oracle from the Lord (vv. 6–8)—perhaps recalling an already ancient word from the time of the conquest. If so, it may have been preserved in the "Book of the Wars of the LORD" (Nu 21:14). In any event, the Lord is depicted as Israel's triumphant Warrior-King (see Ex 15:3,13–18).

60:5 *those you love.* The Hebrew for this expression is here a word of special endearment, as in 127:2; 2Sa 12:25; Jer 11:15.

60:6 *parcel out ... measure off.* Divide his conquered territory among his servant people who were with him in the battles. *Shechem ... Succoth.* Places representative of the territory west and east of the Jordan taken over by the Lord and Israel (see Ge 33:17–18; 1Ki 12:25).

60:7 Israel is the Lord's kingdom—both the land he conquered and his people he settled in it. *Gilead ... Manasseh.* Half of Manasseh was established in Gilead, east of the Jordan, and half of it west of the Jordan, just north of Ephraim (see Jos 13:29–31; 17:5–11). This once again showed that the Lord's kingdom included territory both east and west of the Jordan. *Ephraim ... Judah.* The two leading tribes of Israel, the one representative of the Rachel tribes (Ephraim) in the north, the other of the Leah tribes (Judah) in the south; see Ge 48:13–20; 49:8–12; Nu 2:3,18; Jos 15–16. Together they rep-

[8]Moab is my washbasin,
upon Edom I toss my sandal;
over Philistia I shout in triumph.[a]"
[9]Who will bring me to the fortified city?
Who will lead me to Edom?
[10]Is it not you, O God, you who have
rejected us
and no longer go out with our
armies?[b]
[11]Give us aid against the enemy,
for the help of man is worthless.[c]
[12]With God we will gain the victory,
and he will trample down our
enemies.[d]

Psalm 61

For the director of music.
With stringed instruments. Of David.

[1]Hear my cry, O God;[e]
listen to my prayer.[f]
[2]From the ends of the earth I call to
you,
I call as my heart grows faint;[g]
lead me to the rock[h] that is higher
than I.
[3]For you have been my refuge,[i]
a strong tower against the foe.[j]
[4]I long to dwell[k] in your tent forever
and take refuge in the shelter of
your wings.[l] *Selah*
[5]For you have heard my vows,[m] O God;
you have given me the heritage of
those who fear your name.[n]
[6]Increase the days of the king's life,[o]
his years for many generations.[p]
[7]May he be enthroned in God's
presence forever;[q]
appoint your love and faithfulness to
protect him.[r]
[8]Then will I ever sing praise to your
name[s]
and fulfill my vows day after day.[t]

60:8 [a]S 2Sa 8:1 **60:10** [b]S Jos 7:12 **60:11** [c]Ps 146:3; Pr 3:5 **60:12** [d]S Job 40:12; Ps 44:5 **61:1** [e]Ps 64:1 [f]Ps 4:1; 86:6 **61:2** [g]S Ps 6:2 [h]Ps 18:2; 31:2; 94:22 **61:3** [i]Ps 9:9; S 46:1; 62:7 [j]Ps 59:9; Pr 18:10 **61:4** [k]S Ps 15:1 [l]S Dt 32:11; S Mt 23:37 **61:5** [m]S Nu 30:2; Ps 56:12 [n]S Ex 6:3; S Dt 33:9; Ne 1:11; Ps 102:15; Isa 59:19; Mt 6:9 **61:6** [o]1Ki 3:14 [p]S Ps 21:4 **61:7** [q]S Ps 41:12; Lk 22:69; Eph 1:20; Col 3:1 [r]Ps 40:11 **61:8** [s]S Ex 15:1; Ps 7:17; 30:4 [t]S Nu 30:2; S Dt 23:21

resented all Israel (Isa 11:13; Zec 9:13). *helmet.* As a powerful and aggressive tribe (Dt 33:17; Jdg 7:24—8:3; 12:1), Ephraim figuratively represents the Lord's helmet. *scepter.* Called such because from Judah would come (Ge 49:10)—and had now come (1Sa 16:1–13)—the Lord's chosen earthly regent over his people (see 2Sa 7).
60:8 *Moab ... Edom ... Philistia.* Perpetual enemies on Israel's eastern, southern and western borders respectively (see Ex 15:14–15; see also Ex 13:17; Nu 20:14–21; 22–24). *is my washbasin.* Is reduced to a household vessel in which the Lord washes his feet (Ge 18:4). The metaphor is perhaps suggested by the fact that Moab lay along the east shore of the Dead Sea. *toss my sandal.* Perhaps refers to the conventional symbolic act by which one claimed possession of land (cf. Ru 4:7).
60:9–12 The closing stanza, expressing confidence of victory (see note on 3:8).
60:9 *me ... me.* Possibly referring to the king (see introduction), though the praying community may be referring to itself collectively (see note on Ps 30 title). *lead me.* As God went before his people into battle in the desert (Ex 13:21) and during the conquest (Ex 23:27–28; 33:2; Dt 9:3; 31:8).
60:10 *rejected.* See v. 1.
60:11 *help.* Lit. "salvation" (see v. 5, "Save"). *of man.* See 33:17.
60:12 *gain the victory.* Lit. "do mighty things." With God's help Israel will achieve in a manner similar to that of the Lord himself (see 118:15–16) and will triumph over Edom (see Nu 24:18, "grow strong"). *trample down.* Like a victorious warrior (see Isa 14:19,25; Jer 12:10; Zec 10:5).
Ps 61–64 A series of four psalms linked together by the common theme of strong reliance on God for deliverance in the face of great—perhaps mortal—danger. Two make explicit reference to the king (Ps 61; 63), and the other two (62; 64) may also represent a royal voice, though this is disputed. All have been crafted with considerable care.
Ps 61 A prayer for restoration to God's presence. The circumstances appear to be similar to those referred to in Ps 42–43. Here, however, a king is involved (v. 6), and if the author was David, he may have composed this prayer at the time of his flight from Absalom (see 2Sa 17:21–29). For another possibility see note on v. 2. Structurally, the prayer is framed by a cry to God (v. 1) and a vow to praise (v. 8). The body of the psalm is composed of three couplets: vv. 2–3,4–5,6–7.
61 title See note on Ps 4 title.
61:1 Initial plea for God to hear.
61:2–3 The prayer.
61:2 *ends of the earth.* So it seemed (see 42:6). Possibly the phrase here refers to the brink of the netherworld, i.e., the grave (see 63:9); the psalmist feels himself near death. *heart.* See note on 4:7. *lead me.* See 23:2. *rock.* Secure place (see 27:5; 40:2). *higher than I.* The place of security that he seeks is beyond his reach; only God can bring him to it. Since God is often confessed by the psalmists to be their "rock of refuge" (31:2; 71:3; see also 18:2; 62:2,6–7; 94:22), it may be that God himself is that higher "rock" (the secure refuge) that the psalmist pleads for (see v. 3). Or it may be the secure refuge of God's sanctuary (see v. 4; see also 27:5).
61:3 The reason he appeals to God: God has never failed him as a refuge. *foe.* If this is a prayer when faced with death, death is the present foe (see 68:20; 141:8; Job 33:22; Isa 25:8; 28:15; Jer 9:21; Hos 13:14; see also 1Co 15:26). See note on 49:14.
61:4–5 Longing for the security of God's sanctuary (see 27:5 and note).
61:4 *dwell in.* See note on 15:1. *tent.* Residence (see 2Sa 6:17; 7:2; 1Ki 1:39; 2:28–30). *shelter of your wings.* See note on 17:8.
61:5 The reason for his longing: Either (1) because God has been so responsive to him in the past, or (2) confidence that his longing is about to be satisfied. *my vows.* The vows that accompanied his prayers (see 50:14; 66:14; see also note on 7:17). *heritage.* A place with God's people in the promised land, together with all that the Lord had promised to give and to be to his people (see 16:6; 37:18; 135:12; 136:21–22). *those who fear.* See 60:4 and note. *your name.* See note on 5:11.
61:6–7 Prayer for the king's long life. The king himself may have made this prayer—such transitions to the third person are known from the literature of the ancient Near East—or it may be the prayer of the people, perhaps voiced by a priest or Levite. Later Jewish interpretations (e.g., in the Aramaic Targums) applied these verses to the Messiah. They are fulfilled in Christ, David's great Son.
61:6 May the king live forever (see note on 45:6).
61:7 *enthroned in God's presence.* See note on 41:12. *love and faithfulness.* Personified as God's agents (see notes on 23:6; 43:3; see also note on 26:3).
61:8 The vow to praise (see note on 7:17).

Psalm 62

For the director of music. For Jeduthun.
A psalm of David.

[1]My soul finds rest[u] in God alone;[v]
my salvation comes from him.
[2]He alone is my rock[w] and my salvation;[x]
he is my fortress,[y] I will never be
shaken.[z]

[3]How long will you assault a man?
Would all of you throw him down —
this leaning wall,[a] this tottering
fence?
[4]They fully intend to topple him
from his lofty place;
they take delight in lies.
With their mouths they bless,
but in their hearts they curse.[b] *Selah*

[5]Find rest, O my soul, in God alone;[c]
my hope comes from him.
[6]He alone is my rock and my salvation;
he is my fortress, I will not be
shaken.
[7]My salvation and my honor depend on
God[a];
he is my mighty rock, my refuge.[d]
[8]Trust in him at all times, O people;[e]
pour out your hearts to him,[f]
for God is our refuge. *Selah*

[9]Lowborn men[g] are but a breath,[h]
the highborn are but a lie;
if weighed on a balance,[i] they are
nothing;
together they are only a breath.
[10]Do not trust in extortion[j]
or take pride in stolen goods;[k]
though your riches increase,
do not set your heart on them.[l]

[11]One thing God has spoken,
two things have I heard:
that you, O God, are strong,[m]
[12]and that you, O Lord, are loving.[n]
Surely you will reward each
person
according to what he has done.[o]

62:1 [u]S Ps 5:3 [v]ver 5 **62:2** [w]Ps 18:31; 89:26 [x]S Ex 15:2 [y]S Ps 59:9 [z]S Job 29:18 **62:3** [a]Isa 30:13 **62:4** [b]Ps 28:3; 55:21 **62:5** [c]ver 1 **62:7** [d]S Ps 61:3 **62:8** [e]Ps 37:5; Isa 26:4 [f]1Sa 1:15; Ps 42:4; Mt 26:36-46 **62:9** [g]Ps 49:2 [h]S Job 7:7 [i]Isa 40:15 **62:10** [j]S Ps 12:5; 1Ti 6:17 [k]Isa 61:8; Eze 22:29; Na 3:1 [l]S Job 31:25; Mt 19:23-24; 1Ti 6:6-10 **62:11** [m]S 1Ch 29:11; Rev 19:1 **62:12** [n]Ps 86:5; 103:8; 130:7 [o]S Job 21:31; Ps 28:4; S Mt 16:27; Ro 2:6*; 1Co 3:8; Col 3:25 **63:1** [p]Ps 42:2; 84:2 [q]Ps 143:6

Psalm 63

A psalm of David. When he was in
the Desert of Judah.

[1]O God, you are my God,
earnestly I seek you;
my soul thirsts for you,[p]
my body longs for you,
in a dry and weary land
where there is no water.[q]

[a] 7 Or / *God Most High is my salvation and my honor*

Ps 62 The psalmist commits himself to God when threatened by the assaults of conspirators who wish to "topple him from his lofty place" (v. 4). The author may have been a king. If it was David, the circumstances could well have been the efforts of the family of Saul to topple him. Verse 3 suggests a time of weakness and may indicate advanced age. Implicitly the psalm is an appeal to God to uphold him. No psalm surpasses it in its expression of simple trust in God (see Ps 31 and introduction to Ps 61). The psalm is composed of three parts (vv. 3 – 4,5 – 8,9 – 10), framed by a confession of tranquil resting in God (vv. 1 – 2) and the reason for such trust (vv. 11 – 12). The middle stanza constitutes a thematic hinge: Its first two verses (vv. 5 – 6) echo the opening couplet while the last two verses (vv. 7 – 8) anticipate the closing couplet. The other two stanzas (vv. 3 – 4,9 – 10) speak of those who threaten.

62 title See note on Ps 39 title.

62:1 – 2 Profession of complete trust in God for protection.

62:1 *My soul.* See note on 6:3. *finds rest.* Lit. "is silence," i.e., is in repose.

62:2,6 *shaken.* See note on 10:6.

62:3 – 4 The threatening activities of the enemies.

62:3 Question to the assailants: Will you never give up? *leaning wall … tottering fence.* A metaphor for the psalmist's fragile condition: either (1) a confession that he has no strength in himself, or (2) an acknowledgment that he is in a weakened condition — or, perhaps, (3) a reflection on how his enemies perceive him, a "pushover."

62:4 *lofty place.* Possibly the throne. *lies … curse.* See note on 10:7. *bless.* For example, "Long live the king" (1Sa 10:24; 2Sa 16:16; see also 1Ki 1:25,34,39). *curse.* Call down curses (see note on Ge 12:3).

62:5 – 8 Trust in God: an exhortation to himself (v. 5) and to the people (v. 8).

62:5 *Find rest.* See note on v. 1; faith encouraging faith (see 27:13 – 14; 42:5,11; 43:5).

62:8 Exhortation to God's people (see 31:23 – 24). *pour out your hearts.* In earnest prayer (see La 2:19). *hearts.* See note on 4:7.

62:9 – 10 Humans, as a threat, are nothing (see note on 10:18).

62:9 *Lowborn … highborn.* Persons of every condition. *breath … lie.* People appear to be much more than they really are (see 37:2,20; 39:5 and notes), especially the rich and powerful.

62:10 A warning to those (including those conspiring against him) who trust in their own devices to get what they want (by fair means or foul) rather than trusting in God to sustain them — a virtual summary of Ps 49. *heart.* See note on 4:7.

62:11 – 12 The climax: recollection of God's reassuring word to his people. *strong … loving.* He is able to do all that he has promised and is committed to his people's salvation and blessedness.

62:11 *One thing … two things.* See note on Am 1:3.

62:12 *loving.* See note on 6:4. *Surely.* Ultimately every person will experience God's righteousness (see note on 4:1). *reward … according to.* See notes on Jer 17:10; 32:19.

Ps 63 A confession of longing for God and for the security his presence offers when deadly enemies threaten. That longing is vividly described by the metaphor of thirst (v. 1) and hunger (v. 5; see 42:1 – 2). Like Ps 62 this psalm is an implicit prayer. It is linked to that psalm also by the advancement from hearing (62:11) to seeing (v. 2; see 48:8 and note). The imagery of the night of danger (v. 6) and the morning of salvation (see note on v. 1) once more occurs (see introduction to Ps 57). In the early church this psalm was prescribed for daily public prayers. In its structure, the initial expression of longing (v. 1) gives way at the end to the expectation of joy (v. 11) — the literary frame of the psalm. Verse 6 provides the key thematic link connecting vv. 1 and 11. It stands at the center between two precisely balanced stanzas

[2]I have seen you in the sanctuary[r]
and beheld your power and your glory.[s]
[3]Because your love is better than life,[t]
my lips will glorify you.
[4]I will praise you as long as I live,[u]
and in your name I will lift up my hands.[v]
[5]My soul will be satisfied as with the richest of foods;[w]
with singing lips my mouth will praise you.
[6]On my bed I remember you;
I think of you through the watches of the night.[x]
[7]Because you are my help,[y]
I sing in the shadow of your wings.[z]
[8]My soul clings to you;[a]
your right hand upholds me.[b]
[9]They who seek my life will be destroyed;[c]
they will go down to the depths of the earth.[d]
[10]They will be given over to the sword[e]
and become food for jackals.[f]
[11]But the king will rejoice in God;
all who swear by God's name will praise him,[g]
while the mouths of liars will be silenced.[h]

Psalm 64

For the director of music.
A psalm of David.

[1]Hear me, O God, as I voice my complaint;[i]
protect my life from the threat of the enemy.[j]
[2]Hide me from the conspiracy[k] of the wicked,[l]
from that noisy crowd of evildoers.
[3]They sharpen their tongues like swords[m]

63:2 [r]S Ps 15:1; 27:4; 68:24 [s]S Ex 16:7 **63:3** [t]Ps 36:7; 69:16; 106:45; 109:21 **63:4** [u]Ps 104:33; 146:2; Isa 38:20 [v]S Ps 28:2; 1Ti 2:8 **63:5** [w]S Ps 36:8; Mt 5:6 **63:6** [x]Dt 6:4-9; Ps 16:7; 119:148; Mt 14:25 **63:7** [y]Ps 27:9; 118:7 [z]S Ru 2:12 **63:8** [a]S Nu 32:12; Hos 6:3 [b]S Ps 41:12 **63:9** [c]Ps 40:14 [d]Ps 55:15; 71:20; 95:4; 139:15 **63:10** [e]Jer 18:21; Eze 35:5; Am 1:11 [f]La 5:18 **63:11** [g]Ps 21:1; Isa 19:18; 45:23; 65:16 [h]S Job 5:16; Ro 3:19 **64:1** [i]Ps 142:2 [j]Ps 140:1 **64:2** [k]S Ex 1:10 [l]Ps 56:6; 59:2 **64:3** [m]S Ps 55:21; Isa 49:2

(vv. 2–5,7–10), each having four verses and each made up of 27 Hebrew words. The psalmist's night meditations (v. 6) nurture his longing for God (v. 1; cf. 143:5–6) and reinforce his expectations (v. 11). For the thematic links between the two major stanzas see following notes.

63 title See note on Ps 3 title. *When.* If this tradition is correct, the reference is probably to 2Sa 15:23–28; 16:2,14; 17:16,29 since the psalmist is referred to as king (see v. 11).

63:1 Intense longing for God in a time of need. *earnestly.* Lit. "at dawn," "in the morning." *my soul ... my body.* I, with my whole being (see note on 6:3). *dry and weary land.* A metaphor (see 143:6; Isa 32:2) for his situation of need, in which he does not taste "the richest of foods" (v. 5) supplied by the "river whose streams make glad the city of God" (46:4; see note there).

63:2–5 Comforting reflection on what he had seen in the sanctuary; it awakens joyful expectations.

63:2 See 27:4; 48:8 and notes.

63:3 *love.* See note on 6:4.

63:4 *name.* See note on 5:11. *lift up my hands.* While lifting the hands to God usually signifies prayer, it also—though rarely in Biblical reference—accompanied praise (see 134:2).

63:5 *soul.* See note on 6:3. *the richest of foods.* Lit. "fat and fatness" (for a similar idea see Isa 25:6).

63:6 A centering line (see introduction to this psalm): night reflections, remembering what he had seen "in the sanctuary" (v. 2). *On my bed.* At night as he expectantly awaits the dawning of the morning of deliverance. *watches of the night.* See note on Jdg 7:19; see also 119:148; La 2:19.

63:7–10 The great contrast between "my" prospects (vv. 7–8) and theirs (vv. 9–10). As will be noted, each of these four verses has some kind of thematic link with the corresponding verse in the four-verse stanza with which it is balanced (vv. 2–5; see introduction to this psalm).

63:7 *shadow of your wings.* See note on 17:8. God's saving help brings the psalmist back to the sanctuary (see v. 2) with songs of praise.

63:8 He has experienced God's "love," which is "better than life" (v. 3).

63:9 His enemies will get what they deserve; in seeking his life they forfeit their own (see Ge 9:5; Ex 21:23; Dt 19:21; see also note on Ps 5:10). The final end of the enemies stands in sharp contrast with the psalmist's prospects as anticipated in vv. 7–8—but also as voiced in v. 4: "I will praise," but "they will go down" to the place of silence (see v. 11). *depths.* See note on 30:1. *earth.* Here, the netherworld or grave (see note on 61:2).

63:10 *food for jackals.* Like bodies of enemies left unburied on the battlefield to add to their disgrace (see note on 53:5). Note the vivid portrayal of the contrast between the two prospects: I "will be satisfied with the richest of foods" (v. 5); "they will ... become food for jackals."

63:11 The closing frame (see introduction to this psalm), in which the speaker is finally identified as the king. *all who swear by God's name.* Those who revere and trust God (see Dt 6:13 and note). *mouths of liars.* Those who live by falsehood (see 5:6; 58:3; 101:7 and note on 5:9).

Ps 64 Confident prayer to God for protection when threatened by a conspiracy (see introduction to Ps 61–64). The circumstances may be similar to those reflected in Ps 62 (see introduction to that psalm), but here there is no allusion to the king's weakened condition, and it is not clear whether the conspirators come from within or outside Israel (see note on v. 2). As so often in the prayers of the Psalter, the enemy's tongue is his main weapon (see note on 5:9). The prayer is framed by an initial plea for protection from an enemy (v. 1) and a concluding call to rejoicing and praise (v. 10)—linked by a wordplay (see notes on these verses). Two carefully balanced stanzas spell out David's prayer and the adversaries' threat (vv. 2–4) and God's anticipated counteraction and its effect on all who hear about it (vv. 7–9). The point-counterpoint relationship of these two stanzas is highlighted by the use of key words that occur in corresponding positions in the Hebrew poetic lines—in reverse order: "-doers" (v. 2), "tongues" (v. 3), "shoot ... suddenly" (v. 4), "shoot ... suddenly" (v. 7), "tongues" (v. 8), "works" (v. 9: in Hebrew the same word as for "-doers" in v. 2). At the center, vv. 5–6 describe the disdainful confidence of the conspirators.

64 title See note on Ps 4 title.

64:1 Initial appeal for God to hear. *Hear.* In Hebrew a wordplay on the word for "rejoice" in v. 10 (see note there).

64:2–4 The petition and the threat.

64:2 *noisy crowd.* The Hebrew root underlying this expression is the same as that for "conspire" in 2:1.

64:3 *tongues.* See note on 5:9. *swords ... deadly arrows.* See 59:7 and note.

and aim their words like deadly
arrows.[n]
4 They shoot from ambush at the
innocent man;[o]
they shoot at him suddenly, without
fear.[p]
5 They encourage each other in evil
plans,
they talk about hiding their snares;[q]
they say, "Who will see them[a]?"[r]
6 They plot injustice and say,
"We have devised a perfect plan!"
Surely the mind and heart of man
are cunning.

7 But God will shoot them with arrows;
suddenly they will be struck
down.
8 He will turn their own tongues against
them[s]
and bring them to ruin;
all who see them will shake their
heads[t] in scorn.[u]
9 All mankind will fear;[v]
they will proclaim the works of God
and ponder what he has done.[w]
10 Let the righteous rejoice in the LORD[x]
and take refuge in him;[y]
let all the upright in heart praise
him![z]

Psalm 65

For the director of music.
A psalm of David. A song.

1 Praise awaits[b] you, O God, in Zion;[a]
to you our vows will be fulfilled.[b]
2 O you who hear prayer,
to you all men will come.[c]
3 When we were overwhelmed by sins,[d]
you forgave[c] our transgressions.[e]
4 Blessed are those you choose[f]
and bring near[g] to live in your
courts!
We are filled with the good things of
your house,[h]
of your holy temple.

5 You answer us with awesome deeds of
righteousness,[i]
O God our Savior,[j]
the hope of all the ends of the earth[k]
and of the farthest seas,[l]

64:3 [n] S Ps 7:13; S 58:7 **64:4** [o] S Job 9:23; Ps 10:8; 11:2 [p] S Ps 55:19 **64:5** [q] Ps 91:3; 119:110; 140:5; 141:9 [r] S Job 22:13 **64:8** [s] S Ps 59:12; Pr 18:7 [t] S 2Ki 19:21; Ps 109:25 [u] S Dt 28:37 **64:9** [v] S Ps 40:3 [w] Jer 51:10 **64:10** [x] S Job 22:19 [y] Ps 11:1; 25:20; 31:2 [z] Ps 32:11 **65:1** [a] Ps 2:6 [b] S Dt 23:21; Ps 116:18 **65:2** [c] Ps 86:9; Isa 66:23 **65:3** [d] S Ps 40:12 [e] Ps 79:9; Ro 3:25; Heb 9:14 **65:4** [f] S Ps 33:12 [g] S Nu 16:5 [h] S Ps 36:8 **65:5** [i] S Dt 4:34; S Ps 45:4; 106:22; Isa 64:3 [j] Ps 18:46; 68:19; 85:4 [k] S Ps 48:10 [l] Ps 107:23

[a] 5 Or *us* [b] 1 Or *befits*; the meaning of the Hebrew for this word is uncertain. [c] 3 Or *made atonement for*

64:4 *without fear.* They feel themselves secure from exposure and retaliation (see Ps 10 and notes on 10:6,11), but see vv. 7–8.
64:5–6 The enemies' contemptuous self-confidence.
64:5 *hiding their snares.* See note on 9:15.
64:6 *heart.* See note on 4:7. *cunning.* Lit. "deep" (see Pr 18:4; 20:5).
64:7–9 Confidence in God's righteous judgment—he will do to the adversaries what they had intended to do to David (see vv. 3–4)—and its effect on those who hear about it. For the links between this stanza and vv. 2–4 see introduction to this psalm.
64:7 *shoot…arrows.* See note on Ge 9:13.
64:8 *shake their heads.* See 44:14.
64:9 All people will fear, proclaim and ponder how God's "works" undo and judge the doings of the "evildoers" (v. 2; see note on 46:10; see also 40:3; 58:11; 65:8).
64:10 Framing conclusion (see v. 1): The righteous will rejoice, take refuge and praise. *righteous.* See note on 1:5. *rejoice.* In Hebrew this is the first word of the line and is a wordplay on the Hebrew for "Hear," which is the first word of the first verse.
Ps 65–68 Four psalms dominated by the theme of praise and linked by the shared recognition that God's "awesome" deeds evoke the wonder of "all the ends of the earth" and move (or should move) "all the earth" to join Israel in singing the praise of her God (see note on 46:10). In these four psalms, the occasions—and reasons—for this universal praise include (1) God's mighty acts in maintaining the creation order and making it fruitful so that humans are richly blessed, and (2) God's saving acts in behalf of his people. These are significantly brought together here by alternating the focus; Ps 65 and 67 speak of the former, and Ps 66 and 68 speak of the latter. Thus in this short series all of God's benevolent acts are brought into purview, and the whole human race is encompassed in the community of praise.
Ps 65 A hymn in praise of God's great goodness to his people. In answer to their prayers (1) he pardons their sins so that they continue to enjoy the "good things" that accompany their fellowship with him at his temple (vv. 1–4); (2) as the One who established the secure order of the creation, he also orders the affairs of the world so that international turbulence is put to rest and Israel is secure in her land (vv. 5–8); and (3) he turns the promised land into a veritable Garden of Eden (vv. 9–13). In all this, he is hailed as "the hope" of all humankind. His wondrous deeds evoke their "fear" and move them to "songs of joy."
65 title See notes on Ps 4; 30 titles.
65:1–2 Introductory commitment to praise.
65:1 *awaits.* Or "is silent before" (see note on 62:1; see also NIV text note here). Perhaps the imagery is that of praise personified as a permanent resident of the temple, lying quietly at rest, whom the people will awaken when they come to make good their vows (see 57:8). *our vows.* Those made in conjunction with their prayers in time of need (see 66:14 and note on 7:17).
65:2 *all men.* Lit. "all flesh," perhaps referring to all God's people, as in Joel 2:28 ("all people"). Most interpreters believe (in light of vv. 5,8) that the reference is more universal, as in 64:9; 66:1,4,8; 67:3–5 and elsewhere. *will come.* To praise God as the (only) God who hears and graciously answers prayers.
65:3–4 The crucial act of divine mercy that opens the way for the benefits spelled out in the two remaining stanzas.
65:3 *forgave our transgressions.* Accepted the atonement sacrifices you appointed and so forgave our sins (see NIV text note; see also 32:1–2; 78:38; 79:9 and notes on Lev 16:20–22; 17:11; Heb 2:17; 9:5,7).
65:4 *Blessed.* See note on 1:1. *those you choose and bring near.* Everyone belonging to Israel as God's chosen people (see, e.g., 33:12; Dt 4:37) and whom God accepts at his temple. *live in your courts.* See note on 15:1; see also 23:6. *good things of your house.* All the blessings that flow from God's presence (see 36:8 and note).
65:5–8 God, who continues to uphold the creation order, stills the nations and makes Israel secure in answer to her prayers.
65:5 *awesome deeds.* Acts of God such as were associated with his deliverance of Israel from Egypt and the conquest of Canaan, acts of power that made Israel's enemies cringe

[6]who formed the mountains[m] by your
power,
having armed yourself with
strength,[n]
[7]who stilled the roaring of the seas,[o]
the roaring of their waves,
and the turmoil of the nations.[p]
[8]Those living far away fear your
wonders;
where morning dawns and evening
fades
you call forth songs of joy.[q]
[9]You care for the land and water it;[r]
you enrich it abundantly.[s]
The streams of God are filled with
water
to provide the people with grain,[t]
for so you have ordained it.[a]
[10]You drench its furrows
and level its ridges;
you soften it with showers[u]
and bless its crops.
[11]You crown the year with your bounty,[v]
and your carts overflow with
abundance.[w]
[12]The grasslands of the desert overflow;[x]
the hills are clothed with gladness.[y]

65:6 [m]Am 4:13 [n]S Ps 18:1; 93:1; Isa 51:9 **65:7** [o]Ps 89:9; 93:3-4; 107:29; S Mt 8:26 [p]Dt 32:41; Ps 2:1; 74:23; 139:20; Isa 17:12-13 **65:8** [q]Ps 100:2; 107:22; 126:2; Isa 24:16; 52:9 **65:9** [r]S Lev 26:4 [s]Ps 104:24 [t]S Ge 27:28; S Dt 32:14; Ps 104:14 **65:10** [u]S Dt 32:2; S 2Sa 1:21; S Job 36:28; Ac 14:17 **65:11** [v]S Dt 28:12; Ps 104:28; Jn 10:10 [w]Job 36:28; Ps 147:14; Lk 6:38 **65:12** [x]S Job 28:26; Joel 2:22 [y]Ps 98:8 **65:13** [z]Ps 144:13; Isa 30:23; Zec 8:12

[13]The meadows are covered with flocks[z]
and the valleys are mantled with
grain;[a]
they shout for joy and sing.[b]

Psalm 66

For the director of music.
A song. A psalm.

[1]Shout with joy to God, all the earth![c]
[2]Sing the glory of his name;[d]
make his praise glorious![e]
[3]Say to God, "How awesome are your
deeds![f]
So great is your power
that your enemies cringe[g] before you.
[4]All the earth bows down[h] to you;
they sing praise[i] to you,
they sing praise to your name." *Selah*
[5]Come and see what God has done,
how awesome his works[j] in man's
behalf!

[a] 9 Or *for that is how you prepare the land*

[a]Ps 72:16 [b]Ps 98:8; Isa 14:8; 44:23; 49:13; 55:12 **66:1** [c]Ps 81:1; 84:8; 95:1; 98:4; 100:1 **66:2** [d]Ps 79:9; 86:9 [e]Isa 42:8,12; 43:21 **66:3** [f]S Dt 7:21; S 10:21; Ps 65:5; 106:22; 111:6; 145:6 [g]S 2Sa 22:45 **66:4** [h]Ps 22:27 [i]Ps 7:17; 67:3 **66:5** [j]ver 3; Ps 106:22

(see 66:3; see also 106:22; 145:6; Dt 10:21; 2Sa 7:23; Isa 64:3). *righteousness.* Saving acts by which God kept his covenanted promises to Israel (see note on 4:1). *hope of all.* Even if the nations of the world did not yet fully realize it.

65:6–7 The God of creation, who by his power brought order to the world out of the earlier chaos (see Ge 1), similarly in the redemption of his people establishes a peaceful order among nations (see Isa 2:4; 11:6–9; Mic 4:3–4) so that Israel may be at rest in the promised land (see also Ps 33; 46). God's mighty acts in redemption are often compared by OT poets with his mighty acts in creation (see 74:12–17; 89:9–18; Isa 27:1; 40:6–14,21–31; 51:9–11), since his power as Creator guaranteed his power as Redeemer. *formed the mountains … stilled … the seas.* Gave order to the whole creation (see 95:4–5).

65:7 *turmoil of the nations.* God's stilling the turbulence of the nations—which often threatened Israel—is compared to his taming the turbulence of the primeval waters of chaos (see notes on 32:6; 33:7).

65:8 All peoples will (ultimately) see God's saving acts in behalf of his people and will be moved to fear (see note on 46:10). And all creation will rejoice (see v. 13). *wonders.* Or "signs," referring to God's great saving acts, such as those he performed when he delivered Israel out of Egypt (Dt 4:34; see Ps 78:43; 105:27; 135:9). As "signs" they indicated that God was at work (see Jn 2:11 and note).

65:9–13 God blesses the promised land with all good things in answer to Israel's prayers.

65:9 *streams of God.* See note on 36:8.

65:11 *bounty.* Lit. "goodness" (see 68:10; see also 31:19 and note).

65:13 *they shout for joy and sing.* In the exuberant language of the psalmists, all creation—even its inanimate elements—joins the human chorus to celebrate the goodness of God in creation, blessing and redemption (see 89:12; 96:11–13; 98:8–9; 103:22; 145:10; 148:3–4,7–10; see also Job 38:7; Isa 44:23; 49:13; 55:12).

Ps 66 A psalm of praise for God's answer to prayer—probably delivering the psalmist from an enemy threat. It has often been suggested that the psalm speaks of Judah's remarkable deliverance from the Assyrians (see 2Ki 19). But the occasion may have been a more private crisis, which comes specifically into focus in vv. 13–20. If that is the case, the psalmist has set his personal experience of God's saving help as one of God's people in the larger context of his help of Israel in the exodus. The praise is offered at the temple in fulfillment of a vow (vv. 13–14; see note on 7:17). Such praise was often climaxed by a call for others to take up the praise (see note on 9:1). Here the psalmist exuberantly begins with that call and, as often elsewhere (e.g., 67:3–5; 68:32; 98:4; 99:1–3; 100:1; 117:1), addresses it even to the far corners of the earth. This psalm is the second in a series of four (see introduction to Ps 65–68). It is framed by a call to praise (vv. 1–2) and a declaration of the present occasion for praise (vv. 19–20, in Hebrew involving a play on words—the Hebrew for "praise" and "prayer" sound very much alike). The opening stanza (vv. 1–4) is followed by two thematic sequences having the same structure: a three-verse stanza (vv. 5–7,13–15) followed by a five-verse stanza (vv. 8–12,16–20). The first line of the first stanza of the first sequence (v. 5) begins with "Come and see"; the first line of the second stanza of the second sequence (v. 16) begins with "Come and listen."

66 title See notes on Ps 4; 30 titles.

66:1–4 Calling all the earth to joyful praise.

66:1 *all the earth.* See note on 65:2.

66:2 *name.* See note on 5:11.

66:3 *awesome.* See v. 5; see also note on 65:5. *cringe.* See 18:44; cf. Jos 5:1; 2Ch 20:29.

66:4 See note on 46:10.

66:5–7 Recollection of God's deliverance of Israel at the Red Sea as a sign of his power to rule over the nations. The psalmist portrays his deliverance (see introduction above) both as similar to this Red Sea rescue in its manifestation of God's saving power (see 65:5–7 for a comparison of God's mighty saving acts with his mighty acts of creation) and as a continuation of God's same saving purposes.

66:5 *Come and see.* See introduction to this psalm. God's saving acts of old can still be "seen" at his temple, where they are

6He turned the sea into dry land,[k]
they passed through[l] the waters on foot—
come, let us rejoice[m] in him.
7He rules forever[n] by his power,
his eyes watch[o] the nations—
let not the rebellious[p] rise up against him. *Selah*

8Praise[q] our God, O peoples,
let the sound of his praise be heard;
9he has preserved our lives[r]
and kept our feet from slipping.[s]
10For you, O God, tested[t] us;
you refined us like silver.[u]
11You brought us into prison[v]
and laid burdens[w] on our backs.
12You let men ride over our heads;[x]
we went through fire and water,
but you brought us to a place of abundance.[y]

13I will come to your temple with burnt offerings[z]
and fulfill my vows[a] to you—
14vows my lips promised and my mouth spoke
when I was in trouble.
15I will sacrifice fat animals to you
and an offering of rams;
I will offer bulls and goats.[b] *Selah*

16Come and listen,[c] all you who fear God;
let me tell[d] you what he has done for me.
17I cried out to him with my mouth;
his praise was on my tongue.
18If I had cherished sin in my heart,
the Lord would not have listened;[e]
19but God has surely listened
and heard my voice[f] in prayer.
20Praise be to God,
who has not rejected[g] my prayer
or withheld his love from me!

66:6 [k]S Ge 8:1; S Ex 14:22 [l]1Co 10:1 [m]S Lev 23:40 **66:7** [n]S Ex 15:18; Ps 145:13 [o]S Ex 3:16; S Ps 11:4 [p]S Nu 17:10; Ps 112:10; 140:8 **66:8** [q]S Ps 22:23 **66:9** [r]Ps 30:3 [s]S Dt 32:35; S Job 12:5 **66:10** [t]S Ex 15:25 [u]S Job 6:29; S 28:1; S Ps 12:6 **66:11** [v]Ps 142:7; 146:7; Isa 42:7,22; 61:1 [w]S Ge 3:17; S Ex 1:14; Ps 38:4; Isa 10:27 **66:12** [x]Isa 51:23 [y]Ps 18:19 **66:13** [z]S Ps 51:19 [a]Ps 22:25; 50:14; 116:14; Ecc 5:4; Jnh 2:9 **66:15** [b]S Lev 16:5; Ps 51:19 **66:16** [c]Ps 34:11 [d]Ps 71:15,24 **66:18** [e]S Dt 1:45; S 1Sa 8:18; Jas 4:3 **66:19** [f]S Ps 18:6 **66:20** [g]Ps 22:24

Psalm 67

For the director of music.
With stringed instruments. A psalm.
A song.

1May God be gracious to us and bless us
and make his face shine upon us,[h] *Selah*
2that your ways may be known on earth,
your salvation[i] among all nations.[j]

3May the peoples praise you, O God;
may all the peoples praise you.[k]
4May the nations be glad and sing for joy,[l]

67:1 [h]Nu 6:24-26 **67:2** [i]Isa 40:5; 52:10; 62:1 [j]Ps 98:2; Isa 62:2; Ac 10:35; Tit 2:11 **67:3** [k]ver 5 **67:4** [l]Ps 100:1-2

continually celebrated (see 46:8; 48:8–9 and notes). *in man's behalf.* Specifically for his people.

66:6 *waters.* Possibly the Jordan, but more likely a parallel reference to the Red Sea.

66:7 *rebellious.* Nations that are in revolt against God's rule (see 68:6).

66:8–12 Praise of God's deliverance of his people.

66:8 *peoples.* Here probably the grateful throng of worshipers (see 2Ch 20:27–28).

66:9 *from slipping.* See note on 38:16.

66:10 *tested ... refined.* From one point of view, times of distress constitute a testing of God's people as to their trust in and loyalty to God. The metaphor is borrowed from the technology of refining precious metals, which included heating the metals in a crucible to see if all impurities had been removed (see 12:6 and note; 17:3).

66:11–12 *You ... You.* God's rule is all-pervasive; even when enemies maliciously oppress his people, God is not a mere passive observer but has his own holy purposes in it (see Isa 45:7; Am 3:6). *prison ... burdens ... ride over.* Probably recalling the Egyptian oppression from which the exodus brought relief.

66:12 *fire and water.* Conventional metaphors for severe trials (see Isa 43:2). *to a place of abundance.* Lit. "to an overflowing" (see 23:5). They were brought out of a situation of distress into a situation of overflowing blessings: the promised land.

66:13–15 Announcement of fulfillment of vows: addressed to God (see note on 7:17; see also 50:14; 116:17–19).

66:13 *I.* The king.

66:16–20 Proclamation of what God has done for the psalmist—in praise of God and addressed to the worshiping congregation (cf. 34:1–7).

66:16 *Come and listen.* See introduction. *fear God.* See notes on 15:4; Ge 20:11; Pr 1:7; Lk 12:5.

66:17 *his praise.* Prayer and praise belonged together in the OT (see also Php 4:6; 1Ti 2:1).

66:20 *Praise be to God.* See v. 8. *love.* See note on 6:4.

Ps 67 A communal prayer for God's blessing. Its content, form and brevity suggest that it served as a liturgical prayer of the people at the conclusion of worship, perhaps just prior to (or immediately after) the priestly benediction (see note on v. 1). God's blessing of his people (as well as his saving acts in their behalf) will catch the attention of the nations and move them to praise (see 65:2). This psalm is the third in a series of four having special thematic links with Ps 65 (see introduction to Ps 65–68). It has a completely symmetrical structure: Two verses at the beginning contain the prayer, while the two verses of the concluding stanza speak of the effects of God's answer. In the intervening stanza, framed by a refrain (vv. 3,5), the people seek to motivate God's answer by referring to the worldwide praise that his mercies to his people will awaken.

67 title See notes on Ps 4; 30 titles.

67:1–2 The prayer.

67:1 The heart of the prayer, anticipating (or echoing) the priestly benediction (see Nu 6:24–26). *make his face shine.* See notes on 4:6; 13:1.

67:2 May God's favors to his people be so obvious that all the world takes notice (see note on 46:10).

67:3–5 The motivation. Elaborating on v. 2, the people speak of the worldwide praise that will resound to God when he graciously blesses his people. Their wish is twofold: (1) that God's blessings may be so abundant that the people will be moved to praise, and (2) that the nations may indeed add their praise to that of Israel—an appropriate expression at this climax of the liturgy of worship.

67:4 May the nations rejoice in the Lord when they see how benevolent the rule of God is (see 65:7–8; 98:4–6; 100:1).

for you rule the peoples justly[m]
and guide the nations of the earth.[n]
Selah
5 May the peoples praise you, O God;
may all the peoples praise you.

6 Then the land will yield its harvest,[o]
and God, our God, will bless us.[p]
7 God will bless us,
and all the ends of the earth[q] will
fear him.[r]

Psalm 68

For the director of music. Of David.
A psalm. A song.

1 May God arise,[s] may his enemies be
scattered;[t]
may his foes flee[u] before him.
2 As smoke[v] is blown away by the
wind,
may you blow them away;
as wax melts[w] before the fire,
may the wicked perish[x] before God.
3 But may the righteous be glad
and rejoice[y] before God;
may they be happy and joyful.

4 Sing to God, sing praise to his name,[z]
extol him who rides on the
clouds[a][a] —
his name is the LORD[b] —
and rejoice before him.
5 A father to the fatherless,[c] a defender
of widows,[d]
is God in his holy dwelling.[e]
6 God sets the lonely[f] in families,[b][g]
he leads forth the prisoners[h] with
singing;
but the rebellious live in a sun-
scorched land.[i]

7 When you went out[j] before your
people, O God,
when you marched through the
wasteland,[k] *Selah*
8 the earth shook,[l]
the heavens poured down rain,[m]
before God, the One of Sinai,[n]
before God, the God of Israel.[o]

[a] 4 Or / *prepare the way for him who rides through the deserts* [b] 6 Or *the desolate in a homeland*

67:4 [m]S Ps 9:4; 96:10-13 [n]Ps 68:32 **67:6** [o]S Ge 8:22; S Lev 26:4; Ps 85:12; Isa 55:10; Eze 34:27; Zec 8:12 [p]S Ge 12:2 **67:7** [q]S Ps 2:8 [r]Ps 33:8 **68:1** [s]Ps 12:5; 132:8 [t]Ps 18:14; 89:10; 92:9; 144:6 [u]Nu 10:35; Isa 17:13; 21:15; 33:3 **68:2** [v]S Ps 37:20 [w]S Ps 22:14 [x]S Nu 10:35; Ps 9:3; 80:16 **68:3** [y]Ps 64:10; 97:12 **68:4** [z]S 2Sa 22:50; Ps 7:17; S 30:4; 66:2; 96:2; 100:4; 135:3 [a]ver 33; S Ex 20:21; S Dt 33:26 [b]S Ex 6:3; Ps 83:18 **68:5** [c]Ps 10:14 [d]S Ex 22:22; S Dt 10:18 [e]S Dt 26:15; Jer 25:30 **68:6** [f]Ps 25:16 [g]Ps 113:9 [h]Ps 79:11; 102:20; 146:7; Isa 61:1; Lk 4:18 [i]Isa 35:7; 49:10; 58:11 **67:7** [j]S Ex 13:21 [k]Ps 78:40; 106:14 **68:8** [l]S 2Sa 22:8 [m]S Jdg 5:4; 2Sa 21:10; Ecc 11:3 [n]S Dt 33:2 [o]S Jdg 5:5

67:6 – 7 The effects of God's blessing his people.
67:6 The promised land will yield its abundance (see 65:9 – 13).
67:7 *all the ... earth.* See 65:8 and note. *fear.* See note on 66:16.
Ps 68 A hymn celebrating the triumphal march of Israel's God from Mount Sinai to Mount Zion. Interwoven in it is a prayer that this mighty display of God's power be continued until all God's people are rescued and secure and all kingdoms of the earth bring tribute to and sing the praises of the God of Israel. The voice heard here is that of the worshiping community, and the psalm may originally have accompanied a liturgical procession of the people up to the temple in Jerusalem (see introductions to Ps 24; 47; 118; 132). The first half of the psalm (vv. 1 – 18: 19 Hebrew poetic lines) contains many clear references to God's triumphal march from Mount Sinai (in the days of Moses) to Mount Zion (in the days of David). The events at Mount Sinai marked the birth of the kingdom of God among his people Israel; the placement of the ark of the covenant (symbol of God's throne) in the temple in Jerusalem marked the establishment of God's redemptive kingdom among the nations of the earth, with Jerusalem as its royal city. The second half of the psalm (vv. 19 – 35: 19 Hebrew poetic lines) is framed by the cry "Praise be to the Lord/God" and looks forward with expectations of God's continuing triumphs until the redemption of his people is complete and his kingly rule is universally acknowledged with songs of praise. The early church, taking its cue from Eph 4:8 – 13, understood this psalm to foreshadow the resurrection, ascension and present rule of Christ and the final triumph of his church over the hostile world. Ps 68 is the last in a series of four (see introduction to Ps 65 – 68).

The psalm is composed of nine stanzas (vv. 19 – 20 should probably be joined with vv. 21 – 23), with a concluding doxology. The first stanza (vv. 1 – 3) suggests the beginning of a liturgical procession, and the last (vv. 32 – 35) its conclusion, with God enthroned in his sanctuary. The seventh (vv. 24 – 27) speaks expressly of a procession coming into view and entering the sanctuary. In light of these clear references, the third stanza (vv. 7 – 10) suggests a stage in the procession recalling the desert journey from Sinai to the promised land, while the fifth (vv. 15 – 18) marks that stage in which the Lord ascends Mount Zion. On the other hand, the second stanza (vv. 4 – 6) reflects on the benevolence of God's rule; the fourth (vv. 11 – 14) recalls his victories over the kings of Canaan; the sixth (vv. 19 – 23) speaks reassuringly of God's future victories; and the eighth (vv. 28 – 31) contains prayers that God may muster his power to subdue the enemy as he had done before.
68 title See notes on Ps 4; 30 titles.
68:1 – 3 The start of the procession, liturgically recalling the beginning of God's march with his people in army formation from Sinai (see Nu 10:33 – 35).
68:1 *enemies be scattered.* See note on v. 30.
68:3 *righteous.* Israel as the committed people of God in distinction from those opposed to the coming of God's kingdom (the "wicked" of v. 2); see 1:5 and note.
68:4 – 6 A call to praise God for the benevolence of his rule.
68:4 *name.* See note on 5:11. *who rides on the clouds.* An epithet of Baal found in Canaanite literature is used to make the point that the Lord (Yahweh, not Baal) is the exalted One who truly makes the storm cloud his chariot (see v. 33; 18:9; 104:3; Dt 33:26; Isa 19:1; Mt 26:64).
68:5 – 6 God is the defender of the powerless (see 10:14; 146:7 – 9; 147:6; Dt 10:18).
68:6 *sets the lonely in families.* See Ex 1:21; Ru 4:14 – 17; 1Sa 2:5. *leads forth the prisoners.* As he led Israel out of Egypt (see 69:33; 107:10,14). *rebellious.* See notes on v. 18; 66:7. *sun-scorched land.* A place utterly barren, lacking even soil for vegetation (see Eze 26:4,14).
68:7 – 10 Recollection of God's march through the desert from Sinai into the promised land (see Jdg 5:4 – 5; Hab 3:3 – 6).
68:8 *earth shook.* A reference to the quaking of Mount Sinai (Ex 19:18). *heavens poured down rain.* The Pentateuch preserves no tradition of rain during the desert wanderings, but here (and in Jdg 5:4) rain is closely associated with the quaking of the earth as a manifestation of the majesty of God. Perhaps the "thunder and lightning, with a thick cloud" over Mount Sinai (Ex 19:16) were accompanied by rain. But see also v. 9, which suggests rains that refreshed the people on their journey (cf. 77:17 – 18 and note on 77:16 – 19).

9 You gave abundant showers,[p] O God;
you refreshed your weary inheritance.
10 Your people settled in it,
and from your bounty,[q] O God, you
provided[r] for the poor.

11 The Lord announced the word,
and great was the company[s] of those
who proclaimed it:
12 "Kings and armies flee[t] in haste;
in the camps men divide the
plunder.[u]
13 Even while you sleep among the
campfires,[a][v]
the wings of ⌞my⌟ dove are sheathed
with silver,
its feathers with shining gold."
14 When the Almighty[b] scattered[w] the
kings in the land,
it was like snow fallen on Zalmon.[x]

15 The mountains of Bashan[y] are majestic
mountains;[z]
rugged are the mountains of Bashan.
16 Why gaze in envy, O rugged
mountains,
at the mountain where God chooses[a]
to reign,
where the LORD himself will dwell
forever?[b]
17 The chariots[c] of God are tens of
thousands
and thousands of thousands;[d]
the Lord ⌞has come⌟ from Sinai into
his sanctuary.
18 When you ascended[e] on high,[f]
you led captives[g] in your train;
you received gifts from men,[h]
even from[c] the rebellious[i]—
that you,[d] O LORD God, might dwell
there.

19 Praise be to the Lord, to God our Savior,[j]
who daily bears our burdens.[k] *Selah*
20 Our God is a God who saves;[l]
from the Sovereign LORD comes
escape from death.[m]

21 Surely God will crush the heads[n] of his
enemies,
the hairy crowns of those who go on
in their sins.
22 The Lord says, "I will bring them from
Bashan;
I will bring them from the depths of
the sea,[o]
23 that you may plunge your feet in the
blood of your foes,[p]
while the tongues of your dogs[q] have
their share."

[a] 13 Or *saddlebags* [b] 14 Hebrew *Shaddai* [c] 18 Or *gifts for men, / even* [d] 18 Or *they*

68:9 [p] S Dt 32:2; S Job 36:28; S Eze 34:26 **68:10** [q] S Dt 28:12 [r] Ps 65:9 **68:11** [s] Lk 2:13 **68:12** [t] Jos 10:16 [u] S Jdg 5:30 **68:13** [v] S Ge 49:14 **68:14** [w] 2Sa 22:15 [x] Jdg 9:48 **68:15** [y] ver 22; Nu 21:33; Jer 22:20 [z] S Ps 36:6 **68:16** [a] Dt 12:5; S Ps 2:6; 132:13 [b] Ps 132:14 **68:17** [c] S 2Ki 2:11; Isa 66:15; Hab 3:8 [d] Da 7:10 **68:18** [e] S Ps 47:5 [f] Ps 7:7 [g] Jdg 5:12 [h] Eph 4:8* [i] S Nu 17:10 **68:19** [j] S Ps 65:5 [k] Ps 81:6 **68:20** [l] S 1Sa 10:19 [m] Ps 56:13; Jer 45:5; Eze 6:8 **68:21** [n] Ps 74:14; 110:5; Hab 3:13 **68:22** [o] S Job 36:30; Mt 18:6 **68:23** [p] Ps 58:10 [q] S 1Ki 21:19; S 2Ki 9:36

68:9 *your ... inheritance.* The people of Israel (see Dt 9:29).
68:10 *it.* Probably refers to the promised land. *bounty.* Lit. "goodness" (see 65:11 and note). *provided.* From the produce of Canaan (see Jos 5:11–12). *poor.* Israel as a people dependent on God.
68:11–14 Recollection of God's victories over the kings of Canaan.
68:11 *announced the word.* God declared beforehand that he would be victorious over the Canaanite kings (see Ex 23:22–23,27–28,31; Dt 7:10–24; 11:23–25; Jos 1:2–6). *proclaimed it.* Celebrated God's victories (see Ex 15:1–21; 1Sa 18:6–7; 2Ch 20:26–28). *proclaimed.* See 40:9 and note.
68:13 *sleep among the campfires.* Rest in camp (see Jdg 5:16; see also NIV text note on Ge 49:14). *wings of ⌞my⌟ dove are sheathed.* Israel, God's "dove" (see 74:19 and note; cf. Hos 7:11), is enriched with the silver and gold of plunder from the kings of Canaan even though she still remains in camp. This poetic hyperbole (a figure of speech that uses exaggeration for emphasis) celebrates the fact that God had defeated the kings even before Israel met them in battle (see Jos 2:8–11; 5:1; 6:16; see also 2Sa 5:24; 2Ki 7:5–7; 19:35; 2Ch 20:22–30).
68:14 *Almighty.* See NIV text note; see also note on Ge 17:1. *like snow fallen on Zalmon.* There was a mountain near Shechem that bore this name (see Jdg 9:46–48), but some identify the mountain referred to here as Jebel Druze, a dark volcanic mountain east of Bashan. Its name appears to mean "the dark one"—in distinction from the Lebanon ("the white one") range, composed of limestone—and the figure may involve the contrast of white snow scattered on "Dark Mountain." The reference may then be to abandoned weapons littering the field from which the kings have fled headlong (see 2Ki 7:15).
68:15–18 Celebration of God's ascent to Mount Zion.
68:15–16 The mountains surrounding Bashan, including the towering Mount Hermon, are portrayed as being jealous because God has chosen Mount Zion as the seat of his rule, making it the "highest" of mountains (see 48:2 and note).
68:17 *chariots of God.* God's great heavenly host, here likened to a vast chariot force (see 2Ki 6:17; Hab 3:8,15). In the time of the Roman empire Jesus referred to God's host in terms of "legions" (Mt 26:53).
68:18 *ascended on high.* Went up to your place of enthronement on Mount Zion (see 47:5–6 and note; see also 7:7). *led captives ... received gifts.* Like a victorious king after triumphs on the field of battle. *rebellious.* Those who had opposed the kingdom of God (see v. 6 and note on 66:7) are compelled to submit to him and bring tribute. *that you ... might dwell there.* Grammatically completes the clause, "When you ascended on high." Paul applies this verse (as translated in the Septuagint, the pre-Christian Greek translation of the OT) to the ascended Christ (Eph 4:8–13; see notes on Eph 4:8–9,11), thereby implying that Christ's ascension was a continuation of, and a fulfillment of, God's establishment of his kingdom in his royal city Jerusalem (see introduction to this psalm).
68:19–23 Joyous confession of hope that God's victorious campaigns will continue until the salvation of his people is complete.
68:19 *bears our burdens.* Releases us from bearing the burdens that enslavement to our enemies would impose on us (see 81:6; Isa 9:4; 10:27). But some associate this line with such passages as 55:22; Isa 46:4.
68:20 *escape from death.* At the hand of our enemies—implicitly, perhaps, also from death itself as the last great enemy (see notes on 6:5; 11:7; 16:9–11; 17:15; 49:14–15).
68:21 As God assures the life of his people (see v. 20), so he will crush those who oppose him. *crush the heads.* See Nu 24:17; Jer 48:45–46 and note.
68:22 *them.* The enemies who fled at the victorious onward march of God and his host (see vv. 12,17). *Bashan ... depths of the sea.* The former (see also v. 15) was the high plateau east of the Jordan, the latter the Mediterranean Sea—none of the enemies will escape (see Am 9:1–4).
68:23 See note on 58:10.

[24]Your procession has come into view,
O God,
the procession of my God and King
into the sanctuary.[r]
[25]In front are the singers,[s] after them the
musicians;[t]
with them are the maidens playing
tambourines.[u]
[26]Praise God in the great congregation;[v]
praise the LORD in the assembly of
Israel.[w]
[27]There is the little tribe[x] of Benjamin,[y]
leading them,
there the great throng of Judah's
princes,
and there the princes of Zebulun and
of Naphtali.[z]

[28]Summon your power,[a] O God[a];
show us your strength,[b] O God, as
you have done[c] before.
[29]Because of your temple at Jerusalem
kings will bring you gifts.[d]
[30]Rebuke the beast[e] among the reeds,[f]
the herd of bulls[g] among the calves
of the nations.
Humbled, may it bring bars of silver.
Scatter the nations[h] who delight in
war.[i]
[31]Envoys will come from Egypt;[j]
Cush[b][k] will submit herself to God.

[32]Sing to God, O kingdoms of the
earth,[l]
sing praise[m] to the Lord, *Selah*
[33]to him who rides[n] the ancient skies
above,
who thunders[o] with mighty
voice.[p]
[34]Proclaim the power[q] of God,
whose majesty[r] is over Israel,
whose power is in the skies.
[35]You are awesome,[s] O God, in your
sanctuary;[t]
the God of Israel gives power and
strength[u] to his people.[v]

Praise be to God![w]

Psalm 69

For the director of music.
To ⌊the tune of⌋ "Lilies." Of David.

[1]Save me, O God,
for the waters[x] have come up to my
neck.[y]

[a] *28* Many Hebrew manuscripts, Septuagint and Syriac; most Hebrew manuscripts *Your God has summoned power for you* [b] *31* That is, the upper Nile region

68:24 [r]S Ps 63:2 **68:25** [s]S 1Ch 15:16 [t]S 1Ch 6:31; S 2Ch 5:12; Rev 18:22 [u]S Ge 31:27; S Isa 5:12 **68:26** [v]S Ps 22:22; Heb 2:12 [w]S Lev 19:2 **68:27** [x]S 1Sa 9:21 [y]S Nu 34:21 [z]S Jdg 5:18 **68:28** [a]S Ex 9:16 [b]Ps 29:11 [c]Isa 26:12; 29:23; 45:11; 60:21; 64:8 **68:29** [d]S 2Ch 9:24; S 32:23 **68:30** [e]Isa 27:1; 51:9; Eze 29:3 [f]S Job 40:21 [g]Ps 22:12; Isa 34:7; Jer 50:27 [h]Ps 18:14; 89:10 [i]Ps 120:7; 140:2 **68:31** [j]Isa 19:19; 43:3; 45:14 [k]Isa 11:11; 18:1; Zep 3:10 **68:32** [l]S Ps 46:6; 67:4 [m]Ps 7:17 **68:33** [n]S Dt 33:26 [o]S Ex 9:23; S Ps 29:3 [p]Ps 29:4; Isa 30:30; 33:3; 66:6 **68:34** [q]ver 28 [r]Ps 45:3 **68:35** [s]S Dt 7:21 [t]S Ge 28:17 [u]Ps 18:1; Isa 40:29; 41:10; 50:2 [v]S Ps 29:11 [w]Ps 28:6; 66:20; 2Co 1:3 **69:1** [x]S Ps 42:7 [y]Ps 32:6; Jnh 2:5

68:24–27 The liturgical procession approaches the temple (see Ps 24; 47).
68:25 *maidens playing tambourines.* See note on Jer 31:4.
68:27 All Israel is represented, from little Benjamin to powerful Judah, and tribes from the north as well as the south. *Benjamin, leading.* Perhaps reflecting the fact that from the tribe of Benjamin came the first king (Saul; see 1Sa 9:1–2), who began the royal victories over Israel's enemies (see 1Sa 11:11; 14:20–23).
68:28–31 Prayer for God to continue his conquest of the threatening powers.
68:28 *Summon your power.* Or, perhaps, "Command your power to act."
68:29 *Because of your temple.* Because your earthly royal house has been established in Jerusalem. *bring you gifts.* Acknowledge you by bringing tribute, as subjected kings brought tribute to their conquerors (see 2Sa 8:2,6,10; 2Ki 3:4).
68:30 *Rebuke.* See note on 76:6. *beast among the reeds.* The pharaoh (see Eze 29:3). *herd of bulls among the calves.* Powerful princes supporting the pharaoh, and the lesser princes of other nations. Egypt is singled out here as representative of the hostile nations—because of Israel's past experiences with that world power. It may also be that at the time the psalm was composed Egypt was the one great empire on Israel's immediate horizons. *Scatter the nations.* See v. 1; so that Israel may have peace (see 46:9; 48:4–7; 65:7; 76:3).
68:32–35 Climax of the liturgical procession: a call for all kingdoms to hail with praise the God of Israel as the God who reigns in heaven and has established his earthly throne in the temple in Jerusalem (see Ps 47).
68:33 See v. 4 and note. *thunders with mighty voice.* See note on 29:3–9.
68:35 *awesome.* See 45:4 and note. *gives power and strength to his people.* The Lord of all has made Israel his people (his "kingdom"; see Ex 19:5–6), and his rule among them makes them participants in his victorious power (see 29:10–11).
Ps 69–72 Book II of the Psalter closes with a cluster of three prayers and an attached royal psalm—in perfect balance with its beginning (see note on Ps 42–45). These three prayers were originally all pleas of a king in Israel for deliverance from enemies (apparently internal) determined to do away with him. They all contain certain key words that are found elsewhere in Book II only in Ps 42–44 and in the seven psalms (54–60) placed at the center of the Book. Another link between Ps 69–71 and 42–44 is the placement of a short psalm at the center of each triad. These placements have the appearance of deliberate editorial design. In the former cluster Ps 43 has been artificially separated from 42 (see introduction to Ps 42–43), while in the latter cluster Ps 70 repeats (with some revision) Ps 40:13–17 and was probably intended to serve as an introduction to Ps 71. The attached prayer for the king (Ps 72) stands in similar relationship to Ps 69–71 as Ps 45 stands to Ps 42–44 and brings Book II to its conclusion. Thus, as with Ps 45, its placement hints at a Messianic reading of the psalm already by the editors of the Psalter (see also introduction to Ps 72). It should be further noted that in Ps 65–68 all peoples on earth are drawn into the community of those praising God (see note on Ps 65–68). Here in Ps 69 all creation is called to join that chorus (v. 34), and Ps 72 envisions that all peoples and kings will submit to the son of David (vv. 8–11) and be blessed through his reign (v. 17).
Ps 69 A plea for God to have mercy and to save from a host of enemies: the prayer of a godly king when under vicious attack by a widespread conspiracy at a time when God had wounded him (see v. 26) for some sin in his life (see v. 5). If, as tradition claims, David authored the original psalm (see title), the occasion is unknown. In its present form the prayer suggests a later son of David who ruled over the southern kingdom of Judah (see v. 35). That king may have been Hezekiah (see 2Ki 18–20; 2Ch 29–32). This psalm begins a series

2 I sink in the miry depths,[z]
where there is no foothold.
I have come into the deep waters;
the floods engulf me.
3 I am worn out calling for help;[a]
my throat is parched.
My eyes fail,[b]
looking for my God.
4 Those who hate me[c] without reason[d]
outnumber the hairs of my head;
many are my enemies without
cause,[e]
those who seek to destroy me.[f]
I am forced to restore
what I did not steal.

5 You know my folly,[g] O God;
my guilt is not hidden from you.[h]

6 May those who hope in you
not be disgraced because of me,
O Lord, the LORD Almighty;
may those who seek you
not be put to shame because of me,
O God of Israel.
7 For I endure scorn[i] for your sake,[j]
and shame covers my face.[k]
8 I am a stranger to my brothers,
an alien to my own mother's sons;[l]
9 for zeal for your house consumes me,[m]
and the insults of those who insult
you fall on me.[n]
10 When I weep and fast,[o]
I must endure scorn;
11 when I put on sackcloth,[p]
people make sport of me.
12 Those who sit at the gate[q] mock me,
and I am the song of the drunkards.[r]

13 But I pray to you, O LORD,
in the time of your favor;[s]
in your great love,[t] O God,
answer me with your sure salvation.
14 Rescue me from the mire,
do not let me sink;
deliver me from those who hate me,
from the deep waters.[u]
15 Do not let the floodwaters[v] engulf me
or the depths swallow me up[w]
or the pit close its mouth over me.[x]
16 Answer me, O LORD, out of the
goodness of your love;[y]
in your great mercy turn to me.
17 Do not hide your face[z] from your
servant;
answer me quickly,[a] for I am in
trouble.[b]
18 Come near and rescue me;
redeem[c] me because of my foes.

19 You know how I am scorned,[d]
disgraced and shamed;
all my enemies are before you.

69:2 [z]S Job 30:19 **69:3** [a]Ps 6:6 [b]Ps 119:82 **69:4** [c]S Ps 25:19 [d]Jn 15:25* [e]S Ps 35:19; 38:19 [f]Ps 40:14; 119:95; Isa 32:7 **69:5** [g]Ps 38:5 [h]S Ps 44:21 **69:7** [i]S Ps 39:8 [j]Jer 15:15 [k]Ps 44:15 **69:8** [l]Job 19:13-15; Ps 31:11; 38:11; Isa 53:3; Jn 7:5 **69:9** [m]Jn 2:17* [n]Ps 89:50-51; Ro 15:3* **69:10** [o]S Ps 35:13 **69:11** [p]S 2Sa 3:31; S Ps 35:13 **69:12** [q]S Ge 18:1; S 23:10 [r]Job 30:9 **69:13** [s]Isa 49:8; 2Co 6:2 [t]S Ps 17:7; 51:1 **69:14** [u]ver 2; Ps 144:7 **69:15** [v]Ps 124:4-5 [w]Nu 16:33 [x]Ps 28:1 **69:16** [y]S Ps 63:3 **69:17** [z]S Ps 22:24 [a]Ps 143:7 [b]S Ps 50:15; 66:14 **69:18** [c]Ps 49:15 **69:19** [d]S Ps 22:6

of three prayers for deliverance when threatened by enemies (see introduction to Ps 69–72). Structurally, this psalm is composed of two halves of 22 lines each (22 being the number of letters in the Hebrew alphabet; see introduction to Ps 33). The first half (vv. 1–15) ends with petitions that echo the descriptions of distress at the beginning. It should also be noted that v. 5 stands at the center of vv. 1–12 and v. 29 stands at the center of vv. 22–36. The "centering" of these two verses accounts for why they both stand thematically somewhat apart from their immediate contexts (for this literary device see note on 6:6; for the thematic relationship of these two verses see notes below). The authors of the NT viewed this cry of a godly sufferer as foreshadowing the sufferings of Christ; no psalm, except Ps 22, is quoted more frequently in the NT.
69 title *For the director of music.* See note on Ps 4 title. *To ⌞the tune of⌟.* See note on Ps 9 title. *Lilies.* See note on Ps 45 title.
69:1–4 Description of the dire distress that evokes the psalmist's prayer.
69:1–2 *waters … miry depths … deep waters … floods.* Conventional imagery for great distress (see notes on 30:1; 32:6)—here the results of God's wounding (see v. 26), but especially of the attacks of the enemies (see vv. 14–15,29).
69:3 *throat is parched.* See 22:15. *eyes fail.* See 6:7 and note.
69:4 *without reason … without cause.* Those whom he has not wronged are pitted against him (see 35:19 and note). *outnumber the hairs of my head.* See note on 40:12. *I am forced.* An illustrative way of saying that his enemies are spreading false accusations about him (see 5:9 and note).
69:5 A confession of personal guilt—the reason why God has wounded him (v. 26) and why he is "in pain and distress" (v. 29). *folly.* See NIV text note on 14:1.
69:6–12 Prayer that God's discipline of his godly servant may not bring disgrace on all those who trustingly look to the Lord. The author acknowledges that God's wounding of him has been occasioned by some sin in his life (but he has not sinned against those who have become his enemies). Because of his present suffering, his enemies mock his deep commitment to the Lord (see 22:6–8; 42:3; 79:10; 115:2; Job 2:9). Implicitly he prays that God will restore him again and vindicate his trust in him.
69:8 Even those nearest him dissociate themselves from him (see 31:11–12 and note).
69:9 *zeal for your house.* What was true of the author was even more true of Jesus (see Jn 2:17). *insults of those who insult you.* Those who mock God also mock his servant who trusts in him (see 74:18,22–23; 2Ki 18:31–35), as Christ also experienced (see Ro 15:3).
69:10–11 *weep and fast … put on sackcloth.* As tokens of humbling himself before the Lord in repentance as he prays for God to have mercy and restore him (see 35:13 and note; see also Ge 37:34; 2Sa 12:16–17; Joel 1:13–14; 2:15–17; Jnh 3:5).
69:12 *Those who sit at the gate … drunkards.* Everyone, from the elders of the city to the town drunks.
69:13–15 Though they mock, I pray to you.
69:13 *time of your favor.* When God is near to save (see 32:6 and note; see also Isa 49:8; 61:2; 2Co 6:2). *great love.* See note on 6:4.
69:14–15 *mire … deep waters … floodwaters … depths.* See note on vv. 1–2. The psalmists' petitions commonly echo their earlier descriptions of the distress that occasions the prayer. Here the return to the beginning marks the end of the first half of the psalmist's appeal to God.
69:15 *swallow me.* See note on 49:14. *pit.* See note on 30:1.
69:16–18 An appeal for God to hear—such as commonly begins the prayers brought together in the Psalter.
69:16 *love.* See note on 6:4.
69:17 *hide your face.* See note on 13:1.
69:18 *redeem.* See note on 25:22.
69:19–21 In my trouble they heaped on scorn instead of bringing comfort (see 35:11–16; see also 142:4; Job 13:4; 16:2; 21:34).

20 Scorn has broken my heart
and has left me helpless;
I looked for sympathy, but there was none,
for comforters,[e] but I found none.[f]
21 They put gall in my food
and gave me vinegar[g] for my thirst.[h]
22 May the table set before them become a snare;
may it become retribution and[a] a trap.[i]
23 May their eyes be darkened so they cannot see,
and their backs be bent forever.[j]
24 Pour out your wrath[k] on them;
let your fierce anger overtake them.
25 May their place be deserted;[l]
let there be no one to dwell in their tents.[m]
26 For they persecute those you wound
and talk about the pain of those you hurt.[n]
27 Charge them with crime upon crime;[o]
do not let them share in your salvation.[p]
28 May they be blotted out of the book of life[q]
and not be listed with the righteous.[r]
29 I am in pain and distress;
may your salvation, O God, protect me.[s]

30 I will praise God's name in song[t]
and glorify him[u] with thanksgiving.
31 This will please the LORD more than an ox,
more than a bull with its horns and hoofs.[v]
32 The poor will see and be glad[w]—
you who seek God, may your hearts live![x]
33 The LORD hears the needy[y]
and does not despise his captive people.

34 Let heaven and earth praise him,
the seas and all that move in them,[z]
35 for God will save Zion[a]
and rebuild the cities of Judah.[b]
Then people will settle there and possess it;
36 the children of his servants will inherit it,[c]
and those who love his name will dwell there.[d]

Psalm 70

70:1-5pp — Ps 40:13-17

For the director of music. Of David. A petition.

1 Hasten, O God, to save me;
O LORD, come quickly to help me.[e]

[a] 22 Or *snare / and their fellowship become*

69:20 [e] Job 16:2 [f] Ps 142:4; Isa 63:5 **69:21** [g] S Nu 6:3; Mt 27:48; Mk 15:36; Lk 23:36 [h] Mt 27:34; Mk 15:23; Jn 19:28-30 **69:22** [i] S 1Sa 28:9; S Job 18:10 **69:23** [j] Ro 11:9-10* **69:24** [k] Ps 79:6; Jer 10:25 **69:25** [l] S Lev 26:43; Mt 23:38 [m] Ac 1:20* **69:26** [n] S Job 19:22; Zec 1:15 **69:27** [o] Ne 4:5 [p] Ps 109:14 **69:28** [q] Ex 32:32-33; S Lk 10:20 [r] Eze 13:9 **69:29** [s] S Ps 20:1 **69:30** [t] Ps 28:7 [u] Ps 34:3 **69:31** [v] Ps 50:9-13; 51:16 **69:32** [w] S Ps 34:2 [x] Ps 22:26 **69:33** [y] Ps 12:5 **69:34** [z] Ps 96:11; 98:7; Isa 44:23 **69:35** [a] Ob 1:17 [b] S Ezr 9:9; S Ps 51:18 **69:36** [c] Ps 25:13 [d] S Ps 37:29 **70:1** [e] Ps 22:19; 71:12

69:20 *heart.* See note on 4:7.

69:21 *gall in my food ... vinegar for my thirst.* Vivid metaphors for the bitter scorn they made him eat and drink when his whole being craved the nourishment and refreshment of comfort. The authors of the Gospels, especially Matthew, suggest that the suffering expressed in this verse foreshadowed Christ's suffering on the cross (see Mt 27:34,48; Mk 15:23,36; Lk 23:36; Jn 19:29).

69:22 – 28 Prayer for God to redress the wrongs committed (see note on 5:10).

69:22 – 23 For Paul's application of these verses to the Jews who rejected the Christ see Ro 11:9 – 10.

69:22 They had set his table with "gall" and "vinegar" (v. 21). *table set before them.* Reference may be to the meal accompanying the sealing of a covenant (see note on 23:5). In that case, this verse alludes to a pact uniting the enemies and calls on God to turn it against them. *become a snare ... a trap.* Note the unusual use of this imagery (see note on 9:15).

69:23 They mocked him for his "wound" (v. 26); now may they experience the same failing of the eyes (see v. 3 and note on 6:7) and bending of the back (from weakness and pain; see 38:5 – 8). *May ... their backs be bent.* Lit. "May ... their loins give way." "Loins" refers to the belly and lower part of the back; they were viewed as the back's center of strength (see 66:11; see also Job 40:16).

69:24 *wrath ... anger.* See note on 2:5. *overtake them.* Like a flash flood.

69:25 They sought to remove him from his place; may they be removed. Cf. Peter's application of this judgment to Judas (Ac 1:20).

69:26 The great wrong committed by his enemies against him and to which reference has repeatedly been made.

69:27 They have falsely charged him with crimes (v. 4); may their real crimes all be charged against them.

69:28 They had plotted his death; may death be their destiny. *book of life.* God's royal list of the righteous, whom he blesses with life (see 1:3; 7:9; 11:7; 34:12; 37:17,29; 55:22; 75:10; 92:12 – 14; 140:13). For other references to God's books see notes on 9:5; 51:1. In the NT the "book of life" refers to God's list of those destined for eternal life (see Php 4:3; Rev 3:5 and note; 13:8; 17:8; 20:12,15; 21:27; cf. Lk 10:20; Heb 12:23 and notes).

69:29 A summary renewal of the prayer just prior to the vow to praise (see note on v. 5). *pain.* An echo of v. 26. *your salvation.* Cf. vv. 13,27. *protect me.* Lit. "raise me to a high, secure place."

69:30 – 33 A vow to praise (see note on 7:17) out of assurance that the prayer will be heard (see note on 3:8).

69:30 *God's name.* See v. 36 and note on 5:11.

69:32 *poor.* See note on 34:6. *see and be glad.* See 22:26 and note. *hearts.* See note on 4:7. *live.* Bubble over with the joy of life, because the Lord does hear the prayers of his people in need — contrary to the mocking of scoffers.

69:34 – 36 A call for all creation to take up the praise of the Lord (see note on 9:1), a call that confidently anticipates that God will restore Judah and assure his people's inheritance in the promised land. This stanza appears to indicate that in its final form this royal prayer was used at a time when not only the king was in trouble but the kingdom of Judah had also suffered devastating defeat.

69:34 See 148:1 – 13; Isa 49:13.

69:35 – 36 *people ... children.* God's people and their children through the generations, specifically "those who love his name."

69:35 *Zion.* See note on 9:11.

Ps 70 An urgent prayer for God's help when threatened by enemies — a somewhat revised duplicate of 40:13 – 17 (see notes there). This is the second in a series of three such

[2]May those who seek my life[f]
be put to shame and confusion;
may all who desire my ruin
be turned back in disgrace.[g]
[3]May those who say to me, "Aha! Aha!"[h]
turn back because of their shame.
[4]But may all who seek you[i]
rejoice and be glad[j] in you;
may those who love your salvation
always say,
"Let God be exalted!"[k]

[5]Yet I am poor and needy;[l]
come quickly to me,[m] O God.
You are my help[n] and my deliverer;[o]
O LORD, do not delay.[p]

Psalm 71

71:1-3pp — Ps 31:1-4

[1]In you, O LORD, I have taken refuge;[q]
let me never be put to shame.[r]
[2]Rescue me and deliver me in your
righteousness;
turn your ear[s] to me and save me.
[3]Be my rock of refuge,
to which I can always go;
give the command to save me,
for you are my rock and my fortress.[t]
[4]Deliver[u] me, O my God, from the hand
of the wicked,[v]
from the grasp of evil and cruel
men.[w]

70:2 [f]Ps 35:4 [g]Ps 6:10; 35:26; 71:13; 109:29; 129:5 **70:3** [h]S Ps 35:21 **70:4** [i]Ps 9:10 [j]Ps 31:6-7; 32:11; 118:24 [k]Ps 35:27 **70:5** [l]Ps 86:1; 109:22 [m]Ps 141:1 [n]Ps 30:10; 33:20 [o]Ps 18:2 [p]Ps 119:60 **71:1** [q]S Dt 23:15; Ru 2:12 [r]S Ps 22:5 **71:2** [s]S 2Ki 19:16 **71:3** [t]Ps 18:2 **71:4** [u]S 2Ki 19:19 [v]Ps 140:4 [w]S Ge 48:16 **71:5** [x]S Ps 9:18; S 25:5 [y]S Job 4:6; Jer 17:7 **71:6** [z]S Ps 22:10 [a]S Job 3:16; S Ps 22:9 [b]Ps 9:1; 34:1; 52:9; 119:164; 145:2 **71:7** [c]S Dt 28:46; Isa 8:18; 1Co 4:9 [d]S 2Sa 22:3; Ps 61:3 **71:8** [e]ver 15; Ps 51:15; 63:5 [f]Ps 96:6; 104:1 **71:9** [g]S Ps 51:11 [h]Ps 92:14; Isa 46:4 [i]S Dt 4:31; S 31:6

[5]For you have been my hope,[x]
O Sovereign LORD,
my confidence[y] since my youth.
[6]From birth[z] I have relied on you;
you brought me forth from my
mother's womb.[a]
I will ever praise[b] you.
[7]I have become like a portent[c] to many,
but you are my strong refuge.[d]
[8]My mouth[e] is filled with your praise,
declaring your splendor[f] all day
long.

[9]Do not cast[g] me away when I am
old;[h]
do not forsake[i] me when my
strength is gone.
[10]For my enemies[j] speak against me;
those who wait to kill[k] me conspire[l]
together.
[11]They say, "God has forsaken[m] him;
pursue him and seize him,
for no one will rescue[n] him."
[12]Be not far[o] from me, O God;
come quickly, O my God, to help[p]
me.
[13]May my accusers[q] perish in shame;[r]
may those who want to harm me
be covered with scorn and disgrace.[s]

71:10 [j]Ps 3:7 [k]S Ps 10:8; 59:3; Pr 1:18 [l]S Ex 1:10; S Ps 31:13; S Mt 12:14 **71:11** [m]S Ps 9:10; Isa 40:27; 54:7; La 5:20; Mt 27:46 [n]S Ps 7:2 **71:12** [o]S Ps 38:21 [p]Ps 22:19; 38:22 **71:13** [q]Jer 18:19 [r]S Job 8:22; Ps 25:3 [s]S Ps 70:2

prayers; its language has many links with that of Ps 71. For this psalm's placement in the Psalter see introduction to Ps 69–72; for its special relationship to Ps 71 see introduction to that psalm. The prayer is framed by pleas for God to "come quickly" with his help (vv. 1,5). The rest of the prayer focuses on the effects of God's saving help: (1) upon those "who seek my life" (vv. 2–3) and (2) for those "who seek you" (v. 4).

70 title See note on Ps 4 title. *A petition.* See note on Ps 38 title.

70:4 God's deliverance of his servant will give joy to all who trust in the Lord, because they see in it the assurance of their own salvation. *Let God be exalted!* Because his saving help is sure and effective (contrast v. 3).

70:5 This verse echoes most of the language of v. 1: "God," "LORD," "come quickly," "(my) help (me)."

Ps 71 A prayer for God's help in old age when enemies threaten because they see that the king's strength is waning (see note on 5:9). The psalm bears no title, but it may well be that Ps 70 was viewed by the editors of the Psalms as the introduction to Ps 71 (compare vv. 1,12–13 with 70:1–2,5), in which case the psalm is ascribed to David (in his old age; see vv. 9,18). This suggestion gains support from the fact that Ps 72 is identified as a prayer by and/or for King Solomon (see introduction to that psalm). This is the third in a series of three prayers (see introduction to Ps 69–72); its dominant theme is hope (see v. 14). Formally symmetrical, the psalm is composed of six stanzas, having a five-four-five, five-four-five (in Hebrew) line pattern: vv. 1–4 (five lines), vv. 5–8 (four lines), vv. 9–13 (five lines); vv. 15–18 (five lines), vv. 19–21 (four lines), vv. 22–24 (five lines). Thus each half is made up of 14 lines. At the center (v. 14; see note on 6:6) stands a confident confession of hope. The whole is framed by an appeal for help (vv. 1–4) and a vow to praise in anticipation of deliverance (vv. 22–24). The second and fifth stanzas are linked by references to the troubles the king has experienced; stanzas three and four are linked by references to old age. This psalm appears to contain an unusual number of echoes of other psalms, though these alleged "echoes" may simply reflect a well-established prayer tradition (for particulars see notes below).

71:1–4 The initial appeal for God's help. Verses 1–3 differ only a little from 31:1–3a.

71:2 *your righteousness.* See vv. 15–16,19,24; see also note on 4:1.

71:3 *give the command to save.* In Hebrew a noteworthy verbal link with 44:4 ("who decrees victories"). The Hebrew phraseology occurs only in these two places in the OT.

71:5–8 A confession that the Lord has always been his hope (see vv. 14,19–21).

71:5–6 Cf. 22:10–11.

71:7 *like a portent.* The troubles of his life (see v. 20) have been viewed by others as holding some special significance—especially since the Lord has been his "strong refuge" through them all.

71:8 *My mouth is filled with your praise ... your splendor.* Because of the Lord's faithful care, the psalmist has been moved to fulfill in his life the high purpose of God in saving and blessing his people (see Jer 13:11; 33:9).

71:9–13 A prayer for God's continuing help in the waning years of his life.

71:10 *enemies speak against me.* See notes on 3:2; 5:9.

71:12 *Be not far from me.* Cf. 22:11,19; 35:22; 38:21. *come quickly ... to help me.* Cf. 22:19; 38:22; 40:13; 70:1; cf. also 70:5; 141:1.

71:13 A plea for redress (see note on 5:10). Key words in this closing verse of the first half of the psalm are echoed in the last verse of the second half. Similar language is found in 35:4,26; 40:14–15; 70:2–3; 83:17; 109:28–29.

[14]But as for me, I will always have
hope;[t]
I will praise you more and more.
[15]My mouth will tell[u] of your
righteousness,[v]
of your salvation all day long,
though I know not its measure.
[16]I will come and proclaim your mighty
acts,[w] O Sovereign LORD;
I will proclaim your righteousness,
yours alone.
[17]Since my youth, O God, you have
taught[x] me,
and to this day I declare your
marvelous deeds.[y]
[18]Even when I am old and gray,[z]
do not forsake me, O God,
till I declare your power[a] to the next
generation,
your might to all who are to come.[b]

[19]Your righteousness reaches to the
skies,[c] O God,
you who have done great things.[d]
Who, O God, is like you?[e]
[20]Though you have made me see
troubles,[f] many and bitter,
you will restore[g] my life again;
from the depths of the earth[h]
you will again bring me up.
[21]You will increase my honor[i]
and comfort[j] me once again.

[22]I will praise you with the harp[k]
for your faithfulness, O my God;
I will sing praise to you with the lyre,[l]
O Holy One of Israel.[m]
[23]My lips will shout for joy[n]
when I sing praise to you—
I, whom you have redeemed.[o]
[24]My tongue will tell of your righteous
acts
all day long,[p]
for those who wanted to harm me[q]
have been put to shame and
confusion.[r]

Psalm 72

Of Solomon.

[1]Endow the king with your justice,[s]
O God,
the royal son with your
righteousness.
[2]He will[a] judge your people in
righteousness,[t]
your afflicted ones with justice.
[3]The mountains will bring prosperity to
the people,
the hills the fruit of righteousness.

[a] 2 Or *May he*; similarly in verses 3-11 and 17

71:14 [t]Ps 25:3; 42:5; 130:7; 131:3 **71:15** [u]S ver 8; S Ps 66:16 [v]S Ps 51:14 **71:16** [w]Ps 9:1; 77:12; 106:2; 118:15; 145:4 **71:17** [x]S Dt 4:5; S Jer 7:13 [y]S Job 5:9; Ps 26:7; 86:10; 96:3 **71:18** [z]Isa 46:4 [a]S Ex 9:16 [b]Job 8:8; Ps 22:30,31; 78:4; 145:4; Joel 1:3 **71:19** [c]S Ps 36:5 [d]Ps 126:2; Lk 1:49 [e]Ps 35:10; 77:13; 89:8 **71:20** [f]Ps 25:17 [g]Ps 80:3, 19; 85:4; Hos 6:2 [h]S Ps 63:9 **71:21** [i]Ps 18:35 [j]Ps 23:4; 86:17; Isa 12:1; 40:1-2; 49:13; 54:10 **71:22** [k]Ps 33:2 [l]S Job 21:12; Ps 92:3; 144:9 [m]S 2Ki 19:22 **71:23** [n]Ps 20:5 [o]S Ex 15:13 **71:24** [p]S Ps 35:28 [q]ver 13 [r]S Est 9:2

72:1 [s]S Dt 1:16; S Ps 9:8 **72:2** [t]Isa 9:7; 11:4-5; 16:5; 32:1; 59:17; 63:1; Jer 23:5; 33:15

71:14 A centered confession of unfaltering hope—providing a striking link with Ps 42–43 (see 42:8 and note; see also note on 6:6).
71:15–18 A vow to praise, accompanying the renewal of his prayer (v. 18); see note on 7:17.
71:15 *tell … righteousness … salvation.* Here one of the righteous deeds the psalmist vows to "tell," i.e., to recount, is God's act of deliverance in answer to the psalmist's prayer (see notes on vv. 16–17; 4:1).
71:16–17 *mighty acts … righteousness … marvelous deeds.* God's "mighty (marvelous) acts" in behalf of his people are expressions of his righteousness; see also his "righteous acts" (v. 24).
71:16 *come.* To the temple, where God's people assemble for worship.
71:19–21 A confession that the Lord is still his hope, in the face of all his troubles (see vv. 5–8,14).
71:19 *reaches to the skies.* Is as expansive as all space above the earth (see also 36:5 and note). *Who, O God, is like you?* See Mic 7:18 and note.
71:20 *you have made me see troubles.* The "troubles" referred to are not specified. That God is somehow involved the psalmist does not question; he shares the mature and robust faith that all things are in the hands of the one sovereign God (see Dt 6:4 and note), the God to whom he turns in prayer (cf. 1Sa 16:11–12; Isa 45:5–7; Am 3:6). *restore my life again.* He who gave him life (see v. 6) will renew his life. *depths of the earth.* The realm of the dead, of which the grave is the portal (see note on 30:1).
71:22–24 A vow to praise in confident anticipation of God's saving help (see notes on 3:8; 7:17).
71:22 *harp … lyre.* See note on 57:8. *Holy One of Israel.* See 78:41; 89:18; see also 2Ki 19:22 and note.
71:23 *redeemed.* Here, as often, a synonym for "delivered." See notes on 65:6–7; Ex 6:6–8; 13:13; see also Introduction to Exodus: Themes and Theology.
71:24 *righteous acts.* God's saving acts in behalf of his people according to his covenant promises (see 88:12; Jdg 5:11; 1Sa 12:7 and note; Da 9:16; Mic 6:5; Rev 15:4).
Ps 72 A prayer for the king, a son of David who rules on David's throne as God's earthly regent over his people. It may have been used at the time of the king's coronation (as were Ps 2; 110). These verses express the desire of the nation that the king's reign will, as a consequence of God's endowment of his servant, be characterized by justice and righteousness, the supreme virtues of kingship. The prayer reflects the ideal concept of the king and the glorious effects of his reign. See Jeremiah's indictment of some of the last Davidic kings (e.g., Jer 22:2–3,13,15) and the prophetic announcement of the Messiah's righteous rule (see Isa 9:7; 11:4–5; Jer 23:5–6; 33:15–16; Zec 9:9). Later Jewish tradition saw in this psalm a description of the Messiah, as did the early church. The last three verses do not belong to the prayer (see notes there). For this psalm's function within Book II of the Psalter see introduction to Ps 69–72.
72 title *Of Solomon.* Either by him or for him—of course, both may be true. Undoubtedly it was also used by Israel (Judah) as a prayer for later Davidic kings.
72:1 The basic prayer. *justice … righteousness.* May the king be endowed with the gift for and the love of justice and righteousness so that his reign reflects the rule of God himself. Solomon asked for the necessary wisdom so he could govern God's people justly (see 1Ki 3:9,11–12; see also Pr 16:12). *righteousness.* See note on 4:1.
72:2–7 The quality of his reign: May it be righteous, prosperous and enduring.
72:3 Righteousness in the realm will be like fertilizing rain on the land, for then the Lord will bless his people with abun-

4He will defend the afflicted[u] among the
people
and save the children of the needy;[v]
he will crush the oppressor.[w]

5He will endure[a][x] as long as the sun,
as long as the moon, through all
generations.[y]
6He will be like rain[z] falling on a mown
field,
like showers watering the earth.
7In his days the righteous will flourish;[a]
prosperity will abound till the moon
is no more.

8He will rule from sea to sea
and from the River[b][b] to the ends of
the earth.[c][c]
9The desert tribes will bow before him
and his enemies will lick the dust.
10The kings of Tarshish[d] and of distant
shores[e]
will bring tribute to him;
the kings of Sheba[f] and Seba
will present him gifts.[g]
11All kings will bow down[h] to him
and all nations will serve[i] him.

12For he will deliver the needy who cry
out,
the afflicted who have no one to
help.
13He will take pity[j] on the weak and the
needy
and save the needy from death.
14He will rescue[k] them from oppression
and violence,
for precious[l] is their blood in his
sight.

15Long may he live!
May gold from Sheba[m] be given him.
May people ever pray for him
and bless him all day long.[n]
16Let grain[o] abound throughout the land;
on the tops of the hills may it sway.
Let its fruit[p] flourish like Lebanon;[q]
let it thrive like the grass of the field.[r]
17May his name endure forever;[s]
may it continue as long as the sun.[t]

All nations will be blessed through
him,
and they will call him blessed.[u]

18Praise be to the LORD God, the God of
Israel,[v]
who alone does marvelous deeds.[w]
19Praise be to his glorious name[x] forever;
may the whole earth be filled with
his glory.[y]
Amen and Amen.[z]

20This concludes the prayers of David
son of Jesse.[a]

BOOK III

Psalms 73–89

Psalm 73

A psalm of Asaph.

1Surely God is good to Israel,
to those who are pure in heart.[b]

72:4 [u]S Ps 9:12; 76:9; Isa 49:13 [v]ver 13; Isa 11:4; 29:19; 32:7 [w]S Ps 27:11 **72:5** [x]1Sa 13:13 [y]Ps 33:11 **72:6** [z]S Dt 32:2 **72:7** [a]Ps 92:12; Pr 14:11 **72:8** [b]S Ex 23:31; S 1Ki 4:21 [c]Zec 9:10 **72:10** [d]S Ge 10:4 [e]S Est 10:1 [f]S Ge 10:7 [g]S 1Ki 9:16; S 2Ch 9:24 **72:11** [h]S Ge 27:29 [i]S Ezr 1:2 **72:13** [j]Isa 60:10; Joel 2:18; Lk 10:33 **72:14** [k]Ps 69:18; Eze 13:23; 34:10 [l]1Sa 26:21 **72:15** [m]S Ge 10:7 [n]S Ps 35:28 **72:16** [o]S Ge 27:28; Ps 4:7 [p]Isa 4:2; 27:6; Eze 34:27 [q]Ps 92:12; 104:16 [r]S Nu 22:4; Isa 44:4; 58:11; 66:14 **72:17** [s]S Ex 3:15 [t]Ps 89:36 [u]S Ge 12:3; Lk 1:48 **72:18** [v]1Ch 29:10; Ps 41:13; 106:48; Lk 1:68 [w]S Job 5:9 **72:19** [x]S 2Sa 7:26

[a] 5 Septuagint; Hebrew *You will be feared* [b] 8 That is, the Euphrates [c] 8 Or *the end of the land*

[y]Nu 14:21 [z]S Ps 41:13 **72:20** [a]S Ru 4:17 **73:1** [b]S Ps 24:4; Mt 5:8

dance (see vv. 6–7; 5:12; 65:9–13; 133:3; Lev 25:19; Dt 28:8).

72:5 *endure as long as the sun.* See 21:4 and note.

72:6 See v. 3 and note; see also v. 7. For another vivid metaphor expressive of the significance of the Lord's anointed for the realm see La 4:20.

72:7 *righteous.* See note on 1:5. *will flourish.* Because the king supports and protects them, but uses all his royal power to suppress the wicked (see Ps 101).

72:8–14 The extent of his domain (vv. 8–11) as the result of his righteous rule (vv. 12–14).

72:8 His kingdom and authority will extend throughout the world (see vv. 9–11; cf. 110:2 and note). Ideally and potentially, as God's earthly regent, he possesses royal authority that extends on earth as far as God's—an expectation that is fulfilled in Christ. See Zec 9:10 and note.

72:9 The tribes of the Arabian Desert to the east will yield to him. *lick the dust.* See Mic 7:17 and note.

72:10 The kings whose lands border the Mediterranean Sea to the west will acknowledge him as overlord, as will those who rule in south Arabia and along the eastern African coast. *Tarshish.* A distant Mediterranean seaport, perhaps as far west as modern Spain. *Sheba.* See notes on Ge 10:28; 1Ki 10:1; Joel 3:8. *Seba.* Elsewhere in the OT associated with Cush (Ge 10:7; Isa 43:3); it may refer to a region in modern Sudan, south of Egypt.

72:15–17 Concluding summation: May the king enjoy a long, prosperous, world-renowned reign—one that blesses all the nations.

72:17 *All nations.* The language recalls the promise to Abraham (see Ge 12:3; 22:18) and suggests that it will be fulfilled through the royal son of David—ultimately the Messiah.

72:18–19 A doxology at the conclusion of Book II of the Psalter (see 41:13 and note). It is the people's response, their "Amen," to the contents of Book II (see note on Ps 4 title).

72:19 *filled with his glory.* See note on 85:9.

72:20 An editorial notation probably carried over from an earlier collection of psalms ascribed exclusively to David. *prayers of David.* See titles of Ps 86; 142.

Ps 73–78 Book III consists of three groupings of psalms, having an overall symmetrical pattern (six psalms [73–78], five psalms [79–83], six psalms [84–89]) and at its center (Ps 81) an urgent exhortation to fundamental covenant loyalty to the Lord (see introduction to Ps 79–83, introduction to Ps 84–89 and introduction to Ps 81). The first group is framed by psalms of instruction. Ps 73 is a word of godly wisdom based on an individual's life experience, while Ps 78 is a psalm of instruction based on Israel's communal experience in its historical pilgrimage with God. Within this frame, Ps 74 (a communal prayer) is linked with Ps 77 (a prayer of an individual) by the common experience of seeming to be rejected by God (see 74:1; 77:7) and by an extended evocation of God's saving act in Israel's exodus from Egypt (see 74:13–15; 77:16–19). At the center, two psalms (75; 76) express joyful assurance that Israel's God (his "Name is near," 75:1; "his name is great in Israel," 76:1) calls the arrogant wicked to account and rescues

[2]But as for me, my feet had almost
slipped;[c]
I had nearly lost my foothold.[d]
[3]For I envied[e] the arrogant
when I saw the prosperity of the
wicked.[f]

[4]They have no struggles;
their bodies are healthy and
strong.[a]
[5]They are free[g] from the burdens
common to man;
they are not plagued by human ills.
[6]Therefore pride[h] is their necklace;[i]
they clothe themselves with
violence.[j]
[7]From their callous hearts[k] comes
iniquity[b];
the evil conceits of their minds know
no limits.
[8]They scoff, and speak with malice;[l]
in their arrogance[m] they threaten
oppression.[n]
[9]Their mouths lay claim to heaven,
and their tongues take possession of
the earth.
[10]Therefore their people turn to them
and drink up waters in abundance.[c]
[11]They say, "How can God know?
Does the Most High have
knowledge?"

[12]This is what the wicked are like—
always carefree,[o] they increase in
wealth.[p]

[13]Surely in vain[q] have I kept my heart
pure;
in vain have I washed my hands
in innocence.[r]
[14]All day long I have been plagued;[s]
I have been punished every
morning.

[15]If I had said, "I will speak thus,"
I would have betrayed your
children.
[16]When I tried to understand[t] all this,
it was oppressive to me
[17]till I entered the sanctuary[u] of God;
then I understood their final
destiny.[v]

73:2 [c]S Dt 32:35 [d]Ps 69:2; Eph 4:27 **73:3** [e]Pr 3:31; 23:17; 24:1-2 [f]S Job 9:24; S 21:7; Jer 12:1; Mal 3:15 **73:5** [g]ver 12; Eze 23:42 **73:6** [h]S Lev 26:19 [i]S Ge 41:42; SS 4:9; Eze 16:11 [j]S Ge 6:11; S Pr 4:17 **73:7** [k]S Ps 17:10 **73:8** [l]Ps 41:5; Eze 25:15; Col 3:8 [m]Ps 17:10 [n]S Ps 10:7; S 12:5 **73:12** [o]S ver 5 [p]S Ps 49:6 **73:13** [q]S Job 9:29-31; S 21:15 [r]S Ge 44:16 **73:14** [s]ver 5 **73:16** [t]Ecc 8:17 **73:17** [u]Ex 15:17; Ps 15:1 [v]S Job 8:13; Php 3:19

[a] *4* With a different word division of the Hebrew; Masoretic Text *struggles at their death; / their bodies are healthy* [b] *7* Syriac (see also Septuagint); Hebrew *Their eyes bulge with fat* [c] *10* The meaning of the Hebrew for this verse is uncertain.

their victims; he cuts off "the horns of all the wicked" (75:10) and breaks "the spirit of rulers" (76:12).

Ps 73 A word of godly wisdom concerning the destinies of the righteous and the wicked (see introduction to Ps 73–78). Placed at the beginning of Book III, this psalm voices the faith (confessed [v. 1], tested [vv. 2–26] and reaffirmed [vv. 27–28]) that undergirds the following collection. It serves in Book III as Ps 1–2 serve in Book I (see introduction to Ps 1–2). Here the psalmist addresses one of the most disturbing problems of God's people in the OT: How is it that the wicked so often prosper while the godly suffer so much? Thematically the psalm has many links with Ps 49 (see introduction to that psalm; see also Ps 37). Its date may be as late as the postexilic era. Thematic development divides the psalm's structure into two halves of 14 verses each. Apart from the opening profession of faith (v. 1), the first half is framed by two couplets (vv. 2–3,13–14) that focus on the psalmist's condition—which is sharply contrasted with the perceived condition of the wicked (vv. 4–12). The psalm as a whole is framed by the equally sharp contrast between v. 1 and v. 27.
73 title The psalm is ascribed to Asaph, leader of one of David's three Levitical choirs (the other two leaders were Heman and Jeduthun/Ethan; these three represented the families and descendants of the three sons of Levi; see notes on Ps 39; 42; 50 titles). It begins a collection of 11 Asaphite psalms (Ps 73–83), to which Ps 50 at one time probably belonged. In view of the fact that the collection clearly contains prayers from a later date (e.g., Ps 74; 79; 83), references to Asaph in these titles must sometimes include descendants of Asaph who functioned in his place (see note on Ps 50 title). The Asaphite psalms are dominated by the theme of God's rule over his people and the nations. Apart from an introductory word of instruction (Ps 73) the collection is bracketed by prayers for God to rescue his people from foreign oppression (Ps 74; 83). The rest of the collection (Ps 75–82) appears to reflect thematic pairing: (1) The God who brings down the wicked and exalts the righteous (Ps 75) is the God and Savior of Israel (Ps 76). (2) God's saving acts in behalf of his people are remembered (Ps 77–78). (3) God is petitioned for help against the devastating attacks of Israel's enemies (Ps 79–80). (4) God is portrayed as presiding in judgment over his people (Ps 81) and over the world powers (Ps 82). This pairing, however, as is true of the whole Asaph collection, has been subsumed under another ordering principle (see introduction to Ps 73–78).

73:1–14 An almost fatal trial of faith: In the midst of many troubles a godly Israelite lets his eyes become fixed on the prosperity of the wicked.
73:1 *pure in heart.* See v. 13; see also note on 24:4. *heart.* See note on 4:7.
73:2 *feet had almost slipped.* From the path of truth and godliness (see 37:31 and note).
73:4–12 A description of the prosperous state of the wicked and the haughty self-reliance such prosperity engenders—hardly an objective account; it is rather the exaggerated picture that envious and troubled eyes perceived (see the description of the wicked in 10:2–11; cf. Job's anguished portrayal of the prosperity of the wicked in Job 21).
73:6 *pride is their necklace.* Contrast Pr 1:9; 3:3,22. *clothe themselves with.* See note on 109:29.
73:11 *They say.* Their speech as well as their actions show that they live "far from" God (v. 27). *God ... Most High.* That is, God Most High (see 57:2; see also note on 3:7). *Most High.* See note on Ge 14:19.
73:13–14 The thoughts that plagued the psalmist when he compared the state of the wicked with his own troubled lot.
73:13 *heart pure.* See note on v. 1.
73:14 *punished.* As children are by their parents to keep them in the right way (see Pr 3:12; 23:13–14).

73:15–28 The renewal of faith: In the temple, where God's ways are celebrated and taught, the psalmist sees the destiny God has appointed for the wicked (see v. 17).
73:15 *If I had said.* If the psalmist had given public expression to his thoughts as embodying true insight. *your children.* People characterized by a humble reliance on and commitment to God.

[18]Surely you place them on slippery
ground;[w]
you cast them down to ruin.[x]
[19]How suddenly[y] are they destroyed,
completely swept away[z] by terrors!
[20]As a dream[a] when one awakes,[b]
so when you arise, O Lord,
you will despise them as fantasies.[c]

[21]When my heart was grieved
and my spirit embittered,
[22]I was senseless[d] and ignorant;
I was a brute beast[e] before you.
[23]Yet I am always with you;
you hold me by my right hand.[f]
[24]You guide[g] me with your counsel,[h]
and afterward you will take me into
glory.
[25]Whom have I in heaven but you?[i]
And earth has nothing I desire
besides you.[j]
[26]My flesh and my heart[k] may fail,[l]
but God is the strength[m] of my heart
and my portion[n] forever.

[27]Those who are far from you will
perish;[o]
you destroy all who are unfaithful[p]
to you.
[28]But as for me, it is good to be near
God.[q]
I have made the Sovereign LORD my
refuge;[r]
I will tell of all your deeds.[s]

Psalm 74

A *maskil*[a] of Asaph.

[1]Why have you rejected[t] us forever,[u]
O God?
Why does your anger smolder
against the sheep of your
pasture?[v]
[2]Remember the people you purchased[w]
of old,[x]
the tribe of your inheritance,[y] whom
you redeemed[z]—
Mount Zion,[a] where you dwelt.[b]

[a] Title: Probably a literary or musical term

73:18 [w]S Dt 32:35; Ps 35:6 [x]S Ps 17:13 **73:19** [y]Dt 28:20; Pr 24:22; Isa 47:11 [z]S Ge 19:15 **73:20** [a]S Job 20:8 [b]Ps 78:65; Isa 29:8 [c]Pr 12:11; 28:19 **73:22** [d]Ps 49:10; 92:6; 94:8 [e]Ps 49:12, 20; Ecc 3:18; 9:12 **73:23** [f]S Ge 48:13 **73:24** [g]S Ps 48:14 [h]S 1Ki 22:5 **73:25** [i]Ps 16:2 [j]Php 3:8 **73:26** [k]Ps 84:2 [l]S Ps 31:10; 40:12 [m]Ps 18:1 [n]S Dt 32:9 **73:27** [o]S Ps 34:21 [p]S Lev 6:2; Jer 5:11; Hos 4:12; 9:1 **73:28** [q]Zep 3:2; Heb 10:22; Jas 4:8 [r]Ps 9:9 [s]Ps 26:7; 40:5 **74:1** [t]S Ps 43:2 [u]S Ps 44:23 [v]Ps 79:13; 95:7; 100:3 **74:2** [w]S Ex 15:16; S 1Co 6:20 [x]S Dt 32:7 [y]S Ex 34:9 [z]S Ex 15:13; S Isa 48:20 [a]Ps 2:6 [b]Ps 43:3; 68:16; Isa 46:13; Joel 3:17, 21; Ob 1:17

73:18–20 Though the wicked seem to prosper, God has made their position precarious; without warning they are swept away. The psalmist does not reflect on their state after death but leaves it as his final word that the wicked fall utterly and inevitably from their state of proud prosperity (see Ps 49; cf. the final state of the godly in v. 24).

73:20 When God arouses himself as from sleep (see note on 7:6) and deals with the wicked, they vanish like the shadowy characters of a dream.

73:21 *heart.* See note on 4:7. *spirit.* Lit. "kidneys" (see note on 7:9).

73:22 *a brute beast.* As stupid as a beast (see Job 18:3).

73:23–26 Although the psalmist had (almost) fallen to the level of beastly stupidity, God has not, will not, let him go—ever!

73:24 God's counsel has overcome his folly and will guide him through all the pitfalls of life (see 16:7; 32:8; 107:11). *take me into glory.* At the end of the believer's pilgrimage (see 49:15 and note).

73:25 Though he has envied the prosperity of the wicked, he now confesses that nothing in heaven or on earth is more desirable than God.

73:26 *My flesh … heart.* My whole being (see 84:2). *heart.* See note on 4:7. *portion.* Since the psalmist was a Levite, the Lord was his portion in the promised land in that he lived by the people's tithes dedicated to the Lord (see Nu 18:21–24; Dt 10:9; 18:1–2). But here he confesses more—what every godly Israelite could confess: The Lord himself is the sustainer and preserver of the life of those who put their trust in him (see note on 16:5–6).

73:27–28 See 34:21–22; 37:18–20; Pr 24:16.

73:27 *all who are unfaithful.* Lit. "all who commit (spiritual) prostitution/adultery." Although this expression elsewhere refers to blatant idolatry (as, e.g., in Dt 31:16; Jer 2:20; Hos 2:5 [see note there]) or to political alliance with any world power rather than relying on the Lord for security (as, e.g., in Eze 16:26–29), here it refers to the reliance of the wicked on their predatory economic and political practices, the "violence" with which they accumulated their wealth at the expense of others (vv. 6–11). See Isa 1:21 and note.

73:28 *I will tell of all your deeds.* A concluding vow to praise God for all his mercies to him (see note on 7:17).

Ps 74 A prayer for God to come to the aid of his people and defend his cause in the face of the mocking of the enemies—the Lord's relation to his people is like that of a king to his nation. The psalm dates from the time of the exile when Israel had been destroyed as a nation, the promised land devastated and the temple reduced to ruins (see Ps 79; La 2). Its relationship to the ministries of Jeremiah and Ezekiel is uncertain (see note on v. 9). Thematically the psalm divides into two halves of 11 verses each, with v. 12 (the center line; see note there) highlighting the primary thematic element that unifies the prayer. Verses 1–11 are framed by the "Why's" of the people's complaint (vv. 1,11); the whole psalm is framed by pleas for God to "remember" (vv. 2,22). Note also that the "they's" of vv. 4–8 have their counterpoint in the "you's" of vv. 13–17 (highlighted in Hebrew by seven emphatic pronouns)—the mighty acts of God are appealed to against the destructive and haughty deeds of the enemies. For the placement of this psalm in the Psalter and its relationship to the psalms around it see introduction to Ps 73–78.

74 title *maskil.* See note on Ps 32 title. *Asaph.* See note on Ps 73 title.

74:1–2 Initial complaint and appeal.

74:1 *Why … ? Why … ?* Cf. "How long …?" (v. 10) and "Why …?" (v. 11). See note on 6:3. *forever.* So it seemed, since no relief was in sight. *anger.* See note on 2:5. *sheep … pasture.* Metaphors related to the basic figure of a king as the shepherd of his realm (see notes on 23:1; 95:7; see also 79:13; 100:3).

74:2 *purchased.* Or "acquired"; or "created." *tribe.* Here referring to all Israel. *your inheritance.* See Dt 9:29. *redeemed.* Here, as often, a synonym for "delivered" (see note on 71:23). *Mount Zion.* See note on 9:11. This verse recalls the victory song of Ex 15 (see especially vv. 13–17, and compare the center verse of this psalm, v. 12, with the last verse of the song, Ex 15:18) and thus sets the stage for the other exodus recollections that follow. The Babylonian destruction of Zion seems to be the undoing of God's great victory over Egypt when he redeemed his people.

3 Turn your steps toward these
everlasting ruins,[c]
all this destruction the enemy has
brought on the sanctuary.
4 Your foes roared[d] in the place where
you met with us;
they set up their standards[e] as
signs.
5 They behaved like men wielding axes
to cut through a thicket of trees.[f]
6 They smashed all the carved[g] paneling
with their axes and hatchets.
7 They burned your sanctuary to the
ground;
they defiled[h] the dwelling place[i] of
your Name.[j]
8 They said in their hearts, "We will
crush[k] them completely!"
They burned[l] every place where God
was worshiped in the land.
9 We are given no miraculous signs;[m]
no prophets[n] are left,
and none of us knows how long this
will be.
10 How long[o] will the enemy mock[p] you,
O God?
Will the foe revile[q] your name
forever?
11 Why do you hold back your hand,
your right hand?[r]
Take it from the folds of your
garment[s] and destroy them!

12 But you, O God, are my king[t] from of
old;
you bring salvation[u] upon the earth.
13 It was you who split open the sea[v] by
your power;
you broke the heads of the monster[w]
in the waters.
14 It was you who crushed the heads of
Leviathan[x]
and gave him as food to the
creatures of the desert.[y]
15 It was you who opened up springs[z]
and streams;
you dried up[a] the ever flowing
rivers.
16 The day is yours, and yours also the
night;
you established the sun and moon.[b]
17 It was you who set all the boundaries[c]
of the earth;
you made both summer and
winter.[d]

18 Remember how the enemy has mocked
you, O LORD,
how foolish people[e] have reviled
your name.
19 Do not hand over the life of your dove[f]
to wild beasts;
do not forget the lives of your
afflicted[g] people forever.

74:3 [c] Isa 44:26; 52:9 **74:4** [d] La 2:7 [e] S Nu 2:2; S Jer 4:6 **74:5** [f] Jer 46:22 **74:6** [g] S 1Ki 6:18 **74:7** [h] S Lev 20:3; Ac 21:28 [i] S Lev 15:31 [j] Ps 75:1 **74:8** [k] Ps 94:5 [l] 2Ki 25:9; 2Ch 36:19; Jer 21:10; 34:22; 52:13 **74:9** [m] S Ex 4:17; S 10:1 [n] S 1Sa 3:1 **74:10** [o] Ps 6:3; 79:5; 80:4 [p] ver 22 [q] S Ps 44:16 **74:11** [r] S Ex 15:6 [s] Ne 5:13; Eze 5:3 **74:12** [t] Ps 2:6; S 24:7; 68:24 [u] Ps 27:1 **74:13** [v] S Ex 14:21 [w] Isa 27:1; 51:9; Eze 29:3; 32:2 **74:14** [x] S Job 3:8 [y] Isa 13:21; 23:13; 34:14; Jer 50:39 **74:15** [z] S Ex 17:6; S Nu 20:11 [a] S Ex 14:29; S Jos 2:10 **74:16** [b] S Ge 1:16; Ps 136:7-9 **74:17** [c] Dt 32:8; Ac 17:26 [d] S Ge 8:22 **74:18** [e] Dt 32:6 **74:19** [f] S Ge 8:8; S Isa 59:11 [g] S Ps 9:18

74:3–8 The Babylonians' high-handed destruction of the Lord's temple.
74:3 *Turn your steps toward.* Hurry to restore.
74:4 *standards.* Probably troop standards (see Nu 1:52; Isa 31:9; Jer 4:21). *as signs.* Signifying their triumph.
74:6 *carved paneling.* See 1Ki 6:15.
74:7 *your Name.* See note on 5:11. The NIV capitalizes "Name" when it stands for God's presence at the sanctuary (see Dt 12:5).
74:8 *They said.* See note on 10:11. *every place where God was worshiped.* Lit. "all the meeting places of God" (see v. 4). The reference is uncertain. At the time of the Babylonian attacks there may have been a number of (illegitimate) places in Judah where people went to worship God (see notes on 1Ki 3:2; 2Ki 18:4).
74:9–11 The complaint and prayer renewed (see vv. 1–2).
74:9 *no miraculous signs.* As there were at the time of the exodus (see vv. 13–15; 78:43). *no prophets.* Jeremiah had been taken to Egypt (see Jer 43:6–7), but whether Ezekiel was no longer prophesying is unknown. Perhaps this psalm was composed by an Asaphite who remained in Israel, part of a small group overlooked by Johanan when that army officer led the remnant to Egypt (see Jer 43:4–7).
74:10 *mock you … revile your name.* See v. 18; see also v. 22; 2Ki 18:32–35; Isa 37:6,23.
74:12 The center verse (center line in the Hebrew text; see note on 6:6). The whole psalm presupposes the truth confessed here: God is Israel's King, her hope and Savior; Israel is God's people (kingdom). This accounts for both the complaint and the prayer, and why the destruction of Israel brings with it the mocking of God. *my.* Communal use of the singular pronoun (see note on Ps 30 title). *from of old.* From the days of the exodus (see Ex 3:7; 19:5–6).
74:13–17 The Lord is the mighty God of salvation and creation (see 65:6–7 and note).
74:13–14 Recollection of God's mighty acts when he delivered his people from Egypt. The imagery is borrowed from ancient Near Eastern creation myths, in which the primeval chaotic waters were depicted as a many-headed monster that the creator-god overcame, after which he established the world order (see note on 32:6). The poet here interweaves creation and salvation themes to celebrate the fact that the God of Israel has shown by his saving acts (his opening of the Red Sea for his people and his destruction of the Egyptians) that he is able to overcome all hostile powers to redeem his people and establish his new order in the world. For poetic use of this imagery (1) to celebrate God's creation works see 89:10; Job 9:13; 26:12–13; (2) to celebrate the deliverance from Egypt see Isa 51:9; (3) to announce a future deliverance of Israel see Isa 27:1. Echoes of the same imagery are present in the judgment announced against Egypt in Eze 29:3–5; 32:2–6.
74:15 Recollection of God's water miracles at the Red Sea, in the desert and at the Jordan.
74:16–17 God is the One who established the orders of creation; he (alone) is able to effect redemption and establish his kingdom in the world against all creaturely opposition.
74:18–23 A prayer for God to defend his cause and restore his people.
74:18 See vv. 2,10. *foolish people.* The "foes" of v. 10 are here called fools for their contempt of God (see v. 22; see also NIV text note on 14:1).
74:19 *your dove.* Israel—probably a figure of endearment (see SS 2:14; 5:2; 6:9; see also Ps 68:13 and note). *wild beasts.* See note on 7:2.

[20]Have regard for your covenant,[h]
because haunts of violence fill the
dark places[i] of the land.
[21]Do not let the oppressed[j] retreat in
disgrace;
may the poor and needy[k] praise your
name.
[22]Rise up,[l] O God, and defend your
cause;
remember how fools[m] mock you all
day long.
[23]Do not ignore the clamor[n] of your
adversaries,[o]
the uproar[p] of your enemies,[q] which
rises continually.

Psalm 75

For the director of music. ⌞To the tune of⌟
"Do Not Destroy." A psalm of Asaph.
A song.

[1]We give thanks to you, O God,
we give thanks, for your Name is
near;[r]
men tell of your wonderful deeds.[s]
[2]You say, "I choose the appointed time;[t]
it is I who judge uprightly.[u]
[3]When the earth and all its people
quake,[v]
it is I who hold its pillars[w] firm.
Selah
[4]To the arrogant[x] I say, 'Boast no
more,'[y]
and to the wicked, 'Do not lift up
your horns.[z]
[5]Do not lift your horns against heaven;
do not speak with outstretched
neck.[a]' "
[6]No one from the east or the west
or from the desert can exalt a man.
[7]But it is God who judges:[b]
He brings one down, he exalts
another.[c]
[8]In the hand of the LORD is a cup
full of foaming wine mixed[d] with
spices;
he pours it out, and all the wicked of
the earth
drink it down to its very dregs.[e]
[9]As for me, I will declare[f] this forever;
I will sing[g] praise to the God of
Jacob.[h]
[10]I will cut off the horns of all the
wicked,
but the horns of the righteous will
be lifted up.[i]

74:20 [h]S Ge 6:18 [i]Job 34:22 **74:21** [j]Ps 9:9; 10:18; 103:6; Isa 58:10 [k]S Ps 35:10 **74:22** [l]Ps 17:13 [m]S Ps 53:1 **74:23** [n]Isa 31:4 [o]S Ps 65:7 [p]S Ps 46:6 [q]S Nu 25:17 **75:1** [r]Ps 145:18 [s]S Jos 3:5; Ps 44:1; S 71:16; 77:12; 105:2; 107:8,15; 145:5,12 **75:2** [t]S Ex 13:10 [u]S Ps 7:11 **75:3** [v]Isa 24:19 [w]1Sa 2:8; S 2Sa 22:8 **75:4** [x]S Ps 5:5 [y]S 1Sa 2:3 [z]Zec 1:21 **75:5** [a]S Job 15:25 **75:7** [b]S Ge 16:5; Ps 50:6; 58:11; Rev 18:8 [c]1Sa 2:7; S Job 5:11; Ps 147:6; Eze 21:26; Da 2:21 **75:8** [d]Pr 23:30 [e]Isa 51:17; Jer 25:15; Zec 12:2 **75:9** [f]Ps 40:10 [g]Ps 108:1 [h]S Ge 24:12; Ps 76:6 **75:10** [i]Ps 89:17; 92:10; 112:9; 148:14

74:20 *your covenant.* God's covenant to be the God of Israel, who makes them secure and richly blessed in the promised land (see Ex 19:5–6; 23:27–31; 34:10–11; Lev 26:11–12,42,44–45; Dt 28:1–14; see also Ps 105:8–11; 106:45; 111:5,9; Isa 54:10; Jer 14:21; Eze 16:60).
74:21 *poor and needy.* See note on 34:6. *praise your name.* May they have cause to do so.
74:22 *Rise up.* See note on 3:7.
74:23 *clamor … uproar.* See 64:2.
Ps 75 A song of reassurance when arrogant worldly powers threaten Israel's security. The psalm may date from the time of the Assyrian menace (see 2Ki 18:13—19:37). See also Ps 11; 76. Thematic parallels to the song of Hannah (1Sa 2:1–10) are numerous. The worshiping congregation speaks (v. 1), perhaps led in its praise by one of the descendants of Asaph (v. 9). The psalm is framed by thanksgiving (v. 1) and praise (vv. 9–10). Two stanzas of four (Hebrew) lines each form the body of the psalm, and each stanza is composed of two couplets. The first stanza contains a reassuring word from heaven; the second contains a triumphant response from earth. For this psalm's relationship to those around it, especially to Ps 76, see introduction to Ps 73–78.
75 title *For the director of music.* See note on Ps 4 title. ⌞*To the tune of*⌟. See note on Ps 9 title. *Do Not Destroy.* See Ps 57; 58; 59 titles. *Asaph.* See note on Ps 73 title. *song.* See note on Ps 30 title.
75:1 The congregation begins with thanksgiving in the form of praise (see 7:17; 28:7; 30:12; 35:18). *Name.* See notes on 5:11; 74:7. *wonderful deeds.* See note on 9:1.
75:2–5 A reassuring word from above: God will not fail to call the arrogant to account. It is not clear whether a new word from the Lord is heard or whether these verses recall (and perhaps summarize) earlier prophetic words (such as those of Isaiah in 2Ki 19:21–34).
75:2 God will not fail to judge (see Ps 96; 98)—but in his own time.
75:3 When, because of the upsurge of evil powers, the whole moral order of the world seems to have crumbled, God still guarantees its stability (see note on 11:3). *pillars.* A figure for that which stabilizes the world order (see note on 24:2).
75:4 *arrogant … wicked.* To the psalmists the wicked are both arrogant (see especially Ps 10; 73:4–12; 94:4; see also note on 31:23) and foolish (see 14:1; 74:18,22; 92:6; 94:8). *lift up your horns.* A figure for defiant opposition, based on the action of attacking bulls. "Horn" (see also v. 10) is a common Biblical metaphor for vigor or strength (see NIV text note on 18:2).
75:5 *outstretched neck.* A sign of defiance.
75:6–8 Triumphant echo from earth: perhaps spoken by the Levitical song leader in elaboration of the comforting word from God.
75:8 *cup.* See note on 16:5. *mixed with spices.* The spices used increased the intoxicating effect (see Pr 9:2,5; 23:29–30; SS 8:2; Isa 65:11). *drink it down.* Because God pours it out, they have no choice.
75:9 Concluding vow to praise God forever (see note on 7:17) for his righteous judgments. *me.* Probably the Levitical song leader speaking representatively for the people, but the pronoun may be a communal use of the singular, as in 74:12 (see note on Ps 30 title). *Jacob.* A synonym for Israel (see Ge 32:28).
75:10 It is unclear who is speaking. The action pledged appears unlikely for a Levite but appropriate for a king (see Ps 101). This is not, however, a royal psalm. It seems best, then, to suppose that the speaker(s) of v. 9 recall(s) another word from the Lord. The connection would be: " … the God of Jacob/(who declares,) 'I will …'" *righteous.* See note on 1:5. *lifted up.* See v. 7; see also note on v. 4.

Psalm 76

For the director of music. With stringed instruments. A psalm of Asaph. A song.

[1] In Judah God is known;
his name is great[j] in Israel.
[2] His tent is in Salem,[k]
his dwelling place in Zion.[l]
[3] There he broke the flashing arrows,[m]
the shields and the swords, the weapons of war.[n] *Selah*
[4] You are resplendent with light,[o]
more majestic than mountains rich with game.
[5] Valiant men[p] lie plundered,
they sleep their last sleep;[q]
not one of the warriors
can lift his hands.
[6] At your rebuke,[r] O God of Jacob,
both horse and chariot[s] lie still.
[7] You alone are to be feared.[t]
Who can stand[u] before you when you are angry?[v]
[8] From heaven you pronounced judgment,
and the land feared[w] and was quiet—
[9] when you, O God, rose up to judge,[x]
to save all the afflicted[y] of the land. *Selah*
[10] Surely your wrath against men brings you praise,[z]
and the survivors of your wrath are restrained.[a]
[11] Make vows to the LORD your God and fulfill them;[a]
let all the neighboring lands
bring gifts[b] to the One to be feared.
[12] He breaks the spirit of rulers;
he is feared by the kings of the earth.

Psalm 77

For the director of music. For Jeduthun. Of Asaph. A psalm.

[1] I cried out to God[c] for help;
I cried out to God to hear me.

[a] 10 Or *Surely the wrath of men brings you praise, / and with the remainder of wrath you arm yourself*

76:1 [j] Ps 99:3 **76:2** [k] S Ge 14:18; Heb 7:1 [l] S 2Sa 5:7; Ps 2:6 **76:3** [m] Eze 39:9 [n] Ps 46:9 **76:4** [o] S Ps 36:9 **76:5** [p] S Jdg 20:44 [q] S Ps 13:3; S Mt 9:24 **76:6** [r] S Ps 50:21 [s] S Ex 15:1 **76:7** [t] S 1Ch 16:25 [u] S Ezr 9:15; Rev 6:17 [v] Ps 2:5; Na 1:6 **76:8** [w] S 1Ch 16:30; Eze 38:20 **76:9** [x] S Ps 9:8; 58:11; 74:22; 82:8; 96:13 [y] S Ps 72:4 **76:10** [z] Ex 9:16; Ro 9:17 **76:11** [a] S Lev 22:18; S Ps 50:14; Ecc 5:4-5 [b] S 2Ch 32:23 **77:1** [c] S 1Ki 8:52

Ps 76 A celebration of the Lord's invincible power in defense of Jerusalem, his royal city. The psalm is thematically related to Ps 46; 48; 87 (see introduction to Ps 46). The ancient tradition may well be correct that the psalm was composed after the Lord's destruction of Sennacherib's army when it threatened Jerusalem (see 2Ki 19:35). Structurally, the opening (vv. 1–3) and closing (vv. 11–12) stanzas contain the main theme. Between them, two four-line (in Hebrew) stanzas of praise addressed to God (vv. 4–6,7–10) celebrate his awesome act of judgment. For this psalm's relationship to those around it, especially to Ps 75, see introduction to Ps 73–78.
76 title *For the director of music.* See note on Ps 4 title. *With stringed instruments.* See note on Ps 4 title. *Asaph.* See note on Ps 73 title. *song.* See note on Ps 30 title.
76:1–3 God's crushing defeat of the enemy in defense of Zion.
76:1 *is known.* Now especially—as a result of his marvelous act. *Israel.* The poet probably does not intend to distinguish between the two kingdoms (Judah and Israel) but only, by joining their names together, to refer to the whole of God's covenant people. Moreover, as a result of the Assyrian invasions, many displaced Israelites from the northern kingdom now resided in and around Jerusalem.
76:2 *tent … dwelling place.* Since the two Hebrew words for these nouns frequently refer to a lion's den, covert or lair (see 10:9; 104:22; Job 38:40; Jer 25:38; Am 3:4), it may be that the psalmist is here depicting Israel's God as a lion overpowering its prey. In that case, an alternative rendering of v. 4 should be considered (see note on that verse). *Salem.* Jerusalem, as the parallelism makes clear (see note on Ge 14:18). *Zion.* See note on 9:11.
76:4–10 Praise of God's awesome majesty, whose mighty judgment evokes fearful reverence (see introduction).
76:4 *more majestic … with game.* If the nouns in v. 2 refer to a lion's den (see note there), this line should be rendered something like "the majestic One from the mountains rich with game."
76:5–6 Perhaps echoes also God's victory over the Egyptians at the Red Sea (see Ex 14:28,30; 15:4–5,10).
76:6 *rebuke.* This word, when predicated of God, usually refers to either (1) the thunder of his fierce majesty by which he wields his sovereign control over cosmic entities (see 18:15; 104:7; 106:9; Job 26:11; Isa 50:2; Na 1:4) or repulses his enemies (as here; see also 9:5; 68:30; Isa 17:13), or (2) the thunder of his wrath (see 80:16; Isa 51:20; 54:9; 66:15; Mal 2:3). *God of Jacob.* A link with Ps 75 (see 75:9 and note).
76:7 *You alone … you.* This first line of the second four-line stanza echoes the emphatic "you" with which the first four-line stanza begins (v. 4).
76:8 *From heaven.* Though God is present in Zion (see v. 2), he sovereignly rules from heaven.
76:10 *wrath.* See note on 2:5. *brings you praise.* When his judgments bring deliverance, those rescued praise him. If the alternative translation in the NIV text note is taken, "the wrath of men brings you praise" would mean that when people rise up against God's kingdom, he crushes them in wrath to his own praise as Victor and Deliverer. And "the remainder of wrath" would indicate that particular judgments do not exhaust his wrath; a remainder is left to deal with other hostile powers.
76:11–12 Let Israel acknowledge God's help with grateful vows; let the nations acknowledge his sovereign rule with tribute.
76:11 *Make vows … fulfill.* See note on 50:14.
76:12 *spirit of rulers.* Their bold rebelliousness.
Ps 77 Comforting reflections in a time of great distress. For the relationship of this psalm to Ps 74 see introduction to Ps 73–78. The interplay of verb forms in vv. 1–6 makes it uncertain whether the psalm is a prayer (in which case the verbs of these verses would have to be rendered in the present tense) or the recollection of a past experience (as the NIV understands it). The distress appears to be personal rather than national. Comparison of vv. 16–19 with Hab 3:8–10 suggests, but does not prove, a time late in the monarchy. The poetic development advances from anguished bewilderment (vv. 1–9) to comforting recollection (vv. 10–20). A striking and dramatic feature is the insertion of a four-verse stanza (vv. 16–19) between the third and fourth verses of another four-verse stanza (vv. 13–15,20).
77 title *For the director of music.* See note on Ps 4 title. *Jeduthun.* See note on Ps 39 title. *Asaph.* See note on Ps 73 title.
77:1–9 Anguished perplexity over God's apparent inaction,

[2]When I was in distress,[d] I sought the
Lord;
at night[e] I stretched out untiring
hands[f]
and my soul refused to be
comforted.[g]

[3]I remembered[h] you, O God, and I
groaned;[i]
I mused, and my spirit grew faint.[j]
Selah
[4]You kept my eyes from closing;
I was too troubled to speak.[k]
[5]I thought about the former days,[l]
the years of long ago;
[6]I remembered my songs in the night.
My heart mused and my spirit
inquired:

[7]"Will the Lord reject forever?[m]
Will he never show his favor[n] again?
[8]Has his unfailing love[o] vanished
forever?
Has his promise[p] failed for all time?
[9]Has God forgotten to be merciful?[q]
Has he in anger withheld his
compassion?[r]" *Selah*

[10]Then I thought, "To this I will appeal:
the years of the right hand[s] of the
Most High."
[11]I will remember the deeds of the LORD;
yes, I will remember your miracles[t]
of long ago.
[12]I will meditate[u] on all your works
and consider all your mighty deeds.[v]
[13]Your ways, O God, are holy.
What god is so great as our God?[w]
[14]You are the God who performs
miracles;[x]
you display your power among the
peoples.
[15]With your mighty arm you redeemed
your people,[y]
the descendants of Jacob and
Joseph. *Selah*

[16]The waters[z] saw you, O God,
the waters saw you and writhed;[a]
the very depths were convulsed.
[17]The clouds poured down water,[b]
the skies resounded with thunder;[c]
your arrows[d] flashed back and forth.
[18]Your thunder was heard in the
whirlwind,[e]
your lightning[f] lit up the world;
the earth trembled and quaked.[g]
[19]Your path[h] led through the sea,[i]
your way through the mighty
waters,
though your footprints were not
seen.

[20]You led your people[j] like a flock[k]
by the hand of Moses and Aaron.[l]

Psalm 78

A *maskil*[a] of Asaph.

[1]O my people, hear my teaching;[m]
listen to the words of my mouth.

[a] Title: Probably a literary or musical term

77:2 [d]S Ge 32:7; S 2Sa 22:7; S Ps 118:5 [e]Ps 6:6; 22:2; 88:1 [f]S Ex 9:29; S Job 11:13 [g]S Ge 37:35; Mt 2:18 **77:3** [h]Ps 78:35 [i]Ex 2:23; S Ps 6:6; Jer 45:3 [j]S Ps 6:2 **77:4** [k]S Ps 39:2 **77:5** [l]Dt 32:7; Ps 44:1; 143:5; Ecc 7:10 **77:7** [m]S 1Ch 28:9 [n]Ps 85:1; 102:13; 106:4 **77:8** [o]S Ps 6:4; 90:14 [p]2Pe 3:9 **77:9** [q]Ps 25:6; 40:11; 51:1 [r]Isa 49:15 **77:10** [s]S Ex 15:6 **77:11** [t]S Ne 9:17 **77:12** [u]S Ge 24:63 [v]Ps 143:5 **77:13** [w]S Ex 15:11; S Ps 71:19; 86:8 **77:14** [x]S Ex 3:20; S 34:10 **77:15** [y]S Ex 6:6 **77:16** [z]Ex 14:21,28; Isa 50:2; Hab 3:8 [a]Ps 114:4; Hab 3:10 **77:17** [b]S Jdg 5:4 [c]S Ex 9:23; S Ps 29:3 [d]S Dt 32:23 **77:18** [e]S Ps 55:8 [f]S 2Sa 22:13 [g]S Jdg 5:4 **77:19** [h]S Ex 14:22 [i]S Job 9:8 **77:20** [j]S Ex 13:21 [k]Ps 78:52; Isa 63:11 [l]S Ex 4:16; S Nu 33:1 **78:1** [m]Isa 51:4; 55:3

when he seemingly fails to respond to unceasing and urgent prayers.

77:2 *soul.* See note on 6:3.

77:3–6 Remembrance of God's past mercies intensifies the present perplexity (as also in 22:1–11). God's failure to act now is so troubling that the psalmist cannot sleep (cf. 3:5; 4:8) and words fail (but see vv. 10–20).

77:6 *heart.* See note on 4:7.

77:7–9 Though words fail (v. 4), troubled thoughts will not go away.

77:8 *unfailing love.* See note on 6:4.

77:9 *anger.* See note on 2:5.

77:10–20 Reassuring recollection of God's mighty acts in behalf of Israel in the exodus.

77:10–12 Faith's decision to look beyond the present troubles—and God's bewildering inactivity—to draw hope anew from God's saving acts of old.

77:10 *Most High.* See note on Ge 14:19.

77:11,14 *miracles.* See note on 9:1 ("wonders").

77:13–20 God's mighty acts in the exodus recalled.

77:13 Appears to echo Ex 15:11. *are holy.* Or "are seen in the sanctuary" (see 63:2).

77:15 *redeemed.* Here, as often, a synonym for "delivered" (see note on 71:23). *Joseph.* OT authors sometimes refer to the northern kingdom as "Joseph" (or "Ephraim," Joseph's son) in distinction from the southern kingdom of Judah (see 78:67; 2Sa 19:20; 1Ki 11:28; Eze 37:16,19; Am 5:6,15; 6:6; Zec 10:6). However, here and elsewhere (see 80:1; 81:5; Ob 18) Joseph—the one elevated to the position of firstborn (see Ge 48:5 and note; Jos 16:1–4; 1Ch 5:2; Eze 47:13)—represents the whole of his generation and thus also all the descendants of Jacob.

77:16–19 A poetically heightened description of the majesty of God displayed when he opened a way through the Red Sea (see 74:13–15). Verses 16,19 speak expressly of that event; the intervening verses (vv. 17–18) evoke the majesty of God displayed in the thunderstorm and earthquake. Ex 14:19 speaks only of God's cloud, not of a thunderstorm or earthquake, but the Hebrew poets often associated either or both with the Lord's coming to effect redemption or judgment—no doubt because these were the two most fearsome displays of power known to them (see 18:12–14; 68:8; Jdg 5:4–5; Hab 3:6,10). Here the psalmist declares: It was the God of thunderstorm and earthquake who made his majestic way through the mighty waters of the sea to bring his people out of bondage. For Christians the display of God's power in behalf of his people now includes the resurrection of Jesus Christ from the dead (see Mt 28:2; cf. Eph 1:18–23 and note on 1:19).

77:17 *arrows.* Lightning bolts (see note on Ge 9:13).

77:20 Completes the thought of v. 15 (see introduction). *led your people.* Through the Desert of Sinai. *like a flock.* See 23:1; 74:1 and notes.

Ps 78 A psalm of instruction—of warnings not to repeat Israel's sins of the past but to remember God's saving acts and marvelously persistent grace and, remembering, to keep faith with him and his covenant. Here as elsewhere (pervasively in the OT), trust in and loyalty to God on the part of

[2]I will open my mouth in parables,[n]
I will utter hidden things, things
from of old—
[3]what we have heard and known,
what our fathers have told us.[o]
[4]We will not hide them from their
children;[p]
we will tell the next generation[q]
the praiseworthy deeds[r] of the LORD,
his power, and the wonders[s] he has
done.
[5]He decreed statutes[t] for Jacob[u]
and established the law in Israel,
which he commanded our forefathers
to teach their children,
[6]so the next generation would know
them,
even the children yet to be born,[v]
and they in turn would tell their
children.
[7]Then they would put their trust in
God
and would not forget[w] his deeds
but would keep his commands.[x]
[8]They would not be like their
forefathers[y]—
a stubborn[z] and rebellious[a]
generation,
whose hearts were not loyal to God,
whose spirits were not faithful to
him.

[9]The men of Ephraim, though armed
with bows,[b]
turned back on the day of battle;[c]
[10]they did not keep God's covenant[d]
and refused to live by his law.[e]
[11]They forgot what he had done,[f]
the wonders he had shown them.
[12]He did miracles[g] in the sight of their
fathers
in the land of Egypt,[h] in the region
of Zoan.[i]
[13]He divided the sea[j] and led them
through;
he made the water stand firm like a
wall.[k]

78:2 [n]S Ps 49:4; S Mt 13:35* **78:3** [o]S Jdg 6:13 **78:4** [p]S Dt 11:19 [q]S Dt 32:7; S Ps 71:18 [r]Ps 26:7; 71:17 [s]S Job 5:9 **78:5** [t]Ps 19:7; 81:5 [u]Ps 147:19 **78:6** [v]S Ps 22:31 **78:7** [w]S Dt 6:12 [x]S Dt 5:29 **78:8** [y]S 2Ch 30:7 [z]S Ex 32:9 [a]S Ex 23:21; S Dt 21:18; Isa 30:9; 65:2 **78:9** [b]ver 57; 1Ch 12:2; Hos 7:16 [c]S Jdg 20:39 **78:10** [d]S Jos 7:11; S 2Ki 17:15 [e]S Ex 16:28; S Jer 11:8 **78:11** [f]Ps 106:13 **78:12** [g]S Ne 9:17; Ps 106:22 [h]Ex 11:9 [i]S Nu 13:22 **78:13** [j]S Ex 14:21; Ps 66:6; 136:13 [k]S Ex 14:22; S 15:8

God's people are covenant matters. They do not spring from abstract principles (such as the formal structure of the God-human relationship) or from general human consciousness (such as feelings of dependence on "God" or a sense of awe in the presence of the "holy"), but they result from remembering God's mighty saving acts. Correspondingly, unfaithfulness is the more blameworthy because it contemptuously disregards all God's wonderful acts in his people's behalf (see Ps 105–106).

The psalm probably dates from the period of the divided monarchy and may have been composed about the time of the prophet Hosea (both Hosea and Isaiah speak frequently of the northern kingdom as Ephraim since it was the dominant tribe of that realm). Israel's unfaithfulness is here epitomized in the sin of Ephraim (v. 9); the psalm concludes by recalling the rejection of "Israel" (v. 59) and the abandonment of Shiloh (v. 60), but the election of Judah and Mount Zion (v. 68). Coming, as may be assumed, from the pen of an Asaphite, the psalm was no doubt a warning to worshipers at Jerusalem not to fall away after the manner of the Israelites to the north.

By placing this psalm next to Ps 77, the editors of the Psalter ranked David alongside Moses (and Aaron) as the Lord's shepherd over his people (see vv. 70–72; 77:20) who brought the exodus to its (provisionally) climactic fruition by completing the conquest of the promised land—a perspective apparently shared by the author of the psalm.

The psalm is composed of 77 (Hebrew) lines (72 numbered verses) and seven stanzas—with an 11-line introduction. After the introduction, the structure of the stanzas is symmetrical: 8 lines, 16 lines, 9 lines, 16 lines, 9 lines, 8 lines. The two sequences of 16 lines–9 lines constitute a thematic cycle, while the two 8-line stanzas frame the double cycle and underscore the contrast between the sin of Israel ("Ephraim," vv. 9–16) and the unending mercy of God to his people—mercy that is evidenced in his victory over his enemies and his election of Zion (in Judah) and David (vv. 65–72). For this psalm's relationship to Ps 73 in the arrangement of the Psalter see introduction to Ps 73–78.

78 title *maskil.* See note on Ps 32 title. *Asaph.* See note on Ps 73 title.

78:1–8 Our children must hear what our fathers have told us, so that they may be faithful to the Lord.

78:1–2 This introduction is written in the style of a wisdom writer (see essay, p. 727; see also Ps 49:1–4).

78:2 *parables ... hidden things.* While both terms had specialized uses, they apparently also became conventionalized more generally for instruction in a wide variety of forms (see note on 49:4). *things from of old.* Things for instruction from the past. Mt 13:35 refers to this verse as a prophecy of Jesus' parabolic teaching. Matthew apparently perceived in this psalm a prophetic voice anticipating that of the great Prophet. The "parables" of the psalm are, however, more like the teaching of Stephen (Ac 7) than that of Jesus.

78:4–5 The Lord's saving acts and his covenant statutes—both must be taught, and in relationship, for together they remain the focal point for faith and obedience down through the generations (see vv. 7–8).

78:4 *not hide them.* See Job 15:18.

78:5 *teach their children.* See, e.g., Ex 10:2; 12:26–27; 13:8,14; Dt 4:9; 6:7,20–21.

78:8 *stubborn and rebellious.* Like a rebellious son (see Dt 9:6–7,24; 31:27). *generation.* Reference here is to a people with certain shared characteristics (see 24:6; Dt 32:5,20), thus not limited to the exodus generation (see vv. 9–11,56–64). *hearts.* See note on 4:7.

78:9–16 The northern kingdom has violated God's covenant, not remembering his saving acts (a message emphasized by the prophets Amos and Hosea). Israel's history with God has been a long series of rebellions on her part (vv. 9–16,32–39,56–64), beginning already in the desert (vv. 17–31,40–55).

78:9 *men of Ephraim.* The northern kingdom, dominated by the tribe of Ephraim (see introduction). *turned back.* Neither the tribe of Ephraim nor the northern kingdom had a reputation for cowardice or ineffectiveness in battle (see, e.g., Dt 33:17). This verse is best understood as a metaphor for Israel's betrayal of God's covenant (see v. 10), related to the figure of the "faulty bow" (v. 57).

78:12–16 A summary reference to the plagues in Egypt and to the water miracles at the Red Sea and in the desert. In the two cycles that follow (vv. 17–39,40–64), further elaboration intensifies the indictment.

78:12 See Ex 7–12. *Zoan.* A city in the northeast part of the Nile delta (see v. 43; see also Nu 13:22 and note).

78:13 See Ex 14:1—15:21.

[14]He guided them with the cloud by day
and with light from the fire all
night.[l]
[15]He split the rocks[m] in the desert
and gave them water as abundant as
the seas;
[16]he brought streams out of a rocky crag
and made water flow down like
rivers.

[17]But they continued to sin[n] against him,
rebelling in the desert against the
Most High.
[18]They willfully put God to the test[o]
by demanding the food they craved.[p]
[19]They spoke against God,[q] saying,
"Can God spread a table in the
desert?
[20]When he struck the rock, water gushed
out,[r]
and streams flowed abundantly.
But can he also give us food?
Can he supply meat[s] for his people?"
[21]When the LORD heard them, he was
very angry;
his fire broke out[t] against Jacob,
and his wrath rose against Israel,
[22]for they did not believe in God
or trust[u] in his deliverance.
[23]Yet he gave a command to the skies
above
and opened the doors of the
heavens;[v]
[24]he rained down manna[w] for the people
to eat,
he gave them the grain of heaven.
[25]Men ate the bread of angels;
he sent them all the food they could
eat.
[26]He let loose the east wind[x] from the
heavens
and led forth the south wind by his
power.
[27]He rained meat down on them like
dust,
flying birds[y] like sand on the
seashore.
[28]He made them come down inside their
camp,
all around their tents.
[29]They ate till they had more than
enough,[z]
for he had given them what they
craved.
[30]But before they turned from the food
they craved,
even while it was still in their
mouths,[a]
[31]God's anger rose against them;
he put to death the sturdiest[b] among
them,
cutting down the young men of
Israel.

[32]In spite of all this, they kept on
sinning;[c]
in spite of his wonders,[d] they did not
believe.[e]
[33]So he ended their days in futility[f]
and their years in terror.
[34]Whenever God slew them, they would
seek[g] him;
they eagerly turned to him again.
[35]They remembered that God was their
Rock,[h]
that God Most High was their
Redeemer.[i]
[36]But then they would flatter him with
their mouths,[j]
lying to him with their tongues;
[37]their hearts were not loyal[k] to him,
they were not faithful to his
covenant.
[38]Yet he was merciful;[l]
he forgave[m] their iniquities[n]
and did not destroy them.

78:14 [l]Ex 13:21; Ps 105:39 **78:15** [m]S Nu 20:11; 1Co 10:4 **78:17** [n]ver 32,40; Dt 9:22; Isa 30:1; 63:10; Heb 3:16 **78:18** [o]S Ex 17:2; 1Co 10:9 [p]S Ex 15:24; Nu 11:4 **78:19** [q]Nu 21:5 **78:20** [r]S Nu 20:11; S Isa 35:6 [s]Nu 11:18 **78:21** [t]S Nu 11:1 **78:22** [u]S Dt 1:32; Heb 3:19 **78:23** [v]Ge 7:11; S 2Ki 7:2 **78:24** [w]Ex 16:4; Jn 6:31* **78:26** [x]S Nu 11:31 **78:27** [y]S Ex 16:13; Nu 11:31 **78:29** [z]S Nu 11:20 **78:30** [a]S Nu 11:33 **78:31** [b]Isa 10:16 **78:32** [c]S ver 17 [d]ver 11 [e]ver 22 **78:33** [f]Nu 14:29,35 **78:34** [g]S Dt 4:29; Hos 5:15 **78:35** [h]S Ge 49:24 [i]S Dt 9:26 **78:36** [j]Eze 33:31 **78:37** [k]ver 8; Ac 8:21 **78:38** [l]S Ex 34:6 [m]Isa 1:25; 27:9; 48:10; Da 11:35 [n]Ps 25:11; 85:2

78:15–16 See v. 20; Ex 17:6; Nu 20:8,10–11.
78:17–31 Israel's rebelliousness in the desert; God's marvelous provision of food—and his anger.
78:17 *continued.* Although no sin in the desert has yet been mentioned, the poet probably expected his readers to recall (in conjunction with the miraculous provisions of water just mentioned) how the people grumbled at Marah because of lack of water (see Ex 15:24). *Most High.* See vv. 35,56; see also note on Ge 14:19.
78:18 See Ex 16:2–3. *put God to the test.* See vv. 41,56; see also note on Ex 17:2.
78:19 *Can God spread a table ...?* For a different use of the same imagery see 23:5.
78:20 *food ... meat.* The poet is probably combining and compressing two episodes (Ex 16:2–3; Nu 11:4).
78:21 *wrath.* See vv. 31,49–50,58–59,62; see also note on 2:5.
78:23 *opened the doors of the heavens.* For this imagery see Ge 7:11; 2Ki 7:2; Mal 3:10.
78:25 *bread of angels.* So called because it came down from heaven. *angels.* Lit. "mighty ones." The Hebrew word is used only here of the angels, but reference is clearly to heavenly beings (see 103:20).
78:26–28 See Ex 16:13; Nu 11:31.
78:26 *east wind ... south wind.* Since the quail were migrating from Egypt at this time, the south wind may have carried them north and the east wind may have diverted them to the desert area occupied by the Israelites (the book of Numbers does not provide wind directions).
78:27 *like dust ... like sand.* Similes for a huge number (see note on Ge 13:16).
78:30–31 See Nu 11:33.
78:32–39 Rebelliousness, which became Israel's way of life, showed itself early in the desert wandering (vv. 17–31) and continued throughout that journey.
78:32 *did not believe.* That God could give them victory over the Canaanites (see Nu 14:11).
78:33 The exodus generation was condemned to die in the desert (see Nu 14:22–23,28–35; cf. note on Heb 3:16–19).
78:34–37 A cycle repeated frequently during the period of the judges (see note on Jdg 2:6—3:6).
78:35 *Rock.* See note on 18:2. *Redeemer.* Deliverer (see note on 71:23).
78:36 See Isa 29:13.
78:37 *hearts.* See note on 4:7.
78:38 See Ex 32:14; Nu 14:20. *forgave.* See note on 65:3.

Time after time he restrained his
anger[o]
and did not stir up his full wrath.
39 He remembered that they were but
flesh,[p]
a passing breeze[q] that does not
return.

40 How often they rebelled[r] against him
in the desert[s]
and grieved him[t] in the wasteland!
41 Again and again they put God to the
test;[u]
they vexed the Holy One of Israel.[v]
42 They did not remember[w] his power —
the day he redeemed them from the
oppressor,[x]
43 the day he displayed his miraculous
signs[y] in Egypt,
his wonders[z] in the region of Zoan.
44 He turned their rivers to blood;[a]
they could not drink from their
streams.
45 He sent swarms of flies[b] that devoured
them,
and frogs[c] that devastated them.
46 He gave their crops to the
grasshopper,[d]
their produce to the locust.[e]
47 He destroyed their vines with hail[f]
and their sycamore-figs with sleet.
48 He gave over their cattle to the hail,
their livestock[g] to bolts of
lightning.
49 He unleashed against them his hot
anger,[h]
his wrath, indignation and
hostility —
a band of destroying angels.[i]
50 He prepared a path for his anger;
he did not spare them from death
but gave them over to the plague.
51 He struck down all the firstborn of
Egypt,[j]
the firstfruits of manhood in the
tents of Ham.[k]
52 But he brought his people out like a
flock;[l]
he led them like sheep through the
desert.
53 He guided them safely, so they were
unafraid;
but the sea engulfed[m] their enemies.[n]
54 Thus he brought them to the border of
his holy land,
to the hill country his right hand[o]
had taken.
55 He drove out nations[p] before them
and allotted their lands to them as
an inheritance;[q]
he settled the tribes of Israel in their
homes.

56 But they put God to the test
and rebelled against the Most High;
they did not keep his statutes.
57 Like their fathers[r] they were disloyal
and faithless,
as unreliable as a faulty bow.[s]
58 They angered him[t] with their high
places;[u]
they aroused his jealousy with their
idols.[v]
59 When God heard[w] them, he was very
angry;[x]
he rejected Israel[y] completely.
60 He abandoned the tabernacle of
Shiloh,[z]
the tent he had set up among men.[a]
61 He sent ⌊the ark of⌋ his might[b] into
captivity,[c]
his splendor into the hands of the
enemy.
62 He gave his people over to the sword;[d]
he was very angry with his
inheritance.[e]

78:38 [o]S Job 9:13; S Isa 30:18 **78:39** [p]S Ge 6:3; S Isa 29:5 [q]S Job 7:7; Jas 4:14 **78:40** [r]S Ex 23:21 [s]Ps 95:8; 106:14 [t]Eph 4:30 **78:41** [u]S Ex 17:2 [v]S 2Ki 19:22; Ps 71:22; 89:18 **78:42** [w]S Jdg 3:7; S Ne 9:17 [x]S Ps 27:11 **78:43** [y]Ex 10:1 [z]S Ex 3:20 **78:44** [a]Ex 7:20-21; Ps 105:29 **78:45** [b]Ex 8:24; Ps 105:31 [c]S Ex 8:2,6 **78:46** [d]Na 3:15 [e]S Ex 10:13 **78:47** [f]Ex 9:23; Ps 105:32; 147:17 **78:48** [g]Ex 9:25 **78:49** [h]Ex 15:7 [i]S Ge 19:13; 1Co 10:10 **78:51** [j]S Ex 12:12; Ps 135:8 [k]Ps 105:23; 106:22 **78:52** [l]Job 21:11; S Ps 28:9; 77:20 **78:53** [m]S Ex 14:28 [n]Ex 15:7; Ps 106:10 **78:54** [o]Ps 44:3 **78:55** [p]Ps 44:2 [q]S Dt 1:38; S Jos 13:7; Ac 13:19 **78:57** [r]S 2Ch 30:7; Eze 20:27 [s]S ver 9 **78:58** [t]S Jdg 2:12 [u]S Lev 26:30 [v]Ex 20:4; S Dt 5:8; 32:21 **78:59** [w]Ps 55:19 [x]S Lev 26:28; S Nu 32:14 [y]S Dt 32:19 **78:60** [z]S Jos 18:1 [a]Eze 8:6 **78:61** [b]Ps 132:8 [c]S 1Sa 4:17 **78:62** [d]S Dt 28:25 [e]S 1Sa 10:1

78:39 See 103:14; see also 39:5; 62:9; 144:4 and notes.
78:40–64 The second cycle (the first is vv. 17–39).
78:40–55 Israel's rebelliousness began in the desert; they did not remember how they had been delivered from oppression by God's plagues upon Egypt (see v. 12). Yet he brought them through the sea and the desert and established them in the promised land.
78:41 *Holy One of Israel.* See 71:22; 89:18; see also 2Ki 19:22; Isa 1:4 and notes.
78:44–51 The plagues upon Egypt (see Ex 7–12): The sequence in Exodus is followed only in the first and last; the third, fifth, sixth and ninth plagues are not mentioned.
78:47 *sycamore-figs.* See note on Am 7:14.
78:49 *destroying angels.* The poet personifies God's wrath, indignation and hostility as agents of his anger.
78:51 *tents.* Dwellings. *Ham.* For the association of Ham with Egypt see 105:23,27; 106:21–22; Ge 10:6 and note.
78:52 *like a flock.* See 77:20 and note.
78:53 *sea.* Red Sea (see Ex 15:1–21 and notes).
78:54 *holy land.* See note on Zec 2:12.
78:55 Summarizes the story told in Joshua.
78:56–64 Rebelliousness continued to be Israel's way of life in the promised land (a recurring theme of Judges; see also 1Sa 2:12—7:2), so God rejected Israel (v. 59; see Jer 7:15).
78:57 *faulty bow.* See note on v. 9.
78:58 *high places.* See note on 1Sa 9:12. *jealousy.* God's intense reaction to disloyalty to him (see note on Ex 20:5).
78:59 *rejected Israel completely.* Abandoned her to her enemies. The psalmist does not speak of a permanent casting off of Israel, not even of the ten northern tribes.
78:60 *Shiloh.* The center of worship since the time of Joshua (see Jos 18:1,8; 21:1–2; Jdg 18:31; 1Sa 1:3; Jer 7:12), it was located in Ephraim between Bethel and Shechem (see Jdg 21:19; see also map No. 6 at the end of this study Bible). Apparently it was destroyed by the Philistines when they captured the ark or shortly afterward (see note on Jer 7:12).
78:61 *his might … his splendor.* The ark is here so called because it was the sign of God's kingship in Israel and the focal point for the display of his power and glory (see 26:8; 63:2; 1Sa 4:3,21–22).
78:62,71 *his inheritance.* See Dt 9:29.

63 Fire consumed[f] their young men,
and their maidens had no wedding songs;[g]
64 their priests were put to the sword,[h]
and their widows could not weep.
65 Then the Lord awoke as from sleep,[i]
as a man wakes from the stupor of wine.
66 He beat back his enemies;
he put them to everlasting shame.[j]
67 Then he rejected the tents of Joseph,
he did not choose the tribe of Ephraim;[k]
68 but he chose the tribe of Judah,[l]
Mount Zion,[m] which he loved.
69 He built his sanctuary[n] like the heights,
like the earth that he established forever.
70 He chose David[o] his servant
and took him from the sheep pens;
71 from tending the sheep[p] he brought him
to be the shepherd[q] of his people Jacob,
of Israel his inheritance.
72 And David shepherded them with integrity of heart;[r]
with skillful hands he led them.

78:63 [f] S Nu 11:1 [g] S 1Ki 4:32; Jer 7:34; 16:9; 25:10 **78:64** [h] 1Sa 4:17 **78:65** [i] Ps 44:23 **78:66** [j] 1Sa 5:6 **78:67** [k] Jer 7:15; Hos 9:13; 12:1 **78:68** [l] S Nu 1:7; Ps 108:8 [m] S Ex 15:17; S Ps 68:16 **78:69** [n] S Ps 15:1 **78:70** [o] S 1Sa 16:1 **78:71** [p] S Ge 37:2 [q] S Ps 28:9 **78:72** [r] S Ge 17:1 **79:1** [s] S Ex 34:9 [t] S Lev 20:3 [u] S 2Ki 25:9; S Ne 4:2; S Isa 6:11

Psalm 79

A psalm of Asaph.

1 O God, the nations have invaded your inheritance;[s]
they have defiled[t] your holy temple,
they have reduced Jerusalem to rubble.[u]

78:63 *Fire.* Often associated with the sword (see vv. 62,64) as the two primary instruments of destruction in ancient warfare. *no wedding songs.* So great was the catastrophe that both the wedding songs of the brides and the wailing of the widows (see v. 64) were silenced in the land.

78:64 *priests were put to the sword.* See 1Sa 4:11.

78:65–72 The Lord's election of Judah (instead of Ephraim) as the leading tribe in Israel (anticipated in Jacob's deathbed blessing of his sons, Ge 49:8–12), of Mount Zion (instead of Shiloh) as the place of his sanctuary (royal seat), and of David as his regent to shepherd his people. By these acts the Lord established his people securely as his kingdom in the promised land, following the long period of Israel's troubles from the death of Joshua to the death of Saul—by then God's salvation of Israel begun in the exodus reached its climactic (if provisional) fulfillment (see introduction to Ps 68 and the combination of echoes of God's saving act in the exodus and through David in Isaiah's prophecy of Israel's future deliverance, Isa 11:11–16).

78:65 *awoke as from sleep.* Poetic hyperbole to highlight the contrast between God's action in behalf of his people in the days of David and the preceding time of Israel's troubles (see note on 7:6).

78:66–72 The saving events noted have two focal points: (1) God's decisive victory over his enemies (thus securing his realm) and the establishment of Zion as his royal city, and (2) the appointment of David to be the shepherd of his people.

78:67 *tents of Joseph.* A figure for the tribe of Ephraim (for the figurative use of "tents" see v. 51; see also 69:25; 83:6; 84:10; 120:5; Ge 9:27; Dt 33:18; 1Ki 12:16; Job 8:22; 12:6; Hab 3:7; Mal 2:12).

78:68,70 *he chose ... Mount Zion ... He chose David.* See Ps 132.

78:69 *heights ... earth.* The verse is subject to two interpretations: (1) The Lord built his sanctuary as impregnable as a mountain fortress and as enduring and unmovable as the age-old earth, or (2) the Lord built his sanctuary as secure and enduring as the heavens and the earth (see note on 24:2) and there manifests himself as the Lord of glory (see 24:7–10; 26:8; 63:2; 96:6), even as he does in the creation (see 19:1; 29:9; 97:6).

78:70–71 See 1Sa 16:11–13; 2Sa 7:8.

78:70 *his servant.* Here an official title marking David as a member of God's royal administration (see notes on Ex 14:31; Ps 18 title; Isa 41:8–9; 42:1). For David as God's "servant" see also 89:3,20,39; 132:10; 144:20.

78:71 *shepherd.* See v. 72; see also note on 23:1.

78:72 Israel under the care of the Lord's royal shepherd from the house of David was for the prophets the hope of God's people (see Eze 34:23; 37:24; Mic 5:4—fulfilled in Jesus Christ, Mt 2:6; Jn 10:11; Rev 7:17). *shepherded.* See note on 23:1.

Ps 79–83 A group of five psalms at the center of Book III that are framed by two urgent prayers of the community when the nation has been invaded by powerful enemies (for the different events alluded to see introduction to Ps 79; 83). These two prayers share four thematic links: (1) In 79:4 the Israelites complain that they have become the "objects of reproach ... scorn and derision" to their enemies, while in 83:17 they pray that their enemies may "ever be ashamed and dismayed" and "perish in disgrace." (2) In 79:11 they appeal to God to effect deliverance by the "strength" of his arm, while in 83:8 they charge that Assyria lends "strength" to the invaders. (3) In 79:5 they express anguish over the fact that they continue to feel God's anger "burn like fire," while in 83:14 they pray that God will pursue their enemies like a "fire" that "consumes" a forest. (4) Most significantly, in 79:6 they pray that God will pour out his wrath on "the nations that do not acknowledge [know] you, on the kingdoms that do not call on your name," while in 83:16,18 they pray that God will so overwhelm the foreign invaders that they will "seek your name" and will "know" that the Lord is "the Most High over all the earth."

In the center of this group (Ps 81)—thus also at the center of Book III—stands an urgent admonition to wayward Israel, reminding them that only if they are faithful to the Lord, who brought them out of Egypt, will he preserve them or rescue them from the ravaging of their enemies.

Bracketing this center on one side is a communal prayer for God to "restore" his "flock" and revive his once thriving "vine" that has been decimated by enemies (Ps 80) and on the other a prayer that the God who judges all kings and possesses all nations will arouse himself to "judge the earth" (Ps 82). Notably, Ps 80 is linked with Ps 79 by a shared use of the shepherd-sheep metaphor (see 79:13; 80:1), and Ps 82 is linked with Ps 83 by their shared references to "the Most High" (82:6; 83:18).

Ps 79 Israel's prayer for God's forgiveness and help and for his judgment on the nations that have so cruelly de-

[2]They have given the dead bodies of
your servants
as food to the birds of the air,[v]
the flesh of your saints to the
beasts of the earth.[w]
[3]They have poured out blood like
water
all around Jerusalem,
and there is no one to bury[x] the
dead.[y]
[4]We are objects of reproach to our
neighbors,
of scorn[z] and derision to those
around us.[a]
[5]How long,[b] O LORD? Will you be
angry[c] forever?
How long will your jealousy burn
like fire?[d]
[6]Pour out your wrath[e] on the
nations
that do not acknowledge[f] you,
on the kingdoms
that do not call on your name;[g]
[7]for they have devoured[h] Jacob
and destroyed his homeland.
[8]Do not hold against us the sins of
the fathers;[i]
may your mercy come quickly to
meet us,
for we are in desperate need.[j]
[9]Help us,[k] O God our Savior,
for the glory of your name;
deliver us and forgive our sins
for your name's sake.[l]
[10]Why should the nations say,
"Where is their God?"[m]
Before our eyes, make known among
the nations
that you avenge[n] the outpoured
blood[o] of your servants.
[11]May the groans of the prisoners come
before you;
by the strength of your arm
preserve those condemned to die.
[12]Pay back into the laps[p] of our
neighbors seven times[q]
the reproach they have hurled at
you, O Lord.
[13]Then we your people, the sheep of
your pasture,[r]
will praise you forever;[s]
from generation to generation
we will recount your praise.

79:2 [v]Rev 19:17-18 [w]S Dt 28:26; Jer 7:33 **79:3** [x]Jer 25:33; Rev 11:9 [y]Jer 16:4 **79:4** [z]S Ps 39:8; S Eze 5:14 [a]Ps 44:13; 80:6 **79:5** [b]S Ps 74:10 [c]Ps 74:1; 85:5 [d]S Dt 29:20; Ps 89:46; Zep 3:8 **79:6** [e]S Ps 2:5; 69:24; 110:5; Rev 16:1 [f]Ps 147:20; Jer 10:25 [g]S Ps 14:4 **79:7** [h]Isa 9:12; Jer 10:25 **79:8** [i]S Ge 9:25; Jer 44:21 [j]Ps 116:6; 142:6 **79:9** [k]S 2Ch 14:11 [l]Ps 25:11; 31:3; Jer 14:7 **79:10** [m]S Ps 42:3 [n]Ps 94:1; S Rev 6:10 [o]ver 3 **79:12** [p]Isa 65:6; Jer 32:18 [q]S Ge 4:15 **79:13** [r]S Ps 74:1 [s]Ps 44:8

stroyed her, showing utter contempt for both the Lord and his people. For the relationship of this psalm to Ps 80 – 83 in the arrangement of the Psalter see introduction to Ps 79 – 83. Like Ps 74, with which it has many thematic links, Ps 79 dates from the time of the exile. The poignancy of its appeal is heightened by its juxtaposition to Ps 77 (recalling God's saving acts under Moses) and Ps 78 (recalling God's saving acts under David), two psalms with which it is significantly linked by the shepherd-sheep figure and other thematic elements. Israel acknowledges that the Lord has used the nations to punish her for her sins, so she pleads for pardon. But she knows too that the nations have acted out of their hostility to and disdain for God and his people; that warrants her plea for God's judgment on them (see Isa 10:5 – 11; 47:6 – 7). Daniel's prayer (Da 9:4 – 19) contains much that is similar to the elements of penitence in this psalm.

79 title *Asaph.* See note on Ps 73 title.

79:1 – 4 What the nations have done: They have attacked God's own special domain, violated his temple, destroyed his royal city, slaughtered his people, degraded them in death (by withholding burial — see note on 53:5 — and leaving their bodies as carrion for birds and beasts) and reduced them to the scorn of the world.

79:1 *your inheritance.* Cf. 78:62,71. Here reference is to Israel's homeland as the Lord's domain (see note on 2:8). *holy temple.* See note on 78:69.

79:2 *your servants.* Though banished from the Lord's land for sins that cannot be denied, the exiles plead their special covenant relationship with God (see "your saints," here, and "your people, the sheep of your pasture," v. 13). *saints.* See note on 4:3.

79:3 *poured out blood … all around Jerusalem.* Cf. 2Ki 21:16.

79:5 – 8 A prayer for God to relent and deal with the nations who do not acknowledge him.

79:5 *How long … ?* See note on 6:3. *angry.* See v. 6 ("wrath"); see also note on 2:5. *jealousy.* See note on 78:58. *burn like fire.* See Dt 4:24; 6:15; Zep 1:18; 3:8.

79:6 – 7 See Jer 10:25 and note. Perhaps the psalmist is quoting Jeremiah here.

79:6 *Pour out your wrath.* As they "poured out" (v. 3) the blood of your people. The exiles plead with God to redress the wrongs committed against them (see note on 5:10).

79:7 *devoured.* Like wild beasts (see 44:11; 74:19 and note on 7:2). *Jacob.* A synonym for Israel (see Ge 32:28).

79:8 *sins of the fathers.* Israel suffered exile because of the accumulated sins of the nation (see 2Ki 17:7 – 23; 23:26 – 27; 24:3 – 4; Da 9:4 – 14), from which she did not repent until the judgment of God had fallen on her. The exiles here pray that God will take notice of their penitence and not continue to hold the sins of past generations against his now repentant people. *mercy.* Here personified as God's agent sent to bring relief (see notes on 23:6; 43:3).

79:9 – 11 A prayer for God to help and forgive his people and to redress the violent acts of the enemies.

79:9 *for the glory of your name.* As the desolation of God's people brings reproach to God (see v. 10), so their salvation and prosperity bring him glory (see note on 23:3). *forgive.* See note on 65:3.

79:10 *Where is their God?* See note on 3:2. *avenge.* Redress (see Dt 32:35,43).

79:11 *prisoners … those condemned to die.* The exiles, as imperial captives in Babylonia (see 102:20) — not actually in prisons, but under threat of death should they seek to return to their homeland.

79:12 – 13 Concluding prayer and vow to praise.

79:12 *Pay back into the laps.* See note on Jer 32:18. *seven times.* In full measure; the number seven symbolized completeness. *reproach … at you.* The enemies' violent action against Israel was above all a high-handed reviling of God (see vv. 1,10; 2Ki 19:10 – 12,22 – 23; Isa 52:5).

79:13 *sheep of your pasture.* See 23:2; 74:1 and notes; see also 77:20; 78:72; 80:1. *will praise you forever.* See note on 7:17. *from generation to generation.* See 78:4.

Psalm 80

For the director of music. To ⌞the tune of⌟ "The Lilies of the Covenant." Of Asaph. A psalm.

[1]Hear us, O Shepherd of Israel,
you who lead Joseph like a flock;[t]
you who sit enthroned between the cherubim,[u] shine forth
[2] before Ephraim, Benjamin and Manasseh.[v]
Awaken[w] your might;
come and save us.[x]

[3]Restore[y] us,[z] O God;
make your face shine upon us,
that we may be saved.[a]

[4]O LORD God Almighty,
how long[b] will your anger smolder[c]
against the prayers of your people?
[5]You have fed them with the bread of tears;[d]
you have made them drink tears by the bowlful.[e]
[6]You have made us a source of contention to our neighbors,
and our enemies mock us.[f]

[7]Restore us, O God Almighty;
make your face shine upon us,
that we may be saved.[g]

[8]You brought a vine[h] out of Egypt;
you drove out[i] the nations and planted[j] it.
[9]You cleared the ground for it,
and it took root and filled the land.
[10]The mountains were covered with its shade,
the mighty cedars with its branches.
[11]It sent out its boughs to the Sea,[a]
its shoots as far as the River.[b][k]

[12]Why have you broken down its walls[l]
so that all who pass by pick its grapes?
[13]Boars from the forest ravage[m] it
and the creatures of the field feed on it.
[14]Return to us, O God Almighty!
Look down from heaven and see![n]
Watch over this vine,

80:1 [t]Ps 77:20 [u]S Ex 25:22 **80:2** [v]Nu 2:18-24 [w]S Ps 35:23 [x]Ps 54:1; 69:1; 71:2; 109:26; 116:4; 119:94 **80:3** [y]S Ps 71:20; 85:4; Jer 31:18; La 5:21 [z]S Nu 6:25 [a]ver 7,19 **80:4** [b]S Ps 74:10 [c]S Dt 29:20 **80:5** [d]S Job 3:24 [e]Isa 30:20 **80:6** [f]S Ps 79:4 **80:7** [g]ver 3 **80:8** [h]Isa 5:1-2; Jer 2:21; Mt 21:33-41 [i]Ex 23:28-30; S Jos 13:6; Ac 7:45 [j]S Ex 15:17 **80:11** [k]Ps 72:8 **80:12** [l]Ps 89:40; Isa 5:5; 30:13; Jer 39:8 **80:13** [m]Jer 5:6 **80:14** [n]S Dt 26:15

[a] *11* Probably the Mediterranean [b] *11* That is, the Euphrates

Ps 80 Israel's prayer for restoration when she had been ravaged by a foreign power. For the relationship of this psalm to the others in its group see introduction to Ps 79–83. It seems likely that "Ephraim, Benjamin and Manasseh" (v. 2) here represent the northern kingdom. If Jeroboam was indeed given ten tribes (see 1Ki 11:29–36), leaving only one to Rehoboam—Judah (see 1Ki 12:20), which was actually two tribes because Simeon was located within Judah (see Jos 19:1–9)—then Benjamin belonged to the northern kingdom. However, part of Benjamin must always have remained with the southern kingdom since its territory actually bordered on Jerusalem itself, and the southern kingdom continued to control Jerusalem's environs (see 1Ki 12:21). This suggests that the disaster suffered was the Assyrian campaign that swept the northern kingdom away (see 2Ki 17:1–6). Recent archaeological surveys of the Holy Land have shown that Jerusalem and the surrounding countryside experienced a dramatic increase of population at this time, no doubt the result of a massive influx of displaced persons from the north fleeing the Assyrian conquerors. This could account for the presence of "Ephraim, Benjamin and Manasseh" at the Jerusalem sanctuary, and for a national prayer for restoration with special focus on these tribes (see notes below). The prayer has five stanzas of four (Hebrew) lines each. A recurring petition climaxes the first, second and last (for other refrains see introduction to Ps 42–43), with a progressing urgency of appeal: "O God" (v. 3); "O God Almighty" (v. 7); "O LORD God Almighty" (v. 19).

80 title *For the director of music.* See note on Ps 4 title. *To ⌞the tune of⌟.* See note on Ps 9 title. *Lilies.* See note on Ps 45 title. *Asaph.* See note on Ps 73 title.

80:1–3 An appeal for God to arouse himself and go before his people again with all his glory and might as he did of old in the desert.

80:1 See the shepherd-flock motif in 74:1; 77:20; 78:52, 71–72; 79:13; see also 23:1–2 and notes. *Joseph.* See note on 77:15. *enthroned between the cherubim.* See note on Ex 25:18. *shine forth.* Let your glory be seen again, as in the desert journey (see Ex 24:16–17; 40:34–35), but now especially through your new saving act (see 102:15–16; Ex 14:4,17–18; Nu 14:22; Isa 40:5; 44:23; 60:1–2).

80:2 *before Ephraim, Benjamin and Manasseh.* March against the nations as you marched in the midst of your army from Sinai into the promised land (in that march the ark of the covenant advanced in front of the troops of these three tribes; see Nu 10:21–24; see also introduction to Ps 68). *Awaken.* See note on 7:6.

80:3 *make your face shine.* See vv. 7,19; an echo of the priestly benediction (see Nu 6:25; see also notes on 4:6; 13:1).

80:4–7 A lament over the Lord's severe punishment of his people.

80:4 *LORD ... Almighty.* See vv. 7,14,19; see also note on 1Sa 1:3. *how long ...?* See note on 6:3. *anger.* See note on 2:5.

80:5 God has now given them tears to eat and tears to drink rather than "the bread of angels" and water from the rock (see 78:20,25).

80:8–16 This use of the vine-vineyard metaphor (here to describe Israel's changed condition) is found also in the prophets (see Isa 3:14; 5:1–7; 27:2; Jer 2:21; 12:10; Eze 17:6–8; 19:10–14; Hos 10:1; 14:7; Mic 7:1; see also Ge 49:22; Mt 20:1–16; Mk 12:1–9; Lk 20:9–16; Jn 15:1–5).

80:8–11 Israel was once God's flourishing transplanted vine.

80:8 *brought.* See 78:52; here the Hebrew for this verb has the sense of "uprooted" (as in Job 19:10). *drove out the nations and planted.* See 44:2. *planted.* Transplanted.

80:9 *cleared the ground.* See Isa 5:2.

80:10 *mighty cedars.* Lit. "cedars of God" (the Hebrew word for "God" is sometimes used in the sense of "mighty"; see, e.g., note on 29:1).

80:11 *Sea ... River.* See NIV text notes; see also Ex 23:31 and note.

80:12–15 A prayer for God to renew his care for his ravaged vine.

80:12 *Why ...?* Israel's anguished perplexity over God's abandonment (see note on 6:3). *broken down its walls.* Taken away its defenses.

80:14 *Watch over.* See Ex 3:16. But the Hebrew for this phrase

15 the root your right hand has planted,
the son[a] you have raised up for
yourself.

16 Your vine is cut down, it is burned
with fire;[o]
at your rebuke[p] your people perish.
17 Let your hand rest on the man at your
right hand,
the son of man[q] you have raised up
for yourself.
18 Then we will not turn away from you;
revive[r] us, and we will call on your
name.

19 Restore us, O LORD God Almighty;
make your face shine upon us,
that we may be saved.

Psalm 81

For the director of music. According to *gittith*.[b] Of Asaph.

1 Sing for joy to God our strength;
shout aloud to the God of Jacob![s]
2 Begin the music, strike the
tambourine,[t]
play the melodious harp[u] and lyre.[v]

3 Sound the ram's horn[w] at the New
Moon,[x]
and when the moon is full, on the
day of our Feast;
4 this is a decree for Israel,
an ordinance of the God of Jacob.[y]
5 He established it as a statute for
Joseph
when he went out against Egypt,[z]
where we heard a language we did
not understand.[c][a]

6 He says, "I removed the burden[b] from
their shoulders;[c]
their hands were set free from the
basket.

80:16 [o] Ps 79:1 [p] S Dt 28:20 **80:17** [q] S Job 25:6 **80:18** [r] Ps 85:6; Isa 57:15; Hos 6:2 **81:1** [s] S Ps 66:1 **81:2** [t] S Ex 15:20 [u] Ps 92:3 [v] S Job 21:12 **81:3** [w] S Ex 19:13 [x] S Ne 10:33 **81:4** [y] ver 1 **81:5** [z] S Ex 11:4 [a] Ps 114:1 **81:6** [b] S Ex 1:14 [c] Isa 9:4; 52:2

[a] *15* Or *branch* [b] Title: Probably a musical term
[c] *5* Or */ and we heard a voice we had not known*

may have the sense here that it has in Ru 1:6: "Come to the aid of."
80:15 *son.* Israel (see Ex 4:22–23; Hos 11:1). But "son" may sometimes be used also to refer to a vine branch (see NIV text note; see also note on Ge 49:22). That may be the case here, thus yielding the conventional pair "root and branch," a figure for the whole vine (see Job 18:16; 29:19; Eze 17:7; Mal 4:1; see also Isa 5:24; 27:6; 37:31; Eze 17:9; 31:7; Hos 9:16; Am 2:9; Ro 11:16). *raised up.* See v. 17; lit. "made vigorous."
80:16–19 Concluding prayer for restoration.
80:16 *rebuke.* See 9:5 and note on 76:6.
80:17 *Let your hand rest on.* Show your favor to (see Ezr 7:6,9,28; 8:18,22,31; Ne 2:8,18). *at.* Lit. "of." *your right hand.* Reference may be to the Davidic king as the Lord's anointed, seated in the place of honor in God's presence (see 110:1) and the one in whom the hope of the nation rested (see 2:7–9; 72:8–11; 89:21–25). But v. 15 strongly suggests another sense: that "the man" is Jacob/Israel and that he is "of" God's "right hand" in that he has been "planted" and "raised up" by him.
80:18 A vow to be loyal to God and to trust in him alone. It occurs in a place where it would be more common to find a vow to praise (see note on 7:17).
Ps 81 A festival song. But it is unclear whether the festival is Passover/Unleavened Bread (v. 5; see Ex 12:14–17) or the Jewish New Year (v. 3; see Lev 23:24; Nu 29:1) or the Feast of Tabernacles (v. 3; see Lev 23:34; Nu 29:12). It may have been used at all three. But more likely it was composed for use at both New Year (the first day of the month, "New Moon") and the beginning of Tabernacles (the 15th day of the month, full moon); see notes below. Whether the psalm is preexilic or postexilic cannot be determined, but it clearly shows the grand significance of Israel's annual religious festivals (see chart, pp. 178–179). As memorials of God's saving acts they called Israel to celebration, remembrance and recommitment (see Ps 95). For the significant placement of this psalm within Book III of the Psalter see introduction to Ps 73–78 and introduction to Ps 79–83.

Though the psalm falls into two main parts (vv. 1–5,6–16), thematic development follows a symmetrical pattern: two verses, three verses; two verses, three verses; two verses, four verses. Note also the contrast between vv. 6–7 and vv. 11–12, and the thematic link between v. 10c and v. 16.
81 title *For the director of music.* See note on Ps 4 title. *According to.* See note on Ps 6 title. *gittith.* See note on Ps 8 title. *Asaph.* See note on Ps 73 title.
81:1–5 A summons to celebrate the appointed sacred feast.
81:1 *Jacob.* A synonym for Israel (see Ge 32:28).
81:2 *tambourine.* See note on Jer 31:4. *harp and lyre.* See note on 57:8.
81:3 *ram's horn.* The ram's-horn trumpet (see Ex 19:13). *our Feast.* Probably the Feast of Tabernacles, often called simply "the feast/festival" (see 1Ki 8:2,65; 12:32; 2Ch 5:3; 7:8; Ne 8:14,18; Eze 45:25; see also Dt 16:14). As the great seven-day autumn festival, beginning on the 15th of the month (full moon), it followed shortly after the Day of Atonement (observed on the tenth of the month, Lev 16:29), recalled God's care for his people during the desert journey (see Lev 23:43), served as a feast of thanksgiving for the harvest (see Lev 23:39–40; Dt 16:13–15) and marked the conclusion of the annual cycle of religious festivals that began with Passover and Unleavened Bread six months earlier (see Ex 23:14–17; Lev 23; Dt 16:16; see also note on Zec 14:16). Every seventh year at this festival the covenant law was to be read to all the people (see Dt 31:9–13; Ne 8:2,15). The first day of this month ("New Moon") was commemorated with trumpets (see Lev 23:24). It later came to be known as New Year since the seventh month marked the end of harvest and the beginning of the rainy season, when the new crops were planted.
81:4–5 *decree ... ordinance ... statute.* See the passages referred to in note on v. 3.
81:5 *Joseph.* See note on 77:15. *when he went out against Egypt.* Some believe this indicates that the festival referred to is Passover and Unleavened Bread (see Ex 12:14,42). More likely it serves as a reference to the whole exodus period, while highlighting especially God's triumph over Egypt by which he had set his people free (see vv. 6–7). *heard a language we did not understand.* Were aliens in a foreign land (see 114:1; see also Dt 28:49; Isa 19:18; 33:19; Jer 5:15; Eze 3:5–6). If the alternative translation in the NIV text note is taken, the "voice" is the "thunder" of God's judgment against Egypt (see v. 7), which the Levitical author then proceeds to interpret as to its present reference for the celebrating congregation (vv. 6–16).
81:6–10 God heard and delivered and now summons his people to loyalty.
81:6 *burden ... basket.* The forced labor to which the Israelites were subjected in Egypt (see Ex 1:11–14).

[7]In your distress you called[d] and I
rescued you,
I answered[e] you out of a
thundercloud;
I tested you at the waters of
Meribah.[f] *Selah*
[8]"Hear, O my people,[g] and I will warn
you—
if you would but listen to me,
O Israel!
[9]You shall have no foreign god[h] among
you;
you shall not bow down to an alien
god.
[10]I am the LORD your God,
who brought you up out of Egypt.[i]
Open[j] wide your mouth and I will
fill[k] it.

[11]"But my people would not listen to me;
Israel would not submit to me.[l]
[12]So I gave them over[m] to their stubborn
hearts
to follow their own devices.

[13]"If my people would but listen to me,[n]
if Israel would follow my ways,
[14]how quickly would I subdue[o] their
enemies
and turn my hand against[p] their foes!
[15]Those who hate the LORD would
cringe[q] before him,
and their punishment would last
forever.
[16]But you would be fed with the finest of
wheat;[r]
with honey from the rock I would
satisfy you."

Psalm 82

A psalm of Asaph.

[1]God presides in the great assembly;
he gives judgment[s] among the
"gods":[t]

[2]"How long will you[a] defend the unjust
and show partiality[u] to the wicked?[v]
Selah
[3]Defend the cause of the weak and
fatherless;[w]
maintain the rights of the poor[x] and
oppressed.
[4]Rescue the weak and needy;
deliver them from the hand of the
wicked.

[5]"They know nothing, they understand
nothing.[y]
They walk about in darkness;[z]
all the foundations[a] of the earth are
shaken.

81:7 [d]S Ex 2:23 [e]Ex 19:19 [f]S Ex 17:7; S Dt 33:8 **81:8** [g]Ps 50:7; 78:1 **81:9** [h]S Ex 20:3 **81:10** [i]S Ex 6:6; S 13:3; S 29:46 [j]Eze 2:8 [k]Ps 107:9 **81:11** [l]Ex 32:1-6 **81:12** [m]Eze 20:25; Ac 7:42; Ro 1:24 **81:13** [n]S Dt 5:29 **81:14** [o]Ps 47:3 [p]Am 1:8 **81:15** [q]S 2Sa 22:45 **81:16** [r]S Dt 32:14 **82:1** [s]Ps 7:8; 58:11; Isa 3:13; 66:16; Joel 3:12 [t]S Job 21:22 **82:2** [u]Dt 1:17 [v]Ps 58:1-2; Pr 18:5 **82:3** [w]S Dt 24:17 [x]Ps 140:12; Jer 5:28; 22:16 **82:5** [y]S Ps 14:4; S 53:2 [z]Job 30:26; Isa 5:30; 8:21-22; 9:2; 59:9; 60:2; Jer 13:16; 23:12; La 3:2 [a]S Jdg 5:4; S Ps 11:3

[a] 2 The Hebrew is plural.

81:7 *you called and I rescued.* See Ex 3:7–10. *out of a thundercloud.* See 106:9; Ex 14:21,24; 15:8,10; see also note on 76:6. *I tested you.* See Ex 17:1–7.
81:8–10 God heard his people in their distress (vv. 6–7); now they must listen to him.
81:9–10 See Ex 19:4–5; 20:2–4; Dt 4:15–20.
81:10 *Open wide your mouth.* Trust in the Lord alone for all of life's needs. *I will fill it.* See v. 16; as he did in the desert (see 78:23–29; see also 37:3–4; Dt 11:13–15; 28:1–4).
81:11–16 Israel has not listened—if only they would! See Eze 18:23,32; 33:11.
81:11 See 78:10,17,32,40,56; Dt 9:7,24; Jer 7:24–26.
81:12 It is God who "circumcises" the heart (see Dt 30:6; see also 1Ki 8:58; Jer 31:33; Eze 11:19; 36:26). Thus for God to abandon his people to their sins is the most fearful of punishments (see 78:29; Isa 6:9–10; 29:10; 63:17; cf. Ro 1:24,26,28).
81:13–16 See the promised covenant blessings outlined in Ex 23:22–27; Lev 26:3–13; Dt 7:12–26; 28:1–14.
81:13 *my ways.* See 25:4 and note.
81:16 *honey from the rock.* See note on Dt 32:13.
Ps 82 A word of judgment on unjust rulers and judges. The Levitical author of this psalm evokes a vision of God presiding over his heavenly court—analogous to the experiences of the prophets (see 1Ki 22:19–22; Isa 6:1–7; Jer 23:18, 22; see also Job 15:8). As the Great King (see introduction to Ps 47) and the Judge of all the earth (see 50:6 and note; 94:2; Ge 18:25; 1Sa 2:10) who "loves justice" (99:4) and judges the nations in righteousness (see 9:8; 96:13; 98:9), he is seen calling to account those responsible for defending the weak and oppressed on earth. An early rabbinic interpretation (see Jn 10:34–35) understood the "gods" (vv. 1,6) to be unjust rulers and judges in Israel, of whom there were many (see 1Sa 8:3; Isa 1:16–17; 3:13–15; Jer 21:12; 22:3; Eze 34:4,21; Mic 3:1–3; 7:3). Today many identify the "gods" as the kings of surrounding nations who encouraged the conceit that they were actually or virtually divine beings but who ruled with lofty disregard for justice—though honoring it as a royal ideal. Others hold that the "gods" are the divine beings in whose names the kings claimed to rule (see 95:3). In any event, rulers and judges here are confronted by their King and Judge (see Ps 58). Structurally, the words of the Levite (vv. 1,6) frame the words of God. At the very center (see note on v. 5) stands the most devastating judgment of all. For this psalm's placement in Book III of the Psalter see introduction to Ps 79–83.
82 title See note on Ps 73 title.
82:1 *great assembly.* The assembly in the great Hall of Justice (cf. 1Ki 7:7) in heaven (see 89:5; 1Ki 22:19; Job 1:6; 2:1; Isa 6:1–4). As if in a vision, the psalmist sees the rulers and judges gathered before the Great King to give account of their administration of justice. *gods.* See v. 6. In the language of the OT—and in accordance with the conceptual world of the ancient Near East—rulers and judges, as deputies of the heavenly King, could be given the honorific title "god" (see note on 45:6; see also NIV text notes on Ex 21:6; 22:8) or be called "son of God" (see 2:7 and note).
82:3–4 In the OT a first-order task of kings and judges was to protect the powerless against all who would exploit or oppress them (see 72:2,4,12–14; Pr 31:8–9; Isa 11:4; Jer 22:3,16).
82:5 *They know . . . nothing.* The center of the poem (see note on 6:6). They ought to have shared in the wisdom of God (see 1Ki 3:9; Pr 8:14–16; Isa 11:2), but they are utterly devoid of true understanding of moral issues or of the moral order that God's rule sustains (see Isa 44:18; Jer 3:15; 9:24). *foundations . . . are shaken.* When such people are the wardens of justice, the whole world order crumbles (see 11:3; 75:3 and notes).

[6]"I said, 'You are "gods";[b]
you are all sons of the Most High.'
[7]But you will die[c] like mere men;
you will fall like every other ruler."

[8]Rise up,[d] O God, judge[e] the earth,
for all the nations are your
inheritance.[f]

Psalm 83

A song. A psalm of Asaph.

[1]O God, do not keep silent;[g]
be not quiet, O God, be not still.
[2]See how your enemies are astir,[h]
how your foes rear their heads.[i]
[3]With cunning they conspire[j] against
your people;
they plot against those you cherish.[k]
[4]"Come," they say, "let us destroy[l] them
as a nation,[m]
that the name of Israel be
remembered[n] no more."

[5]With one mind they plot together;[o]
they form an alliance against you—
[6]the tents of Edom[p] and the Ishmaelites,
of Moab[q] and the Hagrites,[r]
[7]Gebal,[a][s] Ammon[t] and Amalek,[u]
Philistia,[v] with the people of Tyre.[w]
[8]Even Assyria[x] has joined them
to lend strength to the descendants
of Lot.[y] *Selah*

[9]Do to them as you did to Midian,[z]
as you did to Sisera[a] and Jabin[b] at
the river Kishon,[c]
[10]who perished at Endor[d]
and became like refuse[e] on the
ground.
[11]Make their nobles like Oreb and Zeeb,[f]
all their princes like Zebah and
Zalmunna,[g]
[12]who said, "Let us take possession[h]
of the pasturelands of God."

[13]Make them like tumbleweed, O my God,
like chaff[i] before the wind.
[14]As fire consumes the forest
or a flame sets the mountains
ablaze,[j]
[15]so pursue them with your tempest[k]
and terrify them with your storm.[l]

[a] *7* That is, Byblos

82:6 [b]Jn 10:34* **82:7** [c]Ps 49:12; Eze 31:14 **82:8** [d]Ps 12:5 [e]S Ps 76:9 [f]Ps 2:8 **83:1** [g]Ps 28:1; 35:22; Isa 42:14; 57:11; 62:1; 64:12 **83:2** [h]Ps 2:1; Isa 17:12 [i]Jdg 8:28 **83:3** [j]S Ex 1:10; S Ps 31:13 [k]Ps 17:14 **83:4** [l]S Est 3:6 [m]Jer 33:24 [n]Jer 11:19 **83:5** [o]Ps 2:2 **83:6** [p]Ps 137:7; Isa 34:5; Jer 49:7; Am 1:11 [q]2Ch 20:1 [r]S Ge 25:16 **83:7** [s]S Jos 13:5 [t]Ge 19:38 [u]S Ge 14:7; S Ex 17:14 [v]Ex 15:14 [w]Isa 23:3; Eze 27:3 **83:8** [x]S Ge 10:11 [y]S Dt 2:9 **83:9** [z]S Ge 25:2; Jdg 7:1-23 [a]S Jdg 4:2 [b]S Jos 11:1 [c]S Jdg 4:23-24 **83:10** [d]S 1Sa 28:7 [e]S 2Ki 9:37; Isa 5:25; Jer 8:2; 9:22; 16:4; 25:33; Zep 1:17 **83:11** [f]Jdg 7:25 [g]S Jdg 8:5 **83:12** [h]2Ch 20:11; Eze 35:10 **83:13** [i]S Job 13:25 **83:14** [j]Dt 32:22; Isa 9:18 **83:15** [k]S Ps 50:3 [l]S Job 9:17

82:6 *I said.* Those who rule (or judge) do so by God's appointment (see 2:7; Isa 44:28) and thus they are his representatives—whether they acknowledge him or not (see Ex 9:16; Jer 27:6; Da 2:21; 4:17,32; 5:18; Jn 19:11; Ro 13:1). *gods.* See notes on v. 1; Jn 10:34. *sons of.* See note on v. 1. *Most High.* See note on Ge 14:19.
82:7 However exalted their position, these corrupt "gods" will be brought low by the same judgment as other human beings. *fall.* See note on 13:4.
82:8 Having seen the prospect in store, the psalmist prays for God's judgment to hasten and for the perfect reign of God to come quickly to the whole world. *Rise up.* See note on 3:7. *inheritance.* Domain (see note on 79:1).
Ps 83 Israel's prayer for God to crush his enemies when the whole world—or so it seemed—was arrayed against his people. For this psalm's relationship to those around it see introduction to Ps 79–83. Neither Kings nor Chronicles tells of a confederacy as extensive as that described here. Perhaps only some of the nations mentioned were actually attacking, while the rest of Israel's historic enemies were more passively supporting the campaign. If so, the occasion may have been that reported in 2Ch 20, when Moab, Ammon, Edom and their allies were invading Judah. In any event, the psalm must date from sometime after the reign of Solomon and before the great thrust of Assyria in the time of King Menahem (see 2Ki 15:19).
Each of the two main divisions (vv. 1–8,9–18) consists of two four-verse stanzas, with the latter division being extended by a two-verse stanza that brings the prayer to its climactic conclusion.
83 title *song.* See note on Ps 30 title. *Asaph.* See note on Ps 73 title.
83:1–4 An appeal to God to act in the face of Israel's imminent danger.
83:1 *do not keep silent.* Do not remain inactive (see 35:22; 109:1).
83:2 *are astir.* In Hebrew the same verb as for "are in uproar" in 46:6 and for "snarling" in 59:6,14.
83:4 *they say.* See note on 3:2. *let us destroy them.* Israel's very existence is at stake (see v. 12).
83:5–8 The array of nations allied against Israel—threat from every quarter.
83:6 *Hagrites.* Either Ishmaelites (descendants of Hagar) or a group mentioned in Assyrian inscriptions as an Aramean confederacy (see 1Ch 5:10,18–22; 27:31).
83:7 *Gebal.* See 1Ki 5:18; Eze 27:9. Gebal was an important Phoenician city (see NIV text note). Some interpreters, however, conclude that reference here is to a place or region in Edom, south of the Dead Sea near Petra. *Amalek.* See note on Ge 14:7
83:8 *Assyria.* Since it is mentioned only as an ally of Moab and Ammon (the descendants of Lot; see note on Ge 19:36–38), Assyria, though distantly active in the region, must not yet have become a major threat in its own right.
83:9–12 A plea for God to destroy his enemies as he did of old in the time of the judges. Those who hurl themselves against the kingdom of God to destroy it from the earth—so that the godless powers are left to shape the destiny of the world as they will—must be crushed if God's kingdom of righteousness and peace is to come and be at rest (see note on 5:10).
83:9 *as you did to Midian.* In Gideon's great victory (see Jdg 7). *as you did to Sisera and Jabin.* In Barak's defeat of the Canaanite coalition (see Jdg 4).
83:10 *Endor.* See Jos 17:11 and note; northeast of where the main battle was fought—apparently where much of the fleeing army was overtaken and decimated.
83:11 *Oreb and Zeeb … Zebah and Zalmunna.* Leaders of the Midianite host destroyed by Gideon.
83:12 See v. 4.
83:13–16 The plea renewed, with vivid imagery of fleeing armies and of God's fearsome power.
83:15 Imagery of the heavenly Warrior attacking his enemies out of the thunderstorm (see 18:7–15; 68:33; 77:17–18; Ex 15:7–10; Jos 10:11; Jdg 5:4,20–21; 1Sa 2:10; 7:10; Isa 29:5–6; 33:3). For the storm cloud as God's chariot see 68:4 and note.

16 Cover their faces with shame[m]
so that men will seek your name,
O LORD.
17 May they ever be ashamed and
dismayed;[n]
may they perish in disgrace.[o]
18 Let them know that you, whose name
is the LORD[p]—
that you alone are the Most High[q]
over all the earth.[r]

Psalm 84

For the director of music. According to *gittith*.[a] Of the Sons of Korah. A psalm.

1 How lovely is your dwelling place,[s]
O LORD Almighty!
2 My soul yearns,[t] even faints,
for the courts of the LORD;
my heart and my flesh cry out
for the living God.[u]
3 Even the sparrow has found a home,
and the swallow a nest for herself,
where she may have her young—
a place near your altar,[v]
O LORD Almighty,[w] my King[x] and
my God.[y]
4 Blessed are those who dwell in your
house;
they are ever praising you. *Selah*
5 Blessed are those whose strength[z] is in
you,
who have set their hearts on
pilgrimage.[a]
6 As they pass through the Valley of
Baca,
they make it a place of springs;[b]
the autumn[c] rains also cover it with
pools.[b]

83:16 [m] S Ps 34:5; 109:29; 132:18 **83:17** [n] S 2Ki 19:26 [o] S Ps 35:4 **83:18** [p] S Ps 68:4 [q] Ps 7:8; 18:13 [r] S Job 34:29 **84:1** [s] S Dt 33:27; Ps 27:4; 43:3; 90:1; 132:5 **84:2** [t] S Job 19:27 [u] S Jos 3:10 **84:3** [v] S Ps 43:4 [w] Jer 44:11 [x] Ps 2:6 [y] Ps 5:2 **84:5** [z] Ps 81:1 [a] Jer 31:6 **84:6** [b] S Job 38:26 [c] Joel 2:23

[a] Title: Probably a musical term [b] 6 Or *blessings*

83:16 *will seek.* See note on v. 18. *name.* See note on 5:11.
83:17–18 The prayer's climactic conclusion.
83:18 The ultimate goal of God's warfare is not merely the security of Israel and the destruction of Israel's (and God's) enemies but the worldwide acknowledgment of the true God and of his rule, even to the point of seeking him as his people do (see v. 16; see also 40:9; 47:9; 58:11; 59:13 and notes). *Most High.* See note on Ge 14:19.
Ps 84–89 The first of the six psalms that make up the final group of Book III (see introduction to Ps 73–78) expresses yearning for fellowship with God, who dwells in his temple in Zion and from whom alone come security and blessing. References to God as "LORD Almighty" and a prayer for "our shield," the Lord's "anointed one," form distinctive links with the final psalm of the group (for the former see 84:1,3,8,12 and 89:8; for the latter see 84:9 and 89:18,38,51). The five psalms thus introduced are four cries of distress arranged around a central song (Ps 87) that celebrates God's special love of Zion and the care he has for all its citizens. Of these four, the first (Ps 85) and the last (Ps 89) are communal prayers, and the remaining two (Ps 86; 88) are prayers of individuals. They all make much of God's "love" and "faithfulness" (see 85:7,10–11; 86:5,13,15; 88:11; 89:1–2,5,8,14,24,28,33,49) and his saving help (see 85:4,7,9; 86:2,16; 88:1; 89:26). And three of them share another key concept, "righteousness/righteous deeds" (see 85:10–11,13; 88:12; 89:14). The two final prayers (Ps 88; 89) both end unrelieved by the usual expression of confidence that God will hear and act (see note on 3:8). However, the editors of Book III have placed them under the near shadow of Ps 87, the more distant shadow of Ps 84 and the still more distant shadow of Ps 82. From these psalms they should not be disassociated.
Ps 84 A prayer of longing for the house of the Lord. In tone and perspective it stands close to Ps 42 and may reflect similar circumstances. If so, the author (presumably a Levite who normally functioned in the temple service), now barred from access to God's house (perhaps when Sennacherib was ravaging Judah; see 2Ki 18:13–16), gives voice to his longing for the sweet nearness to God in his temple that he had known in the past. Reference to God and his temple and to the blessedness (see vv. 4–5,12) of those having free access to both dominates the prayer and highlights its central themes. For its placement in the arrangement of the Psalter see introduction to Ps 84–89. Whatever its origin, the psalm now voices the devotion to and reliance on God that motivate the remaining prayers of the group it introduces.
The psalm has three main divisions and a conclusion (v. 12). In the Hebrew text, a six-line unit (vv. 1–4) precedes and another six-line unit (vv. 8–11) follows a three-line reflection (vv. 5–7) on the blessedness of those free to make pilgrimage to Zion. Each of these six-line divisions contains three references to the "LORD," while the seventh reference (symbolizing fullness or wholeness) appears in the conclusion.
84 title *For the director of music.* See note on Ps 4 title. *According to.* See note on Ps 6 title. *gittith.* See note on Ps 8 title. *Of the Sons of Korah.* See note on Ps 42 title.
84:1–4 A confession of deep longing for the house of the Lord.
84:1 *lovely.* The traditional rendering of the Hebrew here, but perhaps better translated "beloved" or "loved." *LORD Almighty.* See vv. 3,8,12; see also note on 1Sa 1:3.
84:2 *My soul.* I (see note on 6:3). *courts.* Of the temple (see v. 10; 2Ki 21:5; 23:11–12). *my heart ... flesh.* My whole being (see 73:26). *heart.* See note on 4:7. *living God.* See Dt 5:26.
84:3 The psalmist envies the small birds that have such unhindered access to the temple and the altar. They are able even to build their nests there for their young—the place where Israel was to have communion with God.
84:4–5,12 *Blessed.* See note on 1:1.
84:4 *who dwell in your house.* See note on 15:1.
84:5–7 The joyful blessedness of those who are free to make pilgrimage to Zion—them, too, the psalmist envies.
84:5 *those whose strength is in you.* Those who have come to know the Lord as their deliverer and the sustainer of their lives. *who have set their hearts on pilgrimage.* Lit. "in whose hearts are (the) highways," i.e., the highways the Israelites took to observe the religious festivals at Jerusalem (Zion, v. 7). *hearts.* See note on 4:7.
84:6 *As they pass.* On their way to the temple. *Baca.* Means either "weeping" or "balsam trees" (common in arid valleys). The place is unknown and may be figurative (see 23:4) for arid stretches the pilgrims had to traverse. *place of springs.* The joyful expectations of the pilgrims transform the difficult ways into places of refreshment. *autumn rains.* These gentle early showers were greeted as harbingers of the winter rains that covered Israel's sun-scorched hills once more with flourishing vegetation (104:13–15) and mantled the valleys with grain (65:9–13; see also Joel 2:23–24). Reference to these rains suggests that the psalmist had in mind especially the pilgrimage to observe the Feast of Tabernacles (see chart, pp. 178–179). *pools.* The Hebrew for this word may refer to "blessings" or to "pools" (see NIV text note); it is likely that both are intended. By God's benevolent care over his pilgrims, the

7 They go from strength to strength,[d]
till each appears[e] before God in
Zion.[f]

8 Hear my prayer,[g] O LORD God Almighty;
listen to me, O God of Jacob. *Selah*
9 Look upon our shield,[a h] O God;
look with favor on your anointed
one.[i]

10 Better is one day in your courts
than a thousand elsewhere;
I would rather be a doorkeeper[j] in the
house of my God
than dwell in the tents of the
wicked.
11 For the LORD God is a sun[k] and shield;[l]
the LORD bestows favor and honor;
no good thing does he withhold[m]
from those whose walk is blameless.

12 O LORD Almighty,
blessed[n] is the man who trusts in you.

Psalm 85

For the director of music. Of the Sons of
Korah. A psalm.

1 You showed favor to your land,
O LORD;
you restored the fortunes[o] of Jacob.
2 You forgave[p] the iniquity[q] of your
people
and covered all their sins. *Selah*
3 You set aside all your wrath[r]
and turned from your fierce
anger.[s]

4 Restore[t] us again, O God our
Savior,[u]
and put away your displeasure
toward us.
5 Will you be angry with us forever?[v]
Will you prolong your anger
through all generations?
6 Will you not revive[w] us again,
that your people may rejoice[x] in
you?
7 Show us your unfailing love,[y]
O LORD,
and grant us your salvation.[z]

8 I will listen to what God the LORD
will say;
he promises peace[a] to his people,
his saints—
but let them not return to
folly.[b]

84:7 [d] S Job 17:9 [e] S Dt 16:16 [f] 1Ki 8:1 **84:8** [g] Ps 4:1 **84:9** [h] S Ps 59:11 [i] 1Sa 16:6; Ps 2:2; 18:50; 132:17 **84:10** [j] 1Ch 23:5 **84:11** [k] Isa 60:19; Jer 43:13; Rev 21:23 [l] S Ge 15:1 [m] Ps 34:10 **84:12** [n] Ps 2:12 **85:1** [o] S Dt 30:3; Ps 14:7 **85:2** [p] S Nu 14:19 [q] S Ex 32:30; S Ps 78:38 **85:3** [r] Ps 106:23; Da 9:16 [s] Ex 32:12; Dt 13:17; Ps 78:38; Jnh 3:9 **85:4** [t] S Ps 71:20 [u] S Ps 65:5 **85:5** [v] S Ps 50:21 **85:6** [w] S Ps 80:18 [x] Php 3:1 **85:7** [y] S Ps 6:4 [z] Ps 27:1 **85:8** [a] S Lev 26:6; S Isa 60:17; S Jn 14:27; 2Th 3:16 [b] Pr 26:11; 27:22

[a] 9 Or *sovereign*

vale of weeping (or balsam trees), already transformed by the glad hearts of the expectant wayfarers, is turned into a valley of praise (see 2Ch 20:26). God's people on their hopeful way to Zion experience anew the bountiful hand of God as their ancestors did on their way through the Desert of Sinai to the promised land (see 78:15–16; 105:41; 114:8)—and as their descendants would on their return to Zion from Babylonian exile (see Isa 41:17–20; 43:19–20; 49:10).

84:7 *from strength to strength.* Whatever the toils and hardships of the journey (see Isa 40:31). *Zion.* See 9:11 and note.

84:8–11 A prayer for the king, and its motivation: Only as God blesses the king in Jerusalem will the psalmist once more realize his great desire to return to his accustomed service in the temple (see introduction).

84:8 *LORD God Almighty ... God of Jacob.* That is, LORD God Almighty, the God of Jacob (see 59:5; see also note on 3:7). *Jacob.* A synonym for Israel (see Ge 32:28).

84:9 *our shield.* The king in Jerusalem (see NIV text note; see also note on 3:3). *anointed one.* God's earthly regent over his people (from David's line—perhaps Hezekiah [see introduction to this psalm]); see note on 2:2.

84:10 *doorkeeper.* Probably the psalmist's normal (and humble) service at the temple (see 2Ki 22:4). *dwell in the tents of the wicked.* Share in the life of those who do not honor the God of Zion. Perhaps reference is to the peoples imported by Sargon II (see 2Ki 17:24–33), among whom the psalmist was forced at the time to live.

84:11 *sun.* The glorious source of the light of life (see note on 27:1). *shield.* See note on 3:3. *blameless.* See 15:2; Ge 17:1 and notes.

84:12 The sum of it all (see 40:4).

Ps 85 A communal prayer for the renewal of God's mercies to his people at a time when they are once more suffering distress. Many believe that vv. 1–3 refer to the return from exile and that the troubles experienced are those alluded to by Nehemiah and Malachi. Verse 12 suggests that a drought has ravaged the land and may reflect the drought with which the Lord chastened his people in the time of Haggai (see Hag 1:5–11). For this prayer's placement in the Psalter and its relationship to the psalms of its group see introduction to Ps 84–89. Christian liturgical usage has often employed this psalm in the Christmas season. The psalm has two main divisions of seven (Hebrew) lines each: (1) the prayer (vv. 1–7); (2) a reassuring word (vv. 8–13). Each division contains a three-line stanza followed by a four-line stanza, with the corresponding stanzas of the second half answering to those of the first: Verses 1–3 speak of mercies granted, while vv. 8–9 speak of mercies soon to come; vv. 4–7 voice the prayer, and vv. 10–13 offer the blessed reassurance that the prayer will be heard. Each of the four stanzas contains one reference to the "LORD."

85 title *For the director of music.* See note on Ps 4 title. *Of the Sons of Korah.* See note on Ps 42 title.

85:1–7 Prayer for the renewal of God's favor.

85:1–3 Israel begins her prayer by appealing to the Lord's past mercies, recalling how he has forgiven and restored them before (perhaps a reference to the restoration from exile).

85:1 *restored the fortunes of Jacob.* Or "brought Jacob back from exile" (see Jer 29:14 and NIV text note). *Jacob.* A synonym for Israel (see Ge 32:28).

85:3 *wrath ... anger.* See v. 5; see also note on 2:5.

85:4–7 The prayer acknowledges that the present troubles are indicative of God's displeasure. No confession of sin is expressed, but in the light of v. 3 (and possibly v. 8; see below) it is probably implicit.

85:7 *unfailing love.* See v. 10; see also note on 6:4.

85:8–13 God's reassuring answer to the prayer, conveyed through a priest or Levite, perhaps one of the Korahites (see note on 12:5–6; see also 2Ch 20:14).

85:8–9 The assurance that God will again bless his people.

85:8 *I will listen.* The speaker awaits the word from the Lord. *promises peace.* The word from the Lord perhaps takes the form of the priestly benediction (see Nu 6:22–26). *saints.* See

9 Surely his salvation[c] is near those who fear him,
that his glory[d] may dwell in our land.
10 Love and faithfulness[e] meet together;
righteousness[f] and peace kiss each other.
11 Faithfulness springs forth from the earth,
and righteousness[g] looks down from heaven.
12 The LORD will indeed give what is good,[h]
and our land will yield[i] its harvest.
13 Righteousness goes before him
and prepares the way for his steps.

Psalm 86

A prayer of David.

1 Hear, O LORD, and answer[j] me,
for I am poor and needy.
2 Guard my life, for I am devoted to you.
You are my God; save your servant
who trusts in you.[k]
3 Have mercy[l] on me, O Lord,
for I call[m] to you all day long.
4 Bring joy to your servant,
for to you, O Lord,
I lift[n] up my soul.
5 You are forgiving and good, O Lord,
abounding in love[o] to all who call to you.
6 Hear my prayer, O LORD;
listen to my cry[p] for mercy.
7 In the day of my trouble[q] I will call[r] to you,
for you will answer[s] me.
8 Among the gods[t] there is none like you,[u] O Lord;
no deeds can compare with yours.

85:9 [c] Ps 27:1; Isa 43:3; 45:8; 46:13; 51:5; 56:1; 62:11 [d] S Ex 29:43; Isa 60:19; Hag 2:9; Zec 2:5 **85:10** [e] Ps 89:14; 115:1; Pr 3:3 [f] Ps 72:2-3; Isa 32:17 **85:11** [g] Isa 45:8 **85:12** [h] Ps 84:11; Jas 1:17 [i] Lev 26:4; S Ps 67:6; Zec 8:12 **86:1** [j] Ps 17:6 **86:2** [k] Ps 25:2; 31:14 **86:3** [l] Ps 4:1; S 9:13; 57:1 [m] Ps 88:9 **86:4** [n] Ps 46:5; 143:8 **86:5** [o] Ex 34:6; Ne 9:17; Ps 103:8; 145:8; Joel 2:13; Jnh 4:2 **86:6** [p] Ps 5:2; 17:1 **86:7** [q] Ps 27:5; S 50:15; 94:13; Hab 3:16 [r] Job 22:27; Ps 4:3; 80:18; 91:15; Isa 30:19; 58:9; 65:24; Zec 13:9 [s] Ps 3:4 **86:8** [t] S Ex 8:10; S Job 21:22 [u] S Ps 18:31

note on 4:3. *but let them not return to folly.* And so provoke God's displeasure again. But it is also possible to translate the clause: "and to those who turn from folly." *folly.* See NIV text note on 14:1.

85:9 *glory.* Wherever God's saving power is displayed, his glory is revealed (see 57:5 and note; 72:18–19; Ex 14:4,17–18; Nu 14:22; Isa 6:3 and note; 40:5 and note; 44:23; 66:19; Eze 39:21).

85:10–13 God's sure mercies to his people spring from his covenant love, to which in his faithfulness and righteousness he remains true, and that assures his people's welfare (peace). Cf. 40:9–10.

85:10 *Love and faithfulness … righteousness and peace.* These expressions of God's favor toward his people are here personified (see note on 23:6), and the vivid portrayal of their meeting and embracing offers one of the most beautiful images in all Scripture of God's gracious dealings with his covenant people. *righteousness.* See vv. 11,13; see also note on 4:1. *peace.* See notes on Nu 6:26; Eze 34:25; Lk 2:14; Ro 1:7.

85:11 *Faithfulness springs forth.* As new growth springs from the earth to bless all living things with plenty. *righteousness looks down.* It shines down benevolently. (With "disaster" as subject, the Hebrew for "looks down" indicates the opposite effect: Jer 6:1, "looms.") From heaven and from earth God's covenant blessings will abound till Israel's cup overflows.

85:12 *what is good.* See 4:6 and note. *will yield its harvest.* See 67:6 and note.

85:13 *Righteousness goes before.* Again the psalmist personifies. Acting either as herald or guide, righteousness leads the way and marks the course for God's engagement in his people's behalf—and righteousness is God's perfect faithfulness to all his covenant commitments (see note on 4:1).

Ps 86 The prayer of an individual for God's help when attacked by enemies, whose fierce onslaughts betray their disdain for the Lord. Whether or not David was the author (see Introduction: Authorship and Titles), the psalmist's identification of himself as God's "servant" (v. 2) suggests his royal status and thus his special relationship with the Lord (see 2Sa 7:5,8 and note on Ps 18 title). The enemies may then be either those within the kingdom who refuse to acknowledge him as the Lord's anointed, or foreign powers that are attempting to remove him from the international scene. For the placement of this psalm in the arrangement of the Psalter see introduction to Ps 84–89.

This carefully designed poetic prayer is composed of five stanzas, having a symmetrical verse pattern (four, three, three, three, four). The author identifies himself as the Lord's servant in the first and last stanzas, which also contain the prayer for God's mercy and deliverance from the enemy threat. The second stanza (vv. 5–7) adds a profession of assurance; the fourth stanza (vv. 11–13) adds a vow to praise. These are linked by references to God's "love" (see note on 6:4) in vv. 5,13. The center stanza (vv. 8–10) hails the Lord as the incomparable, the only God, whom all the nations will someday worship. Verse 9 is the center verse (see note on 6:6). Yahweh ("LORD") occurs four times (once each in stanzas 1,2,4,5), Elohim ("God") occurs four times, and Adonai ("Lord") occurs seven times. Here and elsewhere such numbers appear to be deliberate.

86 title *prayer.* See note on Ps 17 title; see also note on 72:20. *of David.* This is the only psalm in Book III (Ps 73–89) that is ascribed to David. Perhaps its placement among the Korahite psalms is in part because those who arranged the Psalter perceived a thematic link between v. 9 and 87:4.

86:1–4 Initial prayer for God to have mercy and protect the life of his servant.

86:1 *poor and needy.* See 35:10; see also 34:6 and note.

86:2 *devoted to you.* The Hebrew for this phrase is *hasid* (see note on 4:3). *You are my God.* Not that David has chosen him, but that he has chosen David to be his servant (see 1Sa 13:14; 15:28; 16:12; 2Sa 7:8). David's devotion to God and God's commitment to him are deliberately juxtaposed. *your servant.* See vv. 4,16; see also introduction.

86:4 *my soul.* See note on 6:3.

86:5–7 In his need David prays to the Lord because he is confident that, out of his kindness and love, God answers prayer.

86:5 *love.* See vv. 13,15; see also note on 6:4.

86:7 *I will call … you will answer.* See note on 118:5.

86:8–10 At the center of his prayer David gives expression to his fundamental belief (see also 115:3–7; 135:13–17 and related notes) and makes clear why he appeals to Yahweh in the surrounding stanzas.

9 All the nations you have made
will come[v] and worship[w] before you,
O Lord;
they will bring glory[x] to your name.
10 For you are great[y] and do marvelous
deeds;[z]
you alone[a] are God.

11 Teach me your way,[b] O LORD,
and I will walk in your truth;[c]
give me an undivided[d] heart,
that I may fear[e] your name.
12 I will praise you, O Lord my God, with
all my heart;[f]
I will glorify your name forever.
13 For great is your love toward me;
you have delivered me[g] from the
depths of the grave.[a][h]

14 The arrogant are attacking me, O God;
a band of ruthless men seeks my
life—
men without regard for you.[i]
15 But you, O Lord, are a compassionate
and gracious[j] God,
slow to anger,[k] abounding[l] in love
and faithfulness.[m]
16 Turn to me[n] and have mercy[o] on me;
grant your strength[p] to your servant
and save the son of your
maidservant.[b][q]
17 Give me a sign[r] of your goodness,
that my enemies may see it and be
put to shame,
for you, O LORD, have helped me and
comforted me.

86:9 [v]S Ps 65:2 [w]Ps 66:4; Isa 19:21; 27:13; 49:7; Zec 8:20-22; 14:16; Rev 15:4 [x]Isa 43:7; 44:23 **86:10** [y]S 2Sa 7:22; S Ps 48:1 [z]S Ex 3:20; S Ps 71:17; 72:18 [a]S Dt 6:4; S Isa 43:10; Mk 12:29; 1Co 8:4 **86:11** [b]S Ex 33:13; S 1Sa 12:23; Ps 25:5 [c]S Ps 26:3 [d]Jer 24:7; 32:39; Eze 11:19; 1Co 7:35 [e]S Dt 6:24 **86:12** [f]S Ps 9:1 **86:13** [g]S Ps 34:4; 49:15; 116:8 [h]S Ps 16:10; S 56:13 **86:14** [i]Ps 54:3 **86:15** [j]S Ps 51:1; 103:8; 111:4; 116:5; 145:8 [k]Nu 14:18 [l]ver 5 [m]S Ex 34:6; S Ne 9:17; Joel 2:13 **86:16** [n]S Ps 6:4 [o]S Ps 9:13

Psalm 87

Of the Sons of Korah. A psalm. A song.

1 He has set his foundation on the holy
mountain;[s]
2 the LORD loves the gates of Zion[t]
more than all the dwellings of Jacob.
3 Glorious things are said of you,
O city of God:[u] *Selah*
4 "I will record Rahab[c][v] and Babylon
among those who acknowledge
me—
Philistia[w] too, and Tyre[x], along with
Cush[d]—

[a] *13* Hebrew *Sheol* [b] *16* Or *save your faithful son*
[c] *4* A poetic name for Egypt [d] *4* That is, the upper Nile region

[p]Ps 18:1 [q]Ps 116:16 **86:17** [r]S Ex 3:12; Mt 24:3; S Jn 2:11
87:1 [s]S Ps 48:1 **87:2** [t]Ps 2:6 **87:3** [u]S Ps 46:4
87:4 [v]S Job 9:13 [w]S 2Sa 8:1; Ps 83:7 [x]Ps 45:12; Joel 3:4

86:9 *All the nations.* See note on 46:10. This is the center verse of the psalm (see note on 6:6) and contains the psalm's most exalted confession of faith concerning God's sovereign and universal rule. *they will bring glory.* As David vows to do (v. 12). *your name.* See vv. 11–12; see also note on 5:11.
86:10 *marvelous deeds.* See note on 9:1.
86:11–13 A prayer for godliness and a vow to praise.
86:11 *Teach me ... give me.* What would be the benefit if God saved him from his enemies but abandoned him to his own waywardness? David's dependence on God is complete, and so is his devotion to God—save me from the enemy outside but also from my frailty within (see 25:5; 51:7,10 and notes). Only one who is thus devoted to God may expect God's help and will truly fulfill the vow (v. 12). *undivided heart.* See Eze 11:19 and note; see also 1Ch 12:33; 1Co 7:35. *heart.* See note on 4:7.
86:12 Vow to praise (see note on 7:17).
86:13 David anticipates the answer to his prayer (see note on 3:8). *depths.* See note on 30:1.
86:14–17 Conclusion: the prayer renewed.
86:14 *ruthless.* The Hebrew for this word suggests also ferocity. *men without regard for you.* In their arrogance they dismiss the heavenly Warrior, who is David's defender (see note on 10:11; see also Jer 20:11).
86:15 Echoes v. 5, but is even more similar to Ex 34:6 (see note on Ex 34:6–7).
86:16 *grant your strength.* Exert your power in my behalf. *son of your maidservant.* That is, one born and raised in the household—and thus the Lord's servant from infancy. See NIV text note; see also 116:16 and NIV text note.
86:17 *goodness.* Covenanted favors (see 27:13 and note). *may see it.* May see that you stand with me and help me (see 31:19 and note).
Ps 87 A celebration of Zion as the "city of God" (v. 3), the special object of his love and the royal city of his kingdom (see introductions to Ps 46; 48; 76). According to the ancient and consistent interpretation of Jewish and Christian interpreters alike, this psalm stands in lonely isolation in the Psalter (but see 47:9) in that it foresees the ingathering of the nations into Zion as fellow citizens with Israel in the kingdom of God—after the manner of such prophetic visions as Isa 2:2–4; 19:19–25; 25:6; 45:14,22–24; 56:6–8; 60:3; 66:23; Da 7:14; Mic 4:1–3; Zec 8:23; 14:16. (Accordingly, some have assigned it to the time of Isaiah and Micah, while others have thought it to be postexilic.) So interpreted, this psalm stands in sharpest possible contrast with the other Zion songs of the Psalter (see Ps 46; 48; 76; 125; 129; 137). The key to its main thrust lies in v. 4. It may be that its historic interpretation has sprung from the failure of tradition to preserve memory of the Hebrew poetic device of interrupted syntax (which occurs elsewhere) and that the references to foreign nations should be read as vocatives (see NIV text note on v. 4). With this reading, the psalm stands in thematic accord with the other Zion songs, celebrating God's special love for Zion—which is thrown into the teeth of Zion's historic enemies (see note on v. 4). Placed at the center of four prayers arising from deep crises—two of individuals (Ps 86; 88) and two of the community (Ps 85; 89)—it offers reassurance that God will surely answer such prayers (see introduction to Ps 84–89).
87 title *Of the Sons of Korah.* See note on Ps 42 title. *song.* See note on Ps 30 title.
87:1 *his foundation.* The Lord himself has laid the foundations of Zion (see Isa 14:32) and of the temple as his royal house. *mountain.* The Hebrew for this word is plural, emphasizing the majesty of the holy mountain on which God's throne has been set (see 48:2 and note).
87:2 *loves ... more than.* As the city of his founding, his chosen seat of rule over his people, Zion is the Lord's most cherished city, even among the towns of Israel (see 9:11 and note; 78:68; 132:13–14). *Jacob.* A synonym for Israel (see Ge 32:28).
87:4 *I will record ... This one was born in Zion.* God will list them in his royal register (see notes on 9:5; 51:1; 69:28) as those who are native (-born) citizens of his royal city, having all the privileges and enjoying all the benefits and security of such citizenship. *Rahab.* Whereas elsewhere this name is applied to

and will say, 'This[a] one was born in
Zion.[y]' "
5 Indeed, of Zion it will be said,
"This one and that one were born in
her,
and the Most High himself will
establish her."
6 The LORD will write in the register[z] of
the peoples:
"This one was born in Zion." *Selah*
7 As they make music[a] they will sing,
"All my fountains[b] are in you."

Psalm 88

A song. A psalm of the Sons of Korah. For the director of music. According to *mahalath leannoth.* [b] A *maskil*[c] of Heman the Ezrahite.

1 O LORD, the God who saves me,[c]
day and night I cry out[d] before you.
2 May my prayer come before you;
turn your ear to my cry.
3 For my soul is full of trouble[e]
and my life draws near the grave.[d f]
4 I am counted among those who go
down to the pit;[g]
I am like a man without strength.[h]
5 I am set apart with the dead,
like the slain who lie in the grave,
whom you remember no more,
who are cut off[i] from your care.
6 You have put me in the lowest pit,
in the darkest depths.[j]
7 Your wrath[k] lies heavily upon me;
you have overwhelmed me with
all your waves.[l] *Selah*
8 You have taken from me my closest
friends[m]
and have made me repulsive to
them.

87:4 [y]Isa 19:25 **87:6** [z]Ex 32:32; Ps 69:28; Isa 4:3; Mal 3:16 **87:7** [a]Ps 149:3 [b]S Ps 36:9 **88:1** [c]S Ps 51:14 [d]Ps 3:4; 22:2; Lk 18:7 **88:3** [e]Ps 6:3; 25:17 [f]S Job 33:22 **88:4** [g]S Ps 31:12 [h]Ps 18:1 **88:5** [i]S Ps 31:22 **88:6** [j]Ps 30:1; S 69:15; La 3:55; Jnh 2:3 **88:7** [k]Ps 7:11 [l]S Ps 42:7 **88:8** [m]S Job 19:13; Ps 31:11

[a] 4 Or *"O Rahab and Babylon, / Philistia, Tyre and Cush, / I will record concerning those who acknowledge me: / 'This* [b] Title: Possibly a tune, "The Suffering of Affliction" [c] Title: Probably a literary or musical term [d] 3 Hebrew *Sheol*

the mythical monster of the deep (see 89:10; see also notes on 32:6; Job 9:13), here the reference is to Egypt (see NIV text note), as in Isa 30:7 (see note there); 51:9. The nations listed are representative of all Gentile peoples. As usually interpreted, the psalm here foresees a widespread conversion to the Lord from the peoples who from time immemorial had been hostile to him and to his kingdom (see Isa 19:21; 26:18 and note). But if the NIV text note is correct (see also v. 5), the Lord is here portrayed as carefully recording the names of all his people, those who acknowledge him as their covenant Lord (Hos 6:3), so as to take them under his protection as the citizens of his royal city. Ominously he warns the nations (as in Isa 14:28–32) that he has carefully registered his people one and all and will hold the nations accountable for the harm they do to any one of them (see 105:15).

87:5 *This one and that one.* Wherever they may be dispersed among the nations. *Most High.* See note on Ge 14:19.

87:7 *All my fountains.* All that refreshes them is found in the city of God, a possible allusion to God's "river of delights" (36:8) "whose streams make glad the city of God" (46:4); see notes on those passages. Alternatively, "fountains" may be a metaphor for sources; the sense of the line would then be: We all spring from you. *my.* Communal use of the singular pronoun (see note on Ps 30 title).

Ps 88 A cry out of the depths, the prayer of one on the edge of death, whose whole life has been lived, as it were, in the near vicinity of the grave (see also Ps 90). So troubled have been his years that he seems to have known only the back of God's hand (God's "wrath," v. 7), and even those nearest him have withdrawn themselves as from one with a defiling skin disease (see v. 8). No expressions of hopeful expectation (as in most prayers of the Psalter; but see Ps 44; 89) burst from these lips; the last word speaks of darkness as "my closest friend." And yet the prayer begins, "O LORD, the God who saves me." The psalm recalls the fact that although sometimes godly persons live lives of unremitting trouble (see 73:14), they can still grasp the hope that God is Savior (see also Ps 87 and introduction to Ps 84–89). Many early church leaders interpreted this psalm as a prayer of the suffering Christ (as they did Ps 22); for that reason it became part of the Good Friday liturgy.

Structurally, the prayer ends (vv. 13–18) as it began (vv. 1–5), each section with two Hebrew poetic lines of petition (vv. 1–2,13–14) followed by four lines describing the psalmist's distress (vv. 3–5,15–18). Between the beginning and the end are two stanzas of four lines each (vv. 6–9a,9b–12). In the first of these the psalmist expresses his recognition that what has happened to him is God's doing. In the second he appeals to God to consider the consequences if he does not deliver the petitioner from death.

88 title The psalm bears a double title, perhaps representing two different traditions. *song.* See note on Ps 30 title. *of the Sons of Korah.* See note on Ps 42 title. *For the director of music.* See note on Ps 4 title. *According to.* See note on Ps 6 title. *maskil.* See note on Ps 32 title. *Heman.* See note on Ps 39 title. *Ezrahite.* The reference appears to be to Zerah, one of Judah's sons, who is recorded as having a Heman and an Ethan (see Ps 89 title) among his sons (see 1Ch 2:6). If so, the title here represents a confusion in the tradition, arising from the similarity between these two Judahite names and those of two famous Korahite choir leaders, Heman and Ethan (Jeduthun; see note on Ps 39 title).

88:1–2 Opening appeal to the Lord as "the God who saves me."

88:3–5 Living on the brink of death. Whether the psalmist lies mortally ill or experiences some analogous trouble or peril cannot be known.

88:3 *my soul.* See note on 6:3.

88:4 *pit.* See 28:1; 30:3,9; 143:7.

88:5 *remember no more.* From the perspective of this life, death cuts off from God's care; there is no remembering by God of the needy sufferer to rescue and restore (see 25:7; 74:2; 106:4). In his dark mood the author portrays his situation in bleakest colors (see note on 6:5; cf. Job's experiences).

88:6–9a You, God, have done this! The psalmist knows no reason for it (see v. 14; cf. Ps 44), but he knows God's hand is in it (see Ru 1:20–21; Am 3:6). That his Savior-God shows him the face of wrath deepens his anguish and helplessness. But he does not try to resolve the dark enigma; he simply pleads his case—and it is to his Savior-God that he can appeal (see v. 1).

88:6 *lowest pit . . . darkest depths.* See note on 30:1.

88:7 *wrath.* See v. 16; see also note on 2:5. *all your waves.* See note on 32:6.

88:8 *my closest friends.* See v. 18 and note on 31:11–12.

I am confined[n] and cannot escape;[o]
9 my eyes[p] are dim with grief.

I call[q] to you, O LORD, every day;
I spread out my hands[r] to you.
10 Do you show your wonders to the dead?
Do those who are dead rise up and praise you?[s] *Selah*
11 Is your love declared in the grave,
your faithfulness[t] in Destruction[a]?
12 Are your wonders known in the place of darkness,
or your righteous deeds in the land of oblivion?

13 But I cry to you for help,[u] O LORD;
in the morning[v] my prayer comes before you.[w]
14 Why, O LORD, do you reject[x] me
and hide your face[y] from me?

15 From my youth[z] I have been afflicted[a] and close to death;
I have suffered your terrors[b] and am in despair.[c]
16 Your wrath[d] has swept over me;
your terrors[e] have destroyed me.
17 All day long they surround me like a flood;[f]
they have completely engulfed me.
18 You have taken my companions[g] and loved ones from me;
the darkness is my closest friend.

Psalm 89

A *maskil*[b] of Ethan the Ezrahite.

1 I will sing[h] of the LORD's great love forever;
with my mouth I will make your faithfulness known[i] through all generations.
2 I will declare that your love stands firm forever,
that you established your faithfulness in heaven itself.[j]
3 You said, "I have made a covenant with my chosen one,
I have sworn to David my servant,
4 'I will establish your line forever
and make your throne firm through all generations.'"[k] *Selah*

5 The heavens[l] praise your wonders, O LORD,
your faithfulness too, in the assembly[m] of the holy ones.

[a] *11* Hebrew *Abaddon* [b] Title: Probably a literary or musical term

88:8 [n] Jer 32:2; 33:1 [o] S Job 3:23 **88:9** [p] S Ps 38:10 [q] Ps 5:2 [r] Job 11:13; Ps 143:6 **88:10** [s] S Ps 6:5 **88:11** [t] S Ps 30:9 **88:13** [u] S Ps 30:2 [v] Ps 5:3; S 55:17 [w] Ps 119:147 **88:14** [x] S Ps 43:2 [y] Ps 13:1 **88:15** [z] Ps 129:1; Jer 22:21; Eze 16:22; Hos 2:15 [a] Ps 9:12 [b] Job 6:4; S 18:11 [c] 2Co 4:8 **88:16** [d] Ps 7:11 [e] Job 6:4 **88:17** [f] Ps 124:4 **88:18** [g] ver 8; Ps 38:11 **89:1** [h] Ps 59:16 [i] S Ps 36:5; 40:10 **89:2** [j] S Ps 36:5 **89:4** [k] 2Sa 7:12-16; 1Ki 8:16; Ps 132:11-12; Isa 9:7; Eze 37:24-25; S Mt 1:1; S Lk 1:33 **89:5** [l] S Ps 19:1 [m] S Ps 1:5

88:9 *eyes are dim.* See note on 6:7.
88:9b – 12 Appeal to God to help before the psalmist sinks into "the land of oblivion" (see note on v. 5).
88:10,12 *wonders.* God's saving acts in behalf of his people (see note on 9:1).
88:10 *rise up.* In the realm of the dead (not in the resurrection); see Isa 14:9. *praise you.* See 6:5; 30:9; 115:17 and notes.
88:11 *love … faithfulness.* That is, love-and-faithfulness (see note on 36:5; see also note on 3:7). *love.* See note on 6:4.
88:12 *righteous deeds.* See 71:24 and note.
88:13 – 14 Concluding prayer — with echoes of the initial petition in vv. 1 – 2.
88:13 *in the morning.* See 101:8 and note.
88:14 *Why … ?* See note on 6:3. *hide your face.* See note on 13:1.
88:15 – 18 The psalmist has been no stranger to trouble; all his life he has suffered the terrors of God (cf. Ps 90).
88:17 *like a flood.* See v. 7; see also note on 32:6.
Ps 89 A prayer that mourns the downfall of the Davidic dynasty and pleads for its restoration. The bitter shock of that event (reflected in the sudden transition at v. 38) is almost unbearable — that God, the faithful and almighty One, has abandoned his anointed and made him the mockery of the nations, in seeming violation of his firm covenant with David — and it evokes from the psalmist a lament that borders on reproach (vv. 38 – 45). The event may have been the attack on Jerusalem by Nebuchadnezzar and the exile of King Jehoiachin in 597 B.C. (see 2Ki 24:8 – 17). Although like Ps 44 and 88 this prayer ends in unrelieved perplexity and lamentation over the deep crisis God's rejection has brought about (see v. 38; cf. 44:9; 88:14), in the arrangement of the Psalter it has been brought into relationship with the reassuring themes of Ps 84; 87 (see introduction to Ps 84 – 89).
As with Ps 44 (see introduction to that psalm), a massive foundation is laid for the prayer with which the psalm concludes. An introduction (vv. 1 – 4) sings of God's love and faithfulness (vv. 1 – 2) and his covenant with David (vv. 3 – 4). These two themes are then jubilantly expanded in order: vv. 5 – 18, God's love and faithfulness; vv. 19 – 37, his covenant with David. Suddenly jubilation turns to lament, and the psalmist recounts in detail how God has rejected his anointed (vv. 38 – 45). Thus he comes to his prayer, impatient and urgent, that God will remember once more his covenant with David (vv. 46 – 51). (Verse 52 concludes not the psalm but Book III of the Psalter.)
89 title *maskil.* See note on Ps 32 title. *Ethan.* Jeduthun (see note on Ps 39 title). The author was no doubt a Levite (perhaps a descendant of Jeduthun) who voiced this agonizing prayer as spokesman for the nation. *Ezrahite.* See note on Ps 88 title.
89:1 – 2 God's love and faithfulness celebrated.
89:1 *love … faithfulness.* See vv. 2,33,49; that is, love-and-faithfulness (see v. 14); see note on 36:5. *love.* See vv. 2,14,24,28,33,49; see also note on 6:4. It is God's love and faithfulness that appear to have failed in his rejection (see vv. 38 – 45) of the Davidic king. The author repeats each of these words precisely seven times (in v. 14 the Hebrew uses a different — but related — word for "faithfulness").
89:2 *in heaven itself.* God's love and faithfulness have been made sure in the highest seat of power and authority (see vv. 5 – 8).
89:3 – 4 God's covenant with David celebrated (see 2Sa 7:8 – 16).
89:3 *servant.* See vv. 20,39,50; here an official title (see note on 78:70).
89:5 – 8 The Lord's faithfulness and awesome power set him apart among all the powers in the heavenly realm, and they acknowledge him with praise and reverence.
89:5 *The heavens.* All beings belonging to the divine realm in the heavens. *wonders.* God's mighty acts in creation and redemption (see note on 9:1). *assembly of the holy ones.* The divine council in heaven (see v. 7; see also note on 82:1).

6 For who in the skies above can
compare with the LORD?
Who is like the LORD among the
heavenly beings?[n]
7 In the council[o] of the holy ones[p] God is
greatly feared;
he is more awesome than all who
surround him.[q]
8 O LORD God Almighty,[r] who is like
you?[s]
You are mighty, O LORD, and your
faithfulness surrounds you.

9 You rule over the surging sea;
when its waves mount up, you still
them.[t]
10 You crushed Rahab[u] like one of the
slain;
with your strong arm you scattered[v]
your enemies.
11 The heavens are yours,[w] and yours also
the earth;[x]
you founded the world and all that is
in it.[y]
12 You created the north and the south;
Tabor[z] and Hermon[a] sing for joy[b] at
your name.
13 Your arm is endued with power;
your hand is strong, your right hand
exalted.[c]

14 Righteousness and justice are the
foundation of your throne;[d]
love and faithfulness go before you.[e]
15 Blessed are those who have learned to
acclaim you,
who walk[f] in the light[g] of your
presence, O LORD.
16 They rejoice in your name[h] all day
long;
they exult in your righteousness.
17 For you are their glory and strength,[i]
and by your favor you exalt our
horn.[a][j]
18 Indeed, our shield[b][k] belongs to the
LORD,
our king[l] to the Holy One of Israel.

19 Once you spoke in a vision,
to your faithful people you said:
"I have bestowed strength on a
warrior;
I have exalted a young man from
among the people.
20 I have found David[m] my servant;[n]
with my sacred oil[o] I have anointed[p]
him.
21 My hand will sustain him;
surely my arm will strengthen him.[q]
22 No enemy will subject him to tribute;[r]
no wicked man will oppress[s] him.
23 I will crush his foes before him[t]
and strike down his adversaries.[u]
24 My faithful love will be with him,[v]
and through my name his horn[c] will
be exalted.
25 I will set his hand over the sea,
his right hand over the rivers.[w]
26 He will call out to me, 'You are my
Father,[x]
my God, the Rock[y] my Savior.'[z]
27 I will also appoint him my firstborn,[a]
the most exalted[b] of the kings[c] of the
earth.
28 I will maintain my love to him forever,
and my covenant with him will
never fail.[d]

[a] *17 Horn* here symbolizes strong one. [b] *18* Or *sovereign* [c] *24 Horn* here symbolizes strength.

89:6 [n]S Ge 1:26; S Ex 9:14; S Ps 18:31; 113:5 **89:7** [o]Ps 111:1 [p]S Job 5:1 [q]Ps 47:2 **89:8** [r]Isa 6:3 [s]S Ps 71:19 **89:9** [t]S Ps 65:7 **89:10** [u]S Job 9:13 [v]S Ps 59:11; S 68:1; 92:9 **89:11** [w]S Dt 10:14; Ps 115:16 [x]1Ch 29:11; S Ps 24:1 [y]S Ge 1:1 **89:12** [z]S Jos 19:22 [a]S Dt 3:8; S 4:48 [b]Ps 98:8 **89:13** [c]S Jos 4:24 **89:14** [d]Ps 97:2 [e]Ps 85:10-11 **89:15** [f]Ps 1:1 [g]Ps 44:3 **89:16** [h]Ps 30:4; 105:3 **89:17** [i]Ps 18:1 [j]ver 24; Ps 75:10; 92:10; 112:9; 148:14 **89:18** [k]Ps 18:2 [l]Ps 47:9; Isa 16:5; 33:17,22 **89:20** [m]Ac 13:22 [n]Ps 78:70 [o]S Ex 29:7; S 1Ki 1:39 [p]S 1Sa 2:35; S 2Sa 22:51 **89:21** [q]ver 13; Ps 18:35 **89:22** [r]S Jdg 3:15 [s]2Sa 7:10 **89:23** [t]Ps 18:40 [u]2Sa 7:9 **89:24** [v]S 2Sa 7:15 **89:25** [w]Ps 72:8 **89:26** [x]S 2Sa 7:14; S Jer 3:4; Heb 1:5 [y]S Ps 62:2 [z]S 2Sa 22:47 **89:27** [a]S Col 1:18 [b]S Nu 24:7 [c]Ps 2:6; Rev 1:5; 19:16 **89:28** [d]ver 33-34; Isa 55:3

89:6 *heavenly beings.* Lit. "sons of god(s)" (see 29:1 and note).
89:8 LORD *... Almighty.* See note on 1Sa 1:3. *your faithfulness surrounds you.* It also surrounds this stanza (see v. 5).
89:9 – 13 The Lord's power as Creator — and creation's joy in him.
89:9 – 10 Poetic imagery borrowed from ancient Near Eastern myths of creation, here celebrating God's power in ordering the primeval chaotic waters so that the creation order could be established (see Ge 1:6 – 10; see also notes on 65:6 – 7; 74:13 – 14).
89:10 *Rahab.* Mythical monster of the deep (see notes on 32:6; 87:4), probably another name for Leviathan (see 74:14; 104:26). The last half of this verse is probably echoed in Lk 1:51.
89:12 *the north and the south.* Reference may be to two mountains, here parallel to Hermon and Tabor: "Mount North" (Zaphon; see 48:2 and note) and Mount Amana (see SS 4:8). *Tabor.* See note on Jdg 4:6. *Hermon.* See note on Dt 3:8. *sing for joy.* See note on 65:13. *name.* See vv. 16,24; see also note on 5:11.
89:14 – 18 The Lord's righteousness and faithfulness in his rule in behalf of his people — and their joy in him.
89:14 Righteousness and justice are the foundation stones of God's throne (see 97:2 and note; cf. Pr 16:12; 25:5; 29:14). Love and faithfulness are personified as throne attendants that herald his royal movements (see note on 23:6). *Righteousness.* See v. 16; see also note on 4:1.
89:17 *horn.* King (see NIV text note; see also v. 18).
89:18 *Holy One of Israel.* See 71:22; 78:41; 2Ki 19:22 and note.
89:19 – 29 The Lord's election of David to be his regent over his people, and his everlasting covenant with him. The thought is developed by couplets: (1) introduction (v. 19); (2) I have anointed David as my servant and will sustain him (vv. 20 – 21); (3) I will crush all his foes (vv. 22 – 23); (4) I will extend his realm (vv. 24 – 25); (5) I will make him first among the kings (vv. 26 – 27); (6) I will cause his dynasty to endure forever (vv. 28 – 29) — a promise fulfilled in the eternal reign of Jesus Christ (see Jn 12:34).
89:19 *vision.* Reference is to the revelation to Samuel (see 1Sa 16:12) and/or to Nathan (see 2Sa 7:4 – 16). *faithful people.* See note on 4:3.
89:25 *sea ... rivers.* David's rule will reach from the Mediterranean Sea to the Euphrates River (see 72:8; 80:11 and note on Ex 23:31). But the author uses imagery that underscores the fact that, as his royal "son" (see v. 26) and regent, David's rule will be a reflection of God's (see vv. 9 – 10 and notes; also compare v. 23 with v. 10).
89:27 *firstborn.* The royal son of highest privilege and position in the kingdom of God (see 2:7 – 12; 45:6 – 9; 72:8 – 11; 110), thus "the most exalted of the kings of the earth" (see Rev

29 I will establish his line forever,
his throne as long as the heavens
endure.[e]
30 "If his sons forsake my law
and do not follow my statutes,
31 if they violate my decrees
and fail to keep my commands,
32 I will punish their sin with the rod,
their iniquity with flogging;[f]
33 but I will not take my love from him,[g]
nor will I ever betray my
faithfulness.
34 I will not violate my covenant
or alter what my lips have uttered.[h]
35 Once for all, I have sworn by my
holiness—
and I will not lie to David—
36 that his line will continue forever
and his throne endure before me like
the sun;[i]
37 it will be established forever like the
moon,
the faithful witness in the sky."[j]
Selah
38 But you have rejected,[k] you have
spurned,
you have been very angry with your
anointed one.
39 You have renounced the covenant with
your servant
and have defiled his crown in the
dust.[l]
40 You have broken through all his walls[m]
and reduced his strongholds[n] to ruins.
41 All who pass by have plundered[o] him;
he has become the scorn of his
neighbors.[p]
42 You have exalted the right hand of his
foes;
you have made all his enemies
rejoice.[q]
43 You have turned back the edge of his
sword
and have not supported him in
battle.[r]
44 You have put an end to his splendor
and cast his throne to the ground.
45 You have cut short[s] the days of his
youth;
you have covered him with a mantle
of shame.[t] *Selah*
46 How long, O LORD? Will you hide
yourself forever?
How long will your wrath burn like
fire?[u]
47 Remember how fleeting is my life.[v]
For what futility you have created all
men!
48 What man can live and not see death,
or save himself from the power of
the grave[a]?[w] *Selah*
49 O Lord, where is your former great
love,
which in your faithfulness you swore
to David?
50 Remember, Lord, how your servant
has[b] been mocked,[x]
how I bear in my heart the taunts of
all the nations,
51 the taunts with which your enemies
have mocked, O LORD,
with which they have mocked every
step of your anointed one.[y]
52 Praise be to the LORD forever!
Amen and Amen.[z]

BOOK IV
Psalms 90–106

Psalm 90

A prayer of Moses the man of God.

1 Lord, you have been our dwelling
place[a]
throughout all generations.

89:29 [e] ver 4,36 **89:32** [f] 2Sa 7:14 **89:33** [g] S 2Sa 7:15 **89:34** [h] S Nu 23:19 **89:36** [i] ver 4 **89:37** [j] Jer 33:20-21 **89:38** [k] 1Ch 28:9; Ps 44:9; 78:59 **89:39** [l] La 5:16 **89:40** [m] S Ps 80:12 [n] Isa 22:5; La 2:2 **89:41** [o] S Jdg 2:14 [p] S Ps 44:13 **89:42** [q] Ps 13:2; 80:6 **89:43** [r] Ps 44:10 **89:45** [s] S Ps 39:5 [t] Ps 44:15; 109:29 **89:46** [u] Ps 79:5 **89:47** [v] S Ge 47:9; S Job 7:7; Ps 39:5; 1Pe 1:24 **89:48** [w] S Ge 5:24; Ps 22:29 **89:50** [x] Ps 69:19 **89:51** [y] Ps 74:10 **89:52** [z] S Ps 41:13; S 72:19 **90:1** [a] S Dt 33:27; Eph 2:22; Rev 21:3

[a] 48 Hebrew *Sheol* [b] 50 Or *your servants have*

1:5). So the words may speak of universal rule—ultimately fulfilled in Christ.

89:29 *as long as the heavens endure.* See vv. 36–37.

89:30–37 The Lord's covenant with David and his dynasty (see note on 2Sa 7:1–29; see also chart, p. 19) was everlasting (see vv. 28–29) and unconditional—though if any of his royal descendants is unfaithful, he will individually suffer under God's rod (to the detriment of the entire nation).

89:38–45 God's present rejection of David's son, and all its fearful consequences—the undoing of all that had been promised and assured by covenant (see especially vv. 19–29). To fully appreciate the poignancy of this lament cf. Ps 18.

89:46–51 The prayer, an appeal—in spite of all—to God's faithfulness to his covenant with David. In this dark hour, that remains the psalmist's hope.

89:46 *How long . . . ?* See note on 6:3. *wrath.* See note on 2:5.

89:47 *how fleeting is my life.* See 37:20; 39:4–6 and notes. The shortness of human life adds urgency to the prayer. *futility.* Because humans have limited powers and are subject to death, they are dependent on God's involvement in the world (see 60:11; 90:5–6 and note; 108:12; 127:1–2; see also Job 7:1–3; Ecc 1:2 and note).

89:49 *former great love.* The love referred to in v. 1.

89:50 *Remember.* See v. 47.

89:52 A brief doxology with which the final editors concluded Book III of the Psalter (see note on 41:13).

Ps 90–100 A series of 11 psalms arranged within the frame "you have been our dwelling place throughout all generations" (90:1) and "his faithfulness continues through all generations" (100:5)—a series that begins with prayer and ends with praise. The first two of these psalms (90–91) are thematically connected (point and counterpoint); the next three (92–94) form a trilogy that serves as a transition to the final thematic cluster (95–99). At the very middle, Ps 95 anticipates the four following psalms and adds a warning for the celebrants of Yahweh's reign that echoes the warning of Moses in Dt 6:13–18. Evidently the editors of the Psalter

[2]Before the mountains were born[b]
or you brought forth the earth and
the world,
from everlasting to everlasting[c] you
are God.[d]

[3]You turn men back to dust,
saying, "Return to dust, O sons of
men."[e]
[4]For a thousand years in your sight
are like a day that has just gone by,
or like a watch in the night.[f]
[5]You sweep men away[g] in the sleep of
death;
they are like the new grass of the
morning—
[6]though in the morning it springs up
new,
by evening it is dry and withered.[h]

[7]We are consumed by your anger
and terrified by your indignation.
[8]You have set our iniquities before
you,
our secret sins[i] in the light of your
presence.[j]
[9]All our days pass away under your
wrath;
we finish our years with a moan.[k]
[10]The length of our days is seventy
years[l]—
or eighty,[m] if we have the strength;
yet their span[a] is but trouble and
sorrow,[n]
for they quickly pass, and we fly
away.[o]
[11]Who knows the power of your anger?
For your wrath[p] is as great as the
fear that is due you.[q]
[12]Teach us to number our days[r] aright,
that we may gain a heart of wisdom.[s]
[13]Relent, O LORD! How long[t] will it be?
Have compassion on your servants.[u]

[a] 10 Or *yet the best of them*

90:2 [b]S Job 15:7 [c]Isa 9:6; 57:15 [d]S Ge 21:33; S Job 10:5; Ps 102:24-27; Pr 8:23-26 **90:3** [e]S Ge 2:7; S Job 7:21; 34:15; 1Co 15:47 **90:4** [f]S Job 10:5; 2Pe 3:8 **90:5** [g]S Ge 19:15 **90:6** [h]Isa 40:6-8; Mt 6:30; Jas 1:10 **90:8** [i]S Ps 19:12; 2Co 4:2; Eph 5:12 [j]S Heb 4:13 **90:9** [k]Ps 78:33 **90:10** [l]Isa 23:15,17; Jer 25:11 [m]2Sa 19:35 [n]S Job 5:7 [o]S Job 20:8; S 34:15 **90:11** [p]Ps 7:11 [q]Ps 76:7 **90:12** [r]Ps 39:4; 139:16; Pr 16:9; 20:24 [s]Dt 32:29 **90:13** [t]Ps 6:3 [u]S Dt 32:36

intended readers of this group of psalms to hear echoes of the voice of Moses as interceder (Ps 90) and as admonisher (95:8–11), through which ministries (shared also by Aaron and Samuel) Israel had been blessed under the reign of the Great King, Yahweh (see 99:6–8). See further the introductions to the several psalms of this group.

Ps 90 A prayer to the everlasting God to have compassion on his servants, who through the ages have known him to be their safe haven (v. 1; see also 91:9) but who also painfully experience his wrath because of their sin and his sentence of death that cuts short their lives—a plea that through this long night of his displeasure God will teach them true wisdom (see v. 12 and note) and, in the morning after, bless them in equal measure with expressions of his love so that joy may yet fill their days and the days of their children and their daily labors be blessed. This psalm has many links with Ps 39.

So that the melancholy depiction of the human state found here might not stand alone, the editors of the Psalter have followed it immediately with a psalm that speaks in counterpoint of the happy condition of those who dwell "in the shelter of the Most High" (91:1) and "make the Most High [their] dwelling" (91:9; see also 92:13). To isolate Ps 90 from this context is to distort its intended function in the Psalter collection. See also Ps 103.

Two stanzas descriptive of the human condition under God's aggrieved anger (vv. 3–6,7–10) are framed by two couplets (vv. 1–2,11–12) that, by their implicit contrasts, highlight the major polarities over which the intervening stanzas brood: (1) The Lord, who has ever been our "dwelling place" (v. 1), has shown us the power of his wrath (v. 7). (2) God is the Everlasting One (v. 2), while we must come to terms with the small number of our days (v. 12). These reflections lead to the prayer with which the psalm concludes (vv. 13–17).

90 title *A prayer.* See note on Ps 17 title. *Moses.* Tradition has assigned this psalm to Moses—perhaps because (1) it shares some language with Dt 32–33; (2) as an intercessory prayer it fits well on the lips of Moses, the great interceder for Israel (see Ex 32:11–13; 34:9; Nu 14:13–19; Dt 9:25–29; Ps 106:23; Jer 15:1; see also Ps 99:6); and (3) elsewhere only Moses asks God directly to "relent" from his anger toward Israel (v. 13; see Ex 32:12). *man of God.* A phrase normally applied in the OT to prophets (see note on 1Sa 2:27), including Moses (see, e.g., Jos 14:6).

90:1 *dwelling place.* See 91:9. The Hebrew for this phrase is translated "refuge" in 71:3. Here and in 91:9 it has the connotation of "home" or "safe haven."

90:3–6 Human beings live under God's sentence of death—"dust … to dust" (Ge 3:19).

90:4–5 *For … You.* Perhaps better "Though …, you": Though for God 1,000 years are like a mere watch in the night (three to four hours), he cuts human life short like new grass that shows itself at dawn's light but is withered away by the hot Canaanite sun before evening falls.

90:4 *a thousand years … are like a day.* Cf. 2Pe 3:8 and note. *watch in the night.* See note on Jdg 7:19.

90:5–6 The shortness of human life frequently occupied the thoughts of Biblical writers (see 37:2,20,36; 39:5,11; 62:9; 78:39; 89:47; 102:3,11; 103:15–16; 109:23; 144:4; Job 8:9; 14:1–2; Ecc 6:12; Isa 40:6–8; Jas 1:10–11; 1Pe 1:24–25).

90:7–10 Even life's short span is filled with trouble, as God ferrets out every sin and makes the sinner feel his righteous anger.

90:7 *anger … indignation.* See vv. 9,11; see also note on 2:5.

90:8 *light of your presence.* The holy light of God that illumines the hidden corners of the heart and exposes its dark secrets.

90:10 *eighty.* Hebrew poetic convention called for 80 following 70 in parallel construction (see note on Am 1:3). *if we have the strength.* If God gives us the strength to live that long. *their span.* The Hebrew is difficult. If the reading offered in the NIV text note is preferred, the reference is either to the best of the days or to what people prize most in their years—these are all soured by trouble and sorrow (or disappointment).

90:11–12 *Who knows …? … Teach us.* No one has taken the measure of God's anger. But everyone ought to know the measure of their (few) days or they will play the arrogant fool, with no thought of their mortality or of their accountability to God (see Ps 10; 30:6; 49; 73:4–12; see also Dt 8).

90:11 *fear that is due you.* See note on 15:4.

90:12 *gain a heart of wisdom.* God's discipline humbles arrogant sinners and teaches them true wisdom (see 39; 94:12; Pr 3:1–12; Heb 12:7–11; cf. Ps 92:6–7; 94:8–10).

90:13–17 Prayer for God to be compassionate and restore the joys of life. The good hope with which such a prayer may be uttered comes to expression in Ps 91; 92; see also 94:12–14.

90:13 *Relent.* Lit. "Turn" (cf. v. 3). *How long …?* See note on 6:3.

[14]Satisfy[v] us in the morning with your
unfailing love,[w]
that we may sing for joy[x] and be
glad all our days.[y]
[15]Make us glad for as many days as you
have afflicted us,
for as many years as we have seen
trouble.
[16]May your deeds be shown to your
servants,
your splendor to their children.[z]

[17]May the favor[a] of the Lord our God
rest upon us;
establish the work of our hands for
us—
yes, establish the work of our
hands.[a]

Psalm 91

[1]He who dwells in the shelter[b] of the
Most High
will rest in the shadow[c] of the
Almighty.[b]
[2]I will say[c] of the LORD, "He is my
refuge[d] and my fortress,[e]
my God, in whom I trust."

[3]Surely he will save you from the
fowler's snare[f]
and from the deadly pestilence.[g]
[4]He will cover you with his
feathers,
and under his wings you will find
refuge;[h]
his faithfulness will be your shield[i]
and rampart.
[5]You will not fear[j] the terror of night,
nor the arrow that flies by day,
[6]nor the pestilence that stalks in the
darkness,
nor the plague that destroys at
midday.
[7]A thousand may fall at your side,
ten thousand at your right hand,
but it will not come near you.
[8]You will only observe with your
eyes
and see the punishment of the
wicked.[k]

[9]If you make the Most High your
dwelling—
even the LORD, who is my
refuge—
[10]then no harm[l] will befall you,
no disaster will come near your
tent.
[11]For he will command his angels[m]
concerning you
to guard you in all your ways;[n]
[12]they will lift you up in their hands,
so that you will not strike your foot
against a stone.[o]
[13]You will tread upon the lion and the
cobra;
you will trample the great lion and
the serpent.[p]

90:14 [v]Ps 103:5; 107:9; 145:16, 19 [w]S Ps 77:8; 143:8 [x]S Ps 5:11 [y]Ps 31:7 **90:16** [z]Ps 44:1; Hab 3:2 **90:17** [a]Isa 26:12 **91:1** [b]S Ex 33:22 [c]Ps 63:7; Isa 49:2; La 4:20 **91:2** [d]ver 9; S 2Sa 22:3; Ps 9:9 [e]S 2Sa 22:2 **91:3** [f]Ps 124:7; Pr 6:5 [g]1Ki 8:37 **91:4** [h]S Ru 2:12; Ps 17:8 [i]S Dt 32:10; Ps 35:2; Isa 27:3; 31:5; Zec 12:8 **91:5** [j]S Job 5:21 **91:8** [k]Ps 37:34; S 58:10 **91:10** [l]Pr 12:21 **91:11** [m]S Ge 32:1; Heb 1:14 [n]Ps 34:7 **91:12** [o]Mt 4:6*; Lk 4:10-11* **91:13** [p]Da 6:22; Lk 10:19

[a] 17 Or *beauty* [b] 1 Hebrew *Shaddai* [c] 2 Or *He says*

90:14 *in the morning.* Let there be for us a dawning of your love to relieve this long, dark night of your anger (see introduction to Ps 57). The final answer to this prayer comes with the resurrection (see Ro 5:2–5; 8:18; 2Co 4:16–18). *unfailing love.* See note on 6:4.
90:16 *deeds ... splendor.* That is, deeds-of-splendor (see 111:3; see also note on 3:7). For a fuller description of such deeds see the whole of Ps 111. *to their children.* As to past generations (v. 1).
90:17 *favor.* See NIV text note; see also 27:4 and note. *establish.* As only you have been our security in the world (see v. 1), so also make our labors to be effective and enduring—though we are so transient.
Ps 91 A glowing testimony to the security of those who trust in God—set beside Ps 90 as a counterpoint to the dismal depiction of the human condition found there (see introduction to that psalm). It was probably written by one of the temple personnel (a priest or Levite) as a word of assurance to godly worshipers. Because the "you" of vv. 3–13 applies to any who "make the Most High your dwelling" (v. 9; see 90:1), the devil applied vv. 11–12 to Jesus (see Mt 4:6; Lk 4:10–11).
Structurally, the psalm is divided into two halves of eight verses each, with the opening couplet of the second half (vv. 9–10) echoing the theme of vv. 1–2. In the first half, the godly are assured of security from four threats (vv. 5–6)—though thousands fall (v. 7). In the second half, they are assured of triumphing over four menacing beasts (v. 13). The oracle of vv. 14–16 offers climactic assurance.
91:1 *shelter.* The temple (as in 27:5; 31:20; see also 23:6; 27:4), where the godly find safety under the protective wings of the Lord (see v. 4; 61:4). *Most High.* See v. 9; see also note on Ge 14:19. *shadow.* See note on 17:8. *Almighty.* See NIV text note; see also note on Ge 17:1.
91:3 *fowler's snare.* Metaphor for danger from human enemies (see 124:7; see also note on 9:15). *pestilence.* Danger to life from disease. These two threats are further elaborated in vv. 5–6.
91:4 *with his feathers ... wings.* See note on 17:8.
91:5 *terror.* As in 64:1 ("threat"), reference is to attack by enemies; thus it is paired with "arrow." These two references to threats from war are arrayed alongside "pestilence" and "plague" (v. 6), two references to mortal diseases that often reached epidemic proportions. *night ... day.* At whatever time of day or night the threat may come, you will be kept safe—the time references are not specific to their respective phrases (see also v. 6).
91:7 *ten thousand.* Hebrew poetic convention called for 10,000 following 1,000 in parallel construction (see notes on 90:10; 1Sa 18:7; Am 1:3).
91:9 *dwelling.* See 90:1 and note.
91:11–12 Quoted by Satan in Mt 4:6; Lk 4:10–11.
91:11 *his angels.* See note on 34:7.
91:12 *against a stone.* On the stony trails of Canaan (see Pr 3:23).
91:13 *lion ... cobra ... great lion ... serpent.* These double references to lions and to poisonous snakes balance the double references of vv. 5–6, and complete the illustrative roster of mortal threats (see Am 5:19).

[14]"Because he loves me," says the LORD,
"I will rescue him;
I will protect him, for he
acknowledges my name.
[15]He will call upon me, and I will answer
him;
I will be with him in trouble,
I will deliver him and honor him.[q]
[16]With long life[r] will I satisfy him
and show him my salvation.[s]"

Psalm 92

A psalm. A song.
For the Sabbath day.

[1]It is good to praise the LORD
and make music[t] to your name,[u]
O Most High,[v]
[2]to proclaim your love in the morning[w]
and your faithfulness at night,
[3]to the music of the ten-stringed lyre[x]
and the melody of the harp.[y]

[4]For you make me glad by your deeds,
O LORD;
I sing for joy[z] at the works of your
hands.[a]
[5]How great are your works,[b] O LORD,
how profound your thoughts![c]
[6]The senseless man[d] does not know,
fools do not understand,
[7]that though the wicked spring up like
grass
and all evildoers flourish,
they will be forever destroyed.[e]

[8]But you, O LORD, are exalted forever.

[9]For surely your enemies[f], O LORD,
surely your enemies will perish;
all evildoers will be scattered.[g]
[10]You have exalted my horn[a][h] like that of
a wild ox;[i]
fine oils[j] have been poured upon me.
[11]My eyes have seen the defeat of my
adversaries;
my ears have heard the rout of my
wicked foes.[k]

[12]The righteous will flourish[l] like a palm
tree,
they will grow like a cedar of
Lebanon;[m]
[13]planted in the house of the LORD,
they will flourish in the courts of our
God.[n]
[14]They will still bear fruit[o] in old age,
they will stay fresh and green,
[15]proclaiming, "The LORD is upright;
he is my Rock, and there is no
wickedness in him.[p]"

91:15 [q]S 1Sa 2:30; Jn 12:26 **91:16** [r]Dt 6:2; S Ps 21:4 [s]S Ps 50:23 **92:1** [t]S Ps 27:6 [u]S Ps 9:2; 147:1 [v]Ps 135:3 **92:2** [w]S Ps 55:17 **92:3** [x]S Ps 71:22 [y]S 1Sa 10:5; S Ne 12:27; S Ps 33:2; 81:2 **92:4** [z]S Ps 5:11; 27:6 [a]S Ps 8:6; 111:7; 143:5 **92:5** [b]S Job 36:24; Rev 15:3 [c]Ps 40:5; 139:17; Isa 28:29; 31:2; Ro 11:33 **92:6** [d]S Ps 73:22 **92:7** [e]S Ps 37:2 **92:9** [f]S Ps 45:5 [g]S Ps 68:1; S 89:10 **92:10** [h]S Ps 89:17 [i]S Ps 29:6 [j]S Ps 23:5 **92:11** [k]S Ps 54:7; 91:8 **92:12** [l]S Ps 72:7 [m]S Ps 1:3; 52:8; Jer 17:8; Hos 14:6 **92:13** [n]Ps 135:2 **92:14** [o]S Ps 1:3; S Jn 15:2 **92:15** [p]S Job 34:10

[a] *10 Horn* here symbolizes strength.

91:14–16 Employing the form of a prophetic oracle, the author (see introduction) supports his testimony by assuring the godly that it is confirmed by all the promises of God to those who truly love and trust him.
91:14 *protect him.* Lit. "raise him to a high, secure place." *acknowledges my name.* See 9:10 ("know your name") and note. *my name.* See note on 5:11.
91:15 *He will call ... I will answer.* See note on 118:5.
91:16 *With long life.* The climactic counterpoint to Ps 90.
Ps 92 A joyful celebration of the righteous rule of God. Its testimony to the prosperity of the righteous, "planted in the house of the LORD" (v. 13), links it thematically with Ps 91 (see introduction to that psalm), while its joy over God's righteous reign relates it to the cluster of psalms that follow (Ps 93–100; see especially Ps 94). There are, in fact, reasons to believe that the editors of the Psalter brought together Ps 92–94 as a trilogy that serves as a bridge between Ps 90–91 and 95–99 (see introductions to Ps 93; 94). Notably, God's name Yahweh ("LORD") occurs seven times in this psalm. Verses 10–11 suggest that the author may have been one of Israel's kings.
Following the introduction on praise (vv. 1–3), vv. 4–5 offer the motivation for the praise ("me," "I"), which is picked up again in vv. 10–11 ("my," "me," "My," "my," "my," "my"). Verses 6–9 expound the folly and destiny of evildoers, while vv. 12–15 expound the prosperity of the righteous. Notice also the link between v. 7 and v. 13. The NIV text offers a different analysis of the psalm's structure.
92 title *A song.* See note on Ps 30 title. *For the Sabbath day.* In the postexilic liturgy of the temple, this psalm came to be sung at the time of the morning sacrifice on the Sabbath. (The rest of the weekly schedule was: first day, Ps 24; second day, Ps 48; third day, Ps 82; fourth day, Ps 94; fifth day, Ps 81; sixth day, Ps 93.)
92:1–3 Hymnic introduction.
92:1 *LORD ... Most High.* That is, LORD Most High (see 7:17; see also note on 3:7). *name.* See note on 5:11. *Most High.* A link with Ps 91 (see vv. 1,9 of that psalm). For the title see note on Ge 14:19.
92:2 *love ... faithfulness.* That is, love-and-faithfulness (see note on 36:5; see also note on 3:7). *love.* See note on 6:4. *morning ... night.* Continuously.
92:3 *lyre ... harp.* See note on 57:8. *harp.* See note on Ge 31:27.
92:4–5 Joy over God's saving acts (see vv. 10–11).
92:5 *profound.* Lit. "deep." *your thoughts.* As shown by your deeds.
92:6–9 The fatal folly of evildoers (contrast vv. 12–15).
92:6 *senseless ... fools.* See NIV text note on 14:1; see also 49:10—and note especially 94:8–11. They do not know that the Lord rules righteously. They see the wicked flourishing, but do not see the Lord or foresee the end he has appointed for them. The author thus characterizes his "wicked foes" (v. 11), whom the Lord has routed.
92:7 A condensed statement of what is expounded more fully in Ps 73 (see also 37:2; 62:9; 90:5–6 and notes).
92:8 *exalted forever.* God's eternal exaltation assures the destruction of his enemies.
92:9 *enemies.* Here the evildoers, referred to also in v. 7.
92:10–11 Joy over God's favors (see vv. 4–5): God has made him triumphant (see 89:24) and anointed him with "the oil of joy" (45:7; see also 23:5) by giving him victory over all his enemies.
92:12–15 The secure prosperity of the righteous (contrast vv. 6–9).
92:13 *planted in the house of the LORD.* Though the wicked may "spring up like grass," their end is sure (see v. 7). But the righteous are planted in a secure place (see Ps 91) and so retain the vigor of youth into old age, rejoicing in God's just discrimination (see v. 15). *courts.* Of the temple (see 84:2,10; 2Ki 21:5; 23:11–12).
92:15 *upright ... Rock ... no wickedness in him.* See Dt 32:4 and note.

Psalm 93

1 The LORD reigns,[q] he is robed in
majesty;[r]
the LORD is robed in majesty
and is armed with strength.[s]
The world is firmly established;[t]
it cannot be moved.[u]
2 Your throne was established[v] long
ago;
you are from all eternity.[w]

3 The seas[x] have lifted up, O LORD,
the seas have lifted up their voice;[y]
the seas have lifted up their
pounding waves.[z]
4 Mightier than the thunder[a] of the great
waters,
mightier than the breakers[b] of the
sea—
the LORD on high is mighty.[c]

5 Your statutes stand firm;
holiness[d] adorns your house[e]
for endless days, O LORD.

Psalm 94

1 O LORD, the God who avenges,[f]
O God who avenges, shine forth.[g]
2 Rise up,[h] O Judge[i] of the earth;
pay back[j] to the proud what they
deserve.
3 How long will the wicked, O LORD,
how long will the wicked be
jubilant?[k]

4 They pour out arrogant[l] words;
all the evildoers are full of
boasting.[m]
5 They crush your people,[n] O LORD;
they oppress your inheritance.[o]
6 They slay the widow[p] and the alien;
they murder the fatherless.[q]
7 They say, "The LORD does not see;[r]
the God of Jacob[s] pays no heed."

8 Take heed, you senseless ones[t] among
the people;
you fools, when will you become
wise?
9 Does he who implanted the ear not
hear?
Does he who formed the eye not
see?[u]

93:1 [q]S 1Ch 16:31; S Ps 97:1 [r]S Job 40:10; S Ps 21:5 [s]S Ps 65:6 [t]Ps 24:2; 78:69; 119:90 [u]1Ch 16:30; Ps 96:10 **93:2** [v]S 2Sa 7:16 [w]S Ge 21:33 **93:3** [x]Ps 96:11; 98:7; Isa 5:30; 17:12-13; Jer 6:23 [y]S Ps 46:3 [z]Job 9:8; Ps 107:25, 29; Isa 51:15; Jer 31:35; Hab 3:10 **93:4** [a]Ps 65:7; Jer 6:23 [b]S Ps 18:4; Jnh 1:15 [c]S Ne 9:32; S Job 9:4 **93:5** [d]Ps 29:2; 96:9 [e]Ps 5:7; 23:6 **94:1** [f]S Ge 4:24; Ro 12:19 [g]S Dt 33:2; Ps 80:1 **94:2** [h]S Nu 10:35 [i]S Ge 18:25; Heb 12:23; S Jas 5:9 [j]S Ps 31:23 **94:3** [k]Ps 13:2 **94:4** [l]Jer 43:2 [m]S Ps 52:1 **94:5** [n]Ps 44:2; 74:8; Isa 3:15; Jer 8:21 [o]Ps 28:9 **94:6** [p]S Dt 10:18; S Isa 1:17 [q]Dt 24:19 **94:7** [r]S Job 22:14 [s]S Ge 24:12 **94:8** [t]S Dt 32:6; S Ps 73:22 **94:9** [u]Ex 4:11; Pr 20:12

Ps 93 A hymn to the eternal, universal and invincible reign of the Lord, a theme it shares with Ps 47; 95–99. Together these hymns offer a majestic confession of faith in and hope for the kingdom of God on earth. They were probably composed for the liturgy of a high religious festival in which the kingship of the Lord—over the cosmic order, over the nations and in a special sense over Israel—was annually celebrated (see introduction to Ps 47). And implicitly, where not explicitly, the Lord's kingship is hailed in contrast to the claims of all other gods; he is "the great King above all gods" (95:3). These hymns may all have been composed by temple personnel and spoken by them in the liturgy. They probably date from the preexilic era. Ps 93 appears to have been separated from Ps 95–99 to serve as a thematic pivot between Ps 92 and 94 (as Ps 47 was used as a pivot between Ps 46 and 48). It celebrates Yahweh's secure cosmic rule that grounds his righteous and effective rule over human affairs—which is the joy (Ps 92) and the hope (Ps 94) of those who rely on him for protection against the assaults of the godless fools who live by violence. Structurally, the psalm has two short stanzas (vv. 1–2,3–4) and a conclusion (v. 5).

93:1–2 The Lord's reign, by which the creation order has been and will be secure throughout the ages, is from eternity (see Ge 1:1). Though Israel as a nation has come late on the scene, her God has been King since before the creation of the world.

93:1 *The LORD reigns.* The ultimate truth, and first article, in Israel's creed (see 96:10; 97:1; 99:1; see also Zec 14:9 and note, as well as Introduction: Theology: Major Themes).

93:3–4 Both at and since his founding of the world, the Lord has shown himself to be mightier than all the forces of disorder that threaten his kingdom.

93:3 *seas.* Reference is to the primeval chaotic waters, tamed and assigned a place by the Lord's creative word (see 33:7; 104:7–9; Ge 1:6–10; Job 38:8–11). Implicitly they symbolize all that opposes the coming of the Lord's kingdom (see 65:6–7; 74:13–14 and notes).

93:4 The thunder of the chaotic waters is no match for the thunder of the Lord's ordering word (see 104:7).

93:5 *statutes.* He whose indisputable rule has made the world secure has given his people life directives that are stable and reliable (see 19:7)—and that they must honor (see 95:8–11). *your house.* His earthly temple—but also the heavenly. *for endless days.* Qualifies both clauses.

Ps 94 An appeal to the Lord, as "Judge of the earth" (v. 2), to redress the wrongs perpetrated against the weak by arrogant and wicked persons who occupy seats of power. The psalm has links with Ps 92 (see introductions to Ps 92; 93), but is the voice of the oppressed within Israel, seeking redress at God's throne for injustices done them by the "fools" smugly established in the power structures of the nation. Thus it is unique within the Ps 90–100 group of psalms and stands here as representative of the many cries of the oppressed found in Books I–III of the Psalter. Following a three-verse introduction, the thought advances regularly in five stanzas of four verses each, with the main thematic shift coming at v. 12.

94:1–3 Initial appeal to God, the Judge.

94:1 *avenges.* Redresses wrongs (see note on 5:10; see also Dt 32:35,41 and note on 32:35). To avenge is the function of a king in his role as chief executive of the realm. Thus a direct conceptual link with Ps 47; 93; 95–99 is established at the outset. *shine forth.* Cf. notes on 50:2; 80:1.

94:2 *the proud.* See vv. 4–7 for a description of them.

94:3 *How long . . . ?* See note on 6:3.

94:4–7 Indictment of the wicked.

94:4 *arrogant words . . . boasting.* For similar expressions of the arrogance of the wicked see 10:2–11 and notes.

94:5 *your people . . . your inheritance.* Those among them who are vulnerable (see v. 6).

94:7 *They say.* See note on 3:2. *Jacob.* A synonym for Israel (see Ge 32:28).

94:8–11 Warning to the wicked—those "senseless . . . fools" (see 92:6–9; see also NIV text note on 14:1).

10 Does he who disciplines[v] nations not
punish?
Does he who teaches[w] man lack
knowledge?
11 The LORD knows the thoughts[x] of man;
he knows that they are futile.[y]

12 Blessed is the man you discipline,[z]
O LORD,
the man you teach[a] from your law;
13 you grant him relief from days of
trouble,[b]
till a pit[c] is dug for the wicked.
14 For the LORD will not reject his people;[d]
he will never forsake his inheritance.
15 Judgment will again be founded on
righteousness,[e]
and all the upright in heart[f] will
follow it.

16 Who will rise up[g] for me against the
wicked?
Who will take a stand for me against
evildoers?[h]
17 Unless the LORD had given me help,[i]
I would soon have dwelt in the
silence of death.[j]
18 When I said, "My foot is slipping,[k]"
your love, O LORD, supported me.
19 When anxiety[l] was great within me,
your consolation[m] brought joy to my
soul.

20 Can a corrupt throne[n] be allied with
you—
one that brings on misery by its
decrees?[o]
21 They band together[p] against the
righteous
and condemn the innocent[q] to
death.[r]
22 But the LORD has become my fortress,
and my God the rock[s] in whom I
take refuge.[t]
23 He will repay[u] them for their sins
and destroy[v] them for their
wickedness;
the LORD our God will destroy them.

Psalm 95

1 Come,[w] let us sing for joy[x] to the LORD;
let us shout aloud[y] to the Rock[z] of
our salvation.
2 Let us come before him[a] with
thanksgiving[b]
and extol him with music[c] and song.

3 For the LORD is the great God,[d]
the great King[e] above all gods.[f]
4 In his hand are the depths of the
earth,[g]
and the mountain peaks belong to
him.

94:10 [v]S Ps 39:11 [w]S Ex 35:34; Job 35:11; Isa 28:26 **94:11** [x]Ps 139:2; Pr 15:26; S Mt 9:4 [y]1Co 3:20* **94:12** [z]S Job 5:17; 1Co 11:32; Heb 12:5 [a]S Dt 8:3; S 1Sa 12:23 **94:13** [b]S Ps 86:7 [c]S Ps 7:15; S 55:23 **94:14** [d]S Dt 31:6; Ps 37:28; Ro 11:2 **94:15** [e]Ps 97:2 [f]Ps 7:10; 11:2; S 36:10 **94:16** [g]Nu 10:35; Ps 17:13; Isa 14:22 [h]S Ps 59:2 **94:17** [i]Ps 124:2 [j]S Ps 31:17 **94:18** [k]S Dt 32:35; S Job 12:5 **94:19** [l]Ecc 11:10 [m]S Job 6:10 **94:20** [n]Jer 22:30; 36:30 [o]S Ps 58:2 **94:21** [p]S Ps 56:6 [q]Ps 106:38; Pr 17:15, 26; 28:21; Isa 5:20, 23; Mt 27:4 [r]S Ge 18:23 **94:22** [s]S Ps 61:2 [t]S 2Sa 22:3; S Ps 18:2 **94:23** [u]S Ex 32:34; S Ps 54:5 [v]Ps 9:5; 37:38; 145:20 **95:1** [w]Ps 34:11; 80:2 [x]S Ps 5:11 [y]Ps 81:1; Isa 44:23; Zep 3:14 [z]S 2Sa 22:47 **95:2** [a]Ps 100:2; Mic 6:6 [b]S Ps 42:4 [c]Ps 81:2; S Eph 5:19 **95:3** [d]Ps 48:1; 86:10; 145:3; 147:5 [e]S Ps 47:2 [f]Ps 96:4; 97:9 **95:4** [g]S Ps 63:9

94:10 *disciplines.* Keeps them in line by means of punishment (see Lev 26:18; Jer 31:18). *teaches.* Gives human beings some knowledge of the creation order (see Isa 28:26).
94:11 *The LORD knows.* Contrary to their foolish supposition (see v. 7).
94:12–15 Here the focus shifts from the arrogance and folly of the wicked to the happy state of those who count themselves among the Lord's people and who live under his discipline and rely on his royal protection.
94:12 *Blessed.* See note on 1:1. *discipline ... teach.* See v. 10 and note. Here the author speaks of God's correcting and teaching his people in the ways of his law.
94:14 *people ... inheritance.* See v. 5. The Lord will not abandon the powerless among his people to the injustice of their oppressors. Paul may be echoing this verse in Ro 11:1–2.
94:15 However this difficult verse is to be translated, the author appears to say that God's righteous rule will restore justice for those who have been wrongfully treated while being themselves innocent—described as "the upright in heart" (see also v. 21). *heart.* See note on 4:7.
94:16–19 The Lord is the only sure court of appeal.
94:17 *silence of death.* See note on 30:1. Without God's help the wicked would have silenced the psalmist in the grave, but now it is the wicked for whom the pit will be dug (see v. 13).
94:18 *When I said.* When feeling about to be overwhelmed by the wicked (see note on 38:16). *love.* See note on 6:4.
94:19 *soul.* See note on 6:3.
94:20–23 Confidence that the Lord's justice will prevail. Cf. note on 89:14.
94:20 *corrupt throne.* A seat of authority that works mischief. The author speaks of injustice at the center of power.
94:21 *righteous.* Here referring to those who have not wronged anyone—i.e., "the innocent" (see note on v. 15). For the basic concept see note on 1:5.
Ps 95 A call to worship the Lord, spoken by a priest or Levite to the assembled Israelites at the temple. (See introduction to Ps 93.) Placed at the center of its group (Ps 90–100) and at the beginning of a series of psalms celebrating the universal reign of Israel's God (Ps 95–99), Ps 95 contains a sharp reminder that Israel's sense of security under Yahweh's rule—from which spring both their prayers (as in Ps 90; 94) and their praise (as in Ps 91–93; 95–100)—is warranted only if they show themselves to be Yahweh's loyal and obedient servants. Its function in context is similar to that of Ps 81 (see introduction to Ps 79–83).

The psalm is composed of two parts: (1) a call to praise the Lord of all the earth (vv. 1–5); (2) a call to acknowledge by submissive attitude and obedient heart the Lord's kingship over his people (vv. 6–11). Each part also has two subdivisions, the latter of which forms the climax. Cf. the structure of Ps 96.
95:1–2 The call to praise.
95:1 *Rock of our salvation.* See note on 18:2.
95:3–5 Why Israel is to praise the Lord—because he is above all gods, and there is no corner of the universe that is not in his hand. The ancient pagan world had different gods for different peoples, different geographical areas, different cosmic regions (heaven, earth, netherworld) and different aspects of life (e.g., war, fertility, crafts).
95:4–5 *depths ... mountain peaks ... sea ... dry land.* All the world—the extremes and all that lies between and all that is in them.

[5]The sea is his, for he made it,
and his hands formed the dry land.[h]
[6]Come, let us bow down[i] in worship,[j]
let us kneel[k] before the LORD our Maker;[l]
[7]for he is our God
and we are the people of his pasture,[m]
the flock under his care.

Today, if you hear his voice,
[8] do not harden your hearts[n] as you did at Meribah,[a o]
as you did that day at Massah[b] in the desert,[p]
[9]where your fathers tested[q] and tried me,
though they had seen what I did.
[10]For forty years[r] I was angry with that generation;
I said, "They are a people whose hearts go astray,[s]
and they have not known my ways."[t]
[11]So I declared on oath[u] in my anger,
"They shall never enter my rest."[v]

Psalm 96

96:1-13pp — 1Ch 16:23-33

[1]Sing to the LORD[w] a new song;[x]
sing to the LORD, all the earth.
[2]Sing to the LORD, praise his name;[y]
proclaim his salvation[z] day after day.
[3]Declare his glory[a] among the nations,
his marvelous deeds[b] among all peoples.
[4]For great is the LORD and most worthy of praise;[c]
he is to be feared[d] above all gods.[e]
[5]For all the gods of the nations are idols,[f]
but the LORD made the heavens.[g]

[a] *8 Meribah* means *quarreling.* [b] *8 Massah* means *testing.*

95:5 [h]S Ge 1:9; Ps 146:6 **95:6** [i]S 2Sa 12:16; Php 2:10 [j]S Ps 22:29 [k]2Ch 6:13 [l]Ps 100:3; 149:2; Isa 17:7; 54:5; Da 6:10-11; Hos 8:14 **95:7** [m]S Ps 74:1 **95:8** [n]Mk 10:5; Heb 3:8 [o]S Ex 17:7; S Dt 33:8; Heb 3:15*; 4:7 [p]S Ps 78:40 **95:9** [q]S Nu 14:22; 1Co 10:9 **95:10** [r]S Ex 16:35; S Nu 14:34; Ac 7:36; Heb 3:17 [s]Ps 58:3; 119:67, 176; Pr 12:26; 16:29; Isa 53:6; Jer 31:19; 50:6; Eze 34:6 [t]S Dt 8:6 **95:11** [u]S Nu 14:23 [v]Dt 1:35; Heb 3:7-11*; 4:3* **96:1** [w]Ps 30:4 [x]Ps 33:3; S 40:3; 98:1; 144:9; 149:1; Isa 42:10; S Rev 5:9 **96:2** [y]S Ps 68:4 [z]Ps 27:1; 71:15 **96:3** [a]Ps 8:1 [b]S Ps 71:17; Rev 15:3 **96:4** [c]S Ps 48:1 [d]S Dt 28:58; S 1Ch 16:25; Ps 89:7 [e]S Ps 95:3 **96:5** [f]S Lev 19:4 [g]S Ge 1:1; S 2Ch 2:12

95:6–11 The exhortation to submit to the Lord with obedient hearts—a bent knee is not enough. For a NT reflection on these verses in the light of the advent of Christ see Heb 3:7—4:13.
95:6–7 The call to confess submission to the Lord by kneeling before him.
95:6 *our Maker.* Both as Creator of all things (see Ge 1) and as Israel's Redeemer, he has made them what they are: the people of the Lord in the earth (see Isa 45:9–13; 51:12–16).
95:7 *people of his pasture.* See 100:3; Jer 23:1; Eze 34:17–23. Since kings were commonly called the "shepherds" of their people (see notes on 23:1; 74:1), their realms could be referred to as their "pastures" (see Jer 25:36; 49:20; 50:45). *if you hear his voice.* In the liturgy of the religious festival, possibly in some such manner as Ps 50 and/or 78. The concern expressed in what follows echoes that of Moses in Dt 6:16–19.
95:8 *Meribah ... Massah.* See NIV text notes. The leader of the liturgy reminds Israel of times of her rebellion in the desert (see Ex 17:7; Nu 20:13).
95:9 *me.* Official representatives of the Lord, when speaking for him, could shift to first person (see 50:5,7–15; see also note on Ge 16:7). *had seen what I did.* In Egypt and at the Red Sea—and his provision of food in the desert (see Ex 16; see also Nu 14:11).
95:10 *forty years.* The climax of Israel's rebellion came when they faithlessly refused to undertake the conquest of Canaan and considered returning to Egypt (see Nu 14:1–4). It was then that God condemned them to a 40-year stay in the desert (see Nu 14:34). *angry.* See note on 2:5. *that generation.* The (adult) Israelites who came out of Egypt and covenanted with God at Sinai (see Nu 32:13). *They are a people ... my ways.* A restatement of the Lord's word in Nu 14:11. *hearts.* See note on 4:7. *my ways.* See 25:4 and note.
95:11 *on oath.* See Nu 14:28; Dt 1:34–35. *never enter my rest.* The language of Nu 14:30 is "Not one of you will enter the land," but since the promised land was also called the place where God will give his people "rest" (Jos 1:13,15; see Ex 33:14; Dt 12:10; 25:19), the two statements are equivalent. *rest.* A rich concept indicating Israel's possession of a place with God in the earth where they are secure from all external threats and internal calamities (see Dt 3:20; 1Ki 5:4 and notes).

Ps 96 A call to all nations to praise the Lord as the only God and to proclaim the glory of his reign throughout the world—an OT anticipation of the world mission of the NT people of God (see Mt 28:16–20). (See introductions to Ps 93; 95.) This psalm appears in slightly altered form in 1Ch 16:23–33. Here in the Psalter it is paired with Ps 98, with which it shares much in form, language and theme (compare especially their opening and closing stanzas). Each of these in turn is followed by a hymn that celebrates Yahweh's reign (cf. 97:1; 99:1) and its special benefits for Israel (cf. 97:8–12; 99:4–9). This arrangement suggests that Ps 97 has been linked with 96 and Ps 99 with 98 to form a pair of thematic couplets—introduced by Ps 95.
The psalm is composed of two parts: (1) The first begins with a threefold call to all nations to "sing to the LORD" in praise of his "name" (vv. 1–6); (2) the second begins with a threefold call to all nations to "ascribe to the LORD glory ... the glory due his name" (vv. 7–13). Each part has two subdivisions, the last of which forms the climax to the whole psalm. Cf. the structure of Ps 95.
96:1–3 The call to all the earth to sing the praise of the Lord among the nations. Triple repetition ("Sing ... sing ... Sing") was a common feature in OT liturgical calls to worship (see vv. 7–9 and note; see also 103:20–22; 118:2–4; 135:1; 136:1–3).
96:1 *new song.* See note on 33:3. *all the earth.* See v. 9; or "all the land," in which case the call is addressed to all Israel. However, the worldwide perspective of this psalm (see especially v. 7) suggests that here the psalmist has in view broader horizons (see 97:1; 100:1 and note; 117:1; see also note on 9:1).
96:2 *name.* See v. 8; see also note on 5:11. *proclaim his salvation.* Proclaim as good news (see 40:9 and note) the Lord's saving acts in Israel's behalf (see 3:8; see also 85:9).
96:3 *glory.* See note on 85:9. *marvelous deeds.* See note on 71:16–17.
96:4–6 Why "all the earth" is to praise the Lord: He alone is God (see Ps 115).
96:4 *feared.* See note on 15:4.
96:5 *made the heavens.* As the Maker of the heavenly realm, in pagan eyes the abode of the gods, the Lord is greater than all the gods (see 97:7).

[6]Splendor and majesty[h] are before him;
strength and glory[i] are in his sanctuary.

[7]Ascribe to the LORD,[j] O families of nations,[k]
ascribe to the LORD glory and strength.
[8]Ascribe to the LORD the glory due his name;
bring an offering[l] and come into his courts.[m]
[9]Worship the LORD[n] in the splendor of his[a] holiness;[o]
tremble[p] before him, all the earth.[q]

[10]Say among the nations, "The LORD reigns.[r]"
The world is firmly established,[s] it cannot be moved;[t]
he will judge[u] the peoples with equity.[v]
[11]Let the heavens rejoice,[w] let the earth be glad;[x]
let the sea resound, and all that is in it;
[12]let the fields be jubilant, and everything in them.
Then all the trees of the forest[y] will sing for joy;[z]
[13]they will sing before the LORD, for he comes,
he comes to judge[a] the earth.
He will judge the world in righteousness[b]
and the peoples in his truth.[c]

96:6 [h]S Ps 21:5 [i]Ps 29:1; 89:17 **96:7** [j]Ps 29:1 [k]Ps 22:27 **96:8** [l]Ps 45:12; S 51:19; 72:10 [m]Ps 65:4; 84:10; 92:13; 100:4 **96:9** [n]Ex 23:25; Jnh 1:9 [o]S Ps 93:5 [p]S Ex 15:14; Ps 114:7 [q]Ps 33:8 **96:10** [r]Ps 97:1 [s]Ps 24:2; 78:69; 119:90 [t]S Ps 93:1 [u]Ps 58:11 [v]Ps 67:4; 98:9 **96:11** [w]S Rev 12:12 [x]Ps 97:1; Isa 49:13 **96:12** [y]Isa 44:23; 55:12; Eze 17:24 [z]Ps 65:13 **96:13** [a]Rev 19:11 [b]S Ps 7:11; Ac 17:31 [c]Ps 86:11 **97:1** [d]Ex 15:18; Ps 93:1; 96:10; 99:1; Isa 24:23; 52:7 [e]S Ps 96:11 [f]S Est 10:1

Psalm 97

[1]The LORD reigns,[d] let the earth be glad;[e]
let the distant shores[f] rejoice.
[2]Clouds[g] and thick darkness[h] surround him;
righteousness and justice are the foundation of his throne.[i]
[3]Fire[j] goes before[k] him
and consumes[l] his foes on every side.

[a] 9 Or *LORD with the splendor of*

97:2 [g]S Job 22:14 [h]S Ex 19:9 [i]Ps 89:14 **97:3** [j]Isa 9:19; Da 7:10; Joel 1:19; 2:3 [k]Hab 3:5 [l]S 2Sa 22:9

96:6 *Splendor and majesty ... strength and glory.* Two pairs of divine attributes personified as throne attendants whose presence before the Lord heralds the exalted nature of the one, universal King. For similar personifications see 23:6 and note. *glory.* The Hebrew for this word here connotes radiant beauty.
96:7–9 The call to all nations to worship the Lord (see 29:1–2 and note). The two half-sentences of 29:2 have been expanded in this psalm.
96:8 *courts.* Of the temple (see 84:2,10; 2Ki 21:5; 23:11–12).
96:9 *splendor of his holiness.* See note on 29:2. *tremble.* In reverent awe, equivalent to "fear" (see v. 4).
96:10–13 The call to all nations to proclaim among the nations the righteous reign of the Lord.
96:10 *The LORD reigns.* See 93:1 and note. *The world ... with equity.* In OT perspective, the world order is one, embracing both its physical and moral aspects because both have been established by God as aspects of his one kingdom and both are upheld by his one rule. Therefore God's rule over creation and over human affairs (also his acts of creation and redemption) is often spoken of in one breath, and righteousness, faithfulness and love are equally ascribable to both. And since the creation order is secure in its goodness (see Ge 1), it often serves in OT poetry (as it does here) as a manifest assurance that God's rule over human affairs will also be "with equity," "in righteousness" and "in ... truth" (v. 13; see also 9:7–8; 11:3; 33:4–11; 36:5–9; 57:10; 58:11; 65:6–7; 71:19; 74:13–14,16–17; 75:2; 82:5; 93:3–4; 98:9; 99:4; 119:89–91 and notes). *will judge.* See v. 13 and note.
96:11–12 Because God's kingdom is one (see v. 10 and note), all his creatures will rejoice when God's rule over humankind brings righteousness to full expression in his cosmic kingdom (see note on 65:13; see also 97:7–9). For the present state of the creation as it awaits the fullness of redemption see Ro 8:21–22 and notes.
96:13 *comes ... comes ... will judge.* Because God reigns over all things and is the Lord of history, Israel lived in hope (as the prophets announced) of the coming of God—his future acts by which he would decisively deal with all wickedness and establish his righteousness in the earth. *righteousness.* See note on 4:1.

Ps 97 A joyful celebration of the Lord's righteous reign over all the earth (see introductions to Ps 93; 95), with special attention to the benefits of the Lord's reign enjoyed by Israel (see introduction to Ps 96). The psalm's two main divisions (vv. 1–6,8–12—closely balanced, having 42 and 43 Hebrew words respectively) are joined by a centered verse (v. 7; see note on 6:6) that serves as a counterpoint to the main theme. The opening verses of the two main divisions are thematically linked: v. 1, "be glad ... rejoice"; v. 8, "rejoices ... are glad"—in reverse order, a frequent stylistic device in OT poetry. The first major division is framed by references to "the earth" (v. 1) and "the heavens" (v. 6), the second by references to "Zion ... the villages of Judah" (v. 8) and the "righteous" (v. 12).
97:1–6 A testimony to the nations—that they too have seen God's majesty displayed (vv. 2–6) and ought to rejoice with Israel that the Lord reigns supreme.
97:1 *The LORD reigns.* See 93:1 and note. *earth.* See 96:1; 99:1; 117:1; see also note on 9:1. *distant shores.* Even distant lands reached by the far-ranging ships that sail the seas (see 1Ki 9:26–28; 10:22; Isa 60:9; Jnh 1:3).
97:2–6 The Lord's majestic glory revealed in the sky's awesome displays, especially in the thunderstorm (see 18:7–15 and note; see also introduction to Ps 29).
97:2 *Clouds and thick darkness.* The dark storm clouds that hide the sun and cast a veil across the sky are dramatic visual reminders that the fierce heat and brilliance (also metaphors) of God's naked glory must be veiled from creaturely eyes (see Ex 19:9; 1Ki 8:12). Thus also a curtain closed off the Most Holy Place in the tabernacle and temple (see Ex 26:33; 2Ch 3:14), veiling it in darkness. *righteousness.* See v. 6; see also note on 4:1. *foundation of his throne.* God rules by his power (see 66:7), but his reign is founded on righteousness and justice, which also the heavens proclaim (see v. 6 and note). That a throne was established by righteousness and justice was proverbial in Israel (see Pr 16:2; 25:5; 29:14; cf. Ps 9:7–8; 103:6,19 and notes).
97:3 *Fire.* Manifested in the storm cloud's lightning bolts (see v. 4), fire often signified God's judicial wrath (see, e.g., 21:9; 50:3; 83:14; Dt 4:24; 9:3; 32:22; 1Ki 19:12; Isa 10:17; 30:27,30; see also note on La 1:13).

4 His lightning[m] lights up the world;
the earth[n] sees and trembles.[o]
5 The mountains melt[p] like wax[q] before
the LORD,
before the Lord of all the earth.[r]
6 The heavens proclaim his
righteousness,[s]
and all the peoples see his glory.[t]

7 All who worship images[u] are put to
shame,[v]
those who boast in idols[w]—
worship him,[x] all you gods![y]

8 Zion hears and rejoices
and the villages of Judah are glad[z]
because of your judgments,[a] O LORD.
9 For you, O LORD, are the Most High[b]
over all the earth;[c]
you are exalted[d] far above all gods.

10 Let those who love the LORD hate evil,[e]
for he guards[f] the lives of his faithful
ones[g]
and delivers[h] them from the hand of
the wicked.[i]
11 Light is shed[j] upon the righteous[k]
and joy on the upright in heart.[l]
12 Rejoice in the LORD,[m] you who are
righteous,
and praise his holy name.[n]

Psalm 98

A psalm.

1 Sing to the LORD[o] a new song,[p]
for he has done marvelous things;[q]
his right hand[r] and his holy arm[s]
have worked salvation[t] for him.
2 The LORD has made his salvation
known[u]
and revealed his righteousness[v] to
the nations.[w]
3 He has remembered[x] his love
and his faithfulness to the house of
Israel;
all the ends of the earth[y] have seen
the salvation of our God.[z]

4 Shout for joy[a] to the LORD, all the
earth,
burst into jubilant song with music;
5 make music to the LORD with the
harp,[b]
with the harp and the sound of
singing,[c]
6 with trumpets[d] and the blast of the
ram's horn[e]—
shout for joy[f] before the LORD, the
King.[g]

7 Let the sea[h] resound, and everything
in it,
the world, and all who live in it.[i]
8 Let the rivers clap their hands,[j]
let the mountains[k] sing together for
joy;

97:4 [m]S Job 36:30 [n]S 2Sa 22:8 [o]S Ps 18:7; 104:32; S Rev 6:12 **97:5** [p]S Ps 46:2,6 [q]S Ps 22:14 [r]S Jos 3:11 **97:6** [s]Ps 50:6; 98:2 [t]S Ps 19:1 **97:7** [u]S Lev 26:1 [v]Isa 42:17; Jer 10:14 [w]S Dt 5:8 [x]Heb 1:6 [y]Ex 12:12; Ps 16:4 **97:8** [z]S Ps 9:2 [a]Ps 48:11 **97:9** [b]Ps 7:8 [c]S Job 34:29 [d]S Ps 47:9 **97:10** [e]S Job 28:28; Am 5:15; Ro 12:9 [f]Ps 145:20 [g]Ps 31:23; 37:28; Pr 2:8 [h]S Ps 34:7; Da 3:28; 6:16 [i]Ps 37:40; Jer 15:21; 20:13 **97:11** [j]S Job 22:28 [k]Ps 11:5 [l]Ps 7:10 **97:12** [m]S Job 22:19; Ps 104:34; Isa 41:16; Php 4:4 [n]S Ex 3:15; S Ps 99:3 **98:1** [o]Ps 30:4 [p]S Ps 96:1 [q]Ex 15:1; Ps 96:3; Isa 12:5; Lk 1:51 [r]S Ex 15:6 [s]S Jos 4:24; Job 40:9; Isa 51:9; 52:10; 53:1; 63:5 [t]S Ps 44:3; Isa 59:16 **98:2** [u]Isa 52:10; Lk 3:6 [v]S Ps 97:6 [w]S Ps 67:2 **98:3** [x]S 1Ch 16:15 [y]S Ge 49:10; S Ps 48:10 [z]S Ps 50:23 **98:4** [a]Ps 20:5; Isa 12:6; 44:23; 52:9; 54:1; 55:12 **98:5** [b]Ps 33:2; 92:3; 147:7 [c]Isa 51:3 **98:6** [d]S Nu 10:2; S 2Sa 6:15 [e]S Ex 19:13 [f]Ps 20:5; 100:1; Isa 12:6 [g]Ps 2:6; 47:7 **98:7** [h]S Ps 93:3 [i]S Ps 24:1 **98:8** [j]S 2Ki 11:12 [k]Ps 148:9; Isa 44:23; 55:12

97:4 *earth.* Here the land realm (the continents) personified.
97:6 *proclaim his righteousness.* The stable order of the heaven's vast array speaks (see 19:1–4); it declares that God's reign similarly upholds the moral order (see note on 96:10). *all the peoples see.* Verses 2–6 have spoken of general revelation (cf. 19:1–6).
97:7 The center verse (see note on 6:6) and counterpoint of the psalm: joy to all who acknowledge the Lord; shame and disgrace to those who trust in false gods. *worship him.* With biting irony the psalm calls on all the gods that people foolishly worship to bow in worship before the Lord (see v. 9; see also 29:1 and note).
97:8–12 A declaration of Zion's joy that the Lord reigns (vv. 8–9), and a reminder that only those who hate evil have real cause to rejoice in his righteous rule (vv. 10–12).
97:8 *Zion hears.* That "the LORD reigns" (v. 1) in "righteousness" (v. 6). *judgments.* The executive and judicial acts of the Lord who reigns (v. 1) over all human affairs (see 105:7; Isa 26:9), especially his saving acts in Israel's behalf (see 48:11; 105:5; Dt 33:21).
97:9 *Most High.* See note on Ge 14:19.
97:10 *faithful ones.* See note on 4:3.
97:11 *Light.* See 27:1 and note; see also 36:9. *righteous.* See v. 12; see also note on 1:5. *heart.* See note on 4:7.
97:12 *name.* See note on 30:4.
Ps 98 A call to celebrate with joy the righteous reign of the Lord (see introductions to Ps 93; 95). Its beginning and end echo Ps 96, with which it has been paired (see introduction to Ps 96). The three stanzas progressively extend the call to ever wider circles: (1) the worshiping congregation at the temple; (2) all the peoples of the earth; (3) the whole creation. The first stanza recalls God's revelation of his righteousness (v. 2) in the past; the last stanza speaks confidently of his coming rule "in righteousness" (v. 9); the middle stanza is enclosed by the jubilant cry, "Shout for joy" (vv. 4,6).
98:1–3 The call to celebrate in song God's saving acts in behalf of his people.
98:1 *new song.* See note on 33:3. *marvelous things.* See note on 9:1 ("wonders").
98:2 *made ... known ... revealed ... to the nations.* God's saving acts in behalf of his people are also his self-revelation to the nations; in this sense God is his own evangelist (see 77:14 and note on 46:10; see also Isa 52:10). *salvation ... righteousness.* God's saving acts reveal his righteousness (see notes on 4:1; 71:24).
98:3 *love ... faithfulness.* That is, love-and-faithfulness (see note on 36:5; see also note on 3:7). This compound expression often sums up God's covenant commitment to his people (see note on 6:4).
98:4–6 The call to all the earth to join in the celebration.
98:4 See 100:1. *all the earth.* The peoples of the earth (see 96:1 and note; see also 99:1).
98:5 *harp.* See note on Ge 31:27.
98:6 *trumpets.* The special long, straight trumpets of the sanctuary (referred to only here in Psalms; see notes on Nu 10:2–3,10). *ram's horn.* The more common trumpet (referred to also in 47:5; 81:3; 150:3; see note on Joel 2:1).
98:7–9 The call to the whole creation to celebrate (see note on 96:11–12).
98:7 *sea ... world.* The two great regions of creaturely life.
98:8 *rivers ... mountains.* From the rivers to the mountains, let every feature of the whole earth clap and sing (see note on 65:13).

9 let them sing before the LORD,
for he comes to judge the earth.
He will judge the world in
righteousness
and the peoples with equity.[l]

Psalm 99

1 The LORD reigns,[m]
let the nations tremble;[n]
he sits enthroned[o] between the
cherubim,[p]
let the earth shake.
2 Great is the LORD[q] in Zion;[r]
he is exalted[s] over all the nations.
3 Let them praise[t] your great and
awesome name[u]—
he is holy.[v]

4 The King[w] is mighty, he loves
justice[x]—
you have established equity;[y]
in Jacob you have done
what is just and right.[z]
5 Exalt[a] the LORD our God
and worship at his footstool;
he is holy.

6 Moses[b] and Aaron[c] were among his
priests,
Samuel[d] was among those who
called on his name;
they called on the LORD
and he answered[e] them.
7 He spoke to them from the pillar of
cloud;[f]
they kept his statutes and the
decrees he gave them.

8 O LORD our God,
you answered them;
you were to Israel[a] a forgiving
God,[g]
though you punished[h] their
misdeeds.[b]
9 Exalt the LORD our God
and worship at his holy
mountain,
for the LORD our God is holy.

[a] 8 Hebrew *them* [b] 8 Or / *an avenger of the wrongs done to them*

98:9 [l] S Ps 96:10
99:1 [m] S 1Ch 16:31; S Ps 97:1 [n] S Ex 15:14; S 1Ch 16:30 [o] S 2Sa 6:2 [p] S Ex 25:22
99:2 [q] S Ps 48:1 [r] Ps 2:6 [s] Ex 15:1; Ps 46:10; 97:9; 113:4; 148:13
99:3 [t] Ps 30:4; 33:21; 97:12; 103:1; 106:47; 111:9; 145:21; 148:5 [u] Ps 76:1 [v] S Ex 15:11; S Lev 11:44; Rev 4:8
99:4 [w] Ps 2:6 [x] S 1Ki 10:9 [y] Ps 98:9 [z] S Ge 18:19; Rev 15:3
99:5 [a] S Ex 15:2
99:6 [b] S Ex 24:6 [c] S Ex 28:1 [d] 1Sa 7:5 [e] Ps 4:3; 91:15
99:7 [f] S Ex 13:21; S 19:9; S Nu 11:25
99:8 [g] S Ex 22:27; S Nu 14:20 [h] S Lev 26:18

98:9 *comes to judge.* See 96:13 and note. Israel in faith lived between the past (see vv. 1–3) and the future righteous (saving) acts of God. *righteousness … equity.* See 96:10 and note.

Ps 99 A hymn celebrating the Lord as the great and holy King in Zion—with special emphasis on the benefits of the Lord's reign for Israel, a feature it shares with Ps 97 (see introduction to Ps 96). In developing his theme, the poet makes striking use of the symbolic significance (completeness) of the number seven: Seven times he speaks of the "LORD," and seven times he refers to him by means of independent personal pronouns (Hebrew). (See introduction to Ps 93.)

The form is symmetrical, with four stanzas of three Hebrew poetic lines each and two main divisions (marked by a refrain) that are closely balanced, having 42 and 41 Hebrew words respectively—a formal feature it shares with Ps 97 (see introduction to that psalm). The lesser refrain, "he is holy" (vv. 3,5, and expanded in v. 9), probably reflects a traditional threefold liturgical rubric (see Isa 6:3; Rev 4:8; see also Ps 96:1–3,7–9 and notes for further evidence of a liturgical penchant for triple repetition). The second half of the psalm develops the theme introduced in the second stanza.

99:1–3 The God enthroned in Zion is ruler over all the nations—let them acknowledge him.

99:1 *The LORD reigns.* See 93:1 and note. *tremble … shake.* In reverent awe before God. *cherubim.* See 80:1; see also notes on Ex 25:18; Eze 1:5.

99:3 *Let them praise.* As the Great King, he ought to be shown the fear (v. 1) and honor that are his due. *name.* See v. 6; see also note on 5:11. *holy.* See vv. 5,9; see also Introduction to Leviticus: Theological Themes and note on Lev 11:44.

99:4–5 The Lord has shown the quality of his rule by what he has done for Israel.

99:4 *is mighty … loves justice.* Two chief characteristics of God's reign. *established equity.* That is, created conditions in the world that embody equity—especially for Israel (see 96:10 and note). *Jacob.* A synonym for Israel (see Ge 32:28). *just and right.* Justice and righteousness, as in 97:2. Though even the heavens proclaim God's righteousness (see 97:6 and note), it is in the whole complex of his saving acts in and for Israel that the righteousness of God's reign is especially disclosed (see 98:2 and note).

99:5 See also v. 9. For other refrains in the Psalms see introduction to Ps 42–43. *footstool.* God's royal footstool (see 2Ch 9:18), here a metaphor linking the heavenly throne with the earthly; when God sits on his heavenly throne, his earthly throne is his footstool (here "his holy mountain," v. 9; see 132:7; 1Ch 28:2; La 2:1).

99:6–7 In Israel the Lord provided priestly intermediaries, who (1) were appointed to intercede with him on behalf of his faltering people (v. 6) and (2) were given knowledge of his will so they could instruct Israel.

99:6 *Moses … Aaron … Samuel.* These three no doubt serve here as representatives of all those the Lord used as intermediaries with his people in times of great crises. *priests … who called on his name.* The priestly function of intercession is highlighted (see Ex 17:11 and note; 32:11–13,31–32; Nu 14:13–19; 21:7; 1Sa 7:5,8–9; 12:19,23; Jer 15:1). *they called … he answered.* See note on 118:5. *answered them.* See v. 8; see also the Lord's responses to the intercessions referred to in the note on vv. 6–7.

99:7 *spoke to them from the pillar of cloud.* Though reference may be to all Israel ("them"), more likely the hymn recalls God's speaking with Moses (see Ex 33:9) and Aaron (see Nu 12:5–6). But that special mode of revelation in the desert may also be generalized here to include God's revelations to Samuel, who was called to his prophetic ministry at the sanctuary, "where the ark of God was" (1Sa 3:3; see also 1Sa 12:23). *they kept.* However imperfectly, it was in Israel that God's righteous statutes and decrees were kept because only in Israel had they been made known (see 147:19–20; Dt 4:5–8).

99:8–9 The justice and righteousness of God's rule in Israel (see v. 4) have been especially shown in the manner in which he has dealt with their sins (see Ex 34:6–7; see also note on 4:1).

99:9 *holy mountain.* See v. 5 and note. *the LORD our God is holy.* Climactic expansion of the secondary refrain.

Psalm 100

A psalm. For giving thanks.

[1]Shout for joy[i] to the LORD, all the earth.
[2] Worship the LORD[j] with gladness;
come before him[k] with joyful songs.
[3]Know that the LORD is God.[l]
It is he who made us,[m] and we are his[a];
we are his people,[n] the sheep of his pasture.[o]

[4]Enter his gates with thanksgiving[p]
and his courts[q] with praise;
give thanks to him and praise his name.[r]
[5]For the LORD is good[s] and his love endures forever;[t]
his faithfulness[u] continues through all generations.

Psalm 101

Of David. A psalm.

[1]I will sing of your love[v] and justice;
to you, O LORD, I will sing praise.
[2]I will be careful to lead a blameless life[w]—
when will you come to me?

I will walk[x] in my house
with blameless heart.

100:1 [i]S Ps 98:6 **100:2** [j]S Dt 10:12 [k]S Ps 95:2 **100:3** [l]S 1Ki 18:21; S Ps 46:10 [m]S Job 10:3 [n]Ps 79:13; Isa 19:25; 63:8,17-19; 64:9 [o]S 2Sa 24:17; S Ps 74:1 **100:4** [p]S Ps 42:4 [q]S Ps 96:8 [r]Ps 116:17 **100:5** [s]S 1Ch 16:34 [t]S Ezr 3:11; Ps 106:1 [u]Ps 108:4; 119:90 **101:1** [v]Ps 33:1; 51:14; 89:1; 145:7 **101:2** [w]S Ge 17:1; Php 1:10 [x]S 1Ki 3:14

[a] 3 Or *and not we ourselves*

Ps 100 A call to praise the Lord. Whether or not it was composed for that purpose, the final editors of the Psalter used it to close the series that begins with Ps 90. It has special affinity with 95:1–2,6–7; see also Ps 117. (See introduction to Ps 93.) The second main division (vv. 4–5) parallels the structure of the first (vv. 1–3), namely, a call to praise followed by a declaration of why the Lord is worthy of praise—the corresponding elements of the two divisions are complementary.

100 title *thanks.* Grateful praise (see v. 4; see also note on 75:1). Perhaps it indicates that the psalm was to accompany a thank offering (see Lev 7:12).

100:1 *all the earth.* Though vv. 3,5 clearly speak of God's special relationship with Israel, the call to worship goes out to the whole world, which ought to acknowledge the Lord because of what he has done for his people (see also Ps 98–99; 117).

100:3 *Know.* Acknowledge. *made us.* See 95:6 and note. *sheep of his pasture.* See 95:7 and note; see also note on 23:1.

100:4 *his gates.* The gates of the temple (see 24:7 and note). *courts.* Of the temple (see 84:2,10; 2Ki 21:5; 23:11–12).

100:5 *the LORD is good.* In that his love-and-faithfulness (see note on 36:5) are unfailing through all time (see 98:3 and note). *love.* See note on 6:4.

Ps 101–110 A collection of ten psalms located between two other groups (see introductions to Ps 90–100; 111–119) and framed by two psalms that pertain to the king (the first, the king's vow to pattern his reign after God's righteous rule; the last, God's commitment to maintain the king—his anointed—and give him victories over all his enemies). This little psalter-within-the-Psalter is concentrically arranged. Inside the frame, Ps 102 and 109 are prayers of individuals in times of intense distress; Ps 103 and 108 praise the Lord for his "great ... love" that reaches to the heavens (103:11; 108:4); Ps 104 and 107 are complements, with 104 celebrating God's many wise and benevolent acts in creation and 107 celebrating God's "wonderful deeds" (vv. 8,15,21,24,31) for people through his lordship over creation; and the remaining two are also complements, with Ps 105 reciting the history of Israel's redemption and 106 reciting the same history as a history of Israel's rebellion. This little psalter includes most of the forms and themes found in the rest of the Psalter. Its outer frame is devoted to royal psalms and its center pair to recitals of Israel's history with God. Meanwhile, its themes range from creation and God's eternal enthronement to the covenant with Abraham, Isaac and Jacob, Israel's exodus from Egypt and entrance into Canaan, their exile and restoration, and finally the ultimate triumph of the Lord's anointed. As a collection it bears a distinctively redemption-history stamp and evokes recollection of all the salient elements of the OT message. (For the problem of the Book division at Ps 107 see introduction to that psalm.)

Ps 101 A king's pledge to reign righteously (see 2Ki 23:3), after the pattern of God's rule. For its relationship to Ps 110 see introduction to Ps 101–110. If authored by David (see title), it may have been composed before the ark of God was successfully brought into Jerusalem (see note on v. 2a; see also 2Sa 6). Only Christ, the great Son of David, has perfectly fulfilled these commitments.

Composed of seven couplets (the number of completeness), the psalm begins with a twofold introduction (vv. 1–3a; see notes below), followed by a five-stanza (vv. 3b–8) elaboration of the theme of the second stanza. Of these five stanzas, the middle one (v. 6) speaks of the king's commitment to the "faithful" and "blameless," while the other four (vv. 3b–4,5,7,8) declare his repudiation of all the "faithless" and "wicked" in the land. (For the parallel relationship of stanzas six and seven with three and four see notes below.) The middle stanza is linked with stanzas one and two also by the catchword "blameless." (For centering in the Psalms see note on 6:6.) The whole psalm is framed by references to the "LORD" in the first and last stanzas (see vv. 1,8). The second stanza from the end echoes two phrases found in the second stanza from the beginning ("in my house" [vv. 2,7] and "in my presence" [v. 7]—in Hebrew the same as for "before my eyes" [v. 3]), thus forming an inner frame. For other doublets see notes below.

101:1–2a Celebration of the pattern of God's reign, which the king makes the model for his own.

101:1 *love and justice.* Two of the chief qualities of God's rule (see 6:4; 99:4 and notes). For this particular combination see Hos 12:6; Mic 6:8; cf. Zec 7:9. The present phrase is probably a shortened form of "love and faithfulness" combined with "righteousness and justice" (as in 89:14; cf. 33:5; 36:5–6; 48:9–11; Isa 16:5; Hos 2:19).

101:2a *blameless.* See vv. 2b,6; see also note on Ge 17:1. *when ...?* Perhaps expressive of David's yearning for the presence of the ark of the Lord in his royal city as the sign of God's readiness to be with him and sustain him in his pledge to reign as he ought (see 2Sa 6 and note on 6:2). For later kings it would be a plea for divine enablement relative to the pledge given in vv. 1–2 (cf. Ps 72; 1Ki 3:7–9).

101:2b–3a The essential commitment. *heart ... eyes.* In OT understanding, a person follows the dictates of the heart—the inmost being (see note on 4:7)—and/or the attractions of the eye—external influences (see 119:37; Jdg 14:1–2; 2Sa 11:2; 2Ki 16:10; Job 31:1; Pr 4:25; 17:24). For the combination heart-eyes see v. 5; Nu 15:39; Job 31:7; Pr 21:4; Ecc 2:10; Jer 22:17.

101:2b *house.* Royal administration (also in v. 7).

[3] I will set before my eyes
no vile thing.[y]

The deeds of faithless men I hate;[z]
they will not cling to me.
[4] Men of perverse heart[a] shall be far
from me;
I will have nothing to do with evil.
[5] Whoever slanders his neighbor[b] in
secret,
him will I put to silence;
whoever has haughty eyes[c] and a
proud heart,
him will I not endure.

[6] My eyes will be on the faithful in the
land,
that they may dwell with me;
he whose walk is blameless[d]
will minister to me.

[7] No one who practices deceit
will dwell in my house;
no one who speaks falsely
will stand in my presence.

[8] Every morning[e] I will put to silence
all the wicked[f] in the land;
I will cut off every evildoer[g]
from the city of the LORD.[h]

Psalm 102

A prayer of an afflicted man. When he is faint and pours out his lament before the LORD.

[1] Hear my prayer,[i] O LORD;
let my cry for help[j] come to you.
[2] Do not hide your face[k] from me
when I am in distress.
Turn your ear[l] to me;
when I call, answer me quickly.

[3] For my days vanish like smoke;[m]
my bones[n] burn like glowing
embers.
[4] My heart is blighted and withered like
grass;[o]
I forget to eat my food.[p]

101:3 [y] Jer 16:18; Eze 11:21; Hos 9:10 [z] S Ps 5:5 **101:4** [a] Pr 3:32; 6:16-19; 11:20 **101:5** [b] S Ex 20:16; S Lev 19:16 [c] S Ps 10:5 **101:6** [d] ver 2; Ps 119:1 **101:8** [e] Ps 5:3; Jer 21:12 [f] Ps 75:10 [g] S 2Sa 3:39; Ps 118:10-12 [h] S Ps 46:4 **102:1** [i] Ps 4:1 [j] S Ex 2:23 **102:2** [k] S Ps 22:24 [l] S 2Ki 19:16; Ps 31:2; 88:2 **102:3** [m] S Ps 37:20; S Jas 4:14 [n] La 1:13 **102:4** [o] S Ps 37:2; 90:5-6 [p] S 1Sa 1:7; S Ezr 10:6; S Job 33:20

101:3a *vile.* "Belial" (2Co 6:15) is derived from the Hebrew for this word (see note on Dt 13:13).
101:3b–4 A repudiation of evil deeds and those who promote them (see v. 7).
101:3b *faithless.* Those who rebel against what is right (see Hos 5:2, "rebels").
101:4 *perverse.* The opposite of "blameless" (see 18:26, "crooked"; see also Pr 11:20; 19:1; 28:6). A perverse heart and a deceitful tongue (see v. 7) are root and fruit (see Pr 17:20).
101:5 A pledge to remove from his presence all slanderous and all arrogant persons (see v. 8). *put to silence.* Destroy (as in 54:5; 94:23). See v. 8. *haughty eyes … proud heart.* See vv. 2b–3a and note; called "the lamp of the wicked" in Pr 21:4; cf. Ps 131:1; Isa 10:12. The arrogant tend to be ruthless (see Isa 10:12) and are a law to themselves (see note on 31:23).
101:6 A pledge to surround himself in his reign with the faithful and blameless. *My eyes will be on.* I will look with favor on (see 33:18; 34:15). *the faithful.* Those who maintain moral integrity. *minister to me.* Serve as my aide (see Ex 24:13), attendant (see Ge 39:4; 1Ki 19:21), personal servant (see 2Ki 4:43), commander and official (see 1 Ch 27:1; 2Ch 17:19; Pr 29:12).
101:7 A repudiation of all those who make their way by double-dealing (see vv. 3b–4).
101:8 A pledge to remove all the wicked from the Lord's kingdom (see v. 5). *Every morning.* With diligence and persistence (see Jer 21:12; Zep 3:5). It appears to have been customary for kings to hear judicial cases in the morning — when the mind is fresh and the air cool. That is when victims looked for deliverance from those oppressing them (cf. 88:13; 143:8; Isa 33:2). *city of the LORD.* See Ps 46; 48; 87; see also note on 3:4.
Ps 102 The prayer of an individual in a time of great distress. For its relationship to Ps 109 in the arrangement of the Psalter see introduction to Ps 101–110. The author may have been someone caught up in a great national calamity (see note on title). If this is the case, the voice heard here would be like one of the "we/us" of Ps 90 speaking for himself (for thematic links between these two psalms see notes below). Some interpreters believe that the "I" of vv. 1–11,23–24 is a communal "I" (see the latter part of the note on Ps 30 title), but that does not seem necessary. In early Christian worship this psalm came to be used as a penitential prayer (see introduction to Ps 6), even though it contains no explicit confession of sin.
The main body of the psalm (vv. 1–22) is developed in four stanzas (initial appeal for God to hear, vv. 1–2; description of distress, vv. 3–11; assurance that the Lord will surely hear, vv. 12–17; call for the Lord's certain deliverance to be recorded for his enduring praise, vv. 18–22), followed by a concluding recapitulation (vv. 23–28).
102 title Unique in the Psalter (no author named and no liturgical or historical notes), the title identifies only the life situation in which the prayer is to be used, and in accordance with vv. 1–11,23–24 it designates the prayer as that of an individual. But vv. 12–22,28 clearly indicate national involvement in the calamity. It may be that the distress suffered by the individual, while its description suggests physical illness, is the result of his sharing in a national disaster such as the exile — a suggestion supported by references to the restoration of Zion. Because of the close relationship of the fortunes of king and nation and because of the many themes shared by this and some of the royal psalms, it has been plausibly suggested that the prayer was originally that of a Davidic king, or of a member of the Davidic royal house, while in Babylonian exile. *prayer.* See vv. 1,17. *faint.* See 61:2; 77:3; 142:3; 143:4; see also 107:5; Jnh 2:7. *lament.* The Hebrew for this word is translated "complaint" in 64:1; 142:2; Job 7:13; 9:27; 10:1; 21:4. See Introduction: Psalm Types; Introduction to Lamentations: Themes and Theology.
102:1–2 Initial appeal for God to hear.
102:2 *hide your face.* See note on 13:1. *when I call, answer me.* See note on 118:5.
102:3–11 The description of distress — a suffering so great that it withers body and spirit — brought on by a visitation of God's wrath (v. 10) and making him the mockery of his enemies (v. 8). For the framing imagery that binds this section together see vv. 3–4 and v. 11.
102:3 *my days vanish like smoke.* See also vv. 11,23. *bones burn.* As if a fire is consuming his physical frame (see 31:10; 32:3; 42:10).
102:4 *heart.* See note on 4:7. Here "heart" is used in combination with "bones" (v. 3) to refer to the whole person (body and spirit); see 22:14; Pr 14:30; 15:30; Isa 66:14 ("and you" represents the Hebrew for "and your bones"); Jer 20:9; 23:9. *blighted.* Or "scorched" (by the hot sun); see 121:6. *withered like grass.* See v. 11; see also note on 90:5–6.

5 Because of my loud groaning[q]
I am reduced to skin and bones.
6 I am like a desert owl,[r]
like an owl among the ruins.
7 I lie awake;[s] I have become
like a bird alone[t] on a roof.
8 All day long my enemies[u] taunt me;[v]
those who rail against me use my
name as a curse.[w]
9 For I eat ashes[x] as my food
and mingle my drink with tears[y]
10 because of your great wrath,[z]
for you have taken me up and
thrown me aside.
11 My days are like the evening shadow;[a]
I wither[b] away like grass.

12 But you, O LORD, sit enthroned
forever;[c]
your renown endures[d] through all
generations.[e]
13 You will arise[f] and have compassion[g]
on Zion,
for it is time[h] to show favor[i] to her;
the appointed time[j] has come.
14 For her stones are dear to your
servants;
her very dust moves them to pity.
15 The nations will fear[k] the name of the
LORD,
all the kings[l] of the earth will revere
your glory.
16 For the LORD will rebuild Zion[m]
and appear in his glory.[n]
17 He will respond to the prayer[o] of the
destitute;
he will not despise their plea.

18 Let this be written[p] for a future
generation,
that a people not yet created[q] may
praise the LORD:
19 "The LORD looked down[r] from his
sanctuary on high,
from heaven he viewed the earth,
20 to hear the groans of the prisoners[s]
and release those condemned to
death."
21 So the name of the LORD will be
declared[t] in Zion
and his praise[u] in Jerusalem
22 when the peoples and the kingdoms
assemble to worship[v] the LORD.

23 In the course of my life[a] he broke my
strength;
he cut short my days.[w]

[a] 23 Or *By his power*

102:5 [q] S Ps 6:6 **102:6** [r] S Dt 14:15-17; Job 30:29; Isa 34:11; Zep 2:14 **102:7** [s] Ps 77:4 [t] Ps 38:11 **102:8** [u] S Ps 31:11 [v] S Ps 42:10; Lk 22:63-65; 23:35-37 [w] S Ex 22:28; Isa 65:15; Jer 24:9; 25:18; 42:18; 44:12; Eze 14:8; Zec 8:13 **102:9** [x] Isa 44:20 [y] Ps 6:6; 42:3; 80:5 **102:10** [z] Ps 7:11; 38:3 **102:11** [a] S 1Ch 29:15; S Job 14:2; S Ps 39:6 [b] S Job 8:12; Jas 1:10 **102:12** [c] S Ex 15:18 [d] Ps 135:13; Isa 55:13; 63:12 [e] S Ex 3:15 **102:13** [f] S Ps 44:26 [g] S Dt 32:36; S 1Ki 3:26; Isa 54:8; 60:10; Zec 10:6 [h] Ps 119:126 [i] S Ps 77:7 [j] S Ex 13:10; Da 8:19; Ac 1:7 **102:15** [k] 1Ki 8:43; Ps 67:7; Isa 2:2 [l] Ps 76:12; 138:4; 148:11 **102:16** [m] S Ps 51:18 [n] Ps 8:1; Isa 60:1-2 **102:17** [o] S 1Ki 8:29; Ps 4:1; 6:9 **102:18** [p] S Ro 4:24 [q] S Ps 22:31 **102:19** [r] Ps 53:2 **102:20** [s] S Ps 68:6; S Lk 4:19 **102:21** [t] Ps 22:22 [u] Ps 9:14 **102:22** [v] S Ps 22:27; Isa 49:22-23; Zec 8:20-23 **102:23** [w] S Ps 39:5

102:6 *owl ... owl.* Translations of two different Hebrew words (cf. Lev 11:16–18). The owl was associated with desert areas and ruins (see Isa 34:11,15; Jer 50:39; Zep 2:14).

102:8 *enemies taunt me.* See 109:25; see also notes on 5:9; 39:8. *use my name as a curse.* Their curse takes the form, "May you suffer like that one (the one named) does."

102:9 *drink ... tears.* For tears as food and drink see 42:3; 80:5.

102:10 *wrath.* See note on 2:5.

102:11 An echo of vv. 3–4. *shadow.* See 109:23; 144:4; Job 8:9; 14:2; Ecc 6:12. *grass.* See 37:20; 90:5–6 and notes.

102:12–17 Assurance that heaven's eternal King will surely hear the prayer of the destitute (v. 17) and restore Zion. For such expressions of assurance in the prayers of the Psalter see note on 3:8. This six-verse stanza weaves its themes in a balanced *a-b-c/a-b-c* pattern (see notes on vv. 15–17).

102:12 *sit enthroned forever.* A central theme of the preceding collection (Ps 90–100). Because God reigns forever and remains the same (see v. 27), his mercies to those who look to him for salvation will not fail. *renown.* See note on 30:4 ("name"). For elaborate celebrations of the Lord's renown see Ps 111; 135; 145.

102:13 This verse and v. 16 (see also v. 14) suggest that the psalmist's distress was occasioned by the Babylonian exile. *arise.* See note on 3:7. *appointed time.* The time set by God for judgment and deliverance (see 75:2; Ex 9:5; 2Sa 24:15; Da 11:27,35). Perhaps the psalmist is referring to a time announced by a prophet.

102:14 *dear to your servants.* If Zion, the city of God (see 46:4; 48:1–2,8; 87:3; 101:8; 132:13), is so loved by the Lord's servants (see Ps 126; 137), how much more is she cherished by the Lord!

102:15 *nations will fear.* See notes on 25:12; 46:10. *the name of the LORD.* An echo of reference to the "LORD's" "renown" (see note on 30:4 ["name"]). Yahweh's "renown" that "endures through all generations" (v. 12) will evoke the awe of earth's most powerful inhabitants. *name.* See note on 5:11.

102:16 *will rebuild Zion.* Yahweh will "have compassion" on Zion (v. 13) by rebuilding her. *and appear in his glory.* Or "and thus appear in his glory" (see v. 15 and note on 46:10; see also Isa 40:1–5). This hope will find its fullest expression in the "new Jerusalem" (see Rev 21:2 and note).

102:17 *the destitute.* Reference is to "your servants" (v. 14). *their plea.* Expressive of the pity they feel for their beloved Zion now lying in ruins (v. 14).

102:18–22 Let God's certain deliverance of his people be recorded for his continual praise (v. 8)—until that great day when the worshiping community celebrating Zion's redemption has expanded to include representatives of the "peoples" and "kingdoms" of the world (v. 22). See introduction to Ps 117; see also Rev. 15:4; 21:24,26.

102:18 *written.* Only here does a psalmist call for memory to be sustained by a written record of God's saving act; usually oral transmission suffices (see 22:30; 44:1; 78:1–4). *created.* Brought into being by God's sovereign act (see 51:10; 104:30; 139:13).

102:20 *prisoners ... those condemned to death.* Perhaps prisoners of war, but more likely the exiles in Babylon (see 79:11 and note).

102:21 *praise.* See note on 9:1.

102:22 See note on 46:10; see also 47:9 and note; 96; 98; 100. The expectation here expressed may also be influenced by such prophecies as Isa 2:2–4; Mic 4:1–3.

102:23–28 Concluding recapitulation. The stanza is framed by the radical contrast expressed in vv. 23,28. That human life is cut short (v. 23) by the One whose own being spans all ages (vv. 25–27) adds to the psalmist's sense of loss on the one hand but also to his hope on the other (v. 28) and thus to the urgency of his prayer—as in 90:1–6 (see note on 90:4–5).

102:23–24a See vv. 3–11.

24 So I said:
"Do not take me away, O my God, in
the midst of my days;
your years go on[x] through all
generations.
25 In the beginning[y] you laid the
foundations of the earth,
and the heavens[z] are the work of
your hands.[a]
26 They will perish,[b] but you remain;
they will all wear out like a
garment.
Like clothing you will change them
and they will be discarded.
27 But you remain the same,[c]
and your years will never end.[d]
28 The children of your servants[e] will live
in your presence;
their descendants[f] will be
established before you."

Psalm 103

Of David.

1 Praise the LORD,[g] O my soul;[h]
all my inmost being, praise his holy
name.[i]
2 Praise the LORD,[j] O my soul,
and forget not[k] all his benefits—
3 who forgives all your sins[l]
and heals[m] all your diseases,
4 who redeems your life[n] from the pit
and crowns you with love and
compassion,[o]
5 who satisfies[p] your desires with good
things
so that your youth is renewed[q] like
the eagle's.[r]
6 The LORD works righteousness[s]
and justice for all the oppressed.[t]
7 He made known[u] his ways[v] to Moses,
his deeds[w] to the people of Israel:
8 The LORD is compassionate and
gracious,[x]
slow to anger, abounding in love.
9 He will not always accuse,
nor will he harbor his anger forever;[y]
10 he does not treat us as our sins
deserve[z]
or repay us according to our
iniquities.
11 For as high as the heavens are above
the earth,
so great is his love[a] for those who
fear him;[b]
12 as far as the east is from the west,
so far has he removed our
transgressions[c] from us.

102:24 [x]S Ge 21:33; Job 36:26; Ps 90:2 **102:25** [y]S Ge 1:1; Heb 1:10-12* [z]S 2Ch 2:12 [a]S Ps 8:3 **102:26** [b]Isa 13:10, 13; 34:4; 51:6; Eze 32:8; Joel 2:10; Mt 24:35; 2Pe 3:7-10; Rev 20:11 **102:27** [c]S Nu 23:19; Heb 13:8; Jas 1:17 [d]Ps 9:7 **102:28** [e]Ps 69:36 [f]Ps 25:13; 89:4 **103:1** [g]Ps 28:6 [h]Ps 104:1 [i]S Ps 30:4 **103:2** [j]Ps 106:1; 117:1 [k]S Dt 6:12; Ps 77:11 **103:3** [l]S Ex 34:7 [m]S Ex 15:26; Col 3:13; 1Pe 2:24; 1Jn 1:9 **103:4** [n]Ps 34:22; 56:13; Isa 43:1 [o]S Ps 8:5; 23:6 **103:5** [p]S Ps 90:14; S 104:28 [q]Job 33:25; Ps 119:25, 93; 2Co 4:16 [r]S Ex 19:4 **103:6** [s]Ps 9:8; 65:5; Isa 9:7 [t]S Ps 74:21; S Lk 4:19 **103:7** [u]Ps 99:7; 147:19 [v]S Ex 33:13 [w]Ps 106:22 **103:8** [x]S Ex 22:27; S Ps 86:15; Mic 7:18-19; Jas 5:11 **103:9** [y]Ps 30:5; 79:5; Isa 57:16; Jer 3:5, 12; Mic 7:18 **103:10** [z]S Ezr 9:13; Ro 6:23 **103:11** [a]Ps 13:5; 57:10; 100:5; 106:45; 117:2; La 3:22; Eph 3:18 [b]S 2Ch 6:31 **103:12** [c]S 2Sa 12:13; Ro 4:7; Eph 2:5

102:24b–27 See v. 12 and note. For a NT application of vv. 25–27 to Christ see Heb 1:10–12 and note on 1:10.
102:26 *Like clothing.* With his first creation God clothed himself with the manifestation of his glory (see 8:1,3–4; 19:1; 29:3–9; 104:1,31; Isa 6:3; see also Job 38–41, especially 40:10). But he is more enduring than what he has made—and the first creation will give way to a new creation (see Isa 65:17; 66:22).
102:28 Because the Lord does not change (see v. 27), Israel's future is secure (see Mal 3:6). *live in your presence.* Or "dwell in the (promised) land" (see 69:36; see also 37:3,29; Isa 65:9). *established before you.* See 2Sa 7:24.
Ps 103 A hymn to God's love and compassion toward his people. For its relationship to Ps 108 in the arrangement of the Psalter see introduction to Ps 101–110. Calls to praise frame the body of the hymn (vv. 1–2,20–22) and set its tone. The recital of praise falls into two unequal parts: (1) a three-verse celebration of personal benefits received (vv. 3–5) and (2) a 14-verse recollection of God's mercies to his people Israel (vv. 6–19). The major division (vv. 6–19) is composed of six couplets framed by the breakup of a seventh couplet (vv. 6,19) that describes the general character of God's reign. Thematic development divides the six framed couplets into two equal parts (vv. 7–12,13–18), of which the first celebrates God's compassion on his people as sinners while the second sings of his compassion on them as frail mortals (see also 78:38–39). The concluding couplets of these two parts proclaim the vastness of his love (vv. 11–12) and its unending perseverance (vv. 17–18). As with the hymn found in Ps 33, the length of the psalm has been determined by the number of letters in the Hebrew alphabet (see introduction to Ps 33).
103:1–2 Call to praise, directed inward (cf. vv. 20–22).
103:1–2,22 *O my soul.* A conventional Hebrew way of addressing oneself (see 104:1,35; 116:7). *soul.* See note on 6:3.
103:3–5 Recital of personal blessings received.
103:3 *forgives ... heals.* These two "benefits" (v. 2) are further elaborated in the two stanzas that make up the main body of the psalm: vv. 7–12 and 13–18 (see notes there; see also Mt 9:2,5 and parallels).
103:4 *redeems.* A synonym for "delivers" (see note on 71:23). *pit.* A metaphor for the grave (see note on 30:1). *love and compassion.* The key words of the hymn (see vv. 8,11,13,17). *love.* See vv. 8,11,17; see also note on 6:4.
103:5 *like the eagle's.* The vigor of youth is restored to match the proverbial unflagging strength of the eagle (see Isa 40:30–31).
103:6–19 God's love and compassion toward his people.
103:6 Together with v. 19 (the second verse of a split couplet, providing the other side of the literary frame), v. 6 characterizes the reign of God under which Israel has been so graciously blessed. Read as a (split) couplet, these two verses echo a theme found frequently in Proverbs (see Pr 16:12 and note; 25:5; 29:14; cf. Ps 9:7–8; 97:2; Isa 9:7). *righteousness.* See v. 17; see also note on 4:1.
103:7–12 God's compassion on his people as sinners.
103:7–8 See Ex 33:13; see also note on Ex 34:6–7.
103:7 *his ways.* See 25:10 and note.
103:9 *anger.* See note on 2:5.
103:10,12 *sins ... iniquities ... transgressions.* See 32:5 and note.
103:11–12 The vastness of God's love (note the spatial imagery) is supremely shown in his forgiving Israel's sins.
103:11 See 36:5–9. *so great is.* So prevails. *those who fear him.* See vv. 13,17–18; see also note on 66:16.
103:12 See Isa 1:18; 38:17; 43:25; Jer 31:34; 50:20; Mic 7:18–19.

13 As a father has compassion[d] on his
children,
so the LORD has compassion on
those who fear him;
14 for he knows how we are formed,[e]
he remembers that we are dust.[f]
15 As for man, his days are like grass,[g]
he flourishes like a flower[h] of the
field;
16 the wind blows[i] over it and it is gone,
and its place[j] remembers it no more.
17 But from everlasting to everlasting
the LORD's love is with those who
fear him,
and his righteousness with their
children's children[k]—
18 with those who keep his covenant[l]
and remember[m] to obey his
precepts.[n]

19 The LORD has established his throne[o] in
heaven,
and his kingdom rules[p] over all.

20 Praise the LORD,[q] you his angels,[r]
you mighty ones[s] who do his
bidding,[t]
who obey his word.
21 Praise the LORD, all his heavenly
hosts,[u]
you his servants[v] who do his will.
22 Praise the LORD, all his works[w]
everywhere in his dominion.

Praise the LORD, O my soul.[x]

Psalm 104

1 Praise the LORD, O my soul.[y]

O LORD my God, you are very great;
you are clothed with splendor and
majesty.[z]
2 He wraps[a] himself in light[b] as with a
garment;
he stretches[c] out the heavens[d] like a
tent[e]
3 and lays the beams[f] of his upper
chambers on their waters.[g]
He makes the clouds[h] his chariot[i]
and rides on the wings of the
wind.[j]

103:13 [d]Mal 3:17; 1Jn 3:1 **103:14** [e]Ps 119:73; 139:13-15; Isa 29:16 [f]S Ge 2:7; S Ps 146:4 **103:15** [g]Ps 37:2; 90:5; 102:11; Isa 40:6 [h]S Job 14:2; Jas 1:10 **103:16** [i]Isa 40:7; Hag 1:9 [j]S Job 7:8 **103:17** [k]S Ge 48:11; S Ezr 9:12 **103:18** [l]S Dt 29:9 [m]Ps 119:52 [n]S Nu 15:40; Jn 14:15 **103:19** [o]Ps 47:8; 80:1; 113:5 [p]Ps 22:28; 66:7; Da 4:17 **103:20** [q]Ps 28:6 [r]S Ne 9:6; Lk 2:13; Heb 1:14 [s]S Ps 29:1 [t]Ps 107:25; 135:7; 148:8 **103:21** [u]S 1Ki 22:19 [v]S Ne 7:73 **103:22** [w]Ps 19:1; 67:3; 145:10; 150:6 [x]ver 1; Ps 104:1 **104:1** [y]S Ps 103:22 [z]S Job 40:10 **104:2** [a]Isa 49:18; Jer 43:12 [b]Ps 18:12; 1Ti 6:16 [c]Job 9:8; Jer 51:15 [d]Job 37:18; Isa 40:22; 42:5; 44:24; Zec 12:1 [e]S Ps 19:4 **104:3** [f]Am 9:6 [g]S Ps 24:2 [h]S Dt 33:26; Isa 19:1; Na 1:3 [i]S 2Ki 2:11 [j]Ps 18:10

103:13–18 God's compassion on his people as frail mortals (see 78:39).
103:13–14 In Hebrew the initial words of these two verses strikingly echo the sounds of the initial words of vv. 11–12, thereby effecting a tight rhetorical bond between vv. 7–12 and vv. 13–18.
103:14 *we are dust.* See Ge 2:7; 3:19.
103:15–16 See note on 90:5–6.
103:17–18 The infinite temporal span of God's love (cf. the spatial imagery in vv. 11–12).
103:17 *everlasting to everlasting ... their children's children.* God's love outlasts anyone's little time in this life (cf. note on 109:12).
103:18 *who keep his covenant ... obey his precepts.* See 25:10; Ex 19:5 and note; 20:6 and note; Dt 4:40; 29:9.
103:19 See v. 6 and note; see also 9:4,7; 11:4; 47:2,7–8; 123:1.
103:20–22 Concluding call to praise, directed to all creatures—from the psalmist's inner self (vv. 1–2) to the creatures who serve God in heaven. A call to praise is often the climax of praise in the Psalter (as also of the whole collection; see Ps 148–150). See note on 9:1. *Praise ... Praise ... Praise.* See note on 96:1–3. (The final line was probably added by the editors of the Psalter; see 104:1,35.)
103:20 *who do his bidding.* See 91:11; Heb 1:14.
103:21 *heavenly hosts.* Uniquely here and in 148:2 the Hebrew for "hosts" is masculine, and in both places the "hosts" are associated with "angels." *servants.* Translates the participle of the Hebrew verb for "minister" in 101:6 (see note there; see also note on 104:4).
103:22 *all his works.* See 65:13; 96:11–12 and notes.
Ps 104 A hymn to the Creator. For its relationship to Ps 108 in the arrangement of the Psalter see introduction to Ps 101–110. The preexilic author has adapted Ge 1 to his own quite different purpose and has subordinated its sequence somewhat to his own design (see next paragraph). Ge 1 recounts God's acts of creation as his first work at the beginning, but the poet views the created world displayed before his eyes and sings the glory of its Maker and Sustainer. Surprisingly, he only hints at the angelic world (v. 4) and mentions humans only in passing (vv. 14,23); his theme is the visible creation, which he views as the radiant and stately robe with which the invisible Creator has clothed himself to display his glory.

Following his one-verse introduction, the poet designed the main body of his poem concentrically, with stanzas of three-five-nine-five-three verses. The first stanza speaks of the celestial realm above (vv. 2–4) and the fifth of the nautical realm below (vv. 24–26)—the two realms that bracket the "earth" (see note on v. 5). The second sings of the earth's solid foundations and secure boundaries (vv. 5–9) and the fourth of the orderly cycles of life on earth governed by sun and moon (vv. 19–23). At the center a nine-verse stanza (composed of three triplets) celebrates the luxuriation of life in the earth (vv. 10–18). To the poem's main body he added a four-verse stanza that recites how God maintains life on earth (vv. 27–30), a two-verse conclusion (vv. 31–32—which together with v. 1 frames the whole), and a three-verse epilogue (vv. 33–35). The outer frame ("Praise the LORD, O my soul") was probably added by the editors of the Psalter when they inserted the Book division after Ps 106—thus concluding Book IV with doxologies (see the liturgical frames added to Ps 105–106 and the similar conclusion to Book V: Ps 146–150).
104:1–2 *clothed with ... wraps himself in.* See note on 109:29.
104:1 Introduction: the theme of the hymn.
104:2–4 The celestial realm above.
104:2 *light.* Cf. the first day of creation in Ge 1. *heavens.* Cf. the second day of creation in Ge 1. *like a tent.* Over the earth and the luminaries that give it light.
104:3 *upper chambers.* Vivid imagery for the heavenly abode of God (see v. 13). In the singular, the Hebrew for this phrase usually refers to the upper-level room of a house (as in 1Ki 17:19; 2Ki 1:2). *their waters.* The waters above the "tent" (v. 2; see Ge 1:7), from which, in the imagery of the OT, God gives the rain (see v. 13; see also 36:8 and note). *clouds his chariot.* See 18:7–15; 68:4; 77:16–19 and notes.

4 He makes winds his messengers,[a] [k]
flames of fire[l] his servants.

5 He set the earth[m] on its foundations;[n]
it can never be moved.
6 You covered it[o] with the deep[p] as with
a garment;
the waters stood[q] above the
mountains.
7 But at your rebuke[r] the waters fled,
at the sound of your thunder[s] they
took to flight;
8 they flowed over the mountains,
they went down into the valleys,
to the place you assigned[t] for them.
9 You set a boundary[u] they cannot cross;
never again will they cover the earth.

10 He makes springs[v] pour water into the
ravines;
it flows between the mountains.
11 They give water[w] to all the beasts of
the field;
the wild donkeys[x] quench their
thirst.
12 The birds of the air[y] nest by the
waters;
they sing among the branches.[z]
13 He waters the mountains[a] from his
upper chambers;[b]
the earth is satisfied by the fruit of
his work.[c]
14 He makes grass grow[d] for the cattle,
and plants for man to cultivate—
bringing forth food[e] from the earth:
15 wine[f] that gladdens the heart of man,
oil[g] to make his face shine,
and bread that sustains[h] his heart.
16 The trees of the LORD[i] are well watered,
the cedars of Lebanon[j] that he
planted.

17 There the birds[k] make their nests;
the stork has its home in the pine
trees.
18 The high mountains belong to the wild
goats;[l]
the crags are a refuge for the
coneys.[b] [m]

19 The moon marks off the seasons,[n]
and the sun[o] knows when to go
down.
20 You bring darkness,[p] it becomes
night,[q]
and all the beasts of the forest[r]
prowl.
21 The lions roar for their prey[s]
and seek their food from God.[t]
22 The sun rises, and they steal away;
they return and lie down in their
dens.[u]
23 Then man goes out to his work,[v]
to his labor until evening.[w]

24 How many are your works,[x] O LORD!
In wisdom you made[y] them all;
the earth is full of your creatures.[z]
25 There is the sea,[a] vast and spacious,
teeming with creatures beyond
number—
living things both large and
small.[b]
26 There the ships[c] go to and fro,
and the leviathan,[d] which you
formed to frolic[e] there.[f]

104:4 [k] Ps 148:8; Heb 1:7* [l] Ge 3:24; 2Ki 2:11 **104:5** [m] Ex 31:17; Job 26:7; Ps 24:1-2; 102:25; 121:2 [n] S 1Sa 2:8 **104:6** [o] Ge 7:19 [p] S Ge 1:2 [q] 2Pe 3:6 **104:7** [r] S Ps 18:15 [s] S Ex 9:23; Ps 29:3 **104:8** [t] Ps 33:7 **104:9** [u] S Ge 1:9; S Ps 16:6 **104:10** [v] Ps 107:33; Isa 41:18 **104:11** [w] ver 13 [x] S Ge 16:12; Isa 32:14; Jer 14:6 **104:12** [y] ver 17; Mt 8:20 [z] Mt 13:32 **104:13** [a] Ps 135:7; 147:8; Jer 10:13; Zec 10:1 [b] S Lev 26:4 [c] Am 9:6 **104:14** [d] S Job 38:27; Ps 147:8 [e] S Ge 1:30; S Job 28:5 **104:15** [f] S Ge 14:18; S Jdg 9:13 [g] Ps 23:5; 92:10; Lk 7:46 [h] S Dt 8:3; Mt 6:11 **104:16** [i] Ge 1:11 [j] S Ps 72:16 **104:17** [k] ver 12 **104:18** [l] S Dt 14:5 [m] Pr 30:26 **104:19** [n] S Ge 1:14 [o] Ps 19:6 **104:20** [p] Isa 45:7; Am 5:8 [q] Ps 74:16 [r] S Ps 50:10 **104:21** [s] Am 3:4 [t] Ps 145:15; Joel 1:20; S Mt 6:26 **104:22** [u] S Job 37:8 **104:23** [v] S Ge 3:19 [w] Jdg 19:16 **104:24** [x] Ps 40:5 [y] S Ge 1:31 [z] Ps 24:1; 50:10-11 **104:25** [a] Ps 69:34 [b] Eze 47:10 **104:26** [c] Ps 107:23; Eze 27:9; Jnh 1:3 [d] S Job 3:8; 41:1 [e] Job 40:20 [f] S Ge 1:21

[a] 4 Or *angels* [b] 18 That is, the hyrax or rock badger

104:4 *winds ... flames of fire.* The winds and lightning bolts of the thunderstorm, here personified as the agents of God's purposes (see 148:8; cf. 103:21; see also Heb 1:7 and note).
104:5–9 The earth realm (the spatial element) made secure. Verses 5,9 frame the stanza, highlighting its two main themes.
104:5 *earth.* Land in distinction from sky and seas, not the earth as a planet (see Ge 1:10). *foundations.* See 24:2 and note. *can never be moved.* Firmly founded (see 93:1; 96:10), it will not give way (cf. v. 9).
104:7 *rebuke.* See note on 76:6. *waters fled.* Cf. the third day of creation in Ge 1.
104:9 *set a boundary.* So that the land ("earth") will never be overwhelmed by the sea (cf. v. 5; see 33:7 and note; see also Ge 9:15).
104:10–18 The earth a flourishing garden of life—the center of the psalm and the focal point of the author's contemplation of the creation (the earth, bounded by sky, vv. 2–4, and sea, vv. 24–26). Cf. the third and sixth days of creation in Ge 1.
104:10–12 The gift of water from below—watering the ravines of the Negev, south of Israel's heartland.
104:11 *wild donkeys.* Properly wild asses (onagers); see Job 6:5 and note.
104:13–15 The gift of water from above—watering the uplands of Israel's heartland with its cultivated fields.
104:13 *upper chambers.* See v. 3 and note.
104:15 *heart ... heart.* See note on 4:7. *oil.* Olive oil. *make his face shine.* As food (see 1Ki 17:12), causing a person's face to glow with health, and/or as cosmetic (see Est 2:12).
104:16–18 Well-watered Lebanon (north of Israel's heartland), with its great trees, its hordes of birds and its alpine animals, the very epitome of God's earthly parkland (see 72:16; 2Ki 14:9; 19:23; Isa 10:34; 35:2; 40:16; 60:13; Jer 22:6; Hos 14:7).
104:19–23 The orderly cycles of life (the temporal element; see notes on vv. 2–4,5–9; see also introduction) on earth, governed by the moon and sun. Cf. the fourth day of creation in Ge 1.
104:21,23 *lions ... man.* The one (representing the animal world), lord of the night; the other, lord of the day.
104:24–26 The nautical realm below (see note on vv. 19–23). Cf. the fifth day of creation in Ge 1. The realm of the sea is structurally balanced with the celestial realm (vv. 2–4) as the other boundary to the realm of earth.
104:24 A pause to recapitulate before treating the sea.
104:25 *teeming.* See Ge 1:20–21.
104:26 *leviathan.* That fearsome mythological monster of the deep (see Job 3:8 and note) is here portrayed as nothing more than God's harmless pet playing in the ocean.

27 These all look to you
to give them their food[g] at the proper time.
28 When you give it to them,
they gather it up;
when you open your hand,
they are satisfied[h] with good things.
29 When you hide your face,[i]
they are terrified;
when you take away their breath,
they die and return to the dust.[j]
30 When you send your Spirit,[k]
they are created,
and you renew the face of the earth.

31 May the glory of the LORD[l] endure forever;
may the LORD rejoice in his works[m]—
32 he who looks at the earth, and it trembles,[n]
who touches the mountains,[o] and they smoke.[p]

33 I will sing[q] to the LORD all my life;
I will sing praise to my God as long as I live.
34 May my meditation be pleasing to him,
as I rejoice[r] in the LORD.
35 But may sinners vanish[s] from the earth
and the wicked be no more.[t]
Praise the LORD, O my soul.
Praise the LORD.[a][u]

104:27 [g] Job 36:31; Ps 145:15; 147:9 **104:28** [h] Ps 103:5; 145:16; Isa 58:11 **104:29** [i] S Dt 31:17 [j] S Job 7:21 **104:30** [k] S Ge 1:2 **104:31** [l] Ex 40:35; Ps 8:1; S Ro 11:36 [m] S Ge 1:4 **104:32** [n] S Ps 97:4 [o] S Ex 19:18 [p] Ps 144:5 **104:33** [q] S Ex 15:1; Ps 108:1 **104:34** [r] S Ps 2:11; 9:2; 32:11 **104:35** [s] Ps 37:38 [t] S Job 7:10 [u] Ps 28:6; 105:45; 106:48

Psalm 105

105:1-15pp — 1Ch 16:8-22

1 Give thanks to the LORD,[v] call on his name;[w]
make known among the nations what he has done.
2 Sing to him,[x] sing praise[y] to him;
tell of all his wonderful acts.[z]
3 Glory in his holy name;[a]
let the hearts of those who seek the LORD rejoice.
4 Look to the LORD and his strength;
seek his face[b] always.

5 Remember the wonders[c] he has done,
his miracles, and the judgments he pronounced,[d]
6 O descendants of Abraham his servant,[e]
O sons of Jacob, his chosen[f] ones.
7 He is the LORD our God;
his judgments are in all the earth.

8 He remembers his covenant[g] forever,
the word he commanded, for a thousand generations,

105:1 [v] S 1Ch 16:34 [w] Ps 80:18; 99:6; 116:13; Joel 2:32; Ac 2:21 **105:2** [x] Ps 30:4; 33:3; 96:1 [y] Ps 7:17; 18:49; 27:6; 59:17; 71:22; 146:2 [z] S Ps 75:1 **105:3** [a] S Ps 89:16

[a] *35* Hebrew *Hallelu Yah*; in the Septuagint this line stands at the beginning of Psalm 105.

105:4 [b] S Ps 24:6 **105:5** [c] S Ps 40:5 [d] S Dt 7:18 **105:6** [e] ver 42 [f] S Dt 10:15; Ps 106:5 **105:8** [g] S Ge 9:15; Ps 106:45; 111:5; Eze 16:60; S Lk 1:72

104:27 – 30 By God's benevolent care this zoological garden flourishes. Cf. the sixth day of creation in Ge 1.
104:29 *hide your face.* See note on 13:1.
104:30 *your Spirit.* See note on 51:11. *created.* See note on 102:18.
104:31 *glory of the LORD.* Such as is displayed in his creation (see 19:1 – 4a and note).
104:32 He is so much greater than his creation that with a look or a touch he could undo it.
104:33 – 35 A concluding expression of the psalmist's devotion to Yahweh (cf. NIV text note on v. 35).
104:33 A vow to praise — here attached to a hymn of praise (see note on 7:17).
104:34 *my meditation.* The preceding hymn (see 19:14 and note).
104:35 May the earth be purged of that which alone mars it (cf. Rev 21:27). *Praise the LORD* (last occurrence). Probably belonged originally to Ps 105 (see NIV text note and 105:45; 106:1,48).
Ps 105 An exhortation to Israel to worship and trust in the Lord because of all his saving acts in fulfillment of his covenant with Abraham to give his descendants the land of Canaan. It was composed to be addressed to Israel by a Levite (see 1Ch 16:7 and compare vv. 1 – 15 with 1Ch 16:8 – 22) on one of Israel's annual religious fes tivals (see chart, pp. 178 – 179), possibly the Feast of Tabernacles (see Lev 23:34) but more likely the Feast of Weeks or Pentecost (see Ex 23:16; Lev 23:15 – 21; Nu 28:26; Dt 16:9 – 12; see also Dt 26:1 – 11). For other recitals of the same history (but for different purposes) see Ps 78; 106; Jos 24:2 – 13; Ne 9:7 – 25. For the relationship of this psalm to Ps 106 in the arrangement of the Psalter see introduction to Ps 101 – 110.
The introduction is composed of seven verses in two parts: (1) an exhortation (with ten imperatives) to worship the Lord (vv. 1 – 4); (2) a call to remember what the Lord has done (vv. 5 – 7). The main body that follows is framed by two four-verse stanzas (vv. 8 – 11,42 – 45) that summarize — as introduction and conclusion — its main theme: The Lord has remembered his covenant with Abraham. The editors of the Psalter have added an outer frame of "Hallelujahs" (see introduction to Ps 104; see also note on 104:35).
105:1 – 4 The exhortation to worship and trust.
105:1 *Give thanks.* Through praise (see note on Ps 100 title). *call on.* In prayer (see v. 4). The first two imperatives highlight the two themes of the ten imperatives of the exhortation: praise and prayer as expressions of devotion to the Lord (celebration of his past saving acts; trust in him for future deliverance and blessing). *his name.* See v. 3; see also note on 5:11. *make known among the nations.* As an integral part of praise (see note on 9:1).
105:2 *wonderful acts.* See v. 5 ("wonders"); see also note on 9:1.
105:3,25 *hearts.* See note on 4:7.
105:5 – 7 Exhortation to remember God's saving acts.
105:5 *Remember.* As a motivation for and focus of worship and the basis for trust — remember how the Lord has remembered (see vv. 8 – 11). *judgments.* See v. 7; see also notes on 48:11; 97:8. *pronounced.* As Lord, he commands and it is done (see 7:6 ["decree justice"]; 33:9; 71:3; 78:23; 147:15,18; 148:5; Isa 5:6; 55:11; Jer 1:12; Am 9:3 – 4).
105:6,9 *Abraham ... Jacob ... Isaac.* While "Jacob" occurs 34 times in the Psalter, Abraham is recalled by name in Psalms only here (see also v. 42) and in 47:9. Reference to Isaac occurs in Psalms only here.
105:8 – 11 The Lord remembers his covenant with Abraham (see vv. 42 – 45).
105:8 *covenant.* The promissory covenant of Ge 15:9 – 21 (see chart, p. 19). This verse and v. 9 may be echoed in Lk 1:72 – 73. *thousand generations.* See Ex 20:6; Dt 7:9; 1Ch 16:15.

9 the covenant he made with Abraham,[h]
the oath he swore to Isaac.
10 He confirmed it[i] to Jacob as a decree,
to Israel as an everlasting
covenant:[j]
11 "To you I will give the land of Canaan[k]
as the portion you will inherit."[l]

12 When they were but few in number,[m]
few indeed, and strangers in it,[n]
13 they wandered from nation to nation,[o]
from one kingdom to another.
14 He allowed no one to oppress[p] them;
for their sake he rebuked kings:[q]
15 "Do not touch[r] my anointed ones;
do my prophets[s] no harm."

16 He called down famine[t] on the land
and destroyed all their supplies of
food;
17 and he sent a man before them—
Joseph, sold as a slave.[u]
18 They bruised his feet with shackles,[v]
his neck was put in irons,
19 till what he foretold[w] came to pass,
till the word[x] of the LORD proved him
true.
20 The king sent and released him,
the ruler of peoples set him free.[y]
21 He made him master of his
household,
ruler over all he possessed,
22 to instruct his princes[z] as he pleased
and teach his elders wisdom.[a]

23 Then Israel entered Egypt;[b]
Jacob lived[c] as an alien in the land
of Ham.[d]
24 The LORD made his people very fruitful;
he made them too numerous[e] for
their foes,
25 whose hearts he turned[f] to hate his
people,
to conspire[g] against his servants.
26 He sent Moses[h] his servant,
and Aaron,[i] whom he had chosen.[j]

105:9 [h]Ge 12:7; S 15:18; S 22:16-18; Lk 1:73; Gal 3:15-18 **105:10** [i]Ge 28:13-15 [j]Isa 55:3 **105:11** [k]S Ge 12:7 [l]S Nu 34:2 **105:12** [m]Dt 7:7 [n]Ge 23:4; Heb 11:9 **105:13** [o]Ge 15:13-16; Nu 32:13; 33:3-49 **105:14** [p]Ge 35:5 [q]Ge 12:17-20; S 20:3; S Ps 9:5 **105:15** [r]S Ge 26:11; S 1Sa 12:3 [s]S Ge 20:7 **105:16** [t]S Ge 12:10; S Lev 26:26; Isa 3:1; Eze 4:16 **105:17** [u]S Ge 37:28; Ac 7:9 **105:18** [v]S Ge 40:15 **105:19** [w]S Ge 12:10; 40:20-22 [x]Ge 41:40 **105:20** [y]Ge 41:14 **105:22** [z]Ge 41:43-44 [a]S Ge 41:40 **105:23** [b]Ge 46:6; Ac 7:15; 13:17 [c]Ge 47:28 [d]S Ps 78:51 **105:24** [e]Ex 1:7,9; Ac 7:17 **105:25** [f]S Ex 4:21 [g]Ex 1:6-10; Ac 7:19 **105:26** [h]S Ex 3:10 [i]S Ex 4:16; S Nu 33:1 [j]S Nu 16:5; 17:5-8 **105:27** [k]ver 28-37;

27 They performed[k] his miraculous signs[l]
among them,
his wonders[m] in the land of Ham.
28 He sent darkness[n] and made the land
dark—
for had they not rebelled against[o] his
words?
29 He turned their waters into blood,[p]
causing their fish to die.[q]
30 Their land teemed with frogs,[r]
which went up into the bedrooms of
their rulers.
31 He spoke,[s] and there came swarms of
flies,[t]
and gnats[u] throughout their country.
32 He turned their rain into hail,[v]
with lightning throughout their land;
33 he struck down their vines[w] and fig
trees[x]
and shattered the trees of their
country.
34 He spoke,[y] and the locusts came,[z]
grasshoppers[a] without number;[b]
35 they ate up every green thing in their
land,
ate up the produce of their soil.
36 Then he struck down all the firstborn[c]
in their land,
the firstfruits of all their manhood.
37 He brought out Israel, laden with silver
and gold,[d]
and from among their tribes no one
faltered.
38 Egypt was glad when they left,
because dread of Israel[e] had fallen
on them.
39 He spread out a cloud[f] as a covering,
and a fire to give light at night.[g]

Ex 7:8-12:51 [l]S Ex 4:17; S 10:1 [m]S Ex 3:20; Da 4:3 **105:28** [n]S Ge 1:4; S Ex 10:22 [o]S Ex 7:22 **105:29** [p]S Ps 78:44 [q]Ex 7:21 **105:30** [r]S Ex 8:2,6 **105:31** [s]Ps 107:25; 148:8 [t]Ex 8:21-24; S Ps 78:45 [u]Ex 8:16-18 **105:32** [v]Ex 9:22-25; S Job 38:22; S Ps 78:47 **105:33** [w]Ps 78:47 [x]Ex 10:5,12 **105:34** [y]Ps 107:25 [z]S Ex 10:4,12-15 [a]S 1Ki 8:37 [b]Joel 1:6 **105:36** [c]S Ex 4:23; S 12:12 **105:37** [d]S Ex 3:21,22 **105:38** [e]Ex 15:16 **105:39** [f]S Ex 13:21; 1Co 10:1 [g]S Ps 78:14

105:10 *as a decree.* As a fixed policy governing his future actions (see note on v. 45).

105:12–41 A recital of God's saving acts in Israel's behalf from the granting of the covenant (see v. 11; Ge 15:9–21) to its fulfillment (see v. 44; Jos 21:43). Cf. the recital prescribed by Moses in conjunction with the offering of firstfruits (Dt 26:1–11).

105:14–15 See Ge 20:2–7 and note on 20:7.

105:18 *shackles ... irons.* That is, shackles of iron (see 149:8; see also note on 3:7). The poet takes the freedom to use a later conventional description of prisoners (see Job 13:27; 33:11). (Shackles are not spoken of in Ge 39:20–23, and iron came into common use for them at a later time—earlier shackles were made of bronze; see Jdg 16:21.)

105:22 *instruct.* Lit. "bind," i.e., govern or control. He whose "neck" (v. 18; Hebrew *nephesh*) had been shackled was given authority to "bind" the pharaoh's princes "as he pleased" (Hebrew "with his *nephesh*"—here meaning his will). *elders.* The pharaoh's counselors, conventionally older men of wide experience and learning (see note on Ex 3:16).

105:23,27 *land of Ham.* See 78:51 and note.

105:25 *turned.* In OT perspective God's sovereign control over Israel's destiny is so complete that it governs—mysteriously—even the evil that others commit against them; hence the bold language used here (see Ex 4:21; 7:3; Jos 11:20; 2Sa 24:1; Isa 10:5–7; 37:26–27; Jer 34:22).

105:26,42 *servant.* See 78:70 and note.

105:28–36 Recital of the plagues against Egypt. In this poetic recollection seven plagues (symbolizing completeness) represent the ten plagues of Ex 7–11. Apart from omissions (the plagues of livestock disease and boils) the poet follows the order of Exodus except that he combines the third and fourth plagues (gnats and flies)—in reverse order—to stay within the number seven. He also places the ninth plague (darkness) first in order to frame his recital with mention of the two plagues that climaxed the series.

105:37 *laden with silver and gold.* See Ex 3:22 and note; 12:35–36.

105:39 *as a covering.* Elsewhere it is said that the cloud (symbolic of God's presence) served (1) as a guide for Israel in her desert journeys (see 78:14; Ex 13:21; Nu 9:17; Ne

40 They asked,[h] and he brought them
quail[i]
and satisfied them with the bread of
heaven.[j]
41 He opened the rock,[k] and water gushed
out;
like a river it flowed in the desert.
42 For he remembered his holy promise[l]
given to his servant Abraham.
43 He brought out his people with
rejoicing,[m]
his chosen ones with shouts of joy;
44 he gave them the lands of the nations,[n]
and they fell heir to what others had
toiled[o] for —
45 that they might keep his precepts
and observe his laws.[p]

Praise the LORD.[a][q]

Psalm 106

106:1,47-48pp — 1Ch 16:34-36

1 Praise the LORD.[b][r]

Give thanks to the LORD, for he is
good;[s]
his love endures forever.[t]
2 Who can proclaim the mighty acts[u] of
the LORD
or fully declare his praise?
3 Blessed are they who maintain justice,[v]
who constantly do what is right.[w]
4 Remember me,[x] O LORD, when you
show favor[y] to your people,
come to my aid[z] when you save
them,
5 that I may enjoy the prosperity[a] of your
chosen ones,[b]
that I may share in the joy[c] of your
nation
and join your inheritance[d] in giving
praise.

105:40 [h]Ps 78:18,24 [i]S Ex 16:13 [j]S Ex 16:4; Jn 6:31 **105:41** [k]S Nu 20:11; 1Co 10:4 **105:42** [l]Ge 12:1-3; 13:14-17; 15:13-16 **105:43** [m]Ex 15:1-18; Ps 106:12 **105:44** [n]Ex 32:13; Jos 11:16-23; 12:8; 13:6-7; Ps 111:6 [o]Dt 6:10-11; Ps 78:55 **105:45** [p]S Dt 4:40; 6:21-24; Ps 78:5-7 [q]S Ps 104:35 **106:1** [r]S Ps 22:23; S 103:2 [s]S Ps 119:68 [t]S Ezr 3:11; Ps 136:1-26; Jer 33:11 **106:2** [u]S Ps 71:16 **106:3** [v]Ps 112:5; Hos 12:6 [w]Ps 15:2 **106:4** [x]Ps 25:6,7 [y]S Ps 77:7 [z]S Ge 50:24 **106:5** [a]S Dt 30:15; Ps 1:3 [b]S Ps 105:6 [c]Ps 20:5; 27:6; 47:5; 118:15 [d]S Ex 34:9

[a] *45* Hebrew *Hallelu Yah* [b] *1* Hebrew *Hallelu Yah*; also in verse 48

9:12,19), (2) as a shield of darkness to protect Israel from the pursuing Egyptians (see Ex 14:19–20) and (3) as a covering for the fiery manifestations of God's glorious presence (see Ex 16:10; 24:16; 34:5; 40:34–35,38; Nu 11:25; 12:5; 16:42; Dt 31:15; 1Ki 8:11). The psalmist appears to highlight yet another function: God's protective cover over his people in the desert, perhaps as his shading "wings" (17:8; see note there), so that the sun would not harm them by day (see 121:5–6).

105:40 *bread of heaven.* See 78:24–25 and note on 78:25.

105:41 *like a river.* Poetically heightened imagery to evoke due wonder for the event. This miracle of the desert wanderings concludes the recital and has been placed in climactic position as one of the most striking manifestations of God's redeeming power and benevolence (see 114:8; Isa 43:19–20; cf. Isa 50:2).

105:42–45 Concluding summary (balancing the introduction to the recital: vv. 8–11).

105:44 *gave them the lands.* See v. 11.

105:45 *precepts.* God has kept his "decree" (v. 10) so that Israel might keep his "precepts" — the Hebrew word is the same (see note on v. 5: "remember"). God's redemptive working in fulfillment of his covenant promise has as its goal the creating of a people in the earth who conform their lives to his holy will (see Isa 5:1–7). Thus the list of appropriate responses begun in v. 1 — praise and prayer (trust) — is completed by the third: obedience (see Ge 18:19).

Ps 106 A confession of Israel's long history of rebellion and a prayer for God to once again save his people. In length, poetic style and shared themes it has much affinity with Ps 105 even while it contrasts with it by reciting the past as a history of rebellion (see Ps 78; Ne 9:5–37). It was most likely authored by a Levite in Jerusalem sometime after the return of some of the exiles. The first verse and the last two verses seem to have been taken over from an earlier composition (see 1Ch 16:34–36). These may have been added (along with the "Hallelujah"; see NIV text note) by the editors of the Psalter (borrowing from an earlier Davidic psalter) when they set the Book divisions between Ps 106 and 107. See further the introduction to Ps 101–110.

In the final edited form of the Psalter, the psalm is set between two liturgical calls to praise ("Hallelujah!"). Within this outer frame stands another, also drawn from the liturgical language of praise (vv. 1b,48a; see notes there). And still a third frame (formed by two couplets devoted to prayer [vv. 4–5,47; see notes there]) encloses the main body of the psalm. Verses 2–3 are transitional. While the recital character of the central theme (as in Ps 105; see also Ps 78) controls the basic outline, attention to symmetry brings to light the carefully designed pattern of thematic development. The recital begins with 14 Hebrew poetic lines devoted to the period of the exodus and the desert wanderings (vv. 6–18) and ends with 14 Hebrew lines devoted to Israel's time in the promised land (34–46). The intervening verses (19–33) make up three stanzas with a six-four-six line pattern. In the two six-line stanzas, instances of Israel's engagement in idolatry in the desert period are recalled (the golden calf at Mt. Horeb [vv. 19–23]; the Baal of Peor in the plains of Moab [vv. 28–33]). These stanzas each end with a word about Moses: In the first, Moses intercedes for Israel and wards off God's wrath; in the second, Israel so vexes Moses that he acts rashly and loses his opportunity to enter the promised land — a most poignant contrast. At the center, a four-line stanza recalls Israel's refusal to take over the promised land and Yahweh's condemnation of that generation to die in the desert (see Nu 14:1–23; cf. Heb 3:16–19 and note).

106:1–5 Introduction.

106:1 *Give thanks.* With praise (see note on Ps 100 title); a conventional liturgical call to praise (see 107:1; 118:1,29; 136:1). *love.* See note on 6:4.

106:2–3 Transition to the main body of the psalm — question and answer.

106:2 *Who can …?* With integrity. *his praise.* Praise for his mighty acts (see v. 47; see also note on 9:1).

106:3 *Blessed.* See note on 1:1. *justice … what is right.* That is, justice-and-righteousness (see 36:6 and note; see also notes on 3:7; 119:121). This verse answers the question posed in v. 2.

106:4–5 A poetic couplet, voicing the prayer of an individual (cf. v. 47).

106:4 *Remember me.* As one committed to the way of life described in v. 3. *when you show favor.* Or "with the favor you show" (see vv. 44–46). *when you save them.* Or "with your salvation." The psalmist prays that God will include him in all the mercies of his "great love" (v. 45), which he shows to his people. Thus the inner logic of the prayer seems to be completed at v. 46.

106:5 *prosperity … joy … praise.* A progressive sequence of cause and effect. *your inheritance.* See v. 40.

[6] We have sinned,[e] even as our fathers[f] did;
we have done wrong and acted wickedly.[g]
[7] When our fathers were in Egypt,
they gave no thought[h] to your miracles;
they did not remember[i] your many kindnesses,
and they rebelled by the sea,[j] the Red Sea.[a]
[8] Yet he saved them[k] for his name's sake,[l]
to make his mighty power[m] known.
[9] He rebuked[n] the Red Sea, and it dried up;[o]
he led them through[p] the depths as through a desert.
[10] He saved them[q] from the hand of the foe;[r]
from the hand of the enemy he redeemed them.[s]
[11] The waters covered[t] their adversaries;
not one of them survived.
[12] Then they believed his promises
and sang his praise.[u]

[13] But they soon forgot[v] what he had done
and did not wait for his counsel.[w]
[14] In the desert[x] they gave in to their craving;
in the wasteland[y] they put God to the test.[z]
[15] So he gave them[a] what they asked for,
but sent a wasting disease[b] upon them.
[16] In the camp they grew envious[c] of Moses
and of Aaron, who was consecrated to the LORD.
[17] The earth opened[d] up and swallowed Dathan;[e]
it buried the company of Abiram.[f]
[18] Fire blazed[g] among their followers;
a flame consumed the wicked.

106:6 [e] S 1Ki 8:47; S Ro 3:9 [f] S 2Ch 30:7 [g] Ne 1:7 **106:7** [h] S Jdg 3:7 [i] Ps 78:11,42 [j] Ex 14:11-12 **106:8** [k] Ex 14:30; S Ps 80:3; 107:13; Isa 25:9; Joel 2:32 [l] S Ex 9:16; S Ps 23:3 [m] S Ex 14:31 **106:9** [n] Ps 18:15; Isa 50:2 [o] S Ex 14:21; Na 1:4 [p] Ps 78:13; Isa 63:11-14 **106:10** [q] Ex 14:30; Ps 107:13 [r] S Ps 78:53 [s] Ps 78:42; 107:2; Isa 35:9; 62:12 **106:11** [t] S Ex 14:28 **106:12** [u] Ex 15:1-21; S Ps 105:43 **106:13** [v] S Ex 15:24 [w] S Ex 16:28; S Nu 27:21 **106:14** [x] S Ps 78:40 [y] S Ps 68:7 [z] S Ex 17:2; 1Co 10:9 **106:15** [a] S Ex 16:13; Ps 78:29 [b] S Nu 11:33 **106:16** [c] Nu 16:1-3 **106:17** [d] Dt 11:6 [e] S Ex 15:12 [f] S Nu 16:1 **106:18** [g] S Lev 10:2 **106:19** [h] S Ex 32:4; Ac 7:41 **106:20** [i] Jer 2:11; Ro 1:23 **106:21** [j] Ps 78:11 [k] Dt 10:21; Ps 75:1 **106:22** [l] S Ps 78:51 [m] S Ex 3:20; S Dt 4:34 **106:23** [n] S Ex 32:10

[19] At Horeb they made a calf[h]
and worshiped an idol cast from metal.
[20] They exchanged their Glory[i]
for an image of a bull, which eats grass.
[21] They forgot the God[j] who saved them,
who had done great things[k] in Egypt,
[22] miracles in the land of Ham[l]
and awesome deeds[m] by the Red Sea.
[23] So he said he would destroy[n] them—
had not Moses, his chosen one,
stood in the breach[o] before him
to keep his wrath from destroying them.

[24] Then they despised[p] the pleasant land;[q]
they did not believe[r] his promise.
[25] They grumbled[s] in their tents
and did not obey the LORD.
[26] So he swore[t] to them with uplifted hand
that he would make them fall in the desert,[u]
[27] make their descendants fall among the nations
and scatter[v] them throughout the lands.

[28] They yoked themselves to the Baal of Peor[w]
and ate sacrifices offered to lifeless gods;
[29] they provoked the LORD to anger[x] by their wicked deeds,[y]
and a plague[z] broke out among them.
[30] But Phinehas[a] stood up and intervened,
and the plague was checked.[b]

[a] 7 Hebrew *Yam Suph*; that is, Sea of Reeds; also in verses 9 and 22

[o] Ex 32:11-14; S Nu 11:2; S Dt 9:19 **106:24** [p] Nu 14:30-31 [q] S Dt 8:7; S Jer 3:19 [r] S Nu 14:11; Heb 3:18-19 **106:25** [s] S Ex 15:24; Dt 1:27; 1Co 10:10 **106:26** [t] S Nu 14:23; Heb 4:3 [u] S Dt 2:14; Heb 3:17 **106:27** [v] S Lev 26:33 **106:28** [w] S Nu 23:28 **106:29** [x] Nu 25:3 [y] S Ps 64:2; 141:4 [z] S Nu 16:46; 25:8 **106:30** [a] S Ex 6:25 [b] Nu 25:8

106:6–12 Israel's rebelliousness and the Lord's mercy in the exodus event.
106:6 A general confession of sin introducing the recital. *We.* The author identifies himself with Israel in her rebellion even as he prays for inclusion in God's mercies toward his people (see Ezr 9:6–7).
106:7,22 *miracles.* For example, the plagues against Egypt (see note on 9:1, "wonders").
106:10 *redeemed.* Here, as often, a synonym for "delivered" (see note on 71:23).
106:12 *sang his praise.* See Ex 15:1–21.
106:13–18 Israel's discontent and the Lord's judgments.
106:13–15 Discontent with the Lord's provisions (see Ex 16; Nu 11).
106:13 *his counsel.* The working out of his plan.
106:16–18 Discontent with the Lord's leadership arrangements (see Nu 16:1–35).
106:19–23 Idolatry at Mt. Horeb and Moses' intercession.
106:19 *Horeb.* See note on Ex 3:1.
106:20 *Glory.* Glorious One (see 1Sa 15:29; Jer 2:11 and notes; Hos 4:7).
106:22 *land of Ham.* See 78:51 and note.
106:23 *stood in the breach.* See Ex 32:11–14,31–32. *wrath.* See note on 2:5.
106:24–27 Israel's lack of faith at the border of the promised land and the Lord's judgment (see Nu 14:1–23).
106:24 *pleasant land.* So described in Jer 3:19; 12:10; Zec 7:14; see also Dt 8:7–9; Eze 20:6.
106:26–27 *fall.* See note on 13:4.
106:27 *scatter them throughout the lands.* See Lev 26:33; Dt 28:36–37,64 and note; Eze 20:23.
106:28–33 Idolatry at Peor—and Moses' loss.
106:28 *yoked themselves to.* See Nu 25:3,5 ("joined in worshiping").

[31]This was credited to him[c] as
righteousness
for endless generations[d] to come.
[32]By the waters of Meribah[e] they angered
the LORD,
and trouble came to Moses because
of them;
[33]for they rebelled[f] against the Spirit[g] of
God,
and rash words came from Moses'
lips.[a h]
[34]They did not destroy[i] the peoples
as the LORD had commanded[j] them,
[35]but they mingled[k] with the nations
and adopted their customs.
[36]They worshiped their idols,[l]
which became a snare[m] to them.
[37]They sacrificed their sons[n]
and their daughters to demons.[o]
[38]They shed innocent blood,
the blood of their sons[p] and
daughters,
whom they sacrificed to the idols of
Canaan,
and the land was desecrated by their
blood.
[39]They defiled themselves[q] by what they
did;
by their deeds they prostituted[r]
themselves.
[40]Therefore the LORD was angry[s] with his
people
and abhorred his inheritance.[t]

106:31 [c]S Ge 15:6; S Nu 25:11-13 [d]Ps 49:11 **106:32** [e]S Ex 17:7; Nu 20:2-13 **106:33** [f]S Ex 23:21; Ps 107:11 [g]S Ps 51:11; Isa 63:10 [h]Ex 17:4-7; Nu 20:8-12 **106:34** [i]S Jos 9:15; Jdg 1:27-36 [j]Ex 23:24; S Dt 2:34; 7:16; 20:17 **106:35** [k]Jdg 3:5-6; Ezr 9:1-2 **106:36** [l]S Dt 7:16 [m]S Ex 10:7 **106:37** [n]S Lev 18:21; S Dt 12:31; Eze 16:20-21 [o]S Ex 22:20; S Dt 32:17; 1Co 10:20 **106:38** [p]S Lev 18:21; S Dt 18:10; S 2Ki 3:27 **106:39** [q]S Ge 3:17; Lev 18:24; Eze 20:18 [r]S Nu 15:39 **106:40** [s]S Lev 26:28 [t]S Ex 34:9; S Dt 9:29 **106:41** [u]S Jdg 2:14

[41]He handed them over[u] to the nations,
and their foes ruled over them.
[42]Their enemies oppressed[v] them
and subjected them to their power.
[43]Many times he delivered them,[w]
but they were bent on rebellion[x]
and they wasted away in their sin.

[44]But he took note of their distress
when he heard their cry;[y]
[45]for their sake he remembered his
covenant[z]
and out of his great love[a] he
relented.[b]
[46]He caused them to be pitied[c]
by all who held them captive.

[47]Save us,[d] O LORD our God,
and gather us[e] from the nations,
that we may give thanks[f] to your holy
name[g]
and glory in your praise.

[48]Praise be to the LORD, the God of
Israel,
from everlasting to everlasting.
Let all the people say, "Amen!"[h]
Praise the LORD.

[a] 33 Or *against his spirit, / and rash words came from his lips*

106:42 [v]S Jdg 4:3 **106:43** [w]S Jos 10:14; Jdg 7:1-25; S Ne 9:28; Ps 81:13-14 [x]S Jdg 2:16-19; 6:1-7 **106:44** [y]S Jdg 3:9 **106:45** [z]S Ge 9:15; Ps 105:8; S Lk 1:72 [a]S Ps 17:7; S 103:11 [b]S Ex 32:14 **106:46** [c]S Ex 3:21; S 1Ki 8:50 **106:47** [d]S Ps 28:9 [e]Ps 107:3; 147:2; Isa 11:12; 27:13; 56:8; 66:20; Jer 31:8; Eze 20:34; Mic 4:6 [f]Ps 105:1 [g]Ps 30:4; S 99:3 **106:48** [h]S Ps 41:13; S 72:19

106:31 *credited to him as righteousness.* As Abram's faith was "credited to him as righteousness" (Ge 15:6), so, says the psalmist, was Phinehas's priestly zeal for the Lord (see Nu 25:7–8). *for endless generations.* The psalmist refers to the "covenant of a lasting priesthood" (Nu 25:13) that the Lord granted Phinehas as a gracious reward for his zealous act. It was the granting of this promissory covenant that warranted the statement about crediting righteousness, for God's granting of a promissory covenant to Abram had followed upon his crediting Abram's faith to him as righteousness (see Ge 15:9–21). Similarly, God's promissory covenants with Noah (see Ge 9:9–17) and with David (see 2Sa 7:5–16) followed upon God's testimony to their righteousness (see Ge 7:1; 1Sa 13:14). See chart, p. 19.
106:32 *Meribah.* See note on Ex 17:7.
106:33 *against the Spirit of God.* For a literal rendering of the Hebrew see NIV text note. The interpretation embodied in the NIV text appears warranted by Isa 63:10 (see also Ps 78:40). For the Spirit of God present and at work in the desert wanderings see Ex 31:3; Nu 11:17; 24:2; Ne 9:20; Isa 63:10–14. See also note on 51:11.
106:34–39 A general description of Israel's rebelliousness in the promised land, applicable from the time of the judges to the Babylonian exile.
106:36 *became a snare to them.* See Ex 23:33; Dt 7:16; Jdg 2:3; 8:27; cf. Ex 10:7; 34:12; 1Sa 18:21; cf. also note on 9:15.
106:37 *demons.* The Hebrew for this word occurs elsewhere in the OT only in Dt 32:17, where it refers to false gods. It is related to a Babylonian word referring to (pagan) protective spirits.
106:38 Cf. Jer 19:4–5. *innocent blood.* The blood of anyone not guilty of a capital crime. *desecrated.* The very land itself is defiled by the slaughter of innocents (see Nu 35:33; Jer 3:2,9).
106:39 *defiled.* See Lev 18:24; Jer 2:23; Eze 20:30–31; 22:3–4. *prostituted themselves.* See Ex 34:15 and note.
106:40–46 God's stern measures against his rebellious people (vv. 40–43), but at the same time his gracious remembering of his covenant (vv. 44–46). The judgments here recalled focus particularly on God's most severe covenant sanctions (see Lev 26:25–26,33,38–39; Dt 28:25,36–37,48–57,64–68).
106:40 *angry.* See note on 2:5. *abhorred.* See 5:6.
106:44 *heard their cry.* See Ex 2:23; 3:7–9; Nu 20:16; Jdg 3:9,15; 4:3; 6:6–7; 10:10; 1Sa 9:16; 2Ch 20:6–12; Ne 9:27–28.
106:45 *remembered his covenant.* See 105:8,42; Ex 2:24; Lev 26:42,45. *love.* See note on 6:4.
106:46 *pitied by all who held them captive.* Makes clear that the author's recital includes the Babylonian captivity (see 1Ki 8:50; 2Ch 30:9; Ezr 9:9; Jer 42:12). Although there were earlier captivities of Israelite communities, no other captive group was said to have been shown pity.
106:47 A communal prayer for deliverance and restoration from dispersion (see introduction and note on v. 4). *name.* See note on 5:11. *glory in.* Triumphantly celebrate. The Hebrew for this phrase is found elsewhere only in the parallel in 1Ch 16:35. *praise.* See note on 9:1.
106:48a A conventional word of praise, serving as the doxology to close the psalm and Book IV (see 41:13 and note; see also introduction to this psalm and note on v. 1).
106:48b *Let all the people say.* 1Ch 16:36 sets off the closing exclamations somewhat differently. *Amen!* See Dt 27:15 and note; 1Ch 16:36; Ne 5:13; Jer 11:5; Rom 1:25 and note; 1Co 14:16.

BOOK V

Psalms 107–150

Psalm 107

1 Give thanks to the LORD,[i] for he is good;[j]
his love endures forever.
2 Let the redeemed[k] of the LORD say this—
those he redeemed from the hand of the foe,
3 those he gathered[l] from the lands,
from east and west, from north and south.[a]
4 Some wandered in desert[m] wastelands,
finding no way to a city[n] where they could settle.
5 They were hungry[o] and thirsty,[p]
and their lives ebbed away.
6 Then they cried out[q] to the LORD in their trouble,
and he delivered them from their distress.
7 He led them by a straight way[r]
to a city[s] where they could settle.
8 Let them give thanks[t] to the LORD for his unfailing love[u]
and his wonderful deeds[v] for men,
9 for he satisfies[w] the thirsty
and fills the hungry with good things.[x]
10 Some sat in darkness[y] and the deepest gloom,
prisoners suffering[z] in iron chains,[a]
11 for they had rebelled[b] against the words of God
and despised[c] the counsel[d] of the Most High.

107:1 [i] S 1Ch 16:8; S 2Ch 5:13 [j] S 2Ch 7:3 **107:2** [k] S Ps 106:10; S Isa 35:9 **107:3** [l] S Ne 1:9 **107:4** [m] S Jos 5:6 [n] ver 36 **107:5** [o] Ex 16:3 [p] S Ex 15:22; S 17:2 **107:6** [q] S Ex 14:10 **107:7** [r] S Ezr 8:21 [s] ver 36 **107:8** [t] Ps 105:1 [u] Ps 6:4 [v] S Ps 75:1 **107:9** [w] Ps 22:26; 63:5; Isa 58:11; Mt 5:6; Lk 1:53 [x] S Ps 23:1; Jer 31:25 **107:10** [y] ver 14; Ps 88:6; 143:3; Isa 9:2; 42:7,16; 49:9; Mic 7:9 [z] Ps 102:20; Isa 61:1 [a] S Job 36:8 **107:11** [b] S Ps 5:10 [c] S Nu 14:11 [d] S 1Ki 22:5; 2Ch 36:16

[a] 3 Hebrew *north and the sea*

Ps 107 An exhortation to praise the Lord for his unfailing love in that he hears the prayers of those in need and saves them (see next paragraph—on structure). It was composed for liturgical use at one of Israel's annual religious festivals. Interpretations vary widely, but the following is most likely: Having experienced anew God's mercies in her return from Babylonian exile (v. 3; see Jer 33:11), Israel is led by a Levite in celebrating God's unfailing benevolence toward those who have cried to him in the crises of their lives. In its recitational style the psalm is closely related to Ps 104–106, and in its language to Ps 105–106. For that reason it has been seriously proposed that with these last two psalms it forms a trilogy from the same author. Whether or not this is so, its affinity with the preceding psalms strongly suggests that it was associated with them before the insertion of a Book division between Ps 106 and 107 and that it was intended to conclude the little series, Ps 104–107. Its recital of God's "wonderful deeds for men" (v. 8)—which climaxes Ps 105–106—balances the recital of his many wise works in creation (see 104:2–26) and his benevolent care over the animal world (see 104:27–30). The editors may have inserted a Book division between Ps 106 and 107 with a view to a fivefold division of the Psalter (see Introduction: Collection, Arrangement and Date). See further the introduction to Ps 101–110.

The introduction (vv. 1–3) and conclusion (v. 43) enclose six stanzas, of which the last two (vv. 33–38,39–42) stand apart as an instructive supplement focusing in a more general way on reversals in fortunes—which, however, end up with God restoring the "hungry" (v. 36) and the "needy" (v. 41). Of the four remaining stanzas (marked by recurring refrains: vv. 6,13,19,28; vv. 8,15,21,31), the first and last refer to God's deliverance of those lost in the trackless desert (vv. 4–9) and those imperiled on the boisterous sea (vv. 23–32). The two central stanzas celebrate deliverance from the punishment of foreign bondage (vv. 10–16) and from the punishment of disease (vv. 17–22). Of the concluding lines to these four stanzas, the first two (vv. 9,16) and the last two (vv. 22,32) are similar. The verse pattern of these four stanzas (six-seven-six-ten) makes deliberate use of the significant numbers seven and ten.

107:1–3 Introductory call to praise.

107:1 A conventional liturgical call to praise (see 106:1; 118:1,29; 136:1; Jer 33:11). *Give thanks.* See vv. 8,15,21,31; see also note on Ps 100 title. *love.* See vv. 8,15,21,31,43; see also note on 6:4.

107:2 *redeemed.* Here, as often, a synonym for "delivered" (see note on 71:23).

107:3 *from the lands.* From the dispersion resulting from the Assyrian (see 2Ki 17:6) and Babylonian captivities (see 2Ki 24:14,16; 25:11,26; Jer 52:28–30; see also Ne 1:8; Est 8:5,9,13; Isa 11:12; 43:5–6; Eze 11:17; 20:34). *south.* Lit. "(the) sea" (see NIV text note), i.e., the west, as in Isa 49:12. But perhaps the final letter of the Hebrew word has been lost, which if supplied yields "south."

107:4–9 Deliverance for those lost in the trackless desert. No reference is made to rebellion (as in the third and fourth stanzas), but since Israel had journeyed through the desert on her way to Canaan she had firsthand experience of the terrors of the desert. She was, moreover, bounded on the east by the great Arabian Desert (as on the west by the Mediterranean Sea; see vv. 23–32), across which her merchant caravans traveled.

107:4,7,36 *city where they could settle.* Lit. "city of habitation," i.e., where people live and where a steady supply of food and water makes human life secure.

107:6 *they cried out.* The author uses the same Hebrew verb in v. 28, thus linking the fifth stanza with the second. In vv. 13,19 he uses a different (but similar-sounding) Hebrew verb, linking the third and fourth stanzas. Just as Israel's history was a history of divine deliverance (see Ps 105) and a history of rebellion (see Ps 106), so also it was a history of crying out to the Lord in distress (see references in note on 106:44).

107:7 *straight way.* Direct route, clear of dangerous and difficult obstacles.

107:8 For other refrains see introduction to Ps 42–43. *wonderful deeds.* See vv. 15,21,24,31; see also note on 9:1 ("wonders").

107:9 *satisfies the thirsty ... fills the hungry.* See v. 5; see also 105:40–41.

107:10–16 Deliverance from the punishment of foreign bondage. God even delivers those who cry to him when their distress is a result of his discipline for their sins (see vv. 17–20,33–41).

107:10 *sat in darkness ... deepest gloom.* Vivid imagery for distress (see 18:28; Isa 5:30; 8:22; 59:9; see also note on 44:19). *prisoners.* While reference is no doubt to foreign bondage, the imagery of being bound was also used by OT poets to refer to other forms of distress (see Job 36:8; Isa 28:22; La 3:7); so the reference may be deliberately ambiguous.

107:11 *God ... Most High.* That is, God Most High (see Ge 14:19

12 So he subjected them to bitter labor;
they stumbled, and there was no one
to help.[e]
13 Then they cried to the LORD in their
trouble,
and he saved them[f] from their
distress.
14 He brought them out of darkness[g] and
the deepest gloom[h]
and broke away their chains.[i]
15 Let them give thanks[j] to the LORD for
his unfailing love[k]
and his wonderful deeds[l] for men,
16 for he breaks down gates of bronze
and cuts through bars of iron.

17 Some became fools[m] through their
rebellious ways[n]
and suffered affliction[o] because of
their iniquities.
18 They loathed all food[p]
and drew near the gates of death.[q]
19 Then they cried[r] to the LORD in their
trouble,
and he saved them[s] from their
distress.
20 He sent forth his word[t] and healed
them;[u]
he rescued[v] them from the grave.[w]
21 Let them give thanks[x] to the LORD for
his unfailing love[y]
and his wonderful deeds[z] for men.
22 Let them sacrifice thank offerings[a]
and tell of his works[b] with songs of
joy.[c]

23 Others went out on the sea[d] in ships;[e]
they were merchants on the mighty
waters.
24 They saw the works of the LORD,[f]
his wonderful deeds in the deep.
25 For he spoke[g] and stirred up a
tempest[h]
that lifted high the waves.[i]
26 They mounted up to the heavens and
went down to the depths;
in their peril[j] their courage melted[k]
away.
27 They reeled[l] and staggered like
drunken men;
they were at their wits' end.
28 Then they cried[m] out to the LORD in
their trouble,
and he brought them out of their
distress.[n]
29 He stilled the storm[o] to a whisper;
the waves[p] of the sea were
hushed.[q]
30 They were glad when it grew calm,
and he guided them[r] to their desired
haven.
31 Let them give thanks[s] to the LORD for
his unfailing love[t]
and his wonderful deeds[u] for men.
32 Let them exalt[v] him in the assembly[w]
of the people
and praise him in the council of the
elders.

33 He turned rivers into a desert,[x]
flowing springs[y] into thirsty ground,

107:12 [e]S 2Ki 14:26; Ps 72:12 **107:13** [f]S Ps 106:8 **107:14** [g]S ver 10; Isa 9:2; 42:7; 50:10; 59:9; 60:2; S Lk 1:79 [h]Ps 86:13; Isa 29:18 [i]S Job 36:8; Ps 116:16; Ac 12:7 **107:15** [j]ver 8,21,31; Ps 105:1 [k]Ps 6:4 [l]S Ps 75:1 **107:17** [m]S Ps 53:1 [n]S Ps 25:7 [o]S Lev 26:16; Isa 65:6-7; Jer 30:14-15; Gal 6:7-8 **107:18** [p]S Job 3:24; S 6:6 [q]S Job 17:16; S 33:22 **107:19** [r]ver 28; Ps 5:2 [s]ver 13; Ps 34:4 **107:20** [t]S Dt 32:2; Ps 147:15; Mt 8:8; Lk 7:7 [u]S Ex 15:26 [v]S Job 33:28 [w]Ps 16:10; 30:3; S 56:13 **107:21** [x]S ver 15 [y]Ps 6:4 [z]Ps 75:1 **107:22** [a]S Lev 7:12 [b]Ps 9:11; 73:28; 118:17 [c]S Job 8:21; S Ps 65:8 **107:23** [d]Isa 42:10 [e]S Ps 104:26 **107:24** [f]Ps 64:9; 111:2; 143:5 **107:25** [g]S Ps 105:31 [h]S Ps 50:3 [i]S Ps 93:3 **107:26** [j]Lk 8:23 [k]S Jos 2:11 **107:27** [l]Isa 19:14; 24:20; 28:7 **107:28** [m]S ver 19 [n]Ps 4:1; Jnh 1:6 **107:29** [o]Lk 8:24 [p]S Ps 93:3 [q]S Ps 65:7; Jnh 1:15 **107:30** [r]ver 7 **107:31** [s]S ver 15 [t]Ps 6:4 [u]Ps 75:1; 106:2 **107:32** [v]Ps 30:1; 34:3; 99:5 [w]S Ps 1:5; 22:22,25; 26:12; 35:18 **107:33** [x]1Ki 17:1; Ps 74:15; Isa 41:15; 42:15; 50:2 [y]S Ps 104:10

and note; see also note on 3:7). *counsel.* God's wise directives embodied in his words (see 73:24 and note).

107:12 *subjected them to bitter labor.* Lit. "brought down their heart with labor," i.e., a labor so burdensome it broke their spirit. *stumbled.* Their strength failed (see 31:10; 109:24; Ne 4:10; Isa 40:30; Zec 12:8).

107:13 *cried to.* See note on v. 6.

107:16 Either this verse is quoted from Isa 45:2, or both verses quote an established saying. *gates of bronze.* City gates—normally of wood; here proverbially of bronze, the strongest gates then imaginable (see 1Ki 4:13; cf. Jer 1:18). *bars of iron.* Bars that secured city gates (see Dt 3:5; Jer 51:30). "Can a man break iron … or bronze?" was a proverb of the time (see Jer 15:12).

107:17–22 Deliverance from the punishment of wasting disease (see note on vv. 10–16).

107:17 *fools.* See Jer 4:22; see also NIV text note on 14:1. "Fools despise wisdom and discipline" (Pr 1:7; see v. 43). *affliction because of their iniquities.* See Lev 26:16,25; Dt 28:20–22,35,58–61.

107:18 *gates of death.* The realm of the dead was sometimes depicted as a netherworld city with a series of concentric walls and gates (seven, each inside the other, according to ancient Near Eastern mythology) to keep those descending there from returning to the land of the living (see 9:13 and note on Job 38:17; see also Mt 16:18).

107:19 *cried to.* See note on v. 6. *saved.* See v. 13 (another link between the second and third stanzas); cf. vv. 6,28.

107:20 *his word.* His command, here personified as the agent of his purpose (see 147:15,18; see also note on 23:6).

107:22 *thank offerings.* See Lev 7:12–15; 22:29–30. *tell of his works.* See note on 7:17. In their concluding lines, stanzas four and five are linked, as are stanzas two and three. *songs of joy.* See, e.g., Ps 116.

107:23–32 Deliverance from the perils of the sea (see note on vv. 4–9). Israel's merchants also braved the sea in pursuit of trade (see Ge 49:13; Jdg 5:17; 1Ki 9:26–28; 10:22).

107:23 *mighty waters.* See 29:3.

107:24 *wonderful deeds in the deep.* Since the peoples of the eastern Mediterranean coastlands associated the "mighty waters" (v. 23) of the sea with the primeval chaotic waters (see note on 32:6), the Lord's total control of them was always for Israel a cause of wonder and a sense of security. Therefore the terrifying storms that sometimes swept the Mediterranean (see Jnh 1; Ac 27) are here included among his wonderful deeds.

107:27 *they were at their wits' end.* Lit. "all their wisdom/skill was swallowed up."

107:30 *haven.* Perhaps trading center.

107:32 See v. 22. *elders.* See note on Ex 3:16.

107:33–42 A twofold instructive supplement recalling how the Lord sometimes disciplined his people by turning the fruitful land (v. 34) into a virtual desert (see 1Ki 17:1–7; 2Ki 8:1) but then restored the land again (see Ru 1:6; 1Ki 18:44–45), so that the hungry (v. 36) could live there and prosper in the midst of plenty. But then he sent powerful

34 and fruitful land into a salt waste,[z]
because of the wickedness of those
who lived there.
35 He turned the desert into pools of
water[a]
and the parched ground into flowing
springs;[b]
36 there he brought the hungry to live,
and they founded a city where they
could settle.
37 They sowed fields and planted
vineyards[c]
that yielded a fruitful harvest;
38 he blessed them, and their numbers
greatly increased,[d]
and he did not let their herds
diminish.[e]

39 Then their numbers decreased,[f] and
they were humbled[g]
by oppression, calamity and sorrow;
40 he who pours contempt on nobles[h]
made them wander in a trackless
waste.[i]
41 But he lifted the needy[j] out of their
affliction
and increased their families like
flocks.[k]
42 The upright see and rejoice,[l]
but all the wicked shut their
mouths.[m]

43 Whoever is wise,[n] let him heed these
things
and consider the great love[o] of the
LORD.

Psalm 108

108:1-5pp — Ps 57:7-11
108:6-13pp — Ps 60:5-12

A song. A psalm of David.

1 My heart is steadfast,[p] O God;
I will sing[q] and make music with all
my soul.
2 Awake, harp and lyre![r]
I will awaken the dawn.
3 I will praise you, O LORD, among the
nations;
I will sing of you among the
peoples.
4 For great is your love,[s] higher than the
heavens;
your faithfulness[t] reaches to the
skies.[u]
5 Be exalted, O God, above the
heavens,[v]
and let your glory be over all the
earth.[w]

6 Save us and help us with your right
hand,[x]
that those you love may be
delivered.
7 God has spoken[y] from his sanctuary:[z]
"In triumph I will parcel out
Shechem[a]
and measure off the Valley of
Succoth.[b]
8 Gilead is mine, Manasseh is mine;
Ephraim is my helmet,
Judah[c] my scepter.
9 Moab[d] is my washbasin,
upon Edom[e] I toss my sandal;
over Philistia[f] I shout in triumph."
10 Who will bring me to the fortified
city?
Who will lead me to Edom?
11 Is it not you, O God, you who have
rejected us
and no longer go out with our
armies?[g]
12 Give us aid against the enemy,
for the help of man is worthless.[h]
13 With God we will gain the victory,
and he will trample down[i] our
enemies.

107:34 [z]S Ge 13:10 **107:35** [a]S 2Ki 3:17; Ps 105:41; 126:4; Isa 43:19; 51:3 [b]S Job 38:26; S Isa 35:7 **107:37** [c]S 2Ki 19:29; S Isa 37:30 **107:38** [d]S Ge 12:2; S Dt 7:13 [e]S Ge 49:25 **107:39** [f]S 2Ki 10:32; Eze 5:12 [g]S Ps 44:9 **107:40** [h]S Job 12:18 [i]S Dt 32:10 **107:41** [j]S 1Sa 2:8; Ps 113:7-9 [k]S Job 21:11 **107:42** [l]S Job 22:19; Ps 97:10-12 [m]S Job 5:16; Ro 3:19 **107:43** [n]Jer 9:12; Hos 14:9 [o]Ps 103:11 **108:1** [p]Ps 112:7; 119:30,112 [q]S Ps 18:49 **108:2** [r]S Job 21:12 **108:4** [s]Nu 14:18; Ps 106:45 [t]S Ex 34:6 [u]S Ps 36:5 **108:5** [v]S Ps 8:1 [w]S Ps 57:5 **108:6** [x]S Job 40:14 **108:7** [y]Ps 89:35 [z]Ps 68:35; 102:19 [a]S Ge 12:6 [b]S Ge 33:17 **108:8** [c]S Ps 78:68 **108:9** [d]S Ge 19:37 [e]S 2Sa 8:13-14 [f]S 2Sa 8:1 **108:11** [g]S Ps 44:9 **108:12** [h]Ps 118:8; 146:3; Isa 10:3; 30:5; 31:3; Jer 2:36; 17:5 **108:13** [i]Ps 44:5; Isa 22:5; 63:3,6

armies against them (such as the Assyrians, 2Ki 17:3–6, and the Babylonians, 2Ki 24:10–17; 25:1–26) that devastated the land once more and deported its people; yet afterward he restored the needy (v. 41). But the poet generalizes upon these experiences in the manner of the wisdom teachers.

107:33–35 The imagery is similar to that found in Isa 35:6–7; 41:18; 42:15; 43:19–20; 50:2 and may indicate that the author has been influenced by Isaiah.

107:40 Perhaps quoted from Job 12:21,24. In their prosperity the people, led by their nobles, grow proud and turn their backs on the God who has blessed them (see Dt 31:20; 32:15), so he returns them to the desert (see Dt 32:10; Hos 2:3,14).

107:41 *needy.* Those in need of help (see v. 39; see also 9:18 and note).

107:42 Conclusion to the instruction (vv. 33–41); perhaps an echo of Job 5:16. *upright ... wicked.* A frequent contrast in OT wisdom literature (see Pr 2:21–22; 11:6–7; 12:6; 14:11; 15:8; 21:18,29; 29:27 — but the Hebrew for "wicked" here is shared more often with Job).

107:43 Conclusion to the psalm. *Whoever is wise.* See Dt 32:29; Hos 14:9. *these things.* The instruction in vv. 33–42. *consider the great love of the LORD.* The theme of vv. 4–32, emphatically reiterated.

Ps 108 Praise of God's love, and prayer for his help against the enemies — a combination (with very slight modifications) of 57:7–11 and 60:5–12. For a similar composition of a new psalm by combination of portions from several psalms see 1Ch 16:8–36. The celebration of the greatness of God's love (v. 4) links this psalm thematically with Ps 103 (see 103:11). See introduction to Ps 101–110.

108 title *song.* See note on Ps 30 title. *of David.* Both sources (Ps 57; 60) were credited to him.

108:1–5 Praise of God's love, possibly intended to function here as an expression of trust in God (the God of vv. 7–9,11), to whom appeal is to be made (vv. 6,12); see 109:1 and note. For this stanza see notes on 57:7–11.

108:1 *soul.* Lit. "glory" (see note on 7:5).

108:6–13 Prayer for God's help against enemies (see notes on 60:5–12).

Psalm 109

For the director of music.
Of David. A psalm.

[1]O God, whom I praise,[j]
do not remain silent,[k]
[2]for wicked and deceitful men[l]
have opened their mouths against me;
they have spoken against me with
lying tongues.[m]
[3]With words of hatred[n] they surround
me;
they attack me without cause.[o]
[4]In return for my friendship they accuse
me,
but I am a man of prayer.[p]
[5]They repay me evil for good,[q]
and hatred for my friendship.

[6]Appoint[a] an evil man[b] to oppose him;
let an accuser[c][r] stand at his right
hand.
[7]When he is tried, let him be found
guilty,[s]
and may his prayers condemn[t] him.
[8]May his days be few;[u]
may another take his place[v] of
leadership.
[9]May his children be fatherless
and his wife a widow.[w]
[10]May his children be wandering
beggars;[x]
may they be driven[d] from their
ruined homes.
[11]May a creditor[y] seize all he has;
may strangers plunder[z] the fruits of
his labor.[a]
[12]May no one extend kindness to him
or take pity[b] on his fatherless
children.
[13]May his descendants be cut off,[c]
their names blotted out[d] from the
next generation.
[14]May the iniquity of his fathers[e] be
remembered before the LORD;
may the sin of his mother never be
blotted out.
[15]May their sins always remain before[f]
the LORD,
that he may cut off the memory[g] of
them from the earth.
[16]For he never thought of doing a
kindness,
but hounded to death the poor

109:1 [j]S Ex 15:2; Jer 17:14 [k]S Job 34:29 **109:2** [l]S Ps 43:1 [m]S Ps 52:4 **109:3** [n]Ps 69:4 [o]Ps 35:7; Jn 15:25 **109:4** [p]Ps 69:13; 141:5 **109:5** [q]S Ge 44:4 **109:6** [r]1Ch 21:1; Job 1:6; Zec 3:1 **109:7** [s]Ps 1:5 [t]Pr 28:9; Isa 41:24 **109:8** [u]S Job 15:32 [v]Ac 1:20* **109:9** [w]Ex 22:24; Jer 18:21 **109:10** [x]S Ge 4:12 **109:11** [y]Ne 5:3 [z]S Nu 14:3; Isa 1:7; 6:11; 36:1; La 5:2 [a]Job 20:18 **109:12** [b]S Job 5:4 **109:13** [c]Job 18:19; Ps 21:10 [d]S Nu 14:12; Ps 9:5; Pr 10:7 **109:14** [e]Ex 20:5; Nu 14:18; Isa 65:6-7; Jer 32:18 **109:15** [f]Ps 90:8 [g]S Ex 17:14; S Dt 32:26

[a] 6 Or ⌞*They say:*⌟ *"Appoint* (with quotation marks at the end of verse 19) [b] 6 Or *the Evil One* [c] 6 Or *let Satan* [d] 10 Septuagint; Hebrew *sought*

Ps 109 A prayer for God to deliver from false accusers. The author speaks of his enemies in the singular in vv. 6–19 but in the plural elsewhere. Some therefore suppose that vv. 6–19 contain the enemies' curses pronounced against the author (see NIV text note on v. 6). But it is more likely that either (1) the author shifts here to a collective mode of speaking, or (2) the enemies are united under a leader whose personal animosity toward the psalmist has fired the antagonism of others and so is singled out for special attention. Traditional attempts to isolate a distinct class of psalms called "imprecatory" (and then identify Ps 109 as the climax of the series) are mistaken (see note on vv. 6–15). Thematically, this prayer has much affinity with Ps 35. Within the cluster in which it stands its affinity is with Ps 102 (see introduction to Ps 101–110) — and it is only one line longer than that psalm.

Two (Hebrew) four-line stanzas of petition frame the whole (vv. 1–5,26–29), followed by a two-line conclusion (vv. 30–31). The remaining 20 lines fall into two main divisions of ten lines each (vv. 6–15,16–25). Of these, the second is thematically divided into two parts of five lines each, the first of which (vv. 16–20) catalogues what "he" has done while the second (vv. 21–25) describes how "I" am suffering.

109 title See note on Ps 4 title.

109:1–5 Appeal to God to deliver David from false accusers.

109:1 *whom I praise.* The one he publicly praises as his trustworthy deliverer and defender (see 22:3 and note; see also 35:18; 74:21; 76:10; 79:13; 102:18). *silent.* (Judicially) inactive (see 28:1; 35:22; 50:3,21; 83:1).

109:2–5 The particulars of his case, which he presents before the heavenly bar of justice (see 35:11–16).

109:2 *opened their mouths against me.* See note on 5:9.

109:4 *but I am a man of prayer.* In contrast to the enemy (see vv. 16–18). The intent may be: But I have prayed for them (as in 35:13–14).

109:6–15 Appeal for judicial redress — that the Lord will deal with them in accordance with their malicious intent against him, matching punishment with crime (see note on 5:10; see also 35:4–10 and note).

109:6 *evil man ... accuser.* It may well be that the alternative translations in the NIV text notes are to be preferred (see note on Job 1:6). The psalmist's enemy falsely accused him in order to bring him down; now let the enemy be confronted by an accuser.

109:7 *his prayers.* The petitions he offers in his defense.

109:8 *days be few.* The false accuser was no doubt seeking to effect David's death (see 1Ki 21:8–15). *another take his place of leadership.* The enemy held some official position and was perhaps plotting a coup. For a NT application of these words to Judas see Ac 1:20.

109:10–11 May he also be deprived of all his property so that he has no inheritance to pass on to his children.

109:12 *no one extend kindness.* See v. 16. *his ... children.* The close identity of a man with his children and of children with their parents, resulting from the tightly bonded unity of the three- or four-generation households of that ancient society, is alien to the modern reader, whose sense of self is highly individualistic. But that deep, profoundly human bond accounts for the ancient legal principle of "punishing the children for the sin of the fathers to the third and fourth generation" (see Ex 20:5; but see also 103:17; Ge 18:19).

109:13 Since a man lived on in his children (see previous note), the focus of judgment remains on the false accuser (see 21:10; 37:28). *names blotted out.* See note on 9:5.

109:14–15 *iniquity of his fathers ... sin of his mother ... their sins.* These verses return to the theme of vv. 7–8 (and thus form a frame around the stanza): May the indictment the accuser lodges against him include the sins of his parents (see note on v. 12).

109:15 *cut off the memory of them.* May this slanderer be the last of their family line.

109:16–20 The ruthless character of the enemy — may he be made to suffer the due consequences (see 10:2–15; 59:12–13). Accusation of the adversary is a common feature

and the needy[h] and the
brokenhearted.[i]
[17] He loved to pronounce a curse—
may it[a] come on him;[j]
he found no pleasure in blessing—
may it be[b] far from him.
[18] He wore cursing[k] as his garment;
it entered into his body like
water,[l]
into his bones like oil.
[19] May it be like a cloak wrapped[m] about
him,
like a belt tied forever around him.
[20] May this be the LORD's payment[n] to
my accusers,
to those who speak evil[o] of me.

[21] But you, O Sovereign LORD,
deal well with me for your name's
sake;[p]
out of the goodness of your love,[q]
deliver me.[r]
[22] For I am poor and needy,
and my heart is wounded within
me.
[23] I fade away like an evening shadow;[s]
I am shaken off like a locust.
[24] My knees give[t] way from fasting;[u]
my body is thin and gaunt.[v]
[25] I am an object of scorn[w] to my
accusers;
when they see me, they shake their
heads.[x]

[26] Help me,[y] O LORD my God;
save me in accordance with your
love.
[27] Let them know[z] that it is your hand,
that you, O LORD, have done it.
[28] They may curse,[a] but you will bless;
when they attack they will be put to
shame,
but your servant will rejoice.[b]
[29] My accusers will be clothed with
disgrace
and wrapped in shame[c] as in a
cloak.
[30] With my mouth I will greatly extol the
LORD;
in the great throng[d] I will praise him.
[31] For he stands at the right hand[e] of the
needy one,
to save his life from those who
condemn him.

Psalm 110

Of David. A psalm.

[1] The LORD says[f] to my Lord:
"Sit at my right hand[g]
until I make your enemies
a footstool for your feet."[h]

109:16 [h] S Job 20:19; S Ps 35:10 [i] S Ps 34:18 **109:17** [j] Pr 28:27; S Mt 7:2 **109:18** [k] Ps 10:7 [l] Nu 5:22 **109:19** [m] ver 29; Ps 73:6; Eze 7:27 **109:20** [n] S Ex 32:34; Ps 54:5; 94:23; Isa 3:11; 2Ti 4:14 [o] Ps 71:10 **109:21** [p] S Ex 9:16; S Ps 23:3 [q] Ps 69:16 [r] S Ps 3:7 **109:23** [s] S Job 14:2 **109:24** [t] Heb 12:12 [u] S Ps 35:13 [v] S Job 16:8 **109:25** [w] S Ps 22:6 [x] S Job 16:4; S Mt 27:39; Mk 15:29 **109:26** [y] Ps 12:1; 119:86 **109:27** [z] S Job 37:7 **109:28** [a] S 2Sa 16:12 [b] Ps 66:4; Isa 35:10; 51:11; 54:1; 65:14 **109:29** [c] S Ps 35:26 **109:30** [d] S Ps 35:18 **109:31** [e] Ps 16:8; 108:6 **110:1** [f] Mt 22:44*; Mk 12:36*; Lk 20:42*; Ac 2:34* [g] S Mk 16:19; Heb 1:13*; 12:2 [h] S Jos 10:24; S 1Ki 5:3; 1Co 15:25

[a] 17 Or *curse, / and it has* [b] 17 Or *blessing, / and it is*

in psalms that are appeals to the heavenly Judge (see, e.g., 5:9–10; 10:2–11; 17:10–12).

109:17 *pronounce a curse.* The enemy added curses to lies (see note on Ge 12:3).

109:18–19 *garment ... cloak wrapped.* See note on v. 29.

109:18 *into his body like water, into his bones like oil.* Pronouncing curses on others was his food and drink as well as his clothing; he lived by such cursing (cf. Pr 4:17 and note).

109:20 *the LORD's payment.* See 54:5; 94:23; Isa 3:11; 2Ti 4:14.

109:21–25 The intensity of "my" suffering—Lord, deliver me!

109:21 *for your name's sake.* See notes on 5:11; 23:3. *love.* See v. 26; see also note on 6:4.

109:22 The psalmist's description of his situation echoes the words of v. 16. *poor and needy.* Dependent on the Lord (see note on 34:6). *heart.* See note on 4:7. *is wounded.* The Hebrew for this phrase sounds like the Hebrew for "curse" in vv. 17–18, a deliberate wordplay—while he lives by cursing, I live with deep inward pain.

109:23 *I fade away.* Apparently the psalmist suffers a life-sapping affliction, which is the occasion for his enemies to turn on him (see vv. 24–25; see also note on 5:9). *like an evening shadow.* See 102:11. *shaken off.* See Ne 5:13; Job 38:13.

109:26–29 Concluding petition, with many echoes of preceding themes.

109:28 *servant.* Perhaps identifies the psalmist as the Lord's anointed (see title; see also 78:70 and note).

109:29 *clothed with ... wrapped in.* For other uses of this imagery see vv. 18–19; 35:26; 45:3; 73:6; 104:1–2; 132:9,16,18; Job 8:22; 29:14; 40:10; Pr 31:25; Isa 59:17; 61:3,10; Eze 7:27; 26:16; 31:15; Zec 6:13; Lk 24:19; Ro 13:14; 1Co 15:53–54; Gal 3:27; Col 3:12; 1Pe 5:5.

109:30–31 A vow to praise the Lord for his deliverance (see note on 7:17).

Ps 110 Oracles concerning the Messianic King-Priest. This psalm (specifically its two brief oracles, vv. 1,4) is frequently referred to in the NT testimony to Christ. Like Ps 2, it has the marks of a coronation psalm, composed for use at the enthronement of a new Davidic king. Before the Christian era Jews already viewed it as Messianic. Because of the manner in which it has been interpreted in the NT—especially by Jesus (see Mt 22:43–45; Mk 12:36–37; Lk 20:42–44), but also by Peter (see Ac 2:34–36) and the author of Hebrews (see especially Heb 1:13; 5:6–10; 7:11–28)—Christians have generally held that this is the most directly "prophetic" of all the psalms. If so, David, speaking prophetically (see 2Sa 23:2), composed a coronation psalm for his great future Son, of whom the prophets did not speak until later. It may be, however, that David composed the psalm for the coronation of his son Solomon, that he called him "my Lord" (v. 1) in view of his new status, which placed him above the aged David, and that in so doing he spoke a word that had far larger meaning than he knew. This would seem to be in more accord with what we know of David from Samuel, Kings and Chronicles. For this psalm's setting in the Psalter see introduction to Ps 101–110.

The psalm falls into two precisely balanced halves (vv. 1–3,4–7). Each of the two brief oracles (vv. 1,4) is followed by thematically and structurally similar elaboration: As v. 4 is to v. 1, so v. 5 is to v. 2 and vv. 6–7 are to v. 3 (a poetic couplet).

110:1–3 The Lord's decree, establishing his anointed as his regent in the face of all opposition (see 2:7–12).

110:1 The first oracle (see note on v. 4). *my Lord.* My sovereign, therefore superior to David (see Mt 22:44–45; Mk 12:36–37; Lk 20:42–44; Ac 2:34–35; Heb 1:13 and their contexts). *Sit.* Sit enthroned. *right hand.* The place of honor

[2]The LORD will extend your mighty
scepter[i] from Zion;[j]
you will rule[k] in the midst of your
enemies.
[3]Your troops will be willing
on your day of battle.
Arrayed in holy majesty,[l]
from the womb of the dawn
you will receive the dew of your
youth.[a m]
[4]The LORD has sworn
and will not change his mind:[n]
"You are a priest forever,[o]
in the order of Melchizedek.[p]"
[5]The Lord is at your right hand;[q]
he will crush kings[r] on the day of his
wrath.[s]
[6]He will judge the nations,[t] heaping up
the dead[u]
and crushing the rulers[v] of the whole
earth.
[7]He will drink from a brook beside the
way[b];
therefore he will lift up his head.[w]

110:2 [i]S Ge 49:10; Ps 45:6; Isa 14:5; Jer 48:17 [j]S Ps 2:6 [k]Ps 72:8 **110:3** [l]S Ex 15:11 [m]Mic 5:7 **110:4** [n]S Nu 23:19 [o]Zec 6:13; Heb 5:6*; 7:21* [p]S Ge 14:18; Heb 5:10; 7:15-17* **110:5** [q]Ps 16:8 [r]S Dt 7:24; Ps 2:12; 68:21; 76:12; Isa 60:12; Da 2:44 [s]S Ps 2:5; Ro 2:5; Rev 6:17; 11:18 **110:6** [t]S Ps 9:19 [u]Isa 5:25; 34:3; 66:24 [v]S Ps 18:38 **110:7** [w]Ps 3:3; 27:6

Psalm 111[c]

[1]Praise the LORD.[d]

I will extol the LORD[x] with all my heart[y]
in the council[z] of the upright and in
the assembly.[a]

[a] 3 Or / *your young men will come to you like the dew* [b] 7 Or / *The One who grants succession will set him in authority* [c] This psalm is an acrostic poem, the lines of which begin with the successive letters of the Hebrew alphabet. [d] 1 Hebrew *Hallelu Yah*

111:1 [x]Ps 34:1; 109:30; 115:18; 145:10 [y]S Ps 9:1 [z]Ps 89:7 [a]S Ps 1:5

beside a king (see 45:9; 1Ki 2:19); thus he is made second in authority to God himself. NT references to Jesus' exaltation to this position are many (see Mt 26:64; Mk 14:62; 16:19; Lk 22:69; Ac 2:33; 5:31; 7:55–56; Ro 8:34; Eph 1:20; Col 3:1; Heb 1:3; 8:1; 10:12; 12:2). *enemies.* See note on 2:1–3. *footstool for your feet.* See Heb 10:12–13. Ancient kings often had themselves portrayed as placing their feet on vanquished enemies (see Jos 10:24). For a royal footstool as part of the throne see 2Ch 9:18. For the thought here see 1Ki 5:3. Paul applies this word to Christ in 1Co 15:25; Eph 1:22.

110:2 *extend your mighty scepter.* Expand your reign in ever-widening circles until no foe remains to oppose your rule. *Zion.* David's royal city (see 2Sa 5:7,9), but also God's (see 9:11 and note), where he rules as the Great King (see Ps 46; 48; 132:13–18). The Lord's anointed is his regent over his emerging kingdom in the world.

110:3 *willing.* Lit. "freewill offerings," i.e., they will offer themselves as dedicated warriors to support you on the battlefield (see Jdg 5:2)—as the Israelites offered of their treasures for the building of the tabernacle in the desert (see Ex 35:29; 36:3; see also Ezr 1:4; 2:68). Accordingly, Paul speaks of Christ's followers offering their bodies "as living sacrifices" (Ro 12:1) and of himself as a "drink offering" (Php 2:17); see also 2Co 8:5. *Arrayed ... your youth.* If the text is descriptive of the Lord's anointed, it depicts him as clothed in royal majesty and glory and perpetually preserving the bloom of youth even as the "womb of the dawn" gives birth each morning to the dew (for a different use of this imagery see Isa 26:19). If it speaks of the young warriors who flock to him (see NIV text note), it apparently describes them as dressed in priestly garb, ready for participation in a holy war (see 1Sa 21:4–5; 25:28; 2Ch 13:8,12; 20:15,21; Isa 13:3–4; Jer 6:4; 51:27), and pouring into his camp morning by morning as copious as the dew (see 2Sa 17:11–12). *holy majesty.* See note on 29:2.

110:4–7 The Lord's oath establishing his anointed as king-priest in Zion and assuring him victory over all powers that oppose him.

110:4 The second oracle (see note on v. 1). *has sworn.* In accordance also with his sworn covenant to maintain David's royal line forever (see 89:35–37). The force of this oath is elaborated by the author of Hebrews (Heb 6:16–18; 7:20–22). *priest ... in the order of Melchizedek.* David and his royal sons, as chief representatives of the rule of God, performed many worship-focused activities, such as overseeing the ark of the covenant (see 2Sa 6:1–15, especially v. 14; 1Ki 8:1), building and overseeing the temple (see 1Ki 5–7; 2Ki 12:4–7; 22:3–7; 23:4–7; 2Ch 15:8; 24:4–12; 29:3–11; 34:8) and overseeing the work of the priests and Levites and the temple liturgy (see 1Ch 6:31; 15:11–16; 16:4–42; 23:3–31; 25:1; 2Ch 17:7–9; 19:8–11; 29:25,30; 31:2; 35:15–16; Ezr 3:10; 8:20; Ne 12:24,36,45). In all these duties they exercised authority over even the high priest. But they could not engage in those specifically priestly functions that had been assigned to the Aaronic priesthood (see 2Ch 26:16–18). In the present oracle the son of David is installed by God as king-priest in Zion after the manner of Melchizedek, the king-priest of God Most High at Jerusalem in the days of Abraham (see Ge 14:18,20 and notes). As such a king-priest, he was appointed to a higher order of priesthood than that of Aaron and his sons. (For the union of king and priest in one person see Zec 6:13 and note.) What this means for Christ's priesthood is the main theme of Heb 7. *forever.* Permanently and irrevocably; perhaps alluded to in Jn 12:34.

110:5 *The Lord is at your right hand.* God is near to assist you in your warfare (see v. 2; cf. 109:31). Some take these words as an address to God: The Lord (David's superior son) is at your (God's) right hand (as in v. 1). *on the day of his wrath.* See 2:5 and note.

110:6 *He.* The Lord's anointed. *heaping up the dead.* Battlefield imagery (borrowed from David's victories) that depicts the victory of the Lord's anointed over all powers that oppose the kingdom of God (see 2:9; Rev 19:11–21).

110:7 *drink from a brook.* Even in the heat of battle he will find refreshment and lift up his head with undiminished vigor (see note on v. 3). For another possible but less likely rendering of this line see NIV text note.

Ps 111–119 A cluster of nine psalms framed by unusual alphabetic acrostics (see introductions to Ps 111; 119) that enclose the "Egyptian Hallel" (see introduction to Ps 113–118). The framing psalms that enclose the celebration of redemption contained in the Hallel offer instruction in the piety that must characterize those who join in the celebration of God's saving acts in behalf of his people.

Ps 111 Praise of God for his unfailing righteousness. The psalm combines hymnic praise with wisdom instruction, as its first and last verses indicate. Close comparison with Ps 112 shows that these two psalms are twins, probably written by the same author and intended to be kept together. The two psalms are most likely postexilic. For the relationship of these psalms with those that follow see introduction to Ps 111–119.

Structurally, both Ps 111 and Ps 112 are alphabetic acrostics (see NIV text note), but unique in that each (Hebrew) half-line advances the alphabet. Both psalms are framed by first

2 Great are the works[b] of the LORD;
they are pondered by all[c] who
delight in them.
3 Glorious and majestic are his deeds,
and his righteousness endures[d]
forever.
4 He has caused his wonders to be
remembered;
the LORD is gracious and
compassionate.[e]
5 He provides food[f] for those who fear
him;[g]
he remembers his covenant[h]
forever.
6 He has shown his people the power of
his works,[i]
giving them the lands of other
nations.[j]
7 The works of his hands[k] are faithful
and just;
all his precepts are trustworthy.[l]
8 They are steadfast for ever[m] and ever,
done in faithfulness and uprightness.
9 He provided redemption[n] for his
people;
he ordained his covenant forever—
holy and awesome[o] is his name.
10 The fear of the LORD[p] is the beginning
of wisdom;[q]
all who follow his precepts have
good understanding.[r]
To him belongs eternal praise.[s]

Psalm 112[a]

1 Praise the LORD.[b][t]

Blessed is the man[u] who fears the
LORD,[v]
who finds great delight[w] in his
commands.

2 His children[x] will be mighty in the
land;
the generation of the upright will be
blessed.
3 Wealth and riches[y] are in his house,
and his righteousness endures[z]
forever.
4 Even in darkness light dawns[a] for the
upright,
for the gracious and compassionate
and righteous[b] man.[c]

111:2 [b] S Job 36:24; Ps 143:5; Rev 15:3 [c] Ps 64:9 **111:3** [d] Ps 112:3,9; 119:142 **111:4** [e] S Dt 4:31; S Ps 86:15 **111:5** [f] S Ge 1:30; S Ps 37:25; Mt 6:26,31-33 [g] Ps 103:11 [h] S 1Ch 16:15; S Ps 105:8 **111:6** [i] Ps 64:9; S 66:3,5 [j] S Ps 105:44 **111:7** [k] S Ps 92:4 [l] Ps 19:7; 119:128 **111:8** [m] Ps 119:89,152,160; Isa 40:8; S Mt 5:18 **111:9** [n] Ps 34:22; S 103:4; 130:7; Lk 1:68 [o] Ps 30:4; 99:3; Lk 1:49 **111:10** [p] S Job 23:15; S Ps 19:9 [q] Dt 4:6 [r] S Dt 4:6; Ps 119:98,104,130 [s] Ps 28:6; 89:52 **112:1** [t] Ps 33:2; 103:1; 150:1 [u] Ps 1:1-2 [v] S Job 1:8; Ps 103:11; 115:13; 128:1 [w] S Ps 1:2; 119:14,16,47,92 **112:2** [x] Ps 25:13; 37:26; 128:2-4 **112:3** [y] S Dt 8:18 [z] S Ps 37:6; S 111:3 **112:4** [a] S Ps 18:28 [b] Ps 5:12

[a] This psalm is an acrostic poem, the lines of which begin with the successive letters of the Hebrew alphabet. [b] *1* Hebrew *Hallelu Yah* [c] *4* Or / *for ⌞the LORD⌟ is gracious and compassionate and righteous*

and last verses that highlight their primary themes, and in both psalms the main body develops the theme introduced by the first verse, while the closing verse adds a counterpoint. In both psalms the main body of eight verses falls thematically into two halves of four verses each, with the corresponding verses of each half containing certain thematic links (compare, e.g., 111:2 and 111:6; also vv. 5 and 9). Corresponding verses of the two psalms also tend to share common themes (compare, e.g., 111:3–5 with 112:3–5). Both of these twin psalms are composed of the same number of Hebrew syllables.

111:1 *I will extol.* Introductory to the praise that follows in vv. 2–9. *with all my heart.* A verbal link with a recurring phrase in Ps 119 (see vv. 2,10,34,58,69,145). *council of the upright.* Probably a more intimate circle than the assembly (see 107:32 for a similar distinction) and referring to those who are truly godly—such as the "upright" of 112:2,4 (see 11:7; 33:1; 49:14; 97:11; 107:42; 140:13). *in the assembly.* See note on 9:1.

111:2–5 The stanza is framed by references to the Lord's "works" and "his covenant" (see vv. 6–9 and note).

111:2 *works of the LORD.* The hymn focuses especially on what God has done for his people. Verses 5,9 sum it up. *pondered.* Reflectively examined (see Ezr 10:16, "investigate"; Ecc 1:13, "study").

111:3 *righteousness.* As embodied in his deeds (see note on 4:1).

111:4 *wonders.* See note on 9:1. *gracious and compassionate.* See Ex 34:6–7 and note.

111:5 *provides food.* Illustrative of his bountiful provisions for the daily needs of his people (as in the Lord's prayer: "Give us today our daily bread," Mt 6:11). *fear.* See v. 10 and note. *his covenant.* The Lord remembers "forever" the covenant he "ordained … forever" (v. 9; see also 105:8–11).

111:6–9 The stanza is framed by references to the Lord's "works" and "his covenant" (see vv. 2–5 and note).

111:7 *faithful and just.* Cf. "Glorious and majestic" (v. 3). *precepts are trustworthy.* See note on 93:5.

111:8 *They.* "The works of his hands" (v. 7). *faithfulness and uprightness.* Cf. "gracious and compassionate" (v. 4).

111:9 *provided redemption.* The other great benefit of God's deeds in behalf of his people (cf. "provides food," v. 5). *holy and awesome.* As shown by his works. *name.* See note on 5:11.

111:10 Concluding word of godly wisdom. *The fear of the LORD is the beginning of wisdom.* The classic OT statement concerning the religious basis of what it means to be wise (see Job 28:28; Pr 1:7; 9:10; see also note on 66:16). *who follow his precepts.* Lit. "who do them." The plural Hebrew pronoun refers back to "precepts" in v. 7 (see 19:7–9, where "The fear of the LORD" stands parallel to "statutes," "precepts," "commands," "ordinances"; see also 112:1).

Ps 112 A eulogy to the godly man—in the spirit of Ps 1 but formed after the pattern of Ps 111 and likely intended as its complement (see introduction to Ps 111).

112:1 The basic theme, developed more fully in vv. 2–9. Verse 10 states its converse. See 1:1–2; 128:1. *Blessed.* See note on 1:1. *fears the LORD.* See 66:16 and note. *delight … commands.* A verbal and conceptual link with Ps 119 (see 119:35).

112:2–5 The stanza is framed by references to the godly man's children and his generosity (see vv. 6–9 and note).

112:2 *children.* The godly bring blessing to their children and to themselves—not least in the fact that through their children they are "remembered" in the community (see v. 6; see also Dt 25:6; Ru 4:10; see further Ps 37:26; 127:3–5; 128:3 and note on 109:12). *will be mighty.* Will be persons of influence and reputation.

112:3 Cf. 111:3. *Wealth and riches.* See 1:3; 128:2. *righteousness.* See v. 9; see also note on 1:5. *endures.* It is not an occasional characteristic of his actions (see "steadfast," v. 7).

112:4 *darkness.* A metaphor for calamitous times (see 107:10 and note). *light.* See note on 27:1. *gracious and compassionate.* See 111:4; cf. Ex 34:6–7 and note. *righteous.* Cf. what is said of the Lord in 116:5; 145:8,17.

5 Good will come to him who is
generous and lends freely,[c]
who conducts his affairs with
justice.
6 Surely he will never be shaken;[d]
a righteous man will be
remembered[e] forever.
7 He will have no fear of bad news;
his heart is steadfast,[f] trusting in
the LORD.[g]
8 His heart is secure, he will have no
fear;[h]
in the end he will look in triumph
on his foes.[i]
9 He has scattered abroad his gifts to the
poor,[j]
his righteousness endures[k]
forever;
his horn[a] will be lifted[l] high in
honor.

10 The wicked man will see[m] and be
vexed,
he will gnash his teeth[n] and waste
away;[o]
the longings of the wicked will come
to nothing.[p]

112:5 [c]S Ps 37:21,26; Lk 6:35 **112:6** [d]S Ps 15:5; S 55:22 [e]Pr 10:7; Ecc 2:16 **112:7** [f]Ps 57:7; 108:1 [g]S Ps 28:7; 56:3-4; S Isa 12:2 **112:8** [h]Ps 3:6; 27:1; 56:11; Pr 1:33; Isa 12:2 [i]S Ps 54:7 **112:9** [j]Lk 19:8; Ac 9:36; 2Co 9:9* [k]S Ps 111:3 [l]S Ps 75:10 **112:10** [m]Ps 86:17 [n]S Ps 37:12; S Mt 8:12 [o]S Ps 34:21 [p]S Job 8:13

113:1 [q]S Ps 22:23 [r]Ps 34:22; S 103:21; 134:1 **113:2** [s]S Ps 30:4; 48:10; 145:21; 148:13; 149:3; Isa 12:4 [t]Ps 115:18; 131:3; Da 2:20 **113:3** [u]Isa 24:15; 45:6; 59:19; Mal 1:11

Psalm 113

1 Praise the LORD.[b][q]

Praise, O servants of the LORD,[r]
praise the name of the LORD.
2 Let the name of the LORD be praised,[s]
both now and forevermore.[t]
3 From the rising of the sun[u] to the place
where it sets,
the name of the LORD is to be praised.
4 The LORD is exalted[v] over all the
nations,
his glory above the heavens.[w]
5 Who is like the LORD our God,[x]
the One who sits enthroned[y] on
high,[z]
6 who stoops down to look[a]
on the heavens and the earth?

7 He raises the poor[b] from the dust
and lifts the needy[c] from the ash
heap;

[a] 9 *Horn* here symbolizes dignity. [b] 1 Hebrew *Hallelu Yah*; also in verse 9

113:4 [v]S Ps 99:2 [w]S Ps 8:1; S 57:11 **113:5** [x]S Ex 8:10; S Ps 35:10 [y]S Ps 103:19 [z]S Job 16:19 **113:6** [a]Ps 11:4; 138:6; Isa 57:15 **113:7** [b]1Sa 2:8; Ps 35:10; 68:10; 140:12 [c]Ps 107:41

112:5 *Good.* Well-being and prosperity (see 34:8–14 and note). *is generous and lends freely.* See v. 9; see also 111:5.
112:6–9 The stanza is framed by reference to the righteous man being "remembered" (see note on v. 2) and his generosity (see note on vv. 2–5).
112:6 *shaken.* See note on 10:6.
112:7 Shares with 111:7 the basic theme of reliability. *heart.* See v. 8; see also note on 4:7. *trusting.* His trust in God will be as steadfast as his righteousness is enduring (see v. 3). For trust and obedience to God's righteous will as the sum of true godliness see 34:8–14 and note.
112:8 *secure.* In Hebrew a verbal echo of "steadfast" in 111:8. *will look in triumph.* "Even in darkness light dawns" (v. 4).
112:9 See 2Co 9:9 and note. *gifts to the poor.* See v. 5. *his righteousness.* Just as the Lord remembers his covenant (111:5,9), so the righteous person acts according to "justice" (v. 5) and "righteousness" (v. 9), two of the prime moral virtues the Lord requires of his covenant servant (see Ge 18:19; Ps 106:3; Isa 5:7; 56:1; Eze 18:5,21; 33:14,16,19; 45:9; Am 5:24; 6:12; see also 2Sa 8:15; Pr 1:3; 21:3; Jer 22:15; 32:15—sometimes rendered "just" and "right"). *lifted high in honor.* As God's name is held in holy awe (see 111:9), so the godly will be held in honor.
112:10 The counterpoint—like 111:10. *see and be vexed.* Godliness is the way to blessedness whereas the way the wicked have chosen leads to a dead end (see 10:2–11; 107:42). *come to nothing.* See 1:4–6; see also Ps 37; Pr 10:28.
Ps 113–118 The "Egyptian Hallel," which came to be used in Jewish liturgy at the great religious festivals (Passover, Weeks, Tabernacles, Dedication, New Moon; see Lev 23; Nu 10:10; Jn 10:22; see also chart, pp. 178–179). At Passover, Ps 113 and 114 were sung before the meal (before the second cup was passed) and Ps 115–118 after the meal (when the fourth cup had been filled). For the frame within which the "Hallel" has been set see introduction to Ps 111–119.
Ps 113 A hymn to the Lord celebrating his high majesty and his mercies to the lowly (see 138:6). It was probably composed originally for the temple liturgy. Thematically the psalm has strong links with the song of Hannah (1Sa 2:1–15) and the song of Mary (Lk 1:46–55).

Three precisely balanced stanzas (each having three verses) give the psalm a pleasing symmetry. With seven (the number of completeness) verbs the author celebrates God's praise in stanzas two and three ("is exalted," "sits ... on high," "stoops down," "raises," "lifts," "seats," "settles")—and note the fourfold praise in the first stanza. At the center (v. 5; see note on 6:6) a rhetorical question focuses and heightens the hymnic theme.
113:1b–3 The fourfold call to praise.
113:1 *name of the LORD.* See vv. 2–3. Triple repetition was a common liturgical convention (see note on 96:1–3). *name.* See note on 5:11.
113:2 *now and forevermore.* The praise of those who truly praise the Lord cannot rest content until it fills all time—and space (v. 3).
113:3 The psalmist employs an ancient formula for indicating universal space. Canaanite Amarna letter No. 288 reads as follows: "Behold, the king, my lord, has set his name at the rising of the sun and at the setting of the sun" (see chart, p. xxii; cf. Ps 139:9 and note).
113:4–6 The Lord is enthroned on high, exalted over all creation.
113:4 See the refrain in 57:5,11. *exalted over all the nations.* And implicitly over all their gods (see 95:3; 96:4–5; 97:9; see also 47:2,7–8). Accordingly, those who receive his saving help "exalt" him in grateful praise (118:28)—a thematic frame to the "Hallel." *above the heavens.* Above even the most exalted aspect of the creation (see v. 6; 148:13).
113:5 The rhetorical center (see note on 6:6). *Who is like the LORD ...?* See note on Mic 1:1. *our God.* What grace, that he has covenanted to be "our" God (see Ge 17:7; Ex 19:5–6; 20:2)!
113:7–9 The Lord exalts the lowly—the God of highest majesty does not ally himself with the high and mighty of the earth but stands with and raises up the poor and needy (see 1Sa 2:3–8; Lk 1:46–55). Cf. the deliverance celebrated in Ps 118.
113:7–8 Repeated almost verbatim from 1Sa 2:8.
113:7 *poor ... needy.* See 9:18; 34:6 and notes. *dust ... ash*

8 he seats them[d] with princes,
with the princes of their people.
9 He settles the barren[e] woman in her
home
as a happy mother of children.

Praise the LORD.

Psalm 114

1 When Israel came out of Egypt,[f]
the house of Jacob from a people of
foreign tongue,
2 Judah[g] became God's sanctuary,[h]
Israel his dominion.
3 The sea looked and fled,[i]
the Jordan turned back;[j]
4 the mountains skipped[k] like rams,
the hills like lambs.

5 Why was it, O sea, that you fled,[l]
O Jordan, that you turned back,
6 you mountains, that you skipped like
rams,
you hills, like lambs?
7 Tremble, O earth,[m] at the presence of
the Lord,
at the presence of the God of Jacob,
8 who turned the rock into a pool,
the hard rock into springs of water.[n]

Psalm 115

115:4-11pp — Ps 135:15-20

1 Not to us, O LORD, not to us
but to your name be the glory,[o]
because of your love and
faithfulness.[p]
2 Why do the nations say,
"Where is their God?"[q]
3 Our God is in heaven;[r]
he does whatever pleases him.[s]
4 But their idols are silver and gold,[t]
made by the hands of men.[u]
5 They have mouths, but cannot
speak,[v]
eyes, but they cannot see;

113:8 [d]S 2Sa 9:11 **113:9** [e]S 1Sa 2:5 **114:1** [f]S Ex 13:3; S 29:46 **114:2** [g]Ps 76:1 [h]S Ex 15:17; Ps 78:68-69 **114:3** [i]Ex 14:21; Ps 77:16 [j]S Ex 15:8; S Jos 3:16 **114:4** [k]S Jdg 5:5 **114:5** [l]S Ex 14:21 **114:7** [m]S Ex 15:14; S 1Ch 16:30 **114:8** [n]S Ex 17:6; S Nu 20:11 **115:1** [o]Ps 29:2; 66:2; 96:8 [p]S Ex 34:6 **115:2** [q]S Ps 42:3 **115:3** [r]Ezr 5:11; Ne 1:4; Ps 103:19; 136:26; Mt 6:9 [s]Ps 135:6 **115:4** [t]Rev 9:20 [u]S 2Ki 19:18; S 2Ch 32:19; Jer 10:3-5; Ac 19:26 **115:5** [v]Jer 10:5

heap. Symbolic of a humble status (see Ge 18:27; 1Ki 16:2), but here probably also of extreme distress and need (see Job 30:19; 42:6; Isa 47:1; Jer 25:34).

113:9 *barren woman.* In that ancient society barrenness was the greatest disgrace and the deepest tragedy for a woman (see Ge 30:1; 1Sa 1:6–7,10); in her old age she would be as desolate as Naomi because she would have no one to sustain her (see Ru 1:11–13; see also 2Ki 4:14). *home.* Family circle. *happy mother.* Because of God's gracious provision, as in the case of Sarah (see Ge 21:2), Rebekah (see Ge 25:21), Rachel (see Ge 30:23), Hannah (see 1Sa 1:20), the Shunammite (see 2Ki 4:17) and others.

Ps 114 A hymnic celebration of the exodus, the second psalm in the "Egyptian Hallel" (see introduction to Ps 113–118). It is one of the most exquisitely fashioned songs of the Psalter. It probably dates from the period of the monarchy sometime after the division of the kingdom (see v. 2). No doubt it was composed for liturgical use at the temple during one of the annual religious festivals (see introduction to Ps 113). The theme is progressively developed through four balanced stanzas, reaching its climax in the fourth. The first two stanzas (vv. 1–4) recall the great events of the exodus; the last two (vv. 5–8) celebrate their continuing significance.

114:1–2 The great OT redemptive event.

114:1 *Israel … house of Jacob.* Synonyms (see Ex 19:3). *came out of Egypt.* Recalls the exodus and all the great events of the desert journey.

114:2 *Judah … Israel.* The southern and northern kingdoms, viewed here as the one people of God. *became.* The crucial event was the establishment of the covenant at Sinai, where Israel became bound to the Lord as a "kingdom of priests and a holy nation" (Ex 19:3–6). *God's.* Lit. "his." The "antecedent" is not expressed until the climax (v. 7). *sanctuary.* His temple in which he took up his residence in the world—symbolized by the tabernacle, later the temple. In Ex 15:17 the promised land is similarly called God's sanctuary. *dominion.* The special realm over which he ruled as King. This, rather than the exodus itself, was the great wonder of God's grace.

114:3–4 The author evokes a fearsome scene such as that portrayed by other poets (see 18:7–15; 68:7–8; 77:16–19; Jdg 5:4–5; Hab 3:3–10).

114:3 *sea … Jordan.* The Red Sea and the Jordan River, through which the Lord brought his people—here they are personified. *looked and fled.* Saw the mighty God approach in his awesome pillar of cloud and fled.

114:4 *skipped.* Or "leaped"; the mountains and hills quaked at God's approach (see 29:6).

114:7–8 The Lord of yesterday (vv. 5–6)—the God of Jacob—is still with us.

114:7 *Tremble.* In awesome recognition. *earth.* All creation. *Jacob.* A synonym for Israel (see Ge 32:28).

114:8 *turned the rock into a pool.* Thus sustaining and refreshing life (see Ex 17:6; Nu 20:11).

115 This third psalm in the "Egyptian Hallel" (see introduction to Ps 113–118) offers praise to the Lord, the one true God, for his love and faithfulness toward his people. It was composed as a liturgy of praise for the temple worship. It may have been written for use at the dedication of the second temple (see Ezr 6:16) when Israel was beginning to revive after the disruption of the exile. See introduction to Ps 113. Structurally, the song advances in five movements involving a liturgical exchange between the people and temple personnel: (1) vv. 1–8: the people; (2) vv. 9–11: Levitical choir leader (the refrain perhaps spoken by the Levitical choir); (3) vv. 12–13: the people; (4) vv. 14–15: the priests; (5) vv. 16–18: the people.

115:1–8 Praise of God's love and faithfulness toward his people, which silences the taunts of the nations.

115:1 *Not to us … not to us.* The introductory confession of faith. Israel's existence, and now her revival, is not her own achievement. *name.* See note on 5:11. *love and faithfulness.* The most common OT expression for God's covenant benefits (see note on 26:3). *love.* See note on 6:4.

115:2 *Where is their God?* The taunt of the nations when Israel is decimated by natural disasters (see Joel 2:17) or crushed by enemies, especially when Judah is destroyed and the temple of God razed (see 3:2; 10:11 and notes; 79:10; Mic 7:10).

115:3 *is in heaven.* Sits enthroned (see 113:5) in the "highest heavens" (v. 16). *whatever pleases him.* If Israel is decimated or destroyed, it is God's doing; it is not his failure or inability to act, nor is it the achievement of the idols the nations worship. And when Israel is revived, that is also God's doing, and no other god can oppose him.

115:4–7 Whatever glory and power the false gods are thought to have (as symbolized in the images made to represent them), they are mere figments of human imagination and utterly worthless (see 135:15–18; Isa 46:1–7).

[6]they have ears, but cannot hear,
noses, but they cannot smell;
[7]they have hands, but cannot feel,
feet, but they cannot walk;
nor can they utter a sound with their
throats.
[8]Those who make them will be like
them,
and so will all who trust in them.

[9]O house of Israel, trust[w] in the LORD—
he is their help and shield.
[10]O house of Aaron,[x] trust in the LORD—
he is their help and shield.
[11]You who fear him,[y] trust in the LORD—
he is their help and shield.

[12]The LORD remembers[z] us and will bless
us:[a]
He will bless the house of Israel,
he will bless the house of Aaron,
[13]he will bless those who fear[b] the
LORD—
small and great alike.

[14]May the LORD make you increase,[c]
both you and your children.
[15]May you be blessed by the LORD,
the Maker of heaven[d] and earth.

[16]The highest heavens belong to the
LORD,[e]
but the earth he has given[f] to
man.
[17]It is not the dead[g] who praise the LORD,
those who go down to silence;
[18]it is we who extol the LORD,[h]
both now and forevermore.[i]

Praise the LORD.[a j]

Psalm 116

[1]I love the LORD,[k] for he heard my voice;
he heard my cry[l] for mercy.[m]
[2]Because he turned his ear[n] to me,
I will call on him as long as I live.

[3]The cords of death[o] entangled me,
the anguish of the grave[b] came upon
me;
I was overcome by trouble and
sorrow.
[4]Then I called on the name[p] of the
LORD:
"O LORD, save me![q]"
[5]The LORD is gracious and righteous;[r]
our God is full of compassion.[s]
[6]The LORD protects the simplehearted;
when I was in great need,[t] he saved
me.[u]

[7]Be at rest[v] once more, O my soul,
for the LORD has been good[w] to you.

[a] 18 Hebrew *Hallelu Yah* [b] 3 Hebrew *Sheol*

115:9 [w]Ps 37:3; 62:8 **115:10** [x]Ex 30:30; Ps 118:3 **115:11** [y]Ps 22:23; 103:11; 118:4 **115:12** [z]S 1Ch 16:15 [a]S Ge 12:2 **115:13** [b]S Ps 112:1 **115:14** [c]Dt 1:11 **115:15** [d]S Ge 1:1; Ac 14:15; S Rev 10:6 **115:16** [e]S Ps 89:11 [f]S Ge 1:28; Ps 8:6-8 **115:17** [g]Ps 88:10-12 **115:18** [h]S Ps 111:1 [i]S Ps 113:2 [j]Ps 28:6; 33:2; 103:1 **116:1** [k]Ps 18:1 [l]S Ps 31:22; S 40:1 [m]S Ps 6:9; S 28:2 **116:2** [n]S Ps 5:1 **116:3** [o]S 2Sa 22:6; Ps 18:4-5 **116:4** [p]Ps 80:18; 118:5 [q]S Ps 80:2 **116:5** [r]S Ex 9:27; S 2Ch 12:6; S Ezr 9:15 [s]S Ex 22:27; S Ps 86:15 **116:6** [t]S Ps 79:8 [u]Ps 18:3; 22:5; 107:13 **116:7** [v]Ps 46:10; 62:1; 131:2; Mt 11:29 [w]Ps 13:6; 106:1; 142:7

115:8 *Those who make them.* The taunting nations (cf. v. 2). *like them.* Powerless and ineffectual. For a graphic elaboration of this truth see Isa 44:9–20.
115:9–11 The call to trust in the Lord, not in idols (see v. 8). For triple repetition as a liturgical convention see note on 96:1–3. For the same groupings see 118:2–4; see also 135:19–20.
115:11 *You who fear him.* Perhaps proselytes (see 1Ki 8:41–43; Ezr 6:21; Ne 10:28).
115:12–13 The people's confession of trust.
115:14–15 The priestly blessing.
115:14 *make you increase.* In numbers, wealth and strength (cf. Ecc 2:9: "became greater by far than"—lit. "increased more than").
115:16–18 The people's concluding doxology.
115:16 *highest heavens ... earth.* The one the exclusive realm of the exalted, all-sovereign God; the other the divinely appointed place for human beings, where they live under God's rule and care, enjoy his abundant blessings (vv. 12–13) and celebrate his praise (v. 18).
115:17 *not the dead.* The dead no longer live in "the earth" (v. 16) but have descended to the silent realm below, where blessings are no longer enjoyed and hence praise is absent (see notes on 6:5; 30:1).
Ps 116 Praise of the Lord for deliverance from death. It may have been written by a king (see v. 16 and note; cf. also Hezekiah's thanksgiving, Isa 38:10–20); its language echoes many of the psalms of David. In Jewish liturgy (see introduction to Ps 113–118), the singular personal pronoun must have been used corporately (see note on Ps 30 title), and the references to "death" may have been understood as alluding to the Egyptian bondage and/or the exile.
Structurally, the psalm is so designed that the second half (vv. 10–19) mirrors the first half (vv. 1–9)—which may be why the Septuagint (the pre-Christian Greek translation of the OT) divides the psalm into two. Basically the theme is developed in a series of couplets (vv. 1–2,3–4,5–6,8–9// 10–11,13–14,15–16,17–19—the final couplet being expanded into a triplet). Verse 7 (between the last two couplets of the first half) and v. 12 (between the first two couplets of the second half) have striking verbal and thematic links (see notes on those verses). Further, the divine name Yahweh ("LORD") occurs seven times in each half of the psalm (in v. 8 "LORD" has been supplied by the translators for clarity; in v. 19 the second instance belongs to the appended liturgical formula).
116:1–2 I love the Lord because he has heard and saved me (cf. 18:1).
116:2 *I will call on him.* In him I will trust and my prayers will ever be to him. "I will call/I called" is a key thematic phrase (in Hebrew one word, and always in the same form as here), occurring twice in each half of the psalm (vv. 2,4,13,17).
116:3–4 The deadly threat (see 18:4–6).
116:3 *cords of death.* See note on 18:5.
116:5–6 Testimony to God's goodness—echoing Ex 34:6.
116:5 *gracious ... righteous ... compassion.* See 145:8,17; cf. 112:4. *our God.* The author is conscious of those about him; he is praising the Lord "in the presence of all his people" (vv. 14,18).
116:6 *simplehearted.* Those who are childlike in their sense of dependence on and trust in the Lord (see note on 19:7).
116:7 *Be at rest ... soul.* Lit. "Return, my soul, to your rest." *rest.* A state of unthreatened well-being (cf. Jer 6:16; see 1Ki 5:4; see also note on 23:2, "quiet waters"). *O my soul.* See note on 103:1–2,22. *has been good.* See v. 12 and note.

[8]For you, O LORD, have delivered my
soul[x] from death,
my eyes from tears,
my feet from stumbling,
[9]that I may walk before the LORD[y]
in the land of the living.[z]
[10]I believed;[a] therefore[a] I said,
"I am greatly afflicted."[b]
[11]And in my dismay I said,
"All men are liars."[c]

[12]How can I repay the LORD
for all his goodness[d] to me?
[13]I will lift up the cup of salvation
and call on the name[e] of the LORD.
[14]I will fulfill my vows[f] to the LORD
in the presence of all his people.

[15]Precious in the sight[g] of the LORD
is the death of his saints.[h]
[16]O LORD, truly I am your servant;[i]
I am your servant, the son of your
maidservant[b];[j]
you have freed me from my
chains.[k]

[17]I will sacrifice a thank offering[l] to you
and call on the name of the LORD.
[18]I will fulfill my vows[m] to the LORD
in the presence of all his people,
[19]in the courts[n] of the house of the
LORD—
in your midst, O Jerusalem.[o]

Praise the LORD.[c]

Psalm 117

[1]Praise the LORD,[p] all you nations;[q]
extol him, all you peoples.
[2]For great is his love[r] toward us,
and the faithfulness of the LORD[s]
endures forever.

Praise the LORD.[c]

Psalm 118

[1]Give thanks to the LORD,[t] for he is
good;[u]
his love endures forever.[v]

116:8 [x]S Ps 86:13 **116:9** [y]S Ge 5:22; Ps 56:13; 89:15 [z]S Job 28:13; Ps 27:13; Isa 38:11; Jer 11:19 **116:10** [a]2Co 4:13* [b]Ps 9:18; 72:2; S 107:17; 119:67,71,75 **116:11** [c]Jer 9:3-5; Hos 7:13; Mic 6:12; Ro 3:4 **116:12** [d]Ps 103:2; 106:1 **116:13** [e]S Ps 105:1 **116:14** [f]S Nu 30:2; S Ps 66:13 **116:15** [g]Ps 72:14 [h]S Nu 23:10 **116:16** [i]Ps 119:125; 143:12 [j]S Ps 86:16 [k]S Job 12:18 **116:17** [l]S Lev 7:12; S Ezr 1:4 **116:18** [m]ver 14; S Lev 22:18 **116:19** [n]Ps 92:13; 96:8; 100:4; 135:2 [o]Ps 102:21 **117:1** [p]S Ps 22:23; S 103:2 [q]Ro 15:11* **117:2** [r]S Ps 17:7; S 103:11 [s]Ps 119:90; 146:6 **118:1** [t]S 1Ch 16:8 [u]S 2Ch 5:13; S 7:3 [v]S Ezr 3:11

[a] 10 Or *believed even when* [b] 16 Or *servant, your faithful son* [c] 19,2 Hebrew *Hallelu Yah*

116:8–9 The deliverance experienced—a return to the theme of vv. 3–4.
116:8 *my soul.* Me (see note on 6:3).
116:10–11 Introduction to the second half of the psalm, an elaboration on the introduction to the first half (vv. 1–2).
116:10 *I believed.* The author speaks of his faith that moved him to call on the Lord when he was threatened. *I am greatly afflicted.* This and the quotation in v. 11 should perhaps be taken, together with the one in v. 4, as a brief recollection of the prayer offered when the psalmist was in distress. The threat of death from which he had been delivered was brought on by the false accusations of enemies, as in Ps 109 (see notes on 5:9; 10:7). (For another interpretation see following note.)
116:11 *All men are liars.* The heart of the accusation he had lodged against his false accusers (for examples of similar accusations see 5:9–10; 35:11,15; 109:2–4). Others interpret these words as a declaration that all people offer but a false hope for deliverance (see 60:11; 118:8–9)—therefore the psalmist called on the Lord.
116:12 *How can I repay the LORD ...?* Lit. "What can I return to the LORD ...?" *goodness.* The Hebrew for this word occurs only here in the OT, but represents the same basic root as "has been good" in v. 7. Verses 7,12, taken together, concisely focus the central movement of the psalm's theme.
116:13–14 Answer to the question in v. 12: By offering to the Lord those expressions of devotion he desires (compare vv. 13–14,17–18 with 50:14–15,23).
116:13 *cup of salvation.* Often thought to be related to the cup of the Passover meal referred to in Mt 26:27 and parallels, but far more likely the cup of wine drunk at the festal meal that climaxed a thank offering (cf. 22:26,29; Lev 7:11–21)—called the "cup of salvation" because the thank offering and its meal celebrated deliverance by the Lord. See the parallel with "sacrifice a thank offering" in the corresponding series in vv. 17–18.
116:14 *vows.* To praise the Lord (see note on 7:17).
116:15–16 Elaboration on vv. 3–4. Note the references to "death" in vv. 3,15; cf. vv. 8–9.
116:15 *Precious ... is the death.* Not in the sense of highly valued but of that which is carefully watched over; cf. the analogous expression, "precious is their blood in his sight" (72:14). *saints.* See note on 4:3.
116:16 *your servant.* This may identify the psalmist as the Lord's anointed (see 78:70), but in any event as one devoted to the Lord (see 19:11,13). *son of your maidservant.* See NIV text note; see also 86:16 and note, as well as the NIV text note there.
116:17–19 Reiteration of the vows of vv. 13–14.
116:17 *sacrifice a thank offering.* See note on v. 13.
116:19 *courts.* Of the temple (see 84:2,10; 2Ki 21:5; 23:11–12).
Ps 117 The shortest psalm in the Psalter—and the shortest chapter in the Bible—Ps 117 is an expanded Hallelujah (sometimes joined with Ps 118). It may originally have served as the conclusion to the preceding collection of Hallelujah psalms (Ps 111–116)—of which it is the seventh. All nations and peoples are called on to praise the Lord (as in 47:1; 67:3–5; 96:7; 98:4; 100:1; see note on 9:1) for his great love and enduring faithfulness toward Israel (see Isa 12:4–6). Thus the Hallelujahs of the OT Psalter, when fully expounded, express that great truth, so often emphasized in the OT, that the destiny of all peoples is involved in what God was doing in and for his people Israel (see, e.g., 2:8–12; 47:9; 67:2; 72:17; 102:15; 110; Ge 12:3; Dt 32:43; 1Ki 8:41–43; Isa 2:2–4; 11:10; 14:2; 25:6–7; 52:15; 56:7; 60:3; 66:18–24; Jer 3:17; 16:19–21; 33:9; Am 9:11–12; Mic 5:7–9; Zep 3:8–9; Hag 2:7; Zec 2:10–11; 8:20–23; 9:9–10; 14:2–3; Mal 3:12). See introduction to Ps 113–118.
117:1 Quoted in Ro 15:11 as proof that the salvation of Gentiles and the glorifying of God by Gentiles was not a divine afterthought.
117:2 The reason for the praise. *love ... faithfulness.* That is, love-and-faithfulness (see 36:5 and note; see also note on 3:7). *love.* See note on 6:4.
Ps 118 A hymn of thanksgiving for deliverance from enemies. Of the many interpretations of this psalm, three have gained the most adherents (but with much varia-

[2]Let Israel say:[w]
"His love endures forever."[x]
[3]Let the house of Aaron say:[y]
"His love endures forever."
[4]Let those who fear the LORD[z] say:
"His love endures forever."

[5]In my anguish[a] I cried to the LORD,
and he answered[b] by setting me free.
[6]The LORD is with me;[c] I will not be afraid.
What can man do to me?[d]
[7]The LORD is with me; he is my helper.[e]
I will look in triumph on my enemies.[f]

[8]It is better to take refuge in the LORD[g]
than to trust in man.[h]
[9]It is better to take refuge in the LORD
than to trust in princes.[i]
[10]All the nations surrounded me,
but in the name of the LORD I cut them off.[j]
[11]They surrounded me[k] on every side,[l]
but in the name of the LORD I cut them off.
[12]They swarmed around me like bees,[m]
but they died out as quickly as burning thorns;[n]
in the name of the LORD I cut them off.[o]
[13]I was pushed back and about to fall,
but the LORD helped me.[p]
[14]The LORD is my strength[q] and my song;
he has become my salvation.[r]

[15]Shouts of joy[s] and victory
resound in the tents of the righteous:
"The LORD's right hand[t] has done mighty things![u]
[16]The LORD's right hand is lifted high;
the LORD's right hand has done mighty things!"

[17]I will not die[v] but live,
and will proclaim[w] what the LORD has done.
[18]The LORD has chastened[x] me severely,
but he has not given me over to death.[y]

[19]Open for me the gates[z] of righteousness;
I will enter[a] and give thanks to the LORD.

118:2 [w]Ps 115:9 [x]Ps 106:1; 136:1-26 **118:3** [y]Ex 30:30; Ps 115:10 **118:4** [z]S Ps 115:11 **118:5** [a]Ps 18:6; 31:7; 77:2; 120:1 [b]ver 21; Ps 34:4; 86:7; 116:1; 138:3 **118:6** [c]S Dt 31:6; Heb 13:6* [d]S Ps 56:4 **118:7** [e]S Dt 33:29 [f]S Ps 54:7 **118:8** [g]Ps 2:12; 5:11; 9:9; 37:3; 40:4; Isa 25:4; 57:13 [h]2Ch 32:7-8; S Ps 108:12; S Isa 2:22 **118:9** [i]Ps 146:3 **118:10** [j]S Ps 37:9 **118:11** [k]Ps 88:17 [l]Ps 3:6 **118:12** [m]Dt 1:44 [n]S Ps 58:9 [o]Ps 37:9 **118:13** [p]ver 7; 2Ch 18:31; Ps 86:17 **118:14** [q]S Ex 15:2 [r]S Ps 62:2 **118:15** [s]S Job 8:21; S Ps 106:5 [t]S Ex 15:6; Ps 89:13; 108:6 [u]Lk 1:51 **118:17** [v]Hab 1:12 [w]S Dt 32:3; Ps 64:9; 71:16; 73:28 **118:18** [x]Jer 31:18; 1Co 11:32; Heb 12:5 [y]Ps 86:13 **118:19** [z]S Ps 24:7 [a]Ps 100:4

tion in detail): (1) A Davidic king leads the nation in a liturgy of thanksgiving for deliverance and victory after a hard-fought battle with a powerful confederacy of nations (cf. 2Ch 20:27–28; see note on v. 19). (2) Israel celebrates—probably at the Feast of Tabernacles—her deliverance from Egypt and victory over the Canaanites. (3) The postexilic Jews celebrate deliverance from their enemies, either at the dedication of the second temple (see Ezr 6:16) or at the dedication of the rebuilt walls of Jerusalem (see Ne 12:37–43). According to the first interpretation, the speaker in vv. 5–21 is the king; according to the second and third, the speaker is the Levitical (or priestly) leader of the liturgy, speaking (representatively) on behalf of the people. The notes that follow assume the first interpretation. In the postexilic liturgy developed for the annual festivals (see introduction to Ps 113), the song was used as a thanksgiving for national deliverance. As the last song of that liturgy, it may have been the hymn sung by Jesus and his disciples at the conclusion of the Last Supper (see Mt 26:30).

Following a liturgical call to praise (vv. 1–4), the king offers a song of thanksgiving for deliverance and victory in battle (vv. 5–21). A three-verse stanza (vv. 5–7) summarizing the main theme is followed by two seven-verse composite stanzas (vv. 8–14,15–21) of elaboration, each closing with the refrain: "has/have become my salvation." In vv. 22–27 the people rejoice over what the Lord has done. Thereafter, the king speaks his final word of praise (v. 28), and a liturgical conclusion (v. 29) repeats the opening call to praise, thus framing the whole. In the two seven-verse stanzas (vv. 8–14,15–21) the divine name Yahweh (or its shortened form, Yah) occurs seven times, in the six-verse stanza (vv. 22–27) it occurs seven times, and in the remaining verses (1–7,28–29) it occurs seven times.

118:1–4 The liturgical call to praise.

118:1 A conventional call to praise (shared in whole or in part with Ps 105–107; 136; 1Ch 16:8,34; 2Ch 20:21). *Give thanks.* See note on Ps 100 title. This, together with vv. 2–4 (except for the refrain) and 29, may have been by the same voice that speaks in vv. 5–21. *love.* See vv. 2–4,29; see also note on 6:4.

118:2–4 *Israel ... house of Aaron ... those who fear the LORD.* See 115:9–11 and note. Triple repetition is a common feature in this psalm (see note on 96:1–3).

118:4 *fear the LORD.* See note on 66:16.

118:5–21 The king's song of thanksgiving for deliverance and victory.

118:5–7 The introduction: I cried to the Lord, he answered, I need fear no one.

118:5 *I cried ... he answered.* For the conjunction of this appeal and response elsewhere see 3:4; 4:1; 17:6; 22:2; 27:7; 86:7; 91:15; 99:6; 102:2; 120:1; 138:3; 1Ki 18:24; Pr 21:13; Isa 65:24; Jer 33:3; Jnh 2:2—all these passages share the same Hebrew terms. *free.* Lit. "in a broad place"; see 18:19 and note ("spacious place").

118:7 *I will look.* Or "I look."

118:8–14 Reflection on the experience of the Lord's saving help—framed by vv. 8–9 and v. 14.

118:8–9 See 33:16–19; see also Ps 62; 146.

118:10 *in the name of the LORD.* See 1Sa 17:45. *name.* See vv. 11–12,26; see also note on 5:11.

118:12 *as burning thorns.* See 58:9 and note.

118:13 *fall.* Be killed (see vv. 17–18; see also note on 13:4).

118:14 Perhaps recalls the triumph song of Ex 15, but more likely the verse had become a widely used testimony of praise (see Isa 12:2).

118:15–21 Celebration of the Lord's deliverance—framed by vv. 15–16 and v. 21.

118:15 *tents.* Dwellings. *righteous.* Israel as the people (ideally) committed in heart and life to the Lord (see v. 20; see also 68:3 and note). Cf. "the tents of the wicked" (84:10).

118:17 *live, and ... proclaim.* See 115:17–18; see also note on 6:5.

118:18 *chastened me.* The king acknowledges that the grave threat through which he has passed has also served God's purpose—to discipline him and teach him humble godliness (see 6:1; 38:1; 94:12; Dt 4:36; 8:5).

118:19 *Open for me.* This line suggests a liturgical procession (see v. 27) in which the king approaches the inner court of the

[20]This is the gate of the LORD[b]
through which the righteous may
enter.[c]
[21]I will give you thanks, for you
answered me;[d]
you have become my salvation.[e]
[22]The stone[f] the builders rejected
has become the capstone;[g]
[23]the LORD has done this,
and it is marvelous[h] in our eyes.
[24]This is the day the LORD has made;
let us rejoice and be glad[i] in it.

[25]O LORD, save us;[j]
O LORD, grant us success.
[26]Blessed is he who comes[k] in the name
of the LORD.
From the house of the LORD we bless
you.[a][l]
[27]The LORD is God,[m]
and he has made his light shine[n]
upon us.
With boughs in hand,[o] join in the
festal procession
up[b] to the horns of the altar.[p]

[28]You are my God, and I will give you
thanks;
you are my God,[q] and I will exalt[r]
you.

[29]Give thanks to the LORD, for he is
good;
his love endures forever.

Psalm 119[c]

א Aleph

[1]Blessed are they whose ways are
blameless,[s]
who walk[t] according to the law of
the LORD.[u]

118:20 [b]Ps 122:1-2 [c]Ps 15:1-2; 24:3-4; Rev 22:14 **118:21** [d]S ver 5 [e]Ps 27:1 **118:22** [f]Isa 8:14 [g]Isa 17:10; 19:13; 28:16; Zec 4:7; 10:4; Mt 21:42; Mk 12:10; Lk 20:17*; S Ac 4:11*; 1Pe 2:7* **118:23** [h]Mt 21:42*; Mk 12:11* **118:24** [i]S Ps 70:4 **118:25** [j]S Ps 28:9; 116:4 **118:26** [k]S Mt 11:3; 21:9*; 23:39*; Mk 11:9*; Lk 13:35*; 19:38*; Jn 12:13* [l]Ps 129:8 **118:27** [m]S 1Ki 18:21 [n]Ps 27:1; Isa 58:10; 60:1,19,20; Mal 4:2; 1Pe 2:9 [o]S Lev 23:40 [p]Ex 27:2 **118:28** [q]S Ge 28:21; S Ps 16:2; 63:1; Isa 25:1 [r]S Ex 15:2 **119:1** [s]S Ge 17:1; S Dt 18:13; Pr 11:20 [t]Ps 128:1 [u]S Ps 1:2

[a] *26* The Hebrew is plural. [b] *27* Or *Bind the festal sacrifice with ropes / and take it* [c] This psalm is an acrostic poem; the verses of each stanza begin with the same letter of the Hebrew alphabet.

temple at the head of the jubilant worshipers (see Ps 24; 68). *gates.* Those leading to the inner temple court. *of righteousness.* Often thought to be the name of a particular gateway, but more likely only descriptive here of the gate "through which the righteous may enter" (v. 20). It is possible that the procession began outside the city and that "the gates of righteousness" are the gates of Jerusalem, the city of God (see note on 24:7; see also Isa 26:2).

118:21 This closing verse of the thanksgiving song echoes the "Give thanks" of v. 1, the "answered ... me" of v. 5 and the testimony of v. 14.

118:22–27 The people's exultation.

118:22 *The stone the builders rejected.* Most likely a reference to the king (whose deliverance and victory are being celebrated), who had been looked on with disdain by the kings invading his realm—the builders of worldly empires. Others suppose that the stone refers to Israel, a nation held in contempt by the world powers. *capstone.* Lit. "head of the corner"—either a capstone over a door (a large stone used as a lintel), or a large stone used to anchor and align the corner of a wall, or the keystone of an arch (see Zec 4:7; 10:4). By a wordplay (pun) the author hints at "chief ruler" (the Hebrew word for "corner" is sometimes used as a metaphor for leader/ruler; see Isa 19:13; see also Jdg 20:2; 1Sa 14:38). This stone, disdained by the worldly powers, has become the most important stone in the structure of the new world order that God is bringing about through Israel. Jesus applied this verse (and v. 23) to himself (see Mt 21:42; Mk 12:10–11; Lk 20:17; see also Ac 4:11; Eph 2:20; 1Pe 2:7).

118:24 *day the LORD has made ... rejoice.* This day of rejoicing was made possible by God's deliverance in the victory being celebrated. Others suppose a reference to Passover or the Feast of Tabernacles. *has made.* Or "has done it" (see vv. 15–17,23)—has made the "stone" the "capstone" (v. 22).

118:25 Prayer for the Lord to continue to save and sustain his people (cf. note on Mt 21:9).

118:26 *who comes in the name of the LORD.* The one who with God's help had defeated the enemies "in the name of the LORD" (see vv. 10–12). *From the house of the LORD.* From God's very presence (see 134:3). *you.* The plural (see NIV text note) may have been used to exalt the king (the plural was often used with reference to God), whom God had so singularly blessed (see NIV text note on 1Ki 9:6). Alternatively, it may refer to those who have come with the king victoriously from the battle. The crowds who greeted Jesus at his Triumphal Entry into Jerusalem used the words of vv. 25–26 (see Jn 12:13).

118:27 *made his light shine upon us.* An echo of the priestly benediction (see Nu 6:25 and note). *With boughs ... up.* Apparently a call to complete the climax of the liturgy of a thank offering (see Lev 7:11–21), though others suggest the liturgy of the Feast of Tabernacles.

118:28 The king's closing reiteration of his vow in v. 21.

118:29 Renewal of the opening call to grateful praise (see v. 1 and note).

Ps 119 A devotional on the word of God. The author was an Israelite of exemplary piety (probably postexilic) who (1) was passionately devoted to the word of God as the word of life; (2) humbly acknowledged, nevertheless, the errant ways of his heart and life; (3) knew the pain—but also the fruits—of God's corrective discipline; and (4) had suffered much at the hands of those who arrogantly disregarded God's word and made him the target of their hostility, ridicule and slander. It is possible that he was a priest (see notes on vv. 23,57)—and the psalm might well be a vehicle for priestly instruction in godliness. He elaborated on the themes of 19:7–13 and interwove with them many prayers for deliverance, composing a massive alphabetic acrostic (see NIV text note) that demands patient, meditative reading. In regard to length, form and type it stands alone in the Psalter. And of all the psalms, this one is the most likely to have been composed originally in writing and intended to be read rather than sung or recited. Most of its lines are addressed to God, mingling prayers with professions of devotion to God's law. Yet, as the opening verses (and perhaps also its elaborate acrostic form) make clear, it was intended for godly instruction (in the manner of Ps 1; see v. 9 and note). It was included in the Psalter no doubt as a model of piety. For its placement in the Psalter see introduction to Ps 111–119. See also notes on 111:1; 112:1.

Whereas elsewhere in the Psalter the focus falls primarily on God's mighty acts of creation and redemption and his rule over all the world, here devotion to the word of God (and the God of the word) is the dominant theme. The au-

2 Blessed[v] are they who keep his
statutes[w]
and seek him[x] with all their heart.[y]
3 They do nothing wrong;[z]
they walk in his ways.[a]
4 You have laid down precepts[b]
that are to be fully obeyed.[c]
5 Oh, that my ways were steadfast
in obeying your decrees![d]
6 Then I would not be put to shame[e]
when I consider all your
commands.[f]
7 I will praise you with an upright
heart
as I learn your righteous laws.
8 I will obey your decrees;
do not utterly forsake me.[g]

ב Beth

9 How can a young man keep his
way pure?[h]
By living according to your
word.[i]
10 I seek you with all my heart;[j]
do not let me stray from your
commands.[k]
11 I have hidden your word in my
heart[l]
that I might not sin[m] against you.
12 Praise be[n] to you, O LORD;
teach me[o] your decrees.[p]

119:2 [v]Ps 112:1; Isa 56:2 [w]ver 146; Ps 99:7 [x]S 1Ch 16:11; S Ps 40:16 [y]S Dt 10:12 **119:3** [z]S Ps 59:4; 1Jn 3:9; 5:18 [a]Ps 128:1; Jer 6:16; 7:23 **119:4** [b]Ps 103:18 [c]S ver 56; S Dt 6:17 **119:5** [d]S Lev 19:37 **119:6** [e]ver 46,80 [f]ver 117 **119:8** [g]S Ps 38:21 **119:9** [h]S Ps 39:1 [i]ver 65,169 **119:10** [j]S Ps 9:1 [k]ver 21,118 **119:11** [l]S Dt 6:6; S Job 22:22 [m]ver 133,165; Ps 18:22-23; 19:13; Pr 3:23; Isa 63:13 **119:12** [n]Ps 28:6 [o]Ps 143:8,10 [p]S Ex 18:20

thor highlights two aspects of that word: (1) God's directives for life and (2) God's promises — the one calling for obedience, the other for faith (the two elements of true godliness; see 34:8 – 14 and note). In referring to these, he makes use of eight Hebrew terms supplied him by OT traditions: *torah,* "law"; *'edot,* "statutes"; *piqqudim,* "precepts"; *miṣwot,* "commands, commandments"; *mishpaṭim,* "laws" (all shared with 19:7 – 9; *mishpaṭim* is translated "ordinances" in 19:9); *ḥuqqim,* "decrees"; *dabar,* "word" (sometimes in the sense of "law," sometimes in the sense of "promise"); *'imrah,* "word," but more often "promise." These terms he distributes throughout the 22 stanzas (using all eight in *He, Waw, Heth, Yodh, Kaph, Pe* — never using less than six), employing a different order in each stanza. It may be that the availability of these eight terms determined (in large part) for the author the decision to devote eight verses to each letter of the alphabet. The alphabetic acrostic form, especially one as elaborate as this, may appear arbitrary and artificial to a modern reader (as if the author merely selected a traditional form from the poet's workshop and then labored to fill it with pious sentences), but a sympathetic and reflective reading of this devotional will compel a more favorable judgment. The author had a theme that filled his soul, a theme as big as life, that ranged the length and breadth and height and depth of a person's walk with God. Nothing less than the use of the full power of language would suffice, and of that the alphabet was a most apt symbol.

Apart from the obvious formal structure dictated by the chosen acrostic form, little need (or can) be said. It must be noted, however, that the first three and the last three verses were designed as introduction and conclusion to the whole. The former sets the tone of instruction in godly wisdom; the latter succinctly restates and summarizes the main themes. It may also be observed that the middle of the psalm has been marked by a similar three-verse introduction to the second half (see note on vv. 89 – 91). For the rest, the thought meanders, turns back upon itself and repeats (with varied nuances). The following notes point out continuities of thought and possible structure within stanzas.

119:1 – 3 General introduction.

119:1 – 2 *Blessed.* See note on 1:1.

119:1 *whose ways are blameless.* This opening general description is further elaborated in the rest of the introduction, which concludes with an equally general statement: "they walk in his ways" (v. 3). See Ge 17:1; cf. Ge 26:5 and note. *law.* Hebrew *torah,* a collective term for God's covenant directives for his people (see Dt 4:44). "Law" often came, especially later, to have a broader reference — the whole Pentateuch (see Lk 24:44 and note) or even the whole OT (see Jn 10:34; 12:34; 15:25; 1Co 14:21 and notes) — but here it is limited by the synonyms with which it is used interchangeably.

119:2 *statutes.* Hebrew *'edot,* a specifically covenantal term referring to stipulations laid down by the covenant Lord (see 25:10, "demands"; Dt 4:45, "stipulations"). *seek him with all their heart.* See Dt 4:29 and note. *heart.* See v. 7; see also note on 4:7.

119:3 *ways.* The Hebrew for this word occurs only rarely in this psalm, but is common in Deuteronomy and elsewhere as a general reference to God's covenant requirements (see note on 25:4) — used here to balance "ways" in v. 1.

119:4 – 8 Those who obey God's law (see vv. 4 – 5,8) can hope for God's help (see vv. 6 – 8).

119:4 *precepts.* Hebrew *piqqudim,* covenant regulations laid down by the Lord (see 19:8; 111:7).

119:5 *decrees.* Hebrew *ḥuqqim,* covenant directives (see Dt 6:2; 28:15,45; 30:10,16; 1Ki 11:11), emphasizing their fixed character.

119:6 *not be put to shame.* The psalmist would not suffer poverty or sickness, or humiliation at the hands of his enemies, and so become the object of sneers (see vv. 31,46,80; 25:2 – 3,20; see also introduction to this psalm), but he would have reason to praise the Lord (see v. 7) for blessings received and deliverances granted because the Lord does not forsake him (see v. 8). *consider.* Respect, have regard for (see v. 15; 74:20). *commands.* Hebrew *miṣwot,* covenant directives (see Ex 20:6; 24:12; Dt 4:2), designated specifically as that which God has commanded.

119:7 *righteous.* One of the author's favorite characterizations of God's law (see vv. 62,75,106,123,138,144,160,164,172; see also 19:9). *laws.* Hebrew *mishpaṭim,* covenant directives (see Ex 21:1; 24:3; Dt 4:1), as the laws laid down by a ruler (king).

119:8 *not ... forsake me.* To poverty, sickness or my enemies (cf. 9:10; 22:1; 27:9 – 10; 38:21; 71:9,11,18).

119:9 *young man.* Some have thought this a characterization of the author, but more likely it indicates instruction addressed to the young after the manner of the wisdom teachers (see 34:11; Pr 1:4; Ecc 11:9; 12:1; see also the first two paragraphs of Introduction to Proverbs: Purpose and Teaching). *pure.* Free from all moral taint (see 73:13). *word.* Hebrew *dabar,* a general designation for God's (word) revelation, but here used with special reference to his law (sometimes promises).

119:10 *I seek you.* The author's devotion is first of all to the God of the law and the promises; they have meaning for him only because they are God's word of life for him. *heart.* See v. 11; see also note on 4:7.

119:11 *word.* Hebrew *'imrah,* a synonym of *dabar* ("word"; see note on v. 9; see also Dt 33:9; Pr 30:5). Except where noted, as here, "word" in this psalm is *dabar*; *'imrah* is usually translated "promise."

[13]With my lips I recount
all the laws that come from your mouth.[q]
[14]I rejoice in following your statutes[r]
as one rejoices in great riches.
[15]I meditate on your precepts[s]
and consider your ways.
[16]I delight[t] in your decrees;
I will not neglect your word.

ג Gimel

[17]Do good to your servant,[u] and I will live;
I will obey your word.[v]
[18]Open my eyes that I may see
wonderful things in your law.
[19]I am a stranger on earth;[w]
do not hide your commands from me.
[20]My soul is consumed[x] with longing
for your laws[y] at all times.
[21]You rebuke the arrogant,[z] who are cursed[a]
and who stray[b] from your commands.
[22]Remove from me scorn[c] and contempt,
for I keep your statutes.[d]
[23]Though rulers sit together and slander me,
your servant will meditate on your decrees.
[24]Your statutes are my delight;
they are my counselors.

119:13 [q]ver 72 **119:14** [r]ver 111 **119:15** [s]ver 97,148; Ps 1:2 **119:16** [t]S Ps 112:1 **119:17** [u]Ps 13:6; 116:7 [v]ver 67; Ps 103:20 **119:19** [w]S Ge 23:4; Heb 11:13 **119:20** [x]Ps 42:2; 84:2 [y]ver 131; S Ps 63:1; Isa 26:9 **119:21** [z]ver 51; Job 30:1; Ps 5:5; Jer 20:7; 50:32; Da 4:37; Mal 3:15 [a]Dt 27:26 [b]S ver 10 **119:22** [c]Ps 39:8 [d]ver 2

119:25 [e]Ps 44:25 [f]ver 50,107; Ps 143:11 [g]ver 9 **119:26** [h]Ps 25:4; 27:11; 86:11 **119:27** [i]Ps 105:2; 145:5 **119:28** [j]Ps 6:7; 116:3; Isa 51:11; Jer 45:3 [k]Ps 18:1; Isa 40:29; 41:10 [l]ver 9 **119:29** [m]Ps 26:4 [n]S Nu 6:25 **119:30** [o]S Jos 24:22 [p]S Ps 26:3 [q]S Ps 108:1 **119:31** [r]S Dt 10:20

ד Daleth

[25]I am laid low in the dust;[e]
preserve my life[f] according to your word.[g]
[26]I recounted my ways and you answered me;
teach me your decrees.[h]
[27]Let me understand the teaching of your precepts;
then I will meditate on your wonders.[i]
[28]My soul is weary with sorrow;[j]
strengthen me[k] according to your word.[l]
[29]Keep me from deceitful ways;[m]
be gracious to me[n] through your law.
[30]I have chosen[o] the way of truth;[p]
I have set my heart[q] on your laws.
[31]I hold fast[r] to your statutes, O LORD;
do not let me be put to shame.
[32]I run in the path of your commands,
for you have set my heart free.

ה He

[33]Teach me,[s] O LORD, to follow your decrees;
then I will keep them to the end.
[34]Give me understanding,[t] and I will keep your law[u]
and obey it with all my heart.[v]

119:33 [s]ver 12 **119:34** [t]ver 27,73,144,169; S Job 32:8; Pr 2:6; Da 2:21; Jas 1:5 [u]S Dt 6:25 [v]ver 69

119:13 *recount.* Either in meditation or in liturgies of covenant commitment to the Lord (see 50:16, "recite").

119:14 *as one rejoices in great riches.* See vv. 72,111,162.

119:15 *ways.* The Hebrew for this word is a synonym of the Hebrew for "ways" in v. 3 (see 25:4 and note).

119:17–24 Devotion to God's law marks the Lord's servant, but alienates him from the arrogant (v. 21) of the world.

119:17 *I will obey.* Out of gratitude for God's care and blessing.

119:18 *wonderful things.* Usually ascribed to God's redeeming acts (see 9:1 and note)—but God's law also contains wonders (see v. 27) to contemplate, if only God opens a person's eyes.

119:19 *stranger on earth.* As a servant of the Lord, i.e., a citizen of his kingdom, the psalmist is not at home in any of the kingdoms of the world (see 39:12 and note; see also note on v. 54).

119:20 *My soul is.* I am (see vv. 28,81; see also note on 6:3).

119:21 *the arrogant.* Those who are a law to themselves, most fully described in 10:2–11 (see vv. 51,69,78,85,122; see also note on 31:23). The author has suffered much from their hostility because of his zeal for God and his law, as the next two verses and many others indicate. *cursed.* Ripe for God's judgment.

119:22 *scorn and contempt.* Of the arrogant.

119:23 *rulers.* Because the author mentions also speaking "before kings" (v. 46) and being persecuted by "rulers" (v. 161), it may be that he held some official position, such as priest (one of whose functions it would have been to teach God's law; see Lev 10:11; Ezr 7:6; Ne 8:2–8; Jer 2:8; 18:18; Mal 2:7; see also note on v. 57). The kings and rulers referred to may have been Israelite in the time of the monarchy, but more likely were local rulers in the postexilic Persian imperial system. *sit.* As those securely settled in the world—not as strangers (cf. v. 19). *together and slander.* As they share their worldly counsels, they speak derisively of the one who stands apart because he delights in God's statutes and makes them his "counselors" (v. 24).

119:25–32 Whether "laid low" (v. 25) or "set ... free" (v. 32), he is determined to "hold fast" (v. 31) to God's word.

119:25 *laid low.* The author speaks much of his sorrow, suffering and affliction (see vv. 28,50,67,71,75, 83,92,107,143,153). It is likely that the ridicule, slander and persecution from his adversaries are usually occasioned by this suffering of God's devoted servant, who makes God's word (his law and promises) the hope of his life (see vv. 42,51,65,69,78, 85,95,110,134,141,150,154,157,161; see also notes on v. 6; 5:9; 31:11–12). *in the dust.* See 44:25 and note. *word.* Especially its promises, as also in vv. 28,37,42,49,65,74,81,107,114,147.

119:27 *wonders.* See note on v. 18.

119:29 *deceitful ways.* Ways that seem right but lead to death (see Pr 14:12 and note)—in contrast to the ways prescribed by God's law, which are trustworthy (see vv. 86,138) and true (see vv. 142,151,160). *through your law.* By keeping me true to your law, let me enjoy your blessings.

119:30 *way of truth.* See note on v. 29.

119:31 *put to shame.* See note on v. 6.

119:32 *set my heart free.* Lit. "enlarged my heart," i.e., expanded it with joy (see Isa 60:5, "swell with joy"). Others translate it "increased my understanding" (see 1Ki 4:29, "breadth of understanding"). *heart.* See note on 4:7.

119:33–40 Prayer for instruction in God's will as he longs for his precepts.

119:34 *heart.* See v. 36; see also note on 4:7.

35 Direct me[w] in the path of your
commands,[x]
for there I find delight.[y]
36 Turn my heart[z] toward your statutes
and not toward selfish gain.[a]
37 Turn my eyes away from worthless
things;
preserve my life[b] according to your
word.[a c]
38 Fulfill your promise[d] to your servant,
so that you may be feared.
39 Take away the disgrace[e] I dread,
for your laws are good.
40 How I long[f] for your precepts!
Preserve my life[g] in your
righteousness.

ו Waw

41 May your unfailing love[h] come to me,
O LORD,
your salvation according to your
promise;[i]
42 then I will answer[j] the one who taunts
me,[k]
for I trust in your word.
43 Do not snatch the word of truth from
my mouth,[l]
for I have put my hope[m] in your
laws.
44 I will always obey your law,[n]
for ever and ever.
45 I will walk about in freedom,
for I have sought out your precepts.[o]
46 I will speak of your statutes before
kings[p]
and will not be put to shame,[q]
47 for I delight[r] in your commands
because I love them.[s]
48 I lift up my hands to[b] your commands,
which I love,
and I meditate[t] on your decrees.

ז Zayin

49 Remember your word[u] to your servant,
for you have given me hope.[v]
50 My comfort in my suffering is this:
Your promise preserves my life.[w]
51 The arrogant mock me[x] without
restraint,
but I do not turn[y] from your law.
52 I remember[z] your ancient laws,
O LORD,
and I find comfort in them.
53 Indignation grips me[a] because of the
wicked,
who have forsaken your law.[b]
54 Your decrees are the theme of my song[c]
wherever I lodge.
55 In the night I remember[d] your name,
O LORD,
and I will keep your law.[e]
56 This has been my practice:
I obey your precepts.[f]

ח Heth

57 You are my portion,[g] O LORD;
I have promised to obey your
words.[h]
58 I have sought[i] your face with all my
heart;
be gracious to me[j] according to your
promise.[k]
59 I have considered my ways[l]
and have turned my steps to your
statutes.

[a] *37* Two manuscripts of the Masoretic Text and Dead Sea Scrolls; most manuscripts of the Masoretic Text *life in your way* [b] *48* Or *for*

119:35 [w]Ps 25:4-5 [x]ver 32 [y]S Ps 1:2 **119:36** [z]S Jos 24:23 [a]Eze 33:31 **119:37** [b]ver 25; Ps 71:20 [c]ver 9 **119:38** [d]S Nu 23:19 **119:39** [e]ver 22; Ps 69:9; 89:51; Isa 25:8; 51:7; 54:4 **119:40** [f]ver 20 [g]ver 25,149,154 **119:41** [h]S Ps 6:4 [i]ver 76,116,154, 170 **119:42** [j]Pr 27:11 [k]S Ps 42:10 **119:43** [l]S 1Ki 17:24 [m]ver 74,81,114, 147 **119:44** [n]ver 33,34,55; S Dt 6:25 **119:45** [o]ver 94,155 **119:46** [p]Mt 10:18; Ac 26:1-2 [q]S ver 6 **119:47** [r]ver 77,143; S Ps 112:1 [s]ver 97,127,159, 163,165 **119:48** [t]S Ge 24:63 **119:49** [u]ver 9 [v]ver 43 **119:50** [w]S ver 25 **119:51** [x]S ver 21; S Job 16:10; S 17:2 [y]S Job 23:11 **119:52** [z]Ps 103:18 **119:53** [a]S Ex 32:19; S 33:4 [b]Ps 89:30 **119:54** [c]ver 172; Ps 101:1; 138:5 **119:55** [d]ver 62,72; Ps 1:2; 42:8; S 63:6; 77:2; Isa 26:9; Ac 16:25 [e]S ver 44 **119:56** [f]ver 4,100,134,168; S Nu 15:40 **119:57** [g]S Dt 32:9; Jer 51:19; La 3:24 [h]ver 17,67,101 **119:58** [i]S Dt 4:29; S 1Ch 16:11; Ps 34:4 [j]S Ge 43:29; S Ezr 9:8 [k]ver 41 **119:59** [l]Jos 24:14-15; S Ps 39:1

119:36–37 *heart ... eyes.* See 101:2b–3a and note.
119:38 *that you may be feared.* The Lord's saving acts in fulfillment of his promises contribute to the recognition that he is the true God (see 130:4; 2Sa 7:25–26; 1Ki 8:39–40; Jer 33:8–9).
119:39 *disgrace I dread.* See notes on vv. 6,25.
119:40 *righteousness.* See note on 4:1.
119:41–48 May the Lord deliver me and not take his truth from my mouth; then I will honor his law in my life and speak of it before kings, for I love his commands.
119:41 *love.* See vv. 64,76,88,124,149,159; see also note on 6:4.
119:42 *one who taunts me.* See note on v. 25 ("laid low"). *word.* See note on v. 25.
119:43 *word of truth from my mouth.* See v. 13 and note; see also v. 46.
119:45 *freedom.* Lit. "a wide space," i.e., unconfined by affliction or oppression (see 18:19 and note).
119:46 *before kings.* Such will be his boldness (see note on v. 23).
119:48 *I lift up my hands to.* An act accompanying praise (as in 63:4; 134:2); so the sense may be: I praise.
119:49–56 God's word is my comfort and my guide whatever my circumstances.
119:49 *word.* See note on v. 25.
119:50–51 *in my suffering ... The arrogant mock.* See note on v. 25 ("laid low").
119:51 *arrogant.* See note on v. 21.
119:52 *ancient.* God's law is not fickle but is grounded firmly in his unchanging moral character. This is a major source of the author's comfort and one of the main reasons he cherishes the law so highly (see vv. 89,144,152,160).
119:53 *Indignation grips me.* Zeal for God's law (see vv. 136,139) awakens righteous anger against those who reject it (see vv. 113,115,158), and it brings abhorrence of all that is contrary to it (see vv. 104,128,163); but it draws together those who honor it (see v. 63).
119:54 *wherever I lodge.* Lit. "in my temporary house." The sense may be that of v. 19 (see note there).
119:55 *name.* See note on 5:11.
119:57–64 The Lord is the psalmist's true homestead because it is God's law that fills the earth with all that makes life secure and joyous. So God's promises are his hope, and God's righteous laws his delight.
119:57 *portion.* May identify the author as a priest or Levite (see 73:26 and note).
119:58 *heart.* See note on 4:7.

60 I will hasten and not delay
to obey your commands.[m]
61 Though the wicked bind me with ropes,
I will not forget[n] your law.
62 At midnight[o] I rise to give you thanks
for your righteous laws.[p]
63 I am a friend to all who fear you,[q]
to all who follow your precepts.[r]
64 The earth is filled with your love,[s] O LORD;
teach me your decrees.[t]

ט Teth

65 Do good[u] to your servant
according to your word,[v] O LORD.
66 Teach me knowledge[w] and good judgment,
for I believe in your commands.
67 Before I was afflicted[x] I went astray,[y]
but now I obey your word.[z]
68 You are good,[a] and what you do is good;
teach me your decrees.[b]
69 Though the arrogant have smeared me with lies,[c]
I keep your precepts with all my heart.
70 Their hearts are callous[d] and unfeeling,
but I delight in your law.
71 It was good for me to be afflicted[e]
so that I might learn your decrees.
72 The law from your mouth is more precious to me
than thousands of pieces of silver and gold.[f]

י Yodh

73 Your hands made me[g] and formed me;
give me understanding to learn your commands.
74 May those who fear you rejoice[h] when they see me,
for I have put my hope in your word.[i]
75 I know, O LORD, that your laws are righteous,[j]
and in faithfulness[k] you have afflicted me.
76 May your unfailing love[l] be my comfort,
according to your promise[m] to your servant.
77 Let your compassion[n] come to me that I may live,
for your law is my delight.[o]
78 May the arrogant[p] be put to shame for wronging me without cause;[q]
but I will meditate on your precepts.
79 May those who fear you turn to me,
those who understand your statutes.[r]
80 May my heart be blameless[s] toward your decrees,[t]
that I may not be put to shame.[u]

כ Kaph

81 My soul faints[v] with longing for your salvation,[w]
but I have put my hope[x] in your word.
82 My eyes fail,[y] looking for your promise;[z]
I say, "When will you comfort me?"

119:60 [m]ver 115 **119:61** [n]ver 83, 109, 153, 176 **119:62** [o]S ver 55; Ac 16:25 [p]ver 7 **119:63** [q]Ps 15:4; 101:6-7; 103:11 [r]ver 56; Ps 111:10 **119:64** [s]Ps 33:5 [t]ver 12, 108 **119:65** [u]ver 17; Ps 125:4; Isa 50:2; 59:1; Mic 2:7 [v]S ver 9 **119:66** [w]S Ps 51:6 **119:67** [x]S Ps 116:10 [y]S Ps 95:10; S Jer 8:4 [z]S ver 17 **119:68** [a]Ps 100:5; 106:1; 107:1; 135:3 [b]S Ex 18:20 **119:69** [c]Job 13:4; Ps 109:2 **119:70** [d]S Ps 17:10; Isa 29:13; Ac 28:27 **119:71** [e]ver 67, 75 **119:72** [f]S Job 28:17; S Ps 19:10 **119:73** [g]S Ge 1:27; S Job 4:17; 10:8; Ps 138:8; 139:13-16 **119:74** [h]S Ps 34:2 [i]ver 9; Ps 130:5 **119:75** [j]ver 7, 138, 172 [k]Heb 12:5-11 **119:76** [l]Ps 6:4 [m]S ver 41 **119:77** [n]Ps 90:13; 103:13 [o]S ver 47 **119:78** [p]ver 51; Jer 50:32 [q]ver 86, 161; Ps 35:19 **119:79** [r]ver 27, 125 **119:80** [s]ver 1; S 1Ki 8:61 [t]S Ge 26:5 [u]S ver 6 **119:81** [v]ver 20; Ps 84:2 [w]ver 123 [x]S ver 43 **119:82** [y]S Ps 6:7; 69:3; La 2:11 [z]ver 41, 123

119:61 *bind me with ropes.* Oppress me.
119:62 *give you thanks.* See note on Ps 100 title. *righteous.* See note on v. 7.
119:63 *friend.* See note on v. 53.
119:65–72 Do good to me in accordance with your goodness, even if that means affliction, because your affliction is good for me; it teaches me knowledge and good judgment from your law.
119:65 *Do good.* Cf. v. 68; see 31:19; 86:17 and notes. *word.* See note on v. 25.
119:66 *believe in.* Have confidence in; God's commands are not deceitful (see note on v. 29) or fickle (see note on v. 52).
119:67 *afflicted.* At the hands of God (see v. 71; see also note on v. 25, "laid low"). *word.* See note on v. 11.
119:69 *arrogant.* See note on v. 21.
119:70 *callous and unfeeling.* Lit. "fat as grease." Similar expressions occur also in Isa 6:10; Jer 5:28 (see also 17:10).
119:72 *than thousands ... of silver and gold.* See vv. 14,57, 111,162.
119:73–80 Complete your forming of me by helping me to conform to your righteous laws so that the arrogant may be put to shame and those who fear you may rejoice with me. (The stanza has a concentric structure; compare vv. 73 and 80, 74 and 79, 75 and 78, 76 and 77.)
119:73 *understanding.* What I need to perfect the work you began when you formed me.
119:74 *fear you.* See v. 79; see also note on 34:8–14. *when they see me.* When I am perfectly formed and enjoying the blessings of the godly. *word.* See note on v. 25.
119:75 *laws.* Here the Hebrew for this word (*mishpatim*) may refer to God's just decisions in dealing with his servant, as the rest of the verse implies (see v. 84 and note). *you have afflicted me.* See vv. 67,71.
119:76 *unfailing love.* See note on 6:4. *my comfort.* In my affliction.
119:77 *that I may live.* And not perish in my affliction.
119:78 *the arrogant.* See note on v. 21. *be put to shame.* As they have subjected me to shame (see note on 5:10). *for wronging me.* See note on v. 25 ("laid low").
119:79 *turn to me.* See v. 63 and note on v. 53.
119:80 *heart.* See note on 4:7. *not be put to shame.* See note on v. 6.
119:81–88 Save me from my affliction and my persecutors, according to your promises, and I will obey your statutes. This last stanza of the first half of the psalm, like the closing stanza, is dominated by prayer for God's help (see note on v. 25).
119:81 *soul.* See note on 6:3.
119:82 *My eyes fail.* See note on 6:7.

[83]Though I am like a wineskin in the smoke,
I do not forget[a] your decrees.
[84]How long[b] must your servant wait?
When will you punish my persecutors?[c]
[85]The arrogant[d] dig pitfalls[e] for me,
contrary to your law.
[86]All your commands are trustworthy;[f]
help me,[g] for men persecute me[h]
without cause.[i]
[87]They almost wiped me from the earth,
but I have not forsaken[j] your precepts.
[88]Preserve my life[k] according to your love,[l]
and I will obey the statutes[m] of your mouth.

ל Lamedh

[89]Your word, O LORD, is eternal;[n]
it stands firm in the heavens.
[90]Your faithfulness[o] continues through all generations;[p]
you established the earth, and it endures.[q]
[91]Your laws endure[r] to this day,
for all things serve you.[s]
[92]If your law had not been my delight,[t]
I would have perished in my affliction.[u]
[93]I will never forget[v] your precepts,
for by them you have preserved my life.[w]
[94]Save me,[x] for I am yours;
I have sought out your precepts.[y]
[95]The wicked are waiting to destroy me,[z]
but I will ponder your statutes.[a]
[96]To all perfection I see a limit;
but your commands are boundless.[b]

מ Mem

[97]Oh, how I love your law![c]
I meditate[d] on it all day long.
[98]Your commands make me wiser[e] than my enemies,
for they are ever with me.
[99]I have more insight than all my teachers,
for I meditate on your statutes.[f]
[100]I have more understanding than the elders,
for I obey your precepts.[g]
[101]I have kept my feet[h] from every evil path
so that I might obey your word.[i]
[102]I have not departed from your laws,[j]
for you yourself have taught[k] me.
[103]How sweet are your words to my taste,
sweeter than honey[l] to my mouth![m]
[104]I gain understanding[n] from your precepts;
therefore I hate every wrong path.[o]

נ Nun

[105]Your word is a lamp[p] to my feet
and a light[q] for my path.

119:83 [a]S ver 61 **119:84** [b]Ps 6:3; Rev 6:10 [c]ver 51; Jer 12:3; 15:15; 20:11 **119:85** [d]ver 51 [e]Ps 35:7; 57:6; Jer 18:20,22 **119:86** [f]ver 138 [g]S Ps 109:26 [h]S Ps 7:1 [i]S ver 78 **119:87** [j]ver 150; Isa 1:4,28; 58:2; 59:13 **119:88** [k]S Ps 41:2 [l]ver 124; Ps 51:1; 109:26 [m]ver 2,100,129, 134,168 **119:89** [n]ver 111,144; S Ps 111:8; Isa 51:6; S Mt 5:18; 1Pe 1:25 **119:90** [o]S Ps 36:5 [p]S Ps 45:17 [q]S Job 8:19; Ps 148:6 **119:91** [r]Jer 33:25 [s]Ps 104:2-4; Jer 31:35 **119:92** [t]Ps 37:4; S 112:1 [u]ver 50,67 **119:93** [v]ver 83 [w]S Ps 103:5 **119:94** [x]ver 146; Ps 54:1; 116:4; Jer 17:14; 31:18; 42:11 [y]S ver 45 **119:95** [z]S Ps 69:4 [a]ver 99 **119:96** [b]Ps 19:7

119:97 [c]S ver 47 [d]S ver 15 **119:98** [e]ver 130; S Dt 4:6; Ps 19:7; 2Ti 3:15 **119:99** [f]ver 15 **119:100** [g]S ver 56; S Dt 6:17 **119:101** [h]Pr 1:15 [i]S ver 57 **119:102** [j]S Dt 17:20 [k]S Dt 4:5 **119:103** [l]S Ps 19:10 [m]Pr 24:13-14 **119:104** [n]S Ps 111:10 [o]ver 128 **119:105** [p]Pr 20:27; 2Pe 1:19 [q]ver 130; Pr 6:23

119:83 *like a wineskin in the smoke.* As a wineskin hanging in the smoke and heat above a fire becomes smudged and shriveled, so the psalmist bears the marks of his affliction.
119:84 *How long … wait?* Lit. "How (many are) the days of your servant?" That is, do not delay the punishment of my persecutors, because my life is short. *punish.* Lit. "effect justice upon" (the Hebrew for "justice" is *mishpaṭ*; see note on v. 7, "laws"; see also note on 5:10).
119:85 *The arrogant.* See note on v. 21. *dig pitfalls.* Probably referring to slander—public accusations that the psalmist must be guilty of vile sins or he would not be suffering such affliction (see notes on 5:9; 9:15). *contrary to your law.* See Ex 20:16.
119:86 *trustworthy.* See note on v. 29 ("deceitful ways").
119:88 *love.* See note on 6:4.
119:89–91 God's sovereign and unchanging word governs and maintains all creation. (These first three verses of the second half of the psalm teach a general truth; cf. vv. 1–3.)
119:89 *Your word.* Here God's word by which he created, maintains and governs all things (see 33:4,6; 107:20; 147:15,18). *stands firm in the heavens.* The secure order of the heavens and the earth (v. 90) declares (19:1–4) the reassuring truth that God's word (his "laws," v. 91), by which he upholds and governs all things, is enduring (eternal) and trustworthy ("Your faithfulness," v. 90). And that is the larger truth that confirms the confidence of the godly in the trustworthiness of God's word (his laws and promises) of special revelation (see notes on 93:5; 96:10; see also note on v. 29, "deceitful ways").
119:90 *Your faithfulness.* An indirect reference to God's word (see v. 89 and note).
119:92 *would have perished in my affliction.* Would not have learned the way of life (see v. 93) from your law (see vv. 67,71 and note on vv. 65–72).
119:95 *The wicked.* See note on v. 21 ("the arrogant"). *waiting to destroy me.* See note on v. 25 ("laid low").
119:96 *perfection.* Probably that which has been perfected in the sense of completed, given fixed bounds so that it is no longer open-ended. *boundless.* Lit. "very broad," i.e., an inexhaustible source of wise counsel for life (see vv. 97–100).
119:97–104 Meditation on God's law yields the highest wisdom.
119:98 *my enemies.* Those arrogant ones (see note on v. 21) who place confidence in worldly wisdom. *they.* Your commands.
119:99 *teachers.* Merely human teachers.
119:100 *elders.* Old men, taught by experience (see note on Ex 3:16).
119:102 *you … have taught me.* Through your laws.
119:103 *words.* Perhaps better understood here as "laws" (see vv. 67,133,158,172 and note on v. 11).
119:104 *hate every wrong path.* See note on v. 53.
119:105 *lamp … light.* Apart from which I could only grope about in the darkness.

[106]I have taken an oath[r] and confirmed it,
that I will follow your righteous
laws.[s]
[107]I have suffered much;
preserve my life,[t] O LORD, according
to your word.
[108]Accept, O LORD, the willing praise of
my mouth,[u]
and teach me your laws.[v]
[109]Though I constantly take my life in my
hands,[w]
I will not forget[x] your law.
[110]The wicked have set a snare[y] for me,
but I have not strayed[z] from your
precepts.
[111]Your statutes are my heritage forever;
they are the joy of my heart.[a]
[112]My heart is set[b] on keeping your
decrees
to the very end.[c]

ס Samekh

[113]I hate double-minded men,[d]
but I love your law.[e]
[114]You are my refuge and my shield;[f]
I have put my hope[g] in your word.
[115]Away from me,[h] you evildoers,
that I may keep the commands of
my God!
[116]Sustain me[i] according to your promise,[j]
and I will live;
do not let my hopes be dashed.[k]
[117]Uphold me,[l] and I will be delivered;[m]
I will always have regard for your
decrees.[n]
[118]You reject all who stray[o] from your
decrees,
for their deceitfulness is in vain.
[119]All the wicked of the earth you discard
like dross;[p]
therefore I love your statutes.[q]
[120]My flesh trembles[r] in fear of you;[s]
I stand in awe[t] of your laws.

ע Ayin

[121]I have done what is righteous and
just;[u]
do not leave me to my oppressors.
[122]Ensure your servant's well-being;[v]
let not the arrogant oppress me.[w]
[123]My eyes fail,[x] looking for your
salvation,[y]
looking for your righteous promise.[z]
[124]Deal with your servant according to
your love[a]
and teach me your decrees.[b]
[125]I am your servant;[c] give me
discernment
that I may understand your
statutes.[d]
[126]It is time for you to act, O LORD;
your law is being broken.[e]
[127]Because I love your commands[f]
more than gold,[g] more than pure
gold,[h]
[128]and because I consider all your
precepts right,[i]
I hate every wrong path.[j]

פ Pe

[129]Your statutes are wonderful;[k]
therefore I obey them.[l]
[130]The unfolding of your words gives
light;[m]
it gives understanding to the simple.[n]
[131]I open my mouth and pant,[o]
longing for your commands.[p]

119:106 [r]S Ne 10:29 [s]ver 7 **119:107** [t]S ver 25 **119:108** [u]Ps 51:15; 63:5; 71:8; 109:30 [v]S ver 64 **119:109** [w]S Jdg 12:3 [x]S ver 61 **119:110** [y]Ps 25:15; S 64:5; Isa 8:14; Am 3:5 [z]ver 10 **119:111** [a]ver 14,162 **119:112** [b]S Ps 108:1 [c]ver 33 **119:113** [d]S 1Ki 18:21; Jas 1:8; 4:8 [e]ver 47 **119:114** [f]S Ge 15:1; S Ps 18:2 [g]S ver 43 **119:115** [h]S Ps 6:8 **119:116** [i]S Ps 18:35; 41:3; 55:22; Isa 46:4 [j]S ver 41 [k]Ro 5:5 **119:117** [l]Isa 41:10; 46:4 [m]Ps 34:4 [n]ver 6 **119:118** [o]S ver 10 **119:119** [p]Isa 1:22,25; Eze 22:18,19 [q]ver 47 **119:120** [r]S Job 4:14; S Isa 64:2 [s]S Jos 24:14 [t]Jer 10:7; Hab 3:2 **119:121** [u]S 2Sa 8:15; S Job 27:6 **119:122** [v]S Job 17:3 [w]ver 21,121,134; Ps 106:42 **119:123** [x]Isa 38:14 [y]ver 81 [z]S ver 82 **119:124** [a]S ver 88; S Ps 25:7 [b]ver 12 **119:125** [c]S Ps 116:16 [d]S ver 79 **119:126** [e]S Nu 15:31 **119:127** [f]S ver 47 [g]Ps 19:10 [h]S Job 3:21 **119:128** [i]S Ps 19:8 [j]ver 104,163; Ps 31:6; Pr 13:5 **119:129** [k]ver 18 [l]ver 22, S 88 **119:130** [m]S ver 105 [n]S Ps 19:7 **119:131** [o]Ps 42:1 [p]S ver 20

119:106 *have taken an oath and confirmed it.* Have covenanted (see Ne 10:29).
119:107 See v. 25 and note.
119:109 *take my life in my hands.* By publicly honoring God's law even in the face of threats and hostility (see especially vv. 23,46,161).
119:110 *set a snare.* See v. 85 and note.
119:111–112 *heart.* See note on 4:7.
119:111 *my heritage.* The possession I have received from God as my homestead and that from which I draw the provisions for my life (see note on vv. 57–64).
119:113 *hate double-minded men.* See v. 115; see also note on v. 53. Double-minded people are unstable in all they do (Jas 1:8).
119:114 *word.* See note on v. 25.
119:118 *reject.* Or "shake off" or "make light of." *their deceitfulness.* Probably their ways, which are deceitful (see note on v. 29).
119:119 *dross.* Scum removed from molten ore or metal. The Hebrew for this word is a pun on the word for "stray" in v. 118: Those who stray are treated like dross.
119:120 *My flesh trembles.* He quivers out of his deep reverence for God.
119:121–128 As your faithful servant I pray for deliverance from my oppressors—another stanza in which prayer for deliverance is dominant (see vv. 81–88 and note; see also note on v. 25, "laid low").
119:121 *what is righteous and just.* A phrase commonly used to sum up the whole will of God for moral action (see 106:3; Ge 18:19; 2Sa 8:15; Pr 1:3; 21:3; Isa 56:1; Jer 22:15; 33:15; Eze 18:5,19,21,17; 33:14,16,19; 45:9).
119:122 The only verse in this psalm that does not have either a direct or an indirect (as in vv. 90,121,132; see note on v. 75) reference to God's word. *the arrogant.* See note on v. 21.
119:123 *My eyes fail.* See note on 6:7.
119:124 *love.* See note on 6:4.
119:126 *act.* Either in defense of his servant, or in judgment on the lawbreakers, or both.
119:127 *more than gold.* See vv. 14,57,72,111.
119:128 *I hate every wrong path.* See note on v. 53.
119:129 *wonderful.* See v. 18 and note.
119:130 *unfolding.* Lit. "opening," here meaning (1) the revelation of your words, (2) the interpretation (see "expound," 49:4) of your words, or (3) the entering of your words into the heart. *the simple.* See 19:7 and note.

132 Turn to me[q] and have mercy[r] on me,
as you always do to those who love
your name.[s]
133 Direct my footsteps according to your
word;[t]
let no sin rule[u] over me.
134 Redeem me from the oppression of
men,[v]
that I may obey your precepts.[w]
135 Make your face shine[x] upon your
servant
and teach me your decrees.[y]
136 Streams of tears[z] flow from my
eyes,
for your law is not obeyed.[a]

צ Tsadhe

137 Righteous are you,[b] O LORD,
and your laws are right.[c]
138 The statutes you have laid down are
righteous;[d]
they are fully trustworthy.[e]
139 My zeal wears me out,[f]
for my enemies ignore your words.
140 Your promises[g] have been thoroughly
tested,[h]
and your servant loves them.[i]
141 Though I am lowly and despised,[j]
I do not forget your precepts.[k]
142 Your righteousness is everlasting
and your law is true.[l]
143 Trouble and distress have come
upon me,
but your commands are my
delight.[m]
144 Your statutes are forever right;
give me understanding[n] that I may
live.

ק Qoph

145 I call with all my heart;[o] answer me,
O LORD,
and I will obey your decrees.[p]
146 I call out to you; save me[q]
and I will keep your statutes.
147 I rise before dawn[r] and cry for help;
I have put my hope in your word.
148 My eyes stay open through the watches
of the night,[s]
that I may meditate on your
promises.
149 Hear my voice[t] in accordance with
your love;[u]
preserve my life,[v] O LORD, according
to your laws.
150 Those who devise wicked schemes[w]
are near,
but they are far from your law.
151 Yet you are near,[x] O LORD,
and all your commands are true.[y]
152 Long ago I learned from your
statutes[z]
that you established them to last
forever.[a]

ר Resh

153 Look upon my suffering[b] and
deliver me,[c]
for I have not forgotten[d] your law.
154 Defend my cause[e] and redeem me;[f]
preserve my life[g] according to your
promise.[h]
155 Salvation is far from the wicked,
for they do not seek out[i] your
decrees.
156 Your compassion is great,[j] O LORD;
preserve my life[k] according to your
laws.[l]
157 Many are the foes who persecute
me,[m]
but I have not turned[n] from your
statutes.
158 I look on the faithless with loathing,[o]
for they do not obey your word.[p]
159 See how I love your precepts;
preserve my life,[q] O LORD, according
to your love.
160 All your words are true;
all your righteous laws are
eternal.[r]

119:132 [q] S Ps 6:4 [r] S 2Sa 24:14; S Ps 9:13 [s] S Ps 5:11 **119:133** [t] ver 9 [u] S ver 11; S Ro 6:16 **119:134** [v] S ver 122 [w] S ver 56, S 88 **119:135** [x] S Nu 6:25; Ps 4:6; 67:1; 80:3 [y] ver 12 **119:136** [z] Ps 6:6; Isa 22:4; Jer 9:1, 18; 13:17; 14:17; La 1:16; 3:48 [a] ver 158; Ps 106:25; Isa 42:24; Eze 9:4 **119:137** [b] S Ex 9:27; S Ezr 9:15 [c] S Ne 9:13 **119:138** [d] S ver 75; S Ps 19:7 [e] ver 86 **119:139** [f] Ps 69:9; Jn 2:17 **119:140** [g] S Jos 23:14 [h] Ps 12:6 [i] ver 47 **119:141** [j] S Ps 22:6 [k] ver 61, 134 **119:142** [l] ver 151, 160; Ps 19:7 **119:143** [m] ver 24, S 47 **119:144** [n] S ver 34 **119:145** [o] ver 10 [p] ver 22, 55 **119:146** [q] S ver 94 **119:147** [r] Ps 5:3; 57:8; 108:2 **119:148** [s] S Ps 63:6 **119:149** [t] S Ps 27:7 [u] ver 124 [v] S ver 40 **119:150** [w] S Ps 37:7 **119:151** [x] S Ps 34:18; Php 4:5 [y] S ver 142 **119:152** [z] ver 7, 73 [a] S ver 89; S Ps 111:8; Lk 21:33 **119:153** [b] S Ps 13:3 [c] S Ps 3:7 [d] S Ps 44:17 **119:154** [e] Ps 35:1; Jer 50:34; Mic 7:9 [f] S 1Sa 24:15 [g] ver 25 [h] S ver 41 **119:155** [i] ver 94, 118 **119:156** [j] S Ne 9:27; Jas 5:11 [k] ver 25 [l] ver 149 **119:157** [m] S Ps 7:1 [n] S Ps 44:18 **119:158** [o] ver 104; S Ex 32:19 [p] S ver 136 **119:159** [q] ver 25; S Ps 41:2 **119:160** [r] S ver 89; S Ps 111:8

119:132 *as you always do.* Lit. "as is (your) manner" (the Hebrew for "manner" is *mishpaṭ*); hence an indirect reference (see note on v. 122) to God's law (see note on v. 7).
119:134,154 *Redeem.* Here, as often, a synonym for "deliver."
119:134 *oppression.* See note on v. 25 ("laid low").
119:135 *your face shine.* See note on 13:1 ("hide your face").
119:136 See v. 53 and note.
119:137 – 144 The Lord and his laws are righteous.
119:137 *Righteous.* See note on 4:1.
119:138 *trustworthy.* See v. 142; see also note on v. 29 ("deceitful ways").
119:139 *My zeal.* See note on v. 53.
119:140 *promises.* Hebrew *'imrah*; perhaps better rendered "word" here (see note on v. 11). *tested.* Lit. "refined," i.e., God's word contains nothing worthless or useless.
119:141 *lowly and despised.* Cf. v. 143; see also note on v. 25.
119:145 – 152 Save me, Lord, and I will keep your law. As the psalm draws to a close, prayer for deliverance becomes more dominant (see note on v. 25, "laid low").
119:148 *watches of the night.* See note on Jdg 7:19; see also La 2:19.
119:149 *love.* See note on 6:4. *your laws.* Or "your justice" (complementing "your love"); Hebrew *mishpaṭ* (see note on v. 75).
119:150 *far from your law.* See vv. 21,53,85,118,126,139,155, 158.
119:151 *are true.* See note on v. 29 ("deceitful ways").
119:152 *last forever.* See note on v. 52.
119:153 – 160 See note on vv. 145 – 152.
119:155 *the wicked.* See note on v. 21 ("the arrogant").
119:156 *your laws.* See v. 149 and note.
119:158 *word.* Hebrew *'imrah* (see note on v. 11).
119:160 *All.* Lit. "The sum of" (as in 139:17). *true.* See note on v. 29 ("deceitful ways"). *eternal.* See note on v. 52.

שׁ Sin and Shin

[161]Rulers persecute me[s] without cause,
but my heart trembles[t] at your word.
[162]I rejoice[u] in your promise
like one who finds great spoil.[v]
[163]I hate and abhor[w] falsehood
but I love your law.[x]
[164]Seven times a day I praise you
for your righteous laws.[y]
[165]Great peace[z] have they who love your law,
and nothing can make them stumble.[a]
[166]I wait for your salvation,[b] O LORD,
and I follow your commands.
[167]I obey your statutes,
for I love them[c] greatly.
[168]I obey your precepts[d] and your statutes,[e]
for all my ways are known[f] to you.

ת Taw

[169]May my cry come[g] before you, O LORD;
give me understanding[h] according to your word.[i]
[170]May my supplication come[j] before you;
deliver me[k] according to your promise.[l]
[171]May my lips overflow with praise,[m]
for you teach me[n] your decrees.
[172]May my tongue sing[o] of your word,
for all your commands are righteous.[p]
[173]May your hand be ready to help[q] me,
for I have chosen[r] your precepts.
[174]I long for your salvation,[s] O LORD,
and your law is my delight.[t]
[175]Let me live[u] that I may praise you,
and may your laws sustain me.
[176]I have strayed like a lost sheep.[v]
Seek your servant,
for I have not forgotten[w] your commands.

Psalm 120

A song of ascents.

[1]I call on the LORD[x] in my distress,[y]
and he answers me.
[2]Save me, O LORD, from lying lips[z]
and from deceitful tongues.[a]

[3]What will he do to you,
and what more besides, O deceitful tongue?

119:161 [s]ver 23,122,157; 1Sa 24:14-15 [t]ver 120 **119:162** [u]S ver 111 [v]1Sa 30:16; Isa 9:3; 53:12 **119:163** [w]S ver 128 [x]ver 47 **119:164** [y]ver 7,160 **119:165** [z]Ps 37:11; Isa 26:3,12; 27:5; 32:17; 57:19; 66:12 [a]S ver 11; S Ps 37:24; 1Jn 2:10 **119:166** [b]ver 81 **119:167** [c]ver 47 **119:168** [d]S ver 56, S 88 [e]ver 2,22 [f]S Job 10:4; S 23:10; Ps 139:3; Pr 5:21 **119:169** [g]S Job 16:18 [h]S ver 34 [i]S ver 9 **119:170** [j]1Ki 8:30; 2Ch 6:24; Ps 28:2; 140:6; 143:1 [k]Ps 3:7; 22:20; 59:1 [l]S ver 41 **119:171** [m]Ps 51:15; 63:3 [n]Ps 94:12; Isa 2:3; Mic 4:2

119:172 [o]Ps 51:14 [p]ver 7, S 75 **119:173** [q]Ps 37:24; 73:23; Isa 41:10 [r]S Jos 24:22 **119:174** [s]ver 166 [t]ver 16,24 **119:175** [u]ver 116,159; Isa 55:3 **119:176** [v]ver 10; S Ps 95:10; Jer 50:17; Eze 34:11; S Lk 15:4 [w]S Ps 44:17 **120:1** [x]S Ps 18:6 [y]S 2Sa 22:7; S Ps 118:5 **120:2** [z]S Ps 31:18 [a]S Ps 52:4

119:161–168 See note on vv. 145–152.
119:161 *Rulers.* See note on v. 23. *heart.* See note on 4:7.
119:162 *great spoil.* See vv. 14,72,111.
119:163 *I hate.* See note on v. 53. *falsehood.* Or "that which is (ways that are) deceitful" (see v. 29 and note).
119:164 *Seven.* A number signifying completeness—he praises God throughout the day.
119:165 *Great peace.* Complete security and well-being.
119:169–176 See note on vv. 145–152.
119:171 *overflow with praise.* Because you have delivered me.
119:172 *righteous.* See note on v. 7.
119:174–176 The conclusion to the psalm.
119:176 *I have strayed.* See Isa 53:6; the clearest expression of the author's acknowledgment that, for all his devotion to God's law, he has again and again wandered into other (deceitful) ways and, like a lost sheep, must be brought back by his heavenly Shepherd. For one who has made God's law the guide and dearest treasure of his life, the last word can only be such a confession—and such a prayer.
Ps 120–137 A collection of 15 psalms (120–134), each bearing the title "song of ascents," to which has been attached Ps 135–137. Ps 120–136 have been referred to in some Jewish traditions as the "Great Hallel" (in distinction from the "Egyptian Hallel"; see introduction to Ps 113–118). Ps 137, expressive of deep devotion to Zion/Jerusalem, the city containing the great symbols of the Lord's presence with his people, brings the collection to its close. Some have thought that the Hebrew for "ascents" refers to 15 steps leading up to the temple so that the title means "A song of the stairs" and indicates that these songs were to be used in a liturgical procession up to the temple (probably at the Feast of Tabernacles). Most, however, believe that it refers to the annual religious pilgrimages to Jerusalem (see 84:5–7; Ex 23:14–17; Dt 16:16; Mic 4:2; Zec 14:16 and note), which brought the worshipers singing to Mount Zion (Isa 30:29)—a view that does not exclude the use of these psalms also in the temple liturgy. The title no doubt reflects postexilic usage rather than the original purpose of the composition of each of the several psalms bearing it. The spirit of Ps 84 pervades the collection (see also Ps 42–43).

Whether an overall thematic (or some other) scheme controls the arrangement of the "ascents" psalms is unclear, though it is probably not coincidental that they begin with a prayer that evokes the experience of being far from home and beset by barbarians and end with a call to praise in the sanctuary. It has been pointed out that in the main Hebrew text tradition the middle psalm (127) is ascribed to Solomon while four of the others (122; 124; 131; 133), two on each side of the middle, are ascribed to David. But little can be made of this since the Septuagint (the pre-Christian Greek translation of the OT) reflects a text tradition in which none of the "ascents" psalms is ascribed to a named author. For further observations relative to arrangement within this collection see introductions to the individual psalms.
Ps 120 The prayer of an individual for deliverance from false accusers (see 5:9 and note). The reference to "war" (v. 7) is probably metaphorical. The theme is developed in three short stanzas: The prayer uttered (vv. 1–2), the adversaries addressed (vv. 3–4), the circumstances lamented (vv. 5–7).
120 title See introduction to Ps 120–137.
120:1–2 The prayer.
120:1 *I call ... he answers.* See note on 118:5.
120:2,6 *me ... I.* Lit. "my soul" (see note on 6:3).
120:2 *lying lips ... deceitful tongues.* See note on 5:9.
120:3–4 Assurance that God will act (see 6:8–10 and note on 3:8).
120:3 *he.* The Lord. *what more besides.* An echo of a common oath formula (see 1Sa 3:17 and note), thus suggesting the certainty and severity of God's judgment on the enemies.

[4]He will punish you with a warrior's
sharp arrows,[b]
with burning coals of the broom
tree.
[5]Woe to me that I dwell in Meshech,
that I live among the tents of Kedar![c]
[6]Too long have I lived
among those who hate peace.
[7]I am a man of peace;
but when I speak, they are for war.

Psalm 121

A song of ascents.

[1]I lift up my eyes to the hills—
where does my help come from?
[2]My help comes from the LORD,
the Maker of heaven[d] and earth.[e]

[3]He will not let your foot slip—
he who watches over you will not
slumber;
[4]indeed, he who watches[f] over Israel
will neither slumber nor sleep.

[5]The LORD watches over[g] you—
the LORD is your shade at your right
hand;
[6]the sun[h] will not harm you by day,
nor the moon by night.
[7]The LORD will keep you from all
harm[i]—
he will watch over your life;
[8]the LORD will watch over your coming
and going
both now and forevermore.[j]

Psalm 122

A song of ascents. Of David.

[1]I rejoiced with those who said
to me,
"Let us go to the house of the
LORD."
[2]Our feet are standing
in your gates, O Jerusalem.
[3]Jerusalem is built like a city
that is closely compacted together.

120:4 [b]S Dt 32:23 **120:5** [c]S Ge 25:13; Jer 2:10 **121:2** [d]S Ge 1:1 [e]S Ps 104:5; Ps 115:15 **121:4** [f]Ps 127:1 **121:5** [g]S Ps 1:6 **121:6** [h]Isa 49:10 **121:7** [i]S Ps 9:9 **121:8** [j]Dt 28:6

120:4 *sharp arrows ... burning coals.* As a weapon, the tongue is a sharp arrow (see Pr 25:18; Jer 9:8; see also 57:4; 64:3) and a searing fire (see Pr 16:27; Jas 3:6), and God's judgment will answer in kind (see 7:11–13; 11:6; 64:7). For judgment in kind see 63:9–10; 64:7–8 and notes. *broom tree.* A desert shrub, sometimes large enough to provide shade. Charcoal made from its wood produced an especially hot and durable fire.
120:5–7 Complaint over prolonged harassment.
120:5 *Meshech ... Kedar.* The former was in central Asia Minor (see note on Ge 10:2), the latter in Arabia (see note on Isa 21:16). Besieged by slanderers, the psalmist feels as if far from home, surrounded by barbarians.
Ps 121 A dialogue (perhaps liturgical) of confession and assurance. Its use as a pilgrimage song provides the key to its understanding. Whether the dialogue takes place in a single heart (cf. the refrain in Ps 42–43) or between individuals in the caravan is of no great consequence since all would share the same convictions. The comforting assurance expressed (see Ps 33) is equally appropriate for the pilgrimage to Jerusalem and for the pilgrimage of life to the "glory" into which the faithful will be received (see notes on 49:15; 73:24). The psalm is composed of four couplets, each having an introductory line, which the rest of the couplet develops. Key terms are "the LORD" and "watch(es) over," each occurring five times.
121 title See introduction to Ps 120–137.
121:1–2 Confession of trust in the Lord.
121:1 *hills.* Those in the vicinity of Jerusalem, of which Mount Zion is one (125:2), or, if the plural indicates majesty (as in the Hebrew in 87:1; 133:3), Mount Zion itself.
121:2 *Maker of heaven and earth.* The one true God, the King of all creation (see 124:8; 134:3; see also 33:6; 89:11–13; 96:4–5; 104:2–9; 136:4–9).
121:3–4 Assurance concerning the unsleeping guardian over Israel.
121:3 *not let your foot slip.* Not even where the way is treacherous. *not slumber.* Like the pagan god Baal (see 1Ki 18:27)—though sometimes he seemed to (see 44:23; 78:65).
121:4 *he who watches over Israel.* The Lord of all creation and the guardian over Israel—the One in whom the faithful may put unfaltering trust.
121:5–6 Assurance concerning unfailing protection.
121:5 *shade.* See 91:1 ("shadow") and note on 17:8. *at your right hand.* See 16:8 and note.
121:6 *sun ... moon.* Here, in agreement with the "shade" metaphor, these serve as figures for all that distresses or threatens, day or night (see Isa 4:6; 25:4–5; 49:10; Jnh 4:8).
121:7–8 Assurance concerning all of life.
121:8 *your coming and going.* Lit. "your going and coming." Although the Hebrew order is like that in such military contexts as 1Sa 29:6 ("to have you serve"); 2Sa 3:25 ("your movements"), the sense here is similar to that in Dt 28:6.
Ps 122 A hymn of joy over Jerusalem (see Ps 42–43; 46; 48; 84; 87; 137 and the introductions to those psalms). Sung by a pilgrim in Jerusalem (very likely at one of the three annual festivals, Dt 16:16), it expresses deep joy over the city and offers a prayer for its welfare. As the third of the pilgrimage psalms (see introduction to Ps 120–137), it shares many dominant themes with Ps 132, the third from the end of this collection—possibly a deliberate arrangement. Structurally, a two-verse introduction locates the worshiper with the festival throng in the city of his joy, and the major themes are developed in two closely balanced stanzas of four verses each (in Hebrew the first has a total of 57 syllables, the second, 60 syllables; see also introductions to Ps 127; 128; 129). References to "the house of the LORD" (vv. 1,9) frame the song.
122 title *ascents.* See introduction to Ps 120–137. *Of David.* This element is not present in all ancient witnesses to the text, and the content suggests a later date (see note on v. 1).
122:1–2 Joy for having joined the pilgrimage to Jerusalem.
122:1 *the house of the LORD.* The temple (2Sa 7:5,13; 1Ki 5:3,5, "temple"; 8:10, "temple"). That Jerusalem became the city of pilgrimage before the dedication of the temple is doubtful in light of 1Ki 3:4; 8:1–11.
122:2 *gates.* Gateways.
122:3–5 Jerusalem's significance for the faithful.
122:3 *closely compacted together.* Perhaps refers to the city's well-knit construction (see Ps 48) and probably echoes the account of the construction of the tabernacle (cf. Ex 26:11, "fasten ... together as a unit"). If so, Jerusalem is being celebrated as the earthly residence of God (see note on 9:11; see also Isa 4:5).

4 That is where the tribes go up,
the tribes of the LORD,
to praise the name of the LORD
according to the statute given to
Israel.
5 There the thrones for judgment stand,
the thrones of the house of David.

6 Pray for the peace of Jerusalem:
"May those who love[k] you be secure.
7 May there be peace[l] within your walls
and security within your citadels.[m]"
8 For the sake of my brothers and
friends,
I will say, "Peace be within you."
9 For the sake of the house of the LORD
our God,
I will seek your prosperity.[n]

Psalm 123

A song of ascents.

1 I lift up my eyes to you,
to you whose throne[o] is in heaven.
2 As the eyes of slaves look to the hand
of their master,
as the eyes of a maid look to the
hand of her mistress,
so our eyes look to the LORD[p] our God,
till he shows us his mercy.
3 Have mercy on us, O LORD, have mercy
on us,
for we have endured much
contempt.
4 We have endured much ridicule from
the proud,
much contempt from the arrogant.

Psalm 124

A song of ascents. Of David.

1 If the LORD had not been on our side—
let Israel say[q]—
2 if the LORD had not been on our side
when men attacked us,
3 when their anger flared against us,
they would have swallowed us alive;
4 the flood[r] would have engulfed us,
the torrent[s] would have swept over
us,
5 the raging waters
would have swept us away.

6 Praise be to the LORD,
who has not let us be torn by their
teeth.
7 We have escaped like a bird
out of the fowler's snare;[t]
the snare has been broken,[u]
and we have escaped.

122:6 [k] S Ps 26:8 **122:7** [l] S 1Sa 25:6 [m] S Ps 48:3 **122:9** [n] Ps 128:5 **123:1** [o] S Ps 68:5; Isa 6:1; 63:15 **123:2** [p] S Ps 25:15
124:1 [q] Ps 129:1 **124:4** [r] Ps 88:17 [s] S Ps 18:4 **124:7** [t] S Ps 91:3 [u] Ps 25:15

122:4 *to praise.* For God's saving acts in behalf of Israel and his blessings on the nation. *name.* See note on 5:11. *statute given to Israel.* See 81:3–5; Dt 16:1–17.
122:5 *There ... the thrones of the house of David.* Jerusalem is both the city of the Lord and the royal city of his chosen dynasty, through which he (ideally) protects and governs the nation (see 2:2,6–7; 89:3–4,19–37; 110; 2Sa 7:8–16 and notes). In postexilic times it remained, though now in Messianic hope, the city of David.
122:6–9 Prayers for Jerusalem's peace.
122:6 In Hebrew a beautiful wordplay tightly binds together "Pray," "peace," "Jerusalem" and "be secure." *peace.* See vv. 7–8; includes both security and prosperity. *those who love you.* The psalmist, those referred to in vv. 1,8 and all who love Jerusalem because they are devoted to the Lord and his chosen king. These constitute a loving fellowship of those who worship together, pray together and seek each other's welfare as the people of God (see Ps 133).
122:7 *walls ... citadels.* See 48:13 ("ramparts ... citadels").
122:8–9 *For the sake of ... For the sake of.* Because Jerusalem is the place supreme where God and his people meet together in fruitful communion, the psalmist vows to seek the city's peace.
122:9 *the house of the LORD.* See v. 1 and note; the phrase provides a literary frame for the psalm.
Ps 123 A prayer of God's humble people for him to show mercy and so foil the contempt of the proud. See introduction to Ps 124. As to its structure, a one-verse introduction is followed by two brief stanzas, each developing its own theme.
123 title See introduction to Ps 120–137.
123:1 *I lift up my eyes.* The psalmist speaks as a representative member of or as spokesperson for the community—see the first-person plurals that follow. *whose throne is in heaven.* The same God whose earthly throne is in the temple on Mount Zion (see 122:5 and note; see also 2:4; 9:11; 11:4; 80:1; 99:1; 113:5; 132:14).
123:2 With the use of two similes drawn from domestic life, the faithful (men and women alike) present themselves as dependent and confidently reliant on God.
123:4 *the proud ... the arrogant.* Those who live by their own wits and strength (see notes on 10:2–11; 31:23) and pour contempt on those who humbly rely on the Lord. For examples see those with whom King Hezekiah (2Ki 18:17—19:19) or Governor Nehemiah (Ne 4; 6:1–4) had to contend.
Ps 124 Israel's praise of the Lord for deliverance from powerful enemies—an appropriate sequel to Ps 123. Very likely a Levite speaks in vv. 1–5, while the worshipers answer in vv. 6–8. That it shares with Ps 129 a similar introduction and a theme focused on Zion's deliverance from powerful enemies suggests that these two psalms were arranged to frame the intervening four (see note on 125:5).
124 title *ascents.* See introduction to Ps 120–137. *Of David.* Not all ancient witnesses to the text contain this element, and both language and theme suggest a postexilic date (see note on Ps 122 title). It may have been assigned to David because of supposed echoes of Ps 18; 69.
124:1–5 Let Israel acknowledge that the Lord alone has saved her from extinction (see 20:7; 94:17).
124:2 *men attacked.* Proud and arrogant people (123:4) may attack, but the Lord is Israel's help (v. 8).
124:3 *swallowed us.* Like death (see note on 49:14). But see 69:15.
124:4–5 *flood ... torrent ... raging waters.* See 18:16; see also 32:6; 69:1–2 and notes.
124:6–8 Response of praise for deliverance—with a vivid enrichment of the imagery.
124:6 *torn by their teeth.* As by wild beasts (see note on 7:2).
124:7 *escaped like a bird out of the fowler's snare.* A most apt figure for Israel's release from Babylonian captivity (cf. note on 9:15).

[8]Our help is in the name[v] of the LORD,
the Maker of heaven[w] and earth.

Psalm 125

A song of ascents.

[1]Those who trust in the LORD are like
Mount Zion,[x]
which cannot be shaken[y] but
endures forever.
[2]As the mountains surround
Jerusalem,[z]
so the LORD surrounds[a] his
people
both now and forevermore.
[3]The scepter[b] of the wicked will not
remain[c]
over the land allotted to the
righteous,
for then the righteous might use
their hands to do evil.[d]

[4]Do good, O LORD,[e] to those who are
good,
to those who are upright in heart.[f]
[5]But those who turn[g] to crooked ways[h]
the LORD will banish[i] with the
evildoers.

Peace be upon Israel.[j]

124:8 [v]S 1Sa 17:45 [w]Ge 1:1; Ps 115:15; 121:2; 134:3 **125:1** [x]Ps 48:12; Isa 33:20 [y]Ps 46:5; 48:2-5 **125:2** [z]S 1Ch 21:15 [a]Ps 32:10; Zec 2:4-5 **125:3** [b]S Est 4:11 [c]Ps 89:22; Pr 22:8; Isa 13:11; 14:5 [d]1Sa 24:10 **125:4** [e]S Ps 119:65 [f]S Ps 36:10 **125:5** [g]S Job 23:11 [h]Pr 2:15; Isa 59:8 [i]Ps 92:7 [j]Ps 128:6; Gal 6:16

126:1 [k]Ezr 1:1-3; Ps 85:1; Hos 6:11 **126:2** [l]S Ge 21:6 [m]S Job 8:21; S Ps 65:8 [n]S Dt 10:21; Ps 71:19; Lk 1:49 **126:3** [o]Ps 106:21; Joel 2:21,26 [p]S Ps 9:2; 16:11 **126:4** [q]S Dt 30:3 [r]S Ps 107:35; Isa 43:19; 51:3

Psalm 126

A song of ascents.

[1]When the LORD brought back[k] the
captives to[a] Zion,
we were like men who dreamed.[b]
[2]Our mouths were filled with
laughter,[l]
our tongues with songs of joy.[m]
Then it was said among the
nations,
"The LORD has done great things[n]
for them."
[3]The LORD has done great things[o]
for us,
and we are filled with joy.[p]

[4]Restore our fortunes,[c][q] O LORD,
like streams in the Negev.[r]
[5]Those who sow in tears[s]
will reap[t] with songs of joy.[u]
[6]He who goes out weeping,[v]
carrying seed to sow,
will return with songs of joy,
carrying sheaves with him.

[a] *1* Or *LORD restored the fortunes of* [b] *1* Or *men restored to health* [c] *4* Or *Bring back our captives*

126:5 [s]Ps 6:6; 80:5; Jer 50:4 [t]Gal 6:9 [u]Ps 16:11; 20:5; 23:6; Isa 35:10; 51:11; 60:15; 61:7; Jer 31:6-7, 12 **126:6** [v]S Nu 25:6; S Ps 30:5

124:8 In climax, the great confession (see 121:2 and note).

Ps 125 Israel's security celebrated in testimony, prayer and benediction. The psalm is most likely postexilic and was probably spoken in the temple liturgy by a Levite. Ps 125 and 126 are thematically linked and precisely balanced, each being composed (in Hebrew) of 116 syllables. Their juxtaposition was no doubt deliberate.

125 title See introduction to Ps 120 – 137.

125:1 – 2 The solid security of God's people.

125:1 *Those who trust in the LORD.* God's "people" (v. 2) are also characterized as "the righteous" (v. 3) and "those who are good," "who are upright in heart" (v. 4). For a similar description of the "righteous" see 34:8 – 14 and note. *like Mount Zion.* In their security (see Ps 46; 48).

125:2 *mountains surround Jerusalem.* Though Jerusalem is not surrounded by a ring of peaks, the city is located in what OT writers called a mountainous region. *so the LORD surrounds his people.* As surely, as substantially and as immovably (see 2Ki 6:17; Zec 2:5).

125:3 Wicked rulers, whether by example or by oppression, tend to corrupt even the righteous, but the Lord will preserve his people also from this corrosive threat. *scepter of the wicked.* Probably referring to Persian rule (see Ne 9:36 – 37) and its invidious underlings, such as those Nehemiah had to contend with (see Ne 2:19; 4:1 – 3,7 – 8; 6:1 – 14,17 – 19; 13:7 – 8,28). *land allotted to the righteous.* The promised land (see 78:55).

125:4 – 5 To everyone as they are and do — that is God's way (see 18:25 – 27); thus the confident prayer (v. 4) and the equally confident assertion (v. 5).

125:4 *heart.* See note on 4:7.

125:5 *Peace be upon Israel.* Perhaps a concise form of the priestly benediction (Nu 6:24 – 26; see notes there). This benediction has its counterpart in the prayer of 126:4 – 6. Its repetition at the end of Ps 128 suggests a frame around the four closely balanced psalms (made up of two pairs: 125 – 126; 127 – 128).

Ps 126 A song of joy for restoration to Zion. If not composed for those who returned from Babylonian exile (see Ezra and Nehemiah) — the place of exile is not named — it surely served to voice the joy of that restored community (cf. Ps 42 – 43; 84; 137). The psalm divides into two stanzas of four (Hebrew) lines each, with their initial lines sharing a common theme. Thematic unity is further served by repetition (cf. vv. 2 – 3) and other key words ("the LORD," "songs of joy," "carrying"). References to God's action (vv. 1,3) frame the first stanza, while v. 2 offers exposition. For this psalm's relationship to Ps 125 see introduction to that psalm.

126 title See introduction to Ps 120 – 137.

126:1 – 3 Joy over restoration experienced.

126:1 *brought back the captives.* This translation and its alternative (see NIV text note here and on v. 4) have essentially the same result. *dreamed.* The wonder and joy of the reality were so marvelous that they hardly dared believe it. It seemed more like the dreams with which they had so long been tantalized.

126:2 The twofold effect: joy for those who returned and honor for God among the nations (see note on 46:10).

126:4 – 6 Prayer for restoration to be completed.

126:4 *Restore our fortunes.* Either complete the repatriation of exiles or fully restore the security and prosperity of former times. *like streams in the Negev.* Which are bone-dry in summer, until the winter rains renew their flow.

126:5 – 6 An apt metaphorical portrayal of the joy already experienced and the joy anticipated. *in tears … weeping.* Even when sowing is accompanied by trouble or sorrow, harvest brings joy. For a related figure see 20:5.

Psalm 127

A song of ascents. Of Solomon.

1 Unless the LORD builds[w] the house,
its builders labor in vain.
Unless the LORD watches[x] over the city,
the watchmen stand guard in vain.
2 In vain you rise early
and stay up late,
toiling for food[y] to eat—
for he grants sleep[z] to[a] those he loves.[a]
3 Sons are a heritage from the LORD,
children a reward[b] from him.
4 Like arrows[c] in the hands of a warrior
are sons born in one's youth.
5 Blessed is the man
whose quiver is full of them.[d]
They will not be put to shame
when they contend with their enemies[e] in the gate.[f]

Psalm 128

A song of ascents.

1 Blessed are all who fear the LORD,[g]
who walk in his ways.[h]
2 You will eat the fruit of your labor;[i]
blessings and prosperity[j] will be yours.
3 Your wife will be like a fruitful vine[k]
within your house;
your sons[l] will be like olive shoots[m]
around your table.
4 Thus is the man blessed[n]
who fears the LORD.[o]

5 May the LORD bless you from Zion[p]
all the days of your life;
may you see the prosperity of Jerusalem,[q]
6 and may you live to see your children's children.[r]

Peace be upon Israel.[s]

Psalm 129

A song of ascents.

1 They have greatly oppressed[t] me from my youth[u]—
let Israel say[v]—

127:1 [w]Ps 78:69 [x]Ps 121:4
127:2 [y]S Ge 3:17 [z]S Nu 6:26; S Job 11:18 [a]S Dt 33:12; Ecc 2:25
127:3 [b]S Ge 1:28
127:4 [c]Ps 112:2
127:5 [d]Ps 128:2-3 [e]S Ge 24:60 [f]S Ge 23:10
128:1 [g]Ps 103:11; S 112:1 [h]Ps 119:1-3
128:2 [i]S Ps 58:11; 109:11; Isa 3:10 [j]S Ge 39:3; Pr 10:22
128:3 [k]S Ge 49:22 [l]S Job 29:5 [m]Ps 52:8; 144:12
128:4 [n]S Ps 1:1 [o]Ps 112:1
128:5 [p]S Ps 20:2 [q]Ps 122:9
128:6 [r]S Ge 48:11 [s]S Ps 125:5
129:1 [t]S Ex 1:13 [u]S Ps 88:15 [v]Ps 124:1

[a] 2 Or *eat— / for while they sleep he provides for*

Ps 127 Godly wisdom concerning home and hearth. Its theme is timeless; it reminded the pilgrims on their way to Jerusalem that all of life's securities and blessings are gifts from God rather than their own achievements (see Dt 28:1–14). Two precisely balanced stanzas (in Hebrew having four poetic lines each, and each composed of 57 syllables) develop, respectively, two distinct but related themes. Since this psalm shares with Ps 128 the theme of domestic happiness and is structurally very similar to it, their juxtaposition appears to be deliberate.
127 title *ascents.* See introduction to Ps 120–137. *Of Solomon.* If Solomon was not the author (not all witnesses to the text ascribe it to him), it is easy to see why some thought him so.
127:1–2 It is the Lord who provides shelter, security and sustenance.
127:1 *house.* Domestic shelter. *builders.* The Hebrew for this word is a pun on that for "Sons" in v. 3. *watches over.* See 121:3–8. *city.* The center of power, the refuge when enemies invade the land. *watchmen.* See 2Sa 13:34; 18:24–27; SS 3:3; 5:7.
127:2 *he grants sleep.* A good harvest is not the achievement of endless toil but the result of God's blessing (see Pr 10:22; Mt 6:25–34; 1Pe 5:7). *those he loves.* See especially Dt 33:12; Jer 11:15.
127:3–5 Children are God's gift and a sign of his favor.
127:3 *Sons.* See note on v. 1. Children too are a gift—not the mere product of virility and fertility (see 113:9 and note; Ge 30:2). *heritage.* Emphasis here is on gift rather than possession. But perhaps more is implied. In the OT economy, an Israelite's "inheritance" from the Lord was first of all property in the promised land (Nu 26:53; Jos 11:23; Jdg 2:6), which provided a sure place in the life and "rest" (Jos 1:13) of the Lord's kingdom. But without children the inheritance in the land would be lost (Nu 27:8–11), so that offspring were a heritage in a double sense. *reward from him.* Bestowed by God on one who stands in his favor because he has been faithful.
127:5 *when they contend with their enemies.* Fathers with many sons have many defenders when falsely accused in court. Moreover, the very fact that they have many sons as God's "reward" (v. 3) testifies to God's favor toward them (in effect, they are God-provided character witnesses; see 128:3–4). *in the gate.* For "(city) gate" as court see Dt 17:5; 21:19; 22:15,24; 25:7; Ru 4:1; Isa 29:21 ("court"); Am 5:12 ("courts").
Ps 128 The blessedness of the godly man; another word of wisdom concerning hearth and home (see introduction to Ps 127). The concluding benediction suggests that the psalm originally served as a Levitical (or priestly) word of instruction to those assembled from their homes to worship in Jerusalem. Its date may well be preexilic. Structurally, the frame ("who fear[s] the LORD") around vv. 1–4 sets off those verses as the main body of the psalm.
128 title See introduction to Ps 120–137.
128:1–4 Blessedness affirmed.
128:1 *Blessed.* See note on 1:1. *fear the LORD.* See v. 4; see also note on 66:16. *his ways.* See note on 25:4.
128:2 Blessings upon labor.
128:3 A faithful and fruitful wife. *vine.* Symbol of fruitfulness (Ge 49:22)—and perhaps also of sexual charms (SS 7:8–12) and festivity (Jdg 9:13). *within your house.* She is not like the faithless wife whose "feet never stay at home" (Pr 7:11). *olive shoots.* Ever green and with the promises of both long life and productivity (of staples: wood, fruit, oil). The vine and the olive tree are frequently paired in the OT (as, e.g., in Ex 23:11). Both were especially long-lived, and they produced the wine and the oil that played such a central role in the lives of the people. *around your table.* Converting each family meal into a banquet of domestic joys.
128:5–6 The benediction pronounced—completing the scope of true blessedness: unbroken prosperity, secure relationship with God and secure national existence (the prosperity of Jerusalem entailed both), and long life.
128:5 *from Zion.* See 9:11 and note; 20:2; 135:21.
128:6 *Peace be upon Israel.* See 125:5 and note.
Ps 129 Israel's prayer for the continued withering of all her powerful enemies. The rescue celebrated (v. 4) is probably from Babylonian exile. Against the background of Ps 124–128, this prayer for the withholding of God's blessing (v. 8) is set in sharp relief. Like Ps 127, its two main stanzas

2 they have greatly oppressed me from
my youth,
but they have not gained the
victory[w] over me.
3 Plowmen have plowed my back
and made their furrows long.
4 But the LORD is righteous;[x]
he has cut me free[y] from the cords of
the wicked.[z]
5 May all who hate Zion[a]
be turned back in shame.[b]
6 May they be like grass on the roof,[c]
which withers[d] before it can grow;
7 with it the reaper cannot fill his
hands,[e]
nor the one who gathers fill his
arms.
8 May those who pass by not say,
"The blessing of the LORD be upon
you;
we bless you[f] in the name of the
LORD."

Psalm 130

A song of ascents.

1 Out of the depths[g] I cry to you,[h]
O LORD;
2 O Lord, hear my voice.[i]
Let your ears be attentive[j]
to my cry for mercy.[k]

129:2 [w] Jer 1:19; 15:20; 20:11; Mt 16:18 **129:4** [x] S Ex 9:27 [y] Ps 37:9 [z] Ps 140:5 **129:5** [a] Mic 4:11 [b] S Ps 70:2 **129:6** [c] Isa 37:27 [d] S 2Ki 19:26; Ps 102:11 **129:7** [e] S Dt 28:38; Ps 79:12 **129:8** [f] Ps 118:26 **130:1** [g] S Job 30:19; Ps 42:7; La 3:55 [h] Ps 22:2; 55:17; 142:5 **130:2** [i] S Ps 27:7; 28:2 [j] S 2Ch 6:40 [k] S Ps 28:6; 31:22; 86:6; 140:6 **130:3** [l] S 1Sa 6:20; S Ezr 9:15; Ps 143:2; Na 1:6; Rev 6:17 **130:4** [m] S Ex 34:7; S 2Sa 24:14; S Jer 31:34 [n] S 1Ki 8:40 **130:5** [o] S Ps 27:14; Isa 8:17; 26:8; 30:18; 49:23 [p] S Ps 5:3 [q] S Ps 119:74 **130:6** [r] Ps 63:6 [s] S 2Sa 23:4

3 If you, O LORD, kept a record of sins,
O Lord, who could stand?[l]
4 But with you there is forgiveness;[m]
therefore you are feared.[n]
5 I wait for the LORD,[o] my soul waits,[p]
and in his word[q] I put my hope.
6 My soul waits for the Lord
more than watchmen[r] wait for the
morning,
more than watchmen wait for the
morning.[s]
7 O Israel, put your hope[t] in the
LORD,
for with the LORD is unfailing
love[u]
and with him is full redemption.[v]
8 He himself will redeem[w] Israel
from all their sins.[x]

Psalm 131

A song of ascents. Of David.

1 My heart is not proud,[y] O LORD,
my eyes are not haughty;[z]
I do not concern myself with great
matters[a]
or things too wonderful for me.[b]

130:7 [t] S Ps 25:5; S 71:14 [u] S 1Ch 21:13 [v] S Ps 111:9; S Ro 3:24 **130:8** [w] Lk 1:68 [x] S Ex 34:7; S Mt 1:21 **131:1** [y] Ps 101:5; Isa 2:12; Ro 12:16 [z] S 2Sa 22:28; S Job 41:34 [a] Jer 45:5 [b] S Job 5:9; Ps 139:6

(vv. 1–4,5–8a) are perfectly balanced, having a total of 59 Hebrew syllables each. Its total syllable count (127) closely matches that of Ps 130 (128 syllables). For its apparent link with Ps 124 see introduction to that psalm.

129 title See introduction to Ps 120–137.

129:1–4 The wicked oppressors have not prevailed.

129:1 *from my youth.* From the time Israel was enslaved in Egypt, she has suffered much at the hands of hostile powers.

129:2 *have not gained the victory.* Have not succeeded in their efforts to destroy Israel totally or to hold her permanently in bondage.

129:4 *righteous.* See note on 4:1.

129:5–8 May all those oppressors who have shown hatred toward Zion wither away (see Ps 137).

129:5 See note on 5:10.

129:6 *like grass on the roof.* May those who would plow the backs of Israel (see v. 3) wither like grass that sprouts on the flat, sunbaked housetops, where no plow can prepare a nurturing soil to sustain the young shoots—and so there is no harvest (v. 7).

129:8 *those who pass by.* Whoever may pass by the harvesters in the fields will exchange no joyful greetings (Ru 2:4) because the hands of the harvesters will be empty.

Ps 130 A testimony of trust in the Lord—by one who knows that even though he is a sinner, the Lord hears his cry out of the depths. The language of the psalm suggests a postexilic date. This is the sixth of seven penitential psalms (see introduction to Ps 6). Composed of four couplets, the psalm further divides into two halves of two couplets each. Its total syllable count closely matches that of Ps 129 (see introduction to that psalm).

130 title See introduction to Ps 120–137.

130:1–4 A prayer for mercy, and grounds for assurance.

130:1 *the depths.* As in 69:2 (see notes on 30:1; 32:6; cf. 121:1; 123:1).

130:4 *there is forgiveness.* No doubt recalling such reassuring words as Ex 34:6–7. *feared.* Honored, worshiped, trusted and served as the one true God (see Ps 34:8–14 and note). If God were not forgiving, people could only flee from him in terror.

130:5–8 Trust in the Lord: a personal testimony, expanding into a reassuring invitation (see 131:3).

130:5 *I wait.* In hopeful expectation. *my soul.* See note on 6:3. *his word.* Especially his covenant promises (see 119:25,28,37, 42,49,65,74,81,107,114,147).

130:6 *watchmen.* See 127:1; 2Sa 13:34; 18:24–27; SS 3:3; 5:7. *the morning.* See introduction to Ps 57; see also note on 59:9.

130:7 See 131:3. *unfailing love.* See note on 6:4.

130:8 *from all their sins.* From the root of trouble—but also from all its consequences. This greatest of all hopes has been fulfilled in Christ.

Ps 131 A confession of humble trust in the Lord—appropriately placed next to Ps 130.

131 title *ascents.* See introduction to Ps 120–137. *Of David.* Not all ancient witnesses to the text contain this element (see notes on the titles of Ps 122; 124; 127; 133). It may have been assigned to David because its tone matches the traditional view of David the psalmist.

131:1 *heart.* See note on 4:7. *proud … haughty.* Pride in humanity's presumed ability to master the whole creation, design its own moral world and control its own destiny (of which Babel is the prime Biblical example; see Ge 11:1–9) is that which, more than all else, alienates humans from God (see note on 31:23). *concern myself with.* (Presume to) walk among, live among, be party to. *great matters … too wonderful for me.* Heroic exploits or achievements to rival, if not

[2]But I have stilled and quieted my soul;[c]
like a weaned child with its mother,
like a weaned child is my soul[d] within me.

[3]O Israel, put your hope[e] in the LORD
both now and forevermore.[f]

Psalm 132

132:8-10pp — 2Ch 6:41-42

A song of ascents.

[1]O LORD, remember David
and all the hardships he endured.[g]

[2]He swore an oath to the LORD
and made a vow to the Mighty One of Jacob:[h]
[3]"I will not enter my house[i]
or go to my bed—
[4]I will allow no sleep to my eyes,
no slumber to my eyelids,
[5]till I find a place[j] for the LORD,
a dwelling for the Mighty One of Jacob."

[6]We heard it in Ephrathah,[k]
we came upon it in the fields of Jaar[a]:[b][l]
[7]"Let us go to his dwelling place;[m]
let us worship at his footstool[n]—
[8]arise, O LORD,[o] and come to your resting place,
you and the ark of your might.
[9]May your priests be clothed with righteousness;[p]
may your saints[q] sing for joy."

[10]For the sake of David your servant,
do not reject your anointed one.

[a] 6 That is, Kiriath Jearim [b] 6 Or *heard of it in Ephrathah, / we found it in the fields of Jaar.* (And no quotes around verses 7-9)

131:2 [c]S Ps 116:7 [d]Mt 18:3; 1Co 13:11; 14:20 **131:3** [e]S Ps 25:5; 119:43; 130:7 [f]S Ps 113:2 **132:1** [g]1Sa 18:11; S 2Sa 15:14 **132:2** [h]S Ge 49:24; Isa 49:26; 60:16 **132:3** [i]S 2Sa 7:2,27 **132:5** [j]S 1Ki 8:17; Ac 7:46 **132:6** [k]S 1Sa 17:12 [l]S Jos 9:17; S 1Sa 7:2 **132:7** [m]S 2Sa 15:25; Ps 5:7; 122:1 [n]S 1Ch 28:2 **132:8** [o]S Nu 10:35 **132:9** [p]S Job 27:6; Isa 61:3,10; Zec 3:4; Mal 3:3; Eph 6:14 [q]Ps 16:3; 30:4; 149:5

substitute for, the mighty works of God. The focus seems to be on not claiming Godlike powers (thus trusting in God for deliverance and blessing) rather than on seeking (or claiming) Godlike understanding.

131:2 *soul.* See note on 6:3. *weaned child.* A child of four or five who walks trustingly beside its mother.

131:3 As the psalmist, so ought all Israel (see 130:7)—for all time.

Ps 132 A prayer for God's favor on the reigning son of David and on the regime that David founded—as the structure makes clear (and see note on v. 10). Its language suggests a date early in the monarchy. The venerable belief that it was composed for the dedication of the temple may be correct (compare vv. 8–10 with 2Ch 6:41–42), but the possibility cannot be ruled out that it was used in the coronation ritual (cf. Ps 2; 72; 110). The author of Chronicles places the prayer (or a portion of it) on the lips of the king himself. As used in postexilic liturgies it had Messianic implications.

Two verses of petition (vv. 1,10) are each followed (in Hebrew) by two four-line stanzas, all having an identical form: an introductory line followed by a three-line quotation (see the structure of these quotations). A final couplet brings the prayer to its climactic conclusion. The four stanzas, together with the final couplet, ground the prayer made in vv. 1,10. Verses 2–9 appeal to David's oath to the Lord to find a "place" for the Lord and to his bringing the ark to its "resting place," while vv. 11–18 appeal to the Lord's oath to David and to his election of Zion as his "resting place" (but see note on v. 10).

132 title See introduction to Ps 120–137.

132:1 The initial petition (see v. 10). *remember.* See 20:3; see also 1Ki 11:12–13; 15:4–5. *hardships.* Those he took on himself in his vow (vv. 2–5; see Nu 30:13, where the same technical term for a self-denying oath is used).

132:2–5 David's oath concerning a temple for the Lord is recalled.

132:2 *He swore an oath.* This prayer for David's son is grounded in the special relationship between David and the Lord, as epitomized in their mutual oaths (see vv. 11–12). In 2Sa 6–7, which narrates the events here recalled, David's oath is not mentioned. *LORD ... Mighty One of Jacob.* See v. 5; Isa 1:24; see also note on 3:7. *Jacob.* A synonym for Israel (see Ge 32:28).

132:6–9 Moments in the people's procession to the temple for worship are recalled.

132:6 *it ... it.* Often thought to refer to the ark (see second NIV text note), but more likely it refers to the call to worship that follows (in Hebrew the pronoun is feminine, but the Hebrew for "ark" is masculine). *Ephrathah.* The region around Bethlehem, David's hometown (see Ru 4:11; Mic 5:2). *fields of Jaar.* See first NIV text note; see also 2Sa 6:2 and first NIV text note there. The call to worship is depicted as emanating from David's city and the city where the ark had been since the days of Samuel (see 1Sa 7:1). The call appears to come from a time after the temple had been built—thus involving a poetic compression of events.

132:7 *footstool.* See 99:5 and note.

132:8 *arise.* Although (in accordance with a common feature in Hebrew poetry) the Hebrew omits an introductory word, such as "saying," vv. 8–9 are probably words on the lips of the worshipers. See introduction to Ps 24. *resting place.* As the promised land was Israel's place of rest at the end of her wanderings (see Nu 10:33; Jos 1:13; Mic 2:10), so the temple was the Lord's resting place after he had been moving about in a tent (see 2Sa 7:6; see also 1Ch 28:2). The expression may suggest that the temple was the place of God's throne (v. 14). *ark of your might.* See note on 78:61.

132:9 *clothed with.* Beyond their normal priestly garb—may their ministry be characterized by, i.e., result in. See note on 109:29. *righteousness.* Since the corresponding word in v. 16 is "salvation," the same word used by the author of Chronicles when quoting this verse (2Ch 6:41), and since "righteousness" and "salvation" are often paralleled (40:10; 51:14; 71:15; 98:2; Isa 45:8; 46:13; 51:5–6; 56:1; 59:17; 60:17–18; 61:10; 62:1), the reference is clearly to God's righteousness that effects the salvation of his people (see note on 4:1). *saints.* See note on 4:3.

132:10 The second petition (see v. 1). *your servant.* See note on Ps 18 title. *do not reject.* Do not refuse his petitions (as in 1Ki 2:16–17,20; see 1Ki 8:59; 2Ch 6:41–42). If, as some have proposed, the petitions in vv. 1,10 form a frame around the first half of the psalm, the second half offers assurance that the prayer will be heard (perhaps spoken by a priest or Levite). In any event, David's vow to provide the Lord a dwelling place, which would be for his royal sons and for Israel a house of prayer (see 1Ki 8:27–53; 9:3; 2Ch 7:15–16; Isa 56:7), is made the basis for the appeal that God will hear his anointed's prayer. *your anointed one.* See note on 2:2.

11 The LORD swore an oath to David,[r]
a sure oath that he will not revoke:
"One of your own descendants[s]
I will place on your throne—
12 if your sons keep my covenant[t]
and the statutes I teach them,
then their sons will sit
on your throne[u] for ever and ever."

13 For the LORD has chosen Zion,[v]
he has desired it for his dwelling:[w]
14 "This is my resting place for ever and ever;[x]
here I will sit enthroned,[y] for I have desired it—
15 I will bless her with abundant provisions;
her poor will I satisfy with food.[z]
16 I will clothe her priests[a] with salvation,
and her saints will ever sing for joy.[b]

17 "Here I will make a horn[a] grow[c] for David
and set up a lamp[d] for my anointed one.[e]
18 I will clothe his enemies with shame,[f]
but the crown on his head[g] will be resplendent."

132:11 [r]S Ps 89:3-4,35 [s]S 1Ch 17:11-14; S Mt 1:1; Lk 3:31 **132:12** [t]2Ch 6:16; S Ps 25:10 [u]Lk 1:32; Ac 2:30 **132:13** [v]S Ex 15:17; Ps 48:1-2; S 68:16 [w]S 1Ki 8:13 **132:14** [x]ver 8; Ps 68:16 [y]S 2Sa 6:2; Ps 80:1 **132:15** [z]Ps 107:9; 147:14 **132:16** [a]S 2Ch 6:41 [b]S Job 8:21; Ps 149:5 **132:17** [c]S 1Sa 2:10; Ps 92:10; Eze 29:21; S Lk 1:69 [d]1Ki 11:36; 2Ki 8:19; 2Ch 21:7; Ps 18:28 [e]S Ps 84:9 **132:18** [f]S Job 8:22 [g]S 2Sa 12:30

133:1 [h]S Ge 13:8; S Ro 12:10 [i]Jn 17:11 **133:2** [j]S Ex 29:7

Psalm 133

A song of ascents. Of David.

1 How good and pleasant it is
when brothers live together[h] in unity![i]
2 It is like precious oil poured on the head,[j]
running down on the beard,
running down on Aaron's beard,
down upon the collar of his robes.
3 It is as if the dew[k] of Hermon[l]
were falling on Mount Zion.[m]
For there the LORD bestows his blessing,[n]
even life forevermore.[o]

Psalm 134

A song of ascents.

1 Praise the LORD, all you servants[p] of the LORD
who minister[q] by night[r] in the house of the LORD.

[a] *17 Horn* here symbolizes strong one, that is, king.

133:3 [k]Job 29:19; Pr 19:12; Isa 18:4; 26:19; 45:8; Hos 14:5; Mic 5:7 [l]S Dt 3:8; S 4:48 [m]S Ex 15:17; S Ps 2:6; 74:2 [n]S Lev 25:21 [o]S Ps 21:4 **134:1** [p]S Ps 113:1; 135:1-2; Rev 19:5 [q]S Nu 16:9; S 1Ch 15:2 [r]S 1Ch 23:30

132:11–12 The Lord's covenant with David is recalled, as grounds for the prayer. These and vv. 13–18 are a poetic recollection of 1Ki 9:1–5 (see 2Ch 7:11–18).
132:11 *swore an oath.* See v. 2 and note. 2Sa 7 does not mention an oath, but elsewhere God's promise to David is called a covenant (89:3,28,34,39; 2Sa 23:5; Isa 55:3), and covenants were made on oath. *will not revoke.* See 110:4.
132:12 *covenant ... statutes.* The stipulations of the Sinai covenant, which all Israelites were to keep (see 1Sa 10:25 and note; see also 1Ki 2:3–4).
132:13–16 The Lord's election of Zion recalled, as grounds for the prayer.
132:13 *desired it for his dwelling.* David's and the Lord's desires harmonize (see Dt 12:5–14).
132:15 The Lord enthroned in his resting place (see vv. 8,14) will bless the land, making it a place of rest for his people (see Dt 12:9; Jos 1:13; 1Ki 5:4 and note).
132:16 See note on v. 9.
132:17–18 Concluding word of assurance, which addresses the petition (vv. 1,10) directly and climactically.
132:17 *horn.* The Lord's anointed (see NIV text note). *grow.* Like a plant or branch. *set up a lamp for.* See note on 1Ki 11:36.
132:18 *clothe ... with.* See note on 109:29. *with shame.* In contrast with v. 16. *be resplendent.* Lit. "blossom"—subtly evoking the imagery: grow (v. 17) and blossom.
Ps 133 A song in praise of unity among the people of God. If David was the author (but see note on title), he may have been moved to write it by some such occasion as when, after many years of conflict, all Israel came to Hebron to make him king (2Sa 5:1–3). Other historical possibilities are after the influx of many refugees from the northern tribes into the kingdom of Judah during the great Assyrian invasions (see introduction to Ps 80) or the postexilic regathering of representatives of "all Israel" as reflected in Ezra and Nehemiah (see Ezr 8:25; Ne 12:47). The first and last (Hebrew) lines (vv. 1,3b) frame the whole with the song's main theme. Next to these an inner frame (lines 2,4) elaborates with two striking complementary similes (vv. 2a,3a). The center line (v. 2b) extends the first simile.
133 title *ascents.* See introduction to Ps 120–137. *Of David.* Not all ancient textual sources ascribe the psalm to David (see notes on titles of Ps 122; 124; 127; 131).
133:1 *good and pleasant.* See 135:3; 147:1.
133:2 *like precious oil ... on Aaron's beard ... upon the collar of his robes.* The oil of Aaron's anointing (Ex 29:7; Lev 21:10) saturated all the hair of his beard and ran down on his priestly robes, signifying his total consecration to holy service. Similarly, communal harmony sanctifies God's people.
133:3 *dew of Hermon ... on Mount Zion.* A dew as profuse as that of Mount Hermon would make Mount Zion (or the mountains of Zion) richly fruitful (see Ge 27:28; Hag 1:10; Zec 8:12). So would communal unity make Israel richly fruitful. The two similes (vv. 2–3) are well chosen: God's blessings flowed to Israel through the priestly ministrations at the sanctuary (Ex 29:44–46; Lev 9:22–24; Nu 6:24–26)—epitomizing God's redemptive mercies—and through heaven's dew that sustained life in the fields—epitomizing God's providential mercies in the creation order. *life.* The great covenant blessing (see Dt 30:15,19–20; 32:47).
Ps 134 A liturgy of praise—a brief exchange between the worshipers, as they are about to leave the temple after the evening service, and the Levites, who kept the temple watch through the night. In the Psalter it concludes the "songs of ascent," as Ps 117 concludes a collection of Hallelujah psalms (Ps 111–117). Its date is probably postexilic.
134 title See introduction to Ps 120–137.
134:1–2 The departing worshipers call on the Levites to continue the praise of the Lord through the night (see 1Ch 9:33).

2 Lift up your hands[s] in the sanctuary[t]
and praise the LORD.[u]

3 May the LORD, the Maker of heaven[v]
and earth,
bless you from Zion.[w]

Psalm 135

135:15-20pp — Ps 115:4-11

1 Praise the LORD.[a]

Praise the name of the LORD;
praise him, you servants[x] of the LORD,
2 you who minister in the house[y] of the LORD,
in the courts[z] of the house of our God.

3 Praise the LORD, for the LORD is good;[a]
sing praise to his name,[b] for that is pleasant.[c]
4 For the LORD has chosen Jacob[d] to be his own,
Israel to be his treasured possession.[e]

5 I know that the LORD is great,[f]
that our Lord is greater than all gods.[g]
6 The LORD does whatever pleases him,[h]
in the heavens and on the earth,[i]
in the seas and all their depths.
7 He makes clouds rise from the ends of the earth;
he sends lightning with the rain[j]
and brings out the wind[k] from his storehouses.[l]

8 He struck down the firstborn[m] of Egypt,
the firstborn of men and animals.
9 He sent his signs[n] and wonders into your midst, O Egypt,
against Pharaoh and all his servants.[o]
10 He struck down many[p] nations
and killed mighty kings—
11 Sihon[q] king of the Amorites,[r]
Og king of Bashan[s]
and all the kings of Canaan[t]—
12 and he gave their land as an inheritance,[u]
an inheritance to his people Israel.

13 Your name, O LORD, endures forever,[v]
your renown,[w] O LORD, through all generations.
14 For the LORD will vindicate his people[x]
and have compassion on his servants.[y]

15 The idols of the nations[z] are silver and gold,
made by the hands of men.[a]
16 They have mouths, but cannot speak,[b]
eyes, but they cannot see;
17 they have ears, but cannot hear,
nor is there breath[c] in their mouths.
18 Those who make them will be like them,
and so will all who trust in them.

19 O house of Israel, praise the LORD;[d]
O house of Aaron, praise the LORD;

a 1 Hebrew *Hallelu Yah*; also in verses 3 and 21

134:2 [s]S Ps 28:2; 1Ti 2:8 [t]Ps 15:1 [u]Ps 33:2; 103:1 **134:3** [v]S Ps 124:8 [w]S Lev 25:21; S Ps 20:2 **135:1** [x]Ne 7:73 **135:2** [y]S 1Ch 15:2; Lk 2:37 [z]S Ps 116:19 **135:3** [a]S 1Ch 16:34; S Ps 119:68 [b]S Ps 68:4 [c]S Ps 92:1; 147:1 **135:4** [d]S Dt 10:15 [e]Ex 19:5; Dt 7:6; Mal 3:17; S Tit 2:14 **135:5** [f]S Ps 48:1; 145:3 [g]S Ex 12:12; S 1Ch 16:25; S Job 21:22 **135:6** [h]Ps 115:3; Da 4:35 [i]Mt 6:10 **135:7** [j]S Job 5:10; Ps 68:9; Isa 30:23; Jer 10:13; 51:16; Joel 2:23; Zec 10:1 [k]Am 4:13 [l]S Dt 28:12 **135:8** [m]S Ex 4:23; S 12:12 **135:9** [n]S Ex 7:9 [o]Ps 136:10-15 **135:10** [p]Nu 21:21-25; Jos 24:8-11; Ps 44:2; 78:55; 136:17-21 **135:11** [q]S Nu 21:21 [r]S Nu 21:26 [s]S Nu 21:33 [t]S Jos 12:7-24; 24:12 **135:12** [u]S Dt 29:8 **135:13** [v]S Ex 3:15 [w]S Ps 102:12 **135:14** [x]S 1Sa 24:15; Heb 10:30* [y]S Dt 32:36 **135:15** [z]Ps 96:5; Rev 9:20 [a]Isa 2:8; 31:7; 37:19; 40:19; Jer 1:16; 10:5 **135:16** [b]S 1Ki 18:26 **135:17** [c]Jer 10:14; Hab 2:19 **135:19** [d]S Ps 22:23

134:2 *Lift up your hands.* See 63:4 and note.

134:3 One of the Levites responds with a benediction on the worshipers (see note on 121:2; see also 124:8; 128:5).

Ps 135 A call to praise the Lord—the one true God: Lord of all creation, Lord over all the nations, Israel's Redeemer. No doubt postexilic, it echoes many lines found elsewhere in the OT. It was clearly composed for the temple liturgy. For its place in the Great Hallel see introduction to Ps 120–137. Framed with "Hallelujahs" (as are also Ps 146–150), its first and last stanzas are also calls to praise. Recital of God's saving acts for Israel in Egypt and Canaan (vv. 8–12) makes up the middle of seven stanzas, while the remaining four constitute two pairs related to each other by theme and language (vv. 3–4,13–14; vv. 5–7,15–18).

135:1–2 Initial call to praise, addressed to priests and Levites (see 134:1–2).

135:1,3,13 *name.* See note on 5:11.

135:3–4 A central reason for Israel to praise the Lord (see vv. 13–14).

135:3 *that is pleasant.* See 133:1. Or "he (the Lord) is beautiful" (see 27:4 and note).

135:4 *Jacob.* A synonym for Israel (see Ge 32:28). *his treasured possession.* See Ex 19:5 and note.

135:5–7 The Lord is great as well as good (v. 3); he is the absolute Lord in all creation (cf. the word about idols in vv. 15–18; see Jer 10:11–16; see also 115:3 and 96:5; 97:7 and notes).

135:6 *does whatever pleases him.* The idols can do nothing (vv. 16–17); they are themselves "done" (made) by their worshipers (v. 18). *heavens ... earth ... seas.* The three great domains of the visible creation, as the ancients viewed it (see Ge 1:8–10 and introduction to Ps 104).

135:7 *He makes clouds.* The Lord, not Baal or any other god, brings the life-giving rains (see Ps 29 and its introduction; see also Jer 14:22; Zec 10:1 and notes). *wind.* See 104:4; 148:8. The idols do not even have any wind ("breath") in their mouths (v. 17). *storehouses.* See 33:7 and note; Job 38:22.

135:8–12 The Lord's triumph over Egypt and over the kings whose lands became Israel's inheritance, a concise recollection of Ex 7–14; Nu 21:21–35; Joshua.

135:13–14 See vv. 3–4 and note.

135:14 *vindicate.* Uphold against all attacks by the world powers both Israel's cause and her claim that the Lord is the only true God. *have compassion on.* See Ex 34:6–7 and note. *his servants.* His covenant people.

135:15–18 The powerlessness of the false gods and of those who trust in them (see vv. 5–7 and note; see also 115:4–8 and notes).

135:19–21 Concluding call to praise, addressed to all who are assembled at the temple (see 115:9–11; 118:2–4).

[20]O house of Levi, praise the LORD;
you who fear him, praise the LORD.
[21]Praise be to the LORD from Zion,[e]
to him who dwells in Jerusalem.[f]

Praise the LORD.

Psalm 136

[1]Give thanks[g] to the LORD, for he is
good.[h]
His love endures forever.[i]
[2]Give thanks[j] to the God of gods.[k]
His love endures forever.
[3]Give thanks[l] to the Lord of lords:[m]
His love endures forever.

[4]to him who alone does great
wonders,[n]
His love endures forever.
[5]who by his understanding[o] made the
heavens,[p]
His love endures forever.
[6]who spread out the earth[q] upon the
waters,[r]
His love endures forever.
[7]who made the great lights[s]—
His love endures forever.
[8]the sun to govern[t] the day,
His love endures forever.
[9]the moon and stars to govern the
night;
His love endures forever.

[10]to him who struck down the firstborn[u]
of Egypt
His love endures forever.
[11]and brought Israel out[v] from among
them
His love endures forever.
[12]with a mighty hand[w] and outstretched
arm;[x]
His love endures forever.

[13]to him who divided the Red Sea[a][y]
asunder
His love endures forever.
[14]and brought Israel through[z] the midst
of it,
His love endures forever.
[15]but swept Pharaoh and his army into
the Red Sea;[a]
His love endures forever.

[16]to him who led his people through the
desert,[b]
His love endures forever.

[17]who struck down great kings,[c]
His love endures forever.
[18]and killed mighty kings[d]—
His love endures forever.
[19]Sihon king of the Amorites[e]
His love endures forever.
[20]and Og king of Bashan[f]—
His love endures forever.
[21]and gave their land[g] as an inheritance,[h]
His love endures forever.
[22]an inheritance[i] to his servant Israel;[j]
His love endures forever.

[23]to the One who remembered us[k] in our
low estate
His love endures forever.
[24]and freed us[l] from our enemies,[m]
His love endures forever.
[25]and who gives food[n] to every creature.
His love endures forever.

[26]Give thanks[o] to the God of heaven.[p]
His love endures forever.[q]

Psalm 137

[1]By the rivers of Babylon[r] we sat and
wept[s]
when we remembered Zion.[t]

135:21 [e]Ps 128:5; 134:3 [f]S 1Ki 8:13; S 2Ch 6:2 **136:1** [g]Ps 105:1 [h]Ps 100:5; 106:1; 145:9; Jer 33:11; Na 1:7 [i]ver 2-26; S 2Ch 5:13; S Ezr 3:11; Ps 118:1-4 **136:2** [j]Ps 105:1 [k]S Dt 10:17 **136:3** [l]Ps 105:1 [m]S Dt 10:17; S 1Ti 6:15 **136:4** [n]S Ex 3:20; S Job 9:10 **136:5** [o]Pr 3:19; Jer 51:15 [p]S Ge 1:1 **136:6** [q]S Ge 1:1; Isa 42:5; Jer 10:12; 33:2 [r]S Ge 1:6 **136:7** [s]Ge 1:14,16; Ps 74:16; Jas 1:17 **136:8** [t]S Ge 1:16 **136:10** [u]S Ex 4:23; S 12:12 **136:11** [v]S Ex 6:6; 13:3; Ps 105:43 **136:12** [w]S Ex 3:20; S Dt 5:15 [x]S Dt 9:29 **136:13** [y]S Ps 78:13 **136:14** [z]Ex 14:22; Ps 106:9 **136:15** [a]S Ex 14:27 **136:16** [b]S Ex 13:18; Ps 78:52 **136:17** [c]Nu 21:23-25; Jos 24:8-11; Ps 78:55; 135:9-12 **136:18** [d]Dt 29:7; S Jos 12:7-24 **136:19** [e]Nu 21:21-25 **136:20** [f]Nu 21:33-35

[a] *13* Hebrew *Yam Suph*; that is, Sea of Reeds; also in verse 15

136:21 [g]Jos 12:1 [h]S Dt 1:38; S Jos 14:1 **136:22** [i]S Dt 29:8; Ps 78:55 [j]Isa 20:3; 41:8; 42:19; 43:10; 44:1,21; 45:4; 49:5-7 **136:23** [k]Ps 78:39; 103:14; 115:12 **136:24** [l]S Jos 10:14; S Ne 9:28 [m]S Dt 6:19 **136:25** [n]S Ge 1:30; S Mt 6:26 **136:26** [o]Ps 105:1 [p]S Ps 115:3 [q]S Ezr 3:11 **137:1** [r]Eze 1:1,3; 3:15; 10:15 [s]Ne 1:4 [t]Isa 3:26; La 1:4

135:20 *house of Levi.* Mentioned expressly only here in the Psalter (cf. 1Ch 23:4,30–31; 25:1; 2Ch 20:19,21).
135:21 *from Zion.* Not only in Zion but also from Zion—to the ends of the earth (see notes on 9:1; 22:22–31).
Ps 136 A liturgy of praise to the Lord as Creator and as Israel's Redeemer. Its theme and many of its verses parallel much of Ps 135. Most likely a Levitical song leader led the recital, while the Levitical choir (1Ch 16:41; 2Ch 5:13; Ezr 3:11) or the worshipers (2Ch 7:3,6; 20:21) responded with the refrain (see 106:1; 107:1; 118:1–4,29). This liturgy concludes the Great Hallel (see introduction to Ps 120–137).

Following the initial call to praise (vv. 1–3), the recital devotes six verses to God's creation acts (vv. 4–9), six to his deliverance of Israel out of Egypt (vv. 10–15), one to the desert journey (v. 16) and six to the conquest (vv. 17–22). The four concluding verses return to the same basic themes in reverse order: God's action in history in behalf of his people (vv. 23–24), God's action in the creation order (v. 25) and a closing call to praise (v. 26). The echoing response (*"His love endures forever"*) occurs 26 times, the numerical value of the divine name Yahweh (when the Hebrew letters were used as numbers).
136:1–3,26 *Give thanks to.* Or "Praise" (see 7:17 and note).
136:2 *the God of gods.* See Dt 10:17; see also 135:5.
136:5 *by his understanding.* See Pr 3:19; Jer 10:12.
136:6 *upon the waters.* See 24:2 and note.
136:7–9 Direct echoes of Ge 1:16.
136:23–24 Probably a concluding summary of the deliverance recalled above, but may allude also to the deliverances experienced during the period of the judges and the reign of David.
136:26 *the God of heaven.* A Persian title for God (see note on Ezr 1:2) found frequently in Ezra, Nehemiah and Daniel. Its intent is similar to that of the language of vv. 2–3.
Ps 137 A plaintive song of the exile—perhaps of one who has recently returned from Babylon but in whose soul there lingers the bitter memory of the years in a foreign land and of the cruel events that led to that enforced stay. Here speaks the same deep love of Zion as that found in Ps 42–43; 46; 48; 84; 122; 126. The editors of the Psalter attached this song

[2]There on the poplars[u]
we hung our harps,[v]
[3]for there our captors[w] asked us for
songs,
our tormentors demanded[x] songs of
joy;
they said, "Sing us one of the songs
of Zion!"[y]

[4]How can we sing the songs of the
LORD[z]
while in a foreign land?
[5]If I forget you,[a] O Jerusalem,
may my right hand forget ⌊its skill⌋.
[6]May my tongue cling to the roof[b] of my
mouth
if I do not remember[c] you,
if I do not consider Jerusalem[d]
my highest joy.

[7]Remember, O LORD, what the
Edomites[e] did
on the day Jerusalem fell.[f]
"Tear it down," they cried,
"tear it down to its foundations!"[g]

[8]O Daughter of Babylon, doomed to
destruction,[h]
happy is he who repays you
for what you have done to us—
[9]he who seizes your infants
and dashes them[i] against the rocks.

Psalm 138

Of David.

[1]I will praise you, O LORD, with all my
heart;
before the "gods"[j] I will sing[k] your
praise.
[2]I will bow down toward your holy
temple[l]
and will praise your name[m]
for your love and your faithfulness,[n]
for you have exalted above all things
your name and your word.[o]

137:2 [u]S Lev 23:40 [v]Job 30:31; Isa 24:8; Eze 26:13; Am 6:5 **137:3** [w]Ps 79:1-4; La 1:5 [x]S Job 30:9; Ps 80:6 [y]Eze 16:57; 22:4; 34:29 **137:4** [z]S Ne 12:46 **137:5** [a]Isa 2:3; 56:7; 65:11; 66:20 **137:6** [b]S Ps 22:15 [c]Ne 2:3 [d]S Dt 4:29; Jer 51:50; Eze 6:9 **137:7** [e]S Ge 25:30; S 2Ch 28:17; S Ps 83:6; La 4:21-22 [f]2Ki 25:1-10; Ob 1:11 [g]Ps 74:8 **137:8** [h]Isa 13:1, 19; 47:1-15; Jer 25:12, 26; 50:1; 50:2-51:58 **137:9** [i]S 2Ki 8:12; S Isa 13:16; Lk 19:44 **138:1** [j]Ps 95:3; 96:4 [k]Ps 27:6; 108:1 **138:2** [l]S 1Ki 8:29; S Ps 5:7 [m]Ps 74:21; 97:12; 140:13 [n]Ps 108:4; 115:1 [o]Ps 119:9

to the Great Hallel as a closing expression of supreme devotion to the city at the center of Israel's worship of the Lord (see introduction to Ps 120–137). The 12 poetic lines of the Hebrew song divide symmetrically into three stanzas of four lines each: the remembered sorrow and torment (vv. 1–3), an oath of total commitment to Jerusalem (vv. 4–6), a call for retribution on Edom and Babylon (vv. 7–9).

137:1 *rivers.* The Tigris and Euphrates and the many canals associated with them. *we sat.* Again and again the thought of their forced separation from Zion brought them down to the posture of mourning (see Job 2:8,13; La 2:10).

137:2 *we hung our harps.* "The joyful harp is silent" (Isa 24:8) because the callous Babylonians demanded exotic entertainment with the joyful songs of distant Zion, while the exiles' instruments were only "tuned to mourning" (Job 30:31).

137:4–6 Only someone whose heart had disowned the Lord and his holy city Jerusalem could play the puppet on a Babylonian stage. But may I never play the harp again or sing another syllable if I am untrue to that beloved city!

137:7–9 Lord, remember Edom; and as for you, Babylon, I bless whoever does to you what you did to Jerusalem: a passionate call for redress from a loyal son of the ravaged city (see note on 5:10).

137:7 *Edomites.* The agelong animosity of Edom—descendants of Esau, Jacob's brother—showed its most dastardly face in Jerusalem's darkest hour. No doubt the author knew the Lord's judgments against that nation announced by the prophets (Isa 63:1–4; Jer 49:7–22; Eze 25:8,12–14; 35; Obadiah). *Tear it down.* Lit. "Strip her"—cities were conventionally portrayed as women. La 4:21 anticipates that Edom will be punished by suffering the same humiliation.

137:8 *Daughter of Babylon.* A personification of Babylon (see note on 2Ki 19:21). *doomed to destruction.* The author and those who took up this psalm surely knew of the Lord's announced judgments on this cruel destroyer (Isa 13; 47; Jer 50–51). In the day of the Lord's judgment, Babylon was to receive what she had done to others (see Jer 50:15,29; 51:24,35,49; cf. Rev 18:5–6). For the principle involved see note on Ob 15. *happy is he.* Because a cruel international predator has been removed from the earth (see Isa 14:3–8 and notes; cf. Jer 51:47–48; Rev 19:1–3).

137:9 *your infants.* War was as cruel then as now; women and children were not spared (see 2Ki 8:12; 15:16; Isa 13:16,18; Hos 10:14; 13:16; Am 1:13; Na 3:10). For the final announcement of the destruction of the "Babylon" that persists in its warfare against the City of God, and the joy with which that announcement is greeted, see Rev 14:8 and note; 18:1—19:4.

Ps 138–145 A final collection of eight "Davidic" psalms brings the Psalter toward its close. While much in some of these psalms points to a later, even postexilic, date, they clearly stand in the tradition of psalmody of which David was the reputed father and echo the language and concerns of the earlier Davidic psalms. The collection is framed by songs of praise (Ps 138; 145). The first of these extols the greatness of the Lord's glory as displayed in his answering the prayer (call) of the "lowly" when suffering at the hands of the "proud." The last, employing a grand and intricately woven alphabetic acrostic design, extols the "glorious ... majesty" of the Lord as displayed in his benevolent care over all his creatures—especially those who call on him (look to him in every need). Within this frame have been placed six prayers—with certain interlocking themes that will be pointed out in the notes on the individual psalms.

This final "Davidic" collection contains the Psalter's two most magnificent expositions of the greatness and goodness of God, one of them (Ps 139) focusing on his relationship with an individual, the other (Ps 145) on his relationship with his whole creation.

Ps 138 A song of praise for God's saving help against threatening foes—understood by many to have been originally on the lips of a king. In some respects it is like Ps 18, though in style and scope much less grand. Two (Hebrew) four-line stanzas (vv. 1–3,6–8) develop the main theme; at the center a two-line stanza (vv. 4–5) expands the company of those who praise the Lord to "all the kings of the earth." The psalm shares nearly a third of its vocabulary with Ps 145.

138 title See introduction to Ps 138–145.

138:1–3 Praise for God's faithful love shown in answer to prayers for help.

138:1 *heart.* See note on 4:7. *gods.* Either pagan kings (see vv. 4–5) or the gods they claimed to represent (see introduction to Ps 82; see also note on 82:1).

138:2 *your holy temple.* If David is in fact the author, reference is to the tent he set up for the ark (2Sa 6:17)—many psalms ascribed to David refer to the "temple" (see, e.g., 5:7; 11:4; 18:6; 27:4; see also Ps 30 title). *name.*

3 When I called,[p] you answered me;[q]
you made me bold[r] and
stouthearted.[s]

4 May all the kings of the earth[t] praise
you, O LORD,
when they hear the words of your
mouth.
5 May they sing[u] of the ways of the LORD,
for the glory of the LORD[v] is great.

6 Though the LORD is on high, he looks
upon the lowly,[w]
but the proud[x] he knows from afar.
7 Though I walk[y] in the midst of trouble,
you preserve my life;[z]
you stretch out your hand[a] against the
anger of my foes,[b]
with your right hand[c] you save me.[d]
8 The LORD will fulfill ⌊his purpose⌋[e] for
me;
your love, O LORD, endures forever[f]—
do not abandon[g] the works of your
hands.[h]

Psalm 139

For the director of music.
Of David. A psalm.

1 O LORD, you have searched me[i]
and you know[j] me.
2 You know when I sit and when
I rise;[k]
you perceive my thoughts[l] from
afar.
3 You discern my going out[m] and my
lying down;
you are familiar with all my ways.[n]
4 Before a word is on my tongue
you know it completely,[o] O LORD.
5 You hem me in[p]—behind and
before;
you have laid your hand upon
me.
6 Such knowledge is too wonderful for
me,[q]
too lofty[r] for me to attain.
7 Where can I go from your Spirit?
Where can I flee[s] from your
presence?
8 If I go up to the heavens,[t] you are
there;
if I make my bed[u] in the depths,[a]
you are there.
9 If I rise on the wings of the dawn,
if I settle on the far side of the sea,

138:3 [p] Ps 18:6; 30:2; 99:6; 116:4 [q] S Ps 118:5 [r] Pr 28:1; S Ac 4:29 [s] Ps 28:7 **138:4** [t] Ps 72:11; 102:15 **138:5** [u] S Ps 51:14; 71:16; 145:7 [v] Ps 21:5 **138:6** [w] S Ps 113:6 [x] S Ps 40:4; S Mt 23:12 **138:7** [y] Ps 23:4 [z] S Ps 41:2 [a] S Ex 7:5 [b] Ps 7:6 [c] Ps 20:6; 60:5; 108:6 [d] Ps 17:7, 14 **138:8** [e] Php 1:6 [f] S Ezr 3:11; Ps 100:5 [g] S Ps 51:11 [h] S Job 10:3, 8 **139:1** [i] S Ps 17:3; Ro 8:27 [j] Ps 44:21 **139:2** [k] 2Ki 19:27 [l] Ps 94:11; Pr 24:12; Jer 12:3 **139:3** [m] 2Ki 19:27 [n] S Job 31:4 **139:4** [o] S Heb 4:13 **139:5** [p] S 1Sa 25:16; Ps 32:10; 34:7; 125:2 **139:6** [q] S Ps 131:1 [r] Ro 11:33 **139:7** [s] Jer 23:24; Jnh 1:3 **139:8** [t] Dt 30:12-15; Am 9:2-3 [u] Job 17:13

[a] 8 Hebrew *Sheol*

See note on 5:11. *love and ... faithfulness.* See note on 36:5. *love.* See v. 8; see also note on 6:4. *your word.* Perhaps God's "word" of command that effects his purposes in the world (see 147:15), but more likely his promises (see v. 4 and note). God's display of his love and faithfulness in his answers to prayer (v. 3) has made his name and promises more magnificent than anything else that even kings may prize.

138:3 *I called, you answered.* See note on 118:5.

138:4–5 The center of the poem (see note on 6:6): a wish that all the kings of earth may come to join in the praise of the Lord (see note on 9:1). The verbs, however, could be read as simple futures. In that case, these verses voice a confident expectation.

138:4 *words of your mouth.* God's grand commitments either to his people or to the royal house of David (see 18:30 and note; there, too, God's "words" and "ways" [v. 5] are linked).

138:5 *ways of the LORD.* See 25:10 and note. God's words and his ways are in harmony, and together they display his great glory (cf. Ps 145).

138:6–8 A testimony to God's condescending and faithful love, concluded with a prayer.

138:6 See 113:4–9 and notes. *looks.* With favor. *the proud.* See notes on 31:23; 101:5; 131:1. *knows from afar.* Already from a great distance recognizes them for what they are and so does not let them "see his face" (see note on 11:7). Cf. the acknowledgment of the psalmist in 139:2.

138:8 *will fulfill ⌊his purpose⌋.* See 57:2 and note. *do not abandon the works of your hands.* A concluding prayer that the enduring "love" of God celebrated here will continue until his "purpose" and "works" are completed.

Ps 139 A prayer for God to examine the heart and see its true devotion. Like Job, the author firmly claims his loyalty to the Lord. Nowhere (outside Job) does one find expressed such profound awareness of how awesome it is to ask God to examine not only one's life but also one's soul—God, who knows every thought, word and deed, from whom there is no hiding, who has been privy even to one's formation in the dark concealment of the womb. The thought progresses steadily in four poetic paragraphs of six verses each (vv. 1–6,7–12,13–18,19–24), and each paragraph concludes with a couplet that elaborates on the unit's central theme. References to God's searching and knowing begin and end the prayer.

139 title *For the director of music.* See note on Ps 4 title. *Of David.* See introduction to Ps 138–145.

139:1–6 God, you know me perfectly, far beyond my knowledge of myself: my every action (v. 2a), my every undertaking (v. 3a) and the manner in which I pursue it (v. 3b), even my thoughts before they are fully crystallized (v. 2b) and my words before they are uttered (v. 4). See also v. 23.

139:2 *perceive ... from afar.* See the contrast in 138:8 (see also note there). *my thoughts.* Those that pertain to my wishes, desires and/or plans.

139:5–6 The psalmist's response to the fact that God knows him so well.

139:5 *You hem me in.* To keep me under scrutiny. *laid your hand upon me.* So that I do not escape you. The figures are different in Job 13:27, but the thought is much the same. *hand.* Or "hands."

139:6 *too wonderful for me.* Yours is a "wonder" knowledge, beyond my human capacity—the Hebrew term regularly applies to God's wondrous acts (see 77:11,14, "miracles"; Ex 15:11).

139:7–12 There is no hiding from you—here no abstract doctrine of divine omnipresence but an awed confession that God cannot be escaped (see Jer 23:23–24).

139:7 *your Spirit ... your presence.* See 51:11 and note; Isa 63:9–10; Eze 39:29 ("face ... Spirit").

139:8 *the heavens ... the depths.* The two vertical extremes (see NIV text note).

139:9 *wings of the dawn ... far side of the sea.* The two horizontal extremes: east and west (the sea is the Mediterranean). Us-

10 even there your hand will guide me,[v]
your right hand[w] will hold me fast.

11 If I say, "Surely the darkness will
hide me
and the light become night around
me,"
12 even the darkness will not be dark[x] to
you;
the night will shine like the day,
for darkness is as light to you.

13 For you created my inmost being;[y]
you knit me together[z] in my
mother's womb.[a]
14 I praise you[b] because I am fearfully
and wonderfully made;
your works are wonderful,[c]
I know that full well.
15 My frame was not hidden from you
when I was made[d] in the secret
place.
When I was woven together[e] in the
depths of the earth,[f]
16 your eyes saw my unformed body.
All the days ordained[g] for me
were written in your book
before one of them came to be.

17 How precious to[a] me are your
thoughts,[h] O God![i]
How vast is the sum of them!
18 Were I to count them,[j]
they would outnumber the grains
of sand.[k]
When I awake,[l]
I am still with you.

19 If only you would slay the wicked,[m]
O God!
Away from me,[n] you bloodthirsty
men![o]
20 They speak of you with evil intent;
your adversaries[p] misuse your
name.[q]
21 Do I not hate those[r] who hate you,
O LORD,
and abhor[s] those who rise up against
you?
22 I have nothing but hatred for them;
I count them my enemies.[t]

23 Search me,[u] O God, and know my
heart;[v]
test me and know my anxious
thoughts.
24 See if there is any offensive way[w]
in me,
and lead me[x] in the way everlasting.

[a] 17 Or *concerning*

139:10 [v]Ps 23:3 [w]Ps 108:6; Isa 41:10
139:12 [x]Job 34:22; Da 2:22
139:13 [y]Ps 119:73 [z]S Job 10:11 [a]Isa 44:2,24; 46:3; 49:5; Jer 1:5
139:14 [b]Ps 119:164; 145:10 [c]S Job 40:19
139:15 [d]Ecc 11:5 [e]S Job 10:11 [f]S Ps 63:9
139:16 [g]S Job 33:29; S Ps 90:12
139:17 [h]S Ps 92:5 [i]S Job 5:9
139:18 [j]Ps 40:5 [k]S Job 29:18 [l]S Ps 3:5
139:19 [m]Ps 5:6; Isa 11:4 [n]S Ps 6:8 [o]S Ps 59:2
139:20 [p]S Ps 65:7 [q]S Dt 5:11
139:21 [r]2Ch 19:2; Ps 31:6; 119:113 [s]S Ps 26:5
139:22 [t]Mt 5:43
139:23 [u]Job 31:6 [v]S 1Sa 16:7; S 1Ch 29:17; S Ps 7:9; Pr 17:3; Jer 11:20; S Rev 2:23
139:24 [w]Jer 25:5; 36:3 [x]Ps 5:8; 23:2; 143:10

ing a literary figure in which the totality is denoted by referring to its two extremes (merism), vv. 8–9 specify all spatial reality, the whole creation.

139:10 *guide me ... hold me fast.* Though this language occurs in 73:23–24 to indicate God's solicitous care, it here denotes God's inescapable supervision, not unlike the thought of v. 5.

139:11–12 Just as the whole creation offers no hiding place (vv. 8–9), neither does the darkness of night (see Job 34:22).

139:13–18 You yourself put me together in the womb and ordained the span of my life before I was born. You know me so thoroughly because you made me.

139:13 *created.* The Hebrew for this verb is the same as in Ge 14:19,22; Pr 8:22 ("brought ... forth"), not as in Ge 1:1,21,27. *inmost being.* Lit. "kidneys"—in Hebrew idiom, the innermost center of emotions and of moral sensitivity—that which God tests and examines when he "searches" a person (see note on 7:9).

139:14 *fearfully ... wonderfully ... wonderful.* You know me as the One who formed me (see vv. 15–16), but I cannot begin to comprehend this creature you have fashioned. I can only look upon him with awe and wonder (see note on v. 6)—and praise you (see Ecc 11:5).

139:15 *secret place ... depths of the earth.* Reference is to the womb: called "the secret place" because it normally conceals (see 2Sa 12:12), and it shares with "the depths of the earth" (see note on 30:1) associations with darkness, dampness and separation from the visible realm of life. Moreover, both phrases refer to the place of the dead (63:9; Job 14:13; Isa 44:23; 45:19), with which on one level the womb appears to have been associated: Humans come from the dust and return to the dust (90:3; Ge 3:19; Ecc 3:20; 12:7), and the womb is the "depth"-like place where they are formed (see Isa 44:2,24; 49:5; Jer 1:5).

139:16 *All the days ordained.* The span of life sovereignly determined. *your book.* The heavenly royal register of God's decisions (see note on 56:8).

139:17–18 The psalmist's response: God's thoughts of him are vast and precious.

139:17 *your thoughts.* As expressed in his works—and in contrast with "my thoughts" (v. 2; see note there).

139:18 *When I awake.* The sleep of exhaustion overcomes every attempt to count God's thoughts/works (see 63:6; 119:148), and waking only floods my soul once more with the sense of the presence of this God. On the other hand, reference may be to "awaking" from the sleep of death, as in Ps 17:15 (see also 2Ki 4:31; Job 14:12; Isa 26:9; Jer 51:39,57; Da 12:2). If so, the psalmist extends the sphere of God's presence to beyond the "gates of death" (Job 17:16; see note there).

139:19–24 My zeal for you and loyalty to you set me against all your adversaries.

139:19 *If only.* Jealous impatience with God's patience toward the wicked—whose end will come (Isa 11:4). But the psalmist leaves it to God (cf. note on 5:10).

139:20 *misuse your name.* Perhaps by calling down curses on those trying to be the faithful servants of God.

139:21–22 A declaration of loyalty that echoes the pledge required by ancient Near Eastern kings of their vassals (e.g., "With my friend you shall be friend, and with my enemy you shall be enemy," from a treaty between Mursilis II, a Hittite king, and Tette of Nuhassi, 14th century B.C.).

139:23–24 Examine me, see the integrity of my devotion and keep me true (see 17:3–5 and note). Cf. vv. 1–2.

139:23 *heart.* See note on 4:7. *anxious thoughts.* See 94:19. It is no light matter to be examined by God.

139:24 *the way everlasting.* See note on 16:9–11.

Psalm 140

For the director of music.
A psalm of David.

[1]Rescue me,[y] O LORD, from evil men;
protect me from men of violence,[z]
[2]who devise evil plans[a] in their hearts
and stir up war[b] every day.
[3]They make their tongues as sharp as[c] a serpent's;
the poison of vipers[d] is on their lips. *Selah*

[4]Keep me,[e] O LORD, from the hands of the wicked;[f]
protect me from men of violence
who plan to trip my feet.
[5]Proud men have hidden a snare[g] for me;
they have spread out the cords of their net[h]
and have set traps[i] for me along my path. *Selah*

[6]O LORD, I say to you, "You are my God."[j]
Hear, O LORD, my cry for mercy.[k]
[7]O Sovereign LORD,[l] my strong deliverer,
who shields my head in the day of battle—
[8]do not grant the wicked[m] their desires, O LORD;
do not let their plans succeed,
or they will become proud. *Selah*

[9]Let the heads of those who surround me
be covered with the trouble their lips have caused.[n]
[10]Let burning coals fall upon them;
may they be thrown into the fire,[o]
into miry pits, never to rise.
[11]Let slanderers not be established in the land;
may disaster hunt down men of violence.[p]

[12]I know that the LORD secures justice for the poor[q]
and upholds the cause[r] of the needy.[s]
[13]Surely the righteous will praise your name[t]
and the upright will live[u] before you.[v]

Psalm 141

A psalm of David.

[1]O LORD, I call to you; come quickly[w] to me.
Hear my voice[x] when I call to you.
[2]May my prayer be set before you like incense;[y]
may the lifting up of my hands[z] be like the evening sacrifice.[a]

[3]Set a guard over my mouth,[b] O LORD;
keep watch over the door of my lips.[c]

140:1 [y]Ps 17:13; S 25:20; 59:2; 71:4; 142:6; 143:9 [z]ver 11; Ps 86:14 **140:2** [a]Ps 36:4; 52:2; Pr 6:14; 16:27; Isa 59:4; Hos 7:15 [b]S Ps 68:30 **140:3** [c]Ps 57:4 [d]Ps 58:4; Ro 3:13*; Jas 3:8 **140:4** [e]Ps 141:9 [f]S Ps 36:11 **140:5** [g]S Job 34:30; S Ps 119:110 [h]S Job 18:8 [i]Job 18:9; Ps 31:4; S 38:12 **140:6** [j]S Ps 16:2 [k]S Ps 28:2, 6 **140:7** [l]Ps 68:20 **140:8** [m]Ps 10:2-3; S 66:7 **140:9** [n]Pr 18:7 **140:10** [o]Ps 11:6; 21:9; S Mt 3:10; Lk 12:49; Rev 20:15 **140:11** [p]S Ps 34:21 **140:12** [q]S Ps 82:3 [r]S 1Ki 8:45 [s]S Ps 35:10 **140:13** [t]S Ps 138:2 [u]S Ps 11:7 [v]Ps 16:11 **141:1** [w]S Ps 22:19 [x]S Ps 4:1; 5:1-2; 27:7; 143:1 **141:2** [y]S Lk 1:9; Rev 5:8; 8:3 [z]S Ps 28:2; 63:4; 1Ti 2:8 [a]S Ex 29:39, 41; 30:8 **141:3** [b]S Ps 34:13; Jas 1:26; 3:8 [c]S Ps 12:2

Ps 140 A prayer for deliverance from the plots and slander of unscrupulous enemies. It recalls Ps 58 and 64 but employs a number of words found nowhere else in the OT. Four well-balanced stanzas are followed by a two-verse conclusion. The prayer is strikingly rich in physiological allusions: heart, head, tongue, lips, hands, feet—also ears (lit. "Give ear to," v. 6) and teeth (by a wordplay on the Hebrew for "make ... sharp," v. 3). See introduction to Ps 141; see also introduction to Ps 138–145.
140 title *For the director of music.* See note on Ps 4 title. *of David.* See note on Ps 138 title.
140:1–3 Rescue me from those "vipers."
140:1 *LORD.* Hebrew *Yahweh;* this divine name occurs seven times in this psalm.
140:2 *hearts.* See note on 4:7.
140:3 *tongues.* See note on 5:9. *poison of vipers.* See 58:4 and note.
140:4–5 Protect me from those proud and wicked hunters (see 10:2–11 and notes).
140:5 *Proud men.* See note on 31:23. *snare ... net ... traps.* See 141:9–10.
140:6–8 Do not let these wicked men attain their evil designs against me.
140:6 *Hear, O LORD, my cry for mercy.* A thematic and verbal link with 141:1; 142:1; 143:1.
140:9–11 Let the harm they plot against me recoil on their heads (see note on 5:10).
140:9 *heads ... be covered with the trouble.* Cf. 141:5.
140:10 *burning coals.* For the reference see Lev. 16:12; Job 41:21; Pr 6:28; Isa 47:14; Eze 24:11. Other examples of this imagery for divine judgment may be found in Ps 18:8; 120:4; Eze 10:2. *fire ... miry pits.* This combination, together with the conjunction of fire and darkness in Job 15:30; 20:26, suggests the idea that the fire of God's judgment (see, e.g., 21:9; 97:3; Isa 1:31; 26:11; 33:14) reaches even into the realm of the dead (see Job 31:12 and note on Ps 30:1). *never to rise.* See 36:12; Isa 26:14.
140:11 *hunt down.* May the ruin these hunters (vv. 4–5) intended to bring on me hunt them down.
140:12–13 Confidence in God's just judgment (see note on 3:8).
140:12 *poor ... needy.* See notes on 9:18; 34:6.
140:13 *the righteous.* See note on 1:5. *will praise.* Having experienced God's help (see notes on 7:17; 9:1). *will live before you.* In contrast to the wicked (v. 10; see notes on 11:7; 16:9–11).
Ps 141 A prayer for deliverance from the wicked and their evil ways. The stanza structure of the first half (two Hebrew lines plus three lines) is repeated in the second half, while at the center a couplet develops a complementary theme (see note on v. 5). Like Ps 140, the prayer is profuse in its physiological allusions: hands, mouth, lips, heart, head, bones, eyes (see introduction to that psalm).
141 title See introduction to Ps 138–145.
141:1–2 Initial appeal for God to hear.
141:1 *Hear my voice when I call.* See 140:6 and note.
141:2 *my prayer ... like incense.* See notes on Ex 30:1; Lk 1:9; Rev 5:8. *like the evening sacrifice.* See Ex 29:38–41; Nu 28:3–8. These sacrifices are frequently mentioned (see 1Ki 18:29; 2Ki 16:15; 1Ch 16:40; 2Ch 13:11; 31:3; Ezr 3:3; 9:4–5; Da 9:21).
141:3–4 A plea that God will keep him from speaking, desiring or doing what is evil.

[4]Let not my heart[d] be drawn to what is
evil,
to take part in wicked deeds[e]
with men who are evildoers;
let me not eat of their delicacies.[f]

[5]Let a righteous man[a] strike me—it is a
kindness;
let him rebuke me[g]—it is oil on my
head.[h]
My head will not refuse it.

Yet my prayer is ever against the deeds
of evildoers;
[6]their rulers will be thrown down
from the cliffs,[i]
and the wicked will learn that my
words were well spoken.
[7]⌊They will say,⌋ "As one plows[j] and
breaks up the earth,[k]
so our bones have been scattered at
the mouth[l] of the grave.[b]"

[8]But my eyes are fixed[m] on you,
O Sovereign LORD;
in you I take refuge[n]—do not give
me over to death.
[9]Keep me[o] from the snares they have
laid[p] for me,
from the traps set[q] by evildoers.
[10]Let the wicked fall[r] into their own
nets,
while I pass by in safety.[s]

141:4 [d]S Jos 24:23 [e]S Ps 106:29 [f]Pr 23:1-3 **141:5** [g]Pr 9:8; 19:25; 25:12; Ecc 7:5 [h]S Ex 29:7; Ps 23:5 **141:6** [i]S 2Ch 25:12 **141:7** [j]Ps 129:3 [k]Nu 16:32-33 [l]S Nu 16:30 **141:8** [m]Ps 123:2 [n]Ps 2:12; 11:1 **141:9** [o]Ps 140:4 [p]S Ps 64:5 [q]S Ps 38:12 **141:10** [r]Ps 7:15; 35:8; 57:6 [s]Ps 124:7

142:Title [t]1Sa 22:1; 24:3; Ps 57 Title **142:1** [u]S 1Ki 8:52; Ps 3:4 [v]Ps 30:8 **142:2** [w]Ps 64:1 [x]S Ps 50:15 **142:3** [y]Ps 6:2; 77:3; 84:2; 88:4; 143:4,7; Jer 8:18; La 1:22 **142:4** [z]Jer 25:35 [a]Jer 30:17 **142:5** [b]S Ps 46:1 [c]S Dt 32:9; Ps 16:5 [d]S Job 28:13; Ps 27:13 **142:6** [e]S Ps 17:1 [f]S Ps 79:8

Psalm 142

A *maskil*[c] of David. When he was in
the cave.[t] A prayer.

[1]I cry aloud[u] to the LORD;
I lift up my voice to the LORD for
mercy.[v]
[2]I pour out my complaint[w] before him;
before him I tell my trouble.[x]

[3]When my spirit grows faint[y] within
me,
it is you who know my way.
In the path where I walk
men have hidden a snare for me.
[4]Look to my right and see;
no one is concerned for me.
I have no refuge;[z]
no one cares[a] for my life.

[5]I cry to you, O LORD;
I say, "You are my refuge,[b]
my portion[c] in the land of the
living."[d]
[6]Listen to my cry,[e]
for I am in desperate need;[f]
rescue me[g] from those who pursue
me,
for they are too strong[h] for me.

[a] 5 Or *Let the Righteous One* [b] 7 Hebrew *Sheol*
[c] Title: Probably a literary or musical term

[g]S Ps 25:20 [h]Jer 31:11

141:4 *Let not my heart.* Keep me from yielding to the example and urgings of the wicked (see Pr 1:10–16). *heart.* See note on 4:7. *their delicacies.* Usually taken to refer to the luxuriant tables the wicked set from their unjust gains—thus a prayer that the psalmist be kept from acquiring an appetite for such unholy dainties. But the noun occurs only here, and it may refer to the pleasant sounding, but deceptive and evil, words of the wicked—thus a prayer that the psalmist be kept from taking into his mouth the talk of the wicked that corresponds with their evil way of life (cf. v. 6 and note). Words related to this noun are elsewhere used to characterize words/thoughts (see Pr 15:26; 16:21; 23:8).
141:5 The center of the poem (see note on 6:6). *Let a righteous man strike me.* The disciplining blows and rebukes of the righteous are the true "kindness" (Hebrew *hesed,* meaning "love" or "acts of authentic friendship"; see Pr 27:6; see also note on Ps 6:4). *oil on my head.* See note on 23:5. *My head … deeds of evildoers.* Perhaps better: "Let my head not refuse it (this 'oil' from the righteous),/for my prayer is still against their (the wicked's) evil deeds."
141:6–7 The destiny of the wicked. *their rulers will be thrown down … the wicked will learn … ⌊They will say⌋.* Perhaps better: "let their rulers be thrown down … let the wicked learn … ⌊Let them say⌋."
141:6 *my words.* Of commitment to righteousness, as in vv. 3–5. *well spoken.* Good and right.
141:8–10 A plea that God will deliver from the designs of the wicked.
141:8 *do not give me over to death.* As you do the wicked (see v. 7; see also 73:18–20,23–26 and notes).
141:9 *snares … traps.* Perhaps, as usual, the plots of men to bring him down (as in 38:12; 64:5; 91:3; 140:5; 142:3; see note on 9:15)—note this link with Ps 140; 142.
141:10 *Let the wicked fall.* See note on 5:10. *fall into their own nets.* In Hebrew a verbal echo of 140:10 ("thrown into … miry pits").
Ps 142 A plaintive prayer for deliverance from powerful enemies—when powerless, alone and without refuge. Much of its language echoes that of other psalms (see notes below). Apart from the introduction (vv. 1–2) and conclusion (v. 7b), the prayer (in Hebrew) is composed of two four-line stanzas (vv. 3–4,5–7a).
142 title *maskil.* See note on Ps 32 title. *of David.* See introduction to Ps 138–145. *When … cave.* See note on Ps 57 title. *A prayer.* See note on Ps 17 title.
142:1–2 Initial appeal—using the formal third person (as was often done when addressing kings), equivalent to: "I cry aloud to you, O LORD."
142:1 Very similar to 77:1. *lift up my voice to the LORD for mercy.* See 140:6 and note.
142:2 *I pour out my complaint before him.* Very similar to language found in the title of Ps 102.
142:3–4 Description of his "desperate need" (v. 6).
142:3 *When my spirit grows faint.* Because he is overwhelmed by his situation (see 22:14–15)—a thematic and verbal link with 143:6 (see also 77:3; Ps 102 title; Jnh 2:7). *you who know.* And are concerned about (cf. v. 4). *hidden a snare for me.* A thematic and verbal link with 140:5; 141:9–10 (see note on 9:15).
142:4 *to my right.* To my right hand, where one's helper or defender stands (see 16:8 and note). *is concerned.* In Hebrew a less common synonym of "know" (v. 3); see Ru 2:10,19 ("notice"). *cares for.* See Dt 11:12.
142:5–7 Prayer for rescue.
142:5 *You are my refuge.* See 71:7; Jer 17:17. *portion.* The sustainer and preserver of his life (see 73:26 and note). *in the land of the living.* See 27:13 and note; 52:5; 116:9.
142:6 *Listen to my cry.* See 17:1. *rescue me.* See 143:9; 144:7.

7 Set me free from my prison,[i]
that I may praise your name.[j]
Then the righteous will gather about me
because of your goodness to me.[k]

Psalm 143

A psalm of David.

1 O LORD, hear my prayer,[l]
listen to my cry for mercy;[m]
in your faithfulness[n] and righteousness[o]
come to my relief.
2 Do not bring your servant into judgment,
for no one living is righteous[p] before you.

3 The enemy pursues me,
he crushes me to the ground;
he makes me dwell in darkness[q]
like those long dead.[r]
4 So my spirit grows faint within me;
my heart within me is dismayed.[s]

5 I remember[t] the days of long ago;
I meditate[u] on all your works
and consider what your hands have done.
6 I spread out my hands[v] to you;
my soul thirsts for you like a parched land. *Selah*

7 Answer me quickly,[w] O LORD;
my spirit fails.[x]
Do not hide your face[y] from me
or I will be like those who go down to the pit.
8 Let the morning bring me word of your unfailing love,[z]
for I have put my trust in you.
Show me the way[a] I should go,
for to you I lift up my soul.[b]
9 Rescue me[c] from my enemies,[d] O LORD,
for I hide myself in you.
10 Teach me[e] to do your will,
for you are my God;[f]
may your good Spirit
lead[g] me on level ground.[h]

11 For your name's sake,[i] O LORD,
preserve my life;[j]
in your righteousness,[k] bring me out of trouble.
12 In your unfailing love, silence my enemies;[l]
destroy all my foes,[m]
for I am your servant.[n]

Psalm 144

Of David.

1 Praise be to the LORD my Rock,[o]
who trains my hands for war,
my fingers for battle.

142:7 [i]S Ps 66:11 [j]Ps 7:17; 9:2 [k]S 2Ch 6:41 **143:1** [l]S Ps 141:1 [m]S Ps 28:2; 130:2 [n]S Ex 34:6; Ps 89:1-2 [o]Ps 71:2 **143:2** [p]S Ps 14:3; Ro 3:10 **143:3** [q]S Ps 107:10 [r]La 3:6 **143:4** [s]Ps 30:7 **143:5** [t]Ps 77:6 [u]S Ge 24:63 **143:6** [v]S Ex 9:29; S Job 11:13 **143:7** [w]S Ps 69:17 [x]S Ps 142:3 [y]S Ps 22:24; 27:9; 30:7 **143:8** [z]Ps 6:4; 90:14 [a]S Ex 33:13; S Job 34:32; Ps 27:11; 32:8 [b]Ps 25:1-2; S 86:4 **143:9** [c]S Ps 140:1 [d]S Ps 18:17; 31:15 **143:10** [e]S Ps 119:12 [f]Ps 31:14 [g]S Ne 9:20; Ps 25:4-5 [h]Ps 26:12 **143:11** [i]Ps 25:11 [j]S Ps 41:2 [k]Ps 31:1; 71:2 **143:12** [l]Ps 8:2 [m]Ps 54:5 [n]S Ps 116:16 **144:1** [o]S Ge 49:24

142:7 *prison.* Metaphor for the sense of being fettered by affliction (see note on 18:19; see also Job 36:8). *that I may praise.* In celebration of God's saving help (see note on 7:17). *name.* See note on 5:11. *righteous.* See note on 1:5. *will gather about me.* He will no longer be alone. The conclusion expresses an expectant word of confidence (see note on 3:8). *your goodness to me.* See 13:6; 116:7.

Ps 143 A prayer for deliverance from enemies and for divine leading. This is the seventh and final penitential psalm (see introduction to Ps 6). The psalm is composed of two balanced divisions of seven Hebrew lines each (vv. 1 – 6,7 – 10) and a two-line concluding reiteration of the basic appeal of the prayer (vv. 11 – 12). The three middle lines (vv. 3 – 4) of the first division describe the psalmist's distress, while the three middle lines (vv. 8 – 9) of the second division express the psalmist's trust in the Lord to deliver him from his distress. Appeal to God's righteousness (vv. 1,11) and the author's self-identification as "your servant" (vv. 2,12) enclose the prayer. See also his appeal to God's faithfulness (v. 1) and unfailing love (v. 12), which together form a frequent pair (see note on 36:5). For another enclosure see note on v. 7.

143 title See introduction to Ps 138 – 145.

143:1 – 2 Initial appeal.

143:1 *my cry for mercy.* See 140:6 and note. *righteousness.* See note on 4:1.

143:2 As he begins his prayer, he pleads that God not sit in judgment over his servant (he knows his own failings; see also v. 10) but that he focus his judicial attention on the enemy's harsh and unwarranted attacks. *your servant.* A verbal link with 144:10 — which suggests why this psalm was traditionally ascribed to David (see also 78:70; 132:10 and notes).

143:3 – 4 The distress he suffers.

143:3 The last half of this verse appears almost verbatim in La 3:6. *in darkness.* As one cut off from the enjoyments of life (see v. 7; see also notes on 27:1; 30:1).

143:4 *my spirit grows faint.* See note on 142:3. *heart.* See note on 4:7.

143:5 – 6 Remembrance of God's past acts of deliverance encourages him in his appeal.

143:6 *spread out my hands.* In prayer (see 44:20; 88:9; Ex 9:29). *soul.* See v. 8; see also note on 6:3. *thirsts for you.* See note on 63:1.

143:7 – 10 The prayer.

143:7 *my spirit fails.* Or perhaps: "my spirit faints with longing," which parallels that in 119:81; in view of the next line the thought appears closer to that of 104:29 (where "breath" translates the same Hebrew word as that for "spirit" here). Ultimately, the failing of "my spirit" will be healed by the leading of "your good Spirit" (v. 10) — the two references enclose the prayer. *hide your face.* See note on 13:1. *the pit.* See v. 3 and note on 30:1.

143:8 *the morning.* Of salvation from the present "darkness" (v. 3; see introduction to Ps 57; see also note on 101:8). *unfailing love.* See v. 12; see also note on 6:4. *I have put my trust in you ... to you I lift up my soul.* See 25:1 – 2; see also 24:4 and note. *Show me the way.* See v. 10. Deliverance from the enemy is not enough — either for God's "servant" (vv. 2,12) or for entrance into life.

143:10 *level ground.* See note on 26:12.

143:11 – 12 Concluding reiteration of the prayer (see introduction). Note how "your righteousness" and "your servant" establish links with vv. 1 – 2.

143:11 *For your name's sake.* See note on 23:3.

143:12 *destroy all my foes.* See note on 5:10.

Ps 144 A prayer for deliverance from treacherous enemies, composed in the mode of a royal prayer. Verses 1 – 10 show

2 He is my loving God and my fortress,[p]
my stronghold[q] and my deliverer,
my shield,[r] in whom I take refuge,
who subdues peoples[a][s] under me.

3 O LORD, what is man[t] that you care for him,
the son of man that you think of him?
4 Man is like a breath;[u]
his days are like a fleeting shadow.[v]

5 Part your heavens,[w] O LORD, and come down;[x]
touch the mountains, so that they smoke.[y]
6 Send forth lightning[z] and scatter[a] ⌞the enemies⌟;
shoot your arrows[b] and rout them.
7 Reach down your hand from on high;[c]
deliver me and rescue me[d]
from the mighty waters,[e]
from the hands of foreigners[f]
8 whose mouths are full of lies,[g]
whose right hands[h] are deceitful.[i]

9 I will sing a new song[j] to you, O God;
on the ten-stringed lyre[k] I will make music to you,
10 to the One who gives victory to kings,[l]
who delivers his servant David[m]
from the deadly sword.[n]

11 Deliver me and rescue me[o]
from the hands of foreigners[p]
whose mouths are full of lies,[q]
whose right hands are deceitful.[r]

144:2 [p] Ps 59:9; 91:2 [q] Ps 27:1; 37:39; 43:2 [r] S Ge 15:1; S Ps 18:2 [s] S Jdg 4:23; S Ps 18:39
144:3 [t] Heb 2:6
144:4 [u] S Job 7:7; 27:3; Isa 2:22 [v] S 1Ch 29:15; S Job 14:2; S Jas 4:14
144:5 [w] Ps 18:9; Isa 64:1 [x] S Ge 11:5; S Ps 57:3 [y] Ps 104:32
144:6 [z] Hab 3:11; Zec 9:14 [a] S Ps 59:11; S 68:1 [b] Ps 7:12-13; 18:14
144:7 [c] S 2Sa 22:17 [d] Ps 3:7; S 57:3 [e] Ps 69:2 [f] S Ps 18:44
144:8 [g] Ps 12:2; 41:6 [h] Ge 14:22; Dt 32:40 [i] S Ps 36:3
144:9 [j] S Ps 28:7; S 96:1 [k] Ps 33:2-3; S 71:22
144:10 [l] S 2Sa 8:14 [m] Ps 18:50 [n] S Job 5:20
144:11 [o] Ps 3:7; S 25:20 [p] S Ps 18:44 [q] Ps 41:6-7 [r] Ps 12:2; S 36:3; 106:26;

12 Then our sons in their youth
will be like well-nurtured plants,[s]
and our daughters will be like pillars[t]
carved to adorn a palace.
13 Our barns will be filled[u]
with every kind of provision.
Our sheep will increase by thousands,
by tens of thousands in our fields;
14 our oxen[v] will draw heavy loads.[b]
There will be no breaching of walls,[w]
no going into captivity,
no cry of distress in our streets.[x]

15 Blessed are the people[y] of whom this is true;
blessed are the people whose God is the LORD.

Psalm 145[c]

A psalm of praise. Of David.

1 I will exalt you,[z] my God the King;[a]
I will praise your name[b] for ever and ever.

[a] *2* Many manuscripts of the Masoretic Text, Dead Sea Scrolls, Aquila, Jerome and Syriac; most manuscripts of the Masoretic Text *subdues my people* [b] *14* Or *our chieftains will be firmly established* [c] This psalm is an acrostic poem, the verses of which (including verse 13b) begin with the successive letters of the Hebrew alphabet.

Isa 44:20 **144:12** [s] Ps 92:12-14; S 128:3 [t] SS 4:4; 7:4 **144:13** [u] Pr 3:10 **144:14** [v] Pr 14:4 [w] 2Ki 25:11 [x] Isa 24:11; Jer 14:2-3 **144:15** [y] Dt 28:3 **145:1** [z] Ps 30:1; 34:1 [a] Ps 2:6; 5:2 [b] S Ps 54:6

much affinity to Ps 18 with vv. 5–7 all appearing to be variations on lines found there (see notes below). The remaining lines of this section contain similar echoes of other psalms, and the author may have drawn directly on them. This first part of the psalm is fairly typical of the prayers of the Psalter. What follows is clearly composite: Verse 11 recapitulates the prayer of vv. 5–8; vv. 12–14 describe a people enjoying ideal conditions; v. 15 closes the psalm with an echo of 33:12. For thematic continuities see notes below.
144 title See introduction to Ps 138–145.
144:1–2 Praise of the Lord. As the opening words of a prayer, it seems to function both as an initial appeal (see 143:1–2) and as a confession of confidence that the prayer will be heard. The unusual piling up of epithets for God echoes Ps 18 (see note on 18:2).
144:2 *my loving God.* Lit. "my unfailing love" (see note on 6:4); so called because God is the source of benevolent acts of love that David can count on—just as God can be called "my salvation" because he is the source of salvation (see 27:1; 35:3; 62:2).
144:3–4 Acknowledgment of the relative insignificance of human beings and an expression of wonder that God cares for them.
144:3 A variation of 8:4.
144:4 *breath.* See 39:4–6 and notes. *shadow.* See 102:11 and note.
144:5–8 Prayer for deliverance.
144:5 See 18:9 and note on 18:7–15; see also Isa 64:1 and note.
144:6 See 18:14 and note.
144:7 See 18:16–17 and note on 32:6.
144:8 *mouths.* See note on 5:9. *right hands.* Hands raised to swear covenant oaths of allegiance or submission (see 106:26; Ex 6:8; Dt 32:40).
144:9–10 Vow to praise (see note on 7:17).
144:9 *new song.* See note on 33:3.
144:10 *his servant David.* See 143:2 and note.
144:11 Repetition of the prayer in vv. 7–8, apparently to serve as transition to what follows: If God will deliver his servant David, the realm will prosper and be secure.
144:12–15 Many believe this to be a separate prayer ("May our sons ..."), unrelated to vv. 1–11, but the apparently transitional function of v. 11 supports the NIV rendering.
144:12–14 Possibly a postexilic echo of Dt 28:3–8.
144:12 *daughters ... like pillars carved.* Temple columns in the shape of women were not uncommon (e.g., on the Acropolis in Athens).
144:14 *our oxen will draw heavy loads.* Or "our oxen will be heavy with flesh" or "our oxen will be heavy with young" (see also NIV text note).
144:15 *Blessed.* See note on 1:1. *the people of whom this is true.* Cf. 33:12; see Dt 28:3–8; 1Ki 5:4 and note.
Ps 145 A magnificent hymn to the Lord, the Great King, for his mighty acts and benevolent virtues, which are the glory of his kingly rule. It exploits to the full the traditional language of praise and, as an alphabetic acrostic, reflects the care of studied composition. This care can be seen also in the manner in which the whole is structured. Between the two-line introduction (vv. 1–2) and one-line conclusion (v. 21), four main stanzas (vv. 3–7,9–13a,13b–16,17–20) develop as many themes, each introduced by a thematic line. The first two of these stanzas are each composed of five poetic lines, the last two of four lines. Centered between the first two is an additional thematic line (v. 8) echoing Ex 34:6–7. This signifi-

[2] Every day I will praise[c] you
and extol your name[d] for ever and ever.
[3] Great is the LORD[e] and most worthy of praise;[f]
his greatness no one can fathom.[g]
[4] One generation[h] will commend your works to another;
they will tell[i] of your mighty acts.[j]
[5] They will speak of the glorious splendor[k] of your majesty,
and I will meditate on your wonderful works.[a][l]
[6] They will tell[m] of the power of your awesome works,[n]
and I will proclaim[o] your great deeds.[p]
[7] They will celebrate your abundant goodness[q]
and joyfully sing[r] of your righteousness.[s]
[8] The LORD is gracious and compassionate,[t]
slow to anger and rich in love.[u]
[9] The LORD is good[v] to all;
he has compassion[w] on all he has made.
[10] All you have made will praise you,[x] O LORD;
your saints will extol[y] you.[z]
[11] They will tell of the glory of your kingdom[a]
and speak of your might,[b]
[12] so that all men may know of your mighty acts[c]
and the glorious splendor of your kingdom.[d]
[13] Your kingdom is an everlasting kingdom,[e]
and your dominion endures through all generations.
The LORD is faithful[f] to all his promises[g]
and loving toward all he has made.[b]
[14] The LORD upholds[h] all those who fall
and lifts up all[i] who are bowed down.[j]
[15] The eyes of all look to you,
and you give them their food[k] at the proper time.
[16] You open your hand
and satisfy the desires[l] of every living thing.
[17] The LORD is righteous[m] in all his ways
and loving toward all he has made.[n]
[18] The LORD is near[o] to all who call on him,[p]
to all who call on him in truth.
[19] He fulfills the desires[q] of those who fear him;[r]
he hears their cry[s] and saves them.[t]
[20] The LORD watches over[u] all who love him,[v]
but all the wicked he will destroy.[w]
[21] My mouth will speak[x] in praise of the LORD.
Let every creature[y] praise his holy name[z]
for ever and ever.

Psalm 146

[1] Praise the LORD.[c]

Praise the LORD,[a] O my soul.

145:2 [c]S Ps 71:6 [d]Ps 34:1; Isa 25:1; 26:8 **145:3** [e]S Ps 95:3 [f]S 2Sa 22:4; Ps 96:4 [g]S Job 5:9 **145:4** [h]Ps 22:30 [i]S Dt 11:19 [j]S Ps 71:16 **145:5** [k]Ps 96:6; 148:13 [l]S Ps 75:1 **145:6** [m]Ps 78:4 [n]S Ps 66:3 [o]S Dt 32:3 [p]Ps 75:1; 106:22 **145:7** [q]S Ex 18:9; S Ps 27:13 [r]S Ps 5:11; S 101:1 [s]S Ps 138:5 **145:8** [t]S Ps 86:15; 103:8 [u]S Ps 86:5 **145:9** [v]S 1Ch 16:34; S Ps 136:1; Mt 19:17; Mk 10:18 [w]Ps 103:13-14 **145:10** [x]S Ps 8:6; S 103:22; S 139:14 [y]Ps 30:4; 148:14; 149:9 [z]Ps 115:17-18 **145:11** [a]ver 12-13; S Ex 15:2; Mt 6:33 [b]Ps 21:13 **145:12** [c]S Ps 75:1; 105:1 [d]ver 11; Ps 103:19; Isa 2:10, 19, 21 **145:13** [e]S Ex 15:18; 1Ti 1:17; 2Pe 1:11; Rev 11:15 [f]S Dt 7:9; S 1Co 1:9 [g]S Jos 23:14 **145:14** [h]S Ps 37:17 [i]S 1Sa 2:8; Ps 146:8 [j]S Ps 38:6 **145:15** [k]S Ge 1:30; S Job 28:5; S Ps 37:25; S Mt 6:26 **145:16** [l]S Ps 90:14; S 104:28 **145:17** [m]S Ex 9:27; S Ezr 9:15 [n]ver 13 **145:18** [o]S Nu 23:21; S Ps 46:1; Php 4:5 [p]Ps 18:6; 80:18 **145:19** [q]S Ps 20:4 [r]S Job 22:28 [s]S Ps 31:22; S 40:1 [t]S 1Sa 10:19; Ps 7:10; 34:18 **145:20** [u]S Ps 1:6 [v]Ps 31:23; 91:14; 97:10 [w]S Ps 94:23 **145:21** [x]Ps 71:8 [y]Ps 65:2; 150:6 [z]S Ex 3:15; S Ps 30:4; S 99:3 **146:1** [a]Ps 103:1; 104:1

[a] *5* Dead Sea Scrolls and Syriac (see also Septuagint); Masoretic Text *On the glorious splendor of your majesty / and on your wonderful works I will meditate* [b] *13* One manuscript of the Masoretic Text, Dead Sea Scrolls and Syriac (see also Septuagint); most manuscripts of the Masoretic Text do not have the last two lines of verse 13. [c] *1* Hebrew *Hallelu Yah*; also in verse 10

cant theme is centered (see note on 6:6) and not elaborated here (but see 86:15; 103:8–12; 111:4–5; 116:5–6) to allow the author to remain within the 22-line limits of the Hebrew alphabet. Further, the first two stanzas (vv. 3–13a) highlight the commending, telling, celebrating, singing and extolling the glory of the Lord's reign, while the last two (vv. 13b–20) focus on what it is he does that is worthy of praise.

145 title *praise.* Hebrew *tehillah,* occurring only here in the psalm titles, but from a plural form (*tehillim*) has come the traditional Hebrew name of the Psalter. *Of David.* See introduction to Ps 138–145.

145:1–2 Initial commitment to praise. *name.* See v. 21, thus framing the psalm (see note on 5:11).

145:3–7 Praise of God's mighty acts, which display his greatness (v. 3) and his goodness (v. 7)—as the author underscores by framing the paragraph with these two references. For the same combination see 86:10,17; 135:3,5.

145:4 *will commend ... will tell.* See vv. 5–7,10–12,21; see also note on 9:1. *your works.* In creation, providence and redemption.

145:7 *righteousness.* See v. 17; see also note on 4:1.

145:8 This centered line (see introduction above) is equal in thematic importance to vv. 3,9,13b,17.

145:9–13a Praise of God's benevolent virtues, which move all creatures to celebrate the glory of his kingdom.

145:10 *All you have made will praise you.* See v. 21; see also note on 65:13. *saints.* See note on 4:3.

145:13b–16 Praise of God's faithfulness.

145:13b,17 *loving.* See note on 6:4. For the combination "faithful ... and loving" see note on 36:5.

145:17–20 Praise of God's righteousness.

145:18 *in truth.* With godly integrity.

145:21 The praise of God must continue, and every creature take it up—forever. *every creature.* Or perhaps "every human" (lit. "all flesh"; see 65:2, "all men"; but see also 150:6).

Ps 146–150 A final cluster of five hymns (probably postexilic) all bracketed by shouts of "Hallelujah!" ("Praise Yahweh")—which may have been added by the final editors (see introductions to Ps 105–106; see also Ps 111–117). The Psalter collection begins with two psalms that address the reader and whose function is to identify those to whom the collections specifically belong (see introduction to Ps 1–2). Here, at the collection's

2 I will praise the LORD all my life;[b]
I will sing praise[c] to my God as long
as I live.[d]

3 Do not put your trust in princes,[e]
in mortal men,[f] who cannot save.
4 When their spirit departs, they return
to the ground;[g]
on that very day their plans come
to nothing.[h]

5 Blessed is he[i] whose help[j] is the God
of Jacob,
whose hope is in the LORD his God,
6 the Maker of heaven[k] and earth,
the sea, and everything in them—
the LORD, who remains faithful[l]
forever.
7 He upholds[m] the cause of the
oppressed[n]
and gives food to the hungry.[o]
The LORD sets prisoners free,[p]
8 the LORD gives sight[q] to the blind,[r]
the LORD lifts up those who are bowed
down,[s]
the LORD loves the righteous.[t]
9 The LORD watches over the alien[u]
and sustains the fatherless[v] and the
widow,[w]
but he frustrates the ways of the
wicked.

146:2 [b]Ps 104:33 [c]S Ps 105:2 [d]S Ps 63:4 **146:3** [e]Ps 118:9 [f]Ps 60:11; S 108:12; Isa 2:22 **146:4** [g]S Ge 3:19; S Job 7:21; Ps 103:14; Ecc 12:7 [h]Ps 33:10; 1Co 2:6 **146:5** [i]Ps 33:18; 37:9; 119:43; 144:15; Jer 17:7 [j]Ps 70:5; 71:5; 121:2 **146:6** [k]S 2Ch 2:12; Ps 115:15; Ac 14:15; S Rev 10:6 [l]S Dt 7:9; S Ps 18:25; 108:4; 117:2 **146:7** [m]S Ps 37:17 [n]Ps 103:6 [o]Ps 107:9; 145:15 [p]S Ps 66:11; S 68:6 **146:8** [q]Pr 20:12; Isa 29:18; 32:3; 35:5; 42:7, 18-19; 43:8; Mt 11:5 [r]S Ex 4:11 [s]S Ps 38:6 [t]S Dt 7:13; S Job 23:10

10 The LORD reigns[x] forever,
your God, O Zion, for all generations.

Praise the LORD.

Psalm 147

1 Praise the LORD.[a]

How good it is to sing praises to our
God,
how pleasant[y] and fitting to praise
him![z]

2 The LORD builds up Jerusalem;[a]
he gathers the exiles[b] of Israel.
3 He heals the brokenhearted[c]
and binds up their wounds.[d]

4 He determines the number of the stars[e]
and calls them each by name.
5 Great is our Lord[f] and mighty in
power;[g]
his understanding has no limit.[h]
6 The LORD sustains the humble[i]
but casts the wicked[j] to the ground.

[a] *1* Hebrew *Hallelu Yah*; also in verse 20

146:9 [u]S Lev 19:34 [v]S Ps 10:18 [w]S Ex 22:22; Jas 1:27
146:10 [x]S Ge 21:33; S 1Ch 16:31; Ps 93:1; 99:1; Rev 11:15
147:1 [y]S Ps 135:3 [z]Ps 33:1 **147:2** [a]S Ps 51:18 [b]S Ps 106:47
147:3 [c]S Ps 34:18 [d]S Nu 12:13; S Job 5:18; Isa 1:6; Eze 34:16
147:4 [e]S Ge 15:5 **147:5** [f]S Ps 48:1 [g]S Ex 14:31 [h]Ps 145:3; Isa 40:28
147:6 [i]S 2Ch 33:23; Ps 146:8-9 [j]Ps 37:9-10; 145:20

end, that congregation gives voice to its final themes. They are the themes of praise—and calls to praise—of Zion's heavenly King (see 146:10; 147:12; 149:2), the Maker, Sustainer and Lord over all creation (see 146:6; 147:4,8–9,15–18; 148:5–6); the one sure hope of those who in their need and vulnerability look to him for help (see 146:5–9; 147:2–3,6,11,13–14; 149:4); the Lord of history whose commitment to his people is their security and the guarantee that, as his kingdom people (see especially 147:19–20), they will ultimately triumph over all the forces of his world arrayed against them (see 146:3,10; 147:2,6,10,13–14; 148:14; 149:4–9).

Ps 146 A hymn in praise of Zion's heavenly King, with special focus on his powerful and trustworthy care for Zion's citizens who look to him when oppressed, broken or vulnerable. It has many thematic links with Ps 33; 62; 145. For its placement see introduction to Ps 146–150.

146:1–2 Initial vow to praise—as long as life continues (see 145:21).

146:1 *Praise the LORD, O my soul.* See the frames around Ps 103–104. *soul.* See note on 6:3.

146:3–4 A call to trust ultimately in the Lord rather than in any human help (see 118:10–11 and note; 147:10–11).

146:5–9 Encouragement to trust in the covenant God of Jacob (see note on 14:7), who as Creator is Lord over all, as the Faithful One defends the defenseless and provides for the needy, and as the Righteous One shows favor to the righteous but checks the wicked in their pursuits.

146:6 *Maker of heaven and earth.* See note on 121:2.

146:7 *upholds the cause of the oppressed.* See 9:9; 10:18; 103:6. *gives food to the hungry.* See 17:14; 34:10; 107:9; cf. Isa 49:10. *sets prisoners free.* See 68:6; 79:11; 102:20; 107:10,14; cf. Isa 42:7 and note; 61:1.

146:8 *gives sight to the blind.* See Isa 29:18; 35:5; cf. Isa 42:7; 43:8. *lifts up those who are bowed down.* See 145:14. *righteous.* See note on 1:5.

146:9 *watches over the alien ... fatherless ... widow.* See Dt 10:18; cf. Isa 1:17; 9:17 and notes; cf. also Jer 22:16; Jas 1:17. *frustrates the ways of the wicked.* Cf. 104:35; 145:20.

146:10 Concluding exultant testimony to the citizens of God's royal city. *The LORD reigns forever.* See 93:1 and note. *Zion.* See note on 9:11.

Ps 147 Praise of God, the Creator and Lord over all, for his special mercies to Israel—possibly composed for the Levitical choirs on the joyous occasion of the dedication of the rebuilt walls of Jerusalem (see Ne 12:27–43). The Septuagint (the pre-Christian Greek translation of the OT) plausibly divides the work into two separate psalms (vv. 1–11,12–20). However, the form of the psalm as handed down in the Hebrew text tradition also has the appearance of a rhetorical whole. Following the introduction (v. 1), two couplets in which the Lord's unique favors to Israel are celebrated (vv. 2–3,19–20) frame its main body, while at the center another couplet (vv. 10–11) highlights the Lord's special pleasure in those who rely finally on him rather than on any of his creatures. In the balanced stanzas that intervene (vv. 4–9,12–18), this thematic core is placed in the larger context of God's works and ways. See introduction to Ps 146–150.

147:1 See note on 135:3.

147:2 *builds up.* Refers to the postexilic rebuilding of Jerusalem. *exiles.* Translates an unusual Hebrew word found also in Isa 11:12; 56:8—all of which speak of gathering (restoring) "the exiles of Israel."

147:3 *brokenhearted.* Such as the exiles (see Ps 137; cf. Ps 126) and those who struggled in the face of great opposition to rebuild Jerusalem's walls (Ne 2:17–20; 4:1–23).

147:4–6 He whose power and understanding are such that he fixes the number of (or counts) the stars and names them is able to sustain his humble ones and bring the wicked down (see 20:8; 146:9; see also Isa 40:26–29).

147:6 *humble.* Those who acknowledge that they are without resources to deliver or maintain themselves—those who, as God's people, put their trust in him

7 Sing to the LORD[k] with thanksgiving;[l]
make music[m] to our God on the harp.[n]
8 He covers the sky with clouds;[o]
he supplies the earth with rain[p]
and makes grass grow[q] on the hills.
9 He provides food[r] for the cattle
and for the young ravens[s] when they call.
10 His pleasure is not in the strength[t] of the horse,[u]
nor his delight in the legs of a man;
11 the LORD delights[v] in those who fear him,[w]
who put their hope[x] in his unfailing love.[y]

12 Extol the LORD, O Jerusalem;[z]
praise your God, O Zion,
13 for he strengthens the bars of your gates[a]
and blesses your people[b] within you.
14 He grants peace[c] to your borders
and satisfies you[d] with the finest of wheat.[e]

15 He sends his command[f] to the earth;
his word runs[g] swiftly.
16 He spreads the snow[h] like wool
and scatters the frost[i] like ashes.
17 He hurls down his hail[j] like pebbles.
Who can withstand his icy blast?
18 He sends his word[k] and melts them;
he stirs up his breezes,[l] and the waters flow.

19 He has revealed his word[m] to Jacob,[n]
his laws and decrees[o] to Israel.
20 He has done this for no other nation;[p]
they do not know[q] his laws.

Praise the LORD.[r]

Psalm 148

1 Praise the LORD.[a][s]

Praise the LORD from the heavens,[t]
praise him in the heights above.
2 Praise him, all his angels,[u]
praise him, all his heavenly hosts.[v]
3 Praise him, sun[w] and moon,
praise him, all you shining stars.
4 Praise him, you highest heavens[x]
and you waters above the skies.[y]
5 Let them praise the name[z] of the LORD,
for he commanded[a] and they were created.
6 He set them in place for ever and ever;
he gave a decree[b] that will never pass away.

7 Praise the LORD[c] from the earth,
you great sea creatures[d] and all ocean depths,[e]
8 lightning and hail,[f] snow and clouds,
stormy winds that do his bidding,[g]
9 you mountains and all hills,[h]
fruit trees and all cedars,

[a] *1* Hebrew *Hallelu Yah*; also in verse 14

147:7 [k]Ps 30:4; 33:3 [l]S Ps 42:4 [m]S Ps 27:6 [n]S Ps 98:5 **147:8** [o]S Job 26:8 [p]S Dt 11:14; S 32:2; S 2Sa 1:21; S Job 5:10 [q]S Job 28:26; S Ps 104:14 **147:9** [r]S Ge 1:30; Ps 104:27-28; S Mt 6:26 [s]S Ge 8:7 **147:10** [t]S 1Sa 16:7 [u]S Job 39:11; Ps 33:16-17 **147:11** [v]S Ps 35:27 [w]Ps 33:18; 103:11 [x]Ps 119:43 [y]Ps 6:4 **147:12** [z]Ps 48:1 **147:13** [a]S Dt 33:25 [b]S Lev 25:21; Ps 128:5; 134:3 **147:14** [c]S Lev 26:6; S 2Sa 7:10; S Isa 48:18 [d]S Ps 132:15 [e]S Dt 32:14 **147:15** [f]Job 37:12; Ps 33:9; 148:5 [g]Isa 55:11 **147:16** [h]Ps 148:8 [i]S Job 37:12; 38:29 **147:17** [j]Ex 9:22-23; S Job 38:22; S Ps 78:47 **147:18** [k]ver 15; Ps 33:9; 107:20 [l]S Ps 50:3 **147:19** [m]S Ex 20:1; Ro 3:2 [n]Ps 78:5 [o]S Dt 33:4; Jos 1:8; 2Ki 22:8; Mal 4:4; Ro 9:4 **147:20** [p]Dt 4:7-8, 32-34 [q]S Ps 79:6 [r]Ps 33:2; 103:1 **148:1** [s]Ps 33:2; 103:1 [t]Ps 19:1; 69:34; 150:1 **148:2** [u]Ps 103:20 [v]S 1Ki 22:19 **148:3** [w]S Ps 19:1 **148:4** [x]S Dt 10:14 [y]S Ge 1:7 **148:5** [z]Ps 145:21 [a]S Ps 147:15 **148:6** [b]Jer 31:35-36; 33:25 **148:7** [c]Ps 33:2 [d]S Ge 1:21; Ps 74:13-14 [e]S Dt 33:13 **148:8** [f]S Ex 9:18; S Jos 10:11 [g]Job 37:11-12; S Ps 103:20; 147:15-18 **148:9** [h]Isa 44:23; 49:13; 55:12

(see 149:4; see also 22:26, "the poor"; 37:11, "the meek," and note; 69:32, "the poor"). *ground.* Probably the grave (see note on 61:2).

147:7–9 Israel's God is Lord of creation, the one who provides for all living things.

147:10–11 The central couplet (see note on 6:6), thematically linked with vv. 2–3 and vv. 19–20 (see introduction above). Israel's God is not particularly impressed by the creaturely capacities that humans are prone to rely on (cf. 146:3–4 and note); it gives him delight when his people rely on him (cf. 146:5–9).

147:11 *fear.* See note on 34:8–14. *unfailing love.* See note on 6:4.

147:12–18 The Lord of all creation, Zion's God, secures his people's defenses and prosperity, their peace and abundant provision. The verses mention clouds and rain (v. 8); snow, frost and hail (vv. 16–17); icy winds and warm breezes (vv. 17–18)—the whole range of weather.

147:15 *his command ... his word.* Personified as messengers commissioned to carry out a divine order (see v. 18; see also notes on 23:6; 33:4; 104:4).

147:19–20 God's most unique gift to Israel: his other word, his redemptive word, by which he makes known his program of salvation and his holy will. These verses constitute the end frame, thematically linked with vv. 2–3 and vv. 10–11 (see introduction above and note on vv. 10–11).

Ps 148 A call to all things in all creation to praise the Lord. Whatever its original liturgical purpose, its placement here at the center of the five concluding hymns serves to complete the scope of the calls to praise with which the Psalter closes (see introduction to Ps 146–150). Two similarly constructed stanzas call on all creatures in the heavens (vv. 1–6) and all creatures beneath the heavens (vv. 7–14) to join in the chorus of praise (see 103:20–22 and note). Both stanzas end with a couplet setting forth the motivation for praise. The second of these (vv. 12–14), made up of extended lines, clearly constitutes the climax.

148:1–6 Let all creatures in the heavens praise the Lord.

148:2 *heavenly hosts.* See 103:21 and note.

148:3 *sun and moon ... shining stars.* See note on 65:13.

148:4 *waters above the skies.* See Ge 1:7; cf. "ocean depths" in v. 7; see also note on 42:7.

148:5–6 Motivation for the heavenly creatures to praise the Lord (cf. vv. 13–14).

148:5,13 *name of the LORD.* See note on 5:11. They are to praise the Lord because he has created them and made their existence secure.

148:7–14 Let all creatures on earth praise the Lord. "The earth and the heavens" (v. 13) are the sum of all creation; see 89:11; 113:6; 136:5–6; Ge 2:1,4.

148:7 *sea creatures and all ocean depths.* Likely with Ge 1 in mind (see Ge 1:7,10,21), the call begins with these and moves toward the human components. This and the pairs that follow employ a figure of speech that refers to all reality pertaining to the sphere to which they belong—here, all creatures great and small that belong to the realm of lakes and seas.

148:8 *his bidding.* Lit. "his word" (see 147:15 and note).

10 wild animals[i] and all cattle,
small creatures and flying birds,
11 kings[j] of the earth and all nations,
you princes and all rulers on earth,
12 young men and maidens,
old men and children.

13 Let them praise the name of the LORD,[k]
for his name alone is exalted;
his splendor[l] is above the earth and
the heavens.[m]
14 He has raised up for his people a
horn,[a n]
the praise[o] of all his saints,[p]
of Israel, the people close to his
heart.[q]

Praise the LORD.

Psalm 149

1 Praise the LORD.[b r]

Sing to the LORD a new song,[s]
his praise in the assembly[t] of the
saints.

2 Let Israel rejoice[u] in their Maker;[v]
let the people of Zion be glad in
their King.[w]
3 Let them praise his name with
dancing[x]
and make music to him with
tambourine and harp.[y]

4 For the LORD takes delight[z] in his
people;
he crowns the humble with
salvation.[a]
5 Let the saints rejoice[b] in this honor
and sing for joy on their beds.[c]

6 May the praise of God be in their
mouths[d]
and a double-edged[e] sword in their
hands,[f]
7 to inflict vengeance[g] on the nations
and punishment[h] on the peoples,
8 to bind their kings with fetters,[i]
their nobles with shackles of iron,[j]
9 to carry out the sentence written
against them.[k]
This is the glory of all his saints.[l]

Praise the LORD.

Psalm 150

1 Praise the LORD.[c m]

Praise God in his sanctuary;[n]
praise him in his mighty heavens.[o]

[a] 14 *Horn* here symbolizes strong one, that is, king.
[b] 1 Hebrew *Hallelu Yah*; also in verse 9 [c] 1 Hebrew *Hallelu Yah*; also in verse 6

148:10 [i]Isa 43:20; Hos 2:18 **148:11** [j]S Ps 102:15 **148:13** [k]S Ps 113:2; 138:4 [l]S Ps 145:5 [m]S Ps 8:1 **148:14** [n]S 1Sa 2:1 [o]S Ex 15:2; Ps 22:3 [p]S Ps 145:10 [q]S Dt 26:19 **149:1** [r]Ps 33:2; 103:1 [s]S Ps 28:7; S 96:1; Rev 5:9 [t]S Ps 1:5 **149:2** [u]Isa 13:3; Jer 51:48 [v]S Job 10:3; Ps 95:6; Isa 44:2; 45:11; 54:5 [w]Ps 10:16; 47:6; Isa 32:1; Zec 9:9 **149:3** [x]S Ex 15:20 [y]S Ps 57:8 **149:4** [z]Ps 35:27; 147:11 [a]Ps 132:16 **149:5** [b]S Ps 132:16 [c]Job 35:10; Ps 42:8 **149:6** [d]Ps 66:17 [e]Heb 4:12; Rev 1:16 [f]Ne 4:17 **149:7** [g]S Nu 31:3; S Dt 32:41 [h]Ps 81:15 **149:8** [i]S 2Sa 3:34; S Isa 14:1-2 [j]2Ch 33:11 **149:9** [k]Dt 7:1; Eze 28:26 [l]S Ps 145:10 **150:1** [m]S Ps 112:1 [n]Ps 68:24-26; 73:17; 102:19 [o]S Ps 148:1

148:13 – 14 Climactic conclusion, with focus again on motivation for praise (cf. vv. 5 – 6).
148:13 *his name ... his splendor.* As shown in the glory of his creation. *is above.* The glory of the Creator is greater than the glory of the creation.
148:14 *horn.* The Lord's anointed (see NIV text note; see also notes on 2:2; Ps 18 title). It may be, however, that "horn" here represents the strength and vigor of God's people (see 92:10; 1Sa 2:1; Jer 48:25; La 2:17). In any event, reference is to God's saving acts for Israel — God is to be praised for his works in creation and redemption (see note on 65:6 – 7). *praise.* See 22:3 and note.
Ps 149 Praise of God for the high honor bestowed on his people Israel. Israel's unique honor has two sides: She was granted salvation (in fact and in promise), and, under the particular administration of the emerging kingdom of God that was put in place in the inauguration of the Sinai covenant (see chart, p. 19), she was armed to execute God's sentence of judgment on the world powers that have launched attacks against the kingdom of God. Under that arrangement, she served as the earthly contingent of the armies of the King of heaven (see 68:17 and note; see also Jos 5:14; 2Sa 5:23 – 24; 2Ch 20:15 – 17,22; Hab 3:3 – 15). This next-to-last psalm should be read in the light of the second psalm (see introduction to Ps 2; see also introduction to Ps 146 – 150).
Following an introductory verse, the two main themes are developed in two balanced stanzas of four verses each. References to God's "saints" enclose the song (see also v. 5). The common pair of synonyms, "honor" (v. 5) and "glory" (v. 9), effectively link the two stanzas (see 8:5; 21:5, "glory ... majesty"; 104:1,31, "majesty ... glory"; 145:5,12, "glorious splendor"; Isa 35:2, "glory ... splendor").
149:1 *new song.* See note on 33:3. *in the assembly.* See note on 9:1. *saints.* See vv. 5,9; see also note on 4:3.
149:2 – 5 Let Israel rejoice in their King, who has crowned them with the honor of salvation.
149:3 *his name.* See note on 5:11.
149:4 *crowns.* Endows with splendor (see Isa 55:5; 60:9; 61:3). *humble.* Those who acknowledge that they are without resources (see 147:6 and note).
149:5 *on their beds.* The salvation (v. 4) so tangible in the daytime evokes songs in the night (see 42:8; 63:6; 77:6).
149:6 – 9 Let Israel praise their God, who has given them the glory of bearing the sword as his army in service (cf. Ps 137; 139:19 – 22; Am 9:12; Eze 38 – 39; Da 2:44; 7:22,26 – 27).
149:7 *vengeance.* God's just retribution on those who have attacked his kingdom. Of this divine retribution the OT speaks often: 58:10; 79:10; 94:1; Nu 31:2; Dt 32:35,41,43; 2Ki 9:7; Isa 34:8; 35:4; 47:3; 59:17; 61:2; 63:4; Jer 46:10; 50:15,28; 51:6,11,36; Eze 25:14,17; Mic 5:15; Na 1:2. In the NT age, however, God's people are armed with the "sword of the Spirit" (Eph 6:17) for overcoming the powers arrayed against God's kingdom (see 2Co 6:7; 10:4; Eph 6:12; Heb 4:12); their participation in God's retribution on the world awaits the final judgment (see 1Co 6:2 – 3).
149:9 *sentence written.* God's firmly determined judgment (see 139:16 and note).
Ps 150 The final great Hallelujah — perhaps composed specifically to close the Psalter. See the conclusions to the first four Books: 41:13; 72:18 – 19; 89:52; 106:48. This final call to praise moves powerfully by stages from place to themes to orchestra to choir, framed with Hallelujahs. See introduction to Ps 146 – 150.
150:1 *Where* God should be praised. *his sanctuary.* At Jerusalem. *his mighty heavens.* Lit. "the expanse of his power" (see 19:1, "skies"; Ge 1:6), i.e., the expanse that displays or symbolizes his power or in which his power resides. Usually thought to refer to God's heavenly temple (see 11:4), it may signify

[2]Praise him for his acts of power;[p]
praise him for his surpassing greatness.[q]
[3]Praise him with the sounding of the trumpet,[r]
praise him with the harp and lyre,[s]
[4]praise him with tambourine and dancing,[t]
praise him with the strings[u] and flute,[v]
[5]praise him with the clash of cymbals,[w]
praise him with resounding cymbals.

[6]Let everything[x] that has breath praise the LORD.

Praise the LORD.

150:2 [p]S Dt 3:24 [q]S Ex 15:7 **150:3** [r]S Nu 10:2 [s]S Ps 57:8 **150:4** [t]S Ex 15:20 [u]S Ps 45:8 [v]S Ge 4:21 **150:5** [w]S 2Sa 6:5 **150:6** [x]S Ps 103:22

the vaulted ceiling of the visible universe viewed as a cosmic temple.
150:2 *Why* God should be praised. *his acts of power.* What he does (in creation and redemption). *his surpassing greatness.* Who he is.
150:3–5 *How* God should be praised—with the whole orchestra (eight instruments: wind, string, percussion), with dancing aptly placed at the middle.
150:6 *Who* should praise God. The choir, with articulate expression, celebrates God's mighty acts and surpassing greatness.

Proverbs

INTRODUCTION

Authors

Although the book begins with a title ascribing the proverbs to Solomon, it is clear from later chapters that he was not the only author of the book. Pr 22:17 refers to the "sayings of the wise," and 24:23 mentions additional "sayings of the wise." The presence of an introduction in 22:17 – 21 further indicates that these sections stem from a circle of wise men, not from Solomon himself. Ch. 30 is attributed to Agur son of Jakeh and 31:1 – 9 to King Lemuel, neither of whom is mentioned elsewhere. Lemuel's sayings contain several Aramaic spellings that may point to a non-Israelite background.

Most of the book, however, is closely linked with Solomon. The headings in 10:1 and 25:1 again include his name, though 25:1 states that these proverbs were "copied by the men of Hezekiah king of Judah." This indicates that a group of wise men or scribes compiled these proverbs as editors and added chs. 25 – 29 to the earlier collections. Solomon's ability to produce proverbs is specified in 1Ki 4:32, where 3,000 proverbs are attributed to him. Coupled with statements about his unparalleled wisdom (1Ki 4:29 – 31,34; 10:1 – 13,23 – 24), it is quite likely that he was the source of most of Proverbs. The book contains a short prologue (1:1 – 7) and a longer epilogue (31:10 – 31), which may have been added to the other materials. It is possible that the discourses in the large opening section (1:8 — 9:18) were the work of a compiler or editor, but the similarities of ch. 6 in this section with other chapters (compare 6:1 with 11:15; 17:18; 20:16; 27:13; compare 6:14,19 with 10:12; 15:18; 16:28; 28:25; 29:22; compare 6:19 with 14:5,25; 19:5) fit a Solomonic origin equally well. The emphasis on the "fear of the LORD" (1:7) throughout the book ties the various segments together.

Date

If Solomon is granted a prominent role in the book, most of Proverbs would stem from the tenth century B.C. during the time of Israel's united kingdom. The peace and prosperity that characterized that era accord well with the development of reflective wisdom and the production of literary works. Moreover, several interpreters have noted that the 30 sayings of the wise in 22:17 — 24:22 (especially the first ten) contain similarities to the 30 sections of the Egyptian "Wisdom of Amenemope," an instructional piece that is roughly contemporary with the time of Solomon (see chart, p. xxii). Likewise, the personification of wisdom so prominent in chs. 1 – 9 (see 1:20 and note; 3:15 – 18; 8:1 – 36; 9:1 – 12) can be compared with the personification of abstract ideas in both Mesopotamian and Egyptian writings of the second millennium B.C.

The role of Hezekiah's men (see 25:1) indicates that important sections of Proverbs were compiled and edited from 715 to 686 B.C. This was a time of spiritual renewal led by the king, who also showed great interest in the writings of David and Asaph (see 2Ch 29:30). Perhaps it was also at this time that the sayings of Agur (ch. 30) and Lemuel (31:1 – 9) and the other "sayings of the wise" (22:17 — 24:22; 24:23 – 34) were added to the Solomonic collections, though it is possible that the task of compilation was not completed until after the reign of Hezekiah.

The Nature of a Proverb

Proverbs, such as those contained in this book, are not to be interpreted as prophecies or their statements about effects and results as promises. For instance, 10:27 says that the years of the wicked are cut short, while the righteous live long and prosperous lives (see 3:2 and note). The righteous have abundant food (10:3), but the wicked will go hungry (13:25). While such statements are generally true, there are enough exceptions to indicate that sometimes the righteous suffer and the wicked prosper (see note on 3:2). Normally the righteous and wicked "receive their due on earth" (11:31), but at other times reward and punishment lie beyond the grave.

The Hebrew word translated "proverb" is also translated "oracle" (Nu 23:7,18), "taunt" (Isa 14:4) and "parable" (Eze 17:2), so its meaning is considerably broader than the English term. This may help explain the presence of the longer discourse sections in chs. 1 – 9. Most proverbs are short, compact statements that express truths about human behavior. Often there is repetition of a word or sound that aids memorization. In 30:33, e.g., the same Hebrew verb is translated "churning," "twisting" and "stirring up."

In the longest section of the book (10:1 — 22:16) most of the proverbs are two lines long, and those in chs. 10 – 15 almost always express a contrast. Sometimes the writer simply makes a general observation, such as "A bribe is a charm to the one who gives it" (17:8; cf. 14:20), but usually he evaluates conduct: "he who hates bribes will live" (15:27). Many proverbs, in fact, describe the consequences of a particular action or character trait: "A wise son brings joy to his father" (10:1). Since the proverbs were written primarily for instruction, often they are initiated with an imperatival statement: "Do not love sleep or you will grow poor" (20:13). Even where the imperative form is not used, the desired action is quite clear (see 14:5).

A Quick Look

Author:
King Solomon and other wise men

Audience:
The people of Israel

Date:
Primarily during Solomon's reign (970 – 930 B.C.)

Theme:
Proverbs describes the importance of living wisely and in the fear of the Lord as opposed to following the seductive path of folly.

A common feature of the proverbs is the use of figurative language: "Like cold water to a weary soul / is good news from a distant land" (25:25). In ch. 25 alone there are 11 verses that begin with "like" or "as." These similes make the proverbs more vivid and powerful. Occasionally the simile is used in a humorous or sarcastic way: "Like a gold ring in a pig's snout / is a beautiful woman who shows no discretion" (11:22; cf. 26:9), or, "As a door turns on its hinges, / so a sluggard turns on his bed" (26:14). Equally effective is the use of metaphors: "The teaching of the wise is a fountain of life" (13:14), and "the tongue that brings healing is a tree of life" (15:4). According to 16:24, "pleasant words are a honeycomb." The figure of sowing and reaping is used in both a positive and a negative way (cf. 11:18; 22:8).

In order to develop a proper set of values, a number of proverbs use direct comparisons: "Better a poor man whose walk is blameless / than a rich man whose ways are perverse" (28:6). This "better . . . than" pattern can be seen also in 15:16 – 17; 16:19,32; 17:1,12; a modified form occurs in 22:1. Another pattern found in the book is the so-called numerical proverb. Used for the first time in 6:16 (see note there), this type of saying normally has the number three in the first line and four in the second (cf. 30:15,18,21,29).

The repetition of entire proverbs (compare 6:10 – 11 with 24:33 – 34; 14:12 with 16:25; 18:8 with

26:22; 20:16 with 27:13; 21:19 with 25:24) or parts of proverbs may serve a poetic purpose. A slight variation allows the writer(s) to use the same image to make a related point (as in 17:3; 27:21) or to substitute a word or two to achieve greater clarity or a different emphasis (cf. 19:1; 28:6). In 26:4–5 the same line is repeated in a seemingly contradictory way, but this was designed to make two different points (see notes there).

At times the book of Proverbs is very direct and earthy (cf. 6:6; 21:9; 25:16; 26:3). This is the nature of wisdom literature as it seeks pedagogically effective ways to illumine life situations and to guide the unwise (or not yet wise) into wise choices concerning how to shape their lives as members of the human community that lives under the scrutiny and the providential rule and care of the Creator (see essay, p. 727).

Purpose and Teaching

According to the prologue (1:1–7), Proverbs was written to give "prudence to the simple, knowledge and discretion to the young" (1:4), and to make the wise even wiser (1:5). The frequent references to "my son(s)" (1:8,10; 2:1; 3:1; 4:1; 5:1) emphasize instructing the young and guiding them in a way of life that yields rewarding ends. Acquiring wisdom and knowing how to avoid the pitfalls of folly lead to personal well-being, happy family relationships, fruitful labors and good standing in the community (see chart, p. 957). Although Proverbs is a practical book dealing with the art of living, it bases its practical wisdom solidly on the fear of the Lord (1:7; see Ps 34:8–14 and note). Throughout the book reverence for God and reliance on him are set forth as the path to life, prosperity and security (cf. 3:5–10; 9:10–12; 14:26–27; 16:3,6–7; 18:10; 19:23; 20:22; 22:4; 28:25; 29:25). Such godly wisdom is a virtual "tree of life" (3:18; 11:30; 13:12; 15:4) that yields the happy life that God fashioned the creation to produce.

In the initial cycle of instruction (1:8—9:18) the writer urges the young man to choose the way of wisdom (that leads to life) and shun the ways of folly (that, however tempting they may be, lead to death). The author chooses two prime exemplifications of folly to give concreteness to his exhortations: (1) to get ahead in the world by exploiting (even oppressing) others rather than by diligent and honest labor, and (2) to find sexual pleasure outside the bonds and responsibilities of marriage. Temptation to the one comes from the young man's male peers (1:10–19); temptation to the other comes from the adulterous woman (ch. 5; 6:20–35; ch. 7). Together, these two temptations illustrate the pervasiveness and power of the allurements to folly that the young man will face in life and must be prepared to resist (see also Literary Structure below).

The major collections of proverbs that follow range widely across the broad spectrum of human situations, relationships and responsibilities offering insights, warnings, instructions and counsels along with frequent motivations to heed them. The range and variety of these defy summation. However, an illustrative section can convey the general character, moral tone and scope of the collections. In a variety of situations and relationships the reader is exhorted to honesty, integrity, diligence, kindness, generosity, readiness to forgive, truthfulness, patience, humility, cheerfulness, loyalty, temperance, self-control and the prudent consideration of consequences that flow from attitudes, choices and/or actions. Anger should be held in check, violence and quarrelsomeness shunned, gossip avoided, arrogance repudiated. Drunkenness, gluttony, envy and greed should all be renounced. The poor are not to be exploited, the courts are not to be unjustly manipulated, legitimate authorities are to be honored. Parents should care for the proper instruction and discipline of their children, and children should duly honor their parents and bring no disgrace on them. Human observation and experience have taught the wise that a certain order is in place in God's creation. To honor it leads to known positive effects; to defy it leads only to unhappy consequences. All of life should be lived in conscious awareness of the unfailing scrutiny of the Lord of creation and in reliance on his generous providence.

Although Proverbs is more practical than theological, God's work as Creator is especially highlighted. The role of wisdom in creation is the subject of 8:22–31 (see notes there), where wisdom as an attribute of God is personified. God is called the Maker of the poor (14:31; 17:5; 22:2). He sovereignly directs the steps of people (cf. 16:9; 20:24)—even the actions of kings (21:1)—and his eyes observe all that humans do (cf. 5:21; 15:3). All history moves forward under his control (see 16:4,33 and notes).

In summary, Proverbs provides instruction on how to live wisely and successfully in the "fear of the LORD" (1:7; 9:10) within the theocratic arrangement. The fear of the Lord includes reverence for, trust in and commitment to the Lord and his will as disclosed in his creation and as revealed in his word. Wisdom in this context, then, is basically following the benevolent King's design for human happiness within the creation order — resulting in quality of mind (1:2) and quality of life (1:3).

Literary Structure

The sectional headings found in the NIV text itself divide the book into well-defined units. A short prologue (stating the purpose and theme, 1:1 – 7) opens the book, and a longer epilogue (identifiable by its subject matter and its alphabetic form, 31:10 – 31) closes it. The first nine chapters contain a series of discourses that contrast the way and benefits of wisdom with the way of the fool. Except for the sections where personified wisdom speaks (1:20; 8:1; 9:1), each discourse begins with "my son" or "my sons."

Although Proverbs is more practical than theological, God's work as Creator is especially highlighted, and wisdom as an attribute of God is personified.

A key feature in the introductory discourses of Proverbs is the personification of both wisdom and folly as women, each of whom (by appeals and warnings on the part of Lady Wisdom, by enticements on the part of Lady Folly) seeks to persuade "simple" youths to follow her ways. These discourses are strikingly organized. Beginning (1:8 – 33) and ending (chs. 8 – 9) with direct enticements and appeals, the main body of the discourses is made up of two nicely balanced sections, one devoted to the commendation of wisdom (chs. 2 – 4) and the other to warnings against folly (chs. 5 – 7). In these discourses the young man is depicted as being enticed to folly by men who try to get ahead in the world by exploiting others (1:10 – 19) and by women who seek sexual pleasure outside the bond of marriage (ch. 5; 6:20 – 35; ch. 7). In the social structures of that day, these were the two great temptations for young men. The second especially functions here as illustrative and emblematic of the appeal of Lady Folly.

The main collection of Solomon's proverbs in 10:1 — 22:16 consists of individual couplets, many of which express a contrast. On the surface, there does not seem to be any discernible arrangement, though occasionally two or three proverbs deal with the same subject. For example, 11:24 – 25 deals with generosity, 16:12 – 15 mentions kings, and 19:4,6 – 7 talks about friendship. However, there is growing evidence that arrangements of larger units were deliberate. Further study of this possibility is necessary. The second Solomonic collection (chs. 25 – 29) continues the pattern of two-line verses, but there are also examples of proverbs with three (25:13; 27:10,22,27) or four (25:4 – 5,21 – 22; 26:18 – 19) lines. The last five verses of ch. 27 (vv. 23 – 27) present a short discourse on the benefits of raising flocks and herds.

In the "thirty sayings" of the wise (22:17 — 24:22) and the "further sayings" of 24:23 – 34, there is a prevalence of two- or three-verse units and something of a return to the style of chs. 1 – 9 (see especially 23:29 – 35). These sections have been appended to the preceding and contain some proverbs similar to those included in the foregoing collections (compare 24:6 with 11:14; 24:16 with 11:5). One finds even stronger links with chs. 1 – 9 (compare 23:27 with 2:16; 24:33 – 34 with 6:10 – 11).

At the end of the book the editor(s) has (have) attached three additional pieces, diverse in form and content: the "sayings of Agur," the "sayings of King Lemuel" and a description of "a wife of noble character." The first of these (ch. 30) is dominated by numerical proverbs (30:15,18,21,24,29; see note on 6:16). The second (31:1 – 9) is devoted exclusively to instruction for kings. The third (31:10 – 31), effectively an epilogue to the whole, is an impressive acrostic poem honoring the wife of noble character (cf. Ru 3:11 and note). She demonstrates, and thus epitomizes, many of the qualities and values identified with wisdom throughout the book. In view of the fact that Proverbs is primarily addressed to young men on the threshold of mature life, this focus on the ideal wife appears surprising. But its purpose may be twofold: (1) to offer counsel on the kind of wife a young man ought to seek, and (2) in a subtle way to advise the young man (again) to marry Lady Wisdom, thus returning to the theme of chs. 1 – 9 (as climaxed in ch. 9; compare the description of Lady Wisdom in 9:1 – 2 with the virtues of the wife in 31:10 – 31). In any event, the concluding epitomizing of wisdom in the wife of noble character forms a literary frame with the opening discourses, where wisdom is personified as a woman.

Outline

- I. Prologue: Purpose and Theme (1:1 – 7)
- II. The Superiority of the Way of Wisdom (1:8 — 9:18)
  - A. Appeals and Warnings Confronting Youth (1:8 – 33)
    1. Enticements to secure happiness by violence (1:8 – 19)
    2. Warnings against rejecting wisdom (1:20 – 33)
  - B. Commendation of Wisdom (chs. 2 – 4)
    1. Benefits of accepting wisdom's instructions (ch. 2)
    2. Wisdom bestows well-being (3:1 – 20)
    3. Wisdom's instructions and benefits (3:21 – 35)
    4. Challenge to hold on to wisdom (ch. 4)
  - C. Warnings against Folly (chs. 5 – 7)
    1. Warning against adultery (ch. 5)
    2. Warning against perverse ways (6:1 – 19)
    3. Cost of committing adultery (6:20 – 35)
    4. Warning against the enticements of an adulteress (ch. 7)
  - D. Appeals Addressed to Youth (chs. 8 – 9)
    1. Wisdom's appeal (ch. 8)
    2. Invitations of wisdom and folly (ch. 9)
- III. The Main Collection of Solomon's Proverbs (10:1 — 22:16)
- IV. The Thirty Sayings of the Wise (22:17 — 24:22)
- V. Additional Sayings of the Wise (24:23 – 34)
- VI. Hezekiah's Collection of Solomon's Proverbs (chs. 25 – 29)
- VII. The Sayings of Agur (ch. 30)
- VIII. The Sayings of King Lemuel (31:1 – 9)
- IX. Epilogue: The Ideal Wife (31:10 – 31)

The Wise Man According to Proverbs: An Outline

I. His Character

- A. He Is Teachable, Not Intractable
  - 1. He receives and loves instruction (18:15; 19:20)
  - 2. He grows in wisdom (1:5; 9:9; 10:14)
- B. He Is Righteous, Not Wicked
  - 1. He fears the Lord (1:7; 14:16; see below under relationship to the Lord)
  - 2. He hates what is false (13:5)
  - 3. He shuns evil (3:7; 14:16; 16:6)
  - 4. He does what is righteous (2:20)
  - 5. He speaks the truth (22:21)
- C. He Is Humble, Not Proud (15:33)
- D. He Is Self-controlled, Not Rash
  - 1. His temperament
    - a. He is self-controlled (29:11)
    - b. He has a calm spirit (17:27)
    - c. He is slow to become angry (29:8,11)
  - 2. His actions
    - a. He is cautious, not hasty (19:2)
    - b. He thinks before he acts (13:16; 14:8)
    - c. He thinks before he speaks (12:23; 15:2)
- E. He Is Forgiving, Not Vindictive
  - 1. He is patient (19:11)
  - 2. He is concerned about goodwill/peace (14:9)
  - 3. He forgives those who wrong him (10:12; 17:9)
  - 4.He is not vindictive (20:22; 24:29)

II. His Relationships

- A. To the Lord
  - 1. He fears the Lord (9:10; 14:16; 15:33)
  - 2. He trusts in the Lord (3:5; 16:3,20)
  - 3. He is ever mindful of the Lord (3:6)
  - 4. He chooses the Lord's way/wisdom (8:10-11; 17:24)
  - 5. He submits to the Lord's discipline (1:2-3; 3:11)
  - 6. He confesses his sin (28:13)
- B. To His Family
  - 1. To his parents
    - a. He respects them (17:6; contrast 30:17)
    - b. He listens to them (23:22; cf. 1:8; 4:1)
    - c. He seeks to bring them honor and joy
      - 1) By being wise (10:1; 15:20; 29:3)
      - 2) By being righteous (23:24)
      - 3) By being diligent (10:5)
  - 2. To his wife
    - a. He appreciates her
      - 1) As a gift from the Lord (18:22; 19:14)
      - 2) As his crowning glory (12:4; 31:10-31)
    - b. He praises her (31:28)
    - c. He trusts her (31:11)
    - d. He is faithful to her (5:15-20)
  - 3. To his children
    - a. He loves them (3:12; 13:24)
    - b. He is concerned about them (1:8–9:18)
    - c. He trains them (22:6)
      - 1) Reasons for training them
        - a) Own peace of mind and joy (29:17)
        - b) Child's honor and well-being (1:8-9; 4:9; 19:18; 23:13-14)
      - 2) By teaching/instructing them (1:10; chs. 5-7; 28:7; cf. 4:1-9)
      - 3) By disciplining them
        - a) By verbal correction (13:1)
        - b) By physical discipline (13:24; 23:13-14)
    - d. He provides for their
      - 1) Physical needs (21:20; cf. 27:23-27)
      - 2) Spiritual heritage (14:26; 20:7)
- C. To His Friends and Neighbors
  - 1. To his friends
    - a. He values them (27:10)
    - b. He is constant to them (17:17; 18:24)
    - c. He gives them counsel (27:9,17; cf. 27:6; 28:23)
  - 2. To his neighbors
    - a. He fulfills his obligations (3:27-28)
    - b. He strives for peace (3:29-30)
    - c. He does not outstay his welcome (25:17)
    - d. He does not deceive or mislead them (16:29; 26:18-19)

III. His Words

- A. The Power of His Words
  - 1. Their power
    - a. The power of life and death (12:6; 13:14; 15:4; 18:21)
    - b. The power to heal or to wound (11:9,11; 12:18; 15:4,30; 16:24)
  - 2. Their limitation
    - a. No substitute for deeds (14:23)
    - b. Cannot alter the facts (26:23-26)
    - c. Cannot compel response (29:19)
- B. The Character of His Words
  - 1. They are honest, not false (12:22; 16:13)
  - 2. They are few, not many (10:19)
    - a. Not boastful (27:2)
    - b. Not argumentative (17:14)
    - c. Not contentious (29:9)
    - d. Not a gossip
      - 1) Revealing secrets (11:13; 20:19)
      - 2) Spreading slander (10:18; 26:20-22)
  - 3. They are calm, not emotional
    - a. Rational (15:28; 17:27)
    - b. Gentle and peaceable (15:1,18)
    - c. Yet persuasive (25:15)
  - 4. They are apt, not untimely (15:23; 25:11)
- C. The Source of His Words
  - 1. His heart/character (compare 4:23 with Mt 12:33-35)
    - a. Positively, he is righteous (cf. 10:11; 13:14)
    - b. Negatively, he is not
      - 1) Proud (13:10; cf. 6:16-19)
      - 2) Hateful (26:24,28)
  - 2. His companions (13:20; 27:17)
  - 3. Reflections (15:28)

Prologue: Purpose and Theme

1 The proverbs[a] of Solomon[b] son of David, king of Israel:[c]

[2]for attaining wisdom and discipline;
for understanding words of insight;
[3]for acquiring a disciplined and prudent life,
doing what is right and just and fair;
[4]for giving prudence to the simple,[d]
knowledge and discretion[e] to the young—
[5]let the wise listen and add to their learning,[f]
and let the discerning get guidance—
[6]for understanding proverbs and parables,[g]
the sayings and riddles[h] of the wise.[i]

[7]The fear of the LORD[j] is the beginning of knowledge,
but fools[a] despise wisdom[k] and discipline.[l]

Exhortations to Embrace Wisdom

Warning Against Enticement

[8]Listen, my son,[m] to your father's[n] instruction
and do not forsake your mother's teaching.[o]
[9]They will be a garland to grace your head
and a chain to adorn your neck.[p]

[10]My son, if sinners entice[q] you,
do not give in[r] to them.[s]
[11]If they say, "Come along with us;
let's lie in wait[t] for someone's blood,
let's waylay some harmless soul;
[12]let's swallow[u] them alive, like the grave,[b]
and whole, like those who go down to the pit;[v]
[13]we will get all sorts of valuable things
and fill our houses with plunder;
[14]throw in your lot with us,
and we will share a common purse[w]"—
[15]my son, do not go along with them,
do not set foot[x] on their paths;[y]
[16]for their feet rush into sin,[z]
they are swift to shed blood.[a]
[17]How useless to spread a net
in full view of all the birds!

1:1 [a]Mt 13:3 [b]1Ki 4:29-34 [c]Pr 10:1; 25:1; Ecc 1:1 **1:4** [d]Pr 8:5 [e]Pr 8:12 **1:5** [f]Pr 9:9 **1:6** [g]S Ps 49:4; Mt 13:10-17 [h]S Nu 12:8; S Jdg 14:12 [i]Pr 22:17; 24:23 **1:7** [j]S Ex 20:20; S Job 23:15; Ps 34:4-22; S 112:1; Pr 9:10; 15:33; Isa 33:6; 50:10; 59:19 [k]S Dt 4:6; Jer 8:9 [l]Pr 8:33-36; 9:7-9; 12:1; 13:18; 15:32 **1:8** [m]ver 8-9; Pr 2:1; 3:1; 4:1; 5:1; 6:1; 7:1; 19:27; 22:17; 23:26-28 [n]Jer 35:8 [o]S Dt 21:18; Pr 6:20 **1:9** [p]Pr 3:21-22; 4:1-9 **1:10** [q]S Job 24:15 [r]Dt 13:8 [s]ver 15; Ps 1:1; Pr 16:29 **1:11** [t]S Ps 10:8 **1:12** [u]S Ps 35:25 [v]ver 16-18; S Job 33:18; S Ps 30:3 **1:14** [w]ver 19 **1:15** [x]S Ps 119:101 [y]S Ge 49:6; Pr 4:14 **1:16** [z]S Job 15:31 [a]Pr 6:18; Isa 59:7

[a] 7 The Hebrew words rendered *fool* in Proverbs, and often elsewhere in the Old Testament, denote one who is morally deficient. [b] 12 Hebrew *Sheol*

1:1 *Solomon.* His wisdom and prolific production of proverbs and songs are mentioned in 1Ki 4:29–34 (see notes there). His name occurs again in the headings of 10:1 and 25:1. Cf. SS 1:1.

1:2–4 Verses 2–3 apply to the son (or student); v. 4 refers to the father (or teacher). In Hebrew the terms for "father" and "son" are also used to refer to a teacher and his student.

1:2 *wisdom and discipline.* The two primary virtues in the long list that articulates the purpose of the book (vv. 2–6). Repeated at the end of v. 7, the phrase thus frames the entire prologue (vv. 2–7). *wisdom.* This key term occurs more than 40 times in the book. It includes skill in living—following God's design and thus avoiding moral pitfalls; living and working in accordance with the grain of the created universe and thus avoiding failure. A craftsman can be called a wise (skillful) man (Ex 31:3). Proverbs urges people to get wisdom (4:5; cf. Jas 1:5 and note), for it is worth more than silver or gold (3:13–14) or even rubies (see 3:15 and note). The NT refers to Christ as "wisdom from God" (1Co 1:30; cf. Col 2:3).

1:3 *right and just and fair.* See 2:9; Ps 119:121 and note; Php 4:8.

1:4 *prudence.* Good judgment or good sense (see 15:5; 19:25). Outside Proverbs the Hebrew word is used in the negative sense of "crafty" (Ge 3:1; Job 5:12). *simple.* Another key word in Proverbs, occurring about 15 times. It denotes those who are easily led astray and who "lack judgment" (9:4,16), who are immature, inexperienced and naive (cf. Ps 19:7 and note). See NIV text note on 1:22.

1:6 *riddles.* The Hebrew for this word can sometimes refer to allegories (cf. Eze 17:2).

1:7 The theme of the book (see 9:10; 31:30; cf. Job 28:28; Ps 111:10 and note). *fear of the LORD.* Reliance on the Lord in all circumstances and humble submission to his lordship (see Ps 34:8–14 and note; see also Introduction: Purpose and Teaching). See note on Ge 20:11. *fools.* See NIV text note. "Fools" are those who "hate knowledge" (v. 22) and correction of any kind (12:1), who are "quick to quarrel" (20:3) and give "full vent" to their anger (29:11), who are complacent (1:32) and who trust in themselves (28:26) rather than in God (Ps 14:1). *despise wisdom and discipline.* See 5:12 and note.

1:8 A typical introduction to an instruction speech in Proverbs, evoking a domestic situation of a father preparing his son for life in the world. Here and in 6:20 the mother is also depicted as teacher.

1:9 *to grace ... to adorn.* See 4:9; 6:21. Those who follow wisdom add beauty and honor to their lives.

1:10 *entice.* The Hebrew word is related to the Hebrew noun translated "simple" (see v. 4 and note). One who is "simple" is easily enticed. See Ps 19:7 and note.

1:11 *Come along.* But the father wisely advises, "Do not go along" (v. 15). Cf. Lady Wisdom's appeal in 9:4–6. *lie in wait for ... blood.* Their goal is personal enrichment by theft or oppression (vv. 13,19), even if they have to commit murder. The author uses two major enticements that confronted the young man (in that culture) as examples of the way of folly: (1) to get rich by exploiting others (here) and (2) to be drawn into illicit sexual pleasure by immoral women who fail to honor their marriage vows (5:1–6; 6:24; 7:5; cf. 2:12–19).

1:12 *swallow ... like the grave.* Vivid poetic imagery for shamelessly victimizing others (cf. Ps 49:14 and note).

1:13 *valuable things.* By contrast, the book of Proverbs teaches that wisdom brings the greatest riches people could ever gain (3:13–16; 16:16; see also Job 28:12–19).

1:15 *paths.* Cf. the destructive paths of the adulteress in 2:18 (see note there); 7:25.

1:16 The same as the first two lines of Isa 59:7 and partially quoted in Ro 3:15. Cf. Pr 6:17–18.

1:17 *net.* Nets were used to catch birds and animals (see 6:5; 7:23; Ecc 9:12; Isa 51:20; Jer 5:26; cf. Ps 9:15 and note).

18 These men lie in wait[b] for their own
blood;
they waylay only themselves![c]
19 Such is the end of all who go after ill-
gotten gain;
it takes away the lives of those who
get it.[d]

Warning Against Rejecting Wisdom

20 Wisdom calls aloud[e] in the street,
she raises her voice in the public
squares;
21 at the head of the noisy streets[a] she
cries out,
in the gateways of the city she
makes her speech:
22 "How long will you simple ones[b][f] love
your simple ways?
How long will mockers delight in
mockery
and fools hate[g] knowledge?
23 If you had responded to my rebuke,
I would have poured out my heart to
you
and made my thoughts known to
you.
24 But since you rejected[h] me when I
called[i]
and no one gave heed[j] when I
stretched out my hand,
25 since you ignored all my advice
and would not accept my rebuke,
26 I in turn will laugh[k] at your disaster;[l]
I will mock[m] when calamity
overtakes you[n]—
27 when calamity overtakes you like a
storm,
when disaster[o] sweeps over you like
a whirlwind,
when distress and trouble
overwhelm you.
28 "Then they will call to me but I will
not answer;[p]
they will look for me but will not
find me.[q]
29 Since they hated knowledge
and did not choose to fear the LORD,[r]
30 since they would not accept my advice
and spurned my rebuke,[s]
31 they will eat the fruit of their ways
and be filled with the fruit of their
schemes.[t]
32 For the waywardness of the simple will
kill them,
and the complacency of fools will
destroy them;[u]
33 but whoever listens to me will live in
safety[v]
and be at ease, without fear of
harm."[w]

1:18 [b] S Ps 71:10 [c] S ver 11-12 **1:19** [d] S ver 13-14; Pr 4:14-17; 11:19 **1:20** [e] S Job 28:12; Pr 7:10-13; 9:1-3, 13-15 **1:22** [f] Pr 6:32; 7:7; 8:5; 9:4,16 [g] Ps 50:17 **1:24** [h] Jer 26:5; 35:17; 36:31 [i] Isa 65:12; 66:4; Jer 7:13 [j] S 1Sa 8:19 **1:26** [k] S Ps 2:4 [l] ver 33; S Ps 59:8 [m] S 2Ki 19:21 [n] Dt 28:63 **1:27** [o] S Ps 18:18; Pr 5:12-14 **1:28** [p] S Dt 1:45; S 1Sa 8:18; S Jer 11:11 [q] S Job 27:9; Pr 8:17; Eze 8:18; Hos 5:6; Zec 7:13 **1:29** [r] S Job 21:14 **1:30** [s] ver 25 **1:31** [t] S 2Ch 36:16; Pr 14:14; Jer 6:19; 14:16; 21:14; 30:15 **1:32** [u] Pr 5:22; 15:10; Isa 66:4 **1:33** [v] S Nu 24:21; S Dt 33:28; Pr 3:23 [w] S ver 21-26; S Ps 112:8

[a] *21* Hebrew; Septuagint / *on the tops of the walls*
[b] *22* The Hebrew word rendered *simple* in Proverbs generally denotes one without moral direction and inclined to evil.

1:18 *waylay only themselves.* See v. 11. The wicked unintentionally spread a net for their own feet (29:6; Ps 35:8), so they are less intelligent than birds (see 7:22–23).

1:19 *go after ill-gotten gain.* According to Isa 17:14, destruction is the fate of those who plunder God's people. Contrast the long life enjoyed by the one who "hates ill-gotten gain" (28:16).

1:20 *Wisdom calls aloud.* Personified wisdom also calls out to the simple in 8:1–5; 9:4–6 (see note on 8:1–36). *public squares.* Open areas inside the gate of a walled city (see 8:3).

1:21 *gateways.* Where the leaders of the city met to hold court (see 31:23; see also Ge 19:1; Ru 4:1; Job 29:7 and notes) and where the marketplace was located (2Ki 7:1). As a young man confronts life in its social context, two voices lure him, appeal for his allegiance, and seek to shape his life: (1) the voice of wisdom (as exemplified in the instructions of the teachers of wisdom) and (2) the voice of folly (as exemplified in the sinners of vv. 10–19 and in the adulteress of 5:3; 6:24; 7:5). Thus in the midst of life the youth must learn to exercise discretion. Here and in chs. 8–9 wisdom makes her appeal. She speaks neither out of heaven (by special revelation, as do the prophets) nor out of the earth (through voices from the dead—necromancy; see Lev 19:31; Dt 18:11; 1Sa 28:7–19), but out of the center of the life of the city, where communal experience of the creation order (established by God's wisdom, 8:22–31) is concentrated (see, e.g., 11:10 and note). And it is there also that the godly, the truly wise, test human experience in the crucible of faith and afterward give divine wisdom a human voice in their wise instructions—as in Proverbs.

1:22 *mockers.* Those who are "proud and arrogant" (21:24), who are full of insults, hatred and strife (9:7–8; 22:10; 29:8), who resist correction (13:1; 15:12).

1:23 *poured out my heart.* Wisdom is like a fountain. Her words constantly refresh and strengthen (see 18:4 and note). *heart.* See 2:2; 3:1; 4:4; 5:12; 6:14, etc.; see also Ps 4:7 and note.

1:24 *rejected me.* As Israel rejected the Lord (see Isa 1:4; 5:24; Hos 2:13; 11:2), who brought forth wisdom "as the first of his works" (8:22), and as the people of Jerusalem rejected Jesus (see Mt 23:37), the embodiment and supreme manifestation of God's wisdom (see Jn 1:1–14; 1Co 1:24; Col 1:15–17; 2:3; Heb 1:1–4 and notes). *stretched out my hand.* Cf. Isa 65:2, where God held out his hands all day long to "an obstinate people."

1:25 *ignored … advice.* Cf. 8:33.

1:26 *laugh at your disaster.* Not an expression of heartlessness but a reaction to the absurdity of fools, who laugh at wisdom, choose folly and bring disaster on themselves. Cf. the Lord's response to kings who think they can rebel against him (Ps 2:4). *calamity overtakes you.* Also the fate of "a scoundrel and villain" (6:12–15).

1:27 *like a storm.* See 10:25 and note. *distress and trouble.* See Isa 8:22.

1:28 *I will not answer.* Just as God refused to listen to Israel when the people sinned (see Dt 1:45; Isa 1:15 and note). *find me.* Those who find wisdom find life and blessing (see v. 33; 3:13; 8:17,35).

1:29 *fear the LORD.* See v. 7 and note.

1:31 *eat … be filled with the fruit.* The consequences flow from their actions (see 12:14 and note; 18:20; 31:31; Isa 3:10–11). People reap what they sow (Gal 6:7). *schemes.* To refuse wisdom's "advice" (v. 30) is to suffer the consequences of one's own foolish "schemes" (the Hebrew for "advice" and "schemes" is the same).

1:32 *complacency.* A false sense of security (see Isa 32:9; Am 6:1 and notes; see also Ps 10; 14; Zep 1:12 and notes; cf. Job 21:23; Jer 49:31; Eze 23:42).

1:33 *in safety … at ease.* Words used of places that enjoy God's protection (see Isa 32:18; Eze 34:27).

Moral Benefits of Wisdom

2 My son,[x] if you accept my words
and store up my commands within
you,
2 turning your ear to wisdom
and applying your heart to
understanding,[y]
3 and if you call out for insight[z]
and cry aloud for understanding,
4 and if you look for it as for silver
and search for it as for hidden
treasure,[a]
5 then you will understand the fear of
the LORD
and find the knowledge of God.[b]
6 For the LORD gives wisdom,[c]
and from his mouth come
knowledge and understanding.[d]
7 He holds victory in store for the
upright,
he is a shield[e] to those whose walk
is blameless,[f]
8 for he guards the course of the just
and protects the way of his faithful
ones.[g]

9 Then you will understand[h] what is
right and just
and fair — every good path.
10 For wisdom will enter your heart,[i]
and knowledge will be pleasant to
your soul.
11 Discretion will protect you,
and understanding will guard you.[j]
12 Wisdom will save[k] you from the ways
of wicked men,
from men whose words are perverse,
13 who leave the straight paths
to walk in dark ways,[l]
14 who delight in doing wrong
and rejoice in the perverseness of
evil,[m]
15 whose paths are crooked[n]
and who are devious in their ways.[o]

16 It will save you also from the
adulteress,[p]
from the wayward wife with her
seductive words,
17 who has left the partner of her youth
and ignored the covenant she made
before God.[a][q]
18 For her house leads down to death
and her paths to the spirits of the
dead.[r]
19 None who go to her return
or attain the paths of life.[s]

20 Thus you will walk in the ways of good
men
and keep to the paths of the
righteous.
21 For the upright will live in the land,[t]
and the blameless will remain in it;
22 but the wicked[u] will be cut off from the
land,[v]
and the unfaithful will be torn from
it.[w]

2:1 [x]S Pr 1:8 **2:2** [y]Pr 22:17; 23:12 **2:3** [z]Jas 1:5 **2:4** [a]S Job 3:21; Mt 13:44 **2:5** [b]S Dt 4:6 **2:6** [c]S Job 12:13; S Ps 119:34 [d]S Job 9:4; S 22:22 **2:7** [e]S Ge 15:1; Pr 30:5-6 [f]S Ge 6:9; Ps 84:11 **2:8** [g]1Sa 2:9; S Ps 18:25; S 97:10 **2:9** [h]S Dt 1:16 **2:10** [i]Pr 14:33 **2:11** [j]Pr 4:6

2:12 [k]ver 16; Pr 3:13-18; 4:5 **2:13** [l]Pr 4:19 **2:14** [m]Pr 10:23; 15:21 **2:15** [n]S Ps 125:5 [o]Pr 21:8 **2:16** [p]Pr 5:1-6; 6:20-29; 7:5-27 **2:17** [q]Mal 2:14 **2:18** [r]Pr 5:5; 7:27; 9:18 **2:19** [s]Pr 3:16-18; 5:8; Ecc 7:26 **2:21** [t]S Ps 37:29 **2:22** [u]S Ps 5:4 [v]S Job 18:17 [w]Dt 28:63; S 29:28; Ps 37:9,28-29; Pr 10:30

[a] 17 Or *covenant of her God*

2:1 *store up ... within you.* Just as the psalmist hid God's word in his heart to avoid sin (Ps 119:11).
2:2 *turning your ear.* Listening implies attentiveness and obedience (4:20; 5:1; Isa 32:3; see also Isa 55:3; Jer 13:15). *heart.* See note on 1:23.
2:4 *silver ... hidden treasure.* Job 28:1 – 11 describes ancient mining techniques, comparing the search for wisdom with mining (see Job 28:12,20).
2:5 *fear of the LORD.* See note on 1:7. *knowledge of God.* See 9:10; 30:3; see also Hos 2:20 and note; cf. Isa 1:3.
2:7 *holds ... in store.* For those who "store up" his commands (v. 1). *shield.* Associated with victory also in Ps 18:2,35; cf. Pr 30:5. See Ps 3:3 and note. *blameless.* Having spiritual and moral integrity. This does not imply sinlessness (see 19:1). See v. 21; see also Job 1:1; Ps 15:2 and notes.
2:8 *guards ... protects.* See Ps 91:3 – 7,11 – 12.
2:9 – 11 Those who know the Lord and the wisdom he gives will know what course of action to follow (cf. Heb 5:11 – 14).
2:9 *right and just and fair.* See 1:3 and note. *good path.* Cf. "paths of righteousness" in Ps 23:3 (and see note there).
2:10 *pleasant to your soul.* Just as the words of the wise are "sweet to the soul" of another (see 16:24 and note; cf. 3:17).
2:11 *protect ... guard.* As God guards the faithful (v. 8).
2:12 – 19 Wisdom will save from the enticements of men to follow perverse ways (vv. 12 – 15) and from the "seductive words" of the adulteress (vv. 16 – 19). See note on 1:11.
2:12 *words are perverse.* Cf. v. 14. For other references to deceitful human speech see 6:12,17; 8:13; 10:31 – 32; 17:20; 19:28.
2:13 *straight paths.* See 3:6 and note; 9:15. *dark ways.* The wicked love darkness instead of light (see Job 24:13 – 17 and note; Ecc 2:14; Isa 5:20; 29:15; Eze 8:12; cf. Jn 3:19 – 21; Ro 13:12).
2:14 *delight ... rejoice in ... evil.* Like the sinners of 1:10 – 19.
2:15 *paths are crooked.* See Isa 59:7 – 8.
2:16 *adulteress ... wayward wife.* The Hebrew for these terms occurs again in 5:20 and 7:5. The terms mean lit. "stranger" and "foreigner" (cf. 5:10) because anyone other than one's own wife was to be considered off limits, like a foreigner who worshiped another god (cf. 1Ki 11:1 – 2). "Wayward wife" is parallel to "immoral woman" in 6:24 and "prostitute" in 23:27. *seductive words.* Equal to the "smooth tongue" of 6:24 and the "smooth talk" of 7:21. Cf. 5:3 and note.
2:17 *partner of her youth.* Her husband, whom she married when she was a young woman (cf. Isa 54:6). *covenant ... before God.* Probably the marriage covenant, spoken in God's presence (see Eze 16:8; Mal 2:14). Alternatively, the breaking of the seventh commandment (Ex 20:14) may be indicated (see NIV text note).
2:18 *leads down to death.* According to 7:27, "her house is a highway to the grave." A life of immorality leads to the destruction and death of all who are involved (cf. 5:5; 9:18). *spirits of the dead.* See Job 26:5 and note. The deceased are in the grave (or Sheol), "the chambers of death" (7:27; see also note on Ps 30:1).
2:21 *live in the land.* Abraham's descendants had been promised the land of Canaan (Ge 12:7; 17:8; Dt 4:1), and Ps 37:29 says that "the righteous will inherit the land" (see Ps 37:9,11; Mt 5:5). *blameless.* See note on v. 7.
2:22 *cut off from the land ... torn from it.* In Dt 28:63 God warned that if the people refuse to obey him, they "will

Further Benefits of Wisdom

3 My son,[x] do not forget my teaching,[y]
but keep my commands in your heart,
2 for they will prolong your life many years[z]
and bring you prosperity.[a]
3 Let love and faithfulness[b] never leave you;
bind them around your neck,
write them on the tablet of your heart.[c]
4 Then you will win favor and a good name
in the sight of God and man.[d]
5 Trust in the LORD[e] with all your heart
and lean not on your own understanding;
6 in all your ways acknowledge him,
and he will make your paths[f] straight.[a g]
7 Do not be wise in your own eyes;[h]
fear the LORD[i] and shun evil.[j]
8 This will bring health to your body[k]
and nourishment to your bones.[l]
9 Honor the LORD with your wealth,
with the firstfruits[m] of all your crops;
10 then your barns will be filled[n] to overflowing,
and your vats will brim over with new wine.[o]
11 My son,[p] do not despise the LORD's discipline[q]
and do not resent his rebuke,
12 because the LORD disciplines those he loves,[r]
as a father[b] the son he delights in.[s]
13 Blessed is the man who finds wisdom,
the man who gains understanding,
14 for she is more profitable than silver
and yields better returns than gold.[t]
15 She is more precious than rubies;[u]
nothing you desire can compare with her.[v]
16 Long life is in her right hand;[w]
in her left hand are riches and honor.[x]
17 Her ways are pleasant ways,
and all her paths are peace.[y]
18 She is a tree of life[z] to those who embrace her;
those who lay hold of her will be blessed.[a]

3:1 [x]S Pr 1:8 [y]S Ps 44:17 **3:2** [z]S Dt 11:21 [a]S Dt 5:16; S 30:15, 16; S 1Ki 3:13, 14; Pr 9:6, 10-11 **3:3** [b]S Ps 85:10 [c]S Ex 13:9; S Dt 6:6; Pr 6:21; 7:3; S 2Co 3:3 **3:4** [d]S 1Sa 2:26; Lk 2:52 **3:5** [e]S Ps 4:5 **3:6** [f]S Job 33:11; S Isa 30:11 [g]Ps 5:8; Pr 16:3; Isa 40:3; Jer 42:3 **3:7** [h]Pr 26:5, 12; Isa 5:21 [i]Ps 111:10 [j]S Ex 20:20; S Dt 4:6; S Job 1:1 **3:8** [k]S Ps 38:3; Pr 4:22 [l]Job 21:24 **3:9** [m]S Ex 22:29; Dt 26:1-15 **3:10** [n]Ps 144:13 [o]S Job 22:21; Joel 2:24; Mal 3:10-12 **3:11** [p]Pr 1:8-9 [q]S Job 5:17 **3:12** [r]Pr 13:24; Rev 3:19 [s]S Dt 8:5; S Job 5:17; Heb 12:5-6* **3:14** [t]S Job 28:15; Pr 8:19; 16:16 **3:15** [u]S Job 28:18 [v]S Job 28:17-19 **3:16** [w]S Ge 15:15 [x]S 1Ki 3:13, 14 **3:17** [y]Mt 11:28-30 **3:18** [z]S Ge 2:9; S Pr 10:11; S Rev 2:7 [a]S Pr 2:12; 4:3-9, 8; 8:17-21

[a] 6 Or *will direct your paths* [b] 12 Hebrew; Septuagint / *and he punishes*

be uprooted from the land." The wicked and their offspring will be cut off (Ps 37:9,28).

3:2 *prolong your life.* Fear of the Lord (19:23) brings health to the body (v. 8) and "adds length to life" (10:27; see also 9:10–11). *prosperity.* When Solomon prayed for wisdom (1Ki 3:9), God promised him riches as well as long life if he obeyed God's commands (1Ki 3:13–14). Normally the righteous are prosperous and happy (12:21), but sometimes it is the wicked who are strong and prosperous (Ps 73:3,12), temporary though that may be (Ps 37:10,20,35–36; 73:17–19). Job 1–2 also shows how disaster and death can strike a godly person (see note on vv. 11–12).

3:3 *love and faithfulness.* See Ps 26:3 and note. *bind ... neck.* Like a beautiful necklace (cf. v. 22; 1:9; 3:22). *write them on the tablet of your heart.* See 7:3; cf. Jer 31:33 and note. These instructions are not to be taken literally (see Ex 13:9; Dt 6:8–9 and notes).

3:4 *favor.* See 8:35; 12:2; Ge 6:8. *God and man.* See 1Sa 2:26; Lk 2:52; Ro 12:17 and note; 2Co 8:21.

3:5 *Trust in the LORD.* "Commit your way to the LORD" (Ps 37:5), like Israel's forefathers, who trusted in God and were rescued (Ps 22:4–5). *with all your heart.* Like Caleb (Nu 14:24; Dt 1:36; Jos 14:6–14) or the godly King Hezekiah (Isa 38:3). David challenged Solomon to serve God "with wholehearted devotion" (1Ch 28:9).

3:6 *acknowledge him.* Be ever mindful of God and serve him with a willing and faithful heart (see 1Ch 28:9; Hos 4:1; 6:3,6). *will make your paths straight.* Will remove the obstacles from your pathway and bring you to your desired goal (see 11:5; Isa 40:3; 45:13).

3:7 *fear the LORD and shun evil.* Cf. Job, who was thus "blameless and upright" and "shunned evil" (Job 1:1; cf. Job 28:28). See note on 1:7.

3:8 *bones.* The whole body. Elsewhere, good news and pleasant words bring health to the "bones" (15:30; 16:24; cf. 12:4; 14:30; 17:22).

3:9 *firstfruits.* The Israelites were required to give to the priests the first of the olive oil, wine and grain produced each year (see Lev 23:10; Nu 18:12–13).

3:10 *filled to overflowing.* For those who bring to the Lord the appointed tithes and offerings, God promises to pour out more blessing than they have room for (see Mal 3:10; see also Dt 28:8,12; 2Co 9:6–11). *vats.* See note on Hag 2:16.

3:11–12 An acknowledgment that the righteous sometimes suffer various troubles and afflictions (see v. 2 and note). Through times of testing and affliction, God is teaching them (see 12:1; Ps 119:71). Heb 12:5–6 quotes both of these verses to encourage believers to endure hardship (Heb 12:7). "God disciplines us for our good" (Heb 12:10).

3:12 *as a father.* See 13:24; Ps 94:10 and notes; see also Zep 3:7; cf. Job 5:17.

3:13–18 A poem setting forth the rich benefits of wisdom—framed by references to those who are "blessed."

3:13 *the man who finds wisdom.* Cf. note on 31:10–31.

3:14 *more profitable than silver ... gold.* The psalmist makes the same claim for the commands and precepts of the Lord (Ps 19:10; 119:72,127).

3:15–18 Wisdom is personified, as in 8:1—9:6.

3:15 *rubies.* See 8:11; 20:15. Although rubies were the most priceless jewels in the ancient world, they are considered of less value than wisdom—as also in Job 28:18. The "wife of noble character" is "worth far more than rubies" (31:10; see note on 31:10–31).

3:16 *Long life.* See note on v. 2. *riches and honor.* See 8:18; 22:4.

3:17 *peace.* Hebrew *shalom;* an echo of the Hebrew for "prosperity" in v. 2 (see 16:7; Ps 119:165).

3:18 *tree of life.* Source of life. This figure of speech (see also 11:30; 13:12; 15:4) may recall the tree in the Garden of Eden (see Ge 2:9 and note; see also Introduction: Purpose and Teaching).

19 By wisdom[b] the LORD laid the earth's
foundations,[c]
by understanding he set the
heavens[d] in place;
20 by his knowledge the deeps were
divided,
and the clouds let drop the dew.

21 My son,[e] preserve sound judgment and
discernment,
do not let them out of your sight;[f]
22 they will be life for you,[g]
an ornament to grace your neck.[h]
23 Then you will go on your way in
safety,[i]
and your foot will not stumble;[j]
24 when you lie down,[k] you will not be
afraid;[l]
when you lie down, your sleep[m] will
be sweet.
25 Have no fear of sudden disaster
or of the ruin that overtakes the
wicked,
26 for the LORD will be your confidence[n]
and will keep your foot[o] from being
snared.[p]

27 Do not withhold good from those who
deserve it,
when it is in your power to act.
28 Do not say to your neighbor,
"Come back later; I'll give it
tomorrow"—
when you now have it with you.[q]
29 Do not plot harm against your
neighbor,
who lives trustfully near you.[r]
30 Do not accuse a man for no reason—
when he has done you no harm.

3:19 [b]S Ge 1:31; Ps 136:5-9 [c]S Job 28:25-27 [d]Pr 8:27-29 **3:21** [e]Pr 1:8-9; 6:20 [f]Pr 4:20-22 **3:22** [g]S Dt 30:20; Pr 4:13 [h]S Pr 1:8-9 **3:23** [i]S Pr 1:33 [j]S Ps 37:24; S 119:11; Pr 4:12 **3:24** [k]S Lev 26:6 [l]Ps 91:5; 112:8 [m]S Job 11:18; Jer 31:26 **3:26** [n]S 2Ki 18:5; S Job 4:6 [o]S 1Sa 2:9 [p]S Job 5:19 **3:28** [q]Lev 19:13; Dt 24:15; Lk 10:25-37 **3:29** [r]Zec 8:17
3:31 [s]S Ps 37:1; Pr 24:1-2 **3:32** [t]S Ps 101:4 [u]S Job 29:4 **3:33** [v]S Job 5:3 [w]Zec 5:4 [x]Ps 37:22; Pr 14:11 **3:34** [y]S 2Ki 19:21 [z]S Ps 40:4 [a]S Ps 18:25-27; S Mt 23:12; Jas 4:6*; 1Pe 5:5* **4:1** [b]S Pr 1:8 [c]Pr 19:20 [d]S Job 8:10 **4:4** [e]S 1Ki 9:4 [f]Pr 7:2 **4:5** [g]S Pr 2:12; 3:13-18 **4:6** [h]2Th 2:10 [i]S Pr 2:11

31 Do not envy[s] a violent man
or choose any of his ways,
32 for the LORD detests a perverse man[t]
but takes the upright into his
confidence.[u]

33 The LORD's curse[v] is on the house of
the wicked,[w]
but he blesses the home of the
righteous.[x]
34 He mocks[y] proud mockers[z]
but gives grace to the humble.[a]
35 The wise inherit honor,
but fools he holds up to shame.

Wisdom Is Supreme

4 Listen, my sons,[b] to a father's
instruction;[c]
pay attention and gain
understanding.[d]
2 I give you sound learning,
so do not forsake my teaching.
3 When I was a boy in my father's
house,
still tender, and an only child of my
mother,
4 he taught me and said,
"Lay hold[e] of my words with all
your heart;
keep my commands and you will
live.[f]
5 Get wisdom,[g] get understanding;
do not forget my words or swerve
from them.
6 Do not forsake wisdom, and she will
protect you;[h]
love her, and she will watch over
you.[i]

3:19–20 The role of wisdom in creation is described more fully in 8:22–31 (see notes there). Divine wisdom guided the Creator and now permeates the whole creation. To live by wisdom is to imitate the Lord and conform to the divinely appointed creation order.
3:19 *earth's foundations.* See 8:29. God's work in creation is compared to the construction of a building (see 1Ki 5:17; 6:37; see also Job 38:4–6; Ps 24:2 and note; 104:5; Zec 12:1). *set the heavens in place.* See Isa 42:5; 48:13 and note; 51:16.
3:20 *divided.* In this creation context reference is most likely to the dividing of the waters above from the waters below (see Ge 1:7). *dew.* See Dt 33:13; cf. notes on Ps 36:8; 42:7.
3:22 *ornament to grace your neck.* Like a beautiful necklace (see v. 3 and note).
3:23 *in safety, and your foot will not stumble.* See v. 26; cf. 10:9.
3:24 *when you lie down, you will not be afraid.* Also listed among the covenant blessings (see Lev 26:6; cf. Job 11:18–19; Mic 4:4; Zep 3:13; see also Pr 1:33). *your sleep will be sweet.* See 6:22; Ps 4:8.
3:25 *disaster ... ruin.* The Lord shields the godly from deadly arrows and plagues (see 10:25; Ps 91:3–8; Job 5:21).
3:26 *will keep your foot from being snared.* Contrast the fate of the fool in 1:18; 7:22–23.
3:27 *withhold good.* See Ac 9:36; Gal 6:10; 1Jn 3:17–18. *those who deserve it.* Especially the poor and needy.
3:28 See Lk 11:5–8; Jas 2:15–16.
3:30 *Do not accuse ... for no reason.* See Job 2:3; cf. note on Ps 5:9.
3:31 *Do not envy.* See 23:17; 24:19; Ps 37:1,7. *violent man.* Like the sinners of 1:10–19 (cf. 16:29).
3:32 *detests.* A word that elsewhere expresses abhorrence of pagan practices (see Dt 18:9,12) and moral abuses. It is common in Proverbs (e.g., 6:16; 8:7; 11:20). *takes the upright into his confidence.* See Ge 18:17; Job 29:4; Ps 25:14 and notes; cf. Jn 15:15.
3:33 This contrast is seen also in Dt 11:26–28. *The LORD's curse is on the house of the wicked.* See Jos 7:24–25; Zec 5:3–4. *blesses the home of the righteous.* See Ps 127; 128; cf. Job 42:12–14.
3:34 *mocks proud mockers.* See note on 1:26; see also Ps 18:26 and note. *gives grace.* Shows favor (see v. 4). James and Peter both quote this verse (Jas 4:6; 1Pe 5:5).
4:3 *still tender.* Cf. David's words about Solomon, who was "young and inexperienced" (1Ch 22:5; 29:1). This is part of an autobiographical statement, such as was sometimes used by the wisdom teachers (see 24:30–34; see also the book of Ecclesiastes). *only child.* Therefore deeply loved (cf. Ge 37:3; Jer 6:26 and note; Zec 12:10).
4:4 *with all your heart.* See note on 3:5.
4:6 *protect ... watch over.* The Hebrew words for these two verbs occur together also in 2:8,11. *love her.* To love wisdom is to prosper (8:21); to hate wisdom is to "love death" (8:36).

7 Wisdom is supreme; therefore get
wisdom.
Though it cost all[j] you have,[a] get
understanding.[k]
8 Esteem her, and she will exalt you;
embrace her, and she will honor you.[l]
9 She will set a garland of grace on your
head
and present you with a crown of
splendor.[m]"
10 Listen, my son,[n] accept what I say,
and the years of your life will be
many.[o]
11 I guide[p] you in the way of wisdom
and lead you along straight paths.[q]
12 When you walk, your steps will not be
hampered;
when you run, you will not
stumble.[r]
13 Hold on to instruction, do not let it go;
guard it well, for it is your life.[s]
14 Do not set foot on the path of the
wicked
or walk in the way of evil men.[t]
15 Avoid it, do not travel on it;
turn from it and go on your way.
16 For they cannot sleep till they do evil;[u]
they are robbed of slumber till they
make someone fall.
17 They eat the bread of wickedness
and drink the wine of violence.[v]
18 The path of the righteous[w] is like the
first gleam of dawn,[x]
shining ever brighter till the full light
of day.[y]
19 But the way of the wicked is like deep
darkness;[z]
they do not know what makes them
stumble.[a]

4:7 [j]Mt 13:44-46 [k]Pr 23:23 **4:8** [l]S Pr 3:18 **4:9** [m]S Pr 1:8-9 **4:10** [n]Ps 34:11-16; Pr 1:8-9 [o]S Dt 11:21 **4:11** [p]S 1Sa 12:23 [q]2Sa 22:37; Ps 5:8 **4:12** [r]S Job 18:7; Pr 3:23 **4:13** [s]S Pr 3:22 **4:14** [t]Ps 1:1; S Pr 1:15 **4:16** [u]Ps 36:4; Mic 7:3 **4:17** [v]Ge 49:5; Ps 73:6; Pr 1:10-19; 14:22; Isa 59:6; Jer 22:3; Hab 1:2; Mal 2:16 **4:18** [w]Job 17:9 [x]S Job 22:28 [y]S 2Sa 23:4; Da 12:3; Mt 5:14; Jn 8:12; Php 2:15 **4:19** [z]S Pr 2:13 [a]S Dt 32:35; S Job 3:23; Pr 13:9; S Isa 8:15 **4:20** [b]Ps 34:11-16; Pr 1:8-9 [c]Pr 5:1 **4:21** [d]Pr 3:21 **4:22** [e]S Pr 3:8 **4:23** [f]S 2Ki 10:31 [g]Pr 10:11; Lk 6:45 **4:25** [h]S Job 31:1 **4:26** [i]Heb 12:13* **4:27** [j]S Lev 10:11; S Dt 5:32 **5:1** [k]S Pr 1:8 [l]Pr 4:20 **5:3** [m]S Ps 55:21; Pr 7:5 **5:4** [n]Ecc 7:26

20 My son,[b] pay attention to what I say;
listen closely to my words.[c]
21 Do not let them out of your sight,[d]
keep them within your heart;
22 for they are life to those who find
them
and health to a man's whole body.[e]
23 Above all else, guard[f] your heart,
for it is the wellspring of life.[g]
24 Put away perversity from your mouth;
keep corrupt talk far from your lips.
25 Let your eyes[h] look straight ahead,
fix your gaze directly before you.
26 Make level[b] paths for your feet[i]
and take only ways that are firm.
27 Do not swerve to the right or the left;[j]
keep your foot from evil.

Warning Against Adultery

5 My son,[k] pay attention to my wisdom,
listen well to my words[l] of insight,
2 that you may maintain discretion
and your lips may preserve
knowledge.
3 For the lips of an adulteress drip
honey,
and her speech is smoother than
oil;[m]
4 but in the end she is bitter as gall,[n]
sharp as a double-edged sword.
5 Her feet go down to death;
her steps lead straight to the grave.[c] [o]
6 She gives no thought to the way of
life;
her paths are crooked, but she
knows it not.[p]

[a] 7 Or *Whatever else you get* [b] 26 Or *Consider the* [c] 5 Hebrew *Sheol*

5:5 [o]S Ps 9:17; S Pr 2:18; 7:26-27 **5:6** [p]Pr 9:13; 30:20

4:7 *is supreme.* Or "ranks first"; translated "is the beginning" in 1:7. *Though it cost all you have.* Cf. the parables of the hidden treasure and the pearl in Mt 13:44–46 (see note there).
4:9 *crown of splendor.* Wreaths or crowns were worn at joyous occasions, such as weddings or feasts (see SS 3:11; Eze 16:12; 23:42; cf. 1Pe 5:4).
4:10 *years ... will be many.* See note on 3:2.
4:11 *straight paths.* Right paths (see notes on 3:6; Ps 23:3).
4:12 *you will not stumble.* Because of some obstacle or lack of light (see v. 19; 3:23; 10:9; Ps 18:36; Isa 5:27; 40:30–31).
4:14 *path of the wicked.* Cf. the destructive paths of the adulteress in 2:18; 7:25; see Ps 1:1; 17:4–5.
4:16 *cannot sleep till they do evil.* See Ps 36:4 and note; Mic 2:1. Contrast the attitude of David, who would not sleep until he found a permanent place for God's house (Ps 132:3–5).
4:17 *eat the bread ... drink the wine.* They thrive on wickedness and violence (see 13:2; Job 15:16; cf. Ps 109:18 and note).
4:18 *path of the righteous is ... shining ever brighter.* The godly have all the guidance and protection they need (see vv. 11–12) and are able to lead others to righteousness (Da 12:3).
4:19 *deep darkness.* A dangerous path that leads to destruction (see note on 2:13; see also Isa 59:9–10; Jer 23:12; Jn 11:10).
4:21 *heart.* See 3:1,3.
4:22 *health.* Physical, psychological and spiritual (see 3:8 and note).
4:23 *wellspring of life.* If we store up good things (2:1) in our hearts, our words and actions will be good. "Out of the overflow of the heart the mouth speaks" (Mt 12:34; cf. Mk 7:21).
4:24 *Put away perversity from your mouth.* See note on 2:12; see also 19:1. *corrupt talk.* See 6:12; 19:28; Eph 4:29 and note; Jas 3:6.
4:25 *look straight ahead.* Not at "worthless things" (Ps 119:37).
4:26 *Make level paths.* Remove every moral hindrance (see vv. 11–12). Heb 12:13 quotes the first half of this verse (see note there).
4:27 *Do not swerve to the right or the left.* For similar warnings see Dt 5:32–33; 28:14; Jos 1:7. *foot from evil.* See 1:15.
5:3 *lips ... drip honey.* A reference to the pleasant-sounding talk (cf. 16:24) of the adulteress. *adulteress.* See note on 2:16. *smoother than oil.* See 2:16. Her words are soothing (see Ps 55:21) but full of flattery (Pr 26:28) and hypocrisy (see Ps 5:9 and note).
5:4 *gall.* A bitter herb (see Dt 29:18; La 3:15,19; Am 6:12). *double-edged sword.* A lethal weapon (see Jdg 3:16 and note; see also Ps 55:21; 149:6; Heb 4:12).
5:5 *down to death.* Her immorality hastens her end (see note on 2:18).
5:6 *paths are crooked.* See 2:15; 10:9. *knows it not.* Or "does not acknowledge it."

[7]Now then, my sons, listen[q] to me;
do not turn aside from what I say.
[8]Keep to a path far from her,[r]
do not go near the door of her
house,
[9]lest you give your best strength to
others
and your years to one who is cruel,
[10]lest strangers feast on your wealth
and your toil enrich another man's
house.[s]
[11]At the end of your life you will groan,
when your flesh and body are
spent.
[12]You will say, "How I hated discipline!
How my heart spurned correction![t]
[13]I would not obey my teachers
or listen to my instructors.
[14]I have come to the brink of utter ruin[u]
in the midst of the whole
assembly."[v]
[15]Drink water from your own cistern,
running water from your own well.
[16]Should your springs overflow in the
streets,
your streams of water in the public
squares?
[17]Let them be yours alone,
never to be shared with strangers.
[18]May your fountain[w] be blessed,
and may you rejoice in the wife of
your youth.[x]
[19]A loving doe, a graceful deer[y]—
may her breasts satisfy you always,
may you ever be captivated by her
love.
[20]Why be captivated, my son, by an
adulteress?
Why embrace the bosom of another
man's wife?
[21]For a man's ways are in full view[z] of
the LORD,
and he examines[a] all his paths.[b]
[22]The evil deeds of a wicked man
ensnare him;[c]
the cords of his sin hold him fast.[d]
[23]He will die for lack of discipline,[e]
led astray by his own great folly.[f]

Warnings Against Folly

6 My son,[g] if you have put up security[h]
for your neighbor,[i]
if you have struck hands in pledge[j]
for another,
[2]if you have been trapped by what you
said,
ensnared by the words of your
mouth,
[3]then do this, my son, to free yourself,
since you have fallen into your
neighbor's hands:
Go and humble yourself;
press your plea with your neighbor!

5:7 [q]Pr 1:8-9 **5:8** [r]S Pr 2:16-19; 6:20-29; 7:1-27 **5:10** [s]Pr 29:3 **5:12** [t]Pr 12:1 **5:14** [u]Pr 1:24-27; 6:33 [v]Pr 31:3 **5:18** [w]SS 4:12-15 [x]S Dt 20:7; Pr 2:17; Ecc 9:9; Mal 2:14 **5:19** [y]SS 4:5; 8:14 **5:21** [z]S Ps 119:168 [a]Jer 29:23 [b]S Job 10:4; S 14:16; Pr 15:3; Jer 32:19; S Heb 4:13 **5:22** [c]Ps 9:16 [d]Nu 32:23; S Job 18:9; Ps 7:15-16; S Pr 1:31-32 **5:23** [e]S Job 4:21; Pr 10:21 [f]Job 34:21-25; Pr 11:5 **6:1** [g]S Pr 1:8 [h]Job 17:3 [i]Pr 17:18 [j]Pr 11:15; 22:26-27

5:7–14 The father (teacher) warns the son (student) about the high cost of marital infidelity.
5:8 *far from her.* See Ge 39:12. *door of her house.* Cf. 7:27; 9:14.
5:9 *one who is cruel.* Possibly the vengeful husband (see 6:34–35).
5:10 *strangers feast on your wealth.* Contrast the riches and honor that come to those who embrace wisdom (3:16–18). Immorality eventually reduces one "to a loaf of bread" (6:26; see note there).
5:11 *flesh and body are spent.* Possibly because of the debilitating effects of sexual immorality (see 1Co 6:18; cf. Pr 3:8; 4:22), but more likely referring to the loss of vigor that accompanies old age.
5:12 *hated discipline ... spurned correction.* In old age he will look back and sadly acknowledge that he has played the fool (see 1:7 and note; see also 1:22,29–30).
5:13 *would not obey.* In spite of the repeated urging to "pay attention" or "listen" to their instruction (cf. vv. 1,7; 1:8; 4:1; 5:1).
5:14 *utter ruin.* Physical, financial and social. *in the midst of the whole assembly.* The offender was subject to "blows and disgrace" (6:33) or even death (see Lev 20:10; Dt 22:22).
5:15 *your own cistern ... your own well.* Your own wife (see SS 4:12,15). Let your own wife be your source of pleasure, as water refreshes a thirsty man. Wells and cisterns were privately owned (Jer 38:6) and of great value (2Ki 18:31).
5:16 *springs ... streams of water.* Like "cistern" and "well" in v. 15 and "fountain" in v. 18, these also refer to the wife (see SS 4:12,15). *in the public squares.* The wife may become promiscuous if the husband is unfaithful.
5:18 *wife of your youth.* Chosen by you (or for you) when you were young.
5:19 *doe ... deer.* Descriptive of the wife, perhaps because of the delicate beauty of the doe's limbs (see SS 2:9). *may her breasts satisfy you always.* See SS 7:7–8. *captivated.* Or "exhilarated," "intoxicated." Marital love is portrayed as better than wine in SS 4:10 (cf. SS 7:9).
5:20 *Why ...?* In light of the sheer joy found within the bonds of marriage and the "utter ruin" (v. 14) outside it, why commit adultery? *adulteress.* See v. 3; 2:16 and note.
5:21 *in full view of the LORD.* See 15:3; Job 31:4; 34:21; Jer 16:17; 32:19. *examines all his paths.* See Job 7:18; 34:23; Ps 11:4; 26:2; 139:23; Jer 11:20; 12:3; 17:10.
5:22 *ensnare him.* See 1:18 and note; Dt 7:25; 12:30. In Ecc 7:26 the sinner is ensnared by a woman "whose heart is a trap." *cords of his sin.* See Job 36:8; Ecc 4:12; Isa 5:18; cf. Hos 11:4 and note.
5:23 The death of the fool is described in similar terms in 1:29–32; 7:21–27; cf. Job 36:12. *discipline.* See v. 12 and note.
6:1 *put up security ... struck hands in pledge.* Refers to responsibility for someone else's debt (cf. 22:26) or for some other obligation. It can end in abject poverty (cf. 22:27) or even slavery if you cannot pay. For example, Judah volunteered to personally guarantee the safe return of Benjamin to Jacob (Ge 43:9), and when this seemed impossible, he had to offer himself to Joseph as a slave (Ge 44:32–33). Such an arrangement was sealed by "striking hands," equivalent to our handshake (see 11:15; 17:18; 20:16; 22:26; cf. Job 17:3).
6:2 *trapped ... ensnared.* Cf. v. 5; see also 1:18; 5:22 and notes.
6:3 *to free yourself.* To gain release from the obligation. *fallen into your neighbor's hands.* Assumed responsibility for his obligation. *press your plea.* Be as persistent as the man in Lk 11:8.

[4]Allow no sleep to your eyes,
no slumber to your eyelids.[k]
[5]Free yourself, like a gazelle[l] from the
hand of the hunter,[m]
like a bird from the snare of the
fowler.[n]
[6]Go to the ant, you sluggard;[o]
consider its ways and be wise!
[7]It has no commander,
no overseer or ruler,
[8]yet it stores its provisions in summer[p]
and gathers its food at harvest.[q]

[9]How long will you lie there, you
sluggard?[r]
When will you get up from your
sleep?
[10]A little sleep, a little slumber,
a little folding of the hands to rest[s]—
[11]and poverty[t] will come on you like a
bandit
and scarcity like an armed man.[a]
[12]A scoundrel and villain,
who goes about with a corrupt
mouth,
13 who winks with his eye,[u]
signals with his feet
and motions with his fingers,[v]
14 who plots evil[w] with deceit in his
heart—
he always stirs up dissension.[x]
[15]Therefore disaster will overtake him in
an instant;[y]
he will suddenly[z] be destroyed—
without remedy.[a]

6:4 [k]Ps 132:4
6:5 [l]S 2Sa 2:18 [m]Isa 13:14 [n]S Ps 91:3
6:6 [o]ver 6-11; Pr 20:4
6:8 [p]Pr 30:24-25 [q]Pr 10:4
6:9 [r]Pr 24:30-34; 26:13-16
6:10 [s]Pr 24:33; Ecc 4:5
6:11 [t]ver 10-11; Pr 20:13; 24:30-34
6:13 [u]S Ps 35:19; Pr 16:30 [v]Isa 58:9
6:14 [w]S Ps 140:2 [x]ver 16-19
6:15 [y]S Ps 55:15 [z]Job 5:3 [a]Pr 14:32; 29:1
6:16 [b]ver 16-19; Pr 3:32; 8:13; 15:8,9,26; 16:5
6:17 [c]S Job 41:34; S Ps 10:5 [d]Pr 12:22 [e]S Dt 19:10; Pr 1:16; Isa 1:21; 59:7; Jer 2:34; Mic 7:2
6:18 [f]S Job 15:31
6:19 [g]S Dt 19:16 [h]S Ps 12:2 [i]ver 12-15; Pr 15:18; Zec 8:17
6:20 [j]S Pr 3:21 [k]Pr 1:8
6:21 [l]Dt 6:8; S Pr 3:3; 7:1-3
6:23 [m]S Ps 119:105 [n]Pr 10:17

[16]There are six things the LORD hates,[b]
seven that are detestable to him:
17 haughty eyes,[c]
a lying tongue,[d]
hands that shed innocent blood,[e]
18 a heart that devises wicked
schemes,
feet that are quick to rush into
evil,[f]
19 a false witness[g] who pours out
lies[h]
and a man who stirs up dissension
among brothers.[i]

Warning Against Adultery

[20]My son,[j] keep your father's
commands
and do not forsake your mother's
teaching.[k]
[21]Bind them upon your heart forever;
fasten them around your neck.[l]
[22]When you walk, they will guide
you;
when you sleep, they will watch
over you;
when you awake, they will speak to
you.
[23]For these commands are a lamp,
this teaching is a light,[m]
and the corrections of discipline
are the way to life,[n]

[a] *11* Or *like a vagrant / and scarcity like a beggar*

6:4 *no sleep ... no slumber.* Like David in Ps 132:4.
6:5 *snare of the fowler.* See Ps 124:7.
6:6 *ant.* A creature referred to elsewhere in the Bible only in 30:25, where it stores up its food in the summer (as here; see v. 8). The ant is mentioned also in Canaanite Amarna letter 252.15–19, again in a proverbial context (see chart, p. xxii). *sluggard.* A lazy individual who refuses to work and whose desires are not met (see 10:26; 13:4; 15:19; 19:24; 20:4; 21:25; 22:13; 24:30; 26:13–16).
6:7 *no commander.* Cf. the locust in 30:27.
6:9 *How long will you lie there, you sluggard?* His love for sleep is described also in 26:14 (see note there).
6:10–11 Repeated in 24:33–34.
6:11 *poverty ... scarcity.* Connected with too much sleep also in 10:5; 19:15; 20:13. Hard work is an antidote to poverty (see 12:11; 14:23; 28:19). *like a bandit ... an armed man.* Poverty will come when it is too late to do anything about it (cf. Mt 24:43).
6:12–14 A vivid description of one who uses mouth, eyes, feet and fingers (all of a person's means of communication) in devious ways to achieve the deceitful plots of the heart—here especially to spread slander to destroy someone.
6:12 *scoundrel.* A worthless, wicked person (16:27; Jdg 19:22; 1Sa 25:25; Job 34:18). See note on Dt 13:13. *corrupt mouth.* See 2:12 and note; 19:28.
6:13 *winks with his eye.* To make insinuations (see 10:10; 16:30).
6:14 *plots evil.* See v. 18; 3:29; Mic 2:1. *stirs up dissension.* Through slander such people create distrust that culminates in alienation and conflict (see v. 19; 10:12; 15:18; 16:28; 28:25; 29:22; cf. Ps 5:9 and note).
6:15 *disaster will overtake him in an instant.* Usually a sign of God's judgment (see 1:26; 24:22 and notes; Job 34:20). *suddenly be destroyed—without remedy.* Such scoundrels will suffer the same fate they thought to bring upon others—their punishment will fit their crime (see Ex 21:24; Lev 24:19–20 and notes; cf. Gal 6:7–8). *without remedy.* See 29:1 and note.
6:16–19 A further elaboration on the theme of vv. 12–15, explaining why "disaster will overtake" (v. 15) the scoundrel described here.
6:16 *six ... seven.* A way of handling numbers in synonymous parallelism in Hebrew poetry (see Introduction: The Nature of a Proverb). Such catalogues of items are frequent in the wisdom literature of the OT (see 30:15,18,21,29; see also Job 5:19 and note). In all such cases in Proverbs, the higher number is the operative one. *detestable.* See 3:32 and note.
6:17 *haughty eyes.* They reflect a proud heart, and God will judge them (see 21:4; 30:13; Ps 18:27; 101:5). *lying tongue.* See 2:12 and note; 12:19; 17:7; 21:6. *hands that shed innocent blood.* See 1:11 and note; see also 1:16; 28:17.
6:18 *heart that devises wicked schemes.* See 1:31; 24:2; Ge 6:5. *feet that ... rush into evil.* See 1:16 and note.
6:19 *false witness.* See Ex 20:16; Dt 19:16–19. Proverbs emphasizes the damage done by false witnesses (12:17–18; 25:18; see note on Ps 5:9) and the punishment they receive (see note on v. 15; see also 19:5,9; 21:28). *pours out lies.* See 14:5,25. *stirs up dissension.* See note on v. 14.
6:20 See 1:8 and note.
6:21 See 1:9 and note.
6:22 *walk.* Cf. 4:11. *when you sleep.* See note on 3:24. *watch over you.* See 4:6.
6:23 *lamp ... light.* Just as the word of God "is a lamp to my feet and a light for my path" (Ps 119:105; cf. Ps 19:8). *way to*

[24]keeping you from the immoral
woman,
from the smooth tongue of the
wayward wife.[o]
[25]Do not lust in your heart after her
beauty
or let her captivate you with her
eyes,
[26]for the prostitute reduces you to a loaf
of bread,
and the adulteress preys upon your
very life.[p]
[27]Can a man scoop fire into his lap
without his clothes being burned?
[28]Can a man walk on hot coals
without his feet being scorched?
[29]So is he who sleeps[q] with another
man's wife;[r]
no one who touches her will go
unpunished.

[30]Men do not despise a thief if he
steals
to satisfy his hunger when he is
starving.
[31]Yet if he is caught, he must pay
sevenfold,[s]
though it costs him all the wealth of
his house.
[32]But a man who commits adultery[t]
lacks judgment;[u]
whoever does so destroys himself.
[33]Blows and disgrace are his lot,
and his shame will never[v] be wiped
away;
[34]for jealousy[w] arouses a husband's
fury,[x]
and he will show no mercy when
he takes revenge.
[35]He will not accept any compensation;
he will refuse the bribe, however
great it is.[y]

6:24 [o]Ge 39:8; S Ps 55:21; Pr 2:16; 7:5 **6:26** [p]Pr 7:22-23 **6:29** [q]S Ex 20:14 [r]Pr 2:16-19; S 5:8 **6:31** [s]Ex 22:1-14 **6:32** [t]S Ex 20:14 [u]Pr 7:7; 9:4,16 **6:33** [v]Pr 5:9-14 **6:34** [w]S Nu 5:14 [x]S Ge 34:7 **6:35** [y]Job 31:9-11; SS 8:7

Warning Against the Adulteress

7 My son,[z] keep my words
and store up my commands within
you.
[2]Keep my commands and you will live;[a]
guard my teachings as the apple of
your eye.
[3]Bind them on your fingers;
write them on the tablet of your
heart.[b]
[4]Say to wisdom, "You are my sister,"
and call understanding your
kinsman;
[5]they will keep you from the adulteress,
from the wayward wife with her
seductive words.[c]

[6]At the window of my house
I looked out through the lattice.
[7]I saw among the simple,
I noticed among the young men,
a youth who lacked judgment.[d]
[8]He was going down the street near her
corner,
walking along in the direction of her
house
[9]at twilight,[e] as the day was fading,
as the dark of night set in.
[10]Then out came a woman to meet him,
dressed like a prostitute and with
crafty intent.
[11](She is loud[f] and defiant,
her feet never stay at home;
[12]now in the street, now in the squares,
at every corner she lurks.)[g]
[13]She took hold of him[h] and kissed him
and with a brazen face she said:[i]
[14]"I have fellowship offerings[a][j] at home;
today I fulfilled my vows.

7:1 [z]S Pr 1:8 **7:2** [a]Pr 4:4 **7:3** [b]S Pr 3:3 **7:5** [c]ver 21; S Job 31:9; S Pr 2:16; 6:24 **7:7** [d]S Pr 1:22; S 6:32 **7:9** [e]Job 24:15 **7:11** [f]Pr 9:13 **7:12** [g]Pr 8:1-36; 23:26-28 **7:13** [h]S Ge 39:12 [i]S Pr 1:20 **7:14** [j]S Lev 7:11-18

[a] 14 Traditionally *peace offerings*

life. See 3:22; 4:22; 10:17. Contrast the way to death for the one who hates discipline (see 5:23 and note).
6:24 See notes on 2:16; 5:3.
6:25 *Do not lust.* Jesus shows the close connection between lust and adultery (Mt 5:28; cf. Ex 20:14,17 and notes). *captivate you.* See 5:20.
6:26 *reduces you to a loaf of bread.* Both the prostitute (29:3) and the adulteress (see 5:10 and note) reduce a man to poverty (cf. 1Sa 2:36).
6:29 *no one … will go unpunished.* See vv. 33–34; see also note on 5:14.
6:31 *sevenfold.* Hebrew law demanded no more than fivefold payment as a penalty for any theft (Ex 22:1–9). The number seven is here symbolic—the thief will pay in full.
6:32 *destroys himself.* See 5:14; 7:22–23 and notes.
6:33 *disgrace.* Followed Amnon's rape of Tamar (2Sa 13:13).
6:34 *jealousy.* Its strength is also illustrated in 27:4; SS 8:6.
7:1 See Ps. 119:11.
7:2 *apple of your eye.* See Dt 32:10 and note.
7:3 *Bind them on your fingers.* As a reminder (see 6:21; Dt 6:8). *tablet of your heart.* See 3:3; Jer 31:33 and note.
7:4 *wisdom.* As embodied in the instructions of the wisdom teacher (vv. 1–3). *my sister … kinsman.* Make wisdom your most intimate companion. "Sister" may be used here in the sense of "bride" (see SS 4:9–10,12; 5:1–2).
7:5 See notes on 2:16; 5:3.
7:7 *simple.* See note on 1:4. *who lacked judgment.* See 6:32; 9:4,16.
7:8 *in the direction of her house.* See 5:8.
7:9 *dark of night.* He was hoping no one would see him (see 2:13 and note).
7:10 *dressed like a prostitute.* Perhaps in a gaudy manner (see Eze 16:16) and heavily veiled (see Ge 38:14–15).
7:11 *loud.* Applied to the "woman Folly" in 9:13 (see note there).
7:12 *she lurks.* Ready to catch her prey (see vv. 22–33).
7:13 *kissed him.* A bold greeting (see Ge 29:11).
7:14 *fellowship offerings.* Part of the meat could be eaten by the one who brought the offering and by his (or her) family (Lev 7:12–15). *today I fulfilled my vows.* An offering made as the result of a vow was one of the fellowship offerings, and the meat had to be eaten on the first or second day (see Lev 7:15–16). So the young man had an opportunity to enjoy a sumptuous feast, one that ironically had a religious significance (cf. 1Sa 1:21 and note).

[15]So I came out to meet you;
I looked for you and have found you!
[16]I have covered my bed
with colored linens from Egypt.
[17]I have perfumed my bed[k]
with myrrh,[l] aloes and cinnamon.
[18]Come, let's drink deep of love till morning;
let's enjoy ourselves with love![m]
[19]My husband is not at home;
he has gone on a long journey.
[20]He took his purse filled with money
and will not be home till full moon."
[21]With persuasive words she led him astray;
she seduced him with her smooth talk.[n]
[22]All at once he followed her
like an ox going to the slaughter,
like a deer[a] stepping into a noose[b][o]
[23]till an arrow pierces[p] his liver,
like a bird darting into a snare,
little knowing it will cost him his life.[q]

[24]Now then, my sons, listen[r] to me;
pay attention to what I say.
[25]Do not let your heart turn to her ways
or stray into her paths.[s]
[26]Many are the victims she has brought down;
her slain are a mighty throng.
[27]Her house is a highway to the grave,[c]
leading down to the chambers of death.[t]

Wisdom's Call

8 Does not wisdom call out?[u]
Does not understanding raise her voice?
[2]On the heights along the way,
where the paths meet, she takes her stand;
[3]beside the gates leading into the city,
at the entrances, she cries aloud:[v]
[4]"To you, O men, I call out;[w]
I raise my voice to all mankind.
[5]You who are simple,[x] gain prudence;[y]
you who are foolish, gain understanding.
[6]Listen, for I have worthy things to say;
I open my lips to speak what is right.
[7]My mouth speaks what is true,[z]
for my lips detest wickedness.
[8]All the words of my mouth are just;
none of them is crooked or perverse.
[9]To the discerning all of them are right;
they are faultless to those who have knowledge.
[10]Choose my instruction instead of silver,
knowledge rather than choice gold,[a]
[11]for wisdom is more precious[b] than rubies,
and nothing you desire can compare with her.[c]

[12]"I, wisdom, dwell together with prudence;
I possess knowledge and discretion.[d]
[13]To fear the LORD[e] is to hate evil;[f]
I hate[g] pride and arrogance,
evil behavior and perverse speech.
[14]Counsel and sound judgment are mine;
I have understanding and power.[h]

7:17 [k]S Est 1:6; Isa 57:7; Eze 23:41; Am 6:4 [l]S Ge 37:25 **7:18** [m]S Ge 39:7 **7:21** [n]S ver 5 **7:22** [o]S Job 18:10 **7:23** [p]S Job 15:22; S 16:13 [q]S Pr 6:26; Ecc 7:26 **7:24** [r]Pr 1:8-9; 8:32 **7:25** [s]Pr 5:7-8 **7:27** [t]Jdg 16:19; S Pr 2:18; Rev 22:15 **8:1** [u]S Job 28:12 **8:3** [v]Pr 7:6-13 **8:4** [w]Isa 42:2 **8:5** [x]S Pr 1:22 [y]Pr 1:4 **8:7** [z]Jn 8:14 **8:10** [a]S Job 28:17; S Ps 19:10 **8:11** [b]ver 19; S Job 28:17-19 [c]Pr 3:13-15 **8:12** [d]Pr 1:4 **8:13** [e]S Ge 22:12 [f]S Ex 20:20; S Job 28:28 [g]Jer 44:4 **8:14** [h]S Job 9:4; Pr 21:22; Ecc 7:19

[a] 22 Syriac (see also Septuagint); Hebrew *fool*
[b] 22 The meaning of the Hebrew for this line is uncertain.
[c] 27 Hebrew *Sheol*

7:16 *colored linens from Egypt.* Linen is associated with the wealthy in 31:22. Egyptian linen was of great value (see Isa 19:9 and note; Eze 27:7).
7:17 *myrrh, aloes and cinnamon.* Fragrant perfumes that are linked with making love (see SS 1:3; 4:14; 5:5 and notes; see also Ps 45:8).
7:18 *drink deep of love.* Making love is compared to eating and drinking also in 9:17; 30:20; SS 4:16; 5:1. *enjoy ourselves.* See SS 4:10.
7:19 *not at home.* So he will never know (cf. 6:34–35). *long journey.* Perhaps he was a wealthy merchant.
7:20 *money.* Pieces of silver of various weights were a common medium of exchange, but not in the form of coins until a later period (see note on Ge 20:16).
7:21 *persuasive words ... smooth talk.* See notes on 2:16; 5:3; see also 6:24; 7:5. *led him astray.* Cf. 5:23.
7:22 *like an ox going to the slaughter.* Totally oblivious of the fate that awaits him. *noose.* Cf. Isa 51:20.
7:23 *pierces his liver.* The terrible fate of the wicked is similarly described in Job 20:24–25. *darting into a snare.* See notes on 1:17–18; 5:22.
7:24 See 5:7.
7:25 *her paths.* See 1:15.
7:26 *Many are the victims.* See 9:18; 23:28; Isa 5:14 and note.
7:27 *highway to the grave.* See notes on 2:18; 5:5; see also 14:12; 16:25; Mt 7:13; cf. 1Co 6:9–10.
8:1–36 Wisdom is personified (see note on 1:20) as she addresses humankind in preparation for the final plea from both "Wisdom" and "Folly" in ch. 9.
8:1 *call out ... raise her voice.* See 1:20 and note.
8:2–3 See notes on 1:20–21.
8:4 *mankind.* See v. 31 and note.
8:5 *simple ... foolish.* Both are addressed in wisdom's speech in 1:22,32. *simple, gain prudence.* See note on 1:4.
8:6 *worthy things ... what is right.* See Php 4:8.
8:7 *my lips detest wickedness.* See 3:32 and note; 12:22.
8:8 *crooked or perverse.* See Php 2:15; cf. Pr 2:15.
8:9 *To the discerning.* The wiser they are the more they appreciate words of wisdom. *who have knowledge.* Especially the knowledge of God (see note on 2:5).
8:10 *silver ... gold.* See v. 19; 2:4; 3:14 and note.
8:11 Almost identical with 3:15 (see note there).
8:12 *dwell together with prudence.* Cf. Job 28:20. *prudence ... knowledge and discretion.* See 1:4 and note.
8:13 *To fear the LORD is to hate evil.* See 3:7 and note; 16:6. *I hate pride and arrogance.* See 16:18; 1Sa 2:3; Isa 13:11; see also Ps 10:2–11 and note. *evil behavior and perverse speech.* See note on 2:12; see also 6:12–19.
8:14 *Counsel and sound judgment ... understanding and power.* These characterize the Lord (2:6–7; Job 12:13,16; Isa 40:13–14; Ro 16:27) and the Spirit of the Lord (Isa 11:2). *Counsel.* See 1:25; 19:20. *power.* Cf. Ecc 9:16.

15 By me kings reign
and rulers[i] make laws that are just;
16 by me princes govern,[j]
and all nobles who rule on earth.[a]
17 I love those who love me,[k]
and those who seek me find me.[l]
18 With me are riches and honor,[m]
enduring wealth and prosperity.[n]
19 My fruit is better than fine gold;[o]
what I yield surpasses choice
silver.[p]
20 I walk in the way of righteousness,[q]
along the paths of justice,
21 bestowing wealth on those who
love me
and making their treasuries full.[r]

22 "The LORD brought me forth as the first
of his works,[b,c]
before his deeds of old;
23 I was appointed[d] from eternity,
from the beginning, before the world
began.
24 When there were no oceans, I was
given birth,
when there were no springs
abounding with water;[s]
25 before the mountains were settled in
place,[t]
before the hills, I was given birth,[u]
26 before he made the earth or its fields
or any of the dust of the world.[v]
27 I was there when he set the heavens in
place,[w]
when he marked out the horizon[x] on
the face of the deep,
28 when he established the clouds
above[y]
and fixed securely the fountains of
the deep,[z]
29 when he gave the sea its boundary[a]
so the waters would not overstep
his command,[b]
and when he marked out the
foundations of the earth.[c]
30 Then I was the craftsman at his
side.[d]
I was filled with delight day after
day,
rejoicing always in his presence,
31 rejoicing in his whole world
and delighting in mankind.[e]

32 "Now then, my sons, listen[f] to me;
blessed are[g] those who keep my
ways.[h]
33 Listen to my instruction and be wise;
do not ignore it.
34 Blessed is the man who listens[i] to me,
watching daily at my doors,
waiting at my doorway.
35 For whoever finds me[j] finds life[k]
and receives favor from the LORD.[l]
36 But whoever fails to find me harms
himself;[m]
all who hate me love death."[n]

[a] *16* Many Hebrew manuscripts and Septuagint; most Hebrew manuscripts *and nobles—all righteous rulers* [b] *22* Or *way*; or *dominion* [c] *22* Or *The LORD possessed me at the beginning of his work*; or *The LORD brought me forth at the beginning of his work* [d] *23* Or *fashioned*

8:15 [i]S Ps 2:10 **8:16** [j]S 2Ch 1:10; Pr 29:4 **8:17** [k]S 1Sa 2:30; Jn 14:21-24 [l]S 1Ch 16:11; S Pr 1:28; 3:13-18; Mt 7:7-11 **8:18** [m]S 1Ki 3:13 [n]S Dt 8:18 **8:19** [o]S Job 28:17-19 [p]S Pr 3:13-14 **8:20** [q]S Ps 5:8 **8:21** [r]Pr 15:6; 24:4 **8:24** [s]S Ge 7:11 **8:25** [t]S Job 38:6 [u]S Job 15:7 **8:26** [v]S Ps 90:2 **8:27** [w]S Job 26:7 [x]S Job 22:14 **8:28** [y]S Job 36:29 [z]S Ge 1:7; S Job 9:8; S 26:10 **8:29** [a]S Ge 1:9; S Ps 16:6 [b]S Job 38:8 [c]S 1Sa 2:8; S Job 38:5 **8:30** [d]Pr 3:19-20; Rev 3:14 **8:31** [e]S Job 28:25-27; 38:4-38; Ps 104:1-30; Pr 30:4; Jn 1:1-4; Col 1:15-20 **8:32** [f]S Pr 7:24 [g]Lk 11:28 [h]S 2Sa 22:22; S Ps 18:21 **8:34** [i]1Ki 10:8 **8:35** [j]Pr 3:13-18 [k]Pr 9:6; Jn 5:39-40 [l]S Job 33:26 **8:36** [m]Pr 15:32; Isa 3:9; Jer 40:2 [n]S Job 28:22

8:15 *By me kings reign.* See 29:4. Solomon prayed for wisdom to govern Israel (see 1Ki 3:9; 2Ch 1:10).
8:17 *I love.* I pour out my benefits on (see 4:6 and note; see also Jn 14:21). *those who seek me find me.* See 2:4–5; Isa 55:6; Jas 1:5. Verse 35 completes the thought: "whoever finds me finds life."
8:18 *riches and honor.* See v. 21; 3:16; 22:4. *prosperity.* See note on 3:2; see also 21:21.
8:19 *My fruit.* Wisdom is called a "tree of life" in 3:18 (see note there). *fine gold … choice silver.* See v. 10; Job 28:15; see also 3:14 and note.
8:20 *walk in the way.* See introduction to Ps 1; see also note on Ps 1:6. *way … paths.* See 3:17. *justice.* See v. 15.
8:21 *bestowing wealth.* See v. 18; Zec 8:12 and note. *making their treasuries full.* See 3:10; 24:4 and notes.
8:22–31 A hymn describing wisdom's role in creation. Wisdom is here personified, as in 1:20–33; 3:13–18; 9:1–12. Therefore these verses should not be interpreted as a direct description of Christ. Yet they provide part of the background for the NT portrayal of Christ as the divine Word (Jn 1:1–5) and as the wisdom of God (see note on 1:24). Here, wisdom is an attribute of God, personified and depicted as involved with him in creation.
8:22 *brought … forth.* The Hebrew for this verb is also used in Ge 4:1; 14:19,22 ("Creator"); Dt 32:6 ("Creator"). *me.* Wisdom (see 3:19 and note; Ps 104:24). *as the first of his works.* Cf. Job 40:19 and note.
8:23 *from eternity.* Descriptive also of Christ (see Jn 1:1; cf. Mic 5:2). *before the world began.* Wisdom was already there before God began to create the world (cf. Christ's statement in Jn 17:5).
8:24 *I was given birth.* Elsewhere it is the sea (Job 38:8–9) and the mountains and earth that are "brought forth" (Job 15:7; Ps 90:2). *springs abounding with water.* See Ps 104:10.
8:27 *set the heavens in place.* See 3:19 and note. *when he marked out the horizon on the face of the deep.* See Job 26:10.
8:28 *fountains of the deep.* Earth's springs and streams (see note on 3:20; cf. Ge 7:11).
8:29 *the sea its boundary.* See Ge 1:9 and note; Job 38:10–11; Ps 104:9. *foundations of the earth.* See note on 3:19.
8:30 *craftsman.* Those skilled in various crafts were sometimes called "wise." See, e.g., Bezalel, who designed and built the tabernacle (Ex 31:3; see note on Pr 1:2). Here the term stresses the skill demonstrated in creation. *filled with delight … rejoicing.* Cf. the joyful shouts of the angels at the time of creation (Job 38:7).
8:31 *delighting in mankind.* Cf. v. 4. Humans, made in the image of God, represented the climax of creation (see Ge 1:26–28; Ps 8:5 and notes).
8:32 *blessed.* The blessings associated with gaining wisdom are given in 3:13–18; see Ps 1:1–3 and notes; 119:1–2; 128:1.
8:34 *watching daily at my doors.* Contrast the warning not to go near the door of the adulteress's house (5:8).
8:35 *finds life.* See 1:28; 3:2; 4:22 and notes. Cf. Jn 1:4. *favor.* See 3:4; 12:2; 18:22 and note.
8:36 *all who hate me love death.* See 1:28–33; 5:12,23; 7:27 and notes.

Invitations of Wisdom and of Folly

9 Wisdom has built[o] her house;
she has hewn out its seven pillars.
2 She has prepared her meat and mixed
her wine;[p]
she has also set her table.[q]
3 She has sent out her maids, and she
calls[r]
from the highest point of the city.[s]
4 "Let all who are simple[t] come in here!"
she says to those who lack
judgment.[u]
5 "Come,[v] eat my food
and drink the wine I have mixed.[w]
6 Leave your simple ways and you will
live;[x]
walk in the way of understanding.[y]
7 "Whoever corrects a mocker invites
insult;
whoever rebukes a wicked man
incurs abuse.[z]
8 Do not rebuke a mocker[a] or he will
hate you;
rebuke a wise man and he will love
you.[b]
9 Instruct a wise man and he will be
wiser still;
teach a righteous man and he will
add to his learning.[c]
10 "The fear of the LORD[d] is the beginning
of wisdom,
and knowledge of the Holy One[e] is
understanding.[f]

9:1 [o]Eph 2:20-22; 1Pe 2:5
9:2 [p]Isa 25:6; 62:8 [q]Lk 14:16-23
9:3 [r]S Pr 1:20; 8:1-3 [s]ver 14
9:4 [t]S Pr 1:22 [u]ver 16; S Pr 6:32
9:5 [v]Jn 7:37-38 [w]S Ps 42:2; 63:1; 143:6; Isa 44:3; 55:1
9:6 [x]S Pr 8:35 [y]S Pr 3:1-2
9:7 [z]Pr 23:9; Mt 7:6
9:8 [a]Pr 15:12 [b]Ps 141:5
9:9 [c]Pr 1:5,7; 12:15; 13:10; 14:6; 15:31; 19:25
9:10 [d]S Pr 1:7 [e]Ps 22:3; Pr 30:3 [f]S Dt 4:6
9:11 [g]S Ge 15:15; S Dt 11:21; S Pr 3:1-2; 10:27
9:13 [h]Pr 7:11 [i]S Pr 5:6
9:14 [j]ver 3; Eze 16:25
9:15 [k]S Pr 1:20
9:16 [l]S Pr 1:22
9:17 [m]Pr 20:17
9:18 [n]S Pr 2:18; 7:26-27
10:1 [o]S 1Ki 4:32 [p]S Pr 1:1 [q]Pr 15:20; 17:21; 19:13; 23:22-25; 27:11; 29:3

11 For through me your days will be
many,
and years will be added to your life.[g]
12 If you are wise, your wisdom will
reward you;
if you are a mocker, you alone will
suffer."
13 The woman Folly is loud;[h]
she is undisciplined and without
knowledge.[i]
14 She sits at the door of her house,
on a seat at the highest point of the
city,[j]
15 calling out[k] to those who pass by,
who go straight on their way.
16 "Let all who are simple come in here!"
she says to those who lack
judgment.[l]
17 "Stolen water is sweet;
food eaten in secret is delicious![m]"
18 But little do they know that the dead
are there,
that her guests are in the depths of
the grave.[a][n]

Proverbs of Solomon

10 The proverbs[o] of Solomon:[p]
A wise son brings joy to his father,[q]
but a foolish son grief to his mother.

[a] 18 Hebrew *Sheol*

9:1 *has built her house.* See 14:1 and note; cf. 24:3 and note; 31:10–27. Both wisdom and folly have a house to which humans are invited (see v. 14; 5:8; 7:8; 8:34). *seven pillars.* Perhaps "seven" refers symbolically to the perfection of wisdom's work.
9:2 See v. 17 and note. The banquet prepared by wisdom contrasts with the perfumed bed made ready by the adulteress in 7:17. *mixed her wine.* With spices, to make it tastier (see SS 8:2).
9:3 *she calls from the highest point of the city.* See the description of Folly in v. 14; see also 8:1–3.
9:4 The same invitation is given by Folly in v. 16. *simple.* See 1:4; 8:5 and notes. *lack judgment.* See 6:32; 7:7.
9:5 *Come.* Wisdom's invitation counters the enticements of sinners in 1:10–11 (see note on 1:11). *eat … drink.* As in v. 2, wisdom's gifts are described symbolically as a great banquet (cf. Isa 55:1–2 and notes; Jn 6:27,35,51,55).
9:6 *Leave your simple ways.* See 1:22; see also 1:10–11 and notes. *you will live.* See v. 11; 8:35; see also note on 3:2; cf. 3:18 and note.
9:7 *Whoever corrects a mocker invites insult.* See 1:22 and note; cf. 1:30. *incurs abuse.* Cf. 1Pe 4:4.
9:8 *he will hate you.* See 15:12,32. *rebuke a wise man and he will love you.* See 10:8; 17:10.
9:9 *he will be wiser still.* See 18:15; 21:11.
9:10–12 Wisdom's final words summarize the heart of the message in chs. 1–9.
9:10 *The fear of the LORD is the beginning of wisdom.* See 1:7 and note. *knowledge of the Holy One.* See note on 2:5. *Holy One.* Occurs elsewhere in Proverbs only in 30:3. See note on Lev 11:44.
9:11 *years will be added to your life.* See note on 3:2; see also 3:16; 10:27; 14:27; 19:23.
9:12 *your wisdom will reward you.* Some of wisdom's rewards are given in 3:16–18; 4:22; 8:35; 14:14. *mocker.* See v. 7; see also note on 1:22. *will suffer.* See 1:26 and note; 19:29.
9:13 *The woman Folly is loud.* "Loud" links the personified "Folly" with the adulteress, the wayward wife of 2:16; 7:11. *undisciplined and without knowledge.* She lacks good judgment, prudence and the fear of the Lord (see 1:3–4,22,29; 5:6).
9:14 *sits.* Cf. wisdom's building her house (v. 1). *at the door of her house.* See v. 1 and note. *at the highest point of the city.* Cf. the position of wisdom in v. 3; 8:2.
9:15 *calling out.* Cf. the appeal of Lady Wisdom in v. 3; 8:1,4.
9:16 Her invitation is identical to wisdom's (v. 4; see note on 1:21).
9:17 *Stolen water … food eaten in secret.* The banquet prepared by Lady Folly seems poorer than the wine and meat of wisdom (v. 2). And it was stolen at that! This meal refers to stolen pleasures, exemplified by the illicit sex offered by the adulteress (see 7:18 and note; cf. 5:15–16). *sweet.* But see Job 20:12–15 and note.
9:18 *the dead are there … her guests are in the depths of the grave.* Similar to 2:18; 5:5; 7:27 (see notes there).
10:1 *The proverbs of Solomon.* The title of a collection of proverbs that extends through 22:16. The numerical values of the consonants in the Hebrew word for "Solomon" total 375—the exact number of verses in 10:1—22:16. At the very center of this section is a verse that highlights one of its dominant themes (see 16:4 and note). *wise son.* See v. 5; 15:20; 17:21,25. In later collections he is described as

2 Ill-gotten treasures are of no value,[r]
but righteousness delivers from
death.[s]

3 The LORD does not let the righteous go
hungry[t]
but he thwarts the craving of the
wicked.[u]

4 Lazy hands make a man poor,[v]
but diligent hands bring wealth.[w]

5 He who gathers crops in summer is a
wise son,
but he who sleeps during harvest is
a disgraceful son.[x]

6 Blessings crown the head of the
righteous,
but violence overwhelms the mouth
of the wicked.[a][y]

7 The memory of the righteous[z] will be a
blessing,
but the name of the wicked[a] will
rot.[b]

8 The wise in heart accept commands,
but a chattering fool comes to ruin.[c]

9 The man of integrity[d] walks securely,[e]
but he who takes crooked paths will
be found out.[f]

10 He who winks maliciously[g] causes
grief,
and a chattering fool comes to ruin.

11 The mouth of the righteous is a
fountain of life,[h]
but violence overwhelms the mouth
of the wicked.[i]

12 Hatred stirs up dissension,
but love covers over all wrongs.[j]

13 Wisdom is found on the lips of the
discerning,[k]
but a rod is for the back of him who
lacks judgment.[l]

14 Wise men store up knowledge,[m]
but the mouth of a fool invites ruin.[n]

15 The wealth of the rich is their fortified
city,[o]
but poverty is the ruin of the poor.[p]

16 The wages of the righteous bring them
life,[q]
but the income of the wicked brings
them punishment.[r]

17 He who heeds discipline shows the
way to life,[s]
but whoever ignores correction leads
others astray.

18 He who conceals his hatred has lying
lips,[t]
and whoever spreads slander is a fool.

19 When words are many, sin is not
absent,
but he who holds his tongue is wise.[u]

20 The tongue of the righteous is choice
silver,
but the heart of the wicked is of little
value.

10:2 [r]Pr 13:11; 21:6 [s]ver 16; Pr 11:4,19; 12:28 **10:3** [t]Mt 6:25-34 [u]Pr 13:25 **10:4** [v]Pr 6:6-8; 19:15; 24:30-34 [w]Pr 12:24; 21:5 **10:5** [x]Pr 24:30-34 **10:6** [y]ver 8,11,14; Pr 12:13; 13:3; Ecc 10:12 **10:7** [z]S Ps 112:6 [a]S Job 18:17; S Ps 109:13 [b]S Job 18:17; Ps 9:6 **10:8** [c]ver 14; S Job 33:33; Mt 7:24-27 **10:9** [d]S Ps 25:21 [e]S Ps 37:24 [f]Pr 28:18 **10:10** [g]S Ps 35:19 **10:11** [h]ver 27; S Pr 3:18; S 4:23; 11:30; 13:12,14,19; 14:27; 15:4; 16:22 [i]S ver 6 **10:12** [j]Pr 17:9; 1Co 13:4-7; 1Pe 4:8 **10:13** [k]ver 31; S Ps 37:30; Pr 15:7 [l]S Dt 25:2; Pr 14:3; 26:3 **10:14** [m]Pr 11:13; 12:23 [n]S ver 6; S Ps 59:12; S Pr 14:3; 18:6,7; S Mt 12:37 **10:15** [o]Pr 18:11 [p]Pr 19:7 **10:16** [q]S Dt 30:15 [r]Pr 11:18-19; 15:6; S Ro 6:23 **10:17** [s]Pr 6:23; 15:5 **10:18** [t]S Ps 31:18 **10:19** [u]S Job 1:22; S 6:24; Pr 17:28; S 20:25; 21:23; Jas 1:19; 3:2-12

[a] 6 Or *but the mouth of the wicked conceals violence;* also in verse 11

a "righteous man" (23:24) and as one "who keeps the law" (28:7).

10:2 *Ill-gotten treasures are of no value.* They are fleeting (21:6) and result in God's judgment (see v. 16; 1:19 and note). *righteousness delivers from death.* Repeated in 11:4 (see also 2:16–18; 3:2; 13:21; cf. 12:28; 21:21).

10:3 *not let the righteous go hungry.* See 13:25; Ps 34:9–10; 37:19,25–26. *righteous.* See Ps 1:5 and note. *thwarts the craving of the wicked.* See Nu 11:34; Ps 112:10 and note.

10:4 Many proverbs praise diligence and the profit it brings, and they condemn laziness as a cause of hunger and poverty (see 6:6–11 and notes; 12:11,24,27; 13:4; 14:23; 18:9; 27:23–27; 28:19).

10:5 *sleeps during harvest.* Sleeping when there is work to be done is condemned also in 6:9–11; 19:15; 20:13. *disgraceful son.* See 17:2; 19:26; 28:7; 29:15.

10:6 *Blessings.* God's gifts and favors (see 3:13–18; 28:20; Ge 49:26; Dt 33:16). *crown.* See 11:26. *violence overwhelms the mouth of the wicked.* The trouble caused by their lips will eventually ruin them (see v. 11 and note; see also Ps 140:9).

10:7 *memory of the righteous.* Remembering the righteous. *name ... will rot.* See 22:1 and note.

10:8 *The wise ... accept commands.* See 9:8–9. *chattering fool comes to ruin.* See vv. 10,14,18,19.

10:9 *man of integrity walks securely.* See 2:7; 3:23; 13:6; Isa 33:15–16. *he who takes crooked paths will be found out.* See 26:26; cf. 1Ti 5:24–25; 2Ti 3:9.

10:10 *winks maliciously.* See note on 6:13. *chattering fool.* See v. 8.

10:11 *fountain of life.* A source of life-giving wisdom (see 13:14; 14:27; 16:22; see also Ps 37:30). *violence overwhelms.* See v. 6 and note.

10:12 *stirs up dissension.* See note on 6:14. *covers over all wrongs.* Promotes forgiveness (see 17:9). This line is quoted in Jas 5:20; 1Pe 4:8.

10:13 *rod is for the back.* See 14:3; 19:29; 26:3.

10:14 *store up knowledge.* Rather than babbling folly—and so the wise prosper. See 2:1 and note. *invites ruin.* Quick with his mouth, the fool only brings ruin on himself (see vv. 8,10; 13:3).

10:15 *wealth ... is their fortified city.* Repeated in 18:11. Wealth brings friends (14:20; 19:4) and power (18:23; 22:7). *poverty is the ruin of the poor.* Poverty has no security—as it has no influence (18:23), or friends (19:4,7). See v. 4 and note.

10:16 *wages of the righteous bring them life.* Not wealth (v. 15) but righteousness assures life (see note on 3:2; see also 3:16; 4:22). *income of the wicked brings them punishment.* See 15:6; see also 1:13,31 and notes. "The wages of sin is death" (Ro 6:23).

10:17 *way to life.* See 6:23; 12:28 and notes. *whoever ignores correction.* See 5:12; 15:10.

10:18 *conceals his hatred.* By pretending friendliness (see 26:24,26,28).

10:19 *holds his tongue.* See 11:12; 21:23; see also 13:3; Jas 3:2–6 and notes.

10:20 *choice silver.* What the righteous say has great value (see 3:14; 8:10; 25:11). *heart of the wicked.* Their thoughts and schemes (see 6:14,18).

[21]The lips of the righteous nourish many,
but fools die for lack of judgment.[v]

[22]The blessing of the LORD[w] brings
wealth,[x]
and he adds no trouble to it.[y]

[23]A fool finds pleasure in evil conduct,[z]
but a man of understanding delights
in wisdom.

[24]What the wicked dreads[a] will overtake
him;[b]
what the righteous desire will be
granted.[c]

[25]When the storm has swept by, the
wicked are gone,
but the righteous stand firm[d] forever.[e]

[26]As vinegar to the teeth and smoke[f] to
the eyes,
so is a sluggard to those who send
him.[g]

[27]The fear of the LORD adds length to life,[h]
but the years of the wicked are cut
short.[i]

[28]The prospect of the righteous is joy,
but the hopes of the wicked come to
nothing.[j]

[29]The way of the LORD is a refuge for the
righteous,
but it is the ruin of those who do
evil.[k]

[30]The righteous will never be uprooted,
but the wicked will not remain in
the land.[l]

[31]The mouth of the righteous brings
forth wisdom,[m]
but a perverse tongue[n] will be cut
out.

[32]The lips of the righteous know what is
fitting,[o]
but the mouth of the wicked only
what is perverse.[p]

11 The LORD abhors dishonest scales,[q]
but accurate weights are his
delight.[r]

[2]When pride comes, then comes
disgrace,[s]
but with humility comes wisdom.[t]

[3]The integrity of the upright guides
them,
but the unfaithful are destroyed by
their duplicity.[u]

[4]Wealth[v] is worthless in the day of
wrath,[w]
but righteousness delivers from
death.[x]

[5]The righteousness of the blameless
makes a straight way[y] for them,
but the wicked are brought down by
their own wickedness.[z]

[6]The righteousness of the upright
delivers them,
but the unfaithful are trapped by evil
desires.[a]

[7]When a wicked man dies, his hope
perishes;[b]
all he expected from his power
comes to nothing.[c]

10:21 [v]Pr 5:22-23; Isa 5:13; Jer 5:4; Hos 4:1,6,14 **10:22** [w]S Ps 128:2 [x]S Ge 13:2; S 49:25; S Dt 8:18 [y]S 2Ch 25:9 **10:23** [z]S Pr 2:14 **10:24** [a]Isa 65:7; 66:4 [b]S Ge 42:36 [c]S Ps 37:4; 145:17-19; Eze 11:8 **10:25** [d]S Ps 20:8 [e]Pr 12:3,7; Mt 7:24-27 **10:26** [f]Isa 65:5 [g]Pr 13:17; 25:13; 26:6 **10:27** [h]S ver 11; Dt 11:9; Pr 9:10-11; 19:23; 22:4 [i]S Job 15:32 **10:28** [j]Est 7:10; S Job 8:13; Ps 112:10; Pr 11:7 **10:29** [k]Pr 21:15; Hos 14:9 **10:30** [l]Ps 37:9,28-29; S Pr 2:20-22 **10:31** [m]S ver 13; S Pr 15:2; 31:26 [n]S Ps 52:4 **10:32** [o]Ecc 10:12 [p]S Ps 59:7 **11:1** [q]S Lev 19:36; Dt 25:13-16; S Job 6:2; Pr 20:10,23 [r]Pr 16:11; Eze 45:10 **11:2** [s]Pr 16:18 [t]Pr 18:12; 29:23 **11:3** [u]ver 5; Pr 13:6 **11:4** [v]Eze 27:27 [w]S Job 20:20; S Eze 7:19 [x]S Pr 10:2 **11:5** [y]S 1Ki 8:36 [z]S ver 3; Pr 5:21-23; 13:6; 21:7 **11:6** [a]S Est 7:9 **11:7** [b]S Job 8:13 [c]S Pr 10:28

10:21 *nourish many.* See v. 11 and note. *die for lack of judgment.* See 5:23 and note; 7:7; 9:16.
10:22 *blessing of the LORD brings wealth.* Wealth is a gift from God, not a product of human attainment (see notes on v. 6; 3:10; see also 8:21; cf. Ge 24:35; 26:12; Lev 26:3–5,10; Dt 28:1–14). *adds no trouble to it.* Unlike the "ill-gotten treasures" of v. 2 (see note there); cf. 15:6.
10:23 *finds pleasure in evil conduct.* See 2:14; 15:21; 26:19.
10:24 *What the wicked dreads.* Calamity and distress (see 1:26–27 and notes; 3:25; Job 15:21; Isa 66:4). *what the righteous desire.* See Ps 37:4; 145:19; Mt 5:6.
10:25 Cf. the wise man who built his house on a rock, and the foolish man who built his on the sand (Mt 7:24–27). *the wicked are gone.* See Ps 37:10; Isa 28:18. *the righteous stand firm.* Unshakable, immovable (see 3:25 and note; see also 12:3,7; 14:11; Ps 15:5).
10:26 *vinegar.* See Ps 69:21. *sluggard.* See note on 6:6. *who send him.* As a messenger (cf. 13:17 and note; 25:13; 26:6 and note) or worker.
10:27 *fear of the LORD.* See note on 1:7. *adds length to life.* See note on 3:2. *years … are cut short.* See Job 22:16; Ps 37:36; 55:23.
10:28 *prospect of the righteous.* See v. 24 and note. *joy.* Of fulfillment (cf. 11:23). *hopes of the wicked come to nothing.* See 11:7,23.
10:29 *way of the LORD.* The way he prescribes, the life of wisdom (see Ps 27:11; 143:8). *ruin of those who do evil.* Since judgment comes to those who refuse God's way.
10:30 *never be uprooted.* See v. 25; 2:21 and note; 12:3; cf. Ps 1:3; 125:1 and notes. *not remain in the land.* See note on 2:22.
10:31 *perverse tongue.* See note on 2:12. *cut out.* See Ps 12:3; cf. Mt 5:29–30 and notes.
11:1 *abhors dishonest scales.* Similar denunciation is found in the Law (see Lev 19:35 and note) and the Prophets (Hos 12:7; Am 8:5; Mic 6:11). See also 16:11; 20:10,23. *accurate weights.* See note on 16:11. Silver was weighed on scales balanced against a stone weight. Weights with dishonest labels were used for cheating.
11:2 *When pride comes, then comes disgrace.* Along with destruction (see 16:18; cf. the humbling of proud Assyria in Isa 10:12; cf. also Isa 14:13–15). *with humility comes wisdom.* Along with honor (see note on 15:33).
11:3 *integrity … guides them.* Cf. the actions of Joseph in Ge 39:6–12. *unfaithful are destroyed.* See v. 6; 2:22 and note; 19:3. *duplicity.* See v. 5; cf. 13:6.
11:4 *day of wrath.* The day of judgment (see Isa 10:3; Zep 1:18). *righteousness delivers from death.* See 2:16–18; 3:2; 10:2; 13:21.
11:5 *blameless.* See note on 2:7. *makes a straight way for them.* So that they reach their desired goal (see v. 3; 3:6 and note).
11:6 *righteousness … delivers them.* See vv. 3–4. *trapped.* See 5:22 and note.
11:7 *his hope perishes.* See v. 23; 10:28.

[8]The righteous man is rescued from
trouble,
and it comes on the wicked instead.[d]
[9]With his mouth the godless destroys
his neighbor,
but through knowledge the righteous
escape.[e]
[10]When the righteous prosper, the city
rejoices;[f]
when the wicked perish, there are
shouts of joy.[g]

[11]Through the blessing of the upright a
city is exalted,[h]
but by the mouth of the wicked it is
destroyed.[i]

[12]A man who lacks judgment derides his
neighbor,[j]
but a man of understanding holds
his tongue.[k]

[13]A gossip betrays a confidence,[l]
but a trustworthy man keeps a
secret.[m]

[14]For lack of guidance a nation falls,[n]
but many advisers make victory sure.[o]

[15]He who puts up security[p] for another
will surely suffer,
but whoever refuses to strike hands
in pledge is safe.[q]

[16]A kindhearted woman gains respect,[r]
but ruthless men gain only wealth.

[17]A kind man benefits himself,
but a cruel man brings trouble on
himself.

[18]The wicked man earns deceptive
wages,
but he who sows righteousness
reaps a sure reward.[s]

[19]The truly righteous man attains
life,[t]
but he who pursues evil goes to his
death.[u]

[20]The LORD detests men of perverse
heart[v]
but he delights[w] in those whose
ways are blameless.[x]

[21]Be sure of this: The wicked will not go
unpunished,
but those who are righteous will go
free.[y]

[22]Like a gold ring in a pig's snout
is a beautiful woman who shows no
discretion.

[23]The desire of the righteous ends only
in good,
but the hope of the wicked only in
wrath.

[24]One man gives freely, yet gains even
more;
another withholds unduly, but
comes to poverty.

[25]A generous[z] man will prosper;
he who refreshes others will himself
be refreshed.[a]

[26]People curse the man who hoards
grain,
but blessing crowns him who is
willing to sell.

[27]He who seeks good finds goodwill,
but evil comes to him who searches
for it.[b]

11:8 [d]Pr 21:18 **11:9** [e]Pr 12:6; Jer 45:5 **11:10** [f]S 2Ki 11:20 [g]S Est 8:17 **11:11** [h]Pr 14:34 [i]Pr 29:8 **11:12** [j]Pr 14:21 [k]S Job 6:24 **11:13** [l]Pr 20:19 [m]S Pr 10:14 **11:14** [n]Pr 20:18 [o]S 2Sa 15:34; Pr 15:22; 24:6 **11:15** [p]S Pr 6:1 [q]Pr 17:18; 22:26-27 **11:16** [r]Pr 31:31 **11:18** [s]S Ex 1:20; S Job 4:8; Hos 10:12-13 **11:19** [t]S Dt 30:15; S Pr 10:2 [u]1Sa 2:6; Ps 89:48; Pr 1:18-19; Ecc 7:2; Jer 43:11 **11:20** [v]Pr 3:32 [w]S Nu 14:8 [x]S 1Ch 29:17; S Ps 15:2; 101:1-4; S 119:1; Pr 12:2,22; 15:9 **11:21** [y]Pr 16:5 **11:25** [z]1Ch 29:17; Isa 32:8 [a]Pr 22:9; 2Co 9:6-9 **11:27** [b]Ps 7:15-16

11:8 Cf. the rescue of Mordecai and the execution of Haman in Est 5:14; 7:10.
11:9 *destroys his neighbor.* By spreading slander (see note on Ps 5:9). *through knowledge.* Perhaps the knowledge of the schemes and distortions of the godless (cf. Jn 2:25).
11:10 *city rejoices.* See 28:12; 29:2. Thus life in the city is itself a teacher of wisdom (see 8:1–4; 9:3 and note on 1:21).
11:11 *blessing of the upright.* Their good influence and desire for justice as well as their prosperity (v. 10) bring honor to the city. *mouth of the wicked.* Their deceit, dishonesty and sowing of discord (see v. 9; 6:12–14 and notes).
11:12 *derides his neighbor.* Shows his contempt openly (see 10:18; 14:21). *holds his tongue.* See 10:19 and note.
11:14 See the close parallels in 15:22; 20:18; 24:6. *advisers.* See 2Sa 16:23; Isa 1:26.
11:15 See note on 6:1.
11:16 Assumes that "a good name is more desirable than great riches" (22:1; see note there) and insightfully observes that a woman, if she is kindhearted, will be accorded more respect than wealthy men if they are ruthless. *kindhearted woman.* See 31:28,30.
11:17 *benefits himself.* See Mt 5:7. *brings trouble on himself.* Cf. Ge 34:25–30; 49:7.
11:18 *deceptive wages.* Because they do not last (see notes on 10:2,16; cf. Hag 1:6 and note). *reaps a sure reward.* See 10:24; Gal 6:8–9; Jas 3:18.
11:19 *attains life.* See 10:16 and note; 12:28; 19:23. *goes to his death.* See 5:23; 21:16; Jas 1:15; cf. Ro 6:23.
11:20 *detests men of perverse heart.* See 3:32 and note; 16:5. *blameless.* See note on 2:7.
11:21 *will not go unpunished.* See 6:29. *will go free.* See Ps 118:5.
11:22 *gold ring.* Commonly worn by women on their noses (see Ge 24:47; Eze 16:12 and note). *shows no discretion.* Abigail was praised by David for her display of "good judgment" (1Sa 25:33).
11:23 See 10:24,28. *wrath.* Judgment (see v. 4; Isa 10:3; Zep 1:18; Ro 2:8–9).
11:24 Generosity is the path to blessing and further prosperity (see 3:9–10 and notes; Ecc 11:1–2 and notes; cf. Ps 112:2–9; 2Co 9:6–9). By contrast, the stingy do not make friends and hurt themselves in the long run (21:13).
11:25 *generous man will prosper.* "For he shares his food with the poor" (22:9). "Whoever sows generously will also reap generously" (2Co 9:6; cf. Lk 6:38). *be refreshed.* See Ro 1:12 and note; 15:32.
11:26 *hoards grain.* Probably in times of scarcity to raise the price. *blessing crowns him.* See 10:6.
11:27 *He who seeks good finds goodwill.* Like the man in v. 25 (cf. Mt 7:12). *evil comes to him who searches for it.* His wicked schemes will backfire (see v. 8; 1:18 and notes).

[28]Whoever trusts in his riches will fall,[c]
but the righteous will thrive like a
green leaf.[d]

[29]He who brings trouble on his family
will inherit only wind,
and the fool will be servant to the
wise.[e]

[30]The fruit of the righteous is a tree of
life,[f]
and he who wins souls is wise.

[31]If the righteous receive their due[g] on
earth,
how much more the ungodly and the
sinner!

12 Whoever loves discipline loves
knowledge,
but he who hates correction is
stupid.[h]

[2]A good man obtains favor from the
LORD,[i]
but the LORD condemns a crafty
man.[j]

[3]A man cannot be established through
wickedness,
but the righteous cannot be
uprooted.[k]

[4]A wife of noble character[l] is her
husband's crown,
but a disgraceful wife is like decay in
his bones.[m]

[5]The plans of the righteous are just,
but the advice of the wicked is
deceitful.

[6]The words of the wicked lie in wait for
blood,
but the speech of the upright rescues
them.[n]

[7]Wicked men are overthrown and are
no more,[o]
but the house of the righteous stands
firm.[p]

[8]A man is praised according to his
wisdom,
but men with warped[q] minds are
despised.

[9]Better to be a nobody and yet have a
servant
than pretend to be somebody and
have no food.

[10]A righteous man cares for the needs of
his animal,[r]
but the kindest acts of the wicked
are cruel.

[11]He who works his land will have
abundant food,
but he who chases fantasies lacks
judgment.[s]

[12]The wicked desire the plunder of evil
men,
but the root of the righteous
flourishes.

[13]An evil man is trapped by his sinful
talk,[t]
but a righteous man escapes
trouble.[u]

[14]From the fruit of his lips a man is filled
with good things[v]
as surely as the work of his hands
rewards him.[w]

11:28 [c]Job 31:24-28; S Ps 49:6; S 52:7; 62:10; Jer 9:23; 48:7 [d]Ps 52:8; 92:12-14 **11:29** [e]Pr 14:19 **11:30** [f]S Ge 2:9; S Pr 10:11 **11:31** [g]Jer 25:29; 49:12; 1Pe 4:18 **12:1** [h]Pr 5:11-14; S 9:7-9; 13:1,18; 15:5,10,12,32 **12:2** [i]S Job 33:26; Ps 84:11 [j]2Sa 15:3; S Pr 11:20 **12:3** [k]S Pr 10:25 **12:4** [l]S Ru 3:11; Pr 31:10-11 [m]Pr 18:22

12:6 [n]S Pr 11:9; 14:3 **12:7** [o]S Ps 37:36 [p]S Pr 10:25; 14:11; 15:25 **12:8** [q]Isa 19:14; 29:24 **12:10** [r]S Nu 22:29 **12:11** [s]Pr 28:19 **12:13** [t]S Ps 59:12; S Pr 10:6; 18:7 [u]Pr 21:23 **12:14** [v]Pr 13:2; 15:23; 18:20 [w]Pr 14:14

11:28 *Whoever trusts in his riches.* Usually said of the wicked (see Ps 49:6; 62:10 and note; cf. 1Ti 6:17). *like a green leaf.* See Ps 1:3 and note; Ge 49:22; Jer 17:8.
11:29 *He who brings trouble on his family will inherit only wind.* The inheritance of Levi and Simeon was affected because of their cruelty against Shechem (Ge 34:25–30; 49:5–7). See 15:27 and note. *servant to the wise.* As those who are evil serve those who are good (14:19; cf. 17:2).
11:30 *fruit of the righteous.* What the wise produce (8:18–19). *tree of life.* See note on 3:18. *wins souls.* Wins people over to wisdom and righteousness (see Da 12:3; 1Co 9:19–22; Jas 5:20). However, the Hebrew for this expression is unusual so that its translation is somewhat uncertain.
11:31 *the righteous receive their due.* Even Moses and David were punished for their sins (see Nu 20:11–12; 2Sa 12:10 and notes). *how much more the ungodly and the sinner!* See 1:18,31 and notes; Ps 11:6; 73:18–19.
12:1 *loves discipline loves knowledge.* See 1:7; 10:17; see also 6:23 and note. *hates correction is stupid.* See 1:22; 5:12 and note.
12:2 *obtains favor.* See 3:4; 8:35. *condemns a crafty man.* Cf. 14:17; Job 5:12–13; 1Co 3:19.
12:3 *cannot be established.* See 11:5. *righteous cannot be uprooted.* See 2:21; 10:25,30 and notes.
12:4 *wife of noble character.* Someone like Ruth (Ru 3:11). Such a woman is fully described in 31:10–31. *her husband's crown.* She brings him honor and joy (see 4:9 and note). *decay.* See Hab 3:16 and note. *his bones.* See note on 3:8.
12:5 *advice of the wicked is deceitful.* See 1:10–19 and notes; cf. Ps 1:1.
12:6 *lie in wait for blood.* See note on 1:11; see also 1:16. *speech of the upright rescues them.* See 11:3–4,6,9.
12:7 See 10:25 and note.
12:8 *praised according to his wisdom.* See 3:4 and note. *warped minds.* See Tit 3:11 and note.
12:9 *yet have a servant.* Even people of moderate means had servants (see Jdg 6:15,27). *pretend to be somebody.* Cf. 13:7.
12:10 *cares for the needs of his animal.* See 27:23; Dt 25:4; Mt 12:11; see also chart, p. 268 (item 16). *kindest acts of the wicked are cruel.* Probably to both people and animals.
12:11 Repeated with slight variation in 28:19. *chases fantasies.* Schemes for making easy money.
12:12 *desire the plunder of evil men.* See 1:13 and note; 21:10. *root of the righteous flourishes.* They bear fruit, like firmly rooted trees (see vv. 3,7; 11:30; Ps 1:3; see also 10:25 and note).
12:13 *trapped by his sinful talk.* See 1:18 and note; 29:6. *righteous man escapes trouble.* See 11:8–9 and notes; 21:23; 2Pe 2:9.
12:14 Those who speak with wisdom will reap a harvest from their words, just as farmers enjoy the harvest of their crops (see 1:31 and note; Job 34:11).

[15]The way of a fool seems right to him,[x]
but a wise man listens to advice.[y]

[16]A fool[z] shows his annoyance at once,[a]
but a prudent man overlooks an insult.[b]

[17]A truthful witness gives honest testimony,
but a false witness tells lies.[c]

[18]Reckless words pierce like a sword,[d]
but the tongue of the wise brings healing.[e]

[19]Truthful lips endure forever,
but a lying tongue lasts only a moment.

[20]There is deceit in the hearts of those who plot evil,
but joy for those who promote peace.[f]

[21]No harm befalls the righteous,[g]
but the wicked have their fill of trouble.

[22]The LORD detests lying lips,[h]
but he delights[i] in men who are truthful.[j]

[23]A prudent man keeps his knowledge to himself,[k]
but the heart of fools blurts out folly.[l]

[24]Diligent hands will rule,
but laziness ends in slave labor.[m]

[25]An anxious heart weighs a man down,[n]
but a kind word cheers him up.

[26]A righteous man is cautious in friendship,[a]
but the way of the wicked leads them astray.[o]

[27]The lazy man does not roast[b] his game,
but the diligent man prizes his possessions.

[28]In the way of righteousness there is life;[p]
along that path is immortality.

13 A wise son heeds his father's instruction,
but a mocker does not listen to rebuke.[q]

[2]From the fruit of his lips a man enjoys good things,[r]
but the unfaithful have a craving for violence.

[3]He who guards his lips[s] guards his life,[t]
but he who speaks rashly will come to ruin.[u]

[4]The sluggard craves and gets nothing,[v]
but the desires of the diligent are fully satisfied.

[5]The righteous hate what is false,[w]
but the wicked bring shame and disgrace.

[6]Righteousness guards the man of integrity,
but wickedness overthrows the sinner.[x]

[7]One man pretends to be rich, yet has nothing;[y]
another pretends to be poor, yet has great wealth.[z]

[a] 26 Or *man is a guide to his neighbor* [b] 27 The meaning of the Hebrew for this word is uncertain.

12:15 [x]Pr 14:12; 16:2,25 [y]S Pr 9:7-9; 19:20 **12:16** [z]S 1Sa 25:25 [a]S Job 5:2 [b]Pr 29:11 **12:17** [c]S Ps 12:2; Pr 14:5,25 **12:18** [d]S Ps 55:21; Pr 25:18 [e]Pr 15:4 **12:20** [f]S Ro 14:19 **12:21** [g]S Job 4:7 **12:22** [h]1Ki 13:18; Pr 6:17 [i]Ps 18:19 [j]S Pr 11:20 **12:23** [k]S Pr 10:14 [l]S Ps 38:5; S 59:7; Pr 18:2 **12:24** [m]S Pr 10:4 **12:25** [n]Pr 15:13 **12:26** [o]S Ps 95:10 **12:28** [p]S Dt 30:15; S Pr 10:2 **13:1** [q]S Pr 12:1; 15:5 **13:2** [r]S Pr 12:14 **13:3** [s]S Ps 12:2; S 34:13 [t]S Pr 10:6; 21:23 [u]S Job 1:22; Pr 18:7,20-21 **13:4** [v]Pr 21:25-26 **13:5** [w]S Ps 119:128 **13:6** [x]S Pr 11:3,5; Jer 44:5 **13:7** [y]Rev 3:17 [z]2Co 6:10

12:15 *seems right.* But ends in death (see 1:25,30; 14:12; 16:25).
12:16 *overlooks an insult.* Does not strike back in kind (see 29:11; cf. 2Sa 16:11–12).
12:17 *false witness tells lies.* See note on 6:19.
12:18 *Reckless words.* Cf. Ps 106:33. *pierce like a sword.* See note on Ps 5:9. *tongue of the wise brings healing.* With soothing, comforting words (see 4:20–22; 15:4).
12:19 *Truthful lips ... lying tongue.* See 19:9; Ps 52:4–5.
12:20 *deceit in the hearts.* See 6:14. *plot evil.* See 24:2 and note. *joy for those who promote peace.* "Blessed are the peacemakers" (Mt 5:9).
12:21 *No harm.* See 1:33 and note; 2:8; Ps 91:9–13; 121:7. *their fill of trouble.* See 1:31 and note; 11:5,8; 22:8; Job 4:8.
12:22 Compare the structure of this verse with that of 11:1,20. *detests.* See note on 3:32. *men who are truthful.* See 16:13.
12:23 *keeps his knowledge to himself.* See 10:14 and note. *blurts out folly.* See v. 16; 13:16; 15:2,7,28; 29:11.
12:24 *Diligent hands ... laziness.* Contrasted also in 10:4 (see note there). *will rule.* Cf. 17:2. *slave labor.* Cf. Jdg 1:28; 2Sa 20:24 and notes.
12:25 *anxious heart.* See Ps 94:19. *kind word cheers him up.* See 15:23.
12:26 *is cautious in friendship.* Chooses friends with care (see 13:20; 18:24; 22:24). *leads them astray.* See 5:23; 14:22.
12:27 *does not roast his game.* And is too lazy to lift the food from the dish to his mouth (19:24). *prizes his possessions.* Cf. Ecc 5:19.
12:28 See 10:2 and note. *there is life.* Cf. 3:2 and note; 11:4. *immortality.* Lit. "no death." The way or path of righteousness does not lead to death. Cf. the identification of wisdom with the "tree of life" (3:18 [see note there]; cf. 14:32).
13:1 *heeds his father's instruction.* See 1:8 and note; 4:1. *mocker does not listen to rebuke.* See 1:22; 9:7–8 and notes.
13:2 See 12:14 and note. *have a craving for violence.* See 4:17 and note.
13:3 *He who guards his lips guards his life.* "The tongue has the power of life and death" (18:21). The ability to control the tongue is one of the clearest marks of wisdom. See 10:19 and note. *he who speaks rashly will come to ruin.* See 10:14; 12:18 and note; 18:7.
13:4 *sluggard.* See 6:6 and note. *craves and gets nothing.* Is never satisfied, yet refuses to work (see 21:25–26). *desires of the diligent are fully satisfied.* Diligence yields a profit (see 6:6; see also notes on 10:4,24).
13:5 *bring shame and disgrace.* Like a lazy son (10:5; cf. 19:26).
13:6 This contrast repeats the thought of 2:21–22; 10:9; 11:3,5 (see notes there); cf. 21:12; Ps 25:21.
13:7 Both pretenses are folly and lead to folly (see 14:8 and note; see also 11:24 and note; 12:9).

[8]A man's riches may ransom his life,
but a poor man hears no threat.[a]
[9]The light of the righteous shines
brightly,
but the lamp of the wicked is
snuffed out.[b]
[10]Pride only breeds quarrels,
but wisdom is found in those who
take advice.[c]
[11]Dishonest money dwindles away,[d]
but he who gathers money little by
little makes it grow.
[12]Hope deferred makes the heart sick,
but a longing fulfilled is a tree of
life.[e]
[13]He who scorns instruction will pay for
it,[f]
but he who respects[g] a command is
rewarded.[h]
[14]The teaching of the wise is a fountain
of life,[i]
turning a man from the snares of
death.[j]
[15]Good understanding wins favor,
but the way of the unfaithful is
hard.[a]
[16]Every prudent man acts out of
knowledge,
but a fool exposes[k] his folly.[l]
[17]A wicked messenger falls into trouble,[m]
but a trustworthy envoy brings
healing.[n]
[18]He who ignores discipline comes to
poverty and shame,[o]
but whoever heeds correction is
honored.[p]
[19]A longing fulfilled is sweet to the soul,[q]
but fools detest turning from evil.
[20]He who walks with the wise grows
wise,
but a companion of fools suffers
harm.[r]
[21]Misfortune pursues the sinner,[s]
but prosperity[t] is the reward of the
righteous.[u]
[22]A good man leaves an inheritance for
his children's children,
but a sinner's wealth is stored up for
the righteous.[v]
[23]A poor man's field may produce
abundant food,
but injustice sweeps it away.
[24]He who spares the rod[w] hates his son,
but he who loves him is careful to
discipline[x] him.[y]
[25]The righteous eat to their hearts'
content,
but the stomach of the wicked goes
hungry.[z]

14 The wise woman builds her house,[a]
but with her own hands the foolish
one tears hers down.
[2]He whose walk is upright fears the
LORD,
but he whose ways are devious
despises him.

13:8 [a]Pr 15:16 **13:9** [b]S Job 18:5; S Pr 4:18-19 **13:10** [c]S Jdg 19:30; S Pr 9:9 **13:11** [d]S Pr 10:2 **13:12** [e]S Pr 10:11 **13:13** [f]S Nu 15:31 [g]Ex 9:20 [h]Pr 16:20 **13:14** [i]S Pr 10:11 [j]Pr 14:27 **13:16** [k]Ecc 10:3 [l]Est 5:11; S Ps 38:5 **13:17** [m]S Pr 10:26 [n]Pr 25:13 **13:18** [o]S Pr 1:7; S 12:1 [p]Ps 141:5; Pr 25:12; Ecc 7:5 **13:19** [q]S Pr 10:11 **13:20** [r]2Ch 10:8 **13:21** [s]2Sa 3:39; Jer 40:3; 50:7; Eze 14:13; 18:4 [t]Ps 25:13 [u]Ps 32:10 **13:22** [v]S Est 8:2; S Job 27:17; Ecc 2:26 **13:24** [w]S 2Sa 7:14 [x]S Pr 3:12 [y]Pr 19:18; 22:15; 23:13-14; 29:15,17; Eph 6:4; Heb 12:7 **13:25** [z]Pr 10:3 **14:1** [a]S Ru 3:11; Pr 24:3

[a] 15 Or *unfaithful does not endure*

13:8 *may ransom his life.* Has the means to pay off robbers or enemies (see 10:15 and note; Jer 41:8). *poor man hears no threat.* Even poverty has its advantages.
13:9 *light ... lamp.* Symbols of life (cf. Job 3:20). *shines brightly.* There is joy and prosperity (see note on 4:18). *lamp of the wicked is snuffed out.* Their lives will end (see 20:20; 24:20; Job 18:5; 21:17).
13:10 *Pride.* See 11:2 and note.
13:11 *Dishonest money dwindles away.* Such as wealth gained by extortion (Ps 62:10) or deceit (Pr 21:6). See note on 10:2; see also Jer 17:11. *makes it grow.* See note on 10:4.
13:12 *Hope deferred makes the heart sick.* Cf. Ge 30:1. *longing fulfilled is a tree of life.* It revives and strengthens (see note on 3:18; see also 10:28; 13:19).
13:13 *who scorns instruction will pay for it.* See 1:29–31; 5:12 and note. *who respects a command is rewarded.* With the benefits wisdom gives (see 3:2 and note; 3:16–18; 16:20; cf. 13:21).
13:14 *fountain of life.* See note on 10:11. *from the snares of death.* See notes on 1:17; 5:22; see also 7:23; 22:5.
13:15 *wins favor.* See 3:4; 8:35. *is hard.* See v. 13 and note.
13:16 See 12:23 and note.
13:17 *falls into trouble.* Perhaps by misrepresenting the sender. *brings healing.* A tactful, honest approach benefits both parties (see 25:13; cf. 12:18; 15:4).
13:18 *comes to poverty and shame.* See 5:10–12 and notes. *whoever heeds correction is honored.* See v. 1; 3:16–18; 8:35; 10:17.
13:19 *longing fulfilled.* See v. 12. *fools detest turning from evil.* Cf. their hatred of correction in 5:12.
13:20 *who walks with the wise grows wise.* So choose your friends with care (see 2:20; 12:26). *companion of fools suffers harm.* See 1:10,18; 2:12; 16:29; 22:24–25.
13:21 See v. 13 and note.
13:22 *is stored up for the righteous.* Job agrees that this is often what happens to the possessions of the wicked (Job 27:16–17; cf. Pr 28:8; Ecc 2:26).
13:23 *injustice sweeps it away.* Probably a case of the rich and powerful oppressing the poor (see Am 2:6–7 and notes; cf. Ps 35:10).
13:24 *who spares the rod hates his son.* Parents are counseled to discipline their children so that they do not persist in foolish ways (22:15) that can only lead to their destruction (19:18; 23:13–14). Discipline "imparts wisdom" (29:15) and promotes a healthy and happy family (29:17). It is rooted in love (see 3:11–12 and note). *rod.* A concrete figure of speech for caring discipline of any kind.
13:25 States more specifically the teaching of vv. 13,18,21; see 10:3 and note.
14:1 *wise woman builds her house.* She is a source of strength and an example of diligence for her family (see 31:10–31). Cf. the house built by wisdom in 9:1.
14:2 *fears the LORD.* See note on 1:7.

3 A fool's talk brings a rod to his back,[b]
but the lips of the wise protect
them.[c]
4 Where there are no oxen, the manger
is empty,
but from the strength of an ox[d]
comes an abundant harvest.
5 A truthful witness does not deceive,
but a false witness pours out lies.[e]
6 The mocker seeks wisdom and finds
none,
but knowledge comes easily to the
discerning.[f]
7 Stay away from a foolish man,
for you will not find knowledge on
his lips.
8 The wisdom of the prudent is to give
thought to their ways,[g]
but the folly of fools is deception.[h]
9 Fools mock at making amends for
sin,
but goodwill is found among the
upright.
10 Each heart knows its own bitterness,
and no one else can share its joy.
11 The house of the wicked will be
destroyed,[i]
but the tent of the upright will
flourish.[j]
12 There is a way that seems right to a
man,[k]
but in the end it leads to death.[l]
13 Even in laughter[m] the heart may ache,
and joy may end in grief.
14 The faithless will be fully repaid for
their ways,[n]
and the good man rewarded for his.[o]
15 A simple man believes anything,
but a prudent man gives thought to
his steps.[p]
16 A wise man fears the LORD and shuns
evil,[q]
but a fool[r] is hotheaded and
reckless.
17 A quick-tempered[s] man does foolish
things,[t]
and a crafty man is hated.[u]
18 The simple inherit folly,
but the prudent are crowned with
knowledge.
19 Evil men will bow down in the
presence of the good,
and the wicked at the gates of the
righteous.[v]
20 The poor are shunned even by their
neighbors,
but the rich have many friends.[w]
21 He who despises his neighbor sins,[x]
but blessed is he who is kind to the
needy.[y]
22 Do not those who plot evil go astray?[z]
But those who plan what is good
find[a] love and faithfulness.
23 All hard work brings a profit,
but mere talk leads only to poverty.
24 The wealth of the wise is their crown,
but the folly of fools yields folly.[a]

14:3 [b] S Pr 10:14; Ecc 10:12 [c] S Pr 10:13; S 12:6 **14:4** [d] Ps 144:14 **14:5** [e] S Ps 12:2; S Pr 12:17 **14:6** [f] S Pr 9:9 **14:8** [g] ver 15; Pr 15:28; 21:29 [h] ver 24 **14:11** [i] S Job 8:22; Pr 21:12 [j] S Ps 72:7; S Pr 3:33; S 12:7 **14:12** [k] S Pr 12:15 [l] Pr 16:25 **14:13** [m] Ecc 2:2; 7:3,6 **14:14** [n] S Pr 1:31 [o] S 2Ch 15:7; Pr 12:14 **14:15** [p] S ver 8 **14:16** [q] S Ex 20:20; Pr 22:3 [r] S 1Sa 25:25 **14:17** [s] S 2Ki 5:12 [t] ver 29; Pr 15:18; 16:28; 26:21; 28:25; 29:22 [u] S Est 5:9 **14:19** [v] Pr 11:29 **14:20** [w] Pr 19:4,7 **14:21** [x] Pr 11:12 [y] Pr 19:17 **14:22** [z] Pr 4:16-17 **14:24** [a] ver 8

[a] 22 Or *show*

14:3 *rod to his back.* See 10:13; 19:29; 26:3.
14:4 *oxen.* Used as draft animals in tilling the soil and bringing in the harvest (cf. 27:23).
14:5 See note on 6:19.
14:6 *mocker.* See 1:22 and note. *seeks wisdom and finds none.* Because of refusal to fear the Lord or accept any correction.
14:8 *folly of fools is deception.* What fools believe to be prudent is really folly; it does not bring success but leads to their ruin.
14:9 *mock at making amends for sin.* Cf. 19:28. *goodwill … among the upright.* See 11:27.
14:10 Each human heart has experiences of sorrows and joys that are so personal and unique that others cannot fully share them—but to God every human heart is an open book (see 15:11 and note).
14:11 See 10:25 and note.
14:12 Repeated in 16:25. *in the end it leads to death.* See 5:4,23; 7:21–27; Mt 7:13–14.
14:13 *in laughter the heart may ache.* Cf. Ezr 3:11–12. *joy may end in grief.* As the death of Rachel in childbirth (Ge 35:16–18).
14:14 See 1:31; 12:14 and notes; see also 11:5,8; 18:20; 22:8; Job 4:8.
14:15 *simple man.* See note on 1:4. *gives thought to his steps.* See 4:26 and note; 21:29.
14:16 *fears the LORD and shuns evil.* See notes on 1:7; 3:7. *hotheaded.* Cf. 21:24. *reckless.* In words (12:18; 13:3) and actions (Jdg 9:4).
14:17 *quick-tempered.* See v. 29; Tit 1:7. *crafty.* Cf. 12:2; Job 5:12–13.
14:18 *crowned with knowledge.* Adorned and blessed with knowledge (cf. v. 24 and note).
14:19 *Evil men will bow down.* Cf. 17:2. *at the gates of the righteous.* Perhaps to beg for a favor (cf. 1Sa 2:36).
14:20 *shunned even by their neighbors.* And sometimes by their relatives (see 19:7).
14:21 *blessed is he who is kind to the needy.* Sharing food (22:9), lending money (28:8) and defending rights (31:9) are ways one can show kindness. Such a person "honors God" (v. 31; cf. 17:5) and "will lack nothing" (28:27). Cf. 21:13; Ps 41:1; 112.
14:22 *plot evil.* See 3:29; 6:14,18; Mic 2:1. *go astray.* See 5:23; 12:26. *find love and faithfulness.* Receive the support and care of faithful friends (cf. 3:3; 16:6; 20:28)—perhaps God's support and care are also implied here. *love and faithfulness.* See Ps 26:3 and note.
14:23 *hard work brings a profit.* See note on 10:4; see also 21:5.
14:24 *wealth … is their crown.* The wise obtain wealth, and it adorns them like a crown (see 10:22 and note). *yields folly.* An empty inheritance (see v. 18; 3:35).

25 A truthful witness saves lives,
but a false witness is deceitful.[b]

26 He who fears the LORD has a secure
fortress,[c]
and for his children it will be a
refuge.[d]

27 The fear of the LORD is a fountain of
life,[e]
turning a man from the snares of
death.[f]

28 A large population is a king's glory,
but without subjects a prince is
ruined.[g]

29 A patient man has great
understanding,[h]
but a quick-tempered man displays
folly.[i]

30 A heart at peace gives life to the body,
but envy rots the bones.[j]

31 He who oppresses the poor shows
contempt for their Maker,[k]
but whoever is kind to the needy
honors God.[l]

32 When calamity comes, the wicked are
brought down,[m]
but even in death the righteous have
a refuge.[n]

33 Wisdom reposes in the heart of the
discerning[o]
and even among fools she lets
herself be known.[a]

34 Righteousness exalts a nation,[p]
but sin is a disgrace to any people.

35 A king delights in a wise servant,
but a shameful servant incurs his
wrath.[q]

15 A gentle answer[r] turns away wrath,[s]
but a harsh word stirs up anger.

2 The tongue of the wise commends
knowledge,[t]
but the mouth of the fool gushes
folly.[u]

3 The eyes[v] of the LORD are everywhere,[w]
keeping watch on the wicked and
the good.[x]

4 The tongue[y] that brings healing is a
tree of life,[z]
but a deceitful tongue crushes the
spirit.[a]

5 A fool spurns his father's discipline,
but whoever heeds correction shows
prudence.[b]

6 The house of the righteous contains
great treasure,[c]
but the income of the wicked brings
them trouble.[d]

7 The lips of the wise spread
knowledge;[e]
not so the hearts of fools.

8 The LORD detests the sacrifice[f] of the
wicked,[g]
but the prayer of the upright pleases
him.[h]

9 The LORD detests the way of the
wicked[i]
but he loves those who pursue
righteousness.[j]

[a] 33 Hebrew; Septuagint and Syriac / *but in the heart of fools she is not known*

14:25 [b]S Pr 12:17 **14:26** [c]Pr 18:10 [d]Ps 9:9 **14:27** [e]S Pr 10:11 [f]Ps 18:5; Pr 13:14 **14:28** [g]S 2Sa 19:7 **14:29** [h]S 2Ki 5:12; Pr 17:27 [i]S ver 17; Ecc 7:8-9 **14:30** [j]Pr 17:22 **14:31** [k]Pr 17:5 [l]S Dt 24:14; S Job 20:19; S Mt 10:42 **14:32** [m]S Ps 34:21; S Pr 6:15 [n]S Job 13:15 **14:33** [o]Pr 2:6-10 **14:34** [p]Pr 11:11 **14:35** [q]S Est 8:2; Mt 24:45-51; 25:14-30
15:1 [r]1Ki 12:7; 2Ch 10:7 [s]Pr 25:15 **15:2** [t]ver 7; S Pr 10:31 [u]S Ps 59:7; Ecc 10:12 **15:3** [v]S 2Ch 16:9 [w]S Job 10:4; S 31:4; S Heb 4:13 [x]S Job 34:21; Pr 5:21; Jer 16:17 **15:4** [y]S Ps 5:9 [z]S Pr 10:11 [a]Pr 12:18 **15:5** [b]S Pr 10:17; S 12:1; S 13:1 **15:6** [c]S Pr 8:21 [d]S Pr 10:16 **15:7** [e]S ver 2; S Pr 10:13 **15:8** [f]S Ps 51:17; S Isa 1:13 [g]S Pr 6:16; 21:27 [h]ver 29; Job 35:13; Pr 28:9; S Jn 9:31 **15:9** [i]S Pr 6:16 [j]S Dt 7:13; S Pr 11:20

14:25 See v. 5; 12:17; see also note on 6:19.
14:26 *fears the LORD.* See 1:7; 3:7 and notes. *secure fortress ... refuge.* Means either that the godliness of parents will result in blessing for themselves and their children (see 20:7) or that the "fear of the LORD" will be a strong tower where the children also can find refuge (see Isa 33:6).
14:27 See note on 10:11; see also 13:14.
14:29 *patient.* See 15:18; 16:32; 19:11; Jas 1:19. *quick-tempered.* See v. 17; cf. Eph 4:26.
14:30 *gives life to the body.* Cf. the healthy effects of fearing the Lord and walking in wisdom in 3:7–8,16–18. *envy rots the bones.* See note on 3:8; see also 12:4; Ps 37:7–8.
14:31 *shows contempt for their Maker.* Because God created both the rich and the poor in his image (see 17:5; 22:2; Ge 1:26 and note; Job 31:15; Jas 3:9). *kind to the needy.* See note on v. 21. *honors God.* Does God's will, and in a sense gives gifts to God himself (see 19:17 and note; Mt 25:40).
14:32 *wicked are brought down.* See 1:26 and note; 11:5; 24:16. *even in death the righteous have a refuge.* Their faith in God gives them hope beyond the grave (see 12:28; see also notes on Ps 16:9–11; 49:15).
14:33 *even among fools she lets herself be known.* Perhaps means that even fools occasionally display a bit of wisdom (cf. Ac 17:27–28; Ro 1:19–20), but see NIV text note.
14:34 *Righteousness exalts a nation.* See note on 11:11. Israel was promised prosperity and prestige if she obeyed God's laws (see Dt 28:1–14). *sin is a disgrace to any people.* The Canaanites were driven out because of their terrible sin (Lev 18:24–25), and Israel later received the same curse (Dt 28:15–68; cf. 2Sa 12:10).
14:35 *incurs his wrath.* See 16:14 and note; 19:12; Da 2:12.
15:1 *gentle answer turns away wrath.* Cf. the way Gideon calmed the anger of the men of Ephraim in Jdg 8:1–3 (cf. also Pr 15:18; Ecc 10:4). *harsh word stirs up anger.* Nabal's sarcastic response put David in a fighting mood (1Sa 25:10–13).
15:2 *gushes folly.* See vv. 7,28; 12:23; 13:16.
15:3 *eyes of the LORD are everywhere.* See 5:21; Job 31:4; 34:21; Jer 16:17; 32:19.
15:4 *tongue that brings healing.* See note on 12:18. *tree of life.* See note on 3:18. *deceitful tongue crushes the spirit.* Especially false testimony in court (see 6:19 and note; 22:22), or slander in the community.
15:6 See 10:2,16,22 and notes. *great treasure.* See 3:10 and note; cf. 8:18,21; 24:4; Zec 8:12 and note.
15:8 *detests the sacrifice of the wicked.* Those whose hearts are not right with God gain nothing by offering sacrifices (see Ecc 5:1; see also Pr 21:3; Isa 1:11–15; Jer 6:20 and notes). *prayer of the upright.* See 3:32.
15:9 *who pursue righteousness.* See 11:20; Ps 15:2; cf. Pr 21:21.

Character Traits in Proverbs

Traits to be promoted		Traits to be avoided	
avoiding strife	20:3	anger	29:22
compassion for animals	12:10	antisocial behavior	18:1
contentment	13:25; 14:30; 15:27	beauty without discretion	11:22
diligence	6:6-13; 12:24,27; 13:4	blaming God	19:3
faithful love	20:6	dishonesty	24:28
faithfulness	3:5-6; 5:15-17; 25:13; 28:20	distasteful	14:17
generosity	21:26; 22:9	greed	28:25
honesty	16:11; 24:26	hatred	29:27
humility	11:2; 16:19; 25:6-7; 29:23	hot temper	19:19
integrity	11:3; 25:26; 28:18	immorality	6:20-35
kindness to others	11:16-17	inappropriate desire	27:7
kindness to enemies	25:21-22	injustice	22:16
leadership	30:19-31	jealousy	27:4
loyalty	19:22	laziness	6:6-11; 18:9; 19:15; 20:4; 24:30-34; 26:13-15
noble wife	12:4; 31:10,29	maliciousness	6:27
patience	15:18; 16:32	meddling	26:17; 30:10
peaceful	16:7	pride	15:5; 16:18; 21:4,24; 29:23; 30:13
praiseworthy	27:21	quarrelsomeness	26:21
righteousness	4:26-27; 11:5-6,30; 12:28; 13:6; 29:2	self-conceit	26:12,16
self-control	17:27; 25:28; 29:11	self-deceit	28:11
strength and honor	20:29	self-glory	25:27
strength in adversity	24:10	self-righteousness	30:12
teachable	15:31	social disruption	19:10
truthfulness	12:19,22; 23:23	stubbornness	29:1
		unfaithfulness	25:19
		unneighborliness	3:27-30
		unmerciful	21:13
		vengeance	24:28-29
		wickedness	21:10
		wicked expressions	16:30

[10]Stern discipline awaits him who leaves
the path;
he who hates correction will die.[k]

[11]Death and Destruction[a] lie open before
the LORD[l]—
how much more the hearts of men![m]

[12]A mocker resents correction;[n]
he will not consult the wise.

[13]A happy heart makes the face
cheerful,[o]
but heartache crushes the spirit.[p]

[14]The discerning heart seeks
knowledge,[q]
but the mouth of a fool feeds on
folly.

[15]All the days of the oppressed are
wretched,
but the cheerful heart has a
continual feast.[r]

[16]Better a little with the fear of the LORD
than great wealth with turmoil.[s]

[17]Better a meal of vegetables where there
is love
than a fattened calf with hatred.[t]

[18]A hot-tempered man stirs up
dissension,[u]
but a patient man calms a quarrel.[v]

[19]The way of the sluggard is blocked
with thorns,[w]
but the path of the upright is a
highway.

[20]A wise son brings joy to his father,[x]
but a foolish man despises his
mother.

[21]Folly delights a man who lacks
judgment,[y]
but a man of understanding keeps a
straight course.

[22]Plans fail for lack of counsel,[z]
but with many advisers[a] they
succeed.[b]

[23]A man finds joy in giving an apt
reply[c]—
and how good is a timely
word![d]

[24]The path of life leads upward for
the wise
to keep him from going down to the
grave.[b]

[25]The LORD tears down the proud man's
house[e]
but he keeps the widow's
boundaries intact.[f]

[26]The LORD detests the thoughts[g] of the
wicked,[h]
but those of the pure[i] are pleasing to
him.

[27]A greedy man brings trouble to his
family,
but he who hates bribes will live.[j]

[28]The heart of the righteous weighs its
answers,[k]
but the mouth of the wicked gushes
evil.[l]

[29]The LORD is far from the wicked
but he hears the prayer of the
righteous.[m]

[30]A cheerful look brings joy to the
heart,
and good news gives health to the
bones.[n]

15:10 [k]S Pr 1:31-32; S 12:1 **15:11** [l]S Job 26:6 [m]S 1Sa 2:3; S 2Ch 6:30; S Ps 44:21; S Rev 2:23 **15:12** [n]S Pr 9:8; S 12:1 **15:13** [o]ver 15 [p]S Pr 12:25; 17:22; 18:14 **15:14** [q]Pr 18:15 **15:15** [r]ver 13 **15:16** [s]ver 17; Ps 37:16-17; Pr 13:8; 16:8; 17:1 **15:17** [t]S ver 16; Pr 17:1; Ecc 4:6 **15:18** [u]S Pr 6:16-19; S 14:17 [v]S Ge 13:8 **15:19** [w]Pr 22:5 **15:20** [x]S Pr 10:1 **15:21** [y]S Pr 2:14 **15:22** [z]S Ps 16:7 [a]1Ki 1:12; Pr 24:6 [b]S Pr 11:14 **15:23** [c]S Pr 12:14 [d]Pr 25:11 **15:25** [e]S Pr 12:7 [f]S Dt 19:14; Pr 23:10-11 **15:26** [g]S Ps 94:11 [h]S Pr 6:16 [i]S Ps 18:26 **15:27** [j]S Ex 23:8; S Ps 15:5; Isa 1:23; 33:15 **15:28** [k]S Pr 14:8 [l]S Ps 59:7 **15:29** [m]S ver 8; S Job 15:31; Ps 145:18-19; Isa 59:2; S Jn 9:31 **15:30** [n]Pr 25:25

[a] *11* Hebrew *Sheol and Abaddon* [b] *24* Hebrew *Sheol*

15:10 *the path.* The right (or "straight") path (see 2:13). *who hates correction will die.* See 5:12,23 and notes.
15:11 *Death and Destruction.* See 27:20. *lie open before the LORD.* Not even the grave, the netherworld, is inaccessible to God (see Job 26:6 and note; Ps 139:8). Therefore he knows the secrets of everyone's inmost being (cf. 1Sa 16:7 and note).
15:12 See 1:30; 10:8; 13:1; 17:10. *mocker.* See note on 1:22.
15:13 *happy heart makes the face cheerful.* Cf. 14:30. *heartache crushes the spirit.* Cf. the great sorrow of Job (Job 3) and David (Ps 51:8,10).
15:15 *cheerful heart has a continual feast.* Life is as joyful and satisfying as the days of a festival (see v. 13; 14:30; cf. Lev 23:39–41).
15:16 *fear of the LORD.* See 1:7 and note. *great wealth with turmoil.* The "ill-gotten treasures" of 10:2 (see note there).
15:17 *fattened calf.* Such meat was something of a luxury, reserved for special occasions (cf. 7:14; Mt 22:4; Lk 15:23).
15:18 *stirs up dissension.* See note on 6:14. *patient man.* See 14:29; 16:32; 19:11; Jas 1:19.
15:19 *sluggard.* See note on 6:6. *blocked with thorns.* Mainly because he was too lazy to remove them (see 24:30–31; Hos 2:6). *highway.* The upright can make progress and reach their goals (see note on 3:6).
15:20 See 10:1 and note.
15:21 A variation of 10:23.
15:22 See the close parallels in 11:14; 20:18; 24:6.
15:23 *apt reply.* Cf. Isa 50:4. *how good is a timely word!* Cf. 24:26.
15:24 *leads upward.* Along the "highway" (v. 19), the "straight course" (v. 21) that leads to life. *to keep him from going down to the grave.* See note on 2:18.
15:25 *tears down the proud man's house.* See 2:22; 14:11; see also 10:25 and note. *keeps the widow's boundaries intact.* In ancient times boundary stones marked a person's property. Anyone who moved such a stone was, in effect, stealing land (see 22:28; 23:10; Job 24:2; Dt 19:14 and note).
15:26 *detests the thoughts of the wicked.* Cf. vv. 8–9. *those of the pure.* See 22:11; Ps 24:4 and note.
15:27 *greedy man brings trouble to his family.* See 1:19; 11:29; 28:25. Achan's whole family perished because of his greed at Jericho (see Jos 7:24 and note). *he who hates bribes will live.* See 17:8 and note; 28:16.
15:28 *weighs its answers.* Cf. 10:32; 1Pe 3:15. *gushes evil.* See v. 2; see also v. 7; 12:23.
15:29 *far from the wicked.* See 1:28 and note.
15:30 *cheerful look brings joy.* Cf. v. 13; 16:15; Job 29:24. *good news gives health to the bones.* See 3:8 and note; see also Php 2:19.

[31]He who listens to a life-giving
rebuke
will be at home among the wise.[o]
[32]He who ignores discipline despises
himself,[p]
but whoever heeds correction gains
understanding.[q]
[33]The fear of the LORD[r] teaches a man
wisdom,[a]
and humility comes before honor.[s]

16

To man belong the plans of the
heart,
but from the LORD comes the reply
of the tongue.[t]
[2]All a man's ways seem innocent to
him,[u]
but motives are weighed[v] by the
LORD.[w]
[3]Commit to the LORD whatever
you do,
and your plans will succeed.[x]
[4]The LORD works out everything for his
own ends[y]—
even the wicked for a day of
disaster.[z]
[5]The LORD detests all the proud of
heart.[a]
Be sure of this: They will not go
unpunished.[b]
[6]Through love and faithfulness sin is
atoned for;
through the fear of the LORD[c] a man
avoids evil.[d]
[7]When a man's ways are pleasing to the
LORD,
he makes even his enemies live at
peace[e] with him.[f]
[8]Better a little with righteousness
than much gain[g] with injustice.[h]
[9]In his heart a man plans his course,
but the LORD determines his steps.[i]
[10]The lips of a king speak as an oracle,
and his mouth should not betray
justice.[j]
[11]Honest scales and balances are from
the LORD;
all the weights in the bag are of his
making.[k]
[12]Kings detest wrongdoing,
for a throne is established through
righteousness.[l]
[13]Kings take pleasure in honest lips;
they value a man who speaks the
truth.[m]

[a] 33 Or *Wisdom teaches the fear of the LORD*

15:31 [o]S Pr 9:7-9; S 12:1 **15:32** [p]S Pr 1:7; S 12:1 [q]S Pr 9:7-9; S 12:1; Ecc 7:5 **15:33** [r]S Pr 1:7 [s]Pr 16:18; 18:12; 22:4; 29:23; Isa 66:2 **16:1** [t]ver 9; Pr 19:21 **16:2** [u]S Pr 12:15; 30:12 [v]S 1Sa 2:3 [w]S 2Ch 6:30; Pr 20:27; 21:2; Lk 16:15 **16:3** [x]S 2Ch 20:20; S Ps 20:4; 37:5-6; S Pr 3:5-6 **16:4** [y]Ex 9:16 [z]S 2Ch 34:24; S Ps 18:18; Ro 9:22 **16:5** [a]S Ps 40:4; S Pr 6:16 [b]Pr 11:20-21 **16:6** [c]S Ge 20:11; S Ex 1:17 [d]S Ex 20:20 **16:7** [e]S Ge 39:21 [f]Ps 105:15; Jer 39:12; 40:1; 42:12; Da 1:9 **16:8** [g]S Ps 37:16 [h]S Pr 15:16; 17:1; Ecc 4:6 **16:9** [i]S ver 1; S Job 33:29; S Ps 90:12 **16:10** [j]Pr 17:7 **16:11** [k]S Pr 11:1; Eze 45:10 **16:12** [l]Pr 26:28; 25:5; 29:14; 31:5 **16:13** [m]Pr 22:11

15:31 *who listens to a life-giving rebuke.* See 1:23; 6:23 and note.
15:32 *who ignores discipline despises himself.* See note on 5:12; see also 1:7; 5:23; 8:36. *whoever heeds correction.* Cf. vv. 5,31.
15:33 *fear of the LORD.* See note on 1:7. *humility comes before honor.* See 18:12; 25:6–7; Mt 23:12; Lk 14:11 and note; 18:14; 1Pe 5:6. Wisdom also comes with humility (11:2; 13:10).
16:1 *from the LORD comes the reply of the tongue.* Either an acknowledgment that God must give the ability to articulate and accomplish those plans or, more likely, that God's sovereign governance of human affairs overrides human intentions (see vv. 4,9 and notes; cf. 19:21; see also Ge 50:20 and the experience of Balaam [Nu 22–24]).
16:2 *seem innocent.* See 14:12. *motives are weighed by the LORD.* See 21:2; 24:12 and notes; Ps 139:23; 1Co 4:4–5; Heb 4:12.
16:3 *Commit.* See 1Pe 5:7. *plans will succeed.* Goals will be reached (see 3:5–6 and notes; Ps 1:3; 55:22; 90:17).
16:4 The middle verse of this section of Proverbs (10:1—22:16), aptly summarizing the Lord's sovereignty over every human thought and action. The verse also occupies the central position in a series of seven verses (1–7). Each of the seven verses features the name Yahweh, again stressing his supreme position as Lord over all. *works out everything for his own ends.* God is sovereign in every life and in all of history (see vv. 1,9 and notes; cf. Ecc 7:14; Ac 3:17–18; Ro 8:28). *the wicked for a day of disaster.* God displays his power even through the wicked (cf. Ex 9:16), and all evil will be judged (cf. Eze 38:22–23; Ro 2:5–11).
16:5 See 11:20–21.
16:6 *Through love and faithfulness sin is atoned for.* The moral quality of conduct that God desires is sometimes summed up as "love and faithfulness" (3:3; see Ps 26:3; Hos 4:1 and notes). When his people repent of sin and bring their lives into accord with his will, God forgives and withdraws his judgment (see Isa 1:18–19; 55:7; Jer 3:22; 18:7–10 and note; Eze 18:23,30–32; 33:11–12,14–16; Hos 14:1–2,4). Thus it can be said that love and faithfulness, in a manner of speaking, "atone for" sin, i.e., they turn away God's wrath against it. *fear of the LORD.* See note on 1:7. *avoids evil.* See 3:7 and note.
16:7 *makes even his enemies live at peace with him.* As in the reigns of godly Asa and Jehoshaphat (2Ch 14:6–7; 17:10). *peace.* See 3:17; Ro 12:18 and notes; Heb 12:14.
16:8 See 10:2 and note.
16:9 *the LORD determines his steps.* Verses 1,4 (see notes there) also emphasize God's control of people's lives (see 19:21; 20:24; Ps 37:23; Jer 10:23).
16:10 *speak as an oracle.* In judging cases brought before him, a king functioned as God's representative (see Dt 1:17). Therefore he needed the divine gift of wisdom to discern between right and wrong in order to render God's judgment (see 1Ki 3:9). When he did so, his judgment was tantamount to a divine oracle for the people (see 2Sa 14:17; 1Ki 3:28 and notes).
16:11 See note on 11:1. *Honest scales ... from the LORD.* Cf. 21:2; 24:12; Job 6:2; 31:6. *all the weights in the bag.* Merchants carried stones of different sizes with them to weigh and measure quantities of silver for payment (cf. Mic 6:11).
16:12–15 A series of four proverbs highlighting the role of the king as chief political executive in the life of the community (cf. v. 10).
16:12 *throne is established through righteousness.* When the king "judges the poor with fairness" (29:14), refuses to take bribes (29:4) and removes any wicked advisers (25:5). See note on Ps 103:6; see also Ps 9:7–8; 97:2; Isa 16:5.
16:13 *in honest lips.* Rather than in flattering lips (cf. 26:28).

[14] A king's wrath is a messenger of
death,[n]
but a wise man will appease it.[o]

[15] When a king's face brightens, it means
life;[p]
his favor is like a rain cloud in
spring.[q]

[16] How much better to get wisdom than
gold,
to choose understanding[r] rather than
silver![s]

[17] The highway of the upright avoids evil;
he who guards his way guards his
life.[t]

[18] Pride[u] goes before destruction,
a haughty spirit[v] before a fall.[w]

[19] Better to be lowly in spirit and among
the oppressed
than to share plunder with the
proud.

[20] Whoever gives heed to instruction
prospers,[x]
and blessed is he who trusts in the
LORD.[y]

[21] The wise in heart are called discerning,
and pleasant words promote
instruction.[a][z]

[22] Understanding is a fountain of life to
those who have it,[a]
but folly brings punishment to
fools.

[23] A wise man's heart guides his mouth,[b]
and his lips promote instruction.[b][c]

[24] Pleasant words are a honeycomb,[d]
sweet to the soul and healing to the
bones.[e]

[25] There is a way that seems right to a
man,[f]
but in the end it leads to death.[g]

[26] The laborer's appetite works for him;
his hunger drives him on.

[27] A scoundrel[h] plots evil,
and his speech is like a scorching
fire.[i]

[28] A perverse man stirs up dissension,[j]
and a gossip separates close friends.[k]

[29] A violent man entices his neighbor
and leads him down a path that is
not good.[l]

[30] He who winks[m] with his eye is plotting
perversity;
he who purses his lips is bent on
evil.

[31] Gray hair is a crown of splendor;[n]
it is attained by a righteous life.

[32] Better a patient man than a warrior,
a man who controls his temper than
one who takes a city.

[33] The lot is cast[o] into the lap,
but its every decision[p] is from the
LORD.[q]

16:14 [n] S Ge 40:2; S Job 29:24; Pr 20:2 [o] Pr 25:15; 29:8; Ecc 10:4
16:15 [p] S Ge 40:2; S Job 29:24 [q] Pr 19:12; 25:2-7
16:16 [r] Ps 49:20 [s] S Job 28:15; S Pr 3:13-14
16:17 [t] Pr 19:16
16:18 [u] S 1Sa 17:42 [v] Ps 18:27; Isa 13:11; Jer 48:29 [w] S Est 5:12; Pr 11:2; S 15:33; 18:12; 29:23
16:20 [x] Pr 13:13 [y] S Ps 32:10; 40:4; Pr 19:8; 29:25; Jer 17:7
16:21 [z] ver 23
16:22 [a] S Pr 10:11
16:23 [b] Job 15:5 [c] ver 21
16:24 [d] S 1Sa 14:27 [e] Pr 24:13-14
16:25 [f] S Pr 12:15 [g] Est 3:6; Pr 14:12
16:27 [h] S Ps 140:2 [i] Jas 3:6
16:28 [j] S Pr 14:17 [k] Pr 17:9
16:29 [l] S Pr 1:10; 12:26
16:30 [m] S Pr 6:13
16:31 [n] Pr 20:29
16:33 [o] S Lev 16:8; S 1Sa 10:21; Eze 21:21 [p] 1Sa 14:41 [q] Jos 7:14; Pr 18:18; 29:26; Jnh 1:7

[a] 21 Or *words make a man persuasive* [b] 23 Or *mouth / and makes his lips persuasive*

16:14 *messenger of death.* Any angry king can pronounce death quickly and effectively (see 19:12; Est 7:7–10; Mt 22:7; Lk 19:27). *wise man will appease it.* Cf. Daniel's response to the rage of Nebuchadnezzar (Da 2:12–16).
16:15 *face brightens.* Cf. Nu 6:25 and note; La 4:20. *his favor is like a rain cloud in spring.* The spring rain was essential for the full development of barley and wheat; it was therefore a sign of good things to come. Cf. the "dew" of 19:12; see Ps 72:6.
16:16 See 1:13; 3:14 and notes; 8:10,19.
16:17 *highway of the upright.* See notes on 3:6; 15:19. *avoids evil.* Cf. the thorns and snares in the paths of the wicked (22:5).
16:18 See 11:2 and note; cf. 1Co 10:12.
16:19 *Better to be lowly in spirit.* See 3:34; Isa 57:15; Mt 5:3 and note. *share plunder with the proud.* See 1:13–14.
16:20 *prospers.* See 13:13; 28:25 and notes. *blessed is he who trusts in the LORD.* See v. 3; 3:5–6; Ps 34:8 and note on 34:8–14; 37:4–5; 40:4; 84:12.
16:21 *pleasant words promote instruction.* Cf. the last line of v. 23. "Pleasant" (lit. "sweet") is expanded in the last line of v. 24. Cf. the persuasive but destructive words of the adulteress in 7:21.
16:22 *fountain of life.* See note on 10:11. *punishment to fools.* See 13:13 and note; see also 7:22; 13:15; 15:10.
16:23 *guides his mouth.* See 22:17–18.
16:24 *Pleasant words are a honeycomb.* They are good for you (see 24:13–14), and they taste good (cf. 2:10; Ps 19:10). *healing to the bones.* See notes on 4:22; 12:18; 15:30. *bones.* See note on 3:8.
16:25 See 14:12 and note.
16:26 Cf. Ecc 6:7.
16:27 *scoundrel.* See 6:12 and note. *plots evil.* See 6:12–14; cf. 3:29. *scorching fire.* His speech is inflammatory and destructive (see Jas 3:6).
16:28 *stirs up dissension.* See note on 6:14. *gossip.* See 11:13.
16:29 See 1:10–19 and notes; cf. Ro 1:32.
16:30 *winks with his eye.* See note on 6:13. *purses his lips.* Thereby making insinuations (see note on 6:12–14).
16:31 *Gray hair is a crown of splendor.* Because it signifies a long life—which is attained only by God's blessing (see Ps 91:16; 92:12–14; cf. 128:6; Pr 17:6). *by a righteous life.* See 3:1–2,16.
16:32 *patient man ... warrior.* See 14:29; 15:18; 19:11; Jas 1:19. "Wisdom is better than weapons of war" (Ecc 9:18). *man who controls his temper than one who takes a city.* Although one who practices patience and self-control receives far less attention and acclaim than a warrior who takes a city, he accomplishes better things.
16:33 *The lot is cast into the lap.* Here the lot may have been several pebbles held in the fold of a garment and then drawn out or shaken to the ground (see note on Jnh 1:7). Casting lots was commonly used in making decisions (see notes on Ex 28:30; Nu 26:53; Ne 11:1; Ac 1:26; see also Ps 22:18). *every decision is from the LORD.* God, not chance, is in control (see vv. 1,3–4,9).

17 Better a dry crust with peace and quiet
than a house full of feasting,[a] with strife.[r]

[2]A wise servant will rule over a disgraceful son,
and will share the inheritance as one of the brothers.

[3]The crucible for silver and the furnace for gold,[s]
but the LORD tests the heart.[t]

[4]A wicked man listens to evil lips;
a liar pays attention to a malicious tongue.

[5]He who mocks the poor[u] shows contempt for their Maker;[v]
whoever gloats over disaster[w] will not go unpunished.[x]

[6]Children's children[y] are a crown to the aged,
and parents are the pride of their children.

[7]Arrogant[b] lips are unsuited to a fool—
how much worse lying lips to a ruler![z]

[8]A bribe is a charm to the one who gives it;
wherever he turns, he succeeds.[a]

[9]He who covers over an offense promotes love,[b]
but whoever repeats the matter separates close friends.[c]

17:1 [r]S Pr 15:16, 17; S 16:8 **17:3** [s]Pr 27:21 [t]S 1Ch 29:17; Ps 26:2; S 139:23; 1Pe 1:7 **17:5** [u]S Job 5:16 [v]Pr 14:31 [w]S Job 31:29 [x]Eze 25:3; Ob 1:12 **17:6** [y]S Ps 128:5-6 **17:7** [z]Pr 16:10 **17:8** [a]S Ex 23:8; Pr 19:6 **17:9** [b]S Pr 10:12 [c]Pr 16:28 **17:12** [d]S 1Sa 25:25 **17:13** [e]S 1Sa 19:4 [f]S Ge 44:4; S Ps 35:12 **17:14** [g]Mt 5:25-26 **17:15** [h]S Ps 94:21; S Pr 18:5 [i]Ex 23:6-7; Isa 5:23; La 3:34-36 **17:16** [j]Pr 23:23 **17:17** [k]S 2Sa 15:21; Pr 27:10 **17:18** [l]Pr 6:1-5; S 11:15; 22:26-27

[10]A rebuke impresses a man of discernment
more than a hundred lashes a fool.

[11]An evil man is bent only on rebellion;
a merciless official will be sent against him.

[12]Better to meet a bear robbed of her cubs
than a fool in his folly.[d]

[13]If a man pays back evil[e] for good,[f]
evil will never leave his house.

[14]Starting a quarrel is like breaching a dam;
so drop the matter before a dispute breaks out.[g]

[15]Acquitting the guilty and condemning the innocent[h]—
the LORD detests them both.[i]

[16]Of what use is money in the hand of a fool,
since he has no desire to get wisdom?[j]

[17]A friend loves at all times,
and a brother is born for adversity.[k]

[18]A man lacking in judgment strikes hands in pledge
and puts up security for his neighbor.[l]

[19]He who loves a quarrel loves sin;
he who builds a high gate invites destruction.

[a] *1* Hebrew *sacrifices* [b] *7* Or *Eloquent*

17:2 *A wise servant will rule over a disgraceful son.* See 11:29 and note. *disgraceful son.* See 10:5; 19:26; 28:7; 29:15.
17:3 The first line of this verse is repeated in 27:21. *The crucible ... the furnace.* Silver and gold were refined to remove their impurities (see Ps 12:6 and note). *tests the heart.* See 15:11; 16:2 and notes; Jer 17:10.
17:5 *who mocks the poor shows contempt for their Maker.* See 14:31 and note. *whoever gloats over disaster will not go unpunished.* The people of Edom in particular were condemned for gloating over the collapse of "brother" Jacob/Israel (Ob 10; see Eze 35:12,15; see also Pr 24:17).
17:6 *crown to the aged.* Cf. the "gray hair" of 16:31. To live to see one's grandchildren was considered a great blessing (see Ge 48:11; see also note on Pr 16:31). *parents are the pride of their children.* See Ge 47:7.
17:7 For the structure of this verse cf. 15:11; 19:7,10; 21:27. *Arrogant.* See NIV text note. *lying lips to a ruler.* The right to rule depends on honesty and justice (see 12:22; 16:12–13; cf. Ps 101:5,7).
17:8 *A bribe is a charm.* A sad commentary on human behavior (see 18:16; 21:14; Ecc 10:19). Elsewhere, bribes are condemned (see v. 23; 15:27; 28:16; Ex 23:8; Dt 16:19; 1Sa 12:3; Ecc 7:7; Isa 1:23; Am 5:12; 1Ti 6:10).
17:9 *He who covers over an offense promotes love.* See 10:12 and note.
17:10 *rebuke impresses a man of discernment.* See 9:8–9. *a hundred lashes a fool.* Fools (see note on 1:7) often committed acts that caused them to deserve and receive flogging (cf. 10:13; 19:25,29; 26:3; Dt 25:2–3).
17:11 *merciless official.* See 16:14 and note; cf. the dispatching of Abishai and Joab to end Sheba's rebellion against David (2Sa 20:1–22; see 1Ki 2:25,29,46).
17:12 *bear robbed of her cubs.* Sure to attack you (see 2Sa 17:8; Hos 13:8; cf. the raging of the fool in 29:9).
17:13 *pays back evil for good.* Like Nabal, who refused to reward David's men (1Sa 25:21; see Ps 109:5; Ro 12:17–21). *evil will never leave his house.* The fate of David's family after his affair with Bathsheba and the murder of Uriah (see 2Sa 12:10–11 and notes; cf. Jer 18:20–23).
17:15 *Acquitting the guilty.* Perhaps because of a bribe (see v. 8; 24:24).
17:16 *money in the hand of a fool.* Perhaps to pay the fee for his schooling.
17:17 *friend loves at all times.* See 18:24; cf. David's friendship with Jonathan (2Sa 1:26; see Lev 19:18 and note; Ru 1:16; cf. 1Co 13:4–7).
17:18 See 6:1 and note.
17:19 *who loves a quarrel loves sin.* A hot-tempered person "commits many sins" (29:22). *who builds a high gate.* To build strong defenses (to protect something precious) invites attacks. Some, however, render the ambiguous Hebrew "who opens his mouth wide," meaning "brags too much" and so "invites destruction," including his own (cf. 16:18; 29:23).

[20]A man of perverse heart does not
prosper;
he whose tongue is deceitful falls
into trouble.

[21]To have a fool for a son brings grief;
there is no joy for the father of a
fool.[m]

[22]A cheerful heart is good medicine,
but a crushed[n] spirit dries up the
bones.[o]

[23]A wicked man accepts a bribe[p] in
secret
to pervert the course of justice.[q]

[24]A discerning man keeps wisdom in
view,
but a fool's eyes[r] wander to the ends
of the earth.

[25]A foolish son brings grief to his father
and bitterness to the one who bore
him.[s]

[26]It is not good to punish an innocent
man,[t]
or to flog officials for their integrity.

[27]A man of knowledge uses words with
restraint,[u]
and a man of understanding is even-
tempered.[v]

[28]Even a fool is thought wise if he keeps
silent,
and discerning if he holds his
tongue.[w]

18

An unfriendly man pursues selfish
ends;
he defies all sound judgment.

[2]A fool finds no pleasure in
understanding
but delights in airing his own
opinions.[x]

[3]When wickedness comes, so does
contempt,
and with shame comes disgrace.

[4]The words of a man's mouth are deep
waters,[y]
but the fountain of wisdom is a
bubbling brook.

[5]It is not good to be partial to the
wicked[z]
or to deprive the innocent of justice.[a]

[6]A fool's lips bring him strife,
and his mouth invites a beating.[b]

[7]A fool's mouth is his undoing,
and his lips are a snare[c] to his soul.[d]

[8]The words of a gossip are like choice
morsels;
they go down to a man's inmost
parts.[e]

[9]One who is slack in his work
is brother to one who destroys.[f]

[10]The name of the LORD is a strong
tower;[g]
the righteous run to it and are safe.[h]

[11]The wealth of the rich is their fortified
city;[i]
they imagine it an unscalable wall.

[12]Before his downfall a man's heart is
proud,
but humility comes before honor.[j]

[13]He who answers before listening—
that is his folly and his shame.[k]

[14]A man's spirit sustains him in sickness,
but a crushed spirit who can bear?[l]

17:21 [m]S Pr 10:1
17:22 [n]S Ps 38:8 [o]S Ex 12:46; Pr 14:30; S 15:13; 18:14
17:23 [p]S Ex 18:21; S 23:8; S 1Sa 8:3 [q]S Job 34:33
17:24 [r]S Job 31:1
17:25 [s]S Pr 10:1
17:26 [t]S Ps 94:21
17:27 [u]S Job 6:24 [v]S Pr 14:29
17:28 [w]S Job 2:13; 13:5; S Pr 10:19
18:2 [x]S Pr 12:23
18:4 [y]S Ps 18:16
18:5 [z]Pr 24:23-25; 28:21 [a]S Ps 82:2; S Pr 17:15
18:6 [b]S Pr 10:14
18:7 [c]Ps 140:9 [d]S Ps 64:8; S Pr 10:14; S 12:13; S 13:3; Ecc 10:12
18:8 [e]Pr 26:22
18:9 [f]Pr 28:24
18:10 [g]S Ps 61:3 [h]S Ps 20:1; Pr 14:26
18:11 [i]Pr 10:15
18:12 [j]S Pr 11:2; 15:33; S 16:18
18:13 [k]Pr 20:25
18:14 [l]S Pr 15:13; S 17:22

17:20 *does not prosper.* Contrast 16:20. *whose tongue is deceitful.* See note on 2:12.
17:21 *grief ... no joy.* See v. 25; 19:13.
17:22 *cheerful heart.* See 14:30; 15:13,30; 16:15. *crushed spirit dries up the bones.* See notes on 3:8; 14:30; see also 12:4; Ps 32:3.
17:23 *accepts a bribe.* See note on v. 8.
17:24 *wander to the ends of the earth.* The fool "chases fantasies" (12:11) and is interested in everything except wisdom (cf. Dt 30:11–14).
17:25 See v. 21. *bitterness.* See 14:10 and note.
17:26 *punish an innocent man.* See v. 15. *flog officials.* See v. 10 and note; cf. the beating and disgrace endured by Jeremiah (Jer 20:2; 38:1–6).
17:27 *uses words with restraint.* See 10:19. *even-tempered.* See 16:32 and note.
17:28 *a fool is thought wise if he keeps silent.* Cf. Job's sarcastic comment in Job 13:5 (see note there).
18:1 *pursues selfish ends.* He is quarrelsome and hot-tempered (cf. 17:14).
18:2 *airing his own opinions.* See Ecc 10:3.
18:3 *shame ... disgrace.* Cf. 3:35; 6:33; 10:5; 11:2; Ps 31:17.
18:4 *deep waters.* Profound or obscure (cf. 20:5). *fountain of wisdom is a bubbling brook.* A wise person's words are refreshing and a source of life (see 1:23; 10:11 and notes).
18:5 *partial to the wicked.* See 17:15 and note. Favoritism of any kind was condemned in the law (see Lev 19:15; Dt 1:17; 16:19). *to deprive the innocent of justice.* See 17:26; 31:5; Ps 94:21; Isa 5:23; Am 2:6; 5:7,12; Zec 8:16 and note.
18:6 *bring him strife.* A fool is quick to quarrel (see 17:14,19; 20:3). *invites a beating.* By a rod on his back (see 10:13; 19:29).
18:7 See 10:14 and note.
18:8 Repeated in 26:22. *words of a gossip are like choice morsels.* They are as pleasant as words of wisdom (cf. 16:21,23), but they promote dissension (see 11:13; 26:20). *they go down to a man's inmost parts.* Where they are thoroughly digested and so are carried about and live on and on.
18:9 *who is slack in his work.* See 10:4 and note.
18:10 *name of the LORD.* His "name" often equals his "person," since it expresses his nature and qualities (see Ex 3:14–15 and notes). *strong tower.* See Ps 18:2 and note; 91:2; 144:2. *safe.* See 29:25; Ps 27:5.
18:11 *wealth ... is their fortified city.* Identical to the first line in 10:15 (see note there). *unscalable wall.* But God can bring it down (see Isa 25:12).
18:12 *humility comes before honor.* Identical to the first line in 15:33 (see note there).
18:14 See 15:13; 17:22 and notes.

[15]The heart of the discerning acquires
knowledge;[m]
the ears of the wise seek it out.

[16]A gift[n] opens the way for the giver
and ushers him into the presence of
the great.

[17]The first to present his case seems
right,
till another comes forward and
questions him.

[18]Casting the lot settles disputes[o]
and keeps strong opponents apart.

[19]An offended[p] brother is more
unyielding than a fortified
city,
and disputes are like the barred
gates of a citadel.

[20]From the fruit of his mouth a man's
stomach is filled;
with the harvest from his lips he is
satisfied.[q]

[21]The tongue has the power of life and
death,[r]
and those who love it will eat its
fruit.[s]

[22]He who finds a wife finds what is
good[t]
and receives favor from the LORD.[u]

[23]A poor man pleads for mercy,
but a rich man answers harshly.

[24]A man of many companions may come
to ruin,
but there is a friend who sticks
closer than a brother.[v]

19 Better a poor man whose walk is
blameless
than a fool whose lips are perverse.[w]

[2]It is not good to have zeal without
knowledge,
nor to be hasty and miss the way.[x]

[3]A man's own folly[y] ruins his life,
yet his heart rages against the LORD.[z]

[4]Wealth brings many friends,
but a poor man's friend deserts
him.[a]

[5]A false witness[b] will not go
unpunished,[c]
and he who pours out lies will not
go free.[d]

[6]Many curry favor with a ruler,[e]
and everyone is the friend of a man
who gives gifts.[f]

[7]A poor man is shunned by all his
relatives—
how much more do his friends avoid
him![g]
Though he pursues them with
pleading,
they are nowhere to be found.[a h]

[8]He who gets wisdom loves his own
soul;
he who cherishes understanding
prospers.[i]

[9]A false witness will not go unpunished,
and he who pours out lies will
perish.[j]

[10]It is not fitting for a fool[k] to live in
luxury—
how much worse for a slave to rule
over princes![l]

[11]A man's wisdom gives him patience;[m]
it is to his glory to overlook an
offense.

[12]A king's rage is like the roar of a lion,[n]
but his favor is like dew[o] on the
grass.[p]

[13]A foolish son is his father's ruin,[q]
and a quarrelsome wife is like a
constant dripping.[r]

[a] 7 The meaning of the Hebrew for this sentence is uncertain.

18:15 [m]S Pr 15:14 **18:16** [n]S Ge 32:13; S 1Sa 10:4; Pr 19:6 **18:18** [o]S Pr 16:33 **18:19** [p]S 1Sa 17:28 **18:20** [q]S Pr 12:14 **18:21** [r]S Ps 12:4 [s]Pr 13:2-3; S Mt 12:37 **18:22** [t]S Pr 12:4 [u]S Job 33:26; Pr 19:14; 31:10 **18:24** [v]S 1Sa 20:42; Jn 15:13-15 **19:1** [w]Pr 28:6 **19:2** [x]Pr 29:20 **19:3** [y]Ps 14:1; Pr 9:13; 24:9; Isa 32:6 [z]Jas 1:13-15 **19:4** [a]ver 7; Pr 14:20 **19:5** [b]S Ex 23:1 [c]S Ps 56:7 [d]ver 9; S Dt 19:19; Pr 21:28 **19:6** [e]Pr 29:26 [f]S Pr 17:8; S 18:16 **19:7** [g]Pr 10:15 [h]S ver 4 **19:8** [i]S Pr 16:20 **19:9** [j]S ver 5; S Dt 19:19 **19:10** [k]Pr 26:1 [l]Pr 30:21-23; Ecc 10:5-7 **19:11** [m]S 2Ki 5:12 **19:12** [n]Pr 20:2 [o]S Ps 133:3 [p]S Est 1:12; S 7:7; Ps 72:5-6; Pr 16:14-15 **19:13** [q]S Pr 10:1 [r]S Est 1:18; Pr 21:9

18:17 A warning to judges to hear both sides of a case (cf. Dt 1:16), but applicable to many situations.
18:18 *Casting the lot settles disputes.* See 16:33 and note.
18:19 *An offended brother.* Cf. Esau's anger because of the blessing Jacob received from Isaac (Ge 27:41).
18:20 See 12:14 and note.
18:21 *tongue has the power of life and death.* See notes on 10:19; 13:3. *its fruit.* See v. 20.
18:22 *who finds a wife finds what is good.* See 12:4 and note; 19:14; 31:10. *receives favor from the LORD.* Identical to the second line in 8:35—where finding wisdom brings the Lord's favor.
18:24 *man of many companions may come to ruin.* One must choose friends carefully (see 12:26 and note; 17:17).
19:1 Almost identical to 28:6. *blameless.* See note on 2:7. *than a fool.* Even if the fool becomes rich (see 28:6).
19:2 *zeal without knowledge.* Cf. Ro 10:2. *nor to be hasty.* Haste can lead to poverty (21:5) or folly (29:20). *miss the way.* Fail to achieve one's goal.
19:3 *his heart rages against the LORD.* He blames God for his troubles (see Ge 4:5; Isa 8:21; cf. La 3:39).
19:4 See v. 7; 14:20.
19:5,9 See 6:19 and note.
19:6 *curry favor.* Cf. Job 11:19. *friend of a man who gives gifts.* Generosity (v. 4) or bribery (17:8) could be in view.
19:7 *poor man is shunned.* See v. 4; 14:20.
19:8 *loves his own soul.* Cf. 8:35–36. *prospers.* See 13:13 and note.
19:10 *not fitting for a fool to live in luxury.* Or to have honor (26:1).
19:11 *patience.* See 14:29; 15:18; 16:32; Ecc 7:9; Jas 1:19. *overlook an offense.* See 12:16; 29:11; 2Sa 16:11–12.
19:12 See 16:14–15 and notes. *A king's rage is like the roar of a lion.* Almost identical to the first line of 20:2.
19:13 *foolish son.* See 17:21,25. *quarrelsome wife.* Also denounced in 21:9,19; 25:24; 27:15. Stirring up dissension is condemned throughout Proverbs (see 6:14 and note).

[14]Houses and wealth are inherited from
parents,[s]
but a prudent wife is from the
LORD.[t]

[15]Laziness brings on deep sleep,
and the shiftless man goes hungry.[u]

[16]He who obeys instructions guards his
life,
but he who is contemptuous of his
ways will die.[v]

[17]He who is kind to the poor lends to the
LORD,[w]
and he will reward him for what he
has done.[x]

[18]Discipline your son, for in that there is
hope;
do not be a willing party to his
death.[y]

[19]A hot-tempered man must pay the
penalty;
if you rescue him, you will have to
do it again.

[20]Listen to advice and accept
instruction,[z]
and in the end you will be wise.[a]

[21]Many are the plans in a man's heart,
but it is the LORD's purpose that
prevails.[b]

[22]What a man desires is unfailing love[a];
better to be poor than a liar.

[23]The fear of the LORD leads to life:
Then one rests content, untouched
by trouble.[c]

[24]The sluggard buries his hand in the
dish;
he will not even bring it back to his
mouth![d]

[25]Flog a mocker, and the simple will
learn prudence;
rebuke a discerning man,[e] and he
will gain knowledge.[f]

[26]He who robs his father and drives out
his mother[g]
is a son who brings shame and
disgrace.

[27]Stop listening to instruction, my son,[h]
and you will stray from the words of
knowledge.

[28]A corrupt witness mocks at justice,
and the mouth of the wicked gulps
down evil.[i]

[29]Penalties are prepared for mockers,
and beatings for the backs of fools.[j]

20 Wine[k] is a mocker[l] and beer a
brawler;
whoever is led astray[m] by them is
not wise.[n]

[2]A king's wrath is like the roar of a
lion;[o]
he who angers him forfeits his life.[p]

[3]It is to a man's honor to avoid strife,
but every fool[q] is quick to quarrel.[r]

[4]A sluggard[s] does not plow in season;
so at harvest time he looks but finds
nothing.[t]

[5]The purposes of a man's heart are
deep waters,[u]
but a man of understanding draws
them out.

[6]Many a man claims to have unfailing
love,
but a faithful man who can find?[v]

19:14 [s]2Co 12:14 [t]S Pr 18:22 **19:15** [u]S Pr 10:4; 20:13 **19:16** [v]S Pr 16:17; S Ro 10:5 **19:17** [w]S Dt 24:14 [x]S Dt 24:19; Pr 14:21; 22:9; S Mt 10:42 **19:18** [y]S Pr 13:24; 23:13-14 **19:20** [z]Pr 4:1 [a]S Pr 12:15 **19:21** [b]Ps 33:11; Pr 16:9; 20:24; Isa 8:10; 14:24,27; 31:2; 40:8; 46:10; 48:14; 55:11; Jer 44:29; La 3:37 **19:23** [c]S Job 4:7; S Pr 10:27 **19:24** [d]Pr 26:15 **19:25** [e]S Ps 141:5 [f]S Pr 9:9; 21:11 **19:26** [g]Pr 28:24 **19:27** [h]S Pr 1:8 **19:28** [i]S Job 15:16 **19:29** [j]S Dt 25:2 **20:1** [k]S Lev 10:9; Hab 2:5 [l]S 1Sa 25:36 [m]1Ki 20:16 [n]Pr 31:4 **20:2** [o]S Pr 19:12 [p]S Est 7:7; S Pr 16:14 **20:3** [q]S 1Sa 25:25 [r]S Ge 13:8 **20:4** [s]S Pr 6:6 [t]Ecc 10:18 **20:5** [u]S Ps 18:16 **20:6** [v]Ps 12:1

[a] 22 Or *A man's greed is his shame*

19:14 *prudent wife.* See 12:4 and note; see also 18:22.
19:15 See 6:11; 10:4 and notes.
19:16 See 13:13; 15:10; 16:17 and notes.
19:17 *who is kind to the poor.* See note on 14:21; see also 14:31. *lends to the LORD.* The Lord regards it as a gift to him (see note on 14:31; cf. Mt 25:40).
19:18 *Discipline your son … not … to his death.* See note on 13:24.
19:19 *hot-tempered.* Cf. 14:16–17,29; 15:18.
19:21 See 16:1,4,9 and notes.
19:22 *desires … unfailing love.* But such loyalty is difficult to find (cf. 14:22; 20:6). *better to be poor than a liar.* See vv. 1,28; 6:12.
19:23 *fear of the LORD.* See note on 1:7. *leads to life.* See note on 10:11. *untouched by trouble.* See 3:2; 14:26 and notes.
19:24 Almost identical to 26:15. *sluggard.* See note on 6:6.
19:25 *Flog a mocker.* See v. 29; 14:3; 21:11; see also notes on 1:22; 17:10; 21:24. *the simple.* Not to be confused with the mocker (see note on 1:4).
19:26 *robs … father and drives out … mother.* Children were expected to take care of their parents when they were sick or elderly (cf. Isa 51:18). Robbing them (cf. Jdg 17:1–2) and attacking or calling down curses on them (Ex 21:15,17) were serious crimes (see note on Ex 21:17). *shame and disgrace.* See 10:5; 13:5.
19:27 See 5:1–2.
19:28 *corrupt witness.* See v. 5; see also note on 6:19. *gulps down evil.* Cf. the description of someone "who drinks up evil like water" (Job 15:16; see Job 34:7).
19:29 *Penalties … for mockers.* See v. 25. *beatings for the backs of fools.* See 10:13; 14:3; 26:3.
20:1 *Wine is a mocker and beer a brawler.* Those who overindulge become mockers and brawlers (see Hos 7:5 and note). Proverbs associates drunkenness with poverty (see 23:20–21 and note), strife (23:29–30) and injustice (31:4–5). *led astray.* See Ge 9:21 and note; Isa 28:7.
20:2 See 16:14; 19:12 and notes.
20:3 *quick to quarrel.* See 6:14; 17:14,19; 18:6.
20:4 *sluggard.* See note on 6:6. *but finds nothing.* See 13:4; 21:25–26.
20:5 *purposes.* Or "motives" (cf. 16:1–2). *deep waters.* Cf. 18:4. *draws them out.* As if from a well.
20:6 *unfailing love.* See notes on 19:22; Ps 6:4. *a faithful man who can find?* Cf. Ecc 7:28–29.

[7]The righteous man leads a blameless
life;[w]
blessed are his children after him.[x]

[8]When a king sits on his throne to
judge,[y]
he winnows out all evil with his
eyes.[z]

[9]Who can say, "I have kept my heart
pure;[a]
I am clean and without sin"?[b]

[10]Differing weights and differing
measures —
the LORD detests them both.[c]

[11]Even a child is known by his actions,
by whether his conduct is pure[d] and
right.

[12]Ears that hear and eyes that see —
the LORD has made them both.[e]

[13]Do not love sleep or you will grow
poor;[f]
stay awake and you will have food
to spare.

[14]"It's no good, it's no good!" says the
buyer;
then off he goes and boasts about
his purchase.

[15]Gold there is, and rubies in abundance,
but lips that speak knowledge are a
rare jewel.

[16]Take the garment of one who puts up
security for a stranger;
hold it in pledge[g] if he does it for a
wayward woman.[h]

[17]Food gained by fraud tastes sweet to a
man,[i]
but he ends up with a mouth full of
gravel.[j]

[18]Make plans by seeking advice;
if you wage war, obtain guidance.[k]

[19]A gossip betrays a confidence;[l]
so avoid a man who talks too
much.

[20]If a man curses his father or mother,[m]
his lamp will be snuffed out in pitch
darkness.[n]

[21]An inheritance quickly gained at the
beginning
will not be blessed at the end.

[22]Do not say, "I'll pay you back for this
wrong!"[o]
Wait for the LORD, and he will
deliver you.[p]

[23]The LORD detests differing weights,
and dishonest scales do not please
him.[q]

[24]A man's steps are directed[r] by the
LORD.[s]
How then can anyone understand
his own way?[t]

[25]It is a trap for a man to dedicate
something rashly
and only later to consider his vows.[u]

[26]A wise king winnows out the wicked;
he drives the threshing wheel over
them.[v]

[27]The lamp of the LORD[w] searches the
spirit of a man[a];
it searches out his inmost being.[x]

20:7 [w] S Ps 26:1 [x] Ps 37:25-26; 112:2 **20:8** [y] S 1Ki 7:7 [z] ver 26; Pr 25:4-5 **20:9** [a] S Job 15:14 [b] 1Ki 8:46; Ecc 7:20; 1Jn 1:8 **20:10** [c] ver 23; S Pr 11:1 **20:11** [d] S Ps 39:1 **20:12** [e] S Ps 94:9 **20:13** [f] S Pr 6:11; S 19:15 **20:16** [g] S Ex 22:26 [h] Pr 27:13 **20:17** [i] Pr 9:17 [j] Job 20:14; La 3:16 **20:18** [k] Pr 11:14; 24:6 **20:19** [l] Pr 11:13 **20:20** [m] Pr 30:11 [n] Ex 21:17; S Job 18:5 **20:22** [o] Pr 24:29 [p] Isa 37:20; Jer 1:19; 42:11; Ro 12:19 **20:23** [q] S ver 10; S Dt 25:13 **20:24** [r] S Ps 90:12 [s] S Job 33:29 [t] S Pr 19:21; Jer 10:23 **20:25** [u] S Pr 10:19; 18:13; Ecc 5:2,4-5; Jer 44:25 **20:26** [v] S ver 8 **20:27** [w] S Ps 119:105 [x] S Pr 16:2

[a] 27 Or *The spirit of man is the LORD's lamp*

20:7 *blameless life.* See note on 2:7. *blessed are his children.* See 13:22; see also note on 14:26.
20:8 See v. 26 and note. *winnows out all evil.* See 16:10; Ps 11:4.
20:9 *pure ... clean ... without sin.* No one is without sin (cf. Job 14:4; Ro 3:23) — but those whose sins have been forgiven have "clean hands and a pure heart" (Ps 24:4; see also 51:1 – 2,9 – 10).
20:10 See note on 11:1; cf. 16:11.
20:12 See Ex 4:11; Ps 94:8 – 9.
20:13 *sleep ... grow poor.* See 24:33 – 34.
20:14 *It's no good, it's no good!* Prices were often agreed upon by bargaining, so the buyer is questioning the quality of the article in order to buy it more cheaply.
20:15 *Gold ... rubies.* Wisdom is valued more highly than gold or rubies (3:14 – 15; 8:10 – 11).
20:16 Repeated in 27:13. See note on 6:1. *Take the garment.* A garment could be taken as security for a debt (Dt 24:10 – 13). Anyone who foolishly assumes responsibility for the debt of a stranger, whose reliability is unknown, or of a wayward woman, whose unreliability is known, ought to be held accountable, even to the degree of taking his garment as a pledge.
20:17 *tastes sweet to a man.* Cf. the sweet "food" prepared by the adulteress in 9:17. Zophar observes that evil is sweet in the mouth of the wicked, but it turns sour in their stomachs (Job 20:12 – 18). See note on 10:2.
20:18 *advice ... guidance.* See 15:22; Lk 14:31.
20:20 *curses his father or mother.* Punishable by death (see Ex 21:17 and note; Lev 20:9; cf. Pr 30:11,17). *his lamp ... snuffed out.* He will die (see note on 13:9).
20:21 *inheritance quickly gained ... will not be blessed.* Cf. 19:26; see the sad experience of the son who "squandered his wealth in wild living" (see Lk 15:12 – 13 and notes).
20:22 *I'll pay you back.* Vengeance was God's prerogative. He would repay the wicked for their actions (see 24:12,29; Dt 32:35; Ps 94:1 and notes). *Wait for the LORD.* See Ps 27:14 and note; 37:34.
20:23 See v. 10 and note.
20:24 See notes on 3:5 – 6; 16:9.
20:25 *dedicate something.* Promise to make a special gift to the Lord if he answers an earnest request (see Lev 27:1 – 25; 1Sa 1:11). *rashly.* See Dt 23:21; Jdg 11:30 – 31,34 – 35 and note on 11:30. When a vow was made hastily it was sometimes not carried out (cf. Ecc 5:4 – 6).
20:26 See v. 8. *winnows.* See note on Ru 1:22. *threshing wheel.* The wheel of the threshing cart that separated the grain from the husk (cf. Isa 28:27 – 28). The wicked will be separated from the righteous and duly punished.
20:27 *lamp of the LORD.* Perhaps his eyes (cf. 5:21; 15:3; 21:4 and note) or word (see 6:23 and note; cf. Heb 4:12 – 13 and notes). *searches the spirit ... his inmost being.* See note on 15:11.

[28]Love and faithfulness keep a king safe;
through love[y] his throne is made secure.[z]

[29]The glory of young men is their strength,
gray hair the splendor of the old.[a]

[30]Blows and wounds cleanse[b] away evil,
and beatings[c] purge the inmost being.

21

The king's heart is in the hand of the LORD;
he directs it like a watercourse wherever he pleases.[d]

[2]All a man's ways seem right to him,
but the LORD weighs the heart.[e]

[3]To do what is right and just
is more acceptable to the LORD than sacrifice.[f]

[4]Haughty eyes[g] and a proud heart,
the lamp of the wicked, are sin!

[5]The plans of the diligent lead to profit[h]
as surely as haste leads to poverty.

[6]A fortune made by a lying tongue
is a fleeting vapor and a deadly snare.[a][i]

[7]The violence of the wicked will drag them away,[j]
for they refuse to do what is right.

[8]The way of the guilty is devious,[k]
but the conduct of the innocent is upright.

[9]Better to live on a corner of the roof
than share a house with a quarrelsome wife.[l]

[10]The wicked man craves evil;
his neighbor gets no mercy from him.

[11]When a mocker is punished, the simple gain wisdom;
when a wise man is instructed, he gets knowledge.[m]

[12]The Righteous One[b] takes note of the house of the wicked
and brings the wicked to ruin.[n]

[13]If a man shuts his ears to the cry of the poor,
he too will cry out[o] and not be answered.[p]

[14]A gift given in secret soothes anger,
and a bribe concealed in the cloak pacifies great wrath.[q]

[15]When justice is done, it brings joy to the righteous
but terror to evildoers.[r]

[16]A man who strays from the path of understanding
comes to rest in the company of the dead.[s]

[17]He who loves pleasure will become poor;
whoever loves wine and oil will never be rich.[t]

20:28 [y]Ps 40:11 [z]S Pr 16:12; Isa 16:5 **20:29** [a]Pr 16:31 **20:30** [b]S Ps 51:2; Pr 22:15 [c]Isa 1:5 **21:1** [d]Est 5:1; Jer 39:11-12 **21:2** [e]S Pr 16:2 **21:3** [f]S 1Sa 15:22; Isa 1:11; Mic 6:6-8 **21:4** [g]S Job 41:34 **21:5** [h]S Pr 10:4 **21:6** [i]S Pr 10:2 **21:7** [j]S Pr 11:5 **21:8** [k]S Pr 2:15 **21:9** [l]ver 19; Pr 19:13; 25:24 **21:11** [m]S Pr 19:25 **21:12** [n]S Pr 14:11 **21:13** [o]S Ex 11:6 [p]S Job 29:12 **21:14** [q]S Ge 32:20 **21:15** [r]S Pr 10:29 **21:16** [s]Eze 18:24 **21:17** [t]Pr 23:20-21, 29-35

[a] 6 Some Hebrew manuscripts, Septuagint and Vulgate; most Hebrew manuscripts *vapor for those who seek death* [b] 12 Or *The righteous man*

20:28 *Love and faithfulness.* See 3:3; 14:22; Ps 26:3 and note. *keep a king safe ... secure.* Benevolence and kindness endear a king to his people and encourage them to be loyal subjects (cf. 16:12 and note).

20:29 *their strength.* Cf. Jer 9:23. *gray hair the splendor of the old.* See 16:31 and note.

20:30 *Blows and wounds cleanse away evil.* Stern punishment is necessary to restrain evil. Proverbs often refers to fools whose backs are beaten (10:13; 14:3; 19:29; 26:3), but even then, because they are fools, they may not change their ways (cf. 17:10; see 27:22 and note).

21:1 *king's heart is in the hand of the LORD.* God controls the lives and actions even of kings, such as Nebuchadnezzar (Da 4:31–32,35) and Cyrus (Isa 45:1–7; cf. Ezr 6:22). *directs it ... wherever he pleases.* See 16:1,4,9 and notes.

21:2 *seem right.* See 14:12; 16:2. *weighs the heart.* See 16:2; 24:12; Job 31:6 and notes. Ancient Egyptian paintings depict a deity weighing a human heart on scales to determine whether the weight of its sins is heavier than a feather.

21:3 *what is right and just.* See note on Ps 119:121. *more acceptable ... than sacrifice.* A theme also found in the prophets (see Isa 1:11–15 and note). See v. 27; see also note on 15:8.

21:4 *Haughty eyes.* See note on 6:17. *proud heart.* See 16:5,18. *lamp.* Eyes (see 20:27 and note; Lk 11:34).

21:5 *plans of the diligent lead to profit.* See note on 10:4. *haste.* Either rash actions (see 19:2 and note) or a desire to get rich quick (see 13:11 and note; 20:21; 28:20).

21:6 *fortune made by a lying tongue.* See note on 10:2; cf. 19:1. *fleeting vapor.* See 13:11; Ecc 1:14 and notes. *deadly snare.* Cf. 5:22; 7:23.

21:7 *violence of the wicked will drag them away.* See 1:18–19 and notes.

21:9 Repeated in 25:24. *corner of the roof.* Roofs were flat, and small rooms could be built there (see 2Ki 4:10). *quarrelsome wife.* See 19:13 and note.

21:10 *craves evil.* See 4:16; 10:23. *his neighbor gets no mercy.* Cf. 14:21.

21:11 See 19:25 and note.

21:12 Cf. Job 34:17. *house of the wicked ... to ruin.* See 10:25 and note; 14:11.

21:13 *cry of the poor.* See note on 14:21; see also 28:27. *he too will cry out and not be answered.* See note on 1:28. Cf. the fate of the rich man (Lk 16:19–31) and the unmerciful servant (Mt 18:23–35). Contrast Ps 118:5 (see note there).

21:14 *gift ... bribe.* See note on 17:8; see also 18:16; 19:6. *soothes anger ... wrath.* Perhaps that of an offended party (see 6:34–35).

21:15 *joy to the righteous.* See 11:10 and note. *terror to evildoers.* See 10:29 and note; Ro 13:3.

21:16 Graphically illustrated by the man who succumbs to the adulteress (see 2:18 and note; 5:23; 7:22–23; 9:18).

21:17 *wine and oil.* Both were associated with lavish feasting (see 23:20–21; Am 6:6). Olive oil was used in various lotions or perfumes, some of which were very expensive (Jn 12:5).

[18]The wicked become a ransom[u] for the righteous,
and the unfaithful for the upright.

[19]Better to live in a desert
than with a quarrelsome and ill-tempered wife.[v]

[20]In the house of the wise are stores of choice food and oil,
but a foolish man devours all he has.

[21]He who pursues righteousness and love
finds life, prosperity[a][w] and honor.[x]

[22]A wise man attacks the city of the mighty[y]
and pulls down the stronghold in which they trust.

[23]He who guards his mouth[z] and his tongue
keeps himself from calamity.[a]

[24]The proud and arrogant[b] man—"Mocker" is his name;
he behaves with overweening pride.

[25]The sluggard's craving will be the death of him,[c]
because his hands refuse to work.

[26]All day long he craves for more,
but the righteous[d] give without sparing.[e]

[27]The sacrifice of the wicked is detestable[f]—
how much more so when brought with evil intent![g]

[28]A false witness[h] will perish,[i]
and whoever listens to him will be destroyed forever.[b]

[29]A wicked man puts up a bold front,
but an upright man gives thought to his ways.[j]

[30]There is no wisdom,[k] no insight, no plan
that can succeed against the LORD.[l]

[31]The horse is made ready for the day of battle,
but victory rests with the LORD.[m]

22

A good name is more desirable than great riches;
to be esteemed is better than silver or gold.[n]

[2]Rich and poor have this in common:
The LORD is the Maker of them all.[o]

[3]A prudent man sees danger and takes refuge,[p]
but the simple keep going and suffer for it.[q]

[4]Humility and the fear of the LORD
bring wealth and honor[r] and life.[s]

[5]In the paths of the wicked lie thorns and snares,[t]
but he who guards his soul stays far from them.

[6]Train[c][u] a child in the way he should go,[v]
and when he is old he will not turn from it.[w]

[7]The rich rule over the poor,
and the borrower is servant to the lender.

21:18 [u]Pr 11:8; Isa 43:3 **21:19** [v]S ver 9 **21:21** [w]Ps 25:13 [x]Mt 5:6 **21:22** [y]S Pr 8:14 **21:23** [z]S Ps 34:13 [a]S Pr 10:19; 12:13; S 13:3 **21:24** [b]Jer 43:2 **21:25** [c]Pr 13:4 **21:26** [d]S 2Sa 17:27 [e]S Lev 25:35 **21:27** [f]S 1Ki 14:24 [g]S Pr 15:8 **21:28** [h]Isa 29:21 [i]S Pr 19:5 **21:29** [j]S Pr 14:8 **21:30** [k]S Job 12:13; S 15:25 [l]S 2Ch 13:12; S Job 5:13; Isa 8:10 **21:31** [m]Ps 33:12-19; Isa 31:1 **22:1** [n]Ecc 7:1 **22:2** [o]S Job 31:15; Pr 29:13; Mt 5:45 **22:3** [p]S Pr 14:16 [q]Pr 27:12 **22:4** [r]S Pr 15:33 [s]S Pr 10:27; Da 4:36 **22:5** [t]Pr 15:19 **22:6** [u]S Ge 14:14 [v]Eph 6:4 [w]S Dt 6:7

[a] 21 Or *righteousness* [b] 28 Or / *but the words of an obedient man will live on* [c] 6 Or *Start*

21:18 *The wicked become a ransom for the righteous.* Close to the thought of 11:8. In Isa 43:3–4 God gave three nations to Persia in exchange for Persia's willingness to release the exiles of Judah (see note on Isa 43:3).
21:19 See 19:13 and note.
21:20 *stores of choice food.* See 3:10 and note; 8:21. *oil.* See note on v. 17; see also Dt 7:13.
21:21 *pursues righteousness.* See 15:9 and note. *finds life.* See 10:2 and note. *life, prosperity and honor.* Benefits for those who seek wisdom (see note on 3:2; see also 3:16; 8:18; cf. 22:4).
21:22 *wise man ... pulls down the stronghold.* Probably another way of saying, "Wisdom is better than strength" (Ecc 9:16). Cf. 24:5; cf. also 2Co 10:4, where spiritual weapons "have divine power to demolish strongholds."
21:23 See 13:3 and note; 18:21.
21:24 *"Mocker" is his name.* See note on 1:22. God mocks and punishes him for his "overweening pride" (cf. v. 11; 3:34; 19:25,29).
21:25 *sluggard's craving.* See notes on 6:6; 13:4.
21:26 *give without sparing.* The righteous are prosperous, so they can share with those in need (see Ps 37:25–26; 112:9; cf. Eph 4:28).
21:27 *The sacrifice of the wicked is detestable.* See notes on v. 3; 15:8.
21:28 *false witness will perish.* See 19:5,9; see also note on 6:19.
21:29 *bold front.* Cf. the behavior of the adulteress in 7:13.
21:30 *no plan that can succeed against the LORD.* Because he is sovereign and controls people and nations (see v. 1; 16:4,9 and notes; 19:21; 1Co 3:19–20).
21:31 *horse.* God often cautions against trusting in horses and chariots for victory (e.g., Ps 20:7; Hos 1:7; cf. Dt 17:16; Isa 31:1–3). *victory rests with the LORD.* See 1Sa 17:47; Ps 3:8 and notes.
22:1 *good name.* Its value is recognized also in 3:4; 10:7; Ecc 7:1. *better than silver or gold.* Like the possession of wisdom (see 3:14 and note; 16:16).
22:2 *Maker of them all.* See 14:31 and note.
22:3 *prudent man ... takes refuge.* Cf. 14:8. *simple.* See note on 1:4; see also 9:16.
22:4 See 18:12. *Humility and the fear of the LORD.* Associated also in 15:33 (see note on 1:7). *wealth and honor and life.* Benefits for those who seek wisdom (see note on 3:2; see also 3:16; 8:18; cf. 21:21).
22:5 *thorns and snares.* Evil (cf. 15:19). *stays far from them.* By taking the "highway of the upright" (16:17).
22:6 A proverb, not a prophecy or promise (see Introduction: The Nature of a Proverb). *Train.* Or "Dedicate," as in 1Ki 8:63; see also NIV text note; cf. Ge 18:19. Instruction (1:8) and discipline (22:15) are primarily involved. *way he should go.* The right way, the way of wisdom (see 4:11 and note). *old.* Or "grown."
22:7 *The rich.* See note on 10:15. *the borrower is servant to the*

8 He who sows wickedness reaps trouble,[x]
and the rod of his fury will be destroyed.[y]
9 A generous man will himself be blessed,[z]
for he shares his food with the poor.[a]
10 Drive out the mocker, and out goes strife;
quarrels and insults are ended.[b]
11 He who loves a pure heart and whose speech is gracious
will have the king for his friend.[c]
12 The eyes of the LORD keep watch over knowledge,
but he frustrates the words of the unfaithful.
13 The sluggard says, "There is a lion outside!"[d]
or, "I will be murdered in the streets!"
14 The mouth of an adulteress is a deep pit;[e]
he who is under the LORD's wrath will fall into it.[f]
15 Folly is bound up in the heart of a child,
but the rod of discipline will drive it far from him.[g]
16 He who oppresses the poor to increase his wealth
and he who gives gifts to the rich—both come to poverty.

Sayings of the Wise

17 Pay attention[h] and listen to the sayings of the wise;[i]
apply your heart to what I teach,[j]
18 for it is pleasing when you keep them in your heart
and have all of them ready on your lips.
19 So that your trust may be in the LORD,
I teach you today, even you.
20 Have I not written thirty[a] sayings for you,
sayings of counsel and knowledge,
21 teaching you true and reliable words,[k]
so that you can give sound answers to him who sent you?

22 Do not exploit the poor[l] because they are poor
and do not crush the needy in court,[m]
23 for the LORD will take up their case[n]
and will plunder those who plunder them.[o]

24 Do not make friends with a hot-tempered man,
do not associate with one easily angered,
25 or you may learn his ways
and get yourself ensnared.[p]

26 Do not be a man who strikes hands in pledge[q]
or puts up security for debts;

22:8 [x]S Ex 1:20; S Job 4:8; Gal 6:7-8 [y]Hos 8:7 22:9 [z]S Dt 14:29 [a]S Pr 11:25; S 19:17; 28:27 22:10 [b]Pr 26:20 22:11 [c]Pr 16:13; Mt 5:8 22:13 [d]Pr 26:13 22:14 [e]S Pr 5:3-5; 23:27 [f]Ecc 7:26 22:15 [g]S Pr 13:24; S 20:30 22:17 [h]S Pr 1:8 [i]S Pr 1:6; 30:1; 31:1 [j]S Pr 2:2 22:21 [k]Ecc 12:10 22:22 [l]S Lev 25:17; S Job 5:16 [m]S Ex 23:6 22:23 [n]S Job 29:16; Ps 140:12 [o]Est 8:1; S 9:1; Pr 23:10-11 22:25 [p]1Co 15:33 22:26 [q]Pr 6:1-5

[a] 20 Or *not formerly written*; or *not written excellent*

lender. One of the reasons why putting up security for someone else (v. 26) was frowned upon (cf. Ne 5:4–5).

22:8 *sows wickedness reaps trouble.* See 12:21. "A man reaps what he sows" (Gal 6:7; see also Hos 8:7 and note). *rod of his fury.* His ability to oppress others (see Ps 125:3 and note; Isa 14:5–6).

22:9 *generous man will … be blessed.* See note on 11:25. *shares his food.* See 14:21 and note; see also Dt 15:7–11.

22:10 *Drive out the mocker.* See note on 1:22; cf. Ge 21:9–10. *out goes strife … insults.* Cf. 17:14; 18:3; 20:3.

22:11 *pure heart.* Cf. Ps 24:4. *whose speech is gracious.* Characteristic of the wise in Ecc 10:12. *king for his friend.* Cf. v. 29.

22:12 *The eyes of the LORD keep watch.* See 5:21; 15:3; Job 31:4; 34:21; Ps 121:3–8; Jer 16:17; Heb 4:13. *over knowledge.* Reference may be to knowledge of the truth about God and his world, but others understand the reference to be to God's knowledge (as in Ps 1:6; 34:15). *frustrates … the unfaithful.* Overrules their plans and desires (see 16:9; 21:30 and notes).

22:13 The sluggard (see note on 6:6) creates excuses to avoid work (see 26:13).

22:14 *mouth of an adulteress.* Her seductive words (see note on 5:3; see also 2:16; 7:5). *deep pit.* Perhaps a well or a hunter's trap (see 5:22 and note; 7:22; 23:27).

22:15 *rod of discipline.* See note on 13:24.

22:16 *oppresses the poor.* Condemned also in 14:31; 28:3. *gives gifts to the rich.* Perhaps bribes (see 17:8 and note; 18:16; 19:6). *poverty.* See 21:5; 28:22 and note.

22:17—24:22 A new section that returns more to the style of chs. 1–9. For its relationship to the Egyptian "Wisdom of Amenemope" see Introduction: Date. Pr 22:17–21 forms the introduction to this section. It emphasizes the importance of wisdom (v. 17) and "knowledge" (v. 20): "Teach" (vv. 17,19) and "teaching" (v. 21) are derived from the same Hebrew root as "knowledge."

22:17 *Pay attention and listen.* See 4:20; 5:1. *sayings of the wise.* See 24:23; a title, like "proverbs of Solomon" in 10:1. *apply your heart to.* See 23:12 and note; see also 2:2 and note; 24:32. *heart.* See note on Ps 4:7.

22:18 *it is pleasing.* See 2:10; 16:24 and notes.

22:19 *that your trust may be in the LORD.* See note on 3:5.

22:20 *thirty sayings.* There are 30 units (divided into three sections of ten units each) in 22:22—24:22. The separate units are marked off by spaces in the NIV text. Most of the sayings are two or three verses long, but see 23:29–35. The Egyptian "Wisdom of Amenemope" also contains 30 sections.

22:22 *Do not exploit the poor.* See v. 16; 14:31. *do not crush the needy in court.* See Isa 1:17 and note.

22:23 *the LORD will take up their case.* See 23:11 and note; Ps 12:5; 140:12; Isa 3:13–15; Mal 3:5. *will plunder those who plunder them.* See Ex 22:21–27 and note.

22:24 *Do not make friends.* Cf. 12:26. *hot-tempered man.* His characteristics are given in 14:16–17; 15:18; 29:22.

22:25 *may learn his ways.* "Bad company corrupts good character" (1Co 15:33). *ensnared.* See note on 5:22; see also 12:13; 13:14; 29:6.

22:26 See note on 6:1.

27 if you lack the means to pay,
your very bed will be snatched from under you.[r]

28 Do not move an ancient boundary stone[s]
set up by your forefathers.

29 Do you see a man skilled[t] in his work?
He will serve[u] before kings;[v]
he will not serve before obscure men.

23 When you sit to dine with a ruler,
note well what[a] is before you,
2 and put a knife to your throat
if you are given to gluttony.
3 Do not crave his delicacies,[w]
for that food is deceptive.

4 Do not wear yourself out to get rich;
have the wisdom to show restraint.
5 Cast but a glance at riches, and they are gone,[x]
for they will surely sprout wings
and fly off to the sky like an eagle.[y]

6 Do not eat the food of a stingy man,
do not crave his delicacies;[z]
7 for he is the kind of man
who is always thinking about the cost.[b]
"Eat and drink," he says to you,
but his heart is not with you.
8 You will vomit up the little you have eaten
and will have wasted your compliments.

9 Do not speak to a fool,
for he will scorn the wisdom of your words.[a]

10 Do not move an ancient boundary stone[b]
or encroach on the fields of the fatherless,
11 for their Defender[c] is strong;[d]
he will take up their case against you.[e]

12 Apply your heart to instruction[f]
and your ears to words of knowledge.

13 Do not withhold discipline from a child;
if you punish him with the rod, he will not die.
14 Punish him with the rod
and save his soul from death.[c][g]

15 My son, if your heart is wise,
then my heart will be glad;
16 my inmost being will rejoice
when your lips speak what is right.[h]

17 Do not let your heart envy[i] sinners,
but always be zealous for the fear of the LORD.
18 There is surely a future hope for you,
and your hope will not be cut off.[j]

19 Listen, my son,[k] and be wise,
and keep your heart on the right path.
20 Do not join those who drink too much wine[l]
or gorge themselves on meat,

22:27 [r]S Pr 11:15; S 17:18 **22:28** [s]S Dt 19:14 **22:29** [t]S 1Ki 11:28 [u]S Ge 41:46 [v]S Ge 39:4 **23:3** [w]ver 6-8; Ps 141:4 **23:5** [x]S Mt 6:19 [y]Pr 27:24 **23:6** [z]ver 1-3; Ps 141:4 **23:9** [a]S Pr 9:7 **23:10** [b]S Dt 19:14 **23:11** [c]S Job 19:25 [d]Ps 24:8 [e]Ex 22:22-24; Pr 15:25; 22:22-23 **23:12** [f]S Pr 2:2 **23:14** [g]S Pr 13:24; S 19:18 **23:16** [h]ver 24; Pr 27:11; 29:3 **23:17** [i]S Ps 37:1; S 73:3 **23:18** [j]S Ps 9:18; 37:1-4; Pr 24:14, 19-20 **23:19** [k]Dt 4:9; Pr 28:7 **23:20** [l]Isa 5:11, 22; 56:12; Hab 2:15

[a] 1 Or *who* [b] 7 Or *for as he thinks within himself, / so he is*; or *for as he puts on a feast, / so he is* [c] 14 Hebrew *Sheol*

22:27 *your very bed will be snatched.* You will be reduced to poverty.
22:28 *ancient boundary stone.* See note on 15:25.
22:29 *skilled in his work.* Skilled craftsmen were considered to be "wise" in the area(s) of their expertise (see note on 8:30; see also Ex 35:30—36:2). *serve before kings.* Like Joseph, an administrator (Ge 41:46); David, a musician (1Sa 16:21–23); and Huram, a worker in bronze (1Ki 7:13–14).
23:2 *gluttony.* Cf. the similar warning in vv. 20–21.
23:3 *Do not crave his delicacies.* Repeated in a different context in v. 6. *deceptive.* Perhaps the meaning is that the ruler wants to obligate you in some way, even to influence you to support a wicked scheme (cf. Ps 141:4).
23:4 *Do not wear yourself out to get rich.* The desire to get rich can ruin a person physically and spiritually. "For the love of money is a root of all kinds of evil" (1Ti 6:10; cf. 15:27; 28:20; Heb 13:5).
23:5 *riches ... are gone.* One must trust in God, not in riches (see Jer 17:11; Lk 12:20–21; 1Ti 6:17).
23:6 *stingy man.* One "eager to get rich" (28:22).
23:7 See NIV text note. *his heart is not with you.* Cf. 26:24–25. *heart.* See vv. 12,15,17,19,26; Ps 4:7 and note.
23:8 *vomit.* The greedy host's attitude will sicken you and cause you to want to eat your complimentary words.
23:9 *scorn the wisdom of your words.* Fools "despise wisdom" (1:7) and hate knowledge and correction (1:22; 12:1). They heap abuse on one who rebukes them (9:7).
23:10 *ancient boundary stone.* See note on 15:25; see also 22:28. *fatherless.* Oppressing the widow and the fatherless—the powerless—is strongly denounced (see Isa 10:2; Jer 22:3; Zec 7:10 and note).
23:11 *Defender.* Kinsman-Redeemer, someone who helped close relatives regain land (see Lev 25:25 and note) or who avenged their death (Nu 35:12,19). God is a "father to the fatherless, a defender of widows" (Ps 68:5). See notes on Ru 2:20; Jer 31:11; see also Jer 50:34. *will take up their case.* See Ps 12:5; 140:12; Isa 3:13–15; Mal 3:5.
23:12 *Apply your heart to.* An echo of 22:17, signaling the beginning of the second of the three main sections that comprise "the sayings of the wise" (see note on 22:20).
23:13–14 See 13:24 and note.
23:15 See 10:1 and note; see also v. 24; 27:11; 29:3. *My son.* See 1:8 and note.
23:16 *what is right.* The Hebrew word for this phrase is translated "smoothly" in v. 31. The same lips can be blessed by producing "right" speech or cursed by savoring wine that goes down "smoothly."
23:17 *Do not ... envy sinners.* See 3:31; 24:1,19. *fear of the LORD.* See notes on 1:7; 3:7.
23:18 *future hope.* See 24:14,20; Ps 37:37; Jer 29:11; cf. Ps 17:15; 49:15; 73:24 and notes.
23:19 *right path.* Cf. 4:25–26.
23:20 *Do not join.* See 1:15; 12:26 and note. *those who drink too much wine.* Drunkenness is also condemned

[21]for drunkards and gluttons become
poor,[m]
and drowsiness clothes them in rags.
[22]Listen to your father, who gave you
life,
and do not despise your mother
when she is old.[n]
[23]Buy the truth and do not sell it;
get wisdom, discipline and
understanding.[o]
[24]The father of a righteous man has great
joy;
he who has a wise son delights in
him.[p]
[25]May your father and mother be glad;
may she who gave you birth
rejoice![q]

[26]My son,[r] give me your heart
and let your eyes keep to my ways,[s]
[27]for a prostitute is a deep pit[t]
and a wayward wife is a narrow
well.
[28]Like a bandit she lies in wait,[u]
and multiplies the unfaithful among
men.

[29]Who has woe? Who has sorrow?
Who has strife? Who has
complaints?
Who has needless bruises? Who has
bloodshot eyes?
[30]Those who linger over wine,[v]
who go to sample bowls of mixed
wine.
[31]Do not gaze at wine when it is red,
when it sparkles in the cup,
when it goes down smoothly!
[32]In the end it bites like a snake
and poisons like a viper.
[33]Your eyes will see strange sights
and your mind imagine confusing
things.
[34]You will be like one sleeping on the
high seas,
lying on top of the rigging.
[35]"They hit me," you will say, "but I'm
not hurt!
They beat me, but I don't feel it!
When will I wake up
so I can find another drink?"[w]

24 Do not envy[x] wicked men,
do not desire their company;
[2]for their hearts plot violence,[y]
and their lips talk about making
trouble.[z]

[3]By wisdom a house is built,[a]
and through understanding it is
established;
[4]through knowledge its rooms are
filled
with rare and beautiful treasures.[b]

[5]A wise man has great power,
and a man of knowledge increases
strength;
[6]for waging war you need guidance,
and for victory many advisers.[c]

[7]Wisdom is too high for a fool;
in the assembly at the gate he has
nothing to say.

[8]He who plots evil
will be known as a schemer.
[9]The schemes of folly are sin,
and men detest a mocker.

[10]If you falter in times of trouble,
how small is your strength![d]

23:21 [m]S Pr 21:17 **23:22** [n]S Lev 19:32 **23:23** [o]Pr 4:7; 17:16 **23:24** [p]S ver 15-16 **23:25** [q]S Pr 10:1 **23:26** [r]Pr 5:1-6 [s]S Ps 18:21 **23:27** [t]S Pr 22:14 **23:28** [u]Pr 7:11-12 **23:30** [v]ver 20-21; Isa 5:11 **23:35** [w]Pr 20:1 **24:1** [x]Pr 3:31-32; 23:17-18 **24:2** [y]S Ps 2:1; Isa 32:6; 55:7-8; 59:7; 65:2; 66:18; Hos 4:1 [z]Ps 10:7 **24:3** [a]S Pr 14:1 **24:4** [b]S Pr 8:21 **24:6** [c]S Pr 11:14; S 20:18; Lk 14:31 **24:10** [d]S Job 4:5

in vv. 29–35; 20:1 (see note there); cf. Dt 21:20; Mt 24:49; Lk 21:34; Ro 13:13; Eph 5:18; 1Ti 3:3.
23:21 *gluttons.* See v. 2; 28:7; cf. Mt 11:19. *become poor.* See 21:17. *drowsiness.* Cf. the poverty that overtakes the sluggard in 6:9–11 (see notes there).
23:22 *do not despise your mother.* Cf. 1:8; 10:1; 15:20; 30:17.
23:23 *Buy the truth … get wisdom … understanding.* See 4:5; see also 4:7 and note.
23:24–25 See v. 15; 27:11; see also 10:1 and note.
23:27 *deep pit … narrow well.* From which it is difficult to escape. The same metaphors are used of women in general in the Akkadian "Pessimistic Dialogue" (see chart, p. xxiii). *deep pit.* See note on 22:14. *wayward wife.* See note on 2:16; see also 5:20; 7:18–20.
23:28 *lies in wait.* See 6:26; 7:12; Ecc 7:26. *multiplies the unfaithful.* Cf. 7:26.
23:29–35 A vivid description of the physical and psychological effects of drunkenness.
23:29 *Who has woe?* Cf. the woes pronounced on drunkards in Isa 5:11,22. *strife.* See 20:1 and note. *bruises.* Cf. the "beatings for the backs of fools" in 19:29.
23:30 *linger over wine.* See 1Sa 25:36. *mixed wine.* Wine mixed with spices (see 9:2; Ps 75:8; Isa 5:22 and notes).
23:32 *bites like a snake.* Death will be the result (cf. Nu 21:6).
23:33 *see strange sights … imagine confusing things.* Perhaps a reference to the delirium that afflicts the alcoholic.
23:34 *You will be like one sleeping on the high seas.* Your head will be spinning.
23:35 *They beat me, but I don't feel it!* Cf. the condition of Israel in Jer 5:3. *so I can find another drink.* Pain and misery do not prevent drunkards from repeating their folly (cf. 26:11; 27:22; Isa 56:12; Am 4:1).
24:1 *Do not envy.* See v. 19; Ps 37:1. *do not desire their company.* See 1:15; 12:26 and note; 23:20.
24:2 *plot violence.* See 1:11; 6:14; Job 15:35; Ps 5:9 and notes; 38:12.
24:3 *house.* Symbolic of the life of an individual or a family. *is built.* Cf. the similar expression in 9:1.
24:4 *rare and beautiful treasures.* Wisdom promises to bestow wealth on those who love her (8:21).
24:5 *wise … knowledge.* An echo of 22:17–21, signaling the beginning of the third of the three main sections that comprise "the sayings of the wise" (see note on 22:20). *has great power.* See note on 21:22.
24:7 *gate.* See note on 1:21.
24:8 *plots evil.* See v. 2 and note. *schemer.* Cf. the "crafty man" in 12:2; 14:17.
24:9 *schemes of folly are sin.* Cf. 1:10–19; 9:13–18. *men detest a mocker.* Because he is proud, insulting (9:7) and quarrelsome (22:10). See note on 1:22.
24:10 Cf. Jer 12:5; Gal 6:9.

[11]Rescue those being led away to death;
hold back those staggering toward
slaughter.[e]
[12]If you say, "But we knew nothing
about this,"
does not he who weighs[f g] the heart
perceive it?
Does not he who guards your life
know it?
Will he not repay[h] each person
according to what he has done?[i]

[13]Eat honey, my son, for it is good;
honey from the comb is sweet to
your taste.
[14]Know also that wisdom is sweet to
your soul;
if you find it, there is a future hope
for you,
and your hope will not be cut off.[j k]

[15]Do not lie in wait like an outlaw
against a righteous man's
house,
do not raid his dwelling place;
[16]for though a righteous man falls seven
times, he rises again,
but the wicked are brought down by
calamity.[l]
[17]Do not gloat[m] when your enemy falls;
when he stumbles, do not let your
heart rejoice,[n]
[18]or the LORD will see and disapprove
and turn his wrath away from him.[o]

[19]Do not fret[p] because of evil men
or be envious of the wicked,
[20]for the evil man has no future hope,
and the lamp of the wicked will be
snuffed out.[q]

[21]Fear the LORD and the king,[r] my son,
and do not join with the rebellious,
[22]for those two will send sudden
destruction[s] upon them,
and who knows what calamities
they can bring?

Further Sayings of the Wise

[23]These also are sayings of the wise:[t]

To show partiality[u] in judging is not
good:[v]
[24]Whoever says to the guilty, "You are
innocent"[w]—
peoples will curse him and nations
denounce him.
[25]But it will go well with those who
convict the guilty,
and rich blessing will come upon
them.

[26]An honest answer
is like a kiss on the lips.

[27]Finish your outdoor work
and get your fields ready;
after that, build your house.

[28]Do not testify against your neighbor
without cause,[x]
or use your lips to deceive.
[29]Do not say, "I'll do to him as he has
done to me;
I'll pay that man back for what he
did."[y]

[30]I went past the field of the sluggard,[z]
past the vineyard of the man who
lacks judgment;
[31]thorns had come up everywhere,
the ground was covered with weeds,
and the stone wall was in ruins.
[32]I applied my heart to what I observed
and learned a lesson from what I
saw:

24:11 [e]Ps 82:4 **24:12** [f]S Ps 139:2 [g]S 1Sa 2:3 [h]S Ps 54:5 [i]Job 34:11; Ps 62:12; S Mt 16:27; Ro 2:6* **24:14** [j]Ps 119:103; Pr 16:24 [k]Pr 23:18 **24:16** [l]S Job 5:19; S Ps 34:21 **24:17** [m]Ob 1:12 [n]S 2Sa 3:32; Mic 7:8 **24:18** [o]S Job 31:29 **24:19** [p]Ps 37:1 **24:20** [q]S Job 18:5; S Pr 23:17-18 **24:21** [r]Ro 13:1-5 **24:22** [s]S Ps 73:19 **24:23** [t]S Pr 1:6 [u]S Ex 18:16; S Lev 19:15 [v]Ps 72:2; Pr 28:21; 31:8-9; Jer 22:16 **24:24** [w]S Pr 17:15 **24:28** [x]S Ps 7:4 **24:29** [y]Pr 20:22; Mt 5:38-41 **24:30** [z]Pr 6:6-11; 26:13-16

24:11 *those being led away to death.* Perhaps the innocent condemned to die (cf. 17:15; Isa 58:6–7).

24:12 *we knew nothing about this.* See Jas 4:17. *does not he who weighs the heart perceive it?* God knows even our thoughts and motives (see 16:2; 21:2 and note; Ps 94:9–11). *repay each person.* See v. 29; 20:22; Ps 5:10 and notes.

24:14 *wisdom is sweet to your soul.* It nourishes and brings healing (see 16:24 and note). *future hope.* See 23:18 and note; contrast 24:20.

24:15 *lie in wait.* See 1:11 and note; 12:6; Ps 10:9–10.

24:16 *seven times.* Many times (see 6:16; Job 5:19 and note; cf. Pr 26:16). *rises again.* The righteous may live in the hope that God will deliver and uphold them (cf. Ps 34:19; 37:24). *wicked are brought down.* See v. 22; 4:19; 6:15 and note; 11:3,5.

24:17 *Do not gloat.* See 17:5 and note.

24:19 Almost identical to Ps 37:1; see v. 1; 3:31; 23:17.

24:20 *no future hope.* For himself or his posterity (contrast v. 14; 23:18; see Ps 37:2,28,38). *lamp … will be snuffed out.* See note on 13:9.

24:21 *Fear the LORD and the king.* Submission to civil authority is also commanded in Ecc 8:2–5. 1Pe 2:17 says, "fear God, honor the king," and Ro 13:1–7 urges the same obedience (see notes there). These passages all view the king as a terror to the wicked (cf. 20:8,26).

24:22 *those two.* God and the king. *sudden destruction … calamities.* God's judgment is more common (see 6:15; 11:3,5), but the power of the king is seen in 20:8,26.

24:23–34 An appendix to 22:17—24:22, giving five additional sayings of the wise.

24:23 *partiality in judging is not good.* See 18:5 and note.

24:24 *You are innocent.* See 17:15 and note. *peoples will curse him.* Just as they "curse the man who hoards grain" (11:26).

24:25 *rich blessing.* See 10:6 and note; Dt 16:20.

24:26 *honest answer.* Cf. 16:13. *like a kiss.* Cf. the "pleasant words" that are "sweet to the soul" in 16:24.

24:27 *get your fields ready.* Plan carefully and acquire the means as you build your house. *build your house.* See v. 3 and note.

24:28 *testify … without cause.* See 3:30; Job 2:3. *use your lips to deceive.* See 6:19 and note; 12:17; 25:18.

24:29 *I'll pay that man back.* See v. 12. A spirit of revenge is also warned against in 20:22 (see note there); cf. 25:21–22; Mt 5:43–45; Ro 12:17.

24:30 *sluggard.* See note on 6:6.

24:31 *thorns … weeds.* See 15:19 and note; cf. Isa 34:13.

24:32 *I applied my heart to.* See 22:17; 23:12 and note; Ps 4:7 and note.

[33]A little slumber, a little slumber,
a little folding of the hands to rest[a]—
[34]and poverty will come on you like a bandit
and scarcity like an armed man. *[a][b]*

More Proverbs of Solomon

25 These are more proverbs[c] of Solomon, copied by the men of Hezekiah king of Judah:[d]

[2]It is the glory of God to conceal a matter;
to search out a matter is the glory of kings.[e]
[3]As the heavens are high and the earth is deep,
so the hearts of kings are unsearchable.
[4]Remove the dross from the silver,
and out comes material for *[b]* the silversmith;
[5]remove the wicked from the king's presence,[f]
and his throne will be established[g] through righteousness.[h]
[6]Do not exalt yourself in the king's presence,
and do not claim a place among great men;
[7]it is better for him to say to you, "Come up here,"[i]
than for him to humiliate you before a nobleman.

What you have seen with your eyes
[8] do not bring *[c]* hastily to court,
for what will you do in the end
if your neighbor puts you to shame?[j]
[9]If you argue your case with a neighbor,
do not betray another man's confidence,
[10]or he who hears it may shame you
and you will never lose your bad reputation.
[11]A word aptly spoken
is like apples of gold in settings of silver.[k]
[12]Like an earring of gold or an ornament of fine gold
is a wise man's rebuke to a listening ear.[l]
[13]Like the coolness of snow at harvest time
is a trustworthy messenger to those who send him;
he refreshes the spirit of his masters.[m]
[14]Like clouds and wind without rain
is a man who boasts of gifts he does not give.
[15]Through patience a ruler can be persuaded,[n]
and a gentle tongue can break a bone.[o]

24:33 [a]S Pr 6:10 24:34 [b]S Pr 10:4; Ecc 10:18 25:1 [c]S 1Ki 4:32 [d]S Pr 1:1 25:2 [e]Pr 16:10-15 25:5 [f]S Pr 20:8 [g]S 2Sa 7:13 [h]S Pr 16:12; 29:14 25:7 [i]Lk 14:7-10 25:8 [j]Mt 5:25-26 25:11 [k]ver 12; Pr 15:23 25:12 [l]S ver 11; Ps 141:5; S Pr 13:18 25:13 [m]S Pr 10:26; 13:17 25:15 [n]Ecc 10:4 [o]Pr 15:1

[a] 34 Or *like a vagrant / and scarcity like a beggar*
[b] 4 Or *comes a vessel from*
[c] 7,8 Or *nobleman / on whom you had set your eyes. / [8]Do not go*

24:33–34 See 6:10–11 and note on 6:11.
25:1—29:27 Another collection of Solomon's proverbs similar to 10:1—22:16. It is widely agreed that this "collection" is actually made up of two distinguishable collections: 25:2—27:27 and 28:1—29:27.
25:1 *proverbs of Solomon.* See notes on 1:1; 10:1. *copied by the men of Hezekiah.* There was a great revival in the reign of Hezekiah (c. 715–686 B.C.), who restored the singing of hymns to its proper place. His interest in "the words of David" (2Ch 29:30) corresponds to his support of this compilation of Solomon's proverbs. Solomon was the last king to rule over all Israel during the united monarchy; Hezekiah was the first king to rule over all Israel (now restricted to the southern kingdom) after the destruction of the divided monarchy's northern kingdom. Nothing more is known about this activity of King Hezekiah's court personnel, but the latest editors of Proverbs make a similar connection between Hezekiah and Solomon as the postexilic author of 1,2 Chronicles (see note on 2Ch 29:1—32:33).
25:2–7 Appropriately enough, kings are the subject of this initial series of proverbs compiled by King Hezekiah's men to honor King Solomon.
25:2 *to conceal a matter.* God gets glory because humans cannot fully understand his universe or the way he rules it (see Dt 29:29; Job 26:14 and note; Isa 40:12–24; Ro 11:33–36). *to search out a matter.* A king gets glory if he can uncover the truth and administer justice (see 1Ki 3:9; 4:34).
25:3 *are unsearchable.* Cannot be understood—like the four things in 30:18–19. Yet God controls the hearts of kings (see note on 21:1).
25:4 *Remove the dross from the silver.* A process compared to the purification of society in general and rulers in particular in Isa 1:22–25; Eze 22:18; Zec 13:8–9; Mal 3:2–3.
25:5 *his throne will be established through righteousness.* See note on 16:12.
25:6 *in the king's presence.* Probably at a feast (cf. 23:1). Jesus spoke about the place of honor at a wedding feast (Lk 14:7–11).
25:7 *Come up here.* Cf. "Friend, move up to a better place" (Lk 14:10); contrast Isa 22:15–19.
25:8 *do not bring hastily to court.* A warning about the seriousness of disputes (see 17:14) and the need to exercise caution (see 24:28). *puts you to shame.* Exposes your claims against him to be without grounds.
25:9 *do not betray another man's confidence.* If you do, you are a gossip (see 11:13; 20:19; cf. Ro 1:29; 2Co 12:20).
25:10 *bad reputation.* A good name is one of life's most valuable possessions (see 22:1 and note).
25:11 *gold ... silver.* Cf. the fruit of wisdom in 8:19.
25:12 *earring of gold.* Comparable to the beautiful wreath and necklace that represent the adornment of wisdom and sound teaching (see 1:9; 3:22; 4:9). *wise man's rebuke.* Cf. the "life-giving rebuke" of 15:31.
25:13 *coolness of snow.* Probably a drink cooled by snow from the Lebanon mountains; it did not snow at harvest time in Israel's heartland. See 26:1; contrast 10:26. *trustworthy messenger.* See 13:17 and note.
25:14 *clouds ... without rain.* An image applied to false teachers in Jude 12 (see note on Jude 12–13).
25:15 *Through patience a ruler can be persuaded.* Cf. 14:29. *gentle tongue.* See note on 15:1.

16 If you find honey, eat just enough—
too much of it, and you will vomit.[p]
17 Seldom set foot in your neighbor's house—
too much of you, and he will hate you.

18 Like a club or a sword or a sharp arrow
is the man who gives false testimony against his neighbor.[q]

19 Like a bad tooth or a lame foot
is reliance on the unfaithful in times of trouble.

20 Like one who takes away a garment on a cold day,
or like vinegar poured on soda,
is one who sings songs to a heavy heart.

21 If your enemy is hungry, give him food to eat;
if he is thirsty, give him water to drink.
22 In doing this, you will heap burning coals[r] on his head,
and the LORD will reward you.[s]

23 As a north wind brings rain,
so a sly tongue brings angry looks.

24 Better to live on a corner of the roof
than share a house with a quarrelsome wife.[t]

25 Like cold water to a weary soul
is good news from a distant land.[u]

26 Like a muddied spring or a polluted well
is a righteous man who gives way to the wicked.

27 It is not good to eat too much honey,[v]
nor is it honorable to seek one's own honor.[w]

28 Like a city whose walls are broken down
is a man who lacks self-control.

26 Like snow in summer or rain[x] in harvest,
honor is not fitting for a fool.[y]

2 Like a fluttering sparrow or a darting swallow,
an undeserved curse does not come to rest.[z]

3 A whip for the horse, a halter for the donkey,[a]
and a rod for the backs of fools![b]

4 Do not answer a fool according to his folly,
or you will be like him yourself.[c]

5 Answer a fool according to his folly,
or he will be wise in his own eyes.[d]

6 Like cutting off one's feet or drinking violence
is the sending of a message by the hand of a fool.[e]

7 Like a lame man's legs that hang limp
is a proverb in the mouth of a fool.[f]

25:16 [p]ver 27 **25:18** [q]S Pr 12:18 **25:22** [r]S Ps 18:8 [s]S 2Ch 28:15; Mt 5:44; Ro 12:20* **25:24** [t]S Pr 21:9 **25:25** [u]Pr 15:30 **25:27** [v]ver 16 [w]Pr 27:2; S Mt 23:12 **26:1** [x]S 1Sa 12:17 [y]ver 8; Pr 19:10 **26:2** [z]S Dt 23:5 **26:3** [a]Ps 32:9 [b]S Pr 10:13 **26:4** [c]ver 5; Isa 36:21 **26:5** [d]ver 4; S Pr 3:7 **26:6** [e]S Pr 10:26 **26:7** [f]ver 9

25:16 *honey.* See v. 27.
25:18 *club … sword … arrow.* Cf. Ps 5:9 and note; Jer 9:8. *false testimony.* See note on 6:19; see also 24:28; Ex 20:16.
25:19 *bad tooth … lame foot.* Relying on Egypt was like leaning on a splintered reed (Isa 36:6).
25:20 *soda.* See Jer 2:22; probably sodium carbonate. A vigorous reaction occurs when vinegar is poured on it. *sings songs to a heavy heart.* The exiles were reluctant to sing the songs of Zion (Ps 137:3–4).
25:21–22 Quoted in Ro 12:20.
25:21 Kindness to one's enemy is encouraged in 20:22; Ex 23:4–5 (see note there). *give him food … water.* At Elisha's request, a trapped Aramean army was given a great feast and then sent home (2Ki 6:21–23; cf. 2Ch 28:15).
25:22 *heap burning coals on his head.* Horrible punishment reserved for the wicked (see Ps 140:10). Here, however, it is kindness that will hurt the enemy (cf. the broken bone of v. 15) but perhaps win him over. Alternatively, the expression may reflect an Egyptian expiation ritual, in which a guilty person, as a sign of his repentance, carried a basin of glowing coals on his head. The meaning here, then, would be that in returning good for evil—and so being kind to your enemy (see Ro 12:20)—you may cause him to repent or change. *the Lord will reward you.* Even if the enemy remains hostile (cf. 11:18; 19:17).
25:23 *north.* Perhaps northwest (cf. Lk 12:54). *sly tongue.* One that spreads slander (cf. 10:18).
25:24 Echoed from 21:9 (see note there).
25:25 *good news from a distant land.* See Ge 45:25–28; cf. Isa 52:7.
25:26 *muddied spring.* Cf. Eze 34:18–19. *righteous man who gives way.* Perhaps through bribery (cf. 17:8; 29:4; Isa 1:21–23).
25:27 *too much honey.* See v. 16. *to seek one's own honor.* See vv. 6–7 and notes.
25:28 *city whose walls are broken down.* Defenseless and disgraced (cf. Ne 1:3 and note). *man who lacks self-control.* See 16:32 and note.
26:1–12 As kings are the subject of the series of proverbs that begin ch. 25 (see note on 25:2–7), so fools are the subject at the beginning of ch. 26.
26:1 *rain in harvest.* It rarely rains in the Holy Land from June through September (cf. 25:13 and note). *honor is not fitting for a fool.* See v. 8.
26:2 *undeserved curse does not come to rest.* When David was cursed by Shimei, he realized that the curse would not take effect because he was innocent of the charge of murdering members of Saul's family (2Sa 16:8,12).
26:3 *rod for the backs of fools.* See 14:3; 19:29.
26:4 *Do not answer a fool according to his folly.* Do not stoop to his level (see 23:9; Mt 7:6 and notes).
26:5 *Answer a fool according to his folly.* Sometimes folly must be plainly exposed and denounced. Thus vv. 4–5 do not contradict each other, as is often thought.
26:6 *drinking violence.* See 4:17 and note; Job 34:7. *sending of a message by the hand of a fool.* He will likely misrepresent the one who sends him, or in some other manner frustrate the sender's purpose (see 13:17 and note).

8 Like tying a stone in a sling
is the giving of honor to a fool.[g]
9 Like a thornbush in a drunkard's hand
is a proverb in the mouth of a fool.[h]
10 Like an archer who wounds at random
is he who hires a fool or any
passer-by.
11 As a dog returns to its vomit,[i]
so a fool repeats his folly.[j]
12 Do you see a man wise in his own
eyes?[k]
There is more hope for a fool than
for him.[l]
13 The sluggard says,[m] "There is a lion in
the road,
a fierce lion roaming the streets!"[n]
14 As a door turns on its hinges,
so a sluggard turns on his bed.[o]
15 The sluggard buries his hand in the
dish;
he is too lazy to bring it back to his
mouth.[p]
16 The sluggard is wiser in his own eyes
than seven men who answer
discreetly.
17 Like one who seizes a dog by the ears
is a passer-by who meddles in a
quarrel not his own.
18 Like a madman shooting
firebrands or deadly arrows
19 is a man who deceives his neighbor
and says, "I was only joking!"
20 Without wood a fire goes out;
without gossip a quarrel dies down.[q]
21 As charcoal to embers and as wood to
fire,
so is a quarrelsome man for kindling
strife.[r]
22 The words of a gossip are like choice
morsels;
they go down to a man's inmost
parts.[s]
23 Like a coating of glaze[a] over
earthenware
are fervent lips with an evil heart.
24 A malicious man disguises himself
with his lips,[t]
but in his heart he harbors deceit.[u]
25 Though his speech is charming,[v] do
not believe him,
for seven abominations fill his
heart.[w]
26 His malice may be concealed by
deception,
but his wickedness will be exposed
in the assembly.
27 If a man digs a pit,[x] he will fall into it;[y]
if a man rolls a stone, it will roll
back on him.[z]
28 A lying tongue hates those it hurts,
and a flattering mouth[a] works ruin.

27 Do not boast[b] about tomorrow,
for you do not know what a day
may bring forth.[c]
2 Let another praise you, and not your
own mouth;
someone else, and not your own
lips.[d]
3 Stone is heavy and sand[e] a burden,
but provocation by a fool is heavier
than both.

26:8 [g]S ver 1 **26:9** [h]ver 7 **26:11** [i]2Pe 2:22* [j]S Ps 85:8 **26:12** [k]S Pr 3:7 [l]Pr 29:20 **26:13** [m]Pr 6:6-11; 24:30-34 [n]Pr 22:13 **26:14** [o]S Pr 6:9 **26:15** [p]Pr 19:24 **26:20** [q]Pr 22:10 **26:21** [r]S Pr 14:17 **26:22** [s]Pr 18:8 **26:24** [t]S Ps 31:18 [u]Ps 41:6 **26:25** [v]Ps 28:3 [w]Jer 9:4-8 **26:27** [x]S Ps 7:15 [y]S Est 6:13 [z]S Est 2:23; S 7:9; Ps 35:8; 141:10; Pr 28:10; 29:6; Isa 50:11 **26:28** [a]S Ps 12:3; Pr 29:5 **27:1** [b]S 1Ki 20:11 [c]Mt 6:34; Jas 4:13-16 **27:2** [d]S Pr 25:27 **27:3** [e]S Job 6:3

[a] *23* With a different word division of the Hebrew; Masoretic Text *of silver dross*

26:8 *Like tying a stone in a sling.* A fool with authority wields a formidable weapon, but it is useless in his hands — as useless as a stone that is tied, not placed loosely, in a sling. *honor to a fool.* See v. 1.
26:9 Fools reciting proverbs will do as much damage to themselves and others as a drunkard wielding a thornbush.
26:10 *he who hires a fool or any passer-by.* Can no more be assured of good service than an archer who shoots without aiming.
26:11 *As a dog returns to its vomit.* Quoted in 2Pe 2:22 with reference to false teachers (see note there). *fool repeats his folly.* Drunkards return to their drinks (see 23:35 and note).
26:12 *wise in his own eyes.* This conceit is applied to the sluggard in v. 16 and the rich in 28:11; cf. 26:5. *There is more hope ... him.* Repeated in 29:20.
26:13 – 16 A series of proverbs that focuses on the sluggard (see notes on 25:2 – 7; 26:1 – 12).
26:13 See 22:13 and note.
26:14 As a door turns on its hinges but goes nowhere, so a sluggard just turns over in bed and does not go to attend to his affairs.
26:15 See 19:24 and note.
26:16 *wiser in his own eyes.* See v. 12 and note. *seven.* Many (see note on 24:16).
26:17 *seizes a dog by the ears.* To do so is to immediately create a disturbance.
26:18 *Like a madman shooting.* Cf. the archer in v. 10. *firebrands.* Could easily ignite sheaves of grain (cf. Zec 12:6).
26:19 *I was only joking!* A lame excuse does not undo the damage done.
26:21 *kindling strife.* See 6:14 and note.
26:22 Identical to 18:8 (see note there).
26:23 *coating of glaze over earthenware.* Cf. the clean outside of the cup and dish (Lk 11:39; cf. Mt 23:27). *fervent lips with an evil heart.* The speech of the adulteress is seductive (see 2:16; 5:3 and notes).
26:24 *in his heart he harbors deceit.* See 12:20.
26:25 *his speech is charming.* See Jer 9:8. *seven.* See note on v. 16. For seven things the Lord detests see 6:16 – 19.
26:26 *exposed in the assembly.* See 5:14; Lk 8:17.
26:27 *If a man digs a pit, he will fall into it.* "The trouble he causes recoils on himself" (Ps 7:16). See 1:18 and note; 28:10; 29:6; Est 7:10; Ps 7:15; Ecc 10:8 – 9; Ob 15 and note.
26:28 *lying tongue hates those it hurts.* See 10:18. *flattering mouth works ruin.* See 29:5; cf. 16:13.
27:1 Cf. the words of the rich fool and God's response in Lk 12:19 – 20; cf. also Pr 16:9; Isa 56:12; Jas 4:13 – 16.
27:2 *Let another praise you.* See 2Co 10:12,18.

4 Anger is cruel and fury overwhelming,
but who can stand before jealousy?[f]
5 Better is open rebuke
than hidden love.
6 Wounds from a friend can be trusted,
but an enemy multiplies kisses.[g]
7 He who is full loathes honey,
but to the hungry even what is bitter
tastes sweet.
8 Like a bird that strays from its nest[h]
is a man who strays from his
home.
9 Perfume[i] and incense bring joy to the
heart,
and the pleasantness of one's
friend springs from his earnest
counsel.
10 Do not forsake your friend and the
friend of your father,
and do not go to your brother's
house when disaster[j] strikes
you —
better a neighbor nearby than a
brother far away.
11 Be wise, my son, and bring joy to my
heart;[k]
then I can answer anyone who treats
me with contempt.[l]
12 The prudent see danger and take
refuge,
but the simple keep going and suffer
for it.[m]
13 Take the garment of one who puts up
security for a stranger;
hold it in pledge if he does it for a
wayward woman.[n]
14 If a man loudly blesses his neighbor
early in the morning,
it will be taken as a curse.
15 A quarrelsome wife is like
a constant dripping[o] on a rainy day;
16 restraining her is like restraining the
wind
or grasping oil with the hand.
17 As iron sharpens iron,
so one man sharpens another.
18 He who tends a fig tree will eat its
fruit,[p]
and he who looks after his master
will be honored.[q]
19 As water reflects a face,
so a man's heart reflects the man.
20 Death and Destruction[a] are never
satisfied,[r]
and neither are the eyes of man.[s]
21 The crucible for silver and the furnace
for gold,[t]
but man is tested by the praise he
receives.
22 Though you grind a fool in a mortar,
grinding him like grain with a pestle,
you will not remove his folly from
him.
23 Be sure you know the condition of
your flocks,[u]
give careful attention to your herds;

27:4 [f] S Nu 5:14
27:6 [g] Ps 141:5; Pr 28:23
27:8 [h] Isa 16:2
27:9 [i] S Est 2:12; S Ps 45:8
27:10 [j] S Pr 17:17
27:11 [k] S Pr 10:1; S 23:15-16 [l] S Ge 24:60
27:12 [m] Pr 22:3
27:13 [n] Pr 20:16
27:15 [o] S Est 1:18
27:18 [p] 1Co 9:7 [q] Lk 19:12-27
27:20 [r] Pr 30:15-16; Hab 2:5 [s] Ecc 1:8; 6:7
27:21 [t] S Pr 17:3
27:23 [u] Pr 12:10

[a] 20 Hebrew *Sheol and Abaddon*

27:4 *who can stand before jealousy?* See 6:34; SS 8:6.
27:5 *open rebuke.* Called "life-giving rebuke" in 15:31; cf. Gal 2:14.
27:6 See 28:23. *Wounds from a friend.* Called a "kindness" in Ps 141:5 (see note there). *enemy multiplies kisses.* See 5:3 and note; Mt 26:49.
27:7 *loathes honey.* Cf. 25:16,27.
27:8 *man who strays from his home.* He has lost his security and may be vulnerable to temptation (cf. 7:21 – 23).
27:9 *Perfume.* See note on 21:17. *incense.* Cf. the one "perfumed with myrrh and incense" (SS 3:6). *bring joy to the heart.* See v. 11. *pleasantness of one's friend.* See 16:21,24 and notes.
27:10 Do not fail a friend in need; when in need rely on friendship rather than on mere family relationships. *brother far away.* Either physically or emotionally.
27:11 *Be wise, my son.* See 10:1 and note. *then I can answer anyone who treats me with contempt.* A wise son (or student) serves as a powerful testimony that the father (or teacher) who has shaped him has shown himself to be a man of worth.
27:12 *the simple.* See note on 1:4. *keep going and suffer for it.* See 7:22 – 23; 9:16 – 18.
27:13 Identical to 20:16 (see note there).
27:14 *blesses his neighbor.* Perhaps to win the neighbor's favor (cf. Ps 12:2).
27:15 See 19:13 and note.
27:17 *sharpens another.* Develops and molds the other's character.
27:18 *will eat its fruit.* Cf. 2Ti 2:6.
27:19 *a man's heart reflects the man.* The condition of one's heart indicates one's true character (see Mt 5:8).
27:20 *Death and Destruction.* See note on Job 26:6; see also Pr 15:11. *are never satisfied.* Their appetite is insatiable (see 30:15 – 16; Isa 5:14; Hab 2:5). *neither are the eyes of man.* See Ecc 4:8.
27:21 *crucible … gold.* See 17:3; Ps 12:6 and note. *man is tested by the praise he receives.* If praise is received from honorable people, the person is shown to be honorable; if from dishonorable people, the person is shown to be of like kind.
27:22 *mortar.* A deep bowl-shaped container, probably made of stone. *pestle.* A club-like tool for pounding grain in a mortar. *you will not remove his folly.* In spite of severe punishment, fools refuse to change (see note on 20:30; see also 26:11; Jer 5:3 and note).
27:23 – 27 A section praising the basic security afforded by agricultural pursuits — reflecting the agricultural base of the ancient economy.
27:23 *give careful attention to your herds.* Like Jacob, with Laban's flocks (Ge 31:38 – 40).

[24]for riches do not endure forever,[v]
and a crown is not secure for all
generations.
[25]When the hay is removed and new
growth appears
and the grass from the hills is
gathered in,
[26]the lambs will provide you with
clothing,
and the goats with the price of a
field.
[27]You will have plenty of goats' milk
to feed you and your family
and to nourish your servant
girls.

28 The wicked man flees[w] though no
one pursues,[x]
but the righteous are as bold as a
lion.[y]

[2]When a country is rebellious, it has
many rulers,
but a man of understanding and
knowledge maintains order.

[3]A ruler[a] who oppresses the poor
is like a driving rain that leaves no
crops.

[4]Those who forsake the law praise the
wicked,
but those who keep the law resist
them.

[5]Evil men do not understand justice,
but those who seek the LORD
understand it fully.

[6]Better a poor man whose walk is
blameless
than a rich man whose ways are
perverse.[z]

[7]He who keeps the law is a discerning
son,
but a companion of gluttons
disgraces his father.[a]

[8]He who increases his wealth by
exorbitant interest[b]
amasses it for another,[c] who will be
kind to the poor.[d]

[9]If anyone turns a deaf ear to the law,
even his prayers are detestable.[e]

[10]He who leads the upright along an evil
path
will fall into his own trap,[f]
but the blameless will receive a good
inheritance.

[11]A rich man may be wise in his own
eyes,
but a poor man who has
discernment sees through him.

[12]When the righteous triumph, there is
great elation;[g]
but when the wicked rise to power,
men go into hiding.[h]

[13]He who conceals his sins[i] does not
prosper,
but whoever confesses[j] and
renounces them finds mercy.[k]

[14]Blessed is the man who always fears
the LORD,
but he who hardens his heart falls
into trouble.

[15]Like a roaring lion or a charging bear
is a wicked man ruling over a
helpless people.

27:24 [v]Pr 23:5 **28:1** [w]S 2Ki 7:7 [x]S Lev 26:17 [y]S Ps 138:3 **28:6** [z]Pr 19:1 **28:7** [a]Pr 23:19-21 **28:8** [b]S Ex 18:21; Eze 18:8 [c]S Job 27:17 [d]S Job 3:15; Ps 112:9; Lk 14:12-14 **28:9** [e]S Ps 109:7; S Pr 15:8; S Isa 1:13 **28:10** [f]S Ps 57:6; S Pr 26:27 **28:12** [g]S 2Ki 11:20 [h]ver 28; Job 24:4; Pr 29:2 **28:13** [i]S 2Sa 12:13; S Job 31:33 [j]S Lev 5:5 [k]Ps 32:1-5; Da 4:27; 1Jn 1:9

[a] 3 Or *A poor man*

27:24 *riches do not endure.* See notes on 23:5; Mt 6:19. *crown is not secure.* Cf. 29:14. Even kings may lose their wealth and power (see Job 19:9; La 5:16).
27:25 *hay is removed.* This began in March or April.
27:26 *price of a field.* See 31:16.
27:27 *goats' milk.* Drunk as commonly as cows' milk (see note on Jdg 4:19; see also Isa 7:21 – 22). *servant girls.* See 31:15.
28:1 *wicked man flees.* See Lev 26:17; Ps 53:5 and notes. *bold as a lion.* See 30:30; 2Sa 17:10; cf. Nu 27:24; Jer 25:38; Mic 5:8.
28:2 *it has many rulers.* Israel's rebellion often brought frequent and rapid change in leadership (see 1Ki 16:8 – 28; 2Ki 15:8 – 14; 23:29 — 24:17). *man of understanding ... maintains order.* A wise ruler will be successful (see 8:15 – 16; 16:12 and note; 24:5; 29:4).
28:3 *who oppresses the poor.* See 14:31 and note. *driving rain.* Describes the destructive power of Assyria's king in Isa 28:2 (see note there; cf. 1Sa 12:17 – 18). In Ps 72:6 a righteous king is compared to a gentle rain.
28:4 *law.* The law of Moses (see Ps 119:53; cf. Ps 1). *praise the wicked.* Cf. Ro 1:32 and note. *who keep the law.* See v. 7; 29:18; cf. v. 9. *resist them.* See Eph 5:7,11.
28:5 *who seek the LORD.* Who fear him (see note on 1:7). *understand it fully.* They know "what is right and just and fair" (2:9).
28:6 *blameless.* See v. 18; 2:7; Ps 15:2 and notes.
28:7 *who keeps the law.* See note on v. 4. *companion of gluttons.* See 23:20 – 21 and notes.
28:8 *exorbitant interest.* Prohibited in Ex 22:25 (see notes on Ex 22:21 – 27; Lev 25:36; Eze 18:8). *amasses it for another.* See 13:22 and note; cf. Lk 12:20. *kind to the poor.* See 14:31 and note.
28:9 *law.* See note on v. 4. *his prayers are detestable.* Like the sacrifice of the wicked in 15:8 (see note there; see 3:32 and note; see also Ps 66:18; Isa 1:15; 59:1 – 2; Jer 11:14).
28:10 *into his own trap.* See note on 26:27. *blameless.* See note on 2:7. *good inheritance.* See 3:35; Ps 37; cf. 1Pe 3:9.
28:11 *rich man may be wise in his own eyes.* Like the fool (26:5) or the sluggard (26:16).
28:12 *there is great elation.* See 11:10 and note. *men go into hiding.* See v. 28; Ps 55:6 – 8 and note.
28:13 *He who conceals his sins does not prosper.* See Ps 32:3 – 5 and note. *whoever confesses and renounces them finds mercy.* Note the joy of forgiveness in Ps 32:5,10 – 11; see 1Jn 1:9 and note.
28:14 *who hardens his heart.* Like the pharaoh (Ex 7:13), and like the Israelites who tested the Lord at Meribah and Massah (see Ps 95:8 and note; Ro 2:5).
28:15 *roaring lion.* Full of rage and murderous intent (cf. 19:12; Jdg 14:5). *charging bear.* See 17:12 and note. *wicked man ruling.* See v. 12; cf. Mt 2:16.

16 A tyrannical ruler lacks judgment,
but he who hates ill-gotten gain will enjoy a long life.

17 A man tormented by the guilt of murder
will be a fugitive[l] till death;
let no one support him.

18 He whose walk is blameless is kept safe,[m]
but he whose ways are perverse will suddenly fall.[n]

19 He who works his land will have abundant food,
but the one who chases fantasies will have his fill of poverty.[o]

20 A faithful man will be richly blessed,
but one eager to get rich will not go unpunished.[p]

21 To show partiality[q] is not good[r]—
yet a man will do wrong for a piece of bread.[s]

22 A stingy man is eager to get rich
and is unaware that poverty awaits him.[t]

23 He who rebukes a man will in the end gain more favor
than he who has a flattering tongue.[u]

24 He who robs his father or mother[v]
and says, "It's not wrong"—
he is partner to him who destroys.[w]

25 A greedy man stirs up dissension,[x]
but he who trusts in the LORD[y] will prosper.

26 He who trusts in himself is a fool,[z]
but he who walks in wisdom is kept safe.[a]

27 He who gives to the poor will lack nothing,[b]
but he who closes his eyes to them receives many curses.[c]

28 When the wicked rise to power, people go into hiding;[d]
but when the wicked perish, the righteous thrive.

29 A man who remains stiff-necked[e] after many rebukes
will suddenly be destroyed[f]—
without remedy.[g]

2 When the righteous thrive, the people rejoice;[h]
when the wicked rule,[i] the people groan.[j]

3 A man who loves wisdom brings joy to his father,[k]
but a companion of prostitutes squanders his wealth.[l]

4 By justice a king gives a country stability,[m]
but one who is greedy for bribes tears it down.

5 Whoever flatters his neighbor
is spreading a net for his feet.[n]

6 An evil man is snared by his own sin,[o]
but a righteous one can sing and be glad.

7 The righteous care about justice for the poor,[p]
but the wicked have no such concern.

8 Mockers stir up a city,
but wise men turn away anger.[q]

28:17 [l]1Sa 30:17; 1Ki 20:20; Jer 41:15; 44:14 **28:18** [m]Jer 39:18 [n]S Est 6:13; Pr 10:9 **28:19** [o]Pr 12:11 **28:20** [p]ver 22 **28:21** [q]S Lev 19:15 [r]S Ps 94:21; S Pr 18:5 [s]Eze 13:19 **28:22** [t]ver 20 **28:23** [u]S Pr 27:5-6 **28:24** [v]Pr 19:26 [w]S Pr 18:9 **28:25** [x]S Pr 14:17 [y]Pr 29:25 **28:26** [z]S Ps 4:5; Pr 3:5 [a]1Co 3:18 **28:27** [b]S Dt 24:19; S Pr 22:9 [c]S Ps 109:17 **28:28** [d]S ver 12; S Job 20:19 **29:1** [e]S Ex 32:9; S Dt 9:27 [f]Jer 19:15; 36:31; Hab 2:7 [g]S 2Ch 36:16; Pr 6:15 **29:2** [h]S 2Ki 11:20 [i]Pr 30:22; Ecc 10:6 [j]S Pr 28:12 **29:3** [k]S Pr 10:1; S 23:15-16 [l]Pr 5:8-10; Lk 15:11-32 **29:4** [m]ver 14; S Pr 8:15-16 **29:5** [n]S Job 32:21; S Pr 26:28 **29:6** [o]S Job 5:13; S Pr 26:27; Ecc 9:12 **29:7** [p]Pr 31:8-9 **29:8** [q]Pr 11:11; S 16:14

28:16 *he who hates ill-gotten gain will enjoy a long life.* Unlike those who love such gain (see 1:19 and note).
28:17 *will be a fugitive till death.* Cain was a "restless wanderer" in fear of his life (Ge 4:14). Murder was punishable by death (see Ge 9:6; Ex 21:14 and note).
28:18 *blameless … perverse.* Contrasted also in v. 6; 19:1. *will suddenly fall.* Cf. 11:5.
28:19 *chases fantasies.* See 12:11 and note.
28:20 *richly blessed.* With God's gifts and favors (see 3:13–18; 10:6; Ge 49:26; Dt 33:16). *one eager to get rich will not go unpunished.* Cf. similar warnings in 20:21; 23:4 (see notes there).
28:21 *To show partiality is not good.* See 18:5 and note; 24:23. *a piece of bread.* Perhaps reference is to a bribe, however small.
28:22 *stingy man.* See 23:6. *eager to get rich.* A warning to him is given in v. 20; cf. similar warnings in 20:21; 23:4 (see note there). *poverty awaits him.* Because it is the generous who prosper (see 11:24–25 and notes).
28:23 *He who rebukes a man.* See 15:31; 25:12; cf. Gal 2:14. *who has a flattering tongue.* See 26:28; 29:5; cf. 16:13.
28:24 *who robs his father or mother.* See note on 19:26; cf. Mt 15:4–6; Mk 7:10–12.
28:25 *stirs up dissension.* See note on 6:14. *will prosper.* As does also the generous person (see note on v. 22) and the one who is diligent (13:4, lit. "the desires of the diligent prosper").
28:26 *who walks in wisdom.* Equals "whoever trusts in the LORD" in 29:25; cf. 3:5–6.
28:27 *gives to the poor.* See note on 14:21. *will lack nothing.* Generosity is the path to blessing (see 11:24; 14:21 and notes; 19:17). *closes his eyes to them.* See 21:13.
28:28 *people go into hiding.* See v. 12 and note. *righteous thrive.* See 11:10; 29:2.
29:1 *stiff-necked.* See note on Ex 32:9. *after many rebukes.* Cf. 1:25–30. Eli's sons died because of their stubbornness (see 1Sa 2:25 and note). *will suddenly be destroyed—without remedy.* Identical to 6:15. Cf. the fate of the mockers in 1:22–27.
29:2 *When the righteous thrive, the people rejoice.* See 11:10 and note. *when the wicked rule, the people groan.* See 28:12 and note.
29:3 *man who loves wisdom brings joy to his father.* See 10:1 and note. *companion of prostitutes squanders his wealth.* See 5:10; 6:26 and notes; cf. Lk 15:13 and note.
29:4 *By justice a king gives a country stability.* See 16:12 and note. *bribes.* See 17:8 and note.
29:5 *Whoever flatters his neighbor.* See 28:23.
29:6 *snared by his own sin.* See 1:18 and note; 22:5.
29:7 *The righteous care about justice for the poor.* As Job did (Job 29:16); see Jer 22:16 and note; cf. Jas 1:27; Pr 22:22.
29:8 *Mockers stir up a city.* See notes on 6:14; 11:11; see also 26:21. *Mockers.* See 1:22 and note. *wise men turn away anger.* See Jas 3:17–18.

[9]If a wise man goes to court with a fool,
the fool rages and scoffs, and there
is no peace.

[10]Bloodthirsty men hate a man of
integrity
and seek to kill the upright.[r]

[11]A fool gives full vent to his anger,[s]
but a wise man keeps himself under
control.[t]

[12]If a ruler[u] listens to lies,
all his officials become wicked.[v]

[13]The poor man and the oppressor have
this in common:
The LORD gives sight to the eyes of
both.[w]

[14]If a king judges the poor with fairness,
his throne will always be secure.[x]

[15]The rod of correction imparts wisdom,
but a child left to himself disgraces
his mother.[y]

[16]When the wicked thrive, so does sin,
but the righteous will see their
downfall.[z]

[17]Discipline your son, and he will give
you peace;
he will bring delight to your soul.[a]

[18]Where there is no revelation, the
people cast off restraint;
but blessed is he who keeps the
law.[b]

[19]A servant cannot be corrected by mere
words;
though he understands, he will not
respond.

[20]Do you see a man who speaks in
haste?
There is more hope for a fool than
for him.[c]

[21]If a man pampers his servant from
youth,
he will bring grief[a] in the end.

[22]An angry man stirs up dissension,
and a hot-tempered one commits
many sins.[d]

[23]A man's pride brings him low,[e]
but a man of lowly spirit gains honor.[f]

[24]The accomplice of a thief is his own
enemy;
he is put under oath and dare not
testify.[g]

[25]Fear[h] of man will prove to be a snare,
but whoever trusts in the LORD[i] is
kept safe.[j]

[26]Many seek an audience with a ruler,[k]
but it is from the LORD that man gets
justice.[l]

[27]The righteous detest the dishonest;
the wicked detest the upright.[m]

Sayings of Agur

30 The sayings[n] of Agur son of Jakeh—
an oracle[b]:

This man declared to Ithiel,
to Ithiel and to Ucal:[c]

[2]"I am the most ignorant of men;
I do not have a man's
understanding.

29:10 [r]ver 27; 1Jn 3:12 **29:11** [s]S Job 15:13 [t]Pr 12:16 **29:12** [u]2Ki 21:9 [v]S Job 34:30 **29:13** [w]S Pr 22:2; Mt 5:45 **29:14** [x]S ver 4; Ps 72:1-5; S Pr 16:12 **29:15** [y]ver 17; S Pr 13:24 **29:16** [z]S Ps 91:8; S 92:11 **29:17** [a]S ver 15 **29:18** [b]Ps 1:1-2; 19:11; 119:1-2 **29:20** [c]Pr 19:2; 26:12 **29:22** [d]S Pr 14:17 **29:23** [e]S Est 5:12 [f]S Pr 11:2; S 15:33; S 16:18 **29:24** [g]S Lev 5:1 **29:25** [h]S 1Sa 15:24 [i]Pr 28:25 [j]S Pr 16:20 **29:26** [k]Pr 19:6 [l]S Pr 16:33 **29:27** [m]S ver 10 **30:1** [n]S Pr 22:17

[a] *21* The meaning of the Hebrew for this word is uncertain. [b] *1* Or *Jakeh of Massa* [c] *1* Masoretic Text; with a different word division of the Hebrew *declared, "I am weary, O God; / I am weary, O God, and faint.*

29:10 *Bloodthirsty men hate a man of integrity.* Their schemes are described in 1:11–16; cf. Ps 5:6 and note on 5:9.
29:11 *gives full vent to his anger.* See v. 9; 14:16–17. *keeps himself under control.* See 16:32 and note.
29:12 *all his officials become wicked.* Cf. Isa 1:23.
29:13 *The LORD gives sight.* See Ex 4:11; Ps 94:9; cf. Pr 22:2.
29:14 See 16:12 and note.
29:15 *rod of correction.* See note on 13:24.
29:16 *When the wicked thrive.* See v. 2; 11:11 and note; 28:12,28. *righteous will see their downfall.* See 10:25 and note; 14:11; 21:12.
29:17 *Discipline your son.* Teach him and train him (see 13:24 and note; 22:6).
29:18 *revelation.* A message from God given through a prophet; a prophetic vision (see 1Sa 3:1; Isa 1:1; Ob 1). *people cast off restraint.* Possibly an allusion to the sinful actions of the Israelites while Moses was on Mount Sinai (see Ex 32:25 and note). *blessed is he who keeps the law.* See 28:4 and note.
29:19 *cannot be corrected by mere words.* Servants, like sons (vv. 15,17), must be disciplined (see note on 22:6).
29:20 *who speaks in haste.* See 10:19; 17:27–28; Jas 1:19,26. *There is more hope ... him.* Identical to 26:12.
29:21 *pampers his servant.* See v. 19 and note.
29:22 *angry man stirs up dissension.* See note on 6:14; see also 15:18.
29:23 See 15:33 and note; see also 18:12.
29:24 *he is put under oath.* He will be held responsible for failing to testify (see Lev 5:1).
29:25 *Fear of man.* Cf. 1Sa 15:24; Isa 51:12; Jn 12:42–43. *whoever trusts in the LORD is kept safe.* See 18:10; 28:26 and notes; cf. 3:5–6.
29:26 *Many seek an audience.* See 1Ki 10:24. *it is from the LORD that man gets justice.* The Lord is a more reliable source of justice than human kings or judges.
29:27 The final proverb in this second Solomonic collection (chs. 25–29) highlights in the starkest terms the opposing perspectives that characterize the righteous and the wicked.
30:1–33 The first of two chapters that serve as an appendix to Proverbs.
30:1 *sayings.* See 22:17; 24:23. *Agur son of Jakeh.* Probably a non-Israelite wise man like Job and his friends. *oracle.* An inspired utterance—usually the message of a prophet (see note on Isa 13:1). If "oracle" is taken as the place name "Massa" (see NIV text note), Agur would then be associated with an Ishmaelite people (cf. Ge 25:13–14). *Ithiel ... Ucal.* Perhaps students of Agur, but see NIV text note.

[3]I have not learned wisdom,
nor have I knowledge of the Holy One.[o]
[4]Who has gone up[p] to heaven and come down?
Who has gathered up the wind in the hollow[q] of his hands?
Who has wrapped up the waters[r] in his cloak?[s]
Who has established all the ends of the earth?
What is his name,[t] and the name of his son?
Tell me if you know!

[5]"Every word of God is flawless;[u]
he is a shield[v] to those who take refuge in him.
[6]Do not add[w] to his words,
or he will rebuke you and prove you a liar.

[7]"Two things I ask of you, O LORD;
do not refuse me before I die:
[8]Keep falsehood and lies far from me;
give me neither poverty nor riches,
but give me only my daily bread.[x]
[9]Otherwise, I may have too much and disown[y] you
and say, 'Who is the LORD?'[z]
Or I may become poor and steal,
and so dishonor the name of my God.[a]

[10]"Do not slander a servant to his master,
or he will curse you, and you will pay for it.

30:3 [o]S Pr 9:10 **30:4** [p]Dt 30:12; Ps 24:1-2; S Pr 8:22-31; Jn 3:13; Eph 4:7-10 [q]Isa 40:12 [r]Job 26:8 [s]S Ge 1:2 [t]Rev 19:12 **30:5** [u]S Ps 12:6; S 18:30 [v]S Ge 15:1 **30:6** [w]S Dt 4:2 **30:8** [x]Mt 6:11 **30:9** [y]Jos 24:27; Isa 1:4; 59:13 [z]Dt 6:12; 8:10-14; Hos 13:6 [a]S Dt 8:12

30:11 [b]S Pr 20:20 **30:12** [c]S Pr 16:2 [d]Jer 2:23,35 **30:13** [e]S 2Sa 22:28; S Job 41:34 **30:14** [f]S Job 4:11; S Ps 3:7 [g]Ps 57:4 [h]S Job 24:9 [i]Am 8:4; Mic 2:2 [j]S Job 19:22 **30:15** [k]Pr 27:20 **30:16** [l]Isa 5:14; 14:9,11; Hab 2:5 **30:17** [m]Dt 21:18-21 [n]S Job 15:23

[11]"There are those who curse their fathers
and do not bless their mothers;[b]
[12]those who are pure in their own eyes[c]
and yet are not cleansed of their filth;[d]
[13]those whose eyes are ever so haughty,[e]
whose glances are so disdainful;
[14]those whose teeth[f] are swords
and whose jaws are set with knives[g]
to devour[h] the poor[i] from the earth,
the needy from among mankind.[j]

[15]"The leech has two daughters.
'Give! Give!' they cry.

"There are three things that are never satisfied,[k]
four that never say, 'Enough!':
[16]the grave,[a][l] the barren womb,
land, which is never satisfied with water,
and fire, which never says, 'Enough!'

[17]"The eye that mocks[m] a father,
that scorns obedience to a mother,
will be pecked out by the ravens of the valley,
will be eaten by the vultures.[n]

[18]"There are three things that are too amazing for me,
four that I do not understand:
[19]the way of an eagle in the sky,
the way of a snake on a rock,
the way of a ship on the high seas,
and the way of a man with a maiden.

[a] *16* Hebrew *Sheol*

30:3 *knowledge of the Holy One.* See 9:10 and note.
30:4 The use of rhetorical questions to express God's greatness as Creator occurs also in Job 38:4—39:30; Isa 40:12–31 (see note there). *gathered up the wind.* Cf. Ps 135:7. *wrapped up the waters in his cloak.* See Job 26:8; 38:8–9; cf. Ps 33:7; 97:2. *What is ... the name of his son?* This question has been understood in several different ways. It perhaps was intended as a riddle, the meaning of which remains obscure. *Tell me if you know!* God similarly challenged Job (see Job 38:4–5 and note).
30:5 Almost identical to Ps 18:30. *shield.* See notes on 2:7; Ps 3:3. *those who take refuge in him.* See 14:32; 18:10.
30:6 *Do not add to his words.* Cf. Moses' warning to the Israelites in Dt 4:2 (see note there); cf. also Rev 22:18–19 and note.
30:7 *Two things.* The use of lists characterizes Agur's sayings (see vv. 15,18,21,24,29).
30:8 *my daily bread.* Cf. Job 23:12 and the Lord's Prayer (see Mt 6:11 and note).
30:9 *I may have too much and disown you.* Moses predicted that Israel would forget God when their food was plentiful and their herds large (Dt 8:12–17; 31:20). *Who is the LORD?* Or, Why should I serve him (see Job 21:14–15)? *become poor and steal.* Cf. 6:30.
30:10 *you will pay for it.* Since the accusation is false, the servant's curse will be effective (cf. 26:2 and note)—so do not suppose you can take advantage of a servant's lowly position.
30:11 *curse their fathers.* Cf. v. 17; see 20:20 and note.
30:12 *those who are pure in their own eyes.* Like the Pharisee in Lk 18:11 (cf. Pr 12:15; 16:2).
30:13 *whose eyes are ... haughty.* See note on 6:17; see also Isa 3:16.
30:14 *whose teeth are swords ... whose jaws are ... knives.* See note on Ps 5:9. The wicked are like ravenous beasts that devour the prey (see Job 29:17). *to devour the poor ... the needy.* Cf. Ps 14:4; Mic 3:2–3 and notes.
30:15,18,21,29 *three ... four.* See note on 6:16.
30:15 *leech has two daughters.* The "two daughters" are the two suckers with which this parasite draws blood from its victims.
30:16 *grave.* Its appetite is never satisfied (Isa 5:14; Hab 2:5). *barren womb.* In ancient Israel, a wife without children was desolate, even desperate (cf. Ge 16:2 and note; 30:1; Ru 1:11–13,20–21; 1Sa 1:6,10–11; 2Ki 4:14 and note).
30:17 *The eye.* Haughty and disdainful (see v. 13). *mocks a father ... a mother.* See v. 11 and note; 15:20. *will be pecked out by the ravens ... the vultures.* The loss of an eye was a terrible curse (see the story of Samson in Jdg 16:21). Since vultures normally devoured the dead (see Jer 7:33 and note; Mt 24:28), the meaning may be that the body of a disgraceful son will lie unburied and exposed.
30:18–19 These four "ways" are difficult to understand because none of them leaves a track that can be readily followed.
30:19 *way of an eagle.* Soaring and swooping majestically (cf. Job 39:27; Jer 48:40; 49:22). *way of a man with a maiden.* Prob-

20 "This is the way of an adulteress:
She eats and wipes her mouth
and says, 'I've done nothing
wrong.'[o]

21 "Under three things the earth
trembles,
under four it cannot bear up:
22 a servant who becomes king,[p]
a fool who is full of food,
23 an unloved woman who is married,
and a maidservant who displaces
her mistress.

24 "Four things on earth are small,
yet they are extremely wise:
25 Ants are creatures of little strength,
yet they store up their food in the
summer;[q]
26 coneys[a][r] are creatures of little power,
yet they make their home in the
crags;
27 locusts[s] have no king,
yet they advance together in ranks;
28 a lizard can be caught with the hand,
yet it is found in kings' palaces.

29 "There are three things that are stately
in their stride,
four that move with stately bearing:
30 a lion, mighty among beasts,
who retreats before nothing;
31 a strutting rooster, a he-goat,
and a king with his army around
him.[b]

32 "If you have played the fool and
exalted yourself,
or if you have planned evil,
clap your hand over your mouth![t]
33 For as churning the milk produces
butter,
and as twisting the nose produces
blood,
so stirring up anger produces strife."

Sayings of King Lemuel

31 The sayings[u] of King Lemuel—an oracle[c] his mother taught him:

2 "O my son, O son of my womb,
O son of my vows,[d][v]
3 do not spend your strength on women,
your vigor on those who ruin
kings.[w]

4 "It is not for kings, O Lemuel—
not for kings to drink wine,[x]
not for rulers to crave beer,
5 lest they drink[y] and forget what the
law decrees,[z]
and deprive all the oppressed of
their rights.
6 Give beer to those who are perishing,
wine[a] to those who are in anguish;
7 let them drink[b] and forget their
poverty
and remember their misery no more.

8 "Speak[c] up for those who cannot speak
for themselves,
for the rights of all who are destitute.
9 Speak up and judge fairly;
defend the rights of the poor and
needy."[d]

30:20 [o] Pr 5:6 **30:22** [p] S Pr 19:10; S 29:2 **30:25** [q] Pr 6:6-8 **30:26** [r] S Ps 104:18 **30:27** [s] S Ex 10:4 **30:32** [t] S Job 29:9

31:1 [u] S Pr 22:17 **31:2** [v] S Jdg 11:30 **31:3** [w] S Dt 17:17; S 1Ki 11:3; Pr 5:1-14 **31:4** [x] S Pr 20:1; Ecc 10:16-17; Isa 5:22 **31:5** [y] S 1Ki 16:9 [z] S Pr 16:12 **31:6** [a] S Ge 14:18 **31:7** [b] S Est 1:10 **31:8** [c] S 1Sa 19:4 **31:9** [d] S Pr 24:23; 29:7

[a] *26* That is, the hyrax or rock badger [b] *31* Or *king secure against revolt* [c] *1* Or *of Lemuel king of Massa, which* [d] *2* Or */ the answer to my prayers*

ably a reference to the mystery of courting and how it leads to consummation.

30:20 *adulteress.* See 2:16 and note. *She eats and wipes her mouth.* Eating food is used as a metaphor for making love also in 9:17 (see note there; see also 7:18 and note).

30:22 *servant who becomes king.* See 19:10.

30:23 *unloved woman who is married.* Probably one of several wives, who is miserable because her husband does not love her (cf. Leah in Ge 29:31–32). *maidservant who displaces her mistress.* Perhaps because she was able to bear a child, whereas the wife was barren (cf. Hagar and Sarah in Ge 16:1–6).

30:25 *Ants.* See note on 6:6.

30:26 *in the crags.* Which provide a refuge for them (see Ps 104:18).

30:27 *locusts have no king.* Cf. the ant in 6:6–7. *advance together in ranks.* Locusts are portrayed as a mighty army in Joel 2:2–9 (see note on Joel 2:2).

30:28 *found in kings' palaces.* Lizards climb stone walls easily.

30:30 *lion, mighty among beasts.* See 2Sa 1:23; Mic 5:8.

30:31 *he-goat.* Goats were used to lead flocks of sheep (see Jer 50:8).

30:32 *exalted yourself.* Pride is condemned in 8:13; 11:2; 16:18. *planned evil.* Cf. 6:14; 16:27. *clap your hand over your mouth.* Stop your plotting immediately (cf. Job 21:5; 40:4).

30:33 *churning ... twisting ... stirring up.* For these three English verbs the Hebrew proverb uses the same verb, rhetorically linking the three clauses. *stirring up anger produces strife.* See notes on 6:14; 15:1; see also 29:22.

31:1–9 This brief section, consisting of three proverbs, is also of non-Israelite origin (see note on 30:1). King Lemuel is otherwise unknown. The threefold advice Lemuel's mother gives him highlights two major temptations of royalty (overindulgence in sexual activity with their many wives [vv. 2–3] and drunkenness [vv. 4–7]) as well as one of its primary obligations (defending the poor and needy [vv. 8–9; see Jer 22:15–16 and notes]).

31:1 *oracle.* See note on 30:1. *his mother.* In the ancient Near East, the queen mother was often an influential figure (see 1Ki 1:11–13 and note on 1:11).

31:2 *son of my vows.* Cf. Hannah's vow as she prayed for a son (see 1Sa 1:11 and note). *vows.* See 20:25 and note.

31:3 *your strength on women.* A warning against accumulating a large harem and indulging in sexual pleasures (see 5:9–11; 1Ki 11:1; Ne 13:26 and notes).

31:4 *It is not for kings ... to drink wine.* Woe to the land whose rulers are drunkards (Ecc 10:16–17; cf. Pr 20:1 and note; see Hos 7:5 and note)!

31:5 *deprive all the oppressed of their rights.* See 30:14 and note; see also 17:15; Isa 5:23; 10:2.

31:8–9 The king represents God as the defender of the poor and needy (see 16:10 and note; Ps 82:3; cf. Lev 19:15; Job 29:12–17; Isa 1:17 and note).

Epilogue: The Wife of Noble Character

10 [a] A wife of noble character[e] who can
find?[f]
She is worth far more than rubies.
11 Her husband[g] has full confidence in her
and lacks nothing of value.[h]
12 She brings him good, not harm,
all the days of her life.
13 She selects wool and flax
and works with eager hands.[i]
14 She is like the merchant ships,
bringing her food from afar.
15 She gets up while it is still dark;
she provides food for her family
and portions for her servant girls.
16 She considers a field and buys it;
out of her earnings she plants a
vineyard.
17 She sets about her work vigorously;
her arms are strong for her tasks.
18 She sees that her trading is profitable,
and her lamp does not go out at
night.
19 In her hand she holds the distaff
and grasps the spindle with her
fingers.
20 She opens her arms to the poor
and extends her hands to the needy.[j]
21 When it snows, she has no fear for her
household;
for all of them are clothed in scarlet.
22 She makes coverings for her bed;
she is clothed in fine linen and purple.
23 Her husband is respected at the city
gate,
where he takes his seat among the
elders[k] of the land.
24 She makes linen garments and sells
them,
and supplies the merchants with
sashes.
25 She is clothed with strength and dignity;
she can laugh at the days to come.
26 She speaks with wisdom,
and faithful instruction is on her
tongue.[l]
27 She watches over the affairs of her
household
and does not eat the bread of
idleness.
28 Her children arise and call her blessed;
her husband also, and he praises
her:
29 "Many women do noble things,
but you surpass them all."
30 Charm is deceptive, and beauty is
fleeting;
but a woman who fears the LORD is
to be praised.
31 Give her the reward she has earned,
and let her works bring her praise[m]
at the city gate.

31:10 [e] S Ru 3:11; S Pr 18:22 [f] Pr 8:35 **31:11** [g] S Ge 2:18 [h] S Pr 12:4 **31:13** [i] 1Ti 2:9-10 **31:20** [j] Dt 15:11 **31:23** [k] S Ex 3:16 **31:26** [l] S Pr 10:31 **31:31** [m] Pr 11:16

[a] *10* Verses 10-31 are an acrostic, each verse beginning with a successive letter of the Hebrew alphabet.

31:10–31 The epilogue: an acrostic poem (see NIV text note) praising the "wife of noble character" (v. 10). It corresponds to 1:1–7 (the prologue) as it describes a "woman who fears the LORD" (v. 30; see note on 1:7). Such a wife is almost a personification of wisdom. Like wisdom, she is "worth far more than rubies" (v. 10; cf. 3:15; 8:11), and he who finds her "receives favor from the LORD" (8:35; 18:22). See Introduction: Literary Structure.

31:10 *wife of noble character.* Like Ruth (Ru 3:11). She is "her husband's crown" (12:4; see note there).

31:12 *She brings him good.* See 18:22; 19:14.

31:13 *flax.* Its fibers were made into linen (see note on Ex 25:4; see also Pr 31:19,22,24; Isa 19:9).

31:14 *like the merchant ships.* She is an enterprising person (see v. 18).

31:15 *She gets up while it is still dark.* She is the opposite of the sluggard (see 6:9–10; 26:14 and note). *portions for her servant girls.* See 27:27; Lk 12:42.

31:16 *considers a field ... plants a vineyard.* She shows good judgment—unlike the sluggard, whose vineyard is overgrown with thorns and weeds (24:30–31).

31:17 *sets about her work vigorously.* See 10:4 and note.

31:18 *her trading is profitable.* Like wisdom, she is "worth far more than rubies" (v. 10; see note there). Wisdom "is more profitable than silver" (3:14; see note there).

31:19 *distaff ... spindle.* Spinning thread was women's work.

31:20 *opens her arms to the poor.* See note on 14:21; see also 22:9; Job 31:16–22.

31:21 *clothed in scarlet.* Of high quality, probably made of wool (cf. 2Sa 1:24; Rev 18:16).

31:22 *fine linen.* Associated with nobility (see notes on 7:16; Ex 25:4; see also Ge 41:42). *purple.* Linked with kings (Jdg 8:26; SS 3:10) or the rich (Lk 16:19; Rev 18:16).

31:23 *city gate.* The court (see note on 1:21).

31:24 *linen garments.* See Jdg 14:12 and note; Isa 3:23. *merchants.* Cf. v. 18.

31:25 *clothed with strength and dignity.* See note on Ps 109:29; cf. Isa 52:1; 1Ti 2:9–10. The opposite is to be "clothed with shame and disgrace" (Ps 35:26; 109:29). *she can laugh at the days to come.* She is free of anxiety and worry (cf. Job 39:7).

31:26 *faithful instruction.* Given to her children and friends. She is a wise and loving counselor (see 1:8; 6:20).

31:27 *She watches over.* Hebrew *sophiyyah*, a rare participial form, perhaps chosen here as a pun on *sophia*, the Greek word for "wisdom." If so, an alternative translation for the verse would read: "The ways of her household are wisdom, / and she does not eat the bread of idleness." This revised rendering of v. 27a would balance the statement in v. 26a ("She speaks with wisdom") and would clinch the argument that the "wife of noble character" personifies wisdom (see note on vv. 10–31) in word and deed.

31:28 *blessed.* That is, one who is seen to enjoy extremely happy circumstances. See Ge 30:13; Ps 72:17; SS 6:9; Mal 3:12; cf. Ru 4:14–15.

31:29 *do noble things.* The husband's reference to his wife's "noble" deeds climaxes the main body of the poem (vv. 10–29) that celebrates her "noble" character (v. 10). He further asserts that she surpasses all other women—she is, indeed, "worth far more than rubies" (v. 10).

31:30–31 A concluding reflection on the main body of the poem.

31:30 *Charm is deceptive.* Cf. 5:3 and note. *beauty is fleeting.* See 1Pe 3:3–5 and notes; cf. Job 14:2. *who fears the LORD.* See note on 1:7.

31:31 *reward she has earned.* See v. 16; 12:14 and notes. *bring her praise.* Honor comes through "humility and the fear of the LORD" (22:4). *city gate.* See v. 23 and note.

Ecclesiastes

INTRODUCTION

Author and Date

No time period or writer's name is mentioned in the book, but several passages suggest that King Solomon may be the author (1:1,12,16; 2:4–9; 7:26–29; 12:9; cf. 1Ki 2:9; 3:12; 4:29–34; 5:12; 10:1–8). On the other hand, the writer's title ("Teacher," Hebrew *qoheleth;* see note on 1:1), his unique style of Hebrew and his attitude toward rulers (suggesting that of a subject rather than a monarch — see, e.g., 4:1–2; 5:8–9; 8:2–4; 10:20) may point to another person and a later period (see note on 1:1).

A Quick Look

Author:
Unknown; possibly King Solomon

Audience:
The people of Israel

Date:
Unknown; possibly as early as the tenth century B.C.

Theme:
This wisdom teacher reveals what he has discovered about the meaninglessness of every human endeavor without God at the center of one's life.

Purpose and Teaching

The author of Ecclesiastes puts his powers of wisdom to work to examine the human experience and assess the human condition. His perspective is limited to what happens "under the sun" (as is that of all the wisdom teachers). He considers life as he has experienced and observed it between the horizons of birth and death — life within the boundaries of this visible world. His wisdom cannot penetrate beyond that last horizon; he can only observe the phenomenon of death and perceive the limits it places on human beings. Within the limits of human experience and observation, he is concerned to spell out what is good for people to do. And he represents a devout wisdom. Life in the world is under God — for all its enigmas. Hence what begins with "Meaningless! Meaningless!" (1:2) ends with "Remember your Creator" (12:1) and "Fear God and keep his commandments" (12:13).

With a wisdom matured by many years, the author takes the measure of human beings, examining their limits and their lot. He has attempted to see what human wisdom can do (1:13,16–18; 7:24; 8:16) and has discovered that human wisdom, even when it has its beginning in "the fear of the LORD" (Pr 1:7), has limits to its powers when it attempts to go it alone — limits that circumscribe its perspectives and relativize its counsel. Most significantly, it cannot find out the larger purposes of God or the ultimate meaning of human existence. With respect to these it can only pose questions.

Nevertheless, he does take a hard look at the human enterprise — an enterprise in which he himself has fully participated. He sees a busy, busy human anthill in mad pursuit of many things, trying now this, now that, laboring away as if by dint of effort humans could master the world, lay bare its deepest secrets, change its fundamental structures, somehow burst through the bounds of human limitations, build for themselves enduring monuments, control their destiny, achieve a state of secure and lasting happiness — people laboring at life with an overblown conception of human powers and consequently pursuing unrealistic hopes and aspirations.

He takes a hard look and concludes that human life in this mode is "meaningless," its efforts all futile.

What, then, does wisdom teach him?

1. Humans cannot by all their striving achieve anything of ultimate or enduring significance. Nothing appears to be going anywhere (1:5 – 11), and people cannot by all their efforts break out of this caged treadmill (1:2 – 4; 2:1 – 11); they cannot fundamentally change anything (1:12 – 15; 6:10; 7:13). Hence they often toil foolishly (4:4,7 – 8; 5:10 – 17; 6:7 – 9). All their striving "under the sun" (1:3) after unreal goals leads only to disillusionment.

With a wisdom matured by many years, the author takes the measure of human beings, examining their limits and their lot. He has attempted to see what human wisdom can do and has discovered that its powers are limited.

2. Wisdom is better than folly (2:13 – 14; 7:1 – 6,11 – 12,19; 8:1,5; 9:17 – 18; 10:1 – 3,12 – 15; 12:11) — it is God's gift to those who please him (2:26). But it is unwarranted to expect too much even from such wisdom — to expect that human wisdom is capable of solving all problems (1:16 – 18) or of securing for itself enduring rewards or advantages (2:12 – 17; 4:13 – 16; 9:13 – 16).

3. Experience confronts humans with many apparent disharmonies and anomalies that wisdom cannot unravel. Of these the greatest of all is this: Human life comes to the same end as that of the animals — death (2:15; 3:16 – 17; 7:15; 8:14; 9:1 – 3; 10:5 – 7).

4. Although God made humankind upright, people have gone in search of many "schemes" (for getting ahead by taking advantage of others; see 7:29; cf. Ps 10:2; 36:4; 140:2). So even humans are a disappointment (7:24 – 29).

5. People cannot know or control what will come after them, or even what lies in the more immediate future; therefore all their efforts remain balanced on the razor's edge of uncertainty (2:18; 6:12; 7:14; 9:2).

6. God keeps humans in their place (3:16 – 22).

7. God has ordered all things (3:1 – 15; 5:19; 6:1 – 6; 9:1), and a human being cannot change God's appointments or fully understand them or anticipate them (3:1; 7; 11:1 – 6). But the world is not fundamentally chaotic or irrational. It is ordered by God, and it is for humans to accept matters as they are by God's appointments, including their own limitations. Everything has its "time" and is good in its time (ch. 3).

Therefore wisdom counsels:

1. Accept the human condition as it is shaped by God's appointments and enjoy the life you have been given as fully as you can.

2. Don't trouble yourself with unrealistic goals — know the measure of human capabilities.

3. Be prudent in all your ways — follow wisdom's leading.

4. "Fear God and keep his commandments" (12:13), beginning already in your youth before the fleeting days of life's enjoyments are gone and "the days of trouble" (12:1) come when the infirmities of advanced age vex you and hinder you from tasting, seeing and feeling the good things of life.

To sum up, Ecclesiastes provides instruction on how to live meaningfully, purposefully and joyfully within the theocratic arrangement — primarily by placing God at the center of one's life, work and activities, by contentedly accepting one's divinely appointed lot in life, and by reverently trusting in and obeying the Creator-King. Note particularly 2:24–26; 3:11–14,22; 5:18–20; 8:15; 9:7–10; 11:7—12:1; 12:9–14 (see also any pertinent notes on these passages).

Literary Features

The argument of Ecclesiastes does not flow smoothly. It meanders, with jumps and starts, through the general messiness of human experience, to which it is a response. There is also an intermingling of poetry and prose. Nevertheless, the following outline seeks to reflect, at least in a general way, the structure of the book and its main discourses. The announced theme of "meaninglessness" (futility) provides a literary frame around the whole (1:2; 12:8). And the movement from the unrelieved disillusionment of chs. 1–2 to the more serene tone and sober instructions for life in chs. 11–12 marks a development in matured wisdom's coming to terms with the human condition.

A striking feature of the book is its frequent use of key words and phrases: e.g., "meaningless" (see notes on 1:2; 2:24–25), "work/labor/toil" (see note on 2:10), "good/better" (see note on 2:1), "gift/give" (see note on 2:26), "under the sun" (see note on1:3), "chasing after the wind" (see note on 1:14). Also to be noted is the presence of passages interwoven throughout the book that serve as key indicators of the author's theme and purpose: 1:2–3,14,17; 2:10–11,17,24–26; 3:12–13,22; 4:4,6,16; 5:18–20; 6:9,12; 7:14,24; 8:7,15,17; 9:7,12; 10:14; 11:2,5–6,8–9; 12:1,8,13–14 (see notes on these passages where present). The enjoyment of life as God gives it is a key concept in the book (see 2:24–26 and note on 2:24–25; 3:12–13,22 and note on 3:12–13; 5:18–20; 7:14; 8:15 and note; 9:7–9; 11:8–9).

Outline

- I. Author (1:1)
- II. Theme: The meaninglessness of human efforts on earth apart from God (1:2)
- III. Introduction: The profitlessness of human toil to accumulate things in order to achieve happiness (1:3–11)
- IV. Discourse, Part 1: In spite of life's apparent enigmas and meaninglessness, it is to be enjoyed as a gift from God (1:12—11:6)
  - A. Since human wisdom and endeavors are meaningless, people should enjoy their life and work and its fruits as gifts from God (1:12—6:9)
    - 1. Introduction (1:12–18)
      - a. Human endeavors are meaningless (1:12–15)
      - b. Pursuing human wisdom is meaningless (1:16–18)
    - 2. Seeking pleasure is meaningless (2:1–11)
    - 3. Human wisdom is meaningless (2:12–17)
    - 4. Toiling to accumulate things is meaningless (2:18—6:9)
      - a. Because people must leave the fruits of their labor to others (2:18–26)
      - b. Because all human efforts remain under the government of God's sovereign appointments, which people cannot fully know and which all their toil cannot change (3:1—4:3)
      - c. Because there are things better for people than the envy, greed and ambition that motivate such toil (4:4–16)
      - d. Because the fruits of human labor can be lost, resulting in frustration (5:1—6:9)
  - B. Since people cannot fully know what is best to do or what the future holds for them, they should enjoy now the life and work God has given them (6:10—11:6)
    - 1. Introduction: What is predetermined by God is unalterable, and people cannot fully know what is best or what the future holds (6:10–12)
    - 2. People cannot fully know what is best to do (chs. 7–8)
    - 3. People cannot fully know what the future holds (9:1—11:6)
- V. Discourse, Part 2: Since old age and death will soon come, people should enjoy life in their youth, remembering that God will judge (11:7—12:7)

A. People should enjoy their life on earth because their future after death is mysterious, and in that sense is meaningless for their present life (11:7–8)

B. People should enjoy the fleeting joys of youth, but remember that God will judge (11:9–10)

C. People should remember their Creator (and his gifts) in their youth, before the deteriorations of old age and the dissolution of the body come (12:1–7)

VI. Theme Repeated (12:8)

VII. Conclusion: Reverently trust in and obey God (12:9–14)

Everything Is Meaningless

1 The words of the Teacher,[a][a] son of David, king in Jerusalem:[b]

[2] "Meaningless! Meaningless!"
says the Teacher.
"Utterly meaningless!
Everything is meaningless."[c]
[3] What does man gain from all his labor
at which he toils under the sun?[d]
[4] Generations come and generations go,
but the earth remains forever.[e]
[5] The sun rises and the sun sets,
and hurries back to where it rises.[f]
[6] The wind blows to the south
and turns to the north;
round and round it goes,
ever returning on its course.
[7] All streams flow into the sea,
yet the sea is never full.
To the place the streams come from,
there they return again.[g]
[8] All things are wearisome,
more than one can say.
The eye never has enough of seeing,[h]
nor the ear its fill of hearing.
[9] What has been will be again,
what has been done will be done again;[i]
there is nothing new under the sun.
[10] Is there anything of which one can say,
"Look! This is something new"?
It was here already, long ago;
it was here before our time.
[11] There is no remembrance of men of old,[j]
and even those who are yet to come
will not be remembered
by those who follow.[k]

Wisdom Is Meaningless

[12] I, the Teacher,[l] was king over Israel in
Jerusalem.[m] [13] I devoted myself to study
and to explore by wisdom all that is done
under heaven.[n] What a heavy burden God
has laid on men![o] [14] I have seen all the
things that are done under the sun; all of
them are meaningless, a chasing after the
wind.[p]

[15] What is twisted cannot be straightened;[q]
what is lacking cannot be counted.

[16] I thought to myself, "Look, I have
grown and increased in wisdom more
than anyone who has ruled over Jerusalem before me;[r] I have experienced much
of wisdom and knowledge." [17] Then I
applied myself to the understanding of

1:1 [a] ver 12; Ecc 7:27; 12:10 [b] S Pr 1:1 **1:2** [c] Ps 39:5-6; 62:9; Ecc 12:8; Ro 8:20-21 **1:3** [d] Ecc 2:11,22; 3:9; 5:15-16 **1:4** [e] S Job 8:19 **1:5** [f] Ps 19:5-6 **1:7** [g] Job 36:28 **1:8** [h] Pr 27:20 **1:9** [i] Ecc 2:12; 3:15 **1:11** [j] Ge 40:23; Ecc 9:15 [k] Ps 88:12; Ecc 2:16; 8:10; 9:5 **1:12** [l] S ver 1 [m] Ecc 2:9 **1:13** [n] S Job 28:3 [o] S Ge 3:17; Ecc 3:10 **1:14** [p] Ecc 2:11,17; 4:4; 6:9 **1:15** [q] Ecc 7:13 **1:16** [r] S 1Ki 3:12

[a] 1 Or *leader of the assembly*; also in verses 2 and 12

1:1 *Teacher.* The teacher of wisdom (12:9). The Hebrew term for "Teacher" (*qoheleth*) is related to that for "assembly" (see NIV text note; Ex 16:3; Nu 16:3). Perhaps the Teacher, whose work is described in 12:9–10, also held an office in the assembly. The Septuagint (the pre-Christian Greek translation of the OT) word for "Teacher" is *ekklesiastes,* from which most English titles of the book are taken, and from which such English words as "ecclesiastical" are derived. *son of David.* Suggests Solomon, though his name occurs nowhere in the book. The Hebrew word for "son" can refer to a descendant (even many generations removed)—or even to someone who follows in the footsteps of another (see Ge 4:21; see also Introduction: Author and Date).

1:2 Briefly states the author's theme (see 12:8 and note). *Meaningless!* This key term occurs 39 times in the book. The Hebrew for it originally meant "breath" (see Ps 39:5,11; 62:9; 144:4; cf. Ge 4:2 and note). The basic thrust of Ecclesiastes is that all of life is meaningless (useless, hollow, futile, vain) if it is not rightly related to God. Only when based on God and his word is life worthwhile. *Everything.* See v. 8; whatever human beings undertake apart from God.

1:3–11 The author elaborates his theme that human effort appears to be without benefit or purpose—and therefore without meaning.

1:3 Jesus expands on this question in Mk 8:36–38. *under the sun.* Another key expression (used 29 times), which refers to this present world and the limits of what it offers. "Under heaven" and "on earth" though occuring less frequently (v. 13; 2:3; 3:1), is used synonymously.

1:4–9 Toiling is profitless (v. 3) because humans live in a world of repetitiveness and sameness—one without apparent progress and meaning. This is seen in the endless succession and impermanence of human generations (v. 4) and in the behavior patterns of the sun (v. 5), the wind (v. 6) and the streams (v. 7). Hence the conclusion that "all things are wearisome" (v. 8) and "there is nothing new under the sun" (v. 9).

1:4 *earth remains forever.* By contrast, human life is fleeting.

1:8 *All things.* Everything mentioned in vv. 4–7 (see note on v. 2).

1:10 *something new.* Many things seem to be new simply because the past is easily and quickly forgotten. The old ways reappear in new guises.

1:12–18 Having set forth his theme that all human striving seems futile (see especially vv. 3,11, which frame that section), the Teacher now shows that both human endeavor (vv. 12–15; cf. 2:1–11) and the pursuit of human wisdom (vv. 16–18; cf. 2:12–17) are futile and meaningless.

1:12 *I.* The author shifts to the first person, returning to the third person only in the conclusion (12:9–14).

1:13 *under heaven.* See note on v. 3. *God.* The only Hebrew word the writer uses for God is *Elohim* (used almost 30 times), which emphasizes his absolute sovereignty. He does not use the covenant name, *Yahweh* (translated "LORD"; see notes on Ge 2:4; Ex 3:14–15).

1:14 *chasing after the wind.* A graphic illustration of futility and meaninglessness (see Introduction: Purpose and Teaching). These words are used nine times in the first half of the discourse (here; v. 17; 2:11,17,26; 4:4,6,16; 6:9; see also 5:16).

1:15 See 7:13 and note. Because of the unalterableness of events, human effort is meaningless and hopeless. We should therefore learn to happily accept things the way they are and to accept our divinely appointed lot in life, as the Teacher later counsels.

1:16 *anyone who has ruled over Jerusalem before me.* See 2:7,9. This does not necessarily exclude Solomon as the Teacher. The reference could include kings prior to David, such as Melchizedek (Ge 14:18), Adoni-Zedek (Jos 10:1) and Abdi-Khepa (mentioned in the Canaanite Amarna letters from Egypt; see chart, p. xxii).

wisdom,[s] and also of madness and folly,[t]
but I learned that this, too, is a chasing
after the wind.

18For with much wisdom comes much
sorrow;[u]
the more knowledge, the more grief.[v]

Pleasures Are Meaningless

2 I thought in my heart, "Come now, I
will test you with pleasure[w] to find out
what is good." But that also proved to be
meaningless. 2"Laughter,"[x] I said, "is foolish. And what does pleasure accomplish?"
3I tried cheering myself with wine,[y] and
embracing folly[z]—my mind still guiding
me with wisdom. I wanted to see what
was worthwhile for men to do under heav-
en during the few days of their lives.
4I undertook great projects: I built houses for myself[a] and planted vineyards.[b] 5I
made gardens and parks and planted all
kinds of fruit trees in them. 6I made reser-
voirs to water groves of flourishing trees.
7I bought male and female slaves and had
other slaves[c] who were born in my house.
I also owned more herds and flocks than
anyone in Jerusalem before me. 8I amassed
silver and gold[d] for myself, and the treasure of kings and provinces.[e] I acquired
men and women singers,[f] and a harem[a] as
well—the delights of the heart of man. 9I
became greater by far than anyone in Jerusalem[g] before me.[h] In all this my wisdom
stayed with me.

10I denied myself nothing my eyes
desired;
I refused my heart no pleasure.
My heart took delight in all my work,
and this was the reward for all my
labor.
11Yet when I surveyed all that my hands
had done
and what I had toiled to achieve,
everything was meaningless, a chasing
after the wind;[i]
nothing was gained under the sun.[j]

Wisdom and Folly Are Meaningless

12Then I turned my thoughts to consider
wisdom,
and also madness and folly.[k]
What more can the king's successor do
than what has already been done?[l]
13I saw that wisdom[m] is better than
folly,[n]
just as light is better than darkness.
14The wise man has eyes in his head,
while the fool walks in the
darkness;
but I came to realize
that the same fate overtakes them
both.[o]

15Then I thought in my heart,
"The fate of the fool will overtake me
also.
What then do I gain by being
wise?"[p]
I said in my heart,
"This too is meaningless."
16For the wise man, like the fool, will
not be long remembered;[q]
in days to come both will be
forgotten.[r]
Like the fool, the wise man too must
die![s]

Toil Is Meaningless

17So I hated life, because the work that
is done under the sun was grievous to me.
All of it is meaningless, a chasing after the
wind.[t] 18I hated all the things I had toiled
for under the sun, because I must leave
them to the one who comes after me.[u]

1:17 [s] Ecc 7:23; 8:16 [t] Ecc 2:3, 12; 7:25
1:18 [u] Jer 45:3 [v] Ecc 2:23; 12:12
2:1 [w] ver 24; Ecc 7:4; 8:15
2:2 [x] S Pr 14:13
2:3 [y] ver 24-25; S Jdg 9:13; Ru 3:3; Ecc 3:12-13; 5:18; 8:15 [z] S Ecc 1:17
2:4 [a] 2Ch 2:1; 8:1-6 [b] SS 8:11
2:7 [c] 2Ch 8:7-8
2:8 [d] S 1Ki 9:28 [e] S Jdg 3:15 [f] S 2Sa 19:35
2:9 [g] Ecc 1:12 [h] 1Ch 29:25
2:11 [i] S Ecc 1:14 [j] S Ecc 1:3
2:12 [k] S Ecc 1:17 [l] S Ecc 1:9
2:13 [m] Ecc 7:19; 9:18 [n] Ecc 7:11-12
2:14 [o] Ps 49:10; Ecc 3:19; 6:6; 7:2; 9:3, 11-12
2:15 [p] ver 19; Ecc 6:8
2:16 [q] S Ps 112:6 [r] S Ecc 1:11 [s] Ps 49:10
2:17 [t] S Ecc 1:14
2:18 [u] Ps 39:6; 49:10

[a] 8 The meaning of the Hebrew for this phrase is uncertain.

1:18 Wisdom without God leads to grief and sorrow (cf. 2:23; Jer 45:3).

2:1–11 The Teacher now shows that mere pleasure cannot give meaning or satisfaction (see 1:12–15; see also note on 1:12–18).

2:1–3 The pursuit of pleasure does not bring the fulfillment that human beings seek.

2:1 *I thought in my heart.* See v. 15; 1:16. *good.* A key term in the book ("good" and "better" occur about 40 times).

2:3 *my mind still guiding me with wisdom.* From first to last (v. 9) the author used wisdom to discover the good (v. 1) and the worthwhile (v. 3). *under heaven.* See note on 1:3.

2:4–9 See 1Ki 4–11, which tells of Solomon's splendor and of his wives.

2:8 *provinces.* Probably the neighboring territories from which tribute was collected. *harem.* The Hebrew for this word occurs only here in Scripture (see NIV text note). The meaning seems to be indicated in an early Egyptian letter that uses a similar Canaanite term for concubines. It fits the situation of Solomon, who had 300 concubines in addition to 700 wives (1Ki 11:3).

2:9 See 1:16.

2:10 *work ... labor.* A key thought in Ecclesiastes is the meaninglessness (v. 11), apart from God, of toil, labor, work—words that occur about 40 times.

2:12–17 The Teacher returns to the folly of trying to find satisfaction in merely human wisdom (see 1:16–18; see also note on 1:12–18).

2:12 *king's successor.* Either the Teacher himself (see 1:1) or one who would come after him (cf. 4:15–16).

2:13 *wisdom is better than folly.* Even secular wisdom is better than folly, but in the end it is of no value, since "the same fate overtakes them both" (i.e., overtakes both the wise believer and the foolish unbeliever, v. 14; see Ps 49:10). *better.* See note on 2:1.

2:14 *eyes.* Understanding.

2:16 People tend to soon forget even the greatest leaders and heroes (see 1:11).

2:17–23 To pursue human fulfillment through work done "under the sun" (vv. 17–20,22; see 1:3 and note) is grievous and meaningless and leads to despair; its fruits must be left to others, whose character one cannot predict.

2:18 *leave them to the one who comes after me.* See v. 21; Ps 39:6; Lk 12:20.

19And who knows whether he will be a
wise man or a fool?[v] Yet he will have control over all the work into which I have
poured my effort and skill under the sun.
This too is meaningless. 20So my heart began to despair over all my toilsome labor
under the sun. 21For a man may do his
work with wisdom, knowledge and skill,
and then he must leave all he owns to
someone who has not worked for it. This
too is meaningless and a great misfortune.
22What does a man get for all the toil and
anxious striving with which he labors under the sun?[w] 23All his days his work is
pain and grief;[x] even at night his mind
does not rest.[y] This too is meaningless.

24A man can do nothing better than to
eat and drink[z] and find satisfaction in his
work.[a] This too, I see, is from the hand
of God,[b] 25for without him, who can eat
or find enjoyment?[c] 26To the man who
pleases him, God gives wisdom,[d] knowledge and happiness, but to the sinner he
gives the task of gathering and storing up
wealth[e] to hand it over to the one who
pleases God.[f] This too is meaningless, a
chasing after the wind.

A Time for Everything

3 There is a time[g] for everything,
and a season for every activity under heaven:

2 a time to be born and a time to die,
a time to plant and a time to uproot,[h]
3 a time to kill[i] and a time to heal,
a time to tear down and a time to build,
4 a time to weep and a time to laugh,
a time to mourn and a time to dance,
5 a time to scatter stones and a time to gather them,
a time to embrace and a time to refrain,
6 a time to search and a time to give up,
a time to keep and a time to throw away,
7 a time to tear and a time to mend,
a time to be silent[j] and a time to speak,
8 a time to love and a time to hate,
a time for war and a time for peace.

9What does the worker gain from his
toil?[k] 10I have seen the burden God has laid
on men.[l] 11He has made everything beautiful in its time.[m] He has also set eternity in
the hearts of men; yet they cannot fathom[n]
what God has done from beginning to end.[o]
12I know that there is nothing better for men
than to be happy and do good while they
live. 13That everyone may eat and drink,[p]
and find satisfaction[q] in all his toil—this
is the gift of God.[r] 14I know that everything
God does will endure forever; nothing can
be added to it and nothing taken from it.
God does it so that men will revere him.[s]

15Whatever is has already been,[t]
and what will be has been before;[u]
and God will call the past to account.[a]

16And I saw something else under the
sun:

In the place of judgment—wickedness was there,
in the place of justice—wickedness was there.

17I thought in my heart,

"God will bring to judgment[v]
both the righteous and the wicked,
for there will be a time for every activity,
a time for every deed."[w]

18I also thought, "As for men, God tests
them so that they may see that they are

2:19 [v] S ver 15
2:22 [w] S Ecc 1:3
2:23 [x] S Ecc 1:18
[y] S Ge 3:17; S Job 7:2
2:24 [z] ver 3; 1Co 15:32
[a] S ver 1; Ecc 3:22
[b] S Job 2:10; Ecc 3:12-13; 5:17-19; 7:14; 9:7-10; 11:7-10
2:25 [c] S Ps 127:2
2:26 [d] S Job 9:4
[e] S Job 27:17
[f] S Pr 13:22
3:1 [g] ver 11,17; Ecc 8:6
3:2 [h] Isa 28:24
3:3 [i] S Dt 5:17
3:7 [j] S Est 4:14
3:9 [k] S Ecc 1:3
3:10 [l] S Ecc 1:13
3:11 [m] S ver 1
[n] S Job 11:7
[o] S Job 28:23; Ro 11:33
3:13 [p] Ecc 2:3
[q] Ps 34:12
[r] S Dt 12:7,18; S Ecc 2:24
3:14 [s] S Job 23:15; Ecc 5:7; 7:18; 8:12-13
3:15 [t] Ecc 6:10
[u] S Ecc 1:9
3:17 [v] S Job 19:29; Ecc 11:9; 12:14
[w] ver 1

[a] 15 Or *God calls back the past*

2:19 *who knows ...?* For a more searching "Who knows ...?" for secular people see 3:21.

2:24–25 The heart of Ecclesiastes, a theme repeated in 3:12–13,22; 5:18–20; 8:15; 9:7 and climaxed in 12:13. Only in God does life have meaning and true pleasure. Without him nothing satisfies, but with him we find satisfaction and enjoyment. True pleasure comes only when we acknowledge and revere God (12:13).

2:26 *God gives ... gives.* A key thought in this book (see 3:13 and note on 3:12–13; 5:19; 6:2 and note on 6:2–3,6; 8:15; 9:9). *but to the sinner.* For exceptions to this general principle see 8:14; Ps 73:1–12.

3:1–22 Humans have little or no control over times and changes. The eternal God sovereignly determines all of life's activities (e.g., the 14 opposites of vv. 2–8).

3:1 Cf. 8:6. *under heaven.* See note on 1:3.

3:2 *a time.* Divinely appointed (see Ps 31:15; Pr 16:1–9).

3:9 See note on 2:17–23.

3:11 The chapter summarized: God's beautiful but tantalizing world is too big for us, yet its satisfactions are too small. Since we were made for eternity, the things of time cannot fully and permanently satisfy.

3:12–13 A pointer to the book's conclusion. God's people find meaning in life when they cheerfully accept it from the hand of God.

3:14 *revere him.* A virtual summation of the message of the book (cf. 12:13).

3:15 See 1:9.

3:17 *judgment.* God's true judgments are the answer to cynicism about human injustices. "The past" (v. 15) is not meaningless (as people dismiss it as being, 1:11), and God will override the perverse judgments (v. 16) of people (see 12:14). *the righteous and the wicked.* No one will escape divine judgment (cf. Ro 14:10; 2Co 5:10 and notes; cf. also Rev 20:12–13).

3:18 *like the animals.* Humans "under the sun" are as mortal as any animal; but, unlike animals, they must be made to see this condition and, through their dim awareness of eternity (v. 11), be distressed.

like the animals.[x] 19Man's fate[y] is like that
of the animals; the same fate awaits them
both: As one dies, so dies the other. All
have the same breath[a]; man has no advantage over the animal. Everything is
meaningless. 20All go to the same place;
all come from dust, and to dust all return.[z]
21Who knows if the spirit of man rises upward[a] and if the spirit of the animal[b] goes
down into the earth?"
22So I saw that there is nothing better for
a man than to enjoy his work,[b] because
that is his lot.[c] For who can bring him to
see what will happen after him?

Oppression, Toil, Friendlessness

4 Again I looked and saw all the oppression[d] that was taking place under the
sun:

I saw the tears of the oppressed—
and they have no comforter;
power was on the side of their
oppressors—
and they have no comforter.[e]
2And I declared that the dead,[f]
who had already died,
are happier than the living,
who are still alive.[g]
3But better than both
is he who has not yet been,[h]
who has not seen the evil
that is done under the sun.[i]

4And I saw that all labor and all achievement spring from man's envy of his neighbor. This too is meaningless, a chasing after the wind.[j]

5The fool folds his hands[k]
and ruins himself.
6Better one handful with tranquillity
than two handfuls with toil[l]
and chasing after the wind.

7Again I saw something meaningless
under the sun:

8There was a man all alone;
he had neither son nor brother.
There was no end to his toil,
yet his eyes were not content[m] with
his wealth.
"For whom am I toiling," he asked,
"and why am I depriving myself of
enjoyment?"
This too is meaningless—
a miserable business!

9Two are better than one,
because they have a good return for
their work:
10If one falls down,
his friend can help him up.
But pity the man who falls
and has no one to help him up!
11Also, if two lie down together, they
will keep warm.
But how can one keep warm alone?
12Though one may be overpowered,
two can defend themselves.
A cord of three strands is not quickly
broken.

Advancement Is Meaningless

13Better a poor but wise youth than an
old but foolish king who no longer knows
how to take warning. 14The youth may
have come from prison to the kingship, or
he may have been born in poverty within his kingdom. 15I saw that all who lived
and walked under the sun followed the
youth, the king's successor. 16There was
no end to all the people who were before
them. But those who came later were not
pleased with the successor. This too is
meaningless, a chasing after the wind.

Stand in Awe of God

5 Guard your steps when you go to the
house of God. Go near to listen rather

[a] 19 Or *spirit* [b] 21 Or *Who knows the spirit of man, which rises upward, or the spirit of the animal, which*

3:18 [x] S Ps 73:22 **3:19** [y] S Ecc 2:14 **3:20** [z] S Ge 2:7; S Job 34:15 **3:21** [a] Ecc 12:7 **3:22** [b] S Ecc 2:24 [c] S Job 31:2 **4:1** [d] S Ps 12:5 [e] La 1:16 **4:2** [f] Jer 20:17-18; 22:10 [g] S Job 3:17; S 10:18 **4:3** [h] S Job 3:16 [i] S Job 3:22 **4:4** [j] S Ecc 1:14 **4:5** [k] S Pr 6:10 **4:6** [l] Pr 15:16-17; S 16:8 **4:8** [m] Pr 27:20

3:19 *same breath.* See Ps 104:29–30.

3:20 *to the same place.* Not heaven or hell but humankind's observable destination, which is a return to dust, just like the animals. Death is the great leveler of all living things (see Ge 3:19; Ps 103:14).

3:21 *Who knows . . . ?* See 2:19 and note; cf. 12:7. On their own, human beings cannot know; they can only guess. The answer, revealed at first in glimpses (see e.g., Ps 16:9–11; 49:15; 73:23–26; Isa 26:19; Da 12:2 and note), was brought fully "to light through the gospel" (2Ti 1:10; see also Jn 5:24–29).

3:22 *nothing better.* As an end in itself, work too is meaningless (see 4:4; 9:9). Only receiving it as a gift from God (v. 13) gives it enduring worth (v. 14).

4:1 *oppression.* A theme already touched on (3:16) and another ingredient in the human tragedy. To find life meaningless is sad enough, but to taste its cruelty is bitter beyond words.

4:2 *happier than the living.* See Job 3; Jer 20:14–18. For faith that sees a bigger picture see Ro 8:35–39.

4:4–6 Neither hard work (motivated by envy) nor idleness brings happiness, meaning or fulfillment.

4:4 *all labor and all achievement.* This too is meaningless unless done with God's blessing (see 3:13; cf. the selfless success of Joseph, Ge 39).

4:5 The ruin of the idle person is vividly pictured in 10:18; Pr 6:6–11; 24:30–34.

4:6 *tranquillity.* See Pr 30:7–9. Paul says the last word on this subject (Php 4:11–13).

4:7–12 Those who toil only for themselves—for whatever reason—lead meaningless and difficult lives.

4:12 *two . . . three.* A climactic construction.

4:13–16 Advancement without God is another example of the meaninglessness of secularism.

4:16 *were before them.* Stood before them and served them. *those who came later.* The next generation.

5:1–7 The theme of this section is the meaninglessness of superficial religion, as reflected in making rash vows.

5:1 *Guard your steps.* Think about what you ought to say and do. *house of God.* Here probably a reference

than to offer the sacrifice of fools, who do not know that they do wrong.

2 Do not be quick with your mouth,
  do not be hasty in your heart
  to utter anything before God.[n]
God is in heaven
  and you are on earth,
  so let your words be few.[o]
3 As a dream[p] comes when there are
    many cares,
  so the speech of a fool when there
    are many words.[q]

4 When you make a vow to God, do not
delay in fulfilling it.[r] He has no pleasure in
fools; fulfill your vow.[s] 5 It is better not to
vow than to make a vow and not fulfill it.[t]
6 Do not let your mouth lead you into sin.
And do not protest to the ⌊temple⌋ messenger, "My vow was a mistake." Why should
God be angry at what you say and destroy
the work of your hands? 7 Much dreaming
and many words are meaningless. Therefore stand in awe of God.[u]

Riches Are Meaningless

8 If you see the poor oppressed[v] in a district, and justice and rights denied, do not
be surprised at such things; for one official
is eyed by a higher one, and over them
both are others higher still. 9 The increase
from the land is taken by all; the king himself profits from the fields.

10 Whoever loves money never has
    money enough;
  whoever loves wealth is never
    satisfied with his income.
This too is meaningless.

11 As goods increase,
  so do those who consume them.
And what benefit are they to the owner
  except to feast his eyes on them?

12 The sleep of a laborer is sweet,
  whether he eats little or much,
  but the abundance of a rich man
  permits him no sleep.[w]

13 I have seen a grievous evil under the sun:[x]

wealth hoarded to the harm of its
    owner,
14 or wealth lost through some
    misfortune,
so that when he has a son
  there is nothing left for him.
15 Naked a man comes from his mother's
    womb,
  and as he comes, so he departs.[y]
He takes nothing from his labor[z]
  that he can carry in his hand.[a]

16 This too is a grievous evil:

As a man comes, so he departs,
  and what does he gain,
  since he toils for the wind?[b]
17 All his days he eats in darkness,
  with great frustration, affliction and
    anger.

18 Then I realized that it is good and
proper for a man to eat and drink,[c] and to
find satisfaction in his toilsome labor[d] under the sun during the few days of life God
has given him—for this is his lot. 19 Moreover, when God gives any man wealth
and possessions,[e] and enables him to enjoy them,[f] to accept his lot[g] and be happy
in his work—this is a gift of God.[h] 20 He
seldom reflects on the days of his life, because God keeps him occupied with gladness of heart.[i]

6 I have seen another evil under the
sun, and it weighs heavily on men:
2 God gives a man wealth, possessions and
honor, so that he lacks nothing his heart
desires, but God does not enable him to
enjoy them,[j] and a stranger enjoys them
instead. This is meaningless, a grievous
evil.[k]

5:2 [n] S Jdg 11:35 [o] S Job 6:24; S Pr 20:25 **5:3** [p] S Job 20:8 [q] Ecc 10:14 **5:4** [r] S Dt 23:21; S Jdg 11:35; Ps 119:60 [s] S Nu 30:2; Ps 66:13-14 **5:5** [t] Nu 30:2-4; Jnh 2:9 **5:7** [u] Ecc 3:14 **5:8** [v] S Ps 12:5 **5:12** [w] Job 20:20 **5:13** [x] Ecc 6:1-2 **5:15** [y] S Job 1:21 [z] Ps 49:17; 1Ti 6:7 [a] Ecc 1:3 **5:16** [b] S Ecc 1:3 **5:18** [c] S Ecc 2:3 [d] Ecc 2:10, 24 **5:19** [e] S 1Ch 29:12 [f] Ecc 6:2 [g] S Job 31:2 [h] S Ecc 2:24 **5:20** [i] S Dt 12:7, 18 **6:2** [j] Ecc 5:19 [k] Ecc 5:13

---

to Solomon's temple. *listen.* Obey. 1Sa 15:22 uses the same Hebrew verb and makes the same contrast between real and superficial worship. *sacrifice.* Probably connected with the vow of vv. 4–6.

5:2 *quick with your mouth.* As in a rash vow. *God ... heaven ... you ... earth.* Highlights the contrast between God and humankind.

5:3 A proverb. In context it suggests that in the midst of cares one dreams of bliss (as a starving person dreams of a banquet), and in anticipation may offer rash vows ("many words") to God (see v. 7).

5:4 *vow.* See Dt 23:21–23; 1Sa 1:11,24–28. *no pleasure in fools.* In Scripture the fool is not one who cannot learn, but one who refuses to learn (see Pr 1:20–27; see also NIV text note on Pr 1:7).

5:6 *⌊temple⌋ messenger.* Probably the priest (see Mal 2:7 and note). *Why should God be angry ...?* To break a vow is a serious matter (see Nu 30:2 and note on 30:1–16) and can have disastrous consequences (see Dt 23:21–23).

5:8 *do not be surprised.* For other frank appraisals of human society see 4:1–3. This teacher, like Jesus, who "knew what was in a man" (Jn 2:25), had no illusions or utopian schemes.

5:9 *king ... profits from the fields.* See note on Am 7:1.

5:10 Greater wealth does not bring satisfaction (see 1Ti 6:6–8; see also Php 4:11–12 and notes).

5:11–12 Greater wealth brings greater anxiety (see vv. 13–14 and note on v. 13; Mt 13:22; 1Ti 6:9–10,17–19).

5:11 *those who consume them.* Human parasites.

5:13 *harm.* Including worry about one's possessions.

5:15 *He takes nothing.* See Lk 12:13–21.

5:18–20 See note on 2:24–25.

6:2–3,6 *enjoy.* Comparing v. 2 with 5:19 demonstrates that the ability to enjoy God's blessings is a bonus—a gift of God, not a right or guarantee. God calls the person who forgets this truth a fool (Lk 12:20).

6:2 *a stranger enjoys them instead.* For example, when people are robbed of their wealth or die without heirs.

3 A man may have a hundred children
and live many years; yet no matter how
long he lives, if he cannot enjoy his prosperity and does not receive proper burial, I
say that a stillborn[l] child is better off than
he.[m] 4 It comes without meaning, it departs
in darkness, and in darkness its name is
shrouded. 5 Though it never saw the sun or
knew anything, it has more rest than does
that man— 6 even if he lives a thousand
years twice over but fails to enjoy his prosperity. Do not all go to the same place?[n]

7 All man's efforts are for his mouth,
yet his appetite is never satisfied.[o]
8 What advantage has a wise man
over a fool?[p]
What does a poor man gain
by knowing how to conduct himself
before others?
9 Better what the eye sees
than the roving of the appetite.
This too is meaningless,
a chasing after the wind.[q]

10 Whatever exists has already been
named,[r]
and what man is has been known;
no man can contend
with one who is stronger than he.
11 The more the words,
the less the meaning,
and how does that profit anyone?

12 For who knows what is good for a
man in life, during the few and meaningless days[s] he passes through like a shadow?[t] Who can tell him what will happen
under the sun after he is gone?

Wisdom

7 A good name is better than fine
perfume,[u]
and the day of death better than the
day of birth.[v]
2 It is better to go to a house of
mourning
than to go to a house of feasting,
for death[w] is the destiny[x] of every man;
the living should take this to heart.
3 Sorrow is better than laughter,[y]
because a sad face is good for the
heart.
4 The heart of the wise is in the house of
mourning,
but the heart of fools is in the house
of pleasure.[z]
5 It is better to heed a wise man's rebuke[a]
than to listen to the song of fools.
6 Like the crackling of thorns[b] under the
pot,
so is the laughter[c] of fools.
This too is meaningless.

7 Extortion turns a wise man into a fool,
and a bribe[d] corrupts the heart.
8 The end of a matter is better than its
beginning,
and patience[e] is better than pride.
9 Do not be quickly provoked[f] in your
spirit,
for anger resides in the lap of fools.[g]

10 Do not say, "Why were the old days[h]
better than these?"
For it is not wise to ask such
questions.
11 Wisdom, like an inheritance, is a good
thing[i]
and benefits those who see the sun.[j]
12 Wisdom is a shelter
as money is a shelter,
but the advantage of knowledge is this:
that wisdom preserves the life of its
possessor.

13 Consider what God has done:[k]

Who can straighten
what he has made crooked?[l]
14 When times are good, be happy;
but when times are bad, consider:
God has made the one
as well as the other.[m]
Therefore, a man cannot discover
anything about his future.

6:3 [l]S Job 3:16 [m]S Job 3:3 **6:6** [n]Ecc 2:14 **6:7** [o]S Pr 27:20 **6:8** [p]S Ecc 2:15 **6:9** [q]S Ecc 1:14 **6:10** [r]Ecc 3:15 **6:12** [s]S Job 10:20; S 20:8 [t]S 1Ch 29:15; S Job 14:2; S Ps 39:6 **7:1** [u]Pr 22:1; SS 1:3 [v]S Job 10:18 **7:2** [w]S Pr 11:19 [x]S Ecc 2:14 **7:3** [y]S Pr 14:13 **7:4** [z]S Ecc 2:1; Jer 16:8 **7:5** [a]S Pr 13:18; 15:31-32 **7:6** [b]S Ps 58:9 [c]S Pr 14:13 **7:7** [d]S Ex 18:21; S 23:8 **7:8** [e]Pr 14:29 **7:9** [f]S Mt 5:22 [g]S Pr 14:29 **7:10** [h]S Ps 77:5 **7:11** [i]Ecc 2:13 [j]Ecc 11:7 **7:13** [k]Ecc 2:24 [l]Ecc 1:15 **7:14** [m]S Job 1:21; S Ecc 2:24

6:3 *does not receive proper burial.* Dies unlamented or dishonored, like King Jehoiakim (Jer 22:18–19). *stillborn child.* For the secularist, life is a pointless journey to extinction, to which being stillborn is the quickest and easiest route (cf. Job 3:16; Ps 58:8).

6:6 *to the same place.* Still talking in terms of what we can observe (that all people die), not of what lies beyond death (see v. 12; 3:21).

6:7–12 In confronting complacency, the Teacher gives several causes for concern: the short-lived (v. 7), debatable (v. 8) and elusive (v. 9) rewards of life; the limits of our creativity, power and wisdom (vv. 10–11); and the unreliability of merely human values and predictions (v. 12).

6:9 It is better to be content with what one has than to nurture unrestrained desires (cf. Php 4:11–12 and note on 4:12; 1Ti 6:6,8).

6:10 *named.* Predetermined by God. *known.* Foreknown by God. *one who is stronger.* God.

6:12 *like a shadow.* See Job 8:9 and note.

7:1 *day of death better.* The Christian has ample reason to say this (2Co 5:1–10; Php 1:21–23). But the Teacher's point is valid, as explained in vv. 2–6, namely, that happy times generally teach us less than hard times.

7:6 *crackling of thorns.* The "laughter of fools" is likened to a noisy, but short-lived, fire (see Ps 58:9 and note).

7:7 *bribe.* See Mt 28:11–15; Lk 22:4–6.

7:9 *anger.* See, e.g., Pr 16:32; 17:14; 1Co 13:4–5.

7:11 *see the sun.* Are alive.

7:12 *preserves the life.* The Hebrew for this expression can also mean "gives life" or "renews life" (cf. Pr 3:13–18; 13:14).

7:13 *Who can straighten . . . ?* Not fatalism, but a reminder that mere mortals cannot change what God determines (see note on 1:15; cf. also note on 3:1–22).

7:14 *God has made the one* [bad times] *as well as the other* [good times]. Cf. Ro 8:28–29.

[15]In this meaningless life[n] of mine I have seen both of these:

a righteous man perishing in his righteousness,
and a wicked man living long in his wickedness.[o]
[16]Do not be overrighteous,
neither be overwise—
why destroy yourself?
[17]Do not be overwicked,
and do not be a fool—
why die before your time?[p]
[18]It is good to grasp the one
and not let go of the other.
The man who fears God[q] will avoid all ⌞extremes⌟.[a]
[19]Wisdom[r] makes one wise man more powerful[s]
than ten rulers in a city.
[20]There is not a righteous man[t] on earth
who does what is right and never sins.[u]
[21]Do not pay attention to every word people say,
or you[v] may hear your servant cursing you—
[22]for you know in your heart
that many times you yourself have cursed others.

[23]All this I tested by wisdom and I said,

"I am determined to be wise"[w]—
but this was beyond me.
[24]Whatever wisdom may be,
it is far off and most profound—
who can discover it?[x]
[25]So I turned my mind to understand,
to investigate and to search out wisdom and the scheme of things[y]
and to understand the stupidity of wickedness
and the madness of folly.[z]
[26]I find more bitter than death
the woman who is a snare,[a]
whose heart is a trap
and whose hands are chains.
The man who pleases God will escape her,
but the sinner she will ensnare.[b]

[27]"Look," says the Teacher,[b][c] "this is what I have discovered:

"Adding one thing to another to discover the scheme of things—
[28]while I was still searching
but not finding—
I found one ⌞upright⌟ man among a thousand,
but not one ⌞upright⌟ woman[d] among them all.
[29]This only have I found:
God made mankind upright,
but men have gone in search of many schemes."

8 Who is like the wise man?
Who knows the explanation of things?
Wisdom brightens a man's face
and changes its hard appearance.

Obey the King

[2]Obey the king's command, I say, because you took an oath before God. [3]Do not be in a hurry to leave the king's presence.[e] Do not stand up for a bad cause, for he will do whatever he pleases. [4]Since a king's word is supreme, who can say to him, "What are you doing?[f]"

[5]Whoever obeys his command will come to no harm,
and the wise heart will know the proper time and procedure.
[6]For there is a proper time and procedure for every matter,[g]
though a man's misery weighs heavily upon him.

[a] *18* Or *will follow them both* [b] *27* Or *leader of the assembly*

7:15 [n]S Job 7:7 [o]S Job 21:7; Ecc 8:12-14; Jer 12:1 **7:17** [p]Job 15:32 **7:18** [q]S Ecc 3:14 **7:19** [r]S Ecc 2:13 [s]S Pr 8:14 **7:20** [t]S Ps 14:3 [u]S 2Ch 6:36; S Job 4:17; S Pr 20:9; Ro 3:12 **7:21** [v]Pr 30:10 **7:23** [w]S Ecc 1:17 **7:24** [x]S Job 28:12 **7:25** [y]S Job 28:3 [z]S Ecc 1:17 **7:26** [a]S Ex 10:7; S Jdg 14:15 [b]S Pr 2:16-19; 5:3-5; S 7:23; 22:14 **7:27** [c]S Ecc 1:1 **7:28** [d]1Ki 11:3 **8:3** [e]Ecc 10:4 **8:4** [f]Est 1:19 **8:6** [g]Ecc 3:1

7:15 *righteous man perishing.* Righteousness is no sure protection against hard times or an early death.
7:16 *not ... overrighteous ... overwise.* If true righteousness and wisdom do not necessarily prevent ruin, then extreme, legalistic righteousness and wisdom will surely not help.
7:17 *not ... overwicked.* Extreme wickedness is even more foolhardy.
7:18 *the one ... the other.* The God-fearing person will avoid both extremes (legalism and libertinism) and lead a balanced—truly righteous and wise—life (cf. Ro 6:14).
7:20 *not a righteous man on earth.* A sober Biblical truth (see Ro 3:10–20,23).
7:24 See Job 28:12–28; 1Co 2:9–16.
7:26 See Pr 7:6–27.
7:27 *Teacher.* See note on 1:1. *Adding one thing to another to discover the scheme of things.* This inductive method can never be complete, nor can we reliably interpret all that we manage to observe (3:11b). Human wisdom and understanding must always yield to revealed truth.
7:28 *one ⌞upright⌟ man ... but not one ⌞upright⌟ woman.* According to the Teacher's experience. Scripture nowhere declares that women are morally inferior.
7:29 *God made mankind upright, but.* See Ge 3:1–6; Ro 5:12.
8:2 *king's command.* Both principle (v. 2) and prudence (vv. 3–6) set limits on our freedom. *took an oath.* Of loyalty to the king (as seen, e.g., in 1Ch 29:24).
8:3 *hurry to leave the king's presence.* To do so would show lack of respect—even disloyalty—to him.
8:4 *who can say ..., "What are you doing?"* Cf. Isa 45:9; Ro 9:20.
8:5 *Whoever obeys ... will come to no harm.* See Ro 13:3–5 and notes.
8:6 *a man's misery.* People should put the king's command above their own misery.

7 Since no man knows the future,
who can tell him what is to come?
8 No man has power over the wind to
contain it[a];
so no one has power over the day of
his death.
As no one is discharged in time of war,
so wickedness will not release those
who practice it.

9 All this I saw, as I applied my mind to
everything done under the sun. There is
a time when a man lords it over others to
his own[b] hurt. 10 Then too, I saw the wicked buried[h]—those who used to come and
go from the holy place and receive praise[c]
in the city where they did this. This too is
meaningless.
11 When the sentence for a crime is not
quickly carried out, the hearts of the people are filled with schemes to do wrong.
12 Although a wicked man commits a hundred crimes and still lives a long time, I
know that it will go better[i] with God-fearing men,[j] who are reverent before God.[k]
13 Yet because the wicked do not fear God,[l]
it will not go well with them, and their
days[m] will not lengthen like a shadow.
14 There is something else meaningless
that occurs on earth: righteous men who
get what the wicked deserve, and wicked
men who get what the righteous deserve.[n]
This too, I say, is meaningless.[o] 15 So I
commend the enjoyment of life[p], because
nothing is better for a man under the sun
than to eat and drink[q] and be glad.[r] Then
joy will accompany him in his work all the
days of the life God has given him under
the sun.
16 When I applied my mind to know
wisdom[s] and to observe man's labor on
earth[t]—his eyes not seeing sleep day
or night— 17 then I saw all that God has
done.[u] No one can comprehend what goes
on under the sun. Despite all his efforts
to search it out, man cannot discover its
meaning. Even if a wise man claims he
knows, he cannot really comprehend it.[v]

8:10 [h] S Ecc 1:11
8:12 [i] S Dt 12:28
[j] S Ex 1:20
[k] Ecc 3:14
8:13 [l] Ecc 3:14
[m] Dt 4:40; Job 5:26; Ps 34:12; Isa 65:20
8:14 [n] S Job 21:7
[o] S Ecc 7:15
8:15 [p] S Ps 42:8
[q] S Ex 32:6; S Ecc 2:3
[r] S Ecc 2:1
8:16 [s] S Ecc 1:17
[t] Ecc 1:13
8:17 [u] S Job 28:3
[v] S Job 28:23; Ro 11:33
9:1 [w] Ecc 10:14
9:2 [x] Job 9:22; Ecc 2:14
9:3 [y] S Job 9:22; S Ecc 2:14
[z] Jer 11:8; 13:10; 16:12; 17:9
[a] S Job 21:26
9:5 [b] S Job 14:21
[c] S Ps 9:6
[d] S Ecc 1:11
9:6 [e] S Job 21:21
9:7 [f] S Nu 6:20
[g] S Ecc 2:24

A Common Destiny for All

9 So I reflected on all this and concluded that the righteous and the wise and
what they do are in God's hands, but no
man knows whether love or hate awaits
him.[w] 2 All share a common destiny—the
righteous and the wicked, the good and the
bad,[d] the clean and the unclean, those who
offer sacrifices and those who do not.

As it is with the good man,
so with the sinner;
as it is with those who take oaths,
so with those who are afraid to take
them.[x]

3 This is the evil in everything that happens under the sun: The same destiny
overtakes all.[y] The hearts of men, moreover, are full of evil and there is madness
in their hearts while they live,[z] and afterward they join the dead.[a] 4 Anyone who is
among the living has hope[e]—even a live
dog is better off than a dead lion!

5 For the living know that they will die,
but the dead know nothing;[b]
they have no further reward,
and even the memory of them[c] is
forgotten.[d]
6 Their love, their hate
and their jealousy have long since
vanished;
never again will they have a part
in anything that happens under the
sun.[e]

7 Go, eat your food with gladness, and
drink your wine[f] with a joyful heart,[g] for
it is now that God favors what you do.

[a] 8 Or *over his spirit to retain it* [b] 9 Or *to their*
[c] 10 Some Hebrew manuscripts and Septuagint (Aquila); most Hebrew manuscripts *and are forgotten*
[d] 2 Septuagint (Aquila), Vulgate and Syriac; Hebrew does not have *and the bad.* [e] 4 Or *What then is to be chosen? With all who live, there is hope*

8:7–8 *no man knows ... No man has power.* See Ps 31:15; Mt 6:34; 2Cor 5:1–10; Jas 4:13–16.

8:8 *wickedness will not release.* Moral evil has great power to enslave (see Ro 7:15–24 and note on 7:17). But see Ro 7:25 and note.

8:10 *the wicked buried.* In this context it implies undeserved respect (see note on 6:3; cf. Job 21:28–33; Lk 16:22).

8:11 Delayed punishment tends to induce more wrongdoing.

8:12 *I know.* Here the Teacher speaks from mature faith, not as one "still searching but not finding" (7:28). For similar declarations see 3:17; 11:9; 12:14.

8:14 Job 21–24 enlarges on this; Ps 73 draws the sting of it; and Jn 5:28–29 gives the final explanation.

8:15 *eat ... drink ... be glad.* Spoken gratefully (see 5:19; 9:7; Dt 8). For such words spoken arrogantly see Lk 12:19–20; 1Co 15:32.

8:17 *No one can comprehend.* Dt 29:29 sums up what we are allowed and not allowed to know (cf. Ro 11:33).

9:1 *whether love or hate.* The future is under God's control, and no one knows whether that future will be good or bad.

9:2 *common destiny.* See v. 3. Not only the wise and foolish (2:14), but also the good and the bad are seen leveled, in the sense noted at 3:20. For the Teacher's conviction (beyond mere observation) that God ultimately will see justice done see note on 8:12.

9:3 *evil ... evil.* The apparently common destiny (both the righteous and the wicked die) encourages some people to sin.

9:5 *no further reward.* The dead have lost all opportunity in this life for enjoyment and reward from labor (see v. 6).

9:7–9 The Babylonian *Epic of Gilgamesh* contains a section (10.3.6–14) remarkably similar to this passage, illustrating the international flavor of ancient wisdom literature (see chart, p. xxii, and essay, p. 727).

9:7 See note on 8:15.

8Always be clothed in white,[h] and always
anoint your head with oil. 9Enjoy life with
your wife,[i] whom you love, all the days of
this meaningless life that God has given
you under the sun—all your meaningless
days. For this is your lot[j] in life and in your
toilsome labor under the sun. 10Whatever[k]
your hand finds to do, do it with all your
might,[l] for in the grave,[a][m] where you are
going, there is neither working nor planning nor knowledge nor wisdom.[n]

11I have seen something else under the
sun:

The race is not to the swift
  or the battle to the strong,[o]
nor does food come to the wise[p]
  or wealth to the brilliant
  or favor to the learned;
but time and chance[q] happen to them
    all.[r]

12Moreover, no man knows when his
hour will come:

As fish are caught in a cruel net,
  or birds are taken in a snare,
so men are trapped by evil times[s]
  that fall unexpectedly upon them.[t]

Wisdom Better Than Folly

13I also saw under the sun this example of wisdom[u] that greatly impressed me:
14There was once a small city with only
a few people in it. And a powerful king
came against it, surrounded it and built
huge siegeworks against it. 15Now there
lived in that city a man poor but wise, and
he saved the city by his wisdom. But nobody remembered that poor man.[v] 16So I
said, "Wisdom is better than strength."
But the poor man's wisdom is despised,
and his words are no longer heeded.[w]

17The quiet words of the wise are more
    to be heeded
  than the shouts of a ruler of fools.
18Wisdom[x] is better than weapons of
    war,
  but one sinner destroys much good.

10 As dead flies give perfume a bad
    smell,
  so a little folly[y] outweighs wisdom
    and honor.
2The heart of the wise inclines to the
    right,
  but the heart of the fool to the left.
3Even as he walks along the road,
  the fool lacks sense
  and shows everyone[z] how stupid
    he is.
4If a ruler's anger rises against you,
  do not leave your post;[a]
  calmness can lay great errors to
    rest.[b]

5There is an evil I have seen under the
    sun,
  the sort of error that arises from a
    ruler:
6Fools are put in many high positions,[c]
  while the rich occupy the low ones.
7I have seen slaves on horseback,
  while princes go on foot like slaves.[d]

8Whoever digs a pit may fall into it;[e]
  whoever breaks through a wall may
    be bitten by a snake.[f]
9Whoever quarries stones may be
    injured by them;
  whoever splits logs may be
    endangered by them.[g]

10If the ax is dull
  and its edge unsharpened,
more strength is needed
  but skill will bring success.

11If a snake bites before it is charmed,
  there is no profit for the charmer.[h]
12Words from a wise man's mouth are
    gracious,[i]
  but a fool is consumed by his own
    lips.[j]
13At the beginning his words are folly;
  at the end they are wicked madness—
14 and the fool multiplies words.[k]

No one knows what is coming—
  who can tell him what will happen
    after him?[l]

15A fool's work wearies him;
  he does not know the way to town.

9:8 [h]S Rev 3:4
9:9 [i]S Pr 5:18 [j]S Job 31:2
9:10 [k]S 1Sa 10:7 [l]Ecc 11:6 [m]Nu 16:33; S Ps 6:5; Isa 38:18 [n]S Ecc 2:24
9:11 [o]Am 2:14-15 [p]Job 32:13; Isa 47:10; Jer 9:23 [q]Ecc 2:14 [r]S Dt 8:18
9:12 [s]S Pr 29:6 [t]S Ps 73:22; S Ecc 2:14
9:13 [u]S 2Sa 20:22
9:15 [v]S Ge 40:14; S Ecc 1:11
9:16 [w]Est 6:3
9:18 [x]S Ecc 2:13
10:1 [y]Pr 13:16; 18:2
10:3 [z]Pr 13:16
10:4 [a]Ecc 8:3 [b]S Pr 16:14
10:6 [c]S Pr 29:2
10:7 [d]Pr 19:10
10:8 [e]S Ps 57:6 [f]S Est 2:23; Ps 9:16; Am 5:19
10:9 [g]S Pr 26:27
10:11 [h]S Ps 58:5; S Isa 3:3
10:12 [i]Pr 10:32 [j]S Pr 10:6; S 14:3; S 15:2; S 18:7
10:14 [k]Ecc 5:3 [l]Ecc 9:1

[a] 10 Hebrew *Sheol*

9:8 *be clothed in white ... anoint your head with oil.* Expressions of joy.
9:10 Cf. Col 3:23.
9:11 *time and chance.* Success is uncertain—more evidence that ultimately humans do not control events.
9:12 *hour.* Of disaster. *men are trapped.* Success is unpredictable, because people are not wise enough to know when misfortune may overtake them.
9:15 *But nobody remembered.* Further warning against placing too high hopes on one's wisdom. Its reputation fades, its good is soon undone (v. 18b), and it has no answer to death (2:15–16).
10:1 *a little folly outweighs.* 2Ki 20:12–19 presents a striking example.
10:2 *the right ... the left.* These can stand for the greater and the lesser good (cf. Ge 48:13–20); or perhaps here, as in some later Jewish writings, for what is good and what is evil (cf. Mt 25:33–34,41).
10:5 *error ... from a ruler.* For the Teacher's observations on human regimes see vv. 4,6–7,16–17,20; 3:16; 4:1–3,13–16; 5:8–9; 8:2–6,10–11; 9:17.
10:6–7 See Pr 19:10 and note; 30:21–22.
10:12 *Words.* A favorite topic in wisdom literature (see, e.g., Pr 15; Jas 3:2–12). *is consumed by his own lips.* A striking wordplay for graphically asserting that what a fool spouts from his lips will ultimately destroy him.
10:15 *does not know the way to town.* Since in Scripture a fool is one who refuses God's teaching (see note on

[16]Woe to you, O land whose king was a
servant[a m]
and whose princes feast in the
morning.
[17]Blessed are you, O land whose king is
of noble birth
and whose princes eat at a proper
time—
for strength and not for drunkenness.[n]
[18]If a man is lazy, the rafters sag;
if his hands are idle, the house
leaks.[o]

[19]A feast is made for laughter,
and wine[p] makes life merry,
but money is the answer for
everything.

[20]Do not revile the king[q] even in your
thoughts,
or curse the rich in your bedroom,
because a bird of the air may carry
your words,
and a bird on the wing may report
what you say.

Bread Upon the Waters

11 Cast[r] your bread upon the waters,
for after many days you will find it
again.[s]
[2]Give portions to seven, yes to eight,
for you do not know what disaster
may come upon the land.

[3]If clouds are full of water,
they pour rain upon the earth.
Whether a tree falls to the south or to
the north,
in the place where it falls, there will
it lie.
[4]Whoever watches the wind will not
plant;
whoever looks at the clouds will not
reap.

[5]As you do not know the path of the
wind,[t]
or how the body is formed[b] in a
mother's womb,[u]
so you cannot understand the work of
God,
the Maker of all things.
[6]Sow your seed in the morning,
and at evening let not your hands be
idle,[v]
for you do not know which will
succeed,
whether this or that,
or whether both will do equally
well.

Remember Your Creator While Young

[7]Light is sweet,
and it pleases the eyes to see the
sun.[w]
[8]However many years a man may
live,
let him enjoy them all.
But let him remember[x] the days of
darkness,
for they will be many.
Everything to come is meaningless.
[9]Be happy, young man, while you are
young,
and let your heart give you joy in
the days of your youth.
Follow the ways of your heart
and whatever your eyes see,
but know that for all these things
God will bring you to judgment.[y]
[10]So then, banish anxiety[z] from your
heart
and cast off the troubles of your
body,
for youth and vigor are
meaningless.[a]

12 Remember[b] your Creator
in the days of your youth,

[a] 16 Or *king is a child* [b] 5 Or *know how life* (or *the spirit*) / *enters the body being formed*

10:16 [m]Isa 3:4-5, 12 **10:17** [n]S Dt 14:26; S 1Sa 25:36; S Pr 31:4 **10:18** [o]Pr 20:4; S 24:30-34 **10:19** [p]S Ge 14:18; S Jdg 9:13 **10:20** [q]S Ex 22:28 **11:1** [r]ver 6; Isa 32:20; Hos 10:12 [s]S Dt 24:19 **11:5** [t]Jn 3:8-10 [u]Ps 139:14-16 **11:6** [v]S Ecc 9:10 **11:7** [w]Ecc 7:11 **11:8** [x]Ecc 12:1 **11:9** [y]S Job 19:29; S Ecc 2:24; S 3:17 **11:10** [z]Ps 94:19 [a]S Ecc 2:24 **12:1** [b]Ecc 11:8

5:4), this caustic saying (probably proverbial) refers to more than mere stupidity.

10:16 *whose king was a servant.* A small-minded upstart, not a "poor but wise youth" as in 4:13. See 2Ki 15:8–25; Hos 7:3–7, which portray some of the short-lived usurpers and vicious courtiers who hastened the downfall of Israel.

10:18 *lazy … idle.* See note on 4:5.

10:19 *money is the answer for everything.* Can be read at various levels—as a wry comment on human values, as sober advice to earn a good living rather than have a good time (see the first two lines) or as stating the great versatility of money (cf. Lk 16:9 and note).

11:1 Probably means "Ship your grain across the sea, / for after many days you may receive a return." That is, be adventurous, like those who accept the risks and reap the benefits of seaborne trade. Do not always play it safe (see Pr 11:24 and note).

11:2 Probably means "Invest in seven ventures, yes in eight, / for you do not know …" That is, diversify your efforts because you never know which ventures may fail. "Don't put all your eggs in one basket." Diversify your undertakings and reduce the risks.

11:3–6 *clouds … tree … wind … seed.* Do not toy with maybes and might-have-beens. Start where you can, and recognize how limited your role (or knowledge) is.

11:5 *wind.* See NIV text note; cf. Jn 3:8 ("wind" and "spirit" translate the same word in the original in both verses).

11:7–10 Live life to the fullest (cf. Jn 10:10; Php 1:21 and notes).

11:8,10 *meaningless.* Warns against letting the wonderful gifts mentioned in vv. 7–10 dazzle and distract us. Verse 9 sets us on the true course.

11:9 *judgment.* See 12:14 and note. The prospect of divine praise or blame makes every detail of life significant rather than meaningless. To know this gives direction to our heart and discrimination to our eyes. The stage is set for ch. 12.

12:1 *days of your youth.* Cf. La 3:27.

before the days of trouble[c] come
and the years approach when you will say,
"I find no pleasure in them"—
2 before the sun and the light
and the moon and the stars grow dark,
and the clouds return after the rain;
3 when the keepers of the house tremble,
and the strong men stoop,
when the grinders cease because they are few,
and those looking through the windows grow dim;
4 when the doors to the street are closed
and the sound of grinding fades;
when men rise up at the sound of birds,
but all their songs grow faint;[d]
5 when men are afraid of heights
and of dangers in the streets;
when the almond tree blossoms
and the grasshopper drags himself along
and desire no longer is stirred.
Then man goes to his eternal home[e]
and mourners[f] go about the streets.

6 Remember him—before the silver cord is severed,
or the golden bowl is broken;
before the pitcher is shattered at the spring,
or the wheel broken at the well,
7 and the dust returns[g] to the ground it came from,
and the spirit returns to God[h] who gave it.[i]

8 "Meaningless! Meaningless!" says the Teacher.[a j]
"Everything is meaningless![k]"

The Conclusion of the Matter

9 Not only was the Teacher wise, but also he imparted knowledge to the people. He pondered and searched out and set in order many proverbs.[l] 10 The Teacher[m] searched to find just the right words, and what he wrote was upright and true.[n]

11 The words of the wise are like goads, their collected sayings like firmly embedded nails[o]—given by one Shepherd. 12 Be warned, my son, of anything in addition to them.

Of making many books there is no end, and much study wearies the body.[p]

13 Now all has been heard;
here is the conclusion of the matter:
Fear God[q] and keep his commandments,[r]
for this is the whole ˻duty˼ of man.[s]
14 For God will bring every deed into judgment,[t]
including every hidden thing,[u]
whether it is good or evil.

12:1 [c] S 2Sa 19:35 **12:4** [d] Jer 25:10 **12:5** [e] S Job 10:21 [f] Jer 9:17; Am 5:16 **12:7** [g] S Ge 2:7; S Ps 146:4 [h] Ecc 3:21 [i] S Job 20:8 **12:8** [j] Ecc 1:1 [k] S Ecc 1:2 **12:9** [l] 1Ki 4:32 **12:10** [m] S Ecc 1:1 [n] Pr 22:20-21 **12:11** [o] S Ezr 9:8; S Job 6:25 **12:12** [p] S Ecc 1:18 **12:13** [q] S Ex 20:20; S 1Sa 12:24; S Job 23:15; S Ps 19:9 [r] S Dt 4:2 [s] S Dt 4:6; S Job 37:24 **12:14** [t] S Job 19:29; S Ecc 3:17 [u] S Job 34:21; S Ps 19:12; Jer 16:17; 23:24

[a] 8 Or *the leader of the assembly*; also in verses 9 and 10

12:2–5 A graphic description of progressive deterioration; an allegory about aging.
12:3 *keepers of the house.* This and the other metaphors may refer to parts of the body (hands, legs, etc.). But the imagery should not be pressed to the extent that it destroys the poetry, which moves freely between figures such as darkness, storm, a house in decline and a deserted well, and such literal descriptions as in v. 5a.
12:5 *almond tree.* Its pale blossom possibly suggests the white hair of age. *grasshopper.* Normally agile, its slow movements on a cold morning (cf. Na 3:17) recall the stiffness of old age. *eternal home.* In context, probably points simply to the grave, not beyond it (see Job 10:21 and note; 17:13).
12:6 *silver cord ... golden bowl.* A hanging lamp suspended by a silver chain. If only one link snaps, this light and beauty will perish, suggesting how fragile life is.
12:8 *Meaningless!* See 1:2 and note; see also Introduction: Literary Features. Such is life "under the sun" (on earth, apart from God), ending in brokenness. But with a relationship to our Creator already demanded (v. 1), and with the fact of his judgment affirmed (11:9), meaninglessness is not the last word. *Teacher.* See note on 1:1.
12:9 *pondered and searched.* A rigorous process, with no pains spared in seeking truth and comprehension.
12:11 *given by one Shepherd.* The other side of the matter, recognizing that Scripture is in a class of its own, as v. 12 insists.
12:13 *Fear God.* Loving reverence is the foundation of wisdom (see Ps 111:10; Pr 1:7 and notes), as well as its content (Job 28:28) and its goal and conclusion. *the whole ˻duty˼ of man.* Here is our fulfillment, our all—a far cry from "meaninglessness."
12:14 *every deed into judgment.* Glimpses of this truth are given at intervals in the book: see 3:17; 8:12–13; 11:9 and note; see also Mt 12:36; 1Co 3:12–15 and notes; 2Co 5:9–10; Heb 4:12–13. *every hidden thing.* See Ro 2:16.

Song of Songs

I N T R O D U C T I O N

Title

The title in the Hebrew text is "Solomon's Song of Songs," meaning a song by, for, or about Solomon. The phrase "Song of Songs" means the greatest of songs (cf. Dt 10:17, "God of gods and Lord of lords"; 1Ti 6:15, "King of kings").

Author and Date

Verse 1 appears to ascribe authorship to Solomon (see note on 1:1; but see also Title above). Solomon is referred to seven times (1:1,5; 3:7,9,11; 8:11 – 12), and several verses speak of the "king" (1:4,12; 7:5), but whether he was the author remains an open question.

To date the Song in the tenth century B.C. during Solomon's reign is not impossible. In fact, mention of Tirzah and Jerusalem in one breath (6:4; see note there) has been used to prove a date prior to King Omri (885 – 874 B.C.; see 1Ki 16:23 – 24), though the reason for Tirzah's mention is not clear. On the other hand, many have appealed to the language of the Song as proof of a much later date, but on present evidence the linguistic data are ambiguous.

Consistency of language, style, tone, perspective and recurring refrains seems to argue for a single author. However, many who have doubted that the Song came from one pen, or even from one time or place, explain this consistency by ascribing all the Song's parts to a single literary tradition, since Near Eastern traditions were very careful to maintain stylistic uniformity.

A Quick Look

Author:
Unknown; possibly King Solomon

Audience:
The people of Israel

Date:
Unknown; possibly as early as the tenth century B.C.

Theme:
This wisdom writer celebrates the sexual union between a man and a woman as a joyful part of marital life in God's good creation.

Interpretation

To find the key for unlocking the Song, interpreters have looked to prophetic, wisdom and apocalyptic passages of Scripture, as well as to ancient Egyptian and Babylonian love songs, traditional Semitic wedding songs and songs related to ancient Mesopotamian fertility religions. The closest parallels appear to be those found in Proverbs (see Pr 5:15 – 20; 6:24 – 29; 7:6 – 23). The description of love in 8:6 – 7 (cf. the descriptions of wisdom found in Pr 1 – 9 and Job 28) seems to confirm that the Song belongs to Biblical wisdom literature and that it is wisdom's description of an amorous relationship. The Bible speaks of both love and wisdom as gifts of God, to be received with gratitude and celebration.

The Song belongs to Biblical wisdom literature, which speaks about both love and wisdom as gifts of God, to be received with gratitude and celebration.

This understanding of the Song contrasts with the long-held view that the Song is an allegory of the love relationship between God and Israel, or between Christ and the church, or between Christ and the soul (the NT nowhere quotes from or even alludes to the Song). It is also distinct from more modern interpretations of the Song, such as that which sees it as a poetic drama celebrating the triumph of a maiden's pure, spontaneous love for her rustic shepherd lover over the courtly blandishments of Solomon, who sought to win her for his royal harem. Rather, it views the Song as a linked chain of lyrics depicting love in all its spontaneity, beauty, power and exclusiveness — experienced in its varied moments of separation and intimacy, anguish and ecstasy, tension and contentment. The Song shares with the love poetry of many cultures its extensive use of highly sensuous and suggestive imagery drawn from nature.

Theme and Theology

In ancient Israel everything human came to expression in words: reverence, gratitude, anger, sorrow, suffering, trust, friendship, commitment, loyalty, hope, wisdom, moral outrage, repentance. In the Song, it is love that finds words — inspired words that disclose its exquisite charm and beauty as one of God's choicest gifts. The voice of love in the Song, like that of wisdom in Pr 8:1 — 9:12, is a woman's voice, suggesting that love and wisdom draw men powerfully with the subtlety and mystery of a woman's allurements.

This feminine voice speaks profoundly of love. She portrays its beauty and delights. She claims its exclusiveness ("My lover is mine and I am his," 2:16) and insists on the necessity of its pure spontaneity ("Do not arouse or awaken love until it so desires," 2:7). She also proclaims its overwhelming power — it rivals that of the fearsome enemy, death; it burns with the intensity of a blazing fire; it is unquenchable even by the ocean depths (8:6 – 7a). She affirms its preciousness: All that one possesses cannot purchase it, nor (alternatively) should it be exchanged for it (8:7b). She hints, without saying so explicitly (see the last NIV text note on 8:6), that it is the Lord's gift.

God intends that such love — grossly distorted and abused by both ancient and modern people — be a normal part of marital life in his good creation (see Ge 1:26 – 31; 2:24). Indeed, in the Song the faithful Israelite could ascertain how to live lovingly within the theocratic arrangement. Such marital love is designed by the Creator-King to come to natural expression within his realm.

Literary Features

No one who reads the Song with care can question the artistry of the poet. The subtle delicacy with which he evokes intense sensuous awareness while avoiding crude titillation is one of the chief marks of his achievement. This he accomplishes largely by indirection, by analogy and by bringing to the foreground the sensuous in the world of nature (or in food, drink, cosmetics and jewelry). To liken a lover's enjoyment of his beloved to a gazelle "that browses among the lilies" (2:16), or her breasts to "twin fawns of a gazelle that browse among the lilies" (4:5), or the beloved herself to a garden filled with choice fruits inviting the lover to feast (4:12 – 16) — these combine exquisite artistry and fine sensitivity.

Whether the Song has the unity of a single dramatic line linking all the subunits into a continuing story is a matter of ongoing debate among interpreters. There do appear to be connected scenes in the love relationship (see Outline).

Virtually all agree that the literary climax of the Song is found in 8:6 – 7, where the unsurpassed power and value of love — the love that draws man and woman together — are finally expressly asserted. Literary relaxation follows the intenseness of that declaration. A final expression of mutual desire between the lovers brings the Song to an end, suggesting that love goes on. This last segment (8:8–14) is in some sense also a return to the beginning, as references to the beloved's brothers, to her vineyard and to Solomon (the king) link 8:8–12 with 1:2–6. In this song of love the voice of the beloved is dominant. It is her experience of love, both as the one who loves and as the one who is loved, that is most clearly expressed. The Song begins with her wish for the lover's kiss and ends with her urgent invitation to him for love's intimacy.

Outline

I. Title (1:1)
II. The First Meeting (1:2—2:7)
III. The Second Meeting (2:8—3:5)
IV. The Third Meeting (3:6—5:1)
V. The Fourth Meeting (5:2—6:3)
VI. The Fifth Meeting (6:4—8:4)
VII. The Literary Climax (8:5–7)
VIII. The Conclusion (8:8–14)

1 Solomon's Song of Songs.[a]

Beloved[a]

2 Let him kiss me with the kisses of his
mouth—
for your love[b] is more delightful than
wine.[c]
3 Pleasing is the fragrance of your
perfumes;[d]
your name[e] is like perfume poured
out.
No wonder the maidens[f] love you!
4 Take me away with you—let us
hurry!
Let the king bring me into his
chambers.[g]

Friends

We rejoice and delight[h] in you[b];
we will praise your love[i] more than
wine.

Beloved

How right they are to adore you!

5 Dark am I, yet lovely,[j]
O daughters of Jerusalem,[k]
dark like the tents of Kedar,[l]
like the tent curtains of Solomon.[c]
6 Do not stare at me because I am dark,
because I am darkened by the sun.
My mother's sons were angry with me
and made me take care of the
vineyards;[m]
my own vineyard I have neglected.
7 Tell me, you whom I love, where you
graze your flock
and where you rest your sheep[n] at
midday.
Why should I be like a veiled[o] woman
beside the flocks of your friends?

Friends

8 If you do not know, most beautiful of
women,[p]
follow the tracks of the sheep
and graze your young goats
by the tents of the shepherds.

Lover

9 I liken you, my darling, to a mare
harnessed to one of the chariots[q] of
Pharaoh.
10 Your cheeks[r] are beautiful with
earrings,
your neck with strings of jewels.[s]
11 We will make you earrings of gold,
studded with silver.

Beloved

12 While the king was at his table,
my perfume spread its fragrance.[t]
13 My lover is to me a sachet of myrrh[u]
resting between my breasts.

1:1 [a]S 1Ki 4:32; Ps 45 Title **1:2** [b]ver 4; SS 4:10; 8:6 [c]S Ge 14:18; S Jdg 9:13 **1:3** [d]S Est 2:12; S Ps 45:8 [e]S Ecc 7:1 [f]Ps 45:14 **1:4** [g]Ps 45:15 [h]SS 2:3 [i]S ver 2 **1:5** [j]SS 2:14; 4:3 [k]SS 5:16 [l]S Ge 25:13 **1:6** [m]SS 2:15; 7:12; 8:12 **1:7** [n]Isa 13:20 [o]S Ge 24:65 **1:8** [p]SS 5:9; 6:1 **1:9** [q]2Ch 1:17 **1:10** [r]SS 5:13 [s]Isa 61:10 **1:12** [t]SS 4:11-14 **1:13** [u]S Ge 37:25

[a] Primarily on the basis of the gender of the Hebrew pronouns used, male and female speakers are indicated in the margins by the captions *Lover* and *Beloved* respectively. The words of others are marked *Friends.* In some instances the divisions and their captions are debatable. [b] *4* The Hebrew is masculine singular. [c] *5* Or *Salma*

1:1 *Solomon's.* See Introduction: Title; Author and Date. *Song of Songs.* Greatest of songs (see Introduction: Title). 1Ki 4:32 says that Solomon wrote 1,005 songs.
1:2–3 *kisses ... your love ... your perfumes.* Cf. 4:10–11, "your love ... your perfume ... Your lips."
1:2 *him ... his ... your.* These pronouns all refer to the same person, the lover (Solomon). *love.* Expressions of love—caresses, embraces and consummation (see v. 4; 4:10; 7:12; see also Pr 7:18; Eze 16:8; 23:17). *more delightful than wine.* See v. 4. In 4:10 the lover speaks similarly of the beloved's love.
1:3 *perfumes.* Aromatic spices and gums blended in cosmetic olive oil. *your name.* The very mention of the lover's name fills the air as with a pleasant aroma. The Hebrew words for "name" and "perfume" sound alike. *maidens.* Probably young women of the court or of the royal city (see 6:8–9).
1:4 *king.* Solomon. (The notes refer to the lover as Solomon, though it must be remembered that this identification is not certain; see Introduction: Interpretation.) *his chambers.* The king's private quarters. *We.* Probably the maidens of v. 3. *praise your love more than wine.* For the reason given in v. 2.
1:5 *Dark.* Deeply browned by the sun (see v. 6); not considered desirable. *daughters of Jerusalem.* Probably the maidens of v. 3 and usually the "Friends" in the sectional headings. *tents ... tent curtains.* Handwoven from black goat hair. *Kedar.* See note on Isa 21:16.
1:6 *mother's.* Mothers are referred to seven times in the Song (here; 3:4,11; 6:9; 8:1–2,5); fathers are never mentioned. *my own vineyard.* Her body, as in 8:12 (see 2:15). Vineyard is an apt metaphor since it yields wine, and the excitements of love are compared with those produced by wine (see note on v. 2). The beloved is also compared to a garden, yielding precious fruits for the lover (see note on 4:12).
1:7 *whom I love.* See 3:1. *where you graze your flock.* The lover is portrayed as a shepherd. In v. 8 the beloved is depicted as a shepherdess. *midday.* A time of rest in warm climates. *veiled woman.* Prostitute (see Ge 38:14–15). The beloved does not wish to look for her lover among the shepherds, appearing as though she were a prostitute.
1:8 *beautiful.* The beloved; also in v. 15; 2:10,13; 4:1,7; 5:9; 6:1,4,10 ("fair"). The lover is called "handsome" in v. 16 (in Hebrew the same word as that for "beautiful"). *your young goats.* The beloved is pictured as a shepherdess (see v. 7). *by the tents of the shepherds.* The beloved is instructed to learn where the lover is by joining the shepherds in the fields.
1:9 *my darling.* Used only of the beloved (see note on v. 13). *mare.* A flattering comparison, similar to Theocritus's praise of the beautiful Helen of Troy (*Idyl,* 18.30–31). *harnessed to one of the chariots of Pharaoh.* Her beauty attracts attention the way a mare would among the Egyptian chariot stallions. According to 1Ki 10:28, Solomon imported horses from Egypt.
1:11 *We.* Perhaps the "daughters of Jerusalem" (v. 5).
1:12 *king.* Solomon. *at his table.* Reclining on his couch at the table. *my perfume.* Nard, an aromatic oil extracted from the roots of a perennial herb that grows in India (see 4:13–14; Mk 14:3; Jn 12:3).
1:13 *My lover.* Used only of the lover (see note on v. 9). *myrrh.* An aromatic gum exuding from the bark of a balsam tree that grows in Arabia, Ethiopia and India. It was commonly used as an alluring feminine perfume (Est 2:12; Pr 7:17). It was also used to perfume royal nuptial robes (Ps 45:8) and as an ingredient in the holy anointing oil (Ex 30:23). The Magi brought myrrh to the young Jesus as a gift fit for a king (Mt 2:2,11).

[14]My lover[v] is to me a cluster of henna[w] blossoms
from the vineyards of En Gedi.[x]

Lover

[15]How beautiful[y] you are, my darling!
Oh, how beautiful!
Your eyes are doves.[z]

Beloved

[16]How handsome you are, my lover![a]
Oh, how charming!
And our bed is verdant.

Lover

[17]The beams of our house are cedars;[b]
our rafters are firs.

Beloved[a]

2 I am a rose[b][c] of Sharon,[d]
a lily[e] of the valleys.

Lover

[2]Like a lily among thorns
is my darling among the maidens.

Beloved

[3]Like an apple tree among the trees of the forest
is my lover[f] among the young men.
I delight[g] to sit in his shade,
and his fruit is sweet to my taste.[h]
[4]He has taken me to the banquet hall,[i]
and his banner[j] over me is love.
[5]Strengthen me with raisins,
refresh me with apples,[k]
for I am faint with love.[l]
[6]His left arm is under my head,
and his right arm embraces me.[m]
[7]Daughters of Jerusalem, I charge you[n]
by the gazelles and by the does of the field:
Do not arouse or awaken love
until it so desires.[o]

[8]Listen! My lover!
Look! Here he comes,
leaping across the mountains,
bounding over the hills.[p]
[9]My lover is like a gazelle[q] or a young stag.[r]
Look! There he stands behind our wall,
gazing through the windows,
peering through the lattice.
[10]My lover spoke and said to me,
"Arise, my darling,
my beautiful one, and come with me.
[11]See! The winter is past;
the rains are over and gone.
[12]Flowers appear on the earth;
the season of singing has come,
the cooing of doves
is heard in our land.
[13]The fig tree forms its early fruit;[s]
the blossoming[t] vines spread their fragrance.
Arise, come, my darling;
my beautiful one, come with me."

Lover

[14]My dove[u] in the clefts of the rock,
in the hiding places on the mountainside,
show me your face,
let me hear your voice;
for your voice is sweet,
and your face is lovely.[v]
[15]Catch for us the foxes,[w]
the little foxes
that ruin the vineyards,[x]
our vineyards that are in bloom.[y]

1:14 [v]ver 16; SS 2:3,17; 5:8 [w]SS 4:13 [x]S 1Sa 23:29; S 2Ch 20:2 **1:15** [y]SS 4:7; 7:6 [z]Ps 74:19; SS 2:14; 4:1; 5:2,12; 6:9; Jer 48:28 **1:16** [a]S ver 14 **1:17** [b]1Ki 6:9 **2:1** [c]Isa 35:1 [d]S 1Ch 27:29 [e]SS 5:13; Hos 14:5 **2:3** [f]S SS 1:14 [g]SS 1:4 [h]SS 4:16 **2:4** [i]Est 1:11 [j]S Nu 1:52 **2:5** [k]SS 7:8 [l]SS 5:8 **2:6** [m]SS 8:3 **2:7** [n]SS 5:8 [o]SS 3:5; 8:4 **2:8** [p]ver 17; SS 8:14 **2:9** [q]S 2Sa 2:18 [r]ver 17; SS 8:14 **2:13** [s]Isa 28:4; Jer 24:2; Hos 9:10; Mic 7:1; Na 3:12 [t]SS 7:12 **2:14** [u]S Ge 8:8; S SS 1:15 [v]S SS 1:5 **2:15** [w]Jdg 15:4 [x]S SS 1:6 [y]SS 7:12

[a] Or *Lover* [b] *1* Possibly a member of the crocus family

1:14 *henna.* A shrub (perhaps the cypress) with tightly clustered, aromatic blossoms. *En Gedi.* An oasis watered by a spring, located on the west side of the Dead Sea (see map, p. 418). David sought refuge there from King Saul (1Sa 24:1).
1:15 *How beautiful ... darling!* See 4:1; 6:4; cf. v. 16. *my darling.* See note on v. 9. *doves.* Probably refers to the shape and cosmetic highlighting of her eyes (see 4:1).
1:16 *handsome.* See note on v. 8 ("beautiful"). *verdant.* The lovers lie together in the field under the trees.
2:1 *rose.* See NIV text note and Isa 35:1–2. *Sharon.* The fertile coastal plain south of Mount Carmel (see map No. 2 at the end of this study Bible). *lily.* Probably either lotus or anemone.
2:2 *my darling.* See note on 1:9. *maidens.* See note on 1:3.
2:3 *apple tree.* The precise nature of this fruit tree is uncertain. *his fruit.* Probably a metaphor for the lover's intimacies (see v. 5 and note).
2:4 *banner.* See 6:4; Nu 2:2; Ps 20:5. The king's love for her is displayed for all to see, like a large military banner.
2:5 *raisins ... apples.* Probably metaphors for love's caresses and embraces.
2:7 A recurring refrain in the Song (see 3:5; 8:4; cf. 5:8). It is always spoken by the beloved and always in a context of physical intimacy with her lover. *Daughters of Jerusalem.* See note on 1:5. *charge.* Place under oath. *gazelles ... does.* Perhaps in the imaginative language of love the gazelles and does are portrayed as witnesses to the oath. This would be in harmony with the author's frequent reference to nature. *until it so desires.* Out of the beloved's experience of love comes wise admonition that love is not to be artificially stimulated; utter spontaneity is essential to its genuine truth and beauty.
2:9 *gazelle.* Celebrated for its form and beauty. *young stag.* An apt simile for youthful vigor (cf. Isa 35:6). *gazing ... lattice.* The eager lover tries to catch sight of the beloved while she is still preparing herself for their meeting.
2:10 *Arise ... with me.* See v. 13; cf. 7:11–13. *my beautiful one.* See note on 1:8.
2:11–13 The first signs of spring appear (see 6:11; 7:12)—the time of love.
2:14 *dove ... on the mountainside.* Cf. Ps 55:6–8; Jer 48:28.
2:15 Perhaps spoken by the beloved. *vineyards.* As in 1:6 ("my own vineyard"), probably a metaphor for the lovers' physical beauty. Thus the desire is expressed that the lovers be kept safe from whatever ("foxes") might mar their mutual attractiveness. *in bloom.* Their attractiveness is in its prime.

Beloved

16 My lover is mine and I am his;[z]
he browses among the lilies.[a]
17 Until the day breaks
and the shadows flee,[b]
turn, my lover,[c]
and be like a gazelle
or like a young stag[d]
on the rugged hills.[a][e]

3 All night long on my bed
I looked[f] for the one my heart loves;
I looked for him but did not find
him.
2 I will get up now and go about the city,
through its streets and squares;
I will search for the one my heart
loves.
So I looked for him but did not find
him.
3 The watchmen found me
as they made their rounds in the
city.[g]
"Have you seen the one my heart
loves?"
4 Scarcely had I passed them
when I found the one my heart
loves.
I held him and would not let him go
till I had brought him to my
mother's house,[h]
to the room of the one who
conceived me.[i]
5 Daughters of Jerusalem, I charge you[j]
by the gazelles and by the does of
the field:
Do not arouse or awaken love
until it so desires.[k]

6 Who is this coming up from the desert[l]
like a column of smoke,
perfumed with myrrh[m] and incense
made from all the spices[n] of the
merchant?
7 Look! It is Solomon's carriage,
escorted by sixty warriors,[o]
the noblest of Israel,
8 all of them wearing the sword,
all experienced in battle,
each with his sword at his side,
prepared for the terrors of the night.[p]
9 King Solomon made for himself the
carriage;
he made it of wood from Lebanon.
10 Its posts he made of silver,
its base of gold.
Its seat was upholstered with purple,
its interior lovingly inlaid
by[b] the daughters of Jerusalem.
11 Come out, you daughters of Zion,[q]
and look at King Solomon wearing
the crown,
the crown with which his mother
crowned him
on the day of his wedding,
the day his heart rejoiced.[r]

Lover

4 How beautiful you are, my darling!
Oh, how beautiful!
Your eyes behind your veil[s] are
doves.[t]
Your hair is like a flock of goats
descending from Mount Gilead.[u]
2 Your teeth are like a flock of sheep just
shorn,
coming up from the washing.
Each has its twin;
not one of them is alone.[v]
3 Your lips are like a scarlet ribbon;
your mouth[w] is lovely.[x]

2:16 [z] SS 7:10 [a] SS 4:5; 6:3 **2:17** [b] SS 4:6 [c] S SS 1:14 [d] S ver 9 [e] S ver 8 **3:1** [f] SS 5:6 **3:3** [g] SS 5:7 **3:4** [h] SS 8:2 [i] SS 6:9; 8:5 **3:5** [j] S SS 2:7 [k] SS 8:4 **3:6** [l] SS 8:5 [m] SS 4:6, 14 [n] Ex 30:34 **3:7** [o] S 1Sa 8:11 **3:8** [p] S Job 15:22; Ps 91:5 **3:11** [q] Isa 3:16; 4:4; 32:9-13 [r] Isa 54:5; 62:5; Jer 3:14 **4:1** [s] S Ge 24:65 [t] S SS 1:15 [u] Ge 37:25; Nu 32:1; SS 6:5; Jer 22:6; Mic 7:14 **4:2** [v] SS 6:6 **4:3** [w] SS 5:16 [x] S SS 1:5

[a] *17* Or *the hills of Bether* [b] *10* Or *its inlaid interior a gift of love / from*

2:16 *My lover is mine and I am his.* See 6:3; 7:10. They belong to each other exclusively in a relationship that allows no intrusion. *browses among the lilies.* The lover is compared to a gazelle (see v. 17). The browsing is a metaphor for the lover's intimate enjoyment of her charms (see 6:2–3).
3:1 This verse begins a new moment in love's experience. *All night long.* Night, with its freedom from the distractions of the day, allows the heart to be filled with its own preoccupations.
3:3 *watchmen.* Were stationed at the city gates (see Ne 3:29; 11:19; 13:22) and on the walls (see 5:7; 2Sa 13:34; 18:24–27; 2Ki 9:17–20; Ps 127:1; Isa 52:8; 62:6). Apparently they also patrolled the streets at night (see 5:7).
3:4 *mother's.* See note on 1:6.
3:5 See note on 2:7. Once again this charge occurs at the moment of intimacy.
3:6–11 Perhaps spoken by the friends (see 8:5). If so, this section probably portrays the wedding procession of Solomon and his bride approaching the city.
3:6 This verse begins a new moment in the relationship. *Who ... desert ...?* See 8:5, where the reference is to the beloved. *desert.* Uncultivated seasonal grasslands. *smoke.* Incense (see note on Ex 30:34). *of the merchant.* Imported.
3:7 *carriage.* A richly adorned royal conveyance, a palanquin (see vv. 9–10).
3:8 *terrors of the night.* See Ps 91:5.
3:9 *wood from Lebanon.* See 5:15 and note.
3:10 *posts.* Supporting the canopy. *silver ... gold.* Probably metals that overlay the Lebanon wood. *purple.* See notes on 7:5; Ex 25:4.
3:11 *daughters of Zion.* Elsewhere "daughters of Jerusalem" (see note on 1:5). *crown.* A wedding wreath (see Isa 61:10). *mother.* Bathsheba (but see note on 1:4).
4:1–7 For other exuberant descriptions of the beloved's beauty see 6:4–9; 7:1–7.
4:1b–2 See 6:5b–6.
4:1 *How beautiful ... darling!* See 1:15 and note. *eyes behind your veil.* With the rest of her face concealed, the lover's attention is focused on the beloved's eyes. *doves.* See 1:15 and note. *flock of goats.* The goats of Canaan were usually black (see note on 1:5). The lover's hair was also black (5:11). *descending from Mount Gilead.* The beloved's black tresses flowing from her head remind the lover of a flock of sleek black goats streaming down one of the hills of Gilead (noted for its good pasturage).
4:2 *just shorn.* Clean and white. *coming up from the washing.* Still wet, like moistened teeth.
4:3 *Your lips ... scarlet.* Perhaps the beloved painted her lips, as Egyptian women did. *temples behind ... veil.* See note on

Your temples behind your veil
are like the halves of a
pomegranate.[y]
4 Your neck is like the tower[z] of
David,
built with elegance[a];
on it hang a thousand shields,[a]
all of them shields of warriors.
5 Your two breasts[b] are like two fawns,
like twin fawns of a gazelle[c]
that browse among the lilies.[d]
6 Until the day breaks
and the shadows flee,[e]
I will go to the mountain of myrrh[f]
and to the hill of incense.
7 All beautiful[g] you are, my darling;
there is no flaw[h] in you.

8 Come with me from Lebanon, my
bride,[i]
come with me from Lebanon.
Descend from the crest of Amana,
from the top of Senir,[j] the summit
of Hermon,[k]
from the lions' dens
and the mountain haunts of the
leopards.
9 You have stolen my heart, my sister,
my bride;[l]
you have stolen my heart
with one glance of your eyes,
with one jewel of your necklace.[m]
10 How delightful[n] is your love[o], my
sister, my bride!
How much more pleasing is your
love than wine,[p]
and the fragrance of your perfume[q]
than any spice!
11 Your lips drop sweetness as the
honeycomb, my bride;
milk and honey are under your
tongue.[r]
The fragrance of your garments is
like that of Lebanon.[s]
12 You are a garden[t] locked up, my sister,
my bride;[u]
you are a spring enclosed, a sealed
fountain.[v]
13 Your plants are an orchard of
pomegranates[w]
with choice fruits,
with henna[x] and nard,
14 nard and saffron,
calamus and cinnamon,[y]
with every kind of incense tree,
with myrrh[z] and aloes[a]
and all the finest spices.[b]
15 You are[b] a garden[c] fountain,[d]
a well of flowing water
streaming down from Lebanon.

Beloved

16 Awake, north wind,
and come, south wind!
Blow on my garden,[e]
that its fragrance[f] may spread
abroad.
Let my lover[g] come into his garden
and taste its choice fruits.[h]

4:3 [y]SS 6:7 **4:4** [z]S Ps 144:12 [a]Eze 27:10 **4:5** [b]SS 7:3 [c]S Pr 5:19 [d]S SS 2:16 **4:6** [e]SS 2:17 [f]S SS 3:6 **4:7** [g]S SS 1:15 [h]SS 5:2 **4:8** [i]ver 9, 12; SS 5:1 [j]S Dt 3:9 [k]S 1Ch 5:23 **4:9** [l]S ver 8 [m]S Ge 41:42; S Ps 73:6 **4:10** [n]SS 7:6 [o]S SS 1:2 [p]S Jdg 9:13 [q]ver 16; S Ps 45:8; Isa 57:9 **4:11** [r]S Ps 19:10; SS 5:1 [s]Hos 14:6 **4:12** [t]ver 16; SS 5:1; 6:2; Isa 5:7 [u]S ver 8 [v]Pr 5:15-18 **4:13** [w]SS 7:12 [x]SS 1:14 **4:14** [y]S Ex 30:23 [z]S SS 3:6 [a]S Nu 24:6 [b]SS 1:12 **4:15** [c]Isa 27:2; 58:11; Jer 31:12 [d]Pr 5:18 **4:16** [e]S ver 12 [f]S ver 10 [g]SS 7:13 [h]SS 2:3

[a] *4* The meaning of the Hebrew for this word is uncertain. [b] *15* Or *I am* (spoken by the *Beloved*)

v. 1. *halves of a pomegranate.* Round and blushed with red.
4:4 The beloved's erect, bespangled neck is like a tower on the city wall adorned with warriors' shields (cf. 7:4).
4:5 See 7:3. *fawns.* Representing tender, delicate beauty, and promise rather than full growth (cf. 8:8). *gazelle.* See note on 2:9. Elsewhere the simile is used of the lover. *browse among the lilies.* For a different use of this phrase see 2:16 and note.
4:6 *Until ... shadows flee.* See 2:17. *mountain of myrrh ... hill of incense.* Metaphors for lovers' intimacy.
4:8 To the lover the beloved seems to have withdrawn as if to a remote mountain. *Lebanon ... Amana ... Hermon.* Mountain peaks on the northern horizon. *Senir.* Amorite name for Mount Hermon (Dt 3:9).
4:9 *my sister.* For lovers to address each other as "brother" and "sister" was common in the love poetry of the ancient Near East (see vv. 10,12; 5:1). *one glance of your eyes.* See 6:5 and note.
4:10 *more pleasing ... than wine.* See note on 1:2. *fragrance of your perfume.* See 1:3. *spice.* See v. 14; 5:1,13; 6:2; 8:14. Spice was an imported luxury item (see 1Ki 10:2,10,25; Eze 27:22). Spices were used for fragrance in the holy anointing oil (Ex 25:6; 30:23–25; 35:8) and for fragrant incense (Ex 25:6; 35:8) as well as for perfume.
4:11 *Your lips drop sweetness.* The beloved speaks to him of love (cf. Pr 5:3; 16:24). People in the ancient Near East associated sweetness with the delights of love. *milk and honey.* Perhaps reminiscent of the description of the promised land (see note on Ex 3:8). *under your tongue.* See Job 20:12; Ps 10:7.
4:12 *garden.* A place of sensual delights (see v. 16; 5:1; 6:2; see also note on 1:6). *locked up ... enclosed ... sealed.* Metaphors for the beloved's virginity — or perhaps for the fact that she keeps herself exclusively for her husband. *spring ... fountain.* Sources of refreshment; metaphors for the beloved as a sexual partner, as in Pr 5:15–20 (see notes on Pr 5:15–16).
4:13–15 Verses 13–14 elaborate on the garden metaphor of v. 12a, and v. 15 on the fountain metaphor of v. 12b. The trees and spices in vv. 13–14 are mostly exotic, referring to the beloved's charms.
4:13 *Your plants.* All the beloved's features that delight the lover. *orchard.* Hebrew *pardes* (from which the English word "paradise" comes), a loanword from Old Persian meaning "enclosure" or "park." In Ne 2:8 and Ecc 2:5 it refers to royal parks and forests. *henna.* See note on 1:14. *nard.* See note on 1:12.
4:14 *saffron.* A plant of the crocus family bearing purple or white flowers, parts of which, when dried, were used as a cooking spice. *calamus.* An imported (see Jer 6:20 and note), aromatic spice cane, used also in the holy anointing oil (Ex 30:23, "cane") and in incense (Isa 43:23–24). *cinnamon.* Used in the holy anointing oil (Ex 30:23). *myrrh.* See note on 1:13. *aloes.* Aromatic aloes, used to perfume royal nuptial robes (Ps 45:8). Pr 7:17 says that the adulteress perfumed her bed "with myrrh, aloes and cinnamon."
4:15 *flowing.* Fresh, not stagnant. *streaming ... from Lebanon.* Fresh, cool, sparkling water from the snowfields on the Lebanon mountains.
4:16 May the fragrance of my charms be wafted about to draw my lover to me so that we may enjoy love's intimacies. *his garden.* She belongs to him and she yields herself to her lover (see 6:2).

Lover

5 I have come into my garden,[i] my
sister, my bride;[j]
I have gathered my myrrh with my
spice.
I have eaten my honeycomb and my
honey;
I have drunk my wine and my milk.[k]

Friends

Eat, O friends, and drink;
drink your fill, O lovers.

Beloved

[2]I slept but my heart was awake.
Listen! My lover is knocking:
"Open to me, my sister, my darling,
my dove,[l] my flawless[m] one.[n]
My head is drenched with dew,
my hair with the dampness of the
night."
[3]I have taken off my robe—
must I put it on again?
I have washed my feet—
must I soil them again?
[4]My lover thrust his hand through the
latch-opening;
my heart began to pound for him.
[5]I arose to open for my lover,
and my hands dripped with myrrh,[o]
my fingers with flowing myrrh,
on the handles of the lock.
[6]I opened for my lover,[p]
but my lover had left; he was gone.[q]
My heart sank at his departure.[a]
I looked[r] for him but did not find him.
I called him but he did not answer.
[7]The watchmen found me
as they made their rounds in the
city.[s]
They beat me, they bruised me;
they took away my cloak,
those watchmen of the walls!
[8]O daughters of Jerusalem, I charge
you[t]—
if you find my lover,[u]
what will you tell him?
Tell him I am faint with love.[v]

Friends

[9]How is your beloved better than
others,
most beautiful of women?[w]
How is your beloved better than
others,
that you charge us so?

Beloved

[10]My lover is radiant and ruddy,
outstanding among ten thousand.[x]
[11]His head is purest gold;
his hair is wavy
and black as a raven.
[12]His eyes are like doves[y]
by the water streams,
washed in milk,[z]
mounted like jewels.
[13]His cheeks[a] are like beds of spice[b]
yielding perfume.
His lips are like lilies[c]
dripping with myrrh.[d]
[14]His arms are rods of gold
set with chrysolite.
His body is like polished ivory
decorated with sapphires.[b][e]
[15]His legs are pillars of marble
set on bases of pure gold.
His appearance is like Lebanon,[f]
choice as its cedars.
[16]His mouth[g] is sweetness itself;
he is altogether lovely.
This is my lover,[h] this my friend,
O daughters of Jerusalem.[i]

Friends

6 Where has your lover[j] gone,
most beautiful of women?[k]
Which way did your lover turn,
that we may look for him with you?

5:1 [i]S SS 4:12 [j]S SS 4:8 [k]S SS 4:11; Isa 55:1; Joel 3:18
5:2 [l]S SS 1:15 [m]SS 4:7 [n]SS 6:9
5:5 [o]ver 13
5:6 [p]SS 6:1 [q]SS 6:2 [r]S SS 3:1
5:7 [s]SS 3:3
5:8 [t]S SS 2:7 [u]S SS 1:14
[v]SS 2:5
5:9 [w]S SS 1:8
5:10 [x]Ps 45:2
5:12 [y]S SS 1:15 [z]Ge 49:12
5:13 [a]SS 1:10 [b]SS 6:2 [c]S SS 2:1 [d]ver 5
5:14 [e]S Job 28:6
5:15 [f]1Ki 4:33; SS 7:4
5:16 [g]SS 4:3 [h]SS 7:9 [i]SS 1:5
6:1 [j]SS 5:6 [k]S SS 1:8

[a] 6 Or *heart had gone out to him when he spoke*
[b] 14 Or *lapis lazuli*

5:1 The lover claims the beloved as his garden and enjoys all her delights. *my sister.* See note on 4:9. *Eat ... O lovers.* The friends of the lovers applaud their enjoyment of love.
5:2–8 See 3:1–5 and note on 3:1.
5:2 *I slept ... was awake.* Love holds sway even in sleep—just as a new mother sleeps with an ear open to her baby's slightest whimper.
5:3 Instinctive reaction raises a foolish complaint before the language of love takes over.
5:5 *my hands ... flowing myrrh.* Love's eager imagination extravagantly lotioned the beloved's hands with perfume.
5:9 The friends' question provides an opportunity for the beloved to describe the beauty of her lover—which she does only here.
5:10 *ruddy.* See 1Sa 16:12.
5:11 *black.* The beloved's hair was also black (see note on 4:1).
5:12 *doves.* See note on 1:15. *by the water streams.* The lover's eyes sparkle. *washed in milk.* Describing the white of the eye.
5:13 *spice ... lilies.* These similes probably compare sensuous effects rather than appearances, as do the following similes and metaphors, at least in part. *lilies.* See note on 2:1. *dripping with myrrh.* Love's pleasant excitements are aroused by the lover's lips.
5:14 *chrysolite.* See note on Eze 1:16. *sapphires.* Hebrew *sappir* (from which the English word "sapphire" comes). See NIV text note.
5:15 *appearance is like Lebanon.* Awesome and majestic. *choice as its cedars.* The cedars of Lebanon were renowned throughout the ancient Near East, and their wood was desired for adorning temples and palaces (see 3:9; 1Ki 5:16 and note).
5:16 *mouth.* The lover's kisses and loving speech. *daughters of Jerusalem.* See note on 1:5.
6:1 The question asked by the friends forms a transition from the beloved's description of the lover to her delighted acknowledgment of his intimacy with her and the exclusiveness of their relationship.

Beloved

[2]My lover has gone[l] down to his
garden,[m]
to the beds of spices,[n]
to browse in the gardens
and to gather lilies.
[3]I am my lover's and my lover is
mine;[o]
he browses among the lilies.[p]

Lover

[4]You are beautiful, my darling, as
Tirzah,[q]
lovely as Jerusalem,[r]
majestic as troops with banners.[s]
[5]Turn your eyes from me;
they overwhelm me.
Your hair is like a flock of goats
descending from Gilead.[t]
[6]Your teeth are like a flock of sheep
coming up from the washing.
Each has its twin,
not one of them is alone.[u]
[7]Your temples behind your veil[v]
are like the halves of a
pomegranate.[w]
[8]Sixty queens[x] there may be,
and eighty concubines,[y]
and virgins beyond number;
[9]but my dove,[z] my perfect one,[a] is
unique,
the only daughter of her mother,
the favorite of the one who bore
her.[b]
The maidens saw her and called her
blessed;
the queens and concubines praised
her.

Friends

[10]Who is this that appears like the dawn,
fair as the moon, bright as the sun,
majestic as the stars in procession?

Lover

[11]I went down to the grove of nut trees
to look at the new growth in the
valley,
to see if the vines had budded
or the pomegranates were in
bloom.[c]
[12]Before I realized it,
my desire set me among the royal
chariots of my people.[a]

Friends

[13]Come back, come back, O Shulammite;
come back, come back, that we may
gaze on you!

Lover

Why would you gaze on the
Shulammite
as on the dance[d] of Mahanaim?

7 How beautiful your sandaled feet,
O prince's[e] daughter!
Your graceful legs are like jewels,
the work of a craftsman's hands.
[2]Your navel is a rounded goblet
that never lacks blended wine.
Your waist is a mound of wheat
encircled by lilies.
[3]Your breasts[f] are like two fawns,
twins of a gazelle.

6:2 [l] S SS 5:6 [m] S SS 4:12 [n] SS 5:13 **6:3** [o] SS 7:10 [p] S SS 2:16 **6:4** [q] S Jos 12:24; S 1Ki 15:33 [r] Ps 48:2; 50:2 [s] S Nu 1:52 **6:5** [t] S SS 4:1 **6:6** [u] SS 4:2 **6:7** [v] S Ge 24:65 [w] SS 4:3 **6:8** [x] Ps 45:9 [y] S Ge 22:24; S Est 2:14 **6:9** [z] S SS 1:15 [a] SS 5:2 [b] S SS 3:4 **6:11** [c] SS 7:12 **6:13** [d] S Ex 15:20 **7:1** [e] Ps 45:13 **7:3** [f] SS 4:5

[a] 12 Or *among the chariots of Amminadab*; or *among the chariots of the people of the prince*

6:2 *his garden.* The beloved. *beds of spices.* Her sensuous attractions (cf. 5:13). *browse.* Enjoy (see note on 2:16). *gather lilies.* See note on 2:1. The lover, enjoying intimacies with the beloved, is compared to a graceful gazelle (see notes on 2:7,9) nibbling from lily to lily in undisturbed enjoyment of exotic delicacies.

6:3 *I … mine.* See note on 2:16. Notice the reversal; here her yielding to her lover is emphasized.

6:4 *Tirzah.* An old Canaanite city in the middle of the land (see Jos 12:24). It was chosen by Jeroboam I (930–909 B.C.) as the first royal city of the northern kingdom (see 1Ki 14:17; see also 1Ki 15:21; 16:23–24). The meaning of its name ("pleasure, beauty") suggests that it was a beautiful site, perhaps explaining why the author here sets it alongside Jerusalem (though what constituted the beauty of Tirzah is not known). Comparison of the beloved's beauty to that of cities was perhaps not so unusual in the ancient Near East, since cities were regularly depicted as women (see note on 2Ki 19:21). *majestic.* See v. 10. *as troops with banners.* The beloved's noble beauty evoked in the lover emotions like those aroused by a troop marching under its banners.

6:5–7 See 4:1–3 and notes.

6:5 *your eyes … overwhelm me.* The beloved's eyes awaken in the lover such intensity of love that he is held captive (see 4:9).

6:8 *queens … concubines … virgins.* The reference is either to Solomon's harem or to all the beautiful women of the realm.

6:9 *perfect one.* Cf. "flawless one" in 5:2. *only daughter.* Not literally, but the one uniquely loved (cf. Ge 22:2 and note; Jdg 11:34; Pr 4:3). *maidens … praised her.* All the other women praised her beauty (see 1:8; 5:9; 6:1).

6:10 See 5:9; 6:1.

6:11 *nut.* Perhaps walnut. *look … in the valley.* For the first signs of spring (see note on 2:11–13).

6:12 The most obscure verse in the Song. See NIV text note for other possible translations. *chariots.* Solomon was famous for his chariots (1Ki 10:26).

6:13 *Shulammite.* The beloved. It is either a variant of "Shunammite" (see 1Ki 1:3), i.e., a young woman from Shunem (see Jos 19:18), or a feminine form of the word "Solomon," meaning "Solomon's girl." In ancient Semitic languages the letters *l* and *n* were sometimes interchanged. *Mahanaim.* Perhaps the town in Gilead (see note on 2Sa 2:8).

7:1–7 Here the description moves up from the feet rather than down from the head (cf. 5:11–15).

7:1 Cf. v. 6. *prince's daughter.* Alludes to the nobility of her beauty (see Ps 45:13). *graceful.* The Hebrew for this word suggests "curvaceous."

7:2 *goblet.* A large, two-handled, ring-based bowl (see Ex 24:6; Isa 22:24; see also Am 6:6). *encircled by lilies.* The beloved perhaps wore a loose garland of flowers around her waist.

7:3 See note on 4:5.

[4] Your neck is like an ivory tower.[g]
Your eyes are the pools of Heshbon[h]
by the gate of Bath Rabbim.
Your nose is like the tower of Lebanon[i]
looking toward Damascus.
[5] Your head crowns you like Mount
Carmel.[j]
Your hair is like royal tapestry;
the king is held captive by its
tresses.
[6] How beautiful[k] you are and how
pleasing,
O love, with your delights![l]
[7] Your stature is like that of the palm,
and your breasts[m] like clusters of
fruit.
[8] I said, "I will climb the palm tree;
I will take hold of its fruit."
May your breasts be like the clusters of
the vine,
the fragrance of your breath like
apples,[n]
[9] and your mouth like the best wine.

Beloved

May the wine go straight to my lover,[o]
flowing gently over lips and teeth.[a]
[10] I belong to my lover,
and his desire[p] is for me.[q]
[11] Come, my lover, let us go to the
countryside,
let us spend the night in the villages.[b]
[12] Let us go early to the vineyards[r]
to see if the vines have budded,[s]
if their blossoms[t] have opened,
and if the pomegranates[u] are in
bloom[v]—
there I will give you my love.
[13] The mandrakes[w] send out their
fragrance,
and at our door is every delicacy,
both new and old,
that I have stored up for you, my
lover.[x]

8 If only you were to me like a brother,
who was nursed at my mother's
breasts!
Then, if I found you outside,
I would kiss you,
and no one would despise me.
[2] I would lead you
and bring you to my mother's
house[y]—
she who has taught me.
I would give you spiced wine to drink,
the nectar of my pomegranates.
[3] His left arm is under my head
and his right arm embraces me.[z]
[4] Daughters of Jerusalem, I charge you:
Do not arouse or awaken love
until it so desires.[a]

Friends

[5] Who is this coming up from the desert[b]
leaning on her lover?

Beloved

Under the apple tree I roused you;
there your mother conceived[c] you,
there she who was in labor gave you
birth.
[6] Place me like a seal over your heart,
like a seal on your arm;
for love[d] is as strong as death,
its jealousy[c][e] unyielding as the
grave.[d]

7:4 [g] S Ps 144:12 [h] Nu 21:26 [i] S SS 5:15 **7:5** [j] Isa 35:2 **7:6** [k] S SS 1:15 [l] SS 4:10 **7:7** [m] SS 4:5 **7:8** [n] SS 2:5 **7:9** [o] SS 5:16 **7:10** [p] Ps 45:11 [q] SS 2:16; 6:3 **7:12** [r] S SS 1:6 [s] SS 2:15 [t] SS 2:13 [u] S SS 4:13 [v] SS 6:11 **7:13** [w] S Ge 30:14 [x] SS 4:16 **8:2** [y] SS 3:4 **8:3** [z] SS 2:6 **8:4** [a] SS 2:7; S 3:5 **8:5** [b] SS 3:6 [c] S SS 3:4 **8:6** [d] S SS 1:2 [e] S Nu 5:14

[a] 9 Septuagint, Aquila, Vulgate and Syriac; Hebrew *lips of sleepers* [b] 11 Or *henna bushes* [c] 6 Or *ardor* [d] 6 Hebrew *Sheol*

7:4 *ivory tower.* Mixed imagery, referring to shape as well as to color and texture. *pools.* The beloved's eyes reflect like the surface of a pool; or the imagery may depict serenity and gentleness. *Heshbon.* Once the royal city of King Sihon (Nu 21:26), it was blessed with an abundant supply of spring water. *Bath Rabbim.* Means "daughter of many"; perhaps a popular name for Heshbon. *tower of Lebanon.* Perhaps a military tower on the northern frontier of Solomon's kingdom, but more likely the beautiful, towering Lebanon mountain range.
7:5 *Mount Carmel.* A promontory midway along the western coast of the kingdom, with a wooded summit and known for its beauty. *royal tapestry.* A reference to purple, royal cloth, as in 3:10 (see note on Ex 25:4). *king.* Solomon. *tresses.* The Hebrew for this word suggests a similarity to flowing water (cf. 4:1; 6:5).
7:7 *palm.* The stately date palm.
7:8 *I said.* To myself. *I will climb.* The beloved's beauty draws him irresistibly. *vine.* Grape. *apples.* Perhaps the fragrance of apple blossoms (but see note on 2:3).
7:9 *May the wine … to my lover.* The beloved offers the wine (see 5:1) of her love to her lover.
7:10 *I belong.* See notes on 2:16; 6:3. *desire.* Cf. Ge 3:16.
7:11–12 In 2:10–13 the beloved reports a similar invitation from her lover.
7:12 *I will give you my love.* She offers herself completely to her lover.
7:13 *mandrakes.* Short-stemmed herbs associated with fertility (see note on Ge 30:14). The odor of its blossom is pungent. *at our door.* Where the lovers meet. *every delicacy.* Metaphor for the delights the beloved has for her lover from her "garden" (see 4:12–15). *both new and old.* Those already shared and those still to be enjoyed.
8:1 *no one would despise me.* The beloved could openly show affection without any public disgrace.
8:2 *I would give you.* She would offer her lover the delights of her love. *nectar.* The Hebrew for this word refers to intoxicating juices.
8:4 See 2:7 and note.
8:5 *Who … desert … ?* See 3:6 and note. *Under the apple tree.* In the ancient world, sexual union and birth were often associated with fruit trees.
8:6–7 *love is … grave. It burns … flame. Many waters … away.* These three wisdom statements (see essay, p. 727) characterize marital love as the strongest, most unyielding and invincible force in human experience. With these statements the Song reaches its literary climax and discloses its purpose.
8:6 *seal.* Seals were precious to their owners, as personal as their names (see note on Ge 38:18). *arm.* Probably

It burns like blazing fire,
like a mighty flame.[a]
7 Many waters cannot quench love;
rivers cannot wash it away.
If one were to give
all the wealth of his house for love,
it[b] would be utterly scorned.[f]

Friends

8 We have a young sister,
and her breasts are not yet grown.
What shall we do for our sister
for the day she is spoken for?
9 If she is a wall,
we will build towers of silver on her.
If she is a door,
we will enclose her with panels of cedar.

Beloved

10 I am a wall,
and my breasts are like towers.
Thus I have become in his eyes
like one bringing contentment.
11 Solomon had a vineyard[g] in Baal Hamon;
he let out his vineyard to tenants.
Each was to bring for its fruit
a thousand shekels[c h] of silver.
12 But my own vineyard[i] is mine to give;
the thousand shekels are for you,
O Solomon,
and two hundred[d] are for those who tend its fruit.

Lover

13 You who dwell in the gardens
with friends in attendance,
let me hear your voice!

Beloved

14 Come away, my lover,
and be like a gazelle[j]
or like a young stag[k]
on the spice-laden mountains.[l]

8:7 [f] S Pr 6:35
8:11 [g] Ecc 2:4 [h] Isa 7:23
8:12 [i] S SS 1:6
8:14 [j] S Pr 5:19 [k] S SS 2:9 [l] S SS 2:8, 17

[a] *6* Or */ like the very flame of the* LORD [b] *7* Or *he*
[c] *11* That is, about 25 pounds (about 11.5 kilograms); also in verse 12 [d] *12* That is, about 5 pounds (about 2.3 kilograms)

a poetic synonym for "hand." *unyielding as the grave.* As the grave will not give up the dead, so love will not surrender the loved one. *mighty flame.* The Hebrew expression conveys the idea of a most intense flame, hinting that it has been kindled by the Lord (see NIV text note).

8:7 *Many waters.* Words that suggest not only the ocean depths (see Ps 107:23) but also the primeval waters that the people of the ancient Near East regarded as a permanent threat to the world (see note on Ps 32:6). The waters were also associated with the realm of the dead (see note on Ps 30:1). *If one … scorned.* A fourth wisdom statement (see note on vv. 6 – 7), declaring love's unsurpassed worth.

8:8 – 14 In the closing lines of the Song, the words of the brothers (vv. 8 – 9), the beloved's reference to her own vineyard (v. 12) and her final reference to Solomon (vv. 11 – 12) suggest a return to the beginning of the Song (see 1:2 – 7; see also Introduction: Literary Features). The lines may recall the beloved's development into the age for love and marriage and the blossoming of her relationship with her lover.

8:8 In the ancient Near East, brothers often were guardians of their sisters, especially in matters pertaining to marriage (see Ge 24:50 – 60; 34:13 – 27). *the day she is spoken for.* Marriage was often contracted at an early age.

8:9 This imaginative verse probably expresses the brothers' determination to defend their young sister (the beloved) until her proper time for love and marriage has come. Or it may mean that the brothers are concerned to see that she is properly adorned for marriage before she is spoken for.

8:10 *I … like towers.* In contrast to the time when she was watched over by her brothers, the beloved rejoices in her maturity (cf. Eze 16:7 – 8). *his.* The lover's.

8:11 – 12 *thousand shekels … two hundred.* Whether these figures are to be taken literally (see Isa 7:23) is uncertain.

8:11 *Baal Hamon.* Location unknown. The Hebrew *hamon* sometimes means "wealth" or "abundance"; hence Baal (i.e., "lord") Hamon could mean "lord of abundance," bringing to mind Solomon's great wealth.

8:12 *my own vineyard.* Her body (see note on 1:6). *mine to give.* As Solomon is master of his vineyard, so the beloved is mistress of her attractions to dispense them as she will. She offers Solomon the owner's portion of her vineyard.

8:13 *in the gardens.* In 7:11 – 12 the beloved invites her lover to accompany her to the countryside and the vineyards. Here the imagery places her appropriately in a garden. *friends.* Male; perhaps the companions of the lover (see 1:7). *let me hear your voice.* See 2:14.

8:14 *be like a gazelle or … stag.* Display your virile strength and agility for my delight (see note on 2:9). *on the spice-laden mountains.* Cf. 2:17.

Isaiah

I N T R O D U C T I O N

Position in the Hebrew Bible

In the Hebrew Bible the book of Isaiah initiates a division called the Latter Prophets (for the Former Prophets see Introduction to Joshua: Title and Theological Theme), including also Jeremiah, Ezekiel and the Twelve Minor Prophets (so called because of their small size by comparison with the major prophetic books of Isaiah, Jeremiah and Ezekiel, and not at all suggesting that they are of minor importance; see essay, p. 1333). Thus Isaiah occupies pride of place among the Latter Prophets. This is fitting since he is sometimes referred to as the prince of the prophets.

> **A Quick Look**
>
> **Author:**
> The prophet Isaiah
>
> **Audience:**
> The people of Judah and Israel
>
> **Date:**
> Between 740 and 680 B.C.
>
> **Theme:**
> Isaiah prophesied imminent judgment — but eventual restoration — for the people of Judah and Jerusalem.

Author

Isaiah son of Amoz is often thought of as the greatest of the writing prophets. His name means "The LORD saves." He was a contemporary of Amos, Hosea and Micah, beginning his ministry in 740 B.C., the year King Uzziah died (see note on 6:1). According to an unsubstantiated Jewish tradition (*The Ascension of Isaiah*), he was sawed in half during the reign of Manasseh (cf. Heb 11:37). Isaiah was married and had at least two sons, Shear-Jashub (7:3) and Maher-Shalal-Hash-Baz (8:3). He probably spent most of his life in Jerusalem, enjoying his greatest influence under King Hezekiah (see 37:1 – 2). Isaiah is also credited with writing a history of the reign of King Uzziah (2Ch 26:22).

Many scholars today challenge the claim that Isaiah wrote the entire book that bears his name. Yet his is the only name attached to it (see 1:1; 2:1; 13:1). The strongest argument for the unity of Isaiah is the expression "the Holy One of Israel," a title for God that occurs 12 times in chs. 1 – 39 and 14 times in chs. 40 – 66. Outside Isaiah it appears in the OT only 6 times. There are other striking verbal parallels between chs. 1 – 39 and chs. 40 – 66. Compare the following verses:

1:2	66:24
1:5 – 6	53:4 – 5
5:27	40:30

6:1	52:13; 57:15
6:11–12	62:4
11:1	53:2
11:6–9	65:25
11:12	49:22
35:10	51:11

Altogether, there are at least 25 Hebrew words or forms found in Isaiah (i.e., in both major divisions of the book) that occur in no other prophetic writing.

Isaiah's use of fire as a figure of punishment (see 1:31; 10:17; 26:11; 33:11–14; 34:9–10; 66:24), his references to the "holy mountain" of Jerusalem (see note on 2:2–4) and his mention of the highway to Jerusalem (see note on 11:16) are themes that recur throughout the book.

The structure of Isaiah also argues for its unity. Chs. 36–39 constitute a historical interlude, which concludes chs. 1–35 and introduces chs. 40–66 (see note on 36:1).

Several NT verses refer to the prophet Isaiah in connection with various parts of the book: Mt 12:17–21 (Isa 42:1–4); Mt 3:3 and Lk 3:4 (Isa 40:3); Ro 10:16,20 (Isa 53:1; 65:1); see especially Jn 12:38–41 (Isa 53:1; 6:10).

Date

Most of the events referred to in chs. 1–39 occurred during Isaiah's ministry (see 6:1; 14:28; 36:1), so these chapters may have been completed not long after 701 B.C., the year the Assyrian army was destroyed and Jerusalem was spared (see note on 10:16). The prophet lived until at least 681 (see note on 37:38) and may have written chs. 40–66 during his later years. Assuming he wrote these chapters, his prophetic vision here looked forward to the Babylonian exile (see note on 40:1—66:24; cf. 39:6–7 and notes), and his message was specifically intended for the Israelites groaning in Babylonian captivity (cf. Ps 137). A parallel might be Ezekiel's visions of God's future for Israel in Eze 40–48.

Background

Isaiah lived during the stormy period marking the expansion of the Assyrian empire and the decline of Israel. Under King Tiglath-Pileser III (745–727 B.C.) the Assyrians swept westward into Aram (Syria) and Canaan. About 733 the kings of Aram and Israel tried to pressure Ahaz king of Judah into joining a coalition against Assyria. Ahaz chose instead to ask Tiglath-Pileser for help, a decision condemned by Isaiah (see note on 7:1). Assyria did assist Judah and conquered the northern kingdom in 722–721. But this made Judah even more vulnerable, and in 701 King Sennacherib of Assyria threatened Jerusalem itself (see 36:1 and note). The godly King Hezekiah prayed earnestly, and Isaiah predicted that God would force the Assyrians to withdraw from the city (37:6–7).

Nevertheless Isaiah warned Judah that her sin would bring captivity at the hands of Babylonia. The visit of the Babylonian king's envoys to Hezekiah set the stage for this prediction (see 39:1,6 and notes). Although the fall of Jerusalem would not take place until 586 B.C., Isaiah's later prophecies assume the destruction of Judah by Babylonia and then proceed to predict the destruction of Babylon by Cyrus the Persian and the restoration of the people from captivity (see 40:2–3 and notes).

Themes and Theology

Isaiah is a book that unveils the full dimension of God's acts of judgment and salvation in behalf of his people Israel. God is "the Holy One of Israel" (see 1:4; 6:1 and notes) who must punish his rebellious people (1:2) but will afterward redeem them (41:14,16). Israel is a nation blind and deaf (6:9–10; 42:7), a vineyard that will be trampled (5:1–7), a people devoid of justice or righteousness (5:7; 10:1–2). The awful judgment that will be unleashed upon Israel and all the nations that defy God is called "the day of the LORD." Although Israel has a foretaste of that day (5:30; 42:25), the nations bear its full power (see 2:11,17,20 and note). It is a day associated in the NT with Christ's second coming and the accompanying judgment (see 24:1,21; 34:1–2 and notes). Throughout the book, God's judgment is referred to as "fire" (see 1:31; 30:33 and notes). He is the

"Sovereign LORD" (see note on 25:8), who reigns over all nations and worldly powers — over the whole creation (40:15 – 24).

Yet God will have compassion on his people (14:1 – 2) and will rescue them from both political and spiritual oppression. Their restoration is like a new exodus out of (Egyptian) bondage (43:2,16 – 19; 52:10 – 12) as God redeems them (see 35:9; 41:14 and notes) and saves them (see 43:3; 49:8 and notes). Israel's mighty Creator (40:21 – 22; 48:13) will make streams spring up in the desert (32:2) as he graciously leads them home. The theme of a highway for the return of the exiles is a prominent one (see 11:16; 40:3 and notes) in both major parts of the book. The Lord raises a banner to summon the nations to bring Israel home (see 5:26 and note).

Peace and safety mark this new time (11:6 – 9). A king descended from David (the Messiah) will reign in righteousness (9:7; 32:1), and all nations will stream to the holy mountain of Jerusalem (see 2:2 – 4 and note). God's people will no longer be oppressed by wicked rulers (11:14; 45:14), and Jerusalem will truly be the "City of the LORD" (60:14).

The Lord calls the Messianic King "my servant" in chs. 42 – 53, a term also applied to Israel as a nation (see 41:8 – 9; 42:1 and notes). It is through the suffering of this servant that salvation in its fullest sense is to be achieved. Cyrus was God's instrument to deliver Israel from Babylon (41:2), but the promised Messiah would deliver humankind from the prison of sin (52:13 — 53:12). He would become a "light for the Gentiles" (42:6), so that those nations that faced judgment (chs. 13 – 23) would also find salvation (55:4 – 5) and become "servants of the LORD" (see 54:17 and note).

God is the "Holy One of Israel" who must punish his rebellious people but will afterward redeem them.

The Lord's kingdom on earth, with its righteous Ruler and his righteous subjects, is the goal toward which the book of Isaiah steadily moves. The restored earth (a new creation: chs. 65 – 66) and the restored people will then conform to the divine ideal, and all will result in the praise and glory of the Holy One of Israel for what he has accomplished.

Literary Features

Isaiah contains both prose and poetry, with the main prose material found in chs. 3 – 9; 36 – 39 — the latter constituting the historical interlude that unites the two parts of the book (see Author). The beauty of Isaiah's poetry is unsurpassed in the OT, extremely rich in imagery and wordplay. And the work as a whole employs a larger Hebrew vocabulary than any other OT book.

One of Isaiah's common techniques is personification. The sun and moon are ashamed (24:23), while the desert and parched land rejoice (see 35:1 and note) and the mountains and forests burst into song (44:23). The trees "clap their hands" (55:12). A favorite basic metaphor often exploited is the vineyard. In 5:7, Israel is the vineyard God has cultivated. Elsewhere, treading the winepress is a picture of divine judgment (see 63:3 and note), and to drink God's "cup of wrath" is to stagger under his punishment (see 51:17 and note). And legendary monsters such as Leviathan and Rahab represent nations (see 27:1; 30:7 and notes; 51:9).

The power of Isaiah's imagery is seen in 30:27 – 33, and he makes full use of sarcasm in his denunciation of idols in 44:9 – 20. A forceful example of wordplay appears in 5:7 (see note there), and alliteration and assonance in 24:16 – 17 (see note there). The "overwhelming scourge" of 28:15,18 is an illustration of mixed metaphor.

Isaiah often alludes to earlier events in Israel's history, especially the exodus from Egypt. The crossing of the Red Sea forms the background for 11:15 and 43:2,16 – 17, and other allusions occur in 4:5 – 6; 31:5; 37:36 (see notes on these verses). He also refers to the overthrow of Sodom and Gomorrah (1:9), and Gideon's victory over Midian is mentioned in 9:4; 10:26 (see also 28:21). Several times Isaiah draws upon the song of Moses in Dt 32 (compare 1:2 with Dt 32:1; 30:17 with Dt 32:30; and 43:11,13 with Dt 32:39). Isaiah, like Moses, called the nation to repentance and to faith in a holy, all-powerful God. See also note on 49:8.

The refrain in 48:22 and 57:21 divides the last 27 chapters into three sections of nine chapters each (40 – 48; 49 – 57; 58 – 66; see Outline).

Outline

Part 1: The Book of Judgment (chs. 1 – 39)

I. Messages of Rebuke and Promise (chs. 1 – 6)
   A. Introduction: Charges against Judah for Breaking the Covenant (ch. 1)
   B. The Future Discipline and Glory of Judah and Jerusalem (chs. 2 – 4)
      1. Jerusalem's future blessings (2:1 – 5)
      2. The Lord's discipline of Judah (2:6 — 4:1)
      3. The restoration of Zion (4:2 – 6)
   C. The Nation's Judgment and Exile (ch. 5)
   D. Isaiah's Commission (ch. 6)

II. Prophecies Occasioned by the Aramean and Israelite Threat against Judah (chs. 7 – 12)
   A. Ahaz Warned Not to Fear the Aramean and Israelite Alliance (ch. 7)
   B. Isaiah's Son and David's Son (8:1 — 9:7)
   C. Judgment against Israel (9:8 — 10:4)
   D. The Assyrian Empire and the Davidic Kingdom (10:5 — 12:6)
      1. The destruction of Assyria (10:5 – 34)
      2. The establishment of the Davidic king and his kingdom (ch. 11)
      3. Songs of joy for deliverance (ch. 12)

III. Judgment against the Nations (chs. 13 – 23)
   A. Against Assyria and Its Ruler (13:1 — 14:27)
   B. Against Philistia (14:28 – 32)
   C. Against Moab (chs. 15 – 16)
   D. Against Aram and Israel (ch. 17)
   E. Against Cush (ch. 18)
   F. Against Egypt and Cush (chs. 19 – 20)
   G. Against Babylon (21:1 – 10)
   H. Against Dumah (Edom) (21:11 – 12)
   I. Against Arabia (21:13 – 17)
   J. Against the Valley of Vision (Jerusalem) (ch. 22)
   K. Against Tyre (ch. 23)

IV. Judgment and Promise (the Lord's Kingdom) (chs. 24 – 27)
   A. Universal Judgments for Universal Sin (ch. 24)
   B. Deliverance and Blessing (ch. 25)
   C. Praise for the Lord's Sovereign Care (ch. 26)
   D. Israel's Enemies Punished but Israel's Remnant Restored (ch. 27)

V. Six Woes: Five on the Unfaithful in Israel and One on Assyria (chs. 28 – 33)
   A. Woe to Ephraim (Samaria) — and to Judah (ch. 28)
   B. Woe to David's City, Jerusalem (29:1 – 14)
   C. Woe to Those Who Rely on Foreign Alliances (29:15 – 24)
   D. Woe to the Obstinate Nation (ch. 30)
   E. Woe to Those Who Rely on Egypt (chs. 31 – 32)
   F. Woe to Assyria — but Blessing for God's People (ch. 33)

VI. More Prophecies of Judgment and Promise (chs. 34 – 35)
   A. The Destruction of the Nations and the Avenging of God's People (ch. 34)
   B. The Future Blessings of Restored Zion (ch. 35)

VII. A Historical Transition from the Assyrian Threat to the Babylonian Exile (chs. 36 – 39)
   A. Jerusalem Preserved from the Assyrian Threat (chs. 36 – 37)
      1. The siege of Jerusalem by Sennacherib and the Assyrian army (ch. 36)
      2. The Lord's deliverance of Jerusalem (ch. 37)
   B. The Lord's Extension of Hezekiah's Life (ch. 38)
   C. The Babylonian Exile Predicted (ch. 39)

Part 2: The Book of Comfort (chs. 40 – 66)

VIII. The Deliverance and Restoration of Israel (chs. 40 – 48)
   A. The Coming of the Victorious God (40:1 – 26)
   B. Unfailing Strength for the Weary Exiles (40:27 – 31)
   C. The Lord of History (41:1 — 42:9)
   D. Praise and Exhortation (42:10 – 25)
   E. The Regathering and Renewal of Israel (43:1 — 44:5)
   F. The Only God (44:6 — 45:25)
   G. The Lord's Superiority over Babylon's Gods (ch. 46)
   H. The Fall of Babylon (ch. 47)
   I. The Lord's Exhortations to His People (ch. 48)

IX. The Servant's Ministry and Israel's Restoration (chs. 49 – 57)
   A. The Call and Mission of the Servant (49:1 – 13)
   B. The Repopulation of Zion (49:14 – 26)
   C. Israel's Sin and the Servant's Obedience (ch. 50)
   D. The Remnant Comforted Because of Their Glorious Prospect (51:1 — 52:12)
   E. The Sufferings and Glories of the Lord's Righteous Servant (52:13 — 53:12)
   F. The Future Glory of Zion (ch. 54)
   G. The Lord's Call to Salvation and Covenant Blessings (55:1 — 56:8)
   H. The Condemnation of the Wicked in Israel (56:9 — 57:21)

X. Everlasting Deliverance and Everlasting Judgment (chs. 58 – 66)
   A. False and True Worship (ch. 58)
   B. Zion's Confession and Redemption (ch. 59)
   C. Zion's Peace and Prosperity (ch. 60)
   D. The Lord's Favor (ch. 61)
   E. Zion's Restoration and Glory (62:1 — 63:6)
   F. Prayer for Divine Deliverance (63:7 — 64:12)
   G. The Lord's Answer: Mercy and Judgment (ch. 65)
   H. Judgment for False Worshipers and Blessing for True Worshipers (ch. 66)

1 The vision[a] concerning Judah and Jerusalem[b] that Isaiah son of Amoz saw[c]
during the reigns of Uzziah,[d] Jotham,[e]
Ahaz[f] and Hezekiah,[g] kings of Judah.

A Rebellious Nation

2 Hear, O heavens! Listen, O earth![h]
For the LORD has spoken:[i]
"I reared children[j] and brought them up,
but they have rebelled[k] against me.
3 The ox knows[l] his master,
the donkey his owner's manger,[m]
but Israel does not know,[n]
my people do not understand.[o]"

4 Ah, sinful nation,
a people loaded with guilt,[p]
a brood of evildoers,[q]
children given to corruption![r]
They have forsaken[s] the LORD;
they have spurned the Holy One[t] of
Israel
and turned their backs[u] on him.

5 Why should you be beaten[v] anymore?
Why do you persist[w] in rebellion?[x]
Your whole head is injured,
your whole heart[y] afflicted.[z]
6 From the sole of your foot to the top of
your head[a]
there is no soundness[b]—
only wounds and welts[c]
and open sores,
not cleansed or bandaged[d]
or soothed with oil.[e]

7 Your country is desolate,[f]
your cities burned with fire;[g]
your fields are being stripped by
foreigners[h]
right before you,
laid waste as when overthrown by
strangers.[i]
8 The Daughter of Zion[j] is left[k]
like a shelter in a vineyard,
like a hut[l] in a field of melons,
like a city under siege.
9 Unless the LORD Almighty
had left us some survivors,[m]
we would have become like Sodom,
we would have been like
Gomorrah.[n]

10 Hear the word of the LORD,[o]
you rulers of Sodom;[p]
listen to the law[q] of our God,
you people of Gomorrah![r]
11 "The multitude of your sacrifices—
what are they to me?" says the LORD.
"I have more than enough of burnt
offerings,
of rams and the fat of fattened
animals;[s]

1:1 [a] 1Sa 3:1; Isa 22:1,5; Ob 1:1; Na 1:1 [b] Isa 40:9; 44:26 [c] Isa 2:1; 13:1 [d] S 2Ki 14:21; S 2Ch 26:22 [e] S 1Ch 3:12 [f] S 2Ki 16:1 [g] S 1Ch 3:13 **1:2** [h] S Dt 4:26 [i] Jdg 11:10; Jer 42:5; Mic 1:2 [j] Isa 23:4; 63:16 [k] ver 4,23; Isa 24:5,20; 30:1,9; 46:8; 48:8; 57:4; 65:2; 66:24; Eze 24:3; Hag 1:12; Mal 1:6; 3:5 **1:3** [l] Job 12:9 [m] S Ge 42:27 [n] Jer 4:22; 5:4; 9:3,6; Hos 2:8; 4:1 [o] S Dt 32:28; Isa 42:25; 48:8; Hos 4:6; 7:9 **1:4** [p] Isa 5:18 [q] S ver 2; Isa 9:17; 14:20; 31:2; Jer 23:14 [r] Ps 14:3 [s] S Dt 32:15; S Ps 119:87 [t] S 2Ki 19:22; Isa 5:19,24; 31:1; 37:23; 41:14; 43:14; 45:11; 47:4; Eze 39:7 [u] S Pr 30:9; Isa 59:13 **1:5** [v] Pr 20:30 [w] Jer 2:30; 5:3; 8:5 [x] S ver 2; Isa 31:6; Jer 44:16-17; Heb 3:16 [y] La 2:11; 5:17 [z] Isa 30:26; 33:6,24; 58:8; Jer 30:17 **1:6** [a] S Dt 28:35 [b] Ps 38:3 [c] Isa 53:5 [d] S Ps 147:3; Isa 30:26; Jer 8:22; 14:19; 30:17; La 2:13; Eze 34:4 [e] 2Sa 14:2; Ps 23:5; 45:7; 104:15; Isa 61:3; Lk 10:34 **1:7** [f] S Lev 26:34 [g] S Lev 26:31; S Dt 29:23 [h] Lev 26:16; Jdg 6:3-6; Isa 62:8; Jer 5:17 [i] S 2Ki 18:13; S Ps 109:11 **1:8** [j] S Ps 9:14; S Isa 10:32 [k] Isa 30:17; 49:21 [l] S Job 27:18 **1:9** [m] S Ge 45:7; S 2Ki 21:14; Isa 4:2; 6:13; 27:12; 28:5; 37:4,31-32; 45:25; 56:8; Jer 23:3; Joel 2:32 [n] S Ge 19:24; Ro 9:29* **1:10** [o] Isa 28:14 [p] S Ge 13:13; S 18:20; Eze 16:49; Ro 9:29; Rev 11:8 [q] Isa 5:24; 8:20; 30:9 [r] Isa 13:19 **1:11** [s] Ps 50:8; Am 6:4

1:1—6:13 The first section of Isaiah's prophecies, dominated by oracles of judgment and climaxing in Isaiah's commission found in ch. 6 (cf. note on 7:1—12:6).

1:1-31 Compare the indictment of ch. 1 with that of ch. 5; the two enclose the first series of oracles. Ch. 1 also serves as an introduction to the whole book.

1:1 The title of the book. Other headings occur in 2:1; 13:1; 14:28; 15:1; 17:1; 19:1; 21:1,11,13; 22:1; 23:1. *vision.* In the sense of "revelation" or "prophecy" (see Pr 29:18; Ob 1 and notes; see also 1Sa 3:1). *Amoz.* Not to be confused with the prophet Amos. *Uzziah, Jotham, Ahaz and Hezekiah.* These kings reigned from 792 to 686 B.C. None of the kings of Israel is mentioned since Isaiah ministered primarily to the southern kingdom (Judah).

1:2 Isaiah begins and ends (66:24) with a condemnation of those who rebel against God. The prophet calls on the heavens and the earth to testify to the truth of God's accusation against Israel and the rightness of his judgment—since they were called upon to serve as third-party witnesses to his covenant (see Dt 30:19 and note; 31:28; 32:1; Ps 50:1 and note). Cf. Mic 6 and notes on 6:1-16, 6:1-8 and 6:9-16.

1:3 *manger.* Feeding trough. *does not know.* Refusal to acknowledge God or understand his ways resulted later in Judah's exile from her land (5:13; cf. Hos 2:8 and note).

1:4 *Holy One of Israel.* Occurs 26 times in Isaiah (see especially 5:24) and only 6 times elsewhere in the OT (see Introduction: Author; see also note on 2Ki 19:22). *Holy One.* See Ex 3:5; Lev 11:44 and notes.

1:5-6 The pitiable moral and spiritual condition of Israel is transferred to the suffering servant in 53:4-5. The Hebrew words for "beaten," "injured" and "welts" here correspond to those for "smitten," "infirmities" and "wounds" in that later passage.

1:6 The disease ravages the entire body, as with Job (2:7). *oil.* Olive oil was commonly used for treating wounds (see Lk 10:34).

1:7-9 The desolation of the land of Judah is the result of foreign invasion: e.g., by Aram, the northern kingdom of Israel, Edom and Philistia (2Ch 28:5-18); later (701 B.C.), by King Sennacherib and the Assyrian army (36:1-2); still later (605-586), by King Nebuchadnezzar and the Neo-Babylonian army.

1:8 *Daughter of Zion.* A personification of Jerusalem (see note on 2Ki 19:21). *shelter … hut.* Temporary structures used by watchmen (Job 27:18), who were on the lookout for thieves and intruders. Thus Jerusalem was not very defensible. *melons.* Or possibly "cucumbers."

1:9-10 *Sodom … Gomorrah.* Classic examples of sinful cities that were completely destroyed by divine judgment (see 3:9; Ge 13:13; 18:20-21; 19:5,24-25). Just as Jesus addressed Peter as though he were Satan (Mt 16:23), so Isaiah addresses his fellow Israelites as though they were the "rulers of Sodom" and the "people of Gomorrah."

1:9 Quoted in Ro 9:29, where it is linked with Isa 10:22-23. Isaiah often refers to the remnant that will survive God's judgment on the nation and repossess the land (see 10:20-23; 11:11,16; 46:3).

1:11-15 The moral character and conduct of the worshipers are far more important than the number of their religious activities (see 66:3; Jer 6:20; 7:22-23; Hos 6:6; Am 5:21-24; Mic 6:6-8 and notes).

1:11 *fattened animals.* Those kept in confinement for special feeding.

I have no pleasure[t]
in the blood of bulls[u] and lambs and
goats.[v]
12 When you come to appear before me,
who has asked this of you,[w]
this trampling of my courts?
13 Stop bringing meaningless offerings![x]
Your incense[y] is detestable[z] to me.
New Moons,[a] Sabbaths and
convocations[b]—
I cannot bear your evil assemblies.
14 Your New Moon[c] festivals and your
appointed feasts[d]
my soul hates.[e]
They have become a burden to me;[f]
I am weary[g] of bearing them.
15 When you spread out your hands[h] in
prayer,
I will hide[i] my eyes from you;
even if you offer many prayers,
I will not listen.[j]
Your hands[k] are full of blood;[l]
16 wash[m] and make yourselves clean.
Take your evil deeds
out of my sight![n]
Stop doing wrong,[o]
17 learn to do right![p]
Seek justice,[q]
encourage the oppressed.[a][r]
Defend the cause of the fatherless,[s]
plead the case of the widow.[t]

18 "Come now, let us reason together,"[u]
says the LORD.
"Though your sins are like scarlet,
they shall be as white as snow;[v]
though they are red as crimson,
they shall be like wool.[w]
19 If you are willing and obedient,[x]
you will eat the best from the
land;[y]
20 but if you resist and rebel,[z]
you will be devoured by the
sword."[a]
For the mouth of the LORD
has spoken.[b]

21 See how the faithful city
has become a harlot![c]
She once was full of justice;
righteousness[d] used to dwell in
her—
but now murderers![e]
22 Your silver has become dross,[f]
your choice wine is diluted with
water.
23 Your rulers are rebels,[g]
companions of thieves;[h]
they all love bribes[i]
and chase after gifts.
They do not defend the cause of the
fatherless;
the widow's case does not come
before them.[j]
24 Therefore the Lord, the LORD
Almighty,
the Mighty One[k] of Israel, declares:
"Ah, I will get relief from my foes
and avenge[l] myself on my
enemies.[m]
25 I will turn my hand against you;[n]
I will thoroughly purge[o] away your
dross[p]
and remove all your impurities.[q]
26 I will restore your judges as in days of
old,[r]
your counselors as at the beginning.
Afterward you will be called[s]
the City of Righteousness,[t]
the Faithful City.[u]"

[a] 17 Or / *rebuke the oppressor*

1:11 [t] S Job 22:3 [u] Isa 66:3; Jer 6:20 [v] 1Sa 15:22; S Ps 40:6; Mal 1:10; Heb 10:4 **1:12** [w] Ex 23:17; Dt 31:11 **1:13** [x] Pr 15:8; Isa 66:3; Hag 2:14 [y] Jer 7:9; 18:15; 44:8 [z] S 1Ki 14:24; Ps 115:8; Pr 28:9; Isa 41:24; Mal 2:11 [a] S Nu 10:10 [b] 1Ch 23:31 **1:14** [c] S Ne 10:33 [d] Ex 12:16; Lev 23:1-44; Nu 28:11-29:39; Dt 16:1-17; Isa 5:12; 29:1; Hos 2:11 [e] S Ps 11:5 [f] S Job 7:12 [g] Ps 69:3; Isa 7:13; 43:22, 24; Jer 44:22; Mal 2:17; 3:14 **1:15** [h] S Ex 9:29 [i] S Dt 31:17; Isa 57:17; 59:2 [j] S Dt 1:45; S 1Sa 8:18; S Job 15:31; S Jn 9:31 [k] S Job 9:30 [l] Isa 4:4; 59:3; Jer 2:34; Eze 7:23; Hos 4:2; Joel 3:21 **1:16** [m] S Ru 3:3; Mt 27:24; Jas 4:8 [n] Nu 19:11, 16; Isa 52:11 [o] Isa 55:7; Jer 25:5 **1:17** [p] S Ps 34:14 [q] S Ps 72:1; Isa 11:4; 33:5; 56:1; 61:8; Am 5:14-15; Mic 6:8; Zep 2:3 [r] S Dt 14:29 [s] ver 23; Job 22:9; Ps 82:3; 94:6; Isa 10:2 [t] S Ex 22:22; Eze 18:31; 22:7; Lk 18:3; Jas 1:27 **1:18** [u] S 1Sa 2:25; Isa 41:1; 43:9, 26 [v] S Ps 51:7; Rev 7:14 [w] Isa 55:7 **1:19** [x] S Job 36:11; S Isa 50:10 [y] Dt 30:15-16; Ezr 9:12; Ps 34:10; Isa 30:23; 55:2; 58:14; 62:9; 65:13, 21-22 **1:20** [z] S 1Sa 12:15 [a] S Job 15:22; Isa 3:25; 27:1; 65:12; 66:16; Jer 17:27 [b] Nu 23:19; Isa 21:17; 34:16; 40:5; 58:14; Jer 49:13; Mic 4:4; Zec 1:6; Rev 1:16 **1:21** [c] Isa 57:3-9; Jer 2:20; 3:2, 9; 13:27; Eze 23:3; Hos 2:1-13 [d] Isa 5:7; 46:13; 59:14; Am 6:12 [e] S Pr 6:17 **1:22** [f] S Ps 119:119 **1:23** [g] S ver 2 [h] S Dt 19:14; Mic 2:1-2; 6:12 [i] S Ex 23:8; Am 5:12 [j] Isa 10:2; Jer 5:28; Eze 22:6-7; Mic 3:9; Hab 1:4 **1:24** [k] S Ge 49:24 [l] Isa 34:2, 8; 35:4; 47:3; 59:17; 61:2; 63:4; Jer 51:6; Eze 5:13 [m] S Dt 32:43; S Isa 10:3 **1:25** [n] Dt 28:63 [o] S Ps 78:38 [p] S Ps 119:119 [q] 2Ch 29:15; Isa 48:10; Jer 6:29; 9:7; Eze 22:22; Mal 3:3 **1:26** [r] Jer 33:7, 11; Mic 4:8 [s] S Ge 32:28 [t] Isa 32:16; 33:5; 46:13; 48:18; 61:11; 62:1; Jer 31:23; Zec 8:3 [u] Isa 4:3; 48:2; 52:1; 60:14; 62:2; 64:10; Da 9:24

1:14 *New Moon festivals.* Celebrated on the first day of each Hebrew month. Special sacrifices and feasts were part of the observance (see Nu 28:11–15). *appointed feasts.* The annual feasts mandated in the Mosaic law: Passover (and Unleavened Bread), Weeks (Pentecost) and Tabernacles (Ingathering) (Ex 23:14–17; 34:18–25; Lev 23; Dt 16:1–17).

1:15 *hide my eyes.* In 8:17; 59:2 God hides his face from Israel (see also Mic 3:4 and note).

1:17 See 5:7; Jer 22:16 and note; Am 5:14–15; Jas 1:27. *fatherless ... widow.* Represented the weak and often oppressed part of society. Rulers were warned not to take advantage of them (see v. 23; 10:2; Jer 22:3).

1:18 *scarlet ... crimson.* Refers to the blood that has stained the hands of murderers (see vv. 15,21). *white as snow.* A powerful figurative description of the result of forgiveness (see Ps 51:7 and note). This offer of forgiveness is conditioned on the reformation of life called for in v. 19.

1:19–20 *eat ... be devoured.* The vivid contrast is stressed by the use of the same Hebrew verb.

1:21 *become a harlot.* Jerusalem (representing all Judah) has been unfaithful to the Lord. Here her unfaithfulness is specified as social abuse, exploitation of the powerless, and violence against one's neighbor—violating the Lord's moral order for the community of his people (see note on Ps 73:27; cf. note on Ex 34:15).

1:22 *Your silver has become dross.* See Ps 12:6 and note.

1:24 *The Lord, the LORD Almighty, the Mighty One of Israel.* Stressing God's sovereign authority as Judge (cf. Ps 50:1,6; cf. also Jos 22:22 and note). *the LORD Almighty.* See note on 1Sa 1:3.

1:25–26 *turn ... restore.* The use of the same Hebrew verb emphasizes the contrast (see note on vv. 19–20).

1:25 *purge away your dross.* Purifying fire is also mentioned in 4:4; 48:10.

1:26 *Faithful City.* See v. 21. Using a related Hebrew noun, Zec 8:3 similarly refers to the future Jerusalem as the "City of Truth."

27 Zion will be redeemed with justice,
her penitent[v] ones with
righteousness.[w]
28 But rebels and sinners[x] will both be
broken,
and those who forsake[y] the LORD will
perish.[z]

29 "You will be ashamed[a] because of the
sacred oaks[b]
in which you have delighted;
you will be disgraced because of the
gardens[c]
that you have chosen.
30 You will be like an oak with fading
leaves,[d]
like a garden without water.
31 The mighty man will become tinder
and his work a spark;
both will burn together,
with no one to quench the fire.[e]"

The Mountain of the LORD

2:1-4pp — Mic 4:1-3

2 This is what Isaiah son of Amoz saw
concerning Judah and Jerusalem:[f]

2 In the last days[g]

the mountain[h] of the LORD's temple
will be established
as chief among the mountains;[i]
it will be raised[j] above the hills,
and all nations will stream to it.[k]

3 Many peoples[l] will come and say,

"Come, let us go[m] up to the mountain[n]
of the LORD,
to the house of the God of Jacob.
He will teach us his ways,
so that we may walk in his paths."
The law[o] will go out from Zion,
the word of the LORD from
Jerusalem.[p]
4 He will judge[q] between the nations
and will settle disputes[r] for many
peoples.
They will beat their swords into
plowshares
and their spears into pruning
hooks.[s]
Nation will not take up sword against
nation,[t]
nor will they train for war anymore.

5 Come, O house of Jacob,[u]
let us walk in the light[v] of the
LORD.

The Day of the LORD

6 You have abandoned[w] your people,
the house of Jacob.[x]
They are full of superstitions from the
East;
they practice divination[y] like the
Philistines[z]
and clasp hands[a] with pagans.[b]
7 Their land is full of silver and
gold;[c]
there is no end to their treasures.[d]
Their land is full of horses;[e]
there is no end to their chariots.[f]
8 Their land is full of idols;[g]
they bow down[h] to the work of
their hands,[i]
to what their fingers[j] have made.
9 So man will be brought low[k]
and mankind humbled[l]—
do not forgive them.[a][m]

10 Go into the rocks,
hide[n] in the ground
from dread of the LORD
and the splendor of his majesty![o]

[a] 9 Or *not raise them up*

1:27 [v] Isa 30:15; 31:6; 59:20; Eze 18:30 [w] Isa 35:10; 41:14; 43:1; 52:3; 62:12; 63:4; Hos 2:19 **1:28** [x] Isa 33:14; 43:27; 48:8; 50:1; 59:2; Jer 4:18 [y] S Dt 32:15 [z] Ps 9:5; Isa 24:20; 66:24; Jer 16:4; 42:22; 44:12; 2Th 1:8-9 **1:29** [a] Ps 97:7; Isa 42:17; 44:9, 11; 45:16; Jer 10:14 [b] Isa 57:5; Eze 6:13; Hos 4:13 [c] Isa 65:3; 66:17 **1:30** [d] S Ps 1:3 **1:31** [e] Isa 4:4; 5:24; 9:18-19; 10:17; 24:6; 26:11; 30:27, 33; 33:14; 34:10; 66:15-16, 24; Jer 5:14; 7:20; 21:12; Ob 1:18; Mal 3:2; 4:1; S Mt 25:41 **2:1** [f] Isa 1:1 **2:2** [g] Ac 2:17; Heb 1:2 [h] Isa 11:9; 24:23; 25:6, 10; 27:13; 56:7; 57:13; 65:25; 66:20; Jer 31:23; Da 11:45; Joel 3:17; Mic 4:7 [i] Isa 65:9 [j] Zec 14:10 [k] S Ps 102:15; Jer 16:19 **2:3** [l] Isa 45:23; 49:1; 60:3-6, 14; 66:18; Jer 3:17; Joel 3:2; Zep 3:8; Zec 14:2 [m] Isa 45:14; 49:12, 23; 55:5 [n] S Dt 33:19; S Ps 137:5 [o] S Isa 1:10; 33:22; 51:4, 7 [p] Lk 24:47; S Jn 4:22 **2:4** [q] Ps 7:6; S 9:19; 96:13; 98:9; Isa 1:27; 3:13; 9:7; 42:4; 51:4; Joel 3:14 [r] S Ge 49:10 [s] Joel 3:10 [t] Ps 46:9; Isa 9:5; 11:6-9; 32:18; 57:19; 65:25; Jer 30:10; Da 11:45; Hos 2:18; Mic 4:3; Zec 9:10 **2:5** [u] Isa 58:1 [v] Isa 60:1, 19-20; 1Jn 1:5, 7 **2:6** [w] S Dt 31:17 [x] Jer 12:7 [y] S Dt 18:10; S Isa 44:25 [z] S 2Ki 1:2; S 2Ch 26:6 [a] Pr 6:1 [b] S 2Ki 16:7; Mic 5:12 **2:7** [c] S Dt 17:17 [d] S Ps 17:14 [e] S Dt 17:16 [f] S Ge 41:43; Isa 31:1; Mic 5:10 **2:8** [g] Isa 10:9-11; Rev 9:20 [h] Isa 44:17 [i] S 2Ch 32:19; S Ps 135:15; Mic 5:13 [j] Isa 17:8 **2:9** [k] Ps 62:9 [l] ver 11, 17; Isa 5:15; 13:11 [m] S Ne 4:5 **2:10** [n] ver 19; Na 3:11 [o] S Ps 145:12; 2Th 1:9; Rev 6:15-16

1:27–28 This contrast between the redemption of Zion (Jerusalem) as a whole and the perishing of individuals who refuse to repent is developed in 65:8–16.
1:29 *sacred oaks ... gardens.* Pagan sacrifices were offered at such places (see 65:3; 66:17).
1:31 *fire.* A figure of punishment (see 33:11–14; 34:9–10; see also note on La 1:13).
2:1 A second introduction, probably relating to chs. 2–4 or to chs. 2–12 (see 13:1).
2:2–5 See note on 4:2–6.
2:2–4 Almost identical to Mic 4:1–3. The theme of the "mountain of the LORD" (Mount Zion) is common in Isaiah; it occurs in passages that depict the coming of both Jews and Gentiles to Jerusalem (Zion) in the last days (see 11:9; 27:13; 56:7; 57:13; 65:25; 66:20; see also 60:3–5; Zec 14:16 and note). Some believe that the peace described in this passage has been inaugurated through the coming of Christ and the preaching of the gospel, and will be consummated at the return of Christ. Others maintain that it is solely a prophecy of conditions during a future reign of Christ on the earth.
2:2 *the last days.* Can refer to the future generally (see Ge 49:1), but usually it seems to have in view the Messianic era. In a real sense the last days began with the first coming of Christ (see Ac 2:17; Heb 1:1–2 and notes) and will be completely fulfilled at his second coming.
2:4 *swords into plowshares.* The reverse process occurs in Joel 3:10 (see note there). What is here called a plowshare was actually an iron point mounted on a wooden beam. Ancient plows did not have a true plowshare; they broke up the ground but did not turn it over.
2:6 *East.* Probably means Aram (Syria) and Mesopotamia. *divination like the Philistines.* See 1Sa 6:2 and note; see also Dt 18:10–11 for a description of such practices; and see note on Dt 18:9.
2:7 *silver and gold ... horses.* Accumulating large quantities of these was forbidden to the king (see Dt 17:16–17 and note). They usually led to a failure to trust in God (see 30:1–3,7; 31:1–3).
2:10,19,21 These verses contain a refrain that builds to a climax in v. 21. Lines 3–4 of each verse are identical.
2:10 *rocks ... ground.* During times of severe oppression the

11 The eyes of the arrogant[p] man will be humbled[q]
and the pride[r] of men brought low;[s]
the LORD alone will be exalted[t] in that day.[u]
12 The LORD Almighty has a day[v] in store
for all the proud[w] and lofty,[x]
for all that is exalted[y]
(and they will be humbled),[z]
13 for all the cedars of Lebanon,[a] tall and lofty,[b]
and all the oaks of Bashan,[c]
14 for all the towering mountains
and all the high hills,[d]
15 for every lofty tower[e]
and every fortified wall,[f]
16 for every trading ship[a][g]
and every stately vessel.
17 The arrogance of man will be brought low[h]
and the pride of men humbled;[i]
the LORD alone will be exalted in that day,[j]
18 and the idols[k] will totally disappear.[l]
19 Men will flee to caves[m] in the rocks
and to holes in the ground[n]
from dread[o] of the LORD
and the splendor of his majesty,[p]
when he rises to shake the earth.[q]
20 In that day[r] men will throw away
to the rodents and bats[s]
their idols of silver and idols of gold,[t]
which they made to worship.[u]
21 They will flee to caverns in the rocks[v]
and to the overhanging crags
from dread of the LORD
and the splendor of his majesty,[w]
when he rises[x] to shake the earth.[y]

2:11 [p]S Ne 9:29; Hab 2:5 [q]S ver 9 [r]Isa 5:15; 10:12; 37:23; Eze 31:10 [s]S Job 40:11 [t]S Ps 46:10 [u]ver 17,20; Isa 3:7,18; 4:1,2; 5:30; 7:18; 17:4,7; 24:21; 25:9; 26:1; 27:1 **2:12** [v]Isa 13:6,9; 22:5,8,12; 34:8; 61:2; Jer 30:7; La 1:12; Eze 7:7; 30:3; Joel 1:15; 2:11; Am 5:18; Zep 1:14 [w]S Ps 59:12 [x]S 2Sa 22:28 [y]Ps 76:12; Isa 24:4,21; 60:11; Mal 4:1 [z]S Job 40:11 **2:13** [a]S Jdg 9:15; Isa 10:34; 29:17; Eze 27:5 [b]Isa 10:33 [c]S Ps 22:12; Zec 11:2 **2:14** [d]Isa 30:25; 40:4 **2:15** [e]Isa 30:25; 32:14; 33:18 [f]Isa 25:2,12; Zep 1:16 **2:16** [g]*fn* S Ge 10:4; S 1Ki 9:26 **2:17** [h]S 2Sa 22:28; S Job 40:11 [i]S ver 9 [j]S ver 11 **2:18** [k]S 1Sa 5:2; Eze 36:25 [l]S Dt 9:21; Isa 21:9; Jer 10:11; Mic 5:13 **2:19** [m]S Jdg 6:2; Isa 7:19 [n]S Jdg 6:2; S Job 30:6; Lk 23:30; Rev 6:15 [o]S Dt 2:25 [p]S Ps 145:12

22 Stop trusting in man,[z]
who has but a breath[a] in his nostrils.
Of what account is he?[b]

Judgment on Jerusalem and Judah

3 See now, the Lord,
the LORD Almighty,
is about to take from Jerusalem and Judah
both supply and support:[c]
all supplies of food[d] and all supplies of water,[e]
2 the hero and warrior,[f]
the judge and prophet,
the soothsayer[g] and elder,[h]
3 the captain of fifty[i] and man of rank,[j]
the counselor, skilled craftsman[k] and clever enchanter.[l]

4 I will make boys their officials;
mere children will govern them.[m]
5 People will oppress each other—
man against man, neighbor against neighbor.[n]
The young will rise up against the old,
the base against the honorable.

6 A man will seize one of his brothers
at his father's home, and say,
"You have a cloak, you be our leader;
take charge of this heap of ruins!"
7 But in that day[o] he will cry out,
"I have no remedy.[p]

[a] 16 Hebrew *every ship of Tarshish*

[q]ver 21; S Job 9:6; S Isa 14:16; Heb 12:26 **2:20** [r]S ver 11 [s]Lev 11:19 [t]S Job 22:24; Eze 36:25; Rev 9:20 [u]Eze 7:19-20; 14:6 **2:21** [v]S Ex 33:22 [w]S Ps 145:12 [x]Isa 33:10 [y]S ver 19 **2:22** [z]Ps 118:6,8; 146:3; Isa 51:12; Jer 17:5 [a]S Ge 2:7; S Ps 144:4 [b]S Job 12:19; Ps 8:4; 18:42; 144:3; Isa 17:13; 29:5; 40:15; S Jas 4:14 **3:1** [c]S Ps 18:18 [d]S Lev 26:26; Am 4:6 [e]Isa 5:13; 65:13; Eze 4:16 **3:2** [f]Eze 17:13 [g]Dt 18:10 [h]Isa 9:14-15 **3:3** [i]S 2Ki 1:9 [j]S Job 22:8 [k]2Ki 24:14 [l]S Ecc 10:11; Jer 8:17 **3:4** [m]ver 12; Ecc 10:16 *fn* **3:5** [n]Ps 28:3; Isa 9:19; Jer 9:8; Mic 7:2,6 **3:7** [o]S Isa 2:11 [p]Jer 30:12; Eze 34:4; Hos 5:13

Israelites took refuge in caves and holes in the ground (see Jdg 6:1–2; 1Sa 13:6). *majesty.* The Hebrew for this word is translated "pride" when used of people. Pride is their attempt to be their own gods (see 14:13–14).

2:11,17,20 *in that day.* The phrase, which refers to the day of the Lord, occurs seven times in chs. 2–4 (see 3:7,18; 4:1–2) and in chs. 24–27 (see note on 24:21). The day of the Lord (see also v. 12) is a time of judgment and/or blessing as God intervenes decisively in the affairs of the nations (see Joel 1:15; Am 5:18; Zep 1:14—2:3 and notes). Assyria and Babylonia would bring the terror of judgment upon Judah in Isaiah's day (5:30).

2:13 *cedars of Lebanon.* Even inanimate things that people stand in awe of will be humbled so that "the LORD alone will be exalted" (v. 11). *Bashan.* A region east of the Jordan River and north of Gilead. It was famous for its oaks (Eze 27:6) and its livestock (Eze 39:18).

2:16 *trading ship.* These "ships of Tarshish" (see NIV text note) were large vessels such as those used by Solomon (1Ki 10:22) and the Phoenicians (Isa 23:1,14) to ply the sea in far-flung commercial ventures. For the location of Tarshish see notes on 23:6; Eze 27:12.

2:20 The futility of worshiping idols is repeatedly noted by Isaiah (see, e.g., 30:22; 31:7; 40:19–20; 44:9–20; see also note on 40:18–20).

2:22 *Stop trusting in.* Lit. "Cease from" or "Give up on." The verb is used to describe the rejection of the Messiah in 53:3. Ironically, people "rejected," "gave up on," the one Man who should have been trusted and "esteemed" (equals "of what account" here). He alone was worthy of the esteem wrongly given to frail leaders.

3:1–3 Leaders would be taken away by either death or deportation (see 2Ki 24:14; 25:18–21).

3:2–3 *soothsayer ... enchanter.* Occult practitioners and snake charmers (see Dt 18:10 and note on 18:9; Jer 8:17), whose activities were condemned because they involved implicit denial that all things are in the Lord's hands and under his control. Both legitimate and illegitimate kinds of assistance would be removed or deported (see 2Ki 24:14–16; 25:12; Hos 3:4).

3:3 *captain of fifty.* A company of 50 was a common military unit (see 2Ki 1:9). It was also used for civil groupings (Ex 18:25).

3:6 Normally it was unnecessary to force anyone to be a leader. In 4:1 the same social upheaval is seen as seven women "take hold of" one man. *You have a cloak.* Perhaps the one brother was not as poor as the others. *heap of ruins.* Probably Jerusalem (v. 8).

3:7,18 *in that day.* See note on 2:11,17,20.

I have no food[q] or clothing in my
house;
do not make me the leader of the
people."[r]

[8]Jerusalem staggers,
Judah is falling;[s]
their words[t] and deeds[u] are against the
LORD,
defying[v] his glorious presence.
[9]The look on their faces testifies[w]
against them;
they parade their sin like Sodom;[x]
they do not hide it.
Woe to them!
They have brought disaster[y] upon
themselves.
[10]Tell the righteous it will be well[z] with
them,
for they will enjoy the fruit of their
deeds.[a]
[11]Woe to the wicked![b] Disaster[c] is upon
them!
They will be paid back[d] for what their
hands have done.[e]

[12]Youths[f] oppress my people,
women rule over them.
O my people, your guides lead you
astray;[g]
they turn you from the path.

[13]The LORD takes his place in court;[h]
he rises to judge[i] the people.
[14]The LORD enters into judgment[j]
against the elders and leaders of his
people:
"It is you who have ruined my
vineyard;
the plunder[k] from the poor[l] is in
your houses.
[15]What do you mean by crushing my
people[m]
and grinding[n] the faces of the
poor?"[o]
declares the Lord,
the LORD Almighty.[p]

[16]The LORD says,
"The women of Zion[q] are haughty,
walking along with outstretched
necks,[r]
flirting with their eyes,
tripping along with mincing
steps,
with ornaments jingling on their
ankles.
[17]Therefore the Lord will bring sores
on the heads of the women
of Zion;
the LORD will make their scalps
bald.[s]"

[18]In that day[t] the Lord will snatch away
their finery: the bangles and headbands
and crescent necklaces,[u] [19]the earrings
and bracelets[v] and veils,[w] [20]the headdresses[x] and ankle chains and sashes, the perfume bottles and charms, [21]the signet rings
and nose rings,[y] [22]the fine robes and the
capes and cloaks,[z] the purses [23]and mirrors, and the linen garments[a] and tiaras[b]
and shawls.

[24]Instead of fragrance[c] there will be a
stench;[d]
instead of a sash,[e] a rope;
instead of well-dressed hair,
baldness;[f]
instead of fine clothing,
sackcloth;[g]
instead of beauty,[h] branding.[i]
[25]Your men will fall by the sword,[j]
your warriors in battle.[k]
[26]The gates[l] of Zion will lament and
mourn;[m]
destitute,[n] she will sit on the
ground.[o]

4 [1]In that day[p] seven women
will take hold of one man[q]
and say, "We will eat our own food[r]
and provide our own clothes;
only let us be called by your name.
Take away our disgrace!"[s]

3:7 [q]Joel 1:16 [r]Isa 24:2 **3:8** [s]Isa 1:7 [t]Isa 9:15,17; 28:15; 30:9; 59:3,13 [u]2Ch 33:6 [v]S Job 1:11; Ps 73:9,11; Isa 65:7 **3:9** [w]Nu 32:23; Isa 59:12; Jer 14:7; Hos 5:5 [x]S Ge 13:13 [y]S 2Ch 34:24; S Pr 8:36; Ro 6:23 **3:10** [z]S Dt 5:33; S 12:28; 28:1-14; Ps 37:17; Jer 22:15 [a]S Ge 15:1; S Ps 128:2 **3:11** [b]S Job 9:13; Isa 57:20 [c]Dt 28:15-68 [d]S 2Ch 6:23 [e]Jer 21:14; La 5:16; Eze 24:14 **3:12** [f]S ver 4 [g]Isa 9:16; 19:14; 28:7; 29:9; Jer 23:13; 25:16; Mic 3:5 **3:13** [h]S Job 10:2 [i]S Ps 82:1; S Isa 2:4 **3:14** [j]S 1Sa 12:7; S Job 22:4 [k]S Job 24:9; Jas 2:6 [l]Isa 11:4; 25:4 **3:15** [m]S Ps 94:5 [n]S Job 24:14 [o]Isa 10:6; 11:4; 26:6; 29:19; 32:6; 51:23 [p]Isa 5:7 **3:16** [q]S SS 3:11 [r]S Job 15:25 **3:17** [s]ver 24; Eze 27:31; Am 8:10 **3:18** [t]S Isa 2:11 [u]Ge 41:42; S Jdg 8:21 **3:19** [v]S Ge 24:47 [w]Eze 16:11-12 **3:20** [x]Ex 39:28; Eze 24:17,23; 44:18 **3:21** [y]S Ge 24:22 **3:22** [z]Ru 3:15 **3:23** [a]Eze 16:10; 23:26 [b]S Ex 29:6; SS 3:11; Isa 61:3; 62:3 **3:24** [c]S Est 2:12 [d]Isa 4:4 [e]Pr 31:24 [f]S ver 17; S Lev 13:40; S Job 1:20 [g]S Ge 37:34; Job 16:15; Isa 20:2; Jer 4:8; La 2:10; Eze 27:30-31; Jnh 3:5-8 [h]1Pe 3:3 [i]S 2Sa 10:4; Isa 20:4 **3:25** [j]S Isa 1:20 [k]Jer 15:8 **3:26** [l]Isa 14:31; 24:12; 45:2 [m]S Ps 137:1; Isa 24:4,7; 29:2; 33:9; Jer 4:28; 14:2 [n]S Lev 26:31 [o]S Job 2:13; La 4:5 **4:1** [p]S Isa 2:11 [q]Isa 13:12; 32:9 [r]2Th 3:12 [s]S Ge 30:23

3:8 *Judah is falling.* Fulfilled almost 150 years later in 586 B.C.
3:9 *Sodom.* See note on 1:9–10.
3:12 In the Near East, neither the rule of the young nor that of women was looked on with favor.
3:14 *vineyard.* Represents Israel (see 5:1 and note).
3:15 The leaders were crushing the poor, as women grind grain between two millstones (see note on Jdg 9:53).
3:16–24 For NT warnings against preoccupation with outward adornment rather than with moral virtue, see 1Ti 2:9–10; 1Pe 3:3–5 and notes.
3:16 *walking ... tripping along.* Ornaments on ankles made short steps necessary.
3:17 *bald.* Baldness was associated with mourning over catastrophe (see v. 24; 15:2 and note).
3:18 *crescent necklaces.* Probably moon-shaped; they implied veneration of the moon-god.
3:20 *headdresses.* Perhaps a kind of turban (see Eze 24:17, 23).
3:21 *signet rings.* Contained a seal and were a mark of authority (see Ge 41:42; Hag 2:23 and notes). *nose rings.* Made of gold and worn by brides (see Ge 24:22,53).
3:24 *rope ... branding.* Captives were led away by ropes (see notes on 37:29; 2Ki 19:28; Am 4:2) and sometimes branded.
3:26 *gates of Zion.* The gates are personified, as in Ps 24:7,9. They will lament because the crowds that used to assemble there are gone.
4:1–2 *In that day.* See notes on 2:2 and 2:11,17,20. After judgment comes salvation.
4:1 See note on 3:6. War will decimate the male population (3:25; see 13:12 and note), leaving many women with the double disgrace of being widows and childless. See 54:4.

The Branch of the LORD

2 In that day[t] the Branch of the LORD[u] will
be beautiful[v] and glorious, and the fruit[w]
of the land will be the pride and glory[x] of
the survivors[y] in Israel. 3 Those who are
left in Zion,[z] who remain[a] in Jerusalem,
will be called holy,[b] all who are recorded[c]
among the living in Jerusalem. 4 The Lord
will wash away the filth[d] of the women
of Zion;[e] he will cleanse[f] the bloodstains[g]
from Jerusalem by a spirit[a] of judgment[h]
and a spirit[a] of fire.[i] 5 Then the LORD will
create[j] over all of Mount Zion[k] and over
those who assemble there a cloud of
smoke by day and a glow of flaming fire
by night;[l] over all the glory[m] will be a canopy.[n] 6 It will be a shelter[o] and shade from
the heat of the day, and a refuge[p] and hiding place from the storm[q] and rain.

The Song of the Vineyard

5 I will sing for the one I love
a song about his vineyard:[r]
My loved one had a vineyard
on a fertile hillside.
2 He dug it up and cleared it of stones
and planted it with the choicest
vines.[s]
He built a watchtower[t] in it
and cut out a winepress[u] as well.
Then he looked for a crop of good
grapes,
but it yielded only bad fruit.[v]

3 "Now you dwellers in Jerusalem and
men of Judah,
judge between me and my
vineyard.[w]
4 What more could have been done for
my vineyard
than I have done for it?[x]
When I looked for good grapes,
why did it yield only bad?[y]
5 Now I will tell you
what I am going to do to my
vineyard:
I will take away its hedge,
and it will be destroyed;[z]
I will break down its wall,[a]
and it will be trampled.[b]
6 I will make it a wasteland,[c]
neither pruned nor cultivated,
and briers and thorns[d] will grow
there.
I will command the clouds
not to rain[e] on it."

7 The vineyard[f] of the LORD Almighty
is the house of Israel,
and the men of Judah
are the garden of his delight.
And he looked for justice,[g] but saw
bloodshed;
for righteousness,[h] but heard cries of
distress.[i]

Woes and Judgments

8 Woe[j] to you who add house to house
and join field to field[k]
till no space is left
and you live alone in the land.

[a] 4 Or *the Spirit*

4:2 [t]S Isa 2:11 [u]Isa 11:1-5; 52:13; 53:2; Jer 23:5-6; 33:15-16; Eze 17:22; Zec 3:8; 6:12 [v]Isa 33:17; 53:2 [w]S Ps 72:16; Eze 36:8 [x]Isa 60:15; Eze 34:29 [y]S Isa 1:9 **4:3** [z]S Isa 1:26 [a]Isa 1:9; Ro 11:5 [b]S Ex 19:6; Isa 26:2; 45:25; 52:1; 60:21; Joel 3:17; Ob 1:17; Zep 3:13 [c]S Ps 56:8; S 87:6; S Lk 10:20 **4:4** [d]Isa 3:24 [e]S SS 3:11 [f]S Ps 51:2 [g]S Isa 1:15 [h]Isa 28:6 [i]S Isa 1:31; S 30:30; S Zec 13:9; Mt 3:11; Lk 3:17 **4:5** [j]Isa 41:20; 65:18 [k]Rev 14:1 [l]S Ex 13:21 [m]Isa 35:2; 58:8; 60:1 [n]S Ps 18:11; Rev 7:15 **4:6** [o]Lev 23:34-43; Ps 27:5; Isa 8:14; 25:4; Eze 11:16 [p]Isa 14:32; 25:4; 30:2; 57:13 [q]S Ps 55:8 **5:1** [r]Ps 80:8-9; Isa 27:2; Jn 15:1 **5:2** [s]S Ex 15:17; Isa 16:8 [t]1Sa 2:9; Isa 27:3; 31:5; 49:8; Mt 21:33 [u]S Job 24:11 [v]Mt 21:19; Mk 11:13; Lk 13:6 **5:3** [w]Mt 21:40

5:4 [x]S 2Ch 36:15; Jer 2:5-7; Mic 6:3-4; Mt 23:37 [y]Jer 2:21; 24:2; 29:17 **5:5** [z]2Ch 36:21; Isa 6:12; 27:10 [a]S Ps 80:12; S Isa 22:5 [b]Isa 10:6; 26:6; 28:3,18; 41:25; 63:3; Jer 12:10; 34:22; La 1:15; Hos 2:12; Mic 7:10; Mal 4:3; S Lk 21:24 **5:6** [c]S Ge 6:13; S Lev 26:32; Isa 6:13; 49:17,19; 51:3; Joel 1:10 [d]ver 10,17; S 2Sa 23:6; Isa 7:23,24; 32:13; 34:13; 55:13; Eze 28:24; Hos 2:12; Heb 6:8 [e]S Dt 28:24; S 2Sa 1:21; Am 4:7 **5:7** [f]Ps 80:8; Isa 17:10; 18:5; 37:30 [g]Isa 10:2; 29:21; 32:7; 59:15; 61:8; Eze 9:9; 22:29 [h]S Isa 1:21 [i]S Ps 12:5 **5:8** [j]ver 11,18,20; Isa 6:5; 10:1; 24:16; Jer 22:13 [k]Job 20:19; Mic 2:2; Hab 2:9-12

4:2–6 An oracle of redemption just before the long message of indictment and judgment in ch. 5. It balances that found in 2:2–5, which immediately follows the long message of indictment and judgment in ch. 1 (see note on 1:1–31). These two oracles of redemption were intended to complement each other. Cf. 65:18.

4:2–3 *survivors ... are left.* See note on 1:9.

4:2 *Branch.* A Messianic title related to the "shoot" and "Branch" (11:1; 53:2) descended from David (see Jer 23:5 and note; 33:15; Zec 3:8; 6:12 and note)—but some believe that here "branch" refers to Judah. *pride.* A legitimate pride in the fruitfulness of the land that will characterize the Messiah's reign (see Ps 72:3,6,16 and note on 72:3). Contrast the pride of 2:11,17. *glory.* Here the fruitfulness of the land will be Israel's glory; in 46:13 God's salvation will be her glory ("splendor"); in 60:19 God himself will be her glory.

4:3 *holy.* Means "set apart" to God. See 1:26; 6:13 and note; see also Lev 11:44; Zec 14:20–21 and notes.

4:4 *judgment ... fire.* Purifying fire is also mentioned in 1:25 (see 48:10 and note).

4:5–6 *cloud ... fire ... shelter.* These words recall Israel's desert wanderings, when the pillar of cloud and fire guided and protected the people (see Ex 13:21 and note; 14:21–22). Isaiah often refers to the time of the exodus (see 11:15–16; 31:5; 51:10 and notes).

4:5 *the glory.* The manifestation of God's presence represented by a glow of flaming fire (see Ex 16:10; 24:17; 40:34–35). *canopy.* The cloud of smoke.

4:6 God's presence in cloud and fire will protect and preserve redeemed Zion (cf. Ps 121:5–6).

5:1–30 See note on 1:1–31.

5:1 *loved one.* God. *vineyard.* Israel (see v. 7; 3:14; Ps 80:8–16). Jesus' parable of the tenants (Mt 21:33–44; Mk 12:1–11; Lk 20:9–18) is probably based on this song. See Jn 15:1–17.

5:2 *watchtower.* Contrast the more modest "shelter" of 1:8. God's vineyard had every advantage (see Mt 21:33 and note). *winepress.* That is, the wine vat into which the grape juice flowed when grapes were trodden (see 16:10; Hag 2:16 and notes). *he looked for ... but.* The interpretation (v. 7) uses the same expression (cf. also 59:9,11).

5:6 *briers and thorns.* This pair (the Hebrew words are unique to Isaiah) occurs five more times (7:23–25; 9:18; 27:4; cf. 32:13; cf. also Ge 3:18). *not to rain.* The withholding of rain constituted a curse on the land. See Dt 28:23–24; 2Sa 1:21; 1Ki 17:1.

5:7 The song of the vineyard (vv. 1–6) is now interpreted. A powerful play on words makes the point: The words for "justice" and "bloodshed" (*mishpaṭ* and *miśpaḥ*) sound alike, as do those for "righteousness" (*ṣedaqah*) and "distress" (*ṣe'aqah*).

5:8–23 Six woes are pronounced on God's covenant-breaking people (vv. 8,11–12,18–19,20,21,22–23). Three of these are followed by judgment sections (vv. 9–10,13–15,24–25).

5:8 *house to house ... field to field.* Land in Israel could only be

9 The LORD Almighty[l] has declared in my hearing:[m]

"Surely the great houses will become
desolate,[n]
the fine mansions left without
occupants.
10 A ten-acre[a] vineyard will produce only
a bath[b] of wine,
a homer[c] of seed only an ephah[d] of
grain."[o]

11 Woe[p] to those who rise early in the
morning
to run after their drinks,
who stay up late at night
till they are inflamed with wine.[q]
12 They have harps and lyres at their
banquets,
tambourines[r] and flutes[s] and wine,
but they have no regard[t] for the deeds
of the LORD,
no respect for the work of his
hands.[u]
13 Therefore my people will go into
exile[v]
for lack of understanding;[w]
their men of rank[x] will die of hunger
and their masses will be parched
with thirst.[y]
14 Therefore the grave[e][z] enlarges its
appetite
and opens its mouth[a] without limit;
into it will descend their nobles and
masses
with all their brawlers and revelers.[b]
15 So man will be brought low[c]
and mankind humbled,[d]
the eyes of the arrogant[e] humbled.
16 But the LORD Almighty will be exalted[f]
by his justice,[g]
and the holy God will show himself
holy[h] by his righteousness.
17 Then sheep will graze as in their own
pasture;[i]
lambs will feed[f] among the ruins of
the rich.

18 Woe[j] to those who draw sin along with
cords[k] of deceit,
and wickedness[l] as with cart ropes,

5:9 [l] Jer 44:11 [m] Isa 22:14 [n] Isa 6:11-12; Mt 23:38 **5:10** [o] S ver 6; Lev 26:26; S Dt 28:38; Zec 8:10 **5:11** [p] S ver 8 [q] S 1Sa 25:36; S Pr 23:29-30 **5:12** [r] Ps 68:25; Isa 24:8 [s] S Job 21:12 [t] S 1Sa 12:24 [u] Ps 28:5; Eze 26:13 **5:13** [v] Isa 49:21 [w] S Pr 10:21; S Isa 1:3; Hos 4:6 [x] S Job 22:8 [y] S Isa 3:1 **5:14** [z] S Pr 30:16 [a] S Nu 16:30 [b] Isa 22:2, 13; 23:7; 24:8 **5:15** [c] Isa 10:33 [d] S Isa 2:9 [e] S Isa 2:11 **5:16** [f] Ps 97:9; Isa 33:10 [g] Isa 28:17; 30:18; 33:5; 61:8 [h] S Lev 10:3; Isa 29:23; Eze 36:23 **5:17** [i] Isa 7:25; 17:2; 32:14; Zep 2:6, 14 **5:18** [j] S ver 8 [k] Hos 11:4 [l] Isa 59:4-8; Jer 23:14

5:19 [m] Isa 60:22 [n] S Isa 1:4; 29:23; 30:11, 12 [o] Jer 17:15; Eze 12:22; 2Pe 3:4 **5:20** [p] S ver 8 [q] S Ge 18:25; S 1Ki 22:8 [r] S Ps 94:21 [s] S Job 24:13; Mt 6:22-23; Lk 11:34-35 [t] Am 5:7 **5:21** [u] S Pr 3:7; Isa 47:10; Ro 12:16; 1Co 3:18-20 **5:22** [v] S 1Sa 25:36; S Pr 23:20; S Isa 22:13 [w] S Pr 31:4; Isa 65:11; Jer 7:18

19 to those who say, "Let God hurry,
let him hasten[m] his work
so we may see it.
Let it approach,
let the plan of the Holy One[n] of
Israel come,
so we may know it."[o]

20 Woe[p] to those who call evil good[q]
and good evil,[r]
who put darkness for light
and light for darkness,[s]
who put bitter for sweet
and sweet for bitter.[t]

21 Woe to those who are wise in their
own eyes[u]
and clever in their own sight.

22 Woe to those who are heroes at
drinking wine[v]
and champions at mixing
drinks,[w]
23 who acquit the guilty for a bribe,[x]
but deny justice[y] to the innocent.[z]
24 Therefore, as tongues of fire[a] lick up
straw[b]
and as dry grass sinks down in the
flames,
so their roots will decay[c]
and their flowers blow away like
dust;[d]
for they have rejected the law of the
LORD Almighty
and spurned the word[e] of the Holy
One[f] of Israel.
25 Therefore the LORD's anger[g] burns
against his people;
his hand is raised and he strikes
them down.

[a] *10* Hebrew *ten-yoke,* that is, the land plowed by 10 yoke of oxen in one day [b] *10* That is, probably about 6 gallons (about 22 liters) [c] *10* That is, probably about 6 bushels (about 220 liters) [d] *10* That is, probably about 3/5 bushel (about 22 liters) [e] *14* Hebrew *Sheol* [f] *17* Septuagint; Hebrew / *strangers will eat*

5:23 [x] S Ex 23:8; S Eze 22:12 [y] ver 7; S Isa 1:17; 10:2; 29:21; 59:4, 13-15 [z] S Ps 94:21; Am 5:12; Jas 5:6 **5:24** [a] S Isa 1:31 [b] Isa 47:14; Na 1:10 [c] S 2Ki 19:30; S Job 18:16 [d] S Job 24:24; Isa 40:8 [e] Ps 107:11; Isa 8:6; 30:9, 12 [f] Job 6:10; Isa 1:4; 10:20; 12:6 **5:25** [g] S 2Ki 22:13; S Job 40:11; Isa 10:17; 26:11; 31:9; 66:15; S Jer 6:12

leased, never sold, because parcels had been permanently assigned to individual families (see Nu 27:7–11; 1Ki 21:1–3 and note on 21:3).

5:10 *ephah.* A tenth of a homer (see Eze 45:11). Meager crops often served as judgment on national sin (Dt 28:38–39; Hag 2:16–17). The amount of wine and grain is only a tiny fraction of what a "ten-acre vineyard" and a "homer of seed" would normally produce.

5:11–13 See Am 4:1–3; 6:4–7, where a lifestyle characterized by drunkenness and revelry is likewise condemned.

5:14 *grave.* See note on Ge 37:35. The grave has an insatiable appetite (see Ps 49:14; Pr 30:16 and notes).

5:16 *show himself holy.* See Lev 10:3 and note.

5:18 *cords of deceit.* See Pr 5:22 and note.

5:19 The Hebrew for the words "hurry" and "hasten" corresponds to that of the first and third elements of the name Maher-Shalal-Hash-Baz (see 8:1 and NIV text note). When Isaiah named his son (8:3), he may have been responding to the sarcastic taunts of these sinners. God did bring swift judgment, according to 5:26. *Holy One of Israel.* See 1:4 and note.

5:22 *mixing drinks.* Spices were added to beer and wine (see Ps 75:8; Pr 23:30 and notes).

5:23 See 1:23; 10:1–2.

5:24 *spurned ... the Holy One of Israel.* See v. 19; see also 1:4 and note.

5:25 *The mountains shake.* When God takes action, even the mountains tremble (see 64:3; Ps 18:7; Jer 4:24–26; Mic 1:4; Na 1:15; Hab 3:6,10). *Yet ... upraised.* A refrain repeated in 9:12,17,21; 10:4.

The mountains shake,[h]
and the dead bodies[i] are like refuse[j]
in the streets.[k]
Yet for all this, his anger is not turned
away,[l]
his hand is still upraised.[m]

26 He lifts up a banner[n] for the distant
nations,
he whistles[o] for those at the ends of
the earth.[p]
Here they come,
swiftly and speedily!
27 Not one of them grows tired[q] or
stumbles,
not one slumbers or sleeps;
not a belt[r] is loosened at the waist,[s]
not a sandal thong is broken.[t]
28 Their arrows are sharp,[u]
all their bows[v] are strung;
their horses' hoofs[w] seem like flint,
their chariot wheels like a
whirlwind.[x]
29 Their roar is like that of the lion,[y]
they roar like young lions;
they growl as they seize[z] their prey
and carry it off with no one to
rescue.[a]
30 In that day[b] they will roar over it
like the roaring of the sea.[c]
And if one looks at the land,
he will see darkness[d] and distress;[e]
even the light will be darkened[f] by
the clouds.

5:25 [h]S Ex 19:18 [i]S Ps 110:6 [j]S 2Ki 9:37 [k]S 2Sa 22:43 [l]Jer 4:8; Da 9:16 [m]Isa 9:12,17,21; 10:4 **5:26** [n]S Ps 20:5 [o]Isa 7:18; Zec 10:8 [p]Dt 28:49; Isa 13:5; 18:3 **5:27** [q]Isa 14:31; 40:29-31 [r]Isa 22:21; Eze 23:15 [s]S Job 12:18 [t]Joel 2:7-8 **5:28** [u]S Job 39:23; Ps 45:5 [v]S Ps 7:12 [w]Eze 26:11 [x]S 2Ki 2:1; S Job 1:19 **5:29** [y]S 2Ki 17:25; Jer 51:38; Zep 3:3; Zec 11:3 [z]Isa 10:6; 49:24-25 [a]Isa 42:22; Mic 5:8 **5:30** [b]S Isa 2:11 [c]S Ps 93:3; Jer 50:42; Lk 21:25 [d]S 1Sa 2:9; S Job 21:30; Ps 18:28; 44:19; S 82:5 [e]S Jdg 6:2; Isa 22:5; 33:2; Jer 4:23-28 [f]Isa 13:10; 50:3; Joel 2:10

6:1 [g]S 2Ch 26:22,23

Isaiah's Commission

6 In the year that King Uzziah[g] died,[h] I
saw the Lord[i] seated on a throne,[j] high
and exalted,[k] and the train of his robe[l] filled
the temple. 2 Above him were seraphs,[m]
each with six wings: With two wings they
covered their faces, with two they covered
their feet,[n] and with two they were flying.
3 And they were calling to one another:

"Holy, holy[o], holy is the LORD
Almighty;[p]
the whole earth[q] is full of his glory."[r]

4 At the sound of their voices the doorposts
and thresholds shook and the temple was
filled with smoke.[s]
5 "Woe[t] to me!" I cried. "I am ruined![u]
For I am a man of unclean lips,[v][w] and I
live among a people of unclean lips,[x] and
my eyes have seen[y] the King,[z] the LORD
Almighty."[a]
6 Then one of the seraphs flew to me
with a live coal[b] in his hand, which he had
taken with tongs from the altar. 7 With it
he touched my mouth and said, "See, this
has touched your lips;[c] your guilt is taken
away and your sin atoned for.[d]"

[h]S 2Ki 15:7 [i]S Ex 24:10; S Nu 12:8; Jn 12:41 [j]S 1Ki 22:19; S Ps 9:4; S 123:1; S Rev 4:2 [k]Isa 52:13; 53:12 [l]Rev 1:13 **6:2** [m]Eze 1:5; 10:15; Rev 4:8 [n]Eze 1:11 **6:3** [o]S Ex 15:11 [p]Ps 89:8 [q]Isa 11:9; 54:5; Mal 1:11 [r]S Ex 16:7; Nu 14:21; Ps 72:19; Rev 4:8 **6:4** [s]S Ex 19:18; S 40:34; Eze 43:5; 44:4; Rev 15:8 **6:5** [t]S Isa 5:8 [u]S Nu 17:12; S Dt 5:26 [v]Lk 5:8 [w]Ex 6:12 [x]Isa 59:3; Jer 9:3-8 [y]S Ex 24:10 [z]Ps 45:3; Isa 24:23; 32:1; 33:17; Jer 51:57 [a]S Job 42:5 **6:6** [b]S Lev 10:1; Eze 10:2 **6:7** [c]Jer 1:9; Da 10:16 [d]S Lev 26:41; Isa 45:25; Da 12:3; 1Jn 1:7

5:26 *lifts up a banner.* A pole with a banner was often placed on a hill as a signal for gathering troops (13:2) — used metaphorically for Yahweh's summoning the nations (here for judgment on Israel; in 11:10,12; 49:22; 62:10 to bring Israel back home). *distant nations.* Such as Assyria, whose armies struck Israel and Judah in 722 and 701 B.C., and Babylonia, which began its invasions in 605. *those at the ends of the earth.* Nations on Israel's far horizons, such as Egypt and Assyria.
5:27 *Not one ... grows tired or stumbles.* Cf. the use of these terms in 40:29 – 31.
5:30 *In that day.* See note on 2:11,17,20. *darkness and distress.* Similar words describe the horrors of war in 8:22.

6:1 – 13 Isaiah's commission, the climax of the first major section of his prophecies (see note on 1:1 — 6:13). In vv. 1 – 4 he sees the Lord in all his holy glory (v. 1); in vv. 5 – 7 he then sees himself in all his unholy uncleanness (v. 5); in vv. 8 – 13 the prophet, now cleansed and forgiven (v. 7), sees the rebellious people to whom God is sending him to proclaim the divine message of judgment.
6:1 *the year that King Uzziah died.* 740 B.C. (cf. 14:28 and note). Isaiah's commission probably preceded his preaching ministry; the account was postponed to serve as a climax to the opening series of oracles and to provide warrant for the shocking announcements of judgment they contain. The people had mocked the "Holy One of Israel" (5:19), and now he has commissioned Isaiah to call them to account. Uzziah reigned from 792 to 740 and was a godly and powerful king. When he insisted on burning incense in the temple, however, he was struck with "leprosy" and remained "leprous" until his death (see 2Ch 26:16 – 21 and NIV text note on 26:19). He was also called Azariah (2Ki 14:21; 2Ch 26:1). *I saw.* Probably in a vision in the temple. *the Lord.* Israel's Great King (see v. 5; cf. Jn 12:41 and note). *high and exalted.* The same Hebrew words are applied to God also in 57:15, and similar terms are used of the suffering servant in 52:13. *train of his robe.* A long, flowing garment. Cf. the robe of the "son of man" in Rev 1:13. *temple.* Probably the heavenly temple, with which the earthly temple was closely associated. John's vision of God on his throne is similar (Rev 4:1 – 8).
6:2 *seraphs.* See v. 6; heavenly beings not mentioned elsewhere (but cf. Eze 1:5 – 6 and notes). Their actions correspond to those of the "living creatures" of Rev 4:6 – 9, each of whom also had six wings. *covered their faces.* Apparently they could not gaze directly at the glory of God.
6:3 *Holy, holy, holy.* See Lev 11:44 and note; Rev 4:8. The triple repetition underscores God's infinite holiness. Note the triple use of "the temple of the LORD" in Jer 7:4 to stress the people's confidence in the security of Jerusalem because of the presence of that sanctuary. *LORD Almighty.* See note on 1Sa 1:3. *full of his glory.* In Nu 14:21 – 22; Ps 72:18 – 19 the worldwide glory of God is linked with his miraculous signs (cf. note on Eze 1:28).
6:4 *doorposts ... shook ... filled with smoke.* Similarly the power of God's voice terrified the Israelites at Mount Sinai, and the mountain was covered with smoke (see Ex 19:18 – 19; 20:18 – 19).
6:5 *eyes have seen the King.* See v. 1 and note. Isaiah was dismayed because anyone who saw God expected to die immediately (see Ge 16:13; 32:30 and notes; Ex 33:20).
6:6 *live coal.* Coals of fire were taken inside the Most Holy Place on the Day of Atonement (Lev 16:12), when sacrifice was made to atone for sin. See note on 1:25.
6:7 *touched my mouth.* When God commissioned Jeremiah, his hand touched the prophet's mouth (Jer 1:9).

8 Then I heard the voice[e] of the Lord saying, "Whom shall I send?[f] And who will
go for us?[g]"
And I said, "Here am I.[h] Send me!"
9 He said, "Go[i] and tell this people:

" 'Be ever hearing, but never
understanding;
be ever seeing, but never
perceiving.'[j]
10 Make the heart of this people
calloused;[k]
make their ears dull
and close their eyes.[a l]
Otherwise they might see with their
eyes,
hear with their ears,[m]
understand with their hearts,
and turn and be healed."[n]

11 Then I said, "For how long, O Lord?"[o]
And he answered:

"Until the cities lie ruined[p]
and without inhabitant,
until the houses are left deserted[q]
and the fields ruined and ravaged,[r]
12 until the LORD has sent everyone far
away[s]
and the land is utterly forsaken.[t]
13 And though a tenth remains[u] in the
land,
it will again be laid waste.[v]
But as the terebinth and oak
leave stumps[w] when they are cut
down,
so the holy[x] seed will be the stump
in the land."[y]

6:8 [e]S Job 40:9; Ac 9:4 [f]Jer 26:12,15 [g]S Ge 1:26 [h]S Ge 22:1; S Ex 3:4 **6:9** [i]Eze 3:11; Am 7:15; Mt 28:19 [j]Jer 5:21; S Mt 13:15*; Lk 8:10* **6:10** [k]S Ex 4:21; Dt 32:15; Ps 119:70 [l]Isa 29:9; 42:18-20; 43:8; 44:18 [m]S Dt 29:4; Eze 12:2; Mk 8:18 [n]S Dt 32:39; Mt 13:13-15; Mk 4:12*; Jn 12:40* **6:11** [o]Ps 79:5 [p]S Lev 26:31; S Jer 4:13 [q]S Lev 26:43; Isa 24:10 [r]Ps 79:1; S 109:11; Jer 35:17 **6:12** [s]S Dt 28:64 [t]S Isa 5:5,9; 60:15; 62:4; Jer 4:29; 30:17 **6:13** [u]S Isa 1:9; 10:22 [v]S Isa 5:6 [w]S Job 14:8 [x]S Lev 27:30; S Dt 14:2 [y]S Job 14:7

7:1 [z]S 1Ch 3:13 [a]S ver 8; S 2Ki 15:37 [b]2Ch 28:5 [c]S 2Ki 15:25 [d]ver 5,9; Isa 8:6 **7:2** [e]ver 13; S 2Sa 7:11;

The Sign of Immanuel

7 When Ahaz[z] son of Jotham, the son of
Uzziah, was king of Judah, King Rezin[a]
of Aram[b] and Pekah[c] son of Remaliah[d] king
of Israel marched up to fight against Jerusalem, but they could not overpower it.
2 Now the house of David[e] was told,
"Aram has allied itself with[b] Ephraim[f]";
so the hearts of Ahaz and his people were
shaken,[g] as the trees of the forest are shak-
en by the wind.
3 Then the LORD said to Isaiah, "Go out,
you and your son Shear-Jashub,[c h] to meet
Ahaz at the end of the aqueduct of the Upper Pool, on the road to the Washerman's
Field.[i] 4 Say to him, 'Be careful, keep calm[j]
and don't be afraid.[k] Do not lose heart[l]
because of these two smoldering stubs[m] of
firewood—because of the fierce anger[n] of
Rezin and Aram and of the son of Remaliah.[o] 5 Aram, Ephraim and Remaliah's[p] son
have plotted[q] your ruin, saying, 6 "Let us
invade Judah; let us tear it apart and divide it among ourselves, and make the son
of Tabeel king over it." 7 Yet this is what
the Sovereign LORD says:[r]

[a] *9,10* Hebrew; Septuagint *'You will be ever hearing, but never understanding; / you will be ever seeing, but never perceiving.' / 10This people's heart has become calloused; / they hardly hear with their ears, / and they have closed their eyes* [b] *2* Or *has set up camp in* [c] *3* *Shear-Jashub* means *a remnant will return.*

Isa 16:5; 22:22; Jer 21:12; Am 9:11 [f]Isa 9:9; Hos 5:3 [g]Isa 6:4; Da 5:6 **7:3** [h]Isa 10:21-22 [i]2Ki 18:17; Isa 36:2 **7:4** [j]Isa 30:15; La 3:26 [k]S Ge 15:1; S Dt 3:2; Isa 8:12; 12:2; 35:4; 37:6; Mt 24:6 [l]S Dt 20:3; S Isa 21:4 [m]Am 4:11; Zec 3:2 [n]Isa 10:24; 51:13; 54:14 [o]S 2Ki 15:27 **7:5** [p]S ver 1 [q]ver 21042 **7:7** [r]Isa 24:3; 25:8; 28:16

6:8–10 Isaiah's prophetic commission will have the ironic but justly deserved effect of hardening the callous hearts of rebellious Israel—and so rendering the warnings of judgment sure (see vv. 11–13). See also Jer 1:8,19; Eze 2:3–4.

6:8 *for us.* The heavenly King speaks in the divine council (see Ge 1:26; Ps 82:1 and notes). As a true prophet, Isaiah is made privy to that council, as were Micaiah (1Ki 22:19–20) and Jeremiah (23:18,22). Cf. Am 3:7. *Here am I.* See note on Ge 22:1. *Send me!* Isaiah's readiness to serve as Yahweh's messenger of judgment may have sprung, at least in part, from the fact that his name "Yahweh saves" (as, similarly, Joshua and Elisha) would stand as a constant reminder that the God whose words of judgment he proclaimed was also the God of Israel's salvation (see v. 13 and note; cf. 7:3; 8:1,3,18 and notes).

6:9–10 Quoted by Jesus in the parable of the sower (Mt 13:14–15; Mk 4:12; Lk 8:10). See also Ac 28:26–27; Ro 11:7–10,25 and notes. *this people.* In 1:3; 3:15; 5:13 the Lord refers to Israel as "my people." That their persistent and pervasive rebellion (1:1; 66:24) has begun to alienate them from him is indicated by numerous references to them as "this/these people" (e.g., 8:6,12; 29:13–14; cf. Ex 17:4 and note).

6:10 *heart ... ears ... eyes ... eyes ... ears ... hearts.* The *a-b-c/c-b-a* inversion is a common literary device in the OT. *ears dull ... close their eyes.* Israel's deafness and blindness are also mentioned in 29:9; 42:18; 43:8. One day, however, the nation will be able to see and hear (29:18; 35:5).

6:12 *far away.* See 5:13.

6:13 *a tenth.* A remnant—even it will be laid waste. *holy seed.* The few who are faithful in Israel (cf. 1Ki 19:18; see note on 1:9). *stump.* Out of which the nation will grow again. For a similar use of this imagery see 11:1 and note.

7:1—12:6 The second section of Isaiah's prophecies (sometimes called "the book of Immanuel"), climaxing in the songs of praise found in ch. 12 (cf. note on 1:1—6:13).

7:1 The invasion of Rezin and Pekah (probably in 735/734 B.C.) is known as the Syro-Ephraimite War. Aram (Syria) and Israel were trying unsuccessfully to persuade Ahaz to join a coalition against Assyria, which had strong designs on lands to its west. Isaiah was trying to keep Ahaz from forming a counter-alliance with Assyria (see 2Ki 16:5–18; 2Ch 28:16–21). *Pekah.* Ruled 752–732 B.C. (see 2Ki 15:27–31).

7:2 *house of David.* A reference to Ahaz, who belonged to David's dynasty (see 2Sa 7:8–11). *Ephraim.* Another name for Israel, the northern kingdom (see note on Ge 48:19). *hearts ... were shaken.* Ahaz had been defeated by Aram and Israel earlier (2Ch 28:5–8).

7:3 *Shear-Jashub.* See NIV text note; see also 10:20–22 and note. Isaiah gave each of his sons symbolic names (see 8:1,3,18). *aqueduct of the Upper Pool.* See 36:2 and note. Ahaz was probably inspecting the city's water supply. *Washerman's Field.* Clothes were cleaned by trampling on them in cold water and using a kind of soap (soda) or bleach (see Mal 3:2 and note; Mk 9:3).

7:4 *two smoldering stubs.* Damascus (Aram's capital; see v. 8) was crushed by Tiglath-Pileser III in 732 B.C., and Israel was soundly defeated the same year.

7:6 *Tabeel.* An Aramaic name sometimes associated with the "land of Tob" east of the Jordan River (see Jdg 11:3 and note).

"'It will not take place,
it will not happen,[s]
8 for the head of Aram is Damascus,[t]
and the head of Damascus is only
Rezin.[u]
Within sixty-five years
Ephraim will be too shattered[v] to be
a people.
9 The head of Ephraim is Samaria,[w]
and the head of Samaria is only
Remaliah's son.
If you do not stand[x] firm in your faith,[y]
you will not stand at all.' "[z]

10 Again the LORD spoke to Ahaz, 11 "Ask
the LORD your God for a sign,[a] whether
in the deepest depths or in the highest
heights.[b]"
12 But Ahaz said, "I will not ask; I will
not put the LORD to the test.[c]"
13 Then Isaiah said, "Hear now, you
house of David![d] Is it not enough[e] to try
the patience of men? Will you try the patience[f] of my God[g] also? 14 Therefore the
Lord himself will give you[a] a sign:[h] The
virgin[i] will be with child and will give
birth to a son,[j] and[b] will call him Immanuel.[ck] 15 He will eat curds[l] and honey[m] when
he knows enough to reject the wrong and
choose the right. 16 But before the boy
knows[n] enough to reject the wrong and
choose the right,[o] the land of the two kings
you dread will be laid waste.[p] 17 The LORD
will bring on you and on your people and
on the house of your father a time unlike
any since Ephraim broke away[q] from Judah—he will bring the king of Assyria.[r]"
18 In that day[s] the LORD will whistle[t] for
flies from the distant streams of Egypt and
for bees from the land of Assyria.[u] 19 They
will all come and settle in the steep ravines
and in the crevices[v] in the rocks, on all the
thornbushes[w] and at all the water holes.
20 In that day[x] the Lord will use[y] a razor
hired from beyond the River[dz]—the king of
Assyria[a]—to shave your head and the hair
of your legs, and to take off your beards[b]
also.[c] 21 In that day,[d] a man will keep alive a
young cow and two goats.[e] 22 And because
of the abundance of the milk they give, he
will have curds to eat. All who remain in
the land will eat curds[f] and honey.[g] 23 In
that day,[h] in every place where there were
a thousand vines worth a thousand silver shekels,[ei] there will be only briers and
thorns.[j] 24 Men will go there with bow and
arrow, for the land will be covered with briers[k] and thorns. 25 As for all the hills[l] once
cultivated by the hoe, you will no longer
go there for fear of the briers and thorns;[m]
they will become places where cattle are
turned loose and where sheep run.[n]

7:7 [s] Ps 2:1; Isa 8:10; 14:24; 28:18; 40:8; 46:10; Ac 4:25 **7:8** [t] S Ge 14:15 [u] ver 1; Isa 9:11 [v] 2Ki 17:24; Isa 8:4; 17:1-3 **7:9** [w] S 2Ki 15:29; Isa 9:9; 28:1,3 [x] S Ps 20:8; Isa 8:10; 40:8 [y] 2Ch 20:20 [z] Isa 8:6-8; 30:12-14 **7:11** [a] S Ex 7:9; S Dt 13:2 [b] Ps 139:8 **7:12** [c] Dt 4:34 **7:13** [d] S ver 2 [e] S Ge 30:15 [f] S Isa 1:14 [g] Ps 63:1; 118:28; Isa 25:1; 49:4; 61:10 **7:14** [h] S Ex 3:12; S Lk 2:12 [i] S Ge 24:43 [j] S Ge 3:15; Lk 1:31 [k] S Ge 21:22; Isa 8:8, 10; Mt 1:23* **7:15** [l] S Ge 18:8 [m] ver 22 **7:16** [n] Isa 8:4 [o] Dt 1:39 [p] S Dt 13:16; Isa 17:3; Jer 7:15; Hos 5:9, 13; Am 1:3-5 **7:17** [q] 1Ki 12:16 [r] S ver 20; S 2Ch 28:20 **7:18** [s] ver 20, 21; S Isa 2:11 [t] S Isa 5:26 [u] Isa 13:5 **7:19** [v] S Isa 2:19 [w] ver 25; Isa 17:9; 34:13; 55:13 **7:20** [x] S ver 18 [y] Isa 10:15; 29:16 [z] Isa 11:15; Jer 2:18 [a] ver 17; 2Ki 18:16; Isa 8:7; 10:5 [b] S 2Sa 10:4 [c] S Dt 28:49 **7:21** [d] ver 23; Isa 2:17 [e] Jer 39:10 **7:22** [f] S Ge 18:8 [g] ver 15; Isa 14:30 **7:23** [h] ver 21 [i] SS 8:11 [j] S Isa 5:6; Hos 2:12 **7:24** [k] S Isa 5:6 **7:25** [l] Hag 1:11 [m] S ver 19 [n] S Isa 5:17

[a] *14* The Hebrew is plural. [b] *14* Masoretic Text; Dead Sea Scrolls *and he* or *and they* [c] *14* *Immanuel* means *God with us.* [d] *20* That is, the Euphrates [e] *23* That is, about 25 pounds (about 11.5 kilograms)

7:8 *Within sixty-five years.* By c. 670 B.C. Esarhaddon (and, shortly after him, Ashurbanipal) king of Assyria settled foreign colonists in Israel. Their intermarriage with the Israelites who had not been deported resulted in the "Samaritans" (see 2Ki 17:24–34 and note on 17:29) and marked the end of Ephraim as a separate nation.
7:9 *only Remaliah's son.* Pekah was a usurper and hardly worthy to challenge Ahaz, a son of David. Aram (v. 8) and Israel (v. 9) had human "heads." Judah had a divine head; God was with them (v. 14; 8:8,10). *stand firm ... stand.* The use of the same Hebrew verb emphasizes the seriousness of the Lord's warning (see 1:19–20,25–26 and notes).
7:11 *a sign.* God was willing to strengthen the faith of Ahaz through a sign (see Ex 3:12 and note).
7:13 *house of David.* See note on v. 2.
7:14 *sign.* A sign was normally fulfilled within a few years (see 20:3; 37:30; cf. 8:18). *The virgin.* May refer to a young woman betrothed to Isaiah (8:3), who was to become his second wife (his first wife presumably having died after Shear-Jashub was born). In Ge 24:43 the same Hebrew word *('almah)* refers to a woman about to be married (see also Pr 30:19). Mt 1:23 apparently understood the woman mentioned here to be a type (a foreshadowing) of the Virgin Mary. *Immanuel.* The name "God is with us" was meant to convince Ahaz that God could rescue him from his enemies. See Nu 14:9; 2Ch 13:12; Ps 46:7. The Hebrew for "Immanuel" is used again in 8:8,10, and it may be another name for Maher-Shalal-Hash-Baz (8:3). If so, the boy's names had complementary significance (see note on 8:3). Jesus was the final fulfillment of this prophecy, for he was "God with us" in the fullest sense (Mt 1:23; cf. Isa 9:6–7).
7:15 *curds and honey.* Curds (a kind of yogurt) and honey meant a return to the simple diet of those who lived off the land. The Assyrian invasion would devastate the countryside and make farming impossible. (See vv. 22–25 for the significance of the expression.) *when he knows ... wrong ... right.* Suggests the age of moral determination and responsibility under the law—most likely 12 or 13 years of age. Thus, "when" this boy is 12 or 13 (722/721 B.C.), he will be eating curds and honey instead of agricultural products—due to the devastation of Israel by Assyria. Some believe that this expression involves a shorter period of time, identical to that in v. 16 and 8:4.
7:16 *before the boy knows ... land ... laid waste.* See note on v. 4; cf. 8:4. "Before" the boy is 12 or 13 years old, Aram and Israel will be plundered. This happened in 732 B.C., when the boy was about two years old.
7:17 *Ephraim broke away from Judah.* Almost two centuries earlier (930 B.C.; see 1Ki 12:19–20). *king of Assyria.* Ahaz's appeal to Assyria would bring temporary relief (2Ki 16:8–9), but eventually Assyria would attack Judah (see 8:7–8; 36:1 and notes).
7:18,20,23 *In that day.* Their difficulties will be a foretaste of the "day of the LORD." See note on 2:11,17,20.
7:18 *flies ... bees.* See Ex 23:28 and note.
7:19 *crevices in the rocks.* See note on 2:10. It will be impossible to escape from the invaders.
7:20 *shave ... head ... legs ... beards.* Such forcible shaving was considered a great insult (see 2Sa 10:4 and note). *hair of your legs.* Pubic hair.
7:23 *briers and thorns.* See note on 5:6. The destruction of the vineyards and the farmlands would fulfill 5:5–6.

Assyria, the Lord's Instrument

8 The LORD said to me, "Take a large
scroll[o] and write on it with an ordinary
pen: Maher-Shalal-Hash-Baz.[a] [p] 2And I
will call in Uriah[q] the priest and Zechariah son of Jeberekiah as reliable witnesses[r]
for me."
3Then I went to the prophetess,[s] and she
conceived and gave birth to a son.[t] And the
LORD said to me, "Name him Maher-Shalal-
Hash-Baz.[u] 4Before the boy knows[v] how to
say 'My father' or 'My mother,' the wealth
of Damascus[w] and the plunder of Samaria
will be carried off by the king of Assyria.[x]"
5The LORD spoke to me again:

6"Because this people has rejected[y]
the gently flowing waters of Shiloah[z]
and rejoices over Rezin
and the son of Remaliah,[a]
7therefore the Lord is about to bring
against them
the mighty floodwaters[b] of the
River[b]—
the king of Assyria[c] with all his
pomp.[d]
It will overflow all its channels,
run over all its banks[e]
8and sweep on into Judah, swirling
over it,[f]
passing through it and reaching up
to the neck.
Its outspread wings[g] will cover the
breadth of your land,
O Immanuel[c]!"[h]

9Raise the war cry,[d] [i] you nations, and
be shattered![j]
Listen, all you distant lands.
Prepare[k] for battle, and be shattered!
Prepare for battle, and be shattered!
10Devise your strategy, but it will be
thwarted;[l]
propose your plan, but it will not
stand,[m]
for God is with us.[e] [n]

Fear God

11The LORD spoke to me with his strong
hand upon me,[o] warning me not to follow[p]
the way of this people. He said:

12"Do not call conspiracy[q]
everything that these people call
conspiracy[f];
do not fear what they fear,[r]
and do not dread it.[s]
13The LORD Almighty is the one you are
to regard as holy,[t]
he is the one you are to fear,[u]
he is the one you are to dread,[v]
14and he will be a sanctuary;[w]
but for both houses of Israel he will
be
a stone[x] that causes men to stumble[y]
and a rock that makes them fall.[z]
And for the people of Jerusalem he
will be
a trap and a snare.[a]

8:1 [o]S Dt 27:8; Job 19:23; Isa 30:8; Jer 51:60 [p]ver 3; Hab 2:2; Jer 20:3; Hos 1:4 **8:2** [q]S 2Ki 16:10 [r]ver 16; S Jos 24:22; S Ru 4:9; Jer 32:10, 12, 25, 44 **8:3** [s]S Ex 15:20 [t]S Ge 3:15 [u]S ver 1 **8:4** [v]Isa 7:16 [w]S Ge 14:15 [x]S Isa 7:8 **8:6** [y]S Isa 5:24 [z]S Ne 3:15; Jn 9:7 [a]S Isa 7:1 **8:7** [b]Isa 17:12-13; 28:2, 17; 30:28; 43:2; Da 11:40; Na 1:8 [c]S 2Ch 28:20; S Isa 7:20 [d]Isa 10:16 [e]S Jos 3:15 **8:8** [f]Isa 28:15 [g]Isa 18:6; 46:11; Jer 4:13; 48:40 [h]S Isa 7:14 **8:9** [i]S Jos 6:5; Isa 17:12-13 [j]S Job 34:24 [k]Jer 6:4; 46:3; 51:12, 27-28; Eze 38:7; Joel 3:9; Zec 14:2-3 **8:10** [l]S Job 5:12 [m]S Pr 19:21; S 21:30; S Isa 7:7 [n]S Isa 7:14; Mt 1:23; Ro 8:31 **8:11** [o]Eze 1:3; 3:14 [p]Eze 2:8 **8:12** [q]Isa 7:2; 20:5; 30:1; 36:6 [r]S Isa 7:4; Mt 10:28 [s]1Pe 3:14* **8:13** [t]S Nu 20:12 [u]S Ex 20:20 [v]Isa 29:23 **8:14** [w]S Isa 4:6 [x]S Ps 118:22 [y]Jer 6:21; Eze 3:20; 14:3, 7; Lk 20:18 [z]S Lk 2:34; Ro 9:33*; 1Pe 2:8* [a]S Ps 119:110; Isa 24:17-18

[a] 1 *Maher-Shalal-Hash-Baz* means *quick to the plunder, swift to the spoil*; also in verse 3. [b] 7 That is, the Euphrates [c] 8 *Immanuel* means *God with us.* [d] 9 Or *Do your worst* [e] 10 Hebrew *Immanuel* [f] 12 Or *Do not call for a treaty / every time these people call for a treaty*

8:1–2 *scroll … witnesses.* The witnesses would attest to a legal transaction, either the marriage of Isaiah (see note on 7:14) or a symbolic deed connected with Maher-Shalal-Hash-Baz. The Hebrew word for "scroll" is related to the word for "unsealed copy" in Jer 32:11.

8:2 *Uriah the priest.* Served under King Ahaz (see 2Ki 16:10–11).

8:3–10 See 7:14–17 and notes.

8:3 *prophetess … son.* Probably the initial fulfillment of 7:14. Note the repetition of "conceive," "give birth to," "son" and "call/name" from 7:14. The young woman may be called a prophetess here because she had become the wife of a prophet. *Maher-Shalal-Hash-Baz.* This symbolic name (see NIV text note on v. 1) meant that Ahaz's enemies would be plundered (see v. 4 and note on 7:4), but it also implied that Judah would suffer (see vv. 7–8).

8:4 *knows how to say.* At about age two. The time period is identical to that in 7:16 (see notes on 7:4,16). *plunder of Samaria will be carried off.* The first stage of the destruction of the northern kingdom (see note on 7:4), which was not completed until 722–721 B.C. (see note on 7:15).

8:6 *waters of Shiloah.* See NIV text note on Ne 3:15. The water in Jerusalem that flows from the Gihon spring (see 2Ch 32:30) to the Pool of Siloam (see Jn 9:7 and note) may be intended (see Ne 3:15 and note). Here it symbolizes the sustaining power of the Lord. *Rezin and the son of Remaliah.* Rezin and Pekah both died in 732 B.C. (see 2Ki 16:9; see note on Isa 7:1).

8:7–8 *floodwaters … sweep on.* Mighty rivers were often used to symbolize a powerful invading army (see 17:12 and note; 28:17–19).

8:8 *up to the neck.* See 30:28 and note. Sennacherib's invasion in 701 B.C. overwhelmed all the cities of Judah except Jerusalem (see 1:7–9 and note), the head of Judah (cf. the initial references to Damascus and Samaria in 7:8–9). *outspread wings.* The figure changes to a powerful bird of prey. *Immanuel.* All seems lost, but "God is with us" (v. 10) and he defeats the enemy (see note on 7:14).

8:9 *nations … be shattered.* Just as Aram and Israel would be shattered (7:7–9), so Assyria and Babylon would eventually fall.

8:10 *it will not stand.* Only God's plans and purposes will last. *God is with us.* See NIV text note; see also 2Ch 13:12.

8:11 *his strong hand upon me.* See Eze 1:3 and note; 37:1; 40:1. The prophets were conscious of God's presence in and control over their lives.

8:12 The Lord warns the people not to rely on Assyria (see note on 7:1).

8:13 *the one you are to fear.* See 7:2; Pr 1:7 and note.

8:14 *sanctuary … stone … fall.* Either the Lord is the cornerstone of our lives (see 28:16) or he is a rock over which we fall. See Ro 9:33; 1Pe 2:6 and note for an application to Christ. *both houses.* The northern and southern kingdoms, Israel and Judah.

15 Many of them will stumble;[b]
they will fall and be broken,
they will be snared and captured."

16 Bind up the testimony[c]
and seal[d] up the law among my
disciples.
17 I will wait[e] for the LORD,
who is hiding[f] his face from the
house of Jacob.
I will put my trust in him.[g]

18 Here am I, and the children the LORD
has given me.[h] We are signs[i] and symbols[j]
in Israel from the LORD Almighty, who
dwells on Mount Zion.[k]
19 When men tell you to consult[l] mediums and spiritists,[m] who whisper and
mutter,[n] should not a people inquire[o] of
their God? Why consult the dead on behalf of the living? 20 To the law[p] and to the
testimony![q] If they do not speak according to this word, they have no light[r] of
dawn. 21 Distressed and hungry,[s] they will
roam through the land;[t] when they are
famished, they will become enraged and,
looking upward, will curse[u] their king and
their God. 22 Then they will look toward
the earth and see only distress and darkness and fearful gloom,[v] and they will be
thrust into utter darkness.[w]

8:15 [b] Pr 4:19; Isa 28:13; 59:10; Ro 9:32 **8:16** [c] S Ru 4:7 [d] Isa 29:11-12; Jer 32:14; Da 8:26; 12:4 **8:17** [e] S Ps 27:14 [f] S Dt 31:17 [g] S Ps 22:5; Heb 2:13* **8:18** [h] S Ge 33:5; Heb 2:13* [i] S Ex 3:12; Eze 4:3; 12:6; 24:24; Lk 2:34 [j] S Dt 28:46; S Eze 12:11 [k] Ps 9:11 **8:19** [l] S 1Sa 28:8 [m] S Lev 19:31 [n] Isa 29:4 [o] S Nu 27:21 **8:20** [p] S Isa 1:10; Lk 16:29 [q] S Ru 4:7 [r] ver 22; Isa 9:2; 59:9; 60:2; Mic 3:6 **8:21** [s] S Job 18:12 [t] Job 30:3 [u] S Ex 22:28; Rev 16:11 **8:22** [v] S Job 15:24 [w] S ver 20; S Job 3:13; S Isa 5:30; S Joel 2:2; Mt 25:30; Rev 16:10 **9:1** [x] S Job 15:24 [y] S 2Ki 15:29

To Us a Child Is Born

9 Nevertheless, there will be no more
gloom[x] for those who were in distress.
In the past he humbled the land of Zebulun and the land of Naphtali,[y] but in the
future he will honor Galilee of the Gentiles,
by the way of the sea, along the Jordan—

2 The people walking in darkness[z]
have seen a great light;[a]
on those living in the land of the
shadow of death[a][b]
a light has dawned.[c]
3 You have enlarged the nation[d]
and increased their joy;[e]
they rejoice before you
as people rejoice at the harvest,
as men rejoice
when dividing the plunder.[f]
4 For as in the day of Midian's defeat,[g]
you have shattered[h]
the yoke[i] that burdens them,
the bar across their shoulders,[j]
the rod of their oppressor.[k]
5 Every warrior's boot used in battle
and every garment rolled in
blood
will be destined for burning,[l]
will be fuel for the fire.
6 For to us a child is born,[m]
to us a son is given,[n]
and the government[o] will be on his
shoulders.[p]
And he will be called
Wonderful Counselor,[b][q] Mighty
God,[r]
Everlasting[s] Father,[t] Prince of
Peace.[u]

[a] 2 Or *land of darkness* [b] 6 Or *Wonderful, Counselor*

9:2 [z] S Ps 82:5; S 107:10, 14; S Isa 8:20 [a] S Ps 36:9; Isa 42:6; 49:6; 60:19; Mal 4:2; Eph 5:8 [b] S Lk 1:79 [c] Isa 58:8; Mt 4:15-16* **9:3** [d] S Job 12:23 [e] S Ps 4:7; S Isa 25:9 [f] S Ex 15:9; S Jos 22:8; S Ps 119:162 **9:4** [g] S Jdg 7:25 [h] S Job 34:24; Isa 37:36-38 [i] Isa 14:25; 58:6, 9; Jer 2:20; 30:8; Eze 30:18; Na 1:13; Mt 11:30 [j] S Ps 81:6; S Isa 10:27 [k] Isa 14:4; 16:4; 29:5, 20; 49:26; 51:13; 54:14; 60:18 **9:5** [l] S Isa 2:4 **9:6** [m] S Ge 3:15; Isa 53:2; Lk 2:11 [n] Jn 3:16 [o] S Mt 28:18 [p] Isa 22:22 [q] S Job 15:8; Isa 28:29 [r] S Dt 7:21; Ps 24:8; Isa 10:21; 11:2; 42:13 [s] S Ps 90:2 [t] S Ex 4:22; Isa 64:8; Jn 14:9-10 [u] Isa 26:3, 12; 53:5; 66:12; Jer 33:6; Mic 5:5; S Lk 2:14

8:16 Perhaps a reference to the legal transaction connected with vv. 1–2 (see note there). *testimony.* See v. 20. This term occurs elsewhere only in Ru 4:7, where it is rendered "method of legalizing transactions." *law.* See v. 20. The Hebrew for this word can also mean "teaching" or "instruction." The legal document containing Isaiah's teaching about Assyria's invasion was tied and sealed and then given to the prophet's followers, who were to preserve it until the time of its fulfillment, when God would authenticate it by the events of history (see Jer 32:12–14,44).

8:17–18 *I will put ... given me.* In Heb 2:13 these words are put on Jesus' lips.

8:17 *hiding his face.* See 1:15 and note; 59:2; Mic 3:4 and note.

8:18 *signs and symbols.* See notes on 7:3,14; cf. 20:3.

8:19 *mediums and spiritists.* See Dt 18:9–12 and note on 18:9. In the present crisis, people were turning to the spirits of the dead, as King Saul did when he went to a medium to contact Samuel (1Sa 28:8–11) and learn about the future. See note on 3:2–3.

8:20 *law ... testimony.* See v. 16 and note. Only by heeding the Lord's word through Isaiah—reinforced by the "signs and symbols" (v. 18) that Isaiah and his sons represented—would the light dawn for Israel.

8:21–22 The Assyrian invasion would bring deep distress on all Israel.

8:21 *curse ... king and ... God.* Because of their terrible suffering (cf. Pr 19:3)—but severe punishment awaited anyone who cursed God or a ruler (Ex 22:28; Lev 24:15–16).

9:1 *Naphtali.* This tribe in northern Israel suffered greatly when the Assyrian Tiglath-Pileser III attacked in 734 and 732 B.C. (2Ki 15:29). *will honor Galilee.* Fulfilled when Jesus ministered in Capernaum—near the major highway from Egypt to Damascus, called the Way of the Sea (Mt 4:13–16).

9:2 *great light.* Jesus and his salvation would be a "light for the Gentiles" (42:6; 49:6; cf. Mt 4:15–16 and note; Lk 2:32).

9:4 *Midian's defeat.* Gideon defeated the hordes of Midian and broke their domination over Israel (Jdg 7:22–25). *yoke.* In 10:26–27 Isaiah predicts that God will destroy the Assyrian army and their oppressive yoke. This was fulfilled in 701 B.C. (see 37:36–38 and notes).

9:5 *boot ... garment.* Military equipment will no longer be needed. See notes on 2:2–4; Mic 5:10–15.

9:6 *son.* A royal son, a son of David (see v. 7; see also 2Sa 7:14; Ps 2:7; Mt 1:1; 3:17; Lk 1:32; Jn 3:16 and notes). *Wonderful Counselor.* In Hebrew each of the four throne names of the Messiah consists of two elements (cf. 7:14 ["Immanuel"]). "Counselor" points to the Messiah as a king (see Mic 4:9) who determines upon and carries out a program of action (see 14:27, "purposed"; Ps 20:4, "plans"). As Wonderful Counselor, the coming Son of David will carry out a royal program that will cause all the world to marvel. What that program will be is spelled out in ch. 11, and more fully in chs. 24–27 (see

[7] Of the increase of his government[v] and
peace[w]
there will be no end.[x]
He will reign[y] on David's throne
and over his kingdom,
establishing and upholding it
with justice[z] and righteousness[a]
from that time on and forever.[b]
The zeal[c] of the LORD Almighty
will accomplish this.

The LORD's Anger Against Israel

[8] The Lord has sent a message[d] against
Jacob;
it will fall on Israel.
[9] All the people will know it —
Ephraim[e] and the inhabitants of
Samaria[f] —
who say with pride
and arrogance[g] of heart,
[10] "The bricks have fallen down,
but we will rebuild with dressed
stone;[h]
the fig[i] trees have been felled,
but we will replace them with
cedars.[j]"
[11] But the LORD has strengthened Rezin's[k]
foes against them
and has spurred their enemies on.
[12] Arameans[l] from the east and
Philistines[m] from the west
have devoured[n] Israel with open
mouth.

Yet for all this, his anger[o] is not turned
away,
his hand is still upraised.[p]
[13] But the people have not returned[q] to
him who struck[r] them,
nor have they sought[s] the LORD
Almighty.
[14] So the LORD will cut off from Israel
both head and tail,
both palm branch and reed[t] in a
single day;[u]
[15] the elders[v] and prominent men[w] are
the head,
the prophets[x] who teach lies[y] are the
tail.
[16] Those who guide[z] this people mislead
them,
and those who are guided are led
astray.[a]
[17] Therefore the Lord will take no
pleasure in the young men,[b]
nor will he pity[c] the fatherless and
widows,
for everyone is ungodly[d] and
wicked,[e]
every mouth speaks vileness.[f]

Yet for all this, his anger is not turned
away,
his hand is still upraised.[g]
[18] Surely wickedness burns like a fire;[h]
it consumes briers and thorns,[i]
it sets the forest thickets ablaze,[j]
so that it rolls upward in a column
of smoke.
[19] By the wrath[k] of the LORD Almighty
the land will be scorched[l]
and the people will be fuel for the
fire;[m]
no one will spare his brother.[n]
[20] On the right they will devour,
but still be hungry;[o]
on the left they will eat,[p]
but not be satisfied.
Each will feed on the flesh of his own
offspring[a]:
[21] Manasseh will feed on Ephraim, and
Ephraim on Manasseh;[q]
together they will turn against
Judah.[r]

[a] 20 Or *arm*

9:7 [v] S Isa 2:4 [w] S Ps 85:8; 119:165; Isa 11:9; 26:3,12; 32:17; 48:18 [x] Da 2:44; 4:3; S Lk 1:33; Jn 12:34 [y] Isa 1:26; 32:1; 60:17; 1Co 15:25 [z] Isa 11:4; 16:5; 32:1,16; 33:5; 42:1; Jer 23:5; 33:14 [a] S Ps 72:2 [b] S 2Sa 7:13 [c] 2Ki 19:31; Isa 26:11; 37:32; 42:13; 59:17; 63:15 **9:8** [d] S Dt 32:2 **9:9** [e] S Isa 7:2 [f] S Isa 7:9 [g] Isa 46:12; 48:4; Eze 2:4; Zec 7:11 **9:10** [h] S Ge 11:3 [i] Am 7:14; Lk 19:4 [j] 1Ki 7:2-3 **9:11** [k] S Isa 7:8 **9:12** [l] 2Ki 16:6 [m] S 2Ch 28:18 [n] S Ps 79:7 [o] S Job 40:11 [p] S Isa 5:25 **9:13** [q] S 2Ch 28:22; Am 4:9; Zep 3:7; Hag 2:17 [r] Jer 5:3; Eze 7:9 [s] Isa 2:3; 17:7; 31:1; 55:6; Jer 50:4; Da 9:13; Hos 3:5; 7:7,10; Am 4:6,10; Zep 1:6 **9:14** [t] ver 14-15; Isa 19:15 [u] Rev 18:8 **9:15** [v] Isa 3:2-3 [w] S Isa 5:13 [x] Isa 28:7; Eze 13:2 [y] S Job 13:4; S Isa 3:8; 44:20; Eze 13:22; Mt 24:24 **9:16** [z] Mt 15:14; 23:16,24 [a] S Isa 3:12 **9:17** [b] Jer 9:21; 11:22; 18:21; 48:15; 49:26; Am 4:10; 8:13 [c] S Job 5:4; Isa 27:11; Jer 13:14 [d] Isa 10:6; 32:6; Mic 7:2 [e] S Isa 1:4 [f] S Isa 3:8; Mt 12:34; Ro 3:13-14 [g] S Isa 5:25 **9:18** [h] S Dt 29:23; S Isa 1:31 [i] S Isa 5:6 [j] S Ps 83:14 **9:19** [k] S Job 40:11; Isa 13:9,13 [l] Jer 17:27 [m] S Ps 97:3; S Isa 1:31 [n] S Isa 3:5 **9:20** [o] S Lev 26:26; S Job 18:12 [p] Isa 49:26; Zec 11:9 **9:21** [q] S Jdg 7:22; S 12:4 [r] S 2Ch 28:6

25:1 — "marvelous things, things planned [counseled] long ago"). In 28:29 the same two Hebrew words underlying "Wonderful Counselor" describe the Lord as being "wonderful in counsel" (see also Jdg 13:18 and note). *Mighty God.* See 10:21. His divine power as a warrior is stressed. *Everlasting Father.* He will be an enduring, compassionate provider and protector (cf. 40:9 – 11). *Prince of Peace.* His rule will bring wholeness and well-being to individuals and to society (see 11:6 – 9).

9:7 *David's throne ... righteousness ... forever.* In spite of the sins of kings like Ahaz, Christ will be a descendant of David who will rule in righteousness forever (see 11:3 – 5; 2Sa 7:12 – 13,16; Jer 33:15,20 – 22). *The zeal ... this.* Repeated in 37:32. God is like a jealous lover who will not abandon his people.

9:8 — 10:4 Although Isaiah's prophetic message was primarily "concerning Judah and Jerusalem" (1:1), he also occasionally mediated Yahweh's word to "Ephraim and the inhabitants of Samaria" (9:9). This section is an oracle of divine judgment against the northern kingdom. It consists of four balanced stanzas (vv. 8 – 12,13 – 17,18 – 21; 10:1 – 4), each of which ends with the same refrain (see note on 9:12,17,21).

9:9 *Ephraim.* See note on 7:2.

9:10 *bricks have fallen down.* Bricks made of clay and dried by the sun crumbled easily. *dressed stone.* Amos denounces the stone mansions of the wicked (Am 5:11). *cedars.* The cedars of Lebanon provided the most valuable wood in the ancient Near East (see 1Ki 7:2 – 3).

9:11 *Rezin's foes.* The Assyrians (see note on 7:1).

9:12,17,21 *Yet ... upraised.* See 5:25. This refrain is repeated in 10:4, where the anger of the Lord reaches a climax in the captivity of his people.

9:14 *head and tail ... palm branch and reed.* The leaders of Israel (see also 3:1 – 3). These two pairs refer to Egyptian leaders in 19:15.

9:17 *fatherless and widows.* They often suffered at the hands of the powerful (see note on 1:17), but now even they are wicked.

9:18 *briers and thorns.* See note on 5:6.

9:19 *fuel for the fire.* Contrast v. 5.

9:21 *Manasseh ... Ephraim.* These two prominent tribes in the

Yet for all this, his anger is not turned away,
his hand is still upraised.[s]

10 Woe[t] to those who make unjust laws,
to those who issue oppressive decrees,[u]
2 to deprive[v] the poor of their rights
and withhold justice from the oppressed of my people,[w]
making widows their prey
and robbing the fatherless.[x]
3 What will you do on the day of reckoning,[y]
when disaster[z] comes from afar?
To whom will you run for help?[a]
Where will you leave your riches?
4 Nothing will remain but to cringe among the captives[b]
or fall among the slain.[c]

Yet for all this, his anger is not turned away,[d]
his hand is still upraised.

God's Judgment on Assyria

5 "Woe[e] to the Assyrian,[f] the rod[g] of my anger,
in whose hand is the club[h] of my wrath![i]
6 I send him against a godless[j] nation,
I dispatch[k] him against a people who anger me,[l]
to seize loot and snatch plunder,[m]
and to trample[n] them down like mud in the streets.
7 But this is not what he intends,[o]
this is not what he has in mind;
his purpose is to destroy,
to put an end to many nations.
8 'Are not my commanders[p] all kings?'
he says.
9 'Has not Calno[q] fared like Carchemish?[r]
Is not Hamath[s] like Arpad,[t]
and Samaria[u] like Damascus?[v]
10 As my hand seized the kingdoms of the idols,[w]
kingdoms whose images excelled those of Jerusalem and Samaria—
11 shall I not deal with Jerusalem and her images
as I dealt with Samaria and her idols?[x]' "

12 When the Lord has finished all his
work[y] against Mount Zion[z] and Jerusalem, he will say, "I will punish the king of
Assyria[a] for the willful pride[b] of his heart
and the haughty look[c] in his eyes. 13 For
he says:

" 'By the strength of my hand[d] I have done this,[e]
and by my wisdom, because I have understanding.
I removed the boundaries of nations,
I plundered their treasures;[f]
like a mighty one I subdued[a] their kings.[g]
14 As one reaches into a nest,[h]
so my hand reached for the wealth[i] of the nations;
as men gather abandoned eggs,
so I gathered all the countries;[j]
not one flapped a wing,
or opened its mouth to chirp.[k]' "
15 Does the ax raise itself above him who swings it,
or the saw boast against him who uses it?[l]
As if a rod were to wield him who lifts it up,
or a club[m] brandish him who is not wood!

[a] 13 Or / I subdued the mighty,

9:21 [s]S Isa 5:25 10:1 [t]S Isa 5:8 [u]S Ps 58:2 10:2 [v]Isa 3:14 [w]S Isa 5:23 [x]S Dt 10:18; S Job 6:27; S Isa 1:17 10:3 [y]S Job 31:14 [z]ver 25; Ps 59:5; Isa 1:24; 13:6; 14:23; 24:6; 26:14; 47:11; Jer 5:9; 9:9; 50:15; Lk 19:44 [a]S Ps 108:12; Isa 20:6; 30:7; 31:3 10:4 [b]Isa 24:22; Zec 9:11 [c]Isa 22:2; 34:3; 66:16; Jer 39:6; Na 3:3 [d]S Isa 5:25; 12:1; 63:10; 64:5; Jer 4:8; 30:24; La 1:12 10:5 [e]S 2Ki 19:21; S Isa 28:1 [f]ver 12, 18; S Isa 7:20; 14:25; 31:8; 37:7; Zep 2:13 [g]Isa 14:5; 54:16 [h]ver 15, 24; Isa 30:31; 41:15; 45:1; Jer 50:23; 51:20 [i]Isa 9:4; 13:3, 5, 13; 26:20; 30:30; 34:2; 63:6; 66:14; Eze 30:24-25 10:6 [j]S Isa 9:17 [k]Hab 1:12 [l]S 2Ch 28:9; Isa 9:19 [m]S Jdg 6:4; S Isa 5:29; 8:1 [n]S 2Sa 22:43; S Ps 7:5; S Isa 5:5; 37:26-27 10:7 [o]S Ge 50:20; Ac 4:23-28 10:8 [p]2Ki 18:24 10:9 [q]S Ge 10:10 [r]S 2Ch 35:20 [s]S Nu 34:8; 2Ch 8:4; Isa 11:11 [t]2Ki 18:34 [u]2Ki 17:6 [v]S Ge 14:15; 2Ki 16:9; Jer 49:24 10:10 [w]2Ki 19:18 10:11 [x]S 2Ki 19:13; S Isa 2:8; 36:18-20; 37:10-13 10:12 [y]Isa 28:21-22; 65:7; 66:4; Jer 5:29 [z]2Ki 19:31 [a]S ver 5; S 2Ki 19:7; Isa 30:31-33; 37:36-38; Jer 50:18 [b]S Isa 2:11; S Eze 28:17 [c]Ps 18:27 10:13 [d]S Dt 8:17 [e]S Dt 32:26-27; Isa 47:7; Da 4:30 [f]Eze 28:4 [g]Isa 14:13-14 10:14 [h]Jer 49:16; Ob 1:4; Hab 2:6-11 [i]S Job 31:25 [j]Isa 14:6 [k]2Ki 19:22-24; Isa 37:24-25 10:15 [l]S Isa 7:20; 45:9; Ro 9:20-21 [m]S ver 5

northern kingdom were descended from the two sons of Joseph (see Ge 46:20; see also Ge 48:5–6 and notes). They had fought each other centuries earlier (Jdg 12:4).
10:1 *Woe.* Cf. the series of woes in 5:8–23.
10:2 *the poor.* See note on Ex 22:21–27; cf. Jer 22:15–16. *widows ... fatherless.* See notes on 1:17; 9:17.
10:4 *captives ... slain.* Jer 39:6–7 similarly describes the plight of Judah's rulers when Nebuchadnezzar captured Jerusalem in 586 B.C. *Yet ... upraised.* See note on 9:12,17,21.
10:5 *rod ... club.* See 9:4 and note. Babylonia also was a hammer or club used by God to punish other nations (Jer 50:23; 51:20; Hab 1:6).
10:6 *godless nation.* Judah (see v. 10). *loot ... plunder.* The last part of the fulfillment symbolized by Maher-Shalal-Hash-Baz ("loot" here is the translation of Hebrew *shalal,* and "plunder" is the translation of *baz*). See 8:1–4 and note on 8:3.
10:9 *Calno.* A region in northern Aram (Syria). See Calneh in Am 6:2 (see note there). *Carchemish.* The great fortress on the Euphrates River east of Calno (see Jer 46:2 and note). *Hamath.* A city on the Orontes River that marked the northern extent of Solomon's rule (2Ch 8:4). See note on 2Ki 17:24. *Arpad.* A city near Hamath and just south of Calno. All these areas submitted to Assyria by c. 717 B.C. (see 36:19).
10:10,14 *my hand seized ... my hand reached.* The Hebrew verb is the same in both verses. The repetition of the phrase underscores the unquenchable greed of the Assyrian king.
10:10 *images ... of Jerusalem and Samaria.* No Israelite was supposed to worship idols (see Ex 20:4 and note), but the land was full of them (2:8). Samaria fell to Shalmaneser V (2Ki 17:3–6) and Sargon II in 722–721 B.C.
10:12 The Lord's instruments of judgment are not themselves exempt from his judgment. *pride.* Judgment against the proud was announced in 2:11,17.
10:13–14 *my ... I.* The king of Assyria boastfully refers to himself nine times. Cf. 14:13–14; Eze 28:2–5.
10:15 *ax ... saw ... rod ... club.* See v. 5; 9:4 and notes.

16 Therefore, the Lord, the LORD Almighty,
will send a wasting disease[n] upon
his sturdy warriors;[o]
under his pomp[p] a fire[q] will be kindled
like a blazing flame.
17 The Light of Israel will become a fire,[r]
their Holy One[s] a flame;
in a single day it will burn and
consume
his thorns[t] and his briers.[u]
18 The splendor of his forests[v] and fertile
fields
it will completely destroy,[w]
as when a sick man wastes away.
19 And the remaining trees of his forests[x]
will be so few[y]
that a child could write them
down.

The Remnant of Israel

20 In that day[z] the remnant of Israel,
the survivors[a] of the house of Jacob,
will no longer rely[b] on him
who struck them down[c]
but will truly rely[d] on the LORD,
the Holy One of Israel.[e]
21 A remnant[f] will return,[a][g] a remnant of
Jacob
will return to the Mighty God.[h]
22 Though your people, O Israel, be like
the sand[i] by the sea,
only a remnant will return.[j]
Destruction has been decreed,[k]
overwhelming and righteous.
23 The Lord, the LORD Almighty, will
carry out
the destruction decreed[l] upon the
whole land.[m]

24 Therefore, this is what the Lord, the
LORD Almighty, says:

"O my people who live in Zion,[n]
do not be afraid[o] of the Assyrians,
who beat[p] you with a rod[q]
and lift up a club against you, as
Egypt did.
25 Very soon[r] my anger against you will
end
and my wrath[s] will be directed to
their destruction.[t]"

26 The LORD Almighty will lash[u] them
with a whip,
as when he struck down Midian[v] at
the rock of Oreb;
and he will raise his staff[w] over the
waters,[x]
as he did in Egypt.
27 In that day[y] their burden[z] will be lifted
from your shoulders,
their yoke[a] from your neck;[b]
the yoke[c] will be broken
because you have grown so fat.[b]
28 They enter Aiath;
they pass through Migron;[d]
they store supplies[e] at Micmash.[f]
29 They go over the pass, and say,
"We will camp overnight at Geba.[g]"
Ramah[h] trembles;
Gibeah[i] of Saul flees.[j]
30 Cry out, O Daughter of Gallim![k]
Listen, O Laishah!
Poor Anathoth![l]

[a] *21* Hebrew *shear-jashub*; also in verse 22
[b] *27* Hebrew; Septuagint *broken / from your shoulders*

10:16 [n] ver 18; S Nu 11:33; Isa 17:4 [o] Ps 78:31 [p] S Isa 8:7 [q] Jer 21:14 **10:17** [r] S Job 41:21; S Isa 1:31; 31:9; Zec 2:5 [s] Isa 37:23 [t] S Nu 11:1-3; S 2Sa 23:6 [u] S Isa 9:18 **10:18** [v] S 2Ki 19:23 [w] S ver 5 **10:19** [x] ver 33-34; Isa 32:19 [y] Isa 17:6; 21:17; 27:13; Jer 44:28 **10:20** [z] ver 27; Isa 11:10, 11; 12:1, 4; 19:18, 19; 24:21; 28:5; 52:6; Zec 9:16 [a] S Isa 1:9; Eze 7:16 [b] S 2Ki 16:7 [c] 2Ch 28:20 [d] 2Ch 14:11; Isa 17:7; 48:2; 50:10; Jer 21:2; Hos 3:5; 6:1; Mic 3:11; 7:7 [e] S Isa 5:24 **10:21** [f] S Ge 45:7; Isa 6:13; Zep 3:13 [g] Isa 7:3 [h] S Isa 9:6 **10:22** [i] S Ge 12:2; Isa 48:19; Jer 33:22 [j] Ezr 1:4; Isa 11:11; 46:3 [k] ver 23; Isa 28:22; Jer 40:2; Da 9:27 **10:23** [l] S ver 22 [m] Isa 6:12; 28:22; Ro 9:27-28* **10:24** [n] Ps 87:5-6 [o] S Isa 7:4 [p] S Ex 5:14 [q] S ver 5

10:25 [r] Isa 17:14; 29:17; Hag 2:6 [s] ver 5; Ps 30:5; Isa 13:5; 24:21; 26:20; 30:30; 34:2; 66:14; Da 8:19; 11:36 [t] S ver 3; Mic 5:6 **10:26** [u] Isa 37:36-38 [v] S Isa 9:4 [w] Isa 30:32 [x] S Ex 14:16 **10:27** [y] S ver 20 [z] S Ps 66:11 [a] S Lev 26:13; S Isa 9:4 [b] Isa 14:25; 47:6; 52:2 [c] Jer 30:8 **10:28** [d] S 1Sa 14:2 [e] S Jos 1:11 [f] 1Sa 13:2 **10:29** [g] S Jos 18:24; S Ne 11:31 [h] S Jos 18:25 [i] S Jdg 19:14 [j] Isa 15:5 **10:30** [k] 1Sa 25:44 [l] S Ne 11:32

10:16 *the Lord, the LORD Almighty.* See 1:24 and note. *wasting disease.* When the angel put to death 185,000 soldiers of the Assyrian king Sennacherib in 701 B.C., he may have used a rapidly spreading plague (see note on 37:36; see also 2Sa 24:15–16; 1Ch 21:22,27).
10:17,20 *Holy One.* See note on 1:4.
10:18–19 *forests.* A reference to the Assyrian army. See vv. 33–34 and note on v. 33.
10:19 Probably fulfilled between 612 B.C. (fall of Nineveh) and 605 (battle of Carchemish).
10:20,27 *In that day.* The day of victory and joy, the positive aspect of the "day of the LORD" (see notes on 2:11,17,20; 9:4). Israel is restored and the people praise God. Ch. 11 connects this "day" with the Messianic age (see 11:10–11 and notes; see also 12:1,4).
10:20–22 *remnant.* See note on 1:9. "A remnant will return" was the name of Isaiah's first son (see NIV text note on 7:3). A faithful remnant led by Hezekiah survived the Assyrian invasion of 701 B.C. (see 37:4 and note). Later, a remnant returned from Babylonian exile.
10:20 *him who struck them.* The king of Assyria (see note on 7:17).
10:21 *Mighty God.* See note on 9:6.
10:22 *the sand by the sea.* See notes on Ge 13:16; 22:17. *Destruction ... decreed.* Because of Israel's sin, God would punish the nation through foreign invaders.
10:23–24 *The Lord, the LORD Almighty.* See 1:24 and note.
10:24 *rod ... club.* See v. 5; 9:4 and notes.
10:26–27 *Midian ... burden ... yoke.* See note on 9:4.
10:26 *Oreb.* One of the Midianite leaders (Jdg 7:25). *the waters ... in Egypt.* When Moses stretched out his hand over the Red Sea, the waters engulfed the chariots of the pharaoh (see Ex 14:26–28).
10:27 *fat.* Like a sturdy animal, Israel is able to break the yoke.
10:28–32 As if seeing a vision, Isaiah describes the approach of the Assyrian army to Jerusalem from about ten miles north of the city. Cf. Mic 1:8–16 and notes.
10:28 *Micmash.* Located about seven miles north of Jerusalem.
10:29 *Ramah.* The home of Samuel. It was about five miles from Jerusalem (1Sa 7:17; see note on 1Sa 1:1). *Gibeah of Saul.* About three miles from Jerusalem. It had been the capital of Israel's first king (see 1Sa 10:26).
10:30 *Daughter of Gallim.* A personification of a Benjamite town of Saulide association (see 1Sa 25:44; see also note on 2Ki 19:21). *Poor Anathoth.* Jeremiah's hometown (see Jer 1:1 and note). The Hebrew for "poor" sounds like the word "Anathoth," thus a wordplay.

31 Madmenah is in flight;
the people of Gebim take cover.
32 This day they will halt at Nob;[m]
they will shake their fist[n]
at the mount of the Daughter of
Zion,[o]
at the hill of Jerusalem.

33 See, the Lord, the LORD Almighty,
will lop off[p] the boughs with great
power.
The lofty trees will be felled,[q]
the tall[r] ones will be brought low.[s]
34 He will cut down[t] the forest thickets
with an ax;
Lebanon[u] will fall before the Mighty
One.[v]

The Branch From Jesse

11 A shoot[w] will come up from the
stump[x] of Jesse;[y]
from his roots a Branch[z] will bear
fruit.[a]
2 The Spirit[b] of the LORD will rest on
him—
the Spirit of wisdom[c] and of
understanding,
the Spirit of counsel and of power,[d]
the Spirit of knowledge and of the
fear of the LORD—
3 and he will delight in the fear[e] of the
LORD.

He will not judge by what he sees with
his eyes,[f]
or decide by what he hears with his
ears;[g]
4 but with righteousness[h] he will judge
the needy,[i]
with justice[j] he will give decisions
for the poor[k] of the earth.
He will strike[l] the earth with the rod of
his mouth;[m]
with the breath[n] of his lips he will
slay the wicked.[o]

10:32 [m]S 1Sa 21:1 [n]S Job 15:25 [o]S Ps 9:14; Isa 16:1; Jer 6:23 **10:33** [p]Isa 18:5; 27:11; Eze 17:4 [q]S Ex 12:12 [r]Isa 2:13; Am 2:9 [s]Isa 5:15 **10:34** [t]Na 1:12; Zec 11:2 [u]S 2Ki 19:23 [v]S Ge 49:24; Ps 93:4; Isa 33:21 **11:1** [w]S 2Ki 19:26; S Job 14:7 [x]S Job 14:8 [y]ver 10; Isa 9:7; S Mt 1:1; S Rev 5:5 [z]S Isa 4:2 [a]S 2Ki 19:30; S Isa 27:6 **11:2** [b]S Jdg 3:10; Isa 32:15; 42:1; 44:3; 48:16; 59:21; 61:1; Eze 37:14; 39:29; Joel 2:28; Mt 3:16; Jn 1:32-33; 16:13 [c]S Ex 28:3; S Eph 1:17; S Col 2:3 [d]S Isa 9:6; 2Ti 1:7 **11:3** [e]Isa 33:6 [f]Jn 7:24 [g]Jn 2:25 **11:4** [h]S Ps 72:2 [i]S Ps 72:4; S Isa 14:30 [j]S Isa 9:7; Rev 19:11 [k]S Job 5:16; S Isa 3:14 [l]Isa 27:7; 30:31; Zec 14:12; Mal 4:6 [m]S Job 40:18; Ps 2:9; Rev 19:15 [n]S Job 4:9; Ps 18:8; Isa 30:28, 33; 40:24; 59:19; Eze 21:31; 2Th 2:8 [o]S Ps 139:19 **11:5** [p]Ex 12:11; 1Ki 18:46 [q]Isa 25:1

5 Righteousness will be his belt[p]
and faithfulness[q] the sash around his
waist.[r]

6 The wolf will live with the lamb,[s]
the leopard will lie down with the
goat,
the calf and the lion and the yearling[a]
together;
and a little child will lead them.
7 The cow will feed with the bear,
their young will lie down together,
and the lion will eat straw like the
ox.[t]
8 The infant[u] will play near the hole of
the cobra,
and the young child put his hand
into the viper's[v] nest.
9 They will neither harm nor destroy[w]
on all my holy mountain,[x]
for the earth[y] will be full of the
knowledge[z] of the LORD
as the waters cover the sea.

10 In that day[a] the Root of Jesse[b] will
stand as a banner[c] for the peoples; the nations[d] will rally to him,[e] and his place of
rest[f] will be glorious.[g]
11 In that day[h] the
Lord will reach out his hand a second time
to reclaim the remnant[i] that is left of his
people from Assyria,[j] from Lower Egypt,
from Upper Egypt,[b][k] from Cush,[c][l] from
Elam,[m] from Babylonia,[d] from Hamath[n]
and from the islands[o] of the sea.[p]

[a] 6 Hebrew; Septuagint *lion will feed* [b] 11 Hebrew *from Pathros* [c] 11 That is, the upper Nile region [d] 11 Hebrew *Shinar*

[r]Eph 6:14 **11:6** [s]Isa 65:25 **11:7** [t]S Job 40:15 **11:8** [u]Isa 65:20 [v]Isa 14:29; 30:6; 59:5 **11:9** [w]S Nu 25:12; S Isa 2:4; S 9:7 [x]S Ps 48:1; S Isa 2:2 [y]1Sa 17:46; Ps 98:2-3; Isa 45:22; 48:20; 52:10 [z]Ex 7:5; Isa 19:21; 45:6, 14; 49:26; Jer 24:7; 31:34; Hab 2:14 **11:10** [a]S Isa 10:20 [b]S ver 1 [c]S Ps 20:5; Isa 18:3; Jer 4:6; Jn 12:32 [d]Isa 2:4; 14:1; 49:23; 56:3, 6; 60:5, 10; Lk 2:32; Ac 11:18 [e]Ro 15:12* [f]S Ps 116:7; Isa 14:3; 28:12; 32:17-18; 40:2; Jer 6:16; 30:10; 46:27 [g]Hag 2:9; Zec 2:5 **11:11** [h]S Isa 10:20 [i]S Dt 30:4; S Isa 1:9 [j]Isa 19:24; Hos 11:11; Mic 7:12; Zec 10:10 [k]Jer 44:1, 15; Eze 29:14; 30:14 [l]S Ge 10:6; Ac 8:27 [m]S Ge 10:22 [n]S Isa 10:9 [o]Isa 24:15; 41:1, 5; 42:4, 10, 12; 49:1; 51:5; 59:18; 60:9; 66:19 [p]Isa 49:12; Jer 16:15; 46:27; Eze 38:8; Zec 8:7

10:32 *Nob.* Perhaps on Mount Scopus, on the outskirts of Jerusalem. *Daughter of Zion.* A personification of Jerusalem (see note on 2Ki 19:21).
10:33 *the Lord, the LORD Almighty.* See 1:24 and note. *boughs … trees.* Sennacherib and his armies will fall (see vv. 16–19 and notes).
10:34 *Lebanon.* Refers to the famed cedars of Lebanon (see notes on 2:13; 9:10; 14:8).
11:1 *shoot … stump.* The Assyrians all but destroyed Judah, but it was the Babylonian exile that brought the kingdom of Judah to an end in 586 B.C. The Messiah will grow as a shoot from that stump of David's dynasty. See 6:13 and note. *Jesse.* David's father (see 1Sa 16:10–13). *Branch.* See notes on 4:2; Mt 2:23.
11:2 *The Spirit … will rest on him.* The Messiah, like David (1Sa 16:13), will be empowered by the Holy Spirit (see 61:1 and note). *counsel … power.* The Spirit will endow him with the wisdom to undertake wise purposes and with the power to carry them out (see note on 9:6). *fear of the LORD.* See Pr 1:7 and note.
11:3 *delight in the fear of the LORD.* See Jn 8:29.
11:4 *righteousness … justice.* The rulers of Isaiah's day lacked these qualities (see 1:17; 5:7; see also note on 9:7). *rod of his mouth.* Assyria was God's rod in 10:5,24, but the Messiah will rule the nations with an iron scepter (see Ps 2:9; Rev 2:27 and notes; 19:13–15).
11:5 *belt.* When a man prepared for vigorous action, he tied up his loose, flowing garments with a belt (see 5:27).
11:6–9 The peace and safety of the Messianic age are reflected in the fact that little children will be unharmed as they play with formerly dangerous animals. Such conditions are a description of the future consummation of the Messianic kingdom. See 2:2–4; 35:9; 65:20–25 and notes; Eze 34:25–29.
11:9 *my holy mountain.* See 2:2–4 and note. *full of the knowledge.* See 2:3, where the word of the Lord is taught in Jerusalem (see also Hab 2:14 and note).
11:10 *In that day.* See note on 10:20,27. *Root of Jesse.* A Messianic title closely connected with v. 1 (see also 53:2; Ro 15:12; Rev 5:5; 22:16 and notes). *banner.* See 5:26 and note.
11:11 *second time.* The first time was the exodus from Egypt (see v. 16). The second is probably the return from Assyrian

12 He will raise a banner[q] for the nations
and gather[r] the exiles of Israel;[s]
he will assemble the scattered people[t]
of Judah
from the four quarters of the earth.[u]
13 Ephraim's jealousy will vanish,
and Judah's enemies[a] will be cut off;
Ephraim will not be jealous of Judah,
nor Judah hostile toward Ephraim.[v]
14 They will swoop down on the slopes of
Philistia[w] to the west;
together they will plunder the people
to the east.[x]
They will lay hands on Edom[y] and
Moab,[z]
and the Ammonites[a] will be subject
to them.[b]
15 The LORD will dry up[c]
the gulf of the Egyptian sea;
with a scorching wind[d] he will sweep
his hand[e]
over the Euphrates River.[b][f]
He will break it up into seven streams
so that men can cross over in
sandals.[g]
16 There will be a highway[h] for the
remnant[i] of his people
that is left from Assyria,[j]
as there was for Israel
when they came up from Egypt.[k]

Songs of Praise

12 In that day[l] you will say:

"I will praise[m] you, O LORD.
Although you were angry with me,
your anger has turned away[n]
and you have comforted[o] me.
2 Surely God is my salvation;[p]
I will trust[q] and not be afraid.
The LORD, the LORD,[r] is my strength[s]
and my song;
he has become my salvation.[t]"
3 With joy you will draw water[u]
from the wells[v] of salvation.

4 In that day[w] you will say:

"Give thanks to the LORD, call on his
name;[x]
make known among the nations[y]
what he has done,
and proclaim that his name is
exalted.[z]
5 Sing[a] to the LORD, for he has done
glorious things;[b]
let this be known to all the world.
6 Shout aloud and sing for joy,[c] people of
Zion,
for great[d] is the Holy One of Israel[e]
among you.[f]"

A Prophecy Against Babylon

13 An oracle[g] concerning Babylon[h] that
Isaiah son of Amoz[i] saw:[j]

[a] 13 Or *hostility* [b] 15 Hebrew *the River*

11:12 [q]S Ps 20:5 [r]Isa 14:2; 43:5; 49:22; 54:7; Jer 16:15; 31:10; 32:37 [s]S Ne 1:9; S Ps 106:47; Isa 14:1; 41:14; 49:5 [t]Eze 28:25; Zep 3:10 [u]S Ps 48:10; 67:7; Isa 41:5; Rev 7:1 **11:13** [v]S 2Ch 28:6; Jer 3:18; Eze 37:16-17,22; Hos 1:11 **11:14** [w]S 2Ch 26:6; S 28:18 [x]S Jdg 6:3 [y]S Nu 24:18; S Ps 137:7; Isa 34:5-6; 63:1; Jer 49:22; Eze 25:12; Da 11:41; Joel 3:19; Ob 1:1; Mal 1:4 [z]Isa 15:1; 16:14; 25:10; Jer 48:40; Zep 2:8-11 [a]Jdg 11:14-18 [b]Isa 25:3; 60:12 **11:15** [c]S Ex 14:22; S Dt 11:10; Isa 37:25; 42:15; Jer 50:38; 51:36 [d]S Ge 41:6 [e]Isa 19:16; 30:32 [f]S Isa 7:20 [g]S Ex 14:29 **11:16** [h]Isa 19:23; 35:8; 40:3; 49:11; 51:10; 57:14; 62:10; Jer 50:5 [i]S Ge 45:7 [j]S ver 11 [k]Ex 14:26-31 **12:1** [l]S Isa 10:20 [m]Ps 9:1; Isa 25:1 [n]S Job 13:16 [o]S Ps 71:21 **12:2** [p]Isa 17:10; 25:9; 33:6; 45:17; 51:5,6; 54:8; 59:16; 61:10; 62:11 [q]S Job 13:15; S Ps 26:1; S 112:7; Isa 26:3; Da 6:23 [r]Isa 26:4; 38:11 [s]S Ps 18:1 [t]S Ex 15:2 **12:3** [u]S 2Ki 3:17; Ps 36:9; Jer 2:13; 17:13; Jn 4:10,14 [v]Ex 15:25 **12:4** [w]S Isa 10:20 [x]Ex 3:15; Ps 80:18; 105:1; Isa 24:15; 25:1; 26:8,13; Hos 12:5 [y]Isa 54:5; 60:3; Jer 10:7; Zep 2:11; Mal 1:11 [z]S Ps 113:2 **12:5** [a]S Ex 15:1 [b]S Ps 98:1 **12:6** [c]S Ge 21:6; S Ps 98:4; Isa 24:14; 48:20; 52:8; Jer 20:13; 31:7; Zec 2:10 [d]Ps 48:1 [e]S Ps 78:41; 99:2; Isa 1:24; 10:20; 17:7; 29:19; 37:23; 43:3,14; 45:11; 49:26; 55:5; Eze 39:7 [f]S Ps 46:5; Zep 3:14-17 **13:1** [g]Isa 14:28; 15:1; 21:1; Na 1:1; Hab 1:1; Zec 9:1; 12:1; Mal 1:1 [h]ver 19; S Ge 10:10; Isa 14:4; 21:9; 46:1-2; 48:14; Jer 24:1; 25:12; Rev 14:8 [i]Isa 20:2; 37:2 [j]S Isa 1:1

and Babylonian exile, though some interpreters, who believe that the passage refers to the dispersion after the destruction of Jerusalem in A.D. 70, place the regathering at Christ's second coming. *remnant.* See notes on 1:9; 10:20–22. *Lower Egypt.* The delta region of the Nile, in the north. *Upper Egypt.* Southern Egypt, upstream from the delta. *Elam.* The land northeast of the lower Tigris Valley (see 21:2 and note; Jer 49:34–39; Da 8:2). *Hamath.* See note on 10:9. *islands of the sea.* The coastlands and islands of the Mediterranean are probably intended (see 41:1,5; 42:4; Ge 10:5).

11:12 *gather the exiles.* See 27:13; 49:22; 56:8; 62:10; 66:20. *four quarters.* Lit. "four wings." "Four quarters of the earth" is equivalent to "ends of the earth" (24:16; Job 37:3).

11:13 *Ephraim's jealousy.* See note on 7:2. Prior to the exile, Ephraim and Judah were frequently fighting each other (see 9:21 and note).

11:14 *people to the east.* Perhaps the Midianites, who plundered Israel, along with other eastern peoples (see 9:4). *Edom ... Moab ... Ammonites.* After the exodus, Israel did not attack these nations (see Jdg 11:14–18). Israel's future political domination is also referred to in 14:2; 49:23; 60:12 (see also 25:10; 34:5).

11:15 *dry up ... the Egyptian sea.* An allusion to the drying up of the Red Sea during the exodus (see Ex 14:21–22). *gulf.* Lit. "tongue" (see "bay" in Jos 15:2,5). *Euphrates.* Rev 16:12 refers to the drying up of the Euphrates, perhaps symbolizing the removal of barriers preventing the coming of "the kings from the East."

11:16 *highway.* The removal of obstacles and the building of a highway leading to Jerusalem are also described in 57:14; 62:10 (cf. 35:8–10 and note on 35:8; 40:3–4 and note on 40:3).

12:1–6 Two short psalms of praise for deliverance (vv. 1–3,4–6) climax chs. 7–11 (see note on 7:1—12:6; see also note on 6:1).

12:1,4 *In that day.* See note on 10:20,27.

12:1 *I will praise you.* The "I" is probably the nation, praising the Lord for the deliverance he is sure to bring. *your anger has turned away.* See note on 9:12,17,21. After God punishes Israel, his anger will be directed against nations like Assyria and Babylonia.

12:2 *The LORD, the LORD.* See notes on Ex 3:15; 34:6–7; Dt 28:58. *The LORD ... salvation.* These lines echo Ex 15:2, a verse commemorating the defeat of the Egyptians at the Red Sea. See also Ps 118:14 and note.

12:3 *wells.* Perhaps an allusion to God's abundant provision of water for Israel during the desert wanderings (cf. Ex 15:25,27). But here God's future saving act is itself the "well" from which Israel will draw life-giving water (see Ps 36:9; Jer 2:13; Jn 4:10 and notes).

12:6 *Shout aloud and sing for joy.* These two imperatives occur again in 54:1, where Zion rejoices over the restoration of her people. *Holy One of Israel.* See notes on 1:4; 6:1.

13:1—23:18 A series of prophecies against the nations (see also Jer 46–51; Eze 25–32; Am 1–2; Zep 2:4–15 and notes). They begin with Babylon (13:1—14:23) and Assyria

[2]Raise a banner[k] on a bare hilltop,
shout to them;
beckon to them
to enter the gates[l] of the nobles.
[3]I have commanded my holy ones;
I have summoned my warriors[m] to
carry out my wrath[n]—
those who rejoice[o] in my triumph.

[4]Listen, a noise on the mountains,
like that of a great multitude![p]
Listen, an uproar[q] among the kingdoms,
like nations massing together!
The LORD Almighty[r] is mustering[s]
an army for war.
[5]They come from faraway lands,
from the ends of the heavens[t]—
the LORD and the weapons[u] of his
wrath[v]—
to destroy[w] the whole country.

[6]Wail,[x] for the day[y] of the LORD is near;
it will come like destruction[z] from
the Almighty.[a][a]
[7]Because of this, all hands will go
limp,[b]
every man's heart will melt.[c]
[8]Terror[d] will seize them,
pain and anguish will grip[e] them;
they will writhe like a woman in
labor.[f]
They will look aghast at each other,
their faces aflame.[g]

[9]See, the day[h] of the LORD is coming
—a cruel[i] day, with wrath[j] and
fierce anger[k]—
to make the land desolate
and destroy the sinners within it.
[10]The stars of heaven and their
constellations
will not show their light.[l]
The rising sun[m] will be darkened[n]
and the moon will not give its light.[o]
[11]I will punish[p] the world for its evil,
the wicked[q] for their sins.
I will put an end to the arrogance of
the haughty[r]
and will humble[s] the pride of the
ruthless.[t]
[12]I will make man[u] scarcer than pure
gold,
more rare than the gold of Ophir.[v]
[13]Therefore I will make the heavens
tremble;[w]
and the earth will shake[x] from its
place
at the wrath[y] of the LORD Almighty,
in the day of his burning anger.[z]

[14]Like a hunted[a] gazelle,
like sheep without a shepherd,[b]
each will return to his own people,
each will flee[c] to his native land.[d]

[a] 6 Hebrew *Shaddai*

13:2 [k]S Ps 20:5; Jer 50:2; 51:27 [l]Isa 24:12; 45:2; Jer 51:58 **13:3** [m]ver 17; Isa 21:2; Jer 51:11; Da 5:28,31; Joel 3:11 [n]S Job 40:11; S Isa 10:5 [o]S Ps 149:2 **13:4** [p]Joel 3:14 [q]S Ps 46:6 [r]Isa 47:4; 51:15 [s]Isa 42:13; Jer 50:41 **13:5** [t]S Isa 5:26 [u]Isa 45:1; 54:16; Jer 50:25 [v]S Isa 10:25 [w]S Jos 6:17; Isa 24:1; 30:25; 34:2 **13:6** [x]Isa 14:31; 15:2; 16:7; 23:1; Eze 30:2; Jas 5:1 [y]S Isa 2:12 [z]S Isa 10:3; S 14:15 [a]S Ge 17:1 **13:7** [b]S 2Ki 19:26; S Job 4:3; S Jer 47:3 [c]S Jos 2:11; Eze 21:7 **13:8** [d]S Ps 31:13; S 48:5; S Isa 21:4 [e]Ex 15:14 [f]S Ge 3:16; S Jn 16:21 [g]Joel 2:6; Na 2:10 **13:9** [h]S Isa 2:12; Jer 51:2 [i]Jer 6:23 [j]S Isa 9:19 [k]Isa 26:21; 66:16; Jer 25:31; Joel 3:2 **13:10** [l]S Job 9:7 [m]Isa 24:23; Zec 14:7 [n]S Ex 10:22; S Isa 5:30; Rev 8:12 [o]Eze 32:7; Am 5:20; 8:9; S Mt 24:29*; Mk 13:24* **13:11** [p]Isa 3:11; 11:4; 26:21; 65:6-7; 66:16 [q]S Ps 125:3 [r]S Ps 10:5; S Pr 16:18; Da 5:23 [s]S Isa 2:9; 23:9; Eze 28:2; Da 4:37 [t]Isa 25:3,5; 29:5,20; 49:25,26 **13:12** [u]S Isa 4:1 [v]S Ge 10:29 **13:13** [w]S Ps 102:26; Isa 34:4; 51:6 [x]S Job 9:6; S Isa 14:16; Mt 24:7; Mk 13:8 [y]S Isa 9:19 [z]S Job 9:5 **13:14** [a]Pr 6:5 [b]S 1Ki 22:17; S Mt 9:36; S Jn 10:11 [c]S Ge 11:9; Isa 17:13; 21:15; 22:3; 33:3; Jer 4:9 [d]Jer 46:16; 50:16; 51:9; Na 3:7

(14:24–27) before moving on to smaller nations. God's coming judgment (see 2:12–22) will fall not only on Israel but also on all the other nations of the world (see Jer 25:29). In fact, God's judgments on the nations are often a part of his salvation of his people (see, e.g., 10:12).

13:1—14:27 Since in Isaiah's day Babylon was part of the Assyrian empire, indeed one of its most important cities, it may be that this prophecy against Babylon is actually a prophecy also against the Assyrian empire (see 14:24–27).

13:1 See note on 1:1. *oracle.* The Hebrew for this word is related to a Hebrew verb meaning "to lift up, carry" and is possibly to be understood as either lifting up one's voice or carrying a burden. Such an "oracle" often contains a message of doom. *Babylon.* See 21:1–9; 46:1–2; 47:1–15; Jer 50–51 and notes. Its judgment is announced first probably because Babylon would later bring about the downfall of Judah and Jerusalem between 605 and 586 B.C. Babylon was conquered by Cyrus the Persian (see 45:1; 47:1) in 539. Subsequently it came to symbolize the world powers arrayed against God's kingdom (cf. 1Pe 5:13), and its final destruction is announced in Rev 14:8; 16:19; 17–18.

13:2 *Raise a banner.* See note on 5:26.

13:3 *my holy ones.* Or "those I have prepared for war." Here the reference is probably to the Persians under Cyrus the Great (see note on v. 1). Cf. 10:5, where the Lord calls Assyria "the rod of my anger" (see note there; see also v. 5; 45:1 and notes). *wrath.* God's anger is no longer turned against Israel (see 5:25; 9:12,17,21; 10:4) but against her enemies (see vv. 5,9,13; cf. 30:27). God must punish sin, particularly arrogance (see v. 11).

13:4 *The LORD Almighty is mustering an army.* See note on 1Sa 1:3. The Hebrew for "army" is the singular form of the word for "Almighty." God is the head of the armies of Israel (1Sa 17:45), of angelic powers (1Ki 22:19; Lk 2:13) and, here, of the armies that will destroy Babylon.

13:5 *weapons of his wrath.* Assyria was the club in God's hand during Isaiah's day, and Babylon itself would later serve as God's weapon (see v. 3 and note).

13:6,9 *day of the LORD.* See note on 2:11,17,20.

13:6 *destruction.* Hebrew *shod,* forming a wordplay on "Almighty" (Hebrew *Shaddai*)—as also in Joel 1:15. Cf. note on 5:7. For *Shaddai* see note on Ge 17:1.

13:7 *hands will go limp.* Courage will fail. See Jer 6:24.

13:8 *Terror.* Note the bitter irony; the Lord's warfare in behalf of his people usually brings panic to their enemies (see Ex 15:14–16; Jdg 7:22 and note). *pain … labor.* The prophets often compare the suffering of judgment and war with the pain and anguish that frequently accompany childbirth (see 26:17; Jer 4:31; 6:24).

13:10 *stars … sun … moon.* Cosmic darkness (the undoing of creation) is often associated with the day of the Lord (see 34:4; Joel 2:10,31 and notes; cf. Rev 6:12–13).

13:11 *arrogance … pride.* Cf. 2:9,11,17; 5:15.

13:12 *scarcer … rare.* War will reduce the male population drastically (see 4:1 and note). *Ophir.* Solomon imported large quantities of gold from this place (see 1Ki 9:28; 10:11 and notes).

13:13 *heavens tremble … earth … shake.* Thunderstorms and earthquakes often accompanied the powerful presence of the Lord (see notes on v. 10; Ex 19:16; Ps 77:16–19). Hail may also be involved (cf. 30:30; Jos 10:11).

13:14 *flee.* From parts of the Assyrian empire.

15 Whoever is captured will be thrust through;
all who are caught will fall[e] by the sword.[f]
16 Their infants[g] will be dashed to pieces before their eyes;
their houses will be looted and their wives ravished.[h]

17 See, I will stir up[i] against them the Medes,[j]
who do not care for silver
and have no delight in gold.[k]
18 Their bows[l] will strike down the young men;[m]
they will have no mercy[n] on infants
nor will they look with compassion on children.[o]
19 Babylon,[p] the jewel of kingdoms,[q]
the glory[r] of the Babylonians'[a] pride,
will be overthrown[s] by God
like Sodom and Gomorrah.[t]
20 She will never be inhabited[u]
or lived in through all generations;
no Arab[v] will pitch his tent there,
no shepherd will rest his flocks there.
21 But desert creatures[w] will lie there,
jackals[x] will fill her houses;
there the owls[y] will dwell,
and there the wild goats[z] will leap about.
22 Hyenas[a] will howl in her strongholds,[b]
jackals[c] in her luxurious palaces.
Her time is at hand,[d]
and her days will not be prolonged.[e]

14 The LORD will have compassion[f] on Jacob;
once again he will choose[g] Israel
and will settle them in their own land.[h]
Aliens[i] will join them
and unite with the house of Jacob.
2 Nations will take them
and bring[j] them to their own place.
And the house of Israel will possess the nations[k]
as menservants and maidservants in the LORD's land.
They will make captives[l] of their captors
and rule over their oppressors.[m]

3 On the day the LORD gives you relief[n]
from suffering and turmoil[o] and cruel
bondage,[p] 4 you will take up this taunt[q]
against the king of Babylon:[r]

How the oppressor[s] has come to an end!
How his fury[b] has ended!
5 The LORD has broken the rod[t] of the wicked,[u]
the scepter[v] of the rulers,
6 which in anger struck down peoples[w]
with unceasing blows,
and in fury subdued[x] nations
with relentless aggression.[y]

[a] *19* Or *Chaldeans'* [b] *4* Dead Sea Scrolls, Septuagint and Syriac; the meaning of the word in the Masoretic Text is uncertain.

13:15 [e] Jer 51:4 [f] Isa 14:19; Jer 50:25 **13:16** [g] ver 18; S Nu 16:27; S 2Ki 8:12 [h] S Ge 34:29; S Hos 13:16 **13:17** [i] Jer 50:9, 41; 51:1 [j] S ver 3 [k] 2Ki 18:14-16; Pr 6:34-35 **13:18** [l] S Ps 7:12; Isa 41:2; Jer 50:9, 14, 29 [m] S Dt 32:25; Jer 49:26; 50:30; 51:4 [n] Isa 47:6; Jer 6:23; 50:42 [o] S ver 16; Isa 14:22; 47:9 **13:19** [p] S ver 1 [q] Isa 47:5; Da 2:37-38 [r] Da 4:30 [s] S Ps 137:8; S Rev 14:8 [t] S Ge 19:25; Isa 1:9-10; Ro 9:29 **13:20** [u] Isa 14:23; 34:10-15; Jer 51:29, 37-43, 62 [v] 2Ch 17:11 **13:21** [w] S Ps 74:14; Rev 18:2 [x] Jer 14:6 [y] S Lev 11:16-18; S Dt 14:15-17 [z] Lev 17:7; 2Ch 11:15 **13:22** [a] Isa 34:14 [b] Isa 25:2; 32:14 [c] Isa 34:13; 35:7; 43:20; Jer 9:11; 49:33; 51:37; Mal 1:3 [d] Dt 32:35; Jer 48:16; 51:33 [e] Jer 50:39 **14:1** [f] Ps 102:13; Isa 49:10, 13; 54:7-8, 10; Jer 33:26; Zec 10:6 [g] Ge 18:19; 2Ch 6:6; Isa 41:8; 42:1; 44:1; 45:4; 49:7; 65:9, 22; Zec 1:17; 2:12; 3:2 [h] Jer 3:18; 16:15; 23:8 [i] S Ex 12:43; S Isa 11:10; Eze 47:22; Zec 8:22-23; Eph 2:12-19 **14:2** [j] S Isa 11:12; 60:9 [k] S Ps 49:14; Isa 26:15; 43:14; 49:7, 23; 54:3 [l] Ps 149:8; Isa 45:14; 49:25; 60:12; Jer 40:1 [m] Isa 60:14; 61:5; Jer 30:16; 49:2; Eze 39:10; Zep 3:19; Zec 2:9 **14:3** [n] S Isa 11:10 [o] S Job 3:17 [p] S Ex 1:14 **14:4** [q] Mic 2:4; Hab 2:6 [r] S Isa 13:1 [s] S Isa 9:4 **14:5** [t] S Isa 10:15 [u] S Ps 125:3 [v] S Ps 110:2 **14:6** [w] Isa 10:14 [x] S Ps 47:3 [y] S 2Ki 15:29; Isa 47:6; Hab 1:17

13:16 *infants ... dashed to pieces.* Invading armies often slaughtered infants and children so that there would be no future warriors, nor would there be a remnant through which the city (or country or people) might be revived (see Ps 137:8–9; Hos 10:14 and notes; Na 3:10). *wives ravished.* Women also suffered greatly in war. With their husbands killed, they were often used as prostitutes (see note on Am 7:17).

13:17 *Medes.* Inhabited what is today northwestern Iran. There was conflict between Assyria and Media during the eighth century B.C. Some, however, relate the fulfillment of this verse to the period when the Medes joined the Babylonians in defeating Assyria in 612–609 but later united with Cyrus to conquer Babylon in 539. See Ezr 6:2 and note; Jer 51:11,28; Da 5:31; 6:28.

13:19 *glory ... pride.* Babylon with its temples and palaces became a very beautiful city (see Da 4:29–30 and note on 4:30). The hanging gardens of Nebuchadnezzar were one of the seven wonders of the ancient world. In 4:2 the Hebrew words for "glory" and "pride" were used to describe the "Branch of the LORD." *Babylonians.* The Neo-Babylonian empire of 612–539 B.C. was led by the Chaldean people of southern Babylonia. Nabopolassar welded the tribes together c. 626, and his son Nebuchadnezzar became their most powerful ruler (605–562). *Sodom and Gomorrah.* Previously Isaiah compared Judah to these cities (see 1:9–10 and note).

13:20–22 See the similar description of the desolation of Edom in 34:10–15. Cf. Rev 18:2.

13:20 *never be inhabited.* Babylon was almost totally destroyed for the last time by the Persian king Xerxes I in 478 B.C. Then, after the time of Alexander the Great in 330, the city was basically deserted and fell into complete disrepair and ruin, and has remained that way ever since.

13:21 *wild goats.* This term is connected with demons ("goat idols") in Lev 17:7; 2Ch 11:15. In Rev 18:2 fallen Babylon is described as a home for demons and evil spirits.

14:1 *will have compassion ... will settle them.* Babylon's fall will be linked with Israel's restoration. God's compassion on his people is the theme of chs. 40–66 (see 40:1 and note). *in their own land.* See 2:2–4; 11:10–12 and notes. *Aliens will join them.* See 11:10; 56:6–7; 60:3 and note.

14:2 *Nations ... place.* See note on 5:26. *will possess the nations.* See note on 11:14.

14:3–21 However exalted (and almost divine) the king of Babylon may have thought himself (see vv. 12–14), he will go the way of all world rulers—down to the grave.

14:3 *suffering ... cruel bondage.* The Babylonian captivity was much like Israel's experience in Egypt (see Ex 1:14 and note).

14:4 *taunt.* Cf. 21:9; 47; Jer 25:12–14; 50–51; also the taunts against Babylon in Rev 18. *king of Babylon.* A title also used by the king of Assyria at this time.

14:5 *rod ... scepter.* See 10:5 and note; see also 10:24.

7 All the lands are at rest and at peace;[z]
they break into singing.[a]
8 Even the pine trees[b] and the cedars of Lebanon
exult over you and say,
"Now that you have been laid low,
no woodsman comes to cut us down."[c]

9 The grave[a][d] below is all astir
to meet you at your coming;
it rouses the spirits of the departed[e] to greet you —
all those who were leaders[f] in the world;
it makes them rise from their thrones —
all those who were kings over the nations.[g]
10 They will all respond,
they will say to you,
"You also have become weak, as we are;
you have become like us."[h]
11 All your pomp has been brought down to the grave,[i]
along with the noise of your harps;[j]
maggots are spread out beneath you
and worms[k] cover you.[l]

12 How you have fallen[m] from heaven,
O morning star,[n] son of the dawn!
You have been cast down to the earth,
you who once laid low the nations![o]
13 You said in your heart,
"I will ascend[p] to heaven;
I will raise my throne[q]
above the stars of God;
I will sit enthroned on the mount of assembly,[r]
on the utmost heights[s] of the sacred mountain.[b]
14 I will ascend above the tops of the clouds;[t]
I will make myself like the Most High."[u]
15 But you are brought down[v] to the grave,[w]
to the depths[x] of the pit.[y]

16 Those who see you stare at you,
they ponder your fate:[z]
"Is this the man who shook[a] the earth
and made kingdoms tremble,
17 the man who made the world a desert,[b]
who overthrew[c] its cities
and would not let his captives go home?"[d]

18 All the kings of the nations lie in state,
each in his own tomb.[e]
19 But you are cast out[f] of your tomb
like a rejected branch;
you are covered with the slain,[g]
with those pierced by the sword,[h]
those who descend to the stones of the pit.[i]
Like a corpse trampled underfoot,
20 you will not join them in burial,[j]
for you have destroyed your land
and killed your people.

The offspring[k] of the wicked[l]
will never be mentioned[m] again.
21 Prepare a place to slaughter his sons[n]
for the sins of their forefathers;[o]
they are not to rise to inherit the land
and cover the earth with their cities.

[a] 9 Hebrew *Sheol*; also in verses 11 and 15 [b] 13 Or *the north*; Hebrew *Zaphon*

14:7 [z]S Nu 6:26; Jer 50:34; Zec 1:11 [a]Ps 98:1; 126:1-3; Isa 12:6 **14:8** [b]S 1Ch 16:33; S Ps 65:13; Eze 31:16 [c]S 2Ki 19:23; Isa 37:24 **14:9** [d]S Pr 30:16; Eze 32:21 [e]S Job 26:5 [f]Zec 10:3 [g]S Job 3:14 **14:10** [h]Eze 26:20; 32:21 **14:11** [i]S Nu 16:30; S Pr 30:16 [j]Isa 5:12; Eze 26:13; Am 6:5 [k]S Job 7:5; 24:20; Isa 51:8; 66:24 [l]S Job 21:26 **14:12** [m]Lk 10:18 [n]2Pe 1:19; Rev 2:28; 8:10; 9:1 [o]Eze 26:17 **14:13** [p]Da 5:23; 8:10; Ob 1:4; Mt 11:23 [q]Eze 28:2; 2Th 2:4 [r]Ps 82:1 [s]Isa 37:24 **14:14** [t]S Job 20:6 [u]S Ge 3:5; S Nu 24:16; Isa 10:13; 47:8; Jer 50:29; 51:53; Da 11:36; 2Th 2:4 **14:15** [v]Isa 13:6; 45:7; 47:11; Jer 51:8, 43 [w]S Job 21:13 [x]Mt 11:23; Lk 10:15 [y]S Ps 55:23; Eze 31:16; 32:23 **14:16** [z]Jer 50:23; Rev 18:9 [a]S Isa 2:19; 13:13; Joel 3:16; Hag 2:6, 21 **14:17** [b]Isa 15:6; Joel 2:3 [c]Ps 52:7 [d]Ex 7:14; S 2Ki 15:29; Jer 50:33; Rev 18:18 **14:18** [e]Job 21:32 **14:19** [f]Isa 22:16-18; Jer 8:1; 36:30 [g]Isa 34:3 [h]S Isa 13:15 [i]Jer 41:7-9 **14:20** [j]S 1Ki 21:19 [k]S Job 18:19 [l]S Isa 1:4 [m]S Dt 32:26 **14:21** [n]S Nu 16:27 [o]S Ge 9:25; S Lev 26:39

14:7 *break into singing.* See 12:6 and note.
14:8 *pine trees ... cedars.* Isaiah often personified nature. The trees along with the mountains burst into song in 44:23 (cf. 55:12). *cedars of Lebanon.* These highly prized woods were hauled away by the kings of Assyria and Babylonia for centuries (see notes on 2:13; 9:10).
14:9 *leaders.* Lit. "goats"; a goat often led a flock of sheep (see Jer 50:8 and note). In Zec 10:3 the term is parallel to "shepherds." *rise from their thrones.* Conditions among the dead are described in terms of their roles on earth. *kings over the nations.* See v. 18. Even the greatest and most powerful must go down to "the grave below."
14:11 *brought down to the grave.* Repeated in v. 15. *pomp ... grave.* Cf. 5:14. *noise of your harps.* Music was sometimes a sign of luxury and pleasure (see Am 6:5 – 6).
14:12 – 15 Some believe that Isaiah is giving a description of the fall of Satan (cf. Lk 10:18 — where, however, Jesus is referring to an event contemporary with himself). But the passage clearly applies to the king of Babylon, who is later used as a type (prefiguration) of the "beast" who will lead the Babylon of the last days (see Rev 13:4; 17:3). Cf. the description of the king of Tyre in Eze 28.
14:12 *morning star.* The Hebrew for this expression is translated *lucifer* (lit. "light-bearer") in the Latin Vulgate, the origin of "Lucifer" in early English translations of this verse. For the true Morning Star see Rev 22:16 (see also 2Pe 1:19; cf. Nu 24:17 and note).
14:13 *utmost heights.* Babylon's king is destined for the "depths" of the pit (v. 15; the Hebrew word for "utmost heights" and "depths" is the same) — though he aspires to be "like the Most High" (v. 14). *sacred mountain.* Mount Zaphon (but see NIV text note), also called Mount Casius, was located in northern Syria. The Canaanites considered it the dwelling and meeting place of the gods, much like Mount Olympus for the Greeks (see Ps 48:2 and note). Cf. Ps 82:1 and note.
14:16 – 20a These verses seem to take place on earth, not in the realm of the dead (Sheol) — probably also vv. 9 – 10.
14:17 *captives go home.* Babylonia, like Assyria, deported large segments of defeated populations to subdue the rebellious among them (see 2Ki 24:14 – 16).
14:18 *kings of the nations.* See note on v. 9.
14:19 *cast out of your tomb.* A proper burial was considered important. To have one's body simply discarded was a terrible fate (see Jer 22:19 and note). *corpse trampled.* See 5:25.
14:21 *slaughter his sons.* A man's children, as well as his tombstone, were his memorial (cf. 2Sa 18:18). The king of Babylon would have neither (cf. 47:9).

[22] "I will rise up[p] against them,"
declares the LORD Almighty.
"I will cut off from Babylon her name[q]
and survivors,
her offspring and descendants,[r]"
declares the LORD.
[23] "I will turn her into a place for
owls[s]
and into swampland;
I will sweep her with the broom of
destruction,[t]"
declares the LORD Almighty.[u]

A Prophecy Against Assyria

[24] The LORD Almighty has sworn,[v]

"Surely, as I have planned,[w] so it will
be,
and as I have purposed, so it will
stand.[x]
[25] I will crush the Assyrian[y] in my land;
on my mountains I will trample him
down.
His yoke[z] will be taken from my
people,
and his burden removed from their
shoulders.[a]"
[26] This is the plan[b] determined for the
whole world;
this is the hand[c] stretched out over
all nations.
[27] For the LORD Almighty has purposed,[d]
and who can thwart him?
His hand[e] is stretched out, and who
can turn it back?[f]

A Prophecy Against the Philistines

[28] This oracle[g] came in the year[h] King
Ahaz[i] died:

[29] Do not rejoice, all you Philistines,[j]
that the rod that struck you is
broken;
from the root of that snake will spring
up a viper,[k]
its fruit will be a darting, venomous
serpent.[l]
[30] The poorest of the poor will find
pasture,
and the needy[m] will lie down in
safety.[n]
But your root I will destroy by famine;[o]
it will slay[p] your survivors.[q]
[31] Wail,[r] O gate![s] Howl, O city!
Melt away, all you Philistines![t]
A cloud of smoke comes from the
north,[u]
and there is not a straggler in its
ranks.[v]
[32] What answer shall be given
to the envoys[w] of that nation?
"The LORD has established Zion,[x]
and in her his afflicted people will
find refuge.[y]"

A Prophecy Against Moab

16:6-12pp — Jer 48:29-36

15 An oracle[z] concerning Moab:[a]

Ar[b] in Moab is ruined,[c]
destroyed in a night!
Kir[d] in Moab is ruined,
destroyed in a night!

14:22 [p] S Ps 94:16 [q] S Job 18:17; Ps 109:13; Na 1:14 [r] 2Sa 18:18; 1Ki 14:10; Job 18:19; S Ps 9:6; S Isa 13:18 **14:23** [s] S Lev 11:16-18; Isa 34:11-15; Zep 2:14 [t] S Isa 10:3; Jer 25:12 [u] Jer 50:3; 51:62 **14:24** [v] Isa 45:23; 49:18; 54:9; 62:8 [w] Isa 19:12, 17; 23:8-9; 25:1; Da 4:35 [x] S Job 9:3; S Isa 7:7; 46:10-11; Eze 12:25; Ac 4:28 **14:25** [y] S Isa 10:5, 12; 37:36-38 [z] S Isa 9:4 [a] S Isa 10:27 **14:26** [b] Isa 23:9 [c] Ex 15:12; S Job 30:21 **14:27** [d] Jer 49:20 [e] S Ex 14:21 [f] S 2Ch 20:6; Isa 43:13; Da 4:35 **14:28** [g] S Isa 13:1 [h] S 2Ki 15:7 [i] S 2Ki 16:1 **14:29** [j] S Jos 13:3; S 2Ki 1:2; S 2Ch 26:6 [k] S Isa 11:8 [l] S Dt 8:15 **14:30** [m] Isa 3:15; 25:4 [n] S Isa 7:21-22 [o] Isa 8:21; 9:20; 51:19 [p] Jer 25:16; Zec 9:5-6 [q] Eze 25:15-17; Zep 2:5 **14:31** [r] S Isa 13:6 [s] S Isa 3:26 [t] S Ge 10:14 [u] Isa 41:25; Jer 1:14; 4:6; 6:1, 22; 10:22; 13:20; 25:9; 46:20, 24; 47:2; 50:41; Eze 32:30 [v] S Isa 5:27 **14:32** [w] Isa 37:9 [x] S Ps 51:18; 87:2, 5; Isa 2:2; 26:1; 28:16; 31:5; 33:5, 20; 44:28; 51:21; 54:11 [y] S Isa 4:6; Jas 2:5 **15:1** [z] S Isa 13:1 [a] Nu 22:3-6; S Dt 23:6; S Isa 11:14 [b] S Nu 21:15 [c] S Nu 17:12; Isa 25:12; 26:5; Jer 48:24, 41; 51:58 [d] S 2Ki 3:25

14:22–23 The taunt is extended to include Babylon itself (see note on vv. 3–21); fulfilled, at least partially, through Sennacherib's destruction of Babylon in 689 B.C.—ultimately by the Medes and Persians after they took Babylon in 539.
14:22 *survivors.* A remnant; Israel will survive through a remnant (see 10:20–22 and note; 11:11,16), but Babylon will not.
14:23 See 13:20–22 and notes. *swampland.* Southern Babylonia, where the Chaldean tribes (see note on Ezr 5:12) once lived, was a region of marshlands.
14:24–27 See Zep 2:13–15 and notes; see also note on Isa 13:1—14:27.
14:24 *it will stand.* See 8:10 and note. God's sovereign purposes regarding Assyria and Babylonia will be carried out.
14:25 *yoke … burden.* See 9:4 and note.
14:26–27 *hand stretched out.* See 9:12; 12:1 and notes. God's hand was stretched out against Egypt at the Red Sea (see Ex 15:12).
14:28–32 See Jer 47; Eze 25:15–17; Am 1:6–8; Zep 2:4–7 and notes.
14:28 *oracle.* See note on 13:1. *the year.* Perhaps 715 B.C. *King Ahaz died.* Cf. 6:1 and note. The occasion appears to be the Philistine revolt against Assyria while King Sargon (see 20:1) was too preoccupied with serious revolts elsewhere to give much attention to Canaan.
14:29 *Philistines.* See note on Ge 10:14. Philistine territory was vulnerable to attack by the great empires (Egypt and Assyria) since it lay along the main route from Egypt to Mesopotamia. *the rod.* Probably Sargon of Assyria. *is broken.* If the rod was Sargon, reference is to the threats to his empire by a series of revolts in Babylonia and Asia Minor. *root … fruit.* A figure of speech that refers to the whole (tree) by speaking of its two extremes. After Sargon will come other Assyrian kings: Sennacherib, Esarhaddon, Ashurbanipal.
14:30 *poor … needy.* Israelites (see v. 32).
14:31 *Wail.* Cf. the similar reaction in 13:6; 15:2; 16:7; 23:1. *cloud of smoke.* The dust raised by the marching feet and the chariots of the Assyrians—who always invaded Canaan from the north. *not a straggler.* A longer description is found in 5:26–29.
14:32 *has established Zion.* God will protect Jerusalem from the Assyrians (compare 31:4–5 with 2:2).
15:1—16:14 See Jer 48; Eze 25:8–11; Am 2:1–3; Zep 2:8–11 and notes.
15:1 *oracle.* See note on 13:1. *Moab.* A country east of the Dead Sea that was a perpetual enemy of Israel (see 25:10 and note; 2Ki 13:20). *ruined.* The same word describes Isaiah's feelings about himself in 6:5. The destruction of Moab probably resulted from an invasion by Sargon II of Assyria in 715/713 B.C. Cf. Jer 48:1–17. *Kir.* Probably Kir Hareseth (see note on 2Ki 3:25). Kir means "city."

2 Dibon[e] goes up to its temple,
to its high places[f] to weep;
Moab wails[g] over Nebo[h] and
Medeba.
Every head is shaved[i]
and every beard cut off.[j]
3 In the streets they wear sackcloth;[k]
on the roofs[l] and in the public
squares[m]
they all wail,[n]
prostrate with weeping.[o]
4 Heshbon[p] and Elealeh[q] cry out,
their voices are heard all the way to
Jahaz.[r]
Therefore the armed men of Moab cry
out,
and their hearts are faint.

5 My heart cries out[s] over Moab;[t]
her fugitives[u] flee as far as Zoar,[v]
as far as Eglath Shelishiyah.
They go up the way to Luhith,
weeping as they go;
on the road to Horonaim[w]
they lament their destruction.[x]
6 The waters of Nimrim are dried up[y]
and the grass is withered;[z]
the vegetation is gone[a]
and nothing green is left.[b]
7 So the wealth they have acquired[c] and
stored up
they carry away over the Ravine of
the Poplars.
8 Their outcry echoes along the border
of Moab;
their wailing reaches as far as
Eglaim,
their lamentation as far as Beer[d]
Elim.
9 Dimon's[a] waters are full of blood,
but I will bring still more upon
Dimon[a] —
a lion[e] upon the fugitives of Moab[f]
and upon those who remain in the
land.

16 Send lambs[g] as tribute[h]
to the ruler of the land,
from Sela,[i] across the desert,
to the mount of the Daughter of
Zion.[j]
2 Like fluttering birds
pushed from the nest,[k]
so are the women of Moab[l]
at the fords[m] of the Arnon.[n]

3 "Give us counsel,
render a decision.
Make your shadow like night —
at high noon.
Hide the fugitives,[o]
do not betray the refugees.
4 Let the Moabite fugitives stay with
you;
be their shelter[p] from the destroyer."

The oppressor[q] will come to an end,
and destruction will cease;[r]
the aggressor will vanish from the
land.
5 In love a throne[s] will be established;[t]
in faithfulness a man will sit on it —
one from the house[b] of David[u] —
one who in judging seeks justice[v]
and speeds the cause of
righteousness.

15:2 [e] S Nu 21:30 [f] 1Ki 11:7; Isa 16:12; Jer 48:35 [g] S Isa 13:6; 65:14 [h] S Nu 32:38 [i] S Lev 13:40; S Job 1:20 [j] S 2Sa 10:4 **15:3** [k] S Isa 3:24 [l] S Jos 2:8 [m] Jer 48:38 [n] Isa 14:31; Jer 47:2 [o] ver 5; Isa 16:9; 22:4; La 2:11; Eze 7:18; Mic 1:8 **15:4** [p] S Nu 21:25; S Jos 13:26 [q] S Nu 32:3 [r] S Nu 21:23 **15:5** [s] S ver 3 [t] Isa 16:11; Jer 48:31 [u] S Nu 21:29 [v] S Ge 13:10 [w] Jer 48:3, 34 [x] Jer 4:20; 48:5 **15:6** [y] Isa 19:5-7; Jer 48:34 [z] Ps 37:2; Isa 16:8; 24:4, 7, 11; 33:9; 34:4; 37:27; 40:7; 51:6, 12; Hos 4:3; Joel 1:12 [a] S Isa 14:17 [b] Jer 14:5 **15:7** [c] Isa 30:6; Jer 48:36 **15:8** [d] S Nu 21:16 **15:9** [e] S 2Ki 17:25 [f] Eze 25:8-11 **16:1** [g] S 2Ki 3:4 [h] S 2Ch 32:23 [i] S Jdg 1:36; Ob 1:3 *fn* [j] S Isa 10:32 **16:2** [k] Pr 27:8 [l] Nu 21:29 [m] Jdg 12:5 [n] Nu 21:13-14; Jer 48:20 **16:3** [o] S 1Ki 18:4 **16:4** [p] Isa 58:7 [q] S Isa 9:4 [r] Isa 2:2-4 **16:5** [s] S 1Sa 13:14; Da 7:14; Mic 4:7 [t] S Pr 20:28 [u] S Isa 7:2; Lk 1:32 [v] S Isa 9:7

[a] *9* Masoretic Text; Dead Sea Scrolls, some Septuagint manuscripts and Vulgate *Dibon* [b] *5* Hebrew *tent*

15:2 *Dibon.* Located four miles north of the Arnon River and given to the tribe of Gad at one time (see Nu 32:34). *high places.* Shrines originally built on hilltops and usually associated with pagan worship (see note on 1Ki 3:2). *Nebo.* North of the Arnon River, perhaps near Mount Nebo (Dt 34:1). *Medeba.* About six miles south of Heshbon (see v. 4) and once captured by Israel from Sihon (see Nu 21:26,30). *head is shaved ... beard cut off.* Characteristic of intense mourning (Jer 48:37).
15:3 *sackcloth.* The coarse garb of mourners (see notes on Ge 37:34; Rev 11:3). *roofs.* Perhaps chosen because incense was sometimes offered there (see Jer 19:13 and note).
15:4 *Heshbon.* Located about 18 miles east of the northern tip of the Dead Sea. See also Jer 48:34. It was King Sihon's capital before Israel captured it (see Nu 21:23–26). *Elealeh.* About a mile north of Heshbon and always mentioned with it. *Jahaz.* Just north of the Arnon River and about 20 miles from Heshbon (Nu 21:23; Jer 48:34).
15:5 *Zoar.* Probably located near the southern end of the Dead Sea. Lot fled there from Sodom (see Ge 14:2; 19:23,30).
15:6 *waters of Nimrim.* Perhaps to be identified with the Wadi en-Numeirah, ten miles from the southern end of the Dead Sea (cf. Jer 48:34).
15:7 *Ravine of the Poplars.* Probably at the border between Moab and Edom (see v. 8).
15:8 *Eglaim.* Perhaps near the northern border of Moab. *Beer Elim.* Beer means "well" (cf. Nu 21:16). This site may have been close to the southern border.
15:9 *Dimon's waters ... blood.* The Hebrew for "blood" (*dam*) sounds like "Dimon." This is probably also a wordplay on the name "Dibon" (v. 2), close to the Arnon River. Many Moabites will die in the conflict. *lion.* A reference to either the Assyrian army (cf. 5:29; Jer 50:17) or actual lions (cf. 13:21–22).
16:1 *lambs as tribute.* As King Mesha sent 100,000 lambs to King Ahab of Israel each year (see 2Ki 3:4 and note), so now proud Moab, which has often oppressed Israel, is advised in her crisis to submit to the king in Jerusalem. *Sela.* The naturally fortified capital of the Edomites south of the Dead Sea, situated on a rocky plateau that towers 1,000 feet above the nearby Petra (cf. 42:11). The name means "cliff." The tribute would be sent around the southern end of the Dead Sea. *Daughter of Zion.* A personification of Jerusalem (see note on 2Ki 19:21).
16:2 *fords of the Arnon.* The women were fleeing south (see note on Jos 12:1), away from the northern invader.
16:3 *Hide the fugitives.* The Moabites are asking Judah for refuge (contrast Ru 1:1; 1Sa 22:3–4 and note on 22:3). See map, p. 367.
16:4 *destroyer.* Probably Assyria (see notes on 15:1; 33:1). *oppressor.* Moab.
16:5 *house of David.* See 9:7; 2Sa 7:11–16; 1Ki 12:19; Am 9:11

[6]We have heard of Moab's[w] pride[x]—
her overweening pride and conceit,
her pride and her insolence—
but her boasts are empty.
[7]Therefore the Moabites wail,[y]
they wail together for Moab.
Lament and grieve
for the men[a z] of Kir Hareseth.[a]
[8]The fields of Heshbon[b] wither,[c]
the vines of Sibmah[d] also.
The rulers of the nations
have trampled down the choicest
vines,[e]
which once reached Jazer[f]
and spread toward the desert.
Their shoots spread out[g]
and went as far as the sea.[h]
[9]So I weep,[i] as Jazer weeps,
for the vines of Sibmah.
O Heshbon, O Elealeh,[j]
I drench you with tears![k]
The shouts of joy[l] over your ripened
fruit
and over your harvests[m] have been
stilled.
[10]Joy and gladness are taken away from
the orchards;[n]
no one sings or shouts[o] in the
vineyards;
no one treads[p] out wine at the presses,[q]
for I have put an end to the
shouting.
[11]My heart laments for Moab[r] like a
harp,[s]
my inmost being[t] for Kir Hareseth.
[12]When Moab appears at her high
place,[u]
she only wears herself out;
when she goes to her shrine[v] to pray,
it is to no avail.[w]

[13]This is the word the LORD has already
spoken concerning Moab. [14]But now the
LORD says: "Within three years,[x] as a servant bound by contract[y] would count
them,[z] Moab's splendor and all her many
people will be despised,[a] and her survivors will be very few and feeble."[b]

An Oracle Against Damascus

17 An oracle[c] concerning Damascus:[d]

"See, Damascus will no longer be a
city
but will become a heap of ruins.[e]
[2]The cities of Aroer[f] will be deserted
and left to flocks,[g] which will lie
down,[h]
with no one to make them afraid.[i]
[3]The fortified[j] city will disappear from
Ephraim,
and royal power from Damascus;
the remnant of Aram will be
like the glory[k] of the Israelites,"[l]
declares the LORD Almighty.

[4]"In that day[m] the glory[n] of Jacob
will fade;
the fat of his body will waste[o]
away.

16:6 [w]Jer 25:21; Eze 25:8; Am 2:1; Zep 2:8 [x]S Lev 26:19; S Job 20:6; Jer 49:16; Ob 1:3; Zep 2:10 **16:7** [y]S Isa 13:6; Jer 48:20; 49:3 [z]S 1Ch 16:3 [a]S 2Ki 3:25 **16:8** [b]S Nu 21:25 [c]S Isa 15:6 [d]S Nu 32:3 [e]S Isa 5:2 [f]S Nu 21:32 [g]S Job 8:16 [h]Ps 80:11 **16:9** [i]S Isa 15:3; Eze 27:31 [j]S Nu 32:3 [k]S Job 7:3 [l]S Ezr 3:13 [m]Jer 40:12 **16:10** [n]Isa 24:7-8 [o]Jer 25:30 [p]S Jdg 9:27 [q]S Job 24:11; S Isa 5:2 **16:11** [r]S Isa 15:5 [s]S Job 30:31 [t]Isa 63:15; Hos 11:8; Php 2:1 **16:12** [u]1Ki 11:7 [v]S Isa 15:2 [w]S 1Ki 18:29; Ps 115:4-7; Isa 44:17-18; 1Co 8:4 **16:14** [x]Isa 20:3; 37:30 [y]S Lev 25:50 [z]S Lev 19:13 [a]Isa 25:10; Jer 48:42 [b]Isa 21:17 **17:1** [c]Isa 13:1 [d]S Ge 14:15; Ac 9:2 [e]S Dt 13:16; S Isa 25:2 **17:2** [f]S 2Ki 10:33 [g]S Isa 5:17; 7:21; Eze 25:5 [h]Isa 27:10 [i]S Lev 26:6; Jer 7:33; Mic 4:4 **17:3** [j]Isa 25:2,12; Hos 10:14 [k]ver 4; Isa 21:16; Hos 9:11 [l]Isa 7:8,16; 8:4 **17:4** [m]S Isa 2:11 [n]S ver 3 [o]S Isa 10:16

[a] 7 Or *"raisin cakes,"* a wordplay

and notes. "House" equals "dynasty" (see note on 7:2). *in judging seeks justice.* See 11:2–4 and notes. The Messiah is again in view.

16:6 *Moab's pride.* Though a small nation, Moab is proud and defiant like Assyria and Babylon. Cf. 10:12; 14:13; 25:11; Jer 48:42.

16:7 *men.* See NIV text note. *Kir Hareseth.* See note on 15:1. The four cities in vv. 7–8 appear in inverted (*a-b-c-d/d-c-b-a*) order in vv. 9–11.

16:8 *Heshbon.* See note on 15:4. *Sibmah.* Perhaps three miles west of Heshbon. See Jer 48:32. *choicest vines.* The poet shifts to a metaphor, comparing Moab to a vineyard (cf. 5:1–7 and notes). He returns to a literal description again in v. 10. *Jazer.* Possibly located about 15 miles north of the Dead Sea. *desert.* On the eastern edge of Moab. *shoots spread out.* This is figurative language, as in Ps 80:11, where Israel is the vine. *sea.* Probably the Dead Sea.

16:9–11 *I … I … I … My … my.* The Lord (and/or Isaiah) weeps and laments over the destruction brought on proud Moab to humble her.

16:9 *Elealeh.* See note on 15:4.

16:10 *treads out wine.* The grapes were trampled on, and the juice flowed into the wine vat (see note on 5:2; cf. Jer 48:33; Am 9:13; Hag 2:16 and note).

16:11 Cf. Jer 48:36.

16:12 *high place.* See 15:2 and note. *pray … to no avail.* Moab's god, Chemosh, was a mere idol (see 44:17–20 and notes; 1Ki 11:7).

16:13–14 An epilogue to 15:1—16:12.

16:14 *Within three years.* Other signs that have a three-year limit are given in 20:3; 37:30; see also notes on 7:14,16. Moab's three years were over by c. 715 B.C. (see note on 15:1). *servant bound by contract.* Cf. 21:16–17, where the prophecy against Kedar follows the pattern of this verse.

17:1–14 See Jer 49:23–27; Am 1:3–5 and notes.

17:1 *oracle.* See note on 13:1. *Damascus.* The capital of Aram (Syria), located northeast of Mount Hermon on strategic trade routes between Mesopotamia, Egypt and Arabia. Since the time of David, the Arameans of Damascus were frequent enemies of Israel (see 2Sa 8:5; 1Ki 22:31).

17:2 *Aroer.* About 14 miles east of the Dead Sea on the Arnon River. It marked the southern boundary of Aram's sphere of control (see 2Ki 10:32–33 and notes).

17:3 *Ephraim.* The northern kingdom (see note on 7:2) is mentioned here because of its alliance with Damascus against Assyria (see note on 7:1). *royal power.* In 732 B.C. Tiglath-Pileser III captured Damascus and made it an Assyrian province. Many of the cities of Israel were also captured (see note on 9:1). *remnant of Aram … like the glory of the Israelites.* Like Israel, Aram will be reduced to a remnant.

17:4–11 The prophet shifts from Damascus to Israel (likely the northern kingdom)—a shift prepared for at the end of v. 3. This association of judgment on Damascus and Israel reflects the same linkage as that in ch. 7.

17:4,7,9 *In that day.* See notes on 2:11,17,20; 10:20,27.

[5]It will be as when a reaper gathers the
standing grain
and harvests[p] the grain with his
arm—
as when a man gleans heads of grain[q]
in the Valley of Rephaim.[r]
[6]Yet some gleanings will remain,[s]
as when an olive tree is beaten,[t]
leaving two or three olives on the
topmost branches,
four or five on the fruitful boughs,"
declares the LORD,
the God of Israel.

[7]In that day[u] men will look[v] to their
Maker[w]
and turn their eyes to the Holy One[x]
of Israel.
[8]They will not look to the altars,[y]
the work of their hands,[z]
and they will have no regard for the
Asherah poles[a][a]
and the incense altars their fingers[b]
have made.

[9]In that day their strong cities, which
they left because of the Israelites, will be
like places abandoned to thickets and undergrowth.[c] And all will be desolation.

[10]You have forgotten[d] God your Savior;[e]
you have not remembered the Rock,[f]
your fortress.[g]
Therefore, though you set out the
finest plants
and plant imported vines,[h]
[11]though on the day you set them out,
you make them grow,
and on the morning[i] when you
plant them, you bring them to
bud,
yet the harvest[j] will be as nothing[k]
in the day of disease and incurable[l]
pain.[m]

[12]Oh, the raging[n] of many nations—
they rage like the raging sea![o]
Oh, the uproar[p] of the peoples—
they roar like the roaring of great
waters![q]
[13]Although the peoples roar[r] like the roar
of surging waters,
when he rebukes[s] them they flee[t] far
away,
driven before the wind like chaff[u] on
the hills,
like tumbleweed before a gale.[v]
[14]In the evening, sudden[w] terror![x]
Before the morning, they are gone![y]
This is the portion of those who loot
us,
the lot of those who plunder us.

A Prophecy Against Cush

18 Woe[z] to the land of whirring wings[b]
along the rivers of Cush,[c][a]
[2]which sends envoys[b] by sea
in papyrus[c] boats over the water.

Go, swift messengers,
to a people tall and smooth-skinned,[d]
to a people feared far and wide,
an aggressive[e] nation of strange
speech,
whose land is divided by rivers.[f]
[3]All you people of the world,[g]
you who live on the earth,
when a banner[h] is raised on the
mountains,
you will see it,

a *8* That is, symbols of the goddess Asherah *b* *1* Or *of locusts* *c* *1* That is, the upper Nile region

17:5 [p]ver 11; Isa 33:4; Jer 51:33; Joel 3:13; Mt 13:30 [q]Job 24:24 [r]S Jos 17:15; S 1Ch 11:15 **17:6** [s]S Dt 4:27; S Isa 10:19; S 24:13 [t]ver 11; Isa 27:12 **17:7** [u]S Isa 2:11 [v]S Isa 9:13; S 10:20 [w]S Ps 95:6 [x]S Isa 12:6 **17:8** [y]S Lev 26:30 [z]S 2Ch 32:19; Isa 2:18, 20; 30:22; 46:6; Rev 9:20 [a]S Jdg 3:7; S 2Ki 17:10 [b]Isa 2:8 **17:9** [c]S Isa 7:19 **17:10** [d]S Dt 6:12; 8:11; Ps 50:22; 106:21; Isa 51:13; 57:11; Jer 2:32; 3:21; 13:25; 18:15; Eze 22:12; 23:35; Hos 8:14; 13:6 [e]S Isa 12:2; S Lk 1:47 [f]S Ge 49:24 [g]S Ps 18:2 [h]S Isa 5:7 **17:11** [i]Ps 90:6 [j]S ver 5 [k]S Lev 26:20; Hos 8:7; Joel 1:11; Hag 1:6 [l]Jer 10:19; 30:12 [m]S Dt 28:39; S Job 4:8 **17:12** [n]ver 13; Isa 41:11 [o]S Ps 18:4; Lk 21:25 [p]S Ps 46:6; Isa 8:9 [q]Isa 8:7 **17:13** [r]S Ps 46:3 [s]S Dt 28:20; S Ps 9:5 [t]S Ps 68:1; S Isa 13:14 [u]S Job 13:25; S Isa 2:22; 41:2, 15-16; Da 2:35 [v]Job 21:18; S Ps 65:7 **17:14** [w]Isa 29:5; 30:13; 47:11; 48:3 [x]Isa 33:18; 54:14 [y]S 2Ki 19:35 **18:1** [z]Isa 5:8 [a]S Ge 10:6; S Ps 68:31; S Eze 29:10 **18:2** [b]Ob 1:1 [c]Ex 2:3; Job 9:26 [d]S Ge 41:14 [e]S Ge 10:8-9; S 2Ch 12:3 [f]ver 7 **18:3** [g]S Ps 33:8 [h]S Ps 60:4; Isa 5:26; 11:10; 13:2; 31:9; Jer 4:21

17:5 *harvests the grain.* Harvest here signifies a time of judgment (see Joel 3:13 and note). *Valley of Rephaim.* A fertile area west and southwest of Jerusalem (Jos 15:8) and the scene of Philistine raids (1Ch 14:9).
17:7–8 Cf. 2:20; 10:20.
17:7 *Holy One of Israel.* See note on 1:4.
17:8 *altars.* Probably altars for Baal (cf. 1Ki 16:32). *Asherah poles.* See notes on Ex 34:13; Jdg 2:13; see also NIV text note here. *incense altars.* Associated with high places in Lev 26:30 and with altars for Baal in 2Ch 34:4.
17:9 *they.* Perhaps the Canaanites, whose religious practices are referred to in v. 8. *thickets and undergrowth.* Cf. 7:23–25.
17:10 *Rock.* See 26:4; 30:29; 44:8; Ge 49:24 and note; Dt 32:4,15,18; Ps 18:2 and note; 19:14. *vines.* Probably representing the people of Israel (see 5:7; 18:5; 37:30–31; see also notes on Ps 80:8–16 and 80:8–11).
17:11 *disease and incurable pain.* Brought by the Assyrian invasions.
17:12–14 The same sequence of a powerful invader that is quickly cut down occurs in 10:28–34. Both passages may refer to Sennacherib's invasion of 701 B.C. (see 37:36–37 and notes). But it is more likely that the prophet here speaks more generally of Israel's experience of the world of nations as a perpetual threat to her existence.
17:12 *raging sea.* Assyria is called "floodwaters" in 8:7 (see notes on 8:7–8).
17:13 *chaff … tumbleweed.* Symbolic of the enemy also in 29:5; 41:15–16; Ps 83:13.
18:1–7 See Zep 2:12 and note.
18:1 *whirring wings.* Either a reference to insects (perhaps locusts) or a figurative description of the armies of Cush (see 7:18–19). *Cush.* Nubia or ancient Ethiopia (not to be confused with modern Ethiopia, which is located farther to the southeast), south of Egypt. In 715 B.C. a Cushite named Shabako gained control of Egypt and founded the 25th dynasty.
18:2 *sea.* Perhaps the Nile River (cf. 19:5; Na 3:8, where the same Hebrew word is translated "river"). *papyrus boats.* See note on Ex 2:3. *Go, swift messengers.* With the message contained in vv. 3–6. *people tall and smooth-skinned.* See v. 7; probably the peoples of Cush and Egypt. Unlike Semites, they were clean-shaven (see note on Ge 41:14). *rivers.* The Nile and its tributaries.
18:3 *All you people of the world.* All the nations arrayed against God's people Israel (see 17:12–14 and note). *banner.* See 5:26 and note. *trumpet.* Used to summon troops (see, e.g., Jdg 3:27; 6:34; 2Sa 2:28).

and when a trumpet[i] sounds,
you will hear it.
4This is what the LORD says to me:
"I will remain quiet[j] and will look on
from my dwelling place,[k]
like shimmering heat in the sunshine,[l]
like a cloud of dew[m] in the heat of
harvest."
5For, before the harvest, when the
blossom is gone
and the flower becomes a ripening
grape,
he will cut off[n] the shoots with pruning
knives,
and cut down and take away the
spreading branches.[o]
6They will all be left to the mountain
birds of prey[p]
and to the wild animals;[q]
the birds will feed on them all summer,
the wild animals all winter.

7At that time gifts[r] will be brought to the
LORD Almighty

from a people tall and smooth-skinned,[s]
from a people feared[t] far and wide,
an aggressive nation of strange speech,
whose land is divided by rivers[u]—

the gifts will be brought to Mount Zion, the
place of the Name of the LORD Almighty.[v]

A Prophecy About Egypt

19 An oracle[w] concerning Egypt:[x][y]

See, the LORD rides on a swift cloud[z]
and is coming to Egypt.
The idols of Egypt tremble before him,
and the hearts of the Egyptians melt[a]
within them.

2"I will stir up Egyptian against
Egyptian—
brother will fight against brother,[b]
neighbor against neighbor,
city against city,
kingdom against kingdom.[c]

3The Egyptians will lose heart,[d]
and I will bring their plans[e] to
nothing;[f]
they will consult the idols and the
spirits of the dead,
the mediums and the spiritists.[g]
4I will hand the Egyptians over
to the power of a cruel master,
and a fierce king[h] will rule over
them,"
declares the Lord, the LORD
Almighty.

5The waters of the river will dry up,[i]
and the riverbed will be parched and
dry.[j]
6The canals will stink;[k]
the streams of Egypt will dwindle
and dry up.[l]
The reeds[m] and rushes will wither,[n]
7 also the plants[o] along the Nile,
at the mouth of the river.
Every sown field[p] along the Nile
will become parched, will blow
away and be no more.[q]
8The fishermen[r] will groan and
lament,
all who cast hooks[s] into the Nile;
those who throw nets on the water
will pine away.
9Those who work with combed flax[t]
will despair,
the weavers of fine linen[u] will lose
hope.
10The workers in cloth will be dejected,
and all the wage earners will be sick
at heart.
11The officials of Zoan[v] are nothing but
fools;
the wise counselors[w] of Pharaoh give
senseless advice.[x]
How can you say to Pharaoh,
"I am one of the wise men,[y]
a disciple of the ancient kings"?

18:3 [i]S Jos 6:20; S Jdg 3:27 **18:4** [j]Isa 62:1; 64:12 [k]Isa 26:21; Hos 5:15; Mic 1:3 [l]S Jdg 5:31; S Ps 18:12; Hab 3:4 [m]2Sa 1:21; S Ps 133:3; Isa 26:19; Hos 14:5 **18:5** [n]S Isa 10:33 [o]Isa 17:10-11; Eze 17:6 **18:6** [p]S Isa 8:8 [q]Isa 37:36; 56:9; Jer 7:33; Eze 32:4; 39:17 **18:7** [r]S 2Ch 9:24; S Isa 60:7 [s]S Ge 41:14 [t]Hab 1:7 [u]ver 2 [v]Ps 68:31 **19:1** [w]Isa 13:1 [x]Isa 20:3; Joel 3:19 [y]S Ex 12:12; S Jer 44:3 [z]S Dt 10:14; S 2Sa 22:10; S Rev 1:7 [a]S Jos 2:11 **19:2** [b]S Jdg 7:22; S 12:4; Mt 10:21,36 [c]S 2Ch 15:6; 20:23; Mt 24:7; Mk 13:8; Lk 21:10 **19:3** [d]Ps 18:45 [e]ver 11; S Job 5:12 [f]1Ch 10:13 [g]S Lev 19:31; Isa 47:13; Da 2:2,10; 3:8; 5:7 **19:4** [h]Isa 20:4; Jer 46:26; Eze 29:19; 32:11 **19:5** [i]Isa 44:27; 50:2; Jer 50:38; 51:36 [j]S 2Sa 14:14 **19:6** [k]Ex 7:18 [l]Isa 37:25; Eze 30:12 [m]S Ge 41:2; S Job 8:11 [n]Isa 15:6 **19:7** [o]Nu 11:5 [p]Dt 29:23; Isa 23:3 [q]Zec 10:11 **19:8** [r]Nu 11:5; Eze 47:10 [s]Am 4:2; Hab 1:15 **19:9** [t]S Jos 2:6 [u]Pr 7:16; Eze 16:10; 27:7 **19:11** [v]S Nu 13:22 [w]S Ge 41:37 [x]S ver 3 [y]S 1Ki 4:30; Ac 7:22

18:4 *remain quiet.* In the face of the hostility of the nations, the Lord will not act immediately; but when they are in the full growth of summer (v. 5), he will cut them down.
18:6 *birds of prey ... wild animals.* Cf. 56:9; see Jer 7:33; Eze 32:4; 39:17–20; Rev 19:17 and notes.
18:7 See v. 2 and note. *gifts.* According to 2Ch 32:23 gifts were brought to Hezekiah after Sennacherib's death. The Moabites were asked to send tribute to Mount Zion in 16:1 (cf. 45:14; Zep 3:10). *place of the Name.* See Dt 12:5 and note.
19:1—20:6 See Jer 46; Eze 29–32 and notes.
19:1 *oracle.* See note on 13:1. *rides on a swift cloud.* A metaphor used also in Ps 68:4 (see note there); 104:3; cf. Mt 26:64. *idols ... tremble.* See Jer 50:2 and note. God had also previously judged Egypt's idols during the ten plagues (see Ex 12:12 and note). *hearts ... melt.* See 13:7.
19:2 *Egyptian against Egyptian.* Cf. 9:21. The Libyan dynasty clashed with the Cushites (see note on 18:1) and with the Saites of Dynasty 24.
19:3 *consult ... spiritists.* Israel also did so in desperate times (see 8:19 and note).
19:4 *cruel master.* The king of Assyria (see 20:4). Esarhaddon conquered Egypt in 670 B.C.
19:5 *river will dry up.* The Nile was the lifeline of Egypt; its annual flooding provided essential water and produced the only fertile soil there.
19:6 *canals.* For irrigation.
19:7 *sown field.* Egypt's crops were normally abundant, and some were exported.
19:8 *fishermen.* Fish were usually plentiful (see Nu 11:5 and note).
19:9 *work with ... flax.* Large amounts of water were needed to process flax. *fine linen.* A well-known Egyptian export (see Pr 7:16 and note).
19:11 *Zoan.* A city (possibly Tanis) in the northeastern part of the Nile delta, familiar to the Israelites during their years in Egypt (see Nu 13:22; Ps 78:12,43). It was the northern capital

12 Where are your wise men[z] now?
Let them show you and make known
what the LORD Almighty
has planned[a] against Egypt.
13 The officials of Zoan[b] have become
fools,
the leaders of Memphis[a c] are
deceived;
the cornerstones[d] of her peoples
have led Egypt astray.
14 The LORD has poured into them
a spirit of dizziness;[e]
they make Egypt stagger in all that she
does,
as a drunkard staggers[f] around in his
vomit.
15 There is nothing Egypt can do —
head or tail, palm branch or reed.[g]

16 In that day[h] the Egyptians will be like
women.[i] They will shudder with fear[j] at
the uplifted hand[k] that the LORD Almighty
raises against them. 17 And the land of Judah will bring terror to the Egyptians; everyone to whom Judah is mentioned will
be terrified,[l] because of what the LORD Almighty is planning[m] against them.
18 In that day[n] five cities[o] in Egypt will
speak the language of Canaan and swear
allegiance[p] to the LORD Almighty. One of
them will be called the City of Destruction.[b q]
19 In that day[r] there will be an altar[s] to the

19:12 [z] 1Co 1:20 [a] S Isa 14:24; Ro 9:17 **19:13** [b] S Nu 13:22 [c] Jer 2:16; 44:1; 46:14,19; Eze 30:13,16; Hos 9:6 [d] S Ps 118:22 **19:14** [e] S Pr 12:8; Mt 17:17 [f] S Ps 107:27 **19:15** [g] S Isa 9:14 **19:16** [h] Isa 2:17; 11:10 [i] Jer 50:37; 51:30; Na 3:13 [j] S Dt 2:25; Heb 10:31 [k] S Isa 11:15 **19:17** [l] S Ge 35:5 [m] S Isa 14:24 **19:18** [n] S Isa 10:20 [o] Jer 44:1 [p] Ps 22:27; S 63:11; Isa 48:1; Jer 4:2; Zep 3:9 [q] Isa 17:1; 24:12; 32:19; *fn* Jer 43:13 **19:19** [r] S Isa 10:20 [s] S Jos 22:10 [t] S Ps 68:31 [u] S Ge 28:18 **19:20** [v] S Ge 21:30 [w] S Dt 28:29; S Jdg 2:18; S Isa 25:9 [x] Isa 49:24-26

LORD in the heart of Egypt,[t] and a monument[u] to the LORD at its border. 20 It will be
a sign and witness[v] to the LORD Almighty
in the land of Egypt. When they cry out
to the LORD because of their oppressors,
he will send them a savior[w] and defender,
and he will rescue[x] them. 21 So the LORD
will make himself known to the Egyptians,
and in that day they will acknowledge[y] the
LORD. They will worship[z] with sacrifices
and grain offerings; they will make vows
to the LORD and keep them.[a] 22 The LORD
will strike[b] Egypt with a plague;[c] he will
strike them and heal them. They will turn[d]
to the LORD, and he will respond to their
pleas and heal[e] them.
23 In that day[f] there will be a highway[g]
from Egypt to Assyria.[h] The Assyrians will
go to Egypt and the Egyptians to Assyria. The Egyptians and Assyrians will worship[i] together. 24 In that day[j] Israel will be
the third, along with Egypt and Assyria,[k]
a blessing[l] on the earth. 25 The LORD Almighty will bless[m] them, saying, "Blessed

[a] 13 Hebrew *Noph* [b] 18 Most manuscripts of the Masoretic Text; some manuscripts of the Masoretic Text, Dead Sea Scrolls and Vulgate *City of the Sun* (that is, Heliopolis)

19:21 [y] S Isa 11:9; S 43:10 [z] ver 19; S Ge 27:29; S Ps 86:9; Isa 56:7; 60:7; Mal 1:11 [a] S Nu 30:2; S Dt 23:21 **19:22** [b] Ex 12:23; Heb 12:11 [c] Ex 11:10 [d] Isa 45:14; Eze 33:11; Hos 6:1; 10:12; 12:6; 14:1; Joel 2:13 [e] S Dt 32:39 **19:23** [f] S ver 16,24; Isa 20:6 [g] S Isa 11:16 [h] Mic 7:12 [i] S Ge 27:29; Isa 2:3; 27:13; 66:23 **19:24** [j] S ver 23 [k] S Isa 11:11 [l] S Ge 12:2 **19:25** [m] S Ge 12:3; Eph 2:11-14

for the 25th dynasty (see note on 18:1). *wise men.* See v. 12. Egypt was famous for its wise men (see 1Ki 4:30 and note).

19:13 *Memphis.* An important city 15 miles south of the delta that was the capital during the Old Kingdom (c. 2686 – 2160 B.C.). *cornerstones.* Prophets and priests, as well as political leaders (see 9:15 – 16 and note).

19:14 *drunkard staggers.* Israel's leaders stagger in 28:7 – 8.

19:15 *head or tail, palm branch or reed.* Egypt's leaders. The same two pairs are used of Israel's leaders in 9:14 – 15 (see note on 9:14).

19:16 – 25 A chain of four announcements of coming events associated with "that day": (1) An act of divine judgment will cause Egypt to "shudder with fear" (v. 16) and be in terror of Judah (vv. 16 – 17). (2) "Five cities" in Egypt will "swear allegiance" to the Lord (v. 18). (3) Because of a divine act of deliverance and healing in Egypt, an altar will be erected in Egypt where Egyptians will offer sacrifices to the Lord (vv. 19 – 22). (4) Egypt, Assyria and Israel will be linked into one people of the Lord (vv. 23 – 25). The prophet looks well beyond the present realities in which the world powers do not acknowledge the true God and proudly pursue their own destinies, running roughshod over the people of the Lord. He foresees a series of divine acts that will bring about the conversion of the nations.

19:16,18 – 19,23 – 24 *In that day.* The coming day of the Lord (see 10:20,27 and note; cf. 11:10 – 11).

19:16 *shudder with fear.* Like the people of Jericho (Jos 2:9,11). *hand ... the LORD ... raises.* See 14:26 – 27 and note.

19:17 *land of Judah.* The Egyptians will somehow recognize (perhaps through court contacts with Hezekiah) that it is the God of Judah who has brought judgment upon them.

19:18 *five.* Perhaps in the sense of "many." *speak the language of Canaan.* Either a symbolic reference to Egypt's allegiance to the Lord (see vv. 21 – 22,25) or a literal reference to Jews living in Egypt. After the fall of Jerusalem in 586 B.C., many Jews fled to Egypt (see Jer 44:1 and note). *City of Destruction.* Probably a reference to Heliopolis, city of the sun-god; it was destroyed by Nebuchadnezzar (see Jer 43:13 and note). The Hebrew for "destruction" is almost identical to the Hebrew for "sun."

19:19 *altar.* Some relate this to the temple built in Egypt in the time of Ptolemy VI (181 – 146 B.C.) by the Jewish high priest Onias IV, who fled to Egypt in the second century B.C., but the reference appears to be to a conversion to the Lord of a significant number of Egyptians.

19:20 *sign and witness.* Cf. the purpose of the altar built near the Jordan River by the Transjordan tribes in Jos 22:26 – 27. *oppressors ... savior.* The language of the book of Judges (see Jdg 2:18 and note). It is uncertain who this savior and defender is, but the prophet may well have in mind the promised Son of the house of David (see 11:1 – 10 and notes).

19:21 *make himself known.* Cf. Ex 7:5. *worship with sacrifices.* Offerings of foreigners are also mentioned in 56:7; 60:7 (cf. Zec 14:16 – 19 and note on 14:16).

19:22 *strike Egypt with a plague.* Oppression (see v. 20) and plague were two common forms of divine affliction. Contrast the results of the plague on the firstborn in Ex 12:23. *turn ... heal.* Cf. 6:10; here parallel to sending Egypt a "savior and defender" (v. 20). Earlier a hardhearted pharaoh had not turned to the Lord (Ex 9:34 – 35).

19:23 *highway.* Cf. the highway to Jerusalem in 11:16; 35:8 – 10 (see notes there). For centuries Egyptians and Assyrians had fought each other (see 20:4), but in the future they would be linked in a bond of friendship sealed by their common allegiance to the Lord (cf. 25:3). *worship together.* This description of peace and of unity in worship is similar to 2:2 – 4 (see note there; see also note on 19:21).

19:25 *will bless them.* A fulfillment of Ge 12:3 (see note on Ge 12:2 – 3). *Egypt my people.* Such a universal vision

be Egypt my people,[n] Assyria my handiwork,[o] and Israel my inheritance.[p]"

A Prophecy Against Egypt and Cush

20 In the year that the supreme commander,[q] sent by Sargon king of Assyria, came to Ashdod[r] and attacked and
captured it — 2 at that time the LORD spoke
through Isaiah son of Amoz.[s] He said to
him, "Take off the sackcloth[t] from your
body and the sandals[u] from your feet."
And he did so, going around stripped[v] and
barefoot.[w]
3 Then the LORD said, "Just as my servant[x] Isaiah has gone stripped and barefoot for three years,[y] as a sign[z] and portent[a] against Egypt[b] and Cush,[a][c] 4 so the
king[d] of Assyria will lead away stripped[e]
and barefoot the Egyptian captives[f] and
Cushite[g] exiles, young and old, with buttocks bared[h] — to Egypt's shame.[i] 5 Those
who trusted[j] in Cush[k] and boasted in
Egypt[l] will be afraid and put to shame.[m]
6 In that day[n] the people who live on this
coast will say, 'See what has happened[o] to
those we relied on,[p] those we fled to for
help[q] and deliverance from the king of Assyria! How then can we escape?[r]' "

A Prophecy Against Babylon

21 An oracle[s] concerning the Desert[t] by
the Sea:

Like whirlwinds[u] sweeping through the
southland,[v]
an invader comes from the desert,
from a land of terror.

2 A dire[w] vision has been shown to me:
The traitor betrays,[x] the looter takes
loot.
Elam,[y] attack! Media,[z] lay siege!
I will bring to an end all the
groaning she caused.

3 At this my body is racked with pain,[a]
pangs seize me, like those of a
woman in labor;[b]
I am staggered by what I hear,
I am bewildered[c] by what I see.
4 My heart[d] falters,
fear makes me tremble;[e]
the twilight I longed for
has become a horror[f] to me.
5 They set the tables,
they spread the rugs,
they eat, they drink![g]
Get up, you officers,
oil the shields![h]

6 This is what the Lord says to me:

"Go, post a lookout[i]
and have him report what he sees.
7 When he sees chariots[j]
with teams of horses,
riders on donkeys
or riders on camels,[k]
let him be alert,
fully alert."

8 And the lookout[b][l] shouted,

"Day after day, my lord, I stand on the
watchtower;

[a] *3* That is, the upper Nile region; also in verse 5
[b] *8* Dead Sea Scrolls and Syriac; Masoretic Text *A lion*

19:25 [n] Ps 87:4; S 100:3 [o] Isa 29:23; 43:7; 45:11; 60:21; 64:8; Eph 2:10 [p] S Ex 34:9; Jer 30:22; Hos 2:23 **20:1** [q] 2Ki 18:17 [r] S Jos 11:22; S 13:3 **20:2** [s] S Isa 13:1 [t] 2Ki 1:8; S Isa 3:24; Zec 13:4; Mt 3:4 [u] Eze 24:17,23 [v] S 1Sa 19:24 [w] Eze 4:1-12; Mic 1:8 **20:3** [x] Isa 22:20; 41:8-9; 42:1; 43:10; 49:3,5-7; 50:10; 52:13; 53:11; Jer 7:25; Hag 2:23; Zec 4:14 [y] S Isa 16:14 [z] S Ex 3:12; S Isa 8:18; 37:30; 38:7; Ac 21:11 [a] S Dt 28:46 [b] S Isa 19:1 [c] ver 5; S Ge 10:6; Isa 37:9; 43:3 **20:4** [d] S Isa 19:4 [e] S Job 12:17 [f] Jer 46:19; Na 3:10 [g] Isa 18:1; Zep 2:12 [h] S Isa 3:24 [i] Isa 47:3; Jer 13:22,26; Na 3:5 **20:5** [j] S Isa 8:12 [k] S ver 3 [l] S 2Ki 18:21; S Isa 30:5 [m] Eze 29:16 **20:6** [n] Isa 2:11; S 19:23 [o] S 2Ki 18:21 [p] Jer 46:25 [q] S Isa 10:3 [r] Jer 30:15-17; 31:2; Mt 23:33; 1Th 5:3; Heb 2:3

21:1 [s] S Isa 13:1 [t] Isa 13:21; Jer 50:12; 51:43 [u] S Job 1:19 [v] Da 11:40; Zec 9:14 **21:2** [w] Ps 60:3 [x] Isa 24:16; 33:1 [y] S Ge 10:22; Isa 22:6 [z] S Isa 13:3; Jer 25:25; 51:28 **21:3** [a] S Job 14:22 [b] S Ge 3:16; Ps 48:6; Isa 26:17; 37:3; Jer 30:6; 48:41; 49:22; Jn 16:21 [c] Da 7:28; 8:27; 10:16 **21:4** [d] Isa 7:4; 35:4 [e] S Isa 13:8; Da 5:9 [f] S Ps 55:5 **21:5** [g] Isa 5:12; 22:2,13; 23:7; 24:8; 32:13; Jer 25:16,27; 51:39,57; Da 5:2 [h] 2Sa 1:21; 1Ki 10:16-17; Jer 46:3; 51:11 **21:6** [i] S 2Ki 9:17 **21:7** [j] ver 9 [k] S Jdg 6:5 **21:8** [l] Mic 7:7; Hab 2:1

seems possible for Isaiah only in the light of what has been said about the "shoot ... from the stump of Jesse" (11:1; see 11:1 – 10). Cf. 45:14; Eph 2:11 – 13.

20:1 – 6 An epilogue to chs. 18 – 19, as 16:13 – 14 is to 15:1 — 16:12.

20:1 *the year.* Probably 712 B.C. *Sargon.* Sargon II, who reigned 721 – 705 B.C. (see chart, p. 472). He is mentioned by name only here in the OT. *Ashdod.* One of the five Philistine cities (see map, p. 331), Ashdod was located near the Mediterranean Sea about 18 miles northeast of Gaza. The city had rebelled against Assyria in 713 under King Azuri. In 1963 three small fragments of at least one Assyrian monument commemorating Sargon's victory (in 711) were discovered at Ashdod.

20:2 *sackcloth.* See 15:3 and note; sometimes the garb of prophets (see 2Ki 1:8 and note; Zec 13:4 – 6). *stripped and barefoot.* See vv. 3 – 4; cf. 2Ch 28:15; Mic 1:8 and note.

20:3 *my servant.* See note on 41:8 – 9. *three years.* See 16:14 and note. *sign and portent.* See 8:18; see also 7:3,14 and notes. The prophet Ezekiel's behavior also had symbolic significance (Eze 24:24,27; cf. Zec 3:8). *Egypt and Cush.* See 18:1; 19:1 and notes.

20:5 *trusted in Cush ... Egypt.* After Assyria conquered the northern kingdom of Israel in 722 – 721 B.C., King Hezekiah of Judah was under great pressure to make an alliance with Egypt. Isaiah urgently warned against such a policy (cf. 30:1 – 2; 31:1 and notes).

21:1 *oracle.* See note on 13:1. *Desert.* The coming judgment would eventually turn Babylon (see v. 9) into a wasteland (cf. 13:20 – 22). *the Sea.* Refers either to the Persian Gulf, which was southeast of Babylon, or to the plain laid down by the Euphrates and Tigris rivers and their tributaries. *whirlwinds ... desert.* The desert sometimes spawns powerful winds (see Hos 13:15). *an invader.* Lit. "it"; it is not clear whether "comes from the desert, from a land of terror" is ascribed to an invader or continues the description of the whirlwinds.

21:2 *Elam.* See note on 11:11; see also Jer 49:34 – 39. The Elamites were perpetual enemies of Assyria and Babylon. Much later, they were part of the Persian army that conquered Babylon under Cyrus in 539 B.C. *Media.* See note on 13:17. *she.* Babylon.

21:3 *racked with pain, pangs seize me.* See note on 16:9 – 11; see also Daniel's reaction to visions in Da 8:27; 10:16 – 17.

21:4 *twilight.* Perhaps the end of the Babylonian empire (see note on v. 12). *a horror to me.* The devastation is beyond even what he had desired.

21:5 *eat ... drink.* With the kind of confident assurance reflected in Belshazzar's feast (see Da 5:1). *Get up ... !* Rhetorically the prophet, who has seen in a vision the coming attack on Babylon, calls on the officers of Babylon to prepare. *oil the shields.* See note on 2Sa 1:21.

21:6 *Go, post a lookout.* Probably on the walls of Jerusalem.

21:7 *chariots ... donkeys ... camels.* Bearing messengers from afar.

every night I stay at my post.
9 Look, here comes a man in a chariot[m]
with a team of horses.
And he gives back the answer:
'Babylon[n] has fallen,[o] has fallen!
All the images of its gods[p]
lie shattered[q] on the ground!' "

10 O my people, crushed on the threshing
floor,[r]
I tell you what I have heard
from the LORD Almighty,
from the God of Israel.

A Prophecy Against Edom

11 An oracle concerning Dumah[a]:[s]

Someone calls to me from Seir,[t]
"Watchman, what is left of the
night?
Watchman, what is left of the
night?"
12 The watchman replies,
"Morning is coming, but also the
night.
If you would ask, then ask;
and come back yet again."

A Prophecy Against Arabia

13 An oracle[u] concerning Arabia:[v]

You caravans of Dedanites,[w]
who camp in the thickets of Arabia,
14 bring water for the thirsty;
you who live in Tema,[x]
bring food for the fugitives.
15 They flee[y] from the sword,[z]
from the drawn sword,
from the bent bow
and from the heat of battle.

16 This is what the Lord says to me:
"Within one year, as a servant bound by
contract[a] would count it, all the pomp[b] of
Kedar[c] will come to an end. 17 The survivors of the bowmen, the warriors of Kedar,
will be few.[d]" The LORD, the God of Israel,
has spoken.[e]

A Prophecy About Jerusalem

22 An oracle[f] concerning the Valley[g] of
Vision:[h]

What troubles you now,
that you have all gone up on the
roofs,[i]
2 O town full of commotion,
O city of tumult[j] and revelry?[k]
Your slain[l] were not killed by the
sword,[m]
nor did they die in battle.
3 All your leaders have fled[n] together;
they have been captured[o] without
using the bow.
All you who were caught were taken
prisoner together,
having fled while the enemy was
still far away.
4 Therefore I said, "Turn away from me;
let me weep[p] bitterly.
Do not try to console me
over the destruction of my people."[q]

5 The Lord, the LORD Almighty, has a day[r]
of tumult and trampling[s] and terror[t]
in the Valley of Vision,[u]

[a] 11 *Dumah* means *silence* or *stillness,* a wordplay on *Edom.*

21:9 [m] ver 7 [n] S Isa 13:1; 47:1,5; S Rev 14:8 [o] Isa 47:11; Jer 51:8; Da 5:30 [p] S Lev 26:30; Isa 46:1; Jer 50:2; 51:44 [q] S Isa 2:18 **21:10** [r] Isa 27:12; 28:27,28; 41:15; Jer 51:33; Mic 4:13; Hab 3:12; Mt 3:12 **21:11** [s] S Ge 25:14; S Isa 34:11 [t] Ge 32:3 **21:13** [u] Isa 13:1 [v] S 2Ch 9:14 [w] S Ge 10:7; S 25:3 **21:14** [x] S Ge 25:15 **21:15** [y] S Isa 13:14 [z] Isa 31:8 **21:16** [a] S Lev 25:50 [b] S Isa 17:3 [c] S Ge 25:13 **21:17** [d] S Dt 4:27; S Isa 10:19 [e] S Isa 1:20; 16:14 **22:1** [f] Isa 13:1 [g] Ps 125:2; Jer 21:13; Joel 3:2,12,14 [h] S Isa 1:1 [i] S Jos 2:8; Jer 48:38 **22:2** [j] Eze 22:5 [k] S Isa 5:14; S 21:5 [l] S Isa 10:4 [m] S 2Ki 25:3 **22:3** [n] S Isa 13:14 [o] S 2Ki 25:6 **22:4** [p] S Isa 15:3; S La 1:16; Eze 21:6; Lk 19:41 [q] Jer 9:1 **22:5** [r] S Isa 2:12 [s] S Job 40:12; S Ps 108:13 [t] S 2Sa 22:43; Isa 13:3; Jer 30:7; La 1:5; Eze 8:17-18; 9:9-10; Joel 2:31; Am 5:18-20; Zep 1:15 [u] S Isa 1:1

21:9 *Babylon has fallen.* See 13:19. Babylon fell in 689 B.C. and again in 539. These words were adapted by John in Rev 14:8; 18:2. *its gods lie shattered.* The fall of a kingdom meant the disgrace of its gods (cf. 46:1–2; 1Sa 5:3–7 and notes).
21:10 *crushed.* Judah would be punished by the Babylonians and taken into captivity (see 39:5–7 and notes). *on the threshing floor.* Threshing was a common metaphor for judgment or destruction from war (see Am 1:3 and note).
21:11–12 See Jer 49:7–22; Eze 25:12–14; Am 1:11–12; Obadiah and notes.
21:11 *oracle.* See note on 13:1. *Seir.* A synonym for Edom (Ge 32:3), homeland of Esau's descendants, south of the Dead Sea. Edom is dealt with more extensively in 34:5–15 (see notes there; cf. 63:1 and note).
21:12 *Morning ... but also the night.* Perhaps meaning that the long night of Assyrian oppression is almost over, but only a short "morning" will precede Babylonian domination (see v. 4 and note).
21:13–17 See Jer 49:28–33 and notes.
21:13 *oracle.* See note on 13:1. *Dedanites.* An Arabian tribe whose merchant activities are mentioned also in Eze 27:20; 38:13. *thickets.* The caravans had to hide from the invader (cf. Jdg 5:6). The Assyrians began to attack the Arabs in 732 B.C., and the Babylonians did the same under Nebuchadnezzar (see Jer 25:17,23–24).
21:14 *Tema.* An oasis in northern Arabia about 400 miles southwest of Babylon (cf. Job 6:19; Jer 25:23).
21:15 *sword ... bow.* The simple bows of the Arabs were ineffective against the swords and composite bows of Assyria.
21:16 *servant bound by contract.* See 16:14 and note. *pomp.* See 14:11; 16:14. *Kedar.* The home of nomadic tribes in the Arabian Desert. Kedar was known for its flocks (60:7; Eze 27:21). Nebuchadnezzar defeated the people of Kedar (Jer 49:28–29; cf. Jer 2:10 and note).
21:17 *survivors ... will be few.* Cf. 10:19; 16:14; 17:6.
22:1–13 The notes on this prophecy assume that it refers primarily to the final Babylonian siege of Jerusalem in 588–586 B.C. But it is also possible that the primary reference is to the siege by the Assyrian king Sennacherib in 701.
22:1 *oracle.* See note on 13:1. *Valley of Vision.* A valley where God revealed himself in visions, probably one of the valleys near Jerusalem (see note on v. 7). See also v. 5. *roofs.* See 15:3 and note.
22:2 *tumult and revelry.* See v. 13; 5:11–13 and note; 32:13. Jerusalem is behaving just like Babylon (see 21:5 and note; cf. 23:7). *not killed by the sword.* Perhaps a reference to death from disease and famine when the Babylonians besieged Jerusalem in 586 B.C.
22:3 *leaders have fled.* King Zedekiah and his army fled Jerusalem but were captured near Jericho (see 2Ki 25:4–6).
22:4 *my people.* Lit. "the Daughter of my people" (see note on 2Ki 19:21).
22:5 *has a day.* See 2:12 and note on 2:11,17,20. Also cf. "in

a day of battering down walls[v]
and of crying out to the mountains.
6 Elam[w] takes up the quiver,[x]
with her charioteers and horses;
Kir[y] uncovers the shield.
7 Your choicest valleys[z] are full of
chariots,
and horsemen are posted at the city
gates;[a]
8 the defenses of Judah are stripped
away.

And you looked in that day[b]
to the weapons[c] in the Palace of the
Forest;[d]
9 you saw that the City of David
had many breaches[e] in its defenses;
you stored up water
in the Lower Pool.[f]
10 You counted the buildings in Jerusalem
and tore down houses[g] to strengthen
the wall.[h]
11 You built a reservoir between the two
walls[i]
for the water of the Old Pool,[j]
but you did not look to the One who
made it,
or have regard[k] for the One who
planned[l] it long ago.

12 The Lord, the LORD Almighty,
called you on that day[m]
to weep[n] and to wail,
to tear out your hair[o] and put on
sackcloth.[p]
13 But see, there is joy and revelry,[q]
slaughtering of cattle and killing of
sheep,
eating of meat and drinking of
wine![r]
"Let us eat and drink," you say,
"for tomorrow we die!"[s]

14 The LORD Almighty has revealed this
in my hearing:[t] "Till your dying day this
sin will not be atoned[u] for," says the Lord,
the LORD Almighty.

15 This is what the Lord, the LORD Almighty, says:

"Go, say to this steward,
to Shebna,[v] who is in charge[w] of the
palace:[x]
16 What are you doing here and who gave
you permission
to cut out a grave[y] for yourself[z] here,
hewing your grave on the height
and chiseling your resting place in
the rock?

17 "Beware, the LORD is about to take firm
hold of you
and hurl[a] you away, O you mighty
man.
18 He will roll you up tightly like a ball
and throw[b] you into a large country.
There you will die
and there your splendid chariots[c]
will remain—
you disgrace to your master's house!
19 I will depose you from your office,
and you will be ousted[d] from your
position.[e]

20 "In that day[f] I will summon my servant,[g] Eliakim[h] son of Hilkiah. 21 I will
clothe him with your robe and fasten your
sash[i] around him and hand your authority[j] over to him. He will be a father to those
who live in Jerusalem and to the house
of Judah. 22 I will place on his shoulder[k]
the key[l] to the house of David;[m] what he

22:5 [v] Ne 6:15; S Ps 89:40; Isa 5:5; Jer 39:8; Eze 13:14 **22:6** [w] S Isa 21:2 [x] Ps 46:9; Jer 49:35; 51:56 [y] S 2Ki 16:9 **22:7** [z] Jos 15:8 [a] S 2Ch 32:1-2 **22:8** [b] S Isa 2:12 [c] S 2Ch 32:5 [d] S 1Ki 7:2 **22:9** [e] S Ne 1:3 [f] S 2Ki 18:17; S 2Ch 32:4 **22:10** [g] Jer 33:4 [h] S 2Ch 32:5 **22:11** [i] 2Ki 25:4; 2Ch 32:5; Jer 39:4 [j] S 2Ch 32:4 [k] S 1Sa 12:24 [l] 2Ki 19:25 **22:12** [m] S Isa 2:12 [n] Joel 1:9; 2:17 [o] S Lev 13:40; Mic 1:16 [p] S Isa 3:24 **22:13** [q] S Isa 21:5 [r] S 1Sa 25:36; Ecc 8:15; Isa 5:22; 28:7-8; 56:12; Lk 17:26-29 [s] 1Co 15:32* **22:14** [t] Isa 5:9 [u] S 1Sa 2:25; Isa 13:11; 26:21; 30:13-14; Eze 24:13 **22:15** [v] S 2Ki 6:30; S 18:18 [w] ver 21 [x] S Ge 41:40 **22:16** [y] Mt 27:60 [z] S Ge 50:5; S Nu 32:42 **22:17** [a] Jer 10:18; 13:18; 22:26 **22:18** [b] S Job 18:11; Isa 14:19; 17:13 [c] S Ge 41:43 **22:19** [d] S 1Sa 2:7; S Ps 52:5 [e] Lk 16:3 **22:20** [f] ver 25 [g] S Isa 20:3 [h] S 2Ki 18:18; S Isa 36:3 **22:21** [i] S Isa 5:27 [j] ver 15 **22:22** [k] Isa 9:6 [l] 1Ch 9:27; Mt 16:19; Rev 3:7 [m] S Isa 7:2

that day" in v. 8 and "on that day" in v. 12. *tumult.* A fulfillment of the curse of Dt 28:20.

22:6 *Elam.* See note on 11:11; see also Jer 49:34–39. Elamites probably fought in the Babylonian army. *takes up the quiver.* See Jer 49:35. *Kir.* Perhaps another name for Media (see 21:2; Am 1:5 and note).

22:7 *choicest valleys.* The Kidron Valley lay east of Jerusalem, the Hinnom Valley to the south and west (see map, p. 477).

22:8 *Palace of the Forest.* Built by King Solomon out of cedars from Lebanon (see 1Ki 7:2–6 and notes; 10:17,21).

22:9 *City of David.* See 2Sa 5:6–7,9 and notes; cf. Isa 29:1. *Lower Pool.* Probably the same as the "Old Pool" of v. 11. Hezekiah made a pool and a tunnel as a precaution against Sennacherib's invasion (see 2Ki 20:20 and note). The "Upper Pool" is mentioned in 7:3; 36:2.

22:10 *strengthen the wall.* Cf. Hezekiah's preparations in 2Ch 32:5.

22:11 *did not look to the One.* In 31:1 those who look to horses and chariots rather than to God are similarly condemned.

22:12 *tear out your hair.* The hair was either torn out or shaved off (cf. Jer 16:6; Eze 27:31).

22:13 *joy and revelry.* The same Hebrew phrase is translated "gladness and joy" in 35:10; 51:11, passages depicting great hope in connection with restoration. But this was a time to mourn (Ecc 3:4). See note on v. 2. *Let us eat … we die.* Quoted by Paul in 1Co 15:32 to underscore the utter futility of life without a belief in resurrection from the dead. Cf. Lk 12:19; cf. also Ecc 8:15 and note.

22:15 *Shebna.* Apparently a foreigner, possibly Egyptian; a contemporary of King Hezekiah. *in charge of the palace.* A position second only to the king (see note on v. 21; cf. 36:3; 1Ki 4:6; 2Ki 15:5).

22:16 *cut out a grave.* One's place of burial was considered very important, and Shebna coveted a tomb worthy of a king (cf. 2Ch 16:14).

22:17 *hurl you away.* Cf. Jer 22:24–26 and notes.

22:18 *There you will die.* Apparently without an honorable burial (see note on 14:19). *chariots.* A sign of high office (see Ge 41:43).

22:20 *In that day.* When the Lord acts in judgment (see vv. 17–19). *my servant.* See note on 20:3. *Eliakim.* See 36:3,11,22; 37:2.

22:21 *hand your authority over to him.* By 701 B.C. (see 36:3) Eliakim had replaced Shebna, who was demoted to "secretary."

22:22 Quoted in part in Rev 3:7 (see note there). The mention of "father" (v. 21) and of the responsibility "on his shoulder"

opens no one can shut, and what he shuts
no one can open.[n] 23I will drive him like a
peg[o] into a firm place;[p] he will be a seat[a]
of honor[q] for the house of his father. 24All
the glory of his family will hang on him:
its offspring and offshoots — all its lesser
vessels, from the bowls to all the jars.

25"In that day,[r]" declares the LORD Almighty, "the peg[s] driven into the firm
place will give way; it will be sheared off
and will fall, and the load hanging on it
will be cut down." The LORD has spoken.[t]

A Prophecy About Tyre

23 An oracle concerning Tyre:[u]

Wail,[v] O ships[w] of Tarshish![x]
For Tyre is destroyed[y]
and left without house or harbor.
From the land of Cyprus[b]
word has come to them.

2Be silent,[z] you people of the island
and you merchants[a] of Sidon,[b]
whom the seafarers have enriched.
3On the great waters
came the grain of the Shihor;[c]
the harvest of the Nile[c][d] was the
revenue of Tyre,[e]
and she became the marketplace of
the nations.

4Be ashamed, O Sidon,[f] and you,
O fortress of the sea,
for the sea has spoken:
"I have neither been in labor nor given
birth;[g]
I have neither reared sons nor
brought up daughters."

5When word comes to Egypt,
they will be in anguish[h] at the report
from Tyre.[i]

6Cross over to Tarshish;[j]
wail, you people of the island.
7Is this your city of revelry,[k]
the old, old city,
whose feet have taken her
to settle in far-off lands?
8Who planned this against Tyre,
the bestower of crowns,
whose merchants[l] are princes,
whose traders[m] are renowned in the
earth?
9The LORD Almighty planned[n] it,
to bring low[o] the pride of all glory
and to humble[p] all who are
renowned[q] on the earth.

10Till[d] your land as along the Nile,
O Daughter of Tarshish,
for you no longer have a harbor.
11The LORD has stretched out his hand[r]
over the sea
and made its kingdoms tremble.[s]
He has given an order concerning
Phoenicia[e]
that her fortresses be destroyed.[t]
12He said, "No more of your reveling,[u]
O Virgin Daughter[v] of Sidon, now
crushed!

[a] 23 Or *throne* [b] 1 Hebrew *Kittim* [c] 2,3 Masoretic Text; one Dead Sea Scroll *Sidon, / who cross over the sea; / your envoys* 3*are on the great waters. / The grain of the Shihor, / the harvest of the Nile,* [d] 10 Dead Sea Scrolls and some Septuagint manuscripts; Masoretic Text *Go through* [e] 11 Hebrew *Canaan*

22:22 [n]S Job 12:14 **22:23** [o]ver 25; Eze 15:3; Zec 10:4 [p]S Ezr 9:8; S Job 6:25 [q]S 1Sa 2:7-8; S Job 36:7 **22:25** [r]ver 20 [s]S ver 23 [t]Isa 46:11; Mic 4:4 **23:1** [u]Jos 19:29; 1Ki 5:1; Jer 47:4; Joel 3:4-8; Am 1:9-10 [v]S Isa 13:6 [w]S 1Ki 10:22 [x]S Ge 10:4; Isa 2:16 *fn* [y]S Ge 1:2; Eze 26:4 **23:2** [z]S Job 2:13 [a]Eze 27:5-24 [b]Jdg 1:31 **23:3** [c]S Ge 41:5 [d]S Isa 19:7 [e]S Ps 83:7 **23:4** [f]S Ge 10:15, 19 [g]Isa 54:1 **23:5** [h]Eze 30:9 [i]Eze 26:17-18 **23:6** [j]S Ge 10:4 **23:7** [k]ver 12; S Isa 5:14; S 21:5; 32:13; Eze 26:13 **23:8** [l]Na 3:16 [m]Eze 28:5; Rev 18:23 **23:9** [n]S Isa 14:24 [o]S Job 40:11 [p]S Isa 13:11 [q]Isa 5:13; 9:15; Eze 27:3 **23:11** [r]S Ex 14:21 [s]S Ps 46:6 [t]ver 14; Isa 25:2; Eze 26:4; Zec 9:3-4 **23:12** [u]S ver 7; Rev 18:22 [v]Isa 37:22; 47:1; Jer 14:17; 46:11; La 2:13; Zep 3:14; Zec 2:10

recalls the words about the Messiah in 9:6. *key to the house of David.* The authority delegated to him by the king, who belongs to David's dynasty — perhaps controlling entrance into the royal palace. Cf. the "keys of the kingdom" given to Peter (Mt 16:19; see note there).

22:23 *peg.* Normally the Hebrew for this word refers to a tent peg, but here to a peg driven into wood (see Eze 15:3; Zec 10:4 and note). *seat of honor.* Cf. 1Sa 2:8.

22:25 *In that day.* Another (unspecified) day when the Lord will come in judgment. *peg ... will give way.* Eliakim, like Shebna, will eventually fall from power.

23:1 – 18 See Eze 26:1 — 28:19; Am 1:9 – 10 and notes.

23:1 *oracle.* See note on 13:1. *Tyre.* The main seaport along the Phoenician coast, about 35 miles north of Mount Carmel. Part of the city was built on two rocky islands about half a mile from the shore. King Hiram of Tyre supplied cedars and craftsmen for the temple (see 1Ki 5:8 – 9) and sailors for Solomon's commercial fleet (1Ki 9:27). *Wail, O ships.* See v. 14. *ships of Tarshish.* Trading ships (see note on 2:16). *destroyed.* Fulfilled through Assyria, Nebuchadnezzar and Alexander. Nebuchadnezzar captured the mainland city in 572 B.C. (see Eze 26:7 – 11), but the island fortress was not taken until Alexander the Great destroyed it in 332 (cf. Eze 26:3 – 5; see Zec 9:3 and note). *Cyprus.* An island in the eastern Mediterranean that had close ties with Tyre (see Eze 27:6 and note).

23:2,4,12 *Sidon.* See Eze 28:20 – 26 and notes; the other prominent Phoenician city, about 25 miles north of Tyre.

23:2 *island.* Tyre (see v. 1 and note). *merchants ... seafarers.* Tyre's commercial ventures affected the entire Mediterranean world (see vv. 3,8).

23:3 *Shihor.* Probably the easternmost branch of the Nile (see NIV text note on Jer 2:18). *harvest of the Nile.* See 19:7 and note.

23:4 *fortress of the sea.* Tyre (see note on v. 1). *labor ... birth.* Contrast 54:1 (see note there).

23:6 *Tarshish.* Perhaps Tartessus in Spain (see note on Eze 27:12), or an island in the western Mediterranean, or a site on the coast of North Africa.

23:7 *revelry.* See note on 22:2. *old, old city.* Tyre was founded before 2000 B.C. *settle in far-off lands.* Carthage in North Africa was a colony of Tyre. Tarshish may have been another.

23:8 – 9 *planned.* See 14:24,26 – 27; 25:1 and notes.

23:8 *bestower of crowns.* Tyre crowned kings in her colonies. *traders are renowned.* See Eze 28:4 – 5.

23:9 *pride of all glory.* See Eze 27:3 – 4 and notes.

23:10 *Daughter of Tarshish.* A personification of Tarshish (see note on 2Ki 19:21).

23:11 *stretched out his hand.* See note on 14:26 – 27. *Phoenicia.* Roughly the same as modern Lebanon.

23:12 *Virgin Daughter of Sidon.* A personification of Sidon (see note on 2Ki 19:21). *now crushed.* Sidon was captured by Esarhaddon in the seventh century B.C. and later by Nebuchadnezzar c. 587 (cf. Jer 25:22,26 and notes).

"Up, cross over to Cyprus[a];[w]
even there you will find no rest."
13 Look at the land of the Babylonians,[b][x]
this people that is now of no
account!
The Assyrians[y] have made it
a place for desert creatures;[z]
they raised up their siege towers,[a]
they stripped its fortresses bare
and turned it into a ruin.[b]
14 Wail, you ships[c] of Tarshish;[d]
your fortress is destroyed![e]

15 At that time Tyre[f] will be forgotten for
seventy years,[g] the span of a king's life.
But at the end of these seventy years, it
will happen to Tyre as in the song of the
prostitute:

16 "Take up a harp, walk through the
city,
O prostitute[h] forgotten;
play the harp well, sing many a song,
so that you will be remembered."

17 At the end of seventy years,[i] the LORD
will deal with Tyre. She will return to her
hire as a prostitute[j] and will ply her trade
with all the kingdoms on the face of the
earth.[k] 18 Yet her profit and her earnings
will be set apart for the LORD;[l] they will
not be stored up or hoarded. Her profits
will go to those who live before the LORD,[m]
for abundant food and fine clothes.[n]

The LORD's Devastation of the Earth

24 See, the LORD is going to lay waste
the earth[o]
and devastate[p] it;
he will ruin its face
and scatter[q] its inhabitants—
2 it will be the same
for priest as for people,[r]
for master as for servant,
for mistress as for maid,
for seller as for buyer,[s]
for borrower as for lender,
for debtor as for creditor.[t]
3 The earth will be completely laid waste[u]
and totally plundered.[v]
The LORD has spoken[w]
this word.

4 The earth dries up[x] and withers,[y]
the world languishes and withers,
the exalted[z] of the earth languish.[a]
5 The earth is defiled[b] by its people;
they have disobeyed[c] the laws,
violated the statutes
and broken the everlasting covenant.[d]
6 Therefore a curse[e] consumes the earth;
its people must bear their guilt.
Therefore earth's inhabitants are
burned up,[f]
and very few are left.
7 The new wine dries up[g] and the vine
withers;[h]
all the merrymakers groan.[i]
8 The gaiety of the tambourines[j] is
stilled,
the noise[k] of the revelers[l] has
stopped,
the joyful harp[m] is silent.[n]
9 No longer do they drink wine[o] with a
song;
the beer is bitter[p] to its drinkers.

[a] 12 Hebrew *Kittim* [b] 13 Or *Chaldeans*

23:12 [w] S Ge 10:4 **23:13** [x] Isa 43:14; Jer 51:12 [y] Isa 10:5 [z] S Ps 74:14; Isa 18:6 [a] S 2Ki 25:1 [b] Isa 10:7 **23:14** [c] S 1Ki 10:22 [d] S Ge 10:4; Isa 2:16 *fn* [e] S ver 11 **23:15** [f] Jer 25:22 [g] S Ps 90:10 **23:16** [h] Pr 7:10 **23:17** [i] S Ps 90:10 [j] Dt 23:17-18; Eze 16:26; Na 3:4; Rev 17:1; 18:3,9 [k] Jer 25:26 **23:18** [l] Ex 28:36; S 39:30; Jos 6:17-19; Ps 72:10 [m] Isa 18:7; 60:5-9; 61:6; Mic 4:13 [n] Am 1:9-10; Zec 14:1,14 **24:1** [o] ver 20; Isa 2:19-21; 33:9; Jer 25:29 [p] S Jos 6:17; S Isa 13:5 [q] S Ge 11:9 **24:2** [r] Hos 4:9 [s] Eze 7:12; 1Co 7:29-31 [t] S Lev 25:35-37; Dt 23:19-20; Isa 3:1-7 **24:3** [u] S Ge 6:13 [v] Isa 6:11-12; 10:6 [w] S Isa 7:7 **24:4** [x] Jer 12:11; 14:4; Joel 1:10 [y] S Isa 15:6 [z] S Isa 2:12 [a] S Isa 3:26 **24:5** [b] S Ge 3:17 [c] S Isa 1:2; 9:17; 10:6; 59:12; Jer 7:28 [d] S Ge 9:11; S Jer 11:10 **24:6** [e] S Jos 23:15 [f] S Isa 1:31 **24:7** [g] Jer 48:33; Joel 1:5 [h] Isa 7:23; S 15:6; 32:10 [i] S Isa 3:26; 16:8-10 **24:8** [j] S Ge 31:27; S Isa 5:12 [k] Jer 7:34; 16:9; 25:10; 33:11; Hos 2:11 [l] S Isa 5:14; S 21:5 [m] S Ps 137:2; Rev 18:22 [n] La 5:14; Eze 26:13 **24:9** [o] Isa 5:11,22 [p] Isa 5:20

23:13 *Assyrians.* Sennacherib destroyed the city of Babylon in 689 B.C. Phoenicia would look like the Babylon of that time. *desert creatures.* Cf. 13:21. *siege towers.* See note on 2Ki 25:1.
23:14 See v. 1 and note.
23:15 *seventy years.* Also the length of the Babylonian captivity (see Jer 25:11–12; 29:10 and notes), and the length of time the Babylonian god Marduk (according to an inscription of King Esarhaddon) decreed that Babylon should remain devastated.
23:16 Cf. Pr 7:10–15.
23:17 *her hire as a prostitute.* A "prostitute" nation was one that sought to make the highest profits, regardless of the means. Self-gratification was the key (cf. Rev 14:8; 17:5 and notes).
23:18 *set apart for the LORD.* The earnings of a prostitute could not be given to the Lord (Dt 23:18), but the silver and gold of a city that is devoted to destruction (see note on Dt 2:34) were placed in the Lord's treasury (see Jos 6:17,19 and note on 6:17; cf. Mic 4:13). *to those.* Israel will one day receive the wealth of the nations (see note on 18:7; cf. 60:5–11 and notes; 61:6).
24:1—27:13 Chs. 24–27 deal with judgment and blessing in the last days, the time of God's final victory over the forces of evil. These chapters form a conclusion to chs. 13–23 just as chs. 34–35 form a conclusion to chs. 28–33.
24:1 *lay waste the earth.* Cf. 2:10,19,21; see also 13:13 and note. *scatter its inhabitants.* See Ge 11:8–9 and notes.
24:2 Social distinctions will provide no escape from the judgment (cf. 3:1–3 and notes).
24:4 *dries up and withers.* Words applied to Moab in 15:6; 16:8. Cf. 34:4.
24:5 *broken the everlasting covenant.* Which covenant Isaiah refers to here is uncertain. He possibly has in mind the covenant of Ge 9:8–17 (see chart, p. 19; Ge 9:11 and note), but it is difficult to see how that covenant could be "broken" by humans since it is strictly a covenant of unconditional divine commitment. It is possible that Isaiah read Ge 9:5–6 as an implied condition (see v. 5 here), but it appears more likely that in this word of judgment upon all nations Israel is included along with them because she has broken the Sinaitic covenant with its "laws" and "statutes." Although God's covenants are everlasting from his viewpoint, they can be broken by sinful people (see Jer 31:32 and note).
24:6 *curse.* Because of the intensification of evil in the world, God's devastating curse will burn up the earth's inhabitants—not another universal judgment by flood (cf. Ge 9:8–17) but a judgment by fire (cf. Jer 17:27; Zep 1:2–3 and notes).
24:7 *vine withers.* See v. 4 and note.
24:8 *gaiety ... is stilled.* Cf. 22:2,13; 23:7.
24:9 *wine with a song.* Characteristic of Judah in 5:11–13 (see note there).

[10]The ruined city[q] lies desolate;[r]
the entrance to every house is barred.
[11]In the streets they cry out[s] for wine;[t]
all joy turns to gloom,[u]
all gaiety is banished from the earth.
[12]The city is left in ruins,[v]
its gate[w] is battered to pieces.
[13]So will it be on the earth
and among the nations,
as when an olive tree is beaten,[x]
or as when gleanings are left after
the grape harvest.[y]

[14]They raise their voices, they shout for
joy;[z]
from the west[a] they acclaim the
LORD's majesty.
[15]Therefore in the east[b] give glory[c] to the
LORD;
exalt[d] the name[e] of the LORD, the
God of Israel,
in the islands[f] of the sea.
[16]From the ends of the earth[g] we hear
singing:[h]
"Glory[i] to the Righteous One."[j]

But I said, "I waste away, I waste
away![k]
Woe[l] to me!
The treacherous[m] betray!
With treachery the treacherous
betray![n]"
[17]Terror[o] and pit and snare[p] await you,
O people of the earth.[q]
[18]Whoever flees[r] at the sound of terror
will fall into a pit;[s]
whoever climbs out of the pit
will be caught in a snare.[t]

The floodgates of the heavens[u] are
opened,
the foundations of the earth shake.[v]
[19]The earth is broken up,[w]
the earth is split asunder,[x]
the earth is thoroughly shaken.

[20]The earth reels like a drunkard,[y]
it sways like a hut[z] in the wind;
so heavy upon it is the guilt of its
rebellion[a]
that it falls[b]—never to rise again.[c]

[21]In that day[d] the LORD will punish[e]
the powers[f] in the heavens above
and the kings[g] on the earth below.
[22]They will be herded together
like prisoners[h] bound in a dungeon;[i]
they will be shut up in prison
and be punished[a] after many days.[j]
[23]The moon will be abashed, the sun[k]
ashamed;
for the LORD Almighty will reign[l]
on Mount Zion[m] and in Jerusalem,
and before its elders, gloriously.[n]

Praise to the LORD

25 O LORD, you are my God;[o]
I will exalt you and praise your
name,[p]
for in perfect faithfulness[q]
you have done marvelous things,[r]
things planned[s] long ago.
[2]You have made the city a heap of
rubble,[t]
the fortified[u] town a ruin,[v]
the foreigners' stronghold[w] a city no
more;
it will never be rebuilt.[x]
[3]Therefore strong peoples will honor
you;[y]
cities of ruthless[z] nations will revere
you.

[a] 22 Or *released*

24:10 [q]Isa 25:2; 26:5 [r]S Ge 1:2; S Isa 6:11 **24:11** [s]S Ps 144:14 [t]La 2:12 [u]S Isa 15:6; 16:10; 32:13; Jer 14:3 **24:12** [v]S Isa 19:18 [w]S Isa 3:26; S 13:2 **24:13** [x]S Dt 30:4; S Isa 17:6 [y]Ob 1:5; Mic 7:1 **24:14** [z]S Isa 12:6 [a]Isa 43:5; 49:12 **24:15** [b]S Ps 113:3 [c]Isa 42:12; 66:19; 2Th 1:12 [d]S Ex 15:2; Isa 25:3; 59:19; Mal 1:11 [e]S Isa 12:4 [f]S Isa 11:11 **24:16** [g]S Ps 48:10 [h]S Ps 65:8 [i]Isa 28:5; 60:1,19 [j]S Ezr 9:15 [k]S Lev 26:39 [l]1Sa 4:8; S Isa 5:8; Jer 10:19; 45:3 [m]S Ps 25:3 [n]Isa 21:2; 33:1; Jer 3:6,20; 5:11; 9:2; Hos 5:7; 9:1 **24:17** [o]Dt 32:23-25 [p]Isa 8:14; Jer 48:43 [q]Lk 21:35 **24:18** [r]S Job 20:24 [s]Isa 42:22 [t]S Job 18:9; S Isa 8:14; La 3:47; Eze 12:13 [u]S Ge 7:11 [v]S Jdg 5:4; S Job 9:6; S Ps 11:3; S Eze 38:19 **24:19** [w]S Ps 46:2 [x]S Dt 11:6 **24:20** [y]S Job 12:25 [z]S Job 27:18 [a]S Isa 1:2,28; 43:27; 58:1 [b]S Ps 46:2 [c]S Job 12:14 **24:21** [d]S Isa 2:11; S 10:20; Rev 16:14 [e]Isa 10:12; 13:11; Jer 25:29 [f]1Co 6:3; Eph 6:11-12 [g]S Isa 2:12 **24:22** [h]S Isa 10:4 [i]Isa 42:7,22; Lk 8:31; Rev 20:7-10 [j]Eze 38:8 **24:23** [k]S Isa 13:10 [l]S Ps 97:1; Rev 22:5 [m]S Isa 2:2; Heb 12:22 [n]Isa 28:5; 41:16; 45:25; 60:19; Eze 48:35; Zec 2:5; Rev 21:23 **25:1** [o]S Isa 7:13 [p]S Ps 145:2; S Isa 12:1,4 [q]Isa 11:5 [r]Ps 40:5; 98:1; Joel 2:21,26 [s]Nu 23:19; S Isa 14:24; 37:26; 46:11; Eph 1:11 **25:2** [t]Isa 17:1; 26:5; 37:26 [u]S Isa 17:3 [v]S Dt 13:16 [w]S Isa 13:22 [x]S Job 12:14 **25:3** [y]S Ex 6:2; S Ps 22:23; S Isa 11:14 [z]S Isa 13:11

24:10 *ruined city.* The same idea appears in 25:2; 26:5; 27:10 (cf. 17:1; 19:18). It is probably a composite of all the cities opposed to God—such as Babylon, Tyre, Jerusalem and Rome.
24:13 Only a few olives and grapes will be left (see v. 6; 17:6,11).
24:14 *They.* The godly remnant that survives the judgment.
24:15 *islands.* See note on 11:11.
24:16 *ends of the earth.* See note on 11:12. *I.* Probably collective for the godly community that wastes away because of the villainy of the treacherous nations that seek to crush the people of God. *I waste away … betray!* In the Hebrew text these last four lines of the verse (*Razi li, razi li! 'Oy li! Bogedim bagadu! Ubeged bogedim bagadu!*) contain powerful examples of alliteration and assonance (see 5:7 and note; see also Introduction: Literary Features). *Woe to me!* Isaiah had the same reaction in 6:5. *The treacherous.* The enemies of God's people.
24:17–18 Cf. Am 5:19–20 and note.
24:17 *Terror and pit and snare.* Another example (see note on v. 16) of alliteration and assonance (see note on Jer 48:43). The Hebrew words are *paḥad, paḥat* and *paḥ.*
24:18a God's judgment is inescapable (cf. Am 5:19–20; 9:2–4 and notes).
24:18b *floodgates of the heavens.* An echo of Noah's flood (Ge 7:11; 8:2). *foundations … shake.* Earthquakes and thunder (see note on 13:13; cf. Joel 3:16).
24:20 *like a drunkard.* Cf. 19:14. *like a hut.* See 1:8 and note.
24:21 *In that day.* The phrase, which refers to the day of the Lord (see notes on 2:11,17,20; 10:20,27), occurs seven times in chs. 24–27 (see 25:9; 26:1; 27:1–2,12–13). *powers in the heavens … kings.* All powers in the creation that exalt themselves against God (see 2:6–21; Eph 6:11–12).
24:22 *shut up in prison.* Cf. Rev 20:2. *punished after many days.* See NIV text note; cf. Rev 20:7–10.
24:23 *moon … abashed, the sun ashamed.* The sun and moon do not shine during judgment (see note on 13:10) or when the Lord is the "everlasting light" (60:19–20; cf. Rev 21:23; 22:5). *reign on Mount Zion.* See 2:2–4 and note.
25:1–5 A song of praise celebrating the deliverance brought about by the judgments of ch. 24 (see 24:14–16; see also ch. 12).
25:1 *planned long ago.* See 14:24,26–27; 23:8–9.
25:2 *the city … a ruin.* See 24:10 and note. *never be rebuilt.* Cf. 24:20.
25:3 *strong peoples … ruthless nations.* Such as Egypt and

[4]You have been a refuge[a] for the poor,[b]
a refuge for the needy[c] in his distress,
a shelter from the storm[d]
and a shade from the heat.
For the breath of the ruthless[e]
is like a storm driving against a wall
5 and like the heat of the desert.
You silence[f] the uproar of foreigners;[g]
as heat is reduced by the shadow of a cloud,
so the song of the ruthless[h] is stilled.

[6]On this mountain[i] the LORD Almighty will prepare
a feast[j] of rich food for all peoples,
a banquet of aged wine—
the best of meats and the finest of wines.[k]
[7]On this mountain he will destroy
the shroud[l] that enfolds all peoples,[m]
the sheet that covers all nations;
8 he will swallow up death[n] forever.
The Sovereign LORD will wipe away the tears[o]
from all faces;
he will remove the disgrace[p] of his people
from all the earth.
The LORD has spoken.[q]

[9]In that day[r] they will say,

"Surely this is our God;[s]
we trusted[t] in him, and he saved[u] us.
This is the LORD, we trusted in him;
let us rejoice[v] and be glad in his salvation."[w]

[10]The hand of the LORD will rest on this mountain;[x]
but Moab[y] will be trampled under him
as straw is trampled down in the manure.
[11]They will spread out their hands in it,
as a swimmer spreads out his hands to swim.
God will bring down[z] their pride[a]
despite the cleverness[a] of their hands.
[12]He will bring down your high fortified walls[b]
and lay them low;[c]
he will bring them down to the ground,
to the very dust.

A Song of Praise

26 In that day[d] this song will be sung[e] in the land of Judah:

We have a strong city;[f]
God makes salvation
its walls[g] and ramparts.[h]
[2]Open the gates[i]
that the righteous[j] nation may enter,
the nation that keeps faith.
[3]You will keep in perfect peace[k]
him whose mind is steadfast,
because he trusts[l] in you.
[4]Trust[m] in the LORD forever,[n]
for the LORD, the LORD, is the Rock[o] eternal.
[5]He humbles those who dwell on high,
he lays the lofty city low;
he levels it to the ground[p]
and casts it down to the dust.[q]

[a] *11* The meaning of the Hebrew for this word is uncertain.

25:4 [a]S 2Sa 22:3; S Ps 118:8; S Isa 4:6; 17:10; 27:5; 33:16; Joel 3:16 [b]S Isa 3:14 [c]S Isa 14:30; 29:19 [d]S Ps 55:8 [e]Isa 29:5; 49:25 **25:5** [f]Jer 51:55 [g]S Ps 18:44 [h]S Isa 13:11 **25:6** [i]S Isa 2:2 [j]S Ge 29:22; 1Ki 1:25; Isa 1:19; 55:1-2; 66:11; Joel 3:18; Mt 8:11; 22:4; Rev 19:9 [k]S Ps 36:8; S Pr 9:2 **25:7** [l]2Co 3:15-16; Eph 4:18 [m]S Job 4:9 **25:8** [n]Isa 26:19; Hos 13:14; 1Co 15:54-55* [o]Isa 15:3; 30:19; 35:10; 51:11; 65:19; Jer 31:16; Rev 7:17; 21:4 [p]S Ge 30:23; S Ps 119:39; Mt 5:11; 1Pe 4:14; Rev 7:14 [q]S Isa 7:7 **25:9** [r]S Isa 2:11; S 10:20 [s]Isa 40:9 [t]S Ps 22:5; S Isa 12:2 [u]Ps 145:19; Isa 19:20; 33:22; 35:4; 43:3,11; 45:15,21; 49:25-26; 60:16; 63:8; Jer 14:8 [v]S Dt 32:43; S Ps 9:2; Isa 9:3; 35:2,10; 41:16; 51:3; 61:7,10; 66:14 [w]S Ps 13:5; S Isa 12:2 **25:10** [x]S Isa 2:2 [y]S Ge 19:37; S Nu 21:29; S Dt 23:6; S Isa 11:14; Am 2:1-3 **25:11** [z]Isa 5:25; 14:26; 16:14 [a]S Lev 26:19; S Job 40:12 **25:12** [b]S Isa 2:15 [c]S Job 40:11; S Isa 15:1; S Jer 51:44 **26:1** [d]S Isa 10:20 [e]Isa 30:29 [f]S Isa 14:32 [g]Isa 32:18; 60:18; Zec 2:5; 9:8 [h]S Ps 48:13 **26:2** [i]S Ps 24:7 [j]Ps 24:3-4; 85:13; S Isa 1:26; S 4:3; 9:7; 50:8; 53:11; 54:14; 58:8; 62:2 **26:3** [k]S Job 22:21; S Isa 9:6,7; Php 4:7 [l]S 1Ch 5:20; S Ps 22:5; S 28:7; S Isa 12:2 **26:4** [m]S Isa 12:2; 50:10 [n]S Ps 62:8 [o]S Ge 49:24 **26:5** [p]S Isa 25:12; Eze 26:11 [q]S Isa 25:2

Assyria (see 19:18–25 and notes). *honor you ... revere you.* See 24:15–16.

25:4–5 *refuge ... shelter ... shade ... cloud.* See 4:5–6 and note; cf. 32:2.

25:6–8 The eschatological feast of God (see Mt 8:11; Lk 14:15 and notes).

25:6–7,10 *this mountain.* Mount Zion. See 2:2–4 and note; cf. 24:23.

25:6 *feast ... banquet.* Associated with a coronation (1Ki 1:25) or wedding (see Jdg 14:10 and note); cf. the "wedding supper of the Lamb" (Rev 19:9). *rich food.* Symbolic of great spiritual blessings (see 55:2 and note). *aged wine.* The best wine—aged while being left on its dregs (see Jer 48:11 and note; Zep 1:12).

25:7–8 Christ has brought about the ultimate destruction of death itself (see 2Ti 1:10; cf. Heb 2:14–15 and notes).

25:7 *shroud ... sheet.* Or "covering ... veil," with which faces were covered in mourning—in any event, the associations are with death.

25:8 Quoted in part in 1Co 15:54. *swallow up death.* Death, the great swallower (see Ps 49:14 and note), will be swallowed up. *Sovereign LORD.* See 7:7; 28:16; 30:15; 40:10; 49:22; 52:4; 61:11; 65:13. *wipe away the tears.* See Rev 7:17; 21:4. *remove the disgrace.* See 54:4.

25:9 Another brief song of praise. *In that day.* See 12:1,4; 24:21; see also 10:20,27 and note. *we trusted ... he saved.* Cf. Ps 22:4–5. *rejoice and be glad.* Cf. 35:10; 51:11; 66:10.

25:10–12 An elaboration on the theme of judgment.

25:10 *Moab.* Representative of all the enemies of God, like Edom in 34:5–17. See note on 15:1.

25:11 *pride.* See note on 16:6.

25:12 *high fortified walls.* See v. 2; 2:15; 2Ki 3:27; Jer 51:44 and note, 58.

26:1–15 Another song of praise for God's deliverance (see note on 25:1–5).

26:1 *In that day.* See 12:1,4; 24:21; 25:9; see also note on 10:20,27. *salvation its walls and ramparts.* God's saving acts are Zion's security and strength (cf. Ps 46; 48). *ramparts.* Sloping fortifications of earth or stone (cf. 2Sa 20:15).

26:3 See 30:15 and note. *perfect peace.* Hebrew *shalom, shalom*, the repetition stressing the idea; hence, "perfect." *mind is steadfast.* Cf. Ps 112:6–8 and notes. *trusts.* Cf. 25:9.

26:4 *Rock.* See 17:10; Ps 18:2 and notes.

26:5 *lofty city.* See note on 24:10. *levels it ... to the dust.* Cf. 25:2,12.

6 Feet trample[r] it down—
the feet of the oppressed,[s]
the footsteps of the poor.[t]
7 The path of the righteous is level;[u]
O upright One,[v] you make the way
of the righteous smooth.[w]
8 Yes, LORD, walking in the way of your
laws,[a][x]
we wait[y] for you;
your name[z] and renown
are the desire of our hearts.
9 My soul yearns for you in the night;[a]
in the morning my spirit longs[b] for
you.
When your judgments[c] come upon the
earth,
the people of the world learn
righteousness.[d]
10 Though grace is shown to the wicked,[e]
they do not learn righteousness;
even in a land of uprightness they go
on doing evil[f]
and regard[g] not the majesty of the
LORD.
11 O LORD, your hand is lifted high,[h]
but they do not see[i] it.
Let them see your zeal[j] for your people
and be put to shame;[k]
let the fire[l] reserved for your
enemies consume them.
12 LORD, you establish peace[m] for us;
all that we have accomplished you
have done[n] for us.
13 O LORD, our God, other lords[o] besides
you have ruled over us,
but your name[p] alone do we honor.[q]
14 They are now dead,[r] they live no
more;
those departed spirits[s] do not rise.
You punished them and brought them
to ruin;[t]
you wiped out all memory of them.[u]
15 You have enlarged the nation, O LORD;
you have enlarged the nation.[v]
You have gained glory for yourself;
you have extended all the borders[w]
of the land.
16 LORD, they came to you in their
distress;[x]
when you disciplined[y] them,
they could barely whisper[z] a prayer.[b]
17 As a woman with child and about to
give birth[a]
writhes and cries out in her pain,
so were we in your presence, O LORD.
18 We were with child, we writhed in
pain,
but we gave birth[b] to wind.
We have not brought salvation[c] to the
earth;
we have not given birth to people of
the world.[d]
19 But your dead[e] will live;
their bodies will rise.
You who dwell in the dust,[f]
wake up and shout for joy.
Your dew[g] is like the dew of the
morning;
the earth will give birth to her dead.[h]
20 Go, my people, enter your rooms
and shut the doors[i] behind you;
hide[j] yourselves for a little while
until his wrath[k] has passed by.[l]
21 See, the LORD is coming[m] out of his
dwelling[n]
to punish[o] the people of the earth for
their sins.
The earth will disclose the blood[p] shed
upon her;
she will conceal her slain no longer.

[a] *8* Or *judgments* [b] *16* The meaning of the Hebrew for this clause is uncertain.

26:6 [r]S Isa 5:5 [s]Isa 49:26 [t]S Isa 3:15; S 14:30 **26:7** [u]S Ps 26:12 [v]S Ps 25:8 [w]S Ex 14:19; Isa 40:4; 42:16 **26:8** [x]S Dt 18:18; Ps 1:2; Isa 56:1; 64:5 [y]S Ps 37:9; S 130:5 [z]S Ps 145:2; S Isa 12:4 **26:9** [a]S Ps 119:55 [b]Ps 42:1-3; 63:1; 78:34; Isa 55:6 [c]S 1Ch 16:14 [d]Mt 6:33 **26:10** [e]Mt 5:45 [f]Isa 32:6; 59:7, 13 [g]S 1Sa 12:24; Isa 22:12-13; Jer 2:19; Hos 11:7; Jn 5:37-38; Ro 2:4 **26:11** [h]S Ps 10:12 [i]Isa 18:3; 44:9, 18 [j]S Isa 9:7; Joel 2:18; Zec 1:14 [k]Mic 7:16 [l]S Isa 1:31; Heb 10:27 **26:12** [m]S Ps 119:165; S Isa 9:6 [n]S Ps 68:28 **26:13** [o]Isa 2:8; 10:5, 11 [p]S Isa 12:4 [q]Isa 42:8; 63:7 **26:14** [r]S Dt 4:28 [s]S Job 26:5 [t]S Ps 9:5; S Isa 10:3 [u]S Ps 9:6 **26:15** [v]S Job 12:23; S Isa 14:2 [w]Isa 33:17 **26:16** [x]S Jdg 6:2; S Isa 5:30 [y]S Ps 39:11 [z]Isa 29:4 **26:17** [a]S Isa 21:3; S Jn 16:21; Rev 12:2 **26:18** [b]Isa 33:11; 59:4 [c]S Ge 49:10; Ps 17:14 [d]Isa 42:6; 49:6; 51:4; Jer 12:16 **26:19** [e]S Isa 25:8; Eph 5:14 [f]Ps 22:29 [g]S Ge 27:28; S Isa 18:4 [h]Isa 66:24; Eze 37:1-14; Da 12:2 **26:20** [i]Ex 12:23 [j]Ps 91:1, 4 [k]S Isa 10:25; S 30:27 [l]S Job 14:13 **26:21** [m]Isa 29:6; Jude 1:14 [n]S Isa 18:4 [o]S Isa 13:9, 11; 30:12-14 [p]S Job 16:18; Lk 11:50-51

26:6 *feet of the oppressed.* The oppressors are humiliated also in 49:24–26; 51:22–23 (contrast 3:14–15).
26:7 *path … level; … way … smooth.* A theme found also in 40:3–4; 42:16; 45:13 (see notes there; contrast La 3:9).
26:8 A desire for God to reveal his power in their behalf (see Hos 12:5–6). *name and renown.* See v. 13; 24:15; 25:1.
26:9 *judgments.* Punishment (cf. 4:4).
26:10 *grace.* Such as the blessings of harvest and general prosperity (cf. Mt. 5:45 and note).
26:11 *hand is lifted high.* A sign of power. See 9:12,17,21 and note; Ps 89:13. *zeal.* See 9:7 and note; cf. 37:32; 63:15. *fire.* See note on 1:31.
26:12 *peace.* See v. 3.
26:13 *other lords.* Foreign rulers, such as those of Egypt or Assyria.
26:14 *They are now dead … departed spirits do not rise.* Cf. the fate of the king of Babylon in 14:9–10—and contrast the resurrection scene in 26:19 (see note there).
26:15 *enlarged the nation.* Applied to the return from Babylonian exile in 54:2–3; cf. also 9:3; Zec 2:4 and note.
26:16–18 The prophet speaks to the Lord on behalf of God's people.
26:16 *distress.* Perhaps the Assyrian oppression, described in 5:30; 8:21–22 (see notes there). The period of the judges is also possible (see Jdg 6:2,6).
26:17–18 *give birth writhes … in pain.* See 13:8 and note (cf. 37:3).
26:18 *salvation to the earth.* See 49:6.
26:19–21 The prophet speaks a word of reassurance to God's people.
26:19 *your dead will live … bodies will rise.* A reference to the restoration of Israel (see Eze 37:11–12,14 and notes)—perhaps including the resurrection of the body (see Da 12:2 and note). Cf. 25:8; contrast 26:14. *dew.* Here a symbol of fruitfulness (see 2Sa 1:21; Hos 14:5 and note).
26:20–21 See 24:21–22 and note on 2:11,17,20.
26:20 *a little while … wrath.* See 10:25; 54:7–8 and notes; cf. Ps 30:5 and note. Assyrian tyranny and Babylonian exile, as well as all other oppressions, will end.
26:21 *punish.* See 66:14–16 and notes. *will disclose … will con-*

Deliverance of Israel

27 In that day,[q]
the LORD will punish with his sword,[r]
his fierce, great and powerful sword,
Leviathan[s] the gliding serpent,[t]
Leviathan the coiling serpent;
he will slay the monster[u] of the sea.

2In that day[v]—
"Sing[w] about a fruitful vineyard:[x]
3 I, the LORD, watch over it;
I water[y] it continually.
I guard[z] it day and night
so that no one may harm[a] it.
4 I am not angry.
If only there were briers and thorns
confronting me!
I would march against them in
battle;
I would set them all on fire.[b]
5Or else let them come to me for
refuge;[c]
let them make peace[d] with me,
yes, let them make peace with me."

6In days to come Jacob will take root,[e]
Israel will bud and blossom[f]
and fill all the world with fruit.[g]

7Has ⌊the LORD⌋ struck her
as he struck[h] down those who struck
her?
Has she been killed
as those were killed who killed her?
8By warfare[a] and exile[i] you contend
with her—
with his fierce blast he drives her
out,
as on a day the east wind[j] blows.
9By this, then, will Jacob's guilt be
atoned[k] for,
and this will be the full fruitage of
the removal of his sin:[l]
When he makes all the altar stones[m]
to be like chalk stones crushed to
pieces,
no Asherah poles[b][n] or incense
altars[o]
will be left standing.
10The fortified city stands desolate,[p]
an abandoned settlement, forsaken[q]
like the desert;
there the calves graze,[r]
there they lie down;[s]
they strip its branches bare.
11 When its twigs are dry, they are
broken off[t]
and women come and make fires[u]
with them.
For this is a people without
understanding;[v]
so their Maker has no compassion
on them,
and their Creator[w] shows them no
favor.[x]

12In that day the LORD will thresh[y] from
the flowing Euphrates[c] to the Wadi of
Egypt,[z] and you, O Israelites, will be gathered[a] up one by one. 13And in that day[b]
a great trumpet[c] will sound. Those who
were perishing in Assyria and those who
were exiled[d] in Egypt[e] will come and worship[f] the LORD on the holy mountain[g] in
Jerusalem.

[a] *8* See Septuagint; the meaning of the Hebrew for this word is uncertain. [b] *9* That is, wooden symbols of the goddess Asherah [c] *12* Hebrew *River*

27:1 [q]ver 13; S Isa 2:11; 28:5 [r]S Ge 3:24; S Dt 32:41; Isa 31:8; 34:6; 65:12; 66:16; Eze 21:3; Na 3:15 [s]S Job 3:8 [t]Job 26:13 [u]S Ps 68:30; S 74:13; Rev 12:9 **27:2** [v]Isa 24:21 [w]S Isa 5:1 [x]Jer 2:21 **27:3** [y]Isa 58:11 [z]S Ps 91:4; S Isa 5:2 [a]S Jn 6:39 **27:4** [b]S ver 11; S Isa 10:17; Mt 3:12; Heb 6:8 **27:5** [c]S Isa 25:4 [d]S Job 22:21; S Ps 119:165; Ro 5:1; 2Co 5:20 **27:6** [e]S 2Ki 19:30; Isa 11:10 [f]S Ge 40:10 [g]S Ps 72:16; Isa 11:1; 37:31; Eze 17:23; 36:8; Hos 14:8 **27:7** [h]Isa 10:26; S 11:4; 37:36-38 **27:8** [i]Isa 49:14; 50:1; 54:7 [j]S Ge 41:6 **27:9** [k]S Ps 78:38 [l]Ro 11:27* [m]S Ex 23:24 [n]S Ex 34:13 [o]S Lev 26:30; S 2Ch 14:5 **27:10** [p]S Ge 1:2; S Dt 13:16; Isa 5:6; 32:14; Jer 10:22; 26:6; La 1:4; 5:18 [q]S Isa 5:5 [r]S Isa 5:17 [s]Isa 17:2 **27:11** [t]S Isa 10:33 [u]S ver 4; Isa 33:12 [v]S Dt 32:28; S Isa 1:3 [w]Dt 32:18; Isa 41:8; 43:1,7,15; 44:1-2,21,24 [x]S Isa 9:17; Jer 11:16 **27:12** [y]S Isa 21:10; Mt 3:12 [z]S Ge 15:18 [a]S Dt 30:4; S Isa 1:9; S 11:12; S 17:6 **27:13** [b]S ver 1 [c]S Lev 25:9; S Jdg 3:27; S Mt 24:31 [d]S Ps 106:47 [e]S Isa 10:19; 19:21,25 [f]S Ge 27:29; S Ps 22:29; S 86:9 [g]S Isa 2:2

ceal ... no longer. The blood and bodies of the innocent/righteous who have been slaughtered by the oppressive powers will no longer be hidden in the ground, but will be brought forth to testify against their murderers, so that God may in judgment avenge their deaths (see Ge 4:10 and note).

27:1–2,12–13 *In that day.* See 10:20,27; 24:21 and notes; see also 12:1,4; 25:9; 26:1.

27:1 The climactic word of judgment in 24:1—27:13 (see note there). *his sword.* See Ps 7:12–13 and note. *Leviathan ... monster.* A symbol (drawn from Canaanite myths) of wicked nations, such as Egypt (see 30:7 ["Rahab"]; 51:9; Eze 29:3; 32:2 and notes). *gliding ... coiling serpent.* Cf. Job 3:8; 41:1; Ps 74:13–14.

27:2–6 A second vineyard song (see 5:1–7 and notes).

27:2 *vineyard.* Israel.

27:4–5 A picture of Israel's lukewarmness toward the Lord—not "briers and thorns" (v. 4) like the other nations, but not fully trusting in the Lord either (see 29:13 and note).

27:4 *briers and thorns.* See 5:6 and note.

27:6 *take root.* See 11:1,10 and notes. *bud and blossom.* See 4:2 and note. The Messianic age is in view. *fill all the world.* Contrast 26:18.

27:7–11 What the Lord is going to do with Israel in the judgments that are about to overtake her in Isaiah's day.

27:7 *struck her.* Cf. 10:24–26.

27:8 *exile.* Probably the Babylonian captivity. *east wind.* A hot wind from the desert (see Jer 4:11 and note; Eze 19:12).

27:9 *atoned for.* Israel (Jacob) will have to atone for her guilt through the coming judgment. *altar ... Asherah poles ... incense altars.* See 17:8 and note. *crushed to pieces.* See Ex 34:13 and note.

27:10 *fortified city.* Jerusalem. *desolate ... forsaken.* Cf. 6:11–12. *calves graze.* Cf. 5:5; 7:25.

27:12–13 The redemption that lies beyond the coming judgment.

27:12 *will thresh.* Judgment on the nations into which Israel has been dispersed (see note on 21:10). The threshing will separate Israelites from Gentiles. *Wadi of Egypt.* Probably the Wadi el-Arish, the southern border of the promised land (see map No. 2 and map No. 5 at the end of this study Bible; the Euphrates is the northern border). See Ge 15:18; 1Ki 4:21; 8:65 and notes.

27:13 *great trumpet.* Used especially to summon troops (see 1Sa 13:3). *Assyria ... Egypt.* See 11:11–12 and notes. *holy mountain.* Mount Zion (see 2:2–4 and note; see also 11:6–9; 24:23; 25:6–7,10 and note; 65:25).

Woe to Ephraim

28 Woe[h] to that wreath, the pride of
Ephraim's[i] drunkards,
to the fading flower, his glorious
beauty,
set on the head of a fertile valley[j]—
to that city, the pride of those laid
low by wine![k]
2 See, the Lord has one who is powerful[l]
and strong.
Like a hailstorm[m] and a destructive
wind,[n]
like a driving rain and a flooding[o]
downpour,
he will throw it forcefully to the
ground.
3 That wreath, the pride of Ephraim's[p]
drunkards,
will be trampled[q] underfoot.
4 That fading flower, his glorious beauty,
set on the head of a fertile valley,[r]
will be like a fig[s] ripe before harvest—
as soon as someone sees it and takes
it in his hand,
he swallows it.

5 In that day[t] the LORD Almighty
will be a glorious[u] crown,[v]
a beautiful wreath
for the remnant[w] of his people.
6 He will be a spirit of justice[x]
to him who sits in judgment,[y]
a source of strength
to those who turn back the battle[z] at
the gate.

7 And these also stagger[a] from wine[b]
and reel[c] from beer:
Priests[d] and prophets[e] stagger from
beer
and are befuddled with wine;
they reel from beer,
they stagger when seeing visions,[f]
they stumble when rendering
decisions.
8 All the tables are covered with vomit[g]
and there is not a spot without filth.

28:1 [h] Isa 10:5; 29:1; 30:1; 31:1; 33:1 [i] ver 3; Isa 7:2; 9:9 [j] ver 4 [k] S Lev 10:9; Isa 5:11; Hos 7:5; Am 6:6 **28:2** [l] Isa 40:10 [m] S Jos 10:11 [n] Isa 29:6 [o] S Isa 8:7; S Da 9:26 **28:3** [p] S ver 1 [q] S Job 40:12; S Isa 5:5 **28:4** [r] ver 1 [s] S SS 2:13; Hos 9:10; Na 3:12 **28:5** [t] S Isa 10:20; S 27:1; 29:18; 30:23 [u] S Isa 24:16,23 [v] Isa 62:3; Jer 13:18; Eze 16:12; 21:26; Zec 9:16 [w] S Isa 1:9 **28:6** [x] S 2Sa 14:20; Isa 11:2-4; 32:1,16; 33:5 [y] Isa 4:4; Jn 5:30 [z] Jdg 9:44-45; S 2Ch 32:8 **28:7** [a] S Isa 3:12 [b] S Lev 10:9; S Isa 22:13; S Eph 5:18 [c] S Ps 107:27 [d] Isa 24:2 [e] S Isa 9:15 [f] S Isa 1:1; 29:11 **28:8** [g] Jer 48:26
28:9 [h] ver 26; Ps 32:8; Isa 2:3; 30:20; 48:17; 50:4; 54:13; Jer 31:34; 32:33 [i] Isa 52:7; 53:1 [j] Ps 131:2 [k] Heb 5:12-13; 1Pe 2:2 **28:10** [l] ver 13 **28:11** [m] S Ge 11:7; Isa 33:19; Jer 5:15 [n] Eze 3:5; 1Co 14:21* **28:12** [o] S Ex 14:14; S Jos 1:13; S Job 11:18; S Isa 11:10; Mt 11:28-29 **28:13** [p] ver 10 [q] Mt 21:44 [r] S Isa 8:15 **28:14** [s] Isa 1:10 [t] 2Ch 36:16 **28:15** [u] S Job 5:23; Isa 8:19 [v] ver 2, 18; Isa 8:7-8; 10:26; 29:6; 30:28; Da 11:22 [w] S Isa 9:15 [x] S Jdg 9:35; Isa 29:15; Jer 23:24

9 "Who is it he is trying to teach?[h]
To whom is he explaining his
message?[i]
To children weaned[j] from their milk,[k]
to those just taken from the
breast?
10 For it is:
Do and do, do and do,
rule on rule, rule on rule[a];
a little here, a little there.[l]"

11 Very well then, with foreign lips and
strange tongues[m]
God will speak to this people,[n]
12 to whom he said,
"This is the resting place, let the
weary rest";[o]
and, "This is the place of repose"—
but they would not listen.
13 So then, the word of the LORD to them
will become:
Do and do, do and do,
rule on rule, rule on rule;
a little here, a little there[p]—
so that they will go and fall backward,
be injured[q] and snared and
captured.[r]

14 Therefore hear the word of the LORD,[s]
you scoffers[t]
who rule this people in Jerusalem.
15 You boast, "We have entered into a
covenant with death,[u]
with the grave[b] we have made an
agreement.
When an overwhelming scourge
sweeps by,[v]
it cannot touch us,
for we have made a lie[w] our refuge
and falsehood[c] our hiding place.[x]"

[a] 10 Hebrew *sav lasav sav lasav / kav lakav kav lakav* (possibly meaningless sounds; perhaps a mimicking of the prophet's words); also in verse 13 [b] 15 Hebrew *Sheol*; also in verse 18 [c] 15 Or *false gods*

28:1—35:10 A series of six woes (28:1; 29:1; 29:15; 30:1; 31:1; 33:1), ending with an announcement of judgment on the nations (ch. 34) and a song celebrating the joy of the redeemed (ch. 35). Cf. the six woes in ch. 5 (see note on 5:8–23).
28:1 *wreath.* Samaria, the capital of the northern kingdom, was a beautiful city on a prominent hill (see note on 1Ki 16:24). *pride.* See v. 3 and note on 16:6. *Ephraim's.* See note on 7:2. *drunkards.* In the eighth century B.C. Samaria was a city of luxury and indulgence. See 5:11–13; Am 3:12 and notes; 6:4–7. *fertile valley.* Cf. 5:1.
28:2 *one who is powerful.* The king of Assyria. *hailstorm ... flooding downpour.* See v. 17; 8:7–8 and note; 17:12 and note. Cf. 30:30; 32:19.
28:5 *In that day.* See 4:1–2; 10:20,27 and note; 12:1,4; 24:21 and note. *glorious ... beautiful.* See 4:2 and note. *remnant.* See note on 1:9.
28:6 *spirit of justice.* See 11:2–4 and notes. *gate.* The most vulnerable part of a city.
28:7 *wine ... beer.* The religious leaders should have been filled with the Spirit, not with wine. See Lev 10:9; see also Nu 11:29; Eph 5:18 and notes.
28:8 *vomit.* Cf. Jer 25:16,27.
28:9–10 The mocking response of Isaiah's hearers (see NIV text note on v. 10). Cf. the mocking tones of 5:19.
28:11–12 Quoted in part in 1Co 14:21 (see note on 1Co 14:21–22).
28:11 *foreign lips.* The language of the Assyrians.
28:12 *resting place.* The land given to them by the Lord, in whom they were to trust (see 26:3; 30:15; 40:31; Jos 1:13 and notes). *would not listen.* Cf. Jer 6:16 and note.
28:13 *will become.* They say the prophet is speaking nonsense (vv. 9–10), so the word of the Lord that he speaks will remain nonsense to them (see 6:9–10 and notes).
28:15,18 *covenant with death.* By using a vivid figure of speech, Isaiah mocks their sense of assurance against national calamity, placing on their lips a claim to have a covenant

16So this is what the Sovereign LORD says:

"See, I lay a stone in Zion,[y]
a tested stone,[z]
a precious cornerstone for a sure foundation;[a]
the one who trusts will never be dismayed.[b]
17I will make justice[c] the measuring line
and righteousness the plumb line;[d]
hail[e] will sweep away your refuge, the lie,
and water will overflow[f] your hiding place.
18Your covenant with death will be annulled;
your agreement with the grave will not stand.[g]
When the overwhelming scourge sweeps by,[h]
you will be beaten down[i] by it.
19As often as it comes it will carry you away;[j]
morning after morning,[k] by day and by night,
it will sweep through."

The understanding of this message
will bring sheer terror.[l]
20The bed is too short to stretch out on,
the blanket too narrow to wrap around you.[m]
21The LORD will rise up as he did at Mount Perazim,[n]
he will rouse himself as in the Valley of Gibeon[o]—
to do his work,[p] his strange work,
and perform his task, his alien task.
22Now stop your mocking,[q]
or your chains will become heavier;
the Lord, the LORD Almighty, has told me
of the destruction decreed[r] against the whole land.[s]

23Listen[t] and hear my voice;
pay attention and hear what I say.

28:16 [y]S Isa 14:32 [z]Ps 118:22; Isa 8:14-15; Da 2:34-35,45; Zec 12:3; S Ac 4:11 [a]Jer 51:26; 1Co 3:11; 2Ti 2:19 [b]Isa 29:22; 45:17; 50:7; 54:4; Ro 9:33*; 10:11*; 1Pe 2:6* **28:17** [c]S Ps 11:7; S Isa 5:16 [d]S 2Ki 21:13 [e]S Jos 10:11 [f]S Isa 8:7 **28:18** [g]S Isa 7:7 [h]S ver 15 [i]S Isa 5:5; 63:18; Da 8:13 **28:19** [j]2Ki 24:2 [k]S Ps 5:3 [l]S Job 18:11 **28:20** [m]Isa 59:6 **28:21** [n]S Ge 38:29; S 1Ch 14:11 [o]S Jos 9:3 [p]Isa 10:12; 65:7; Lk 19:41-44 **28:22** [q]S 2Ch 36:16; Jer 29:18; La 2:15; Zep 2:15 [r]S Isa 10:22 [s]S Isa 10:23 **28:23** [t]Isa 32:9

28:24 [u]Ecc 3:2 **28:25** [v]Mt 23:23 [w]S Ex 9:31 [x]Ex 9:32; Eze 4:9 **28:26** [y]S Ps 94:10 **28:27** [z]S Isa 21:10 [a]S Job 41:30 [b]Isa 10:5 **28:28** [c]S Isa 21:10 **28:29** [d]S Isa 9:6 [e]S Ps 92:5; Ro 11:33 **29:1** [f]Isa 22:12-13; S 28:1 [g]ver 2,7 [h]S 2Sa 5:7 [i]S Isa 1:14 **29:2** [j]S ver 1 [k]S Isa 3:26; La 2:5 [l]Eze 43:15

24When a farmer plows for planting,[u]
does he plow continually?
Does he keep on breaking up and harrowing the soil?
25When he has leveled the surface,
does he not sow caraway and scatter cummin?[v]
Does he not plant wheat in its place,[a]
barley[w] in its plot,[a]
and spelt[x] in its field?
26His God instructs him
and teaches[y] him the right way.

27Caraway is not threshed[z] with a sledge,[a]
nor is a cartwheel rolled over cummin;
caraway is beaten out with a rod,[b]
and cummin with a stick.
28Grain must be ground to make bread;
so one does not go on threshing it forever.
Though he drives the wheels of his threshing cart[c] over it,
his horses do not grind it.
29All this also comes from the LORD Almighty,
wonderful in counsel[d] and magnificent in wisdom.[e]

Woe to David's City

29 Woe[f] to you, Ariel, Ariel,[g]
the city[h] where David settled!
Add year to year
and let your cycle of festivals[i] go on.
2Yet I will besiege Ariel;[j]
she will mourn and lament,[k]
she will be to me like an altar hearth.[b][l]
3I will encamp against you all around;
I will encircle[m] you with towers
and set up my siege works[n] against you.

a 25 The meaning of the Hebrew for this word is uncertain. *b* 2 The Hebrew for *altar hearth* sounds like the Hebrew for *Ariel.*

29:3 [m]Lk 19:43-44 [n]S 2Ki 25:1

with death that it will not harm them (cf. Hos 2:18 and note). *overwhelming scourge.* A mixed metaphor referring to the armies of Assyria and Babylonia. "Overwhelming" pictures an army as a flooding river (see 8:7–8 and note); a "scourge" is a whip (10:26).

28:16 *stone.* The Lord (see 8:14; 17:10 and notes). *cornerstone.* Cf. the "capstone" of Ps 118:22 (see note there). *sure foundation.* See 1Co 3:11; cf. 1Pe 2:4–8 and notes.

28:17 *measuring line … plumb line.* The standards and tests the Lord will apply are his "justice" and "righteousness" (cf. 34:11 and note). *hail.* See v. 2; 30:30; 32:19.

28:20 *too short … too narrow.* Israel was unprepared both militarily and spiritually.

28:21 *Mount Perazim.* Where God had "broken out" against the Philistines (see 2Sa 5:20 and note). *Valley of Gibeon.* Where God sent hail to demolish the Amorites (see Jos 10:10–13 and notes). *strange work … alien task.* This time God would fight against Israel.

28:22 *destruction decreed.* See 10:22–23 and note on 10:22.

28:23–29 A wisdom poem (a poetic parable) in two stanzas, each ending in a verse that praises the wisdom of God. In the context, and since "threshing" is emphasized (vv. 27–28), the point may be that though God must punish Israel, his actions will be as measured and as well-timed as a farmer's. See 27:12 and note.

28:25 *cummin.* An herb for seasoning (see Mt 23:23 and note). *spelt.* A kind of wheat (see note on Ex 9:32).

28:27 *rod.* See 10:5 and note.

28:29 *wonderful in counsel.* See 9:6 and note.

29:1–2,7 *Ariel.* Jerusalem (Ariel may mean "City of God"). Fighting and bloodshed will turn the city into a virtual "altar hearth" (Hebrew *'ari'el*; see NIV text note on v. 2).

29:1 *Woe.* See note on 28:1. *city where David settled.* See 2Sa 5:6–9 and notes; cf. Isa 22:9. *cycle of festivals.* See 1:13–14 and note on 1:14.

29:3 *towers.* Pushed up to the city wall by attackers so they could fight the defenders on the same level.

[4]Brought low, you will speak from the ground;
your speech will mumble[o] out of the dust.[p]
Your voice will come ghostlike[q] from the earth;
out of the dust your speech will whisper.[r]

[5]But your many enemies will become like fine dust,[s]
the ruthless[t] hordes like blown chaff.[u]
Suddenly,[v] in an instant,
6 the LORD Almighty will come[w]
with thunder[x] and earthquake[y] and great noise,
with windstorm and tempest[z] and flames of a devouring fire.[a]
[7]Then the hordes of all the nations[b] that fight against Ariel,[c]
that attack her and her fortress and besiege her,
will be as it is with a dream,[d]
with a vision in the night—
[8]as when a hungry man dreams that he is eating,
but he awakens,[e] and his hunger remains;
as when a thirsty man dreams that he is drinking,
but he awakens faint, with his thirst unquenched.[f]
So will it be with the hordes of all the nations
that fight against Mount Zion.[g]

[9]Be stunned and amazed,[h]
blind yourselves and be sightless;[i]
be drunk,[j] but not from wine,[k]
stagger,[l] but not from beer.
[10]The LORD has brought over you a deep sleep:[m]
He has sealed your eyes[n] (the prophets);[o]
he has covered your heads (the seers).[p]

[11]For you this whole vision[q] is nothing but words sealed[r] in a scroll. And if you give the scroll to someone who can read, and say to him, "Read this, please," he will answer, "I can't; it is sealed." [12]Or if you give the scroll to someone who cannot read, and say, "Read this, please," he will answer, "I don't know how to read."

[13]The Lord says:

"These people[s] come near to me with their mouth
and honor me with their lips,[t]
but their hearts are far from me.[u]
Their worship of me
is made up only of rules taught by men.[a][v]
[14]Therefore once more I will astound these people
with wonder upon wonder;[w]
the wisdom of the wise[x] will perish,
the intelligence of the intelligent will vanish.[y]"
[15]Woe to those who go to great depths
to hide[z] their plans from the LORD,
who do their work in darkness and think,
"Who sees us?[a] Who will know?"[b]
[16]You turn things upside down,
as if the potter were thought to be like the clay![c]
Shall what is formed say to him who formed[d] it,
"He did not make me"?
Can the pot say of the potter,[e]
"He knows nothing"?[f]

[a] 13 Hebrew; Septuagint *They worship me in vain; / their teachings are but rules taught by men*

29:4 [o]Isa 8:19 [p]Isa 47:1; 52:2 [q]S Lev 19:31 [r]Isa 26:16 **29:5** [s]S Dt 9:21; Ps 78:39; 103:15; S Isa 2:22; 37:27; 40:6; 51:12 [t]S Isa 13:11 [u]S Isa 17:13 [v]S Ps 55:15; S Isa 17:14; 1Th 5:3 **29:6** [w]S Isa 26:21; Zec 14:1-5 [x]S Ex 19:16 [y]Mt 24:7; Mk 13:8; Lk 21:11; S Rev 6:12; 11:19 [z]S Ps 50:3; S 55:8; S Isa 28:15 [a]S Lev 10:2; Ps 83:13-15 **29:7** [b]Mic 4:11-12; Zec 12:9 [c]S ver 1 [d]S Job 20:8 **29:8** [e]S Ps 73:20 [f]ver 5,7; Isa 41:11,15; Jer 30:16; Zec 12:3 [g]Isa 17:12-14; 54:17 **29:9** [h]ver 14; Jer 4:9; Hab 1:5 [i]S Isa 6:10 [j]Isa 51:17; 63:6; Jer 13:13; 25:27 [k]S Lev 10:9; Isa 28:1; 51:21-22 [l]S Ps 60:3; S Isa 3:12 **29:10** [m]S Jdg 4:21; Jnh 1:5 [n]Ps 69:23; S Isa 6:9-10; 44:18; Ro 11:8*; 2Th 2:9-11 [o]Mic 3:6 [p]S 1Sa 9:9 **29:11** [q]S Isa 28:7 [r]S Isa 8:16; Da 8:26; 12:9; Mt 13:11; Rev 5:1-2 **29:13** [s]Jer 14:11; Hag 1:2; 2:14 [t]S Ps 50:16 [u]S Ps 119:70; Isa 58:2; Jer 12:2; Eze 33:31 [v]Mt 15:8-9*; Mk 7:6-7*; Col 2:22 **29:14** [w]S Job 10:16 [x]S Job 5:13; Jer 8:9; 49:7 [y]Isa 6:9-10; 1Co 1:19* **29:15** [z]S Ge 3:8; S Isa 28:15 [a]S Job 8:3; Ps 10:11-13; 94:7; Isa 47:10; 57:12; Eze 8:12; 9:9 [b]S 2Ki 21:16; S Job 22:13 **29:16** [c]S Job 10:9; S Isa 10:15 [d]S Ge 2:7 [e]Isa 45:9; 64:8; Jer 18:6; Ro 9:20-21* [f]S Job 9:12

29:4 *whisper.* Used of mediums and spiritists in 8:19. Judah speaks as from the realm of the dead ("ground ... dust ... earth")—so much for their covenant with death (see 28:15,18 and note).
29:5–8 In God's time, those nations that devastate Jerusalem will be devastated (see 10:5–19; 27:1; cf. Ge 12:2–3 and note). The sudden destruction of the enemy resembles that of Assyria's army in 701 B.C. (see 10:16 and note).
29:5 *chaff.* See 17:13; Ps 1:4 and notes.
29:6 *thunder and earthquake ... windstorm and tempest.* As in Jdg 5:4–5; Ps 18:7–15; Hab 3:3–7; see also 28:2; Ps 83:13–15 and notes.
29:9–14 Isaiah speaks again of Israel's spiritual state and warns of the Lord's impending judgment.
29:9 *blind yourselves ... be drunk.* Refers to spiritual stupor (see 6:10 and note; cf. 28:1,7 and note).
29:10 Quoted in part in Ro 11:8 (see note there). *seers.* See 1Sa 9:9 and note; 2Ki 17:13.
29:11–12 God's revelation to Isaiah here is a closed book ("sealed," v. 11) to all the people.
29:13 Quoted in part by Jesus to show the hypocrisy of the Pharisees (see Mk 7:6 and note). *These people.* Not "my people" (cf. 6:9; 8:6,11–12; cf. also Ex 17:4; Jer 14:10–11; Hag 1:2 and notes).
29:14 Quoted in part in 1Co 1:19 (see note there). *wonder upon wonder.* He who showed them wonders in the exodus (see Ex 15:11; Ps 78:12–16 and note) will now show them wonders in judgment. *wisdom ... will perish.* Cf. 44:25; Jer 8:9.
29:15 *Woe.* A new woe begins (see note on 28:1—35:10). *their plans.* Perhaps the alliance between Ahaz and Assyria or between Hezekiah and Egypt (see 30:1–2 and notes). *Who sees us?* See note on Ps 10:11.
29:16 See 45:9; 64:8; see also notes on Jer 18:1–6. This verse is quoted in part in Ro 9:20 (see notes on Ro 9:20–21). Cf. the creation of Adam in Ge 2:7 (see note there); also cf. Isa 10:15; Ps 139.

17 In a very short time,[g] will not
Lebanon[h] be turned into a
fertile field[i]
and the fertile field seem like a
forest?[j]
18 In that day[k] the deaf[l] will hear the
words of the scroll,
and out of gloom and darkness[m]
the eyes of the blind will see.[n]
19 Once more the humble[o] will rejoice in
the LORD;
the needy[p] will rejoice in the Holy
One[q] of Israel.
20 The ruthless[r] will vanish,[s]
the mockers[t] will disappear,
and all who have an eye for evil[u]
will be cut down—
21 those who with a word make a man
out to be guilty,
who ensnare the defender in court[v]
and with false testimony[w] deprive
the innocent of justice.[x]

22 Therefore this is what the LORD, who
redeemed[y] Abraham,[z] says to the house of
Jacob:

"No longer will Jacob be ashamed;[a]
no longer will their faces grow pale.[b]
23 When they see among them their
children,[c]
the work of my hands,[d]
they will keep my name holy;[e]
they will acknowledge the holiness
of the Holy One[f] of Jacob,
and will stand in awe of the God of
Israel.
24 Those who are wayward[g] in spirit will
gain understanding;[h]
those who complain will accept
instruction."[i]

29:17 [g]S Isa 10:25 [h]S Isa 2:13 [i]Ps 84:6; 107:33 [j]Isa 32:15 **29:18** [k]S Isa 28:5 [l]Mk 7:37 [m]S Ps 107:14 [n]S Ps 146:8; S Isa 32:3; Mt 11:5; Lk 7:22 **29:19** [o]Ps 25:9; 37:11; Isa 61:1; Mt 5:5; 11:29 [p]S Ps 72:4; S Isa 3:15; S 14:30; Mt 11:5; Lk 7:22; Jas 1:9; 2:5 [q]ver 23; Isa 1:4; S 5:19; S 12:6; 30:11 **29:20** [r]S Isa 9:4; S 13:11 [s]Isa 34:12 [t]S 2Ch 36:16; Isa 28:22 [u]S Job 15:35; Ps 7:14; Isa 32:7; 33:11; 59:4; Eze 11:2; Mic 2:1; Na 1:11 **29:21** [v]Am 5:10,15 [w]Pr 21:28 [x]S Isa 5:23; 32:7; Hab 1:4 **29:22** [y]S Ex 6:6 [z]Ge 17:16; Isa 41:8; 51:2; 63:16 [a]Ps 22:5; 25:3; S Isa 28:16; 49:23; 61:7; Joel 2:26; Zep 3:11 [b]Jer 30:6,10; Joel 2:6,21; Na 2:10 **29:23** [c]Isa 49:20-26; 53:10; 54:1-3 [d]S Ps 8:6; S Isa 19:25 [e]Mt 6:9 [f]S ver 19; S Isa 5:19 **29:24** [g]Ps 95:10; S Pr 12:8; Isa 28:7;

Woe to the Obstinate Nation

30 "Woe[j] to the obstinate children,"[k]
declares the LORD,
"to those who carry out plans that are
not mine,
forming an alliance,[l] but not by my
Spirit,
heaping sin upon sin;
2 who go down to Egypt[m]
without consulting[n] me;
who look for help to Pharaoh's
protection,[o]
to Egypt's shade for refuge.[p]
3 But Pharaoh's protection will be to
your shame,
Egypt's shade[q] will bring you
disgrace.[r]
4 Though they have officials in Zoan[s]
and their envoys have arrived in
Hanes,
5 everyone will be put to shame
because of a people[t] useless[u] to
them,
who bring neither help[v] nor advantage,
but only shame and disgrace.[w]"

6 An oracle[x] concerning the animals of
the Negev:[y]

Through a land of hardship and
distress,[z]
of lions[a] and lionesses,
of adders and darting snakes,[b]
the envoys carry their riches on
donkeys'[c] backs,

Heb 5:2 [h]Isa 1:3; 32:4; 41:20; 60:16 [i]Isa 30:21; 42:16 **30:1** [j]S Isa 28:1 [k]S Dt 21:18; S Isa 1:2 [l]S 2Ki 17:4; S Isa 8:12 **30:2** [m]2Ki 25:26; Isa 31:1; 36:6; Jer 2:18,36; 42:14; Eze 17:15; 29:16 [n]S Ge 25:22; S Nu 27:21 [o]Isa 36:9 [p]S Isa 4:6 **30:3** [q]Jdg 9:8-15 [r]ver 5; S Ps 44:13; Isa 20:4-5; 36:6 **30:4** [s]S Nu 13:22 **30:5** [t]ver 7; Isa 20:5; 31:1; 36:6 [u]S 2Ki 18:21 [v]S Ps 108:12; Jer 37:3-5 [w]S ver 3; S 2Ki 18:21; Eze 17:15 **30:6** [x]Isa 13:1 [y]S Jdg 1:9 [z]S Ex 1:13; 5:10,21; Isa 5:30; 8:22; Jer 11:4 [a]S Isa 5:29; 35:9 [b]S Dt 8:15 [c]S Ge 42:26; S 1Sa 25:18

29:17–24 Another sudden shift to the theme of redemption, as in 28:5–8.
29:17 *Lebanon.* Perhaps symbolic of Assyria (see 10:34). The forests of Lebanon were unequaled (see 2:13 and note), so "fertile field" represents a lesser status (see 32:15 and note).
29:18 *In that day.* See notes on 10:20,27; 26:1. Beyond the day of Assyria's destruction lies the day of Israel's restoration. *deaf will hear … blind will see.* The opposite of 6:9; linked with the Messianic age in 35:5.
29:19 *needy.* See 11:4. *Holy One of Israel.* See Introduction: Author; see also note on 1:4.
29:20 *ruthless.* See v. 21. *mockers.* Cf. 28:14,22.
29:21 *deprive … of justice.* See 1:17; 9:17 and notes; see also 10:2; Am 5:10,12,24 and note.
29:22 *redeemed.* Normally used of the deliverance of Israel from Egypt (see Ex 6:6 and note; 15:13). Cf. 43:1,3,14. But Abraham also had an "exodus" out of a pagan world (see Ge 12:1; Jos 24:2–3,14–15 and notes). *be ashamed.* Cf. 45:17; 50:7; 54:4. *grow pale.* From fear of the enemy.
29:23 *see … their children.* Cf. 49:20–21; 54:1–2 and notes. Restoration from exile may be in view. See also 53:10 and note. *children, the work of my hands.* See 45:11 (cf. Eph 2:10 and note). *acknowledge the holiness … stand in awe.* See 8:13. Isaiah's contemporaries showed little respect for the Lord. *Holy One of Jacob.* Cf. v. 19; see note on 1:4.
29:24 *wayward in spirit.* See 19:14. *gain understanding.* Contrast 1:3 (see also note there).
30:1 *Woe.* See note on 28:1—35:10. *obstinate children.* See 1:2 and note. *plans … not mine.* See 29:15 and note. *alliance.* After Shabako became pharaoh in 715 B.C., the smaller nations in Aram (Syria) and Canaan sought his help against Assyria. Judah apparently joined them (see 20:5 and note). *my Spirit.* Who spoke through his prophet.
30:2 Hezekiah did this (see 2Ki 18:21 and note). *shade.* A metaphor for a king as one who provides protection (see Jdg 9:15; La 4:20 and notes). The Lord should have been Israel's "shade" (cf. 49:2; 51:16; see Ps 91:1; 121:5 and notes).
30:4 *Zoan.* Ironically, where the Israelites once served as slaves; see 19:11 and note. *Hanes.* Possibly Heracleopolis Magna, about 50 miles south of Cairo, or perhaps a city in the Nile delta, close to Zoan.
30:6 *oracle.* See 13:1 and note. *Negev.* The dry region in the southern part of the Holy Land (see Ge 12:9 and note; cf. Jdg 1:9). *hardship and distress.* Perhaps it was necessary to use back roads because the Assyrians had control of the main coastal road (see Dt 8:15; Jdg 5:6 and note). *darting snakes.* See 14:29.

their treasures[d] on the humps of
camels,
to that unprofitable nation,
[7] to Egypt, whose help is utterly
useless.[e]
Therefore I call her
Rahab[f] the Do-Nothing.

[8]Go now, write it on a tablet[g] for them,
inscribe it on a scroll,[h]
that for the days to come
it may be an everlasting witness.[i]
[9]These are rebellious[j] people, deceitful[k]
children,
children unwilling to listen to the
LORD's instruction.[l]
[10]They say to the seers,[m]
"See no more visions[n]!"
and to the prophets,
"Give us no more visions of what is
right!
Tell us pleasant things,[o]
prophesy illusions.[p]
[11]Leave this way,[q]
get off this path,
and stop confronting[r] us
with the Holy One[s] of Israel!"

[12]Therefore, this is what the Holy One[t]
of Israel says:

"Because you have rejected this
message,[u]
relied on oppression[v]
and depended on deceit,
[13]this sin will become for you
like a high wall,[w] cracked and
bulging,
that collapses[x] suddenly,[y] in an
instant.
[14]It will break in pieces like pottery,[z]
shattered so mercilessly
that among its pieces not a fragment
will be found
for taking coals from a hearth
or scooping water out of a cistern."

[15]This is what the Sovereign[a] LORD, the
Holy One[b] of Israel, says:

"In repentance and rest[c] is your
salvation,
in quietness and trust[d] is your
strength,
but you would have none of it.[e]
[16]You said, 'No, we will flee[f] on
horses.'[g]
Therefore you will flee!
You said, 'We will ride off on swift
horses.'
Therefore your pursuers will be
swift!
[17]A thousand will flee
at the threat of one;
at the threat of five[h]
you will all flee[i] away,
till you are left[j]
like a flagstaff on a mountaintop,
like a banner[k] on a hill."

[18]Yet the LORD longs[l] to be gracious to
you;
he rises to show you compassion.[m]
For the LORD is a God of justice.[n]
Blessed are all who wait for him![o]

[19]O people of Zion, who live in Jerusalem, you will weep no more.[p] How gracious he will be when you cry for help![q]
As soon as he hears, he will answer[r] you.
[20]Although the Lord gives you the bread[s]
of adversity and the water of affliction,
your teachers[t] will be hidden[u] no more;
with your own eyes you will see them.
[21]Whether you turn to the right or to the
left, your ears will hear a voice[v] behind
you, saying, "This is the way;[w] walk in it."
[22]Then you will defile your idols[x] overlaid
with silver and your images covered with
gold;[y] you will throw them away like a
menstrual[z] cloth and say to them, "Away
with you![a]"

30:6 [d]S Isa 15:7 **30:7** [e]S 2Ki 18:21; S Jer 2:36 [f]S Job 9:13 **30:8** [g]S Dt 27:8 [h]S Ex 17:14; S Isa 8:1; Jer 25:13; 30:2; 36:28; Hab 2:2 [i]Jos 24:26-27 **30:9** [j]S Ps 78:8; S Isa 1:2; S Eze 2:6 [k]Isa 28:15; 59:3-4 [l]S Isa 1:10 **30:10** [m]S 1Sa 9:9 [n]Jer 11:21; 32:3; Am 7:13 [o]S 1Ki 22:8; S Jer 4:10 [p]Jer 23:26; 25:9; 26:9; 36:29; Eze 13:7; Ro 16:18; 2Ti 4:3-4 **30:11** [q]ver 21; Pr 3:6; Isa 35:8-9; 48:17 [r]S Job 21:14 [s]S Isa 29:19 **30:12** [t]ver 15; S Isa 5:19; 31:1 [u]S Isa 5:24 [v]S Ps 10:7; S 12:5; S Isa 5:7 **30:13** [w]S Ne 2:17; Ps 62:3; S 80:12 [x]S 1Ki 20:30 [y]S Isa 17:14 **30:14** [z]S Ps 2:9 **30:15** [a]Jer 7:20; Eze 3:11 [b]S ver 12 [c]S Ex 14:14; S Jos 1:13 [d]S 2Ch 20:12; Isa 32:17 [e]Isa 8:6; 42:24; 57:17 **30:16** [f]Jer 46:6 [g]S Dt 17:16; 1Ki 10:28-29; S Ps 20:7; Isa 31:1,3; 36:8 **30:17** [h]S Lev 26:8 [i]Lev 26:36; Dt 28:25; S 2Ki 7:7 [j]S Isa 1:8 [k]S Ps 20:5 **30:18** [l]S Ge 43:31; Isa 42:14; 2Pe 3:9,15 [m]Ps 78:38; Isa 48:9; Jnh 3:10 [n]S Ps 11:7; S Isa 5:16 [o]S Ps 27:14; Isa 25:9; 33:2; 40:31; 64:4; La 3:25; Da 12:12 **30:19** [p]S Isa 25:8; 60:20; 61:3 [q]S Job 24:12 [r]Job 22:27; Ps 50:15; S 86:7; Isa 41:17; 58:9; 65:24; Zec 13:9; Mt 7:7-11 **30:20** [s]1Ki 22:27 [t]S Isa 28:9 [u]Ps 74:9; Am 8:11 **30:21** [v]S Isa 29:24 [w]S ver 11; S Job 33:11 **30:22** [x]S Ex 32:4; S Isa 17:8 [y]S Job 22:24; Isa 31:7 [z]Lev 15:19-23 [a]Eze 7:19-20

30:7 *Rahab.* A mythical sea monster, here symbolic of Egypt. The name itself means "storm," and also "arrogance." See 27:1 ("Leviathan") and note.
30:8 *write it.* Probably the name "Rahab the Do-Nothing."
30:9 *rebellious people.* See v. 1; see also 1:2 and note.
30:10 *seers.* See 1Sa 9:9 and note; 2Ki 17:13. *See no more visions.* Cf. Am 2:12; 7:13,16; Mic 2:6. *Tell us pleasant things.* As false prophets do (see 1Ki 22:13; Jer 6:14; 8:11; 23:16–17,26; Mic 2:11; 3:5,11 and notes; cf. 2Ti 4:3–4 and note on 4:3).
30:11–12,15 *Holy One of Israel.* See 1:4 and note.
30:12 *oppression.* Especially in their domestic policy (see 1:15–17,23; 5:7; 29:21; 58:3–4; 59:3,6–8,13). *deceit.* Especially in their foreign policy (see vv. 1–2; 29:15).
30:13 *like a high wall.* Oppression and deceit (v. 12) had been the "wall" they built to assure their safety and prosperity, but it will be shattered to pieces.
30:15 See 26:3. *repentance and rest.* The true way to salvation and security.
30:16 *horses.* See Ps 20:7–8 and note; 33:17; Pr 21:31 and note.
30:17 *A thousand will flee.* A fulfillment of the curse of Dt 32:30. *flagstaff … banner.* See 5:26 and note (see also 1:8 and note).
30:18 *longs to be gracious.* After punishing Israel, God will once again bless them (cf. 40:2 and note).
30:19 *weep no more.* See 25:8 and note. God's response is similar to his zeal for the vineyard (Israel) in 27:2–6 (see notes there).
30:20 *bread of adversity … water of affliction.* Prisoners' food (see 1Ki 22:27). *teachers.* Prophets, like Isaiah. Or the Hebrew for "teachers" can be rendered "Teacher" and be referred to the Lord, who will instruct them, and this time they will respond with obedience (vv. 21–22); cf. Jer 31:31–34; Eze 11:19–20; 36:25–27.
30:21 *This is the way; walk in it.* See Dt 5:32–33. Contrast the attitude shown in v. 9 (cf. 29:24; Jer 6:16 and note).
30:22 *defile your idols.* In repentance, not in despair as in 2:20 (see note there).

23He will also send you rain[b] for the
seed you sow in the ground, and the food
that comes from the land will be rich[c] and
plentiful.[d] In that day[e] your cattle will
graze in broad meadows.[f] 24The oxen[g]
and donkeys that work the soil will eat
fodder[h] and mash, spread out with fork[i]
and shovel. 25In the day of great slaughter,[j] when the towers[k] fall, streams of water will flow[l] on every high mountain and
every lofty hill. 26The moon will shine like
the sun,[m] and the sunlight will be seven
times brighter, like the light of seven full
days, when the LORD binds up the bruises
of his people and heals[n] the wounds he
inflicted.

27See, the Name[o] of the LORD comes from
afar,
with burning anger[p] and dense
clouds of smoke;
his lips are full of wrath,[q]
and his tongue is a consuming
fire.[r]
28His breath[s] is like a rushing torrent,[t]
rising up to the neck.[u]
He shakes the nations in the sieve[v]
of destruction;
he places in the jaws of the peoples
a bit[w] that leads them astray.
29And you will sing
as on the night you celebrate a
holy festival;[x]
your hearts will rejoice[y]
as when people go up with
flutes[z]
to the mountain[a] of the LORD,
to the Rock[b] of Israel.
30The LORD will cause men to hear
his majestic voice[c]
and will make them see his arm[d]
coming down
with raging anger[e] and consuming
fire,[f]
with cloudburst, thunderstorm[g]
and hail.[h]
31The voice of the LORD will shatter
Assyria;[i]
with his scepter he will strike[j] them
down.
32Every stroke the LORD lays on them
with his punishing rod[k]
will be to the music of tambourines[l]
and harps,
as he fights them in battle with the
blows of his arm.[m]
33Topheth[n] has long been prepared;
it has been made ready for the
king.
Its fire pit has been made deep and
wide,
with an abundance of fire and
wood;
the breath[o] of the LORD,
like a stream of burning sulfur,[p]
sets it ablaze.[q]

Woe to Those Who Rely on Egypt

31 Woe[r] to those who go down to
Egypt[s] for help,
who rely on horses,[t]
who trust in the multitude of their
chariots[u]
and in the great strength of their
horsemen,
but do not look to the Holy One[v] of
Israel,
or seek help from the LORD.[w]

30:23 [b]S Dt 28:12; Isa 65:21-22 [c]Isa 25:6; 55:2; Jer 31:14 [d]S Job 36:31; Isa 62:8 [e]S Isa 28:5 [f]S Ps 65:13 **30:24** [g]Isa 32:14, 20 [h]S Job 6:5 [i]Mt 3:12; Lk 3:17 **30:25** [j]S Isa 13:5; 34:6; 65:12; Jer 25:32; 50:27 [k]S Isa 2:15 [l]S Ex 17:6; Isa 32:2; 41:18; Joel 3:18; Zec 14:8 **30:26** [m]Isa 24:23; 60:19-20; Zec 14:7; Rev 21:23; 22:5 [n]S Dt 32:39; S 2Ch 7:14; Ps 107:20; S Isa 1:5; Jer 3:22; 17:14; Hos 14:4 **30:27** [o]1Ki 18:24; Ps 20:1; Isa 59:19; 64:2 [p]Isa 26:20; 66:14; Eze 22:31 [q]Isa 10:5; 13:5 [r]S ver 30; S Job 41:21 **30:28** [s]S Isa 11:4 [t]S Ps 50:3; S Isa 28:15 [u]S Isa 8:8 [v]Am 9:9 [w]2Ki 19:28 **30:29** [x]Isa 25:6 [y]Isa 12:1 [z]S 1Sa 10:5 [a]S Ps 42:4; Mt 26:30 [b]S Ge 49:24 **30:30** [c]S Ps 68:33 [d]Isa 9:12; 40:10; 51:9; 52:10; 53:1; 59:16; 62:8; 63:12

[e]S ver 27; S Isa 10:25 [f]S Isa 4:4; 47:14 [g]Ex 20:18; Ps 29:3 [h]S Ex 9:18 **30:31** [i]S Isa 10:5, 12 [j]S Isa 11:4 **30:32** [k]Isa 10:26 [l]S Ex 15:20 [m]S Isa 11:15; Eze 32:10 **30:33** [n]S 2Ki 23:10 [o]S Ex 15:10; S 2Sa 22:16 [p]S Ge 19:24; S Rev 9:17 [q]S Isa 1:31 **31:1** [r]S Isa 28:1 [s]S Dt 17:16; S Isa 30:2, 5; S Jer 37:5 [t]S Isa 30:16 [u]S Isa 2:7 [v]Job 6:10; S Isa 1:4; S 30:12 [w]S Dt 20:1; S Pr 21:31; S Isa 9:13; Jer 46:9; Eze 29:16

30:23 *rain ... food ... rich and plentiful.* Part of the covenant blessings promised in Dt 28:11–12. See 5:6 and note. *In that day.* Cf. 29:18; see notes on 10:20,27; 26:1. *cattle will graze.* Cf. 32:20 and note.
30:24 *mash.* Seasoned, tasty fodder.
30:25 *day of great slaughter.* Cf. 24:1; 34:2,6 and note. Assyria's fall (v. 31) is one illustration. *streams ... on every high mountain.* Paradise-like conditions will return to the land (see 41:18; Ps 104:13–15 and notes).
30:26 *moon ... brighter.* The darkness will be past: Night will be like the day, and day will be illumined with sevenfold light. *binds up the bruises ... heals the wounds.* Israel was bruised politically because of the sins of the people (see 1:5–6; 61:1; Jer 33:6 and notes).
30:27 *the Name.* The revelation of God, especially his power and glory. *anger ... clouds of smoke.* The language of theophany (a manifestation or appearance of God). God is portrayed as coming in a storm (see v. 30; see also 28:2; 29:6; Job 38:1; Ps 18:7–15 and notes). *consuming fire.* Perhaps lightning.
30:28 *rising up to the neck.* The army of Assyria was similarly described in 8:8 (see note there). *bit.* Cf. 37:29.
30:29 *sing ... holy festival.* Perhaps the Passover, alluded to in 31:5 (cf. Mt 26:30). *mountain of the LORD.* Zion, where the temple was (see 2:2–4 and note). *Rock.* God himself (see 17:10 and note).
30:30–31 *voice.* Associated with thunder in Ex 20:18–19; Ps 29:3–9 (see note there).
30:30 *arm coming down.* See 9:12,17,21; 51:9 and notes. *cloudburst ... hail.* See 28:2.
30:31 *voice of the LORD will shatter.* Cf. 10:5; Ps 29:5–9.
30:32 *his punishing rod.* See 11:4 and note. *music of tambourines.* After a great victory the women rejoiced with singing and dancing (see Ex 15:20–21; Jdg 11:34 and notes; 1Sa 18:6).
30:33 *Topheth.* A region outside Jerusalem where children were sacrificed to Molech (see 2Ki 23:10; Jer 7:31–32; 19:6,11–14 and notes), the god of the Ammonites (see 1Ki 11:7). Thus it was a place of burning. *king.* Of Assyria (or perhaps a reference to Molech; see note on Jdg 10:6). *burning sulfur.* See 1:31; Ge 19:24 and notes.
31:1 See 30:1 and note. In shorter form, ch. 31 recapitulates the structure and content of ch. 30. *go down to Egypt.* See Ge 26:2. *horses ... chariots.* Egypt had large numbers of horses and chariots (see 1Ki 10:28–29 and notes). *Holy One of Israel.* See 1:4 and note.

2 Yet he too is wise[x] and can bring
disaster;[y]
he does not take back his words.[z]
He will rise up against the house of the
wicked,[a]
against those who help evildoers.
3 But the Egyptians[b] are men and not
God;[c]
their horses[d] are flesh and not spirit.
When the LORD stretches out his hand,[e]
he who helps will stumble,
he who is helped[f] will fall;
both will perish together.[g]

4 This is what the LORD says to me:

"As a lion[h] growls,
a great lion over his prey —
and though a whole band of
shepherds[i]
is called together against him,
he is not frightened by their shouts
or disturbed by their clamor[j] —
so the LORD Almighty will come down[k]
to do battle on Mount Zion and on
its heights.
5 Like birds hovering[l] overhead,
the LORD Almighty will shield[m]
Jerusalem;
he will shield it and deliver[n] it,
he will 'pass over'[o] it and will rescue
it."

6 Return[p] to him you have so greatly revolted[q] against, O Israelites. 7 For in that
day[r] every one of you will reject the idols
of silver and gold[s] your sinful hands have
made.[t]

8 "Assyria[u] will fall by a sword that is
not of man;
a sword, not of mortals, will devour[v]
them.
They will flee before the sword
and their young men will be put to
forced labor.[w]

31:2 [x]S Ps 92:5; Ro 16:27 [y]Isa 45:7; 47:11; Am 3:6 [z]Nu 23:19; S Pr 19:21 [a]S Isa 1:4; 29:15; 32:6 **31:3** [b]Isa 20:5; 36:9 [c]S Ps 9:20; Eze 28:9; 2Th 2:4 [d]S Isa 30:16 [e]Ne 1:10; S Job 30:21; Isa 9:17,21; Jer 51:25; Eze 20:34 [f]Isa 10:3; 30:5-7 [g]S Isa 20:6; Jer 17:5 **31:4** [h]Nu 24:9; S 1Sa 17:34; Hos 11:10; Am 3:8 [i]Jer 3:15; 23:4; Eze 34:23; Na 3:18 [j]Ps 74:23 [k]Isa 42:13 **31:5** [l]S Ge 1:2; S Mt 23:37 [m]S Ps 91:4; S Isa 5:2; S Zec 9:15 [n]S Ps 34:7; Isa 37:35; 38:6 [o]S Ex 12:23 **31:6** [p]S Job 22:23; S Isa 1:27 [q]S Isa 1:5 **31:7** [r]Isa 29:18 [s]S Isa 30:22 [t]S Ps 135:15 **31:8** [u]S Isa 10:12 [v]S Ex 12:12; Isa 10:12; 14:25; S 27:1; 33:1; 37:7; Jer 25:12; Hab 2:8 [w]S Ge 49:15; S Dt 20:11 **31:9** [x]Dt 32:31,37 [y]S Isa 18:3; S Jer 4:6 [z]Jer 51:9; Na 3:7 [a]S Isa 10:17 [b]Ps 21:9; Mal 4:1 **32:1** [c]S Ps 149:2; S Isa 6:5; 55:4; Eze 37:24

9 Their stronghold[x] will fall because of
terror;
at sight of the battle standard[y] their
commanders will panic,[z]"
declares the LORD,
whose fire[a] is in Zion,
whose furnace[b] is in Jerusalem.

The Kingdom of Righteousness

32 See, a king[c] will reign in
righteousness
and rulers will rule with justice.[d]
2 Each man will be like a shelter[e] from
the wind
and a refuge from the storm,[f]
like streams of water[g] in the desert[h]
and the shadow of a great rock in a
thirsty land.
3 Then the eyes of those who see will no
longer be closed,[i]
and the ears[j] of those who hear will
listen.
4 The mind of the rash will know and
understand,[k]
and the stammering tongue[l] will be
fluent and clear.
5 No longer will the fool[m] be called
noble
nor the scoundrel be highly
respected.
6 For the fool speaks folly,[n]
his mind is busy with evil:[o]
He practices ungodliness[p]
and spreads error[q] concerning the
LORD;
the hungry he leaves empty[r]
and from the thirsty he withholds
water.

[d]Ps 72:1-4; S Isa 9:7; S 28:6 **32:2** [e]S 1Ki 18:4 [f]S Ps 55:8 [g]S Ps 23:2; S Isa 30:25; 49:10; Jer 31:9 [h]S Ps 107:35; Isa 44:3 **32:3** [i]S Isa 29:18; 35:5; 42:7,16 [j]S Dt 29:4 **32:4** [k]Isa 6:10; S 29:24 [l]Isa 35:6 **32:5** [m]S 1Sa 25:25 **32:6** [n]S Pr 19:3 [o]S Pr 24:2; S Isa 26:10 [p]S Isa 9:17 [q]Isa 3:12; 9:16 [r]S Isa 3:15

31:2 *he too is wise.* People had questioned God's wisdom in 29:14–16 (see notes there).
31:3 *Egyptians are men and not God.* Cf. Hos 11:9. *God ... spirit.* See Jn 4:24 and note. *stretches out his hand.* Cf. the refrain in 5:25 (see note there); 9:12,17,21; 10:4. *he who helps will stumble.* Cf. 30:3,5.
31:4 *lion.* A simile, but perhaps also an allusion to the Assyrian king (see notes on 15:9; Jer 2:15). *shepherds.* Perhaps an allusion to the rulers of the nations (see NIV text note on Na 3:18).
31:5 *birds ... will shield.* Cf. Dt 32:10–11. *pass over.* The technical word used of the destroying angel who "passed over" every house in Egypt that had blood on the doorposts (see Ex 12:13,23 and notes). Cf. Isa 37:35.
31:6 *greatly revolted.* See 1:2 and note.
31:7 *reject the idols.* See 2:20 and note.
31:8 *sword, not of mortals.* The angel of the Lord struck down 185,000 soldiers (see 37:36 and note; see also Ps 7:12–13 and note). *put to forced labor.* As prisoners of war.
31:9 *stronghold.* Nineveh was destroyed by the Medes and Babylonians in 612 B.C. (see Na 3:7). *commanders will panic.* Cf. Na 2:10 and note. *fire ... furnace.* The Lord's glory resides in Zion, and from that center of his people his fire of judgment breaks out upon the wicked (see 10:17; 30:33 and note; cf. Lev 10:2; Joel 3:16 and note; Am 1:2 and note).
32:1 *king ... in righteousness.* The Messianic age is again in view (see 9:7; 11:4; 16:5 and notes). Cf. vv. 16–17; 33:17 and note.
32:2 *Each man will be like.* The Lord's redeemed, as sources of protection and blessing, will reflect him (see the rest of this note; see also vv. 3–8). *shelter ... refuge ... shadow.* Similar terms are applied to the Lord in 25:4 (see 4:5–6 and note). *streams ... in the desert.* See 35:6–7; 41:18; 49:10 and notes.
32:3 *eyes ... no longer be closed ... ears ... listen.* See 35:5 and note (contrast 6:9–10; see notes there).
32:5–8 The redeemed will no longer be among the fools. The contrast between the fool and the wise or noble is characteristic of wisdom literature (compare Pr 9:1–6 with Pr 9:13–18).
32:6 A full explication of what the OT calls a "fool" (see Pr 1:7 and note; see also NIV text note there). *fool speaks folly.* Cf. 9:16–17; Ps 14:1 and note; 53:1.

[7]The scoundrel's methods are wicked,[s]
he makes up evil schemes[t]
to destroy the poor with lies,
even when the plea of the needy[u] is
just.[v]
[8]But the noble man makes noble plans,
and by noble deeds[w] he stands.[x]

The Women of Jerusalem

[9]You women[y] who are so complacent,
rise up and listen[z] to me;
you daughters who feel secure,[a]
hear what I have to say!
[10]In little more than a year[b]
you who feel secure will tremble;
the grape harvest will fail,[c]
and the harvest of fruit will not come.
[11]Tremble,[d] you complacent women;
shudder, you daughters who feel
secure![e]
Strip off your clothes,[f]
put sackcloth[g] around your waists.
[12]Beat your breasts[h] for the pleasant
fields,
for the fruitful vines[i]
[13]and for the land of my people,
a land overgrown with thorns and
briers[j]—
yes, mourn[k] for all houses of
merriment
and for this city of revelry.[l]
[14]The fortress[m] will be abandoned,
the noisy city deserted;[n]
citadel and watchtower[o] will become a
wasteland forever,
the delight of donkeys,[p] a pasture for
flocks,[q]
[15]till the Spirit[r] is poured upon us from
on high,
and the desert becomes a fertile
field,[s]
and the fertile field seems like a
forest.[t]
[16]Justice[u] will dwell in the desert[v]
and righteousness[w] live in the fertile
field.
[17]The fruit of righteousness[x] will be
peace;[y]
the effect of righteousness will be
quietness and confidence[z]
forever.
[18]My people will live in peaceful[a]
dwelling places,
in secure homes,[b]
in undisturbed places of rest.[c]
[19]Though hail[d] flattens the forest[e]
and the city is leveled[f] completely,
[20]how blessed you will be,
sowing[g] your seed by every stream,[h]
and letting your cattle and donkeys
range free.[i]

Distress and Help

33 Woe[j] to you, O destroyer,
you who have not been destroyed!
Woe to you, O traitor,
you who have not been betrayed!
When you stop destroying,
you will be destroyed;[k]
when you stop betraying,
you will be betrayed.[l]
[2]O LORD, be gracious[m] to us;
we long for you.
Be our strength[n] every morning,
our salvation[o] in time of distress.[p]
[3]At the thunder of your voice,[q] the
peoples flee;[r]
when you rise up,[s] the nations
scatter.

32:7 [s]Jer 5:26-28; Da 12:10 [t]S Isa 29:20; Mic 7:3 [u]S Ps 72:4; Isa 29:19; 61:1 [v]S Isa 29:21 **32:8** [w]1Ch 29:9; S Pr 11:25 [x]Isa 14:24 **32:9** [y]S Isa 4:1 [z]Isa 28:23 [a]ver 11; Isa 47:8; Da 4:4; Am 6:1; Zep 2:15 **32:10** [b]Isa 37:30 [c]Isa 5:5-6; S 24:7 **32:11** [d]Isa 33:14 [e]S ver 9 [f]Isa 47:2; Mic 1:8; Na 3:5 [g]S Isa 3:24 **32:12** [h]Na 2:7 [i]Isa 16:9 **32:13** [j]S Isa 5:6; Hos 10:8 [k]S Isa 24:11 [l]S Isa 23:7 **32:14** [m]S Isa 13:22 [n]S Isa 6:11; S 27:10 [o]S Isa 2:15; 34:13 [p]S Ps 104:11 [q]S Isa 5:17 **32:15** [r]S Isa 11:2; S Eze 37:9 [s]Ps 107:35; Isa 35:1-2 [t]Isa 29:17 **32:16** [u]S Isa 9:7; S 28:6 [v]Isa 35:1,6; 42:11 [w]S Ps 48:1; S Isa 1:26 **32:17** [x]S Ps 85:10 [y]S Ps 119:165; S Isa 9:7; Ro 14:17; Heb 12:11; Jas 3:18 [z]S Isa 30:15 **32:18** [a]S Isa 2:4 [b]S Isa 26:1; 33:20; 37:33; 65:21; 66:14; Am 9:14

[c]S Jos 1:13; S Job 11:18; Hos 2:18-23 **32:19** [d]Isa 28:17 [e]S Isa 10:19; Zec 11:2 [f]S Job 40:11; S Isa 19:18; 24:10; 27:10 **32:20** [g]S Ecc 11:1 [h]S Dt 28:12 [i]Job 39:8; S Isa 30:24 **33:1** [j]S 2Ki 19:21; S Isa 28:1 [k]S Isa 31:8; S Mt 7:2 [l]S Isa 21:2; Jer 30:16; Eze 39:10 **33:2** [m]S Ge 43:29; S Ezr 9:8 [n]Isa 40:10; 51:9; 59:16; 63:5 [o]S Ps 13:5; S Isa 12:2 [p]S Isa 5:30 **33:3** [q]S Ps 46:6; S 68:33 [r]S Ps 68:1; S Isa 13:14 [s]ver 10; Nu 10:35; Ps 12:5; Isa 59:16-18

32:7 *plea of the needy.* See 1:17 and note.
32:8 *plans ... stands.* See 8:10 and note.
32:9 *women.* Cf. 3:16—4:1 and notes. *complacent ... feel secure.* See v. 11; Am 6:1 and note. These words are used in a good sense in v. 18 (the Hebrew for "undisturbed" is the same as that for "complacent").
32:10 *a year.* Perhaps the invasion of Sennacherib (701 B.C.) is in view. *grape harvest will fail.* Cf. 37:30. The armies of Assyria would bring widespread destruction, ruining the summer fruit.
32:11 *Strip.* Cf. 47:2–3 and notes. *sackcloth.* Cf. 3:24; 22:12; see notes on Ge 37:34; Rev 11:3.
32:12 *Beat your breasts.* Like the slave girls of Nineveh (Na 2:7). *for the fruitful vines.* Cf. the Lord's weeping in 16:9.
32:13 *thorns and briers.* See 5:6; 7:23 and notes. *merriment ... revelry.* See 22:2 and note; cf. Jer 16:8–9.
32:14 *fortress ... noisy city.* Assyria's invasion is a warning that Jerusalem (see 24:10 and note) will one day be destroyed. *donkeys ... flocks.* Cf. 7:25; 13:21–22; 34:13.
32:15 *till the Spirit is poured upon.* The outpouring of the Spirit is linked with abundance also in 44:3 (see note there; see also 11:2; Joel 2:28–32 and notes). *fertile field ... forest.* The forest probably stands for Lebanon (see 29:17 and note; cf. 35:1–2 and notes).
32:16 *Justice ... righteousness.* See v. 1 and note.
32:17 *peace.* Cf. 9:7; 11:6–9 and note. *quietness and confidence.* Contrast 30:15 ("you would have none of it").
32:18 *secure ... undisturbed.* See note on v. 9. *places of rest.* See 28:12 and note.
32:19 *hail.* Cf. 28:2. *forest.* Probably Assyria. See 10:33–34 and notes. *city.* See 24:10 and note.
32:20 The abundance of the day of the Lord is described (see 30:23–24 and notes).
33:1 *Woe.* See note on 28:1—35:10. *destroyer ... traitor.* Probably Assyria—depicted as treacherous (see 10:5–6; 16:4; 21:2; 24:16 and notes).
33:2–9 A prayer asking the Lord to bring about the promised destruction of Assyria.
33:2 *be gracious.* See 30:18 and note; cf. Nu 6:25. *strength ... salvation.* See 12:2 and note; cf. 59:16 and note. *every morning.* See Ps 88:13; 143:8 and note; see also introduction to Ps 57. *distress.* See 37:3.
33:3 *thunder of your voice.* See 30:30–31 and note. *rise up ... scatter.* An allusion to Nu 10:35–36 (see notes there); cf. Ps 68:1 and note.

4 Your plunder,[t] O nations, is harvested[u]
as by young locusts;[v]
like a swarm of locusts men pounce
on it.
5 The LORD is exalted,[w] for he dwells on
high;[x]
he will fill Zion with justice[y] and
righteousness.[z]
6 He will be the sure foundation for
your times,
a rich store of salvation[a] and
wisdom and knowledge;
the fear[b] of the LORD is the key to
this treasure.[a][c]
7 Look, their brave men[d] cry aloud in
the streets;
the envoys[e] of peace weep bitterly.
8 The highways are deserted,
no travelers[f] are on the roads.[g]
The treaty is broken,[h]
its witnesses[b] are despised,
no one is respected.
9 The land mourns[c][i] and wastes away,
Lebanon[j] is ashamed and
withers;[k]
Sharon[l] is like the Arabah,
and Bashan[m] and Carmel[n] drop
their leaves.
10 "Now will I arise,[o]" says the LORD.
"Now will I be exalted;[p]
now will I be lifted up.
11 You conceive[q] chaff,
you give birth[r] to straw;
your breath is a fire[s] that consumes
you.
12 The peoples will be burned as if to
lime;[t]
like cut thornbushes[u] they will be set
ablaze.[v]"

33:4 [t]S Nu 14:3; S 2Ki 7:16 [u]S Isa 17:5; Joel 3:13 [v]Joel 1:4 **33:5** [w]S Isa 5:16 [x]S Job 16:19 [y]S Isa 9:7; S 28:6 [z]S Isa 1:26 **33:6** [a]S Isa 12:2; 26:1; 51:6; 60:18 [b]S Pr 1:7; Isa 11:2-3; Mt 6:33 [c]S Ge 39:3; S Job 22:25 **33:7** [d]Isa 10:34 [e]S 2Ki 18:37 **33:8** [f]Isa 60:15; Zec 7:14 [g]S Jdg 5:6; Isa 30:21; 35:8 [h]S 2Ki 18:14 **33:9** [i]S Isa 3:26 [j]S 2Ki 19:23; Isa 2:13; 35:2; 37:24; Jer 22:6 [k]S Isa 15:6 [l]S 1Ch 27:29 [m]Mic 7:14 [n]1Ki 18:19; Isa 35:2; Na 1:4 **33:10** [o]S ver 3; Isa 2:21 [p]S Isa 5:16 **33:11** [q]Ps 7:14; Isa 59:4; Jas 1:15 [r]S Isa 26:18 [s]Isa 1:31 **33:12** [t]Am 2:1 [u]S Isa 5:6 [v]S Isa 10:17; S 27:11 **33:13** [w]Ps 48:10; 49:1 [x]Isa 34:1; 48:16; 49:1 **33:14** [y]S Isa 1:28 [z]S Isa 32:11 [a]S Isa 1:31; S 30:30; S Zec 13:9; Heb 12:29 **33:15** [b]Isa 58:8 [c]Ps 15:2; 24:4 [d]Eze 22:13; 33:31 [e]S Pr 15:27

13 You who are far away,[w] hear[x] what I
have done;
you who are near, acknowledge my
power!
14 The sinners[y] in Zion are terrified;
trembling[z] grips the godless:
"Who of us can dwell with the
consuming fire?[a]
Who of us can dwell with everlasting
burning?"
15 He who walks righteously[b]
and speaks what is right,[c]
who rejects gain from extortion[d]
and keeps his hand from accepting
bribes,[e]
who stops his ears against plots of
murder
and shuts his eyes[f] against
contemplating evil—
16 this is the man who will dwell on the
heights,[g]
whose refuge[h] will be the mountain
fortress.[i]
His bread will be supplied,
and water will not fail[j] him.
17 Your eyes will see the king[k] in his
beauty[l]
and view a land that stretches afar.[m]
18 In your thoughts you will ponder the
former terror:[n]
"Where is that chief officer?
Where is the one who took the
revenue?
Where is the officer in charge of
the towers?[o]"

[a] 6 Or *is a treasure from him* [b] 8 Dead Sea Scrolls; Masoretic Text / *the cities* [c] 9 Or *dries up*

[f]Ps 119:37 **33:16** [g]S Dt 32:13 [h]S Ps 46:1; S Isa 25:4 [i]Ps 18:1-2; Isa 26:1 [j]Isa 48:21; 49:10; 65:13 **33:17** [k]S Isa 6:5 [l]S Isa 4:2 [m]S Isa 26:15 **33:18** [n]S Isa 17:14 [o]S Isa 2:15

33:5 *fill … righteousness.* See 1:26; 32:1 and note.
33:6 *wisdom … knowledge … fear of the LORD.* Terms linked with the Messiah in 11:2 (see note there). See 9:6; Pr 1:7 and notes.
33:7 *their brave men.* The men of Judah, during Sennacherib's invasion of 701 B.C. (see 10:28–34 and notes). *envoys of peace.* Perhaps the three officials who conferred with the Assyrian field commander (see 36:3,22).
33:8 *highways are deserted.* Travel and trade were impossible, creating economic hardship (see Jdg 5:6 and note). *treaty.* Perhaps the agreement made when Hezekiah paid large sums to Sennacherib (see 2Ki 18:14 and note).
33:9 *land … wastes away.* Farmland and pastures were ruined by the invaders. See 24:4 and note. *Lebanon.* Renowned for its cedars (2:13) and wildlife (40:16). *Sharon.* A plain along the Mediterranean coast north of Joppa, known for its beautiful foliage and superb grazing land (see 35:2 and note; 65:10; 1Ch 27:29). *Arabah.* A very dry area along the lower Jordan River and the Dead Sea (see Dt 1:1; 2:8 and notes). *Bashan.* See 2:13 and note. *Carmel.* See note on 1Ki 18:19; means "fertile field" (as in 29:17; 32:15) or "orchards" (as in 16:10) and is also associated with lush pasturelands (see 35:2 and note; Mic 7:14 and NIV text note; Na 1:4 and note).
33:10 *be exalted.* Through the judgment he brings on his rebellious people (see v. 14 and note).
33:11 *conceive … give birth.* Cf. 26:18. *breath is a fire.* They only produce what results in their destruction.
33:12 *to lime.* The burning will be complete (see Am 2:1). *thornbushes.* They burn very quickly (see 27:4; 2Sa 23:6–7).
33:13 *hear … acknowledge.* Cf. 34:1.
33:14 *sinners in Zion.* See 1:27–28 and note; 4:4. *consuming fire.* The presence of the God of judgment (see 29:6; 30:27,30; Ex 24:17; Dt 4:24; 9:3; 2Sa 22:9; Ps 18:8; Heb 12:29).
33:15 Similar requirements are found in Ps 15:2–5; 24:3–6 (see notes there). *bribes.* See 1:23.
33:16 *heights … fortress.* Symbolic of the security found in God (cf. Ps 18:2 and note). *bread … water.* Cf. 49:10.
33:17 *king.* See 32:1 and note; cf. 6:1,5 and notes. *in his beauty.* Reflecting on the splendor and majesty of a Davidic king; probably a foreshadowing of the Messianic kingdom (cf. 4:2; Ps 45:3–5 and notes; contrast Isa 53:2–3 [see notes there]). *land … afar.* See 26:15 and note.
33:18 *former terror.* The Assyrian invasion (see 17:12–14 and note). *revenue.* Forced tribute (see note on v. 8). *towers.* Judah's fortifications were probably under strict Assyrian control (see 2:15).

[19] You will see those arrogant people[p] no more,
those people of an obscure speech,
with their strange, incomprehensible tongue.[q]

[20] Look upon Zion,[r] the city of our festivals;
your eyes will see Jerusalem,
a peaceful abode,[s] a tent[t] that will not be moved;[u]
its stakes will never be pulled up,
nor any of its ropes broken.
[21] There the LORD will be our Mighty[v] One.
It will be like a place of broad rivers and streams.[w]
No galley with oars will ride them,
no mighty ship[x] will sail them.
[22] For the LORD is our judge,[y]
the LORD is our lawgiver,[z]
the LORD is our king;[a]
it is he who will save[b] us.

[23] Your rigging hangs loose:
The mast is not held secure,
the sail is not spread.
Then an abundance of spoils will be divided
and even the lame[c] will carry off plunder.[d]
[24] No one living in Zion will say, "I am ill";[e]
and the sins of those who dwell there will be forgiven.[f]

Judgment Against the Nations

34 Come near, you nations, and listen;[g]
pay attention, you peoples![h]
Let the earth[i] hear, and all that is in it,
the world, and all that comes out of it![j]
[2] The LORD is angry with all nations;
his wrath[k] is upon all their armies.
He will totally destroy[a][l] them,
he will give them over to slaughter.[m]
[3] Their slain[n] will be thrown out,
their dead bodies[o] will send up a stench;[p]
the mountains will be soaked with their blood.[q]
[4] All the stars of the heavens will be dissolved[r]
and the sky rolled up[s] like a scroll;
all the starry host will fall[t]
like withered[u] leaves from the vine,
like shriveled figs from the fig tree.

[5] My sword[v] has drunk its fill in the heavens;
see, it descends in judgment on Edom,[w]
the people I have totally destroyed.[x]
[6] The sword[y] of the LORD is bathed in blood,
it is covered with fat—
the blood of lambs and goats,
fat from the kidneys of rams.
For the LORD has a sacrifice[z] in Bozrah[a]
and a great slaughter[b] in Edom.

a 2 The Hebrew term refers to the irrevocable giving over of things or persons to the LORD, often by totally destroying them; also in verse 5.

33:19 [p] S Ps 5:5 [q] S Ge 11:7; S Isa 28:11 **33:20** [r] S Ps 125:1 [s] S Isa 32:18 [t] S Ge 26:22 [u] ver 6; Ps 46:5 **33:21** [v] S Isa 10:34 [w] S Ex 17:6; S Ps 1:3; Isa 32:2; 41:18; 48:18; 49:10; 66:12; Na 3:8 [x] Isa 23:1 **33:22** [y] Isa 11:4 [z] S Isa 2:3; Jas 4:12 [a] S Ps 89:18 [b] S Isa 25:9 **33:23** [c] S 2Ki 7:8 [d] S 2Ki 7:16 **33:24** [e] S Isa 30:26 [f] S Nu 23:21; S 2Ch 6:21; Isa 43:1; 48:20; Jer 31:34; 33:8; 1Jn 1:7-9 **34:1** [g] S Isa 33:13 [h] Isa 41:1; 43:9 [i] S Dt 4:26; Ps 49:1 [j] Ps 24:1 **34:2** [k] S Isa 10:25 [l] S Isa 13:5; S Zec 5:3 [m] S Isa 30:25 **34:3** [n] S Isa 5:25; S 10:4 [o] S Ps 110:6; Eze 39:11 [p] Joel 2:20; Am 4:10 [q] ver 7; S 2Sa 1:22; Isa 63:6; Eze 5:17; 14:19; 32:6; 35:6; 38:22 **34:4** [r] S Job 9:7; S Isa 13:13; 2Pe 3:10 [s] Isa 38:12; Heb 1:12 [t] S Mt 24:29*; Mk 13:25* [u] S Job 8:12; S Isa 15:6; Mt 21:19 **34:5** [v] Dt 32:41-42; Jer 47:6; Eze 21:5; Zec 13:7 [w] S 2Sa 8:13-14; S 2Ch 28:17; Am 1:11-12 [x] S Dt 13:15; S Jos 6:17; Isa 24:6; Am 3:14-15; 6:11 **34:6** [y] S Dt 32:41; S Isa 27:1 [z] S Lev 3:9 [a] S Ge 36:33 [b] S Isa 30:25; S Jer 25:34; Rev 19:17

33:19 *arrogant.* Cf. 10:12 and note. *obscure speech.* The Assyrian language was related to Hebrew but was different enough to sound strange to Israelite ears. See 28:11; Dt 28:49.
33:20 *Look upon Zion.* The redeemed city, in contrast to the city described in vv. 7–9. *festivals.* See 1:14 and note. *peaceful abode.* See 32:17–18 and notes. *tent … not … moved.* Her exile will be over. *stakes … ropes.* Cf. the similar description of Jerusalem in 54:2.
33:21 *Mighty One.* See 10:34 (cf. Ps 93:3–4 and notes). *broad rivers.* To prevent easy access to her borders—thus like Tyre (23:1) or Thebes (see Na 3:8 and note).
33:22 *our judge.* See 2:4; 11:4 and note. *our lawgiver.* See 2:3; 51:4 and note. *our king.* See v. 17; 32:1 and notes; see also Ps 46; 48. *save.* See Jdg 2:16–19 and note.
33:23 *rigging.* Jerusalem is pictured as a ship, unprepared to sail into battle against Assyria. *Then.* When God strikes down the Assyrian army (see 10:33–34; 37:36 and notes). *plunder.* See v. 4.
33:24 Looking beyond Isaiah's own day to the physically and spiritually whole Jerusalem of vv. 17,20–22.
34:1—35:10 Chs. 34–35 conclude chs. 28–33 and comprise an eschatological section corresponding to chs. 24–27, which conclude chs. 13–23 (see note on 24:1—27:13).
34:2 *angry … wrath.* In the day of the Lord (see 2:11,17,20; 26:20–21 and notes). See also 13:3,13 and notes. *totally destroy.* The kind of destruction visited on the Canaanites. See NIV text note; see also v. 5; Jos 6:17 and note. *slaughter.* See 30:25 and note.
34:3 *thrown out.* Not to have a proper burial was considered a disgrace (see 14:19 and note).
34:4 *stars … dissolved.* Disturbances in the heavens characterize the day of the Lord (see 13:10,13 and notes; cf. Eze 32:7–8). *sky … scroll … starry host will fall.* Referred to in Mk 13:25 (see note on 13:24–25); Rev 6:13–14 in connection with the "great distress" (Mt 24:21) and the second coming of Christ. *withered leaves.* Cf. 24:4; 40:7–8.
34:5–6 *My sword … The sword of the LORD.* See Ps 7:12–13 and note.
34:5 *drunk its fill.* Cf. Eze 39:18–20 and notes. *Edom.* Symbolic of all the enemies of God and his people, like Moab in 25:10–12 (see note on 25:10). See note on 21:11. The Edomites were driven from their homeland by the Nabatean Arabs, perhaps as early as 500 B.C.
34:6 *fat.* Considered the best part of the meat, and therefore offered to the Lord in the sacrifices (see Lev 3:9–11). *lambs and goats.* Symbolizing the people. *sacrifice.* Battles are often compared to sacrifices (see Jer 46:10 and note; 50:27; Eze 39:17–19 and notes; cf. Rev 19:17–18). *Bozrah.* An important city of Edom and a sheepherding center, it was located about 25 miles southeast of the southern end of the Dead Sea. The name means "grape-gathering" (cf. 63:1–3).

7 And the wild oxen[c] will fall with them,
the bull calves and the great bulls.[d]
Their land will be drenched with
blood,[e]
and the dust will be soaked with fat.
8 For the LORD has a day[f] of vengeance,[g]
a year of retribution,[h] to uphold
Zion's cause.
9 Edom's streams will be turned into
pitch,
her dust into burning sulfur;[i]
her land will become blazing pitch!
10 It will not be quenched[j] night and day;
its smoke will rise forever.[k]
From generation to generation[l] it will
lie desolate;[m]
no one will ever pass through it
again.
11 The desert owl[a][n] and screech owl[a] will
possess it;
the great owl[a] and the raven[o] will
nest there.
God will stretch out over Edom[p]
the measuring line of chaos[q]
and the plumb line[r] of desolation.
12 Her nobles will have nothing there to
be called a kingdom,
all her princes[s] will vanish[t] away.
13 Thorns[u] will overrun her citadels,
nettles and brambles her strongholds.[v]
She will become a haunt for jackals,[w]
a home for owls.[x]
14 Desert creatures[y] will meet with
hyenas,[z]
and wild goats will bleat to each
other;
there the night creatures[a] will also
repose
and find for themselves places of
rest.
15 The owl will nest there and lay eggs,
she will hatch them, and care for her
young under the shadow of her
wings;[b]
there also the falcons[c] will gather,
each with its mate.

16 Look in the scroll[d] of the LORD and
read:

None of these will be missing,[e]
not one will lack her mate.
For it is his mouth[f] that has given the
order,[g]
and his Spirit will gather them
together.
17 He allots their portions;[h]
his hand distributes them by
measure.
They will possess it forever
and dwell there from generation to
generation.[i]

Joy of the Redeemed

35 The desert[j] and the parched land
will be glad;
the wilderness will rejoice and
blossom.[k]
Like the crocus,[l] 2 it will burst into
bloom;
it will rejoice greatly and shout for
joy.[m]
The glory of Lebanon[n] will be given
to it,
the splendor of Carmel[o] and Sharon;[p]
they will see the glory[q] of the LORD,
the splendor of our God.[r]

3 Strengthen the feeble hands,
steady the knees[s] that give way;
4 say[t] to those with fearful hearts,[u]
"Be strong, do not fear;[v]
your God will come,[w]
he will come with vengeance;[x]

34:7 [c]S Nu 23:22 [d]S Ps 68:30 [e]S 2Sa 1:22 **34:8** [f]S Isa 2:12 [g]S Isa 1:24; 35:4; 47:3; 63:4 [h]Isa 59:18; Eze 25:12-17; Joel 3:4; Am 1:6-8, 9-10 **34:9** [i]S Ge 19:24 **34:10** [j]S Isa 1:31 [k]Rev 14:10-11; 19:3 [l]ver 17 [m]Isa 13:20; 24:1; Jer 49:18; Eze 29:12; 35:3; Mal 1:3 **34:11** [n]S Lev 11:16-18; S Dt 14:15-17; Rev 18:2 [o]S Ge 8:7 [p]Isa 21:11; Eze 35:15; Joel 3:19; Ob 1:1; Mal 1:4 [q]S Ge 1:2 [r]S 2Ki 21:13; Am 7:8 **34:12** [s]Job 12:21; Ps 107:40; Isa 40:23; Jer 21:7; 27:20; 39:6; Eze 24:5 [t]Isa 29:20; 41:11-12 **34:13** [u]S Isa 5:6; S 7:19 [v]S Isa 13:22 [w]Ps 44:19; S Isa 13:22; Jer 9:11; 10:22 [x]S Lev 11:16-18 **34:14** [y]S Ps 74:14 [z]Isa 13:22 [a]Rev 18:2 **34:15** [b]S Ps 17:8 [c]Dt 14:13 **34:16** [d]Isa 30:8 [e]Isa 40:26; 48:13 [f]Isa 1:20; 58:14 [g]S Isa 1:20 **34:17** [h]Isa 17:14; Jer 13:25 [i]ver 10 **35:1** [j]Isa 27:10; 32:15, 16; 41:18-19 [k]Isa 27:6; 51:3 [l]SS 2:1

[a] *11* The precise identification of these birds is uncertain.

35:2 [m]S Ge 21:6; Ps 105:43; Isa 12:6; S 25:9; 44:23; 51:11; 52:9; 55:12 [n]S Ezr 3:7; S Isa 33:9 [o]SS 7:5 [p]S 1Ch 27:29; Isa 65:10 [q]S Ex 16:7; S Isa 4:5; S 59:19 [r]S Isa 25:9 **35:3** [s]S Job 4:4; Heb 12:12 **35:4** [t]2Ch 32:6; Isa 40:2; Zec 1:13 [u]S Dt 20:3; S Isa 21:4 [v]S Jos 1:9; S Isa 7:4; Da 10:19 [w]Isa 40:9, 10-11; 51:5; 62:11; Rev 22:12 [x]S Isa 1:24; S 34:8

34:7 *wild oxen ... great bulls.* Symbolizing the troops and/or leaders of the nations. *drenched with blood.* See v. 3.
34:8 *day of vengeance.* See 35:4; 61:2. The Edomites opposed Israel at every opportunity (see 2Sa 8:13–14) and rejoiced when Jerusalem was destroyed (see La 4:21; see also Ps 137:7; Jer 49:8 and notes). But Edom's day would come (see 63:1–4 and notes).
34:9 *burning sulfur.* Edom's destruction is compared with the overthrow of Sodom and Gomorrah (see Jer 49:17–18 and notes). See also 1:31; Ge 19:24 and notes.
34:10 *smoke ... forever.* Applied to Babylon in Rev 19:3 (see also Rev 14:10–11 and notes). *lie desolate.* See 13:20–22; Mal 1:3–4 and notes.
34:11 *desert owl ... screech owl ... great owl ... raven.* Ceremonially unclean birds (see Dt 14:14–17). Such birds would also live in the ruins of Babylon (13:21) and Nineveh (Zep 2:14). *measuring line ... plumb line.* Cf. 28:17 and note. *chaos ... desolation.* The Hebrew for these words is used in Ge 1:2 (see note there) to describe the earth in its "formless" and "empty" state (see also Jer 4:23 and note).
34:13 *Thorns ... nettles.* Cf. 7:24–25.
34:14 *Desert creatures ... hyenas.* See 13:20–22 and note. *wild goats.* Sometimes connected with demons (see note on 13:21).
34:15 *owl ... falcons.* Ceremonially unclean (see v. 11 and note; Dt 14:13,15–17).
34:16 *scroll.* After the destruction of Edom, people will read this prophecy given by Isaiah. *these.* The creatures just listed.
34:17 *allots their portions.* God will give the creatures of vv. 11,13–15 clear title to the land of Edom.
35:1 *desert ... will be glad.* The personification of nature is common in Isaiah (see 33:9; 44:23; 55:12). *wilderness.* The Arabah (see note on 33:9). *crocus.* See NIV text note on SS 2:1.
35:2 *rejoice ... shout for joy.* See 54:1 and note. *Lebanon ... Carmel ... Sharon.* Fertile areas renowned for their beautiful trees and foliage (see note on 33:9). *glory of the LORD.* In the great transformation just announced. See 6:3 and note.
35:3 See Heb 12:12.
35:4 *Be strong, do not fear.* Cf. God's words of encouragement to Joshua in Jos 1:6–7,9 (see note on Jos 1:18). *God will come.*

with divine retribution
he will come to save[y] you."

5 Then will the eyes of the blind be
opened[z]
and the ears of the deaf[a] unstopped.
6 Then will the lame[b] leap like a deer,[c]
and the mute tongue[d] shout for joy.[e]
Water will gush forth in the wilderness
and streams[f] in the desert.
7 The burning sand will become a pool,
the thirsty ground[g] bubbling
springs.[h]
In the haunts where jackals[i] once lay,
grass and reeds[j] and papyrus will
grow.
8 And a highway[k] will be there;
it will be called the Way of Holiness.[l]
The unclean[m] will not journey on it;
it will be for those who walk in that
Way;
wicked fools will not go about on it.[a]
9 No lion[n] will be there,
nor will any ferocious beast[o] get up
on it;
they will not be found there.
But only the redeemed[p] will walk
there,
10 and the ransomed[q] of the LORD will
return.
They will enter Zion with singing;[r]
everlasting joy[s] will crown their
heads.
Gladness[t] and joy will overtake them,
and sorrow and sighing will flee
away.[u]

35:4 [y]S Isa 25:9 **35:5** [z]S Ps 146:8; Jn 9:6-7; Ac 26:18 [a]Isa 29:18; 42:18; 50:4 **35:6** [b]Mt 15:30; Lk 7:22; Jn 5:8-9; Ac 3:8 [c]S 2Sa 22:34 [d]Isa 32:4; Mt 9:32-33; 12:22; Mk 7:35; Lk 11:14 [e]Ps 20:5 [f]S Ex 17:6; Jn 7:38 **35:7** [g]S Ps 68:6; Isa 41:17; 44:3; 55:1 [h]Ps 107:35; Isa 49:10; 58:11 [i]S Isa 13:22 [j]S Job 8:11; S 40:21 **35:8** [k]S Isa 11:16; S 33:8; S Jer 31:21; Mt 7:13-14 [l]Isa 4:3; 1Pe 1:15 [m]Isa 52:1 **35:9** [n]S Isa 30:6 [o]Isa 11:6; 13:22; 34:14 [p]S Ex 6:6; Lev 25:47-55; Isa 51:11; 62:12; 63:4 **35:10** [q]S Job 19:25; S Isa 1:27 [r]Isa 30:29 [s]S Ps 4:7; S 126:5; S Isa 25:9 [t]S Ps 51:8; S Isa 51:3 [u]S Isa 30:19; Rev 7:17; 21:4

36:1 [v]S 2Ki 18:9 [w]S 2Ch 32:1 [x]S Ps 109:11

Sennacherib Threatens Jerusalem

36:1-22pp — 2Ki 18:13,17-37; 2Ch 32:9-19

36 In the fourteenth year of King Hezekiah's[v] reign, Sennacherib[w] king of
Assyria attacked all the fortified cities of
Judah and captured them.[x] 2 Then the king
of Assyria sent his field commander with
a large army from Lachish[y] to King Hezekiah at Jerusalem. When the commander
stopped at the aqueduct of the Upper Pool,
on the road to the Washerman's Field,[z]
3 Eliakim[a] son of Hilkiah the palace administrator,[b] Shebna[c] the secretary,[d] and
Joah[e] son of Asaph the recorder[f] went out
to him.
4 The field commander said to them,
"Tell Hezekiah,

" 'This is what the great king, the
king of Assyria, says: On what are
you basing this confidence of yours?
5 You say you have strategy and military strength — but you speak only
empty words. On whom are you
depending, that you rebel[g] against
me? 6 Look now, you are depending[h]
on Egypt,[i][j] that splintered reed[k] of a
staff, which pierces a man's hand and
wounds him if he leans on it! Such is
Pharaoh king of Egypt to all who depend on him. 7 And if you say to me,

[a] 8 Or / *the simple will not stray from it*

36:2 [y]S Jos 10:3 [z]S Isa 7:3 **36:3** [a]Isa 22:20-21; 37:2 [b]S Ge 41:40 [c]S 2Ki 18:18 [d]S 2Sa 8:17 [e]ver 11 [f]S 2Sa 8:16 **36:5** [g]S 2Ki 18:7 **36:6** [h]S 2Ki 17:4; S Isa 8:12 [i]Eze 17:17 [j]S Isa 30:2,5 [k]Isa 42:3; 58:5; Eze 29:6-7

Cf. 40:9 – 10. Similar language is used of the coming of the Messiah (see 62:11 and note; cf. Rev 22:12,20 and notes). *vengeance … retribution.* See note on 34:8.

35:5 *eyes … ears.* See 29:18; 32:3; 42:7 and notes. Spiritual and physical healing are also linked together in Christ's ministry (see Lk 7:22 and note).

35:6 *lame leap … mute tongue shout.* Signs of the Messianic age (see Mt 12:22; Ac 3:7 – 8). *Water … streams.* See 32:2 and note. Cf. God's provision of water in Ex 17:6; 2Ki 3:15 – 20 (see note on 2Ki 3:17).

35:7 *springs.* Cf. 41:18. *reeds and papyrus.* Plants that grow in marshes and lakes (cf. 19:6 – 7).

35:8 *highway.* A road built up to make travel easier (see 11:16; 40:3 and notes). *the Way of Holiness.* The way set apart for those who are holy; only the redeemed (v. 9) could use it. In ancient times, certain roads between temples were open only to those who were ceremonially pure.

35:9 *lion … beast.* Sometimes wild animals made travel dangerous (see Dt 8:15; Jdg 14:5 and note). *redeemed.* Those the Lord has delivered from bondage (cf. 1:27; 51:10; 62:12; Ex 6:6 – 8 and notes; Lev 25:47 – 48; Dt 7:8).

35:10 Repeated in 51:11. *enter Zion with singing.* As the Israelites did when they returned from Babylonian exile (see introduction to Ps 126). *overtake them.* They will be pursued, not by wild animals (v. 9) but by gladness and joy (cf. Ps 23:6 and note). *sorrow … will flee.* Cf. 25:8; 65:19.

36:1 — 39:8 Much of chs. 36 – 39 is paralleled, sometimes verbatim, in 2Ki 18:13 — 20:19 (see notes there). The compiler of 2 Kings may have used Isa 36 – 39 as one of his sources, or both may have drawn on a common source. Chs. 36 – 37 describe the fulfillment of many predictions about Assyria's collapse, while chs. 38 – 39 point toward the Babylonian context of chs. 40 – 66.

36:1 *fourteenth year of … Hezekiah's reign.* 701 B.C., the 14th year of his sole reign. Hezekiah ruled as sole king from 715 to 686 but was a coregent from c. 729 (see notes on 2Ki 18:1; Pr 25:1). *Sennacherib.* Reigned over Assyria from 705 to 681 (see chart, p. 472). *all the … cities.* In his annals Sennacherib lists 46 such cities (see note on 2Ki 18:13).

36:2 *large army.* Cf. 37:36 and note. *Lachish.* An important city about 30 miles southwest of Jerusalem that guarded the main approach to Judah's capital from that quarter (see Jer 34:7 and note). *aqueduct … Field.* See 7:3 and note; see also note on 2Ki 18:17.

36:3 *Eliakim.* See 22:20 – 21 and notes. *palace administrator.* In charge of the palace (see 22:15 and note). *Shebna.* See 22:15 and note. *secretary.* Perhaps equivalent to secretary of state (see Jer 36:12; see also note on 2Sa 8:17). *recorder.* An official position also associated elsewhere with "secretary" (see 1Ki 4:3). See also note on 2Sa 8:16.

36:4,13 *great king.* See note on 2Ki 18:19.

36:5 *rebel.* By refusing to pay the expected tribute (see 2Ki 17:4; 18:7 and note).

36:6,9 *depending on Egypt.* Cf. 10:20.

36:6 *Egypt.* Hezekiah had been under pressure to make an alliance with Egypt since 715 B.C. or earlier (see 20:5; 30:1 and notes). *splintered reed.* Egypt is compared to a reed again in Eze 29:6 – 7 (see note on 29:6). *Such is Pharaoh.* Cf. 30:3,7.

36:7 *high places and altars.* Hezekiah had destroyed these popular shrines often dedicated to Baal worship (see note on

"We are depending[l] on the LORD our
God"—isn't he the one whose high
places and altars Hezekiah removed,[m]
saying to Judah and Jerusalem, "You
must worship before this altar"?[n]
8" 'Come now, make a bargain with
my master, the king of Assyria: I will
give you two thousand horses[o]—if
you can put riders on them! 9How
then can you repulse one officer of
the least of my master's officials, even
though you are depending on Egypt[p]
for chariots[q] and horsemen?[r] 10Fur-
thermore, have I come to attack and
destroy this land without the LORD?
The LORD himself told[s] me to march
against this country and destroy it.' "

11Then Eliakim, Shebna and Joah[t] said
to the field commander, "Please speak to
your servants in Aramaic,[u] since we understand it. Don't speak to us in Hebrew
in the hearing of the people on the wall."
12But the commander replied, "Was it
only to your master and you that my master sent me to say these things, and not
to the men sitting on the wall—who, like
you, will have to eat their own filth and
drink their own urine?[v]"
13Then the commander stood and
called out in Hebrew,[w] "Hear the words
of the great king, the king of Assyria![x]
14This is what the king says: Do not let
Hezekiah deceive[y] you. He cannot deliver
you! 15Do not let Hezekiah persuade you
to trust in the LORD when he says, 'The
LORD will surely deliver[z] us; this city will
not be given into the hand of the king of
Assyria.'[a]
16"Do not listen to Hezekiah. This is
what the king of Assyria says: Make peace
with me and come out to me. Then every
one of you will eat from his own vine and
fig tree[b] and drink water from his own cistern,[c] 17until I come and take you to a land
like your own[d]—a land of grain and new
wine,[e] a land of bread and vineyards.
18"Do not let Hezekiah mislead you
when he says, 'The LORD will deliver us.'
Has the god of any nation ever delivered his land from the hand of the king
of Assyria? 19Where are the gods of Hamath and Arpad?[f] Where are the gods of
Sepharvaim?[g] Have they rescued Samaria[h]
from my hand? 20Who of all the gods[i] of
these countries has been able to save his
land from me? How then can the LORD deliver Jerusalem from my hand?"[j]
21But the people remained silent and
said nothing in reply, because the king
had commanded, "Do not answer him."[k]
22Then Eliakim[l] son of Hilkiah the palace administrator, Shebna the secretary,
and Joah son of Asaph the recorder[m] went
to Hezekiah, with their clothes torn,[n] and
told him what the field commander had
said.

Jerusalem's Deliverance Foretold

37:1-13pp — 2Ki 19:1-13

37 When King Hezekiah heard this, he
tore his clothes[o] and put on sackcloth[p] and went into the temple[q] of the
LORD. 2He sent Eliakim[r] the palace administrator, Shebna[s] the secretary, and the
leading priests, all wearing sackcloth, to
the prophet Isaiah son of Amoz.[t] 3They
told him, "This is what Hezekiah says:
This day is a day of distress[u] and rebuke
and disgrace, as when children come to
the point of birth[v] and there is no strength

36:7 [l]Ps 22:8; Mt 27:43 [m]S 2Ki 18:4 [n]Dt 12:2-5; S 2Ch 31:1 **36:8** [o]S Ps 20:7; S Isa 30:16 **36:9** [p]S Isa 31:3 [q]Isa 37:24 [r]S Ps 20:7; Isa 30:2-5 **36:10** [s]S 1Ki 13:18; Isa 10:5-7 **36:11** [t]ver 3 [u]S Ezr 4:7 **36:12** [v]2Ki 6:25; Eze 4:12 **36:13** [w]S 2Ch 32:18 [x]Isa 37:4 **36:14** [y]S 2Ch 32:15 **36:15** [z]S Ps 3:2,7 [a]Isa 37:10 **36:16** [b]S 1Ki 4:25 [c]Pr 5:15 **36:17** [d]S 2Ki 15:29 [e]S Ge 27:28; S Dt 28:51 **36:19** [f]S 2Ki 18:34 [g]S 2Ki 17:24 [h]S 2Ki 15:29 **36:20** [i]S 1Ki 20:23 [j]Ex 5:2; 2Ch 25:15; Isa 10:8-11; 37:10-13,18-20; 40:18; Da 3:15 **36:21** [k]Pr 9:7-8; S 26:4 **36:22** [l]S 2Ki 18:18 [m]S 2Sa 8:16 [n]S Ge 37:29; S 2Ch 34:19 **37:1** [o]S Ge 37:29; S 2Ch 34:19 [p]S Ge 37:34 [q]S ver 14; S 1Ki 8:33; Mt 21:13 **37:2** [r]S 2Ki 18:18; S Isa 36:3 [s]S 2Ki 18:18 [t]ver 21; Isa 1:1; S 13:1; 38:1 **37:3** [u]S Jdg 6:2; S Isa 5:30 [v]Isa 26:18; 66:9; Hos 13:13

2Ki 18:4; see also 2Ch 31:1). *this altar.* In Solomon's temple.
36:8 *two thousand horses.* A sizable number for any army. Horses and chariots were highly prized (see note on 30:16). *if you can put riders on them!* See note on 2Ki 18:23.
36:10 *The LORD ... told me.* The Lord had used Assyria to punish Israel (see 10:5–6), but now it was Assyria's turn to be judged. Pharaoh Neco claimed God's approval on his mission according to 2Ch 35:21.
36:11 *Eliakim ... Joah.* See v. 3 and note. *Aramaic.* The diplomatic language of that day (see note on 2Ki 18:26). *Don't speak ... in Hebrew.* The officials feared that the commander's speech might damage the people's morale.
36:12 *eat ... filth ... drink ... urine.* A crude way of describing the horrors of famine if Jerusalem were to be besieged (cf. 2Ki 6:25 and note). Contrast v. 16 (see note there).
36:14 *deceive you.* Cf. 37:10 and note.
36:16 *own vine and fig tree.* Symbols of security and prosperity in the best of times (see 1Ki 4:25; Mic 4:4 and note; Zec 3:10 and note).
36:17 *come and take you.* The Assyrians deported rebellious peoples to reduce their will to revolt (see 2Ki 15:29; 17:6 and notes). *grain and new wine.* Two of the staples of Israel (cf. Dt 28:51; Hag 1:11 and note).
36:18–20 The commander's words echo the boasts of the proud Assyrians in 10:8–11. See note on 2Ki 18:33–35.
36:19 *Hamath and Arpad.* See 10:9 and note. *Sepharvaim.* Probably located in northern Aram (Syria) not far from Hamath. Residents of Sepharvaim were deported to Samaria, though they still worshiped the gods Adrammelech and Anammelech. See 2Ki 17:24 and note, 31. *Samaria.* The Assyrians assumed that each people had its own gods and so did not associate the God of Judah with that of Samaria.
36:21 *people remained silent.* The Assyrians had hoped that the masterful psychology of vv. 4–20 would produce panic.
36:22 See v. 3 and note. *clothes torn.* See note on 2Ki 18:37.
37:1 *clothes ... sackcloth.* See Ge 37:34 and note; see also note on 2Ki 18:37. *temple.* Designated as a place of prayer by Solomon (see 1Ki 8:33). The Assyrian references to Hezekiah's dependence on the Lord (36:7,15,18) were true (see note on 36:7).
37:2 *Eliakim ... Shebna.* See note on 36:3. *leading priests.* See note on 2Ki 19:2. *Isaiah son of Amoz.* See note on 1:1. Prophet, priests and king join in supplication.
37:3 *day of distress.* See 5:30; 26:16; 33:2 and notes. *point of birth.* An even more vivid description than that of the pains of childbirth (see 13:8 and note).

to deliver them. 4It may be that the LORD your God will hear the words of the field commander, whom his master, the king of Assyria, has sent to ridicule[w] the living God,[x] and that he will rebuke him for the words the LORD your God has heard.[y] Therefore pray[z] for the remnant[a] that still survives."

5When King Hezekiah's officials came to Isaiah, 6Isaiah said to them, "Tell your master, 'This is what the LORD says: Do not be afraid[b] of what you have heard—those words with which the underlings of the king of Assyria have blasphemed[c] me. 7Listen! I am going to put a spirit[d] in him so that when he hears a certain report,[e] he will return to his own country, and there I will have him cut down[f] with the sword.' "

8When the field commander heard that the king of Assyria had left Lachish,[g] he withdrew and found the king fighting against Libnah.[h]

9Now Sennacherib[i] received a report[j] that Tirhakah, the Cushite[a][k] king ⌞of Egypt⌟, was marching out to fight against him. When he heard it, he sent messengers to Hezekiah with this word: 10"Say to Hezekiah king of Judah: Do not let the god you depend on deceive[l] you when he says, 'Jerusalem will not be handed over to the king of Assyria.'[m] 11Surely you have heard what the kings of Assyria have done to all the countries, destroying them completely. And will you be delivered?[n] 12Did the gods of the nations that were destroyed by my forefathers[o] deliver them—the gods of Gozan, Haran,[p] Rezeph and the people of Eden[q] who were in Tel Assar? 13Where is the king of Hamath, the king of Arpad,[r] the king of the city of Sepharvaim,[s] or of Hena or Ivvah?"[t]

37:4 [w] ver 23-24; S 2Ch 32:17 [x] S Jos 3:10 [y] Isa 36:13, 18-20 [z] S 1Sa 7:8 [a] S Isa 1:9; Am 7:2 **37:6** [b] S Jos 1:9; S Isa 7:4 [c] S Nu 15:30 **37:7** [d] 1Ch 5:26 [e] ver 9 [f] S Isa 31:8 **37:8** [g] S Jos 10:3 [h] S Nu 33:20 **37:9** [i] S 2Ch 32:1 [j] ver 7 [k] S Isa 20:3 **37:10** [l] 2Ch 32:11,15 [m] Isa 36:15 **37:11** [n] Isa 36:18-20 **37:12** [o] 2Ki 18:11 [p] Ge 11:31; 12:1-4; Ac 7:2 [q] Eze 27:23; Am 1:5 **37:13** [r] Isa 10:9 [s] S 2Ki 17:24 [t] S Isa 36:20 **37:14** [u] 2Ch 32:17 [v] ver 1,38; S 1Ki 8:33 **37:15** [w] S 2Ch 32:20 **37:16** [x] S Ps 2:4 [y] S Ge 3:24 [z] Dt 10:17; S Ps 46:10; 86:10; 136:2-3 [a] Da 4:34 [b] S Ge 1:1; S Isa 11:12; 41:9; 43:6; Ac 4:24 **37:17** [c] S 1Ki 8:29; S 2Ch 6:40 [d] Jer 25:29; Da 9:18 [e] S 2Ch 32:1 [f] S 2Ch 32:17 [g] S Jos 3:10 **37:18** [h] S 2Ki 15:29; Na 2:11-12 **37:19** [i] S Jos 7:15 [j] Isa 26:14; 36:20 [k] 2Ch 13:9; Isa 40:17; 41:24,29; Jer 2:11; 5:7; 16:20; Gal 4:8 [l] S 2Ch 32:19; S Ps 135:15; Isa 40:18-20; 44:9-11 **37:20** [m] S Ps 3:2,7; S Pr 20:22 [n] S Jos 4:24 [o] S 1Sa 17:46; S Ps 46:10 **37:21** [p] S ver 2 **37:22** [q] S Isa 23:12 [r] S Isa 10:32

Hezekiah's Prayer

37:14-20pp — 2Ki 19:14-19

14Hezekiah received the letter[u] from the messengers and read it. Then he went up to the temple[v] of the LORD and spread it out before the LORD. 15And Hezekiah prayed[w] to the LORD: 16"O LORD Almighty, God of Israel, enthroned[x] between the cherubim,[y] you alone are God[z] over all the kingdoms[a] of the earth. You have made heaven and earth.[b] 17Give ear, O LORD, and hear;[c] open your eyes, O LORD, and see;[d] listen to all the words Sennacherib[e] has sent to insult[f] the living God.[g]

18"It is true, O LORD, that the Assyrian kings have laid waste all these peoples and their lands.[h] 19They have thrown their gods into the fire[i] and destroyed them,[j] for they were not gods[k] but only wood and stone, fashioned by human hands.[l] 20Now, O LORD our God, deliver[m] us from his hand, so that all kingdoms on earth[n] may know that you alone, O LORD, are God.[b][o]"

Sennacherib's Fall

37:21-38pp — 2Ki 19:20-37; 2Ch 32:20-21

21Then Isaiah son of Amoz[p] sent a message to Hezekiah: "This is what the LORD, the God of Israel, says: Because you have prayed to me concerning Sennacherib king of Assyria, 22this is the word the LORD has spoken against him:

"The Virgin Daughter[q] of Zion[r]
despises and mocks you.

[a] *9* That is, from the upper Nile region [b] *20* Dead Sea Scrolls (see also 2 Kings 19:19); Masoretic Text *alone are the LORD*

37:4 *ridicule.* The Hebrew is translated "insult" in vv. 17,23–24. *pray.* See note on 2Ki 19:4. *remnant.* Jerusalem was left almost alone (see 36:1 and notes on 1:9; 2Ki 19:4; see also 10:20–22 and note).
37:6 *Do not be afraid.* Cf. 7:4; see 35:4 and note.
37:7 *spirit.* Perhaps a compulsion or a disposition (cf. 1Ch 5:26). *report.* See note on 2Ki 19:7. *return … cut down with the sword.* See vv. 37–38 and note on v. 38.
37:8 *Lachish.* See note on 36:2. *Libnah.* See note on 2Ki 8:22; see also Jos 10:31.
37:9 *Tirhakah, the Cushite king.* In 701 B.C. he was actually a prince (the "lieutenant" of the new pharaoh Shebitku, who sent him with an army to help Hezekiah withstand the Assyrian invasion); he did not become king until 690. But this part of Isaiah was not written before 681 (see note on v. 38), so it was natural at that time to speak of Tirhakah as king. See 18:1 and note.
37:10 *god … deceive.* See 36:14–15,18. The message of vv. 10–13 is similar to that of 36:18–20 (see note there).
37:12 *Gozan.* A city in northern Mesopotamia to which some of the Israelites had been deported by the Assyrians (see 2Ki 17:6 and note). *Haran.* A city west of Gozan where Abraham lived for a number of years (see Ge 11:31 and note). *Rezeph.* A city between Haran and the Euphrates River. *Eden.* The state of Bit Adini, located between the Euphrates and Balikh rivers (see note on 2Ki 19:12).
37:13 *Hamath … Arpad.* See 10:9 and note. *Sepharvaim.* See 36:19; 2Ki 17:24 and notes.
37:14 *temple.* See v. 1 and note. *spread it out.* Contrast the hypocritical spreading out of hands to pray in 1:15 (see note on 1:11–15).
37:16 *LORD Almighty.* See 13:4 and note. *enthroned … cherubim.* See notes on 1Sa 4:4; 2Sa 6:2. *all the kingdoms.* Cf. 40:17 and note. *made heaven and earth.* The role of God as Creator is emphasized also in 40:26,28; 42:5; 45:12 (see note on 40:21).
37:17 *Give ear … open your eyes.* Cf. Solomon's prayer in 1Ki 8:52; 2Ch 6:40. *insult the living God.* See v. 4 and note.
37:19 *not gods.* See 36:19 and note. *wood and stone.* Cf. 2:8; 44:9–20 and notes.
37:20 *that all kingdoms on earth may know.* See note on 2Ki 19:19. *you alone … are God.* Cf. v. 16; 43:11; 45:18,21–22; see note on Ex 20:3; see also note and NIV text note on Dt 6:4.
37:22 *Virgin Daughter of Zion … Daughter of Jerusalem.* A personification of Jerusalem (see note on 2Ki 19:21). *tosses her head.* A gesture of mocking (see Ps 22:7; 44:14 and notes).

The Daughter of Jerusalem
tosses her head[s] as you flee.
23 Who is it you have insulted and
blasphemed?[t]
Against whom have you raised your
voice[u]
and lifted your eyes in pride?[v]
Against the Holy One[w] of Israel!
24 By your messengers
you have heaped insults on the Lord.
And you have said,
'With my many chariots[x]
I have ascended the heights of the
mountains,
the utmost heights[y] of Lebanon.[z]
I have cut down its tallest cedars,
the choicest of its pines.[a]
I have reached its remotest heights,
the finest of its forests.
25 I have dug wells in foreign lands[a]
and drunk the water there.
With the soles of my feet
I have dried up[b] all the streams of
Egypt.[c]'

26 "Have you not heard?
Long ago I ordained[d] it.
In days of old I planned[e] it;
now I have brought it to pass,
that you have turned fortified cities
into piles of stone.[f]
27 Their people, drained of power,
are dismayed and put to shame.
They are like plants in the field,
like tender green shoots,
like grass[g] sprouting on the roof,[h]
scorched[b] before it grows up.
28 "But I know where you stay
and when you come and go[i]
and how you rage[j] against me.
29 Because you rage against me
and because your insolence[k] has
reached my ears,
I will put my hook[l] in your nose[m]
and my bit in your mouth,
and I will make you return
by the way you came.[n]

30 "This will be the sign[o] for you, O Hezekiah:

"This year[p] you will eat what grows by
itself,
and the second year what springs
from that.
But in the third year[q] sow and reap,
plant vineyards[r] and eat their fruit.[s]
31 Once more a remnant of the house of
Judah
will take root[t] below and bear fruit[u]
above.
32 For out of Jerusalem will come a
remnant,[v]
and out of Mount Zion a band of
survivors.[w]
The zeal[x] of the LORD Almighty
will accomplish this.

33 "Therefore this is what the LORD says
concerning the king of Assyria:

"He will not enter this city[y]
or shoot an arrow here.
He will not come before it with shield
or build a siege ramp[z] against it.
34 By the way that he came he will
return;[a]
he will not enter this city,"
declares the LORD.
35 "I will defend[b] this city and save it,
for my sake[c] and for the sake of
David[d] my servant!"

36 Then the angel[e] of the LORD went
out and put to death[f] a hundred and
eighty-five thousand men in the Assyrian[g]

37:22 [s]S Job 16:4 **37:23** [t]ver 4; S Nu 15:30; Isa 52:5; Eze 36:20,23; Da 7:25 [u]S Job 15:25 [v]S Isa 2:11 [w]S Isa 1:4; S 12:6 **37:24** [x]Isa 36:9 [y]Isa 14:13 [z]S 1Ki 7:2; S Isa 14:8; S 33:9 [a]1Ki 5:8-10; Isa 41:19; 55:13; 60:13; Hos 14:8 **37:25** [b]S Isa 19:6; 44:27 [c]S Dt 11:10; S Isa 10:14; Da 4:30 **37:26** [d]Ac 2:23; 4:27-28; 1Pe 2:8 [e]Isa 10:6; S 25:1 [f]S Dt 13:16; S Isa 25:2 **37:27** [g]S Isa 15:6 [h]Ps 129:6 **37:28** [i]Ps 139:1-3 [j]Ps 2:1 **37:29** [k]Isa 10:12 [l]S 2Ch 33:11 [m]S Job 40:24 [n]ver 34 **37:30** [o]S Isa 20:3 [p]Isa 32:10 [q]S Isa 16:14 [r]S Lev 25:4 [s]Ps 107:37; Isa 30:23; 65:21; Jer 31:5 **37:31** [t]Isa 11:10 [u]S Isa 27:6 **37:32** [v]S Isa 11:11 [w]S Isa 1:9 [x]S Isa 9:7 **37:33** [y]S Isa 32:18 [z]S 2Sa 20:15 **37:34** [a]ver 29 **37:35** [b]S Isa 31:5 [c]Isa 43:25; 48:9,11; Eze 36:21-22 [d]S 1Ch 17:19 **37:36** [e]S Ex 12:23 [f]S Ex 12:12 [g]S Isa 10:12

[a] *25* Dead Sea Scrolls (see also 2 Kings 19:24); Masoretic Text does not have *in foreign lands.* [b] *27* Some manuscripts of the Masoretic Text, Dead Sea Scrolls and some Septuagint manuscripts (see also 2 Kings 19:26); most manuscripts of the Masoretic Text *roof / and terraced fields*

37:23 *lifted … in pride.* Assyria's great pride had been condemned earlier (see 10:12 and note). *Holy One of Israel.* A designation of the God of Israel characteristic of Isaiah (see 1:4 and note).
37:24 *many chariots.* See 36:8 and note. *ascended the heights.* Cf. the words of the king of Babylon in 14:13–14. *Lebanon.* See 33:9; 35:2 and notes. *cut down … cedars.* For many centuries the kings of Mesopotamia had used the cedars of Lebanon in their royal buildings (see notes on 2:13; 9:10; 14:8; cf. 1Ki 5:8–10).
37:25 *dug wells.* Desert lands could not stop him. *dried up all the streams.* The branches of the Nile were no obstacle either. This boast was almost a claim to deity. See 11:15; 44:27 and notes.
37:26 *ordained … planned … brought it to pass.* See Ps 33:10–11. Cf. 40:21 and note. *cities into piles of stone.* Assyria had been God's tool of judgment against the nations (see 10:5–6 and note on 10:5).
37:27 See 40:6–8 and notes; Ps 37:1–2. *grass … on the roof.* Roofs in the Near East were flat (cf. 2Sa 11:2 and note).
37:29 *hook in your nose.* The Assyrians often led away captives by tying ropes to rings placed in their noses (see note on 2Ki 19:28). *bit.* Cf. 30:28.
37:30 *sign.* See 7:11,14 and notes. *what grows by itself.* See note on 2Ki 19:29. *second … third year.* See note on 2Ki 19:29. Probably the second year was to begin shortly, so the total time was less than 36 months. Another three-year sign was given in 20:3. *plant vineyards and eat.* The response to Assyria's proposal in 36:16 (see note there).
37:31–32 *remnant.* See notes on v. 4; 1:9; 2Ki 19:4,30–31.
37:31 *take root … bear fruit.* See 4:2; 11:1,10; 27:6 and notes.
37:32 *The zeal … this.* See 9:7 and note.
37:33 *siege ramp.* To help the invaders bring up battering rams and scale the walls (see 2Sa 20:15).
37:35 *sake of David.* God had promised David an enduring throne in Jerusalem (see 9:7; 55:3; 2Sa 7:16 and notes).
37:36 *angel of the LORD … put to death.* The Lord often sent his angel as his agent to bring plagues. Cf. the striking down of the firstborn in Egypt (Ex 12:12–13) and the angel's sword poised against Jerusalem (see 2Sa 24:15–16 and note on

camp. When the people got up the next
morning — there were all the dead bodies!
37 So Sennacherib[h] king of Assyria broke
camp and withdrew. He returned to Nineveh[i] and stayed there.
38 One day, while he was worshiping in
the temple[j] of his god Nisroch, his sons
Adrammelech and Sharezer cut him down
with the sword, and they escaped to the
land of Ararat.[k] And Esarhaddon[l] his son
succeeded him as king.[m]

Hezekiah's Illness

38:1-8pp — 2Ki 20:1-11; 2Ch 32:24-26

38 In those days Hezekiah became ill
and was at the point of death. The
prophet Isaiah son of Amoz[n] went to him
and said, "This is what the LORD says: Put
your house in order,[o] because you are going to die; you will not recover."[p]
2 Hezekiah turned his face to the wall
and prayed to the LORD, 3 "Remember,
O LORD, how I have walked[q] before you
faithfully and with wholehearted devotion[r] and have done what is good in your
eyes.[s]" And Hezekiah wept[t] bitterly.
4 Then the word[u] of the LORD came to
Isaiah: 5 "Go and tell Hezekiah, 'This is
what the LORD, the God of your father David,[v] says: I have heard your prayer and
seen your tears;[w] I will add fifteen years[x]
to your life. 6 And I will deliver you and
this city from the hand of the king of Assyria. I will defend[y] this city.
7 " 'This is the LORD's sign[z] to you that
the LORD will do what he has promised: 8 I
will make the shadow cast by the sun go
back the ten steps it has gone down on the
stairway of Ahaz.' " So the sunlight went
back the ten steps it had gone down.[a]

9 A writing of Hezekiah king of Judah
after his illness and recovery:

37:37 [h]S 2Ch 32:1 [i]S Ge 10:11; S Na 1:1 **37:38** [j]S ver 14 [k]Ge 8:4; Jer 51:27 [l]S 2Ki 17:24 [m]S Isa 9:4; 10:26; S 14:25 **38:1** [n]S Isa 37:2 [o]2Sa 17:23 [p]2Ki 8:10 **38:3** [q]Ps 26:3 [r]S 1Ki 8:61; S 1Ch 29:19 [s]S Dt 6:18; S 10:20 [t]Ps 6:8 **38:4** [u]1Sa 13:13; Isa 39:5 **38:5** [v]2Ki 18:3 [w]Ps 6:6 [x]S 2Ki 18:2 **38:6** [y]S Isa 31:5 **38:7** [z]S Ge 24:14; S 2Ch 32:31; Isa 7:11,14; S 20:3 **38:8** [a]Jos 10:13 **38:10** [b]Ps 102:24 [c]S Job 17:16; Ps 107:18; 2Co 1:9 [d]S Job 17:11 **38:11** [e]S Isa 12:2 [f]S Job 28:13; S Ps 116:9 **38:12** [g]Isa 33:20; 2Co 5:1,4; 2Pe 1:13-14 [h]S Job 4:21 [i]S Isa 34:4; Heb 1:12 [j]S Nu 11:15; S Job 7:6; S Ps 31:22 [k]ver 13; Ps 32:4; 73:14 **38:13** [l]S Ps 37:7 [m]S Job 9:17; Ps 51:8 [n]S Job 10:16; Jer 34:17; La 3:4; Da 6:24 [o]S ver 12

10 I said, "In the prime of my life[b]
must I go through the gates of
death[a][c]
and be robbed of the rest of my
years?[d]"
11 I said, "I will not again see the LORD,
the LORD,[e] in the land of the living;[f]
no longer will I look on mankind,
or be with those who now dwell in
this world.[b]
12 Like a shepherd's tent[g] my house
has been pulled down[h] and taken
from me.
Like a weaver I have rolled[i] up my
life,
and he has cut me off from the
loom;[j]
day and night[k] you made an end
of me.
13 I waited patiently[l] till dawn,
but like a lion he broke[m] all my
bones;[n]
day and night[o] you made an end
of me.
14 I cried like a swift or thrush,
I moaned like a mourning dove.[p]
My eyes grew weak[q] as I looked to the
heavens.
I am troubled; O Lord, come to my
aid!"[r]
15 But what can I say?[s]
He has spoken to me, and he himself
has done this.[t]
I will walk humbly[u] all my years
because of this anguish of my soul.[v]
16 Lord, by such things men live;
and my spirit finds life in them too.

[a] 10 Hebrew *Sheol* [b] 11 A few Hebrew manuscripts; most Hebrew manuscripts *in the place of cessation*

38:14 [p]S Ge 8:8; S Isa 59:11 [q]S Ps 6:7 [r]S Ge 50:24; S Job 17:3 **38:15** [s]2Sa 7:20 [t]S Ps 39:9 [u]1Ki 21:27 [v]S Job 7:11

24:16; 1Ch 21:22,27). The Greek historian Herodotus attributed this destruction to a bubonic plague. The death of these soldiers fulfills the prophecies of 10:33–34 (see notes there); 30:31; 31:8 (see note there).
37:37 *Nineveh.* The capital of Assyria (see Jnh 1:2 and note).
37:38 *in the temple.* Hezekiah had gone to the Lord's temple and gained strength (vv. 1,14). Twenty years later (681 B.C.) Sennacherib went to the temple of his god and was killed (see note on 2Ki 19:37). *Ararat.* Urartu, north of Assyria in Armenia (see note on Ge 8:4). *Esarhaddon.* Reigned 681–669 (see chart, p. 472; see also 2Ki 19:37 and note; Ezr 4:2).
38:1 *In those days.* Sometime before Sennacherib's invasion of 701 B.C. (see v. 6). *Isaiah.* He is prominent in this historical interlude (chs. 36–39). *Put your house in order.* See note on 2Ki 20:1. *you are going to die.* See note on 2Ki 20:1. Elisha similarly predicted the death of Ben-Hadad (see 2Ki 8:9–10 and notes). *you will not recover.* See v. 21 and note.
38:2 *wall.* Perhaps of the nearby temple. *prayed.* Cf. also Hezekiah's prayer of thanksgiving in vv. 10–20 (see note there).
38:3 *wholehearted devotion.* Like David (1Ki 11:4), Hezekiah was truly faithful (see 36:7; 2Ki 18:3–5 and notes).
38:5 *fifteen years.* See note on 2Ki 20:6.
38:6 *deliver … this city.* See 31:5; 37:35 and notes.
38:7 *sign.* See 7:11,14 and notes.
38:8 *stairway of Ahaz.* See note on 2Ki 20:11. *sunlight went back.* Perhaps the miracle involved the refraction of light. See 2Ki 20:9–11 and notes; Jos 10:12–14 and note on 10:13.
38:10–20 A hymn of thanksgiving in two stanzas, similar to many of the psalms. Hezekiah was deeply interested in the psalms of David and Asaph (see 2Ch 29:30).
38:10–14 Hezekiah voices his complaint about his past affliction (v. 1).
38:11 *the LORD, the LORD.* See 26:4. *land of the living.* Cf. Ps 27:13 and note.
38:12 *rolled up my life.* Cf. the rolling up of the sky like a scroll in 34:4 (see also Heb 1:12).
38:13 *broke all my bones.* Physical or spiritual distress is often described in terms of aching or broken bones (see Ps 6:2; 32:3).
38:15–20 Hezekiah offers praise for God's healing (see v. 5).
38:15 *what can I say?* Hezekiah wonders how he can praise God (cf. 2Sa 7:20).
38:16 *by such things.* Perhaps referring to God's promises and gracious acts, though his gracious acts can include such experiences as sickness and peril.

You restored me to health
and let me live.[w]
17 Surely it was for my benefit[x]
that I suffered such anguish.[y]
In your love you kept me
from the pit[z] of destruction;
you have put all my sins[a]
behind your back.[b]
18 For the grave[a][c] cannot praise you,
death cannot sing your praise;[d]
those who go down to the pit[e]
cannot hope for your faithfulness.
19 The living, the living—they praise[f]
you,
as I am doing today;
fathers tell their children[g]
about your faithfulness.
20 The LORD will save me,
and we will sing[h] with stringed
instruments[i]
all the days of our lives[j]
in the temple[k] of the LORD.

21 Isaiah had said, "Prepare a poultice of figs and apply it to the boil, and he will recover."

22 Hezekiah had asked, "What will be the sign[l] that I will go up to the temple of the LORD?"

Envoys From Babylon

39:1-8pp — 2Ki 20:12-19

39 At that time Merodach-Baladan son of Baladan king of Babylon[m] sent Hezekiah letters and a gift, because he had heard of his illness and recovery. 2 Hezeki-
ah received the envoys[n] gladly and showed them what was in his storehouses—the silver, the gold,[o] the spices, the fine oil, his entire armory and everything found among his treasures.[p] There was nothing in his palace or in all his kingdom that Hezekiah did not show them.

3 Then Isaiah the prophet went to King Hezekiah and asked, "What did those men say, and where did they come from?"

"From a distant land,[q]" Hezekiah replied. "They came to me from Babylon."

4 The prophet asked, "What did they see in your palace?"

"They saw everything in my palace," Hezekiah said. "There is nothing among my treasures that I did not show them."

5 Then Isaiah said to Hezekiah, "Hear
the word[r] of the LORD Almighty: 6 The
time will surely come when everything in your palace, and all that your fathers have stored up until this day, will be carried off to Babylon.[s] Nothing will be left,
says the LORD. 7 And some of your descen-
dants, your own flesh and blood who will be born to you, will be taken away, and they will become eunuchs in the palace of the king of Babylon.[t]"

8 "The word of the LORD you have spoken is good,[u]" Hezekiah replied. For he thought, "There will be peace and security in my lifetime.[v]"

Comfort for God's People

40 Comfort, comfort[w] my people,
says your God.

38:16 [w] Ps 119:25; Heb 12:9
38:17 [x] Ro 8:28; Heb 12:11 [y] S Job 7:11; Ps 119:71,75 [z] S Job 17:16; S Ps 30:3 [a] Ps 103:3; Jer 31:34 [b] S Ps 103:12; Isa 43:25; Mic 7:19
38:18 [c] S Nu 16:30; S Ecc 9:10 [d] Ps 6:5; 88:10-11; 115:17 [e] S Ps 30:9
38:19 [f] Ps 118:17; 119:175 [g] S Dt 11:19
38:20 [h] Ps 68:25 [i] S Ps 33:2; S 45:8 [j] Ps 23:6; S 63:4; 116:2 [k] Ps 116:17-19
38:22 [l] S 2Ch 32:31
39:1 [m] S 2Ch 32:31
39:2 [n] 2Ch 32:31 [o] S 2Ki 18:15 [p] 2Ch 32:27-29
39:3 [q] S Dt 28:49
39:5 [r] S Isa 38:4
39:6 [s] S Jdg 6:4; S 2Ki 24:13
39:7 [t] S 2Ki 24:15; Da 1:1-7
39:8 [u] S Jdg 10:15; Job 1:21; Ps 39:9 [v] S 2Ch 32:26
40:1 [w] Isa 12:1; 49:13; 51:3, 12; 52:9; 57:18; 61:2; 66:13; Jer 31:13; Zep 3:14-17; Zec 1:17; 2Co 1:3

[a] 18 Hebrew *Sheol*

38:17 *pit of destruction.* The grave (see Ps 55:23 and note). *all my sins.* Physical and spiritual healing are sometimes linked together (see 53:4–5 and notes). *sins behind your back.* God not only puts our sins out of sight; he also puts them out of reach (Ps 103:12; Mic 7:19), out of mind (Jer 31:34) and out of existence (Isa 43:25; 44:22; Ps 51:1,9; Jer 50:20; Ac 3:19).

38:18 *cannot hope.* Knowledge about the afterlife was limited in the OT period, but the gospel of Christ has "brought ... immortality to light" (2Ti 1:10).

38:20 *sing with stringed instruments.* Instrumental music and hymns of praise were closely linked in worship (cf. Ps 33:1–3; 150). *all ... our lives in the temple.* Hezekiah, like David (Ps 23:6), loved God's house.

38:21 *Prepare ... apply.* The verbs are plural (probably addressed to the court physicians). *poultice of figs.* Figs were used for medicinal purposes in ancient Ugarit. *he will recover.* Contrast v. 1. God answered Hezekiah's prayer for healing (see v. 5).

38:22 *sign.* Perhaps the healing of the boil (see v. 21).

39:1 *Merodach-Baladan.* Reigned 721–710 B.C. and again in 703 (see note on 2Ki 20:12). *Babylon.* See note on 13:1. *sent ... letters and a gift.* Merodach-Baladan probably wanted Hezekiah's support in a campaign against Assyria. During his career, he organized several revolts against his hated neighbors. See note on 2Ki 20:12.

39:2 *silver ... gold ... treasures.* See 2Ch 32:27–29,31 and notes. Probably Hezekiah was seeking help from the Babylonians against the Assyrian threat (see note on 2Ki 20:13). But the information gained during this ill-advised tour escorted by Hezekiah would be valuable to Merodach-Baladan's powerful successors (vv. 5–7).

39:3 *Isaiah the prophet.* Earlier God had sent Isaiah to confront Ahaz (7:3); cf. also Nathan's rebuke of David (see 2Sa 12:1 and note, 7).

39:5 *word of the LORD.* Contrast the word of hope in 38:4–6.

39:6 *carried off to Babylon.* The first mention of Babylon as Jerusalem's conqueror, though 14:3–4 implied the Babylonian exile (see notes there). The wickedness of Hezekiah's son Manasseh was a major cause of the captivity (see 2Ki 21:11–15). See also notes on 2Ki 20:17; 21:15.

39:7 *your descendants.* Such as King Jehoiachin (see 2Ki 24:15 and note). *eunuchs.* Cf. Da 1:3–6, where the Hebrew for "court officials" (Da 1:3) can also be translated "eunuchs." *king of Babylon.* Nebuchadnezzar.

39:8 *word ... is good.* See note on 2Ki 20:19. *peace ... in my lifetime.* See 2Ki 22:20 and note. "Peace" recurs in a refrain in 48:22; 57:21, dividing the last 27 chapters into 3 sections of 9 chapters each (40–48; 49–57; 58–66).

40:1—66:24 In chs. 1–35 Isaiah prophesied against the backdrop of the Assyrian threat against Judah and Jerusalem, and in chs. 36–39 he recorded Assyria's failure and warned about the future rise of Babylon; chs. 40–66 assume that the Babylonian exile of Judah is almost over (see Introduction: Author).

40:1 *Comfort, comfort.* That is, comfort greatly. The double imperative for emphasis is found also in 51:9,17; 52:1,11; 57:14; 62:10.

[2]Speak tenderly[x] to Jerusalem,
and proclaim to her
that her hard service[y] has been
completed,[z]
that her sin has been paid for,[a]
that she has received from the LORD's
hand
double[b] for all her sins.

[3]A voice of one calling:
"In the desert prepare
the way[c] for the LORD[a];
make straight[d] in the wilderness
a highway for our God.[b][e]
[4]Every valley shall be raised up,[f]
every mountain and hill[g] made low;
the rough ground shall become level,[h]
the rugged places a plain.
[5]And the glory[i] of the LORD will be
revealed,
and all mankind together will see it.[j]
For the mouth of the LORD
has spoken."[k]

[6]A voice says, "Cry out."
And I said, "What shall I cry?"
"All men are like grass,[l]
and all their glory is like the flowers
of the field.
[7]The grass withers[m] and the flowers
fall,
because the breath[n] of the LORD
blows[o] on them.
Surely the people are grass.
[8]The grass withers and the flowers[p]
fall,
but the word[q] of our God stands[r]
forever.[s]"

40:2 [x]S Ge 34:3; S Isa 35:4 [y]S Job 7:1 [z]Isa 41:11-13; 49:25 [a]S Lev 26:41 [b]Isa 51:19; 61:7; Jer 16:18; 17:18; Zec 9:12; Rev 18:6
40:3 [c]S Isa 11:16; 43:19; Mal 3:1 [d]S Pr 3:5-6 [e]Mt 3:3*; Mk 1:3*; Jn 1:23*
40:4 [f]Isa 49:11 [g]S Isa 2:14 [h]S Ps 26:12; S Isa 26:7; 45:2,13; Jer 31:9
40:5 [i]S Ex 16:7; S Nu 14:21; S Isa 59:19 [j]Isa 52:10; 62:2; Lk 2:30; 3:4-6* [k]S Isa 1:20; 58:14
40:6 [l]S Ge 6:3; S Isa 29:5
40:7 [m]S Job 8:12; S Isa 15:6 [n]S Ex 15:10; S Job 41:21 [o]S Ps 103:16; S Eze 22:21
40:8 [p]S Isa 5:24; Jas 1:10 [q]Isa 55:11; 59:21 [r]S Pr 19:21; S Isa 7:7,9; S Jer 39:16 [s]S Ps 119:89; S Mt 5:18; 1Pe 1:24-25*
40:9 [t]Isa 41:27; 44:28; 52:7-10; 61:1; Na 1:15; S Ac 13:32; Ro 10:15; 1Co 15:1-4

[9]You who bring good tidings[t] to Zion,
go up on a high mountain.
You who bring good tidings to
Jerusalem,[c][u]
lift up your voice with a shout,
lift it up, do not be afraid;
say to the towns of Judah,
"Here is your God!"[v]
[10]See, the Sovereign LORD comes[w] with
power,[x]
and his arm[y] rules[z] for him.
See, his reward[a] is with him,
and his recompense accompanies
him.
[11]He tends his flock like a shepherd:[b]
He gathers the lambs in his arms[c]
and carries them close to his heart;[d]
he gently leads[e] those that have
young.[f]

[12]Who has measured the waters[g] in the
hollow of his hand,[h]
or with the breadth of his hand
marked off the heavens?[i]
Who has held the dust of the earth in a
basket,
or weighed the mountains on the
scales
and the hills in a balance?[j]

[a] 3 Or *A voice of one calling in the desert: / "Prepare the way for the LORD* [b] 3 Hebrew; Septuagint *make straight the paths of our God* [c] 9 Or *O Zion, bringer of good tidings, / go up on a high mountain. / O Jerusalem, bringer of good tidings*

[u]S Isa 1:1 [v]Isa 25:9 **40:10** [w]Isa 35:4; 59:20; Mt 21:5; Rev 22:7 [x]Isa 28:2 [y]S Ps 44:3; S Isa 30:30; S 33:2 [z]Isa 9:6-7 [a]S Isa 35:4; Rev 22:12
40:11 [b]S Ge 48:15; S Ps 28:9; S Mic 5:4; S Jn 10:11 [c]S Nu 11:12 [d]S Dt 26:19 [e]Isa 49:10 [f]S Ge 33:13; S Dt 30:4 **40:12** [g]S Job 12:15; S 38:10 [h]Pr 30:4 [i]S Job 38:5; Heb 1:10-12 [j]S Job 38:18; Pr 16:11

40:2 *Speak tenderly.* The Hebrew for this phrase is used also in 2Ch 32:6, where Hezekiah "encouraged" Judah to trust in God in spite of the Assyrian invasion. *hard service.* The exile in Babylonia (cf. Ps 137:1–6; La 1:1–2,9,16–17,21). *sin ... paid for.* By enduring the punishment of captivity (see Lev 26:41). *double.* Full (or enough) punishment. Cf. the "double calamities" of 51:19.

40:3–5 See 35:1–2 and note on 35:2.

40:3 *voice.* Three voices are mentioned (vv. 3,6,9), each showing how the comfort of v. 1 will come about. The NT links the voice of v. 3 with John the Baptist in Mt 3:3; Lk 3:4; Jn 1:23 (see notes there). *prepare the way.* Clear obstacles out of the road (cf. 57:14; 62:10). The language of vv. 3–4 has in view the ancient Near Eastern custom of sending representatives ahead to prepare the way for the visit of a monarch. The picture is that of preparing a processional highway for the Lord's coming to Jerusalem. In Mt 3:1–8 John declares that repentance is necessary to prepare the way for Christ. *make straight ... a highway.* See 11:16; 35:8 and notes.

40:4 *rough ground ... level.* See 26:7 and note.

40:5 *glory ... revealed.* God (through Cyrus king of Persia) would redeem Israel from Babylonia (see 35:9–10; 44:23–24), and all the nations would see the deliverance (see 52:10 and note; cf. Lk 3:6 and note). Ultimately the glory of the redeeming God would be seen in Jesus Christ (see Jn 1:14; 11:4; 17:4 and notes; see also Heb 1:3 and note on 1:2–3), especially at his return (Mt 16:27; 24:30; 25:31; Rev 1:7)—but also in the redeemed (see 1Co 10:31; 2Co 3:18; Eph 3:21 and notes). See also Isa 6:3 and note.

40:6,8 Quoted in part in 1Pe 1:24–25.

40:6 *like grass.* See 37:27 and note; 51:12. *all their glory ... field.* Even the power of Assyria and Babylonia would soon vanish.

40:8 *word of our God stands.* The plans and purposes of the nations will not prevail (see 8:10; Ps 119:89 and notes).

40:9 *good tidings.* The news that God is leading his people back to Judah (vv. 10–11). He cares for his people and will redeem them (see 52:7–10; 61:1 and notes). The NT expands this "good news" or "gospel" to refer to the salvation that Christ brings to all people (see 1Co 15:2–3 and notes). See NIV text note for an alternative translation. *Here is your God!* The Lord is returning to Jerusalem (see v. 10). These words apply to the return from exile (see 52:7–9 and notes), the first coming of Christ (Mt 21:5) and the second coming of Christ (62:11; Rev 22:12). See 35:4 and note.

40:10 *arm rules.* Cf. 51:9; 59:16 and notes. He is characterized by both strength and gentleness (v. 11). *reward ... recompense.* His delivered people, the flock of v. 11 (see 62:11–12 and notes).

40:11 *tends his flock.* Cf. Jer 31:10; Eze 34:11–16 and notes.

40:12–31 Rhetorical questions are used to persuade the people to trust in the Lord, who has the ability to deliver, strengthen and restore his people.

40:12 *measured the waters.* See Job 28:25; 38:8. In Job 38–41 the Lord overwhelms Job with a description of his greatness. *marked off the heavens.* See 48:13 and note.

13 Who has understood the mind[a][k] of the LORD,
or instructed him as his counselor?[l]
14 Whom did the LORD consult to enlighten him,
and who taught him the right way?
Who was it that taught him knowledge[m]
or showed him the path of understanding?[n]

15 Surely the nations are like a drop in a bucket;
they are regarded as dust on the scales;[o]
he weighs the islands as though they were fine dust.[p]
16 Lebanon[q] is not sufficient for altar fires,
nor its animals[r] enough for burnt offerings.
17 Before him all the nations[s] are as nothing;[t]
they are regarded by him as worthless
and less than nothing.[u]

18 To whom, then, will you compare God?[v]
What image[w] will you compare him to?
19 As for an idol,[x] a craftsman casts it,
and a goldsmith[y] overlays it with gold[z]
and fashions silver chains for it.
20 A man too poor to present such an offering
selects wood[a] that will not rot.
He looks for a skilled craftsman
to set up an idol[b] that will not topple.[c]

21 Do you not know?
Have you not heard?[d]
Has it not been told[e] you from the beginning?[f]
Have you not understood[g] since the earth was founded?[h]
22 He sits enthroned[i] above the circle of the earth,
and its people are like grasshoppers.[j]
He stretches out the heavens[k] like a canopy,[l]
and spreads them out like a tent[m] to live in.[n]
23 He brings princes[o] to naught
and reduces the rulers of this world to nothing.[p]
24 No sooner are they planted,
no sooner are they sown,
no sooner do they take root[q] in the ground,
than he blows[r] on them and they wither,[s]
and a whirlwind sweeps them away like chaff.[t]

25 "To whom will you compare me?[u]
Or who is my equal?" says the Holy One.[v]
26 Lift your eyes and look to the heavens:[w]
Who created[x] all these?
He who brings out the starry host[y] one by one,
and calls them each by name.
Because of his great power and mighty strength,[z]
not one of them is missing.[a]

27 Why do you say, O Jacob,
and complain, O Israel,
"My way is hidden from the LORD;
my cause is disregarded by my God"?[b]

40:13 [k]Isa 11:2; 42:1 [l]S Job 15:8; Ro 11:34*; 1Co 2:16* **40:14** [m]Job 21:22; Col 2:3 [n]S Job 12:13; S 34:13; Isa 55:9 **40:15** [o]S Ps 62:9 [p]S Dt 9:21; Isa 2:22 **40:16** [q]Isa 33:9; 37:24 [r]Ps 50:9-11; Mic 6:7; Heb 10:5-9 **40:17** [s]Isa 30:28 [t]S Job 12:19; Isa 29:7 [u]S Isa 37:19; Da 4:35 **40:18** [v]S Ex 8:10; S 1Sa 2:2 [w]S Dt 4:15; Ac 17:29 **40:19** [x]S Ex 20:4; Ps 115:4; S Isa 37:19; 42:17; Jer 2:8, 28; 10:8; 16:19; Hab 2:18; Zec 10:2 [y]Isa 41:7; 46:6; Jer 10:3 [z]Isa 2:20; 31:7 **40:20** [a]Isa 44:19 [b]S 1Sa 12:21 [c]S 1Sa 5:3 **40:21** [d]ver 28; 2Ki 19:25; Isa 41:22; 42:9; 44:8; 48:3, 5 [e]Ps 19:1; 50:6; Ac 14:17 [f]S Ge 1:1 [g]Ro 1:19 [h]Isa 48:13; 51:13 **40:22** [i]S 2Ch 6:18; S Ps 2:4 [j]S Nu 13:33 [k]S Ge 1:1; S Isa 48:13 [l]S Ge 1:8; S Job 22:14 [m]S Job 36:29

[a] 13 Or *Spirit*; or *spirit*

[n]S Job 26:7 **40:23** [o]S Job 12:18; S Isa 34:12 [p]S Job 12:19; Am 2:3 **40:24** [q]S Job 5:3 [r]S 2Sa 22:16; S Isa 11:4; 41:16 [s]S Job 8:12; S 18:16 [t]S Job 24:24; S Isa 41:2 **40:25** [u]S 1Sa 2:2; S 1Ch 16:25 [v]Isa 1:4; 37:23 **40:26** [w]Isa 51:6 [x]ver 28; Ps 89:11-13; Isa 42:5; 66:2 [y]S 2Ki 17:16; S Ne 9:6; S Job 38:32 [z]S Job 9:4; S Isa 45:24; Eph 1:19 [a]S Isa 34:16 **40:27** [b]S Job 6:29; S 27:2; Lk 18:7-8

40:13 Quoted in Ro 11:34; 1Co 2:16. *counselor.* See 9:6 and note.
40:15 *nations ... a drop in a bucket.* See note on v. 6. *dust.* See 17:13 and note; 29:5.
40:16 *Lebanon.* The wood of its cedar trees. *its animals.* Cf. Ps 104:16–18 and note. Sacrifices, however numerous, could never do justice to the greatness of God.
40:17 *nothing ... worthless.* In spite of the temporary splendor they might possess (see 13:19 and note).
40:18–20 More than any other prophet, Isaiah shows the folly of worshiping idols. His sarcastic caricature, satire and denunciation of these false gods reach a peak in 44:9–20 (see notes there; see also 41:7,22–24; 42:17; 46:5–7; 48:5 and note).
40:18 *To whom ... compare God?* See v. 25 and note; 46:5.
40:19 *craftsman ... goldsmith.* See 41:7; 44:10–12. *gold ... silver.* See 2:20; Hab 2:18–19 and notes.
40:20 *wood.* See 44:14–16,19 and notes. *that will not topple.* See 41:7; cf. 46:7; 1Sa 5:3–4.
40:21 *from the beginning.* God's work as Creator is emphasized in the rest of the chapter (cf. 37:26; 41:4,26).
40:22 *sits enthroned.* Cf. 66:1; see 37:16 and note. *circle.* Or "horizon." See Job 22:14; Pr 8:27. *stretches out the heavens ... like a tent.* See 42:5; 44:24; 51:13; Ps 104:2; see also note on Ps 19:4b–6.
40:23 *princes ... rulers ... to nothing.* See v. 17; 2:22 and notes; cf. Jer 25:17–26; Da 2:21.
40:24 *whirlwind ... like chaff.* See 17:13 and note; 41:15–16.
40:25 See v. 18. Apparently some Israelite doubters were comparing their God with the gods of their captors, and they believed that the Lord was failing the test. *Holy One.* See 1:4 and note.
40:26 *created.* See vv. 21–22 and notes. *brings out.* The Hebrew for this expression is used for bringing forth the constellations in Job 38:32. *starry host.* Also worshiped by the people (see 47:13; Jer 19:13 and note). *each by name.* See note on Ps 147:4–6. *not one ... missing.* See 34:16 and note.
40:27–31 As in many psalms of praise, Isaiah now stresses the goodness of God after describing his majesty (vv. 12–26). Such a God is able to deliver and restore his distressed people if they will wait in faith for him to act. They are to trust in him and draw strength from him.
40:27 *way.* Condition. *hidden ... disregarded.* Cf. 49:14; 54:8.

28 Do you not know?
Have you not heard?[c]
The LORD is the everlasting[d] God,
the Creator[e] of the ends of the earth.[f]
He will not grow tired or weary,[g]
and his understanding no one can fathom.[h]
29 He gives strength[i] to the weary[j]
and increases the power of the weak.
30 Even youths grow tired and weary,
and young men[k] stumble and fall;[l]
31 but those who hope[m] in the LORD
will renew their strength.[n]
They will soar on wings like eagles;[o]
they will run and not grow weary,
they will walk and not be faint.[p]

The Helper of Israel

41 "Be silent[q] before me, you islands![r]
Let the nations renew their strength![s]
Let them come forward[t] and speak;
let us meet together[u] at the place of judgment.
2 "Who has stirred[v] up one from the east,[w]
calling him in righteousness[x] to his service[a]?[y]
He hands nations over to him
and subdues kings before him.
He turns them to dust[z] with his sword,
to windblown chaff[a] with his bow.[b]
3 He pursues them and moves on unscathed,[c]
by a path his feet have not traveled before.
4 Who has done this and carried it through,
calling[d] forth the generations from the beginning?[e]
I, the LORD—with the first of them
and with the last[f]—I am he.[g]"
5 The islands[h] have seen it and fear;
the ends of the earth[i] tremble.
They approach and come forward;
6 each helps the other
and says to his brother, "Be strong![j]"
7 The craftsman[k] encourages the goldsmith,[l]
and he who smooths with the hammer
spurs on him who strikes the anvil.
He says of the welding, "It is good."
He nails down the idol so it will not topple.[m]
8 "But you, O Israel, my servant,[n]
Jacob, whom I have chosen,[o]
you descendants of Abraham[p] my friend,[q]
9 I took you from the ends of the earth,[r]
from its farthest corners I called[s] you.
I said, 'You are my servant';[t]
I have chosen[u] you and have not rejected you.
10 So do not fear,[v] for I am with you;[w]
do not be dismayed, for I am your God.

[a] 2 Or / *whom victory meets at every step*

40:28 [c]S ver 21 [d]S Dt 33:27; S Ps 90:2 [e]S ver 26 [f]S Isa 37:16 [g]Isa 44:12 [h]S Ps 147:5; Ro 11:33 **40:29** [i]S Ge 18:14; S Ps 68:35; S 119:28 [j]Isa 50:4; 57:19; Jer 31:25 **40:30** [k]Isa 9:17; Jer 6:11; 9:21 [l]S Ps 20:8; Isa 5:27 **40:31** [m]S Ps 37:9; 40:1; S Isa 30:18; Lk 18:1 [n]S 1Sa 2:4; S 2Ki 6:33; S 2Co 4:16 [o]S Ex 19:4 [p]2Co 4:1; Heb 12:1-3 **41:1** [q]Ps 37:7; Hab 2:20; Zep 1:7; Zec 2:13 [r]S Isa 11:11 [s]S 1Sa 2:4 [t]Isa 48:16; 57:3 [u]S Isa 1:18; 34:1; 50:8 **41:2** [v]S Ezr 1:2 [w]ver 25; Isa 13:4, 17; 44:28; 45:1, 13; 48:14; Jer 50:3; 51:11 [x]Isa 45:8, 13 [y]Isa 44:28; Jer 25:9 [z]S 2Sa 22:43 [a]Ps 1:4; Isa 40:24 [b]S Isa 13:18 **41:3** [c]Da 8:4 **41:4** [d]ver 9; Isa 43:7 [e]ver 26; S Ge 1:1; Isa 46:10 [f]Isa 44:6; 48:12; Rev 1:8, 17 [g]S Dt 32:39 **41:5** [h]S Isa 11:11; Eze 26:17-18 [i]S Dt 30:4; S Isa 11:12 **41:6** [j]S Jos 1:6 **41:7** [k]Isa 44:13; Jer 10:3-5 [l]S Isa 40:19 [m]S 1Sa 5:3; Isa 46:7 **41:8** [n]S Ps 136:22; S Isa 27:11 [o]S Isa 14:1 [p]S Isa 29:22; 51:2; 63:16 [q]2Ch 20:7; Jas 2:23 **41:9** [r]Isa 11:12; S 37:16 [s]S ver 4 [t]S Isa 20:3 [u]S Dt 7:6 **41:10** [v]S Ge 15:1 [w]S Dt 3:22; Jos 1:9; Isa 43:2, 5; Jer 30:10; 46:27-28; Ro 8:31

40:28 *everlasting God.* See 9:6. *Creator.* See vv. 21–22 and notes. *ends of the earth.* See 11:12 and note; cf. 5:26; 41:9; 43:6. *not grow tired.* Contrast 44:12.
40:30 *grow tired ... stumble.* See note on 5:27.
40:31 *hope in.* Trust in or look expectantly to (see 5:2; 49:23). *renew.* See 41:1 and note. Their human weakness will give way to God's strength (v. 29). *eagles.* Known for their vigor (see Ps 103:5 and note) and speed (Jer 4:13; 48:40).
41:1,5 *islands.* Or "coastlands" (see 11:11 and note).
41:1 *renew their strength.* See 40:31 and note. The nations and their gods are challenged to display the same power and wisdom as Israel's God (see vv. 21–24).
41:2 *one from the east.* Cyrus the Great, king of Persia (559–530 B.C.), who conquered Babylon in 539 (see 13:17 and note) and issued the decree allowing the Jews to return to Jerusalem (see Ezr 1:1–4; 6:3–5). Cyrus is referred to also in v. 25; 44:28—45:5,13; 46:11. *calling him in righteousness.* Like the servant of the Lord in 42:6, Cyrus was chosen to carry out God's righteous purposes. *subdues kings.* Such as Croesus king of Lydia in Asia Minor. *windblown chaff.* See 17:13 and note. *his bow.* The Persians were renowned for their ability as archers.
41:4 *from the beginning.* See 40:21 and note. *with the first ... with the last.* Since the Lord was present with the first of the generations and will still be there with the last of them, he is the eternal Lord of history and nations (see Heb 13:8; Rev 1:8,17; 2:8; 21:6; 22:13).
41:5–7 By 546 B.C. Cyrus had fought his way victoriously to the west coast of Asia Minor, where his leading opponent was Croesus king of Lydia. Sarcasm and satire are used in the description of the frantic efforts in vv. 6–7—all of them futile (cf. 40:19–20).
41:5 *ends of the earth.* See 11:12 and note.
41:6 *Be strong!* See 35:4 and note.
41:7 *hammer.* Cf. 44:12. *so it will not topple.* See 40:18–20 and notes.
41:8–9 *my servant.* A significant term in chs. 41–53, referring sometimes to the nation of Israel and other times to an individual. In these passages the title refers to one who occupies a special position in God's royal administration of his kingdom, as in "my servant Moses" (Nu 12:7), "my servant David" (2Sa 3:18; 7:5,8), "my servants the prophets" (2Ki 17:13; Jer 7:25). See note on 42:1; see also 20:3; 22:20; 42:1,19; 43:10; 44:1–2,21; 45:4; 49:3,5–7; 50:10; 52:13; 53:11.
41:8 *But.* In contrast to the nations of vv. 5–7, Israel does not need to be afraid (v. 10). *Abraham my friend.* See Ge 18; 2Ch 20:7; Jas 2:23 and note.
41:9 *ends of the earth.* See v. 5; probably a reference to Mesopotamia and Egypt (see Ge 11:31; 12:1; 15:7; Ps 114:1–2; Jer 31:32).
41:10 *do not fear ... be dismayed.* See vv. 13–14; 43:1,5; see also 35:4 and note. *strengthen ... help you.* As one called to

I will strengthen[x] you and help[y] you;
I will uphold you[z] with my righteous
right hand.[a]

11 "All who rage[b] against you
will surely be ashamed and
disgraced;[c]
those who oppose[d] you
will be as nothing and perish.[e]
12 Though you search for your enemies,
you will not find them.[f]
Those who wage war against you
will be as nothing[g] at all.
13 For I am the LORD, your God,
who takes hold of your right hand[h]
and says to you, Do not fear;
I will help[i] you.
14 Do not be afraid,[j] O worm[k] Jacob,
O little Israel,
for I myself will help[l] you," declares
the LORD,
your Redeemer,[m] the Holy One[n] of
Israel.
15 "See, I will make you into a threshing
sledge,[o]
new and sharp, with many teeth.
You will thresh the mountains[p] and
crush them,
and reduce the hills to chaff.[q]
16 You will winnow[r] them, the wind will
pick them up,
and a gale[s] will blow them away.[t]
But you will rejoice[u] in the LORD
and glory[v] in the Holy One[w] of
Israel.
17 "The poor and needy search for water,[x]
but there is none;
their tongues are parched with
thirst.[y]
But I the LORD will answer[z] them;
I, the God of Israel, will not forsake[a]
them.

41:10 [x]S Ps 68:35; S 119:28 [y]ver 13-14; Isa 44:2; 49:8; 50:7,9 [z]S Ps 18:35; S 119:117 [a]S Ex 3:20; S Job 40:14 **41:11** [b]S Isa 17:12 [c]Isa 29:22; 45:24; 54:17 [d]S Ex 23:22 [e]S Isa 29:8; S Jer 2:3 **41:12** [f]Ps 37:35-36; S Isa 34:12 [g]S Job 7:8; Isa 17:14; 29:20 **41:13** [h]Ps 73:23; Isa 42:6; 45:1; 51:18 [i]ver 10 **41:14** [j]S Ge 15:1 [k]S Job 4:19; S Ps 22:6 [l]S ver 10 [m]S Ex 15:13; S Job 19:25; S Isa 1:27 [n]ver 16,20; S Isa 1:4 **41:15** [o]S Job 41:30; S Isa 10:5; S 21:10 [p]S Ex 19:18; S Ps 107:33; Jer 9:10; Eze 33:28 [q]S ver 2 **41:16** [r]Jer 15:7; 51:2 [s]Isa 40:24 [t]Da 2:35 [u]S Isa 25:9 [v]Isa 45:25; 60:19 [w]S ver 14; S Mk 1:24 **41:17** [x]Isa 43:20 [y]S Isa 35:7 [z]S Isa 30:19 [a]S Dt 31:6; S Ps 27:9 **41:18** [b]S Isa 30:25 [c]Isa 43:19 [d]S 2Ki 3:17

18 I will make rivers flow[b] on barren
heights,
and springs within the valleys.
I will turn the desert[c] into pools of
water,[d]
and the parched ground into springs.[e]
19 I will put in the desert[f]
the cedar and the acacia,[g] the myrtle
and the olive.
I will set pines[h] in the wasteland,
the fir and the cypress[i] together,[j]
20 so that people may see and know,[k]
may consider and understand,[l]
that the hand[m] of the LORD has done
this,
that the Holy One[n] of Israel has
created[o] it.

21 "Present your case,[p]" says the LORD.
"Set forth your arguments," says
Jacob's King.[q]
22 "Bring in ˛your idols˛ to tell us
what is going to happen.[r]
Tell us what the former things[s] were,
so that we may consider them
and know their final outcome.
Or declare to us the things to come,[t]
23 tell us what the future holds,
so we may know[u] that you are gods.
Do something, whether good or bad,[v]
so that we will be dismayed[w] and
filled with fear.
24 But you are less than nothing[x]
and your works are utterly
worthless;[y]
he who chooses you is detestable.[z]

[e]S Job 38:26; S Isa 35:7 **41:19** [f]S Isa 35:1; 51:3 [g]Ex 25:5, 10, 13 [h]S Isa 37:24 [i]Isa 44:14 [j]Isa 60:13 **41:20** [k]S Ex 6:7 [l]S Isa 29:24 [m]Ezr 7:6; 8:31; Isa 50:2; 51:9; 59:1; 66:14; Jer 32:17 [n]S ver 14; Isa 43:3, 14 [o]S Isa 4:5 **41:21** [p]S ver 1 [q]Isa 43:15; 44:6 **41:22** [r]ver 26; Isa 43:9; 44:7; 45:21; 48:14 [s]Isa 43:18, 26; 46:9; 48:3 [t]Isa 42:9; 43:19; 46:10; 48:6; 65:17; Jn 13:19 **41:23** [u]Isa 45:3 [v]Jer 10:5 [w]S 2Ki 19:26 **41:24** [x]S Isa 37:19; 1Co 8:4 [y]S 1Sa 12:21; Jer 8:19; 10:5, 8, 15 [z]S Ps 109:7; S Isa 1:13; S 48:8

God's service (see vv. 9,15–16). See also v. 14; 40:29; 44:2; 49:8. *right hand.* A hand of power and salvation (see Ex 15:6,12; Ps 20:6; 48:10; 89:13; 98:1).

41:11 *be ashamed and disgraced.* Cf. 45:17; 50:7; 54:4. *will be as nothing.* See vv. 15–16 and notes.

41:13 *takes hold ... right hand.* To strengthen them and keep them from stumbling. *Do not fear.* See v. 10 and note.

41:14 *worm.* A reference to their feeble and despised condition in exile (cf. Job 25:6; Ps 22:6). *Redeemer.* Deliverer from Babylonian exile (in a new exodus). The Hebrew for this word refers to an obligated family protector and thus portrays the Lord as the family protector of Israel. He is related to Israel as father (63:16; 64:8) and husband (54:5). As Redeemer (or family protector), he redeems their property (for he regathers them to their land, 54:1–8), guarantees their freedom (35:9; 43:1–4; 48:20; 52:11–12), avenges them against their tormentors (47:3–4; 49:25–26; 64:4) and secures their posterity for the future (61:8–9). See note on Ru 2:20. *Holy One of Israel.* See vv. 16,20; see also 1:4 and note. The title occurs with "Redeemer" also in 43:14; 47:4; 48:17; 49:7; 54:5.

41:15 *threshing sledge.* Cf. 28:27; Am 1:3 and note; Mic 4:13; Hab 3:12. *mountains ... hills.* Probably represents the nations. See 2:14. *reduce ... to chaff.* See v. 2; 17:13 and note; 29:5–6.

41:16 *winnow.* A figure of judgment used also in Jer 51:2 (see note on Ru 1:22). *rejoice.* Cf. 25:9; 35:10; 51:11.

41:17 *poor and needy.* Israel in exile or on the way home (cf. v. 14; 32:7). *will answer.* See 30:19 and note.

41:18 *rivers ... on barren heights.* See 30:25 and note. *desert into pools ... springs.* See 32:2; 35:6–7 and notes.

41:19 These trees will beautify the desert (cf. 35:1–2). Several are named in 60:13 in connection with adorning the place of God's sanctuary. Acacia wood was used for the tabernacle (see Ex 25:5 and note, 10,13). The pine tree and myrtle replace thorns and briers in 55:13.

41:20 *created it.* These fruitful conditions are part of God's new creation in behalf of his people (see 48:7; 57:19; 65:17–18).

41:21–22 God takes the nations and their idols to court (see v. 1 and note).

41:22 *former things.* Earlier divine predictions or accomplishments (see 42:9; 43:9,18; 46:9; 48:3).

41:23 *Do something ... good or bad.* See note on 40:18–20.

41:24 *less than nothing ... worthless.* Like the nations that worship them. See 40:17; 44:9; Hos 9:10. *detestable.* Like those who marry idolaters (see Mal 2:11 and note).

25 "I have stirred[a] up one from the north,[b]
and he comes—
one from the rising sun who calls on my name.
He treads[c] on rulers as if they were mortar,
as if he were a potter treading the clay.
26 Who told of this from the beginning,[d]
so we could know,
or beforehand, so we could say, 'He was right'?
No one told of this,
no one foretold[e] it,
no one heard any words[f] from you.
27 I was the first to tell[g] Zion, 'Look, here they are!'
I gave to Jerusalem a messenger of good tidings.[h]
28 I look but there is no one[i]—
no one among them to give counsel,[j]
no one to give answer[k] when I ask them.
29 See, they are all false!
Their deeds amount to nothing;[l]
their images[m] are but wind[n] and confusion.

The Servant of the LORD

42 "Here is my servant,[o] whom I uphold,
my chosen one[p] in whom I delight;[q]
I will put my Spirit[r] on him
and he will bring justice[s] to the nations.[t]
2 He will not shout or cry out,[u]
or raise his voice in the streets.
3 A bruised reed[v] he will not break,[w]
and a smoldering wick he will not snuff out.[x]
In faithfulness he will bring forth justice;[y]
4 he will not falter or be discouraged
till he establishes justice[z] on earth.
In his law[a] the islands[b] will put their hope."[c]

5 This is what God the LORD says—
he who created the heavens[d] and stretched them out,
who spread out the earth[e] and all that comes out of it,[f]
who gives breath[g] to its people,
and life to those who walk on it:
6 "I, the LORD, have called[h] you in righteousness;[i]
I will take hold of your hand.[j]
I will keep[k] you and will make you
to be a covenant[l] for the people
and a light[m] for the Gentiles,[n]
7 to open eyes that are blind,[o]
to free[p] captives from prison[q]
and to release from the dungeon
those who sit in darkness.[r]

8 "I am the LORD;[s] that is my name![t]
I will not give my glory to another[u]
or my praise to idols.[v]

41:25 [a]S Ezr 1:2 [b]S ver 2; Jer 50:9,41; 51:48 [c]S 2Sa 22:43; S Isa 5:5; Na 3:14 **41:26** [d]S ver 4 [e]S ver 22; Isa 52:6 [f]S 1Ki 18:26; Hab 2:18-19 **41:27** [g]Isa 48:3,16 [h]S Isa 40:9 **41:28** [i]Ps 22:11; Isa 50:2; 59:16; 63:5; 64:7; Eze 22:30 [j]Isa 40:13-14 [k]S 1Ki 18:26; Isa 65:12; 66:4; Jer 25:4 **41:29** [l]S 1Sa 12:21 [m]S Isa 37:19 [n]Jer 5:13 **42:1** [o]S Isa 20:3; S Mt 20:28 [p]S Isa 14:1; Lk 9:35; 23:35; 1Pe 2:4,6 [q]Mt 3:17 [r]S Isa 11:2; S 44:3; Mt 3:16-17; S Jn 3:34 [s]S Isa 9:7 [t]S Ge 49:10 **42:2** [u]Pr 8:1-4 **42:3** [v]S Isa 36:6 [w]S Job 30:24 [x]S Job 13:25 [y]Ps 72:2; 96:13 **42:4** [z]S Isa 2:4 [a]ver 21; Ex 34:29; Isa 51:4 [b]S Isa 11:11 [c]S Ge 49:10; Mt 12:18-21* **42:5** [d]S Ge 1:6; Ps 102:25; Isa 48:13 [e]S Ge 1:1 [f]Ps 24:2; Ac 17:24 [g]S Ge 2:7; Ac 17:25 **42:6** [h]Ex 31:2; S Jdg 4:10; Isa 41:9-10; 43:1 [i]Isa 45:24; Jer 23:6; Da 9:7 [j]Isa 41:13; 45:1 [k]Isa 26:3; 27:3 [l]Isa 49:8; 54:10; 59:21; 61:8; Jer 31:31; 32:40; Mal 3:1; S Lk 22:20 [m]S Isa 9:2 [n]S Isa 26:18; S Lk 2:32 **42:7** [o]S Ps 146:8; S Isa 32:3; Mt 11:5 [p]Isa 49:9; 51:14; 52:2; Zec 2:7 [q]S Ps 66:11; S Isa 24:22; 48:20; Zec 9:11; S Lk 4:19; 2Ti 2:26; Heb 2:14-15 [r]S Ps 107:10,14; Ac 26:18 **42:8** [s]Ps 81:10; Isa 43:3,11,15; 46:9; 49:23 [t]S Ex 3:15; S 6:3 [u]Isa 48:11 [v]S Ex 8:10; S 20:4

41:25 *stirred up.* See v. 2 and note. *from the north.* Cyrus came from the east (v. 2) but conquered a number of kingdoms north of Babylon early in his reign. From the perspective of those living in Jerusalem, invasions came primarily from the north (see 14:31; Jer 1:14; 6:1,22; 10:22; 46:20; 50:3,9,41; 51:48). *calls on my name.* Cyrus used the Lord's name in his decree (Ezr 1:2) but did not acknowledge him (see 45:4–5 and note on 45:4). *treads on … mortar … clay.* Similar to Assyria in 10:6. Cf. Mic 7:10; Na 3:14.
41:26 *from the beginning.* Before these events began to unfold (cf. v. 4). *you.* Idols or their worshipers.
41:27 *here they are.* Words about the deliverance from Babylon. *messenger of good tidings.* The prophet. See 40:9; 52:7 and notes.
41:28 *no one to give answer.* See 46:7.
41:29 *amount to nothing.* See v. 24.
42:1–4 Quoted in part in Mt 12:18–21 (see note there) with reference to Christ. There are four "servant songs" in which the servant is the Messiah: 42:1–4 (or 42:1–7 or 42:1–9); 49:1–6 (or 49:1–7 or 49:1–13); 50:4–9 (or 50:4–11); 52:13—53:12; cf. 61:1–2 and notes. He is "Israel" in its ideal form (49:3). The nation was to be a kingdom of priests (see Ex 19:6 and note), but the Messiah would be the high priest who would atone for the sins of the world (53:4–12). Cyrus was introduced in ch. 41 as a deliverer from Babylon, but the servant would deliver the world from its bondage to sin (see v. 7).
42:1 *my servant.* See 41:8–9; Zec 3:8 and notes. In the royal terminology of the ancient Near East "servant" meant something like "trusted envoy" or "confidential representative." *chosen one.* See 41:8–9 and note. *delight.* Cf. Lk 3:22. *my Spirit on him.* Like the "Branch" of 11:1–2 (see note on 11:2); cf. 61:1. *justice.* A righteous world order (see v. 4); see also 9:7; 11:4 and notes.
42:2 *not shout or cry out.* He will bring peace (see 9:6).
42:3 *bruised reed.* Someone who is weak (see Ps 72:2,4). The servant will mend broken lives.
42:4 *falter.* Cf. 40:28. *justice.* Perfect order (see v. 1 and note). *In his law … hope.* As do the nations in 2:2–4. The servant will be a new Moses (see Dt 18:15–18; Ac 3:21–23,26). *islands.* See note on 11:11.
42:5 *created the heavens … stretched.* See 40:22 and note. *gives breath … life.* Cf. 57:15.
42:6 *called … righteousness.* Similar to the call of Cyrus (see 41:2 and note). *take hold of your hand.* See 41:13 and note. *covenant.* See 49:8. Through the Messiah as king, the Davidic covenant (see 2Sa 7:12–16; cf. Isa 55:3 and note) would be fulfilled (9:7), and he would institute the new covenant by his death (see Jer 31:31–34; Heb 8:6–13; 9:15 and notes). *people.* Probably the Israelites (see 49:8; Ac 26:17–18). *light for the Gentiles.* See note on 9:2. *light.* Parallel to "salvation" in 49:6 (cf. 51:4).
42:7 *open eyes.* See 29:18; 32:3; 35:5 and notes. *free … from prison.* From the prison of Babylonia and also from spiritual and moral bondage (compare 61:1 with Lk 4:18).
42:8 *my glory.* See 40:5 and note.

[9]See, the former things[w] have taken
place,
and new things I declare;
before they spring into being
I announce[x] them to you."

Song of Praise to the LORD

[10]Sing[y] to the LORD a new song,[z]
his praise[a] from the ends of the
earth,[b]
you who go down to the sea, and all
that is in it,[c]
you islands,[d] and all who live in
them.
[11]Let the desert[e] and its towns raise their
voices;
let the settlements where Kedar[f]
lives rejoice.
Let the people of Sela[g] sing for joy;
let them shout from the
mountaintops.[h]
[12]Let them give glory[i] to the LORD
and proclaim his praise[j] in the
islands.[k]
[13]The LORD will march out like a mighty[l]
man,
like a warrior[m] he will stir up his
zeal;[n]
with a shout[o] he will raise the battle cry
and will triumph over his enemies.[p]
[14]"For a long time I have kept silent,[q]
I have been quiet and held myself
back.[r]
But now, like a woman in childbirth,
I cry out, I gasp and pant.[s]
[15]I will lay waste[t] the mountains[u] and
hills
and dry up all their vegetation;
I will turn rivers into islands
and dry up[v] the pools.
[16]I will lead[w] the blind[x] by ways they
have not known,
along unfamiliar paths I will guide
them;
I will turn the darkness into light[y]
before them
and make the rough places smooth.[z]
These are the things I will do;
I will not forsake[a] them.
[17]But those who trust in idols,
who say to images, 'You are our
gods,'[b]
will be turned back in utter shame.[c]

Israel Blind and Deaf

[18]"Hear, you deaf;[d]
look, you blind, and see!
[19]Who is blind[e] but my servant,[f]
and deaf like the messenger[g] I send?
Who is blind like the one committed[h]
to me,
blind like the servant of the LORD?
[20]You have seen many things, but have
paid no attention;
your ears are open, but you hear
nothing."
[21]It pleased the LORD
for the sake[j] of his righteousness
to make his law[k] great and
glorious.
[22]But this is a people plundered[l] and
looted,
all of them trapped in pits[m]
or hidden away in prisons.[n]
They have become plunder,
with no one to rescue them;[o]
they have been made loot,
with no one to say, "Send them
back."
[23]Which of you will listen to this
or pay close attention[p] in time to
come?
[24]Who handed Jacob over to become
loot,
and Israel to the plunderers?[q]
Was it not the LORD,[r]
against whom we have sinned?
For they would not follow[s] his ways;
they did not obey his law.[t]

42:9 [w]S Isa 41:22 [x]S Isa 40:21; Eze 2:4 **42:10** [y]S Ex 15:1 [z]S Ps 96:1 [a]1Ki 10:9; Isa 60:6 [b]S Dt 30:4; S Ps 48:10; 65:5; Isa 49:6 [c]S 1Ch 16:32; Ps 96:11 [d]S Isa 11:11 **42:11** [e]S Isa 32:16 [f]S Ge 25:13; Isa 60:7 [g]S Jdg 1:36 [h]Isa 52:7; Na 1:15 **42:12** [i]S 1Ch 16:24; S Isa 24:15 [j]S Ps 26:7; S 66:2; 1Pe 2:9 [k]S Isa 11:11 **42:13** [l]S Isa 9:6 [m]S Ex 14:14 [n]S Isa 26:11 [o]S Jos 6:5; Jer 25:30; Hos 11:10; Joel 3:16; Am 1:2; 3:4,8 [p]Isa 66:14 **42:14** [q]S Est 4:14; S Ps 50:21 [r]S Ge 43:31; Lk 18:7; 2Pe 3:9 [s]Jer 4:31 **42:15** [t]Eze 38:20 [u]S Ps 107:33 [v]S Isa 11:15; 50:2; Na 1:4-6 **42:16** [w]S Isa 29:24; 40:11; 57:18; 58:11; Jer 31:8-9; Lk 1:78-79 [x]S Isa 32:3 [y]S Ps 18:28; Isa 58:8, 10; S Ac 26:18 [z]S Isa 26:7; Lk 3:5 [a]S Dt 4:31; Heb 13:5 **42:17** [b]S Ex 32:4 [c]S Ps 97:7; S Isa 1:29 **42:18** [d]S Isa 35:5 **42:19** [e]Isa 43:8; Eze 12:2 [f]Isa 41:8-9 [g]Isa 44:26; Hag 1:13 [h]Isa 26:3 **42:20** [i]Isa 6:9-10; 43:8; Jer 5:21; 6:10 **42:21** [j]Isa 43:25 [k]S ver 4; 2Co 3:7 **42:22** [l]S Jdg 6:4; S 2Ki 24:13 [m]S Isa 24:18 [n]S Ps 66:11; S Isa 24:22 [o]S Isa 5:29 **42:23** [p]Dt 32:29; Ps 81:13; Isa 47:7; 48:18; 57:11 **42:24** [q]S 2Ki 17:6; Isa 43:28; 47:6 [r]Isa 10:5-6 [s]S Isa 30:15 [t]S Jos 1:7; S Ps 119:136; Isa 5:24; Jer 44:10

42:9 *former things.* See 41:22 and note. *new things.* The restoration of Israel (43:19). Cf. 48:6.
42:10 *new song.* To celebrate the "new things" of v. 9. *ends of the earth.* See 11:12 and note; 41:5. *islands.* See v. 12; 11:11 and note.
42:11 *desert.* See 35:1 and note. *Kedar.* See note on 21:16. *Sela.* See note on 16:1.
42:12 *give glory ... praise.* See 24:14–16.
42:13 *mighty man.* God will fight as he did at the Red Sea (Ex 15:3); see 9:6 and note. *zeal.* Cf. 9:7; 37:32; 59:17; 63:15. *raise the battle cry.* To cause panic among the enemy (see 1Sa 4:5–8).
42:14 *For a long time.* During Israel's humiliation and exile. *held myself back.* See 63:15; 64:12. The Hebrew verb is also used of Joseph, who controlled his emotions while he tested his brothers (Ge 43:31; 45:1). See 30:18 and note.
42:15 *lay waste ... dry up.* The opposite of 35:1–2; 41:18. *rivers into islands.* Perhaps to make travel easier. See 37:25; 44:27.
42:16 *blind.* Israel (vv. 19–20). *rough places smooth.* See note on 26:7. *not forsake.* Cf. 40:27; 49:14; 54:8.
42:18 *deaf ... blind.* See 6:10 and note.
42:19 *my servant.* Israel. See note on 41:8–9. *messenger I send.* A term associated with prophets (see Hag 1:13; cf. Isa 44:26; Mal 3:1).
42:21 *law great and glorious.* Especially the law of Moses, given in the awesome setting of Mount Sinai (see Ex 34:29).
42:22 *plundered and looted.* By the Assyrians (see 10:6 and note) and the Babylonians (see 39:6). *trapped in pits ... prisons.* See v. 7 and note. Cf. Jdg 6:2–4.
42:24 *Who handed Jacob over ...?* Babylonia conquered Israel, not because their gods were stronger than the Lord (see 40:17–18; 1Ki 20:23 and note), but because the Lord was punishing his people.

25 So he poured out on them his burning
anger,[u]
the violence of war.
It enveloped them in flames,[v] yet they
did not understand;[w]
it consumed them, but they did not
take it to heart.[x]

Israel's Only Savior

43 But now, this is what the LORD says—
he who created[y] you, O Jacob,
he who formed[z] you, O Israel:[a]
"Fear not, for I have redeemed[b] you;
I have summoned you by name;[c] you
are mine.[d]
2 When you pass through the waters,[e]
I will be with you;[f]
and when you pass through the rivers,
they will not sweep over you.
When you walk through the fire,[g]
you will not be burned;
the flames will not set you ablaze.[h]
3 For I am the LORD, your God,[i]
the Holy One[j] of Israel, your Savior;[k]
I give Egypt[l] for your ransom,
Cush[a][m] and Seba[n] in your stead.[o]
4 Since you are precious and honored[p]
in my sight,
and because I love[q] you,
I will give men in exchange for you,
and people in exchange for your life.
5 Do not be afraid,[r] for I am with you;[s]
I will bring your children[t] from the
east
and gather[u] you from the west.[v]
6 I will say to the north, 'Give them up!'
and to the south,[w] 'Do not hold
them back.'
Bring my sons from afar
and my daughters[x] from the ends of
the earth[y]—
7 everyone who is called by my name,[z]
whom I created[a] for my glory,[b]
whom I formed and made.[c]"
8 Lead out those who have eyes but are
blind,[d]
who have ears but are deaf.[e]
9 All the nations gather together[f]
and the peoples assemble.
Which of them foretold[g] this
and proclaimed to us the former
things?
Let them bring in their witnesses to
prove they were right,
so that others may hear and say, "It
is true."
10 "You are my witnesses,[h]" declares the
LORD,
"and my servant[i] whom I have
chosen,
so that you may know[j] and believe me
and understand that I am he.
Before me no god[k] was formed,
nor will there be one after me.[l]
11 I, even I, am the LORD,[m]
and apart from me there is no
savior.[n]
12 I have revealed and saved and
proclaimed—
I, and not some foreign god[o] among
you.
You are my witnesses,[p]" declares the
LORD, "that I am God.

[a] *3* That is, the upper Nile region

42:25 [u] S 2Ki 22:13; S Job 40:11; S Isa 51:17; S Eze 7:19 [v] 2Ki 25:9; Isa 66:15; Jer 4:4; 21:12; La 2:3; Na 1:6 [w] S Isa 1:3 [x] Isa 29:13; 47:7; 57:1,11; Hos 7:9 **43:1** [y] S Isa 27:11 [z] S ver 7; S Ge 2:7 [a] Ge 32:28; Isa 44:21 [b] S Ex 6:6; S Job 19:25 [c] S Isa 42:6; 45:3-4; 49:1 [d] S Dt 7:6; Mal 3:17 **43:2** [e] S Isa 8:7 [f] S Ge 26:3; S Ex 14:22 [g] Isa 29:6; 30:27 [h] Ps 66:12; Da 3:25-27 **43:3** [i] S Ex 20:2 [j] S Isa 41:20 [k] S Ex 14:30; S Jdg 2:18; S Ps 3:8; S Isa 25:9 [l] S Ps 68:31; Isa 19:1; Eze 29:20 [m] S Isa 20:3 [n] S Ge 10:7 [o] S Pr 21:18 **43:4** [p] Ex 19:5; Isa 49:5 [q] Isa 63:9; Rev 3:9 **43:5** [r] S Ge 15:1; Isa 44:2 [s] S Ge 21:22; S Ex 14:22; Jer 30:10-11 [t] Isa 41:8; 54:3; 61:9; 66:22 [u] S Isa 11:12; S 49:18 [v] S Isa 24:14; Zec 8:7; S Mt 8:11 **43:6** [w] Ps 107:3 [x] Isa 60:4; Eze 16:61; 2Co 6:18 [y] S Dt 30:4; S Isa 11:12; Jer 23:8; Eze 36:24 **43:7** [z] Isa 48:1; 56:5; 62:2; 63:19; 65:1; Jer 15:16; Jas 2:7 [a] S Isa 27:11 [b] S Ps 86:9 [c] ver 1,21; Ps 100:3; S Isa 19:25 **43:8** [d] S Isa 6:9-10 [e] S Isa 42:20; Eze 12:2 **43:9** [f] S Isa 41:1; 45:20; 48:14 [g] S Isa 41:26 **43:10** [h] ver 12; S Jos 24:22 [i] S Isa 20:3; 41:8-9 [j] S Ex 6:7 [k] ver 11; S Ps 86:10; Isa 19:21; 44:6,8; 45:5-6,14 [l] S Dt 4:35; S 32:39; Jer 14:22 **43:11** [m] S Ex 6:2; S Isa 42:8 [n] S ver 10; S Ps 3:8; S 18:31; S Isa 25:9; 64:4 **43:12** [o] S Dt 32:12 [p] S ver 10

42:25 *poured out … anger.* Israel had a foretaste of the day of the Lord (see 5:25; 9:12,17,21; 13:3; 34:2 and notes; cf. Joel 1:15; Am 5:18 and notes).

43:1 *created … formed.* God made the nation Israel as surely as he made the first man and woman (see Ge 1:27 and note; see also Isa 43:7,15,21; 44:2,24). *Fear not.* See 41:10 and note. *redeemed you.* See notes on 35:9; 41:14. The verb is also used in 29:22; 44:22–23; 48:20 (cf. Ex 15:13). *summoned … by name.* God chose Israel to serve him in a special way. See 45:3–4 (Cyrus). In Ex 31:2; 35:30 the Hebrew underlying this expression is translated "chosen."

43:2 *waters … rivers.* Probably an allusion to crossing the Red Sea (Ex 14:21–22) and the Jordan River (Jos 3:14–17). Cf. Ps 66:6,12. *walk through the fire.* Cf. the experience of Shadrach, Meshach and Abednego (Da 3:25–27). Contrast 42:25.

43:3 *Holy One of Israel.* See notes on 1:4; 41:14. *Savior.* Who delivers from the oppression of Egypt or Babylonia and from the spiritual oppression of sin (see 19:20 and note; 25:9 and note; 33:22; 35:4 and note; 43:11–12; 45:15,21–22; 49:25; 60:16; 63:8–9). *ransom.* The Persians conquered Egypt, Cush and Seba, and perhaps this was a reward or ransom for Persia's kindness to Israel (see note on 41:2; cf. Eze 29:19–20). *Cush.* See note on 18:1. *Seba.* A land near Cush (cf. 45:14) or Sheba (Ps 72:10). It was probably either in south Arabia (see Ge 10:7 and note; see also Eze 27:21–22) or in east Africa.

43:5 *Do not be afraid.* See 41:10 and note. *east.* Especially Assyria and Babylonia. See 11:11–12 and notes; cf. Ps 107:3. *west.* For example, the "islands" of 11:11 (see also 24:14–15; 49:12).

43:6 *north.* For example, Hamath (see 10:9 and note; 11:11). *south.* Egypt. *ends of the earth.* See note on 11:12 (cf. 41:5; 42:10).

43:7 *called by my name.* People belonging to God. *created … formed.* See v. 1 and note.

43:8 *blind … deaf.* Probably referring to Israel (see 6:10 and note; 42:18–20).

43:9–13 A court scene; see also 41:21–22.

43:9 *nations … peoples assemble.* See 41:1 and note. *foretold.* See 41:26 and note. *former things.* See 41:22 and note. *witnesses.* To verify the accuracy of earlier predictions by idols or their worshipers (see 41:26).

43:10 *You are my witnesses.* See also v. 12; 44:8. God's work in behalf of Israel is proof of his saving power. *my servant.* See 41:8–9 and note.

43:11 The main thrust is repeated in 44:6,8; 45:5–6,18,21–22; 46:9 (see also Dt 32:39). *savior.* See v. 3 and note.

43:12 *foreign god.* Cf. Dt 32:12,16. Israel repeatedly worshiped other gods (see Jdg 2:12–13 and notes). *witnesses.* See v. 10 and note.

13 Yes, and from ancient days[q] I am he.[r]
No one can deliver out of my hand.
When I act, who can reverse it?"[s]

God's Mercy and Israel's Unfaithfulness

14 This is what the LORD says—
your Redeemer,[t] the Holy One[u] of Israel:
"For your sake I will send to Babylon
and bring down as fugitives[v] all the Babylonians,[a][w]
in the ships in which they took pride.
15 I am the LORD,[x] your Holy One,
Israel's Creator,[y] your King.[z]"

16 This is what the LORD says—
he who made a way through the sea,
a path through the mighty waters,[a]
17 who drew out[b] the chariots and horses,[c]
the army and reinforcements together,[d]
and they lay[e] there, never to rise again,
extinguished, snuffed out like a wick:[f]
18 "Forget the former things;[g]
do not dwell on the past.
19 See, I am doing a new thing![h]
Now it springs up; do you not perceive it?
I am making a way in the desert[i]
and streams in the wasteland.[j]
20 The wild animals[k] honor me,
the jackals[l] and the owls,
because I provide water[m] in the desert
and streams in the wasteland,
to give drink to my people, my chosen,
21 the people I formed[n] for myself[o]
that they may proclaim my praise.[p]

22 "Yet you have not called upon me,
O Jacob,
you have not wearied[q] yourselves for me, O Israel.[r]
23 You have not brought me sheep for burnt offerings,[s]
nor honored[t] me with your sacrifices.[u]
I have not burdened[v] you with grain offerings
nor wearied you with demands[w] for incense.[x]
24 You have not bought any fragrant calamus[y] for me,
or lavished on me the fat[z] of your sacrifices.
But you have burdened me with your sins
and wearied[a] me with your offenses.[b]

25 "I, even I, am he who blots out
your transgressions,[c] for my own sake,[d]
and remembers your sins[e] no more.[f]
26 Review the past for me,
let us argue the matter together;[g]
state the case[h] for your innocence.
27 Your first father[i] sinned;
your spokesmen[j] rebelled[k] against me.
28 So I will disgrace the dignitaries of your temple,
and I will consign Jacob to destruction[b][l]
and Israel to scorn.[m]

[a] 14 Or *Chaldeans* [b] 28 The Hebrew term refers to the irrevocable giving over of things or persons to the LORD, often by totally destroying them.

43:13 [q]Ps 90:2 [r]S Dt 32:39; Isa 46:4; 48:12 [s]S Nu 23:8; S Job 9:12 **43:14** [t]S Ex 15:13; S Job 19:25 [u]S Isa 1:4; S 41:20 [v]Isa 13:14-15 [w]S Isa 23:13 **43:15** [x]S Isa 42:8 [y]S Isa 27:11; 45:11 [z]S Isa 41:21 **43:16** [a]S Ex 14:29; S 15:8; S Isa 11:15 **43:17** [b]Ps 118:12; Isa 1:31 [c]S Ex 14:22 [d]S Ex 14:9 [e]Ps 76:5-6 [f]S Job 13:25; Jer 51:21; Eze 38:4 **43:18** [g]S Isa 41:22 **43:19** [h]S Isa 41:22; Jer 16:14-15; 23:7-8; 2Co 5:17; Rev 21:5 [i]S Isa 40:3 [j]S Ps 126:4; S Isa 33:21; S 35:7 **43:20** [k]S Ps 148:10 [l]S Isa 13:22 [m]S Nu 20:8 **43:21** [n]S ver 7; S Ge 2:7 [o]Mal 3:17 [p]S Ps 66:2; 102:18; 1Pe 2:9 **43:22** [q]S Jos 22:5; S Isa 1:14 [r]Isa 30:11 **43:23** [s]S Ex 29:41 [t]Zec 7:5-6; Mal 1:6-8 [u]Am 5:25 [v]Mic 6:3; Mal 1:12-13 [w]Jer 7:22 [x]Ex 30:35; S Lev 2:1 **43:24** [y]S Ex 30:23 [z]Lev 3:9 [a]S Isa 1:14; S 7:13; S Jer 8:21 [b]Jer 44:22; Mal 2:17 **43:25** [c]S 2Sa 12:13; S 2Ch 6:21; Mk 2:7; Lk 5:21; Ac 3:19 [d]S Isa 37:35; S Eze 20:44 [e]Isa 64:9; Mic 7:18 [f]S Job 7:21; S Isa 38:17 **43:26** [g]S Isa 1:18 [h]S Isa 41:1; 49:25; 50:8 **43:27** [i]S Ge 12:18 [j]Isa 9:15; 28:7; Jer 5:31 [k]S Isa 24:20; S 48:8 **43:28** [l]S Nu 5:27; S Dt 13:15; S Isa 42:24; S Zec 5:3 [m]S Ps 39:8; Jer 24:9; Eze 5:15

43:13 See v. 11. *No one can deliver ... hand.* Identical to Dt 32:39.

43:14 *Redeemer.* See 41:14 and note. *Holy One of Israel.* See 1:4; 41:14 and notes. *Babylon.* See note on 13:1. *fugitives ... in the ships.* The Babylonians used the Persian Gulf, as well as the Tigris and Euphrates rivers, for trading purposes. But their splendid ships (cf. 2:16) would one day become their means of flight (cf. Jer 51:13).

43:15 *Creator.* See v. 1 and note. *King.* God was called "king over Jeshurun" (Israel) in Dt 33:5 (contrast 1Sa 8:7).

43:16–17 A reference to crossing the Red Sea (see v. 2 and note). The pharaoh's chariots and horsemen were destroyed as Israel's God fought against them (see 51:10; Ex 14:28; 15:4).

43:17 *snuffed out like a wick.* Contrast 42:3.

43:18–19 *former things ... new thing.* See 41:22; 42:9 and notes.

43:19 *way in the desert.* See 35:8; 40:3 and notes. *streams in the wasteland.* See v. 20; 32:2 and note. Contrast 42:15 and note.

43:20 *jackals ... owls.* Creatures of the desert (see 13:21–22; 34:13–15; 35:7).

43:21 *people ... proclaim my praise.* Cf. 42:12.

43:22–24 The Israelites may have brought sacrifices (see 1:11–15 and note), but their hearts were not right with God.

43:22 *not called ... not wearied.* Apparently their prayers were halfhearted (contrast Ps 69:3).

43:23 *not burdened ... nor wearied.* God did not make excessive demands on his people.

43:24 *calamus.* Linked with incense (see v. 23) also in SS 4:14; Jer 6:20. *fat.* See note on 34:6. *burdened ... wearied.* See 1:14.

43:25 *blots out ... transgressions.* See Ps 51:1 and note. In spite of the punishment Israel must suffer (v. 28), God is eager to forgive and restore his people (see 1:18; 44:22–23; see also 40:2 and note).

43:26 *state the case.* The Lord takes Israel to court, as he did the nations in 41:21–22.

43:27 *first father.* Either (1) Adam (the ultimate father; see Ge 5:3 and note; see also note on Lk 3:23–38) or (2) Abraham (the more immediate father; see 51:2) or most likely (3) Jacob (the even more immediate father; cf. vv. 22,28). All were sinners, the main point for the present sinful generation. *spokesmen.* Probably the priests and prophets.

43:28 *consign ... to destruction.* See NIV text note; see also note on 34:2. Any town of Israel that harbored

Israel the Chosen

44 "But now listen, O Jacob, my
servant,[n]
Israel, whom I have chosen.[o]
2 This is what the LORD says—
he who made[p] you, who formed you
in the womb,[q]
and who will help[r] you:
Do not be afraid,[s] O Jacob, my
servant,[t]
Jeshurun,[u] whom I have chosen.
3 For I will pour water[v] on the thirsty
land,
and streams on the dry ground;[w]
I will pour out my Spirit[x] on your
offspring,
and my blessing[y] on your
descendants.[z]
4 They will spring up like grass[a] in a
meadow,
like poplar trees[b] by flowing
streams.[c]
5 One will say, 'I belong[d] to the LORD';
another will call himself by the
name of Jacob;
still another will write on his hand,[e]
'The LORD's,'[f]
and will take the name Israel.

The LORD, Not Idols

6 "This is what the LORD says—
Israel's King[g] and Redeemer,[h] the
LORD Almighty:
I am the first and I am the last;[i]
apart from me there is no God.[j]
7 Who then is like me?[k] Let him
proclaim it.
Let him declare and lay out before
me
what has happened since I established
my ancient people,
and what is yet to come—
yes, let him foretell[l] what will come.
8 Do not tremble, do not be afraid.
Did I not proclaim[m] this and foretell
it long ago?
You are my witnesses. Is there any
God[n] besides me?
No, there is no other Rock;[o] I know
not one."
9 All who make idols[p] are nothing,
and the things they treasure are
worthless.[q]
Those who would speak up for them
are blind;[r]
they are ignorant, to their own
shame.[s]
10 Who shapes a god and casts an idol,[t]
which can profit him nothing?[u]
11 He and his kind will be put to shame;[v]
craftsmen are nothing but men.
Let them all come together and take
their stand;
they will be brought down to terror
and infamy.[w]

12 The blacksmith[x] takes a tool
and works with it in the coals;
he shapes an idol with hammers,
he forges it with the might of his
arm.[y]
He gets hungry and loses his strength;
he drinks no water and grows faint.[z]
13 The carpenter[a] measures with a line
and makes an outline with a marker;
he roughs it out with chisels
and marks it with compasses.
He shapes it in the form of man,[b]
of man in all his glory,
that it may dwell in a shrine.[c]
14 He cut down cedars,
or perhaps took a cypress or oak.
He let it grow among the trees of the
forest,
or planted a pine,[d] and the rain
made it grow.

44:1 [n]ver 21 [o]S Ge 16:11; S Isa 14:1 **44:2** [p]ver 21; S Ps 149:2 [q]S Ge 2:7; S Ps 139:13; S Isa 27:11 [r]S Isa 41:10 [s]S Isa 43:5 [t]Jer 30:10; 46:27 [u]S Nu 23:21; S Dt 32:15 **44:3** [v]Joel 3:18; Jn 4:10 [w]S Pr 9:5; S Isa 32:2; S 35:7 [x]S Isa 11:2; Eze 36:27; S Mk 1:8; S Ac 2:17 [y]Mal 3:10 [z]Isa 61:9; 65:23 **44:4** [a]S Job 5:25; S Ps 72:16 [b]S Lev 23:40 [c]S Job 40:22 **44:5** [d]Ps 116:16; Isa 19:21; Jer 50:5 [e]Ex 13:9 [f]Isa 60:3; 66:23; Zec 8:20-22; 13:9; 14:16 **44:6** [g]S Isa 41:21 [h]S Job 19:25; Isa 43:1 [i]S Isa 41:4; Rev 1:8,17 [j]S Dt 6:4; S 1Ch 17:20; S Ps 18:31; S Isa 43:10 **44:7** [k]S Dt 32:39 [l]S Isa 41:22,26 **44:8** [m]S Isa 40:21; S 42:9 [n]S Isa 43:10 [o]S Ge 49:24 **44:9** [p]S Ex 20:4; S Lev 19:4; Isa 40:19 [q]S Isa 41:24 [r]S Isa 26:11 [s]S Isa 1:29; 65:13; 66:5; Jer 22:22 **44:10** [t]S Isa 40:19 [u]Isa 41:29; Jer 10:5; Ac 19:26 **44:11** [v]S ver 9; S Isa 1:29 [w]S 2Ki 19:18; S Isa 37:19 **44:12** [x]S Isa 40:19; 41:6-7; 54:16 [y]Ac 17:29 [z]Isa 40:28 **44:13** [a]S Isa 41:7 [b]Ps 115:4-7 [c]S Jdg 17:4-5 **44:14** [d]S Isa 41:19

idolatry was to receive this fate (Dt 13:12–15). Jerusalem suffered destruction at the hands of the Babylonians (2Ki 25:8–9) because of idolatry (see Eze 7:15–22).

44:1–2 *my servant.* See 41:8–9 and note.

44:2 *formed you.* See 43:1 and note. *in the womb.* See v. 24. The tenderness of the Creator is shown (see also 49:5; Jer 1:5 and note). *Do not be afraid.* See v. 8; 41:10 and note. *Jeshurun.* Israel (see v. 1); found elsewhere only in Dt 32:15 (see NIV text note there); 33:5,26.

44:3 *pour water … streams.* See 30:25; 32:2; 35:6–7 and notes; see also 41:18. *pour out my Spirit.* Associated with the Messianic age in 32:15; Joel 2:28 (see notes there; see also note on Zec 12:10).

44:4 *grass.* A symbol of luxuriant growth also in 35:7 (contrast 37:27; 40:6–8).

44:5 *call … by the name.* A willingness to identify with Jacob, the Lord's people. See 43:7 and note. *write on his hand.* Perhaps a mark of ownership (cf. 49:16; Rev 13:16) or a reminder of one's allegiance (cf. Ex 13:9,16).

44:6 *King.* See 43:15 and note. *Redeemer.* See v. 24; 41:14 and note. *first … last.* See 41:4 and note. *apart … God.* See 43:11; Ex 20:3 and notes.

44:7 *foretell.* See 41:22,26 and notes.

44:8 *You are my witnesses.* See 43:10 and note. *Rock.* See 17:10 and note. As in v. 2; 43:11–13, Isaiah may be drawing on the song of Moses, which describes God as "the Rock" (Dt 32:4,15,30–31), but the metaphor is also common in the Psalms (see note on Ps 18:2).

44:9–20 A satire on the folly of idolatry (see 40:18–20 and note).

44:9 *nothing … worthless.* Like the nations and their idols (see 40:17; 41:24 and notes). *shame.* Cf. v. 11; 42:17; 45:16.

44:11 *craftsmen.* See 40:19 and note.

44:12–13 *blacksmith … carpenter.* See 48:5.

44:12 *grows faint.* But God never gets tired (40:28).

44:13 *in the form of man.* Human beings were made in the image of God (see Ge 1:26–27 and notes), but an idol is made in their image (see Dt 4:16; Ro 1:23 and note).

44:14 *cedars … cypress … oak.* The most valuable kinds of wood then known. See 2:13; 9:10; 14:8 and notes.

15 It is man's fuel[e] for burning;
some of it he takes and warms himself,
he kindles a fire and bakes bread.
But he also fashions a god and worships[f] it;
he makes an idol and bows[g] down to it.
16 Half of the wood he burns in the fire;
over it he prepares his meal,
he roasts his meat and eats his fill.
He also warms himself and says,
"Ah! I am warm; I see the fire.[h]"
17 From the rest he makes a god, his idol;
he bows down to it and worships.[i]
He prays[j] to it and says,
"Save[k] me; you are my god."
18 They know nothing, they understand[l] nothing;
their eyes[m] are plastered over so they cannot see,
and their minds closed so they cannot understand.
19 No one stops to think,
no one has the knowledge or understanding[n] to say,
"Half of it I used for fuel;[o]
I even baked bread over its coals,
I roasted meat and I ate.
Shall I make a detestable[p] thing from what is left?
Shall I bow down to a block of wood?"[q]
20 He feeds on ashes,[r] a deluded[s] heart misleads him;
he cannot save himself, or say,
"Is not this thing in my right hand a lie?[t][u]"

21 "Remember[v] these things, O Jacob,
for you are my servant, O Israel.[w]
I have made you, you are my servant;[x]
O Israel, I will not forget you.[y]

44:15 [e] ver 19 [f] S Ex 20:5; Rev 9:20 [g] S 2Ch 25:14 **44:16** [h] Isa 47:14 **44:17** [i] S Ex 20:5; Isa 2:8; Jer 1:16 [j] S 1Ki 18:26 [k] S Jdg 10:14; Isa 45:20; 46:7; 47:15 **44:18** [l] Isa 1:3; S 16:12; Jer 4:22; 10:8, 14, 14-15 [m] S Isa 6:9-10; S 29:10 **44:19** [n] ver 18-19; Isa 5:13; 27:11; 45:20 [o] ver 15 [p] S Dt 27:15 [q] Isa 40:20 **44:20** [r] Ps 102:9 [s] S Job 15:31; Ro 1:21-23, 28; 2Th 2:11; 2Ti 3:13 [t] S Dt 4:28; Hos 10:5; 13:2 [u] Isa 59:3, 4, 13; Jer 9:3; 10:14; 51:17; Ro 1:25 **44:21** [v] Isa 46:8; Zec 10:9 [w] S Isa 43:1 [x] S Ps 136:22; S Isa 27:11 [y] Ps 27:10; Isa 49:15; Jer 31:20 **44:22** [z] S 2Sa 12:13; S 2Ch 6:21; Ac 3:19 [a] S Job 22:23; Isa 45:22; 55:7; Jer 36:3; Mal 3:7 [b] S Isa 33:24; S Mt 20:28; 1Co 6:20 **44:23** [c] S Ps 98:4; S Isa 12:6 [d] S 1Ch 16:31; Ps 148:7 [e] S Ps 98:8 [f] S Ps 65:13 [g] S Ex 6:6; Isa 51:11; 62:12 [h] S Ex 16:7; S Lev 10:3; S Isa 4:2; 43:7;

22 I have swept away[z] your offenses like a cloud,
your sins like the morning mist.
Return[a] to me,
for I have redeemed[b] you."

23 Sing for joy,[c] O heavens, for the LORD has done this;
shout aloud, O earth[d] beneath.
Burst into song, you mountains,[e]
you forests and all your trees,[f]
for the LORD has redeemed[g] Jacob,
he displays his glory[h] in Israel.

Jerusalem to Be Inhabited

24 "This is what the LORD says—
your Redeemer,[i] who formed[j] you in the womb:[k]

I am the LORD,
who has made all things,
who alone stretched out the heavens,[l]
who spread out the earth[m] by myself,
25 who foils[n] the signs of false prophets
and makes fools of diviners,[o]
who overthrows the learning of the wise[p]
and turns it into nonsense,[q]
26 who carries out the words[r] of his servants
and fulfills[s] the predictions of his messengers,

who says of Jerusalem,[t] 'It shall be inhabited,'
of the towns of Judah, 'They shall be built,'
and of their ruins,[u] 'I will restore them,'[v]

46:13; 49:3; 52:1; 55:5; 60:9, 21; 61:3; Jer 30:19 **44:24** [i] S Job 19:25; Isa 43:14 [j] S Isa 27:11 [k] S Ps 139:13 [l] S Ge 2:1; S Isa 42:5 [m] S Ge 1:1 **44:25** [n] Ps 33:10 [o] Lev 19:26; 1Sa 6:2; Isa 2:6; 8:19; 47:13; Jer 27:9; Da 2:2, 10; 4:7; Mic 3:7; Zec 10:2 [p] S Job 5:13; 1Co 1:27 [q] 2Sa 15:31; 1Co 1:19-20 **44:26** [r] Isa 59:21; Zec 1:6 [s] Isa 46:10; 55:11; Jer 23:20; 39:16; La 2:17; Da 9:12; S Mt 5:18 [t] S Isa 1:1 [u] S Ps 74:3; S Isa 51:3 [v] S Ezr 9:9; S Ps 51:18; Isa 49:8-21; S 61:4

44:15 *worships ... bows down.* Repeated in vv. 17,19; see 2:8,20.

44:16 *roasts his meat ... warms himself.* Although wood serves common purposes, it is also made into an idol (see v. 19).

44:17 *Save me.* King Amaziah was condemned for worshiping the gods of Seir (Edom), a nation he had defeated in battle (see note on 2Ch 25:14–25). Isaiah denounces such idolatry as totally irrational (see 45:20). Whereas those who worshiped idols associated the god with the idol, for Isaiah there was no god for the idol to represent, so he depicts idolatry as worship of a mere "block of wood" (v. 19).

44:18 *eyes are plastered ... minds closed.* Israel's condition in 6:9–10 (see note there). The description ironically characterizes both the idols and those who worship them. See also Ps 82:5; 115:4–8 and notes.

44:19 *detestable thing.* The Lord detests idols (see Dt 27:15). In 1Ki 11:5,7; 2Ki 23:13 Molech and Chemosh are called detestable gods. Those who worship idols are also called detestable (see 41:24 and note).

44:20 *feeds on ashes.* Even devoted worship does not benefit the idolater. Cf. Hos 12:1. *lie.* Or "fraud." See 2Th 2:11 and note.

44:21 *my servant.* See vv. 1–2; 41:8–9 and note.

44:22 *swept away your offenses.* As in 40:2 (see note there), the suffering of Israel has paved the way for forgiveness and the restoration of the nation (see 43:25 and note). *Return to me.* Cf. Jer 31:18; Zec 1:3 and note. *redeemed.* Cf. v. 23; see notes on 35:9; 41:14; 43:1.

44:23 *Sing for joy ... shout aloud.* The whole creation is called on to join in praise (see also 35:1; 49:13). *Burst into song, you mountains.* See 49:13; 55:12. *displays his glory.* See 35:2; 40:5 and notes.

44:24 *Redeemer.* See 41:14 and note. *stretched out ... spread out.* See 40:22 and note; cf. 51:13.

44:25 *signs of false prophets.* See Dt 13:1–5 and notes. *diviners.* The Hebrew for this word is used of Balaam (see Jos 13:22 and note), the medium at Endor (1Sa 28:8) and false prophets (see Jer 27:9 and note). It is linked with soothsaying and sorcery (see 3:2–3 and note; Dt 18:9–11 and note on 18:9). *overthrows ... the wise.* See 29:14 and note.

44:26 *servants ... messengers.* The true prophets (see 42:19; Jer 7:25 and notes). *inhabited ... built.* See Jer 32:15; cf. Isa 58:12; 61:4. *ruins ... restore.* Contrast 6:11.

[27]who says to the watery deep, 'Be dry,
and I will dry up[w] your streams,'
[28]who says of Cyrus,[x] 'He is my
shepherd
and will accomplish all that I
please;
he will say of Jerusalem,[y] "Let it be
rebuilt,"
and of the temple,[z] "Let its
foundations[a] be laid." '

45

"This is what the LORD says to his
anointed,[b]
to Cyrus,[c] whose right hand I take
hold[d] of
to subdue nations[e] before him
and to strip kings of their armor,
to open doors before him
so that gates will not be shut:
[2]I will go before you[f]
and will level[g] the mountains[a];
I will break down gates[h] of bronze
and cut through bars of iron.[i]
[3]I will give you the treasures[j] of
darkness,
riches stored in secret places,[k]
so that you may know[l] that I am the
LORD,
the God of Israel, who summons you
by name.[m]
[4]For the sake of Jacob my servant,[n]
of Israel my chosen,
I summon you by name
and bestow on you a title of honor,
though you do not acknowledge[o]
me.
[5]I am the LORD, and there is no other;[p]
apart from me there is no God.[q]
I will strengthen you,[r]
though you have not acknowledged
me,
[6]so that from the rising of the sun
to the place of its setting[s]
men may know[t] there is none besides
me.[u]
I am the LORD, and there is no
other.
[7]I form the light and create darkness,[v]
I bring prosperity and create
disaster;[w]
I, the LORD, do all these things.
[8]"You heavens above, rain[x] down
righteousness;[y]
let the clouds shower it down.
Let the earth open wide,
let salvation[z] spring up,
let righteousness grow with it;
I, the LORD, have created it.
[9]"Woe to him who quarrels[a] with his
Maker,[b]
to him who is but a potsherd[c] among
the potsherds on the ground.
Does the clay say to the potter,[d]
'What are you making?'[e]
Does your work say,
'He has no hands'?[f]
[10]Woe to him who says to his father,
'What have you begotten?'
or to his mother,
'What have you brought to birth?'
[11]"This is what the LORD says—
the Holy One[g] of Israel, and its
Maker:[h]
Concerning things to come,
do you question me about my
children,
or give me orders about the work of
my hands?[i]

[a] *2* Dead Sea Scrolls and Septuagint; the meaning of the word in the Masoretic Text is uncertain.

44:27 [w]S Isa 11:15; S 19:5; Rev 16:12 **44:28** [x]S 2Ch 36:22; S Isa 41:2 [y]S Isa 14:32 [z]Ezr 1:2-4 [a]S Isa 28:16; 58:12 **45:1** [b]S Ps 45:7 [c]S 2Ch 36:22; S Isa 41:2 [d]Ps 73:23; Isa 41:13; 42:6 [e]Isa 48:14; Jer 50:35; 51:20, 24; Mic 4:13 **45:2** [f]Ex 23:20 [g]S Isa 40:4 [h]S Isa 13:2 [i]Ps 107:16; 147:13; Jer 51:30; La 2:9; Na 3:13 **45:3** [j]S 2Ki 24:13; Jer 50:37; 51:13 [k]Jer 41:8 [l]Isa 41:23 [m]S Ex 33:12; S Isa 43:1 **45:4** [n]S Isa 14:1; 41:8-9 [o]Ac 17:23 **45:5** [p]S Isa 44:8 [q]S Dt 32:12; S Ps 18:31; S Isa 43:10 [r]S Ps 18:39; Eze 30:24-25 **45:6** [s]S Ps 113:3; Isa 43:5 [t]S Isa 11:9 [u]ver 5, 18; Isa 14:13-14; 47:8, 10; Zep 2:15 **45:7** [v]S Ge 1:4; S Ex 10:22 [w]S Isa 14:15; S 31:2; La 3:38 **45:8** [x]Ps 72:6; S 133:3; Joel 3:18 [y]ver 24; Ps 85:11; S Isa 41:2; 46:13; 48:18; 60:21; 61:10, 11; 62:1; Hos 10:12; Joel 2:23; Am 5:24; Mal 4:2 [z]S Ps 85:9; Isa 12:3 **45:9** [a]S Job 12:13; S 15:25; S 27:2; 1Co 10:22 [b]S Job 33:13 [c]Ps 22:15 [d]S Isa 29:16; Ro 9:20-21* [e]S Job 9:12; Da 4:35 [f]S Isa 10:15 **45:11** [g]S Isa 1:4 [h]S Ps 149:2; S Isa 51:13 [i]S Ps 8:6; S Isa 19:25

44:27 *Be dry.* A reference to the crossing of the Red Sea (see 11:15; 37:25; 43:16–17 and notes; cf. 50:2; 51:10).

44:28 *Cyrus.* See 41:2 and note; see also chart, p. 472. *shepherd.* Often applied to rulers (see 2Sa 5:2; Jer 23:2). *Jerusalem ... temple.* The decree of Cyrus (Ezr 1:2–4; 6:3–5) authorized the rebuilding of the temple, which would lead to a restored Jerusalem (see 45:13).

45:1 *anointed.* "Messiah" comes from the Hebrew for this word. Cyrus, a foreign emperor, is called "his anointed" just as he is called "my shepherd" (44:28), because God has appointed him to carry out a divine commission in his role as king. Nebuchadnezzar is similarly called "my servant" (see Jer 25:9 and note; 27:6; 43:10). The servant—Christ (see note on 42:1–4)—is called "the Anointed One" in Da 9:25–26 (see NIV text note on Mt 1:17). See also Ps 2:2 and note. *right hand I ... hold.* See 41:13 and note.

45:2 *gates of bronze ... bars of iron.* Normally the doors of city gates were made of wood, and the bars were metal (see Jdg 16:3 and note).

45:3 *that you may know.* God's actions reveal his power (cf. Eze 6:7; 7:27). *summons you by name.* To indicate God's control of Cyrus's activities. See v. 4; see also note on 43:1.

45:4 *my servant.* See 41:8–9 and note. *title of honor.* Perhaps "anointed" (v. 1). *though ... not acknowledge me.* See v. 5. Cyrus apparently worshiped the chief Babylonian deity, Marduk, whom he praised in his inscriptions.

45:5 *I ... there is no other.* See vv. 6,14,18,21–22; 43:11 and note.

45:6 *rising ... to ... setting.* The whole earth (see Mal 1:11 and note).

45:7 *darkness ... disaster.* Such as the darkness that plagued the Egyptians (see Ex 10:21–23; Ps 105:28; cf. Isa 47:11; Am 3:6).

45:8 *heavens ... earth.* Let all creation serve to advance God's "righteousness" and "salvation." *rain down ... shower.* A picture of abundance (see Hos 10:12 and note). *righteousness.* In v. 13; 41:2 Cyrus is mentioned in connection with God's righteousness. God is making things right through the Persian king. *let salvation spring up.* God will deliver his people. *righteousness grow.* Peace and justice will prevail (cf. 11:4).

45:9 *clay say to the potter.* See 29:16 and note; cf. 64:8; Jer 18:6; see also Ro 9:20–21 and notes.

45:11 *Holy One of Israel.* See 1:4 and note. *children ... work of my hands.* See 29:23 and note.

12 It is I who made the earth[j]
and created mankind upon it.
My own hands stretched out the
heavens;[k]
I marshaled their starry hosts.[l]
13 I will raise up Cyrus[a][m] in my
righteousness:
I will make all his ways straight.[n]
He will rebuild my city[o]
and set my exiles free,
but not for a price or reward,[p]
says the LORD Almighty."
14 This is what the LORD says:

"The products[q] of Egypt and the
merchandise of Cush,[b]
and those tall Sabeans[r]—
they will come over to you[s]
and will be yours;
they will trudge behind you,[t]
coming over to you in chains.[u]
They will bow down before you
and plead[v] with you, saying,
'Surely God is with you,[w] and there is
no other;
there is no other god.[x]'"
15 Truly you are a God who hides[y]
himself,
O God and Savior[z] of Israel.
16 All the makers of idols will be put to
shame and disgraced;[a]
they will go off into disgrace
together.
17 But Israel will be saved[b] by the LORD
with an everlasting salvation;[c]
you will never be put to shame or
disgraced,[d]
to ages everlasting.
18 For this is what the LORD says—
he who created the heavens,
he is God;
he who fashioned and made the
earth,[e]
he founded it;
he did not create it to be empty,[f]
but formed it to be inhabited[g]—
he says:
"I am the LORD,
and there is no other.[h]
19 I have not spoken in secret,[i]
from somewhere in a land of
darkness;[j]
I have not said to Jacob's
descendants,[k]
'Seek[l] me in vain.'
I, the LORD, speak the truth;
I declare what is right.[m]
20 "Gather together[n] and come;
assemble, you fugitives from the
nations.
Ignorant[o] are those who carry[p] about
idols of wood,
who pray to gods that cannot save.[q]
21 Declare what is to be, present it—
let them take counsel together.
Who foretold[r] this long ago,
who declared it from the distant
past?[s]
Was it not I, the LORD?
And there is no God apart from me,[t]
a righteous God[u] and a Savior;[v]
there is none but me.
22 "Turn[w] to me and be saved,[x]
all you ends of the earth;[y]
for I am God, and there is no
other.[z]
23 By myself I have sworn,[a]
my mouth has uttered in all
integrity[b]
a word that will not be revoked:[c]
Before me every knee will bow;[d]
by me every tongue will swear.[e]

[a] 13 Hebrew *him* [b] 14 That is, the upper Nile region

45:12 [j] S Ge 1:1 [k] S Ge 2:1; S Isa 48:13 [l] S Ne 9:6; S Job 38:32 **45:13** [m] S 2Ch 36:22; S Isa 41:2 [n] S 1Ki 8:36; S Ps 26:12; S Isa 40:4 [o] S Ezr 1:2 [p] Isa 52:3 **45:14** [q] 2Sa 8:2; Isa 18:7; 60:5 [r] S Isa 2:3; 60:11; 62:2; Zec 8:20-22 [s] S Isa 2:3 [t] S Ge 27:29 [u] S 2Sa 3:34; S Isa 14:1-2 [v] Jer 16:19; Zec 8:20-23 [w] 1Co 14:25 [x] S Ps 18:31; S Isa 11:9; S 43:10 **45:15** [y] S Dt 31:17; Ps 44:24; S Isa 1:15 [z] S Isa 25:9 **45:16** [a] S Ps 35:4; S Isa 1:29 **45:17** [b] Jer 23:6; 33:16; Ro 11:26 [c] S Isa 12:2 [d] S Ge 30:23; S Isa 29:22; S 41:11 **45:18** [e] S Ge 1:1 [f] S Ge 1:2 [g] S Ge 1:26 [h] ver 5; Dt 4:35 **45:19** [i] Isa 48:16; 65:4 [j] Jer 2:31 [k] ver 25; Isa 41:8; 65:9; Jer 31:36 [l] S Dt 4:29; S 2Ch 15:2 [m] S Dt 30:11 **45:20** [n] S Isa 43:9 [o] S Isa 44:19 [p] Ps 115:7; Isa 46:1; Jer 10:5 [q] Dt 32:37; S Isa 44:17; Jer 1:16; 2:28 **45:21** [r] S Isa 41:22 [s] Isa 46:10 [t] ver 5; S Ps 46:10; Isa 46:9; Mk 12:32 [u] Ps 11:7 [v] S Ps 3:8; S Isa 25:9 **45:22** [w] S Isa 44:22; Zec 12:10 [x] Nu 21:8-9; S 2Ch 20:12 [y] S Ge 49:10; S Isa 11:9,12; 49:6,12 [z] Hos 13:4 **45:23** [a] S Ge 22:16; S Isa 14:24 [b] S Dt 30:11; Heb 6:13 [c] Isa 55:11 [d] S ver 14 [e] S Ps 63:11; S Isa 19:18; Ro 14:11*; Php 2:10-11

45:12 *stretched ... heavens.* See 40:22 and note. *marshaled ... starry hosts.* See 40:26 and note.

45:13 *Cyrus in my righteousness.* See note on 41:2. *make ... ways straight.* Enabling him to reach his goals (see v. 2; see also 40:3 and note; cf. Pr 3:6 and note). *rebuild my city.* See note on 44:28. *not for a price.* Since God had not received a payment when he sold them (see 52:3 and note; contrast note on 43:3).

45:14 *products ... merchandise.* See 18:7 and note. *Egypt ... Cush ... Sabeans.* See notes on 18:1; 43:3. *coming over to you ... bow down.* See Ps 68:31. Israel's future domination over her former enemies has been mentioned in 11:14; 14:1–2 (see note on 14:1); it is also the theme of 49:23; 54:3; 60:11–14. *Surely God is with you.* One day the nations will acknowledge Israel's God (see v. 23; 19:23,25; Zec 8:20–23 and notes).

45:15 *hides himself.* God's plans and actions are a mystery to humans (cf. 54:8; 55:8–9). *Savior.* See v. 21 and note on 43:3.

45:16 *put to shame.* See 42:17; 44:9.

45:17 *everlasting salvation.* Cf. the "everlasting kindness" of 54:8. *never be put to shame.* See 29:22 and note.

45:18 *created ... fashioned.* See 40:21–22 and notes. *empty.* Or "formless" or "chaotic" (see Ge 1:2 and note). *to be inhabited.* The Holy Land was now empty (see 6:11; Jer 4:23–26) and chaotic but would soon have inhabitants (see 44:26,28) and be orderly again.

45:19 *in secret ... darkness.* Probably an allusion to the clandestine ways of mediums and spiritists (see 8:19–20 and notes; 29:4). *Seek me in vain.* Cf. Jer 29:13–14.

45:20 *Ignorant ... save.* See 44:17–18 and notes.

45:21 *Declare ... present.* See 41:21–22 and note. *foretold ... distant past.* See 41:26 and note.

45:22 An important theme verse in chs. 40–48. *Turn ... be saved.* See 49:6 and note; see also the invitation of 55:7. *ends of the earth.* See 11:12 and note; 42:10.

45:23 *By myself I have sworn.* Explained in Heb 6:13 (see note there). See also 62:8. *word ... not ... revoked.* See 55:10–11. *every knee ... every tongue.* See v. 14 and note. Paul quotes this portion of Isaiah in Ro 14:11 and Php 2:10–11 to describe Christ's exalted position.

24 They will say of me, 'In the LORD
alone
are righteousness[f] and strength.[g]' "
All who have raged against him
will come to him and be put to
shame.[h]
25 But in the LORD all the descendants[i] of
Israel
will be found righteous[j] and will
exult.[k]

Gods of Babylon

46 Bel[l] bows down, Nebo stoops low;
their idols[m] are borne by beasts of
burden.[a]
The images that are carried[n] about are
burdensome,
a burden for the weary.
2 They stoop and bow down together;
unable to rescue the burden,
they themselves go off into
captivity.[o]

3 "Listen[p] to me, O house of Jacob,
all you who remain[q] of the house of
Israel,
you whom I have upheld since you
were conceived,[r]
and have carried[s] since your birth.[t]
4 Even to your old age and gray hairs[u]
I am he,[v] I am he who will sustain
you.
I have made you and I will carry you;
I will sustain[w] you and I will rescue
you.

5 "To whom will you compare me or
count me equal?
To whom will you liken me that we
may be compared?[x]
6 Some pour out gold from their bags
and weigh out silver on the scales;
they hire a goldsmith[y] to make it into a
god,
and they bow down and worship it.[z]
7 They lift it to their shoulders and
carry[a] it;
they set it up in its place, and there
it stands.
From that spot it cannot move.[b]
Though one cries out to it, it does not
answer;[c]
it cannot save[d] him from his troubles.

8 "Remember[e] this, fix it in mind,
take it to heart, you rebels.[f]
9 Remember the former things,[g] those of
long ago;[h]
I am God, and there is no other;
I am God, and there is none like me.[i]
10 I make known the end from the
beginning,[j]
from ancient times,[k] what is still to
come.[l]
I say: My purpose will stand,[m]
and I will do all that I please.
11 From the east I summon[n] a bird of
prey;[o]
from a far-off land, a man to fulfill
my purpose.
What I have said, that will I bring
about;
what I have planned,[p] that will I do.[q]
12 Listen[r] to me, you stubborn-hearted,[s]
you who are far from righteousness.[t]
13 I am bringing my righteousness[u] near,
it is not far away;
and my salvation[v] will not be
delayed.
I will grant salvation to Zion,[w]
my splendor[x] to Israel.

The Fall of Babylon

47 "Go down, sit in the dust,[y]
Virgin Daughter[z] of Babylon;
sit on the ground without a throne,
Daughter of the Babylonians.[b][a]

45:24 [f]S ver 8; Jer 33:16 [g]S Dt 33:29; S Ps 18:39; S Isa 40:26; 63:1 [h]S Isa 41:11 **45:25** [i]S ver 19 [j]S Isa 4:3; S 49:4 [k]S Isa 24:23; S 41:16 **46:1** [l]S Isa 21:9; Jer 50:2; 51:44 [m]S 1Sa 5:2 [n]ver 7; S Isa 45:20 **46:2** [o]S Jdg 18:17-18; S 2Sa 5:21; Jer 51:47 **46:3** [p]ver 12; Isa 48:12; 51:1 [q]S Isa 1:9 [r]S Ps 139:13; Isa 44:2 [s]S Dt 1:31; S Ps 28:9 [t]S Ps 22:10 **46:4** [u]Ps 71:18 [v]S Dt 32:39; S Isa 43:13 [w]S Ps 18:35; S 119:117 **46:5** [x]S Ex 15:11; Job 41:10; Isa 40:18,25; Jer 49:19 **46:6** [y]S Isa 40:19 [z]S Ex 20:5; Isa 44:17; Hos 13:2 **46:7** [a]S ver 1 [b]S 1Sa 5:3; S Isa 41:7 [c]S 1Ki 18:26 [d]S Isa 44:17; S 47:13 **46:8** [e]S Isa 44:21 [f]S Isa 1:2 **46:9** [g]S Isa 41:22 [h]S Dt 32:7 [i]S Ex 8:10; S Isa 45:5,21; Mk 12:32 **46:10** [j]S Isa 41:4 [k]S Isa 45:21 [l]S Isa 41:22 [m]S Pr 19:21; S Isa 7:7,9; S 44:26; Ac 5:39; Eph 1:11 **46:11** [n]S Jdg 4:10; S Ezr 1:2 [o]S Isa 8:8 [p]S Isa 25:1 [q]S Ge 41:25; Jer 44:28 **46:12** [r]S ver 3 [s]S Ex 32:9; S Isa 9:9 [t]Ps 119:150; Isa 48:1; Jer 2:5 **46:13** [u]S Isa 1:26; S 45:8; Ro 3:21 [v]S Ps 85:9 [w]S Ps 74:2; Joel 2:32 [x]S Isa 44:23 **47:1** [y]S Job 2:13; S Isa 29:4 [z]S Isa 21:9; S 23:12 [a]Ps 137:8; Jer 50:42; 51:33; Zec 2:7

[a] 1 Or *are but beasts and cattle* [b] 1 Or *Chaldeans*; also in verse 5

45:24 *In the LORD alone … strength.* See v. 5 and note. This is the climax of the refrain that runs through the chapter. *All … put to shame.* Very similar to 41:11 except for "against you" (Israel).
45:25 *exult.* The Hebrew for this verb is translated "glory" in 41:16.
46:1 *Bel.* Another name for Marduk, the chief deity of Babylon. The name "Bel" is equivalent to Canaanite "Baal" and means "lord." *bows down … stoops.* In disgrace (see v. 2; 21:9 and note). *Nebo.* Nabu, the god of learning and writing who was the son of Marduk, the chief god in the Babylonian pantheon.
46:2 *go off into captivity.* The idols join their worshipers in exile (see Jer 48:7 and note; 49:3; Hos 10:5; Am 1:15).
46:3 *who remain.* The remnant (see 1:9 and note). *since … conceived … since … birth.* See 44:2 and note.
46:4 *old age and gray hairs.* Cf. Ps 37:25. *sustain … made … rescue.* Unlike the helpless idols of vv. 1–2. See 41:10,13; 43:1–2 and notes.
46:5–7 See 40:18–20 and note.
46:6 *bow down and worship.* See 44:15,17,19.
46:7 *carry.* See v. 1. *cannot save.* See 44:17 and note.
46:8 *rebels.* Israel. See 1:2 and note; cf. 1:20,23,28; 30:1; 57:4.
46:9 *former things.* See 41:22 and note. *there is no other.* See 43:11 and note.
46:10–11 *My purpose.* Especially God's purposes and plans regarding Babylon and Israel (see 8:9–10; 14:24; 48:14 and notes). Cf. Ps 33:11.
46:10 *from the beginning.* See 41:26 and note.
46:11 *east … bird of prey.* Cyrus king of Persia (see 41:2 and note). The swiftness and power of a bird of prey are in view (see 8:8 and note; Jer 49:22; cf. Da 8:4).
46:12 *stubborn-hearted.* See v. 8; 48:4; Eze 2:4.
46:13 *righteousness.* Here equivalent to salvation. See 41:2; 45:8 and notes. *salvation.* See note on 43:3. *splendor.* See 35:2; 40:5 and notes; see also 44:23; 49:3.
47:1 *sit in the dust … on the ground.* A sign of mourning (see 3:26). *Virgin Daughter of Babylon … Daughter of the Babylo-*

No more will you be called
tender or delicate.[b]
2 Take millstones[c] and grind[d] flour;
take off your veil.[e]
Lift up your skirts,[f] bare your legs,
and wade through the streams.
3 Your nakedness[g] will be exposed
and your shame[h] uncovered.
I will take vengeance;[i]
I will spare no one.[j]"

4 Our Redeemer[k]—the LORD Almighty[l] is
his name[m]—
is the Holy One[n] of Israel.

5 "Sit in silence,[o] go into darkness,[p]
Daughter of the Babylonians;[q]
no more will you be called
queen[r] of kingdoms.[s]
6 I was angry[t] with my people
and desecrated my inheritance;[u]
I gave them into your hand,[v]
and you showed them no mercy.[w]
Even on the aged
you laid a very heavy yoke.
7 You said, 'I will continue forever[x]—
the eternal queen!'[y]
But you did not consider these things
or reflect[z] on what might happen.[a]

8 "Now then, listen, you wanton
creature,
lounging in your security[b]
and saying to yourself,
'I am, and there is none besides
me.[c]
I will never be a widow[d]
or suffer the loss of children.'
9 Both of these will overtake you
in a moment,[e] on a single day:
loss of children[f] and widowhood.[g]
They will come upon you in full
measure,
in spite of your many sorceries[h]
and all your potent spells.[i]
10 You have trusted[j] in your wickedness
and have said, 'No one sees me.'[k]
Your wisdom[l] and knowledge mislead[m]
you
when you say to yourself,
'I am, and there is none besides me.'
11 Disaster[n] will come upon you,
and you will not know how to
conjure it away.
A calamity will fall upon you
that you cannot ward off with a
ransom;
a catastrophe you cannot foresee
will suddenly[o] come upon you.

12 "Keep on, then, with your magic
spells
and with your many sorceries,[p]
which you have labored at since
childhood.
Perhaps you will succeed,
perhaps you will cause terror.
13 All the counsel you have received has
only worn you out![q]
Let your astrologers[r] come forward,
those stargazers who make predictions
month by month,
let them save[s] you from what is
coming upon you.
14 Surely they are like stubble;[t]
the fire[u] will burn them up.
They cannot even save themselves
from the power of the flame.[v]
Here are no coals to warm anyone;
here is no fire to sit by.
15 That is all they can do for you—
these you have labored with
and trafficked[w] with since childhood.
Each of them goes on in his error;
there is not one that can save[x] you.

47:1 [b]Dt 28:56 **47:2** [c]Ex 11:5; Mt 24:41 [d]S Jdg 16:21 [e]S Ge 24:65 [f]S Isa 32:11 **47:3** [g]S Ge 2:25; Eze 16:37; Na 3:5 [h]S Isa 20:4 [i]S Isa 1:24; S 34:8 [j]Isa 13:18-19 **47:4** [k]S Job 19:25 [l]S Isa 13:4 [m]Isa 48:2; Jer 50:34; Am 4:13 [n]S Isa 1:4; 48:17 **47:5** [o]S Job 2:13 [p]Isa 9:2; 13:10 [q]S Isa 21:9 [r]ver 7; La 1:1; Rev 18:7 [s]S Isa 13:19; Rev 17:18 **47:6** [t]S 2Ch 28:9 [u]S Dt 13:15; S Isa 42:24; Jer 2:7; 50:11 [v]Isa 10:13 [w]S Isa 14:6 **47:7** [x]S Isa 10:13; Da 4:30 [y]S ver 5; Rev 18:7 [z]S Isa 42:23, 25 [a]S Dt 32:29 **47:8** [b]S Isa 32:9 [c]S Isa 45:6 [d]Isa 49:21; 54:4; La 1:1; Rev 18:7 **47:9** [e]S Ps 55:15; 73:19; 1Th 5:3; Rev 18:8-10 [f]S Isa 13:18 [g]Isa 4:1; Jer 15:8; 18:21 [h]ver 12; Na 3:4; Mal 3:5 [i]Dt 18:10-11; Rev 9:21; 18:23 **47:10** [j]S Job 15:31; Ps 52:7; 62:10 [k]S 2Ki 21:16; S Isa 29:15 [l]S Isa 5:21 [m]Isa 44:20 **47:11** [n]S Isa 10:3; S 14:15; S 21:9; S 31:2; Lk 17:27 [o]S Ps 55:15; S Isa 17:14; 1Th 5:3 **47:12** [p]S ver 9; S Ex 7:11 **47:13** [q]Isa 57:10; Jer 51:58; Hab 2:13 [r]S Isa 19:3; S 44:25 [s]ver 15; S Isa 5:29; 43:13; 46:7 **47:14** [t]S Isa 5:24 [u]S Isa 30:30 [v]Isa 10:17; Jer 51:30, 32, 58 **47:15** [w]Rev 18:11 [x]S ver 13; S Isa 44:17

nians. A personification of the city of Babylon (see note on 2Ki 19:21).
47:2 *millstones and grind.* A menial task performed by women (see Ex 11:5; Jdg 9:53 and notes). *through the streams.* Probably on the way to exile.
47:3 *nakedness will be exposed.* See Eze 16:36. Babylon is no longer a queen (see vv. 5,7); she is reduced to a servant girl or a prostitute (see v. 8). *take vengeance.* See 34:8 and note. *spare no one.* See 13:18–20.
47:4 *Redeemer.* See note on 41:14. *LORD Almighty.* See 13:4 and note. *Holy One of Israel.* See 1:4; 41:14 and notes.
47:5 *Daughter of the Babylonians.* See note on v. 1. *queen of kingdoms.* Babylon was a very beautiful city (see 13:19 and note).
47:6 *angry ... desecrated my inheritance.* See 10:5–6 (where Assyria is God's tool); 42:24 and note; 43:28 and note; La 2:2. *Even on the aged.* Their suffering fulfilled Moses' curse for covenant disobedience (Dt 28:49–50).
47:7 *I will continue forever.* Cf. the arrogant words of Nebuchadnezzar in Da 4:30.
47:8,10 *I am ... none besides me.* Almost a claim of deity (cf. the Lord's words in 43:11; 45:5–6,18,22; cf. also Ex 3:14–15; 20:3; Dt 6:4 and notes; see also Isa 14:12–15 and note).
47:8 *lounging in your security.* Similar language is used of the complacent women of Jerusalem in 32:9,11. Cf. also Am 6:1,4,7. *widow.* Deserted and distressed. *loss of children.* See v. 9; 13:16,18; 14:22.
47:9,12 *sorceries ... spells.* Magical practices to avoid danger and to inflict harm on the enemy (see 3:2–3 and note).
47:10 *No one sees me.* See 29:15 and note.
47:11 *with a ransom.* The Medes and Persians would not accept any settlement short of surrender (see 13:17).
47:13 *astrologers ... stargazers.* Babylonia probably utilized their services more than any other nation (see Da 2:2,10).
47:14 *stubble.* This will be a rapid, powerful fire. See note on 1:31; cf. Mal 4:1 and note. *cannot ... save themselves.* In contrast to the mighty Savior of Israel (see 43:3 and note), astrologers and sorcerers are as helpless as idols (see 44:17 and note). *no coals to warm anyone.* A subtle reference to firewood, a material from which pagans sometimes made idols (see 44:15).

Stubborn Israel

48 "Listen to this, O house of Jacob,
you who are called by the name of
Israel[y]
and come from the line of Judah,[z]
you who take oaths[a] in the name of
the LORD[b]
and invoke[c] the God of Israel—
but not in truth[d] or righteousness—
2 you who call yourselves citizens of the
holy city[e]
and rely[f] on the God of Israel—
the LORD Almighty is his name:[g]
3 I foretold the former things[h] long ago,
my mouth announced[i] them and I
made them known;
then suddenly[j] I acted, and they
came to pass.
4 For I knew how stubborn[k] you were;
the sinews of your neck[l] were
iron,
your forehead[m] was bronze.
5 Therefore I told you these things long
ago;
before they happened I announced[n]
them to you
so that you could not say,
'My idols did them;[o]
my wooden image and metal god
ordained them.'
6 You have heard these things; look at
them all.
Will you not admit them?

"From now on I will tell you of new
things,[p]
of hidden things unknown to you.
7 They are created[q] now, and not long
ago;[r]
you have not heard of them before
today.
So you cannot say,
'Yes, I knew[s] of them.'
8 You have neither heard nor
understood;[t]
from of old your ear[u] has not been
open.
Well do I know how treacherous[v] you
are;
you were called a rebel[w] from
birth.
9 For my own name's sake[x] I delay
my wrath;[y]
for the sake of my praise I hold it
back from you,
so as not to cut you off.[z]
10 See, I have refined[a] you, though not
as silver;
I have tested[b] you in the furnace[c] of
affliction.
11 For my own sake,[d] for my own sake,
I do this.
How can I let myself be defamed?[e]
I will not yield my glory to
another.[f]

Israel Freed

12 "Listen[g] to me, O Jacob,
Israel, whom I have called:[h]
I am he;[i]
I am the first and I am the last.[j]
13 My own hand laid the foundations of
the earth,[k]
and my right hand spread out the
heavens;[l]
when I summon them,
they all stand up together.[m]

14 "Come together,[n] all of you, and
listen:
Which of ⌞the idols⌟ has foretold[o]
these things?

48:1 [y] S Ge 17:5 [z] S Ge 29:35 [a] S Isa 19:18 [b] S 1Sa 20:42; S Isa 43:7 [c] Ex 23:13; 2Sa 14:11; Ps 50:16; Isa 58:2; Jer 7:9-10; 44:26 [d] Isa 59:14; Jer 4:2; 5:2; Da 8:12; Zec 8:3 **48:2** [e] S Ne 11:1; S Isa 1:26; S Mt 4:5 [f] S Isa 10:20; Ro 2:17 [g] S Isa 47:4 **48:3** [h] S Isa 41:22 [i] S Isa 40:21; 45:21 [j] S Isa 17:14; 30:13 **48:4** [k] S Isa 9:9 [l] S Ex 32:9; S Dt 9:27; Ac 7:51 [m] Eze 3:9 **48:5** [n] S Isa 40:21; S 42:9 [o] Jer 44:15-18 **48:6** [p] S Isa 41:22; S Ro 16:25 **48:7** [q] Isa 65:18 [r] Isa 45:21 [s] S Ex 6:7 **48:8** [t] S Isa 1:3 [u] S Dt 29:4 [v] Isa 41:24; Mal 2:11,14 [w] Dt 9:7,24; Ps 58:3; S Isa 1:2; 43:27; 58:1 **48:9** [x] S 1Sa 12:22; S Isa 37:35 [y] S Job 9:13; S Isa 30:18 [z] S Ne 9:31 **48:10** [a] S Isa 1:25; Zec 13:9; Mal 3:3; 1Pe 1:7 [b] S Ex 15:25 [c] S Ex 1:13; S 1Ki 8:51 **48:11** [d] S 1Sa 12:22; S Isa 37:35 [e] S Lev 18:21; Dt 32:27; Jer 14:7,21; Eze 20:9,14,22,44 [f] Isa 42:8 **48:12** [g] S Isa 46:3 [h] Isa 41:8; 42:6; 43:1 [i] S Isa 43:13 [j] S Isa 41:4; S Rev 1:17 **48:13** [k] Heb 1:10-12 [l] S Ge 2:1; Ex 20:11; Job 9:8; Isa 40:22; S 42:5; 45:18; 51:16; 65:17 [m] S Isa 34:16 **48:14** [n] S Isa 43:9 [o] S Isa 41:22

48:1 *called by the name.* They belong to Israel (see 43:7 and note). *Israel.* See Ge 32:28 and note. *Judah.* The main tribe of the southern kingdom. See Ge 49:8 and note. *not in truth.* Contrast the oaths of 65:16 (see note there).
48:2 *holy city.* Jerusalem, where the temple was located (see 2:2–4 and note; 52:1; 56:7; 57:13; 64:10–11; 65:11). See also 1:26; 4:3 and notes; Da 9:24. *rely on … God.* Superficially (see 10:20; contrast 31:1; 36:6,9; Eze 29:6–7). *LORD Almighty.* See 13:4 and note.
48:3 *former things.* See 41:22 and note. *they came to pass.* See 42:9.
48:4 *stubborn … bronze.* See Jer 6:28; cf. Eze 3:7.
48:5 *My idols did them.* See Isaiah's harsh words about idolatry in 44:17–20 (see notes there). *wooden image and metal god.* See note on 44:12–13.
48:6 *new things.* For example, Israel's restoration (see 42:9 and note). The Messianic age and the new heavens and new earth may also be in view (cf. 65:17). *hidden things.* Cf. Ro 16:25–26 and notes.
48:7 *created now.* Now given substance in the prophetic announcement of their coming.
48:8 *neither heard nor understood.* See 1:3. *ear … not … open.* See 6:10 and note. *rebel.* See 1:2; 46:8 and notes.
48:9 *delay my wrath.* Cf. Ps 78:38. *my praise.* The praise God is worthy of (cf. Ps 22:3 and note).
48:10 *refined … tested.* Images of judgment (see Ps 12:6; Jer 9:7; Eze 22:18 and notes). Purifying fire is also mentioned in 1:25; 4:4. *furnace of affliction.* For Israel, Egypt had been an "iron-smelting furnace" (Dt 4:20 [see note there]; 1Ki 8:51; Jer 11:4). The fall of Jerusalem and the Babylonian exile were for the Israelites a similar "furnace" experience.
48:11 *For … defamed.* Jerusalem's fall and God's scattered people had brought dishonor to God's name (see Eze 36:20–23 and notes). *my glory.* See 40:5 and note.
48:12 *called.* To be God's servant, his chosen people. See 42:6; see also 41:2; 43:1 and notes. *first and … last.* See 41:4 and note.
48:13 *laid the foundations … spread out the heavens.* Isaiah often refers to God as Creator (see 40:21–22; 42:5; 51:13 and notes). Cf. Ps 102:25. *when I summon … all stand up.* All creation does God's bidding (see 40:26 and note).
48:14 ⌞*the idols*⌟ *… foretold.* See 41:21–23,26; 43:9 and notes. *chosen ally.* Cyrus the Great (see 41:2 and note). *his purpose.* See 46:10–11 and note. *Babylon.* See 13:1 and note.

The LORD's chosen ally[p]
will carry out his purpose[q] against
Babylon;[r]
his arm will be against the
Babylonians.[a]
15 I, even I, have spoken;
yes, I have called[s] him.
I will bring him,
and he will succeed[t] in his mission.

16 "Come near[u] me and listen[v] to this:

"From the first announcement I have
not spoken in secret;[w]
at the time it happens, I am there."

And now the Sovereign LORD[x] has sent[y]
me,
with his Spirit.[z]
17 This is what the LORD says—
your Redeemer,[a] the Holy One[b] of
Israel:
"I am the LORD your God,
who teaches[c] you what is best for
you,
who directs[d] you in the way[e] you
should go.
18 If only you had paid attention[f] to my
commands,
your peace[g] would have been like a
river,[h]
your righteousness[i] like the waves of
the sea.
19 Your descendants[j] would have been
like the sand,[k]
your children like its numberless
grains;[l]
their name would never be cut off[m]
nor destroyed from before me."

20 Leave Babylon,
flee[n] from the Babylonians!
Announce this with shouts of joy[o]
and proclaim it.
Send it out to the ends of the earth;[p]
say, "The LORD has redeemed[q] his
servant Jacob."
21 They did not thirst[r] when he led them
through the deserts;
he made water flow[s] for them from
the rock;
he split the rock
and water gushed out.[t]

22 "There is no peace," [u] says the LORD,
"for the wicked."[v]

The Servant of the LORD

49 Listen[w] to me, you islands;[x]
hear this, you distant nations:
Before I was born[y] the LORD called[z] me;
from my birth he has made mention
of my name.[a]
2 He made my mouth[b] like a sharpened
sword,[c]
in the shadow of his hand[d] he hid
me;
he made me into a polished arrow[e]
and concealed me in his quiver.
3 He said to me, "You are my servant,[f]
Israel, in whom I will display my
splendor.[g]"

[a] *14* Or *Chaldeans*; also in verse 20

48:14 [p]S Isa 41:2 [q]Isa 46:10-11 [r]S Isa 21:9; S 45:1; Jer 50:45 **48:15** [s]S Jdg 4:10; Isa 45:1 [t]Isa 44:28-45:4 **48:16** [u]S Isa 41:1 [v]S Isa 33:13 [w]S Isa 45:19 [x]Isa 50:5,7,9 [y]Zec 2:9,11 [z]S Isa 11:2 **48:17** [a]S Job 19:25; Isa 49:7; 54:8 [b]S Isa 47:4 [c]S Isa 28:9; S Jer 7:13 [d]Isa 49:10; 57:18; 58:11 [e]S Isa 30:11 **48:18** [f]S Isa 42:23 [g]Ps 147:14; S Isa 9:7; 54:13; 66:12 [h]S Isa 33:21 [i]S Isa 1:26; S 45:8 **48:19** [j]Isa 43:5; 44:3; 61:9 [k]S Ge 12:2 [l]S Job 5:25 [m]Isa 56:5; 65:23; 66:22; Jer 35:19 **48:20** [n]Isa 52:11; Jer 48:6; 50:8; 51:6,45; Zec 2:6-7; Rev 18:4 [o]S Isa 12:6; 49:13; 51:11 [p]S Ge 49:10; S Dt 30:4; S Jer 25:22 [q]S Ex 6:6; S Isa 33:24; 52:9; 63:9; Mic 4:10 **48:21** [r]S Isa 33:16 [s]S Isa 30:25 [t]S Nu 20:11; S Isa 35:6 **48:22** [u]S Job 3:26 [v]S Isa 3:11; 57:21 **49:1** [w]S Isa 33:13 [x]S Isa 11:11 [y]Isa 44:24; 46:3; Mt 1:20 [z]Isa 7:14; 9:6; 44:2; Jer 1:5; Gal 1:15 [a]S Ex 33:12; S Isa 43:1 **49:2** [b]S Job 40:18 [c]S Ps 64:3; Eph 6:17; S Rev 1:16 [d]S Ex 33:22; S Ps 91:1 [e]S Dt 32:23; Zec 9:13 **49:3** [f]S Isa 20:3; Zec 3:8 [g]S Lev 10:3; S Isa 44:23

48:15 *called him.* Cyrus (see 41:2 and note). *will succeed.* See 44:28; 45:1–4 and notes.
48:16 *first announcement.* The prediction about Cyrus and his mission (see 41:25–27 and notes). *not spoken in secret.* See 45:19 and note. *has sent me.* A reference to either the prophet or the servant of the Lord. *with his Spirit.* The Spirit of the Lord comes upon the servant in 42:1 (see note there) and upon the Messianic prophet of 61:1 (see note there).
48:17 *Redeemer, the Holy One of Israel.* See 41:14 and note. *teaches you … the way you should go.* Through the prophets or priests (see 30:20–21; Ps 32:8–10 and notes).
48:18 *peace … like a river, righteousness like the waves.* Abundant and overflowing peace and righteousness (see 45:8; Am 5:24 and notes). Peace and righteousness are also linked in 9:7; 32:17; 54:13–14; 60:17; Ps 85:10 (see note there); Heb 7:2; Jas 3:18.
48:19 *descendants … like the sand.* See 10:22; see also Ge 13:16 and note; Ge 22:17; Jer 33:22 and note. *name … never be cut off.* Israel's name would not be completely obliterated (see v. 9; 54:3; Jer 31:36).
48:20 *Leave Babylon, flee.* Although the Jews did not have to flee (see 52:12), they were encouraged to depart quickly because of the judgment coming on Babylon (cf. Rev 18:4). This is the last mention of Babylon by name in Isaiah. *shouts of joy.* See 44:23; 49:13; 52:9 and notes. *ends of the earth.* See 11:12; 42:10 and notes. *redeemed.* See 43:1 and note. *his servant.* See 41:8–9 and note.
48:21 *did not thirst … water … from the rock.* A reference to God's provision after the exodus (see Ex 17:6 and note; Nu 20:11; see also Isa 32:2; 35:6; 43:19; 49:10 and notes). God's people would have water on the way home from Babylonian exile also.
48:22 Repeated almost verbatim in 57:21. *peace.* See 39:8 and note; see also Introduction: Literary Features. *wicked.* Those who rebel against the Lord (see note on 1:2).
49:1–6 (or **1–7** or **1–13)** The second of the four servant songs (see note on 42:1–4).
49:1 *islands.* Or "coastlands." In 42:4 the islands "put their hope" in the servant's law. *Before I was born … called me.* Cf. v. 5. The language is similar to that of the call of the prophet Jeremiah (see Jer 1:5 and note) and of the apostle Paul (Gal 1:15). Cf. 41:9. *made mention of my name.* See 43:1 and note.
49:2 *my mouth … sharpened sword.* See Rev 1:16; 2:12,16; 19:15,21; cf. Isa 11:4; Eph 6:17; Heb 4:12. *shadow of his hand.* Descriptive of protection (see 30:2–3; 51:16). *polished arrow.* Arrows are used of God's judgment in Dt 32:23,42; Job 6:4 (see note there), of the deadly words of the wicked in Ps 64:3–4 and of Satan's schemes and temptations in Eph 6:11,16.
49:3 *my servant, Israel.* See notes on 41:8–9; 42:1–4; 42:1. "Servant" here cannot mean literally national Israel, since in v. 5 this servant has a mission to Israel. Rather, the Messianic servant is the ideal Israel through whom the Lord will be glorified. He will succeed where national Israel failed. *display my splendor.* Through the redemption he will accomplish (see notes on 35:2; 40:5).

4 But I said, "I have labored to no purpose;
I have spent my strength in vain[h] and for nothing.
Yet what is due me is in the LORD's hand,[i]
and my reward[j] is with my God."[k]

5 And now the LORD says—
he who formed me in the womb[l] to be his servant
to bring Jacob back to him
and gather Israel[m] to himself,
for I am honored[n] in the eyes of the LORD
and my God has been my strength[o]—
6 he says:
"It is too small a thing for you to be my servant[p]
to restore the tribes of Jacob
and bring back those of Israel I have kept.[q]
I will also make you a light[r] for the Gentiles,[s]
that you may bring my salvation to the ends of the earth."[t]

7 This is what the LORD says—
the Redeemer and Holy One of Israel[u]—
to him who was despised[v] and abhorred by the nation,
to the servant of rulers:
"Kings[w] will see you and rise up,
princes will see and bow down,[x]
because of the LORD, who is faithful,[y]
the Holy One of Israel, who has chosen[z] you."

49:4 [h] S Lev 26:20; Isa 55:2; 65:23 [i] Isa 45:25; 50:8; 53:10; 54:17 [j] S Isa 35:4 [k] S Job 27:2 **49:5** [l] S Ps 139:13; Gal 1:15 [m] S Dt 30:4; S Isa 11:12 [n] S Isa 43:4 [o] S Ps 18:1 **49:6** [p] S ver 3 [q] Isa 1:9 [r] S Isa 9:2; Jn 1:9 [s] S Isa 26:18; 55:5; Zec 8:22; S Lk 2:32 [t] S Dt 30:4; S Ps 48:10; S Mt 28:19; Jn 11:52; Ac 13:47* **49:7** [u] S Isa 48:17 [v] S Ps 22:6; 69:7-9 [w] S Ezr 1:2; Isa 52:15 [x] S Ge 27:29; S Ps 22:29; S 86:9 [y] S Dt 7:9; S 1Co 1:9 [z] S Isa 14:1

49:8 [a] Ps 69:13; Isa 60:10; 61:2 [b] S Isa 41:10; 2Co 6:2* [c] S Isa 5:2; 26:3 [d] S Isa 42:6 [e] Lev 25:10; S Ps 37:9; Isa 44:26; 58:12; 61:4; Eze 36:10, 33; Am 9:11, 14 [f] S Nu 34:13; S Isa 60:21 **49:9** [g] Isa 42:7; 61:1; S Lk 4:19 [h] S Ps 107:10 [i] Isa 41:18 **49:10** [j] S Isa 33:16

Restoration of Israel

8 This is what the LORD says:

"In the time of my favor[a] I will answer you,
and in the day of salvation I will help you;[b]
I will keep[c] you and will make you
to be a covenant for the people,[d]
to restore the land[e]
and to reassign its desolate inheritances,[f]
9 to say to the captives,[g] 'Come out,'
and to those in darkness,[h] 'Be free!'

"They will feed beside the roads
and find pasture on every barren hill.[i]
10 They will neither hunger nor thirst,[j]
nor will the desert heat or the sun beat upon them.[k]
He who has compassion[l] on them will guide[m] them
and lead them beside springs[n] of water.
11 I will turn all my mountains into roads,
and my highways[o] will be raised up.[p]
12 See, they will come from afar[q]—
some from the north, some from the west,[r]
some from the region of Aswan.[a]"

13 Shout for joy,[s] O heavens;
rejoice, O earth;[t]
burst into song, O mountains![u]

[a] *12* Dead Sea Scrolls; Masoretic Text *Sinim*

[k] Ps 121:6; Rev 7:16 [l] S Isa 14:1 [m] S Ps 48:14; S Isa 42:16; S 48:17 [n] S Isa 33:21; S 35:7 **49:11** [o] S Isa 11:16 [p] Isa 40:4; Jer 31:9 **49:12** [q] S Isa 2:3; S 11:11; 43:5-6 [r] Isa 59:19; S Mt 8:11 **49:13** [s] S Isa 48:20 [t] S Ps 96:11 [u] S Ps 65:12-13; 98:4; Isa 44:23

49:4 *labored to no purpose ... in vain.* Just as the nation Israel had toiled in vain (see 65:23), so Christ would encounter strong opposition during his ministry and would temporarily suffer apparent failure. The "suffering servant" theme is developed in the third and fourth of the four servant songs (50:4–9 or 50:4–11; 52:13—53:12). *what is due me ... my reward.* Perhaps referring to the spiritual offspring of the servant (see 53:10)—Jews and Gentiles alike who believe in him (vv. 5–6); see 40:10 and note. In any case, he will be vindicated and rewarded (50:8; 53:10–12; 1Ti 3:16).

49:5 *formed me in the womb.* See v. 1; 44:2 and notes. *bring Jacob back ... gather Israel.* A prophecy of release from captivity in Babylon (see vv. 9–12,22; 41:2 and note) and from the greater captivity of sin (see 42:7 and note). *my strength.* See 12:2.

49:6 Together with Ge 12:1–3; Ex 19:5–6, this verse is sometimes called the "great commission of the OT" and is quoted in part by Paul and Barnabas in Ac 13:47. *those ... I have kept.* Probably referring to the remnant (see 1:9 and note). *light for the Gentiles.* See 9:2; 42:6 and notes; Ac 26:23. Christ is the light of the world (Lk 2:30–32; Jn 8:12; 9:5), and Christians are to reflect his light (Mt 5:14). *ends of the earth.* See 11:12 and note; see also 41:5; 42:10; 48:20.

49:7 *Redeemer and Holy One of Israel.* See 41:14 and note. *despised.* Applied twice to the suffering servant in 53:3. In 60:14 Zion is despised by her enemies. *nation.* Refers to either Israel (1:4) or Gentiles. *Kings will see ... bow down.* See v. 23. This reaction to the servant is similar to that of 52:15. Former oppressors bow before a restored Jerusalem in 60:14 (cf. 45:14; 60:11–12; 66:23). *chosen you.* See 41:8–9; 42:1 and notes.

49:8 Quoted in part in 2Co 6:2. *time of my favor ... day of salvation.* The background of this verse is probably the Year of Jubilee (see 61:1–2; Lev 25:10). The return from exile will bring the same restoration of land for the people as that year of liberty did. *keep you ... to be a covenant.* See 42:6 and note. *reassign its desolate inheritances.* See 44:26. It was under Joshua that the land had been divided among individual tribes and families (Jos 14:1–5). The Messianic servant will be a new Joshua—as well as a new Moses (see vv. 9–10, which echo Israel's deliverance from Egypt and her desert experiences under Moses during the period of the exodus).

49:9 *captives.* The exiles. See 42:7 and note. *barren hill.* See 41:18 and note.

49:10 *neither hunger nor thirst.* See 48:21 and note. *has compassion.* See 14:1 and note. *will guide them.* As a shepherd (see 40:11 and note). This whole verse is also a picture of heaven according to Rev 7:16–17.

49:11 *mountains into roads.* See 26:7 and note. *highways ... raised up.* See 11:16; 35:8; 40:3; 62:10 and notes.

49:12 *come from afar.* See 11:11 and note; 60:4. *north ... west.* See 43:5–6 and notes. *Aswan.* See Eze 29:10 and note; 30:6; located in the most southern part of Egypt.

49:13 *Shout for joy ... mountains.* Nature is personified often

For the LORD comforts[v] his people
and will have compassion[w] on his
afflicted ones.[x]

14 But Zion[y] said, "The LORD has
forsaken[z] me,
the Lord has forgotten me."

15 "Can a mother forget the baby at her
breast
and have no compassion on the
child[a] she has borne?
Though she may forget,
I will not forget you![b]
16 See, I have engraved[c] you on the palms
of my hands;
your walls[d] are ever before me.
17 Your sons hasten back,
and those who laid you waste[e]
depart from you.
18 Lift up your eyes and look around;
all your sons gather[f] and come to
you.
As surely as I live,[g]" declares the LORD,
"you will wear[h] them all as
ornaments;
you will put them on, like a bride.

19 "Though you were ruined and made
desolate[i]
and your land laid waste,[j]
now you will be too small for your
people,[k]
and those who devoured[l] you will be
far away.
20 The children born during your
bereavement
will yet say in your hearing,
'This place is too small for us;
give us more space to live in.'[m]
21 Then you will say in your heart,
'Who bore me these?[n]
I was bereaved[o] and barren;
I was exiled and rejected.[p]
Who brought these[q] up?
I was left[r] all alone,[s]
but these—where have they come
from?'"

22 This is what the Sovereign LORD[t]
says:

"See, I will beckon to the Gentiles,
I will lift up my banner[u] to the
peoples;
they will bring[v] your sons in their arms
and carry your daughters on their
shoulders.[w]
23 Kings[x] will be your foster fathers,
and their queens your nursing
mothers.[y]
They will bow down[z] before you with
their faces to the ground;
they will lick the dust[a] at your feet.
Then you will know that I am the
LORD;[b]
those who hope[c] in me will not be
disappointed.[d]"

24 Can plunder be taken from warriors,[e]
or captives rescued from the fierce[a]?

25 But this is what the LORD says:

"Yes, captives[f] will be taken from
warriors,[g]
and plunder retrieved from the
fierce;[h]
I will contend with those who contend
with you,[i][j]
and your children I will save.[k]
26 I will make your oppressors[l] eat[m] their
own flesh;
they will be drunk on their own
blood,[n] as with wine.

49:13 [v]S Ps 71:21; S Isa 40:1; S 2Co 1:4 [w]S Isa 14:1 [x]S Ps 9:12 **49:14** [y]Isa 40:9 [z]S Ps 9:10; S 71:11; S Isa 27:8 **49:15** [a]S 1Ki 3:26; Isa 66:13 [b]S Isa 44:21 **49:16** [c]S Ge 38:18; S Ex 28:9 [d]Ps 48:12-13; Isa 62:6 **49:17** [e]S Isa 5:6; 10:6; 37:18 **49:18** [f]S Isa 11:12; 14:1; 43:5; 51:3; 54:7 [g]S Nu 14:21; Isa 45:23; 54:9; 62:8; Ro 14:11* [h]Isa 52:1; 61:10; Jer 2:32 **49:19** [i]S Lev 26:33; Isa 54:1,3; 60:18; 62:4 [j]S Isa 5:6 [k]Eze 36:10-11; Zec 10:10 [l]S Isa 1:20 **49:20** [m]Isa 54:1-3; Zec 2:4; 10:10 **49:21** [n]Isa 29:23; 66:7-8 [o]S Isa 47:8; 54:1 [p]Isa 5:13; 54:6 [q]Isa 60:8 [r]S Isa 1:8 [s]S Ps 142:4; Isa 51:18; Jer 10:20 **49:22** [t]S Ge 15:2 [u]S Isa 11:10 [v]S Isa 11:12; S 14:2 [w]Lk 15:5 **49:23** [x]Isa 60:3,10-11 [y]S Nu 11:12; S Isa 60:16 [z]S Ge 27:29; Rev 3:9 [a]S Ge 3:14; Ps 72:9 [b]S Ex 6:2; S Ps 22:23; S Isa 42:8 [c]S Ps 37:9; S 130:5 [d]S Ps 22:5; S Isa 29:22; S 41:11 **49:24** [e]Mt 12:29; Mk 3:27; Lk 11:21 **49:25** [f]S Isa 14:2 [g]Jer 50:33-34; Mk 3:27 [h]S Isa 13:11; S 25:4 [i]Isa 25:5; S 43:26; 51:22; Jer 50:34 [j]S 1Sa 24:15 [k]Isa 25:9; 33:22; 35:4 **49:26** [l]S Isa 9:4; S 13:11 [m]S Isa 9:20 [n]Nu 23:24; Jer 25:27; Na 1:10; 3:11; Rev 16:6

[a] *24* Dead Sea Scrolls, Vulgate and Syriac (see also Septuagint and verse 25); Masoretic Text *righteous*

in Isaiah. See 44:23 and note. *comforts his people.* As he redeems and saves them. Cf. 2Co 1:3–4. *will have compassion.* See v. 10 and note; 54:7–10.

49:14 *forsaken … forgotten.* See 40:27; 54:7; La 5:20–22.

49:15 *Can a mother forget … ?* Cf. Ps 27:10.

49:16 *engraved you on … my hands.* As the names of the tribes of Israel were engraved on stones and fastened to the ephod of the high priest as a memorial before the Lord (Ex 28:9–12; cf. SS 8:6). *ever before me.* Cf. Ps 137:5–6.

49:17 *sons.* Or "builders," following the reading of the Dead Sea Scrolls and some ancient versions (cf. note on 62:5).

49:18 *sons gather.* See vv. 5,12 and notes. *ornaments.* Beautiful clothes and jewels symbolize strength and joy.

49:19–20 *too small.* The restoration of Israel will be astonishing and complete. The prophecy was partially fulfilled in the return from Babylon (see note on 11:11) and may include spiritual offspring among both Jews and Gentiles (see 54:17 and note).

49:19 *ruined … desolate.* Cf. v. 8; see 44:26 and note.

49:20 Cf. Zec 2:4 and note.

49:21 *bereaved and barren.* The concept of Israel as a barren woman is stressed in 54:1 (cf. Ps 113:9 and note).

49:22 *lift up my banner.* See 5:26 and note; 13:2. *bring your sons … daughters.* See 11:12 and note. The nations bring Israel back also in 14:2; 43:6; 60:9. *in their arms.* Cf. 60:4; see 40:11 and note.

49:23 *Kings … will bow down.* See v. 7; 11:14 and notes. *know that I am the LORD.* See v. 26; 60:16; Eze 12:20; 13:9; 36:38. *hope in me.* See 40:31 and note. *not be disappointed.* See 29:22 and note.

49:24 *warriors … fierce.* The Babylonians (see 51:13).

49:25 *captives will be taken.* See Ezr 2:1,64–65; Jer 50:33–34; 52:27–30. *I will contend.* God takes up the case of his people. He will "defend their cause" (Jer 50:34). *I will save.* See 35:4 and note.

49:26 *oppressors.* See 14:4; 16:4; 51:13. *eat their own flesh.* During the siege of Jerusalem its people were reduced to cannibalism (La 4:10; cf. Zec 11:9 and note). *drunk on their own blood.* Cf. 51:22–23. *mankind will know.* See v. 23 and note. *Savior.* See 43:3 and note; 60:16. *Redeemer.* See 41:14 and note. *Mighty One of Jacob.* See 1:24 and note; 60:16.

Then all mankind will know[o]
that I, the LORD, am your Savior,[p]
your Redeemer,[q] the Mighty One of
Jacob.[r]"

Israel's Sin and the Servant's Obedience

50 This is what the LORD says:

"Where is your mother's certificate of
divorce[s]
with which I sent her away?
Or to which of my creditors
did I sell[t] you?
Because of your sins[u] you were sold;[v]
because of your transgressions your
mother was sent away.
2 When I came, why was there no one?
When I called, why was there no
one to answer?[w]
Was my arm too short[x] to ransom you?
Do I lack the strength[y] to rescue
you?
By a mere rebuke[z] I dry up the sea,[a]
I turn rivers into a desert;[b]
their fish rot for lack of water
and die of thirst.
3 I clothe the sky with darkness[c]
and make sackcloth[d] its covering."

4 The Sovereign LORD[e] has given me an
instructed tongue,[f]
to know the word that sustains the
weary.[g]
He wakens me morning by morning,[h]
wakens my ear to listen like one
being taught.[i]
5 The Sovereign LORD[j] has opened my
ears,[k]
and I have not been rebellious;[l]
I have not drawn back.
6 I offered my back to those who beat[m]
me,
my cheeks to those who pulled out
my beard;[n]
I did not hide my face
from mocking and spitting.[o]
7 Because the Sovereign LORD[p] helps[q]
me,
I will not be disgraced.
Therefore have I set my face like flint,[r]
and I know I will not be put to
shame.[s]
8 He who vindicates[t] me is near.[u]
Who then will bring charges against
me?[v]
Let us face each other![w]
Who is my accuser?
Let him confront me!
9 It is the Sovereign LORD[x] who helps[y]
me.
Who is he that will condemn[z] me?
They will all wear out like a garment;
the moths[a] will eat them up.

10 Who among you fears[b] the LORD
and obeys[c] the word of his
servant?[d]
Let him who walks in the dark,
who has no light,[e]
trust[f] in the name of the LORD
and rely on his God.

49:26 [o]Ex 6:7; S Isa 11:9; Eze 39:7 [p]S Isa 25:9 [q]S Job 19:25; S Isa 48:17 [r]S Ge 49:24; S Ps 132:2 **50:1** [s]S Dt 24:1; Hos 2:2; Mt 19:7; Mk 10:4 [t]S Ne 5:5; S Mt 18:25 [u]S Isa 1:28 [v]S Dt 32:30; S Jdg 3:8 **50:2** [w]S 1Sa 8:19; S Isa 41:28 [x]Nu 11:23; Isa 59:1 [y]S Ge 18:14; S Ps 68:35; Jer 14:9 [z]S Ps 18:15 [a]S Ex 14:22 [b]S Ps 107:33 **50:3** [c]S Ex 10:22; S Isa 5:30 [d]Rev 6:12 **50:4** [e]ver 5; Isa 61:1 [f]S Ex 4:12 [g]S Isa 40:29; Mt 11:28 [h]Ps 5:3; 88:13; 119:147; 143:8 [i]S Isa 28:9 **50:5** [j]S Isa 48:16 [k]Isa 35:5 [l]Eze 2:8; 24:3; S Mt 26:39; Jn 8:29; 14:31; 15:10; Ac 26:19; Heb 5:8 **50:6** [m]Isa 53:5; Mt 27:30; Mk 14:65; 15:19; Lk 22:63; Jn 19:1 [n]S 2Sa 10:4 [o]S Nu 12:14; La 3:30; Mt 26:67; Mk 10:34 **50:7** [p]S Isa 48:16 [q]S Isa 41:10; 42:1 [r]Jer 1:18; 15:20; Eze 3:8-9 [s]S Isa 28:16; S 29:22 **50:8** [t]S Isa 26:2; S 49:4 [u]S Ps 34:18 [v]S Job 13:19; S Isa 43:26; Ro 8:32-34 [w]S Isa 41:1 **50:9** [x]S Isa 48:16 [y]S Isa 41:10 [z]Ro 8:1,34 [a]S Job 13:28; S Isa 51:8 **50:10** [b]S Pr 1:7 [c]Isa 1:19; Hag 1:12 [d]S Isa 49:3 [e]S Ps 107:14; Ac 26:18 [f]S Isa 10:20; S 26:4

50:1 *certificate of divorce.* A husband was required to give this to a wife he wished to divorce (see Dt 24:1–4; Mt 19:3; Mk 10:2,5–6 and notes). According to Jer 3:8 God gave the northern kingdom of Israel her certificate of divorce, and Isa 54:6–7 indicates that God had left Judah (see 62:4). Perhaps the prophet's point is that God did not initiate the divorce; Judah broke her relationship with him. The exile, then, was actually a temporary period of separation (see 54:7) rather than a divorce. *my creditors.* If a man's debts were not paid, his children could be sold into slavery (see 2Ki 4:1 and note). But God has no creditors. *you were sold.* Cf. 45:13; 52:3.
50:2 *I came ... called.* Through his servants the prophets (see Jer 7:25 and note). *no one to answer.* Israel was deaf toward God (see 6:10 and note; 66:4). *arm too short.* The arm represented power. *dry up the sea.* An allusion to the crossing of the Red Sea (see 43:16–17 and notes; Ps 106:9). *rivers into a desert.* See 42:15 and note. *fish rot.* Perhaps an allusion to one of the plagues in Egypt (see 19:5–6,8; Ex 7:18).
50:3 *sky with darkness.* Perhaps an allusion to the plague of darkness (Ex 10:21); but see 13:10 and note.
50:4–9 (or **4–11**) The third of the four servant songs (see note on 42:1–4).
50:4–5,7,9 *Sovereign LORD.* The only uses of this title in the servant songs.
50:4 *word that sustains the weary.* In 42:3 the servant assisted the weak (contrast 49:2). Cf. Jer 31:25. *wakens my ear.* Unlike Israel (see v. 2), the servant was responsive to God.
50:5 *opened my ears.* A sign of obedience (see 1:19; Ps 40:6 and note). *not been rebellious.* Unlike Israel (see 1:2 and note; 1:20).
50:6 *my back to those who beat me.* Beatings were for criminals or fools (see Pr 10:13; 19:29; 26:3; Mt 27:26; Jn 19:1). *pulled out my beard.* A sign of disrespect and contempt (see 2Sa 10:4–5; Ne 13:25). *mocking and spitting.* To show hatred (Job 30:10) or to insult or disgrace (Dt 25:9; Job 17:6; Mt 27:30). This treatment of the servant anticipates his ultimate suffering in 52:13—53:12.
50:7 *helps me.* See v. 9; 49:8. *not be disgraced ... put to shame.* See 29:22 and note. Ultimately the servant will be honored (see 49:7; 52:13; 53:10–12). *my face like flint.* Like the prophets, the servant will endure with great resolution. Cf. Lk 9:51, where Jesus "resolutely set out for Jerusalem" (lit. "resolutely set his face to go to Jerusalem").
50:8 *vindicates me.* The Lord will find him righteous (see 45:25; for its ultimate fulfillment see 1Ti 3:16). *bring charges.* See 49:25 and note. Because Christ was sinless, he also nullifies the charges brought against any who believe in him (see Ro 8:31–34 and notes). *my accuser.* Cf. 54:17.
50:9 *Who ... will condemn me?* Cf. the similar language Paul uses in Ro 8:34. *wear out like a garment; the moths.* Those who falsely accuse the righteous succumb to moths in 51:8 (i.e., they will be destroyed).
50:10 *fears the LORD.* See Ge 20:11; Pr 1:7 and notes. Cf. 25:3; 59:19. *in the dark.* Perhaps trouble or distress, similar to the experience of the servant (cf. 8:22). *trust ... rely.* The Lord encouraged such trust in 12:2; 31:1.

11 But now, all you who light fires
and provide yourselves with flaming torches,[g]
go, walk in the light of your fires[h]
and of the torches you have set ablaze.
This is what you shall receive from my hand:[i]
You will lie down in torment.[j]

Everlasting Salvation for Zion

51 "Listen[k] to me, you who pursue righteousness[l]
and who seek[m] the LORD:
Look to the rock[n] from which you were cut
and to the quarry from which you were hewn;
2 look to Abraham,[o] your father,
and to Sarah, who gave you birth.
When I called him he was but one,
and I blessed him and made him many.[p]
3 The LORD will surely comfort[q] Zion[r]
and will look with compassion on all her ruins;[s]
he will make her deserts like Eden,[t]
her wastelands[u] like the garden of the LORD.
Joy and gladness[v] will be found in her,
thanksgiving[w] and the sound of singing.

4 "Listen to me, my people;[x]
hear me,[y] my nation:
The law[z] will go out from me;
my justice[a] will become a light to the nations.[b]
5 My righteousness draws near speedily,
my salvation[c] is on the way,[d]
and my arm[e] will bring justice to the nations.
The islands[f] will look to me
and wait in hope[g] for my arm.
6 Lift up your eyes to the heavens,
look at the earth beneath;
the heavens will vanish like smoke,[h]
the earth will wear out like a garment[i]
and its inhabitants die like flies.
But my salvation[j] will last forever,[k]
my righteousness will never fail.[l]

7 "Hear me, you who know what is right,[m]
you people who have my law in your hearts:[n]
Do not fear the reproach of men
or be terrified by their insults.[o]
8 For the moth will eat them up like a garment;[p]
the worm[q] will devour them like wool.
But my righteousness will last forever,[r]
my salvation through all generations."

9 Awake, awake![s] Clothe yourself with strength,[t]
O arm[u] of the LORD;
awake, as in days gone by,
as in generations of old.[v]
Was it not you who cut Rahab[w] to pieces,
who pierced that monster[x] through?
10 Was it not you who dried up the sea,[y]
the waters of the great deep,[z]
who made a road in the depths of the sea[a]
so that the redeemed[b] might cross over?
11 The ransomed[c] of the LORD will return.
They will enter Zion with singing;[d]
everlasting joy will crown their heads.

50:11 [g]Pr 26:18 [h]Isa 1:31; Jas 3:6 [i]S Dt 21:22-23; S Pr 26:27 [j]S Job 15:20; Isa 65:13-15 **51:1** [k]S Isa 46:3 [l]ver 7; S Dt 7:13; 16:20; Ps 94:15; Isa 63:8; Ro 9:30-31 [m]Isa 55:6; 65:10 [n]Isa 17:10 **51:2** [o]S Ge 17:6; S Isa 29:22; Ro 4:16; Heb 11:11 [p]S Ge 12:2 **51:3** [q]S Isa 40:1 [r]S Ps 51:18; S Isa 61:4 [s]Isa 44:26; 52:9; 61:4 [t]S Ge 2:8 [u]S Isa 5:6; S 41:19 [v]S Isa 25:9; 35:10; 65:18; 66:10; Jer 16:9 [w]Jer 17:26; 30:19; 33:11 **51:4** [x]Ex 6:7; Ps 50:7; Isa 3:15; 63:8; 64:9 [y]S Ps 78:1 [z]S Dt 18:18 [a]S Isa 2:4 [b]S Isa 26:18; S 49:6 **51:5** [c]S Ps 85:9; S Isa 12:2 [d]S Isa 35:4 [e]Ps 98:1; Isa 40:10; 50:2; 52:10; 59:16; 63:1,5 [f]S Isa 11:11 [g]S Ge 49:10; S Ps 37:9 **51:6** [h]S Ps 37:20; S 102:26; Mt 24:35; Lk 21:33; 2Pe 3:10 [i]Ps 102:25-26; Heb 1:10-12 [j]S Isa 12:2 [k]ver 8; S Ps 119:89 [l]Ps 89:33; Isa 54:10 **51:7** [m]S ver 1 [n]S Dt 6:6; Ps 119:11 [o]S Ps 119:39; Isa 50:7; 54:4; Mt 5:11; Lk 6:22; Ac 5:41 **51:8** [p]S Job 13:28; Jas 5:2 [q]S Isa 14:11 [r]S ver 6 **51:9** [s]S Jdg 5:12 [t]S Ge 18:14; S Ps 65:6; Isa 40:31; 52:1 [u]S Ps 98:1; S Isa 30:30; S 33:2 [v]Ex 6:6; Dt 4:34; S 32:7 [w]S Job 9:13 [x]S Ps 68:30; S 74:13 **51:10** [y]S Ex 14:22; Zec 10:11; Rev 16:12 [z]Ex 15:5,8 [a]S Job 36:30 [b]S Ex 15:13 **51:11** [c]S Isa 35:9; S 44:23 [d]S Ps 109:28; Isa 65:14; Jer 30:19; Zep 3:14

50:11 *light fires . . . flaming torches.* Perhaps a reference to wicked practices that will ultimately destroy those who engage in them. Fire is a frequent figure of punishment (see 1:31 and note; cf. 9:18; 47:14; Ps 7:13). *torment.* Cf. 66:24.
51:1 *Listen to me.* See vv. 4,7. *who pursue righteousness.* Cf. v. 7; Dt 16:20; Pr 15:9. *rock.* Abraham (v. 2).
51:2 *was but one.* See Ge 12:1; Eze 33:24. *blessed him and made him many.* See Ge 12:2 – 3; 13:16; 15:5; 17:5 and note; 22:17.
51:3 *comfort . . . compassion.* See 49:13 and note. *deserts like Eden.* See 35:1 – 2. The contrast between the lush splendor of Eden and the barrenness of the desert is found also in Joel 2:3 (see note there). Cf. Ge 2:8,10. *Joy and gladness.* See v. 11; 25:9 and note.
51:4 *law . . . my justice.* The rule of the servant would bring justice also (see 2:2 – 4; 42:4 and notes). *light to the nations.* The servant is the light in 42:6; 49:6.
51:5 *righteousness draws near.* In the deliverance from exile. Ultimately, salvation through Christ will come to all nations. See 46:13 and note. *arm.* Symbolizes power. *islands.* See 11:11 and note. *look to me . . . hope.* See 40:31; 42:4 and notes.
51:6 *Lift . . . to the heavens.* See 40:26. *heavens will vanish.* See 34:4 and note. *earth will wear out like a garment.* See 24:4; Heb 1:10 – 11; cf. Isa 50:9. *last forever.* See v. 8; 45:17. The word of God will also endure forever (see 40:8 and note; Mt 24:35; Lk 21:33).
51:7 *who know what is right.* See v. 1 and note. *who have my law in your hearts.* See Ps 37:31; Jer 31:33 and note. *reproach . . . insults.* Such as those borne by the servant in 50:6 – 7.
51:8 *moth . . . like a garment.* See 50:9 and note; cf. 51:6.
51:9,17; 52:1 *Awake, awake!* See 40:1 and note.
51:9 *Clothe . . . with strength.* Cf. 50:2; see note on 40:31. *arm of the LORD.* Symbol of God's power (cf. v. 5). See 30:30; 50:2 and notes; 52:10; 53:1; 63:12. *Rahab . . . monster.* Egypt. See 27:1; 30:7 and notes.
51:10 *sea.* The Red Sea (see 50:2 and note). *the redeemed.* See 35:9 and note.
51:11 Identical to 35:10 (see note there).

Gladness and joy[e] will overtake them,
and sorrow and sighing will flee
away.[f]

12 "I, even I, am he who comforts[g] you.
Who are you that you fear[h] mortal
men,[i]
the sons of men, who are but grass,[j]
13 that you forget[k] the LORD your Maker,[l]
who stretched out the heavens[m]
and laid the foundations of the
earth,
that you live in constant terror[n] every
day
because of the wrath of the
oppressor,
who is bent on destruction?
For where is the wrath of the
oppressor?[o]
14 The cowering prisoners will soon be
set free;[p]
they will not die in their dungeon,
nor will they lack bread.[q]
15 For I am the LORD your God,
who churns up the sea[r] so that its
waves roar[s]—
the LORD Almighty[t] is his name.
16 I have put my words in your mouth[u]
and covered you with the shadow
of my hand[v]—
I who set the heavens in place,
who laid the foundations of the
earth,[w]
and who say to Zion, 'You are my
people.[x]'"

The Cup of the LORD's Wrath

17 Awake, awake![y]
Rise up, O Jerusalem,
you who have drunk from the hand
of the LORD
the cup[z] of his wrath,[a]
you who have drained to its dregs[b]
the goblet that makes men
stagger.[c]
18 Of all the sons[d] she bore
there was none to guide her;[e]

51:11 [e] S Isa 48:20; Jer 33:11 [f] S Isa 30:19; Jer 31:13; S Rev 7:17
51:12 [g] S Isa 40:1; S 2Co 1:4 [h] S 2Ki 1:15 [i] S Isa 2:22 [j] S Isa 15:6; 40:6-7; 1Pe 1:24
51:13 [k] S Job 8:13; S Isa 17:10 [l] S Job 4:17; Isa 17:7; 45:11; 54:5 [m] S Ge 1:1; S Isa 48:13 [n] S Isa 7:4 [o] S Isa 9:4
51:14 [p] S Isa 42:7 [q] Isa 49:10
51:15 [r] S Ex 14:21 [s] S Ps 93:3 [t] S Isa 13:4
51:16 [u] S Ex 4:12, 15 [v] S Ex 33:22 [w] S Isa 48:13 [x] Jer 7:23; 11:4; 24:7; Eze 14:11; Zec 8:8
51:17 [y] S Jdg 5:12; Isa 52:1 [z] S ver 22; S Ps 16:5; S Mt 20:22 [a] ver 20; Job 21:20; Isa 42:25; 66:15; Rev 14:10; 16:19 [b] S Ps 75:8 [c] S ver 23; S Ps 60:3
51:18 [d] Ps 88:18 [e] S Job 31:18; S Isa 49:21 [f] S Isa 41:13
51:19 [g] S Isa 40:2; 47:9 [h] Isa 49:13; 54:11; Jer 15:5; Na 3:7 [i] Isa 60:18; 62:4; Jer 48:3; La 3:47 [j] S Isa 14:30 [k] Jer 14:12; 24:10
51:20 [l] Isa 5:25; Jer 14:16; La 2:19 [m] S Job 18:10

of all the sons she reared
there was none to take her by the
hand.[f]
19 These double calamities[g] have come
upon you—
who can comfort you?[h]—
ruin and destruction,[i] famine[j] and
sword[k]—
who can[a] console you?
20 Your sons have fainted;
they lie at the head of every street,[l]
like antelope caught in a net.[m]
They are filled with the wrath[n] of the
LORD
and the rebuke[o] of your God.
21 Therefore hear this, you afflicted[p] one,
made drunk,[q] but not with wine.
22 This is what your Sovereign LORD says,
your God, who defends[r] his people:
"See, I have taken out of your hand
the cup[s] that made you stagger;
from that cup, the goblet of my wrath,
you will never drink again.
23 I will put it into the hands of your
tormentors,[t]
who said to you,
'Fall prostrate[u] that we may walk[v]
over you.'
And you made your back like the
ground,
like a street to be walked over."[w]

52 Awake, awake,[x] O Zion,
clothe yourself with strength.[y]
Put on your garments of splendor,[z]
O Jerusalem, the holy city.[a]
The uncircumcised[b] and defiled[c]
will not enter you again.[d]

[a] *19* Dead Sea Scrolls, Septuagint, Vulgate and Syriac; Masoretic Text / *how can I*

[n] S ver 17; S Job 40:11; Jer 44:6 [o] S Dt 28:20 **51:21** [p] S Isa 14:32 [q] ver 17; S Isa 29:9 **51:22** [r] S Isa 49:25 [s] S ver 17; Jer 25:15; 51:7; Hab 2:16; S Mt 20:22 **51:23** [t] Isa 14:4; 49:26; Jer 25:15-17, 26, 28; 49:12 [u] ver 17; Zec 12:2 [v] S Jos 10:24 [w] Ps 66:12; Mic 7:10
52:1 [x] S Isa 51:17 [y] S 1Sa 2:4; S Isa 51:9 [z] Ex 28:2, 40; Est 6:8; Ps 110:3; Isa 49:18; 61:10; Zec 3:4 [a] S Ne 11:1; S Isa 1:26; Mt 4:5; S Rev 21:2 [b] S Ge 34:14 [c] S Isa 35:8 [d] Joel 3:17; Na 1:15; Zec 9:8; Rev 21:27

51:12 *who comforts.* See v. 3; 49:13 and note. *grass.* See 37:27; 40:6 and notes.
51:13 *stretched out the heavens and ... earth.* See v. 16; 48:13 and note. *wrath of the oppressor.* See 49:26 and note. Babylon's wrath was insignificant beside the mighty wrath of God (cf. 13:3,5; 30:27).
51:14 *prisoners ... set free.* The exiles in Babylon (see 42:7 and note; 49:9). *in their dungeon.* Cf. 42:7; Jer 37:16.
51:15 *churns up the sea.* Cf. Job 26:12; Ps 107:25; Jer 31:35. *LORD Almighty.* See 13:4 and note.
51:16 *my words.* Primarily the law of Moses, mentioned in v. 7. Like the servant of 49:2, the people are responding to God's word (cf. 59:21; Jos 1:8). *shadow of my hand.* See 49:2 and note. *set the heavens ... earth.* See v. 13 and note.
51:17 *cup of his wrath.* See vv. 20–22; 13:3 and note. Experiencing God's judgment is often compared to becoming drunk on strong wine. It is the fate of wicked nations in particular. See 29:9; 63:6; Ps 60:3 and note; 75:8; Jer 25:15–16 and notes; La 4:21; Eze 23:31 and note; Hab 2:16 and note; Zec 12:2; cf. Jn 18:11.
51:18 Children were expected to take care of parents who were sick or unsteady (cf. 1Ti 5:8).
51:19 *who can comfort you?* A question also asked in Jer 15:5. Contrast v. 3.
51:20 *caught in a net.* Cf. Pr 7:22. *rebuke.* See 17:13; 54:9; 66:15.
51:21 *afflicted one.* Jerusalem (see 54:11). *made drunk.* On God's wrath (see v. 17 and note).
51:22 *defends his people.* See 49:25 and note. *cup ... of my wrath.* See v. 17 and note.
51:23 *your tormentors.* The Babylonians. See vv. 13–14; 14:4. *your back like the ground.* Perhaps figurative, but cf. Jos 10:24 and note.
52:1 *Awake, awake.* See 51:9,17. *garments of splendor.* Perhaps the robes of the priests, which belong to Jerusalem as a "holy city." See 49:18 and note. *holy city.* See 48:2 and note.

[2]Shake off your dust;[e]
rise up,[f] sit enthroned, O Jerusalem.
Free yourself from the chains on your neck,[g]
O captive Daughter of Zion.[h]

[3]For this is what the LORD says:

"You were sold for nothing,[i]
and without money[j] you will be redeemed.[k]"

[4]For this is what the Sovereign LORD says:

"At first my people went down to Egypt[l] to live;
lately, Assyria[m] has oppressed them.

[5]"And now what do I have here?" declares the LORD.

"For my people have been taken away for nothing,
and those who rule them mock,[a]"
declares the LORD.
"And all day long
my name is constantly blasphemed.[n]
[6]Therefore my people will know[o] my name;[p]
therefore in that day[q] they will know
that it is I who foretold[r] it.
Yes, it is I."

[7]How beautiful on the mountains[s]
are the feet of those who bring good news,[t]
who proclaim peace,[u]
who bring good tidings,
who proclaim salvation,
who say to Zion,
"Your God reigns!"[v]

52:2 [e]S Isa 29:4 [f]Isa 60:1 [g]S Ps 81:6; S Isa 10:27 [h]Ps 9:14 **52:3** [i]S Ps 44:12 [j]Isa 45:13 [k]S Isa 1:27; 1Pe 1:18 **52:4** [l]S Ge 46:6 [m]Isa 10:24 **52:5** [n]S Isa 37:23; Ro 2:24* **52:6** [o]S Isa 49:23 [p]S Ex 6:3 [q]S Isa 10:20 [r]S Isa 41:26 **52:7** [s]S Isa 42:11 [t]S 2Sa 18:26; S Isa 40:9; Ro 10:15* [u]Na 1:15; Lk 2:14; Eph 6:15 [v]S 1Ch 16:31; S Ps 97:1; 1Co 15:24-25

52:8 [w]S 1Sa 14:16; Isa 56:10; 62:6; Jer 6:17; 31:6; Eze 3:17; 33:7 [x]Isa 40:9 [y]S Isa 12:6 [z]S Nu 10:36 [a]Isa 59:20; Zec 8:3 **52:9** [b]S Ps 98:4; S Isa 35:2 [c]S Ps 74:3; S Isa 51:3 [d]S Isa 40:1; Lk 2:25 [e]S Ezr 9:9; S Isa 48:20 **52:10** [f]S 2Ch 32:8; S Ps 44:3; S Isa 30:30 [g]Isa 66:18 [h]S Jos 4:24; S Isa 11:9

[8]Listen! Your watchmen[w] lift up their voices;[x]
together they shout for joy.[y]
When the LORD returns[z] to Zion,[a]
they will see it with their own eyes.
[9]Burst into songs of joy[b] together,
you ruins[c] of Jerusalem,
for the LORD has comforted[d] his people,
he has redeemed Jerusalem.[e]
[10]The LORD will lay bare his holy arm[f]
in the sight of all the nations,[g]
and all the ends of the earth[h] will see
the salvation[i] of our God.

[11]Depart,[j] depart, go out from there!
Touch no unclean thing![k]
Come out from it and be pure,[l]
you who carry the vessels[m] of the LORD.
[12]But you will not leave in haste[n]
or go in flight;
for the LORD will go before you,[o]
the God of Israel will be your rear guard.[p]

The Suffering and Glory of the Servant

[13]See, my servant[q] will act wisely[b];
he will be raised and lifted up and highly exalted.[r]

[a] 5 Dead Sea Scrolls and Vulgate; Masoretic Text *wail*
[b] 13 Or *will prosper*

[i]S Ps 67:2; Lk 2:30; 3:6 **52:11** [j]S Isa 48:20 [k]S Isa 1:16; 2Co 6:17* [l]S Nu 8:6; 2Ti 2:19 [m]S 2Ch 36:10 **52:12** [n]S Ex 12:11 [o]Mic 2:13; Jn 10:4 [p]S Ex 14:19 **52:13** [q]S Jos 1:8; S Isa 4:2; S 20:3 [r]S Isa 6:1; 57:15; Ac 3:13; S Php 2:9

uncircumcised and defiled. Foreign invaders. See 35:8; Jdg 14:3 and notes.

52:2 *Shake off your dust.* Contrast the fate of Babylon in 47:1 (see note there). *Free yourself.* See 42:7 and note; 49:9; 51:14. *Daughter of Zion.* A personification of Jerusalem (see note on 2Ki 19:21).

52:3 *sold for nothing.* The enemy paid the Lord nothing for acquiring Jerusalem. See 45:13; 50:1 and notes. *without money ... redeemed.* See 41:14 and note; 43:1; 45:13.

52:4 *Assyria ... oppressed them.* See 9:4 and note.

52:5 Quoted in part in Ro 2:24. *for nothing.* See v. 3 and note. *my name is ... blasphemed.* The captivity brought disrespect to the God of helpless Jerusalem (see Eze 36:20–23 and notes). Cf. Assyria's blasphemy in 37:23–24.

52:6 *know my name.* See 49:26 and note. *in that day.* The day of deliverance from Babylon. See 10:20,27 and note. *foretold it.* The return from exile.

52:7 *feet of those who bring good news.* A reference to messengers who ran from the scene of a battle to bring news of the outcome to a waiting king and people (see 2Sa 18:26; Na 1:15 and note). Here the news refers to the return from exile (vv. 11–12; see 40:9 and note; 41:27), a deliverance that prefigures Christ's deliverance from sin. See Ro 10:15; Eph 6:15 and notes. *salvation.* See 49:8 and note. *Your God reigns!* See Ps 93:1 and note. The return of God's people to Jerusalem emphasizes his sovereign rule over the world (see 40:9 and note). God's kingdom will come more fully at the second coming of Christ (see Rev 19:6).

52:8 *watchmen.* Stationed on Jerusalem's walls (see 62:6–7; Ps 127:1 and note).

52:9 *Burst into songs.* See 44:23 and note. *comforted.* See 49:13 and note. *redeemed.* See v. 3 and note.

52:10 *holy arm.* See 51:9 and note. God's arm is often associated with redemption and salvation (see Ex 6:6). *all the ends of the earth.* Equivalent to all humankind (see note on 40:5). Cf. 45:22.

52:11 Quoted in part in 2Co 6:17. *Depart, depart ...!* See note on 40:1. *unclean thing.* Perhaps referring to pagan religious objects (cf. Ge 31:19; 35:2). *you who carry the vessels.* Cyrus allowed the people to take back the articles of the temple seized by Nebuchadnezzar (Ezr 1:7–11). The priests and Levites were responsible for them (see Nu 3:6–8; 2Ch 5:4–7).

52:12 *not leave in haste.* See 48:20 and note. *go before you ... be your rear guard.* As he did for the Israelites when they were freed from Egypt (see Ex 13:21; 14:19–20 and notes; cf. Isa 42:16; 49:10; 58:8).

52:13—53:12 The fourth and longest of the four servant songs (see note on 42:1–4). It constitutes the central and most important unit in chs. 40–66 as well as in chs. 49–57 (see note on 39:8). The song contains five stanzas of three numbered verses each. It is quoted more frequently in the NT than any other OT passage and is often referred to as the "gospel in the OT."

52:13 *my servant.* See note on 42:1. *act wisely.* A mark of God's blessing (see 1Sa 18:14) and of obedience to

[14]Just as there were many who were
appalled[s] at him[a]—
his appearance was so disfigured[t]
beyond that of any man
and his form marred beyond human
likeness[u]—
[15]so will he sprinkle[v] many nations,[b]
and kings[w] will shut their mouths[x]
because of him.
For what they were not told, they will
see,
and what they have not heard, they
will understand.[y]

53 Who has believed our message[z]
and to whom has the arm[a] of the
LORD been revealed?[b]
[2]He grew up before him like a tender
shoot,[c]
and like a root[d] out of dry ground.
He had no beauty or majesty to attract
us to him,
nothing in his appearance[e] that we
should desire him.
[3]He was despised and rejected by men,
a man of sorrows,[f] and familiar with
suffering.[g]
Like one from whom men hide[h] their
faces
he was despised,[i] and we esteemed
him not.
[4]Surely he took up our infirmities
and carried our sorrows,[j]
yet we considered him stricken by
God,[k]
smitten by him, and afflicted.[l]
[5]But he was pierced[m] for our
transgressions,[n]
he was crushed[o] for our iniquities;
the punishment[p] that brought us
peace[q] was upon him,
and by his wounds[r] we are healed.[s]
[6]We all, like sheep, have gone astray,[t]
each of us has turned to his own
way;[u]
and the LORD has laid on him
the iniquity[v] of us all.
[7]He was oppressed[w] and afflicted,
yet he did not open his mouth;[x]
he was led like a lamb[y] to the
slaughter,[z]
and as a sheep before her shearers is
silent,
so he did not open his mouth.
[8]By oppression[c] and judgment[a] he was
taken away.
And who can speak of his
descendants?

52:14 [s]S Lev 26:32; S Job 18:20 [t]S 2Sa 10:4 [u]S Job 2:12; S 16:16 **52:15** [v]S Lev 14:7; S 16:14-15 [w]S Isa 49:7 [x]S Jdg 18:19; Ps 107:42 [y]Ro 15:21*; Eph 3:4-5 **53:1** [z]S Isa 28:9; Ro 10:16* [a]S Ps 98:1; S Isa 30:30 [b]Jn 12:38* **53:2** [c]S 2Ki 19:26; S Job 14:7; S Isa 4:2 [d]S Isa 11:10 [e]Isa 52:14 **53:3** [f]Ps 69:29 [g]ver 4, 10; S Ex 1:10; S Mt 16:21; Lk 18:31-33; Heb 5:8 [h]S Dt 31:17; Isa 1:15 [i]S 1Sa 2:30; S Ps 22:6; Mt 27:29; Jn 1:10-11 **53:4** [j]Mt 8:17* [k]S Dt 5:24; S Job 4:5; Jer 23:5-6; 25:34; Eze 34:23-24; Mic 5:2-4; Zec 13:7; Jn 19:7 [l]S ver 3; S Ge 12:17; S Ru 1:21 **53:5** [m]S Ps 22:16 [n]S Ex 28:38; S Ps 39:8; S Jn 3:17; Ro 4:25; 1Co 15:3; Heb 9:28 [o]Ps 34:18 [p]S Isa 50:6 [q]S Isa 9:6; Ro 5:1 [r]Isa 1:6; Mt 27:26; Jn 19:1 [s]S Dt 32:39; S 2Ch 7:14; 1Pe 2:24-25 **53:6** [t]S Ps 95:10; 1Pe 2:24-25 [u]S 1Sa 8:3; Isa 56:11; 57:17; Mic 3:5 [v]ver 12; S Ex 28:38; Ro 4:25 **53:7** [w]Isa 49:26 [x]S Mk 14:61; 1Pe 2:23 [y]Mt 27:31; S Jn 1:29 [z]S Ps 44:22 **53:8** [a]Mk 14:49

[a] *14* Hebrew *you* [b] *15* Hebrew; Septuagint *so will many nations marvel at him* [c] *8* Or *From arrest*

God's word (see Jos 1:8). The Messianic King will "reign wisely" (Jer 23:5). Cf. 53:10. *raised and lifted up.* Words that describe the Lord in Isaiah's vision (see 6:1 and note; 57:15). Christ's exaltation is referred to in Ac 2:33; 3:13; Eph 1:20–23; Php 2:9–11 (see also 1Pe 1:10–11 and note on 1:11).

52:14 *appalled at him.* When they saw Christ's suffering on the cross. Cf. the reaction to the ruined city of Tyre (Eze 27:35). *disfigured.* A term used of a "blemished animal," which should not be offered to the Lord (Mal 1:14). Cf. the disgraceful treatment of the servant (see 50:6 and note). *beyond that of any man.* Cf. Ps 22:6. His treatment was inhuman.

52:15 *sprinkle many nations.* With the sprinkling of cleansing (see Lev 14:7; Nu 8:7; 19:18–19) and/or of consecration (see Ex 29:21; Lev 8:11,30). But see NIV text note. *kings will shut their mouths.* In astonishment at the suffering and exaltation of the servant (see 49:6–7 and notes). Cf. Job 21:5. *For what … understand.* Quoted in Ro 15:21. Even though they have not heard the prophetic word, kings will understand the mission of the servant when they see his humiliation and exaltation (contrast 6:9–10).

53:1 Quoted in whole in Jn 12:38 and in part in Ro 10:16. *our message.* The good news about salvation, given by the prophets to Israel and the nations (see 52:7,10). *arm of the LORD.* See 51:9 and note.

53:2 *tender shoot.* The Messiah would grow from the "stump of Jesse" (11:1; see note there; cf. 4:2; Zec 3:8 and notes). His beginnings would be humble. *root.* See 11:10 and note. *beauty.* The Hebrew for this word is used of David in 1Sa 16:18, where it is translated "fine-looking." *majesty.* Christ had nothing of the bearing or trappings of royalty.

53:3 *despised.* See 49:7 and note; Ps 22:6. *rejected … esteemed.* The Hebrew words used here occur together also in 2:22 (see note there). Cf. Jn 1:10–11. *sorrows.* The Hebrew for this word is used of both physical and mental pain (see v. 4; Ex 3:7). *hide their faces.* See 1:15 and note; 8:17.

53:4 Quoted in part in Mt 8:17 with reference to Jesus' healing ministry. *infirmities.* Diseases often result from sinful living and are ultimately the consequences of original (Adamic) sin. See 1:5–6 and note. *stricken by God.* With a terrible disease (see Ge 12:17; 2Ki 15:5). People (Israel in particular) thought the servant was suffering for his own sins. *afflicted.* Or "humbled," or "oppressed" (see v. 7; 58:10).

53:5 *pierced.* See Ps 22:16; Zec 12:10; Jn 19:34 and notes. *crushed.* In spirit (see Ps 34:18; cf. Isa 57:15). The sins of the world weighed heavily upon him. *healed.* Here probably equivalent to "forgiven" (see 6:10; Jer 30:17; see also note on 1Pe 2:24).

53:6 *have gone astray.* Cf. Ps 119:176 and note; Jer 50:6; Eze 34:4–6,16; 1Pe 2:25 and note. *laid on him the iniquity of us all.* Just as the priest laid his hands on the scapegoat and symbolically put Israel's sins on it (see Lev 16:20–22 and note). See 1Pe 2:24 and note.

53:7–8 Verses read by the Ethiopian eunuch in the presence of Philip (see Ac 8:34 and note).

53:7 *oppressed.* Like Israel. See 49:26 and note. The Hebrew for this word is translated "slave drivers" in Ex 5:6. *lamb to the slaughter.* Cf. Ps 44:22; Rev 5:6 and note. John the Baptist called Jesus "the Lamb of God" (Jn 1:29,36; see note on 1:29). *did not open his mouth.* Jesus remained silent before the chief priests and Pilate (Mt 27:12–14; Mk 14:60–61; 15:4–5; Jn 19:8–9) and before Herod (Lk 23:8–9).

53:8 *By oppression and judgment.* Jesus was given an unfair trial. *his descendants.* To die without children was considered a tragedy (2Sa 18:18). Cf. also v. 10. But see second NIV text note here.

For he was cut off from the land of the
living;[b]
for the transgression[c] of my people
he was stricken.[a]
9 He was assigned a grave with the
wicked,[d]
and with the rich[e] in his death,
though he had done no violence,[f]
nor was any deceit in his mouth.[g]

10 Yet it was the LORD's will[h] to crush[i]
him and cause him to suffer,[j]
and though the LORD makes[b] his life
a guilt offering,[k]
he will see his offspring[l] and prolong
his days,
and the will of the LORD will
prosper[m] in his hand.
11 After the suffering[n] of his soul,
he will see the light[o] ⌞of life⌟[c] and be
satisfied[d];
by his knowledge[e] my righteous
servant[p] will justify[q] many,
and he will bear their iniquities.[r]
12 Therefore I will give him a portion
among the great,[f s]
and he will divide the spoils[t] with
the strong,[g]
because he poured out his life unto
death,[u]
and was numbered with the
transgressors.[v]
For he bore[w] the sin of many,[x]
and made intercession[y] for the
transgressors.

53:8 [b] Ps 88:5; Da 9:26; Ac 8:32-33* [c] ver 12; S Ps 39:8 **53:9** [d] Mt 27:38; Mk 15:27; Lk 23:32; Jn 19:18 [e] Mt 27:57-60; Mk 15:43-46; Lk 23:50-53; Jn 19:38-41 [f] Isa 42:1-3 [g] S Job 16:17; 1Pe 2:22*; 1Jn 3:5; Rev 14:5 **53:10** [h] Isa 46:10; 55:11; Ac 2:23 [i] ver 5 [j] S ver 3; S Ge 12:17 [k] S Lev 5:15; Jn 3:17 [l] S Ps 22:30 [m] S Jos 1:8; S Isa 49:4 **53:11** [n] Jn 10:14-18 [o] S Job 33:30 [p] S Isa 20:3; Ac 7:52 [q] S Isa 6:7; Jn 1:29; Ac 10:43; S Ro 4:25 [r] S Ex 28:38 **53:12** [s] S Isa 6:1; S Php 2:9 [t] S Ex 15:9; S Ps 119:162; Lk 11:22 [u] Mt 26:28,38, 39,42 [v] Mt 27:38; Mk 15:27*; Lk 22:37*; 23:32 [w] S ver 6; 1Pe 2:24 [x] Heb 9:28 [y] Isa 59:16; S Ro 8:34

The Future Glory of Zion

54 "Sing, O barren woman,[z]
you who never bore a child;
burst into song, shout for joy,[a]
you who were never in labor;[b]
because more are the children[c] of the
desolate[d] woman
than of her who has a husband,[e]"
says the LORD.
2 "Enlarge the place of your tent,[f]
stretch your tent curtains wide,
do not hold back;
lengthen your cords,
strengthen your stakes.[g]
3 For you will spread out to the right and
to the left;
your descendants[h] will dispossess
nations[i]
and settle in their desolate[j] cities.

4 "Do not be afraid;[k] you will not suffer
shame.[l]
Do not fear disgrace;[m] you will not
be humiliated.

[a] 8 Or *away. / Yet who of his generation considered / that he was cut off from the land of the living / for the transgression of my people, / to whom the blow was due?* [b] 10 Hebrew *though you make* [c] 11 Dead Sea Scrolls (see also Septuagint); Masoretic Text does not have *the light ⌞of life⌟.* [d] 11 Or (with Masoretic Text) [11] *He will see the result of the suffering of his soul / and be satisfied* [e] 11 Or *by knowledge of him* [f] 12 Or *many* [g] 12 Or *numerous*

54:1 [z] S Ge 30:1 [a] S Ge 21:6; S Ps 98:4 [b] Isa 66:7 [c] Isa 49:20 [d] S Isa 49:19 [e] S 1Sa 2:5; Gal 4:27* **54:2** [f] S Ge 26:22; Isa 26:15; 49:19-20 [g] Ex 35:18; 39:40 **54:3** [h] S Ge 13:14; S Isa 48:19 [i] S Job 12:23; S Isa 14:2; 60:4-11 [j] S Isa 49:19 **54:4** [k] Jer 30:10; Joel 2:21 [l] S Isa 28:16; S 29:22 [m] S Ge 30:23; S Ps 119:39; S Isa 41:11

53:9 *the wicked.* The manner of his death would indicate that, as far as those who condemned him were concerned, he was to be buried with executed criminals. *the rich.* Not as a burial with honor. The parallelism (with its effective wordplay in Hebrew) makes clear that Isaiah here associates the rich with the wicked, as do many OT writers — because they acquired their wealth by wicked means and/or trusted in their wealth rather than in God (see, e.g., Ps 37:16,35; Pr 18:23; 28:6,20; Jer 5:26 – 27; Mic 6:10,12). According to the Gospels (Mt 27:57 – 60 and parallels), the wealthy Joseph of Arimathea gave Jesus an honorable burial by placing his body in his own tomb. But this was undoubtedly an act of love growing out of his awareness that he had been forgiven much (see Lk 7:47). Thus the fulfillment fitted but also transcended the prophecy. *he had done no violence, nor … deceit in his mouth.* Peter quotes these lines as he encourages believers to endure unjust suffering (1Pe 2:22).
53:10 *crush him.* See v. 5 and note. *guilt offering.* An offering where restitution was usually required and the offender sacrificed a ram (see note on Lev 5:15). *his offspring.* Spiritual progeny. *prolong his days.* Christ would live forever (see 9:7 and note). *prosper.* See 52:13 and NIV text note there.
53:11 *light ⌞of life⌟.* A reference to the resurrection of Christ; see 1Co 15:4 (but see also the first two NIV text notes here). For "of life" see Job 33:30 and note; Ps 49:19; 56:13 and note. *be satisfied.* In 1:11, where the same Hebrew word appears, God had "more than enough" of innumerable sacrifices that accomplished nothing. Here the one sacrifice of Christ brings perfect satisfaction. *his knowledge.* His true knowledge of the true God (see 1:3; 6:9; 43:10; 45:4 – 5; 52:6; 56:10). The Spirit of knowledge (11:2) rested on the Messiah (but see the third NIV text note here). Cf. 52:13. *my … servant.* See 41:8 – 9; 42:1 and notes. *justify.* Cause many to be declared righteous. See 5:23 ("acquit"); Ro 5:19 and note. *many.* See NIV text notes on v. 12; see also 52:15; Da 12:3.
53:12 *among the great … with the strong.* God will reward his servant as if he were a king sharing in the spoils of a great victory (see 52:15). *divide the spoils.* God's gift to his suffering servant (cf. 9:3). *poured out his life.* As a sacrifice (see v. 10). *unto death.* See Php 2:8 and note. *and was numbered with the transgressors.* Quoted in Lk 22:37 with reference to Jesus (see note there). *bore.* The Hebrew for this verb is translated "took up" in v. 4. *made intercession.* See Jer 7:16 ("pray"); 27:18 ("plead"). Cf. 59:16; Heb 7:25.
54:1 This verse is applied by Paul to Sarah and the covenant of promise, representing "the Jerusalem that is above" (Gal 4:26 – 27; see notes there). *Sing … burst into song.* See 12:6; 44:23; 52:9 and notes. *barren woman.* Jerusalem (representing Israel), especially during the exile (see 49:21). In the Near East, barrenness was considered a disgrace (see 4:1 and note). *more are the children of the desolate woman.* See 49:19 – 20 and note. Israel will be restored both physically and spiritually (cf. 62:4). *husband.* See 50:1 and note.
54:2 See 26:15; 33:20 and notes. *your tent.* Jerusalem is viewed as a woman living in her own tent.
54:3 *spread out.* See 49:19 – 20 and note; cf. Ge 28:14. *dispossess nations.* See 11:14; 49:7 and notes.
54:4 *not suffer shame … disgrace.* See 29:22 and note; 45:17. *shame of your youth.* Probably the period of slavery in Egypt. Cf. Jer 31:19; Eze 16:60. *reproach of your widowhood.* Probably referring to the exile, when Israel was alone, like a widow (vv. 6 – 7).

You will forget the shame of your
youth[n]
and remember no more the
reproach[o] of your widowhood.[p]
5For your Maker[q] is your husband[r]—
the LORD Almighty is his name—
the Holy One[s] of Israel is your
Redeemer;[t]
he is called the God of all the earth.[u]
6The LORD will call you back[v]
as if you were a wife deserted[w] and
distressed in spirit—
a wife who married young,[x]
only to be rejected," says your
God.
7"For a brief moment[y] I abandoned[z]
you,
but with deep compassion[a] I will
bring you back.[b]
8In a surge of anger[c]
I hid[d] my face from you for a
moment,
but with everlasting kindness[e]
I will have compassion[f] on you,"
says the LORD your Redeemer.[g]

9"To me this is like the days of Noah,
when I swore that the waters of
Noah would never again cover
the earth.[h]
So now I have sworn[i] not to be angry[j]
with you,
never to rebuke[k] you again.
10Though the mountains be shaken[l][m]
and the hills be removed,
yet my unfailing love[n] for you will not
be shaken[o]
nor my covenant[p] of peace[q] be
removed,"
says the LORD, who has compassion[r]
on you.

11"O afflicted[s] city, lashed by storms[t]
and not comforted,[u]
I will build you with stones of
turquoise,[a][v]
your foundations[w] with sapphires.[b][x]
12I will make your battlements of rubies,
your gates[y] of sparkling jewels,
and all your walls of precious stones.
13All your sons will be taught by the
LORD,[z]
and great will be your children's
peace.[a]
14In righteousness[b] you will be
established:[c]
Tyranny[d] will be far from you;
you will have nothing to fear.[e]
Terror[f] will be far removed;
it will not come near you.
15If anyone does attack you, it will not
be my doing;
whoever attacks you will surrender[g]
to you.

16"See, it is I who created the
blacksmith[h]
who fans the coals into flame
and forges a weapon[i] fit for its work.
And it is I who have created the
destroyer[j] to work havoc;
17 no weapon forged against you will
prevail,[k]
and you will refute[l] every tongue
that accuses you.
This is the heritage of the servants[m] of
the LORD,
and this is their vindication[n] from
me,"
declares the LORD.

54:4 [n]S Ps 25:7; S Jer 2:2; S 22:21 [o]S Isa 51:7 [p]S Isa 47:8 **54:5** [q]S Ps 95:6; S 149:2; S Isa 51:13 [r]S SS 3:11; Jer 3:14; 31:32; Hos 2:7,16 [s]S Isa 1:4; 49:7; 55:5; 60:9 [t]S Isa 48:17 [u]S Isa 6:3; S 12:4 **54:6** [v]Isa 49:14-21 [w]ver 6-7; Isa 1:4; 50:1-2; 60:15; 62:4,12; Jer 44:2; Hos 1:10 [x]S Ex 20:14; Mal 2:15 **54:7** [y]S Job 14:13; Isa 26:20 [z]S Ps 71:11; S Isa 27:8 [a]S Ps 51:1 [b]S Isa 49:18 **54:8** [c]Isa 9:12; 26:20; 60:10 [d]S Isa 1:15 [e]ver 10; S Ps 25:6; 92:2; Isa 55:3; 63:7 [f]S Ps 102:13; S Isa 14:1; Hos 2:19 [g]S Isa 48:17 **54:9** [h]S Ge 8:21 [i]S Isa 14:24; S 49:18 [j]Ps 13:1; 103:9; Isa 12:1; 57:16; Jer 3:5,12; Eze 39:29; Mic 7:18 [k]S Dt 28:20 **54:10** [l]Rev 6:14 [m]S Ps 46:2 [n]S Ps 6:4 [o]S Isa 51:6; Heb 12:27 [p]S Ge 9:16; Ex 34:10; Ps 89:34; S Isa 42:6 [q]S Nu 25:12 [r]ver 8; S Isa 14:1; 55:7 **54:11** [s]S Isa 14:32

[a] *11* The meaning of the Hebrew for this word is uncertain. [b] *11* Or *lapis lazuli*

[t]Isa 28:2; 29:6 [u]S Isa 51:19 [v]1Ch 29:2; Rev 21:18 [w]S Isa 28:16; Rev 21:19-20 [x]S Ex 24:10; S Job 28:6 **54:12** [y]Rev 21:21 **54:13** [z]S Isa 28:9; Mic 4:2; Jn 6:45*; Heb 8:11 [a]S Lev 26:6; S Isa 48:18 **54:14** [b]S Isa 26:2 [c]Jer 30:20 [d]S 2Sa 7:10; S Isa 9:4 [e]Zep 3:15; Zec 9:8 [f]S Isa 17:14 **54:15** [g]Isa 41:11-16 **54:16** [h]S Isa 44:12 [i]S Isa 10:5 [j]S Isa 13:5 **54:17** [k]S Isa 29:8 [l]S Isa 41:11 [m]Isa 56:6-8; 63:17; 65:8,9,13-15; 66:14 [n]S Ps 17:2; Zec 1:20-21

54:5 *husband.* See 62:4–5. *Holy One of Israel ... Redeemer.* See 1:4; 41:14 and notes.

54:6–7 *wife deserted ... abandoned.* Israel's experience in exile (see 49:14; 50:1 and note; 62:4).

54:7–8,10 *compassion.* See 14:1; 49:10,13; 51:3.

54:7 *brief moment.* The Babylonian exile was relatively brief (see 26:20; 50:1 and notes).

54:8 *surge of anger.* See 9:12,17,21 and note; 60:10. *hid my face.* See 1:15 and note. *everlasting kindness.* See v. 10; 55:3 and note. Cf. 45:17. *Redeemer.* See v. 5.

54:9 *never again cover the earth.* See Ge 9:11 and note. *not to be angry.* Cf. 12:1 and note. *never to rebuke you again.* As I did when I sent you into exile.

54:10 *mountains ... be removed.* Cf. 51:6; Ps 46:2; 102:26–27. *unfailing love ... covenant of peace.* A reference to God's covenantal commitments to Israel, embodied in the Abrahamic, Sinaitic, Davidic and new covenants (see chart, p. 19). Cf. Jer 33:20–21; for the language see Nu 25:11–13.

54:11–12 A figurative description of restored Jerusalem, echoed in the description of the new Jerusalem in Rev 21:10,18–21.

54:11 *afflicted city.* Jerusalem. See 51:21. *lashed by storms.* See 28:2 and note. *turquoise.* A bluish-green stone. It was used in Solomon's temple (1Ch 29:2). *sapphires.* Cf. the "pavement made of sapphire" (a blue stone) in Ex 24:10 (see also Eze 1:26; 10:1).

54:12 *battlements.* Parapets on the top of walls. *walls.* Cf. 26:1.

54:13–14 *peace ... righteousness.* See 48:18 and note.

54:13 Quoted in part in Jn 6:45. *taught by the LORD.* Like the servant of the Lord in 50:4. Cf. Jer 31:34 and note.

54:14 *Tyranny ... Terror ... far removed.* Cf. 14:4; 33:18–19.

54:15 *surrender to you.* See v. 3.

54:16 *created the destroyer.* God raised up nations such as Assyria and Babylonia to punish Israel (see 10:5; 33:1 and notes).

54:17 *refute every tongue.* Just as no legitimate charges could be brought against the servant of 50:8–9. *servants of the LORD.* After ch. 53 the singular "servant" no longer occurs in Isaiah. The "servants" (see 63:17; 65:8–9,13–15; 66:14) are true believers—both Jew and Gentile (see 56:6–8)—who are faithful to the Lord. They are in a sense the "offspring" of the servant (53:10). See 49:19–20 and note.

Invitation to the Thirsty

55 "Come, all you who are thirsty,[o]
come to the waters;[p]
and you who have no money,
come, buy[q] and eat!
Come, buy wine and milk[r]
without money and without cost.[s]
2 Why spend money on what is not
bread,
and your labor on what does not
satisfy?[t]
Listen, listen to me, and eat what is
good,[u]
and your soul will delight in the
richest[v] of fare.
3 Give ear and come to me;
hear[w] me, that your soul may live.[x]
I will make an everlasting covenant[y]
with you,
my faithful love[z] promised to David.[a]
4 See, I have made him a witness[b] to the
peoples,
a leader and commander[c] of the
peoples.
5 Surely you will summon nations[d] you
know not,
and nations that do not know you
will hasten to you,[e]
because of the LORD your God,
the Holy One[f] of Israel,
for he has endowed you with
splendor."[g]

6 Seek[h] the LORD while he may be
found;[i]
call[j] on him while he is near.
7 Let the wicked forsake[k] his way
and the evil man his thoughts.[l]
Let him turn[m] to the LORD, and he will
have mercy[n] on him,
and to our God, for he will freely
pardon.[o]

8 "For my thoughts[p] are not your
thoughts,
neither are your ways my ways,"[q]
declares the LORD.
9 "As the heavens are higher than the
earth,[r]
so are my ways higher than your
ways
and my thoughts than your
thoughts.[s]
10 As the rain[t] and the snow
come down from heaven,
and do not return to it
without watering the earth
and making it bud and flourish,[u]
so that it yields seed[v] for the sower
and bread for the eater,[w]
11 so is my word[x] that goes out from my
mouth:
It will not return to me empty,[y]
but will accomplish what I desire
and achieve the purpose[z] for which I
sent it.
12 You will go out in joy[a]
and be led forth in peace;[b]
the mountains and hills
will burst into song[c] before you,
and all the trees[d] of the field
will clap their hands.[e]
13 Instead of the thornbush will grow the
pine tree,
and instead of briers[f] the myrtle[g]
will grow.
This will be for the LORD's renown,[h]
for an everlasting sign,
which will not be destroyed."

55:1 [o] S Pr 9:5; S Isa 35:7; Mt 5:6; Lk 6:21; Jn 4:14; 7:37 [p] Jer 2:13; Eze 47:1, 12; Zec 14:8 [q] La 5:4; Mt 13:44; Rev 3:18 [r] S SS 5:1; 1Pe 2:2 [s] Hos 14:4; Mt 10:8; Rev 21:6; 22:17 **55:2** [t] Ps 22:26; Ecc 6:2; Isa 49:4; Jer 12:13; Hos 4:10; 8:7; Mic 6:14; Hag 1:6 [u] S Isa 1:19 [v] S Isa 30:23 **55:3** [w] S Ps 78:1 [x] S Lev 18:5; S Jn 6:27; Ro 10:5 [y] S Ge 9:16; S Isa 54:10; S Heb 13:20 [z] S Isa 54:8 [a] Ac 13:34* **55:4** [b] Rev 1:5 [c] S 1Sa 13:14; S 2Ch 7:18; S Isa 32:1 **55:5** [d] S Isa 49:6 [e] S Isa 2:3 [f] S Isa 12:6; S 54:5 [g] S Isa 44:23 **55:6** [h] S Dt 4:29; S 2Ch 15:2; S Isa 9:13 [i] Ps 32:6; Isa 49:8; Ac 17:27; 2Co 6:1-2 [j] S Ps 50:15; Isa 65:24; Jer 29:12; 33:3 **55:7** [k] S 2Ch 7:14; S 30:9; Eze 18:27-28 [l] Isa 32:7; 59:7 [m] S Isa 44:22; S Jer 26:3; S Eze 18:32 [n] S Isa 54:10 [o] S 2Ch 6:21; Isa 1:18; 40:2 **55:8** [p] Php 2:5; 4:8 [q] Isa 53:6; Mic 4:12

55:9 [r] S Job 11:8; Ps 103:11 [s] S Nu 23:19; S Isa 40:13-14 **55:10** [t] Isa 30:23 [u] S Lev 25:19; S Job 14:9; S Ps 67:6 [v] S Ge 47:23 [w] 2Co 9:10 **55:11** [x] S Dt 32:2; Jn 1:1 [y] Isa 40:8; 45:23; S Mt 5:18; Heb 4:12 [z] S Pr 19:21; S Isa 44:26; Eze 12:25 **55:12** [a] S Ps 98:4; S Isa 35:2 [b] Isa 54:10, 13 [c] S Ps 65:12-13; S 96:12-13 [d] S 1Ch 16:33 [e] Ps 98:8 **55:13** [f] S Nu 33:55; S Isa 5:6 [g] Isa 41:19 [h] S Ps 102:12; Isa 63:12; Jer 32:20; 33:9

55:1 The exiles are summoned to return and be restored. *thirsty.* Spiritual thirst is primarily in view (see 41:17; 44:3; Ps 42:1–2 and notes; 63:1). *waters.* Figurative for spiritual refreshment. Cf. wisdom's invitation in Pr 9:5 (see note there). Christ similarly invited people to drink the water of life (see Jn 4:14 and note; 7:37; cf. Rev 22:17). *no money.* In hard times even water had to be purchased (see La 5:4). *wine and milk.* Symbols of abundance, enjoyment and nourishment. *without money.* The death of the servant (53:5–9) paid for the free gift of life (see Ro 6:23 and note).

55:2 *what is not bread.* Perhaps the husks of pagan religious practices. Cf. Dt 8:3 and note. *richest of fare.* Great spiritual blessings are compared to a banquet (see 25:6 and note; Ps 22:26; 34:8; Jer 31:14).

55:3 *everlasting covenant.* David had been promised an unending dynasty, one that would culminate in the Messiah (see 9:7; 54:10; 61:8; 2Sa 7:14–16 and notes). *faithful love.* Assuring the continuation of the nation. See 54:8 and note. Christ's resurrection was further proof of God's faithfulness to David (see Ac 13:34, which quotes from this verse).

55:4 *witness to the peoples.* A reference either to David, who exalted the Lord among the nations (see Ps 18:43,49–50 and notes), or to David's Son, the Messiah, who was a light to the nations (see 42:6; 49:6 and notes). *leader … of the peoples.* Similar titles are used of David (1Sa 13:14; 25:30) and the Messiah (Da 9:25).

55:5 *you will summon nations.* The attraction of nations to Zion and to the God of Israel is a major Biblical theme (see, e.g., 2:2–4; 45:14; Zec 8:22 and notes). *Holy One of Israel.* See 1:4; 41:14 and notes. *endowed … with splendor.* See 4:2; 60:9. The nation will be restored physically and spiritually.

55:6 *Seek the LORD.* See Jer 29:13–14; Hos 3:5; Am 5:4,6,14 (contrast the hypocritical seeking of 58:2).

55:7 *wicked forsake.* See 1:16. *turn to the LORD … freely pardon.* See 43:25; 44:22 and notes.

55:9 *my ways higher.* See Ps 145:3.

55:11 *my word.* Especially the promises of vv. 3,5,12. The word is viewed as a messenger also in 9:8; Ps 107:20 (see note there). Cf. Jn 1:1 and note. *achieve the purpose.* See 46:10–11 and note; cf. 40:8; Heb 4:12 and note.

55:12 *go out in joy.* The departure from Babylon provides the background (see 35:10; 52:9–12 and notes). *mountains … will burst into song.* See 44:23 and note. *hands.* Branches. The language is figurative (cf. 1Ch 16:33; Ps 98:8 and note; 114:3–6).

55:13 *thornbush … pine tree … briers … myrtle.* The reverse of the desolation Isaiah had prophesied about earlier (5:6;

Salvation for Others

56 This is what the LORD says:

"Maintain justice[i]
and do what is right,[j]
for my salvation[k] is close at hand
and my righteousness[l] will soon be revealed.
2 Blessed[m] is the man who does this,
the man who holds it fast,
who keeps the Sabbath[n] without desecrating it,
and keeps his hand from doing any evil."

3 Let no foreigner[o] who has bound himself to the LORD say,
"The LORD will surely exclude me from his people."[p]
And let not any eunuch[q] complain,
"I am only a dry tree."

4 For this is what the LORD says:
"To the eunuchs[r] who keep my Sabbaths,
who choose what pleases me
and hold fast to my covenant[s]—
5 to them I will give within my temple
and its walls[t]
a memorial[u] and a name
better than sons and daughters;
I will give them an everlasting name[v]
that will not be cut off.[w]
6 And foreigners[x] who bind themselves
to the LORD
to serve[y] him,
to love the name[z] of the LORD,
and to worship him,
all who keep the Sabbath[a] without desecrating it
and who hold fast to my covenant—
7 these I will bring to my holy mountain[b]
and give them joy in my house of prayer.
Their burnt offerings and sacrifices[c]
will be accepted on my altar;
for my house will be called
a house of prayer for all nations."[d][e]
8 The Sovereign LORD declares—
he who gathers the exiles of Israel:
"I will gather[f] still others to them
besides those already gathered."

God's Accusation Against the Wicked

9 Come, all you beasts of the field,[g]
come and devour, all you beasts of the forest!
10 Israel's watchmen[h] are blind,
they all lack knowledge;[i]
they are all mute dogs,
they cannot bark;
they lie around and dream,
they love to sleep.[j]
11 They are dogs with mighty appetites;
they never have enough.
They are shepherds[k] who lack understanding;[l]
they all turn to their own way,[m]
each seeks his own gain.[n]
12 "Come," each one cries, "let me get wine![o]
Let us drink our fill of beer!
And tomorrow will be like today,
or even far better."[p]

56:1 [i]S Ps 11:7; S Isa 1:17; S Jer 22:3 [j]S Isa 26:8 [k]S Ps 85:9 [l]Jer 23:6; Da 9:24 **56:2** [m]S Ps 119:2 [n]S Ex 20:8, 10 **56:3** [o]S Ex 12:43; S 1Ki 8:41; S Isa 11:10; Zec 8:20-23 [p]Dt 23:3 [q]S Lev 21:20; Jer 38:7 *fn*; Ac 8:27 **56:4** [r]Jer 38:7 *fn* [s]S Ex 31:13 **56:5** [t]Isa 26:1; 60:18 [u]S Nu 32:42; 1Sa 15:12 [v]S Isa 43:7 [w]S Isa 48:19; 55:13 **56:6** [x]S Ex 12:43; S 1Ki 8:41 [y]S 1Ch 22:2; Isa 60:7, 10; 61:5 [z]Mal 1:11 [a]ver 2, 4 **56:7** [b]S Isa 2:2; Eze 20:40 [c]S Isa 19:21; Ro 12:1; Php 4:18; Heb 13:15 [d]Mt 21:13*; Lk 19:46* [e]Mk 11:17* **56:8** [f]S Dt 30:4; S Isa 1:9; S 11:12; 60:3-11; Eze 34:12; Jn 10:16 **56:9** [g]Isa 18:6; Jer 12:9; Eze 34:5, 8; 39:17-20 **56:10** [h]S Isa 52:8; 62:6; Jer 6:17; 31:6; Eze 3:17; 33:7 [i]Jer 2:8; 10:21; 14:13-14 [j]Na 3:18 **56:11** [k]Jer 23:1; Eze 34:2 [l]Isa 1:3 [m]S Isa 53:6; Hos 4:7-8 [n]Isa 57:17; Jer 6:13; 8:10; 22:17; Eze 13:19; Mic 3:11 **56:12** [o]S Lev 10:9; S Pr 23:20; S Isa 22:13 [p]Ps 10:6; Lk 12:18-19

32:13). For the significance of trees see 35:2; see also 41:19 and note. *LORD's renown.* Similar to God's fame in the exodus (see 63:12,14). *everlasting sign.* God's deliverance would never be forgotten. Cf. 19:20; 56:5.

56:1 *justice ... what is right.* See note on Ps 119:121. *salvation ... righteousness.* See 45:8; 46:13; 51:5 and notes.

56:2 *keeps the Sabbath.* See vv. 4,6. Just as the Sabbath had been instituted after the exodus from Egypt (see notes on Ex 20:8–10) as a sign of the Sinaitic covenant (see Ex 31:13–17 and notes), so God's new deliverance (55:12) afforded an opportunity to obey him fully, an obedience summed up in "keeps the Sabbath" (see 58:13; 66:23; Jer 17:21–27 and notes; Eze 20:20–21).

56:3 *foreigner.* See vv. 6–7. Members of certain nations who came to live among the Israelites had been excluded from worship, at least for several generations (see Ex 12:43; Dt 23:3,7–8). But the work of the servant of the Lord would change this (see 49:19–20; 54:17; 60:10 and notes). Cf. 14:1. *eunuch.* See v. 4; Mt 19:12 and note. Eunuchs were also excluded from the assembly of the Lord (see Dt 23:1 and note), but they could still be part of God's people (see Ac 8:27,38–40).

56:4,6 *hold fast to my covenant.* Keeping the Sabbath was a sign of the Sinaitic covenant (see note on v. 2; see also Eze 20:12 and note, 20; cf. notes on Ge 9:12–13; 17:11).

56:5 *memorial.* Absalom built a "Monument" (same Hebrew word) as a memorial since he had no surviving sons (2Sa 18:18). *name.* The Hebrew for this word is translated "renown" in 55:13. The Hebrew for "a memorial and a name" (*yad vashem*) was chosen from v. 5 as the name of the main Holocaust monument in Jerusalem in modern Israel. *that will not be cut off.* An idiom sometimes referring to the preserving of a name through one's descendants.

56:6 *serve.* Cf. 60:7,10.

56:7 *my holy mountain.* See 2:2–4 and note. *offerings ... accepted on my altar.* Cf. 60:7; contrast 1:11–13. *my house ... for all nations.* Quoted by Jesus in Mk 11:17 and parallels. *house of prayer for all nations.* Solomon may have anticipated this in his prayer of dedication for the temple (see 1Ki 8:41–42 and notes).

56:8 *gathers the exiles.* See 11:11–12 and notes. *gather still others.* Including Gentiles (see v. 3 and note; cf. Jn 10:16 and note).

56:9—59:15 Many verses in these sections could apply to conditions before or during the Babylonian exile.

56:9 *beasts.* Foreign invaders (see 18:6 and note).

56:10 *watchmen.* The prophets (see note on Eze 3:17; cf. note on Isa 52:8). *blind ... love to sleep.* Cf. 29:9–10. *mute dogs.* Watchdogs who guarded the sheep (cf. Job 30:1).

56:11 *mighty appetites.* They devour the sheep. See Eze 34:3. *shepherds.* Rulers may be included. See Eze 34:2–5 and notes.

56:12 *wine ... beer.* Cf. the behavior of priests and prophets in 28:7. *tomorrow will be ... far better.* Cf. the words of the rich fool in Lk 12:19.

57 The righteous perish,[q]
and no one ponders it in his heart;[r]
devout men are taken away,
and no one understands
that the righteous are taken away
to be spared from evil.[s]
2 Those who walk uprightly[t]
enter into peace;
they find rest[u] as they lie in death.

3 "But you—come here, you sons of a sorceress,[v]
you offspring of adulterers[w] and prostitutes![x]
4 Whom are you mocking?
At whom do you sneer
and stick out your tongue?
Are you not a brood of rebels,[y]
the offspring of liars?
5 You burn with lust among the oaks[z]
and under every spreading tree;[a]
you sacrifice your children[b] in the ravines
and under the overhanging crags.
6 ⌊The idols⌋[c] among the smooth stones of the ravines are your portion;
they, they are your lot.
Yes, to them you have poured out drink offerings[d]
and offered grain offerings.
In the light of these things, should I relent?[e]
7 You have made your bed on a high and lofty hill;[f]
there you went up to offer your sacrifices.[g]
8 Behind your doors and your doorposts
you have put your pagan symbols.
Forsaking me, you uncovered your bed,
you climbed into it and opened it wide;
you made a pact with those whose beds you love,[h]
and you looked on their nakedness.[i]
9 You went to Molech[a][j] with olive oil
and increased your perfumes.[k]
You sent your ambassadors[b][l] far away;
you descended to the grave[c][m] itself!
10 You were wearied[n] by all your ways,
but you would not say, 'It is hopeless.'[o]
You found renewal of your strength,[p]
and so you did not faint.

11 "Whom have you so dreaded and feared[q]
that you have been false to me,
and have neither remembered[r] me
nor pondered[s] this in your hearts?
Is it not because I have long been silent[t]
that you do not fear me?
12 I will expose your righteousness and your works,[u]
and they will not benefit you.
13 When you cry out[v] for help,
let your collection ⌊of idols⌋ save[w] you!
The wind will carry all of them off,
a mere breath will blow[x] them away.
But the man who makes me his refuge[y]
will inherit the land[z]
and possess my holy mountain."[a]

Comfort for the Contrite

14 And it will be said:

"Build up, build up, prepare the road![b]
Remove the obstacles out of the way of my people."[c]
15 For this is what the high and lofty[d] One says—
he who lives forever,[e] whose name is holy:
"I live in a high[f] and holy place,
but also with him who is contrite[g]
and lowly in spirit,[h]

57:1 [q]S Ps 12:1; Eze 21:3 [r]S Isa 42:25 [s]S 2Ki 22:20 **57:2** [t]Isa 26:7 [u]Da 12:13 **57:3** [v]S Ex 22:18; Mal 3:5 [w]ver 7-8; Mt 16:4; Jas 4:4 [x]Isa 1:21; Jer 2:20 **57:4** [y]S Isa 1:2 **57:5** [z]S Isa 1:29 [a]S Dt 12:2; 2Ki 16:4 [b]S Lev 18:21; S Dt 18:10; Ps 106:37-38; Eze 16:20 **57:6** [c]S 2Ki 17:10; Jer 3:9; Hab 2:19 [d]Jer 7:18; 19:13; 44:18 [e]Jer 5:9, 29; 9:9 **57:7** [f]Jer 3:6; Eze 6:3; 16:16; 20:29 [g]Isa 65:7; Jer 13:27; Eze 6:13; 20:27-28 **57:8** [h]Eze 16:26; 23:7 [i]Eze 16:15, 36; 23:18 **57:9** [j]S Lev 18:21; S 1Ki 11:5 [k]S SS 4:10 [l]Eze 23:16, 40 [m]S Isa 8:19 **57:10** [n]S Isa 47:13 [o]Jer 2:25; 18:12; Mal 3:14 [p]S 1Sa 2:4 **57:11** [q]S 2Ki 1:15; Pr 29:25; Isa 7:2 [r]S Isa 17:10; Jer 2:32; 3:21; 13:25; 18:15; Eze 22:12 [s]S Isa 42:23 [t]S Est 4:14; S Ps 50:21; S 83:1 **57:12** [u]Isa 29:15; 58:1; 59:6, 12; 65:7; 66:18; Eze 16:2; Mic 3:2-4, 8 **57:13** [v]Jer 22:20; 30:15 [w]S Jdg 10:14 [x]Isa 40:7, 24 [y]S Ps 118:8 [z]S Ps 37:9 [a]Isa 2:2-3; 56:7; 65:9-11 **57:14** [b]S Isa 11:16 [c]Isa 62:10; Jer 18:15 **57:15** [d]S Isa 52:13 [e]S Dt 33:27; S Ps 90:2 [f]S Job 16:19 [g]Ps 147:3 [h]Ps 34:18; 51:17; Isa 66:2; Mic 6:8; Mt 5:3

[a] 9 Or *to the king* [b] 9 Or *idols* [c] 9 Hebrew *Sheol*

57:1 *spared from evil.* Huldah explained that righteous King Josiah would die before disaster struck (2Ki 22:19–20).
57:2 *peace.* Contrast v. 21. *find rest.* Cf. Paul's words in Php 1:21,23.
57:3 *sorceress.* A woman who practices magic or consults evil spirits (see 3:2–3 and note; 47:12; Dt 18:10). *adulterers and prostitutes.* Spiritual adultery (idolatry) is in view (see vv. 5–8; see also Ex 34:15 and note).
57:4 *mocking … sneer.* The people mocked Isaiah in 28:9,14. *brood of rebels.* See 1:4; 46:8 and note.
57:5 *oaks.* Sacred trees (see 1:29 and note). *spreading tree.* Associated with high places of pagan worship in 1Ki 14:23. Cf. Jer 2:20 and note; 3:13. *sacrifice your children.* Often associated with the worship of Molech (cf. v. 9; see note on 30:33) or Baal (Jer 19:5; see notes on Jer 7:31–32). Ps 106:37–38 says that children were sacrificed to idols and demons.
57:6 *ravines.* Possibly the Hinnom Valley (see Jer 7:31 and note). *drink offerings.* These pagan libations were especially popular.
57:7 *high and lofty hill.* "High places" or "mountain shrines" (see Jer 3:6; Eze 6:3 and note; 16:16; 22:9).
57:8 *those … you love.* Pagan deities or idols.
57:9 *Molech.* The main god of the Ammonites (see v. 5; 1Ki 11:5 and notes). *olive oil.* Used as an ointment for perfume. See SS 4:10, where the Hebrew word for "oil" is translated "perfume." *to the grave.* Cf. 8:19.
57:10 *It is hopeless.* Ironically, the people said that turning away from their own plans or from foreign gods was hopeless. *renewal of your strength.* Cf. 40:31 and note.
57:11 *so dreaded and feared.* They feared mere mortals (see 51:12). *neither remembered me.* See 51:13. *long been silent.* God had not acted in judgment (see 42:14 and note).
57:12 *righteousness.* See 58:2–3; 64:6.
57:13 *collection ⌊of idols⌋ save you.* See 44:9,17 and notes. *wind will carry … breath will blow.* Idols are no stronger than their worshipers. *me his refuge.* See 25:4. *inherit the land.* See 49:8 and note. *my holy mountain.* See 2:2–4 and note.
57:14 *Build up, build up.* See note on 40:1. *prepare the road.* See 40:3 and note.
57:15 *high and lofty One.* See 6:1; 52:13 and notes; cf. 33:5. *contrite.* Or "crushed" (see 53:5).

to revive the spirit of the lowly
and to revive the heart of the
contrite.[i]
16 I will not accuse[j] forever,
nor will I always be angry,[k]
for then the spirit of man would grow
faint before me —
the breath[l] of man that I have
created.
17 I was enraged by his sinful greed;[m]
I punished him, and hid[n] my face in
anger,
yet he kept on in his willful ways.[o]
18 I have seen his ways, but I will heal[p]
him;
I will guide[q] him and restore
comfort[r] to him,
19 creating praise on the lips[s] of the
mourners in Israel.
Peace, peace,[t] to those far and near,"[u]
says the LORD. "And I will heal
them."
20 But the wicked[v] are like the tossing
sea,[w]
which cannot rest,
whose waves cast up mire[x] and mud.
21 "There is no peace,"[y] says my God,
"for the wicked."[z]

True Fasting

58 "Shout it aloud,[a] do not hold back.
Raise your voice like a trumpet.[b]
Declare to my people their rebellion[c]
and to the house of Jacob their sins.[d]
2 For day after day they seek[e] me out;
they seem eager to know my ways,
as if they were a nation that does what
is right
and has not forsaken[f] the commands
of its God.
They ask me for just decisions
and seem eager for God to come
near[g] them.
3 'Why have we fasted,'[h] they say,
'and you have not seen it?
Why have we humbled[i] ourselves,
and you have not noticed?'[j]

"Yet on the day of your fasting, you do
as you please[k]
and exploit all your workers.
4 Your fasting ends in quarreling and
strife,[l]
and in striking each other with
wicked fists.
You cannot fast as you do today
and expect your voice to be heard[m]
on high.
5 Is this the kind of fast[n] I have chosen,
only a day for a man to humble[o]
himself?
Is it only for bowing one's head like a
reed[p]
and for lying on sackcloth and
ashes?[q]
Is that what you call a fast,
a day acceptable to the LORD?

6 "Is not this the kind of fasting[r] I have
chosen:
to loose the chains of injustice[s]
and untie the cords of the yoke,
to set the oppressed[t] free
and break every yoke?[u]
7 Is it not to share your food with the
hungry[v]
and to provide the poor wanderer
with shelter[w] —
when you see the naked, to clothe[x]
him,
and not to turn away from your own
flesh and blood?[y]

57:15 [i] S 2Ki 22:19; S Job 5:18; S Mt 23:12 **57:16** [j] S Ps 50:21; Isa 3:13-14 [k] S Ps 103:9; S Isa 54:9 [l] S Ge 2:7; Zec 12:1 **57:17** [m] S Isa 56:11; Jer 8:10 [n] S Isa 1:15 [o] Isa 1:4; S 30:15; S 53:6; 66:3 **57:18** [p] S Dt 32:39; S 2Ch 7:14; S Isa 30:26 [q] S Ps 48:14; S Isa 42:16; S 48:17 [r] Isa 49:13; 61:1-3 **57:19** [s] Isa 6:7; 51:16; 59:21; Heb 13:15 [t] S Isa 2:4; 26:3, 12; 32:17; S Lk 2:14 [u] Ac 2:39 **57:20** [v] Job 18:5-21 [w] S Ge 49:4; Eph 4:14; Jude 1:13 [x] Ps 69:14 **57:21** [y] S Isa 26:3; 59:8; Eze 13:16 [z] S Isa 48:22 **58:1** [a] Isa 40:6 [b] S Ex 20:18 [c] S Isa 24:20; S 48:8 [d] S Isa 57:12; Eze 3:17 **58:2** [e] S Isa 48:1; Tit 1:16; Jas 4:8 [f] S Dt 32:15; S Ps 119:87 [g] Isa 29:13 **58:3** [h] S Lev 16:29 [i] S Ex 10:3; S 2Ch 6:37; Jer 44:10 [j] Mal 3:14 [k] Isa 22:13; Zec 7:5-6 **58:4** [l] 1Ki 21:9-13; Isa 59:6; Jer 6:7; Eze 7:11; Mal 2:16 [m] S 1Sa 8:18; Isa 59:2; La 3:44; Eze 8:18; Mic 3:4 **58:5** [n] Zec 7:5 [o] 1Ki 21:27; Mt 6:16 [p] S Isa 36:6 [q] S Job 2:8 **58:6** [r] Joel 2:12-14 [s] Ne 5:10-11 [t] S Dt 14:29; Isa 61:1; Jer 34:9; Am 4:1; S Lk 4:19 [u] S Isa 9:4 **58:7** [v] S Job 22:7; Eze 18:16; Lk 3:11 [w] Isa 16:4; Heb 13:2 [x] Job 31:19-20; S Mt 25:36 [y] S Ge 29:14; Lk 10:31-32

57:16 *not accuse forever.* He had taken Israel to court repeatedly (see 3:13 – 14). *nor ... be angry.* See 54:9 and note; Jer 3:12.
57:17 *hid my face in anger.* See 54:8; see also 1:15 and note.
57:18 *heal him.* See v. 19; 6:10; 30:26; Jer 3:22. God will forgive and restore his people. *guide.* Cf. 40:11; 42:16; 49:10. *restore comfort.* See 49:13 and note.
57:19 *mourners.* Those mourning the judgment on Jerusalem (see 66:10). *Peace, peace.* Contrast Jer 6:13 – 14 (see note on 6:14). *those far.* Either Gentiles or exiled Jews. Paul probably had this verse in mind in Eph 2:17.
57:20 *like the tossing sea.* See Jer 49:23. *cannot rest.* Contrast v. 2.
57:21 Almost identical to 48:22 (see note there; see also 39:8 and note).
58:1 *voice like a trumpet.* God's powerful voice is compared to a trumpet blast at Mount Sinai (see Ex 19:19; 20:18 – 19). *rebellion.* See 1:2 and note. *sins.* See 1:4; 59:12 – 13.
58:2 *seek me out.* See 55:6 and note. Cf. the frequent sacrifices of 1:11. *eager for God to come near.* The same hypocrisy is mentioned in 29:13 (see note there).
58:3 *fasted ... fasting.* See v. 6; a time of self-denial, self-humbling and repentance for sin. After the fall of Jerusalem, the number of days for fasting increased (see Lev 16:29 and NIV text note; see also Zec 8:19 and note). *humbled ourselves.* Cf. 2Ch 7:14; 1Ki 21:29. *you have not noticed.* The same attitude is seen in Mal 3:14 (see note there; cf. Lk 18:12). *exploit all your workers.* See 3:14 – 15; 10:2.
58:4 *to be heard on high.* Such hypocritical religious activity is actually a hindrance to prayer (see 1:11 – 15; 59:2 and notes).
58:5 *fast ... humble himself.* See Mt 6:16 – 18. *like a reed.* A sign of weakness and humility (see 42:3 and note). *sackcloth and ashes ... fast.* See notes on Ge 37:34; Ezr 8:23; 10:6; Joel 1:13 – 14; Jnh 3:5 – 6; Rev 11:3. *acceptable.* A term often applied to sacrifices (see 56:7; 60:7; Lev 1:3; cf. Ro 12:1).
58:6 *chains of injustice.* During the siege of Jerusalem, Hebrew slaves were rightly released — only to be reclaimed by their masters (see Jer 34:8 – 11 and notes). *yoke.* See v. 9; 9:4; 10:27, where the yoke imposed by Assyria is mentioned. *oppressed.* See 1:17.
58:7 *share your food ... provide ... shelter ... clothe.* The outward evidence of genuine righteousness. See Job 31:17 – 20; Eze 18:7,16 and Jesus' identification with the hun-

8 Then your light will break forth like the dawn,[z]
and your healing[a] will quickly appear;
then your righteousness[a b] will go before you,
and the glory of the LORD will be your rear guard.[c]
9 Then you will call,[d] and the LORD will answer;[e]
you will cry for help, and he will say: Here am I.

"If you do away with the yoke of oppression,
with the pointing finger[f] and malicious talk,[g]
10 and if you spend yourselves in behalf of the hungry
and satisfy the needs of the oppressed,[h]
then your light[i] will rise in the darkness,
and your night will become like the noonday.[j]
11 The LORD will guide[k] you always;
he will satisfy your needs[l] in a sun-scorched land[m]
and will strengthen[n] your frame.
You will be like a well-watered garden,[o]
like a spring[p] whose waters never fail.
12 Your people will rebuild the ancient ruins[q]
and will raise up the age-old foundations;[r]
you will be called Repairer of Broken Walls,[s]
Restorer of Streets with Dwellings.

13 "If you keep your feet from breaking the Sabbath[t]
and from doing as you please on my holy day,
if you call the Sabbath a delight[u]
and the LORD's holy day honorable,
and if you honor it by not going your own way
and not doing as you please or speaking idle words,[v]
14 then you will find your joy[w] in the LORD,
and I will cause you to ride on the heights[x] of the land
and to feast on the inheritance[y] of your father Jacob."
The mouth of the LORD has spoken.[z]

Sin, Confession and Redemption

59 Surely the arm[a] of the LORD is not too short[b] to save,
nor his ear too dull to hear.[c]
2 But your iniquities have separated[d] you from your God;
your sins have hidden his face from you,
so that he will not hear.[e]
3 For your hands are stained with blood,[f]
your fingers with guilt.[g]
Your lips have spoken lies,[h]
and your tongue mutters wicked things.
4 No one calls for justice;[i]
no one pleads his case with integrity.
They rely[j] on empty arguments and speak lies;[k]
they conceive trouble and give birth to evil.[l]
5 They hatch the eggs of vipers[m]
and spin a spider's web.[n]

58:8 [z]S Job 11:17; S Isa 9:2 [a]S Isa 1:5; S 30:26 [b]S Isa 26:2 [c]S Ex 14:19 **58:9** [d]S Ps 50:15 [e]S Job 8:6; S Isa 30:19; Da 9:20; S Zec 10:6 [f]S Pr 6:13 [g]Ps 12:2; Isa 59:13 **58:10** [h]Dt 15:7-8 [i]S Isa 42:16 [j]S Job 11:17 **58:11** [k]S Ps 48:14; S Isa 42:16; S 48:17 [l]S Ps 104:28; S 107:9 [m]S Ps 68:6 [n]S Ps 72:16 [o]S SS 4:15 [p]S Isa 35:7; Jn 4:14 **58:12** [q]S Isa 49:8 [r]S Isa 44:28 [s]Ne 2:17 **58:13** [t]S Ex 20:8 [u]Ps 37:4; 42:4; 84:2,10 [v]Isa 59:3 **58:14** [w]S Job 22:26 [x]S Dt 32:13 [y]Ps 105:10-11 [z]S Isa 1:20 **59:1** [a]S Isa 41:20 [b]S Isa 50:2 [c]Isa 30:19; 58:9; 65:24 **59:2** [d]Jer 5:25; Eze 39:23 [e]S Ps 18:41; S Isa 58:4; S Jer 11:11; S Jn 9:31 **59:3** [f]S 2Ki 21:16; S Isa 1:15; S Eze 22:9 [g]Ps 7:3 [h]S Isa 3:8 **59:4** [i]S Isa 5:23 [j]S Job 15:31 [k]S Isa 44:20 [l]S Job 4:8; S Isa 29:20; Jas 1:15 **59:5** [m]S Isa 11:8; Mt 3:7 [n]S Job 8:14

[a] 8 Or *your righteous One*

gry and naked in Mt 25:34–40 (see notes there). *flesh and blood.* Probably refers to close relatives (Ge 37:27), but see 2Sa 5:1 and note.

58:8 *light.* The joy, prosperity and salvation brought by the Lord (see 9:2; 60:1–3; Ps 27:1 and note). *healing.* See 57:18 and note. *go before you … be your rear guard.* See 52:12 and note. The Lord will protect them and guide them. *glory of the LORD.* Probably an allusion to the pillar of cloud and fire in the desert (see 4:5–6; Ex 13:21; 14:20 and notes).

58:9 *LORD will answer.* See 30:19 and note. *Here am I.* See 65:1. *pointing finger.* A gesture of either contempt or accusation (see note on Pr 6:12–14). *malicious talk.* See Pr 2:12; 6:12,17,19 and notes.

58:10 *hungry … oppressed.* See vv. 6–7 and notes. *light.* See v. 8 and note.

58:11 *guide you.* See 57:18 and note. *needs.* Both material and spiritual (see note on 32:2). *sun-scorched land.* See 35:7; 49:10. *well-watered garden.* In 1:30 Jerusalem was a garden without water. *spring … never fail.* Contrast Jer 15:18 (see note there). Cf. the "living water" Jesus gives in Jn 4:10,14 (see notes there).

58:12 *ancient ruins … age-old foundations.* See 44:26,28 and notes; 61:4; Eze 36:10; Am 9:11,13–15 and notes. *Repairer of Broken Walls.* Cf. the work of Nehemiah in Ne 2:17 (see note there).

58:13 *Sabbath.* See 56:2 and note. *my holy day.* A day set apart to God (see Ex 3:5 and note). *delight.* They were also to delight themselves in the Lord (Ps 37:4) and in his law (see Ps 1:2 and note). *going your own way.* Perhaps to engage in business (see Am 8:5).

58:14 *joy in the LORD.* See 61:10. *ride on the heights.* Thus controlling the land. See 33:16 and note; see also Hab 3:19. *feast on the inheritance.* Enjoying plentiful food in the promised land (see Dt 32:13–14). *mouth … has spoken.* See 40:5 and note.

59:1 *arm … too short.* See 51:9 and note. *too dull to hear.* See 30:19 and note.

59:2 *hidden his face … he will not hear.* See 1:15 and note.

59:3–4 *lies.* See v. 13; 28:15; Hos 4:2 and note.

59:3 *stained with blood.* See v. 7; 1:15,21; Eze 7:23; see also notes on Eze 18:4,21.

59:4 *justice … pleads his case.* The poor and helpless could not receive fair trials (see v. 14; 1:17–23; 5:7,23). *they conceive … evil.* Identical to Job 15:35 (see note there). Cf. Isa 33:11; Ps 7:14.

59:5 *spider's web.* Verse 6 and Job 8:14–15 stress how fragile it is.

Whoever eats their eggs will die,
and when one is broken, an adder is hatched.
[6]Their cobwebs are useless for clothing;
they cannot cover themselves with what they make.[o]
Their deeds are evil deeds,
and acts of violence[p] are in their hands.
[7]Their feet rush into sin;
they are swift to shed innocent blood.[q]
Their thoughts are evil thoughts;[r]
ruin and destruction mark their ways.[s]
[8]The way of peace they do not know;[t]
there is no justice in their paths.
They have turned them into crooked roads;[u]
no one who walks in them will know peace.[v]

[9]So justice is far from us,
and righteousness does not reach us.
We look for light, but all is darkness;[w]
for brightness, but we walk in deep shadows.
[10]Like the blind[x] we grope along the wall,
feeling our way like men without eyes.
At midday we stumble[y] as if it were twilight;
among the strong, we are like the dead.[z]
[11]We all growl like bears;
we moan mournfully like doves.[a]
We look for justice, but find none;
for deliverance, but it is far away.

[12]For our offenses[b] are many in your sight,
and our sins testify[c] against us.
Our offenses are ever with us,
and we acknowledge our iniquities:[d]
[13]rebellion[e] and treachery against the LORD,
turning our backs[f] on our God,
fomenting oppression[g] and revolt,
uttering lies[h] our hearts have conceived.
[14]So justice[i] is driven back,
and righteousness[j] stands at a distance;
truth[k] has stumbled in the streets,
honesty cannot enter.
[15]Truth[l] is nowhere to be found,
and whoever shuns evil becomes a prey.

The LORD looked and was displeased
that there was no justice.[m]
[16]He saw that there was no one,[n]
he was appalled that there was no one to intervene;[o]
so his own arm worked salvation[p] for him,
and his own righteousness[q] sustained him.
[17]He put on righteousness as his breastplate,[r]
and the helmet[s] of salvation on his head;
he put on the garments[t] of vengeance[u]
and wrapped himself in zeal[v] as in a cloak.
[18]According to what they have done,
so will he repay[w]
wrath to his enemies
and retribution to his foes;
he will repay the islands[x] their due.

59:6 [o]Isa 28:20 [p]S Ps 55:9; S Pr 4:17; S Isa 58:4 **59:7** [q]S 2Ki 21:16; S Pr 6:17; S Mic 3:10 [r]S Pr 24:2; S Isa 26:10; Mk 7:21-22 [s]Ro 3:15-17* **59:8** [t]Ro 3:15-17* [u]S Jdg 5:6 [v]S Isa 57:21; Lk 1:79 **59:9** [w]S Job 19:8; S Ps 107:14; S Isa 5:30; S 8:20; S Lk 1:79 **59:10** [x]Dt 28:29; S Isa 6:9-10; 56:10; La 4:14; Zep 1:17 [y]S Job 3:23; S Isa 8:15; Jn 11:9-10 [z]La 3:6 **59:11** [a]S Ge 8:8; Ps 74:19; Isa 38:14; Jer 48:28; Eze 7:16; Na 2:7 **59:12** [b]S Ezr 9:6; S Isa 57:12 [c]S Ge 4:7; S Isa 3:9; S Jer 2:19 [d]Ps 51:3 **59:13** [e]Isa 46:8; 48:8 [f]S Nu 11:20; S Pr 30:9; Mt 10:33; Tit 1:16 [g]S Ps 12:5; S Isa 5:7 [h]S Isa 3:8; S 44:20; Mk 7:21-22 **59:14** [i]S Isa 29:21 [j]S Isa 1:21 [k]S Isa 48:1; S Jer 33:16 **59:15** [l]Jer 7:28; 9:5; Da 8:12 [m]S Isa 5:7 **59:16** [n]S Isa 41:28 [o]S Isa 53:12 [p]S Isa 51:5 [q]Isa 45:8, 13; 46:13 **59:17** [r]Eph 6:14; 1Th 5:8 [s]Eph 6:17; 1Th 5:8 [t]S Job 27:6; Isa 63:3 [u]S Isa 1:24 [v]S Isa 9:7; Eze 5:13 **59:18** [w]S Lev 26:28; S Nu 10:35; S Isa 34:8; S Mt 16:27 [x]Isa 11:11; 41:5

59:6 *acts of violence.* See v. 3; Jer 6:7; Eze 7:11.
59:7–8 Quoted in part in Ro 3:15–17 by Paul to show the universality of sin.
59:7 *Their feet rush … to shed innocent blood.* This sentence appears in Pr 1:16 (see note there). *evil thoughts.* God's thoughts are different (see 55:7–9). *ruin and destruction.* Contrast 60:18.
59:8 *way of peace.* Cf. 26:3,12; 57:20–21; Lk 1:79. *crooked roads.* Unsafe (see Jdg 5:6 and note).
59:9 *us … We.* The prophet includes himself with the people. *justice … righteousness.* Personified here and in v. 14. See v. 4 and note; 1:21. *We look for … but.* See v. 11; cf. note on 5:2. *darkness … deep shadows.* Similar language describes conditions when Assyria invaded Israel (see 5:30; 8:21–22; 9:1–2). Contrast 58:8.
59:10 *Like the blind we grope … At midday.* The fulfillment of the curse for disobedience in Dt 28:29. Cf. Job 5:14. *strong.* Perhaps enemies or oppressors.
59:11 *growl like bears.* Impatient and frustrated.
59:12 *offenses … sins … iniquities.* In Hebrew the three most common OT words for evil thoughts and deeds (see Ps 32:5 and note). *offenses are many.* See 58:1. *we acknowledge our iniquities.* Like Ezra (9:6–7), the prophet confesses the sins of the nation.
59:13 *rebellion and treachery.* See 46:8; 48:8 and notes. *turning our backs.* See 1:4. *oppression.* See 30:12. *lies.* See vv. 3–4.
59:14 *justice … truth.* Cf. the personification of wisdom in Pr 8:1—9:12 (see note on 8:1–36). *righteousness stands at a distance.* Cf. v. 9; contrast 46:13 (see note there).
59:15 *becomes a prey.* See 32:7.
59:16 *there was no one.* To help (see 63:5, a parallel to the whole verse). Cf. Eze 22:30 and note. *appalled.* Cf. the reaction to the servant in 52:14. *intervene.* Cf. the intercession of the servant in 53:12 (see note there). *his own arm worked salvation.* See 51:9; 52:10. For the meaning of salvation see 43:3; 49:8; 52:7 and notes. *righteousness.* For the relationship between righteousness and salvation see 45:8; 46:13 and notes.
59:17 *put on … wrapped himself in.* See note on Ps 109:29. *righteousness … breastplate … helmet … salvation.* This imagery is echoed in Paul's description of "the full armor of God" (Eph 6:11) that believers are to put on in their warfare against Satan (see Eph 6:14,17 and notes). *garments of vengeance.* Cf. the blood-spattered garments of 63:1–3. God's vengeance is described also in 34:8 (see note there); 63:4. It is part of the day of the Lord (see 34:2 and note). *zeal.* God's jealous love (see 9:7 and note; 37:32; 42:13).
59:18 *enemies … foes.* God will judge the nations, but he must also punish wicked Israelites (see 65:6–7; 66:6; Jer

19 From the west,[y] men will fear the
name of the LORD,
and from the rising of the sun,[z] they
will revere his glory.[a]
For he will come like a pent-up flood
that the breath[b] of the LORD drives
along.[a]

20 "The Redeemer[c] will come to Zion,[d]
to those in Jacob who repent of their
sins,"[e]
declares the LORD.

21 "As for me, this is my covenant[f] with
them," says the LORD. "My Spirit,[g] who
is on you, and my words that I have put
in your mouth[h] will not depart from your
mouth,[i] or from the mouths of your children, or from the mouths of their descendants from this time on and forever," says
the LORD.

The Glory of Zion

60 "Arise,[j] shine, for your light[k] has
come,
and the glory[l] of the LORD rises upon
you.
2 See, darkness[m] covers the earth
and thick darkness[n] is over the
peoples,
but the LORD rises upon you
and his glory appears over you.
3 Nations[o] will come to your light,[p]
and kings[q] to the brightness of your
dawn.

4 "Lift up your eyes and look about you:
All assemble[r] and come to you;
your sons come from afar,[s]
and your daughters[t] are carried on
the arm.[u]
5 Then you will look and be radiant,[v]
your heart will throb and swell with
joy;[w]
the wealth[x] on the seas will be brought
to you,
to you the riches of the nations will
come.
6 Herds of camels[y] will cover your
land,
young camels of Midian[z] and
Ephah.[a]
And all from Sheba[b] will come,
bearing gold and incense[c]
and proclaiming the praise[d] of the
LORD.
7 All Kedar's[e] flocks will be gathered to
you,
the rams of Nebaioth will serve
you;
they will be accepted as offerings[f] on
my altar,[g]
and I will adorn my glorious
temple.[h]

8 "Who are these[i] that fly along like
clouds,[j]
like doves to their nests?

[a] 19 Or *When the enemy comes in like a flood, / the Spirit of the LORD will put him to flight*

59:19 [y]S Isa 49:12; S Mt 8:11 [z]S Ps 113:3 [a]Ps 97:6; S Isa 24:15; 35:2; 40:5; 52:10; 66:18 [b]S Isa 11:4 **59:20** [c]S Job 19:25; Isa 60:16; 63:16 [d]S Isa 52:8; S Joel 3:21 [e]S Job 22:23; S Isa 1:27; S Jer 35:15; Ac 2:38-39; Ro 11:26-27* **59:21** [f]S Ge 9:16; S Dt 29:14; S Isa 42:6 [g]S Isa 11:2; S 44:3 [h]S Ex 4:15 [i]S Jos 1:8 **60:1** [j]Isa 52:2 [k]S Ps 36:9; S 118:27; S Isa 9:2; Jn 8:12; Eph 5:14 [l]S Ex 16:7; S Isa 4:5; Rev 21:11 **60:2** [m]S 1Sa 2:9; S Ps 82:5; S 107:14; S Isa 8:20 [n]Jer 13:16; Col 1:13 **60:3** [o]S Isa 44:5; S 45:14; Mt 2:1-11; Rev 21:24 [p]S Isa 9:2; 42:6 [q]S Isa 49:23 **60:4** [r]S Isa 11:12 [s]S Isa 2:3; Jer 30:10 [t]S Isa 43:6 [u]Isa 49:20-22

60:5 [v]S Ex 34:29 [w]Isa 35:2; 65:13; 66:14; Zec 10:7 [x]S Dt 33:19; S Jdg 3:15; Rev 21:26 **60:6** [y]S Jdg 6:5 [z]S Ge 25:2 [a]Ge 25:4 [b]S Ge 10:7,28 [c]Isa 43:23; Jer 6:20; Mt 2:11 [d]S 1Ki 5:7; S Isa 42:10 **60:7** [e]S Ge 25:13 [f]Isa 18:7; Eze 20:40; 43:27; Zep 3:10 [g]S Isa 19:21 [h]ver 13; Hag 2:3,7,9 **60:8** [i]Isa 49:21 [j]Isa 19:1

25:29). Only the remnant will be blessed (see v. 20; see also 1:9 and note). *islands.* See note on 11:11.

59:19 *From the west ... rising of the sun.* All nations will see God's saving work in behalf of his people (see 40:5; 45:6; 52:10 and notes). *name.* See 30:27 and note. *pent-up flood.* The coming of the Lord will be irresistible, "like a rushing torrent" (30:28) that overwhelms the enemy.

59:20 *Redeemer.* See 41:14 and note. *come to Zion.* In the return from exile, but more fully in the person of Christ (see Ro 11:26–27 and notes). See 35:4; 40:9; 52:7 and notes. Cf. Zec 8:3. *those ... who repent.* See 1:27–28 and note; 30:15; 31:6; see also Eze 18:30–32 and notes.

59:21 *covenant.* The description fits the "new covenant" best (see 42:6; Jer 31:31–34 and notes). *My Spirit.* See 11:2; 32:15; Eze 36:27; Jn 16:13 and notes. *you ... your ... your ... your.* In Hebrew the pronouns are singular but are probably intended in a collective sense—the citizens of Zion. *my words ... in your mouth.* Then Israel will truly be God's people (see 51:16; Jer 31:33 and notes). *not depart from your mouth.* See Jos 1:8.

60:1–2 *glory.* Probably an allusion to the pillar of cloud, but announcing a new manifestation of God's redeeming glory (see 58:8 and note). See also 35:2 and note.

60:1 *light.* See 58:8 and note. Here the Lord himself is viewed as the light (see vv. 19–20).

60:2 *darkness.* A symbol of gloom, oppression, sin and judgment (see 8:22; 9:2; 59:9).

60:3 *Nations will come.* See vv. 5,10–12 and notes. This theme was first mentioned in 2:2–4 (see note there). *light.* See 42:6; 49:6 and notes.

60:4 The first two lines are almost identical to the beginning of 49:18, the last two to the end of 49:22 (see note there). The setting there was the return from exile, but here much broader implications are involved. *afar.* See v. 9; 49:12 and note.

60:5 *wealth on the seas.* Jerusalem will be enriched by the nations (see v. 11; 61:6; 66:12; see also 18:7; 23:18; 45:14 and notes). The contribution of King Darius to Zerubbabel's temple may be a partial fulfillment (see Ezr 6:8–9 and notes). Some interpret this verse as referring to conditions during the future phase of the Messianic kingdom, while others apply it to the influx of Gentiles into the church (see note on 2:2–4). See Rev 21:26 (the new Jerusalem); see also Hag 2:7; Zec 14:14 and notes.

60:6 *camels will cover your land.* As caravans bringing goods. Ironically it was on camels that the Midianites once devastated Israel (see 9:4; Jdg 6:1–6 and notes). *Midian.* Abraham's son through Keturah (Ge 25:2). The Midianites roamed the deserts of Transjordan. *Ephah.* A son of Midian (Ge 25:4). *Sheba.* A wealthy land in southern Arabia, perhaps roughly equal to modern Yemen (see 1Ki 10:1 and note). *gold and incense.* The queen of Sheba brought gold and spices to Solomon (1Ki 10:2). Jer 6:20 mentions the incense of Sheba. Cf. Ps 72:10; Mt 2:11. *proclaiming the praise.* Cf. the queen's words in 1Ki 10:9 (but see note there).

60:7 *Kedar's flocks.* See note on 21:16. *Nebaioth.* The firstborn son of Ishmael (Ge 25:13). The name is probably preserved in that of the later Nabatean kingdom. *serve.* See v. 10; 56:6. *accepted as offerings.* See 56:7; 58:5 and notes.

[9]Surely the islands[k] look to me;
in the lead are the ships of
Tarshish,[a][l]
bringing[m] your sons from afar,
with their silver and gold,[n]
to the honor[o] of the LORD your God,
the Holy One[p] of Israel,
for he has endowed you with
splendor.[q]

[10]"Foreigners[r] will rebuild your walls,
and their kings[s] will serve you.
Though in anger I struck you,
in favor[t] I will show you
compassion.[u]
[11]Your gates[v] will always stand open,
they will never be shut, day or
night,
so that men may bring you the wealth
of the nations[w]—
their kings[x] led in triumphal
procession.
[12]For the nation or kingdom that will not
serve[y] you will perish;
it will be utterly ruined.[z]
[13]"The glory of Lebanon[a] will come to
you,
the pine, the fir and the cypress
together,[b]
to adorn the place of my sanctuary;[c]
and I will glorify the place of my
feet.[d]
[14]The sons of your oppressors[e] will come
bowing before you;
all who despise you will bow down[f]
at your feet
and will call you the City[g] of the LORD,
Zion[h] of the Holy One[i] of Israel.

[15]"Although you have been forsaken[j] and
hated,
with no one traveling[k] through,
I will make you the everlasting pride[l]
and the joy[m] of all generations.
[16]You will drink the milk of nations
and be nursed[n] at royal breasts.
Then you will know[o] that I, the LORD,
am your Savior,[p]
your Redeemer,[q] the Mighty One
of Jacob.[r]
[17]Instead of bronze I will bring you
gold,[s]
and silver in place of iron.
Instead of wood I will bring you
bronze,
and iron in place of stones.
I will make peace[t] your governor
and righteousness your ruler.[u]
[18]No longer will violence[v] be heard in
your land,
nor ruin or destruction[w] within your
borders,
but you will call your walls Salvation[x]
and your gates Praise.[y]
[19]The sun will no more be your light by
day,
nor will the brightness of the moon
shine on you,
for the LORD will be your everlasting
light,[z]
and your God will be your glory.[a]
[20]Your sun[b] will never set again,
and your moon will wane no more;
the LORD will be your everlasting
light,
and your days of sorrow[c] will end.
[21]Then will all your people be
righteous[d]

[a] 9 Or *the trading ships*

60:9 [k]S Isa 11:11 [l]S Ge 10:4; Isa 2:16 *fn* [m]S Isa 14:2; S 43:6 [n]S 1Ki 10:22 [o]S Ps 22:23 [p]ver 14; Isa 1:4; S 54:5 [q]S Isa 44:23; 55:5; Jer 30:19 **60:10** [r]S Ex 1:11; S Isa 14:1-2; S 56:6 [s]S Ezr 1:2; Rev 21:24 [t]S Isa 49:8 [u]S Ps 102:13 **60:11** [v]ver 18; S Ps 24:7; Isa 62:10; Mic 2:13; Rev 21:25 [w]S ver 5; Isa 61:6; Rev 21:26 [x]Ps 149:8; S Isa 2:12 **60:12** [y]S Isa 11:14; S 14:2 [z]S Ge 27:29; S Ps 110:5; Da 2:34 **60:13** [a]S Ezr 3:7 [b]Isa 41:19 [c]S ver 7 [d]S 1Ch 28:2 **60:14** [e]S Isa 14:2 [f]S Ge 27:29; S Isa 2:3; Rev 3:9 [g]S Ge 32:28; S Isa 1:26 [h]Heb 12:22 [i]S ver 9 **60:15** [j]Isa 1:7-9; S 6:12; S 54:6 [k]S Isa 33:8 [l]S Isa 4:2 [m]S Ps 126:5; Isa 65:18 **60:16** [n]S Ex 6:2; Isa 49:23; 66:11,12 [o]S Ex 6:7 [p]S Ex 14:30; S Isa 25:9 [q]S Job 19:25; S Isa 59:20 [r]S Ge 49:24; S Ps 132:2 **60:17** [s]1Ki 10:21 [t]S Ps 85:8; Isa 66:12; Hag 2:9 [u]S Isa 9:7 **60:18** [v]S Lev 26:6; S 2Sa 7:10; S Isa 9:4 [w]S Isa 49:19; S 51:19 [x]S Isa 33:6 [y]Isa 61:11; 62:7; Jer 33:9; Zep 3:20 **60:19** [z]S Ps 36:9; S 118:27; Rev 22:5 [a]S Ps 85:9; S Isa 24:16,23; Rev 21:23 **60:20** [b]Isa 30:26 [c]S Isa 30:19; S 35:10; S Rev 7:17 **60:21** [d]S Isa 4:3; S 26:2; Rev 21:27

60:9 *islands look to me.* See 11:11 and note. *ships of Tarshish.* See note on 2:16. *bringing your sons.* See 49:22 and note. *silver and gold.* Ships of Tarshish had brought these to Solomon every three years (1Ki 10:22). *Holy One of Israel.* See v. 14; 1:4 and note. *endowed ... with splendor.* See 55:5 and note.
60:10 *Foreigners ... kings.* See vv. 12,14; 49:7,23; 61:5. *will rebuild your walls.* In 444 B.C. King Artaxerxes issued the decree allowing Nehemiah to rebuild the walls of Jerusalem (Ne 2:8). Some also apply the rebuilt walls to the building up of the church through Gentile believers (Ac 15:14–16). *Though in anger ... compassion.* See 54:7–8 and notes.
60:11 *gates ... always ... open.* As are the gates of the new Jerusalem (Rev 21:25). *wealth.* See v. 5.
60:12 *nation ... will perish.* Israel's future political domination is referred to also in 11:14; 14:2; 49:23 (cf. vv. 10,14).
60:13 *glory of Lebanon.* Its magnificent cedar trees, which were used in the construction of Solomon's temple, along with pine trees (1Ki 5:10,18). See also 35:2. The glory of Solomon's era would return. *pine ... fir ... cypress.* See 41:19 and note. *adorn ... sanctuary.* See v. 7. *place of my feet.* The temple, and especially the ark of the covenant, God's "footstool."
60:14 *oppressors ... bow down.* See 49:7,23 and notes. Cf. vv. 10,12. *City of the LORD.* Cf. the names for the future Jerusalem in 1:26; 62:4; Eze 48:35; Zec 8:3; Heb 12:22 (see notes there).
60:15 *forsaken and hated.* See 6:11–12; 62:4; Jer 30:17. *pride ... joy.* See 4:2 and note.
60:16 *nursed at royal breasts.* The "riches of the nations" (v. 5) will nourish Jerusalem and restore her to vigorous health. *Then ... Jacob.* For this sentence see 49:26 and note.
60:17 *gold ... silver.* As in Solomon's day gold and silver were plentiful (1Ki 10:21,27), so the future Jerusalem will have the most valuable metals as well as the strongest (*iron*). Cf. 9:10. *peace ... righteousness.* Both are also present in the rule of the Messianic king in 9:7. See note on 48:18.
60:18 *No longer ... violence.* Cf. 54:14. *ruin or destruction.* See 51:19 and note. *walls Salvation.* See 26:1.
60:19 *sun ... moon.* According to Rev 21:23; 22:5 their light will no longer be needed in the new Jerusalem, since God and the Lamb will be the "everlasting light." *glory.* See vv. 1–2 and note; Zec 2:5; cf. notes on Ex 40:34; Ps 26:8.
60:20 *sun will never set.* There will be no night there (cf. Rev 22:5) but only the light of joy and salvation (see 58:8 and note). *sorrow will end.* See 25:8; 35:10; 51:11; 65:19; Rev 21:4.

and they will possess[e] the land
forever.
They are the shoot I have planted,[f]
the work of my hands,[g]
for the display of my splendor.[h]
22 The least of you will become a
thousand,
the smallest a mighty nation.[i]
I am the LORD;
in its time I will do this swiftly."[j]

The Year of the LORD's Favor

61 The Spirit[k] of the Sovereign LORD[l] is
on me,
because the LORD has anointed[m] me
to preach good news[n] to the poor.[o]
He has sent me to bind up[p] the
brokenhearted,
to proclaim freedom[q] for the
captives[r]
and release from darkness for the
prisoners,[a]
2 to proclaim the year of the LORD's
favor[s]
and the day of vengeance[t] of our
God,
to comfort[u] all who mourn,[v]
3 and provide for those who grieve in
Zion—
to bestow on them a crown[w] of beauty
instead of ashes,[x]
the oil[y] of gladness
instead of mourning,[z]
and a garment of praise
instead of a spirit of despair.
They will be called oaks of
righteousness,
a planting[a] of the LORD
for the display of his splendor.[b]
4 They will rebuild the ancient ruins[c]
and restore the places long
devastated;
they will renew the ruined cities
that have been devastated for
generations.
5 Aliens[d] will shepherd your flocks;
foreigners will work your fields and
vineyards.
6 And you will be called priests[e] of the
LORD,
you will be named ministers of our
God.
You will feed on the wealth[f] of nations,
and in their riches you will boast.
7 Instead of their shame[g]
my people will receive a double[h]
portion,
and instead of disgrace
they will rejoice in their inheritance;
and so they will inherit[i] a double
portion in their land,
and everlasting joy[j] will be theirs.
8 "For I, the LORD, love justice;[k]
I hate robbery and iniquity.
In my faithfulness I will reward them
and make an everlasting covenant[l]
with them.

60:21 [e]Ps 37:11,22; Isa 49:8; 57:13; 61:7; 65:9; Zec 8:12 [f]S Ex 15:17; Ps 44:2; 80:8-11; Jer 32:41; Am 9:15; Mt 15:13 [g]S Job 10:3; S Ps 8:6; S Isa 19:25; Eph 2:10 [h]S Lev 10:3; S Isa 44:23 **60:22** [i]S Ge 12:2; S Dt 1:10 [j]Isa 5:19 **61:1** [k]S Isa 11:2; 2Co 3:17 [l]S Isa 50:4 [m]S Ps 45:7; S Da 9:24-26; S Ac 4:26 [n]S 2Sa 18:26; S Isa 40:9 [o]S Job 5:16; S Mt 11:5; Lk 7:22 [p]S 2Ki 22:19; S Job 5:18 [q]S Lev 25:10 [r]S Ps 68:6; S Isa 49:9 **61:2** [s]S Isa 49:8; S Lk 4:18-19* [t]S Isa 1:24 [u]S Isa 40:1; Mt 5:4 [v]S Job 5:11; Lk 6:21 **61:3** [w]S Isa 3:23 [x]S Job 2:8 [y]S Ru 3:3; S Isa 1:6; Heb 1:9 [z]Jer 31:13; Mt 5:4 [a]Ps 1:3; 92:12-13; Mt 15:13; 1Co 3:9 [b]S Isa 44:23 **61:4** [c]S Isa 44:26; 51:3; 65:21; Eze 36:33; Am 9:14; Zec 1:16-17 **61:5** [d]S Isa 14:1-2; S 56:6 **61:6** [e]S Ex 19:6; 1Pe 2:5 [f]Dt 33:19; S Isa 60:11 **61:7** [g]S Isa 29:22; S 41:11 [h]S Dt 21:17; S Isa 40:2 [i]S Isa 60:21 [j]S Ps 126:5; S Isa 25:9 **61:8** [k]S Ps 11:7; S Isa 1:17; S 5:16 [l]S Ge 9:16; S Isa 42:6; S Heb 13:20

[a] *1* Hebrew; Septuagint *the blind*

60:21 *people be righteous.* Only the redeemed will be there (see 4:3; 35:8; Rev 21:27). *possess the land forever.* Enter into full blessing (see 49:8 and note; see also 57:13; 61:7; Ps 37:11,22). *shoot I have planted.* Cf. the vineyard of 5:2,7 (see also 11:1). *work of my hands.* God made them as a potter forms clay (see 64:8; see also 29:23; 45:11). *display of my splendor.* They are the evidence of God's redemptive work. See 49:3; 61:3; see also notes on 35:2; 40:5.

60:22 *least ... will become a thousand.* See 51:2; 54:3 and notes. The blessing of Lev 26:8 is similar. *do this swiftly.* Cf. 5:19, where the same Hebrew verb is translated "hasten."

61:1–2 Jesus applied these verses to himself in the synagogue at Nazareth (see Lk 4:16–20 and notes; cf. Mt 11:5).

61:1 *Spirit ... is on me.* The statement may refer to the prophet in a limited sense, but the Messianic servant is the main figure intended (cf. what is said of him in 42:1; see 11:2; 48:16 and notes). *Sovereign LORD.* See 50:4–5,7,9 and note. *anointed me.* See 45:1 and note. *good news.* See 40:9 and note. *poor.* Cf. 11:4; 29:19. *bind up the brokenhearted.* See 30:26 and note. *freedom for the captives.* Freedom is proclaimed in the Year of Jubilee in Lev 25:10 (see 49:8 and note).

61:2 *year of the LORD's favor.* Corresponds to the "day of salvation" in 49:8 (see note there) and the "year of my redemption" in 63:4. Christ ended his quotation at this point (Lk 4:19–20), probably because the "day of vengeance" will not occur until his second coming. *day of vengeance.* See 34:2,8 and notes. *comfort all who mourn.* See 49:13; 57:19 and notes; 66:10; Jer 31:13; Mt 5:4.

61:3 *bestow on them ... a garment of praise.* See note on Ps 109:29. *crown of beauty.* A "turban" (as the Hebrew for this phrase is translated in Eze 24:17) or headdress. In 3:20 the women of Jerusalem were to lose their beautiful headdresses. *oil of gladness.* Anointing with olive oil was common on joyous occasions (see Ps 23:5; 45:7 and notes; 104:15; 133:1–2; cf. 2Sa 14:2). See also 1:6 and note. *garment of praise.* Contrast the "garments of vengeance" in 59:17. *oaks of righteousness.* Perhaps signifying flourishing oaks; contrast the oaks of 1:30. *planting ... for the display.* See 60:21 and note.

61:4 *rebuild the ancient ruins ... ruined cities.* See 58:12 and note.

61:5 *Aliens ... foreigners.* See 14:1–2; 56:3; 60:10 and notes.

61:6 *priests of the LORD.* See 66:21. True Israel will be a "kingdom of priests" among the Gentiles (see Ex 19:6; Zec 3:1–10 and notes). *ministers.* Priests. See 1Ki 8:11, where the Hebrew word for "minister" is translated "perform their service." *wealth of nations.* See 60:5 and note.

61:7 *shame ... disgrace.* See 45:17; 54:4. *double portion.* The firstborn son received a double share of the inheritance (see Dt 21:17; Zec 9:12 and notes). Contrast the "double" punishment Israel received (40:2). *everlasting joy.* See 35:10; 51:11; cf. Ps 16:11.

61:8 *love justice.* Cf. 30:18; 59:15. *robbery and iniquity.* Israel had been mistreated by her conquerors. Cf. 42:24; 59:18. *everlasting covenant.* Probably the new covenant (see 55:3; 59:21 and notes; cf. Jer 31:35–37; 32:40 and notes).

[9]Their descendants[m] will be known
among the nations
and their offspring among the
peoples.
All who see them will acknowledge
that they are a people the LORD has
blessed."[n]

[10]I delight greatly in the LORD;
my soul rejoices[o] in my God.
For he has clothed me with garments
of salvation
and arrayed me in a robe of
righteousness,[p]
as a bridegroom adorns his head[q] like
a priest,
and as a bride[r] adorns herself with
her jewels.
[11]For as the soil makes the sprout
come up
and a garden[s] causes seeds to grow,
so the Sovereign LORD will make
righteousness[t] and praise
spring up before all nations.

Zion's New Name

62 For Zion's sake I will not keep
silent,[u]
for Jerusalem's sake I will not
remain quiet,
till her righteousness[v] shines out like
the dawn,[w]
her salvation[x] like a blazing torch.
[2]The nations[y] will see your
righteousness,
and all kings your glory;
you will be called by a new name[z]
that the mouth of the LORD will
bestow.
[3]You will be a crown[a] of splendor in the
LORD's hand,
a royal diadem in the hand of your
God.
[4]No longer will they call you Deserted,[b]
or name your land Desolate.[c]
But you will be called Hephzibah,[a][d]
and your land Beulah[b];
for the LORD will take delight[e] in you,
and your land will be married.[f]
[5]As a young man marries a maiden,
so will your sons[c] marry you;
as a bridegroom[g] rejoices over his
bride,
so will your God rejoice[h] over you.
[6]I have posted watchmen[i] on your
walls, O Jerusalem;
they will never be silent day or night.
You who call on the LORD,
give yourselves no rest,[j]
[7]and give him no rest[k] till he establishes
Jerusalem
and makes her the praise[l] of the
earth.
[8]The LORD has sworn[m] by his right hand
and by his mighty arm:
"Never again will I give your grain[n]
as food for your enemies,
and never again will foreigners drink
the new wine
for which you have toiled;
[9]but those who harvest it will eat[o] it
and praise the LORD,[p]
and those who gather the grapes will
drink it
in the courts of my sanctuary."[q]
[10]Pass through, pass through the gates![r]
Prepare the way for the people.
Build up, build up the highway![s][t]
Remove the stones.
Raise a banner[u] for the nations.

61:9 [m]S Isa 43:5; S 48:19 [n]S Ge 12:2; S Dt 28:3-12 **61:10** [o]S Ps 2:11; S Isa 7:13; S 25:9; Hab 3:18; S Lk 1:47 [p]S Job 27:6; S Ps 132:9; S Isa 52:1; Rev 19:8 [q]S Ex 39:28 [r]S Isa 49:18; Rev 21:2 **61:11** [s]S Ge 47:23; Isa 58:11 [t]S Isa 45:8 **62:1** [u]S Est 4:14; S Ps 50:21; S 83:1 [v]S Isa 1:26; S 45:8 [w]S Job 11:17 [x]S Ps 67:2 **62:2** [y]S Ps 67:2; S Isa 40:5; S 45:14; 52:10 [z]S Ge 32:28; S Isa 1:26; Rev 2:17; 3:12 **62:3** [a]S Isa 28:5; 1Th 2:19 **62:4** [b]S Lev 26:43; S Isa 6:12; S 54:6 [c]S Isa 49:19; S 51:19 [d]2Ki 21:1 [e]Isa 65:19; Jer 32:41; Zep 3:17; Mal 3:12 [f]Isa 54:5; Jer 3:14; Hos 2:19 **62:5** [g]S SS 3:11 [h]S Dt 28:63; Isa 65:19; Jer 31:12; Zep 3:17 **62:6** [i]S Isa 52:8; Heb 13:17 [j]Ps 132:4 **62:7** [k]Mt 15:21-28; Lk 18:1-8 [l]S Dt 26:19; S Isa 60:18 **62:8** [m]S Ge 22:16; S Isa 14:24; S 49:18 [n]Dt 28:30-33; S Isa 1:7 **62:9** [o]S Isa 1:19; Am 9:14 [p]S Dt 12:7; Joel 2:26 [q]Lev 23:39 **62:10** [r]S Ps 24:7; S Isa 60:11 [s]Isa 57:14 [t]S Isa 11:16 [u]S Isa 11:10

[a] 4 *Hephzibah* means *my delight is in her.* [b] 4 *Beulah* means *married.* [c] 5 Or *Builder*

61:9 *people the LORD has blessed.* See 44:3; 65:23 and the promises to Abraham in Ge 12:1–3 (see notes there).
61:10 Zion is probably the speaker. *clothed me with … arrayed me in.* See note on Ps 109:29. *garments of salvation.* See v. 3; 52:1 and note. *head like a priest.* Putting on a turban or headband (see note on v. 3). *bride … with her jewels.* See 49:18 and note.
61:11 *sprout … grow.* Cf. 55:10. *righteousness and praise spring up.* See 45:8 and note.
62:1 *not keep silent … quiet.* See v. 6; 42:14; 57:11 and note; 64:12; 65:6; see also Ps 28:1 and note. *righteousness … salvation.* See 46:13 and note. *dawn.* Cf. 58:8.
62:2 *nations will see … glory.* See 52:10; see also 40:5; 60:3 and notes. *your.* Jerusalem's (see vv. 1,6). *new name.* To reflect a new status (see vv. 4,12; see also 1:26; 60:14; Ge 32:28 and notes).
62:3 *crown of splendor.* In 28:5 the Lord is a "glorious crown" for his people (cf. Zec 9:16).
62:4 *Deserted … Desolate.* See 54:6–7; 60:15 and note. *Hephzibah.* Also the name of Hezekiah's wife (2Ki 21:1). *married.* Israel's relationship with the Lord will be restored. See 50:1 and note.
62:5 *sons marry you.* The Israelites will again possess the land once deserted. Cf. 54:1. Or the Hebrew for "sons" could be read as "Builder," referring to God (see note on 49:17).
62:6 *watchmen.* Probably those (the prophets especially; see note on 56:10) waiting for the messenger with good news (see 52:8 and note). *never be silent.* They will be praying that God will not be silent (see v. 1) but will restore Jerusalem. *give yourselves no rest.* Cf. David's intense prayer as he searched for a home for the ark (Ps 132:1–5).
62:7 *praise of the earth.* Cf. Jer 33:9; Zep 3:19–20; see 60:3 and note.
62:8 *has sworn.* Cf. 45:23; 54:9. *mighty arm.* See 51:9 and note. *grain … for your enemies … foreigners drink the new wine.* Punishment Moses warned about in Lev 26:16; Dt 28:33. See also 52:1 and note; Jer 5:17.
62:9 *eat it … drink it.* See 65:13,21–23. *in the courts of my sanctuary.* During a festival, or when they brought the tithe to the Lord (Lev 23:39–40; Dt 14:22–26).
62:10 *Pass through, pass through.* See note on 40:1. *gates.* Probably of Babylon (cf. 48:20; Mic 2:12–13). *Prepare the way … build up the highway.* See 40:3; 49:11 and notes. *Remove the stones.* See 57:14. *banner.* See 5:26 and note.

[11]The Lord has made proclamation
to the ends of the earth:[v]
"Say to the Daughter of Zion,[w]
'See, your Savior comes![x]
See, his reward is with him,
and his recompense accompanies
him.' "[y]
[12]They will be called[z] the Holy People,[a]
the Redeemed[b] of the Lord;
and you will be called Sought After,
the City No Longer Deserted.[c]

God's Day of Vengeance and Redemption

63 Who is this coming from Edom,[d]
from Bozrah,[e] with his garments
stained crimson?[f]
Who is this, robed in splendor,
striding forward in the greatness of
his strength?[g]
"It is I, speaking in righteousness,
mighty to save."[h]

[2]Why are your garments red,
like those of one treading the
winepress?[i]

[3]"I have trodden the winepress[j] alone;
from the nations no one was with
me.
I trampled[k] them in my anger
and trod them down in my wrath;[l]
their blood spattered my garments,[m]
and I stained all my clothing.
[4]For the day of vengeance[n] was in my
heart,
and the year of my redemption has
come.
[5]I looked, but there was no one[o] to
help,
I was appalled that no one gave
support;
so my own arm[p] worked salvation for
me,
and my own wrath sustained me.[q]
[6]I trampled[r] the nations in my anger;
in my wrath I made them drunk[s]
and poured their blood[t] on the
ground."

Praise and Prayer

[7]I will tell of the kindnesses[u] of the
Lord,
the deeds for which he is to be
praised,
according to all the Lord has done
for us—
yes, the many good things[v] he has
done
for the house of Israel,
according to his compassion[w] and
many kindnesses.
[8]He said, "Surely they are my people,[x]
sons who will not be false to me";
and so he became their Savior.[y]
[9]In all their distress he too was
distressed,
and the angel[z] of his presence[a]
saved them.
In his love and mercy he redeemed[b]
them;
he lifted them up and carried[c] them
all the days of old.[d]
[10]Yet they rebelled[e]
and grieved his Holy Spirit.[f]
So he turned and became their
enemy[g]
and he himself fought[h] against
them.

62:11 [v]S Dt 30:4 [w]S Ps 9:14; Zec 9:9; Mt 21:5 [x]S Isa 35:4; Rev 22:12 [y]S Isa 40:10 **62:12** [z]S Ge 32:28 [a]S Ex 19:6; 1Pe 2:9 [b]S Ps 106:10; S Isa 35:9; S 44:23 [c]S Ps 27:9; Isa 42:16; S 54:6 **63:1** [d]S 2Ch 28:17; S Isa 11:14 [e]S Ge 36:33; Am 1:12 [f]Rev 19:13 [g]S Job 9:4; S Isa 45:24 [h]ver 5; Isa 46:13; S 51:5; Jer 42:11; Zep 3:17 **63:2** [i]S Ge 49:11 **63:3** [j]S Jdg 6:11; S Rev 14:20 [k]S Job 40:12; S Ps 108:13; S Isa 5:5 [l]S Isa 22:5 [m]Rev 19:13 **63:4** [n]S Isa 1:24; S Jer 50:15 **63:5** [o]S 2Ki 14:26; S Isa 41:28 [p]S Ps 44:3; S 98:1; S Isa 33:2 [q]Isa 59:16 **63:6** [r]S Job 40:12; S Ps 108:13 [s]S Isa 29:9; La 4:21 [t]S Isa 34:3 **63:7** [u]S Isa 54:8 [v]S Ex 18:9 [w]S Ps 51:1; Eph 2:4 **63:8** [x]S Ps 100:3; S Isa 51:4 [y]S Ex 14:30; S Isa 25:9 **63:9** [z]S Ex 14:19 [a]S Ex 33:14 [b]Dt 7:7-8; S Ezr 9:9; S Isa 48:20 [c]S Dt 1:31; S Ps 28:9 [d]S Dt 32:7; S Job 37:23 **63:10** [e]S Ps 78:17; Eze 20:8; Ac 7:39-42 [f]S Ps 51:11; Ac 7:51; Eph 4:30 [g]Ps 106:40; S Isa 10:4 [h]S Jos 10:14

62:11 *ends of the earth.* See 11:12; 49:6 and notes. *Daughter of Zion.* A personification of Jerusalem (see note on 2Ki 19:21). *your Savior comes!* See 40:9; 43:3; Zec 9:9 and notes; Mt 21:5. *reward ... recompense.* See 40:10 and note; cf. Rev 22:12.

62:12 *Holy People.* See 4:3; Ex 19:6 and notes. *Redeemed.* See 35:9 and note. *Sought After ... No Longer Deserted.* See v. 4.

63:1 *Edom.* See 21:11; 34:5 and notes. Edom here symbolizes a world that hates God's people. *Bozrah.* See 34:6 and note. *stained crimson.* Cf. Christ's robe "dipped in blood" (Rev 19:13; see note there) as he wages war at his second coming. *righteousness, mighty to save.* See 45:8; 46:13; 59:16 and notes.

63:2 *Why ... ?* The prophet responds with a question. *treading the winepress.* See 16:10 and note.

63:3 *trodden the winepress.* A figure of judgment (see notes on La 1:15; Joel 3:13; Rev 14:19; 19:15). *in my anger ... wrath.* On the day of the Lord. See v. 6; 13:3; 34:2 and notes.

63:4 *day of vengeance ... year of my redemption.* See 61:2 and note. The day of judging the enemy marks the time of redemption for God's people. See 35:9; 41:14 and notes.

63:5 See 59:16 (a parallel to the whole verse) and note. *wrath.* In 59:16 "righteousness" is used. God's righteousness and holiness resulted in his wrath.

63:6 *made them drunk.* They drank the "cup of his wrath" (see 51:17 and note). *poured their blood.* Here the battle is compared to a sacrifice, as in 34:6.

63:7—64:12 The prophet's prayer, asking the Lord to bring about the redemption he has promised—as one of the "watchmen" the Lord has posted on the walls of Jerusalem (see 62:6 and note). It is similar to a national lament (see, e.g., Ps 44).

63:7 *kindnesses.* Demonstrations of God's unfailing love as he stood true to his covenant with Israel (see note on Ps 6:4). *many good things.* Cf. Jos 21:45; 1Ki 8:66. *compassion.* See 54:7–8,10 and note.

63:8 *my people, sons who will not be false.* But see 1:2–4. *Savior.* See 43:3 and note.

63:9 *In all their distress ... distressed.* The suffering in Egypt and during the period of the judges is probably in view (see Jdg 10:16). *angel of his presence.* See Ex 23:20–23; 33:14–15. *redeemed.* See 41:14; 43:1 and notes. *lifted ... carried.* Like a father (see Dt 1:31; 32:10–12).

63:10 *rebelled.* In the desert (see 1:2 and note; 30:1; Nu 20:10; Ps 78:40–55 and note). *grieved his Holy Spirit.* See Ps 106:33 and note; cf. Isa 11:1–2; 42:1; Eph 4:30 and note. *became their enemy.* See 43:28 and note.

11 Then his people recalled[a] the days of old,
the days of Moses and his people —
where is he who brought them through the sea,[i]
with the shepherd of his flock?[j]
Where is he who set
his Holy Spirit[k] among them,
12 who sent his glorious arm[l] of power
to be at Moses' right hand,
who divided the waters[m] before them,
to gain for himself everlasting renown,[n]
13 who led[o] them through the depths?[p]
Like a horse in open country,
they did not stumble;[q]
14 like cattle that go down to the plain,
they were given rest[r] by the Spirit of the LORD.
This is how you guided your people
to make for yourself a glorious name.
15 Look down from heaven[s] and see
from your lofty throne,[t] holy and glorious.
Where are your zeal[u] and your might?
Your tenderness and compassion[v]
are withheld[w] from us.
16 But you are our Father,[x]
though Abraham does not know us
or Israel acknowledge[y] us;
you, O LORD, are our Father,
our Redeemer[z] from of old is your name.
17 Why, O LORD, do you make us
wander[a] from your ways
and harden our hearts[b] so we do not revere[c] you?
Return[d] for the sake of your servants,
the tribes that are your inheritance.[e]
18 For a little while[f] your people
possessed your holy place,
but now our enemies have trampled[g]
down your sanctuary.[h]
19 We are yours from of old;
but you have not ruled over them,
they have not been called by your name.[b][i]

64 Oh, that you would rend the heavens[j] and come down,[k]
that the mountains[l] would tremble before you!
2 As when fire sets twigs ablaze
and causes water to boil,
come down to make your name[m]
known to your enemies
and cause the nations to quake[n]
before you!
3 For when you did awesome[o] things
that we did not expect,
you came down, and the mountains
trembled[p] before you.
4 Since ancient times no one has heard,
no ear has perceived,
no eye has seen any God besides you,[q]
who acts on behalf of those who
wait for him.[r]
5 You come to the help of those who
gladly do right,[s]
who remember your ways.
But when we continued to sin against them,
you were angry.[t]
How then can we be saved?
6 All of us have become like one who is unclean,[u]
and all our righteous[v] acts are like
filthy rags;

63:11 [i] S Ex 14:22,30 [j] S Ps 77:20 [k] S Nu 11:17 **63:12** [l] S Ge 49:24; S Ex 3:20 [m] Ex 14:21-22; Isa 11:15 [n] S Ps 102:12; S Isa 55:13; S Jer 13:11 **63:13** [o] S Dt 32:12 [p] S Ex 14:22 [q] S Ps 119:11; Jer 31:9 **63:14** [r] S Ex 33:14; S Dt 12:9 **63:15** [s] S Dt 26:15; La 3:50 [t] S 1Ki 22:19; S Ps 123:1 [u] S Isa 9:7; S 26:11 [v] S 1Ki 3:26; S Ps 25:6 [w] S Ge 43:31; Isa 64:12 **63:16** [x] S Ex 4:22; S Jer 3:4; Jn 8:41 [y] S Job 14:21 [z] Isa 41:14; 44:6; S 59:20 **63:17** [a] S Ge 20:13; La 3:9 [b] S Ex 4:21 [c] Isa 29:13 [d] S Nu 10:36 [e] S Ex 34:9 **63:18** [f] Dt 4:26; 11:17 [g] S Isa 28:18; Da 8:13; S Lk 21:24 [h] S Lev 26:31; S 2Ki 25:9 **63:19** [i] S Isa 43:7; S Jer 14:9 **64:1** [j] Ps 18:9; 144:5 [k] ver 3; Mic 1:3 [l] S Ex 19:18 **64:2** [m] S Isa 30:27 [n] Ps 99:1; 119:120; Jer 5:22; 33:9 **64:3** [o] S Ps 65:5 [p] S Ps 18:7 **64:4** [q] S Isa 43:10-11 [r] S Isa 30:18; 1Co 2:9* **64:5** [s] S Isa 26:8 [t] S Isa 10:4 **64:6** [u] S Lev 5:2; S 12:2 [v] Isa 46:12; 48:1

[a] 11 Or *But may he recall* [b] 19 Or *We are like those you have never ruled, / like those never called by your name*

63:11 *sea.* The Red Sea (see 50:2 and note; 51:10). *shepherd.* Moses. *Holy Spirit.* See note on Ps 51:11. The Spirit rested on Moses and 70 elders (Nu 11:17,25). See also v. 14.
63:12 *arm of power.* See 51:9 and note; Ex 15:16. *divided the waters.* See Ex 14:21; cf. Isa 11:15; 51:10. *everlasting renown.* See 55:13 and note.
63:13 *depths.* Of the Red Sea (see Ex 15:5,8; Ps 106:9). But the crossing of the Jordan (Jos 3) may be intended as well (see v. 14 and note).
63:14 *to the plain.* To find the best pasturage. *given rest.* They found a home in Canaan, the promised land (see Dt 12:9; Jos 1:13 and note; 21:44).
63:15 *lofty throne.* See 6:1. *zeal.* See 9:7; 42:13 and notes. *tenderness and compassion.* Cf. Hos 11:8. *withheld.* See 42:14 and note.
63:16 *Father.* See 64:8; Dt 32:6; Jer 3:4 and note. *Abraham does not know.* Even if their human fathers — Israel's patriarchal ancestors — refuse to own them, God will not (cf. 49:14–15 and notes). *Redeemer.* See 41:14 and note.
63:17 *make us wander.* When Israel went astray (see 53:6), God let them wander. *harden our hearts.* The people's hearts were hard (see 6:10; Ps 95:8), and the Lord confirmed that condition (see 6:10; Ex 4:21 and notes). *servants.* True believers (see 54:17 and note).
63:18 *enemies.* The Babylonians. *trampled down your sanctuary.* Graphically described in Ps 74:3–8 (see notes there); cf. Isa 64:11. Since it was God's sanctuary, his honor was at stake (cf. 48:11).
63:19 *called by your name.* See 43:7 and note.
64:1 *rend the heavens.* The sky is compared to a tent. For this and the further description of the cosmic effects of God's coming in judgment and redemption see Jdg 5:4–5; Ps 18:7–15; 144:5; Na 1:5; Hab 3:3–7 and notes.
64:2 *make your name known.* See 30:27 and note.
64:3 *awesome things.* See Ps 66:3,5–7 and notes.
64:4 *no … God besides you.* See 43:11 and note. *wait for him.* See 30:18; see also 40:31 and note.
64:5 *do right.* See 56:1. *you were angry.* See 9:12,17,21 and note. God's anger culminated in the exile. *saved.* Or "delivered" (see 43:3 and note).
64:6 *unclean.* Ceremonially unclean, like a person with a defiling skin disease (see 6:5; see also notes on Lev 4:12; 11:2; 13:2,45–46; cf. Introduction to Leviticus: Theological Themes). *righteous acts.* See 57:12 and note. *filthy rags.* The

we all shrivel up like a leaf,[w]
  and like the wind our sins sweep us
    away.[x]
7 No one[y] calls on your name[z]
  or strives to lay hold of you;
for you have hidden[a] your face from us
  and made us waste away[b] because
    of our sins.

8 Yet, O LORD, you are our Father.[c]
  We are the clay, you are the potter;[d]
  we are all the work of your hand.[e]
9 Do not be angry[f] beyond measure,
    O LORD;
  do not remember our sins[g] forever.
Oh, look upon us, we pray,
  for we are all your people.[h]
10 Your sacred cities[i] have become a desert;
  even Zion is a desert, Jerusalem a
    desolation.[j]
11 Our holy and glorious temple,[k] where
    our fathers praised you,
  has been burned with fire,
  and all that we treasured[l] lies in ruins.
12 After all this, O LORD, will you hold
    yourself back?[m]
  Will you keep silent[n] and punish us
    beyond measure?

Judgment and Salvation

65 "I revealed myself to those who did
    not ask for me;
  I was found by those who did not
    seek me.[o]
To a nation[p] that did not call on my
    name,[q]
  I said, 'Here am I, here am I.'
2 All day long I have held out my hands
  to an obstinate people,[r]
who walk in ways not good,
  pursuing their own imaginations[s]—
3 a people who continually provoke me
  to my very face,[t]
offering sacrifices in gardens[u]
  and burning incense[v] on altars of
    brick;
4 who sit among the graves[w]
  and spend their nights keeping
    secret vigil;
who eat the flesh of pigs,[x]
  and whose pots hold broth of
    unclean meat;
5 who say, 'Keep away; don't come near
    me,
  for I am too sacred[y] for you!'
Such people are smoke[z] in my nostrils,
  a fire that keeps burning all day.

6 "See, it stands written before me:
  I will not keep silent[a] but will pay
    back[b] in full;
  I will pay it back into their laps[c]—
7 both your sins[d] and the sins of your
    fathers,"[e]
  says the LORD.
"Because they burned sacrifices on the
    mountains
  and defied me on the hills,[f]
I will measure into their laps
  the full payment[g] for their former
    deeds."

8 This is what the LORD says:

"As when juice is still found in a
    cluster of grapes[h]
  and men say, 'Don't destroy it,
  there is yet some good in it,'
so will I do in behalf of my servants;[i]
  I will not destroy them all.

64:6 [w]S Ps 1:3; 90:5-6 [x]Ps 1:4; Jer 4:12 **64:7** [y]S Isa 41:28; 59:4; 63:5; Jer 8:6; Eze 22:30 [z]S Ps 14:4 [a]Dt 31:18; Isa 1:15; 54:8 [b]S Isa 9:18; Eze 22:18-22 **64:8** [c]S Ex 4:22; S Jer 3:4 [d]S Isa 29:16; Ro 9:20-21 [e]S Job 10:3; S Isa 19:25 **64:9** [f]Isa 54:8; 57:17; 60:10; La 5:22 [g]S Isa 43:25 [h]S Ps 100:3; S Isa 51:4 **64:10** [i]Ps 78:54; S Isa 1:26 [j]S Dt 29:23 **64:11** [k]S Lev 26:31; S 2Ki 25:9; Ps 74:3-7; La 2:7 [l]ver 10-11; La 1:7,10 **64:12** [m]S Ge 43:31; Ps 74:10-11 [n]S Est 4:14; S Ps 50:21; S 83:1 **65:1** [o]Hos 1:10; Ro 9:24-26; 10:20* [p]Ro 9:30; Eph 2:12 [q]S Ps 14:4; S Isa 43:7 **65:2** [r]S Ps 78:8; S Isa 1:2,23; Ro 10:21* [s]Ps 81:11-12; S Pr 24:2; Isa 66:18 **65:3** [t]S Job 1:11 [u]S Isa 1:29 [v]S Lev 2:2; Jer 41:5; 44:17; Eze 23:41 **65:4** [w]S Lev 19:31; S Isa 8:19 [x]S Lev 11:7 **65:5** [y]S Ps 40:4; Mt 9:11; Lk 7:39; 18:9-12 [z]Pr 10:26 **65:6** [a]S Ps 50:3 [b]S 2Ch 6:23; Isa 59:18; Jer 16:18 [c]S Ps 79:12; Eze 9:10; Lk 6:38 **65:7** [d]S Isa 22:14 [e]Ex 20:5; Jer 32:18 [f]S Isa 57:7 [g]S Pr 10:24; S Isa 10:12 **65:8** [h]Isa 5:2 [i]S Isa 54:17

cloths a woman uses during her period, a time when she is "unclean" (see Lev 15:19–24; Eze 36:17). *shrivel up like a leaf.* A figure used also in 1:30. *like the wind.* Which blows away the chaff (see 17:13; 40:24; Ps 1:4 and notes).

64:7 *No one calls on your name.* The Lord urges earnest prayer in times of distress (see, e.g., 2Ch 7:14). *hidden your face.* See 1:15 and note.

64:8 *Father.* See 63:16 and note. *clay … potter.* See 29:16 and note. *work of your hand.* See 60:21 and note.

64:9 *Do not be angry.* Cf. the promise to end that anger in 54:7–8 (see notes there). *do not remember our sins.* See 43:25 and note; Jer 31:34; Mic 7:18. *your people.* See 63:17–19; Ps 79:13.

64:10 *sacred cities.* Sacred because Israel was the "holy land" (Zec 2:12 [see note there]; cf. Ps 78:54). Jerusalem is often called the "holy city" (see 48:2 and note). *Zion is a desert … desolation.* See 1:7–9 and note; 6:11; Jer 12:11.

64:11 *holy and glorious temple.* See 60:7; 63:15. *burned with fire.* The prophet here reaches the climax of his lament. See 63:18 and note.

64:12 *hold yourself back … keep silent.* See 42:14; 57:11; 62:1,6–7 and notes.

65:1—66:24 The grand conclusion to chs. 58–66, as well as to chs. 40–66 and to the whole book.

65:1–2 *I revealed … people.* Paul makes use of these prophetic words in Ro 10:20–21. *a nation … an obstinate people.* See v. 3; see also note on 6:9–10.

65:1 *did not ask … did not seek.* The Lord now proceeds to answer the prophet's prayer. Israel failed to stay close to the Lord, though they sought him in a superficial way (see 55:6; 58:2 and notes). *did not call on my name.* See 64:7. *Here am I.* See 58:9.

65:2 *obstinate people.* See 1:2; 30:1,9 and notes. *imaginations.* See 59:7 and note.

65:3 *provoke me.* By worshiping idols (see Jdg 2:12–13 and notes). *to my very face.* Defiantly (cf. 3:8–9). *gardens.* See 1:29 and note. *burning incense.* As when worshiping the Queen of Heaven (see Jer 44:17–19 and notes).

65:4 *sit among the graves.* Perhaps to consult the dead (see 8:19 and note; 57:9; Dt 18:11). *flesh of pigs.* Considered ceremonially unclean (see 66:3,17; Lev 11:7–8).

65:5 *I am too sacred for you.* Those who engaged in pagan rituals often believed they were "holier" than others (see 66:17 and note).

65:6 *not keep silent.* The answer to 64:12. *pay back.* See 59:18 and note.

65:7 *burned sacrifices on the mountains.* Offered to Baal on the high places (see 57:7; Hos 2:13 and note). *defied me.* See Eze 20:27–28.

65:8 *cluster of grapes.* Israel was a vineyard that had produced

9 I will bring forth descendants[j] from
Jacob,
and from Judah those who will
possess[k] my mountains;
my chosen[l] people will inherit them,
and there will my servants live.[m]
10 Sharon[n] will become a pasture for
flocks,[o]
and the Valley of Achor[p] a resting
place for herds,
for my people who seek[q] me.
11 "But as for you who forsake[r] the LORD
and forget my holy mountain,[s]
who spread a table for Fortune
and fill bowls of mixed wine[t] for
Destiny,
12 I will destine you for the sword,[u]
and you will all bend down for the
slaughter;[v]
for I called but you did not answer,[w]
I spoke but you did not listen.[x]
You did evil in my sight
and chose what displeases me."[y]

13 Therefore this is what the Sovereign
LORD says:

"My servants will eat,[z]
but you will go hungry;[a]
my servants will drink,[b]
but you will go thirsty;[c]
my servants will rejoice,[d]
but you will be put to shame.[e]
14 My servants will sing[f]
out of the joy of their hearts,
but you will cry out[g]
from anguish of heart
and wail in brokenness of spirit.
15 You will leave your name
to my chosen ones as a curse;[h]
the Sovereign LORD will put you to
death,
but to his servants he will give
another name.[i]
16 Whoever invokes a blessing[j] in the
land
will do so by the God of truth;[k]
he who takes an oath in the land
will swear[l] by the God of truth.
For the past troubles[m] will be forgotten
and hidden from my eyes.

New Heavens and a New Earth

17 "Behold, I will create
new heavens and a new earth.[n]
The former things will not be
remembered,[o]
nor will they come to mind.
18 But be glad and rejoice[p] forever
in what I will create,
for I will create Jerusalem[q] to be a
delight
and its people a joy.
19 I will rejoice[r] over Jerusalem
and take delight[s] in my people;
the sound of weeping and of crying[t]
will be heard in it no more.

20 "Never again will there be in it
an infant[u] who lives but a few days,
or an old man who does not live out
his years;[v]

65:9 [j]S Isa 45:19 [k]S Nu 34:13; S Isa 60:21; Jer 50:19; Am 9:11-15 [l]S Isa 14:1 [m]Isa 32:18 **65:10** [n]S 1Ch 27:29; S Isa 35:2; Ac 9:35 [o]Jer 31:12; 33:12; Eze 34:13-14 [p]S Jos 7:26 [q]S Isa 51:1 **65:11** [r]Dt 28:20; 29:24-25; S 32:15; Isa 1:28; Jer 2:13; 19:4 [s]S Dt 33:19; S Ps 137:5 [t]S Isa 5:22 **65:12** [u]S Isa 1:20; S 27:1 [v]S Isa 30:25 [w]S Pr 1:24-25; S Isa 41:28; 66:4; Jer 7:27 [x]2Ch 36:15-16; Jer 7:13; 13:11; 25:3; 26:5 [y]Ps 149:7; Isa 1:24; 66:4; Mic 5:15 **65:13** [z]S Isa 1:19 [a]S Job 18:12; Lk 6:25 [b]S Isa 33:16 [c]S Isa 3:1; 41:17 [d]S Isa 60:5; 61:7 [e]S Isa 44:9 **65:14** [f]S Ps 109:28; Zep 3:14-20; Jas 5:13 [g]S Isa 15:2; Mt 8:12; Lk 13:28 **65:15** [h]S Nu 5:27; S Ps 102:8 [i]S Ge 32:28; Rev 2:17 **65:16** [j]S Dt 29:19 [k]Ps 31:5; Rev 3:14 [l]S Ps 63:11; S Isa 19:18 [m]S Job 11:16 **65:17** [n]S Isa 41:22; 66:22; 2Co 5:17; S 2Pe 3:13 [o]Isa 43:18; Jer 3:16; S Rev 7:17 **65:18** [p]S Dt 32:43; Ps 98:1-9; S Isa 25:9 [q]Rev 21:2 **65:19** [r]S Isa 35:10; S 62:5 [s]S Dt 30:9 [t]S Isa 25:8; Rev 7:17 **65:20** [u]Isa 11:8 [v]Ge 5:1-32; S 15:15; S Ecc 8:13; Zec 8:4

bad grapes (5:2,4,7). *my servants.* See vv. 9,13–14; 54:17 and note. Here the Lord's servants are equivalent to the remnant (see 1:9 and note).

65:9 *descendants.* See Jer 31:36 and note. *Jacob ... Judah.* The northern and southern kingdoms respectively. *possess my mountains.* See 49:8; 60:21 and notes. "Mountains" refers to the whole land, since so much of it was hilly (see Jdg 1:9; Eze 6:2–3). *chosen people.* See 41:8–9 and note. *inherit.* See 57:13 and note.

65:10 *Sharon.* See 33:9 and note. *Valley of Achor.* A valley near Jericho (see Jos 7:24,26; Hos 2:15 and notes). Since Sharon and Achor are on the western and eastern edges of the land respectively, they probably represent the whole country. *seek me.* See v. 1; 51:1 and notes.

65:11 *forsake the LORD.* See 1:4. *holy mountain.* See 2:2–4 and note. *spread a table ... mixed wine.* A meal and drink offering presented to deities. See note on 5:22; cf. v. 3; Jer 7:18 and note. *Fortune ... Destiny.* The pagan gods of good fortune and fate. See Jos 11:17, where "Gad" may mean "Fortune."

65:12 *sword.* Designed for God's enemies, such as Edom (34:5–6), but the wicked of Israel would also suffer (see 1:20; 59:18 and note; 66:16). *called ... not answer.* See 50:2; 2Ch 24:19 and notes. *chose what displeases me.* Contrast the faithfulness of the eunuchs in 56:4. The last four lines of v. 12 are almost identical to those of 66:4.

65:13 *eat ... drink.* See 41:17–18; 49:10. *go hungry ... thirsty.* See 5:13; 8:21. *rejoice.* See 61:7 and note; 66:14. *put to shame.* See 42:17; 44:9,11; Ps 25:2–3; 31:17.

65:14 *sing out of ... joy.* See 35:10; 54:1 and notes. *brokenness of spirit.* They had refused God's healing. See 61:1 and note.

65:15 *chosen ones.* See v. 9 and note. *as a curse.* The rebellious Israelites will be used as an example when curses are uttered (see Jer 29:22). *another name.* Perhaps the "new name" of 62:2 (see note there).

65:16 *invokes a blessing.* See 48:1; Dt 29:19. *the God of truth.* God is faithful to his promises. The Hebrew word for "truth" here is *amen* (see Dt 27:15; Ro 1:25; 1Co 14:15–17; 2Co 1:20; Rev 3:14 and notes). Alternatively, the Hebrew for this phrase is understood by some to mean "the true God." *swear by.* See 45:23. Perhaps a contrast is intended with those who took oaths in the name of Baal (see Jer 12:16; cf. Dt 6:13 and note).

65:17 *new heavens and a new earth.* See 66:22; the climax of the "new things" Isaiah has been promising (see 42:9; 48:6; 2Pe 3:13 and notes). *former things.* The "old order of things" (Rev 21:4), including pain and sorrow.

65:18 *be glad and rejoice.* See 66:10; see also 51:3 and note. *create Jerusalem.* John links the notion of a new heaven and a new earth with the "new Jerusalem" (Rev 21:1–2). A restored Jerusalem after the exile points toward this greater Jerusalem. See note on 54:11–12.

65:19 *rejoice ... take delight.* See 62:4–5 and notes. *weeping ... crying.* See 25:8 and note; 35:10.

65:20–25 See 11:6–9 and note.

65:20 *hundred ... mere youth.* Comparable to the longevity of Adam and his early descendants. See the genealogy of Ge 5 (but see note on Ge 5:5).

he who dies at a hundred
will be thought a mere youth;
he who fails to reach[a] a hundred
will be considered accursed.
21 They will build houses[w] and dwell in
them;
they will plant vineyards and eat
their fruit.[x]
22 No longer will they build houses and
others live in them,[y]
or plant and others eat.
For as the days of a tree,[z]
so will be the days[a] of my people;
my chosen[b] ones will long enjoy
the works of their hands.
23 They will not toil in vain[c]
or bear children doomed to
misfortune;[d]
for they will be a people blessed[e] by
the LORD,
they and their descendants[f] with
them.
24 Before they call[g] I will answer;[h]
while they are still speaking[i] I will
hear.
25 The wolf and the lamb[j] will feed
together,
and the lion will eat straw like the
ox,[k]
but dust will be the serpent's[l] food.
They will neither harm nor destroy
on all my holy mountain,"[m]
says the LORD.

Judgment and Hope

66 This is what the LORD says:

"Heaven is my throne,[n]
and the earth is my footstool.[o]
Where is the house[p] you will build for
me?
Where will my resting place be?
2 Has not my hand made all these
things,[q]
and so they came into being?"
declares the LORD.

"This is the one I esteem:
he who is humble and contrite in
spirit,[r]
and trembles at my word.[s]
3 But whoever sacrifices a bull[t]
is like one who kills a man,
and whoever offers a lamb,
like one who breaks a dog's neck;
whoever makes a grain offering
is like one who presents pig's[u]
blood,
and whoever burns memorial incense,[v]
like one who worships an idol.
They have chosen their own ways,[w]
and their souls delight in their
abominations;[x]
4 so I also will choose harsh treatment
for them
and will bring upon them what they
dread.[y]
For when I called, no one answered,[z]
when I spoke, no one listened.
They did evil[a] in my sight
and chose what displeases me."[b]

5 Hear the word of the LORD,
you who tremble at his word:[c]
"Your brothers who hate[d] you,
and exclude you because of my
name, have said,
'Let the LORD be glorified,
that we may see your joy!'
Yet they will be put to shame.[e]
6 Hear that uproar from the city,
hear that noise from the temple!
It is the sound[f] of the LORD
repaying[g] his enemies all they
deserve.

7 "Before she goes into labor,[h]
she gives birth;
before the pains come upon her,
she delivers a son.[i]

65:21 [w]S Isa 32:18; S 61:4 [x]S 2Ki 19:29; S Isa 37:30; Eze 28:26; Am 9:14 **65:22** [y]S Dt 28:30 [z]Ps 1:3; 92:12-14 [a]Ps 21:4; 91:16 [b]S Isa 14:1 **65:23** [c]S Isa 49:4; 1Co 15:58 [d]Dt 28:32,41; Jer 16:3-4 [e]S Ge 12:2; S Dt 28:3-12 [f]S Isa 44:3; Ac 2:39 **65:24** [g]S Isa 55:6; Mt 6:8 [h]S Job 8:6; S Isa 30:19; S Zec 10:6 [i]Da 9:20-23; 10:12 **65:25** [j]Isa 11:6 [k]S Job 40:15 [l]Ge 3:14; Mic 7:17 [m]S Job 5:23; S Isa 2:4 **66:1** [n]S 2Ch 6:18; S Ps 2:4; S 9:7; Mt 23:22 [o]S 1Ki 8:27; Mt 5:34-35 [p]S 2Sa 7:7; Jn 4:20-21; Ac 7:49*; 17:24 **66:2** [q]S Isa 40:26; Ac 7:50*; 17:24 [r]S Isa 57:15; Mt 5:3-4; Lk 18:13-14 [s]S Ezr 9:4 **66:3** [t]S Isa 1:11 [u]S Lev 11:7 [v]S Lev 2:2 [w]S Isa 57:17 [x]ver 17; S Dt 27:15; Eze 8:9-13 **66:4** [y]S Pr 10:24; S Isa 10:12 [z]S 1Sa 8:19; S Isa 41:28 [a]2Ki 21:2,4,6; Isa 59:12 [b]S Isa 65:12 **66:5** [c]S Ezr 9:4 [d]Ps 38:20; Isa 60:15; Jn 15:21 [e]S Isa 44:9; Lk 13:17 **66:6** [f]S 1Sa 2:10; S Ps 68:33 [g]S Lev 26:28; Isa 65:6; Joel 3:7 **66:7** [h]S Isa 54:1 [i]Rev 12:5

[a] 20 Or / *the sinner who reaches*

65:21–22 Contrast Moses' curse for disobedience in Dt 28:30; cf. the same contrast in Am 5:11; 9:14; cf. also Mic 6:15.
65:21 *plant vineyards.* See 62:8–9.
65:22 *days of a tree.* Cf. the righteous in Ps 1:3 (see note there); 92:12–14. *chosen ones.* See 41:8–9 and note. *long enjoy.* Cf. Ps 91:16.
65:23 *toil in vain.* See 49:4 and note. *misfortune.* Such as death or captivity. *people blessed by the LORD.* See 61:9 and note.
65:24 *Before they call I will answer.* See 30:19; 58:9; Ps 118:5 and note; Mt 6:8.
65:25 *wolf ... lamb ... lion.* See 11:6–9 and notes. *dust ... serpent's food.* See Ge 3:14 and note. The serpent will be harmless (see 11:8). *They ... mountain.* Identical to the first two lines of 11:9.
66:1 *throne ... footstool.* See 40:22 and note. *Where is the house ...?* Solomon realized that God could not be localized in a temple built by humans, magnificent though it may be (see 1Ki 8:27 and note).
66:2 *made all these things.* See 40:26 and note. *humble and contrite.* See 57:15 and note.
66:3 Cf. Isaiah's harsh words about ineffective sacrifices in 1:11–14. *breaks a dog's neck.* The dog was ceremonially unclean and not used in offerings. Cf. the law about breaking a donkey's neck in Ex 13:13. *pig's blood.* See 65:4 and note. The dog and pig are mentioned together also in Mt 7:6; 2Pe 2:22 (see note there). *worships an idol.* See 44:19 and note. *abominations.* Probably idols (see Jer 4:1).
66:4 *choose harsh treatment.* Cf. 65:7. *For when ... displeases me.* For these last four lines see 65:12 and note.
66:5 *tremble.* See v. 2. *Your brothers.* Fellow Israelites (see Ac 11:1 and note). *Let ... joy.* Apparently spoken sarcastically, much as in 5:19; Ps 22:8.
66:6 *city.* Probably Jerusalem. *repaying his enemies.* See 59:18 and note; 65:6–7.
66:7 *Before ... labor.* See 54:1 (and note), where Zion was barren.

8 Who has ever heard of such a thing?
Who has ever seen[j] such things?
Can a country be born in a day[k]
or a nation be brought forth in a
moment?
Yet no sooner is Zion in labor
than she gives birth to her children.[l]
9 Do I bring to the moment of birth[m]
and not give delivery?" says the
LORD.
"Do I close up the womb
when I bring to delivery?" says your
God.
10 "Rejoice[n] with Jerusalem and be glad
for her,
all you who love[o] her;
rejoice greatly with her,
all you who mourn[p] over her.
11 For you will nurse[q] and be satisfied
at her comforting breasts;[r]
you will drink deeply
and delight in her overflowing
abundance."[s]

12 For this is what the LORD says:

"I will extend peace[t] to her like a
river,[u]
and the wealth[v] of nations like a
flooding stream;
you will nurse and be carried[w] on her
arm
and dandled on her knees.
13 As a mother comforts her child,[x]
so will I comfort[y] you;
and you will be comforted over
Jerusalem."

14 When you see this, your heart will
rejoice[z]
and you will flourish[a] like grass;
the hand[b] of the LORD will be made
known to his servants,[c]
but his fury[d] will be shown to his
foes.
15 See, the LORD is coming with fire,[e]
and his chariots[f] are like a
whirlwind;[g]
he will bring down his anger with fury,
and his rebuke[h] with flames of fire.
16 For with fire[i] and with his sword[j]
the LORD will execute judgment[k]
upon all men,
and many will be those slain[l] by the
LORD.

17 "Those who consecrate and purify
themselves to go into the gardens,[m] following the one in the midst of[a] those who
eat the flesh of pigs[n] and rats[o] and other
abominable things—they will meet their
end[p] together," declares the LORD.
18 "And I, because of their actions and
their imaginations,[q] am about to come[b]
and gather all nations[r] and tongues, and
they will come and see my glory.[s]
19 "I will set a sign[t] among them, and
I will send some of those who survive[u]
to the nations—to Tarshish,[v] to the Libyans[c] and Lydians[w] (famous as archers),
to Tubal[x] and Greece,[y] and to the distant
islands[z] that have not heard of my fame
or seen my glory.[a] They will proclaim my
glory among the nations. 20 And they will
bring[b] all your brothers, from all the nations, to my holy mountain[c] in Jerusalem

[a] 17 Or *gardens behind one of your temples, and*
[b] 18 The meaning of the Hebrew for this clause is uncertain.
[c] 19 Some Septuagint manuscripts *Put* (Libyans); Hebrew *Pul*

66:8 [j] Isa 64:4; Jer 18:13 [k] S Isa 49:20 [l] S Isa 49:21 **66:9** [m] S Isa 37:3 **66:10** [n] S Dt 32:43; S Isa 25:9; Ro 15:10 [o] S Ps 26:8 [p] Isa 57:19; 61:2 **66:11** [q] S Nu 11:12; S Isa 60:16 [r] Ge 49:25 [s] S Nu 25:1; S Isa 25:6 **66:12** [t] S Ps 119:165; S Isa 9:6 [u] S Isa 33:21 [v] Ps 72:3; Isa 60:5; 61:6 [w] S Nu 11:12; Isa 60:4 **66:13** [x] S Isa 49:15; 1Th 2:7 [y] S Isa 40:1; S 2Co 1:4 **66:14** [z] S Isa 25:9; S 60:5; S Joel 2:23 [a] S Ps 72:16 [b] S Ezr 5:5; S Isa 41:20 [c] S Isa 54:17 [d] S Isa 10:5; S 30:27 **66:15** [e] S Isa 1:31; S 42:25 [f] S 2Ki 2:11; S Ps 68:17 [g] S 2Ki 2:1 [h] S Dt 28:20; S Ps 9:5; S 39:11 **66:16** [i] Isa 30:30; Am 7:4; Mal 4:1 [j] S Isa 1:20; S 27:1; S Eze 14:21 [k] S Isa 13:9, 11; S Jer 2:35; S Eze 36:5 [l] S Isa 10:4

66:17 [m] S Isa 1:29 [n] S Lev 11:7 [o] Lev 11:29 [p] Ps 37:20; Isa 1:28 **66:18** [q] S Pr 24:2; S Isa 65:2 [r] S Isa 2:3; S Zec 12:3 [s] S Ex 16:7; S Isa 59:19 **66:19** [t] Isa 11:10; 49:22; Mt 24:30 [u] S 2Ki 19:31 [v] S Isa 2:16 [w] Jer 46:9; Eze 27:10 [x] S Ge 10:2 [y] Jer 31:10; Da 11:18 [z] Isa 11:11 [a] S 1Ch 16:24; S Isa 24:15 **66:20** [b] S Isa 11:12; S Jer 25:22; Eze 34:13 [c] S Dt 33:19; S Isa 2:2; Jer 31:23

66:8 *country … born in a day.* See 49:19–20 and note.
66:9 *moment of birth.* See 37:3 and note.
66:10 *Rejoice … be glad.* See 65:18 and note. *all … who love her.* Cf. Ps 137:6. *who mourn.* See 57:19; 61:2 and notes.
66:11 *nurse and be satisfied.* In 60:16 (see note there) Jerusalem was drinking the milk of nations. Here she is the mother (cf. v. 12; 49:23).
66:12 *peace … like a river.* See 48:18 and note. *wealth of nations.* See 60:5 and note. *flooding stream.* Contrast the destructive flood of 8:7–8 (see note there). *on her arm.* See 40:11.
66:13 *comforted over Jerusalem.* See 40:1; 49:13 and notes. Cf. 2Co 1:3–4.
66:14 *heart will rejoice.* See 60:5. *grass.* Usually a symbol of weakness. See 37:27 and note; 51:12; but contrast 44:4. *hand of the LORD.* Cf. Ezr 7:9; 8:31. *servants.* See 54:17 and note. *fury.* See v. 15; 13:3 and note.
66:15–16 *fire.* A figure of judgment (see 1:31 and note; 30:27).
66:15 *chariots … like a whirlwind.* See 5:28; 2Ki 2:11 and note; 6:17; Ps 68:17 and note. *anger.* See 34:2; 42:25 and notes. *rebuke.* See 51:20 and note.
66:16 *sword.* See 27:1; 31:8; 35:5–6 and note on Ps 7:12–13. *execute judgment.* The day of the Lord (see note on 2:11,17,20; cf. Eze 38:21–22).
66:17 *consecrate and purify themselves.* By special rituals required by their pagan religion. Cf. 2Ch 30:17. *gardens.* See 1:29 and note. *flesh of pigs.* See 65:4 and note.
66:18 *their imaginations.* See 65:2 and note. Wicked Israelites may be the antecedent. *gather all nations.* Cf. Joel 3:2 and note; Zep 3:8; Zec 12:3 and note. *see my glory.* Usually linked with God's deliverance of his people (see 35:2–4; 40:5 and notes).
66:19 *sign.* Possibly the banner of 11:10,12 (see note on 5:26; cf. Ps 74:4). Cf. the "sign of the Son of Man" (Mt 24:30) at the second coming. *those who survive.* After the judgment of v. 16. Cf. Zec 14:16. *Tarshish.* See 23:6 and note. *Libyans.* People who lived west of Egypt. See Na 3:9. *Lydians.* People probably from western Asia Minor (see Ge 10:13 and note). *archers.* See Jer 46:9. *Tubal.* Usually mentioned with Meshech (see Ge 10:2; Eze 27:13; 38:2–3; 39:1 and notes). It was probably a region southeast of the Black Sea. For the location of several of these nations see map, p. 22. *islands.* See 11:11 and note. *proclaim my glory.* See 42:12; 1Ch 16:24.
66:20 *bring all your brothers.* Gentiles will bring back the remnant (see 11:11–12; 49:22; 60:4 and notes). *holy mountain.* See 2:2–4 and note. *as an offering … to the temple.* As the Israelites were to bring their tithes and offerings (see Dt 12:5–7).

as an offering to the LORD—on horses, in
chariots and wagons, and on mules and
camels,"[d] says the LORD. "They will bring
them, as the Israelites bring their grain offerings, to the temple of the LORD in ceremonially clean vessels.[e] 21 And I will select
some of them also to be priests[f] and Levites," says the LORD.

22 "As the new heavens and the new
earth[g] that I make will endure before me,"
declares the LORD, "so will your name and
descendants endure.[h] 23 From one New
Moon to another and from one Sabbath[i] to
another, all mankind will come and bow
down[j] before me," says the LORD. 24 "And
they will go out and look upon the dead
bodies[k] of those who rebelled[l] against me;
their worm[m] will not die, nor will their fire
be quenched,[n] and they will be loathsome
to all mankind."

66:20 [d] S Ezr 2:66 [e] Isa 52:11 **66:21** [f] S Ex 19:6; 1Pe 2:5,9 **66:22** [g] S Isa 65:17; Heb 12:26-27; S 2Pe 3:13 [h] S Isa 48:19; Jn 10:27-29; 1Pe 1:4-5 **66:23** [i] Eze 46:1-3 [j] S Ps 22:29; S Isa 19:21; S 44:5; Rev 15:4 **66:24** [k] S Ps 110:6 [l] S Isa 1:2 [m] S Isa 14:11 [n] S Isa 1:31; S Mt 25:41; Mk 9:48*

66:21 *some of them.* A reference either to believing Jews (see 61:6 and note) or to Gentiles as part of the church or Messianic kingdom (see 1Pe 2:5,9 and notes).
66:22 *new heavens ... new earth.* See 65:17 and note. *name and descendants endure.* See 48:19 and note.
66:23 *New Moon.* See 1:14 and note. *all mankind ... bow down.* See 19:21; Zec 14:16 and notes.
66:24 Quoted in part in Mk 9:48 (see note there; see also Mk 9:43,45,47, where "hell" renders Greek *gehenna*). The Valley of Hinnom (Hebrew *ge' hinnom,* from which the word Gehenna comes) was located southwest of Jerusalem and became a picture of hell (see note on Mt 5:22). See Ne 11:30; Jer 7:31 and note. *dead bodies.* See 5:25; 34:3. *rebelled.* See 1:2 and note; 24:20. *worm will not die.* There will be everlasting torment. See 14:11; 48:22; 50:11; 57:21. *fire ... quenched.* See 1:31 and note; Mt 3:12. *loathsome.* The Hebrew for this word is translated "contempt" in Da 12:2.

Jeremiah

INTRODUCTION

Author and Date

The book preserves an account of the prophetic ministry of Jeremiah (1:1), whose personal life and struggles are shown to us in greater depth and detail than those of any other OT prophet. The meaning of his name is uncertain. Suggestions include "The LORD exalts" and "The LORD establishes," but a more likely proposal is "The LORD throws," either in the sense of "hurling" the prophet into a hostile world or of "throwing down" the nations in divine judgment for their sins. Jeremiah's prophetic ministry began in 626 B.C. and ended sometime after 586 (see notes on 1:2–3). His ministry was immediately preceded by that of Zephaniah. Habakkuk was a contemporary, and Joel and Obadiah may have been also. Since Ezekiel began his ministry in Babylon in 593, he too was a late contemporary of the great prophet in Jerusalem. How and when Jeremiah died is not known; Jewish tradition, however, asserts that while living in Egypt he was put to death by stoning (cf. Heb 11:37).

Jeremiah was a member of the priestly household of Hilkiah. His hometown was Anathoth (1:1), so he may have been a descendant of Abiathar (1Ki 2:26), a priest during the days of King Solomon. The Lord commanded Jeremiah not to marry and raise children because the impending divine judgment on Judah would sweep away the next generation (see 16:1–4 and note on 16:2). Primarily a prophet of doom, he attracted only a few friends, among whom were Ahikam (26:24), Gedaliah (Ahikam's son, 39:14) and Ebed-Melech (38:7–13; cf. 39:15–18). Jeremiah's closest companion was his faithful secretary, Baruch, who wrote down Jeremiah's words as the prophet dictated them (36:4–32). Baruch was advised by Jeremiah not to succumb to the temptations of ambition but to be content with his lot (ch. 45). He also received from Jeremiah and deposited for safekeeping a deed of purchase (32:11–16), and he accompanied the prophet on the long road to exile in Egypt (43:6–7). It is possible that Baruch was also responsible for the final compilation of the book of Jeremiah itself, since no event recorded in chs. 1–51 occurred after 580 B.C. (ch. 52 is an appendix added by a later hand).

Given to self-analysis and self-criticism (10:24), Jeremiah has revealed a great deal about himself. Although timid by nature (1:6), he received the Lord's assurance that he would become strong and courageous (1:18; 6:27; 15:20). In his "confessions" (see 11:18–23; 12:1–4; 15:10–21; 17:12–18; 18:18–23; 20:7–18 and notes) he laid bare the deep struggles of his inmost being, sometimes making startling statements about his feelings toward God (12:1; 15:18). On occasion, he engaged in calling for redress against his personal enemies (12:1–3; 15:15; 17:18; 18:19–23;

see note on Ps 5:10) — a practice that explains the origin of the English word "jeremiad," referring to a denunciatory tirade or complaint. Jeremiah, so often expressing his anguish of spirit (4:19; 9:1; 10:19 – 20; 23:9), has justly been called the "weeping prophet." But it is also true that the memory of his divine call (1:17) and the Lord's frequent reaffirmations of his commissioning as a prophet (see, e.g., 3:12; 7:2,27 – 28; 11:2,6; 13:12 – 13; 15:19 – 21; 17:19 – 20) made Jeremiah fearless and faithful in the service of his God (cf. 15:20).

Background

Jeremiah began prophesying in Judah halfway through the reign of Josiah (640 – 609 B.C.) and continued throughout the reigns of Jehoahaz (609), Jehoiakim (609 – 598), Jehoiachin (598 – 597) and Zedekiah (597 – 586). It was a period of storm and stress when the doom of entire nations — including Judah itself — was being sealed. The smaller states of western Asia were often pawns in the power plays of such imperial giants as Egypt, Assyria and Babylonia, and the time of Jeremiah's ministry was no exception. Ashurbanipal, last of the great Assyrian rulers, died in 627. His successors were no match for Nabopolassar, the founder of the Neo-Babylonian empire, who began his rule in 626 (the year of Jeremiah's call to prophesy). Soon after Assyria's capital city Nineveh fell under the onslaught of a coalition of Babylonians and Medes in 612, Egypt (no friend of Babylonia) marched northward in an attempt to rescue Assyria, which would soon be destroyed. King Josiah of Judah made the mistake of trying to stop the Egyptian advance, and his untimely death near Megiddo in 609 at the hands of Pharaoh Neco II was the sad result (2Ch 35:20 – 24). Jeremiah, who had found a kindred spirit in the godly Josiah and perhaps had proclaimed the messages recorded in 11:1 – 8; 17:19 – 27 during the king's reformation movement, lamented Josiah's death (see 2Ch 35:25 and note).

Josiah's son Jehoahaz (see NIV text note on 22:11), also known as Shallum, is mentioned only briefly in the book of Jeremiah (22:10b – 12), and then in an unfavorable way. Neco put Jehoahaz in chains and made Eliakim, another of Josiah's sons, king in his place, renaming him Jehoiakim. Jehoahaz had ruled for a scant three months (2Ch 36:2), and his reign marks the turning point in the king's attitude toward Jeremiah. Once the friend and confidant of the king, the prophet now entered a dreary round of persecution and imprisonment, alternating with only brief periods of freedom (20:1 – 2; 26:8 – 9; 32:2 – 3; 33:1; 36:26; 37:12 – 21; 38:6 – 13,28).

Jehoiakim remained relentlessly hostile toward Jeremiah. On one occasion, when an early draft of the prophet's writings was being read to Jehoiakim (36:21), the king used a scribe's knife to cut the scroll apart, three or four columns at a time, and threw it piece by piece into the firepot in his winter apartment (vv. 22 – 23). At the Lord's command, however, Jeremiah simply dictated his prophecies to Baruch a second time, adding "many similar words" to them (v. 32) — doubtless including intimations of Jehoiakim's eventual downfall.

Just prior to this episode in Jeremiah's life, an event of extraordinary importance took place that changed the course of history: In 605 B.C., the Egyptians were crushed at Carchemish on the Euphrates by Nebuchadnezzar (46:2), the gifted general who succeeded his father Nabopolassar as ruler of Babylonia that same year. Neco returned to Egypt after heavy losses, and Babylonia was given a virtually free hand in western Asia for the next 70 years. Nebuchadnezzar besieged Jerusalem in 605, humiliating Jehoiakim (Da 1:1 – 2) and carrying off Daniel and his three companions to Babylon (Da 1:3 – 6). Later, in 598 – 597, Nebuchadnezzar attacked Jerusalem again, and the rebellious Jehoiakim was heard of no more. His son Jehoiachin ruled Judah for only three months (2Ch 36:9). Jeremiah foretold the captivity of Jehoiachin and his followers (22:24 – 30), a prediction that was soon fulfilled (24:1; 29:1 – 2).

A Quick Look

Author:
Jeremiah

Audience:
The people of Judah and Jerusalem during the reigns of their last five kings.

Date:
Between 626 and 586 B.C.

Theme:
Jeremiah, the prophet of the new covenant, predicts Judah's Babylonian exile and ultimate restoration under the Davidic Messiah.

Mattaniah, Jehoiachin's uncle and a son of Josiah, was renamed Zedekiah and placed on Judah's throne by Nebuchadnezzar in 597 B.C. (37:1; 2Ch 36:9 – 14). Zedekiah, a weak and vacillating ruler, sometimes befriended Jeremiah and sought his advice but at other times allowed the prophet's enemies to mistreat and imprison him. Near the end of Zedekiah's reign, Jeremiah entered into an agreement with him to reveal God's will to him in exchange for his own personal safety (38:14 – 27). Even then the prophet was under virtual house arrest until Jerusalem was captured in 586 (38:28).

While trying to flee the city, Zedekiah was overtaken by the pursuing Babylonians. In his presence his sons were executed, after which he himself was blinded by Nebuchadnezzar (39:1 – 7). Nebuzaradan, commander of the imperial guard, advised Jeremiah to stay with Gedaliah, whom Nebuchadnezzar had made governor over Judah (40:1 – 6). After a brief term of office, Gedaliah was murdered by his opponents (41:1 – 9). Others in Judah feared Babylonian reprisal and fled to Egypt, taking Jeremiah and Baruch with them (43:4 – 7). By that time the prophet was probably over 70 years old. His last recorded words are found in 44:24 – 30, the last verse of which is the only explicit reference in the Bible to Pharaoh Hophra, who ruled Egypt from 589 to 570 B.C.

Theological Themes and Message

Referred to frequently as "Jeremiah the prophet" in the book that bears his name (20:2; 25:2; 28:5,10 – 12,15; 29:1,29; 32:2; 34:6; 36:8,26; 37:2,3,6; 38:9 – 10,14; 42:2,4; 43:6; 45:1; 46:1,13; 47:1; 49:34; 50:1) and elsewhere (2Ch 36:12; Da 9:2; Mt 2:17; 27:9; see Mt 16:14), Jeremiah was ever conscious of his call from the Lord (1:5; 15:19) to be a prophet. As such, he proclaimed words given him by God himself (19:2) and therefore certain of fulfillment (28:9; 32:24). Jeremiah had only contempt for false prophets (14:13 – 18; 23:13 – 40; 27:14 – 18) like Hananiah (ch. 28) and Shemaiah (29:24 – 32). Many of his own predictions were fulfilled in the short term (e.g., 16:15; 20:4; 25:11 – 14; 27:19 – 22; 29:10; 34:4 – 5; 43:10 – 11; 44:30; 46:13), and others were — or will yet be — fulfilled in the long term (e.g., 23:5 – 6; 30:8 – 9; 31:31 – 34; 33:15 – 16).

As hinted earlier, an aura of conflict surrounded Jeremiah almost from the beginning. He lashed out against the sins of his countrymen (44:23), scoring them severely for their idolatry (16:10 – 13,20; 22:9; 32:29; 44:2 – 3,8,17 – 19,25) — which sometimes even involved sacrificing their children to foreign gods (see 7:30 – 34 and notes). But Jeremiah loved the people of Judah in spite of their sins, and he prayed for them (14:7,20) even when the Lord told him not to (7:16; 11:14; 14:11).

Called to the unhappy task of announcing the destruction of the kingdom of Judah, Jeremiah is commissioned by God to lodge his indictment against his people and proclaim the end of an era.

Judgment is one of the all-pervasive themes in Jeremiah's writings, though he was careful to point out that repentance, if sincere, would postpone the otherwise inevitable. His counsel of submission to Babylon and his message of "life as usual" for the exiles of the early deportations branded him as a traitor in the eyes of many. Actually, of course, his advice not to rebel against Babylon marked him as a true patriot, a man who loved his own people too much to stand by silently and watch them destroy themselves. By warning them to submit and not rebel, Jeremiah was revealing God's will to them — always the most sensible prospect under any circumstances.

For Jeremiah, God was ultimate. The prophet's theology conceived of the Lord as the Creator of all that exists (10:12 – 16; 51:15 – 19), as all-powerful (32:27; 48:15; 51:57), as everywhere present (23:24). Jeremiah ascribed the most elevated attributes to the God whom he served (32:17 – 25), viewing him as the Lord not only of Judah but also of the nations (5:15; 18:7 – 10; 25:17 – 28; chs. 46 – 51).

At the same time, God is very much concerned about individual people and their accountability to him. Jeremiah's emphasis in this regard (see, e.g., 31:29 – 30) is similar to that of Ezekiel (see Eze 18:2 – 4), and the two men have become known as the "prophets of individual responsibility." The undeniable relationship between sin and its consequences, so visible to Jeremiah as he watched his beloved Judah in her death throes, made him — in the pursuit of his divine vocation — a fiery preacher (5:14; 20:9; 23:29) of righteousness, and his oracles have lost none of their power with the passing of the centuries.

Called to the unhappy task of announcing the destruction of the kingdom of Judah (thoroughly corrupted by the long and evil reign of Manasseh and only superficially affected by Josiah's efforts at reform), Jeremiah is commissioned by God to lodge his indictment against his people and proclaim the end of an era. At long last, the Lord was about to inflict on the remnant of his people the ultimate covenant curse (see Lev 26:31 – 33; Dt 28:49 – 68). This sad fact, perhaps more than any other, explains Jeremiah's continuous allusions to God's demands for covenant obedience as reflected primarily in the book of Deuteronomy (see study notes throughout Jeremiah). God would undo all that he had done for them since the day he brought them out of Egypt. It would then seem that the end had come, that Israel's stubborn and uncircumcised (unconsecrated) heart (see 4:4 and note) had sealed her final destiny, that God's chosen people had been cast off, that all the ancient promises and covenants had come to nothing.

But God's judgment of his people (and the nations), though terrible, was not to be the last word, the final work of God in history. Mercy and covenant faithfulness would triumph over wrath. Beyond the judgment would come restoration and renewal. Israel would be restored, the nations that crushed her would be crushed, and the old covenants (with Israel, David and the Levites) would be honored. God would make a new covenant with his people in which he would write his law on their hearts (see 31:31 – 34 and notes; see also Heb 8:8 – 12 and note) and thus consecrate them to his service. The new covenant was cast in the form of ancient Near Eastern royal grant treaties and contained unconditional, gracious and profoundly spiritual, moral, ethical and relational promises (see chart, p. 19). The house of David would rule God's people in righteousness, and faithful priests would serve. God's commitment to Israel's redemption was as unfailing as the secure order of creation (ch. 33).

Jeremiah's message illumined the distant as well as the near horizon. It was false prophets who proclaimed peace to a rebellious nation, as though the God of Israel's peace was indifferent to her unfaithfulness. But the very God who compelled Jeremiah to denounce sin and pronounce judgment was the God who authorized him to announce that the divine wrath had its bounds, its 70 years. Afterward forgiveness and cleansing would come — and a new day, in which all the old expectations, aroused by God's past acts and his promises and covenants, would yet be fulfilled in a manner transcending all God's mercies of old.

Literary Features

Jeremiah is the longest book in the Bible, containing more words than any other book. Although a number of chapters were written mainly in prose (chs. 7; 11; 16; 19; 21; 24 – 29; 32 – 45), including the appendix (ch. 52), most sections are predominantly poetic in form. Jeremiah's poetry is lofty and lyrical. A creator of beautiful phrases, he has given us an abundance of memorable passages (e.g., 2:13,26 – 28; 7:4,11,34; 8:20,22; 9:23 – 24; 10:6 – 7,10,12 – 13; 13:23; 15:20; 17:5 – 9; 20:13; 29:13; 30:7,22; 31:3,15,29 – 30,31 – 34; 33:3; 51:10).

Poetic repetition was used by Jeremiah with particular skill (see, e.g., 4:23 – 26; 51:20 – 23). He understood the effectiveness of repeating a striking phrase over and over. An example is "sword, famine and plague," found in 15 separate verses (14:12; 21:7,9; 24:10; 27:8,13; 29:17 – 18; 32:24,36; 34:17; 38:2; 42:17,22; 44:13). He made use of cryptograms (see NIV text notes on 25:26; 51:1,41) on appropriate occasions. Alliteration and assonance were also a part of his literary style, examples being *zarim wezeruha* ("foreigners ... to winnow her," 51:2) and *paḥad wapaḥat wapaḥ* ("Terror and pit and snare," 48:43; see note on Isa 24:17). Like Ezekiel, Jeremiah was often instructed to use symbolism to highlight his message: a ruined and useless belt (13:1 – 11), a smashed clay jar (19:1 – 12), a yoke of straps and crossbars (ch. 27), large stones in a brick pavement (43:8 – 13). Symbolic value is also seen in the Lord's commands to Jeremiah not to marry and raise children (16:1 – 4), not to enter a house where there is a funeral meal or where there is feasting (16:5 – 9), and to buy a field in his hometown, Anathoth (32:6 – 15). Similarly, the Lord used visual aids in conveying his message to Jeremiah: potter's clay (18:1 – 10), two baskets of figs (ch. 24).

Outline

Unlike Ezekiel, the oracles in Jeremiah are not arranged in chronological order. Had they been so arranged, the sequence of sections within the book would have been approximately as follows: 1:1 — 7:15; ch. 26; 7:16 — 20:18; ch. 25; chs. 46 – 51; 36:1 – 8; ch. 45; 36:9 – 32; ch. 35; chs. 21 – 24; chs. 27 – 31; 34:1 – 7; 37:1 – 10; 34:8 – 22; 37:11 — 38:13; 39:15 – 18; chs. 32 – 33; 38:14 — 39:14; 52:1 – 30; chs. 40 – 44; 52:31 – 34. The outline below represents an analysis of the book of Jeremiah in its present canonical order.

- I. Call of the Prophet (ch. 1)
- II. Warnings and Exhortations to Judah (chs. 2 – 35)
  - A. Earliest Discourses (chs. 2 – 6)
  - B. Temple Message (chs. 7 – 10)
  - C. Covenant and Conspiracy (chs. 11 – 13)
  - D. Messages Concerning the Drought (chs. 14 – 15)
  - E. Disaster and Comfort (16:1 — 17:18)
  - F. Command to Keep the Sabbath Holy (17:19 – 27)
  - G. Lessons from the Potter (chs. 18 – 20)
  - H. Condemnation of Kings, Prophets and People (chs. 21 – 24)
  - I. Foretelling the Babylonian Exile (chs. 25 – 29)
  - J. Promises of Restoration (chs. 30 – 33)
  - K. Historical Appendix (chs. 34 – 35)
- III. Sufferings and Persecutions of the Prophet (chs. 36 – 38)
  - A. Burning Jeremiah's Scroll (ch. 36)
  - B. Imprisoning Jeremiah (chs. 37 – 38)
- IV. The Fall of Jerusalem and Its Aftermath (chs. 39 – 45)
  - A. The Fall Itself (ch. 39)
  - B. Accession and Assassination of Gedaliah (40:1 — 41:15)
  - C. Migration to Egypt (41:16 — 43:13)
  - D. Prophecy against Those in Egypt (ch. 44)
  - E. Historical Appendix: Promise to Baruch (ch. 45)
- V. Judgment against the Nations (chs. 46 – 51)
  - A. Against Egypt (ch. 46)
  - B. Against Philistia (ch. 47)
  - C. Against Moab (ch. 48)
  - D. Against Ammon (49:1 – 6)
  - E. Against Edom (49:7 – 22)
  - F. Against Damascus (49:23 – 27)
  - G. Against Kedar and Hazor (Arabia) (49:28 – 33)
  - H. Against Elam (49:34 – 39)
  - I. Against Babylonia (chs. 50 – 51)
- VI. Historical Appendix (ch. 52)

1 The words of Jeremiah son of Hilkiah, one of the priests at Anathoth[a] in
the territory of Benjamin. 2 The word of
the LORD came[b] to him in the thirteenth
year of the reign of Josiah[c] son of Amon
king of Judah, 3 and through the reign of
Jehoiakim[d] son of Josiah king of Judah,
down to the fifth month of the eleventh
year of Zedekiah[e] son of Josiah king of Judah, when the people of Jerusalem went
into exile.[f]

The Call of Jeremiah

4 The word of the LORD came to me, saying,

5 "Before I formed you in the womb[g] I
knew[a][h] you,
before you were born[i] I set you
apart;[j]
I appointed you as a prophet to the
nations.[k]"

6 "Ah, Sovereign LORD," I said, "I do not
know how to speak;[l] I am only a child."[m]
7 But the LORD said to me, "Do not say,
'I am only a child.' You must go to everyone I send you to and say whatever I command you. 8 Do not be afraid[n] of them, for
I am with you[o] and will rescue[p] you," declares the LORD.[q]
9 Then the LORD reached out his hand
and touched[r] my mouth and said to
me, "Now, I have put my words in your
mouth.[s] 10 See, today I appoint you over
nations[t] and kingdoms to uproot[u] and tear
down, to destroy and overthrow, to build
and to plant."[v]

[a] 5 Or *chose*

1:1 [a] S Jos 21:18 **1:2** [b] Eze 1:3; Hos 1:1; Joel 1:1 [c] S 2Ki 22:1 **1:3** [d] S 2Ki 23:34 [e] S 2Ki 24:17 [f] Ezr 5:12; Jer 52:15 **1:5** [g] S Ps 139:13 [h] Ps 139:16 [i] S Isa 49:1 [j] Jn 10:36 [k] ver 10; Jer 25:15-26 **1:6** [l] S Ex 3:11; S 6:12 [m] 1Ki 3:7 **1:8** [n] S Ge 15:1; S Jos 8:1 [o] S Ge 26:3; S Jos 1:5; Jer 15:20 [p] ver 19; Jer 15:21; 26:24; 36:26; 42:11 [q] Jer 20:11 **1:9** [r] S Isa 6:7 [s] S Ex 4:12 **1:10** [t] Jer 25:17; 46:1 [u] Jer 12:17 [v] Jer 18:7-10; 24:6; 31:4,28

1:1–3 The background and setting of Jeremiah's call are stated concisely but comprehensively.

1:1 *The words of.* See 36:10; see also Ne 1:1; Ecc 1:1; Am 1:1; cf. Dt 1:1. *Jeremiah.* For the meaning of the name see Introduction: Author and Date. Nine other OT men had the same name (see 1Ch 5:24; 12:4,10,13; Ne 10:2; 12:1,12,34), two of whom were the prophet's contemporaries (Jer 35:3; 52:1). *Hilkiah.* Means "The LORD is my portion." For Hilkiah's possible relationship to a priestly house dating back to King Solomon see Introduction: Author and Date. Two other men named Hilkiah (a common OT name) were also Jeremiah's contemporaries (see 29:3; Ezr 7:1 and note). *priests.* Like Ezekiel (Eze 1:3) and Zechariah (see Introduction to Zechariah: Author), Jeremiah was both a prophet and a member of a priestly family. *Anathoth.* See 11:21–23; 32:6–9. The Hebrew word is the plural form of the name of the Canaanite deity Anat(h), goddess of war. Anathoth had had priestly connections in Israel as early as the times of Joshua (Jos 21:18) and Solomon (1Ki 2:26), and its pagan origins had presumably been almost forgotten by Jeremiah's time. Present-day Anata, three miles northeast of Jerusalem, preserves the ancient name and may be the ancient site itself. *Benjamin.* Anathoth was one of the four Levitical towns in the tribal territory of Benjamin (Jos 21:17–18), and after the exile Benjamites settled there again (Ne 11:31–32).

1:2 *The word of the LORD came.* The most common way of introducing a divine oracle at the beginning of a prophetic book (see Eze 1:3; Jnh 1:1 and note; Hag 1:1; Zec 1:1 and note; cf. Hos 1:1; Joel 1:1 and note; Mic 1:1; Zep 1:1). *to him.* Beginning in v. 4, Jeremiah speaks in the first person (see, e.g., vv. 11,13; 2:1). *thirteenth year.* 626 B.C. (see 25:3). *Josiah.* See 3:6; 36:2. He was the last good and godly king of Judah. Jeremiah sympathized with and supported his attempts at spiritual reformation and renewal (see 22:15b–16), which began in earnest in 621 (see 2Ki 22:3—23:25; 2Ch 34:8—35:19; cf. 2Ch 34:3–7).

1:3 *Jehoiakim.* His predecessor (Jehoahaz) and successor (Jehoiachin) are not mentioned, since they each reigned only three months. In contrast to his father Josiah, Jehoiakim was a wicked ruler (see 2Ki 23:36–37; 2Ch 36:5)—as Jeremiah discovered almost immediately (see Introduction: Background; see also 22:13–15a,17–19; 26:20–23). *fifth month of the eleventh year.* Ab (July-August), 586 B.C. (see 52:12). *Zedekiah.* The last king of Judah (see Introduction: Background), as wicked in his own way as Jehoiakim (see 52:1–2; 2Ch 36:11–14; see also Jer 24:8; 37:1–2). *exile.* The main captivity of Judah's people coincided with the destruction of Jerusalem and Solomon's temple by Nebuchadnezzar in 586 (see 2Ki 25:8–11).

1:4–19 The account of Jeremiah's call includes two prophetic visions (vv. 10–16) and some closing words of exhortation and encouragement (vv. 17–19).

1:4 See note on v. 2.

1:5 *I formed you.* See Isa 49:5. God's creative act (see Ge 2:7; Ps 119:73) is the basis of his sovereign right (see 18:4–6; Isa 43:21) to call Jeremiah into his service. *I knew you.* In the sense of making Jeremiah the object of his choice (see NIV text note). The Hebrew verb used here is translated "chosen" in Ge 18:19; Am 3:2. *I set you apart.* I consecrated you (cf. Jdg 13:5; Isa 49:1; Ro 1:1; Gal 1:15 and note). *I appointed you.* The Hebrew for this verb is not the same as that in v. 10, but both refer to the commissioning of the prophet. *prophet.* Lit. "one who has been called" to be God's spokesman (see Ex 7:1–2; 1Sa 9:9 and notes). *nations.* Although Judah's neighbors are probably the primary focus (see 25:8–38; chs. 46–51), Judah herself is not excluded.

1:6 *not know how to speak.* Like Moses (see Ex 4:10 and note), Jeremiah claimed inability to be a prophet; God nevertheless made him his spokesman (15:19). *only a child.* See 1Ki 3:7. Jeremiah's objection is denied immediately by the Lord (v. 7).

1:7 Youth and inexperience do not disqualify when God calls (see 1Ti 4:12); he equips and sustains those he commissions.

1:8 *Do not be afraid.* See 10:5; 30:10; 40:9; 42:11; 46:27–28; 51:46; see also Isa 35:4 and note; 41:10,13–14; 43:1; Zep 3:11; Hag 2:5. *I am with you.* See v. 19; 15:20. God's promise of his continuing presence should calm the fears of the most reluctant of prophets (see Ge 26:3; Ex 3:12–15; Jos 1:5 and notes). *rescue.* See v. 19; 15:20; 39:17. The Lord does not promise that Jeremiah will not be persecuted or imprisoned, but that no serious physical harm will come to him.

1:9 *touched my mouth.* Either in prophetic vision (see note on v. 11) or figuratively—or both (cf. Isa 6:7). *I have put my words in your mouth.* Continues the figure of speech begun earlier in the verse and provides a classic description of the relationship between the Lord and his prophet (see 5:14; Ex 4:15; Nu 22:38; 23:5,12,16; Dt 18:18; Isa 51:16; cf. 2Pe 1:21).

1:10 *appoint.* See note on v. 5. *uproot and tear down ... destroy and overthrow ... build and ... plant.* See 12:14–15,17; 18:7–10; 24:6; 31:28; 42:10; 45:4. The first two pairs of verbs are negative, stressing the fact that Jeremiah is to be primarily a prophet of doom, while the last pair is positive, indicating that he is also to be a prophet of restoration—even if

11 The word of the LORD came to me:
"What do you see, Jeremiah?"[w]
"I see the branch of an almond tree," I
replied.
12 The LORD said to me, "You have seen
correctly, for I am watching[a][x] to see that
my word is fulfilled."
13 The word of the LORD came to me
again: "What do you see?"[y]
"I see a boiling pot, tilting away from
the north," I answered.
14 The LORD said to me, "From the north[z]
disaster will be poured out on all who live
in the land. 15 I am about to summon all
the peoples of the northern kingdoms,"
declares the LORD.

"Their kings will come and set up their
thrones
in the entrance of the gates of
Jerusalem;
they will come against all her
surrounding walls
and against all the towns of Judah.[a]
16 I will pronounce my judgments[b] on my
people
because of their wickedness[c] in
forsaking me,[d]
in burning incense to other gods[e]
and in worshiping[f] what their hands
have made.[g]

17 "Get yourself ready! Stand up and
say[h] to them whatever I command you.
Do not be terrified[i] by them, or I will terrify you before them. 18 Today I have made
you[j] a fortified city, an iron pillar and a
bronze wall to stand against the whole
land—against the kings of Judah, its officials, its priests and the people of the land.
19 They will fight against you but will not
overcome[k] you, for I am with you[l] and will
rescue[m] you," declares the LORD.

Israel Forsakes God

2 The word[n] of the LORD came to me:
2 "Go and proclaim in the hearing of Jerusalem:

" 'I remember the devotion of your
youth,[o]
how as a bride you loved me
and followed me through the desert,[p]
through a land not sown.
3 Israel was holy[q] to the LORD,[r]
the firstfruits[s] of his harvest;
all who devoured[t] her were held
guilty,[u]
and disaster overtook them,' "
declares the LORD.

1:11 [w] Jer 24:3; Am 7:8 **1:12** [x] S Job 29:2; Jer 44:27 **1:13** [y] Jer 24:3; Zec 4:2; 5:2 **1:14** [z] S Isa 14:31 **1:15** [a] Jer 4:16; 9:11; 10:22 **1:16** [b] Jer 4:12 [c] S Ge 6:5; Jer 44:5 [d] Jer 2:13; 17:13 [e] S Ex 20:3; Jer 7:9; 19:4; 44:3 [f] S Nu 25:3 [g] Ps 115:4-8; S 135:15 **1:17** [h] ver 7; Jer 7:27; 26:2, 15; 42:4 [i] S Dt 31:6; S 2Ki 1:15 **1:18** [j] S Isa 50:7 **1:19** [k] S Ps 129:2 [l] S Ge 26:3; Isa 43:2; Jer 20:11 [m] S ver 8; S Pr 20:22; Ac 26:17 **2:1** [n] Isa 38:4; Eze 1:3; Mic 1:1 **2:2** [o] Ps 71:17; Isa 54:4; Jer 3:4; Eze 16:8-14, 60; Hos 2:15; 11:1; Rev 2:4 [p] S Ex 13:21; S Dt 1:19 **2:3** [q] S Dt 7:6 [r] S Ex 19:6; S Dt 7:6

[a] *12* The Hebrew for *watching* sounds like the Hebrew for *almond tree.*

[s] Lev 23:9-14; Jas 1:18; Rev 14:4 [t] Isa 41:11; Jer 10:25; 30:16 [u] Jer 50:7

only secondarily. The first verb ("uproot") is the opposite of the last ("plant"), and fully half of the verbs ("tear down," "destroy," "overthrow") are the opposite of "build."

1:11 *What do you see ...?* Often spoken by the Lord (or his representative) to introduce a prophetic vision (see v. 13; Am 7:8; 8:2; Zec 4:2; 5:2).

1:12 *watching.* See NIV text note. Just as the almond tree (v. 11) blooms first in the year (and therefore "wakes up" early—the Hebrew word for "watching" means to be wakeful), so the Lord is ever watchful to make sure that his word is fulfilled.

1:13 *pot.* The Hebrew for this word is translated "caldron" in Job 41:31 and stresses its large size (see Eze 24:3–5).

1:14 *From the north disaster.* See note on Isa 41:25. *will be poured out.* The Hebrew for this word has a sound similar to that for "boiling" in v. 13. *land.* Judah (see v. 15).

1:15 *northern kingdoms.* Since Assyria posed only a minimal threat to Judah after the death of Ashurbanipal in 627 B.C., reference is most likely to Babylon and her allies. *set up their thrones in ... the gates of Jerusalem.* For the fulfillment see 39:3. Since the gateway of a city was the place where its ruling council sat (see notes on Ge 19:1; Ru 4:1), the Babylonians replaced Judah's royal authority with their own (cf. 43:10; 49:38).

1:16 *my judgments on my people.* God, sovereign over his own, judges his own for their sins, using the Babylonians as his agents of judgment. *burning incense to other gods.* A common feature of pagan worship (e.g., 7:9; 11:12–13,17; 18:15; 19:13; 32:29; 44:17). *what their hands have made.* Idols (see 16:19–20; 25:6; 2Ki 22:17; 2Ch 33:22; Isa 46:6).

1:17 *Get yourself ready!* Lit. "Tighten your belt around your waist!" For related expressions see Ex 12:11; 1Ki 18:46; 2Ki 4:29; 9:1; Job 38:3; 40:7.

1:18 *fortified city.* A symbol of security and impregnability (see 5:17; Pr 18:11,19). *iron pillar.* Unique in the OT, the expression signifies dignity and strength. *bronze wall.* See 15:20. Jeremiah would be able to withstand the abuse and persecution that his divine commission would evoke, even though his enemies themselves would be "bronze and iron" (6:28). *kings ... officials ... priests ... people.* The whole nation would defy the prophet and his God (see, e.g., 2:26; 23:8; 32:32).

1:19 See note on v. 8; see also 15:20.

2:1—6:30 It is generally agreed that these chapters are among Jeremiah's earliest discourses, delivered during the reign of Josiah (3:6). The basic theme is the virtually total apostasy of Judah (chs. 2–5), leading inevitably to divine retribution through foreign invasion (ch. 6).

2:1—3:5 The wickedness and backsliding of God's people are vividly portrayed in numerous colorful figures of speech.

2:1 See note on 1:2.

2:2 *devotion.* The Hebrew for this word refers to the most intimate degree of loyalty, love and faithfulness that can exist between two people or between an individual and the Lord. *youth ... as a bride.* Early in her history, Israel had enjoyed a close and cordial relationship with the Lord, who is often described figuratively as Israel's husband (3:14; 31:32; Isa 54:5; Hos 2:16). *you loved me.* But later God's people forsook him and loved "foreign gods" (v. 25), tragically abandoning their first love (cf. Rev 2:4). *followed me.* But later they followed "worthless idols" (vv. 5,8), "the Baals" (v. 23). *desert.* Sinai (see v. 6).

2:3 *holy to the LORD.* Set apart to him and his service (see notes on Ex 3:5; Lev 11:44; Dt 7:6). *firstfruits.* Just as the "best of the firstfruits" of Israel's crops were to be brought to the Lord (Ex 23:19; see Nu 18:12; 2Ch 31:5; Eze 44:30), so also the people themselves were his first and choicest treasure (cf. Jas 1:18; Rev 14:4 and note). *disaster overtook them.* See, e.g., Ex 17:8–16.

4 Hear the word of the LORD, O house of
Jacob,
all you clans of the house of Israel.

5 This is what the LORD says:

"What fault did your fathers find
in me,
that they strayed so far from me?
They followed worthless idols[v]
and became worthless[w] themselves.
6 They did not ask, 'Where is the LORD,
who brought us up out of Egypt[x]
and led us through the barren
wilderness,
through a land of deserts[y] and
rifts,[z]
a land of drought and darkness,[a]
a land where no one travels[a] and
no one lives?'
7 I brought you into a fertile land
to eat its fruit and rich produce.[b]
But you came and defiled my land
and made my inheritance
detestable.[c]
8 The priests did not ask,
'Where is the LORD?'
Those who deal with the law did not
know me;[d]
the leaders[e] rebelled against me.
The prophets prophesied by Baal,[f]
following worthless idols.[g]

2:5 [v] S Dt 32:21; S 1Sa 12:21; Ps 31:6 [w] 2Ki 17:15 **2:6** [x] S Ex 6:6; Hos 13:4 [y] S Dt 1:19 [z] S Dt 32:10 [a] Jer 51:43 **2:7** [b] S Nu 13:27; Dt 8:7-9; 11:10-12 [c] Ps 106:34-39; Jer 3:9; 7:30; 16:18; Eze 11:21; 36:17 **2:8** [d] S 1Sa 2:12; Jer 4:22 [e] Jer 3:15; 23:1; 25:34; 50:6 [f] S 1Ki 18:22 [g] ver 25; S Isa 40:19; S 56:10; Jer 5:19; 9:14; 16:19; 22:9 **2:9** [h] Jer 25:31; Hos 4:1; Mic 6:2 **2:10** [i] S Ge 10:4 [j] S Ge 25:13 **2:11** [k] S Isa 37:19; Jer 16:20; Gal 4:8 [l] S 1Sa 4:21; Ro 1:23 **2:13** [m] S Dt 31:16; S Isa 65:11 [n] S Isa 12:3; Jn 4:14 **2:14** [o] Ex 4:22; Jer 31:9

9 "Therefore I bring charges[h] against you
again,"
declares the LORD.
"And I will bring charges against
your children's children.
10 Cross over to the coasts of Kittim[b][i] and
look,
send to Kedar[c][j] and observe closely;
see if there has ever been anything
like this:
11 Has a nation ever changed its gods?
(Yet they are not gods[k] at all.)
But my people have exchanged their[d]
Glory[l]
for worthless idols.
12 Be appalled at this, O heavens,
and shudder with great horror,"
declares the LORD.
13 "My people have committed two
sins:
They have forsaken[m] me,
the spring of living water,[n]
and have dug their own cisterns,
broken cisterns that cannot hold
water.
14 Is Israel a servant, a slave[o] by birth?
Why then has he become plunder?

[a] *6* Or *and the shadow of death* [b] *10* That is, Cyprus and western coastlands [c] *10* The home of Bedouin tribes in the Syro-Arabian desert [d] *11* Masoretic Text; an ancient Hebrew scribal tradition *my*

2:4 *Hear.* A common divine imperative in prophetic writings, summoning God's people—as well as the nations—into his courts to remind them of their legal obligations to him and, when necessary, to pass judgment on them (see, e.g., 7:2; 17:20; 19:3; 21:11; 22:2,29; 31:10; 42:15; 44:24,26; Isa 1:10; Eze 13:2; Hos 4:1; Am 7:16).

2:5 *This is what the LORD says.* The so-called messenger formula, introducing God's word through the prophet. Actually such a messenger formula was an integral part of the "word" that was to be proclaimed (cf. Nu 23:16; Jdg 11:15). Though frequent in overall occurrence, its use is restricted to Jeremiah, Isaiah (e.g., 7:7), Ezekiel (e.g., 2:4), Amos (e.g., 1:3), Obadiah (1), Micah (3:5), Nahum (1:12), Haggai (e.g., 1:2), Zechariah (e.g., 1:3) and Malachi (1:4). *strayed.* See 4:1; 23:13,32; 31:19; 50:6; Isa 53:6; Eze 34:4–6,16; 1Pe 2:25. *followed worthless idols.* See vv. 8,23; see also note on v. 2. "Worthless" is Jeremiah's favorite way of describing idols (8:19; 10:8,15; 14:22; 16:19; 51:18). *became worthless themselves.* See 2Ki 17:15. Idolaters are no better than the idols they worship (see Ps 115:8 and note).

2:6 *LORD ... brought us up out of Egypt.* The Lord, Israel's Redeemer (see notes on Ge 2:4; Ex 3:15), freed his people from Egyptian bondage so that they might serve him alone (Ex 20:2–6). *led us.* As a shepherd leads sheep (see v. 17; Dt 8:15; Ps 23:2–3). *land of deserts ... land of ... darkness.* The desert was often used to symbolize a place of darkness with its attendant dangers, including death (see v. 31 and note; 9:10; 12:12; 17:6; 23:10; Ps 44:19).

2:7 *fertile.* The Hebrew for this word is *karmel,* translated "orchards" in 48:33 and also used as the name of a place (see Isa 33:9 and note). Rendered "fruitful land" in 4:26, it is the opposite of a desert. *defiled my land.* Made it ceremonially unclean (see 3:1–2,9; 16:18; see also note on Lev 4:12). *inheritance.* The promised land, given by God to Israel as a legacy and often intimately associated with the people themselves (see especially 12:7–9,14–15). *detestable.* See note on Lev 7:21.

2:8 No one consulted the Lord (see v. 6). *priests ... leaders ... prophets.* See note on 1:18. *Those who deal with the law.* Priests (see Dt 31:11 and note). *leaders.* Lit. "shepherds," a term used elsewhere to denote rulers (23:1–4; 49:19; 50:44; see especially Eze 34:1–10,23–24). *by Baal.* In the name of Baal (cf. 11:21; 14:15; 23:25; 26:9; see note on Jdg 2:13). *following worthless idols.* See v. 23. *worthless.* Lit. "unprofitable." See v. 11.

2:9 *bring charges against.* See note on v. 4; see also 25:31; Hos 4:1; 12:2; Mic 6:2.

2:10 *Kittim.* See the first NIV text note on this verse; see also Nu 24:24; Eze 27:6 and notes. *Kedar.* Represents the eastern nations and regions (see NIV text note; see also 49:28; Isa 21:16 and note).

2:11 *Has ... gods?* A rhetorical question, clearly expecting a negative answer and emphasizing how incredible is Judah's practice of substituting idolatry for the worship of the Lord. *their Glory.* God (see Ps 106:20; Hos 4:7; see also 1Sa 15:29). *worthless.* See note on v. 8.

2:12 *Be appalled ... O heavens.* See note on Isa 1:2; see also Mic 6:1–2 and note. The Hebrew for these phrases offers a striking play on words: *shommu shamayim.*

2:13 See 1:16. *forsaken me.* See v. 19. *me, the spring of living water.* See 17:13. God himself provides life-giving power to his people (see Ps 36:9; see also note on Jn 4:10; Isa 55:1 and note; Rev 21:6). *broken cisterns.* Watertight plaster was used to keep cisterns from losing water. Idols, like broken cisterns, will always fail their worshipers; by contrast, God provides life abundant and unfailing.

2:14 *Is ... birth?* Another rhetorical question (see note on v. 11), again expecting a negative answer in the light of God's redemptive acts during the period of the exodus (see Ex 6:6; 20:2). *plunder.* To Assyria and Egypt (see vv. 15–16).

15 Lions[p] have roared;
they have growled at him.
They have laid waste[q] his land;
his towns are burned[r] and deserted.[s]
16 Also, the men of Memphis[a][t] and
Tahpanhes[u]
have shaved the crown of your
head.[b]
17 Have you not brought this on
yourselves[v]
by forsaking[w] the LORD your God
when he led you in the way?
18 Now why go to Egypt[x]
to drink water from the Shihor[c]?[y]
And why go to Assyria[z]
to drink water from the River[d]?[a]
19 Your wickedness will punish you;
your backsliding[b] will rebuke[c] you.
Consider then and realize
how evil and bitter[d] it is for you
when you forsake[e] the LORD your God
and have no awe[f] of me,"
declares the Lord,
the LORD Almighty.

20 "Long ago you broke off your yoke[g]
and tore off your bonds;[h]
you said, 'I will not serve you!'[i]
Indeed, on every high hill[j]
and under every spreading tree[k]
you lay down as a prostitute.[l]
21 I had planted[m] you like a choice vine[n]
of sound and reliable stock.
How then did you turn against me
into a corrupt,[o] wild vine?
22 Although you wash[p] yourself with
soda[q]
and use an abundance of soap,
the stain of your guilt is still before
me,"
declares the Sovereign LORD.[r]
23 "How can you say, 'I am not defiled;[s]
I have not run after the Baals'?[t]
See how you behaved in the valley;[u]
consider what you have done.
You are a swift she-camel
running[v] here and there,
24 a wild donkey[w] accustomed to the
desert,[x]
sniffing the wind in her craving —
in her heat who can restrain her?
Any males that pursue her need not
tire themselves;
at mating time they will find her.
25 Do not run until your feet are bare
and your throat is dry.
But you said, 'It's no use![y]
I love foreign gods,[z]
and I must go after them.'[a]

26 "As a thief is disgraced[b] when he is
caught,
so the house of Israel is disgraced —

2:15 [p]Jer 4:7; 50:17 [q]S Isa 1:7 [r]S 2Ki 25:9 [s]S Lev 26:43 **2:16** [t]S Isa 19:13 [u]Jer 43:7-9 **2:17** [v]Jer 4:18 [w]S Isa 1:28; Jer 17:13; 19:4 **2:18** [x]S Isa 30:2 [y]S Jos 13:3 [z]S 2Ki 16:7; Hos 5:13; 7:11; 8:9 [a]S Isa 7:20 **2:19** [b]Jer 3:11,22; 7:24; 11:10; 14:7; Hos 14:4 [c]Isa 3:9; 59:12; Hos 5:5 [d]S Job 20:14; Am 8:10 [e]Jer 19:4 [f]S Ps 36:1 **2:20** [g]S Lev 26:13 [h]Ps 2:3; Jer 5:5 [i]S Job 21:14 [j]Isa 57:7; Jer 3:23; 17:2 [k]S Dt 12:2 [l]S Isa 1:21; Eze 16:15 **2:21** [m]S Ex 15:17 [n]S Ps 80:8 [o]S Isa 5:4 **2:22** [p]S Ps 51:2; La 1:8,17 [q]S Job 9:30 [r]Jer 17:1 **2:23** [s]S Pr 30:12 [t]ver 25; Jer 9:14; 23:27 [u]S 2Ki 23:10; Jer 7:31; 19:2; 31:40 [v]ver 33; Jer 31:22 **2:24** [w]S Ge 16:12; Jer 14:6 [x]S Job 39:6 **2:25** [y]S Isa 57:10 [z]Dt 32:16; Jer 3:13; 14:10 [a]S ver 8, S ver 23 **2:26** [b]Jer 48:27; La 1:7; Eze 16:54; 36:4

[a] *16* Hebrew *Noph* [b] *16* Or *have cracked your skull* [c] *18* That is, a branch of the Nile [d] *18* That is, the Euphrates

2:15 *Lions.* Probably symbolizing Assyria (see v. 18; 50:17; see also notes on 4:7; Isa 15:9). *roared ... growled.* See Am 3:4. *laid waste his land.* See 4:7; 18:16; 50:3. *towns are burned and deserted.* The Hebrew for this phrase is very similar to that in 4:7, rendered there "towns will lie in ruins without inhabitant" (cf. 22:6).
2:16 *Memphis.* See 44:1; 46:14,19; see also note on Isa 19:13. *Tahpanhes.* Probably the city later called Daphnai by the Greeks, located just south of Lake Menzaleh in the eastern delta region of Egypt and known today as Tell Defneh (see 43:7–9; 44:1; 46:14; Eze 30:18). *shaved the crown of your head.* Figurative for bringing disgrace and devastation (see 47:5; 48:37; see also notes on Isa 3:17; 7:20).
2:17 *he led you.* See note on v. 6. *the way.* See Ex 18:8; 23:20; Dt 1:33.
2:18 See v. 36. The tendency of Israel or Judah to seek help alternately from Egypt and Assyria was not restricted to Jeremiah's time (see, e.g., Hos 7:11; 12:2). *drink water.* Provided by enemies, whether national or spiritual, rather than by God (see v. 13; Isa 8:6–8 and notes).
2:19 *backsliding.* See 3:22; 5:6; 14:7. The word implies repeated apostasy. *LORD Almighty.* A title for God occurring about 75 times in Jeremiah — more than in any other OT book (see note on 1Sa 1:3).
2:20 — 3:6 The rebellion of Judah against God is vividly portrayed by Jeremiah with the use of numerous figures of speech.
2:20 Like a stubborn draft animal (see Hos 4:16), Judah refuses to obey the Lord's commands. *broke off your yoke and tore off your bonds.* See 5:5; see also 31:18; cf. Ps 2:3. Judah has broken God's law and violated his covenant. *on every high hill and under every spreading tree.* Locales of pagan worship (see 1Ki 14:23; 2Ki 17:10; Eze 6:13). *as a prostitute.* See v. 2; Ex 34:15 and notes.
2:21 See Isa 5:1–7; see also Ps 80:8–16; Eze 17:1–10; Hos 10:1–2; cf. Jn 15:1–8. *choice vine.* See Isa 5:2. The Hebrew for this word refers to a grape of exceptional quality. *wild.* Lit. "foreign." A vine symbolizing Israel should not be like a vine symbolizing Israel's enemies (see Dt 32:32).
2:22 *soda ... soap.* Mineral alkali and vegetable alkali respectively. Sins can be removed and forgiven (see Ps 51:2,7; Isa 1:18), but only when the sinner repents and confesses (see Pr 28:13; cf. 1Jn 1:7,9).
2:23 *defiled.* Ceremonially unclean (see 19:13; see also note on Lev 4:12). *run after.* See note on v. 2; see also v. 25. *Baals.* See 9:14; see also notes on Jdg 2:11,13. *the valley.* Probably the Hinnom Valley (see note on Jos 15:5), known also as the Valley of Ben Hinnom (7:31–32; 19:2,6; 32:35). *running here and there.* Instead, the people of Judah should have been obeying the Lord, not turning aside either "to the right or to the left" (Dt 28:14).
2:24 *wild donkey.* Properly the wild ass, an unruly (see Ge 16:12) and intractable (see Job 39:5–8) animal. *accustomed to the desert.* See 14:6; Job 24:5. *sniffing the wind.* The picture is one of active searching, not passive waiting (see Hos 2:7,13).
2:25 *your feet are bare.* You wear out your sandals. *It's no use!* See 18:12 and note. *I love foreign gods.* As opposed to the love Judah was expected to express toward God under the terms of their covenant relationship (see, e.g., Dt 6:5; 7:9; Hos 2:16; see also Ex 34:15 and note). *go after them.* See v. 23; see also note on v. 2.
2:26 *disgraced when he is caught.* See, e.g., Ex 22:3–4. The Hebrew word underlying "disgraced" means lit. "shame," a term often used as a pejorative synonym for the name of Baal, the

they, their kings and their officials,
their priests[c] and their prophets.[d]
27 They say to wood,[e] 'You are my father,'
and to stone,[f] 'You gave me birth.'
They have turned their backs[g] to me
and not their faces;[h]
yet when they are in trouble,[i] they say,
'Come and save[j] us!'
28 Where then are the gods[k] you made for
yourselves?
Let them come if they can save you
when you are in trouble![l]
For you have as many gods
as you have towns,[m] O Judah.

29 "Why do you bring charges against
me?
You have all[n] rebelled against me,"
declares the LORD.
30 "In vain I punished your people;
they did not respond to correction.[o]
Your sword has devoured your
prophets[p]
like a ravening lion.

31 "You of this generation, consider the
word of the LORD:

"Have I been a desert to Israel
or a land of great darkness?[q]
Why do my people say, 'We are free to
roam;
we will come to you no more'?[r]
32 Does a maiden forget her jewelry,
a bride her wedding ornaments?
Yet my people have forgotten[s] me,
days without number.
33 How skilled you are at pursuing[t] love!
Even the worst of women can learn
from your ways.
34 On your clothes men find
the lifeblood[u] of the innocent poor,
though you did not catch them
breaking in.[v]
Yet in spite of all this
35 you say, 'I am innocent;[w]
he is not angry with me.'
But I will pass judgment[x] on you
because you say, 'I have not
sinned.'[y]
36 Why do you go about so much,
changing[z] your ways?
You will be disappointed by Egypt[a]
as you were by Assyria.
37 You will also leave that place
with your hands on your head,[b]
for the LORD has rejected those you
trust;
you will not be helped[c] by them.

3

"If a man divorces[d] his wife
and she leaves him and marries
another man,
should he return to her again?
Would not the land be completely
defiled?[e]
But you have lived as a prostitute with
many lovers[f]—
would you now return to me?"[g]
declares the LORD.
2 "Look up to the barren heights[h] and
see.
Is there any place where you have
not been ravished?
By the roadside[i] you sat waiting for
lovers,
sat like a nomad[a] in the desert.
You have defiled the land[j]
with your prostitution[k] and
wickedness.

[a] 2 Or *an Arab*

2:26 [c] Eze 22:26 [d] Jer 32:32; 44:17,21 **2:27** [e] Jer 10:8 [f] Jer 3:9 [g] S 1Ki 14:9; S 2Ch 29:6; Ps 14:3; Eze 8:16 [h] Jer 18:17; 32:33; Eze 7:22 [i] Jdg 10:10; Isa 26:16 [j] Isa 37:20; Hos 5:15 **2:28** [k] S Isa 45:20 [l] S Dt 32:37; S Isa 40:19 [m] S 2Ki 17:29 **2:29** [n] Jer 5:1; 6:13; Da 9:11; Mic 3:11; 7:2 **2:30** [o] S Lev 26:23 [p] S Ne 9:26; S Jer 11:21; Ac 7:52; 1Th 2:15 **2:31** [q] Isa 45:19 [r] S Job 21:14 **2:32** [s] S Dt 32:18; S Isa 57:11 **2:33** [t] S ver 23 **2:34** [u] S 2Ki 21:16; S Pr 6:17 [v] S Ex 22:2 **2:35** [w] S Pr 30:12 [x] Isa 66:16; Jer 25:31; 39:7; 45:5; Eze 17:20; 20:35; Joel 3:2 [y] S 2Sa 12:13; 1Jn 1:8,10 **2:36** [z] Jer 31:22 [a] S Ps 108:12; S Isa 30:2,3,7; Jer 37:7 **2:37** [b] 2Sa 13:19 [c] Jer 37:7 **3:1** [d] Dt 24:1-4 [e] S Ge 3:17 [f] S 2Ki 16:7; S Isa 1:21; Jer 2:20,25; 4:30; La 1:2; Eze 16:26,29; Hos 2:5,12; 3:1 [g] Hos 2:7

3:2 [h] ver 21 [i] Ge 38:14; Eze 16:25 [j] ver 9 [k] S Nu 15:39; S Isa 1:21

chief god of Canaan (see 11:13 and note; Hos 9:10; see also note on Jdg 6:32). *kings ... officials ... priests ... prophets.* See note on 1:18.

2:27 See Isa 44:13–17; contrast Dt 32:6,18; Isa 64:8; Mal 2:10. *wood ... stone.* Materials used to make idols (see 3:9 and note). *Come ... save.* See v. 28.

2:28 *as many gods as ... towns.* See 11:13; cf. 1Co 8:5. Every ancient Near Eastern town of any importance had its own patron deity (cf. Ac 19:28,34–35), and many towns were named after deities (see, e.g., note on 1:1).

2:29 *bring charges against.* Cf. v. 9; see 12:1; Job 33:13.

2:30 *I punished your people.* Cf. Heb 12:6. *did not respond to correction.* See 5:3. *sword has devoured your prophets.* See, e.g., 26:20–23; 2Ki 21:16; 24:4; see also Ne 9:26.

2:31 *generation.* Often has negative connotations (see, e.g., Dt 1:35; 32:5; Mt 12:39; 16:4; 17:17; Ac 2:40; Php 2:15; Heb 3:10). *Have I been a desert ... a land of great darkness?* On the contrary, the Lord led his people through the desert and its darkness (v. 6). The phrase "great darkness" translates the Hebrew for "darkness of the LORD" (i.e., darkness sent by the Lord; cf. 1Sa 26:12), just as "mighty flame" in SS 8:6 translates "flame of the LORD" (see NIV text note there).

2:32 See Isa 49:15,18 and notes. *bride.* Cf. v. 2. *my people have forgotten me.* See 18:15; see also 3:21; 13:25; Isa 17:10; Eze 22:12; 23:35; Hos 8:14. Israel was always to "remember" the Lord and all that he had done for her (Dt 7:18; 8:18) and so trust and worship him alone, but she often "forgot" him—put him out of mind (Hos 2:13; cf. Jdg 2:10).

2:33 *love.* See v. 25 and note.

2:34 See Am 2:6–8; 4:1; 5:11–12. *catch them breaking in.* See Ex 22:2 and note.

2:36 *disappointed by Egypt ... by Assyria.* See vv. 15–18 and notes. The days of Ahaz (see 2Ch 28:21), and perhaps the days of Zedekiah (see 37:7), are in view here.

2:37 *with your hands on your head.* Ancient reliefs depict captives with wrists tied together above their heads. *those you trust.* Egypt and Assyria.

3:1 *If ... defiled?* Cf. Dt 24:1–4. Divorce and remarriage on a widespread scale defiles not only the participants but also the Lord's land in which they live (cf. v. 2; Lev 18:25–28). *lived as a prostitute with many lovers.* A metaphor carried forward from ch. 2 and used throughout ch. 3 (see 2:20,25,33 and note on 2:25). *many.* See note on 2:28. *return to me.* Or "turn to me"—for deliverance from your present distresses (see vv. 10–11).

3:2 *barren heights.* Places where pagan gods were consulted and worshiped (see v. 21; 12:12; Nu 23:3). *ravished.* Cf. Dt 28:30. *By the roadside you sat.* See Ge 38:14 and note; Pr 7:10,12. *like a nomad in the desert.* Waiting in ambush to waylay a traveler (cf. Lk 10:30). *defiled the land.* See v. 9.

3Therefore the showers have been
withheld,[l]
and no spring rains[m] have fallen.
Yet you have the brazen[n] look of a
prostitute;
you refuse to blush with shame.[o]
4Have you not just called to me:
'My Father,[p] my friend from my
youth,[q]
5will you always be angry?[r]
Will your wrath continue forever?'
This is how you talk,
but you do all the evil you can."

Unfaithful Israel

6During the reign of King Josiah,[s] the
LORD said to me, "Have you seen what
faithless[t] Israel has done? She has gone
up on every high hill and under every
spreading tree[u] and has committed adultery[v] there. 7I thought that after she had
done all this she would return to me but
she did not, and her unfaithful sister[w] Judah saw it.[x] 8I gave faithless Israel[y] her
certificate of divorce[z] and sent her away
because of all her adulteries. Yet I saw that
her unfaithful sister Judah had no fear;[a]
she also went out and committed adultery.
9Because Israel's immorality mattered so
little to her, she defiled the land[b] and committed adultery[c] with stone[d] and wood.[e]
10In spite of all this, her unfaithful sister
Judah did not return[f] to me with all her
heart, but only in pretense,[g]" declares the
LORD.[h]
11The LORD said to me, "Faithless Israel
is more righteous[i] than unfaithful[j] Judah.[k]

3:3 [l]Lev 26:19; Jer 5:25; Am 4:7 [m]S Dt 11:14; Jer 14:4; Joel 1:10 [n]Eze 3:7; 16:30 [o]Jer 6:15; 8:12; Zep 2:1; 3:5 **3:4** [p]ver 19; S Dt 32:6; S Ps 89:26; Isa 63:16; 64:8; Jer 31:9 [q]S Jer 2:2 **3:5** [r]S Ps 103:9; S Isa 54:9 **3:6** [s]S 1Ch 3:14 [t]ver 12, 22; S Isa 24:16; Jer 31:22; 49:4 [u]S Dt 12:2; Jer 17:2; Eze 20:28; Hos 4:13 [v]S Lev 17:7; Jer 2:20 **3:7** [w]Eze 16:46; 23:2, 11 [x]Am 4:8 **3:8** [y]Jer 11:10 [z]S Dt 4:27; S 24:1 [a]Eze 16:47; 23:11 **3:9** [b]ver 2 [c]S Lev 17:7; S Isa 1:21 [d]S Isa 57:6 [e]Jer 2:27 **3:10** [f]Isa 31:6; Am 4:9; Hag 2:17 [g]Jer 12:2; Eze 33:31 [h]S 2Ki 17:19 **3:11** [i]Eze 16:52; 23:11 [j]ver 7 [k]S Jer 2:19 **3:12** [l]2Ki 17:3-6 [m]ver 14; S Dt 4:30; Jer 31:21, 22; Eze 14:6; 33:11;

12Go, proclaim this message toward the
north:[l]

"'Return,[m] faithless[n] Israel,' declares
the LORD,
'I will frown on you no longer,
for I am merciful,'[o] declares the LORD,
'I will not be angry[p] forever.
13Only acknowledge[q] your guilt—
you have rebelled against the LORD
your God,
you have scattered your favors to
foreign gods[r]
under every spreading tree,[s]
and have not obeyed[t] me,'"
declares the LORD.

14"Return,[u] faithless people," declares
the LORD, "for I am your husband.[v] I will
choose you—one from a town and two
from a clan—and bring you to Zion.
15Then I will give you shepherds[w] after my
own heart,[x] who will lead you with knowledge and understanding. 16In those days,
when your numbers have increased greatly
in the land," declares the LORD, "men will
no longer say, 'The ark[y] of the covenant of
the LORD.' It will never enter their minds
or be remembered;[z] it will not be missed,
nor will another one be made. 17At that
time they will call Jerusalem The Throne[a]
of the LORD, and all nations[b] will gather in
Jerusalem to honor[c] the name of the LORD.

Hos 14:1 [n]S ver 6 [o]S 1Ki 3:26; S Ps 6:2 [p]S Ps 103:9; S Isa 54:9 **3:13** [q]Dt 30:1-3; Jer 14:20; 1Jn 1:9 [r]S Jer 2:25 [s]S Dt 12:2 [t]ver 25; Jer 22:21 **3:14** [u]S ver 12; S Job 22:23; Jer 4:1 [v]S Isa 54:5 **3:15** [w]S Isa 31:4 [x]Ac 13:22 **3:16** [y]S Nu 3:31; S 1Ch 15:25 [z]S Isa 65:17 **3:17** [a]S Ps 47:8; Jer 17:12; 33:16; Eze 1:26; 43:7; 48:35 [b]S Isa 2:3; Mic 4:1 [c]S Ps 22:23; Jer 13:11; 33:9

3:3 *showers have been withheld.* See 14:1–6; Am 4:7–8. This is the reverse of God's gracious response to his people in Hos 2:21; 6:3. *spring rains.* See notes on Dt 11:14; Jas 5:7. *brazen look.* See Pr 7:13.

3:4 *My Father.* See v. 19; contrast 2:27 and see note there. Compared to the NT, the title "Father" for God is relatively rare in the OT. However, it often occurs in personal names—compound names that begin with Abi- (e.g., Abinadab and Abiram) refer to God as "(my) Father." *my friend.* Claiming intimate association (see Ps 55:13; Pr 16:28; 17:9; Mic 7:5); perhaps even claiming to be the Lord's faithful wife (cf. Pr 2:17). *from my youth.* See note on 2:2.

3:5 *Will your wrath continue forever?* Not if God's people truly repent (vv. 12–13).

3:6—6:30 The unfaithfulness of Judah (3:6—5:31) will ultimately bring the Babylonians as God's instrument of judgment (ch. 6).

3:6 *King Josiah.* See Introduction: Background; see also note on 1:2. *faithless Israel.* The northern kingdom, destroyed in 722–721 B.C. (see vv. 8,11–12).

3:7 *her unfaithful sister Judah.* The southern kingdom (see vv. 8,10–11). Samaria (Israel's capital) and Jerusalem (Judah's capital) are similarly compared as adulterous sisters in Eze 23. *it.* Israel's adultery.

3:8 *certificate of divorce.* See v. 1 and note; see also Dt 24:1–4; Isa 50:1 and notes. *sent her away.* Into exile in 721 B.C. *Judah had no fear.* She refused to learn from Israel's tragic experience.

3:9 *committed adultery with stone and wood.* Worshiped pagan deities (see notes on 2:27; Ex 34:15).

3:10 *in pretense.* Judah's response to Josiah's reform measures (see note on 1:2) was superficial and hypocritical.

3:11 *Israel is more righteous than ... Judah.* See note on v. 8; see also Eze 16:51–52; 23:11.

3:12 *Go, proclaim.* See 2:2. *north.* Assyria's northern provinces, to which many Israelites had been exiled. *Return.* Repent (see v. 13). *merciful.* The Hebrew for this word is used of God elsewhere only in Ps 145:13,17, where it is translated "loving." *not be angry forever.* See note on v. 5.

3:13 *scattered your favors.* See Eze 16:15,33–34 and note on 16:33. *foreign gods.* See note on 2:25. *under every spreading tree.* See note on 2:20.

3:14 *husband.* See 31:32; Hos 2:16–17. The Hebrew root underlying this word is *ba'al.* Instead of allowing God to be their husband, his people followed "the Baals" (2:23; see note on Jdg 2:11). *one ... two.* A remnant will return (see note on Isa 10:20–22). *Zion.* Jerusalem.

3:15 See 23:4. *shepherds.* Rulers (see note on 2:8). *after my own heart.* Like David (see 1Sa 13:14; see also Eze 34:23; Hos 3:5).

3:16 *In those days.* In the days of the Messiah (see v. 18; 31:29). *numbers have increased.* See 23:3; Eze 36:11. For the fuller meaning of the Hebrew underlying this phrase see note on Ge 1:28. *nor will another one be made.* The ark of the covenant, formerly symbolizing God's royal presence (see 1Sa 4:3 and NIV text note), will be irrelevant when the Messiah comes.

3:17 *Throne.* The Lord sat "enthroned between the cherubim" above the ark (see 1Sa 4:4 and note), but Jerusa-

No longer will they follow the stubbornness of their evil hearts.[d] 18In those days
the house of Judah will join the house of
Israel,[e] and together[f] they will come from
a northern[g] land to the land[h] I gave your
forefathers as an inheritance.

19"I myself said,

" 'How gladly would I treat you like
sons
and give you a desirable land,[i]
the most beautiful inheritance[j] of
any nation.'
I thought you would call me 'Father'[k]
and not turn away from following
me.
20But like a woman unfaithful to her
husband,
so you have been unfaithful[l] to me,
O house of Israel,"
declares the LORD.

21A cry is heard on the barren heights,[m]
the weeping[n] and pleading of the
people of Israel,
because they have perverted their ways
and have forgotten[o] the LORD their
God.

22"Return,[p] faithless people;
I will cure[q] you of backsliding."[r]

"Yes, we will come to you,
for you are the LORD our God.
23Surely the ⌊idolatrous⌋ commotion on
the hills[s]
and mountains is a deception;
surely in the LORD our God
is the salvation[t] of Israel.
24From our youth shameful[u] gods have
consumed
the fruits of our fathers' labor—

3:17 [d]Ps 81:12; Jer 7:24; 9:14; 11:8; 13:10; 16:12; 18:12 **3:18** [e]Jer 30:3; Eze 37:19 [f]S Isa 11:13; Jer 50:4 [g]Jer 16:15; 31:8 [h]Dt 31:7; S Isa 14:1; Eze 11:17; 37:22; Am 9:15 **3:19** [i]S Dt 8:7 [j]Ps 106:24; Eze 20:6 [k]S ver 4; S Ex 4:22; S 2Sa 7:14 **3:20** [l]S Isa 24:16 **3:21** [m]ver 2 [n]Jer 31:18 [o]S Isa 57:11 **3:22** [p]S ver 12; S Job 22:23 [q]S Isa 30:26; 57:18; Jer 33:6; Hos 6:1 [r]S Jer 2:19 **3:23** [s]S Jer 2:20 [t]Ps 3:8; Jer 17:14 **3:24** [u]Jer 11:13; Hos 9:10 **3:25** [v]S Ezr 9:6; Jer 31:19; Da 9:7 [w]S Jdg 10:10; S 1Ki 8:47 [x]Jer 14:20 [y]S Ps 25:7; S Jer 22:21 [z]S ver 13; Eze 2:3 **4:1** [a]S Dt 4:30; S 2Ki 17:13; S Hos 12:6 [b]S 2Ki 21:4; Jer 16:18; 35:15; Eze 8:5 **4:2** [c]Dt 10:20; S Isa 19:18; 65:16 [d]S Nu 14:21; Jer 5:2; 12:16; 44:26; Hos 4:15 [e]S Ge 12:2; Gal 3:8 [f]Jer 9:24 **4:3** [g]Hos 10:12 [h]Mk 4:18

their flocks and herds,
their sons and daughters.
25Let us lie down in our shame,[v]
and let our disgrace cover us.
We have sinned[w] against the LORD our
God,
both we and our fathers;[x]
from our youth[y] till this day
we have not obeyed[z] the LORD our
God."

4 "If you will return[a], O Israel,
return to me,"
declares the LORD.
"If you put your detestable idols[b] out
of my sight
and no longer go astray,
2and if in a truthful, just and righteous
way
you swear,[c] 'As surely as the LORD
lives,'[d]
then the nations will be blessed[e] by
him
and in him they will glory.[f]"

3This is what the LORD says to the men
of Judah and to Jerusalem:

"Break up your unplowed ground[g]
and do not sow among thorns.[h]
4Circumcise yourselves to the LORD,
circumcise your hearts,[i]
you men of Judah and people of
Jerusalem,
or my wrath[j] will break out and burn
like fire[k]
because of the evil[l] you have
done—
burn with no one to quench[m] it.

4:4 [i]S Lev 26:41 [j]Zep 1:18; 2:2 [k]S Job 41:21 [l]S Ex 32:22 [m]Isa 1:31; Am 5:6

lem itself would someday be his throne. *all nations will gather.* See Zec 2:11; see also note on Isa 2:2–4. *they.* Israel. *follow the stubbornness of their evil hearts.* A stock phrase referring to Israel's disobedience and often involving the worship of pagan gods (see 9:14; 11:8; 13:10; 16:12; 18:12; 23:17).

3:18 *Judah will join ... Israel.* In the Messianic age God's divided people will again be united (see, e.g., 31:31; Isa 11:12; Eze 37:15–23; Hos 1:11). *northern land.* Where they had been exiles (see note on v. 12; see also 31:8). *land I gave ... as an inheritance.* See note on 2:7.

3:19 *sons.* Israel was the Lord's firstborn (see Ex 4:22; cf. Hos 11:1). *desirable land.* Or "pleasant land," as in Ps 106:24; Zec 7:14. *beautiful inheritance.* Judah, Jerusalem, the people themselves—ideally, all were beautiful in God's eyes (see 6:2; 11:16). *Father.* See note on v. 4.

3:20 A concise summary of the story told in Hos 1–3 (see note on Ex 34:15).

3:21 *barren heights.* See note on v. 2. *weeping and pleading.* A description of repentance, verbalized in vv. 22b–25. *forgotten.* See note on 2:32.

3:22 See v. 14. *Return, faithless ... backsliding.* Each of these three words is derived from the same Hebrew root, producing a striking series of puns. *I will cure you.* See 30:17; 33:6; Hos 6:1; 14:4. *Yes.* The people's repentance begins.

3:23 *commotion.* See, e.g., 1Ki 18:25–29. *in the LORD ... is ... salvation.* See Ge 49:18; Ps 3:8; Jnh 2:9 and note.

3:24 *our youth.* The period of the judges. *shameful gods.* See notes on 2:26; 11:13. *consumed the fruits.* False worship was costly for Israel, both economically and spiritually. *sons and daughters.* Often sacrificed to pagan gods (see note on 7:31).

3:25 *shame.* The Hebrew for this word is the same as that for "shameful gods" in v. 24—a pointed wordplay.

4:2 *truthful, just and righteous.* The piling up of qualifying words underscores the need for repentance that is sincere and not perfunctory. *As surely as the LORD lives.* See Dt 6:13 and note. *nations will be blessed by him.* Reflects the language of the seventh of God's great promises to Abram (see Ge 12:2–3 and note). Israel's repentance is a necessary precondition for the ultimate blessing of the nations.

4:3 *Break up your unplowed ground.* Probably quoted from Hos 10:12. *do not sow among thorns.* See Mt 13:7,22. Openness to the Lord's overtures is necessary, as is total commitment to him (see Eze 18:31).

4:4 *circumcise your hearts.* Consecrate your hearts (see 6:10 and NIV text note; 9:26; see also Ge 17:10 and note; Dt 10:16; 30:6; cf. Ro 2:29 and note; 1Co 7:19; Col 2:11). *wrath will ... burn with no one to quench it.* See 21:12; see also Isa 1:31; Am 5:6 and note. *because of the evil you have done.* Probably quoted from Dt 28:20.

Disaster From the North

[5]"Announce in Judah and proclaim[n] in
Jerusalem and say:
'Sound the trumpet[o] throughout the
land!'
Cry aloud and say:
'Gather together!
Let us flee to the fortified cities!'[p]
6Raise the signal[q] to go to Zion!
Flee for safety without delay!
For I am bringing disaster[r] from the
north,[s]
even terrible destruction."

7A lion[t] has come out of his lair;[u]
a destroyer[v] of nations has set out.
He has left his place
to lay waste[w] your land.
Your towns will lie in ruins[x]
without inhabitant.
8So put on sackcloth,[y]
lament[z] and wail,
for the fierce anger[a] of the LORD
has not turned away from us.

9"In that day," declares the LORD,
"the king and the officials will lose
heart,[b]
the priests will be horrified,
and the prophets will be appalled."[c]

10Then I said, "Ah, Sovereign LORD, how
completely you have deceived[d] this people
and Jerusalem by saying, 'You will have
peace,'[e] when the sword is at our throats."
11At that time this people and Jerusalem
will be told, "A scorching wind[f] from the
barren heights in the desert blows toward
my people, but not to winnow or cleanse;
12a wind[g] too strong for that comes from
me.[a] Now I pronounce my judgments[h]
against them."

13Look! He advances like the clouds,[i]
his chariots[j] come like a whirlwind,[k]
his horses[l] are swifter than eagles.[m]
Woe to us! We are ruined![n]
14O Jerusalem, wash[o] the evil from your
heart and be saved.[p]
How long[q] will you harbor wicked
thoughts?
15A voice is announcing from Dan,[r]
proclaiming disaster from the hills of
Ephraim.[s]
16"Tell this to the nations,
proclaim it to Jerusalem:
'A besieging army is coming from a
distant land,[t]
raising a war cry[u] against the cities
of Judah.[v]
17They surround[w] her like men guarding
a field,
because she has rebelled[x] against
me,'"
declares the LORD.
18"Your own conduct and actions[y]
have brought this upon you.[z]
This is your punishment.
How bitter[a] it is!
How it pierces to the heart!"

19Oh, my anguish, my anguish![b]
I writhe in pain.[c]

[a] 12 Or *comes at my command*

4:5 [n]Jer 5:20; 11:2,6 [o]S ver 21; S Nu 10:2, 7; S Job 39:24 [p]S Jos 10:20 **4:6** [q]ver 21; Ps 74:4; S Isa 11:10; 31:9; Jer 50:2 [r]Jer 11:11; 18:11 [s]S Isa 14:31; Jer 50:3 **4:7** [t]S 2Ki 24:1; S Jer 2:15 [u]Jer 25:38; Hos 5:14; 13:7; Na 2:12 [v]Jer 6:26; 15:8; 22:7; 48:8; 51:1,53; Eze 21:31; 25:7 [w]S Isa 1:7; Eze 12:20 [x]ver 29; S Lev 26:31; S Isa 6:11 **4:8** [y]1Ki 21:27; S Isa 3:24; Jer 6:26; Eze 7:18; Joel 1:8 [z]Jer 7:29; 9:20; Am 5:1 [a]S Isa 10:4; S Jer 30:24 **4:9** [b]S 1Sa 17:32 [c]S Isa 29:9 **4:10** [d]S Ex 5:23; 2Th 2:11 [e]Isa 30:10; Jer 6:14; 8:11; 14:13; 23:17; Eze 13:10; Mic 3:5; 1Th 5:3 **4:11** [f]S Ge 41:6; S Lev 26:33; S Job 1:19 **4:12** [g]S Isa 64:6 [h]Jer 1:16 **4:13** [i]S 2Sa 22:10; Isa 19:1 [j]Isa 66:15; Eze 26:10; Na 2:4 [k]S 2Ki 2:1 [l]Hab 3:8 [m]S Dt 28:49; Hab 1:8 [n]ver 20, 27; Isa 6:11; 24:3; Jer 7:34; 9:11, 19; 12:11; 25:11; 44:6; Mic 2:4 **4:14** [o]S Ru 3:3; S Ps 51:2; Jas 4:8 [p]Isa 45:22 [q]S Ps 6:3 **4:15** [r]S Ge 30:6 [s]Jer 31:6 **4:16** [t]S Dt 28:49 [u]ver 19; Eze 21:22 [v]S Jer 1:15 **4:17** [w]S 2Ki 25:1, 4 [x]S 1Sa 12:15; Jer 5:23 **4:18** [y]Ps 107:17; S Isa 1:28; Jer 5:25 [z]Jer 2:17 [a]Jer 2:19 **4:19** [b]Isa 22:4; Jer 6:24; 9:10; La 1:20 [c]S Job 6:10; S 14:22; Jer 10:19

4:5–31 The invaders from the north will bring God's judgment against his unrepentant people (see ch. 6).
4:5 *Sound the trumpet.* To warn of impending doom (see 6:1; see also note on Joel 2:1). *flee to the fortified cities.* See v. 6. To avoid capture by hostile troops, people living in the countryside would take refuge in the nearest walled town (see 5:17; 8:14; 34:7; 48:18).
4:6 See 6:1. *Raise the signal.* See note on Isa 5:26. *disaster from the north.* See 1:14; 6:22; the Babylonians (see 25:9; Isa 41:25 and notes). *terrible destruction.* See 6:1; cf. 48:3; 50:22; 51:54.
4:7 *lion.* A symbol of Babylonia (see note on 2:15). *destroyer.* Usually refers to Babylonia (6:26; 15:8; 48:8,32), but in 51:1,56 it refers to Persia and her allies (see 51:48,53). *towns ... without inhabitant.* See note on 2:15; see also v. 25; 46:19.
4:8 *sackcloth.* See notes on Ge 37:34; Rev 11:3. *anger ... has not turned away.* Contrast 2:35.
4:9 *In that day.* See note on Isa 2:11,17,20. *king ... officials ... priests ... prophets.* See note on 1:18.
4:10 *you have deceived.* Not directly, but through false prophets (see, e.g., 1Ki 22:20–23 and note on 22:23). *You will have peace.* Here the words of false prophets, not of God (see 14:13; 23:17; see also 6:13–14; 8:10–11). *throats.* The Hebrew for this word is usually translated "soul" or "life," but originally it had the meaning "throat, neck" (see, e.g., Ps 69:1).
4:11 *scorching wind.* The sirocco or khamsin, a hot, dry wind that brings sand and dust (see Ps 11:6; Isa 11:15; Jnh 4:8). *winnow.* See note on Ru 1:22.
4:12 *too strong for that.* Neither winnowing (separating grain from chaff) nor cleansing (blowing dust from the grain), God's judgments will sweep away good and bad alike.
4:13 *advances like the clouds.* Cf. Eze 38:16. *chariots ... like a whirlwind.* See 2Ki 2:11; 6:17; Ps 68:17; Isa 66:15. *horses are swifter than eagles.* See Hab 1:8, where the Babylonians (Hab 1:6) use horses that are "swifter than leopards" and employ cavalry that "fly like a vulture" (or "eagle," as here; see also Dt 28:49). *ruined.* See v. 20; 9:19; 48:1.
4:14 *Jerusalem.* As the royal city of Judah and the most important metropolis of the nation, Jerusalem is addressed as representative of the nation. *wash.* See 2:22 and note. *wicked thoughts.* Against other people (see Pr 6:18; Isa 59:7).
4:15 *Dan.* On the northern border of Israel (see 8:16). *Ephraim.* A few miles north of Jerusalem. In the mind's eye of the prophet, the enemy is making fearfully rapid progress toward the holy city.
4:16 *besieging army.* See Isa 1:8. *distant land.* Babylon. *raising a war cry.* A verbal link with 2:15, where the Hebrew for this phrase is translated "growled."
4:17 *surround her.* See 1:15.
4:19–26 A brief personal interlude, broken only by the divine complaint in v. 22. Jeremiah voices his agony at the approaching destruction of his beloved land and its people.
4:19 See 10:19–20. *anguish.* Often associated with labor pangs, as here (see 6:24; 49:24; 50:43). *heart pounds.* See Job

Oh, the agony of my heart!
My heart pounds[d] within me,
I cannot keep silent.[e]
For I have heard the sound of the
trumpet;[f]
I have heard the battle cry.[g]
20 Disaster follows disaster;[h]
the whole land lies in ruins.[i]
In an instant my tents[j] are destroyed,
my shelter in a moment.
21 How long must I see the battle
standard[k]
and hear the sound of the
trumpet?[l]

22 "My people are fools;[m]
they do not know me.[n]
They are senseless children;
they have no understanding.[o]
They are skilled in doing evil;[p]
they know not how to do good."[q]

23 I looked at the earth,
and it was formless and empty;[r]
and at the heavens,
and their light[s] was gone.
24 I looked at the mountains,
and they were quaking;[t]
all the hills were swaying.
25 I looked, and there were no people;
every bird in the sky had flown
away.[u]
26 I looked, and the fruitful land was a
desert;[v]
all its towns lay in ruins[w]
before the LORD, before his fierce
anger.[x]

27 This is what the LORD says:

"The whole land will be ruined,[y]
though I will not destroy[z] it
completely.
28 Therefore the earth will mourn[a]
and the heavens above grow dark,[b]
because I have spoken and will not
relent,[c]
I have decided and will not turn
back."[d]

29 At the sound of horsemen and
archers[e]
every town takes to flight.[f]
Some go into the thickets;
some climb up among the rocks.[g]
All the towns are deserted;[h]
no one lives in them.

30 What are you doing,[i] O devastated
one?
Why dress yourself in scarlet
and put on jewels[j] of gold?
Why shade your eyes with paint?[k]
You adorn yourself in vain.
Your lovers[l] despise you;
they seek your life.[m]

31 I hear a cry as of a woman in labor,[n]
a groan as of one bearing her first
child—
the cry of the Daughter of Zion[o]
gasping for breath,[p]
stretching out her hands[q] and
saying,
"Alas! I am fainting;
my life is given over to murderers."[r]

4:19 [d]S Job 37:1; Jer 23:9 [e]S Job 4:2; Jer 20:9 [f]S ver 21; S Nu 10:2; S Job 39:24 [g]S ver 16; Nu 10:9; Jer 49:2; Zep 1:16 **4:20** [h]S Dt 31:17 [i]S ver 13 [j]S Nu 24:5; Jer 10:20; La 2:4 **4:21** [k]S ver 6; S Nu 2:2; S Isa 18:3 [l]ver 5, 19; S Jos 6:20; Jer 6:1; Hos 5:8; Am 3:6; Zep 1:16 **4:22** [m]Jer 5:21; 10:8 [n]S Isa 1:3; 27:11; Jer 2:8; 8:7; Hos 5:4; 6:6 [o]S Ps 14:4; S 53:2 [p]Jer 13:23; S 1Co 14:20 [q]S Ps 36:3 **4:23** [r]S Ge 1:2 [s]ver 28; S Job 9:7; 30:26; S Isa 5:30; 59:9; La 3:2 **4:24** [t]S Ex 19:18; S Job 9:6 **4:25** [u]Jer 7:20; 9:10; 12:4; Hos 4:3; Zep 1:3 **4:26** [v]S Ge 13:10; Jer 12:4; 23:10 [w]S Isa 6:11 [x]Jer 12:13; 25:38 **4:27** [y]S ver 13 [z]S Lev 26:44; Jer 5:10, 18; 12:12; 30:11; 46:28; Eze 20:17; Am 9:8 **4:28** [a]Jer 12:4, 11; 14:2; Hos 4:3 [b]S ver 23 [c]S Nu 23:19 [d]ver 8; Jer 23:20; 30:24 **4:29** [e]S ver 13; Jer 6:23; 8:16 [f]2Ki 25:4 [g]S Ex 33:22; S 1Sa 26:20 [h]S ver 7; S Isa 6:12 **4:30** [i]Isa 10:3-4 [j]Eze 16:11; 23:40 [k]S 2Ki 9:30 [l]Job 19:14; La 1:2; Eze 23:9, 22 [m]S Ps 35:4 **4:31** [n]S Ge 3:16; Jer 6:24; 13:21; 22:23; 30:6; Mic 4:10 [o]S Ps 9:14 [p]Isa 42:14 [q]Isa 1:15; La 1:17 [r]S Dt 32:25; La 2:21

37:1; Ps 38:10; Hab 3:16. *sound of the trumpet.* See note on v. 5.
4:20 *lies in ruins.* See v. 13; 9:19; 48:1. *shelter.* Lit. "tent curtains" (as in Isa 54:2), usually made of goat hair (see Ex 26:7) and therefore strong enough to protect from cold and rain (see 10:20).
4:21 *battle standard ... sound of the trumpet.* See notes on vv. 5–6.
4:22 The Lord speaks. *fools.* See NIV text note on Pr 1:7. *do not know me.* See 2:8. Leaders and people alike had committed the ultimate sin (see Isa 1:2–3; Hos 4:1). *senseless.* See 5:21; 10:8,14,21; 51:17. *skilled in doing evil.* See Mic 7:3. *know not how to do good.* See Ps 14:1–3 and note on 14:1.
4:23–26 The striking repetition of "I looked" at the beginning of each verse ties this poem together and underscores its visionary character, as the prophet sees his beloved land in ruins after the Babylonian onslaught. God's creating acts have been, as it were, reversed.
4:23 *formless and empty.* The phrase occurs elsewhere only in Ge 1:2 (see note there). In Jeremiah's vision, the primeval chaos has returned. *light was gone.* Contrast Ge 1:3.
4:24 See Na 1:5.
4:25 *there were no people.* The Hebrew underlying this phrase occurs elsewhere only in Ge 2:5, where it is translated "there was no man." Again, uncreation has replaced creation.
4:26 *fruitful land.* See note on 2:7. *fierce anger.* See v. 8; Isa 13:13; Na 1:6.
4:27 *not destroy it completely.* See 5:10,18; 30:11; 46:28. God's mercy tempers the total judgment envisioned by Jeremiah in vv. 23–26.
4:28 *will not relent.* Unless his people repent (see 18:7–10 and note).
4:29 *archers.* Babylonia's evil deeds against Judah will someday recoil on her (see 50:29). *Some go.* See Jdg 6:2; 1Sa 13:6; Isa 2:19,21. Even people living in fortified towns feel unsafe. *deserted.* Contrast Isa 62:4.
4:30 *you ... yourself.* All the second-person pronouns in this verse represent feminine pronouns or verbs in Hebrew, indicating that Jerusalem is being addressed (see v. 14 and note). She is here portrayed as an adulterous wife trying to allure her lovers. *paint.* Antimony, a black powder used to enlarge the eyes and make them more attractive (see 2Ki 9:30; Eze 23:40). *lovers.* The Hebrew root underlying this word is found elsewhere only in Eze 23:5,7,9,12,16,20, where it is used of Samaria and Jerusalem, the adulterous sisters (see notes on Jer 2:25; 3:1,7) who "lusted" after foreign nations and their gods. *seek your life.* They are intent only on murdering you (see v. 31).
4:31 *woman in labor.* See 6:24; 13:21; 22:23; 30:6; 31:8; 48:41; 49:22,24; 50:43; see also v. 19; Isa 13:8 and notes. *Daughter of Zion.* A personification of Jerusalem (see note on 2Ki 19:21). *stretching out her hands.* In prayer for help (see Job 11:13).

Not One Is Upright

5 "Go up and down[s] the streets of
Jerusalem,
look around and consider,[t]
search through her squares.
If you can find but one person[u]
who deals honestly[v] and seeks the
truth,
I will forgive[w] this city.
2 Although they say, 'As surely as the
LORD lives,'[x]
still they are swearing falsely.[y]"
3 O LORD, do not your eyes[z] look for truth?
You struck[a] them, but they felt no
pain;
you crushed them, but they refused
correction.[b]
They made their faces harder than
stone[c]
and refused to repent.[d]
4 I thought, "These are only the poor;
they are foolish,[e]
for they do not know[f] the way of the
LORD,
the requirements of their God.
5 So I will go to the leaders[g]
and speak to them;
surely they know the way of the LORD,
the requirements of their God."
But with one accord they too had
broken off the yoke
and torn off the bonds.[h]
6 Therefore a lion from the forest[i] will
attack them,
a wolf from the desert will ravage[j]
them,
a leopard[k] will lie in wait near their
towns
to tear to pieces any who venture out,
for their rebellion is great
and their backslidings many.[l]

5:1 [s]2Ch 16:9; Eze 22:30 [t]Ps 45:10 [u]Ge 18:32; S Jer 2:29 [v]ver 31; Jer 14:14; Eze 13:6 [w]S Ge 18:24 **5:2** [x]S Jer 4:2 [y]S Lev 19:12 **5:3** [z]2Ch 16:9 [a]S Isa 9:13 [b]S Lev 26:23 [c]Jer 7:26; 19:15; Eze 3:8-9; 36:26; Zec 7:12 [d]S 2Ch 28:22; S Isa 1:5; Eze 2:4-5; Am 4:6; Zec 7:11 **5:4** [e]S ver 21; S Jer 4:22 [f]S Pr 10:21; S Isa 1:3 **5:5** [g]Mic 3:1,9 [h]S Jer 2:20 **5:6** [i]S Ps 17:12 [j]S Lev 26:22 [k]Hos 13:7 [l]Jer 14:7; 30:14

5:7 [m]S Jos 23:7 [n]Dt 32:21; Jer 2:11; 16:20; Gal 4:8 [o]S Nu 25:1 [p]Jer 13:27 **5:8** [q]Jer 29:23; Eze 22:11; 33:26 **5:9** [r]ver 29; Jer 9:9 [s]S Isa 57:6 **5:10** [t]S Jer 4:27; Am 9:8 **5:11** [u]S 1Ki 19:10; S Ps 73:27; S Isa 24:16 **5:12** [v]Isa 28:15 [w]Jer 23:17 [x]Jer 14:13; 27:8 **5:13** [y]Jer 14:15 [z]S 2Ch 36:16; S Job 6:26 **5:14** [a]Hos 6:5 [b]S Ps 39:3; Jer 23:29 [c]S Isa 1:31

7 "Why should I forgive you?
Your children have forsaken me
and sworn[m] by gods that are not
gods.[n]
I supplied all their needs,
yet they committed adultery[o]
and thronged to the houses of
prostitutes.[p]
8 They are well-fed, lusty stallions,
each neighing for another man's
wife.[q]
9 Should I not punish them for this?"[r]
declares the LORD.
"Should I not avenge[s] myself
on such a nation as this?
10 "Go through her vineyards and ravage
them,
but do not destroy them completely.[t]
Strip off her branches,
for these people do not belong to the
LORD.
11 The house of Israel and the house of
Judah
have been utterly unfaithful[u] to me,"
declares the LORD.
12 They have lied[v] about the LORD;
they said, "He will do nothing!
No harm will come to us;[w]
we will never see sword or famine.[x]
13 The prophets[y] are but wind[z]
and the word is not in them;
so let what they say be done to
them."

14 Therefore this is what the LORD God
Almighty says:

"Because the people have spoken these
words,
I will make my words in your
mouth[a] a fire[b]
and these people the wood it
consumes.[c]

5:1–31 Jeremiah resumes his vivid description of the wickedness of the people of Judah and Jerusalem.
5:1 See Zep 1:12. The Lord challenges anyone to find just one righteous person in Israel—a rhetorical way of charging that corruption pervaded the city (see Ps 14:1–3; Isa 64:6–7; Hos 4:1–2; Mic 7:2). *If you can find ... I will forgive.* See Ge 18:26–32.
5:2 *As surely as the LORD lives.* See 4:2 and note. *they are swearing falsely.* In violation of Lev 19:12 (see note on Ex 20:7). The Hebrew underlying this phrase is translated "commit ... perjury" in 7:9 (see NIV text note there).
5:3 *refused correction.* See 2:30. *made their faces harder than stone.* A striking portrayal of rebellion (see Eze 3:7–9).
5:4 *poor.* Concerned about basic physical needs (cf. 39:10; 40:7), they are uninformed about God's word and way. *foolish.* See 4:22; see also Nu 12:11 and NIV text note on Pr 1:7. *do not know ... requirements of their God.* They are more ignorant than the birds of the heavens (see 8:7).
5:5 *leaders.* Lit. "great ones." Although possessing every advantage, they were no more righteous than the poorest of the common people. *broken ... bonds.* See note on 2:20.
5:6 *lion ... wolf ... leopard.* See Lev 26:22; Eze 14:15; cf. 2Ki 17:25–26. *backslidings.* See 2:19 and note; 3:22; 14:7.
5:7 *Why should I forgive you?* See v. 1. *Your children.* Jerusalem is depicted as the mother city of the nation. *gods that are not gods.* Idols (see 2:11). *I supplied ... yet they.* See Dt 32:15–16; Hos 2:8. *committed adultery.* See 2:25 and note.
5:8 *lusty stallions.* See 13:27; 50:11; Eze 23:20.
5:9 *Should I not punish ... such a nation as this?* Repeated in v. 29; 9:9.
5:10 *Go.* Addressed to Israel's enemies (see v. 15). *vineyards.* Vines and vineyards are often symbolic of Israel (see notes on 2:21; Isa 5:1). *not destroy them completely.* See v. 18; see also note on 4:27. *Strip off her branches.* See Isa 18:5; Jn 15:2,6. *these people do not belong to the LORD.* See Hos 1:9.
5:11 See note on 3:7.
5:12 *He will do nothing.* Either good or bad (see Ps 10:11 and note; Zep 1:12). *sword or famine.* Jeremiah introduces us to the first two elements of his characteristic triad: "sword, famine and plague" (see note on 14:12).
5:13 *prophets are but wind.* Like images of false gods (see Isa 41:29). *let what they say be done to them.* See note on 4:29; see also Ps 7:16; 54:5.
5:14 *my words in your mouth a fire.* In contrast to the total lack of God's word in the mouths of false prophets (v. 13). Cf. 2Ki 1:10–12. *consumes.* See note on Isa 1:31.

15 "O house of Israel," declares the LORD,
"I am bringing a distant nation[d]
against you—
an ancient and enduring nation,
a people whose language[e] you do
not know,
whose speech you do not
understand.
16 Their quivers[f] are like an open grave;
all of them are mighty warriors.
17 They will devour[g h] your harvests and
food,
devour[i j] your sons and daughters;
they will devour[k] your flocks and
herds,
devour your vines and fig trees.[l]
With the sword[m] they will destroy
the fortified cities[n] in which you
trust.[o]

18 "Yet even in those days," declares the
LORD, "I will not destroy[p] you completely.
19 And when the people ask,[q] 'Why has the
LORD our God done all this to us?' you will
tell them, 'As you have forsaken me and
served foreign gods[r] in your own land, so
now you will serve foreigners[s] in a land
not your own.'

20 "Announce this to the house of Jacob
and proclaim[t] it in Judah:
21 Hear this, you foolish and senseless
people,[u]
who have eyes[v] but do not see,
who have ears but do not hear:[w]
22 Should you not fear[x] me?" declares the
LORD.
"Should you not tremble[y] in my
presence?
I made the sand a boundary for the
sea,[z]
an everlasting barrier it cannot cross.
The waves may roll, but they cannot
prevail;
they may roar,[a] but they cannot
cross it.
23 But these people have stubborn and
rebellious[b] hearts;
they have turned aside[c] and gone
away.
24 They do not say to themselves,
'Let us fear[d] the LORD our God,
who gives autumn and spring rains[e]
in season,
who assures us of the regular weeks
of harvest.'[f]
25 Your wrongdoings have kept these
away;
your sins have deprived you of
good.[g]

26 "Among my people are wicked[h]
men
who lie in wait[i] like men who
snare birds
and like those who set traps[j] to
catch men.
27 Like cages full of birds,
their houses are full of deceit;[k]
they have become rich[l] and
powerful
28 and have grown fat[m] and sleek.
Their evil deeds have no limit;
they do not plead the case of the
fatherless[n] to win it,
they do not defend the rights of the
poor.[o]
29 Should I not punish them for this?"
declares the LORD.
"Should I not avenge[p] myself
on such a nation as this?

30 "A horrible[q] and shocking thing
has happened in the land:
31 The prophets prophesy lies,[r]
the priests[s] rule by their own
authority,
and my people love it this way.
But what will you do in the end?[t]

5:15 [d] S Dt 28:49; S 2Ki 24:2 [e] S Ge 11:7; S Isa 28:11 **5:16** [f] S Job 39:23 **5:17** [g] S Isa 1:7; Jer 8:16; 30:16 [h] Lev 26:16 [i] Jer 50:7,17 [j] Dt 28:32 [k] Dt 28:31 [l] S Nu 16:14; Jer 8:13; Hos 2:12 [m] S Lev 26:25 [n] S Jos 10:20 [o] Dt 28:33 **5:18** [p] S Jer 4:27 **5:19** [q] S Dt 4:28; S 1Ki 9:9 [r] S Jer 2:8; 15:14; 16:13; 17:4 [s] Dt 28:48 **5:20** [t] S Jer 4:5 **5:21** [u] ver 4; S Dt 32:6; S Jer 4:22; Hab 2:18 [v] Isa 6:10; Eze 12:2 [w] S Dt 29:4; S Isa 42:20; S Mt 13:15; Mk 8:18 **5:22** [x] S Dt 28:58 [y] S Job 4:14; S Isa 64:2 [z] S Ge 1:9 [a] S Ps 46:3 **5:23** [b] S Dt 21:18 [c] Ps 14:3 **5:24** [d] Dt 6:24 [e] S Lev 26:4; S 2Sa 1:21; Jas 5:7 [f] S Ge 8:22; Ac 14:17 **5:25** [g] Ps 84:11 **5:26** [h] S Mt 7:15 [i] S Ps 10:8 [j] Ecc 9:12; Jer 9:8; Hos 5:1; Mic 7:2 **5:27** [k] Jer 8:5; 9:6 [l] Jer 12:1 **5:28** [m] S Dt 32:15 [n] Zec 7:10 [o] Ex 22:21-24; S Ps 82:3; S Isa 1:23; Jer 7:6; Eze 16:49; Am 5:12 **5:29** [p] S Isa 57:6 **5:30** [q] ver 30-31; Jer 18:13; 23:14; Hos 6:10 **5:31** [r] S ver 1; Mic 2:11 [s] La 4:13 [t] Hos 9:5

5:15 *distant nation.* See note on 4:16. *ancient and enduring nation.* The history of Babylonia reached back 2,000 years and more. *whose language you do not know.* See Dt 28:49 and note.
5:16 *open grave.* Symbolizing insatiability, destruction and death (see Ps 5:9; Pr 30:15–16).
5:17 *devour your sons and daughters.* Either as sacrifices to pagan gods (see note on 3:24), or as casualties of war (see 10:25). *fortified cities in which you trust.* See note on 4:5; see also Dt 28:52.
5:18 See v. 10; see also note on 4:27.
5:21 *Hear this.* See note on 2:4. *foolish and senseless.* See 4:22; see also NIV text note on Pr 1:7. *who have eyes … do not hear.* See note on Isa 6:10; see also Dt 29:4; Ps 115:4–8; 135:15–18.
5:22 *fear me.* See note on Ge 20:11. *boundary for the sea.* See Job 38:8–11; Ps 104:6–9.
5:23 Though the sea never crosses its divinely appointed boundaries, God's people have violated the limits he has set for them.
5:24 *God, who gives.* See v. 7 and note. *autumn and spring rains.* See 3:3; see also note on Dt 11:14. *regular weeks of harvest.* Perhaps the seven weeks between Passover and the Feast of Weeks (see Lev 23:15–16).
5:26 *traps.* Lit. "destroyer" (see, e.g., Ex 12:23) or "destruction" (see, e.g., Eze 21:31). *men.* Innocent (see Isa 29:21), godly, upright people (see Mic 7:2).
5:27 *cages.* Traps woven of wicker; the Hebrew for this word is translated "basket" in Am 8:1–2. *deceit.* Riches gained through extortion and deception (see Hab 2:6).
5:28 *grown fat and sleek.* Symbolic of prosperity (see Dt 32:15; Jas 5:5 and note). *evil deeds have no limit.* See Ps 73:7. *they do not plead the case.* What the wicked will not do, God must do (see Dt 10:18)—and so must those who truly know and serve him (see 22:16; Jas 1:27).
5:29 Repeated from v. 9; see also 9:9.
5:31 See 1:18 and note. *prophesy lies.* See 20:6 (often, and arrogantly, in God's name; see 23:25; 27:15; 29:9). *my people love it this way.* See note on Am 4:5.

Jerusalem Under Siege

6 "Flee for safety, people of Benjamin!
Flee from Jerusalem!
Sound the trumpet[u] in Tekoa![v]
Raise the signal over Beth
Hakkerem![w]
For disaster looms out of the north,[x]
even terrible destruction.
2 I will destroy the Daughter of Zion,[y]
so beautiful and delicate.[z]
3 Shepherds[a] with their flocks will come
against her;
they will pitch their tents around[b]
her,
each tending his own portion."

4 "Prepare for battle against her!
Arise, let us attack at noon![c]
But, alas, the daylight is fading,
and the shadows of evening grow
long.
5 So arise, let us attack at night
and destroy her fortresses!"

6 This is what the LORD Almighty says:

"Cut down the trees[d]
and build siege ramps[e] against
Jerusalem.
This city must be punished;
it is filled with oppression.[f]
7 As a well pours out its water,
so she pours out her wickedness.
Violence[g] and destruction[h] resound in
her;
her sickness and wounds are ever
before me.
8 Take warning, O Jerusalem,
or I will turn away[i] from you
and make your land desolate
so no one can live in it."

9 This is what the LORD Almighty says:

"Let them glean the remnant[j] of Israel
as thoroughly as a vine;
pass your hand over the branches
again,
like one gathering grapes."

10 To whom can I speak and give
warning?
Who will listen[k] to me?
Their ears are closed[a][l]
so they cannot hear.[m]
The word[n] of the LORD is offensive to
them;
they find no pleasure in it.
11 But I am full of the wrath[o] of the LORD,
and I cannot hold it in.[p]

"Pour it out on the children in the
street
and on the young men[q] gathered
together;
both husband and wife will be caught
in it,
and the old, those weighed down
with years.[r]

[a] 10 Hebrew *uncircumcised*

6:1 [u] S Nu 10:7; S Jer 4:21 [v] 2Ch 11:6; Am 1:1 [w] Ne 3:14 [x] S Jer 4:6 **6:2** [y] S Ps 9:14 [z] La 4:5 **6:3** [a] Jer 12:10 [b] S 2Ki 25:4; Lk 19:43 **6:4** [c] Jer 15:8; 22:7 **6:6** [d] Dt 20:19-20 [e] S 2Sa 20:15; Jer 32:24; 52:4; Eze 26:8 [f] S Dt 28:33; Jer 25:38; Zep 3:1 **6:7** [g] S Ps 55:9; S Isa 58:4 [h] Jer 20:8 **6:8** [i] Eze 23:18 **6:9** [j] S Ge 45:7 **6:10** [k] Jer 7:13, 24; 35:15 [l] Jer 4:4; Ac 7:51 [m] S Isa 42:20 [n] Jer 15:10, 15; 20:8 **6:11** [o] Jer 7:20; 15:17 [p] Job 32:20; Jer 20:9 [q] S 2Ch 36:17; S Isa 40:30 [r] La 2:21

6:1 – 30 The prophet envisions the future Babylonian attack on Jerusalem.

6:1 The Lord speaks in vv. 1 – 3. Verse 1 is strongly reminiscent of 4:6 (see note there). But whereas in 4:6 the command was to seek protection in Jerusalem, in 6:1 the people are to flee from Jerusalem, because no place — not even the holy city itself — will be safe from the invader. *Benjamin.* The tribal territory bordering Judah north of Jerusalem. Jeremiah himself was from Benjamite territory (see 1:1). *Sound ... Tekoa.* In the Hebrew there is a play on these words. Tekoa was the hometown of Amos (see Introduction to Amos: Author). *Raise ... signal.* In the Hebrew there is a play on words, made possible by using a different Hebrew word (found also in Lachish Letter 4:10) for "signal" (caused by the smoke of a fire; see Jdg 20:38,40) than the one used in 4:6. *Beth Hakkerem.* Mentioned elsewhere only in Ne 3:14 (see note there). *disaster ... out of the north.* See 1:14 and note.
6:2 *Daughter of Zion.* A personification of Jerusalem (see note on 2Ki 19:21). *delicate.* Used to describe the city of Babylon in Isa 47:1.
6:3 See 1:15. *Shepherds with their flocks.* Rulers (see note on 2:8) with their troops. *pitch.* The Hebrew for this verb continues the pun on "Tekoa" in v. 1 (see note on v. 8). *each ... his own portion.* The Hebrew for this phrase is used similarly ("each ... his own place") in Nu 2:17. *tending.* Grazing or depasturing, and thus destroying.
6:4 The invaders speak in vv. 4 – 5. *Prepare for.* Lit. "Consecrate" (also in Joel 3:9; Mic 3:5). Since ancient battles had religious connotations, soldiers had to prepare themselves ritually as well as militarily (see Dt 20:2 – 4; 1Sa 21:4 and note). *at noon.* To take advantage of the element of surprise, since the usual time of attack was early in the morning (see, e.g., Jos 8:10,14).
6:5 *at night.* Since attacking soldiers normally retired for the night and resumed siege the following morning, the phrase underscores their eagerness and determination (see Jdg 7:19 and note).
6:6 The Lord addresses the Babylonian troops. *siege ramps.* To help them bring up battering rams and scale Jerusalem's walls (see 33:4). *oppression.* Against its own people (see note on Isa 30:12).
6:7 *sickness and wounds.* Jerusalem suffers from spiritual decay and disease (see v. 14; cf. Isa 1:5 – 6 and notes) and is not aware of it.
6:8 *Take warning.* The better part of wisdom (see v. 10; Ps 2:10). *turn away.* In sorrow, but also in disgust. The Hebrew for this phrase continues the pun on "Tekoa" in v. 1 (see note on v. 3). *desolate so no one can live in it.* See 22:6.
6:9 *glean.* See notes on Ru 2:2; Isa 17:5. *remnant.* See 11:23; 23:3; 31:7; 40:11,15; 42:2,15,19; 43:5; 44:7,12,14,28; 50:20; see also note on Isa 10:20 – 22. *thoroughly.* Stopping just short of complete destruction (see 4:27; 5:10,18; 30:11; 46:28). *vine.* Symbolic of Israel (see 2:21 and note; 5:10).
6:10 Jeremiah speaks. *give warning.* See note on v. 8. *ears are closed.* See NIV text note; see also 4:4 and note. The imagery of uncircumcised ears is found elsewhere only in Ac 7:51 (see note there).
6:11 The prophet speaks, then the Lord resumes his speech (through v. 23). *full of the wrath.* See 25:15 and note. *children ... young men ... husband and wife ... old.* All will be judged, from youngest to oldest (see v. 13). *in the street.* Where children play (see 9:21; Zec 8:5).

[12]Their houses will be turned over to
others,[s]
together with their fields and their
wives,[t]
when I stretch out my hand[u]
against those who live in the land,"
declares the LORD.
[13]"From the least to the greatest,
all[v] are greedy for gain;[w]
prophets and priests alike,
all practice deceit.[x]
[14]They dress the wound of my people
as though it were not serious.
'Peace, peace,' they say,
when there is no peace.[y]
[15]Are they ashamed of their loathsome
conduct?
No, they have no shame at all;
they do not even know how to
blush.[z]
So they will fall among the fallen;
they will be brought down when I
punish[a] them,"
says the LORD.

[16]This is what the LORD says:

"Stand at the crossroads and look;
ask for the ancient paths,[b]
ask where the good way[c] is, and walk
in it,
and you will find rest[d] for your
souls.
But you said, 'We will not walk
in it.'
[17]I appointed watchmen[e] over you and
said,
'Listen to the sound of the trumpet!'[f]
But you said, 'We will not listen.'[g]
[18]Therefore hear, O nations;
observe, O witnesses,
what will happen to them.
[19]Hear, O earth:[h]
I am bringing disaster[i] on this people,
the fruit of their schemes,[j]
because they have not listened to my
words[k]
and have rejected my law.[l]
[20]What do I care about incense from
Sheba[m]
or sweet calamus[n] from a distant
land?
Your burnt offerings are not
acceptable;[o]
your sacrifices[p] do not please me."[q]

[21]Therefore this is what the LORD says:

"I will put obstacles before this people.
Fathers and sons alike will stumble[r]
over them;
neighbors and friends will perish."

[22]This is what the LORD says:

"Look, an army is coming
from the land of the north;[s]
a great nation is being stirred up
from the ends of the earth.[t]
[23]They are armed with bow and spear;
they are cruel and show no mercy.[u]
They sound like the roaring sea[v]
as they ride on their horses;[w]
they come like men in battle formation
to attack you, O Daughter of Zion."[x]

[24]We have heard reports about them,
and our hands hang limp.[y]
Anguish[z] has gripped us,
pain like that of a woman in labor.[a]
[25]Do not go out to the fields
or walk on the roads,
for the enemy has a sword,
and there is terror on every side.[b]

6:12 [s]S Dt 28:30; Mic 2:4 [t]1Ki 11:4; Jer 8:10; 29:23; 38:22; 43:6; 44:9, 15 [u]Isa 5:25; Jer 21:5; 32:21; Eze 6:14; 35:3; Zep 1:4 **6:13** [v]S Jer 2:29 [w]S Isa 56:11 [x]La 4:13 **6:14** [y]S Isa 30:10; S Jer 4:10 **6:15** [z]Jer 3:3; 8:10-12; Mic 3:7; Zec 13:4 [a]2Ch 25:16; Jer 27:15 **6:16** [b]Jer 18:15 [c]S 1Ki 8:36; S Ps 119:3 [d]S Jos 1:13; S Isa 11:10; Mt 11:29 **6:17** [e]S Isa 52:8 [f]S Ex 20:18 [g]Jer 11:7-8; Eze 33:4; Zec 1:4 **6:19** [h]S Dt 4:26; Jer 22:29; Mic 1:2 [i]S Jos 23:15; Jer 11:11; 19:3 [j]Pr 1:31 [k]Jer 29:19 [l]Jer 8:9; Eze 20:13; Am 2:4 **6:20** [m]S Ge 10:7 [n]S Ex 30:23 [o]Am 5:22; Mal 1:9 [p]Ps 50:8-10; Jer 7:21; Mic 6:7-8 [q]S Isa 1:11; Jer 14:12; Hos 8:13; 9:4 **6:21** [r]S Lev 26:37; S Isa 8:14 **6:22** [s]S Jer 4:6 [t]S Dt 28:49 **6:23** [u]S Isa 13:18 [v]S Ps 18:4; S 93:3 [w]S Jer 4:29 [x]S Isa 10:32 **6:24** [y]Isa 13:7 [z]S Jer 4:19 [a]S Jer 4:31; 50:41-43 **6:25** [b]S Job 15:21; S Ps 31:13; Jer 49:29

6:12–15 Repeated almost verbatim in 8:10–12.
6:12 *houses . . . fields . . . wives.* Cf. Ex 20:17; Dt 5:21. *turned over to others.* As Dt 28:30 warned—one of the covenant curses. *stretch out my hand against.* To destroy (see 15:6).
6:13 See 1:18 and note.
6:14 *wound.* See note on v. 7. *Peace . . . when there is no peace.* A common message of false and greedy prophets (see Eze 13:10; Mic 3:5). The wicked, in any case, cannot expect to enjoy peace (Isa 48:22; 57:21).
6:16 *ancient paths.* The tried and true ways of Judah's godly ancestors (see 18:15; Dt 32:7). *walk in it.* See Isa 30:21. *you will find rest for your souls.* Quoted by Jesus in Mt 11:29 (see Isa 28:12; cf. Ps 119:165).
6:17 *watchmen.* True prophets (see Eze 3:17 and note; Hab 2:1). *sound of the trumpet.* To warn of approaching danger (see v. 1; see also note on Joel 2:1).
6:18 *hear, O nations.* See Mic 1:2.
6:19 *rejected my law.* Disobeyed the law of Moses (see 8:8–9).
6:20 *Sheba.* Located in southwestern Arabia, it was the center of the spice trade (see Isa 60:6 and note). *calamus.* See SS 4:14; Isa 43:24 and notes. The Hebrew for this word is translated "cane" in Ex 30:23; calamus, which probably came from India, was an ingredient in the sacred anointing oil (Ex 30:25). *burnt offerings are not acceptable.* The attitude of one's heart and the manner of one's life are far more important than the ritual of sacrifice (see note on Isa 1:11–15).
6:21 *obstacles.* The Babylonian invaders (see v. 22).
6:22–24 Repeated almost verbatim in 50:41–43.
6:22 *land of the north.* Babylonia (see 4:6; Isa 41:25 and notes). *from the ends of the earth.* See 25:32; 31:8.
6:23 *spear.* The Hebrew for this word is translated "javelin" in 1Sa 17:6. Another possibility is "sword," as attested in *The War of the Sons of Light against the Sons of Darkness,* one of the Dead Sea Scrolls (see essay, pp. 1452–1453). *like the roaring sea.* See Isa 5:30; see also Isa 17:12 and note. *horses.* See note on 4:13; see also 8:16. *Daughter of Zion.* See v. 2 and note.
6:24–26 The prophet speaks to, and on behalf of, the people of Judah.
6:24 *hands hang limp.* Courage fails (see 47:3; Isa 13:7 and notes). *Anguish.* See note on 4:19. *woman in labor.* See note on 4:31.
6:25 *terror on every side.* A favorite expression of Jeremiah (20:10; 46:5; 49:29; cf. La 2:22). The Hebrew for this phrase is used once as a proper name, "Magor-Missabib" (20:3; see NIV text note there).

26O my people, put on sackcloth[c]
and roll in ashes;[d]
mourn with bitter wailing[e]
as for an only son,[f]
for suddenly the destroyer[g]
will come upon us.
27"I have made you a tester[h] of metals
and my people the ore,
that you may observe
and test their ways.
28They are all hardened rebels,[i]
going about to slander.[j]
They are bronze and iron;[k]
they all act corruptly.
29The bellows blow fiercely
to burn away the lead with fire,
but the refining[l] goes on in vain;
the wicked are not purged out.
30They are called rejected silver,[m]
because the LORD has rejected them."[n]

False Religion Worthless

7 This is the word that came to Jeremiah
from the LORD: 2"Stand[o] at the gate of
the LORD's house and there proclaim this
message:
" 'Hear the word of the LORD, all you
people of Judah who come through these
gates to worship the LORD. 3This is what
the LORD Almighty, the God of Israel, says:
Reform your ways[p] and your actions, and
I will let you live[q] in this place. 4Do not
trust[r] in deceptive[s] words and say, "This
is the temple of the LORD, the temple of
the LORD, the temple of the LORD!" 5If you
really change[t] your ways and your actions
and deal with each other justly,[u] 6if you
do not oppress[v] the alien, the fatherless
or the widow and do not shed innocent
blood[w] in this place, and if you do not follow other gods[x] to your own harm, 7then I
will let you live in this place, in the land[y]
I gave your forefathers[z] for ever and ever.
8But look, you are trusting[a] in deceptive[b]
words that are worthless.
9" 'Will you steal[c] and murder,[d] commit
adultery[e] and perjury,[a][f] burn incense to
Baal[g][h] and follow other gods[i] you have
not known, 10and then come and stand[j]
before me in this house,[k] which bears my
Name, and say, "We are safe"—safe to
do all these detestable things?[l] 11Has this
house,[m] which bears my Name, become

[a] 9 Or *and swear by false gods*

6:26 [c]S Jer 4:8 [d]S Job 2:8; Jer 25:34; Eze 27:30; Jnh 3:6 [e]Jer 9:1; 18:22; 20:16; 25:36 [f]S Ge 21:16 [g]S Ex 12:23; S Jer 4:7 **6:27** [h]Jer 9:7; Zec 13:9 **6:28** [i]Jer 5:23 [j]S Lev 19:16 [k]Eze 22:18 **6:29** [l]Mal 3:3 **6:30** [m]Pr 17:3; Eze 22:18 [n]Ps 53:5; 119:119; Jer 7:29; La 5:22; Hos 9:17 **7:2** [o]Jer 17:19 **7:3** [p]Jer 18:11; 26:13; 35:15 [q]ver 7 **7:4** [r]S Job 15:31 [s]ver 8; Jer 28:15; Mic 3:11 **7:5** [t]ver 3; Jer 18:11; 26:13; 35:15 [u]S Ex 22:22; S Lev 25:17; S Isa 1:17 **7:6** [v]S Jer 5:28; Eze 22:7 [w]S 2Ki 21:16; Jer 2:34; 19:4; 22:3 [x]S Ex 20:3; S Dt 8:19 **7:7** [y]S Dt 4:40 [z]S Jos 1:6 **7:8** [a]S Job 15:31 [b]S ver 4 **7:9** [c]Ex 20:15 [d]Ex 20:13 [e]Ex 20:14; S Nu 25:1 [f]Ex 20:16; S Lev 19:12; Zec 8:17; Mal 3:5 [g]S Isa 1:13 [h]Jer 11:13, 17; 32:29 [i]S Ex 20:3; Hos 2:13 **7:10** [j]S Isa 48:1 [k]ver 30; 2Ki 21:4-5; Jer 23:11; 32:34; Eze 23:38-39 [l]Eze 33:25 **7:11** [m]Isa 56:7

6:26 *put on sackcloth.* See 4:8; see also note on Ge 37:34. *roll in ashes; mourn.* See Eze 27:30–31; cf. Mic 1:10. *only son.* A father's most precious possession (see Ge 22:12,16; Am 8:10; Zec 12:10; Ro 8:32). *destroyer.* Babylonia (see note on 4:7).

6:27–30 The Lord speaks to Jeremiah and appoints him to test the people of Judah as a refiner tests metals (see 9:7; Ps 12:6 and note; Isa 1:25; Mal 3:2–3).

6:27 *tester of metals.* See Job 23:10.

6:28 *going about to slander.* Contrary to Lev 19:16. *bronze and iron.* Base metals when compared to gold and silver. *act corruptly.* See Dt 31:29; Isa 1:4.

6:29 In ancient times, lead was added to silver ore in the refining process. When the crucible was heated, the lead oxidized and acted as a flux to remove the alloys. Here the process fails because the ore is not pure enough (cf. Eze 24:11–13).

6:30 *They are … rejected.* The "hardened rebels" (v. 28), the "wicked" (v. 29), have failed to pass the Lord's test. Nothing worthwhile can be made of them.

7:1—10:25 A series of temple messages delivered by Jeremiah, perhaps over a period of several years. Since 26:2–6,12–15 is very similar in content to ch. 7, it is possible that chs. 7–10 (or at least ch. 7) date to the reign of Jehoiakim (see 26:1). On the other hand, Jeremiah may have repeated various themes on several occasions during his lengthy ministry. In any event, nothing in chs. 7–10 is inappropriate to the time of King Josiah.

7:1—8:3 The straightforward narrative of this section asserts that Solomon's temple in Jerusalem will not escape the fate of the earlier sanctuary at Shiloh if the people of Judah persist in worshiping false gods.

7:1 *the word that came.* See 1:2 and note; 1:4,11,13; 2:1.

7:2 *gate.* In the wall between the inner and outer courts of the temple, perhaps the so-called New Gate (26:10; 36:10). *Hear.* See note on 2:4. *all you people … who come … to worship.* Perhaps during one of the three annual pilgrimage festivals (see Dt 16:16 and note). *gates.* Leading into the outer court.

7:3 *this place.* Used almost 30 times in Jeremiah to designate the land God had given them (see, e.g., v. 7; 14:13,15; 24:5–6).

7:4 *deceptive words.* Spoken by false prophets. The idea that God would not destroy Jerusalem simply because his dwelling, the temple, was located there was a delusion, fostered in part by the miraculous deliverance of the city during the reign of Hezekiah (see 2Ki 19:32–36; cf. 2Sa 7:11b–13; Ps 132:13–14). In the light of Judah's sinful rebellion against the Lord such an idea was "worthless" (v. 8; see Mic 3:11). *This is.* Lit. "They are," referring to the buildings that constituted the entire temple complex. *temple … temple … temple.* Vain and repetitious babbling (cf. Mt 6:7). Often such a threefold repeating of a word or phrase is for emphasis (see 22:29; see also note on Isa 6:3).

7:6 Rulers and people alike needed to hear and act on these prophetic words (see 22:2–3). *alien … fatherless … widow.* See Dt 16:11,14; 24:19–21; 26:12–13; 27:19; cf. Jas 1:27. *innocent blood.* See 19:4; 22:17; 26:15; see also the frightening example of King Manasseh (2Ki 21:16).

7:7 *land … for ever and ever.* See Ge 17:8 and note.

7:8 *deceptive words.* See note on v. 4.

7:9 This one verse mentions the violation of fully half of the Ten Commandments (cf. Hos 4:2 and note). *burn incense to Baal.* See note on 1:16. *follow other gods you have not known.* See 19:4. Tragically, such sins would be the cause of their exile to lands they had not known (see 9:14,16; 16:11,13).

7:10 *house, which bears my Name.* See vv. 11,14,30; 25:29; 32:34; 34:15; Dt 12:5 and note; 1Ki 8:16 and note; 2Ch 6:33; 20:9; Da 9:18. The "Name" of God is equivalent to his gracious presence in such passages (see vv. 12,15; see also note on Ps 5:11). *We are safe.* See 12:12. *detestable.* See 2:7; see also note on Lev 7:21.

7:11 Together with the last half of Isa 56:7, part of this verse is quoted by Jesus in Mt 21:13; Mk 11:17; Lk 19:46.

a den of robbers[n] to you? But I have been
watching![o] declares the LORD.
12“ ‘Go now to the place in Shiloh[p] where
I first made a dwelling[q] for my Name,[r] and
see what I did[s] to it because of the wickedness of my people Israel. 13While you were
doing all these things, declares the LORD, I
spoke[t] to you again and again,[u] but you did
not listen;[v] I called[w] you, but you did not
answer.[x] 14Therefore, what I did to Shiloh[y]
I will now do to the house that bears my
Name,[z] the temple[a] you trust in, the place I
gave to you and your fathers. 15I will thrust
you from my presence,[b] just as I did all
your brothers, the people of Ephraim.’[c]
16“So do not pray for this people nor offer any plea[d] or petition for them; do not
plead with me, for I will not listen[e] to you.
17Do you not see what they are doing in
the towns of Judah and in the streets of Jerusalem? 18The children gather wood, the
fathers light the fire, and the women knead
the dough and make cakes of bread for the
Queen of Heaven.[f] They pour out drink offerings[g] to other gods to provoke[h] me to
anger. 19But am I the one they are provoking?[i] declares the LORD. Are they not rather
harming themselves, to their own shame?[j]
20“ ‘Therefore this is what the Sovereign[k]
LORD says: My anger[l] and my wrath will
be poured[m] out on this place, on man and
beast, on the trees of the field and on the
fruit of the ground, and it will burn and
not be quenched.[n]

7:11 [n]Mt 21:13*; Mk 11:17*; Lk 19:46* [o]Ge 31:50; Jdg 11:10; Jer 29:23; 42:5 **7:12** [p]S Jos 18:1; S 1Sa 2:32 [q]S Ex 40:2; S Jos 18:10 [r]Da 9:18 [s]S 1Sa 4:10-11, 22; Ps 78:60-64 **7:13** [t]Ps 71:17; Isa 48:17; Jer 32:33 [u]S 2Ch 36:15 [v]S ver 26; S Isa 65:12 [w]S Pr 1:24 [x]Jer 35:17 **7:14** [y]S Jdg 18:31; S 1Sa 2:32 [z]S 1Ki 9:7 [a]ver 4; Eze 24:21 **7:15** [b]S Ge 4:14; S Ex 33:15; S 2Ki 17:20; Jer 23:39 [c]S Ps 78:67 **7:16** [d]S Ex 32:10; Dt 9:14; Jer 15:1 [e]S Nu 23:19 **7:18** [f]Jer 44:17-19 [g]S Isa 57:6 [h]S Dt 31:17; S 1Ki 14:9 **7:19** [i]Dt 32:21; Jer 44:3 [j]S Job 7:20; Jer 9:19; 20:11; 22:22 **7:20** [k]S Isa 30:15 [l]S Job 40:11; Jer 42:18;

21“ ‘This is what the LORD Almighty, the
God of Israel, says: Go ahead, add your
burnt offerings to your other sacrifices[o]
and eat[p] the meat yourselves! 22For when
I brought your forefathers out of Egypt and
spoke to them, I did not just give them
commands[q] about burnt offerings and sacrifices,[r] 23but I gave them this command:[s]
Obey[t] me, and I will be your God and you
will be my people.[u] Walk in all the ways[v]
I command you, that it may go well[w] with
you. 24But they did not listen[x] or pay attention;[y] instead, they followed the stubborn
inclinations of their evil hearts.[z] They
went backward[a] and not forward. 25From
the time your forefathers left Egypt until now, day after day, again and again[b] I
sent you my servants[c] the prophets.[d] 26But
they did not listen to me or pay attention.[e]
They were stiff-necked[f] and did more evil
than their forefathers.’[g]
27“When you tell[h] them all this, they
will not listen[i] to you; when you call to
them, they will not answer.[j] 28Therefore
say to them, ‘This is the nation that has
not obeyed the LORD its God or responded
to correction.[k] Truth[l] has perished; it has

La 2:3-5 [m]Jer 6:11-12; La 4:11 [n]S Isa 1:31; Jer 11:16; 13:14; 15:6, 14; 17:4, 27; Eze 20:47-48 **7:21** [o]S Jer 6:20; Am 5:21-22 [p]S 1Sa 2:12-17; Hos 8:13 **7:22** [q]Isa 43:23 [r]S 1Sa 15:22 **7:23** [s]1Jn 3:23 [t]S Ex 19:5 [u]S Lev 26:12; S Isa 51:16 [v]S 1Ki 8:36; S Ps 119:3 [w]S Dt 5:33 **7:24** [x]S Jer 6:10 [y]Jer 11:8; 17:23; 34:14 [z]S Jer 3:17 [a]S Jer 2:19; Eze 37:23 **7:25** [b]S 2Ch 36:15 [c]S Isa 20:3 [d]S Nu 11:29; Jer 25:4; 35:15 **7:26** [e]ver 13, 24; S 2Ch 36:16; Ps 81:11; Jer 13:11; 22:21; 25:3; 35:15; Eze 20:8, 21 [f]S Ex 32:9; Ac 7:51 [g]Jer 16:12; Mal 3:7; Lk 11:47 **7:27** [h]Eze 2:7 [i]ver 13; Eze 3:7; Zec 7:13 [j]S Isa 65:12 **7:28** [k]S Lev 26:23; Zep 3:7 [l]S Ps 15:2; S Isa 59:15

den of robbers. As thieves hide in caves and think they are safe, so the people of Judah falsely trust in the temple to protect them in spite of their sins.

7:12 See note on 7:1—8:3. *place in Shiloh ... see what I did to it.* See v. 14; 26:6,9; Ps 78:60–61. The tabernacle had been set up in Shiloh after the conquest of Canaan (Jos 18:1) and was still there at the end of the period of the judges (see 1Sa 1:9 and NIV text note). Modern Seilun, near a main highway about 18 miles north of Jerusalem, preserves the name of the ancient site. Archaeological excavations there indicate that it was destroyed by the Philistines c. 1050 B.C. The tabernacle itself was not included in that destruction, since it was still in existence at Gibeon during David's reign (see 1Ch 21:29). One or more auxiliary buildings had apparently been erected at Shiloh near the tabernacle in connection with various aspects of public worship there (cf. the reference to the "doors of the house of the LORD" in 1Sa 3:15; see note on 1Sa 1:9). Such structures would have been destroyed with the city itself, perhaps sometime after the events of 1Sa 4.

7:13 *again and again.* The Hebrew idiom underlying this phrase is found frequently in Jeremiah (v. 25; 11:7; 25:3–4; 26:5; 29:19; 32:33; 35:14–15; 44:4), but appears nowhere else in the OT.

7:15 *thrust you from my presence.* Into exile (see Dt 29:28). *just as I did all your brothers.* God sent Israel, the northern kingdom, into captivity in 721 B.C. (see 2Ki 17:20). *Ephraim.* Another name for Israel (see, e.g., 31:9)—and, ironically, the tribal territory in which Shiloh was located.

7:16 Perhaps the events of ch. 26 belong chronologically between vv. 15 and 16 (see Introduction: Outline). *do not pray for this people.* As a true prophet would (see 27:18; Ex 32:31–32; 1Sa 12:23). See 11:14; 14:11; cf. 15:1 and note. There is virtually no hope for them (cf. Eze 14:14,20). On various occasions, however, Jeremiah prayed for his countrymen (see, e.g., 18:20). *this people.* See note on Ex 17:4.

7:18 *children ... fathers ... women.* Entire families participate in idolatrous worship. *cakes of bread.* See 44:19. *Queen of Heaven.* A Babylonian title for Ishtar, an important goddess in the Babylonian pantheon (see 44:17–19,25). *drink offerings to other gods.* And sometimes to the Queen of Heaven herself (see 44:19,25). *provoke me to anger.* See Dt 31:29.

7:19 *their own shame.* See 3:25.

7:20 All nature suffers when God judges sinners (see 5:17; Ro 8:20–22). *burn and not be quenched.* See 4:4; 21:12; see also Isa 1:31; Am 5:6.

7:21 Because of your sinful deeds your sacrifices are worthless, so you might as well eat them yourselves.

7:22–23 Sacrifices are valid only when accompanied by sincere repentance and joyful obedience (see 6:20; Isa 1:11–15 and notes).

7:23 *your God ... my people.* The most basic summary of the relationship between God and Israel implied in the covenant at Sinai (see Ex 6:7; Lev 26:12; Zec 8:8 and notes; Dt 26:17–18).

7:24 *followed ... evil hearts.* See note on 3:17; see also Ge 6:5 and note.

7:25 *again and again.* See note on v. 13. *my servants the prophets.* See 25:4; 26:5; 29:19; 35:15; 44:4; see also Zec 1:6 and note. God had promised that Moses would be the first in a long line of prophets who would speak in the Lord's name and serve him faithfully (see Dt 18:15–22 and notes).

7:26 *stiff-necked.* See 17:23; 19:15; Ex 32:9 and note.

7:28 *not ... responded to correction.* See 2:30; 5:3. *Truth ... has vanished from their lips.* No one seeks the truth (see 5:1 and note).

vanished from their lips. 29Cut off[m] your
hair and throw it away; take up a lament[n]
on the barren heights, for the LORD has
rejected and abandoned[o] this generation
that is under his wrath.

The Valley of Slaughter

30“ ‘The people of Judah have done
evil[p] in my eyes, declares the LORD. They
have set up their detestable idols[q] in the
house that bears my Name and have defiled[r] it. 31They have built the high places
of Topheth[s] in the Valley of Ben Hinnom[t]
to burn their sons and daughters[u] in the
fire—something I did not command, nor
did it enter my mind.[v] 32So beware, the
days are coming, declares the LORD, when
people will no longer call it Topheth or the
Valley of Ben Hinnom, but the Valley of
Slaughter,[w] for they will bury[x] the dead
in Topheth until there is no more room.
33Then the carcasses[y] of this people will
become food[z] for the birds of the air and
the beasts of the earth, and there will be
no one to frighten them away.[a] 34I will
bring an end to the sounds[b] of joy and
gladness and to the voices of bride and
bridegroom[c] in the towns of Judah and the
streets of Jerusalem,[d] for the land will become desolate.[e]

7:29 [m]S Lev 21:5; S Job 1:20 [n]S Jer 4:8; S Eze 19:1 [o]S Jer 6:30; 12:7; Hos 11:8; Mic 5:3 **7:30** [p]S ver 10; S Lev 18:21 [q]S Jer 2:7; S 4:1; Eze 7:20-22 [r]S Lev 20:3; Jer 32:34 **7:31** [s]S 2Ki 23:10 [t]S Jos 15:8; 2Ch 33:6 [u]S Lev 18:21; Eze 16:20 [v]Jer 19:5; 32:35; Eze 20:31; Mic 6:7 **7:32** [w]Jer 19:6 [x]Jer 19:11 **7:33** [y]S Ge 15:11 [z]S Dt 28:26; Eze 29:5 [a]Jer 6:11; 14:16 **7:34** [b]S Isa 24:8 [c]Rev 18:23 [d]Isa 24:7-12; Jer 33:10 [e]S Lev 26:34; Zec 7:14; Mt 23:38

8:1 [f]S Ps 53:5 [g]S Isa 14:19 **8:2** [h]S 2Ki 23:5; Jer 19:13; Zep 1:5; Ac 7:42

8 “ ‘At that time, declares the LORD, the
bones of the kings and officials of Judah, the bones of the priests and prophets,
and the bones[f] of the people of Jerusalem
will be removed[g] from their graves. 2They
will be exposed to the sun and the moon
and all the stars of the heavens, which
they have loved and served[h] and which
they have followed and consulted and
worshiped.[i] They will not be gathered up
or buried,[j] but will be like refuse lying on
the ground.[k] 3Wherever I banish them,[l] all
the survivors of this evil nation will prefer
death to life,[m] declares the LORD Almighty.’

Sin and Punishment

4“Say to them, ‘This is what the LORD
says:

“ ‘When men fall down, do they not
get up?[n]
When a man turns away,[o] does he
not return?
5Why then have these people turned
away?
Why does Jerusalem always turn
away?

[i]S Job 31:27 [j]Jer 14:16; Eze 29:5; 37:1 [k]S 2Ki 9:37; Jer 31:40; 36:30 **8:3** [l]Dt 29:28 [m]S Job 3:22; Rev 9:6 **8:4** [n]Pr 24:16; Mic 7:8 [o]Ps 119:67; Jer 31:19

7:29 Addressed to Jerusalem. *Cut off your hair.* A sign of mourning (see Job 1:20; Mic 1:16). The Hebrew for the word "hair" is related to the word "Nazirite" (see Nu 6:2) and referred originally to the diadem worn by the high priest (see Ex 29:6). The Nazirites' hair was the symbol of their separation or consecration (Nu 6:7). As the Nazirites were commanded to cut off their hair when they became ceremonially unclean (Nu 6:9), so also Jerusalem must cut off her hair because of her sins. *lament on the barren heights.* See 3:21; see also note on 3:2.

7:30 *set up their ... idols in the house.* Manasseh had put a carved Asherah pole (see NIV text note on 2Ki 13:6) in the temple (2Ki 21:7). Jeremiah's contemporary, the good King Josiah, removed the pole and other accessories to idol worship (2Ki 23:4–7). But less than 20 years after Josiah's death, Ezekiel reported that there were numerous idols in the temple courts (see Eze 8:3,5–6,10,12). *defiled it.* See note on 2:7.

7:31 *high places.* Pagan shrines, usually (but not here) located on natural heights (see 1Sa 9:13–14; 10:5; 1Ki 11:7). *Topheth.* See v. 32; 19:6,11–14; see also note on Isa 30:33. The word is of Aramaic origin and means "fireplace," though in cultures outside Israel it was used as a common noun meaning "place of child sacrifice." Its vowel pattern was perhaps intentionally conformed to that of Hebrew *bosheth,* "shameful thing" (see note on Jdg 6:32), often used in connection with idol worship (see notes on 2:26; 3:25). The OT Topheth had a fire pit (see Isa 30:33), into which the hapless children were apparently thrown. *Valley of Ben Hinnom.* See v. 32; 19:2,6; 32:35; see also note on Jos 15:5. It was used as a trash dump and also as a place for sacrificing children to pagan gods. The abbreviated Hebrew name *ge' hinnom* ("Valley of Hinnom"; see Ne 11:30 and note) became "Gehenna" (Greek *geenna*), consistently translated in the NT as "hell," the place of eternal, fiery punishment (see Mt 5:22 and note; 18:9; Mk 9:47–48). *burn their sons and daughters in the fire.* A horrible ritual, prohibited in the law of Moses (see Lev 18:21 and note; Dt 18:10) but practiced by Ahaz (see 2Ki 16:2–3) and Manasseh (2Ki 21:1,6). *nor did it enter my mind.* Stresses how terribly evil such an act is to God (see 19:5; 32:35).

7:32 *So beware ... Valley of Slaughter.* Repeated almost verbatim in 19:6. Their place of sacrifice would become their cemetery when the people of Judah were slaughtered by the Babylonian invaders.

7:33 The punishment announced here is one of the curses for covenant disobedience (see Dt 28:26). *food for the birds ... of the earth.* See 16:4; 19:7; see also 34:20, where the same judgment is the result of violating God's covenant (34:18–19). To remain unburied was an unspeakable abomination in ancient times (cf. 22:19 and note).

7:34 See 16:9; 25:10; contrast 33:10–11. *land will become desolate.* Another covenant curse (Lev 26:31,33).

8:1 *bones ... removed from their graves.* A gross indignity and sacrilege (see 2Ki 23:16,18; Am 2:1 and note). *kings ... officials ... priests ... prophets.* See 2:26; see also note on 1:18.

8:2 *exposed to the sun ... moon ... stars.* To hasten their disintegration, and perhaps also to demonstrate that the heavenly bodies, which had been worshiped by some of Judah's kings (see 2Ki 21:3,5; 23:11), among others, were powerless to help. *loved and served and ... followed and consulted and worshiped.* Acts of homage and adoration that should have been given to God alone. *They.* The bones. *not be gathered up or buried.* Contrast 2Sa 21:13–14. *refuse.* Lit. "dung" (see 9:22; 16:4; 25:33).

8:3 *survivors.* See note on 6:9.

8:4—9:26 In contrast to 7:1—8:3, this section is almost completely in poetic form. Jeremiah resumes his extended commentary on the inevitability of divine judgment against sinners.

8:4 *Say to them.* Connects this section with the previous (see 7:28). *turns away ... return.* The Hebrew for these two verbs is identical, forming a play on words.

8:5 The general truths stated in v. 4 are routinely and per-

They cling to deceit;[p]
they refuse to return.[q]
[6]I have listened[r] attentively,
but they do not say what is right.
No one repents[s] of his wickedness,
saying, "What have I done?"
Each pursues his own course[t]
like a horse charging into battle.
[7]Even the stork in the sky
knows her appointed seasons,
and the dove, the swift and the thrush
observe the time of their migration.
But my people do not know[u]
the requirements of the LORD.

[8]" 'How can you say, "We are wise,
for we have the law[v] of the LORD,"
when actually the lying pen of the scribes
has handled it falsely?
[9]The wise[w] will be put to shame;
they will be dismayed[x] and trapped.[y]
Since they have rejected the word[z] of the LORD,
what kind of wisdom[a] do they have?
[10]Therefore I will give their wives to other men
and their fields to new owners.[b]
From the least to the greatest,
all are greedy for gain;[c]
prophets[d] and priests alike,
all practice deceit.[e]
[11]They dress the wound of my people
as though it were not serious.
"Peace, peace," they say,
when there is no peace.[f]
[12]Are they ashamed of their loathsome conduct?
No, they have no shame[g] at all;
they do not even know how to blush.
So they will fall among the fallen;
they will be brought down when they are punished,[h]
says the LORD.[i]

[13]" 'I will take away their harvest,
declares the LORD.
There will be no grapes on the vine.[j]
There will be no figs[k] on the tree,
and their leaves will wither.[l]
What I have given them
will be taken[m] from them.[a]' "

[14]"Why are we sitting here?
Gather together!
Let us flee to the fortified cities[n]
and perish there!
For the LORD our God has doomed us to perish
and given us poisoned water[o] to drink,
because we have sinned[p] against him.
[15]We hoped for peace[q]
but no good has come,
for a time of healing
but there was only terror.[r]
[16]The snorting of the enemy's horses[s]
is heard from Dan;[t]
at the neighing of their stallions
the whole land trembles.[u]
They have come to devour[v]
the land and everything in it,
the city and all who live there."

[17]"See, I will send venomous snakes[w] among you,
vipers that cannot be charmed,[x]
and they will bite you,"
declares the LORD.

8:5 [p]S Jer 5:27 [q]Zec 7:11 **8:6** [r]Mal 3:16 [s]Rev 9:20 [t]Ps 14:1-3 **8:7** [u]S Dt 32:28; S Jer 4:22 **8:8** [v]Ro 2:17 **8:9** [w]S Isa 29:14 [x]S 2Ki 19:26 [y]S Job 5:13 [z]S Jer 6:19 [a]Pr 1:7; 1Co 1:20 **8:10** [b]S Jer 6:12 [c]S Isa 56:11 [d]Jer 14:14; La 2:14 [e]Jer 23:11,15 **8:11** [f]ver 15; S Jer 4:10; Eze 7:25 **8:12** [g]S Jer 3:3 [h]Ps 52:5-7; Isa 3:9 [i]S Jer 6:15 **8:13** [j]Hos 2:12; Joel 1:7 [k]Lk 13:6 [l]Mt 21:19 [m]S Jer 5:17 **8:14** [n]S Jos 10:20; Jer 4:5; 35:11 [o]S Dt 29:18; Jer 9:15; 23:15 [p]Jer 14:7,20; Da 9:5 **8:15** [q]S ver 11 [r]S Job 19:8; Jer 14:19 **8:16** [s]S Jer 4:29 [t]S Ge 30:6 [u]Jer 51:29 [v]S Jer 5:17 **8:17** [w]Nu 21:6; S Dt 32:24 [x]S Ps 58:5; S Isa 3:3

[a] *13* The meaning of the Hebrew for this sentence is uncertain.

versely violated by the people of Jerusalem. *turned away ... turn away ... return.* Continuing the wordplay of v. 4.

8:6 *I.* The Lord. *pursues.* The Hebrew for this word continues the wordplay of vv. 4–5. *his own course.* And therefore evil (see 23:10).

8:7 See Isa 1:3. Although migratory birds obey their God-given instincts, God's rebellious people refuse to obey his laws. *swift.* Of similar build and habit as the swallow but not related to it (see 38:14, where it is also linked with the thrush). *do not know ... requirements of the LORD.* See note on 5:4.

8:8–9 *law of the LORD ... word of the LORD.* Misinterpreting and manipulating the first (the written law of Moses) leads to rejection of the second (God's truth as found in the law and proclaimed by his servants the prophets).

8:8 *lying pen.* Symbolizes mistreatment of the written law. *scribes.* The earliest mention of them as a recognizable group. They were apparently organized on the basis of families (see 1Ch 2:55; 2Ch 34:13; see also note on Ezr 7:6). *handled it falsely.* Contrast 2Ti 2:15.

8:9 *rejected ... wisdom.* Contrast Dt 4:5–6.

8:10–12 See 6:12–15 and notes.

8:11 *my people.* Lit. "the Daughter of my people" (also in v. 21; see Isa 22:4 and note).

8:13—9:24 This section is read aloud in synagogues every year on the ninth of Ab (see chart, p. 104), the very day the temple in Jerusalem was destroyed by the Babylonians in 586 B.C. and by the Romans in A.D. 70.

8:13 *vine.* Israel (see 2:21 and note). *grapes ... figs.* Symbolic of individual people also in Mic 7:1; see ch. 24. *leaves will wither.* Contrast 17:8; Ps 1:3.

8:14–16 On behalf of the people the prophet speaks, envisioning the Babylonian invasion.

8:14 *Gather together!* See 4:5. The Hebrew for this phrase forms a wordplay with the Hebrew for "take away" and "harvest" in v. 13. *flee to the fortified cities.* See note on 4:5. *poisoned water.* The phrase is unique to the prophet Jeremiah (see 9:15; 23:15; cf. 25:15).

8:15 Repeated almost verbatim in 14:19. *peace.* Under the circumstances, a false hope (see notes on 4:10; 6:14). *healing.* See note on 6:7.

8:16 *the enemy's horses.* See note on 4:13. *Dan.* Close to the northern border of Israel. It would be the first to feel the effects of the Babylonian invasion. *stallions.* Lit. "mighty ones"; the Hebrew word is translated "stallions" again in 50:11, "steeds" in 47:3. *city.* See note on 46:8.

8:17 *vipers that cannot be charmed.* Such are the wicked always (see Ps 58:4–5).

18 O my Comforter[a] in sorrow,
my heart is faint[y] within me.
19 Listen to the cry of my people
from a land far away:[z]
"Is the LORD not in Zion?
Is her King[a] no longer there?"

"Why have they provoked[b] me to anger
with their images,
with their worthless[c] foreign idols?"[d]

20 "The harvest is past,
the summer has ended,
and we are not saved."

21 Since my people are crushed,[e] I am
crushed;
I mourn,[f] and horror grips me.
22 Is there no balm in Gilead?[g]
Is there no physician[h] there?
Why then is there no healing[i]
for the wound of my people?

9 1 Oh, that my head were a spring of
water
and my eyes a fountain of tears![j]
I would weep[k] day and night
for the slain of my people.[l]
2 Oh, that I had in the desert[m]
a lodging place for travelers,
so that I might leave my people
and go away from them;
for they are all adulterers,[n]
a crowd of unfaithful[o] people.

3 "They make ready their tongue
like a bow, to shoot lies;[p]
it is not by truth
that they triumph[b] in the land.
They go from one sin to another;
they do not acknowledge[q] me,"
declares the LORD.

4 "Beware of your friends;[r]
do not trust your brothers.[s]
For every brother is a deceiver,[c t]
and every friend a slanderer.[u]
5 Friend deceives friend,[v]
and no one speaks the truth.[w]
They have taught their tongues to lie;[x]
they weary themselves with sinning.
6 You[d] live in the midst of deception;[y]
in their deceit they refuse to
acknowledge me,"
declares the LORD.

7 Therefore this is what the LORD Almighty says:

"See, I will refine[z] and test[a] them,
for what else can I do
because of the sin of my people?
8 Their tongue[b] is a deadly arrow;
it speaks with deceit.
With his mouth each speaks cordially
to his neighbor,[c]
but in his heart he sets a trap[d] for
him.[e]
9 Should I not punish them for this?"
declares the LORD.
"Should I not avenge[f] myself
on such a nation as this?"

10 I will weep and wail for the mountains
and take up a lament concerning the
desert pastures.[g]
They are desolate and untraveled,
and the lowing of cattle is not heard.

a 18 The meaning of the Hebrew for this word is uncertain. *b* 3 Or *lies; / they are not valiant for truth* *c* 4 Or *a deceiving Jacob* *d* 6 That is, Jeremiah (the Hebrew is singular)

8:18 [y] La 5:17 **8:19** [z] Dt 28:64; Jer 9:16 [a] Mic 4:9 [b] Jer 44:3 [c] S Isa 41:24 [d] S Dt 32:21 **8:21** [e] S Ps 94:5 [f] Ps 78:40; Isa 43:24; Jer 4:19; 10:19; 14:17; 30:14; La 2:13; Eze 6:9 **8:22** [g] S Ge 37:25 [h] Job 13:4 [i] S Isa 1:6; Jer 30:12 **9:1** [j] S Ps 119:136 [k] Jer 13:17; 14:17; La 2:11,18; 3:48 [l] Isa 22:4 **9:2** [m] Ps 55:7 [n] S Nu 25:1; Jer 23:10; Hos 4:2; 7:4 [o] S 1Ki 19:10; S Isa 24:16 **9:3** [p] ver 8; S Ex 20:16; Ps 64:3; S Isa 44:20; Jer 18:18; Mic 6:12 [q] S Isa 1:3 **9:4** [r] S 2Sa 15:12 [s] Mic 7:5-6 [t] S Ge 27:35 [u] S Ex 20:16; S Lev 19:16 **9:5** [v] S Lev 6:2 [w] S Ps 15:2; S Isa 59:15 [x] S Ps 52:3 **9:6** [y] S Jer 5:27 **9:7** [z] S Job 28:1; S Isa 1:25 [a] S Jer 6:27 **9:8** [b] S ver 3; S Ps 35:20 [c] S Isa 3:5 [d] S Jer 5:26 [e] ver 4 **9:9** [f] S Dt 32:43; S Isa 10:3 **9:10** [g] Jer 23:10; Joel 1:19

8:18 The prophet speaks. *my heart is faint.* See La 1:22; 5:17.
8:19 The prophet speaks in the first part of the verse, the Lord in the last part. *my people from a land far away.* Judah in Babylonian exile (see Ps 137:1–4) as Jeremiah envisions the future. *Is the LORD not in Zion?* Cf. Mic 3:11. The people are perplexed at their fate, still wondering how God could have permitted the destruction of his land and temple (see note on 7:4). *King.* God (see Isa 33:22 and note). *provoked me to anger.* See 7:18; Dt 31:29. *worthless … idols.* See note on 2:5.
8:20 The people speak from the hopelessness of their exile. *we are not saved.* We have been captured by the enemy.
8:21 Jeremiah identifies himself with his exiled countrymen. *grips me.* See 6:24.
8:22 *balm in Gilead.* See 46:11; cf. 51:8. The territory of Gilead was an important source of spices and medicinal herbs (see Ge 37:25 and note). *no healing for the wound.* Contrast 30:17.
9:1–2 The prophet's frustration is highlighted as he speaks of his countrymen with tender sympathy in v. 1 and with indignant disgust in v. 2.
9:1 Jeremiah is often called the "weeping prophet"—a well-deserved title (see v. 10; the book of Lamentations; cf. 2Sa 18:33; Lk 19:41; Ro 9:2–4; 10:1).
9:2 The prophet wants to get as far away from his wicked countrymen as possible (cf. Ps 55:6–8). *adulterers … unfaithful people.* See v. 14; see also Ex 34:15 and note. *crowd.* The Hebrew for this word is always used elsewhere in the OT in the sense of a solemn religious assembly (see, e.g., Dt 16:8), sometimes perverted by the worshipers and therefore falling under divine judgment (see Isa 1:13; Am 5:21).
9:3–9 The Lord speaks.
9:3 *tongue like a bow.* See vv. 5,8; see also Ps 64:3–4; cf. Jas 3:5–12. *do not acknowledge me.* See v. 6; Jdg 2:10; 1Sa 2:12; Job 18:21; Hos 4:1 and note; Ro 1:28; contrast Hos 6:3.
9:4 *deceiver.* See NIV text note; Ge 25:26 and note; NIV text note on Ge 27:36; Hos 12:2–3 and NIV text note on 12:2.
9:6 *refuse to acknowledge me.* The situation has deteriorated even further (v. 3 says simply "do not acknowledge me").
9:7 *refine and test.* See 6:27–30 and notes. The Lord will test his people "in the furnace of affliction" (Isa 48:10; see note there).
9:8 *tongue … deceit.* See v. 3 and note. *With his mouth … but in his heart.* See Ps 55:21. *cordially.* The Hebrew for this word is translated "peace" in 6:14 (see note there).
9:9 Repeated from 5:9,29.
9:10 The prophet speaks. See 4:23–26 and notes. *weep and wail.* See v. 18; see also note on v. 1. *desert pastures.* Good only for poor grazing by sheep and goats at best (see 1Sa 17:28; cf. Ex 3:1). *desolate.* Lit. "burned" (as in 2:15); here parched by the blazing sun. *untraveled.* See v. 12; Jdg 5:6 and note; Eze 33:28.

The birds of the air[h] have fled
and the animals are gone.

11 "I will make Jerusalem a heap[i] of
ruins,
a haunt of jackals;[j]
and I will lay waste the towns of
Judah[k]
so no one can live there."[l]

12What man is wise[m] enough to understand this? Who has been instructed by
the LORD and can explain it? Why has the
land been ruined and laid waste like a desert that no one can cross?
13The LORD said, "It is because they have
forsaken my law, which I set before them;
they have not obeyed me or followed my
law.[n] 14Instead, they have followed[o] the
stubbornness of their hearts;[p] they have
followed the Baals, as their fathers taught
them." 15Therefore, this is what the LORD
Almighty, the God of Israel, says: "See,
I will make this people eat bitter food[q]
and drink poisoned water.[r] 16I will scatter them among nations[s] that neither they
nor their fathers have known,[t] and I will
pursue them with the sword[u] until I have
destroyed them."[v]

17This is what the LORD Almighty says:

"Consider now! Call for the wailing
women[w] to come;
send for the most skillful of them.
18 Let them come quickly
and wail over us
till our eyes overflow with tears
and water streams from our eyelids.[x]
19 The sound of wailing is heard from
Zion:
'How ruined[y] we are!
How great is our shame!
We must leave our land
because our houses are in ruins.' "

20 Now, O women, hear the word of the
LORD;
open your ears to the words of his
mouth.[z]
Teach your daughters how to wail;
teach one another a lament.[a]
21 Death has climbed in through our
windows[b]
and has entered our fortresses;
it has cut off the children from the
streets
and the young men[c] from the public
squares.

22Say, "This is what the LORD declares:

" 'The dead bodies of men will lie
like refuse[d] on the open field,
like cut grain behind the reaper,
with no one to gather them.' "

23This is what the LORD says:

"Let not the wise man boast of his
wisdom[e]
or the strong man boast of his
strength[f]
or the rich man boast of his riches,[g]
24 but let him who boasts boast[h] about
this:
that he understands and knows[i] me,
that I am the LORD,[j] who exercises
kindness,[k]
justice and righteousness[l] on earth,
for in these I delight,"
declares the LORD.

25"The days are coming," declares the
LORD, "when I will punish all who are cir-

9:10 [h]S Jer 4:25; 12:4; Hos 4:3; Joel 1:18 **9:11** [i]Jer 26:18 [j]S Job 30:29; S Isa 34:13 [k]S Jer 1:15 [l]S Lev 26:31; Isa 25:2; S Jer 4:13; 26:9; 33:10; 50:3, 13; 51:62; La 1:4 **9:12** [m]S Ps 107:43 **9:13** [n]S 2Ch 7:19; S Ps 89:30-32 **9:14** [o]S Jer 2:8, 23; Am 2:4 [p]S Jer 3:17; S 7:24 **9:15** [q]La 3:15 [r]S Jer 8:14 **9:16** [s]S Lev 26:33 [t]S Dt 4:32; S Jer 8:19 [u]Jer 14:12; 24:10; Eze 5:2 [v]Jer 44:27; Eze 5:12 **9:17** [w]S Ecc 12:5 **9:18** [x]S Ps 119:136; La 3:48 **9:19** [y]S Jer 4:13 **9:20** [z]Jer 23:16 [a]Isa 32:9-13 **9:21** [b]Joel 2:9 [c]S 2Ch 36:17; S Isa 40:30; S Jer 16:6 **9:22** [d]S 2Ki 9:37 **9:23** [e]S Job 4:12; S Ecc 9:11 [f]S 1Ki 20:11 [g]Ps 62:10; S Pr 11:28; Jer 48:7; 49:4; Eze 28:4-5 **9:24** [h]S Ps 34:2; 1Co 1:31*; Gal 6:14 [i]S Ps 36:10 [j]2Co 10:17* [k]Ps 51:1 [l]Ps 36:6

9:11 The Lord speaks. *haunt of jackals.* See 10:22; 49:33; 51:37; Ps 44:19; Isa 13:21–22; La 5:18; Eze 13:4; Mal 1:3; contrast Isa 35:7. *no one can live there.* See 2:15; 4:7 and notes.
9:12 The prophet asks a series of questions. *What man is wise ...?* See Hos 14:9.
9:13 The Lord answers the prophet and then continues to speak through v. 19. *law, which I set before them.* In the days of Moses (see Dt 4:8).
9:14 *stubbornness.* See note on 3:17. *Baals.* See 2:23 and note.
9:15 *eat bitter food and drink poisoned water.* Repeated in 23:15; see note on 8:14. Centuries earlier, Moses had warned the Israelites concerning just such a fate (see Dt 29:18).
9:16 *I will scatter them.* See 13:24; 18:17; 30:11; 46:28. This warning was given in Dt 28:64 as one of the curses for persistent covenant unfaithfulness. *pursue them with the sword.* See 42:16. *destroyed them.* But not to the last man (see note on 4:27; see especially 44:27–28).
9:17 *wailing women.* Professionals, paid to mourn at funerals and other sorrowful occasions (see 2Ch 35:25; Ecc 12:5; Am 5:16).
9:18 *wail.* See v. 10. *eyes overflow with tears.* See v. 1.
9:19 *How ruined we are!* See 4:13,20; cf. 48:1.
9:20–21 The prophet speaks.
9:20 The wailing women will have to teach their daughters how to lament, so great will be the need for their services.
9:21 *Death.* Personified here (as in Hab 2:5). Canaanite mythology included a deity named Mot (a word related to the Hebrew word for "death"), the god of infertility and the netherworld. *climbed in through our windows.* Said of enemy soldiers in Joel 2:9. *children ... young men.* See 6:11.
9:22 *dead bodies.* See 7:33 and note. *like refuse.* See note on 8:2. *reaper.* The concept of death as the Grim Reaper comes largely from this verse.
9:23 *Let not ... the rich man boast of his riches.* An almost exact parallel occurs in the Aramaic *Words of Ahiqar,* written about a century after Jeremiah's time: "Let not the rich man say, 'In my riches I am glorious.'"
9:24 1Co 1:31 summarizes: "Let him who boasts boast in the Lord." *this ... these.* Ultimately, only God and our knowledge of and love for him are worthwhile. *understands and knows.* See 3:15; see also note on 4:22. *I am the LORD.* Ex 6:2–8, a key passage on the doctrine of redemption, begins and ends with this statement of divine self-disclosure. *kindness.* The Hebrew for this word is translated "devotion" in 2:2 (see note there). *in these I delight.* See Ps 11:7; 33:5; 99:4; 103:6; Mic 6:8; 7:18.
9:25–26 See Ro 2:25–29; see also note on Ge 17:10.

cumcised only in the flesh[m]— [26]Egypt, Judah, Edom, Ammon, Moab and all who
live in the desert in distant places.[a][n] For
all these nations are really uncircumcised,[o]
and even the whole house of Israel is uncircumcised in heart.[p]"

God and Idols

10:12-16pp — Jer 51:15-19

10 Hear what the LORD says to you,
O house of Israel. [2]This is what the
LORD says:

"Do not learn the ways of the nations[q]
or be terrified by signs[r] in the sky,
though the nations are terrified by
them.
[3]For the customs of the peoples are
worthless;
they cut a tree out of the forest,
and a craftsman[s] shapes it with his
chisel.[t]
[4]They adorn it with silver[u] and gold;
they fasten it with hammer and nails
so it will not totter.[v]
[5]Like a scarecrow in a melon patch,
their idols cannot speak;[w]
they must be carried
because they cannot walk.[x]
Do not fear them;
they can do no harm[y]
nor can they do any good."[z]
[6]No one is like you,[a] O LORD;
you are great,[b]
and your name is mighty in power.
[7]Who should not revere[c] you,
O King of the nations?[d]
This is your due.
Among all the wise men of the nations
and in all their kingdoms,
there is no one like you.
[8]They are all senseless[e] and foolish;[f]
they are taught by worthless wooden
idols.[g]
[9]Hammered silver is brought from
Tarshish[h]
and gold from Uphaz.
What the craftsman and goldsmith
have made[i]
is then dressed in blue and purple—
all made by skilled workers.
[10]But the LORD is the true God;
he is the living God,[j] the eternal
King.[k]
When he is angry,[l] the earth trembles;[m]
the nations cannot endure his
wrath.[n]

[11]"Tell them this: 'These gods, who did
not make the heavens and the earth, will
perish[o] from the earth and from under the
heavens.'"[b]

[12]But God made[p] the earth[q] by his
power;
he founded the world by his
wisdom[r]

[a] *26* Or *desert and who clip the hair by their foreheads*
[b] *11* The text of this verse is in Aramaic.

9:25 [m]S Lev 26:41; Ro 2:25 **9:26** [n]Jer 25:23; 49:32 [o]S 1Sa 14:6; Eze 31:18 [p]Ac 7:51 **10:2** [q]S Ex 23:24; S Lev 20:23 [r]S Ge 1:14 **10:3** [s]S Isa 40:19 [t]Dt 9:21; S 1Ki 8:36; Jer 44:8; Eze 7:20 **10:4** [u]Ps 135:15; Hos 13:2; Hab 2:19 [v]S 1Sa 5:3; Isa 41:7 **10:5** [w]S 1Ki 18:26; 1Co 12:2 [x]S Isa 45:20 [y]Isa 41:23 [z]S Isa 41:24; 44:9-20; 46:7; Ac 19:26 **10:6** [a]S Ex 8:10 [b]S 2Sa 7:22; S Ps 48:1 **10:7** [c]Jer 5:22 [d]Ps 22:28; S Isa 12:4; Rev 15:4 **10:8** [e]S Isa 44:18 [f]S Isa 40:19; S Jer 4:22 [g]S Dt 32:21 **10:9** [h]S Ge 10:4 [i]Ps 115:4; S Isa 40:19 **10:10** [j]S Jos 3:10; S Mt 16:16 [k]S Ge 21:33; Da 6:26 [l]S Ps 18:7 [m]S Jdg 5:4; S Job 9:6; Ps 29:8 [n]Ps 76:7; Jer 21:12; Na 1:6 **10:11** [o]S Isa 2:18 **10:12** [p]S 1Sa 2:8 [q]S ver 16 [r]S Ge 1:31

9:26 *who live ... in distant places.* Arab tribes (see 25:23; 49:32), later to be attacked by the Babylonians under Nebuchadnezzar (see 49:28–33). With the NIV text note contrast Lev 19:27. *uncircumcised in heart.* See 4:4 and note.

10:1–25 Jeremiah concludes his series of temple messages with a poetic section that focuses primarily on the vast difference between idols and the Lord (vv. 2–16). idols and their worshipers are condemned in vv. 2–5,8–9,11,14–15, while the one true God is praised in the alternate passages (vv. 6–7,10,12–13,16). See Isa 40:18–20 and note; 41:7; 44:9–20; 46:5–7.

10:1 *Hear.* See note on 2:4.

10:2 *Do not ... be terrified.* See 1:17. *ways.* The Hebrew for this word is singular and refers to the religious practices of the nations. The early Christians often called their distinctive beliefs and lifestyle the "Way" (see Ac 9:2; 19:9,23; 22:4; 24:14,22). *signs in the sky.* The heavenly bodies were created by the Lord for purposes other than idolatrous worship (see Ge 1:14–18 and notes). *nations are terrified.* Not only by the heavenly bodies themselves but also by unusual phenomena associated with them (such as comets, meteors and eclipses).

10:3 *worthless.* See note on 2:5. *cut a tree.* See Isa 44:14–15. *craftsman.* The word is often used of idol-makers who work usually—but not always (see Isa 40:19)—with wood (see Isa 41:7). *chisel.* Cf. Isa 44:13.

10:4 *silver and gold.* Wooden idols were plated with precious metals to beautify them (see Isa 30:22; 40:19). *fasten it ... so it will not totter.* See Isa 40:20; 41:7; cf. 46:7; contrast 1Sa 5:2–4.

10:5 The impotence of idols is described in classic form in Ps 115:4–7; 135:15–18. *scarecrow.* Verse 70 in the Apocryphal *Letter of Jeremiah* uses the same imagery. *melon patch.* See Isa 1:8 and note. *must be carried.* Usually on the backs of animals. See Isa 46:1. *harm nor ... good.* Idols can do nothing at all (see Isa 41:22–24).

10:6 *No one.* Among the gods (see Ps 86:8). *your name is mighty in power.* See 16:21.

10:7 *revere you, O King of the nations.* See Ps 47:8–9 and notes; 96:10; Rev 15:3–4 and notes. Unlike the tribal deities, limited to their own territories, the Lord is King over all. *This.* Reverence. *Among all the wise men ... no one like you.* See Isa 19:12; 29:14; 1Co 1:20.

10:8 *senseless and foolish.* See vv. 14,21; 5:21; see also NIV text note on Pr 1:7. *taught by ... idols.* Instead of by the Lord (see Dt 11:2; Job 5:17; Pr 3:11, where the Hebrew word for "taught by" is translated "discipline"). *worthless.* See note on v. 3.

10:9 *silver ... from Tarshish.* See Eze 27:12; see also note on Isa 23:6. *Uphaz.* Mentioned only here; location unknown. *craftsman and goldsmith.* See Isa 40:19 and note. *dressed in blue and purple.* To make it look regal. *all.* The idols.

10:10 Everything that idols are not, the Lord is. *true.* See 1Th 1:9. *living God.* See 23:36; Dt 5:26; 2Ki 19:4 and note. *eternal.* See Ex 15:18; Ps 10:16; 29:10. *When ... wrath.* See Ps 97:5; Na 1:5.

10:11 See NIV text note. The other major Aramaic passages in the OT are Ezr 4:8—6:18; 7:12–26; Da 2:4—7:28. *them.* Pagan idolaters, who would have been more likely to understand Aramaic (the language of diplomacy during this period) than Hebrew.

10:12–16 Repeated almost verbatim in 51:15–19.

10:12 *But God.* In contrast to the false gods of v. 11. *stretched out the heavens.* Like a tent or canopy (see Ps 104:2; Isa 40:22 and note).

and stretched out the heavens[s] by
his understanding.
13 When he thunders,[t] the waters in the
heavens roar;
he makes clouds rise from the ends
of the earth.
He sends lightning[u] with the rain[v]
and brings out the wind from his
storehouses.[w]

14 Everyone is senseless and without
knowledge;
every goldsmith is shamed[x] by his
idols.
His images are a fraud;[y]
they have no breath in them.
15 They are worthless,[z] the objects of
mockery;
when their judgment comes, they
will perish.
16 He who is the Portion[a] of Jacob is not
like these,
for he is the Maker of all things,[b]
including Israel, the tribe of his
inheritance[c]—
the LORD Almighty is his name.[d]

Coming Destruction

17 Gather up your belongings[e] to leave
the land,
you who live under siege.
18 For this is what the LORD says:
"At this time I will hurl[f] out
those who live in this land;
I will bring distress[g] on them
so that they may be captured."

19 Woe to me because of my injury!
My wound[h] is incurable!
Yet I said to myself,
"This is my sickness, and I must
endure[i] it."

20 My tent[j] is destroyed;
all its ropes are snapped.
My sons are gone from me and are no
more;[k]
no one is left now to pitch my tent
or to set up my shelter.
21 The shepherds[l] are senseless[m]
and do not inquire of the LORD;[n]
so they do not prosper[o]
and all their flock is scattered.[p]
22 Listen! The report is coming—
a great commotion from the land of
the north![q]
It will make the towns of Judah
desolate,[r]
a haunt of jackals.[s]

Jeremiah's Prayer

23 I know, O LORD, that a man's life is not
his own;
it is not for man to direct his steps.[t]
24 Correct me, LORD, but only with
justice—
not in your anger,[u]
lest you reduce me to nothing.[v w]
25 Pour out your wrath on the nations[x]
that do not acknowledge you,
on the peoples who do not call on
your name.[y]
For they have devoured[z] Jacob;
they have devoured him completely
and destroyed his homeland.[a]

The Covenant Is Broken

11 This is the word that came to Jeremiah from the LORD: 2 "Listen to the
terms of this covenant[b] and tell them to
the people of Judah and to those who live

10:12 [s] S Ge 1:1,8 **10:13** [t] S Job 36:29 [u] S Job 36:30 [v] S Ps 104:13; S 135:7 [w] S Dt 28:12 **10:14** [x] S Ps 97:7; S Isa 1:29 [y] S Isa 44:20 **10:15** [z] S Isa 41:24; S Jer 14:22 **10:16** [a] S Dt 32:9; S Ps 119:57 [b] ver 12; Jer 32:17; 33:2 [c] S Ex 34:9; Ps 74:2 [d] Jer 31:35; 32:18 **10:17** [e] Eze 12:3-12 **10:18** [f] S 1Sa 25:29; S Isa 22:17 [g] S Dt 28:52 **10:19** [h] Job 34:6; Jer 14:17; 15:18; 30:12,15; La 2:13; Mic 1:9; Na 3:19 [i] Mic 7:9 **10:20** [j] S Jer 4:20 [k] Jer 31:15; La 1:5 **10:21** [l] Jer 22:22; 23:1; 25:34; 50:6 [m] ver 8 [n] S Isa 56:10 [o] Jer 22:30 [p] Jer 23:2; Eze 34:6 **10:22** [q] Jer 6:22; 27:6; 49:28,30 [r] Eze 12:19 [s] S Isa 34:13 **10:23** [t] S Job 33:29; S Pr 3:5-6; 20:24 **10:24** [u] Ps 6:1; 38:1; S Jer 7:20; 18:23 [v] Jer 46:28 [w] Jer 30:11 **10:25** [x] S Ps 69:24; Zep 2:2; 3:8 [y] S Ps 14:4 [z] S Ps 79:7; S Jer 2:3 [a] Ps 79:6-7 **11:2** [b] S Dt 5:2

10:13 *he makes clouds ... his storehouses.* Repeated in Ps 135:7, where the one true God is contrasted to false gods (see Ps 135:5,15–17); cf. Job 38:22.
10:14 *senseless.* See vv. 8,21; see also note on 4:22. *images.* Cast in metal; the Hebrew for this word is translated "metal god" in Isa 48:5 and "metal images" in Da 11:8. *no breath.* See Ps 135:17.
10:15 *worthless.* See note on v. 3.
10:16 *Portion of Jacob.* A title for God, used again only in 51:19 (see Ps 73:26 and note; 119:57; 142:5; La 3:24). *tribe of his inheritance.* See Isa 63:17. *the LORD Almighty is his name.* See 2:19 and note; Isa 54:5; Am 4:13.
10:17–22 Destruction and exile are imminent.
10:18 *hurl out.* As from a sling (cf. 1Sa 25:29).
10:19–20 On behalf of his countrymen, the prophet bemoans their fate and his own (see 4:19–21).
10:20 *My sons.* The people of Judah and Jerusalem (Jeremiah never married or had children; see 16:2). *shelter.* See note on 4:20.
10:21 *shepherds ... flock.* Rulers and people (see note on 2:8). *senseless.* See vv. 8,14; see also note on 4:22. *do not inquire of the LORD.* Instead, they consult the heavenly bodies (see 8:2). *scattered.* See note on 9:16.
10:22 *great commotion.* The sound of the invaders (see 6:23; 8:16). *land of the north.* Babylonia (see 4:6; 6:22; see also note on Isa 41:25). *haunt of jackals.* See 9:11 and note.
10:23–25 On the people's behalf, the prophet prays for divine justice.
10:23 Only the Lord can direct people's steps (see Ps 37:23; Pr 16:9 and note).
10:25 Repeated almost verbatim in Ps 79:6–7, where the context (see Ps 79:1–5) shows that the prayer is not vengeful but is an appeal for God's justice (see note on Ps 5:10). The verse is recited annually by Jews during their Passover service.
11:1—13:27 Because of Judah's violations of its covenant obligations, the people will be exiled to Babylonia. The section is perhaps to be dated to the reign of Josiah (but see note on 13:18).
11:1–17 God's people have broken his covenant with them.
11:2 *Listen.* See note on 2:4. *terms.* Lit. "words," a technical term for covenant stipulations (see vv. 3–4,6; 34:18; see also note on Ex 20:1). *this covenant.* See vv. 3,6,8,10; Dt 29:9. Reference is to the covenant established by God with Israel through Moses at Mount Sinai (see v. 4; Ex 19–24). *tell them.* Periodic public reading of covenants was a common and necessary practice (see Dt 31:10–13; Jos 8:34–35).

in Jerusalem. 3Tell them that this is what
the LORD, the God of Israel, says: 'Cursed[c]
is the man who does not obey the terms
of this covenant— 4the terms I commanded your forefathers when I brought them
out of Egypt,[d] out of the iron-smelting furnace.[e]' I said, 'Obey[f] me and do everything
I command you, and you will be my people,[g] and I will be your God. 5Then I will
fulfill the oath I swore[h] to your forefathers,
to give them a land flowing with milk and
honey'[i]—the land you possess today."
I answered, "Amen,[j] LORD."
6The LORD said to me, "Proclaim[k] all
these words in the towns of Judah and
in the streets of Jerusalem: 'Listen to the
terms of this covenant and follow[l] them.
7From the time I brought your forefathers
up from Egypt until today, I warned them
again and again,[m] saying, "Obey me." 8But
they did not listen or pay attention;[n] instead, they followed the stubbornness of
their evil hearts.[o] So I brought on them
all the curses[p] of the covenant I had commanded them to follow but that they did
not keep.[q]' "
9Then the LORD said to me, "There is
a conspiracy[r] among the people of Judah
and those who live in Jerusalem. 10They
have returned to the sins of their forefathers,[s] who refused to listen to my words.[t]
They have followed other gods[u] to serve
them.[v] Both the house of Israel and the
house of Judah have broken the covenant[w]
I made with their forefathers. 11Therefore
this is what the LORD says: 'I will bring
on them a disaster[x] they cannot escape.[y]
Although they cry[z] out to me, I will not
listen[a] to them. 12The towns of Judah and
the people of Jerusalem will go and cry
out to the gods to whom they burn incense,[b] but they will not help them at all
when disaster[c] strikes. 13You have as many
gods[d] as you have towns,[e] O Judah; and
the altars you have set up to burn incense[f]
to that shameful[g] god Baal are as many as
the streets of Jerusalem.'
14"Do not pray[h] for this people nor offer
any plea or petition for them, because I
will not listen[i] when they call to me in the
time of their distress.

15"What is my beloved doing in my
temple
as she works out her evil schemes
with many?
Can consecrated meat[j] avert ⌞your
punishment⌟?[k]
When you engage in your wickedness,
then you rejoice.[a]"

16The LORD called you a thriving olive
tree[l]
with fruit beautiful in form.
But with the roar of a mighty storm
he will set it on fire,[m]
and its branches will be broken.[n]

17The LORD Almighty, who planted[o] you,
has decreed disaster[p] for you, because the
house of Israel and the house of Judah
have done evil and provoked[q] me to anger
by burning incense to Baal.[r]

Plot Against Jeremiah

18Because the LORD revealed their plot to
me, I knew it, for at that time he showed
me what they were doing. 19I had been like
a gentle lamb led to the slaughter;[s] I did
not realize that they had plotted[t] against
me, saying,

[a] 15 Or *Could consecrated meat avert your punishment? / Then you would rejoice*

11:3 [c]Dt 11:26-28; 27:26; 28:15-68; Gal 3:10 **11:4** [d]ver 7 [e]S 1Ki 8:51 [f]S Ex 24:8; Jer 7:23 [g]Jer 7:23; 31:33; Eze 11:20 **11:5** [h]S Ex 6:8; 13:5; Dt 7:12; Ps 105:8-11 [i]S Ex 3:8 [j]S Dt 27:26 **11:6** [k]S Jer 4:5 [l]S Ex 15:26; S Dt 15:5; Jas 1:22 **11:7** [m]S 2Ch 36:15 **11:8** [n]S Jer 7:26 [o]S Ecc 9:3; S Jer 3:17 [p]Lev 26:14-43; Dt 28:15-68; S Jos 23:15 [q]S 2Ch 7:19; Ps 78:10; Jer 26:4; 32:23; 44:10 **11:9** [r]Eze 22:25 **11:10** [s]Dt 9:7; S 2Ch 30:7 [t]Zec 7:11 [u]S Jdg 2:12-13; S 10:13 [v]Jer 16:11; Eze 20:8 [w]Isa 24:5; Jer 34:18; Hos 6:7; 8:1 **11:11** [x]S 2Ki 22:16; S Jer 4:6 [y]S Job 11:20; La 2:22 [z]S Job 27:9; Jer 14:12; Eze 8:18; Mal 2:13 [a]ver 14; S Ps 66:18; Pr 1:28; S Isa 1:15; 59:2; Eze 8:8; Zec 7:13 **11:12** [b]S Dt 32:38; S Jer 44:17 [c]S Dt 32:37; S Jdg 10:14

11:13 [d]S Ex 20:3; Jer 19:4 [e]S 2Ki 17:29 [f]S Jer 7:9; 44:21 [g]S Jer 3:24
11:14 [h]S Ex 32:10 [i]S ver 11 **11:15** [j]Hag 2:12 [k]S Jer 7:9-10
11:16 [l]S Ps 1:3; Hos 14:6 [m]S Jer 7:20; 21:14 [n]S Isa 27:11; Ro 11:17-24
11:17 [o]S Ex 15:17; Isa 5:2; Jer 12:2; 45:4 [p]ver 11 [q]Jer 7:18 [r]S Jer 7:9
11:19 [s]S Ps 44:22 [t]ver 21; S Ps 44:16; 54:3; 71:10; Jer 18:18; 20:10

11:3 *Cursed is the man.* The phrase appears at the beginning of every covenant curse in Dt 27:15–26, and the people respond to each of the curses with their "Amen." Blessings resulted from obedience to the covenant (see Dt 28:1–14); curses resulted from disobedience (see Dt 28:15–68; see also Dt 11:26–28; 29:20–21).

11:4 *out of Egypt ... the iron-smelting furnace.* See note on Dt 4:20. *Obey me.* See v. 7; 7:23; Ex 19:5. *my people ... your God.* See note on 7:23.

11:5 *land flowing with milk and honey.* See 32:22; see also note on Ex 3:8. *Amen.* See note on v. 3. *fulfill the oath I swore.* See Ge 15:17–18 and notes; 22:16–18; Dt 7:8.

11:6 *Proclaim.* See 2:2; 3:12.

11:7 *again and again.* See note on 7:13.

11:8 See 7:24. *stubbornness of their evil hearts.* See note on 3:17. *curses of the covenant.* See note on v. 3. *So I brought on them.* See 2Ki 17:18–23.

11:9 *conspiracy.* Against the intended reforms of Josiah (see Introduction: Background; see also note on 1:2).

11:10 *refused.* Their sin was deliberate (see note on 9:6). *the covenant.* Lit. "my covenant," emphasizing its origin in God himself.

11:11 *I will bring on them.* Judah will be judged, just as Israel had been judged earlier (see v. 10; see also 2Ki 17:18–23).

11:12 *burn incense.* See vv. 13,17; see also note on 1:16.

11:13 *as many gods as ... towns.* See note on 2:28. *altars ... as many as the streets.* See 2Ch 28:24. *to that shameful god Baal.* See 3:24; see also notes on 2:26; Jdg 6:32.

11:14 *Do not pray for this people.* See note on 7:16; cf. 1Jn 5:16.

11:15 See 7:10–11,21–24. *my beloved.* Judah (see 12:7; cf. Dt 33:12, where Benjamin is called the "beloved of the LORD").

11:16 *called you ... olive tree.* See Ps 52:8; 128:3. *storm.* The Hebrew for this word appears elsewhere only in Eze 1:24, where it is translated "tumult" in reference to the noise made by an army (see Isa 13:4). *branches will be broken.* See Eze 31:12.

11:17 Fulfilled when Judah was destroyed in 586 B.C. (see 44:2–3). *provoked me to anger.* See 8:19; Dt 31:29.

11:18–23 The first of Jeremiah's six "confessions" (see Introduction: Author and Date).

11:18 *their ... they.* Jeremiah's personal enemies, the "men of Anathoth" (vv. 21,23), his hometown.

11:19 *lamb led to the slaughter.* See 51:40; see also Isa 53:7 and note. *destroy the tree and its fruit.* Contrast 12:2. *cut him*

"Let us destroy the tree and its fruit;
let us cut him off from the land of the living,[u]
that his name be remembered[v] no more."
20 But, O LORD Almighty, you who judge righteously[w]
and test the heart[x] and mind,[y]
let me see your vengeance[z] upon them,
for to you I have committed my cause.

21 "Therefore this is what the LORD says
about the men of Anathoth[a] who are seeking your life[b] and saying, 'Do not prophesy[c] in the name of the LORD or you will
die[d] by our hands' — 22 therefore this is
what the LORD Almighty says: 'I will punish them. Their young men[e] will die by
the sword, their sons and daughters by
famine. 23 Not even a remnant[f] will be left
to them, because I will bring disaster on
the men of Anathoth in the year of their
punishment.[g]' "

Jeremiah's Complaint

12 You are always righteous,[h] O LORD,
when I bring a case[i] before you.
Yet I would speak with you about your justice:[j]
Why does the way of the wicked prosper?[k]
Why do all the faithless live at ease?
2 You have planted[l] them, and they have taken root;
they grow and bear fruit.[m]
You are always on their lips
but far from their hearts.[n]
3 Yet you know me, O LORD;
you see me and test[o] my thoughts about you.
Drag them off like sheep[p] to be butchered!
Set them apart for the day of slaughter![q]
4 How long will the land lie parched[a][r]
and the grass in every field be withered?[s]
Because those who live in it are wicked,
the animals and birds have perished.[t]
Moreover, the people are saying,
"He will not see what happens to us."

God's Answer

5 "If you have raced with men on foot
and they have worn you out,
how can you compete with horses?
If you stumble in safe country,[b]
how will you manage in the thickets[u] by[c] the Jordan?
6 Your brothers, your own family—
even they have betrayed you;
they have raised a loud cry against you.[v]
Do not trust them,
though they speak well of you.[w]

[a] 4 Or *land mourn* [b] 5 Or *If you put your trust in a land of safety* [c] 5 Or *the flooding of*

11:19 [u]S Job 28:13; S Ps 116:9; Isa 53:8 [v]Ps 83:4 **11:20** [w]Ps 7:11 [x]S 1Sa 2:3; S 1Ch 29:17 [y]S Ps 26:2 [z]S Ps 58:10; La 3:60 **11:21** [a]S Jos 21:18 [b]S ver 19; Jer 12:6; 21:7; 34:20 [c]S Isa 30:10 [d]Jer 2:30; 18:23; 26:8,11; 38:4 **11:22** [e]S Isa 9:17; Jer 18:21 **11:23** [f]Jer 6:9 [g]Jer 23:12 **12:1** [h]S Ezr 9:15; Job 8:3; Da 9:14 [i]S Job 5:8 [j]Eze 18:25 [k]S Job 21:7,13; Ps 37:7; Jer 5:27-28 **12:2** [l]S Jer 11:17 [m]S Job 5:3 [n]S Isa 29:13; S Jer 3:10; S Eze 22:27; Mt 15:8; Mk 7:6; Tit 1:16 **12:3** [o]Ps 7:9; 11:5; 139:1-4 [p]S Ps 44:11 [q]Jer 16:18; 17:18; 20:11 **12:4** [r]S Jer 4:28 [s]S ver 11; S Jer 4:26; Joel 1:10-12; Am 1:2 [t]Dt 28:15-18; S Jer 4:25; S 9:10 **12:5** [u]Jer 49:19; 50:44 **12:6** [v]S Pr 26:24-25; Jer 9:4 [w]Ps 12:2

off from the land of the living. See Isa 53:8; contrast Ps 27:13. *name.* Since Jeremiah had no children (see 16:2), his name would die with him. *be remembered no more.* As though he were evil (see Job 24:20; Eze 21:32).

11:20 Repeated almost verbatim in 20:12; see also 17:10. *you who judge righteously.* See note on Ge 18:25. *let me see your vengeance upon them.* See notes on Dt 32:35; Ps 5:10.

11:21 *men of Anathoth who are seeking your life.* See 12:6. "A man's enemies are the members of his own household" (Mic 7:6, quoted by Jesus in Mt 10:36).

11:22 *sword … famine.* See note on 5:12.

11:23 *remnant.* See 6:9; Isa 10:20–22 and notes. *them.* The conspirators in Anathoth, not its entire population, since 128 men of Anathoth returned to their hometown after the exile (see Ezr 2:23).

12:1–4 The second of Jeremiah's "confessions" (see Introduction: Author and Date), continuing and closely related to the first (11:18–23). Jeremiah speaks in vv. 1–4, and God responds in vv. 5–6.

12:1 *You are … righteous.* See note on Ge 18:25; see also 11:20; Ps 51:4; Ro 3:4. Because God is righteous, he is a dependable arbiter and judge. *Yet.* He is nevertheless ready to listen to our questions and complaints. *Why does … the wicked prosper?* The question is not unique to Jeremiah (see, e.g., Job 21:7–15; Mal 3:15). The Lord replies that ultimately the wicked in Judah will perish (vv. 7–13) and that the wicked invaders who destroy them will themselves be destroyed (vv. 14–17).

12:2 *You have planted them.* But a sovereign God can always reconsider his intentions if conditions warrant a change (see 18:9–10). *bear fruit.* The wicked flourish, while Jeremiah's fellow citizens plot to destroy his own "fruit" (see 11:19). *on their lips … far from their hearts.* Quoted in part by Jesus in Mt 15:8–9.

12:3 *test my thoughts.* See 11:20. *like sheep to be butchered.* Jeremiah asks that his wicked countrymen receive the fate mentioned for himself in 11:19. His request arises not so much out of a desire for revenge as for the vindication of God's righteousness (see note on 10:25). *day of slaughter.* An expression found elsewhere only in Jas 5:5 (see note there).

12:4 *parched … withered.* See 23:10; see also 3:3; 14:1 and note. Apparently there was a series of droughts in Judah during Jeremiah's ministry. *He will not see.* The prophet's enemies do not believe that his predictions will be fulfilled. Or they believe that if they are, Jeremiah will not live to see their fulfillment.

12:5 The Lord warns Jeremiah that in the future his troubles will increase (see, e.g., 38:4–6). *stumble.* The Hebrew for this word, which usually means "trust" (see NIV text note), has a negative meaning in a few passages (see, e.g., Pr 14:16, where it is translated "reckless"). *thickets.* Providing cover for lions (see 49:19; 50:44; Zec 11:3). If the Hebrew for this word means "flooding" (see NIV text note) here, an ancient example is described in Jos 3:15.

12:6 *family.* Lit. "house," linking this verse verbally with the following context (see v. 7). Apparently, members of Jeremiah's own family were included in the "men of Anathoth" (11:21,23) who wanted to kill him.

7 "I will forsake[x] my house,
abandon[y] my inheritance;
I will give the one I love[z]
into the hands of her enemies.[a]
8 My inheritance has become to me
like a lion[b] in the forest.
She roars at me;
therefore I hate her.[c]
9 Has not my inheritance become to me
like a speckled bird of prey
that other birds of prey surround and
attack?
Go and gather all the wild beasts;
bring them to devour.[d]
10 Many shepherds[e] will ruin my vineyard
and trample down my field;
they will turn my pleasant field
into a desolate wasteland.[f]
11 It will be made a wasteland,[g]
parched and desolate before me;[h]
the whole land will be laid waste
because there is no one who cares.
12 Over all the barren heights in the
desert
destroyers will swarm,
for the sword[i] of the LORD[j] will
devour[k]
from one end of the land to the
other;[l]
no one will be safe.[m]
13 They will sow wheat but reap thorns;
they will wear themselves out but
gain nothing.[n]
So bear the shame of your harvest
because of the LORD's fierce
anger."[o]

14 This is what the LORD says: "As for all
my wicked neighbors who seize the inheritance[p] I gave my people Israel, I will
uproot[q] them from their lands and I will
uproot[r] the house of Judah from among
them. 15 But after I uproot them, I will
again have compassion[s] and will bring[t]
each of them back to his own inheritance
and his own country. 16 And if they learn[u]
well the ways of my people and swear by
my name, saying, 'As surely as the LORD
lives'[v]—even as they once taught my
people to swear by Baal[w]—then they will
be established among my people.[x] 17 But
if any nation does not listen, I will completely uproot and destroy[y] it," declares
the LORD.

A Linen Belt

13 This is what the LORD said to me:
"Go and buy a linen belt and put it
around your waist, but do not let it touch
water." 2 So I bought a belt, as the LORD directed, and put it around my waist.
3 Then the word of the LORD came to me
a second time:[z] 4 "Take the belt you bought
and are wearing around your waist, and
go now to Perath[a][a] and hide it there in a
crevice in the rocks." 5 So I went and hid it
at Perath, as the LORD told me.[b]
6 Many days later the LORD said to me,
"Go now to Perath and get the belt I told

[a] 4 Or possibly *the Euphrates*; also in verses 5-7

12:7 [x] S 2Ki 21:14 [y] S Jer 7:29 [z] Isa 5:1 [a] Jer 17:4 **12:8** [b] S Ps 17:12 [c] Ps 5:5; Hos 9:15; Am 6:8 **12:9** [d] S Dt 28:26; Isa 56:9; Jer 15:3; Eze 23:25; 39:17-20 **12:10** [e] Jer 23:1; 25:34; Eze 34:2-10 [f] Isa 5:1-7; Jer 9:10; 25:11 **12:11** [g] S Isa 5:6; S 24:4 [h] ver 4; Jer 9:12; 14:4; 23:10 **12:12** [i] Eze 21:3-4 [j] S Dt 32:41; Isa 31:8; Jer 46:10; 47:6; Eze 14:17; 21:28; 33:2 [k] S Dt 32:42 [l] Jer 3:2 [m] Jer 7:10 **12:13** [n] S Lev 26:20; S Dt 28:38 [o] S Ex 15:7; S Jer 4:26 **12:14** [p] S Dt 29:28; S 2Ch 7:20 [q] S Ps 9:6; Zec 2:7-9 [r] S Dt 28:63 **12:15** [s] S Ps 6:2 [t] S Dt 30:3; Am 9:14-15 **12:16** [u] Jer 18:8 [v] S Jer 4:2 [w] S Jos 23:7 [x] S Isa 26:18; 49:6; Jer 3:17 **12:17** [y] S Ge 27:29 **13:3** [z] Jer 33:1 **13:4** [a] S Ge 2:14 **13:5** [b] Ex 40:16

12:7 – 17 The Lord will judge Judah (vv. 7 – 13) as well as the wicked neighboring nations (vv. 14 – 17).
12:7 *house.* Judah (see, e.g., 11:17). *inheritance.* God's land and people (see vv. 8 – 9,14 – 15; see also Ex 15:17 and note; Dt 4:20; Isa 19:25; 47:6). *the one I love.* See note on 11:15.
12:8 *I hate her.* I will withdraw my love from her by giving her "into the hands of her enemies" (v. 7; see Mal 1:3 and note).
12:9 *other birds of prey ... wild beasts.* Judah's enemies (see Isa 56:9 and note).
12:10 *shepherds.* Rulers (see note on 2:8). *my vineyard.* Judah (see 2:21 and note). *pleasant field.* See 3:19 and note.
12:11 *parched.* See v. 4 and note. A total of seven *s*-sounds and seven *m*-sounds in the Hebrew of this brief verse punctuates its theme and provides a striking example of Jeremiah's literary gifts (see Introduction: Literary Features).
12:12 *barren heights.* Places of idolatrous worship (see 3:2; Nu 23:3). *destroyers.* The Babylonians (see note on 4:7). *sword of the LORD.* Symbolizing God's instruments of judgment (see 25:29; 47:6 and note on Ps 7:12 – 13). *from one end ... to the other.* See 25:33. *no one will be safe.* Lit. "there will be no peace/safety for anyone" (see 6:14 and note).
12:13 See 14:2 – 4.
12:14 *wicked neighbors.* See, e.g., 2Ki 24:2. *seize.* Lit. "touch," used in the context of attack and plunder in Zec 2:8. *uproot.* Carry off into exile (see, e.g., 1Ki 14:15).
12:15 The exiles from Judah, and those from the neighboring nations, will eventually be brought back to their respective lands (see v. 16; 32:37,44; 33:26; 48:47; 49:6).
12:16 To be fulfilled in the times of the Messiah (see Isa 56:6 – 7 and note on 56:7). *ways.* See note on 10:2. *swear by my name.* See Dt 6:13 and note. *Baal.* See note on Jdg 2:13. *be established.* Or, perhaps, "prosper," as in Mal 3:15.
13:1 – 27 A series of five warnings, the first two (vv. 1 – 11, 12 – 14) written in prose and the last three (vv. 15 – 17, 18 – 19,20 – 27) in poetry.
13:1 – 11 The story of the ruined, useless belt is the first major example of the Lord's commanding Jeremiah to perform symbolic acts to illustrate his message (see Introduction: Literary Features).
13:1 – 2,4 – 7 *Go and buy ... So I bought ... Take the belt ... and hide it ... So I went and hid it ... Go now to Perath and get the belt ... So I went to Perath and dug up the belt.* Like his spiritual ancestor Abraham (see note on Ge 12:4), Jeremiah was characterized by prompt obedience.
13:1 *linen.* The material of which the priests' garments were made (see Eze 44:17 – 18), symbolic of Israel's holiness as a "kingdom of priests" (see Ex 19:6 and note). The linen belt is a symbol of the formerly intimate relationship between God and Judah (see v. 11). *do not let it touch water.* Do not wash it — symbolic of Judah's sinful pride (see v. 9).
13:3 *Then.* Some time later.
13:4 *Perath.* Perhaps the same as Parah (Jos 18:23), near the modern Wadi Farah, three miles northeast of Anathoth. Since in other contexts the Hebrew for Perath refers to the river Euphrates (see NIV text note), it serves as an appropriate symbol of the corrupting Assyrian and Babylonian influence on Judah that began during the reign of Ahaz (see 2Ki 16). *crevice in the rocks.* See note on 16:16.
13:6 *Many days later.* Perhaps a reference to the lengthy Babylonian exile.

you to hide there." 7So I went to Perath
and dug up the belt and took it from the
place where I had hidden it, but now it
was ruined and completely useless.
8Then the word of the LORD came to
me: 9"This is what the LORD says: 'In the
same way I will ruin the pride of Judah
and the great pride[c] of Jerusalem. 10These
wicked people, who refuse to listen[d] to
my words, who follow the stubbornness
of their hearts[e] and go after other gods[f] to
serve and worship them,[g] will be like this
belt — completely useless![h] 11For as a belt
is bound around a man's waist, so I bound
the whole house of Israel and the whole
house of Judah to me,' declares the LORD,
'to be my people for my renown[i] and praise
and honor.[j] But they have not listened.'[k]

Wineskins

12"Say to them: 'This is what the LORD,
the God of Israel, says: Every wineskin
should be filled with wine.' And if they say
to you, 'Don't we know that every wineskin should be filled with wine?' 13then
tell them, 'This is what the LORD says: I am
going to fill with drunkenness[l] all who live
in this land, including the kings who sit on
David's throne, the priests, the prophets
and all those living in Jerusalem. 14I will
smash them one against the other, fathers
and sons alike, declares the LORD. I will allow no pity[m] or mercy or compassion[n] to
keep me from destroying[o] them.' "

Threat of Captivity

15Hear and pay attention,
do not be arrogant,
for the LORD has spoken.[p]
16Give glory[q] to the LORD your God
before he brings the darkness,
before your feet stumble[r]
on the darkening hills.
You hope for light,
but he will turn it to thick darkness
and change it to deep gloom.[s]
17But if you do not listen,[t]
I will weep in secret
because of your pride;
my eyes will weep bitterly,
overflowing with tears,[u]
because the LORD's flock[v] will be
taken captive.[w]
18Say to the king[x] and to the queen
mother,[y]
"Come down from your thrones,
for your glorious crowns[z]
will fall from your heads."
19The cities in the Negev will be shut up,
and there will be no one to open
them.
All Judah[a] will be carried into exile,
carried completely away.
20Lift up your eyes and see
those who are coming from the
north.[b]
Where is the flock[c] that was entrusted
to you,
the sheep of which you boasted?
21What will you say when ⌞the LORD⌟ sets
over you
those you cultivated as your special
allies?[d]
Will not pain grip you
like that of a woman in labor?[e]

13:9 [c]S Lev 26:19; S Mt 23:12; S Lk 1:51 **13:10** [d]Jer 22:21 [e]S Ecc 9:3; S Jer 3:17 [f]S Dt 8:19; Jer 9:14 [g]S Jdg 10:13 [h]Eze 15:3 **13:11** [i]Isa 63:12; Jer 32:20 [j]Ex 19:5-6; Isa 43:21; S Jer 3:17 [k]S Isa 65:12; S Jer 7:26 **13:13** [l]Ps 60:3; 75:8; S Isa 29:9; Jer 25:18; 51:57 **13:14** [m]Eze 7:4; 8:18; 9:5,10; 24:14; Zec 11:6 [n]S Isa 9:17; Jer 16:5 [o]Dt 29:20; Isa 9:19-21; S Jer 7:20; 49:32,36; La 2:21; Eze 5:10 **13:15** [p]S Ex 23:21; Ps 95:7-8 **13:16** [q]S Jos 7:19 [r]S Lev 26:37; S Job 3:23; Isa 51:17; Jer 23:12 [s]S 1Sa 2:9; S Job 3:5; S Ps 82:5 **13:17** [t]Mal 2:2 [u]S Jer 9:1 [v]Ps 80:1; Jer 23:1 [w]Jer 14:18; 29:1 **13:18** [x]Jer 21:11; 22:1 [y]S 1Ki 2:19; S 2Ki 24:8; S Isa 22:17 [z]S 2Sa 12:30; La 5:16; Eze 16:12; 21:26 **13:19** [a]Jer 20:4; 52:30; La 1:3 **13:20** [b]Jer 6:22; Hab 1:6 [c]Jer 23:2 **13:21** [d]S Ps 41:9; Jer 4:30; 20:10; 38:22; Ob 1:7 [e]S Jer 4:31

13:7 *dug up.* The belt had either been buried by the prophet or silted over by the water of the wadi. *it was ruined.* As foreseen in Lev 26:39, God's people in exile would waste away because of their sins and the sins of their ancestors.
13:9 *pride ... great pride.* Contrast 9:23–24. Judah's vaunted pride would be a cause of her downfall and exile (see vv. 15,17), as foreshadowed in Lev 26:19.
13:10 *refuse to listen.* See note on 9:6. *stubbornness of their hearts.* See note on 3:17. *completely useless.* See 24:8.
13:11 *But they have not listened.* And therefore the promise of Dt 26:19 can no longer be fulfilled in them.
13:12–14 The Lord uses the imagery of filled wineskins to point toward the eventual destruction of Judah's leaders and people.
13:13 *drunkenness.* In a literal sense (see, e.g., Isa 28:7), but also symbolizing the effects of the wine of God's wrath (see 25:15–29; Ps 60:3; Isa 51:17–23; Eze 23:32–34). *kings ... priests ... prophets ... all those living in Jerusalem.* See 26:16; see also note on 1:18.
13:14 *smash them one against the other.* The various factions in Judah produced only confusion and chaos in the face of determined outside enemies. *no pity or mercy or compassion.* See 21:7; see also Eze 5:11.
13:15–17 Sinful pride carries the seeds of its own destruction, says the prophet.
13:15 *Hear.* See note on 2:4. *do not be arrogant.* See v. 17; see also note on v. 9.
13:16 *Give glory to ... God.* Confess your sins (see Jos 7:19; Jn 9:24 and NIV text notes). *You hope for light, but.* Cf. the description of the day of the Lord in Am 5:18–20; 8:9.
13:17 *I will weep.* See note on 9:1. *pride.* See v. 15; see also note on v. 9. *flock.* The Israelites living in the kingdom of Judah (see v. 20; Zec 10:3; see also note on 10:21). *taken captive.* Into exile (see v. 19).
13:18–19 The prophet speaks: Exile is imminent.
13:18 *king and ... queen mother.* Probably Jehoiachin and Nehushta (2Ki 24:8). If so, the date is 597 B.C., about 12 years after Josiah's death (see note on 11:1 — 13:27). *your ... crowns will fall.* See 22:24–26; 29:2; 2Ki 24:15; cf. Eze 21:25–27 and notes.
13:19 *Negev.* The dry southland (see note on Ge 12:9). *shut up.* Blocked by debris (see Isa 24:10). *All Judah.* The nation as a whole. *carried completely away.* Cf. Am 1:6,9 ("whole communities").
13:20–27 First the prophet speaks (vv. 20–23), then the Lord (vv. 24–27). Judah's willful rebellion has made exile inevitable.
13:20 *your ... you ... you.* Jerusalem, personified as a woman (see vv. 21–22,26–27), is being addressed. *the north.* Babylonia (see 4:6; see also note on Isa 41:25). *flock ... sheep.* See note on v. 17.
13:21 *special allies.* Perhaps Egypt and Babylonia, who alter-

[22]And if you ask yourself,
"Why has this happened to me?"[f]—
it is because of your many sins[g]
that your skirts have been torn off[h]
and your body mistreated.[i]
[23]Can the Ethiopian[a] change his skin
or the leopard its spots?
Neither can you do good
who are accustomed to doing evil.[j]

[24]"I will scatter you like chaff[k]
driven by the desert wind.[l]
[25]This is your lot,
the portion[m] I have decreed for you,"
declares the LORD,
"because you have forgotten[n] me
and trusted in false gods.[o]
[26]I will pull up your skirts over your face
that your shame may be seen[p]—
[27]your adulteries and lustful neighings,
your shameless prostitution![q]
I have seen your detestable acts
on the hills and in the fields.[r]
Woe to you, O Jerusalem!
How long will you be unclean?"[s]

Drought, Famine, Sword

14 This is the word of the LORD to Jeremiah concerning the drought:[t]

[2]"Judah mourns,[u]
her cities languish;
they wail for the land,
and a cry goes up from Jerusalem.
[3]The nobles send their servants for
water;
they go to the cisterns
but find no water.[v]
They return with their jars unfilled;
dismayed and despairing,
they cover their heads.[w]
[4]The ground is cracked
because there is no rain in the
land;[x]
the farmers are dismayed
and cover their heads.
[5]Even the doe in the field
deserts her newborn fawn
because there is no grass.[y]
[6]Wild donkeys stand on the barren
heights[z]
and pant like jackals;
their eyesight fails
for lack of pasture."[a]
[7]Although our sins testify[b] against us,
O LORD, do something for the sake
of your name.[c]
For our backsliding[d] is great;
we have sinned[e] against you.
[8]O Hope[f] of Israel,
its Savior[g] in times of distress,[h]
why are you like a stranger in the
land,
like a traveler who stays only a
night?
[9]Why are you like a man taken by
surprise,
like a warrior powerless to save?
You are among[j] us, O LORD,
and we bear your name;[k]
do not forsake[l] us!

[10]This is what the LORD says about this people:

"They greatly love to wander;
they do not restrain their feet.[m]

[a] 23 Hebrew *Cushite* (probably a person from the upper Nile region)

13:22 [f]S 1Ki 9:9 [g]Jer 9:2-6; 16:10-12 [h]S Isa 20:4 [i]La 1:8; Eze 16:37; 23:26; Na 3:5-6 **13:23** [j]S 2Ch 6:36 **13:24** [k]S Ps 1:4 [l]S Lev 26:33; S Job 1:19; S 27:21 **13:25** [m]S Job 20:29; Mt 24:51 [n]S Isa 17:10 [o]S Dt 31:20; S Ps 4:2; 106:19-21 **13:26** [p]La 1:8; Eze 16:37; Na 3:5 **13:27** [q]Eze 23:29 [r]S Isa 57:7; Eze 6:13 [s]Hos 8:5 **14:1** [t]S Dt 28:22; S Isa 5:6 **14:2** [u]S Isa 3:26 **14:3** [v]S Dt 28:48; S 2Ki 18:31; Job 6:19-20 [w]S Est 6:12 **14:4** [x]S Jer 3:3; S 12:11; Am 4:8; Zec 14:17 **14:5** [y]Isa 15:6 **14:6** [z]S Job 39:5-6; S Ps 104:11; S Jer 2:24 [a]S Ge 47:4 **14:7** [b]S Isa 3:9; Hos 5:5 [c]S 1Sa 12:22; S Ps 79:9 [d]S Jer 2:19; 5:6 [e]S Jer 8:14 **14:8** [f]S Ps 9:18; Jer 17:13; 50:7 [g]Ps 18:46; S Isa 25:9 [h]Ps 46:1 **14:9** [i]S Isa 50:2 [j]S Ge 17:7; Jer 8:19 [k]Isa 63:19; Jer 15:16 [l]S Ps 27:9 **14:10** [m]Ps 119:101; Jer 2:25

nated in dominating Judah (see Introduction: Background). *like … a woman in labor.* See note on 4:31.
13:22 *skirts … torn off.* Disgraced publicly, like a common prostitute (see vv. 26–27; Isa 47:2–3; Hos 2:3,10).
13:23 *Can … spots?* A rhetorical question, expecting a negative answer (see 17:9).
13:24 *like chaff driven.* The fate of the wicked (see, e.g., Ps 1:4). *desert wind.* See note on 4:11.
13:25 *forgotten me.* See 2:32 and note.
13:26 See v. 22 and note.
13:27 *adulteries and lustful neighings.* See note on 5:8. *shameless prostitution.* See Eze 16:26; see also Ex 34:15 and note. *How long …?* There is yet hope, however slender, to postpone the divine wrath (cf., e.g., 12:14–16).
14:1 — 15:21 Messages delivered by Jeremiah during an especially severe drought, the date of which is unknown.
14:1 — 15:9 After an initial vivid description of the drought (14:2–6), Jeremiah alternately prays (14:7–9,13,19–22) and God responds (14:10–12,14–18; 15:1–9).
14:1 *drought.* See 17:8. Unlike that in 3:3; 12:4, the suffering is increased because an enemy has invaded the land (see v. 18). Drought was one of the curses threatened (see 23:10) for disobedience to the covenant (see Lev 26:19–20; Dt 28:22–24).
14:2 *cities.* Lit. "gates" (see note on Ge 22:17); see 15:7.
14:3 *nobles.* A drought is no respecter of class distinctions. *cover their heads.* In mourning (see v. 4; 2Sa 15:30; cf. 2Sa 19:4).
14:4 *because there is no rain.* See 1Ki 17:7. Unlike Egypt, where the mighty Nile waters the ground, the Holy Land depends on adequate rainfall.
14:6 *pant.* The Hebrew underlying this word is translated "sniffing the wind" in 2:24. There a female wild donkey (Jerusalem) was in the heat of desire, while here the male wild donkeys are panting because of a drought brought on by Judah's sin. *eyesight fails.* See Ps 6:7 and note.
14:7–9 The prophet prays on behalf of the people (see v. 11).
14:7 *for the sake of your name.* See v. 21; Jos 7:9; Isa 48:9–11. *backsliding.* See 2:19; 3:22; 5:6. The word implies apostasy.
14:8 *O Hope of Israel.* See v. 22; 17:13; 50:7; Ac 28:20.
14:9 *we bear your name.* We belong to you, our ever-present Savior (see note on 7:10).
14:10–12 The Lord responds.
14:10–11 *this people.* God does not acknowledge them as his own (see Isa 6:9–10; 8:6,11–12; see also note on Ex 17:4).
14:10 *wander.* After false gods (see 2:23,31). *the LORD does not … their sins.* The Hebrew for these three lines is quoted verbatim from Hos 8:13 (cf. Hos 9:9).

So the LORD does not accept[n] them;
he will now remember[o] their
wickedness
and punish them for their sins."[p]

11 Then the LORD said to me, "Do not
pray[q] for the well-being of this people.
12 Although they fast, I will not listen to
their cry;[r] though they offer burnt offerings[s] and grain offerings,[t] I will not accept[u] them. Instead, I will destroy them
with the sword,[v] famine[w] and plague."[x]
13 But I said, "Ah, Sovereign LORD, the
prophets[y] keep telling them, 'You will not
see the sword or suffer famine.[z] Indeed, I
will give you lasting peace[a] in this place.' "
14 Then the LORD said to me, "The prophets are prophesying lies[b] in my name. I
have not sent[c] them or appointed them or
spoken to them. They are prophesying to
you false visions,[d] divinations,[e] idolatries[a]
and the delusions of their own minds.
15 Therefore, this is what the LORD says
about the prophets who are prophesying
in my name: I did not send them, yet they
are saying, 'No sword or famine will touch
this land.' Those same prophets will perish[f] by sword and famine.[g] 16 And the people they are prophesying to will be thrown
out into the streets of Jerusalem because
of the famine and sword. There will be
no one to bury[h] them or their wives, their
sons or their daughters.[i] I will pour out on
them the calamity they deserve.[j]

17 "Speak this word to them:

" 'Let my eyes overflow with tears[k]
night and day without ceasing;
for my virgin[l] daughter—my
people—
has suffered a grievous wound,
a crushing blow.[m]
18 If I go into the country,
I see those slain by the sword;
if I go into the city,
I see the ravages of famine.[n]
Both prophet and priest
have gone to a land they know not.[o]' "

19 Have you rejected Judah completely?[p]
Do you despise Zion?
Why have you afflicted us
so that we cannot be healed?[q]
We hoped for peace
but no good has come,
for a time of healing
but there is only terror.[r]
20 O LORD, we acknowledge[s] our
wickedness
and the guilt of our fathers;[t]
we have indeed sinned[u] against you.
21 For the sake of your name[v] do not
despise us;
do not dishonor your glorious
throne.[w]
Remember your covenant[x] with us
and do not break it.
22 Do any of the worthless idols[y] of the
nations bring rain?[z]
Do the skies themselves send down
showers?
No, it is you, O LORD our God.
Therefore our hope is in you,
for you are the one who does all
this.[a]

15
1 Then the LORD said to me: "Even if
Moses[b] and Samuel[c] were to stand
before me, my heart would not go out to
this people.[d] Send them away from my
presence![e] Let them go! 2 And if they ask
you, 'Where shall we go?' tell them, 'This
is what the LORD says:

[a] 14 Or *visions, worthless divinations*

14:10 [n] Jer 6:20; Am 5:22 [o] Hos 7:2; 9:9; Am 8:7 [p] Jer 44:21-23; Hos 8:13; Am 3:2 **14:11** [q] S Ex 32:10; S 1Sa 2:25 **14:12** [r] S Dt 1:45; S 1Sa 8:18; S Jer 11:11 [s] Lev 1:1-17; Jer 7:21 [t] S Lev 2:1-16 [u] Am 5:22 [v] S Isa 51:19; S Jer 9:16 [w] Jer 15:2; 16:4 [x] Jer 21:6; 27:8,13; 32:24; 34:17; Eze 14:21 **14:13** [y] Dt 18:22; Jer 27:14; 37:19 [z] S Jer 5:12 [a] S Isa 30:10; S Jer 4:10 **14:14** [b] S Jer 5:1; 23:25; 27:14; Eze 13:2 [c] Jer 23:21,32; 29:31; Eze 13:6 [d] Jer 23:16; La 2:9 [e] Eze 12:24 **14:15** [f] Jer 20:6; Eze 14:9 [g] Jer 5:12-13; 16:4; La 1:19 **14:16** [h] Ps 79:3 [i] S Jer 7:33 [j] S Pr 1:31; S Jer 17:10 **14:17** [k] S Ps 119:136 [l] S 2Ki 19:21; S Isa 23:12 [m] S Jer 8:21 **14:18** [n] Eze 7:15 [o] S 2Ch 36:10; S Jer 13:17 **14:19** [p] Jer 7:29 [q] S Isa 1:6; Jer 30:12-13 [r] S Job 19:8; S Jer 8:15 **14:20** [s] S Jer 3:13 [t] S Lev 26:40; S 1Ki 8:47; S Ezr 9:6 [u] S Jdg 10:10; Da 9:7-8 **14:21** [v] ver 7; S Jos 7:9 [w] Isa 62:7; Jer 3:17 [x] S Ex 2:24 **14:22** [y] S Isa 41:24; S 44:10; Jer 10:15; 16:19; Hab 2:18 [z] S 1Ki 8:36; S Ps 135:7 [a] S Isa 43:10 **15:1** [b] S Ex 32:11; Nu 14:13-20 [c] S 1Sa 1:20; S 7:8 [d] S 1Sa 2:25; S Jer 7:16 [e] S 2Ki 17:20; Jer 16:13

14:11 *Do not pray.* See note on 7:16; cf. 1Sa 7:8; 12:19.

14:12 *not accept them.* See v. 10. Sacrifice is to no avail when unaccompanied by repentance (see note on 6:20). *sword, famine and plague.* Curses for violating God's covenant (see Lev 26:25–26); the first occurrence of this triad, which occurs 15 times in Jeremiah (see Introduction: Literary Features; see also Eze 5:16–17 and note).

14:13 Jeremiah reminds the Lord of what the false prophets are saying. *not ... sword or ... famine.* See 5:12. *lasting peace.* Jeremiah's elaboration of the false prophets' "Peace, peace" (see 6:14; 8:11).

14:14–18 The Lord responds.

14:14 *lies.* See 5:12. *in my name.* See Dt 18:20,22. *delusions of their own minds.* See 23:26.

14:15 *Those ... prophets will perish.* See 28:15–17; Dt 18:20.

14:16 *no one to bury them.* See note on 7:33. *wives ... sons ... daughters.* All would perish, because all had worshiped false gods (see note on 7:18).

14:17 *my eyes overflow with tears.* See 9:18; 13:17. *virgin daughter—my people.* Lit. "the virgin of the daughter of my people" (see 8:11; Isa 22:4 and note on 2Ki 19:21).

14:19–22 The prophet prays on behalf of the people.

14:20 *guilt of our fathers.* See 2:5–6; 7:25–26. *we have ... sinned.* Repentance brings restoration (see Dt 30:2–3).

14:21 *For the sake of your name.* See Eze 20:9 and note. *your glorious throne.* The Jerusalem temple (see 17:12; 2Ki 19:14–15; Ps 99:1–2). *Remember your covenant ... do not break it.* Jeremiah pleads the ancient promise of God found in Lev 26:44–45.

14:22 See Hos 2:8,21–22. *worthless idols.* See note on 2:5. *it is you.* Only the Lord (not Baal) can send the showers to end the drought (see v. 1). *our hope is in you.* See note on v. 8.

15:1–9 The Lord responds, concluding this section (see note on 14:1—15:9).

15:1 *Moses and Samuel.* Very special agents of God's rule over Israel who were also famed for their intercessions for sinful Israel (see Ex 32:11–14,30–34; Nu 14:13–23; Dt 9:18–20,25–29; 1Sa 7:5–9; 12:19–25; Ps 99:6–8). *Send them away.* The people are so wicked that God refuses to hear prayers offered on their behalf. They are beyond divine help (see notes on 7:16; 14:11–12).

15:2 See Eze 14:21; 33:27. *death.* Probably by plague; see 14:12 (and note), where "sword, famine and plague" are God's three agents of destruction, paralleling the first three here

" 'Those destined for death, to death;
those for the sword, to the sword;[f]
those for starvation, to starvation;[g]
those for captivity, to captivity.'[h]

3"I will send four kinds of destroyers[i]
against them," declares the LORD, "the
sword[j] to kill and the dogs[k] to drag away
and the birds[l] of the air and the beasts of
the earth to devour and destroy.[m] 4I will
make them abhorrent[n] to all the kingdoms
of the earth[o] because of what Manasseh[p]
son of Hezekiah king of Judah did in Jerusalem.

5"Who will have pity[q] on you,
O Jerusalem?
Who will mourn for you?
Who will stop to ask how you are?
6You have rejected[r] me," declares the LORD.
"You keep on backsliding.
So I will lay hands[s] on you and destroy you;
I can no longer show compassion.[t]
7I will winnow[u] them with a winnowing fork
at the city gates of the land.
I will bring bereavement[v] and destruction on my people,[w]
for they have not changed their ways.[x]
8I will make their widows[y] more numerous
than the sand of the sea.
At midday I will bring a destroyer[z]
against the mothers of their young men;
suddenly I will bring down on them
anguish and terror.[a]
9The mother of seven will grow faint[b]
and breathe her last.[c]
Her sun will set while it is still day;
she will be disgraced[d] and humiliated.
I will put the survivors to the sword[e]
before their enemies,"[f]
declares the LORD.

10Alas, my mother, that you gave me birth,[g]
a man with whom the whole land
strives and contends![h]
I have neither lent[i] nor borrowed,
yet everyone curses[j] me.
11The LORD said,

"Surely I will deliver you[k] for a good purpose;
surely I will make your enemies
plead[l] with you
in times of disaster and times of distress.
12"Can a man break iron—
iron from the north[m]—or bronze?
13Your wealth[n] and your treasures
I will give as plunder,[o] without charge,[p]
because of all your sins
throughout your country.[q]

15:2 [f] Jer 42:22; 43:11; 44:13 [g] S Dt 28:26; S Jer 14:12; La 4:9 [h] Eze 12:11; Rev 13:10 **15:3** [i] S Nu 33:4 [j] S Lev 26:25 [k] S 1Ki 21:19; S 2Ki 9:36 [l] S Dt 28:26 [m] S Lev 26:22; Eze 14:21; 33:27 **15:4** [n] Jer 24:9; 29:18; 34:17 [o] S Dt 28:25; S Job 17:6 [p] S 2Ki 21:2; 23:26-27 **15:5** [q] Isa 27:11; 51:19; S Jer 13:14; 16:13; 21:7; Na 3:7 **15:6** [r] S Dt 32:15; Jer 6:19 [s] Isa 31:3; Zep 1:4 [t] S Jer 7:20; Am 7:8 **15:7** [u] S Isa 41:16 [v] Isa 3:26 [w] Jer 18:21 [x] S 2Ch 28:22 **15:8** [y] S Isa 47:9 [z] S Jer 4:7; S 6:4 [a] S Job 18:11 **15:9** [b] 1Sa 2:5 [c] S Job 8:13 [d] Jer 7:19 [e] Jer 21:7; 25:31 [f] 2Ki 25:7; Jer 19:7 **15:10** [g] S Job 3:1; S 10:18-19 [h] Jer 1:19 [i] S Lev 25:36; Ne 5:1-12 [j] S Jer 6:10 **15:11** [k] ver 21; Jer 40:4 [l] Jer 21:1-2; 37:3; 42:1-3 **15:12** [m] S Dt 28:48; Jer 28:14; La 1:14; Hos 10:11 **15:13** [n] S 2Ki 25:15 [o] S 2Ki 24:13; Eze 38:12-13 [p] S Ps 44:12 [q] Jer 17:3

(the Hebrew word for "starvation" here is the same as that for "famine" in 14:12).

15:3–4 Foreseen in Dt 28:25–26.

15:3 *four kinds.* Not the same four as in v. 2, but an elaboration of three of the fates awaiting the corpses of those killed by the sword. The seventh-century B.C. vassal treaties of Esarhaddon present similar curses: "May Ninurta, leader of the gods, fell you with his fierce arrow, fill the plain with your corpses, and give your flesh to the eagles and vultures to feed on … May dogs and pigs eat your flesh." *dogs.* See 1Ki 21:23. *beasts of the earth.* See Rev 6:8.

15:4 *abhorrent.* Cf. "a thing of horror" in Dt 28:25. *what Manasseh … did in Jerusalem.* Manasseh, good King Josiah's grandfather, was the most wicked king in Judah's long history (see 2Ki 21:1–11,16). His sins were a primary cause of Judah's eventual destruction (see 2Ki 21:12–15; 23:26–27; 24:3–4).

15:5–9 A poem concerning the forthcoming destruction of Jerusalem in 586 B.C (see La 1:1,12,21; 2:13,20).

15:5 Cf. Mt 23:37.

15:6 *You keep on backsliding.* Lit. "You go backward" (cf. 7:24; see note on 2:19).

15:7 *winnow.* See note on Ru 1:22. Winnowing as a figure of judgment is found also in 51:2; Pr 20:8,26; Isa 41:16. *bereavement … on my people.* The young men will fall in battle, and Judah and Jerusalem will be left childless (see Eze 5:17). *not changed.* Lit. "not repented of," reminiscent of the refrain in Am 4:6,8–11: "yet you have not returned to me," where the same Hebrew verb is used (see note on 3:1).

15:8 *widows more numerous than the sand of the sea.* A tragic reversal of the covenant promise of innumerable offspring (see Ge 22:17 and note). *At midday … suddenly.* Military attacks at noon were unexpected (see note on 6:4). *destroyer.* Babylon (see note on 4:7). *anguish.* See note on 4:19.

15:9 *seven.* The complete, ideal number of sons (see Ru 4:15 and note)—soon to be destroyed. *sun will set while it is still day.* See Am 8:9; cf. Mt 27:45 and note. *survivors.* Lit. "remnant" (see note on 6:9). Even they will be put to the sword (see Mic 6:14).

15:10–21 The third of Jeremiah's "confessions" (see Introduction: Author and Date), including in this case two responses by the Lord (vv. 11–14,19–21).

15:10 See 20:14–15 and notes; Job 3:3–10. *have neither lent nor borrowed.* Have not become involved in matters likely to evoke dispute or difference of opinion.

15:11–14 The Lord speaks, first to Jeremiah (v. 11), then to the people of Judah (vv. 12–14).

15:11 God encourages Jeremiah. *I will make your enemies plead with you.* Fulfilled, e.g., in 21:1–2; 37:3; 38:14–26; 42:1–3.

15:12 A rhetorical question assuming a negative answer. *iron.* Symbolic of great strength (see 28:13). *from the north.* From Babylonia (see note on Isa 41:25).

15:13–14 Repeated in large part in 17:3–4.

15:13 Fulfilled in 52:17–23. *without charge.* Cf. Isa 55:1. People and plunder alike would be free for the taking (see note on Isa 52:3).

[14]I will enslave you to your enemies
in[a] a land you do not know,[r]
for my anger will kindle a fire[s]
that will burn against you."

[15]You understand, O LORD;
remember me and care for me.
Avenge me on my persecutors.[t]
You are long-suffering[u]—do not take
me away;
think of how I suffer reproach for
your sake.[v]
[16]When your words came, I ate[w] them;
they were my joy and my heart's
delight,[x]
for I bear your name,[y]
O LORD God Almighty.
[17]I never sat[z] in the company of revelers,
never made merry with them;
I sat alone because your hand[a] was
on me
and you had filled me with
indignation.
[18]Why is my pain unending
and my wound grievous and
incurable?[b]
Will you be to me like a deceptive
brook,
like a spring that fails?[c]

[19]Therefore this is what the LORD says:

"If you repent, I will restore you
that you may serve[d] me;
if you utter worthy, not worthless,
words,
you will be my spokesman.[e]
Let this people turn to you,
but you must not turn to them.

15:14 [r]S Dt 28:36; S Jer 5:19 [s]S Ps 21:9
15:15 [t]Jdg 16:28; S Ps 119:84 [u]S Ex 34:6 [v]Ps 44:22; 69:7-9; S Jer 6:10
15:16 [w]Eze 2:8; 3:3; Rev 10:10 [x]S Job 15:11; Ps 119:72,103 [y]S Isa 43:7; S Jer 14:9
15:17 [z]Ru 3:3; Ps 1:1; 26:4-5; Jer 16:8 [a]S 2Ki 3:15
15:18 [b]S Job 6:4; S Jer 10:19; 30:12; Mic 1:9 [c]S Job 6:15; S Ps 9:10
15:19 [d]Zec 3:7 [e]S Ex 4:16
15:20 [f]S Isa 50:7 [g]S Ps 129:2 [h]S Jer 1:8; 20:11; 42:11; Eze 3:8
15:21 [i]S Jer 1:8 [j]S Ps 97:10 [k]Jer 50:34 [l]S Ge 48:16
16:2 [m]Mt 19:12; 1Co 7:26-27
16:3 [n]Jer 6:21
16:4 [o]ver 6; Jer 25:33 [p]S Jer 9:22 [q]S Jer 14:15 [r]S Dt 28:26; Ps 79:1-3; S Jer 14:12; 19:7
16:5 [s]S Jer 15:5
16:6 [t]Jer 9:21; Eze 9:5-6 [u]S ver 4 [v]S Lev 19:28 [w]S Lev 21:5; S Job 1:20

[20]I will make you a wall[f] to this people,
a fortified wall of bronze;
they will fight against you
but will not overcome[g] you,
for I am with you
to rescue and save you,"[h]
declares the LORD.
[21]"I will save[i] you from the hands of the
wicked[j]
and redeem[k] you from the grasp of
the cruel."[l]

Day of Disaster

16 Then the word of the LORD came to
me: [2]"You must not marry[m] and have
sons or daughters in this place." [3]For this
is what the LORD says about the sons and
daughters born in this land and about the
women who are their mothers and the
men who are their fathers:[n] [4]"They will
die of deadly diseases. They will not be
mourned or buried[o] but will be like refuse
lying on the ground.[p] They will perish by
sword and famine,[q] and their dead bodies
will become food for the birds of the air
and the beasts of the earth."[r]
[5]For this is what the LORD says: "Do
not enter a house where there is a funeral
meal; do not go to mourn or show sympathy, because I have withdrawn my blessing, my love and my pity[s] from this people," declares the LORD. [6]"Both high and
low will die in this land.[t] They will not
be buried or mourned,[u] and no one will
cut[v] himself or shave[w] his head for them.

[a] 14 Some Hebrew manuscripts, Septuagint and Syriac (see also Jer. 17:4); most Hebrew manuscripts *I will cause your enemies to bring you / into*

15:14 *for my anger will kindle a fire.* Quoted verbatim from Dt 32:22, where the Hebrew is translated "For a fire has been kindled by my wrath."
15:15 *You understand.* The Lord is aware of what Jeremiah has suffered (see v. 10). *remember.* Express concern for (see note on Ge 8:1).
15:16 *your words ... I ate them.* I digested them, I assimilated them, I made them a part of me (see Eze 2:8—3:3; Rev 10:9–10). *came.* Lit. "were found"—perhaps referring to the discovery of the Book of the Law in the temple during the reign of Josiah in 621 B.C. (see 2Ki 22:13; 23:2; see also note on 1:2). *they were ... my heart's delight.* See Ps 1:2. *I bear your name.* See 14:9. I belong to you (see note on 7:10).
15:17 *sat alone.* Jeremiah never married (see 16:2), and he attracted only a few friends (see Introduction: Author and Date). *your hand.* Divine constraint (see 2Ki 3:15; Isa 8:11 and note; Eze 1:3; 3:14,22; 37:1; 40:1). *indignation.* At the sins of Judah (see 6:11).
15:18 Two rhetorical questions used by Jeremiah to express his nagging doubts about himself, his mission and God's faithfulness. *pain unending ... wound grievous and incurable.* Jerusalem is similarly described in 30:12–15, together with God's promise of healing in 30:17. *deceptive brook.* See Mic 1:14, where also "deceptive" probably refers to the kind of intermittent streams described in Job 6:15–20. Jeremiah here accuses God of being undependable, in contrast to the Lord's own earlier description of himself as a "spring of living water" (see 2:13 and note).

15:19–21 The Lord commands Jeremiah to repent, then encourages him and renews his call.
15:19 *repent ... restore ... turn ... turn.* The Hebrew root is the same for all four words (see notes on 3:1; Isa 1:25–26). *serve.* Lit. "stand before"—the appropriate posture for the obedient servant (Nu 16:9; Dt 10:8). *spokesman.* Lit. "mouth" (see 1:9 and note; Ex 4:15–16; see also note on Ex 7:1–2).
15:20 See 1:8,18–19 and notes.
15:21 *save you from ... the wicked.* See, e.g., 36:26; 38:6–13.
16:1—17:18 Messages of disaster and comfort, with the note of disaster predominating (16:1–13,16–18; 16:21—17:6; 17:9–13,18). The first half of the section is prose (16:1–18), the second half poetry (16:19—17:18).
16:2 Jeremiah's ministry was such that he had to face life alone (see note on 15:17), without the comfort and support a family can provide. *You must not.* The Hebrew underlying this phrase is used for the most forceful of negative commands, as, e.g., in the Ten Commandments (see Ex 20:3–4,7,13–17). *this place.* Judah and Jerusalem, especially the latter (see, e.g., Zep 1:4).
16:4 *not be mourned or buried.* See v. 6; 7:33 and note; 8:2; 14:16; 25:33. *refuse.* Lit. "dung" (see 8:2; 9:22; 25:33). *perish by sword and famine.* See 14:15–16; see also note on 5:12. *food for the birds ... and the beasts.* See note on 7:33.
16:5 *do not go to mourn.* See the similar command of God in Eze 24:16–17,22–23.
16:6 *cut himself ... shave his head.* Actions forbidden in the law (see Lev 19:28; 21:5 and note; Dt 14:1 and note), but

7 No one will offer food[x] to comfort those
who mourn[y] for the dead—not even for a
father or a mother—nor will anyone give
them a drink to console[z] them.
8 "And do not enter a house where there
is feasting and sit down to eat and drink.[a]
9 For this is what the LORD Almighty, the
God of Israel, says: Before your eyes and in
your days I will bring an end to the sounds[b]
of joy and gladness and to the voices of
bride[c] and bridegroom in this place.[d]
10 "When you tell these people all this
and they ask you, 'Why has the LORD decreed such a great disaster against us?
What wrong have we done? What sin have
we committed against the LORD our God?'[e]
11 then say to them, 'It is because your fathers forsook me,' declares the LORD, 'and
followed other gods and served and worshiped[f] them. They forsook me and did
not keep my law.[g]
12 But you have behaved
more wickedly than your fathers.[h] See how
each of you is following the stubbornness
of his evil heart[i] instead of obeying me.
13 So I will throw you out of this land[j] into
a land neither you nor your fathers have
known,[k] and there you will serve other
gods[l] day and night, for I will show you
no favor.'[m]
14 "However, the days are coming,"[n] declares the LORD, "when men will no longer say, 'As surely as the LORD lives, who
brought the Israelites up out of Egypt,'[o]
15 but they will say, 'As surely as the LORD
lives, who brought the Israelites up out of
the land of the north[p] and out of all the
countries where he had banished them.'[q]

16:7 [x] S 2Sa 3:35 [y] Jer 22:10; Eze 24:17; Hos 9:4 [z] La 1:9,16 **16:8** [a] S Ex 32:6; S Ecc 7:2-4; S Jer 15:17 **16:9** [b] S Isa 24:8; S 51:3; Eze 26:13; Am 6:4-7 [c] S Ps 78:63 [d] Isa 22:12-14; Rev 18:23 **16:10** [e] S Dt 29:24; Jer 5:19 **16:11** [f] S Job 31:27 [g] Dt 29:25-26; S 1Ki 9:9; Ps 106:35-43 **16:12** [h] S Ex 32:8; S Jer 7:26; Eze 20:30; Am 2:4 [i] S Ecc 9:3; S Jer 3:17 **16:13** [j] S 2Ch 7:20 [k] S Dt 28:36; S Jer 5:19 [l] S Dt 4:28; S 1Ki 9:9 [m] S Jer 15:5 **16:14** [n] Jer 29:10; 30:3; 31:27,38 [o] S Dt 15:15 **16:15** [p] S Jer 3:18 [q] S Isa 11:11; Jer 23:8 [r] Ps 53:6; S Isa 11:12; Jer 30:3; 32:44; Eze 38:14; Joel 3:1 [s] S Dt 30:3; S Isa 14:1

For I will restore[r] them to the land I gave
their forefathers.[s]
16 "But now I will send for many fishermen," declares the LORD, "and they will
catch them.[t] After that I will send for many
hunters, and they will hunt[u] them down
on every mountain and hill and from the
crevices of the rocks.[v]
17 My eyes are on all
their ways; they are not hidden[w] from me,
nor is their sin concealed from my eyes.[x]
18 I will repay[y] them double[z] for their wickedness and their sin, because they have
defiled my land[a] with the lifeless forms of
their vile images[b] and have filled my inheritance with their detestable idols.[c]"[d]

19 O LORD, my strength and my fortress,
my refuge[e] in time of distress,
to you the nations will come[f]
from the ends of the earth and say,
"Our fathers possessed nothing but
false gods,[g]
worthless idols[h] that did them no
good.[i]
20 Do men make their own gods?
Yes, but they are not gods!"[j]

21 "Therefore I will teach them—
this time I will teach them
my power and might.
Then they will know
that my name[k] is the LORD.

16:16 [t] Am 4:2; Hab 1:14-15 [u] Am 9:3; Mic 7:2 [v] S 1Sa 26:20 **16:17** [w] S Ge 3:8; S Ecc 12:14; S Mk 4:22; 1Co 4:5; S Heb 4:13 [x] S Ps 51:9; Pr 15:3; Zep 1:12 **16:18** [y] S Isa 65:6 [z] S Isa 40:2; S Jer 12:3; Rev 18:6 [a] Nu 35:34; Jer 2:7 [b] S Ps 101:3 [c] S 1Ki 14:24 [d] S Jer 2:7; S 4:1; Eze 5:11; 8:10 **16:19** [e] S 2Sa 22:3; S Ps 46:1 [f] S Isa 2:2; Jer 3:17 [g] S Ps 4:2 [h] S Dt 32:21; S 1Sa 12:21 [i] S Isa 40:19; S Jer 14:22 **16:20** [j] Ps 115:4-7; S Jer 2:11; Ro 1:23 **16:21** [k] S Ex 3:15

sometimes practiced by Israelites as a sign of mourning (see 41:5; Eze 7:18; Mic 1:16).

16:7 Food was customarily offered to mourners (see 2Sa 3:35; 12:16–17; Eze 24:17,22; Hos 9:4). *drink to console them.* Lit. "cup of consolation," in later Judaism a special cup of wine for the chief mourner.

16:8 *do not enter a house where there is.* The present crisis is a time for neither feasting nor mourning (see v. 5).

16:9 See 7:34; 25:10; contrast 33:10–11.

16:10–13 The same question but a more elaborate answer than in 5:19 (see 9:12–16; 22:8–9; Dt 29:24–28; 1Ki 9:8–9).

16:10 Cf. the similar questions in Mal 1:6–7; 2:17; 3:7–8,13.

16:11 See 11:10, where committing sins like those mentioned here is called breaking the Lord's covenant.

16:12 *behaved more wickedly than your fathers.* See 1Ki 14:9. The coming judgment cannot be blamed on the sins of previous generations (see 31:29–30 and notes; Eze 18:2–4). *following the stubbornness of his evil heart.* See note on 3:17; see also 7:24.

16:13 See Dt 28:36,64. *I will throw you out.* Into exile (see 7:15; 22:26; Dt 29:28). *land neither you nor your fathers have known.* Babylonia (see 9:16).

16:14–15 Repeated almost verbatim in 23:7–8, the passage outlines nearly 1,000 years of Israelite history: exodus (c. 1446 B.C.), exile (586), restoration (537). See Isa 43:16–21; 48:20–21; 51:9–11. *As surely as the LORD lives.* See note on Ge 42:15.

16:15 *land of the north.* Babylonia (see note on Isa 41:25).

16:16 *fishermen ... hunters.* Symbolic of conquerors (see Eze 12:13; 29:4; Am 4:2 and note). *mountain and hill.* To which the people would flee in vain (see 4:29 and note). *crevices of the rocks.* The phrase occurs outside Jeremiah only in Isa 7:19. The Lord may be recalling here the episode of the ruined linen belt, hidden in a "crevice in the rocks" (13:4).

16:17 *My eyes are on all their ways.* See 32:19. *they are not hidden from me.* See 23:24 and note.

16:18 *repay them double.* See 17:18; Isa 40:2 and note. *defiled my land.* Made it ceremonially unclean (see 2:7; 3:1–2; see also note on Lev 4:12). *lifeless forms of their vile images.* See Lev 26:30. Idols have no life in them (see Ps 115:4–7; 135:15–17). *my inheritance.* God's land (see 17:4; see also note on 2:7). *detestable.* Abominable in the Lord's eyes (see 2:7; see also note on Lev 7:21).

16:19–20 The prophet interjects a few brief words of hope.

16:19 *strength ... fortress ... refuge in time of distress.* Such descriptions of God's dependability and protecting power are common in the Psalms (see, e.g., Ps 18:1–2; 28:7–8; 59:9,16–17). *to you the nations will come.* See 4:2 and note; see also Isa 2:2–4; 42:4; 45:14; 49:6; Zec 8:20–23; 14:16. *worthless idols.* See note on 2:5. *did them no good.* Were unprofitable to them (see note on 2:8).

16:20 *not gods.* See 5:7.

16:21—17:4 The Lord responds to Jeremiah and continues his solemn warnings that began in v. 1.

16:21 *teach ... teach ... know.* The same Hebrew root underlies each of these words. God would "cause them to know," and then they would surely "know." *them ... they.* Probably includes Judah as well as the nations (see Eze 36:23; 37:14). *know that my name is the LORD.* "Name" often means "person"

17 "Judah's sin is engraved with an
iron tool,[l]
inscribed with a flint point,
on the tablets of their hearts[m]
and on the horns[n] of their altars.
2 Even their children remember
their altars and Asherah poles[a o]
beside the spreading trees
and on the high hills.[p]
3 My mountain in the land
and your[b] wealth and all your
treasures
I will give away as plunder,[q]
together with your high places,[r]
because of sin throughout your
country.[s]
4 Through your own fault you will lose
the inheritance[t] I gave you.
I will enslave you to your enemies[u]
in a land[v] you do not know,
for you have kindled my anger,
and it will burn[w] forever."

5 This is what the LORD says:

"Cursed is the one who trusts in
man,[x]
who depends on flesh for his
strength
and whose heart turns away from
the LORD.[y]
6 He will be like a bush in the
wastelands;
he will not see prosperity when it
comes.
He will dwell in the parched places[z] of
the desert,
in a salt[a] land where no one lives.
7 "But blessed[b] is the man who trusts[c] in
the LORD,
whose confidence is in him.
8 He will be like a tree planted by the
water
that sends out its roots by the
stream.[d]
It does not fear when heat comes;
its leaves are always green.
It has no worries in a year of drought[e]
and never fails to bear fruit."[f]

9 The heart[g] is deceitful above all things
and beyond cure.
Who can understand it?

10 "I the LORD search the heart[h]
and examine the mind,[i]
to reward[j] a man according to his
conduct,
according to what his deeds
deserve."[k]

11 Like a partridge that hatches eggs it did
not lay
is the man who gains riches by
unjust means.
When his life is half gone, they will
desert him,
and in the end he will prove to be a
fool.[l]

12 A glorious throne,[m] exalted from the
beginning,
is the place of our sanctuary.

[a] *2* That is, wooden symbols of the goddess Asherah
[b] *2,3* Or *hills / [3]and the mountains of the land. / Your*

17:1 [l] Job 19:24 [m] S Dt 6:6; S 2Co 3:3 [n] S Ex 27:2 **17:2** [o] S 2Ch 24:18 [p] S Jer 2:20 **17:3** [q] S 2Ki 24:13 [r] Jer 26:18; Mic 3:12 [s] Jer 15:13 **17:4** [t] La 5:2 [u] Dt 28:48; S Jer 12:7 [v] Jer 16:13; 22:28 [w] S Jer 7:20 **17:5** [x] S Ps 108:12; S Isa 2:22 [y] 2Co 1:9 **17:6** [z] Job 30:3 [a] Dt 29:23; S Job 39:6; Ps 107:34; Jer 48:9 **17:7** [b] S Ps 146:5 [c] S Ps 26:1; 34:8; 40:4; Pr 16:20; Jer 39:18 **17:8** [d] S Job 14:9 [e] Jer 14:1-6 [f] Ps 1:3; 92:12-14; Eze 19:10; 47:12 **17:9** [g] S Ecc 9:3; Mt 13:15; Mk 7:21-22 **17:10** [h] S Jos 22:22; S 2Ch 6:30; S Rev 2:23 [i] Ps 17:3; 139:23; Jer 11:20; 20:12; Eze 11:5; 38:10 [j] S Lev 26:28; Ps 62:12; Jer 32:19; S Mt 16:27 [k] Jer 12:13; 14:16; 21:14; 32:19 **17:11** [l] Lk 12:20 **17:12** [m] S Jer 3:17

or "being" in the OT (see note on Ps 5:11). Ezekiel's equivalent of Jeremiah's phrase is "know that I am the LORD," found in his prophecy about 70 times (see Introduction to Ezekiel: Themes; see also note on Eze 5:13).

17:1 *engraved with an iron tool.* The method used to inscribe the most permanent of records (see Job 19:24). *flint.* An extremely hard stone from which tools and weapons were made (see notes on Ex 4:25; Jos 5:2; see also Eze 3:9; Zec 7:12). *tablets of their hearts.* For the same imagery see Pr 3:3; 7:3. *horns of their altars.* The people of Judah have backslid so badly that their sins are engraved not only on their hearts but also on their altars—to be remembered by God rather than to be atoned for (see Lev 16:18).

17:2 *altars and Asherah poles.* See notes on Ex 34:13; Dt 7:5. *spreading trees ... high hills.* See note on 2:20.

17:3–4 Repeated in large part from 15:13–14 (see notes there).

17:3 *My mountain.* Mount Zion, the location of the temple in Jerusalem (see Ps 24:3; Isa 2:3; Zec 8:3). *high places.* Locales of idolatrous worship (see note on 1Ki 3:2).

17:4 *inheritance.* The land of Canaan (see 16:18; see also note on 2:7).

17:5–8 See Ps 1 and notes.

17:5 *Cursed.* See note on 11:3. *flesh.* The opposite of "spirit" (see Isa 31:3; cf. Job 10:4).

17:6 *bush.* The Hebrew for this word suggests destitution (see Ps 102:17, "destitute"). *prosperity.* Lit. "good." The Hebrew for this word is translated "bounty" in Dt 28:12, where it refers to rain. *salt land.* An evidence of God's curse also in Dt 29:23.

17:7 *trusts ... confidence.* The same Hebrew root underlies both words.

17:8 *planted.* Or "transplanted." *stream.* See Isa 44:4, where the same Hebrew root is used again to illustrate the source of the righteous person's strength. *drought.* See note on 14:1. *bear fruit.* The Lord's answer to Jeremiah's complaint in 12:1–2 (see notes there).

17:9 The prophet makes an observation, then asks a rhetorical question. *heart.* The "wellspring of life" (Pr 4:23), in which wickedness must not be allowed to take root (see Ps 4:7 and note). *deceitful.* The Hebrew root for this word is the basis of the name Jacob (see NIV text notes on 9:4; Ge 27:36).

17:10 The Lord responds to Jeremiah's question. *search ... examine.* See 11:20; 12:3. *mind.* Lit. "kidneys" (see 11:20). The Hebrew for this word is translated "heart(s)" in 12:2. *what his deeds deserve.* Lit. "the fruit of his deeds" (cf. 6:19).

17:11 The prophet uses a proverb to make his point (as in v. 9). *partridge.* Mentioned elsewhere in the OT only in 1Sa 26:20. *fool.* Morally and spiritually bankrupt (see note on Pr 1:7).

17:12–18 The fourth of Jeremiah's "confessions" (see Introduction: Author and Date).

17:12 *glorious throne.* See note on 14:21; see also Isa 6:1. The Lord is often represented as sitting on a throne between the cherubim on the ark of the covenant in the temple (see 1Sa 4:4 and note). *exalted.* Mount Zion is the "high mountain of Israel" (Eze 20:40). *from the beginning.* From time immemorial, Zion had been chosen by God as the place of his sanctuary (see Ex 15:17).

13O LORD, the hope[n] of Israel,
all who forsake[o] you will be put to shame.
Those who turn away from you will be written in the dust[p]
because they have forsaken the LORD,
the spring of living water.[q]

14Heal me, O LORD, and I will be healed;[r]
save[s] me and I will be saved,
for you are the one I praise.[t]
15They keep saying to me,
“Where is the word of the LORD?
Let it now be fulfilled!”[u]
16I have not run away from being your shepherd;
you know I have not desired the day of despair.
What passes my lips[v] is open before you.
17Do not be a terror[w] to me;
you are my refuge[x] in the day of disaster.[y]
18Let my persecutors be put to shame,
but keep me from shame;
let them be terrified,
but keep me from terror.
Bring on them the day of disaster;
destroy them with double destruction.[z]

Keeping the Sabbath Holy

19This is what the LORD said to me:
“Go and stand at the gate of the people,
through which the kings of Judah go in
and out; stand also at all the other gates
of Jerusalem.[a] 20Say to them, ‘Hear the
word of the LORD, O kings of Judah and all
people of Judah and everyone living in Jerusalem[b] who come through these gates.[c]
21This is what the LORD says: Be careful
not to carry a load on the Sabbath[d] day
or bring it through the gates of Jerusalem.
22Do not bring a load out of your houses or
do any work on the Sabbath, but keep the
Sabbath day holy, as I commanded your
forefathers.[e] 23Yet they did not listen or
pay attention;[f] they were stiff-necked[g] and
would not listen or respond to discipline.[h]
24But if you are careful to obey me, declares the LORD, and bring no load through
the gates of this city on the Sabbath, but
keep the Sabbath day holy[i] by not doing
any work on it, 25then kings who sit on David’s throne[j] will come through the gates
of this city with their officials. They and
their officials will come riding in chariots
and on horses, accompanied by the men of
Judah and those living in Jerusalem, and
this city will be inhabited forever.[k] 26Peo-
ple will come from the towns of Judah
and the villages around Jerusalem, from
the territory of Benjamin and the western
foothills, from the hill country and the
Negev,[l] bringing burnt offerings and sacrifices, grain offerings, incense and thank

17:13 [n]Ps 71:5; Jer 14:8 [o]S Jer 2:17 [p]S Ps 69:28; 87:6; Eze 13:9; Da 12:1 [q]S Isa 12:3; Jn 4:10 **17:14** [r]S Isa 30:26; Jer 15:18 [s]S Ps 119:94 [t]S Ex 15:2; S Ps 109:1 **17:15** [u]S Isa 5:19; 2Pe 3:4 **17:16** [v]Ps 139:4 **17:17** [w]Ps 88:15-16 [x]S Ps 46:1; Jer 16:19; Na 1:7 [y]S Ps 18:18 **17:18** [z]Ps 35:1-8; S Isa 40:2; S Jer 12:3 **17:19** [a]Jer 7:2; 26:2 **17:20** [b]Jer 19:3 [c]Jer 22:2 **17:21** [d]Nu 15:32-36; S Dt 5:14; Ne 13:15-21; Jn 5:10 **17:22** [e]S Ge 2:3; S Ex 20:8; Isa 56:2-6 **17:23** [f]Jer 7:26 [g]Jer 19:15 [h]S 2Ch 28:22; S Jer 7:28; Zec 7:11 **17:24** [i]ver 22 **17:25** [j]S 2Sa 7:13; Isa 9:7; Jer 22:2, 4; Lk 1:32 [k]Jer 30:10; 33:16; Eze 28:26 **17:26** [l]Jer 32:44; 33:13; Zec 7:7

17:13 *hope of Israel.* See note on 14:8. *dust.* Lit. “earth,” sometimes referring to the netherworld (see note on Ps 61:2; see also note on Job 7:21), as also in Canaanite and Mesopotamian literature. “Written in the dust” would then mean “destined for death,” the opposite of “written in the book” of life (see Da 12:1; see also Ex 32:32; Ps 69:28; Lk 10:20; Rev 3:5 and notes). *forsaken ... spring of living water.* Contrast 15:18; see note on 2:13.

17:14 *Heal me.* See 15:18; Ps 6:2. *you are the one I praise.* Lit. “you are my praise” (see Ps 22:3 and note).

17:15 See 20:8. Jeremiah’s enemies accuse him of being a false prophet (see Dt 18:21–22). The accusation must have been voiced before the first invasion of Judah by the Babylonians in 605 B.C. after the battle of Carchemish (see 46:2; see also Introduction: Background).

17:16 *shepherd.* Symbolic of leadership and therefore of Jeremiah’s role as a prophet (see notes on 2:8; Ps 23:1; Jn 10:1–30).

17:17 *my refuge.* See 16:19 and note. *day of disaster.* See v. 18; 15:11.

17:18 *my persecutors.* See 15:15. *double.* See 16:18; Isa 40:2 and note.

17:19–27 An extended commentary on the Sabbath-day commandment (the covenant sign of God’s relationship with Israel; see Ex 31:13–17; Eze 20:12), probably the version recorded in Dt 5:12–15 (see note on v. 22 below).

17:19 *people.* Lit. “sons of the people.” The Hebrew for this word is translated “common people” in 26:23; 2Ki 23:6 and “lay people” in 2Ch 35:5,7. The latter meaning seems intended here, and therefore the “gate of the people” is likely the east gate of the temple, where the people assembled in large numbers and which the kings would be expected to use frequently.

17:20 *kings of Judah.* The current king and all subsequent ruling members of David’s dynasty (see, e.g., v. 25; 1:18; 2:26; 13:13; 19:3).

17:21 *Be careful.* See Jos 23:11. The Hebrew underlying this phrase is translated “watch yourselves ... carefully” in Dt 4:15, and a similar expression is translated “guard yourself in your spirit” in Mal 2:15, stressing the urgency and solemnity of the Lord’s command.

17:22 *Do not.* See note on 16:2. The Hebrew for this negative expression is stronger than that in v. 21. *not ... do any work ... keep the Sabbath day holy.* Specific references to the Sabbath-day commandment of Ex 20:8,10; Dt 5:12,14. *as I commanded.* The Hebrew underlying this phrase is unique to the Ten Commandments as recorded in Deuteronomy (see Dt 5:12,15–16; see note on vv. 19–27).

17:23 *did not listen ... were stiff-necked.* Repeated from 7:26 (see note there; see also 11:10). *not ... respond to discipline.* See 2:30; 5:3.

17:25 Repeated in part in 22:4. King David’s dynasty will last forever (see 23:5–6; 30:9; 33:15; 2Sa 7:12–17), and Jerusalem will be inhabited for all time (31:38–40; Zec 2:2–12; 8:3; 14:11), if the people of Judah obey the Lord (see v. 27)—and they will, according to 31:33–34.

17:26 *territory of Benjamin.* Jeremiah’s hometown was located there (see 1:1). *western foothills ... hill country.* See note on Dt 1:7. *Negev.* See note on Ge 12:9. *thank offerings.* Lit. “bringing thank offerings.” This repetition of “bringing” (see earlier in the verse) suggests that the sense of the Hebrew is “bringing burnt offerings ... and incense as thank offerings” (as intended also in 33:11).

offerings to the house of the LORD. 27But if you do not obey[m] me to keep the Sabbath[n] day holy by not carrying any load as you come through the gates of Jerusalem on the Sabbath day, then I will kindle an unquenchable fire[o] in the gates of Jerusalem that will consume her fortresses.' "[p]

At the Potter's House

18 This is the word that came to Jeremiah from the LORD: 2"Go down to the potter's house, and there I will give you my message." 3So I went down to the potter's house, and I saw him working at the wheel. 4But the pot he was shaping from the clay was marred in his hands; so the potter formed it into another pot, shaping it as seemed best to him.

5Then the word of the LORD came to me: 6"O house of Israel, can I not do with you as this potter does?" declares the LORD. "Like clay[q] in the hand of the potter, so are you in my hand,[r] O house of Israel. 7If at any time I announce that a nation or kingdom is to be uprooted,[s] torn down and destroyed, 8and if that nation I warned repents of its evil, then I will relent[t] and not inflict on it the disaster[u] I had planned. 9And if at another time I announce that a nation or kingdom is to be built[v] up and planted, 10and if it does evil[w] in my sight and does not obey me, then I will reconsider[x] the good I had intended to do for it.[y]

11"Now therefore say to the people of Judah and those living in Jerusalem, 'This is what the LORD says: Look! I am preparing a disaster[z] for you and devising a plan[a] against you. So turn[b] from your evil ways,[c] each one of you, and reform your ways and your actions.'[d] 12But they will reply, 'It's no use.[e] We will continue with our own plans; each of us will follow the stubbornness of his evil heart.[f]' "

13Therefore this is what the LORD says:

"Inquire among the nations:
Who has ever heard anything like this?[g]
A most horrible[h] thing has been done
by Virgin[i] Israel.
14Does the snow of Lebanon
ever vanish from its rocky slopes?
Do its cool waters from distant sources
ever cease to flow?[a]
15Yet my people have forgotten[j] me;
they burn incense[k] to worthless idols,[l]
which made them stumble[m] in their ways
and in the ancient paths.[n]
They made them walk in bypaths
and on roads not built up.[o]
16Their land will be laid waste,[p]
an object of lasting scorn;[q]
all who pass by will be appalled[r]
and will shake their heads.[s]

[a] 14 The meaning of the Hebrew for this sentence is uncertain.

17:27 [m]S 1Ki 9:6; Jer 22:5 [n]S Ne 10:31 [o]S Jer 7:20 [p]S 2Ki 25:9; Hos 8:14; Am 2:5 **18:6** [q]S Isa 29:16; 45:9; Ro 9:20-21 [r]S Ge 2:7 **18:7** [s]Jer 1:10 **18:8** [t]S Ex 32:14; Ps 25:11; Jer 26:13; 36:3; Jnh 3:8-10 [u]Jer 31:28; 42:10; Da 9:14; Hos 11:8-9; Joel 2:13; Jnh 4:2 **18:9** [v]Jer 1:10; 31:28 **18:10** [w]Eze 33:18 [x]1Sa 2:29-30; 13:13 [y]S Jer 1:10 **18:11** [z]S 2Ki 22:16; S Jer 4:6 [a]ver 18 [b]S Dt 4:30; S 2Ki 17:13; Isa 1:16-19 [c]S Jer 7:3 [d]S Job 16:17 **18:12** [e]S Isa 57:10 [f]S Jer 3:17 **18:13** [g]S Isa 66:8 [h]S Jer 5:30 [i]S 2Ki 19:21 **18:15** [j]S Isa 17:10 [k]S Isa 1:13; Jer 44:15,19 [l]Jer 10:15; 51:18; Hos 11:2 [m]Eze 44:12; Mal 2:8 [n]Jer 6:16 [o]S Isa 57:14; 62:10 **18:16** [p]S Dt 28:37; Jer 25:9; Eze 33:28-29 [q]Jer 19:8; 42:18 [r]S Lev 26:32 [s]S 2Ki 19:21; S Job 16:4; Ps 22:7; La 1:12

17:27 Disobedience will bring disaster and will negate—at least temporarily—the promises of vv. 24–26. *gates of Jerusalem.* The symbols of Sabbath violation would be the first structures destroyed. *kindle ... fire ... consume her fortresses.* Common prophetic language for divine judgment against rebellious cities (see 49:27; 50:32; Am 1:4,7,10,12,14; 2:2,5; cf. Jer 21:14).

18:1—20:18 Three chapters focusing on lessons the Lord taught Jeremiah at the potter's workshop, probably before 605 B.C. (see note on 17:15).

18:1–17 As the potter controls what he does with the clay, so the Lord is sovereign over the people of Judah.

18:2 *Go down.* The potter's workshop was probably located on the slopes of the Valley of Ben Hinnom near the Potsherd Gate (see 19:2 and note).

18:3 *wheel.* Lit. "two stones." Both wheels were attached to a single upright shaft, one end of which was sunk permanently in the ground. The potter would spin the lower wheel with his foot and would work the clay on the upper wheel; the process is described in the Apocryphal book of Ecclesiasticus (38:29–30).

18:4 *marred.* The Hebrew for this word is translated "ruined" in 13:7 with respect to the linen belt that Jeremiah had hidden (see note there). *as seemed best to him.* The flaw was in the clay itself, not in the potter's skill.

18:6 *Like clay ... so are you.* Biblical imagery often pictures humankind as made of clay by a potter (see Job 4:19 and note; Ro 9:20–21). *potter.* The Hebrew for this word is translated "Maker" in 10:16 with reference to God.

18:7–10 *If ... if ... if ... if.* God's promises and threats are conditioned on human actions. God, who himself does not change (see Nu 23:19; Mal 3:6; Jas 1:17), nevertheless does change his preannounced response to people, depending on what they do (see note on 4:28; see also Joel 2:13; Jnh 3:8—4:2 and note on 3:9; 4:11).

18:7 *uprooted, torn down and destroyed.* See 1:10 and note.

18:8 See 26:3. *evil ... disaster.* The Hebrew is the same for both words (also in v. 11).

18:9 *built up and planted.* See 1:10 and note.

18:11 *devising a plan.* See Est 8:3; 9:25; Eze 38:10. *turn from.* The Hebrew phrase underlying this phrase is translated "repents of" in v. 8.

18:12 *It's no use.* See 2:25; see also note on Isa 57:10. *follow the stubbornness of his evil heart.* See note on 3:17.

18:13–17 See 2:10–13.

18:13 *horrible thing.* See 5:30; 23:14; Hos 6:10. *Virgin Israel.* See note on 2Ki 19:21.

18:14–15 Although nature is reliable (v. 14), Judah is fickle and unfaithful (v. 15).

18:14 *Lebanon.* One of the highest of the northern mountains (see 22:6), reaching an altitude of over 10,000 feet.

18:15 *my people have forgotten me.* Repeated from 2:32 (see note there). *burn incense.* See note on 1:16. *worthless idols.* Lit. "nothing" (see 2:8 and note; Ps 31:6). *which made them stumble.* See 2Ch 28:23. *ancient paths.* See note on 6:16. *roads not built up.* See note on Isa 35:8.

18:16 *waste ... appalled.* The same Hebrew root underlies both words. *object of ... scorn.* See 19:8; 25:9,18; 29:18; 51:37.

17 Like a wind[t] from the east,
I will scatter them before their
enemies;
I will show them my back and not
my face[u]
in the day of their disaster."

18 They said, "Come, let's make plans[v]
against Jeremiah; for the teaching of the
law by the priest[w] will not be lost, nor will
counsel from the wise,[x] nor the word from
the prophets.[y] So come, let's attack him
with our tongues[z] and pay no attention to
anything he says."

19 Listen to me, O LORD;
hear what my accusers[a] are saying!
20 Should good be repaid with evil?[b]
Yet they have dug a pit[c] for me.
Remember that I stood[d] before you
and spoke in their behalf[e]
to turn your wrath away from
them.
21 So give their children over to famine;[f]
hand them over to the power of the
sword.[g]
Let their wives be made childless and
widows;[h]
let their men be put to death,
their young men[i] slain by the sword
in battle.
22 Let a cry[j] be heard from their houses
when you suddenly bring invaders
against them,
for they have dug a pit[k] to capture me
and have hidden snares[l] for my feet.
23 But you know, O LORD,
all their plots to kill[m] me.
Do not forgive[n] their crimes
or blot out their sins from your sight.
Let them be overthrown before you;
deal with them in the time of your
anger.[o]

19 This is what the LORD says: "Go and
buy a clay jar from a potter.[p] Take
along some of the elders[q] of the people
and of the priests 2 and go out to the Valley
of Ben Hinnom,[r] near the entrance of the
Potsherd Gate. There proclaim the words
I tell you, 3 and say, 'Hear the word of the
LORD, O kings[s] of Judah and people of Jerusalem. This is what the LORD Almighty,
the God of Israel, says: Listen! I am going
to bring a disaster[t] on this place that will
make the ears of everyone who hears of it
tingle.[u] 4 For they have forsaken[v] me and
made this a place of foreign gods[w]; they
have burned sacrifices[x] in it to gods that
neither they nor their fathers nor the kings
of Judah ever knew, and they have filled
this place with the blood of the innocent.[y]
5 They have built the high places of Baal to
burn their sons[z] in the fire as offerings to

18:17 [t]S Job 7:10; Jer 13:24 [u]S 2Ch 29:6; S Jer 2:27 **18:18** [v]ver 11; Jer 11:19 [w]Jer 2:8; Hag 2:11; Mal 2:7 [x]S Job 5:13; Eze 7:26 [y]Jer 5:13 [z]Ps 52:2; 64:2-8; S Jer 9:3 **18:19** [a]Ps 71:13 **18:20** [b]S Ge 44:4 [c]Ps 35:7; 57:6; S 119:85 [d]Jer 15:1 [e]S Ge 20:7; S Dt 9:19; Ps 106:23; Jer 14:7-9 **18:21** [f]Jer 11:22; 14:16 [g]S Ps 63:10 [h]S 1Sa 15:33; Ps 109:9; S Isa 47:9; La 5:3 [i]S Isa 9:17 **18:22** [j]S Jer 6:26 [k]S Ps 119:85 [l]Ps 35:15; 140:5; Jer 5:26; 20:10 **18:23** [m]S Jer 11:21; 37:15 [n]S Ne 4:5 [o]Ps 59:5; S Jer 10:24 **19:1** [p]Jer 18:2 [q]S Nu 11:17; 1Ki 8:1 **19:2** [r]S Jos 15:8 **19:3** [s]Jer 17:20

[t]S Jer 6:19 [u]S 1Sa 3:11 **19:4** [v]S Dt 31:16; Dt 28:20; S Isa 65:11 [w]S Ex 20:3; S Jer 1:16 [x]S Lev 18:21 [y]S 2Ki 21:16 **19:5** [z]S Lev 18:21; S 2Ki 3:27; Ps 106:37-38

The phrase implies hissing or whistling to express shock, ridicule and contempt. *all ... appalled.* See 19:8; 1Ki 9:8. *shake their heads.* See 48:27; Job 16:4 and note; see also Ps 44:14; 109:25.

18:17 *wind from the east.* See 4:11; Ps 48:7 and notes. *show them my back and not my face.* As the people themselves had done to God (see 2:27). His face symbolizes his gracious blessing and favor (see Nu 6:24–26 and note on 6:25).

18:18–23 The fifth of Jeremiah's "confessions" (see Introduction: Author and Date).

18:18 *They.* Jeremiah's enemies (see note on 17:15). *plans against Jeremiah.* See v. 12; 11:18–23; 12:6; 15:10–11,15–21. *teaching of the law.* Assigned to the priests (see note on Hos 4:4–9). *priest ... wise ... prophets.* Despite Jeremiah's prophecies to the contrary (see 6:13–15; cf. 23:9–40; Eze 7:26 and note), the people thought that the various sources for receiving guidance from the Lord would continue as usual. *attack him with our tongues.* See note on 9:3.

18:20 *good ... repaid with evil.* See Ps 35:12. *dug a pit.* Symbolic of his enemies' plots against him (see v. 22; Ps 57:6 and note; Pr 22:14; 23:27). *stood before you.* See note on 15:1. *spoke in their behalf.* See 14:7–9,21.

18:21 *hand them over to the power of the sword.* The Hebrew underlying this phrase occurs also in Ps 63:10; Eze 35:5. *be put to death.* Lit. "be slain by death," probably referring to plague, as in 15:2 (see note there).

18:22–23 See Ps 141:8–10.

18:22 *hidden snares.* See Ps 140:5; 142:3.

18:23 *you know, O LORD.* See 12:3; 15:15. *Do not forgive their crimes ... Let them be overthrown before you.* A prayer not for human vengeance but for divine vindication (see note on 10:25). *blot out their sins.* See Ps 51:1–2 and notes.

19:1–15 A jar deliberately broken by Jeremiah (vv. 1–10) symbolizes the forthcoming destruction of Judah and Jerusalem (vv. 11–15). In ch. 18, the potter's clay was still moist and pliable, making it possible to reshape and rework it (see 18:1–11). In ch. 19, however, the clay jar is hard and, if unsuitable for the owner's use, can only be destroyed (see v. 11).

19:1 *jar.* The Hebrew for this word implies a vessel with a narrow neck, perhaps the water decanter frequently found in excavations and ranging from 5 to 12 inches high. *elders.* See note on Ex 3:16. *of the people.* See 1Ki 8:1–3. *of the priests.* See 2Ki 19:2, "leading priests" (lit. "elders of the priests"). Elders in Israel were of two kinds, one performing primarily civil functions and the other primarily religious functions.

19:2 *Valley of Ben Hinnom.* See note on 7:31. *Potsherd Gate.* The Jerusalem Targum (an ancient Aramaic paraphrase) identifies the Potsherd Gate (so called because it overlooked the main dump for broken pottery) with the Dung Gate of Ne 2:13 (see note there); 3:13–14; 12:31.

19:3 *kings.* See note on 17:20. *disaster ... make the ears ... tingle.* Echoed from 2Ki 21:12 (see 1Sa 3:11). The phrase refers to the shock of hearing an announcement of threatened punishment.

19:4 *they.* All who tried to combine the worship of idols with the worship of the one true God. *this ... place.* Jerusalem. *burned sacrifices.* The Hebrew for this phrase is always translated "burned incense" elsewhere in Jeremiah (see note on 1:16). *filled this place with the blood of the innocent.* The blood of godly people (see 2:34; 7:6; 22:3,17; 26:15), specifically as shed by wicked King Manasseh (see 15:4 and note; see also 2Ki 21:16).

19:5–6 Repeated in large part from 7:31–32 (see notes there).

Baal—something I did not command or
mention, nor did it enter my mind.[a] 6So
beware, the days are coming, declares the
LORD, when people will no longer call this
place Topheth[b] or the Valley of Ben Hinnom,[c] but the Valley of Slaughter.[d]
7" 'In this place I will ruin[a] the plans[e]
of Judah and Jerusalem. I will make them
fall by the sword before their enemies,[f] at
the hands of those who seek their lives,
and I will give their carcasses[g] as food[h]
to the birds of the air and the beasts of
the earth. 8I will devastate this city and
make it an object of scorn;[i] all who pass
by will be appalled[j] and will scoff because
of all its wounds.[k] 9I will make them eat[l]
the flesh of their sons and daughters, and
they will eat one another's flesh during
the stress of the siege imposed on them
by the enemies[m] who seek their lives.'
10"Then break the jar[n] while those who
go with you are watching, 11and say to
them, 'This is what the LORD Almighty
says: I will smash[o] this nation and this
city just as this potter's jar is smashed
and cannot be repaired. They will bury[p]
the dead in Topheth until there is no more
room. 12This is what I will do to this place
and to those who live here, declares the
LORD. I will make this city like Topheth.
13The houses[q] in Jerusalem and those of
the kings of Judah will be defiled[r] like
this place, Topheth—all the houses where
they burned incense on the roofs[s] to all
the starry hosts[t] and poured out drink offerings[u] to other gods.' "
14Jeremiah then returned from Topheth,
where the LORD had sent him to prophesy,
and stood in the court[v] of the LORD's temple and said to all the people, 15"This is
what the LORD Almighty, the God of Israel,
says: 'Listen! I am going to bring on this
city and the villages around it every disaster[w] I pronounced against them, because
they were stiff-necked[x] and would not listen[y] to my words.' "

19:5 [a]S Jer 7:31; Eze 16:36 **19:6** [b]S 2Ki 23:10 [c]S Jos 15:8 [d]Jer 7:32 **19:7** [e]Ps 33:10-11 [f]S ver 9; S Lev 26:17; S Dt 28:25 [g]S Jer 16:4; 34:20 [h]S Dt 28:26 **19:8** [i]S Dt 28:37; S Jer 18:16; 25:9 [j]S Lev 26:32; La 2:15-16 [k]S Dt 29:22 **19:9** [l]S Lev 26:29; Dt 28:49-57; La 4:10 [m]S ver 7; Jer 21:7; 34:20 **19:10** [n]ver 1; S Ps 2:9; Jer 13:14 **19:11** [o]Ps 2:9; Isa 30:14 [p]Jer 7:32 **19:13** [q]Jer 32:29; 52:13; Eze 16:41 [r]Ps 74:7 [s]S 2Ki 23:12 [t]Dt 4:19; S 2Ki 17:16; S Job 38:32; Jer 8:2; Ac 7:42 [u]S Isa 57:6; Eze 20:28 **19:14** [v]2Ch 20:5; S Jer 7:2; 26:2

Jeremiah and Pashhur

20 When the priest Pashhur son of Immer,[z] the chief officer[a] in the temple
of the LORD, heard Jeremiah prophesying
these things, 2he had Jeremiah the prophet
beaten[b] and put in the stocks[c] at the Upper
Gate of Benjamin[d] at the LORD's temple.
3The next day, when Pashhur released him
from the stocks, Jeremiah said to him,
"The LORD's name[e] for you is not Pashhur,

[a] *7* The Hebrew for *ruin* sounds like the Hebrew for *jar* (see verses 1 and 10).

19:15 [w]ver 3; Jer 11:11 [x]S Ne 9:16; Ac 7:51 [y]Jer 22:21 **20:1** [z]S 1Ch 24:14 [a]2Ki 25:18; Lk 22:52 **20:2** [b]Dt 25:2-3; S Jer 1:19; 15:15; 37:15; 2Co 11:24 [c]S Job 13:27; Jer 29:26; Ac 16:24; Heb 11:36 [d]S Job 29:7; Jer 37:13; 38:7; Zec 14:10 **20:3** [e]Hos 1:4

19:7 *ruin.* Lit. "pour out"; see NIV text note (see also note on v. 1). As Jeremiah was saying this, he may have been pouring water from the jar to the ground (cf. 2Sa 14:14). *fall by the sword before their enemies.* The Babylonians are the instruments of the divine threat (see 20:6). *carcasses as food … beasts of the earth.* See 7:33 and note.

19:8 Echoes the language of 18:16 (see note there; see also Eze 27:35; Zep 2:15). *devastate … appalled.* The same Hebrew root underlies both words—the devastation of the city will have a similar effect on those who see its ruins. *scorn … scoff.* The same Hebrew root underlies both words.

19:9 One of the covenant curses (see Lev 26:29; Dt 28:53–57). *eat the flesh of their sons and daughters … eat one another's flesh.* When Jerusalem's food supply ran out during the Babylonian siege in 586 B.C., cannibalism resulted (see La 2:20; 4:10; Eze 5:10). Such shocking activity was not unprecedented in Israel (see 2Ki 6:28–29), and it would occur again in A.D. 70 during the Roman siege of Jerusalem (see Zec 11:9 and note): "A woman … who … had fled to Jerusalem … killed her son, roasted him, and ate one half, concealing and saving the rest" (Josephus, *Wars*, 6.3.4).

19:11 *smash this nation … as this potter's jar is smashed.* Egyptians of the 12th Dynasty (1991–1786 B.C.) inscribed the names of their enemies on pottery bowls and then smashed them, hoping to break the power of their enemies by so doing. *cannot be repaired.* See note on vv. 1–15.

19:13 *will be defiled like … Topheth.* King Josiah had earlier "desecrated Topheth" (2Ki 23:10). *burned incense.* See note on 1:16. *on the roofs.* See 32:29; see also note on Isa 15:3. The kings of Judah had built pagan altars on the roof of the palace in Jerusalem (see 2Ki 23:12). The Ugaritic Keret epic of the 14th century B.C. (see chart, p. xxiii) describes a similar practice: "Go to the top of a tower, bestride the top of the wall … Honor Baal with your sacrifice … Then descend … from the housetops." *starry hosts.* Worship of the sun, moon and stars was common in Judah throughout much of the later history of the monarchy (see, e.g., 2Ki 17:16; 21:3,5; 23:4–5; Zep 1:5). *drink offerings to other gods.* See note on 7:18.

19:14 *all the people.* A much larger audience than the elders of v. 1.

19:15 *the villages around it.* The towns of Judah that were dependent on Jerusalem (see 1:15; 9:11). *were stiff-necked and would not listen.* Repeated from 7:26 (see note there; see also 11:10).

20:1–6 Pashhur's response to Jeremiah's symbolic act (vv. 1–2), and Jeremiah's rejoinder (vv. 3–6).

20:1 *Pashhur.* One or more different men with the same name appear in 21:1; 38:1. *Immer.* Perhaps a descendant of the head of the 16th division of priests in the Jerusalem temple (see 1Ch 24:14). *chief officer.* The priest in charge of punishing troublemakers, real or imagined, in the temple courts (see v. 2; 29:26). The position was second only to that of the chief priest himself (compare 29:25–26 with 52:24).

20:2 The first of many recorded acts of physical violence against Jeremiah. *the prophet.* The first time Jeremiah is so called in the book (see Introduction: Theological Themes and Message), here to stress the enormity of Pashhur's actions. *beaten.* Probably in accordance with the Mosaic law of Dt 25:2–3 (see note on Dt 25:3). *stocks.* Lit. "restraint, confinement." *Upper Gate of Benjamin.* Probably the same as the "north gate of the inner court" (Eze 8:3; see 2Ki 15:35; see also Eze 9:2). *at the LORD's temple.* This qualifying phrase distinguishes the temple's Gate of Benjamin from the "Benjamin Gate" in the city wall (37:13; 38:7). Both gates were in the northern part of the city, facing the territory of Benjamin.

20:3 *Magor-Missabib.* See NIV text note; see also note on 6:25.

but Magor-Missabib.[a][f] 4For this is what
the LORD says: 'I will make you a terror to
yourself and to all your friends; with your
own eyes[g] you will see them fall by the
sword of their enemies. I will hand[h] all Judah over to the king of Babylon, who will
carry[i] them away to Babylon or put them
to the sword. 5I will hand over to their
enemies all the wealth[j] of this city—all
its products, all its valuables and all the
treasures of the kings of Judah. They will
take it away[k] as plunder and carry it off
to Babylon. 6And you, Pashhur, and all
who live in your house will go into exile
to Babylon. There you will die and be buried, you and all your friends to whom you
have prophesied[l] lies.' "

Jeremiah's Complaint

7O LORD, you deceived[b][m] me, and I was
  deceived[b];
 you overpowered[n] me and prevailed.
I am ridiculed[o] all day long;
 everyone mocks[p] me.
8Whenever I speak, I cry out
 proclaiming violence and
  destruction.[q]
So the word of the LORD has brought me
 insult and reproach[r] all day long.
9But if I say, "I will not mention him
 or speak any more in his name,"[s]
his word is in my heart like a fire,[t]
 a fire shut up in my bones.
I am weary of holding it in;[u]
 indeed, I cannot.

10I hear many whispering,
 "Terror[v] on every side!
 Report[w] him! Let's report him!"
All my friends[x]
 are waiting for me to slip,[y] saying,
"Perhaps he will be deceived;
 then we will prevail[z] over him
 and take our revenge[a] on him."

11But the LORD[b] is with me like a mighty
  warrior;
 so my persecutors[c] will stumble and
  not prevail.[d]
They will fail and be thoroughly
  disgraced;[e]
 their dishonor will never be
  forgotten.
12O LORD Almighty, you who examine
  the righteous
 and probe the heart and mind,[f]
let me see your vengeance[g] upon them,
 for to you I have committed[h] my
  cause.

13Sing[i] to the LORD!
 Give praise to the LORD!
He rescues[j] the life of the needy
 from the hands of the wicked.[k]

14Cursed be the day I was born![l]
 May the day my mother bore me not
  be blessed!

[a] *3 Magor-Missabib* means *terror on every side.*
[b] *7* Or *persuaded*

20:3 [f] S ver 10; S Ps 31:13 **20:4** [g] Jer 29:21 [h] Jer 21:10; 25:9 [i] Jer 13:19; 39:9; 52:27 **20:5** [j] S 2Ki 25:15; Jer 17:3 [k] S 2Ki 20:17 **20:6** [l] S Jer 14:15; La 2:14 **20:7** [m] S Ex 5:23; 22:16 [n] Isa 8:11; Am 3:8; 1Co 9:16 [o] Job 12:4 [p] S Job 17:2; S Ps 119:21 **20:8** [q] Jer 6:7; 28:8 [r] S 2Ch 36:16; S Jer 6:10 **20:9** [s] Jer 44:16 [t] S Ps 39:3; S Jer 4:19 [u] S Job 4:2; S Jer 6:11; Am 3:8; Ac 4:20 **20:10** [v] Jer 6:25 [w] Ne 6:6-13; Isa 29:21 [x] S Job 19:14; S Jer 13:21 [y] S Ps 57:4; S Jer 18:22; Lk 11:53-54 [z] S 1Ki 19:2 [a] S 1Sa 18:25; S Jer 11:19 **20:11** [b] Jer 1:8; Ro 8:31 [c] Jer 15:15; 17:18 [d] S Ps 129:2 [e] S Jer 7:19; 23:40 **20:12** [f] S Ps 7:9; S Jer 17:10 [g] Dt 32:35; S Ro 12:19 [h] Ps 62:8; Jer 11:20 **20:13** [i] S Isa 12:6 [j] Ps 34:6; 35:10 [k] S Ps 97:10 **20:14** [l] S Job 3:8, 16; Jer 15:10

20:4 Pashhur's new name symbolizes terror to all Judah, whose people will be exiled to Babylonia or put to death. *friends.* Associates and allies in the sense of covenant partners (see v. 6). *king of Babylon.* Nebuchadnezzar, who acceded to the Babylonian throne in 605 B.C. (see notes on 17:15; 18:1—20:18).

20:5 Fulfilled in 597 B.C. (see 2Ki 24:13) and in 586 (see 52:17–23; 2Ki 25:13–17).

20:6 *you, Pashhur, ... will go into exile.* Probably in 597 B.C., because shortly after that year (see 29:2) two other men in succession had replaced Pashhur as chief officer in the temple (see 29:25–26). *you have prophesied lies.* The priest Pashhur had pretended to be a prophet.

20:7–18 The sixth, last and longest of Jeremiah's "confessions" (see Introduction: Author and Date; see also note on 11:18–23). In some respects, it is the most daring and bitter of them all.

20:7 Cf. 15:18. *deceived.* Lit. "seduced" (Ex 22:16) or "enticed" (1Ki 22:20–22); see v. 10. Jeremiah feels that when the Lord originally called him to be a prophet, he had overly persuaded him (see NIV text note; see also 1:7–8,17–19; cf. Eze 14:9).

20:8 Jeremiah attributes his suffering to the Lord's demands on his life. *violence and destruction.* The prophet's message echoes the Lord's word (see 6:7). *reproach.* See Ps 44:13; 79:4.

20:9 A classic description of prophetic reluctance overcome by divine compulsion (see 1:6–8; Am 3:8; Ac 4:20; 1Co 9:16). *his word is ... like a fire.* See 23:29. The figure is unique to the prophet Jeremiah (see also La 1:13).

20:10 The Hebrew of the first two lines is identical with that of the first two lines of Ps 31:13. *Terror on every side!* See note on 6:25. The phrase is here used to mock Jeremiah in the light of his doleful message. *friends.* Lit. "men of my peace/welfare" (cf. Ps 41:9 and note). *waiting for me to slip.* See Ps 35:15; 38:16. *deceived.* See v. 7 and note. *we will prevail over him.* Or so they think (see v. 11). *take our revenge on him.* His enemies will not give up, no matter what it takes (see 11:19; 12:6; 26:11; cf. Ps 56:5–6; 71:10).

20:11 *the LORD is with me.* See 1:8 and note. *mighty.* The Hebrew for this word is translated "cruel" in 15:21, where it describes Jeremiah's enemies. Here it has a different nuance and is applied to God, whose might overcomes all cruelty. *warrior.* See notes on Ex 14:14; 15:3.

20:12 *vengeance.* See 11:20 and notes on Dt 32:35; Ps 5:10.

20:13 *Sing ... Give praise.* See 31:7; see also introduction to Ps 9. *rescues ... from the hands of the wicked.* See 15:21; 21:12. *needy.* See 22:16. By Jeremiah's time, "poor/needy" had become virtually synonymous with "righteous" (see Am 2:6; see also notes on Ps 9:18; 34:6).

20:14–18 See Job 3:3–19. From the heights of exultation (v. 13), Jeremiah now sinks to the depths of despair. The irreversibility of his divine call (v. 9), the betrayal of his friends (v. 10), the relentless pursuit of his enemies (vv. 7,11), the negative and condemnatory nature of his message (v. 8)—all have combined to bring to his lips a startling expression of despondency and hopelessness. The passage serves also as a transition to the next major section of the book. Judah and Jerusalem, Jeremiah will soon say, are now irrevocably doomed (see 21:1–10).

20:14 *Cursed be the day I was born!* See note on Job 3:3. The prophet questions the very basis of his divine commission (see 1:5).

15 Cursed be the man who brought my
father the news,
who made him very glad, saying,
"A child is born to you — a son!"
16 May that man be like the towns[m]
the LORD overthrew without pity.
May he hear wailing[n] in the morning,
a battle cry at noon.
17 For he did not kill me in the womb,[o]
with my mother as my grave,
her womb enlarged forever.
18 Why did I ever come out of the womb[p]
to see trouble[q] and sorrow
and to end my days in shame?[r]

God Rejects Zedekiah's Request

21 The word came to Jeremiah from
the LORD when King Zedekiah[s] sent
to him Pashhur[t] son of Malkijah and the
priest Zephaniah[u] son of Maaseiah. They
said: 2 "Inquire[v] now of the LORD for us because Nebuchadnezzar[a][w] king of Babylon[x]
is attacking us. Perhaps the LORD will perform wonders[y] for us as in times past so
that he will withdraw from us."
3 But Jeremiah answered them, "Tell
Zedekiah, 4 'This is what the LORD, the
God of Israel, says: I am about to turn[z]
against you the weapons of war that are in
your hands, which you are using to fight
the king of Babylon and the Babylonians[b]
who are outside the wall besieging[a] you.
And I will gather them inside this city. 5 I
myself will fight[b] against you with an outstretched hand[c] and a mighty arm[d] in anger and fury and great wrath. 6 I will strike[e]
down those who live in this city — both
men and animals — and they will die of a
terrible plague.[f] 7 After that, declares the
LORD, I will hand over Zedekiah[g] king of
Judah, his officials and the people in this
city who survive the plague,[h] sword and
famine, to Nebuchadnezzar king of Babylon[i] and to their enemies[j] who seek their
lives.[k] He will put them to the sword;[l] he
will show them no mercy or pity or compassion.'[m]
8 "Furthermore, tell the people, 'This is
what the LORD says: See, I am setting before you the way of life[n] and the way of
death. 9 Whoever stays in this city will die
by the sword, famine or plague.[o] But whoever goes out and surrenders[p] to the Babylonians who are besieging you will live;

20:16 [m]S Ge 19:25 [n]S Jer 6:26 **20:17** [o]S Job 3:16; S 10:18-19 **20:18** [p]S Job 3:10-11; S Ecc 4:2 [q]S Ge 3:17; S Job 5:7 [r]S 1Ki 19:4; Ps 90:9; 102:3 **21:1** [s]2Ki 24:18; Jer 52:1 [t]S 1Ch 9:12 [u]S 2Ki 25:18 **21:2** [v]S Ge 25:22; S 2Ki 22:18 [w]S 2Ki 25:1 [x]S Ge 10:10 [y]Ps 44:1-4; Jer 32:17 **21:4** [z]Jer 32:5 [a]Jer 37:8-10 **21:5** [b]S Jos 10:14; Eze 5:8 [c]S 2Ki 22:13; S Jer 6:12 [d]S Ex 3:20 **21:6** [e]S Jer 7:20 [f]S Jer 14:12 **21:7** [g]S 2Ki 25:7; Jer 52:9; Eze 12:14 [h]Jer 14:12; 27:8 [i]S 2Ch 36:10; Jer 27:6; 32:4; 34:3; 37:17; 38:18; 39:5; Eze 29:19 [j]S Lev 26:17; S Jer 19:9 [k]S Jer 11:21 [l]S Jer 15:9 [m]S 2Ch 36:17; S Jer 15:5; Eze 7:9; Hab 1:6 **21:8** [n]S Dt 30:15 **21:9** [o]Jer 14:12; Eze 5:12 [p]Jer 27:11; 40:9

[a] 2 Hebrew *Nebuchadrezzar,* of which *Nebuchadnezzar* is a variant; here and often in Jeremiah and Ezekiel
[b] 4 Or *Chaldeans*; also in verse 9

20:15 News of the birth of a son, normally a blessing in ancient times (see, e.g., Ge 29:31 – 35), Jeremiah sees as a curse in his own case. *Cursed be the man.* A rhetorical curse, not directed against the man personally.
20:16 *towns the LORD overthrew.* Sodom and Gomorrah (see Ge 19:24 – 25,29). By Jeremiah's time, their wickedness had long been proverbial (see 23:14; Dt 29:23; see also note on Isa 1:9 – 10). *battle cry.* See 4:19. *at noon.* See note on 6:4.
20:17 *enlarged.* Lit. "pregnant." In his anguish, Jeremiah wishes that his mother's womb, which gave him birth, had been instead his eternal tomb.
21:1 — 24:10 The prophet denounces Judah's rulers (21:1 — 23:7), false prophets (23:8 – 40) and sinful people (ch. 24). Although for the most part chs. 1 – 20 relate events in chronological order, chs. 21 – 52 are arranged on the basis of subject matter rather than chronology (see 24:1; 25:1; 26:1; 27:1; 29:2; 32:1; 35:1; 36:1; 37:1; 45:1; 49:34; 51:59; 52:4).
21:1 — 23:7 The rulers of Judah, who bear the primary responsibility for the nation's economic, social and spiritual ills, are the first to be denounced by Jeremiah.
21:1 *The word came.* The phrase does not appear again until 25:1, suggesting that chs. 21 – 24 constitute an integral section in the book. *Zedekiah.* Means "The LORD is my righteousness." See Introduction: Background. *Pashhur son of Malkijah.* Not the same as the Pashhur of 20:1 – 6 (see 38:1). *the priest Zephaniah son of Maaseiah.* Not the same as the prophet Zephaniah (see 29:25,29; 37:3; 52:24; see also Zep 1:1).
21:2 *Inquire ... of the LORD.* A request for knowledge or information (see Ge 25:22; 2Ki 22:13), not necessarily for help. *Nebuchadnezzar.* See NIV text note; see also chart, p. 472, and note on 2Ki 24:1. *is attacking.* About 588, because the brash Zedekiah had rebelled against Babylon (see 52:3). *us.* Jerusalem. *perform wonders ... as in times past.* For example, in the days of Hezekiah (see Isa 37:36). *he will withdraw.* See Isa 37:37.
21:4 *turn against you the weapons.* Your defense of Jerusalem will fail. *Babylonians.* See NIV text note; see also note on Job 1:17. *gather them inside this city.* Either (1) the weapons, meaning that Judah's troops would be totally unable to defend the approaches to the city, or (2) the Babylonians, meaning that Jerusalem's defeat is imminent and inevitable.
21:5 *I myself will fight against you.* The Lord, usually his people's defender, will now destroy them and seal their doom. *with an outstretched hand and a mighty arm.* See 27:5; 32:17. A similar phrase is used to describe God's powerful redemption of Israel at the exodus (see 32:21; Dt 4:34; 5:15; 7:19; 26:8), but here God turns his wrath against his own people. *in anger and fury and great wrath.* Probably quoted from Dt 29:28, where the Hebrew for this phrase is translated "in furious anger and in great wrath."
21:7 *I will hand over Zedekiah ... his officials and the people.* Fulfilled in 52:8 – 11,24 – 27 (see Eze 12:13 – 14). *plague, sword and famine.* See v. 9. For this triad see note on 14:12. *no mercy or pity or compassion.* For this triad see 13:14; see also Eze 5:11. The three triads here heighten the literary effect of the passage.
21:8 – 10 See 27:12 – 13. Similar advice is offered in 38:2 – 3, 17 – 18 (see Dt 30:15 – 20).
21:8 *See, I am setting before you.* See Dt 11:26. The people are offered a choice, but few of them will make the right decision. *the way of life and the way of death.* See Dt 30:15,19; see also Pr 6:23.
21:9 Repeated almost verbatim in 38:2. Jeremiah's counsel of surrender branded him as a traitor in the eyes of many (see 37:13), but he was in fact a true patriot who wanted to stay in Judah even after Jerusalem was destroyed (see 37:14; 40:6; 42:7 – 22). *whoever ... surrenders to the Babylonians ... will live.* Fulfilled in 39:9; 52:15. *he will escape with his life.* Lit. "his life will be his (only) booty." The victorious in battle can expect to share plunder; the defeated are fortunate indeed if their lives are spared.

he will escape with his life.[q] [10]I have determined to do this city harm[r] and not good,
declares the LORD. It will be given into the
hands[s] of the king of Babylon, and he will
destroy it with fire.'[t]

[11]"Moreover, say to the royal house[u] of Judah, 'Hear the word of the LORD; [12]O house
of David, this is what the LORD says:

" 'Administer justice[v] every morning;
rescue from the hand of his
oppressor[w]
the one who has been robbed,
or my wrath will break out and burn
like fire[x]
because of the evil[y] you have done—
burn with no one to quench[z] it.
[13]I am against[a] you, ⌞Jerusalem,⌟
you who live above this valley[b]
on the rocky plateau,
declares the LORD—
you who say, "Who can come against
us?
Who can enter our refuge?"[c]
[14]I will punish you as your deeds[d]
deserve,
declares the LORD.
I will kindle a fire[e] in your forests[f]
that will consume everything around
you.' "

Judgment Against Evil Kings

22 This is what the LORD says: "Go down
to the palace of the king[g] of Judah
and proclaim this message there: [2]'Hear[h]
the word of the LORD, O king of Judah, you
who sit on David's throne[i]—you, your officials and your people who come through
these gates.[j] [3]This is what the LORD says:
Do what is just[k] and right. Rescue from the
hand of his oppressor[l] the one who has
been robbed. Do no wrong or violence to
the alien, the fatherless or the widow,[m] and
do not shed innocent blood[n] in this place.
[4]For if you are careful to carry out these
commands, then kings[o] who sit on David's
throne will come through the gates of this
palace, riding in chariots and on horses,
accompanied by their officials and their
people. [5]But if you do not obey[p] these commands, declares the LORD, I swear[q] by myself that this palace will become a ruin.' "

[6]For this is what the LORD says about the
palace of the king of Judah:

"Though you are like Gilead[r] to me,
like the summit of Lebanon,[s]
I will surely make you like a desert,[t]
like towns not inhabited.
[7]I will send destroyers[u] against you,
each man with his weapons,
and they will cut[v] up your fine cedar
beams
and throw them into the fire.[w]

[8]"People from many nations will pass
by this city and will ask one another,
'Why has the LORD done such a thing to
this great city?'[x] [9]And the answer will be:
'Because they have forsaken the covenant
of the LORD their God and have worshiped
and served other gods.[y]' "

21:9 [q]Jer 27:12; 38:2,17; 39:18; 45:5 **21:10** [r]Jer 44:11,27; Am 9:4 [s]S Jer 20:4; 32:28; 38:2-3 [t]S 2Ki 25:9; S 2Ch 36:19 **21:11** [u]S Jer 13:18 **21:12** [v]S Ex 22:22; S Lev 25:17 [w]S Ps 27:11 [x]S Isa 42:25; S Jer 10:10 [y]Jer 23:2 [z]S Isa 1:31 **21:13** [a]Jer 23:30; 50:31; 51:25; Eze 5:8; 13:8; 21:3; 29:10; 34:10; Na 2:13; 3:5 [b]Ps 125:2 [c]2Sa 5:6-7; Jer 49:4; La 4:12; Ob 1:3-4 **21:14** [d]S Pr 1:31; S Isa 3:10-11; S Jer 17:10 [e]S 2Ch 36:19; La 2:3 [f]S 2Ki 19:23; Eze 20:47 **22:1** [g]S Jer 13:18; 34:2 **22:2** [h]Am 7:16 [i]S Jer 17:25; Lk 1:32 [j]Jer 17:20 **22:3** [k]S Lev 25:17; Isa 56:1; Jer 5:1; Eze 33:14; 45:9; Hos 12:6; Am 5:24; Mic 6:8; Zec 7:9 [l]Ps 72:4; Jer 21:12 [m]S Ex 22:22; S Isa 1:17; Jer 5:28 [n]S Jer 7:6 **22:4** [o]S Jer 17:25 **22:5** [p]S Jer 17:27 [q]S Ge 22:16; Heb 6:13 **22:6** [r]S Ge 31:21; S SS 4:1 [s]S 1Ki 7:2; S Isa 33:9 [t]Mic 3:12 **22:7** [u]S Jer 4:7; S 6:4 [v]Ps 74:5; Isa 10:34 [w]S 2Ch 36:19; Zec 11:1 **22:8** [x]Dt 29:25-26; 1Ki 9:8-9; Jer 16:10-11 **22:9** [y]S 1Ki 9:9; Jer 16:11; Eze 39:23

21:10 *determined.* Lit. "set my face" (see 44:11; Isa 50:7 and notes). *harm and not good.* See Am 9:4; contrast Jer 24:6. *It will be given ... destroy it with fire.* See 34:2.

21:12 *Administer justice.* See 5:28; 22:16; 1Ki 3:28; La 3:59. The king was obliged and expected to do so, as was the future Messiah (see 23:5; 33:15). *every morning.* When the mind is clear and the day is cool (see Ps 101:8 and note). *rescue ... robbed.* Repeated in 22:3. *or my wrath ... no one to quench it.* Repeated verbatim from 4:4 (see Am 5:6). *wrath will ... burn.* See 15:14; 17:4,27.

21:13 *valley.* Jerusalem, surrounded on three sides by valleys (see note on Isa 22:7), is called the "Valley of Vision" in Isa 22:1,5. *rocky plateau.* Mount Zion. *you who say.* The pronouns are plural in the second half of the verse (referring to Jerusalem's inhabitants), singular in the first half (referring to Jerusalem personified). *Who can come against us?* The people think that no one can successfully besiege them (see notes on 7:4; 8:19).

21:14 *as your deeds deserve.* See note on 17:10. *kindle a fire ... consume.* See note on 17:27. *forests.* The Hebrew for this word is singular and perhaps refers figuratively to Jerusalem's royal palace, called the "Palace of the Forest of Lebanon" (1Ki 7:2; 10:17,21; see Isa 22:8) because of the cedar (see 22:7,14,15,23) used in its construction. The palace (see 22:1) is compared to the "summit of Lebanon" in 22:6 (see 22:23 and NIV text note).

22:1 *Go down.* The palace was at a lower elevation than the temple (see 26:10; 36:10–12). *king of Judah.* Probably Zedekiah (see 21:3,7; compare v. 3 with 21:12), whose predecessors are mentioned in sequence later in the chapter (Josiah, vv. 10a,15b–16; Jehoahaz/Shallum, vv. 10b–12; Jehoiakim, vv. 13–15a,17–19; Jehoiachin/Coniah, vv. 24–30).

22:2 *David's throne.* Though all the kings of the Davidic dynasty failed to a greater or lesser degree, the victorious Messiah would someday appear as the culmination of David's royal line (see 23:5 and NIV text note; 33:15; Eze 34:23–24; Mt 1:1). *who come through these gates.* See 17:25 and note.

22:3 Contrast Isa 11:3–5 with Eze 22:6–7.

22:4 Repeated in part from 17:25.

22:5 See 17:27 and note. *swear by myself.* See notes on Ge 22:16; Isa 45:23; see also 49:13; 51:14; cf. 44:26. *become a ruin.* Fulfilled in 52:13 (see 27:17).

22:6 *Gilead ... Lebanon.* Renowned for their forests. Lebanon in particular supplied cedar for the royal palace (see note on 21:14; see also 1Ki 5:6,8–10; 7:2–3; 10:27).

22:7 *send.* Lit. "consecrate" (see note on 6:4). *destroyers.* The Babylonians (see note on 4:7; see also 12:12). *each man with his weapons.* See Eze 9:2. *cut up your ... cedar.* Cf. Isa 10:33–34; cf. especially the vivid description of the Babylonian troops smashing the carved paneling of the Jerusalem temple with their axes and hatchets (Ps 74:3–6).

22:8–9 Echoed in 1Ki 9:8–9; see Dt 29:24–26.

22:9 *forsaken the covenant ... and served other gods.* A gross violation of the first and second stipulations of the Sinaitic covenant (see Ex 20:3–5 and notes).

10 Do not weep for the dead[z] ⌞king⌟ or
mourn[a] his loss;
rather, weep bitterly for him who is
exiled,
because he will never return[b]
nor see his native land again.

11 For this is what the LORD says about Shallum[a][c] son of Josiah, who succeeded his
father as king of Judah but has gone from
this place: "He will never return. 12 He will
die[d] in the place where they have led him
captive; he will not see this land again."

13 "Woe[e] to him who builds[f] his palace
by unrighteousness,
his upper rooms by injustice,
making his countrymen work for
nothing,
not paying[g] them for their labor.
14 He says, 'I will build myself a great
palace[h]
with spacious upper rooms.'
So he makes large windows in it,
panels it with cedar[i]
and decorates it in red.[j]

15 "Does it make you a king
to have more and more cedar?
Did not your father have food and
drink?
He did what was right and just,[k]
so all went well[l] with him.
16 He defended the cause of the poor and
needy,[m]
and so all went well.

22:10 [z] S Ecc 4:2 [a] ver 18; Eze 24:16 [b] ver 27; Jer 24:9; 29:18; 42:18 **22:11** [c] S 2Ki 23:31 **22:12** [d] 2Ki 23:34 **22:13** [e] S Isa 5:8 [f] Mic 3:10; Hab 2:9 [g] S Lev 19:13; Jas 5:4 **22:14** [h] Isa 5:8-9 [i] S 2Sa 7:2 [j] Eze 23:14 **22:15** [k] 2Ki 23:25 [l] Ps 128:2; S Isa 3:10 **22:16** [m] Ps 72:1-4, 12-13; S 82:3; S Pr 24:23 [n] S Ps 36:10 **22:17** [o] S Isa 56:11 [p] S 2Ki 24:4 [q] S Dt 28:33; Eze 18:12; Mic 2:2 **22:18** [r] S 2Sa 1:26 **22:19** [s] 2Ki 24:6 [t] Jer 8:2; 36:30 **22:20** [u] S Isa 57:13 [v] S Ps 68:15 [w] S Nu 27:12 [x] ver 22; Jer 30:14; La 1:19; Eze 16:33-34; Hos 8:9 **22:21** [y] Zec 7:7 [z] Dt 9:7; Ps 25:7;

Is that not what it means to know[n]
me?"
declares the LORD.
17 "But your eyes and your heart
are set only on dishonest gain,[o]
on shedding innocent blood[p]
and on oppression and extortion."[q]

18 Therefore this is what the LORD says about
Jehoiakim son of Josiah king of Judah:

"They will not mourn[r] for him:
'Alas, my brother! Alas, my sister!'
They will not mourn for him:
'Alas, my master! Alas, his
splendor!'
19 He will have the burial[s] of a donkey—
dragged away and thrown[t]
outside the gates of Jerusalem."

20 "Go up to Lebanon and cry out,[u]
let your voice be heard in Bashan,[v]
cry out from Abarim,[w]
for all your allies[x] are crushed.
21 I warned you when you felt secure,[y]
but you said, 'I will not listen!'
This has been your way from your
youth;[z]
you have not obeyed[a] me.
22 The wind[b] will drive all your
shepherds[c] away,
and your allies[d] will go into exile.

[a] *11* Also called *Jehoahaz*

Isa 54:4; Jer 3:25; 31:19; 32:30 [a] S Jer 3:13; 7:23-28; Zep 3:2 **22:22** [b] S Dt 28:64; S Job 27:21 [c] S Jer 10:21 [d] S ver 20

22:10 *weep for the dead ⌞king⌟.* Josiah, who was mourned long after his death (see 2Ch 35:24–25). *him who is exiled.* Jehoahaz/Shallum. In 609 B.C., the Egyptian pharaoh Neco "carried him off to Egypt, and there he died" (2Ki 23:34).
22:11 *Shallum.* See 1Ch 3:15. Shallum was his personal name, Jehoahaz his throne name (the latter means "The LORD seizes").
22:12 *the place where they have led him captive.* Egypt (see note on v. 10).
22:13–19 A scathing denunciation of King Jehoiakim, who is described in the third person (vv. 13–14), then rhetorically addressed in the second person (vv. 15,17), then identified by name (v. 18), meaning "The LORD raises up." Good King Josiah is referred to in vv. 15b–16 by way of contrast.
22:13 *Woe to him who builds.* See Hab 2:9,12. *by unrighteousness ... by injustice.* Contrast v. 3; 21:12. *upper rooms.* See note on Jdg 3:20. *making his countrymen work for nothing.* Contrary to the law (see Lev 25:39; Dt 24:14–15). Jehoiakim's refusal to pay them may have been due partly to inability, since Judah was under heavy tribute to Egypt during the early part of his reign (see 2Ki 23:35).
22:14 *large windows.* The windows described here may well be the same as those found in the ruins of Beth Hakkerem (see 6:1; see also note on Ne 3:14) by archaeologists in the early 1960s. *panels.* Haggai similarly deplores the use of paneling as an extravagant and unneeded luxury in certain situations (see Hag 1:4).
22:15 *your father.* Josiah. *have food and drink.* Enjoy life (see Ecc 2:24–25; 3:12–13). *did what was right and just.* Like his ancestor David (see 2Sa 8:15); contrast v. 13 (see note there; see also note on Ps 119:121).
22:16 James defines a proper relationship to God in similar terms (Jas 1:27); contrast Jer 5:28 (see note there). *poor and needy.* See note on 20:13. *to know me.* To love God fully, which results in living a pious life and serving those in need (see Dt 10:12–13; Hos 6:6; Mic 6:8).
22:17 *your.* Jehoiakim's (see v. 18). *dishonest gain.* See 6:13; 8:10. *shedding innocent blood.* See note on 19:4; for an illustration of Jehoiakim's cruelty in this regard see 26:20–23. *oppression.* See v. 3; 6:6; 21:12.
22:18 Contrast 2Ch 35:24–25. *They will not mourn for him: "Alas, my brother!"* Contrast 1Ki 13:30.
22:19 *burial of a donkey.* Tantamount to no burial at all (see 36:30); fulfilled in 2Ki 24:6, where no burial is described and where it says that Jehoiakim "rested with his fathers," a euphemism for dying (see notes on Ge 25:8; 1Ki 1:21). *dragged away.* See 15:3.
22:20–23 The Lord speaks to Jerusalem, which is personified as a woman (see v. 23).
22:20 *Lebanon ... Bashan ... Abarim.* Mountainous regions (see v. 6; Nu 27:12; 33:47–48; Dt 32:49; Jdg 3:3; Ps 68:15), the first two in the north and the third in the south, suitable heights from which the whole land of Israel could be rhetorically addressed. *allies.* Lit. "lovers" (see 4:30 and note), here referring to nations joined together by treaty. Judah's onetime allies included Egypt, Assyria (see 2:36), Edom, Moab, Ammon and Phoenicia (see 27:3), all of whom had been—or soon would be—conquered by Babylonia (see 27:6–7; 28:14). *crushed.* See 14:17.
22:21 *not listen ... not obeyed me.* See 7:22–26; 11:7–8. *your youth.* The days of Israel's early history in Egypt (see 2:2 and note; Hos 2:15).
22:22 *wind will drive ... away.* See 13:24; Job 27:21; Isa 27:8. *shepherds.* See 2:8 and note; 10:21; 23:1–4. The initial fulfillment of this verse took place in 597 B.C. (see 2Ki 24:12–16).

Then you will be ashamed and
disgraced[e]
because of all your wickedness.
23 You who live in 'Lebanon,[a f]'
who are nestled in cedar buildings,
how you will groan when pangs come
upon you,
pain[g] like that of a woman in labor!

24 "As surely as I live," declares the LORD,
"even if you, Jehoiachin[b h] son of Jehoiakim king of Judah, were a signet ring[i] on
my right hand, I would still pull you off.
25 I will hand you over[j] to those who seek
your life, those you fear—to Nebuchadnezzar king of Babylon and to the Babylonians.[c] 26 I will hurl[k] you and the mother[l]
who gave you birth into another country,
where neither of you was born, and there
you both will die. 27 You will never come
back to the land you long to return[m] to."

28 Is this man Jehoiachin[n] a despised,
broken pot,[o]
an object no one wants?
Why will he and his children be
hurled[p] out,
cast into a land[q] they do not know?
29 O land,[r] land, land,
hear the word of the LORD!
30 This is what the LORD says:
"Record this man as if childless,[s]
a man who will not prosper[t] in his
lifetime,
for none of his offspring[u] will prosper,
none will sit on the throne[v] of David
or rule anymore in Judah."

22:22 [e]S Jer 7:19 **22:23** [f]S 1Ki 7:2; Eze 17:3 [g]S Jer 4:31 **22:24** [h]S 2Ki 24:6,8 [i]S Ge 38:18 **22:25** [j]S 2Ki 24:16; S 2Ch 36:10 **22:26** [k]S 1Sa 25:29; S 2Ki 24:8; 2Ch 36:10; S Isa 22:17; Eze 19:9-14 [l]S 1Ki 2:19 **22:27** [m]S ver 10 **22:28** [n]S 2Ki 24:6 [o]Ps 31:12; S Jer 19:10; 25:34; 48:38 [p]Jer 15:1 [q]S Jer 17:4 **22:29** [r]S Jer 6:19 **22:30** [s]1Ch 3:18; Jer 38:23; 52:10; Mt 1:12 [t]Jer 10:21 [u]S Job 18:19 [v]S Ps 94:20

23:1 [w]Jer 10:21; 12:10; 25:36; Eze 34:1-10; Zec 10:2; Zec 11:15-17 [x]S Isa 56:11 [y]Ps 100:3; S Jer 13:17; Eze 34:31 **23:2** [z]Jn 10:8 [a]S Jer 10:21; 13:20 [b]Jer 21:12; Eze 34:8-10 **23:3** [c]Isa 11:10-12; Jer 32:37; Eze 34:11-16 [d]S 1Ki 8:48 **23:4** [e]S Ge 48:15; S Isa 31:4; Jer 31:10 [f]Jer 30:10; 46:27-28 [g]S Jn 6:39 **23:5** [h]S 2Ki 19:26; S Isa 4:2; Eze 17:22 [i]S Mt 2:2 [j]Isa 9:7; S Mt 1:1 [k]S Ge 18:19

The Righteous Branch

23 "Woe to the shepherds[w] who are destroying and scattering[x] the sheep of
my pasture!"[y] declares the LORD. 2 Therefore this is what the LORD, the God of Israel, says to the shepherds[z] who tend my
people: "Because you have scattered my
flock[a] and driven them away and have
not bestowed care on them, I will bestow
punishment on you for the evil[b] you have
done," declares the LORD. 3 "I myself will
gather the remnant[c] of my flock out of
all the countries where I have driven
them and will bring them back to their
pasture,[d] where they will be fruitful and
increase in number. 4 I will place shepherds[e] over them who will tend them,
and they will no longer be afraid[f] or terrified, nor will any be missing,[g]" declares
the LORD.

5 "The days are coming," declares the
LORD,
"when I will raise up to David[d] a
righteous Branch,[h]
a King[i] who will reign[j] wisely
and do what is just and right[k] in the
land.

[a] *23* That is, the palace in Jerusalem (see 1 Kings 7:2) [b] *24* Hebrew *Coniah,* a variant of *Jehoiachin*; also in verse 28 [c] *25* Or *Chaldeans* [d] *5* Or *up from David's line*

22:23 *Lebanon ... cedar.* See NIV text note; see also 21:14 and note; Eze 17:3–4,12. *pain like that of a woman in labor.* See 4:19,31 and notes.

22:24–30 A prophecy against King Jehoiachin (fulfilled in 24:1; 29:2), who was also known as Coniah (see NIV text note on v. 24), a shortened form of Jeconiah (see NIV text note on 24:1); see Introduction: Background. All three forms of the name mean "The LORD establishes."

22:24 *As surely as I live.* See note on Ge 42:15. *even if you ... were a signet ring.* The curse on Jehoiachin is apparently reversed in Hag 2:23 (see note there).

22:25 *hand you over to ... those you fear.* Contrast 39:17.

22:26 Fulfilled in 597 B.C. (see 29:2; 2Ki 24:15). *hurl ... into another country.* Send into exile in Babylonia (see 7:15; 16:13; Dt 29:28). *you and the mother who gave you birth.* Jehoiachin and Nehushta (see note on 13:18).

22:28 Two rhetorical questions, answered in v. 30. *broken pot ... hurled out.* Jehoiachin and his descendants, like Judah itself (see 19:10–11), are under God's judgment. *he and his children.* Though Jehoiachin was only 18 years old at the time of his exile (see 2Ki 24:8), he already had more than one wife (see 2Ki 24:15) and therefore probably one or more children.

22:29 *land, land, land.* The repetition implies the strongest possible emphasis and intensity (see 7:4 and note; 23:30–32; Isa 6:3 and note; Eze 21:27).

22:30 *as if childless.* Not in the sense of Jehoiachin's having no children at all (he had at least seven; see 1Ch 3:17–18), but of having none to sit on the throne of David in Judah. Jehoiachin's grandson Zerubbabel (1Ch 3:17–19; Mt 1:12) became governor of Judah (see Hag 1:1), but not king. Zedekiah was a son of Josiah (see 37:1), not of Jehoiachin, and he and his sons died before the latter (see 52:10–11). Jehoiachin therefore was Judah's last surviving Davidic king—until Christ.

23:1–8 A summary statement (probably dating to Zedekiah's reign; see note on v. 6) that includes God's intention to judge the wicked rulers and leaders of Judah (vv. 1–2), to ultimately bring his people back from exile (vv. 3–4,7–8), and to raise up an ideal Davidic King (vv. 5–6).

23:1 See 10:21 and note. *sheep.* The people of Judah (see v. 2).

23:2 *bestowed care ... bestow punishment.* The same Hebrew root underlies both phrases (see v. 4 and note). What Judah's rulers had failed to do is summarized in Eze 34:4.

23:3 *remnant.* See note on 6:9. *I have driven.* Although Judah's sins and the sins of their leaders had caused them to be "driven ... away" (v. 2) into exile, the Lord himself ultimately carried out the results of his people's repeated violations of their covenant commitments. *be fruitful and increase.* See note on Ge 1:28.

23:4 *be afraid ... terrified.* The absence of a concerned shepherd invites attacks by wild animals (see Eze 34:8). *be missing.* See Nu 31:49. The Hebrew root underlying this phrase is the same as that for "bestowed care" and "bestow punishment" in v. 2 (see note there).

23:5–6 One of the most important Messianic passages in Jeremiah, echoed in 33:15–16.

23:5 *raise up.* See 2Sa 7:12; see also 30:9; Eze 34:23–24; 37:24. The Hebrew for this phrase is translated "place" in v. 4. *to David.* See NIV text note; see also Mt 1:1 and NIV text

6In his days Judah will be saved
and Israel will live in safety.[l]
This is the name[m] by which he will be called:
The LORD Our Righteousness.[n]

7"So then, the days are coming,"[o] declares
the LORD, "when people will no longer
say, 'As surely as the LORD lives, who
brought the Israelites up out of Egypt,'[p]
8but they will say, 'As surely as the LORD
lives, who brought the descendants of Israel up out of the land of the north and
out of all the countries where he had banished them.' Then they will live in their
own land."[q]

Lying Prophets

9Concerning the prophets:

My heart[r] is broken within me;
all my bones tremble.[s]
I am like a drunken man,
like a man overcome by wine,
because of the LORD
and his holy words.[t]
10The land is full of adulterers;[u]
because of the curse[a][v] the land lies parched[b]
and the pastures[w] in the desert are withered.[x]
The ⌞prophets⌟ follow an evil course
and use their power unjustly.

11"Both prophet and priest are godless;[y]
even in my temple[z] I find their wickedness,"
declares the LORD.
12"Therefore their path will become slippery;[a]
they will be banished to darkness
and there they will fall.
I will bring disaster on them
in the year they are punished,[b]"
declares the LORD.

13"Among the prophets of Samaria
I saw this repulsive thing:
They prophesied by Baal[c]
and led my people Israel astray.[d]
14And among the prophets of Jerusalem
I have seen something horrible:[e]
They commit adultery and live a lie.[f]
They strengthen the hands of evildoers,[g]
so that no one turns from his wickedness.[h]
They are all like Sodom[i] to me;
the people of Jerusalem are like Gomorrah."[j]

15Therefore, this is what the LORD Almighty says concerning the prophets:

"I will make them eat bitter food
and drink poisoned water,[k]
because from the prophets of Jerusalem
ungodliness[l] has spread throughout the land."

16This is what the LORD Almighty says:

"Do not listen[m] to what the prophets
are prophesying to you;
they fill you with false hopes.
They speak visions[n] from their own minds,
not from the mouth[o] of the LORD.
17They keep saying[p] to those who despise me,
'The LORD says: You will have peace.'[q]

[a] 10 Or *because of these things* [b] 10 Or *land mourns*

23:6 [l]S Lev 25:18; S Dt 32:8; Hos 2:18 [m]Ex 23:21; Jer 33:16; Mt 1:21-23 [n]S Ezr 9:15; S Isa 42:6; Ro 3:21-22; S 1Co 1:30 **23:7** [o]Jer 30:3 [p]S Dt 15:15 **23:8** [q]S Isa 14:1; S 43:5-6; Jer 30:10; Eze 20:42; 34:13; Am 9:14-15 **23:9** [r]S Jer 4:19 [s]S Job 4:14 [t]Jer 20:8-9 **23:10** [u]S Jer 9:2 [v]Dt 28:23-24 [w]Ps 107:34; S Jer 9:10 [x]S Jer 4:26; S 12:11 **23:11** [y]Jer 6:13; S 8:10; Zep 3:4 [z]S 2Ki 21:4; S Jer 7:10 **23:12** [a]S Dt 32:35; S Job 3:23; Jer 13:16 [b]Jer 11:23 **23:13** [c]S 1Ki 18:22 [d]ver 32; S Isa 3:12; Eze 13:10 **23:14** [e]S Jer 5:30; Hos 6:10 [f]Jer 29:23 [g]ver 22 [h]S Isa 5:18 [i]S Ge 18:20; Mt 11:24 [j]Jer 20:16; Am 4:11 **23:15** [k]S Jer 8:14; 9:15 [l]S Jer 8:10 **23:16** [m]Jer 27:9-10, 14; S Mt 7:15 [n]S Jer 14:14; Eze 13:3 [o]Jer 9:20 **23:17** [p]ver 31 [q]S 1Ki 22:8; S Jer 4:10

note on Mt 1:17. The Messiah, unlike any previous descendant of David, would be the ideal King. He would sum up in himself all the finest qualities of the best rulers, and infinitely more. *Branch.* A Messianic title (see notes on Isa 4:2; Zec 3:8; 6:12). The Targum (ancient Aramaic paraphrase) reads "Messiah" here. *reign wisely.* See note on Isa 52:13. *do what is just and right.* See 22:3,15; said also of King David (see 2Sa 8:15).

23:6 *Judah ... and Israel.* God's reunited people will be restored (see 31:31 and note; Eze 37:15–22). *be saved ... live in safety.* The deliverance will be both spiritual and physical (see Dt 33:28–29). *The LORD Our Righteousness.* Although Zedekiah did not live up to the meaning of his name, "The LORD is my righteousness," the Messiah would bestow on his people the abundant blessings (see Eze 34:25–31) that come from the hands of a King who does "what is just and right" (v. 5).

23:7–8 Repeated almost verbatim from 16:14–15 (see notes there).

23:9–40 False prophets denounced (see 2:8; 4:9; 5:30–31; 6:13–15; 8:10–12; 14:13–15; 18:18–23; 26:8,11,16; 27–28; Isa 28:7–13; Eze 13; Mic 3:5–12).

23:9 *Concerning.* Introduces headings also in 46:2; 48:1; 49:1,7,23,28. *his holy words.* Contrast the unholy words of the false prophets (see vv. 16–18).

23:10 See Isa 24:4–6. *adulterers.* See 5:7–8; 9:2 and notes. *curse.* Brought on by violating the Lord's covenant (see 11:3 and note; 11:8). *parched ... withered.* See 12:4 and note. To worship other gods is to deny to the land the fertility that only the Lord can bring (see Hos 2:5–8,21–22; Am 4:4–9). *pastures in the desert.* See note on 9:10. *evil course.* Evil because it is their own and not God's (see 8:6).

23:11 *even in my temple ... wickedness.* For examples see 32:34; 2Ki 16:10–14; 21:5; Eze 8:5,10,14,16.

23:12 *their path will become slippery ... banished to darkness.* See Ps 35:5–6; see also Ps 73:18.

23:13 *prophesied by Baal.* See 2:8 and note; see also 1Ki 18:19–40.

23:14 *They ... live a lie.* See 14:13 and note; cf. 1Jn 1:6. *strengthen the hands of.* The Hebrew underlying this phrase is translated "encouraged" in Eze 13:22. *no one turns from his wickedness.* See Eze 13:22. *like Sodom ... like Gomorrah.* See note on 20:16.

23:15 *I will make ... poisoned water.* Repeated almost verbatim from 9:15 (see note there). *ungodliness.* See v. 11.

23:16 *visions.* "Revelations" or "prophecies" (see 1Sa 3:1; Pr 29:18; Isa 1:1; Ob 1 and notes). *from their own minds.* See v. 26; 14:14. False prophets are like preachers of a "different gospel" (Gal 1:6–9).

23:17 *You will have peace.* The essential message of the false prophets (see 6:14 and note; 8:11; 14:13 and note; cf. 28:8–9). *stubbornness of their hearts.* See note on 3:17.

And to all who follow the
stubbornness[r] of their hearts
they say, 'No harm[s] will come to you.'
18 But which of them has stood in the
council[t] of the LORD
to see or to hear his word?
Who has listened and heard his
word?
19 See, the storm[u] of the LORD
will burst out in wrath,
a whirlwind[v] swirling down
on the heads of the wicked.
20 The anger[w] of the LORD will not turn
back[x]
until he fully accomplishes
the purposes of his heart.
In days to come
you will understand it clearly.
21 I did not send[y] these prophets,
yet they have run with their
message;
I did not speak to them,
yet they have prophesied.
22 But if they had stood in my council,[z]
they would have proclaimed[a] my
words to my people
and would have turned[b] them from
their evil ways
and from their evil deeds.[c]

23 "Am I only a God nearby,[d]"
declares the LORD,
"and not a God far away?
24 Can anyone hide[e] in secret places
so that I cannot see him?"
declares the LORD.
"Do not I fill heaven and earth?"[f]
declares the LORD.

25 "I have heard what the prophets say
who prophesy lies[g] in my name. They say,
'I had a dream![h] I had a dream!' 26 How
long will this continue in the hearts of
these lying prophets, who prophesy the
delusions[i] of their own minds?[j] 27 They
think the dreams they tell one another
will make my people forget[k] my name, just
as their fathers forgot[l] my name through
Baal worship.[m] 28 Let the prophet who has
a dream[n] tell his dream, but let the one
who has my word[o] speak it faithfully. For
what has straw to do with grain?" declares
the LORD. 29 "Is not my word like fire,"[p] declares the LORD, "and like a hammer[q] that
breaks a rock in pieces?

30 "Therefore," declares the LORD, "I
am against[r] the prophets[s] who steal from
one another words supposedly from me.
31 Yes," declares the LORD, "I am against
the prophets who wag their own tongues
and yet declare, 'The LORD declares.'[t] 32 Indeed, I am against those who prophesy
false dreams,[u]" declares the LORD. "They
tell them and lead my people astray[v] with
their reckless lies,[w] yet I did not send[x] or
appoint them. They do not benefit[y] these
people in the least," declares the LORD.

False Oracles and False Prophets

33 "When these people, or a prophet or
a priest, ask you, 'What is the oracle[a][z] of
the LORD?' say to them, 'What oracle?[b] I
will forsake[a] you, declares the LORD.' 34 If a
prophet or a priest or anyone else claims,

[a] *33* Or *burden* (see Septuagint and Vulgate)
[b] *33* Hebrew; Septuagint and Vulgate *'You are the burden.* (The Hebrew for *oracle* and *burden* is the same.)

23:17 [r]S Jer 13:10 [s]Jer 5:12; Am 9:10; Mic 3:11 **23:18** [t]S 1Ki 22:19; S Ro 11:34 **23:19** [u]Isa 30:30; Jer 25:32; 30:23 [v]Zec 7:14 **23:20** [w]S 2Ki 23:26 [x]S Jer 4:28 **23:21** [y]S Jer 14:14; 27:15 **23:22** [z]S 1Ki 22:19 [a]S Dt 33:10 [b]S 2Ki 17:13; Jer 25:5; Zec 1:4 [c]ver 14; Am 3:7 **23:23** [d]Ps 139:1-10 **23:24** [e]S Ge 3:8; S Job 11:20; 22:12-14; S Ecc 12:14; S Isa 28:15; 1Co 4:5 [f]S 1Ki 8:27 **23:25** [g]ver 16; Jer 14:14; 27:10 [h]ver 28, 32; S Dt 13:1; Jer 27:9; 29:8 **23:26** [i]S Isa 30:10; 1Ti 4:1-2 [j]Jer 14:14; Eze 13:2 **23:27** [k]Dt 13:1-3; Jer 29:8 [l]S Jdg 3:7; S 8:33-34 [m]S Jer 2:23 **23:28** [n]S ver 25 [o]S 1Sa 3:17 **23:29** [p]S Ps 39:3; Jer 5:14; S 1Co 3:13 [q]Heb 4:12 **23:30** [r]S Ps 34:16 [s]ver 2; Dt 18:20; Jer 14:15; S 21:13 **23:31** [t]ver 17 **23:32** [u]S ver 25 [v]S ver 13; S Jer 50:6 [w]S Job 13:4; Eze 13:3; 22:28 [x]S Jer 14:14 [y]Jer 7:8; La 2:14 **23:33** [z]Mal 1:1 [a]S 2Ki 21:14

23:18 *council of the LORD.* God's heavenly confidants (see v. 22; Job 15:7–10 and note; see also 1Ki 22:19–22; Job 1:6; 2:1; 29:4 and note; Ps 89:7). In Am 3:7 the Hebrew for "council" is translated "plan," the purposes that God has promised to reveal to his chosen servants (see v. 20). **23:19–20** Repeated almost verbatim in 30:23–24. **23:19** *storm ... whirlwind.* A vivid image of God's wrath. **23:20** *you will understand it clearly.* Unlike the false prophets, who continued to mislead their hearers even in Babylonia after the exile of 597 B.C. (see 29:20–23). **23:21** *I did not send.* See v. 32; 29:9; contrast 1:7; Isa 6:8; Eze 3:5. *did not speak to them.* See 29:23. **23:22** *my council.* See note on v. 18. **23:23** *God nearby ... God far away.* God is both immanent and transcendent; he lives "in a high and holy place, but also with him who is ... lowly in spirit" (Isa 57:15). **23:24** *hide ... so that I cannot see him.* See Job 26:6; Ps 139:7–12; Am 9:2–4. *I fill heaven and earth.* See Isa 66:1. **23:25** *lies.* See 5:12. *in my name.* See Dt 18:20,22. *dream.* An infrequent mode of divine revelation to a true prophet (see 27:9; Dt 13:1–3; 1Sa 28:6; Zec 10:2; but cf. Nu 12:6; Joel 2:28). **23:26** *hearts ... minds.* The Hebrew is the same for both words (see note on Ps 4:7). *their own minds.* See note on v. 16. **23:27** *my name.* To forget the Lord's name is tantamount to forgetting him (see note on Ps 5:11). *forgot ... through Baal worship.* When Judah's ancestors forgot God, they began to serve Baal (see Jdg 3:7; 1Sa 12:9–10). *forgot.* See Ps 9:17 and note. **23:28–29** The true word of God is symbolized in three figures of speech (grain, fire, hammer). **23:28** *straw ... grain.* Of the two, only grain can feed and nourish (see note on 15:16). **23:29** *like fire.* See note on 20:9. The fire of the divine word ultimately tests "the quality of each man's work" (1Co 3:13; see note there). *like a hammer.* Similarly, the divine word works relentlessly, like a sword or hammer, to judge "the thoughts and attitudes of the heart" (Heb 4:12; see note there). **23:30–32** *I am against.* The threefold statement is for emphasis (see note on 22:29). **23:31** *prophets who ... declare.* False prophets are claiming that their own prophecies are the oracles of God. The Hebrew for this verb is used only here with someone other than God as the subject. The phrase "declares the LORD" or its equivalent occurs hundreds of times in the OT, more frequently in Jeremiah (over 175 times) than in any other book. **23:32** *did not send.* See v. 21 and note. **23:33** *oracle.* The Hebrew for this word can also mean "burden" (see NIV text note), a term that may refer to a burdensome message from the Lord (see, e.g., Na 1:1).

'This is the oracle[b] of the LORD,' I will punish[c] that man and his household. 35This
is what each of you keeps on saying to
his friend or relative: 'What is the LORD's
answer?'[d] or 'What has the LORD spoken?'
36But you must not mention 'the oracle
of the LORD' again, because every man's
own word becomes his oracle and so you
distort[e] the words of the living God,[f] the
LORD Almighty, our God. 37This is what
you keep saying to a prophet: 'What is the
LORD's answer to you?' or 'What has the
LORD spoken?' 38Although you claim, 'This
is the oracle of the LORD,' this is what the
LORD says: You used the words, 'This is the
oracle of the LORD,' even though I told you
that you must not claim, 'This is the oracle
of the LORD.' 39Therefore, I will surely forget you and cast[g] you out of my presence
along with the city I gave to you and your
fathers. 40I will bring upon you everlasting
disgrace[h]—everlasting shame that will not
be forgotten."

Two Baskets of Figs

24 After Jehoiachin[a][i] son of Jehoiakim
king of Judah and the officials, the
craftsmen and the artisans of Judah were
carried into exile from Jerusalem to Babylon by Nebuchadnezzar king of Babylon,
the LORD showed me two baskets of figs[j]
placed in front of the temple of the LORD.
2One basket had very good figs, like those
that ripen early;[k] the other basket had very
poor[l] figs, so bad they could not be eaten.
3Then the LORD asked me, "What do you
see,[m] Jeremiah?"
"Figs," I answered. "The good ones are
very good, but the poor ones are so bad
they cannot be eaten."
4Then the word of the LORD came to me:
5"This is what the LORD, the God of Israel, says: 'Like these good figs, I regard as
good the exiles from Judah, whom I sent[n]
away from this place to the land of the
Babylonians.[b] 6My eyes will watch over
them for their good, and I will bring them
back[o] to this land. I will build[p] them up
and not tear them down; I will plant[q] them
and not uproot them. 7I will give them a
heart to know[r] me, that I am the LORD.
They will be my people,[s] and I will be
their God, for they will return[t] to me with
all their heart.[u]
8" 'But like the poor[v] figs, which are so
bad they cannot be eaten,' says the LORD,
'so will I deal with Zedekiah[w] king of Judah, his officials[x] and the survivors[y] from
Jerusalem, whether they remain in this
land or live in Egypt.[z] 9I will make them
abhorrent[a] and an offense to all the kingdoms of the earth, a reproach and a byword,[b] an object of ridicule and cursing,[c]
wherever I banish[d] them. 10I will send the
sword,[e] famine[f] and plague[g] against them
until they are destroyed from the land I
gave to them and their fathers.[h]' "

Seventy Years of Captivity

25 The word came to Jeremiah concerning all the people of Judah in
the fourth year of Jehoiakim[i] son of Jo-

[a] *1* Hebrew *Jeconiah,* a variant of *Jehoiachin*
[b] *5* Or *Chaldeans*

23:34 [b]La 2:14 [c]Zec 13:3 **23:35** [d]Jer 33:3; 42:4 **23:36** [e]Gal 1:7-8; 2Pe 3:16 [f]S Jos 3:10 **23:39** [g]S Jer 7:15 **23:40** [h]S Jer 20:11; Eze 5:14-15 **24:1** [i]S 2Ki 24:16; S 2Ch 36:9 [j]Ex 23:19; Dt 26:2; Am 8:1-2 **24:2** [k]S SS 2:13 [l]S Isa 5:4 **24:3** [m]Jer 1:11; Am 8:2 **24:5** [n]Jer 29:4,20 **24:6** [o]S Dt 30:3; Jer 27:22; 29:10; 30:3; Eze 11:17 [p]Jer 33:7; 42:10 [q]S Dt 30:9; S Jer 1:10; Am 9:14-15 **24:7** [r]S Isa 11:9 [s]S Lev 26:12; S Isa 51:16; S Zec 2:11; Heb 8:10 [t]Jer 32:40 [u]S 2Ch 6:37; Eze 11:19 **24:8** [v]Jer 29:17 [w]Jer 32:4-5; 38:18,23; 39:5; 44:30 [x]Jer 39:6 [y]Jer 39:9 [z]Jer 44:1,26; 46:14 **24:9** [a]S Jer 15:4; 25:18 [b]S Dt 28:25; S 1Ki 9:7 [c]S 2Ki 22:19; S Jer 29:18 [d]S Dt 28:37; Da 9:7 **24:10** [e]S Isa 51:19; S Jer 9:16; Rev 6:8 [f]Jer 15:2 [g]Jer 27:8 [h]S Dt 28:21 **25:1** [i]S 2Ki 24:2

23:36 The three divine titles at the end of the verse enhance the solemnity of what is being said. *living God.* See 10:10; Dt 5:26.

23:39 *forget.* The Hebrew for this word is a pun on the Hebrew for the word "oracle" in vv. 33–34,36,38—by which Jeremiah highlights his word of judgment. *the city.* Jerusalem.

23:40 Echoed from 20:11.

24:1–10 See Am 8:1–3. Having denounced Judah's leaders (21:1—23:8) and false prophets (23:9–40), Jeremiah now describes the division of Judah's people into good and bad (24:1–3) and summarizes the Lord's determination to restore the good (vv. 4–7) but destroy the bad (vv. 8–10).

24:1 *Jehoiachin … and the officials … were carried into exile.* In 597 B.C. *craftsmen and … artisans.* See 29:2; 2Ki 24:14,16. Only the poorest and weakest people were left behind in Judah (see 2Ki 24:14; for the later period [586] cf. Jer 39:10). *the LORD showed me.* A common way of introducing prophetic visions (see Am 7:1,4,7). *figs.* See note on 8:13. *placed.* The Hebrew root underlying this word is translated "meet" in Ex 29:42–43. As the Lord desired to "meet" with the Israelites at the entrance to the tabernacle, so the figs (symbolizing the people of Judah) would be "met" by him in front of the Jerusalem temple.

24:2 *very good figs … that ripen early.* The first figs in June are especially juicy and delicious (see Isa 28:4; Hos 9:10; Mic 7:1; Na 3:12).

24:3 *What do you see … ?* See note on 1:11.

24:5–6 Just as good figs should be protected and preserved by their owner, so also the exiles of 597 B.C., who were the best of Judah's leaders and craftsmen (see 2Ki 24:14–16), would be watched over and cared for by the Lord (see 29:4–14).

24:6 *My eyes will watch over them for their good.* Contrast the word of judgment in Am 9:4. *bring them back.* In 538/537 B.C. *build them up … tear them down … plant … uproot.* See 1:10 and note.

24:7 *a heart to know me.* For a more comprehensive prediction including the same promise see 31:31–34. *my people … their God.* The classic statement of covenant relationship (see 31:33; 32:38; see also notes on Ge 17:7; Zec 8:8). *with all their heart.* See 29:13.

24:8 *live in Egypt.* Perhaps those deported with Jehoahaz in 609 B.C. (see 22:10b–12 and notes; 2Ki 23:31–34) and/or those who fled to Egypt after the Babylonians defeated the Egyptians in the battle of Carchemish in 605 (see 46:2).

24:9 *abhorrent … to all the kingdoms.* See 34:17. *reproach … object of ridicule.* See Dt 28:37. *byword.* See notes on 1Ki 9:7; Job 17:6.

24:10 *sword, famine and plague.* See note on 14:12. *destroyed from the land.* In 586 B.C. (see 52:4–27).

25:1—29:32 The dominant theme in chs. 25–29 is the forthcoming destruction of Jerusalem and exile to Babylonia in 586 B.C. (hinted at briefly in 24:10).

25:1–38 Divine judgment will descend not only on Judah

siah king of Judah, which was the first
year of Nebuchadnezzar[j] king of Babylon.
2So Jeremiah the prophet said to all the
people of Judah[k] and to all those living in
Jerusalem: 3For twenty-three years—from
the thirteenth year of Josiah[l] son of Amon
king of Judah until this very day—the
word of the LORD has come to me and I
have spoken to you again and again,[m] but
you have not listened.[n]
4And though the LORD has sent all his
servants the prophets[o] to you again and
again, you have not listened or paid any
attention.[p] 5They said, "Turn[q] now, each
of you, from your evil ways and your evil
practices, and you can stay in the land[r] the
LORD gave to you and your fathers for ever
and ever. 6Do not follow other gods[s] to
serve and worship them; do not provoke
me to anger with what your hands have
made. Then I will not harm you."
7"But you did not listen to me," declares
the LORD, "and you have provoked[t] me
with what your hands have made,[u] and
you have brought harm[v] to yourselves."
8Therefore the LORD Almighty says
this: "Because you have not listened to
my words, 9I will summon[w] all the peoples of the north[x] and my servant[y] Nebuchadnezzar[z] king of Babylon," declares
the LORD, "and I will bring them against
this land and its inhabitants and against
all the surrounding nations. I will completely destroy[a][a] them and make them an
object of horror and scorn,[b] and an everlasting ruin.[c] 10I will banish from them the
sounds[d] of joy and gladness, the voices of
bride and bridegroom,[e] the sound of millstones[f] and the light of the lamp.[g] 11This
whole country will become a desolate
wasteland,[h] and these nations will serve[i]
the king of Babylon seventy years.[j]
12"But when the seventy years[k] are fulfilled, I will punish the king of Babylon[l]
and his nation, the land of the Babylonians,[b] for their guilt," declares the LORD,
"and will make it desolate[m] forever. 13I will
bring upon that land all the things I have
spoken against it, all that are written[n] in
this book and prophesied by Jeremiah
against all the nations. 14They themselves
will be enslaved[o] by many nations[p] and
great kings; I will repay[q] them according to their deeds and the work of their
hands."

The Cup of God's Wrath

15This is what the LORD, the God of
Israel, said to me: "Take from my hand
this cup[r] filled with the wine of my wrath
and make all the nations to whom I send[s]
you drink it. 16When they drink[t] it, they
will stagger[u] and go mad[v] because of the
sword[w] I will send among them."

25:1 [j]S 2Ki 24:1 **25:2** [k]Jer 18:11 **25:3** [l]S 1Ch 3:14 [m]Jer 11:7; 26:5 [n]S Isa 65:12; S Jer 7:26 **25:4** [o]Jer 6:17; S 7:25; 29:19 [p]S Jer 7:26; 34:14; 44:5 **25:5** [q]S Jdg 6:8; S 2Ch 7:14; S 30:9; S Jer 23:22 [r]S Ge 12:7; S Dt 4:40 **25:6** [s]S Ex 20:3; S Dt 8:19 **25:7** [t]Jer 30:14; 32:35; 44:5 [u]Dt 32:21 [v]2Ki 17:20; 21:15 **25:9** [w]Isa 13:3-5 [x]S Isa 14:31 [y]S Isa 41:2; Jer 27:6 [z]S 2Ch 36:6 [a]S Nu 21:2 [b]S 2Ch 29:8 [c]S Jer 19:8; S 20:4; Eze 12:20 **25:10** [d]S Isa 24:8; Eze 26:13 [e]Jer 7:34; 33:11 [f]Ecc 12:3-4 [g]S Job 18:5; La 5:15; Rev 18:22-23 **25:11** [h]S Lev 26:31,32; Jer 4:26-27; 12:11-12 [i]Jer 28:14 [j]S 2Ch 36:21 **25:12** [k]Jer 27:7; 29:10 [l]S Ge 10:10; S Ps 137:8 [m]S Isa 13:19-22; 14:22-23 **25:13** [n]S Isa 30:8 **25:14** [o]Isa 14:6; Jer 27:7 [p]Jer 50:9; 51:27-28 [q]S Dt 32:41; S Job 21:19; S Jer 51:6 **25:15** [r]S Isa 51:17; Jer 49:12; La 4:21; Eze 23:31; Rev 14:10 [s]Jer 1:5 **25:16** [t]ver 26 [u]S Ps 60:3 [v]Jer 51:7 [w]ver 27-29

[a] *9* The Hebrew term refers to the irrevocable giving over of things or persons to the LORD, often by totally destroying them. [b] *12* Or *Chaldeans*

but on "all the surrounding nations" (v. 9) as well (see notes on Isa 13:1—23:18; Am 1:3—2:16; 5:18, Mic 1:2; Zep 2:4—3:8).

25:1 *fourth year of Jehoiakim ... first year of Nebuchadnezzar.* The synchronism yields the date 605 B.C. (see note on Da 1:1).

25:3 *twenty-three years.* Nineteen under Josiah and four under Jehoiakim (see v. 1). *thirteenth year of Josiah.* 626 B.C. (or possibly as early as 627); see 1:2. *again and again.* See v. 4; see also note on 7:13. *you have not listened.* Jeremiah, now halfway through his prophetic ministry, had been warned at the time of his call that the people of Judah would oppose him (see 1:17–19).

25:4 Echoed from 7:25–26; see also 35:15. *his servants the prophets.* See note on 7:25.

25:5 *stay in the land the LORD gave ... your fathers for ever and ever.* Echoed from 7:7; see Ge 17:8 and note.

25:6 *provoke me to anger.* See 7:18; Dt 31:29. *what your hands have made.* Idols (see note on 1:16).

25:7 *brought harm to yourselves.* See 7:6.

25:9 *peoples of the north.* Babylonia and her allies (see 1:15 and note). *my servant Nebuchadnezzar.* See 27:6; 43:10. "Servant" is used here not in the sense of "worshiper" but of "vassal" or "agent of judgment," just as the pagan ruler Cyrus is called the Lord's "shepherd" in Isa 44:28 and his "anointed" in Isa 45:1 (see note there). *this land.* Judah. *surrounding nations.* Named in vv. 19–26. *completely destroy.* See NIV text note; 50:21,26; 51:3; see also note on Dt 2:34. *object of horror and scorn.* See note on 18:16. *everlasting ruin.* See 49:13; Ps 74:3; Isa 58:12 and note.

25:11–12 *seventy years.* This round number (as in Ps 90:10; Isa 23:15) represents the period from 605 (see notes on v. 1; Da 1:1) to 538/537 B.C., which marked the beginning of Judah's return from exile (see 2Ch 36:20–23; see also notes on Da 9:1–2). The 70 years of Zec 1:12 are not necessarily the same as those here and in 29:10. They probably represent the period from 586 (when Solomon's temple was destroyed) to 516 (when Zerubbabel's temple was completed). See note on Zec 7:5.

25:11 *This ... country ... and these nations.* Judah and the nations named in vv. 19–26.

25:12 *punish the king ... and his nation.* See 50:18. The city of Babylon was captured by the Medes and Persians in 539 B.C. (near the end of Jeremiah's 70 years; see note on vv. 11–12). *for their guilt.* See 50:11,31–32; 51:6,49,53,56; Isa 13:19. *make it desolate forever.* See 50:12–13; 51:26; see also note on Isa 13:20.

25:13 *book.* After this word, the Septuagint (the pre-Christian Greek translation of the OT) inserts the material found in chs. 46–51, though rearranged.

25:14 *many nations.* Media, Persia and their allies. *great kings.* Cyrus and his associates. *repay them according to their deeds.* See 50:29; 51:24.

25:15 *cup filled with the wine of my wrath.* Symbolic of divine judgment, especially against wicked nations (see Isa 51:17 and note; see also 51:7; Rev 18:6). *nations to whom I send you.* See 1:5 and note.

25:16 *stagger and go mad.* See 13:12–14 and notes; Rev 14:8. *because of the sword.* As the sting of wine causes people to stagger, so the stroke of the sword causes them to fall, never to rise again (see v. 27).

17So I took the cup from the LORD's hand
and made all the nations to whom he sent[x]
me drink it: 18Jerusalem[y] and the towns
of Judah, its kings and officials, to make
them a ruin[z] and an object of horror and
scorn[a] and cursing,[b] as they are today;[c]
19Pharaoh king[d] of Egypt,[e] his attendants,
his officials and all his people, 20and all
the foreign people there; all the kings of
Uz;[f] all the kings of the Philistines[g] (those
of Ashkelon,[h] Gaza,[i] Ekron, and the people left at Ashdod); 21Edom,[j] Moab[k] and
Ammon;[l] 22all the kings of Tyre[m] and Sidon;[n] the kings of the coastlands[o] across
the sea; 23Dedan,[p] Tema,[q] Buz[r] and all
who are in distant places[a];[s] 24all the kings
of Arabia[t] and all the kings of the foreign
people[u] who live in the desert; 25all the
kings of Zimri,[v] Elam[w] and Media;[x] 26and
all the kings of the north,[y] near and far,
one after the other—all the kingdoms[z] on
the face of the earth. And after all of them,
the king of Sheshach[b][a] will drink it too.

27"Then tell them, 'This is what the
LORD Almighty, the God of Israel, says:
Drink, get drunk[b] and vomit, and fall to
rise no more because of the sword[c] I will
send among you.' 28But if they refuse to
take the cup from your hand and drink[d],
tell them, 'This is what the LORD Almighty
says: You must drink it! 29See, I am beginning to bring disaster[e] on the city that
bears my Name,[f] and will you indeed go
unpunished?[g] You will not go unpunished,
for I am calling down a sword[h] upon all[i]
who live on the earth,[j] declares the LORD
Almighty.'

30"Now prophesy all these words against
them and say to them:

" 'The LORD will roar[k] from on high;
he will thunder[l] from his holy
dwelling[m]
and roar mightily against his land.
He will shout like those who tread[n] the
grapes,
shout against all who live on the
earth.
31The tumult[o] will resound to the ends of
the earth,
for the LORD will bring charges[p]
against the nations;
he will bring judgment[q] on all[r]
mankind
and put the wicked to the sword,[s]' "
declares the LORD.

32This is what the LORD Almighty says:
"Look! Disaster[t] is spreading
from nation to nation;[u]
a mighty storm[v] is rising
from the ends of the earth."[w]

[a] 23 Or *who clip the hair by their foreheads*
[b] 26 *Sheshach* is a cryptogram for Babylon.

25:17 [x]Jer 1:10; 27:3 **25:18** [y]S Jer 13:13 [z]S Job 12:19 [a]S 2Ch 29:8 [b]S Jer 24:9 [c]S Ge 19:13; Jer 44:22 **25:19** [d]S 2Ki 18:21 [e]Isa 19:1; 20:3; Jer 44:30; Eze 29:2 **25:20** [f]S Ge 10:23 [g]S Jos 13:3; S 2Ch 26:6; S 28:18; Zep 2:4-7 [h]Jer 47:5; Am 1:7-8 [i]S Ge 10:19 **25:21** [j]S Ge 25:30 [k]S Ge 19:37; S Dt 23:6 [l]S Ge 19:38; Jer 27:3; 49:1 **25:22** [m]S Jos 19:29 [n]S Ge 10:15 [o]Isa 11:11; 48:20; 66:20; Jer 31:10; Eze 27:15; 39:6; Da 11:18 **25:23** [p]S Ge 25:3 [q]S Ge 25:15 [r]S Ge 2 2:21 [s]Jer 9:26; 49:32 **25:24** [t]S 2Ch 9:14 [u]ver 20 **25:25** [v]Ge 25:2 [w]S Ge 10:22 [x]S Isa 21:2 **25:26** [y]ver 9; Jer 50:3,9; 51:11,48 [z]Isa 23:17 [a]Jer 51:41 **25:27** [b]ver 16,28; S Isa 29:9; S 49:26; Jer 51:57; Eze 23:32-34; Na 3:18; Hab 2:16 [c]S Jer 12:12; Eze 14:17; 21:4 **25:28** [d]S Isa 51:23 **25:29** [e]S 2Sa 5:7; Isa 10:12; Jer 13:12-14; 39:1 [f]S Dt 28:10; S Isa 37:17 [g]S Pr 11:31 [h]ver 27 [i]ver 30-31; Isa 34:2 [j]S Isa 24:1 **25:30** [k]Isa 16:10; S 42:13 [l]S Ps 46:6 [m]S Ps 68:5 [n]Isa 63:3; Joel 3:13; Rev 14:19-20 **25:31** [o]Jer 23:19 [p]S Jer 2:9 [q]S 1Sa 12:7; S Jer 2:35; S Eze 36:5 [r]S ver 29 [s]S Jer 15:9 **25:32** [t]S Isa 30:25 [u]Isa 34:2 [v]S Jer 23:19 [w]S Dt 28:49

25:17 A symbolic description of Jeremiah's announcement of divine judgment against the nations.

25:18 *Jerusalem and ... Judah.* God's own people are to be judged first (see v. 29; see also Eze 9:6; 1Pe 4:17). *its kings.* See note on 17:20. *ruin ... horror ... scorn ... cursing.* See vv. 9,11; 18:16; 19:8.

25:19–26 The roster of nations begins with Egypt and ends with Babylonia, as in chs. 46–51; but Damascus (see 49:23–27) is omitted, and a few other regions are added.

25:19 *Egypt.* See 46:2–28.

25:20 *foreign people.* See v. 24; Ne 13:3. *Uz.* See note on Job 1:1. *Philistines.* See ch. 47; see also note on Ge 10:14. *Ashkelon, Gaza, Ekron.* See note on Jdg 1:18; see also map, p. 331. *people left at Ashdod.* According to the Greek historian Herodotus (2.157), the Egyptian pharaoh Psammetichus I (664–610 B.C.) destroyed Ashdod after a long siege. By Nehemiah's time, it was inhabited again (see note on Ne 4:7). The fifth main Philistine city, Gath (see Jos 13:3), though important earlier (see, e.g., 1Sa 21:10–12), was destroyed and apparently not rebuilt (in later centuries it is not mentioned with the other four cities; see Am 1:6–8; Zep 2:4; Zec 9:5–6).

25:21–22 See 27:3–5.

25:21 *Edom.* See 49:7–22; see also note on Ge 36:1. *Moab and Ammon.* See 48:1—49:6; see also note on Ge 19:36–38.

25:22 *Tyre and Sidon.* See 47:4; see also notes on Isa 23:1–2,4,12. *coastlands across the sea.* Mediterranean islands and maritime regions, some of them Phoenician colonies (see Eze 27:15; Da 11:18 and notes).

25:23 *Dedan.* See 49:8; see also notes on Isa 21:13; Eze 25:13. *Tema.* See note on Isa 21:14. *Buz.* A desert region in the east, the homeland of Elihu (see Job 32:2 and note). *who are in distant places.* See note on 9:26.

25:24 *Arabia.* See 49:28–33; see also 3:2 and NIV text note. *foreign people.* See v. 20; Ne 13:3. The same Hebrew root underlies "Arabia" and "foreign people."

25:25 *Zimri.* Not to be confused with the Israelite king of that name, Zimri is perhaps the same as Zimran, whom Keturah bore to Abraham (see Ge 25:1–2). The region known as Zimri (location unknown) would then have been named after him. *Elam.* See 49:34–39; see also note on Ge 10:22. *Media.* Later to join the Persians in conquering Babylon (see 51:11,28; see also note on Isa 13:17).

25:26 *Sheshach.* See NIV text note. The cryptogram is formed by substituting the first consonant of the Hebrew alphabet for the last, the second for the next-to-last, etc. Its purpose is not fully understood, though in some cases the cryptogram itself bears a suitable meaning (see note on 51:1). *will drink it too.* The Lord's agents of judgment are not themselves exempt from his judgment (see 51:48–49).

25:27 *fall ... because of the sword.* See note on v. 16.

25:29 *beginning.* See note on v. 18. *city that bears my Name.* Jerusalem (see note on 7:10). *sword.* See note on 12:12.

25:30 *The LORD will roar ... thunder.* An echo of Joel 3:16; Am 1:2 (see note there; see also Hos 11:10; Am 3:8). *his land.* Judah. *shout like those who tread the grapes.* See Isa 9:3; 16:9–10; 63:3 and note; see also Isa 16:10 and note.

25:31 *tumult.* The sounds of war (see Am 2:2). *bring charges ... bring judgment.* See note on 2:9; see also 2:35; 12:1.

25:32 *mighty storm ... from the ends of the earth.* The wrath of God (see 23:19), mediated through the coming invasion of the Babylonians (see note on Isa 41:25).

[33]At that time those slain[x] by the LORD will
be everywhere — from one end of the earth
to the other. They will not be mourned or
gathered[y] up or buried,[z] but will be like
refuse lying on the ground.

[34]Weep and wail, you shepherds;[a]
roll[b] in the dust, you leaders of the
flock.
For your time to be slaughtered[c] has
come;
you will fall and be shattered like
fine pottery.[d]
[35]The shepherds will have nowhere to
flee,
the leaders of the flock no place to
escape.[e]
[36]Hear the cry[f] of the shepherds,[g]
the wailing of the leaders of the
flock,
for the LORD is destroying their
pasture.
[37]The peaceful meadows will be laid
waste
because of the fierce anger of the
LORD.
[38]Like a lion[h] he will leave his lair,
and their land will become desolate[i]
because of the sword[a] of the
oppressor[j]
and because of the LORD's fierce
anger.[k]

Jeremiah Threatened With Death

26 Early in the reign of Jehoiakim[l] son
of Josiah king of Judah, this word
came from the LORD: [2]"This is what the
LORD says: Stand in the courtyard[m] of the
LORD's house and speak to all the people
of the towns of Judah who come to worship in the house of the LORD.[n] Tell[o] them
everything I command you; do not omit[p]
a word. [3]Perhaps they will listen and each
will turn[q] from his evil way. Then I will
relent[r] and not bring on them the disaster
I was planning because of the evil they
have done. [4]Say to them, 'This is what the
LORD says: If you do not listen[s] to me and
follow my law,[t] which I have set before
you, [5]and if you do not listen to the words
of my servants the prophets, whom I have
sent to you again and again (though you
have not listened[u]), [6]then I will make this
house like Shiloh[v] and this city an object
of cursing[w] among all the nations of the
earth.' "

[7]The priests, the prophets and all the
people heard Jeremiah speak these words
in the house of the LORD. [8]But as soon as
Jeremiah finished telling all the people everything the LORD had commanded[x] him
to say, the priests, the prophets and all the
people seized[y] him and said, "You must
die![z] [9]Why do you prophesy in the LORD's
name that this house will be like Shiloh
and this city will be desolate and deserted?"[a] And all the people crowded[b] around
Jeremiah in the house of the LORD.

[10]When the officials[c] of Judah heard
about these things, they went up from
the royal palace to the house of the LORD
and took their places at the entrance of
the New Gate[d] of the LORD's house. [11]Then
the priests and the prophets said to the
officials and all the people, "This man
should be sentenced to death[e] because he
has prophesied against this city. You have
heard it with your own ears!"[f]

[12]Then Jeremiah said to all the officials[g]
and all the people: "The LORD sent me
to prophesy[h] against this house and this

[a] *38* Some Hebrew manuscripts and Septuagint (see also Jer. 46:16 and 50:16); most Hebrew manuscripts *anger*

25:33 [x]Isa 66:16; Eze 39:17-20 [y]S Jer 8:2 [z]S Ps 79:3 **25:34** [a]S Jer 2:8; Zec 10:3 [b]S Jer 6:26 [c]S Ps 44:22; S Isa 34:6; Jer 50:27; 51:40; Zec 11:4,7 [d]S Jer 22:28 **25:35** [e]S Job 11:20 **25:36** [f]S Jer 6:26 [g]S Jer 23:1; Zec 11:3 **25:38** [h]S Job 10:16; S Jer 4:7 [i]Jer 44:22 [j]Jer 46:16; 50:16 [k]S Ex 15:7; S Jer 4:26 **26:1** [l]2Ki 23:36 **26:2** [m]Jer 19:14 [n]S Jer 17:19 [o]S ver 12; S Jer 1:17; Mt 28:20; Ac 20:27 [p]Dt 4:2 **26:3** [q]Dt 30:2; 2Ch 33:12-13; Isa 55:7; Jer 35:15; 36:7 [r]S Jer 18:8 **26:4** [s]Lev 26:14; Jer 25:3 [t]Ex 20:1-23:33; S 1Ki 9:6; S Jer 11:8 **26:5** [u]S Pr 1:24; S Isa 65:12; Jer 25:4; 44:5 **26:6** [v]S Jos 18:1; S Jdg 18:31 [w]S Dt 28:25; S 2Ki 22:19 **26:8** [x]Jer 43:1 [y]Ac 6:12; 21:27 [z]Lev 24:15-16; S Ne 9:26; S Jer 11:21 **26:9** [a]S Lev 26:32; S Jer 9:11 [b]Ac 21:32 **26:10** [c]ver 16; Jer 34:19; Eze 22:27 [d]S Ge 23:10 **26:11** [e]Dt 18:20; S Jer 11:21; 18:23; Mt 26:66; Ac 6:11 [f]S Ps 44:1 **26:12** [g]Jer 1:18 [h]S Isa 6:8; Am 7:15; Ac 4:18-20; 5:29

25:33 *not be mourned ... like refuse lying on the ground.* Repeated from 8:2 (see note there); 16:4.
25:34 – 36 *shepherds ... leaders of the flock.* See 2:8 and note; 10:21; 22:22; Eze 34:2 and note.
25:34 *roll in the dust.* Or "roll in ashes" (as in 6:26). *your time ... has come.* See La 4:18. *shattered like fine pottery.* Cf. the description of Jehoiachin in 22:28.
25:36 *their pasture.* The land of Judah.
26:1 – 24 A summary (vv. 2 – 6) — and its results (vv. 7 – 24) — of one of Jeremiah's temple messages in ch. 7 (see note on 7:1 — 10:25).
26:1 *Early in the reign.* See 27:1. The Babylonian equivalent of the Hebrew for this phrase implies that the first year of King Jehoiakim (609 – 608 B.C.) is probably meant.
26:2 *courtyard of the LORD's house.* Perhaps near the New Gate (see v. 10; see also note on 7:2). *who come to worship.* See 7:2 and note. *do not omit a word.* See Dt 4:2 and note.
26:3 See 7:3,5 – 7. *relent.* See vv. 13,19; see also notes on 4:28; 18:7 – 10.
26:4 *If you do not listen.* See v. 5; 7:13. *my law.* See 7:6,9 and notes.
26:5 See 7:13,25 – 26. *my servants the prophets.* See note on 7:25. *again and again.* See note on 7:13.
26:6 *make this house like Shiloh.* See v. 9; see also note on 7:12. *this city.* Jerusalem. *object of cursing.* See 24:9; 25:18; see also note on Zec 8:13.
26:8 *You must die!* A similar phrase describes the ultimate penalty for gross violations of the law of Moses (see, e.g., Ex 21:15 – 17; Lev 24:16 – 17,21; Dt 18:20; cf. 1Ki 21:13).
26:9 *crowded around.* With hostile intent (see Nu 16:3).
26:10 *officials of Judah.* Those responsible for making legal decisions concerning disputes taking place in the temple precincts. The priests and (false) prophets, who had a vested interest in Jerusalem and its temple, felt that Jeremiah should be sentenced to death because he was predicting the destruction of both the city and the Lord's house (see vv. 8 – 9,11). After hearing Jeremiah's defense (vv. 12 – 15), the officials decided in his favor (v. 16). The people, fickle and easily swayed, first opposed Jeremiah (vv. 8 – 9), then supported him (v. 16). *New Gate.* See 36:10; possibly the same as the "Upper Gate of Benjamin" (see 20:2 and note).
26:11 Jeremiah's enemies judge him before he has a chance to defend himself (cf. Dt 19:6; Jos 20:1 – 9 and note).
26:12 *The LORD sent me.* Contrast 23:21.

city all the things you have heard.[i] 13 Now
reform[j] your ways and your actions and
obey[k] the LORD your God. Then the LORD
will relent[l] and not bring the disaster he
has pronounced against you. 14 As for me,
I am in your hands;[m] do with me whatever
you think is good and right. 15 Be assured,
however, that if you put me to death, you
will bring the guilt of innocent blood[n] on
yourselves and on this city and on those
who live in it, for in truth the LORD has
sent me to you to speak all these words[o]
in your hearing."

16 Then the officials[p] and all the people
said to the priests and the prophets, "This
man should not be sentenced to death![q]
He has spoken to us in the name of the
LORD our God."

17 Some of the elders of the land stepped
forward and said to the entire assembly
of people, 18 "Micah[r] of Moresheth prophesied in the days of Hezekiah king of Judah. He told all the people of Judah, 'This
is what the LORD Almighty says:

"'Zion[s] will be plowed like a field,
Jerusalem will become a heap of
rubble,[t]
the temple hill[u] a mound overgrown
with thickets.'[a v]

19 "Did Hezekiah king of Judah or anyone else in Judah put him to death? Did
not Hezekiah[w] fear the LORD and seek[x]

26:12 [i] S ver 2, 15 **26:13** [j] S Jer 7:5; Joel 2:12-14 [k] Jer 11:4 [l] S Jer 18:8 **26:14** [m] Jos 9:25; Jer 38:5 **26:15** [n] S Dt 19:10 [o] S ver 12; S Jer 1:17 **26:16** [p] S ver 10; S Ac 23:9 [q] Ac 23:29 **26:18** [r] Mic 1:1 [s] Isa 2:3 [t] S 2Ki 25:9; S Ne 4:2; Jer 9:11 [u] Mic 4:1; Zec 8:3 [v] S Jer 17:3 **26:19** [w] S 1Ch 3:13; 2Ch 32:24-26; Isa 37:14-20 [x] S 1Sa 13:12 [y] S Ex 32:14; S Jer 18:8 [z] Jer 44:7 [a] Hab 2:10 **26:20** [b] S Jos 9:17 **26:21** [c] S 1Ki 19:2 [d] ver 10 [e] Jer 2:30; Mt 23:37 [f] S Ge 31:21; Mt 10:23 **26:22** [g] Jer 36:12, 25 **26:23** [h] Heb 11:37 [i] 2Ki 23:6 **26:24** [j] S 2Ki 22:12

his favor? And did not the LORD relent,[y]
so that he did not bring the disaster[z] he
pronounced against them? We are about
to bring a terrible disaster[a] on ourselves!"

20 (Now Uriah son of Shemaiah from Kiriath Jearim[b] was another man who prophesied in the name of the LORD; he prophesied the same things against this city and
this land as Jeremiah did. 21 When King Jehoiakim[c] and all his officers and officials[d]
heard his words, the king sought to put
him to death.[e] But Uriah heard of it and
fled[f] in fear to Egypt. 22 King Jehoiakim,
however, sent Elnathan[g] son of Acbor to
Egypt, along with some other men. 23 They
brought Uriah out of Egypt and took him
to King Jehoiakim, who had him struck
down with a sword[h] and his body thrown
into the burial place of the common people.)[i]

24 Furthermore, Ahikam[j] son of Shaphan
supported Jeremiah, and so he was not
handed over to the people to be put to
death.

Judah to Serve Nebuchadnezzar

27 Early in the reign of Zedekiah[b k] son
of Josiah king of Judah, this word

[a] *18* Micah 3:12 [b] *1* A few Hebrew manuscripts and Syriac (see also Jer. 27:3,12 and 28:1); most Hebrew manuscripts *Jehoiakim* (Most Septuagint manuscripts do not have this verse.)

27:1 [k] S 2Ch 36:11

26:13 *reform your ways and your actions.* Repeated from 7:3 (see also 18:11; 35:15). *relent.* See vv. 3,19; see also notes on 4:28; 18:7–10.

26:15 *innocent blood.* See 7:6 and note; see also Mt 27:24–25; Ac 5:28.

26:16 Contrast v. 11; see note on v. 10.

26:17 *elders.* See 19:1 and note.

26:18–19 The elders cite the precedent of Micah, who lived a century earlier and who (together with Isaiah) convinced King Hezekiah to pray for forgiveness on behalf of his people. The Lord answered the prayers of the king and the prophets, and in 701 B.C. Jerusalem and the temple were spared (see Isa 37:33–37).

26:18 *Micah of Moresheth.* See Introduction to Micah: Author. *Zion will be plowed ... overgrown with thickets.* Quoted verbatim from Mic 3:12 (see note there)—the only place in the OT where one prophet quotes another and identifies his source.

26:19 *seek his favor.* Lit. "stroke his face" (cf. Ps 119:58), "pat his cheek" (see Ex 32:11; 1Sa 13:12; 2Ki 13:4). *relent.* See vv. 3,13; see also notes on 4:28; 18:7–10.

26:20–23 A parenthesis, cited as an example of the contrast between how a good king, Hezekiah, treated the Lord's prophets and how a wicked king, Jehoiakim, was known to have treated them.

26:20 *Uriah.* Not mentioned elsewhere in the OT, though it has been claimed (but not substantiated) that he appears in one of the Lachish letters (see note on 34:7; see also chart, p. xxii).

26:21 *officers.* Lit. "strong men" (perhaps the royal bodyguard). *Uriah ... fled ... to Egypt.* A fatal mistake, for now he could be accused of treason and sedition.

26:22 *Elnathan son of Acbor.* One of King Jehoiakim's highest officials (see 36:12), he was impressed on another occasion by Jeremiah's prophecies (see 36:16), "urged the king not to burn" Jeremiah's scroll (36:25), and warned the prophet to hide (see 36:19). An Elnathan (perhaps the same man) was Jehoiakim's father-in-law (see 2Ki 24:6,8). An Acbor (perhaps the father of this Elnathan) was one of King Josiah's officials (see 2Ki 22:12,14; see also note on v. 24).

26:23 *brought Uriah out of Egypt.* Mutual rights of extradition were a part of the treaty imposed on Judah by Egypt when Jehoiakim became the vassal of the Egyptian pharaoh Neco II (see 2Ki 23:34–35). *Jehoiakim ... had him struck down.* Apart from divine intervention, Jeremiah probably would have fallen victim to the same fate (see 36:26). *burial place of the common people.* See note on 17:19. Commoners were buried in the Kidron Valley east of Jerusalem (see 2Ki 23:6).

26:24 *Ahikam son of Shaphan.* One of King Josiah's officials (see 2Ki 22:12,14), along with an Acbor who may have been the father of the Elnathan in v. 22 (see note there). Ahikam was also the father of Gedaliah, who would become governor of Judah after Jerusalem was destroyed in 586 B.C. (see 40:5) and who also befriended Jeremiah (see 39:14). *supported Jeremiah.* Ahikam's high position in Jehoiakim's court was doubtless instrumental in saving the prophet's life.

27:1—29:32 Further attempts by Jeremiah to counteract the teachings of false prophets, who were claiming that Babylon's doom was near and that rebellion against Nebuchadnezzar was therefore warranted and desirable.

27:1–22 Jeremiah tells the nations (vv. 3–11), King Zedekiah (vv. 12–15), and the priests and people of Judah (vv. 16–22) to submit to the Babylonian yoke.

27:1 *Early in the reign.* See note on 26:1. In this case, however, the phrase has been extended in meaning to include Zedekiah's fourth year (593 B.C.; see 28:1).

came to Jeremiah from the LORD: 2This is
what the LORD said to me: "Make a yoke[l]
out of straps and crossbars and put it on
your neck. 3Then send[m] word to the kings
of Edom, Moab, Ammon,[n] Tyre and Sidon[o]
through the envoys who have come to Jerusalem to Zedekiah king of Judah. 4Give
them a message for their masters and say,
'This is what the LORD Almighty, the God
of Israel, says: "Tell this to your masters:
5With my great power and outstretched
arm[p] I made[q] the earth and its people and
the animals[r] that are on it, and I give[s] it
to anyone I please. 6Now I will hand all
your countries over to my servant[t] Nebuchadnezzar[u] king of Babylon; I will make
even the wild animals subject to him.[v] 7All
nations will serve[w] him and his son and
his grandson until the time[x] for his land
comes; then many nations and great kings
will subjugate[y] him.

8" ' "If, however, any nation or kingdom
will not serve Nebuchadnezzar king of Babylon or bow its neck under his yoke, I will
punish[z] that nation with the sword,[a] famine[b] and plague,[c] declares the LORD, until I
destroy it by his hand. 9So do not listen to
your prophets,[d] your diviners,[e] your interpreters of dreams,[f] your mediums[g] or your
sorcerers[h] who tell you, 'You will not serve[i]
the king of Babylon.' 10They prophesy lies[j]
to you that will only serve to remove[k] you
far from your lands; I will banish you and
you will perish. 11But if any nation will
bow its neck under the yoke[l] of the king of
Babylon and serve him, I will let that nation remain in its own land to till it and to
live[m] there, declares the LORD." ' "

12I gave the same message to Zedekiah
king of Judah. I said, "Bow your neck under the yoke[n] of the king of Babylon; serve
him and his people, and you will live.[o]
13Why will you and your people die[p] by
the sword, famine and plague[q] with which
the LORD has threatened any nation that
will not serve the king of Babylon? 14Do
not listen[r] to the words of the prophets[s]
who say to you, 'You will not serve the
king of Babylon,' for they are prophesying lies[t] to you. 15'I have not sent[u] them,'
declares the LORD. 'They are prophesying
lies in my name.[v] Therefore, I will banish
you and you will perish,[w] both you and
the prophets who prophesy to you.' "

16Then I said to the priests and all these
people, "This is what the LORD says: Do
not listen to the prophets who say, 'Very
soon now the articles[x] from the LORD's
house will be brought back from Babylon.'
They are prophesying lies to you. 17Do not
listen[y] to them. Serve the king of Babylon,
and you will live.[z] Why should this city
become a ruin? 18If they are prophets and
have the word of the LORD, let them plead[a]
with the LORD Almighty that the furnishings remaining in the house of the LORD
and in the palace of the king of Judah
and in Jerusalem not be taken to Babylon.
19For this is what the LORD Almighty says
about the pillars, the Sea,[b] the movable
stands and the other furnishings[c] that are
left in this city, 20which Nebuchadnezzar
king of Babylon did not take away when
he carried[d] Jehoiachin[a][e] son of Jehoiakim
king of Judah into exile from Jerusalem
to Babylon, along with all the nobles of

[a] 20 Hebrew *Jeconiah,* a variant of *Jehoiachin*

27:2 [l]S Lev 26:13; S 1Ki 22:11 **27:3** [m]S Jer 25:17 [n]S Jer 25:21 [o]S Ge 10:15; S Jer 25:22 **27:5** [p]S Dt 9:29 [q]S Ge 1:1 [r]S Ge 1:25 [s]Ps 115:16; Da 4:17 **27:6** [t]S Jer 25:9 [u]S Jer 21:7 [v]Jer 28:14; Da 2:37-38 **27:7** [w]S 2Ch 36:20; Da 5:18 [x]S Jer 25:12 [y]S Jer 25:14; 51:47; Da 5:28 **27:8** [z]Jer 9:16 [a]Jer 21:9 [b]S Jer 5:12 [c]S Jer 14:12 **27:9** [d]Eze 13:1-23 [e]S Ge 30:27; S Isa 44:25 [f]S Dt 13:1; S Jer 23:25 [g]S Dt 18:11 [h]S Ex 7:11 [i]Jer 6:14 **27:10** [j]S Jer 23:25; S Mk 13:5 [k]S 2Ki 23:27 **27:11** [l]S Jer 21:9 [m]Dt 6:2 **27:12** [n]Jer 17:4 [o]S Jer 21:9 **27:13** [p]Eze 18:31 [q]S Jer 14:12 **27:14** [r]S Jer 23:16 [s]S Jer 14:13 [t]S Jer 14:14; S Mt 7:15 **27:15** [u]S Jer 23:21 [v]Jer 29:9; 44:16 [w]S Jer 6:15; Mt 15:12-14 **27:16** [x]1Ki 7:48-50; S 2Ki 24:13 **27:17** [y]Jer 23:16 [z]Jer 42:11 **27:18** [a]S Nu 21:7; S 1Sa 7:8 **27:19** [b]1Ki 7:23-26 [c]S 1Ki 7:51; Jer 52:17-23 **27:20** [d]S Dt 28:36; S 2Ch 36:10 [e]Jer 22:24; Mt 1:11

27:2 *yoke.* Of the kind worn by oxen, it was a symbol of political submission (see vv. 8,11–12; Lev 26:13). That Jeremiah actually wore such a yoke for a time is clear from 28:10,12.
27:3 *send word.* In his role as a "prophet to the nations" (1:5). *Edom, Moab, Ammon.* Lands east and south of Judah (see 25:21 and note). *Tyre and Sidon.* Prominent cities in Phoenicia, north of Judah (see 25:22 and note). *envoys … have come … to Zedekiah.* Perhaps to discuss rebellion against Babylonia. They may have counted on support from Egypt, where Psammetichus II had become pharaoh a year earlier (594 B.C.). Zedekiah went to Babylon in 593 (see 51:59), perhaps to be interrogated by Nebuchadnezzar. In any case, Zedekiah rebelled against him (see 52:3).
27:5 *great power and outstretched arm.* See note on 21:5.
27:6 *my servant Nebuchadnezzar.* See note on 25:9. *make … wild animals subject to him.* Nothing would be beyond the reach of Nebuchadnezzar's dominion (see 28:14; Da 2:38).
27:7 *him … his son … his grandson.* Three generations of rulers, not necessarily in direct father-son relationships (see note on Da 5:1; see also NIV text notes on Ge 10:2,8). *time for his land comes.* Babylonia will be judged (see note on 25:26). *many nations and great kings.* See note on 25:14.
27:8 *yoke.* See note on v. 2. *sword, famine and plague.* See note on 14:12. *until I destroy.* See 9:16; 24:10.
27:9 See 29:8. *your prophets.* False prophets. *diviners … mediums … sorcerers.* Forbidden in Israel (see Lev 19:26; Dt 18:10–11 and note on 18:9). *interpreters of dreams.* Including prophets and diviners (see 23:25–28; 29:8).
27:10 *prophesy lies.* See note on 5:31; cf. 2Ti 4:3–4.
27:11 *yoke.* See note on v. 2. *serve … till.* The Hebrew underlying both words is the same ("work" is the common denominator in serving and tilling).
27:12 *your neck … serve … live.* The Hebrew for all these words is plural, since Jeremiah is speaking to the people of Judah as well as to Zedekiah (see v. 13). *yoke.* See note on v. 2.
27:13 See v. 8. *sword, famine and plague.* See note on 14:12.
27:14 See vv. 9–10.
27:15 See 14:14; 23:21 and note.
27:16 *prophets who say, 'Very soon now …'* As the prophet Hananiah was saying (see 28:1–3). *articles from the LORD's house.* Some were carried off to Babylon by Nebuchadnezzar in 605 B.C. (see Da 1:1–2), others in 597 (see 2Ki 24:13). Still others would be carried off in 586 (see vv. 21–22; 52:17–23).
27:18 *If they are prophets … let them plead.* If they are true prophets and in communion with the Lord, let them intercede for Judah, because the Lord has announced his intention to judge the nation.
27:19 *the pillars, the Sea, the movable stands.* See 52:17; see also 1Ki 7:15–37 and notes.

Judah and Jerusalem— 21yes, this is what
the LORD Almighty, the God of Israel, says
about the things that are left in the house
of the LORD and in the palace of the king
of Judah and in Jerusalem: 22'They will be
taken[f] to Babylon and there they will remain until the day[g] I come for them,' declares the LORD. 'Then I will bring[h] them
back and restore them to this place.' "

The False Prophet Hananiah

28 In the fifth month of that same year,
the fourth year, early in the reign of
Zedekiah[i] king of Judah, the prophet Hananiah son of Azzur, who was from Gibeon,[j] said to me in the house of the LORD in
the presence of the priests and all the people: 2"This is what the LORD Almighty, the
God of Israel, says: 'I will break the yoke[k]
of the king of Babylon. 3Within two years I
will bring back to this place all the articles[l]
of the LORD's house that Nebuchadnezzar
king of Babylon removed from here and
took to Babylon. 4I will also bring back to
this place Jehoiachin[a][m] son of Jehoiakim
king of Judah and all the other exiles from
Judah who went to Babylon,' declares the
LORD, 'for I will break the yoke of the king
of Babylon.' "[n]

5Then the prophet Jeremiah replied to
the prophet Hananiah before the priests
and all the people who were standing in
the house of the LORD. 6He said, "Amen!
May the LORD do so! May the LORD fulfill
the words you have prophesied by bringing the articles of the LORD's house and all
the exiles back to this place from Babylon.[o]
7Nevertheless, listen to what I have to say
in your hearing and in the hearing of all
the people: 8From early times the prophets
who preceded you and me have prophesied war, disaster and plague[p] against
many countries and great kingdoms. 9But
the prophet who prophesies peace will be
recognized as one truly sent by the LORD
only if his prediction comes true.[q]"

10Then the prophet Hananiah took the
yoke[r] off the neck of the prophet Jeremiah and broke it, 11and he said[s] before all
the people, "This is what the LORD says:
'In the same way will I break the yoke of
Nebuchadnezzar king of Babylon off the
neck of all the nations within two years.' "
At this, the prophet Jeremiah went on his
way.

12Shortly after the prophet Hananiah
had broken the yoke off the neck of the
prophet Jeremiah, the word of the LORD
came to Jeremiah: 13"Go and tell Hananiah, 'This is what the LORD says: You have
broken a wooden yoke, but in its place
you will get a yoke of iron. 14This is what
the LORD Almighty, the God of Israel, says:
I will put an iron yoke[t] on the necks of all
these nations to make them serve[u] Nebuchadnezzar[v] king of Babylon, and they
will serve him. I will even give him control
over the wild animals.[w]' "

15Then the prophet Jeremiah said to
Hananiah the prophet, "Listen, Hananiah! The LORD has not sent[x] you, yet you
have persuaded this nation to trust in lies.[y]
16Therefore, this is what the LORD says: 'I
am about to remove you from the face of
the earth.[z] This very year you are going
to die,[a] because you have preached rebellion[b] against the LORD.' "

[a] 4 Hebrew *Jeconiah,* a variant of *Jehoiachin*

27:22 [f] S 2Ki 20:17; 25:13 [g] S 2Ch 36:21; S Jer 24:6 [h] S Ezr 7:19
28:1 [i] S 2Ch 36:11 [j] S Jos 9:3
28:2 [k] Jer 27:12
28:3 [l] S 2Ki 24:13
28:4 [m] S 2Ki 25:30; Jer 22:24-27 [n] Hos 7:3
28:6 [o] Zec 6:10
28:8 [p] Lev 26:14-17; Isa 5:5-7; Na 1:14
28:9 [q] S Dt 18:22; Eze 33:33
28:10 [r] S Lev 26:13; S 1Ki 22:11
28:11 [s] Jer 14:14; 27:10
28:14 [t] S Dt 28:48; S Jer 15:12 [u] Jer 25:11 [v] Jer 39:1; Da 1:1; 5:18 [w] S Jer 27:6
28:15 [x] Jer 29:31 [y] S Jer 7:4; 20:6; 29:21; La 2:14; Eze 13:6
28:16 [z] S Ge 7:4 [a] Dt 18:20; Zec 13:3 [b] Dt 13:5; Jer 29:32

27:22 *They will be taken to Babylon.* In 586 B.C. (see 52:17–23). *I will bring them back.* In 538/537 and shortly afterward (see Ezr 1:7–11).

28:1–17 The true prophet Jeremiah confronts the false prophet Hananiah.

28:1 *fourth year . . . of Zedekiah.* 593 B.C. *early in the reign.* See notes on 26:1; 27:1. *prophet.* The word is used for all prophets, whether true (vv. 5,10–12,15) or false (vv. 1,5,10,12,15,17). *Hananiah.* Means "The LORD is gracious," an appropriate name for a prophet who believed strongly (though mistakenly) that the Lord would soon bring back the exiles of Judah and the temple articles (see vv. 3–4,11). *Gibeon.* See 41:12,16; see also note on Jos 9:3.

28:2 *This is what the LORD . . . says.* See v. 11. Though a false prophet, Hananiah claims to have the same authority as Jeremiah (see vv. 13–14,16; see also 23:31). *yoke.* See note on 27:2.

28:3 Hananiah's prediction directly contradicts the words of Jeremiah (see 27:16–22 and notes). *two years.* See v. 11. Contrast Jeremiah's 70 years (25:11–12; 29:10).

28:4 *bring back.* Contradicting Jeremiah's prophecy (see 22:24–27), which was fulfilled (see 52:34). *Jehoiachin . . . went to Babylon.* In 597 B.C. *yoke.* See note on 27:2.

28:6 See 1Ki 1:36. *Amen.* See 11:5 and note. *May the LORD fulfill.* One of the signs of true prophecy (see v. 9; see also Dt 18:21–22 and note). For another sign (or test) see Dt 13:1–5 and note.

28:7 *Nevertheless.* Though in sympathy with what Hananiah is predicting, Jeremiah reminds him that their true predecessors were basically prophets of doom (see v. 8).

28:8 *war, disaster and plague.* An appropriate modification of Jeremiah's usual triad (see note on 14:12).

28:9 *peace.* Ordinarily the message of false prophets (see 6:14 and note).

28:10 *yoke off the neck of the prophet.* See note on 27:2. *broke it.* Perhaps to break symbolically the power of Jeremiah's earlier prophecies (see 25:11–12; 27:7), which contradicted his own.

28:11 *two years.* See note on v. 3.

28:13 *yoke of iron.* The wooden yoke of submission (see note on 27:2) would be exchanged for the iron yoke of servitude (see v. 14; 38:17–23).

28:14 *all these nations . . . will serve him.* See 27:7. *control over the wild animals.* See 27:6 and note.

28:15 *The LORD has not sent you.* A mark of the false prophet (see 23:21 and note).

28:16 *remove.* The Hebrew root underlying this word is the same as that underlying "sent" in v. 15. The Lord had not "sent" Hananiah to prophesy; therefore he would soon be "sent away" to his death. *preached rebellion.* Such activity on the part of false prophets was punishable by death (see Dt 13:5; see also Dt 18:20; cf. Eze 11:13; Ac 5:1–11).

17In the seventh month of that same
year, Hananiah the prophet died.[c]

A Letter to the Exiles

29 This is the text of the letter[d] that the
prophet Jeremiah sent from Jerusalem to the surviving elders among the exiles and to the priests, the prophets and
all the other people Nebuchadnezzar had
carried into exile from Jerusalem to Babylon.[e] 2(This was after King Jehoiachin[a][f]
and the queen mother,[g] the court officials
and the leaders of Judah and Jerusalem,
the craftsmen and the artisans had gone
into exile from Jerusalem.) 3He entrusted
the letter to Elasah son of Shaphan and to
Gemariah son of Hilkiah, whom Zedekiah
king of Judah sent to King Nebuchadnezzar in Babylon. It said:

4This is what the LORD Almighty,
the God of Israel, says to all those I
carried[h] into exile from Jerusalem to
Babylon: 5"Build[i] houses and settle
down; plant gardens and eat what
they produce. 6Marry and have sons
and daughters; find wives for your
sons and give your daughters in marriage, so that they too may have sons
and daughters. Increase in number
there; do not decrease.[j] 7Also, seek[k]
the peace and prosperity of the city
to which I have carried you into exile. Pray[l] to the LORD for it, because
if it prospers, you too will prosper."
8Yes, this is what the LORD Almighty,
the God of Israel, says: "Do not let
the prophets[m] and diviners among
you deceive[n] you. Do not listen to
the dreams[o] you encourage them to
have.[p] 9They are prophesying lies[q]
to you in my name. I have not sent[r]
them," declares the LORD.

10This is what the LORD says: "When
seventy years[s] are completed for Babylon, I will come to you[t] and fulfill
my gracious promise[u] to bring you
back[v] to this place. 11For I know the
plans[w] I have for you," declares the
LORD, "plans to prosper[x] you and
not to harm you, plans to give you
hope and a future.[y] 12Then you will
call[z] upon me and come and pray[a] to
me, and I will listen[b] to you. 13You
will seek[c] me and find me when you
seek me with all your heart.[d] 14I will
be found by you," declares the LORD,
"and will bring you back[e] from captivity.[b] I will gather you from all the
nations and places where I have banished you," declares the LORD, "and
will bring you back to the place from
which I carried you into exile."[f]

15You may say, "The LORD has
raised up prophets for us in Babylon,"
16but this is what the LORD says about
the king who sits on David's throne
and all the people who remain in this
city, your countrymen who did not

28:17 [c]S 2Ki 1:17
29:1 [d]ver 28 [e]S 2Ch 36:10; S Jer 13:17
29:2 [f]S 2Ki 24:12 [g]S 2Ki 24:8
29:4 [h]S Jer 24:5
29:5 [i]ver 28
29:6 [j]Jer 30:19
29:7 [k]S Est 3:8 [l]1Ti 2:1-2
29:8 [m]1Jn 4:1 [n]Jer 37:9 [o]S Dt 13:1; S Jer 23:25 [p]S Jer 23:27
29:9 [q]S Jer 27:15; La 2:14; Eze 13:6 [r]Jer 23:21
29:10 [s]S 2Ch 36:21; S Da 9:2 [t]S Ru 1:6 [u]1Ki 8:56; Jer 32:42; 33:14 [v]S Jer 16:14; S 24:6
29:11 [w]Ps 40:5 [x]Isa 55:12 [y]S Job 8:7; Zec 8:15
29:12 [z]Hos 2:23; Zep 3:12; Zec 13:9 [a]S 1Ki 8:30 [b]Ps 145:19; S Isa 55:6
29:13 [c]Mt 7:7 [d]S Dt 4:29; S 2Ch 6:37
29:14 [e]S Dt 30:3; Jer 30:3; Eze 39:25; Am 9:14; Zep 3:20 [f]Jer 23:3-4; 30:10; 46:27; Eze 37:21

[a] 2 Hebrew *Jeconiah,* a variant of *Jehoiachin* [b] 14 Or *will restore your fortunes*

28:17 *In the seventh month ... Hananiah ... died.* He who had falsely prophesied restoration "within two years" (vv. 3,11) himself died within two months (see v. 1).

29:1–32 Jeremiah's letter to the exiles of 597 B.C. (vv. 4–23) is followed by God's message of judgment against the false prophet Shemaiah (vv. 24–32).

29:2 *queen mother.* Nehushta (see note on 13:18). *craftsmen and ... artisans.* See 24:1 and note.

29:3 *entrusted the letter to.* Placed it in the ancient equivalent of the diplomatic pouch to ensure its safe arrival. *Shaphan.* Perhaps the father also of Ahikam (see 26:24 and note) and/or Gemariah (see 36:10), both of whom were sympathetic to Jeremiah and his mission. *Gemariah.* A common name in Jeremiah's time (see, e.g., 36:10), found on one of the Lachish ostraca (see note on 34:7) as well as in at least two of the Elephantine papyri (see note on 32:11) a century later. *Hilkiah.* Perhaps the Hilkiah who was high priest under Josiah (see 2Ki 22:12, where Hilkiah and one or more Shaphans are mentioned together). *Zedekiah ... sent to King Nebuchadnezzar.* Possibly at or about the same time (593 B.C.) that Zedekiah himself went to Babylon for a brief period (see 51:59). The purpose of the journey(s) is unknown.

29:4 *I.* The Lord (see v. 7). Since it is God who has exiled his people, they are to submit to their captors and not rebel against them.

29:5 *Build ... plant.* Reminiscent of Jeremiah's call (see 1:10), but here used in a literal sense. *settle down.* Ezekiel, e.g., lived in his own house in Babylonia (see Eze 8:1 and note).

29:6 *find wives.* But among the exiles themselves, not among the women of Babylonia (cf. Dt 7:3–4; Ezr 9:1–2).

29:7 An unprecedented and unique concept in the ancient world: working toward and praying for the prosperity of one's captors. *peace and prosperity ... prospers ... prosper.* The Hebrew word is *shalom* in all three cases. *city.* Every place in which the exiles settle down. *Pray ... for it.* See Ezr 6:10 and note; Mt 5:44; in the Apocrypha cf. 1 Maccabees 7:33.

29:8 *prophets and diviners ... dreams.* See 27:9 and note. *among you.* The exiles in Babylonia had their share of false prophets (see vv. 21,31), who had doubtless accompanied them when they were deported in 597 B.C.

29:9 See v. 31; see also notes on 23:16,21.

29:10 *seventy years.* See note on 25:11–12. *bring you back.* See note on 27:22.

29:11 *I know.* See v. 23. Appearances to the contrary notwithstanding, the Lord has not forgotten his people. *prosper.* See note on v. 7. *and not ... harm.* God is the ultimate source of both prosperity and disaster (see Isa 45:7).

29:12–13 Echoed from Dt 4:29–30. The Lord's gracious gift of prosperity is contingent on his people's willingness to repent.

29:14 A summary of Dt 30:3–5. *bring you back from captivity.* See NIV text note; see also 30:3,18; 31:23; 32:44; 33:7,11,26; 48:47; 49:6,39; and note on Ps 126:4.

29:15 *prophets ... in Babylon.* See note on v. 8.

29:16 *the king ... on David's throne.* Zedekiah. *sits ... remain.* The Hebrew for both words is identical. King and people alike are guilty.

go with you into exile — 17yes, this is
what the LORD Almighty says: "I will
send the sword, famine and plague[g]
against them and I will make them
like poor figs[h] that are so bad they
cannot be eaten. 18I will pursue them
with the sword, famine and plague
and will make them abhorrent[i] to all
the kingdoms of the earth and an object of cursing[j] and horror,[k] of scorn[l]
and reproach, among all the nations
where I drive them. 19For they have
not listened to my words,"[m] declares
the LORD, "words that I sent to them
again and again[n] by my servants the
prophets.[o] And you exiles have not
listened either," declares the LORD.
20Therefore, hear the word of the
LORD, all you exiles whom I have sent[p]
away from Jerusalem to Babylon.
21This is what the LORD Almighty, the
God of Israel, says about Ahab son of
Kolaiah and Zedekiah son of Maaseiah, who are prophesying lies[q] to you
in my name: "I will hand them over
to Nebuchadnezzar king of Babylon,
and he will put them to death before
your very eyes. 22Because of them,
all the exiles from Judah who are in
Babylon will use this curse: 'The LORD
treat you like Zedekiah and Ahab,
whom the king of Babylon burned[r] in
the fire.' 23For they have done outrageous things in Israel; they have committed adultery[s] with their neighbors'
wives and in my name have spoken
lies, which I did not tell them to do.
I know[t] it and am a witness[u] to it,"
declares the LORD.

29:17 [g] Jer 27:8 [h] S Isa 5:4 **29:18** [i] S Jer 15:4 [j] S Nu 5:27; S Jer 18:16; S 22:10; 44:12 [k] S Dt 28:25 [l] S Dt 28:37; S Isa 28:22; S Mic 2:6 **29:19** [m] Jer 6:19 [n] Jer 7:25 [o] S Jer 25:4 **29:20** [p] S Jer 24:5 **29:21** [q] ver 9; Jer 14:14 **29:22** [r] Da 3:6 **29:23** [s] S Jer 23:14 [t] S Heb 4:13 [u] S Ge 31:48; S Jer 7:11 **29:25** [v] S 2Ki 25:18 **29:26** [w] S 1Sa 10:11; Hos 9:7; S Jn 10:20 [x] Jer 20:2 **29:28** [y] ver 1 [z] ver 10 [a] ver 5 **29:29** [b] Jer 21:1 **29:31** [c] ver 24 [d] S Jer 14:14 **29:32** [e] S 1Sa 2:30-33 [f] ver 10 [g] S Jer 28:16 **30:2** [h] S Isa 30:8; S Jer 36:2

Message to Shemaiah

24Tell Shemaiah the Nehelamite, 25"This
is what the LORD Almighty, the God of Israel, says: You sent letters in your own name
to all the people in Jerusalem, to Zephaniah[v] son of Maaseiah the priest, and to all
the other priests. You said to Zephaniah,
26'The LORD has appointed you priest in
place of Jehoiada to be in charge of the
house of the LORD; you should put any
madman[w] who acts like a prophet into the
stocks[x] and neck-irons. 27So why have you
not reprimanded Jeremiah from Anathoth,
who poses as a prophet among you? 28He
has sent this message[y] to us in Babylon:
It will be a long time.[z] Therefore build[a]
houses and settle down; plant gardens and
eat what they produce.' "
29Zephaniah[b] the priest, however, read
the letter to Jeremiah the prophet. 30Then
the word of the LORD came to Jeremiah:
31"Send this message to all the exiles:
'This is what the LORD says about Shemaiah[c] the Nehelamite: Because Shemaiah
has prophesied to you, even though I did
not send[d] him, and has led you to believe
a lie, 32this is what the LORD says: I will
surely punish Shemaiah the Nehelamite
and his descendants.[e] He will have no one
left among this people, nor will he see the
good[f] things I will do for my people, declares the LORD, because he has preached
rebellion[g] against me.' "

Restoration of Israel

30 This is the word that came to Jeremiah from the LORD: 2"This is what the
LORD, the God of Israel, says: 'Write[h] in a
book all the words I have spoken to you.

29:17 *sword, famine and plague.* See v. 18; see also note on 14:12. *poor figs . . . so bad they cannot be eaten.* See 24:8.
29:18 See 24:9 and note.
29:19 *again and again.* See note on 7:13. *my servants the prophets.* See note on 7:25. *you exiles have not listened.* See Eze 2:5,7; 3:7,11.
29:21 *Ahab . . . and Zedekiah.* Not the well-known kings (of Israel and Judah respectively); rather, they were false prophets (see note on v. 8).
29:22 *fire.* Used in Babylonia as a method of execution (see Da 3:6,24; this is also evident in the Code of Hammurapi, sections 25; 110; 157).
29:23 *done outrageous things in Israel.* See Ge 34:7 and note. *committed adultery . . . and . . . spoken lies.* See note on 23:10. *I know.* See v. 11.
29:24 *Shemaiah.* A false prophet (see v. 31). *Nehelamite.* The Hebrew root underlying this word is the same as that for "dreams" in v. 8 (see 27:9 and note). Jeremiah is perhaps suggesting that Shemaiah is not a true prophet but a mere dreamer.
29:25 *Zephaniah.* Not the prophet of that name (see note on 21:1).
29:26 *Jehoiada.* Not the same as the priest during the days of King Joash (see 2Ki 12:7). *in charge of the house of the LORD.* See note on 20:1. *madman.* Prophetic behavior sometimes appeared deranged to the casual observer (see 2Ki 9:11). *stocks.* See 20:2 and note.
29:27 *Anathoth.* See note on 1:1.
29:28 See v. 5 and note. *a long time.* Here 70 years (see 25:11–12 and note; see also 2Sa 3:1).
29:29 *Zephaniah . . . however.* He was apparently sympathetic toward Jeremiah (see 21:1–2; 37:3).
29:31–32 The Lord's threat against Shemaiah is similar to that against Hananiah (see 28:15–16).
29:31 *led . . . to believe a lie.* See 28:15.
29:32 *preached rebellion against.* See 28:16 and note.
30:1—33:26 Often called Jeremiah's "book of consolation," the section depicts the ultimate restoration of both Israel (the northern kingdom) and Judah (the southern kingdom) and is the longest sustained passage in Jeremiah concerned with the future hope of the people of God (for other and briefer passages on restoration see 3:14–18; 16:14–15; 23:3–8; 24:4–7). The information in 32:1 may be used to date the entire section to 587 B.C., the year before Jerusalem was destroyed by Nebuchadnezzar and its people exiled to Babylon.
30:1—31:40 Written almost entirely in poetry, these two chapters are filled with optimism as the prophet looks forward to the time when God would redeem his people.
30:1 The heading for chs. 30–31 (and perhaps chs. 32–33 as well).
30:2 *Write.* In order to preserve for future generations the predictions of restoration. *book.* In scroll form (see, e.g., 36:2,4; 45:1; see also Ex 17:14 and note). *all the words I have spoken to*

3The days[i] are coming,' declares the LORD,
'when I will bring[j] my people Israel and
Judah back from captivity[a] and restore[k]
them to the land I gave their forefathers to
possess,' says the LORD."
4These are the words the LORD spoke
concerning Israel and Judah: 5"This is
what the LORD says:

" 'Cries of fear[l] are heard—
terror, not peace.
6Ask and see:
Can a man bear children?
Then why do I see every strong man
with his hands on his stomach like a
woman in labor,[m]
every face turned deathly pale?[n]
7How awful that day[o] will be!
None will be like it.
It will be a time of trouble[p] for Jacob,
but he will be saved[q] out of it.

8" 'In that day,' declares the LORD
Almighty,
'I will break the yoke[r] off their necks
and will tear off their bonds;[s]
no longer will foreigners enslave
them.[t]
9Instead, they will serve the LORD their
God
and David[u] their king,[v]
whom I will raise up for them.

10" 'So do not fear,[w] O Jacob my servant;[x]
do not be dismayed, O Israel,'
declares the LORD.
'I will surely save[y] you out of a distant
place,
your descendants from the land of
their exile.
Jacob will again have peace and
security,[z]
and no one will make him afraid.[a]
11I am with you[b] and will save you,'
declares the LORD.
'Though I completely destroy all the
nations
among which I scatter you,
I will not completely destroy[c] you.
I will discipline[d] you but only with
justice;
I will not let you go entirely
unpunished.'[e]

12"This is what the LORD says:

" 'Your wound[f] is incurable,
your injury beyond healing.[g]
13There is no one to plead your cause,[h]
no remedy for your sore,
no healing[i] for you.
14All your allies[j] have forgotten you;
they care nothing for you.
I have struck you as an enemy[k] would
and punished you as would the cruel,[l]
because your guilt is so great
and your sins[m] so many.
15Why do you cry out over your wound,
your pain that has no cure?[n]
Because of your great guilt and many
sins
I have done these things to you.[o]

16" 'But all who devour[p] you will be
devoured;
all your enemies will go into exile.[q]

30:3 [i]S Jer 16:14; S 24:6 [j]S Jer 29:14 [k]S Jer 16:15 **30:5** [l]Jer 6:25 **30:6** [m]S Jer 4:31 [n]S Isa 29:22 **30:7** [o]S Isa 2:12 [p]S Isa 22:5; Zep 1:15 [q]ver 10; Jer 23:3 **30:8** [r]S Isa 9:4 [s]Ps 107:14 [t]Jer 25:14; 27:7; Eze 34:27 **30:9** [u]S Mt 1:1 [v]ver 21; S 1Sa 13:14; Jer 33:15; Eze 34:23-24; 37:24; Hos 1:11; 3:5 **30:10** [w]S Isa 41:10 [x]S Isa 44:2 [y]S ver 7; S Jer 29:14 [z]Isa 35:9; S Jer 17:25 [a]S Isa 29:22; S 54:4; S Jer 23:4; Eze 34:25-28 **30:11** [b]S Jos 1:5 [c]S Lev 26:44; S Jer 5:18; 46:28 [d]S Jer 10:24 [e]Hos 11:9; Am 9:8 **30:12** [f]S Job 6:4; S Jer 10:19 [g]S Jer 8:22 **30:13** [h]S Jdg 6:31 [i]S Jer 8:22; 14:19; 46:11; Na 3:19 **30:14** [j]S Jer 22:20; La 1:2 [k]S Job 13:24 [l]S Job 30:21 [m]S Jer 25:7 **30:15** [n]S Jer 10:19 [o]S Pr 1:31; La 1:5 **30:16** [p]S Isa 29:8; S 33:1; S Jer 2:3 [q]S Isa 14:2; Joel 3:4-8

[a] 3 *Or will restore the fortunes of my people Israel and Judah*

you. Concerning the future redemption of God's people. The phrase is less comprehensive here than in 36:2.

30:3 *bring ... back from captivity.* See note on 29:14. *Israel and Judah.* The northern and southern kingdoms, the first of which was exiled in 721 B.C. and the second of which would be entering the final stages of its removal to Babylonia in about a year (see note on 30:1—33:26). *restore.* The occurrences of this verb here and in 33:26 serve to identify and frame the main topic of these four chapters (see note on 30:1—33:26).

30:5 *Cries of fear ... terror.* The sounds of battle and destruction.

30:6 *woman in labor.* A symbol of anguish and distress (see notes on 4:19,31).

30:7 A description of the day of the Lord (see notes on Isa 2:11,17,20; Am 5:18; 8:9). Jeremiah's immediate reference is to the foreseeable future (see vv. 8,18)—but a more remote time in the Messianic age may also be in view. *awful.* Lit. "great" (as in Joel 2:11; Zep 1:14; cf. Joel 1:15). *None will be like it.* Cf. Da 12:1; Joel 2:2; Mt 24:21. *time of trouble.* The Hebrew for this phrase is translated "time of distress" in Da 12:1 (see Mt 24:21 and note; Rev 16:18). *Jacob.* Israel (see v. 10).

30:8 *In that day.* See note on Isa 2:11,17,20. *yoke.* See note on 27:2. *tear off their bonds.* The Hebrew underlying this phrase is translated "break their chains" in Ps 2:3, where the nations plot to free themselves from the Lord and his anointed ruler. Here the Lord promises to free his people from enslavement to the nations. *foreigners.* Including, but not limited to, Babylonia.

30:9 *David their king.* The Messiah (see note on 23:5). The Targum (ancient Aramaic paraphrase) here reads "Messiah, the son of David, their king." *raise up.* See 23:5 and note.

30:10–11 Repeated almost verbatim in 46:27–28.

30:10 *Jacob my servant.* See Isa 41:8–9 and note; 44:1–2,21; 45:4; 48:20. *no one will make him afraid.* Contrast v. 5; see Lev 26:6; Job 11:19; Isa 17:2; Eze 34:28; 39:26; Mic 4:4 and note; Zep 3:13.

30:11 *I am with you and will save you.* Words spoken originally to Jeremiah alone (see 1:8,19; 15:20) are now spoken to all God's people. *scatter.* See 9:16 and note; 23:1–2. *not completely destroy.* See 4:27 and note. *not ... go ... unpunished.* See 25:29; 49:12.

30:12–13 See 8:22; Hos 5:13; 6:1; 7:1; 11:3.

30:12 *Your.* Judah's. *wound is incurable.* See 15:18 and note. *injury beyond healing.* See 14:17.

30:13 *plead your cause.* Against your enemies. *no remedy for your sore.* See Hos 5:13.

30:14 *allies.* See note on 22:20. Egypt, e.g., often supported Judah against the Babylonians (see 37:5–7). *because your guilt ... so many.* See 5:6; 13:22. The Hebrew for this clause is repeated verbatim in v. 15.

30:16 *all who devour you.* See 3:24; 5:17; 8:16; 10:25. *will be devoured.* See note on 25:26; see also 51:48–49. *will be plundered.* See Isa 17:14.

Those who plunder[r] you will be
plundered;
all who make spoil of you I will
despoil.
17 But I will restore you to health
and heal[s] your wounds,'
declares the LORD,
'because you are called an outcast,[t]
Zion for whom no one cares.'[u]

18 "This is what the LORD says:

" 'I will restore the fortunes[v] of Jacob's
tents[w]
and have compassion[x] on his
dwellings;
the city will be rebuilt[y] on her ruins,
and the palace will stand in its
proper place.
19 From them will come songs[z] of
thanksgiving[a]
and the sound of rejoicing.[b]
I will add to their numbers,[c]
and they will not be decreased;
I will bring them honor,[d]
and they will not be disdained.
20 Their children[e] will be as in days of old,
and their community will be
established[f] before me;
I will punish[g] all who oppress them.
21 Their leader[h] will be one of their own;
their ruler will arise from among
them.[i]
I will bring him near[j] and he will come
close to me,
for who is he who will devote
himself
to be close to me?'
declares the LORD.

30:16 [r] Jer 49:2; 50:10
30:17 [s] S Isa 1:5; Hos 6:1 [t] S Isa 6:12; Jer 33:24 [u] Ps 142:4
30:18 [v] ver 3; S Dt 30:3; Jer 31:23; 32:44 [w] S Nu 24:5 [x] Ps 102:13; Jer 33:26; Eze 39:25 [y] Jer 31:4, 24, 38; 33:7; Eze 36:10, 33; Am 9:14
30:19 [z] S Ps 9:2; Isa 35:10; S 51:11 [a] S Isa 51:3 [b] Ps 126:1-2; Jer 31:4 [c] S Ge 15:5; 22:17; Jer 33:22; Eze 37:26; Zec 2:4 [d] S Isa 44:23; S 60:9
30:20 [e] Isa 54:13; Jer 31:17; Zec 8:5 [f] Isa 54:14 [g] S Ex 23:22
30:21 [h] S ver 9; Jer 23:5-6 [i] Dt 17:15 [j] Nu 16:5
30:22 [k] S Isa 19:25; Hos 2:23 [l] S Lev 26:12
30:23 [m] S Jer 23:19
30:24 [n] Jer 4:8; La 1:12 [o] S Jer 4:28 [p] Jer 23:19-20
31:1 [q] S Lev 26:12
31:2 [r] Nu 14:20 [s] S Ex 33:14; S Dt 12:9
31:3 [t] S Dt 4:37 [u] Hos 11:4; Jn 6:44
31:4 [v] S Jer 1:10; S 30:18 [w] S 2Ki 19:21 [x] S Ge 31:27 [y] S Ex 15:20 [z] S Jer 30:19

22 " 'So you will be my people,[k]
and I will be your God.[l]' "

23 See, the storm[m] of the LORD
will burst out in wrath,
a driving wind swirling down
on the heads of the wicked.
24 The fierce anger[n] of the LORD will not
turn back[o]
until he fully accomplishes
the purposes of his heart.
In days to come
you will understand[p] this.

31 "At that time," declares the LORD, "I
will be the God[q] of all the clans of
Israel, and they will be my people."
2 This is what the LORD says:

"The people who survive the sword
will find favor[r] in the desert;
I will come to give rest[s] to Israel."

3 The LORD appeared to us in the past,[a]
saying:

"I have loved[t] you with an everlasting
love;
I have drawn[u] you with loving-
kindness.
4 I will build you up again
and you will be rebuilt,[v] O Virgin[w]
Israel.
Again you will take up your
tambourines[x]
and go out to dance[y] with the joyful.[z]

[a] 3 Or *LORD has appeared to us from afar*

30:17 *restore you to health.* Contrast 8:22; see 33:6; Isa 58:8. *Zion.* See note on 2Sa 5:7.

30:18 *restore the fortunes.* See note on 29:14. *the city … the palace.* Lit. "a city … a palace," perhaps referring to Judah's cities and palaces in general (see Am 9:14). It is possible, however, that only Jerusalem and its palace are intended (see 31:38). *ruins.* The Hebrew for this word is *tel(l)*, referring to a mound of ruins resulting from the accumulation of the debris of many years or centuries of occupation and on which successive series of towns were often built (see, e.g., Jos 11:13 and note).

30:19 *songs of thanksgiving.* See 33:11. *rejoicing.* See 31:4 and note; contrast 15:17. *add … not be decreased.* See 29:6; Eze 36:37–38. *honor … not be disdained.* See Isa 9:1.

30:20 *days of old.* Probably the early days of the united kingdom, especially the reign of David. *will be established before me.* See Ps 102:28 and note.

30:21 *leader … ruler.* Although the Aramaic Targum renders "Messiah" here (similarly in v. 9; see note there), the terms probably refer in the first place to the rulers of Judah immediately after the exile. But Jesus Christ ultimately fulfills the promise. *one of their own … from among them.* Not foreigners (cf. Dt 18:15,18). *bring him near … come close.* See Nu 16:5; contrast Ex 24:2. Unauthorized approaches into God's presence were punishable by death (see Ex 19:21; Nu 8:19).

30:22 See 31:1; see also note on 7:23.

30:23–24 Repeated almost verbatim from 23:19–20 (see notes there).

31:1–40 Continuing the theme of restoration begun in 30:1, Jeremiah records the words of the Lord to (1) all the people of God, v. 1 (prose); (2) the restored northern kingdom of Israel, vv. 2–22 (poetry); (3) the restored southern kingdom of Judah, vv. 23–26 (prose); and (4) Israel and Judah together, vv. 27–40 (prose prologue, vv. 27–30; poetic body, vv. 31–37; prose epilogue, vv. 38–40—each section beginning with the words "The days are coming"; see note on v. 31).

31:1 See 30:22; see also note on 7:23. *all the clans of Israel.* All 12 tribes.

31:2 *people who survive the sword.* The remnant (see v. 7; see also note on 6:9), who will return from captivity. *desert.* The Arabian Desert, analogous in the return from exile to the Sinai Desert through which Israel's ancestors marched after the exodus. Return from exile is often pictured as or compared to release from Egyptian slavery at the time of the exodus (see 16:14–15; Isa 35:1–11 and notes; 40:3–4; 42:14–16; 43:18–21; 48:20–21; 51:9–11; cf. Hos 2:14–15). *rest.* See 6:16; contrast Dt 28:65. See notes on Dt 3:20; Jos 1:13. *Israel.* The northern kingdom (see also vv. 4,7,9–10,21). Other names for it are Samaria (v. 5), Ephraim (vv. 6,9,18,20), Jacob (vv. 7,11) and Rachel (v. 15).

31:3 *drawn … with loving-kindness.* The Hebrew underlying this phrase is similar to that which underlies "Continue … love" in Ps 36:10 (see note on Ps 6:4).

31:4 *build.* See 1:10 and note. *Virgin Israel.* See note on 2Ki 19:21. *tambourines.* Used on joyful occasions (see Ps 68:25), especially following a military victory (see Ex 15:20 and note;

5 Again you will plant[a] vineyards
on the hills of Samaria;[b]
the farmers will plant them
and enjoy their fruit.[c]
6 There will be a day when watchmen[d]
cry out
on the hills of Ephraim,
'Come, let us go up to Zion,
to the LORD our God.' "[e]

7 This is what the LORD says:

"Sing[f] with joy for Jacob;
shout for the foremost[g] of the
nations.
Make your praises heard, and say,
'O LORD, save[h] your people,
the remnant[i] of Israel.'
8 See, I will bring them from the land of
the north[j]
and gather[k] them from the ends of
the earth.
Among them will be the blind[l] and the
lame,[m]
expectant mothers and women in
labor;
a great throng will return.
9 They will come with weeping;[n]
they will pray as I bring them back.
I will lead[o] them beside streams of
water[p]
on a level[q] path where they will not
stumble,
because I am Israel's father,[r]
and Ephraim is my firstborn son.

10 "Hear the word of the LORD, O nations;
proclaim it in distant coastlands:[s]
'He who scattered[t] Israel will gather[u]
them
and will watch over his flock like a
shepherd.'[v]
11 For the LORD will ransom Jacob
and redeem[w] them from the hand of
those stronger[x] than they.
12 They will come and shout for joy[y] on
the heights[z] of Zion;
they will rejoice in the bounty[a] of
the LORD—
the grain, the new wine and the oil,[b]
the young of the flocks[c] and herds.
They will be like a well-watered garden,[d]
and they will sorrow[e] no more.
13 Then maidens will dance and be glad,
young men and old as well.
I will turn their mourning[f] into gladness;
I will give them comfort[g] and joy[h]
instead of sorrow.
14 I will satisfy[i] the priests[j] with
abundance,
and my people will be filled with my
bounty,[k]"
declares the LORD.

15 This is what the LORD says:

"A voice is heard in Ramah,[l]
mourning and great weeping,
Rachel weeping for her children
and refusing to be comforted,[m]
because her children are no more."[n]

31:5 [a] S Dt 20:6 [b] Jer 33:13; 50:19; Ob 1:19 [c] S Isa 37:30; Am 9:14 **31:6** [d] S Isa 52:8; S 56:10 [e] ver 12; S Dt 33:19; Jer 50:4-5; Mic 4:2 **31:7** [f] S Isa 12:6 [g] Dt 28:13; Isa 61:9 [h] Ps 14:7; 28:9 [i] S Isa 37:31 **31:8** [j] S Jer 3:18 [k] S Ge 33:13; S Dt 30:4; S Ps 106:47; Eze 34:12-14 [l] Isa 42:16 [m] Eze 34:16; Mic 4:6 **31:9** [n] S Ezr 3:12; Ps 126:5 [o] Isa 63:13 [p] S Nu 20:8; S Ps 1:3; S Isa 32:2 [q] S Isa 40:4; S 49:11 [r] S Ex 4:22; S Jer 3:4 **31:10** [s] Isa 49:1; S 66:19; S Jer 25:22 [t] S Lev 26:33 [u] S Dt 30:4; S Isa 11:12; Jer 50:19 [v] Isa 40:11; Eze 34:12 **31:11** [w] S Ex 6:6; Zec 9:16 [x] Ps 142:6 **31:12** [y] S Ps 126:5 [z] Eze 17:23; 20:40; 40:2; Mic 4:1 [a] S Ps 36:8; Joel 3:18 [b] S Nu 18:12; Hos 2:21-22; Joel 2:19 [c] ver 24; S Isa 65:10 [d] S SS 4:15 [e] S Isa 30:19; S 62:5; Jn 16:22; S Rev 7:17 **31:13** [f] S Isa 61:3 [g] S Isa 40:1 [h] Ps 30:11; S Isa 51:11 **31:14** [i] ver 25 [j] Lev 7:35-36 [k] S Ps 36:8; S Isa 30:23 **31:15** [l] S Jos 18:25 [m] S Ge 37:35 [n] S Jer 10:20; Mt 2:17-18*

Jdg 11:34)—in contrast to Judah's experience during the exile (see Ps 137:1–3). *dance.* See v. 13; often a religious activity in ancient times (see 2Sa 6:14; Ps 149:3; 150:4).
31:5 *plant.* See 1:10 and note. *Samaria.* Conquered in 722–721 B.C. (see 2Ki 17:24), it would someday be resettled by God's people. *plant them and enjoy their fruit.* See Dt 28:30; Isa 62:8–9; 65:21–22. Since the law stipulated that the fruit of a tree could not be eaten until the fifth year after planting it (see Lev 19:23–25), a return to normalcy is envisioned here.
31:6 *watchmen ... on the hills.* Watchmen were stationed in appropriate locations to observe and give notice of the appearance of various phases of the moon to fix the times of the most important feasts (see Dt 16:16 and note). *Ephraim ... to Zion.* In the days of Jeroboam I, the people of the northern kingdom had been required to worship at northern shrines (see 1Ki 12:26–30). In the future, however, they would worship the Lord only in Jerusalem (cf. Jn 4:20). *go up.* In ancient Israel one always went "up" to Jerusalem (see, e.g., Ezr 1:3; 7:7; Isa 2:3; Jn 2:13), not only because its elevation was above the surrounding countryside but also because it was the royal city and the main center of the nation's religious life.
31:7 *foremost of the nations.* See Dt 26:19; Am 6:1. Israel was the greatest nation not because of intrinsic merit but because of divine grace and appointment (see Dt 7:6–8; 2Sa 7:23–24). *save.* The Hebrew for this word is the basis of "Hosanna," the cry of the people of Jerusalem on Palm Sunday (see Mt 21:9 and NIV text note; see also Ps 20:9; 28:9; 86:2; and especially 118:25). *remnant.* See note on 6:9.
31:8 *land of the north.* See 3:18; 4:6 and notes; 6:22; 16:15. *ends of the earth.* See 6:22; 25:32. *blind ... lame.* See Isa 35:5–6 and notes; 42:16. *women in labor.* See note on 4:31.
31:9 *with weeping.* Contrast Ps 126:5–6; Isa 55:12. *lead them.* See Isa 40:11; 48:21; contrast Isa 20:4. *beside streams of water.* See Ps 23:2 and note; Isa 49:10; cf. Isa 41:18. *level path.* See Isa 40:3–4 and notes; 43:16,19. *I am Israel's father.* See 3:4 and note; see also Dt 32:6; Isa 63:16; 64:8. *firstborn son.* Cf. v. 20; see Ex 4:22 and note; Hos 11:1–4.
31:10 *distant coastlands.* Remote areas to the west of Israel (see 2:10; 25:22 and note; 47:4; Ps 72:10; Isa 41:1,5; 42:10,12; 49:1). *scattered Israel ... watch over his flock like a shepherd.* See 23:1–3 and notes.
31:11 *redeem.* See note on Ru 2:20. As the Lord had redeemed (delivered) his people from Egyptian slavery (see Ex 6:6 and note; 15:13; Dt 7:8; 9:26), so now he would redeem their descendants from Babylonian exile (see Isa 41:14; 43:1 and notes; 52:9). *from ... those stronger than they.* See Ps 35:10.
31:12 *heights of Zion.* See note on 17:12. *bounty of the LORD.* Primarily material blessings (see v. 14; Hos 3:5). *grain ... new wine ... oil.* See note on Dt 7:13; see also Hos 2:8. *like a well-watered garden.* See Isa 58:11 and note. *sorrow no more.* See Isa 25:8.
31:14 *abundance.* Either (1) a synonym for God's bounty (see Ps 36:8; 63:5; Isa 55:2) or (2) a reference to the special portions of the sacrificial animal reserved for the priests (see Lev 7:31–36)—sacrifices will once again be brought to the Lord's altar (cf. Joel 1:13).
31:15 Quoted in Mt 2:18, where Herod's orders to kill all the male infants "in Bethlehem and its vicinity" (Mt 2:16)

16 This is what the LORD says:

"Restrain your voice from weeping
and your eyes from tears,[o]
for your work will be rewarded,[p]"
declares the LORD.
"They will return[q] from the land of
the enemy.
17 So there is hope[r] for your future,"
declares the LORD.
"Your children[s] will return to their
own land.

18 "I have surely heard Ephraim's
moaning:
'You disciplined[t] me like an unruly
calf,[u]
and I have been disciplined.
Restore[v] me, and I will return,
because you are the LORD my God.
19 After I strayed,[w]
I repented;
after I came to understand,
I beat[x] my breast.
I was ashamed[y] and humiliated
because I bore the disgrace of my
youth.'[z]
20 Is not Ephraim my dear son,
the child[a] in whom I delight?
Though I often speak against him,
I still remember[b] him.
Therefore my heart yearns for him;
I have great compassion[c] for him,"
declares the LORD.

21 "Set up road signs;
put up guideposts.[d]
Take note of the highway,[e]
the road that you take.

31:16 [o]S Ps 30:5; S Isa 25:8; 30:19 [p]S Ru 2:12; S 2Ch 15:7 [q]Jer 30:3; Eze 11:17 **31:17** [r]S Job 8:7; La 3:29 [s]S Jer 30:20 **31:18** [t]S Job 5:17 [u]Jer 50:11; Hos 4:16; 10:11 [v]S Ps 80:3 **31:19** [w]S Ps 95:10; S Jer 8:4; Eze 36:31 [x]Eze 21:12; Lk 18:13 [y]Ezr 9:6 [z]S Ps 25:7; S Jer 22:21 **31:20** [a]La 3:33 [b]S Isa 44:21 [c]S 1Ki 3:26; S Ps 6:2; Isa 55:7; Mic 7:18 **31:21** [d]Eze 21:19 [e]Isa 35:8; Jer 50:5 [f]Isa 52:11; S Jer 3:12 [g]ver 4 **31:22** [h]S Jer 2:23 [i]S Jer 3:6 [j]Isa 43:19 [k]S Dt 32:10 **31:23** [l]S Jer 30:18 [m]S Ge 28:3; S Nu 6:24 [n]S Isa 1:26 [o]S Ps 48:1; S Isa 2:2 **31:24** [p]S Jer 30:18; Zec 8:4-8 [q]S ver 12 **31:25** [r]S Isa 40:29

Return,[f] O Virgin[g] Israel,
return to your towns.
22 How long will you wander,[h]
O unfaithful[i] daughter?
The LORD will create a new thing[j] on
earth —
a woman will surround[a k] a man."

23 This is what the LORD Almighty, the
God of Israel, says: "When I bring them
back from captivity,[b l] the people in the
land of Judah and in its towns will once
again use these words: 'The LORD bless[m]
you, O righteous dwelling,[n] O sacred mountain.'[o] 24 People will live[p] together in Judah
and all its towns — farmers and those who
move about with their flocks.[q] 25 I will refresh the weary[r] and satisfy the faint."[s]

26 At this I awoke[t] and looked around.
My sleep had been pleasant to me.

27 "The days are coming,"[u] declares the
LORD, "when I will plant[v] the house of Israel and the house of Judah with the offspring of men and of animals. 28 Just as I
watched[w] over them to uproot[x] and tear
down, and to overthrow, destroy and bring
disaster,[y] so I will watch over them to build
and to plant,"[z] declares the LORD. 29 "In
those days people will no longer say,

'The fathers[a] have eaten sour grapes,
and the children's teeth are set on
edge.'[b]

[a] 22 Or *will go about ⌞seeking⌟*; or *will protect*
[b] 23 Or *I restore their fortunes*

[s]Jn 4:14 **31:26** [t]Zec 4:1 **31:27** [u]S Jer 16:14 [v]Hos 2:23 **31:28** [w]S Job 29:2 [x]S Dt 29:28 [y]S Jer 18:8 [z]S Dt 28:63; S 30:9; S Jer 1:10; Eze 36:10-11; Am 9:14 **31:29** [a]S Ge 9:25; Dt 24:16; La 5:7 [b]Eze 18:2

are stated to be a fulfillment of this passage. *Ramah.* Also known as Ramathaim. It was Samuel's hometown and also one of the centers where he held court (see 1Sa 1:1 and note; 2:11; 7:17). Located about five miles north of Jerusalem, it was one of the towns through which Jerusalem's people passed on their way to exile in Babylonia (see 40:1; cf. Isa 10:29; Hos 5:8). *Rachel.* Jacob's favorite wife (see Ge 29:30) and the grandmother of Ephraim and Manasseh (see Ge 30:22–24; 48:1–2), the two most powerful tribes in the northern kingdom. The name is used here to personify that kingdom (see note on v. 2). Some, however, believe that Rachel is referenced here as the mother of Benjamin, in whose tribal territory Ramah was located and from which tribe Israel's first king (Saul) came.
31:16 *for your work will be rewarded.* Echoed in 2Ch 15:7. Here the work is the bearing and raising of children.
31:17 *hope for your future.* See 29:11. *children will return.* Cf. Hos 11:10–11.
31:18–19 *Restore … return … strayed.* The same Hebrew root underlies all three words (see 8:4–5 and notes).
31:18 *like an unruly calf.* See Hos 4:16 and note.
31:19 *beat my breast.* A gesture of mourning and grief (see Eze 21:12). Similar expressions are found in other ancient literature, such as Homer, *Iliad*, 15.397–398; 16.125; *Odyssey*, 13.198–199. *ashamed and humiliated.* See Isa 45:16. *youth.* Early history (see 2:2; 3:24–25; 22:21; 32:30; Isa 54:4; Eze 16:22).
31:20 *child in whom I delight.* Cf. Isa 5:7. *Though … I have great compassion for him.* See Hos 11:1–4,8–9. *my heart yearns.* See Isa 16:11.
31:21 The departing exiles are advised to set up markers along their path to exile so that in due time they will be able to find their way back to Judah (see notes on 30:1—33:26; 32:1). *road signs.* Tombstone-shaped markers (see 2Ki 23:17; Eze 39:15). *Virgin Israel.* See v. 4 and note.
31:22 *unfaithful daughter.* A personification of the people of Judah (see note on 2Ki 19:21), who are apostate (see 3:14,22). *create a new thing.* See Isa 42:9 and note. *surround.* Embrace with tender and unfailing love. Judah would someday return to the Lord and love him as her husband without reservation (see v. 32 and note).
31:23 *bring … back from captivity.* See note on 29:14. *The LORD bless you.* See Ps 128:5; 134:3. *righteous dwelling.* Jerusalem (cf. Isa 1:21,26). *sacred mountain.* The temple hill (see Ps 2:6; 48:1–2; Isa 2:2–3; 11:9; 27:13; 66:20).
31:26 *I awoke.* Jeremiah had evidently received the previous divine revelation (beginning in 30:3) in a dream (for similar examples see Da 10:9; Zec 4:1). *sleep … pleasant.* See Pr 3:24 and note.
31:27 *plant … offspring.* See Eze 36:8–11. The same Hebrew root underlies both words. *Israel and … Judah.* North and south would again be united (see 3:18 and note.)
31:28 *watched … watch.* See note on 1:12. *uproot … tear down … overthrow, destroy … build … plant.* See note on 1:10.
31:29 *The fathers … set on edge.* Repeated in Eze 18:2. This was apparently a popular proverb that originated in a misunderstanding of such passages as Ex 20:5 and Nu 14:18, which teach that sins can have a negative effect on de-

30 Instead, everyone will die for his own sin;[c] whoever eats sour grapes—his own teeth will be set on edge.

31 "The time is coming," declares the LORD,
"when I will make a new covenant[d]
with the house of Israel
and with the house of Judah.
32 It will not be like the covenant[e]
I made with their forefathers[f]
when I took them by the hand
to lead them out of Egypt,[g]
because they broke my covenant,
though I was a husband[h] to[a] them,[b]"
declares the LORD.
33 "This is the covenant I will make with
the house of Israel
after that time," declares the LORD.
"I will put my law in their minds[i]
and write it on their hearts.[j]
I will be their God,
and they will be my people.[k]
34 No longer will a man teach[l] his
neighbor,
or a man his brother, saying, 'Know
the LORD,'
because they will all know[m] me,
from the least of them to the
greatest,"
declares the LORD.
"For I will forgive[n] their wickedness
and will remember their sins[o] no
more."

35 This is what the LORD says,

he who appoints[p] the sun
to shine by day,
who decrees the moon and stars
to shine by night,[q]
who stirs up the sea[r]
so that its waves roar[s]—
the LORD Almighty is his name:[t]
36 "Only if these decrees[u] vanish from my
sight,"
declares the LORD,
"will the descendants[v] of Israel ever
cease
to be a nation before me."

37 This is what the LORD says:

"Only if the heavens above can be
measured[w]
and the foundations of the earth
below be searched out
will I reject[x] all the descendants of
Israel
because of all they have done,"
declares the LORD.

38 "The days are coming," declares the
LORD, "when this city will be rebuilt[y] for
me from the Tower of Hananel[z] to the

31:30 [c]S 2Ki 14:6; S Isa 3:11; Gal 6:7 **31:31** [d]S Dt 29:14; S Isa 42:6; S 54:10; S Lk 22:20; Heb 8:8-12*; 10:16-17 **31:32** [e]S Ex 24:8 [f]Dt 5:3 [g]Jer 11:4 [h]S Isa 54:5 **31:33** [i]S Ex 4:15 [j]S Dt 6:6; S 2Co 3:3 [k]S Jer 11:4; Heb 10:16 **31:34** [l]1Jn 2:27 [m]S Isa 11:9; S Jn 6:45 [n]Ps 85:2; 130:4; Jer 33:8; 50:20 [o]S Job 7:21; S Isa 38:17; Mic 7:19; Heb 10:17* **31:35** [p]Ps 136:7-9 [q]S Ge 1:16 [r]S Ex 14:21 [s]S Ps 93:3 [t]S Jer 10:16 **31:36** [u]S Job 38:33; Jer 33:20-26 [v]Ps 89:36-37 **31:37** [w]S Job 38:5; Jer 33:22 [x]Jer 33:24-26; Ro 11:1-5 **31:38** [y]S Jer 30:18 [z]S Ne 3:1

[a] 32 Hebrew; Septuagint and Syriac / *and I turned away from* [b] 32 Or *was their master*

scendants. In the time of Jeremiah and Ezekiel, many people felt that God's hand of judgment against them was due not to their own sins, but to the sins of their ancestors.

31:30 *everyone will die for his own sin.* See Dt 24:16; Eze 18:3,20; 33:7–18. Although group or collective responsibility is an important concept, Jeremiah and Ezekiel emphasize individual responsibility as both preparation and explanation for the imminent destruction of Jerusalem, which the people might have been tempted to blame on the sins of their ancestors.

31:31–34 The high point of Jeremiah's prophecies, this passage is the longest sequence of OT verses to be quoted in its entirety in the NT (see note on Heb 8:8–12; see also Heb 10:16–17). Verse 31 contains the only OT use of the phrase "new covenant," which (together with its NT echoes) has come down to us (via Latin) as "new testament," the name that would later be applied to the distinctively Christian part of the Biblical canon. See Introduction: Theological Themes and Message.

31:31 *The time is coming.* Lit. "The days are coming" (as in vv. 27,38), a phrase that often refers to the Messianic era. *make.* Lit. "cut" (see notes on 34:18; Ge 15:18). *new covenant.* See note on vv. 31–34. As the old covenant was put into effect with the shedding of the blood of animals (Ex 24:4–8), so the new would be put into effect with the shedding of the blood of Christ (see Mt 26:28 and NIV text note; Mk 14:24; Lk 22:20 and notes; 1Co 11:25; 2Co 3:6; Heb 9:15; 12:24). *house of Israel … house of Judah.* The reunited people of God (see 3:18 and note).

31:32 *covenant I made with their forefathers.* See 7:23; 11:1–8; Ex 19:5; 20:22—23:19 and notes. The covenant at Sinai eventually became known as the "old covenant" (2Co 3:14) or "first covenant" (Heb 8:7; 9:15,18). *took them by the hand.* See Hos 11:3–4. *they broke my covenant.* See 11:10. The people, not God, were responsible for violating his covenant (see note on Isa 24:5). *I was a husband.* See 3:14 and note.

31:33 *house of Israel.* Here includes both Israel and Judah (see v. 31 and note on 3:18). *put my law in their minds.* Internally (see Dt 6:6; 11:18; 30:14; Eze 11:19; 18:31; 36:26–27), in contrast to setting it before them externally (see 9:13; Dt 4:8; 11:32). *write it on their hearts.* So that it effectively governs their lives, in contrast to the ineffectiveness of merely presenting it in writing, though inscribed on durable stone (see Ex 24:4; 31:18; 32:15–16; 34:28–29; Dt 4:13; 5:22; 9:9,11; 10:4). *their God … my people.* See note on 7:23. The "new" covenant fulfills the "old" and achieves its purpose (cf. Mt 5:17 and note).

31:34 *No longer … teach his neighbor.* When the Lord has done his new work, there will no longer be among his people those who are ignorant of him and his will for human lives. True knowledge of the Lord will be shared by all—young and old, the peasant and the powerful (see 5:4–5 and notes; see also 32:38–40; Isa 54:13 and note; Eze 11:19–20; 36:25–27; Eph 3:12; Heb 4:16; 10:19–22). *Know.* In the experiential, not the academic, sense (see Ex 6:3 and note). *I will forgive … their sins.* The glorious basis of the new covenant (see Heb 10:16–18 and notes).

31:35 *appoints the sun … moon … stars.* See Ge 1:16–18 and notes. *who stirs up … is his name.* The same line is found in Isa 51:15 (see Ps 46:3; Isa 17:12).

31:36 See 33:20–21,25–26. Just as God's creation order is established and secure, so also Israel will always have descendants.

31:37 *reject all.* Israel will continue to exist as a remnant (cf. Lev 26:40–45; Ro 11:5,25–29 and notes), even though a terrible judgment is about to sweep the kingdom of Judah away.

31:38–40 See Zec 14:10–11.

31:38 *this city.* Jerusalem. *Tower of Hananel … Corner Gate.*

Corner Gate.[a] 39The measuring line[b] will
stretch from there straight to the hill of Gareb and then turn to Goah. 40The whole
valley[c] where dead bodies[d] and ashes are
thrown, and all the terraces out to the Kidron Valley[e] on the east as far as the corner of the Horse Gate,[f] will be holy[g] to the
LORD. The city will never again be uprooted or demolished."

Jeremiah Buys a Field

32 This is the word that came to Jeremiah from the LORD in the tenth[h] year
of Zedekiah king of Judah, which was the
eighteenth[i] year of Nebuchadnezzar. 2The
army of the king of Babylon was then besieging[j] Jerusalem, and Jeremiah the
prophet was confined[k] in the courtyard of
the guard[l] in the royal palace of Judah.

3Now Zedekiah king of Judah had imprisoned him there, saying, "Why do you
prophesy[m] as you do? You say, 'This is
what the LORD says: I am about to hand
this city over to the king of Babylon, and
he will capture[n] it. 4Zedekiah[o] king of Judah will not escape[p] out of the hands of
the Babylonians[a][q] but will certainly be
handed over to the king of Babylon, and
will speak with him face to face and see
him with his own eyes. 5He will take[r] Zedekiah to Babylon, where he will remain
until I deal with him,[s] declares the LORD.
If you fight against the Babylonians, you
will not succeed.' "[t]

6Jeremiah said, "The word of the LORD
came to me: 7Hanamel son of Shallum your
uncle is going to come to you and say, 'Buy
my field at Anathoth,[u] because as nearest
relative it is your right and duty[v] to buy it.'

8"Then, just as the LORD had said, my
cousin Hanamel came to me in the courtyard of the guard and said, 'Buy my field[w]
at Anathoth in the territory of Benjamin.
Since it is your right to redeem it and possess it, buy it for yourself.'

"I knew that this was the word of the
LORD; 9so I bought the field[x] at Anathoth
from my cousin Hanamel and weighed out
for him seventeen shekels[b] of silver.[y] 10I
signed and sealed the deed,[z] had it witnessed,[a] and weighed out the silver on the
scales. 11I took the deed of purchase—the
sealed copy containing the terms and conditions, as well as the unsealed copy—
12and I gave this deed to Baruch[b] son of
Neriah,[c] the son of Mahseiah, in the presence of my cousin Hanamel and of the
witnesses who had signed the deed and
of all the Jews sitting in the courtyard of
the guard.

13"In their presence I gave Baruch these
instructions: 14'This is what the LORD Almighty, the God of Israel, says: Take these
documents, both the sealed[d] and unsealed
copies of the deed of purchase, and put them
in a clay jar so they will last a long time.

31:38 [a]S 2Ki 14:13; S 2Ch 25:23
31:39 [b]S 1Ki 7:23
31:40 [c]S Jer 2:23; 7:31-32 [d]S Jer 8:2 [e]S 2Sa 15:23; Jn 18:1 [f]S 2Ki 11:16 [g]S Isa 4:3; Joel 3:17; Zec 14:21
32:1 [h]2Ki 25:1 [i]Jer 25:1
32:2 [j]S 2Ki 25:1 [k]S Ps 88:8 [l]S Ne 3:25
32:3 [m]Jer 26:8-9 [n]ver 28; Jer 21:4; 34:2-3
32:4 [o]Jer 34:21; 44:30 [p]S Jer 21:7; 38:18,23; 39:5-7; 52:9 [q]ver 24
32:5 [r]Jer 39:7; Eze 12:13 [s]S 2Ki 25:7 [t]Jer 21:4; La 1:14
32:7 [u]S Jos 21:18 [v]Lev 25:24-25; S Ru 4:3-4; Mt 27:10*
32:8 [w]ver 25
32:9 [x]Jer 37:12 [y]S Ge 23:16
32:10 [z]Ge 23:20 [a]S Ru 4:9; S Isa 8:2
32:12 [b]ver 16; Jer 36:4; 43:3,6; 45:1 [c]Jer 51:59
32:14 [d]S Isa 8:16

[a] 4 Or *Chaldeans*; also in verses 5, 24, 25, 28, 29 and 43
[b] 9 That is, about 7 ounces (about 200 grams)

The eastern and western ends of the northern wall (see note on Zec 14:10).

31:39 *measuring line.* Mentioned in connection with restored Jerusalem also in Eze 40:3; Zec 1:16; 2:1. *Gareb ... Goah.* Probably west of Jerusalem.

31:40 *valley.* Probably the Hinnom Valley (see 2:23 and note). *Horse Gate.* See note on Ne 3:28. *holy to the LORD.* See Zec 14:20 and note. *uprooted ... demolished.* See note on 1:10. Jerusalem, the city of God, will endure. For the ultimate fulfillment cf. Gal 4:26 and note; Rev 21:1–5.

32:1–44 Though with some reluctance (see v. 25), Jeremiah obeys the Lord's command to buy a field in Anathoth from his cousin (see vv. 8–9) even as the Babylonians are besieging Jerusalem (see vv. 2,24).

32:1 *tenth year of Zedekiah ... eighteenth year of Nebuchadnezzar.* 587 B.C., the year before Jerusalem was destroyed by the Babylonians (see 52:12–13). The siege began in 588 (see 39:1; 52:4).

32:2 *confined in the courtyard of the guard.* See Ne 3:25 and note. Jeremiah was imprisoned by King Zedekiah (see 37:21) and remained in the courtyard of the guard until Jerusalem fell (see 38:13,28; 39:14).

32:3–5 See 21:3–7; 34:2–5; 37:17. The fulfillment is recorded in 52:7–14.

32:5 *until I deal with him.* After his capture by the Babylonians, Zedekiah was taken to Babylon, where he eventually died (see 52:11). *you will not succeed.* See note on 29:4.

32:7 *Anathoth.* Jeremiah's hometown (see note on 1:1). *as nearest relative ... duty to buy it.* In accordance with the ancient law of redemption (see Lev 25:23–25 and notes on 25:24–25; see also notes on Ru 2:20; 4:3).

32:8 *came to me in the courtyard.* Though imprisoned, Jeremiah was allowed to have visitors. *in the territory of Benjamin.* Some time earlier, Jeremiah had been on his way home "to get his share of the property" in Benjamin (37:12), but he was arrested, falsely accused of treason, and thrown into prison (see 37:13–16).

32:9 *so I bought.* In obedience to the Lord's command (see v. 7). *weighed out.* Coinage had not yet been invented. *seventeen shekels of silver.* See NIV text note. The size of the field is unknown, but the price was probably not exorbitant (contrast Ge 23:15; see note there).

32:10 *sealed.* Not to attest his signature (as, e.g., in Est 3:12; see note on Ge 38:18) but to guarantee the contents of the deed and keep it from being tampered with (see Isa 8:16; 29:11; Da 12:4,9; Rev 15:1–5).

32:11 *unsealed copy.* For ready reference, the authenticity of which would then be guaranteed by the sealed copy if the unsealed deed should be lost, damaged or changed (deliberately or otherwise). Examples of tied and sealed papyrus documents of the fifth and subsequent centuries B.C. have been found at Elephantine in southern Egypt, in the desert of Judah west of the Dead Sea, and elsewhere (see chart, p. xxii).

32:12 *Baruch.* Means "blessed (by the LORD)." He was Jeremiah's faithful secretary and friend (see Introduction: Author and Date).

32:14 *put them in a clay jar so they will last a long time.* Documents found in clay jars at Elephantine (see note on v. 11) and Qumran (west of the Dead Sea) were preserved almost intact for more than 2,000 years (see essay, p. 1452).

15For this is what the LORD Almighty, the
God of Israel, says: Houses, fields and vineyards will again be bought in this land.'[e]
16"After I had given the deed of purchase to Baruch[f] son of Neriah, I prayed
to the LORD:

17"Ah, Sovereign LORD,[g] you have
made the heavens and the earth[h] by
your great power and outstretched
arm.[i] Nothing is too hard[j] for you.
18You show love[k] to thousands but
bring the punishment for the fathers'
sins into the laps[l] of their children[m]
after them. O great and powerful
God,[n] whose name is the LORD Almighty,[o] 19great are your purposes
and mighty are your deeds.[p] Your
eyes are open to all the ways of men;[q]
you reward everyone according to his
conduct and as his deeds deserve.[r]
20You performed miraculous signs
and wonders[s] in Egypt[t] and have continued them to this day, both in Israel and among all mankind, and have
gained the renown[u] that is still yours.
21You brought your people Israel out
of Egypt with signs and wonders, by
a mighty hand[v] and an outstretched
arm[w] and with great terror.[x] 22You
gave them this land you had sworn to
give their forefathers, a land flowing
with milk and honey.[y] 23They came
in and took possession[z] of it, but they
did not obey you or follow your law;[a]
they did not do what you commanded them to do. So you brought all this
disaster[b] upon them.
24"See how the siege ramps[c] are
built up to take the city. Because of
the sword, famine and plague,[d] the
city will be handed over to the Babylonians who are attacking it. What
you said[e] has happened,[f] as you now
see. 25And though the city will be
handed over to the Babylonians, you,
O Sovereign LORD, say to me, 'Buy the
field[g] with silver and have the transaction witnessed.[h]'"

26Then the word of the LORD came to
Jeremiah: 27"I am the LORD, the God of all
mankind.[i] Is anything too hard for me?[j]
28Therefore, this is what the LORD says: I
am about to hand this city over to the Babylonians and to Nebuchadnezzar[k] king of
Babylon, who will capture it.[l] 29The Babylonians who are attacking this city will
come in and set it on fire; they will burn it
down,[m] along with the houses[n] where the
people provoked me to anger by burning
incense on the roofs to Baal and by pouring out drink offerings[o] to other gods.[p]
30"The people of Israel and Judah have
done nothing but evil in my sight from their
youth;[q] indeed, the people of Israel have
done nothing but provoke[r] me with what
their hands have made,[s] declares the LORD.
31From the day it was built until now, this
city[t] has so aroused my anger and wrath
that I must remove[u] it from my sight. 32The
people of Israel and Judah have provoked[v]
me by all the evil[w] they have done—they,
their kings and officials,[x] their priests and
prophets, the men of Judah and the people
of Jerusalem. 33They turned their backs[y]
to me and not their faces; though I taught[z]
them again and again, they would not lis-

32:15 [e] ver 43-44; Isa 44:26; Jer 30:18; Eze 28:26; Am 9:14-15
32:16 [f] S ver 12
32:17 [g] Jer 1:6 [h] S Ge 1:1; S Jer 10:16 [i] S Dt 9:29; 2Ki 19:15; Ps 102:25 [j] S 2Ki 3:18; Jer 51:15; S Mt 19:26
32:18 [k] S Dt 5:10 [l] S Ps 79:12 [m] S Ex 20:5; S Ps 109:14 [n] Jer 10:6 [o] S Jer 10:16
32:19 [p] S Job 12:13; Da 2:20 [q] S Job 14:16; S Pr 5:21; Jer 16:17 [r] S Job 34:11; S Mt 16:27
32:20 [s] S Ex 3:20; S Job 9:10 [t] Ex 9:16 [u] S Isa 55:13; S Jer 13:11
32:21 [v] S Ex 6:6; Da 9:15 [w] S Dt 5:15; S Jer 6:12 [x] S Dt 26:8
32:22 [y] S Ex 3:8; Eze 20:6
32:23 [z] S Ps 44:2; 78:54-55 [a] S Ex 16:28; S Jos 1:7; S 1Ki 9:6; S Jer 11:8 [b] S Dt 28:64; 31:29; Da 9:14
32:24 [c] S 2Sa 20:15; S Jer 6:6 [d] S Jer 14:12 [e] Dt 4:25-26; Jos 23:15-16 [f] S Dt 28:2
32:25 [g] S ver 8 [h] S Isa 8:2 **32:27** [i] S Nu 16:22 [j] S Ge 18:14; S 2Ki 3:18
32:28 [k] S 2Ch 36:17 [l] S ver 3; S Jer 21:10 **32:29** [m] S 2Ch 36:19 [n] S Jer 19:13 [o] Jer 44:18 [p] S Jer 7:9 **32:30** [q] S Ps 25:7; S Jer 22:21 [r] Jer 8:19 [s] Jer 25:7 **32:31** [t] 1Ki 11:7-8; 2Ki 21:4-5; Mt 23:37 [u] S 2Ki 23:27 **32:32** [v] S 1Ki 14:9 [w] Da 9:8 [x] S Jer 2:26; S 44:9
32:33 [y] S 1Ki 14:9; S Ps 14:3; Jer 2:27; Eze 8:16; Zec 7:11 [z] S Dt 4:5; S Isa 28:9; S Jer 7:13

32:15 Jeremiah's deed of purchase would enable him (or his heirs) to reclaim the field as soon as normal economic activity resumed after the exile.

32:17 See 27:5. *great power and outstretched arm.* See v. 21; see also note on 21:5. *Nothing is too hard for you.* See note on Ge 18:14. The Lord's reply to Jeremiah echoes these words (see v. 27).

32:18 *show love to thousands but ... punishment for the fathers' sins.* See Ex 20:5–6; 34:7; see also note on Ex 20:6. *bring ... into the laps.* A symbol of retribution (see Ps 79:12; Isa 65:6–7; cf. Lk 6:38 and note). *great and powerful God.* See Dt 10:17. *whose name is the LORD Almighty.* See 31:35; Isa 54:5; Am 4:13; see also note on 1Sa 1:3.

32:19 *great are your purposes and ... deeds.* See Ps 66:5; Isa 9:6; 28:29. *you reward everyone ... as his deeds deserve.* Repeated verbatim from 17:10 (see note there; see also Ro 2:6 and note; 1Co 3:8; Eph 6:8).

32:20 *miraculous signs and wonders.* See v. 21; Ex 7:3; see also notes on Ex 3:12; 4:8.

32:21 Echoes Dt 26:8 (see also Dt 4:34). *mighty hand ... outstretched arm.* See v. 17 and note on 21:5. *great terror.* See Ex 15:14–16.

32:22 *land flowing with milk and honey.* See 11:5; see also note on Ex 3:8.

32:24 *siege ramps.* See 6:6; 33:4; see also note on Isa 37:33. *sword, famine and plague.* See note on 14:12.

32:25 Jeremiah expresses his doubts concerning what must seem to him to be an unwise investment. Nevertheless, he remains the obedient servant (see vv. 8–9).

32:27 *the LORD, the God of all mankind.* Echoes Nu 16:22; 27:16, emphasizing God's universal dominion. *Is anything too hard for me?* Responds to the description in Jeremiah's prayer (see v. 17 and note on Ge 18:14), stressing God's omnipotence. God is worthy of obedience because he is always faithful in fulfilling his promises.

32:29 *burn it down.* See 21:10; 34:2; 37:8. *provoked me to anger.* See 7:18; Dt 31:29. *burning incense ... to Baal.* See 1:16 and note. *on the roofs.* See note on 19:13. *drink offerings to other gods.* See 7:18 and note; 19:13.

32:30 Echoes Dt 31:29. *youth.* See note on 31:19. *what their hands have made.* A reference to idols.

32:31 *remove it from my sight.* See 52:3; 2Ki 24:3.

32:32 *kings ... officials ... priests ... prophets.* See 1:18 and note.

32:33 *again and again.* See note on 7:13. *not ... respond to discipline.* See 2:30; 5:3; 7:28; 17:23.

ten or respond to discipline.[a] 34They set up
their abominable idols[b] in the house that
bears my Name[c] and defiled[d] it. 35They
built high places for Baal in the Valley of
Ben Hinnom[e] to sacrifice their sons and
daughters[a] to Molech,[f] though I never
commanded, nor did it enter my mind,[g]
that they should do such a detestable[h]
thing and so make Judah sin.[i]

36"You are saying about this city, 'By the
sword, famine and plague[j] it will be handed over to the king of Babylon'; but this is
what the LORD, the God of Israel, says: 37I
will surely gather[k] them from all the lands
where I banish them in my furious anger[l]
and great wrath; I will bring them back
to this place and let them live in safety.[m]
38They will be my people,[n] and I will be
their God. 39I will give them singleness[o] of
heart and action, so that they will always
fear[p] me for their own good and the good
of their children after them. 40I will make
an everlasting covenant[q] with them: I will
never stop doing good to them, and I will
inspire[r] them to fear me, so that they will
never turn away from me.[s] 41I will rejoice[t]
in doing them good[u] and will assuredly
plant[v] them in this land with all my heart
and soul.[w]

42"This is what the LORD says: As I have
brought all this great calamity[x] on this
people, so I will give them all the prosperity I have promised[y] them. 43Once more
fields will be bought[z] in this land of which
you say, 'It is a desolate[a] waste, without
men or animals, for it has been handed
over to the Babylonians.' 44Fields will
be bought for silver, and deeds[b] will be
signed, sealed and witnessed[c] in the territory of Benjamin, in the villages around
Jerusalem, in the towns of Judah and in
the towns of the hill country, of the western foothills and of the Negev,[d] because I
will restore[e] their fortunes,[b] declares the
LORD."

32:33
[a]S Jer 7:28
32:34
[b]S 2Ki 21:4; Eze 8:3-16
[c]Jer 7:10; 34:15
[d]S Jer 7:30
32:35 [e]Jer 19:2
[f]S Lev 18:21
[g]S Jer 19:5
[h]S 1Ki 14:24
[i]S Jer 25:7
32:36 [j]ver 24
32:37
[k]S Isa 11:12
[l]Jer 21:5
[m]S Lev 25:18; Eze 34:28; 39:26
32:38 [n]Jer 24:7; 2Co 6:16*
32:39
[o]S 2Ch 30:12; S Ps 86:11; Jn 17:21; Ac 4:32
[p]S Dt 6:24; S 10:16
32:40
[q]S Ge 9:16; S Isa 42:6
[r]S Dt 4:10
[s]S Jer 24:7
32:41
[t]S Dt 28:63; S Isa 62:4
[u]S Dt 28:3-12
[v]Jer 24:6; 31:28
[w]Mic 7:18
32:42 [x]La 3:38
[y]S Jer 29:10
32:43 [z]ver 15
[a]Jer 33:12
32:44 [b]ver 10
[c]S Ru 4:9; S Isa 8:2
[d]S Jer 17:26
[e]S Ezr 9:9; Ps 14:7
33:1 [f]S Ps 88:8
[g]Jer 37:21; 38:28

Promise of Restoration

33 While Jeremiah was still confined[f] in
the courtyard[g] of the guard, the word
of the LORD came to him a second time:[h]
2"This is what the LORD says, he who
made the earth,[i] the LORD who formed it
and established it—the LORD is his name:[j]
3'Call[k] to me and I will answer you and tell
you great and unsearchable[l] things you do
not know.' 4For this is what the LORD, the
God of Israel, says about the houses in this
city and the royal palaces of Judah that
have been torn down to be used against
the siege[m] ramps[n] and the sword 5in the
fight with the Babylonians[c]: 'They will be
filled with the dead bodies of the men I
will slay in my anger and wrath.[o] I will
hide my face[p] from this city because of all
its wickedness.

[a] 35 Or *to make their sons and daughters pass through* ⌞*the fire*⌟ [b] 44 Or *will bring them back from captivity* [c] 5 Or *Chaldeans*

[h]Jer 13:3 33:2 [i]S Ps 136:6; S Jer 10:16 [j]S Ex 3:15 33:3 [k]S Isa 55:6 [l]S Job 28:11 33:4 [m]S 2Ki 25:1; Eze 4:2 [n]Jer 32:24; Eze 26:8; Hab 1:10 33:5 [o]Jer 21:4-7 [p]S Dt 31:17; S Isa 8:17

32:34–35 Repeated from 7:30–31 (see notes there).
32:34 *house that bears my Name.* See 7:10 and note.
32:35 *Molech.* The god of the Ammonites (see 49:1,3; see also note on Lev 18:21). *nor did it enter my mind.* See 7:31 and note.
32:36 *You.* The people of Judah as a whole. *sword, famine and plague.* See note on 14:12. *but.* After judgment on the wicked comes restoration for the righteous.
32:37 See Dt 30:1–5. *furious anger and great wrath.* See note on 21:5. *bring them back … let them live.* See Eze 36:11,33; Hos 11:11. The Hebrew underlying the first phrase sounds like that underlying the second.
32:38 See 31:33; see also note on 7:23.
32:39 *singleness of heart.* See 24:7; 31:32 and note; Eze 11:19. *their children after them.* See Dt 4:9–10.
32:40 *everlasting covenant.* See 31:37; 33:17–26; Isa 55:3 and notes; Eze 16:60; 37:26. *inspire them to fear me.* See Dt 6:24; see also note on Ge 20:11. *never turn away from me.* See 26:3; Isa 53:6.
32:41 *rejoice in doing them good.* See Dt 30:9; Isa 62:5; 65:19.
32:43–44 *fields will be bought.* The field purchased by Jeremiah (see v. 9) is symbolic of the many fields that will be purchased in Judah after the Babylonian exile, when economic conditions return to normal (see note on v. 15).
32:43 *you.* See note on v. 36. *desolate waste, without men or animals.* See 4:23–26 and notes.
32:44 *territory of Benjamin.* See 1:1. Here Benjamin is mentioned first because it was the region in which Jeremiah's hometown was located (see vv. 7–8 and notes). *hill country … western foothills.* See note on Dt 1:7. *Negev.* See note on Ge 12:9. *restore their fortunes.* See NIV text note; see also note on 29:14.
33:1–26 Concluding Jeremiah's "book of consolation" (see note on 30:1—33:26), the section is divided into two roughly equal parts: (1) vv. 1–13, which continue and build on ch. 32, and (2) vv. 14–26, which summarize a wider range of earlier passages in Jeremiah and elsewhere. This section is not found in the Septuagint (the pre-Christian Greek translation of the OT).
33:1 *still confined.* In 587 B.C. (see note on 32:1). *courtyard of the guard.* See 32:2 and note. *a second time.* Ch. 32 comprises the first time.
33:2 See 10:12; 32:17; 51:15; see also 31:35 and note.
33:3 *Call … and I will answer.* The prayers of God's people invite—and assure—God's response (see Ps 3:4; 4:3; 18:6; 27:7; 28:1–2; 30:8; 55:17; 118:5 and note; Mt 7:7; contrast 11:14). *great and unsearchable.* Elsewhere this phrase is used to describe the formidable cities of Canaan ("large and fortified" [Nu 13:28; Jos 14:12]; cf. Dt 1:28; 9:1, where "up to the sky" is added). *unsearchable things you do not know.* The Hebrew (with the change of one letter) for this phrase echoes Isa 48:6: "hidden things unknown to you." As the rest of ch. 33 demonstrates, the Lord will first judge his people (vv. 4–5) and then restore them in ways that will be nothing short of incredible (vv. 6–26).
33:4 Jerusalem's houses—including those of the king—were torn down so that their stones could be used to repair the city's battered walls (see Isa 22:10 and note). *siege ramps.* See 6:6 and note.
33:5 *fight with the Babylonians.* See 32:5. *dead bodies.* Of Jerusalem's defenders.

6 “ ‘Nevertheless, I will bring health and
healing to it; I will heal[q] my people and
will let them enjoy abundant peace[r] and
security. 7 I will bring Judah[s] and Israel
back from captivity[a t] and will rebuild[u]
them as they were before.[v] 8 I will cleanse[w]
them from all the sin they have committed
against me and will forgive[x] all their sins
of rebellion against me. 9 Then this city will
bring me renown,[y] joy, praise[z] and honor[a]
before all nations on earth that hear of all
the good things I do for it; and they will be
in awe and will tremble[b] at the abundant
prosperity and peace I provide for it.’
10 “This is what the LORD says: ‘You say
about this place, “It is a desolate waste,
without men or animals.”[c] Yet in the towns
of Judah and the streets of Jerusalem that
are deserted,[d] inhabited by neither men
nor animals, there will be heard once more
11 the sounds of joy and gladness,[e] the voices of bride and bridegroom, and the voices
of those who bring thank offerings[f] to the
house of the LORD, saying,

“Give thanks to the LORD Almighty,
for the LORD is good;[g]
his love endures forever.”[h]

For I will restore the fortunes[i] of the land
as they were before,[j]’ says the LORD.
12 “This is what the LORD Almighty says:
‘In this place, desolate[k] and without men
or animals[l]—in all its towns there will
again be pastures for shepherds to rest
their flocks.[m] 13 In the towns of the hill[n]
country, of the western foothills and of
the Negev,[o] in the territory of Benjamin,
in the villages around Jerusalem and in
the towns of Judah, flocks will again pass
under the hand[p] of the one who counts
them,’ says the LORD.
14 “ ‘The days are coming,’ declares the
LORD, ‘when I will fulfill the gracious
promise[q] I made to the house of Israel and
to the house of Judah.

15 “ ‘In those days and at that time
I will make a righteous[r] Branch[s]
sprout from David’s line;[t]
he will do what is just and right in
the land.
16 In those days Judah will be saved[u]
and Jerusalem will live in safety.[v]
This is the name by which it[b] will be
called:[w]
The LORD Our Righteousness.’[x]

17 For this is what the LORD says: ‘David
will never fail[y] to have a man to sit on the
throne of the house of Israel, 18 nor will the
priests,[z] who are Levites,[a] ever fail to have
a man to stand before me continually to
offer burnt offerings, to burn grain offerings and to present sacrifices.[b]’ ”
19 The word of the LORD came to Jeremiah: 20 “This is what the LORD says: ‘If you
can break my covenant with the day[c] and
my covenant with the night, so that day
and night no longer come at their appointed time,[d] 21 then my covenant[e] with David
my servant—and my covenant with the
Levites[f] who are priests ministering before me—can be broken and David will

33:6 [q]S Dt 32:39; S Isa 30:26 [r]S Isa 9:6 **33:7** [s]Jer 32:44 [t]Jer 30:3; Eze 39:25; Am 9:14 [u]S Jer 24:6 [v]S Isa 1:26 **33:8** [w]S Lev 16:30; Heb 9:13-14 [x]S 2Sa 24:14; S Jer 31:34 **33:9** [y]S Isa 55:13 [z]S Isa 60:18 [a]S Jer 3:17 [b]S Isa 64:2 **33:10** [c]Jer 32:43 [d]S Lev 26:32; S Jer 9:11 **33:11** [e]S Ps 51:8; S Isa 24:8; S 51:3 [f]S Lev 7:12 [g]S 2Ch 7:3; Ps 25:8; S 136:1; Na 1:7 [h]S 1Ch 16:34; 2Ch 5:13; Ps 100:4-5 [i]Ps 14:7 [j]S Isa 1:26 **33:12** [k]Jer 32:43 [l]ver 10 [m]S Isa 65:10; Eze 34:11-15 **33:13** [n]S Jer 31:5 [o]S Jer 17:26; Ob 1:20 [p]S Lev 27:32 **33:14** [q]Dt 28:1-14; S Jos 23:15; S Jer 29:10 **33:15** [r]S Ps 72:2 [s]S Isa 4:2 [t]S 2Sa 7:12 **33:16** [u]S Isa 45:17 [v]S Jer 17:25; S 32:37 [w]Isa 59:14; Jer 3:17; Eze 48:35; Zep 3:13; Zec 8:3, 16 [x]S 1Co 1:30 **33:17** [y]S 2Sa 7:13; S 2Ch 7:18; Ps 89:29-37; S Lk 1:33 **33:18** [z]S Nu 25:11-13; Heb 7:17-22 [a]S Dt 18:1 [b]Heb 13:15 **33:20** [c]Ps 89:36 [d]S Ge 1:14 **33:21** [e]Ps 89:34 [f]S Dt 18:1

[a] 7 Or *will restore the fortunes of Judah and Israel*
[b] 16 Or *he*

33:6–16 The glorious restoration of Jerusalem (see Isa 35:1–10 and notes).
33:6 *health and healing.* See 30:17; contrast 8:22.
33:7 *bring ... back from captivity.* See vv. 11,26; see also note on 29:14. *Judah and Israel.* See note on 3:18.
33:8 *forgive all their sins.* The basis of the institution of the new covenant (see 31:34 and note; see also 50:20; Eze 36:25–26).
33:9 *tremble at the abundant prosperity.* See Hos 3:5 and note.
33:10 See 32:43 and note.
33:11 *joy and gladness ... bride and bridegroom.* The glorious reversal of the judgment proclaimed in 7:34; 16:9; 25:10. *those who bring thank offerings.* See note on 17:26. *restore the fortunes.* See note on 29:14.
33:13 *hill country ... towns of Judah.* See 17:26 and note; 32:44. *flocks ... pass under the hand ... counts them.* See Eze 20:37 and note.
33:15–16 Repeated from 23:5–6 (see notes there).
33:15 *what is just and right.* See note on Ps 119:121.
33:16 *it will be called.* Because of Jerusalem's intimate relationship to the Messiah, it is given the same name by which he is called in 23:6 (see note there; for other examples of similar naming see Jdg 6:24; Eze 48:35). But see NIV text note.
33:17–26 In the face of the impending judgment in which the nation will be swept away and the promised land reduced to a desolate wasteland, all God's past covenants with his people appear to be rendered of no effect—his covenants with Israel, with David and with Phinehas (see chart, p. 19). This series of oracles, however, gives reassurance that the ancient covenants are not being repudiated, that they are as secure as God's covenant concerning the creation order, and that in the future restoration they will all yet be fulfilled.
33:17 See 2Sa 7:12–16; 1Ki 2:4; 8:25; 9:5; 2Ch 6:16; 7:18. This passage is fulfilled ultimately in Jesus (see Lk 1:32–33 and notes).
33:18 See Nu 25:13. The priestly covenant with the Levites, like the royal covenant with David, was not a private grant to the priestly family involving only that family and the Lord. It was rather an integral part of the Lord's dealings with his people in which Israel was assured of the ministry of a priesthood that was acceptable to the Lord and through whose mediation they could enjoy communion with him. That ministry was and is being fulfilled by Jesus, who administers a higher and better priesthood (see Ps 110:4; Heb 5:6–10; 6:19–20; 7:11–25). *priests, who are Levites.* See Dt 17:9,18.
33:20 *covenant with the day and ... the night.* See v. 25; 31:35–36. Although reference may be to God's sovereign establishment of the creation order in the beginning, more likely the covenant of Ge 9:8–17 (see Ge 8:22) is in view.
33:21 *covenant with the Levites.* See Mal 2:4.

no longer have a descendant to reign on
his throne.[g] 22 I will make the descendants
of David my servant and the Levites who
minister before me as countless[h] as the
stars of the sky and as measureless as the
sand on the seashore.’ ”
23 The word of the LORD came to Jeremiah: 24 “Have you not noticed that these
people are saying, ‘The LORD has rejected the two kingdoms[a][i] he chose’? So they
despise[j] my people and no longer regard
them as a nation.[k] 25 This is what the LORD
says: ‘If I have not established my covenant with day and night[l] and the fixed
laws[m] of heaven and earth,[n] 26 then I will
reject[o] the descendants of Jacob[p] and David my servant and will not choose one
of his sons to rule over the descendants
of Abraham, Isaac and Jacob. For I will
restore their fortunes[b][q] and have compassion[r] on them.’ ”

Warning to Zedekiah

34 While Nebuchadnezzar king of Babylon and all his army and all the
kingdoms and peoples[s] in the empire he
ruled were fighting against Jerusalem[t]
and all its surrounding towns, this word
came to Jeremiah from the LORD: 2 “This is
what the LORD, the God of Israel, says: Go
to Zedekiah[u] king of Judah and tell him,
‘This is what the LORD says: I am about
to hand this city over to the king of Babylon, and he will burn it down.[v] 3 You will
not escape from his grasp but will surely be captured and handed over[w] to him.
You will see the king of Babylon with your
own eyes, and he will speak with you face
to face. And you will go to Babylon.
4 “ ‘Yet hear the promise of the LORD,
O Zedekiah king of Judah. This is what the
LORD says concerning you: You will not die
by the sword;[x] 5 you will die peacefully. As
people made a funeral fire[y] in honor of your
fathers, the former kings who preceded
you, so they will make a fire in your hon-
or and lament, “Alas,[z] O master!” I myself
make this promise, declares the LORD.’ ”
6 Then Jeremiah the prophet told all this
to Zedekiah king of Judah, in Jerusalem,
7 while the army of the king of Babylon
was fighting against Jerusalem and the
other cities of Judah that were still holding
out—Lachish[a] and Azekah.[b] These were
the only fortified cities left in Judah.

Freedom for Slaves

8 The word came to Jeremiah from the
LORD after King Zedekiah had made a covenant with all the people[c] in Jerusalem to

33:21 [g] S 2Sa 7:13; S 2Ch 7:18
33:22 [h] S Ge 12:2; S Jer 30:19; Hos 1:10
33:24 [i] Eze 37:22 [j] S Ne 4:4 [k] S Jer 30:17; Eze 36:20
33:25 [l] S Ge 1:18 [m] S Ps 148:6 [n] Ps 74:16-17
33:26 [o] S Lev 26:44 [p] S Isa 14:1 [q] ver 7; Ps 14:7 [r] S Jer 30:18
34:1 [s] Jer 27:7 [t] 2Ki 25:1; Jer 39:1
34:2 [u] S 2Ch 36:11 [v] ver 22; Jer 32:29; 37:8
34:3 [w] S 2Ki 25:7; S Jer 21:7
34:4 [x] Jer 52:11
34:5 [y] S 2Ch 16:14 [z] Jer 22:18
34:7 [a] S Jos 10:3 [b] Jos 10:10; 2Ch 11:9
34:8 [c] S 2Ki 11:17

[a] 24 Or *families* [b] 26 Or *will bring them back from captivity*

33:22 In words that echo the covenant promises to the patriarchs (Abraham, Ge 22:17; Isaac, Ge 26:4; Jacob, Ge 32:12), the Lord assures the flourishing of the two mediatorial (royal and priestly) families and thus the continuation of this ministry in the spiritual commonwealth he has established with his people. This promise of a numerous progeny to both the royal and priestly families is no doubt fulfilled in that great throng who (will) reign with Christ (see Ro 5:17; 8:17; 1Co 6:3; 2Ti 2:12; Rev 3:21; 5:10; 20:5–6; 22:5; see also Mt 19:28; Lk 22:30) and who in Christ have been consecrated to be priests (see 1Pe 2:5,9; Rev 1:6; 5:10; 20:6; see also Isa 66:21; Ro 6:13; 12:1; 15:16; Eph 5:2; Php 4:18; Heb 13:15–16).
33:24 *two kingdoms.* Israel and Judah. But since the Hebrew uses a word here that commonly refers to families (see NIV text note), the reference may be to the two mediatorial (royal and priestly) families, or to the families of "Jacob and David" (v. 26). *he chose.* See Am 3:2 and note.
33:25–26 See v. 20 and note.
33:26 *restore their fortunes and have compassion.* Echoes Dt 30:3; see note on 29:14. *restore.* See 30:3 and note.
34:1—35:19 The first major division of the book (chs. 2–35) now comes to a close. Jeremiah's warnings and exhortations to Judah are concluded with a historical appendix (chs. 34–35), a technique used to conclude the third major division of the book (chs. 39–45) as well (see note on 45:1–5). Ch. 52, written by someone other than Jeremiah, serves as a fitting historical appendix to the entire book.
34:1–22 The chapter divides naturally into two parts (vv. 1–7 and 8–22), each of which dates to 588 B.C. (see notes on vv. 7,21–22).
34:1–7 Jeremiah's warning to King Zedekiah parallels the prophet's similar admonition in 21:1–10 (see notes there).
34:1 *kingdoms and peoples in the empire he ruled.* Nebuchadnezzar's empire was vast (see Eze 26:7; Da 3:2–4; 4:1; cf. the similar description of the Medes in 51:28). *fighting against Jerusalem.* Subject nations were expected to supply troops to fight alongside those of their overlord (see 2Ki 24:2). In a 14th-century B.C. treaty between the Hittite ruler Mursilis II and Duppi-Tessub king of the Amorites, Mursilis says, "If you do not send your son or brother with your foot soldiers and charioteers to help the Hittite king, you act in disregard of the gods of the oath." *all its surrounding towns.* See 19:15 and note.
34:2–3 See 32:3–5 and note; see also 39:4–7; Eze 12:12–13; 17:11–20.
34:4 *not die by the sword.* See 32:5; 38:17,20; 52:11; Eze 17:16.
34:5 *funeral fire in honor of ... the former kings.* Not cremation (see 2Ch 16:14; 21:19; see also note on Am 6:10). *Alas, O master!* Words of mourning at the death of a king (see 22:18; cf. 1Ki 13:30).
34:7 *Lachish and Azekah.* Solomon's son Rehoboam had fortified them (see 2Ch 11:5,9), but Lachish was later besieged (701 B.C.) during Hezekiah's reign by the Assyrian king Sennacherib (see 2Ch 32:9). A contemporary relief depicting Sennacherib's conquest states that he "sat on a throne and passed in review the plunder taken from Lachish." In 1935, 18 ostraca (broken pottery fragments used as writing material) were discovered at Lachish (see chart, p. xxii), nearly all of them in the ruins of the latest occupation level (588 B.C.) of the Israelite gate-tower. Ostracon 4, written to the commander at Lachish shortly after the events described here, ends as follows: "We are watching for the fire-signals of Lachish ... for we cannot see Azekah." See note on 6:1.
34:8–22 Contemporary with the events of 37:4–12 (see note on vv. 21–22).
34:8 *proclaim freedom.* See Lev 25:10 and note. *freedom for the slaves.* In accordance with the general provisions of the law of Moses (see Ex 21:2–11 and notes; Lev 25:39–55; Dt 15:12–18).

proclaim freedom[d] for the slaves. 9Every-
one was to free his Hebrew slaves, both
male and female; no one was to hold a fellow Jew in bondage.[e] 10So all the officials
and people who entered into this covenant
agreed that they would free their male and
female slaves and no longer hold them in
bondage. They agreed, and set them free.
11But afterward they changed their minds[f]
and took back the slaves they had freed
and enslaved them again.

12Then the word of the LORD came to
Jeremiah: 13"This is what the LORD, the
God of Israel, says: I made a covenant with
your forefathers[g] when I brought them out
of Egypt, out of the land of slavery.[h] I said,
14'Every seventh year each of you must free
any fellow Hebrew who has sold himself
to you. After he has served you six years,
you must let him go free.'[a][i] Your fathers,
however, did not listen to me or pay attention[j] to me. 15Recently you repented and
did what is right in my sight: Each of you
proclaimed freedom to his countrymen.[k]
You even made a covenant before me in
the house that bears my Name.[l] 16But now
you have turned around[m] and profaned[n]
my name; each of you has taken back the
male and female slaves you had set free
to go where they wished. You have forced
them to become your slaves again.

17"Therefore, this is what the LORD says:
You have not obeyed me; you have not
proclaimed freedom for your fellow countrymen. So I now proclaim 'freedom' for
you,[o] declares the LORD—'freedom' to fall
by the sword, plague[p] and famine.[q] I will
make you abhorrent to all the kingdoms of
the earth.[r] 18The men who have violated
my covenant[s] and have not fulfilled the
terms of the covenant they made before
me, I will treat like the calf they cut in two
and then walked between its pieces.[t] 19The
leaders of Judah and Jerusalem, the court
officials,[u] the priests and all the people of
the land who walked between the pieces
of the calf, 20I will hand over[v] to their enemies who seek their lives.[w] Their dead
bodies will become food for the birds of
the air and the beasts of the earth.[x]

21"I will hand Zedekiah[y] king of Judah
and his officials[z] over to their enemies[a]
who seek their lives, to the army of the
king of Babylon,[b] which has withdrawn[c]
from you. 22I am going to give the order,
declares the LORD, and I will bring them
back to this city. They will fight against it,
take[d] it and burn[e] it down. And I will lay
waste[f] the towns of Judah so no one can
live there."

The Recabites

35 This is the word that came to Jeremiah from the LORD during the reign
of Jehoiakim[g] son of Josiah king of Judah:
2"Go to the Recabite[h] family and invite
them to come to one of the side rooms[i] of

a 14 Deut. 15:12

34:8 [d]S Ex 21:2; Lev 25:10,39-41; Ne 5:5-8 **34:9** [e]Dt 15:12-18 **34:11** [f]Ps 78:37 **34:13** [g]S Ex 24:8 [h]S Dt 15:15 **34:14** [i]S Ex 21:2 [j]2Ki 17:14; S Jer 7:26 **34:15** [k]ver 8 [l]S Jer 32:34 **34:16** [m]Eze 3:20; 18:24 [n]S Lev 19:12 **34:17** [o]S Mt 7:2; Gal 6:7 [p]Jer 21:7 [q]S Jer 14:12 [r]Jer 15:4; S 24:9; S 29:18 **34:18** [s]S Jer 11:10 [t]S Ge 15:10 **34:19** [u]S Jer 26:10; Zep 3:3-4 **34:20** [v]Jer 21:7; Eze 16:27; 23:28 [w]S Jer 11:21 [x]S Dt 28:26 **34:21** [y]S Jer 32:4 [z]2Ki 25:21; Jer 39:6; 52:24-27 [a]S Jer 21:7 [b]S 2Ch 36:10 [c]Jer 37:5 **34:22** [d]Jer 39:1-2 [e]S Ne 2:17; Jer 38:18; 39:8; Eze 23:47 [f]S Lev 26:32; S Isa 1:7 **35:1** [g]S 2Ch 36:5 **35:2** [h]S 2Ki 10:15 [i]S 1Ki 6:5

34:9 *Hebrew.* See Ex 21:2 and note. *no one … hold a fellow Jew in bondage.* See Lev 25:39,42. *Jew.* A shortened form of "Judahite" (an inhabitant of the kingdom of Judah, where a remnant of the Israelites was still living). Strictly speaking, the term "Jew" is properly applied only to the OT people of God and their descendants from the time of the Babylonian exile on.

34:10 *They … set them free.* To gain God's blessing, and/or in the hope that the freed slaves would be more willing to help defend Jerusalem.

34:11 *afterward.* When the Babylonian siege was temporarily lifted due to Egyptian intervention (see vv. 21–22; 37:5,11). *took back the slaves they had freed.* In violation of Dt 15:12. *enslaved them.* Cf. 2Ch 28:10.

34:13 *land of slavery.* Lit. "house of slaves" (see Ex 13:3,14; 20:2; Dt 5:6; 6:12; 8:14; 13:5; Jos 24:17; Jdg 6:8). The Israelites were to free their slaves because God had earlier freed the Israelites (see Dt 15:15).

34:14 *Every seventh year … let him go free.* A loose quotation of Dt 15:12.

34:15–16 *you repented … you have turned around.* The Hebrew for the two phrases is identical, providing an ironic play on words (see note on v. 18).

34:15 *house that bears my Name.* See 7:10 and note.

34:16 *you have … profaned my name.* By breaking the Lord's covenant. Zedekiah was a man whose word could not be trusted (see Eze 17:15,18). *go where they wished.* See Dt 21:14.

34:17 *sword, plague and famine.* See note on 14:12. *abhorrent to all the kingdoms of the earth.* See 15:4 and note.

34:18 *violated … walked.* The Hebrew root underlying both words is the same, again providing an ironic play on words (see note on vv. 15–16). *made … cut.* The Hebrew for the two words is identical. In ancient times, making a covenant involved a self-maledictory oath ("May thus and so be done to me if I do not keep this covenant"), which was often symbolized by cutting an animal in two and walking between the two halves (see Ge 15:18 and note). *between its pieces.* See note on Ge 15:17.

34:20 *food for the birds … of the earth.* See 7:33 and note.

34:21–22 Because of the arrival of the Egyptians on the scene, the Babylonians in 588 B.C. temporarily lifted the siege of Jerusalem (see notes on v. 11; 37:3).

34:21 *withdrawn from you.* See the hope expressed in 21:2.

34:22 *I will bring them back.* See 37:8.

35:1–19 The family of the Recabites, who obeyed their forefather's command, are an example and rebuke to the people of Judah, who have disobeyed the Lord (see v. 16). The mention of "Babylonian and Aramean armies" (v. 11) dates the chapter to no earlier than the eighth year of King Jehoiakim, who began his reign in 609 B.C., whose capital city of Jerusalem was besieged in 605 (see Da 1:1 and note) by Nebuchadnezzar, and who rebelled against Nebuchadnezzar three or four years later—an unwise act that led to raids on his territory by Babylonians, Arameans and others (see 2Ki 24:1–2). (The raids are perhaps reflected in 12:7–13.)

35:1 *during the reign of Jehoiakim.* Chs. 35–36 (see 36:1) are a flashback to the reign of Jehoiakim (609–598 B.C.; see Introduction: Outline).

35:2 *Recabite family.* A nomadic tribal group related to the Kenites (see 1Ch 2:55), some of whom lived among or near the Israelites (see Jdg 1:16; 4:11; 1Sa 27:10) and were

the house of the LORD and give them wine
to drink."
3So I went to get Jaazaniah son of Jeremiah, the son of Habazziniah, and his
brothers and all his sons — the whole family of the Recabites. 4I brought them into
the house of the LORD, into the room of the
sons of Hanan son of Igdaliah the man of
God.[j] It was next to the room of the officials, which was over that of Maaseiah son
of Shallum[k] the doorkeeper.[l] 5Then I set
bowls full of wine and some cups before
the men of the Recabite family and said to
them, "Drink some wine."
6But they replied, "We do not drink
wine, because our forefather Jonadab[m]
son of Recab gave us this command: 'Neither you nor your descendants must ever
drink wine.[n] 7Also you must never build
houses, sow seed or plant vineyards; you
must never have any of these things, but
must always live in tents.[o] Then you will
live a long time in the land[p] where you
are nomads.' 8We have obeyed everything
our forefather[q] Jonadab son of Recab commanded us. Neither we nor our wives nor
our sons and daughters have ever drunk
wine 9or built houses to live in or had
vineyards, fields or crops.[r] 10We have lived
in tents and have fully obeyed everything
our forefather Jonadab commanded us.
11But when Nebuchadnezzar king of Babylon invaded[s] this land, we said, 'Come,
we must go to Jerusalem[t] to escape the
Babylonian[a] and Aramean armies.' So we
have remained in Jerusalem."
12Then the word of the LORD came to
Jeremiah, saying: 13"This is what the LORD
Almighty, the God of Israel, says: Go and
tell[u] the men of Judah and the people of
Jerusalem, 'Will you not learn a lesson[v]
and obey my words?' declares the LORD.
14'Jonadab son of Recab ordered his sons
not to drink wine and this command has
been kept. To this day they do not drink
wine, because they obey their forefather's
command.[w] But I have spoken to you again
and again,[x] yet you have not obeyed[y] me.
15Again and again I sent all my servants
the prophets[z] to you. They said, "Each of
you must turn[a] from your wicked ways
and reform[b] your actions; do not follow
other gods[c] to serve them. Then you will
live in the land[d] I have given to you and
your fathers." But you have not paid attention or listened[e] to me. 16The descendants
of Jonadab son of Recab have carried out
the command their forefather[f] gave them,
but these people have not obeyed me.'
17"Therefore, this is what the LORD God
Almighty, the God of Israel, says: 'Listen!
I am going to bring on Judah and on everyone living in Jerusalem every disaster[g]
I pronounced against them. I spoke to
them, but they did not listen;[h] I called to
them, but they did not answer.'"[i]
18Then Jeremiah said to the family of
the Recabites, "This is what the LORD Almighty, the God of Israel, says: 'You have
obeyed the command of your forefather[j]
Jonadab and have followed all his instructions and have done everything he ordered.' 19Therefore, this is what the LORD
Almighty, the God of Israel, says: 'Jonadab
son of Recab will never fail[k] to have a man
to serve[l] me.'"

Jehoiakim Burns Jeremiah's Scroll

36 In the fourth year of Jehoiakim[m] son
of Josiah king of Judah, this word

[a] 11 Or *Chaldean*

35:4 [j] S Dt 33:1 [k] 1Ch 9:19 [l] S 2Ki 12:9; S 23:4
35:6 [m] S 2Ki 10:15 [n] S Lev 10:9; Nu 6:2-4; S Lk 1:15
35:7 [o] Heb 11:9 [p] S Ex 20:12; Eph 6:2-3
35:8 [q] Pr 1:8; Col 3:20
35:9 [r] 1Ti 6:6
35:11 [s] 2Ki 24:1 [t] S Jos 10:20; Jer 8:14
35:13 [u] Jer 11:6 [v] Jer 6:10; 32:33
35:14 [w] ver 6-10, 16 [x] S Jer 7:13 [y] Isa 30:9
35:15 [z] S Jer 7:25 [a] S 2Ki 17:13; S Jer 26:3 [b] S Isa 1:16-17; S 59:20; Jer 4:1; 18:11; Eze 14:6; 18:30 [c] S Ex 20:3 [d] S Dt 4:40; Jer 25:5 [e] S Jer 6:10; S 7:26; 44:4-5
35:16 [f] S Lev 20:9; Mal 1:6
35:17 [g] S Jos 23:15; S 1Ki 13:34; Jer 21:4-7 [h] S Pr 1:24; Ro 10:21 [i] Jer 7:13
35:18 [j] S Ge 31:35
35:19 [k] S Isa 48:19; Jer 33:17 [l] Jer 15:19
36:1 [m] S 2Ch 36:5

on friendly terms with them (see 1Sa 15:6; 30:26,29). *side rooms of the house of the LORD.* Used for storage and/or as living quarters (see 1Ki 6:5; 1Ch 28:12; 2Ch 31:11; Ne 13:4–5).

35:3 *Jaazaniah.* Means "The LORD hears." It was a common name in Jeremiah's time (see 40:8; Eze 8:11; 11:1) and appears on a stamp seal (discovered at Tell en-Nasbeh north of Jerusalem and dating c. 600 B.C.) as well as on one of the Lachish ostraca (see note on 34:7). *Jeremiah.* Not the prophet.

35:4 *sons.* Perhaps here in the sense of "disciples" (see Am 7:14 and note). *man of God.* A synonym for "prophet" (see 1Ki 12:22; see also note on 1Sa 9:9), emphasizing his relationship to the One who has called him. *Maaseiah.* Perhaps the man of the same name mentioned in 21:1; 29:25; 37:3. *doorkeeper.* One of three supervisors (see 52:24) over those who guarded the entrances to the temple (see 2Ki 12:9).

35:5 *bowls.* Large vessels, from which smaller cups would be filled.

35:6 *We do not drink wine.* A permanent vow taken by the Recabites; cf. the Nazirites' temporary vow (see Nu 6:2–3,20; Jdg 13:4–7). Malkijah son of Recab may have been a later renegade exception to the Recabite vow, since he was "ruler of the district of Beth Hakkerem" (Ne 3:14), which means "house of the vineyard." *Jonadab.* Spelled "Jehonadab" in 2Ki 10:15,23. Nearly 250 years before the days of Jeremiah, he helped King Jehu destroy Baal worship (at least temporarily) in the northern kingdom.

35:7 *must always live in tents.* Except during times of national emergency (see v. 11). *Then you will live a long time in the land.* An echo of Ex 20:12, where honoring one's parents is commanded.

35:8 *We have obeyed … Jonadab.* Contrast Judah's disobedience toward God (see v. 16).

35:11 See note on vv. 1–19.

35:13 *learn a lesson.* The Hebrew underlying this phrase is translated "respond(ed) to correction" in 2:30; 7:28 (see 5:3; 17:23 and note).

35:14–15 *again and again.* See note on 7:13.

35:15 See 25:4–5 and notes.

35:17 See 11:11.

35:19 *never fail to have a man to serve me.* See 33:18. Various traditions in the Jewish Mishnah (see note on Ne 10:34) claim that the Recabites were later given special duties to perform in connection with the Jerusalem temple built after the return from Babylonian exile.

36:1—38:28 Three chapters united by the common theme of Jeremiah's suffering and persecution.

36:1–32 An account of King Jehoiakim's attempt to destroy Jeremiah's written prophecies.

36:1 *fourth year of Jehoiakim.* 605 B.C.—a critical year in Judah's history (see notes on 25:1; 46:2).

came to Jeremiah from the LORD: 2"Take a
scroll[n] and write on it all the words[o] I have
spoken to you concerning Israel, Judah
and all the other nations from the time I
began speaking to you in the reign of Josiah[p] till now. 3Perhaps[q] when the people
of Judah hear[r] about every disaster I plan
to inflict on them, each of them will turn[s]
from his wicked way; then I will forgive[t]
their wickedness and their sin."
4So Jeremiah called Baruch[u] son of Neriah,[v] and while Jeremiah dictated[w] all
the words the LORD had spoken to him,
Baruch wrote them on the scroll.[x] 5Then
Jeremiah told Baruch, "I am restricted; I
cannot go to the LORD's temple. 6So you
go to the house of the LORD on a day of
fasting[y] and read to the people from the
scroll the words of the LORD that you wrote
as I dictated.[z] Read them to all the people
of Judah[a] who come in from their towns.
7Perhaps they will bring their petition[b] before the LORD, and each will turn[c] from his
wicked ways, for the anger[d] and wrath
pronounced against this people by the
LORD are great."
8Baruch son of Neriah did everything
Jeremiah the prophet told him to do; at
the LORD's temple he read the words of the
LORD from the scroll. 9In the ninth month[e]
of the fifth year of Jehoiakim son of Josiah king of Judah, a time of fasting[f] before
the LORD was proclaimed for all the people in Jerusalem and those who had come
from the towns of Judah. 10From the room
of Gemariah[g] son of Shaphan[h] the secretary,[i] which was in the upper courtyard
at the entrance of the New Gate[j] of the
temple, Baruch read to all the people at
the LORD's temple the words of Jeremiah
from the scroll.
11When Micaiah son of Gemariah, the
son of Shaphan, heard all the words of the
LORD from the scroll, 12he went down to
the secretary's[k] room in the royal palace,
where all the officials were sitting: Elishama the secretary, Delaiah son of Shemaiah,
Elnathan[l] son of Acbor, Gemariah son of
Shaphan, Zedekiah son of Hananiah, and
all the other officials.[m] 13After Micaiah told
them everything he had heard Baruch read
to the people from the scroll, 14all the officials sent Jehudi[n] son of Nethaniah, the
son of Shelemiah, the son of Cushi, to say
to Baruch, "Bring the scroll[o] from which
you have read to the people and come." So
Baruch son of Neriah went to them with
the scroll in his hand. 15They said to him,
"Sit down, please, and read it to us."
So Baruch read it to them. 16When they
heard all these words, they looked at each
other in fear[p] and said to Baruch, "We
must report all these words to the king."
17Then they asked Baruch, "Tell us, how
did you come to write[q] all this? Did Jeremiah dictate it?"
18"Yes," Baruch replied, "he dictated[r] all
these words to me, and I wrote them in
ink on the scroll."
19Then the officials[s] said to Baruch,
"You and Jeremiah, go and hide.[t] Don't let
anyone know where you are."
20After they put the scroll in the room of
Elishama the secretary, they went to the
king in the courtyard and reported everything to him. 21The king sent Jehudi[u] to get
the scroll, and Jehudi brought it from the
room of Elishama the secretary and read it
to the king[v] and all the officials standing
beside him. 22It was the ninth month and
the king was sitting in the winter apartment,[w] with a fire burning in the firepot in
front of him. 23Whenever Jehudi had read
three or four columns of the scroll,[x] the
king cut them off with a scribe's knife and
threw them into the firepot, until the entire

36:2 [n] S ver 4; S Ex 17:14; S Ps 40:7; Jer 30:2; Hab 2:2 [o] Eze 2:7 [p] Jer 1:2; 25:3 **36:3** [q] ver 7; Eze 12:3; Am 5:15 [r] Isa 6:9; Mk 4:12 [s] S 2Ki 17:13; S Isa 44:22; S Jer 26:3; Ac 3:19 [t] S Jer 18:8 **36:4** [u] S Jer 32:12 [v] Jer 51:59 [w] ver 18 [x] ver 2; Eze 2:9; Da 7:1; Zec 5:1 **36:6** [y] ver 9 [z] S Ex 4:16 [a] 2Ch 20:4 **36:7** [b] Jer 37:20; 42:2 [c] S Jer 26:3 [d] S Dt 31:17 **36:9** [e] ver 22 [f] S 2Ch 20:3 **36:10** [g] ver 12, 25; Jer 29:3 [h] Jer 26:24 [i] Jer 52:25 [j] S Ge 23:10 **36:12** [k] S 2Sa 8:17 [l] S Jer 26:22 [m] Jer 38:4 **36:14** [n] ver 21 [o] ver 4 **36:16** [p] S Ps 36:1 **36:17** [q] Jer 30:2 **36:18** [r] ver 4 **36:19** [s] Jer 26:16 [t] S 1Ki 17:3 **36:21** [u] ver 14 [v] 2Ki 22:10 **36:22** [w] Am 3:15 **36:23** [x] ver 2

36:2 *scroll.* See notes on 30:2; Ex 17:14. *write on it.* To preserve Jeremiah's messages for future generations. *all the words I have spoken to you.* This "earliest edition" of Jeremiah's prophecies may have included all or most of chs. 1–26; 46–51. *began speaking to you in the reign of Josiah.* See note on 1:2.
36:3 *Perhaps ... then.* If the people repent, the Lord will relent (see 18:7–10 and note; 26:3).
36:4 *Baruch.* See note on 32:12.
36:5 *I am restricted.* Perhaps because of his unpopular temple message(s) (see 7:2–15; 26:2–6), or perhaps because of the events recorded in 19:1—20:6.
36:6 *day of fasting.* Proclaimed because of a national emergency (cf. Joel 2:15), perhaps in this case the Babylonian attack of 605 B.C. (see Da 1:1 and note).
36:7 See v. 3 and note.
36:8 If the book presented Jeremiah's prophecies in chronological order, ch. 45 would appear after this verse (see Introduction: Outline).
36:9 *ninth month of the fifth year.* December, 604 B.C., during a time of cold weather (see v. 22).
36:10 Cf. 2Ki 23:2. *room.* See note on 35:2. *Gemariah son of Shaphan.* This official's name has been found in Jerusalem on a seal impression. *Shaphan.* Secretary of state under King Josiah (see 2Ki 22:3; see also notes on 26:24; 29:3). *entrance of the New Gate.* See 26:10 and note.
36:12 *Elnathan son of Acbor.* See note on 26:22.
36:18 *ink.* Mentioned only here in the OT (but see also 2Co 3:3; 2Jn 12; 3Jn 13). In ancient times, ink was made from soot or lampblack mixed with gum arabic, oil, or a metallic substance (as in the case of the Lachish ostraca; see note on 34:7).
36:19 The officials were understandably concerned about the safety of Jeremiah and Baruch (cf. 26:20–23).
36:20 *put.* For safekeeping (the Hebrew root for this word is translated "store" in Isa 10:28).
36:22 *ninth month.* See note on v. 9. *winter apartment.* Lit. "winter house" (as in Am 3:15), here probably a large room in the king's palace. *firepot.* A depression or container in the middle of the floor where coals were kept burning to warm the room.
36:23 Contrast King Josiah's desire to know the word of God and obey it (see 2Ki 22:11—23:3; 23:21–24). *columns.* Lit. "doors," so called because of their rectangular shape. *cut.* The Hebrew for this verb is frequently rendered elsewhere "tore"

scroll was burned in the fire.[y] 24The king
and all his attendants who heard all these
words showed no fear,[z] nor did they tear
their clothes.[a] 25Even though Elnathan,
Delaiah[b] and Gemariah[c] urged the king
not to burn the scroll, he would not listen
to them. 26Instead, the king commanded
Jerahmeel, a son of the king, Seraiah son
of Azriel and Shelemiah son of Abdeel to
arrest[d] Baruch the scribe and Jeremiah the
prophet. But the LORD had hidden[e] them.
27After the king burned the scroll containing the words that Baruch had written
at Jeremiah's dictation,[f] the word of the
LORD came to Jeremiah: 28"Take another
scroll[g] and write on it all the words that
were on the first scroll, which Jehoiakim
king of Judah burned up. 29Also tell Jehoiakim king of Judah, 'This is what the
LORD says: You burned that scroll and said,
"Why did you write on it that the king of
Babylon would certainly come and destroy
this land and cut off both men and animals[h] from it?"[i] 30Therefore, this is what
the LORD says about Jehoiakim[j] king of
Judah: He will have no one to sit on the
throne of David; his body will be thrown
out[k] and exposed[l] to the heat by day and
the frost by night.[m] 31I will punish him and
his children[n] and his attendants for their
wickedness; I will bring on them and those
living in Jerusalem and the people of Judah every disaster[o] I pronounced against
them, because they have not listened.[p]' "
32So Jeremiah took another scroll and
gave it to the scribe Baruch son of Neriah,
and as Jeremiah dictated,[q] Baruch wrote[r]
on it all the words of the scroll that Jehoiakim king of Judah had burned[s] in the
fire. And many similar words were added
to them.

36:23 [y] 1Ki 22:8 **36:24** [z] S Ps 36:1 [a] S Ge 37:29; S Nu 14:6 **36:25** [b] ver 12 [c] S ver 10 **36:26** [d] Mt 23:34 [e] S 1Ki 17:3; Ps 11:1; S Jer 1:8; 15:21 **36:27** [f] ver 4 **36:28** [g] ver 2 **36:29** [h] Jer 33:12 [i] S Isa 30:10 **36:30** [j] Jer 52:2 [k] S Isa 14:19 [l] S 2Ki 24:6 [m] S Jer 8:2 **36:31** [n] Ex 20:5 [o] S Pr 29:1 [p] S Pr 1:24 **36:32** [q] ver 4 [r] Ex 34:1; Jer 30:2 [s] ver 23

37:1 [t] S 2Ki 24:17 [u] 1Sa 11:1; Eze 17:13 [v] S 2Ki 24:8, 12; Jer 22:24 **37:2** [w] S 2Ki 24:19 **37:3** [x] ver 17; Jer 38:14 [y] Jer 38:1 [z] S 2Ki 25:18; Jer 29:25; 52:24 [a] S Ex 8:28; S Nu 21:7; 1Sa 12:19; 1Ki 13:6; 2Ki 19:4; Jer 42:2 **37:4** [b] ver 15; Jer 32:2 **37:5** [c] S Ge 15:18; Isa 31:1; Eze 17:15 [d] Jer 34:21 [e] S Isa 30:5; Jer 34:11 **37:7** [f] S Ge 25:22; S 2Ki 22:18 [g] ver 5 [h] S 2Ki 18:21; S Jer 2:36;

Jeremiah in Prison

37 Zedekiah[t] son of Josiah was made
king[u] of Judah by Nebuchadnezzar
king of Babylon; he reigned in place of Jehoiachin[a][v] son of Jehoiakim. 2Neither he
nor his attendants nor the people of the
land paid any attention[w] to the words the
LORD had spoken through Jeremiah the
prophet.
3King Zedekiah, however, sent[x] Jehucal[y]
son of Shelemiah with the priest Zephaniah[z] son of Maaseiah to Jeremiah the
prophet with this message: "Please pray[a]
to the LORD our God for us."
4Now Jeremiah was free to come and
go among the people, for he had not yet
been put in prison.[b] 5Pharaoh's army had
marched out of Egypt,[c] and when the Babylonians[b] who were besieging Jerusalem
heard the report about them, they withdrew[d] from Jerusalem.[e]
6Then the word of the LORD came to
Jeremiah the prophet: 7"This is what the
LORD, the God of Israel, says: Tell the king
of Judah, who sent you to inquire[f] of me,
'Pharaoh's army, which has marched[g] out
to support you, will go back to its own
land, to Egypt.[h] 8Then the Babylonians
will return and attack this city; they will
capture[i] it and burn[j] it down.'
9"This is what the LORD says: Do not
deceive[k] yourselves, thinking, 'The Babylonians will surely leave us.' They will
not! 10Even if you were to defeat the entire Babylonian[c] army that is attacking you
and only wounded men were left in their

[a] *1* Hebrew *Coniah,* a variant of *Jehoiachin* [b] *5* Or *Chaldeans*; also in verses 8, 9, 13 and 14 [c] *10* Or *Chaldean*; also in verse 11

La 1:7; 4:17 **37:8** [i] Jer 38:3 [j] Jer 21:10; 38:18; 39:8 **37:9** [k] Jer 29:8; S Mk 13:5

(as a garment). Instead of tearing his clothes in repentance (see note on v. 24), the king tore the prophet's scroll.

36:24 *attendants ... showed no fear.* See v. 31. Contrast the response of the "officials" (v. 12; see vv. 16,25). *nor did they tear their clothes.* Contrast the response of Jehoiakim's father Josiah (see 2Ki 22:11; cf. 1Ki 21:27).

36:26 *Jerahmeel, a son of the king.* This official's name, along with his title, has been found on a seal impression discovered in a burnt archive near Jerusalem. *son of the king.* Since Jehoiakim was only about 30 years old (see 2Ki 23:36), the phrase probably is not to be understood literally but means "member of the royal court" (as also in 38:6; 1Ki 22:26; Zep 1:8).

36:30 *Jehoiakim ... will have no one to sit on the throne.* His son Jehoiachin (see 2Ki 24:6) ruled only 3 months (see 2Ki 24:8) and then was captured and carried off to exile in Babylonia (see 2Ki 24:15), where he eventually died (see 52:33–34). *his body will be thrown out.* As punishment for the fact that he "threw" (v. 23) the prophet's scroll into the fire (see 22:18–19 and notes).

36:31 See 11:11; 19:15; 35:17. *attendants.* See note on v. 24.

36:32 *another scroll.* Cf. similarly Ex 34:1. *the scribe Baruch son of Neriah.* This precise identification has been found on two seal impressions (made with the same seal) discovered in the same burnt archive mentioned in the note on v. 26.

37:1—38:28 During the last two years of Zedekiah's reign (588–586 B.C.), Jeremiah is imprisoned by the authorities (see 20:2 and note).

37:1 See 2Ki 24:15,17–18. *Zedekiah.* Means "The LORD is my righteousness" (cf. note on 23:6). See Introduction: Background. *reigned in place of Jehoiachin.* In 597 B.C. This fulfills the prophecy concerning Jehoiakim in 36:30.

37:3 *Zedekiah ... sent ... to Jeremiah.* See 21:1. *Jehucal son of Shelemiah.* Later became Jeremiah's enemy (see 38:1,4). *the priest Zephaniah son of Maaseiah.* See 21:1 and note. *pray ... for us.* See 21:2 and note; perhaps to ask the Lord to make the temporary withdrawal of the Babylonians in 588 B.C. permanent (see note on 34:21–22).

37:5 *Pharaoh's army.* The troops of Hophra (see 44:30). *marched out of Egypt.* Probably to help Zedekiah at his request; Lachish ostracon 3 (see note on 34:7) mentions a visit to Egypt made by the commander of Judah's army. All such ploys by Zedekiah would fail, however (see Eze 17:15,17). *Babylonians ... withdrew.* To deal with the Egyptian threat (see 34:21 and note).

37:7 *Pharaoh's army ... will go back ... to Egypt.* Hophra would soon be defeated by Nebuchadnezzar (see note on Eze 30:21).

37:10 *wounded.* Lit. "pierced through," "mortally wounded." Though seriously handicapped, the Babylonians would still destroy Jerusalem.

tents, they would come out and burn[l] this
city down."

11 After the Babylonian army had withdrawn[m] from Jerusalem because of Pharaoh's army, 12 Jeremiah started to leave the
city to go to the territory of Benjamin to
get his share of the property[n] among the
people there. 13 But when he reached the
Benjamin Gate,[o] the captain of the guard,
whose name was Irijah son of Shelemiah,
the son of Hananiah, arrested him and
said, "You are deserting to the Babylonians!"[p]

14 "That's not true!" Jeremiah said. "I
am not deserting to the Babylonians." But
Irijah would not listen to him; instead, he
arrested[q] Jeremiah and brought him to the
officials. 15 They were angry with Jeremiah and had him beaten[r] and imprisoned[s]
in the house[t] of Jonathan the secretary,
which they had made into a prison.

16 Jeremiah was put into a vaulted cell
in a dungeon, where he remained a long
time. 17 Then King Zedekiah sent[u] for him
and had him brought to the palace, where
he asked[v] him privately,[w] "Is there any
word from the LORD?"

"Yes," Jeremiah replied, "you will be
handed over[x] to the king of Babylon."

18 Then Jeremiah said to King Zedekiah,
"What crime[y] have I committed against
you or your officials or this people, that
you have put me in prison? 19 Where are
your prophets[z] who prophesied to you,
'The king of Babylon will not attack you
or this land'? 20 But now, my lord the king,
please listen. Let me bring my petition
before you: Do not send me back to the
house of Jonathan the secretary, or I will
die there."[a]

21 King Zedekiah then gave orders for Jeremiah to be placed in the courtyard of the
guard and given bread from the street of
the bakers each day until all the bread[b] in
the city was gone.[c] So Jeremiah remained
in the courtyard of the guard.[d]

Jeremiah Thrown Into a Cistern

38 Shephatiah son of Mattan, Gedaliah son of Pashhur[e], Jehucal[a][f] son of
Shelemiah, and Pashhur son of Malkijah
heard what Jeremiah was telling all the
people when he said, 2 "This is what the
LORD says: 'Whoever stays in this city will
die by the sword, famine or plague,[g] but
whoever goes over to the Babylonians[b]
will live. He will escape with his life; he
will live.'[h] 3 And this is what the LORD says:
'This city will certainly be handed over to
the army of the king of Babylon, who will
capture it.' "[i]

4 Then the officials[j] said to the king,
"This man should be put to death.[k] He is
discouraging[l] the soldiers who are left in
this city, as well as all the people, by the
things he is saying to them. This man is
not seeking the good of these people but
their ruin."

5 "He is in your hands,"[m] King Zedekiah
answered. "The king can do nothing[n] to
oppose you."

6 So they took Jeremiah and put him
into the cistern of Malkijah, the king's
son, which was in the courtyard of the
guard.[o] They lowered Jeremiah by ropes[p]
into the cistern; it had no water in it,[q]
only mud, and Jeremiah sank down into
the mud.[r]

[a] *1* Hebrew *Jucal,* a variant of *Jehucal* [b] *2* Or *Chaldeans*; also in verses 18, 19 and 23

37:10 [l] Jer 21:10 **37:11** [m] ver 5 **37:12** [n] S Jer 32:9 **37:13** [o] S Jer 20:2 [p] Jer 21:9 **37:14** [q] Isa 58:6; Jer 40:4 **37:15** [r] S Jer 20:2; Heb 11:36 [s] S 1Ki 22:27 [t] ver 20; Jer 38:26 **37:17** [u] S ver 3 [v] S Ge 25:22; Jer 15:11 [w] Jer 38:16 [x] S Jer 21:7 **37:18** [y] S 1Sa 26:18; Jn 10:32; Ac 25:8 **37:19** [z] S Jer 14:13; Eze 13:2 **37:20** [a] S ver 15 **37:21** [b] S Lev 26:26; Isa 33:16; Jer 38:9; La 1:11 [c] S 2Ki 25:3 [d] Jer 32:2; 38:6, 13, 28; 39:13-14 **38:1** [e] S 1Ch 9:12 [f] Jer 37:3 **38:2** [g] Jer 34:17 [h] ver 17; S Jer 21:9; 39:18; 45:5 **38:3** [i] S Jer 21:4, 10 **38:4** [j] S Jer 36:12 [k] S Jer 11:21 [l] S 1Sa 17:32 **38:5** [m] S Jer 26:14 [n] 1Sa 15:24 **38:6** [o] S Jer 37:21 [p] S Jos 2:15 [q] S Ge 37:24 [r] S Job 30:19; La 3:53

37:12 *territory of Benjamin.* Where Jeremiah's hometown, Anathoth, was located (see note on 1:1). *get his share of the property.* While there was a brief lull in the Babylonian invasion, Jeremiah wanted to settle matters of estate with the other members of his family.

37:13 *Benjamin Gate.* See 38:7; see also note on Zec 14:10. *You are deserting to the Babylonians.* Irijah's fear was understandable, since Jeremiah recommended surrendering to the Babylonians (see 21:9; 38:2) and since many Judahites in fact defected (see 38:19; 39:9; 52:15).

37:14 *That's not true!* Lit. "A lie" (see 2Ki 9:12).

37:15 *had him beaten.* See 20:2 and note. *house of Jonathan.* Jeremiah would later look back on this prison as a place of great danger for him (see v. 20; 38:26).

37:16 *dungeon.* Lit. "house of the cistern" (see Ex 12:29).

37:17 *Zedekiah ... asked him privately.* Not wanting to do so in the presence of his officials, whom he apparently feared (see note on 38:5). *you will be handed over to the king of Babylon.* See 32:4; 34:3.

37:19 *your prophets.* False prophets (see Dt 18:22 and note).

37:20 *bring my petition before you.* See 36:7.

37:21 *courtyard of the guard.* A less objectionable prison than the dungeon of v. 16 (see note on 32:2). *street of the bakers.* Perhaps near the Tower of the Ovens (see note on Ne 3:11). *until all the bread ... was gone.* The Hebrew word for "bread" is translated "food" in 52:6.

38:1 *Pashhur.* See note on 20:1. *Jehucal son of Shelemiah.* See note on 37:3. *Pashhur son of Malkijah.* See note on 21:1. *Jeremiah was telling all the people.* Though he was confined in the courtyard of the guard (see 37:21), he was allowed to have visitors and to speak freely to them (see 32:8,12).

38:2 Echoes 21:9 (see note there).

38:3 Echoes 32:28 (see 34:2; 37:8).

38:4 *officials.* Those named in v. 1. *discouraging.* See Ezr 4:4; lit. "weakening the hands of," as in a similar situation in Lachish ostracon 6 (see note on 34:7): "The words of the officials are not good; they serve only to weaken our hands." Contrast Isa 35:3. *seeking the good.* The Hebrew underlying this phrase is translated "seek the peace and prosperity" in 29:7 (see note there). *good ... ruin.* The Hebrew for these words is translated "prosperity ... disaster" in Isa 45:7.

38:5 *The king can do nothing.* Not because of inability or lack of authority but through failure of nerve. He feared his own officials (see vv. 25–26; see also 37:17 and note).

38:6 *cistern.* A pit with a relatively small opening at the top (see 37:16 and note). *king's son.* See note on 36:26. *cistern ... had no water in it.* Zedekiah's officials wanted to kill Jeremiah (see v. 4), but not by taking his life with their own hands (cf. Ge 37:20–24).

7But Ebed-Melech,[s] a Cushite,[a] an official[b t] in the royal palace, heard that they
had put Jeremiah into the cistern. While
the king was sitting in the Benjamin Gate,[u]
8Ebed-Melech went out of the palace and
said to him, 9"My lord the king, these
men have acted wickedly in all they have
done to Jeremiah the prophet. They have
thrown him into a cistern,[v] where he will
starve to death when there is no longer
any bread[w] in the city."
10Then the king commanded Ebed-Melech the Cushite, "Take thirty men from
here with you and lift Jeremiah the prophet out of the cistern before he dies."
11So Ebed-Melech took the men with
him and went to a room under the treasury in the palace. He took some old rags
and worn-out clothes from there and let
them down with ropes[x] to Jeremiah in the
cistern. 12Ebed-Melech the Cushite said to
Jeremiah, "Put these old rags and worn-
out clothes under your arms to pad the
ropes." Jeremiah did so, 13and they pulled
him up with the ropes and lifted him out
of the cistern. And Jeremiah remained in
the courtyard of the guard.[y]

Zedekiah Questions Jeremiah Again

14Then King Zedekiah sent[z] for Jeremiah
the prophet and had him brought to the
third entrance to the temple of the LORD. "I
am going to ask you something," the king
said to Jeremiah. "Do not hide[a] anything
from me."
15Jeremiah said to Zedekiah, "If I give
you an answer, will you not kill me? Even
if I did give you counsel, you would not
listen to me."
16But King Zedekiah swore this oath secretly[b] to Jeremiah: "As surely as the LORD
lives, who has given us breath,[c] I will neither kill you nor hand you over to those
who are seeking your life."[d]

38:7 [s]Jer 39:16 [t]*fn* Isa 56:3-5; Ac 8:27 [u]S Job 29:7 **38:9** [v]S Ge 37:20 [w]S Jer 37:21 **38:11** [x]S Jos 2:15 **38:13** [y]S Jer 37:21 **38:14** [z]S Jer 37:3 [a]S 1Sa 3:17 **38:16** [b]Jer 37:17 [c]Isa 42:5; 57:16 [d]ver 4 **38:17** [e]Jer 27:8 [f]S Jer 21:9 **38:18** [g]ver 3 [h]S Jer 37:8 [i]S Jer 24:8; S 32:4 **38:19** [j]Isa 51:12; Jn 12:42 [k]Jer 39:9; 52:15 **38:20** [l]Jer 11:4 [m]S Dt 5:33; Jer 40:9 [n]Isa 55:3 **38:22** [o]S Jer 6:12 [p]S Job 19:14; S Jer 13:21 [q]S Job 30:19; Ps 69:14 **38:23** [r]S 2Ki 25:6 [s]S Jer 32:4; Eze 17:15 [t]S Jer 24:8 [u]Jer 21:10; 37:8 **38:24** [v]Jer 37:17

17Then Jeremiah said to Zedekiah, "This
is what the LORD God Almighty, the God of
Israel, says: 'If you surrender[e] to the officers of the king of Babylon, your life will
be spared and this city will not be burned
down; you and your family will live.[f] 18But
if you will not surrender to the officers of
the king of Babylon, this city will be handed over[g] to the Babylonians and they will
burn[h] it down; you yourself will not escape[i] from their hands.' "
19King Zedekiah said to Jeremiah, "I am
afraid[j] of the Jews who have gone over[k] to
the Babylonians, for the Babylonians may
hand me over to them and they will mistreat me."
20"They will not hand you over," Jeremiah replied. "Obey[l] the LORD by doing what
I tell you. Then it will go well[m] with you,
and your life[n] will be spared. 21But if you
refuse to surrender, this is what the LORD
has revealed to me: 22All the women[o] left
in the palace of the king of Judah will be
brought out to the officials of the king of
Babylon. Those women will say to you:

" 'They misled you and overcame
you—
those trusted friends[p] of yours.
Your feet are sunk in the mud;[q]
your friends have deserted you.'

23"All your wives and children[r] will be
brought out to the Babylonians. You yourself will not escape[s] from their hands but
will be captured[t] by the king of Babylon;
and this city will[c] be burned down."[u]
24Then Zedekiah said to Jeremiah, "Do
not let anyone know[v] about this conversation, or you may die. 25If the officials hear
that I talked with you, and they come to
you and say, 'Tell us what you said to the
king and what the king said to you; do not

[a] 7 Probably from the upper Nile region [b] 7 Or *a eunuch* [c] 23 Or *and you will cause this city to*

38:7 *Ebed-Melech.* Means "king's servant." *king was sitting in the Benjamin Gate.* See 37:13; see also note on Zec 14:10. Since a city gateway was often used as a courtroom or town hall (see notes on Ge 19:1; Ru 4:1), Zedekiah may have been settling various legal complaints on this occasion (see 2Sa 15:2–4) and would therefore be in a position to help Ebed-Melech.
38:9 *no longer any bread in the city.* See 37:21 and note.
38:10 *thirty men.* The large number was probably to keep the officials (see v. 4) and their friends from trying to prevent Jeremiah's rescue.
38:11 *room under the treasury.* Perhaps a wardrobe storeroom (see 2Ki 10:22).
38:12 *Put these old rags … to pad the ropes.* Ebed-Melech's kindnesses to Jeremiah were evidence that he trusted in the Lord, and the Lord rewarded him (see 39:15–18).
38:13 *remained in the courtyard of the guard.* See note on 32:2.
38:14–26 Jeremiah's final interview with King Zedekiah.
38:14 *third entrance.* Mentioned only here; perhaps the king's private access to the temple.
38:16 *As surely as the LORD lives.* See note on Ge 42:15. *those who are seeking your life.* Zedekiah's officials (see v. 4 and note).
38:17–18 See vv. 2–3; 21:9–10; 32:3–4; 34:2–5. *surrender.* Lit. "come out" (see 2Ki 18:31; 24:12). *officers of the king of Babylon.* Those in charge of the siege of Jerusalem (see 39:3,13).
38:19 *I am afraid.* See v. 5 and note. If Zedekiah had trusted in the Lord, he would not have had to fear either officials or deserters (see Pr 29:25 and note). *gone over to the Babylonians.* See 37:13 and note. *mistreat me.* Do violence to me (see Jdg 19:25; 1Ch 10:4).
38:22 *women … in the palace … brought out to the officials.* Women in a conquered king's harem became the property of the conquerors (cf. 2Sa 16:21–22). *misled you and overcame you—those trusted friends of yours.* Repeated almost verbatim in Ob 7 (see 20:10 and note). Zedekiah's so-called friends were his officials (see v. 4) and false prophets (see 37:19). *feet are sunk in the mud.* Symbolic of great distress (see Ps 69:14).

hide it from us or we will kill you,' 26then tell[w] them, 'I was pleading with the king not to send me back to Jonathan's house[x] to die there.' "

27All the officials did come to Jeremiah and question him, and he told them everything the king had ordered him to say. So they said no more to him, for no one had heard his conversation with the king.

28And Jeremiah remained in the courtyard of the guard[y] until the day Jerusalem was captured.

The Fall of Jerusalem

39:1-10pp — 2Ki 25:1-12; Jer 52:4-16

39 This is how Jerusalem[z] was taken: 1In the ninth year of Zedekiah[a] king of Judah, in the tenth month, Nebuchadnezzar[b] king of Babylon marched against Jerusalem with his whole army and laid siege[c] to it. 2And on the ninth day of the fourth[d] month of Zedekiah's eleventh year, the city wall[e] was broken through.[f] 3Then all the officials[g] of the king of Babylon came and took seats in the Middle Gate: Nergal-Sharezer of Samgar, Nebo-Sarsekim[a] a chief officer, Nergal-Sharezer a high official and all the other officials of the king of Babylon. 4When Zedekiah king of Judah and all the soldiers saw them, they fled; they left the city at night by way of the king's garden, through the gate between the two walls,[h] and headed toward the Arabah.[b][i]

5But the Babylonian[c] army pursued them and overtook Zedekiah[j] in the plains of Jericho. They captured[k] him and took him to Nebuchadnezzar king of Babylon at Riblah[l] in the land of Hamath, where he pronounced sentence on him. 6There at Riblah the king of Babylon slaughtered the sons of Zedekiah before his eyes and also killed all the nobles[m] of Judah. 7Then he put out Zedekiah's eyes[n] and bound him with bronze shackles to take him to Babylon.[o]

8The Babylonians[d] set fire[p] to the royal palace and the houses of the people and broke down the walls[q] of Jerusalem. 9Nebuzaradan commander of the imperial guard carried into exile to Babylon the people who remained in the city, along with those who had gone over to him,[r] and the rest of the people.[s] 10But Nebuzaradan the commander of the guard left behind in the land of Judah some of the poor people, who owned nothing; and at that time he gave them vineyards and fields.

11Now Nebuchadnezzar king of Babylon had given these orders about Jeremiah through Nebuzaradan commander of the imperial guard: 12"Take him and look after him; don't harm[t] him but do for him whatever he asks." 13So Nebuzaradan the commander of the guard, Nebushazban a chief officer, Nergal-Sharezer a high official and all the other officers[u] of the king of Babylon 14sent and had Jeremiah taken out of the courtyard of the guard.[v] They turned him over to Gedaliah[w] son of Ahikam,[x] the son of Shaphan,[y] to take him back to his home. So he remained among his own people.[z]

38:26 [w] 1Sa 16:2 [x] S Jer 37:15 **38:28** [y] S Jer 37:21 **39:1** [z] S Jer 25:29 [a] S 2Ch 36:11 [b] S 2Ki 24:1; S Jer 28:14 [c] S 2Ki 25:1; Jer 52:4; Eze 4:3; 24:2 **39:2** [d] Zec 8:19 [e] S 2Ki 14:13 [f] Eze 33:21 **39:3** [g] ver 13; Jer 21:4 **39:4** [h] S Isa 22:11 [i] Eze 12:12 **39:5** [j] S Jer 24:8; S 32:4 [k] S Jer 21:7 [l] S Nu 34:11 **39:6** [m] S Isa 34:12 **39:7** [n] S Nu 16:14; Eze 12:13 [o] S Jer 2:35 **39:8** [p] S Jer 34:22 [q] S Ne 1:3; S Ps 80:12; S Isa 22:5; La 2:8 **39:9** [r] Jer 21:9 [s] Jer 40:1; La 1:5 **39:12** [t] S Pr 16:7; Jer 15:20-21; 1Pe 3:13 **39:13** [u] S ver 3 **39:14** [v] S Ne 3:25; Jer 37:21 [w] S 2Ki 25:22 [x] S 2Ki 22:12 [y] S 2Ki 22:3 [z] Jer 40:5

[a] 3 Or *Nergal-Sharezer, Samgar-Nebo, Sarsekim* [b] 4 Or *the Jordan Valley* [c] 5 Or *Chaldean* [d] 8 Or *Chaldeans*

38:26 See 37:20. *Jonathan's house.* See 37:15 and note.

38:27 *told them everything the king had ordered him to say.* Jeremiah was not obliged to give the officials the other information, which had been shared in confidence.

38:28 *remained in the courtyard of the guard.* See v. 13; see also note on 32:2.

39:1 — 45:5 The most detailed account in the OT of the Babylonian conquest of Jerusalem and its aftermath. The section concludes with a brief appendix (ch. 45).

39:1 – 10 A vivid summary of the siege and fall of Jerusalem and of the exile of its inhabitants (see 52:4 – 27).

39:1 – 2 Summarizes 52:4 – 7a.

39:1 *ninth year of Zedekiah … tenth month.* The final Babylonian siege of Jerusalem began on the tenth day of the month (see 52:4; 2Ki 25:1; Eze 24:1 – 2), or Jan. 15, 588 B.C.

39:2 *ninth day … fourth month … eleventh year.* July 18, 586 B.C. (see 52:5 – 6; 2Ki 25:2 – 3). The siege lasted just over two and a half years.

39:3 *took seats in the Middle Gate.* In fulfillment of 1:15. The Middle Gate may have been located in the wall separating the citadel of Mount Zion from the lower city, therefore serving as a strategic vantage point for the invaders. *Nergal-Sharezer.* Means "Nergal [a god; see 2Ki 17:30], protect the king." One of the two men so named here (see v. 13) is probably Neriglissar, who later became a successor of Nebuchadnezzar as ruler of Babylonia (560 – 556 B.C.). *Nebo-Sarsekim a chief officer.* In 2007 this man's name, along with his title, was found on a clay tablet in London's British Museum collection. The name means "Nabu [a god; see note on 2Ki 24:1] has preserved his kingship." The date on the tablet is Nebuchadnezzar's tenth year (595 B.C., seven years before the siege of Jerusalem began; see v. 1 and note). *chief officer.* See v. 13; see also note on 2Ki 18:17. *high official.* See v. 13. The Hebrew for this phrase is cognate to Babylonian *rab mu(n)gi,* a high military official who sometimes served as an envoy to foreign rulers.

39:4 – 7 See 52:7 – 11; see also 2Ki 25:4 – 7 and notes.

39:4 *Arabah.* See note on Dt 1:1.

39:5 *plains.* The Hebrew for this word is the plural of the word for "Arabah" (v. 4).

39:8 – 10 See 52:12 – 16; see also 2Ki 25:8 – 12 and notes.

39:12 *look after him.* See note on 40:4.

39:14 *had Jeremiah taken out.* Either (1) a summary statement of Jeremiah's release from prison, the specific details of which are given in 40:1 – 6; or (2) a brief description of the first of two releases, the second of which (made necessary because Jeremiah had been arrested again by mistake in the confusion surrounding the capture and transporting of thousands of exiles) is detailed in 40:1 – 6. *courtyard of the guard.* See note on 32:2. *Gedaliah son of Ahikam, the son of Shaphan.* See note on 26:24. *his home.* The governor's residence. An early sixth-century seal impression found at Lachish reads: "Belonging to Gedaliah [probably the man named in this verse], who is over the house."

15 While Jeremiah had been confined
in the courtyard of the guard, the word
of the LORD came to him: 16 "Go and tell
Ebed-Melech[a] the Cushite, 'This is what
the LORD Almighty, the God of Israel, says:
I am about to fulfill my words[b] against this
city through disaster,[c] not prosperity. At
that time they will be fulfilled before your
eyes. 17 But I will rescue[d] you on that day,
declares the LORD; you will not be handed
over to those you fear. 18 I will save[e] you;
you will not fall by the sword[f] but will escape with your life,[g] because you trust[h] in
me, declares the LORD.' "

Jeremiah Freed

40 The word came to Jeremiah from the
LORD after Nebuzaradan commander
of the imperial guard had released him at
Ramah.[i] He had found Jeremiah bound in
chains among all the captives[j] from Jerusalem and Judah who were being carried
into exile to Babylon. 2 When the commander[k] of the guard found Jeremiah, he
said to him, "The LORD your God decreed[l]
this disaster[m] for this place.[n] 3 And now the
LORD has brought it about; he has done
just as he said he would. All this happened
because you people sinned[o] against the
LORD and did not obey[p] him. 4 But today I
am freeing[q] you from the chains[r] on your
wrists. Come with me to Babylon, if you
like, and I will look after you; but if you do
not want to, then don't come. Look, the
whole country lies before you; go wherever you please."[s] 5 However, before Jeremiah turned to go,[a] Nebuzaradan added,
"Go back to Gedaliah[t] son of Ahikam,[u] the
son of Shaphan, whom the king of Babylon has appointed[v] over the towns[w] of Judah, and live with him among the people,
or go anywhere else you please."[x]

Then the commander gave him provisions and a present[y] and let him go. 6 So
Jeremiah went to Gedaliah son of Ahikam
at Mizpah[z] and stayed with him among the
people who were left behind in the land.

Gedaliah Assassinated

40:7-9; 41:1-3pp — 2Ki 25:22-26

7 When all the army officers and their
men who were still in the open country
heard that the king of Babylon had appointed Gedaliah son of Ahikam as governor[a] over the land and had put him in
charge of the men, women and children
who were the poorest[b] in the land and who
had not been carried into exile to Babylon,
8 they came to Gedaliah at Mizpah[c]—Ishmael[d] son of Nethaniah, Johanan[e] and
Jonathan the sons of Kareah, Seraiah son
of Tanhumeth, the sons of Ephai the Netophathite,[f] and Jaazaniah[b] the son of the
Maacathite,[g] and their men. 9 Gedaliah son
of Ahikam, the son of Shaphan, took an
oath to reassure them and their men. "Do
not be afraid to serve[h] the Babylonians,[c i]"
he said. "Settle down in the land and serve
the king of Babylon, and it will go well
with you.[j] 10 I myself will stay at Mizpah[k]
to represent you before the Babylonians
who come to us, but you are to harvest the
wine,[l] summer fruit and oil, and put them
in your storage jars,[m] and live in the towns
you have taken over."[n]

11 When all the Jews in Moab,[o] Ammon,
Edom[p] and all the other countries[q] heard
that the king of Babylon had left a remnant in Judah and had appointed Gedaliah son of Ahikam, the son of Shaphan, as
governor over them, 12 they all came back
to the land of Judah, to Gedaliah at Mizpah, from all the countries where they had
been scattered.[r] And they harvested an
abundance of wine and summer fruit.

13 Johanan[s] son of Kareah and all the
army officers still in the open country came

[a] 5 Or *Jeremiah answered* [b] 8 Hebrew *Jezaniah,* a variant of *Jaazaniah* [c] 9 Or *Chaldeans*; also in verse 10

39:16 [a] Jer 38:7 [b] Ps 33:11; Isa 14:27; 40:8; Jer 44:28; La 2:17; S Mt 1:22 [c] S Jos 23:15; Jer 21:10 **39:17** [d] Ps 34:22; 41:1-2 **39:18** [e] S 1Sa 17:47; Ac 16:31 [f] S Job 5:20 [g] S Jer 21:9; S 38:2 [h] S Jer 17:7; Ro 10:11 **40:1** [i] S Jos 18:25; 1Sa 8:4; Mt 2:18 [j] S Dt 21:10; S 2Ki 24:1; S 2Ch 36:10; Na 3:10 **40:2** [k] Ro 13:4 [l] S Isa 10:22 [m] S 2Ch 34:24; S Ps 18:18; S Pr 8:36; Gal 6:7-8 [n] S Jos 23:15 **40:3** [o] S Pr 13:21; Ro 6:23; Jas 1:15 [p] S Lev 26:33; Dt 28:45-52; 29:24-28; 31:17-18; S 1Ki 9:9; Jer 22:8-9; Da 9:14; Ac 7:39; Ro 2:5-9 **40:4** [q] Ps 105:18-20; S Jer 37:14 [r] La 3:7 [s] S Ge 13:9 **40:5** [t] S 2Ki 25:22 [u] 2Ki 22:12-14 [v] Ne 5:14; Jer 41:2 [w] Jer 44:2; Zec 1:12 [x] Jer 39:14 [y] S Ge 32:20; S 1Sa 9:7 **40:6** [z] ver 10; Jdg 20:1; 1Sa 7:5-17 **40:7** [a] S Ge 41:41; S Ne 5:14 [b] S 2Ki 24:14; S Ac 24:17; Jas 2:5 **40:8** [c] ver 13 [d] ver 14; Jer 41:1, 2 [e] ver 15; Jer 41:11 [f] S 2Sa 23:28 [g] S Dt 3:14 **40:9** [h] Jer 5:19; 27:11; Ro 13:1-2; Eph 6:5-8 [i] Eze 23:23 [j] S Jer 38:20; La 1:1 **40:10** [k] S ver 6 [l] S Ge 27:28; S Ex 23:16 [m] Ex 7:19; 2Co 4:7 [n] Dt 1:39 **40:11** [o] S Nu 21:11; 25:1 [p] S Ge 25:30 [q] Jer 12:14 **40:12** [r] Jer 43:5 **40:13** [s] Jer 42:1

39:15 – 18 See note on 38:12.

39:16 *Go and tell.* Though confined in prison, Jeremiah was permitted to have visitors (see note on 38:1). *I am about to fulfill my words against this city.* See 19:15.

39:17 *those you fear.* The court officials (see 38:1) who, in Ebed-Melech's judgment, had "acted wickedly" (38:9).

39:18 *escape with your life.* See note on 21:9. *you trust in me.* Ebed-Melech had expressed his faith in God by securing Jeremiah's release from the cistern (see 38:7 – 13; see also note on 38:12).

40:1 — 44:30 A lively narrative of the aftermath of the fall of Jerusalem. Chronologically, the chapters are the latest in the book (although 52:31 – 34 is later, it is part of the appendix and not of the book proper).

40:1 *The word came.* A heading introducing the prophecies of Jeremiah after the exile, just as "The word ... came" (1:2) introduces his prophecies from the time of his call up to the exile (see 1:3). *Nebuzaradan ... released him.* See note on 39:14. *Ramah.* See note on 31:15. *chains.* Manacles that were fastened to the wrists (see v. 4; see also Job 36:8; Isa 45:14).

40:2 – 3 Nebuzaradan doubtless knew the basic content of Jeremiah's prophetic message against Jerusalem, and he here repeats it to the prophet in summary fashion.

40:4 *I will look after you.* Nebuzaradan promises to carry out Nebuchadnezzar's wishes concerning Jeremiah (see 39:12). *the whole country lies before you.* Cf. Abram's offer to Lot in Ge 13:9.

40:5 – 9 See 2Ki 25:22 – 24 and notes.

40:5 *Gedaliah son of Ahikam.* See note on 26:24. *provisions.* The Hebrew for this word is translated "allowance" in 52:34.

40:8 *Jaazaniah.* See note on 2Ki 25:23.

40:10 *harvest the wine, summer fruit and oil.* Nebuzaradan (see 39:9) had arrived in Jerusalem in August of 586 B.C. (see note on 2Ki 25:8). Grapes, figs and olives were harvested in the Holy Land during August and September.

to Gedaliah at Mizpah[t] 14and said to him, "Don't you know that Baalis king of the Ammonites[u] has sent Ishmael[v] son of Nethaniah to take your life?" But Gedaliah son of Ahikam did not believe them.

15Then Johanan[w] son of Kareah said privately to Gedaliah in Mizpah, "Let me go and kill[x] Ishmael son of Nethaniah, and no one will know it. Why should he take your life and cause all the Jews who are gathered around you to be scattered[y] and the remnant[z] of Judah to perish?"

16But Gedaliah son of Ahikam said to Johanan[a] son of Kareah, "Don't do such a thing! What you are saying about Ishmael is not true."

41 In the seventh month Ishmael[b] son of Nethaniah, the son of Elishama, who was of royal blood and had been one of the king's officers, came with ten men to Gedaliah son of Ahikam at Mizpah. While they were eating together there, 2Ishmael[c] son of Nethaniah and the ten men who were with him got up and struck down Gedaliah son of Ahikam, the son of Shaphan, with the sword,[d] killing the one whom the king of Babylon had appointed[e] as governor over the land.[f] 3Ishmael also killed all the Jews who were with Gedaliah at Mizpah, as well as the Babylonian[a] soldiers who were there.

4The day after Gedaliah's assassination, before anyone knew about it, 5eighty men who had shaved off their beards,[g] torn their clothes[h] and cut[i] themselves came from Shechem,[j] Shiloh[k] and Samaria,[l] bringing grain offerings and incense[m] with them to the house of the LORD.[n] 6Ishmael son of Nethaniah went out from Mizpah to meet them, weeping[o] as he went. When he met them, he said, "Come to Gedaliah son of Ahikam."[p] 7When they went into the city, Ishmael son of Nethaniah and the men who were with him slaughtered them and threw them into a cistern.[q] 8But ten of them said to Ishmael, "Don't kill us! We have wheat and barley, oil and honey, hidden in a field."[r] So he let them alone and did not kill them with the others. 9Now the cistern where he threw all the bodies of the men he had killed along with Gedaliah was the one King Asa[s] had made as part of his defense[t] against Baasha[u] king of Israel. Ishmael son of Nethaniah filled it with the dead.

10Ishmael made captives of all the rest of the people[v] who were in Mizpah—the king's daughters[w] along with all the others who were left there, over whom Nebuzaradan commander of the imperial guard had appointed Gedaliah son of Ahikam. Ishmael son of Nethaniah took them captive and set out to cross over to the Ammonites.[x]

11When Johanan[y] son of Kareah and all the army officers who were with him heard about all the crimes Ishmael son of Nethaniah had committed, 12they took all their men and went to fight[z] Ishmael son of Nethaniah. They caught up with him near the great pool[a] in Gibeon. 13When all the people[b] Ishmael had with him saw Johanan son of Kareah and the army officers who were with him, they were glad. 14All

[a] 3 Or *Chaldean*

40:13 [t]ver 8 **40:14** [u]S Ge 19:38; 2Sa 10:1-19; Jer 25:21; 41:10; 49:1 [v]S ver 8 **40:15** [w]S ver 8 [x]S Dt 5:17; Mt 5:21-22 [y]S Ge 11:4; S Lev 26:33; Mt 26:31; Jn 11:52; Jas 1:1 [z]S 2Ki 21:14; S Isa 1:9; Ro 11:5 **40:16** [a]Jer 43:2 **41:1** [b]S Jer 40:8 **41:2** [c]Ps 41:9; 109:5 [d]S Jos 11:10; Jer 40:15; Heb 11:37 [e]S Jer 40:5 [f]2Sa 3:27; 20:9-10; S Jer 40:8 **41:5** [g]S Lev 19:27; Jer 47:5; 48:37 [h]S Ge 37:29; S Lev 10:6; S Mk 14:63 [i]S Lev 19:28 [j]Ge 12:6; 33:18; Jdg 9:1-57; 1Ki 12:1 [k]S Jos 18:1 [l]1Ki 16:24 [m]S Nu 16:40; S Lk 1:9 [n]1Ki 3:2; 6:38; 2Ki 25:9 **41:6** [o]2Sa 3:16 [p]Ps 5:9; Hos 7:11; Rev 20:10 **41:7** [q]S Ge 37:24; 2Ki 10:14 **41:8** [r]Isa 45:3 **41:9** [s]S 1Ki 15:22; S 2Ch 16:6 [t]S Jdg 6:2 [u]S 2Ch 16:1

41:10 [v]Jer 40:7,12 [w]Jer 38:23 [x]S Jer 40:14 **41:11** [y]S Jer 40:8 **41:12** [z]S Ex 14:14; Jn 18:36 [a]S Jos 9:3; Jn 9:7 **41:13** [b]ver 10

40:14 *Baalis.* Three royal inscriptions have been found that may relate to this king: (1) "King Ba'lay," as his name is written on an early sixth-century B.C. bottle discovered in Jordan; (2) "Ba'al-Yasha," an Ammonite king whose name appears on a stamp seal found at Tell el-Umeiri in Jordan in 1984; (3) "Baalis king of [the Ammonites]," as his name reads on an Ammonite stamp seal that came to light in 1998. *Ammonites.* Ammon was among the nations that earlier had been allies against Babylonia (see 27:3 and note; see also Eze 21:18–32).

40:15 *privately.* See note on 38:16. *remnant.* See note on 6:9.

40:16 *not true.* Lit. "a lie" (see 37:14 and note). Gedaliah's naive faith in Ishmael's integrity would cost him his life (see 41:2).

41:1–3 See 2Ki 25:25 and note.

41:1 *one of the king's officers.* Ishmael's loyalty to Zedekiah might explain his assassination of Gedaliah, whom he considered to be a Babylonian puppet ruler. *they were eating together.* Ancient custom with respect to hospitality probably made Gedaliah assume that his guests would not harm him, much less kill him (see note on Jdg 4:21).

41:5 *shaved off their beards, torn their clothes and cut themselves.* Signs of mourning (see 16:6 and note; see also note on Ezr 9:3), probably over the destruction of Jerusalem. *came.* In the "seventh month" (v. 1) to celebrate the Feast of Tabernacles (see note on Ex 23:16). *Shechem, Shiloh and Samaria.* Formerly worship centers in the north (see notes on 7:12; Ge 12:6; see also Jos 24:25–26). After the northern kingdom was destroyed in 722–721 B.C., many Israelites made periodic pilgrimages to Jerusalem, especially during the reform movements of Hezekiah (see 2Ch 30:11) and Josiah (see 2Ch 34:9). *grain offerings and incense.* Bloodless offerings, since the altar of the Jerusalem temple had been destroyed. *house of the LORD.* Though the temple itself was in ruins, the site was still considered holy.

41:6 *weeping.* Pretending to share the sorrow of the mourners from the north.

41:7 *the city.* Mizpah. *cistern.* A favorite place to dispose of victims, whether living or dead (see 37:16 and note; 38:6).

41:8 *wheat and barley, oil and honey.* Supplies that Ishmael perhaps would have taken with him when he fled to Ammon (see v. 15).

41:9 *the cistern ... was the one King Asa had made.* Probably as part of the fortifications Asa had built at Mizpah (see 1Ki 15:22), since cisterns were essential for storing water during times of siege. Archaeologists have discovered numerous cisterns in the ruins of ancient Mizpah (modern Tell en-Nasbeh, seven and a half miles north of Jerusalem).

41:10 *king's daughters.* Women who had been members of King Zedekiah's court, not necessarily daughters of the king himself (see note on 36:26). *Ammonites.* See 40:14 and note.

41:12 *great pool in Gibeon.* Perhaps the same as the one mentioned in 2Sa 2:13 (see note there).

the people Ishmael had taken captive at Mizpah[c] turned and went over to Johanan son of Kareah. 15 But Ishmael son of Nethaniah and eight of his men escaped[d] from Johanan and fled to the Ammonites.

Flight to Egypt

16 Then Johanan son of Kareah and all the army officers[e] who were with him led away all the survivors[f] from Mizpah whom he had recovered from Ishmael son of Nethaniah after he had assassinated Gedaliah son of Ahikam: the soldiers, women, children and court officials he had brought from Gibeon. 17 And they went on, stopping at Geruth Kimham[g] near Bethlehem[h] on their way to Egypt[i] 18 to escape the Babylonians.[a] They were afraid[j] of them because Ishmael son of Nethaniah had killed Gedaliah[k] son of Ahikam, whom the king of Babylon had appointed as governor over the land.

42 Then all the army officers, including Johanan[l] son of Kareah and Jezaniah[b] son of Hoshaiah,[m] and all the people from the least to the greatest[n] approached 2 Jeremiah the prophet and said to him, "Please hear our petition and pray[o] to the LORD your God for this entire remnant.[p] For as you now see, though we were once many, now only a few[q] are left. 3 Pray that the LORD your God will tell us where we should go and what we should do."[r]

4 "I have heard you," replied Jeremiah the prophet. "I will certainly pray[s] to the LORD your God as you have requested; I will tell[t] you everything the LORD says and will keep nothing back from you."[u]

5 Then they said to Jeremiah, "May the LORD be a true[v] and faithful[w] witness[x] against us if we do not act in accordance with everything the LORD your God sends you to tell us. 6 Whether it is favorable or unfavorable, we will obey the LORD our God, to whom we are sending you, so that it will go well[y] with us, for we will obey[z] the LORD our God."

7 Ten days later the word of the LORD came to Jeremiah. 8 So he called together Johanan son of Kareah and all the army officers[a] who were with him and all the people from the least to the greatest.[b] 9 He said to them, "This is what the LORD, the God of Israel, to whom you sent me to present your petition,[c] says:[d] 10 'If you stay in this land,[e] I will build[f] you up and not tear you down; I will plant[g] you and not uproot you,[h] for I am grieved over the disaster I have inflicted on you.[i] 11 Do not be afraid of the king of Babylon,[j] whom you now fear.[k] Do not be afraid of him, declares the LORD, for I am with you and will save[l] you and deliver you from his hands.[m] 12 I will show you compassion[n] so that he will have compassion on you and restore you to your land.'[o]

13 "However, if you say, 'We will not stay in this land,' and so disobey[p] the LORD your God, 14 and if you say, 'No, we will go and live in Egypt,[q] where we will not see war or hear the trumpet[r] or be hungry for bread,'[s] 15 then hear the word of the LORD,[t] O remnant of Judah. This is what the LORD Almighty, the God of Israel, says: 'If you are determined to go to Egypt and you do go to settle there, 16 then the sword[u] you fear[v] will overtake you there, and the famine[w] you dread will follow you into Egypt, and there you will die.[x] 17 Indeed, all who are determined to go to Egypt to settle there will die by the sword, famine and plague;[y] not one of them will survive or escape the disaster I will bring on them.' 18 This is what the LORD Almighty, the God of Israel, says: 'As my anger and wrath[z] have been poured out on those who lived

41:14 [c] Jer 40:6 **41:15** [d] Job 21:30; S Pr 28:17 **41:16** [e] Jer 42:1; 43:2 [f] Isa 1:9; Jer 43:4; Eze 7:16; 14:22; Zep 2:9 **41:17** [g] 2Sa 19:37 [h] Ge 35:19; Mic 5:2 [i] Jer 42:14 **41:18** [j] S Nu 14:9; Isa 51:12; Jer 42:16; Lk 12:4-5 [k] S 2Ki 25:22 **42:1** [l] S Jer 40:13 [m] S Jer 41:16 [n] Jer 6:13; 44:12 **42:2** [o] S Ge 20:7; S Jer 36:7; Ac 8:24; Jas 5:16 [p] S Isa 1:9 [q] S Lev 26:22; La 1:1 **42:3** [r] ver 20; Ps 86:11; S Pr 3:6; S Jer 15:11 **42:4** [s] Ex 8:29; 1Sa 12:23 [t] S Jer 1:17 [u] S Nu 22:18; S 1Sa 3:17 **42:5** [v] 1Ki 22:16; Ps 119:160; Ro 3:4 [w] S Dt 7:9; Jn 8:26; S 1Co 1:9 [x] S Ge 31:48; S Dt 4:26; S Isa 1:2; S Ro 1:9; Rev 1:5 **42:6** [y] Dt 5:29; 6:3; Jer 7:23; 22:15 [z] S ver 19; S Ex 24:7; S Jos 24:24 **42:8** [a] ver 1 [b] Jer 41:16; S Mk 9:35; Lk 7:28; Heb 8:11 **42:9** [c] ver 2 [d] 2Ki 22:15 **42:10** [e] Jer 43:4 [f] S Jer 24:6 [g] S Dt 30:9 [h] S Dt 29:28; Ecc 3:2; Jer 45:4; Eze 36:36; Da 11:4 [i] S 2Ch 34:24; Isa 30:26; S Jer 18:8 **42:11** [j] Jer 27:11 [k] S Nu 14:9; S 1Sa 15:24; Ps 23:4; Mt 10:28; 2Ti 1:7 [l] Ps 18:27; 69:35; S 119:94; S Isa 63:1; Heb 7:25 [m] S Ps 3:7; S Pr 20:22; S Jer 1:8; Ro 8:31 **42:12** [n] S Ex 3:21; S 2Sa 24:14; 2Co 1:3 [o] S Ge 31:3; S Ne 1:9; Ps 106:44-46 **42:13** [p] S Dt 11:28 **42:14** [q] Nu 11:4-5; S Dt 17:16; S Isa 30:2 [r] S Jos 6:20; S Mt 24:31 [s] S Dt 8:3; 1Sa 2:5; Pr 10:3; Isa 65:13; Mt 4:2-4 **42:15** [t] Jer 44:24 **42:16** [u] S Lev 26:33; Eze 11:8; 14:17 [v] S Jer 41:18 [w] S Ge 41:55 [x] S Ge 2:17; 2Ch 25:4; S Job 21:20; Eze 3:19; 18:4 **42:17** [y] ver 22; S Jer 21:7; 44:13 **42:18** [z] Dt 29:18-20; S 2Ch 12:7

[a] 18 Or *Chaldeans* [b] 1 Hebrew; Septuagint (see also 43:2) *Azariah*

41:15 *eight of his men escaped.* Ishmael lost only two of his men (see v. 2) in the fight with Johanan.

41:17 *Geruth Kimham.* Perhaps means "lodging place of Kimham," a friend of David who returned with him to Jerusalem after Absalom's death (see 2Sa 19:37–40).

42:1 *Jezaniah son of Hoshaiah.* Possibly the same as "Jaazaniah the son of the Maacathite" (40:8; see NIV text note there). Apparently Jezaniah was also known as Azariah (see NIV text note; see also 43:2), as was King Uzziah (see NIV text notes on 2Ki 14:21; 2Ch 26:1).

42:2 *Jeremiah.* Had probably been among the "survivors from Mizpah" (41:16). *hear our petition.* See v. 9; 37:20. *remnant.* See vv. 15,19; see also note on 6:9.

42:3 The people may be asking the Lord to confirm what they sincerely believe to be their only option: flight to Egypt (see v. 17; 41:17).

42:6 *we will obey the LORD our God.* Though they twice declare here their desire to do God's will, they soon demonstrate that they have already decided to follow their own inclinations (see 43:2).

42:7 *Ten days later.* Jeremiah does not bring God's word to the people until he is sure of it himself (see 28:10–17).

42:10 *build you up … tear you down … plant … uproot.* See 1:10 and note; see also 31:4,28; 33:7.

42:12 *he will have compassion on you.* For similar examples see Ge 43:14; 1Ki 8:50.

42:16 *the sword you fear will overtake you there.* See 43:11 and note.

42:17–18 See 44:11–14.

42:17 *sword, famine and plague.* See note on 14:12.

42:18 *my anger and wrath have been poured out.* See 7:20; 44:6. *object of cursing … and reproach.* See notes on 24:9; 25:18; see also 29:18. *this place.* Jerusalem.

in Jerusalem,[a] so will my wrath be poured out on you when you go to Egypt. You will be an object of cursing[b] and horror,[c] of condemnation and reproach;[d] you will never see this place again.'[e]

19"O remnant[f] of Judah, the LORD has told you, 'Do not go to Egypt.'[g] Be sure of this: I warn you today 20that you made a fatal mistake[a] when you sent me to the LORD your God and said, 'Pray to the LORD our God for us; tell us everything he says and we will do it.'[h] 21I have told you today, but you still have not obeyed the LORD your God in all he sent me to tell you.[i] 22So now, be sure of this: You will die by the sword, famine[j] and plague[k] in the place where you want to go to settle."[l]

43 When Jeremiah finished telling the people all the words of the LORD their God—everything the LORD had sent him to tell them[m]— 2Azariah son of Hoshaiah[n] and Johanan[o] son of Kareah and all the arrogant[p] men said to Jeremiah, "You are lying![q] The LORD our God has not sent you to say, 'You must not go to Egypt to settle there.'[r] 3But Baruch[s] son of Neriah is inciting you against us to hand us over to the Babylonians,[b] so they may kill us or carry us into exile to Babylon."[t]

4So Johanan son of Kareah and all the army officers and all the people[u] disobeyed the LORD's command[v] to stay in the land of Judah.[w] 5Instead, Johanan son of Kareah and all the army officers led away all the remnant of Judah who had come back to live in the land of Judah from all the nations where they had been scattered.[x] 6They also led away all the men, women[y] and children and the king's daughters whom Nebuzaradan commander of the imperial guard had left with Gedaliah son of Ahikam, the son of Shaphan, and Jeremiah the prophet and Baruch[z] son of Neriah. 7So they entered Egypt[a] in disobedience to the LORD and went as far as Tahpanhes.[b]

8In Tahpanhes[c] the word of the LORD came to Jeremiah: 9"While the Jews are watching, take some large stones[d] with you and bury them in clay in the brick[e] pavement at the entrance to Pharaoh's palace[f] in Tahpanhes. 10Then say to them, 'This is what the LORD Almighty, the God of Israel, says: I will send for my servant[g] Nebuchadnezzar[h] king of Babylon, and I will set his throne[i] over these stones I have buried here; he will spread his royal canopy[j] above them. 11He will come and attack Egypt,[k] bringing death[l] to those destined[m] for death, captivity to those destined for captivity,[n] and the sword to those destined for the sword.[o] 12He[c] will set fire[p] to the temples[q] of the gods[r] of Egypt; he will burn their temples and take their gods captive.[s] As a shepherd wraps[t] his garment around him, so will he wrap Egypt around himself and depart from there unscathed. 13There in the temple of the sun[d][u] in Egypt he will demolish the sacred pillars[v] and will burn down the temples of the gods of Egypt.'"

Disaster Because of Idolatry

44 This word came to Jeremiah concerning all the Jews living in Lower Egypt[w]—in Migdol,[x] Tahpanhes[y] and Memphis[e][z]—and in Upper Egypt[f]:[a] 2"This is what the LORD Almighty, the God of Israel, says: You saw the great disaster[b] I brought

[a] 20 Or *you erred in your hearts* [b] 3 Or *Chaldeans* [c] 12 Or *I* [d] 13 Or *in Heliopolis* [e] 1 Hebrew *Noph* [f] 1 Hebrew *in Pathros*

42:18 [a]S 2Ch 36:19; Jer 39:1-9 [b]S Nu 5:27; S Jer 25:18 [c]S Dt 28:25, 37 [d]S Ps 44:13 [e]S Jer 22:10 **42:19** [f]Jer 40:15 [g]S ver 6; Dt 17:16; Isa 30:7; Jer 43:2; 44:16 **42:20** [h]ver 2; Eze 14:7-8 **42:21** [i]S Ex 24:7; Jer 40:3; Eze 2:7; 12:2; Zec 7:11-12 **42:22** [j]S Isa 1:28 [k]S ver 17; Jer 24:10; Eze 6:11 [l]S Jer 15:2; Hos 9:6 **43:1** [m]Jer 26:8; 42:9-22 **43:2** [n]S Jer 41:16 [o]Jer 40:16 [p]S Ne 9:29; 1Co 4:18-21 [q]S Ge 19:14; S Dt 13:3; Ro 9:1; 2Co 11:31; 1Ti 2:7 [r]S Ex 24:7; 2Ki 25:24; Jer 18:19; S 42:19; Eze 37:14 **43:3** [s]S Jer 32:12 [t]Jer 38:4; 41:18; 52:30 **43:4** [u]S Jer 41:16 [v]2Ch 25:16; Jer 42:5-6 [w]Jer 42:10 **43:5** [x]Jer 40:12 **43:6** [y]S Jer 6:12 [z]S Jer 32:12 **43:7** [a]S 2Ki 25:26 [b]Jer 2:16; 44:1; 46:14; Eze 30:18 **43:8** [c]Ps 139:7; Jer 2:16 **43:9** [d]Ge 31:45-53; Jos 4:1-7; 1Ki 18:31-32 [e]S Ge 11:3 [f]S Ge 47:14 **43:10** [g]Isa 44:28; 45:1; Jer 25:9; 27:6 [h]Jer 46:13 [i]Jer 49:38 [j]S Ps 18:11 **43:11** [k]Jer 46:13-26; Eze 29:19-20 [l]S Pr 11:19; Ro 6:23 [m]S Ps 49:14; Heb 9:27 [n]S Dt 28:64; Rev 13:10 [o]S Jer 15:2; Eze 32:11; Zec 11:9 **43:12** [p]S Jos 7:15 [q]S 1Ki 16:32 [r]ver 13; S Ex 12:12; S Isa 2:18; Jer 46:25; Eze 30:13; Zec 13:2 [s]Da 11:8 [t]S Ps 104:2; 109:18-19 **43:13** [u]S Ge 1:16; Isa 19:18 *fn*; S Dt 4:19 [v]Jer 52:17; Eze 26:11 **44:1** [w]S Dt 32:42; S Jer 24:8 [x]S Ex 14:2 [y]S Jer 43:7, 8 [z]S Isa 19:13 [a]S Isa 11:11 [b]S 2Ch 34:24

42:19 *I warn you.* See 11:7.

43:2 *Azariah.* See note on 42:1. *arrogant men.* They demonstrate themselves to be such by their words.

43:3 *Baruch.* See note on 32:12. Jeremiah's opponents decide to put the blame on someone they consider less spiritually formidable than the prophet himself.

43:5 *remnant of Judah.* Jews who had fled from the Babylonians to neighboring countries (see 40:11–12).

43:6 *king's daughters.* See note on 41:10. *Jeremiah ... and Baruch.* No doubt they went to Egypt unwillingly, in the light of 32:6–15; 40:1–6; 42:13–22.

43:7 *Tahpanhes.* See note on 2:16.

43:9 *Pharaoh's palace.* Not necessarily his main residence. One of the Elephantine papyri (see chart, p. xxii), e.g., mentions the "king's house," apparently a more modest dwelling for the pharaoh's use when he visited Elephantine in southern Egypt.

43:10 *my servant Nebuchadnezzar.* See note on 25:9. *his throne.* Symbolizing his authority.

43:11 See 15:2 and note. *He will ... attack Egypt.* A fragmentary text now owned by the British Museum in London states that Nebuchadnezzar carried out a punitive expedition against Egypt in his 37th year (568–567 B.C.) during the reign of Pharaoh Amasis (see Eze 29:17–20 and notes).

43:12 *As a shepherd wraps ... so will he wrap.* Routinely and confidently.

43:13 *temple of the sun in Egypt.* Lit. "Beth Shemesh in Egypt," not to be confused with "Beth Shemesh in Judah" (2Ki 14:11). The Egyptian city is probably to be identified with Heliopolis (Greek for "city of the sun"; see NIV text note), called *On* in Hebrew (see note on Ge 41:45). *sacred pillars.* Obelisks, for which ancient Heliopolis was famous.

44:1–30 The last of Jeremiah's recorded prophecies (see note on 40:1—44:30).

44:1 *Jews living in ... Egypt.* As a result of previous deportations (see, e.g., 2Ki 23:34) and/or the Jews mentioned in 43:5–7. In either case, some time must have elapsed between chs. 43 and 44 to bring about the gathering mentioned in v. 15. *Lower Egypt ... Upper Egypt.* See note on Isa 11:11. *Migdol.* Probably in northern Egypt (see 46:14). The name means "watchtower." *Tahpanhes and Memphis.* See notes on 2:16; Isa 19:13.

on Jerusalem and on all the towns of Judah.[c] Today they lie deserted and in ruins[d]
3because of the evil[e] they have done. They
provoked me to anger[f] by burning incense[g]
and by worshiping other gods[h] that neither
they nor you nor your fathers[i] ever knew.
4Again and again[j] I sent my servants the
prophets,[k] who said, 'Do not do this detestable[l] thing that I hate!' 5But they did
not listen or pay attention;[m n] they did not
turn from their wickedness[o] or stop burning incense[p] to other gods.[q] 6Therefore,
my fierce anger was poured out;[r] it raged
against the towns of Judah and the streets
of Jerusalem and made them the desolate
ruins[s] they are today.

7"Now this is what the LORD God Almighty, the God of Israel, says: Why bring
such great disaster[t] on yourselves by cutting off from Judah the men and wom-
en,[u] the children and infants, and so leave
yourselves without a remnant?[v] 8Why provoke me to anger with what your hands
have made,[w] burning incense[x] to other
gods in Egypt,[y] where you have come
to live?[z] You will destroy yourselves and
make yourselves an object of cursing and
reproach[a] among all the nations on earth.
9Have you forgotten the wickedness committed by your fathers[b] and by the kings[c]
and queens[d] of Judah and the wickedness
committed by you and your wives[e] in the
land of Judah and the streets of Jerusalem?[f] 10To this day they have not humbled[g]
themselves or shown reverence,[h] nor have
they followed my law[i] and the decrees[j] I
set before you and your fathers.[k]

11"Therefore, this is what the LORD Almighty,[l] the God of Israel, says: I am determined to bring disaster[m] on you and to
destroy all Judah. 12I will take away the
remnant[n] of Judah who were determined
to go to Egypt to settle there. They will
all perish in Egypt; they will fall by the
sword or die from famine. From the least
to the greatest,[o] they will die by sword
or famine.[p] They will become an object
of cursing and horror, of condemnation

44:2 [c]S Jer 40:5 [d]S Lev 26:31; S Dt 29:23; S Isa 6:11 **44:3** [e]S Ex 32:22 [f]S Nu 11:33 [g]S Nu 16:40 [h]ver 8; S Nu 25:3; Dt 13:6-11; 29:26; Isa 19:1 [i]S Jdg 2:19 **44:4** [j]S Jer 7:13 [k]S Nu 11:29 [l]S Dt 18:9; S 1Ki 14:24; 1Pe 4:3 **44:5** [m]Da 9:6 [n]S Jer 25:4 [o]S Ge 6:5; Ro 1:18; 2Ti 2:19 [p]ver 21; Jer 1:16; Eze 8:11; 16:18; 23:41 [q]Jer 11:8-10; S 25:7 **44:6** [r]Eze 8:18; 20:34 [s]S Lev 26:31,34; S Dt 29:23; La 1:13; Zec 7:14 **44:7** [t]Jer 26:19 [u]Jer 51:22 [v]S 2Ki 21:14 **44:8** [w]S Isa 40:18-20; S Jer 10:3; Ro 1:23 [x]ver 17-25; Jer 41:5 [y]S ver 3; S Ex 12:12 [z]S 1Co 10:22 [a]S Ps 44:13 **44:9** [b]S Jdg 2:19 [c]S 2Ki 23:11 [d]1Ki 21:25 [e]S Pr 31:10; S Jer 6:12 [f]ver 17,21; Jer 11:12; 32:32 **44:10** [g]S Dt 8:3; S Mt 23:12; Php 2:8 [h]S Dt 6:13; S Ps 5:7 [i]S Jos 1:7; S Jer 11:8; Mt 5:17-20; Gal 3:19; 1Jn 3:4 [j]S Lev 18:4 [k]1Ki 9:6-9; 2Ki 17:17 **44:11** [l]Rev 4:8 [m]S 2Ch 34:24; Am 9:4 **44:12** [n]ver 7; Jer 40:15 [o]S Jer 42:1 [p]S Isa 1:28

and reproach.[q] 13I will punish[r] those who
live in Egypt with the sword,[s] famine and
plague,[t] as I punished Jerusalem. 14None
of the remnant of Judah who have gone
to live in Egypt will escape or survive to
return to the land of Judah, to which they
long to return and live; none will return
except a few fugitives."[u]

15Then all the men who knew that their
wives[v] were burning incense[w] to other
gods, along with all the women[x] who were
present—a large assembly—and all the
people living in Lower and Upper Egypt,[a y]
said to Jeremiah, 16"We will not listen[z] to
the message you have spoken to us in the
name of the LORD![a] 17We will certainly do
everything we said we would:[b] We will
burn incense[c] to the Queen of Heaven[d]
and will pour out drink offerings to her
just as we and our fathers, our kings and
our officials[e] did in the towns of Judah and
in the streets of Jerusalem.[f] At that time
we had plenty of food[g] and were well off
and suffered no harm.[h] 18But ever since we
stopped burning incense to the Queen of
Heaven and pouring out drink offerings[i] to
her, we have had nothing and have been
perishing by sword and famine.[j k]"

19The women added, "When we burned
incense[l] to the Queen of Heaven[m] and
poured out drink offerings to her, did not
our husbands[n] know that we were making cakes[o] like her image[p] and pouring out
drink offerings to her?"

20Then Jeremiah said to all the people,
both men and women, who were answering him, 21"Did not the LORD remember[q]
and think about the incense[r] burned in
the towns of Judah and the streets of

[a] 15 Hebrew *in Egypt and Pathros*

[q]S Dt 28:25; S Jer 29:18 **44:13** [r]S Ex 32:34; Lev 26:14-17 [s]S Jer 15:2 [t]S Jer 42:17 **44:14** [u]Jer 22:24-27; 49:5; La 4:15; Eze 6:8; S Ro 9:27 **44:15** [v]S Pr 31:10; S Jer 6:12 [w]S Jer 18:15 [x]S Ge 3:6; 1Ti 2:14 [y]S Isa 11:11 **44:16** [z]S 1Sa 8:19; Job 15:25-26; Jer 11:8-10 [a]S Jer 42:19 **44:17** [b]ver 28; Dt 23:23; Zec 1:6 [c]S Isa 65:3 [d]ver 25; Jer 11:12 [e]Ne 9:34 [f]S ver 9; S Jer 2:26 [g]S Ex 16:3; Nu 11:4-6 [h]S Job 21:15; Isa 3:9; Hos 2:5-13; 9:1 **44:18** [i]Lev 23:18 [j]Mal 3:13-15 [k]Jer 42:16 **44:19** [l]S Jer 18:15 [m]Jer 7:18 [n]S Ge 3:6; Eph 5:22 [o]Lev 7:12 [p]S Lev 26:1; Ac 17:29 **44:21** [q]Isa 64:9; S Jer 14:10; Hos 8:13 [r]S Jer 11:13

44:3 See note on 1:16; see also 11:17; 19:4; 32:32.
44:4 See 7:25 and note. *Do not do this detestable thing.* See Jdg 19:24.
44:6 *my fierce anger was poured out.* See 7:20; 42:18.
44:7 *bring … disaster on yourselves.* See 26:19. *men and women, the children and infants.* A stock phrase meaning "everyone" (see 1Sa 15:3; 22:19).
44:8 *what your hands have made.* Idols (see 1:16 and note; see also note on Ex 34:15). *object of cursing and reproach.* See 42:18; see also notes on 24:9; 25:18.
44:9 *wickedness committed by … queens … and your wives.* The women joined their husbands in worshiping the "Queen of Heaven" (v. 19; see v. 15).
44:10 *nor … followed my law.* See 9:13; 26:4; see also 7:9 and note.
44:11–14 See 42:17–18 and notes.
44:11 *am determined.* Lit. "set my face" (see 21:10 and note).
44:15 *wives … women.* See v. 19; see also note on v. 9. *Lower and Upper Egypt.* See v. 1; see also note on Isa 11:11.
44:17 *Queen of Heaven.* See note on 7:18. *At that time we … were well off.* Judah had been relatively prosperous during King Manasseh's lengthy reign.
44:18 *ever since we stopped.* As a result of King Josiah's reform movement, which began in 621 B.C. *we have had nothing.* Beginning with Josiah's death in 609, a series of disasters, including invasion and exile, had struck Judah. The people understandably (though mistakenly) attributed their misfortune to their failure to worship the Queen of Heaven.
44:19 *women.* Since Ishtar (the "Queen of Heaven") was a Babylonian goddess of fertility, women played a major role in her worship. *did not our husbands know …?* To have validity, a religious vow made by a married woman (see v. 25) had to be confirmed by her husband (see Nu 30:10–15). *we were making cakes like her image.* See 7:18.

Jerusalem[s] by you and your fathers,[t] your kings and your officials and the people of the land?[u] 22When the LORD could no longer endure[v] your wicked actions and the detestable things you did, your land became an object of cursing[w] and a desolate waste[x] without inhabitants, as it is today.[y] 23Because you have burned incense and have sinned against the LORD and have not obeyed him or followed[z] his law or his decrees[a] or his stipulations, this disaster[b] has come upon you, as you now see."[c]

24Then Jeremiah said to all the people, including the women,[d] "Hear the word of the LORD, all you people of Judah in Egypt.[e] 25This is what the LORD Almighty, the God of Israel, says: You and your wives[f] have shown by your actions what you promised when you said, 'We will certainly carry out the vows we made to burn incense and pour out drink offerings to the Queen of Heaven.'[g]

"Go ahead then, do what you promised! Keep your vows![h] 26But hear the word of the LORD, all Jews living in Egypt:[i] 'I swear[j] by my great name,' says the LORD, 'that no one from Judah living anywhere in Egypt will ever again invoke my name or swear, "As surely as the Sovereign[k] LORD lives."[l] 27For I am watching[m] over them for harm,[n] not for good; the Jews in Egypt will perish[o] by sword and famine[p] until they are all destroyed.[q] 28Those who escape the sword[r] and return to the land of Judah from Egypt will be very few.[s] Then the whole remnant[t] of Judah who came to live in Egypt will know whose word will stand[u]—mine or theirs.[v]

29" 'This will be the sign[w] to you that I will punish[x] you in this place,' declares the LORD, 'so that you will know that my threats of harm against you will surely stand.'[y] 30This is what the LORD says: 'I am going to hand Pharaoh[z] Hophra king of Egypt over to his enemies who seek his life, just as I handed Zedekiah[a] king of Judah over to Nebuchadnezzar king of Babylon, the enemy who was seeking his life.' "[b]

A Message to Baruch

45 This is what Jeremiah the prophet told Baruch[c] son of Neriah[d] in the fourth year of Jehoiakim[e] son of Josiah king of Judah, after Baruch had written on a scroll[f] the words Jeremiah was then dictating: 2"This is what the LORD, the God of Israel, says to you, Baruch: 3You said, 'Woe[g] to me! The LORD has added sorrow[h] to my pain;[i] I am worn out with groaning[j] and find no rest.' "[k]

4⌞The LORD said,⌟ "Say this to him: 'This is what the LORD says: I will overthrow what I have built and uproot[l] what I have planted,[m] throughout the land.[n] 5Should you then seek great[o] things for yourself? Seek them not.[p] For I will bring disaster[q] on all people,[r] declares the LORD, but wherever you go I will let you escape[s] with your life.' "[t]

A Message About Egypt

46 This is the word of the LORD that came to Jeremiah the prophet concerning the nations:[u]

2Concerning Egypt:[v]

This is the message against the army of Pharaoh Neco[w] king of Egypt, which was

44:21 [s]ver 9 [t]S Ps 79:8 [u]S Jer 2:26 **44:22** [v]S Isa 1:14 [w]S Jer 25:18 [x]S Lev 26:31,32 [y]S Ge 19:13; Ps 107:33-34; Eze 33:28-29 **44:23** [z]S 1Ki 9:6 [a]S Lev 18:4 [b]Jer 40:2 [c]S Lev 26:33; S 1Ki 9:9; Jer 7:13-15; Eze 39:23; Da 9:11-12 **44:24** [d]S Ge 3:6 [e]Jer 43:7 **44:25** [f]S Pr 31:10 [g]S ver 17; S Dt 32:38 [h]S Pr 20:25; Eze 20:39; Jas 1:13-15 **44:26** [i]S Jer 24:8 [j]S Ge 22:16; S Isa 48:1; Ac 19:13; Heb 6:13-17 [k]S Ge 15:2 [l]Dt 32:40; Ps 50:16; S Jer 4:2 **44:27** [m]S Jer 1:12 [n]S Jer 21:10 [o]S Lev 26:38; S Job 15:22; 2Pe 3:9 [p]S Ge 41:55 [q]S Jer 9:16; Da 9:14; Am 9:8 **44:28** [r]Jer 45:5; Eze 6:8 [s]ver 13-14; S Isa 10:19 [t]S 2Ki 21:14 [u]S Isa 7:9; S Jer 39:16; 42:15-18 [v]S ver 17,25-26 **44:29** [w]S Ge 24:14; S Ex 3:12; S Nu 16:38; S Mt 12:38; 24:3 [x]S Ex 32:34

[y]S Pr 19:21 **44:30** [z]S Jer 25:19; 46:26; Eze 30:21; 32:32 [a]2Ki 25:1-7; S Jer 24:8 [b]Jer 43:9-13 **45:1** [c]S Jer 32:12 [d]Jer 51:59 [e]S 2Ch 36:5 [f]S Ex 17:14; S Ps 40:7 **45:3** [g]S Isa 24:16; 1Co 9:16 [h]S Ps 119:28; Mk 14:34; Ro 9:2 [i]S Job 6:10 [j]S Job 23:2; Ps 69:3 [k]S Jos 1:13; Mt 11:28; Heb 4:3 **45:4** [l]S Jer 42:10 [m]S Jer 11:17 [n]S Dt 28:63; S 30:9; Isa 5:5-7; Jer 18:7-10 **45:5** [o]Ps 131:1 [p]Mt 6:25-27,33 [q]Jer 11:11; 40:2 [r]S Jer 2:35 [s]S Ps 68:20; S Jer 44:28 [t]S Jer 21:9 **46:1** [u]S Jer 1:10 **46:2** [v]S Ex 1:8 [w]S 2Ki 23:29

44:22 *object of cursing.* See v. 12. *desolate waste.* See v. 6.
44:23 *stipulations.* Of the Lord's covenant with his people (see Dt 4:45; 6:17,20).
44:25 *Go ahead then.* Spoken in irony (see 7:21 and note).
44:26 *I swear by my great name.* See note on 22:5. *or swear.* See Dt 6:13 and note. *As surely as the Sovereign LORD lives.* See note on Ge 42:15.
44:27 *watching.* See note on 1:12; see also 31:28.
44:28 *very few.* See v. 14.
44:30 *Hophra.* Ruled Egypt 589–570 B.C. (see 37:5 and note). *his enemies who seek his life.* Hophra was killed by his Egyptian rivals during a power struggle. *I handed Zedekiah ... over to Nebuchadnezzar.* See 39:5–7.
45:1–5 A brief message of encouragement to Baruch, Jeremiah's faithful secretary (see note on 32:12). Though out of chronological order, the section provides a suitable historical appendix to chs. 39–44 as well as a smooth transition to chs. 46–51 (see notes on v. 1; 46:2).
45:1 *fourth year of Jehoiakim.* 605 B.C. Ch. 45 fits chronologically between 36:8 and 36:9 (see note on 36:8). *had written on a scroll.* See 36:4; see also 36:2 and note.
45:3 To some extent Baruch shared Jeremiah's anguish, the result of Jeremiah's prophetic call and ministry (see, e.g., 8:18—9:2; 20:7–18). *worn out with groaning.* See Ps 6:6. *find no rest.* See La 5:5.
45:4 *overthrow ... built ... uproot ... planted.* See note on 1:10; see also 2:21; 31:4–5,28,40; 32:41; 33:7. *land.* Or "earth" (see "all people" in v. 5; see also 25:15,31; 46–51).
45:5 *great things ... Seek them not.* See Ps 131:1. Baruch's brother Seraiah would occupy an important position under King Zedekiah (see 32:12; 51:59), but Baruch himself was not to be ambitious or self-seeking. *escape with your life.* See note on 21:9.
46:1—51:64 See notes on 25:1–38; 25:13; 25:19–26. Chs. 46–51 consist of a series of prophecies against the nations (see Isa 13–23; Eze 25–32; Am 1–2; Zep 2:4–15). They begin with Egypt (ch. 46) and end with Babylonia (chs. 50–51), the two powers that vied for control of Judah during Jeremiah's ministry. The arrangement of the prophecies is in a generally west-to-east direction.
46:1 *This is the word of the LORD ... concerning.* See 14:1; 47:1; 49:34; 50:1. *nations.* To whom Jeremiah was called to prophesy (see 1:5 and note).
46:2 *Concerning Egypt.* See Isa 19–20; Eze 29–32. *Neco.* Ruled Egypt 610–595 B.C. *Carchemish.* See 2Ch 35:20; Isa 10:9 and note. The name means "fortress of Chemosh" (chief

defeated at Carchemish[x] on the Euphrates[y]
River by Nebuchadnezzar king of Babylon
in the fourth year of Jehoiakim[z] son of Josiah king of Judah:

3 "Prepare your shields,[a] both large and
small,
and march out for battle!
4 Harness the horses,
mount the steeds!
Take your positions
with helmets on!
Polish[b] your spears,
put on your armor![c]
5 What do I see?
They are terrified,
they are retreating,
their warriors are defeated.
They flee[d] in haste
without looking back,
and there is terror[e] on every side,"
declares the LORD.
6 "The swift cannot flee[f]
nor the strong escape.
In the north by the River Euphrates[g]
they stumble and fall.[h]
7 "Who is this that rises like the Nile,
like rivers of surging waters?[i]
8 Egypt rises like the Nile,[j]
like rivers of surging waters.
She says, 'I will rise and cover the
earth;
I will destroy cities and their
people.'[k]
9 Charge, O horses!
Drive furiously, O charioteers![l]
March on, O warriors—
men of Cush[a][m] and Put who carry
shields,
men of Lydia[n] who draw the bow.

46:2 [x]S 2Ch 35:20 [y]S Ge 2:14 [z]Jer 1:3; 25:1; 35:1; 36:1; 45:1; Da 1:1 **46:3** [a]S Isa 21:5 **46:4** [b]Eze 21:9-11 [c]1Sa 17:5,38; 2Ch 26:14; Ne 4:16 **46:5** [d]ver 21; Jer 48:44 [e]S Ps 31:13; S 48:5 **46:6** [f]Isa 30:16 [g]Ge 2:14; 15:18 [h]ver 12,16; S Ps 20:8 **46:7** [i]Jer 47:2 **46:8** [j]Eze 29:3,9; 30:12; Am 8:8 [k]Da 11:10 **46:9** [l]Jer 47:3; Eze 26:10; Na 3:2 [m]S Ge 10:6 [n]S Isa 66:19 **46:10** [o]Eze 32:10; Joel 1:15; Ob 1:15 [p]S Nu 31:3; S Dt 32:41; 2Ki 23:29-30 [q]S Dt 32:42; S 2Sa 2:26; Zep 2:12 [r]S Dt 32:42 [s]S Lev 3:9; Zep 1:7 [t]Ge 2:14; 15:18 **46:11** [u]S Ge 37:25 [v]S 2Ki 19:21 [w]S Jer 30:13; S Mic 1:9 **46:12** [x]S ver 6; Isa 19:4; Na 3:8-10 **46:13** [y]ver 26; Eze 32:11 [z]Isa 19:1; Jer 27:7 **46:14** [a]S Isa 19:13

10 But that day[o] belongs to the Lord, the
LORD Almighty—
a day of vengeance[p], for vengeance
on his foes.
The sword will devour[q] till it is
satisfied,
till it has quenched its thirst with
blood.[r]
For the Lord, the LORD Almighty, will
offer sacrifice[s]
in the land of the north by the River
Euphrates.[t]
11 "Go up to Gilead and get balm,[u]
O Virgin[v] Daughter of Egypt.
But you multiply remedies in vain;
there is no healing[w] for you.
12 The nations will hear of your shame;
your cries will fill the earth.
One warrior will stumble over another;
both will fall[x] down together."

13 This is the message the LORD spoke to
Jeremiah the prophet about the coming of
Nebuchadnezzar king of Babylon[y] to at-
tack Egypt:[z]

14 "Announce this in Egypt, and proclaim
it in Migdol;
proclaim it also in Memphis[b][a] and
Tahpanhes:[b]
'Take your positions and get ready,
for the sword devours[c] those around
you.'
15 Why will your warriors be laid low?
They cannot stand, for the LORD will
push them down.[d]

a 9 That is, the upper Nile region *b* 14 Hebrew *Noph*; also in verse 19

[b]S Jer 43:8 [c]S Dt 32:42; S 2Sa 2:26; S Jer 24:8 **46:15** [d]S Jos 23:5; Isa 66:15-16

god of Moab; see 2Ki 23:13), as clarified by the Ebla tablets (see Introduction to Genesis: Background; see also chart, p. xxii). *Euphrates River.* See note on Ge 15:18. *by Nebuchadnezzar.* Egypt's defeat by Babylonia at Carchemish was one of the most decisive battles in the ancient world, ending Egypt's agelong claims and pretensions to power in Syro-Palestine. *fourth year of Jehoiakim.* 605 B.C., the first year of Nebuchadnezzar's reign (see 25:1).

46:3 *Prepare.* Spoken to the Egyptians in sarcasm (see, e.g., Na 2:1; 3:14 and notes).

46:4 *horses.* Egypt was a prime source for the finest horses (see 1Ki 10:28). *put on your armor.* See 51:3.

46:5 *terror on every side.* The phrase is used in 6:25 (see note there) with reference to the Babylonian army (see 6:22 and note).

46:7–8 *rivers of surging waters.* In the northern Egyptian delta, where the Nile branches out into numerous streams.

46:8 *rise and cover the earth.* The same metaphor is used of Assyria in Isa 8:7–8 (see note there). *cities.* The Hebrew for this word is in the singular but is used as a generic plural ("city" is generic also in 8:16).

46:9 *Charge.* See note on v. 3; see also 8:6; Na 3:3. *Drive furiously, O charioteers!* See Na 2:4. *Put.* See note on Ge 10:6. *Lydia.* See note on Isa 66:19. Men from Cush, Put and Lydia were mercenaries in the Egyptian army.

46:10 *day of vengeance.* See Isa 34:8 and note. The Lord will avenge Egypt's cruelties toward Judah (see, e.g., 2Ki 23:29,33–35). *sword will devour.* See v. 14. *quenched its thirst with blood … offer sacrifice.* Slaughter in battle is often compared with sacrifices (see Isa 34:5–7 and notes; Zep 1:7–8).

46:11 *Gilead … balm.* See 8:22 and note. *Virgin Daughter of Egypt.* A personification of Egypt (see note on 2Ki 19:21). *remedies in vain … no healing for you.* The statement is ironic in the light of Egypt's reputation for expertise in the healing arts.

46:12 *stumble … fall.* See vv. 6,16.

46:13 *Nebuchadnezzar … to attack Egypt.* In 568–567 B.C. (see note on 43:11), long after the battle of Carchemish (see note on v. 2).

46:14 *Migdol.* See note on 44:1. *Memphis and Tahpanhes.* See 44:1; see also notes on 2:16; Isa 19:13. *Take your positions.* See v. 4. *sword devours.* See v. 10.

46:15 *warriors.* The Hebrew for this word is not the same as that for "warrior" in vv. 5,9,12. It is lit. "strong ones," often referring to powerful animals ("stallions" in 8:16; 50:11; "steeds" in 47:3; Jdg 5:22). In Ps 22:12; 50:13; 68:30; Isa 34:7 the Hebrew word is translated "bulls" (see note on Ps 68:30). *be laid low.* The Hebrew for this phrase is translated "Apis has fled" in the Septuagint (the pre-Christian Greek translation of the OT). Apis was a bull-god worshiped in Egypt, especially at

[16]They will stumble[e] repeatedly;
they will fall[f] over each other.
They will say, 'Get up, let us go back
to our own people[g] and our native
lands,
away from the sword of the
oppressor.'[h]
[17]There they will exclaim,
'Pharaoh king of Egypt is only a loud
noise;[i]
he has missed his opportunity.[j]'

[18]"As surely as I live," declares the King,[k]
whose name is the LORD Almighty,
"one will come who is like Tabor[l]
among the mountains,
like Carmel[m] by the sea.
[19]Pack your belongings for exile,[n]
you who live in Egypt,
for Memphis[o] will be laid waste[p]
and lie in ruins without inhabitant.

[20]"Egypt is a beautiful heifer,
but a gadfly is coming
against her from the north.[q]
[21]The mercenaries[r] in her ranks
are like fattened calves.[s]
They too will turn and flee[t] together,
they will not stand their ground,
for the day[u] of disaster is coming upon
them,
the time[v] for them to be punished.
[22]Egypt will hiss like a fleeing serpent
as the enemy advances in force;
they will come against her with axes,
like men who cut down trees.[w]
[23]They will chop down her forest,"
declares the LORD,
"dense though it be.
They are more numerous than locusts,[x]
they cannot be counted.
[24]The Daughter of Egypt will be put to
shame,
handed over to the people of the
north.[y]"

[25]The LORD Almighty, the God of Israel,
says: "I am about to bring punishment on
Amon god of Thebes,[a z] on Pharaoh,[a] on
Egypt and her gods[b] and her kings, and on
those who rely[c] on Pharaoh. [26]I will hand
them over[d] to those who seek their lives,
to Nebuchadnezzar king[e] of Babylon and
his officers. Later, however, Egypt will be
inhabited[f] as in times past," declares the
LORD.

[27]"Do not fear,[g] O Jacob[h] my servant;[i]
do not be dismayed, O Israel.
I will surely save you out of a distant
place,
your descendants from the land of
their exile.[j]
Jacob will again have peace and
security,
and no one will make him afraid.
[28]Do not fear, O Jacob my servant,
for I am with you,"[k] declares the
LORD.
"Though I completely destroy[l] all the
nations
among which I scatter you,
I will not completely destroy you.
I will discipline you but only with
justice;
I will not let you go entirely
unpunished."

A Message About the Philistines

[47] This is the word of the LORD that
came to Jeremiah the prophet concerning the Philistines[m] before Pharaoh
attacked Gaza:[n]

[a] 25 Hebrew *No*

46:16 [e]S Lev 26:37 [f]S ver 6 [g]S Isa 13:14 [h]S Jer 25:38 **46:17** [i]1Ki 20:10-11 [j]Isa 19:11-16 **46:18** [k]Jer 48:15 [l]S Jos 19:22 [m]1Ki 18:42 **46:19** [n]S Isa 20:4 [o]S Isa 19:13 [p]Eze 29:10, 12; 35:7 **46:20** [q]ver 24; S Isa 14:31; Jer 47:2 **46:21** [r]S 2Ki 7:6 [s]Lk 15:27 [t]S ver 5; S Job 20:24 [u]Ps 18:18; 37:13; Jer 18:17 [v]S Job 18:20 **46:22** [w]Ps 74:5 **46:23** [x]S Dt 28:42; S Jdg 7:12 **46:24** [y]S 2Ki 24:7 **46:25** [z]Eze 30:14; Na 3:8 [a]2Ki 24:7; Eze 30:22 [b]S Jer 43:12 [c]Isa 20:6 **46:26** [d]S Jer 44:30 [e]S ver 13; S Isa 19:4 [f]Eze 29:11-16 **46:27** [g]Isa 43:5; Jer 51:46 [h]Isa 41:8; 44:1; Mal 1:2 [i]S Isa 44:2 [j]S Isa 11:11; S Jer 29:14; 50:19 **46:28** [k]S Ex 14:22; S Nu 14:9; Isa 8:9-10 [l]S Jer 4:27 **47:1** [m]S Ge 10:14; S Jdg 3:31 [n]S Ge 10:19; Zec 9:5-7

Memphis (see v. 14). An alternative translation of v. 15 would then read as follows: "Why did Apis flee? Why did your bull [many manuscripts have the singular form] not stand? Because the LORD pushed him down."
46:16 *They will stumble repeatedly.* See vv. 6,12; lit. "He will make many stumble." *They will say, '... let us go.'* The mercenaries in the pharaoh's army (see v. 9 and note) will decide to return to their homelands. *sword of the oppressor.* See 25:38; 50:16.
46:17 *only a loud noise.* In Isa 30:7, Egypt is called "the Do-Nothing." *missed his opportunity.* After the battle of Carchemish (see v. 2), Nebuchadnezzar returned to Babylonia on learning of his father's death. Egypt failed to press its advantage at that time.
46:18 *As surely as I live.* See notes on Ge 22:16; 42:15. *King.* God is called "King" also in 8:19; 10:7,10; 48:15; 51:57. *one.* Nebuchadnezzar. *Tabor ... Carmel.* Two prominent mountains in Israel (see notes on Jdg 4:6; SS 7:5; Isa 33:9).
46:19 *Pack your belongings for exile.* Echoed in Eze 12:3. *Egypt.* Lit. "Daughter of Egypt" (see v. 11 and note). *laid waste.* Judah is so described in 2:15; 9:12.
46:20 *heifer.* Perhaps an ironic reference to Egyptian bull-worship (see note on v. 15). *gadfly.* Nebuchadnezzar. Insects are often used to symbolize an attacking enemy (see note on Ex 23:28).
46:21 *mercenaries.* See note on v. 9. *calves.* See note on v. 20. *day of disaster.* See 18:17. *time for them to be punished.* See 11:23; 23:12; 50:27.
46:22 *serpent.* Often used by Egyptian pharaohs as a symbol of their sovereignty (see note on Ex 4:3). *the enemy ... like men who cut down trees.* See 21:14; see also Isa 10:18–19,33–34 and notes.
46:23 *more numerous than locusts.* Here an invading army is compared to locusts. In Joel 2:11,25 locusts are compared to an invading army (see also 51:14).
46:24 *Daughter of Egypt.* See v. 11 and note.
46:25 *Amon.* The chief god of Egypt during much of its history. Wicked King Manasseh may have named his son after the Egyptian deity (see 2Ki 21:18; 2Ch 33:22). *Thebes.* The capital of Upper (southern) Egypt (see Eze 30:14–16).
46:26 *Egypt will be inhabited as in times past.* Cf. 48:47; 49:6,39; see also Isa 19:23–25 and notes.
46:27–28 Repeated almost verbatim from 30:10–11 (see notes there).
47:1 *concerning the Philistines.* See Isa 14:28–32; Eze 25:15–17; Am 1:6–8; Zep 2:4–7. *Pharaoh.* It is uncertain

²This is what the LORD says:

"See how the waters are rising in the north;[o]
they will become an overflowing torrent.
They will overflow the land and everything in it,
the towns and those who live in them.
The people will cry out;
all who dwell in the land will wail[p]
³at the sound of the hoofs of galloping steeds,
at the noise of enemy chariots[q]
and the rumble of their wheels.
Fathers will not turn to help their children;
their hands will hang limp.[r]
⁴For the day has come
to destroy all the Philistines
and to cut off all survivors
who could help Tyre[s] and Sidon.[t]
The LORD is about to destroy the Philistines,[u]
the remnant from the coasts of Caphtor.[a v]
⁵Gaza will shave[w] her head in mourning;
Ashkelon[x] will be silenced.
O remnant on the plain,
how long will you cut[y] yourselves?

⁶"'Ah, sword[z] of the LORD,' ⌞you cry,⌟
'how long till you rest?
Return to your scabbard;
cease and be still.'[a]
⁷But how can it rest
when the LORD has commanded it,
when he has ordered it
to attack Ashkelon and the coast?"[b]

47:2 [o]S Isa 14:31 [p]S Isa 15:3 **47:3** [q]S Jer 46:9; S Eze 23:24 [r]Isa 13:7; Jer 50:43; Eze 7:17; 21:7 **47:4** [s]S Isa 23:1; Am 1:9-10; Zec 9:2-4 [t]S Ge 10:15; S Jer 25:22 [u]S Ge 10:14; Joel 3:4 [v]S Dt 2:23 **47:5** [w]S Jer 41:5 [x]S Jer 25:20 [y]S Lev 19:28 **47:6** [z]S Isa 34:5; Jer 12:12; 48:10; 50:35 [a]Eze 21:30 **47:7** [b]Eze 25:15-17

48:1 [c]S Ge 19:37; S Dt 23:6 [d]S Nu 32:38 [e]S Nu 32:37; S Jos 13:19 **48:2** [f]Isa 16:14 [g]S Nu 21:25; S Jos 13:26 [h]ver 42 **48:3** [i]S Isa 15:5 **48:5** [j]Isa 15:5 [k]ver 3 **48:6** [l]S Ge 19:17 [m]Jer 17:6 **48:7** [n]S Ps 49:6; S Pr 11:28 [o]S Nu 21:29 [p]Isa 46:1-2; Jer 49:3 [q]Am 2:3

A Message About Moab

48:29-36pp — Isa 16:6-12

48 Concerning Moab:[c]

This is what the LORD Almighty, the God of Israel, says:

"Woe to Nebo,[d] for it will be ruined.
Kiriathaim[e] will be disgraced and captured;
the stronghold[b] will be disgraced and shattered.
²Moab will be praised[f] no more;
in Heshbon[c g] men will plot her downfall:
'Come, let us put an end to that nation.'[h]
You too, O Madmen,[d] will be silenced;
the sword will pursue you.
³Listen to the cries from Horonaim,[i]
cries of great havoc and destruction.
⁴Moab will be broken;
her little ones will cry out.[e]
⁵They go up the way to Luhith,[j]
weeping bitterly as they go;
on the road down to Horonaim[k]
anguished cries over the destruction are heard.
⁶Flee![l] Run for your lives;
become like a bush[f] in the desert.[m]
⁷Since you trust in your deeds and riches,[n]
you too will be taken captive,
and Chemosh[o] will go into exile,[p]
together with his priests and officials.[q]

[a] 4 That is, Crete [b] 1 Or / *Misgab* [c] 2 The Hebrew for *Heshbon* sounds like the Hebrew for *plot*. [d] 2 The name of the Moabite town Madmen sounds like the Hebrew for *be silenced*. [e] 4 Hebrew; Septuagint / *proclaim it to Zoar* [f] 6 Or *like Aroer*

whether Neco II (see 46:2; see also note on 2Ki 23:29) or Hophra (see notes on 37:5; 44:30) is intended. *Gaza.* See v. 5; 25:20; see also note on Jdg 1:18.

47:2 *waters are rising.* See notes on 46:7–8. *the north.* Babylonia, as in 1:13–14; 46:20. *the land ... live in them.* The Hebrew for this phrase is repeated verbatim from 8:16. *land.* Phoenicia and Philistia. *towns.* See note on 46:8; includes Tyre and Sidon (see v. 4) as well as Gaza, Ashkelon (see v. 5) and other Philistine cities.

47:3 *steeds.* Lit. "strong ones" (see note on 46:15). *hands will hang limp.* Paralyzed by terror (see 6:24; Isa 13:7 and notes).

47:4 *Tyre and Sidon.* See notes on v. 2; 25:22; 27:3. *remnant.* See v. 5; see also 2Ki 19:30–31; Isa 1:9; 10:20–22 and notes. *Caphtor.* Crete (see NIV text note; the Kerethites of Zep 2:5 and elsewhere were probably Cretans), one of many islands in the Mediterranean believed to be the original homeland of the Philistines (see Ge 10:14 and note; see also Dt 2:23).

47:5 *Gaza.* See v. 1; 25:20; see also note on Jdg 1:18. *shave her head in mourning.* See note on 16:6; see also 48:37. *Ashkelon.* See v. 7; 25:20; see also note on Jdg 1:18. *plain.* Roughly equivalent to the modern Gaza Strip, it lay west of the foothills that separated Philistia from Judah. *cut yourselves.* See note on 16:6; see also 48:37.

47:6 *sword.* See 12:12 and note. *you.* The Philistines.

47:7 *attack Ashkelon.* The immediate fulfillment took place under Nebuchadnezzar in 604 B.C. *coast.* See Eze 25:16; the Philistine plain (see note on v. 5).

48:1 *Concerning Moab.* See Isa 15–16; Eze 25:8–11; Am 2:1–3; Zep 2:8–11. Josephus (*Antiquities*, 10.9.7) implies that Jeremiah's prophecy concerning the future destruction of Moab was fulfilled in the "twenty-third year of Nebuchadnezzar's reign" (582 B.C.). *Nebo.* See v. 22; a town originally allotted to the tribe of Reuben (see Nu 32:3,37–38; see also Isa 15:2 and note). *Kiriathaim.* See v. 23. An ancient town (see Ge 14:5), it too was allotted to Reuben (see Jos 13:19). Nebo, Kiriathaim and several other towns referred to in this chapter are mentioned also in an important Moabite inscription written by Mesha king of Moab (see 2Ki 3:4) and discovered in 1868 (see chart, p. xxiii).

48:2 *Heshbon.* See vv. 34,45; 49:3; Nu 21:25. Originally allotted to Reuben (see Nu 32:37; Jos 13:17), it was later reassigned to Gad as a Levitical town (see Jos 21:39). *Madmen.* Perhaps a longer spelling of "Dimon" (Isa 15:9—but see note there). In Isa 25:10, the feminine form of the Hebrew word *madmen* is translated "manure." *sword will pursue you.* See 9:16; 42:16.

48:4 *broken.* Like a clay jar (see 19:11).

48:6 *Flee! Run for your lives.* See 51:6. *like a bush.* See note on 17:6.

48:7 *Chemosh.* See vv. 13,46; the national god of Moab (see 1Ki 11:7,33; 2Ki 23:13). The Hebrew text here implies the alter-

8 The destroyer[r] will come against every
town,
and not a town will escape.
The valley will be ruined
and the plateau[s] destroyed,
because the LORD has spoken.
9 Put salt[t] on Moab,
for she will be laid waste[a];[u]
her towns will become desolate,
with no one to live in them.

10 "A curse on him who is lax in doing
the LORD's work!
A curse on him who keeps his
sword[v] from bloodshed![w]

11 "Moab has been at rest[x] from youth,
like wine left on its dregs,[y]
not poured from one jar to another —
she has not gone into exile.
So she tastes as she did,
and her aroma is unchanged.
12 But days are coming,"
declares the LORD,
"when I will send men who pour from
jars,
and they will pour her out;
they will empty her jars
and smash her jugs.
13 Then Moab will be ashamed[z] of
Chemosh,[a]
as the house of Israel was ashamed
when they trusted in Bethel.[b]

14 "How can you say, 'We are warriors,[c]
men valiant in battle'?
15 Moab will be destroyed and her towns
invaded;
her finest young men[d] will go down
in the slaughter,[e]"
declares the King,[f] whose name is
the LORD Almighty.[g]
16 "The fall of Moab is at hand;[h]
her calamity will come quickly.
17 Mourn for her, all who live around
her,
all who know her fame;[i]
say, 'How broken is the mighty
scepter,[j]
how broken the glorious staff!'

18 "Come down from your glory
and sit on the parched ground,[k]
O inhabitants of the Daughter of
Dibon,[l]
for he who destroys Moab
will come up against you
and ruin your fortified cities.[m]
19 Stand by the road and watch,
you who live in Aroer.[n]
Ask the man fleeing and the woman
escaping,
ask them, 'What has happened?'
20 Moab is disgraced, for she is shattered.
Wail[o] and cry out!
Announce by the Arnon[p]
that Moab is destroyed.
21 Judgment has come to the plateau[q] —
to Holon,[r] Jahzah[s] and Mephaath,[t]
22 to Dibon,[u] Nebo[v] and Beth
Diblathaim,
23 to Kiriathaim,[w] Beth Gamul and Beth
Meon,[x]

48:8 [r] S Ex 12:23; S Jer 4:7 [s] S Jos 13:9 **48:9** [t] Jdg 9:45 [u] Jer 51:29 **48:10** [v] S Jer 47:6 [w] S 1Sa 15:11; 1Ki 20:42; 2Ki 13:15-19 **48:11** [x] Zec 1:15 [y] Zep 1:12 **48:13** [z] Hos 10:6 [a] ver 7 [b] S Jos 7:2 **48:14** [c] Ps 33:16 **48:15** [d] S Isa 9:17 [e] Jer 51:40 [f] S Jer 46:18 [g] Jer 51:57 **48:16** [h] Isa 13:22 **48:17** [i] 2Ki 3:4-5 [j] S Ps 110:2 **48:18** [k] Isa 47:1 [l] S Nu 21:30; S Jos 13:9 [m] ver 8 **48:19** [n] S Nu 32:34 **48:20** [o] S Isa 16:7 [p] S Nu 21:13 **48:21** [q] S Jos 13:9, 21 [r] S Jos 15:51 [s] S Nu 21:23; S Isa 15:4 [t] S Jos 13:18 **48:22** [u] S Nu 21:30; S Jos 13:9, 17 [v] S Nu 32:38 **48:23** [w] S Nu 32:37; S Jos 13:19 [x] S Jos 13:17

[a] 9 Or *Give wings to Moab, / for she will fly away*

nate spelling Chemish, as in "Carchemish" (see note on 46:2). *will go into exile ... and officials.* A stock phrase (see 49:3; Am 1:15). Images of pagan deities were often carried about from place to place (see 43:12; Am 5:26).

48:8 *destroyer.* See v. 32; probably Nebuchadnezzar. *valley ... plateau.* Much of western Moab overlooks the Jordan Valley.

48:9 See 17:6. *Put salt on Moab.* To make its farmland unproductive and barren (see note on Jdg 9:45).

48:10 *lax.* Or "lazy" (as in Pr 10:4; 12:24). Those whom the Lord designates to destroy Moab are urged on in their appointed task.

48:11 A copy of the Hebrew text of this verse has been found inscribed on a large clay seal, dating to the early Christian era and apparently used for stamping the bitumen with which the mouths of wine jars were sealed. *from youth.* From her early history. *like wine.* An apt figure, since Moab was noted for her vineyards (see vv. 32 – 33; Isa 16:8 – 10). *left on its dregs.* In order to improve with age (see Isa 25:6). *she has not gone into exile.* Unlike Israel.

48:12 *days are coming.* Moab will be destroyed (see note on v. 1). *pour from jars.* Ordinarily in order to leave the unwanted sediment in the bottom, but these men will be the agents of divine judgment and will "smash" Moab (see v. 4 and note).

48:13 *house of Israel.* The northern kingdom, destroyed and exiled in 722 – 721 B.C. *Bethel.* Either (1) the well-known town where one of Jeroboam's golden calves was placed (see 1Ki 12:28 – 30) or, (2) in parallelism with Chemosh, the West Semitic deity known from contemporary Babylonian inscriptions as well as from the Elephantine papyri a century later (see chart, p. xxii).

48:14 *How can you say ... ?* See 2:23; 8:8.

48:15 *go down in the slaughter.* See 50:27; for war depicted as the slaughter of sacrificial animals see Isa 34:6 and note. *King.* See note on 46:18. The true King is the Lord, not Chemosh.

48:16 See Dt 32:35.

48:17 *who live around her ... who know her fame.* Nations near and far respectively. *mighty.* At one time Moab had been powerful and feared (see 27:3; 2Ki 1:1; 3:5; 24:2). *scepter ... staff.* Symbols of authority and dominion (see Ge 49:10; Ps 2:9; Eze 19:11,14).

48:18 *Come down ... sit.* See Isa 47:1 and note. *Daughter of Dibon.* A personification of the important (apparently at one time royal) Moabite city of Dibon (see note on 2Ki 19:21), where the famous Moabite Stone of King Mesha was discovered (see chart, p. xxiii; see also Introduction to 1Kings: Theme: Kingship and Covenant). *Dibon.* See v. 22; Nu 21:30; see also note on Isa 15:2.

48:19 *Aroer.* See NIV text note on v. 6; see also Nu 32:34; Dt 2:36.

48:20 *Arnon.* Moab's most important river.

48:21 *plateau.* See note on v. 8. *Holon.* Not the same as the town mentioned in Jos 15:51; 21:15. *Jahzah.* See 1Ch 6:78; elsewhere called Jahaz (see v. 34; see also Isa 15:4 and note).

48:22 *Dibon.* See v. 18. *Nebo.* See note on v. 1. *Beth Diblathaim.* Perhaps the same as, or near, Almon Diblathaim (see Nu 33:46).

48:23 *Kiriathaim.* See note on v. 1. *Beth Gamul.* Modern Khirbet Jumeil, five miles east of Aroer. *Beth Meon.* The same as Baal Meon (see Nu 32:38) and Beth Baal Meon (see Jos 13:17).

[24] to Kerioth[y] and Bozrah[z]—
to all the towns[a] of Moab, far and
near.
[25] Moab's horn[a][b] is cut off;
her arm[c] is broken,"
declares the LORD.

[26] "Make her drunk,[d]
for she has defied[e] the LORD.
Let Moab wallow in her vomit;[f]
let her be an object of ridicule.[g]
[27] Was not Israel the object of your
ridicule?[h]
Was she caught among thieves,[i]
that you shake your head[j] in scorn[k]
whenever you speak of her?
[28] Abandon your towns and dwell among
the rocks,
you who live in Moab.
Be like a dove[l] that makes its nest
at the mouth of a cave.[m]

[29] "We have heard of Moab's pride[n]—
her overweening pride and conceit,
her pride and arrogance
and the haughtiness[o] of her heart.
[30] I know her insolence but it is futile,"
declares the LORD,
"and her boasts[p] accomplish
nothing.
[31] Therefore I wail[q] over Moab,
for all Moab I cry out,
I moan for the men of Kir Hareseth.[r]
[32] I weep for you, as Jazer[s] weeps,
O vines of Sibmah.[t]
Your branches spread as far as the sea;
they reached as far as the sea of
Jazer.
The destroyer has fallen
on your ripened fruit and grapes.
[33] Joy and gladness are gone
from the orchards and fields of
Moab.
I have stopped the flow of wine[u] from
the presses;
no one treads them with shouts of
joy.[v]
Although there are shouts,
they are not shouts of joy.

[34] "The sound of their cry rises
from Heshbon[w] to Elealeh[x] and
Jahaz,[y]
from Zoar[z] as far as Horonaim[a] and
Eglath Shelishiyah,
for even the waters of Nimrim are
dried up.[b]
[35] In Moab I will put an end
to those who make offerings on the
high places[c]
and burn incense[d] to their gods,"
declares the LORD.

[36] "So my heart laments[e] for Moab like a
flute;
it laments like a flute for the men of
Kir Hareseth.[f]
The wealth they acquired[g] is gone.
[37] Every head is shaved[h]
and every beard[i] cut off;
every hand is slashed
and every waist is covered with
sackcloth.[j]
[38] On all the roofs in Moab
and in the public squares[k]
there is nothing but mourning,
for I have broken Moab
like a jar[l] that no one wants,"
declares the LORD.
[39] "How shattered[m] she is! How they
wail!
How Moab turns her back in shame!
Moab has become an object of
ridicule,[n]
an object of horror to all those
around her."

[40] This is what the LORD says:

"Look! An eagle is swooping[o] down,
spreading its wings[p] over Moab.

48:24 [y]Am 2:2 [z]Jer 49:13 [a]S Isa 15:1 **48:25** [b]Ps 75:10 [c]Ps 10:15; 37:17; Eze 30:21 **48:26** [d]Jer 25:16,27; 51:39 [e]ver 42; 1Sa 17:26 [f]S Isa 28:8 [g]ver 39 **48:27** [h]S Jer 2:26 [i]2Ki 17:3-6 [j]S Job 16:4; Ps 44:14; Jer 18:16 [k]S Dt 28:37; Mic 7:8-10; Zep 2:8,10 **48:28** [l]S Ge 8:8; S SS 1:15 [m]S Jdg 6:2 **48:29** [n]S Lev 26:19; S Job 40:12 [o]S Ps 10:5; S Pr 16:18 **48:30** [p]S Ps 10:3 **48:31** [q]ver 36; Isa 15:5-8 [r]S 2Ki 3:25 **48:32** [s]S Jos 13:25 [t]S Nu 32:3 **48:33** [u]S Isa 24:7 [v]Joel 1:12; Am 5:17 **48:34** [w]S Nu 21:25; S Jos 13:26 [x]S Nu 32:3 [y]S Nu 21:23; S Isa 15:4 [z]S Ge 13:10 [a]S Isa 15:5 [b]S Isa 15:6 **48:35** [c]S Isa 15:2 [d]Jer 11:13 **48:36** [e]S ver 31 [f]S 2Ki 3:25 [g]S Isa 15:7 **48:37** [h]Isa 15:2; S Jer 41:5; Eze 27:31; 29:18 [i]S Lev 19:27; S 2Sa 10:4 [j]S Ge 37:34; S Isa 3:24; Jer 16:6; Am 8:10 **48:38** [k]S Isa 15:3 [l]S Jer 22:28 **48:39** [m]Jer 50:23 [n]ver 26 **48:40** [o]S Dt 28:49; Hab 1:8 [p]S Isa 8:8

[a] 25 *Horn* here symbolizes strength.

48:24 *Kerioth.* See note on Am 2:2. *Bozrah.* Not the same as Bozrah in Edom (see 49:13,22), but another name for Bezer in Moab (see note on Dt 4:43).
48:26 The Lord speaks to the Babylonian invaders. *Make her drunk.* By drinking down the cup of God's wrath (see 13:13; 25:15–17,28). *wallow in her vomit.* See 25:27; Isa 19:14. *let her be an object of ridicule.* As she had once ridiculed others (see v. 27; Zep 2:8,10).
48:27 *shake your head in scorn.* See 18:16 and note; see also Ps 64:8.
48:28 *like a dove … mouth of a cave.* See Ps 55:6–8; SS 2:14.
48:29–30 An expanded version of the description of Moab found in Isa 16:6.
48:29 *Moab's pride.* It had long since become proverbial (see Isa 25:10–11; Zep 2:8–10).
48:31–33 See Isa 16:7–10.
48:31–32 *I.* The prophet (as in Isa 16:9; cf. Isa 15:5).
48:31 *moan.* Like a mourning dove (see Isa 38:14; 59:11). *Kir Hareseth.* See Isa 16:7,11; see also note on Isa 15:1.
48:32 *as Jazer.* Or "more than Jazer" (so also in Isa 16:9). *Jazer … Sibmah … sea.* See note on Isa 16:8. *vines.* See note on v. 11. *destroyer.* See v. 8; probably Nebuchadnezzar.
48:33 *orchards.* See note on 2:7. *treads.* See note on Isa 16:10. *not shouts of joy.* Instead, shouts of judgment (see 25:30; 51:14).
48:34 See Isa 15:4–6 and notes.
48:36 See Isa 16:11. *flute.* Played by mourners at funerals (see Mt 9:23–24 and note on 9:23).
48:37 Signs of mourning (see Isa 15:2–3 and notes). *is slashed.* See note on 16:6.
48:38 *broken … like a jar that no one wants.* See v. 4 and note on v. 12; cf. the description of King Jehoiachin in 22:28 (see note there).
48:39 *object of ridicule.* See v. 26 and note.
48:40–41 Echoed in 49:22 with respect to Edom.
48:40 *eagle.* Nebuchadnezzar (as in Eze 17:3); see Dt 28:49 and note.

[41]Kerioth[a q] will be captured
and the strongholds taken.
In that day the hearts of Moab's
warriors[r]
will be like the heart of a woman in
labor.[s]
[42]Moab will be destroyed[t] as a nation[u]
because she defied[v] the LORD.
[43]Terror[w] and pit and snare[x] await you,
O people of Moab,"
declares the LORD.
[44]"Whoever flees[y] from the terror
will fall into a pit,
whoever climbs out of the pit
will be caught in a snare;
for I will bring upon Moab
the year[z] of her punishment,"
declares the LORD.
[45]"In the shadow of Heshbon
the fugitives stand helpless,
for a fire has gone out from Heshbon,
a blaze from the midst of Sihon;[a]
it burns the foreheads of Moab,
the skulls[b] of the noisy boasters.
[46]Woe to you, O Moab![c]
The people of Chemosh are
destroyed;
your sons are taken into exile
and your daughters into captivity.
[47]"Yet I will restore[d] the fortunes of
Moab
in days to come,"
declares the LORD.

Here ends the judgment on Moab.

A Message About Ammon

49 Concerning the Ammonites:[e]

This is what the LORD says:

"Has Israel no sons?
Has she no heirs?
Why then has Molech[b f] taken
possession of Gad?[g]
Why do his people live in its
towns?
[2]But the days are coming,"
declares the LORD,
"when I will sound the battle cry[h]
against Rabbah[i] of the
Ammonites;
it will become a mound of ruins,[j]
and its surrounding villages will
be set on fire.
Then Israel will drive out
those who drove her out,[k]"
says the LORD.
[3]"Wail, O Heshbon,[l] for Ai[m] is
destroyed!
Cry out, O inhabitants of Rabbah!
Put on sackcloth[n] and mourn;
rush here and there inside the
walls,
for Molech[o] will go into exile,[p]
together with his priests and
officials.
[4]Why do you boast of your valleys,
boast of your valleys so fruitful?
O unfaithful daughter,[q]
you trust in your riches[r] and say,
'Who will attack me?'[s]
[5]I will bring terror on you
from all those around you,"
declares the Lord,
the LORD Almighty.
"Every one of you will be driven
away,
and no one will gather the
fugitives.[t]
[6]"Yet afterward, I will restore[u] the
fortunes of the Ammonites,"
declares the LORD.

48:41 [q]S Isa 15:1 [r]Am 2:16 [s]S Isa 21:3 **48:42** [t]S Isa 16:14 [u]ver 2 [v]S ver 26 **48:43** [w]Jer 49:5 [x]S Isa 24:17 **48:44** [y]1Ki 19:17; S Job 20:24; Isa 24:18; S Jer 46:5 [z]Jer 11:23; 23:12 **48:45** [a]S Nu 21:21, 26-28; S Jos 12:2 [b]Nu 24:17 **48:46** [c]S Nu 21:29 **48:47** [d]Ps 14:7; Isa 11:11; Jer 12:15; 49:6,39; Eze 16:53; Da 11:41 **49:1** [e]S Ge 19:38; S 1Sa 11:1-11; 2Sa 10:1-19 [f]S Lev 18:21 [g]Ge 30:11 **49:2** [h]S Jer 4:19 [i]S Dt 3:11 [j]S Dt 13:16 [k]S Isa 14:2; S Jer 30:16; Eze 21:28-32; 25:2-11 **49:3** [l]S Jos 13:26 [m]S Ge 12:8; S Jos 8:28 [n]S Ge 37:34 [o]Zep 1:5 [p]S Jer 48:7 **49:4** [q]S Jer 3:6 [r]S Jer 9:23; 1Ti 6:17 [s]S Jer 21:13 **49:5** [t]S Jer 44:14 **49:6** [u]Jer 12:14-17; S 48:47

[a] *41* Or *The cities* [b] *1* Or *their king*; Hebrew *malcam*; also in verse 3

48:41 *woman in labor.* See note on 4:31.
48:43 *Terror and pit and snare.* The Hebrew original illustrates Jeremiah's fondness for the well-turned phrase (see Introduction: Literary Features)—though in this case Jeremiah was not its creator (see Isa 24:17–18 and note on 24:17).
48:44 *Whoever flees ... will fall ... whoever climbs ... will be caught.* Divine judgment, once determined, is unavoidable (see Am 5:19).
48:45–46 Echoed from Nu 21:28–29; 24:17. Balaam's oracles against Moab are about to be fulfilled.
48:45 *Heshbon.* See note on v. 2. Apparently at this time it was controlled by the Ammonites (see 49:3). *Sihon.* Refers to the associates of Sihon king of the Amorites, whose chief city was Heshbon (see Nu 21:27) during the time of the exodus. *boasters.* See note on v. 29.
48:46 *Chemosh.* See note on v. 7.
48:47 See 46:26. *restore the fortunes.* See note on 29:14. *Here ends.* A note by the final compiler of the book of Jeremiah (see 51:64).
49:1 *Concerning the Ammonites.* See Eze 25:1–7; Am 1:13–15; Zep 2:8–11. Ammon was east of the Jordan and north of Moab (see note on Ge 19:36–38). *Has Israel no ... heirs?* Rhetorical questions to underscore how the Ammonites have humiliated Israel. *Molech.* The chief god of the Ammonites (see 1Ki 11:5,7,33), also known as Milcom (see NIV text note on 1Ki 11:5). Both titles are related to the West Semitic word for "king" (see NIV text note here). *taken possession of Gad.* Probably refers to the aftermath of Tiglath-Pileser III's conquest of Transjordan in 734–732 B.C. The Ammonites later apparently recovered from their defeat and overran some of the territory owned by the Israelite tribe of Gad. *his.* Molech's.
49:2 *battle cry.* See Am 1:14. *Rabbah of the Ammonites.* See note on Dt 3:11. *mound of ruins.* See 30:18 and note.
49:3 *Heshbon.* See note on 48:45; see also Jdg 11:26–27. *Ai.* Not the Ai of Jos 8. *walls.* The Hebrew for this word refers not to city walls but to walls separating vineyards from each other (see Nu 22:24; Isa 5:5). *Molech.* See note on v. 1. *will go into exile ... and officials.* See note on 48:7.
49:4 *unfaithful daughter.* A personification of the Ammonites (see note on 2Ki 19:21); the same language is used of the people of Judah in 31:22. *you trust in your riches.* Spoken to Moab in 48:7. *Who will attack me?* According to Josephus (*Antiquities*, 10.9.7) Nebuchadnezzar destroyed Ammon in the 23rd year of his reign (582 B.C.).

A Message About Edom

49:9-10pp — Ob 5-6
49:14-16pp — Ob 1-4

7 Concerning Edom:[v]

This is what the LORD Almighty says:

"Is there no longer wisdom in Teman?[w]
Has counsel perished from the prudent?
Has their wisdom decayed?
8 Turn and flee, hide in deep caves,[x]
you who live in Dedan,[y]
for I will bring disaster on Esau
at the time I punish him.
9 If grape pickers came to you,
would they not leave a few grapes?
If thieves came during the night,
would they not steal only as much as they wanted?
10 But I will strip Esau bare;
I will uncover his hiding places,[z]
so that he cannot conceal himself.
His children, relatives and neighbors will perish,
and he will be no more.[a]
11 Leave your orphans;[b] I will protect their lives.
Your widows[c] too can trust in me."

12 This is what the LORD says: "If those
who do not deserve to drink the cup[d] must
drink it, why should you go unpunished?[e]
You will not go unpunished, but must
drink it. 13 I swear[f] by myself," declares
the LORD, "that Bozrah[g] will become a ruin
and an object of horror,[h] of reproach[i] and
of cursing; and all its towns will be in ruins forever."[j]

14 I have heard a message from the LORD:
An envoy was sent to the nations to say,
"Assemble yourselves to attack it!
Rise up for battle!"

15 "Now I will make you small among the nations,
despised among men.
16 The terror you inspire
and the pride[k] of your heart have deceived you,
you who live in the clefts of the rocks,[l]
who occupy the heights of the hill.
Though you build your nest[m] as high as the eagle's,
from there I will bring you down,"
declares the LORD.
17 "Edom will become an object of horror;[n]
all who pass by will be appalled and will scoff
because of all its wounds.[o]
18 As Sodom[p] and Gomorrah[q] were overthrown,
along with their neighboring towns,"
says the LORD,
"so no one will live there;
no man will dwell[r] in it.
19 "Like a lion[s] coming up from Jordan's thickets[t]
to a rich pastureland,
I will chase Edom from its land in an instant.
Who is the chosen one I will appoint for this?
Who is like[u] me and who can challenge me?[v]
And what shepherd[w] can stand against me?"
20 Therefore, hear what the LORD has planned against Edom,[x]
what he has purposed[y] against those who live in Teman:[z]

49:7 [v]S Ge 25:30; S Ps 83:6 [w]S Ge 36:11, 15,34 **49:8** [x]S Jdg 6:2 [y]S Ge 10:7; S 25:3 **49:10** [z]S Ge 3:8 [a]Isa 34:10-12; S Jer 11:23; Eze 35:4; Ob 1:18; Mal 1:2-5 **49:11** [b]Hos 14:3 [c]S Dt 10:18; Jas 1:27 **49:12** [d]S Isa 51:23; S Jer 25:15; Mt 20:22 [e]S Pr 11:31 **49:13** [f]S Ge 22:16 [g]S Ge 36:33 [h]ver 17 [i]Jer 42:18 [j]S Jer 19:8; Eze 35:9 **49:16** [k]Eze 35:13; Ob 1:12 [l]S Job 39:28 [m]S Job 39:27 **49:17** [n]ver 13 [o]S Dt 29:22; Eze 35:7 **49:18** [p]Jer 23:14 [q]S Ge 19:24 [r]ver 33; S Isa 34:10 **49:19** [s]S 1Sa 17:34 [t]S Jer 12:5 [u]S Ex 8:10; S 2Ch 20:6; S Isa 46:5 [v]S Job 9:19; Jer 50:44 [w]1Sa 17:35 **49:20** [x]Isa 34:5 [y]Isa 14:27 [z]ver 7; S Ge 36:11

49:7 – 22 Shares many memorable phrases and concepts with the book of Obadiah (see Introduction to Obadiah: Unity and Theme).
49:7 *Concerning Edom.* See Isa 21:11 – 12; Eze 25:12 – 14; Am 1:11 – 12; Ob 1 – 16. *wisdom.* For which Edom was justly famed (see notes on Job 1:1; 2:11). *Teman.* An important Edomite town located south of the Dead Sea (see note on Job 2:11). In v. 20 it is used in parallelism with Edom itself.
49:8 *Turn and flee.* See v. 24; 46:21. *Dedan.* See 25:23; see also notes on Isa 21:13; Eze 25:13. *Esau.* The patriarch Jacob's brother, and another name for Edom (see Ge 25:29 – 30; 36:1), just as Israel was another name for Jacob (see Ge 32:28). The fact that Esau was Jacob's brother made Edom's enmity toward Israel all the more reprehensible (see Am 1:11; Ob 10).
49:9 – 10 Paralleled in Ob 5 – 6 (see notes there).
49:9 *grape pickers.* See note on v. 13. *leave a few grapes.* For the poor to glean (see note on Ru 2:2).
49:10 *strip ... bare.* See note on 13:22. *be no more.* See 31:15; Isa 19:7.
49:11 When the men of Edom go off to war and die, the Lord will protect their widows and orphans.
49:12 Echoed from 25:28 – 29. *those who do not deserve ... must drink it.* Though they are God's chosen ones, the people of Judah will be punished because of their sin (see 25:28; Am 3:2 and notes).
49:13 *swear by myself.* See notes on Ge 22:16; Isa 45:23; see also 22:5; 51:14. *Bozrah.* Not the Bozrah of 48:24 (see note there); the Edomite Bozrah was probably the capital of Edom in the days of Jeremiah (see v. 22; Ge 36:33; see also notes on Isa 34:6; Am 1:12). The Hebrew root underlying Bozrah is the same as that for "grape pickers" in v. 9. *ruin ... cursing.* See 25:18. *towns.* Surrounding villages. *in ruins forever.* See 25:9; Ps 74:3; Isa 58:12 and note.
49:14 – 16 Paralleled in Ob 1 – 4.
49:16 *pride.* Edom's besetting sin (see v. 4; Ob 11 – 13; cf. 48:29 – 30). *heights of the hill.* Edom was noted for its mountain strongholds. In the note on Sela at 2Ki 14:7; see notes on Isa 16:1; Ob 3.
49:17 Echoed from 19:8.
49:18 Repeated almost verbatim in 50:40, and echoed in part in v. 33. *Sodom and Gomorrah were overthrown.* See Ge 19:24 – 25. Later calamities were often compared with the one that befell Sodom and Gomorrah (see note on Am 4:11). *their neighboring towns.* Primarily Admah and Zeboiim (see Ge 14:2,8; Dt 29:23; Hos 11:8 and note).
49:19 – 21 Repeated almost verbatim in the oracle against Babylon (see 50:44 – 46).
49:19 *Jordan's thickets.* See 12:5 and note. *shepherd.* Ruler (see note on 2:8).
49:20 *Teman.* See note on v. 7. *flock.* The people of Edom.

The young of the flock[a] will be dragged
away;
he will completely destroy[b] their
pasture because of them.[c]
21 At the sound of their fall the earth will
tremble;[d]
their cry[e] will resound to the Red
Sea.[a]
22 Look! An eagle will soar and swoop[f]
down,
spreading its wings over Bozrah.[g]
In that day the hearts of Edom's
warriors[h]
will be like the heart of a woman in
labor.[i]

A Message About Damascus

23 Concerning Damascus:[j]

"Hamath[k] and Arpad[l] are dismayed,
for they have heard bad news.
They are disheartened,
troubled like[b] the restless sea.[m]
24 Damascus has become feeble,
she has turned to flee
and panic has gripped her;
anguish and pain have seized her,
pain like that of a woman in labor.[n]
25 Why has the city of renown not been
abandoned,
the town in which I delight?
26 Surely, her young men[o] will fall in the
streets;
all her soldiers will be silenced[p] in
that day,"
declares the LORD Almighty.
27 "I will set fire[q] to the walls of
Damascus;[r]
it will consume[s] the fortresses of
Ben-Hadad.[t]"

A Message About Kedar and Hazor

28 Concerning Kedar[u] and the kingdoms
of Hazor,[v] which Nebuchadnezzar[w] king
of Babylon attacked:

This is what the LORD says:

"Arise, and attack Kedar
and destroy the people of the East.[x]
29 Their tents and their flocks[y] will be
taken;
their shelters will be carried off
with all their goods and camels.
Men will shout to them,
'Terror[z] on every side!'
30 "Flee quickly away!
Stay in deep caves,[a] you who live in
Hazor,[b]"
declares the LORD.
"Nebuchadnezzar[c] king of Babylon has
plotted against you;
he has devised a plan against you.
31 "Arise and attack a nation at ease,
which lives in confidence,"
declares the LORD,
"a nation that has neither gates nor
bars;[d]
its people live alone.
32 Their camels[e] will become plunder,
and their large herds[f] will be booty.
I will scatter to the winds[g] those who
are in distant places[c][h]
and will bring disaster on them from
every side,"
declares the LORD.
33 "Hazor[i] will become a haunt of
jackals,[j]
a desolate[k] place forever.
No one will live there;
no man will dwell[l] in it."

A Message About Elam

34 This is the word of the LORD that
came to Jeremiah the prophet concerning
Elam,[m] early in the reign of Zedekiah[n] king
of Judah:

[a] 21 Hebrew *Yam Suph*; that is, Sea of Reeds
[b] 23 Hebrew *on* or *by* [c] 32 Or *who clip the hair by their foreheads*

49:20 [a] Jer 50:45 [b] ver 10; Ob 1:10; Mal 1:3-4 [c] Jer 50:45 **49:21** [d] Ps 114:7; Eze 26:15; 27:28; 31:16 [e] Jer 50:46; 51:29; Eze 26:18 **49:22** [f] S Dt 28:49; Hos 8:1; Hab 1:8 [g] S Ge 36:33 [h] Jer 50:36; Na 3:13 [i] Isa 13:8 **49:23** [j] S Ge 14:15; 2Ki 14:28; 2Ch 16:2; Ac 9:2 [k] 1Ki 8:65; Isa 10:9; Eze 47:16; Am 6:2; Zec 9:2 [l] S 2Ki 18:34; S 19:13 [m] S Ge 49:4 **49:24** [n] Jer 13:21 **49:26** [o] S Isa 9:17; S 13:18 [p] Isa 17:12-14 **49:27** [q] Jer 21:14; 43:12; 50:32; Eze 30:8; 39:6; Am 1:4 [r] S Ge 14:15 [s] Isa 17:1 [t] S 1Ki 15:18 **49:28** [u] S Ge 25:13 [v] S Jos 11:1 [w] S Jer 10:22 [x] S Jdg 6:3 **49:29** [y] ver 32 [z] S Jer 6:25 **49:30** [a] S Jdg 6:2 [b] Jos 11:1 [c] S Jer 10:22 **49:31** [d] Eze 38:11 **49:32** [e] S Jdg 6:5 [f] ver 29 [g] ver 36; Jer 13:24 [h] S Jer 9:26 **49:33** [i] S Jos 11:1 [j] S Isa 13:22 [k] Jer 48:9 [l] S ver 18; Jer 51:37 **49:34** [m] S Ge 10:22 [n] 2Ki 24:18

49:22 Echoed from 48:40–41. *eagle.* Represents Nebuchadnezzar in 48:40 (see note there), and probably here also. A more complete subjugation of the Edomites, however, was accomplished by Nabatean Arabs (perhaps the "desert jackals" of Mal 1:3) beginning c. 550 B.C. *Bozrah.* See note on v. 13. *woman in labor.* See note on 4:31.
49:23 *Concerning Damascus.* See Isa 17; Am 1:3–5 (see also note on Isa 17:1). *Hamath.* An important city in the kingdom of Aram (see Isa 10:9 and note). *Arpad.* See note on Isa 10:9. *bad news.* The threat of Babylonian invasion. *troubled like the restless sea.* See Isa 57:20.
49:24 *anguish.* See note on 4:19.
49:26 Repeated almost verbatim in 50:30.
49:27 A conventional word of judgment (see note on Am 1:4).
49:28 *Concerning Kedar.* See Isa 21:13–17; see also 2:10 and note. *kingdoms of Hazor.* See vv. 30,33; not the Hazor north of the Sea of Galilee (see Jos 11:1). These kingdoms may have included Dedan, Tema, Buz and other Arab regions (see 25:23–24 and notes), since the Hebrew root of the proper name Hazor often serves as a common noun meaning "settlement" (see especially Isa 42:11; see also Ge 25:16). *Nebuchadnezzar ... attacked.* In 599–598 B.C. *people of the East.* See Jdg 6:3 and note; Job 1:3; Eze 25:4.
49:29 *Terror on every side.* See note on 6:25.
49:30 *Stay in deep caves.* See v. 8.
49:31 *at ease.* Completely secure (see Job 21:23). *in confidence.* In safety, unsuspecting (see Jdg 18:7 and note; Eze 38:11). *has neither gates nor bars.* Lives in unwalled villages (see Dt 3:5; cf. 1Sa 23:7).
49:32 *scatter to the winds.* See Eze 5:12; 12:4. *who are in distant places.* See note on 9:26. *disaster ... from every side.* Contrast the description of Solomon's realm in 1Ki 5:4.
49:33 *haunt of jackals.* See note on 9:11. *No one ... dwell in it.* Echoes v. 18.
49:34 *This is the word of the LORD ... concerning.* See note on 46:1. *Elam.* See note on Isa 11:11.

35 This is what the LORD Almighty says:

"See, I will break the bow[o] of Elam,
the mainstay of their might.
36 I will bring against Elam the four winds[p]
from the four quarters of the heavens;[q]
I will scatter them to the four winds,
and there will not be a nation
where Elam's exiles do not go.
37 I will shatter Elam before their foes,
before those who seek their lives;
I will bring disaster upon them,
even my fierce anger,"[r]
declares the LORD.
"I will pursue them with the sword[s]
until I have made an end of them.
38 I will set my throne in Elam
and destroy her king and officials,"
declares the LORD.

39 "Yet I will restore[t] the fortunes of Elam
in days to come,"
declares the LORD.

A Message About Babylon

51:15-19pp — Jer 10:12-16

50 This is the word the LORD spoke through Jeremiah the prophet concerning Babylon[u] and the land of the Babylonians[a]:

2 "Announce and proclaim[v] among the nations,
lift up a banner[w] and proclaim it;
keep nothing back, but say,
'Babylon will be captured;[x]
Bel[y] will be put to shame,[z]
Marduk[a] filled with terror.
Her images will be put to shame
and her idols[b] filled with terror.'
3 A nation from the north[c] will attack her
and lay waste her land.
No one will live[d] in it;
both men and animals[e] will flee away.

4 "In those days, at that time,"
declares the LORD,
"the people of Israel and the people of Judah together[f]
will go in tears[g] to seek[h] the LORD their God.
5 They will ask the way[i] to Zion
and turn their faces toward it.
They will come[j] and bind themselves to the LORD
in an everlasting covenant[k]
that will not be forgotten.

6 "My people have been lost sheep;[l]
their shepherds[m] have led them astray[n]
and caused them to roam on the mountains.
They wandered over mountain and hill[o]
and forgot their own resting place.[p]
7 Whoever found them devoured[q] them;
their enemies said, 'We are not guilty,[r]
for they sinned against the LORD, their true pasture,
the LORD, the hope[s] of their fathers.'

8 "Flee[t] out of Babylon;[u]
leave the land of the Babylonians,
and be like the goats that lead the flock.

[a] *1* Or *Chaldeans*; also in verses 8, 25, 35 and 45

49:35 [o] S Ps 37:15; S Isa 22:6 **49:36** [p] S ver 32 [q] Da 11:4 **49:37** [r] Jer 30:24 [s] Jer 9:16; Eze 32:24 **49:39** [t] S Jer 48:47 **50:1** [u] S Ge 10:10; S Ps 137:8 **50:2** [v] S Dt 30:4; Jer 4:16 [w] S Ps 20:5; S Isa 13:2 [x] ver 9; Jer 51:31 [y] S Isa 21:9; S 46:1 [z] Ps 97:7; Jer 51:52 [a] ver 38; Isa 46:6; Jer 51:47 [b] S Lev 26:30 **50:3** [c] S ver 26; S Isa 41:25; S Jer 25:26 [d] S ver 13; S Isa 14:22-23; S Jer 9:11 [e] Zep 1:3 **50:4** [f] S Jer 3:18; Eze 37:22 [g] S Ezr 3:12 [h] S Isa 9:13; Eze 37:17; Hos 3:5 **50:5** [i] S Isa 11:16; S Jer 31:21 [j] S 1Sa 29:1; Jer 33:7 [k] S Dt 29:14; Isa 55:3; Jer 32:40; Heb 8:6-10 **50:6** [l] S Ps 119:176; Mt 9:36; 10:6 [m] S Jer 2:8; S 10:21 [n] S Ps 95:10; Jer 23:32; Eze 13:10 [o] Jer 3:6; Eze 34:6 [p] ver 19 **50:7** [q] S Jer 5:17; 10:25; Eze 35:12 [r] Jer 2:3 [s] S Jer 14:8 **50:8** [t] S Isa 48:20 [u] ver 28

49:35 *bow.* The Elamites were skilled archers (see Isa 22:6).
49:36 Contrast Isa 11:12. *to the four winds.* In every direction (see Eze 37:9; Da 7:2; 8:8).
49:37 *I will pursue ... made an end of them.* Echoes 9:16.
49:38 *set my throne in.* See 1:15 and note.
50:1—51:64 See Isa 13:1—14:23; 21:1-9. Jeremiah's prophecy concerning Babylon is by far the longest of his oracles against foreign nations (chs. 46-51) and expands on his earlier and briefer statements (see 25:12-14,26). Its date, in whole or in part, is 593 B.C. (see 51:59 and note). The two chapters divide into three main sections (50:2-28; 50:29—51:26; 51:27-58), each of which begins with a summons concerning war against Babylon, Judah's mortal enemy (see 50:2-3; 50:29-32; 51:27-32).
50:1 *word.* Or "message" (as in 46:13), comprising chs. 50-51. *through.* See 37:2. The message would eventually be sent by the prophet to Babylon itself (see 51:59-61).
50:2 *Announce and proclaim.* See 4:5; 46:14. *lift up a banner.* See note on Isa 5:26. The Hebrew for this phrase is translated "Raise the signal" in 4:6. *Babylon will be captured.* Fulfilled in 539 B.C. *Bel.* See 51:44; Isa 46:1 and note. *put to shame ... filled with terror.* The repetition of each of these phrases emphasizes that the chief god of Babylon and his images and idols are alike doomed. *Her ... her.* Babylon's. *idols.* See note on Lev 26:30. Derogatory references concerning idols and idolatry are common in the OT (see, e.g., Ps 115:4-7; Isa 44:9-20).
50:3 *nation from the north.* In Jeremiah, the foe from the north is almost always Babylonia (see, e.g., 1:14-15). Here, however, the reference is probably to Persia. Babylon's nemesis is expanded to "an alliance of great nations" in v. 9, specified by name in 51:27-28. *men and animals will flee.* Babylon will suffer the same fate as Jerusalem (see 33:12).
50:4 *Israel and ... Judah together.* See note on 3:18. *tears.* Of repentance (see 3:21-22; 31:9).
50:5 *everlasting covenant.* See 32:40 and note; see also 31:31-34; 33:20-21.
50:6 *lost sheep.* See Jesus' parable in Lk 15:3-7. *shepherds.* Rulers (see note on 2:8). *mountain and hill.* Places where pagan gods were worshiped (see note on 2:20). *their own resting place.* The Lord (see v. 7).
50:7 *hope of their fathers.* A phrase found only here (see 14:8,22; cf. Ac 28:20).
50:8 *like the goats that lead the flock.* Judah would be among the first of the captive peoples to be released from exile in Babylon.

9 For I will stir[v] up and bring against
Babylon
an alliance of great nations[w] from
the land of the north.[x]
They will take up their positions
against her,
and from the north she will be
captured.[y]
Their arrows[z] will be like skilled
warriors
who do not return empty-handed.
10 So Babylonia[a] will be plundered;[a]
all who plunder her will have their
fill,"
declares the LORD.
11 "Because you rejoice and are glad,
you who pillage my inheritance,[b]
because you frolic like a heifer[c]
threshing grain
and neigh like stallions,
12 your mother will be greatly ashamed;
she who gave you birth will be
disgraced.[d]
She will be the least of the nations—
a wilderness, a dry land, a desert.[e]
13 Because of the LORD's anger she will
not be inhabited
but will be completely desolate.[f]
All who pass Babylon will be horrified[g]
and scoff[h]
because of all her wounds.[i]
14 "Take up your positions around
Babylon,
all you who draw the bow.[j]
Shoot at her! Spare no arrows,[k]
for she has sinned against the LORD.
15 Shout[l] against her on every side!
She surrenders, her towers fall,
her walls[m] are torn down.
Since this is the vengeance[n] of the
LORD,
take vengeance on her;
do to her[o] as she has done to
others.[p]
16 Cut off from Babylon the sower,
and the reaper with his sickle at
harvest.
Because of the sword[q] of the oppressor
let everyone return to his own
people,[r]
let everyone flee to his own land.[s]
17 "Israel is a scattered flock[t]
that lions[u] have chased away.
The first to devour[v] him
was the king[w] of Assyria;
the last to crush his bones[x]
was Nebuchadnezzar[y] king[z] of
Babylon."

18 Therefore this is what the LORD Almighty, the God of Israel, says:
"I will punish the king of Babylon and
his land
as I punished the king[a] of Assyria.[b]
19 But I will bring[c] Israel back to his own
pasture
and he will graze on Carmel and
Bashan;
his appetite will be satisfied[d]
on the hills[e] of Ephraim and Gilead.[f]
20 In those days, at that time,"
declares the LORD,
"search will be made for Israel's guilt,
but there will be none,[g]
and for the sins[h] of Judah,
but none will be found,
for I will forgive[i] the remnant[j] I spare.
21 "Attack the land of Merathaim
and those who live in Pekod.[k]
Pursue, kill and completely destroy[b]
them,"
declares the LORD.

[a] *10* Or *Chaldea* [b] *21* The Hebrew term refers to the irrevocable giving over of things or persons to the LORD, often by totally destroying them; also in verse 26.

50:9 [v] S Isa 13:17 [w] S Jer 25:14 [x] S Isa 41:25; S Jer 25:26 [y] S ver 2 [z] S Isa 13:18 **50:10** [a] Isa 47:11; S Jer 30:16 **50:11** [b] S Isa 47:6 [c] S Jer 31:18 **50:12** [d] Jer 51:47 [e] ver 13; S Isa 21:1; Jer 25:12; 51:26 **50:13** [f] ver 3, S 12; S Jer 9:11; 48:9; 51:62 [g] Jer 51:41 [h] S Jer 18:16; 51:37; Eze 27:36; Hab 2:6 [i] S Dt 29:22 **50:14** [j] ver 29, 42 [k] S Isa 13:18 **50:15** [l] Jer 51:14 [m] S 2Ki 25:4; S Jer 51:44, 58 [n] ver 28; S Isa 10:3; 63:4; Jer 51:6 [o] ver 29; Ps 137:8; Rev 18:6 [p] Jer 51:24; Hab 2:7-8 **50:16** [q] S Jer 25:38 [r] S Isa 13:14 [s] Jer 51:9 **50:17** [t] S Lev 26:33; S Ps 119:176 [u] S 2Ki 24:1; S Jer 2:15 [v] S Jer 5:17 [w] S Dt 4:27; S 2Ki 15:29 [x] S Nu 24:8; La 3:4 [y] Jer 51:34 [z] S 2Ki 24:17; S 25:7 **50:18** [a] S Isa 10:12 [b] Eze 31:3; Zep 2:13 **50:19** [c] S Jer 31:10; Eze 34:13 [d] Jer 31:14 [e] S Jer 31:5 [f] Mic 7:14; Zec 10:10 **50:20** [g] S Ps 17:3 [h] Ps 103:12; S Isa 38:17; Eze 33:16; Mic 7:18, 19; Zec 3:4, 9 [i] S Isa 33:24 [j] S Ge 45:7; Isa 1:9; 10:20-22; S Ro 9:27 **50:21** [k] Eze 23:23

50:9 *alliance of great nations.* See Isa 13:4. They are named in 51:27–28 (see note on v. 3).
50:11 *you.* Babylonia. *my inheritance.* God's land and people (see 2:7; 12:7 and notes). *frolic like a heifer.* See Mal 4:2. *stallions.* See note on 8:16.
50:12 *mother.* Either (1) the city or, more likely, (2) the land (see Isa 50:1; Hos 2:5). *least.* Lit. "last." As Amalek, "first among the nations" (Nu 24:20) to attack Israel, was destroyed, so Babylonia, the last to attack Israel (up to Jeremiah's time), would be destroyed.
50:13 *not be inhabited.* See Isa 13:20 and note. *All who pass … because of all her wounds.* Said of Jerusalem in 19:8 and of Edom in 49:17.
50:14 *you who draw the bow.* Including the Medes (see Isa 13:17–18).
50:15 *Shout.* Give the battle cry (see Jos 6:16). *vengeance of the LORD.* See v. 28; 51:11. Though originating in his sovereign holiness, it was often carried out by his people (see Nu 31:3). *do to her … to others.* See v. 29; Ob 15 and note; cf. Gal 6:7–8.
50:16 *sword of the oppressor.* See 46:16. *let everyone … to his own land.* The Hebrew for this passage has a parallel in Isa 13:14. The captive peoples are warned to flee Babylon in order to avoid being cut down by her invaders.
50:17 *scattered flock.* See Joel 3:2. *lions.* Symbolic of Assyria and Babylonia (see 4:7; Isa 15:9 and notes). *The first … was the king of Assyria.* The Assyrians destroyed Israel (the northern kingdom) in 722–721 B.C. *the last … was Nebuchadnezzar.* The Babylonians destroyed Judah (the southern kingdom) in 586 B.C.
50:18 *I punished the king of Assyria.* Nineveh, the proud Assyrian capital, fell in 612 B.C., and Assyria herself was conquered by a coalition of Medes and Babylonians in 609.
50:19 *Carmel.* See Isa 33:9 and note. *Bashan.* See note on Isa 2:13. *hills of Ephraim.* The lush mountains of central Israel (see Eze 34:13–14). *Gilead.* See note on Ge 31:21; see also Nu 32:1; Mic 7:14.
50:20 See 33:8 and note; see also 36:3; Mic 7:18–19.
50:21 *Merathaim.* Means "double rebellion [against the Lord]," perhaps referring to vv. 24,29 (see Jdg 3:8; Isa 40:2 and notes). It is probably a pun on the Babylonian

"Do everything I have commanded
you.
22 The noise[l] of battle is in the land,
the noise of great destruction!
23 How broken and shattered
is the hammer[m] of the whole earth![n]
How desolate[o] is Babylon
among the nations!
24 I set a trap[p] for you, O Babylon,
and you were caught before you
knew it;
you were found and captured[q]
because you opposed[r] the LORD.
25 The LORD has opened his arsenal
and brought out the weapons[s] of his
wrath,
for the Sovereign LORD Almighty has
work to do
in the land of the Babylonians.[t]
26 Come against her from afar.[u]
Break open her granaries;
pile her up like heaps of grain.[v]
Completely destroy[w] her
and leave her no remnant.
27 Kill all her young bulls;[x]
let them go down to the slaughter![y]
Woe to them! For their day[z] has come,
the time[a] for them to be punished.
28 Listen to the fugitives[b] and refugees
from Babylon
declaring in Zion[c]
how the LORD our God has taken
vengeance,[d]
vengeance for his temple.[e]
29 "Summon archers against Babylon,
all those who draw the bow.[f]
Encamp all around her;
let no one escape.[g]
Repay[h] her for her deeds;[i]
do to her as she has done.
For she has defied[j] the LORD,
the Holy One[k] of Israel.

30 Therefore, her young men[l] will fall in
the streets;
all her soldiers will be silenced in
that day,"
declares the LORD.
31 "See, I am against[m] you, O arrogant
one,"
declares the Lord, the LORD
Almighty,
"for your day[n] has come,
the time for you to be punished.
32 The arrogant[o] one will stumble and
fall[p]
and no one will help her up;[q]
I will kindle a fire[r] in her towns
that will consume all who are
around her."

33 This is what the LORD Almighty says:

"The people of Israel are oppressed,[s]
and the people of Judah as well.
All their captors hold them fast,
refusing to let them go.[t]
34 Yet their Redeemer[u] is strong;
the LORD Almighty[v] is his name.
He will vigorously defend their cause[w]
so that he may bring rest[x] to their
land,
but unrest to those who live in
Babylon.

35 "A sword[y] against the Babylonians!"[z]
declares the LORD—
"against those who live in Babylon
and against her officials and wise[a]
men!
36 A sword against her false prophets!
They will become fools.
A sword against her warriors![b]
They will be filled with terror.[c]

50:22 [l] Jer 4:19-21; 51:54 **50:23** [m] S Isa 10:5 [n] Jer 51:25 [o] S Isa 14:16 **50:24** [p] Jer 51:12 [q] Jer 51:31 [r] Job 9:4 **50:25** [s] S Isa 13:5 [t] Jer 51:25,55 **50:26** [u] ver 3,41; Jer 51:11 [v] S Ru 3:7 [w] S Isa 14:22-23 **50:27** [x] S Ps 68:30; Jer 48:15 [y] S Isa 30:25; S Jer 25:34 [z] S Job 18:20 [a] Jer 51:6 **50:28** [b] ver 8 [c] Isa 48:20; Jer 51:10 [d] S ver 15 [e] 2Ki 24:13; Jer 51:11; 52:13 **50:29** [f] S ver 14 [g] S Isa 13:18; Jer 51:3 [h] S Dt 32:41; S Job 21:19; S Jer 51:6; Rev 18:6 [i] Eze 35:11; Ob 1:15 [j] S Isa 14:13-14; 47:10; Da 5:23 [k] Ps 78:41; Isa 41:20; Jer 51:5 **50:30** [l] S Isa 13:18 **50:31** [m] S Jer 21:13 [n] S Job 18:20; Rev 18:7-8 **50:32** [o] S Ps 119:21 [p] S Ps 20:8 [q] Am 5:2 [r] S Jer 49:27 **50:33** [s] Isa 58:6 [t] S Isa 14:17 **50:34** [u] S Ex 6:6; S Job 19:25 [v] Jer 31:35; 51:19 [w] S Ps 119:154; S Isa 49:25; Jer 15:21; 51:36; La 3:58 [x] S Isa 14:7 **50:35** [y] S Jer 47:6 [z] S Isa 45:1 [a] Da 5:7 **50:36** [b] S Jer 49:22 [c] Jer 51:30,32

word *marratu,* which sometimes referred to a region in southern Babylonia that was characterized by briny waters. *Pekod.* See Eze 23:23; means "punishment [from the Lord]," a pun on *Puqudu,* the Babylonian name for an Aramean tribe living on the eastern bank of the lower Tigris River. *completely destroy.* See NIV text note; v. 26; 25:9; 51:3; see also note on Dt 2:34.

50:22 *great destruction.* See 4:6; 6:1; cf. 48:3; 51:54.

50:23 *hammer of the whole earth.* See note on Isa 10:5. *How desolate ... among the nations!* The Hebrew for this sentence is repeated verbatim in 51:41.

50:24 *caught before you knew it.* The Persian attack in 539 B.C. would catch the city of Babylon completely by surprise (see 51:8; Isa 47:11).

50:25 *weapons of his wrath.* The nations (see 51:27–28) that the Lord would use to conquer Babylonia (see Isa 13:5 and note). *the ... LORD ... has work to do.* See 48:10.

50:26 *heaps of grain.* The Hebrew for this expression is used in Ne 4:2 to describe heaps of rubble that had been burned. *Completely destroy her.* By burning (see note on v. 21; see also Jos 11:11–13).

50:27 *young bulls.* The people of Babylonia, including especially her fighting men (see Isa 34:6–7 and notes). *go down to the slaughter.* See note on 48:15. *time for them to be punished.* See 11:23; 23:12; 46:21.

50:28 *fugitives and refugees.* Jewish exiles who had fled the destruction overtaking Babylonia. *vengeance, vengeance for his temple.* See v. 15 and note; 46:10; 51:6. The conquest of Babylonia was the Lord's response to Babylonia's burning of the Jerusalem temple.

50:29 *Repay her for her deeds.* Echoed from 25:14 (see 51:24). *do to her as she has done.* See v. 15 and note. *Holy One of Israel.* A title of God found frequently in Isaiah (see note on Isa 1:4), it occurs in Jeremiah only here and in 51:5.

50:30 Echoes 49:26.

50:31–32 A distant echo of 21:13–14, spoken there to Jerusalem but here to Babylonia.

50:33 *their captors.* See Ps 137:3; Isa 14:2. *refusing to let them go.* Reminiscent of the pharaoh's repeated refusals before the exodus (see, e.g., Ex 7:14; 8:2,32; 9:2,7).

50:34 *Redeemer.* See 31:11 and note. *defend their cause.* See 51:36. *bring rest.* See 31:2 and note; see also Isa 14:3,7 and notes on Dt 3:20; Jos 1:13.

50:35–38 Cf. Eze 21.

50:36 *false prophets ... will become fools.* See Isa 44:25; see also Nu 12:11 and NIV text note on Pr 1:7.

37 A sword against her horses and
chariots[d]
and all the foreigners in her ranks!
They will become women.[e]
A sword against her treasures![f]
They will be plundered.
38 A drought on[a] her waters![g]
They will dry[h] up.
For it is a land of idols,[i]
idols that will go mad with terror.

39 "So desert creatures[j] and hyenas will
live there,
and there the owl will dwell.
It will never again be inhabited
or lived in from generation to
generation.[k]
40 As God overthrew Sodom and
Gomorrah[l]
along with their neighboring towns,"
declares the LORD,
"so no one will live there;
no man will dwell in it.[m]

41 "Look! An army is coming from the
north;[n]
a great nation and many kings
are being stirred[o] up from the ends
of the earth.[p]
42 They are armed with bows[q] and
spears;
they are cruel[r] and without mercy.[s]
They sound like the roaring sea[t]
as they ride on their horses;
they come like men in battle formation
to attack you, O Daughter of
Babylon.[u]
43 The king of Babylon has heard reports
about them,
and his hands hang limp.[v]
Anguish has gripped him,
pain like that of a woman in labor.[w]
44 Like a lion coming up from Jordan's
thickets[x]
to a rich pastureland,
I will chase Babylon from its land in an
instant.
Who is the chosen[y] one I will
appoint for this?
Who is like me and who can challenge
me?[z]
And what shepherd can stand
against me?"
45 Therefore, hear what the LORD has
planned against Babylon,
what he has purposed[a] against the
land of the Babylonians:[b]
The young of the flock will be dragged
away;
he will completely destroy their
pasture because of them.
46 At the sound of Babylon's capture the
earth will tremble;[c]
its cry[d] will resound among the
nations.

51 This is what the LORD says:
"See, I will stir[e] up the spirit of a
destroyer
against Babylon[f] and the people of
Leb Kamai.[b]
2 I will send foreigners[g] to Babylon
to winnow[h] her and to devastate her
land;
they will oppose her on every side
in the day[i] of her disaster.
3 Let not the archer string his bow,[j]
nor let him put on his armor.[k]
Do not spare her young men;
completely destroy[c] her army.
4 They will fall[l] down slain in Babylon,[d]
fatally wounded in her streets.[m]
5 For Israel and Judah have not been
forsaken[n]
by their God, the LORD Almighty,
though their land[e] is full of guilt[o]
before the Holy One of Israel.

6 "Flee[p] from Babylon!
Run for your lives!
Do not be destroyed because of her
sins.[q]
It is time[r] for the LORD's vengeance;[s]
he will pay[t] her what she deserves.

50:37 [d] S 2Ki 19:23; Jer 51:21 [e] S Isa 19:16 [f] S Isa 45:3 **50:38** [g] Ps 137:1; Jer 51:13 [h] S Isa 11:15; Jer 51:36 [i] S ver 2 **50:39** [j] S Ps 74:14 [k] Isa 13:19-22; 34:13-15; Jer 51:37; Rev 18:2 **50:40** [l] S Ge 19:24; S Mt 10:15 [m] Jer 51:62 **50:41** [n] S ver 26; S Isa 41:25 [o] S Isa 13:17 [p] S Isa 13:4; Jer 51:22-28 **50:42** [q] S ver 14 [r] S Job 30:21 [s] S Isa 13:18 [t] S Isa 5:30 [u] S Isa 47:1 **50:43** [v] S Jer 47:3 [w] Jer 6:22-24 **50:44** [x] S Jer 12:5 [y] S Nu 16:5 [z] S Job 41:10; Isa 46:9; S Jer 49:19 **50:45** [a] Ps 33:11; Jer 51:11 [b] S Isa 48:14 **50:46** [c] S Jdg 5:4; S Jer 49:21 [d] S Job 24:12; Rev 18:9-10 **51:1** [e] S Isa 13:17 [f] Jer 25:12 **51:2** [g] Isa 13:5 [h] S Isa 41:16; Mt 3:12 [i] S Isa 13:9 **51:3** [j] S Jer 50:29 [k] Jer 46:4 **51:4** [l] Isa 13:15 [m] S Isa 13:18 **51:5** [n] S Lev 26:44; Isa 54:6-8 [o] Hos 4:1 **51:6** [p] S Isa 48:20 [q] Nu 16:26; Rev 18:4 [r] Jer 50:27 [s] S Isa 1:24; S Jer 50:15 [t] ver 24, 56; Dt 32:35; S Job 21:19; Jer 25:14; 50:29; La 3:64

[a] 38 Or *A sword against* [b] 1 *Leb Kamai* is a cryptogram for Chaldea, that is, Babylonia. [c] 3 The Hebrew term refers to the irrevocable giving over of things or persons to the LORD, often by totally destroying them. [d] 4 Or *Chaldea* [e] 5 Or / *and the land ⌞of the Babylonians⌟*

50:37 *against her horses and chariots.* See Isa 43:17; see also Ps 20:7. *foreigners.* See 25:20,24; Ne 13:3. *will become women.* See Na 3:13 and note.
50:38 *idols.* See 51:52; see also note on Isa 21:9. *go mad.* See 25:16 and note.
50:39 See Isa 13:20–22 and notes.
50:40 Echoes 49:18 (see note there).
50:41–43 Echoes 6:22–24 (see notes there). The earlier oracle, referring to Jerusalem, is here applied to Babylon.
50:42 *Daughter of Babylon.* A personification of the city of Babylon (see note on 2Ki 19:21).
50:43 *woman in labor.* See note on 4:31.
50:44–46 Echoes 49:19–21 (see notes there). The oracle against Edom is here applied to Babylon.
51:1 *stir up the spirit.* See 1Ch 5:26; Hag 1:14. The Hebrew underlying this phrase is translated "aroused ... the hostility of" in 2Ch 21:16. *destroyer.* See note on 4:7; here including the "kings of the Medes" (v. 11). *Leb Kamai.* Lit. "the heart of my attackers" (cf. Rev 17:5, where Babylon is called "the mother of prostitutes and of the abominations of the earth"). See NIV text note; see also note on 25:26.
51:3 *completely destroy.* See NIV text note; 25:9; 50:21,26; see also note on Dt 2:34.
51:4 *fall ... in her streets.* See 49:26; 50:30.
51:5 *forsaken.* Lit. "widowed"; contrast Isa 54:4,6–7 and notes. *Holy One of Israel.* See note on 50:29.
51:6 *Flee ... ! Run for your lives!* See v. 45; 48:6. This was spoken to the people of Judah (as in 50:8). *the LORD's vengeance.* See note on 50:15. *pay her what she deserves.* See Isa 59:18; 66:6.

[7]Babylon was a gold cup[u] in the LORD's
hand;
she made the whole earth drunk.
The nations drank her wine;
therefore they have now gone mad.
[8]Babylon will suddenly fall[v] and be
broken.
Wail over her!
Get balm[w] for her pain;
perhaps she can be healed.

[9]" 'We would have healed Babylon,
but she cannot be healed;
let us leave[x] her and each go to his
own land,
for her judgment[y] reaches to the
skies,
it rises as high as the clouds.'
[10]" 'The LORD has vindicated[z] us;
come, let us tell in Zion
what the LORD our God has done.'[a]

[11]"Sharpen the arrows,[b]
take up the shields![c]
The LORD has stirred up the kings[d] of
the Medes,[e]
because his purpose[f] is to destroy
Babylon.
The LORD will take vengeance,[g]
vengeance for his temple.[h]
[12]Lift up a banner[i] against the walls of
Babylon!
Reinforce the guard,
station the watchmen,[j]
prepare an ambush![k]
The LORD will carry out his purpose,[l]
his decree against the people of
Babylon.
[13]You who live by many waters[m]
and are rich in treasures,[n]
your end has come,
the time for you to be cut off.[o]
[14]The LORD Almighty has sworn by
himself:[p]
I will surely fill you with men, as
with a swarm of locusts,[q]
and they will shout[r] in triumph over
you.

51:7 [u]S Isa 51:22; Jer 25:15-16; 49:12; Rev 14:8-10 **51:8** [v]S Isa 14:15; S 21:9; S Rev 14:8 [w]Jer 8:22; 46:11 **51:9** [x]S Isa 13:14; S 31:9; Jer 50:16 [y]Rev 18:4-5 **51:10** [z]Mic 7:9 [a]Ps 64:9; S Jer 50:28 **51:11** [b]Jer 50:9 [c]S Isa 21:5 [d]S Isa 41:2 [e]ver 28; S Isa 13:3; S 41:25 [f]S Jer 50:45 [g]S Lev 26:25 [h]S Jer 50:28 **51:12** [i]ver 27; S Ps 20:5 [j]2Sa 18:24; Eze 33:2 [k]Jer 50:24 [l]S Ps 33:11 **51:13** [m]S Jer 50:38 [n]S Isa 45:3; Eze 22:27; Hab 2:9 [o]Jer 50:3 **51:14** [p]S Ge 22:16; Am 6:8 [q]ver 27; Am 7:1; Na 3:15 [r]Jer 50:15 **51:15** [s]Ps 104:24 [t]S Ge 1:1; S Ps 104:2 [u]S Ps 136:5 **51:16** [v]Ps 18:11-13 [w]S Job 28:26 [x]S Dt 28:12; S Ps 135:7; Jnh 1:4 **51:17** [y]S Isa 44:20; Hab 2:18-19 **51:18** [z]S Jer 18:15 **51:19** [a]S Ps 119:57 [b]S Ex 34:9 **51:20** [c]S Isa 10:5; Zec 9:13 [d]S Job 34:24; Mic 4:13 [e]S Isa 45:1

[15]"He made the earth by his power;
he founded the world by his
wisdom[s]
and stretched[t] out the heavens by
his understanding.[u]
[16]When he thunders,[v] the waters in the
heavens roar;
he makes clouds rise from the ends
of the earth.
He sends lightning with the rain[w]
and brings out the wind from his
storehouses.[x]

[17]"Every man is senseless and without
knowledge;
every goldsmith is shamed by his
idols.
His images are a fraud;[y]
they have no breath in them.
[18]They are worthless,[z] the objects of
mockery;
when their judgment comes, they
will perish.
[19]He who is the Portion[a] of Jacob is not
like these,
for he is the Maker of all things,
including the tribe of his
inheritance[b]—
the LORD Almighty is his name.

[20]"You are my war club,[c]
my weapon for battle—
with you I shatter[d] nations,[e]
with you I destroy kingdoms,
[21]with you I shatter horse and rider,[f]
with you I shatter chariot[g] and
driver,
[22]with you I shatter man and woman,
with you I shatter old man and
youth,
with you I shatter young man and
maiden,[h]
[23]with you I shatter shepherd and flock,
with you I shatter farmer and oxen,
with you I shatter governors and
officials.[i]

51:21 [f]S Ex 15:1 [g]S Isa 43:17; S Jer 50:37 **51:22** [h]S 2Ch 36:17; Isa 13:17-18 **51:23** [i]ver 57

51:7 See 25:15–16 and notes. *Babylon was ... gold.* See note on Da 2:32–43.
51:8 *Babylon will ... fall.* See Isa 21:9 and note. *balm.* See note on 8:22.
51:9 The speakers are the nations conquered by Babylonia. *each go to his own land.* See 50:16 and note. *her judgment.* The judgment on her sin. *reaches to the skies ... high as the clouds.* Poetic exaggeration (see Dt 1:28; Ps 57:10; 108:4).
51:10 Judah speaks (see 50:28). *The LORD has vindicated us.* See Ps 37:6.
51:11 *stirred up.* Lit. "stirred up the spirit of" (see note on v. 1). *Medes.* See v. 28; Isa 13:17 and note; Isa 21:2; Da 5:28,31; 6:8,12,15; 8:20. *vengeance, vengeance for his temple.* See note on 50:28.
51:12 *prepare an ambush.* To keep defenders from retreating to the safety of their fortifications (see Jos 8:14–22; Jdg 20:29–39).
51:13 *many waters.* The "rivers of Babylon" (Ps 137:1), including the mighty Euphrates along with a magnificent system of irrigation canals, were proverbial. *cut off.* Like a thread from the loom (see Isa 38:12).
51:14 *sworn by himself.* See note on Ge 22:16. *as with ... locusts.* See 46:23. *shout in triumph.* See note on 48:33.
51:15–19 Echoes 10:12–16 (see notes there).
51:20–23 Illustrates Jeremiah's fondness for the effective use of repetition (see 4:23–26; see also Introduction: Literary Features).
51:20 *You are my war club.* Cf. Pr 25:18; either (1) Cyrus of Persia, soon to conquer Babylon, or, more likely, (2) Babylonia, destroyer of nations (see 50:23; see also note on Isa 10:5). *shatter.* See vv. 21–23. The Hebrew root for this verb is the same as that for "war club." See also Ex 15:6. The Hebrew verb is translated "dash (to pieces)" in Ps 2:9; 137:9; Hos 10:14; 13:16.

24"Before your eyes I will repay[j] Babylon[k] and all who live in Babylonia[a] for
all the wrong they have done in Zion," declares the LORD.

25"I am against[l] you, O destroying
mountain,
you who destroy the whole earth,"[m]
declares the LORD.
"I will stretch out my hand[n] against
you,
roll you off the cliffs,
and make you a burned-out
mountain.[o]
26No rock will be taken from you for a
cornerstone,
nor any stone for a foundation,
for you will be desolate[p] forever,"
declares the LORD.

27"Lift up a banner[q] in the land!
Blow the trumpet among the
nations!
Prepare the nations for battle against
her;
summon against her these
kingdoms:[r]
Ararat,[s] Minni and Ashkenaz.[t]
Appoint a commander against her;
send up horses like a swarm of
locusts.[u]
28Prepare the nations for battle against
her—
the kings of the Medes,[v]
their governors and all their officials,
and all the countries they rule.[w]
29The land trembles[x] and writhes,
for the LORD's purposes[y] against
Babylon stand—
to lay waste[z] the land of Babylon
so that no one will live there.[a]
30Babylon's warriors[b] have stopped
fighting;
they remain in their strongholds.
Their strength is exhausted;
they have become like women.[c]
Her dwellings are set on fire;[d]
the bars[e] of her gates are broken.
31One courier[f] follows another
and messenger follows messenger
to announce to the king of Babylon
that his entire city is captured,[g]
32the river crossings seized,
the marshes set on fire,[h]
and the soldiers terrified.[i]"

33This is what the LORD Almighty, the
God of Israel, says:

"The Daughter of Babylon[j] is like a
threshing floor[k]
at the time it is trampled;
the time to harvest[l] her will soon
come.[m]"

34"Nebuchadnezzar[n] king of Babylon has
devoured[o] us,[p]
he has thrown us into confusion,
he has made us an empty jar.
Like a serpent he has swallowed us
and filled his stomach with our
delicacies,
and then has spewed[q] us out.
35May the violence[r] done to our flesh[b]
be upon Babylon,"
say the inhabitants of Zion.
"May our blood be on those who live
in Babylonia,"
says Jerusalem.[s]

36Therefore, this is what the LORD says:

"See, I will defend your cause[t]
and avenge[u] you;
I will dry up[v] her sea
and make her springs dry.
37Babylon will be a heap of ruins,
a haunt[w] of jackals,
an object of horror and scorn,[x]
a place where no one lives.[y]

[a] 24 Or *Chaldea*; also in verse 35 [b] 35 Or *done to us and to our children*

51:24 [j]S ver 6,35; S Dt 32:41; S Jer 50:15; La 3:64 [k]S Isa 45:1
51:25 [l]S Jer 21:13 [m]Jer 50:23 [n]S Ex 3:20 [o]Zec 4:7
51:26 [p]ver 29; S Isa 13:19-22; S Jer 50:12
51:27 [q]S Ps 20:5; S Isa 13:2 [r]S Jer 25:14 [s]S Ge 8:4 [t]Ge 10:3 [u]S ver 14
51:28 [v]S ver 11 [w]ver 48
51:29 [x]S Jdg 5:4; S Jer 49:21 [y]S Ps 33:11 [z]Jer 48:9 [a]ver 43; S Isa 13:20
51:30 [b]S Jer 50:36 [c]S Isa 19:16 [d]S Isa 47:14 [e]S Isa 45:2
51:31 [f]2Sa 18:19-31 [g]S Jer 50:2; Da 5:30
51:32 [h]S Isa 47:14 [i]S Jer 50:36
51:33 [j]S Isa 47:1 [k]S Isa 21:10 [l]S Isa 17:5 [m]S Isa 13:22
51:34 [n]S Jer 50:17 [o]Na 2:12 [p]Hos 8:8 [q]ver 44; S Lev 18:25
51:35 [r]Joel 3:19; Hab 2:17 [s]S ver 24; Ps 137:8
51:36 [t]Ps 140:12; Jer 50:34; La 3:58 [u]ver 6; Jer 20:12; S Ro 12:19 [v]S Isa 11:15; S 19:5; Hos 13:15
51:37 [w]S Isa 13:22; Rev 18:2 [x]Na 3:6; Mal 2:9 [y]S Jer 50:13,39

51:24 *your.* Judah's. *repay ... for all the wrong they have done.* See v. 6; 50:15,29 and notes.
51:25 *destroying mountain.* Symbolizes a powerful kingdom (see Da 2:35,44–45), here Babylon. *burned-out mountain.* After being judged by the Lord, Babylon will be like an extinct volcano.
51:26 *desolate forever.* See 25:12; 50:12–13; see also note on Isa 13:20.
51:27 See 50:29. *Lift up a banner ... ! Blow the trumpet ... !* See 4:5–6; 6:1 and notes. *Prepare ... for battle.* Lit. "Consecrate" (see note on 6:4). *these kingdoms.* Allies of the Medes (see v. 11 and note). *Ararat.* See note on Ge 8:4. *Minni.* A region mentioned in Assyrian inscriptions, it was located somewhere in Armenia. *Ashkenaz.* See note on Ge 10:3. *commander.* The Hebrew for this word appears again in the OT only in Na 3:17 ("officials"). It is a Babylonian loanword meaning lit. "scribe." *like ... locusts.* See note on 46:23.
51:28 *Medes.* See note on v. 11. *all the countries they rule.* See note on 34:1; see also 1Ki 9:19.
51:29 *land trembles and writhes.* At the fearful prospect of war.
51:30 *exhausted ... women.* In the Hebrew there is a play on words. *become like women.* See 50:37; Na 3:13 and note.
51:31 *One courier follows another.* They run to the palace from all parts of the city.
51:32 *river crossings.* Fords and ferries (and perhaps bridges). *marshes set on fire.* To destroy the reeds and prevent fugitives from hiding among them.
51:33 *Daughter of Babylon.* A personification of the city of Babylon (see note on 2Ki 19:21). *threshing floor.* The destruction of a city or nation is often depicted as a harvest (see Isa 27:12; Joel 3:13 and notes; Mic 4:12–13; cf. Rev 14:14–20 and note on 14:15).
51:34 *serpent.* The Hebrew for this word is translated "monster" in Isa 51:9, where it symbolizes Egypt (see Ge 1:21 and note). *delicacies.* See Ge 49:20.
51:35 *flesh.* See Mic 3:2–3.
51:36 *avenge you.* See vv. 6,11; see also note on 50:15. *sea ... springs.* See note on v. 13. Babylonia is called the "Desert by the Sea" in Isa 21:1 (see note there).
51:37 See 9:11; 18:16 and notes.

38 Her people all roar like young lions,[z]
they growl like lion cubs.
39 But while they are aroused,
I will set out a feast for them
and make them drunk,[a]
so that they shout with laughter—
then sleep forever[b] and not awake,"
declares the LORD.[c]
40 "I will bring them down
like lambs to the slaughter,
like rams and goats.[d]

41 "How Sheshach[a][e] will be captured,[f]
the boast of the whole earth seized!
What a horror[g] Babylon will be
among the nations!
42 The sea will rise over Babylon;
its roaring waves[h] will cover her.
43 Her towns will be desolate,
a dry and desert[i] land,
a land where no one lives,
through which no man travels.[j]
44 I will punish Bel[k] in Babylon
and make him spew out[l] what he
has swallowed.
The nations will no longer stream to
him.
And the wall[m] of Babylon will fall.
45 "Come out[n] of her, my people!
Run[o] for your lives!
Run from the fierce anger[p] of the
LORD.
46 Do not lose heart[q] or be afraid[r]
when rumors[s] are heard in the land;
one rumor comes this year, another the
next,
rumors of violence in the land
and of ruler against ruler.
47 For the time will surely come
when I will punish the idols[t] of
Babylon;
her whole land will be disgraced[u]
and her slain will all lie fallen within
her.[v]
48 Then heaven and earth and all that is
in them
will shout[w] for joy over Babylon,
for out of the north[x]
destroyers[y] will attack her,"
declares the LORD.

49 "Babylon must fall because of Israel's
slain,
just as the slain in all the earth
have fallen because of Babylon.[z]
50 You who have escaped the sword,
leave[a] and do not linger!
Remember[b] the LORD in a distant land,[c]
and think on Jerusalem."

51 "We are disgraced,[d]
for we have been insulted
and shame covers our faces,
because foreigners have entered
the holy places of the LORD's
house."[e]

52 "But days are coming," declares the
LORD,
"when I will punish her idols,[f]
and throughout her land
the wounded will groan.[g]
53 Even if Babylon reaches the sky[h]
and fortifies her lofty stronghold,
I will send destroyers[i] against her,"
declares the LORD.

54 "The sound of a cry[j] comes from
Babylon,
the sound of great destruction[k]
from the land of the Babylonians.[b]
55 The LORD will destroy Babylon;
he will silence[l] her noisy din.
Waves[m] ⌞of enemies⌟ will rage like great
waters;
the roar of their voices will resound.
56 A destroyer[n] will come against
Babylon;
her warriors will be captured,
and their bows will be broken.[o]
For the LORD is a God of retribution;
he will repay[p] in full.

51:38 [z]S Isa 5:29 **51:39** [a]S Isa 21:5 [b]S Ps 13:3 [c]ver 57; S Jer 50:24 **51:40** [d]Eze 39:18 **51:41** [e]S Jer 25:26 [f]Isa 13:19 [g]Jer 50:13 **51:42** [h]S Ps 18:4; Isa 8:7 **51:43** [i]S Isa 21:1 [j]S ver 29,62; S Isa 13:20; Jer 2:6 **51:44** [k]S Isa 21:9; S 46:1 [l]S ver 34 [m]ver 58; S 2Ki 25:4; Isa 25:12; Jer 50:15 **51:45** [n]ver 50 [o]S Isa 48:20 [p]Ps 76:10; 79:6 **51:46** [q]Ps 18:45 [r]S Jer 46:27 [s]S 2Ki 19:7 **51:47** [t]S Isa 46:1-2; S Jer 50:2 [u]Jer 50:12 [v]S Jer 27:7 **51:48** [w]S Job 3:7; S Ps 149:2; Rev 18:20 [x]ver 11; S Isa 41:25; S Jer 25:26 [y]ver 53,56 **51:49** [z]Ps 137:8; S Jer 50:29 **51:50** [a]ver 45 [b]S Ps 137:6 [c]Jer 23:23 **51:51** [d]Ps 44:13-16; 79:4 [e]La 1:10 **51:52** [f]ver 47 [g]S Job 24:12 **51:53** [h]S Ge 11:4; S Isa 14:13-14 [i]S ver 48; S Job 15:21 **51:54** [j]S Job 24:12 [k]S Jer 50:22 **51:55** [l]Isa 25:5 [m]S Ps 18:4 **51:56** [n]S ver 48; S Job 15:21 [o]Ps 46:9 [p]S ver 6; S Ge 4:24; S Dt 32:41; Ps 94:1-2; Hab 2:8

[a] *41* *Sheshach* is a cryptogram for Babylon.
[b] *54* Or *Chaldeans*

51:38 *roar like young lions.* See 2:15 and note.
51:39 *aroused.* Lit. "heated"; for a similar image see Hos 7:4–7. *drunk.* See v. 57; see also notes on 25:15–16,26.
51:40 *lambs ... rams and goats.* Symbolic of the people (see Isa 34:6; Eze 39:18) of Babylon. *slaughter.* See Isa 53:7 and note.
51:41 *Sheshach.* See note on 25:26.
51:42 *sea ... its roaring waves.* See Isa 17:12 and note; here and in v. 55, Babylon's enemies (see 46:7 and note).
51:43 See 48:9; 49:18,33; 50:12–13.
51:44 *Bel.* See 50:2; Isa 46:1 and note. *what he has swallowed.* Captive peoples (including Judah) and plundered goods (including vessels from the temple in Jerusalem; see Da 5:2–3). *wall of Babylon.* A wall of double construction, the outer wall (12 feet thick) being separated from the inner wall (21 feet thick) by a dry moat 23 feet wide.
51:45 *Run for your lives!* See note on v. 6. *fierce anger.* See 4:8,26; Isa 13:13; Na 1:6.
51:46 *Do not ... be afraid when rumors are heard.* While giving his Olivet discourse, Jesus may have had this passage in mind (see Mt 24:6; Mk 13:7; Lk 21:9).
51:47 *punish the idols of Babylon.* See v. 52; see also note on 50:2.
51:48 *heaven and earth ... will shout for joy.* See Isa 44:23; Rev 18:20; 19:1–3. *out of the north.* See note on 50:3.
51:49 See note on 25:26.
51:50 *leave.* See note on v. 6.
51:51 *foreigners have entered the holy places.* Refers to Nebuchadnezzar's defiling the Jerusalem temple in 586 B.C. The same sacrilege would occur under Antiochus Epiphanes in 168 B.C. and under the Romans in A.D. 70.
51:53 *reaches the sky.* See Ge 11:4 and note; Isa 14:13–15. *destroyers.* See vv. 48,56.
51:54 See 50:46. *great destruction.* See note on 4:6.
51:55 *Waves.* See note on v. 42. *like great waters.* See note on Ps 32:6.
51:56 *God of retribution.* See note on v. 24.

57 I will make her officials[q] and wise[r]
men drunk,[s]
her governors, officers and warriors
as well;
they will sleep[t] forever and not
awake,"
declares the King,[u] whose name is
the LORD Almighty.

58 This is what the LORD Almighty says:
"Babylon's thick wall[v] will be leveled
and her high gates[w] set on fire;
the peoples[x] exhaust[y] themselves for
nothing,
the nations' labor is only fuel for the
flames."[z]

59 This is the message Jeremiah gave to
the staff officer Seraiah son of Neriah,[a] the
son of Mahseiah, when he went to Babylon with Zedekiah[b] king of Judah in the
fourth[c] year of his reign. 60 Jeremiah had
written on a scroll[d] about all the disasters
that would come upon Babylon — all that
had been recorded concerning Babylon.
61 He said to Seraiah, "When you get to
Babylon, see that you read all these words
aloud. 62 Then say, 'O LORD, you have said
you will destroy this place, so that neither
man nor animal will live in it; it will be
desolate[e] forever.' 63 When you finish reading this scroll, tie a stone to it and throw
it into the Euphrates.[f] 64 Then say, 'So will
Babylon sink to rise no more[g] because of
the disaster I will bring upon her. And her
people[h] will fall.' "[i]

The words of Jeremiah end[j] here.

The Fall of Jerusalem

52:1-3pp — 2Ki 24:18-20; 2Ch 36:11-16
52:4-16pp — Jer 39:1-10
52:4-21pp — 2Ki 25:1-21; 2Ch 36:17-20

52 Zedekiah[k] was twenty-one years old
when he became king, and he reigned
in Jerusalem eleven years. His mother's
name was Hamutal daughter of Jeremiah;
she was from Libnah.[l] 2 He did evil in the
eyes of the LORD, just as Jehoiakim[m] had
done. 3 It was because of the LORD's anger
that all this happened to Jerusalem and
Judah,[n] and in the end he thrust them
from his presence.[o]

Now Zedekiah rebelled[p] against the
king of Babylon.

4 So in the ninth year of Zedekiah's reign,
on the tenth[q] day of the tenth month, Nebuchadnezzar king of Babylon marched
against Jerusalem[r] with his whole army.
They camped outside the city and built
siege works[s] all around it.[t] 5 The city was
kept under siege until the eleventh year of
King Zedekiah.

6 By the ninth day of the fourth month
the famine in the city had become so severe that there was no food for the people
to eat.[u] 7 Then the city wall was broken
through, and the whole army fled.[v] They
left the city at night through the gate between the two walls near the king's garden, though the Babylonians[a] were surrounding the city. They fled toward the
Arabah,[b] 8 but the Babylonian[c] army pursued King Zedekiah and overtook him in
the plains of Jericho. All his soldiers were
separated from him and scattered, 9 and he
was captured.[w]

He was taken to the king of Babylon at
Riblah[x] in the land of Hamath,[y] where he
pronounced sentence on him. 10 There at
Riblah the king of Babylon slaughtered the
sons[z] of Zedekiah before his eyes; he also
killed all the officials of Judah. 11 Then he
put out Zedekiah's eyes, bound him with
bronze shackles and took him to Babylon,
where he put him in prison till the day of
his death.[a]

12 On the tenth day of the fifth[b] month,
in the nineteenth year of Nebuchadnezzar
king of Babylon, Nebuzaradan[c] commander of the imperial guard, who served the

51:57 [q] S ver 23 [r] S Job 5:13 [s] S Isa 21:5 [t] S ver 39; Ps 76:5; S Jer 25:27 [u] S Isa 6:5
51:58 [v] S ver 44; S 2Ki 25:4; S Isa 15:1 [w] S Isa 13:2 [x] ver 64 [y] S Isa 47:13 [z] S Isa 47:14
51:59 [a] Jer 36:4 [b] Jer 52:1 [c] Jer 28:1
51:60 [d] S Ex 17:14; Jer 30:2; 36:2
51:62 [e] S Isa 13:20; S Jer 9:11; S 50:13,39
51:63 [f] S Ge 2:14
51:64 [g] Eze 26:21; 28:19 [h] S ver 58 [i] Rev 18:21 [j] S Job 31:40
52:1 [k] S 2Ki 24:17 [l] S Nu 33:20; Jos 10:29; 2Ki 8:22
52:2 [m] S Jer 36:30
52:3 [n] Isa 3:1 [o] S Ge 4:14; S Ex 33:15 [p] Eze 17:12-16
52:4 [q] Zec 8:19 [r] Jer 34:1 [s] S Jer 6:6 [t] Eze 24:1-2
52:6 [u] S Lev 26:26; S Isa 3:1; La 1:11
52:7 [v] La 4:19
52:9 [w] S Jer 21:7; S 32:4 [x] S Nu 34:11 [y] S Nu 13:21
52:10 [z] S Jer 22:30
52:11 [a] Jer 34:4; Eze 12:13; 17:16
52:12 [b] Zec 7:5; 8:19 [c] ver 26

[a] 7 Or *Chaldeans*; also in verse 17 [b] 7 Or *the Jordan Valley* [c] 8 Or *Chaldean*; also in verse 14

51:57 *officials and wise men.* See 50:35. *drunk.* See v. 39; see also notes on 25:15 – 16,26. *King.* See note on 46:18. The true King is the Lord, not Bel/Marduk (see 50:2 and note).

51:58 *thick wall.* See note on v. 44. *high gates.* The famous Ishtar Gate was almost 40 feet high. *the peoples ... fuel for the flames.* Very similar to Hab 2:13.

51:59 – 64 A prose conclusion to the book in general and to the oracle against Babylon in particular.

51:59 *staff officer.* Lit. "resting-place officer" (see Nu 10:33), the official responsible for determining when and where his men on the march should stay overnight. *Seraiah son of Neriah.* An ancient seal has been found that bears the inscription "Belonging to Seraiah son of Neriah," and it no doubt refers to the man mentioned here. He was a brother of Jeremiah's secretary, Baruch (see 32:12). *he.* Seraiah. *Zedekiah ... fourth year.* 593 B.C. Zedekiah may have been summoned to Babylon by Nebuchadnezzar to be interrogated by him (see note on 27:3).

51:60 *scroll.* See note on Ex 17:14. *all that had been recorded concerning Babylon.* Probably the oracle of 50:2 — 51:58 (see note on 50:1).

51:62 *you have said.* See v. 26.

51:64 *The words of Jeremiah end here.* A note by the final compiler of the book of Jeremiah (see 48:47).

52:1 – 27,31 – 34 Paralleled almost verbatim in 2Ki 24:18 — 25:21,27 – 30 (see notes there). (52:4 – 27 is summarized in 39:1 – 10; see notes there.) The writer(s) of Kings and the writer of the appendix to Jeremiah (perhaps Baruch) doubtless had access to the same sources. It is unlikely that either of the two accounts copied from the other, since each has peculiarities characteristic of the larger work that it concludes. In a few passages, Jeremiah is fuller than Kings (compare especially vv. 10 – 11 with 2Ki 25:7; v. 15 with 2Ki 25:11; vv. 19 – 23 with 2Ki 25:15 – 17; v. 31 with 2Ki 25:27; v. 34 with 2Ki 25:30).

52:1 *Jeremiah.* Not the prophet. *Libnah.* See note on 2Ki 8:22.

52:12 *tenth day.* The parallel in 2Ki 25:8 reads "seventh day";

king of Babylon, came to Jerusalem. 13He
set fire[d] to the temple[e] of the LORD, the
royal palace and all the houses[f] of Jerusalem. Every important building he burned
down. 14The whole Babylonian army under the commander of the imperial guard
broke down all the walls[g] around Jerusalem. 15Nebuzaradan the commander of the
guard carried into exile[h] some of the poorest people and those who remained in the
city, along with the rest of the craftsmen[a]
and those who had gone over[i] to the king
of Babylon. 16But Nebuzaradan left behind[j] the rest of the poorest people of the
land to work the vineyards and fields.
17The Babylonians broke up the bronze
pillars,[k] the movable stands[l] and the
bronze Sea[m] that were at the temple of
the LORD and they carried all the bronze to
Babylon.[n] 18They also took away the pots,
shovels, wick trimmers, sprinkling bowls,[o]
dishes and all the bronze articles used in
the temple service.[p] 19The commander of
the imperial guard took away the basins,
censers,[q] sprinkling bowls, pots, lampstands,[r] dishes[s] and bowls used for drink
offerings[t]—all that were made of pure
gold or silver.[u]
20The bronze from the two pillars, the
Sea and the twelve bronze bulls[v] under it,
and the movable stands, which King Solomon had made for the temple of the LORD,
was more than could be weighed.[w] 21Each
of the pillars was eighteen cubits high
and twelve cubits in circumference[b]; each
was four fingers thick, and hollow.[x] 22The
bronze capital[y] on top of the one pillar was
five cubits[c] high and was decorated with a
network and pomegranates[z] of bronze all
around. The other pillar, with its pomegranates, was similar. 23There were ninety-six pomegranates on the sides; the total
number of pomegranates[a] above the surrounding network was a hundred.[b]
24The commander of the guard took as
prisoners Seraiah[c] the chief priest, Zephaniah[d] the priest next in rank and the three
doorkeepers.[e] 25Of those still in the city,
he took the officer in charge of the fighting men, and seven royal advisers. He also
took the secretary[f] who was chief officer
in charge of conscripting the people of the
land and sixty of his men who were found
in the city. 26Nebuzaradan[g] the commander took them all and brought them to the
king of Babylon at Riblah. 27There at Riblah,[h] in the land of Hamath, the king had
them executed.

So Judah went into captivity, away[i] from
her land. 28This is the number of the people Nebuchadnezzar carried into exile:[j]

in the seventh year, 3,023 Jews;
29in Nebuchadnezzar's eighteenth year,
832 people from Jerusalem;
30in his twenty-third year,
745 Jews taken into exile[k] by Nebuzaradan the commander of the
imperial guard.
There were 4,600 people in all.[l]

Jehoiachin Released

52:31-34pp — 2Ki 25:27-30

31In the thirty-seventh year of the exile
of Jehoiachin[m] king of Judah, in the year
Evil-Merodach[d] became king of Babylon,
he released Jehoiachin king of Judah and
freed him from prison on the twenty-fifth
day of the twelfth month. 32He spoke
kindly to him and gave him a seat of hon-
or higher than those of the other kings
who were with him in Babylon. 33So Jehoiachin put aside his prison clothes and
for the rest of his life ate regularly at the
king's table.[n] 34Day by day the king of
Babylon gave Jehoiachin a regular allowance[o] as long as he lived, till the day of
his death.

52:13 [d]S 2Ch 36:19; S Ps 74:8; La 2:6 [e]S Dt 29:24; Ps 79:1; Mic 3:12 [f]S Dt 13:16; S Jer 19:13 **52:14** [g]S Ne 1:3; La 2:8 **52:15** [h]S 2Ki 24:1; S Jer 1:3 [i]S Jer 38:19 **52:16** [j]Jer 40:6 **52:17** [k]S 1Ki 7:15 [l]1Ki 7:27-37 [m]S 1Ki 7:23 [n]Jer 27:19-22 **52:18** [o]S Nu 4:14 [p]S Ex 27:3; 1Ki 7:45 **52:19** [q]S Lev 10:1; S 1Ki 7:50 [r]S Nu 3:31 [s]Ex 25:29 [t]S Nu 4:7 [u]S Ezr 1:7; Da 5:2 **52:20** [v]1Ki 7:25 [w]S 1Ki 7:47 **52:21** [x]S 1Ki 7:15 **52:22** [y]S 1Ki 7:16 [z]S Ex 28:33 **52:23** [a]1Ki 7:20 [b]S ver 17; S Jer 27:19 **52:24** [c]S 2Ki 25:18 [d]S 2Ki 25:18; S Jer 37:3 [e]S 2Ki 12:9 **52:25** [f]Jer 36:10 **52:26** [g]S ver 12 **52:27** [h]S Nu 34:11 [i]S Jer 20:4 **52:28** [j]S Dt 28:36; S 2Ch 36:20; S Ne 1:2 **52:30** [k]S Jer 43:3 [l]S Jer 13:19 **52:31** [m]S 2Ch 36:9 **52:33** [n]S 2Sa 9:7 **52:34** [o]2Sa 9:10

[a] *15* Or *populace* [b] *21* That is, about 27 feet (about 8.1 meters) high and 18 feet (about 5.4 meters) in circumference [c] *22* That is, about 7 1/2 feet (about 2.3 meters) [d] *31* Also called *Amel-Marduk*

one of the numbers is a copyist's error, but we cannot tell which (see vv. 22,25,31 and notes).

52:18–19 See notes on 1Ki 7:40,45,50.

52:20 *twelve bronze bulls.* See note on 2Ch 4:4.

52:21–23 See notes on 1Ki 7:15–23.

52:22 *five.* The parallel in 2Ki 25:17 reads "three" (see NIV text note there), probably a copyist's error.

52:25 *seven.* The parallel in 2Ki 25:19 reads "five"; see note on v. 12.

52:28 *seventh year.* Of Nebuchadnezzar's reign (see vv. 29–30), which was 597 B.C. *3,023.* Probably includes only adult males, since the corresponding figure(s) in 2Ki 24:14,16 are significantly higher.

52:29 *eighteenth year.* 586 B.C. In v. 12 the same year is called the "nineteenth year"; the difference is due to alternate ways of computing regnal years (for a similar case see note on Da 1:1).

52:30 *twenty-third year.* 581 B.C. *taken into exile by Nebuzaradan.* Either (1) to quell further rebellion (see v. 3), or (2) in belated reprisal for Gedaliah's assassination (see 41:1–3).

52:31–34 Paralleled almost verbatim in 2Ki 25:27–30 (see notes there). Jeremiah and Kings thus conclude with the same happy ending.

52:31 *twenty-fifth.* The parallel in 2Ki 25:27 reads "twenty-seventh"; see note on v. 12.

52:32 See 2Ki 25:28 and note.

52:34 *till the day of his death.* See v. 11. Since the phrase does not appear in the parallel verses in 2 Kings in either case, its intention is probably to highlight the contrast between Zedekiah, who remained in prison till the day he died (see v. 11), and Jehoiachin, who was released from prison and was treated well by the Babylonian kings till the day he died (see notes on 2Ki 25:27–28).

Lamentations

INTRODUCTION

Title

The Hebrew title of the book is *'ekah* ("How . . . !"), the first word not only in 1:1 but also in 2:1; 4:1. Because of its subject matter, the book is also referred to in Jewish tradition as *qinot*, "Lamentations," a title taken over by the Septuagint (the pre-Christian Greek translation of the OT) and by the fourth-century Latin Vulgate, as well as by English versions.

Author and Date

Lamentations is anonymous, although ancient Jewish and early Christian traditions ascribe it to Jeremiah. These traditions are based in part on 2Ch 35:25 (though the "Laments" referred to there are not to be identified with the OT book of Lamentations); in part on such texts as Jer 7:29; 8:21; 9:1,10,20; and in part on the similarity of vocabulary and style between Lamentations and the prophecies of Jeremiah. Moreover, such an ascription gains a measure of plausibility from the fact that Jeremiah was an eyewitness to the divine judgment on Jerusalem in 586 B.C., which is so vividly portrayed here. Nevertheless, we cannot be certain who authored these carefully crafted poems or who is responsible for putting them together into a single scroll. Lamentations poignantly expresses the people's overwhelming sense of loss that accompanied the destruction of Jerusalem and the temple as well as the exile of Judah's inhabitants from the land Yahweh had covenanted to give Israel as a perpetual national homeland.

The earliest possible date for the book is 586 B.C., and the latest is 516 (when the rebuilt Jerusalem temple was dedicated). The graphic immediacy of Lamentations argues for an earlier date, probably before 575.

Literary Features

The entire book is poetic. The first, second, fourth and fifth laments all contain 22 verses, reflecting the number of letters in the Hebrew alphabet. In the first and second laments each

A Quick Look

Author:
Probably Jeremiah

Audience:
Jews in Babylonian exile who are lamenting the destruction of Jerusalem

Date:
Shortly after the fall of Jerusalem in 586 B.C.

Theme:
The prophet and his fellow Jews lament the devastation of their beloved city at the hands of the Babylonians.

verse contains three poetic lines; in the fourth each verse contains two lines; and in the fifth each verse contains but one line. The first four laments are alphabetic acrostics (see NIV text notes on 1:1; 2:1; 3:1; 4:1). In the first, second and fourth, each numbered verse begins with the letter of the Hebrew alphabet dictated by the traditional order of that alphabet. The third (middle) lament is distinctive in that while it too is made up of 22 three-line units (like laments 1 and 2), in it the three lines of each unit all begin with the sequenced order of the letters of the alphabet (thus three *aleph* lines followed by three *beth* lines, etc.) — after the manner of Ps 119. The fifth lament continues to use the 22-line structure, but the initial letters of these lines do not follow the alphabetic sequence (see note on 5:1 – 22). Use of the alphabet as a formal structuring element indicates that, however passionate these laments, they were composed with studied care.

The author of these laments understands clearly that the Babylonians are merely the human agents of divine judgment.

Themes and Theology

Lamentations is not the only OT book that contains individual or community laments. (A large number of the Psalms are lament poems, and every prophetic book except Haggai includes one or more examples of the lament genre.) Lamentations is the only book, however, that consists solely of laments.

As a series of laments over the destruction of Jerusalem (the royal city of the Lord's kingdom) in 586 B.C., it stands in a tradition with such ancient non-Biblical writings as the Sumerian "Lamentation over the Destruction of Ur," "Lamentation over the Destruction of Sumer and Ur," and "Lamentation over the Destruction of Nippur." Orthodox Jews customarily read it aloud in its entirety on the ninth day of Ab, the traditional date of the destruction of Solomon's temple in 586 as well as the date of the destruction of Herod's temple in A.D. 70. Many also read it each week at the Western Wall (the "Wailing Wall") in the Old City of Jerusalem. In addition, the book is important in traditional Roman Catholic liturgy, where it is customarily read during the last three days of Holy Week.

This Christian practice reminds us that the book of Lamentations not only bemoans Jerusalem's destruction but also contains profound theological insights. The horrors accompanying the Babylonian destruction of Judah are recited in some detail:

1. Wholesale devastation and slaughter engulfed kings (2:6,9; 4:20), princes (1:6; 2:2,9; 4:7 – 8; 5:12), elders (1:19; 2:10; 4:16; 5:12), priests (1:4,19; 2:6,20; 4:16), prophets (2:9,20) and commoners (2:10 – 12; 3:48; 4:6) alike.
2. Starving mothers were reduced to cannibalism (2:20; 4:10).
3. The flower of Judah's inhabitants were dragged off into ignominious exile (1:3,18).
4. An elaborate system of ceremony and worship came to an end (1:4,10).

But this recital is integrally woven into the fabric of a poetic wrestling with the ways of God who, as the Lord of history, was dealing with his wayward people.

The author of these laments understands clearly that the Babylonians are merely the human agents of divine judgment. It was God himself who had destroyed the city and temple (1:12 – 15; 2:1 – 8,17,22; 4:11). This was not a merely arbitrary act on the Lord's part; blatant, God-defying sin and covenant-breaking rebellion were at the root of his people's woes (1:5,8 – 9; 4:13; 5:7,16). Although weeping (1:16; 2:11,18; 3:48 – 51) is to be expected and cries for redress against the enemy (1:22; 3:59 – 66) are understandable (see note on Ps 5:10), the proper response to judgment is acknowledgment of sin (1:5,8,14,22; 2:14; 3:39; 4:13; 5:7,16) and heartfelt contrition (3:40 – 42). Trust in God's mercies and faithfulness must not falter. The book that begins with lament (1:1 – 2) rightly ends with an appeal to the Lord for restoration (5:21 – 22).

In the middle of the book, the theology of Lamentations reaches its apex as it focuses on the goodness of God. He is the Lord of hope (3:21,24 – 25), of love (3:22), of faithfulness (3:23), of salvation and restoration (3:26). In spite of all evidence to the contrary, "his compassions never fail. / They are new every morning; / great is your faithfulness" (3:22 – 23).

Near the end of the book, faith rises from Jerusalem's lamentable condition to acknowledge

Yahweh's eternal reign: "You, O LORD, reign forever; / your throne endures from generation to generation" (5:19; see introductions to Ps 47; 93; see also note on Ps 102:12).

Outline

I. Jerusalem's Misery and Desolation (ch. 1)
II. The Lord's Anger against His People (ch. 2)
III. Judah's Complaint — and Basis for Consolation (ch. 3)
IV. The Contrast between Zion's Past and Present (ch. 4)
V. Judah's Appeal to the Lord for Forgiveness and Restoration (ch. 5)

1[a] How deserted[a] lies the city,
once so full of people![b]
How like a widow[c] is she,
who once was great[d] among the nations!
She who was queen among the provinces
has now become a slave.[e]

[2]Bitterly she weeps[f] at night,
tears are upon her cheeks.
Among all her lovers[g]
there is none to comfort her.
All her friends have betrayed[h] her;
they have become her enemies.[i]

[3]After affliction and harsh labor,
Judah has gone into exile.[j]
She dwells among the nations;
she finds no resting place.[k]
All who pursue her have overtaken her[l]
in the midst of her distress.

[4]The roads to Zion mourn,[m]
for no one comes to her appointed feasts.
All her gateways are desolate,[n]
her priests groan,
her maidens grieve,
and she is in bitter anguish.[o]

[5]Her foes have become her masters;
her enemies are at ease.
The LORD has brought her grief[p]
because of her many sins.[q]
Her children have gone into exile,[r]
captive before the foe.[s]

[6]All the splendor has departed
from the Daughter of Zion.[t]
Her princes are like deer
that find no pasture;
in weakness they have fled[u]
before the pursuer.

[7]In the days of her affliction and wandering
Jerusalem remembers all the treasures
that were hers in days of old.
When her people fell into enemy hands,
there was no one to help her.[v]
Her enemies looked at her
and laughed[w] at her destruction.

[8]Jerusalem has sinned[x] greatly
and so has become unclean.[y]
All who honored her despise her,
for they have seen her nakedness;[z]
she herself groans[a]
and turns away.

[9]Her filthiness clung to her skirts;
she did not consider her future.[b]
Her fall[c] was astounding;
there was none to comfort[d] her.
"Look, O LORD, on my affliction,[e]
for the enemy has triumphed."

[10]The enemy laid hands
on all her treasures;[f]
she saw pagan nations
enter her sanctuary[g]—
those you had forbidden[h]
to enter your assembly.

1:1 [a]S Lev 26:43 [b]S Jer 42:2 [c]S Isa 47:8 [d]S 1Ki 4:21 [e]Isa 3:26; S Jer 40:9; Eze 5:5 **1:2** [f]Ps 6:6 [g]S Jer 3:1 [h]S Jer 4:30; Mic 7:5 [i]ver 16; S Jer 30:14 **1:3** [j]S Jer 13:19 [k]Dt 28:65 [l]S Ex 15:9 **1:4** [m]S Ps 137:1 [n]S Isa 27:10; S Jer 9:11 [o]ver 21; Joel 1:8-13 **1:5** [p]S Isa 22:5; S Jer 30:15 [q]S Ps 5:10 [r]S Jer 10:20; S 39:9; 52:28-30 [s]S Ps 137:3; La 2:17 **1:6** [t]S Ps 9:14; Jer 13:18 [u]S Lev 26:36 **1:7** [v]S 2Ki 14:26; S Jer 37:7; La 4:17 [w]S Jer 2:26 **1:8** [x]ver 20; Isa 59:2-13 [y]S Jer 2:22 [z]S Jer 13:22,26 [a]ver 21,22; S Ps 6:6; S 38:8 **1:9** [b]Dt 32:28-29; Eze 24:13 [c]Jer 13:18 [d]S Ecc 4:1; S Jer 16:7 [e]Ps 25:18 **1:10** [f]S Isa 64:11 [g]Ps 74:7-8; 79:1; Jer 51:51 [h]Dt 23:3

[a] This chapter is an acrostic poem, the verses of which begin with the successive letters of the Hebrew alphabet.

1:1–22 As is widely done in OT prophecy and psalmody, Jerusalem is here presented as a woman—and represents the nation of which she is the political head and symbolic heart.
1:1–11 In the first half of this first lament, Jerusalem's condition is described by one who speaks of her in the third person—yet as one who bemoans the city's desperate situation. For the transition to Jerusalem's own voice see the quoted words at the end of v. 11.
1:1 *How . . . !* Expresses a mixture of shock and deep dismay (see 2:1; 4:1–2; 2Sa 1:25,27; Jer 9:19; 48:17,39; Eze 26:17). *deserted lies.* The Hebrew underlying this phrase is translated "sat alone" in Jer 15:17. There the prophet sat alone; here his beloved city does the same. *city.* Jerusalem. *once so full of people.* Cf. Isa 1:21. *great among the nations.* Cf. Jer 49:15. *slave.* The Hebrew for this word is translated "forced labor" in Ex 1:11; 1Ki 4:6.
1:2 *Bitterly she weeps.* As did Jeremiah, and for much the same reason (Jer 13:17). *at night.* See 2:18–19. *lovers . . . friends.* International allies to whom the people of Jerusalem and Judah looked for security rather than to the Lord (see Jer 2:36–37; 27:3; Eze 16:26,28–29; 23:11–21; see also Ex 34:15 and note). *none to comfort her.* See vv. 9,16–17,21. *All . . . have betrayed her.* See v. 19; like Edom (4:21–22; Ps 137:7) and Ammon (Jer 40:14; Eze 25:2–3,6). *become her enemies.* See v. 17.
1:3 *gone into exile.* To Babylonia (see Jer 20:4–5 and thereafter in Jeremiah). *among the nations . . . finds no resting place.* As Moses warned in Dt 28:65.
1:4 *mourn.* Are deserted and desolate (see Jdg 5:6; Isa 33:8 and notes). *appointed feasts.* See Ex 23:14–17 and notes; Lev 23:2. *maidens grieve.* A sign of utter defeat (see Jer 9:20; contrast Ex 15:20 and note; 1Sa 18:6; Ps 68:25; Jer 31:13).
1:5 *masters.* Lit. "head"—in accordance with Dt 28:44 (contrast Dt 28:13).
1:6 *Daughter of Zion.* A personification of Jerusalem (see note on 2Ki 19:21). *Her princes . . . have fled before the pursuer.* See Jer 52:7–8. *like deer that find no pasture.* Hence are weakened and become easy prey for predators.
1:7 *affliction and wandering.* See 3:19. *treasures.* See vv. 10–11. *days of old.* For example, the days of David and Solomon. *fell into enemy hands.* See 2Sa 24:14. *destruction.* Lit. "cessation" (see notes on Ge 2:2–3 and NIV text note on 2:2). The Hebrew root for this word is the same as that for "Sabbath"—and may be intended as an ironic pun (see Lev 26:34–35).
1:8 *unclean.* See v. 17 and note. It refers to the ceremonial uncleanness of a woman during her monthly period (see Lev 12:2,5; 15:19). *her nakedness.* See Isa 47:3; Eze 16:37 and notes.
1:9 *filthiness.* Ceremonial uncleanness (see note on Lev 4:12), here caused by willful sin. *did not consider her future.* Just as Babylon did not (Isa 47:7). *Look, O LORD.* Jerusalem's desolation is further depicted by quoting the cry that bursts from her lips (see v. 11 and note). *enemy has triumphed.* See v. 16.
1:10 *forbidden to enter your assembly.* See Eze 44:7,9 and notes.

[11] All her people groan[i]
as they search for bread;[j]
they barter their treasures for food
to keep themselves alive.
"Look, O LORD, and consider,
for I am despised."

[12] "Is it nothing to you, all you who pass
by?[k]
Look around and see.
Is any suffering like my suffering[l]
that was inflicted on me,
that the LORD brought on me
in the day of his fierce anger?[m]

[13] "From on high he sent fire,
sent it down into my bones.[n]
He spread a net[o] for my feet
and turned me back.
He made me desolate,[p]
faint[q] all the day long.

[14] "My sins have been bound into a
yoke[a];[r]
by his hands they were woven
together.
They have come upon my neck
and the Lord has sapped my
strength.
He has handed me over[s]
to those I cannot withstand.

[15] "The Lord has rejected
all the warriors in my midst;[t]
he has summoned an army[u] against
me
to[b] crush my young men.[v]
In his winepress[w] the Lord has
trampled[x]
the Virgin Daughter[y] of Judah.

[16] "This is why I weep
and my eyes overflow with tears.[z]
No one is near to comfort[a] me,
no one to restore my spirit.
My children are destitute
because the enemy has prevailed."[b]

[17] Zion stretches out her hands,[c]
but there is no one to comfort her.
The LORD has decreed for Jacob
that his neighbors become his
foes;[d]
Jerusalem has become
an unclean[e] thing[f] among them.

[18] "The LORD is righteous,[g]
yet I rebelled[h] against his command.
Listen, all you peoples;
look upon my suffering.[i]
My young men and maidens
have gone into exile.[j]

[19] "I called to my allies[k]
but they betrayed me.
My priests and my elders
perished[l] in the city
while they searched for food
to keep themselves alive.

[20] "See, O LORD, how distressed[m] I am!
I am in torment[n] within,
and in my heart I am disturbed,[o]
for I have been most rebellious.[p]
Outside, the sword bereaves;
inside, there is only death.[q]

[21] "People have heard my groaning,[r]
but there is no one to comfort me.[s]
All my enemies have heard of my
distress;
they rejoice[t] at what you have done.
May you bring the day[u] you have
announced
so they may become like me.

1:11 [i]S Ps 6:6; S 38:8 [j]S Jer 37:21; S 52:6 **1:12** [k]S Jer 18:16 [l]ver 18 [m]S Isa 10:4; 13:13; S Jer 30:24 **1:13** [n]S Job 30:30; Ps 102:3 [o]S Job 18:8 [p]S Jer 44:6 [q]Hab 3:16 **1:14** [r]S Dt 28:48; S Isa 47:6; S Jer 15:12 [s]S Jer 32:5 **1:15** [t]Jer 37:10 [u]Isa 41:2 [v]Isa 28:18; S Jer 18:21 [w]S Jdg 6:11 [x]S Isa 5:5 [y]Jer 14:17 **1:16** [z]S Job 7:3; S Ps 119:136; S Isa 22:4; La 2:11, 18; 3:48-49 [a]S Ps 69:20; Ecc 4:1; S Jer 16:7 [b]S ver 2; Jer 13:17; 14:17 **1:17** [c]S Jer 4:31 [d]S Ex 23:21 [e]Jer 2:22 [f]S Lev 18:25-28 **1:18** [g]S Ex 9:27; S Ezr 9:15 [h]S 1Sa 12:14 [i]ver 12 [j]Dt 28:32, 41 **1:19** [k]S Jer 22:20 [l]S Jer 14:15; La 2:20 **1:20** [m]S Jer 4:19 [n]La 2:11 [o]S Job 20:2 [p]S ver 8 [q]S Dt 32:25; Eze 7:15 **1:21** [r]S ver 8; S Ps 6:6; S 38:8 [s]ver 4 [t]La 2:15 [u]Isa 47:11; Jer 30:16

[a] 14 Most Hebrew manuscripts; Septuagint *He kept watch over my sins* [b] 15 Or *has set a time for me / when he will*

1:11 *search for bread.* Food shortages were an ever-present problem during and after the siege of Jerusalem. *keep themselves alive.* See v. 19; 2Ki 6:24–29. *Look, O LORD.* Again, Jerusalem's desperate cry to the Lord is suddenly introduced. From here to the end of this lament, personified Jerusalem speaks.

1:12 *who pass by.* See Jer 18:16 and note. *Look ... like my suffering.* In his magisterial *The Messiah,* Handel borrowed these lines (as they appeared in the KJV: "Behold, and see if there be any sorrow like unto my sorrow") and placed them on the lips of the Messiah—perhaps associating them with Isa 53:4 ("Surely he hath borne our griefs and carried our sorrows ..."); cf. also Isa 53:3 ("man of sorrows"). *fierce anger.* See 2:3,6; 4:11. The expression is common in Jeremiah (see Jer 4:8,26; 12:13; 25:37–38; 44:6; 49:37; 51:45).

1:13 *From on high he sent fire.* The fire of his judgment (see 2:3–4; Lev 10:2; Nu 11:1–3; 16:35; 2Ki 1:10,12; Isa 29:6; 30:30; 66:15–16; Jer 4:4; 21:14; 49:27; 50:32; Am 7:4). *my bones.* The bones of Jerusalem (personified as a woman; see note on v. 8). In a strikingly similar image, the word of the Lord was like fire in the bones of the prophet (see Jer 20:9 and note). *spread a net for my feet.* See Ps 57:6; Pr 29:5. *desolate.* Like Absalom's sister Tamar (see 2Sa 13:20).

1:15 *In his winepress ... trampled.* A common metaphor of divine judgment (see Isa 63:2–3; Joel 3:13; Rev 14:19–20; 19:15). *Virgin Daughter of Judah.* A personification of Judah (see note on 2Ki 19:21).

1:16 *eyes overflow with tears.* See 2:11; 3:48; Jer 9:1 and note, 18; 13:17; 14:17. *enemy has prevailed.* See v. 9.

1:17 *become his foes.* See v. 2. *unclean thing.* See note on v. 8; for the same imagery elsewhere see Ezr 9:11; Isa 30:22; 64:6; Eze 7:19–20; 36:17.

1:18 *is righteous.* Has dealt rightly with me. *yet I rebelled.* Better "for I have rebelled." *Listen ... look.* The nations are called to take note of the Lord's righteous acts of judgment as well as of his righteous acts of deliverance.

1:19 *allies ... betrayed me.* See v. 2 and note. *keep themselves alive.* See note on v. 11.

1:20 *I am in torment within.* Repeated in 2:11. *Outside ... inside.* See Jer 14:18. The Sumerian "Lamentation over the Destruction of Ur" contains a striking parallel: "Inside it we die of famine, outside we are killed by weapons" (lines 403–404).

1:21 *day you have announced.* Day of God's judgment on the nations (see 4:21–22; Jer 25:15–38 and notes).

[22]"Let all their wickedness come before you;
deal with them
as you have dealt with me
because of all my sins.[v]
My groans[w] are many
and my heart is faint."

2 [a] How the Lord has covered the Daughter of Zion
with the cloud of his anger[b]![x]
He has hurled down the splendor of Israel
from heaven to earth;
he has not remembered his footstool[y]
in the day of his anger.[z]

[2]Without pity[a] the Lord has swallowed[b] up
all the dwellings of Jacob;
in his wrath he has torn down
the strongholds[c] of the Daughter of Judah.
He has brought her kingdom and its princes
down to the ground[d] in dishonor.

[3]In fierce anger he has cut off
every horn[c][e] of Israel.
He has withdrawn his right hand[f]
at the approach of the enemy.
He has burned in Jacob like a flaming fire
that consumes everything around it.[g]

[4]Like an enemy he has strung his bow;[h]
his right hand is ready.
Like a foe he has slain
all who were pleasing to the eye;[i]
he has poured out his wrath[j] like fire[k]
on the tent[l] of the Daughter of Zion.

[5]The Lord is like an enemy;[m]
he has swallowed up Israel.
He has swallowed up all her palaces
and destroyed her strongholds.[n]
He has multiplied mourning and lamentation[o]
for the Daughter of Judah.[p]

[6]He has laid waste his dwelling like a garden;
he has destroyed[q] his place of meeting.[r]
The LORD has made Zion forget
her appointed feasts and her Sabbaths;[s]
in his fierce anger he has spurned
both king and priest.[t]

[7]The Lord has rejected his altar
and abandoned his sanctuary.[u]
He has handed over to the enemy
the walls of her palaces;[v]
they have raised a shout in the house of the LORD
as on the day of an appointed feast.[w]

[8]The LORD determined to tear down
the wall around the Daughter of Zion.[x]
He stretched out a measuring line[y]
and did not withhold his hand from destroying.
He made ramparts[z] and walls lament;
together they wasted away.[a]

[9]Her gates[b] have sunk into the ground;
their bars[c] he has broken and destroyed.

1:22 [v]Ne 4:5 [w]S ver 8; S Ps 6:6
2:1 [x]La 3:44 [y]Ps 99:5; 132:7 [z]S Jer 12:7
2:2 [a]ver 17; La 3:43 [b]Ps 21:9 [c]Ps 89:39-40; Mic 5:11 [d]S Isa 25:12
2:3 [e]Ps 75:5,10 [f]Ps 74:11 [g]S Isa 42:25; Jer 21:4-5,14
2:4 [h]S Job 3:23; 16:13; La 3:12-13 [i]S Ps 48:2; Eze 24:16,25 [j]S 2Ch 34:21; Eze 20:34 [k]Isa 42:25; S Jer 7:20 [l]S Jer 4:20
2:5 [m]S Job 13:24 [n]ver 2 [o]S Isa 29:2 [p]S Jer 7:20; 9:17-20
2:6 [q]2Ch 36:19 [r]S Jer 52:13 [s]Zep 3:18 [t]Isa 43:28; S Jer 7:14; La 4:16; 5:12
2:7 [u]S Lev 26:31; S Eze 7:24 [v]Ps 74:7-8; S Isa 64:11; Jer 33:4-5; Eze 7:21-22 [w]Jer 21:4; 52:13
2:8 [x]ver 18 [y]S 2Ki 21:13 [z]S Ps 48:13 [a]Isa 3:26; S Jer 39:8; S 52:14
2:9 [b]S Ne 1:3 [c]S Isa 45:2; Hos 11:6

[a] This chapter is an acrostic poem, the verses of which begin with the successive letters of the Hebrew alphabet. [b] *1* Or *How the Lord in his anger / has treated the Daughter of Zion with contempt* [c] *3* Or */ all the strength*; or *every king*; *horn* here symbolizes strength.

1:22 *wickedness … before you.* See Ps 109:14–15. *my heart is faint.* The same expression is found in Jer 8:18; see La 5:17; Isa 1:5.
2:1–22 Jerusalem is again personified as a woman—and represents the nation (see note on 1:1–22). In vv. 1–10 Jerusalem's experience of God's wrath is described by a voice that speaks of her in the third person. In vv. 12–19 Jerusalem is directly addressed (second-person pronouns abound). At the center (vv. 11–12) the author begins to speak in the first person (see note on 1:1–11). The first-person voice of vv. 20–22 is that of Jerusalem.
2:1 *How …!* See note on 1:1. *Daughter of Zion.* A personification of Jerusalem (see the same or similar idiom in vv. 2, 4–5,8,10,13,15,18; see also note on 2Ki 19:21). *hurled down the splendor of Israel.* The imagery is that of a falling star (as in Isa 14:12). *footstool.* Either (1) the ark of the covenant (see 1Ch 28:2) or, more likely, (2) Mount Zion (see Ps 99:5 and note).
2:2 *swallowed up all the dwellings.* See v. 5. *Daughter of Judah.* See note on v. 1.
2:3 *cut off every horn.* See NIV text note. *flaming fire that consumes.* See 1:13 and note.
2:4 *strung his bow.* See 3:12; Dt 32:42; Ps 7:12–13; Hab 3:9. *poured out.* Widely used imagery in the OT for the display of God's wrath (see Ps 69:24; 79:6; Jer 6:11; 7:20; 10:25; 42:18; 44:6; Hos 5:10; Zep 3:8). *Daughter of Zion.* See note on v. 1.
2:5 *palaces … strongholds.* See Hos 8:14. *multiplied mourning and lamentation.* The Sumerian "Lamentation over the Destruction of Sumer and Ur" offers this parallel: "In the desolate city there was uttered nothing but laments and dirges" (lines 361–362, 486–487). *Daughter of Judah.* See note on v. 1.
2:6 *his dwelling … his place of meeting.* The temple in Jerusalem (see 1Ki 8:29; 9:3; 2Ch 6:2; 7:1–3; Ps 27:7–10 and note; 132:8,13–14). *like a garden.* Cf. Isa 5:5–6; Jer 5:10; 12:10.
2:7 *rejected … abandoned.* These two verbs are found in Ps 89:38–39 ("rejected … renounced") in connection with the Lord's forsaking of the king from the dynasty of David. *raised a shout in the house of the LORD.* See Ps 74:4. *as on the day of an appointed feast.* See Ps 42:4; 47:5; 81:1–4. But there is bitter irony in the fact that the triumphant shouts of the enemy have silenced the joyful shouts of those who had worshiped at the temple.
2:8 *determined to tear down.* See Jer 1:15; 32:31. *stretched out a measuring line.* To destroy with the same standards of precision used in building (see Isa 28:17; Am 7:7–8 and notes). *ramparts … walls.* Cf. Isa 26:1. The ramparts were the outer fortifications (see 2Sa 20:15).
2:9 *the law is no more.* There are no longer any priests (see v. 20) to teach and interpret the covenant law (see Jer 18:18; Hos 4:4–9 and note). *prophets no longer find vi-*

Her king and her princes are exiled[d]
among the nations,
the law[e] is no more,
and her prophets[f] no longer find
visions[g] from the LORD.

10 The elders of the Daughter of Zion
sit on the ground in silence;[h]
they have sprinkled dust[i] on their heads[j]
and put on sackcloth.[k]
The young women of Jerusalem
have bowed their heads to the
ground.[l]

11 My eyes fail from weeping,[m]
I am in torment within,[n]
my heart[o] is poured out[p] on the ground
because my people are destroyed,[q]
because children and infants faint[r]
in the streets of the city.

12 They say to their mothers,
"Where is bread and wine?"[s]
as they faint like wounded men
in the streets of the city,
as their lives ebb away[t]
in their mothers' arms.[u]

13 What can I say for you?[v]
With what can I compare you,
O Daughter[w] of Jerusalem?
To what can I liken you,
that I may comfort you,
O Virgin Daughter of Zion?[x]
Your wound is as deep as the sea.[y]
Who can heal you?

14 The visions of your prophets
were false[z] and worthless;
they did not expose your sin
to ward off your captivity.[a]
The oracles they gave you
were false and misleading.[b]

2:9 [d]Dt 28:36; S 2Ki 24:15; Jer 16:13; Hos 3:4 [e]S 2Ch 15:3 [f]S 1Sa 3:1 [g]S Jer 14:14 **2:10** [h]La 3:28 [i]S Jos 7:6 [j]Job 2:12 [k]S Isa 3:24 [l]S Job 2:13; S Isa 3:26; Eze 27:30-31 **2:11** [m]S Ps 119:82; S Isa 15:3; S La 1:16; 3:48-51 [n]S Job 30:27; La 1:20 [o]S Isa 1:5 [p]ver 19; Ps 22:14 [q]S Jer 9:1 [r]La 4:4 **2:12** [s]Isa 24:11 [t]S Job 3:24 [u]La 4:4 **2:13** [v]S Isa 1:6 [w]S 2Ki 19:21 [x]Isa 37:22 [y]Jer 14:17; 30:12-15; La 1:12 **2:14** [z]S Jer 28:15 [a]Jer 8:11 [b]Jer 2:8; S 20:6; 23:25-32,33-40; S 29:9; Eze 13:3; 22:28 **2:15** [c]S Nu 24:10; Eze 25:6 [d]S Dt 28:37; S Isa 28:22; Jer 19:8; S Na 3:19 [e]S Job 16:4 [f]S La 1:21 [g]Ps 45:11; S 48:2; 50:2; Eze 16:14 [h]Ps 48:2 **2:16** [i]Ps 22:13; La 3:46 [j]S Job 16:9 [k]S Ps 35:25 [l]Eze 36:3; Mic 4:11

15 All who pass your way
clap their hands at you;[c]
they scoff[d] and shake their heads[e]
at the Daughter of Jerusalem:[f]
"Is this the city that was called
the perfection of beauty,[g]
the joy of the whole earth?"[h]

16 All your enemies open their mouths
wide against you;[i]
they scoff and gnash their teeth[j]
and say, "We have swallowed her
up.[k]
This is the day we have waited for;
we have lived to see it."[l]

17 The LORD has done what he planned;
he has fulfilled[m] his word,
which he decreed long ago.[n]
He has overthrown you without pity,[o]
he has let the enemy gloat over
you,[p]
he has exalted the horn[a] of your
foes.[q]

18 The hearts of the people
cry out to the Lord.[r]
O wall of the Daughter of Zion,[s]
let your tears[t] flow like a river
day and night;[u]
give yourself no relief,
your eyes no rest.[v]

19 Arise, cry out in the night,
as the watches of the night begin;
pour out your heart[w] like water
in the presence of the Lord.[x]

[a] *17 Horn* here symbolizes strength.

2:17 [m]S Jer 39:16 [n]Dt 28:15-45 [o]S ver 2; Eze 5:11; 7:9; 8:18 [p]S Ps 22:17 [q]Ps 89:42; S Isa 44:26; S La 1:5; Zec 1:6 **2:18** [r]S Ps 119:145 [s]ver 8 [t]S La 1:16 [u]S Jer 9:1 [v]La 3:49 **2:19** [w]1Sa 1:15 [x]S ver 11; Isa 26:9

sions. The Lord was no longer communicating to his people through prophets (see Ps 74:9; Am 8:11 and note; Mic 3:7).

2:10 *elders.* See note on Ex 3:16. *Daughter of Zion.* See note on v. 1. *sit on the ground in silence ... sprinkled dust on their heads and put on sackcloth ... bowed their heads.* Signs of mourning (see Job 2:12–13; Ps 35:13–14). *young women of Jerusalem.* See 1:4 and note.

2:11 *My ... I ... my ... my.* See note on vv. 1–22. Presumably the speaker is the same as that heard in vv. 1–10 and in 1:1–11 (see note there). He begins at this point with an expression of deep personal grief over Jerusalem's condition, especially that of her little ones (vv. 11–12), and then addresses Jerusalem directly (vv. 13–19). *weeping.* See note on 1:16. *I am in torment within.* Repeated from 1:20. *my people.* Lit. "the daughter of my people" (see note on v. 1). This particular phrase occurs also in 3:48; 4:3,6,10; Isa 22:4; Jer 8:11,21; cf. Jer 14:17.

2:13 *What can I say for you?* The author has no words that can bring comfort to suffering Jerusalem.

2:14 *prophets ... false.* Jeremiah often denounced the false prophets (see Jer 5:12–13; 6:13–14; 8:10–11; 14:13–15; 23:9–40; 27:9—28:17; cf. Jer 26:7–11,16; Eze 22:26,28). *worthless.* Or "mere whitewash"; for an explanation of this image see Eze 13:10–16; 22:28. *misleading.* The unusual Hebrew word underlying this word comes from the same root as that underlying "banish" in Jer 27:10,15: The lies of false prophets "mislead" the people and thus lead to "banishment" by the Lord—so they are "banishing" in their effect.

2:15 *who pass your way.* See 1:12. *clap their hands.* See Job 27:23; 34:37. *scoff.* See v. 16; see also note on Jer 19:8. *shake their heads.* See Job 16:4 and note; Ps 44:14; 64:8; 109:25; Jer 18:16. *was called the perfection of beauty.* As in Ps 50:2 (see note there). *was called ... the joy of the whole earth.* As in Ps 48:2 (see note there; cf. Jer 51:41).

2:16 *open their mouths wide.* To taunt or to devour (see Nu 16:30; Ps 22:13; Isa 5:14; 9:12). *swallowed her up.* See vv. 2,5; Jer 51:34.

2:17 *fulfilled his word.* See Isa 55:11 and note. *long ago.* The days of Moses (see, e.g., the threats of Lev 26:23–39; Dt 28:15–68). *exalted the horn.* Increased the strength (see NIV text note; see also 1Sa 2:1; Ps 75:4).

2:18 See Jer 14:17. *O wall.* A city gate is similarly addressed in Isa 14:31.

2:19 *watches of the night begin.* See note on Jdg 7:19; see also Ps 63:6. *pour out your heart.* In earnest prayer (see Ps 62:8). *like water.* A common simile with "pour out" (see Dt 12:16,24; 15:23; Ps 79:3; Hos 5:10). *Lift up your hands.* In prayer (see Ps 28:2 and note; 1Ti 2:8). *children, who faint from hunger.* See vv. 11–12.

Lift up your hands[y] to him
for the lives of your children,
who faint[z] from hunger
at the head of every street.

20 "Look, O LORD, and consider:
Whom have you ever treated like this?
Should women eat their offspring,[a]
the children they have cared for?[b]
Should priest and prophet be killed[c]
in the sanctuary of the Lord?[d]

21 "Young and old lie together
in the dust of the streets;
my young men and maidens
have fallen by the sword.[e]
You have slain them in the day of your anger;
you have slaughtered them without pity.[f]

22 "As you summon to a feast day,
so you summoned against me
terrors[g] on every side.
In the day of the LORD's anger
no one escaped[h] or survived;
those I cared for and reared,[i]
my enemy has destroyed."

3[a] I am the man who has seen affliction[j]
by the rod of his wrath.[k]
2 He has driven me away and made me walk
in darkness[l] rather than light;
3 indeed, he has turned his hand against me[m]
again and again, all day long.

4 He has made my skin and my flesh grow old[n]
and has broken my bones.[o]
5 He has besieged me and surrounded me
with bitterness[p] and hardship.[q]
6 He has made me dwell in darkness
like those long dead.[r]

7 He has walled me in so I cannot escape;[s]
he has weighed me down with chains.[t]
8 Even when I call out or cry for help,[u]
he shuts out my prayer.[v]
9 He has barred[w] my way with blocks of stone;
he has made my paths crooked.[x]

10 Like a bear lying in wait,
like a lion[y] in hiding,[z]
11 he dragged me from the path and mangled[a] me
and left me without help.
12 He drew his bow[b]
and made me the target[c] for his arrows.[d]

13 He pierced[e] my heart
with arrows from his quiver.[f]
14 I became the laughingstock[g] of all my people;[h]
they mock me in song[i] all day long.

[a] This chapter is an acrostic poem; the verses of each stanza begin with the successive letters of the Hebrew alphabet, and the verses within each stanza begin with the same letter.

2:19 [y]S Ps 28:2 [z]S Isa 51:20 **2:20** [a]S Dt 28:53; Jer 19:9; Eze 5:10 [b]La 4:10 [c]Ps 78:64; S Jer 14:15; 23:11-12 [d]S La 1:19 **2:21** [e]S Dt 32:25; S 2Ch 36:17; Ps 78:62-63; Jer 6:11 [f]S Jer 13:14; La 3:43; Zec 11:6 **2:22** [g]S Ps 31:13; S Jer 20:10 [h]S Jer 11:11 [i]Job 27:14; Hos 9:13 **3:1** [j]Jer 15:17-18 [k]S Job 19:21; Ps 88:7 **3:2** [l]S Job 19:8; S Ps 82:5; S Jer 4:23 **3:3** [m]Ps 38:2; Isa 5:25 **3:4** [n]S Job 30:30; La 4:8 [o]Ps 51:8; S Isa 38:13; S Jer 50:17 **3:5** [p]ver 19 [q]Jer 23:15 **3:6** [r]Ps 88:5-6; 143:3; Isa 59:10 **3:7** [s]S Job 3:23 [t]Jer 40:4 **3:8** [u]Ps 5:2 [v]ver 44; S Dt 1:45; S Job 30:20; Ps 22:2 **3:9** [w]S Job 19:8 [x]S Job 9:24; S Isa 63:17; Hos 2:6 **3:10** [y]S Job 10:16 [z]Hos 13:8; Am 5:18-19 **3:11** [a]Hos 6:1 **3:12** [b]S La 2:4 [c]Job 7:20 [d]S Job 16:12; Ps 7:12-13; 38:2 **3:13** [e]S Job 16:13 [f]Job 6:4 **3:14** [g]S Ge 38:23; Ps 22:6-7; Jer 20:7 [h]S Job 17:2 [i]S Job 30:9

2:20–22 Jerusalem's heartbroken prayer in response to v. 19.
2:20 *women eat their offspring.* See note on Jer 19:9.
2:21 See Jer 6:11 and note.
2:22 *summon to a feast day.* The same Lord who had called Israel to come to him in worship and to celebrate his saving acts in her history (see, e.g., Ps 81; 95; 114) now issues a quite different summons. *summoned against me.* See 1:15. *terrors on every side.* See note on Jer 6:25. *day of the LORD's anger.* The lament ends as it began (see v. 1). *no one escaped or survived.* See Jer 42:17; 44:14. *those I cared for.* Jerusalem's inhabitants.
3:1–66 This lament at the center of the book stands apart in significant ways. As to form: Like chs. 1 and 2, it is an alphabetic acrostic and is made up of 22 three-line units, but here each line of each unit begins with the same letter (see Introduction: Literary Features). That probably accounts for why in this lament each poetic line, rather than each stanza, has traditionally been set off as a grammatical unit and assigned a separate verse number. As to content: It begins (vv. 1–39) like the prayers of individuals found in the Psalter (which it extensively echoes) without any clear reference to the destruction of Jerusalem and the exile of the nation. This extended introduction may have been intended to put the communal lament that follows (vv. 40–66; see note on vv. 48–66) in a context that models how the community should react to its present distress.
3:1 The exact center of the book. The speaker identifies himself as one who exemplifies those who have suffered much under the rod of God's wrath. *affliction.* See v. 19. *rod of his wrath.* See Job 9:34; 21:9; cf. Isa 10:5 and note. *his.* God's.
3:2 *darkness rather than light.* See Job 12:25; Ps 143:3; Isa 50:10; 59:9; cf. Am 5:18 and note.
3:4 *grow old.* See Ps 32:3 ("wasted away"); Ps 49:14 ("decay"). *broken my bones.* See Ps 51:8; Isa 38:13 and note.
3:5 *surrounded me.* See Job 19:6. *bitterness.* Lit. "poison" (see Jer 8:14 and note). *hardship.* See Ex 18:8; Nu 20:14; Ne 9:32.
3:6 See Ps 143:3 and note.
3:7 *walled.* The Hebrew for this word is the same as that for "barred" in v. 9 (see Job 19:8; Hos 2:6). *cannot escape.* See Ps 88:8.
3:8 *shuts out my prayer.* See v. 44; Job 30:20; Ps 18:41; 22:2; Pr 1:28; Jer 7:16 and note.
3:9 *blocks of stone.* Of enormous size, like those used in the foundation of Solomon's temple (see 1Ki 5:17). *made ... crooked.* Rather than level (see Isa 26:7; 45:2; Jer 31:9 and note) or straight (see Ps 5:8; Pr 3:6 and notes; 11:5; Isa 45:13).
3:10 *Like a bear ... like a lion.* See Jer 4:7; 5:6; 49:19; 50:44; Am 1:2 and note; 5:19; cf. Ps 7:2 and note.
3:11 See 1:2.
3:12 *drew his bow.* See note on 2:4. *made me the target.* See note on Job 6:4.
3:13 *heart.* Lit. "kidneys" (as in Job 16:13). *with arrows.* See Ps 38:2 and note.
3:14 See Jeremiah's complaint in Jer 20:7. *mock me in song.* See v. 63; Ps 69:12; see also Ps 22:6–7; cf. Isa 28:9–10 and note.

[15]He has filled me with bitter herbs
and sated me with gall.[j]
[16]He has broken my teeth with gravel;[k]
he has trampled me in the dust.[l]
[17]I have been deprived of peace;
I have forgotten what prosperity is.
[18]So I say, "My splendor is gone
and all that I had hoped from the LORD."[m]
[19]I remember my affliction and my wandering,
the bitterness[n] and the gall.[o]
[20]I well remember them,
and my soul is downcast[p] within me.[q]
[21]Yet this I call to mind
and therefore I have hope:
[22]Because of the LORD's great love[r] we are not consumed,[s]
for his compassions never fail.[t]
[23]They are new every morning;
great is your faithfulness.[u]
[24]I say to myself, "The LORD is my portion;[v]
therefore I will wait for him."
[25]The LORD is good to those whose hope is in him,
to the one who seeks him;[w]
[26]it is good to wait quietly[x]
for the salvation of the LORD.[y]
[27]It is good for a man to bear the yoke
while he is young.
[28]Let him sit alone in silence,[z]
for the LORD has laid it on him.
[29]Let him bury his face in the dust[a]—
there may yet be hope.[b]
[30]Let him offer his cheek to one who would strike him,[c]
and let him be filled with disgrace.[d]
[31]For men are not cast off
by the Lord forever.[e]
[32]Though he brings grief, he will show compassion,
so great is his unfailing love.[f]
[33]For he does not willingly bring affliction
or grief to the children of men.[g]
[34]To crush underfoot
all prisoners in the land,
[35]to deny a man his rights
before the Most High,[h]
[36]to deprive a man of justice—
would not the Lord see such things?[i]
[37]Who can speak and have it happen
if the Lord has not decreed it?[j]

3:15 [j]ver 19; Jer 9:15 **3:16** [k]S Pr 20:17 [l]S Ps 7:5 **3:18** [m]S ver 54; S Job 17:15 **3:19** [n]ver 5 [o]S ver 15 **3:20** [p]S Ps 42:5 [q]Ps 42:11; 43:5 **3:22** [r]S Ps 103:11 [s]S Job 34:15; S Hos 11:9 [t]Ps 78:38; 130:7 **3:23** [u]S Ex 34:6; Zep 3:5 **3:24** [v]S Ps 119:57 **3:25** [w]S Ps 33:18; Isa 25:9; S 30:18 **3:26** [x]S Isa 7:4 [y]Ps 37:7; 40:1 **3:28** [z]Jer 15:17; La 2:10 **3:29** [a]S Job 2:8 [b]S Jer 31:17 **3:30** [c]S Job 16:10; S Isa 50:6 [d]Mic 5:1 **3:31** [e]Ps 94:14; Isa 54:7 **3:32** [f]Ps 78:38; 106:43-45; Hos 11:8; Na 1:12 **3:33** [g]S Job 37:23; S Jer 31:20; Eze 18:23; 33:11 **3:35** [h]Ge 14:18,19,20,22 **3:36** [i]Ps 140:12; S Pr 17:15; S Jer 22:3; Hab 1:13 **3:37** [j]Ps 33:9-11; S Pr 19:21; S 21:30

3:15 *filled me with bitter herbs.* The Hebrew underlying this phrase is translated "overwhelm me with misery" in Job 9:18 (see note on Jer 9:15). For the significance of the bitter herbs eaten during the Passover meal see note on Ex 12:8.
3:16 *broken my teeth with gravel.* Cf. Ps 72:9; Mic 7:17. *trampled me in the dust.* See Ps 7:5.
3:18 *all that I had hoped from the LORD.* See Ps 39:7; the first explicit mention of God in ch. 3.
3:19–20 The author again recalls all his troubles but now in preparation for his words of hope and encouragement in vv. 21–39.
3:19 *affliction and…wandering.* See 1:7. *the bitterness and the gall.* See vv. 5,15; cf. Jer 9:15.
3:21–26 The theological—and spiritual—high point of the book of Lamentations (see Introduction: Themes and Theology).
3:22 *great love.* See v. 32. The Hebrew for this phrase is plural (as also in Ps 107:43) and denotes the Lord's loving faithfulness to his covenant promises (see Ps 89:1). See note on Ps 6:4; see also Isa 63:7 ("kindnesses") and note. *we.* The Lord's people.
3:23 *They.* The "great love" and "compassions" (v. 22) of the Lord. *new every morning.* See Ps 30:5 and note; Isa 33:2. *great is your faithfulness.* It is beyond measure (see note on v. 32; see also Ps 36:5 and note).
3:24 *The LORD is my portion.* See Ps 73:26; 142:5 and notes. He was the inheritance share of the priests and Levites (see Nu 18:20; see also note on Ge 15:1). *therefore I will wait.* See Ps 27:14; 71:14 and notes. The Hebrew for this phrase is the same as that for "therefore I have hope" in v. 21 and serves as a refrain.
3:25 *The LORD is good.* See Ps 34:8 and note on 34:8–14; 86:5. *whose hope is in him.* See Ps 25:3; 33:18; 37:9 and note.
3:26 See Ps 40:1; Isa 26:3; 30:15.
3:27 *It is good.* See Pr 3:11–12 and note. *a man to bear the yoke.* Echoes the thought of v. 1: "the man who has seen affliction." *while…young.* Cf. Ecc 12:1.
3:28 *sit alone.* Patiently suffering the mockery of his enemies (see v. 30). *in silence.* See v. 39; Ps 39:9. *it.* The yoke (see v. 27).
3:29 *bury his face in the dust.* Showing humble submission to God. *there may yet be hope.* See 2Sa 12:22; Job 2:14; Am 5:15; Jnh 3:9.
3:30 *offer his cheek.* See Mt 5:39. *filled with disgrace.* See Ps 123:3–4.
3:31 *men are not cast off…forever.* See Isa 49:14–16; cf. note on Jer 3:5.
3:32 The same God who judges also restores (see Ps 30:5; Isa 54:7–8). *great is his unfailing love.* See note on v. 22; see also "great is your faithfulness" (v. 23)—faithfulness and unfailing love are often used together to sum up God's covenant mercies toward his people (see Ps 25:10; 26:3 and notes).
3:33 *does not willingly bring affliction.* See Eze 18:23,32; Hos 11:8; 2Pe 3:9.
3:34 *crush underfoot.* As the Babylonians had done in 586 B.C.
3:35 *deny…rights.* As the leaders of Judah had done, in direct violation of the law (see Ex 23:6). *before the Most High.* In the presence of those whom the Most High designates to dispense justice (see Ex 22:8–9 and NIV text notes; see also introduction to Ps 82). *Most High.* See note on Ge 14:19.
3:36 *deprive…of justice.* People might, but God never does (see Job 8:3; 34:12). *the Lord see such things.* Contrary to what the wicked think (see Ps 10:11 and note), the Lord does see and will call to account (see Ps 10:13–15).
3:37 *speak and have it happen.* No one is equal to God (see Ge 1:3 and note; Ps 33:9–11 and note on 33:4–11); so no one can override the Lord's governing authority (cf. Job 1:12; 2:6 and notes).

[38]Is it not from the mouth of the Most
High
that both calamities and good things
come?[k]
[39]Why should any living man complain
when punished for his sins?[l]

[40]Let us examine our ways and test
them,[m]
and let us return to the LORD.[n]
[41]Let us lift up our hearts and our hands
to God in heaven,[o] and say:
[42]"We have sinned and rebelled[p]
and you have not forgiven.[q]

[43]"You have covered yourself with anger
and pursued[r] us;
you have slain without pity.[s]
[44]You have covered yourself with a cloud[t]
so that no prayer[u] can get through.[v]
[45]You have made us scum[w] and refuse
among the nations.

[46]"All our enemies have opened their
mouths
wide[x] against us.[y]
[47]We have suffered terror and pitfalls,[z]
ruin and destruction.[a]"
[48]Streams of tears[b] flow from my eyes[c]
because my people are destroyed.[d]

[49]My eyes will flow unceasingly,
without relief,[e]
[50]until the LORD looks down
from heaven and sees.[f]
[51]What I see brings grief to my soul
because of all the women of my city.

[52]Those who were my enemies without
cause
hunted me like a bird.[g]
[53]They tried to end my life in a pit[h]
and threw stones at me;
[54]the waters closed over my head,[i]
and I thought I was about to be cut
off.[j]

[55]I called on your name, O LORD,
from the depths[k] of the pit.[l]
[56]You heard my plea:[m] "Do not close
your ears
to my cry for relief."
[57]You came near[n] when I called you,
and you said, "Do not fear."[o]

[58]O Lord, you took up my case;[p]
you redeemed my life.[q]
[59]You have seen, O LORD, the wrong
done to me.[r]
Uphold my cause![s]
[60]You have seen the depth of their
vengeance,
all their plots against me.[t]

[61]O LORD, you have heard their insults,[u]
all their plots against me—
[62]what my enemies whisper and mutter
against me all day long.[v]
[63]Look at them! Sitting or standing,
they mock me in their songs.[w]
[64]Pay them back what they deserve,
O LORD,
for what their hands have done.[x]
[65]Put a veil over their hearts,[y]
and may your curse be on them!
[66]Pursue[z] them in anger and destroy them
from under the heavens of the LORD.

3:38 [k]S Job 2:10; S Isa 45:7; Jer 32:42 **3:39** [l]S Jer 30:15; Mic 7:9 **3:40** [m]2Co 13:5 [n]Ps 119:59; 139:23-24 **3:41** [o]S Ps 25:1; S 28:2 **3:42** [p]Jer 14:20; Da 9:5 [q]S 2Ki 24:4; Jer 5:7-9 **3:43** [r]ver 66; Ps 35:6 [s]S La 2:2,17,21 **3:44** [t]Ps 97:2; La 2:1 [u]S ver 8; Zec 7:13 [v]S Isa 58:4 **3:45** [w]1Co 4:13 **3:46** [x]Ps 22:13 [y]La 2:16 **3:47** [z]Jer 48:43 [a]S Isa 24:17-18; S 51:19 **3:48** [b]S Ps 119:136 [c]S Jer 9:1,18; La 1:16 [d]La 2:11 **3:49** [e]Jer 14:17; S La 2:18 **3:50** [f]S Ps 14:2; 80:14; S Isa 63:15 **3:52** [g]Ps 35:7

3:53 [h]Jer 37:16; S 38:6 **3:54** [i]Ps 69:2; Jnh 2:3-5 [j]ver 18; Ps 88:5; Eze 37:11 **3:55** [k]S Ps 88:6 [l]Ps 130:1; Jnh 2:2 **3:56** [m]S Ps 55:1; 116:1-2 **3:57** [n]S Ps 46:1 [o]Isa 41:10 **3:58** [p]S Jer 51:36 [q]Ps 34:22; S Jer 50:34 **3:59** [r]Jer 18:19-20 [s]Ps 35:23; 43:1 **3:60** [t]S Jer 11:20; 18:18 **3:61** [u]Ps 89:50; Zep 2:8 **3:62** [v]Eze 36:3 **3:63** [w]S Job 30:9 **3:64** [x]S Ps 28:4; S Jer 51:6 **3:65** [y]Ex 14:8; Dt 2:30; Isa 6:10 **3:66** [z]S ver 43

3:38 See Job 2:10; Pr 3:11–12; Isa 45:7; Am 3:3–6 and notes; see also Jer 32:42.
3:39 *complain.* See v. 28 and note.
3:40–41 Here the voice of the community breaks in, responding to the model set before them in vv. 1–39 (see note on v. 1). Appropriately, the community begins with a confession of sin (see 1:8 and note; see also Ps 32:3–5; 39:7–10; 40:11–12; 41:4).
3:40 *let us return to the LORD.* See Hos 6:1; cf. Jer 3:1; 4:1; Hos 14:1; Joel 2:12–13; Zec 1:3.
3:41 *lift up … hands.* See note on 2:19. *heaven.* Where God is enthroned (see Ps 2:4; Isa 63:15; 66:1).
3:42 *We have sinned and rebelled.* For similar confessions see Ps 106:6; Da 9:5.
3:43 *covered yourself with anger.* Cf. Isa 59:17–18. *pursued us … slain without pity.* See v. 66; 2:21; Jer 29:18.
3:46 See 2:16 and note.
3:48–66 The voice returns to first-person singular. It could be the same voice as that heard in vv. 1–39, but more likely the community now speaks in first-person singular (see, e.g., Ps 44:1,4 and note on 44:4). To its prayer the community adds expressions of assurance of being heard and a call for redress against the enemies who have attacked them "without cause" (v. 52)—both of which are common elements in the prayers of individuals in the Psalter (cf. Ps 5:10; Ps 54 and notes).
3:48 *tears flow from my eyes.* See note on 1:16. *my people.* Lit. "the daughter of my people" (see note on 2:11).
3:50 *looks down … sees.* See 5:1; Ps 80:14; Isa 63:15.
3:51 *women of my city.* See 1:4,18; 2:20–21; 5:11.
3:52 *enemies without cause.* See note on Ps 35:19. *like a bird.* See Ps 124:7.
3:53 *end my life in a pit.* See Ps 35:7. *threw stones at.* See 2Sa 16:6; 1Ki 12:18.
3:54 *waters closed over my head.* See Ps 32:6; 42:7; 69:1–2 and notes. *cut off.* See Ps 31:22; Isa 53:8.
3:55 *from the depths of the pit.* See Ps 30:1 and note.
3:56 *cry for relief.* See Job 32:20; Ps 118:5.
3:57 *near when I called.* See Ps 145:18. *Do not fear.* A frequent reassuring word from God (see Jer 1:8 and note).
3:58 *redeemed my life.* See Ps 25:22; 103:4 and notes.
3:59 *You have seen.* See Ps 10:14; 35:22. *Uphold my cause!* See Ps 35:23; 43:1; 119:154.
3:61 *you have heard.* The Lord has heard as well as seen (vv. 59–60) what the enemies are doing.
3:62 *whisper … mutter.* See Ps 5:9 and note.
3:63 *Sitting or standing.* Engaging in any kind of activity (see Dt 6:7; 11:19; Ps 139:2; Isa 37:28). *mock me in their songs.* See note on v. 14.
3:64 Paralleled in Ps 28:4; see Ps 5:10 and note.
3:65 *Put a veil over their hearts.* So they cannot see the error of their ways or foresee the consequences. *may your curse be on them!* See Ps 109:16–20 and note.
3:66 *Pursue them.* Just as you have pursued us without pity because of our sins (v. 43), so now pursue them without pity for what they have done to us.

4[a] How the gold has lost its luster,
the fine gold become dull!
The sacred gems are scattered
at the head of every street.[a]

2 How the precious sons of Zion,[b]
once worth their weight in gold,
are now considered as pots of clay,
the work of a potter's hands!

3 Even jackals offer their breasts
to nurse their young,
but my people have become heartless
like ostriches in the desert.[c]

4 Because of thirst[d] the infant's tongue
sticks to the roof of its mouth;[e]
the children beg for bread,
but no one gives it to them.[f]

5 Those who once ate delicacies
are destitute in the streets.
Those nurtured in purple[g]
now lie on ash heaps.[h]

6 The punishment of my people
is greater than that of Sodom,[i]
which was overthrown in a moment
without a hand turned to help her.

7 Their princes were brighter than snow
and whiter than milk,
their bodies more ruddy than rubies,
their appearance like sapphires.[b]

8 But now they are blacker[j] than soot;
they are not recognized in the streets.
Their skin has shriveled on their bones;[k]
it has become as dry as a stick.

9 Those killed by the sword are better off
than those who die of famine;[l]
racked with hunger, they waste away
for lack of food from the field.[m]

10 With their own hands compassionate women
have cooked their own children,[n]
who became their food
when my people were destroyed.

11 The LORD has given full vent to his wrath;[o]
he has poured out[p] his fierce anger.[q]
He kindled a fire[r] in Zion
that consumed her foundations.[s]

12 The kings of the earth did not believe,
nor did any of the world's people,
that enemies and foes could enter
the gates of Jerusalem.[t]

13 But it happened because of the sins of her prophets
and the iniquities of her priests,[u]
who shed within her
the blood[v] of the righteous.

14 Now they grope through the streets
like men who are blind.[w]
They are so defiled with blood[x]
that no one dares to touch their garments.

15 "Go away! You are unclean!" men cry to them.
"Away! Away! Don't touch us!"
When they flee and wander[y] about,
people among the nations say,
"They can stay here no longer."[z]

16 The LORD himself has scattered them;
he no longer watches over them.[a]
The priests are shown no honor,
the elders[b] no favor.[c]

17 Moreover, our eyes failed,
looking in vain[d] for help;[e]

4:1 [a] Eze 7:19 **4:2** [b] Isa 51:18 **4:3** [c] S Job 39:16 **4:4** [d] S Dt 28:48; S 2Ki 18:31 [e] S Ps 22:15 [f] La 2:11,12 **4:5** [g] Jer 6:2 [h] S Isa 3:26; Am 6:3-7 **4:6** [i] S Ge 19:25 **4:8** [j] S Job 30:28 [k] Ps 102:3-5; S La 3:4 **4:9** [l] S 2Ki 25:3 [m] S Jer 15:2; S 16:4; La 5:10 **4:10** [n] S Lev 26:29; Dt 28:53-57; Jer 19:9; La 2:20; Eze 5:10 **4:11** [o] S Job 20:23 [p] S 2Ch 34:21 [q] Na 1:6; Zep 2:2; 3:8 [r] Jer 17:27 [s] S Dt 32:22; S Jer 7:20; Eze 22:31 **4:12** [t] S 1Ki 9:9; S Jer 21:13 **4:13** [u] Jer 5:31; 6:13; Eze 22:28; Mic 3:11 [v] S 2Ki 21:16 **4:14** [w] S Isa 59:10 [x] Jer 19:4 **4:15** [y] S Jer 44:14 [z] Lev 13:46; Mic 2:10 **4:16** [a] Isa 9:14-16 [b] La 5:12 [c] S La 2:6 **4:17** [d] S Ge 15:18; S Isa 20:5; Eze 29:16 [e] S La 1:7

[a] This chapter is an acrostic poem, the verses of which begin with the successive letters of the Hebrew alphabet.
[b] 7 Or *lapis lazuli*

4:1–22 Another lamentation over the conquest of Jerusalem by the Babylonians—apparently by someone who had experienced the long siege of the city and the subsequent dispersion of its people. Verses 1–10 describe the terrible conditions of the siege, vv. 11–19 speak of the taking of the city and the fate of the refugees, v. 20 expresses the people's shock and dismay at the crushing of the Davidic king, and vv. 21–22 close the lament with words about the contrasting futures of exultant Edom and desolate Zion.

4:1 *How . . . !* See note on 1:1. *gold . . . gems.* Metaphors for God's chosen people (see v. 2). For similar imagery see SS 5:11–12,14–15; Zec 9:16; see also "The Babylonian Theodicy": "O . . . my precious brother, . . . jewel of gold" (lines 56–57). *at the head of every street.* See 2:19; Isa 51:20.

4:3 *my people.* Lit. "the daughter of my people" (see note on 2:11). *become heartless.* See v. 10 and note. *like ostriches.* See Job 39:14–16.

4:5 *delicacies . . . purple.* See Ge 49:20. Purple was the color of royalty (see, e.g., Jdg 8:26; see also note on SS 7:5); cf. the expressions "born to the purple" and "royal blue." *lie on ash heaps.* See Job 2:8 and note; cf. Jer 6:26 and note.

4:6 *my people.* Lit. "the daughter of my people" (see note on 2:11). *Sodom.* See note on Jer 20:16. *overthrown in a moment.* And therefore spared the suffering of a lengthy siege (like that of Jerusalem).

4:7 *whiter . . . ruddy.* The Hebrew underlying these two words is translated "radiant . . . ruddy" in SS 5:10. *than rubies.* See Job 28:18. *sapphires.* See NIV text note; see also SS 5:14; Isa 54:11 and notes.

4:8 *skin has shriveled on their bones.* See Job 19:20.

4:10 See Jer 19:9 and note. *my people.* Lit. "the daughter of my people" (see note on 2:11).

4:11 *fierce anger.* See 1:12 and note. *kindled a fire . . . consumed.* See Jer 17:27 and note.

4:12 *people.* Or "rulers" (parallel to "kings"); the Hebrew form underlying this word is translated "king" in Am 1:5,8.

4:13 See 2:14 and note; see also Eze 22:26,28.

4:14 *grope . . . like men who are blind.* See Dt 28:28–29; Isa 29:9 and note; 59:10 and note; Zep 1:17. *defiled with blood.* See Isa 59:3.

4:15 *unclean!* The cry of the person with a much dreaded skin disease (see Lev 13:45). *people . . . no longer.* Threatened in Dt 28:65–66.

4:16 As threatened in Dt 28:49–50.

4:17 *our eyes failed.* See Dt 28:28; Ps 69:3. *nation that could not save us.* For example, Egypt (see Eze 29:16).

from our towers we watched
for a nation[f] that could not save us.

18 Men stalked us at every step,
so we could not walk in our
streets.
Our end was near, our days were
numbered,
for our end had come.[g]
19 Our pursuers were swifter
than eagles[h] in the sky;
they chased us[i] over the mountains
and lay in wait for us in the
desert.[j]
20 The LORD's anointed,[k] our very life
breath,
was caught in their traps.[l]
We thought that under his shadow[m]
we would live among the nations.

21 Rejoice and be glad, O Daughter of
Edom,
you who live in the land of Uz.[n]
But to you also the cup[o] will be
passed;
you will be drunk and stripped
naked.[p]
22 O Daughter of Zion, your punishment
will end;[q]
he will not prolong your exile.
But, O Daughter of Edom, he will
punish your sin
and expose your wickedness.[r]

5 Remember, O LORD, what has
happened to us;
look, and see our disgrace.[s]
2 Our inheritance[t] has been turned over
to aliens,[u]
our homes[v] to foreigners.[w]
3 We have become orphans and
fatherless,
our mothers like widows.[x]
4 We must buy the water we drink;[y]
our wood can be had only at a
price.[z]
5 Those who pursue us are at our heels;
we are weary[a] and find no rest.[b]
6 We submitted to Egypt and Assyria[c]
to get enough bread.
7 Our fathers[d] sinned and are no more,
and we bear their punishment.[e]
8 Slaves[f] rule over us,
and there is none to free us from
their hands.[g]
9 We get our bread at the risk of our
lives
because of the sword in the desert.
10 Our skin is hot as an oven,
feverish from hunger.[h]
11 Women have been ravished[i] in Zion,
and virgins in the towns of Judah.
12 Princes have been hung up by their
hands;
elders[j] are shown no respect.[k]

4:17 [f]Jer 37:7 **4:18** [g]Eze 7:2-12; Am 8:2 **4:19** [h]S Dt 28:49 [i]S Lev 26:36; Isa 5:26-28 [j]Jer 52:7 **4:20** [k]S 1Sa 26:9; 2Sa 19:21 [l]Jer 39:5; Eze 12:12-13; 19:4,8 [m]S Ps 91:1 **4:21** [n]S Ge 10:23 [o]S Ps 16:5; S Jer 25:15 [p]Isa 34:6-10; S 63:6; Eze 35:15; Am 1:11-12; Ob 1:16; Hab 2:16 **4:22** [q]Isa 40:2; Jer 33:8 [r]S Ps 137:7; Eze 25:12-14; Mal 1:4
5:1 [s]Ps 44:13-16; 89:50 **5:2** [t]Ps 79:1 [u]S Ps 109:11 [v]Zep 1:13 [w]Jer 17:4 **5:3** [x]S Ex 22:24; Jer 15:8; S 18:21 **5:4** [y]S Isa 55:1; Eze 4:16-17 [z]Isa 3:1 **5:5** [a]S Ne 9:37; Isa 47:6 [b]S Jos 1:13 **5:6** [c]Jer 2:36; Hos 5:13; 7:11; 9:3 **5:7** [d]S Jer 31:29 [e]Jer 14:20; 16:12 **5:8** [f]Ne 5:15 [g]Zec 11:6 **5:10** [h]S Job 30:30; S La 4:8-9 **5:11** [i]S Ge 34:29; Zec 14:2 **5:12** [j]S Lev 19:32 [k]S La 2:6; 4:16

4:19 *eagles.* See Jer 4:13; 48:40 and notes.

4:20 *The LORD's anointed.* King Zedekiah of the dynasty of David—under which the people of Judah felt secure because of God's covenant with David (see 2Sa 7; Ps 89; 132; Isa 55:3 and note). *our very life breath.* Lit. "the breath of our nostrils" (a title used also of Pharaoh Rameses II in an inscription found at Abydos in Egypt). *was caught.* See Jer 39:4–7; 52:7–11. *shadow.* Protection (see Jdg 9:15; Ps 17:8 and notes). This verse beautifully expresses the hope that came to be focused in the promised Messiah—the Anointed One from the house of David.

4:21 *Rejoice and be glad.* Irony—exult for the little time you have left before God's judgment sweeps over you (see v. 22). *Daughter of Edom.* A personification of Edom (see note on 2Ki 19:21). *Edom.* Because of its close relationship with Israel from earliest times and its persistent hostility (see note on Ge 25:26), Edom often served OT writers as representative of all Israel's enemies (see Ps 137:7 and note; Isa 13:1–6 and note on 13:1; 34:5 and note; Jer 49:7–22 and note on 49:8; Am 9:12 and note; Introduction to Obadiah: Unity and Theme; Ob 8 and note). *land of Uz.* See Jer 25:20; see also note on Job 1:1. *cup.* See note on Jer 25:15. *stripped naked.* See 1:8; see also Jer 49:10; Na 3:5.

4:22 *Daughter of Zion.* A personification of Jerusalem (see note on 2Ki 19:21). *will not prolong your exile.* See Jer 31–33. *expose your wickedness.* Contrast Ps 32:1; 85:2.

5:1–22 Although not an explicitly alphabetic acrostic like chs. 1–4, this lament is still controlled by the alphabet in that it is composed of just 22 poetic lines (see introduction to Ps 33). The first-person plural language identifies it as the voice of the community (like Ps 44; 60; 74; 80). The circumstances described suggest the time immediately after the fall of Jerusalem when all was chaotic in the land (see v. 18; see also Jer 40:7—41:45). Some interpreters have suggested that the diminution of formal structure in this final lament may have been chosen to reflect the social disintegration brought on by the Babylonian destruction of the state of Judah.

5:1 *Remember ... see.* Initial appeal to the Lord to give his full attention to the plight of his people (see Ps 44:13; 79:4).

5:2 *Our inheritance.* The land of Judah (see Jer 2:7 and note; 3:18).

5:3 *have become orphans ... like widows.* Are as helpless as these (see notes on Ex 22:21–27; Isa 1:17).

5:4 *We must buy the water ... wood.* Contrast Dt 29:11; Jos 9:21,23,27. *wood.* Firewood.

5:5 *find no rest.* The promised "rest" has been taken from them (see Dt 3:20 and note).

5:6 *submitted.* See 1Ch 29:24; 2Ch 30:8; Jer 50:15; lit. "gave the hand" (as in 2Ki 10:15; Ezr 10:19; Eze 17:18). *Egypt ... Assyria.* By this time a conventional way of referring to the great world powers to which the Israelites had often turned for protective alliances (see Isa 7:18; 11:16; 19:23–25; 52:4; Jer 2:18,36; see also Hos 7:11; 9:3; 11:5,11; 12:1 and notes; cf. Mic 7:12; Zec 10:10 and note).

5:7 Fathers and sons alike are responsible for the calamity that has befallen Jerusalem (see v. 16; Jer 3:25; 16:11–12; 31:29–30; Eze 18:2–4; cf. Isa 65:7).

5:8 *Slaves.* An ironic reference to the Babylonian officials who now rule over Jerusalem (formerly "queen among the provinces," 1:1); see Pr 30:21–22.

5:9 *sword in the desert.* Marauding bandits.

5:12 *hung.* An added indignity following execution (see notes on Dt 21:22–23).

[13]Young men toil at the millstones;
boys stagger under loads of wood.
[14]The elders are gone from the city gate;
the young men have stopped their
music.[l]
[15]Joy is gone from our hearts;
our dancing has turned to
mourning.[m]
[16]The crown[n] has fallen from our head.[o]
Woe to us, for we have sinned![p]
[17]Because of this our hearts[q] are faint,[r]
because of these things our eyes[s]
grow dim[t]
[18]for Mount Zion,[u] which lies desolate,[v]
with jackals prowling over it.

[19]You, O LORD, reign forever;[w]
your throne endures[x] from
generation to generation.
[20]Why do you always forget us?[y]
Why do you forsake[z] us so long?
[21]Restore[a] us to yourself, O LORD, that
we may return;
renew our days as of old
[22]unless you have utterly rejected us[b]
and are angry with us beyond
measure.[c]

5:14 [l]S Isa 24:8; Jer 7:34 **5:15** [m]S Jer 25:10; Am 8:10 **5:16** [n]Ps 89:39; S Jer 13:18 [o]S Job 19:9 [p]S Isa 3:11; Jer 14:20 **5:17** [q]S Isa 1:5 [r]S Jer 8:18 [s]Ps 6:7 [t]S Job 16:8 **5:18** [u]Ps 74:2-3 [v]S Isa 27:10; Mic 3:12 **5:19** [w]S 1Ch 16:31 [x]S Ps 45:6; 102:12, 24-27 **5:20** [y]S Ps 13:1; 44:24 [z]S Ps 71:11 **5:21** [a]S Ps 80:3; Isa 60:20-22 **5:22** [b]S Ps 53:5; 60:1-2; S Jer 6:30 [c]S Isa 64:9

5:13 *toil at the millstones.* Humiliating work (see note on Jdg 9:53; see also Isa 47:2).
5:14 *city gate.* The municipal court (see Jos 20:4), but also a gathering place for conversation and entertainment (cf. 1:4).
5:15 See Jer 7:34; 16:9; 25:10; contrast Ps 30:11; Jer 31:13.
5:16 *crown.* Symbolizes the glory and honor embodied in the city of Jerusalem (see 1:1; 2:15; cf. Isa 28:1,3).
5:17 *hearts are faint.* See note on 1:22. *eyes grow dim.* See 2:11; see also note on Ps 6:7.
5:18 *jackals.* The Hebrew for this word, different from that used in 4:3, can also mean "foxes" (Jdg 15:4). For similar imagery of desolation see Isa 13:21 – 22; 34:11 – 15; Zep 2:13 – 15.
5:19 Paralleled in Ps 102:12 (see note there). Elsewhere also prayer begins with praise (see Ps 44:1 – 8; 74:12 – 14; 80:1 – 2; 89:1 – 18; cf. Ac 24:23 and note). See Introduction: Themes and Theology (last paragraph).
5:20 *Why . . . ? Why . . . ?* See note on Ps 6:3.
5:21 *Restore us to yourself.* This language suggests a prayer for renewed commitment to the Lord (see 1Ki 8:33,48; Ne 1:9; Jer 3:7,10; Hos 7:10). *we may return.* See Jer 31:18 and note on 31:18 – 19. *renew.* See Ps 104:30.
5:22 See Jer 14:19. *unless.* Or "but." A similarly somber ending characterizes not only other laments (e.g., Ps 88) but also other OT books (e.g., Isaiah and Malachi).

Ezekiel

INTRODUCTION

Background

Ezekiel lived during a time of international upheaval. The Assyrian empire that had once conquered the Syro-Palestinian area and destroyed the northern kingdom of Israel (which fell to the Assyrians in 722–721 B.C.) began to crumble under the blows of a resurgent Babylon. In 612 the great Assyrian city of Nineveh fell to a combined force of Babylonians and Medes. Three years later, Pharaoh Neco II of Egypt marched north to assist the Assyrians and to try to reassert Egypt's age-old influence over Canaan and Aram (Syria). At Megiddo, King Josiah of Judah, who may have been an ally of Babylonia as King Hezekiah had been, attempted to intercept the Egyptian forces but was crushed, losing his life in the battle (see 2Ki 23:29–30; 2Ch 35:20–24).

Jehoahaz, a son of Josiah, ruled Judah for only three months, after which Neco installed Jehoiakim, another son of Josiah, as his royal vassal in Jerusalem (609 B.C.). In 605 the Babylonians overwhelmed the Egyptian army at Carchemish (see Jer 46:2), then pressed south as far as the Philistine plain. In the same year, Nebuchadnezzar was elevated to the Babylonian throne and Jehoiakim shifted allegiance to him. When a few years later the Egyptian and Babylonian forces met in a standoff battle, Jehoiakim rebelled against his new overlord.

Nebuchadnezzar soon responded by sending a force against Jerusalem, subduing it in 597 B.C. Jehoiakim's son Jehoiachin and about 10,000 Jews (see 2Ki 24:14), including Ezekiel, were exiled to Babylon, where they joined those who had been exiled in Jehoiakim's "third year" (see Da 1:1 and note). Nebuchadnezzar placed Jehoiachin's uncle, Zedekiah, on the throne in Jerusalem, but within five or six years he too rebelled. The Babylonians laid siege to Jerusalem in 588, and in July, 586, the walls were breached and the city plundered. On Aug. 14, 586, the city and temple were burned.

Under Nebuchadnezzar and his successors, Babylon dominated the international scene until it was crushed by Cyrus the Persian in 539 B.C. With the fall of Jerusalem, the reign of the house of

A Quick Look

Author:
Ezekiel

Audience:
Jews who were taken captive to Babylonia in 597 B.C.

Date:
Between 593 and 571 B.C.

Theme:
Ezekiel the priest assures his fellow Jews that God will one day return them to Jerusalem and restore the temple.

David came to an end; the kingdom of Judah ceased to be an independent nation; Jerusalem and the Lord's temple lay in ruins.

Author

What is known of Ezekiel is derived solely from the book that bears his name. He was among the Jews exiled to Babylonia by Nebuchadnezzar in 597 B.C., and there among the exiles he received his call to become a prophet (see 1:1 – 3). He was married (see 24:15 – 18), lived in a house of his own (see 3:24; 8:1) and along with his fellow exiles, though confined to Babylonia, had a relatively free existence there.

He was of a priestly family (see NIV text note on 1:3) and therefore was eligible to serve as a priest. As a priest-prophet called to minister to the exiles (separated from the temple of the Lord with its symbolism, sacrifices, priestly ministrations and worship rituals), his message had much to do with the temple (see especially chs. 8 – 11; 40 – 48) and its ceremonies.

Ezekiel was obviously a man of broad knowledge, not only of his own national traditions but also of international affairs and history. His acquaintance with general matters of culture, from shipbuilding to literature, is equally amazing. He was gifted with a powerful intellect and was capable of grasping large issues and of dealing with them in grand and compelling images. His style is often detached, but in places it is passionate and earthy (see chs. 16; 23).

More than any other prophet (more even than Hosea and Jeremiah) he was directed to involve himself personally in the divine word by acting it out in prophetic symbolism.

Occasion, Purpose and Summary of Contents

Though Ezekiel lived with his fellow exiles in Babylonia, his divine call forced him to suppress any natural expectations he may have had of an early return to an undamaged Jerusalem. For the first seven years of his ministry (593 – 586 B.C.) he faithfully relayed to his fellow Jews the stern, heart-rending, hope-crushing word of divine judgment: Because of all her sins, Jerusalem would fall (see chs. 1 – 24). The fact that Israel was God's covenant people and that Jerusalem was the city of his temple would not bring their early release from exile or prevent Jerusalem from being destroyed (see Jer 29 – 30). The only hope the prophet was authorized to extend to his hearers was that of living at peace with themselves and with God during their exile.

After being informed by the Lord that Jerusalem was under siege and would surely fall (24:1 – 14), Ezekiel was told that his beloved wife would soon die. The delight of his eyes would be taken from him just as the temple, the delight of Israel's eyes, would be taken from her. He was not to mourn openly for his wife, as a sign to his people not to mourn openly for Jerusalem (24:15 – 27). He was then directed to pronounce a series of judgments on the seven nations of Ammon, Moab, Edom, Philistia, Tyre, Sidon and Egypt (chs. 25 – 32). The day of God's wrath was soon to come, but not on Israel alone.

Once news was received that Jerusalem had fallen, Ezekiel's message turned to the Lord's consoling word of hope for his people — they would experience revival, restoration and a glorious future as the redeemed and perfected kingdom of God in the world (chs. 33 – 48).

Date

Since the book of Ezekiel contains more dates (see chart, p. 1239) than any other OT prophetic book, its prophecies can be dated with considerable precision. In addition, modern scholarship, using archaeology (Babylonian annals on cuneiform tablets) and astronomy (accurate dating of eclipses referred to in ancient archives), provides precise modern calendar equivalents.

Twelve of the 13 dates specify times when Ezekiel received a divine message. The other is the date of the arrival of the messenger who reported the fall of Jerusalem (33:21).

After receiving his call in July, 593 B.C., Ezekiel was active for 22 years, his last dated prophecy being received in April, 571 (see 29:17). If the "thirtieth year" of 1:1 (see note there) refers to Ezekiel's age at the time of his call, his prophetic career exceeded a normal priestly term of service by two years (see Nu 4:3). His period of activity coincides with Jerusalem's darkest hour, preceding the 586 destruction by 7 years and following it by 15.

Dates in Ezekiel

REFERENCE	YEAR	MONTH	DAY	MODERN RECKONING	EVENT
1. 1:1	30	4	5	July 31, 593 B.C.	Inaugural vision
1:2	5	—	5		
3:16	"At the end of seven days"				
2. 8:1	6	6	5	Sept. 17, 592	Transport to Jerusalem
3. 20:1-2	7	5	10	Aug. 14, 591	Negative view of Israel's history
4. 24:1	9	10	10	Jan. 15, 588	Beginning of siege (see also 2 Ki 25:1)
5. 26:1	11	—	1	Apr. 23, 587 to Apr. 13, 586	Oracle against Tyre (see note on 26:1)
6. 29:1	10	10	12	Jan. 7, 587	Oracle against Egypt
7. 29:17	27	1	1	Apr. 26, 571	Egypt in exchange for Tyre
8. 30:20	11	1	7	Apr. 29, 587	Oracle against Pharaoh
9. 31:1	11	3	1	June 21, 587	Oracle against Pharaoh
10. 32:1	12	12	1	Mar. 3, 585	Lament over Pharaoh
11. 32:17	12	—	15	Apr. 13, 586 to Apr. 1, 585	Egypt dead
12. 33:21	12	10	5	Jan. 8, 585	Arrival of first fugitive
13. 40:1	25	1	10	Apr. 28, 573	Vision of the future
40:1	"fourteenth year after the fall of the city"				

Themes

The OT in general and the prophets in particular presuppose and teach God's sovereignty over all creation, over people and nations and the course of history. And nowhere in the Bible are God's initiative and control expressed more clearly and pervasively than in the book of Ezekiel. From the first chapter, which graphically describes the overwhelming invasion of the divine presence into Ezekiel's world, to the last phrase of Ezekiel's vision ("THE LORD IS THERE") the book sounds and echoes God's sovereignty.

This sovereign God resolved that he would be known and acknowledged. Approximately 65 occurrences of the clause (or variations) "Then they will know that I am the LORD" testify to that divine desire and intention (see note on 6:7). Overall, chs. 1 – 24 teach that God will be revealed in the fall of Jerusalem and the destruction of the temple; chs. 25 – 32 teach that the nations likewise will know God through his judgments; and chs. 33 – 48 promise that God will be known through the restoration and spiritual renewal of Israel.

God's total sovereignty is also evident in his mobility. He is not limited to the temple in Jerusalem. He can respond to his people's sin by leaving his sanctuary in Israel, and he can graciously condescend to visit his exiled children in Babylon.

God is free to judge, and he is equally free to be gracious. His stern judgments on Israel ultimately reflect his grace. He allows the total dismemberment of Israel's political and religious life so that her renewed life and his presence with her will be clearly seen as a gift from the Lord of the universe.

Furthermore, as God's spokesman, Ezekiel's "son of man" status (see note on 2:1) testifies to the sovereign God he was commissioned to serve.

See also Theological Significance below.

Literary Features

The three major prophets (Isaiah, Jeremiah, Ezekiel) and Zephaniah all have the same basic sequence of messages: (1) prophecies against Israel, (2) prophecies against the nations, (3) consolation for Israel. In no other book is this pattern clearer than in Ezekiel (see Outline).

Besides clarity of structure, the book of Ezekiel reveals symmetry. The vision of the desecrated temple fit for destruction (chs. 8–11) is balanced by the vision of the restored and purified temple (chs. 40–48). The God presented in agitated wrath (ch. 1) is also shown to be a God of comfort ("THE LORD IS THERE," 48:35). Ezekiel's call to be a watchman announcing divine judgment (ch. 3) is balanced by his call to be a watchman announcing the new age to follow (ch. 33). In one place (ch. 6) the mountains of Israel receive a prophetic rebuke, but in another (ch. 36) they are consoled.

Ezekiel powerfully depicts the grandeur and glory of God's sovereign rule and his holiness, which he jealously safeguards.

Prophetic books are usually largely poetic, the prophets apparently having spoken in imaginative and rhythmic styles. Most of Ezekiel, however, is prose, perhaps due to his priestly background. His repetitions have an unforgettable hammering effect, and his priestly orientation is also reflected in a case-law type of sentence (compare 3:19, "If you do warn the wicked ...," with Ex 21:2, "If you buy a Hebrew servant ...").

The book contains four major visions (chs. 1–3; 8–11; 37:1–14; 40–48) and 12 symbolic acts (3:22–26; 4:1–3; 4:4–8; 4:9–11; 4:12–14; 5:1–3; 12:1–16; 12:17–20; 21:6–7; 21:18–24; 24:15–24; 37:15–28). Five messages are in the form of parables (chs. 15–17; 19; 23).

Theological Significance

Other prophets deal largely with Israel's idolatry, with her moral corruption in public and private affairs, and with her international intrigues and alliances on which she relied instead of the Lord. They announce God's impending judgment on his rebellious nation but speak also about a future redemption: a new exodus, a new covenant, a restored Jerusalem, a revived Davidic dynasty, a worldwide recognition of the Lord and his Messiah and a paradise-like peace.

The contours and sweep of Ezekiel's message are similar, but he focuses uniquely on Israel as the holy people of the holy temple, the holy city and the holy land. By defiling her worship, Israel had rendered herself unclean and had defiled temple, city and land. From such defilement God could only withdraw and judge his people with national destruction.

But God's faithfulness to his covenant and his desire to save were so great that he would revive his people once more, shepherd them with compassion, cleanse them of all their defilement, reconstitute them as a perfect expression of his kingdom under the hand of "David" (34:23–24), overwhelm all the forces and powers arrayed against them, display his glory among the nations and restore the glory of his presence to the holy city.

Ezekiel powerfully depicts the grandeur and glory of God's sovereign rule (see Themes) and his holiness, which he jealously safeguards. The book's theological center is the unfolding of God's saving purposes in the history of the world — from the time in which he must withdraw from the defilement of his covenant people to the culmination of his grand design of redemption. The message of Ezekiel, which is ultimately eschatological, anticipates — even demands — God's future works in history proclaimed by the NT.

Outline

- I. Messages of Judgment against Israel (chs. 1–24)
  - A. Ezekiel's Inaugural Vision (chs. 1–3)
    1. Overwhelming display of the glory of the Lord (ch. 1)
    2. Ezekiel's call to be a prophet (2:1—3:15)
    3. Ezekiel's task as watchman (3:16–21)
    4. Restraints on Ezekiel's prophetic ministry (3:22–27)

B. Symbolic Acts Portraying the Siege of Jerusalem (chs. 4–5)
   1. Ezekiel's symbolic siege of Jerusalem (ch. 4)
   2. God's razor of judgment at work (ch. 5)
C. Messages of Divine Judgment (chs. 6–7)
   1. Doom for the mountains of Israel (ch. 6)
   2. The end has come on the land (ch. 7)
D. Corruption of the Temple and Its Consequences (chs. 8–11)
   1. Idolatry in the temple (ch. 8)
   2. Judgment on the idolaters (ch. 9)
   3. God's glory departs from the temple (ch. 10)
   4. God's sure judgment on Jerusalem (11:1–14)
   5. Those in exile to be restored (11:15–21)
   6. Conclusion of the vision (11:22–25)
E. Ezekiel Symbolizes the Exile of Jerusalem (ch. 12)
   1. An exile's baggage (12:1–16)
   2. Anxious eating (12:17–20)
   3. The nearness of judgment (12:21–28)
F. Messages concerning God's Judgment on Judah (13:1—24:14)
   1. Condemnation of the false prophets (ch. 13)
   2. Condemnation of the idolaters (14:1–11)
   3. No mediators can turn back God's judgment (14:12–23)
   4. Jerusalem likened to a piece of burnt vine (ch. 15)
   5. Jerusalem allegorized as an adulterous wife (ch. 16)
   6. Allegory of two eagles and a vine (ch. 17)
   7. The soul who sins will die (ch. 18)
   8. A lament over the fall of Jerusalem's kings (ch. 19)
   9. Apostate Israel purged and renewed through judgment (20:1–44)
   10. Babylonia, God's sword of judgment (20:45—21:32)
   11. The sins for which Jerusalem is judged (ch. 22)
   12. Jerusalem and Samaria allegorized as adulterous sisters (ch. 23)
   13. Jerusalem cooked over the fire (24:1–14)
G. The Death of Ezekiel's Wife Symbolizes Jerusalem's Fall (24:15–27)

II. Messages of Judgment against the Nations (chs. 25–32)
A. A Prophecy against Ammon (25:1–7)
B. A Prophecy against Moab (25:8–11)
C. A Prophecy against Edom (25:12–14)
D. A Prophecy against Philistia (25:15–17)
E. A Prophecy against Tyre (26:1—28:19)
   1. Tyre's destruction announced (ch. 26)
   2. A lament over Tyre (ch. 27)
   3. A prophecy against the king of Tyre (28:1–19)
F. A Prophecy against Sidon (28:20–24)
   (For Israel, a restoration, 28:25–26)
G. A Prophecy against Egypt (chs. 29–32)
   1. Egypt a doomed monster (29:1–16)
   2. Egypt a payment to Nebuchadnezzar (29:17–21)
   3. Laments over Egypt (30:1–19)
   4. The pharaoh's arms are broken (30:20–26)
   5. The pharaoh a felled Lebanon cedar (ch. 31)
   6. Lament over the pharaoh (32:1–16)
   7. The pharaoh consigned to the realm of the dead (32:17–32)

- III. Messages of Consolation for Israel (chs. 33 – 48)
  - A. Renewal of Ezekiel's Call as Watchman (33:1 – 20)
  - B. Jerusalem's Fall Reported and Its Remnant Condemned (33:21 – 33)
  - C. The Lord to Be Israel's Shepherd (ch. 34)
  - D. A Prophecy against Edom (ch. 35)
  - E. Israel's Complete Restoration Announced (ch. 36)
  - F. Israel's Dry Bones Revived and Unity Restored (ch. 37)
    1. Israel's dry bones restored to life (37:1 – 14)
    2. Again one nation under one king (37:15 – 28)
  - G. The Great Battle of the Ages (chs. 38 – 39)
  - H. The New Order for Purified Israel (chs. 40 – 48)
    1. The temple area restored (40:1 – 47)
    2. The new temple (40:48 — 42:20)
    3. God's glory returns to the temple (43:1 – 12)
    4. Restoration of the great altar (43:13 – 27)
    5. Restoration of the priesthood (ch. 44)
    6. Restoration of the theocratic order (chs. 45 – 46)
    7. The river of life from the temple (47:1 – 12)
    8. The boundaries of the land (47:13 – 23)
    9. The distribution of the land (48:1 – 29)
    10. The twelve gates of the new city (48:30 – 35)

The Living Creatures and the Glory of the LORD

1 In the[a] thirtieth year, in the fourth
month on the fifth day, while I was
among the exiles[a] by the Kebar River,[b] the
heavens were opened[c] and I saw visions[d]
of God.
2On the fifth of the month—it was the
fifth year of the exile of King Jehoiachin[e]—
3the word of the LORD came to Ezekiel[f] the
priest, the son of Buzi,[b] by the Kebar River
in the land of the Babylonians.[c] There the
hand of the LORD was upon him.[g]
4I looked, and I saw a windstorm[h] coming out of the north[i]—an immense cloud
with flashing lightning and surrounded by
brilliant light. The center of the fire looked
like glowing metal,[j] 5and in the fire was
what looked like four living creatures.[k] In
appearance their form was that of a man,[l]
6but each of them had four faces[m] and four
wings. 7Their legs were straight; their feet
were like those of a calf and gleamed like
burnished bronze.[n] 8Under their wings
on their four sides they had the hands of
a man.[o] All four of them had faces and
wings, 9and their wings touched one another. Each one went straight ahead; they
did not turn as they moved.[p]
10Their faces looked like this: Each of
the four had the face of a man, and on the
right side each had the face of a lion, and
on the left the face of an ox; each also had
the face of an eagle.[q] 11Such were their faces. Their wings[r] were spread out upward;
each had two wings, one touching the
wing of another creature on either side,
and two wings covering its body. 12Each
one went straight ahead. Wherever the
spirit would go, they would go, without
turning as they went.[s] 13The appearance of
the living creatures was like burning coals[t]
of fire or like torches. Fire moved back and
forth among the creatures; it was bright,
and lightning[u] flashed out of it. 14The creatures sped back and forth like flashes of
lightning.[v]
15As I looked at the living creatures,[w] I
saw a wheel[x] on the ground beside each
creature with its four faces. 16This was the
appearance and structure of the wheels:
They sparkled like chrysolite,[y] and all four
looked alike. Each appeared to be made
like a wheel intersecting a wheel. 17As
they moved, they would go in any one of
the four directions the creatures faced; the

1:1 [a]S Dt 21:10; Eze 11:24-25 [b]S Ps 137:1 [c]S Mt 3:16 [d]S Ex 24:10 **1:2** [e]S 2Ki 24:15 **1:3** [f]Eze 24:24 [g]S 2Ki 3:15; Isa 8:11; Eze 3:14, 22; 8:1; 33:22; 37:1; 40:1 **1:4** [h]S Job 38:1 [i]Jer 1:14 [j]Eze 8:2 **1:5** [k]S Isa 6:2; Rev 4:6 [l]ver 26; Da 7:13 **1:6** [m]Eze 10:14 **1:7** [n]Eze 40:3; Da 10:6; S Rev 1:15 **1:8** [o]Eze 10:8 **1:9** [p]Eze 10:22 **1:10** [q]Eze 10:14; Rev 4:7 **1:11** [r]Isa 6:2 **1:12** [s]Eze 10:16-19 **1:13** [t]S 2Sa 22:9 [u]Rev 4:5 **1:14** [v]S Ps 29:7 **1:15** [w]Eze 3:13 [x]Eze 10:2; Da 7:9 **1:16** [y]S Ex 28:20

a 1 Or *˻my˼* *b* 3 Or *Ezekiel son of Buzi the priest* *c* 3 Or *Chaldeans*

1:1–28 Forced into Babylonian exile far from the Lord's temple with its symbolic evocations of God's glory (see notes on Ex 26:1; 40:34; Ps 24:2; see also Ps 24:8–10; 26:8; 29:9; 96:6 and notes), Ezekiel is inaugurated into his prophetic mission (see 1:1 and note) with an overwhelming vision of God's glory (see note on 1:28)—much as Isaiah was granted an awesome vision of God enthroned on high and attended by winged "seraphs" (see Isa 6:1–2 and notes) at the inauguration of his prophetic ministry (cf. 1Ki 22:19 and note).

1:1 *thirtieth year.* Probably Ezekiel's age (see NIV text note). According to Nu 4:3, a person entered active priestly ministry in his 30th year. Denied the ministry of the priesthood, Ezekiel received another commission—that of prophet. *Kebar River.* A canal of the Euphrates near the city of Nippur, south of Babylon, and possibly a place of prayer for the exiles (see Ps 137:1; cf. Ac 16:13). *visions of God.* A special term, always in the plural and always with the word "God" (not with the more personal "LORD"). The expression precedes this and the two other major visions of the prophet (8:3; 40:2).

1:2 *fifth year of the exile.* Verses 2–3, written in the third person (the only third-person narrative in the book), clarify the date in v. 1. *King Jehoiachin.* Was forced to accompany an early group of exiles to Babylonia in 597 B.C. (see Introduction: Background). Ezekiel was among them and received his prophetic call in 593.

1:3 *Ezekiel.* The prophet's name occurs elsewhere in the book only in 24:24 (see note there) and thus frames the first major literary unit in his prophecy. His name means "God is strong" (cf. 3:14), "God strengthens" (cf. 30:25; 34:16) or "God makes hard" (cf. 3:8–9). *priest.* Member of a priestly family (see NIV text note). *hand of the LORD.* A phrase occurring seven times in the book (here; 3:14,22; 8:1; 33:22; 37:1; 40:1), indicating an overpowering experience of divine revelation.

1:4 *I looked.* Introduces the first part of the vision: storm and living creatures (vv. 4–14). The "I looked" of v. 15 introduces the second part: wheels and the glory of the Lord. *a windstorm.* A storm cloud—accompanied with wind, lightning and thunder—often served as symbolic of God's powerful and active presence (see Ex 19:16–18; Ps 18:7–15; 77:16–19 and notes; cf. Job 38:1).

1:5 *four living creatures.* "Four," which stands for completeness (cf. the four directions in Ge 13:14 and the four quarters of the earth in Isa 11:12), is used often in this chapter—and over 40 times in the book. The living creatures, called "cherubim" in ch. 10, are throne attendants (see Ex 25:18 and note). Here (see v. 10 and note) they contribute to the whole complex scenario that symbolically represents God's creation. These four creatures (cf. the "seraphs" of Isa 6:2–4) appear again in Rev 4:7. They were often depicted in the paintings and sculptures of the Middle Ages, but in this later use they represent the four Gospels. *their form … a man.* God's noblest creature on earth (see Ge 1:26 and note).

1:6 *four faces.* See v. 10 and note. *four wings.* Signifying their mobility as throne attendants of the heavenly King who is ever on the move through history.

1:7 *like those of a calf.* Perhaps indicates agility (cf. Ps 29:6; Mal 4:2).

1:10 *face of a man.* God's appointed ruler on earth (see Ge 1:26–28; Ps 8:3–8 and notes). *lion.* The most ferocious of wild animals known in Israel and Mesopotamia, and reputedly the strongest of such beasts (see Jdg 14:18). *ox.* The most powerful of domesticated animals. *eagle.* The mightiest of the birds. Cf. Rev 4:7 and note.

1:12 *straight ahead … without turning.* In their mobility they were multidirectional (see v. 14). *the spirit.* The directing presence in the cherubim (see v. 20).

1:13 *like burning coals.* Cf. Ps 18:8. *like torches.* Cf. Ge 15:17.

1:15 *wheel.* Also symbolic of mobility (see note on v. 12).

1:16 *chrysolite.* The precise identification of this stone is uncertain. See Ex 28:20 (and NIV text note), where the stone appears in the priestly breastplate. *a wheel intersecting a wheel.* Probably two wheels intersecting at right angles in order to move in all four directions (see v. 17). The imagery symbolizes the omnipresence of God.

wheels did not turn[z] about[a] as the creatures went. 18 Their rims were high and
awesome, and all four rims were full of
eyes[a] all around.
19 When the living creatures moved, the
wheels beside them moved; and when the
living creatures rose from the ground, the
wheels also rose. 20 Wherever the spirit
would go, they would go,[b] and the wheels
would rise along with them, because the
spirit of the living creatures was in the
wheels. 21 When the creatures moved, they
also moved; when the creatures stood still,
they also stood still; and when the creatures rose from the ground, the wheels
rose along with them, because the spirit
of the living creatures was in the wheels.[c]
22 Spread out above the heads of the
living creatures was what looked like an
expanse,[d] sparkling like ice, and awesome. 23 Under the expanse their wings
were stretched out one toward the other, and each had two wings covering its
body. 24 When the creatures moved, I heard
the sound of their wings, like the roar of
rushing[e] waters, like the voice[f] of the Almighty,[b] like the tumult of an army.[g] When
they stood still, they lowered their wings.
25 Then there came a voice from above
the expanse over their heads as they stood
with lowered wings. 26 Above the expanse
over their heads was what looked like a
throne[h] of sapphire,[c,i] and high above on
the throne was a figure like that of a man.[j]
27 I saw that from what appeared to be his
waist up he looked like glowing metal, as
if full of fire, and that from there down
he looked like fire; and brilliant light surrounded him.[k] 28 Like the appearance of a
rainbow[l] in the clouds on a rainy day, so
was the radiance around him.[m]
This was the appearance of the likeness
of the glory[n] of the LORD. When I saw it,
I fell facedown,[o] and I heard the voice of
one speaking.

Ezekiel's Call

2 He said to me, "Son of man,[p] stand[q] up
on your feet and I will speak to you.[r]"
2 As he spoke, the Spirit came into me and
raised me[s] to my feet, and I heard him
speaking to me.
3 He said: "Son of man, I am sending you
to the Israelites, to a rebellious nation that
has rebelled against me; they and their
fathers have been in revolt against me to
this very day.[t] 4 The people to whom I am
sending you are obstinate and stubborn.[u]
Say to them, 'This is what the Sovereign
LORD says.'[v] 5 And whether they listen or
fail to listen[w]—for they are a rebellious
house[x]—they will know that a prophet
has been among them.[y] 6 And you, son of
man, do not be afraid[z] of them or their
words. Do not be afraid, though briers and
thorns[a] are all around you and you live
among scorpions. Do not be afraid of what
they say or terrified by them, though they
are a rebellious house.[b] 7 You must speak[c]
my words to them, whether they listen
or fail to listen, for they are rebellious.[d]
8 But you, son of man, listen to what I say
to you. Do not rebel[e,f] like that rebellious
house;[g] open your mouth and eat[h] what
I give you."
9 Then I looked, and I saw a hand[i]
stretched out to me. In it was a scroll,[j]

1:17 [z]ver 9
1:18 [a]Rev 4:6
1:20 [b]ver 12
1:21 [c]Eze 10:9-12
1:22 [d]Eze 10:1
1:24 [e]S Ps 46:3; Eze 3:13 [f]Eze 10:5; 43:2; Da 10:6; Rev 1:15; 14:2; 19:6 [g]S 2Ki 7:6
1:26 [h]S 1Ki 22:19; Isa 6:1; S Jer 3:17 [i]S Ex 24:10 [j]S ver 5; S Eze 2:1; S Rev 1:13
1:27 [k]Eze 8:2
1:28 [l]S Ge 9:13; Rev 10:1 [m]S Rev 4:2 [n]S Ex 16:7; S 24:16; Lk 2:9 [o]S Ge 17:3; S Nu 14:5
2:1 [p]S Job 25:6; Ps 8:4; S Eze 1:26; Da 7:13; 8:15 [q]Da 10:11; Ac 14:10; 26:16 [r]Ac 9:6
2:2 [s]Eze 3:24; Da 8:18
2:3 [t]S Jer 3:25; Eze 5:6; 20:8-24; 24:3
2:4 [u]S Ex 32:9; S Isa 9:9; Eze 3:7 [v]Am 7:15
2:5 [w]Eze 3:11 [x]Eze 3:27 [y]S Jer 5:3; Eze 33:33; Jn 15:22
2:6 [z]S Dt 31:6; S 2Ki 1:15 [a]S Nu 33:55; Isa 9:18; Mic 7:4 [b]S Isa 1:2; 30:9; Eze 24:3; 44:6
2:7 [c]Jer 7:27 [d]Jer 1:7; S 42:21; Eze 3:10-11
2:8 [e]Nu 20:10-13 [f]Isa 8:11 [g]S Isa 50:5 [h]Ps 81:10; S Jer 15:16; Rev 10:9
2:9 [i]Eze 8:3 [j]S Ps 40:7; S Jer 36:4; Rev 5:1-5; 10:8-10

[a] 17 Or *aside* [b] 24 Hebrew *Shaddai* [c] 26 Or *lapis lazuli*

1:18 *full of eyes.* Symbolizes God's all-seeing nature (cf. notes on Zec 3:9; 4:10).

1:22 *expanse.* The same word occurs in Ge 1:6–8, where its function is to separate the waters above from the waters below. Here it separates the creatures from the glory of the Lord. *like ice ... awesome.* Cf. Rev 4:6 and note; 15:2.

1:25 *stood with lowered wings.* Awaiting a word from the throne.

1:26 *Above the expanse ... on the throne.* Cf. Ex 24:10. *a figure like that of a man.* Ezekiel is reporting his vision of God, but he carefully avoids saying he saw God directly (see Ge 16:13; Ex 3:6; Jdg 13:22).

1:28 *appearance of the likeness.* See note on v. 26. *glory of the LORD.* See note on 1:1–28. When God's glory was symbolically revealed, it took the form of brilliant light (see Ex 40:34 and note; Isa 6:3). What is remarkable about Ezekiel's experience is that God's glory had for centuries been associated with the temple in Jerusalem (see 1Ki 8:11; Ps 26:8; 63:2; 96:6; 102:16). Now God had left his temple and was appearing to his exiled people in Babylonia—a major theme in the first half of Ezekiel's message (see 10:4; 11:23). In his vision of the restored Jerusalem the prophet saw the glory of the Lord returning (see 43:2 and note). *I fell facedown.* See Ge 17:3; Ex 3:6; cf. Isa 6:5.

2:1—3:15 God does not abandon his covenant people even though he banishes them from the promised land because of their long history of rebellion against him. He commissions Ezekiel to bring his word to those in exile, still calling them by their covenant name "Israel" (see 2:3; 3:4–5,7). Ezekiel's mission to the exiles overlapped that of Jeremiah, another member of a priestly family called to the prophetic office, whose mission was to the Israelites still living in and around Jerusalem.

2:1 *Son of man.* A term used 93 times in Ezekiel, emphasizing the prophet's humanity as he was addressed by the transcendent God (see note on Ps 8:4). Da 7:13 and 8:17 are the only other places where the phrase is used as a title in the OT. Jesus' frequent use of the phrase in referring to himself showed that he was the eschatological figure spoken about in Da 7:13 (see, e.g., Mk 8:31 and note).

2:2 *the Spirit came into me and raised me to my feet.* The Spirit of God governs and empowers the prophet's entire ministry (see 11:5; 36:27; 37:14; 39:29; see also 3:12 and note).

2:3 *to a rebellious nation.* A theme that became a keynote of Ezekiel's preaching.

2:6 *briers and thorns ... scorpions.* Vivid images of those who would make life difficult for the prophet.

10which he unrolled before me. On both
sides of it were written words of lament
and mourning and woe.[k]
3 And he said to me, "Son of man, eat
what is before you, eat this scroll; then
go and speak to the house of Israel." 2So
I opened my mouth, and he gave me the
scroll to eat.
3Then he said to me, "Son of man, eat
this scroll I am giving you and fill your
stomach with it." So I ate[l] it, and it tasted
as sweet as honey[m] in my mouth.
4He then said to me: "Son of man, go
now to the house of Israel and speak my
words to them.[n] 5You are not being sent to
a people of obscure speech and difficult
language,[o] but to the house of Israel—
6not to many peoples of obscure speech
and difficult language, whose words you
cannot understand. Surely if I had sent you
to them, they would have listened to you.[p]
7But the house of Israel is not willing to
listen[q] to you because they are not willing
to listen to me, for the whole house of Israel is hardened and obstinate.[r] 8But I will
make you as unyielding and hardened as
they are.[s] 9I will make your forehead[t] like
the hardest stone, harder than flint.[u] Do
not be afraid of them or terrified by them,
though they are a rebellious house.[v]"
10And he said to me, "Son of man, listen
carefully and take to heart[w] all the words I
speak to you. 11Go[x] now to your countrymen
in exile and speak to them. Say to them,
'This is what the Sovereign LORD says,'[y]
whether they listen or fail to listen.[z]"
12Then the Spirit lifted me up,[a] and
I heard behind me a loud rumbling
sound—May the glory of the LORD be
praised in his dwelling place!— 13the
sound of the wings of the living creatures[b]
brushing against each other and the sound
of the wheels beside them, a loud rumbling sound.[c] 14The Spirit[d] then lifted me
up[e] and took me away, and I went in bitterness and in the anger of my spirit, with
the strong hand of the LORD[f] upon me. 15I
came to the exiles who lived at Tel Abib
near the Kebar River.[g] And there, where
they were living, I sat among them for sev-
en days[h]—overwhelmed.

Warning to Israel

16At the end of seven days the word of
the LORD came to me:[i] 17"Son of man, I
have made you a watchman[j] for the house
of Israel; so hear the word I speak and give
them warning from me.[k] 18When I say to
a wicked man, 'You will surely die,[l]' and
you do not warn him or speak out to dissuade him from his evil ways in order to
save his life, that wicked man will die for[a]
his sin, and I will hold you accountable for
his blood.[m] 19But if you do warn the wicked man and he does not turn[n] from his
wickedness[o] or from his evil ways, he will
die[p] for his sin; but you will have saved
yourself.[q]

[a] *18* Or *in*; also in verses 19 and 20

2:10 [k]Isa 3:11; Rev 8:13 **3:3** [l]S Jer 15:16 [m]S Ps 19:10; Rev 10:9-10 **3:4** [n]Eze 11:4,25 **3:5** [o]S Isa 28:11; Jnh 1:2 **3:6** [p]Jnh 3:5-10; Mt 11:21-23; Ac 13:46-48 **3:7** [q]S Jer 7:27 [r]Isa 48:4; Jer 3:3; S Eze 2:4; Jn 15:20-23 **3:8** [s]Jer 1:18; S 15:20 **3:9** [t]S Isa 48:4 [u]S Jer 5:3 [v]Isa 50:7; Eze 2:6; 44:6; Mic 3:8 **3:10** [w]S Job 22:22 **3:11** [x]S Isa 6:9 [y]ver 27 [z]Eze 2:4-5,7; 11:24-25
3:12 [a]ver 14; Eze 8:3; 43:5 **3:13** [b]Eze 1:15 [c]Eze 1:24; 10:5,16-17 **3:14** [d]S 1Ki 18:12 [e]S ver 12 [f]ver 22; S Isa 8:11; Eze 37:1 **3:15** [g]S Ps 137:1 [h]S Ge 50:10 **3:16** [i]Jer 42:7 **3:17** [j]S Isa 52:8 [k]S Isa 58:1; Jer 1:17; Eze 11:4; Hab 2:1 **3:18** [l]S Ge 2:17; Jn 8:21,24 [m]ver 20 **3:19** [n]S Ps 7:12 [o]S Ge 6:5 [p]S Jer 42:16 [q]S 2Ki 17:13; Eze 14:14,20; Ac 18:6; 20:26; 1Ti 4:14-16

2:10 *On both sides.* Normally, ancient scrolls were written on one side only. See Ex 32:15 and note. *lament and mourning and woe.* Although Ezekiel was later commanded to preach hope (see note on 33:1—48:35), his initial commission (until the fall of Jerusalem) was to declare God's displeasure and the certainty of his judgment on Jerusalem and all of Judah.
3:1 *eat this scroll.* Ezekiel must ingest the Lord's message that he is commissioned to bring to the exiles so that it becomes, as it were, a very part of his being (cf. Jer 15:16 and note).
3:3 *sweet as honey in my mouth.* What Jeremiah experienced emotionally (Jer 15:16) was experienced by Ezekiel in a more sensory way: Words from God are sweet to the taste (see Ps 19:10; 119:103)—even when their content is bitter (see Rev 10:9–10).
3:6 *Surely if I had sent you to them, they would have listened.* For the greater readiness of other peoples to hear and heed the word of God, see Jnh 3:5; Mal 1:10–11; Mt 11:20–24; Ro 10:20–21.
3:9 *I will make your forehead like the hardest stone.* Strength and courage were necessary equipment for a prophet, especially when preaching judgment. Jeremiah was similarly equipped (see Jer 1:18; cf. Isa 50:7).
3:10 *listen carefully and take to heart.* The prophet is to stand in marked contrast to the people, who do not listen.
3:11 *Go now to your countrymen in exile.* Ezekiel's ministry was to the exilic community, most of whom refused to believe that God would abandon Jerusalem and the temple. After the fall of Jerusalem, therefore, they were strongly inclined to despair.
3:12–15 The dramatic conclusion to Ezekiel's call experience, with echoes of his initial vision.
3:12 *the Spirit lifted me up.* See v. 14; 8:3; 11:1,24; 37:1; 43:5; cf. 2:2 and note. *in his dwelling place.* Most likely Ezekiel here refers to God's heavenly dwelling place and the praise that surrounds his presence there (cf. Ps 103:20–21; 148:1–6).
3:14 *in bitterness and in the anger of my spirit.* The prophet, knowing the righteousness of God's anger, personally identified with the divine emotions. *strong hand of the LORD upon me.* See note on 1:3.
3:15 *Tel Abib.* The only mention of the specific place where the exiles lived. In Babylonian the name meant "mound of the deluge" and was used to refer to ancient (antediluvian) cities that had been reduced to mere mounds (*tells*). When used of the modern Israeli city of Tel Aviv, this name (Abib and Aviv are the same word in Hebrew) is understood to mean "hill of new growth" (cf. note on Ex 12:2). *seven days.* The traditional period of mourning (see Ge 50:10; 1Sa 31:13). *overwhelmed.* Because of his horror over Judah's impending doom (cf. Ezr 9:3–4; Job 2:13 and note; Da 8:27).
3:16–21 Ezekiel's appointment to serve as a "watchman" for Israel—a metaphor drawn from urban life. His special task as watchman is spelled out here; its urgency is more fully elaborated in ch. 18.
3:17 *I have made you a watchman.* In ancient Israel, watchmen were stationed on city walls to serve as the eyes of the city (see 2Sa 18:24–27; 2Ki 9:17–20; SS 3:3; 5:7; Isa 52:8; 62:6), especially to warn of approaching danger (see 33:2–3,6; Ps 127:1; Isa 21:6; 56:10; Jer 6:17; Hos 9:8).

20"Again, when a righteous man turns[r]
from his righteousness and does evil, and
I put a stumbling block[s] before him, he
will die. Since you did not warn him, he
will die for his sin. The righteous things
he did will not be remembered, and I will
hold you accountable for his blood.[t] 21But
if you do warn the righteous man not to
sin and he does not sin, he will surely
live because he took warning, and you
will have saved yourself.[u]"
22The hand of the LORD[v] was upon me
there, and he said to me, "Get up and go[w]
out to the plain,[x] and there I will speak
to you." 23So I got up and went out to
the plain. And the glory of the LORD was
standing there, like the glory I had seen
by the Kebar River,[y] and I fell facedown.[z]
24Then the Spirit came into me and
raised me[a] to my feet. He spoke to me
and said: "Go, shut yourself inside your
house.[b] 25And you, son of man, they will
tie with ropes; you will be bound so that
you cannot go out among the people.[c] 26I
will make your tongue stick to the roof[d]
of your mouth so that you will be silent
and unable to rebuke them, though they
are a rebellious house.[e] 27But when I
speak to you, I will open your mouth and
you shall say to them, 'This is what the
Sovereign LORD says.'[f] Whoever will listen
let him listen, and whoever will refuse
let him refuse; for they are a rebellious
house.[g]

3:20 [r] S Jer 34:16 [s] S Lev 26:37; S Isa 8:14; S Eze 7:19 [t] ver 18; Ps 125:5; Eze 18:24; 33:12,18 **3:21** [u] Ac 20:31 **3:22** [v] S ver 14; S Eze 1:3 [w] Ac 9:6 [x] Eze 8:4 **3:23** [y] Eze 1:1 [z] S Ge 17:3 **3:24** [a] S Eze 2:2 [b] Jer 15:17 **3:25** [c] Eze 4:8 **3:26** [d] S Ps 22:15 [e] Eze 2:5; 24:27; 33:22; Hos 4:4 **3:27** [f] ver 11 [g] Eze 2:5; 12:3; 24:27; 29:21; 33:22; Rev 22:11

4:2 [h] S Jer 6:6; Eze 17:17; Da 11:15 [i] S Jer 33:4; Eze 21:22 **4:3** [j] S Lev 2:5 [k] ver 7; Eze 20:46; 21:2 [l] S Isa 8:18; S 20:3; Jer 13:1-7; 18:1-4; 19:1-2; Eze 5:1-4; 12:3-6 [m] S Jer 39:1 **4:6** [n] S Ex 28:38 [o] Nu 14:34; Da 9:24-26; 12:11-12 **4:7** [p] S ver 3; Eze 6:2; S 13:17 **4:8** [q] Eze 3:25 **4:9** [r] S Isa 28:25

Siege of Jerusalem Symbolized

4 "Now, son of man, take a clay tablet,
put it in front of you and draw the city
of Jerusalem on it. 2Then lay siege to it:
Erect siege works against it, build a ramp[h]
up to it, set up camps against it and put
battering rams around it.[i] 3Then take an
iron pan,[j] place it as an iron wall between
you and the city and turn your face toward[k] it. It will be under siege, and you
shall besiege it. This will be a sign[l] to the
house of Israel.[m]
4"Then lie on your left side and put the
sin of the house of Israel upon yourself.[a]
You are to bear their sin for the number of
days you lie on your side. 5I have assigned
you the same number of days as the years
of their sin. So for 390 days you will bear
the sin of the house of Israel.
6"After you have finished this, lie down
again, this time on your right side, and bear
the sin[n] of the house of Judah. I have assigned you 40 days, a day for each year.[o]
7Turn your face[p] toward the siege of Jerusalem and with bared arm prophesy against
her. 8I will tie you up with ropes so that you
cannot turn from one side to the other until
you have finished the days of your siege.[q]
9"Take wheat and barley, beans and lentils, millet and spelt;[r] put them in a storage
jar and use them to make bread for yourself. You are to eat it during the 390 days

[a] 4 Or *your side*

3:20 *I put a stumbling block before him.* Those who have abandoned righteousness and embraced what is evil will be put to the test by the Lord himself (see 14:9; cf. Dt 13:3; 2Sa 24:1 and note; 2Ch 32:31; Ps 66:10 and note; see also Mt 6:13).
3:22–27 God places severe limitations on Ezekiel's freedom to carry out his mission, very likely to signify that the Lord knows that the exiles will not be responsive to his warnings.
3:22 *hand of the LORD.* See note on 1:3.
3:25 *you ... they will tie with ropes.* Perhaps better: "you ... will be tied with ropes" (metaphorically)—the Hebrew construction sometimes is equivalent to a passive. Reference is to the restraints that God will place on Ezekiel's movements (cf. 4:8).
3:26 *you will be silent.* Verses 26–27 indicate that the prophet would be unable to speak except when he had a direct word from the Lord. His enforced silence underscored Israel's stubborn refusal to take God's word seriously—and was itself a part of God's judgment on his rebellious people (see 7:26 and note; 20:3,31). This condition was relieved only after the fall of Jerusalem (24:27; 33:22). From that time on, Ezekiel was given messages of hope, which he continually shared with his fellow exiles.
4:1—5:17 By means of a series of symbolic acts Ezekiel is to portray the siege of Jerusalem and its outcome. In 4:1–3 the siege itself is portrayed; in 4:4–8 Ezekiel symbolically bears the punishment of the people of Israel and Judah; in 4:9–17 Ezekiel's assigned food symbolizes both the limitations of food that those under siege will suffer and the fact that they and the exiles will be forced to eat food the law specified to be ceremonially unclean and therefore prohibited; in 5:1–4 Ezekiel is instructed to shave off his hair and use it to symbolize that only a small remnant of Israel will be left from God's unfolding judgment; in 5:5–17 these symbolic acts are explained.
4:1 *take a clay tablet.* The first of several symbolic acts to be performed by the prophet. After inscribing a likeness of the city of Jerusalem on a moist clay tablet, such as those commonly used in Babylonia, Ezekiel was to place around it models of siege works to represent the city under attack (v. 2). He was then to place an iron pan (perhaps a baking griddle) between himself and the symbolized city (v. 3) to indicate the unbreakable strength of the siege.
4:3 *you shall besiege it.* Ezekiel's own presence in the scene signified that the siege would actually be laid by the Lord himself. *sign.* For Ezekiel as a "sign" see also 12:6,11; 24:24,27. These references to "sign" mark off significant literary transitions in the book (see notes on 12:1–28; 24:15–27).
4:4 *You are to bear their sin.* A representative rather than a substitutionary bearing of sin. The prophet's action symbolized the punishment Israel would suffer for her sins; it did not remove the sins.
4:5 *for 390 days.* The 390 years (see v. 6) may represent the period from the time of Solomon's unfaithfulness to the fall of Jerusalem. Correspondingly, the 40 years of v. 6 may represent the long reign of wicked Manasseh before his repentance (see 2Ki 21:11–15; 23:26–27; 24:3–4; 2Ch 33:12–13).
4:6 *on your right side.* Lying on his left side (v. 4) while facing Jerusalem (v. 7) probably placed Ezekiel to the north of the symbolic city (v. 1); lying on his right side would then have placed him to the south—signifying the northern and southern kingdoms respectively.
4:7 *prophesy against her.* By means of his symbolic actions.
4:9 *Take wheat and barley, beans and lentils, millet and spelt.* A scant, vegetarian diet representing the meager provisions of a besieged city.

you lie on your side. [10]Weigh out twenty shekels[a][s] of food to eat each day and eat it at set times. [11]Also measure out a sixth of a hin[b] of water and drink it at set times.[t] [12]Eat the food as you would a barley cake; bake it in the sight of the people, using human excrement[u] for fuel." [13]The LORD said, "In this way the people of Israel will eat defiled food among the nations where I will drive them."[v]

[14]Then I said, "Not so, Sovereign LORD![w] I have never defiled myself. From my youth until now I have never eaten anything found dead[x] or torn by wild animals. No unclean meat has ever entered my mouth.[y]"

[15]"Very well," he said, "I will let you bake your bread over cow manure instead of human excrement."

[16]He then said to me: "Son of man, I will cut off[z] the supply of food in Jerusalem. The people will eat rationed food in anxiety and drink rationed water in despair,[a] [17]for food and water will be scarce.[b] They will be appalled at the sight of each other and will waste away because of[c] their sin.[c]

5 "Now, son of man, take a sharp sword and use it as a barber's razor[d] to shave[e] your head and your beard.[f] Then take a set of scales and divide up the hair. [2]When the days of your siege come to an end, burn a third[g] of the hair with fire[h] inside the city. Take a third and strike it with the sword all around the city. And scatter a third to the wind.[i] For I will pursue them with drawn sword.[j] [3]But take a few strands of hair and tuck them away in the folds of your garment.[k] [4]Again, take a few of these and throw them into the fire[l] and burn them up. A fire will spread from there to the whole house of Israel.

[5]"This is what the Sovereign LORD says: This is Jerusalem, which I have set in the center of the nations, with countries all around her.[m] [6]Yet in her wickedness she has rebelled against my laws and decrees more than the nations and countries around her. She has rejected my laws and has not followed my decrees.[n]

[7]"Therefore this is what the Sovereign LORD says: You have been more unruly than the nations around you and have not followed my decrees or kept my laws. You have not even[d] conformed to the standards of the nations around you.[o]

[8]"Therefore this is what the Sovereign LORD says: I myself am against you, Jerusalem, and I will inflict punishment on you in the sight of the nations.[p] [9]Because of all your detestable idols, I will do to you what I have never done before and will never do again.[q] [10]Therefore in your midst fathers will eat their children, and children will eat their fathers.[r] I will inflict punishment on you and will scatter all your survivors to the winds.[s] [11]Therefore as surely as I live,[t] declares the Sovereign[u] LORD, because you have defiled my sanctuary[v] with all your vile images[w] and detestable practices,[x] I myself will withdraw my favor; I will not look on you with pity or spare you.[y] [12]A third of your people will die of the plague or perish by famine inside you; a third will fall by the sword outside your walls; and a third I will scatter to the winds[z] and pursue with drawn sword.[a]

[13]"Then my anger will cease and my wrath[b] against them will subside, and I will be avenged.[c] And when I have spent

[a] *10* That is, about 8 ounces (about 0.2 kilogram)
[b] *11* That is, about 2/3 quart (about 0.6 liter)
[c] *17* Or *away in* [d] *7* Most Hebrew manuscripts; some Hebrew manuscripts and Syriac *You have*

4:10 [s]S Ex 30:13 **4:11** [t]ver 16 **4:12** [u]S Isa 36:12 **4:13** [v]Hos 9:3; Am 7:17 **4:14** [w]Jer 1:6; Eze 9:8; 20:49 [x]S Lev 11:39 [y]S Ex 22:31; Dt 14:3; 32:37-38; Da 1:8; Hos 9:3-4 **4:16** [z]S Ps 105:16 [a]ver 10-11; S Lev 26:26; Isa 3:1; Eze 12:19 **4:17** [b]La 5:4; Eze 5:16; 12:18-19; Am 4:8 [c]S Lev 26:39; Eze 24:23; 33:10 **5:1** [d]S Nu 6:5 [e]Eze 44:20 [f]S Lev 21:5; S 2Sa 10:4 **5:2** [g]Zec 13:8 [h]Jer 21:10; Eze 15:7 [i]ver 10; Jer 13:24 [j]ver 12; S Lev 26:33; S Jer 9:16; S 39:1-2 **5:3** [k]2Ki 25:12; S Ps 74:11; Jer 39:10 **5:4** [l]Eze 10:7; 15:7 **5:5** [m]S Dt 4:6; S La 1:1; Eze 16:14 **5:6** [n]S 2Ki 17:15; Ne 9:17; Jer 11:10; S Eze 2:3; 16:47-51; Zec 7:11 **5:7** [o]S 2Ki 21:9; S 2Ch 33:9; Jer 2:10-11; Eze 16:47 **5:8** [p]S Jer 21:5,13; 24:9; Eze 11:9; 15:7; Zec 14:2 **5:9** [q]Da 9:12; S Mt 24:21 **5:10** [r]S Lev 26:29; S La 2:20 [s]S Lev 26:33; S Ps 44:11; S Jer 13:14; Eze 12:14 **5:11** [t]S Nu 14:21 [u]S Ge 15:2 [v]S Lev 15:31 [w]Eze 7:20; 11:18 [x]2Ch 36:14; Eze 8:6 [y]S Job 27:22; S Jer 16:18; S La 2:17; Eze 7:4,9; 8:18; 9:5 **5:12** [z]ver 10; Jer 13:24 [a]S ver 2,17; S Ps 107:39; S Jer 15:2; S 21:9; Eze 6:11-12; 7:15; 12:14; Am 9:4; Zec 13:8; Rev 6:8 **5:13** [b]S 2Ch 12:7; S Job 20:23; Eze 21:17; 24:13 [c]S Isa 1:24

4:15 *cow manure.* When thoroughly dried, it was commonly used in the Near East as a fuel for baking and is still sometimes so used even today. Ezekiel again showed his sensitivity to things ceremonially unclean (see note on 1:3), and God graciously responded to the prophet's objection by allowing this substitute for human excrement.

5:1–17 The fate of the people of Jerusalem in the judgment that is about to overtake them—only the merest remnant will be left (cf. notes on 2Ki 19:30–31; Isa 1:9; 10:20–22).

5:1 *take a sharp sword.* What Isaiah had expressed in a metaphor (Isa 7:20) Ezekiel acted out in prophetic symbolism.

5:2 *with drawn sword.* See 12:14; 21:3–5; 30:25; 32:10; Ps 7:12–13 and note.

5:5 *This is Jerusalem.* After wordlessly acting out the symbols (beginning in 4:1), Ezekiel received and probably related the divine explanations. *center of the nations.* God had chosen for his people Israel and for his earthly temple a place at the crossroads of the continents of Africa, Asia and Europe so that Israel and what he does for them might be a strong witness to the nations that he is the one and only God with whom all peoples have to do and from whom alone come life and blessing. This made Israel's responsibility and judgment all the more severe (see also 38:12 and note).

5:6 *more than the nations ... around her.* See v. 7; 16:47–48; 2Ki 21:9; Am 3:9 and note.

5:8 *I myself am against you.* A short and effective phrase of judgment used often by Ezekiel (see 13:8; 21:3; 26:3; 28:22; 29:3,10; 30:22; 34:10; 35:3; 38:3; 39:1; see also Jer 23:30–32; 50:31; 51:25; Na 2:13; 3:5). *inflict punishment on you in the sight of the nations.* Just as he had acted to bring about Israel's freedom and privileged position as his people (see Lev 26:45; Jos 2:11; 5:1; cf. Isa 52:10).

5:10 *fathers will eat their children.* Cannibalism, the most gruesome extremity of life under siege (see 2Ki 6:28), was threatened as a consequence of breaking the covenant (Dt 28:53; see Jer 19:9 and note; La 2:20; Zec 11:9 and note).

5:11 *as surely as I live.* A divine oath, revealing God's unalterable intention. It is used often in Ezekiel (see 14:16,18,20; 16:48; 17:16,19; 18:3; 20:3,31,33; 33:11,27; 34:8; 35:6,11; see also Heb 6:13 and note). *you have defiled my sanctuary.* See ch. 8.

5:13 *spent my wrath upon.* An expression frequently used by the Lord in this book (see 6:12; 7:8; 13:15; 20:8,21). *they will*

my wrath upon them, they will know that
I the LORD have spoken in my zeal.[d]
14“I will make you a ruin and a reproach
among the nations around you, in the
sight of all who pass by.[e] 15You will be a
reproach[f] and a taunt, a warning[g] and an
object of horror to the nations around you
when I inflict punishment on you in anger
and in wrath and with stinging rebuke.[h]
I the LORD have spoken.[i] 16When I shoot
at you with my deadly and destructive arrows of famine, I will shoot to destroy you.
I will bring more and more famine upon
you and cut off your supply of food.[j] 17I
will send famine and wild beasts[k] against
you, and they will leave you childless.
Plague and bloodshed[l] will sweep through
you, and I will bring the sword against
you. I the LORD have spoken.[m]”

A Prophecy Against the Mountains of Israel

6 The word of the LORD came to me:
2“Son of man, set your face[n] against
the mountains[o] of Israel; prophesy against
them[p] 3and say: ‘O mountains of Israel,
hear the word of the Sovereign LORD. This
is what the Sovereign LORD says to the
mountains and hills, to the ravines and valleys:[q] I am about to bring a sword against
you, and I will destroy your high places.[r]
4Your altars will be demolished and your
incense altars[s] will be smashed; and I will
slay your people in front of your idols.[t] 5I
will lay the dead bodies of the Israelites in
front of their idols, and I will scatter your
bones[u] around your altars.[v] 6Wherever
you live,[w] the towns will be laid waste and
the high places[x] demolished, so that your
altars will be laid waste and devastated,
your idols[y] smashed and ruined, your incense altars[z] broken down, and what you
have made wiped out.[a] 7Your people will
fall slain[b] among you, and you will know
that I am the LORD.[c]
8“ ‘But I will spare some, for some of
you will escape[d] the sword when you are
scattered among the lands and nations.[e]
9Then in the nations where they have
been carried captive, those who escape
will remember[f] me—how I have been
grieved[g] by their adulterous hearts, which
have turned away from me, and by their
eyes, which have lusted after their idols.[h]
They will loathe themselves for the evil[i]
they have done and for all their detestable
practices.[j] 10And they will know that I am
the LORD;[k] I did not threaten in vain to
bring this calamity on them.[l]
11“ ‘This is what the Sovereign LORD
says: Strike your hands together and
stamp your feet and cry out “Alas!” because of all the wicked and detestable
practices of the house of Israel, for they
will fall by the sword, famine and plague.[m]
12He that is far away will die of the plague,
and he that is near will fall by the sword,
and he that survives and is spared will
die of famine. So will I spend my wrath[n]
upon them.[o] 13And they will know that I
am the LORD, when their people lie slain
among their idols[p] around their altars, on
every high hill and on all the mountaintops, under every spreading tree and every leafy oak[q]—places where they offered
fragrant incense to all their idols.[r] 14And
I will stretch out my hand[s] against them
and make the land a desolate waste from

5:13 [d]S Isa 59:17; Eze 16:42; 38:19; Hos 10:10; Zec 6:8 **5:14** [e]S Lev 26:32; Ne 2:17; Ps 74:3-10; 79:1-4; Isa 64:11; Eze 6:6; 22:4; Da 9:16; Mic 3:12 **5:15** [f]S Isa 43:28 [g]S Dt 28:46 [h]S Dt 28:20; S 1Ki 9:7; S Jer 22:8-9; 24:9; Eze 14:8 [i]S Jer 23:40 **5:16** [j]S Lev 26:26; S Dt 32:24 **5:17** [k]Eze 14:15 [l]Eze 38:22 [m]S ver 12; S Lev 26:25; Eze 14:21; 28:23 **6:2** [n]S Eze 4:7 [o]Eze 18:6; Mic 6:1 [p]ver 13 **6:3** [q]Eze 36:4 [r]S Lev 26:30 **6:4** [s]S 2Ch 14:5 [t]Eze 9:6; 14:3; 20:16 **6:5** [u]S Nu 19:16; S Ps 53:5; Jer 8:1-2 [v]ver 13; S Lev 26:30 **6:6** [w]S Ex 12:20 [x]Hos 10:8 [y]Eze 30:13; Mic 1:7; Zec 13:2 [z]S Lev 26:30 [a]S 1Sa 5:4; Isa 6:11; S Eze 5:14 **6:7** [b]Eze 9:7 [c]ver 10, 13, 14; Eze 11:10-12 **6:8** [d]S Ps 68:20; S Jer 44:28 [e]S Ge 11:4; S Ps 44:11; Isa 6:13; S Jer 44:14; Eze 7:16; 12:16; 14:22 **6:9** [f]S Ps 137:6; Zec 10:9 [g]S Isa 7:13; S Jer 8:21 [h]S Ex 22:20; Eze 20:7, 24; Mic 5:13 [i]S Ex 32:22 [j]S Job 42:6; Eze 20:43; 23:14-16; 36:31 **6:10** [k]S ver 7 [l]S Dt 28:52; Jer 40:2 **6:11** [m]S Jer 42:22; Eze 21:14, 17; 22:13; 25:6 **6:12** [n]S Job 20:23 [o]S Eze 5:12; 7:15 **6:13** [p]S Lev 26:30 [q]S Isa 1:29 [r]S 1Ki 14:23; S Jer 2:20; Eze 18:6; 20:28; Hos 4:13 **6:14** [s]S Ex 7:5; S Job 30:21; S Jer 6:12; 51:25; Eze 20:34

know that I the LORD have spoken. See 17:21; 36:36; 37:14. See also 6:7 and note.

5:15 *a reproach and a taunt, a warning and an object of horror.* A fourfold list (see note on 1:5).

5:16–17 These verses contain echoes of the threatened forces of judgment for covenant unfaithfulness found in Dt 32:22–25. Note especially that God's "arrows" of judgment are the four main causes of death among the peoples of the ancient Near East: famine, disease, sword (violent death at human hands), wild beasts (see 14:12–21; see also 6:11–12; 7:15; 12:16; cf. 34:25–31; see also Jer 14:12 and note; cf. Rev 6:8).

5:16 *my ... arrows.* A widely used metaphor for God's judgments (see note on Ge 9:13).

6:1–14 After announcing judgment on Jerusalem (chs. 4–5) Ezekiel is instructed to pronounce judgment on the whole land; the "mountains of Israel" were the heavily cultivated central highlands (see Ps 104:13–15 and note), which also provided the principal sites for the pagan sanctuaries set up to worship the Baals. The judgment Ezekiel is to pronounce echoes Lev 26:27–39.

6:3 *high places.* Open-air sanctuaries of Canaanite origin, condemned throughout the OT. The high places, together with the "altars," "incense altars" and "idols" (v. 4), make up a list of four objects (see note on 1:5).

6:4 *incense altars.* Made of burnt clay, about two feet high, usually inscribed with animal figures and idols of Canaanite gods. *idols.* The Hebrew word is a derisive term (see note on Lev 26:30) used especially by Ezekiel (38 times, as opposed to only 9 times elsewhere in the OT).

6:7 *you will know that I am the LORD.* This assertion that God's mighty acts in history (his dealings with Israel and the nations in judgment and redemption) will result in his being known and acknowledged by Israel and the nations echoes throughout chs. 6–39 (see Introduction: Themes; see also 5:13 and note).

6:9 *those who escape will remember me.* The corrective outcome God intends from the severe judgment to come (see v. 10). *their adulterous hearts ... lusted after their idols.* See Ex 34:15 and note.

6:11 *Strike your hands together and stamp your feet.* A command to Ezekiel to punctuate his words of judgment with symbolic acts (see 21:14,17)—acts of quite different intent from those of Israel's enemies in 25:6. *sword, famine and plague.* See 5:16–17 and note.

6:14 *I will stretch out my hand against.* A common expression in Ezekiel (see 14:9,13; 16:27; 25:7; 35:3). *Diblah.* Perhaps the Beth Diblathaim of Jer 48:22, a city in Moab; or Riblah, a city north of Damascus on the Orontes River (see NIV text note).

the desert to Diblah[a]—wherever they
live. Then they will know that I am the
LORD.[t]"

The End Has Come

7 The word of the LORD came to me:
2"Son of man, this is what the Sovereign LORD says to the land of Israel: The
end![u] The end has come upon the four
corners[v] of the land. 3The end is now upon
you and I will unleash my anger against
you. I will judge you according to your
conduct[w] and repay you for all your detestable practices.[x] 4I will not look on you
with pity[y] or spare you; I will surely repay
you for your conduct and the detestable
practices among you. Then you will know
that I am the LORD.[z]

5"This is what the Sovereign LORD says:
Disaster![a] An unheard-of[b] disaster is coming. 6The end[b] has come! The end has
come! It has roused itself against you. It has
come! 7Doom has come upon you—you
who dwell in the land. The time has come,
the day[c] is near;[d] there is panic, not joy,
upon the mountains. 8I am about to pour
out my wrath[e] on you and spend my anger
against you; I will judge you according to
your conduct and repay you for all your detestable practices.[f] 9I will not look on you
with pity or spare you;[g] I will repay you in
accordance with your conduct and the detestable practices among you.[h] Then you
will know that it is I the LORD who strikes
the blow.[i]

10"The day is here! It has come! Doom
has burst forth, the rod[j] has budded, arrogance has blossomed! 11Violence[k] has
grown into[c] a rod to punish wickedness;
none of the people will be left, none of
that crowd—no wealth, nothing of value.[l] 12The time has come, the day has arrived. Let not the buyer[m] rejoice nor the
seller grieve, for wrath is upon the whole
crowd.[n] 13The seller will not recover the
land he has sold as long as both of them
live, for the vision concerning the whole
crowd will not be reversed. Because of
their sins, not one of them will preserve
his life.[o] 14Though they blow the trumpet[p] and get everything ready, no one will
go into battle, for my wrath[q] is upon the
whole crowd.

15"Outside is the sword, inside are plague
and famine; those in the country will die
by the sword, and those in the city will be
devoured by famine and plague.[r] 16All who
survive[s] and escape will be in the mountains, moaning like doves[t] of the valleys,
each because of his sins.[u] 17Every hand
will go limp,[v] and every knee will become
as weak as water.[w] 18They will put on sackcloth[x] and be clothed with terror.[y] Their
faces will be covered with shame and their
heads will be shaved.[z] 19They will throw
their silver into the streets,[a] and their gold
will be an unclean thing. Their silver and
gold will not be able to save them in the
day of the LORD's wrath.[b] They will not
satisfy[c] their hunger or fill their stomachs
with it, for it has made them stumble[d] into
sin.[e] 20They were proud of their beautiful
jewelry and used it to make[f] their detestable idols and vile images.[g] Therefore I
will turn these into an unclean thing for
them.[h] 21I will hand it all over as plunder[i]
to foreigners and as loot to the wicked of
the earth, and they will defile it.[j] 22I will
turn my face[k] away from them, and they
will desecrate my treasured place; robbers
will enter it and desecrate it.[l]

23"Prepare chains, because the land is
full of bloodshed[m] and the city is full of
violence.[n] 24I will bring the most wicked
of the nations to take possession of their
houses; I will put an end to the pride of
the mighty, and their sanctuaries[o] will be
desecrated.[p] 25When terror comes, they
will seek peace, but there will be none.[q]

6:14 [t]Eze 12:19; 14:13 **7:2** [u]Am 8:2,10 [v]Rev 7:1; 20:8 **7:3** [w]Eze 18:30 [x]S Ge 6:13 **7:4** [y]S Jer 13:14; S Eze 5:11 [z]S Eze 5:11; 23:49 **7:5** [a]S 2Ki 21:12 **7:6** [b]Eze 39:8 **7:7** [c]S Job 18:20; S Isa 2:12; Am 5:18-20 [d]Eze 12:23; 30:3; Zep 1:14; Mal 3:2 **7:8** [e]Isa 42:25; Eze 9:8; 14:19; 22:22; Hos 5:10; Na 1:6 [f]Eze 20:8,21; 36:19 **7:9** [g]S Jer 21:7; S Eze 5:11 [h]Eze 22:31 [i]Dt 32:35; S Ps 39:10; S Isa 9:13 **7:10** [j]Ps 89:32; Isa 10:5 **7:11** [k]S Ps 55:9; S Isa 58:4 [l]Jer 16:6; Zep 1:18 **7:12** [m]S Isa 24:2 [n]ver 7; Isa 5:13-14; Eze 30:3 **7:13** [o]Lev 25:24-28 **7:14** [p]S Job 39:24 [q]Jer 25:38 **7:15** [r]S Dt 32:25; Jer 14:18; S La 1:20; S Eze 5:12; 33:27 **7:16** [s]S Isa 10:20; S Jer 41:16; 42:17 [t]S Ge 8:8; S Isa 59:11 [u]S Ezr 9:15; Jer 9:19; S Eze 6:8 **7:17** [v]S 2Ki 19:26; S Jer 47:3; Eze 21:7; 22:14 [w]Da 5:6 **7:18** [x]S Jer 4:8; 48:37; 49:3 [y]S Ps 55:5 [z]S Isa 15:2-3; Eze 27:31; Am 8:10 **7:19** [a]S La 4:1 [b]Isa 42:25; Eze 13:5; 30:3; Joel 1:15; 2:1; Zep 1:7,18; 2:2 [c]Isa 55:2 [d]Eze 3:20; 14:3; Hos 4:5 [e]S Pr 11:4 **7:20** [f]S Jer 10:3 [g]S Eze 5:11 [h]S Isa 2:20; 30:22; Eze 16:17 **7:21** [i]S Nu 14:3 [j]S 2Ki 24:13 **7:22** [k]S Jer 2:27; Eze 39:23-24 [l]Ps 74:7-8; Jer 19:13; S La 2:7 **7:23** [m]S 2Ki 21:16; S Isa 1:15; S Eze 22:9 [n]S Ge 6:11; Eze 11:6 **7:24** [o]La 2:7; Eze 24:21 [p]2Ch 7:20; Eze 28:7 **7:25** [q]Jer 6:14; S 8:11; Eze 13:10,16

[a] *14* Most Hebrew manuscripts; a few Hebrew manuscripts *Riblah* [b] *5* Most Hebrew manuscripts; some Hebrew manuscripts and Syriac *Disaster after* [c] *11* Or *The violent one has become*

7:1–27 God's word of judgment on the "mountains of Israel" (6:2; see ch. 6 and note on 6:1–14) is elaborated under the fateful declaration that God's patience with Israel's stubborn rebelliousness has run out: "The end! The end has come" (v. 2; see vv. 3,6,24; see also Jer 51:13; La 4:18; cf. Am 7:8; 8:2).
7:7 *the day.* The "day of the LORD's wrath" (v. 19), i.e., the day of reckoning when God brings down his righteous judgments on the wickedness of his people (see also vv. 10,12). Ezekiel's language may be a deliberate echo of the "day of the LORD" of which many of the prophets spoke (see Am 5:18 and note). *panic, not joy.* Cf. Am 5:20 ("darkness, not light").
7:8 *pour out my wrath.* A common expression in Ezekiel (see 9:8; 14:19; 20:8,13,21; 22:31; 30:15; 36:18).
7:12 *Let not the buyer rejoice.* Advice similar to that of Jesus (see Mt 24:17–18).
7:15 *sword ... plague and famine.* See 5:16–17 and note.
7:17 *every knee will become as weak as water.* Or "every knee will be wet with urine."
7:18 *They will put on sackcloth ... their heads will be shaved.* As signs of intense mourning (see Ge 37:34; Job 1:20; Isa 15:2; Rev 11:3 and notes).
7:19 *They will throw their silver.* See Isa 2:20.
7:20 *beautiful jewelry.* See Ex 32:2–4.
7:22 *my treasured place.* The Jerusalem temple.
7:23 *full of bloodshed ... violence.* See 9:9; 11:6; 12:19; see also 2Ki 21:16; 24:4; Jer 19:4; 22:17; La 4:13; Mic 3:10; Hab 1:2–4; cf. Hab 2:8,12,17.
7:24 *pride of the mighty.* The Jerusalem temple, described by the word "pride" (as in 24:21; see also 33:28).

26Calamity upon calamity[r] will come, and
rumor upon rumor. They will try to get a
vision from the prophet;[s] the teaching of
the law by the priest will be lost, as will
the counsel of the elders.[t] 27The king will
mourn, the prince will be clothed with despair,[u] and the hands of the people of the
land will tremble. I will deal with them
according to their conduct,[v] and by their
own standards I will judge them. Then
they will know that I am the LORD.[w]"

Idolatry in the Temple

8 In the sixth year, in the sixth month on
the fifth day, while I was sitting in my
house and the elders[x] of Judah were sitting
before[y] me, the hand of the Sovereign LORD
came upon me there.[z] 2I looked, and I saw
a figure like that of a man.[a] From what
appeared to be his waist down he was like
fire, and from there up his appearance was
as bright as glowing metal.[a] 3He stretched
out what looked like a hand[b] and took me
by the hair of my head. The Spirit lifted
me up[c] between earth and heaven and in
visions[d] of God he took me to Jerusalem,
to the entrance to the north gate of the inner court,[e] where the idol that provokes to
jealousy[f] stood. 4And there before me was
the glory[g] of the God of Israel, as in the
vision I had seen in the plain.[h]
5Then he said to me, "Son of man, look
toward the north." So I looked, and in the
entrance north of the gate of the altar I
saw this idol[i] of jealousy.
6And he said to me, "Son of man, do
you see what they are doing—the utterly
detestable[j] things the house of Israel is doing here, things that will drive me far from
my sanctuary?[k] But you will see things
that are even more detestable."
7Then he brought me to the entrance to
the court. I looked, and I saw a hole in the
wall. 8He said to me, "Son of man, now
dig into the wall." So I dug into the wall
and saw a doorway there.
9And he said to me, "Go in and see the
wicked and detestable things they are doing here." 10So I went in and looked, and I
saw portrayed all over the walls[l] all kinds
of crawling things and detestable[m] animals
and all the idols of the house of Israel.[n]
11In front of them stood seventy elders[o] of
the house of Israel, and Jaazaniah son of
Shaphan was standing among them. Each
had a censer[p] in his hand, and a fragrant
cloud of incense[q] was rising.[r]
12He said to me, "Son of man, have you
seen what the elders of the house of Israel are doing in the darkness,[s] each at
the shrine of his own idol? They say, 'The
LORD does not see[t] us; the LORD has forsak-
en the land.'" 13Again, he said, "You will
see them doing things that are even more
detestable."
14Then he brought me to the entrance
to the north gate of the house of the LORD,
and I saw women sitting there, mourning
for Tammuz.[u] 15He said to me, "Do you see
this, son of man? You will see things that
are even more detestable than this."

[a] 2 Or *saw a fiery figure*

7:26 [r]S Dt 29:21; S 31:17 [s]S 1Sa 3:1 [t]Isa 47:11; S Jer 18:18; Eze 20:1-3; Am 8:11; Mic 3:6 **7:27** [u]S Ps 109:19; Eze 26:16 [v]S Isa 3:11; Eze 18:20 [w]S ver 4 **8:1** [x]S 2Ki 6:32; Eze 14:1 [y]Eze 33:31 [z]Eze 1:1-3; 24:1; 40:1 **8:2** [a]Eze 1:4, 26-27 **8:3** [b]S Eze 2:9 [c]S Eze 3:12; 11:1 [d]S Ex 24:10 [e]ver 16 [f]ver 5; Ex 20:5; Dt 32:16 **8:4** [g]S Ex 24:16 [h]Eze 3:22 **8:5** [i]Ps 78:58; S Jer 4:1; 32:34 **8:6** [j]Ps 78:60; S Eze 5:11 [k]Hos 5:6 **8:10** [l]S Jdg 17:4-5; Eze 23:14 [m]Jer 44:4 [n]Ex 20:4; Dt 4:15-18; S Jer 16:18; Eze 11:12 **8:11** [o]S Ex 3:16 [p]S Lev 10:1; Nu 16:17 [q]Nu 16:35; S Jer 44:5 [r]Eze 11:1-2 **8:12** [s]S Job 22:13 [t]S 2Ki 21:16; Ps 10:11; S Isa 29:15; Eze 9:9; Zep 1:12 **8:14** [u]Eze 11:12

7:26 *prophet ... priest ... elders.* There would be no guidance from God and no direction from the elders (see 1Sa 28:6; Am 8:11–12 and note on 8:11; Mic 3:6–7; see also Jer 18:18 and note).

7:27 *king ... prince.* Here both nouns probably refer to the same person, namely, King Jehoiachin. *clothed with.* See note on Ps 109:29. *people of the land.* The full citizens of Judah (those holding inherited family property and subject to military service; see 12:19; 45:16,22; 46:3).

8:1—11:25 The vision has six movements: (1) God shows Ezekiel the idolatry practiced in the temple in Jerusalem (ch. 8); (2) God pronounces his judgment on the idolaters there (ch. 9); (3) Ezekiel is shown God's glory departing from the temple (ch. 10); (4) God declares that the complacent Jerusalemites will not escape his judgment (11:1–13); (5) God promises that the exiles, whom those still in Jerusalem have written off, will be restored (11:14–21); and (6) the conclusion of the vision (11:22–25).

8:1–8 Ezekiel is shown four examples (see note on 1:5) of idolatrous worship being carried on in the very temple of the Lord: (1) "idol of jealousy" (v. 5), (2) "crawling things and detestable animals" (v. 10), (3) "mourning for Tammuz" (v. 14), and (4) "bowing down to the sun" (v. 16).

8:1 *In the sixth year, in the sixth month on the fifth day.* Sept. 17, 592 B.C.—the second of 13 dates in Ezekiel (see chart, p. 1239). This one, like those in 1:2 and 40:1, introduces a vision. *sitting in my house.* The exiles were free to build houses (see Jer 29:5). *elders of Judah were sitting before me.* They also had freedom of movement, assembly and worship (see 14:1; 20:1). A year and two months after his inaugural vision and preaching, the prophet commanded a hearing. Some have seen in such meetings the beginnings of the synagogue form of worship. *hand of the Sovereign LORD.* See note on 1:3.

8:2 *figure like that of a man.* An angel, similar in appearance to the vision of God in 1:26–27. *like fire ... as bright as glowing metal.* A way of describing the blinding brightness of the divine messenger (see Mt 28:3; cf. Ac 9:3).

8:3 *The Spirit lifted me up.* See 3:12 and note. *took me to Jerusalem.* Ezekiel had been directed to prophesy stern judgments on Jerusalem (chs. 1–7). Now he was transported to Jerusalem in "visions of God" (see 1:1 and note; see also 11:24) and shown the reason for the judgments. *idol that provokes to jealousy.* Any idol in the temple provoked the Lord to jealousy (see Ex 20:5 and note), but this one seems to be a statue of Asherah, the Canaanite goddess of fertility, which Josiah had removed some 30 years previously (see 2Ki 23:6).

8:5 *idol of jealousy.* See note on v. 3.

8:10 *all kinds of crawling things and detestable animals.* Probably reflecting Egyptian influence (cf. 2Ki 23:31–35).

8:11 *Jaazaniah.* Not the same person as in 11:1. Ironically, the name means "The LORD hears," and the irony is sharpened by the quotation in v. 12.

8:14 *Tammuz.* The only Biblical reference to this Babylonian fertility god. The women of Jerusalem were bewailing his dying (which supposedly happened seasonally at the height of the summer heat), which they thought caused the

16He then brought me into the inner
court[v] of the house of the LORD, and there
at the entrance to the temple, between the
portico and the altar,[w] were about twenty-five men. With their backs toward the
temple of the LORD and their faces toward
the east, they were bowing down to the
sun[x] in the east.[y]
17He said to me, "Have you seen this,
son of man? Is it a trivial matter for the
house of Judah to do the detestable things[z]
they are doing here? Must they also fill the
land with violence[a] and continually provoke me to anger?[b] Look at them putting
the branch to their nose! 18Therefore I
will deal with them in anger;[c] I will not
look on them with pity[d] or spare them.
Although they shout in my ears, I will not
listen[e] to them."

Idolaters Killed

9 Then I heard him call out in a loud
voice, "Bring the guards of the city here,
each with a weapon in his hand." 2And I
saw six men coming from the direction of
the upper gate, which faces north, each
with a deadly weapon in his hand. With
them was a man clothed in linen[f] who had
a writing kit at his side. They came in and
stood beside the bronze altar.
3Now the glory[g] of the God of Israel
went up from above the cherubim,[h] where
it had been, and moved to the threshold
of the temple. Then the LORD called to the
man clothed in linen who had the writing kit at his side 4and said to him, "Go
throughout the city of Jerusalem[i] and put
a mark[j] on the foreheads of those who
grieve and lament[k] over all the detestable
things that are done in it.[l]"
5As I listened, he said to the others, "Follow him through the city and kill, without

8:16 [v] ver 3 [w] Joel 2:17 [x] S Ge 1:16 [y] Dt 4:19; S 17:3; S Job 31:28; S Jer 2:27; Eze 9:6; 11:1, 12; 40:6; 43:1 **8:17** [z] Eze 16:2 [a] S Ge 6:11 [b] S Nu 11:33; S 1Ki 14:9; Eze 16:26 **8:18** [c] S Jer 44:6 [d] S Jer 13:14; S Eze 5:11; 9:10; 24:14 [e] S 1Sa 8:18; S Isa 58:4; S Jer 11:11 **9:2** [f] S Lev 16:4; Eze 10:2; Da 10:5; 12:6; Rev 15:6 **9:3** [g] S 1Sa 4:21; Eze 10:4 [h] Eze 11:22 **9:4** [i] Jer 25:29 [j] S Ge 4:15; Ex 12:7; 2Co 1:22; S Rev 7:3 [k] Ps 119:136; Jer 7:29; 13:17; Eze 21:6; Am 6:6 [l] Ps 119:53 **9:5** [m] S Jer 13:14; S Eze 5:11 [n] S Ex 32:27; Isa 13:18 **9:6** [o] Jer 7:32 [p] S Jer 16:6 [q] S Ge 4:15; S Ex 12:7 [r] Eze 8:11-13, 16 [s] S 2Ch 36:17; Jer 25:29; S Eze 6:4; 1Pe 4:17 **9:7** [t] Eze 6:7 **9:8** [u] S Jos 7:6 [v] S Eze 4:14 [w] S Eze 7:8 [x] Eze 11:13; Am 7:1-6 **9:9** [y] S Ps 58:2; Jer 12:1; Eze 22:29;

showing pity[m] or compassion.[n] 6Slaughter[o]
old men, young men and maidens, wom-
en and children,[p] but do not touch anyone
who has the mark.[q] Begin at my sanctuary." So they began with the elders[r] who
were in front of the temple.[s]
7Then he said to them, "Defile the temple and fill the courts with the slain.[t]
Go!" So they went out and began killing
throughout the city. 8While they were killing and I was left alone, I fell facedown,[u]
crying out, "Ah, Sovereign LORD![v] Are you
going to destroy the entire remnant of Israel in this outpouring of your wrath[w] on
Jerusalem?[x]"
9He answered me, "The sin of the house
of Israel and Judah is exceedingly great;
the land is full of bloodshed and the city is
full of injustice.[y] They say, 'The LORD has
forsaken the land; the LORD does not see.'[z]
10So I will not look on them with pity[a] or
spare them, but I will bring down on their
own heads what they have done.[b]"
11Then the man in linen with the writing
kit at his side brought back word, saying,
"I have done as you commanded."

The Glory Departs From the Temple

10 I looked, and I saw the likeness of a
throne[c] of sapphire[a][d] above the expanse[e] that was over the heads of the cherubim.[f] 2The LORD said to the man clothed
in linen,[g] "Go in among the wheels[h] beneath the cherubim. Fill[i] your hands with
burning coals[j] from among the cherubim
and scatter them over the city." And as I
watched, he went in.

[a] *1* Or *lapis lazuli*

Hab 1:4 [z] S Job 22:13; S Eze 8:12; 14:23 **9:10** [a] S Jer 13:14; S Eze 8:18 [b] S Isa 22:5; S 65:6; Eze 11:21; 23:49 **10:1** [c] S Rev 4:2 [d] S Ex 24:10 [e] Eze 1:22 [f] S Ge 3:24 **10:2** [g] S Eze 9:2 [h] S Eze 1:15 [i] Rev 8:5 [j] S 2Sa 22:9

annual summer die-off of the vegetation. According to some interpreters, he is alluded to in Da 11:37 ("the one desired by women"; see note there).

8:16 *twenty-five men.* A representative number (see 11:1). *With their backs toward the temple.* Almost all ancient temples were oriented toward the east. Worshiping the sun as it rose required people to turn their backs to the temple. *bowing down to the sun.* For other references to sun worship see Dt 4:19; 17:3; 2Ki 23:5,11; cf. 2Ki 17:16; 21:3,5; Jer 43:13.

8:17 *fill the land with violence.* See 7:23 and note. *putting the branch to their nose.* A ceremonial gesture in pagan worship, not documented elsewhere in the Bible.

9:1–11 See note on 8:1—11:25.

9:1 *loud voice.* The thunderous voice of God (see Ex 19:19 and NIV text note; see also Ps 29). *guards.* See 44:11; 2Ki 11:18.

9:2 *six men coming from the direction of the upper gate.* These six guardian angels of the city, plus the seventh clothed in linen, came from the place where the idol that provoked to jealousy stood (see 8:3 and note).

9:3 *the glory . . . went up.* God began to vacate the temple, his glory moving to the door (see note on 8:1—11:25).

9:4 *mark.* A *Taw,* the last letter of the Hebrew alphabet, which originally looked like an "x" (see Rev 7:2–4 and note on 7:2; cf. Rev 13:16 and note). For a possible parallel see Ge 4:15 and note. *those who grieve and lament.* The remnant (see 1Ki 19:18).

9:5 *kill, without showing pity.* See La 2:21.

9:6 *Begin at my sanctuary.* Because that was a primary source of the evil that pervaded Jerusalem (see ch. 8). Cf. an echo in 1Pe 4:17.

9:8 *crying out.* See 11:13. As those who served as intermediaries between God and his people, the prophets frequently interceded on behalf of the people when God's judgments threatened (see Ex 32:31; Nu 14:13–19; 1Sa 12:23; Jer 14:19–21; 15:1; Am 7:2,5).

9:9 *land is full of bloodshed.* See 7:23 and note.

9:10 *bring down on their own heads what they have done.* See 16:43; Jer 50:15; Ob 15 and note.

10:1–22 See note on 8:1—11:25.

10:1 *I looked.* Ch. 10 echoes ch. 1, underscoring the identity of what Ezekiel saw at the Kebar River with what he now sees in his vision (see 8:4). The creatures in ch. 1 are here called cherubim (see note on 1:5).

10:2 *burning coals.* While in 1:13 the living creatures looked like burning coals, here there are real coals. *scatter them over the city.* A judgment by fire (see Ge 19:24; Am 7:4).

3Now the cherubim were standing on the
south side of the temple when the man went
in, and a cloud filled the inner court. 4Then
the glory of the LORD[k] rose from above the
cherubim and moved to the threshold of
the temple. The cloud filled the temple, and
the court was full of the radiance of the glory of the LORD. 5The sound of the wings of
the cherubim could be heard as far away
as the outer court, like the voice[l] of God
Almighty[a] when he speaks.[m]
6When the LORD commanded the man in
linen, "Take fire from among the wheels,[n]
from among the cherubim," the man went
in and stood beside a wheel. 7Then one
of the cherubim reached out his hand to
the fire[o] that was among them. He took
up some of it and put it into the hands of
the man in linen, who took it and went
out. 8(Under the wings of the cherubim
could be seen what looked like the hands
of a man.)[p]
9I looked, and I saw beside the cherubim four wheels, one beside each of the
cherubim; the wheels sparkled like chrysolite.[q] 10As for their appearance, the four of
them looked alike; each was like a wheel
intersecting a wheel. 11As they moved,
they would go in any one of the four directions the cherubim faced; the wheels
did not turn about[b] as the cherubim went.
The cherubim went in whatever direction
the head faced, without turning as they
went. 12Their entire bodies, including their
backs, their hands and their wings, were
completely full of eyes,[r] as were their four
wheels.[s] 13I heard the wheels being called
"the whirling wheels." 14Each of the cherubim[t] had four faces:[u] One face was that
of a cherub, the second the face of a man,
the third the face of a lion,[v] and the fourth
the face of an eagle.[w]
15Then the cherubim rose upward.
These were the living creatures[x] I had seen
by the Kebar River.[y] 16When the cherubim
moved, the wheels beside them moved;
and when the cherubim spread their wings
to rise from the ground, the wheels did
not leave their side. 17When the cherubim
stood still, they also stood still; and when
the cherubim rose, they rose with them,
because the spirit of the living creatures
was in them.[z]
18Then the glory[a] of the LORD departed
from over the threshold of the temple and
stopped above the cherubim.[b] 19While I
watched, the cherubim spread their wings
and rose from the ground, and as they
went, the wheels went with them.[c] They
stopped at the entrance to the east gate
of the LORD's house, and the glory[d] of the
God of Israel was above them.
20These were the living creatures I had
seen beneath the God of Israel by the Kebar River,[e] and I realized that they were
cherubim. 21Each had four faces[f] and four
wings,[g] and under their wings was what
looked like the hands of a man. 22Their
faces had the same appearance as those
I had seen by the Kebar River.[h] Each one
went straight ahead.

Judgment on Israel's Leaders

11 Then the Spirit lifted me up and
brought me to the gate of the house
of the LORD that faces east. There at the
entrance to the gate were twenty-five men,
and I saw among them Jaazaniah son of
Azzur and Pelatiah[i] son of Benaiah, leaders[j] of the people.[k] 2The LORD said to me,
"Son of man, these are the men who are
plotting evil[l] and giving wicked advice in
this city.[m] 3They say, 'Will it not soon be
time to build houses?[c] This city is a cooking pot,[n] and we are the meat.'[o] 4Therefore
prophesy[p] against them; prophesy, son of
man."
5Then the Spirit of the LORD came upon
me, and he told me to say: "This is what
the LORD says: That is what you are saying,
O house of Israel, but I know what is going
through your mind.[q] 6You have killed many

10:4 [k] S Ex 24:16; Eze 9:3; 44:4 **10:5** [l] S Job 40:9 [m] S Eze 3:13 **10:6** [n] Da 7:9 **10:7** [o] S Eze 5:4 **10:8** [p] Eze 1:8 **10:9** [q] S Ex 28:20; Rev 21:20 **10:12** [r] Rev 4:6-8 [s] Eze 1:15-21 **10:14** [t] 1Ki 7:36 [u] Eze 1:6 [v] 1Ki 7:29 [w] Eze 1:10; 41:19; Rev 4:7 **10:15** [x] S Isa 6:2 [y] S Ps 137:1 **10:17** [z] S Eze 3:13 **10:18** [a] S 1Sa 4:21 [b] S Ps 18:10 **10:19** [c] Eze 11:1,22 [d] Eze 43:4 **10:20** [e] Eze 1:1 **10:21** [f] Eze 41:18 [g] Eze 1:6 **10:22** [h] Eze 1:1 **11:1** [i] ver 13 [j] Jer 5:5 [k] S Eze 8:16; S 10:19; 43:4-5 **11:2** [l] S Isa 29:20; Na 1:11 [m] Eze 8:11 **11:3** [n] Jer 1:13; Eze 24:3 [o] ver 7,11; Eze 12:22,27; Mic 3:3 **11:4** [p] S Eze 3:4,17 **11:5** [q] S Ps 26:2; S Jer 17:10

[a] 5 Hebrew *El-Shaddai* [b] 11 Or *aside* [c] 3 Or *This is not the time to build houses.*

10:3 *cloud.* The cloud that enclosed the "glory of the LORD" (v. 4), which otherwise would have blinded those who saw it (see 1:4; Ex 16:10; 24:15–17; 40:34–35,38; Nu 9:15–16; 16:42; Dt 5:23; 1Ki 8:10–12; Hag 2:7 and note; cf. Mt 13:5; 24:30; 26:64; Mk 9:7; 13:26; 14:62; Lk 9:34–35; 21:27; Ac 1:9; Rev 1:7; 14:14–16).

10:7 *one of the cherubim reached out his hand.* Though the "man clothed in linen" was initially commanded to get the coals himself (v. 2), he received them from the hand of one of the creatures (see 1:8). *who took it and went out.* No further report is given, but the destructive spreading of the coals over Jerusalem is assumed.

10:14 *One face was that of a cherub.* While the faces of the man, lion and eagle are identical with those in 1:10 (see note on 1:5), the ox is here called a cherub (see note on Ge 3:24).

10:15 *Kebar River.* See 1:1 and note.

10:19 *to the east gate ... and the glory of the God of Israel was above them.* A second movement of the glory, again in an easterly direction (see 9:3; 10:4; see also note on 8:1—11:25). See ch. 43 for the return of the glory of the Lord to the temple by way of the east gate (see note on 43:1–12).

11:1–13 See note on 8:1—11:25.

11:1 *the Spirit lifted me up.* See 3:12 and note. *twenty-five men.* See 8:16 and note. *Jaazaniah.* See note on 8:11. *Pelatiah.* Means "The LORD delivers."

11:3 *soon ... time to build houses?* The residents of Jerusalem who were not exiled by the Babylonians in 597 B.C. felt smugly secure, thinking they had no further Babylonian threat to fear. *cooking pot.* As in ch. 24, Jerusalem is compared to a cooking pot. Those left behind boasted that they were the "meat," the choice portions—the inference being that the exiles in Babylon were the discarded bones (see v. 15).

11:5 *the Spirit of the LORD came upon me.* See 2:2 and note.

11:6 *killed many ... filled its streets with the dead.* See 7:23 and note.

people in this city and filled its streets with
the dead.[r]
7"Therefore this is what the Sovereign
LORD says: The bodies you have thrown
there are the meat and this city is the pot,[s]
but I will drive you out of it.[t] 8You fear the
sword,[u] and the sword is what I will bring
against you, declares the Sovereign LORD.[v]
9I will drive you out of the city and hand
you over[w] to foreigners and inflict punishment on you.[x] 10You will fall by the sword,
and I will execute judgment on you at the
borders of Israel.[y] Then you will know that
I am the LORD. 11This city will not be a pot[z]
for you, nor will you be the meat in it; I
will execute judgment on you at the borders of Israel. 12And you will know that I
am the LORD,[a] for you have not followed
my decrees[b] or kept my laws but have
conformed to the standards of the nations
around you.[c]"
13Now as I was prophesying, Pelatiah[d]
son of Benaiah died. Then I fell facedown
and cried out in a loud voice, "Ah, Sovereign LORD! Will you completely destroy
the remnant of Israel?[e]"
14The word of the LORD came to me:
15"Son of man, your brothers — your brothers who are your blood relatives[a] and the
whole house of Israel — are those of whom
the people of Jerusalem have said, 'They
are[b] far away from the LORD; this land was
given to us as our possession.'[f]

Promised Return of Israel

16"Therefore say: 'This is what the Sovereign LORD says: Although I sent them
far away among the nations and scattered
them among the countries, yet for a little
while I have been a sanctuary[g] for them in
the countries where they have gone.'
17"Therefore say: 'This is what the Sovereign LORD says: I will gather you from
the nations and bring you back from the
countries where you have been scattered,
and I will give you back the land of Israel
again.'[h]
18"They will return to it and remove all
its vile images[i] and detestable idols.[j] 19I
will give them an undivided heart[k] and put
a new spirit in them; I will remove from
them their heart of stone[l] and give them a
heart of flesh.[m] 20Then they will follow my
decrees and be careful to keep my laws.[n]
They will be my people,[o] and I will be
their God.[p] 21But as for those whose hearts
are devoted to their vile images and detestable idols,[q] I will bring down on their
own heads what they have done, declares
the Sovereign LORD.[r]"
22Then the cherubim, with the wheels
beside them, spread their wings, and
the glory[s] of the God of Israel was above
them.[t] 23The glory[u] of the LORD went up
from within the city and stopped above
the mountain[v] east of it. 24The Spirit[w] lifted me up and brought me to the exiles
in Babylonia[c] in the vision[x] given by the
Spirit of God.
Then the vision I had seen went up from
me, 25and I told the exiles everything the
LORD had shown me.[y]

The Exile Symbolized

12 The word of the LORD came to me:
2"Son of man, you are living among
a rebellious people.[z] They have eyes to see
but do not see and ears to hear but do not
hear, for they are a rebellious people.[a]
3"Therefore, son of man, pack your belongings for exile and in the daytime, as
they watch, set out and go from where you
are to another place. Perhaps[b] they will

[a] *15* Or *are in exile with you* (see Septuagint and Syriac)
[b] *15* Or *those to whom the people of Jerusalem have said, 'Stay*
[c] *24* Or *Chaldea*

11:6 [r] S Eze 7:23; 22:6 **11:7** [s] Jer 1:13 [t] ver 3; Eze 24:3-13; Mic 3:2-3 **11:8** [u] S Lev 26:25; S Jer 42:16 [v] S Pr 10:24; Isa 66:4 **11:9** [w] Ps 106:41 [x] Dt 28:36; S Eze 5:8 **11:10** [y] 2Ki 14:25 **11:11** [z] ver 3; Eze 24:6 **11:12** [a] S Eze 6:7 [b] S Lev 18:4; Eze 18:9 [c] Eze 8:10 **11:13** [d] ver 1 [e] S Eze 9:8; Am 7:2 **11:15** [f] Eze 33:24 **11:16** [g] Ps 31:20; 90:1; 91:9; S Isa 4:6 **11:17** [h] S Ne 1:9; S Jer 3:18; 24:5-6; S 31:16; Eze 20:41; 28:25; 34:13; 36:28 **11:18** [i] S Eze 5:11 [j] Eze 37:23 **11:19** [k] S 2Ch 30:12; S Ps 86:11 [l] Zec 7:12; Ro 2:5 [m] Eze 18:31; S 2Co 3:3 **11:20** [n] S Ps 1:2 [o] S Jer 11:4; 32:38 [p] S Ex 6:7; Eze 14:11; 34:30; 36:26-28; Hos 1:9; Zec 8:8; Heb 8:10 **11:21** [q] Jer 16:18 [r] Jer 16:11; S Eze 9:10; 16:43 **11:22** [s] S Ex 24:16 [t] Eze 9:3; S 10:19 **11:23** [u] Eze 1:28; S 10:4 [v] Zec 14:4 **11:24** [w] Eze 37:1; 43:5 [x] 2Co 12:2-4

11:25 [y] S Eze 3:4,11 **12:2** [z] Ps 78:40; S Jer 42:21 [a] S Isa 6:10; S Mt 13:15; Mk 4:12; 8:18 **12:3** [b] S Jer 36:3

11:7 *The bodies you have thrown there are the meat.* The meat, redefined by the prophet, is not those in power in Jerusalem (who will be driven out) but the innocent people they killed.
11:11 *at the borders of Israel.* At Riblah (see 2Ki 25:20 – 21).
11:13 *cried out.* See note on 9:8.
11:14 – 21 See note on 8:1 — 11:25.
11:16 *I have been a sanctuary for them.* A key verse in Ezekiel. Although the exiles had been driven from Jerusalem and its sanctuary (the symbol of God's presence among his people), God himself became their sanctuary, i.e., he was present among them to preserve and bless them.
11:19 *undivided heart ... new spirit.* Inner spiritual and moral transformation that results in single-minded commitment to the Lord and to his will (see 36:26). *remove ... heart of stone ... give ... heart of flesh.* Give Israel a new heart responsive to God's will (see 2Co 3:3 and note).
11:20 *my people ... their God.* The heart of God's covenant promise (see Ex 6:7; Jer 7:23 and notes).
11:21 *bring down on their own heads what they have done.* See note on 9:10.
11:22 – 25 See note on 8:1 — 11:25.
11:23 *The glory of the LORD went up.* The final eastward movement of the glory (as the Lord left his temple), which stopped above the Mount of Olives (see 9:3; 10:4,19; see also note on 8:1 — 11:25). God's glory returns in ch. 43.
11:24 See note on 8:3.
12:1 – 28 The first series of messages concludes with Ezekiel being called on to symbolize by personal actions the coming exile of Jerusalem — just as the second series culminates (24:15 – 27) in Ezekiel suffering the death of his wife as a symbolic representation of the fall of Jerusalem. Verses 1 – 2 and v. 28 frame the chapter; two symbolic acts (vv. 3 – 16,17 – 20) are followed by the refutation of two sayings with which the Jerusalemites vainly try to reassure themselves (vv. 21 – 25,26 – 27).
12:2 *eyes to see but do not see.* The hardening about which the Lord had spoken to Isaiah (see Isa 6:8 – 10 and notes). The Israelites in Jerusalem refuse to recognize that the end has come for them (see v. 28; 7:2 – 6).
12:3 *pack your belongings.* Another symbolic act, which, like those in chs. 4 – 5, follows a vision. *Perhaps they will understand.* Some hope remained that they would change.

understand,[c] though they are a rebellious
house.[d] 4During the daytime, while they
watch, bring out your belongings packed
for exile. Then in the evening, while they
are watching, go out like those who go
into exile.[e] 5While they watch, dig through
the wall[f] and take your belongings out
through it. 6Put them on your shoulder as
they are watching and carry them out at
dusk. Cover your face so that you cannot
see the land, for I have made you a sign[g]
to the house of Israel."

7So I did as I was commanded.[h] During
the day I brought out my things packed for
exile. Then in the evening I dug through
the wall with my hands. I took my belongings out at dusk, carrying them on my
shoulders while they watched.

8In the morning the word of the LORD
came to me: 9"Son of man, did not that
rebellious house of Israel ask you, 'What
are you doing?'[i]

10"Say to them, 'This is what the Sovereign LORD says: This oracle concerns the
prince in Jerusalem and the whole house
of Israel who are there.' 11Say to them, 'I
am a sign[j] to you.'

"As I have done, so it will be done to
them. They will go into exile as captives.[k]

12"The prince among them will put his
things on his shoulder at dusk[l] and leave,
and a hole will be dug in the wall for him
to go through. He will cover his face so
that he cannot see the land.[m] 13I will spread
my net[n] for him, and he will be caught in
my snare;[o] I will bring him to Babylonia,
the land of the Chaldeans,[p] but he will not
see[q] it, and there he will die.[r] 14I will scatter to the winds all those around him—his
staff and all his troops—and I will pursue
them with drawn sword.[s]

15"They will know that I am the LORD,
when I disperse them among the nations[t]
and scatter them through the countries.
16But I will spare a few of them from the
sword, famine and plague, so that in the
nations where they go they may acknowledge all their detestable practices. Then
they will know that I am the LORD.[u]"

17The word of the LORD came to me:
18"Son of man, tremble as you eat your
food,[v] and shudder in fear as you drink
your water. 19Say to the people of the land:
'This is what the Sovereign LORD says about
those living in Jerusalem and in the land
of Israel: They will eat their food in anxiety and drink their water in despair, for
their land will be stripped of everything[w]
in it because of the violence of all who live
there.[x] 20The inhabited towns will be laid
waste and the land will be desolate. Then
you will know that I am the LORD.[y]'"

21The word of the LORD came to me:
22"Son of man, what is this proverb[z] you
have in the land of Israel: 'The days go
by and every vision comes to nothing'?[a]
23Say to them, 'This is what the Sovereign
LORD says: I am going to put an end to this
proverb, and they will no longer quote it
in Israel.' Say to them, 'The days are near[b]
when every vision will be fulfilled.[c] 24For
there will be no more false visions or flattering divinations[d] among the people of Israel. 25But I the LORD will speak what I will,
and it shall be fulfilled without delay.[e] For
in your days, you rebellious house, I will
fulfill[f] whatever I say, declares the Sovereign LORD.[g]'"

26The word of the LORD came to me:
27"Son of man, the house of Israel is saying, 'The vision he sees is for many years
from now, and he prophesies about the
distant future.'[h]

12:3 [c]Jer 26:3 [d]ver 11; S Eze 3:27; 2Ti 2:25-26 **12:4** [e]ver 12; 2Ki 25:4; S Jer 39:4 **12:5** [f]Jer 52:7; Am 4:3 **12:6** [g]ver 12; S Isa 8:18; S 20:3 **12:7** [h]Eze 24:18; 37:10 **12:9** [i]Eze 17:12; 20:49; 24:19 **12:11** [j]Isa 8:18; Zec 3:8 [k]S 2Ki 25:7; S Jer 15:2; 52:15 **12:12** [l]S Jer 39:4 [m]Jer 52:7 **12:13** [n]Eze 17:20; 19:8; 32:3; Hos 7:12 [o]S Isa 24:17-18 [p]Eze 1:3 [q]S Jer 39:7 [r]S Jer 24:8; S 52:11; S La 4:20; Eze 17:16 **12:14** [s]S 2Ki 25:5; S Jer 21:7; S Eze 5:10, 12; 17:21 **12:15** [t]S Lev 26:33 **12:16** [u]S Jer 22:8-9; Eze 6:8-10; 14:22; 36:20 **12:18** [v]La 5:9 **12:19** [w]Jer 10:22; S Eze 6:6-14; Mic 7:13; Zec 7:14 [x]S Eze 4:16; 23:33 **12:20** [y]Isa 7:23-24; S Jer 4:7; S 25:9 **12:22** [z]S Ps 49:4 [a]S Isa 5:19; Eze 11:3; Am 6:3; 2Pe 3:4 **12:23** [b]S Eze 7:7 [c]S Ps 37:13; Eze 18:3; Joel 2:1; Zep 1:14 **12:24** [d]Jer 14:14; Eze 13:23; Mic 3:6; Zec 13:2-4 **12:25** [e]Hab 2:3 [f]S Nu 11:23; Eze 13:6 [g]Nu 14:28-34; S Isa 14:24; S 55:11; Jer 16:9; Hab 1:5 **12:27** [h]S Eze 11:3; Da 10:14; Mt 24:48-50; 2Pe 3:4

12:5 *dig through the wall.* Not the city wall, which was made of stone and was many feet thick, but the sun-dried brick wall of his house.

12:6 *sign.* Prophets were often instructed to perform symbolic acts (see 4:3 and note; cf. 1Ki 11:29–31; 13:23–32; 20:35–43; Isa 8:18; Jer 13:1–11; 16:1–9; 19:1–15; 27:2—28:14; 32:6–15).

12:8 *In the morning.* After Ezekiel "did as ... commanded" (v. 7). Again the divine explanation follows the prophet's unquestioning obedience (see note on 8:3).

12:9 *What are you doing?* The book's first indication of the people's response to the prophet's symbolic acts.

12:10 *prince in Jerusalem.* Zedekiah.

12:13 *Chaldeans.* See notes on 23:23; Ezr 5:12; Job 1:17. *he will not see it.* Nebuchadnezzar's men would put out Zedekiah's eyes (see 2Ki 25:7).

12:14 *with drawn sword.* See 5:2 and note.

12:15 *know that I am the LORD.* See vv. 16,20; see also note on 6:7.

12:16 *sword, famine and plague.* See 5:16–17 and note.

12:18 *tremble as you eat.* Another prophetic symbol. Ezekiel's trembling must have been particularly violent, because the Hebrew word for "tremble" is used elsewhere to describe an earthquake (see 1Ki 19:11; Am 1:1).

12:19 *people of the land.* See note on 7:27. *because of the violence.* See 7:23 and note.

12:22 For more than 30 years Jeremiah had been prophesying Jerusalem's fall, but the city still stood. So among its inhabitants, whose ears were deaf to Jeremiah's warnings (v. 2), a mocking proverb was making the rounds, reinforced by the false prophets (see ch. 13; Jer 23:9–40; 28), which said in effect: "The days go by" and none of the visions of coming disaster have come true, so forget them.

12:23 The Lord refutes the first saying (v. 22) of the Israelites that dismisses his prophet's announcements of impending judgment.

12:24 *no more false visions ... divinations.* Events will silence the false prophets whose "visions are false and their divinations a lie" (13:6).

12:27 Another saying (see note on v. 23) is being passed around among the Israelites, this one apparently among those in exile. It pertains to Ezekiel's visions and dismisses them as having to do only with far-off events that need not concern the present generation.

28“Therefore say to them, ‘This is what
the Sovereign LORD says: None of my
words will be delayed any longer; whatever I say will be fulfilled, declares the Sovereign LORD.’ ”

False Prophets Condemned

13 The word of the LORD came to me:
2“Son of man, prophesy against the
prophets[i] of Israel who are now prophesying. Say to those who prophesy out of
their own imagination:[j] ‘Hear the word
of the LORD![k] 3This is what the Sovereign
LORD says: Woe to the foolish[a] prophets[l]
who follow their own spirit and have seen
nothing![m] 4Your prophets, O Israel, are like
jackals among ruins. 5You have not gone
up to the breaks in the wall to repair[n] it
for the house of Israel so that it will stand
firm in the battle on the day of the LORD.[o]
6Their visions are false[p] and their divinations a lie. They say, “The LORD declares,”
when the LORD has not sent[q] them; yet they
expect their words to be fulfilled.[r] 7Have
you not seen false visions[s] and uttered lying divinations when you say, “The LORD
declares,” though I have not spoken?
8“ ‘Therefore this is what the Sovereign
LORD says: Because of your false words
and lying visions, I am against you,[t] declares the Sovereign LORD. 9My hand will
be against the prophets who see false visions and utter lying[u] divinations. They
will not belong to the council of my people or be listed in the records[v] of the house
of Israel, nor will they enter the land of
Israel. Then you will know that I am the
Sovereign LORD.[w]
10“ ‘Because they lead my people astray,[x]
saying, “Peace,”[y] when there is no peace,
and because, when a flimsy wall is built,
they cover it with whitewash,[z] 11therefore
tell those who cover it with whitewash
that it is going to fall. Rain will come in
torrents, and I will send hailstones[a] hur-
tling down,[b] and violent winds will burst
forth.[c] 12When the wall collapses, will people not ask you, “Where is the whitewash
you covered it with?”
13“ ‘Therefore this is what the Sovereign
LORD says: In my wrath I will unleash a
violent wind, and in my anger hailstones[d]
and torrents of rain[e] will fall with destructive fury.[f] 14I will tear down the wall[g] you
have covered with whitewash and will level it to the ground so that its foundation[h]
will be laid bare. When it[b] falls,[i] you will
be destroyed in it; and you will know that
I am the LORD. 15So I will spend my wrath
against the wall and against those who
covered it with whitewash. I will say to
you, “The wall is gone and so are those
who whitewashed it, 16those prophets of
Israel who prophesied to Jerusalem and
saw visions of peace for her when there
was no peace, declares the Sovereign
LORD.[j]” ’
17“Now, son of man, set your face[k]
against the daughters[l] of your people who
prophesy out of their own imagination.
Prophesy against them[m] 18and say, ‘This
is what the Sovereign LORD says: Woe to
the women who sew magic charms on
all their wrists and make veils of various
lengths for their heads in order to ensnare
people. Will you ensnare the lives of my
people but preserve your own? 19You have
profaned[n] me among my people for a few
handfuls of barley and scraps of bread.[o]

[a] 3 Or *wicked* [b] 14 Or *the city*

13:2 [i]S Isa 9:15 [j]Jer 28:15 [k]ver 17; S Jer 23:16; S 37:19; Eze 22:28 **13:3** [l]S La 2:14; Hos 9:7 [m]S Jer 23:25-32 **13:5** [n]Isa 58:12; Eze 22:30 [o]S Eze 7:19; 30:3 **13:6** [p]S Jer 5:1; 23:16 [q]S Jer 14:14 [r]S Jer 28:15; S 29:9; Eze 12:24-25; 22:28 **13:7** [s]S Isa 30:10 **13:8** [t]S Jer 21:13 **13:9** [u]S Dt 13:3 [v]S Ex 32:32; S Jer 17:13 [w]S Ex 6:2; Jer 20:3-6; Eze 20:38 **13:10** [x]S Jer 23:13; S 50:6 [y]S Jer 4:10 [z]S Eze 7:25; 22:28 **13:11** [a]S Jos 10:11 [b]S Job 38:23 [c]Ps 11:6; Eze 38:22 **13:13** [d]S Jos 10:11; Rev 11:19; 16:21 [e]Job 14:19 [f]S Ex 9:25; S Job 38:23; Isa 30:30 **13:14** [g]S Isa 22:5 [h]Mic 1:6 [i]Jer 6:15 **13:16** [j]S Isa 57:21; Jer 6:14; S Eze 7:25 **13:17** [k]S Eze 4:7; 25:2; 28:21 [l]S Ex 15:20; Rev 2:20 [m]S ver 2 **13:19** [n]Jer 44:26; Eze 20:39; 22:26; 36:20; 39:7 [o]S Isa 56:11

12:28 *None of my words will be delayed any longer.* The Lord also refutes this saying (v. 27) circulating among his “rebellious people” (v. 2; see note on 12:1–28).

13:1–23 The Lord’s condemnation of the false prophets, both men and women—as through Jeremiah in Jerusalem (Jer 23:9–40; 28), so through Ezekiel in Babylonia. This begins a series of prophecies concerning God’s judgment on Judah that concludes with a parable in which Jerusalem is likened to a pot cooking on a fire (24:1–14).

13:2 *out of their own imagination.* Cf. Jer 23:16,26–32.

13:3 *have seen nothing.* No revelation from God was received (cf. 1Sa 3:1 and note; Jer 23:18,22 and note on 23:18).

13:4 *jackals.* Animals that travel in packs and feed on dead flesh—a powerfully negative image (see Ps 63:10; La 5:18).

13:5 *to repair it for the house of Israel.* The function of true prophets is described (cf. 22:30; Ps 106:23). *day of the LORD.* See note on 7:7.

13:6 *Their visions are false.* Whether the false prophets had actual visions is unknown, but they claimed to have received revelations from God when in reality their messages only proclaimed what their hearers wanted to hear (see 12:24 and note; Isa 30:10; Jer 23:9–17; 2Ti 4:3).

13:8 *I am against you.* See 5:8 and note.

13:9 *They will not belong ... land of Israel.* A threefold punishment, resulting in total exclusion from the community. *council of my people.* See Ps 111:1 and note. *records of the house of Israel.* See Ezr 2:62; cf. Da 12:1; see also Ps 69:28 and note.

13:10 *saying, “Peace.”* Very likely in echo of the priestly benediction (see Nu 6:24–26 and note on 6:26), ignoring the fact that God’s promise of “peace” to his people was conditional on their faithfulness to him. *when there is no peace.* See v. 16; Jer 6:14 and note; 8:11. *whitewash.* See vv. 11,14–15; 22:28; an uncommon word used only by Ezekiel, perhaps chosen by him to evoke the like-sounding word rendered “repulsive thing” in Jer 23:13 and “worthless” in La 2:14, both pertaining to the proclamations of the false prophets.

13:11 *Rain will come in torrents.* The violent thunderstorm of God’s judgment (imagery frequently used in the OT) was about to sweep them away (see, e.g., Ps 18:7–15; 77:17–18; 83:15; Isa 28:17; 30:30; Jer 23:19; 30:23).

13:18 *magic charms.* Exactly what the women were doing is not known, but that it was some kind of black magic or voodoo is clear. The Bible consistently avoids explicit description of occult practices.

13:19 *profaned me.* See note on Lev 18:21. *for a few handfuls of barley.* Involvement in religious matters of any kind for mere gain is consistently condemned in the Bible

By lying to my people, who listen to lies,
you have killed those who should not have
died and have spared those who should
not live.[p]
20“ ‘Therefore this is what the Sovereign LORD says: I am against your magic
charms with which you ensnare people
like birds and I will tear them from your
arms; I will set free the people that you ensnare like birds.[q] 21I will tear off your veils
and save my people from your hands, and
they will no longer fall prey to your power.
Then you will know that I am the LORD.[r]
22Because you disheartened the righteous
with your lies,[s] when I had brought them
no grief, and because you encouraged the
wicked not to turn from their evil ways
and so save their lives,[t] 23therefore you
will no longer see false visions[u] or practice
divination.[v] I will save[w] my people from
your hands. And then you will know that
I am the LORD.[x]’ ”

Idolaters Condemned

14 Some of the elders of Israel came to
me and sat down in front of me.[y]
2Then the word of the LORD came to me:
3“Son of man, these men have set up idols
in their hearts[z] and put wicked stumbling blocks[a] before their faces. Should I
let them inquire of me at all?[b] 4Therefore
speak to them and tell them, ‘This is what
the Sovereign LORD says: When any Israelite sets up idols in his heart and puts
a wicked stumbling block before his face
and then goes to a prophet, I the LORD
will answer him myself in keeping with
his great idolatry. 5I will do this to recapture the hearts of the people of Israel, who
have all deserted[c] me for their idols.’[d]
6“Therefore say to the house of Israel,
‘This is what the Sovereign LORD says: Repent![e] Turn from your idols and renounce
all your detestable practices![f]
7“ ‘When any Israelite or any alien[g] living in Israel separates himself from me
and sets up idols in his heart and puts a
wicked stumbling block[h] before his face
and then goes to a prophet to inquire[i] of
me, I the LORD will answer him myself.
8I will set my face against[j] that man and
make him an example[k] and a byword.[l] I
will cut him off from my people. Then you
will know that I am the LORD.[m]
9“ ‘And if the prophet[n] is enticed[o] to utter a prophecy, I the LORD have enticed
that prophet, and I will stretch out my
hand against him and destroy him from
among my people Israel.[p] 10They will bear
their guilt—the prophet will be as guilty
as the one who consults him. 11Then the
people of Israel will no longer stray[q] from
me, nor will they defile themselves anymore with all their sins. They will be my
people,[r] and I will be their God, declares
the Sovereign LORD.[s]’ ”

Judgment Inescapable

12The word of the LORD came to me:
13“Son of man, if a country sins[t] against
me by being unfaithful and I stretch out my
hand against it to cut off its food supply[u]
and send famine upon it and kill its men
and their animals,[v] 14even if these three
men—Noah,[w] Daniel[a][x] and Job[y]—were
in it, they could save only themselves by
their righteousness,[z] declares the Sovereign LORD.
15“Or if I send wild beasts[a] through that
country and they leave it childless and it

[a] 14 Or *Danel*; the Hebrew spelling may suggest a person other than the prophet Daniel; also in verse 20.

13:19 [p] Pr 28:21; Mic 3:11 **13:20** [q] Ps 124:7 **13:21** [r] Ps 91:3 **13:22** [s] S Isa 9:15 [t] Jer 23:14; Eze 18:21; 33:14-16 **13:23** [u] Ne 6:12 [v] S Eze 12:24 [w] S Ps 72:14 [x] Mic 3:6 **14:1** [y] S Eze 8:1; 20:1 **14:3** [z] S Eze 6:4 [a] S ver 7; S Eze 7:19 [b] Isa 1:15; Eze 20:31 **14:5** [c] S Dt 32:15; Eze 16:45; Hos 5:7; Zec 11:8 [d] Jer 2:11 **14:6** [e] Ne 1:9; S Jer 3:12; S 35:15 [f] S Isa 2:20; S 30:22 **14:7** [g] Ex 12:48; 20:10 [h] ver 3; S Isa 8:14; Hos 4:5; 5:5 [i] S Ge 25:22 **14:8** [j] Eze 15:7 [k] S Nu 16:38 [l] S Ps 102:8; S Eze 5:15 [m] S Jer 42:20 **14:9** [n] S Jer 14:15 [o] Isa 63:17; Jer 4:10 [p] 1Ki 22:23; S 2Ch 18:22; Zec 13:3 **14:11** [q] Eze 48:11 [r] S Isa 51:16 [s] S Eze 11:19-20; 37:23 **14:13** [t] S Pr 13:21 [u] S Lev 26:26 [v] S Eze 5:16; 14:6; 15:8 **14:14** [w] Ge 6:8 [x] ver 20; Eze 28:3; Da 1:6; 6:13

[y] S Job 1:1 [z] S Ge 6:9; S Job 42:9; Jer 15:1; S Eze 3:19; 18:20 **14:15** [a] Eze 5:17

(see, e.g., Jer 6:13; 8:10; Mic 3:5,11; Ac 8:9–24; 2Co 2:17; Tit 1:11). For the proper attitude and motivation see 2Co 11:7; 2Th 3:8; 1Ti 3:3. *you have killed.* The women had used their evil powers for unjust ends, involving even matters of life and death.

14:1–11 The idolatry among the Israelites that God here condemns took the form of worshiping the gods of neighboring peoples (see notes on Ge 20:9; Ex 34:15) along with the worship of Yahweh—the people thought they should take all the gods seriously—an apostasy that struck at the very heart of Israel's covenant relationship with Yahweh (see Ex 20:3–5 and notes). And this idolatry was not limited to those still living in Jerusalem; Ezekiel had to confront it also among the exiles.

14:1 *elders of Israel.* Apparently interchangeable with "elders of Judah" (see note on 8:1).

14:3 *idols.* See note on 6:4. *wicked stumbling blocks.* The physical representations of the idols. *inquire.* A technical term for seeking an oracle from a prophet (see 2Ki 1:16; 3:11; 8:8).

14:4 *I the LORD will answer him myself.* Not through a prophet but by direct action. The punishment for idolatry was death (Dt 13:6–18).

14:6 *Repent!* First of three calls for repentance from Ezekiel, who elsewhere proclaims inescapable judgment (see 18:30; 33:11).

14:9 *enticed.* Related to God's testing of his people's loyalty (see 3:20 and note; cf. 1Ki 22:19–23).

14:11 The harsh judgment about to fall on idolatrous Israel has a redemptive purpose: to restore Israel to covenant faithfulness (see 20:32–44; cf. 33:11). *my people ... their God.* Covenant terminology (see note on 11:20).

14:12–23 Israel must know that once God's judgments have been sent upon an unfaithful nation, no one can persuade him to call them back—and that will be even more true of Jerusalem (cf. Jer 15:1 and note). The judgments in view here include the four often mentioned in Ezekiel: famine (v. 13), wild beasts (v. 15), sword (v. 17) and plague (v. 19; see also v. 21 and note on 5:16–17).

14:14,20 *Noah, Daniel and Job.* Three ancient men of renown, selected because of their proverbial righteousness. As the NIV text note indicates, another Daniel may be referred to (Ugaritic literature speaks of an honored "Danel"; see chart, p. xxiii), since the Biblical Daniel's righteousness probably had not become proverbial so soon (Daniel and Ezekiel were contemporaries; see Da 1:1).

becomes desolate so that no one can pass
through it because of the beasts,[b] 16as surely as I live, declares the Sovereign LORD,
even if these three men were in it, they
could not save their own sons or daughters. They alone would be saved, but the
land would be desolate.[c]
17"Or if I bring a sword[d] against that
country and say, 'Let the sword pass
throughout the land,' and I kill its men
and their animals,[e] 18as surely as I live,
declares the Sovereign LORD, even if these
three men were in it, they could not save
their own sons or daughters. They alone
would be saved.
19"Or if I send a plague into that land
and pour out my wrath[f] upon it through
bloodshed,[g] killing its men and their animals,[h] 20as surely as I live, declares the
Sovereign LORD, even if Noah, Daniel and
Job were in it, they could save neither son
nor daughter. They would save only themselves by their righteousness.[i]
21"For this is what the Sovereign LORD
says: How much worse will it be when I
send against Jerusalem my four dreadful
judgments[j]—sword[k] and famine[l] and wild
beasts and plague[m]—to kill its men and
their animals![n] 22Yet there will be some survivors[o]—sons and daughters who will be
brought out of it.[p] They will come to you,
and when you see their conduct[q] and their
actions, you will be consoled[r] regarding
the disaster I have brought upon Jerusalem—every disaster I have brought upon
it. 23You will be consoled when you see
their conduct and their actions, for you will
know that I have done nothing in it without cause, declares the Sovereign LORD.[s]"

14:15 [b]S Lev 26:22 **14:16** [c]S Ge 19:29; Eze 18:20 **14:17** [d]S Lev 26:25; S Jer 25:27; S 42:16 [e]Eze 25:13; Zep 1:3 **14:19** [f]S Eze 7:8 [g]S Isa 34:3 [h]Jer 14:12; Eze 38:22 **14:20** [i]S ver 14 **14:21** [j]S Nu 33:4 [k]Isa 31:8; 34:6; 66:16; Eze 21:3,19 [l]S 2Sa 24:13 [m]S Jer 14:12; 27:8 [n]S Jer 15:3; S Eze 5:17; 33:27; Am 4:6-10; Rev 6:8 **14:22** [o]S Jer 41:16 [p]S Eze 12:16 [q]Eze 20:43 [r]Eze 31:16; 32:31 **14:23** [s]S Jer 22:8-9; Eze 8:6-18; S 9:9

15:2 [t]Ps 80:8-16; Isa 5:1-7; 27:2-6; Jer 2:21; Hos 10:1; S Jn 15:2 **15:3** [u]Jer 13:10 [v]S Isa 22:23 **15:4** [w]Eze 17:3-10; 19:14; Jn 15:6 **15:7** [x]S Lev 26:17; Ps 34:16; Eze 14:8 [y]S Eze 5:2 [z]S Eze 5:4 [a]Isa 24:18; Am 9:1-4

Jerusalem, A Useless Vine

15 The word of the LORD came to me:
2"Son of man, how is the wood of a
vine[t] better than that of a branch on any
of the trees in the forest? 3Is wood ever
taken from it to make anything useful?[u] Do
they make pegs[v] from it to hang things on?
4And after it is thrown on the fire as fuel
and the fire burns both ends and chars
the middle, is it then useful for anything?[w]
5If it was not useful for anything when it
was whole, how much less can it be made
into something useful when the fire has
burned it and it is charred?
6"Therefore this is what the Sovereign
LORD says: As I have given the wood of
the vine among the trees of the forest as
fuel for the fire, so will I treat the people living in Jerusalem. 7I will set my face
against[x] them. Although they have come
out of the fire[y][z], the fire will yet consume
them. And when I set my face against
them, you will know that I am the LORD.[a]
8I will make the land desolate[b] because
they have been unfaithful,[c] declares the
Sovereign LORD."

An Allegory of Unfaithful Jerusalem

16 The word of the LORD came to me:
2"Son of man, confront[d] Jerusalem
with her detestable practices[e] 3and say,
'This is what the Sovereign LORD says to
Jerusalem: Your ancestry[f] and birth were
in the land of the Canaanites; your father[g]
was an Amorite[h] and your mother a Hittite.[i]

15:8 [b]S Eze 14:13 [c]Eze 17:20; 18:24 **16:2** [d]S Isa 57:12; Eze 23:36 [e]Eze 8:17; 20:4; 22:2 **16:3** [f]Ge 11:25-29; Eze 21:30 [g]S Ge 12:18 [h]S Ge 15:16 [i]ver 45; S Ge 10:15; S Dt 7:1; Jos 24:14-15

14:20 *neither son nor daughter.* When God comes in judgment against a nation or people, they cannot count on another's righteousness—not even that of their parents—to deliver them.

14:23 *You.* Plural; i.e., the exiles in Babylonia. *will be consoled.* When the exiles see the wickedness of those brought to Babylonia from Jerusalem, they will know that God's judgment on the city was just.

15:1–8 God compares Jerusalem to a vine (cf. Ps 80:8–16 and note) that yields no grapes and is therefore good for nothing but to be used as fuel.

15:3 *Do they make pegs from it to hang things on?* See Isa 22:23–25.

15:4 *is it then useful for anything?* Whereas Isaiah (5:1–7) and Jeremiah (2:21) express divine disappointment over Israel's failure to produce good fruit, Ezekiel typically laments her total uselessness.

15:7 *Although they have come out of the fire.* A reference to the siege of Jerusalem in 597 B.C., which resulted in the exile of which Ezekiel was a part (see 1:2; 2Ki 24:10–16). *fire will yet consume them.* Prophecy threatening another and more devastating siege—Ezekiel's main message before 586 (see 5:2,4; 10:2,7).

16:1–63 The whole history of God's dealings with Jerusalem is graphically portrayed in an allegory that highlights the Lord's great goodness to the city on the one hand and the depth of the city's unfaithfulness to him on the other. Here Jerusalem as a royal city among the other cities of the world is in focus and serves as an analogue and representative of Israel. She is the city God had chosen to be the site of his temple (see 1Ki 9:3; 2Ch 7:1–3; Ps 68:16; 78:68–69; 132:13–16) and had elevated her, as "the city of the Great King" (Ps 48:2), to be the earthly center of his kingly rule in human affairs. He had married her (see v. 8 and note) and provided for her richly. But she turned to the false gods to supply her needs and allied herself with the great empires around her (Egypt [v. 26], Assyria [v. 28] and Babylonia [v. 29]) to provide her security. So God accuses her of unfaithfulness to him like that of an adulterous wife (see Ex 34:15 and note).

16:3 *Your ancestry and birth.* Jerusalem had a centuries-old, pre-Israelite history (see notes on Ge 14:18; Ecc 1:16), and the city long resisted Israelite conquest (Jos 15:63). It became fully Israelite only after David's conquest (2Sa 5:6–9). *father ... mother.* A reference to Jerusalem's non-Israelite origin generally, not to any specific individuals. *Amorite.* Cf. v. 45. Like the Canaanites, the Amorites were pre-Israelite, Semitic inhabitants of Canaan (see Ge 10:16 and note; 48:22; Jos 5:1 and note; 10:5; Jdg 1:34–36). *Hittite.* The Hittites were non-Semitic residents of Canaan, who earlier had flourished in Asia Minor during the second millennium B.C. (see Ge 10:15 and note; 23:10–20; 26:34; 1Sa 26:6; 2Sa 11:2–27; 1Ki 11:1).

4On the day you were born[j] your cord was
not cut, nor were you washed with water
to make you clean, nor were you rubbed
with salt or wrapped in cloths. 5No one
looked on you with pity or had compassion enough to do any of these things for
you. Rather, you were thrown out into the
open field, for on the day you were born
you were despised.
6" 'Then I passed by and saw you kicking about in your blood, and as you lay
there in your blood I said to you, "Live!"[a][k]
7I made you grow[l] like a plant of the field.
You grew up and developed and became
the most beautiful of jewels.[b] Your breasts
were formed and your hair grew, you who
were naked and bare.[m]
8" 'Later I passed by, and when I looked
at you and saw that you were old enough
for love, I spread the corner of my garment[n] over you and covered your nakedness. I gave you my solemn oath and entered into a covenant[o] with you, declares
the Sovereign LORD, and you became
mine.[p]
9" 'I bathed[c] you with water and washed[q]
the blood from you and put ointments on
you. 10I clothed you with an embroidered[r]
dress and put leather sandals on you. I
dressed you in fine linen[s] and covered
you with costly garments.[t] 11I adorned
you with jewelry:[u] I put bracelets[v] on your
arms and a necklace[w] around your neck,
12and I put a ring on your nose,[x] earrings[y]
on your ears and a beautiful crown[z] on
your head.[a] 13So you were adorned with
gold and silver; your clothes[b] were of fine
linen and costly fabric and embroidered
cloth. Your food was fine flour, honey and
olive oil.[c] You became very beautiful and
rose to be a queen.[d] 14And your fame[e]
spread among the nations on account of
your beauty,[f] because the splendor I had
given you made your beauty perfect, declares the Sovereign LORD.[g]
15" 'But you trusted in your beauty and
used your fame to become a prostitute.
You lavished your favors on anyone who
passed by[h] and your beauty became his.[d][i]
16You took some of your garments to make
gaudy high places,[j] where you carried on
your prostitution.[k] Such things should not
happen, nor should they ever occur. 17You
also took the fine jewelry I gave you, the
jewelry made of my gold and silver, and
you made for yourself male idols and engaged in prostitution with them.[l] 18And
you took your embroidered clothes to
put on them, and you offered my oil and
incense[m] before them. 19Also the food I
provided for you — the fine flour, olive oil
and honey I gave you to eat — you offered
as fragrant incense before them. That is
what happened, declares the Sovereign
LORD.[n]
20" 'And you took your sons and daughters[o] whom you bore to me[p] and sacrificed
them as food to the idols. Was your prostitution not enough?[q] 21You slaughtered my
children and sacrificed them[e] to the idols.[r]
22In all your detestable practices and your
prostitution you did not remember the
days of your youth,[s] when you were naked
and bare,[t] kicking about in your blood.[u]
23" 'Woe![v] Woe to you, declares the Sovereign LORD. In addition to all your other

16:4 [j]Hos 2:3 **16:6** [k]ver 22; S Ex 19:4; Eze 18:23,32 **16:7** [l]S Dt 1:10 [m]S Ex 1:7 **16:8** [n]Ru 3:9 [o]ver 59; S Jer 11:10; Mal 2:14 [p]Jer 2:2; Hos 2:7,19-20 **16:9** [q]S Ru 3:3 **16:10** [r]S Ex 26:36; S Isa 19:9 [s]Eze 27:16 [t]ver 18; S Isa 3:23 **16:11** [u]S Jer 4:30; Eze 23:40 [v]Isa 3:19; Eze 23:42 [w]S Ge 41:42; S Ps 73:6 **16:12** [x]Isa 3:21 [y]S Ge 35:4 [z]S Isa 28:5; S Jer 13:18 [a]Pr 1:9; S Isa 3:19 **16:13** [b]Est 5:1 [c]1Sa 10:1 [d]Dt 32:13-14; S 1Ki 4:21; S Est 2:9,17 **16:14** [e]1Ki 10:24 [f]S Est 1:11; S Ps 48:2; S La 2:15 [g]S Eze 5:5 **16:15** [h]ver 25 [i]S Isa 57:8; S Jer 2:20; Eze 23:3; 27:3 **16:16** [j]S Isa 57:7 [k]S 2Ki 23:7 **16:17** [l]S Eze 7:20; Hos 2:13 **16:18** [m]S Jer 44:5 **16:19** [n]Hos 2:8 **16:20** [o]S Jer 7:31 [p]Ex 13:2 [q]Ps 106:37-38; S Isa 57:5; Eze 23:37 **16:21** [r]S 2Ki 17:17; S Jer 19:5 **16:22** [s]S Ps 25:7; S 88:15; Jer 2:2; Hos 2:15; 11:1 [t]Hos 2:3 [u]ver 6 **16:23** [v]Eze 24:6

[a] 6 A few Hebrew manuscripts, Septuagint and Syriac; most Hebrew manuscripts *"Live!" And as you lay there in your blood I said to you, "Live!"* [b] 7 Or *became mature* [c] 9 Or *I had bathed* [d] 15 Most Hebrew manuscripts; one Hebrew manuscript (see some Septuagint manuscripts) *by. Such a thing should not happen* [e] 21 Or *and made them pass through the fire*

16:4 *rubbed with salt.* This practice has been observed among Arab peasants as late as A.D. 1918. *wrapped in cloths.* Cf. Lk 2:7.

16:5 *thrown out into the open field.* Abandoned to die. Exposure of infants, common in ancient pagan societies, was abhorrent to Israel.

16:6 *blood.* Of childbirth. *Live!* God's basic desire for all people, summed up in one word (see 18:23,32; 1Ti 2:4; 2Pe 3:9).

16:7 *hair.* Pubic hair.

16:8 *spread the corner of my garment.* Symbolic of entering a marriage relationship (see notes on Dt 22:30; Ru 3:9). *covenant.* Since the maiden symbolizes Jerusalem, this does not refer to the Sinai covenant but to marriage as a covenant (see Mal 2:14).

16:9 *blood.* Menstrual blood, indicating sexual maturity (see NIV text note on v. 7).

16:10 *embroidered dress ... leather sandals ... fine linen.* Representative of the very best garments. *embroidered dress.* See 27:16,24; colored, variegated material fit for a queen (see Ps 45:14). *leather sandals.* The same kind of leather was used to cover the tabernacle ("hides of sea cows," Ex 25:5; 26:14).

16:11 *bracelets on your arms.* See Ge 24:22.

16:12 *ring.* Not piercing the nose but worn on the outer part of the nose (see Ge 24:47). *earrings.* Circular ear ornaments, worn by men (Nu 31:50). The Hebrew for this word is not the same as that used in Ge 35:4; Ex 32:2–3. *crown.* The wedding crown (see SS 3:11, where the groom wears it).

16:13 *gold and silver.* Cf. Hos 2:8. *fine flour.* Used in offerings, therefore of high quality (see v. 19; 46:14). *olive oil.* Cf. Hos 2:8. For the combination of honey and oil see Dt 32:13. *You became very beautiful.* Cf. Eph 5:27.

16:14 *your fame spread.* Especially in the time of David and Solomon.

16:15 *favors.* Sexual favors. Verb and noun forms of the Hebrew for this word occur 23 times in this chapter. *anyone who passed by.* Cf. Ge 38:14–16.

16:16 *garments.* All of the Lord's previous gifts were used by Jerusalem in prostituting herself. Cloths of some kind were needed in the Asherah worship practices (see 2Ki 23:7). They may have been used as curtains or as bedding (see Am 2:7–8).

16:20 *sons and daughters ... sacrificed.* See 20:26,31 and note on 20:26; 23:37; 2Ki 21:6; 23:10; Jer 7:31 and note; 19:5; 32:35. For laws against child sacrifice see Lev 18:21; Dt 18:10; cf. Lev 20:2–5; Dt 12:31.

wickedness, 24you built a mound for
yourself and made a lofty shrine[w] in every public square.[x] 25At the head of every
street[y] you built your lofty shrines and
degraded your beauty, offering your body
with increasing promiscuity to anyone
who passed by.[z] 26You engaged in prostitution[a] with the Egyptians,[b] your lustful
neighbors, and provoked[c] me to anger
with your increasing promiscuity.[d] 27So I
stretched out my hand[e] against you and
reduced your territory; I gave you over[f]
to the greed of your enemies, the daughters of the Philistines,[g] who were shocked
by your lewd conduct. 28You engaged in
prostitution with the Assyrians[h] too, because you were insatiable; and even after
that, you still were not satisfied.[i] 29Then
you increased your promiscuity to include
Babylonia,[a][j] a land of merchants, but even
with this you were not satisfied.[k]
30" 'How weak-willed you are, declares
the Sovereign LORD, when you do all these
things, acting like a brazen prostitute![l]
31When you built your mounds at the
head of every street and made your lofty
shrines[m] in every public square, you were
unlike a prostitute, because you scorned
payment.
32" 'You adulterous wife! You prefer
strangers to your own husband! 33Every
prostitute receives a fee,[n] but you give
gifts[o] to all your lovers, bribing them to
come to you from everywhere for your illicit favors.[p] 34So in your prostitution you
are the opposite of others; no one runs after you for your favors. You are the very
opposite, for you give payment and none
is given to you.
35" 'Therefore, you prostitute, hear the
word of the LORD! 36This is what the Sovereign LORD says: Because you poured out
your wealth[b] and exposed your nakedness
in your promiscuity with your lovers, and
because of all your detestable idols, and
because you gave them your children's
blood,[q] 37therefore I am going to gather all
your lovers, with whom you found pleasure, those you loved as well as those you
hated. I will gather them against you from
all around and will strip[r] you in front of
them, and they will see all your nakedness.[s] 38I will sentence you to the punishment of women who commit adultery and
who shed blood;[t] I will bring upon you
the blood vengeance of my wrath and jealous anger.[u] 39Then I will hand you over[v] to
your lovers, and they will tear down your
mounds and destroy your lofty shrines.
They will strip you of your clothes and
take your fine jewelry and leave you naked
and bare.[w] 40They will bring a mob against
you, who will stone[x] you and hack you to
pieces with their swords. 41They will burn
down[y] your houses and inflict punishment
on you in the sight of many women.[z] I
will put a stop[a] to your prostitution, and
you will no longer pay your lovers. 42Then
my wrath against you will subside and my
jealous anger will turn away from you; I
will be calm and no longer angry.[b]
43" 'Because you did not remember[c] the
days of your youth but enraged me with
all these things, I will surely bring down[d]
on your head what you have done, declares the Sovereign LORD. Did you not
add lewdness to all your other detestable
practices?[e]
44" 'Everyone who quotes proverbs[f] will
quote this proverb about you: "Like mother, like daughter." 45You are a true daughter of your mother, who despised[g] her husband[h] and her children; and you are a true
sister of your sisters, who despised their
husbands and their children. Your mother
was a Hittite and your father an Amorite.[i]
46Your older sister[j] was Samaria, who lived
to the north of you with her daughters;

[a] 29 Or *Chaldea* [b] 36 Or *lust*

16:24 [w] ver 31; Isa 57:7 [x] Ps 78:58; S Jer 2:20; 3:2; S 44:21; Eze 20:28 **16:25** [y] S Jer 3:2 [z] ver 15; S Pr 9:14 **16:26** [a] S Isa 23:17 [b] S Jer 3:1 [c] S 1Ki 14:9; S Eze 8:17 [d] S Isa 57:8; Jer 11:15; Eze 20:8; 23:19-21 **16:27** [e] Eze 20:33; 25:13 [f] S Jer 34:20 [g] S 2Ch 28:18 **16:28** [h] S 2Ki 16:7 [i] Isa 57:8 **16:29** [j] S Jer 3:1; Eze 23:14-17 [k] Na 3:4 **16:30** [l] S Jer 3:3 **16:31** [m] S ver 24 **16:33** [n] S Ge 30:15 [o] Isa 30:6; 57:9 [p] Hos 8:9-10 **16:36** [q] S Jer 19:5; Eze 23:10 **16:37** [r] Hos 2:3 [s] S Isa 47:3; S Jer 13:22; Eze 23:22; Hos 2:10; 8:10; Rev 17:16 **16:38** [t] S Ge 38:24 [u] S Lev 20:10; Ps 79:3,5; Eze 23:25; Zep 1:17 **16:39** [v] S 2Ki 18:11 [w] Eze 21:31; Hos 2:3 **16:40** [x] Jn 8:5,7 **16:41** [y] S Dt 13:16; S Jer 19:13 [z] Eze 23:10 [a] Eze 22:15; 23:27,48 **16:42** [b] 2Sa 24:25; Isa 40:1-2; 54:9; S Eze 5:13; 39:29

16:43 [c] S Ex 15:24; Ps 78:42 [d] Eze 22:31 [e] Eze 11:21 **16:44** [f] S Ps 49:4 **16:45** [g] S Eze 14:5 [h] Jer 44:19 [i] ver 3; Eze 23:2 **16:46** [j] S Jer 3:7

16:24 *mound ... lofty shrine.* Centers of idol worship were built not only in the countryside but also in Jerusalem itself.
16:26–29 *Egyptians ... Philistines ... Assyrians ... Babylonia.* The historical sequence of Jerusalem's political alliances with these four powers.
16:26 *lustful.* The Hebrew is more graphic: "having oversized organs." The language reflects both God's and Ezekiel's disgust with Jerusalem's apostasy. *neighbors.* Nowhere else in the OT are the Egyptians called "neighbors."
16:27 *reduced your territory.* After the 701 B.C. siege of Jerusalem, the Assyrian king Sennacherib gave some of Jerusalem's territory to the Philistines. *shocked by your lewd conduct.* Cf. Am 3:9,13 and notes.
16:29 *Babylonia, a land of merchants.* See note on Rev 14:8; see also Rev 18:11–19,23.
16:32 *your own husband.* The Lord himself (see v. 8 and note). Elsewhere the prophets speak about the Lord as the husband of his people (see Jer 3:14; 31:32; Hos 2:16–17 and notes; cf. Ex 34:15 and note).
16:33 *you give gifts to all your lovers.* Jerusalem's perversity is here pictured as worse than adultery and ordinary prostitution (see also v. 34).
16:37 *strip you.* A reversal of the marriage covering (v. 8) and a return to the state described in v. 7.
16:38 *sentence you.* The punishment prescribed in the law was death (see Lev 20:10; Dt 22:22) by stoning (Dt 22:21–24; Jn 8:5–7). *jealous anger.* See v. 42; see also notes on Ex 20:5; Zec 1:14.
16:39 *your mounds ... your lofty shrines.* See vv. 24–25.
16:40 See 23:46–47.
16:43 *bring down on your head what you have done.* See note on Ob 15.
16:44 *Like mother, like daughter.* Referring to Jerusalem's continual and seemingly hereditary tendency toward evil (cf. vv. 3,45).
16:45 *Hittite ... Amorite.* See note on v. 3.
16:46 *Your older sister was Samaria.* Historically, Samaria was not founded as a royal city until after 880 B.C. (see note on 1Ki

and your younger sister, who lived to the
south of you with her daughters, was Sodom.[k] 47You not only walked in their ways
and copied their detestable practices, but
in all your ways you soon became more
depraved than they.[l] 48As surely as I live,
declares the Sovereign[m] LORD, your sister
Sodom[n] and her daughters never did what
you and your daughters have done.[o]
49" 'Now this was the sin of your sister
Sodom:[p] She and her daughters were arrogant,[q] overfed and unconcerned;[r] they did
not help the poor and needy.[s] 50They were
haughty[t] and did detestable things before
me. Therefore I did away with them as you
have seen.[u] 51Samaria did not commit half
the sins you did. You have done more detestable things than they, and have made
your sisters seem righteous by all these
things you have done.[v] 52Bear your disgrace, for you have furnished some justification for your sisters. Because your sins
were more vile than theirs, they appear
more righteous[w] than you. So then, be
ashamed and bear[x] your disgrace, for you
have made your sisters appear righteous.
53" 'However, I will restore[y] the fortunes
of Sodom and her daughters and of Samaria and her daughters, and your fortunes
along with them,[z] 54so that you may bear
your disgrace[a] and be ashamed of all you
have done in giving them comfort. 55And
your sisters, Sodom with her daughters
and Samaria with her daughters, will return to what they were before; and you
and your daughters will return to what
you were before.[b] 56You would not even
mention your sister Sodom in the day of
your pride, 57before your wickedness was
uncovered. Even so, you are now scorned[c]
by the daughters of Edom[a][d] and all her
neighbors and the daughters of the Philistines — all those around you who despise
you. 58You will bear the consequences of
your lewdness and your detestable practices, declares the LORD.[e]
59" 'This is what the Sovereign LORD
says: I will deal with you as you deserve,
because you have despised my oath by
breaking the covenant.[f] 60Yet I will remember the covenant[g] I made with you in the
days of your youth,[h] and I will establish
an everlasting covenant[i] with you. 61Then
you will remember your ways and be
ashamed[j] when you receive your sisters,
both those who are older than you and
those who are younger. I will give them to
you as daughters,[k] but not on the basis of
my covenant with you. 62So I will establish
my covenant[l] with you, and you will know
that I am the LORD.[m] 63Then, when I make
atonement[n] for you for all you have done,
you will remember and be ashamed[o] and
never again open your mouth[p] because of
your humiliation, declares the Sovereign
LORD.[q] ' "

Two Eagles and a Vine

17 The word of the LORD came to me:
2"Son of man, set forth an allegory
and tell the house of Israel a parable.[r] 3Say
to them, 'This is what the Sovereign LORD
says: A great eagle[s] with powerful wings,
long feathers and full plumage of varied
colors came to Lebanon.[t] Taking hold of
the top of a cedar, 4he broke off[u] its topmost shoot and carried it away to a land
of merchants, where he planted it in a city
of traders.

16:46 [k]Ge 13:10-13; S 18:20; Jer 3:8-11; Eze 23:4; Rev 11:8
16:47 [l]S Eze 5:7
16:48 [m]S Ge 15:2 [n]S Ge 19:25 [o]Mt 10:15; 11:23-24
16:49 [p]S Isa 1:10 [q]Ps 138:6; Eze 28:2 [r]Isa 22:13 [s]S Ge 13:13; 19:9; S Jer 5:28; Eze 18:7,12,16; Am 6:4-6; Lk 12:16-20; 16:19; Jas 5:5
16:50 [t]Ps 18:27 [u]Ge 18:20-21; S 19:5
16:51 [v]Jer 3:8-11; Eze 5:6-7; 23:11
16:52 [w]S Jer 3:11 [x]Eze 23:35
16:53 [y]S Dt 30:3; Isa 19:24-25; S Jer 48:47 [z]Eze 39:25
16:54 [a]S Jer 2:26
16:55 [b]Eze 36:11; Mal 3:4
16:57 [c]S Ps 137:3 [d]2Ki 16:6
16:58 [e]Eze 23:49
16:59 [f]S ver 8; Eze 17:19
16:60 [g]S Ge 6:18; S 9:15 [h]S Ps 25:7; S Jer 2:2 [i]S Ge 9:16; Eze 37:26
16:61 [j]ver 63; Eze 20:43; 43:10; 44:13 [k]S Isa 43:6
16:62 [l]S Dt 29:14 [m]S Jer 24:7; Eze 20:37,43-44; 34:25; 37:26; Hos 2:19-20 16:63 [n]Ps 65:3; 78:38; 79:9 [o]Eze 36:31-32 [p]Ro 3:19 [q]Ps 39:9; Da 9:7-8 17:2 [r]S Jdg 14:12; S Eze 20:49 17:3 [s]S Dt 28:49; Jer 49:22; Da 7:4; Hos 8:1 [t]S Jer 22:23 17:4 [u]S Isa 10:33

[a] 57 Many Hebrew manuscripts and Syriac; most Hebrew manuscripts, Septuagint and Vulgate *Aram*

16:24), so "older" in this allegory apparently alludes to the fact that Samaria ruled over a significantly larger kingdom than Jerusalem did. *daughters.* Suburbs or satellite cities.

16:47 *more depraved than they.* The Bible frequently compares a city or people to Sodom (see v. 46) as the epitome of evil and degradation (see Ge 13:10 and note; Dt 29:23; 32:32; Isa 1:9 – 10 and note; 3:9; Jer 23:14; La 4:6; Mt 10:15; 11:23 – 24; Jude 7).

16:49 *sin of your sister Sodom.* Here social injustice rather than sexual perversion (Ge 19) is highlighted.

16:51 – 52 *righteous.* Relatively innocent.

16:56 *day of your pride.* Referring to a time long before Ezekiel, when Jerusalem (as an Israelite city) was still relatively uncorrupted — as in the days of David and the early years of Solomon.

16:57 *scorned by the daughters of Edom.* The OT frequently condemns Edom for this (see 25:12 – 14; 35:5 and note; Isa 63:1; Introduction to Obadiah: Unity and Theme; Ob 10 – 14 and notes).

16:59 – 63 In God's concluding word concerning Jerusalem's future reformation and restoration, the city's role as representative of Israel in the allegory is foregrounded (see note on vv. 1 – 63) so that his words about remembering the covenant and establishing an everlasting covenant (see v. 60; cf. v. 62) parallel what is elsewhere said of Israel itself (see 37:26; Isa 55:3; Jer 32:40 and notes).

16:59 *covenant.* See v. 8 and note.

16:60 *I will remember the covenant.* Though Jerusalem did not (v. 43).

16:61 *will remember ... be ashamed.* See v. 63. Jerusalem (Israel) will remember — to her everlasting shame.

16:63 *when I make atonement for you.* God himself will do for faithless Jerusalem what she cannot do for herself (cf. Ro 3:23; 1Jn 2:2 and notes).

17:1 – 24 An allegory/parable symbolizing King Zedekiah's vacillating royal policy that led to his downfall. The allegory is presented in vv. 1 – 10; its explanation follows in vv. 11 – 21; and vv. 22 – 24 append a promise of better times to come, utilizing the imagery of the allegory.

17:3 *great eagle.* Nebuchadnezzar (see v. 12). *Lebanon.* Jerusalem (see v. 12). *cedar.* David's dynasty; his royal family.

17:4 *topmost shoot.* Jehoiachin. *land of merchants.* The country of Babylonia (see v. 12; 16:29 and note). *city of traders.* Babylon.

5“ ‘He took some of the seed of your
land and put it in fertile soil. He planted
it like a willow by abundant water,[v] 6and
it sprouted and became a low, spreading
vine. Its branches[w] turned toward him, but
its roots remained under it. So it became a
vine and produced branches and put out
leafy boughs.[x]
7“ ‘But there was another great eagle
with powerful wings and full plumage.
The vine now sent out its roots toward
him from the plot where it was planted
and stretched out its branches to him for
water.[y] 8It had been planted in good soil
by abundant water so that it would produce branches,[z] bear fruit and become a
splendid vine.’
9“Say to them, ‘This is what the Sovereign LORD says: Will it thrive? Will it not
be uprooted and stripped of its fruit so that
it withers? All its new growth will wither.
It will not take a strong arm or many people to pull it up by the roots.[a] 10Even if
it[b] is transplanted, will it thrive? Will it
not wither completely when the east wind
strikes it — wither away in the plot where
it grew?[c]’ ”
11Then the word of the LORD came to
me: 12“Say to this rebellious house, ‘Do
you not know what these things mean?[d]’
Say to them: ‘The king of Babylon went
to Jerusalem and carried off her king and
her nobles,[e] bringing them back with him
to Babylon.[f] 13Then he took a member of
the royal family and made a treaty[g] with
him, putting him under oath.[h] He also carried away the leading men[i] of the land,
14so that the kingdom would be brought
low,[j] unable to rise again, surviving only
by keeping his treaty. 15But the king rebelled[k] against him by sending his envoys
to Egypt[l] to get horses and a large army.[m]
Will he succeed? Will he who does such
things escape? Will he break the treaty
and yet escape?[n]

17:5 [v]Dt 8:7-9; Ps 1:3; Isa 44:4; Eze 31:5 **17:6** [w]S Isa 18:5 [x]S Job 5:3 **17:7** [y]Eze 31:4 **17:8** [z]Job 18:19; Mal 4:1 **17:9** [a]Jer 42:10; Am 2:9 **17:10** [b]S Job 1:19; Hos 12:1; 13:15 [c]S Eze 15:4 **17:12** [d]S Eze 12:9 [e]S 2Ki 24:15 [f]S Dt 21:10; S 2Ch 36:10; Eze 24:19 **17:13** [g]S Ex 23:32; S Jer 37:1 [h]2Ch 36:13 [i]Isa 3:2 **17:14** [j]Eze 29:14 **17:15** [k]Jer 52:3 [l]S Isa 30:2; S Jer 37:5 [m]S Dt 17:16 [n]S Ps 56:7; S Isa 30:5; Jer 34:3; 38:18; Eze 29:16 **17:16** [o]S Jer 52:11; Eze 12:13 [p]S 2Ki 24:17 **17:17** [q]Jer 37:7 [r]S Eze 4:2 [s]S Isa 36:6; Jer 37:5; Eze 29:6-7 **17:18** [t]S 2Ki 10:15; 1Ch 29:24 **17:19** [u]Jer 7:9; S Eze 16:59; 21:23; Hos 10:4 **17:20** [v]S Eze 12:13; 32:3 [w]S Jer 2:35 [x]S Eze 15:8 **17:21** [y]S Eze 12:14 [z]2Ki 25:11 [a]S Lev 26:33; S 2Ki 25:5; Zec 2:6 [b]S Jer 27:8

16“ ‘As surely as I live, declares the Sovereign LORD, he shall die[o] in Babylon,
in the land of the king who put him on
the throne, whose oath he despised and
whose treaty he broke.[p] 17Pharaoh[q] with
his mighty army and great horde will be
of no help to him in war, when ramps[r]
are built and siege works erected to destroy many lives.[s] 18He despised the oath
by breaking the covenant. Because he had
given his hand in pledge[t] and yet did all
these things, he shall not escape.
19“ ‘Therefore this is what the Sovereign LORD says: As surely as I live, I will
bring down on his head my oath that he
despised and my covenant that he broke.[u]
20I will spread my net[v] for him, and he will
be caught in my snare. I will bring him
to Babylon and execute judgment[w] upon
him there because he was unfaithful[x] to
me. 21All his fleeing troops will fall by the
sword,[y] and the survivors[z] will be scattered to the winds.[a] Then you will know
that I the LORD have spoken.[b]
22“ ‘This is what the Sovereign LORD says:
I myself will take a shoot[c] from the very
top of a cedar and plant it; I will break
off a tender sprig from its topmost shoots
and plant it on a high and lofty mountain.[d]
23On the mountain heights[e] of Israel I will
plant it; it will produce branches and bear
fruit[f] and become a splendid cedar. Birds
of every kind will nest in it; they will find
shelter in the shade of its branches.[g] 24All
the trees of the field[h] will know that I the
LORD bring down[i] the tall tree and make
the low tree grow tall. I dry up the green
tree and make the dry tree flourish.[j]
“ ‘I the LORD have spoken, and I will
do it.[k]’ ”

17:22 [c]S 2Ki 19:30; S Isa 4:2 [d]ver 23; Isa 2:2; S Jer 23:5; Eze 20:40; 36:1,36; 37:22; 40:2; 43:12 **17:23** [e]S ver 22; S Jer 31:12 [f]S Isa 27:6 [g]Ps 92:12; S Isa 2:2; Eze 31:6; Da 4:12; Hos 14:5-7; S Mt 13:32 **17:24** [h]S Ps 96:12; Isa 2:13 [i]S Ps 52:5 [j]S Nu 17:8; Da 5:21 [k]S 1Sa 2:7-8; Eze 19:12; 21:26; 22:14; 37:13; Am 9:11

17:5 *seed.* Zedekiah son of Josiah; he was the brother of Jehoahaz and Jehoiakim and uncle of Jehoiachin (see 2Ki 23–24). *planted it.* Made him king (2Ki 24:17).

17:6 *low, spreading vine.* No longer a tall cedar, because thousands of Judah's leading citizens had been deported (see 2Ki 24:15–16; see also Jer 52:28). But see note on 15:1–8.

17:7 *another great eagle.* An Egyptian pharaoh, either Psammetichus II (595–589 B.C.) or Hophra (589–570). Hophra, mentioned in Jer 44:30, is probably the pharaoh who offered help to Jerusalem in 586 (see Jer 37:5). If the fact that ch. 17 is located between ch. 8 (dated 592) and ch. 20 (dated 591) is chronologically meaningful, Psammetichus is meant. *sent out its roots toward him.* Zedekiah appealed to Egypt for military aid (v. 15), an act of rebellion against Nebuchadnezzar (see 2Ki 24:20).

17:10 *east wind.* The hot, dry wind known today as the khamsin, which withers vegetation (see 19:12). Here it stands for Nebuchadnezzar and his Babylonian forces.

17:12 *this rebellious house.* See 2:3 and note.

17:15 *Will he break the treaty and yet escape?* The point of the chapter (see vv. 16,18).

17:16 *he shall die in Babylon.* See 2Ki 25:7.

17:19 *my oath ... my covenant.* The king of Judah would have sworn faithfulness to the treaty in the name of the Lord. His oath would have taken some such form as "May the Lord slay me if I do not remain true to this treaty" (a self-maledictory oath; see notes on Ge 9:13; 15:17; 17:10). To swear such an oath and then violate it was to treat the Lord as if he were powerless.

17:22 *I myself.* A beautiful Messianic promise follows, using the previous imagery in a totally new and unexpected way. *shoot.* A member of David's family (cf. Isa 11:1; Zec 3:8; 6:12 and notes). *cedar.* See note on v. 3. *plant it.* Make him king (see v. 5). *high and lofty mountain.* Jerusalem (see Isa 2:2–4 and note).

17:23 *Birds ... will nest in it.* For similar imagery applied to a mighty king see Da 4:10–12,20–22; cf. Mk 4:32.

17:24 *trees of the field.* Kings and rulers of the world. *bring down the tall tree ... make the dry tree flourish.* See 1Sa 2:4–8 and notes; cf. Isa 2:12–18.

The Soul Who Sins Will Die

18 The word of the LORD came to me:
2"What do you people mean by quoting this proverb about the land of Israel:

" 'The fathers eat sour grapes,
and the children's teeth are set on
edge'?[l]

3"As surely as I live, declares the Sovereign LORD, you will no longer quote this
proverb[m] in Israel. 4For every living soul
belongs to me, the father as well as the
son—both alike belong to me. The soul
who sins[n] is the one who will die.[o]

5"Suppose there is a righteous man
who does what is just and right.
6He does not eat at the mountain[p]
shrines
or look to the idols[q] of the house of
Israel.
He does not defile his neighbor's wife
or lie with a woman during her
period.[r]
7He does not oppress[s] anyone,
but returns what he took in pledge[t]
for a loan.
He does not commit robbery[u]
but gives his food to the hungry[v]
and provides clothing for the
naked.[w]
8He does not lend at usury
or take excessive interest.[a][x]
He withholds his hand from doing
wrong
and judges fairly[y] between man and
man.
9He follows my decrees[z]
and faithfully keeps my laws.
That man is righteous;[a]
he will surely live,[b]
declares the Sovereign LORD.

10"Suppose he has a violent son, who
sheds blood[c] or does any of these other
things[b] 11(though the father has done none
of them):

"He eats at the mountain shrines.[d]
He defiles his neighbor's wife.
12He oppresses the poor[e] and needy.
He commits robbery.
He does not return what he took in
pledge.[f]
He looks to the idols.
He does detestable things.[g]
13He lends at usury and takes excessive
interest.[h]
Will such a man live? He will not! Because
he has done all these detestable things, he
will surely be put to death and his blood
will be on his own head.[i]

[a] 8 Or *take interest*; similarly in verses 13 and 17
[b] 10 Or *things to a brother*

18:2 [l]S Job 21:19; Isa 3:15; Jer 31:29 **18:3** [m]S Ps 49:4 **18:4** [n]S 2Ki 14:6; S Pr 13:21 [o]ver 20; S Ge 18:23; S Ex 17:14; S Job 21:20; Isa 42:5; Eze 33:8; S Ro 6:23 **18:6** [p]S Eze 6:2 [q]Dt 4:19; S Eze 6:13; 20:24; Am 5:26 [r]S Lev 12:2; S 15:24 **18:7** [s]Ex 22:21; Mal 3:5; Jas 5:4 [t]S Ex 22:26 [u]S Ex 20:15 [v]S Job 22:7 [w]Dt 15:11; S Eze 16:49; S Mt 25:36; Lk 3:11 **18:8** [x]S Ex 18:21; 22:25; S Lev 25:35-37; Dt 23:19-20 [y]S Jer 22:3; Zec 8:16 **18:9** [z]S Lev 19:37 [a]Hab 2:4 [b]S Lev 18:5; S Eze 11:12; 20:11; Am 5:4 **18:10** [c]Ex 21:12; Eze 22:6 **18:11** [d]Eze 22:9 **18:12** [e]S Ex 22:22; S Job 24:9; Am 4:1 [f]S Ex 22:27 [g]2Ki 21:11; Isa 59:6-7; S Jer 22:17; S Eze 16:49; Hab 2:6 **18:13** [h]Ex 22:25 [i]S Lev 20:9; Eze 33:4-5; Hos 12:14

18:1–32 A word to silence those who complained that they were being made to suffer for the sins of their ancestors rather than for their own sins. The fact that sin and guilt are not always purely individual but often have a communal and thus also a cumulative dimension is the pervasive testimony of the OT (see, e.g., Ex 20:5; Jdg 7:24; 1Ki 14:14–16 and notes; see also Ex 34:7; 1Ki 22:16–20; 23:26–27; 24:1–4; 2Ki 21:10–15; Isa 5:1–7; Jer 1:15–16; 5:1–17; 17:1–4; Am 2:4–16; 5:12). But when the Jerusalemites charged God with injustice as if they themselves were not guilty, that called for a sharp corrective word—they had not turned away from the sinful ways of their ancestors after the manner specified in vv. 14–17,27–28. This justification of God's way with Israel stands at the center of the series of prophecies found in 13:1—24:14 (see note on 13:1–23).

18:2 *this proverb.* Jer 31:29 indicates that the proverb arose first in Jerusalem. Jeremiah predicted the cessation of the proverb, and Ezekiel said its end had come. *about the land of Israel.* And about the fate of those who have suffered loss. *The fathers … on edge.* The proverb expresses self-pity and mocks the justice of God. *set on edge.* The Hebrew for this phrase perhaps means "blunted" or "worn" (cf. Ecc 10:10), but it may refer to the sensation in the mouth when eating something bitter or sour.

18:3 *As surely as I live.* See note on 5:11.

18:4 *The soul who sins is the one who will die.* Or "Only the soul …" Ezekiel spoke out against a false use the people were making of a doctrine of inherited guilt (perhaps based on a false understanding of Ex 20:5; 34:7). What follows is his description of three men, standing for three generations, who break the three/four-generation pattern. *soul.* "Life" or "person," not used here to distinguish spirit from body.

18:5 *righteous man.* The first generation that keeps the law. The following 15 commandments are partly ceremonial but are mostly moral injunctions. See the Ten Commandments in Ex 20 and Dt 5; cf. Ps 15:2–5; 24:3–6; Isa 33:15; cf. also notes on Ps 1:5; 119:121. *just and right.* Emphasized by Ezekiel in chs. 18 (see vv. 19,21,27) and 33 (see vv. 14,16,19; see also note on Ps 119:121).

18:6 *eat at the mountain shrines.* Eating meat sacrificed to idols on the high places (see 6:3; Hos 4:13). *look to.* Seek help from (see 23:27; 33:25; Ps 121:1). *idols.* See note on 6:4. *defile.* Adultery (condemned in Ex 20:14; Dt 22:22; Lev 18:20; 20:10) is here associated with a menstrual prohibition (see Lev 15:19–24; 18:19; 20:18), which is absent from the two listings that follow (cf. vv. 11,15).

18:7 *oppress.* The rich taking advantage of the poor. *returns what he took in pledge.* See Ex 22:26; Dt 24:12–13; Am 2:8. *robbery.* See the commandment against stealing in Ex 20:15; Dt 5:19. This is violent (armed) robbery rather than secret theft or burglary (see Lev 19:13). *food to the hungry.* See Dt 15:7–11; Mt 25:31–46.

18:8 *lend at usury.* See 22:12; see also Ex 22:21–27 and notes.

18:9 *That man is righteous; he will surely live.* After the checklist of commandments has been gone over, the verdict is rendered (cf. Ps 15:5; 24:5). *live.* See note on 16:6. This is life as more than mere existence; it includes communion with God (see Ps 63:3; 73:27–28).

18:10 *violent son.* Evil, second generation. About half (eight) of the previous commandments follow, but in a different order.

18:13 *his blood will be on his own head.* He is held responsible for his own sin (see Lev 20:9,11–12,16,27).

14 “But suppose this son has a son who
sees all the sins his father commits, and
though he sees them, he does not do such
things:[j]

15 “He does not eat at the mountain
shrines[k]
or look to the idols[l] of the house of
Israel.
He does not defile his neighbor’s wife.
16 He does not oppress anyone
or require a pledge for a loan.
He does not commit robbery
but gives his food to the hungry[m]
and provides clothing for the naked.[n]
17 He withholds his hand from sin[a]
and takes no usury or excessive
interest.
He keeps my laws[o] and follows my
decrees.

He will not die for his father’s sin; he will
surely live. 18 But his father will die for
his own sin, because he practiced extortion, robbed his brother and did what was
wrong among his people.

19 “Yet you ask, ‘Why does the son not
share the guilt of his father?’ Since the son
has done what is just and right and has
been careful to keep all my decrees, he
will surely live.[p] 20 The soul who sins is the
one who will die.[q] The son will not share
the guilt of the father, nor will the father
share the guilt of the son. The righteousness of the righteous man will be credited
to him, and the wickedness of the wicked
will be charged against him.[r]

21 “But if[s] a wicked man turns away from
all the sins he has committed and keeps
all my decrees[t] and does what is just and
right, he will surely live; he will not die.[u]
22 None of the offenses he has committed
will be remembered against him. Because
of the righteous things he has done, he
will live.[v] 23 Do I take any pleasure in the
death of the wicked? declares the Sovereign LORD. Rather, am I not pleased[w] when
they turn from their ways and live?[x]

24 “But if a righteous man turns[y] from his
righteousness and commits sin and does
the same detestable things the wicked
man does, will he live? None of the righteous things he has done will be remembered. Because of the unfaithfulness[z] he
is guilty of and because of the sins he has
committed, he will die.[a]

25 “Yet you say, ‘The way of the Lord is
not just.’[b] Hear, O house of Israel: Is my
way unjust?[c] Is it not your ways that are
unjust? 26 If a righteous man turns from his
righteousness and commits sin, he will die
for it; because of the sin he has committed
he will die. 27 But if a wicked man turns
away from the wickedness he has committed and does what is just and right, he will
save his life.[d] 28 Because he considers all
the offenses he has committed and turns
away from them, he will surely live; he
will not die.[e] 29 Yet the house of Israel says,
‘The way of the Lord is not just.’ Are my
ways unjust, O house of Israel? Is it not
your ways that are unjust?

30 “Therefore, O house of Israel, I will
judge you, each one according to his ways,
declares the Sovereign LORD. Repent![f] Turn
away from all your offenses; then sin will
not be your downfall.[g] 31 Rid[h] yourselves of
all the offenses you have committed, and
get a new heart[i] and a new spirit. Why[j] will
you die, O house of Israel?[k] 32 For I take no
pleasure in the death of anyone, declares
the Sovereign LORD. Repent[l] and live![m]

A Lament for Israel’s Princes

19 “Take up a lament[n] concerning the
princes[o] of Israel 2 and say:

[a] 17 Septuagint (see also verse 8); Hebrew *from the poor*

18:14 [j] 2Ch 34:21; S Pr 23:24 **18:15** [k] Eze 22:9 [l] S Ps 24:4 **18:16** [m] Isa 58:7 [n] S Ex 22:27; Ps 41:1; Isa 58:10; S Eze 16:49 **18:17** [o] S Ps 1:2 **18:19** [p] Ex 20:5; Dt 5:9; Jer 15:4; Zec 1:3-6 **18:20** [q] S Nu 15:31 [r] Dt 24:16; S 1Ki 8:32; 2Ki 14:6; Isa 3:11; S Eze 7:27; S 14:14; S Mt 16:27; Jn 9:2 **18:21** [s] Jer 18:8 [t] S Ge 26:5 [u] S Eze 13:22; 36:27 **18:22** [v] Ps 18:20-24; S Isa 43:25; Da 4:27; Mic 7:19 **18:23** [w] Ps 147:11 [x] S Job 37:23; S La 3:33; S Eze 16:6; Mic 7:18; S 1Ti 2:4 **18:24** [y] S Jer 34:16 [z] S Eze 15:8 [a] S 1Sa 15:11; 2Ch 24:17-20; S Job 35:8; Pr 21:16; S Eze 3:20; 20:27; 2Pe 2:20-22 **18:25** [b] Jer 2:29 [c] S Ge 18:25; Jer 12:1; Eze 33:17; Zep 3:5; Mal 2:17; 3:13-15 **18:27** [d] S Isa 1:18; S Eze 13:22 **18:28** [e] S Isa 55:7 **18:30** [f] S Isa 1:27; S Jer 35:15; Mt 3:2 [g] Eze 7:3; 24:14; 33:20; Hos 12:6; 1Pe 1:17 **18:31** [h] S Jdg 6:8 [i] Ps 51:10 [j] Jer 27:13 [k] S Isa 1:16-17; S Eze 11:19; 36:26 **18:32** [l] S Job 22:23; Isa 55:7; Mal 3:7 [m] S 2Ch 7:14; S Job 37:23; S Eze 16:6; 33:11 **19:1** [n] ver 14; Jer 7:29; 9:10, 20; Eze 26:17; 27:2, 32; 28:12; 32:2, 16; Am 5:1 [o] S 2Ki 24:6

18:14 *a son.* Righteous, third generation. Twelve commandments follow.

18:20 *righteousness ... credited to him.* See Ps 106:31 and note.

18:21 *But if a wicked man turns ... and keeps ... he will surely live.* Verses 1–20 indicate that the chain of inherited guilt can be broken, and vv. 21–29 teach that the power of guilt accumulated within a person’s life can be overcome.

18:23 *Do I take any pleasure in the death of the wicked?* In addition to the answer in this verse and in v. 32, see 33:11; Jnh 4:11 and notes (cf. 2Pe 3:9 and note).

18:24 *But if a righteous man turns.* See Heb 2:3; 2Pe 2:20–22 for warnings against those who knowingly and willfully turn from righteousness.

18:25 *Is my way unjust?* See 33:17; cf. Ge 18:25 and note; Dt 32:4; Jer 12:1 and note.

18:26 *If a righteous man.* Verses 26–29 repeat the argument developed in vv. 21–25.

18:30 *Therefore.* Concluding summary oracle. Compare the language of this conclusion with the closing words of the last (the 14th) oracle in this series (24:14). *each one.* While the house of Israel as a whole was guilty, God’s judgment would be just and individual. *Repent!* Second call to repentance (see 14:6 and note).

18:31 *get a new heart.* What had been promised unconditionally (11:19; 36:26) is here portrayed as attainable but not inevitable (cf. the same tension between Php 2:12 and 2:13).

18:32 *I take no pleasure.* Verse 23 is echoed in this final, grand summary, called by some the most important message in the whole book of Ezekiel (see note on 16:6).

19:1–14 A twofold dirge lamenting the fall of the royal family of Judah, one part employing the imagery of a lioness and her brood of whelps (vv. 1–9), the other utilizing the imagery of a once flourishing vine (vv. 10–14).

19:1 *lament.* A chant usually composed for funerals of fallen leaders (as in 2Sa 1:17–27), but often used sarcastically by the OT prophets to lament or to ironically predict the death of a nation (see Isa 14:4–21; Am 5:1–3 and note on 5:1). See also 2:10. *princes.* Kings.

19:2 An allegorical reference to the people of Israel or the nation of Judah.

"'What a lioness[p] was your mother
among the lions!
She lay down among the young lions
and reared her cubs.[q]
3 She brought up one of her cubs,
and he became a strong lion.
He learned to tear the prey
and he devoured men.
4 The nations heard about him,
and he was trapped in their pit.
They led him with hooks[r]
to the land of Egypt.[s]

5 "'When she saw her hope unfulfilled,
her expectation gone,
she took another of her cubs[t]
and made him a strong lion.[u]
6 He prowled among the lions,
for he was now a strong lion.
He learned to tear the prey
and he devoured men.[v]
7 He broke down[a] their strongholds
and devastated[w] their towns.
The land and all who were in it
were terrified by his roaring.
8 Then the nations[x] came against him,
those from regions round about.
They spread their net[y] for him,
and he was trapped in their pit.[z]
9 With hooks[a] they pulled him into a cage
and brought him to the king of Babylon.[b]
They put him in prison,
so his roar[c] was heard no longer
on the mountains of Israel.[d]

10 "'Your mother was like a vine in your vineyard[b][e]
planted by the water;[f]
it was fruitful and full of branches
because of abundant water.[g]
11 Its branches were strong,
fit for a ruler's scepter.
It towered high
above the thick foliage,
conspicuous for its height
and for its many branches.[h]
12 But it was uprooted[i] in fury
and thrown to the ground.
The east wind[j] made it shrivel,
it was stripped of its fruit;
its strong branches withered
and fire consumed them.[k]
13 Now it is planted in the desert,[l]
in a dry and thirsty land.[m]
14 Fire spread from one of its main[c] branches
and consumed[n] its fruit.
No strong branch is left on it
fit for a ruler's scepter.'[o]

This is a lament[p] and is to be used as a
lament."

Rebellious Israel

20 In the seventh year, in the fifth month
on the tenth day, some of the elders
of Israel came to inquire[q] of the LORD, and
they sat down in front of me.[r]
2 Then the word of the LORD came to me:
3 "Son of man, speak to the elders[s] of Israel
and say to them, 'This is what the Sovereign LORD says: Have you come to inquire[t]
of me? As surely as I live, I will not let
you inquire of me, declares the Sovereign
LORD.'[u]
4 "Will you judge them? Will you judge
them, son of man? Then confront them
with the detestable practices of their fathers[v] 5 and say to them: 'This is what the
Sovereign LORD says: On the day I chose[w]
Israel, I swore with uplifted hand[x] to the
descendants of the house of Jacob and re-

19:2 [p] S Nu 23:24 [q] S Ge 49:9 **19:4** [r] S Job 41:2 [s] 2Ki 23:33-34; 2Ch 36:4; S La 4:20 **19:5** [t] S Ge 49:9 [u] 2Ki 23:34 **19:6** [v] 2Ki 24:9; 2Ch 36:9 **19:7** [w] Eze 29:10; 30:12 **19:8** [x] 2Ki 24:2 [y] S Eze 12:13 [z] 2Ki 24:11; S La 4:20 **19:9** [a] S 2Ki 19:28 [b] S 2Ki 25:7; S 2Ch 36:6 [c] Zec 11:3 [d] S 2Ki 24:15 **19:10** [e] S Ge 49:22 [f] S Jer 17:8 [g] Ps 80:8-11 **19:11** [h] Eze 31:3; Da 4:11 **19:12** [i] S Dt 29:28 [j] S Ge 41:6 [k] S Isa 27:11; S Eze 17:24; 28:17; Hos 13:15 **19:13** [l] Eze 20:35; Hos 2:14 [m] Hos 2:3 **19:14** [n] Eze 20:47 [o] S Eze 15:4 [p] S ver 1 **20:1** [q] S Ge 25:22 [r] Eze 1:1-2; S 8:1; 21:1 **20:3** [s] S Eze 7:26 [t] S Ge 25:22; Eze 14:3 [u] S 1Sa 28:6; Isa 1:15; Am 8:12; Mic 3:7 **20:4** [v] S Eze 16:2; 22:2; Mt 23:32 **20:5** [w] S Dt 7:6 [x] S Ge 14:22; S Nu 14:30

[a] 7 Targum (see Septuagint); Hebrew *He knew* [b] 10 Two Hebrew manuscripts; most Hebrew manuscripts *your blood* [c] 14 Or *from under its*

19:3 *one of her cubs.* Jehoahaz (see 2Ki 23:31–34; Jer 22:10–12), who reigned only three months. *devoured men.* A reference to his oppressive policies.

19:5 *another of her cubs.* Perhaps Jehoiachin (who reigned only three months, 2Ki 24:8), but probably Zedekiah (of whom v. 7 appears a more likely description). Both were taken to Babylon (v. 9). If the reference is to Jehoiachin (2Ki 24:15), this was a true lament; if to Zedekiah, it was a prediction (2Ki 25:7).

19:10 *Your mother was like a vine.* The one previously pictured as a lioness (v. 2) is here a vine (for other uses of the vine imagery see 15:1–8; 17:7 and notes).

19:12 *east wind.* Nebuchadnezzar and his army (see note on 17:10).

19:13 *desert.* Babylonia—which to Israel seemed like a desert (see 20:35).

19:14 *Fire.* Rebellion (see 2Ki 24:20). *one of its main branches.* Zedekiah. *to be used as a lament.* Indicates repeated use (see Ps 137:1).

20:1–44 This word to be addressed to the elders of Israel came to Ezekiel on Aug. 14, 591 B.C., some 11 months after the preceding dated vision (see 8:1 and note on 8:1—11:25; see also chart, p. 1239). It begins with an overview of Israel's long history of apostasy (vv. 1–29), which leads into an announcement of the Lord's purpose to purge and renew his apostate people through the judgment now overtaking them (vv. 30–44).

20:1 *seventh year ... fifth month ... tenth day.* The third date (see previous note) supplied in the book of Ezekiel (see 1:2; 8:1). *elders of Israel.* See notes on 8:1; 14:1. *inquire.* See v. 3 and note on 14:3.

20:3 *As surely as I live.* See note on 5:11. *I will not let you inquire of me.* See v. 31; see also 3:26; 7:26 and notes.

20:4 *Will you judge them?... Then confront them.* As the one sent to pronounce God's judgment on Israel, Ezekiel is instructed to spell out the "detestable practices" for which that judgment comes on them (see also 22:2; 23:36).

20:5–26 These verses present Israel's history of apostasy in three acts (Act 1: vv. 5–9, Egypt; Act 2: vv. 10–17, Desert, Part 1; Act 3: vv. 18–26, Desert, Part 2). Each act has four scenes: (1) revelation, (2) rebellion, (3) wrath, (4) reconsideration. But see also note on v. 28.

20:5 *With uplifted hand.* A symbolic act accompanying the swearing of an oath (see vv. 15,23,42; Ge 14:22 and note; Ex 6:8). *I am the LORD your God.* See Ex 3:6,14–15 and notes.

vealed myself to them in Egypt. With uplifted hand I said to them, "I am the LORD
your God.[y]" 6On that day I swore[z] to them
that I would bring them out of Egypt into
a land I had searched out for them, a land
flowing with milk and honey,[a] the most
beautiful of all lands.[b] 7And I said to them,
"Each of you, get rid of the vile images[c]
you have set your eyes on, and do not defile yourselves with the idols[d] of Egypt. I
am the LORD your God.[e]"

8" 'But they rebelled against me and
would not listen to me;[f] they did not get
rid of the vile images they had set their
eyes on, nor did they forsake the idols
of Egypt.[g] So I said I would pour out
my wrath on them and spend my anger
against them in Egypt.[h] 9But for the sake
of my name I did what would keep it from
being profaned[i] in the eyes of the nations
they lived among and in whose sight I had
revealed myself to the Israelites by bringing them out of Egypt.[j] 10Therefore I led
them out of Egypt and brought them into
the desert.[k] 11I gave them my decrees and
made known to them my laws, for the man
who obeys them will live by them.[l] 12Also
I gave them my Sabbaths[m] as a sign[n] between us,[o] so they would know that I the
LORD made them holy.[p]

13" 'Yet the people of Israel rebelled[q]
against me in the desert. They did not follow my decrees but rejected my laws[r]—although the man who obeys them will live
by them—and they utterly desecrated my
Sabbaths.[s] So I said I would pour out my
wrath[t] on them and destroy[u] them in the
desert.[v] 14But for the sake of my name I did
what would keep it from being profaned[w]
in the eyes of the nations in whose sight
I had brought them out.[x] 15Also with uplifted hand I swore[y] to them in the desert
that I would not bring them into the land I
had given them—a land flowing with milk
and honey, most beautiful of all lands[z]—
16because they rejected my laws[a] and did
not follow my decrees and desecrated my
Sabbaths. For their hearts[b] were devoted
to their idols.[c] 17Yet I looked on them with
pity and did not destroy[d] them or put an
end to them in the desert. 18I said to their
children in the desert, "Do not follow the
statutes of your fathers[e] or keep their laws
or defile yourselves[f] with their idols. 19I
am the LORD your God;[g] follow my decrees
and be careful to keep my laws.[h] 20Keep
my Sabbaths[i] holy, that they may be a
sign[j] between us. Then you will know that
I am the LORD your God.[k]"

21" 'But the children rebelled against me:
They did not follow my decrees, they were
not careful to keep my laws[l]—although
the man who obeys them will live by
them—and they desecrated my Sabbaths.
So I said I would pour out my wrath on
them and spend my anger[m] against them
in the desert.[n] 22But I withheld[o] my hand,
and for the sake of my name[p] I did what
would keep it from being profaned in the
eyes of the nations in whose sight I had
brought them out. 23Also with uplifted
hand I swore to them in the desert that I
would disperse them among the nations
and scatter[q] them through the countries,
24because they had not obeyed my laws
but had rejected my decrees[r] and desecrated my Sabbaths,[s] and their eyes ⌊lusted⌋ after[t] their fathers' idols.[u] 25I also gave them
over[v] to statutes that were not good and

20:5 [y]S Lev 11:44 **20:6** [z]S Ex 6:8 [a]S Ex 3:8 [b]S Dt 8:7; Da 8:9; 11:41; Mal 3:12 **20:7** [c]Ex 20:4 [d]S Eze 6:9 [e]S Ex 20:2; Lev 18:3; Dt 29:18 **20:8** [f]S Jer 7:26 [g]S Jer 11:10; S Eze 7:8; S 16:26 [h]S Ex 32:7; Dt 9:7; S Isa 63:10 **20:9** [i]S Isa 48:11 [j]Eze 36:22; 39:7 **20:10** [k]S Ex 13:18; 19:1 **20:11** [l]Ex 20:1-23; Lev 18:5; Dt 4:7-8; S Eze 18:9; S Ro 10:5 **20:12** [m]S Ex 20:10 [n]S Ex 31:13 [o]Jer 17:22 [p]S Lev 20:8 **20:13** [q]Ps 78:40 [r]S Jer 6:19; 11:8 [s]ver 24 [t]S Dt 9:8 [u]S Ex 32:10 [v]Lev 26:15,43; S Nu 14:29; Ps 95:8-10; Isa 56:6 **20:14** [w]S Isa 48:11 [x]Eze 36:23 **20:15** [y]S Dt 1:34 [z]Nu 14:22-23; Ps 95:11; 106:26; Heb 3:11 **20:16** [a]Jer 11:8; Am 2:4 [b]S Nu 15:39 [c]ver 24; S Eze 6:4; Am 5:26 **20:17** [d]S Jer 4:27 **20:18** [e]S 2Ch 30:7; Zec 1:4 [f]S Ps 106:39 **20:19** [g]S Ex 20:2 [h]Dt 5:32-33; 6:1-2; S 8:1; 11:1; S 12:1 **20:20** [i]S Ex 20:10 [j]S Ex 31:13 [k]Jer 17:22 **20:21** [l]S Jer 7:26 [m]Nu 25:3 [n]S Eze 7:8 **20:22** [o]Ps 78:38 [p]S Isa 48:11 **20:23** [q]S Lev 26:33; S Ps 9:11 **20:24** [r]Am 2:4 [s]ver 13 [t]S Eze 6:9 [u]S ver 16; S Eze 2:3; S 18:6 **20:25** [v]S Ps 81:12; Ro 1:28

20:6 *land flowing with milk and honey.* See note on Ex 3:8. *most beautiful of all lands.* Cf. Dt 8:7–10; Jer 3:19 for the land's natural beauty. Its real beauty lay in being selected as God's dwelling place (Dt 12:5,11).
20:7 *idols.* See note on 6:4.
20:8 *But they rebelled.* See vv. 13,21; see also Jos 24:14. *So I said I would pour out my wrath on them.* An internal refrain (see vv. 13,21); see also note on 7:8. *spend my anger against.* See note on 5:13.
20:9 *for the sake of my name.* See vv. 14,22,44. Name and person are closely connected in the Bible. God's name is his identity and reputation—that by which he is known (see note on Ps 5:11). The phrase used here is equivalent to "for my own sake" (cf. Isa 37:35; 43:25). God's acts of deliverance—past and future—identify him, revealing his true nature (see 36:22; Ps 23:3 and notes; Isa 48:9). *profaned.* Made light of—as through ridicule (see Nu 14:15–16).
20:10 *desert.* Act 2 (see note on vv. 5–26).
20:11 *will live.* See vv. 13,21; contrast v. 25. See notes on 16:6; 18:9; see also Lev 18:5 and note.
20:12 *Sabbaths as a sign.* Israel's observance of the Sabbath was to serve as a sign that she was the Lord's holy people (see Ex 31:16–17 and note). Ezekiel highlights the Sabbath (see 22:8,26; 23:38; 44:24; 45:17; 46:3), as did Isaiah (see Isa 56:1–8 and notes) and Jeremiah (Jer 17:19–27; cf. Ne 13:17–18). Jewish legalism later corrupted the Sabbath law (see Mt 12:1–14).
20:13 *desecrated.* By not observing the Sabbath-rest (see Jer 17:21–23) or by not observing it in the manner and spirit God intended (see Am 8:5).
20:15 *land flowing with milk and honey.* See note on Ex 3:8.
20:18 *I said to their children.* Act 3 (see note on vv. 5–26). God began anew with the second generation in the desert (see Nu 14:26–35).
20:25 *I also gave them … laws they could not live by.* Just as God's judgments undo the creation order (see note on Ge 6:9—9:29) and undo human history (see note on Ge 11:1–9), so as an act of judgment he turns the laws he gave as the way to life (see vv. 12–13,21 and note on v. 11) into laws that produced death. This is a hard saying, but it most likely refers to God's requirement that Israel dedicate to him every firstborn male (Ex 13:2; 22:29)—which kings Ahaz and Manasseh, under the influence of the pagan religions of Israel's neighbors, radicalized into a law calling for actual sacrifice of the firstborn (v. 26; cf. Ro 1:24–32 and notes).

laws they could not live by;[w] 26I let them
become defiled through their gifts — the
sacrifice[x] of every firstborn[a] — that I might
fill them with horror so they would know
that I am the LORD.[y]'

27"Therefore, son of man, speak to the
people of Israel and say to them, 'This is
what the Sovereign LORD says: In this also
your fathers[z] blasphemed[a] me by forsaking
me:[b] 28When I brought them into the land[c]
I had sworn to give them and they saw
any high hill or any leafy tree, there they
offered their sacrifices, made offerings that
provoked me to anger, presented their fragrant incense and poured out their drink
offerings.[d] 29Then I said to them: What is
this high place[e] you go to?'" (It is called
Bamah[b] to this day.)

Judgment and Restoration

30"Therefore say to the house of Israel: 'This is what the Sovereign LORD says:
Will you defile yourselves[f] the way your
fathers did and lust after their vile images?[g] 31When you offer your gifts — the
sacrifice of your sons[h] in[c] the fire — you
continue to defile yourselves with all your
idols to this day. Am I to let you inquire of
me, O house of Israel? As surely as I live,
declares the Sovereign LORD, I will not let
you inquire of me.[i]

32"'You say, "We want to be like the nations, like the peoples of the world, who
serve wood and stone." But what you
have in mind will never happen. 33As surely as I live, declares the Sovereign LORD, I
will rule over you with a mighty hand and
an outstretched arm[j] and with outpoured
wrath.[k] 34I will bring you from the nations[l]
and gather[m] you from the countries where
you have been scattered — with a mighty
hand[n] and an outstretched arm and with
outpoured wrath.[o] 35I will bring you into
the desert[p] of the nations and there, face
to face, I will execute judgment[q] upon
you. 36As I judged your fathers in the desert of the land of Egypt, so I will judge
you, declares the Sovereign LORD.[r] 37I will
take note of you as you pass under my
rod,[s] and I will bring you into the bond of
the covenant.[t] 38I will purge[u] you of those
who revolt and rebel against me. Although
I will bring them out of the land where
they are living, yet they will not enter the
land of Israel. Then you will know that I
am the LORD.[v]

39"'As for you, O house of Israel, this
is what the Sovereign LORD says: Go and
serve your idols,[w] every one of you! But
afterward you will surely listen to me and
no longer profane my holy name[x] with
your gifts and idols.[y] 40For on my holy
mountain, the high mountain of Israel,[z]
declares the Sovereign LORD, there in the
land the entire house of Israel will serve
me, and there I will accept them. There
I will require your offerings[a] and your
choice gifts,[d] along with all your holy
sacrifices.[b] 41I will accept you as fragrant
incense[c] when I bring you out from the
nations and gather[d] you from the countries where you have been scattered, and I
will show myself holy[e] among you in the
sight of the nations.[f] 42Then you will know
that I am the LORD,[g] when I bring you into
the land of Israel,[h] the land I had sworn
with uplifted hand to give to your fathers.[i]

[a] 26 Or *—making every firstborn pass through ⌞the fire⌟* [b] 29 *Bamah* means *high place.* [c] 31 Or *—making your sons pass through* [d] 40 Or *and the gifts of your firstfruits*

20:25 [w] Isa 66:4; 2Th 2:11 **20:26** [x] S Lev 18:21 [y] Lev 20:2-5; 2Ki 17:17 **20:27** [z] S Ps 78:57 [a] S Nu 15:30; Ro 2:24 [b] S Eze 18:24 **20:28** [c] Ne 9:23; Ps 78:55,58 [d] S Jer 2:7; S 3:6; S 19:13; S Eze 6:13 **20:29** [e] Eze 16:16; 43:7 **20:30** [f] ver 43 [g] S Jdg 2:16-19; S Jer 16:12 **20:31** [h] S Eze 16:20 [i] Ps 106:37-39; S Jer 7:31; S Eze 14:3; Am 8:12; Zec 7:13 **20:33** [j] S Eze 16:27 [k] Jer 21:5; Eze 25:16 **20:34** [l] 2Co 6:17* [m] S Dt 30:4; S Ps 106:47 [n] S Isa 31:3 [o] Isa 27:12-13; S Jer 44:6; S La 2:4; S Eze 6:14 **20:35** [p] S Eze 19:13 [q] S 1Sa 12:7; S Job 22:4; S Jer 2:35 **20:36** [r] Nu 11:1-35; 14:28-30; 1Co 10:5-10 **20:37** [s] S Lev 27:32 [t] S Eze 16:62 **20:38** [u] Eze 34:17-22; Am 9:9-10 [v] Ps 95:11; Jer 44:14; S Eze 13:9; 23:49; Hos 2:14; Zec 13:8-9; Mal 3:3; 4:1-3; Heb 4:3 **20:39** [w] S Jer 44:25 [x] S Ex 20:7; S Eze 13:19 [y] Eze 43:7; Am 4:4 **20:40** [z] S Eze 17:22; 34:14 [a] S Isa 60:7 [b] S Isa 56:7; Mal 3:4 **20:41** [c] S 2Co 2:14 [d] S Dt 30:4 [e] Eze 28:25; 36:23 [f] S Isa 5:16; S Eze 11:17; 2Co 6:17 **20:42** [g] Eze 38:23 [h] S Jer 23:8; Eze 34:13; 36:24 [i] Jer 30:3; Eze 34:27; 37:21

20:26 *sacrifice of every firstborn.* See v. 31 and note on 16:20. *so they would know that I am the LORD.* God will go to any lengths to get his people to acknowledge him (see note on 6:7).

20:28 *When I brought them into the land.* Apparently Act 4 in Ezekiel's history (see note on vv. 5–26), but it is not carried through with the same schematic consistency.

20:30–44 See note on vv. 1–44.

20:30 *Will you defile yourselves the way your fathers did ...?* See note on vv. 5–26.

20:31 *inquire.* See v. 3 and note.

20:32 *like the nations.* The temptation to lose its uniqueness was always present for Israel (see 1Sa 8:5 and note). *will never happen.* As happened to those who were exiled to Egypt (see Jer 44:15–19). God will not abandon them to their idolatrous ways but will firmly turn them back to the way of covenant faithfulness to him.

20:33 *mighty hand ... outstretched arm.* Terminology of the exodus (cf. Dt 4:34; 5:15; 7:19; 11:2; 26:8).

20:35 *desert of the nations.* Exile among the nations would be for Israel like a return to the desert through which she journeyed on the way to the promised land (see Hos 2:14 and note).

20:37 *pass under my rod.* The way a shepherd counts or separates his flock (see Lev 27:32; Jer 33:13; cf. Mt 25:32–33). *I will bring you into the bond of the covenant.* As he had in the Sinai Desert (see note on 16:59–63).

20:38 *purge.* As in the first desert experience, many were not allowed to enter the land (see Nu 14:26–35 and notes).

20:39 *Go and serve your idols.* Irony, as in Am 4:4. *profane my holy name.* See Lev 18:21 and note.

20:40 *my holy mountain.* Mentioned only here in Ezekiel, it refers to Jerusalem or Zion (see Ps 2:6; Isa 2:2–4 and notes; 65; Ob 16; Zep 3:11). *entire house of Israel.* Includes a remnant of the northern kingdom, which fell in 722–721 B.C. (see 11:15; 36:10 and note). *offerings.* Possibly refers to a prescribed contribution. The other 19 occurrences in Ezekiel of the Hebrew for this word are confined to chs. 44–48, where the reference is to the land set aside for the temple and priests (see 45:1; 48:8–10, "portion[s]") or to the special gifts for the priests (see 44:30). *choice gifts.* Voluntary contributions (but see NIV text note).

20:41 *as fragrant incense.* In a metaphorical sense (as in Eph 5:2). *bring you out.* Cf. v. 34. *show myself holy.* See Lev 10:3 and note.

43There you will remember your conduct[j]
and all the actions by which you have defiled yourselves, and you will loathe yourselves[k] for all the evil you have done.[l]
44You will know that I am the LORD, when
I deal with you for my name's sake[m] and
not according to your evil ways and your
corrupt practices, O house of Israel, declares the Sovereign LORD.[n]' "

Prophecy Against the South

45The word of the LORD came to me:
46"Son of man, set your face toward[o]
the south; preach against the south and
prophesy against[p] the forest of the southland.[q] 47Say to the southern forest:[r] 'Hear
the word of the LORD. This is what the Sovereign LORD says: I am about to set fire to
you, and it will consume[s] all your trees,
both green and dry. The blazing flame
will not be quenched, and every face from
south to north[t] will be scorched by it.[u]
48Everyone will see that I the LORD have
kindled it; it will not be quenched.[v]' "
49Then I said, "Ah, Sovereign LORD![w]
They are saying of me, 'Isn't he just telling
parables?[x]' "

Babylon, God's Sword of Judgment

21 The word of the LORD came to me:[y]
2"Son of man, set your face against[z]
Jerusalem and preach against the sanctuary.[a] Prophesy against[b] the land of Israel
3and say to her: 'This is what the LORD
says: I am against you.[c] I will draw my
sword[d] from its scabbard and cut off from
you both the righteous and the wicked.[e]
4Because I am going to cut off the righteous and the wicked, my sword[f] will be
unsheathed against everyone from south
to north.[g] 5Then all people will know that
I the LORD have drawn my sword[h] from its
scabbard; it will not return[i] again.'[j]
6"Therefore groan, son of man! Groan
before them with broken heart and bitter
grief.[k] 7And when they ask you, 'Why are
you groaning?[l]' you shall say, 'Because of
the news that is coming. Every heart will
melt[m] and every hand go limp;[n] every spirit
will become faint[o] and every knee become
as weak as water.'[p] It is coming! It will surely take place, declares the Sovereign LORD."
8The word of the LORD came to me:
9"Son of man, prophesy and say, 'This is
what the Lord says:

" 'A sword, a sword,
sharpened and polished—
10sharpened for the slaughter,[q]
polished to flash like lightning!

" 'Shall we rejoice in the scepter of my
son ⌞Judah⌟? The sword despises every
such stick.[r]

11" 'The sword is appointed to be
polished,[s]
to be grasped with the hand;
it is sharpened and polished,
made ready for the hand of the slayer.
12Cry out and wail, son of man,
for it is against my people;
it is against all the princes of Israel.

20:43 [j]Eze 14:22 [k]S Lev 26:41 [l]S Eze 6:9; S 16:61; Hos 5:15 **20:44** [m]Ps 109:21; Isa 43:25; Eze 36:22 [n]S Eze 16:62; 36:32 **20:46** [o]S Eze 4:3; S 13:17 [p]Eze 21:2; Am 7:16 [q]Isa 30:6; Jer 13:19 **20:47** [r]S 2Ki 19:23 [s]Eze 19:14 [t]Eze 21:4 [u]Isa 9:18-19; S 13:8 **20:48** [v]S Jer 7:20; Eze 21:5,32; 23:25 **20:49** [w]S Eze 4:14 [x]S Jdg 14:12; S Ps 78:2; S Eze 12:9; Mt 13:13; S Jn 16:25 **21:1** [y]S Eze 20:1 **21:2** [z]S Eze 13:17 [a]Eze 9:6 [b]Jer 26:11-12; S Eze 20:46 **21:3** [c]S Jer 21:13 [d]S Isa 27:1; S Eze 14:21 [e]ver 9-11; S Job 9:22; S Isa 57:1; Jer 47:6-7 **21:4** [f]S Lev 26:25; S Jer 25:27 [g]Eze 20:47 **21:5** [h]S Isa 34:5 [i]ver 30 [j]S Eze 20:47-48; Na 1:9 **21:6** [k]ver 12; S Isa 22:4; Jer 30:6; S Eze 9:4 **21:7** [l]S Job 23:2 [m]S Jos 7:5 [n]S Jer 47:3; Eze 22:14 [o]S Ps 6:2 [p]S Lev 26:36; S Job 11:16 **21:10** [q]Ps 110:5-6; Isa 34:5-6 [r]Dt 32:41 **21:11** [s]Jer 46:4

20:43 *you will remember ... and ... loathe yourselves.* A thorough repentance (see 6:9 and note; 16:63; 36:31; Lk 15:17–19).
20:44 *for my name's sake.* Summarizes and concludes the prophecy (see note on v. 9).
20:45—21:32 Babylon will be God's sword to bring a ruinous destruction as total as that of a forest fire—primarily on Judah and Jerusalem (20:45—21:27), but also on the Ammonites (21:28–29)—and then Babylon, too, will feel God's wrath (21:30–32).
20:46 *set your face.* A posture required eight times of Ezekiel (here; 13:17; 21:2; 25:2; 28:21; 29:2; 35:2; 38:2). *toward the south.* Toward Judah and Jerusalem. Any Babylonian invasion would traverse Israel from north to south (see 26:7 and note).
20:47 *set fire.* Common figurative language for God's devastating judgments (see Isa 10:16–19), which often took the form of invasion by a world power (see Am 1:4 and note). *both green and dry.* All trees (cf. 17:24; Lk 23:31). *from south to north.* Expresses totality, not direction; equivalent to saying, "from the border on the right to that on the left."
20:49 *parables.* See note on 17:1–24; for other ridiculing of the prophet see 12:21–28; 33:32.
21:2 *set your face.* See note on 20:46. *against the sanctuary.* See 9:6 and note.
21:3–5 *my sword ... my sword ... my sword.* See 5:2 and note.
21:3 *I am against you.* See note on 5:8. *my sword.* This is the first of five sword prophecies (see vv. 8–17,18–24,25–27, 28–32). Here the sword refers to Babylonia and Nebuchadnezzar (v. 19). *both the righteous and the wicked.* Indicates the completeness of the judgment that is about to come on Israel. No one will escape its devastating effects, not even the righteous in the land. Contrast God's deliverance of Noah (Ge 6:7–8) and Lot (Ge 18:23; 19:12–13).
21:4 *from south to north.* See note on 20:47.
21:6 *groan ... with broken heart and bitter grief.* Ezekiel's display of intense grief is to serve as another prophetic sign and as an occasion for a new message of impending judgment. This is Ezekiel's seventh symbolic act (see Introduction: Literary Features).
21:7 *every knee become as weak as water.* See 7:17 and note.
21:9 *A sword, a sword.* A sword song (see vv. 3–5 and note), possibly accompanied by dancing or symbolic actions. Such songs may have been sung by warriors about to go into battle (see note on 2Sa 1:18).
21:10 *Shall we rejoice ... every such stick.* To think that the Babylonians would conquer every other country except Judah was a false hope. *scepter.* Represents rule, government or kingdom (see Nu 24:17 and note). *my son ⌞Judah⌟.* Corresponds to "my people" in v. 12 (see Ge 49:9). Perhaps a better rendering would be "my royal son," referring to the reigning king of the house of David (see Ps 2:7 and note). *sword.* Babylonia and Nebuchadnezzar (v. 19).
21:11 *slayer.* Nebuchadnezzar (v. 19).
21:12 *Cry out and wail ... beat your breast.* Eighth symbolic act (see Introduction: Literary Features).

They are thrown to the sword
along with my people.
Therefore beat your breast.[t]

13 "'Testing will surely come. And what
if the scepter ˛of Judah˛, which the sword
despises, does not continue? declares the
Sovereign LORD.'

14 "So then, son of man, prophesy
and strike your hands[u] together.
Let the sword strike twice,
even three times.
It is a sword for slaughter—
a sword for great slaughter,
closing in on them from every side.[v]
15 So that hearts may melt[w]
and the fallen be many,
I have stationed the sword for
slaughter[a]
at all their gates.
Oh! It is made to flash like lightning,
it is grasped for slaughter.[x]
16 O sword, slash to the right,
then to the left,
wherever your blade is turned.
17 I too will strike my hands[y] together,
and my wrath[z] will subside.
I the LORD have spoken.[a]"

18 The word of the LORD came to me:
19 "Son of man, mark out two roads for
the sword[b] of the king of Babylon to take,
both starting from the same country. Make
a signpost[c] where the road branches off
to the city. 20 Mark out one road for the
sword to come against Rabbah of the Ammonites[d] and another against Judah and
fortified Jerusalem. 21 For the king of Babylon will stop at the fork in the road, at
the junction of the two roads, to seek an
omen: He will cast lots[e] with arrows, he
will consult his idols,[f] he will examine the
liver.[g] 22 Into his right hand will come the
lot for Jerusalem, where he is to set up
battering rams, to give the command to
slaughter, to sound the battle cry,[h] to set
battering rams against the gates, to build
a ramp[i] and to erect siege works.[j] 23 It will
seem like a false omen to those who have
sworn allegiance to him, but he will remind[k] them of their guilt[l] and take them
captive.

24 "Therefore this is what the Sovereign LORD says: 'Because you people have
brought to mind your guilt by your open
rebellion, revealing your sins in all that
you do—because you have done this, you
will be taken captive.

25 "'O profane and wicked prince of Israel, whose day has come,[m] whose time
of punishment has reached its climax,[n]
26 this is what the Sovereign LORD says:
Take off the turban, remove the crown.[o]
It will not be as it was: The lowly will be
exalted and the exalted will be brought
low.[p] 27 A ruin! A ruin! I will make it a
ruin! It will not be restored until he
comes to whom it rightfully belongs;[q] to
him I will give it.'[r]

28 "And you, son of man, prophesy and
say, 'This is what the Sovereign LORD says
about the Ammonites[s] and their insults:

"'A sword,[t] a sword,
drawn for the slaughter,
polished to consume
and to flash like lightning!

[a] *15* Septuagint; the meaning of the Hebrew for this word is uncertain.

21:12 [t] Jer 31:19 **21:14** [u] ver 17; S Nu 24:10 [v] S Eze 6:11; 30:24 **21:15** [w] S 2Sa 17:10 [x] Ps 22:14 **21:17** [y] ver 14; Eze 22:13 [z] S Eze 5:13 [a] S Eze 6:11; S 16:42 **21:19** [b] S Eze 14:21; 32:11 [c] Jer 31:21 **21:20** [d] S Dt 3:11 **21:21** [e] S Pr 16:33 [f] Zec 10:2 [g] Nu 22:7; S 23:23 **21:22** [h] S Jer 4:16 [i] Jer 32:24 [j] S 2Ki 25:1; S Eze 4:2; 26:9 **21:23** [k] S Nu 5:15 [l] S Eze 17:19 **21:25** [m] Eze 22:4 [n] Eze 35:5 **21:26** [o] S Isa 28:5; S Jer 13:18 [p] S Ps 75:7; Isa 40:4; S Eze 17:24; S Mt 23:12 **21:27** [q] Ge 49:10 [r] Ps 2:6; Jer 23:5-6; Eze 37:24; Hag 2:21-22 **21:28** [s] S Ge 19:38; Zep 2:8 [t] S Jer 12:12

21:13 *come.* On Judah. *what if the scepter ... does not continue?* See note on v. 10. The question anticipates the final interruption of Davidic kingship, which came in 586 B.C. (see vv. 25–27).
21:14 *strike your hands.* See 6:11 and note. *Let the sword strike twice.* Cf. 2Ki 13:18–19.
21:17 *strike my hands.* As Ezekiel was commanded to do in v. 14.
21:19 *king of Babylon.* Nebuchadnezzar. *same country.* Babylonia, or possibly Aram (Syria)—Nebuchadnezzar headquartered at Riblah in northern Aram (see 2Ki 25:6).
21:20 *Rabbah.* Capital of Ammon (Jer 49:2); modern Amman (capital of Jordan).
21:21 *cast lots with arrows.* Divination with arrows, for the purpose of seeking good omens for the coming campaign—a practice not elsewhere mentioned in the Bible. Apparently arrows were labeled (e.g., "Rabbah," "Jerusalem"), placed into a quiver and drawn out, one with each hand. Right-hand selection was seen as a good omen (see v. 22). *idols.* The Hebrew for this word is translated "household gods" in Ge 31:19 (see note there). Consulting them is referred to in Hos 3:4; Zec 10:2. The household gods of Ge 31:19–35 were small enough to hide in a saddle, but others were life-size (1Sa 19:13–16). *examine the liver.* Looking at the color and configurations of sheep livers to foretell the future was common in ancient Babylonia and Rome, but the practice is not mentioned elsewhere in the Bible.
21:23 *false omen.* The leaders of Jerusalem, once submissive to Nebuchadnezzar but now in rebellion (2Ki 24:20), hoped that the result of the omen-seeking (vv. 21–22) was misleading.
21:25,29 *whose day ... has reached its climax.* The same fate awaits Judah's king that awaits the Ammonites.
21:25 *prince of Israel.* Zedekiah (see note on 7:27).
21:26 *turban.* Only here is it mentioned as royal headwear. Elsewhere it is worn by priests (Ex 28:4,37,39; 29:6; 39:28,31; Lev 8:9; 16:4), as a setting for the crown (Ex 28:36–37; 29:6; 39:31; Lev 8:9). It was made of fine linen (Ex 28:39; 39:28). *lowly ... exalted ... exalted ... brought low.* A common Biblical expression for the reversal of human conditions because of the intervention of the Lord (see 17:24 and note; 1Sa 2:7–8; Lk 1:52–53).
21:27 *A ruin! A ruin! ... a ruin!* Threefold repetition for emphasis (see Isa 6:3; Jer 7:4). *It.* The crown (v. 26), representing dominion (the kingdom of Judah). *until he comes to whom it rightfully belongs.* The Messiah; probably an allusion to Ge 49:10 (see note there).
21:28 *Ammonites.* See v. 20. After judgment on Jerusalem, they too will be dealt with (see 25:1–7; see also Jer 9:26; 49:1–6; Am 1:13–15; Zep 2:8–11). *their insults.* See 25:3,6; cf. also 36:15. *A sword, a sword.* Nebuchadnezzar's (see vv. 9,19 and notes).

29 Despite false visions concerning you
and lying divinations[u] about you,
it will be laid on the necks
of the wicked who are to be slain,
whose day has come,
whose time of punishment has
reached its climax.[v]
30 Return the sword to its scabbard.[w]
In the place where you were created,
in the land of your ancestry,[x]
I will judge you.
31 I will pour out my wrath upon you
and breathe[y] out my fiery anger[z]
against you;
I will hand you over to brutal men,
men skilled in destruction.[a]
32 You will be fuel for the fire,[b]
your blood will be shed in your land,
you will be remembered[c] no more;
for I the LORD have spoken.' "

Jerusalem's Sins

22 The word of the LORD came to me:
2 "Son of man, will you judge her?
Will you judge this city of bloodshed?[d]
Then confront her with all her detestable
practices[e] 3 and say: 'This is what the Sovereign LORD says: O city that brings on herself doom by shedding blood[f] in her midst
and defiles herself by making idols, 4 you
have become guilty because of the blood
you have shed[g] and have become defiled
by the idols you have made. You have
brought your days to a close, and the end
of your years has come.[h] Therefore I will
make you an object of scorn[i] to the nations and a laughingstock to all the countries.[j] 5 Those who are near and those who
are far away will mock you, O infamous
city, full of turmoil.[k]
6 " 'See how each of the princes of Israel who are in you uses his power to shed
blood.[l] 7 In you they have treated father
and mother with contempt;[m] in you they
have oppressed the alien[n] and mistreated
the fatherless and the widow.[o] 8 You have
despised my holy things and desecrated
my Sabbaths.[p] 9 In you are slanderous men[q]
bent on shedding blood;[r] in you are those
who eat at the mountain shrines[s] and commit lewd acts.[t] 10 In you are those who dishonor their fathers' bed;[u] in you are those
who violate women during their period,[v]
when they are ceremonially unclean.[w] 11 In
you one man commits a detestable offense
with his neighbor's wife,[x] another shamefully defiles his daughter-in-law,[y] and another violates his sister,[z] his own father's
daughter.[a] 12 In you men accept bribes[b] to
shed blood; you take usury[c] and excessive
interest[a] and make unjust gain from your
neighbors[d] by extortion. And you have forgotten[e] me, declares the Sovereign LORD.[f]
13 " 'I will surely strike my hands[g] together at the unjust gain[h] you have made and
at the blood[i] you have shed in your midst.[j]
14 Will your courage endure[k] or your hands[l]
be strong in the day I deal with you? I the
LORD have spoken,[m] and I will do it.[n] 15 I
will disperse you among the nations and
scatter[o] you through the countries; and
I will put an end to[p] your uncleanness.[q]
16 When you have been defiled[b] in the eyes
of the nations, you will know that I am
the LORD.' "
17 Then the word of the LORD came to
me: 18 "Son of man, the house of Israel

[a] 12 Or *usury and interest* [b] 16 Or *When I have allotted you your inheritance*

21:29 [u] Jer 27:9 [v] ver 25; Eze 22:28; 35:5 **21:30** [w] ver 5; Jer 47:6 [x] S Eze 16:3 **21:31** [y] Ps 18:15; S Isa 11:4 [z] Ps 79:6; Eze 22:20-21 [a] S Jer 4:7; 51:20-23; S Eze 16:39 **21:32** [b] S Eze 20:47-48; Mal 4:1 [c] Eze 25:10 **22:2** [d] Eze 24:6,9; Hos 4:2; Na 3:1; Hab 2:12 [e] S Eze 16:2; 23:36 **22:3** [f] ver 6,13,27; Eze 23:37,45; 24:6 **22:4** [g] S 2Ki 21:16 [h] Eze 21:25 [i] S Ps 137:3 [j] Ps 44:13-14; S Eze 5:14 **22:5** [k] S Isa 22:2 **22:6** [l] S Eze 11:6; 18:10; 33:25 **22:7** [m] S Dt 5:16; Mic 7:6 [n] S Ex 23:9 [o] S Ex 22:21-22 **22:8** [p] S Ex 20:8; Eze 23:38-39 **22:9** [q] S Lev 19:16 [r] Isa 59:3; S Eze 11:6; Hos 4:2; 6:9 [s] Eze 18:11 [t] Eze 23:29; Hos 4:10,14 **22:10** [u] Lev 18:7 [v] S Lev 12:2 [w] S Lev 18:8,19 **22:11** [x] S Jer 5:8 [y] S Ge 11:31; Lev 18:15 [z] S Lev 18:9; S 2Sa 13:14 [a] Eze 18:6 **22:12** [b] S Ex 18:21; Dt 27:25; Ps 26:10; Isa 5:23; Am 5:12; Mic 7:3 [c] S Eze 18:8 [d] Lev 19:13 [e] Ps 106:21; S Isa 17:10; S 57:11 [f] S Eze 11:6 **22:13** [g] S Nu 24:10; S Eze 21:17 [h] S ver 27; S Isa 33:15 [i] S ver 3 [j] S Eze 6:11 **22:14** [k] Ps 76:7; Joel 2:11; Na 1:6; Mal 3:2 [l] S Eze 7:17 [m] Eze 24:14 [n] S Eze 17:24 **22:15** [o] S Lev 26:33; Dt 4:27; Zec 7:14 [p] S Eze 16:41 [q] Eze 24:11

21:29 *false visions ... lying divinations.* Apparently Ammon also had false prophets of peace (see v. 10 and note; 13:10; Jer 6:14; 8:11–12). *it.* The sword.

21:30–32 When the Lord has accomplished his purpose through the Babylonians, they too will come under his judgment for all their evil ways (see Jer 50:15,27,29,31; 51:6,49; Hab 2:4–20; cf. Isa 10:5–19 and note on 10:12).

21:30 *Return the sword.* Addressing Nebuchadnezzar.

21:31 *brutal men.* The people of the East, as in 25:4.

21:32 *fuel for the fire.* See 20:47 and note.

22:1–31 Ezekiel is instructed to confront Jerusalem (vv. 1–12) and the land of Judah (vv. 23–29) with all the sins of which they are guilty and for which they were about to feel the fiery wrath of Yahweh (vv. 13–22,30–31). Under Manasseh, Amon and Jehoiakim, Jerusalem had become a city of idolatry and pervasive moral corruption (see 2Ki 21:2–26; Jer 22:13–17). In the land of Judah all who held power cruelly exploited the weak.

22:2 *will you judge her?* Cf. 20:4 and note. *this city.* Jerusalem, the usual focal point of Ezekiel's prophecy (see 5:5 and note).

22:3 *shedding blood ... making idols.* Two categories of sins are developed: social injustices and idol worship. *idols.* See note on 6:4.

22:6 *princes of Israel.* Leaders generally, not kings; contrast 21:12 with 19:1.

22:7 *treated father and mother with contempt.* See Mic 7:6 and note. Both passages are the opposite of what God commands in Ex 20:12 (see note there). *alien ... fatherless ... widow.* See Ex 22:21–27 and notes; Dt 10:18; 16:11,14; 24:17; 27:19; Ps 68:5–6 and note; 82:3; Isa 1:17 and note; 23; Jer 7:6; 22:3; Jas 1:27.

22:8 *Sabbaths.* A major concern in Ezekiel (see note on 20:12).

22:9 *eat at the mountain shrines.* See 18:6 and note. *commit lewd acts.* In their pagan worship practices (see Hos 4:14 and note).

22:10 *violate women.* Cf. 18:6 and note.

22:11 *detestable offense.* All the sins mentioned in this verse were specifically forbidden in the law (Lev 18:7–20; 20:10–21; Dt 22:22–23,30; 27:22).

22:12 *usury and excessive interest.* See 18:8 and note.

22:13 *strike my hands.* In anger (see 21:14,17).

22:17–22 Jerusalem will become God's "furnace" in which he melts down all those remaining in and around the city in order to cleanse away the "dross" (see Ps 12:6 and note).

has become dross[r] to me; all of them are
the copper, tin, iron and lead left inside
a furnace.[s] They are but the dross of silver.[t] 19 Therefore this is what the Sovereign
LORD says: 'Because you have all become
dross,[u] I will gather you into Jerusalem.
20 As men gather silver, copper, iron, lead
and tin into a furnace to melt it with a fiery blast, so will I gather you in my anger
and my wrath and put you inside the city
and melt you.[v] 21 I will gather you and I
will blow[w] on you with my fiery wrath,
and you will be melted inside her.[x] 22 As
silver is melted[y] in a furnace, so you will
be melted inside her, and you will know
that I the LORD have poured out my wrath[z]
upon you.' "[a]

23 Again the word of the LORD came to
me: 24 "Son of man, say to the land, 'You
are a land that has had no rain or showers[a] in the day of wrath.'[b] 25 There is a conspiracy[c] of her princes[b] within her like a
roaring lion[d] tearing its prey; they devour
people,[e] take treasures and precious things
and make many widows[f] within her. 26 Her
priests do violence to my law[g] and profane
my holy things; they do not distinguish
between the holy and the common;[h] they
teach that there is no difference between
the unclean and the clean;[i] and they shut
their eyes to the keeping of my Sabbaths,
so that I am profaned[j] among them.[k] 27 Her
officials[l] within her are like wolves[m] tearing their prey; they shed blood and kill
people[n] to make unjust gain.[o] 28 Her prophets whitewash[p] these deeds for them by
false visions and lying divinations.[q] They
say, 'This is what the Sovereign LORD
says'—when the LORD has not spoken.[r]
29 The people of the land practice extortion
and commit robbery;[s] they oppress the
poor and needy and mistreat the alien,[t]
denying them justice.[u]

30 "I looked for a man among them who
would build up the wall[v] and stand before
me in the gap on behalf of the land so I
would not have to destroy it, but I found
none.[w] 31 So I will pour out my wrath on
them and consume them with my fiery anger,[x] bringing down[y] on their own heads
all they have done, declares the Sovereign
LORD.[z]"

Two Adulterous Sisters

23 The word of the LORD came to me:
2 "Son of man, there were two wom-
en, daughters of the same mother.[a] 3 They
became prostitutes in Egypt,[b] engaging
in prostitution[c] from their youth.[d] In that
land their breasts were fondled and their
virgin bosoms caressed.[e] 4 The older was
named Oholah, and her sister was Oholibah. They were mine and gave birth to
sons and daughters. Oholah is Samaria,
and Oholibah is Jerusalem.[f]

5 "Oholah engaged in prostitution while
she was still mine; and she lusted after her
lovers, the Assyrians[g]—warriors[h] 6 clothed
in blue, governors and commanders, all of
them handsome young men, and mounted
horsemen. 7 She gave herself as a prostitute to all the elite of the Assyrians and
defiled herself with all the idols of everyone she lusted after.[i] 8 She did not give up
the prostitution she began in Egypt,[j] when
during her youth men slept with her, caressed her virgin bosom and poured out
their lust upon her.[k]

9 "Therefore I handed her over[l] to her
lovers,[m] the Assyrians, for whom she lusted.[n] 10 They stripped[o] her naked, took away

[a] 24 Septuagint; Hebrew *has not been cleansed or rained on* [b] 25 Septuagint; Hebrew *prophets*

22:18 [r]S Ps 119:119 [s]Isa 48:10 [t]Jer 6:28-30 **22:19** [u]S Ps 119:119 **22:20** [v]Hos 8:10; Mal 3:2 **22:21** [w]Isa 40:7; Hag 1:9 [x]Ps 68:2; Eze 21:31 **22:22** [y]S Isa 1:25 [z]S Eze 7:8 [a]S Isa 64:7 **22:24** [b]Eze 24:13 **22:25** [c]Jer 11:9 [d]S Ps 22:13 [e]Hos 6:9 [f]Jer 15:8; 18:21 **22:26** [g]Hos 9:7-8; Zep 3:4; Mal 2:7-8 [h]Eze 42:20; 44:23 [i]S Lev 20:25 [j]S Lev 18:21; S Eze 13:19 [k]ver 8; S 1Sa 2:12-17; Jer 2:8, 26; Hag 2:11-14 **22:27** [l]S Jer 26:10; Zep 3:3 [m]Mt 7:15 [n]S ver 3; S Eze 11:6; 33:25; 34:2-3; Mic 3:2, 10 [o]ver 13; S Ge 37:24; S Isa 1:23; S Jer 12:2; S 51:13; Eze 33:31 **22:28** [p]S Eze 13:10 [q]S La 2:14; S 4:13; S Eze 21:29 [r]S Eze 13:2, 6-7 **22:29** [s]S Ps 62:10 [t]S Ex 22:21 [u]S Isa 5:7 **22:30** [v]S Eze 13:5 [w]Ps 106:23; S Isa 64:7; Jer 5:1 **22:31** [x]Ex 32:10; S Isa 30:27; S La 4:11 [y]Eze 16:43 [z]Eze 7:8-9; Ro 2:8 **23:2** [a]S Jer 3:7; S Eze 16:45 **23:3** [b]Jos 24:14 [c]S Lev 17:7; S Isa 1:21 [d]S Ps 25:7 [e]S Eze 16:15 **23:4** [f]S Eze 16:46 **23:5** [g]S 2Ki 16:7; Hos 5:13 [h]Hos 8:9 **23:7** [i]Isa 57:8; Hos 5:3; 6:10 **23:8** [j]Ex 32:4 [k]S Eze 16:15 **23:9** [l]S 2Ki 18:11 [m]S Jer 4:30 [n]Hos 11:5 **23:10** [o]Hos 2:10

22:25 *princes.* Ezekiel begins to speak plainly concerning the "dross" of vv. 18–22. All of Jerusalem's leaders and people were included: princes (here), priests (v. 26), officials (v. 27), prophets (v. 28), people (v. 29). *like a roaring lion.* Cf. v. 27; 13:4; Zep 3:3.

22:26 *distinguish between the holy and the common.* One of the main duties of the priests (see 44:23 and note; see also Lev 10:10 and note). *Sabbaths.* See note on v. 8. *I am profaned.* See Lev 18:21 and note.

22:28 *whitewash.* See 13:10 and note.

22:29 *people of the land.* See 7:27 and note.

22:30 *I looked for a man.* Cf. Isa 59:16; 63:5 and notes. *stand before me in the gap.* See 13:5 and note. Some interpret the task here as prophetic intercession with God in behalf of the people (see Ge 20:7; 1Sa 12:23; Jer 37:3; 42:2). Others interpret it as teaching, particularly calling the people to repentance. Cf. the task of the prophetic "watchman" (3:17–21; 33:1–6).

22:31 *bringing down on their own heads all they have done.* See note on 16:43.

23:1–49 This extended allegory depicting in lurid colors the sins of Israel (similar to that found in ch. 16) climaxes the series of prophecies of judgment on Jerusalem and Judah begun in ch. 13 (see notes on 13:1–23; 18:1–32).

23:4 *The older.* See 16:46 and note. *Oholah.* Means "her tent," probably referring to the fact that Samaria had its own unauthorized sanctuary. *Oholibah.* Means "My tent is in her," probably referring to the Lord's sanctuary in Jerusalem. Cf. the two sisters of Jer 3:6–12 and note on 3:7.

23:5 *prostitution.* Here represents political alliances with pagan powers—not idolatry as in ch. 16 (see Ex 34:15 and note). The graphic language of the chapter underscores God's and Ezekiel's disgust with Israel for playing the worldly game of international politics rather than relying on the Lord for her security—as clear a case of religious prostitution as idolatry. *Assyrians.* See 2Ki 15:19 and note.

23:8 *in Egypt.* Cf. 20:5–8. Israel's entire history was marked by unfaithfulness. For her attachment to Egypt see Ex 17:3; Nu 11:5,18,20; 14:2–4; 21:5.

23:10 *stripped her naked.* A reference to the fall of Samaria to the Assyrians in 722–721 B.C.

her sons and daughters and killed her with the sword. She became a byword among women,[p] and punishment was inflicted[q] on her.[r]

11 "Her sister Oholibah saw this,[s] yet in her lust and prostitution she was more depraved than her sister.[t] 12 She too lusted after the Assyrians—governors and commanders, warriors in full dress, mounted horsemen, all handsome young men.[u] 13 I saw that she too defiled herself; both of them went the same way.[v]

14 "But she carried her prostitution still further. She saw men portrayed on a wall,[w] figures of Chaldeans[a] portrayed in red,[x] 15 with belts[y] around their waists and flowing turbans on their heads; all of them looked like Babylonian chariot officers, natives of Chaldea.[b] 16 As soon as she saw them, she lusted after them and sent messengers[z] to them in Chaldea.[a] 17 Then the Babylonians[b] came to her, to the bed of love, and in their lust they defiled her. After she had been defiled by them, she turned away from them in disgust.[c] 18 When she carried on her prostitution openly and exposed her nakedness,[d] I turned away[e] from her in disgust, just as I had turned away from her sister.[f] 19 Yet she became more and more promiscuous as she recalled the days of her youth, when she was a prostitute in Egypt. 20 There she lusted after her lovers, whose genitals were like those of donkeys and whose emission was like that of horses. 21 So you longed for the lewdness of your youth, when in Egypt your bosom was caressed and your young breasts fondled.[c][g]

22 "Therefore, Oholibah, this is what the Sovereign LORD says: I will stir up your lovers[h] against you, those you turned away from in disgust, and I will bring them against you from every side[i]— 23 the Babylonians[j] and all the Chaldeans,[k] the men of Pekod[l] and Shoa and Koa, and all the Assyrians with them, handsome young men, all of them governors and commanders, chariot officers and men of high rank, all mounted on horses.[m] 24 They will come against you with weapons,[d] chariots and wagons[n] and with a throng of people; they will take up positions against you on every side with large and small shields and with helmets. I will turn you over to them for punishment,[o] and they will punish you according to their standards. 25 I will direct my jealous anger[p] against you, and they will deal with you in fury. They will cut off your noses and your ears, and those of you who are left will fall by the sword. They will take away your sons and daughters,[q] and those of you who are left will be consumed by fire.[r] 26 They will also strip[s] you of your clothes and take your fine jewelry.[t] 27 So I will put a stop[u] to the lewdness and prostitution you began in Egypt. You will not look on these things with longing or remember Egypt anymore.

28 "For this is what the Sovereign LORD says: I am about to hand you over[v] to those you hate, to those you turned away from in disgust. 29 They will deal with you in hatred and take away everything you have worked for. They will leave you naked[w] and bare, and the shame of your prostitution will be exposed.[x] Your lewdness[y] and promiscuity[z] 30 have brought this upon you, because you lusted after the nations and defiled yourself with their idols.[a] 31 You have gone the way of your sister; so I will put her cup[b] into your hand.[c]

32 "This is what the Sovereign LORD says:

"You will drink your sister's cup,
a cup large and deep;
it will bring scorn and derision,[d]
for it holds so much.[e]
33 You will be filled with drunkenness
and sorrow,
the cup of ruin and desolation,
the cup of your sister Samaria.[f]
34 You will drink it[g] and drain it dry;
you will dash it to pieces
and tear your breasts.

I have spoken, declares the Sovereign LORD.[h]

23:10 [p] Eze 16:41 [q] Jer 42:10 [r] Eze 16:36 **23:11** [s] S Jer 3:7 [t] Jer 3:8-11; S Eze 16:51 **23:12** [u] 2Ki 16:7-15; S 2Ch 28:16; S Eze 16:15,28 **23:13** [v] S 2Ki 17:19; Hos 12:2 **23:14** [w] S Eze 8:10 [x] Jer 22:14; Na 2:3 **23:15** [y] S Isa 5:27 **23:16** [z] S Isa 57:9 [a] S Eze 6:9 **23:17** [b] Jer 40:9 [c] S Eze 16:29 **23:18** [d] S Isa 57:8 [e] Ps 78:59; 106:40; Jer 6:8 [f] Jer 12:8; Am 5:21 **23:21** [g] S Eze 16:26 **23:22** [h] S Jer 4:30 [i] S Eze 16:37 **23:23** [j] 2Ki 20:14-18; S Jer 40:9 [k] S Ge 11:28 [l] Jer 50:21 [m] S 2Ki 24:2 **23:24** [n] Jer 47:3; Eze 26:7,10; Na 2:4 [o] Jer 39:5-6 **23:25** [p] S Dt 29:20 [q] ver 47; Eze 24:21 [r] S Jer 12:9; S Eze 16:38; S 20:47-48 **23:26** [s] S Jer 13:22 [t] S Isa 3:18-23; S Eze 16:39 **23:27** [u] S Eze 16:41 **23:28** [v] S Jer 34:20 **23:29** [w] Mic 1:11 [x] S Jer 13:27 [y] S Eze 22:9 [z] Dt 28:48; S Eze 16:36 **23:30** [a] Ps 106:37-38; Zep 3:1 **23:31** [b] S Jer 25:15 [c] 2Ki 21:13 **23:32** [d] Ps 44:13; Hos 7:16 [e] Ps 60:3; Isa 51:17; Jer 25:15 **23:33** [f] Jer 25:15-16; S Eze 12:19 **23:34** [g] S Ps 16:5 [h] S Jer 25:27

[a] *14* Or *Babylonians* [b] *15* Or *Babylonia*; also in verse 16 [c] *21* Syriac (see also verse 3); Hebrew *caressed because of your young breasts* [d] *24* The meaning of the Hebrew for this word is uncertain.

23:14 *portrayed in red.* Jeremiah, too, noted red interior decorations with disfavor (Jer 22:14).

23:15 *belts.* Cf. Isa 5:27 for similar Assyrian military equipment.

23:20 *genitals.* See note on 16:26.

23:23 *Babylonians ... Chaldeans.* Often identified with one another (see 1:3 and NIV text note there; 12:13), here distinguished (as in v. 15), probably because the Chaldeans were relative newcomers. *Pekod.* Aramaic people located east of Babylon. *Shoa and Koa.* Babylonian allies of uncertain origin and location.

23:24 *their standards.* Which were cruel and gruesome (see v. 25).

23:25 *jealous anger.* See 16:38 and note. *fire.* See notes on 15:7; 20:47.

23:27 *in Egypt.* See note on v. 8.

23:31 *cup.* Filled with the anger of the Lord. To drink it was to die. For a development of the imagery see Ps 16:5 and note; 75:8; Isa 51:17,22; Jer 25:15 and note; 49:12; La 4:21; Ob 16 and note; Hab 2:16; Mt 20:22; 26:39; Rev 14:10 and note.

23:34 *tear your breasts.* Beating the breasts—a sign of mourning (see 21:12; see also Jer 31:19; Lk 23:48 and notes)—is here poetically intensified to the point of tearing them in a frantic attempt to find relief from intolerable suffering.

35 “Therefore this is what the Sovereign
LORD says: Since you have forgotten[i] me
and thrust me behind your back,[j] you must
bear[k] the consequences of your lewdness
and prostitution.”
36 The LORD said to me: “Son of man, will
you judge Oholah and Oholibah? Then
confront[l] them with their detestable practices,[m] 37 for they have committed adultery
and blood is on their hands. They committed adultery with their idols; they even
sacrificed their children, whom they bore
to me,[a] as food for them.[n] 38 They have
also done this to me: At that same time
they defiled my sanctuary[o] and desecrated my Sabbaths.[p] 39 On the very day they
sacrificed their children to their idols, they
entered my sanctuary and desecrated[q] it.
That is what they did in my house.[r]
40 “They even sent messengers for men
who came from far away,[s] and when they
arrived you bathed yourself for them,
painted your eyes[t] and put on your jewelry.[u] 41 You sat on an elegant couch,[v] with a
table[w] spread before it on which you had
placed the incense[x] and oil that belonged
to me.[y]
42 “The noise of a carefree[z] crowd was
around her; Sabeans[b][a] were brought from
the desert along with men from the rabble, and they put bracelets[b] on the arms
of the woman and her sister and beautiful
crowns on their heads.[c] 43 Then I said about
the one worn out by adultery, ‘Now let
them use her as a prostitute,[d] for that is all
she is.’ 44 And they slept with her. As men
sleep with a prostitute, so they slept with
those lewd women, Oholah and Oholibah.
45 But righteous men will sentence them to
the punishment of women who commit
adultery and shed blood,[e] because they are
adulterous and blood is on their hands.[f]
46 “This is what the Sovereign LORD says:
Bring a mob[g] against them and give them
over to terror and plunder.[h] 47 The mob
will stone them and cut them down with
their swords; they will kill their sons and
daughters[i] and burn[j] down their houses.[k]
48 “So I will put an end[l] to lewdness in the
land, that all women may take warning and
not imitate you.[m] 49 You will suffer the penalty for your lewdness and bear the consequences of your sins of idolatry.[n] Then you
will know that I am the Sovereign LORD.[o]”

The Cooking Pot

24 In the ninth year, in the tenth month
on the tenth day, the word of the
LORD came to me:[p] 2 “Son of man, record[q]
this date, this very date, because the king
of Babylon has laid siege to Jerusalem this
very day.[r] 3 Tell this rebellious house[s] a
parable[t] and say to them: ‘This is what
the Sovereign LORD says:

“ ‘Put on the cooking pot;[u] put it on
and pour water into it.
4 Put into it the pieces of meat,
all the choice pieces — the leg and
the shoulder.
Fill it with the best of these bones;[v]
5 take the pick of the flock.[w]
Pile wood beneath it for the bones;
bring it to a boil
and cook the bones in it.[x]

6 “ ‘For this is what the Sovereign LORD
says:

“ ‘Woe[y] to the city of bloodshed,[z]
to the pot now encrusted,
whose deposit will not go away!
Empty it piece by piece
without casting lots[a] for them.[b]

[a] 37 Or *even made the children they bore to me pass through* ⌞*the fire*⌟ [b] 42 Or *drunkards*

23:35 [i] S Dt 32:18; S Isa 17:10 [j] S 1Ki 14:9; S 2Ch 29:6 [k] Eze 16:52 **23:36** [l] S Eze 16:2 [m] Isa 58:1; S Eze 22:2; Mic 3:8 **23:37** [n] S Eze 16:36 **23:38** [o] S Lev 15:31 [p] S Ne 10:31 **23:39** [q] S 2Ki 21:4 [r] S Jer 7:10; Eze 22:8 **23:40** [s] S Isa 57:9 [t] 2Ki 9:30 [u] S Jer 4:30; Eze 16:13-19; Hos 2:13 **23:41** [v] S Est 1:6; S Pr 7:17 [w] Isa 65:11; Eze 41:22; 44:16; Mal 1:7,12 [x] Isa 57:9; S 65:3; S Jer 44:5 [y] S Nu 18:12 **23:42** [z] S Ps 73:5 [a] S 2Ch 9:1 [b] S Ge 24:30 [c] S Eze 16:11-12 **23:43** [d] ver 3 **23:45** [e] S Eze 22:3 [f] S Lev 20:10; S Eze 16:38; Hos 2:2; 6:5 **23:46** [g] Eze 16:40 [h] S Dt 28:25; S Jer 25:9 **23:47** [i] S ver 25 [j] 2Ch 36:19; S Jer 34:22 [k] S 2Ch 36:17 **23:48** [l] Eze 16:41 [m] 2Pe 2:6 **23:49** [n] Eze 24:13 [o] S Eze 7:4; S 9:10; 16:58; S 20:38 **24:1** [p] S Eze 8:1; 26:1; 29:17 **24:2** [q] Isa 30:8; Hab 2:2 [r] 2Ki 25:1; S Jer 39:1 **24:3** [s] S Isa 1:2; S Eze 2:3,6 [t] S Eze 20:49 [u] S Eze 11:3 **24:4** [v] S Eze 11:7 **24:5** [w] S Isa 34:12; Jer 52:10 [x] Jer 52:24-27; Mic 3:2-3 **24:6** [y] S Eze 16:23 [z] S Eze 22:2 [a] S Job 6:27; Joel 3:3; Ob 1:11; Na 3:10 [b] S Eze 11:11

23:35 *you have forgotten me.* See 22:12; Jer 2:32 and note.
23:37 *sacrificed their children.* See note on 16:20.
23:38 *defiled my sanctuary.* See ch. 8. *Sabbaths.* See note on 22:8.
23:40 *They even sent messengers for men.* Possibly a reference to the Jerusalem summit meeting in Zedekiah's time (Jer 27). *you.* Jerusalem. *painted your eyes.* By daubing them with kohl, a soot-like compound, to draw attention to the eyes.
23:41 *couch, with a table spread before it.* Ready for a banquet (see Isa 21:5; also Pr 9:2).
23:42 *Sabeans.* Men from Sheba, located at the southwest corner of the Arabian peninsula (modern Yemen), known for trading (see 27:22; 38:13; 1Ki 10:1 and note; Job 1:15 and note; 6:19). But see NIV text note.
24:1 – 14 The series of prophecies beginning with ch. 13 (see note on 13:1 – 23) ends with a depiction of Jerusalem as a pot cooking over an open fire, concluding with words that echo the final words of the seventh prophecy in this series (see 18:30; 24:14 and notes).
24:1 *ninth year . . . tenth month . . . tenth day.* Of King Zedekiah's reign (2Ki 25:1); Jan. 15, 588 B.C., some two and a half years after the preceding dated prophecy (see 20:1 and chart, p. 1239); Ezekiel's fourth date (see 1:2; 8:1; 20:1).
24:2 *record this date . . . because.* God revealed to Ezekiel what was happening in Jerusalem.
24:3 *rebellious house.* The last occurrence of this condemning phrase in Ezekiel (see 2:5,6,8; 3:9,26 – 27; 12:2 – 3,9,25; 17:12). Jerusalem's rebellion would soon be crushed. *parable.* Cf. 17:2. *cooking pot.* A reuse of the imagery found in 11:3 – 12. The cooking pot is Jerusalem (cf. 11:3 and note). In what follows, the imagery shifts from cooking the meat and bones in the pot (vv. 4 – 5) to burning away the impurities that adhere to the pot (vv. 6 – 8), and then repeats the cycle (vv. 9 – 10, cooking the meat and bones; vv. 11 – 12, burning off the encrusted impurities).
24:4 *choice pieces.* The people of Jerusalem who thought they were spared the exile in 597 B.C. because of their goodness (see 11:3 and note).
24:5 *wood.* Nebuchadnezzar's siege equipment.
24:6 *city of bloodshed.* Cf. v. 9; 22:2 – 3. *encrusted.* Representing Jerusalem's irredeemable situation. *without casting lots for them.* After the siege of Jerusalem in 597, perhaps the Bab-

7 " 'For the blood she shed is in her
midst:
She poured it on the bare rock;
she did not pour it on the ground,
where the dust would cover it.[c]
8 To stir up wrath and take revenge
I put her blood on the bare rock,
so that it would not be covered.

9 " 'Therefore this is what the Sovereign
LORD says:

" 'Woe to the city of bloodshed!
I, too, will pile the wood high.
10 So heap on the wood
and kindle the fire.
Cook the meat well,
mixing in the spices;
and let the bones be charred.
11 Then set the empty pot on the coals
till it becomes hot and its copper
glows
so its impurities may be melted
and its deposit burned away.[d]
12 It has frustrated all efforts;
its heavy deposit has not been
removed,
not even by fire.

13 " 'Now your impurity is lewdness. Because I tried to cleanse you but you would
not be cleansed[e] from your impurity, you
will not be clean again until my wrath
against you has subsided.[f]

14 " 'I the LORD have spoken.[g] The time
has come for me to act.[h] I will not hold
back; I will not have pity,[i] nor will I relent.[j] You will be judged according to your
conduct and your actions,[k] declares the
Sovereign LORD.[l] ' "

Ezekiel's Wife Dies

15 The word of the LORD came to me:
16 "Son of man, with one blow[m] I am
about to take away from you the delight
of your eyes.[n] Yet do not lament or weep
or shed any tears.[o] 17 Groan quietly;[p] do
not mourn for the dead. Keep your turban[q] fastened and your sandals[r] on
your feet; do not cover the lower part of
your face[s] or eat the customary food ⌞of
mourners⌟.[t]"

18 So I spoke to the people in the morning, and in the evening my wife died. The
next morning I did as I had been commanded.[u]

19 Then the people asked me, "Won't
you tell us what these things have to do
with us?[v]"

20 So I said to them, "The word of the
LORD came to me: 21 Say to the house of
Israel, 'This is what the Sovereign LORD
says: I am about to desecrate my sanctuary[w]—the stronghold in which you
take pride,[x] the delight of your eyes,[y] the
object of your affection. The sons and
daughters[z] you left behind will fall by
the sword.[a] 22 And you will do as I have
done. You will not cover the lower part of
your face[b] or eat the customary food ⌞of
mourners⌟.[c] 23 You will keep your turbans[d]
on your heads and your sandals[e] on your
feet. You will not mourn[f] or weep but will
waste away[g] because of[a] your sins and
groan among yourselves.[h] 24 Ezekiel[i] will
be a sign[j] to you; you will do just as he
has done. When this happens, you will
know that I am the Sovereign LORD.'

25 "And you, son of man, on the day I take
away their stronghold, their joy and glory, the delight of their eyes,[k] their heart's
desire,[l] and their sons and daughters[m] as

[a] 23 Or *away in*

24:7 [c] S Lev 17:13 **24:11** [d] Jer 21:10 **24:13** [e] S Isa 22:14 [f] Jer 6:28-30; La 1:9; S Eze 16:42; 22:24; 23:36-49; Hos 7:1; Zec 6:8 **24:14** [g] Eze 22:14 [h] S Nu 11:23 [i] S Eze 8:18 [j] S Job 27:22 [k] Eze 36:19; Zec 8:14 [l] S Isa 3:11; S Eze 18:30 **24:16** [m] S Ps 39:10 [n] ver 21; Ps 84:1; S La 2:4 [o] Jer 13:17; 16:5; S 22:10 **24:17** [p] Ps 39:9 [q] S Ex 28:39; S Isa 3:20 [r] S Isa 20:2 [s] S Lev 13:45 [t] ver 22; S Jer 16:7 **24:18** [u] S Eze 12:7 **24:19** [v] Eze 12:9; 37:18 **24:21** [w] S Lev 26:31; S Eze 7:24 [x] S Lev 26:19 [y] S ver 16; Ps 27:4 [z] S Eze 23:25 [a] Jer 7:14,15; Hos 9:12,16; Mal 2:12 **24:22** [b] S Lev 13:45 [c] Jer 16:7 **24:23** [d] S Ex 28:39; S Isa 3:20 [e] S Isa 20:2 [f] Ex 33:4 [g] S Lev 26:16 [h] Ps 78:64 **24:24** [i] Eze 1:3 [j] S Isa 20:3; Eze 12:11

24:25 [k] S La 2:4 [l] S Ps 20:4 [m] Dt 28:32; Jer 11:22

ylonians had cast lots to see whom they would take away into exile. Now everyone would go.

24:7 *blood ... on the bare rock.* Jerusalem had brazenly left on display the blood she unjustly shed (cf. Isa 3:9). For uncovered blood see Ge 4:10; Job 16:18 and notes; cf. Lev 17:13–14.

24:8 *wrath.* God's wrath. What Jerusalem had done would be done to her (see 16:43 and note; see also 1Ki 8:32; Isa 3:1; cf. Ex 4:21; 21:23–25; Lev 24:17–22; Dt 19:21 and notes).

24:11 *empty pot.* Jerusalem, emptied of inhabitants, would be set to the torch, in a vain final effort at purification.

24:13 *lewdness.* See 16:1–63; 23:1–49 and notes.

24:14 *The time has come.* See 7:2–3 and note on 7:1–27. *judged according to your conduct and your actions.* See notes on Job 34:11; Ro 2:1–16; 2:6–8; Rev 20:12.

24:15–27 Following the series of prophecies concerning God's judgment on Judah (13:1—24:14) Ezekiel's action upon the death of his wife serves to symbolize how the exiles would react to the fall of Jerusalem, just as his earlier symbolic actions symbolized the exile of the people of Jerusalem (see 12:1–28 and note). These two symbolic acts thus serve as a literary frame around this second series of prophecies in Ezekiel.

24:16 *blow.* Some swiftly fatal disease, one that often reached plague proportions (see Ex 9:14; Nu 14:37). *delight of your eyes.* The object of loving attention (see vv. 21,25)—apparently a conventional way of referring to a man's wife (cf. Jdg 14:3, "She's the right one for me" [lit. "She is right in my eyes"]; see also SS 8:10).

24:17 *Keep your turban fastened.* Mourners normally removed turbans and put dust on their heads (see Jos 7:6; 1Sa 4:12 and notes). *sandals on your feet.* To remove them showed grief (see 2Sa 15:30 and note). *cover ... face.* A gesture of shame (Mic 3:7). *food ⌞of mourners⌟.* The funeral meal (see Jer 16:7 and note).

24:18 *in the evening my wife died.* She died the same day the temple was set on fire (Aug. 14, 586 B.C.; see vv. 25–27; 2Ki 25:8 and note; see also Introduction: Occasion, Purpose and Summary of Contents).

24:19 *Then the people asked me.* The third time the people responded to Ezekiel's behavior (see 12:9; 21:7 and notes).

24:21 *desecrate.* By letting Nebuchadnezzar burn it down.

24:24 *Ezekiel.* The Lord speaks of Ezekiel in the third person. Elsewhere the prophet's name occurs only in 1:3 (see note there). *sign.* See v. 27 and note on 12:6.

well— 26on that day a fugitive will come
to tell you[n] the news. 27At that time your
mouth will be opened; you will speak with
him and will no longer be silent.[o] So you
will be a sign to them, and they will know
that I am the LORD.[p]"

A Prophecy Against Ammon

25 The word of the LORD came to me:
2"Son of man, set your face against[q]
the Ammonites[r] and prophesy against
them.[s] 3Say to them, 'Hear the word of the
Sovereign LORD. This is what the Sovereign
LORD says: Because you said "Aha![t]" over
my sanctuary when it was desecrated[u] and
over the land of Israel when it was laid
waste and over the people of Judah when
they went into exile,[v] 4therefore I am going
to give you to the people of the East[w] as a
possession. They will set up their camps[x]
and pitch their tents among you; they will
eat your fruit and drink your milk.[y] 5I will
turn Rabbah[z] into a pasture for camels and
Ammon into a resting place for sheep.[a]
Then you will know that I am the LORD.
6For this is what the Sovereign LORD says:
Because you have clapped your hands[b]
and stamped your feet, rejoicing with all
the malice of your heart against the land
of Israel,[c] 7therefore I will stretch out my
hand[d] against you and give you as plunder[e] to the nations. I will cut you off from
the nations and exterminate you from the
countries. I will destroy[f] you, and you will
know that I am the LORD.[g]' "

A Prophecy Against Moab

8"This is what the Sovereign LORD says:
'Because Moab[h] and Seir[i] said, "Look, the
house of Judah has become like all the
other nations," 9therefore I will expose
the flank of Moab, beginning at its frontier towns—Beth Jeshimoth[j], Baal Meon[k]
and Kiriathaim[l]—the glory of that land. 10I
will give Moab along with the Ammonites
to the people of the East as a possession,
so that the Ammonites will not be remembered[m] among the nations; 11and I will inflict punishment on Moab. Then they will
know that I am the LORD.' "[n]

A Prophecy Against Edom

12"This is what the Sovereign LORD
says: 'Because Edom[o] took revenge on the
house of Judah and became very guilty
by doing so, 13therefore this is what the
Sovereign LORD says: I will stretch out my
hand[p] against Edom and kill its men and
their animals.[q] I will lay it waste, and from
Teman[r] to Dedan[s] they will fall by the
sword.[t] 14I will take vengeance on Edom
by the hand of my people Israel, and they
will deal with Edom in accordance with
my anger[u] and my wrath; they will know
my vengeance, declares the Sovereign
LORD.' "[v]

24:26 [n]S 1Sa 4:12; Job 1:15-19 **24:27** [o]Da 10:15 [p]S Eze 3:26; 33:22 **25:2** [q]S Eze 13:17; 29:2 [r]S Eze 21:28 [s]Jer 49:1-6 **25:3** [t]S Ps 35:21; Eze 26:2; 36:2 [u]Zep 2:8 [v]S Pr 17:5 **25:4** [w]S Ge 25:6; S Jdg 6:3 [x]S Nu 31:10 [y]Dt 28:33,51; S Jdg 6:33 **25:5** [z]S Dt 3:11 [a]S S Isa 17:2 **25:6** [b]S Nu 24:10 [c]S Eze 6:11; Ob 1:12; Zep 2:8 **25:7** [d]Zep 1:4 [e]S Nu 14:3 [f]Eze 21:31 [g]ver 13-14, 17; Am 1:14-15 **25:8** [h]S Ge 19:37; S Dt 23:6; S Isa 16:6 [i]S Ge 14:6 **25:9** [j]S Nu 33:49 [k]S Nu 32:3; S Jos 13:17 [l]S Nu 32:37; S Jos 13:19 **25:10** [m]Eze 21:32 **25:11** [n]Isa 15:9; 16:1-14; Jer 48:1; Am 2:1-3 **25:12** [o]S 2Sa 8:13-14; S 2Ch 28:17; S Isa 11:14 **25:13** [p]S Ex 7:5; S Eze 16:27 [q]Eze 29:8 [r]S Ge 36:11, 15, 34 [s]Jer 25:23 [t]S Jer 49:10; S Eze 14:17 **25:14** [u]Eze 35:11 [v]S Ps 137:7; Eze 32:29; 35:2-3; 36:5; Am 1:11; Ob 1:1, 10-16; Mal 1:4

24:26 *fugitive.* The first of the exiles of 586 B.C. *news.* About the siege—its beginning (verifying the accuracy of vv. 1–2) and its ending (see note on 33:21).

24:27 *At that time.* When the fugitive arrived from Jerusalem (see 33:21 and note). *no longer be silent.* The muteness that had been imposed on him at the beginning of his ministry was now lifted (see 3:26 and note).

25:1—32:32 Prophecies against the nations. Frequently in the prophets, God's word of judgment on Israel is accompanied by messages of judgment on the nations (see note on Jer 46:1—51:64). These make clear that, while judgment begins "with the family of God" (1Pe 4:17), the pagan nations would not escape God's wrath. Often these judgments are implicit messages of salvation for Israel (see 28:25–26 and notes) since the Lord's victories over hostile powers remove an enemy of his people or punish them for their cruel attacks on his people. In the case of Ezekiel there are seven prophecies (the seventh of which has seven parts, each introduced by the phrase "The word of the LORD came to me"; see Introduction: Outline). The structure of these oracles follows the pattern "Because [introducing the evil committed] ..., therefore [introducing the judgment] ... know that I am the LORD" (e.g., 25:3–7).

25:2 *set your face.* See note on 20:46. *Ammonites.* Ammon (part of modern Jordan) was immediately east of Israel (see 21:20 and note; see also Jer 9:26; 49:1–6; Am 1:13–15; Zep 2:8–11). For hostile Ammonite action during this time and later see 2Ki 24:2; Ne 4:7.

25:3 *Aha!* A cry of malicious joy (cf. 26:2; 36:2; Ps 35:21–25).

25:4 *people of the East.* Probably nomadic tribes of the desert east of Ammon, though this could be a reference to Nebuchadnezzar and his army (see 21:31).

25:5 *Rabbah.* See note on 21:20. *pasture ... resting place.* A common OT description of destroyed cities (see Isa 34:13–15; Zep 2:13–15). The sites were returned to the conditions they were in before the cities were built, representing the undoing of human efforts.

25:6 *clapped your hands.* See 6:11 and note.

25:7 *I will stretch out my hand against.* See note on 6:14. *plunder to the nations.* Cf. 26:5; 34:28. *cut you off.* Cf. v. 16.

25:8 *Moab.* Immediately to the south of Ammon, east of the Dead Sea (see Ge 19:36–38 and note; Isa 15–16; Jer 48; Am 2:1–3; Zep 2:8–11). *Seir.* Edom, a country south of Moab and south of the Dead Sea (see ch. 35, especially v. 15; 36:5; Isa 34:5–17; 63:1–6; Jer 49:7–11; Am 1:11–12). *like all the other nations.* Israel wanted to be like the nations (see 20:32 and note), but when the nations saw Judah in her apparent vulnerability and lost their awe of her, they failed to take her God seriously (cf. La 4:12).

25:9 *flank of Moab.* Lower hills rising from the Dead Sea, visible from Jerusalem. *Beth Jeshimoth.* A town in the plains of Moab. *Baal Meon.* A major Moabite town mentioned in an inscribed monument of Mesha king of Moab (see chart, p. xxiii). *Kiriathaim.* A city also mentioned in the Mesha inscription (cf. 2Ki 3:4–5 and note on 2Ki 1:1).

25:12 *Edom.* See note on v. 8 ("Seir"). *took revenge.* By not harboring Judah's refugees after 586 B.C. (see Ob 11–14 and notes).

25:13 *Teman.* A district near Petra in central Edom (see Jer 49:7,20; Am 1:12; Ob 9; Hab 3:3 and notes). *Dedan.* A tribe and territory in southern Edom (see 27:20; 38:13; Isa 21:13 and note; Jer 49:8).

A Prophecy Against Philistia

15"This is what the Sovereign LORD
says: 'Because the Philistines[w] acted in
vengeance and took revenge with malice[x]
in their hearts, and with ancient hostility
sought to destroy Judah, 16therefore this is
what the Sovereign LORD says: I am about
to stretch out my hand against the Philistines,[y] and I will cut off the Kerethites[z] and
destroy those remaining along the coast.[a]
17I will carry out great vengeance[b] on them
and punish[c] them in my wrath. Then they
will know that I am the LORD,[d] when I take
vengeance on them.[e][f]' "

A Prophecy Against Tyre

26 In the eleventh year, on the first
day of the month, the word of the
LORD came to me:[g] 2"Son of man, because Tyre[h] has said of Jerusalem, 'Aha![i]
The gate to the nations is broken, and its
doors have swung open to me; now that
she lies in ruins I will prosper,' 3therefore
this is what the Sovereign LORD says: I am
against you, O Tyre, and I will bring many
nations against you, like the sea[j] casting up its waves. 4They will destroy[k] the
walls of Tyre[l] and pull down her towers;
I will scrape away her rubble and make
her a bare rock. 5Out in the sea[m] she will
become a place to spread fishnets,[n] for I
have spoken, declares the Sovereign LORD.
She will become plunder[o] for the nations,[p]
6and her settlements on the mainland will
be ravaged by the sword. Then they will
know that I am the LORD.

7"For this is what the Sovereign LORD
says: From the north I am going to bring
against Tyre Nebuchadnezzar[a][q] king of
Babylon, king of kings,[r] with horses and
chariots,[s] with horsemen and a great army.
8He will ravage your settlements on the
mainland with the sword; he will set up
siege works[t] against you, build a ramp[u] up
to your walls and raise his shields against
you. 9He will direct the blows of his battering rams against your walls and demolish your towers with his weapons.[v] 10His
horses will be so many that they will cover
you with dust. Your walls will tremble at
the noise of the war horses, wagons and
chariots[w] when he enters your gates as
men enter a city whose walls have been
broken through. 11The hoofs[x] of his horses will trample all your streets; he will
kill your people with the sword, and your
strong pillars[y] will fall to the ground.[z]
12They will plunder your wealth and loot

[a] 7 Hebrew *Nebuchadrezzar,* of which *Nebuchadnezzar* is a variant; here and often in Ezekiel and Jeremiah

25:15 [w]S Jos 13:3; S 2Ch 28:18 [x]S Ps 73:8 **25:16** [y]S 2Ch 26:6; Am 1:8 [z]S 1Sa 30:14 [a]S Eze 20:33 **25:17** [b]S Nu 31:3 [c]Jer 44:13 [d]S Ex 6:2; S 8:22 [e]S Isa 11:14 [f]S Isa 14:30; Jer 47:7; Joel 3:4 **26:1** [g]S Eze 24:1; 29:1; 30:20 **26:2** [h]S Jos 19:29; 2Sa 5:11 [i]S Eze 25:3 **26:3** [j]ver 19; Isa 5:30; Jer 50:42; 51:42 **26:4** [k]S Isa 23:1,11 [l]Am 1:10 **26:5** [m]Eze 27:32 [n]Eze 47:10 [o]S Nu 14:3; Eze 29:19 [p]Zec 9:2-4 **26:7** [q]Jer 27:6; 39:1 [r]S Ezr 7:12 [s]S Eze 23:24; Na 2:3-4 **26:8** [t]S Jer 6:6 [u]S Jer 33:4 **26:9** [v]S Eze 21:22 **26:10** [w]S Jer 4:13; S 46:9; S Eze 23:24 **26:11** [x]Isa 5:28 [y]S Jer 43:13 [z]S Isa 26:5

25:15 *Philistines.* Inhabitants of the coastal plain along the Mediterranean west of Judah (1Sa 6:17; see note on Ge 10:14) who strove for control of Canaan until subdued by David. Their hostility to Israel continued, however (see Isa 14:29–31; Jer 47; Am 1:6–8; Zep 2:4–7), until Nebuchadnezzar deported them.

25:16 *Kerethites.* Related to, if not identical with, the Philistines (see 1Sa 30:14 and note; 2Sa 8:18; 15:18; 20:7). *coast.* Of the Mediterranean.

26:1—28:19 A series of prophecies against Tyre, the chief seaport of Phoenicia (present-day Lebanon). Tyre was an island fortress that had an additional harbor on the mainland. After Nebuchadnezzar's victory at Carchemish in 605 B.C., it acknowledged the hegemony of the Babylonian king, but in 594 B.C. it joined a coalition of states to throw off the Babylonian yoke (Jer 27:3). Ancient historians relate that Nebuchadnezzar laid siege to Tyre for 15 years (cf. 29:18 and note) and may have succeeded in once more establishing some kind of authority over it, but he did not succeed in destroying the city. The island fortress was not overrun until Alexander the Great conquered it after a seven-month siege in 332 B.C.

26:1 *eleventh year ... first day of the month.* The fifth date in the book (see 1:2; 8:1; 20:1; 24:1). The number of the month is missing. The entire year dates from Apr. 23, 587, to Apr. 13, 586 B.C. This prophecy must date from the end of that year, in the 11th (Feb. 13, 586) or the 12th month (Mar. 15, 586). But there is a problem with these dates: This prophecy describes Tyre's gloating over the destruction of Jerusalem (v. 2), yet Jerusalem did not fall until July 18, 586 (see note on 2Ki 25:2–3), and was not burned until Aug. 14, 586 (see note on 2Ki 25:8)—several months after the date given here for Tyre's celebration of the fact that Jerusalem "now ... lies in ruins" (v. 2). To solve the problem, many interpreters believe that the probable reading of the original Hebrew text was "In the eleventh month of the twelfth year, on the first day of the month," and that the words "month of the twelfth" must have been inadvertently omitted by a copyist. The restored reading would yield the date Feb. 3, 585, which would nicely fit the chronology in 33:21 (see note there). If, on the other hand, the Hebrew text that has come down to us is correct, then the Lord (through Ezekiel) is prophesying what Tyre's response to Jerusalem's fall will be and how the Lord, in turn, will judge Tyre.

26:2 *Tyre.* For other prophecies against Tyre see Isa 23; Jer 25:22; 47:4; Joel 3:4–5; Am 1:9–10; Zec 9:2–4). *Aha!* See note on 25:3. *gate to the nations.* Because of its geographical location, its political importance and the central role it played in international trade. The anti-Babylonian summit meeting was held there (see Jer 27).

26:3 *I am against you.* See note on 5:8. *like the sea casting up its waves.* For invading armies likened to waves of the sea cf. Isa 17:12–13. Since Tyre was mainly a fortified island, the metaphor is especially appropriate here.

26:5 *to spread fishnets.* To dry them by spreading them out flat on the rock or ground (see v. 14; 47:10). Large seine nets were spread into a sea or lake and then dragged onto the shore, where the fish that had been caught would be sorted out (see Mt 13:47–51 and note). *plunder for the nations.* Cf. 25:7; 34:28.

26:6 *know that I am the LORD.* See Introduction: Themes.

26:7 *north.* The direction from which Nebuchadnezzar would descend on Tyre after first marching his army up the Euphrates River valley rather than across the Arabian Desert (cf. Jer 1:13). *I am going to bring.* A clear indication of God's sovereignty over the nations (cf. 28:7; 29:8). *Nebuchadnezzar.* The first of four references to him in Ezekiel (see 29:18–19; 30:10). He ruled from 605 to 562 B.C., and his name means "O (god) Nabu, protect my son/boundary." Jeremiah and Ezekiel both proclaimed that this pagan king would be used by God to do his work (see Jer 25:9 and note; 27:6).

26:8 *siege.* See note on 26:1—28:19.

your merchandise; they will break down
your walls and demolish your fine houses
and throw your stones, timber and rubble
into the sea.[a] 13I will put an end[b] to your
noisy songs,[c] and the music of your harps[d]
will be heard no more.[e] 14I will make you a
bare rock, and you will become a place to
spread fishnets. You will never be rebuilt,[f]
for I the LORD have spoken, declares the
Sovereign LORD.

15"This is what the Sovereign LORD says
to Tyre: Will not the coastlands[g] tremble[h]
at the sound of your fall, when the wounded groan[i] and the slaughter takes place in
you? 16Then all the princes of the coast
will step down from their thrones and lay
aside their robes and take off their embroidered[j] garments. Clothed[k] with terror, they
will sit on the ground,[l] trembling[m] every
moment, appalled[n] at you. 17Then they
will take up a lament[o] concerning you and
say to you:

"'How you are destroyed, O city of
renown,
peopled by men of the sea!
You were a power on the seas,
you and your citizens;
you put your terror
on all who lived there.[p]
18Now the coastlands tremble[q]
on the day of your fall;
the islands in the sea
are terrified at your collapse.'[r]

19"This is what the Sovereign LORD says:
When I make you a desolate city, like cities no longer inhabited, and when I bring
the ocean depths[s] over you and its vast
waters cover you,[t] 20then I will bring you
down with those who go down to the pit,[u]
to the people of long ago. I will make you
dwell in the earth below, as in ancient ruins, with those who go down to the pit,
and you will not return or take your place[a]
in the land of the living.[v] 21I will bring
you to a horrible end and you will be no
more.[w] You will be sought, but you will
never again be found, declares the Sovereign LORD."[x]

A Lament for Tyre

27 The word of the LORD came to me:
2"Son of man, take up a lament[y] concerning Tyre. 3Say to Tyre,[z] situated at the
gateway to the sea,[a] merchant of peoples
on many coasts, 'This is what the Sovereign LORD says:

"'You say, O Tyre,
"I am perfect in beauty."[b]
4Your domain was on the high seas;
your builders brought your beauty
to perfection.[c]
5They made all your timbers
of pine trees from Senir[b];[d]
they took a cedar from Lebanon[e]
to make a mast for you.
6Of oaks[f] from Bashan
they made your oars;
of cypress wood[c] from the coasts of
Cyprus[d g]
they made your deck, inlaid with
ivory.
7Fine embroidered linen[h] from Egypt
was your sail
and served as your banner;
your awnings were of blue and
purple[i]
from the coasts of Elishah.[j]
8Men of Sidon and Arvad[k] were your
oarsmen;
your skilled men, O Tyre, were
aboard as your seamen.[l]
9Veteran craftsmen of Gebal[e m] were on
board
as shipwrights to caulk your seams.

[a] 20 Septuagint; Hebrew *return, and I will give glory* [b] 5 That is, Hermon [c] 6 Targum; the Masoretic Text has a different division of the consonants. [d] 6 Hebrew *Kittim* [e] 9 That is, Byblos

26:12 [a]Isa 23:8; S Jer 4:7; Eze 27:3-27; 28:8; Hab 1:8 **26:13** [b]S Jer 7:34 [c]S Isa 23:7 [d]S Ps 137:2; S Isa 14:11 [e]S Job 30:31; S Jer 16:9; S 25:10; Rev 18:22 **26:14** [f]S Job 12:14; Mal 1:4 **26:15** [g]Isa 41:5; Eze 27:35 [h]S Jer 49:21 [i]S Job 24:12 **26:16** [j]S Ex 26:36 [k]S Job 8:22 [l]S Job 2:8,13 [m]Hos 11:10 [n]S Lev 26:32; Eze 32:10 **26:17** [o]S Eze 19:1 [p]Isa 14:12 **26:18** [q]S Ps 46:6; S Jer 49:21 [r]Isa 23:5; S 41:5; Eze 27:35 **26:19** [s]S Ge 7:11 [t]S ver 3; Isa 8:7-8 **26:20** [u]Nu 16:30; Ps 28:1; 88:6; Eze 31:14; 32:18; Am 9:2; Jnh 2:2,6 [v]S Job 28:13; S Isa 14:9-10; Eze 32:24,30 **26:21** [w]S Jer 51:64; Da 11:19 [x]Jer 20:4; Eze 27:36; 28:19; Rev 18:21 **27:2** [y]S Eze 19:1 **27:3** [z]S Ps 83:7 [a]ver 33; Hos 9:13 [b]S Isa 23:9; S Eze 16:15 **27:4** [c]Eze 28:12 **27:5** [d]S Dt 3:9 [e]S Isa 2:13 **27:6** [f]Nu 21:33; S Ps 29:9; Jer 22:20; Zec 11:2 [g]S Ge 10:4; Isa 23:12 **27:7** [h]S Ex 26:36; S Isa 19:9 [i]Ex 25:4; Jer 10:9 [j]Ge 10:4 **27:8** [k]Ge 10:18 [l]1Ki 9:27 **27:9** [m]S Jos 13:5

26:14 *to spread fishnets.* See v. 5 and note. *never be rebuilt.* Eventually fulfilled by Alexander's devastating siege in 332 B.C. (see note on Isa 23:1).
26:16 *princes of the coast.* Called kings in 27:35, they were probably trading partners with Tyre. *lay aside their robes.* Usually mourners tore their clothes (Job 2:12) and put on sackcloth, but cf. the king of Nineveh (Jnh 3:6). *Clothed with terror.* Because of political shock waves from the fall of such a powerful city (cf. 7:27; Ps 35:26; 109:29 and note).
26:17 *lament.* See note on 19:1.
26:19 *ocean depths.* The primeval, chaotic mass—the "deep" of Ge 1:2. Tyre's collapse into the sea is described in almost cosmic terms.
26:20 *pit.* "The earth below," the realm of the dead (see note on Ps 30:1). *people of long ago.* Those long dead (Ps 143:3; La 3:6). *not return or take your place in the land of the living.* As Israel would (see 37:1–14).
26:21 See 27:36; 28:19.
27:2 *lament.* See note on 19:1.
27:3 *I am perfect in beauty.* See 28:12 and note; cf. 28:2 for a similar prideful statement. Since Tyre is described as a stately ship in the following verses, some translate, "You are a ship, perfect in beauty."
27:4 *brought your beauty to perfection.* See v. 11.
27:5 *Senir.* Amorite name for Hermon, the Anti-Lebanon mountain (or range) famed for cedar.
27:6 *Bashan.* See note on 39:18. *Cyprus.* The Hebrew word *Kittim* (see NIV text note) was originally the name of a town in southern Cyprus colonized by Phoenicia.
27:7 *Elishah.* A city on the east side of Cyprus; also the oldest name for Cyprus (but see note on Ge 10:4).
27:8 *Sidon.* A harbor city 25 miles north of Tyre, which sometimes rivaled her in political and commercial importance (see note on 28:21). *Arvad.* Another Phoenician island-city, off the Mediterranean coast and north of Sidon.
27:9 *Gebal.* Byblos, an important ancient city on the coast between Sidon and Arvad (see NIV text note and 1Ki 5:18; see also map No. 5 at the end of this study Bible).

All the ships of the sea[n] and their
 sailors
 came alongside to trade for your
 wares.

10 " 'Men of Persia,[o] Lydia[p] and Put[q]
 served as soldiers in your army.
They hung their shields[r] and helmets
 on your walls,
 bringing you splendor.
11 Men of Arvad and Helech
 manned your walls on every side;
men of Gammad
 were in your towers.
They hung their shields around your
 walls;
 they brought your beauty to
 perfection.[s]

12 " 'Tarshish[t] did business with you because of your great wealth of goods;[u] they
exchanged silver, iron, tin and lead for
your merchandise.
13 " 'Greece,[v] Tubal and Meshech[w] traded
with you; they exchanged slaves[x] and articles of bronze for your wares.
14 " 'Men of Beth Togarmah[y] exchanged
work horses, war horses and mules for
your merchandise.
15 " 'The men of Rhodes[a][z] traded with
you, and many coastlands[a] were your customers; they paid you with ivory[b] tusks
and ebony.
16 " 'Aram[b][c] did business with you because of your many products; they exchanged turquoise,[d] purple fabric, embroidered work, fine linen,[e] coral[f] and rubies
for your merchandise.
17 " 'Judah and Israel traded with you;
they exchanged wheat[g] from Minnith[h] and
confections,[c] honey, oil and balm[i] for your
wares.[j]
18 " 'Damascus,[k] because of your many
products and great wealth of goods,[l] did
business with you in wine from Helbon
and wool from Zahar.
19 " 'Danites and Greeks[m] from Uzal[n]
bought your merchandise; they exchanged
wrought iron, cassia[o] and calamus for
your wares.
20 " 'Dedan[p] traded in saddle blankets
with you.
21 " 'Arabia[q] and all the princes of Kedar[r]
were your customers; they did business
with you in lambs, rams and goats.
22 " 'The merchants of Sheba[s] and Raamah traded with you; for your merchandise they exchanged the finest of all kinds
of spices[t] and precious stones, and gold.[u]
23 " 'Haran,[v] Canneh and Eden[w] and merchants of Sheba, Asshur[x] and Kilmad traded
with you. 24 In your marketplace they traded
with you beautiful garments, blue fabric,
embroidered work and multicolored rugs
with cords twisted and tightly knotted.

[a] *15* Septuagint; Hebrew *Dedan* [b] *16* Most Hebrew manuscripts; some Hebrew manuscripts and Syriac *Edom* [c] *17* The meaning of the Hebrew for this word is uncertain.

27:9 [n] S Ps 104:26 **27:10** [o] 2Ch 36:20; Ezr 1:1; Eze 38:5; Da 8:20 [p] S Isa 66:19 [q] S Ge 10:6; Eze 30:5; Na 3:9 [r] SS 4:4 **27:11** [s] ver 27 **27:12** [t] S Ge 10:4 [u] ver 18,33 **27:13** [v] Joel 3:6 [w] Ge 10:2; Isa 66:19; Eze 32:26; 38:2; 39:1 [x] Rev 18:13 **27:14** [y] S Ge 10:3 **27:15** [z] S Ge 10:7 [a] S Jer 25:22 [b] 1Ki 10:22; Rev 18:12 **27:16** [c] Jdg 10:6; Isa 7:1-8 [d] Ex 28:18; 39:11; Eze 28:13 [e] S Eze 16:10 [f] Job 28:18 **27:17** [g] S 1Ki 5:9 [h] Jdg 11:33 [i] S Ge 43:11 [j] Ac 12:20 **27:18** [k] S Ge 14:15; Eze 47:16-18 [l] S ver 12 **27:19** [m] S Ge 10:2 [n] Ge 10:27 [o] S Ex 30:24 **27:20** [p] S Ge 10:7 **27:21** [q] S 2Ch 9:14 [r] S Ge 25:13; Isa 21:17 **27:22** [s] S Ge 10:7,28 [t] S Ge 43:11 [u] Rev 18:12 **27:23** [v] S Ge 11:26 [w] S Isa 37:12 [x] S Ge 10:22; S Nu 24:24

27:10 *Persia.* Or Paras (identification uncertain). *Lydia.* In Asia Minor; the Lydians are known to have served as mercenaries for the Egyptians. *Put.* Libya, in North Africa, west of Egypt. *soldiers.* The ship image is abandoned, and Tyre is now described literally—as a city (note references to walls and towers here and in v. 11), complete with a mercenary army gathered from many peoples.
27:11 *Arvad.* See note on v. 8. *Helech.* Cilicia, the mountainous region in southeast Asia Minor. *Gammad.* Either (1) northern Asia Minor, or (2) a coastal town near Arvad.
27:12 *Tarshish.* Traditionally located on the coast of southern Spain, but the island of Sardinia has also been suggested. Passages such as 1Ki 10:22; Jnh 1:3 imply that it was a long distance from the Canaanite coast. The list of places in vv. 12–23 generally follows a west-to-east direction.
27:13 *Tubal and Meshech.* Both in Asia Minor.
27:14 *Beth Togarmah.* In eastern Asia Minor, present-day Armenia (see 38:6). *work horses.* Asia Minor was known for its horses (see 1Ki 10:28 and NIV text note there on "Kue").
27:15 *Rhodes.* A large island off the southwest coast of Asia Minor that served as gateway to the Aegean islands. It was an early major trading center (see Ac 21:1).
27:16 *Aram.* Modern Syria. Since Damascus, the capital of Aram, is mentioned in v. 18, perhaps Edom is meant here (see NIV text note; see also 25:12 and note).
27:17 *Israel traded with you.* In the past. Since 722–721 B.C. Israel had ceased to exist as a political state. *Minnith.* An Ammonite town, apparently famous for its wheat; "wheat from Minnith" possibly denoted a superior quality of wheat. *balm.* Gum or oil from one of several plants; a product of Gilead (see Ge 37:25 and note; Jer 8:22; 46:11).
27:18 *Damascus.* Capital of Aram (see note on v. 16; see also Isa 7:8). *Helbon.* A town north of Damascus, still in existence and still a wine-making center. The name occurs only here in the Bible. *Zahar.* Modern Sahra, an area northwest of Damascus, where grazing is still common today.
27:19 *Danites.* A term that Homer used for Greeks. Some read (as does the Septuagint, the pre-Christian Greek translation of the OT) "and wine from" for "Danites and Greeks from." *Uzal.* See Ge 10:27; 1Ch 1:21; perhaps Yemen or the area between Haran and the Tigris. *cassia.* Similar to the cinnamon tree. The only other Biblical mention of it is in Ex 30:24, where it appears in a list of aromatic plants. *calamus.* An aromatic reed.
27:20 *Dedan.* See note on 25:13.
27:21 *Arabia and ... Kedar.* A general expression for the nomadic tribes from Aram to the Arabian Desert. For Kedar see Isa 21:16 and note; 42:11; 60:7; Jer 49:28.
27:22 *Sheba.* See note on 23:42. *Raamah.* A city in southern Arabia.
27:23 *Haran.* A city east of Carchemish, in present-day eastern Turkey. It was well-known in ancient times as a center both for trade and for the worship of the moon-god Sin. From here Abram moved to Canaan (see Ge 11:31 and note; 12:4). *Canneh.* Of uncertain location, presumably in Mesopotamia. It is often identified with Calneh (Isa 10:9; Am 6:2). *Eden.* A district south of Haran, mentioned in connection with Haran in 2Ki 19:12 (see note there). Cf. Beth Eden in Am 1:5 (but see note there). *Sheba.* See note on 23:42. *Asshur.* Can mean the city, the country (Assyria) or the people (Assyrians). Here it is probably the city south of Nineveh that gave its name to the country. *Kilmad.* If a town, it is yet unidentified; presumably in Mesopotamia. Some read "all Media."

[25]“ ‘The ships of Tarshish[y] serve
as carriers for your wares.
You are filled with heavy cargo
in the heart of the sea.[z]
[26]Your oarsmen take you
out to the high seas.
But the east wind[a] will break you to
pieces
in the heart of the sea.
[27]Your wealth,[b] merchandise and wares,
your mariners, seamen and
shipwrights,
your merchants and all your soldiers,
and everyone else on board
will sink into the heart of the sea[c]
on the day of your shipwreck.
[28]The shorelands will quake[d]
when your seamen cry out.
[29]All who handle the oars
will abandon their ships;
the mariners and all the seamen
will stand on the shore.
[30]They will raise their voice
and cry bitterly over you;
they will sprinkle dust[e] on their heads
and roll[f] in ashes.[g]
[31]They will shave their heads[h] because
of you
and will put on sackcloth.
They will weep[i] over you with anguish
of soul
and with bitter mourning.[j]
[32]As they wail and mourn over you,
they will take up a lament[k]
concerning you:
“Who was ever silenced like Tyre,
surrounded by the sea?[l]”
[33]When your merchandise went out on
the seas,[m]
you satisfied many nations;
with your great wealth[n] and your
wares
you enriched the kings of the
earth.
[34]Now you are shattered by the sea
in the depths of the waters;
your wares and all your company
have gone down with you.[o]
[35]All who live in the coastlands[p]
are appalled[q] at you;
their kings shudder with horror
and their faces are distorted with
fear.[r]
[36]The merchants among the nations hiss
at you;[s]
you have come to a horrible end
and will be no more.[t]’ ”

A Prophecy Against the King of Tyre

28 The word of the LORD came to me:
[2]“Son of man[u], say to the ruler of
Tyre, ‘This is what the Sovereign LORD
says:

“ ‘In the pride of your heart
you say, “I am a god;
I sit on the throne[v] of a god
in the heart of the seas.”[w]
But you are a man and not a god,
though you think you are as wise
as a god.[x]
[3]Are you wiser than Daniel[a]?[y]
Is no secret hidden from you?
[4]By your wisdom and understanding
you have gained wealth for
yourself
and amassed gold and silver
in your treasuries.[z]
[5]By your great skill in trading[a]
you have increased your wealth,[b]
and because of your wealth
your heart has grown proud.[c]

[6]“ ‘Therefore this is what the Sovereign
LORD says:

“ ‘Because you think you are wise,
as wise as a god,
[7]I am going to bring foreigners against
you,
the most ruthless of nations;[d]
they will draw their swords against
your beauty and wisdom[e]
and pierce your shining splendor.[f]
[8]They will bring you down to the pit,[g]
and you will die a violent death[h]
in the heart of the seas.[i]
[9]Will you then say, “I am a god,”
in the presence of those who kill
you?
You will be but a man, not a god,[j]
in the hands of those who slay
you.[k]

[a] 3 Or *Danel*; the Hebrew spelling may suggest a person other than the prophet Daniel.

27:25 [y]S Ge 10:4; Isa 2:16 *fn* [z]Rev 18:3 **27:26** [a]S Ge 41:6; Jer 18:17 **27:27** [b]Pr 11:4 [c]Eze 28:8 **27:28** [d]S Jer 49:21 **27:30** [e]S Jos 7:6; S 2Sa 1:2 [f]S Jer 6:26 [g]Rev 18:18-19 **27:31** [h]S Lev 13:40; S Job 1:20; S Isa 3:17; S Jer 48:37 [i]S Isa 16:9; Rev 18:15 [j]S Est 4:1; Job 3:20; Isa 22:12; Jer 6:26; S La 2:10; S Eze 7:18 **27:32** [k]S Eze 19:1 [l]Isa 23:1-6; Eze 26:5 **27:33** [m]S ver 3 [n]S ver 12; Eze 28:4-5 **27:34** [o]Zec 9:4 **27:35** [p]S Eze 26:15 [q]S Lev 26:32; S Job 18:20 [r]S Eze 26:17-18; 32:10 **27:36** [s]Jer 19:8; S 49:17; S 50:13; Zep 2:15 [t]S Ps 37:10,36; S Eze 26:21 **28:2** [u]S Isa 13:11 [v]S Isa 14:13 [w]Zep 2:15 [x]S Ge 3:5; S Ps 9:20; 82:6-7; S Eze 16:49; 2Th 2:4 **28:3** [y]S Eze 14:14; Da 1:20; 2:20-23,28; 5:11-12 **28:4** [z]Isa 10:13; Zec 9:3 **28:5** [a]S Isa 23:8 [b]S Jer 9:23; S Eze 27:33 [c]S Job 31:25; Ps 52:7; 62:10; Hos 12:8; 13:6 **28:7** [d]Eze 30:11; 31:12; 32:12; Hab 1:6 [e]Jer 9:23 [f]S Eze 7:24 **28:8** [g]S Ps 55:23; Eze 32:30 [h]Rev 18:7 [i]S Eze 26:12; 27:27 **28:9** [j]S Isa 31:3 [k]S Eze 16:49

27:25 *Tarshish.* See note on v. 12. The ship image is resumed (see notes on vv. 3,10).
27:26 *east wind.* Disastrous at sea (Ps 48:7) as well as on land (Jer 18:17). It possibly symbolizes Nebuchadnezzar (as in 17:10; 19:12).
27:30 *dust on their heads.* See 26:16 for a similar scene. *roll in ashes.* Cf. Mic 1:10 and note.
27:31 *shave their heads.* Cf. 7:18; Isa 15:2 and note; 22:12. *sackcloth.* See notes on Ge 37:34; Rev 11:3.
27:36 *horrible end … be no more.* See 26:21; 28:19; see also note on Isa 23:1.
28:2,8 *in the heart of the seas.* Emphasizes Tyre's location as an island fortress and as a dominant force in maritime commerce.
28:2 *ruler of Tyre.* May refer to the city of Tyre as ruler, or to Ethbaal II, Tyre's king (see v. 12), not to be confused with Ethbaal I (see 1Ki 16:31). *pride.* Cf. 27:3; Pr 11:2 and note; 16:18; Ac 12:21–23. *I am a god.* Cf. the proud boasts of the king of Babylon in Isa 14:12–15 (see note there).
28:3 *Daniel.* See note on 14:14.
28:7 *foreigners.* The Babylonians; see next phrase.
28:8 *pit.* Cf. Job 33:22,24; see note on 26:20.

[10]You will die the death of the
uncircumcised[l]
at the hands of foreigners.
I have spoken, declares the Sovereign
LORD.'"

[11]The word of the LORD came to me:
[12]"Son of man, take up a lament[m] concerning the king of Tyre and say to him: 'This is what the Sovereign LORD says:

"'You were the model of perfection,
full of wisdom and perfect in
beauty.[n]
[13]You were in Eden,[o]
the garden of God;[p]
every precious stone[q] adorned you:
ruby, topaz and emerald,
chrysolite, onyx and jasper,
sapphire,[a] turquoise[r] and beryl.[b]
Your settings and mountings[c] were
made of gold;
on the day you were created they
were prepared.[s]
[14]You were anointed[t] as a guardian
cherub,[u]
for so I ordained you.
You were on the holy mount of God;
you walked among the fiery stones.
[15]You were blameless in your ways
from the day you were created
till wickedness was found in you.
[16]Through your widespread trade
you were filled with violence,[v]
and you sinned.
So I drove you in disgrace from the
mount of God,
and I expelled you, O guardian
cherub,[w]
from among the fiery stones.
[17]Your heart became proud[x]
on account of your beauty,
and you corrupted your wisdom
because of your splendor.
So I threw you to the earth;
I made a spectacle of you before
kings.[y]
[18]By your many sins and dishonest
trade
you have desecrated your
sanctuaries.
So I made a fire[z] come out from you,
and it consumed you,
and I reduced you to ashes[a] on the
ground
in the sight of all who were
watching.[b]
[19]All the nations who knew you
are appalled[c] at you;
you have come to a horrible end
and will be no more.[d]'"

A Prophecy Against Sidon

[20]The word of the LORD came to me:
[21]"Son of man, set your face against[e] Sidon;[f] prophesy against her [22]and say: 'This is what the Sovereign LORD says:

"'I am against you, O Sidon,
and I will gain glory[g] within you.
They will know that I am the LORD,
when I inflict punishment[h] on her
and show myself holy[i] within her.
[23]I will send a plague upon her
and make blood flow in her streets.
The slain will fall within her,
with the sword against her on every
side.
Then they will know that I am the
LORD.[j]

[24]"'No longer will the people of Israel have malicious neighbors who are painful briers and sharp thorns.[k] Then they will know that I am the Sovereign LORD.

[a] 13 Or *lapis lazuli* [b] 13 The precise identification of some of these precious stones is uncertain. [c] 13 The meaning of the Hebrew for this phrase is uncertain.

28:10 [l] S 1Sa 14:6; S Jer 9:26; Eze 32:19,24 **28:12** [m] S Eze 19:1 [n] Eze 27:2-4 **28:13** [o] S Ge 2:8 [p] Eze 31:8-9 [q] Rev 17:4 [r] S Eze 27:16 [s] Isa 14:11; Rev 21:20 **28:14** [t] Ex 30:26; 40:9 [u] Ex 25:17-20 **28:16** [v] S Ge 6:11; Hab 2:17 [w] S Ge 3:24 **28:17** [x] Isa 10:12; Eze 16:49; 31:10 [y] S Eze 19:12 **28:18** [z] Ob 1:18 [a] Mal 4:3 [b] Zec 9:2-4 **28:19** [c] S Lev 26:32 [d] S Jer 51:64; S Eze 26:21 **28:21** [e] S Eze 13:17 [f] S Ge 10:15; S Jer 25:22 **28:22** [g] Eze 39:13 [h] Eze 30:19 [i] S Lev 10:3 **28:23** [j] S Eze 5:17; 38:22 **28:24** [k] S Isa 5:6; S Eze 2:6

28:10 *uncircumcised.* Used here in the sense of barbarian or uncouth. The Phoenicians, like the Israelites and the Egyptians, practiced circumcision (see 31:18; 32:19).
28:12 *lament.* See note on 19:1. *king of Tyre.* Cf. v. 2, but see note on Isa 14:12–15. *model of perfection.* "Model" is lit. "seal," as in Hag 2:23, where Zerubbabel is called God's "signet ring." With cutting irony Ezekiel depicts the proud king of Tyre as the first man created, radiant with wisdom and beauty. *perfect in beauty.* See 27:3 and note.
28:13 *You were in Eden.* Like Adam (Ge 2:15). Ezekiel continues to use imagery of the creation and the fall to picture the career of the king of Tyre (see 31:9,16,18). *every precious stone.* Unlike Adam, who was naked (Ge 2:25), the king is pictured as a fully clothed priest, ordained (v. 14) to guard God's holy place. The 9 stones are among the 12 worn by the priest (Ex 28:17–20). (The Septuagint, the pre-Christian Greek translation of the OT, lists all 12.) *settings and mountings.* For the precious stones. *on the day you were created.* Cf. v. 15; Ge 5:2.
28:14 *as a guardian cherub.* Cf. v. 16. The Genesis account has cherubim (plural) stationed at the border of the garden after the expulsion of Adam and Eve (see Ge 3:24 and note). Some read "with" instead of "as." *holy mount of God.* Cf. v. 16. This does not reflect the Genesis story. See Isa 14:13 for the figure of God dwelling on a mountain. *fiery stones.* The precious stones (v. 13; cf. Rev 4:1–6; 21:15–21).
28:15 *You were blameless … till.* The parallel to Ge 2–3 is clear (see Ge 6:9 and note; 17:1).
28:16 *widespread trade … filled with violence.* Tyre's major crime.
28:17 *threw you to the earth.* Expulsion from the heavenly garden.
28:19 *horrible end … be no more.* See note on 27:36.
28:21 *set your face.* See note on 20:46. *Sidon.* See 27:8 and note. This is the only time in the OT that Sidon is mentioned apart from Tyre (cf. Isa 23:1–4; Jer 47:4; Joel 3:4; Zec 9:2).
28:22 *I am against you.* Possibly because of Sidon's involvement in the Jerusalem summit conference (Jer 27:3; see note on 5:8). *I will gain glory within you.* The Lord's glory would be recognized in Sidon's punishment. *show myself holy.* See v. 25; Lev 10:3 and note.
28:24 *painful briers.* For references to Israel's enemies as briers see Nu 33:55; Jos 23:13.

[25]" 'This is what the Sovereign LORD says: When I gather[l] the people of Israel from the nations where they have been scattered,[m] I will show myself holy[n] among them in the sight of the nations. Then they will live in their own land, which I gave to my servant Jacob.[o] [26]They will live there in safety[p] and will build houses and plant[q] vineyards; they will live in safety when I inflict punishment[r] on all their neighbors who maligned them. Then they will know that I am the LORD their God.[s]' "

A Prophecy Against Egypt

29 In the tenth year, in the tenth month on the twelfth day, the word of the LORD came to me:[t] [2]"Son of man, set your face against[u] Pharaoh king of Egypt[v] and prophesy against him and against all Egypt.[w] [3]Speak to him and say: 'This is what the Sovereign LORD says:

" 'I am against you, Pharaoh[x] king of Egypt,
you great monster[y] lying among your streams.
You say, "The Nile[z] is mine;
I made it for myself."
[4]But I will put hooks[a] in your jaws
and make the fish of your streams stick to your scales.
I will pull you out from among your streams,
with all the fish sticking to your scales.[b]
[5]I will leave you in the desert,
you and all the fish of your streams.
You will fall on the open field
and not be gathered[c] or picked up.
I will give you as food
to the beasts of the earth and the birds of the air.[d]

[6]Then all who live in Egypt will know that I am the LORD.

" 'You have been a staff of reed[e] for the house of Israel. [7]When they grasped you with their hands, you splintered[f] and you tore open their shoulders; when they leaned on you, you broke and their backs were wrenched.[a][g]

[8]" 'Therefore this is what the Sovereign LORD says: I will bring a sword against you and kill your men and their animals.[h] [9]Egypt will become a desolate wasteland. Then they will know that I am the LORD.

" 'Because you said, "The Nile[i] is mine; I made it,[j]" [10]therefore I am against you[k] and against your streams, and I will make the land of Egypt[l] a ruin and a desolate waste[m] from Migdol[n] to Aswan,[o] as far as the border of Cush.[b][p] [11]No foot of man or animal will pass through it; no one will live there for forty years.[q] [12]I will make the land of Egypt desolate[r] among devastated lands, and her cities will lie desolate forty years among ruined cities. And I will disperse the Egyptians among the nations and scatter them through the countries.[s]

[13]" 'Yet this is what the Sovereign LORD says: At the end of forty years I will gather the Egyptians from the nations where they were scattered. [14]I will bring them back from captivity and return them to Upper Egypt,[c][t] the land of their ancestry. There they will be a lowly[u] kingdom.[v] [15]It will be the lowliest of kingdoms and will never again exalt itself above the other nations.[w] I will make it so weak that it will never again

[a] 7 Syriac (see also Septuagint and Vulgate); Hebrew *and you caused their backs to stand* [b] 10 That is, the upper Nile region [c] 14 Hebrew *to Pathros*

28:25 [l]Ps 106:47; Jer 32:37 [m]S Isa 11:12 [n]S Eze 20:41 [o]Jer 12:15; 23:8; S Eze 11:17; 34:27; 37:25 **28:26** [p]S Lev 25:18; S 1Ki 4:25; S Jer 17:25 [q]S Dt 20:6 [r]S Ps 149:9 [s]S Isa 65:21; S Jer 32:15; Eze 38:8; 39:26-27; Hos 2:15; 11:11; Am 9:14-15 **29:1** [t]ver 17; S Eze 26:1 **29:2** [u]S Eze 25:2 [v]S Jer 25:19 [w]Isa 19:1-17; Jer 46:2; Eze 30:1-26; 31:1-18; 32:1-32 **29:3** [x]Jer 44:30 [y]S Ps 68:30; S 74:13; Eze 32:2 [z]S Jer 46:8 **29:4** [a]S 2Ki 19:28; S Job 41:2 [b]Eze 38:4 **29:5** [c]S Jer 8:2 [d]S Jer 7:33; 34:20; Eze 31:13; 32:4-6; 39:4 **29:6** [e]S 2Ki 18:21 **29:7** [f]2Ki 18:21; Isa 36:6 [g]Jer 17:5; Eze 17:15-17 **29:8** [h]Eze 25:13; 32:11-13 **29:9** [i]S Jer 46:8 [j]Eze 30:7-8, 13-19 **29:10** [k]S Jer 21:13 [l]S Ex 3:22 [m]S Jer 46:19 [n]S Ex 14:2 [o]Eze 30:6 [p]Isa 18:1; Eze 30:4 **29:11** [q]Eze 32:13 **29:12** [r]S Isa 34:10 [s]S Jer 46:19; Eze 30:7,23,26 **29:14** [t]S Isa 11:11; Eze 30:14 [u]Eze 17:14 [v]S Isa 19:22; Jer 46:26 **29:15** [w]Zec 10:11

28:25 *When I gather … Israel.* A frequent promise in Ezekiel and later (see 11:17; 20:34,41–42; 29:13; 34:13; 36:24; 37:21; 38:8; 39:27; Ne 1:9; Zec 10:8,10). *my servant Jacob.* Cf. 37:25. For the promise see Ge 28:13; 35:12; Ps 105:10–11.

28:26 *live there in safety.* A perennial ideal that had become an especially meaningful promise (cf. 34:28; 38:8,11,14; 39:26; Lev 25:18–19; Jer 23:6; 32:37; 33:16)—closely related to God's promised "rest" (see Dt 3:20 and note). *houses … vineyards.* Basic necessities of the good life (cf. Isa 65:21; Jer 29:5,28; Am 9:14).

29:1—32:32 A series of seven prophecies against Egypt (for their dates see notes below), most of which came during Jerusalem's last years when the Egyptian pharaoh was offering encouragement to King Zedekiah to rebel against Nebuchadnezzar (see 17:15; Jer 37:5–8).

29:1 *tenth year … tenth month … twelfth day.* Jan. 7, 587 B.C.; the sixth date in Ezekiel (see 1:2; 8:1; 20:1; 24:1; 26:1). All the prophecies against Egypt are dated except one (30:1).

29:2 *set your face.* See note on 20:46. *Pharaoh.* Hophra, 589–570 B.C. (see Jer 44:30).

29:3 *I am against you.* See note on 5:8. *great monster.* Or "crocodile"; pictured as being in the Nile. See notes on Job 41:1; Ps 74:13–14; Isa 27:1. *your streams.* Nile delta and canals (cf. Isa 7:18; 19:6; 37:25). *You say.* Boasts inscribed on Egyptian monuments had become proverbial.

29:4 *hooks.* Cf. 19:4. *fish of your streams.* Egypt's conquered territories or mercenaries.

29:5 *food to the beasts.* Particularly frustrating to the pharaoh's great hopes for an afterlife, as symbolized by the pyramids and expressed in the Egyptian Book of the Dead.

29:6 *You have been a staff of reed.* A comparison made earlier (see Isa 36:6 and note). Pharaoh Hophra briefly but unsuccessfully diverted the Babylonians from laying siege to Jerusalem (see Jer 37:1–10).

29:8 *sword.* Nebuchadnezzar's (see 5:2 and note).

29:10 *Migdol.* Probably in northern Egypt (see Jer 44:1 and note). *Aswan.* A town in southern Egypt. "From Migdol to Aswan" (see 30:6) probably indicated all Egypt, just as "from Dan to Beersheba" meant all Israel (see, e.g., Jdg 20:1; 1Sa 3:20 and notes).

29:11 *forty years.* Sometimes used to signify a long and difficult period (cf. 4:6).

29:14 *Upper Egypt.* Southern Egypt (see 30:14; Isa 11:11 and note; Jer 44:1,15).

rule over the nations. [16]Egypt will no longer
be a source of confidence[x] for the people of
Israel but will be a reminder[y] of their sin
in turning to her for help.[z] Then they will
know that I am the Sovereign LORD.[a]' "

[17]In the twenty-seventh year, in the first
month on the first day, the word of the LORD
came to me:[b] [18]"Son of man, Nebuchadnezzar[c] king of Babylon drove his army
in a hard campaign against Tyre; every
head was rubbed bare[d] and every shoulder made raw.[e] Yet he and his army got no
reward from the campaign he led against
Tyre. [19]Therefore this is what the Sovereign
LORD says: I am going to give Egypt to Nebuchadnezzar king[f] of Babylon, and he will
carry off its wealth. He will loot and plunder[g] the land as pay for his army.[h] [20]I have
given him Egypt[i] as a reward for his efforts
because he and his army did it for me, declares the Sovereign LORD.[j]

[21]"On that day I will make a horn[a][k]
grow for the house of Israel, and I will
open your mouth[l] among them. Then they
will know that I am the LORD.[m]"

A Lament for Egypt

30 The word of the LORD came to me:
[2]"Son of man, prophesy and say:
'This is what the Sovereign LORD says:

" 'Wail[n] and say,
"Alas for that day!"
[3]For the day is near,[o]
the day of the LORD[p] is near—
a day of clouds,
a time of doom for the nations.
[4]A sword will come against Egypt,[q]
and anguish will come upon Cush.[b][r]
When the slain fall in Egypt,
her wealth will be carried away
and her foundations torn down.[s]

[5]Cush and Put,[t] Lydia and all Arabia,[u] Libya[c] and the people[v] of the covenant land
will fall by the sword along with Egypt.[w]

29:16 [x]2Ch 32:10 [y]S Nu 5:15 [z]S La 4:17 [a]Isa 20:5; S 30:2; Hos 8:13 **29:17** [b]S ver 1; S Eze 24:1; 30:20; 40:1 **29:18** [c]Jer 27:6; 39:1 [d]S Lev 13:40; S Job 1:20; S Jer 48:37 [e]Ge 49:15 **29:19** [f]S Isa 19:4 [g]S Eze 26:5 [h]Jer 43:10-13; Eze 30:4,10, 24-25; 32:11 **29:20** [i]S Isa 43:3 [j]Isa 10:6-7; 45:1; S Jer 25:9 **29:21** [k]S Ps 132:17; S Lk 1:69 [l]Eze 33:22 [m]S Eze 3:27 **30:2** [n]S Isa 13:6; Jas 5:1 **30:3** [o]S Eze 7:7; Joel 1:15; 2:1,11; Ob 1:15 [p]ver 18; S Eze 7:12,19; 32:7; 34:12 **30:4** [q]Jer 25:19; Da 11:43 [r]S Ge 10:6; S Eze 29:10 [s]S Eze 29:19 **30:5** [t]S Eze 27:10 [u]S 2Ch 9:14 [v]Jer 25:20 [w]Na 3:9 **30:6** [x]Eze 29:10 **30:7** [y]S Eze 29:12 **30:8** [z]S Jer 49:27; Eze 39:6; Am 1:4,7,10; Na 1:6 [a]S Eze 29:9 **30:9** [b]S Ge 10:6 [c]Isa 23:5 [d]Eze 32:9-10; Zep 2:12 **30:10** [e]Jer 39:1 [f]S Eze 29:19 **30:11** [g]S Eze 28:7 [h]ver 24-25

[6]" 'This is what the LORD says:

" 'The allies of Egypt will fall
and her proud strength will fail.
From Migdol to Aswan[x]
they will fall by the sword within
her,
declares the Sovereign LORD.
[7]" 'They will be desolate
among desolate lands,
and their cities will lie
among ruined cities.[y]
[8]Then they will know that I am the
LORD,
when I set fire[z] to Egypt
and all her helpers are crushed.[a]

[9]" 'On that day messengers will go out
from me in ships to frighten Cush[b] out of
her complacency. Anguish[c] will take hold
of them on the day of Egypt's doom, for it
is sure to come.[d]

[10]" 'This is what the Sovereign LORD
says:

" 'I will put an end to the hordes of
Egypt
by the hand of Nebuchadnezzar[e]
king of Babylon.[f]
[11]He and his army—the most ruthless of
nations[g]—
will be brought in to destroy the
land.
They will draw their swords against
Egypt
and fill the land with the slain.[h]
[12]I will dry up[i] the streams of the Nile[j]
and sell the land to evil men;
by the hand of foreigners
I will lay waste[k] the land and
everything in it.

I the LORD have spoken.

[a] *21 Horn* here symbolizes strength. [b] *4* That is, the upper Nile region; also in verses 5 and 9 [c] *5* Hebrew *Cub*

30:12 [i]S Isa 19:6 [j]S Jer 46:8; Eze 29:9 [k]S Eze 19:7

29:17 The second prophecy against Egypt (see note on v. 1). *twenty-seventh year ... first month ... first day.* Apr. 26, 571 B.C.; the seventh date in Ezekiel (see v. 1; 1:2; 8:1; 20:1; 24:1; 26:1). This is the latest date in Ezekiel; accordingly, this prophecy intrudes in the series of dated prophecies against Egypt, all the rest of which come within the years 587–585.

29:18 *hard campaign.* Nebuchadnezzar besieged Tyre for 15 years, from 586 to 571 B.C. (see 26:7–14). *every head was rubbed bare.* Probably from the leather helmets.

29:19 *I am going to give.* God's sovereignty over the nations is again proclaimed.

29:21 *make a horn grow for.* Revive the strength of (see NIV text note). The passage is not a Messianic prophecy. *open your mouth.* Ezekiel's muteness (3:26; 24:27) would be removed, which anticipates 33:22.

30:1 The third prophecy against Egypt (see note on 29:1). No date is given, but it was probably between January and April of 587 B.C. Compare 29:1 with 30:20. Jerusalem was under siege at this time.

30:2–3 *that day ... the day of the LORD.* The day of God's coming in judgment (see 7:7 and note). Egypt's judgment is announced.

30:3 *the day is near.* See 7:2–3,6 and note on 7:1–27; cf. Isa 13:6. *day of clouds.* Cf. Joel 2:2; Zep 1:15.

30:4 *sword.* Nebuchadnezzar's (see 29:8 and note).

30:5 *Put.* Libya, in North Africa (see note on 27:10). *Lydia.* See 27:10 and note. *Libya.* Hebrew *Cub* (see NIV text note), probably best understood as an unidentified place. *people of the covenant land.* Apparently Jews living in Egypt (see Jer 44 and note on 44:1).

30:6 *From Migdol to Aswan.* See note on 29:10.

30:8 *set fire to.* See note on 20:47.

30:9 *messengers ... in ships.* See Isa 18 for a similar oracle on Cush, involving ships on the Nile.

30:11 *most ruthless of nations.* A common phrase for the Babylonians, who were known for their cruelty (see 2Ki 25:7; Hab 1:6).

13" 'This is what the Sovereign LORD says:

" 'I will destroy the idols[l]
and put an end to the images in
Memphis.[a][m]
No longer will there be a prince in
Egypt,[n]
and I will spread fear throughout the
land.
14I will lay[o] waste Upper Egypt,[b]
set fire to Zoan[p]
and inflict punishment on Thebes.[c][q]
15I will pour out my wrath on Pelusium,[d]
the stronghold of Egypt,
and cut off the hordes of Thebes.
16I will set fire[r] to Egypt;
Pelusium will writhe in agony.
Thebes will be taken by storm;
Memphis[s] will be in constant
distress.
17The young men of Heliopolis[e][t] and
Bubastis[f]
will fall by the sword,
and the cities themselves will go into
captivity.
18Dark will be the day at Tahpanhes[u]
when I break the yoke of Egypt;[v]
there her proud strength will come
to an end.
She will be covered with clouds,
and her villages will go into
captivity.[w]
19So I will inflict punishment[x] on Egypt,
and they will know that I am the
LORD.' "

20In the eleventh year, in the first month
on the seventh day, the word of the LORD
came to me:[y] 21"Son of man, I have broken
the arm[z] of Pharaoh[a] king of Egypt. It has
not been bound up for healing[b] or put in
a splint so as to become strong enough to
hold a sword. 22Therefore this is what the
Sovereign LORD says: I am against Pharaoh
king of Egypt.[c] I will break both his arms,
the good arm as well as the broken one,
and make the sword fall from his hand.[d]
23I will disperse the Egyptians among the
nations and scatter them through the
countries.[e] 24I will strengthen[f] the arms of
the king of Babylon and put my sword[g]
in his hand, but I will break the arms of
Pharaoh, and he will groan[h] before him
like a mortally wounded man. 25I will
strengthen the arms of the king of Babylon, but the arms of Pharaoh will fall
limp. Then they will know that I am the
LORD, when I put my sword[i] into the hand
of the king of Babylon and he brandish-
es it against Egypt.[j] 26I will disperse the
Egyptians among the nations and scatter
them through the countries. Then they
will know that I am the LORD.[k]"

A Cedar in Lebanon

31 In the eleventh year,[l] in the third
month on the first day, the word
of the LORD came to me:[m] 2"Son of man,
say to Pharaoh king of Egypt and to his
hordes:

" 'Who can be compared with you in
majesty?
3Consider Assyria,[n] once a cedar in
Lebanon,[o]
with beautiful branches
overshadowing the forest;
it towered on high,
its top above the thick foliage.[p]
4The waters[q] nourished it,
deep springs made it grow tall;
their streams flowed
all around its base
and sent their channels
to all the trees of the field.[r]

30:13 [l]S Jer 43:12; S Eze 6:6 [m]S Isa 19:13 [n]Zec 10:11 **30:14** [o]S Eze 29:14 [p]S Nu 13:22 [q]S Jer 46:25 **30:16** [r]S Jos 7:15 [s]S Isa 19:13 **30:17** [t]Ge 41:45 **30:18** [u]S Jer 43:7 [v]S Lev 26:13; S Isa 9:4 [w]S ver 3 **30:19** [x]Eze 28:22 **30:20** [y]S Eze 26:1; S 29:17; 31:1; 32:1 **30:21** [z]S Jer 48:25 [a]S Jer 44:30 [b]Jer 30:13; 46:11 **30:22** [c]S Ge 15:18; S Jer 46:25 [d]Ps 37:17; Zec 11:17 **30:23** [e]S Eze 29:12 **30:24** [f]Zec 10:6, 12; 12:5 [g]S Eze 21:14; Zep 2:12 [h]Jer 51:52 **30:25** [i]1Ch 21:12 [j]S Isa 10:5; 45:1,5; S Eze 29:19 **30:26** [k]S Eze 29:12 **31:1** [l]Jer 52:5 [m]S Eze 30:20; 32:17 **31:3** [n]S Jer 50:18 [o]S 2Ki 19:23; Hab 2:17; Zec 11:1 [p]Isa 10:34; S Eze 19:11 **31:4** [q]Eze 17:7 [r]Da 4:10

[a] *13* Hebrew *Noph*; also in verse 16 [b] *14* Hebrew *waste Pathros* [c] *14* Hebrew *No*; also in verses 15 and 16 [d] *15* Hebrew *Sin*; also in verse 16 [e] *17* Hebrew *Awen* (or *On*) [f] *17* Hebrew *Pi Beseth*

30:13 *idols.* See note on 6:4. *Memphis.* Located 15 miles south of Cairo, Memphis was a former capital of Egypt and one of her largest cities. The list of towns shows no discernible geographical pattern but is a literary device used to underscore the scope of the destruction (cf. Isa 10:9–11,27–32; Mic 1:10–15; Zep 2:4). *prince.* King.
30:14 *Upper Egypt.* See 29:14 and note. *Zoan.* A city in northeast Egypt in the delta region; also called Tanis (see Isa 19:11; 30:4 and notes). *Thebes.* Capital of Upper Egypt; present-day Luxor and Karnak (see NIV text note).
30:15 *Pelusium.* A fortress in the eastern delta region of the Nile (see NIV text note).
30:17 *Heliopolis.* Greek name (meaning "city of the sun") for On (see NIV text note), located six miles northeast of Cairo. *Bubastis.* At one time the capital of Lower (northern) Egypt; located 40 miles northeast of Cairo.
30:18 *Dark.* A common Biblical metaphor describing ruin, destruction or death. *Tahpanhes.* In extreme northeast Egypt. Johanan son of Kareah and his men fled there after the murder of Gedaliah (see Jer 43:4–7). *covered with clouds.* See v. 3 and note; 32:7.
30:20 The fourth prophecy against Egypt (see note on 29:1). *eleventh year ... first month ... seventh day.* Apr. 29, 587 B.C.; the eighth date in Ezekiel (see 1:2; 8:1; 20:1; 24:1; 26:1; 29:1,17).
30:21 *broken the arm.* Refers to Pharaoh Hophra's defeat by Nebuchadnezzar the previous year (see notes on 29:6; Jer 37:5,7).
30:24 *put my sword in his hand.* See note on 21:3.
30:25 *my sword.* See 5:2 and note.
31:1 The fifth prophecy against Egypt (see note on 29:1). *eleventh year ... third month ... first day.* June 21, 587 B.C.; the ninth date in Ezekiel (see 1:2; 8:1; 20:1; 24:1; 26:1; 29:1,17; 30:20).
31:3 *Consider Assyria.* A great nation that had fallen. In 609 B.C. Pharaoh Neco and his army marched north to help the Assyrians who were reeling from Babylonian attacks. The effort ultimately failed, and Assyria passed from history. *once a cedar.* The beginning of another allegory (see Ezekiel's allegorical use of the cedar in ch. 17). *Lebanon.* Known for its cedars (see vv. 15–18; Jdg 9:15; 1Ki 4:33; 5:6; 2Ki 14:9; Ezr 3:7; Ps 29:5; 92:12; 104:16).
31:4 *waters.* The Tigris and Euphrates. *deep springs.* Or "the deep" (see note on 26:19).

[5]So it towered higher[s]
than all the trees of the field;
its boughs increased
and its branches grew long,
spreading because of abundant
waters.[t]
[6]All the birds of the air
nested in its boughs,
all the beasts of the field
gave birth[u] under its branches;
all the great nations
lived in its shade.[v]
[7]It was majestic in beauty,
with its spreading boughs,
for its roots went down
to abundant waters.[w]
[8]The cedars[x] in the garden of God
could not rival it,
nor could the pine trees
equal its boughs,
nor could the plane trees[y]
compare with its branches —
no tree in the garden of God
could match its beauty.[z]
[9]I made it beautiful
with abundant branches,
the envy of all the trees of Eden[a]
in the garden of God.[b]

[10]" 'Therefore this is what the Sovereign
LORD says: Because it towered on high,
lifting its top above the thick foliage,
and because it was proud[c] of its height,
[11]I handed it over to the ruler of the nations, for him to deal with according to its
wickedness. I cast it aside,[d] [12]and the most
ruthless of foreign nations[e] cut it down
and left it. Its boughs fell on the mountains and in all the valleys;[f] its branches
lay broken in all the ravines of the land.
All the nations of the earth came out from
under its shade and left it.[g] [13]All the birds
of the air settled on the fallen tree, and
all the beasts of the field were among its
branches.[h] [14]Therefore no other trees by
the waters are ever to tower proudly on
high, lifting their tops above the thick foliage. No other trees so well-watered are
ever to reach such a height; they are all
destined[i] for death,[j] for the earth below,
among mortal men, with those who go
down to the pit.[k]

[15]" 'This is what the Sovereign LORD
says: On the day it was brought down to
the grave[a] I covered the deep springs with
mourning for it; I held back its streams,
and its abundant waters were restrained.
Because of it I clothed Lebanon with
gloom, and all the trees of the field withered away.[l] [16]I made the nations tremble[m]
at the sound of its fall when I brought it
down to the grave with those who go down
to the pit. Then all the trees[n] of Eden,[o] the
choicest and best of Lebanon, all the trees
that were well-watered, were consoled[p] in
the earth below.[q] [17]Those who lived in its
shade, its allies among the nations, had
also gone down to the grave with it, joining those killed by the sword.[r]

[18]" 'Which of the trees of Eden can be
compared with you in splendor and majesty? Yet you, too, will be brought down
with the trees of Eden to the earth below;
you will lie among the uncircumcised,[s]
with those killed by the sword.

" 'This is Pharaoh and all his hordes, declares the Sovereign LORD.' "

A Lament for Pharaoh

32 In the twelfth year, in the twelfth
month on the first day, the word of
the LORD came to me:[t] [2]"Son of man, take
up a lament[u] concerning Pharaoh king of
Egypt and say to him:

" 'You are like a lion[v] among the
nations;
you are like a monster[w] in the seas[x]
thrashing about in your streams,
churning the water with your feet
and muddying the streams.[y]

[3]" 'This is what the Sovereign LORD
says:

" 'With a great throng of people
I will cast my net over you,
and they will haul you up in my
net.[z]

31:5 [s]ver 10 [t]S Nu 24:6; S Eze 17:5 **31:6** [u]S Ge 31:7-9 [v]S Eze 17:23; S Mt 13:32 **31:7** [w]S Job 14:9 **31:8** [x]Ps 80:10 [y]S Ge 30:37 [z]Ge 2:8-9 **31:9** [a]S Ge 2:8 [b]S Ge 13:10; Eze 28:13 **31:10** [c]S Isa 2:11; S 14:13-14; S Eze 28:17 **31:11** [d]Da 5:20 **31:12** [e]S Eze 28:7 [f]Eze 32:5; 35:8 [g]Eze 32:11-12; Da 4:14 **31:13** [h]S Isa 18:6; S Eze 29:5; 32:4 **31:14** [i]S Ps 49:14 [j]S Ps 82:7 [k]S Nu 14:11; Ps 63:9; S Eze 26:20; 32:24 **31:15** [l]S 2Sa 1:21 **31:16** [m]S Jer 49:21 [n]S Isa 14:8 [o]S Ge 2:8 [p]S Eze 14:22 [q]S Isa 14:15; Eze 32:18 **31:17** [r]Ps 9:17 **31:18** [s]S Jer 9:26 **32:1** [t]S Eze 31:1; 33:21 **32:2** [u]2Sa 1:17; 3:33; 2Ch 35:25; S Eze 19:1 [v]S 2Ki 24:1; Na 2:11-13 [w]S Job 3:8; S Ps 74:13 [x]S Ge 1:21 [y]ver 13; Job 41:31; S Eze 29:3; 34:18 **32:3** [z]S Eze 12:13; Hab 1:15

[a] *15* Hebrew *Sheol*; also in verses 16 and 17

31:6 *birds of the air.* See 17:23 and note.
31:8 *garden of God.* Cf. 28:13.
31:11 *ruler of the nations.* Probably Nabopolassar, or possibly his son Nebuchadnezzar. *its wickedness.* Pride (see v. 10; Ge 11:1–8).
31:12 *most ruthless.* Babylon (see note on 30:11).
31:14 *pit.* See note on 26:20.
31:15 *deep springs.* See v. 4 and note on 26:19. *clothed ... with gloom.* See note on Ps 109:29.
31:16 *nations tremble.* As at Tyre's fall (see 27:35; 28:19). *were consoled.* Because the mightiest of trees had joined them in the "grave" (Sheol).
31:17 *those killed by the sword.* Those who met a premature death.
31:18 *you.* The Egyptian pharaoh. *you, too.* It would happen to the pharaoh as it had happened to Assyria. *uncircumcised.* See note on 28:10.
32:1 The sixth prophecy against Egypt (see note on 29:1). *twelfth year ... twelfth month ... first day.* Mar. 3, 585 B.C.; the tenth date in Ezekiel (see 1:2; 8:1; 20:1; 24:1; 26:1; 29:1,17; 30:20; 31:1). If the Septuagint (the pre-Christian Greek translation of the OT) is followed ("eleventh year"), then the chronological order of the prophecies against Egypt is preserved (and the date would be Mar. 13, 586). Cf. 29:1; 30:20; 31:1; see v. 17 and note.
32:2 *lament.* See note on 19:1. *lion among the nations.* A figure for royalty and grandeur (see 19:1–9). *monster.* See 29:3 and note. *seas ... streams.* Canals of the Nile (see note on 29:3).
32:3 *cast my net.* Earlier it was Zedekiah over whom God's net was thrown (see 12:13; 17:20; 19:8).

[4]I will throw you on the land
and hurl you on the open field.
I will let all the birds of the air settle
on you
and all the beasts of the earth gorge
themselves on you.[a]
[5]I will spread your flesh on the
mountains
and fill the valleys[b] with your
remains.
[6]I will drench the land with your
flowing blood[c]
all the way to the mountains,
and the ravines will be filled with
your flesh.[d]
[7]When I snuff you out, I will cover the
heavens
and darken their stars;
I will cover the sun with a cloud,
and the moon will not give its light.[e]
[8]All the shining lights in the heavens
I will darken[f] over you;
I will bring darkness over your
land,[g]
declares the Sovereign LORD.
[9]I will trouble the hearts of many
peoples
when I bring about your destruction
among the nations,
among[a] lands you have not known.
[10]I will cause many peoples to be
appalled at you,
and their kings will shudder with
horror because of you
when I brandish my sword[h] before
them.
On the day[i] of your downfall
each of them will tremble
every moment for his life.[j]

[11]" 'For this is what the Sovereign LORD
says:

" 'The sword[k] of the king of Babylon[l]
will come against you.[m]
[12]I will cause your hordes to fall
by the swords of mighty men—
the most ruthless of all nations.[n]
They will shatter the pride of Egypt,
and all her hordes will be
overthrown.[o]

32:4 [a]S Isa 18:6; Eze 31:12-13; 39:4-5,17 **32:5** [b]S Eze 31:12 **32:6** [c]S Isa 34:3 [d]S Eze 29:5 **32:7** [e]S Isa 13:10; 34:4; S Eze 30:3; Joel 2:2,31; 3:15; S Mt 24:29; Rev 8:12 **32:8** [f]S Ps 102:26 [g]S Job 9:7; S Jer 4:23; Joel 2:10 **32:10** [h]S Isa 30:32 [i]S Jer 46:10 [j]S Eze 26:16; S 27:35; 30:9; Rev 18:9-10 **32:11** [k]S Eze 21:19 [l]S Isa 19:4; S Jer 46:13 [m]S Eze 29:19 **32:12** [n]S Eze 28:7 [o]Eze 31:11-12

32:13 [p]S ver 2; S Eze 29:8,11 **32:15** [q]Ex 7:5; S 14:4,18; Ps 107:33-34 **32:16** [r]S Ge 50:10; S Eze 19:1 **32:17** [s]S ver 1 **32:18** [t]Jer 1:10 [u]Eze 26:20; S 31:14,16; Mic 1:8 **32:19** [v]ver 29-30; S Eze 28:10 **32:20** [w]Ps 28:3 [x]Eze 31:17-18 **32:21** [y]S Isa 14:9 [z]Eze 28:10 **32:23** [a]S Isa 14:15 [b]Na 1:14 **32:24** [c]S Ge 10:22 [d]S Jer 49:37 [e]S Job 28:13

[13]I will destroy all her cattle
from beside abundant waters
no longer to be stirred by the foot of
man
or muddied by the hoofs of cattle.[p]
[14]Then I will let her waters settle
and make her streams flow like oil,
declares the Sovereign LORD.
[15]When I make Egypt desolate
and strip the land of everything in it,
when I strike down all who live there,
then they will know that I am the
LORD.[q]'

[16]"This is the lament[r] they will chant for
her. The daughters of the nations will chant
it; for Egypt and all her hordes they will
chant it, declares the Sovereign LORD."

[17]In the twelfth year, on the fifteenth day
of the month, the word of the LORD came
to me:[s] [18]"Son of man, wail for the hordes
of Egypt and consign[t] to the earth below
both her and the daughters of mighty nations, with those who go down to the pit.[u]
[19]Say to them, 'Are you more favored than
others? Go down and be laid among the
uncircumcised.'[v] [20]They will fall among
those killed by the sword. The sword is
drawn; let her be dragged[w] off with all
her hordes.[x] [21]From within the grave[b][y] the
mighty leaders will say of Egypt and her
allies, 'They have come down and they lie
with the uncircumcised,[z] with those killed
by the sword.'
[22]"Assyria is there with her whole army;
she is surrounded by the graves of all her
slain, all who have fallen by the sword.
[23]Their graves are in the depths of the pit[a]
and her army lies around her grave.[b] All
who had spread terror in the land of the
living are slain, fallen by the sword.
[24]"Elam[c] is there, with all her hordes
around her grave. All of them are slain,
fallen by the sword.[d] All who had spread
terror in the land of the living[e] went down
uncircumcised to the earth below. They
bear their shame with those who go down

[a] 9 Hebrew; Septuagint *bring you into captivity among the nations, / to* [b] 21 Hebrew *Sheol*; also in verse 27

32:4 *I will throw.* God's actions here are very similar to those described in 29:3–5.
32:7–8 A piling up of language that evokes the darkness associated with the day of the Lord (see Joel 2:2 and note, 10,31; 3:15; Am 5:18 and note; Zep 1:15).
32:9 *trouble the hearts.* This and the next verse reflect the fear brought about whenever great world powers fall, reminding lesser nations that they are even more vulnerable. Cf. similar feelings aroused by Tyre's fall (26:16–18; 27:35; 28:19).
32:10 *my sword.* See 5:2 and note.
32:11 *king of Babylon.* Nebuchadnezzar (cf. 21:19).
32:12 *most ruthless of all nations.* Babylon (see note on 30:11). *pride of Egypt.* The army in which she took pride ("her hordes"; cf. Am 6:8).
32:14 *streams flow like oil.* Their surface undisturbed by any form of life.
32:16 *daughters of the nations.* A world chorus of professional wailers (see Jer 9:17–18 and notes).
32:17 The seventh and last prophecy against Egypt (see note on 29:1). *twelfth year … fifteenth day.* No month is given (as in 26:1; 40:1). The whole year dates from Apr. 13, 586, to Apr. 1, 585 B.C. The Septuagint (the pre-Christian Greek translation of the OT) suggests the first month, the 15th day of which would be Apr. 27, 586.
32:18 *earth below.* Same as "grave" (Sheol) in 31:15. *daughters of mighty nations.* See note on v. 16.
32:19 *uncircumcised.* See note on 28:10.
32:24 *Elam.* A country east of Assyria; in present-day Iran (see note on Isa 11:11).

to the pit.[f] 25A bed is made for her among
the slain, with all her hordes around her
grave. All of them are uncircumcised,[g]
killed by the sword. Because their terror
had spread in the land of the living, they
bear their shame with those who go down
to the pit; they are laid among the slain.
26"Meshech and Tubal[h] are there, with
all their hordes around their graves. All
of them are uncircumcised, killed by the
sword because they spread their terror in
the land of the living. 27Do they not lie
with the other uncircumcised[i] warriors
who have fallen, who went down to the
grave with their weapons of war, whose
swords were placed under their heads? The
punishment for their sins rested on their
bones, though the terror of these warriors
had stalked through the land of the living.
28"You too, O Pharaoh, will be broken
and will lie among the uncircumcised,
with those killed by the sword.
29"Edom[j] is there, her kings and all her
princes; despite their power, they are laid
with those killed by the sword. They lie
with the uncircumcised, with those who
go down to the pit.[k]
30"All the princes of the north[l] and all
the Sidonians[m] are there; they went down
with the slain in disgrace despite the terror
caused by their power. They lie uncircumcised[n] with those killed by the sword and
bear their shame with those who go down
to the pit.[o]
31"Pharaoh—he and all his army—will
see them and he will be consoled[p] for all
his hordes that were killed by the sword,
declares the Sovereign LORD. 32Although I
had him spread terror in the land of the
living, Pharaoh[q] and all his hordes will be
laid among the uncircumcised, with those
killed by the sword, declares the Sovereign
LORD."[r]

Ezekiel a Watchman

33 The word of the LORD came to me:
2"Son of man, speak to your countrymen and say to them: 'When I bring
the sword[s] against a land, and the people
of the land choose one of their men and
make him their watchman,[t] 3and he sees
the sword coming against the land and
blows the trumpet[u] to warn the people,
4then if anyone hears the trumpet but does
not take warning[v] and the sword comes
and takes his life, his blood will be on his
own head.[w] 5Since he heard the sound of
the trumpet but did not take warning, his
blood will be on his own head.[x] If he had
taken warning, he would have saved himself.[y] 6But if the watchman sees the sword
coming and does not blow the trumpet to
warn the people and the sword comes and
takes the life of one of them, that man will
be taken away because of his sin, but I
will hold the watchman accountable for
his blood.'[z]
7"Son of man, I have made you a watchman[a] for the house of Israel; so hear the
word I speak and give them warning from
me.[b] 8When I say to the wicked, 'O wicked
man, you will surely die,[c]' and you do not
speak out to dissuade him from his ways,
that wicked man will die for[a] his sin, and
I will hold you accountable for his blood.[d]
9But if you do warn the wicked man to
turn from his ways and he does not do so,[e]
he will die for his sin, but you will have
saved yourself.[f]
10"Son of man, say to the house of Israel, 'This is what you are saying: "Our
offenses and sins weigh us down, and
we are wasting away[g] because of[b] them.
How then can we live?[h]" ' 11Say to them,
'As surely as I live, declares the Sovereign
LORD, I take no pleasure in the death of
the wicked, but rather that they turn from
their ways and live.[i] Turn![j] Turn from your
evil ways! Why will you die, O house of
Israel?'[k]
12"Therefore, son of man, say to your
countrymen,[l] 'The righteousness of the
righteous man will not save him when he

[a] 8 Or *in*; also in verse 9 [b] 10 Or *away in*

32:24 [f]S Eze 26:20
32:25 [g]Eze 28:10
32:26 [h]S Eze 27:13
32:27 [i]Eze 28:10
32:29 [j]S Ps 137:7; Isa 34:5-15; Jer 49:7; Eze 35:15; Ob 1:1 [k]Eze 25:12-14
32:30 [l]S Isa 14:31; Jer 25:26; Eze 38:6; 39:2 [m]S Ge 10:15; S Jer 25:22 [n]Eze 28:10 [o]S Eze 26:20; S 28:8
32:31 [p]S Eze 14:22
32:32 [q]S Jer 44:30 [r]S Job 3:14
33:2 [s]S Lev 26:25; S Jer 12:12 [t]S 1Sa 14:16; Isa 21:6-9; S Jer 51:12
33:3 [u]S Ex 20:18; S Nu 10:7; Hos 5:8; 8:1
33:4 [v]2Ch 25:16 [w]S Lev 20:9; S Jer 6:17; Zec 1:4; Ac 18:6
33:5 [x]S Lev 20:9 [y]S Ex 9:21
33:6 [z]Isa 56:10-11; S Eze 3:18
33:7 [a]S Isa 52:8 [b]Jer 1:17; 26:2
33:8 [c]ver 14 [d]S Isa 3:11; S Eze 18:4
33:9 [e]S Ps 7:12 [f]Eze 3:17-19
33:10 [g]S Lev 26:16 [h]S Lev 26:39; S Eze 4:17
33:11 [i]S La 3:33 [j]S 2Ch 30:9; S Isa 19:22; S Jer 3:12 [k]Jer 44:7-8; S Eze 18:23; Hos 11:8; Joel 2:12; S 1Ti 2:4
33:12 [l]ver 2

32:26 *Meshech and Tubal.* Peoples and territories in Asia Minor (see 38:2 and note).
32:29 *Edom.* See note on Ge 36:1,8; see also Isa 34:5; Am 1:11–12; Introduction to Obadiah: Unity and Theme; map, p. 497.
32:30 *Sidonians.* See note on 28:21.
33:1—48:35 A section depicting consolation for Israel (see Introduction: Outline).
33:1—37:28 Sermons and prophecies of comfort following the fall of Jerusalem. Interspersed are words of warning and judgment (e.g., 33:23–33; 34:1–19; 35).
33:1–20 At this juncture, when his message takes on a radically different theme, Ezekiel's call to be a "watchman" for Israel is renewed (see 3:16–19 and note on 3:17).
33:2 *your countrymen.* Fellow Israelites in exile with Ezekiel. *sword.* The invading army (cf. 5:2 and note). *people of the land.* See note on 7:27.
33:3 *trumpet.* An instrument made from a ram's horn (see notes on Jos 6:4–5), used to warn of approaching danger (Ne 4:18–20; Jer 4:19; Am 3:6).
33:4 *his blood will be on his own head.* See note on 18:13.
33:6 *his blood.* His life, blood being the life principle (see Ge 9:5; 42:22; Lev 17:11 and note).
33:7–9 Cf. 3:17–19.
33:10 *Our offenses and sins.* The first time the exiles expressed consciousness of sin. Previously they had blamed their fathers (18:2) and even God (18:19,25).
33:11 *As surely as I live.* See note on 5:11. *I take no pleasure.* The question of 18:23 (see note there) is now a statement. God's basic intention for his creation is life, not death (see note on 16:6). *Turn!* The third call for repentance (see 14:6; 18:30).
33:12–20 Cf. 18:21–29 (see notes there).

disobeys, and the wickedness of the wicked man will not cause him to fall when
he turns from it. The righteous man, if he
sins, will not be allowed to live because
of his former righteousness.'[m] 13If I tell the
righteous man that he will surely live, but
then he trusts in his righteousness and
does evil, none of the righteous things he
has done will be remembered; he will die
for the evil he has done.[n] 14And if I say
to the wicked man, 'You will surely die,'
but he then turns away from his sin and
does what is just[o] and right— 15if he gives
back what he took in pledge[p] for a loan,
returns what he has stolen,[q] follows the
decrees that give life, and does no evil, he
will surely live; he will not die.[r] 16None of
the sins[s] he has committed will be remembered against him. He has done what is
just and right; he will surely live.[t]

17"Yet your countrymen say, 'The way of
the Lord is not just.' But it is their way that
is not just. 18If a righteous man turns from
his righteousness and does evil,[u] he will
die for it.[v] 19And if a wicked man turns
away from his wickedness and does what
is just and right, he will live by doing so.[w]
20Yet, O house of Israel, you say, 'The way
of the Lord is not just.' But I will judge
each of you according to his own ways."[x]

Jerusalem's Fall Explained

21In the twelfth year of our exile, in the
tenth month on the fifth day, a man who
had escaped[y] from Jerusalem came to me
and said, "The city has fallen![z]" 22Now the
evening before the man arrived, the hand
of the LORD was upon me,[a] and he opened
my mouth[b] before the man came to me in
the morning. So my mouth was opened
and I was no longer silent.[c]

23Then the word of the LORD came to
me: 24"Son of man, the people living in
those ruins[d] in the land of Israel are saying, 'Abraham was only one man, yet he
possessed the land. But we are many;[e]
surely the land has been given to us as our
possession.'[f] 25Therefore say to them, 'This
is what the Sovereign LORD says: Since you
eat[g] meat with the blood[h] still in it and
look to your idols and shed blood, should
you then possess the land?[i] 26You rely on
your sword, you do detestable things,[j] and
each of you defiles his neighbor's wife.[k]
Should you then possess the land?'

27"Say this to them: 'This is what the
Sovereign LORD says: As surely as I live,
those who are left in the ruins will fall by
the sword, those out in the country I will
give to the wild animals to be devoured,
and those in strongholds and caves will die
of a plague.[l] 28I will make the land a desolate waste, and her proud strength will
come to an end, and the mountains[m] of
Israel will become desolate so that no one
will cross them.[n] 29Then they will know
that I am the LORD, when I have made the
land a desolate[o] waste because of all the
detestable things they have done.'[p]

30"As for you, son of man, your countrymen are talking together about you by
the walls and at the doors of the houses,
saying to each other, 'Come and hear the
message that has come from the LORD.'
31My people come to you, as they usually
do, and sit before[q] you to listen to your
words, but they do not put them into practice. With their mouths they express devotion, but their hearts are greedy[r] for unjust
gain.[s] 32Indeed, to them you are nothing
more than one who sings love songs[t] with
a beautiful voice and plays an instrument
well, for they hear your words but do not
put them into practice.[u]

33:12 [m]2Ch 7:14; S Eze 3:20; S 18:21 **33:13** [n]Heb 10:38; 2Pe 2:20-21 **33:14** [o]S Jer 22:3 **33:15** [p]S Ex 22:26 [q]Ex 22:1-4; S Lev 6:2-5 [r]Isa 55:7; Jer 18:7-8; S Lk 19:8 **33:16** [s]S Jer 50:20 [t]S Isa 43:25 **33:18** [u]Jer 18:10 [v]S Eze 3:20 **33:19** [w]S ver 14-15 **33:20** [x]S Job 34:11 **33:21** [y]Eze 24:26 [z]S 2Ki 25:4, 10; Jer 39:1-2; 52:4-7; S Eze 32:1 **33:22** [a]S Eze 1:3 [b]Eze 29:21; Lk 1:64 [c]Eze 3:26-27; S 24:27 **33:24** [d]Eze 36:4 [e]S Dt 1:10 [f]Isa 51:2; Jer 40:7; Eze 11:15; Lk 3:8; Ac 7:5 **33:25** [g]Jer 7:21 [h]S Ge 9:4 [i]Jer 7:9-10; S Eze 22:6, 27 **33:26** [j]Jer 41:7 [k]Eze 22:11 **33:27** [l]1Sa 13:6; Isa 2:19; S Jer 42:22; S Eze 7:15; S 14:21; 39:4 **33:28** [m]S Isa 41:15 [n]S Ge 6:7; Jer 9:10 **33:29** [o]S Lev 26:34 [p]S Jer 18:16; S 44:22; Eze 36:4; Mic 7:13 **33:31** [q]S Eze 8:1 [r]Ps 119:36 [s]Ps 78:36-37; S Isa 29:13; S 33:15; S Jer 3:10; S 6:17; S Eze 22:27; Mt 13:22; 1Jn 3:18 **33:32** [t]S 1Ki 4:32 [u]Mk 6:20

33:14 *what is just and right.* See notes on 18:5; Ps 119:121.

33:15 *gives back what he took in pledge … returns what he has stolen.* See note on 18:7. *decrees that give life.* The purpose of God's law was to foster and protect life (see note on 20:11). *he will surely live.* The entire section is Ezekiel's answer to the despairing question of v. 10.

33:17 *The way of the Lord is not just.* See note on 18:25.

33:21–33 When news of Jerusalem's fall reaches Ezekiel, he must still reinforce his earlier word that "the end" had truly come on the city (see note on 7:1–27); even the remnant eking out an existence in the ruins of the city will be destroyed.

33:21 *twelfth year … tenth month … fifth day.* Jan. 8, 585 B.C., five months after the Jerusalem temple was burned down. See date in 2Ki 25:8, which in modern reckoning is Aug. 14, 586. The journey between Jerusalem and Babylon could be made in four months (Ezr 7:9). *man who had escaped.* The first of the exiles of 586 (see 24:26, "fugitive"; see also note there). He had "escaped" alive from the disaster at Jerusalem. *The city has fallen!* With this statement all of Ezekiel's previous prophecies were fulfilled and vindicated. He was then sent with a new mission: pastoral comfort.

33:22 *no longer silent.* See 24:27 and note.

33:24 *people living in those ruins.* The residents of Jerusalem not exiled in 586 B.C. *Abraham was only one man … But we are many.* A boast by the unrepentant, similar to that of 11:15 (cf. Lk 3:8).

33:25 *eat meat with the blood.* Forbidden in Ge 9:4 (see note there; see also note on Lev 17:11). *look to your idols.* See note on 18:6.

33:27 *As surely as I live.* See note on 5:11. *sword … wild animals … plague.* Cf. the threefold threat in 5:12; 7:15; 12:16 and the fourfold threat in 14:12–21 (see note on 5:16–17).

33:29 *know that I am the LORD.* See Introduction: Themes.

33:30–33 Words addressed to Ezekiel, but included here as a rebuke and admonition to the remnant from Jerusalem living in exile.

33:31 *sit before you.* As the elders had (8:1; 14:1). *greedy.* The people were waiting for Ezekiel to tell them how they could personally profit from the situation. They were not interested in God's designs for them (cf. Mt 20:20–28).

33:32 *one who sings.* May indicate that Ezekiel chanted his messages (see 2Ki 3:15; Isa 5:1), but more likely the prophet was using a metaphor. *they hear … but do not … practice.* See Isa 29:13 and note; Mt 21:28–32; cf. Jas 1:22–25.

33“When all this comes true—and it
surely will—then they will know that a
prophet has been among them.[v]”

Shepherds and Sheep

34 The word of the LORD came to me:
2“Son of man, prophesy against the
shepherds of Israel; prophesy and say to
them: ‘This is what the Sovereign LORD
says: Woe to the shepherds of Israel who
only take care of themselves! Should not
shepherds take care of the flock?[w] 3You eat
the curds, clothe yourselves with the wool
and slaughter the choice animals, but you
do not take care of the flock.[x] 4You have
not strengthened the weak or healed[y] the
sick or bound up[z] the injured. You have
not brought back the strays or searched
for the lost. You have ruled them harshly
and brutally.[a] 5So they were scattered because there was no shepherd,[b] and when
they were scattered they became food for
all the wild animals.[c] 6My sheep wandered
over all the mountains and on every high
hill.[d] They were scattered[e] over the whole
earth, and no one searched or looked for
them.[f]

7“ ‘Therefore, you shepherds, hear the
word of the LORD: 8As surely as I live, declares the Sovereign LORD, because my flock
lacks a shepherd and so has been plundered[g] and has become food for all the wild
animals,[h] and because my shepherds did
not search for my flock but cared for themselves rather than for my flock,[i] 9therefore,
O shepherds, hear the word of the LORD:
10This is what the Sovereign LORD says: I am
against[j] the shepherds and will hold them
accountable for my flock. I will remove
them from tending the flock so that the
shepherds can no longer feed themselves.
I will rescue[k] my flock from their mouths,
and it will no longer be food for them.[l]

11“ ‘For this is what the Sovereign LORD
says: I myself will search for my sheep[m]
and look after them. 12As a shepherd[n]
looks after his scattered flock when he is
with them, so will I look after my sheep. I
will rescue them from all the places where
they were scattered on a day of clouds and
darkness.[o] 13I will bring them out from the
nations and gather[p] them from the countries, and I will bring them into their own
land.[q][r][s][t] I will pasture them on the mountains of Israel, in the ravines and in all
the settlements in the land.[u][v][w] 14I will tend
them in a good pasture, and the mountain
heights of Israel[x] will be their grazing land.
There they will lie down in good grazing
land, and there they will feed in a rich
pasture[y] on the mountains of Israel.[z] 15I
myself will tend my sheep and have them
lie down,[a] declares the Sovereign LORD.[b]
16I will search for the lost and bring back
the strays. I will bind up[c] the injured and
strengthen the weak,[d] but the sleek and
the strong I will destroy.[e] I will shepherd
the flock with justice.[f]

17“ ‘As for you, my flock, this is what the
Sovereign LORD says: I will judge between
one sheep and another, and between rams
and goats.[g] 18Is it not enough[h] for you to
feed on the good pasture? Must you also
trample the rest of your pasture with your
feet?[i] Is it not enough for you to drink

33:33 [v]S 1Sa 3:20; S Jer 28:9; S Eze 2:5 **34:2** [w]Ps 78:70-72; Isa 40:11; Jer 3:15; S 23:1; Mic 3:11; Jn 10:11; 21:15-17; Jude 1:12 **34:3** [x]Isa 56:11; S Eze 22:27; Am 6:4; Zec 11:5 **34:4** [y]S Isa 3:7 [z]S Isa 1:6 [a]ver 16; S Lev 25:43; Mic 3:3; Zec 11:15-17 **34:5** [b]S Nu 27:17 [c]ver 28; S Isa 56:9; Ac 20:29 **34:6** [d]S Jer 50:6 [e]S Lev 26:33; S Ps 95:10; S Jer 10:21 [f]2Ch 18:16; Ps 142:4; Hos 7:13; S Mt 9:36; 18:12-13; Lk 15:5; 1Pe 2:25 **34:8** [g]S Jdg 2:14 [h]S Isa 56:9 [i]Jude 1:12 **34:10** [j]S Jer 21:13 [k]S Ps 72:14 [l]1Sa 2:29-30; S Jer 23:2; Zec 10:3 **34:11** [m]S Ps 119:176 **34:12** [n]Isa 40:11; S Jer 31:10; Zec 10:3; Lk 19:10 [o]S Eze 32:7 **34:13** [p]S Ge 48:21; S Dt 30:4 [q]Mic 4:6 [r]S Eze 11:17 [s]S Jer 23:8 [t]S Isa 66:20 [u]S Eze 28:25; 36:24 [v]S Jer 50:19 [w]Jer 23:3 **34:14** [x]S Eze 20:40 [y]Ps 23:2; S 37:3 [z]S Isa 65:10; Eze 36:29-30; 37:22; Am 9:14; Mic 7:14 **34:15** [a]Zep 3:13 [b]Ps 23:1-2; S Jer 33:12; Mic 5:4 **34:16** [c]S Ps 147:3 [d]Mic 4:6; Zep 3:19 [e]Lk 19:10 [f]Isa 10:16; S Jer 31:8; Lk 5:32 **34:17** [g]Mt 25:32-33 **34:18** [h]S Ge 30:15 [i]S Eze 32:2

34:1–31 The Lord gives the Israelites in exile the reassuring word that in the future he will himself be their Shepherd. In vv. 1–10 he denounces Israel's worthless "shepherds"; in vv. 11–16 he promises to seek out his scattered flock; in vv. 17–22 he declares that he will judge the strong sheep who have oppressed the weak; in vv. 23–24 he promises to set over his flock his servant "David"; in vv. 25–31 he speaks climactically of his "covenant of peace" that will secure Israel's blessed state.

34:2 *shepherds of Israel.* Those responsible for providing leadership, especially the kings and their officials (see 2Sa 7:7 and note; Jer 25:18–19), but also the prophets and priests (see Isa 56:11; Jer 23:9–11). Ezekiel had earlier singled out the princes, priests and prophets for special rebuke (ch. 22). To call a king a shepherd was common throughout the ancient Near East (see note on Ps 23:1). For David's rise from shepherd to shepherd-king see Ps 78:70–71. For condemnation of the shepherds cf. Jer 23:1–4.

34:3 *eat … clothe … slaughter.* Legitimate rewards for shepherds. Their crime was that they did not care for the flock.

34:4 *searched for the lost.* Cf. Jer 50:6; Zec 11:15–17; Mt 18:12–14; Lk 15:4; 19:10.

34:5 *scattered.* Often used by Ezekiel to describe Israel's exile and dispersion (11:16–17; 12:15; 20:23,34,41; 22:15; 28:25). *no shepherd.* That is, no true shepherd (cf. Mk 6:34).

34:8 *wild animals.* Hostile foreign nations; but see v. 28, where they are contrasted.

34:10 *I am against the shepherds.* See note on 5:8.

34:11 *I myself will search for my sheep.* Having dealt with the faithless shepherds (vv. 1–10), the Lord committed himself to shepherd his flock (see Jer 23:3–4).

34:12 *from all the places.* Babylonia was not the only place where the Israelites had gone (see Jer 43:1–7). *day of clouds and darkness.* The day of the Lord that had come upon Israel when Jerusalem fell in the summer of 586 B.C. (see 7:7; 32:7 and notes).

34:13 *I will bring them out.* The promises of restoration—begun in 11:17 and repeated in 20:34,41–42; 28:25—find special emphasis in this part (chs. 33–39) of Ezekiel (see 36:24–32 and notes; 37:21; 38:8 and note; 39:27). *mountains of Israel.* Compare the tone of 6:3–7 with judgment now past (see v. 12). The mountains perhaps represented the scene of salvation.

34:14 *I will tend them.* See Isa 40:11; Jn 10:11.

34:16 *the sleek and the strong.* Those with power who had fattened themselves by oppressing the other "sheep" (see vv. 17–22).

34:17 *rams and goats.* People of power and influence who were oppressing poorer Israelites. This prophetic

clear water? Must you also muddy the rest
with your feet? 19Must my flock feed on
what you have trampled and drink what
you have muddied with your feet?
20" 'Therefore this is what the Sovereign
LORD says to them: See, I myself will judge
between the fat sheep and the lean sheep.[j]
21Because you shove with flank and shoulder, butting all the weak sheep with your
horns[k] until you have driven them away,
22I will save my flock, and they will no longer be plundered. I will judge between one
sheep and another.[l] 23I will place over them
one shepherd, my servant David, and he
will tend[m] them; he will tend them and be
their shepherd.[n] 24I the LORD will be their
God,[o] and my servant David[p] will be prince
among them.[q] I the LORD have spoken.[r]
25" 'I will make a covenant[s] of peace[t]
with them and rid the land of wild beasts[u]
so that they may live in the desert and sleep
in the forests in safety.[v] 26I will bless[w] them
and the places surrounding my hill.[a] I will
send down showers in season;[x] there will
be showers of blessing.[y] 27The trees of the
field will yield their fruit[z] and the ground
will yield its crops;[a] the people will be secure[b] in their land. They will know that I
am the LORD, when I break the bars of their
yoke[c] and rescue them from the hands of
those who enslaved them.[d] 28They will no
longer be plundered by the nations, nor
will wild animals devour them. They will
live in safety,[e] and no one will make them
afraid.[f] 29I will provide for them a land renowned[g] for its crops, and they will no
longer be victims of famine[h] in the land or
bear the scorn[i] of the nations.[j] 30Then they
will know that I, the LORD their God, am
with them and that they, the house of Israel, are my people, declares the Sovereign
LORD.[k] 31You my sheep,[l] the sheep of my
pasture,[m] are people, and I am your God,
declares the Sovereign LORD.' "

34:20 [j]Mt 25:32 **34:21** [k]S Dt 33:17 **34:22** [l]Ps 72:12-14; Jer 23:2-3; Eze 20:37-38 **34:23** [m]Isa 40:11 [n]S Isa 31:4; Mic 5:4 **34:24** [o]Eze 36:28 [p]Ps 89:49 [q]S Isa 53:4; Zec 13:7 [r]Jer 23:4-5; S 30:9; S 33:14; Jn 10:16; Rev 7:17 **34:25** [s]S Eze 16:62 [t]S Nu 25:12 [u]Lev 26:6 [v]S Lev 25:18; Isa 11:6-9; Hos 2:18 **34:26** [w]S Ge 12:2 [x]Ps 68:9; Joel 2:23 [y]Dt 11:13-15; S 28:12; Isa 44:3 **34:27** [z]S Ps 72:16 [a]S Job 14:9; S Ps 67:6 [b]S Nu 24:21 [c]S Lev 26:13 [d]S Jer 30:8; S Eze 20:42; S 28:25 **34:28** [e]S Jer 32:37 [f]S Jer 30:10; S Eze 28:26; 39:26; Hos 11:11; Am 9:15; Zep 3:13; Zec 14:11 **34:29** [g]S Isa 4:2 [h]Eze 36:29

A Prophecy Against Edom

35 The word of the LORD came to me:
2"Son of man, set your face against
Mount Seir;[n] prophesy against it 3and say:
'This is what the Sovereign LORD says: I am
against you, Mount Seir, and I will stretch
out my hand[o] against you and make you
a desolate waste.[p] 4I will turn your towns
into ruins[q] and you will be desolate. Then
you will know that I am the LORD.[r]
5" 'Because you harbored an ancient
hostility and delivered the Israelites over
to the sword[s] at the time of their calamity,[t]
the time their punishment reached its climax,[u] 6therefore as surely as I live, declares
the Sovereign LORD, I will give you over to
bloodshed[v] and it will pursue you.[w] Since
you did not hate bloodshed, bloodshed
will pursue you. 7I will make Mount Seir a
desolate waste[x] and cut off from it all who
come and go.[y] 8I will fill your mountains
with the slain; those killed by the sword

[a] 26 Or *I will make them and the places surrounding my hill a blessing*

[i]S Ps 137:3; Eze 36:6; Joel 2:19 [j]Eze 36:15 **34:30** [k]S Eze 14:11; 37:27 **34:31** [l]S Ps 28:9 [m]S Jer 23:1 **35:2** [n]S Ge 14:6 **35:3** [o]S Jer 6:12 [p]S Isa 34:10; Eze 25:12-14 **35:4** [q]Jer 44:2 [r]ver 9; S Jer 49:10 **35:5** [s]S Ps 63:10 [t]Ob 1:13 [u]Ps 137:7; S Eze 21:29 **35:6** [v]S Isa 34:3 [w]Isa 63:2-6 **35:7** [x]S Jer 46:19 [y]S Jer 49:17

word shows the same concern for social justice found elsewhere in the prophets (see Isa 3:13–15; 5:8; Am 5:12; 6:1–7; see also Mic 2:1–5 and notes). Cf. the treatment of slaves Jeremiah observed (Jer 34:8–11).

34:23–24 *my servant David.* A ruler like David and from his line (see Ps 89:4,20,29; see also Jer 23:5–6 and notes).

34:24 *prince.* The Lord announced a kingdom where he would be King and the earthly king a "prince" (cf. 37:25; 44:3; 45:7,16–17,22; 46:2–18; 48:21–22).

34:25 *covenant of peace.* Cf. 37:26. All of God's covenants aim at peace (see Ge 26:28–31; Nu 25:12; Isa 54:10; Mal 2:5). This covenant (the "new covenant" spoken of by Jeremiah, 31:31–34) looks to the final peace, initiated by Christ (Php 4:7) and still awaiting final fulfillment. The "peace" (Hebrew *shalom*) envisioned here is that of a restored relationship with God and the secure enjoyment of a life made full and rich through his blessings. None of the threats to life experienced under God's judgments will mar this "peace" (compare vv. 25–29 with 5:16–17 and note). *sleep in the forests.* Often dangerous (see Ps 104:20–21; Jer 5:6).

34:26 *showers in season.* Autumn rains, which signal the beginning of the rainy season, and spring rains, which come at the end (cf. Jer 5:24). *showers of blessing.* Blessing, the power of life promised to God's people through Abraham (Ge 12:1–3), is beautifully symbolized in the life-giving effects of rain.

34:27 *bars of their yoke.* The bars were wooden pegs inserted down through holes in the yoke and tied below the animal's neck with cords (Isa 58:6) to form a collar (cf. 30:18; Lev 26:13; Jer 27:2; 28:10–13). The entire picture represents foreign domination.

34:29 *scorn of the nations.* See 22:4.

34:30 *their God ... my people.* Covenant language (see 11:20; Ex 6:7; Hos 1:9; Zec 8:8 and notes).

35:1–15 The counterpart of Israel's restoration as the Lord's people is the desolation of her enemies—of which Edom serves here as representative (see 36:5). Given the historic relationship between Israel and Edom (see notes on vv. 2,5), the spiteful treatment of Judah by the Edomites at the time of Jerusalem's fall was especially reprehensible (see Isa 63:1–6 and notes; Introduction to Obadiah: Unity and Theme; see also notes on Am 9:12; Ob 8).

35:2 *set your face against.* See note on 20:46. *Mount Seir.* Edom (v. 15), Israel's relative (Jacob and Esau being twins, Ge 25:21–30) and constant enemy, from whom brotherhood was sought but seldom found (cf. Am 1:11). Edom had to be dealt with before Israel could find peace (cf. Ge 32–33). See 25:12 and note.

35:3 *I am against you.* See note on 5:8.

35:5 *ancient hostility.* Beginning with Jacob's deception of Isaac for Esau's blessing (Ge 27; see especially v. 41) and continuing later (Nu 20:14–21; 2Sa 8:13–14; 1Ki 9:26–28). *time of their calamity.* Edom looted Jerusalem in 586 B.C. (see Ob 11–14 and notes).

35:6 *as surely as I live.* See note on 5:11. *bloodshed will pursue you.* Retributive justice, in accordance with Ge 9:6 (see note there).

will fall on your hills and in your valleys and in all your ravines.[z] 9I will make you desolate forever;[a] your towns will not be inhabited. Then you will know that I am the LORD.[b]

10" 'Because you have said, "These two nations and countries will be ours and we will take possession[c] of them," even though I the LORD was there, 11therefore as surely as I live, declares the Sovereign LORD, I will treat you in accordance with the anger[d] and jealousy you showed in your hatred of them and I will make myself known among them when I judge you.[e] 12Then you will know that I the LORD have heard all the contemptible things you have said against the mountains of Israel. You said, "They have been laid waste and have been given over to us to devour.[f]" 13You boasted[g] against me and spoke against me without restraint, and I heard it.[h] 14This is what the Sovereign LORD says: While the whole earth rejoices, I will make you desolate.[i] 15Because you rejoiced[j] when the inheritance of the house of Israel became desolate, that is how I will treat you. You will be desolate, O Mount Seir,[k] you and all of Edom.[l] Then they will know that I am the LORD.' "

A Prophecy to the Mountains of Israel

36 "Son of man, prophesy to the mountains of Israel[m] and say, 'O mountains of Israel, hear the word of the LORD. 2This is what the Sovereign LORD says:[n] The enemy said of you, "Aha![o] The ancient heights[p] have become our possession.[q]" ' 3Therefore prophesy and say, 'This is what the Sovereign LORD says: Because they ravaged[r] and hounded you from every side so that you became the possession of the rest of the nations and the object of people's malicious talk and slander,[s] 4therefore, O mountains of Israel, hear the word of the Sovereign LORD: This is what the Sovereign LORD says to the mountains and hills, to the ravines and valleys,[t] to the desolate ruins[u] and the deserted[v] towns that have been plundered and ridiculed[w] by the rest of the nations around you[x]— 5this is what the Sovereign LORD says: In my burning[y] zeal I have spoken against the rest of the nations, and against all Edom, for with glee and with malice in their hearts they made my land their own possession so that they might plunder its pastureland.'[z] 6Therefore prophesy concerning the land of Israel and say to the mountains and hills, to the ravines and valleys: 'This is what the Sovereign LORD says: I speak in my jealous wrath because you have suffered the scorn of the nations.[a] 7Therefore this is what the Sovereign LORD says: I swear with uplifted hand[b] that the nations around you will also suffer scorn.[c]

8" 'But you, O mountains of Israel, will produce branches and fruit[d] for my people Israel, for they will soon come home. 9I am concerned for you and will look on you with favor; you will be plowed and sown,[e] 10and I will multiply the number of people upon you, even the whole house of Israel. The towns will be inhabited and the ruins[f] rebuilt.[g] 11I will increase the number of men and animals upon you, and they will be fruitful[h] and become numerous. I will settle people[i] on you as in the past[j]

35:8 [z]S Eze 31:12 **35:9** [a]Ob 1:10 [b]S Isa 34:5-6; S Jer 49:13 **35:10** [c]S Ps 83:12; Eze 36:2,5 **35:11** [d]Eze 25:14 [e]S Ps 9:16; Ob 1:15; S Mt 7:2 **35:12** [f]S Jer 50:7 **35:13** [g]S Jer 49:16 [h]Da 11:36 **35:14** [i]Jer 51:48 **35:15** [j]Eze 36:5; Ob 1:12 [k]ver 3 [l]S Isa 34:5-6,11; Jer 50:11-13; S La 4:21; S Eze 32:29 **36:1** [m]S Eze 17:22 **36:2** [n]Eze 6:2-3 [o]S Eze 25:3 [p]S Dt 32:13 [q]S Eze 35:10 **36:3** [r]Ob 1:13 [s]Ps 44:13-14; S La 2:16; 3:62 **36:4** [t]Eze 6:3 [u]Eze 33:24 [v]S Lev 26:43 [w]S Jer 2:26 [x]Dt 11:11; S Ps 79:4; S Eze 33:28-29 **36:5** [y]S Dt 29:20 [z]Isa 66:16; Jer 25:31; 50:11; Eze 25:12-14; S 35:10,15; 38:22; Joel 3:2,14 **36:6** [a]Ps 123:3-4; Eze 34:29 **36:7** [b]S Nu 14:30 [c]S Jer 25:9 **36:8** [d]S Isa 4:2; S 27:6; Eze 47:12 **36:9** [e]ver 34-36; Jer 31:27 **36:10** [f]S Isa 49:8 [g]Isa 49:17-23; S Jer 30:18 **36:11** [h]S Ge 1:22 [i]S Isa 49:19 [j]Mic 7:14

35:9 *desolate forever.* To experience no restoration like Egypt's (see 29:13–16). *know that I am the LORD.* See Introduction: Themes.

35:10 *These two nations.* Israel and Judah. *I the LORD was there.* See 48:35 and note.

35:13 *You boasted against me.* Cf. Ob 12; Zep 2:8,10; also Ps 35:26; Jer 48:26,42.

36:1–38 How God, whose name has been profaned among the nations, will display his holiness in the restoration of his people: Verses 1–15 set forth God's promise to cause the now desolate land ("mountains") of Israel to prosper once more so that it is a place of blessing for Israel, thereby removing its disgrace; vv. 16–38 spell out God's promise to cleanse and restore his now defiled and scattered people, thereby removing the disgrace that Israel has brought on his name and once again showing to all nations his holiness.

36:1–15 The comforting counterpart to ch. 6. Verses 1–7 announce God's coming judgment on the nations for the scorn they heaped on the land of Israel; vv. 8–15 announce God's future renewal of the prosperity of the land.

36:2 *The enemy said of you.* See 25:3; 26:2. *Aha!* See note on 25:3. *ancient heights.* The promised land, of which the elevated region between the Jordan Valley and the Mediterranean coast was the central core.

36:3 *rest of the nations.* All nations that in the past had conquered parts of Israel—until finally they took full possession.

36:4 *mountains ... hills ... ravines ... valleys.* See 6:3 and note on 1:5.

36:5 *my burning zeal.* The Lord was personally offended by the ridicule of the nations because it was his special land ("my land") they were mocking and plundering. *Edom.* Singled out because of their long-standing hostility to Israel (see ch. 35, especially vv. 2,5 and notes).

36:6 *jealous wrath.* See 16:38 and note.

36:7 *with uplifted hand.* See 20:5 and note.

36:8 *branches and fruit.* Signs of productivity (see 17:8,23) and the Lord's restored favor (see Lev 26:3–5); to be contrasted with Edom's desolation in 35:3,7,15. *soon.* Even as judgment fell, a speedy return of the exiles was announced.

36:9 *I ... will look on you with favor.* Cf. Lev 26:9 for the identical clause in a similar context.

36:10 *even the whole house of Israel.* In this chapter (as in 37:15–23) Ezekiel is speaking of the restoration of all Israel.

36:11 *be fruitful and become numerous.* Identical terminology to the divine blessing at creation (Ge 1:22,28; see Ge 8:17; 9:1,7) and the subsequent covenant blessing (see Ge 17:6; 35:11; 48:3–4; Ex 1:7). *know that I am the LORD.* These words of recognition, used throughout the book to express God's revelation through judgment, here point to God's self-disclosure in salvation (see 35:9 and note).

and will make you prosper more than before.[k] Then you will know that I am the
LORD. 12I will cause people, my people Israel, to walk upon you. They will possess
you, and you will be their inheritance;[l]
you will never again deprive them of their
children.
13"'This is what the Sovereign LORD
says: Because people say to you, "You devour men[m] and deprive your nation of its
children," 14therefore you will no longer
devour men or make your nation childless, declares the Sovereign LORD. 15No
longer will I make you hear the taunts
of the nations, and no longer will you
suffer the scorn of the peoples or cause
your nation to fall, declares the Sovereign
LORD.[n]'"
16Again the word of the LORD came to
me: 17"Son of man, when the people of
Israel were living in their own land, they
defiled it by their conduct and their actions. Their conduct was like a woman's
monthly uncleanness[o] in my sight.[p] 18So
I poured out[q] my wrath on them because
they had shed blood in the land and because they had defiled it with their idols.
19I dispersed them among the nations, and
they were scattered[r] through the countries;
I judged them according to their conduct
and their actions.[s] 20And wherever they
went among the nations they profaned[t]
my holy name, for it was said of them,
'These are the LORD's people, and yet they
had to leave his land.'[u] 21I had concern for
my holy name, which the house of Israel
profaned among the nations where they
had gone.[v]
22"Therefore say to the house of Israel,
'This is what the Sovereign LORD says: It is
not for your sake, O house of Israel, that
I am going to do these things, but for the
sake of my holy name,[w] which you have
profaned[x] among the nations where you
have gone.[y] 23I will show the holiness of
my great name,[z] which has been profaned[a]
among the nations, the name you have
profaned among them. Then the nations
will know that I am the LORD,[b] declares the
Sovereign LORD, when I show myself holy[c]
through you before their eyes.[d]
24"'For I will take you out of the nations; I will gather you from all the countries and bring you back into your own
land.[e] 25I will sprinkle[f] clean water on
you, and you will be clean; I will cleanse[g]
you from all your impurities[h] and from all
your idols.[i] 26I will give you a new heart[j]
and put a new spirit in you; I will remove
from you your heart of stone[k] and give
you a heart of flesh.[l] 27And I will put my
Spirit[m] in you and move you to follow
my decrees[n] and be careful to keep my
laws.[o] 28You will live in the land I gave
your forefathers; you will be my people,[p]

36:11 [k]Lev 26:9; Job 42:13; S Jer 31:28; S Eze 16:55; Zec 10:8 **36:12** [l]Eze 47:14,22 **36:13** [m]S Nu 13:32 **36:15** [n]Ps 89:50-51; Isa 54:4; S Eze 34:29 **36:17** [o]S Lev 5:2; S 12:2 [p]Ps 106:37-38; S Jer 2:7 **36:18** [q]S 2Ch 34:21 **36:19** [r]Dt 28:64 [s]Lev 18:24-28; S Eze 7:8; S 24:14; 39:24 **36:20** [t]S Lev 18:21; S Eze 13:19; Ro 2:24 [u]Isa 52:5; S Jer 33:24; S Eze 12:16 **36:21** [v]Ps 74:18; Isa 48:9 **36:22** [w]S Isa 37:35; S Eze 20:44 [x]Ro 2:24* [y]Dt 9:5-6; Ps 106:8; S Eze 20:9 **36:23** [z]S Nu 6:27 [a]S Isa 37:23 [b]S Ps 46:10 [c]S Eze 20:41 [d]Ps 126:2; S Isa 5:16; Eze 20:14; 38:23; 39:7,27-28

36:24 [e]S Isa 43:5-6; S Eze 34:13; 37:21 **36:25** [f]S Lev 14:7; S 16:14-15; Heb 9:13 [g]S Ps 51:2,7 [h]S Ezr 6:21 [i]Isa 2:18; Joel 3:21; Zec 3:4; 13:2; S Ac 22:16 **36:26** [j]Jer 24:7 [k]S Jer 5:3 [l]S Ps 51:10; S Eze 18:31; S 2Co 3:3 **36:27** [m]S Isa 44:3; Joel 2:29; Jn 3:5 [n]S Eze 18:21 [o]Jer 50:20; 1Th 4:8 **36:28** [p]Jer 30:22; 31:33

36:12 *walk upon you.* The mountains of Israel are still being addressed. *deprive them of their children.* The mountains are poetically pictured as having contributed to the depopulation brought by the exile. This may refer to the fact that the promised land had contained the Canaanites and their religious centers ("high places"; see 1Ki 3:2 and note), which had led Israel astray and so brought God's wrath down on his people (see 6:3 and note).

36:16–38 God's restoration of his defiled and scattered people. Verses 16–23 remind Israel that the nation was exiled from her land because of her uncleanness and that her restoration is for the sake of God's holy name; vv. 24–27 announce God's renewal of defiled Israel and its effects on Israel (vv. 28–32) and on the nations (vv. 33–36); vv. 37–38 provide a concluding summary.

36:18 *shed blood ... defiled it with their idols.* A summary reference to Israel's social injustices and idolatrous religious practices (see 22:3 and note). *idols.* See note on 6:4.

36:20 *they profaned my holy name.* Because Israel had been removed from her land, it seemed to the nations that her God was unable to protect and preserve his people (see 20:9 and note; cf. Nu 14:15–16; 2Ki 18:32–35; 19:10–12).

36:22 *It is not for your sake.* Not because God did not care for Israel, but because they did not deserve what he was about to do (cf. Dt 9:4–6). Statements like these make Ezekiel a preacher of pure grace. *for the sake of my holy name.* The reason given in ch. 20 for the withholding of divine punishment (see 20:9,14,22) is here given as a reason for divine restoration.

36:23 *Then the nations will know that I am the LORD.* The ultimate purpose of God's plans with Israel is that the whole world may know the true God (see 6:7 and note). *show myself holy.* See Lev 10:3 and note.

36:24–27 The four elements in the promised restoration: (1) return of the exiles (v. 24), (2) cleansing from sin (v. 25), (3) renewal of heart (v. 26) and (4) enablement by God's Spirit to live God's way (v. 27).

36:25 *I will sprinkle clean water.* For sprinkling with water as a ritual act of cleansing see Ex 30:19–20; Lev 14:51; Nu 19:18; cf. Zec 13:1; Heb 10:22. *I will cleanse.* See v. 33; 37:23; Jer 33:8. *idols.* See note on 6:4.

36:26–27 Contains "new covenant" terminology (see Jer 31:31–34 and notes).

36:26 *new heart.* See notes on 11:19; 18:31. *put a new spirit in you.* Transform your mind and heart. Here and in 11:19 God declared that he would bring about the change. In 18:31 (see note there) he called on his people to effect the change. What he requires of his people he always provides. *heart of flesh.* "Flesh" in the OT is often a symbol for weakness and frailty (Isa 31:3); in the NT it often stands for the sinful nature as a God-opposing force (as in Ro 8:5–8). Here it stands (in opposition to stone) for a pliable, teachable heart.

36:27 *my Spirit.* God bestows his Spirit to enable the human spirit to do his will (see 37:14 and note on 2:2). Verses 25–27 are closely paralleled in Ps 51:7–11 (see notes there).

36:28–32 The results of Israel's renewal: restoration to prosperity (vv. 28–30) and a deep sense of shame for all her sins (vv. 31–32).

36:28 *my people ... your God.* Covenant language (see 11:20 and note).

and I will be your God.[q] 29I will save you
from all your uncleanness. I will call for
the grain and make it plentiful and will
not bring famine[r] upon you. 30I will increase the fruit of the trees and the crops
of the field, so that you will no longer suffer disgrace among the nations because of
famine.[s] 31Then you will remember your
evil ways and wicked deeds, and you will
loathe yourselves for your sins and detestable practices.[t] 32I want you to know
that I am not doing this for your sake, declares the Sovereign LORD. Be ashamed[u]
and disgraced for your conduct, O house
of Israel![v]
33"'This is what the Sovereign LORD
says: On the day I cleanse[w] you from all
your sins, I will resettle your towns, and
the ruins[x] will be rebuilt.[y] 34The desolate land will be cultivated instead of lying desolate in the sight of all who pass
through it. 35They will say, "This land that
was laid waste has become like the garden of Eden;[z] the cities that were lying
in ruins, desolate and destroyed, are now
fortified and inhabited.[a]" 36Then the nations around you that remain will know
that I the LORD have rebuilt what was
destroyed and have replanted what was
desolate. I the LORD have spoken, and I
will do it.'[b]
37"This is what the Sovereign LORD says:
Once again I will yield to the plea[c] of the
house of Israel and do this for them: I will
make their people as numerous as sheep,[d]
38as numerous as the flocks for offerings[e]
at Jerusalem during her appointed feasts.
So will the ruined cities be filled with
flocks of people. Then they will know that
I am the LORD.[f]"

The Valley of Dry Bones

37 The hand of the LORD was upon me,[g]
and he brought me out by the Spirit[h]
of the LORD and set me in the middle of a
valley;[i] it was full of bones.[j] 2He led me
back and forth among them, and I saw a
great many bones on the floor of the valley, bones that were very dry. 3He asked
me, "Son of man, can these bones live?"
I said, "O Sovereign LORD, you alone
know.[k]"
4Then he said to me, "Prophesy to these
bones and say to them, 'Dry bones, hear
the word of the LORD![l] 5This is what the
Sovereign LORD says to these bones: I will
make breath[a] enter you, and you will
come to life.[m] 6I will attach tendons to you
and make flesh come upon you and cover
you with skin; I will put breath in you,
and you will come to life. Then you will
know that I am the LORD.[n]'"
7So I prophesied as I was commanded. And as I was prophesying, there was
a noise, a rattling sound, and the bones
came together, bone to bone. 8I looked,
and tendons and flesh appeared on them
and skin covered them, but there was no
breath in them.
9Then he said to me, "Prophesy to the
breath;[o] prophesy, son of man, and say to
it, 'This is what the Sovereign LORD says:
Come from the four winds,[p] O breath, and
breathe into these slain, that they may
live.'" 10So I prophesied as he commanded[q] me, and breath entered them; they
came to life and stood up on their feet—a
vast army.[r]

[a] 5 The Hebrew for this word can also mean *wind* or *spirit* (see verses 6-14).

36:28 [q] S Eze 11:17; S 14:11; 34:24; 37:14,27; Zec 8:8 **36:29** [r] Eze 34:29 **36:30** [s] Lev 26:4-5; S Eze 34:13-14; Hos 2:21-22 **36:31** [t] Isa 6:5; S Jer 31:19; S Eze 6:9 **36:32** [u] Eze 16:63 [v] Dt 9:5 **36:33** [w] S Lev 16:30 [x] S Lev 26:31 [y] S Isa 49:8 **36:35** [z] S Ge 2:8 [a] Am 9:14 **36:36** [b] S Jer 42:10; S Eze 17:22; 37:14; 39:27-28 **36:37** [c] Zec 10:6; 13:9 [d] Ps 102:17; Jer 29:12-14 **36:38** [e] 1Ki 8:63; 2Ch 35:7-9 [f] S Ex 6:2

37:1 [g] S Eze 1:3 [h] S Eze 11:24; Lk 4:1; Ac 8:39 [i] Jer 7:32 [j] S Jer 8:2; Eze 40:1 **37:3** [k] Dt 32:39; S 1Sa 2:6; Isa 26:19; 1Co 15:35 **37:4** [l] Jer 22:29 **37:5** [m] S Ge 2:7; Ps 104:29-30; Rev 11:11 **37:6** [n] S Ex 6:2; Eze 38:23 **37:9** [o] ver 14; Ps 104:30; Isa 32:15; Eze 39:29; Zec 12:10 [p] Jer 49:36; Da 7:2; 8:8; 11:4; Zec 2:6; 6:5; Rev 7:1 **37:10** [q] S Eze 12:7 [r] Rev 11:11

36:29 *from all your uncleanness.* From idol worship and moral defilement (see v. 25; 37:23).

36:30 *disgrace.* As in v. 15.

36:31 *Then you will remember.* God's undeserved grace leads to recollection and repentance (cf. 6:9; 16:63; 20:43; Ps 130:4).

36:32 *not … for your sake.* See note on v. 22.

36:33 – 36 The impact of Israel's restoration on the nations.

36:33 *On the day.* Connects the promise of cleansing (vv. 24 – 32) and the promise of repopulation (vv. 33 – 36).

36:35 *garden of Eden.* Cf. 28:13; 31:9. *fortified.* In contrast to 38:11.

36:36 *nations … will know.* See note on v. 23.

36:37 – 38 In summary, Israel's full standing with God will be restored.

36:37 *yield to the plea.* Allowing petitions to come to him again, God reversed his earlier refusals to hear (cf. 14:3; 20:3,31).

36:38 *as numerous as the flocks for offerings.* See 1Ki 8:63; 1Ch 29:21; 2Ch 35:7 for the appropriateness of the comparison.

37:1 – 28 Although one of Ezekiel's major visions, it surprisingly bears no date (see chart, p. 1239). However, it must have come to Ezekiel sometime after 586 B.C. The symbolic vision given to Ezekiel (vv. 1 – 15) is immediately followed by a symbolic act that Ezekiel is instructed to perform (vv. 16 – 28). Both speak of the restoration of Israel, the central theme of chs. 34 – 36.

37:1 *hand of the LORD.* See note on 1:3. *brought me out by the Spirit.* See 3:12 and note. *valley.* The Hebrew for this word is the same as that translated "plain" in 3:22 – 23; 8:4. Ezekiel now received a message of hope, whereas previously he had heard God's word of judgment. *bones.* Verse 11 interprets them as symbolizing Israel's apparently hopeless condition in exile.

37:2 *a great many bones.* Symbolizing the whole community of exiles. *very dry.* Long dead, far beyond the reach of resuscitation (1Ki 17:17 – 24; 2Ki 4:18 – 37; but see 2Ki 13:21).

37:4 *Prophesy to these bones.* Ezekiel had previously prophesied to inanimate objects (mountains, 6:2; 36:1; forests, 20:47); now he prophesies to lifeless bones and "the breath" (v. 9). Cf. Jn 5:25 and note.

37:6 *tendons … flesh … skin … breath.* Lists of four items are common in Ezekiel (see note on 1:5).

37:8 *but there was no breath.* This visionary re-creation of God's people recalls the two-step creation of Adam in Ge 2:7.

37:9 *breath.* See NIV text note on v. 5. *four.* See note on 1:5. *slain.* What Ezekiel saw was a battlefield strewn with the bones of the fallen (see v. 10).

11Then he said to me: "Son of man,
these bones are the whole house of Israel.
They say, 'Our bones are dried up and our
hope is gone; we are cut off.'[s] 12Therefore
prophesy and say to them: 'This is what
the Sovereign LORD says: O my people, I
am going to open your graves and bring
you up from them; I will bring you back
to the land of Israel.[t] 13Then you, my people, will know that I am the LORD,[u] when
I open your graves and bring you up from
them.[v] 14I will put my Spirit[w] in you and
you will live, and I will settle[x] you in your
own land. Then you will know that I the
LORD have spoken, and I have done it, declares the LORD.[y]' "

One Nation Under One King

15The word of the LORD came to me:
16"Son of man, take a stick of wood and
write on it, 'Belonging to Judah and the
Israelites[z] associated with him.[a]' Then
take another stick of wood, and write on
it, 'Ephraim's stick, belonging to Joseph
and all the house of Israel associated with
him.' 17Join them together into one stick so
that they will become one in your hand.[b]
18"When your countrymen ask you,
'Won't you tell us what you mean by
this?'[c] 19say to them, 'This is what the Sovereign LORD says: I am going to take the
stick of Joseph—which is in Ephraim's
hand—and of the Israelite tribes associated with him, and join it to Judah's stick,
making them a single stick of wood, and
they will become one in my hand.'[d] 20Hold
before their eyes the sticks you have written on 21and say to them, 'This is what the
Sovereign LORD says: I will take the Israelites out of the nations where they have
gone. I will gather them from all around
and bring them back into their own land.[e]
22I will make them one nation in the land,
on the mountains of Israel.[f] There will be
one king over all of them and they will
never again be two nations or be divided
into two kingdoms.[g] 23They will no longer defile[h] themselves with their idols and
vile images or with any of their offenses,
for I will save them from all their sinful
backsliding,[a][i] and I will cleanse them.
They will be my people, and I will be their
God.[j]
24" 'My servant David[k] will be king[l] over
them, and they will all have one shepherd.[m]
They will follow my laws and be careful to
keep my decrees.[n] 25They will live in the
land I gave to my servant Jacob, the land
where your fathers lived.[o] They and their
children and their children's children will
live there forever,[p] and David my servant
will be their prince forever.[q] 26I will make
a covenant of peace[r] with them; it will be
an everlasting covenant.[s] I will establish
them and increase their numbers,[t] and I
will put my sanctuary among them[u] forever.[v] 27My dwelling place[w] will be with
them; I will be their God, and they will be
my people.[x] 28Then the nations will know
that I the LORD make Israel holy,[y] when my
sanctuary is among them forever.[z][a]' "

37:11 [s]S Job 17:15; S La 3:54 **37:12** [t]ver 21; Dt 32:39; 1Sa 2:6; Isa 26:19; Jer 29:14; Hos 13:14; Am 9:14-15; Zep 3:20; Zec 8:8 **37:13** [u]S Ex 6:2 [v]S Eze 17:24; Hos 13:14 **37:14** [w]S ver 9; S Isa 11:2; Joel 2:28-29 [x]S Jer 43:2 [y]Eze 36:27-28, 36; Rev 11:11 **37:16** [z]S 1Ki 12:20; 2Ch 10:17-19 [a]Nu 17:2-3; 2Ch 15:9 **37:17** [b]ver 24; Isa 11:13; S Jer 50:4; Hos 1:11 **37:18** [c]S Eze 24:19 **37:19** [d]Zec 10:6 **37:21** [e]S ver 12; S Isa 43:5-6; S Eze 20:42; 39:27; Mic 4:6 **37:22** [f]S Eze 17:22; S 34:13-14 [g]Isa 11:13; Jer 33:24; S 50:4; Hos 1:11 **37:23** [h]Eze 43:7 [i]S Jer 7:24 [j]Eze 11:18; S 36:28; Na 2:2 **37:24** [k]Isa 55:4; Hos 3:5 [l]S 1Sa 13:14; S Isa 32:1 [m]Zec 13:7 [n]Ps 78:70-71; S Jer 30:21; S Eze 21:27

[a] 23 Many Hebrew manuscripts (see also Septuagint); most Hebrew manuscripts *all their dwelling places where they sinned*

37:25 [o]S Eze 28:25 [p]S Ezr 9:12; Am 9:15 [q]S Ps 89:3-4; Isa 11:1; S Eze 34:23-24 **37:26** [r]S Nu 25:12 [s]S Ge 9:16; S Dt 29:14; S Heb 13:20 [t]S Jer 30:19 [u]Lev 26:11 [v]S Eze 16:62 **37:27** [w]S Lev 26:11 [x]S Eze 34:30; S 36:28; S 2Co 6:16* **37:28** [y]S Ex 31:13 [z]Hos 1:10-11 [a]Eze 43:9; Zep 3:15

37:11 *Our bones ... cut off.* A sense of utter despair, to which the vision offers hope.

37:12 *graves.* The imagery shifts from a scattering of bones on a battlefield (see note on v. 9) to a cemetery with sealed graves.

37:14 *I will put my Spirit in you.* See 36:27 and note. *I will settle you in your own land.* These words make it clear that the Lord is not speaking here of a resurrection from the dead but of the national restoration of Israel.

37:16 *take a stick.* Ezekiel's last symbolic act involving a material object (cf. 4:1,3,9; 5:1). *write on it.* Zec 11:7 seems to be based on this passage in Ezekiel.

37:18 *Won't you tell us ...?* The symbolic act successfully aroused the people's curiosity (see 12:9; 21:7; 24:19).

37:19 *they will become one in my hand.* God would duplicate Ezekiel's symbolic act by uniting the two kingdoms separated since Solomon's death (see 1Ki 12). For similar prophecies of the reunion of Israel see 33:23,29; Jer 3:18; 23:5–6; Hos 1:11; Am 9:11.

37:22 *mountains of Israel.* See 6:2–3; 34:13; 36:1. *one king.* Only here and in v. 24 is the word "king" used of the future ruler. Usually "prince" is used (see note on 34:24), as in v. 25. See 7:27 and note; see also 44:3; 45:7–9 and frequently in chs. 45–48, where the ruler in the ideal age is always referred to as "prince."

37:23 *idols.* The old and basic offense (see note on 6:4). *backsliding.* Cf. Jer 2:19; 3:22. *cleanse.* Cf. 36:25 for the same notion. *my people ... their God.* See 11:20 and note.

37:24–26 These verses appear to recall the Davidic covenant (v. 24a), the Sinaitic covenant (v. 24b) and the Abrahamic covenant (v. 25)—all of which will be fulfilled in the "covenant of peace" (v. 26).

37:24 *My servant David.* As in 34:23 (see note on 34:23–24) the coming Messianic ruler is called David because he would be a descendant of David and would achieve for Israel what David had—except more fully. *king.* See note on v. 22. *shepherd.* As in 34:23 the coming ruler is likened to a shepherd who cares for his flock (cf. Jn 10, especially v. 16).

37:25 *my servant Jacob.* See 28:25 and note.

37:26 *covenant of peace.* See 34:25 and note. *everlasting covenant.* See note on 16:59–63. The phrase occurs 16 times in the OT, referring at times to the Noahic covenant (Ge 9:16), the Abrahamic (Ge 17:7,13,19), the Davidic (2Sa 23:5) and the "new" (Jer 31:31; 32:40). Cf. the covenant with Phinehas (Nu 25:12–13). *put my sanctuary among them.* As he had done before. This word is further developed in Ezekiel's vision of the future age, in which the rebuilt sanctuary would have central position (chs. 40–48). See vv. 27–28 and map, p. 1308.

A Prophecy Against Gog

38 The word of the LORD came to me:
2"Son of man, set your face against
Gog,[b] of the land of Magog,[c] the chief
prince of[a] Meshech and Tubal;[d] prophesy
against him 3and say: 'This is what the
Sovereign LORD says: I am against you,
O Gog, chief prince of[b] Meshech and Tubal.[e] 4I will turn you around, put hooks[f]
in your jaws and bring you out with your
whole army—your horses, your horsemen
fully armed, and a great horde with large
and small shields, all of them brandishing
their swords.[g] 5Persia, Cush[c][h] and Put[i] will
be with them, all with shields and helmets,
6also Gomer[j] with all its troops, and Beth
Togarmah[k] from the far north[l] with all its
troops—the many nations with you.
7" 'Get ready; be prepared,[m] you and all
the hordes gathered about you, and take
command of them. 8After many days[n] you
will be called to arms. In future years you
will invade a land that has recovered from
war, whose people were gathered from
many nations[o] to the mountains of Israel,
which had long been desolate. They had
been brought out from the nations, and
now all of them live in safety.[p] 9You and
all your troops and the many nations with
you will go up, advancing like a storm;[q]
you will be like a cloud[r] covering the
land.[s]
10" 'This is what the Sovereign LORD
says: On that day thoughts will come into
your mind[t] and you will devise an evil
scheme.[u] 11You will say, "I will invade a
land of unwalled villages; I will attack a
peaceful and unsuspecting people[v]—all
of them living without walls and without
gates and bars.[w] 12I will plunder and loot
and turn my hand against the resettled ruins and the people gathered from the nations, rich in livestock and goods, living at
the center of the land." 13Sheba[x] and Dedan[y] and the merchants of Tarshish[z] and
all her villages[d] will say to you, "Have you
come to plunder? Have you gathered your
hordes to loot, to carry off silver and gold,
to take away livestock and goods and to
seize much plunder?[a]" '

38:2 [b] ver 14; Eze 39:11 [c] S Ge 10:2 [d] S Eze 27:13 **38:3** [e] Eze 39:1 **38:4** [f] S 2Ki 19:28 [g] S Isa 43:17; Eze 29:4; 39:2; Da 11:40 **38:5** [h] S Ge 10:6 [i] S Ge 10:6; S Eze 27:10 **38:6** [j] S Ge 10:2 [k] S Ge 10:3 [l] S Eze 32:30 **38:7** [m] S Isa 8:9 **38:8** [n] Isa 24:22 [o] S Isa 11:11 [p] ver 14; Jer 23:6; S Eze 28:26; Joel 3:1 **38:9** [q] Isa 25:4; 28:2 [r] ver 16; Jer 4:13; Joel 2:2 [s] Rev 20:8 **38:10** [t] S Jer 17:10 [u] Ps 36:4; Mic 2:1 **38:11** [v] S Ge 34:25 [w] Jer 49:31; Zec 2:4 **38:13** [x] S Ge 10:7 [y] S Ge 25:3 [z] S Ge 10:4 [a] Isa 10:6; 33:23; S Jer 15:13

[a] *2* Or *the prince of Rosh,* [b] *3* Or *Gog, prince of Rosh,* [c] *5* That is, the upper Nile region [d] *13* Or *her strong lions*

38:1—39:29 The great battle of the ages when the future restoration of Israel under the reign of the house of David (ch. 37) evokes a massive coalition of world powers to destroy God's kingdom. The vast host that comes against Jerusalem will end up as dead bodies strewn over the fields of the promised land, which will become the cemetery of all the enemy hordes that invade it (cf. ch. 39). Three prophecies against Gog (38:1–13,14–23; 39:1–16) are followed by the depiction of a great feast in which the enemy warriors are described in terms of sacrificial animals (39:17–20). Two final words put this great battle in the context of God's ways with Israel in exile and restoration: (1) The nations will then know that Israel was carried into exile not because her God was incapable of protecting his own but because he had punished her for being unfaithful to him (39:21–24), and (2) Israel's restoration following her punishment will show the nations that Israel's God is truly the Holy One (39:25–29).

38:1 This statement, repeated often for receiving God's word, stands as an introduction to chs. 38–39, which are a unit.

38:2 *Son of man.* See note on 2:1. *set your face.* See note on 20:46. *Gog.* Apparently a leader or king whose name appears only in chs. 38–39; Rev 20:8. Several identifications have been attempted, notably Gyges, king of Lydia (c. 660 B.C.). Possibly the name is purposely vague, standing for a mysterious, as yet undisclosed, enemy of God's people. *of the land of Magog.* In Ge 10:2; 1Ch 1:5 Magog is one of the sons of Japheth, thus the name of a people. In Eze 39:6 it appears to refer to a people. But since the prefix *ma-* can mean "place of," Magog may here simply mean "land of Gog." Israel had long experienced the hostility of the Hamites and other Semitic peoples; the future coalition here envisioned will include—and in fact be led by—peoples descended from Japheth (cf. Ge 10). *chief prince.* Military commander-in-chief. The NIV text note gives the possible translation "prince of Rosh," and if it is correct, Rosh is probably the name of an unknown people or place. Identification with Russia is unlikely, and in any case cannot be proven. *Meshech and Tubal.* These sons of Japheth (see Ge 10:2 and note; 1Ch 1:5) are probably located in eastern Asia Minor (cf. 27:13; 32:26). They are peoples and territories to the north of Israel (cf. vv. 6,15; 39:2). As in the days of the Assyrians and Babylonians, the major attack will come from the north.

38:3 *I am against you.* See note on 5:8.

38:4 *I will turn you around.* Emphasis is on the fact that God is in complete control of all that is to follow. *put hooks in your jaws.* As with the pharaoh in 29:4, Gog is likened to a beast led around by God.

38:5 *Cush.* See NIV text note. The invading forces from the north (see v. 2 and note) are joined by armies from the south. *Put.* Libya.

38:6 *Gomer.* Another of Gog's northern allies (see note on v. 2), mentioned in Ge 10:3 and 1Ch 1:6 as one of the sons of Japheth. According to non-Biblical sources, these peoples originated north of the Black Sea. *Beth Togarmah.* See note on 27:14. According to Ge 10:3 and 1Ch 1:6 Togarmah is one of the children of Gomer.

38:8 *After many days ... In future years.* After all the events of Israel's restoration described in chs. 34–37 are completed.

38:9 *like a cloud.* Jeremiah similarly describes an invasion from the north in Jer 4:13.

38:10 *On that day.* A phrase also common to other prophetic writings; here it refers to the day of Gog's invasion of Israel. *thoughts will come into your mind.* The divine initiative (v. 4) is paralleled, as it often is in Scripture, by human action (cf. Dt 31:3; Isa 10:6–7). *evil scheme.* A raiding expedition (see v. 12).

38:11 *land of unwalled villages.* Speaks of a blissfully peaceful, ideal future time when walls will no longer be needed. See Zec 2:4–5, which assumes, as does this passage, that the Lord alone is sufficient protection (cf. 36:35–36).

38:12 *center of the land.* The Hebrew for "center" also means "navel," a graphic image for the belief that Israel was the vital link between God and the world (the idea occurs also in 5:5). Since the Hebrew for "land" can also mean "earth," theologically Jerusalem is both the center of the land of Israel and the center of the world.

38:13 *Sheba.* Southwest corner of the Arabian peninsula (modern Yemen), known for trading (Job 6:19; see 23:42;

14“Therefore, son of man, prophesy and
say to Gog: ‘This is what the Sovereign
LORD says: In that day, when my people Israel are living in safety,[b] will you not take
notice of it? 15You will come from your
place in the far north,[c] you and many nations with you, all of them riding on horses, a great horde, a mighty army.[d] 16You
will advance against my people Israel like
a cloud[e] that covers the land.[f] In days to
come, O Gog, I will bring you against my
land, so that the nations may know me
when I show myself holy[g] through you before their eyes.[h]

17“‘This is what the Sovereign LORD
says: Are you not the one I spoke of in
former days by my servants the prophets of Israel? At that time they prophesied
for years that I would bring you against
them. 18This is what will happen in that
day: When Gog attacks the land of Israel, my hot anger will be aroused, declares
the Sovereign LORD. 19In my zeal and fiery
wrath I declare that at that time there shall
be a great earthquake[i] in the land of Israel.[j] 20The fish of the sea, the birds of the
air, the beasts of the field, every creature
that moves along the ground, and all the
people on the face of the earth will tremble[k] at my presence. The mountains will
be overturned,[l] the cliffs will crumble[m]
and every wall will fall to the ground.[n]
21I will summon a sword[o] against Gog on
all my mountains, declares the Sovereign
LORD. Every man’s sword will be against
his brother.[p] 22I will execute judgment[q]
upon him with plague and bloodshed;[r]
I will pour down torrents of rain, hailstones[s] and burning sulfur[t] on him and on
his troops and on the many nations with
him.[u] 23And so I will show my greatness
and my holiness, and I will make myself
known in the sight of many nations. Then
they will know that I am the LORD.[v]’

39 “Son of man, prophesy against Gog[w]
and say: ‘This is what the Sovereign LORD says: I am against you, O Gog,
chief prince of[a] Meshech[x] and Tubal.[y]
2I will turn you around and drag you
along. I will bring you from the far north[z]
and send you against the mountains of Israel.[a] 3Then I will strike your bow[b] from
your left hand and make your arrows[c]
drop from your right hand. 4On the mountains of Israel you will fall, you and all
your troops and the nations with you. I
will give you as food to all kinds of carrion birds[d] and to the wild animals.[e] 5You
will fall in the open field, for I have spoken, declares the Sovereign LORD.[f] 6I will
send fire[g] on Magog[h] and on those who
live in safety in the coastlands,[i] and they
will know[j] that I am the LORD.

7“‘I will make known my holy name
among my people Israel. I will no longer
let my holy name be profaned,[k] and the
nations will know[l] that I the LORD am the
Holy One in Israel.[m] 8It is coming! It will
surely take place, declares the Sovereign
LORD. This is the day[n] I have spoken of.

9“‘Then those who live in the towns
of Israel will go out and use the weapons for fuel and burn them up—the small
and large shields, the bows and arrows,[o]
the war clubs and spears. For seven years
they will use them for fuel.[p] 10They will
not need to gather wood from the fields or
cut it from the forests, because they will
use the weapons for fuel. And they will
plunder[q] those who plundered them and
loot those who looted them, declares the
Sovereign LORD.[r]

11“‘On that day I will give Gog a burial
place in Israel, in the valley of those who
travel east toward[b] the Sea.[c] It will block
the way of travelers, because Gog and all
his hordes will be buried[s] there. So it will
be called the Valley of Hamon Gog.[d][t]

[a] 1 Or *Gog, prince of Rosh,* [b] 11 Or *of* [c] 11 That is, the Dead Sea [d] 11 *Hamon Gog* means *hordes of Gog.*

38:14 [b]S ver 8; S Lev 25:18; S Jer 16:15; Zec 2:5 **38:15** [c]Eze 32:30 [d]Eze 39:2; Rev 20:8 **38:16** [e]S ver 9 [f]Joel 3:11 [g]S Lev 10:3 [h]Isa 29:23; Eze 39:21 **38:19** [i]Isa 24:18; Joel 2:10; 3:16; S Rev 6:12 [j]Ps 18:7; S Eze 5:13; Hag 2:6,21 **38:20** [k]S Ex 15:14 [l]Isa 42:15 [m]Job 14:18 [n]S Ps 76:8; Hos 4:3; Na 1:5 **38:21** [o]Isa 66:16; Jer 25:29 [p]S 1Sa 14:20; S 2Ch 20:23; Hag 2:22 **38:22** [q]Isa 66:16; Jer 25:31; S Eze 36:5 [r]S Eze 14:19; S 28:23 [s]S Ex 9:18; Ps 18:12; Rev 16:21 [t]S Ge 19:24; S Rev 9:17 [u]S Eze 13:11 **38:23** [v]Eze 20:42; S 36:23; S 37:6 **39:1** [w]Rev 20:8 [x]S Ge 10:2 [y]S Eze 27:13; S 38:2,3 **39:2** [z]S Eze 32:30 [a]S Eze 38:4,15 **39:3** [b]Hos 1:5; Am 2:15 [c]Ps 76:3 **39:4** [d]S Ge 40:19 [e]ver 17-20; S Jer 25:33; S Eze 29:5; S 33:27 **39:5** [f]S Eze 32:4 **39:6** [g]S Eze 30:8; Rev 20:9 [h]S Ge 10:2 [i]S Jer 25:22 [j]S Ex 6:7

39:7 [k]S Ex 20:7; S Eze 13:19 [l]S Isa 49:26 [m]S Isa 12:6; S 54:5; S Eze 20:9; S 36:16,23 **39:8** [n]Eze 7:6 **39:9** [o]Ps 76:3 [p]S Ps 46:9 **39:10** [q]S Ex 3:22 [r]S Isa 14:2; S 33:1; Hab 2:8 **39:11** [s]S Isa 34:3 [t]S Eze 38:2

27:22; Ge 10:28 and note). *Dedan.* See note on 25:13. *Tarshish.* See note on 27:12.

38:16 *show myself holy.* See Lev 10:3 and note.

38:17 *Are you not the one I spoke of . . . ?* Probably a general reference to earlier prophecies of divine judgment on the nations arrayed against God and his people.

38:19 *earthquake.* Signaling the mighty presence of God, who comes to overwhelm the great army invading his land.

38:20 The fourfold listing of the animal world indicates the totality of nature (see note on 1:5; cf. Ge 9:2; 1Ki 4:33; Job 12:7–8 for similar listings).

38:21 *I will summon a sword.* God’s sword of judgment (see 5:2 and note). *Every man’s sword will be against his brother.* The coalition of Israel’s enemies will turn on itself, as did the armies that attacked Judah in the time of Jehoshaphat (2Ch 20:22–23).

38:22 The list of divine weapons suggests that God will intervene directly without the benefit of an earthly army.

39:1–16 The same basic events as those of ch. 38 are described, though some new details are added.

39:1 *Gog, chief prince of Meshech.* See note on 38:2.

39:2 *from the far north.* As in 38:6,15.

39:3 *bow.* Cf. Jer 6:23. The Lord will disarm Israel’s enemies before they can shoot an arrow.

39:4 *food to all kinds of carrion birds.* A theme expanded in vv. 17–20.

39:6 *I will send fire.* See 20:47 and note.

39:7 *let my holy name be profaned.* See Lev 18:21 and note. *the Holy One.* See Lev 11:44 and note.

39:9 *seven.* A symbolic number signifying the size of the invading armies and the finality of this great battle against God’s people.

39:11 *toward.* But see first NIV text note. *Hamon Gog.* See third NIV text note.

12“ ‘For seven months the house of Israel will be burying them in order to cleanse the land.[u] 13All the people of the land will bury them, and the day I am glorified[v] will be a memorable day for them, declares the Sovereign LORD.

14“ ‘Men will be regularly employed to cleanse the land. Some will go throughout the land and, in addition to them, others will bury those that remain on the ground. At the end of the seven months they will begin their search. 15As they go through the land and one of them sees a human bone, he will set up a marker beside it until the gravediggers have buried it in the Valley of Hamon Gog. 16(Also a town called Hamonah[a] will be there.) And so they will cleanse the land.’

17“Son of man, this is what the Sovereign LORD says: Call out to every kind of bird[w] and all the wild animals: ‘Assemble and come together from all around to the sacrifice I am preparing for you, the great sacrifice on the mountains of Israel. There you will eat flesh and drink blood.[x] 18You will eat the flesh of mighty men and drink the blood of the princes of the earth as if they were rams and lambs, goats and bulls—all of them fattened animals from Bashan.[y] 19At the sacrifice[z] I am preparing for you, you will eat fat till you are glutted and drink blood till you are drunk. 20At my table you will eat your fill of horses and riders, mighty men and soldiers of every kind,’ declares the Sovereign LORD.[a]

21“I will display my glory among the nations, and all the nations will see the punishment I inflict and the hand I lay upon them.[b] 22From that day forward the house of Israel will know that I am the LORD their God. 23And the nations will know that the people of Israel went into exile for their sin, because they were unfaithful to me. So I hid my face from them and handed them over to their enemies, and they all fell by the sword.[c] 24I dealt with them according to their uncleanness and their offenses, and I hid my face from them.[d]

25“Therefore this is what the Sovereign LORD says: I will now bring Jacob back from captivity[b e] and will have compassion[f] on all the people of Israel, and I will be zealous for my holy name.[g] 26They will forget their shame and all the unfaithfulness they showed toward me when they lived in safety[h] in their land with no one to make them afraid.[i] 27When I have brought them back from the nations and have gathered them from the countries of their enemies, I will show myself holy through them in the sight of many nations.[j] 28Then they will know that I am the LORD their God, for though I sent them into exile among the nations, I will gather them[k] to their own land, not leaving any behind.[l] 29I will no longer hide my face[m] from them, for I will pour out my Spirit[n] on the house of Israel, declares the Sovereign LORD.[o]”

The New Temple Area

40 In the twenty-fifth year of our exile, at the beginning of the year, on the tenth of the month, in the fourteenth year after the fall of the city[p]—on that very day the hand of the LORD was upon me[q] and

39:12 [u] Dt 21:23 **39:13** [v] Eze 28:22 **39:17** [w] S Job 15:23 [x] S Eze 32:4 **39:18** [y] S Ps 22:12; Jer 51:40 **39:19** [z] S Lev 3:9 **39:20** [a] S Isa 56:9; S Jer 12:9; Rev 19:17-18 **39:21** [b] Ex 9:16; Isa 37:20; S Eze 38:16 **39:23** [c] Isa 1:15; 59:2; S Jer 22:8-9; S 44:23 **39:24** [d] 2Ki 17:23; Jer 2:17,19; 4:18; S Eze 7:22; Da 9:7 **39:25** [e] S Jer 33:7 [f] S Jer 30:18 [g] Isa 27:12-13; S Eze 16:53 **39:26** [h] S 1Ki 4:25; S Jer 32:37; S Eze 38:8 [i] Isa 17:2; Eze 34:28; Mic 4:4 **39:27** [j] S Eze 37:21 **39:28** [k] Ps 147:2 [l] S Eze 36:23,36 **39:29** [m] S Dt 31:17 [n] S Isa 11:2; S Eze 37:9; S Ac 2:17 [o] S Eze 16:42 **40:1** [p] S 2Ki 25:7; Jer 39:1-10; 52:4-11 [q] S Eze 1:3; S 29:17

[a] *16 Hamonah* means *horde.* [b] *25* Or *now restore the fortunes of Jacob*

39:12 *seven.* See v. 9 and note. *cleanse the land.* Ritual purity is a basic element in Ezekiel's theology (see 22:26; 24:13; 36:25,33; 37:23). Corpses were especially unclean (see Lev 5:2; 21:1,11; 22:4; Nu 5:2; 6:6–12; 19:16; 31:19).

39:13 *people of the land.* See 7:27 and note, though here a special class may not be implied.

39:14 *Men will be regularly employed.* After the seven-month burial period observed by all the people, special squads will be hired full time to ensure total cleansing of the land—by marking for burial any human bones that may have been missed. Total ritual purity is the aim.

39:17–20 These verses involve a restating of vv. 9–16, employing a different figure (see Isa 34:6 and note; Jer 46:10; Zep 1:7). The metaphor of sacrifice suggests a consecration to the Lord in judgment, as with Jericho (see Jos 6:17 and NIV text note there).

39:18 *You will eat the flesh of mighty men.* A gory description of what birds of prey commonly do (see previous note and Rev 19:17–21). *as if they were.* The bodies of the victims are compared to animals commonly used for sacrifices. *Bashan.* Rich pastureland east of the Sea of Galilee, known for its sleek cattle (Dt 32:14; Ps 22:12; Am 4:1) and its oak trees (27:6; Isa 2:13).

39:19 *eat fat … drink blood.* Further indication that this is the Lord's sacrificial feast, in that fat and blood were normally reserved for God (see 44:15; see also Lev 3:16; 1Sa 2:15; Isa 34:6 and notes).

39:20 *my table.* Sacrificial altar. See 40:38–43 and 41:22 for description of the tables in the new temple.

39:21 *my glory.* God's visible presence in the world (see note on 1:28). Here that visibility is due to divine intervention in history.

39:22–23 *the house of Israel will know … And the nations will know.* As God had made himself known to Israel and the nations through his saving acts in Israel's behalf (see Ex 6:7; 7:5,17; 10:2; 14:18; 16:6–7,12; Jos 3:10; 4:24; cf. Jos 2:9–11; 5:1), so now Israel and the nations see him at work as he judges his people for their sin (see v. 27; 6:7 and note).

39:23 *I hid my face.* Expression of divine displeasure (see Ps 13:1 and note; 30:7; Isa 54:8; 57:17).

39:24 *their uncleanness and their offenses.* Spelled out especially in ch. 22, but also throughout chs. 6–24.

39:25 *Jacob.* The nation of Israel, as in 20:5. *my holy name.* See 20:9 and note.

39:26 *They will forget their shame.* The remembrance of shame previously called for (6:9; 20:43; 36:31) is here erased.

39:27 *I will show myself holy through them.* God will reveal himself anew in a restored, holy people (see Lev 10:3 and note).

39:28 *know that I am the LORD.* See note on vv. 22–23.

39:29 *I will pour out my Spirit.* The gift of God's enabling Spirit (see 36:27; 37:14; see also notes on 2:2; Joel 2:28).

40:1—48:35 The restoration of Israel as a purified people calls for a purified land and a new order in the common-

he took me there. 2In visions[r] of God he
took me to the land of Israel and set me
on a very high mountain,[s] on whose south
side were some buildings that looked like
a city. 3He took me there, and I saw a man
whose appearance was like bronze;[t] he
was standing in the gateway with a linen
cord and a measuring rod[u] in his hand.
4The man said to me, "Son of man, look
with your eyes and hear with your ears
and pay attention to everything I am going to show you,[v] for that is why you have
been brought here. Tell[w] the house of Israel everything you see.[x]"

The East Gate to the Outer Court

5I saw a wall completely surrounding the
temple area. The length of the measuring
rod in the man's hand was six long cubits,
each of which was a cubit[a] and a handbreadth.[b] He measured[y] the wall; it was one
measuring rod thick and one rod high.
6Then he went to the gate facing east.[z]
He climbed its steps and measured the
threshold of the gate; it was one rod deep.[c]
7The alcoves[a] for the guards were one rod
long and one rod wide, and the projecting
walls between the alcoves were five cubits
thick. And the threshold of the gate next
to the portico facing the temple was one
rod deep.
8Then he measured the portico of the
gateway; 9it[d] was eight cubits deep and its
jambs were two cubits thick. The portico
of the gateway faced the temple.
10Inside the east gate were three alcoves
on each side; the three had the same measurements, and the faces of the projecting
walls on each side had the same measurements. 11Then he measured the width of
the entrance to the gateway; it was ten
cubits and its length was thirteen cubits.
12In front of each alcove was a wall one
cubit high, and the alcoves were six cubits square. 13Then he measured the gateway from the top of the rear wall of one
alcove to the top of the opposite one; the
distance was twenty-five cubits from one
parapet opening to the opposite one. 14He
measured along the faces of the projecting walls all around the inside of the gateway—sixty cubits. The measurement was
up to the portico[e] facing the courtyard.[f b]
15The distance from the entrance of the
gateway to the far end of its portico was fifty cubits. 16The alcoves and the projecting
walls inside the gateway were surmounted
by narrow parapet openings all around, as
was the portico; the openings all around
faced inward. The faces of the projecting
walls were decorated with palm trees.[c]

The Outer Court

17Then he brought me into the outer
court.[d] There I saw some rooms and a
pavement that had been constructed all
around the court; there were thirty rooms[e]
along the pavement.[f] 18It abutted the sides

40:2 [r] S Ex 24:10; Da 7:1,7 [s] S Jer 31:12; S Eze 17:22; Rev 21:10 **40:3** [t] S Eze 1:7; Rev 1:15 [u] Eze 47:3; Zec 2:1-2; Rev 11:1; 21:15 **40:4** [v] S Dt 6:6 [w] Jer 26:2 [x] Eze 44:5 **40:5** [y] Eze 42:20 **40:6** [z] S Eze 8:16 **40:7** [a] ver 36 **40:14** [b] S Ex 27:9 **40:16** [c] ver 21-22; 2Ch 3:5; Eze 41:26 **40:17** [d] Rev 11:2 [e] Eze 41:6 [f] Eze 42:1

[a] 5 The common cubit was about 1 1/2 feet (about 0.5 meter). [b] 5 That is, about 3 inches (about 8 centimeters) [c] 6 Septuagint; Hebrew *deep, the first threshold, one rod deep* [d] 8,9 Many Hebrew manuscripts, Septuagint, Vulgate and Syriac; most Hebrew manuscripts *gateway facing the temple; it was one rod deep. 9Then he measured the portico of the gateway; it* [e] 14 Septuagint; Hebrew *projecting wall* [f] 14 The meaning of the Hebrew for this verse is uncertain.

wealth of the people of God. This is the subject of Ezekiel's last vision, which presents an idealized picture of the new order to be put in place. For the basic outline of the vision's various topics see Introduction: Outline under "The New Order for Purified Israel" as well as the summary (overview) notes below.

40:1–47 Restoration of the temple area.

40:1 *twenty-fifth year ... beginning ... tenth.* Apr. 28, 573 B.C. *of our exile.* All the dates in the book of Ezekiel (see chart, p. 1239) are reckoned from the 597 exile, but only here and in 33:21 is the exile specifically mentioned (see 1:2). *the beginning of the year.* Hebrew *Rosh Hashanah,* the well-known Jewish New Year festival. It had long occurred in the fall (in either September or October), but since throughout the book Ezekiel uses a different and older religious calendar, the spring date as given above is correct (see note on Lev 23:24). *hand of the LORD was upon me.* See note on 1:3.

40:2 *visions of God.* Introduces all three of Ezekiel's major visions (see 1:1; 8:3). *very high mountain.* Mount Zion, also seen as extraordinarily high in other prophetic visions (17:22; Isa 2:2; Mic 4:1; Zec 14:10). Height here signifies importance, as the earthly seat of God's reign. *on whose south side.* With the city located on its southern slopes, the mountain is to the north (cf. Ps 48; see Ps 48:2 and note).

40:3 *like bronze.* Indicates the man was other than human. *in the gateway.* Presumably of the outer court (see vv. 17–19). *linen cord.* Used for longer measurements such as those in 47:3. *measuring rod.* Used for shorter measurements—about ten feet and four inches long.

40:5 *wall completely surrounding the temple area.* Separating the sacred from the secular. *six long cubits.* In using the long cubit (seven handbreadths, or about 21 inches), which was older than the shorter cubit (six handbreadths, or about 18 inches), Ezekiel was returning to more ancient standards for the new community (see 2Ch 3:3).

40:6 *gate facing east.* The gate of the outer court. The three gates (east, north, south) of the outer court were similar to the three in the inner court (v. 32), having six alcoves for the guards (three on each side) and a portico (vv. 8–9). Comparable gate plans have been discovered at Megiddo, Gezer and Hazor, all dating from the time of Solomon (see 1Ki 9:15). The guards kept out anyone who might profane the temple area (see Ezr 2:62). *climbed its steps.* The first of three sets of stairs leading to the temple. This one had seven steps (v. 22); the next one (inner court), eight (v. 31); the last (temple), ten (v. 49; see NIV text note)—possibly indicating increasing degrees of holiness (sacredness).

40:9 *portico of the gateway faced the temple.* The reverse position of the porticoes of the inner court gates, which faced away from the temple (v. 34).

40:10 *three alcoves.* The alcoves for the guards, mentioned in v. 7.

40:16 *palm trees.* As in Solomon's temple (see 1Ki 6:29 and note, 32,35).

40:17 *thirty rooms.* The exact location of these rooms is not given. They were probably intended for the people's use (see Jer 35:2 and note, 4).

Ezekiel's Temple

A. Wall (40:5,16-20)
B. East gate (40:6-14,16)
C. Portico (40:8)
D. Outer court (40:17)
E. Pavement (40:17)
F. East inner court (40:19)
G. North gate (40:20-22)
H. North inner court (40:23)
I. South gate (40:24-26)
J. South inner court (40:27)
K. Gateway (40:28-31)
L. Gateway (40:32-34)
M. Gateway (40:35-38)
N. Priests' rooms (40:44-45)
O. Court (40:47)
P. Temple portico (40:48-49)
Q. Outer sanctuary (41:1-2)
R. Most Holy Place (41:3-4)
S. Temple walls (41:5-7,9,11)
T. Base (41:8)
U. Open area (41:10)
V. West building (41:12)
W. Priests' rooms (42:1-10)
X. Altar (43:13-17)
AA. Rooms for preparing sacrifices (40:39-43)
BB. Ovens (46:19-20)
CC. Kitchens (46:21-24)

Ezekiel uses a long or "royal" cubit, c. 21 inches or 52 cm ("cubit and a handbreadth," Eze 40:5) as opposed to the standard Hebrew cubit of c. 18 inches or 45 cm.

Scripture describes a floor plan, but provides few height dimensions. This artwork shows an upward projection of the temple over the floor plan. This temple existed only in a vision of Ezekiel (Eze 40:2), and was never actually built as were the temples of Solomon, Zerubbabel and Herod.

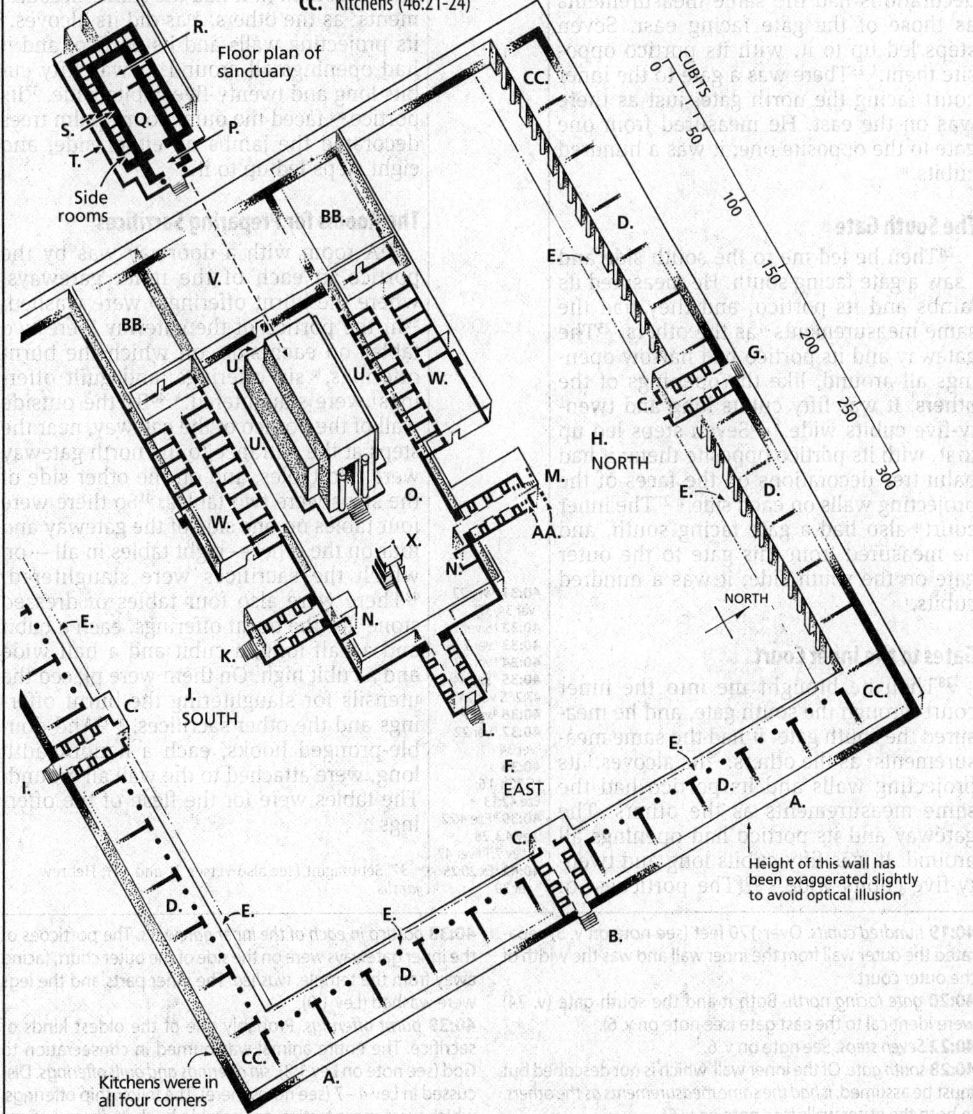

of the gateways and was as wide as they
were long; this was the lower pavement.
19Then he measured the distance from the
inside of the lower gateway to the outside
of the inner court;[g] it was a hundred cubits[h] on the east side as well as on the
north.

The North Gate

20Then he measured the length and
width of the gate facing north, leading
into the outer court. 21Its alcoves[i]—three
on each side—its projecting walls and its
portico[j] had the same measurements as
those of the first gateway. It was fifty cubits long and twenty-five cubits wide. 22Its
openings, its portico[k] and its palm tree
decorations had the same measurements
as those of the gate facing east. Seven
steps led up to it, with its portico opposite them.[l] 23There was a gate to the inner
court facing the north gate, just as there
was on the east. He measured from one
gate to the opposite one; it was a hundred
cubits.[m]

The South Gate

24Then he led me to the south side and
I saw a gate facing south. He measured its
jambs and its portico, and they had the
same measurements[n] as the others. 25The
gateway and its portico had narrow openings all around, like the openings of the
others. It was fifty cubits long and twenty-five cubits wide.[o] 26Seven steps led up
to it, with its portico opposite them; it had
palm tree decorations on the faces of the
projecting walls on each side.[p] 27The inner
court[q] also had a gate facing south, and
he measured from this gate to the outer
gate on the south side; it was a hundred
cubits.[r]

Gates to the Inner Court

28Then he brought me into the inner
court through the south gate, and he measured the south gate; it had the same measurements[s] as the others. 29Its alcoves,[t] its
projecting walls and its portico had the
same measurements as the others. The
gateway and its portico had openings all
around. It was fifty cubits long and twenty-five cubits wide.[u] 30(The porticoes[v] of
the gateways around the inner court were
twenty-five cubits wide and five cubits
deep.) 31Its portico[w] faced the outer court;
palm trees decorated its jambs, and eight
steps led up to it.[x]
32Then he brought me to the inner court
on the east side, and he measured the
gateway; it had the same measurements[y]
as the others. 33Its alcoves,[z] its projecting
walls and its portico had the same measurements as the others. The gateway and
its portico had openings all around. It was
fifty cubits long and twenty-five cubits
wide. 34Its portico[a] faced the outer court;
palm trees decorated the jambs on either
side, and eight steps led up to it.
35Then he brought me to the north gate[b]
and measured it. It had the same measurements[c] as the others, 36as did its alcoves,[d]
its projecting walls and its portico, and it
had openings all around. It was fifty cubits long and twenty-five cubits wide. 37Its
portico[a][e] faced the outer court; palm trees
decorated the jambs on either side, and
eight steps led up to it.[f]

The Rooms for Preparing Sacrifices

38A room with a doorway was by the
portico in each of the inner gateways,
where the burnt offerings[g] were washed.
39In the portico of the gateway were two
tables on each side, on which the burnt
offerings,[h] sin offerings[i] and guilt offerings[j] were slaughtered.[k] 40By the outside
wall of the portico of the gateway, near the
steps at the entrance to the north gateway
were two tables, and on the other side of
the steps were two tables. 41So there were
four tables on one side of the gateway and
four on the other—eight tables in all—on
which the sacrifices were slaughtered.
42There were also four tables of dressed
stone[l] for the burnt offerings, each a cubit
and a half long, a cubit and a half wide
and a cubit high. On them were placed the
utensils for slaughtering the burnt offerings and the other sacrifices.[m] 43And dou-
ble-pronged hooks, each a handbreadth
long, were attached to the wall all around.
The tables were for the flesh of the offerings.

40:19 [g] Eze 46:1 [h] ver 23,27 **40:21** [i] ver 7 [j] ver 30 **40:22** [k] ver 49 [l] S ver 16,26 **40:23** [m] S ver 19 **40:24** [n] ver 32,35 **40:25** [o] ver 33 **40:26** [p] S ver 22 **40:27** [q] ver 32 [r] S ver 19 **40:28** [s] ver 35 **40:29** [t] ver 7 [u] ver 25 **40:30** [v] ver 21 **40:31** [w] ver 22 [x] ver 34,37 **40:32** [y] S ver 24 **40:33** [z] ver 7 **40:34** [a] ver 22 **40:35** [b] Eze 44:4; 47:2 [c] S ver 24 **40:36** [d] ver 7 **40:37** [e] ver 22 [f] ver 34 **40:38** [g] S 2Ch 4:6; Eze 42:13 **40:39** [h] Eze 46:2 [i] Lev 4:3,28 [j] S Lev 7:1 [k] ver 42 **40:42** [l] Ex 20:25 [m] ver 39

[a] *37* Septuagint (see also verses 31 and 34); Hebrew *jambs*

40:19 *hundred cubits.* Over 170 feet (see note on v. 5) separated the outer wall from the inner wall and was the width of the outer court.
40:20 *gate facing north.* Both it and the south gate (v. 24) were identical to the east gate (see note on v. 6).
40:22 *Seven steps.* See note on v. 6.
40:28 *south gate.* Of the inner wall, which is not described but must be assumed. *it had the same measurements as the others.* In both the outer walls (see note on v. 6).
40:34 *eight steps.* See note on v. 6.
40:38 *portico in each of the inner gateways.* The porticoes of the inner gateways were on the side of the outer court, facing away from the temple. *washed.* The inner parts and the legs were washed (Lev 1:9).
40:39 *burnt offerings.* Probably one of the oldest kinds of sacrifice. The entire animal was burned in consecration to God (see note on Lev 1:3). *sin offerings and guilt offerings.* Discussed in Lev 4–7 (see notes there). The fellowship offerings, which were more festive, are notable by their absence from this listing (see 43:27; 45:17; 46:2,12; see also chart, p. 153).

Rooms for the Priests

44 Outside the inner gate, within the inner court, were two rooms, one[a] at the
side of the north gate and facing south,
and another at the side of the south[b] gate
and facing north. 45 He said to me, "The
room facing south is for the priests who
have charge of the temple,[n] 46 and the room
facing north[o] is for the priests who have
charge of the altar.[p] These are the sons
of Zadok,[q] who are the only Levites who
may draw near to the LORD to minister before him.[r]"
47 Then he measured the court: It was
square — a hundred cubits long and a
hundred cubits wide. And the altar was in
front of the temple.[s]

The Temple

48 He brought me to the portico of the
temple[t] and measured the jambs of the
portico; they were five cubits wide on either side. The width of the entrance was
fourteen cubits and its projecting walls
were[c] three cubits wide on either side.
49 The portico[u] was twenty cubits wide,
and twelve[d] cubits from front to back. It
was reached by a flight of stairs,[e] and there
were pillars[v] on each side of the jambs.
41 Then the man brought me to the
outer sanctuary[w] and measured the
jambs; the width of the jambs was six
cubits[f] on each side.[g] 2 The entrance was
ten cubits wide, and the projecting walls
on each side of it were five cubits wide.
He also measured the outer sanctuary; it
was forty cubits long and twenty cubits
wide.[x]
3 Then he went into the inner sanctuary
and measured the jambs of the entrance;
each was two cubits wide. The entrance
was six cubits wide, and the projecting
walls on each side of it were seven cubits wide. 4 And he measured the length of
the inner sanctuary; it was twenty cubits,
and its width was twenty cubits across the
end of the outer sanctuary.[y] He said to me,
"This is the Most Holy Place.[z]"
5 Then he measured the wall of the temple; it was six cubits thick, and each side
room around the temple was four cubits
wide. 6 The side rooms were on three levels, one above another, thirty[a] on each level. There were ledges all around the wall
of the temple to serve as supports for the
side rooms, so that the supports were not
inserted into the wall of the temple.[b] 7 The
side rooms all around the temple were
wider at each successive level. The structure surrounding the temple was built in
ascending stages, so that the rooms wid-
ened as one went upward. A stairway[c]
went up from the lowest floor to the top
floor through the middle floor.
8 I saw that the temple had a raised base
all around it, forming the foundation of
the side rooms. It was the length of the
rod, six long cubits. 9 The outer wall of the
side rooms was five cubits thick. The open
area between the side rooms of the temple
10 and the ⌊priests'⌋ rooms was twenty cubits wide all around the temple. 11 There
were entrances to the side rooms from
the open area, one on the north and another on the south; and the base adjoining the open area was five cubits wide all
around.
12 The building facing the temple courtyard on the west side was seventy cubits
wide. The wall of the building was five
cubits thick all around, and its length was
ninety cubits.
13 Then he measured the temple; it was a
hundred cubits long, and the temple courtyard and the building with its walls were
also a hundred cubits long. 14 The width of
the temple courtyard on the east, including the front of the temple, was a hundred
cubits.[d]
15 Then he measured the length of the
building facing the courtyard at the rear of
the temple, including its galleries[e] on each
side; it was a hundred cubits.

40:45 [n] 1Ch 9:23 **40:46** [o] Eze 42:13 [p] Nu 18:5 [q] S 2Sa 8:17; S Ezr 7:2 [r] Nu 16:5; Eze 43:19; 44:15; 45:4; 48:11 **40:47** [s] Eze 41:13-14 **40:48** [t] 1Ki 6:2 **40:49** [u] ver 22; 1Ki 6:3 [v] S 1Ki 7:15 **41:1** [w] ver 23 **41:2** [x] 2Ch 3:3 **41:4** [y] 1Ki 6:20 [z] S Ex 26:33; Heb 9:3-8

41:6 [a] Eze 40:17 [b] S 1Ki 6:5 **41:7** [c] 1Ki 6:8 **41:14** [d] Eze 40:47 **41:15** [e] Eze 42:3

[a] 44 Septuagint; Hebrew *were rooms for singers, which were* [b] 44 Septuagint; Hebrew *east* [c] 48 Septuagint; Hebrew *entrance was* [d] 49 Septuagint; Hebrew *eleven* [e] 49 Hebrew; Septuagint *Ten steps led up to it* [f] 1 The common cubit was about 1 1/2 feet (about 0.5 meter). [g] 1 One Hebrew manuscript and Septuagint; most Hebrew manuscripts *side, the width of the tent*

40:46 *sons of Zadok.* For the distinction between the sons of Zadok and the Levites see the fuller discussion in the notes on 44:15 – 31.

40:47 *altar.* Described in 43:13 – 17 (see notes there).

40:48 — 42:20 Description of the new temple (see diagram, p. 1297).

40:48 *portico.* Similar to the portico in Solomon's temple but slightly larger (see 1Ki 6:3).

40:49 *pillars.* Called Jakin and Boaz in Solomon's temple (see 1Ki 7:21 and NIV text notes).

41:1 *outer sanctuary.* Or nave, the largest of the three rooms comprising the temple (see 1Ki 6:3 – 5, where it is called the main hall). This outer sanctuary was identical in size to Solomon's (see 1Ki 6:17).

41:3 *he went into the inner sanctuary.* Only the angel, not Ezekiel, entered the Most Holy Place. Lev 16 forbids any but the high priest to enter it, and then only once a year (see Heb 9:7 and note). *six cubits wide.* Note the progressive narrowing of the door openings as one approaches the inner sanctuary (40:48, 14 cubits; 41:2, 10 cubits; here, 6 cubits).

41:4 *Most Holy Place.* See notes on Ex 26:31 – 35; 27:12 – 13; 1Ki 6:2,23; 2Ch 3:8; Ezr 6:15; Ps 28:2; Mt 27:51; Heb 8:2; 10:19 – 20.

41:6 *thirty on each level.* These 90 side rooms were probably storerooms for the priests, possibly for the tithes (see Mal 3:10 and note).

41:13 *hundred.* The 100-cubit symmetry stood for perfection.

The outer sanctuary, the inner sanctuary and the portico facing the court, [16]as well as the thresholds and the narrow windows[f] and galleries around the three of them—everything beyond and including the threshold was covered with wood. The floor, the wall up to the windows, and the windows were covered.[g] [17]In the space above the outside of the entrance to the inner sanctuary and on the walls at regular intervals all around the inner and outer sanctuary [18]were carved[h] cherubim[i] and palm trees.[j] Palm trees alternated with cherubim. Each cherub had two faces:[k] [19]the face of a man toward the palm tree on one side and the face of a lion toward the palm tree on the other. They were carved all around the whole temple.[l] [20]From the floor to the area above the entrance, cherubim and palm trees were carved on the wall of the outer sanctuary.

[21]The outer sanctuary[m] had a rectangular doorframe, and the one at the front of the Most Holy Place was similar. [22]There was a wooden altar[n] three cubits high and two cubits square[a]; its corners, its base[b] and its sides were of wood. The man said to me, "This is the table[o] that is before the LORD." [23]Both the outer sanctuary[p] and the Most Holy Place had double doors.[q] [24]Each door had two leaves—two hinged leaves[r] for each door. [25]And on the doors of the outer sanctuary were carved cherubim and palm trees like those carved on the walls, and there was a wooden overhang on the front of the portico. [26]On the sidewalls of the portico were narrow windows with palm trees carved on each side. The side rooms of the temple also had overhangs.[s]

Rooms for the Priests

42 Then the man led me northward into the outer court and brought me to the rooms[t] opposite the temple courtyard[u] and opposite the outer wall on the north side.[v] [2]The building whose door faced north was a hundred cubits[c] long and fifty cubits wide. [3]Both in the section twenty cubits from the inner court and in the section opposite the pavement of the outer court, gallery[w] faced gallery at the three levels.[x] [4]In front of the rooms was an inner passageway ten cubits wide and a hundred cubits[d] long. Their doors were on the north.[y] [5]Now the upper rooms were narrower, for the galleries took more space from them than from the rooms on the lower and middle floors of the building. [6]The rooms on the third floor had no pillars, as the courts had; so they were smaller in floor space than those on the lower and middle floors. [7]There was an outer wall parallel to the rooms and the outer court; it extended in front of the rooms for fifty cubits. [8]While the row of rooms on the side next to the outer court was fifty cubits long, the row on the side nearest the sanctuary was a hundred cubits long. [9]The lower rooms had an entrance[z] on the east side as one enters them from the outer court.

[10]On the south side[e] along the length of the wall of the outer court, adjoining the temple courtyard[a] and opposite the outer wall, were rooms[b] [11]with a passageway in front of them. These were like the rooms on the north; they had the same length and width, with similar exits and dimensions. Similar to the doorways on the north [12]were the doorways of the rooms on the south. There was a doorway at the beginning of the passageway that was parallel to the corresponding wall extending eastward, by which one enters the rooms.

[13]Then he said to me, "The north[c] and south rooms[d] facing the temple courtyard[e] are the priests' rooms, where the priests who approach the LORD will eat the most holy offerings. There they will put the most holy offerings—the grain offerings,[f] the sin offerings[g] and the guilt offerings[h]—for the place is holy.[i] [14]Once the priests enter the holy precincts, they are not to go into the outer court until they leave behind the garments[j] in which they minister, for these are holy. They are to put on other clothes before they go near the places that are for the people.[k]"

41:16 [f] 1Ki 6:4 [g] ver 25-26; 1Ki 6:15; Eze 42:3 **41:18** [h] S 1Ki 6:18 [i] Ex 37:7; S 2Ch 3:7 [j] S 1Ki 6:29; 7:36 [k] Eze 10:21 **41:19** [l] S Eze 10:14 **41:21** [m] ver 1 **41:22** [n] S Ex 30:1 [o] S Ex 25:23; S Eze 23:41 **41:23** [p] ver 1 [q] 1Ki 6:32 **41:24** [r] 1Ki 6:34 **41:26** [s] ver 15-16; Eze 40:16 **42:1** [t] ver 13 [u] S Ex 27:9; Eze 41:12-14 [v] Eze 40:17 **42:3** [w] Eze 41:15 [x] Eze 41:16 **42:4** [y] Eze 46:19 **42:9** [z] Eze 44:5; 46:19 **42:10** [a] Eze 41:12-14 [b] ver 1 **42:13** [c] Eze 40:46 [d] ver 1 [e] Eze 41:12-14 [f] Jer 41:5 [g] S Lev 10:17 [h] Lev 14:13 [i] S Ex 29:31; S Lev 6:29; 7:6; 10:12-13; Nu 18:9-10 **42:14** [j] Lev 16:23; Eze 44:19 [k] Ex 29:9; S Lev 8:7-9

[a] 22 Septuagint; Hebrew *long* [b] 22 Septuagint; Hebrew *length* [c] 2 The common cubit was about 1 1/2 feet (about 0.5 meter). [d] 4 Septuagint and Syriac; Hebrew *and one cubit* [e] 10 Septuagint; Hebrew *Eastward*

41:16 *everything ... was covered with wood.* As in Solomon's temple (1Ki 6:15).

41:18 *cherubim.* Who served as guards (cf. Ge 3:24 and note). These, as opposed to those mentioned in ch. 10 (see note on 1:5), have only two faces—a man's and a lion's (see 1Ki 6:29,32,35).

41:22 *wooden altar.* As the great altar stood outside the temple proper (43:13–17), so a smaller altar (3'5" square by 5' high) stood outside the Most Holy Place. It served as a table, no doubt to hold the bread of the Presence (see Ex 25:30; Lev 24:5–9; 1Ki 7:48 and notes). Ezekiel makes no mention of an altar of incense or of lampstands, such as were found in Solomon's temple and in the tabernacle before it. Also not included are the "Sea" (1Ki 7:23) and the ark of the covenant (see note on Ezr 6:15).

41:23 *double doors.* Folding doors, so that the entry could be made still narrower.

42:1 *rooms opposite the temple courtyard.* Their function is described in vv. 13–14. They have no parallel in Solomon's temple as described in 1Ki 6.

42:13 *priests who approach the LORD.* The sons of Zadok (see 40:6 and note on 44:15). *eat the most holy offerings.* The priests normally received partial maintenance by being allowed to eat certain sacrifices (see Lev 2:3; 5:13; 6:16,26,29; 7:6,10). *the place is holy.* See note on Lev 11:44; see also Introduction to Leviticus: Theological Themes.

[15]When he had finished measuring what was inside the temple area, he led me out by the east gate[l] and measured the area all around: [16]He measured the east side with the measuring rod; it was five hundred cubits.[a] [17]He measured the north side; it was five hundred cubits[b] by the measuring rod. [18]He measured the south side; it was five hundred cubits by the measuring rod. [19]Then he turned to the west side and measured; it was five hundred cubits by the measuring rod. [20]So he measured[m] the area[n] on all four sides. It had a wall around it,[o] five hundred cubits long and five hundred cubits wide,[p] to separate the holy from the common.[q]

The Glory Returns to the Temple

43 Then the man brought me to the gate facing east,[r] [2]and I saw the glory of the God of Israel coming from the east. His voice was like the roar of rushing waters,[s] and the land was radiant with his glory.[t] [3]The vision I saw was like the vision I had seen when he[c] came to destroy the city and like the visions I had seen by the Kebar River, and I fell facedown. [4]The glory[u] of the LORD entered the temple through the gate facing east.[v] [5]Then the Spirit[w] lifted me up[x] and brought me into the inner court, and the glory[y] of the LORD filled the temple.[z]

[6]While the man was standing beside me, I heard someone speaking to me from inside the temple. [7]He said: "Son of man, this is the place of my throne[a] and the place for the soles of my feet. This is where I will live among the Israelites forever. The house of Israel will never again defile[b] my holy name—neither they nor their kings—by their prostitution[d] and the lifeless idols[e] of their kings at their high places.[c] [8]When they placed their threshold next to my threshold and their doorposts beside my doorposts, with only a wall between me and them, they defiled my holy name by their detestable practices. So I destroyed them in my anger. [9]Now let them put away from me their prostitution and the lifeless idols of their kings, and I will live among them forever.[d]

[10]"Son of man, describe the temple to the people of Israel, that they may be ashamed[e] of their sins. Let them consider the plan, [11]and if they are ashamed of all they have done, make known to them the design of the temple—its arrangement, its exits and entrances—its whole design and all its regulations[f] and laws. Write these down before them so that they may be faithful to its design and follow all its regulations.[f]

[12]"This is the law of the temple: All the surrounding area[g] on top of the mountain will be most holy.[h] Such is the law of the temple.

The Altar

[13]"These are the measurements of the altar[i] in long cubits, that cubit being a cubit[g] and a handbreadth[h]: Its gutter is a cubit deep and a cubit wide, with a rim of one span[i] around the edge. And this is the height of the altar: [14]From the gutter on

42:15 [l]Eze 43:1
42:20 [m]Eze 40:5 [n]Eze 43:12 [o]Zec 2:5 [p]Eze 45:2; Rev 21:16 [q]S Eze 22:26
43:1 [r]S 1Ch 9:18; S Eze 8:16; 42:15; 44:1
43:2 [s]S Ps 18:4; S Rev 1:15 [t]Isa 6:3; Rev 18:1; 21:11
43:4 [u]Eze 1:28 [v]Eze 10:19; 44:2
43:5 [w]S Eze 11:24 [x]S Eze 3:12 [y]S Ex 16:7 [z]S Isa 6:4
43:7 [a]S Jer 3:17 [b]S Eze 37:23 [c]S Lev 26:30; S Eze 20:29, 39
43:9 [d]Eze 37:26-28
43:10 [e]S Eze 16:61
43:11 [f]Eze 44:5
43:12 [g]Eze 42:20 [h]S Eze 17:22
43:13 [i]S Ex 20:24; 2Ch 4:1

[a] *16* See Septuagint of verse 17; Hebrew *rods*; also in verses 18 and 19. [b] *17* Septuagint; Hebrew *rods* [c] *3* Some Hebrew manuscripts and Vulgate; most Hebrew manuscripts *I* [d] *7* Or *their spiritual adultery*; also in verse 9 [e] *7* Or *the corpses*; also in verse 9 [f] *11* Some Hebrew manuscripts and Septuagint; most Hebrew manuscripts *regulations and its whole design* [g] *13* The common cubit was about 1 1/2 feet (about 0.5 meter). [h] *13* That is, about 3 inches (about 8 centimeters) [i] *13* That is, about 9 inches (about 22 centimeters)

42:20 *five hundred cubits long and five hundred cubits wide.* Perfect symmetry in the ideal temple's total area.

43:1–12 God's glory returns to the new temple.

43:2 *I saw the glory.* The high point of chs. 40–48 (see note on 1:28). The temple had been prepared for this moment, and all that follows flows from this appearance. *coming from the east.* The direction Ezekiel had seen God leave (see 11:23 and note). In the book of Ezekiel God's glory is always active (see vv. 4–5; 3:23; 9:3; 10:4,18; 44:4). *like the roar of rushing waters.* Ezekiel experienced an audition as well as a vision. For the comparison see 1:24; Rev 1:15; 14:2; 19:6. *the land was radiant with his glory.* God's visible glory is always described as being very bright (see 10:4; Lk 2:9; Rev 21:11,23).

43:3 *like the vision I had seen.* But somewhat different, for no creatures or wheels are mentioned here. *when he came to destroy the city.* See ch. 9. *Kebar River.* See 1:1 and note. *I fell facedown.* See 1:28; 3:23; 9:8; 11:13; 44:4.

43:4 *through the gate facing east.* See note on v. 2.

43:5 *Then the Spirit lifted me up.* With God being nearer, the function of the guiding angel was taken over by the Spirit of God. Ezekiel was transported into the inner court but not into the temple (cf. 3:12 and note). *filled the temple.* As at the consecration of Solomon's temple (1Ki 8:10–11; see notes on Ex 40:34; 1Ki 8:10; cf. Isa 6:4).

43:6 *someone.* God, but out of reverence not named here, preserving an air of awe and mystery.

43:7 *place of my throne.* See 1Sa 4:4; Ps 47:8 and notes. *place for the soles of my feet.* See 1Ch 28:2; Ps 99:5 and note; 132:7; Isa 60:13 and note; La 2:1. *I will live among the Israelites forever.* Renewing the promise of 37:26–28 (see v. 9; 1Ki 6:13; Zec 2:11). *defile my holy name.* See Lev 18:21 and note. *prostitution.* See note on Ex 34:15. *lifeless idols.* As the NIV text note indicates, the reference is either to idols or to monuments or graves of past kings. Fourteen kings of Judah were buried in Jerusalem, possibly near (too near for Ezekiel) the temple area (see 2Ki 21:18,26; 23:30).

43:8 *their threshold next to my threshold.* Solomon's temple was surrounded by many of his own private structures (see 1Ki 7:1–12). The distinction between God's holy temple and the rest of the world is a central idea in the book of Ezekiel (see v. 12; 44:23). *So I destroyed them.* As elsewhere in Ezekiel, the unstable practices of the people and their kings brought about their destruction (see 5:11; 18:10–12; and especially 22:1–15).

43:12 *This is the law.* Refers to the contents of chs. 40–42.

43:13–27 Restoration of the great altar.

43:13 *altar.* Alluded to in 40:47 and here described in detail. Although the material is not mentioned, dressed stones were probably to be used. Ex 20:24–26 allowed an

the ground up to the lower ledge it is two
cubits high and a cubit wide, and from the
smaller ledge up to the larger ledge it is
four cubits high and a cubit wide. 15The
altar hearth[j] is four cubits high, and four
horns[k] project upward from the hearth.
16The altar hearth is square, twelve cubits
long and twelve cubits wide.[l] 17The upper
ledge[m] also is square, fourteen cubits long
and fourteen cubits wide, with a rim of half
a cubit and a gutter of a cubit all around.
The steps[n] of the altar face east.[o]"

18Then he said to me, "Son of man, this
is what the Sovereign LORD says: These
will be the regulations for sacrificing burnt
offerings[p] and sprinkling blood[q] upon the
altar when it is built: 19You are to give a
young bull[r] as a sin offering to the priests,
who are Levites, of the family of Zadok,[s]
who come near[t] to minister before me,
declares the Sovereign LORD. 20You are to
take some of its blood and put it on the
four horns of the altar[u] and on the four
corners of the upper ledge[v] and all around
the rim, and so purify the altar[w] and make
atonement for it. 21You are to take the bull
for the sin offering and burn it in the designated part of the temple area outside the
sanctuary.[x]

22"On the second day you are to offer a
male goat without defect for a sin offering,
and the altar is to be purified as it was purified with the bull. 23When you have finished purifying it, you are to offer a young
bull and a ram from the flock, both without defect.[y] 24You are to offer them before
the LORD, and the priests are to sprinkle
salt[z] on them and sacrifice them as a burnt
offering to the LORD.

25"For seven days[a] you are to provide a
male goat daily for a sin offering; you are
also to provide a young bull and a ram
from the flock, both without defect.[b] 26For
seven days they are to make atonement for
the altar and cleanse it; thus they will dedicate it. 27At the end of these days, from
the eighth day[c] on, the priests are to present your burnt offerings[d] and fellowship
offerings[a][e] on the altar. Then I will accept
you, declares the Sovereign LORD."

43:15 [j]Isa 29:2 [k]S Ex 27:2 **43:16** [l]Rev 21:16 **43:17** [m]ver 20; Eze 45:19 [n]Ex 20:26 [o]S Ex 27:1 **43:18** [p]Ex 40:29 [q]Lev 1:5,11; Heb 9:21-22 **43:19** [r]S Lev 4:3 [s]S 2Sa 8:17; S Ezr 7:2 [t]Nu 16:40; S Eze 40:46 **43:20** [u]S Lev 4:7 [v]S ver 17 [w]Lev 16:19 **43:21** [x]Ex 29:14; Heb 13:11 **43:23** [y]Ex 29:1; S Lev 22:20 **43:24** [z]S Lev 2:13; Mk 9:49-50 **43:25** [a]S Lev 8:33 [b]S Ex 29:37 **43:27** [c]Lev 9:1 [d]S Isa 60:7 [e]S Ex 32:6; S Lev 17:5 **44:1** [f]S Eze 43:1 **44:2** [g]Eze 43:4-5 **44:3** [h]S Ex 24:9-11 [i]Eze 46:2,8 **44:4** [j]S Eze 40:35 [k]S Isa 6:4; S Eze 10:4; Rev 15:8 [l]Da 8:17 **44:5** [m]S Eze 42:9 [n]Eze 40:4; 43:10-11 **44:6** [o]S Eze 3:9 **44:7** [p]S Lev 26:41

The Prince, the Levites, the Priests

44 Then the man brought me back to
the outer gate of the sanctuary, the
one facing east,[f] and it was shut. 2The
LORD said to me, "This gate is to remain
shut. It must not be opened; no one may
enter through it.[g] It is to remain shut because the LORD, the God of Israel, has entered through it. 3The prince himself is the
only one who may sit inside the gateway
to eat in the presence[h] of the LORD. He is to
enter by way of the portico of the gateway
and go out the same way.[i]"

4Then the man brought me by way of
the north gate[j] to the front of the temple.
I looked and saw the glory of the LORD
filling the temple[k] of the LORD, and I fell
facedown.[l]

5The LORD said to me, "Son of man, look
carefully, listen closely and give attention
to everything I tell you concerning all the
regulations regarding the temple of the
LORD. Give attention to the entrance[m] of
the temple and all the exits of the sanctuary.[n] 6Say to the rebellious house[o] of
Israel, 'This is what the Sovereign LORD
says: Enough of your detestable practices,
O house of Israel! 7In addition to all your
other detestable practices, you brought foreigners uncircumcised in heart[p] and flesh

[a] 27 Traditionally *peace offerings*

altar to be made of earth, but use of dressed stones for those altars was strictly forbidden (see notes on Ex 20:24–25). Solomon's altar was bronze (1Ki 8:64). Ezekiel's altar, much larger than Solomon's, was over 20 feet tall (including the horns, v. 15), made up of three slabs of decreasing size, like an Egyptian pyramid or Babylonian ziggurat: the "lower ledge" (v. 14), two cubits high; the "larger ledge" (v. 14), four cubits high; and the "altar hearth" (v. 15), four cubits high.

43:15 *altar hearth.* The Hebrew for this term appears only here in the OT and may also mean "mountain of God" or "lion of God"; it is a variant of a form that appears in Isa 29:1–2,7 (see note there). *four horns.* Stone projections from each of the four corners of the altar hearth. On earlier altars they afforded a refuge of last resort for an accused person (see Ex 21:12–14; 1Ki 1:50–51; 2:28–29).

43:17 *steps of the altar.* Forbidden in Ex 20:26 but here required because of the size (see note on v. 13).

43:18 *burnt offerings.* See note on 40:39. *sprinkling blood.* See Ex 29:16; Lev 4:6; 5:9.

43:19 *sin offering.* To cleanse the altar from the pollution of human sin (see note on 40:39). *of the family of Zadok.* See note on 44:15.

43:21 *outside the sanctuary.* As prescribed in Ex 29:14; Lev 4:12,21; 8:17; 9:11; 16:27. This action foreshadows one aspect of Christ's sacrifice (see Heb 13:11–13 and notes).

43:22 *purified.* By the sprinkling of the blood (see v. 20).

43:27 *fellowship offerings.* After the seven-day consecration by burnt offerings and sin offerings, the altar was ready for the celebration of the more festive fellowship offerings where the people partook of some of the meat (see note on Lev 3:1).

44:1–31 Restoration of the priesthood.

44:2 *It is to remain shut because.* The reason given here is that God entered through the east gate (43:1–2), thus making it holy. Related reasons may be that God would never again leave as before (10:19; 11:23) and that sun worship would be made impossible (see 8:16). Today the east gate (called the Golden Gate) of the sacred Moslem area (*Haram esh-Sharif,* "The Noble Sanctuary") in Jerusalem is likewise sealed shut as a result of a later but possibly related tradition.

44:3 *prince.* The first mention of the prince in chs. 40–48 (see 34:24 and note). *to eat.* Probably his part of the fellowship offering (see Lev 7:15; Dt 12:7; see also Eze 43:27 and note). While this honor is accorded the prince, it is significant that he is given no other part in the ceremonial functions, reserved now solely for the priests (see 2Ch 26:16–20). *by way of the portico.* From the inside of the outer court.

44:7 *uncircumcised in heart.* Spiritually unfit.

into my sanctuary, desecrating my temple
while you offered me food, fat and blood,
and you broke my covenant.[q] 8 Instead of
carrying out your duty in regard to my
holy things, you put others in charge of
my sanctuary.[r] 9 This is what the Sovereign
LORD says: No foreigner uncircumcised in
heart and flesh is to enter my sanctuary,
not even the foreigners who live among
the Israelites.[s]
10 " 'The Levites who went far from me
when Israel went astray[t] and who wandered from me after their idols must bear
the consequences of their sin.[u] 11 They may
serve in my sanctuary, having charge of
the gates of the temple and serving in it;
they may slaughter the burnt offerings[v]
and sacrifices for the people and stand
before the people and serve them.[w] 12 But
because they served them in the presence
of their idols and made the house of Israel fall[x] into sin, therefore I have sworn
with uplifted hand[y] that they must bear
the consequences of their sin, declares the
Sovereign LORD.[z] 13 They are not to come
near to serve me as priests or come near
any of my holy things or my most holy offerings; they must bear the shame[a] of their
detestable practices.[b] 14 Yet I will put them
in charge of the duties of the temple and
all the work that is to be done in it.[c]
15 " 'But the priests, who are Levites and
descendants of Zadok[d] and who faithfully carried out the duties of my sanctuary
when the Israelites went astray from me,
are to come near to minister before me;
they are to stand before me to offer sacrifices of fat[e] and blood, declares the Sovereign LORD.[f] 16 They alone are to enter my
sanctuary; they alone are to come near my
table[g] to minister before me and perform
my service.[h]
17 " 'When they enter the gates of the inner court, they are to wear linen clothes;[i]
they must not wear any woolen garment
while ministering at the gates of the inner court or inside the temple. 18 They are
to wear linen turbans[j] on their heads and
linen undergarments[k] around their waists.
They must not wear anything that makes
them perspire.[l] 19 When they go out into
the outer court where the people are, they
are to take off the clothes they have been
ministering in and are to leave them in the
sacred rooms, and put on other clothes, so
that they do not consecrate[m] the people by
means of their garments.[n]
20 " 'They must not shave[o] their heads
or let their hair grow long, but they are
to keep the hair of their heads trimmed.[p]
21 No priest is to drink wine when he enters the inner court.[q] 22 They must not marry widows or divorced women; they may
marry only virgins of Israelite descent or
widows of priests.[r] 23 They are to teach my
people the difference between the holy
and the common[s] and show them how to
distinguish between the unclean and the
clean.[t]
24 " 'In any dispute, the priests are to
serve as judges[u] and decide it according
to my ordinances. They are to keep my
laws and my decrees for all my appointed
feasts,[v] and they are to keep my Sabbaths
holy.[w]

44:7 [q]Ge 17:14; Ex 12:48; Lev 22:25 **44:8** [r]Lev 22:2; Nu 18:7 **44:9** [s]Joel 3:17; Zec 14:21 **44:10** [t]Ps 95:10 [u]Nu 18:23 **44:11** [v]2Ch 29:34 [w]Nu 3:5-37; S 16:9; S 1Ch 26:12-19 **44:12** [x]S Jer 18:15 [y]Ps 106:26 [z]2Ki 16:10-16; Jer 14:10 **44:13** [a]S Eze 16:61 [b]Nu 18:3; Hos 5:1 **44:14** [c]1Sa 2:36; 2Ki 23:9; S 1Ch 23:28-32 **44:15** [d]S 2Sa 8:17; S Ezr 7:2 [e]S Ex 29:13 [f]S Jer 33:18; S Eze 40:46; Zec 3:7 **44:16** [g]S Eze 41:22 [h]Lev 3:16-17; 17:5-6; Nu 18:5; S 1Sa 2:35; Zec 3:7 **44:17** [i]Rev 19:8 **44:18** [j]S Ex 28:39; S Isa 3:20 [k]S Ex 28:42 [l]S Lev 16:4 **44:19** [m]S Lev 6:27 [n]Ex 39:27-29; Lev 6:10-11; S Eze 42:14 **44:20** [o]Eze 5:1 [p]S Lev 21:5; Nu 6:5 **44:21** [q]S Lev 10:9 **44:22** [r]Lev 21:7 **44:23** [s]S Eze 22:26 [t]S Ge 7:2; Lev 13:50; 15:31; Jer 15:19; Hag 2:11-13 **44:24** [u]Dt 17:8-9; 19:17; 21:5; S 1Ch 23:4 [v]S Lev 23:2 [w]2Ch 19:8

44:9 *No foreigner uncircumcised ... is to enter my sanctuary.* Nehemiah enforced this restriction when he dismissed Tobiah (Ne 13:8), an Ammonite (Ne 2:10; see Dt 23:3). Foreigners could, however, be a part of Israel (see 47:22).
44:10 *Levites.* Some members of the tribe of Levi served as priests (see Dt 33:8–11; Jdg 17:13). *when Israel went astray.* The reference is mainly to the period of the monarchy, especially to the last years, during which Ezekiel so often criticized the people's idolatry (see 6:3–6; 14:3–11; 16:18–21; 23:36–49; 36:17–18; 37:23).
44:11 *stand before the people and serve them.* Cf. "minister before ... stand before" the Lord as ministers and servants (v. 15); the Levites still had an honorable position.
44:12 *with uplifted hand.* See 20:5 and note.
44:15 *Zadok.* Traced his Levitical lineage to Aaron through Aaron's son Eleazar (1Ch 6:50–53). He served as priest under David, along with Abiathar (see 2Sa 8:17 and note; 15:24–29; 20:25). He supported Solomon (as opposed to Abiathar, who pledged himself to Adonijah) and thus secured for himself and his descendants the privilege of serving in the Jerusalem temple (see 1Ki 1). Later the Zadokites were removed from office, but the Qumran (Dead Sea Scrolls) community remained loyal to them (see essay, pp. 1453–1454). *who faithfully carried out.* A distinction Ezekiel did not make in his prophecies of judgment (see 7:26; 22:26 and the thrust of all of ch. 8). In chs. 40–48, however, the Zadokites received special consideration because of their faithfulness. *fat and blood.* See 39:19 and note.
44:16 *They alone are to enter.* This elevation of the Zadokite priests and demotion of the Levites were part of the concern for ritual purity, a major theme of chs. 40–48. Only the fittest were to serve. *my table.* Either the table that held the bread (see 41:22 and note) or the large altar on which the Lord's food was presented (v. 7).
44:17 *linen.* Cooler than wool (see v. 18).
44:18 *turbans.* Ezekiel wore one (24:17).
44:19 *take off the clothes.* In the interest of ritual purity.
44:20 *must not shave their heads.* Because it was a mourning ritual (7:18) that rendered the mourner unclean (see Lev 21:1–5). *or let their hair grow long.* Because it implied the taking of a vow that might prevent the priest from serving (see Nu 6:5; Ac 21:23–26).
44:23 *difference between the holy and the common.* One of Ezekiel's central concerns. The important task of declaring God's will on matters of ceremonially clean and unclean food, the fitness of sacrificial animals and ritual purity either had been done for pay (see Mic 3:11) or had been neglected altogether (see Jer 2:8; Eze 22:26 and note). See Hag 2:10–13 for a positive example. *distinguish between the unclean and the clean.* See Lev 11; Dt 14:3–21 and notes.
44:24 *priests are to serve as judges.* One of their functions from earliest days (see NIV text note on 1Sa 4:18; see also 2Ch 19:8–11).

25 "'A priest must not defile himself by
going near a dead person; however, if the
dead person was his father or mother, son
or daughter, brother or unmarried sister,
then he may defile himself.[x] 26 After he is
cleansed, he must wait seven days.[y] 27 On
the day he goes into the inner court of the
sanctuary[z] to minister in the sanctuary, he
is to offer a sin offering[a] for himself, declares the Sovereign LORD.
28 "'I am to be the only inheritance[b] the
priests have. You are to give them no possession in Israel; I will be their possession.
29 They will eat[c] the grain offerings, the sin
offerings and the guilt offerings; and everything in Israel devoted[a] to the LORD[d]
will belong to them.[e] 30 The best of all the
firstfruits[f] and of all your special gifts will
belong to the priests. You are to give them
the first portion of your ground meal[g] so
that a blessing[h] may rest on your household.[i] 31 The priests must not eat anything,
bird or animal, found dead[j] or torn by
wild animals.[k]

Division of the Land

45 "'When you allot the land as an inheritance,[l] you are to present to the
LORD a portion of the land as a sacred district, 25,000 cubits long and 20,000[b] cubits
wide; the entire area will be holy.[m] 2 Of this,
a section 500 cubits square[n] is to be for
the sanctuary, with 50 cubits around it for
open land. 3 In the sacred district, measure
off a section 25,000 cubits[c] long and 10,000
cubits[d] wide. In it will be the sanctuary, the
Most Holy Place. 4 It will be the sacred portion of the land for the priests,[o] who minister in the sanctuary and who draw near to
minister before the LORD. It will be a place
for their houses as well as a holy place for
the sanctuary.[p] 5 An area 25,000 cubits long
and 10,000 cubits wide will belong to the
Levites, who serve in the temple, as their
possession for towns to live in.[e][q]
6 "'You are to give the city as its property
an area 5,000 cubits wide and 25,000 cubits long, adjoining the sacred portion; it
will belong to the whole house of Israel.[r]
7 "'The prince will have the land bordering each side of the area formed by the sacred district and the property of the city. It
will extend westward from the west side
and eastward from the east side, running
lengthwise from the western to the eastern
border parallel to one of the tribal portions.[s]
8 This land will be his possession in Israel.
And my princes will no longer oppress my
people but will allow the house of Israel to
possess the land according to their tribes.[t]
9 "'This is what the Sovereign LORD says:
You have gone far enough, O princes of
Israel! Give up your violence and oppression[u] and do what is just and right.[v] Stop
dispossessing my people, declares the
Sovereign LORD. 10 You are to use accurate
scales,[w] an accurate ephah[f][x] and an accurate bath.[g] 11 The ephah[y] and the bath are
to be the same size, the bath containing a
tenth of a homer[h] and the ephah a tenth
of a homer; the homer is to be the standard measure for both. 12 The shekel[i] is to
consist of twenty gerahs.[z] Twenty shekels
plus twenty-five shekels plus fifteen shekels equal one mina.[j]

44:25 [x]Lev 21:1-4 **44:26** [y]Nu 19:14 **44:27** [z]S Nu 3:28 [a]S Lev 4:28; Nu 6:11 **44:28** [b]S Nu 18:20; Dt 18:1-2; S Jos 13:33 **44:29** [c]Lev 6:16 [d]S Lev 27:21 [e]Nu 18:9, 14; S Jos 13:14 **44:30** [f]Nu 18:12-13; S 2Ch 31:5 [g]S Nu 15:18-21 [h]S Lev 25:21 [i]S 2Ch 31:10; Ne 10:35-37 **44:31** [j]S Lev 11:39 [k]S Ex 22:31; S Lev 11:40 **45:1** [l]S Nu 34:13 [m]Eze 48:8-9, 29 **45:2** [n]Eze 42:20 **45:4** [o]S Eze 40:46 [p]Eze 48:10-11 **45:5** [q]Eze 48:13 **45:6** [r]Eze 48:15-18 **45:7** [s]Eze 48:21 **45:8** [t]S Nu 26:53; Eze 46:18 **45:9** [u]Ps 12:5 [v]S Jer 22:3; Zec 7:9-10; 8:16 **45:10** [w]Dt 25:15; S Pr 11:1; Am 8:4-6; Mic 6:10-11 [x]S Lev 19:36 **45:11** [y]Isa 5:10 **45:12** [z]Ex 30:13; Lev 27:25; Nu 3:47

[a] *29* The Hebrew term refers to the irrevocable giving over of things or persons to the LORD. [b] *1* Septuagint (see also verses 3 and 5 and 48:9); Hebrew *10,000* [c] *3* That is, about 7 miles (about 12 kilometers) [d] *3* That is, about 3 miles (about 5 kilometers) [e] *5* Septuagint; Hebrew *temple; they will have as their possession 20 rooms* [f] *10* An ephah was a dry measure. [g] *10* A bath was a liquid measure. [h] *11* A homer was a dry measure. [i] *12* A shekel weighed about 2/5 ounce (about 11.5 grams). [j] *12* That is, 60 shekels; the common mina was 50 shekels.

44:25 *dead person.* Contact with the dead made a person ceremonially unclean (Lev 21:1–3; Hag 2:13).
44:28 *no possession.* The statement that priests were not to own land agrees with Nu 18:20,23–24; Dt 10:9; Jos 13:14,33; 18:7.
44:31 *found dead.* This restriction applied to all Israel according to Lev 7:24.
45:1—46:24 An idealized depiction of the restoration of Israel's theocratic order.
45:1 *When you allot the land.* Envisioned a new acquisition and redistribution of the land. *present to the LORD.* The entire square area in the center of the land was to be set aside for the Lord. *20,000 cubits.* With the 5,000-cubit city area (v. 6) it was a perfect square. *entire area will be holy.* Set apart for the Lord and owned by no tribe.
45:2 *section 500 cubits square.* The temple area discussed in 42:16–20. *open land.* An unoccupied strip of land that served as a buffer between the more holy and the less holy, though the whole area was holy (see 42:20).
45:3 *measure off a section.* The middle strip of the holy square was specifically for the temple (see map, p. 1308).
45:4 *land for the priests.* Not to own (see 44:28) but to live on.
45:5 *area ... to the Levites.* A section of equal size just to the north was for the Levites to dwell on, even though it was in the holy area. The Levites, as opposed to the Zadokite priests, could hold land as a possession.
45:6 *city.* The former Jerusalem contained the temple area. The new holy city would not, but would be adjacent to the temple. *5,000 cubits wide.* The southernmost section of the city completed the perfectly square area. *it will belong to the whole house of Israel.* Not to any one tribe or person as in former days.
45:7 *The prince will have the land.* A considerable portion of territory. In view of the next verse (cf. 46:18) the generous allotment should have kept the prince from greed like that of Ahab (see 1Ki 21). The prince was also responsible for sizable offerings (v. 17).
45:9 *O princes of Israel!* The language of this verse is reminiscent of the preaching Ezekiel did before 586 B.C. (see 22:6). *what is just and right.* See note on 33:14.
45:10 *You are to use accurate scales.* Israel was not to repeat the economic injustices of the past. The OT often warns against cheating in weights and measures (see Lev 19:35 and note; Dt 25:13–16; Mic 6:10–12).
45:11 *same size.* A little more than half a bushel. *homer.* About six bushels.

Offerings and Holy Days

13“ ‘This is the special gift you are to offer: a sixth of an ephah from each homer
of wheat and a sixth of an ephah from
each homer of barley. 14The prescribed
portion of oil, measured by the bath, is
a tenth of a bath from each cor (which
consists of ten baths or one homer, for ten
baths are equivalent to a homer). 15Also
one sheep is to be taken from every flock
of two hundred from the well-watered pastures of Israel. These will be used for the
grain offerings, burnt offerings[a] and fellowship offerings[a] to make atonement[b] for
the people, declares the Sovereign LORD.
16All the people of the land will participate
in this special gift for the use of the prince
in Israel. 17It will be the duty of the prince
to provide the burnt offerings, grain offerings and drink offerings at the festivals,
the New Moons[c] and the Sabbaths[d]—at
all the appointed feasts of the house of
Israel. He will provide the sin offerings,
grain offerings, burnt offerings and fellowship offerings to make atonement for the
house of Israel.[e]

18“ ‘This is what the Sovereign LORD says:
In the first month[f] on the first day you are
to take a young bull without defect[g] and
purify the sanctuary.[h] 19The priest is to
take some of the blood of the sin offering
and put it on the doorposts of the temple, on the four corners of the upper ledge[i]
of the altar[j] and on the gateposts of the
inner court. 20You are to do the same on
the seventh day of the month for anyone
who sins unintentionally[k] or through ignorance; so you are to make atonement
for the temple.

21“ ‘In the first month on the fourteenth
day you are to observe the Passover,[l] a
feast lasting seven days, during which
you shall eat bread made without yeast.
22On that day the prince is to provide a
bull as a sin offering for himself and for
all the people of the land.[m] 23Every day
during the seven days of the Feast he is to
provide seven bulls and seven rams[n] without defect as a burnt offering to the LORD,
and a male goat for a sin offering.[o] 24He is
to provide as a grain offering[p] an ephah
for each bull and an ephah for each ram,
along with a hin[b] of oil for each ephah.[q]

25“ ‘During the seven days of the Feast,[r]
which begins in the seventh month on the
fifteenth day, he is to make the same provision for sin offerings, burnt offerings,
grain offerings and oil.[s]

46 “ ‘This is what the Sovereign LORD
says: The gate of the inner court[t] facing east[u] is to be shut on the six working
days, but on the Sabbath day and on the
day of the New Moon[v] it is to be opened.
2The prince is to enter from the outside
through the portico[w] of the gateway and
stand by the gatepost. The priests are to
sacrifice his burnt offering[x] and his fellowship offerings.[c] He is to worship at the
threshold of the gateway and then go out,
but the gate will not be shut until evening.[y] 3On the Sabbaths[z] and New Moons
the people of the land are to worship in
the presence of the LORD at the entrance
to that gateway.[a] 4The burnt offering the
prince brings to the LORD on the Sabbath
day is to be six male lambs and a ram, all
without defect. 5The grain offering given
with the ram is to be an ephah,[d] and the
grain offering with the lambs is to be as
much as he pleases, along with a hin[b] of
oil for each ephah.[b] 6On the day of the
New Moon[c] he is to offer a young bull, six
lambs and a ram, all without defect.[d] 7He
is to provide as a grain offering one ephah
with the bull, one ephah with the ram,
and with the lambs as much as he wants

45:15 [a]S Lev 1:4 [b]Lev 6:30 **45:17** [c]S Nu 10:10 [d]S Lev 23:38; Isa 66:23 [e]S 1Ki 8:62; S 2Ch 31:3; Eze 46:4-12 **45:18** [f]Ex 12:2 [g]S Lev 22:20; Heb 9:14 [h]S Lev 16:16,33 **45:19** [i]S Eze 43:17 [j]Lev 16:18-19 **45:20** [k]Lev 4:27 **45:21** [l]S Ex 12:11 **45:22** [m]Lev 4:14 **45:23** [n]S Nu 22:40; S Job 42:8 [o]Nu 28:16-25 **45:24** [p]Nu 28:12-13 [q]Eze 46:5-7 **45:25** [r]Dt 16:13 [s]Lev 23:34-43; Nu 29:12-38 **46:1** [t]S Eze 40:19 [u]S 1Ch 9:18 [v]ver 6; Isa 66:23 **46:2** [w]ver 8 [x]Eze 40:39 [y]ver 12; S Eze 44:3 **46:3** [z]S Isa 66:23 [a]Lk 1:10 **46:5** [b]ver 11 **46:6** [c]ver 1; S Nu 10:10 [d]S Lev 22:20

[a] *15* Traditionally *peace offerings*; also in verse 17
[b] *24,5* That is, probably about 4 quarts (about 4 liters)
[c] *2* Traditionally *peace offerings*; also in verse 12
[d] *5* That is, probably about 3/5 bushel (about 22 liters)

45:13 *special gift.* Given to the prince as distinct from the gifts given to the priests (44:30). The prince is to use these gifts in part for the offerings to the Lord (see v. 16).
45:15 *make atonement.* See notes on Ex 25:17; Lev 16:20–22; 17:11; Ro 3:25.
45:16 *people of the land.* See v. 22; 7:27 and note.
45:17 *drink offerings.* Usually wine is meant (see Nu 15:5; Hos 9:4); but wine is not mentioned here, though olive oil is (vv. 14,24).
45:18—46:24 This entire section involves so many variations from Pentateuchal law that the rabbis spent a great deal of effort trying to reconcile them. For example, the provision in 45:18 for an annual purification of the temple does not seem to take into consideration the Day of Atonement ritual of Lev 16.
45:19 *priest.* High priest.
45:20 *sins unintentionally or through ignorance.* See Nu 15:22–30 and notes.
45:22 *sin offering.* See note on 40:39.
45:25 *the Feast, which begins in the seventh month.* In some respects the most important of the festivals—called the Feast of Ingathering (Ex 23:16; 34:22) and the Feast of Tabernacles (Dt 16:16; see note on Zec 14:16).
46:1 *gate of the inner court.* While the east gate of the outer court was permanently closed (44:2), the east gate of the inner court could be opened on festival days.
46:2 *through the portico of the gateway.* The portico of the gate of the inner court faced the outer court. *stand by the gatepost.* Which had been ritually cleansed (45:19). From there the prince could observe the sacrifices being performed on the great altar in the inner court, but he was not allowed into the inner court itself.
46:3 *people of the land.* See note on 7:27. *at the entrance to that gateway.* But in the outer court.
46:4 *six male lambs and a ram.* Another example of a difference from Pentateuchal laws (see note on 45:18—46:24). Nu 28:9 calls for two lambs and no ram on the Sabbath.
46:5 *ephah.* Contrast Nu 28:9.
46:6 *day of the New Moon.* The first day of the month. Contrast the requirement of Nu 28:11.
46:7 *as a grain offering one ephah.* Contrast Nu 28:12.

to give, along with a hin of oil with each
ephah.[e] 8When the prince enters, he is to
go in through the portico[f] of the gateway,
and he is to come out the same way.[g]
9" 'When the people of the land come
before the LORD at the appointed feasts,[h]
whoever enters by the north gate to worship is to go out the south gate; and whoever enters by the south gate is to go out
the north gate. No one is to return through
the gate by which he entered, but each is
to go out the opposite gate. 10The prince is
to be among them, going in when they go
in and going out when they go out.[i]
11" 'At the festivals and the appointed
feasts, the grain offering is to be an ephah
with a bull, an ephah with a ram, and with
the lambs as much as one pleases, along
with a hin of oil for each ephah.[j] 12When
the prince provides[k] a freewill offering[l] to
the LORD—whether a burnt offering or fellowship offerings—the gate facing east is
to be opened for him. He shall offer his
burnt offering or his fellowship offerings
as he does on the Sabbath day. Then he
shall go out, and after he has gone out, the
gate will be shut.[m]
13" 'Every day you are to provide a year-
old lamb without defect for a burnt offering to the LORD; morning by morning[n] you
shall provide it.[o] 14You are also to provide
with it morning by morning a grain offering, consisting of a sixth of an ephah with
a third of a hin of oil[p] to moisten the flour.
The presenting of this grain offering to the
LORD is a lasting ordinance.[q] 15So the lamb
and the grain offering and the oil shall be
provided morning by morning for a regular[r] burnt offering.[s]
16" 'This is what the Sovereign LORD
says: If the prince makes a gift from his
inheritance to one of his sons, it will also
belong to his descendants; it is to be their
property by inheritance.[t] 17If, however, he
makes a gift from his inheritance to one of
his servants, the servant may keep it until
the year of freedom;[u] then it will revert to
the prince. His inheritance belongs to his
sons only; it is theirs. 18The prince must
not take[v] any of the inheritance[w] of the
people, driving them off their property. He
is to give his sons their inheritance out of
his own property, so that none of my people will be separated from his property.' "
19Then the man brought me through the
entrance[x] at the side of the gate to the sacred rooms facing north,[y] which belonged
to the priests, and showed me a place at
the western end. 20He said to me, "This is
the place where the priests will cook the
guilt offering and the sin offering and bake
the grain offering, to avoid bringing them
into the outer court and consecrating[z] the
people."[a]
21He then brought me to the outer court
and led me around to its four corners, and
I saw in each corner another court. 22In
the four corners of the outer court were
enclosed[a] courts, forty cubits long and
thirty cubits wide; each of the courts in the
four corners was the same size. 23Around
the inside of each of the four courts was a
ledge of stone, with places for fire built all
around under the ledge. 24He said to me,
"These are the kitchens where those who
minister at the temple will cook the sacrifices of the people."

The River From the Temple

47 The man brought me back to the
entrance of the temple, and I saw
water[b] coming out from under the threshold of the temple toward the east (for the
temple faced east). The water was coming down from under the south side of
the temple, south of the altar.[c] 2He then
brought me out through the north gate[d]
and led me around the outside to the outer
gate facing east, and the water was flowing from the south side.
3As the man went eastward with a measuring line[e] in his hand, he measured
off a thousand cubits[b] and then led me
through water that was ankle-deep. 4He
measured off another thousand cubits

a 22 The meaning of the Hebrew for this word is uncertain. *b* 3 That is, about 1,500 feet (about 450 meters)

46:7 [e]Eze 45:24 **46:8** [f]ver 2 [g]Eze 44:3 **46:9** [h]S Ex 23:14; S 34:20 **46:10** [i]2Sa 6:14-15; Ps 42:4 **46:11** [j]ver 5 **46:12** [k]S Eze 45:17 [l]S Lev 7:16 [m]ver 2 **46:13** [n]S Ps 5:3 [o]Ex 29:38; S Nu 28:3 **46:14** [p]Nu 15:6 [q]Da 8:11 **46:15** [r]S Ex 29:42 [s]S Ex 29:38; Nu 28:5-6 **46:16** [t]2Ch 21:3 **46:17** [u]S Lev 25:10 **46:18** [v]1Sa 8:14 [w]S Lev 25:23; Eze 45:8; Mic 2:1-2 **46:19** [x]S Eze 42:9 [y]Eze 42:4 **46:20** [z]S Lev 6:27 [a]ver 24; Zec 14:20 **47:1** [b]S Isa 55:1 [c]Ps 46:4; Joel 3:18; Rev 22:1 **47:2** [d]S Eze 40:35 **47:3** [e]S Eze 40:3

46:9 *whoever enters by the north gate.* These appear to be crowd control measures. If so, the new era would see masses of people thronging the sanctuary on the festival day.
46:12 *freewill offering.* Above and beyond what was required of the prince.
46:13 *morning by morning.* Contrast Nu 28:3–8, where the daily sacrifice consists of one lamb in the morning and one in the evening (see 1Ch 16:40; 2Ch 13:11; 31:3). A different custom appears in 2Ki 16:15, where a burnt offering was offered in the mornings, a grain offering in the evenings.
46:14 *sixth of an ephah … third of a hin.* Contrast Nu 28:5.
46:16 *his descendants.* Ezekiel pictured a hereditary rulership.
46:17 *until the year of freedom.* The Year of Jubilee—held, theoretically, every 50th year (see Lev 25:8–15, especially v. 13).
46:18 *The prince must not take.* See note on 45:7.
46:19–24 Fits well after 42:13–14, where other rooms for priests are described. The provisions here are a fitting conclusion to the sacrifice laws. The priests' area (vv. 19–20) was to be kept separate from the cooking areas of the Levites (vv. 21–24).
47:1–12 The river of life flowing from the temple.
47:1 *man.* The angelic guide (40:3), who here appears for the last time, concluded Ezekiel's visionary tour of the new temple. *entrance of the temple.* Ezekiel was standing in the inner court. *water.* The rest of this section (vv. 1–12) makes it clear that healing, life-nurturing water is meant (see Ps 36:8; 46:4 and notes; see also Joel 3:18; Zec 13:1; 14:8; Rev 22:1–2). In the larger background was the river flowing from the Garden of Eden (Ge 2:10).
47:2 *brought me out through the north gate.* Because the east gate was closed (44:2).

and led me through water that was knee-
deep. He measured off another thousand
and led me through water that was up to
the waist. 5He measured off another thousand, but now it was a river[f] that I could
not cross, because the water had risen and
was deep enough to swim in—a river that
no one could cross.[g] 6He asked me, "Son
of man, do you see this?"

Then he led me back to the bank of the
river. 7When I arrived there, I saw a great
number of trees on each side of the river.[h]
8He said to me, "This water flows toward
the eastern region and goes down into the
Arabah,[a][i] where it enters the Sea.[b] When
it empties into the Sea,[b] the water there becomes fresh.[j] 9Swarms of living creatures
will live wherever the river flows. There
will be large numbers of fish, because this
water flows there and makes the salt water
fresh; so where the river flows everything
will live.[k] 10Fishermen[l] will stand along the
shore; from En Gedi[m] to En Eglaim there
will be places for spreading nets.[n] The
fish will be of many kinds[o]—like the fish
of the Great Sea.[c][p] 11But the swamps and
marshes will not become fresh; they will
be left for salt.[q] 12Fruit trees of all kinds
will grow on both banks of the river.[r]
Their leaves will not wither, nor will their
fruit[s] fail. Every month they will bear, because the water from the sanctuary[t] flows
to them. Their fruit will serve for food and
their leaves for healing.[u]"

47:5 [f]S Ge 2:10 [g]Isa 11:9; Hab 2:14
47:7 [h]ver 12; Rev 22:2
47:8 [i]S Dt 1:1; S 3:17 [j]Isa 41:18
47:9 [k]Isa 12:3; 55:1; Jn 4:14; 7:37-38
47:10 [l]S Isa 19:8; Mt 4:19 [m]S Jos 15:62 [n]Eze 26:5 [o]S Ps 104:25; Mt 13:47 [p]S Nu 34:6
47:11 [q]S Dt 29:23
47:12 [r]ver 7; Rev 22:2 [s]S Ps 1:3 [t]S Isa 55:1 [u]S Ge 2:9; S Jer 17:8; Eze 36:8
47:13 [v]Nu 34:2-12 [w]S Ge 48:16; S 49:26
47:14 [x]S Ge 12:7; S Dt 1:8; S Eze 36:12
47:15 [y]Nu 34:2 [z]ver 19; S Nu 34:6 [a]Eze 48:1
47:16 [b]2Sa 8:8 [c]Nu 13:21; S Jer 49:23; Eze 48:1
47:17 [d]Eze 48:1

The Boundaries of the Land

13This is what the Sovereign LORD says:
"These are the boundaries[v] by which you
are to divide the land for an inheritance
among the twelve tribes of Israel, with two
portions for Joseph.[w] 14You are to divide
it equally among them. Because I swore
with uplifted hand to give it to your forefathers, this land will become your inheritance.[x]

15"This is to be the boundary of the
land:[y]

"On the north side it will run from the
Great Sea[z] by the Hethlon road[a] past
Lebo[d] Hamath to Zedad, 16Berothah[e][b]
and Sibraim (which lies on the border
between Damascus and Hamath),[c] as
far as Hazer Hatticon, which is on
the border of Hauran. 17The boundary will extend from the sea to Hazar
Enan,[f] along the northern border of
Damascus, with the border of Hamath to the north. This will be the
north boundary.[d]

18"On the east side the boundary will
run between Hauran and Damascus,
along the Jordan between Gilead and
the land of Israel, to the eastern sea

[a] *8* Or *the Jordan Valley* [b] *8* That is, the Dead Sea [c] *10* That is, the Mediterranean; also in verses 15, 19 and 20 [d] *15* Or *past the entrance to* [e] *15,16* See Septuagint and Ezekiel 48:1; Hebrew *road to go into Zedad, 16Hamath, Berothah* [f] *17* Hebrew *Enon,* a variant of *Enan*

47:5 *measured off another thousand.* For a total of four measurings (see note on 1:5). *river that no one could cross.* Amazing, in that a stream fed by no tributaries does not increase as it flows.

47:7 *great number of trees.* Reminiscent of Eden (Ge 2:9).

47:8 *toward the eastern region.* Contrast Zec 14:8. *Arabah.* Here the waterless region between Jerusalem and the Dead Sea (see NIV text note). *the Sea.* Usually means the Mediterranean Sea, but here obviously the Dead Sea is intended (see NIV text note). *becomes fresh.* The Hebrew says, figuratively, "becomes healed." That this lowest (1,300 feet below sea level) and saltiest (25 percent) body of water in the world should sustain such an abundance of life indicates the wonderful renewing power of this "river of the water of life" (Rev 22:1).

47:9 *Swarms of living creatures.* Overtones of Ge 1:20–21 point to a new creation.

47:10 *En Gedi.* Means "spring of the goat"; a strong spring midway along the western side of the Dead Sea (see note on SS 1:14). *En Eglaim.* Means "spring of the two calves." It is possibly Ain Feshkha, at the northwestern corner of the Dead Sea, though some suggest a location on the east bank. *for spreading nets.* See 26:5 and note. *the Great Sea.* See NIV text note.

47:11 *they will be left for salt.* Perhaps to provide the salt needed in the sacrifices (43:24).

47:12 *Every month they will bear.* A marvelous extension of the promises in 34:27; 36:30 (see Am 9:13; cf. Rev 22:2).

47:13–23 The boundaries of the land in the new order (see map, p. 1308).

47:13 *two portions for Joseph.* Since the tribe of Levi received none (44:28), Ephraim and Manasseh, Joseph's two sons adopted by Jacob (Ge 48:5,17–20), each received an allotment (see 48:4–5).

47:14 *Because I swore.* A reference to the covenant made with Abram (see Ge 15:9–21 and notes; Eze 20:5; 36:28). *with uplifted hand.* See 20:5 and note.

47:15 *This is to be the boundary.* Approximates Israel's borders at the time of David and Solomon, except that Transjordan is not included (see v. 18)—which, in any event, was never within the boundaries of the promised land proper. The following specified boundaries closely resemble those in Nu 34:1–12. *Hethlon road.* Probably situated on the Mediterranean coast, somewhere in present-day Lebanon. *Lebo Hamath.* Lebo should be identified with modern Lebweh, about 15 miles northeast of Baalbek and 20 miles southwest of Kadesh on the Orontes River, near Riblah. At one time Lebo must have served as a fortress guarding the southern route to Hamath. Perhaps the phrase should be translated "Lebo of Hamath." It is often referred to in Scripture as the northern limit of Israel (see v. 20; 48:1; Nu 13:21; 34:8; Jos 13:5; 1Ki 8:65; 2Ki 14:25; Am 6:14). *Zedad.* Mentioned in Nu 34:8 but otherwise unknown.

47:16 *Berothah.* Probably to be identified with the Berothai of 2Sa 8:8, but otherwise unknown. *Sibraim.* Location unknown; probably the Sepharvaim of 2Ki 17:24; 18:34. *Damascus.* Capital of Aram (Syria); according to v. 17 it was included in Israel. *Hamath.* A city about 120 miles north of Damascus on the Orontes River. *Hazer Hatticon.* Means "the middle enclosure." Its location is unknown, but it is possibly the same as Hazar Enan in v. 17.

47:18 *eastern sea.* The Dead Sea (see Joel 2:20; Zec 14:8). *Tamar.* Means "(place of) palms" (see v. 19; 48:28); mentioned in Ge 14:7 (Hazazon Tamar) and 1Ki 9:18 (see NIV

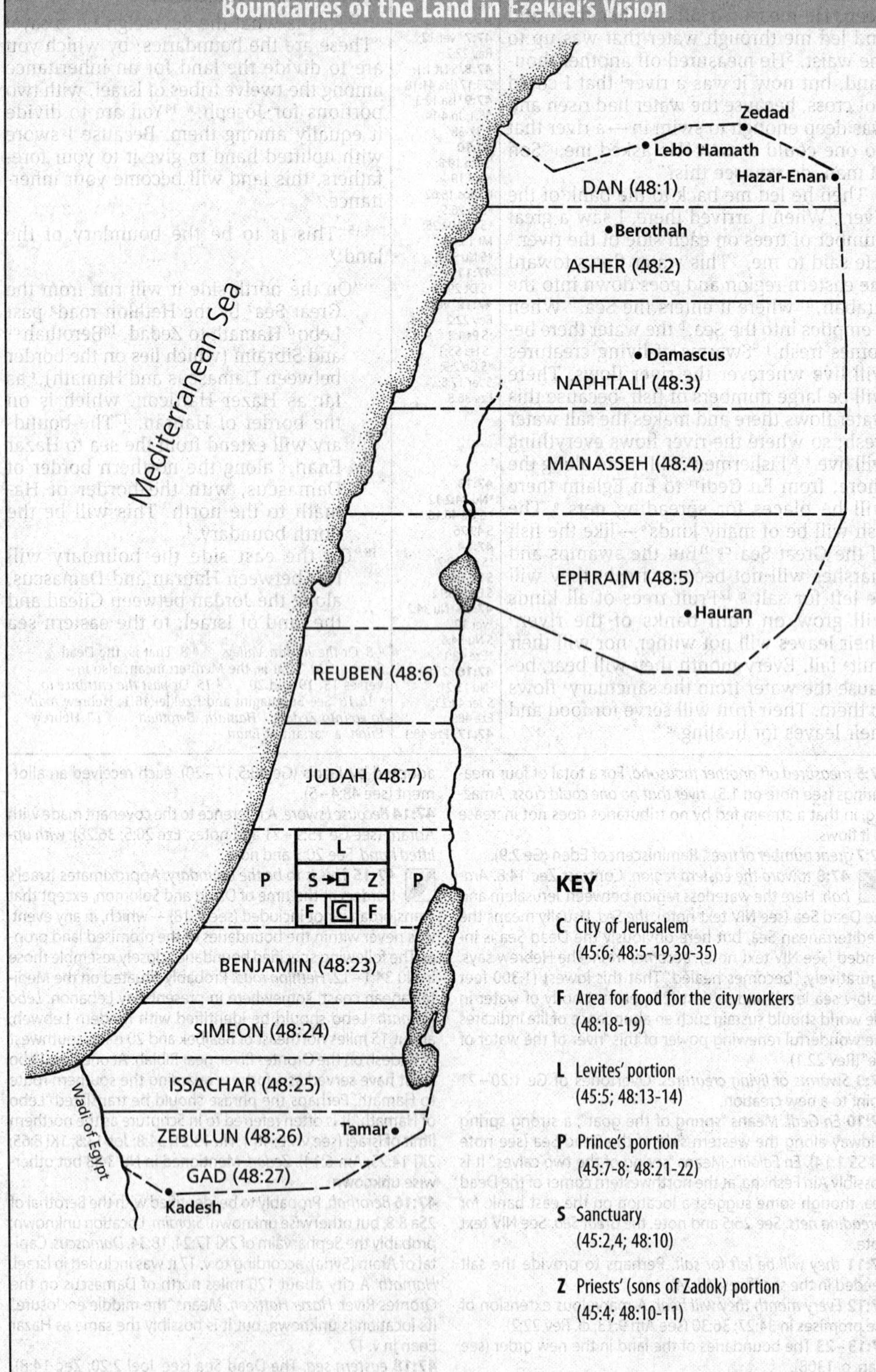

Boundaries of the Land in Ezekiel's Vision
Mediterranean Sea
Zedad
Lebo Hamath
Hazar-Enan
DAN (48:1)
Berothah
ASHER (48:2)
Damascus
NAPHTALI (48:3)
MANASSEH (48:4)
EPHRAIM (48:5)
Hauran
REUBEN (48:6)
JUDAH (48:7)
L
P
S
Z
P
F
C
F
BENJAMIN (48:23)
SIMEON (48:24)
ISSACHAR (48:25)
ZEBULUN (48:26)
Tamar
GAD (48:27)
Kadesh
Wadi of Egypt
KEY
C City of Jerusalem (45:6; 48:5-19,30-35)
F Area for food for the city workers (48:18-19)
L Levites' portion (45:5; 48:13-14)
P Prince's portion (45:7-8; 48:21-22)
S Sanctuary (45:2,4; 48:10)
Z Priests' (sons of Zadok) portion (45:4; 48:10-11)

and as far as Tamar.[a] This will be the
east boundary.[e]
19"On the south side it will run from Tamar as far as the waters of Meribah
Kadesh,[f] then along the Wadi ⌞of
Egypt⌟[g] to the Great Sea.[h] This will be
the south boundary.
20"On the west side, the Great Sea will
be the boundary to a point opposite
Lebo[b] Hamath.[i] This will be the west
boundary.[j]

21"You are to distribute this land among
yourselves according to the tribes of Israel.
22You are to allot it as an inheritance[k] for
yourselves and for the aliens[l] who have
settled among you and who have children.
You are to consider them as native-born
Israelites; along with you they are to be
allotted an inheritance among the tribes
of Israel.[m] 23In whatever tribe the alien settles, there you are to give him his inheritance," declares the Sovereign LORD.[n]

The Division of the Land

48 "These are the tribes, listed by name:
At the northern frontier, Dan[o] will
have one portion; it will follow the Hethlon road[p] to Lebo[c] Hamath;[q] Hazar Enan
and the northern border of Damascus next
to Hamath will be part of its border from
the east side to the west side.
2"Asher[r] will have one portion; it will
border the territory of Dan from east to
west.
3"Naphtali[s] will have one portion; it will
border the territory of Asher from east to
west.
4"Manasseh[t] will have one portion; it
will border the territory of Naphtali from
east to west.
5"Ephraim[u] will have one portion; it will
border the territory of Manasseh[v] from
east to west.[w]
6"Reuben[x] will have one portion; it will
border the territory of Ephraim from east
to west.
7"Judah[y] will have one portion; it will
border the territory of Reuben from east
to west.
8"Bordering the territory of Judah from
east to west will be the portion you are to
present as a special gift. It will be 25,000
cubits[d] wide, and its length from east to
west will equal one of the tribal portions;
the sanctuary will be in the center of it.[z]
9"The special portion you are to offer to
the LORD will be 25,000 cubits long and
10,000 cubits[e] wide.[a] 10This will be the
sacred portion for the priests. It will be
25,000 cubits long on the north side, 10,000
cubits wide on the west side, 10,000 cubits
wide on the east side and 25,000 cubits
long on the south side. In the center of it
will be the sanctuary of the LORD.[b] 11This
will be for the consecrated priests, the Zadokites,[c] who were faithful in serving me[d]
and did not go astray as the Levites did
when the Israelites went astray.[e] 12It will
be a special gift to them from the sacred
portion of the land, a most holy portion,
bordering the territory of the Levites.
13"Alongside the territory of the priests,
the Levites will have an allotment 25,000
cubits long and 10,000 cubits wide. Its
total length will be 25,000 cubits and its
width 10,000 cubits.[f] 14They must not sell
or exchange any of it. This is the best of
the land and must not pass into other
hands, because it is holy to the LORD.[g]
15"The remaining area, 5,000 cubits
wide and 25,000 cubits long, will be for
the common use of the city, for houses

[a] *18* Septuagint and Syriac; Hebrew *Israel. You will measure to the eastern sea* [b] *20* Or *opposite the entrance to* [c] *1* Or *to the entrance to* [d] *8* That is, about 7 miles (about 12 kilometers) [e] *9* That is, about 3 miles (about 5 kilometers)

47:18 [e]S Eze 27:18 **47:19** [f]Dt 32:51 [g]S Ge 15:18; Isa 27:12 [h]S ver 15; Eze 48:28 **47:20** [i]S Nu 13:21; Eze 48:1 [j]Nu 34:6 **47:22** [k]S Eze 36:12 [l]S Dt 24:19; S Isa 14:1; Mal 3:5 [m]S Lev 24:22; Nu 15:29; 26:55-56; Isa 56:6-7; Ro 10:12; Eph 2:12-16; 3:6; Col 3:11 **47:23** [n]S Dt 10:19 **48:1** [o]S Ge 30:6 [p]Eze 47:15-17 [q]S Eze 47:20 **48:2** [r]Jos 19:24-31 **48:3** [s]Jos 19:32-39 **48:4** [t]Jos 17:1-11 **48:5** [u]Jos 16:5-9 [v]Jos 17:7-10 [w]Jos 17:17 **48:6** [x]Jos 13:15-21 **48:7** [y]Jos 15:1-63 **48:8** [z]ver 21 **48:9** [a]S Eze 45:1 **48:10** [b]ver 21; S Eze 45:3-4 **48:11** [c]S 2Sa 8:17 [d]S Lev 8:35 [e]Eze 14:11; S 44:15 **48:13** [f]Eze 45:5 **48:14** [g]S Lev 25:34; 27:10,28

text note) and identified with En Gedi (see note on v. 10) in 2Ch 20:2.

47:19 *Meribah Kadesh.* A district about 50 miles south of Beersheba, identified with Kadesh Barnea in Nu 34:4. *Wadi ⌞of Egypt⌟.* The Wadi el-Arish, a deeply cut riverbed with seasonal flow that runs from the Sinai north-northwest until it enters the Mediterranean, 50 miles south of Gaza. It marked the southernmost extremity of Solomon's kingdom (1Ki 8:65). See map, p. 1308.

47:22 *You are to consider them as native-born Israelites.* A gracious inclusiveness that went beyond the provision of 14:7. It reflects the same universalism that is found in such prophecies as Isa 56:3–8 (see notes there).

48:1–29 The distribution of the land in the new order (see map, p. 1308).

48:1 *Dan.* Occupies its historical location as the northernmost tribe (see the phrase "from Dan to Beersheba," giving northern and southern boundaries—e.g., in Jdg 20:1; 1Sa 3:20). Dan was born to Rachel's maidservant Bilhah (Ge 35:25). *Hethlon ... Lebo Hamath.* See note on 47:15. *Hazar Enan.* See note on 47:16.

48:2 *Asher.* Born to Leah's maidservant Zilpah (Ge 35:26). The tribes descended from maidservants were placed farthest from the sanctuary (see Dan, v. 1; Naphtali, v. 3; Gad, v. 27).

48:3 *Naphtali.* Born to Rachel's maidservant Bilhah (see note on v. 2).

48:4 *Manasseh.* See note on 47:13.

48:5 *Ephraim.* See note on 47:13.

48:6 *Reuben.* Leah's firstborn (Ge 29:31).

48:7 *Judah.* Son of Leah (Ge 35:23). He had the most prestigious place, bordering the central holy portion (v. 8), because his tribe was given the Messianic promise (see Ge 49:8–12 and note on 49:8).

48:8–22 An expansion of 45:1–8 (see notes there).

48:9 *10,000 cubits wide.* The width of the entire sacred district was 20,000 cubits (see 45:1). The present verse must refer to the width of either the priests' or the Levites' area. The Septuagint (the pre-Christian Greek translation of the OT), however, reads "20,000" here.

48:11 *Zadokites, who were faithful.* See note on 44:15.

48:14 *not sell or exchange.* Since it was the Lord's, it was not to be an object of commerce.

and for pastureland. The city will be in
the center of it 16and will have these measurements: the north side 4,500 cubits,
the south side 4,500 cubits, the east side
4,500 cubits, and the west side 4,500 cubits.[h] 17The pastureland for the city will
be 250 cubits on the north, 250 cubits on
the south, 250 cubits on the east, and 250
cubits on the west. 18What remains of the
area, bordering on the sacred portion and
running the length of it, will be 10,000 cubits on the east side and 10,000 cubits on
the west side. Its produce will supply food
for the workers of the city.[i] 19The workers
from the city who farm it will come from
all the tribes of Israel. 20The entire portion
will be a square, 25,000 cubits on each
side. As a special gift you will set aside
the sacred portion, along with the property of the city.
21"What remains on both sides of the
area formed by the sacred portion and the
city property will belong to the prince. It
will extend eastward from the 25,000 cubits of the sacred portion to the eastern
border, and westward from the 25,000 cubits to the western border. Both these areas
running the length of the tribal portions
will belong to the prince, and the sacred
portion with the temple sanctuary will be
in the center of them.[j] 22So the property
of the Levites and the property of the city
will lie in the center of the area that belongs to the prince. The area belonging to
the prince will lie between the border of
Judah and the border of Benjamin.
23"As for the rest of the tribes: Benjamin[k] will have one portion; it will extend
from the east side to the west side.
24"Simeon[l] will have one portion; it will
border the territory of Benjamin from east
to west.
25"Issachar[m] will have one portion; it
will border the territory of Simeon from
east to west.
26"Zebulun[n] will have one portion; it
will border the territory of Issachar from
east to west.
27"Gad[o] will have one portion; it will
border the territory of Zebulun from east
to west.
28"The southern boundary of Gad will
run south from Tamar[p] to the waters of
Meribah Kadesh, then along the Wadi ⌞of
Egypt⌟ to the Great Sea.[a][q]
29"This is the land you are to allot as
an inheritance to the tribes of Israel, and
these will be their portions," declares the
Sovereign LORD.[r]

The Gates of the City

30"These will be the exits of the city: Beginning on the north side, which is 4,500
cubits long, 31the gates of the city will be
named after the tribes of Israel. The three
gates on the north side will be the gate of
Reuben, the gate of Judah and the gate
of Levi.
32"On the east side, which is 4,500 cubits long, will be three gates: the gate of
Joseph, the gate of Benjamin and the gate
of Dan.
33"On the south side, which measures
4,500 cubits, will be three gates: the gate
of Simeon, the gate of Issachar and the
gate of Zebulun.
34"On the west side, which is 4,500 cubits long, will be three gates: the gate of
Gad, the gate of Asher and the gate of
Naphtali.[s]
35"The distance all around will be
18,000 cubits.
"And the name of the city from that time
on will be:

THE LORD IS THERE.[t]"

[a] 28 That is, the Mediterranean

48:16 [h] Rev 21:16 **48:18** [i] Eze 45:6 **48:21** [j] ver 8, 10; Eze 45:7 **48:23** [k] Jos 18:11-28 **48:24** [l] S Ge 29:33; Jos 19:1-9 **48:25** [m] Jos 19:17-23 **48:26** [n] Jos 19:10-16 **48:27** [o] Jos 13:24-28 **48:28** [p] S Ge 14:7 [q] S Nu 34:6; Eze 47:19 **48:29** [r] S Eze 45:1 **48:34** [s] S 2Ch 4:4; Rev 21:12-13 **48:35** [t] S Isa 12:6; S 24:23; S Jer 3:17; 14:9; Joel 3:21; Rev 3:12; S 21:3

48:19 *from all the tribes of Israel.* The sacred district was national property, not the prince's private domain.
48:23 *Benjamin.* Rachel's son (Ge 35:24).
48:24 *Simeon.* Leah's son (Ge 35:23).
48:25 *Issachar.* Leah's son (Ge 35:23).
48:26 *Zebulun.* Leah's son (Ge 35:23).
48:27 *Gad.* Son of Zilpah, Leah's maid (see note on v. 2).
48:28 *Tamar.* See note on 47:18. *Meribah Kadesh.* See note on 47:19. *Wadi ⌞of Egypt⌟.* See note on 47:19.
48:30–35 The 12 gates of the new city of Jerusalem.
48:31 *Reuben . . . Judah . . . Levi.* Reuben (representing the first-born), Judah (the Messianic tribe) and Levi (the tribe of the priesthood) had gates together on the north side. Since Levi was included in this list, Joseph (v. 32) represented Ephraim and Manasseh (see note on 47:13) in order to keep the number at 12. For the gates cf. Rev 21:12–14.
48:35 THE LORD IS THERE. The great decisive word concerning the holy city. The Hebrew for this clause is *Yahweh Shammah,* which may be a wordplay on *Yerushalayim,* the Hebrew pronunciation of Jerusalem. For other names of Jerusalem see 23:4; Isa 1:26; 60:14; 62:2–4,12; Jer 3:17; 33:16; Zec 8:3. The book of Joel has a similar ending (see note on Joel 3:21).

Daniel

I N T R O D U C T I O N

Author, Date and Authenticity

In several passages (such as 9:2; 10:2) the book implies that Daniel was its author. With this, Jesus appears to have concurred, as evidenced by his reference to "'the abomination that causes desolation,' spoken of through the prophet Daniel" (Mt 24:15; see note there), quoting 9:27 (see note there); 11:31; 12:11. The book was probably completed c. 530 B.C., shortly after Cyrus the Great, king of Persia, captured the city of Babylon in 539.

The widely held view that the book of Daniel is largely fictional rests mainly on the modern philosophical assumption that long-range predictive prophecy is impossible. Therefore all fulfilled predictions in Daniel, it is claimed, had to have been composed no earlier than the Maccabean period (second century B.C.), after the fulfillments had taken place. But objective evidence excludes this hypothesis on several counts:

A Quick Look

Author:
Daniel

Audience:
The Jewish exiles in Babylonia

Date:
About 605 – 530 B.C.

Theme:
The Most High God is sovereign over all human kingdoms.

1. To avoid fulfillment of long-range predictive prophecy in the book, the adherents of the late-date view usually maintain that the four empires of chs. 2 and 7 are Babylonia, Media, Persia and Greece. But in the mind of the author, "the Medes and Persians" (5:28; see note there) together constituted the second in the series of four kingdoms (2:32 – 43; see note there). Thus it becomes clear that the four empires are the Babylonian, Medo-Persian, Greek and Roman. See chart, p. 1323.

2. The language itself argues for a date earlier than the second century. Linguistic evidence from the Dead Sea Scrolls (which furnish authentic samples of Hebrew and Aramaic writing from the third and second centuries B.C.; see essay, p. 1452) demonstrates that the Hebrew and Aramaic chapters of Daniel must have been composed centuries earlier. Furthermore, as recently demonstrated, the Persian and Greek words in Daniel do not require a late date. Some of the technical terms appearing in ch. 3 were already so obsolete by the second century B.C. that translators of the Septuagint (the pre-Christian Greek translation of the OT) translated them incorrectly.

3. Several of the fulfillments of prophecies in Daniel could not have taken place by the second century anyway, so the prophetic element cannot be dismissed. The symbolism connected

with the fourth kingdom makes it unmistakably predictive of the Roman empire (see 2:33; 7:7,19), which did not take control of Syro-Palestine until 63 B.C. Also, a plausible interpretation of the prophecy concerning the coming of "the Anointed One, the ruler," approximately 483 years after "the issuing of the decree to restore and rebuild Jerusalem" (9:25; see note on 9:25–27), works out to the time of Jesus' ministry.

Objective evidence, therefore, appears to exclude the late-date hypothesis and indicates that there is insufficient reason to deny Daniel's authorship.

Theological Theme

The theological theme of the book is summarized in 4:17; 5:21: "The Most High (God) is sovereign over the kingdoms of men." Daniel's visions always show God as triumphant (7:11,26–27; 8:25; 9:27). The climax of his sovereign rule is described in Revelation: "The kingdom of the world has become the kingdom of our Lord and of his Christ [i.e., Messiah, 'Anointed One'], and he will reign for ever and ever" (Rev 11:15; see Da 2:44; 7:27 and notes).

Daniel's historical narratives and apocalyptic visions always show God as truimphant.

Literary Form

The book is made up primarily of historical narrative (found mainly in chs. 1–6) and apocalyptic ("revelatory") material (found mainly in chs. 7–12). The latter may be defined as symbolic, visionary, prophetic literature, usually composed during oppressive conditions and being chiefly eschatological in theological content. Apocalyptic literature is primarily a literature of encouragement to the people of God (see Introduction to Zechariah: Literary Form and Themes; see also Introduction to Revelation: Literary Form). For the symbolic use of numbers in apocalyptic literature see Introduction to Revelation: Distinctive Feature.

Outline

- I. Prologue: The Setting (ch. 1; in Hebrew)
  - A. Historical Introduction (1:1–2)
  - B. Daniel and His Friends Are Taken Captive (1:3–7)
  - C. The Young Men Are Faithful (1:8–16)
  - D. The Young Men Are Elevated to High Positions (1:17–21)
- II. The Destinies of the Nations of the World (chs. 2–7; in Aramaic, beginning at 2:4b)
  - A. Nebuchadnezzar's Dream of a Large Statue (ch. 2)
  - B. Nebuchadnezzar's Making of a Gold Image and His Decree That It Be Worshiped (ch. 3)
  - C. Nebuchadnezzar's Dream of an Enormous Tree (ch. 4)
  - D. Belshazzar's and Babylon's Downfall (ch. 5)
  - E. Daniel's Deliverance from the Lion's Den (ch. 6)
  - F. Daniel's Dream of Four Beasts (ch. 7)
- III. The Destiny of the Nation of Israel (chs. 8–12; in Hebrew)
  - A. Daniel's Vision of a Ram and a Goat (ch. 8)
  - B. Daniel's Prayer and His Vision of the 70 "Sevens" (ch. 9)
  - C. Daniel's Vision of Israel's Future (chs. 10–12)
    1. Revelation of things to come (10:1–3)
    2. Revelation from the angelic messenger (10:4—11:1)
    3. Prophecies concerning Persia and Greece (11:2–4)
    4. Prophecies concerning Egypt and Syria (11:5–35)
    5. Prophecies concerning the antichrist (11:36–45)
    6. Distress and deliverance (12:1)
    7. Two resurrections (12:2–3)
    8. Instruction to Daniel (12:4)
    9. Conclusion (12:5–13)

Daniel's Training in Babylon

1 In the third year of the reign of Jehoiakim[a] king of Judah, Nebuchadnezzar[b] king of Babylon[c] came to Jerusalem
and besieged it.[d] 2And the Lord delivered
Jehoiakim king of Judah into his hand,
along with some of the articles from the
temple of God. These he carried[e] off to the
temple of his god in Babylonia[a] and put in
the treasure house of his god.[f]
3Then the king ordered Ashpenaz, chief
of his court officials, to bring in some of
the Israelites from the royal family and the
nobility[g]— 4young men without any physical defect, handsome,[h] showing aptitude
for every kind of learning,[i] well informed,
quick to understand, and qualified to serve
in the king's palace. He was to teach them
the language[j] and literature of the Babylonians.[b] 5The king assigned them a daily
amount of food and wine[k] from the king's
table.[l] They were to be trained for three
years,[m] and after that they were to enter
the king's service.[n]
6Among these were some from Judah:
Daniel,[o] Hananiah, Mishael and Azariah.[p]
7The chief official gave them new names:
to Daniel, the name Belteshazzar;[q] to Hananiah, Shadrach; to Mishael, Meshach;
and to Azariah, Abednego.[r]
8But Daniel resolved not to defile[s] himself with the royal food and wine, and
he asked the chief official for permission
not to defile himself this way. 9Now God
had caused the official to show favor[t] and
sympathy[u] to Daniel, 10but the official told
Daniel, "I am afraid of my lord the king,
who has assigned your[c] food and drink.[v]
Why should he see you looking worse
than the other young men your age? The
king would then have my head because
of you."
11Daniel then said to the guard whom
the chief official had appointed over
Daniel, Hananiah, Mishael and Azariah,
12"Please test[w] your servants for ten days:
Give us nothing but vegetables to eat and
water to drink. 13Then compare our appearance with that of the young men who
eat the royal food, and treat your servants
in accordance with what you see."[x] 14So
he agreed to this and tested[y] them for ten
days.
15At the end of the ten days they looked
healthier and better nourished than any of
the young men who ate the royal food.[z]
16So the guard took away their choice food
and the wine they were to drink and gave
them vegetables instead.[a]
17To these four young men God gave
knowledge and understanding[b] of all
kinds of literature and learning.[c] And Daniel could understand visions and dreams
of all kinds.[d]
18At the end of the time[e] set by the king
to bring them in, the chief official presented them to Nebuchadnezzar. 19The king
talked with them, and he found none equal
to Daniel, Hananiah, Mishael and Azariah;
so they entered the king's service.[f] 20In every matter of wisdom and understanding
about which the king questioned them, he

1:1 [a]S Jer 46:2 [b]S 2Ki 24:1; S Jer 28:14 [c]Jer 50:1 [d]2Ki 24:1; S 2Ch 36:6; Jer 35:11 **1:2** [e]S 2Ki 24:13 [f]S 2Ch 36:7; Jer 27:19-20; Zec 5:5-11 **1:3** [g]S 2Ki 20:18; S 24:15; Isa 39:7 **1:4** [h]S Ge 39:6 [i]ver 17 [j]S Ezr 4:7 **1:5** [k]ver 8, 10 [l]S Est 2:9 [m]ver 18 [n]ver 19; S Est 2:5-6 **1:6** [o]S Eze 14:14 [p]Da 2:17, 25 **1:7** [q]Da 2:26; 4:8; 5:12; 10:1 [r]S Isa 39:7; Da 2:49; 3:12 **1:8** [s]S Eze 4:13-14 **1:9** [t]S Ge 39:21; S Pr 16:7 [u]S 1Ki 8:50 **1:10** [v]ver 5 **1:12** [w]Rev 2:10 **1:13** [x]ver 16 **1:14** [y]Rev 2:10 **1:15** [z]Ex 23:25 **1:16** [a]ver 12-13 **1:17** [b]S Job 12:13 [c]Da 2:23; Col 1:9; Jas 1:5 [d]Da 2:19, 30; 5:11; 7:1; 8:1 **1:18** [e]ver 5 **1:19** [f]S Ge 41:46

[a] 2 Hebrew *Shinar* [b] 4 Or *Chaldeans*
[c] *10* The Hebrew for *your* and *you* in this verse is plural.

1:1 *third year.* According to the Babylonian system of computing the years of a king's reign, the third year of Jehoiakim would have been 605 B.C., since his first full year of kingship began on New Year's Day after his accession in 608. But according to the system in Judah, which counted the year of accession as the first year of reign, this was "the fourth year of Jehoiakim" (Jer 25:1; 46:2; see notes there). *Jehoiakim king of Judah.* See 2Ki 23:34; 2Ch 36:5–8 and notes. *Nebuchadnezzar king of Babylon.* 605 B.C. was also the first year of his reign (see Jer 25:1; 2Ki 24:1 and note; see also chart, p. 472).

1:2 *carried off.* Judah was exiled to Babylonia because she disobeyed God's word regarding covenant-keeping, the sabbath years and idolatry (see Lev 25:4 and note; 26:27–35; Dt 28:15–68; 2Ki 25:1 and note; 2Ch 36:20–21 and note). The first deportation (605 B.C.) included Daniel, and the second (597) included Ezekiel. A third deportation took place in 586, when the Babylonians destroyed the city of Jerusalem and Solomon's temple. *his god.* Marduk (see note on Isa 45:4).

1:4 *language and literature of the Babylonians.* Including the classical literature in Sumerian and Akkadian cuneiform, a complicated syllabic writing system. But the language of normal communication in multiracial Babylon was Aramaic, written in an easily learned alphabetic script (see 2:4 and note).

1:6 *Daniel.* Means "God is (my) Judge." *Hananiah.* Means "The LORD shows grace." *Mishael.* Means "Who is what God is?" *Azariah.* Means "The LORD helps."

1:7 *gave them new names.* Indicating that they were now subject to Nebuchadnezzar's authority (see Ge 17:5; 41:45; 2Ki 23:34; 24:17 and notes). *Belteshazzar.* Probably means, in Babylonian, "Bel (i.e., Marduk), protect his life!" *Shadrach.* Probably means "command of Aku (Sumerian moon-god)." *Meshach.* Probably means "Who is what Aku is?" *Abednego.* Means "servant of Nego/Nebo (i.e., Nabu)."

1:8 *royal food and wine.* Israelites considered food from Nebuchadnezzar's table to be contaminated because the first portion of it was offered to idols. Likewise a portion of the wine was poured out on a pagan altar. Ceremonially unclean animals were used and were neither slaughtered nor prepared according to the regulations of the law. *he asked ... not to defile himself.* He demonstrated the courage of his convictions.

1:9 *God had caused the official to show favor ... to Daniel.* The careers of Joseph and Daniel were similar in many respects (see Ge 39–41).

1:12 *test your servants.* Daniel used good judgment by offering an alternative instead of rebelling. *ten.* Often symbolized completeness.

1:17 With God's help, Daniel and his friends mastered the essential Babylonian literature on astrology and divination by dreams. But in the crucial tests of interpretation and prediction (see 2:2–11; 4:6–7), all the pagan literature proved worthless. Only by God's special revelation (2:17–28) was Daniel able to interpret correctly.

1:20 *ten.* See note on v. 12. *magicians.* See note on Ge 41:8.

found them ten times better than all the
magicians[g] and enchanters in his whole
kingdom.[h]
21And Daniel remained there until the
first year of King Cyrus.[i]

Nebuchadnezzar's Dream

2 In the second year of his reign, Nebuchadnezzar had dreams;[j] his mind was
troubled[k] and he could not sleep.[l] 2So the
king summoned the magicians,[m] enchanters, sorcerers[n] and astrologers[a][o] to tell him
what he had dreamed.[p] When they came
in and stood before the king, 3he said to
them, "I have had a dream that troubles[q]
me and I want to know what it means.[b]"
4Then the astrologers answered the king
in Aramaic,[c][r] "O king, live forever![s] Tell
your servants the dream, and we will interpret it."
5The king replied to the astrologers,
"This is what I have firmly decided:[t] If you
do not tell me what my dream was and
interpret it, I will have you cut into pieces[u] and your houses turned into piles of
rubble.[v] 6But if you tell me the dream and
explain it, you will receive from me gifts
and rewards and great honor.[w] So tell me
the dream and interpret it for me."
7Once more they replied, "Let the king
tell his servants the dream, and we will
interpret it."
8Then the king answered, "I am certain that you are trying to gain time, because you realize that this is what I have
firmly decided: 9If you do not tell me the
dream, there is just one penalty[x] for you.
You have conspired to tell me misleading
and wicked things, hoping the situation
will change. So then, tell me the dream,
and I will know that you can interpret it
for me."[y]
10The astrologers[z] answered the king,
"There is not a man on earth who can do
what the king asks! No king, however great
and mighty, has ever asked such a thing of
any magician or enchanter or astrologer.[a]
11What the king asks is too difficult. No one
can reveal it to the king except the gods,[b]
and they do not live among men."
12This made the king so angry and furious[c] that he ordered the execution[d] of all
the wise men of Babylon. 13So the decree
was issued to put the wise men to death,
and men were sent to look for Daniel and
his friends to put them to death.[e]
14When Arioch, the commander of the
king's guard, had gone out to put to death
the wise men of Babylon, Daniel spoke
to him with wisdom and tact. 15He asked
the king's officer, "Why did the king issue such a harsh decree?" Arioch then
explained the matter to Daniel. 16At this,
Daniel went in to the king and asked for
time, so that he might interpret the dream
for him.
17Then Daniel returned to his house and
explained the matter to his friends Hananiah, Mishael and Azariah.[f] 18He urged
them to plead for mercy[g] from the God of
heaven[h] concerning this mystery,[i] so that
he and his friends might not be executed
with the rest of the wise men of Babylon.
19During the night the mystery[j] was revealed to Daniel in a vision.[k] Then Daniel
praised the God of heaven[l] 20and said:

"Praise be to the name of God for ever
and ever;[m]
wisdom and power[n] are his.
21He changes times and seasons;[o]
he sets up kings[p] and deposes[q]
them.
He gives wisdom[r] to the wise
and knowledge to the discerning.[s]
22He reveals deep and hidden things;[t]
he knows what lies in darkness,[u]
and light[v] dwells with him.

[a] 2 Or *Chaldeans*; also in verses 4, 5 and 10
[b] 3 Or *was*
[c] 4 The text from here through chapter 7 is in Aramaic.

1:20 [g] S Ge 41:8 [h] S 1Ki 4:30; Est 2:15; S Eze 28:3; Da 2:13,28; 4:18; 6:3 **1:21** [i] S 2Ch 36:22; Da 6:28; 10:1 **2:1** [j] ver 3; S Ge 20:3; S Job 33:15,18; Da 4:5 [k] Ge 41:8 [l] S Est 6:1 **2:2** [m] S Ge 41:8 [n] Ex 7:11; Jer 27:9 [o] S ver 10; S Isa 19:3; S 44:25 [p] Da 4:6 **2:3** [q] Da 4:5 **2:4** [r] S Ezr 4:7 [s] S Ne 2:3 **2:5** [t] Ge 41:32 [u] ver 12 [v] Ezr 6:11; Da 3:29 **2:6** [w] ver 48; Da 5:7,16 **2:9** [x] Est 4:11 [y] Isa 41:22-24 **2:10** [z] ver 2; Da 3:8; 4:7 [a] ver 27; Da 5:8 **2:11** [b] S Ge 41:38 **2:12** [c] Da 3:13,19 [d] ver 5 **2:13** [e] S Da 1:20; 5:19 **2:17** [f] S Da 1:6 **2:18** [g] S Isa 37:4 [h] Ezr 1:2; Ne 1:4; Jnh 1:9; Rev 11:13 [i] ver 23; Jer 33:3 **2:19** [j] ver 28 [k] S Job 33:15; S Da 1:17 [l] S Jos 22:33 **2:20** [m] S Ps 113:2; 145:1-2 [n] S Job 9:4; S Jer 32:19 **2:21** [o] Da 7:25 [p] Da 4:17 [q] S Job 12:19; Ps 75:6-7; Ro 13:1 [r] S Ps 119:34; Jas 1:5 [s] S 2Sa 14:17 **2:22** [t] S Ge 40:8; S Job 12:22; Da 5:11; 1Co 2:10 [u] Job 12:22; Ps 139:11-12; Jer 23:24; S Heb 4:13 [v] Isa 45:7; Jas 1:17

1:21 *there.* In Babylonia. *first year of King Cyrus.* Over Babylon (539 B.C.; see chart, p. 472). Daniel spent about 70 years in Babylonia and was still living in the year 537 (10:1), so he saw the return of some of the exiles to Judah from Babylonian captivity.

2:1 *second year of ... Nebuchadnezzar.* 604 B.C. (see 1:1 and note). *he could not sleep.* See 6:18; Est 6:1 and note.

2:2 *magicians, enchanters, sorcerers.* See Dt 18:9 – 14 and note on 18:9.

2:4 *Aramaic.* Since the astrologers were of various racial backgrounds, they communicated in Aramaic, the language everyone understood. From here to the end of ch. 7 the entire narrative is in Aramaic. These six chapters deal with matters of importance to the Gentile nations of the Near East and were written in a language understandable to all. But the last five chapters (8 – 12) revert to Hebrew, since they deal with special concerns of the chosen people. *your servants.* Us.

2:5 See 3:29.

2:10 *not a man on earth who can do what the king asks.* But "God in heaven" can (through Daniel; see vv. 27 – 28).

2:11 *do not live among men.* Are not readily accessible.

2:14 *Arioch.* Also the name of a Mesopotamian king who lived centuries earlier (Ge 14:1,9).

2:18 *God of heaven.* In this chapter this Persian title for a high god (see note on Ezr 1:2) is used to refer to Yahweh, the God of Israel. *mystery.* A key word in Daniel (vv. 19,27 – 30,47; 4:9). It also appears often in the writings (Dead Sea Scrolls) of the Qumran community (see essay, pp. 1452 – 1453). The Greek equivalent is used in the NT to refer to the secret purposes of God that he reveals only to his chosen prophets and apostles (see notes on Ro 11:25; Rev 10:7).

2:21 *He gives wisdom ... to the discerning.* See Pr 1:2 – 5 and note on 1:2.

2:22 *light dwells with him.* See Ps 36:9 and note.

23 I thank and praise you, O God of my
fathers:[w]
You have given me wisdom[x] and
power,
you have made known to me what we
asked of you,
you have made known to us the
dream of the king.[y]"

Daniel Interprets the Dream

24 Then Daniel went to Arioch,[z] whom
the king had appointed to execute the wise
men of Babylon, and said to him, "Do not
execute the wise men of Babylon. Take me
to the king, and I will interpret his dream
for him."
25 Arioch took Daniel to the king at once
and said, "I have found a man among the
exiles[a] from Judah[b] who can tell the king
what his dream means."
26 The king asked Daniel (also called Belteshazzar),[c] "Are you able to tell me what
I saw in my dream and interpret it?"
27 Daniel replied, "No wise man, enchanter, magician or diviner can explain to
the king the mystery he has asked about,[d]
28 but there is a God in heaven who reveals
mysteries.[e] He has shown King Nebuchadnezzar what will happen in days to come.[f]
Your dream and the visions that passed
through your mind[g] as you lay on your
bed[h] are these:[i]
29 "As you were lying there, O king, your
mind turned to things to come, and the
revealer of mysteries showed you what is
going to happen.[j] 30 As for me, this mystery has been revealed[k] to me, not because
I have greater wisdom than other living
men, but so that you, O king, may know
the interpretation and that you may understand what went through your mind.
31 "You looked, O king, and there before
you stood a large statue—an enormous,
dazzling statue,[l] awesome[m] in appearance.
32 The head of the statue was made of pure
gold, its chest and arms of silver, its belly
and thighs of bronze, 33 its legs of iron, its
feet partly of iron and partly of baked clay.
34 While you were watching, a rock was cut
out, but not by human hands.[n] It struck
the statue on its feet of iron and clay and
smashed[o] them.[p] 35 Then the iron, the clay,
the bronze, the silver and the gold were
broken to pieces at the same time and
became like chaff on a threshing floor in
the summer. The wind swept them away[q]
without leaving a trace. But the rock that
struck the statue became a huge mountain[r] and filled the whole earth.[s]
36 "This was the dream, and now we will
interpret it to the king.[t] 37 You, O king, are
the king of kings.[u] The God of heaven has
given you dominion[v] and power and might
and glory; 38 in your hands he has placed
mankind and the beasts of the field and
the birds of the air. Wherever they live, he
has made you ruler over them all.[w] You
are that head of gold.
39 "After you, another kingdom will rise,
inferior to yours. Next, a third kingdom,
one of bronze, will rule over the whole
earth.[x] 40 Finally, there will be a fourth
kingdom, strong as iron—for iron breaks
and smashes everything—and as iron
breaks things to pieces, so it will crush
and break all the others.[y] 41 Just as you saw
that the feet and toes were partly of baked
clay and partly of iron, so this will be a
divided kingdom; yet it will have some of
the strength of iron in it, even as you saw
iron mixed with clay. 42 As the toes were
partly iron and partly clay, so this kingdom will be partly strong and partly brittle. 43 And just as you saw the iron mixed
with baked clay, so the people will be a
mixture and will not remain united, any
more than iron mixes with clay.
44 "In the time of those kings, the God
of heaven will set up a kingdom that will
never be destroyed, nor will it be left to
another people. It will crush[z] all those
kingdoms[a] and bring them to an end,
but it will itself endure forever.[b] 45 This
is the meaning of the vision of the rock[c]
cut out of a mountain, but not by human
hands[d]—a rock that broke the iron, the
bronze, the clay, the silver and the gold
to pieces.

2:23 [w] S Ge 31:5; S Ex 3:15 [x] S Da 1:17 [y] S Eze 28:3
2:24 [z] ver 14
2:25 [a] S Dt 21:10 [b] S Da 1:6; 5:13; 6:13
2:26 [c] S Da 1:7
2:27 [d] S ver 10; S Ge 41:8
2:28 [e] S Ge 40:8; Jer 10:7; Am 4:13 [f] S Ge 49:1; Da 10:14; Mt 24:6; Rev 1:1; 22:6 [g] Da 4:5 [h] S Ps 4:4 [i] S Eze 28:3; S Da 1:20
2:29 [j] S Ge 41:25
2:30 [k] Isa 45:3; S Da 1:17; Am 4:13
2:31 [l] Hab 1:7 [m] Isa 25:3-5
2:34 [n] S Job 12:19; Zec 4:6 [o] S Job 34:24 [p] ver 44-45; Ps 2:9; S Isa 60:12; Da 8:25
2:35 [q] Ps 1:4; 37:10; S Isa 17:13; 41:15-16 [r] Isa 2:3; Mic 4:1 [s] Zec 12:3
2:36 [t] S Ge 40:12
2:37 [u] S Ezr 7:12 [v] S Jer 27:7; Da 4:26
2:38 [w] S Jer 27:6; Da 4:21-22; 5:18
2:39 [x] Da 7:5
2:40 [y] Da 7:7,23
2:44 [z] S Ge 27:29; Ps 2:9; S 110:5; Mt 21:43-44; 1Co 15:24 [a] S 1Sa 9:20; Hag 2:22 [b] Ps 145:13; S Isa 9:7; Da 4:34; 6:26; 7:14,27; Ob 1:21; Mic 4:7,13; S Lk 1:33; Rev 11:15
2:45 [c] S Isa 28:16 [d] Da 8:25

2:29 *the revealer of mysteries.* God (see v. 47).
2:32–43 See map No. 8b and map No. 14 at the end of this study Bible; see also chart, p. 1323. The gold head represents the Neo-Babylonian empire (v. 38; see Jer 51:7 and note; see also map, p. 1318); the silver chest and arms, the Medo-Persian empire established by Cyrus in 539 B.C. (the date of the fall of Babylon); the bronze belly and thighs, the Greek empire established by Alexander the Great c. 330; the iron legs and feet, the Roman empire. The toes (v. 41) are understood by some to represent a later confederation of states occupying the territory formerly controlled by the Roman empire. The diminishing value of the metals from gold to silver to bronze to iron represents the decreasing power and grandeur (v. 39) of the rulers of the successive empires, from the absolute despotism of Nebuchadnezzar to the democratic system of checks and balances that characterized the Roman senates and assemblies. The metals also symbolize a growing degree of toughness and endurance, with each successive empire lasting longer than the preceding one.
2:33 *partly of iron and partly of baked clay.* "Partly strong and partly brittle" (v. 42).
2:35 *broken to pieces.* See Lk 20:18 and note.
2:37 *king of kings.* That is, the greatest king (cf. v. 47; Ezr 7:12 and note; 1Ti 6:15; Rev 17:14 and note; 19:16).
2:44 The fifth kingdom is the eternal kingdom of God (see Rev 11:15), built on the ruins of the sinful empires of the world. Its authority will extend over "the whole earth" (v. 35) and ultimately over "a new heaven and a new earth" (Rev 21:1).

"The great God has shown the king what will take place in the future.[e] The dream is true[f] and the interpretation is trustworthy."

46Then King Nebuchadnezzar fell prostrate[g] before Daniel and paid him honor and ordered that an offering[h] and incense be presented to him. 47The king said to Daniel, "Surely your God is the God of gods[i] and the Lord of kings[j] and a revealer of mysteries,[k] for you were able to reveal this mystery.[l]"

48Then the king placed Daniel in a high[m] position and lavished many gifts on him. He made him ruler over the entire province of Babylon and placed him in charge of all its wise men.[n] 49Moreover, at Daniel's request the king appointed Shadrach, Meshach and Abednego administrators over the province of Babylon,[o] while Daniel himself remained at the royal court.[p]

The Image of Gold and the Fiery Furnace

3 King Nebuchadnezzar made an image[q] of gold, ninety feet high and nine feet[a] wide, and set it up on the plain of Dura in the province of Babylon. 2He then summoned the satraps,[r] prefects, governors, advisers, treasurers, judges, magistrates and all the other provincial officials[s] to come to the dedication of the image he had set up. 3So the satraps, prefects, governors, advisers, treasurers, judges, magistrates and all the other provincial officials assembled for the dedication of the image that King Nebuchadnezzar had set up, and they stood before it.

4Then the herald loudly proclaimed, "This is what you are commanded to do, O peoples, nations and men of every language:[t] 5As soon as you hear the sound of the horn, flute, zither, lyre, harp,[u] pipes and all kinds of music, you must fall down and worship the image[v] of gold that King Nebuchadnezzar has set up.[w] 6Whoever does not fall down and worship will immediately be thrown into a blazing furnace."[x]

7Therefore, as soon as they heard the sound of the horn, flute, zither, lyre, harp and all kinds of music, all the peoples, nations and men of every language fell down and worshiped the image of gold that King Nebuchadnezzar had set up.[y]

8At this time some astrologers[b][z] came forward and denounced the Jews. 9They said to King Nebuchadnezzar, "O king, live forever![a] 10You have issued a decree,[b] O king, that everyone who hears the sound of the horn, flute, zither, lyre, harp, pipes and all kinds of music must fall down and worship the image of gold,[c] 11and that whoever does not fall down and worship will be thrown into a blazing furnace. 12But there are some Jews whom you have set over the affairs of the province of Babylon—Shadrach, Meshach and Abednego[d]—who pay no attention[e] to you, O king. They neither serve your gods nor worship the image of gold you have set up."[f]

13Furious[g] with rage, Nebuchadnezzar summoned Shadrach, Meshach and Abednego. So these men were brought before the king, 14and Nebuchadnezzar said to them, "Is it true, Shadrach, Meshach and Abednego, that you do not serve my gods[h] or worship the image[i] of gold I have set up? 15Now when you hear the sound of the horn, flute, zither, lyre, harp, pipes and all kinds of music, if you are ready to fall down and worship the image I made, very good. But if you do not worship it, you will be thrown immediately into a blazing furnace. Then what god[j] will be able to rescue[k] you from my hand?"

16Shadrach, Meshach and Abednego[l] replied to the king, "O Nebuchadnezzar, we do not need to defend ourselves before you in this matter. 17If we are thrown into the blazing furnace, the God we serve is able to save[m] us from it, and he will rescue[n] us from your hand, O king.

2:45 [e]S Ge 41:25 [f]Rev 22:6 **2:46** [g]Da 8:17; Ac 10:25 [h]Ac 14:13 **2:47** [i]S Dt 10:17; Da 11:36 [j]Da 4:25; 1Ti 6:15 [k]S ver 22, 28 [l]Da 4:9; 1Co 14:25 **2:48** [m]S 2Ki 25:28 [n]S ver 6; S Est 8:2; S Da 1:20; 4:9; 5:11; 8:27 **2:49** [o]S Da 1:7; 3:30 [p]Da 6:2 **3:1** [q]ver 14; S Isa 46:6; Jer 16:20; Hab 2:19 **3:2** [r]S Est 1:1 [s]ver 27; Da 6:7 **3:4** [t]Da 4:1; 6:25; Rev 10:11 **3:5** [u]S Ge 4:21 [v]Rev 13:12 [w]ver 10, 15 **3:6** [x]ver 11, 15, 21; Jer 29:22; Da 5:19; 6:7; Mt 13:42, 50; Rev 13:15 **3:7** [y]S ver 5 **3:8** [z]S Isa 19:3; S Da 2:10 **3:9** [a]S Ne 2:3; Da 5:10; 6:6 **3:10** [b]Da 6:12 [c]ver 4-6 **3:12** [d]S Da 2:49 [e]Da 6:13 [f]S Est 3:3 **3:13** [g]S Da 2:12 **3:14** [h]Isa 46:1; Jer 50:2 [i]S ver 1 **3:15** [j]S Isa 36:18-20 [k]S 2Ch 32:15 **3:16** [l]S Da 1:7 **3:17** [m]S Ge 48:16; S Ps 18:48; 27:1-2 [n]S Job 5:19; Jer 1:8; Da 6:20

[a] 1 Aramaic *sixty cubits high and six cubits wide* (about 27 meters high and 2.7 meters wide)
[b] 8 Or *Chaldeans*

2:46 *offering ... be presented to him.* As to a god (cf. Ac 14:12 and note).

2:48 Cf. the story of Joseph (Ge 41:41–43).

2:49 Daniel requests that his administrative authority be shared with his three Jewish friends.

3:1 *image of gold.* Large statues of this kind were not made of solid gold but were plated with gold. *ninety feet high.* Including the lofty pedestal on which it no doubt stood (cf. Est 5:14 and note). *Dura.* Either the name of a place now marked by a series of mounds (located a few miles south of Babylon) or a common noun meaning "walled enclosure."

3:2 The seven classifications of government officials were to pledge full allegiance to the newly established empire as they stood before the image. The image probably represented the god Nabu, whose name formed the first element in Nebuchadnezzar's name (see note on 2Ki 24:1).

3:4 *every language.* Nebuchadnezzar's Babylon had become a cosmopolitan city whose population included people of many national and ethnic origins (see v. 7).

3:5 The words for "zither," "harp" and "pipes" (or perhaps "small drum") are Greek loanwords in Daniel. Greek musicians and instruments are mentioned in Assyrian inscriptions written before the time of Nebuchadnezzar. *fall down and worship the image.* See Ex 20:4–5 and note on 20:4).

3:8 *Jews.* A shortened form of "Judahites" (see Jer 34:9 and note).

3:12 *They neither serve your gods nor worship the image.* They obeyed the word of God (Ex 20:3–5) above the word of the king.

3:15 *what god will be able to rescue you from my hand?* Such boastful taunts were characteristic of proud Mesopotamian rulers (see Isa 36:18–20 and note).

3:17 See vv. 26–27; Heb 11:34 and note. *the God we serve is able to save us.* For what God is "able" to do

18 But even if he does not, we want you
to know, O king, that we will not serve
your gods or worship the image of gold
you have set up.[o]"
19 Then Nebuchadnezzar was furious
with Shadrach, Meshach and Abednego,
and his attitude toward them changed. He
ordered the furnace heated seven[p] times
hotter than usual 20 and commanded some
of the strongest soldiers in his army to
tie up Shadrach, Meshach and Abednego[q] and throw them into the blazing furnace. 21 So these men, wearing their robes,
trousers, turbans and other clothes, were
bound and thrown into the blazing furnace. 22 The king's command was so urgent and the furnace so hot that the flames
of the fire killed the soldiers who took up
Shadrach, Meshach and Abednego,[r] 23 and
these three men, firmly tied, fell into the
blazing furnace.
24 Then King Nebuchadnezzar leaped to
his feet in amazement and asked his advisers, "Weren't there three men that we
tied up and threw into the fire?"

They replied, "Certainly, O king."
25 He said, "Look! I see four men walking around in the fire, unbound and unharmed, and the fourth looks like a son
of the gods."
26 Nebuchadnezzar then approached the
opening of the blazing furnace and shouted, "Shadrach, Meshach and Abednego,
servants of the Most High God,[s] come out!
Come here!"

So Shadrach, Meshach and Abednego
came out of the fire, 27 and the satraps, prefects, governors and royal advisers[t] crowded around them.[u] They saw that the fire[v]
had not harmed their bodies, nor was a
hair of their heads singed; their robes were
not scorched, and there was no smell of
fire on them.
28 Then Nebuchadnezzar said, "Praise
be to the God of Shadrach, Meshach and
Abednego, who has sent his angel[w] and
rescued[x] his servants! They trusted[y] in
him and defied the king's command and
were willing to give up their lives rather than serve or worship any god except
their own God.[z] 29 Therefore I decree[a] that
the people of any nation or language who
say anything against the God of Shadrach,
Meshach and Abednego be cut into pieces and their houses be turned into piles
of rubble,[b] for no other god can save[c] in
this way."
30 Then the king promoted Shadrach,
Meshach and Abednego in the province of
Babylon.[d]

Nebuchadnezzar's Dream of a Tree

4 King Nebuchadnezzar,

To the peoples, nations and men of
every language,[e] who live in all the
world:

May you prosper greatly![f]

2 It is my pleasure to tell you about
the miraculous signs[g] and wonders
that the Most High God[h] has performed for me.

3 How great are his signs,
how mighty his wonders![i]
His kingdom is an eternal
kingdom;
his dominion endures[j] from
generation to generation.

4 I, Nebuchadnezzar, was at home
in my palace, contented[k] and prosperous. 5 I had a dream[l] that made
me afraid. As I was lying in my bed,[m]
the images and visions that passed
through my mind[n] terrified me.[o] 6 So I
commanded that all the wise men of
Babylon be brought before me to interpret[p] the dream for me. 7 When the
magicians,[q] enchanters, astrologers[a]
and diviners[r] came, I told them the
dream, but they could not interpret it
for me.[s] 8 Finally, Daniel came into my
presence and I told him the dream.
(He is called Belteshazzar,[t] after the
name of my god, and the spirit of the
holy gods[u] is in him.)
9 I said, "Belteshazzar, chief[v] of
the magicians, I know that the spirit
of the holy gods[w] is in you, and no

3:18 [o] ver 28; S Ex 1:17; S Jos 24:15 **3:19** [p] Lev 26:18-28 **3:20** [q] S Da 1:7 **3:22** [r] S Da 1:7 **3:26** [s] Da 4:2, 34 **3:27** [t] ver 2; Da 6:7 [u] Ps 91:3-11; S Isa 43:2; Heb 11:32-34 [v] Da 6:23 **3:28** [w] S Ps 34:7; Da 6:22; Ac 5:19 [x] S Ps 97:10; Ac 12:11 [y] S Dt 31:20; S Job 13:15; S Ps 26:1; 84:12 [z] S ver 18 **3:29** [a] Da 6:26 [b] S Ezr 6:11 [c] Da 6:27 **3:30** [d] S Da 2:49 **4:1** [e] S Da 3:4 [f] Da 6:25 **4:2** [g] Ps 74:9 [h] S Da 3:26 **4:3** [i] S Ps 105:27; Da 6:27 [j] Da 2:44 **4:4** [k] Ps 30:6; S Isa 32:9 **4:5** [l] S Da 2:1 [m] Ps 4:4 [n] Da 2:28 [o] ver 19; S Ge 41:8; S Job 3:26; Da 2:3; 5:6 **4:6** [p] Da 2:2 **4:7** [q] S Ge 41:8 [r] S Isa 44:25; S Da 2:2 [s] S Da 2:10 **4:8** [t] S Da 1:7 [u] S Ge 41:38 **4:9** [v] Da 2:48 [w] Da 5:11-12

[a] 7 Or *Chaldeans*

see, e.g., 4:37; 6:19–22 (cf. Ro 11:23; 2Co 9:8; Heb 7:25; Jude 24–25 and notes).

3:18 *if he does not.* Whether God decides to rescue them (v. 17) or not, their faith is fully resigned to his will.

3:19 *seven times hotter than usual.* Probably figurative for "as hot as possible" (seven signifies completeness).

3:25 See Ps 91:9–12. *son of the gods.* Nebuchadnezzar was speaking as a pagan polytheist and was content to conceive of the fourth figure as a lesser heavenly being ("angel," v. 28) sent by the all-powerful God of the Jews (see also 6:22).

3:26 *Most High God.* Nebuchadnezzar had earlier acknowledged that Daniel's God is "the God of gods and the Lord of kings" (2:47).

3:28 *They trusted in him.* See 6:23 and note; Ps 11; 16; 23; 31; 52; Pr 3:5 and note.

3:29 See 2:5. *no other god can save.* See Isa 40:18–20; 41:24; 44:17 and notes (cf. Jn 14:6 and note).

4:1–3 Nebuchadnezzar reached this conclusion after the experiences of vv. 4–33. The language of his confession may reflect Daniel's influence.

4:3 *His kingdom ... from generation to generation.* See v. 34 and note.

4:8 *after the name of my god.* See note on 1:7. Bel ("lord") was a title for the god Marduk, chief god of the Babylonian pantheon and Nebuchadnezzar's personal god and so his favorite god.

4:9 *chief of the magicians.* See 2:48.

mystery is too difficult for you. Here is
my dream; interpret it for me. [10]These
are the visions I saw while lying in
my bed:[x] I looked, and there before
me stood a tree in the middle of the
land. Its height was enormous.[y] [11]The
tree grew large and strong and its top
touched the sky; it was visible to the
ends of the earth.[z] [12]Its leaves were
beautiful, its fruit abundant, and on it
was food for all. Under it the beasts of
the field found shelter, and the birds
of the air lived in its branches;[a] from
it every creature was fed.

[13]"In the visions I saw while lying in my bed,[b] I looked, and there
before me was a messenger,[a] a holy
one,[c] coming down from heaven. [14]He
called in a loud voice: 'Cut down the
tree[d] and trim off its branches; strip
off its leaves and scatter its fruit. Let
the animals flee from under it and the
birds from its branches.[e] [15]But let the
stump and its roots, bound with iron
and bronze, remain in the ground, in
the grass of the field.

"'Let him be drenched with the
dew of heaven, and let him live with
the animals among the plants of the
earth. [16]Let his mind be changed from
that of a man and let him be given the
mind of an animal, till seven times[b]
pass by for him.[f]

[17]"'The decision is announced by
messengers, the holy ones declare the
verdict, so that the living may know
that the Most High[g] is sovereign[h] over
the kingdoms of men and gives them

4:10 [x]S ver 5; Ps 4:4 [y]Eze 31:3-4 **4:11** [z]S Eze 19:11; 31:5 **4:12** [a]S Eze 17:23; S Mt 13:32 **4:13** [b]ver 10; Da 7:1 [c]S ver 23; S Dt 33:2 **4:14** [d]S Job 24:20 [e]S Eze 31:12; S Mt 3:10 **4:16** [f]ver 23,32 **4:17** [g]ver 2,25; Ps 83:18 [h]S Ps 103:19; Jer 27:5-7; Da 2:21; 5:18-21; Ro 13:1

[a] 13 Or *watchman*; also in verses 17 and 23
[b] 16 Or *years*; also in verses 23, 25 and 32

4:10 *tree.* Interpreted in v. 22.

4:11 *grew large and strong.* In one of Nebuchadnezzar's building inscriptions, Babylon is compared to a spreading tree (cf. v. 22). *its top touched the sky.* A phrase often used of Mesopotamian temple-towers (see Ge 11:4 and note).

4:13 *messenger.* Angel (but see NIV text note).

4:15 *let the stump ... remain.* Implies that the tree will be revived later (see v. 26). *him.* The tree is here personified and later identified (v. 22).

4:16 *seven.* Signifies completeness (i.e., a full measure). *times.* See NIV text note; see also 7:25 and NIV text note. Alternatively, "times" can refer to indefinite periods.

4:17 *messengers.* The agents of God, who is the ultimate source of the "decision" (see v. 24). *the Most High is sovereign.* See Introduction: Theological Theme.

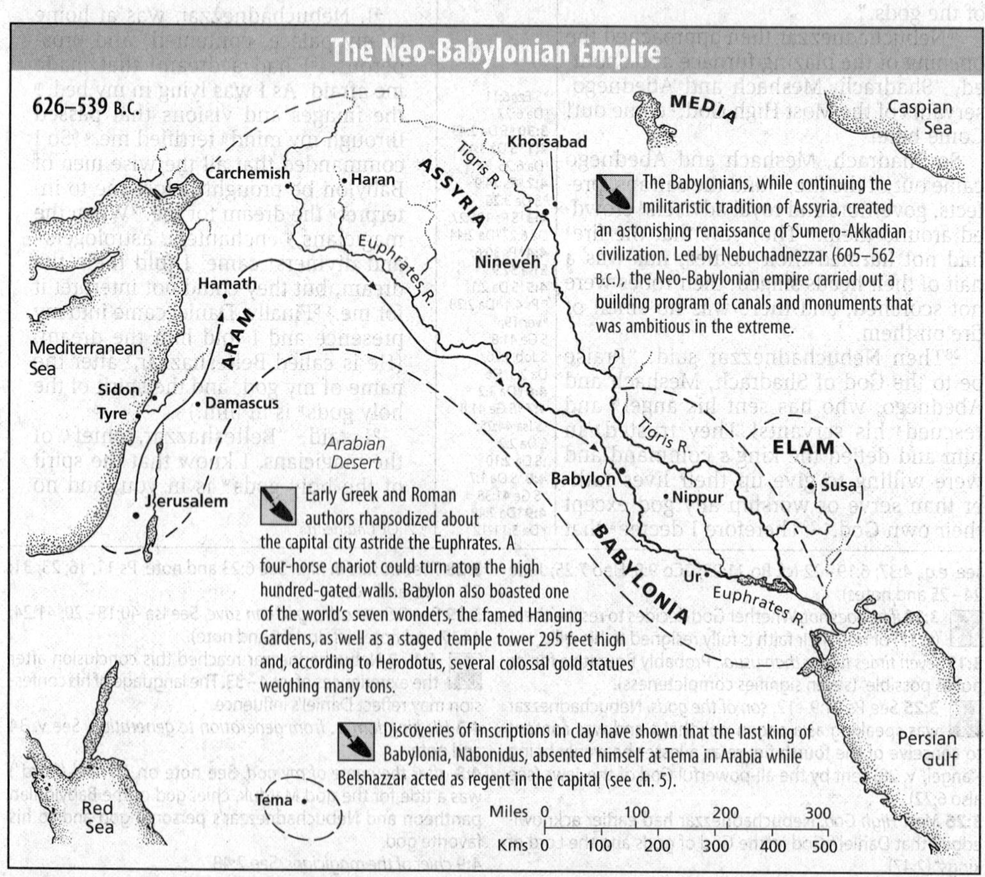
The Neo-Babylonian Empire
626–539 B.C.
MEDIA
Caspian Sea
Khorsabad
Tigris R.
ASSYRIA
Carchemish
Haran
Nineveh
Euphrates R.
Hamath
ARAM
Mediterranean Sea
Sidon
Tyre
Damascus
Arabian Desert
Jerusalem
Tigris R.
ELAM
Babylon
Nippur
Susa
BABYLONIA
Ur
Euphrates R.
Persian Gulf
Red Sea
Tema
Miles 0 100 200 300
Kms 0 100 200 300 400 500
The Babylonians, while continuing the militaristic tradition of Assyria, created an astonishing renaissance of Sumero-Akkadian civilization. Led by Nebuchadnezzar (605–562 B.C.), the Neo-Babylonian empire carried out a building program of canals and monuments that was ambitious in the extreme.
Early Greek and Roman authors rhapsodized about the capital city astride the Euphrates. A four-horse chariot could turn atop the high hundred-gated walls. Babylon also boasted one of the world's seven wonders, the famed Hanging Gardens, as well as a staged temple tower 295 feet high and, according to Herodotus, several colossal gold statues weighing many tons.
Discoveries of inscriptions in clay have shown that the last king of Babylonia, Nabonidus, absented himself at Tema in Arabia while Belshazzar acted as regent in the capital (see ch. 5).

to anyone he wishes and sets over
them the lowliest[i] of men.'
[18]"This is the dream that I, King
Nebuchadnezzar, had. Now, Belteshazzar, tell me what it means, for
none of the wise men in my kingdom
can interpret it for me.[j] But you can,[k]
because the spirit of the holy gods[l] is
in you."[m]

Daniel Interprets the Dream

[19]Then Daniel (also called Belteshazzar) was greatly perplexed for
a time, and his thoughts terrified[n]
him. So the king said, "Belteshazzar,
do not let the dream or its meaning
alarm you."[o]
Belteshazzar answered, "My lord,
if only the dream applied to your enemies and its meaning to your adversaries! [20]The tree you saw, which
grew large and strong, with its top
touching the sky, visible to the whole
earth, [21]with beautiful leaves and
abundant fruit, providing food for
all, giving shelter to the beasts of the
field, and having nesting places in its
branches for the birds of the air[p]—
[22]you, O king, are that tree![q] You have
become great and strong; your greatness has grown until it reaches the
sky, and your dominion extends to
distant parts of the earth.[r]
[23]"You, O king, saw a messenger, a
holy one,[s] coming down from heaven
and saying, 'Cut down the tree and
destroy it, but leave the stump, bound
with iron and bronze, in the grass of
the field, while its roots remain in the
ground. Let him be drenched with the
dew of heaven; let him live like the
wild animals, until seven times pass
by for him.'[t][u]
[24]"This is the interpretation, O king,
and this is the decree[v] the Most High
has issued against my lord the king:
[25]You will be driven away from people
and will live with the wild animals;
you will eat grass like cattle and be
drenched[w] with the dew of heaven.
Seven times will pass by for you until
you acknowledge that the Most High[x]
is sovereign over the kingdoms of men
and gives them to anyone he wishes.[y]
[26]The command to leave the stump
of the tree with its roots[z] means that
your kingdom will be restored to you
when you acknowledge that Heaven
rules.[a] [27]Therefore, O king, be pleased
to accept my advice: Renounce your
sins by doing what is right, and your
wickedness by being kind to the oppressed.[b] It may be that then your
prosperity[c] will continue.[d]"

The Dream Is Fulfilled

[28]All this happened[e] to King Nebuchadnezzar. [29]Twelve months later,
as the king was walking on the roof
of the royal palace of Babylon, [30]he
said, "Is not this the great Babylon I
have built as the royal residence, by
my mighty power and for the glory[f] of
my majesty?"[g]
[31]The words were still on his lips
when a voice came from heaven,
"This is what is decreed for you, King
Nebuchadnezzar: Your royal authority
has been taken from you.[h] [32]You will
be driven away from people and will
live with the wild animals; you will eat
grass like cattle. Seven times will pass
by for you until you acknowledge that
the Most High is sovereign over the
kingdoms of men and gives them to
anyone he wishes."[i]
[33]Immediately what had been said
about Nebuchadnezzar was fulfilled.
He was driven away from people and
ate grass like cattle. His body was
drenched[j] with the dew of heaven
until his hair grew like the feathers of
an eagle and his nails like the claws
of a bird.[k]
[34]At the end of that time, I, Nebuchadnezzar, raised my eyes toward
heaven, and my sanity[l] was restored.
Then I praised the Most High; I honored and glorified him who lives forever.[m]

4:17 [i]Da 11:21; Mt 23:12 **4:18** [j]S Ge 41:8; Da 5:8,15 [k]S Ge 41:15 [l]S Ge 41:38 [m]ver 7-9; S Da 1:20 **4:19** [n]S ver 5; S Ge 41:8; Da 7:15,28; 8:27; 10:16-17 [o]S Ge 40:12 **4:21** [p]S Eze 31:6 **4:22** [q]S 2Sa 12:7 [r]Jer 27:7; Da 5:18-19 **4:23** [s]ver 13; Da 8:13 [t]Da 5:21 [u]S Eze 31:3-4 **4:24** [v]Job 40:12; Ps 107:40; Jer 40:2 **4:25** [w]S Job 24:8 [x]S ver 17 [y]Jer 27:5; S Da 2:47; 5:21 **4:26** [z]ver 15 [a]S Da 2:37 **4:27** [b]Isa 55:6-7 [c]Jer 29:7 [d]S Dt 24:13; 1Ki 21:29; S Ps 41:3; S Pr 28:13; S Eze 18:22 **4:28** [e]Nu 23:19 **4:30** [f]Isa 13:19 [g]S Isa 10:13; S 37:24-25; Da 5:20; Hab 1:11; 2:4 **4:31** [h]S 2Sa 22:28; Da 5:20 **4:32** [i]S Job 9:12 **4:33** [j]S Job 24:8 [k]Da 5:20-21 **4:34** [l]S Job 12:20 [m]Da 12:7

4:19 *Daniel ... was greatly perplexed.* Possibly over how to state the interpretation in an appropriate way. *My lord, if only ... adversaries!* Daniel prepared the king to fear the worst.
4:22 *you, O king, are that tree.* Cf. 2:37–38. *your dominion extends ... the earth.* Nebuchadnezzar's empire was the largest and most powerful in that part of the world up to that time.
4:25 *eat grass like cattle.* Nebuchadnezzar was possibly stricken with a rare mental illness (see v. 34) known as boanthropy, which causes its victims to assume the appearance, habits and posture of cattle (v. 33). *acknowledge that the Most High is sovereign.* He will soon learn that lesson (compare v. 30 with v. 37).
4:26 *Heaven.* A Jewish way of referring to God, later reflected in the NT expression "kingdom of heaven" (compare, e.g., Mt 5:3 with Lk 6:20).
4:28 *All this happened.* But only because Nebuchadnezzar did not follow Daniel's "advice" (v. 27).
4:30 *great Babylon.* Illustrated, e.g., in the city's ramparts, temples and hanging gardens (see note on Isa 13:19; see also map and accompanying text, p. 1318).
4:31 *The words were still on his lips.* See Lk 12:19–20.
4:33 *what had been said ... was fulfilled.* See Pr 11:2 and note; 16:18. *driven away.* Possibly into the palace gardens. His counselors, perhaps led by Daniel (see 2:48–49), could have administered the kingdom efficiently.
4:34 *At the end of that time.* Perhaps as much as seven years (see v. 16 and note). *His dominion ... from generation to generation.* Nebuchadnezzar returns to the grand theme with which he began (see v. 3; see also 6:26; 7:14).

His dominion is an eternal dominion;
his kingdom[n] endures from
generation to generation.[o]
35 All the peoples of the earth
are regarded as nothing.[p]
He does as he pleases[q]
with the powers of heaven
and the peoples of the earth.
No one can hold back[r] his hand[s]
or say to him: "What have you
done?"[t]

36 At the same time that my sanity
was restored, my honor and splendor
were returned to me for the glory of
my kingdom.[u] My advisers and nobles
sought me out, and I was restored to
my throne and became even greater
than before. 37 Now I, Nebuchadnezzar, praise and exalt[v] and glorify[w] the
King of heaven, because everything
he does is right and all his ways are
just.[x] And those who walk in pride[y]
he is able to humble.[z]

The Writing on the Wall

5 King Belshazzar[a] gave a great banquet[b]
for a thousand of his nobles[c] and drank
wine with them. 2 While Belshazzar was
drinking[d] his wine, he gave orders to bring
in the gold and silver goblets[e] that Nebuchadnezzar his father[a] had taken from the
temple in Jerusalem, so that the king and
his nobles, his wives and his concubines[f]
might drink from them.[g] 3 So they brought
in the gold goblets that had been taken
from the temple of God in Jerusalem, and
the king and his nobles, his wives and his
concubines drank from them. 4 As they
drank the wine, they praised the gods[h] of
gold and silver, of bronze, iron, wood and
stone.[i]

5 Suddenly the fingers of a human hand
appeared and wrote on the plaster of the
wall, near the lampstand in the royal
palace. The king watched the hand as it
wrote. 6 His face turned pale[j] and he was
so frightened[k] that his knees knocked[l] together and his legs gave way.[m]

7 The king called out for the enchanters,[n]
astrologers[b][o] and diviners[p] to be brought
and said to these wise[q] men of Babylon,
"Whoever reads this writing and tells me
what it means will be clothed in purple
and have a gold chain placed around his
neck,[r] and he will be made the third[s] highest ruler in the kingdom."[t]

8 Then all the king's wise men[u] came
in, but they could not read the writing or
tell the king what it meant.[v] 9 So King Belshazzar became even more terrified[w] and
his face grew more pale. His nobles were
baffled.

10 The queen,[c] hearing the voices of the
king and his nobles, came into the banquet hall. "O king, live forever!"[x] she said.
"Don't be alarmed! Don't look so pale!
11 There is a man in your kingdom who
has the spirit of the holy gods[y] in him.
In the time of your father he was found
to have insight and intelligence and wisdom[z] like that of the gods.[a] King Nebuchadnezzar your father—your father the
king, I say—appointed him chief of the
magicians, enchanters, astrologers and diviners.[b] 12 This man Daniel, whom the king
called Belteshazzar,[c] was found to have
a keen mind and knowledge and understanding, and also the ability to interpret
dreams, explain riddles[d] and solve difficult
problems.[e] Call for Daniel, and he will tell
you what the writing means.[f]"

13 So Daniel was brought before the king,
and the king said to him, "Are you Daniel, one of the exiles my father the king
brought from Judah?[g] 14 I have heard that
the spirit of the gods[h] is in you and that
you have insight, intelligence and outstanding wisdom.[i] 15 The wise men and enchanters were brought before me to read
this writing and tell me what it means, but
they could not explain it.[j] 16 Now I have
heard that you are able to give interpretations and to solve difficult problems.[k] If
you can read this writing and tell me what
it means, you will be clothed in purple

[a] 2 Or *ancestor*; or *predecessor*; also in verses 11, 13 and 18 [b] 7 Or *Chaldeans*; also in verse 11
[c] 10 Or *queen mother*

4:34 [n]Isa 37:16 [o]Ps 145:13; S Da 2:44; 5:21; 6:26; Lk 1:33 **4:35** [p]S Isa 40:17 [q]Dt 21:8; Ps 115:3; S 135:6; Jnh 1:14 [r]S Isa 14:27 [s]S Dt 32:39 [t]S Job 9:4; S Isa 14:24; S 45:9; Da 5:21; Ro 9:20 **4:36** [u]S Pr 22:4; Da 5:18 **4:37** [v]S Ex 15:2 [w]S Ps 34:3 [x]Dt 32:4; Ps 33:4-5 [y]Ps 18:27; S 119:21 [z]S Job 31:4; 40:11-12; S Isa 13:11; Da 5:20,23; Mt 23:12 **5:1** [a]ver 30; Da 7:1; 8:1 [b]S 1Ki 3:15 [c]Jer 50:35 **5:2** [d]S Isa 21:5 [e]S 2Ki 24:13; S 2Ch 36:10; S Jer 52:19 [f]S Est 2:14 [g]S Est 1:7; Da 1:2 **5:4** [h]Jdg 16:24 [i]S Est 1:10; Ps 135:15-18; Hab 2:19; Rev 9:20 **5:6** [j]S Job 4:15 [k]S Da 4:5 [l]S Isa 7:2 [m]S Ps 22:14; Eze 7:17 **5:7** [n]S Ge 41:8 [o]S Isa 19:3 [p]Isa 44:25 [q]Jer 50:35; Da 4:6-7 [r]S Ge 41:42 [s]Est 10:3 [t]Da 2:5-6,48 **5:8** [u]S Ex 8:18 [v]S Da 2:10,27; S 4:18 **5:9** [w]S Ps 48:5; S Isa 21:4 **5:10** [x]S Ne 2:3; S Da 3:9 **5:11** [y]S Ge 41:38 [z]ver 14; S Da 1:17 [a]S Da 2:22 [b]Da 2:47-48 **5:12** [c]S Da 1:7 [d]S Nu 12:8 [e]ver 14-16; Da 6:3 [f]S Eze 28:3 **5:13** [g]S Est 2:5-6; Da 6:13 **5:14** [h]S Ge 41:38 [i]S Da 2:22 **5:15** [j]S Da 4:18 **5:16** [k]S Ge 41:15

4:35 See Ps 115:3 and note.
4:36 Cf. Job 42:10,12.
4:37 *everything he does is right and ... just.* See note on Eze 18:25. *those who walk in pride he is able to humble.* See Pr 3:34; Jas 4:6,10; 1Pe 5:5–6.
5:1–4 The orgy of revelry and blasphemy on such occasions is mentioned also by the ancient Greek historians Herodotus and Xenophon.
5:1 *King.* Belshazzar (meaning "Bel, protect the king!") was the son and viceroy of Nabonidus (see chart, p. 472). He is called the "son" of Nebuchadnezzar (v. 22), but the Aramaic term could also mean "grandson" or "descendant" or even "successor" (see NIV text note on v. 22). See also note on v. 10 and NIV text note on v. 2.
5:2 *gold ... that Nebuchadnezzar ... had taken from the temple.* In the eighth year of his reign (597 B.C.; see 2Ki 24:12–13 and note on 24:12).
5:5 *Suddenly.* See 4:31; see also Pr 29:1; 1Th 5:3 and notes.
5:7 *third highest ruler in the kingdom.* Nabonidus was first, Belshazzar second (see last notation on map, p. 1318).
5:10 *queen.* See NIV text note. She could have been (1) the wife of Nebuchadnezzar, or (2) the daughter of Nebuchadnezzar and wife of Nabonidus, or (3) the wife of Nabonidus but not the daughter of Nebuchadnezzar.
5:11 *the time of your father.* Nebuchadnezzar had died in 562 B.C.; the year is now 539.
5:16 *third highest ruler.* See v. 7 and note.

and have a gold chain placed around your
neck,[l] and you will be made the third
highest ruler in the kingdom."[m]
17Then Daniel answered the king, "You
may keep your gifts for yourself and give
your rewards to someone else.[n] Nevertheless, I will read the writing for the king
and tell him what it means.
18"O king, the Most High God gave your
father Nebuchadnezzar[o] sovereignty and
greatness and glory and splendor.[p] 19Be-
cause of the high position he gave him, all
the peoples and nations and men of every
language dreaded and feared him. Those
the king wanted to put to death, he put
to death;[q] those he wanted to spare, he
spared; those he wanted to promote, he
promoted; and those he wanted to humble, he humbled.[r] 20But when his heart became arrogant and hardened with pride,[s]
he was deposed from his royal throne[t] and
stripped[u] of his glory.[v] 21He was driven
away from people and given the mind of
an animal; he lived with the wild donkeys
and ate grass like cattle; and his body was
drenched with the dew of heaven, until he
acknowledged that the Most High God is
sovereign[w] over the kingdoms of men and
sets over them anyone he wishes.[x]
22"But you his son,[a] O Belshazzar, have
not humbled[y] yourself, though you knew
all this. 23Instead, you have set yourself up
against[z] the Lord of heaven. You had the
goblets from his temple brought to you,
and you and your nobles, your wives[a] and
your concubines drank wine from them.
You praised the gods of silver and gold,
of bronze, iron, wood and stone, which
cannot see or hear or understand.[b] But
you did not honor the God who holds in
his hand your life[c] and all your ways.[d]
24Therefore he sent the hand that wrote
the inscription.
25"This is the inscription that was written:

MENE, MENE, TEKEL, PARSIN[b]

26"This is what these words mean:

Mene[c]: God has numbered the
days[e] of your reign and
brought it to an end.[f]
27*Tekel*[d]: You have been weighed
on the scales[g] and found
wanting.[h]
28*Peres*[e]: Your kingdom is divided
and given to the Medes[i] and
Persians."[j]

29Then at Belshazzar's command, Daniel was clothed in purple, a gold chain
was placed around his neck,[k] and he was
proclaimed the third highest ruler in the
kingdom.[l]
30That very night Belshazzar,[m] king[n] of
the Babylonians,[f] was slain,[o] 31and Darius[p] the Mede[q] took over the kingdom, at
the age of sixty-two.

Daniel in the Den of Lions

6 It pleased Darius[r] to appoint 120 satraps[s] to rule throughout the kingdom,
2with three administrators over them, one
of whom was Daniel.[t] The satraps were
made accountable[u] to them so that the
king might not suffer loss. 3Now Daniel so
distinguished himself among the administrators and the satraps by his exceptional
qualities that the king planned to set him
over the whole kingdom.[v] 4At this, the administrators and the satraps tried to find
grounds for charges[w] against Daniel in his
conduct of government affairs, but they
were unable to do so. They could find no
corruption in him, because he was trustworthy and neither corrupt nor negligent.
5Finally these men said, "We will never
find any basis for charges against this man

5:16 [l] S Ge 41:42 [m] S Est 5:3; S Da 2:6 **5:17** [n] S 2Ki 5:16 **5:18** [o] S Jer 28:14 [p] S Jer 27:7; S Da 2:37-38; S 4:36 **5:19** [q] Da 2:12-13; S 3:6 [r] S Da 4:22 **5:20** [s] Da 4:30 [t] Jer 43:10 [u] Jer 13:18; S Da 4:31 [v] S Job 40:12; Isa 14:13-15; Eze 31:10-11; Da 8:8 **5:21** [w] S Eze 17:24 [x] Da 4:16-17,35 **5:22** [y] S Ex 10:3 **5:23** [z] S Isa 14:13; S Jer 50:29 [a] Jer 44:9 [b] Ps 115:4-8; Hab 2:19; Rev 9:20 [c] Job 12:10; Ac 17:28 [d] S Job 31:4; S Isa 13:11; Jer 10:23; S 48:26 **5:26** [e] Jer 27:7 [f] Isa 13:6 **5:27** [g] S Job 6:2 [h] Ps 62:9 **5:28** [i] Isa 13:17 [j] S Jer 27:7; 50:41-43; Da 6:28 **5:29** [k] S Ge 41:42 [l] S Da 2:6 **5:30** [m] S ver 1 [n] Jer 50:35 [o] S Isa 21:9; S Jer 51:31 **5:31** [p] Jer 50:41; Da 6:1; 9:1; 11:1 [q] S Isa 13:3 **6:1** [r] S Da 5:31 [s] S Est 1:1 **6:2** [t] Da 2:48-49 [u] Ezr 4:22 **6:3** [v] S Ge 41:41; S Est 10:3; S Da 1:20; 5:12-14 **6:4** [w] Jer 20:10

[a] 22 Or *descendant*; or *successor* [b] 25 Aramaic *UPARSIN* (that is, *AND PARSIN*) [c] 26 *Mene* can mean *numbered* or *mina* (a unit of money). [d] 27 *Tekel* can mean *weighed* or *shekel*. [e] 28 *Peres* (the singular of *Parsin*) can mean *divided* or *Persia* or *a half mina* or *a half shekel*. [f] 30 Or *Chaldeans*

5:17 *keep your gifts for yourself.* See Ge 14:23; 2Ki 5:16 and notes.
5:21 *He was ... given the mind of an animal.* See 4:25 and note. *until he acknowledged.* See note on 4:25. *the Most High God is sovereign over the kingdoms of men.* See Introduction: Theological Theme.
5:22–23 Three charges were brought against Belshazzar: (1) He sinned through disobedience and pride, not through ignorance (v. 22); (2) he defied God by desecrating the sacred vessels (v. 23a); and (3) he praised idols and so did not honor God (v. 23b).
5:23 The stark contrast between the false gods of the nations and the one true God is a pervasive theme in the prophets (see, e.g., 3:29 and note; Isa 41:5–10; 44:6–23; Jer 10:1–16; Eze 8–9; Hos 13:1–8; Hab 2:18–20; see also Ps 115:2–8; 135:15–18).
5:24 *he sent the hand.* Daniel waits until the last moment before informing the king that God himself is the source of the inscription.
5:26–28 See NIV text notes. Three weights (mina, shekel, and half mina/shekel) may be intended, symbolizing three rulers (respectively): (1) Nebuchadnezzar, (2) either Evil-Merodach (see 2Ki 25:27 and note) or Nabonidus, and (3) Belshazzar.
5:27 *weighed on the scales.* Measured in the light of God's standards (see Job 31:6 and note; Ps 62:9).
5:28 *divided ... Persians.* Daniel employs a telling wordplay (see NIV text note). *Medes and Persians.* The second kingdom of the series of four predicted in ch. 2 (see Introduction: Author, Date and Authenticity; see also chart, p. 1323).
5:29 *gold chain was placed around his neck.* As a symbol of authority (see Ge 41:42 and note).
5:30 *That very night.* See Pr 6:15 and note; Lk 12:20.
5:31 *Darius the Mede.* Perhaps another name for Gubaru, referred to in Babylonian inscriptions as the governor that Cyrus put in charge of the newly conquered Babylonian territories. Or "Darius the Mede" may have been Cyrus's throne name in Babylon (see NIV text note on 6:28; see also 1Ch 5:26 and note). *took over the kingdom.* In 539 B.C. The "head of gold" (2:38) is now no more, as predicted in 2:39.

Daniel unless it has something to do with
the law of his God."[x]
6So the administrators and the satraps
went as a group to the king and said:
"O King Darius, live forever![y] 7The royal
administrators, prefects, satraps, advisers
and governors[z] have all agreed that the
king should issue an edict and enforce the
decree that anyone who prays to any god
or man during the next thirty days, except
to you, O king, shall be thrown into the lions' den.[a] 8Now, O king, issue the decree
and put it in writing so that it cannot be
altered—in accordance with the laws of
the Medes and Persians, which cannot be
repealed."[b] 9So King Darius put the decree
in writing.
10Now when Daniel learned that the decree had been published, he went home
to his upstairs room where the windows
opened toward[c] Jerusalem. Three times a
day he got down on his knees[d] and prayed,
giving thanks to his God, just as he had
done before.[e] 11Then these men went as a
group and found Daniel praying and asking God for help.[f] 12So they went to the
king and spoke to him about his royal decree: "Did you not publish a decree that
during the next thirty days anyone who
prays to any god or man except to you,
O king, would be thrown into the lions'
den?"
The king answered, "The decree
stands—in accordance with the laws of
the Medes and Persians, which cannot be
repealed."[g]
13Then they said to the king, "Daniel,
who is one of the exiles from Judah,[h] pays
no attention[i] to you, O king, or to the decree you put in writing. He still prays three
times a day." 14When the king heard this,
he was greatly distressed;[j] he was determined to rescue Daniel and made every
effort until sundown to save him.
15Then the men went as a group to the
king and said to him, "Remember, O king,
that according to the law of the Medes and
Persians no decree or edict that the king
issues can be changed."[k]
16So the king gave the order, and they
brought Daniel and threw him into the lions' den.[l] The king said to Daniel, "May

6:5 [x]Ac 24:13-16 **6:6** [y]S Ne 2:3 **6:7** [z]S Da 3:2 [a]Ps 59:3; 64:2-6; S Da 3:6 **6:8** [b]S Est 1:19 **6:10** [c]S 1Ki 8:29 [d]Ps 95:6 [e]Mt 6:6; Ac 5:29 **6:11** [f]1Ki 8:48-50; Ps 55:17; 1Th 5:17-18 **6:12** [g]S Est 1:19; Da 3:8-12 **6:13** [h]S Eze 14:14; Da 2:25 [i]S Est 3:8 **6:14** [j]Mk 6:26 **6:15** [k]S Est 8:8 **6:16** [l]S ver 7

your God, whom you serve continually,
rescue[m] you!"
17A stone was brought and placed over
the mouth of the den, and the king sealed[n]
it with his own signet ring and with the
rings of his nobles, so that Daniel's situation might not be changed. 18Then the
king returned to his palace and spent the
night without eating[o] and without any entertainment being brought to him. And he
could not sleep.[p]
19At the first light of dawn, the king got
up and hurried to the lions' den. 20When
he came near the den, he called to Daniel
in an anguished voice, "Daniel, servant of
the living God, has your God, whom you
serve continually, been able to rescue you
from the lions?"[q]
21Daniel answered, "O king, live forever![r] 22My God sent his angel,[s] and he shut
the mouths of the lions.[t] They have not
hurt me, because I was found innocent in
his sight.[u] Nor have I ever done any wrong
before you, O king."
23The king was overjoyed and gave
orders to lift Daniel out of the den. And
when Daniel was lifted from the den, no
wound[v] was found on him, because he
had trusted[w] in his God.
24At the king's command, the men who
had falsely accused Daniel were brought
in and thrown into the lions' den,[x] along
with their wives and children.[y] And before they reached the floor of the den, the
lions overpowered them and crushed all
their bones.[z]
25Then King Darius wrote to all the peoples, nations and men of every language[a]
throughout the land:

"May you prosper greatly![b]

26"I issue a decree that in every part
of my kingdom people must fear and
reverence[c] the God of Daniel.[d]

"For he is the living God[e]
and he endures forever;[f]
his kingdom will not be destroyed,
his dominion will never end.[g]
27He rescues and he saves;[h]
he performs signs and wonders[i]
in the heavens and on the earth.
He has rescued Daniel
from the power of the lions."[j]

[m]S Job 5:19; Ps 37:39-40; S 97:10 **6:17** [n]Mt 27:66 **6:18** [o]S 2Sa 12:17; Da 10:3 [p]S Est 6:1 **6:20** [q]S Da 3:17 **6:21** [r]S Ne 2:3; Da 3:9 **6:22** [s]S Ge 32:1; S Da 3:28 [t]ver 27; Ps 91:11-13; Heb 11:33 [u]Ac 12:11; 2Ti 4:17 **6:23** [v]Da 3:27 [w]S 1Ch 5:20; S Isa 12:2 **6:24** [x]Dt 19:18-19; Est 7:9-10; Ps 54:5 [y]Dt 24:16; 2Ki 14:6 [z]S Isa 38:13 **6:25** [a]S Da 3:4 [b]Da 4:1 **6:26** [c]S Ps 5:7 [d]S Est 8:17; Ps 99:1-3; Da 3:29 [e]S Jos 2:11; S 3:10 [f]S Jer 10:10; Da 12:7; Rev 1:18 [g]S Da 2:44 **6:27** [h]Da 3:29 [i]S Da 4:3 [j]S ver 22

6:7 The conspirators lied in stating that "all" the royal administrators supported the proposed decree since they knew that Daniel (totally unaware of the proposal) was the foremost of the three administrators. *lions' den.* A pit with a relatively small opening at the top (see v. 17), making it impossible for a prisoner to escape.

6:8,12 *laws of the Medes and Persians, which cannot be repealed.* See v. 15; see also notes on Est 1:19; 8:8.

6:10 *toward Jerusalem.* See 2Ch 6:38–39. *Three times a day.* Cf. Ps 55:17. *prayed … just as he had done before.* Not even the threat of death could keep Daniel from honoring his customary times of prayer.

6:13 *pays no attention to you.* But see vv. 22,24.

6:16 *serve continually.* See 1Co 15:58 and note.

6:18 *he could not sleep.* See 2:1; Est 6:1 and note.

6:20 *has your God … been able to rescue you …?* See 3:17 and note.

6:23 *no wound was found on him.* See 3:27. *he … trusted in his God.* That the lions were ravenously hungry (v. 24) was no obstacle to the Lord's rewarding Daniel's faith by saving his life (see 3:28 and note).

6:24 *along with their wives and children.* In accordance with Persian custom (cf. Jos 7:24 and note).

28 So Daniel prospered during the reign
of Darius and the reign of Cyrus[a][k] the Persian.[l]

Daniel's Dream of Four Beasts

7 In the first year of Belshazzar[m] king
of Babylon, Daniel had a dream, and
visions[n] passed through his mind[o] as he
was lying on his bed.[p] He wrote[q] down the
substance of his dream.
2 Daniel said: "In my vision at night I
looked, and there before me were the four
winds of heaven[r] churning up the great
sea. 3 Four great beasts,[s] each different
from the others, came up out of the sea.
4 "The first was like a lion,[t] and it had
the wings of an eagle.[u] I watched until its
wings were torn off and it was lifted from
the ground so that it stood on two feet like
a man, and the heart of a man was given
to it.
5 "And there before me was a second
beast, which looked like a bear. It was
raised up on one of its sides, and it had
three ribs in its mouth between its teeth.
It was told, 'Get up and eat your fill of
flesh!'[v]
6 "After that, I looked, and there before
me was another beast, one that looked like
a leopard.[w] And on its back it had four
wings like those of a bird. This beast had
four heads, and it was given authority to
rule.

6:28 [k] S 2Ch 36:22; S Da 1:21 [l] S Da 5:28 **7:1** [m] S Da 5:1 [n] S Eze 40:2 [o] S Da 1:17 [p] Ps 4:4; S Da 4:13 [q] S Jer 36:4 **7:2** [r] S Eze 37:9; Da 8:8; 11:4; Rev 7:1 **7:3** [s] Rev 13:1 **7:4** [t] S 2Ki 24:1; Ps 7:2; Jer 4:7; Rev 13:2 [u] S Eze 17:3 **7:5** [v] Da 2:39 **7:6** [w] Rev 13:2

[a] 28 Or *Darius, that is, the reign of Cyrus*

6:28 See NIV text note.
7:1 *first year of Belshazzar.* Probably 553 B.C. The events of ch. 7 preceded those of ch. 5.
7:2 *the great sea.* The world of nations and peoples (see also vv. 3,17).
7:4–7 The lion with an eagle's wings is a cherub symbolizing the Neo-Babylonian empire (see Ge 3:24 and note). The rest of v. 4 perhaps reflects the humbling of Nebuchadnezzar, as recorded in ch. 4. The bear (v. 5), "raised up on one of its sides," refers to the superior status of the Persians in the Medo-Persian alliance. The three ribs may represent its three principal conquests: Lydia (546 B.C.), Babylon (539) and Egypt (525). The leopard with four wings (v. 6) represents the speedy conquests of Alexander the Great (334–330), and the four heads correspond to the four main divisions into which his empire fell after his untimely death in 323 (see 8:22): Macedon and Greece (under Antipater and Cassander), Thrace and Asia Minor (under Lysimachus), Syria (under Seleucus I), and the Holy Land and Egypt (under Ptolemy I). The fourth beast (v. 7), with its irresistible power and surpassing all its predecessors, points to the Roman empire (cf. 11:30 and note; in the Apocrypha see 2 Esdras 12:11). Its ten horns correspond to the ten toes of 2:41–42 (see note on 2:32–43).

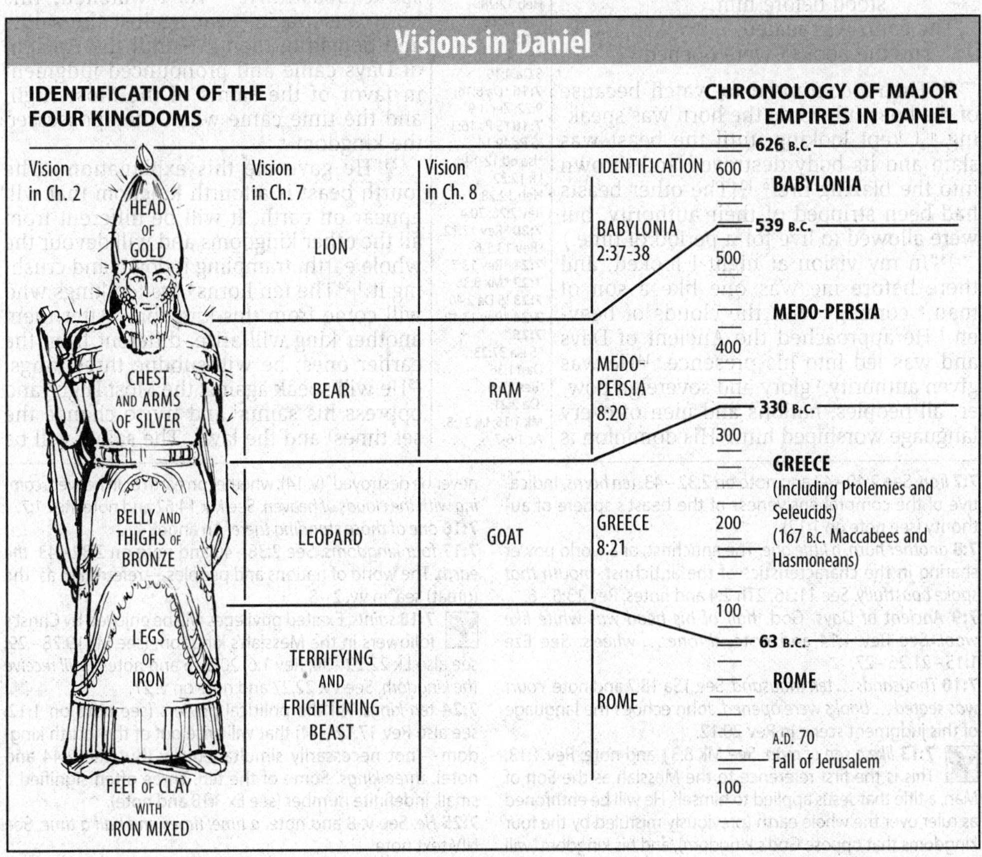

7 “After that, in my vision[x] at night I
looked, and there before me was a fourth
beast — terrifying and frightening and
very powerful. It had large iron[y] teeth;
it crushed and devoured its victims and
trampled[z] underfoot whatever was left.[a] It
was different from all the former beasts,
and it had ten horns.[b]
8 “While I was thinking about the horns,
there before me was another horn, a little[c] one, which came up among them; and
three of the first horns were uprooted before it. This horn had eyes like the eyes
of a man[d] and a mouth that spoke boastfully.[e]
9 “As I looked,

“thrones were set in place,
and the Ancient of Days[f] took his
seat.[g]
His clothing was as white as snow;[h]
the hair of his head was white like
wool.[i]
His throne was flaming with fire,
and its wheels[j] were all ablaze.
10 A river of fire[k] was flowing,
coming out from before him.[l]
Thousands upon thousands attended
him;
ten thousand times ten thousand
stood before him.
The court was seated,
and the books[m] were opened.

11 “Then I continued to watch because
of the boastful words the horn was speaking.[n] I kept looking until the beast was
slain and its body destroyed and thrown
into the blazing fire.[o] 12 (The other beasts
had been stripped of their authority, but
were allowed to live for a period of time.)
13 “In my vision at night I looked, and
there before me was one like a son of
man,[p] coming[q] with the clouds of heav-
en.[r] He approached the Ancient of Days
and was led into his presence. 14 He was
given authority,[s] glory and sovereign power; all peoples, nations and men of every
language worshiped him.[t] His dominion is
an everlasting dominion that will not pass
away, and his kingdom[u] is one that will
never be destroyed.[v]

The Interpretation of the Dream

15 “I, Daniel, was troubled in spirit, and
the visions that passed through my mind
disturbed me.[w] 16 I approached one of
those standing there and asked him the
true meaning of all this.
“So he told me and gave me the interpretation[x] of these things: 17 ‘The four
great beasts are four kingdoms that will
rise from the earth. 18 But the saints[y] of the
Most High will receive the kingdom[z] and
will possess it forever — yes, for ever and
ever.’[a]
19 “Then I wanted to know the true
meaning of the fourth beast, which was
different from all the others and most
terrifying, with its iron teeth and bronze
claws — the beast that crushed and devoured its victims and trampled underfoot whatever was left. 20 I also wanted to
know about the ten horns[b] on its head and
about the other horn that came up, before which three of them fell — the horn
that looked more imposing than the others and that had eyes and a mouth that
spoke boastfully.[c] 21 As I watched, this
horn was waging war against the saints
and defeating them,[d] 22 until the Ancient
of Days came and pronounced judgment
in favor of the saints of the Most High,
and the time came when they possessed
the kingdom.[e]
23 “He gave me this explanation: ‘The
fourth beast is a fourth kingdom that will
appear on earth. It will be different from
all the other kingdoms and will devour the
whole earth, trampling it down and crushing it.[f] 24 The ten horns[g] are ten kings who
will come from this kingdom. After them
another king will arise, different from the
earlier ones; he will subdue three kings.
25 He will speak against the Most High[h] and
oppress his saints[i] and try to change the
set times[j] and the laws. The saints will be

7:7 [x] S Eze 40:2 [y] S Da 2:40 [z] Da 8:10 [a] Da 8:7 [b] S Rev 12:3 **7:8** [c] Da 8:9 [d] Rev 9:7 [e] S Ps 12:3; Rev 13:5-6 **7:9** [f] ver 22 [g] S 1Ki 22:19; 2Ch 18:18; Mt 19:28; Rev 4:2; 20:4 [h] S Mt 28:3 [i] Rev 1:14 [j] S Eze 1:15; 10:6 **7:10** [k] Ps 50:3; 97:3; Isa 30:27 [l] S Dt 33:2; Ps 68:17; Jude 1:14; Rev 5:11 [m] S Ex 32:32; S Ps 56:8; Rev 20:11-15 **7:11** [n] Rev 13:5-6 [o] Rev 19:20 **7:13** [p] S Eze 1:5; S 2:1; Mt 8:20*; Rev 1:13*; 14:14* [q] Isa 13:6; Zep 1:14; Mal 3:2; 4:1 [r] S Dt 33:26; S Rev 1:7 **7:14** [s] S Mt 28:18 [t] Ps 72:11; 102:22 [u] S Isa 16:5 [v] S Da 2:44; Heb 12:28; Rev 11:15 **7:15** [w] S Job 4:15; S Da 4:19 **7:16** [x] Da 8:16; 9:22; Zec 1:9 **7:18** [y] S Ps 16:3 [z] S Ps 49:14 [a] Isa 60:12-14; Lk 12:32; Heb 12:28; Rev 2:26; 20:4 **7:20** [b] Rev 17:12 [c] Rev 13:5-6 **7:21** [d] Rev 13:7 **7:22** [e] Mk 8:35 **7:23** [f] S Da 2:40 **7:24** [g] Rev 17:12 **7:25** [h] S Isa 37:23; Da 11:36 [i] Rev 16:6 [j] Da 2:21; Mk 1:15; Lk 21:8; Ac 1:6-7

7:7 *iron.* See 2:40 – 43 and note on 2:32 – 43. *ten horns.* Indicative of the comprehensiveness of the beast's sphere of authority (see note on 1:12).
7:8 *another horn, a little one.* The antichrist, or a world power sharing in the characteristics of the antichrist. *mouth that spoke boastfully.* See 11:36; 2Th 2:4 and notes; Rev 13:5 – 6.
7:9 *Ancient of Days.* God. *hair of his head was white like wool.* See Rev 1:14 and note. *throne ... wheels.* See Eze 1:15 – 21,26 – 27.
7:10 *Thousands ... ten thousand.* See 1Sa 18:7 and note. *court was seated ... books were opened.* John echoes the language of this judgment scene in Rev 20:12.
7:13 *like a son of man.* See Mk 8:31 and note; Rev 1:13. This is the first reference to the Messiah as the Son of Man, a title that Jesus applied to himself. He will be enthroned as ruler over the whole earth (previously misruled by the four kingdoms that oppose God's kingdom), and his kingdom "will never be destroyed" (v. 14), whether on earth or in heaven. *coming with the clouds of heaven.* See Mk 14:62 and note; Rev 1:7.
7:16 *one of those standing there.* An angel.
7:17 *four kingdoms.* See 2:38 – 40 and note on 2:32 – 43. *the earth.* The world of nations and peoples — referred to as "the (great) sea" in vv. 2 – 3.
7:18 *saints.* Exalted privileges will be enjoyed by Christ's followers in the Messiah's kingdom (see Mt 19:28 – 29; see also Lk 22:29 – 30; Rev 1:6; 20:2 – 6 and notes). *will receive the kingdom.* See vv. 22,27 and note on v. 27.
7:24 *ten kings.* All the political powers (see note on 1:12; see also Rev 17:12 – 14) that will arise out of the fourth kingdom — not necessarily simultaneously (but see 2:44 and note). *three kings.* Some of the ten. Three often signified a small, indefinite number (see Ex 3:18 and note).
7:25 *He.* See v. 8 and note. *a time, times and half a time.* See NIV text note.

handed over to him for a time, times and
half a time.[a][k]
26“ ‘But the court will sit, and his power will be taken away and completely destroyed[l] forever. 27Then the sovereignty,
power and greatness of the kingdoms[m]
under the whole heaven will be handed
over to the saints,[n] the people of the Most
High.[o] His kingdom will be an everlasting[p]
kingdom, and all rulers will worship[q] and
obey him.’
28“This is the end of the matter. I, Daniel, was deeply troubled[r] by my thoughts,[s]
and my face turned pale,[t] but I kept the
matter to myself.”

Daniel's Vision of a Ram and a Goat

8 In the third year of King Belshazzar's[u]
reign, I, Daniel, had a vision,[v] after the
one that had already appeared to me. 2In
my vision I saw myself in the citadel of
Susa[w] in the province of Elam;[x] in the vision I was beside the Ulai Canal. 3I looked
up,[y] and there before me was a ram[z] with
two horns, standing beside the canal, and
the horns were long. One of the horns was
longer than the other but grew up later.
4I watched the ram as he charged toward
the west and the north and the south. No
animal could stand against him, and none
could rescue from his power.[a] He did as he
pleased[b] and became great.
5As I was thinking about this, suddenly a goat with a prominent horn between
his eyes came from the west, crossing the
whole earth without touching the ground.
6He came toward the two-horned ram I
had seen standing beside the canal and
charged at him in great rage. 7I saw him
attack the ram furiously, striking the ram
and shattering his two horns. The ram
was powerless to stand against him; the
goat knocked him to the ground and trampled on him,[c] and none could rescue the
ram from his power.[d] 8The goat became
very great, but at the height of his power
his large horn was broken off,[e] and in its
place four prominent horns grew up toward the four winds of heaven.[f]
9Out of one of them came another horn,
which started small[g] but grew in power to
the south and to the east and toward the
Beautiful Land.[h] 10It grew until it reached[i]
the host of the heavens, and it threw some
of the starry host down to the earth[j] and
trampled[k] on them. 11It set itself up to be
as great as the Prince[l] of the host;[m] it took
away the daily sacrifice[n] from him, and the
place of his sanctuary was brought low.[o]
12Because of rebellion, the host ⌞of the
saints⌟[b] and the daily sacrifice were given
over to it. It prospered in everything it did,
and truth was thrown to the ground.[p]
13Then I heard a holy one[q] speaking,
and another holy one said to him, “How
long will it take for the vision to be fulfilled[r]—the vision concerning the daily
sacrifice, the rebellion that causes desolation, and the surrender of the sanctuary
and of the host that will be trampled[s] underfoot?”
14He said to me, “It will take 2,300 evenings and mornings; then the sanctuary
will be reconsecrated.”[t]

The Interpretation of the Vision

15While I, Daniel, was watching the vision[u] and trying to understand it, there before me stood one who looked like a man.[v]
16And I heard a man's voice from the Ulai[w]
calling, “Gabriel,[x] tell this man the meaning of the vision.”[y]

[a] 25 Or *for a year, two years and half a year*
[b] 12 Or *rebellion, the armies*

7:25 [k]Da 8:24; 12:7; S Rev 11:2 **7:26** [l]Rev 19:20 **7:27** [m]S Isa 14:2 [n]1Co 6:2 [o]Ge 14:18 [p]S 2Sa 7:13; Ps 145:13; S Da 2:44; S 4:34; S Lk 1:33; Rev 11:15; 22:5 [q]S Ps 22:27; 72:11; 86:9 **7:28** [r]S Isa 21:3; S Da 4:19 [s]S Ps 13:2 [t]S Job 4:15 **8:1** [u]S Da 5:1 [v]S Da 1:17 **8:2** [w]S Ezr 4:9; S Est 2:8 [x]S Ge 10:22 **8:3** [y]Da 10:5 [z]Rev 13:11 **8:4** [a]Isa 41:3 [b]Da 11:3, 16 **8:7** [c]S Da 7:7 [d]Da 11:11, 16 **8:8** [e]2Ch 26:16-21; S Da 5:20 [f]S Da 7:2; Rev 7:1 **8:9** [g]Da 7:8 [h]S Eze 20:6; Da 11:16 **8:10** [i]S Isa 14:13 [j]Rev 8:10; 12:4 [k]S Da 7:7 **8:11** [l]ver 25 [m]Da 11:36-37 [n]Eze 46:13-14 [o]Da 11:31; 12:11 **8:12** [p]S Isa 48:1 **8:13** [q]S Dt 33:2; S Da 4:23 [r]Da 12:6 [s]S Isa 28:18; S Lk 21:24; Rev 11:2 **8:14** [t]Da 12:11-12 **8:15** [u]ver 1 [v]S Eze 2:1; Da 10:16-18 **8:16** [w]ver 2 [x]Da 9:21; S Lk 1:19 [y]S Da 7:16

7:27 *handed over to the saints.* For their benefit. God and the Messiah will rule (see Rev 19–22).
8:1—12:13 These chapters are written in Hebrew (see note on 2:4).
8:1 *third year.* About 551 B.C. The events of ch. 8 preceded those of ch. 5. *after the one that had already appeared to me.* Two years earlier (see 7:1 and note).
8:2 *citadel of Susa … Elam.* See notes on Ezr 4:9; Est 1:2.
8:3 The ram represents the Medo-Persian empire (v. 20). The longer of his two horns reflects the predominant position of Persia (see 7:5 and note on 7:4–7).
8:5 The rapidly charging goat is Greece, and the “prominent horn” is Alexander the Great, “the first king” (v. 21; see chart, p. 1323).
8:7 *shattering his two horns.* Greece crushes Medo-Persia.
8:8 *his large horn was broken off.* The death of Alexander the Great at the height of his power (323 B.C.). *four prominent horns.* Equivalent to the “four heads” of 7:6 (see note on 7:4–7).
8:9–12 “Another horn” (v. 9) emerges not from the ten horns belonging to the fourth kingdom (as in 7:8), but rather from one of the four horns belonging to the third kingdom. The horn that “started small” is Antiochus IV Epiphanes, who during the last few years of his reign (168–164 B.C.) made a determined effort to destroy the Jewish faith. He in turn served as a type of the even more ruthless beast of the last days (the antichrist), who is also referred to in 7:8 as a “little” horn. Antiochus was to extend his power over Israel, “the Beautiful Land” (v. 9; see Jer 3:19 and note), and defeat the godly believers there (referred to as “the host of the heavens,” v. 10; see also v. 12), many of whom died for their faith. Then he set himself up to be the equal of God (“the Prince of the host,” v. 11) and ordered the daily sacrifices to end. Eventually the army of Judas Maccabeus recaptured Jerusalem and rededicated the temple (v. 14) to the Lord (December, 165)—the origin of the Feast of Hanukkah (see Jn 10:22 and note), still celebrated by Jews today (in the Apocrypha see 1 Maccabees 1–4; see also bottom of chart, pp. 178–179).
8:13 *a holy one.* An angel.
8:14 There were two daily sacrifices for the continual burnt offering (see 9:21; Ex 29:38–39 and note), representing the atonement required for Israel as a whole. The “2,300 evenings and mornings” probably refer to the number of sacrifices consecutively offered on 1,150 days, the interval between the desecration of the Lord's altar by Antiochus Epiphanes and its reconsecration by Judas Maccabeus on Kislev 25, 165 B.C.
8:16 *Gabriel.* An angel (see Lk 1:19 and note).

17 As he came near the place where I was
standing, I was terrified and fell prostrate.[z]
"Son of man," he said to me, "understand
that the vision concerns the time of the
end."[a]
18 While he was speaking to me, I was in
a deep sleep, with my face to the ground.[b]
Then he touched me and raised me to my
feet.[c]
19 He said: "I am going to tell you what
will happen later in the time of wrath,[d]
because the vision concerns the appointed time[e] of the end.[a f] 20 The two-horned
ram that you saw represents the kings of
Media and Persia.[g] 21 The shaggy goat is
the king of Greece,[h] and the large horn between his eyes is the first king.[i] 22 The four
horns that replaced the one that was broken off represent four kingdoms that will
emerge from his nation but will not have
the same power.
23 "In the latter part of their reign, when
rebels have become completely wicked,
a stern-faced king, a master of intrigue,
will arise. 24 He will become very strong,
but not by his own power. He will cause
astounding devastation and will succeed
in whatever he does. He will destroy the
mighty men and the holy people.[j] 25 He
will cause deceit[k] to prosper, and he will
consider himself superior. When they feel
secure, he will destroy many and take his
stand against the Prince of princes.[l] Yet
he will be destroyed, but not by human
power.[m]
26 "The vision of the evenings and mornings that has been given you is true,[n] but
seal[o] up the vision, for it concerns the distant future."[p]
27 I, Daniel, was exhausted and lay ill[q] for
several days. Then I got up and went about
the king's business.[r] I was appalled[s] by the
vision; it was beyond understanding.

Daniel's Prayer

9 In the first year of Darius[t] son of Xerxes[b u] (a Mede by descent), who was
made ruler over the Babylonian[c] kingdom— 2 in the first year of his reign, I,
Daniel, understood from the Scriptures,
according to the word of the LORD given to
Jeremiah the prophet, that the desolation
of Jerusalem would last seventy[v] years.
3 So I turned to the Lord God and pleaded
with him in prayer and petition, in fasting,[w] and in sackcloth and ashes.[x]
4 I prayed to the LORD my God and confessed:[y]

"O Lord, the great and awesome
God,[z] who keeps his covenant of
love[a] with all who love him and obey
his commands, 5 we have sinned[b] and
done wrong.[c] We have been wicked
and have rebelled; we have turned
away[d] from your commands and
laws.[e] 6 We have not listened[f] to your
servants the prophets,[g] who spoke in
your name to our kings, our princes
and our fathers,[h] and to all the people
of the land.
7 "Lord, you are righteous,[i] but this
day we are covered with shame[j]—the
men of Judah and people of Jerusalem and all Israel, both near and far,
in all the countries where you have
scattered[k] us because of our unfaithfulness[l] to you.[m] 8 O LORD, we and our
kings, our princes and our fathers
are covered with shame because we
have sinned against you.[n] 9 The Lord
our God is merciful and forgiving,[o]
even though we have rebelled against
him;[p] 10 we have not obeyed the LORD
our God or kept the laws he gave us
through his servants the prophets.[q]
11 All Israel has transgressed[r] your
law[s] and turned away, refusing to
obey you.
"Therefore the curses[t] and sworn
judgments[u] written in the Law of Moses, the servant of God, have been
poured out on us, because we have

[a] 19 *Or because the end will be at the appointed time*
[b] 1 Hebrew *Ahasuerus* [c] 1 Or *Chaldean*

8:17 [z] Eze 1:28; 44:4; S Da 2:46; Rev 1:17 [a] ver 19; Hab 2:3 **8:18** [b] Da 10:9 [c] S Eze 2:2; Da 10:16-18; Zec 4:1 **8:19** [d] S Isa 10:25 [e] S Ps 102:13 [f] Hab 2:3 **8:20** [g] S Eze 27:10 **8:21** [h] Da 10:20 [i] Da 11:3 **8:24** [j] S Da 7:25; 11:36 **8:25** [k] Da 11:23 [l] Da 11:36 [m] S Da 2:34; 11:21 **8:26** [n] Da 10:1 [o] S Isa 8:16; S 29:11; Rev 10:4; 22:10 [p] Da 10:14 **8:27** [q] Da 10:8 [r] S Da 2:48 [s] S Isa 21:3; S Da 4:19 **9:1** [t] S Da 5:31 [u] S Ezr 4:6 **9:2** [v] S 2Ch 36:21; Jer 29:10; Zec 1:12; 7:5 **9:3** [w] S 2Ch 20:3 [x] S 2Sa 13:19; S Ne 1:4; Jer 29:12; Da 10:12; Jnh 3:6 **9:4** [y] S 1Ki 8:30 [z] S Dt 7:21 [a] Dt 7:9; S 1Ki 8:23 **9:5** [b] S Jer 8:14 [c] Ps 106:6 [d] Isa 53:6 [e] ver 11; La 1:20; S 3:42 **9:6** [f] S 2Ki 18:12 [g] S 2Ch 36:16; S Jer 44:5; Jas 5:10; Rev 10:7 [h] S 2Ch 29:6 **9:7** [i] S Ezr 9:15; S Isa 42:6 [j] Ezr 9:7; Ps 44:15 [k] Dt 4:27; Am 9:9 [l] S Dt 7:3 [m] S Jer 3:25; S 24:9; S Eze 39:23-24 **9:8** [n] S Ne 9:33; S Jer 14:20; S Eze 16:63 **9:9** [o] S Ex 34:7; S 2Sa 24:14; Jer 42:12 [p] S Ne 9:17; Jer 14:7 **9:10** [q] 2Ki 17:13-15; S 18:12; Rev 10:7 **9:11** [r] S Jer 2:29 [s] 2Ki 22:16 [t] S Dt 11:26; S 13:15; S 28:15 [u] 2Ki 17:23

8:17 *Son of man.* Not to be confused with the "one like a son of man" in 7:13 (see note there; see also note on Eze 2:1).
8:21 See v. 5 and note.
8:22 See v. 8 and note.
8:23–25 A description of Antiochus IV and his rise to power by intrigue and deceit (he was not the rightful successor to the Seleucid throne).
8:25 *consider himself superior.* Antiochus IV called himself Epiphanes ("God manifest"). *Prince of princes.* God. *destroyed, but not by human power.* Antiochus died in 164 B.C. at Tabae in Persia through illness or accident; God "destroyed" him.
8:26 *vision of the evenings and mornings.* See v. 14 and note.
9:1 *first year.* 539–538 B.C. *Darius ... a Mede.* See 5:31 and note. *Xerxes.* See NIV text note; not the later Xerxes of the book of Esther.
9:2 *Jeremiah ... seventy years.* See note on Jer 25:11–12.
9:3–19 Daniel's prayer contains expressions of humility (v. 3), worship (v. 4), confession (vv. 5–15) and petition (vv. 16–19). See similar prayers in Ezr 9:5–15; Ne 9:5–37 (see note there).
9:3 *sackcloth and ashes.* See notes on Ge 37:34; Rev 11:3.
9:4 *who keeps his covenant of love.* See Dt 7:9,12 and note. *who love him and obey his commands.* See Ne 1:5; cf. Ex 20:6 and note.
9:6 *your servants the prophets.* See v. 10; see also Jer 7:25; Zec 1:6 and notes.
9:7 *scattered us because of our unfaithfulness.* See 2Ki 17:7–23 and note; 2Ch 36:15–20.
9:11 *curses ... written in the Law.* See Lev 26:33; Dt 28:64 and note.

sinned[v] against you. 12You have fulfilled[w] the words spoken against us
and against our rulers by bringing
upon us great disaster.[x] Under the
whole heaven nothing has ever been
done like[y] what has been done to
Jerusalem.[z] 13Just as it is written in
the Law of Moses, all this disaster
has come upon us, yet we have not
sought the favor of the LORD[a] our God
by turning from our sins and giving
attention to your truth.[b] 14The LORD
did not hesitate to bring the disaster[c]
upon us, for the LORD our God is righteous in everything he does;[d] yet we
have not obeyed him.[e]
15"Now, O Lord our God, who
brought your people out of Egypt with
a mighty hand[f] and who made for
yourself a name[g] that endures to this
day, we have sinned, we have done
wrong. 16O Lord, in keeping with all
your righteous acts,[h] turn away[i] your
anger and your wrath[j] from Jerusalem,[k] your city, your holy hill.[l] Our
sins and the iniquities of our fathers
have made Jerusalem and your people an object of scorn[m] to all those
around us.
17"Now, our God, hear the prayers
and petitions of your servant. For
your sake, O Lord, look with favor[n]
on your desolate sanctuary. 18Give
ear,[o] O God, and hear;[p] open your
eyes and see[q] the desolation of the
city that bears your Name.[r] We do not
make requests of you because we are
righteous, but because of your great
mercy.[s] 19O Lord, listen! O Lord, forgive![t] O Lord, hear and act! For your
sake,[u] O my God, do not delay, because your city and your people bear
your Name."

9:11 [v]Isa 1:4-6; Jer 8:5-10 **9:12** [w]S Isa 44:26; Zec 1:6 [x]S Jer 44:23 [y]Jer 30:7 [z]Jer 44:2-6; Eze 5:9; Da 12:1; Joel 2:2; Zec 7:12 **9:13** [a]S Dt 4:29; S Isa 31:1 [b]S Isa 9:13; Jer 2:30 **9:14** [c]S Jer 18:8; S 44:27 [d]S Ge 18:25; S 2Ch 12:6; S Jer 12:1 [e]S Ne 9:33; S Jer 32:23; S 40:3 **9:15** [f]S Ex 3:20; S Jer 32:21 [g]S Ne 9:10 **9:16** [h]S Jdg 5:11; Ps 31:1 [i]S Isa 5:25 [j]S Ps 85:3 [k]Jer 32:32 [l]S Ex 15:17; S Ps 48:1 [m]S Ps 39:8; S Eze 5:14 **9:17** [n]Nu 6:24-26; Ps 80:19 **9:18** [o]S Ps 5:1 [p]Ps 116:1 [q]Ps 80:14 [r]S Dt 28:10; S Isa 37:17; Jer 7:10-12; 25:29 [s]Lk 18:13 **9:19** [t]Ps 44:23 [u]S 1Sa 12:22

The Seventy "Sevens"

20While I was speaking and praying,
confessing[v] my sin and the sin of my people Israel and making my request to the
LORD my God for his holy hill[w]— 21while I
was still in prayer, Gabriel,[x] the man I had
seen in the earlier vision, came to me in
swift flight about the time of the evening
sacrifice.[y] 22He instructed me and said to
me, "Daniel, I have now come to give you
insight and understanding.[z] 23As soon as
you began to pray,[a] an answer was given,
which I have come to tell you, for you are
highly esteemed.[b] Therefore, consider the
message and understand the vision:[c]
24"Seventy 'sevens'[a] are decreed for
your people and your holy city[d] to finish[b] transgression, to put an end to sin, to
atone[e] for wickedness, to bring in everlasting righteousness,[f] to seal up vision and
prophecy and to anoint the most holy.[c]
25"Know and understand this: From
the issuing of the decree[d] to restore and
rebuild[g] Jerusalem until the Anointed
One,[e][h] the ruler,[i] comes, there will be sev-
en 'sevens,' and sixty-two 'sevens.' It will
be rebuilt with streets and a trench, but
in times of trouble.[j] 26After the sixty-two
'sevens,' the Anointed One will be cut off[k]
and will have nothing.[f] The people of the
ruler who will come will destroy the city
and the sanctuary. The end will come like
a flood:[l] War will continue until the end,
and desolations[m] have been decreed.[n] 27He
will confirm a covenant with many for one

9:20 [v]S Ezr 10:1 [w]S ver 3; Ps 145:18; S Isa 58:9 **9:21** [x]S Da 8:16; S Lk 1:19 [y]S Ex 29:39 **9:22** [z]S Da 7:16; 10:14; Am 3:7 **9:23** [a]S Isa 65:24 [b]Da 10:19; Lk 1:28 [c]Da 10:11-12; Mt 24:15 **9:24** [d]S Isa 1:26 [e]S Isa 53:10 [f]S Isa 56:1; Heb 9:12 **9:25** [g]S Ezr 4:24; S 6:15 [h]Mt 1:17; Jn 4:25 [i]S 1Sa 13:14 [j]S Ezr 3:3 **9:26** [k]S Isa 53:8; Mt 16:21 [l]Isa 28:2; Da 11:10; Na 1:8 [m]S Ps 46:8 [n]Isa 61:1; S Eze 4:5-6; Hag 2:23; Zec 4:14

[a] 24 Or *'weeks'*; also in verses 25 and 26 [b] 24 Or *restrain* [c] 24 Or *Most Holy Place*; or *most holy One* [d] 25 Or *word* [e] 25 Or *an anointed one*; also in verse 26 [f] 26 Or *off and will have no one*; or *off, but not for himself*

9:14 *the LORD our God is righteous.* See Ps 4:1; Jer 12:1 and notes.

9:18 *city that bears your Name.* Jerusalem (1Ki 11:36; cf. Ps 132:13 and note; see Jer 25:29 and note). *Name.* See Dt 12:5 and note. *because of your great mercy.* God answers prayer because of his grace, not because of our works.

9:20 *While I was speaking.* See Isa 65:24. *holy hill.* Zion (see Ps 2:6 and note).

9:21 *Gabriel.* See 8:16 and note. *evening sacrifice.* See note on Ps 141:2.

9:24 *sevens.* Probably seven-year periods of time, making a total of 490 years, but the numbers may be symbolic. Of the six purposes mentioned (all to be fulfilled through the Messiah), some believe that the last three were not achieved by the crucifixion and resurrection of Christ but await his further action: the establishment of everlasting righteousness (on earth), the complete fulfillment of vision and prophecy, and the anointing of the "most holy" (see NIV text note).

9:25–27 The time between the decree authorizing the rebuilding of Jerusalem (v. 25) and the coming of the Messiah ("the Anointed One") was to be 69 (7 plus 62) "sevens," or 483 years (see note on Ezr 7:11). The "seven 'sevens'" may refer to the period of the complete restoration of Jerusalem (partially narrated in Ezra and Nehemiah) and the "sixty-two 'sevens'" to the period between that restoration and the Messiah's coming to Israel. The final (70th) "seven" is not mentioned specifically until v. 27, following the prophecy of the destruction of Jerusalem by "the people of the ruler who will come" (Titus in A.D. 70). Therefore, while many hold that the 70th "seven" was fulfilled during Christ's earthly ministry and the years immediately following, others conclude that there is an indeterminate interval between the 69th and the 70th "seven"—a period of "war" and "desolations" (v. 26). According to this latter opinion, in the 70th "seven" the little horn or beast (the antichrist) of the last days (referred to here as the one who sets up an "abomination that causes desolation" and whose hostile acts against God's people are similar to those of the Roman general [later, emperor] Titus; see Rev 13:1–8 and notes) will establish a covenant for seven years with the Jews (the "many") but will violate the covenant halfway through that period (but see also note on v. 27). The cutting off of the Anointed One (v. 26) refers to the crucifixion of Christ.

9:27 *He will confirm a covenant ... will put an end to sacrifice.* According to some, a reference to the Messiah's

'seven.'[a] In the middle of the 'seven'[a] he will put an end to sacrifice and offering. And on a wing ⌞of the temple⌟ he will set up an abomination that causes desolation, until the end that is decreed[o] is poured out on him.[b]"[c]

Daniel's Vision of a Man

10 In the third year of Cyrus[p] king of Persia, a revelation was given to Daniel (who was called Belteshazzar).[q] Its message was true[r] and it concerned a great war.[d] The understanding of the message came to him in a vision.

2At that time I, Daniel, mourned[s] for three weeks. 3I ate no choice food; no meat or wine touched my lips;[t] and I used no lotions at all until the three weeks were over.

4On the twenty-fourth day of the first month, as I was standing on the bank[u] of the great river, the Tigris,[v] 5I looked up[w] and there before me was a man dressed in linen,[x] with a belt of the finest gold[y] around his waist. 6His body was like chrysolite,[z] his face like lightning,[a] his eyes like flaming torches,[b] his arms and legs like the gleam of burnished bronze,[c] and his voice[d] like the sound of a multitude.

7I, Daniel, was the only one who saw the vision; the men with me did not see it,[e] but such terror overwhelmed them that they fled and hid themselves. 8So I was left alone,[f] gazing at this great vision; I had no strength left,[g] my face turned deathly pale[h] and I was helpless.[i] 9Then I heard him speaking, and as I listened to him, I fell into a deep sleep, my face to the ground.[j]

10A hand touched me[k] and set me trembling on my hands and knees.[l] 11He said, "Daniel, you who are highly esteemed,[m] consider carefully the words I am about to speak to you, and stand up,[n] for I have now been sent to you." And when he said this to me, I stood up trembling.

12Then he continued, "Do not be afraid,[o] Daniel. Since the first day that you set your mind to gain understanding and to humble[p] yourself before your God, your words[q] were heard, and I have come in response to them.[r] 13But the prince[s] of the Persian kingdom resisted me twenty-one days. Then Michael,[t] one of the chief princes, came to help me, because I was detained there with the king of Persia. 14Now I have come to explain[u] to you what will happen to your people in the future,[v] for the vision concerns a time yet to come.[w]"

15While he was saying this to me, I bowed with my face toward the ground and was speechless.[x] 16Then one who looked like a man[e] touched my lips, and I opened my mouth and began to speak.[y] I said to the one standing before me, "I am overcome with anguish[z] because of the vision, my lord, and I am helpless. 17How can I, your servant, talk with you, my lord? My strength is gone and I can hardly breathe."[a]

18Again the one who looked like a man touched[b] me and gave me strength.[c] 19"Do not be afraid, O man highly esteemed,"[d] he said. "Peace![e] Be strong now; be strong."[f]

When he spoke to me, I was strengthened and said, "Speak, my lord, since you have given me strength."[g]

20So he said, "Do you know why I have come to you? Soon I will return to fight against the prince of Persia, and when I go, the prince of Greece[h] will come; 21but first I will tell you what is written in the Book of Truth.[i] (No one supports me against them except Michael,[j] your prince.

11 1And in the first year of Darius[k] the Mede, I took my stand to support and protect him.)

The Kings of the South and the North

2"Now then, I tell you the truth:[l] Three more kings will appear in Persia, and then a fourth, who will be far richer than all the

9:27 [o]S Isa 10:22 **10:1** [p]S Da 1:21 [q]S Da 1:7 [r]Da 8:26 **10:2** [s]S Ezr 9:4 **10:3** [t]S Da 6:18 **10:4** [u]Da 12:5 [v]S Ge 2:14 **10:5** [w]Da 8:3 [x]S Eze 9:2; Rev 15:6 [y]Jer 10:9 **10:6** [z]S Ex 28:20 [a]Mt 17:2; S 28:3 [b]Job 41:19; Rev 19:12 [c]S Eze 1:7; S Rev 1:15 [d]S Eze 1:24 **10:7** [e]2Ki 6:17-20; Ac 9:7 **10:8** [f]Ge 32:24 [g]S Job 4:14; Da 8:27 [h]S Job 4:15 [i]Hab 3:16 **10:9** [j]Da 8:18; Mt 17:6 **10:10** [k]Jer 1:9 [l]Rev 1:17 **10:11** [m]S Ge 6:9; Da 9:23 [n]S Eze 2:1 **10:12** [o]S Mt 14:27 [p]S Lev 16:31; S Da 9:3 [q]S Isa 65:24 [r]Da 9:20 **10:13** [s]Isa 24:21 [t]ver 21; Da 12:1; S Jude 1:9 **10:14** [u]S Da 9:22 [v]S Eze 12:27 [w]S Da 2:28; 8:26; Hab 2:3 **10:15** [x]Eze 24:27; Lk 1:20 **10:16** [y]S Isa 6:7; Jer 1:9; Da 8:15-18 [z]S Isa 21:3 **10:17** [a]S Da 4:19 **10:18** [b]ver 16 [c]S Da 8:18 **10:19** [d]S Da 9:23 [e]Jdg 6:23; S Isa 35:4 [f]Jos 1:9 [g]Isa 6:1-8 **10:20** [h]Da 8:21; 11:2 **10:21** [i]Da 11:2 [j]S ver 13; S Jude 1:9 **11:1** [k]S Da 5:31 **11:2** [l]Da 10:21

[a] 27 Or *'week'* [b] 27 Or *it* [c] 27 Or *And one who causes desolation will come upon the pinnacle of the abominable ⌞temple⌟, until the end that is decreed is poured out on the desolated ⌞city⌟.* [d] 1 Or *true and burdensome* [e] 16 Most manuscripts of the Masoretic Text; one manuscript of the Masoretic Text, Dead Sea Scrolls and Septuagint *Then something that looked like a man's hand*

("the Anointed One," v. 26) instituting the new covenant and putting "an end" to the OT sacrificial system; according to others, a reference to the antichrist's ("the [ultimate] ruler who will come," v. 26) making a treaty with the Jews in the future and then disrupting their system of worship. *abomination that causes desolation.* See note on 11:31.

10:1 *third year of Cyrus.* 537 B.C. This is the third year after his conquest of Babylonia in 539 (see note on 1:1).

10:3 See 1:8–16 and note on 1:8.

10:5–6 See 7:9; Rev 1:12–16 and notes.

10:7 Cf. Ac 9:7.

10:13 *prince of the Persian kingdom.* Apparently reference is to a spiritual power viewed as exercising influence over the Persian realm in the interests of Satan (see also v. 20 and note). His resistance was finally overcome by the archangel Michael, "the great prince who protects" the people of God (12:1).

10:14 *what will happen to your people in the future.* See chs. 11–12.

10:16 *touched my lips, and I … began to speak.* See Isa 6:7; Jer 1:9 and notes.

10:20 *prince of Greece.* See note on v. 13. This spiritual power will also have to be opposed.

10:21 *Book of Truth.* See 12:1; perhaps a reference to God's book of the destinies of all human beings (see Ex 32:32; Ps 69:28 and notes).

11:1 *Darius the Mede.* See note on 5:31.

11:2 *Three more kings.* Cambyses (530–522 B.C.), Pseudo-Smerdis or Gaumata (522) and Darius I (522–486). *fourth.*

others. When he has gained power by his wealth, he will stir up everyone against the kingdom of Greece.[m] 3Then a mighty king will appear, who will rule with great power and do as he pleases.[n] 4After he has appeared, his empire will be broken up and parceled out toward the four winds of heaven.[o] It will not go to his descendants, nor will it have the power he exercised, because his empire will be uprooted[p] and given to others.

5"The king of the South will become strong, but one of his commanders will become even stronger than he and will rule his own kingdom with great power. 6After some years, they will become allies. The daughter of the king of the South will go to the king of the North to make an alliance, but she will not retain her power, and he and his power[a] will not last. In those days she will be handed over, together with her royal escort and her father[b] and the one who supported her.

7"One from her family line will arise to take her place. He will attack the forces of the king of the North[q] and enter his fortress; he will fight against them and be victorious. 8He will also seize their gods,[r] their metal images and their valuable articles of silver and gold and carry them off to Egypt.[s] For some years he will leave the king of the North alone. 9Then the king of the North will invade the realm of the king of the South but will retreat to his own country. 10His sons will prepare for war and assemble a great army, which will sweep on like an irresistible flood[t] and carry the battle as far as his fortress.

11"Then the king of the South will march out in a rage and fight against the king of the North, who will raise a large army, but it will be defeated.[u] 12When the army is carried off, the king of the South will be filled with pride and will slaughter many thousands, yet he will not remain triumphant. 13For the king of the North will muster another army, larger than the first; and after several years, he will advance with a huge army fully equipped.

14"In those times many will rise against the king of the South. The violent men among your own people will rebel in fulfillment of the vision, but without success. 15Then the king of the North will come and build up siege ramps[v] and will capture a fortified city. The forces of the South will be powerless to resist; even their best troops will not have the strength to stand. 16The invader will do as he pleases;[w] no one will be able to stand against him.[x] He will establish himself in the Beautiful Land and will have the power to destroy it.[y] 17He will determine to come with the might of his entire kingdom and will make an alliance with the king of the South. And he will give him a daughter in marriage in order to overthrow the kingdom, but his plans[c] will not succeed[z] or help him. 18Then he will turn his attention to the coastlands[a] and will take many of them, but a commander will put an end to his insolence and will turn his insolence back upon him.[b] 19After this, he will turn back toward the fortresses of his own country but will stumble and fall,[c] to be seen no more.[d]

20"His successor will send out a tax collector to maintain the royal splendor.[e] In a

11:2 [m]S Da 10:20 **11:3** [n]S Da 8:4,21 **11:4** [o]S Da 7:2; 8:22 [p]S Jer 42:10 **11:7** [q]ver 6 **11:8** [r]Isa 37:19; S 46:1-2 [s]Jer 43:12 **11:10** [t]Isa 8:8; Jer 46:8; S Da 9:26 **11:11** [u]Da 8:7-8 **11:15** [v]S Eze 4:2 **11:16** [w]S Da 8:4 [x]S Jos 1:5; S Da 8:7 [y]S Da 8:9 **11:17** [z]S Ps 20:4 **11:18** [a]S Isa 66:19; S Jer 25:22 [b]Hos 12:14 **11:19** [c]S Ps 27:2; S 46:2 [d]S Ps 37:36; S Eze 26:21 **11:20** [e]Isa 60:17

[a] 6 Or *offspring* [b] 6 Or *child* (see Vulgate and Syriac) [c] 17 Or *but she*

Xerxes I (486–465; see note on Est 1:1), who attempted to conquer Greece in 480.
11:3 *mighty king.* Alexander the Great (336–323).
11:4 *four winds.* See 7:2–3 and note on 7:4–7 (four heads).
11:5 *king of the South.* Ptolemy I Soter (323–285 B.C.) of Egypt (see chart and map, pp. 1330–1331). *one of his commanders.* Seleucus I Nicator (311–280). *his own kingdom.* Initially Babylonia, to which he then added extensive territories both east and west.
11:6 *daughter of the king of the South.* Berenice, daughter of Ptolemy II Philadelphus (285–246 B.C.) of Egypt. *king of the North.* Antiochus II Theos (261–246) of Syria. *alliance.* A treaty cemented by the marriage of Berenice to Antiochus. *she will not retain her power, and he ... will not last.* Antiochus's former wife, Laodice, conspired to have Berenice and Antiochus put to death. *her father.* Berenice's father Ptolemy died at about the same time.
11:7 *One from her family line.* Berenice's brother, Ptolemy III Euergetes (246–221 B.C.) of Egypt, who did away with Laodice. *king of the North.* Seleucus II Callinicus (246–226) of Syria. *his fortress.* Either (1) Seleucia (see Ac 13:4 and note), which was the port of Antioch, or (2) Antioch itself.
11:8 *their gods.* Images of Syrian deities, and also of Egyptian gods that the Persian Cambyses had carried off after conquering Egypt in 525 B.C.
11:10 *His sons.* Seleucus III Ceraunus (226–223 B.C.) and Antiochus III (the Great) (223–187), sons of Seleucus II. *his fortress.* Ptolemy's fortress at Raphia (southwest of Gaza).
11:11 *king of the South.* Ptolemy IV Philopator (221–203 B.C.) of Egypt. *king of the North.* Antiochus III. *defeated.* At Raphia in 217.
11:12 *slaughter many thousands.* The Greek historian Polybius records that Antiochus lost nearly 10,000 infantrymen at Raphia.
11:14 *king of the South.* Ptolemy V Epiphanes (203–181 B.C.) of Egypt. *violent men among your own people.* Jews who joined the forces of Antiochus. *without success.* The Ptolemaic general Scopas crushed the rebellion in 200.
11:15 *fortified city.* The Mediterranean port of Sidon.
11:16 *The invader.* Antiochus, who was in control of the Holy Land by 197 B.C. *Beautiful Land.* See note on 8:9–12.
11:17 *he will give him a daughter in marriage.* Antiochus gave his daughter Cleopatra I in marriage to Ptolemy V in 194 B.C.
11:18 *he.* Antiochus. *coastlands.* Asia Minor and perhaps also mainland Greece. *commander.* The Roman consul Lucius Cornelius Scipio Asiaticus, who defeated Antiochus at Magnesia in Asia Minor in 190 B.C.
11:19 *stumble and fall.* Antiochus died in 187 B.C. while attempting to plunder a temple in the province of Elymais.
11:20 *His successor.* Seleucus IV Philopator (187–175 B.C.),

few years, however, he will be destroyed,
yet not in anger or in battle.
21"He will be succeeded by a contemptible[f] person who has not been given the
honor of royalty.[g] He will invade the kingdom when its people feel secure, and he
will seize it through intrigue. 22Then an
overwhelming army will be swept away[h]
before him; both it and a prince of the covenant will be destroyed.[i] 23After coming to
an agreement with him, he will act deceitfully,[j] and with only a few people he will
rise to power. 24When the richest provinces
feel secure, he will invade them and will
achieve what neither his fathers nor his
forefathers did. He will distribute plunder,
loot and wealth among his followers.[k] He
will plot the overthrow of fortresses—but
only for a time.
25"With a large army he will stir up his
strength and courage against the king of
the South. The king of the South will wage
war with a large and very powerful army,
but he will not be able to stand because
of the plots devised against him. 26Those
who eat from the king's provisions will
try to destroy him; his army will be swept
away, and many will fall in battle. 27The
two kings, with their hearts bent on evil,[l]
will sit at the same table and lie[m] to each
other, but to no avail, because an end will
still come at the appointed time.[n] 28The
king of the North will return to his own
country with great wealth, but his heart
will be set against the holy covenant. He
will take action against it and then return
to his own country.
29"At the appointed time he will invade
the South again, but this time the outcome will be different from what it was
before. 30Ships of the western coastlands[a][o]
will oppose him, and he will lose heart.[p]

11:21 [f]Da 4:17 [g]S Da 8:25
11:22 [h]S Isa 28:15 [i]Da 8:10-11
11:23 [j]Da 8:25
11:24 [k]Ne 9:25
11:27 [l]Ps 64:6 [m]Ps 12:2; Jer 9:5 [n]Hab 2:3
11:30 [o]S Ge 10:4 [p]S 1Sa 17:32

[a] 30 Hebrew *of Kittim*

son and successor of Antiochus the Great. *tax collector.* Seleucus's finance minister, Heliodorus. *he will be destroyed.* Seleucus was the victim of a conspiracy engineered by Heliodorus.

11:21 *contemptible person.* Seleucus's younger brother, Antiochus IV Epiphanes (175–164 B.C.). *not been given the honor of royalty.* Antiochus seized power while the rightful heir to the throne, the son of Seleucus (later to become Demetrius I), was still very young. *kingdom.* Syro-Palestine.

11:22 *prince of the covenant.* Either the high priest Onias III, who was murdered in 170 B.C., or, if the Hebrew for this phrase is translated "confederate prince," Ptolemy VI Philometor (181–146) of Egypt.

11:23 *he.* Antiochus.

11:24 *richest provinces.* Either of the Holy Land or of Egypt. *fortresses.* In Egypt.

11:25 *king of the South.* Ptolemy VI.

11:26 *his army.* That of Ptolemy.

11:27 *two kings.* Antiochus and Ptolemy, who was living in Antiochus's custody.

11:28 *against the holy covenant.* In 169 B.C. Antiochus plundered the temple in Jerusalem, set up a garrison there and massacred many Jews in the city.

11:30 *Ships of the western coastlands.* Roman vessels under the command of Popilius Laenas. *those who forsake the holy covenant.* Apostate Jews (see also v. 32).

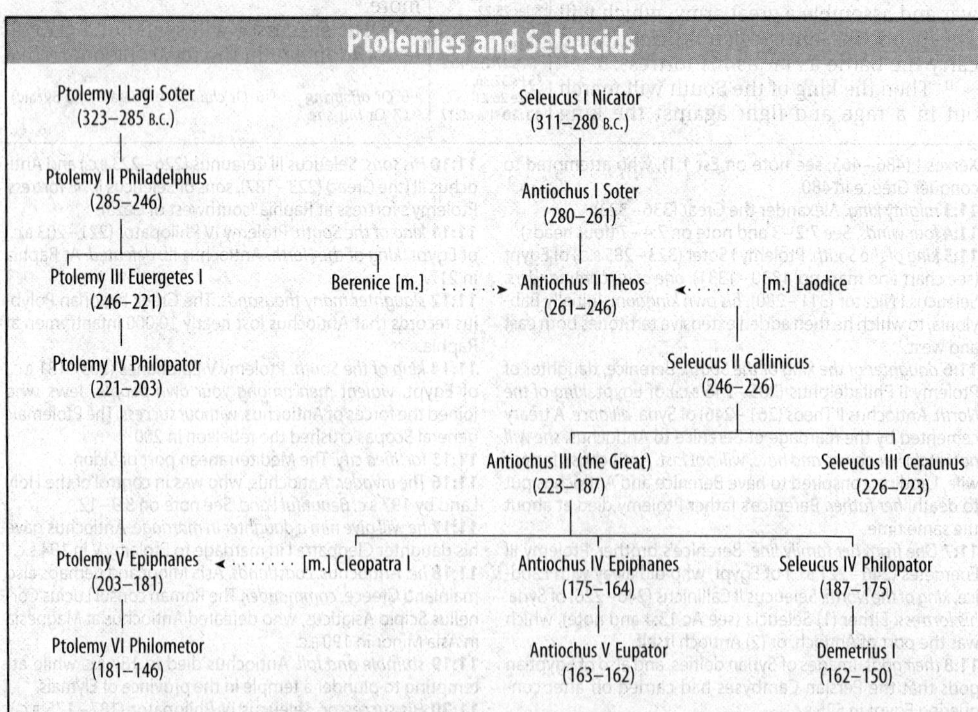

Then he will turn back and vent his fury[q]
against the holy covenant. He will return
and show favor to those who forsake the
holy covenant.
[31]"His armed forces will rise up to desecrate the temple fortress and will abolish
the daily sacrifice.[r] Then they will set up
the abomination that causes desolation.[s]
[32]With flattery he will corrupt those who
have violated the covenant, but the people who know their God will firmly resist[t]
him.
[33]"Those who are wise will instruct[u]
many, though for a time they will fall by
the sword or be burned or captured or
plundered.[v] [34]When they fall, they will receive a little help, and many who are not
sincere[w] will join them. [35]Some of the wise
will stumble, so that they may be refined,[x]
purified and made spotless until the time
of the end, for it will still come at the appointed time.

11:30 [q]S Job 15:13 **11:31** [r]Hos 3:4 [s]S Jer 19:4; Da 8:11-13; S 9:27; Mt 24:15*; Mk 13:14* **11:32** [t]Mic 5:7-9 **11:33** [u]Da 12:3; Mal 2:7 [v]Mt 24:9; Jn 16:2; Heb 11:32-38 **11:34** [w]Mt 7:15; Ro 16:18 **11:35** [x]S Job 28:1; S Ps 78:38; S Isa 48:10; Da 12:10; Zec 13:9; Jn 15:2 **11:36** [y]Jude 1:16 [z]Rev 13:5-6 [a]S Dt 10:17; S Isa 14:13-14; S Da 7:25; 8:11-12, 25; 2Th 2:4 [b]S Isa 10:25; 26:20 [c]Eze 35:13; S Da 8:24

The King Who Exalts Himself

[36]"The king will do as he pleases. He
will exalt and magnify himself[y] above every god and will say unheard-of things[z]
against the God of gods.[a] He will be successful until the time of wrath[b] is completed, for what has been determined must
take place.[c] [37]He will show no regard for
the gods of his fathers or for the one desired by women, nor will he regard any
god, but will exalt himself above them all.
[38]Instead of them, he will honor a god of
fortresses; a god unknown to his fathers
he will honor with gold and silver, with
precious stones and costly gifts. [39]He will
attack the mightiest fortresses with the
help of a foreign god and will greatly hon-
or those who acknowledge him. He will
make them rulers over many people and
will distribute the land at a price.[a]

[a] 39 Or *land for a reward*

11:31 *abomination that causes desolation.* See 9:27; 12:11; the altar to the pagan god Zeus Olympius, set up in 168 B.C. by Antiochus Epiphanes and prefiguring a similar abomination that Jesus predicted would be erected (see Mt 24:15; Lk 21:20 and notes).

11:33 *Those who are wise.* The godly leaders of the Jewish resistance movement, also called the Hasidim. *fall by the sword or be burned or captured or plundered.* See Heb 11:36–38.

11:34 *a little help.* The early successes of the guerrilla uprising (168 B.C.) that originated in Modein, 17 miles northwest of Jerusalem, under the leadership of Mattathias and his son Judas Maccabeus. In December, 165, the altar of the temple was rededicated (see note on 8:9–12).

11:35 *time of the end.* See v. 40; 12:4,9. Daniel concludes his predictions about Antiochus Epiphanes and begins to prophesy concerning the more distant future.

11:36 From here to the end of ch. 11 the antichrist (see notes on 7:8; 9:27) is in view. The details of this section do not fit what is known of Antiochus Epiphanes. See 2Th 2:3–4 and notes; cf. Rev 13:5–8.

11:37 *the one desired by women.* Usually interpreted as either Tammuz (see Eze 8:14 and note) or the Messiah (see Hag 2:7 and note).

Soon after the death of Alexander the Great in 323 B.C., his generals divided his empire into four parts, two of which—Egypt and Syria—were under the rule of the Ptolemies and Seleucids respectively. The Holy Land was controlled from Egypt by the Ptolemaic dynasty from 323 to 198, and was subsequently governed by the Seleucids of Syria from 198 to 142.

The Diadochi, as the successors of Alexander were called, struggled bitterly for power over his domain. At first Ptolemy I seized his own satrapy, Egypt and North Africa, which had splendid resources and natural defense capabilities. Seleucus gained Syria and Mesopotamia, and by 301 Lysimachus held Thrace and Asia Minor while Cassander ruled Macedon. The situation changed again by 277, when only three major Hellenistic kingdoms stabilized in Egypt, in Syria, and in Macedonia under the Antigonids (277–168). Each continued until the eventual triumph of Rome.

Daniel 11 treats the "king of the South" and the "king of the North," describing their conflicts, wars and alliances. Their hostility toward the people of God culminated in the "abomination that causes desolation" (11:31), identified historically with the reign of Antiochus IV Epiphanes (175-164). The Maccabean revolt followed, leading eventually to the founding of the Hasmonean dynasty.

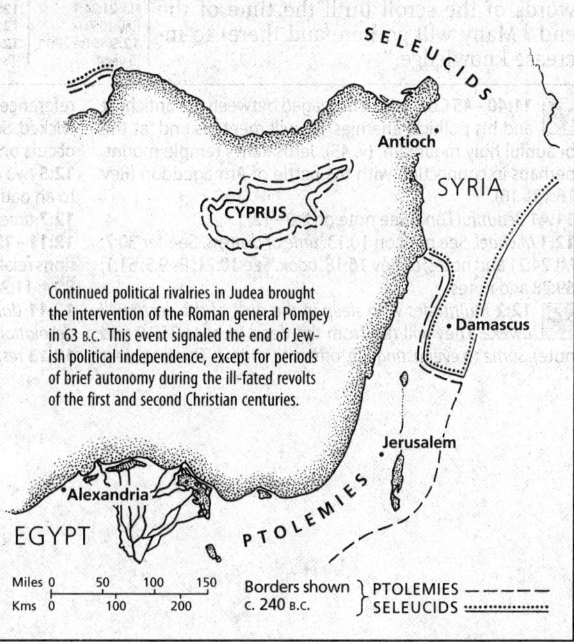

Continued political rivalries in Judea brought the intervention of the Roman general Pompey in 63 B.C. This event signaled the end of Jewish political independence, except for periods of brief autonomy during the ill-fated revolts of the first and second Christian centuries.

40“At the time of the end the king of the
South[d] will engage him in battle, and the
king of the North will storm[e] out against
him with chariots and cavalry and a great
fleet of ships. He will invade many countries and sweep through them like a flood.[f]
41He will also invade the Beautiful Land.[g]
Many countries will fall, but Edom,[h] Moab[i]
and the leaders of Ammon will be delivered from his hand. 42He will extend his
power over many countries; Egypt will not
escape. 43He will gain control of the treasures of gold and silver and all the riches
of Egypt,[j] with the Libyans[k] and Nubians
in submission. 44But reports from the east
and the north will alarm him, and he will
set out in a great rage to destroy and annihilate many. 45He will pitch his royal tents
between the seas at[a] the beautiful holy
mountain.[l] Yet he will come to his end,
and no one will help him.

The End Times

12 “At that time Michael,[m] the great
prince who protects your people,
will arise. There will be a time of distress[n]
such as has not happened from the beginning of nations until then. But at that
time your people — everyone whose name
is found written in the book[o] — will be delivered.[p] 2Multitudes who sleep in the dust
of the earth will awake:[q] some to everlasting life, others to shame and everlasting
contempt.[r] 3Those who are wise[b][s] will
shine[t] like the brightness of the heavens,
and those who lead many to righteousness,[u] like the stars for ever and ever.[v]
4But you, Daniel, close up and seal[w] the
words of the scroll until the time of the
end.[x] Many will go here and there[y] to increase knowledge.”

5Then I, Daniel, looked, and there before me stood two others, one on this bank
of the river and one on the opposite bank.[z]
6One of them said to the man clothed in
linen,[a] who was above the waters of the
river, “How long will it be before these astonishing things are fulfilled?”[b]
7The man clothed in linen, who was
above the waters of the river, lifted his
right hand[c] and his left hand toward heav-
en, and I heard him swear by him who
lives forever,[d] saying, “It will be for a time,
times and half a time.[c][e] When the power
of the holy people[f] has been finally broken, all these things will be completed.[g]”
8I heard, but I did not understand. So I
asked, “My lord, what will the outcome of
all this be?”
9He replied, “Go your way, Daniel, because the words are closed up and sealed[h]
until the time of the end.[i] 10Many will be
purified, made spotless and refined,[j] but
the wicked will continue to be wicked.[k]
None of the wicked will understand, but
those who are wise will understand.[l]
11“From the time that the daily sacrifice[m] is abolished and the abomination
that causes desolation[n] is set up, there
will be 1,290 days.[o] 12Blessed is the one
who waits[p] for and reaches the end of the
1,335 days.[q]
13“As for you, go your way till the end.[r]
You will rest,[s] and then at the end of the
days you will rise to receive your allotted
inheritance.[t][u]”

11:40 [d]S Isa 21:1 [e]Isa 5:28 [f]S Isa 8:7; S Eze 38:4 **11:41** [g]S Eze 20:6; Mal 3:12 [h]S Isa 11:14 [i]S Jer 48:47 **11:43** [j]S Eze 30:4 [k]2Ch 12:3; Na 3:9 **11:45** [l]S Isa 2:2, 4; Da 8:9 **12:1** [m]S Da 10:13; Jude 1:9 [n]S Da 9:12; S Mt 24:21; Mk 13:19; Rev 16:18 [o]S Ex 32:32; S Ps 56:8; S Jer 17:13; S Lk 10:20 [p]Jer 30:7 **12:2** [q]Jn 11:24 [r]S Isa 26:19; Mt 25:46 **12:3** [s]S Da 11:33 [t]Mt 13:43; Jn 5:35; Php 2:15 [u]S Isa 6:7 [v]S Pr 4:18; 1Co 15:42 **12:4** [w]S Isa 8:16 [x]ver 9, 13; Rev 22:10 [y]Jer 5:1 **12:5** [z]Da 10:4 **12:6** [a]S Eze 9:2 [b]Da 8:13 **12:7** [c]S Ge 14:22 [d]S Da 6:26; Rev 10:5-6 [e]S Da 7:25; S Rev 11:2 [f]S Da 8:24 [g]Lk 21:24; Rev 10:7 **12:9** [h]S Isa 29:11 [i]S ver 4 **12:10** [j]S Isa 1:25; S Da 11:35 [k]S Isa 32:7; Rev 22:11 [l]Hos 14:9 **12:11** [m]S Ex 29:38 [n]S Da 8:11; S 9:27; Mt 24:15*; Mk 13:14* [o]Rev 11:2 **12:12** [p]S Isa 30:18 [q]S Eze 4:5-6; Da 8:14 **12:13** [r]S ver 4 [s]Isa 57:2 [t]Ps 16:5; Rev 14:13 [u]Mt 10:22; Jas 1:12

[a] 45 Or *the sea and* [b] 3 Or *who impart wisdom* [c] 7 Or *a year, two years and half a year*

11:40 – 45 Conflicts to be waged between the antichrist and his political enemies. He will meet his end “at the beautiful holy mountain” (v. 45), Jerusalem’s temple mount, perhaps in connection with the battle of Armageddon (Rev 16:13 – 16).
11:41 *Beautiful Land.* See note on 8:9 – 12.
12:1 *Michael.* See note on 10:13. *time of distress.* See Jer 30:7; Mt 24:21 and notes; cf. Rev 16:18. *book.* See 10:21; Ps 9:5; 51:1; 69:28 and notes.
12:2 *Multitudes who sleep in the dust of the earth will awake.* They will rise from the dead (see Isa 26:19 and note). *some to everlasting life, others to shame.* The first clear reference to a resurrection of both the righteous and the wicked. See Jn 5:24 – 29 and notes. *everlasting life.* the phrase occurs only here in the OT.
12:5 *two others.* Two was the minimum number of witnesses to an oath (see v. 7; Dt 17:6 and note; 19:15).
12:7 *time, times and half a time.* See NIV text note; cf. 7:25.
12:11 – 12 Apparently representing either (1) further calculations relating to the persecutions of Antiochus Epiphanes (see 8:14; 11:28 and notes) or (2) further end-time calculations.
12:11 *daily sacrifice is abolished … abomination that causes desolation is set up.* See 11:31 and note.
12:13 *rest.* Die (see Job 3:17).

The Book of the Twelve, or the Minor Prophets

In Ecclesiasticus (an Apocryphal book written c. 190 B.C.), Jesus ben Sira spoke of "the twelve prophets" (Ecclesiasticus 49:10) as a unit parallel to Isaiah, Jeremiah and Ezekiel. He thus indicated that these 12 prophecies were at that time thought of as a unit and were probably already written together on one scroll, as is the case in later times. Josephus (*Against Apion*, 1.8.3) also was aware of this grouping. Augustine (*The City of God*, 18.25) called them the "Minor Prophets," referring to the small size of these books by comparison with the major prophetic books and not at all suggesting that they are of minor importance.

In the traditional Jewish canon these works are arranged in what was thought to be their chronological order: (1) the books that came from the period of Assyrian power (Hosea, Joel, Amos, Obadiah, Jonah, Micah), (2) those written about the time of the decline of Assyria (Nahum, Habakkuk, Zephaniah) and (3) those dating from the postexilic era (Haggai, Zechariah, Malachi). On the other hand, their order in the Septuagint (the pre-Christian Greek translation of the OT) is: Hosea, Amos, Micah, Joel, Obadiah, Jonah, Nahum, Habakkuk, Zephaniah, Haggai, Zechariah, Malachi (the order of the first six was probably determined by length, except for Jonah, which is placed last among them because of its different character).

In any event, it appears that within a century after the composition of Malachi the Jews had brought together the 12 shorter prophecies to form a book (scroll) of prophetic writing, which was received as canonical and paralleled the three major prophetic books of Isaiah, Jeremiah and Ezekiel. The great Greek manuscripts Alexandrinus and Vaticanus place the Twelve before the major prophets, but in the traditional Jewish canon and in all modern versions they appear after them.

Jerusalem During the Time of the Prophets

c. 750–586 B.C.

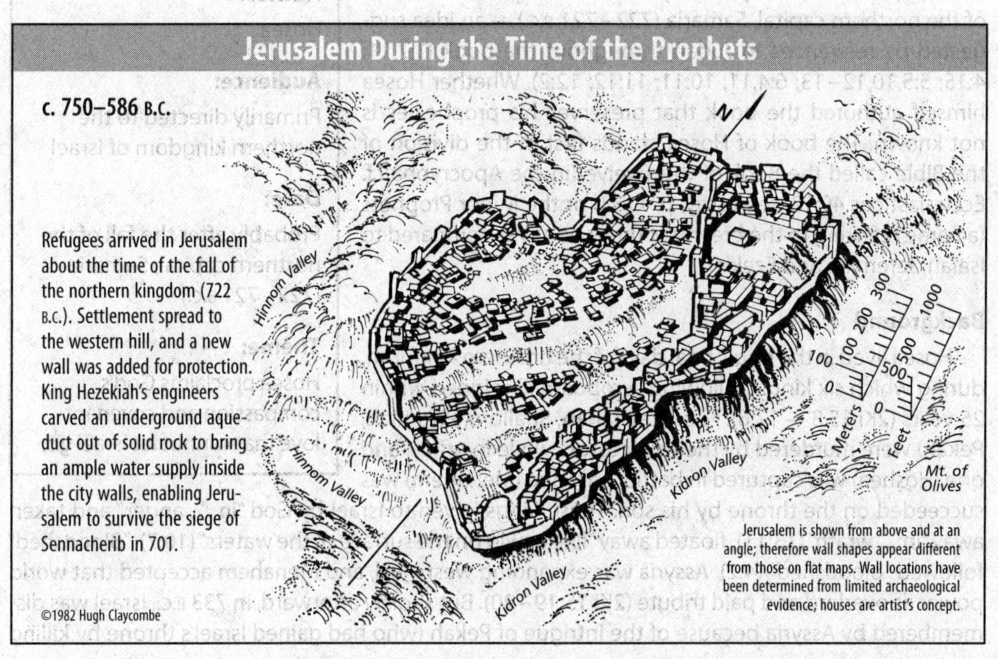

Refugees arrived in Jerusalem about the time of the fall of the northern kingdom (722 B.C.). Settlement spread to the western hill, and a new wall was added for protection. King Hezekiah's engineers carved an underground aqueduct out of solid rock to bring an ample water supply inside the city walls, enabling Jerusalem to survive the siege of Sennacherib in 701.

Jerusalem is shown from above and at an angle; therefore wall shapes appear different from those on flat maps. Wall locations have been determined from limited archaeological evidence; houses are artist's concept.

Hosea

I N T R O D U C T I O N

Author and Date

Hosea son of Beeri prophesied about the middle of the eighth century B.C., his ministry beginning during or shortly after that of Amos. Amos threatened God's judgment on Israel at the hands of an unnamed enemy; Hosea identifies that enemy as Assyria (7:11; 8:9; 10:6; 11:11). Judging from the kings mentioned in 1:1, Hosea must have prophesied for at least 38 years, though almost nothing is known about him from sources outside his book. He was the only one of the writing prophets to come from the northern kingdom (Israel), and his prophecy is primarily directed to that kingdom. But since his prophetic activity is dated by reference to kings of Judah, the book was probably written in Judah after the fall of the northern capital, Samaria (722–721 B.C.)—an idea suggested by references to Judah throughout the book (1:7,11; 4:15; 5:5,10,12–13; 6:4,11; 10:11; 11:12; 12:2). Whether Hosea himself authored the book that preserves his prophecies is not known. The book of Hosea stands first in the division of the Bible called the Book of the Twelve (in the Apocrypha cf. Ecclesiasticus 49:10; see essay, p. 1333) or the Minor Prophets (a name referring to the brevity of these books as compared to Isaiah, Jeremiah and Ezekiel).

A Quick Look

Author:
Hosea

Audience:
Primarily directed to the northern kingdom of Israel

Date:
Probably after the fall of the northern capital, Samaria (722–721 B.C.)

Theme:
Hosea proclaims God's compassion and covenant love that cannot let Israel go.

Background

Hosea lived in the tragic final days of the northern kingdom, during which six kings (following Jeroboam II) reigned within 25 years (2Ki 15:8—17:6). Four (Zechariah, Shallum, Pekahiah, Pekah) were murdered by their successors while in office, and one (Hoshea) was captured in battle; only one (Menahem) was succeeded on the throne by his son. These kings, given to Israel by God "in ... anger" and taken away "in ... wrath" (13:11), floated away "like a twig on the surface of the waters" (10:7). "Bloodshed" followed "bloodshed" (4:2). Assyria was expanding westward, and Menahem accepted that world power as overlord and paid tribute (2Ki 15:19–20). But shortly afterward, in 733 B.C., Israel was dismembered by Assyria because of the intrigue of Pekah (who had gained Israel's throne by killing

Pekahiah, Menahem's son and successor). Only the territories of Ephraim and western Manasseh were left to the king of Israel. Then, because of the disloyalty of Hoshea (Pekah's successor), Samaria was captured and its people exiled in 722–721, bringing the northern kingdom to an end.

Theological Theme and Message

The first part of the book (chs. 1–3) narrates the family life of Hosea as a symbol (similar to the symbolism in the lives of Isaiah, Jeremiah and Ezekiel) to convey the message the prophet had from the Lord for his people. God ordered Hosea to marry an adulterous wife, Gomer, and their three children were each given a symbolic name representing part of the ominous message. Ch. 2 alternates between Hosea's relation to Gomer and its symbolic representation of God's relation to Israel. The children are told to drive the unfaithful mother out of the house; but it was her reform, not her riddance, that was sought. The prophet was ordered to continue loving her, and he took her back and kept her in isolation for a while (ch. 3). The affair graphically represents the Lord's relation to the Israelites (cf. 2:4,9,18), who had been disloyal to him by worshiping Canaanite deities as the source of their abundance. Israel was to go through a period of exile (cf. 7:16; 9:3,6,17; 11:5). Just as Hosea took back his wife Gomer, so the Lord loves his covenant people and longs to take them back. This return is described with imagery recalling the exodus from Egypt and settlement in Canaan (cf. 1:11; 2:14–23; 3:5; 11:10–11; 14:4–7). Hosea saw Israel's past experiences with the Lord as the fundamental pattern, or type, of God's future dealings with his people.

Just as Hosea took back his wife Gomer, so the Lord loves his covenant people and longs to take them back.

The second part of the book (chs. 4–14) gives the details of Israel's involvement in Canaanite religion, but a systematic outline of the material is difficult. Like other prophetic books, Hosea issued a call to repentance. Israel's alternative to destruction was to forsake her idols and return to the Lord (chs. 6; 14). Information gleaned from materials discovered at Ugarit, located some distance north of the northern kingdom of Israel and dating from the 15th century B.C. (see chart, p. xxiii), enables us to know more clearly the religious practices taken over from the Canaanites against which Hosea protested.

Hosea saw the failure to acknowledge God (4:1,6; 8:2–3; 13:4) as Israel's basic problem. God's relation to Israel was that of love (2:19; 4:1; 6:6; 10:12; 12:6). The intimacy of the covenant relationship between God and Israel, illustrated in the first part of the book by the husband-wife relationship, is later amplified by the father-child relationship (11:1–4). Disloyalty to God was spiritual adultery (4:13–14; 5:4; 9:1; cf. Jer 3; see note on Ex 34:15). Israel had turned to Baal worship and had sacrificed at the pagan high places, which included associating with the sacred prostitutes at the sanctuaries (4:14) and worshiping the calf images set up by Jeroboam I (see 1Ki 12:28–29 and notes; cf. Hos 8:5; 10:5–6; 13:2). There were also international intrigue (5:13; 7:8–11) and materialism. Yet despite God's condemnation and the harshness of language with which the unavoidable judgment was announced, the major purpose of the book is to proclaim God's compassion and covenant love that cannot—finally—let Israel go.

Special Problems

The book of Hosea has at least two perplexing problems. The first concerns the nature of the story told in chs. 1–3 and the character of Gomer. While some interpreters have thought the story to be merely an allegory of the relation between God and Israel, others claim, more plausibly, that the story is to be taken literally. Among the latter, some insist that Gomer was faithful at first and later became unfaithful, others that she was a prostitute even before the marriage.

The second problem of the book is the relation of ch. 3 to ch. 1. Despite the fact that no children are mentioned in ch. 3, some interpreters claim that the two chapters are different accounts of the same episode. The traditional interpretation, however, is more likely, namely, that ch. 3 is a sequel to ch. 1—i.e., after Gomer proved unfaithful, Hosea was instructed to take her back.

Outline

- I. Superscription (1:1)
- II. The Unfaithful Wife and the Faithful Husband (1:2 — 3:5)
  - A. The Children as Signs (1:2 — 2:1)
  - B. The Unfaithful Wife (2:2 – 23)
    1. The Lord's judgment of Israel (2:2 – 13)
    2. The Lord's restoration of Israel (2:14 – 23)
  - C. The Faithful Husband (ch. 3)
- III. The Unfaithful Nation and the Faithful God (chs. 4 – 14)
  - A. Israel's Unfaithfulness (4:1 — 6:3)
    1. The general charge (4:1 – 3)
    2. The cause declared and the results described (4:4 – 19)
    3. A special message to the people and leaders (ch. 5)
    4. The people's sorrowful plea (6:1 – 3)
  - B. Israel's Punishment (6:4 — 10:15)
    1. The case stated (6:4 — 7:16)
    2. The judgment pronounced (chs. 8 – 9)
    3. Summary and appeal (ch. 10)
  - C. The Lord's Faithful Love (chs. 11 – 14)
    1. The Lord's fatherly love (11:1 – 11)
    2. Israel's punishment for unfaithfulness (11:12 — 13:16)
    3. Israel's restoration after repentance (ch. 14)

1 The word of the LORD that came[a] to Hosea son of Beeri during the reigns of Uzziah,[b] Jotham,[c] Ahaz[d] and Hezekiah,[e] kings of Judah,[f] and during the reign of Jeroboam[g] son of Jehoash[a] king of Israel:[h]

Hosea's Wife and Children

2When the LORD began to speak through Hosea, the LORD said to him, "Go, take to yourself an adulterous[i] wife and children of unfaithfulness, because the land is guilty of the vilest adultery[j] in departing from the LORD." 3So he married Gomer[k] daughter of Diblaim, and she conceived and bore him a son.

4Then the LORD said to Hosea, "Call him Jezreel,[l] because I will soon punish the house of Jehu for the massacre at Jezreel, and I will put an end to the kingdom of Israel. 5In that day I will break Israel's bow in the Valley of Jezreel.[m]"

6Gomer[n] conceived again and gave birth to a daughter. Then the LORD said to Hosea, "Call her Lo-Ruhamah,[b][o] for I will no longer show love to the house of Israel,[p] that I should at all forgive them. 7Yet I will show love to the house of Judah; and I will save them—not by bow,[q] sword or battle, or by horses and horsemen, but by the LORD their God.[r]"

8After she had weaned Lo-Ruhamah,[s] Gomer had another son. 9Then the LORD said, "Call him Lo-Ammi,[c] for you are not my people, and I am not your God.[t]

10"Yet the Israelites will be like the sand on the seashore, which cannot be measured or counted.[u] In the place where it was said to them, 'You are not my people,' they will be called 'sons of the living God.'[v][w] 11The people of Judah and the people of Israel will be reunited,[x] and they will appoint one leader[y] and will come up out of the land,[z] for great will be the day of Jezreel.[a]

2 "Say of your brothers, 'My people,' and of your sisters, 'My loved one.'[b]

Israel Punished and Restored

2"Rebuke your mother,[c] rebuke her,
for she is not my wife,
and I am not her husband.
Let her remove the adulterous[d] look
from her face
and the unfaithfulness from between
her breasts.
3Otherwise I will strip[e] her naked
and make her as bare as on the day
she was born;[f]
I will make her like a desert,[g]
turn her into a parched land,
and slay her with thirst.

1:1 [a]S Jer 1:2 [b]S 2Ki 14:21 [c]S 1Ch 3:12 [d]S 1Ch 3:13 [e]S 1Ch 3:13 [f]Isa 1:1; Mic 1:1 [g]S 2Ki 13:13 [h]Am 1:1 **1:2** [i]S Jer 3:1; Hos 2:2,5; 3:1 [j]Dt 31:16; Jer 3:14; Eze 23:3-21; Hos 5:3 **1:3** [k]ver 6 **1:4** [l]ver 11; S 1Sa 29:1; 1Ki 18:45; 2Ki 10:1-14; Hos 2:22 **1:5** [m]S Jos 15:56; S 1Sa 29:1; 2Ki 15:29 **1:6** [n]ver 3 [o]ver 8; Hos 2:23 [p]Hos 2:4 **1:7** [q]S Ps 44:6 [r]Zec 4:6 **1:8** [s]S ver 6 **1:9** [t]ver 10; S Eze 11:19-20; 1Pe 2:10 **1:10** [u]S Ge 22:17; S Jer 33:22 [v]S ver 9; Hos 2:23; Ro 9:26* [w]S Jos 3:10 **1:11** [x]S Isa 11:12,13 [y]Jer 23:5-8; 30:9 [z]S Eze 37:15-28 [a]S ver 4 **2:1** [b]ver 23; 1Pe 2:10 **2:2** [c]ver 5; S Isa 50:1; S Hos 1:2; 4:5 [d]S Isa 1:21; S Eze 23:45 **2:3** [e]S Eze 16:37 [f]Eze 16:4,22 [g]Isa 32:13-14

[a] *1* Hebrew *Joash,* a variant of *Jehoash* [b] *6* *Lo-Ruhamah* means *not loved.* [c] *9* *Lo-Ammi* means *not my people.*

1:1 *word of the LORD.* A claim of authority paralleling that of Jeremiah (1:2,4), Ezekiel (1:3), Joel (1:1), Jonah (1:1; 3:1), Micah (1:1), Zephaniah (1:1), Haggai (1:1,3; 2:1,10,20), Zechariah (1:1,7; 9:1; 12:1) and Malachi (1:1). *Hosea.* Means "salvation." *Uzziah.* Reigned 792–740 B.C. *Jotham.* 750–732. *Ahaz.* 735–715. *Hezekiah.* 729–686. All the reigns overlapped, the coregency of Ahaz and Hezekiah being the longest (see note on Isa 36:1). *Jeroboam.* Jeroboam II, 793–753. Hosea was a contemporary of Isaiah, Amos and Micah (see the similar first verse in their prophecies).

1:2 *take ... an adulterous wife.* See Introduction: Special Problems. *unfaithfulness.* The one great sin of which the Lord (through Hosea) accuses Israel.

1:3 *Gomer.* Not mentioned outside this book. *him.* The omission of this word in vv. 6,9 may indicate that Hosea was not the father of Gomer's next two children.

1:4 *Jezreel.* Means "God scatters," here used to reinforce the announcement of judgment on the reigning dynasty (see notes on v. 11; 2:22). Jeroboam II was of the dynasty of Jehu (841–814 B.C.), which was established at Jezreel by the overthrow of Ahab's son Joram (see 2Ki 9:14–29; see also 1Ki 19:16–17 and notes). Jehu's dynasty ended with the murder of Zechariah in 753 (2Ki 15:8–10).

1:5 *Israel's bow.* Israel's military power, broken in 725 B.C., though Samaria held out under siege for three more years (see 2Ki 17:5–6 and notes). *Valley of Jezreel.* Located east of Megiddo, it provides the only major pass through the mountain range that traverses Israel from north to south and was therefore a major battleground in ancient times.

1:6 *Lo-Ruhamah.* See NIV text note. The naming represents a reversal of the love (compassion) that God had earlier shown to Israel (see Ex 33:19; Dt 7:6–8 and note on 7:8) but that later was promised again (see 2:23 and note).

1:7 *Yet.* See v. 10 and note. *Judah ... I will save.* They were saved from Assyria by the Lord in 722–721 B.C. and again in 701 (see 2Ki 19:32–36).

1:9 *Lo-Ammi.* See NIV text note. The naming represents a break in the covenant relationship between the Lord and Israel (see Ex 6:7; Jer 7:23 and note), which later, however, would be restored (v. 10; 2:1,23). The warnings became more severe in moving from the first to the third child.

1:10 Cited in Ro 9:26; 1Pe 2:10 (see note there) and applied to the mission to the Gentiles. *Yet.* The threatened punishment (vv. 4–6,9) would be for only a limited time, and a period of blessing would follow. *sand on the seashore.* See the promise to Abraham and Jacob (Ge 22:17; 32:12; cf. Jer 33:22 and note; Heb 11:12). *sons.* Contrasts with "children of unfaithfulness/adultery" (v. 2; 2:4). *living God.* Contrasts with idols—"which are not God" (Dt 32:17; cf. Ps 115:4–7 and note).

1:11 *reunited.* Israel and Judah would become one nation again. *out of the land.* Possibly the land of exile (cf. Ex 1:10). Another interpretation is that they would spring up from the ground as plants do. *Jezreel.* Here "God scatters" (see note on v. 4) refers to sowing or planting, indicating a reversal of the meaning of the first child's name (see 2:21–23 and notes).

2:1 *My people ... My loved one.* The negatives associated with the names of Hosea's children (see NIV text notes on 1:6,9) are dropped.

2:2 The Lord speaks to Hosea's children, continuing the analogy between Gomer and Israel. *not my wife.* The marriage was broken by unfaithfulness, but reconciliation, not divorce, was sought (cf. vv. 7–15).

2:3 *strip her.* The husband supplied the wife's clothing (see Ex 21:10; Eze 16:10), and here her unfaithfulness was exposed (see Jer 13:26; Eze 16:39). *bare.* As Israel was when the Lord

[4]I will not show my love to her
children,[h]
because they are the children of
adultery.[i]
[5]Their mother has been unfaithful
and has conceived them in disgrace.
She said, 'I will go after my lovers,[j]
who give me my food and my water,
my wool and my linen, my oil and
my drink.'[k]
[6]Therefore I will block her path with
thornbushes;
I will wall her in so that she cannot
find her way.[l]
[7]She will chase after her lovers but not
catch them;
she will look for them but not find
them.[m]
Then she will say,
'I will go back to my husband[n] as at
first,[o]
for then I was better off[p] than now.'
[8]She has not acknowledged[q] that I was
the one
who gave her the grain, the new
wine and oil,[r]
who lavished on her the silver and
gold[s]—
which they used for Baal.[t]

[9]"Therefore I will take away my grain[u]
when it ripens,
and my new wine[v] when it is ready.
I will take back my wool and my linen,
intended to cover her nakedness.
[10]So now I will expose[w] her lewdness
before the eyes of her lovers;[x]
no one will take her out of my
hands.[y]
[11]I will stop[z] all her celebrations:[a]
her yearly festivals, her New Moons,
her Sabbath days—all her appointed
feasts.[b]
[12]I will ruin her vines[c] and her fig trees,[d]
which she said were her pay from
her lovers;[e]
I will make them a thicket,[f]
and wild animals will devour them.[g]
[13]I will punish her for the days
she burned incense[h] to the Baals;[i]
she decked herself with rings and
jewelry,[j]
and went after her lovers,[k]
but me she forgot,[l]"
declares the LORD.[m]

[14]"Therefore I am now going to allure
her;
I will lead her into the desert[n]
and speak tenderly to her.
[15]There I will give her back her
vineyards,
and will make the Valley of Achor[a o]
a door of hope.
There she will sing[b p] as in the days of
her youth,[q]
as in the day she came up out of
Egypt.[r]

[16]"In that day," declares the LORD,
"you will call me 'my husband';[s]

[a] *15 Achor* means *trouble.* [b] *15* Or *respond*

2:4 [h]S Eze 8:18; Hos 1:6 [i]Hos 5:7 **2:5** [j]S Jer 3:6; S Hos 1:2 [k]Jer 44:17-18 **2:6** [l]S Job 3:23; S 19:8; S La 3:9 **2:7** [m]Hos 5:13 [n]S Isa 54:5 [o]Jer 2:2; S 3:1 [p]S Eze 16:8 **2:8** [q]S Isa 1:3 [r]S Nu 18:12 [s]S Dt 8:18 [t]ver 13; Eze 16:15-19; Hos 8:4 **2:9** [u]Hos 8:7 [v]Hos 9:2 **2:10** [w]Eze 23:10 [x]Jer 13:26 [y]S Eze 16:37 **2:11** [z]Jer 7:34 [a]S Isa 24:8 [b]S Isa 1:14; Jer 16:9; Hos 3:4; 9:5; Am 5:21; 8:10 **2:12** [c]S Isa 7:23; S Jer 8:13 [d]S Jer 5:17 [e]S Jer 3:1 [f]S Isa 5:6 [g]Hos 5:7; 13:8 **2:13** [h]Isa 65:7 [i]ver 8; S Jer 7:9; Hos 11:2 [j]S Eze 16:17; S 23:40 [k]Hos 4:13 [l]Hos 4:6; 8:14; 13:6 [m]S Jer 44:17; Hos 13:1 **2:14** [n]S Eze 19:13 **2:15** [o]S Jos 7:24,26 [p]Ex 15:1-18 [q]S Jer 2:2; S Eze 16:22 [r]S Eze 28:26; Hos 12:9 **2:16** [s]S Isa 54:5

found her in Egypt—in slavery and with nothing (cf. Eze 16:4–8; Na 3:5).

2:4 *children of adultery.* See 1:2 and note. This contrasts with being "sons of the living God" (1:10; cf. 11:1).

2:5 *go after.* The wife was chasing other men (see v. 13; Jer 3:2; Eze 16:33–34). *lovers.* See vv. 7,10. The reference is to Canaanite deities (such as Baal), whose worshipers hoped to receive from Baal the fertility of their flocks and fields (see note on Ex 34:15). *who give me my food ... my drink.* Ugaritic texts (see chart, p. xxiii) attribute crops to rain given by Baal. *wool ... linen ... oil ... drink.* The agricultural staples of the Holy Land. Israel does not know the true source of her blessings.

2:6 *block her path ... wall her in.* Rather than punish Israel with death (cf. Dt 22:21; Eze 16:39–40; 23:47; Na 3:5–7), the Lord would isolate her.

2:7 *look for.* See 5:6,15 ("seek"). *not find.* See 5:6 and note. *go back.* The Hebrew for this expression often means "repent." *my husband.* The Lord.

2:8 *She has not acknowledged.* Along with the Canaanites, the Israelites attributed to Baal "the grain, the new wine and oil" (see Dt 7:13; Joel 1:10; Hag 1:11 and notes). *silver and gold.* Used for making idols (see 8:4; 13:2). *Baal.* The Canaanite god who was believed to control the weather and the fertility of crops, animals and people (see note on Jdg 2:13).

2:9 *take away.* By withholding the fruits of field and flock, the Lord made known that he was the true source of those blessings.

2:10 *expose her lewdness.* The unfaithful wife was exposed to public shame (see La 1:8; Eze 16:37; 23:29). *no one will take her.* Baal had no power.

2:11 *stop ... celebrations.* In exile these joyous seasons would be only a memory. *yearly festivals.* See Ex 23:14–17; Dt 16:16 and notes. See also chart, pp. 178–179. *New Moons.* See 2Ki 4:23; Isa 1:14; Am 8:5 and notes. *Sabbath.* See Ex 20:8–11.

2:12 *pay from her lovers.* The prostitute's pay (see v. 5; 9:1; Dt 23:18; Eze 16:33; Mic 1:7). Israel attributed her agricultural products to the false gods she worshiped, rather than to the Lord (see Dt 11:13–14).

2:13 *days.* Festival days. *Baals.* See v. 17; 11:2. Hosea used the plural here, suggesting the idols at the many local shrines (see Jdg 2:11–13 and notes; Jer 2:23,28 and note; 9:14). *went after.* See note on v. 5. *forgot.* The opposite of "acknowledge" (see note on v. 20) in Hosea (see 13:4–6 and note on 13:6; see also note on 1Sa 12:9).

2:14 *into the desert.* For a second betrothal (see vv. 19–20). It refers back to the days of Israel's desert wandering, before she was tempted by the Baals in Canaan. *speak tenderly to.* Reassure, encourage, comfort (cf. Ge 34:3; Ru 2:13; Isa 40:2). God continually shows love in the midst of judgment.

2:15 *Valley of Achor.* Near Jericho (see Jos 7:24,26; Isa 65:10). As the prophet reversed the meaning of the names of his children, so also the meaning of Achor (see NIV text note)—where God first judged his people in the promised land—became a symbol of new opportunity.

2:16–17 *husband ... master ... Baals.* A play on words. Of the two Hebrew words for husband, one (master) is identical with

you will no longer call me 'my
master.[a]'
17 I will remove the names of the Baals
from her lips;[t]
no longer will their names be
invoked.[u]
18 In that day I will make a covenant for
them
with the beasts of the field and the
birds of the air
and the creatures that move along
the ground.[v]
Bow and sword and battle
I will abolish[w] from the land,
so that all may lie down in safety.[x]
19 I will betroth[y] you to me forever;
I will betroth you in[b] righteousness
and justice,[z]
in[c] love and compassion.[a]
20 I will betroth you in faithfulness,
and you will acknowledge[b] the
LORD.[c]

21 "In that day I will respond,"
declares the LORD—
"I will respond[d] to the skies,
and they will respond to the earth;
22 and the earth will respond to the grain,
the new wine and oil,[e]
and they will respond to Jezreel.[d f]
23 I will plant[g] her for myself in the land;
I will show my love to the one I
called 'Not my loved one.[e h]'
I will say to those called 'Not my
people,[f]' 'You are my people';[i]
and they will say, 'You are my
God.[j]'"

Hosea's Reconciliation With His Wife

3 The LORD said to me, "Go, show your
love to your wife again, though she is
loved by another and is an adulteress.[k]
Love her as the LORD loves the Israelites,
though they turn to other gods and love
the sacred raisin cakes.[l]"
2 So I bought her for fifteen shekels[g] of
silver and about a homer and a lethek[h] of
barley. 3 Then I told her, "You are to live
with[i] me many days; you must not be a
prostitute or be intimate with any man,
and I will live with[i] you."
4 For the Israelites will live many days
without king or prince,[m] without sacrifice[n]
or sacred stones,[o] without ephod[p] or idol.[q]
5 Afterward the Israelites will return and
seek[r] the LORD their God and David their
king.[s] They will come trembling[t] to the
LORD and to his blessings in the last days.[u]

[a] 16 Hebrew *baal* [b] 19 Or *with*; also in verse 20
[c] 19 Or *with* [d] 22 *Jezreel* means *God plants.*
[e] 23 Hebrew *Lo-Ruhamah* [f] 23 Hebrew *Lo-Ammi*
[g] 2 That is, about 6 ounces (about 170 grams)
[h] 2 That is, probably about 10 bushels (about 330 liters)
[i] 3 Or *wait for*

2:17 [t]Ex 23:13; Ps 16:4 [u]S Jos 23:7; Zec 13:2 **2:18** [v]S Job 5:22 [w]S Ps 46:9; S Isa 2:4; Zec 9:10 [x]S Job 5:23; S Jer 23:6; Eze 34:25 **2:19** [y]S Isa 62:4; 2Co 11:2 [z]S Isa 1:27 [a]S Isa 54:8 **2:20** [b]Jer 31:34; Hos 4:1; 6:6; 13:4 [c]S Eze 16:8 **2:21** [d]Isa 55:10; Zec 8:12; Mal 3:10-11 **2:22** [e]S Jer 31:12; Hos 14:7; Joel 2:19 [f]S Eze 36:29-30; S Hos 1:4 **2:23** [g]S Jer 31:27 [h]S Hos 1:6 [i]S ver 1; S Isa 19:25; S Hos 1:10 [j]S Jer 29:12; Ro 9:25*; 1Pe 2:10 **3:1** [k]S Hos 1:2 [l]S 2Sa 6:19 **3:4** [m]Hos 13:11 [n]Da 11:31; S Hos 2:11 [o]Hos 10:1 [p]S Ex 25:7 [q]Jdg 17:5-6; 18:14-17; S La 2:9; Zec 10:2 **3:5** [r]S Dt 4:29; S Isa 9:13; S 10:20; Hos 5:15; Mic 4:1-2 [s]S 1Sa 13:14 [t]S Ps 18:45 [u]S Dt 4:30; S Jer 50:4-5; Hos 11:10

the name of the god Baal (see NIV text note on v. 16). There will be such a vigorous reaction against Baal worship that this Hebrew word for "master" will no longer be used of the Lord. **2:18** *make a covenant.* See 6:7; 8:1. Animals, the instruments of destruction in v. 12, as well as birds and insects, would no longer threaten life. Nature and history combine in a picture of peace (see Isa 11:6–9 and note; 65:25). *Bow and sword and battle.* See 1:5,7. War is terminated. *land.* The area occupied by Israel (see 1:2; 4:1,3; 9:3 and note; 10:1). *lie down in safety.* See Jer 33:16; Eze 34:24–28.

2:19–20 Rather than money, these five traits necessary to the covenant relationship make up the bride-price (see Ex 22:16; 1Sa 18:25 and notes).

2:19 *righteousness.* See 10:12; Ps 4:1; Jer 23:6 and notes. *justice.* See Am 5:24 and note. *love.* See 4:1; 6:4; 10:12 and note; 12:6. *compassion.* A reversal of God's threatened withdrawal of compassion (see 1:6 and note). "Lo-Ruhamah" means lit. "not shown compassion" (cf. Ps 51:1; 103:3–14).

2:20 *faithfulness.* Dependability (see Dt 32:4; Ps 88:11). *acknowledge.* The Hebrew for this word can refer to intimate sexual relations (Ge 19:8; Nu 31:17–18,35 ["slept with"]), but it also refers to active acknowledgment of a covenant partner (see 6:3 and note; 8:2; 13:4; cf. 2Sa 7:20 and note).

2:21 *respond.* The woman (Israel) responded to the Lord's overtures (see NIV text note on v. 15); now God responded to her new behavior. The land also responded by becoming productive (vv. 21–22).

2:22 *Jezreel.* Here used in the sense "God plants" (see NIV text note and v. 23; see also 1:4,11 and notes). The threats represented by the names of the children are turned into blessings (see 1:10 and note). The basic statement describing the covenant relationship was "I will be your God and you will be my people" (Jer 7:23; see notes on Ex 6:7; Zec 8:8).

2:23 *my people ... my God.* See note on v. 22. *You are my God.* The people respond to God's graciousness. This verse is quoted in part in Ro 9:25–26 (see note there); 1Pe 2:10 and applied to Gentiles coming into the church.

3:1 *said to me.* Ch. 3 is narrated in the first person, ch. 1 in the third person. *Go ... love ... your wife.* Hosea's love for unfaithful Gomer illustrated God's love for unfaithful Israel. God's love for Israel (see 11:1 and note; 14:4) is the basic theme of the book. *other gods.* See Ex 20:3; Dt 31:20. *raisin cakes.* Offered to Baal in thanksgiving for harvest.

3:2 Gomer had evidently become a slave, and Hosea bought her back. *fifteen shekels.* Half the usual price of a slave (see Ex 21:32 and note) or of the redemption value of a woman's vow (Lev 27:4). *lethek.* See NIV text note. It appears that half her price was paid in money (silver) and half in produce (barley)—for a total value of 30 shekels.

3:3–5 A picture of exile and return.

3:3 *many days.* Not forever. There would be an "afterward" (v. 5), a future (see Jer 29:11). *live with.* Suggests a period of isolation (see NIV text note; see also 2:6 and note), comparable to Israel's exile.

3:4 *king.* See 1:4; 5:1; 8:4,10; 10:15; 13:10–11. *prince.* See 7:3,5; 8:4; 13:10. *without sacrifice.* See 6:6; 8:11,13. *sacred stones.* See 10:1–2; 1Ki 14:23 and note; 2Ki 17:10; Mic 5:13. *ephod.* Here an image associated with idols (see Jdg 8:27; 17:5 and notes). *idol.* See Ge 31:30; 1Sa 19:13,16.

3:5 *return.* A basic word in Hosea's vocabulary (see 2:7 ["go back"]; 5:4; 6:1; 7:10; 11:5; 12:6; 14:1–2). *seek.* Israel's repentance is envisioned (see 5:15 and note)—the reverse of their present stubborn rebellion (7:10). *LORD their God.* See 12:9; 13:4; Jer 50:4. *David their king.* The Messianic king from the dynasty of David (see Jer 30:9; Eze 34:24 and note). After the death of Solomon, Israel (the northern kingdom)

The Charge Against Israel

4 Hear the word of the LORD, you Israelites,
because the LORD has a charge[v] to bring
against you who live in the land:[w]
"There is no faithfulness,[x] no love,
no acknowledgment[y] of God in the land.[z]
2 There is only cursing,[a] lying[a] and murder,[b]
stealing[c] and adultery;[d]
they break all bounds,
and bloodshed follows bloodshed.[e]
3 Because of this the land mourns,[b][f]
and all who live in it waste away;[g]
the beasts of the field and the birds of the air
and the fish of the sea are dying.[h]

4 "But let no man bring a charge,
let no man accuse another,
for your people are like those
who bring charges against a priest.[i]
5 You stumble[j] day and night,
and the prophets stumble with you.
So I will destroy your mother[k] —
6 my people are destroyed from lack of knowledge.[l]

"Because you have rejected knowledge,
I also reject you as my priests;
because you have ignored the law[m] of your God,
I also will ignore your children.
7 The more the priests increased,
the more they sinned against me;
they exchanged[c] their[d] Glory[n] for
something disgraceful.[o]
8 They feed on the sins of my people
and relish their wickedness.[p]
9 And it will be: Like people, like priests.[q]
I will punish both of them for their ways
and repay them for their deeds.[r]

10 "They will eat but not have enough;[s]
they will engage in prostitution[t] but not increase,
because they have deserted[u] the LORD
to give themselves 11 to prostitution,[v]
to old wine[w] and new,
which take away the understanding[x]
12 of my people.
They consult a wooden idol[y]
and are answered by a stick of wood.[z]
A spirit of prostitution[a] leads them astray;[b]
they are unfaithful[c] to their God.
13 They sacrifice on the mountaintops
and burn offerings on the hills,

4:1 [v]S Job 10:2; S Jer 2:9 [w]Joel 1:2,14 [x]S Pr 24:2 [y]S Pr 10:21; S Isa 1:3; Jer 7:28; S Hos 2:20 [z]S Jer 51:5 **4:2** [a]Isa 59:3; Hos 7:3; 10:4; 11:12 [b]Hos 5:2; 6:9 [c]Hos 7:1 [d]S Jer 9:2 [e]S 2Ki 21:16; S Isa 1:15; S Eze 22:2,9; Hos 5:2; 10:13 **4:3** [f]S Jer 4:28 [g]S Isa 15:6; S 33:9 [h]S Jer 4:25; S 9:10; S Eze 38:20; Zep 1:3 **4:4** [i]Dt 17:12; S Eze 3:26 **4:5** [j]S Eze 7:19; S 14:7 [k]S Hos 2:2 **4:6** [l]S Pr 10:21; S Isa 1:3; S Hos 2:13; Mal 2:7-8 [m]Hos 8:1,12 **4:7** [n]Hab 2:16 [o]Hos 9:11; 10:1,6; 13:6 **4:8** [p]S Isa 56:11; Hos 14:1; Mic 3:11 **4:9** [q]S Isa 24:2 [r]Jer 5:31; Hos 8:13; 9:9,15; 10:10; 12:2 **4:10** [s]S Lev 26:26; S Isa 55:2; Mic 6:14 [t]S Eze 22:9 [u]Hos 7:14; 9:17 **4:11** [v]ver 14; Hos 5:4 [w]S Lev 10:9; S 1Sa 25:36 [x]S Pr 20:1 **4:12** [y]Jer 2:27 [z]Hab 2:19 [a]S Nu 15:39 [b]S Isa 44:20 [c]S Ps 73:27

[a] 2 That is, to pronounce a curse upon [b] 3 Or *dries up* [c] 7 Syriac and an ancient Hebrew scribal tradition; Masoretic Text *I will exchange* [d] 7 Masoretic Text; an ancient Hebrew scribal tradition *my*

had abandoned the Davidic kings. *his blessings.* The vineyards and olive groves that had been taken away (see 2:12) and all of God's gifts (cf. Jer 31:12–14). *last days.* The Hebrew for this phrase occurs 13 times in the OT, sometimes simply meaning the future ("days to come," Ge 49:1), but most of the time, as no doubt here, referring to the Messianic age ("afterward," Joel 2:28; cf. Ac 2:17; Heb 1:2).

4:1—14:9 Deals with Israel's involvement in Canaanite religion, her moral sins and her international intrigues.

4:1 *Hear the word.* See Jer 2:4 and note. *charge.* As the Lord's spokesman, Hosea brought charges against unfaithful, covenant-breaking Israel (cf. v. 4; 12:2; Isa 3:13; Jer 2:9; Mic 6:2). *faithfulness.* Loyalty (see 2:20 and note) to the covenant Lord (Jos 24:14) and right dealing with others (cf. Pr 3:3). *love.* See 2:19; 10:12. *acknowledgment of God.* See 2:20; 6:3 and notes.

4:2 *cursing … adultery.* The sins detailed (paralleled in Jer 7:9) transgress several of the Ten Commandments (see Ex 20:13–16 and notes on 20:1–2). *bloodshed.* Includes (1) murder (see 6:8–9), (2) the assassinations following the death of Jeroboam II when three kings reigned in one year (2Ki 15:10–14) and (3) human sacrifice (Ps 106:38; Eze 16:20–21; 23:37). Where God is not acknowledged (v. 1), moral uprightness disappears.

4:3 *land mourns.* God's judgment on human sin affects all living things in the world (see, e.g., Isa 24:3–6; Jer 4:23–28). *waste away.* See Isa 19:8; Jer 14:2; 15:9; Joel 1:10.

4:4–9 An indictment against the priests, whose duty it was to be guardians of God's law and to furnish religious instruction (see Lev 10:11; Dt 31:9–13; 33:10; 2Ch 17:8–9; Ezr 7:6,10; Jer 18:18; Eze 7:26 and note; Zep 3:4; Hag 2:11; Mal 2:7–9). Hosea warned the priests not to lodge charges against the people for bringing God's judgment down on the nation, for they themselves were guilty, and the people could also bring charges against them — as Hosea proceeded to do (see v. 9; cf. Isa 28:7; Jer 2:26; 4:9; 23:11).

4:5 *stumble.* Experience calamity (see 5:5). *prophets.* See Mic 2:6,11; 3:5–7. *your mother.* The nation (see 2:2,5; Isa 50:1).

4:6 *my people.* Israel (see vv. 8,12; 2:1,23; 6:11; 11:7; Mic 6:3,5). *destroyed from lack of knowledge.* Partly because the priests had failed to teach God's word to the people. *rejected knowledge … reject you.* Punishment in kind. *law of your God.* Israel's source of life (see Dt 30:20 and note), which the priests should have been faithfully promoting.

4:7 *their Glory.* God (see Ps 106:20 and note).

4:8 *feed on the sins.* Priests devoured the sacrifices (see 1Sa 2:13–17 and notes), profiting from the continuation of the sin rather than helping to cure it (see 8:13 and note).

4:9 *Like people, like priests.* Without exception, all would be punished for their sins.

4:10 *eat but not have enough.* The punishment (a futility curse; see note on Hag 1:6) fit the sin. *prostitution.* See vv. 12,18; 2:4; 6:10; 9:1; Jdg 2:17 and note; Ps 106:39. Instead of giving themselves to the Lord, they gave themselves to prostitution (vv. 11–15; see notes on Ge 20:9; Ex 34:15; Ps 73:27).

4:11 *old wine.* See 7:5. *new.* See 2:8–9,22; 7:14; 9:2.

4:12 *wooden idol.* An image intended to represent a god (see Jer 2:27; 10:8; Hab 2:19). *stick of wood.* Either the wooden idol or a diviner's rod. *spirit of prostitution.* See 5:4. Hebrew idioms often speak of inner tendencies in terms of "spirit."

4:13 *mountaintops.* Places commonly chosen for pagan altars (see 10:8; Dt 12:2; 1Ki 3:2 and note;

under oak,[d] poplar and terebinth,
where the shade is pleasant.[e]
Therefore your daughters turn to
prostitution[f]
and your daughters-in-law to
adultery.[g]

14 "I will not punish your daughters
when they turn to prostitution,
nor your daughters-in-law
when they commit adultery,
because the men themselves consort
with harlots[h]
and sacrifice with shrine
prostitutes[i]—
a people without understanding[j] will
come to ruin![k]

15 "Though you commit adultery,
O Israel,
let not Judah become guilty.

"Do not go to Gilgal;[l]
do not go up to Beth Aven.[a][m]
And do not swear, 'As surely as the
LORD lives!'[n]

16 The Israelites are stubborn,[o]
like a stubborn heifer.[p]
How then can the LORD pasture them
like lambs[q] in a meadow?

17 Ephraim is joined to idols;
leave him alone!

18 Even when their drinks are gone,
they continue their prostitution;
their rulers dearly love shameful
ways.

19 A whirlwind[r] will sweep them away,
and their sacrifices will bring them
shame.[s]

Judgment Against Israel

5 "Hear this, you priests!
Pay attention, you Israelites!
Listen, O royal house!
This judgment[t] is against you:
You have been a snare[u] at Mizpah,
a net[v] spread out on Tabor.

2 The rebels are deep in slaughter.[w]
I will discipline all of them.[x]

3 I know all about Ephraim;
Israel is not hidden[y] from me.
Ephraim, you have now turned to
prostitution;
Israel is corrupt.[z]

4 "Their deeds do not permit them
to return[a] to their God.
A spirit of prostitution[b] is in their
heart;
they do not acknowledge[c] the LORD.

5 Israel's arrogance testifies[d] against
them;
the Israelites, even Ephraim,
stumble[e] in their sin;
Judah also stumbles with them.[f]

[a] 15 *Beth Aven* means *house of wickedness* (a name for Bethel, which means *house of God*).

4:13 [d] S Isa 1:29 [e] S Jer 3:6; Hos 10:8; 11:2 [f] Jer 2:20; Am 7:17 [g] Hos 2:13 **4:14** [h] S ver 11 [i] S Ge 38:21; Hos 9:10 [j] S Pr 10:21 [k] ver 19 **4:15** [l] Hos 9:15; 12:11; Am 4:4; 5:5 [m] S Jos 7:2; S Hos 5:8 [n] S Jer 4:2 **4:16** [o] S Ex 32:9 [p] S Jer 31:18 [q] Isa 5:17; 7:25 **4:19** [r] Hos 12:1; 13:15 [s] ver 13-14; Isa 1:29 **5:1** [t] S Job 10:2 [u] Hos 6:9; 9:8 [v] S Jer 5:26 **5:2** [w] S Hos 4:2 [x] Hos 9:15 **5:3** [y] Am 5:12 [z] S Eze 23:7; S Hos 1:2; 6:10 **5:4** [a] Hos 7:10 [b] S Hos 4:11 [c] S Jer 4:22; S Hos 4:6 **5:5** [d] S Isa 3:9; S Jer 2:19; Hos 7:10 [e] S Eze 14:7 [f] Hos 14:1

Jer 2:20; 3:6). Clay tablets from Ugarit (see chart, p. xxiii) tell of fertility rites carried out by the Canaanites at the high places. *oak ... terebinth.* Trees noted for their shade. *turn to prostitution.* Canaanite fertility rites involved sexual activity (v. 14) that led to general erosion of sexual morality.

4:14 *not punish.* The men would punish their women for immorality, but God would have no part in their hypocrisy. *harlots.* Common prostitutes (see Ge 34:31; Lev 21:14; Eze 16:31). *shrine prostitutes.* Women of the sanctuaries who served as partners for men in sexual activity that was part of their religious ritual (cf. Ge 38:21 and note; Dt 23:18). *without understanding.* Contrast 14:9.

4:15 *commit adultery.* See notes on Ge 20:9; Ex 34:15. *Judah.* An aside warning (see Introduction: Author and Date). *guilty.* See 10:2; 13:1. *Do not go.* The nation as a whole was addressed. *Gilgal.* A site near Jericho (see 9:15; 12:11; Jos 4:19; 1Sa 11:14 and notes) where the Israelites had established a religious shrine. *Beth Aven.* A sarcastic substitute name for Bethel (see NIV text note; see also 5:8), site of one of the two major worship centers established by Jeroboam I (see 1Ki 12:29 and note). *As surely as the LORD lives.* A form of solemn oath (see Ge 42:15 and note; Jdg 8:19; Ru 3:13; 1Sa 14:39; 26:10,16; Jer 4:2; 38:16). Though proper in itself—since it invoked the true God (Dt 6:13; 10:20; cf. Jos 23:7)—it was here forbidden because it was being used deceitfully, as though the Israelites were truly honoring the Lord (see Jer 5:2 and note).

4:16 *stubborn.* See Ne 9:29; Zec 7:11. *stubborn heifer.* See Jer 2:20; 31:18 and notes; an apt figure for unruly Israel (Hos 10:11; cf. 11:4).

4:17 *Ephraim.* Israel's largest tribe (see notes on 9:11; 13:1), whose name came to be used of the northern kingdom as a whole. *idols.* The golden calf (see 8:5 and note) and the Baals (see 2:8,13 and notes). *leave him alone.* Nothing could be done to help (see 2Sa 16:11; 2Ki 23:18).

4:19 *A whirlwind will sweep them away.* Lit. "The wind will catch them up with its wings," probably a metaphor from the threshing floor (see 13:3; Ru 1:22; Ps 1:4 and notes) for the sudden violence that would bring the exile. Since the Hebrew for the words "wind" and "spirit" is the same, there is a possible wordplay with the "spirit of prostitution" (see v. 12 and note). *shame.* By means of their sacrifices they hoped to flourish, but God's punishment for their idolatry would bring them into disgrace among the nations (see 10:6).

5:1 *priests ... Israelites ... royal house.* The three groups addressed were all responsible for maintaining justice, but it miscarried at their hands. *snare ... net.* Devices for catching animals and birds, here used as metaphors for those who by economic and legal schemes took cruel advantage of innocent people (see Job 18:8–10; Ps 140:5; Pr 29:5–6; La 1:13). *Mizpah.* Either (1) Mizpah in Gilead east of the Jordan (Ge 31:43–49) or (2) Mizpah in Benjamin (see 1Sa 7:5 and note). *Tabor.* A mountain at the southeastern edge of the Jezreel Valley. Reference must have been to well-known events that illustrated Israel's corruption.

5:2 *discipline.* A significant word in the prophets for God's corrective action against his people (see Isa 26:16; Jer 2:30; 5:3; 7:28).

5:3 *Ephraim.* See note on 4:17. *prostitution.* See note on 4:10.

5:4 *Their deeds.* See 4:9; 7:2; 9:15; 12:2. Persistent sin can make repentance impossible (see Jer 13:23; Jn 8:34; Ro 6:6,16). *spirit of prostitution.* See 4:12 and note. *not acknowledge the LORD.* See 4:6; Isa 1:3 and note.

5:5 *arrogance.* Stubborn rebellion against the Lord (see Dt 1:43; 1Sa 15:23; Ne 9:16; Job 35:12; Ps 10:2; Eze 16:56–57). *testifies.* In the case God presented against his people (see 4:1

6 When they go with their flocks and herds
to seek the LORD,[g]
they will not find him;
he has withdrawn[h] himself from them.
7 They are unfaithful[i] to the LORD;
they give birth to illegitimate[j] children.
Now their New Moon festivals[k]
will devour[l] them and their fields.

8 "Sound the trumpet[m] in Gibeah,[n]
the horn in Ramah.[o]
Raise the battle cry in Beth Aven[a];[p]
lead on, O Benjamin.
9 Ephraim will be laid waste[q]
on the day of reckoning.[r]
Among the tribes of Israel
I proclaim what is certain.[s]
10 Judah's leaders are like those
who move boundary stones.[t]
I will pour out my wrath[u] on them
like a flood of water.
11 Ephraim is oppressed,
trampled in judgment,
intent on pursuing idols.[b][v]
12 I am like a moth[w] to Ephraim,
like rot[x] to the people of Judah.

13 "When Ephraim[y] saw his sickness,
and Judah his sores,
then Ephraim turned to Assyria,[z]
and sent to the great king for help.[a]
But he is not able to cure[b] you,
not able to heal your sores.[c]
14 For I will be like a lion[d] to Ephraim,
like a great lion to Judah.
I will tear them to pieces[e] and go away;
I will carry them off, with no one to rescue them.[f]
15 Then I will go back to my place[g]
until they admit their guilt.[h]
And they will seek my face;[i]
in their misery[j] they will earnestly seek me.[k]"

5:6 [g] Mic 6:6-7 [h] S Pr 1:28; Isa 1:15; Eze 8:6; Mal 1:10 **5:7** [i] S Isa 24:16; Hos 6:7 [j] Hos 2:4 [k] Isa 1:14 [l] S Hos 2:11-12 **5:8** [m] S Nu 10:2; S Jer 4:21; S Eze 33:3 [n] Jdg 19:12; Hos 9:9; 10:9 [o] S Isa 10:29 [p] S Jos 7:2; Hos 4:15; 10:5 **5:9** [q] S Isa 7:16 [r] Isa 37:3; Hos 9:11-17 [s] Isa 46:10; Zec 1:6 **5:10** [t] S Dt 19:14 [u] S Eze 7:8 **5:11** [v] Hos 9:16; Mic 6:16 **5:12** [w] S Job 13:28; S Isa 51:8 [x] S Job 18:16 **5:13** [y] S Isa 7:16 [z] S Eze 23:5; Hos 7:11; 8:9; 12:1 [a] S La 5:6; Hos 7:8; 10:6 [b] S Isa 3:7; Hos 14:3 [c] Hos 2:7 **5:14** [d] S Job 10:16; S Jer 4:7; Am 3:4 [e] Hos 6:1 [f] S Dt 32:39; Mic 5:8 **5:15** [g] S Isa 18:4 [h] S Lev 26:40 [i] S Nu 21:7; S Ps 24:6; S Hos 3:5 [j] Ps 50:15; S Jer 2:27 [k] Isa 64:9; S Eze 20:43

Israel Unrepentant

6 "Come, let us return[l] to the LORD.
He has torn us to pieces[m]
but he will heal us;[n]
he has injured us
but he will bind up our wounds.[o]
2 After two days he will revive us;[p]
on the third day[q] he will restore[r] us,
that we may live in his presence.
3 Let us acknowledge the LORD;
let us press on to acknowledge him.
As surely as the sun rises,
he will appear;
he will come to us like the winter rains,[s]
like the spring rains that water the earth.[t]"

4 "What can I do with you, Ephraim?[u]
What can I do with you, Judah?
Your love is like the morning mist,
like the early dew that disappears.[v]

[a] *8* *Beth Aven* means *house of wickedness* (a name for Bethel, which means *house of God*).
[b] *11* The meaning of the Hebrew for this word is uncertain.

6:1 [l] S Isa 10:20; S 19:22 [m] S Job 16:9; La 3:11; Hos 5:14 [n] S Nu 12:13; S Jer 3:22 [o] S Dt 32:39; S Job 5:18; S Jer 30:17; Hos 14:4 **6:2** [p] Ps 30:5; S 80:18 [q] S Mt 16:21 [r] S Ps 71:20 **6:3** [s] S Job 4:3; Joel 2:23 [t] Ps 72:6; Hos 11:10; 12:6 **6:4** [u] Hos 11:8 [v] Hos 7:1; 13:3

and note). *stumble.* See 4:5 and note. *Judah.* See Introduction: Author and Date.

5:6 *seek the LORD.* Go to him with prayer and sacrifices (see 3:5 and note; Am 5:4–5). *not find him.* Offering sacrifices in their situation was useless (see 2:7; cf. Isa 1:10–15; Am 5:21–24; Mic 6:6–8). The Lord would be found by Israel only when she turned to him with integrity of heart (see v. 15; 3:5; Dt 4:29–31; Jer 29:13).

5:7 *unfaithful.* See 1:2 and note. *New Moon.* Usually a festive occasion (see, e.g., 2:11; 1Sa 20:5 and note; Am 8:5; Col 2:16), but now a time of judgment. Or the meaning may be that one month would be sufficient to accomplish their punishment.

5:8 Some interpreters suggest that the Aramean (Syrian)-Ephraimite (Israelite) war (see 2Ki 16:5–9; Isa 7:1–9 and notes) forms the background of the message in chs. 4–5. *trumpet.* Made of a ram's horn, which here sounds the alarm that an army is approaching (see 8:1; Joel 2:1 and note; Am 3:6). *Gibeah.* Two miles north of Jerusalem. *Ramah.* North of Gibeah. *Beth Aven.* See note on 4:15. *lead on, O Benjamin.* Perhaps a Benjamite war cry.

5:9 *laid waste.* See Jer 25:11,38.

5:10 *move boundary stones.* See Dt 19:14 and note; 27:17; Pr 15:25 and note; 23:10; cf. Isa 5:8; Mic 2:2. *my wrath.* See 13:11.

5:12 *moth ... rot.* Both consume (see Job 13:28).

5:13 *sickness ... sores.* Metaphors for the national wounds that Israel and Judah had suffered at the hands of their enemies (see Isa 1:5–6; 17:11; Jer 15:18; 30:12–15). *turned to Assyria.* Assyrian records document the tribute paid to Tiglath-Pileser III by the Israelite kings Menahem and Hoshea (cf. 2Ki 15:19–20; 17:3). *not able to cure.* The alliances were worthless.

5:14 *lion.* See 13:7; Am 1:2 and note; 3:8. The Lord might use human agents (see Isa 10:5 and note), but he would be the one to bring on Israel her punishment, from which there was no escape (see Isa 5:29; 42:22; Am 9:1–4).

5:15 *go back to my place.* God threatened to withdraw from Israel until, out of desperation, she truly repented. This idea sets the stage for the prophet's next theme.

6:1 *let us return.* A shallow (see v. 4) proposal of repentance (using phrases from 5:13–15), in which Israel acknowledged that God, not Assyria (cf. 5:13), was the true physician (cf. 7:1).

6:2 *two days ... third day.* A brief time. Israel supposed that God's wrath would only be temporary.

6:3 *acknowledge the LORD.* A key concept in Hosea (see v. 6; 2:20 and note; 4:1,6; 5:4). *like the winter rains ... spring rains.* Israel believed that, as surely as seasonal rains fell, reviving the earth, God's favor would return and restore her.

6:4 *What can I do ...?* See Isa 5:4. God saw through Israel's superficial repentance. *Ephraim.* See note on 4:17. *Judah.* See Introduction: Author and Date. *love.* See 2:19; see also note on v. 6. *morning mist ... dew.* Figurative for that which is temporary.

[5]Therefore I cut you in pieces with my
prophets,
I killed you with the words of my
mouth;[w]
my judgments flashed like lightning
upon you.[x]
[6]For I desire mercy, not sacrifice,[y]
and acknowledgment[z] of God rather
than burnt offerings.[a]
[7]Like Adam,[a] they have broken the
covenant[b]—
they were unfaithful[c] to me there.
[8]Gilead is a city of wicked men,[d]
stained with footprints of blood.
[9]As marauders lie in ambush for a
man,[e]
so do bands of priests;
they murder[f] on the road to Shechem,
committing shameful crimes.[g]
[10]I have seen a horrible[h] thing
in the house of Israel.
There Ephraim is given to prostitution
and Israel is defiled.[i]

[11]"Also for you, Judah,
a harvest[j] is appointed.

"Whenever I would restore the
fortunes[k] of my people,
7 [1]whenever I would heal Israel,
the sins of Ephraim are exposed
and the crimes of Samaria revealed.[l]
They practice deceit,[m]
thieves break into houses,[n]
bandits rob in the streets;[o]
[2]but they do not realize
that I remember[p] all their evil deeds.[q]
Their sins engulf them;[r]
they are always before me.

[3]"They delight the king with their
wickedness,
the princes with their lies.[s]
[4]They are all adulterers,[t]
burning like an oven
whose fire the baker need not stir
from the kneading of the dough till it
rises.
[5]On the day of the festival of our king
the princes become inflamed with
wine,[u]
and he joins hands with the
mockers.[v]
[6]Their hearts are like an oven;[w]
they approach him with intrigue.
Their passion smolders all night;
in the morning it blazes like a
flaming fire.
[7]All of them are hot as an oven;
they devour their rulers.
All their kings fall,[x]
and none of them calls[y] on me.

[8]"Ephraim mixes[z] with the nations;
Ephraim is a flat cake not turned
over.

[a] 7 Or *As at Adam*; or *Like men*

6:5 [w]Jer 1:9-10; 5:14; 23:29 [x]Heb 4:12 **6:6** [y]S 1Sa 15:22; S Isa 1:11; Mt 9:13*; 12:7*; Mk 12:33 [z]S Jer 4:22; S Hos 2:20 [a]S Ps 40:6; Mic 6:8 **6:7** [b]S Ge 9:11; S Jer 11:10; Hos 8:1 [c]S Hos 5:7 **6:8** [d]Hos 12:11 **6:9** [e]Ps 10:8 [f]S Hos 4:2 [g]Jer 5:30-31; 7:9-10; S Eze 22:9; S Hos 5:1; 7:1 **6:10** [h]S Jer 5:30 [i]S Jer 23:14; S Eze 23:7; S Hos 5:3 **6:11** [j]Jer 51:33; Joel 3:13 [k]S Ps 126:1; Zep 2:7 **7:1** [l]S Eze 24:13; S Hos 6:4 [m]ver 13 [n]S Ex 22:2; Hos 4:2 [o]S Hos 6:9; 12:1 **7:2** [p]S Jer 14:10; S 44:21; S Hos 8:13 [q]S Job 35:15; Hos 9:15 [r]Jer 2:19; 4:18 **7:3** [s]Jer 28:1-4; S Hos 4:2; 10:13; Mic 7:3 **7:4** [t]S Jer 9:2 **7:5** [u]S Isa 28:1,7 [v]S Ps 1:1 **7:6** [w]Ps 21:9 **7:7** [x]Hos 13:10 [y]ver 16; S Ps 14:4; S Isa 9:13; Zep 1:6 **7:8** [z]ver 11; Ps 106:35; S Hos 5:13

6:5 *my prophets.* God's spokesmen had denounced the people's sin. *words of my mouth.* The judgments spoken by the Lord's faithful prophets (see Jer 1:9; 15:19 and notes).

6:6 *mercy.* Hebrew *ḥesed,* a word that can refer to right conduct toward one's neighbor or loyalty to the Lord or both—the sum of what God requires of his servants. Here it perhaps refers to both. The same Hebrew word is translated "love" in v. 4 (see note on Ps 6:4). *not sacrifice.* Sacrifice apart from faithfulness to the Lord's will is wholly unacceptable to him (see 1Sa 15:22–23; Isa 1:11–15; Jer 7:21–23; Am 5:21–24; Mic 6:6–8; Mt 9:13; 12:7). *acknowledgment of God.* See v. 3; 2:20 and notes.

6:7 *Like Adam.* The allusion is uncertain, since Scripture records no covenant with Adam. The NIV text note suggests a place named Adam (Tell ed-Damiyeh) at the Jordan (see Jos 3:16), as suggested by the reference to "there" at the end of the sentence. A third interpretation takes Adam as humankind (see NIV text note). *broken the covenant.* See 8:1; Jos 7:11.

6:8 *Gilead.* See 12:11; Jdg 10:17; 12:7. *footprints of blood.* The allusion is unclear, but Hosea may have been referring to a more recent event than the bloodbath of Jdg 12:1–6—such as Pekah's rebellion against Pekahiah (see 2Ki 15:25).

6:9 *they murder.* The specific event is unknown. *Shechem.* See Ge 33:18 and note.

6:10 *prostitution.* See note on 4:10.

6:11 *harvest.* Figurative for God's judgments (see 8:7; 10:12–13; Jer 51:33; Mt 13:30,39–42; Rev 14:15). *restore the fortunes.* Paralleling "heal" (7:1), the phrase refers to the restoration of the wounded national body (see Joel 3:1; Zep 3:20).

7:1 *heal.* See 5:13; 6:1; 11:3; 14:4; Jer 51:8–9. *sins.* See 4:8; 5:5; 8:13. *Ephraim.* See note on 4:17. *exposed … revealed.* God sees them. *crimes.* See v. 3. *Samaria.* Another name for the northern kingdom, of which Samaria was the royal city, selected by Omri to be the capital of Israel (see 1Ki 16:24 and note). *deceit.* See Jer 6:13; 8:10; probably refers to both feigned repentance and treacherous foreign alliances. *thieves.* See 4:2. *bandits.* See 6:9; Ge 49:19; Jer 18:22.

7:2 See Ps 90:8 and note. *I remember.* Everything is open before the Lord, but the wicked believe that God does not see (see Ps 10:6,11 and notes).

7:3 *delight the king.* Perhaps in conjunction with one of the palace revolts (see 2Ki 15:8–30). They were entertaining and flattering the king and princes while engaging in the "wickedness" of preparing to stab them in the back (vv. 6–7; see note on v. 7). *lies.* See 11:12; Ps 10:7 and note; Na 3:1.

7:4 *adulterers.* See note on 4:15. *fire.* A metaphor for political intrigue (see vv. 6–7). The fire was banked until ready to use; then it broke out. *baker.* Perhaps the leader of the conspiracy.

7:5 *festival of our king.* Probably a coronation or birthday that became a drunken orgy. King Elah died in drunkenness (see 1Ki 16:9 and note). *mockers.* See Pr 1:22 and note. Isaiah (28:1–8,14) condemned Israel's drunkenness and her scoffers.

7:6 The intrigue was kept secret until a suitable time.

7:7 *rulers … kings.* Four kings were assassinated in 20 years, Zechariah and Shallum in a seven-month period (2Ki 15:10–14). *none of them calls on me.* The reason for the shameful situation.

7:8 *mixes with the nations.* See v. 11 and note. *flat cake.* A metaphor describing unwise policies. Baked on hot stones (cf. 1Ki 19:6), the cake was burned on the bottom and undone on the top.

9 Foreigners sap his strength,[a]
but he does not realize it.
His hair is sprinkled with gray,
but he does not notice.
10 Israel's arrogance testifies against him,[b]
but despite all this
he does not return[c] to the LORD his God
or search[d] for him.

11 "Ephraim is like a dove,[e]
easily deceived and senseless—
now calling to Egypt,[f]
now turning to Assyria.[g]
12 When they go, I will throw my net[h]
over them;
I will pull them down like birds of
the air.
When I hear them flocking together,
I will catch them.
13 Woe[i] to them,
because they have strayed[j] from me!
Destruction to them,
because they have rebelled against
me!
I long to redeem them
but they speak lies[k] against me.[l]
14 They do not cry out to me from their
hearts[m]
but wail upon their beds.
They gather together[a] for grain and
new wine[n]
but turn away from me.[o]
15 I trained[p] them and strengthened them,
but they plot evil[q] against me.
16 They do not turn to the Most High;[r]
they are like a faulty bow.[s]
Their leaders will fall by the sword
because of their insolent[t] words.
For this they will be ridiculed[u]
in the land of Egypt.[v]

7:9 [a] Isa 1:7; Hos 8:7 **7:10** [b] Hos 5:5 [c] Hos 5:4 [d] ver 14; S Isa 9:13 **7:11** [e] S Ge 8:8 [f] ver 16; Hos 9:6 [g] S ver 8; S Jer 2:18; S La 5:6; Hos 9:3; 12:1 **7:12** [h] S Eze 12:13; S 32:3 **7:13** [i] Hos 9:12 [j] Jer 14:10; S Eze 34:4-6; Hos 9:17 [k] S Ps 116:11 [l] ver 1; Jer 51:9; Mt 23:37 **7:14** [m] Jer 3:10 [n] Am 2:8 [o] S ver 10; S Hos 4:10; 9:1; 13:16 **7:15** [p] Hos 11:3 [q] Ps 2:1; S 140:2; Na 1:9,11 **7:16** [r] S ver 7 [s] S Ps 78:9,57 [t] Mal 3:14 [u] S Eze 23:32 [v] S ver 11; Hos 9:3; 11:5 **8:1** [w] S Nu 10:2; S Eze 33:3 [x] S Dt 28:49; Jer 4:13 [y] S Jer 11:10 [z] S Hos 4:6; S 6:7 **8:3** [a] S Mt 7:23; Tit 1:16 **8:4** [b] Hos 13:10 [c] S Hos 2:8; 13:1-2 **8:5** [d] ver 6; Hos 10:5 [e] Jer 13:27 **8:6** [f] S Jer 16:20; Hos 14:3 [g] S Ex 32:4 [h] S ver 5

Israel to Reap the Whirlwind

8 "Put the trumpet[w] to your lips!
An eagle[x] is over the house of the
LORD
because the people have broken my
covenant[y]
and rebelled against my law.[z]
2 Israel cries out to me,
'O our God, we acknowledge you!'
3 But Israel has rejected what is good;
an enemy will pursue him.[a]
4 They set up kings without my consent;
they choose princes without my
approval.[b]
With their silver and gold
they make idols[c] for themselves
to their own destruction.
5 Throw out your calf-idol, O Samaria![d]
My anger burns against them.
How long will they be incapable of
purity?[e]
6 They are from Israel!
This calf—a craftsman has made it;
it is not God.[f]
It will be broken in pieces,
that calf[g] of Samaria.[h]

7 "They sow the wind
and reap the whirlwind.[i]
The stalk has no head;
it will produce no flour.[j]

[a] 14 Most Hebrew manuscripts; some Hebrew manuscripts and Septuagint *They slash themselves*

8:7 [i] S Job 4:8; Pr 22:8; Isa 66:15; Hos 10:12-13; Na 1:3; Gal 6:8 [j] S Dt 28:38; S Isa 17:11; Hos 9:16

7:9 *Foreigners sap his strength.* Tribute to Assyria (2Ki 15:19–20) and to Egypt (v. 11) had weakened the country economically. *hair ... gray.* He was old before his time, but ignored the danger signals.
7:10 *return.* See 3:5; 5:4; Am 4:6–11. *search.* See 3:5; 5:6,15 and notes.
7:11 *dove.* See 11:11 and note, where a different image is intended. See also note on Ps 68:13. *senseless.* See Jer 5:21. Menahem turned to Assyria (2Ki 15:19–20); Hoshea alternated in allegiance to Assyria and Egypt (2Ki 17:3–4).
7:12 *my net.* The Lord himself was the hunter—not the nations—and Israel was certain to be caught.
7:13 *Woe.* Often used in conjunction with threats of judgment (see 9:12). *Destruction.* See 9:6; Isa 13:6. *redeem.* See 13:14; also used for deliverance from Egypt (see, e.g., Ex 6:6–8 and notes; Mic 6:4). *lies.* Possibly of ascribing prosperity and destiny to gods other than the Lord.
7:14 *wail.* See Joel 1:13. *They gather together.* See NIV text note; cf. Lev 19:28; 21:5 and notes. *grain and new wine.* See 2:8,22; 9:1–2.
7:15 *I trained them.* As children (see 11:3 and note) or, perhaps, as troops. *strengthened them.* Lit. "strengthened their arms" (see Eze 30:24–25).
7:16 *Most High.* See 11:7; Dt 32:8 and note. *faulty bow.* See Ps 78:57. The arrow missed the mark; Israel missed her purpose for being. *ridiculed.* Egypt would fail to assist Israel and then would belittle God's power (see Dt 9:28). *Egypt.* See 8:13; 11:5 and notes. There is no record of a forced exile of large numbers to Egypt. Some captives were taken there (2Ki 23:34; Jer 22:11–14), and some fugitives voluntarily went there (2Ki 25:26; Jer 42–44). A return from Egypt is envisioned in 11:11; Isa 11:11; 27:13; Zec 10:10.
8:1 *trumpet.* See 5:8 and note. *your.* Hosea's. *eagle.* Or "vulture," referring to Assyria. *house of the LORD.* The land of Israel, not just the temple (see 9:15 and note; cf. Ex 15:17).
8:2 *we acknowledge you.* See 2:20; 6:3 and notes; but their worship of the Lord was thoroughly corrupted by pagan notions and practices, as vv. 3–6 indicate (see Am 2:4,7–8; 3:14; 5:26).
8:3 *an enemy.* The Assyrians.
8:4 *set up kings.* After Jeroboam II, five kings ruled over Israel in 13 years (2Ki 15:8–30), three of whom seized the throne by violence (see 7:7 and note).
8:5 *calf-idol.* See 10:5; 13:2. Jeroboam I (930–909 B.C.) had set up golden calves in Bethel and Dan, saying, "Here are your gods" (see 1Ki 12:28–33 and note on 12:28). *Samaria.* See note on 7:1.
8:6 *a craftsman has made it.* For prophetic satire on idolatry see Isa 40:20; 41:22–24; 44:9–20; see also Ps 115:4–8 and notes. Israel's leaders (Ex 32:4) and Jeroboam I had said, "These are your gods"; but Hosea said, "It is not God."
8:7 *They sow ... whirlwind.* A familiar proverb about the results of doing evil (see 10:13; Job 4:8; Ps 126:5–6; Pr

Were it to yield grain,
foreigners would swallow it up.[k]
8 Israel is swallowed up;[l]
now she is among the nations
like a worthless[m] thing.
9 For they have gone up to Assyria[n]
like a wild donkey[o] wandering
alone.
Ephraim has sold herself to lovers.[p]
10 Although they have sold themselves
among the nations,
I will now gather them together.[q]
They will begin to waste away[r]
under the oppression of the mighty
king.

11 "Though Ephraim built many altars for
sin offerings,
these have become altars for
sinning.[s]
12 I wrote for them the many things of
my law,
but they regarded them as something
alien.[t]
13 They offer sacrifices given to me
and they eat[u] the meat,
but the LORD is not pleased with
them.[v]
Now he will remember[w] their
wickedness
and punish their sins:[x]
They will return to Egypt.[y]
14 Israel has forgotten[z] his Maker[a]
and built palaces;
Judah has fortified many towns.
But I will send fire upon their cities
that will consume their fortresses."[b]

8:7 [k]Hos 2:9; S 7:9 **8:8** [l]Jer 51:34 [m]Jer 22:28 **8:9** [n]S Jer 2:18 [o]S Ge 16:12 [p]S Jer 22:20; Eze 23:5; S Hos 5:13 **8:10** [q]S Eze 16:37; S 22:20 [r]Jer 42:2 **8:11** [s]Hos 10:1; 12:11 **8:12** [t]S ver 1 **8:13** [u]S Jer 7:21 [v]S Jer 6:20; Hos 9:4 [w]Hos 7:2; 9:9; Am 8:7 [x]S Hos 4:9 [y]Hos 9:3,6 **8:14** [z]S Dt 32:18; S Isa 17:10; S Hos 2:13 [a]S Ps 95:6 [b]Jer 5:17; S 17:27; Am 2:5

9:1 [c]Isa 22:12-13 [d]S Ps 73:27; S Isa 24:16; S Hos 7:14; 10:5 [e]S Ge 30:15 **9:2** [f]Isa 24:7; Hos 2:9; Joel 1:10 **9:3** [g]Lev 25:23 [h]S Hos 7:16; S 8:13 [i]Eze 4:13; S Hos 7:11; 10:5; Am 7:17 **9:4** [j]Joel 1:9,13; 2:14 [k]S Hos 8:13 [l]S Jer 16:7 [m]S Dt 26:14; Hag 2:13-14 [n]S Eze 4:13-14 **9:5** [o]Isa 10:3; Jer 5:31 [p]S Hos 2:11 **9:6** [q]S Hos 7:11; S 8:13 [r]S Isa 19:13 [s]S Jer 42:22 [t]Zep 1:11 [u]Isa 5:6; Hos 10:8

Punishment for Israel

9 Do not rejoice, O Israel;
do not be jubilant[c] like the other
nations.
For you have been unfaithful[d] to your
God;
you love the wages of a prostitute[e]
at every threshing floor.
2 Threshing floors and winepresses will
not feed the people;
the new wine[f] will fail them.
3 They will not remain[g] in the LORD's
land;
Ephraim will return to Egypt[h]
and eat unclean[a] food in Assyria.[i]
4 They will not pour out wine offerings[j]
to the LORD,
nor will their sacrifices please[k] him.
Such sacrifices will be to them like the
bread of mourners;[l]
all who eat them will be unclean.[m]
This food will be for themselves;
it will not come into the temple of
the LORD.[n]

5 What will you do[o] on the day of your
appointed feasts,[p]
on the festival days of the LORD?
6 Even if they escape from destruction,
Egypt will gather them,[q]
and Memphis[r] will bury them.[s]
Their treasures of silver[t] will be taken
over by briers,
and thorns[u] will overrun their tents.

[a] 3 That is, ceremonially unclean

11:18; 22:8; 2Co 9:6; Gal 6:7). Israel sowed the wind of idolatry and reaped the whirlwind of Assyria. *stalk ... flour.* The prophet played on the similar sound of the Hebrew words. *foreigners.* Assyria.

8:8 Israel was chosen to be God's own people (see Ex 19:5; Am 3:2 and notes), but since she had conformed to the other nations, she lost her special identity and so became "worthless" to God.

8:9 *wild donkey wandering alone.* See Jer 2:24 and note. *Ephraim.* See note on 4:17. *sold herself to lovers.* For the prostitute's fees (see 9:1 and note) of Assyrian protection. Menahem (2Ki 15:19) and Hoshea (2Ki 17:3), kings of Israel, paid tribute to Assyria.

8:10 Even though Israel paid tribute to Assyria, that would not buy her security, for God would send judgment by the king of Assyria. Israel's real enemy was the Lord himself (see 2:8–13; 7:12 and note).

8:13 *offer sacrifices.* See v. 2 and note. *eat the meat.* Some of the sacrifices were partly eaten by the offerer and priests (see Lev 7:11–18,28–36; Dt 12:7; Jer 7:21). *not pleased with them.* See 6:6 and note. *Egypt.* Israel, who had trusted in Egypt and Assyria, was to go back to "Egypt," i.e., into bondage in a foreign land, primarily Assyria (see 9:3). But see note on 7:16.

8:14 *Israel has forgotten.* The cause of all their problems (see 2:13 and note; cf. Jdg 2:10). *built palaces ... fortified many towns.* Israel's trust was not in her Maker but in what she herself had accomplished. *Judah.* See Introduction: Author and Date. *fire ... that will consume.* See Am 1:4 and note.

9:1 This verse begins a section that was probably spoken at a harvest festival, such as the Feast of Tabernacles (Lev 23:33–43; Dt 16:13–15). *unfaithful.* See 1:2; 2:2–5 and notes). *wages of a prostitute.* See 2:12 and note; not to be taken literally, but in the sense of spiritual adultery (see Ex 34:15 and note). *at every threshing floor.* Since the threshing floor at threshing time was a man's world—the threshers feasted there at the end of the day's labors and stayed all night to protect the grain (see Ru 3:2–3 and notes)—prostitutes were not uncommon visitors.

9:3 *LORD's land.* The promised land, which the Lord claimed as his own (see Lev 25:23; Jos 22:19 and note; Jer 2:7; Eze 38:16; Joel 1:6). *Ephraim.* See note on 4:17. *Egypt ... Assyria.* Israel was threatened with exile to the lands it depended on—where the temple sacrifice could not be offered (see 7:16; 8:13 and notes). *unclean.* A foreign country was ceremonially unclean (see NIV text note; see also Am 7:17 and NIV text note). What grew there was likewise unclean, because it was the product of fertility credited to pagan gods (see 2:5 and note; Eze 4:13).

9:4 *bread of mourners.* Unclean, like bread in a house where there had been a death (see Nu 19:14 and note; Dt 26:14; Jer 16:7). All who touched it became ceremonially unclean. *not come into the temple of the LORD.* In exile Israel would have no place (not even those places established by Jeroboam I; 1Ki 12:28–33) where she could bring sacrifices to the Lord or celebrate her religious festivals in his honor (v. 5).

9:5 *appointed feasts ... festival days.* See 2:11 and note.

9:6 *Egypt.* See 7:16; 8:13; 11:5 and notes. *Memphis.* The capital of Lower (northern) Egypt. *briers, and thorns.* Cf. a similar threat against Edom (Isa 34:13).

7 The days of punishment[v] are coming,
the days of reckoning[w] are at hand.
Let Israel know this.
Because your sins[x] are so many
and your hostility so great,
the prophet is considered a fool,[y]
the inspired man a maniac.[z]
8 The prophet, along with my God,
is the watchman over Ephraim,[a]
yet snares[a] await him on all his paths,
and hostility in the house of his God.[b]
9 They have sunk deep into corruption,[c]
as in the days of Gibeah.[d]
God will remember[e] their wickedness
and punish them for their sins.[f]

10 "When I found Israel,
it was like finding grapes in the desert;
when I saw your fathers,
it was like seeing the early fruit[g] on the fig[h] tree.
But when they came to Baal Peor,[i]
they consecrated themselves to that shameful idol[j]
and became as vile as the thing they loved.
11 Ephraim's glory[k] will fly away like a bird[l]—
no birth, no pregnancy, no conception.[m]
12 Even if they rear children,
I will bereave[n] them of every one.
Woe[o] to them
when I turn away from them![p]
13 I have seen Ephraim,[q] like Tyre,
planted in a pleasant place.[r]
But Ephraim will bring out
their children to the slayer."[s]

14 Give them, O LORD—
what will you give them?
Give them wombs that miscarry
and breasts that are dry.[t]

15 "Because of all their wickedness in Gilgal,[u]
I hated them there.
Because of their sinful deeds,[v]
I will drive them out of my house.
I will no longer love them;[w]
all their leaders are rebellious.[x]
16 Ephraim[y] is blighted,
their root is withered,
they yield no fruit.[z]
Even if they bear children,
I will slay[a] their cherished offspring."

17 My God will reject[b] them
because they have not obeyed[c] him;
they will be wanderers among the nations.[d]

10 Israel was a spreading vine;[e]
he brought forth fruit for himself.
As his fruit increased,
he built more altars;[f]
as his land prospered,[g]
he adorned his sacred stones.[h]
2 Their heart is deceitful,[i]
and now they must bear their guilt.[j]
The LORD will demolish their altars[k]
and destroy their sacred stones.[l]

[a] 8 Or *The prophet is the watchman over Ephraim, / the people of my God*

9:7 [v]Isa 34:8; Jer 10:15; Mic 7:4; Lk 21:22 [w]S Job 31:14 [x]Jer 16:18 [y]S 1Sa 10:11; Isa 44:25; S La 2:14; Eze 14:9-10 [z]S Jer 29:26; Hos 14:1 **9:8** [a]S Hos 5:1 [b]S Eze 22:26 **9:9** [c]Zep 3:7 [d]Jdg 19:16-30; S Hos 5:8 [e]S Hos 8:13 [f]S Hos 4:9 **9:10** [g]S SS 2:13 [h]S Isa 28:4 [i]Nu 25:1-5; Ps 106:28-29 [j]Jer 11:13; S Hos 4:14 **9:11** [k]S Isa 17:3 [l]S Hos 4:7; 10:5 [m]ver 14 **9:12** [n]ver 16; S Eze 24:21 [o]Hos 7:13 [p]S Dt 31:17 **9:13** [q]S Ps 78:67 [r]S Eze 27:3 [s]S Job 15:22; S La 2:22 **9:14** [t]ver 11; Lk 23:29 **9:15** [u]S Hos 4:15 [v]S Hos 7:2 [w]S Jer 12:8 [x]S Isa 1:23; S Hos 4:9; 5:2 **9:16** [y]S Hos 5:11 [z]S Job 15:32; S Hos 8:7 [a]S ver 12 **9:17** [b]S Jer 6:30 [c]S Hos 4:10 [d]S Dt 28:65; S Hos 7:13 **10:1** [e]S Eze 15:2 [f]S 1Ki 14:23 [g]Hos 13:15 [h]Hos 3:4; S 4:7; S 8:11; 12:11 **10:2** [i]1Ki 18:21 [j]Hos 13:16 [k]ver 8 [l]Mic 5:13

9:7 *inspired man.* See Mic 3:8 and note. *maniac.* See 2Ki 9:11; Jer 29:26 and notes; cf. 1Sa 21:15.

9:8 *watchman.* See Eze 3:17; Hab 2:1 and notes. *snares ... hostility.* Israel showed only hostility toward the watchmen (the true prophets) whom God sent to warn his people of the great dangers that threatened (see Jer 1:19; 11:19; 15:10; Am 7:10–13).

9:9 *corruption.* This word was also used of the Israelites who worshiped the golden calf (see Ex 32:7 and note; Dt 9:12). *days of Gibeah.* A reference to the corrupt behavior of the Benjamites so graphically described in Jdg 19–21. *God will remember.* Sins unrepented of are remembered, as well as the accumulated sins of generations (see 13:12).

9:10 *I found Israel ... I saw your fathers.* The covenant relation is traced back to "the desert" (see 2:14–15 and note on 2:14; 13:5; Dt 32:10). *grapes ... fig.* Refreshing delicacies (see SS 2:13; Isa 28:4; Mic 7:1). The images used here (grapes in the desert, early fruit of the fig tree) beautifully convey God's delight in Israel when she, out of all the nations, committed herself to him in covenant at Sinai. *Baal Peor.* Peor was a mountain (Nu 23:28). "Baal Peor" refers to the god of Peor (Nu 25:1–3) and is here used to refer to Beth Peor, "the sanctuary of Peor" (see Dt 3:29 and note; 4:3,46; Jos 13:20). Hosea refers here to the incident in Nu 25. *that shameful idol.* See Jdg 6:32; Jer 2:26 and notes. *became ... vile.* See Isa 5:2,4,7.

9:11 *Ephraim's glory.* Her large population and prosperity. The punishment fit the sin. Prostitution produces no increase (see 4:10; Jdg 2:17 and notes). *fly away like a bird.* Never to return (see Pr 23:5).

9:12 *Woe.* See 7:13 and note.

9:13 *Tyre.* Noted for its wealth, pleasant environment and security (see Eze 27:3–25). *planted.* That is, Ephraim. Tyre was a Mediterranean seaport.

9:14 Hosea did not pray out of hateful vengeance against Israel, but because he shared God's holy wrath against her sins.

9:15 *Gilgal.* See note on 4:15. *drive them out of my house.* As the unfaithful wife was driven from her husband's house, so Israel was driven from God's "house"—i.e., his land (see 8:1 and note). *no longer love them.* Because of their sins. But when they repent and ask the Lord to forgive them (see 14:1–2 and notes), he will "love them freely" (14:4).

9:17 *My God.* Hosea's words alone, for God was no longer Israel's God. *reject.* See 4:6; 2Ki 17:20. *wanderers.* Like Cain (Ge 4:12–16).

10:1 *Israel.* The nation personified and called by the name of its ancestor. *vine.* A frequent metaphor for Israel (see Ps 80:8–16 and note). *prospered.* The prosperity during the period of Jeroboam II (793–753 B.C.) is probably in view. *sacred stones.* See 3:4 and note.

10:2 *Their heart is deceitful.* See Jer 17:9 and note. Israel formally cried out to God, but they dishonored him by pagan worship (see 8:2 and note).

[3]Then they will say, "We have no king
because we did not revere the LORD.
But even if we had a king,
what could he do for us?"
[4]They make many promises,
take false oaths[m]
and make agreements;[n]
therefore lawsuits spring up
like poisonous weeds[o] in a plowed
field.
[5]The people who live in Samaria fear
for the calf-idol[p] of Beth Aven.[a][q]
Its people will mourn over it,
and so will its idolatrous priests,[r]
those who had rejoiced over its
splendor,
because it is taken from them into
exile.[s]
[6]It will be carried to Assyria[t]
as tribute[u] for the great king.[v]
Ephraim will be disgraced;[w]
Israel will be ashamed[x] of its
wooden idols.[b]
[7]Samaria and its king will float away[y]
like a twig on the surface of the
waters.
[8]The high places[z] of wickedness[c][a] will
be destroyed—
it is the sin of Israel.
Thorns[b] and thistles will grow up
and cover their altars.[c]
Then they will say to the mountains,
"Cover us!"[d]
and to the hills, "Fall on us!"[e]
[9]"Since the days of Gibeah,[f] you have
sinned,[g] O Israel,
and there you have remained.[d]
Did not war overtake
the evildoers in Gibeah?
[10]When I please, I will punish[h] them;
nations will be gathered against
them
to put them in bonds for their
double sin.

10:4 [m]S Hos 4:2 [n]S Eze 17:19; Am 5:7 [o]Am 6:12 **10:5** [p]S Ex 32:4; S Isa 44:17-20 [q]ver 8; S Hos 5:8 [r]S 2Ki 23:5; Zep 1:4 [s]S Jdg 18:17-18; S Hos 8:5; S 9:1, 3, 11 **10:6** [t]S 2Ki 16:7; Hos 11:5 [u]S Jdg 3:15 [v]S Hos 5:13 [w]Isa 30:3; S Hos 4:7 [x]Jer 48:13 **10:7** [y]ver 15; Hos 13:11 **10:8** [z]S Eze 6:6 [a]S ver 5; 1Ki 12:28-30; S Hos 4:13 [b]S Hos 9:6 [c]ver 2; S Isa 32:13 [d]S Job 30:6; Am 3:14-15 [e]Am 7:9; Lk 23:30*; Rev 6:16 **10:9** [f]S Hos 5:8 [g]S Jos 7:11 **10:10** [h]S Eze 5:13; S Hos 4:9 **10:11** [i]S Jer 15:12; S 31:18 **10:12** [j]S Ecc 11:1 [k]S Pr 11:18; Jas 3:18 [l]Jer 4:3 [m]S Isa 19:22; Hos 12:6 [n]S Isa 45:8 **10:13** [o]S Job 4:8; S Hos 7:3; 11:12; Gal 6:7-8 [p]S Pr 11:18; S Hos 8:7 [q]Ps 33:16 **10:14** [r]S Isa 17:3; Mic 5:11 [s]S 2Ki 17:3 [t]S Isa 13:16; Hos 13:16 **10:15** [u]S ver 7 **11:1** [v]S Jer 2:2; S Eze 16:22 [w]S Dt 4:37 [x]S Ex 4:22; Hos 12:9, 13; 13:4; Mt 2:15*

[11]Ephraim is a trained heifer
that loves to thresh;
so I will put a yoke[i]
on her fair neck.
I will drive Ephraim,
Judah must plow,
and Jacob must break up the ground.
[12]Sow[j] for yourselves righteousness,[k]
reap the fruit of unfailing love,
and break up your unplowed ground;[l]
for it is time to seek[m] the LORD,
until he comes
and showers righteousness[n] on you.
[13]But you have planted wickedness,
you have reaped evil,[o]
you have eaten the fruit of
deception.[p]
Because you have depended on your
own strength
and on your many warriors,[q]
[14]the roar of battle will rise against your
people,
so that all your fortresses will be
devastated[r]—
as Shalman[s] devastated Beth Arbel on
the day of battle,
when mothers were dashed to the
ground with their children.[t]
[15]Thus will it happen to you, O Bethel,
because your wickedness is great.
When that day dawns,
the king of Israel will be completely
destroyed.[u]

God's Love for Israel

11 "When Israel was a child,[v] I loved[w]
him,
and out of Egypt I called my son.[x]

[a] *5* *Beth Aven* means *house of wickedness* (a name for Bethel, which means *house of God*). [b] *6* Or *its counsel* [c] *8* Hebrew *aven*, a reference to Beth Aven (a derogatory name for Bethel) [d] *9* Or *there a stand was taken*

10:3 *We have no king.* Such would soon be their condition when Assyria destroyed the nation.
10:4 *They make many promises.* The last kings of Israel were notoriously corrupt and deceitful.
10:5 *Samaria.* The royal city of Israel (see note on 7:1). *calf-idol of Beth Aven.* The idol that Jeroboam I had set up at Bethel (see NIV text note; see also 8:5 and note).
10:6 *tribute for the great king.* See 5:13 and note. *Ephraim.* See note on 4:17.
10:8 *high places.* See 4:13–14 and note on 4:13. *wickedness.* See NIV text note. *Cover us!... Fall on us!* Cries of utter despair; quoted by Jesus (see Lk 23:30 and note) and alluded to in Rev 6:16.
10:9 *Gibeah.* See 9:9 and note. As war came on Gibeah, so war and captivity would come on Israel.
10:11 *trained heifer.* Up to now Ephraim (Israel) had been as contented as a young cow that ate while threshing grain. But now God would cause Israel (here called both Ephraim and Jacob) and Judah to do the heavy work of plowing and harrowing under a yoke—a picture of going into the Assyrian and Babylonian captivities. *Judah.* See Introduction: Author and Date.
10:12 *reap the fruit of unfailing love.* If Israel would only do what was right ("unfailing love" translates the Hebrew word *hesed;* see note on 6:6), God would bless her. *break up your unplowed ground.* Be no longer unproductive, but repentant, making a radical new beginning and becoming productive and fruitful. *righteousness.* God's covenant blessings that in righteousness he would shower on his people if they in righteousness were loyal to him, their covenant Lord (see note on Ps 4:1).
10:13 *deception.* Israel had been living a lie—and by lies (see v. 4; 7:3; 11:12; 12:1; cf. 1Jn 1:6).
10:14 *Shalman devastated Beth Arbel.* The event is otherwise unknown, as are the names mentioned—though Shalman may be an abbreviated form of Shalmaneser V, the Assyrian king who laid siege to Samaria in 725 B.C. (see 2Ki 17:3–5). In any event, atrocities against civilians were common in ancient warfare (see 9:13; 13:16; see also Ps 137:9 and note).
10:15 *Bethel.* See v. 8 and NIV text note; 12:4 and note.
11:1 A third appeal to history (see 9:10; 10:9) traces God's choice of Israel back to Egypt, the exodus from that country (cf. 12:9; 13:4) having given birth to the nation.

[2]But the more I[a] called Israel,
the further they went from me.[b][y]
They sacrificed to the Baals[z]
and they burned incense to
images.[a]
[3]It was I who taught Ephraim to walk,
taking them by the arms;[b]
but they did not realize
it was I who healed[c] them.
[4]I led them with cords of human
kindness,
with ties of love;[d]
I lifted the yoke[e] from their neck
and bent down to feed[f] them.[g]

[5]"Will they not return to Egypt[h]
and will not Assyria[i] rule over them
because they refuse to repent?[j]
[6]Swords[k] will flash in their cities,
will destroy the bars[l] of their gates
and put an end to their plans.
[7]My people are determined to turn[m]
from me.[n]
Even if they call to the Most High,
he will by no means exalt them.

[8]"How can I give you up,[o] Ephraim?[p]
How can I hand you over, Israel?
How can I treat you like Admah?
How can I make you like Zeboiim?[q]
My heart is changed within me;
all my compassion[r] is aroused.[s]
[9]I will not carry out my fierce anger,[t]
nor will I turn and devastate[u]
Ephraim.
For I am God, and not man[v]—
the Holy One[w] among you.
I will not come in wrath.[c]

11:2 [y]ver 7 [z]S Hos 2:13 [a]S 2Ki 17:15; Isa 65:7; S Jer 18:15; S Hos 4:13; 13:1 **11:3** [b]S Dt 1:31; S 32:11; Hos 7:15 [c]S Ex 15:26; Jer 30:17 **11:4** [d]Jer 31:2-3 [e]S Lev 26:13 [f]Ex 16:32; Ps 78:25 [g]Jer 31:20 **11:5** [h]S Hos 7:16 [i]S Hos 10:6 [j]S Ex 13:17 **11:6** [k]Hos 13:16 [l]S La 2:9 **11:7** [m]S Isa 26:10 [n]ver 2; Jer 3:6-7; 8:5 **11:8** [o]S Jer 7:29 [p]Hos 6:4 [q]S Ge 14:8; S La 3:32 [r]S 1Ki 3:26; S Ps 25:6 [s]S Eze 33:11; Am 7:3 **11:9** [t]Dt 13:17; S Jer 18:8; S 30:11 [u]La 3:22; Mal 3:6 [v]S Nu 23:19 [w]S 2Ki 19:22; S Isa 31:1 **11:10** [x]S Isa 42:13 [y]S Isa 31:4 [z]S Ps 18:45 [a]S Hos 3:5; S 6:1-3 **11:11** [b]S Ge 8:8 [c]S Isa 11:11 [d]S Eze 28:26; S 34:25-28 **11:12** [e]S Hos 4:2 [f]S Dt 7:9

[10]They will follow the LORD;
he will roar[x] like a lion.[y]
When he roars,
his children will come trembling[z]
from the west.[a]
[11]They will come trembling
like birds from Egypt,
like doves[b] from Assyria.[c]
I will settle them in their homes,"[d]
declares the LORD.

Israel's Sin

[12]Ephraim has surrounded me with lies,[e]
the house of Israel with deceit.
And Judah is unruly against God,
even against the faithful[f] Holy One.[g]

12 [1]Ephraim[h] feeds on the wind;[i]
he pursues the east wind all day
and multiplies lies and violence.[j]
He makes a treaty with Assyria[k]
and sends olive oil to Egypt.[l]
[2]The LORD has a charge[m] to bring
against Judah;[n]
he will punish[o] Jacob[d] according to
his ways
and repay him according to his
deeds.[p]
[3]In the womb he grasped his brother's
heel;[q]
as a man he struggled[r] with God.

[a] 2 Some Septuagint manuscripts; Hebrew *they*
[b] 2 Septuagint; Hebrew *them* [c] 9 Or *come against any city* [d] 2 *Jacob* means *he grasps the heel* (figuratively, *he deceives*).

[g]S Hos 10:13 **12:1** [h]S Ps 78:67 [i]S Ge 41:6; S Eze 17:10 [j]S Hos 4:19; S 7:1 [k]Hos 5:13; S 7:11 [l]S 2Ki 17:4 **12:2** [m]S Job 10:2; Mic 6:2 [n]Am 2:4 [o]S Ex 32:34 [p]S Hos 4:9; S 9:15 **12:3** [q]Ge 25:26 [r]Ge 32:24-29

Israel's response to the Lord is now illustrated by the wayward son rather than by the unfaithful wife (chs. 1–3). Israel is also referred to as God's "son/child" elsewhere (see Ex 4:22–23 and notes; Isa 1:2,4). For God as Israel's "Father" see Dt 32:6; Isa 63:16; 64:8. Hosea saw God's love as the basis (see 3:1 and note) for the election of Israel. Matthew saw in Jesus' return from Egypt a typological fulfillment of Israel's deliverance from Egypt (see Mt 2:15 and note).

11:2 *Baals.* See 2:13 and note. *images.* See Dt 7:25.

11:3 *Ephraim.* See note on 4:17. *walk.* This picture of a father teaching his child to walk is one of the most tender in the OT. *did not realize.* See 2:5–8 and note on 2:8. *healed.* See 5:13; 6:1 and note; 7:1.

11:4 The imagery is unclear, but the figure seems to change to a farmer tending his work animals. Another interpretation sees a continuation of the son image, with the father lifting the son to his cheek. *feed them.* God supplied miraculous food in the desert (see Ex 16; Dt 8:16).

11:5 *Egypt ... Assyria.* See 8:13; 9:3 and notes. The tender tone (vv. 1–4) changes to threat of exile to the two countries between which Israel had vacillated. It is ironic that the people rescued from Egypt should be returned there because of their disloyalty to the one who had rescued them.

11:7 *Most High.* See 7:16 and note.

11:8 The stubborn son was subject to stoning (Dt 21:18–21), but the Lord's compassion overcame his wrath and he refused to destroy Ephraim (Israel). *Admah ... Zeboiim.* Cities of the plain (see Ge 10:19 and note; 14:2,8), overthrown when Sodom was destroyed (Ge 19:24–25; Dt 29:23; Jer 49:18) and symbolizing total destruction (see Am 4:11 and note).

11:9 *God, and not man.* God will not be untrue to the love he has shown toward Israel (see vv. 1–4; 1Sa 15:29; Mal 3:6). Israel was to be punished, but not destroyed. *the Holy One among you.* God's holiness is alluded to in Hosea both here and in v. 12 (see notes on Ex 3:5; Lev 11:44).

11:10 The return from exile. *roar like a lion.* Rather than threatening destruction (cf. 5:14; 13:7), God's roar was now a clear signal to return from exile. *the west.* The islands and coastlands of the Mediterranean Sea.

11:11 *from Egypt ... Assyria.* See 7:16 and note; 9:3. *like birds ... like doves.* Suggests swiftness of return (cf. Isa 60:8) and is not derogatory, as was the earlier comparison to a silly dove (7:11).

11:12 *lies ... deceit.* See 10:13 and note. *Judah.* See Introduction: Author and Date. *unruly against God.* See Jer 2:31. *Holy One.* See v. 9 and note.

12:1 *Ephraim.* See note on 4:17. *wind.* See 8:7; Ecc 1:14. *east wind.* See 13:15; Job 15:2; Jer 18:17. Pursuing the wind symbolized Israel's futile foreign policy, which vacillated between Egypt (2Ki 17:4; Isa 30:6–7) and Assyria (see 5:13; 7:11; 8:9 and notes; 2Ki 17:3).

12:2 *charge.* See 4:1 and note. *Judah.* See Introduction: Author and Date. *Jacob.* Israel (see 10:11). The Lord indicted both kingdoms—all the descendants of Father Jacob. In their deceitfulness, Israel and Judah were living up to the name of their forefather (see NIV text note).

12:3 *In the womb.* See Ge 25:26; 27:36 and notes. *grasped his brother's heel.* See NIV text note on v. 2. God's

4 He struggled with the angel and
overcame him;
he wept and begged for his favor.
He found him at Bethel[s]
and talked with him there—
5 the LORD God Almighty,
the LORD is his name[t] of renown!
6 But you must return[u] to your God;
maintain love and justice,[v]
and wait for your God always.[w]

7 The merchant uses dishonest scales;[x]
he loves to defraud.
8 Ephraim boasts,[y]
"I am very rich; I have become
wealthy.[z]
With all my wealth they will not find
in me
any iniquity or sin."

9 "I am the LORD your God,
⌞who brought you⌟ out of[a] Egypt;[a]
I will make you live in tents[b] again,
as in the days of your appointed
feasts.
10 I spoke to the prophets,
gave them many visions
and told parables[c] through them."[d]

11 Is Gilead wicked?[e]
Its people are worthless!
Do they sacrifice bulls in Gilgal?[f]
Their altars will be like piles of
stones
on a plowed field.[g]

12 Jacob fled to the country of Aram[b];[h]
Israel served to get a wife,
and to pay for her he tended
sheep.[i]
13 The LORD used a prophet to bring
Israel up from Egypt,[j]
by a prophet he cared for him.[k]
14 But Ephraim has bitterly provoked him
to anger;
his Lord will leave upon him the
guilt of his bloodshed[l]
and will repay him for his
contempt.[m]

The LORD's Anger Against Israel

13 When Ephraim spoke, men
trembled;[n]
he was exalted[o] in Israel.
But he became guilty of Baal
worship[p] and died.
2 Now they sin more and more;
they make[q] idols for themselves
from their silver,[r]
cleverly fashioned images,
all of them the work of craftsmen.[s]
It is said of these people,
"They offer human sacrifice
and kiss[c][t] the calf-idols.[u]"

[a] 9 Or *God / ever since you were in* [b] 12 That is, Northwest Mesopotamia [c] 2 Or *"Men who sacrifice / kiss*

12:4 [s]S Ge 12:8; S 35:15 **12:5** [t]S Ex 3:15 **12:6** [u]S Isa 19:22; Jer 4:1; Joel 2:12 [v]S Ps 106:3; S Jer 22:3 [w]S Eze 18:30; Hos 6:1-3; 10:12; Mic 7:7 **12:7** [x]S Lev 19:36; Am 8:5 **12:8** [y]S Eze 28:5 [z]Ps 62:10; Rev 3:17 **12:9** [a]Lev 23:43; S Hos 2:15; S 11:1 [b]S Ne 8:17 **12:10** [c]S Jdg 14:12; S Eze 20:49 [d]2Ki 17:13; Jer 7:25 **12:11** [e]S Hos 6:8 [f]S Hos 4:15 [g]S Hos 8:11 **12:12** [h]Ge 28:5 [i]S Ge 29:18 **12:13** [j]S Hos 11:1 [k]Ex 13:3; 14:19-22; Isa 63:11-14 **12:14** [l]S Eze 18:13 [m]Da 11:18 **13:1** [n]Jdg 12:1 [o]S Jdg 8:1 [p]S Hos 11:2 **13:2** [q]Jer 44:8 [r]S Isa 46:6; S Jer 10:4 [s]Hos 14:3 [t]1Ki 19:18 [u]S Isa 44:17-20; S Hos 8:4

covenant people here relived the experiences of Father Jacob and now had to return to God, just as Jacob was called back to Bethel (Ge 35:1–15).
12:4 *struggled with the angel.* See Ge 32:22–28 and NIV text note on 32:28. *Bethel.* See Ge 28:12–19 and NIV text note on 28:19; 35:1–15. In Hosea's time, Bethel was the most important royal sanctuary in the northern kingdom (cf. Am 7:13).
12:6 *love.* Hebrew *hesed;* see 6:6 ("mercy") and note. *justice.* See Am 5:24; Mic 6:8 and notes.
12:7 *merchant.* As Hosea had played on the meaning of Jacob in v. 2, he here uses a wordplay on Canaan (the Hebrew for "merchant" sounds like Canaan) to charge that Israel was no better than a Canaanite (see note on Zec 14:21). *dishonest scales.* See Lev 19:35; Pr 11:1 and notes.
12:8 *I am very rich.* Riches brought a sense of self-sufficiency (cf. 10:13; Dt 32:15–18; Lk 12:19; Rev 3:17). *not find in me any iniquity.* Like a dishonest merchant, Ephraim (Israel) was confident that her deceitfulness (see 10:13 and note) would not come to light.
12:9 *I am the LORD your God.* See 13:4; Ex 20:2 and note. *tents.* Recalling the desert journey of long ago (cf. 2:14–15). *appointed feasts.* Probably the Feast of Tabernacles (see Lev 23:33–43 and note on 23:42), which commemorated the desert journey.
12:10 *spoke to the prophets.* See 6:5; Am 2:11 and notes; Heb 1:1. There had been ample warning. *visions.* Revelations (see Nu 12:6–8 and note; Am 1:1). *parables.* Containing messages of warning from God (see 2Sa 12:1–4; Ps 78:2; Isa 5:1–7; Eze 17:2; 24:3).
12:11 *Gilead wicked.* See 6:8–9 and notes. Gilead was overrun by Assyria in 734–732 B.C. (2Ki 15:29). *Gilgal.* See 4:15 and note. The Hebrew contains a wordplay between "Gilgal" and "piles" (Hebrew *gallim*). Rather than assuring safety, the altars themselves would be destroyed. *on a plowed field.* Israelite farmers gathered into piles the stones turned up by their plows.
12:12 Jacob fled from Esau to Paddan Aram (Ge 28:2,5), serving Laban seven years for each wife (Ge 29:20–28), and then continued six more years as Laban's herdsman (Ge 30:31; 31:41).
12:13 *prophet.* Moses (cf. Nu 12:6–8; Dt 18:15; 34:10). *cared for him.* As Jacob had cared for Laban's flocks, so the Lord cared for Israel during her desert wandering. Earlier leadership by the prophet Moses stands in contrast with Israel's present disregard for prophets (cf. 4:5; 6:5; 9:7).
12:14 *Ephraim . . . provoked him.* Despite warnings. *bloodshed.* Cf. 1:4; 4:2; 5:2; 6:8. This refers to violence committed against others, including human sacrifice (see 13:2 and note). In legal passages such as Lev 20:11,13,16,27, "their blood will be on their own heads" describes guilt. The prophet drew a contrast between past divine preservation and present divine anger that would bring punishment. *repay.* See Isa 65:7.
13:1 *When Ephraim spoke.* In accordance with Jacob's blessing (Ge 48:10–20), Ephraim became a powerful tribe (Jdg 8:1–3; 12:1–6; 1Sa 1:1–4), from which came such prominent leaders as Joshua (Nu 13:8,16; Jos 24:29–30) and Jeroboam I (1Ki 11:26; 12:20). *Ephraim.* See note on 4:17. *Israel.* The 12 tribes. *died.* The wages of sin was death (cf. Ro 6:23), and the end of the nation was at hand.
13:2 *idols.* See 4:12; 8:5–6 and notes; 11:2. *human sacrifice.* See Lev 18:21; 2Ki 16:13; 17:17; 23:10; Jer 7:31 and notes; Eze 20:26; Mic 6:7. For the sense of the NIV text note see 1Ki 12:26–33. *kiss.* Show homage to (see Ps 2:12 and note). *calf-idols.* See 8:5 and note; 10:5.

³Therefore they will be like the morning mist,
like the early dew that disappears,[v]
like chaff[w] swirling from a threshing floor,[x]
like smoke[y] escaping through a window.

⁴"But I am the LORD your God,
⌞who brought you⌟ out of[a] Egypt.[z]
You shall acknowledge[a] no God but me,[b]
no Savior[c] except me.
⁵I cared for you in the desert,[d]
in the land of burning heat.
⁶When I fed them, they were satisfied;
when they were satisfied, they became proud;[e]
then they forgot[f] me.[g]
⁷So I will come upon them like a lion,[h]
like a leopard I will lurk by the path.
⁸Like a bear robbed of her cubs,[i]
I will attack them and rip them open.
Like a lion[j] I will devour them;
a wild animal will tear them apart.[k]

⁹"You are destroyed, O Israel,
because you are against me,[l] against your helper.[m]
¹⁰Where is your king,[n] that he may save you?
Where are your rulers in all your towns,
of whom you said,
'Give me a king and princes'?[o]
¹¹So in my anger I gave you a king,[p]
and in my wrath I took him away.[q]
¹²The guilt of Ephraim is stored up,
his sins are kept on record.[r]
¹³Pains as of a woman in childbirth[s]
come to him,
but he is a child without wisdom;
when the time[t] arrives,
he does not come to the opening of the womb.[u]

¹⁴"I will ransom them from the power of the grave[b];[v]
I will redeem them from death.[w]
Where, O death, are your plagues?
Where, O grave,[b] is your destruction?[x]

"I will have no compassion,
15 even though he thrives[y] among his brothers.
An east wind[z] from the LORD will come,
blowing in from the desert;
his spring will fail
and his well dry up.[a]
His storehouse will be plundered[b]
of all its treasures.
¹⁶The people of Samaria[c] must bear their guilt,[d]
because they have rebelled[e] against their God.
They will fall by the sword;[f]
their little ones will be dashed[g] to the ground,
their pregnant women[h] ripped open."

Repentance to Bring Blessing

14 Return,[i] O Israel, to the LORD your God.
Your sins[j] have been your downfall![k]

[a] *4* Or *God / ever since you were in* [b] *14* Hebrew *Sheol*

13:3 [v]S Hos 6:4 [w]S Job 13:25; Ps 1:4; S Isa 17:13 [x]Da 2:35 [y]Ps 68:2 **13:4** [z]S Jer 2:6; S Hos 12:9 [a]S Hos 2:20 [b]S Ex 20:3 [c]S Dt 28:29; Ps 18:46; Isa 43:11; 45:21-22 **13:5** [d]S Dt 1:19 **13:6** [e]S Eze 28:5 [f]S Dt 32:18; S Isa 17:10 [g]Dt 32:12-15; S Pr 30:7-9; S Jer 5:7; S Hos 2:13; S 4:7 **13:7** [h]S Job 10:16; S Jer 4:7 **13:8** [i]2Sa 17:8 [j]S 1Sa 17:34; Ps 17:12 [k]Ps 50:22; S La 3:10; S Hos 2:12 **13:9** [l]Jer 2:17-19 [m]S Dt 33:29 **13:10** [n]2Ki 17:4; Hos 7:7 [o]1Sa 8:6; Hos 8:4 **13:11** [p]S Nu 11:20 [q]S Jos 24:20; S 1Sa 13:14; S 1Ki 14:10; Hos 3:4; S 10:7 **13:12** [r]S Dt 32:34 **13:13** [s]Isa 13:8; Mic 4:9-10 [t]2Ki 19:3 [u]Isa 66:9 **13:14** [v]S Ps 16:10; 49:15; S Eze 37:12-13 [w]S Isa 25:8 [x]1Co 15:55* **13:15** [y]S Hos 10:1 [z]S Job 1:19; S Eze 19:12; S Hos 4:19 [a]S Jer 51:36 [b]Jer 20:5 **13:16** [c]2Ki 17:5 [d]Hos 10:2 [e]S Hos 7:14 [f]Hos 11:6 [g]S 2Ki 8:12; S Hos 10:14 [h]2Ki 15:16; Isa 13:16; Am 1:13 **14:1** [i]S Isa 19:22; S Jer 3:12 [j]S Hos 4:8 [k]S Hos 5:5; S 9:7

13:3 "Mist" and "dew" (see 6:4), "chaff" (see Ps 1:4 and note; 35:5; Isa 17:13; 29:5; Zep 2:2) and "smoke" (see Ps 37:20; 68:2; Isa 51:6) are all figurative for Ephraim, which was soon to vanish as a nation.

13:4 *I am the LORD.* See 12:9; Ex 20:2 and note. The contrast is with Jeroboam's declaration, "Here are your gods" (1Ki 12:28). *acknowledge … God.* See 2:20; 6:3 and notes.

13:5 *desert.* See 2:14; 9:10 and notes.

13:6 *satisfied.* See Dt 6:11–12; 8:10–14; 11:15. *forgot me.* See 2:13; Dt 6:10–12 and notes; 8:11,14,19; 32:18.

13:7–8 The Lord, previously pictured as a shepherd (4:16), would attack like the wild beasts that often ravaged the flocks (see Am 1:2 and note).

13:7 *lion.* See 5:14 and note. *leopard.* See Jer 5:6; Rev 13:2.

13:8 *bear robbed of her cubs.* See 2Sa 17:8; Pr 17:12 and note.

13:9 *helper.* See Ps 10:14; 30:10; 54:4.

13:10 *Where is your king …?* Help comes only from the Lord (Ps 121:2), not from kings. The prophet likely alludes to the royal assassinations of his day (see 7:7; 8:4 and notes). *Give me a king.* Though all Israel asked for a king in the days of Samuel (see 1Sa 8:5 and note), the reference here is only to the northern monarchy. Israel selected Jeroboam I (1Ki 12:20) in preference to the Davidic kings.

13:11 Reference is to the kings of the northern kingdom of Israel.

13:12 See 9:9 and note; Job 14:17. *sins … on record.* See 7:2 and note; Dt 32:34.

13:13 *Pains as of … childbirth.* Their helpless situation was comparable to that of a woman in childbirth (see Isa 13:8 and note; 21:3; Jer 13:21; Mic 4:9–10; Mt 24:8) who cannot deliver the child (see 2Ki 19:3) and consequently dies.

13:14 *I will ransom.* A promise of redemption from death. *Where, O death …?* The personified reference is to the death of the nation (see note on v. 1). Paul applies this passage to resurrection (1Co 15:55). *grave.* See NIV text note. For a description of Sheol see Job 3:13–19; Isa 14:9–10; see also note on Ge 37:35.

13:15 *thrives.* In Hebrew a wordplay on Ephraim (meaning "fruitful"). The drought-bringing east wind (see 12:1; Ge 41:7 and note; Job 1:19; Isa 27:8; Jer 4:11; 13:24; 18:17) is here a figure for Assyria, an instrument of the Lord (see Isa 10:5 and note). Assyria invaded the northern kingdom in 734 B.C., then crushed it and exiled its people in 722–721. *all its treasures.* See Na 2:9.

13:16 *Samaria.* See 7:1 and note; 8:5–6; 10:5,7; here, the northern kingdom. *rebelled against.* See Ps 5:10; Isa 1:2 and note; Eze 20:8,13,21. *little ones … women.* For atrocities against women and children see 10:14; Ps 137:9 and notes.

14:1 *Return.* Another appeal for repentance (see 10:12; 12:6). Unlike that of ch. 6, this repentance would have to be sincere in order for the people to receive the gracious

[2]Take words with you
and return to the LORD.
Say to him:
"Forgive[l] all our sins
and receive us graciously,[m]
that we may offer the fruit of our
lips.[a n]
[3]Assyria cannot save us;[o]
we will not mount war-horses.[p]
We will never again say 'Our gods'[q]
to what our own hands have
made,[r]
for in you the fatherless[s] find
compassion."

[4]"I will heal[t] their waywardness[u]
and love them freely,[v]
for my anger has turned away[w] from
them.
[5]I will be like the dew[x] to Israel;
he will blossom like a lily.[y]
Like a cedar of Lebanon[z]
he will send down his roots;[a]
[6]his young shoots will grow.
His splendor will be like an olive tree,[b]
his fragrance like a cedar of
Lebanon.[c]
[7]Men will dwell again in his shade.[d]
He will flourish like the grain.
He will blossom[e] like a vine,
and his fame will be like the wine[f]
from Lebanon.[g]
[8]O Ephraim, what more have I[b] to do
with idols?[h]
I will answer him and care for him.
I am like a green pine[i] tree;
your fruitfulness comes from me."

[9]Who is wise?[j] He will realize these
things.
Who is discerning? He will
understand them.[k]
The ways of the LORD are right;[l]
the righteous walk[m] in them,
but the rebellious stumble in them.

[a] 2 Or *offer our lips as sacrifices of bulls* [b] 8 Or *What more has Ephraim*

14:2 [l]S Ex 34:9 [m]Ps 51:16-17; Mic 7:18-19 [n]Heb 13:15 **14:3** [o]S Hos 5:13 [p]Ps 33:17; S Isa 31:1; Mic 5:10 [q]Hos 8:6 [r]ver 28; Hos 13:2 [s]Ps 10:14; 68:5; Jer 49:11 **14:4** [t]S Isa 30:26; S Hos 6:1 [u]S Jer 2:19 [v]S Isa 55:1; Jer 31:20; Zep 3:17 [w]S Job 13:16 **14:5** [x]S Ge 27:28; S Isa 18:4 [y]S SS 2:1 [z]Isa 35:2 [a]Job 29:19 **14:6** [b]Ps 52:8; S Jer 11:16 [c]S Ps 92:12; S SS 4:11 **14:7** [d]Ps 91:1-4 [e]S Ge 40:10 [f]S Hos 2:22 [g]S Eze 17:23 **14:8** [h]S ver 3 [i]S Isa 37:24 **14:9** [j]S Ps 107:43 [k]S Pr 10:29; S Isa 1:28; Da 12:10 [l]Ps 111:7-8; Zep 3:5; Ac 13:10 [m]Isa 26:7

response from the Lord promised in vv. 4–8 (cf. Ps 130:7–8; Isa 55:6–7).

14:2 *Take words.* None could appear before the Lord empty-handed (Ex 23:15; 34:20), but animal sacrifices would not be enough. Only words of true repentance would be sufficient. *fruit of our lips.* As thank offerings to the Lord (see Heb 13:15).

14:3 *what our own hands have made.* Idols (see v. 8; 13:2 and note). *fatherless.* Penitent Israel (see Ps 10:14; 68:5; La 5:3). *find compassion.* Cf. the name of the child Lo-Ruhamah (see 1:6 and note; see also 2:1,23).

14:4 *heal.* See 11:3 and note. *waywardness.* See 11:7. *love them freely.* That is, love them out of my own free choice (cf. 9:15 and note). *love.* See 3:1; 11:1 and notes. *anger … turned away.* Contrasts with the burning anger that brought destruction (see 8:5).

14:5 *dew.* Here not a symbol of transitoriness (cf. 6:4; 13:3) but of God's blessing (see Dt 33:13; Mic 5:7 and note). *cedar of Lebanon.* See notes on Jdg 9:15; 1Ki 5:6; Isa 9:10. *cedar.* See Ps 80:8–11. *Lebanon.* See Ps 104:16–18 and note.

14:7 *shade.* Protection (see Jdg 9:15 and note; SS 2:3; Eze 31:6). *vine.* See 10:1; Ps 80:8–16 and note.

14:8 *Ephraim.* See note on 4:17. *tree.* Only here in the OT is God compared to a tree. For the point of the imagery see Eze 31:3–7; Da 4:12. *fruitfulness.* Ephraim ("fruitful"; see Ge 41:52 and note) received his fruitfulness from the Lord (cf. 2:8).

14:9 *ways of the* LORD. See Ps 18:21; 25:4 and note. The prophet concludes by offering each reader the alternatives of walking or stumbling (cf. 4:5; 5:5)—of obedience or rebellion.

Joel

INTRODUCTION

Author

The prophet Joel cannot be identified with any of the 12 other figures in the OT who have the same name. He is not mentioned outside the books of Joel and Acts (Ac 2:16). The non-Biblical legends about him are unconvincing. His father, Pethuel (1:1), is also unknown. Judging from his concern with Judah and Jerusalem (see 2:32; 3:1,6,8,16–20), it seems likely that Joel lived in that area. See note on 1:1.

Date

The book contains no references to datable historical events. Many interpreters date it somewhere between the late seventh and early fifth centuries B.C. In any case, its message is not significantly affected by its dating.

The book of Joel has striking linguistic parallels to the language of Amos, Micah, Zephaniah, Jeremiah and Ezekiel. Some scholars maintain that the prophets borrowed phrases from one another; others hold that they drew more or less from the religious literary traditions that they and their readers shared in common — liturgical and otherwise.

> **A Quick Look**
>
> **Author:**
> Joel
>
> **Audience:**
> The people of Judah
>
> **Date:**
> Probably between the late seventh and early fifth centuries B.C.
>
> **Theme:**
> Restoration and blessing will come to the people of Judah only after judgment and repentance.

Theological Message

Joel sees the massive locust plague and severe drought devastating Judah as a harbinger of the "great and dreadful day of the LORD" (2:31). (The locusts he mentions in 1:4; 2:25 are best understood as real insects, not as allegorical representations of the Babylonians, Medo-Persians, Greeks and Romans, as held by some interpreters.) Confronted with this crisis, he calls on everyone to repent: old and young (1:2–3), drunkards (1:5), farmers (1:11) and priests (1:13). He describes the locusts as the Lord's army and sees in their coming a reminder that the day of the Lord is near. He does not voice the popular notion that the day will be one of judgment on the nations but deliverance and blessing for Israel. Instead — with Isaiah (2:10–21), Jeremiah (4:5–9), Amos (5:18–20) and Zephaniah (1:7–18) — he describes the day as one of punishment of unfaithful Israel as well. Restoration and blessing will come only after judgment and repentance.

Joel sees the massive locust plague and severe drought devastating Judah as a harbinger of the "great and dreadful day of the LORD" and calls on everyone to repent.

Outline

I. Title (1:1)
II. Judah Experiences a Foretaste of the Day of the Lord (1:2—2:17)
  A. A Call to Mourning and Prayer (1:2–14)
  B. The Announcement of the Day of the Lord (1:15—2:11)
  C. A Call to Repentance and Prayer (2:12–17)
III. Judah Is Assured of Salvation in the Day of the Lord (2:18—3:21)
  A. The Lord's Restoration of Judah (2:18–27)
  B. The Lord's Renewal of His People (2:28–32)
  C. The Coming of the Day of the Lord (ch. 3)
    1. The nations judged (3:1–16)
    2. God's people blessed (3:17–21)

1 The word of the LORD that came[a] to
Joel[b] son of Pethuel.

An Invasion of Locusts

2 Hear this,[c] you elders;[d]
listen, all who live in the land.[e]
Has anything like this ever happened
in your days
or in the days of your forefathers?[f]
3 Tell it to your children,[g]
and let your children tell it to their
children,
and their children to the next
generation.[h]
4 What the locust[i] swarm has left
the great locusts have eaten;
what the great locusts have left
the young locusts have eaten;
what the young locusts have left[j]
other locusts[a] have eaten.[k]

5 Wake up, you drunkards, and weep!
Wail, all you drinkers of wine;[l]
wail because of the new wine,
for it has been snatched[m] from your
lips.
6 A nation has invaded my land,
powerful and without number;[n]
it has the teeth[o] of a lion,
the fangs of a lioness.
7 It has laid waste[p] my vines
and ruined my fig trees.[q]
It has stripped off their bark
and thrown it away,
leaving their branches white.

8 Mourn like a virgin[b] in sackcloth[r]
grieving for the husband[c] of her
youth.
9 Grain offerings and drink offerings[s]
are cut off from the house of the
LORD.
The priests are in mourning,[t]
those who minister before the LORD.
10 The fields are ruined,
the ground is dried up[d];[u]
the grain is destroyed,
the new wine[v] is dried up,
the oil fails.[w]
11 Despair, you farmers,[x]
wail, you vine growers;
grieve for the wheat and the barley,[y]
because the harvest of the field is
destroyed.[z]
12 The vine is dried up
and the fig tree is withered;[a]
the pomegranate,[b] the palm and the
apple tree—
all the trees of the field—are dried
up.[c]
Surely the joy of mankind
is withered away.

A Call to Repentance

13 Put on sackcloth,[d] O priests, and
mourn;
wail, you who minister[e] before the
altar.
Come, spend the night in sackcloth,
you who minister before my God;
for the grain offerings and drink
offerings[f]
are withheld from the house of your
God.
14 Declare a holy fast;[g]
call a sacred assembly.
Summon the elders
and all who live in the land[h]
to the house of the LORD your God,
and cry out[i] to the LORD.[j]

[a] *4* The precise meaning of the four Hebrew words used here for locusts is uncertain. [b] *8* Or *young woman* [c] *8* Or *betrothed* [d] *10* Or *ground mourns*

1:1 [a]S Jer 1:2 [b]Ac 2:16 **1:2** [c]Hos 5:1 [d]Joel 2:16 [e]S Hos 4:1 [f]Joel 2:2 **1:3** [g]S Ex 10:2 [h]S Ps 71:18 **1:4** [i]S Ex 10:14 [j]S Ex 10:5 [k]S Ex 10:15; S Dt 28:39; Am 7:1; Na 3:15 **1:5** [l]Joel 3:3 [m]S Isa 24:7 **1:6** [n]Ps 105:34; Joel 2:2,11,25 [o]Rev 9:8 **1:7** [p]Isa 5:6 [q]Am 4:9 **1:8** [r]ver 13; Isa 22:12; Am 8:10 **1:9** [s]S Hos 9:4 [t]S Isa 22:12 **1:10** [u]S Isa 5:6; S 24:4; S Jer 3:3 [v]S Hos 9:2 [w]S Nu 18:12 **1:11** [x]S Job 6:20; Am 5:16 [y]S Ex 9:31 [z]S Isa 17:11 **1:12** [a]S Isa 15:6 [b]S Ex 28:33 [c]S Isa 16:8; Hag 2:19 **1:13** [d]S Ge 37:34; S Jer 4:8 [e]Joel 2:17 [f]ver 9; S Hos 9:4; Joel 2:14 **1:14** [g]S 2Ch 20:3 [h]S Hos 4:1 [i]Jnh 3:8 [j]2Ch 20:4

1:1 *word of the LORD.* See Hos 1:1 and note. *Joel.* Means "The LORD is God"; cf. Elijah's name, which means "(My) God is the LORD."

1:2 *elders.* Either the older men of the community or the recognized officials (see v. 14; 2:16,28; see also note on Ex 3:16).

1:4 *locust swarm ... great locusts ... young locusts ... other locusts.* Either (1) various species of locusts or (2) locusts in various stages of their life cycle. See 2:25; Ex 10:4 and note.

1:5 *drunkards.* Although Joel calls for repentance, drunkenness is the only specific sin mentioned in the book. It suggests a self-indulgent lifestyle (cf. Isa 28:7–8; Am 4:1) pursued by those who value material things more than spiritual. *weep.* Various segments of the community (drunkards, here; general population, v. 8; farmers, v. 11; priests, v. 13) are called upon to mourn. The destruction of the vines by the locusts leaves the drunkards without a source of wine.

1:6 The locusts are compared here to a nation; cf. the ants and coneys in Pr 30:25–26, where the Hebrew word for "creatures" means lit. "(a) people." Elsewhere the locusts are called the Lord's "army" (2:11,25). The reverse comparison—that of armies to locusts in regard to numbers—is as old as Ugaritic literature (15th century B.C.; see chart, p. xxiii) and is common in the OT (see Jdg 6:5 and note; Jer 46:23; 51:14,27; Na 3:15). *without number.* A phrase used to describe the locusts in the plague in Egypt (see Ps 105:34; see also Ex 10:4–6,12–15). *teeth.* Joel's comparison of the locusts' teeth to lions' teeth is reflected in Rev 9:8.

1:7 *my.* The personal pronouns here and elsewhere in Joel (vv. 6,13–14; 2:1,13–14,17–18,23,26–27; 3:2–5,17) offer a hint of hope, since they indicate that the people belong to the Lord (cf. Jos 22:19).

1:8 *virgin.* The community is addressed. In Israel, when a woman was pledged to be married to a man, he was called her husband and she his wife, though she was still a virgin (see Dt 22:23–24). This verse refers to such a husband who died before the marriage was consummated. *sackcloth.* See v. 13; Ge 37:34; Rev 11:3 and notes.

1:9 *offerings.* See v. 13; 2:14. The locusts have left nothing that can be offered as sacrifice. The grain offering (Lev 2:1–2) and the drink offering, which was a libation of wine (Lev 23:13), were part of the daily offering (Ex 29:40; Nu 28:5–8).

1:10 *dried up.* The destruction caused by the locusts was intensified by drought. *grain ... new wine ... oil.* An important OT triad, related to the agriculture of that day (see 2:19).

1:13 *my God ... your God.* See note on v. 7. *grain offerings and drink offerings.* See note on v. 9.

1:14 *fast ... assembly.* See 2:15. Fasting, required on the Day of Atonement (see note and NIV text note on Lev

15 Alas for that[k] day!
For the day of the LORD[l] is near;
it will come like destruction from the Almighty.[a][m]

16 Has not the food been cut off[n]
before our very eyes —
joy and gladness[o]
from the house of our God?[p]

17 The seeds are shriveled
beneath the clods.[b][q]
The storehouses are in ruins,
the granaries have been broken down,
for the grain has dried up.

18 How the cattle moan!
The herds mill about
because they have no pasture;[r]
even the flocks of sheep are suffering.[s]

19 To you, O LORD, I call,[t]
for fire[u] has devoured the open pastures[v]
and flames have burned up all the trees of the field.

20 Even the wild animals pant for you;[w]
the streams of water have dried up[x]
and fire has devoured the open pastures.[y]

An Army of Locusts

2 Blow the trumpet[z] in Zion;[a]
sound the alarm on my holy hill.[b]
Let all who live in the land tremble,
for the day of the LORD[c] is coming.
It is close at hand[d] —

2 a day of darkness[e] and gloom,[f][g]
a day of clouds[h] and blackness.[i]
Like dawn spreading across the mountains
a large and mighty army[j] comes,
such as never was of old[k]
nor ever will be in ages to come.

3 Before them fire[l] devours,
behind them a flame blazes.
Before them the land is like the garden of Eden,[m]
behind them, a desert waste[n] —
nothing escapes them.

4 They have the appearance of horses;[o]
they gallop along like cavalry.

5 With a noise like that of chariots[p]
they leap over the mountaintops,
like a crackling fire[q] consuming stubble,
like a mighty army drawn up for battle.

6 At the sight of them, nations are in anguish;[r]
every face turns pale.[s]

[a] 15 Hebrew *Shaddai* [b] 17 The meaning of the Hebrew for this word is uncertain.

1:15 [k] S Isa 2:12; Jer 30:7; S 46:10; S Eze 30:3; Mal 4:5 [l] Joel 2:1,11,31; 3:14; Am 5:18; Zep 1:14; Zec 14:1 [m] S Ge 17:1 **1:16** [n] Isa 3:7 [o] S Ps 51:8 [p] Dt 12:7 **1:17** [q] S Isa 17:10-11 **1:18** [r] S Ge 47:4 [s] S Jer 9:10 **1:19** [t] Ps 50:15 [u] S Ps 97:3; Am 7:4 [v] S Jer 9:10 **1:20** [w] S Ps 42:1; S 104:21 [x] 1Ki 17:7 [y] Joel 2:22 **2:1** [z] S Nu 10:2,7 [a] ver 15 [b] S Ex 15:17 [c] S Joel 1:15; Zep 1:14-16 [d] S Eze 12:23; S 30:3; Ob 1:15 **2:2** [e] ver 10,31; S Job 9:7; S Isa 8:22; S 13:10; Am 5:18 [f] S Da 9:12; S Mt 24:21 [g] S Eze 34:12 [h] S Eze 38:9 [i] Zep 1:15; Rev 9:2 [j] S Joel 1:6 [k] Joel 1:2 **2:3** [l] S Ps 97:3; S Isa 1:31 [m] S Ge 2:8 [n] Ex 10:12-15; Ps 105:34-35; S Isa 14:17 **2:4** [o] Rev 9:7 **2:5** [p] Rev 9:9 [q] Isa 5:24; 30:30 **2:6** [r] S Isa 13:8 [s] S Isa 29:22

16:29) and also practiced in times of calamity (see Jdg 20:26; 2Sa 12:16; Est 4:3,16; Jer 14:12; Jnh 3:4 – 5; Zec 7:3), was a sign of penitence and humility. The Bible speaks against outward signs that do not reflect a corresponding inward belief or attitude (see Mt 6:1 – 8,16 – 18; 23:1 – 36). *elders.* See notes on v. 2; Ex 3:16; 2Sa 3:17.

1:15 *day of the LORD.* See note on Am 5:18. This phrase occurs five times in Joel and is the dominant theme (here; 2:1,11,31; 3:14). Six other prophets also use it: Isaiah (13:6,9), Ezekiel (13:5; 30:3), Amos (5:18,20), Obadiah (15), Zephaniah (1:7,14) and Malachi (4:5); and an equivalent expression occurs in Zec 14:1. Sometimes abbreviated as "that day," the term often refers to the decisive intervention of God in history, such as through the invasion of locusts in Joel or at the battle of Carchemish, 605 B.C. (see Jer 46:2,10). It can also refer to Christ's coming to consummate history (see Mal 4:5; 1Co 5:5; 2Co 1:14; 1Th 5:2 and note; 2Pe 3:10). When the term is not used for divine judgments in the midst of history, it refers to the final day of the Lord, which generally has two aspects: (1) God's triumph over and punishment of his enemies and (2) his granting of rest (security) and blessing to his people. *destruction … Almighty.* See Isa 13:6 and note.

1:18 Cf. the description of a drought in Jer 14:5 – 6. *moan.* The Hebrew for this word is used for the groaning of Israel in Egypt (Ex 2:23) and of others in distress (Pr 29:2; Isa 24:7; La 1:4,8,11,21; Eze 9:4; 21:12). *mill about.* The Hebrew for this verb is used to describe Israel's confused movements in the desert (Ex 14:3). *even … sheep.* Sheep are the last to suffer, because they can even grub the grass roots out of the soil.

1:19 – 20 *fire.* Although the destruction caused by the locusts is elsewhere compared to that of a fire (see 2:3), here the prophet may be describing the effects of a drought. In both cases he evokes the fire of God's judgment (see, e.g., Jer 4:4; 15:14; 17:27 and note; Eze 5:4; 15:6 – 7 and note on 15:7; 20:47; 21:32; Hos 8:14; Am 1:4 and note).

2:1 *trumpet.* See v. 15. Made of a ram's or bull's horn, it was used to signal approaching danger (see Jer 4:5; Eze 33:3 and notes). Its sound brought trembling (from fear) to the people (see Am 3:6). *Zion.* See v. 15; 3:17,21. Here it refers to Jerusalem as the capital of the nation. *day of the LORD.* See 1:15; Isa 2:11,17,20 and notes.

2:2 *day of darkness.* Darkness is a common prophetic figure used of the day of the Lord (see Am 5:18 and note; Zep 1:15) and is generally a metaphor for distress and suffering (see Isa 50:3; 59:9; Jer 2:6; 13:16; La 3:6; Eze 34:12 and notes). *dawn.* Usually suggests relief from sorrow or gloom, the end of darkness (cf. Isa 8:20; 58:8). Here, however, it is used as bitter irony, describing the locust infestation that fans out across the land like the light of dawn, which first lights up the eastern horizon and then spreads across the whole countryside.

2:3 – 11 The staccato character of the poetry is appropriate for the imagery of war (see Na 3:1 – 3).

2:3 *Before them.* Joel creates a special impact by using this phrase three times (twice in v. 3 and once in v. 10), "behind them" twice (v. 3) and "At the sight of them" once (v. 6). *fire.* See note on 1:19 – 20. *Eden.* See Ge 2:8,15 (the garden before the fall); Ge 13:10 (the Jordan Valley before the destruction of Sodom); and Isa 51:3; Eze 31:8 – 9,16,18; 36:35 (all of which describe a desert that has become like Eden).

2:4 *horses.* Whereas the book of Job compares the horse to a locust (Job 39:19 – 20), Joel does the opposite.

2:5 Mountains, though barriers to ordinary horses and chariots, are no deterrent to locusts.

2:6 *At the sight of them.* Parallels "Before them" (vv. 3,10). *in anguish.* Because of the famine that the locusts will cause.

7 They charge like warriors;[t]
they scale walls like soldiers.
They all march in line,[u]
not swerving[v] from their course.
8 They do not jostle each other;
each marches straight ahead.
They plunge through defenses
without breaking ranks.
9 They rush upon the city;
they run along the wall.
They climb into the houses;[w]
like thieves they enter through the windows.[x]
10 Before them the earth shakes,[y]
the sky trembles,[z]
the sun and moon are darkened,[a]
and the stars no longer shine.[b]
11 The LORD[c] thunders[d]
at the head of his army;[e]
his forces are beyond number,
and mighty are those who obey his command.
The day of the LORD is great;[f]
it is dreadful.
Who can endure it?[g]

Rend Your Heart

12 "Even now," declares the LORD,
"return[h] to me with all your heart,[i]
with fasting and weeping and mourning."
13 Rend your heart[j]
and not your garments.[k]
Return[l] to the LORD your God,
for he is gracious and compassionate,[m]
slow to anger and abounding in love,[n]
and he relents from sending calamity.[o]
14 Who knows? He may turn[p] and have pity[q]
and leave behind a blessing[r]—
grain offerings and drink offerings[s]
for the LORD your God.

15 Blow the trumpet[t] in Zion,[u]
declare a holy fast,[v]
call a sacred assembly.[w]
16 Gather the people,
consecrate[x] the assembly;
bring together the elders,[y]
gather the children,
those nursing at the breast.
Let the bridegroom[z] leave his room
and the bride her chamber.
17 Let the priests, who minister[a] before the LORD,
weep[b] between the temple porch and the altar.[c]
Let them say, "Spare your people, O LORD.
Do not make your inheritance an object of scorn,[d]
a byword[e] among the nations.
Why should they say among the peoples,
'Where is their God?[f]'"

The LORD's Answer

18 Then the LORD will be jealous[g] for his land
and take pity[h] on his people.

19 The LORD will reply[a] to them:

[a] *18,19 Or* LORD *was jealous . . . / and took pity . . . / 19The* LORD *replied*

2:7 [t]S Job 16:14 [u]Pr 30:27 [v]Isa 5:27 **2:9** [w]Ex 10:6 [x]Jer 9:21 **2:10** [y]Ps 18:7; Na 1:5 [z]S Eze 38:19 [a]S ver 2; S Isa 5:30; S Mt 24:29; Mk 13:24; Rev 9:2 [b]S Job 9:7; S Ps 102:26; Isa 13:10; S Eze 32:8 **2:11** [c]S Isa 2:12; S Eze 30:3; S Joel 1:15; Ob 1:15 [d]S Ps 29:3 [e]S ver 2,25 [f]Zep 1:14 [g]S Eze 22:14; Zep 2:11; Rev 6:17 **2:12** [h]S Dt 4:30; S Eze 33:11; S Hos 12:6 [i]S 1Sa 7:3 **2:13** [j]Ps 51:17; Isa 57:15 [k]S Ge 37:29; S Nu 14:6; Job 1:20 [l]S Isa 19:22 [m]S Dt 4:31 [n]Ex 34:6; S Ps 86:5,15 [o]S Jer 18:8; Jnh 4:2 **2:14** [p]Jer 26:3; Jnh 3:9 [q]Am 5:15; Jnh 1:6 [r]Jer 31:14; Hag 2:19; Zec 8:13; Mal 3:10 [s]S Joel 1:13 **2:15** [t]S Nu 10:2 [u]ver 1 [v]S 2Ch 20:3; Jer 36:9 [w]S Ex 32:5; Nu 10:3 **2:16** [x]S Ex 19:10,22 [y]Joel 1:2 [z]Ps 19:5 **2:17** [a]Joel 1:13 [b]S Isa 22:12 [c]Eze 8:16; Mt 23:35 [d]Dt 9:26-29; Ps 44:13 [e]S 1Ki 9:7; S Job 17:6 [f]S Ps 42:3 **2:18** [g]S Isa 26:11; Zec 1:14; 8:2 [h]S Ps 72:13

2:9 *climb into the houses.* As in the Egyptian plague of locusts (Ex 10:6). Latticed windows with no glass would not stop them.
2:10 *earth shakes.* See Ps 68:8; 77:18; Isa 24:18–20; Jer 4:24; Am 8:8; Na 1:5. *sky trembles.* See 2Sa 22:8; Isa 13:13; Hag 2:6,21; Heb 12:26–28. *darkened.* Joel links God's judgment through the locusts to the cosmic phenomena of the day of the Lord.
2:11 Just as Isaiah saw the Assyrians (see Isa 10:5 and note) and Jeremiah the Babylonians (Jer 25:9; 43:10) as the Lord's weapons, so Joel sees the locusts as the Lord's army (cf. Jos 5:14; Ps 68:17; Hab 3:8–9)—the army of the Lord with which he will come against his enemies in the day of the Lord (see 3:9–11 and note). This passage parallels Zep 1:14 (cf. v. 31; 3:14; Mal 4:1,5). *thunders.* See 3:16 and note. *great . . . dreadful.* Two ideas often associated in the OT, though sometimes the Hebrew word underlying "dreadful" means "awesome" (see Dt 7:21; 10:21; Ps 106:22). The terms are frequently used to describe the day of the Lord (see v. 31; Mal 4:5). *Who can endure it?* See Na 1:6 and note; Mal 3:2; Rev 6:17. There is no escape except in turning to God.
2:12–17 The first half of the book ends with a call to repentance ("return," vv. 12–13; see Hos 14:1 and note) and prayer (v. 17), balancing the call to mourning and prayer with which the section begins (1:2–14).
2:13 *Rend your heart.* See Ps 51:17 and note. *gracious . . . abounding in love.* Recalls the great self-characterization of God in Ex 34:6–7, which runs like a golden thread through the OT (see note on Ex 34:6–7; see also Dt 4:31; Mic 7:18).
2:14 *grain offerings and drink offerings.* See note on 1:9.
2:15 *trumpet.* Not an alarm as in v. 1, but a call to religious assembly (see Lev 23:24; 25:9; Nu 10:10; Jos 6:4–5; 2Ch 15:14; Ps 98:6 and note). *fast . . . assembly.* See note on 1:14.
2:16 As with the call to mourning in ch. 1, no segment of the community was exempt. *assembly.* The Hebrew for this word refers to the religious community (see Nu 16:3; 2Ch 30:2,4,23–25; Mic 2:5). *elders.* See note on 1:2. *chamber.* The place where the marriage was consummated.
2:17 *your inheritance.* Israel is God's special possession (see Ex 34:9; Jer 3:19 and note). Judah is to plead, not her innocence, but that God's honor is at stake before the world (see Ex 32:12; see also Nu 14:13; Jos 7:9 and notes). *byword.* See note on 1Ki 9:7. *Where is their God?* A rhetorical question with sarcastic intent (see Ps 3:2; 10:11; 115:2 and notes).
2:18 Joel begins a new section by turning from the destruction caused by the locusts to the blessings God will give (or gave; see NIV text note on vv. 18,19) to a repentant people. *jealous.* See note on Ex 20:5. The Lord will respond (or responded) to the prayer of v. 17 and arouse (or aroused) himself to defend his honor and have pity on his people.
2:19 *grain, new wine and oil.* See note on 1:10.

"I am sending you grain, new wine[i]
and oil,[j]
enough to satisfy you fully;[k]
never again will I make you
an object of scorn[l] to the nations.

20 "I will drive the northern army[m] far
from you,
pushing it into a parched and barren
land,
with its front columns going into the
eastern[n] sea[a]
and those in the rear into the
western sea.[b]
And its stench[o] will go up;
its smell will rise."

Surely he has done great things.[c]
21 Be not afraid,[p] O land;
be glad and rejoice.[q]
Surely the LORD has done great
things.[r]
22 Be not afraid, O wild animals,
for the open pastures are becoming
green.[s]
The trees are bearing their fruit;
the fig tree[t] and the vine[u] yield their
riches.[v]
23 Be glad, O people of Zion,
rejoice[w] in the LORD your God,
for he has given you
the autumn rains in righteousness.[d][x]
He sends you abundant showers,[y]
both autumn[z] and spring rains,[a] as
before.
24 The threshing floors will be filled with
grain;
the vats will overflow[b] with new
wine[c] and oil.

25 "I will repay you for the years the
locusts[d] have eaten[e]—
the great locust and the young
locust,
the other locusts and the locust
swarm[e]—
my great army[f] that I sent among you.
26 You will have plenty to eat, until you
are full,[g]
and you will praise[h] the name of the
LORD your God,
who has worked wonders[i] for you;
never again will my people be
shamed.[j]
27 Then you will know[k] that I am in
Israel,
that I am the LORD[l] your God,
and that there is no other;
never again will my people be
shamed.[m]

The Day of the LORD

28 "And afterward,
I will pour out my Spirit[n] on all
people.[o]
Your sons and daughters will
prophesy,[p]
your old men will dream dreams,[q]
your young men will see visions.
29 Even on my servants,[r] both men and
women,
I will pour out my Spirit in those
days.[s]
30 I will show wonders in the heavens[t]
and on the earth,[u]
blood and fire and billows of smoke.

[a] 20 That is, the Dead Sea [b] 20 That is, the Mediterranean [c] 20 Or *rise. / Surely it has done great things."* [d] 23 Or / *the teacher for righteousness:* [e] 25 The precise meaning of the four Hebrew words used here for locusts is uncertain.

2:19 [i]Ps 4:7 [j]S Jer 31:12 [k]S Lev 26:5 [l]S Eze 34:29 **2:20** [m]Jer 1:14-15 [n]Zec 14:8 [o]S Isa 34:3 **2:21** [p]S Isa 29:22; S 54:4; Zep 3:16-17 [q]S Ps 9:2 [r]S Ps 126:3; S Isa 25:1 **2:22** [s]S Ps 65:12 [t]S 1Ki 4:25 [u]S Nu 16:14 [v]Joel 1:18-20; Zec 8:12 **2:23** [w]Ps 33:21; 97:12; 149:2; Isa 12:6; 41:16; 66:14; Hab 3:18; Zec 10:7 [x]S Isa 45:8 [y]S Job 36:28; S Eze 34:26 [z]Ps 84:6 [a]S Lev 26:4; S Ps 135:7; Jas 5:7 **2:24** [b]Lev 26:10; Mal 3:10 [c]S Pr 3:10; Joel 3:18; Am 9:13 **2:25** [d]S Ex 10:14; Am 4:9 [e]S Dt 28:39 [f]S Joel 1:6 **2:26** [g]S Lev 26:5 [h]S Lev 23:40; S Isa 62:9 [i]S Ps 126:3; S Isa 25:1 [j]S Isa 29:22 **2:27** [k]S Ex 6:7 [l]S Ex 6:2; S Isa 44:8; Joel 3:17 [m]Isa 45:17; 54:4; Zep 3:11 **2:28** [n]S Isa 11:2; S 44:3 [o]S Nu 11:17; S Mk 1:8; Gal 3:14 [p]S 1Sa 19:20 [q]Jer 23:25 **2:29** [r]1Co 12:13; Gal 3:28 [s]S Eze 36:27 **2:30** [t]Lk 21:11 [u]Mk 13:24-25

2:20 *northern army.* Since enemies in ancient times did not invade from the sea or across the desert, Canaan's geographical location made her vulnerable only from the south (Egypt) and from the north (Assyria and Babylonia). The hordes of locusts are pictured here as a vast army of Israel's most feared enemies. *stench.* Because the locusts are now dead.

2:21–23 As there was a multiple call to grief (1:5,8,11,13), so there is a multiple call to joy: The land (v. 21), the wild animals (v. 22) and the people (v. 23) are called on to rejoice in the Lord's bounty.

2:22 The wild animals now find green open pastures (cf. 1:19–20). The same land, with its trees that the locusts and drought had devastated (see 1:7,12,19), is now productive.

2:23 *the autumn rains in righteousness.* See NIV text note. The religious sect at Qumran (which produced most of the Dead Sea Scrolls; see essay, p. 1452) hailed their most revered teacher of the law, whom they called the "Teacher of Righteousness," as the fulfillment of this prophecy. The immediate context, however, seems to support the translation in the NIV text.

2:24 *threshing floors.* See note on Ru 1:22. *vats.* See note on Hag 2:16.

2:25 See 1:4 and note.

2:26 *wonders.* God performed wonders for the people when they were in Egypt (see Ex 3:20 and note; 7:3), and now he will work wonders in restoring the devastated land.

2:27 *Israel.* Probably refers to all God's people, with no distinction between the northern and southern kingdoms, as also in 3:2,16. *I am the LORD your God.* This clause recalls the covenant at Sinai (see Ex 20:2 and note). *there is no other.* See note on Dt 4:35.

2:28–32 Quoted by Peter on the day of Pentecost (Ac 2:16–21), but with a few variations from both the Hebrew text and the Septuagint (the pre-Christian Greek translation of the OT).

2:28 *afterward.* In the Messianic period, beyond the restoration just spoken of. *pour out my Spirit.* See v. 29; Isa 32:15; 44:3; Eze 39:29 and note; Zec 12:10—13:1. *all people.* All will participate without regard to gender, age or rank; and then Moses' wish (see Nu 11:29 and note) will be realized (cf. Gal 3:28). Peter extends the "all" of this verse and the "everyone" of v. 32 to the Gentiles ("all who are far off," Ac 2:39; see also note on Ac 2:17), who will not be excluded from the Spirit's outpouring or deliverance (cf. Ro 11:11–24). *prophesy … dream dreams … see visions.* See Nu 12:6.

2:30–31 These cosmic events are often associated with the day of the Lord (see Isa 13:9–10,13; 34:4; Mt 24:29; Rev 6:12–13; 8:8–9; 9:1–19; 14:14–20; 16:4,8–9).

2:30 *blood … fire … smoke.* From war; fire and smoke can also be signs of God's presence (see Ge 15:17 and note).

31 The sun will be turned to darkness[v]
and the moon to blood
before the coming of the great and
dreadful day of the LORD.[w]
32 And everyone who calls
on the name of the LORD[x] will be
saved;[y]
for on Mount Zion[z] and in Jerusalem
there will be deliverance,[a]
as the LORD has said,
among the survivors[b]
whom the LORD calls.[c]

The Nations Judged

3 “In those days and at that time,
when I restore the fortunes[d] of
Judah[e] and Jerusalem,
2 I will gather[f] all nations
and bring them down to the Valley
of Jehoshaphat.[a][g]
There I will enter into judgment[h]
against them
concerning my inheritance, my
people Israel,
for they scattered[i] my people among
the nations
and divided up my land.
3 They cast lots[j] for my people
and traded boys for prostitutes;
they sold girls for wine[k]
that they might drink.

4 “Now what have you against me,
O Tyre and Sidon[l] and all you regions
of Philistia?[m] Are you repaying me for
something I have done? If you are paying me back, I will swiftly and speedily
return on your own heads what you have
done.[n] 5 For you took my silver and my
gold and carried off my finest treasures
to your temples.[o] 6 You sold the people
of Judah and Jerusalem to the Greeks,[p]
that you might send them far from their
homeland.

7 “See, I am going to rouse them out of
the places to which you sold them,[q] and
I will return[r] on your own heads what
you have done. 8 I will sell your sons[s] and
daughters to the people of Judah,[t] and
they will sell them to the Sabeans,[u] a nation far away.” The LORD has spoken.[v]

9 Proclaim this among the nations:
Prepare for war![w]
Rouse the warriors![x]
Let all the fighting men draw near
and attack.
10 Beat your plowshares into swords
and your pruning hooks[y] into
spears.[z]
Let the weakling[a] say,
“I am strong!”[b]
11 Come quickly, all you nations from
every side,
and assemble[c] there.
Bring down your warriors,[d]
O LORD!

[a] 2 *Jehoshaphat* means *the LORD judges*; also in verse 12.

2:31 [v] S ver 2; S Isa 22:5; S Jer 4:23; S Mt 24:29 [w] S Joel 1:15; Ob 1:15; Mal 3:2; 4:1,5 **2:32** [x] S Ge 4:26; S Ps 105:1 [y] S Ps 106:8; Ac 2:17-21*; Ro 10:13* [z] S Isa 46:13 [a] Ob 1:17 [b] S Isa 1:9; 11:11; Mic 4:7; 7:18; S Ro 9:27 [c] Ac 2:39 **3:1** [d] S Dt 30:3; S Jer 16:15; S Eze 38:8; Zep 3:20 [e] Jer 40:5 **3:2** [f] Zep 3:8 [g] ver 12; S Isa 22:1 [h] S Isa 13:9; S Jer 2:35; S Eze 36:5 [i] S Ge 11:4; S Lev 26:33 **3:3** [j] S Job 6:27; S Eze 24:6 [k] Joel 1:5; Am 2:6 **3:4** [l] S Ge 10:15; S Mt 11:21 [m] S Ps 87:4; Isa 14:29-31; Jer 47:1-7 [n] S Lev 26:28; S Isa 34:8; S Eze 25:15-17; Zec 9:5-7 **3:5** [o] S 1Ki 15:18; S 2Ch 21:16-17 **3:6** [p] Eze 27:13; Zec 9:13 **3:7** [q] S Isa 43:5-6; Jer 23:8 [r] S Isa 66:6 **3:8** [s] Isa 60:14 [t] Isa 14:2 [u] S Ge 10:7; S 2Ch 9:1 [v] S Isa 23:1; S Jer 30:16 **3:9** [w] S Isa 8:9 [x] Jer 46:4 **3:10** [y] Isa 2:4 [z] S Nu 25:7 [a] Zec 12:8 [b] S Jos 1:6 **3:11** [c] Eze 38:15-16; Zep 3:8 [d] S Isa 13:3

2:31 *darkness.* See v. 2 and note. *blood.* The moon will become blood-red. *great and dreadful day of the LORD.* See v. 11; 1:15 and notes.

2:32 *calls on the name of the LORD.* Worships God and prays to him (see Ge 4:26; 12:8; Ps 116:4). *saved.* Delivered from the wrath of God's judgment (see Mt 24:13). *as the LORD has said.* Perhaps Joel is recalling the Lord's covenant with David (see 2Sa 7; Ps 132:11–18). *survivors.* See Zec 13:8–9 and notes; 14:2.

3:1 *In those days.* At the time of Israel's final redemption (see v. 18 and note). *restore the fortunes of.* Or "bring back from captivity" (see vv. 6–7; see also note on Jer 29:14 and NIV text note there).

3:2 *Valley of Jehoshaphat.* See v. 12. Called the "valley of decision" in v. 14, it seems to be a symbolic name for a valley near Jerusalem that is here depicted as the place of God's ultimate judgment on the nations gathered against Jerusalem (see NIV text note; cf. Zec 6:1 and note). There King Jehoshaphat had witnessed one of the Lord's historic victories over the nations (see 2Ch 20:1–30). *my inheritance.* See note on 2:17. Eight times in three verses (vv. 2–3,5) God uses "my," emphasizing his covenant relationship with Israel. *Israel.* See note on 2:27.

3:3 *cast lots for my people.* This happened to Judah at the time of the captivity (586 B.C.) and is mentioned in Ob 11. The Israelites were treated by their enemies as mere chattel, to be traded off for the pleasures of prostitution and wine.

3:4–8 A parenthetical interlude. In vv. 1–3,9–16 God announces judgment against the nations hostile to Israel, but here he addresses the nations directly.

3:4 *me.* The Lord. *Tyre … Sidon … Philistia.* Tyre and Philistia had sold Israelites as slaves (see Am 1:6,9 and notes), and Philistia had often plundered Israel (see Jdg 13:1; 1Sa 5:1; 2Ch 21:16–17; Eze 25:15–17 and note on 25:15). God punished them by allowing Sidon to be destroyed and many of its people enslaved by Artaxerxes III c. 345 B.C. and by allowing Tyre to be captured by the Greeks (under Alexander the Great) in 332. *return on your own heads what you have done.* See v. 7; Eze 16:43 and note.

3:6 The Greeks were trading with the Phoenicians as early as 800 B.C.

3:8 *Sabeans.* See Job 1:15 and note; from Sheba, whose queen visited Solomon (see 1Ki 10:1–13 and note on 10:1). *far away.* It was located in the southern part of the Arabian peninsula (present-day Yemen).

3:9–21 In vv. 9–11 Joel is the speaker; in vv. 12–13 God speaks; in vv. 14–16, Joel; and in vv. 17–21, God. When Joel speaks, he does so as the spokesman of the Lord, who has commissioned him to be his prophet.

3:9–11 Joel commands that the nations be told to prepare for battle, for the Lord would come against them with his invincible heavenly army and bring them into judgment (cf. Eze 38–39; Rev 19).

3:10 The first part of this verse is the reverse of Isa 2:4 (see note there) and Mic 4:3, where the peaceful effect of God's reign is portrayed. Here God's enemies are summoned to their last great confrontation with him. *plowshares.* See note on Isa 2:4.

3:11 *assemble there.* In the Valley of Jehoshaphat for judgment (vv. 2,12).

12 "Let the nations be roused;
let them advance into the Valley of Jehoshaphat,[e]
for there I will sit
to judge[f] all the nations on every side.
13 Swing the sickle,[g]
for the harvest[h] is ripe.
Come, trample the grapes,[i]
for the winepress[j] is full
and the vats overflow—
so great is their wickedness!"

14 Multitudes,[k] multitudes
in the valley[l] of decision!
For the day of the LORD[m] is near
in the valley of decision.[n]
15 The sun and moon will be darkened,
and the stars no longer shine.[o]
16 The LORD will roar[p] from Zion
and thunder from Jerusalem;[q]
the earth and the sky will tremble.[r]
But the LORD will be a refuge[s] for his people,
a stronghold[t] for the people of Israel.

Blessings for God's People

17 "Then you will know[u] that I, the LORD your God,[v]
dwell in Zion,[w] my holy hill.[x]
Jerusalem will be holy;[y]
never again will foreigners invade her.[z]

18 "In that day the mountains will drip new wine,[a]
and the hills will flow with milk;[b]
all the ravines of Judah will run with water.[c]
A fountain will flow out of the LORD's house[d]
and will water the valley of acacias.[a][e]
19 But Egypt[f] will be desolate,
Edom[g] a desert waste,
because of violence[h] done to the people of Judah,
in whose land they shed innocent blood.
20 Judah will be inhabited forever[i]
and Jerusalem through all generations.
21 Their bloodguilt,[j] which I have not pardoned,
I will pardon.[k]"

The LORD dwells in Zion![l]

[a] 18 Or *Valley of Shittim*

3:12 [e] S ver 2 [f] S Ps 82:1; S Isa 2:4 **3:13** [g] Mk 4:29 [h] S Isa 17:5; S Hos 6:11; Mt 13:39; Rev 14:15-19 [i] S Jer 25:30 [j] S Jdg 6:11; S Rev 14:20 **3:14** [k] Isa 13:4 [l] S Isa 22:1 [m] Isa 34:2-8; S Joel 1:15; S Zep 1:7 [n] S Isa 2:4; S Eze 36:5 **3:15** [o] S Job 9:7; S Eze 32:7 **3:16** [p] S Isa 42:13 [q] Am 1:2 [r] S Jdg 5:4; S Isa 14:16; S Eze 38:19 [s] S Ps 46:1; S Isa 25:4; Zec 12:8 [t] S 2Sa 22:3; Jer 16:19; Zec 9:12 **3:17** [u] S Ex 6:7 [v] S Joel 2:27 [w] S Ps 74:2; S Isa 4:3 [x] Ps 2:6; S Isa 2:2; S Eze 17:22 [y] S Jer 31:40 [z] S Isa 52:1; S Eze 44:9; Zec 9:8 **3:18** [a] S Joel 2:24 [b] Ex 3:8; S SS 5:1 [c] S Isa 30:25; 35:6; S 44:3 [d] Rev 22:1-2 [e] S Nu 25:1; S Isa 25:6; S Jer 31:12; S Eze 47:1; Am 9:13 **3:19** [f] S Isa 19:1 [g] S Isa 11:14; S 34:11 [h] S Jer 51:35; Ob 1:10 **3:20** [i] S Ezr 9:12; Am 9:15 **3:21** [j] S Isa 1:15 [k] S Eze 36:25 [l] S Ps 74:2; Isa 59:20; S Eze 48:35; Zec 8:3

3:13 As a result of the Lord's great army of locusts that had marched against Judah (see 2:3–11 and note on 2:11), there had been no harvest (2:3). But that harvest was to be restored (2:19,22,24,26). In the final great day of the Lord, there will also be a harvest—the harvest of God's judgment on the nations. Rev 14:14–20 draws heavily on this picture of judgment (see notes on Rev 14:15,18–20). *vats.* See 2:24 and note.

3:14 *valley of decision.* The Valley of Jehoshaphat (judgment) of vv. 2,12. "Jehoshaphat" speaks of God's role as Judge (see note on v. 2). Here "decision" (from a different Hebrew word) refers to the heavenly Judge's decision or judicial decree. The valley is now viewed as the place where that decree will be executed. *day of the LORD.* See 1:15 and note.

3:15 See 2:10 and note.

3:16 *roar.* Like a lion, God will destroy the nations. The first two lines occur also in Am 1:2 (see note there; see also Jer 25:30). *from Zion.* See note on Am 1:2. *thunder.* As God at the head of his army had thundered against Jerusalem (2:11), so he will then thunder against Jerusalem's enemies, and he will do so from his royal city, from which he rules his inheritance (see v. 17; Am 1:2). *the earth and the sky will tremble.* See 2:10 and note. *Israel.* See note on 2:27.

3:17–21 God blesses his people in a dual way: negatively, by destroying their enemies; positively, by giving them good things.

3:17 *dwell in Zion.* The Lord himself will dwell with them (see v. 21). The same picture is found in 2:27; Ps 46:4 (cf. Rev 21:3). The final blessed state of the now unholy and vulnerable city will be God's abiding presence in her (see v. 21 and note; Rev 21). Then she will be holy and impregnable (see Zec 14:21 and note). *Zion.* See 2:1 and note.

3:18 *In that day.* The same as "In those days" of v. 1. The Edenic lushness pictured in this verse is in great contrast to the drought in 1:10 (see Am 9:13). *mountains … hills.* See Ps 104:13–15; Hag 1:11 and notes. *A fountain will flow out of the LORD's house.* Flowing from God's presence, streams of blessing will refresh his people and make their place endlessly fruitful (see Ps 36:8; 46:4 and notes; 87:7; Eze 47:1–12; Rev 22:1–2). *acacias.* See Ex 25:5 and note. Since acacias flourish in dry soil, the picture is that of a well-watered desert.

3:19 *Egypt … Edom.* As old enemies of Israel, they here represent all the nations hostile to God's people (see notes on Eze 35:1–15; Zec 10:10). *desolate … desert waste.* Figures for the removal of all life-sustaining blessings, thus setting in sharp focus the contrasting destinies of God's people and the enemies of God's kingdom. This picture of desolation also recalls the earlier description of Judah's condition (2:3).

3:20 *will be inhabited forever.* When God's judgment and redemption are consummated, his kingdom will endure and flourish eternally.

3:21 This book of judgment ends on a promising and encouraging note: "The LORD dwells in Zion," and therefore all is right with those who trust in God and live with him. The book of Ezekiel has a similar ending (see note on Eze 48:35).

Amos

INTRODUCTION

Author

Amos was from Tekoa (1:1), a small town in Judah about 6 miles south of Bethlehem and 11 miles from Jerusalem. He was not a man of the court like Isaiah, or a member of a priestly family like Jeremiah and Ezekiel. He earned his living from the flock and the sycamore-fig grove (1:1; 7:14–15). Whether he owned the flocks and groves or only worked as a hired hand is not known. His skill with words and the strikingly broad range of his general knowledge of history and the world preclude his being an ignorant peasant. Though his home was in Judah, he was sent to announce God's judgment on the northern kingdom (Israel). He probably ministered for the most part at Bethel (7:10–13; see 1Ki 12:28–30 and notes), Israel's main religious sanctuary, where the upper echelons of the northern kingdom worshiped.

The book brings his prophecies together in a carefully organized form intended to be read as a unit. It offers few, if any, clues as to the chronological order of his spoken messages — he may have repeated them on many occasions to reach everyone who came to worship. The book is ultimately addressed to all Israel (hence the references to Judah and Jerusalem).

A Quick Look

Author:
Amos

Audience:
Primarily the idolatrous and indulgent people of the northern kingdom

Date:
760–750 B.C.

Theme:
The prophet Amos calls for social justice as the indispensable expression of true piety.

Date and Historical Situation

According to the first verse, Amos prophesied during the reigns of Uzziah over Judah (792–740 B.C.) and Jeroboam II over Israel (793–753). The main part of his ministry was probably carried out c. 760–750. Both kingdoms were enjoying great prosperity and had reached new political and military heights (cf. 2Ki 14:23 — 15:7; 2Ch 26). It was also a time of idolatry, extravagant indulgence in luxurious living, immorality, corruption of judicial procedures and oppression of the poor. As a consequence, God would soon bring about the Assyrian captivity of the northern kingdom (722–721).

Israel at the time was politically secure and spiritually smug. About 40 years earlier, at the end of his ministry, Elisha had prophesied the resurgence of Israel's power (2Ki 13:17–19), and more recently Jonah had prophesied her restoration to a glory not known since the days of Solomon (2Ki 14:25). The nation felt sure, therefore, that she was in God's good graces. But prosperity increased Israel's religious and moral corruption. God's past punishments for unfaithfulness were forgotten, and his patience was at an end — which he sent Amos to announce.

Prior to Amos, the Lord sent his prophets primarily to carry messages to the kings in Israel. Beginning with Amos, the messages of the prophets were addressed to the general population — their ministries to the kings after David had proven to be largely fruitless. And with Amos, their messages began to be preserved in permanent form as written compositions that would accompany Israel through the coming times of judgment and beyond. (Since Amos was a contemporary of Hosea and Jonah, see Introductions to those books.)

Amos was a vigorous spokesman for God's justice and righteousness, whereas Hosea emphasized God's love, grace, mercy and forgiveness.

Theological Theme and Message

The dominant theme is clearly stated in 5:24, which calls for social justice as the indispensable expression of true piety. Amos was a vigorous spokesman for God's justice and righteousness, whereas Hosea emphasized God's love, grace, mercy and forgiveness. Amos declared that God was going to judge his unfaithful, disobedient, covenant-breaking people. Despite the Lord's special choice of Israel and his kindnesses to her during the exodus and conquest and in the days of David and Solomon, his people continually failed to honor and obey him. The worship centers that King Jeroboam I had set up in Bethel, Dan and elsewhere (1Ki 12:28 – 33) became thoroughly paganized. The Israelites came to believe that the observance of religious rites at the sacred places was all that God was interested in and that outside their worship activities they could do whatever they pleased — an essentially pagan notion. Without commitment to God's law, they had no basis for standards of conduct. Amos condemns all who make themselves powerful or rich at the expense of others. Those who had acquired great wealth at the expense of the poor and powerless through fraud in the marketplace and corruption of the courts would lose everything.

God's imminent judgment on Israel would not be a mere punitive blow to warn (as often before; see 4:6 – 11 and note), but an almost total destruction. The unthinkable was about to happen: Because they had not faithfully consecrated themselves to his lordship, God would uproot his chosen people by the hands of a pagan nation. Even so, if they would repent, there was hope that "the LORD God Almighty (would) have mercy on the remnant" (5:15; see 5:4 – 6,14). In fact, the Lord had a glorious future for his people, beyond the impending judgment. The house of David would again rule over Israel — even extend its rule over many nations — and Israel would once more be secure in the promised land, feasting on wine and fruit (9:11 – 15). The God of Israel, the Lord of history, would not abandon his chosen people or his chosen program of redemption.

The God for whom Amos speaks is Lord over more than Israel. He is the Great King who rules the whole universe (4:13; 5:8; 9:5 – 6). Because he is all-sovereign, the God of Israel holds the history and destiny of all peoples and of the world in his hands. Israel must know not only that he is the Lord of her future, but also that he is Lord over all, and that he has purposes and concerns that reach far beyond her borders. Israel had a unique, but not an exclusive, claim on God. She needed to remember not only his covenant commitments to her but also her covenant obligations to him. (See further the prophecy of Jonah.)

Outline

I. Superscription (1:1)
II. Introduction to Amos's Message (1:2)
III. Prophecies against the Nations, including Judah and Israel (1:3 — 2:16)
  A. Judgment on Aram (1:3 – 5)
  B. Judgment on Philistia (1:6 – 8)
  C. Judgment on Phoenicia (1:9 – 10)

- D. Judgment on Edom (1:11 – 12)
- E. Judgment on Ammon (1:13 – 15)
- F. Judgment on Moab (2:1 – 3)
- G. Judgment on Judah (2:4 – 5)
- H. Judgment on Israel (2:6 – 16)
  1. Ruthless oppression of the poor (2:6 – 7a)
  2. Unbridled profanation of religion (2:7b – 8)
  3. Contrasted position of the Israelites (2:9 – 12)
  4. The oppressive system will perish (2:13 – 16)

IV. Prophecies against Israel (3:1 — 5:17)

- A. Judgment on the Chosen People (ch. 3)
  1. God's punishment announced (3:1 – 2)
  2. The announcement vindicated (3:3 – 8)
  3. The punishment vindicated (3:9 – 15)
- B. Judgment on an Unrepentant People (ch. 4)
  1. Judgment on the socialites (4:1 – 3)
  2. Perversion of religious life (4:4 – 5)
  3. Past calamities brought no repentance (4:6 – 11)
  4. No hope for a hardened people (4:12 – 13)
- C. Judgment on an Unjust People (5:1 – 17)
  1. The death dirge (5:1 – 3)
  2. Exhortation to life (5:4 – 6)
  3. Indictment of injustices (5:7 – 13)
  4. Exhortation to life (5:14 – 15)
  5. Prosperity will turn to grief (5:16 – 17)

V. Announcements of Exile (5:18 — 6:14)

- A. A Message of Woe against Israel's Perverted Religion (5:18 – 27)
- B. A Message of Woe against Israel's Complacent Pride (6:1 – 7)
- C. A Sworn Judgment on the Proud and Unjust Nation (6:8 – 14)

VI. Visions of Divine Retribution (7:1 — 9:10)

- A. Judgment Relented (7:1 – 6)
  1. A swarm of locusts (7:1 – 3)
  2. A consuming fire (7:4 – 6)
- B. Judgment Unrelented (7:7 — 9:10)
  1. The plumb line (7:7 – 17)
     - a. The vision (7:7 – 9)
     - b. Amos challenged and vindicated (7:10 – 17)
  2. The basket of ripe fruit (ch. 8)
     - a. The vision (8:1 – 3)
     - b. The exposition (8:4 – 14)
  3. The Lord by the altar (9:1 – 10)
     - a. The vision (9:1 – 4)
     - b. The exposition (9:5 – 10)

VII. Restored Israel's Blessed Future (9:11 – 15)

- A. Revival of the House of David (9:11 – 12)
- B. Restoration of Israel to an Edenic Promised Land (9:13 – 15)

1 The words of Amos, one of the shepherds of Tekoa[a] — what he saw concerning Israel two years before the earthquake,[b] when Uzziah[c] was king of Judah
and Jeroboam[d] son of Jehoash[a] was king
of Israel.[e]

2 He said:

"The LORD roars[f] from Zion
and thunders[g] from Jerusalem;[h]
the pastures of the shepherds dry up,[b]
and the top of Carmel[i] withers."[j]

Judgment on Israel's Neighbors

3 This is what the LORD says:

"For three sins of Damascus,[k]
even for four, I will not turn back
⌞my wrath⌟.[l]
Because she threshed Gilead
with sledges having iron teeth,
4 I will send fire[m] upon the house of
Hazael[n]
that will consume the fortresses[o] of
Ben-Hadad.[p]
5 I will break down the gate[q] of
Damascus;
I will destroy the king who is in[c] the
Valley of Aven[d]
and the one who holds the scepter in
Beth Eden.[r]
The people of Aram will go into exile
to Kir,[s]"
says the LORD.[t]

6 This is what the LORD says:

"For three sins of Gaza,[u]
even for four, I will not turn back
⌞my wrath⌟.[v]
Because she took captive whole
communities
and sold them to Edom,[w]
7 I will send fire upon the walls of
Gaza
that will consume her fortresses.
8 I will destroy the king[e] of Ashdod[x]
and the one who holds the scepter
in Ashkelon.

1:1 [a] S 2Sa 14:2 [b] Zec 14:5 [c] S 2Ki 14:21; S 2Ch 26:23 [d] S 2Ki 14:23 [e] S Hos 1:1
1:2 [f] S Isa 42:13 [g] S Ps 29:3 [h] Joel 3:16 [i] Am 9:3 [j] S Jer 12:4
1:3 [k] Isa 7:8; 8:4; 17:1-3 [l] ver 6,9,11,13; Am 2:6
1:4 [m] S Jer 49:27; S Eze 30:8 [n] S 1Ki 19:17; 2Ki 8:7-15 [o] Jer 17:27 [p] 1Ki 20:1; 2Ki 6:24; Jer 49:23-27
1:5 [q] Jer 51:30 [r] S Isa 37:12 [s] S 2Ki 16:9; S Isa 22:6; Zec 9:1 [t] S Isa 7:16; Jer 49:27
1:6 [u] S Ge 10:19; 1Sa 6:17; Zep 2:4 [v] S ver 3 [w] S Ge 14:6; Ob 1:11
1:8 [x] S 2Ch 26:6

[a] *1* Hebrew *Joash,* a variant of *Jehoash* [b] *2* Or *shepherds mourn* [c] *5* Or *the inhabitants of* [d] *5* *Aven* means *wickedness.* [e] *8* Or *inhabitants*

1:1 *Amos.* Apparently a shortened form of a name like Amasiah (2Ch 17:16), meaning "The LORD carries" or "The LORD upholds." *shepherds.* The Hebrew for this word occurs elsewhere in the OT only in reference to the king of Moab (2Ki 3:4, where it is translated "raised sheep"). Cf. 7:14, where a different Hebrew word is used. Amos was not a professional prophet who earned his living from his ministry; he stood outside religious institutions. *Tekoa.* See Introduction: Author. *saw.* Received by divine revelation. *earthquake.* Evidently a major shock, long remembered, and probably the one mentioned in Zec 14:5. Recent geological studies have detected a mammoth seismic event in this area dating to c. 750 B.C. Reference to the earthquake suggests that the author viewed it as a kind of divine reinforcement of the words of judgment. *Uzziah.* See Introduction: Date and Historical Situation; see also note on Isa 6:1. *Jeroboam.* See Introduction: Date and Historical Situation.

1:2 A thematic verse, ominously announcing the main thrust of Amos's message. *roars.* Amos, a shepherd, was sent to Israel to warn her that he had heard a lion roar and that the lion is none other than the Lord himself, who has only wanted to be Israel's shepherd. For the use of this imagery in other contexts see Jer 25:30; Joel 3:16 and note. *from Zion.* The Lord established his earthly throne in Jerusalem, among his special people, and from there he announces his judgments on them, as well as on the other nations. *pastures ... top of Carmel.* See 9:3. From the lowest and driest portions of the land to the highest and greenest, the Lord's judgment will be felt like a severe drought that devastates the whole land.

1:3 — 2:16 A series of prophecies against the nations; for parallel sections in other prophets see Isa 13:1 — 23:18 and note. After pronouncing judgments on Israel's neighbors for various atrocities — judgments that Israel would naturally applaud — Amos announces God's condemnation of his own two kingdoms for despising God's laws. His listing of Israel's sins under the same form of indictment used against the other nations shockingly arrays Israel's sins alongside those of her pagan neighbors.

1:3 *This is what the LORD says.* See vv. 6,9,11,13; 2:1,4,6. Amos, the Lord's spokesman, uses the messenger formula that identifies the actual source of his prophecies. *For three sins ... four.* For their many sins, especially the one named; see also vv. 6,9,11,13; 2:1,4,6. For similar numerical expressions see Job 5:19; Pr 6:16; Mic 5:5 and notes. *Damascus.* Capital of the Aramean state directly north of Israel (see note on Isa 17:1) and a constant enemy in that day. Her crime was brutality to the conquered people of Gilead, Israel's territory east of Galilee. *not turn back ⌞my wrath⌟.* See Isa 9:12,17,21 and note; Jer 23:20. *threshed ... sledges.* Heads of grain were threshed by driving a wooden sledge fitted with sharp teeth over the cut grain (cf. Job 41:30; Isa 28:27; 41:15; Hab 3:12; see 2Ki 13:7 and note on Ru 1:22).

1:4 *fire ... that will consume.* See vv. 7,10,12,14; 2:2,5; a common description of the threat of divine judgment, usually carried out by a devastating war that resulted in the burning of major cities and fortresses (see Jer 17:27 and note; Hos 8:14). *Hazael.* King of Damascus and founder of a new line of kings (see 2Ki 8:7 – 15 and note on 8:15). *fortresses.* See vv. 7,10,12,14; 2:2,5; perhaps referring not only to citadels but also to the fortress-like palatial dwellings of the rich and powerful. *Ben-Hadad.* Son of Hazael (see 2Ki 13:3 and note) and the second (or possibly third) king with this name (cf. 2Ki 8:14 – 15).

1:5 *king.* See v. 8; lit. "one who sits [enthroned]." *Valley of Aven.* Possibly the Beqaa Valley between the Lebanon and Anti-Lebanon mountains, but may refer to the river valley in which Damascus is located (see note on 2Ki 5:12), calling it the "valley of wickedness" (see NIV text note). *Beth Eden.* Probably Damascus, the garden spot of that region. *Aram.* See note on Dt 26:5. *Kir.* An unidentified place, possibly in the vicinity of Elam (see 2Ki 16:9 and note), from which the Arameans are said to have come (9:7).

1:6 *Gaza.* One of the five major Philistine cities (see map, p. 331); it guarded the entry to Canaan from Egypt. *whole communities.* See v. 9; not just warriors captured in battle. The reference may be to villages in south Judah on the trade route from Edom to Gaza. *to Edom.* See v. 9; trading the people like cattle to another country.

1:8 *Ashdod ... Ashkelon ... Ekron.* Three more cities of the Philistine group (see note on v. 6). Gath, the fifth (cf. 6:2), may already have been subdued by Uzziah (see 2Ch 26:6). *the last.* There would be no remnant. Philistia was finally destroyed by Nebuchadnezzar.

I will turn my hand[y] against Ekron,
till the last of the Philistines[z] is dead,"[a]
says the Sovereign LORD.[b]

9This is what the LORD says:

"For three sins of Tyre,[c]
even for four, I will not turn back
⌞my wrath⌟.[d]
Because she sold whole communities
of captives to Edom,
disregarding a treaty of
brotherhood,[e]
10I will send fire upon the walls of Tyre
that will consume her fortresses.[f]"

11This is what the LORD says:

"For three sins of Edom,[g]
even for four, I will not turn back
⌞my wrath⌟.
Because he pursued his brother with a
sword,[h]
stifling all compassion,[a]
because his anger raged continually
and his fury flamed unchecked,[i]
12I will send fire upon Teman[j]
that will consume the fortresses of
Bozrah.[k]"

13This is what the LORD says:

"For three sins of Ammon,[l]
even for four, I will not turn back
⌞my wrath⌟.
Because he ripped open the pregnant
women[m] of Gilead
in order to extend his borders,
14I will set fire to the walls of Rabbah[n]
that will consume[o] her fortresses
amid war cries[p] on the day of battle,
amid violent winds[q] on a stormy day.
15Her king[b] will go into exile,
he and his officials together,[r]"
says the LORD.[s]

1:8 [y]Ps 81:14 [z]S Eze 25:16 [a]S Isa 34:8 [b]Isa 14:28-32; Zep 2:4-7 **1:9** [c]1Ki 5:1; 9:11-14; Jer 25:22; Joel 3:4; S Mt 11:21 [d]ver 3 [e]S 1Ki 5:12 **1:10** [f]Isa 23:1-18; S 34:8; S Jer 47:4; Eze 26:2-4; Zec 9:1-4 **1:11** [g]Nu 20:14-21; S 2Ch 28:17; S Ps 83:6 [h]S Ps 63:10 [i]S Eze 25:12-14; Zec 1:15 **1:12** [j]S Ge 36:11, 15 [k]S Isa 34:5; 63:1-6; Jer 25:21; Eze 25:12-14; 35:1-15; Ob 1:1; Mal 1:2-5 **1:13** [l]S Ge 19:38; S Eze 21:28 [m]S Ge 34:29; S 2Ki 8:12; S Hos 13:16 **1:14** [n]S Dt 3:11 [o]Isa 30:30 [p]S Job 39:25 [q]Jer 23:19 **1:15** [r]S Jer 25:21 [s]1Ch 20:1; S Jer 49:1; Eze 21:28-32; 25:2-7

2:1 [t]S Isa 16:6 [u]Isa 33:12 **2:2** [v]Jer 48:24 [w]S Job 39:25 [x]S Jos 6:20 **2:3** [y]S Ps 2:10 [z]S Isa 40:23 [a]Isa 15:1-9; 16:1-14; S 25:10; Jer 48:1; S Eze 25:8-11; Zep 2:8-9 **2:4** [b]2Ki 17:19; Hos 12:2

2 This is what the LORD says:

"For three sins of Moab,[t]
even for four, I will not turn back
⌞my wrath⌟.
Because he burned, as if to lime,[u]
the bones of Edom's king,
2I will send fire upon Moab
that will consume the fortresses of
Kerioth.[c][v]
Moab will go down in great tumult
amid war cries[w] and the blast of the
trumpet.[x]
3I will destroy her ruler[y]
and kill all her officials with him,"[z]
says the LORD.[a]

4This is what the LORD says:

"For three sins of Judah,[b]
even for four, I will not turn back
⌞my wrath⌟.
Because they have rejected the law[c] of
the LORD
and have not kept his decrees,[d]
because they have been led astray[e] by
false gods,[d][f]
the gods[e] their ancestors followed,[g]
5I will send fire[h] upon Judah
that will consume the fortresses[i] of
Jerusalem.[j]"

Judgment on Israel

6This is what the LORD says:

"For three sins of Israel,
even for four, I will not turn back
⌞my wrath⌟.[k]

[a] *11* Or *sword / and destroyed his allies* [b] *15* Or / *Molech*; Hebrew *malcam* [c] *2* Or *of her cities* [d] *4* Or *by lies* [e] *4* Or *lies*

[c]S Jer 6:19 [d]S Eze 20:24 [e]Isa 9:16 [f]S Ex 34:15; S Dt 31:20; S Ps 4:2 [g]S 2Ki 22:13; S Jer 9:14; S 16:12 **2:5** [h]S 2Ki 25:9; S 2Ch 36:19 [i]Am 3:11 [j]S Jer 17:27; S Hos 8:14 **2:6** [k]S Am 1:3

1:9 *Tyre.* The dominant Phoenician merchant city, allied to Israel by a "treaty of brotherhood" in the days of David (1Ki 5:1), later in the time of Solomon (1Ki 5:12) and later still during the reign of Ahab, whose father-in-law ruled Tyre and Sidon (1Ki 16:30–31). *she sold.* Her crime was like Philistia's (v. 6).
1:10 *walls.* Tyre was an almost impregnable island, boastful of her security (cf. Eze 26:1—28:19).
1:11 *Edom.* The nation descended from Esau (Ge 36; see Ge 25:23–30; 27:39–40 and NIV text note on 25:25). *brother.* Israel (see Ob 8–10 and note on Ob 10). Reference may be to a treaty "brother" (see note on v. 9). Edom's crime was in violating this relationship by persistent hostility.
1:12 *Teman ... Bozrah.* Major cities of Edom, the former thought to be near Petra (see note on Ob 9), the latter now identified with Buseirah, 37 miles to the north. With their destruction, Edom would lose its capacity for continual warfare.
1:13 *Ammon.* Judgment centered on Rabbah (v. 14; see note on Dt 3:11), modern Amman. Greed for land bred a brutal genocide that would be punished by a tumult of men and nature, leaving the state without leaders to continue such practices (see 1Ki 8:12 and note).
1:14 Fulfilled through the Assyrians.
1:15 *Her king.* See NIV text note; see also Jer 49:3 and note on 49:1.
2:1 *Moab.* Located east of the Dead Sea (see note on Isa 15:1). *burned ... the bones of Edom's king.* Thus depriving the king's spirit of the rest that was widely believed to result from decent burial.
2:2 *Kerioth.* Perhaps a plural noun meaning "cities" (see NIV text note) or the name of a major town (see Jer 48:24) and shrine of Chemosh, the national god of Moab (see 1Ki 11:7,33).
2:4 *rejected the law of the LORD.* Judah's sins differed in kind from those of the other nations. Those nations violated the generally recognized laws of humanity, but Judah disobeyed the revealed law of God. These sins may be included in the indictment against Israel that follows.
2:5 *fire ... consume the fortresses.* See 1:4 and note. Judah's punishment is the same as Aram's (1:4), Philistia's (1:7), Phoenicia's (1:10), Edom's (1:12), Ammon's (1:14) and Moab's (2:2)—loss of the defenses and wealth in which they trusted.
2:6–16 The climactic prophecy in this series (see note on 1:3—2:16).
2:6 Israel's sins revealed the general moral deterioration of

They sell the righteous for silver,
and the needy for a pair of sandals.[l]
7 They trample on the heads of the poor
as upon the dust of the ground
and deny justice to the oppressed.
Father and son use the same girl
and so profane my holy name.[m]
8 They lie down beside every altar
on garments taken in pledge.[n]
In the house of their god
they drink wine[o] taken as fines.[p]

9 "I destroyed the Amorite[q] before them,
though he was tall[r] as the cedars
and strong as the oaks.[s]
I destroyed his fruit above
and his roots[t] below.
10 "I brought you up out of Egypt,[u]
and I led[v] you forty years in the
desert[w]
to give you the land of the
Amorites.[x]
11 I also raised up prophets[y] from among
your sons
and Nazirites[z] from among your
young men.
Is this not true, people of Israel?"
declares the LORD.
12 "But you made the Nazirites drink wine
and commanded the prophets not to
prophesy.[a]

13 "Now then, I will crush you
as a cart crushes when loaded with
grain.[b]
14 The swift will not escape,[c]
the strong[d] will not muster their
strength,
and the warrior will not save his
life.[e]
15 The archer[f] will not stand his ground,
the fleet-footed soldier will not get
away,
and the horseman[g] will not save his
life.[h]
16 Even the bravest warriors[i]
will flee naked on that day,"
declares the LORD.

Witnesses Summoned Against Israel

3 Hear this word the LORD has spoken against you,[j] O people of Israel—against the whole family I brought up out of Egypt:[k]

2 "You only have I chosen[l]
of all the families of the earth;
therefore I will punish[m] you
for all your sins.[n]"

3 Do two walk together
unless they have agreed to do so?

2:6 [l] S Joel 3:3; Am 8:6 **2:7** [m] S Lev 18:21; Am 5:11-12; 8:4 **2:8** [n] S Ex 22:26; Dt 24:12-13 [o] Hos 7:14; Am 4:1; 6:6 [p] Hab 2:6 **2:9** [q] Nu 21:23-26; Jos 10:12 [r] S Isa 10:33 [s] S Ps 29:9 [t] S 2Ki 19:30; S Job 18:16; S Eze 17:9 **2:10** [u] S Ex 6:6; 20:2; Am 3:1 [v] S Dt 8:2 [w] S Dt 2:7 [x] S Ex 3:8; S Nu 21:25; S Jos 13:4; Am 9:7 **2:11** [y] Dt 18:18; Jer 7:25 [z] S Jdg 13:5 **2:12** [a] Isa 30:10; Jer 11:21; Am 7:12-13; Mic 2:6 **2:13** [b] Am 7:16-17 **2:14** [c] S Job 11:20 [d] S 1Ki 20:11 [e] Ps 33:16; Isa 30:16-17 **2:15** [f] S Eze 39:3 [g] S Ex 15:21; Zec 10:5 [h] Ecc 9:11 **2:16** [i] Jer 48:41 **3:1** [j] Zep 2:5 [k] S Am 2:10 **3:2** [l] S Ex 19:6; Dt 7:6; Lk 12:47 [m] ver 14 [n] S Jer 14:10; Mic 2:3; 1Pe 4:17

the nation. *the righteous.* Probably those who were not in debt and whom there was no lawful reason to sell (cf. Lev 25:39–43). Alternatively, the "righteous" here may refer to the "poor" (v. 7; cf. 5:12; 8:6) in contrast to the sinfully wicked behavior of the wealthy and powerful (see 4:1–5; 6:1–7). *the needy.* God had commanded that they be helped (see Dt 15:7–11 and note on 15:11), but they were instead sold for failure to repay a (perhaps paltry) debt, for which a "pair of sandals" had been given in pledge (see 8:6).

2:7 *trample.* See 5:11; 8:4. *poor … oppressed.* To care for them and to protect them from injustice were clearly commanded by Israel's law (Ex 23:6–8); also, throughout the ancient Near East, kings were supposed to defend such people. *Father and son use the same girl.* Whether the girl in question was a household servant (in which case father and son used her as a family prostitute) is not clear. In any case, the law required that if there were sexual relations with a girl, marriage was obligatory (Ex 22:16; Dt 22:28–29). For a father and son to have sexual relations with the same girl or woman was strictly forbidden (Lev 18:7–8,15; 20:11–12). *profane my holy name.* Cf. Lev 18:21 and note; 19:12; 20:3; 21:6; 22:2,32; see Jer 34:16; Eze 20:9 and notes; 36:20–23; 39:7.

2:8 *beside every altar … In the house of their god.* Israelites who broke the laws protecting the powerless brazenly used their wrongly gotten gains even in places supposed to be holy. *garments taken in pledge.* The law prohibited keeping a man's cloak overnight as security for a debt (see Ex 22:26–27 and note; Dt 24:12–13), or taking a widow's cloak at all (Dt 24:17). *fines.* Claimed as restitution for damages suffered. Exorbitant claims or even false charges of damage seem to be suggested.

2:9 *I destroyed.* Israel not only had known God's law but had been specially favored by his powerful help. *Amorite.* Here used for all the inhabitants of Canaan (see notes on Ge 10:16; 15:16; Jdg 6:10). *tall … strong.* Neither the size of Canaan's people nor their military power (see Nu 13:27–33) was able to prevent God's victory over them (see Jos 10:5,12–13). *his fruit above and his roots below.* That is, totally.

2:10 *I brought you up.* See 3:1; see also Ex 20:2 and note. God's great blessings to Israel in the past added to her guilt, and now they are recalled as a part of the Lord's indictment against his people.

2:11 *I also raised up prophets … and Nazirites.* Prophets, as God's faithful spokesmen (see Dt 18:15–20 and note on 18:15), and Nazirites, as those uniquely dedicated to him (see Nu 6:1–21 and note on 6:2; Jdg 13:5 and note), are singled out as special gifts to his people. These persons who were outside the priesthood were used by God through word and example to call his people to faithfulness.

2:12 *But you.* Israel showed utter disdain for God's faithful servants and thus demonstrated her callous insensitivity to God's working among them (cf. 7:16).

2:13 A loaded cart crushes anything that falls beneath its wheels.

2:14–16 No one who might be expected to stand their ground or escape would be able to save themselves.

2:16 *that day.* The day God comes in judgment (see 5:18; Joel 1:15 and notes)—as he did through the Assyrian invasion that swept the northern kingdom away.

3:1—5:17 Prophecies that underscore the certainty of God's judgment on Israel.

3:1 *Hear this word.* See 4:1; 5:1. The Lord calls his people to account because of their sins.

3:2 *You only.* Israel's present strength and prosperity gave rise to complacency about her privileged status as the Lord's chosen people. She is shockingly reminded of the long-forgotten responsibilities her privileges entailed.

3:3–6 With these rhetorical questions (involving comparisons) Amos builds up to the statements of vv. 7–8, to explain why he is speaking such terrifying words. Each

4Does a lion roar[o] in the thicket
when he has no prey?[p]
Does he growl in his den
when he has caught nothing?
5Does a bird fall into a trap on the
ground
where no snare[q] has been set?
Does a trap spring up from the earth
when there is nothing to catch?
6When a trumpet[r] sounds in a city,
do not the people tremble?
When disaster[s] comes to a city,
has not the LORD caused it?[t]

7Surely the Sovereign LORD does nothing
without revealing his plan[u]
to his servants the prophets.[v]

8The lion[w] has roared[x]—
who will not fear?
The Sovereign LORD has spoken—
who can but prophesy?[y]

9Proclaim to the fortresses of Ashdod[z]
and to the fortresses of Egypt:
"Assemble yourselves on the
mountains of Samaria;[a]
see the great unrest within her
and the oppression among her
people."

10"They do not know how to do right,[b]"
declares the LORD,
"who hoard plunder[c] and loot in
their fortresses."[d]

11Therefore this is what the Sovereign
LORD says:

"An enemy will overrun the land;
he will pull down your strongholds
and plunder your fortresses.[e]"

3:4 [o]S Isa 42:13 [p]Ps 104:21; S Hos 5:14
3:5 [q]S Ps 119:110
3:6 [r]S Nu 10:2; S Job 39:24; S Jer 4:21 [s]S Isa 31:2 [t]Isa 14:24-27
3:7 [u]Ge 18:17; S 1Sa 3:7; S Da 9:22; Jn 15:15; Rev 10:7 [v]S Jer 23:22
3:8 [w]S Isa 31:4 [x]S Isa 42:13 [y]S Jer 20:9; Jnh 1:1-3; 3:1-3; Ac 4:20
3:9 [z]S Jos 13:3; S 2Ch 26:6 [a]Am 4:1; 6:1
3:10 [b]Am 5:7; 6:12 [c]Hab 2:8 [d]S Ps 36:3; Mic 6:10; Zep 1:9
3:11 [e]Am 2:5; 6:14
3:12 [f]S 1Sa 17:34 [g]S Est 1:6; Am 6:4
3:13 [h]Eze 2:7
3:14 [i]S ver 2; S Lev 26:18 [j]S Ge 12:8; Am 5:5-6 [k]S Ex 27:2
3:15 [l]Jer 36:22 [m]Jdg 3:20 [n]S 1Ki 22:39 [o]Am 5:11; 6:11 [p]S Isa 34:5 [q]Hos 10:5-8, 14-15
4:1 [r]S Ps 22:12 [s]S Am 3:9 [t]S Isa 58:6; S Eze 18:12 [u]S Dt 24:14 [v]Jer 44:19 [w]S Am 2:8; 5:11; 8:6

12This is what the LORD says:

"As a shepherd saves from the lion's[f]
mouth
only two leg bones or a piece of an
ear,
so will the Israelites be saved,
those who sit in Samaria
on the edge of their beds
and in Damascus on their
couches.[a][g]"

13"Hear this and testify[h] against the
house of Jacob," declares the Lord, the
LORD God Almighty.

14"On the day I punish[i] Israel for her
sins,
I will destroy the altars of Bethel;[j]
the horns[k] of the altar will be cut off
and fall to the ground.
15I will tear down the winter house[l]
along with the summer house;[m]
the houses adorned with ivory[n] will be
destroyed
and the mansions[o] will be
demolished,[p]"
declares the LORD.[q]

Israel Has Not Returned to God

4 Hear this word, you cows of Bashan[r]
on Mount Samaria,[s]
you women who oppress the poor[t]
and crush the needy[u]
and say to your husbands,[v] "Bring
us some drinks![w]"

[a] *12* The meaning of the Hebrew for this line is uncertain.

picture is of cause and effect, using figures drawn from daily life—and culminating in divine action (v. 6).

3:7 *his servants the prophets.* See Jer 7:25; Zec 1:6 and notes.

3:8 *lion has roared.* Echoes 1:2 (see note there). *who can but prophesy?* Amos must speak because God has spoken.

3:9 The rich and powerful of Philistia and Egypt are summoned to witness the Lord's indictment against those who store up ill-gotten riches in the fortresses of Samaria (see v. 15). *fortresses.* See note on 1:4. *great unrest.* The result of a violent, selfish power structure that was heedless of the justice called for in God's law.

3:10 *who hoard.* Cf. 2:6–8. The prosperity of Israel's wealthy depended on oppression and robbery. The following verses announce God's judgment on such greed (cf. Hab 2:6–11).

3:11 *enemy.* Assyria. *plunder your fortresses.* Those that Samaria's wealthy had greedily filled with plunder.

3:12 *As a shepherd saves … only two leg bones.* To prove to the owner that the sheep had been eaten by a wild animal, not stolen by the shepherd (see Ex 22:13). *be saved.* Only some mutilated pieces would be "saved." The nation as such would be more than wounded—it would be destroyed. *those who sit.* In idle luxury (see 6:4). *in Damascus on their couches.* See NIV text note. Since at this time Israel had extended its influence over Damascus, the rich merchants of Samaria may have maintained luxurious houses also in Damascus along with market privileges in that city (see 1Ki 20:34 and note).

3:13 *Hear … testify.* Addressed to those summoned in v. 9. The rich and powerful of Philistia and Egypt are called upon to hear the Lord's indictment of the rich and powerful in Samaria and to testify that his indictment is true and that his judgment is warranted. Even these pagans will agree with God's judgment.

3:14 *altars of Bethel.* Israel's sins were rooted in the false shrine built by Jeroboam I at Bethel (1Ki 12:26–33). *horns of the altar.* Even the last refuge for a condemned person (cf. 1Ki 1:50–53 and note on 1:50) will afford Israel no protection.

3:15 *winter house … summer house.* Cf. 6:11; further signs of opulence that would not benefit their owners on the day of God's judgment—nor would expensive imported decorations, carvings and inlays of ivory (cf. 6:4). Many examples of such carvings have been found in ruined palaces in Samaria and other cities (see 1Ki 22:39 and note).

4:1 *Hear this word.* See note on 3:1. *cows of Bashan.* Upper-class women, directly addressed, are compared with the best breed of cattle in ancient Canaan, which were raised (and pampered) in the pastures of northern Transjordan (see Ps 22:12; Eze 39:18 and notes). Whether the metaphor was intended as an insult or as ironic flattery is uncertain. *Mount Samaria.* See 6:1 and note.

[2]The Sovereign LORD has sworn by his
holiness:
"The time[x] will surely come
when you will be taken away[y] with
hooks,[z]
the last of you with fishhooks.
[3]You will each go straight out
through breaks in the wall,[a]
and you will be cast out toward
Harmon,[a]"
declares the LORD.

[4]"Go to Bethel[b] and sin;
go to Gilgal[c] and sin yet more.
Bring your sacrifices every morning,[d]
your tithes[e] every three years.[b][f]
[5]Burn leavened bread[g] as a thank
offering
and brag about your freewill
offerings[h]—
boast about them, you Israelites,
for this is what you love to do,"
declares the Sovereign LORD.

[6]"I gave you empty stomachs[c] in every
city
and lack of bread in every town,
yet you have not returned to me,"
declares the LORD.[i]

[7]"I also withheld[j] rain from you
when the harvest was still three
months away.
I sent rain on one town,
but withheld it from another.[k]
One field had rain;
another had none and dried up.
[8]People staggered from town to town
for water[l]
but did not get enough[m] to drink,
yet you have not returned[n] to me,"
declares the LORD.[o]

[9]"Many times I struck your gardens and
vineyards,
I struck them with blight and
mildew.[p]
Locusts[q] devoured your fig and olive
trees,[r]
yet you have not returned[s] to me,"
declares the LORD.

[10]"I sent plagues[t] among you
as I did to Egypt.[u]
I killed your young men[v] with the sword,
along with your captured horses.
I filled your nostrils with the stench[w] of
your camps,
yet you have not returned to me,"[x]
declares the LORD.[y]

[11]"I overthrew some of you
as I[d] overthrew Sodom and
Gomorrah.[z]
You were like a burning stick[a] snatched
from the fire,
yet you have not returned to me,"
declares the LORD.[b]

[12]"Therefore this is what I will do to you,
Israel,
and because I will do this to you,
prepare to meet your God, O Israel."

[13]He who forms the mountains,[c]
creates the wind,[d]
and reveals his thoughts[e] to man,

4:2 [x]Jer 31:31 [y]Am 6:8 [z]S 2Ki 19:28; S 2Ch 33:11; S Isa 19:8 **4:3** [a]S Eze 12:5 **4:4** [b]S Jos 7:2 [c]S Hos 4:15 [d]S Nu 28:3 [e]Dt 14:28 [f]S Eze 20:39; Am 5:21-22 **4:5** [g]S Lev 7:13 [h]S Lev 22:18-21 **4:6** [i]S Isa 3:1; S 9:13; S Jer 5:3; Hag 2:17 **4:7** [j]S Jer 3:3; Zec 14:17 [k]Ex 9:4,26; Dt 11:17; S 2Ch 7:13; S Isa 5:6 **4:8** [l]S Eze 4:16-17 [m]Hag 1:6 [n]S Jer 3:7 [o]S Job 36:31; S Jer 14:4 **4:9** [p]S Dt 28:22 [q]S Ex 10:13; S Joel 2:25 [r]Joel 1:7 [s]S Isa 9:13; S Jer 3:10 **4:10** [t]S Ex 9:3 [u]Ex 11:5 [v]S Isa 9:17 [w]S Isa 34:3 [x]S Dt 28:21 [y]S Isa 9:13 **4:11** [z]S Ge 19:24; S Jer 23:14 [a]S Isa 7:4; Jude 1:23 [b]S Job 36:13 **4:13** [c]Ps 65:6 [d]Ps 135:7 [e]S Da 2:28

[a] 3 Masoretic Text; with a different word division of the Hebrew (see Septuagint) *out, O mountain of oppression* [b] 4 Or *tithes on the third day* [c] 6 Hebrew *you cleanness of teeth* [d] 11 Hebrew *God*

4:2 *The Sovereign LORD has sworn.* Stresses the solemnity of the situation and the certainty of the events. *by his holiness.* Contrasts with Israel's sin, reminding them of what they could have been (see Ex 19:6 and note) if they had faithfully kept their side of the covenant—as God had his. *hooks.* According to Assyrian reliefs (pictures engraved on stone), prisoners of war were led away with a rope fastened to a hook that pierced the nose or lower lip (see 2Ki 19:28 and note; 2Ch 33:11; Eze 19:4,9; Hab 1:15). The Hebrew word here may, in fact, refer to ropes.
4:3 *breaks in the wall.* Cf. 2Ki 17:5; Eze 13:5. *Harmon.* Appears to be a place-name, though it is not otherwise known (see NIV text note).
4:4–5 Spoken in irony.
4:4 *Bethel ... Gilgal.* These towns had historical importance as places where God's help was commemorated (Ge 35:1–15; Jos 4:20–24), and both were popular places of worship in Amos's day (5:5; see Hos 4:15; 12:4 and notes). *sacrifices every morning.* See Ex 29:38–41. *tithes.* Apparently the special tithe that was to be brought "every three years" (Dt 14:28; see 26:12). *years.* See NIV text note. The Hebrew word for "days" sometimes stands for years.
4:5 *leavened bread.* The burning of leavened bread in the sacrifices was strictly forbidden (see Lev 2:11; 6:17). Either Amos rebukes the Israelites for willful transgression of the law, or he speaks of burning in a general way for offering inappropriate gifts to the Lord. Leavened bread could accompany a fellowship offering (see Lev 7:13). *what you love to do.* They loved the forms and rituals of religion but did not love what God loves—goodness, mercy, kindness, justice (see 5:15; Isa 5:7; 61:8; Hos 6:6 and note; Mic 6:8).
4:6–11 In the past, God had used natural disasters to discipline and warn his people, but those lessons were soon forgotten (cf. the covenant curses in Dt 28:22–24,39–40,42,48,56–57).
4:6 *I.* These were not simply natural disasters; they were direct acts of God (3:6). *yet you have not returned to me.* A recurring accusation that runs like a refrain through vv. 8–11.
4:7–8 Lack of rain three months before harvest would prevent full development of the grain.
4:9 *blight and mildew.* See Hag 2:17 and note. *Locusts.* See Ex 10:14 and note.
4:10 *plagues ... as ... Egypt.* See Ex 7:14—12:30.
4:11 *Sodom and Gomorrah.* Exemplified total destruction, God's judgment on those cities (see Ge 19:24–25) eventually becoming proverbial (see Dt 29:23; Isa 1:9; 13:19; see also Jer 49:18; Zep 2:9 and notes). *burning stick snatched from the fire.* Saved only by God's grace (see Zec 3:2 and note).
4:12 *prepare to meet your God.* Devastated Israel, brought to her knees by the Assyrians, would meet the God she had covenanted with at Sinai and had now so grievously offended.
4:13 See note on 5:8–9. The God of such power and majesty is easily able to execute the judgment announced in v. 12.

he who turns dawn to darkness,
and treads the high places of the earth[f]—
the LORD God Almighty is his name.[g]

A Lament and Call to Repentance

5 Hear this word, O house of Israel, this lament[h] I take up concerning you:

2 "Fallen is Virgin[i] Israel,
never to rise again,
deserted in her own land,
with no one to lift her up.[j]"

3 This is what the Sovereign LORD says:

"The city that marches out a thousand strong for Israel
will have only a hundred left;
the town that marches out a hundred strong
will have only ten left.[k]"

4 This is what the LORD says to the house of Israel:

"Seek[l] me and live;[m]
5 do not seek Bethel,
do not go to Gilgal,[n]
do not journey to Beersheba.[o]
For Gilgal will surely go into exile,
and Bethel will be reduced to nothing.[a][p]"
6 Seek[q] the LORD and live,[r]
or he will sweep through the house of Joseph like a fire;[s]
it will devour,
and Bethel[t] will have no one to quench it.[u]

7 You who turn justice into bitterness[v]
and cast righteousness[w] to the ground[x]
8 (he who made the Pleiades and Orion,[y]
who turns blackness into dawn[z]
and darkens day into night,[a]
who calls for the waters of the sea
and pours them out over the face of the land—
the LORD is his name[b]—
9 he flashes destruction on the stronghold
and brings the fortified city to ruin),[c]
10 you hate the one who reproves in court[d]
and despise him who tells the truth.[e]

11 You trample on the poor[f]
and force him to give you grain.
Therefore, though you have built stone mansions,[g]
you will not live in them;[h]

4:13 [f] Mic 1:3 [g] S Isa 47:4; Am 5:8,27; 9:6 **5:1** [h] S Jer 4:8; S Eze 19:1 **5:2** [i] S 2Ki 19:21; Jer 14:17 [j] Jer 50:32; Am 8:14 **5:3** [k] Isa 6:13; Am 6:9 **5:4** [l] S Dt 4:29 [m] Dt 32:46-47; Isa 55:3; Jer 29:13; S Eze 18:9 **5:5** [n] 1Sa 11:14; S Hos 4:15 [o] Ge 21:31; Am 8:14 [p] S 1Sa 7:16; S 8:2 **5:6** [q] Ps 22:26; 105:4; S Isa 31:1; 55:6; Zep 2:3 [r] ver 14; S Lev 18:5 [s] Dt 4:24 [t] S Am 3:14 [u] S Jer 4:4 **5:7** [v] Isa 5:20; Am 6:12 [w] S Am 3:10 [x] S Hos 10:4 **5:8** [y] S Ge 1:16; S Job 38:31 [z] S Job 38:12; Isa 42:16 [a] S Ps 104:20; Am 8:9 [b] Ps 104:6-9; Jer 16:21; S Am 4:13 **5:9** [c] Mic 5:11 **5:10** [d] S Isa 29:21 [e] 1Ki 22:8; Gal 4:16 **5:11** [f] Am 8:6 [g] S Am 3:15 [h] S Dt 28:30; Mic 1:6

[a] 5 Or *grief*; or *wickedness*; Hebrew *aven*, a reference to Beth Aven (a derogatory name for Bethel)

5:1–17 The climactic prophecy in this series of three (see 3:1; 4:1). Its structure is distinctive: *a* lament over Israel (vv. 1–3); *b* a call to repentance (vv. 4–6); *c* the reasons for God's judgment on Israel (vv. 7–13, and see note on v. 10); *b'* a call to repentance (vv. 14–15); *a'* lament over Israel (vv. 16–17). Here in the middle of the book, calls to repentance in the midst of laments over Israel's destruction and the reasons for God's judgments indicate that Amos's primary purpose for announcing God's coming judgments is to bring about a true repentance among God's people.

5:1 *Hear this word.* See note on 3:1. *this lament.* Amos sorrowfully fashioned a lament as if Israel were already dead.

5:2 *Virgin Israel.* A personification of Israel (see note on 2Ki 19:21). *deserted.* Left like a dead body on the open field (see Jer 8:2; 9:22).

5:3 *city ... town.* The Hebrew expression denotes communities of varying size, all of which would suffer.

5:4 *Seek me and live.* This gracious invitation is expanded in v. 6, and yet again in v. 14, to heighten the rhetorical effect. If the people of Israel would seek the Lord, they (or at least a "remnant," v. 15) could yet escape the violent death anticipated in Amos's lament (see Zep 2:3 and note).

5:5 *Bethel ... Gilgal.* See note on 4:4. *Beersheba.* Located in the south of Judah, it also had evidently become a place of pilgrimage and idolatry (see 8:14). All shrines where the worship of God was abused would be destroyed.

5:6 The places of idolatry were doomed; yet if Israel turned to God, there was hope for her as a nation. Otherwise the people, too, would be destroyed. *Seek ... live.* See v. 4 and note. *house of Joseph.* The northern kingdom of Israel, dominated by the tribe of Ephraim, descendants of Joseph (see v. 15; 6:6; Hos 4:7 and note). *Bethel.* The main religious center of the northern kingdom (see 3:14; 4:4; 7:13; Hos 12:4 and notes). The god the Israelites worshiped there would be powerless to save the place when the true God brought his judgment.

5:7 *You who turn justice into bitterness.* They corrupted the procedures and institutions of justice (the courts), making them instruments of injustice ("bitterness"). Turning God's order upside down is inevitable in a society that ignores his law and despises true religion (see 6:12 and note).

5:8–9 As in 4:13, a brief hymn is inserted (see 9:5–6 and notes). Here Amos highlights the contrast between "you who turn" good into bad (v. 7) and the One "who turns" night into day and governs the order of the universe—and whose power can smash the walls his people hide behind.

5:8 *Pleiades.* A group of seven stars (part of the constellation Taurus); always mentioned in connection with Orion (see note on Job 9:9). *blackness into dawn ... day into night.* The orderly sequence of day and night (see Ge 8:22; Jer 31:35). *waters of the sea.* The waters above the expanse (see 9:6; Ge 1:7; see also notes on Ps 36:8; 42:7; 104:3); alternatively, waters evaporated from the sea and condensed as rain. *the LORD is his name.* The middle of three occurrences of this refrain (see 4:13, where the refrain is expanded; 9:6).

5:10 Continues the sentence begun in v. 7. This poetic paragraph is continued and completed in vv. 12b–13, which (in the Hebrew) use the third person, while the preceding passage (vv. 11–12a) uses the second person. The indictment of vv. 7,10,12b–13 is therefore more objective and descriptive, while that of vv. 11–12a is more direct and pointed. *reproves ... tells the truth.* Those who are concerned that the courts uphold justice.

5:11 *trample on the poor.* Echoes the initial indictment against Israel (2:7). *though you have built.* God would take away their prized possessions acquired through wrongful gain. Their prosperity would be turned to grief (see the covenant curses in Dt 28:30,38–40).

though you have planted lush
vineyards,
you will not drink their wine.[i]
12 For I know how many are your
offenses
and how great your sins.[j]
You oppress the righteous and take
bribes[k]
and you deprive the poor[l] of justice
in the courts.[m]
13 Therefore the prudent man keeps
quiet[n] in such times,
for the times are evil.[o]
14 Seek good, not evil,
that you may live.[p]
Then the LORD God Almighty will be
with you,
just as you say he is.
15 Hate evil,[q] love good;[r]
maintain justice in the courts.[s]
Perhaps[t] the LORD God Almighty will
have mercy[u]
on the remnant[v] of Joseph.

16 Therefore this is what the Lord, the
LORD God Almighty, says:

"There will be wailing[w] in all the
streets[x]
and cries of anguish in every public
square.
The farmers[y] will be summoned to
weep
and the mourners to wail.
17 There will be wailing[z] in all the
vineyards,
for I will pass through[a] your midst,"
says the LORD.[b]

5:11 [i]S Jdg 9:27; S Am 4:1; 9:14; Mic 6:15; Zep 1:13 **5:12** [j]Hos 5:3 [k]S Job 36:18; S Isa 1:23; S Eze 22:12 [l]S Jer 5:28 [m]S Job 5:4; S Isa 5:23; S Am 2:6-7 **5:13** [n]S Est 4:14 [o]Mic 2:3 **5:14** [p]S ver 6 **5:15** [q]S Ps 52:3; S 97:10; Ro 12:9 [r]S Ge 18:25 [s]S Isa 1:17; S 29:21; Zec 8:16 [t]S Jer 36:3 [u]S Joel 2:14 [v]Mic 5:7,8; 7:18 **5:16** [w]Jer 9:17; Am 8:3; Zep 1:10 [x]Jer 7:34 [y]S Joel 1:11 **5:17** [z]S Ex 11:6 [a]Ex 12:12 [b]Isa 16:10; S Jer 48:33

5:18 [c]S Isa 2:12; S Joel 1:15 [d]S Jer 30:5 [e]S 1Sa 2:9; S Joel 2:2 [f]S Job 20:28; Isa 5:19,30; Jer 30:7 **5:19** [g]S La 3:10 [h]S Dt 32:24; Job 20:24; S Ecc 10:8; Isa 24:17-18; Jer 15:2-3; 48:44 **5:20** [i]S 1Sa 2:9 [j]S Isa 13:10; S Eze 7:7; Ob 1:15; Zep 1:15 **5:21** [k]Jer 44:4

The Day of the LORD

18 Woe to you who long
for the day of the LORD![c]
Why do you long for the day of the
LORD?[d]
That day will be darkness,[e] not
light.[f]
19 It will be as though a man fled from a
lion
only to meet a bear,[g]
as though he entered his house
and rested his hand on the wall
only to have a snake bite him.[h]
20 Will not the day of the LORD be
darkness,[i] not light—
pitch-dark, without a ray of
brightness?[j]

21 "I hate,[k] I despise your religious
feasts;[l]
I cannot stand your assemblies.[m]
22 Even though you bring me burnt
offerings[n] and grain offerings,
I will not accept them.[o p]
Though you bring choice fellowship
offerings,[a]
I will have no regard for them.[q r]
23 Away with the noise of your songs!
I will not listen to the music of your
harps.[s]
24 But let justice[t] roll on like a river,
righteousness[u] like a never-failing
stream![v]

[a] 22 Traditionally *peace offerings*

[l]S Lev 26:31; S Hos 2:11 [m]S Eze 23:18 **5:22** [n]Lev 26:31 [o]S Jer 7:21 [p]S Ps 40:6 [q]Jer 14:12; S Am 4:4; Mic 6:6-7 [r]Isa 1:11-16; S 66:3 **5:23** [s]Am 6:5 **5:24** [t]S Jer 22:3 [u]S Isa 45:8 [v]Mic 6:8

5:13 *prudent man.* He knows he cannot change the state of affairs, and therefore only awaits judgment.
5:14 *Seek good.* Cf. "Seek me" (v. 4; see note there; see also Isa 1:16–17 and note on 1:17). *that you may live.* The purpose is more definitely expressed than in vv. 4,6, and the way to change is explicit. *with you.* As your security and source of blessing.
5:15 *Perhaps.* Emphasizes the danger of presuming on God's grace. Even a widespread change of attitude would need the test of time to prove its genuineness. *remnant.* Implies that a change now would benefit the individual survivors of the disaster, though the nation as a whole would perish. *Joseph.* See note on v. 6.
5:16–17 A return to the theme of lament with which this section began (vv. 1–2). *streets ... square ... farmers ... vineyards.* All will be affected by God's punishment. Even farmers, usually too busy for such things, would join the professional mourners in lament, and mourning would overflow from the cities to the vineyards (see Joel 1:5 and note). When the holy God "will pass through" (as he did in Egypt, Ex 12:12), punishment for the unholy and unjust will be inescapable (cf. Isa 6:5).
5:18—6:14 Another series of three prophecies of judgment (5:18–27; 6:1–7; 6:8–14), the last being climactic—as in the two previous series.
5:18 *day of the LORD.* The time when God will show himself the victor over the world, vindicating his claims to be the Lord over all the earth (see notes on 8:9; Isa 2:11,17,20; Joel 1:15). Israel expected to be exalted as his people and longed for that day to come. Amos warned that the day would come, but not as Israel expected—it would be a day of "darkness, not light" (v. 20; see 8:9 and note) for her, because she had not been faithful to God. (Cf. "the day of our Lord Jesus Christ" and variations in 1Co 1:8; 3:12–15; 5:5; 2Co 1:14; Php 1:6,10; 2:16.) Amos speaks primarily of an imminent and decisive judgment on Israel—which would foreshadow God's final judgment.
5:19–20 The two pictures (v. 19) emphasize vividly the inescapability of God's coming judgment.
5:21–27 Again God directly addresses Israel with the charge of unfaithfulness.
5:21–23 These three verses summarize and reject the current practice of religion in Israel. The institutions were not wrong in themselves; it was the worshipers and the ways they corrupted (paganized) their worship that were wrong. The people had no basis on which to come to God, because their conduct reflected disobedience to his law (see Isa 1:11–15 and note).
5:21 *I cannot stand your assemblies.* Or "I cannot stand the odor of your assemblies" (lit. "I cannot smell your assemblies with delight").
5:24 *justice ... righteousness.* Prerequisites for acceptance by God (see Mic 6:8 and note); but these are what Israel had rejected and scorned (cf. vv. 7,10,12b). *river ... never-failing stream.* In contrast to streambeds that are dry much of the year (see Jer 15:18 and note). The simile is

25 “Did you bring me sacrifices[w] and
offerings
forty years[x] in the desert, O house of
Israel?
26 You have lifted up the shrine of your
king,
the pedestal of your idols,[y]
the star of your god[a] —
which you made for yourselves.
27 Therefore I will send you into exile[z]
beyond Damascus,”
says the LORD, whose name is God
Almighty.[a]

Woe to the Complacent

6 Woe to you[b] who are complacent[c] in
Zion,
and to you who feel secure[d] on
Mount Samaria,[e]
you notable men of the foremost
nation,
to whom the people of Israel come![f]
2 Go to Calneh[g] and look at it;
go from there to great Hamath,[h]
and then go down to Gath[i] in
Philistia.
Are they better off than[j] your two
kingdoms?
Is their land larger than yours?
3 You put off the evil day
and bring near a reign of terror.[k]
4 You lie on beds inlaid with ivory
and lounge on your couches.[l]
You dine on choice lambs
and fattened calves.[m]
5 You strum away on your harps[n] like
David
and improvise on musical
instruments.[o]

5:25 [w]S Isa 43:23 [x]S Ex 16:35 **5:26** [y]S Eze 18:6; S 20:16 **5:27** [z]Am 6:7; 7:11,17; Mic 1:16 [a]Dt 32:17-19; Jer 38:17; S Am 4:13; Ac 7:42-43* **6:1** [b]Lk 6:24 [c]Zep 1:12 [d]S Job 24:23 [e]S Am 3:9 [f]Isa 32:9-11 **6:2** [g]S Ge 10:10 [h]S 2Ki 17:24; S Jer 49:23 [i]S Jos 11:22; 2Ch 26:6 [j]Na 3:8 **6:3** [k]S Isa 56:12; S Eze 12:22; Am 9:10 **6:4** [l]S Est 1:6; S Pr 7:17 [m]S Isa 1:11; S Eze 34:2-3; S Am 3:12 **6:5** [n]S Ps 137:2; S Isa 14:11; Am 5:23 [o]S 1Ch 15:16 **6:6** [p]S Isa 28:1; S Am 2:8 [q]S Eze 9:4 [r]S Eze 16:49 **6:7** [s]S Am 5:27 [t]S Jer 16:9; S La 4:5 **6:8** [u]S Ge 22:16; Heb 6:13 [v]S Lev 26:30 [w]S Ps 47:4 [x]S Jer 12:8 [y]Am 4:2 [z]S Lev 26:19; Dt 32:19 **6:9** [a]S Am 5:3 **6:10** [b]S 1Sa 31:12 [c]Am 8:3 **6:11** [d]S Isa 34:5 [e]S Am 3:15

6 You drink wine[p] by the bowlful
and use the finest lotions,
but you do not grieve[q] over the ruin
of Joseph.[r]
7 Therefore you will be among the first
to go into exile;[s]
your feasting and lounging will end.[t]

The LORD Abhors the Pride of Israel

8 The Sovereign LORD has sworn by himself[u] — the LORD God Almighty declares:

“I abhor[v] the pride of Jacob[w]
and detest his fortresses;[x]
I will deliver up[y] the city
and everything in it.[z]”

9 If ten[a] men are left in one house, they
too will die. 10 And if a relative who is to
burn the bodies[b] comes to carry them out
of the house and asks anyone still hiding
there, “Is anyone with you?” and he says,
“No,” then he will say, “Hush![c] We must
not mention the name of the LORD.”

11 For the LORD has given the command,
and he will smash[d] the great house[e]
into pieces
and the small house into bits.[f]
12 Do horses run on the rocky crags?
Does one plow there with oxen?
But you have turned justice into
poison[g]
and the fruit of righteousness[h] into
bitterness[i] —

[a] 26 Or *lifted up Sakkuth your king / and Kaiwan your idols, / your star-gods*; Septuagint *lifted up the shrine of Molech / and the star of your god Rephan, / their idols*

[f]Isa 55:11 **6:12** [g]Hos 10:4 [h]S Am 3:10 [i]S Isa 1:21; S Am 5:7

especially apt: As plant and animal life flourishes where there is water, so human life flourishes where there is justice and righteousness.

5:25 Israel's right relationship with the Lord was never established primarily by sacrifices. It was above all based on obedience (see 1Sa 15:22 and note; cf. Ro 1:5). *forty years in the desert.* See Nu 14:32–35 and note on 14:34.

5:26 The obscure language of this verse speaks of Israelite idolatry, but whether it was in the desert long ago or more recently in the promised land, or both, is not clear. The NIV text note takes two nouns as proper names derived from Akkadian. The Septuagint (the pre-Christian Greek translation of the OT) represents a somewhat different text, which is followed by Ac 7:43.

5:27 This punishment is the final one — exile from the God-given land to remote foreign places.

6:1 *in Zion ... on Mount Samaria.* Although Amos spoke primarily to Israel, Judah and Jerusalem (Zion) also deserved his rebuke (cf. 2:4–5), for Israel properly comprised all 12 tribes. *Mount Samaria.* See 4:1; Israel's capital city, founded by King Omri. It was located on an easily defended lofty hill (see 1Ki 16:24 and note). *foremost nation.* In Israel's self-complacent eyes in this time of her newly recovered power and prosperity (see Introduction: Date and Historical Situation).

6:2 Perhaps Calneh and Hamath had fallen in Jeroboam II's campaign (see 2Ki 14:25,28 and notes), and the wall of Gath had been broken down by Uzziah (2Ch 26:6). These words may have been spoken by the "people of Israel" (v. 1) who, when they came before their notables, flattered their vanity and thus reinforced their arrogant complacency.

6:3 *evil day.* See note on 5:18.

6:4 *lie ... lounge on your couches.* See 3:12 and note. *ivory.* See 3:15 and note.

6:5 *like David.* See 1Sa 16:15–23; 2Sa 23:1.

6:6 *by the bowlful.* To extravagant and intemperate excess. *Joseph.* See note on 5:6.

6:8 *sworn by himself.* See notes on Ge 22:16; Heb 6:13. By this oath God declares that the verdict is final. *the pride of Jacob.* The strongholds in which the people took pride ("his fortresses"; cf. Eze 32:12 and note). *fortresses.* See note on 1:4.

6:10–11 A fearful scene: Apparently a survivor is cowering inside the house, the relative forbidding him even to pray because God's wrath had fallen on the city.

6:10 *burn the bodies.* Reference may be to kindling a memorial fire in honor of the dead (see Jer 34:5 and note). Cremation was not generally practiced, being reserved primarily for serious offenders (see Ge 38:24; Lev 20:14; 21:9; Jos 7:15,25; 1Sa 31:12 and note).

6:11 *great house ... small house.* Cf. perhaps the "summer house" and "winter house" of 3:15.

6:12 *plow there with oxen.* The Hebrew for this phrase is sometimes translated (with a slight textual change) "plow

13 you who rejoice in the conquest of Lo
Debar[a]
and say, "Did we not take Karnaim[b]
by our own strength?[j]"
14 For the LORD God Almighty declares,
"I will stir up a nation[k] against you,
O house of Israel,
that will oppress you all the way
from Lebo[c] Hamath[l] to the valley of
the Arabah.[m]"

Locusts, Fire and a Plumb Line

7 This is what the Sovereign LORD showed
me:[n] He was preparing swarms of locusts[o] after the king's share had been harvested and just as the second crop was
coming up. 2 When they had stripped the
land clean,[p] I cried out, "Sovereign LORD,
forgive! How can Jacob survive?[q] He is so
small![r]"
3 So the LORD relented.[s]
"This will not happen," the LORD said.[t]
4 This is what the Sovereign LORD
showed me: The Sovereign LORD was calling for judgment by fire;[u] it dried up the
great deep and devoured[v] the land. 5 Then
I cried out, "Sovereign LORD, I beg you,
stop! How can Jacob survive? He is so
small![w]"
6 So the LORD relented.[x]
"This will not happen either," the Sovereign LORD said.[y]

6:13 [j] S Job 8:15; Isa 28:14-15 **6:14** [k] Jer 5:15 [l] S Nu 13:21 [m] S Am 3:11 **7:1** [n] ver 7; Am 8:1 [o] Ps 78:46; S Jer 51:14; S Joel 1:4 **7:2** [p] S Ex 10:15 [q] S Isa 37:4 [r] S Eze 11:13; S Am 4:9 **7:3** [s] S Ex 32:14; Dt 32:36; S Jer 18:8; 26:19 [t] S Hos 11:8 **7:4** [u] S Isa 66:16; S Joel 1:19 [v] Dt 32:22 **7:5** [w] S ver 1-2; Joel 2:17 **7:6** [x] S Ex 32:14; S Jer 18:8; Jnh 3:10 [y] Jer 42:10; S Eze 9:8
7:8 [z] Jer 1:11,13 [a] Am 8:2 [b] S 2Ki 21:13 [c] S Jer 15:6; Eze 7:2-9 **7:9** [d] S Lev 26:30 [e] S Lev 26:31 [f] S 1Ki 13:34; 2Ki 15:9; Isa 63:18; S Hos 10:8 **7:10** [g] S Jos 7:2 [h] S 2Ki 14:23 [i] Jer 38:4 [j] 2Ki 14:24; Jer 26:8-11

7 This is what he showed me: The Lord
was standing by a wall that had been built
true to plumb, with a plumb line in his
hand. 8 And the LORD asked me, "What do
you see,[z] Amos?[a]"
"A plumb line,[b]" I replied.
Then the Lord said, "Look, I am setting
a plumb line among my people Israel; I
will spare them no longer.[c]
9 "The high places[d] of Isaac will be
destroyed
and the sanctuaries[e] of Israel will be
ruined;
with my sword I will rise against the
house of Jeroboam.[f]"

Amos and Amaziah

10 Then Amaziah the priest of Bethel[g]
sent a message to Jeroboam[h] king of Israel: "Amos is raising a conspiracy[i] against
you in the very heart of Israel. The land
cannot bear all his words.[j] 11 For this is
what Amos is saying:

" 'Jeroboam will die by the sword,
and Israel will surely go into exile,[k]
away from their native land.' "[l]

[a] *13 Lo Debar* means *nothing.* [b] *13 Karnaim* means *horns*; *horn* here symbolizes strength. [c] *14* Or *from the entrance to*

7:11 [k] S Am 5:27 [l] Jer 36:16

the sea with oxen." Israel's perversion of justice flies in the face of even common human wisdom about the right order of things. See 5:7 and note.

6:13 *Lo Debar ... Karnaim.* See NIV text notes for Amos's ironic play on the meanings of these place names. The towns may have been regained from Hazael by Jehoash (2Ki 10:32–33; 13:25) or by Jeroboam II (see 2Ki 14:25 and note), then taken by the Assyrians soon after Amos's day (2Ki 15:29)—beginning the sequence of events that would lead to the loss of all territory conquered by Jeroboam II.

6:14 *nation.* Assyria. *from Lebo Hamath to the valley of the Arabah.* From the Orontes River in north Lebanon to the Dead Sea—thus the whole land (see 2Ki 14:25).

7:1—9:10 The final series of prophetic messages, made up of three panels (7:1–17; 8:1–14; 9:1–10), each of which begins with a vision (or visions), followed by further elaboration, and again, the third is climactic.

7:1 *showed me.* Introduces reports of visions that convey God's message through things seen as well as heard (see vv. 4,7; 8:1; Jer 1:11 and note; cf. Am 9:1). *locusts.* See 4:9; Ex 10:4 and note. *king's share.* Apparently the earlier crop, from which the royal taxes were taken. *second crop.* The growth that came up in the fields after the grains and early hay were harvested. On these the flocks and herds pastured until the summer dry season stopped all growth.

7:2 See v. 5. *How ... survive?* Mass starvation would afflict all the people. *Jacob.* Israel. *so small.* Powerless to withstand the calamity. Amos makes no appeal to the Lord's covenant with Israel—perhaps because Israel's unfaithfulness had removed all right to such an appeal.

7:3 See v. 6. *the LORD relented.* In response to the prophetic intercession (see Ge 20:7)—but forgiveness is not offered.

7:4 *great deep.* Probably the Mediterranean Sea. *land.* Lit. "portion," probably referring to the promised land or, more precisely, to everything growing on the land (cf. Joel 1:19).

7:5 See note on v. 2.

7:6 See note on v. 3.

7:7 Israel is compared to a wall built "true to plumb"—what she should have been, after all the Lord had done for her.

7:8–9 In vv. 1–6 God proposed wholesale punishments amounting to total destruction, but relented at Amos's prayer—though without promise of forgiveness. Now the Lord is no longer open to such intercession (see Jer 7:16; 15:1 and notes).

7:8 *What do you see ...?* See note on Jer 1:11. *plumb line.* God's people had been "built" (v. 7) according to God's standards. They were expected to be true to those standards, but were completely out of plumb when tested (see 2Ki 21:13 and note). *my people.* Here, for the first time in the book of Amos, the Lord calls Israel "my people" (see v. 15; 8:2; 9:10,14; see also note on Ex 17:4). *spare them no longer.* See 8:2; cf. 9:1–4.

7:9 *high places ... sanctuaries ... house.* The centers of religious and political pretension and of self-righteous pride would be wiped out. *Isaac.* Israel's (Jacob's) father, a way of referring to Israel found only in Amos (see v. 16). *Jeroboam.* The prophecies of chs. 1–6 were spoken to the leading people of Israel and Samaria as a whole; here Amos names one man, King Jeroboam II.

7:11 Amaziah's words summarize Amos's message (see note on v. 17). *Jeroboam.* That is, his "house" (v. 9), the king's name also representing his dynasty. *will die.* Jeroboam died naturally (2Ki 14:29), but his son and successor Zechariah (2Ki 15:8) was assassinated (2Ki 15:10).

12 Then Amaziah said to Amos, "Get out,
you seer![m] Go back to the land of Judah.
Earn your bread there and do your prophesying there.[n] 13 Don't prophesy anymore at
Bethel,[o] because this is the king's sanctuary and the temple[p] of the kingdom.[q]"
14 Amos answered Amaziah, "I was neither a prophet[r] nor a prophet's son, but
I was a shepherd, and I also took care of
sycamore-fig trees.[s] 15 But the LORD took
me from tending the flock[t] and said to
me, 'Go,[u] prophesy[v] to my people Israel.'[w]
16 Now then, hear[x] the word of the LORD.
You say,

"'Do not prophesy against[y] Israel,
and stop preaching against the
house of Isaac.'

17 "Therefore this is what the LORD says:

"'Your wife will become a prostitute[z]
in the city,
and your sons and daughters will fall
by the sword.
Your land will be measured and
divided up,
and you yourself will die in a pagan[a]
country.
And Israel will certainly go into exile,[a]
away from their native land.[b]'"

A Basket of Ripe Fruit

8 This is what the Sovereign LORD showed
me:[c] a basket of ripe fruit. 2 "What do
you see,[d] Amos?[e]" he asked.
"A basket[f] of ripe fruit," I answered.
Then the LORD said to me, "The time is
ripe for my people Israel; I will spare them
no longer.[g]
3 "In that day," declares the Sovereign
LORD, "the songs in the temple will turn
to wailing.[b][h] Many, many bodies—flung
everywhere! Silence![i]"

4 Hear this, you who trample the needy
and do away with the poor[j] of the
land,[k]
5 saying,

"When will the New Moon[l] be over
that we may sell grain,
and the Sabbath be ended
that we may market[m] wheat?"[n]—
skimping the measure,
boosting the price
and cheating[o] with dishonest
scales,[p]
6 buying the poor[q] with silver
and the needy for a pair of sandals,
selling even the sweepings with the
wheat.[r]

7 The LORD has sworn by the Pride of Jacob:[s] "I will never forget[t] anything they
have done.[u]

8 "Will not the land tremble[v] for this,
and all who live in it mourn?
The whole land will rise like the Nile;
it will be stirred up and then sink
like the river of Egypt.[w]

[a] 17 Hebrew *an unclean* [b] 3 Or *"the temple singers will wail*

7:12 [m] S 1Sa 9:9 [n] Mt 8:34 **7:13** [o] S Jos 7:2; S 1Ki 12:29 [p] Jer 36:5 [q] S Jer 20:2; S Am 2:12; Ac 4:18 **7:14** [r] S 1Sa 10:5; 2Ki 2:5; 4:38; Zec 13:5 [s] S 1Ki 10:27; S Isa 9:10 **7:15** [t] S Ge 37:2; S 2Sa 7:8 [u] S Isa 6:9 [v] S Jer 26:12 [w] Jer 7:1-2; S Eze 2:3-4 **7:16** [x] Jer 22:2 [y] S Eze 20:46; Mic 2:6 **7:17** [z] S Hos 4:13 [a] S Am 5:27 [b] S 2Ki 17:6; S Eze 4:13; S Hos 9:3; Am 2:12-13 **8:1** [c] S Am 7:1 **8:2** [d] Jer 1:13; 24:3 [e] Am 7:8 [f] S Ge 40:16 [g] S La 4:18; Eze 7:2-9 **8:3** [h] S Am 5:16 [i] Am 6:10 **8:4** [j] S Pr 30:14 [k] S Job 20:19; S Ps 14:4; S Am 2:7 **8:5** [l] S Nu 10:10 [m] Isa 58:13 [n] S Ne 10:31 [o] S Ge 31:7 [p] Dt 25:15; 2Ki 4:23; Ne 13:15-16; Eze 45:10-12; S Hos 12:7; Mic 6:10-11; Zec 5:6 **8:6** [q] Am 5:11 [r] S Am 2:6; S 4:1 **8:7** [s] S Ps 47:4 [t] S Hos 8:13 [u] S Job 35:15 **8:8** [v] S Job 9:6; Jer 51:29 [w] Ps 18:7; S Jer 46:8; Am 9:5

7:12 *seer.* Amaziah dismissed Amos as a prophet for hire whom he need not take seriously. *Go back to ... Judah ... and do your prophesying there.* Return to your homeland (see Introduction: Author). You have no business or standing among us.

7:13 *king's sanctuary.* Amaziah served the king in Samaria, not Israel's heavenly King; hence he would not allow a prophetic word to be spoken against Jeroboam or his realm at the royal chapel.

7:14 *neither a prophet nor a prophet's son.* Amos denied any previous connection with the prophets or their disciples (see note on 1Ki 20:35). No one had hired him to come and announce judgment on Jeroboam and Israel. *shepherd.* See note on 1:1, but the Hebrew uses a different word here—one not found elsewhere in the OT. The Hebrew for this word is, however, related to a word for "cattle," suggesting that Amos may also have tended cattle. *sycamore-fig trees.* They yield fig-like fruit, though smaller than figs and of inferior quality. To ensure good fruit, the gardener had to slit the top of each fig—which may be the procedure referred to by the obscure Hebrew word here rendered "took care of."

7:15 *tending.* Or "following" (as in 2Sa 7:8), the Hebrew for which stresses the location of the shepherd rather than his activity. *Go.* Amos was in Bethel because God had sent him to prophesy there.

7:16 *Do not prophesy.* Cf. 2:12.

7:17 Amos turned to condemn the priest personally. *prostitute.* With the exile of Amaziah, the death of his children and the loss of the family estate, Amaziah's wife would be reduced to prostitution to survive. *Your land.* Amaziah's private estate would be "divided up" and given to others. *pagan country.* Where his ceremonial purity as a priest would be defiled (see NIV text note). *And Israel ... native land.* Amos repeats—verbatim in the Hebrew—the last two lines of Amaziah's earlier summary of Amos's message (v. 11).

8:1 *showed me.* See note on 7:1.

8:2 *What do you see ... ?* See 7:8 and note. *ripe fruit ... time is ripe.* A wordplay in Hebrew; Israel was ready to be plucked. *my people.* See 7:8 and note. *spare them no longer.* See 7:8.

8:3 *that day.* See 5:18 and note. *wailing ... Silence!* There would be no thanksgiving songs for this harvest (contrast Lev 23:39–41)—only silence in the face of divine judgment (see note on Hab 2:20).

8:4 *Hear this.* See 3:1 and note. *trample.* See 5:11 and note.

8:5 *New Moon ... Sabbath.* The official religious festivals, when commerce ceased (see Nu 28:9–15; 2Ki 4:23 and note). *skimping the measure, boosting the price ... dishonest scales.* See Lev 19:35; Pr 11:1 and notes; Hos 12:7.

8:6 See note on 2:6.

8:7 *The LORD has sworn by the Pride of Jacob.* That is, he has sworn by himself. In ironic fashion, Amos echoes the phrase "pride of Jacob" in 6:8, where it refers not to God (as here) but to the fortresses of Israel.

8:8 See 9:5. *rise like the Nile.* Because of the heavy seasonal rains in Ethiopia, the Nile in Egypt annually rose by as much as 25 feet, flooding the whole valley except for the towns and villages standing above it. Its waters carried a large amount of rich soil, which was deposited on the land—perhaps referred to by the words "stirred up."

[9]"In that day," declares the Sovereign LORD,

"I will make the sun go down at noon
and darken the earth in broad daylight.[x]
[10]I will turn your religious feasts[y] into mourning
and all your singing into weeping.[z]
I will make all of you wear sackcloth[a]
and shave[b] your heads.
I will make that time like mourning for an only son[c]
and the end of it like a bitter day.[d]

[11]"The days are coming,"[e] declares the Sovereign LORD,
"when I will send a famine through the land—
not a famine of food or a thirst for water,
but a famine[f] of hearing the words of the LORD.[g]
[12]Men will stagger from sea to sea
and wander from north to east,
searching for the word of the LORD,
but they will not find it.[h]

[13]"In that day

"the lovely young women and strong young men[i]
will faint because of thirst.[j]
[14]They who swear by the shame[a] of Samaria,[k]
or say, 'As surely as your god lives, O Dan,'[l]
or, 'As surely as the god[b] of Beersheba[m] lives'—
they will fall,[n]
never to rise again.[o]"

8:9 [x]S Job 5:14; Isa 59:9-10; Jer 13:16; 15:9; S Eze 32:7; S Am 5:8; Mic 3:6; Mt 27:45; Mk 15:33; Lk 23:44-45 **8:10** [y]S Lev 26:31 [z]S La 5:15; S Hos 2:11 [a]S Joel 1:8 [b]S Lev 13:40; S Isa 3:17 [c]S Ge 21:16 [d]S Jer 2:19; S Eze 7:18 **8:11** [e]Jer 30:3; 31:27 [f]S Isa 30:20 [g]S 1Sa 3:1; S 28:6; S 2Ch 15:3 **8:12** [h]S Eze 20:3,31 **8:13** [i]S Isa 9:17 [j]Isa 41:17; Hos 2:3 **8:14** [k]Mic 1:5 [l]S 1Ki 12:29 [m]S Am 5:5 [n]S Ps 46:2 [o]S Am 5:2 **9:1** [p]Ps 68:21 [q]Jer 11:11 **9:2** [r]S Job 7:9; S Eze 26:20 [s]Jer 51:53 [t]Ob 1:4 **9:3** [u]Am 1:2 [v]Ps 139:8-10 [w]Ps 68:22 [x]Isa 27:1 [y]Jer 16:16-17 [z]S Ge 49:17; S Job 11:20 **9:4** [a]S Lev 26:33; S Eze 5:12 [b]S Jer 21:10 [c]Jer 39:16; S Eze 15:7 [d]S Jer 44:11

Israel to Be Destroyed

9 I saw the Lord standing by the altar, and he said:

"Strike the tops of the pillars
so that the thresholds shake.
Bring them down on the heads[p] of all the people;
those who are left I will kill with the sword.
Not one will get away,
none will escape.[q]
[2]Though they dig down to the depths of the grave,[c][r]
from there my hand will take them.
Though they climb up to the heavens,[s]
from there I will bring them down.[t]
[3]Though they hide themselves on the top of Carmel,[u]
there I will hunt them down and seize them.[v]
Though they hide from me at the bottom of the sea,[w]
there I will command the serpent[x] to bite them.[y][z]
[4]Though they are driven into exile by their enemies,
there I will command the sword[a] to slay them.
I will fix my eyes upon them
for evil[b] and not for good.[c]"[d]

[a] 14 Or *by Ashima*; or *by the idol* [b] 14 Or *power* [c] 2 Hebrew *to Sheol*

8:9 *that day.* See 5:18 and note. *darken the earth.* As elsewhere, the "day of the LORD" is described as one in which the cosmic (world) order is disrupted and light is turned to darkness (see 5:18,20; Isa 13:10; 24:23; 34:4; 50:3; Eze 32:7–8; Joel 2:2,10,31 and note on 2:2; Mic 3:6; Zep 1:15; Rev 6:12), as if creation is being undone (see Jer 4:23 and note).

8:10 *mourning.* Illustrated by King David (2Sa 18:33). *wear sackcloth ... shave your heads.* Signs of mourning (see Ge 37:34; Isa 15:2–3 and notes). *only son.* On whose life the future of the family depended (cf. 2Sa 18:18). *bitter day.* The opposite of the "day of celebration" (Est 9:22).

8:11 *days.* When God's judgment begins to take effect. *famine of hearing the words of the LORD.* In times of great distress Israel turned to the Lord for a prophetic word of hope or guidance (see, e.g., 2Ki 19:1–4,14–15; 22:13–14; Jer 21:1–2; Eze 14:7), but in the coming judgment the Lord will answer all such appeals with silence—the awful silence of God (see Eze 7:26 and note; 20:1–3; Mic 3:4,7).

8:12 *sea to sea ... north to east.* Throughout the land of Israel, from the Mediterranean to the Dead Sea, even to the Transjordan.

8:13 *thirst.* Both physical and spiritual. Their strength sapped, even the "lovely young women and strong young men" of the nation would faint and fall helpless.

8:14 *They who swear.* By the gods of their various religious centers (see NIV text notes)—the false gods in which they trusted rather than in the Lord (see Dt 6:13 and note). *Samaria.* See note on 6:1. *Dan ... Beersheba.* Cities that not only marked the northern and southern limits of Israel (see note on Jdg 20:1) but also were noted as sites where pagan shrines had been built (see 5:5; 1Ki 12:29 and notes).

9:1 *I saw the Lord.* See notes on 7:1—9:10 and 7:1. God is now poised on earth. *by the altar.* God is about to initiate the destruction from the very place from which the people expect to hear a word of peace and blessing. *tops of the pillars.* God will shatter the temple completely, from the decorated capitals down to the heavy stone "thresholds." The next lines depict the destruction. *Not one ... will escape.* See note on 7:8.

9:2–4 See note on 7:8. These verses emphasize the impossibility of escape from God's impending judgment. The imaginary extremes to which a person might go may be compared with those in Ps 139:7–12 (see note there). God's domain includes every place, even the realm of the grave (v. 2).

9:3 *top of Carmel.* See note on 1:2. *serpent.* In pagan mythology, the fierce monster of the sea (see Ps 74:13–14 and note). If some of "the people" (v. 1) should seek to escape by hiding in the depths, they still could not evade God, for even there all are subject to him.

9:4 *driven ... by their enemies ... I will command.* Even those dispersed among the nations will not escape God's judgment. *I will fix my eyes ... for evil.* Contrast Ps 33:18–19; 34:15.

5 The Lord, the LORD Almighty,
he who touches the earth and it melts,[e]
and all who live in it mourn—
the whole land rises like the Nile,
then sinks like the river of Egypt[f]—
6 he who builds his lofty palace[a][g] in the heavens
and sets its foundation[b] on the earth,
who calls for the waters of the sea
and pours them out over the face of the land—
the LORD is his name.[h]
7 "Are not you Israelites
the same to me as the Cushites[c]?"[i]
declares the LORD.
"Did I not bring Israel up from Egypt,
the Philistines[j] from Caphtor[d][k]
and the Arameans from Kir?[l]
8 "Surely the eyes of the Sovereign LORD
are on the sinful kingdom.
I will destroy[m] it
from the face of the earth—
yet I will not totally destroy
the house of Jacob,"
declares the LORD.[n]
9 "For I will give the command,
and I will shake the house of Israel
among all the nations
as grain[o] is shaken in a sieve,[p]
and not a pebble will reach the ground.[q]
10 All the sinners among my people
will die by the sword,[r]
all those who say,
'Disaster will not overtake or meet us.'[s]

Israel's Restoration

11 "In that day I will restore
David's[t] fallen tent.[u]
I will repair its broken places,
restore its ruins,[v]
and build it as it used to be,[w]
12 so that they may possess the remnant of Edom[x]
and all the nations that bear my name,[e][y]"
declares the LORD,
who will do these things.[z]

13 "The days are coming," [a] declares the LORD,

"when the reaper[b] will be overtaken
by the plowman[c]
and the planter by the one treading[d] grapes.
New wine[e] will drip from the mountains
and flow from all the hills.[f]

9:5 [e] S Ps 46:2 [f] S Am 8:8 **9:6** [g] Jer 43:9 [h] Ps 104:1-3, 5-6, 13; S Am 5:8 **9:7** [i] S 2Ch 12:3; Isa 20:4; 43:3 [j] S Ge 10:14 [k] S Dt 2:23 [l] S 2Ki 16:9; S Isa 22:6; S Am 2:10 **9:8** [m] S Jer 4:27 [n] S Jer 44:27 **9:9** [o] Lk 22:31 [p] Isa 30:28 [q] S Jer 31:36; S Da 9:7 **9:10** [r] Jer 49:37 [s] Jer 5:12; S 23:17; S Eze 20:38; S Am 6:3 **9:11** [t] S Isa 7:2 [u] S Ge 26:22 [v] Ps 53:6; S Isa 49:8 [w] Ps 80:12; S Eze 17:24; Mic 7:8, 11; Zec 12:7; 14:10 **9:12** [x] S Nu 24:18 [y] Isa 43:7; Jer 25:29 [z] Ac 15:16-17* **9:13** [a] Jer 31:38; 33:14 [b] S Ru 2:3 [c] Lev 26:5 [d] S Jdg 9:27 [e] S Joel 2:24 [f] S Joel 3:18

[a] *6* The meaning of the Hebrew for this phrase is uncertain. [b] *6* The meaning of the Hebrew for this word is uncertain. [c] *7* That is, people from the upper Nile region [d] *7* That is, Crete [e] *12* Hebrew; Septuagint *so that the remnant of men / and all the nations that bear my name may seek* ⌞*the Lord*⌟

9:5 *The Lord ... who.* Introduces a hymnic reminder that Israel's God is the Creator and Sustainer of the universe, thus underlining the pronouncements of the previous verses (see 4:13; 5:8–9 and notes). *earth ... melts.* See note on Ps 46:6. *rises like the Nile.* See 8:8 and note.

9:6 *his lofty palace.* Contrasts the scale of God with the scale of human beings, whose structures fall at the movement of the earth (v. 5). See Ps 104:3 and note. *waters of the sea.* See 5:8 and note.

9:7 *Cushites.* See NIV text note; see also notes on 2Ch 14:9; Isa 18:1. *Did I not bring Israel up ... ?* See note on Ex 20:2. Israel could not rely on God's past blessings as an assurance of his future benevolence. Her stubborn rebelliousness robbed the exodus of all special meaning for her; her journey from Egypt is reduced to no more significance than the movements of other peoples. *Philistines from Caphtor.* See note on Jer 47:4. *Kir.* See note on 1:5.

9:8 *sinful kingdom.* Israel, the chosen, whose disobedience was far worse than the sins of other nations (see 1:3—2:16; 3:1–2 and note on 3:2). *yet I will not totally destroy.* See note on v. 11.

9:9 *sieve.* Separates the wheat from small stones and other refuse gathered with it when scooped up from the earthen threshing floor. *not a pebble will reach.* Only the grain drops through, the refuse being screened out to be discarded.

9:10 *All the sinners ... will die.* For their persistent rebellion. *my people.* See 7:8 and note.

9:11–12 Quoted in Ac 15:16–17 (see note on Ac 15:16).

9:11 The verse is also regarded as Messianic in the Jewish Talmud. *I will restore.* Raises a hope underlying Amos's words—one that runs through the whole OT from Ge 3:15 on: God will bring blessing after judgment and will not ultimately reject Israel. *tent.* Or "booth"—that provided shelter (see Isa 1:8; 4:6). While unfaithful Israel sometimes looked to Egypt for protection (see Isa 30:2 and note), faithful Israel always looked to the Lord for shelter (see Ps 91:1; cf. 17:8 and note). They also looked to the Lord's anointed king from the house of David to provide the shade (protection) in which they would live safely among the nations (see La 4:20 and note). That protective booth had now "fallen," but it would be restored. *as it used to be.* In the days of David and Solomon.

9:12 *remnant of Edom.* Whatever is left of Israel's bitter enemy (see note on 1:11) after her punishment. *all the nations that bear my name.* Refers to the extent of the rule of the Lord's anointed future King, recalling that David had reigned over many nations surrounding Israel. It represents the fulfillment of the Abrahamic and Davidic covenants. The Messiah will reign even over former enemies, of whom Edom is symbolic (see notes on Isa 34:5; Joel 3:19; Ob 8). *will do these things.* God does what he says.

9:13–15 After all the forecasts of destruction, dearth and death (see, e.g., 5:9,11,27), Amos's final words picture a glorious Edenic prosperity, when the seasons will run together so that sowing and reaping are without interval, and there will be a continuous supply of fresh produce—a reversal of the conditions portrayed in 4:6–11 (see notes there).

9:13 See Joel 3:18 and note.

[14]I will bring[g] back my exiled[a h] people
Israel;
they will rebuild the ruined cities[i]
and live in them.
They will plant vineyards[j] and drink
their wine;
they will make gardens and eat their
fruit.[k]
[15]I will plant[l] Israel in their own land,[m]
never again to be uprooted[n]
from the land I have given them,"[o]

says the LORD your God.[p]

[a] *14* Or *will restore the fortunes of my*

9:14 [g]S Jer 29:14 [h]S Jer 33:7 [i]S Isa 32:18; S 49:8; S 61:4 [j]S 2Ki 19:29 [k]S Isa 62:9; S Jer 30:18; S 31:28; Eze 28:25-26; S 34:13-14; S Am 5:11

9:15 [l]S Ex 15:17; S Isa 60:21 [m]S Jer 23:8 [n]S Joel 3:20 [o]S Isa 65:9; S Jer 3:18; Ob 1:17 [p]S Jer 18:9; S 24:6; S 32:15; S Eze 28:26; S 34:25-28; S 37:12, 25

9:14 – 15 *I will bring ... they will rebuild ... They will plant ... I will plant.* In the promised land, God will make his people productive, fruitful and secure.
9:14 *my ... people.* See note on 7:8; contrast Hos 1:9, but see Hos 2:23. *rebuild the ruined cities.* See Isa 58:12 and note.
9:15 *never again.* When Israel is finally and fully restored, she will never again be destroyed. *your God.* Contrast Hos 1:9, but see Hos 2:23.

Obadiah

INTRODUCTION

Author

The author's name is Obadiah, which means "servant (or worshiper) of the LORD." His was a common name (see 1Ki 18:3–16; 1Ch 3:21; 7:3; 8:38; 9:16; 12:9; 27:19; 2Ch 17:7; 34:12; Ezr 8:9; Ne 10:5; 12:25). Neither his father's name nor the place of his birth is given.

A Quick Look

Author:
Obadiah

Audience:
The people of Judah suffering the treachery of the Edomites, descendants of Esau

Date:
The time of the Babylonian attacks on Jerusalem (605–586 B.C.)

Theme:
Obadiah prophesies judgment against the proud Edomites, who are gloating over Jerusalem's devastation by foreign powers.

Date and Place of Writing

The date and place of composition are disputed. Dating the prophecy is mainly a matter of relating vv. 11–14 to one of two specific events in Israel's history:

1. The rebellion of Edom against Judah during the reign of Jehoram (853–841 B.C.); see 2Ki 8:20–22; 2Ch 21:8–15. In this case, Obadiah would be a contemporary of Elisha.

2. The Babylonian attacks on Jerusalem (605–586). Obadiah would then be a contemporary of Jeremiah. This alternative seems more likely.

The striking parallels between Ob 1–6 and Jer 49:9–10, 14–16 have caused many to suggest some kind of interdependence between Obadiah and Jeremiah, but it may be that both prophets were drawing on a common source not otherwise known to us.

Unity and Theme

There is no compelling reason to doubt the unity of this brief prophecy, the shortest book in the OT. Its theme is that Edom, proud over her own security, has gloated over Israel's devastation by foreign powers. However, Edom's participation in that disaster will bring on God's wrath. She herself will be destroyed, but Mount Zion and Israel will be delivered, and God's kingdom will triumph.

Edom's hostile activities have spanned the centuries of Israel's existence. The following Biblical references are helpful in understanding the relation of Israel and Edom: Ge 27:41–45; 32:1–21; 33;

36; Ex 15:15; Nu 20:14 – 21; Dt 2:1 – 6; 23:7 – 8; 1Sa 22 with Ps 52; 2Sa 8:13 – 14; 2Ki 8:20 – 22; 14:7; Ps 83; 137:7; Eze 35; Joel 3:18 – 19; Am 1:11 – 12; 9:11 – 12.

Since the Edomites are related to the Israelites (v. 10), their hostility is all the more reprehensible. Edom is fully responsible for her failure to assist Israel and for her open aggression. The fact that God rejected Esau (Ge 25:23; Mal 1:3; Ro 9:13) in no way exonerates the Edomites. Edom, smug in its mountain strongholds, will be dislodged and sacked. But Israel will prosper because God is with her.

Edom will be destroyed, but Israel and Mount Zion will be delivered and God's kingdom will triumph.

Outline

- I. Title and Introduction (1)
- II. Judgment on Edom (2 – 14)
  - A. Edom's Destruction Announced (2 – 7)
    - 1. The humbling of her pride (2 – 4)
    - 2. The completeness of her destruction (5 – 7)
  - B. Edom's Destruction Reaffirmed (8 – 14)
    - 1. Her shame and destruction (8 – 10)
    - 2. Her crimes against Israel (11 – 14)
- III. The Day of the Lord (15 – 21)
  - A. Judgment on the Nations but Deliverance for Zion (15 – 18)
  - B. The Lord's Kingdom Established (19 – 21)

[1]The vision[a] of Obadiah.
1-4pp — Jer 49:14-16
5-6pp — Jer 49:9-10

This is what the Sovereign LORD says about Edom[b]—

We have heard a message from the
LORD:
An envoy[c] was sent to the nations to
say,
"Rise, and let us go against her for
battle"[d]—

[2]"See, I will make you small[e] among the
nations;
you will be utterly despised.
[3]The pride[f] of your heart has deceived
you,
you who live in the clefts of the
rocks[a][g]
and make your home on the heights,
you who say to yourself,
'Who can bring me down to the
ground?'[h]
[4]Though you soar like the eagle
and make your nest[i] among the stars,
from there I will bring you down,"[j]
declares the LORD.[k]
[5]"If thieves came to you,
if robbers in the night—
Oh, what a disaster awaits you—
would they not steal only as much
as they wanted?
If grape pickers came to you,
would they not leave a few grapes?[l]
[6]But how Esau will be ransacked,
his hidden treasures pillaged!
[7]All your allies[m] will force you to the
border;
your friends will deceive and
overpower you;
those who eat your bread[n] will set a
trap for you,[b]
but you will not detect it.
[8]"In that day," declares the LORD,
"will I not destroy[o] the wise men of
Edom,
men of understanding in the
mountains of Esau?
[9]Your warriors, O Teman,[p] will be
terrified,
and everyone in Esau's mountains
will be cut down in the slaughter.
[10]Because of the violence[q] against your
brother Jacob,[r]
you will be covered with shame;
you will be destroyed forever.[s]
[11]On the day you stood aloof
while strangers carried off his
wealth
and foreigners entered his gates
and cast lots[t] for Jerusalem,
you were like one of them.[u]
[12]You should not look down[v] on your
brother
in the day of his misfortune,[w]
nor rejoice[x] over the people of Judah
in the day of their destruction,[y]
nor boast[z] so much
in the day of their trouble.[a]

1 [a]S Isa 1:1 [b]S Ge 25:14; S Isa 11:14; S 34:11; 63:1-6; Jer 49:7-22; S Eze 25:12-14; S 32:29; S Am 1:11-12 [c]Isa 18:2 [d]Jer 6:4-5 **2** [e]Nu 24:18 **3** [f]S Isa 16:6 [g]*fn* Isa 16:1 [h]S 2Ch 25:11-12 **4** [i]S Isa 10:14 [j]S Isa 14:13 [k]S Job 20:6 **5** [l]S Dt 4:27; 24:21; S Isa 24:13 **7** [m]Jer 30:14 [n]S Ps 41:9 **8** [o]Job 5:12; Isa 29:14 **9** [p]S Ge 36:11,34 **10** [q]S Joel 3:19 [r]Ps 137:7; Am 1:11-12 [s]S Ps 137:7; S Eze 25:12-14; 35:9 **11** [t]S Job 6:27; S Eze 24:6 [u]S Am 1:6 **12** [v]Pr 24:17 [w]S Job 31:29 [x]S Eze 35:15 [y]S Pr 17:5 [z]Ps 137:7 [a]S Eze 25:6; Mic 4:11; 7:8

[a] 3 Or *of Sela* [b] 7 The meaning of the Hebrew for this clause is uncertain.

1–4 Paralleled in Jer 49:14–16.
1 *vision.* Commonly used in the OT to designate a revelation from God (see Pr 29:18; Isa 1:1 and notes). *Obadiah.* See Introduction: Author. *We.* Either (1) the editorial "we," or (2) the prophet's association of Israel with himself, or (3) other prophets' pronouncements against Edom. In any case, the rest of the verse sets the stage for Obadiah's prophetic message, which begins with v. 2. *message.* Or "report." An envoy had been sent to the nations, calling them to battle against Edom. Perhaps a conspiracy was under way among some of Edom's allies (v. 7). Although Edom feels secure (trusting in her mountain fortresses and her wise men, vv. 2–4,8–9), Obadiah announces God's judgment on her for her hostility to Israel.
2 *I will make you small.* Cf. the colloquial expression, "cut one down to size."
3 *pride.* See v. 12; Jer 49:16 and note. *rocks.* See NIV text note. Sela was the capital of Edom. Perhaps the later Petra (both Sela and Petra mean "rock" or "cliff"), this rugged site is located some 50 miles south of the southern end of the Dead Sea (see notes on 2Ki 14:7; Isa 16:1).
4 *eagle.* A proud and regal bird, noted for strength, keenness of vision and power of flight (see Dt 28:49; Isa 40:31; Jer 4:13; 49:22; Eze 17:3). *stars.* Hyperbole for high, inaccessible places in the mountains.
5–6 Paralleled in Jer 49:9–10.
5 *leave a few grapes.* See Jer 49:9 and note.
6 *hidden treasures.* The ancient Greek historian Diodorus Siculus indicates that the Edomites put their wealth—accumulated from trade—in vaults in the rocks.
7 *eat your bread.* See Ps 41:9 and note. *set a trap for you.* However the Hebrew for this expression is understood (see NIV text note), it must indicate an act of treachery on the part of previously trusted close friends.
8 *In that day.* The day of Edom's destruction, but the words also have an eschatological ring (see v. 15 and note). Since in OT prophecy Edom was often emblematic of all the world powers hostile to God and his kingdom, her judgment anticipates God's complete removal of all such opposition in that day (see note on Am 9:12). *wise men.* In whom Edom put so much confidence for her security (see Jer 49:7 and note). Eliphaz, one of Job's three friends, was a Temanite (see note on v. 9). Indeed, Job himself was probably an Edomite (see note on Job 1:1). *Esau.* Another name for Edom (see Ge 36:1 and note).
9 *Teman.* A reference to all Edom, as in Jer 49:7,20 (see notes on Jer 49:7; Am 1:12). Teman means "south," and the name probably refers to Edom as the southland.
10 *your brother Jacob.* Edom's violent crimes are all the more reprehensible because they were committed against the brother nation.
11 See Introduction: Date and Place of Writing. *strangers … foreigners.* These terms put in relief the sin of Edom: He did not act like a brother (v. 12) but was like one of the strangers. *cast lots for Jerusalem.* See Eze 24:6 and note.
12–14 A rebuke of Edom's hostile actions. The eight rebukes in this section proceed from the general to the particular. See Ps 137:7; Eze 35:13 for examples of Edom's reactions to Judah's misfortunes (see also note on Ps 137:7).
12 *boast.* See v. 3; Jer 49:16 and note.

[13]You should not march through the
gates of my people
in the day of their disaster,
nor look down on them in their
calamity[b]
in the day of their disaster,
nor seize their wealth
in the day of their disaster.
[14]You should not wait at the crossroads
to cut down their fugitives,[c]
nor hand over their survivors
in the day of their trouble.

[15]"The day of the LORD is near[d]
for all nations.
As you have done, it will be done to
you;
your deeds[e] will return upon your
own head.
[16]Just as you drank[f] on my holy hill,[g]
so all the nations will drink[h]
continually;
they will drink and drink
and be as if they had never been.[i]
[17]But on Mount Zion will be
deliverance;[j]
it will be holy,[k]
and the house of Jacob
will possess its inheritance.[l]
[18]The house of Jacob will be a fire
and the house of Joseph a flame;
the house of Esau will be stubble,
and they will set it on fire[m] and
consume[n] it.
There will be no survivors[o]
from the house of Esau."
The LORD has spoken.

[19]People from the Negev will occupy
the mountains of Esau,
and people from the foothills will
possess
the land of the Philistines.[p]
They will occupy the fields of Ephraim
and Samaria,[q]
and Benjamin[r] will possess Gilead.
[20]This company of Israelite exiles who
are in Canaan
will possess ⌞the land⌟ as far as
Zarephath;[s]
the exiles from Jerusalem who are in
Sepharad
will possess the towns of the Negev.[t]
[21]Deliverers[u] will go up on[a] Mount Zion
to govern the mountains of Esau.
And the kingdom will be the LORD's.[v]

13 [b]S Eze 35:5 **14** [c]S 1Ki 18:4 **15** [d]S Jer 46:10; S Eze 30:3; S Joel 2:31; S Am 5:18 [e]S Jer 50:29; Hab 2:8 **16** [f]Isa 51:17 [g]S Ex 15:17 [h]Jer 25:15; 49:12; S La 4:21-22 [i]S La 4:21; S Eze 25:12-14 **17** [j]S Ps 69:35; S Isa 14:1-2; Joel 2:32; S Am 9:11-15 [k]S Ps 74:2; S Isa 4:3 [l]Zec 8:12 **18** [m]S Isa 1:31 [n]Zec 12:6 [o]S Jer 49:10 **19** [p]Isa 11:14 [q]S Jer 31:5 [r]S Nu 1:36 **20** [s]1Ki 17:9-10; Lk 4:26 [t]S Jer 33:13 **21** [u]S Dt 28:29; S Jdg 3:9 [v]S Ps 22:28; 47:9; 66:4; S Da 2:44; Zec 14:9,16; Mal 1:14; Rev 11:15

[a] 21 Or *from*

15 *The day of the LORD is near for all nations.* If there was an eschatological glimmering in "in that day" (v. 8), it here becomes a strong ray. The day of the Lord brings judgment for the nations (including, but not limited to, Edom) and salvation for the house of Jacob (see v. 17; Joel 1:15; Am 5:18 and notes). *upon your own head.* The situation will be reversed in retribution for Edom's hostility against God's people detailed in vv. 11–14. Ezekiel's denunciation of Edom (ch. 35) reflects a similar punishment-fits-the-crime principle (see Est 7:10 and note; Ps 7:15–16; Eze 16:43).

16 *Just as you drank.* As the Edomites profaned the holy mountain by carousing, so the nations "will drink and drink." Their drinking, however, is that of the bitter potion of God's judgment—which they will be compelled to keep on drinking (cf. Jer 25:15–16; 49:12 and notes).

17 *But on Mount Zion will be deliverance.* Beginning with this verse the blessings on the house of Jacob are mentioned. The future has in store for the nations a contrasting destiny: judgment on God's enemies, blessing on God's people. *inheritance.* The land that God had promised them (see Jer 3:19; 12:7 and notes).

18 *Jacob ... Joseph.* Previously it was stated that the Lord would destroy Edom, using other nations (v. 7); now it is to be done by God's people. *no survivors.* The final word to Esau here is that his house (or nation) will be totally destroyed. Yet compare Am 9:12 with Ac 15:17, and see note and NIV text note on Am 9:12.

19 *People ... will occupy.* With Edom destroyed, others will occupy Edomite territory. Although not expressly identified, these are most likely the remnant of Israel referred to in the lines immediately following. *Negev.* See note on Ge 12:9. *foothills.* See note on Mic 1:10–15. *Philistines.* See note on Ge 10:14. *Gilead.* See notes on Ge 31:21; SS 4:1.

20 *Zarephath.* See note on 1Ki 17:9. *Sepharad.* Usually taken to refer to Sardis in Asia Minor (present-day Turkey), though others have suggested that Persian Sparda, north and west of Media, is meant.

21 *Deliverers.* Having developed the theme of possessing lands around Zion, the prophet now turns to the center. The "deliverers" come from Mount Zion and rule over the mountains of Esau. Mount Zion is exalted over the mountains of Esau. The Messiah, the Deliverer par excellence, may ultimately be in view. *the kingdom will be the LORD's.* The conclusion of the prophecy—and the final outcome of history. The last book of the Bible echoes this theme (Rev 11:15).

Jonah

INTRODUCTION

Title

The book is named after its principal character, whose name means "dove"; see the simile used of Ephraim in Hos 7:11 to portray the northern kingdom as "easily deceived and senseless." See also Ps 68:13; 74:19 and notes.

Authorship and Date

Though the book does not identify its author, tradition has ascribed it to the prophet himself, Jonah son of Amittai (1:1), from Gath Hepher (2Ki 14:25; see note there) in Zebulun (Jos 19:10,13). In view of its many similarities with the narratives about Elijah and Elisha, however, it may come from the same prophetic circles that originally composed the accounts about those prophets, perhaps in the eighth century B.C. (see Introduction to 1 Kings: Author, Sources and Date).

For a number of reasons, including the preaching to Gentiles, the book is often assigned a postexilic date. At least, it is said, the book must have been written after the destruction of Nineveh in 612 B.C. But these considerations are not decisive. The similarity of this narrative to the Elijah-Elisha accounts has already been noted. One may also question whether mention of the repentance of Nineveh and the consequent averted destruction of the city would have had so much significance to the author after Nineveh's overthrow. And to suppose that proclaiming God's word to Gentiles had no relevance in the eighth century is to overlook the fact that already in the previous century Elijah and Elisha had extended their ministries to foreign lands (1Ki 17:7 – 24; 2Ki 8:7 – 15). Moreover, the prophet Amos (c. 760 – 750) set God's redemptive work in behalf of Israel in the context of his dealings with the nations (Am 1:3 — 2:16; 9:7,12). Perhaps the third quarter of the eighth century is the most likely date for the book, after the public ministries of Amos and Hosea and before the fall of Samaria to Assyria in 722 – 721.

Background

In the half-century during which the prophet Jonah ministered (800 – 750 B.C.), a significant event affected the northern kingdom of Israel: King Jeroboam II (793 – 753) restored her traditional borders, ending almost a century of sporadic seesaw conflict between Israel and Damascus.

Jeroboam, in God's good providence (2Ki 14:26 – 27), capitalized on Assyria's defeat of Damascus (in the latter half of the ninth century), which temporarily crushed that center of Aramean power. Prior to that time, not only had Israel been considerably reduced in size, but the king of Damascus had even been able to control internal affairs in the northern kingdom (2Ki 13:7). However, after the Assyrian campaign against Damascus in 797 B.C., Jehoash king of Israel had been able to recover the territory lost to the king of Damascus (2Ki 13:25). Internal troubles in Assyria subsequently allowed Jeroboam to complete the restoration of Israel's northern borders. Nevertheless, Assyria remained the real threat from the north at this time.

The prophets of the Lord were speaking to Israel regarding these events. About 797 B.C. Elisha spoke to the king of Israel concerning future victories over Damascus (2Ki 13:14–19). A few years later Jonah prophesied the restoration that Jeroboam accomplished (2Ki 14:25). But soon after Israel had triumphed, she began to gloat over her newfound power. Because she was relieved of foreign pressures — relief that had come in accordance with encouraging words from Elisha and Jonah — she felt jealously complacent about her favored status with God (Am 6:1). She focused her religion on expectations of the "day of the LORD" (Am 5:18–20), when God's darkness would engulf the other nations, leaving Israel to bask in his light.

It was in such a time that the Lord sent Amos and Hosea to announce to his people Israel that he would "spare them no longer" (Am 7:8; 8:2) but would send them into exile "beyond Damascus" (Am 5:27), i.e., to Assyria (Hos 9:3; 10:6; 11:5). During this time the Lord also sent Jonah to Nineveh to warn it of the imminent danger of divine judgment.

Since Jonah was a contemporary of Amos, see Introduction to Amos: Date and Historical Situation for additional details.

Interpretation

Many have questioned the historicity of the book of Jonah. The frequently alleged legendary character of some of the events (e.g., the episode involving the great fish) has caused them to suggest alternatives to the traditional view that the book is biographical. Although their specific suggestions range from fictional short story to allegory to parable, they share the common assumption that the account sprang essentially from the author's imagination.

Such interpretations, often based in part on doubt about the miraculous as such, too quickly dismiss (1) the similarities between the narrative of Jonah and other parts of the OT and (2) the pervasive concern of the OT writers, especially the prophets, for history. They also fail to realize that OT narrators had a keen ear for recognizing how certain past events in Israel's pilgrimage with God illumine (by way of analogy) later events. (For example, the events surrounding the birth of Moses illumine the exodus, those surrounding Samuel's birth illumine the series of events narrated in the books of Samuel, and the ministries of Moses and Joshua illumine those of Elijah and Elisha.) Similarly, the prophets recognized that the future events they announced could be illumined by reference to analogous events of the past. Overlooking these features in OT narrative and prophecy, many have supposed that a story that too neatly fits the author's purpose must therefore be fictional.

On the other hand, it must be acknowledged that Biblical narrators were more than historians. They interpretatively recounted the past with the unswerving purpose of bringing it to bear on the present and the future. In the portrayal of past events, they used their materials to achieve this purpose effectively. Nonetheless, the integrity with which they treated the past ought not to be questioned. The book of Jonah recounts real events in the life and ministry of the prophet himself.

A Quick Look

Author:
Unknown

Audience:
The northern kingdom of Israel

Date:
Jonah prophesied during the reign of Jeroboam II (793–753 B.C.); the date of the writing of the book is unknown.

Theme:
In this story of God's loving concern for all people, the stubbornly reluctant Jonah represents Israel's jealousy of her favored relationship with God and her unwillingness to share the Lord's compassion with the nations.

Literary Characteristics

Unlike most other prophetic parts of the OT, this book is a narrative account of a single prophetic mission. Its treatment of that mission is thus similar to the accounts of the ministries of Elijah and Elisha found in 1 and 2 Kings, and to certain narrative sections of Isaiah, Jeremiah and Ezekiel.

As is often the case in Biblical narratives, the author has compressed much into a small space; 40 verses tell the entire story (eight additional verses of poetry are devoted to Jonah's prayer of thanksgiving). In its scope (a single extended episode), compactness, vividness and character delineation, it is much like the book of Ruth.

The book depicts the larger scope of God's purpose for Israel: that she might rediscover the truth of his concern for the whole creation and that she might better understand her own role in carrying out that concern.

Also as in Ruth, the author uses structural symmetry effectively. The story is developed in two parallel cycles that call attention to a series of comparisons and contrasts (see Outline). The story's climax is Jonah's grand prayer of confession, "Salvation comes from the LORD"—the middle confession of three from his lips (1:9; 2:9; 4:2). The last sentence emphasizes that the Lord's word is final and decisive, while Jonah is left sitting in the hot, open country outside Nineveh.

The author uses the art of representative roles in a straightforward manner. In this story of God's loving concern for all people, Nineveh, the great menace to Israel, is representative of the Gentiles. Correspondingly, stubbornly reluctant Jonah represents Israel's jealousy of her favored relationship with God and her unwillingness to share the Lord's compassion with the nations.

The book depicts the larger scope of God's purpose for Israel: that she might rediscover the truth of his concern for the whole creation and that she might better understand her own role in carrying out that concern.

Outline

- I. Jonah Flees His Mission (chs. 1–2)
  - A. Jonah's Commission and Flight (1:1–3)
  - B. The Endangered Sailors' Cry to Their Gods (1:4–6)
  - C. Jonah's Disobedience Exposed (1:7–10)
  - D. Jonah's Punishment and Deliverance (1:11—2:1; 2:10)
  - E. His Prayer of Thanksgiving (2:2–9)
- II. Jonah Reluctantly Fulfills His Mission (chs. 3–4)
  - A. Jonah's Renewed Commission and Obedience (3:1–4)
  - B. The Endangered Ninevites' Repentant Appeal to the Lord (3:5–9)
  - C. The Ninevites' Repentance Acknowledged (3:10—4:4)
  - D. Jonah's Deliverance and Rebuke (4:5–11)

Jonah Flees From the LORD

1 The word of the LORD came to Jonah[a]
son of Amittai:[b] 2“Go to the great city
of Nineveh[c] and preach against it, because
its wickedness has come up before me.”
3But Jonah ran[d] away from the LORD and
headed for Tarshish[e]. He went down to
Joppa,[f] where he found a ship bound for
that port. After paying the fare, he went
aboard and sailed for Tarshish to flee from
the LORD.[g]
4Then the LORD sent a great wind on the
sea, and such a violent storm arose that
the ship threatened to break up.[h] 5All the
sailors were afraid and each cried out to
his own god. And they threw the cargo
into the sea to lighten the ship.[i]
But Jonah had gone below deck, where
he lay down and fell into a deep sleep.
6The captain went to him and said, “How
can you sleep? Get up and call[j] on your
god! Maybe he will take notice of us, and
we will not perish.”[k]
7Then the sailors said to each other,
“Come, let us cast lots to find out who is
responsible for this calamity.”[l] They cast
lots and the lot fell on Jonah.[m]
8So they asked him, “Tell us, who is responsible for making all this trouble for
us? What do you do? Where do you come
from? What is your country? From what
people are you?”
9He answered, “I am a Hebrew and I
worship the LORD,[n] the God of heaven,[o]
who made the sea[p] and the land.[q]”
10This terrified them and they asked,
“What have you done?” (They knew he
was running away from the LORD, because
he had already told them so.)
11The sea was getting rougher and rougher. So they asked him, “What should we do
to you to make the sea calm down for us?”
12“Pick me up and throw me into the
sea,” he replied, “and it will become calm.
I know that it is my fault that this great
storm has come upon you.”[r]

1:1 [a]Mt 12:39-41; 16:4; Lk 11:29-32 [b]2Ki 14:25
1:2 [c]S Ge 10:11; S Na 1:1
1:3 [d]Ps 139:7 [e]S Ge 10:4 [f]S Jos 19:46; Ac 9:36,43 [g]Ex 4:13; S Jer 20:9; S Am 3:8
1:4 [h]Ps 107:23-26
1:5 [i]Ac 27:18-19
1:6 [j]Jnh 3:8 [k]S Ps 107:28
1:7 [l]Nu 32:23; Jos 7:10-18; S 1Sa 14:42 [m]S Pr 16:33
1:9 [n]S Ps 96:9 [o]S Da 2:18; Ac 17:24 [p]S Ne 9:6 [q]S Ge 1:9
1:12 [r]2Sa 24:17; 1Ch 21:17

1:1 *word of the LORD.* See 3:1; Hos 1:1 and note. *Jonah.* See Introduction: Title; Author. In his account of Jonah's mission to Nineveh written for Israel's instruction, the author probably presents Jonah as a cameo representation of Israel, the people called out from the nations by God to be the channel of his redemptive purposes for the peoples of the world. In this narrative, the people of Israel are to see themselves as in a mirror: their unique position of privilege as the people to whom God had revealed himself in a special way, their particular vocation as God's chosen kingdom people, their stubborn resistance to fulfilling that vocation, and the reason Israel must die as a nation (the judgment the prophets were announcing) and be raised up again refined and renewed (the more distant future the prophets were envisioning). Cf. note on Jdg 13:1—16:31.

1:2 *great city.* See 3:2; 4:11; see also note on 3:3. According to Ge 10:11, Nineveh was first built by Nimrod and was traditionally known as the "great city" (3:2; 4:11; see Ge 10:12 and note). About 700 B.C. Sennacherib made it the capital of Assyria, which it remained until its fall in 612 (see Introduction to Nahum: Background). Nineveh is over 500 miles from Gath Hepher, Jonah's hometown (see 2Ki 14:25 and note). *its wickedness has come up.* Cf. Sodom and Gomorrah (see Ge 18:20–21 and note on 18:20). Except for the "violence" (3:8) of Nineveh, her "evil ways" (3:8,10) are not described in Jonah. Nahum later states that Nineveh's sins included plotting evil against the Lord, cruelty and plundering in war, prostitution, witchcraft and commercial exploitation (Na 1:11; 2:12–13; 3:1,4,16,19).

1:3 *ran away.* Jonah gives his reason in 4:2. The futility of trying to run away from the Lord is acknowledged in Ps 139:7–12 (see note there). *Tarshish.* Perhaps the city of Tartessus in southern Spain, a Phoenician mining colony near Gibraltar. By heading in the opposite direction from Nineveh (see map, p. 1384), to what seemed like the end of the world, Jonah intended to escape his divinely appointed task. *Joppa.* See note on Ac 9:36.

1:4–16 Probably this account of the storm at sea is intended to be a graphic depiction, in exquisite miniature, of the pagan world of many nations (represented by the sailors) threatened by the judgments of God (represented by the storm) with Israel in their midst (represented by Jonah). If Jonah (Israel) does not fulfill his mission, the sailors (nations) will die calling on their gods. And because he is rebelling against his mission, he must "die" to save them. See note on 1:1; cf. note on Ac 27:13–44.

1:4–5 Although Jonah's mission was to bring God's warning of impending judgment to the pagan world, his refusal to go to Nineveh brings these pagan sailors into peril.

1:4 *the LORD sent a great wind.* God's sovereign working in Jonah's mission is evident at several other points also: the fish (v. 17), the release of Jonah (2:10), the vine (4:6), the worm (4:7) and the "scorching east wind" (4:8).

1:5 *his own god.* Apparently the sailors, who may have come from various ports, worshiped several pagan gods (see note on Ge 28:15).

1:6 *The captain went to him.* The pagan captain's concern for everyone on board contrasts with the believing prophet's refusal to carry God's warning to Nineveh.

1:7 *let us cast lots.* The casting of lots was a custom widely practiced in the ancient Near East. The precise method is unclear, though it appears that, for the most part, sticks or marked pebbles were drawn from a receptacle into which they had been "cast" (see notes on Ex 28:30; Ne 11:1; Pr 16:33; Eze 21:21; Ac 1:26). *lot fell on Jonah.* By the lot of judgment the Lord exposed the guilty one (see Jos 7:14–26 and note on 7:14; 1Sa 14:37–44 and note on 14:37).

1:9 *Hebrew.* See note on Ge 14:13. *God of heaven, who made the sea and the land.* See note on Ezr 1:2. The sailors would have understood Jonah's words as being descriptive of the highest deity. Their present experiences confirmed this truth, since, in the religions of the ancient Near East generally, the supreme god was master of the seas (see note on Jos 3:10). This is Jonah's first confessional statement, and, like those that follow (2:9d; 4:2), it is thoroughly orthodox. Though orthodox in his beliefs, Jonah refuses to fulfill his divine mission to Nineveh.

1:10 *What have you done?* This rhetorical question is really an accusation.

1:12 *throw me into the sea.* Jonah's readiness to die to save the terrified sailors contrasts with his later callous departure from Nineveh to watch from a safe distance while the city perishes—at least he still hoped it would perish (see 4:5 and note).

[13]Instead, the men did their best to row
back to land. But they could not, for the
sea grew even wilder than before.[s] [14]Then
they cried to the LORD, "O LORD, please do
not let us die for taking this man's life.
Do not hold us accountable for killing
an innocent man,[t] for you, O LORD, have
done as you pleased."[u] [15]Then they took
Jonah and threw him overboard, and the
raging sea grew calm.[v] [16]At this the men
greatly feared[w] the LORD, and they offered
a sacrifice to the LORD and made vows[x]
to him.

[17]But the LORD provided[y] a great fish to
swallow Jonah,[z] and Jonah was inside the
fish three days and three nights.

1:13 [s]S Pr 21:30
1:14 [t]Dt 21:8
[u]S Da 4:35
1:15
[v]S Ps 107:29; Lk 8:24
1:16 [w]Mk 4:41
[x]S Nu 30:2; Ps 66:13-14
1:17 [y]Jnh 4:6,7
[z]Mt 12:40; 16:4; Lk 11:30

2:2 [a]La 3:55
[b]Ps 18:6; 120:1
[c]Ps 86:13
2:3 [d]S Ps 88:6
[e]S 2Sa 22:5
[f]S Ps 42:7

Jonah's Prayer

2 From inside the fish Jonah prayed to
the LORD his God. [2]He said:

"In my distress I called[a] to the LORD,[b]
and he answered me.
From the depths of the grave[a][c] I called
for help,
and you listened to my cry.
[3]You hurled me into the deep,[d]
into the very heart of the seas,
and the currents swirled about me;
all your waves[e] and breakers
swept over me.[f]

[a] 2 Hebrew *Sheol*

1:13 *did their best to row.* The Hebrew uses the picturesque word meaning "to dig" (with oars) to indicate strenuous effort. The ship could be driven by sails, oars, or both. The reluctance of the sailors to throw Jonah into the sea stands in sharp contrast to Jonah's reluctance to warn Nineveh of impending judgment.

1:14 *cried to the LORD.* Earlier the sailors had cried out to their own gods (see v. 5 and note), but now in their desperation they plead for help from Jonah's God.

1:16 *greatly feared the LORD.* There is no evidence that the sailors renounced all other gods (contrast Naaman; see 2Ki 5:15 and note). Ancient pagans were ready to recognize the existence and power of many gods. At the least, however, the sailors acknowledged that the God of Israel was in control of the present events, that he was the one who both stirred up and calmed the storm, and that at this moment he was the one to be recognized and worshiped.

1:17 *the LORD provided.* This characteristic phrase occurs also in 4:6–8. *great fish.* The Hebrew here and the Greek of Mt 12:40 are both general terms for a large fish, not necessarily a whale. This great fish is carefully distinguished from the sinister "serpent" of the sea (Am 9:3) — otherwise called "Leviathan" (Isa 27:1), the "monster of the deep" (Job 7:12; see Ps 74:13; Eze 32:2). *three days and three nights.* The phrase used here may, as in Mt 12:40, refer to a period of time including one full day and parts of two others (see notes on Mt 12:40; 1Co 15:4). In any case, the NT clearly uses Jonah's experience as a type (foreshadowing) of the burial and resurrection of Jesus, who was entombed for "three days and three nights" (Mt 12:40; see Mt 16:4; Lk 11:29–30 and note on 11:30).

2:2–9 A psalm of thanksgiving for deliverance from death in the Mediterranean Sea. Jonah recalls his prayer for help as he was sinking into the depths. His gratitude is heightened by his knowledge that he deserved death but that God had shown him extraordinary mercy. The language of this song indicates that Jonah was familiar with the praise literature of the Psalms.

2:2 *I called ... he answered.* See note on Ps 118:5. *grave.* Figurative for Jonah's near-death experience in the sea (see Ps 30:3 and note). See also note on Ge 37:35.

2:3 *You hurled me ... your waves.* Jonah recognizes that the sailors (1:15) were agents of God's judgment.

The Book of Jonah

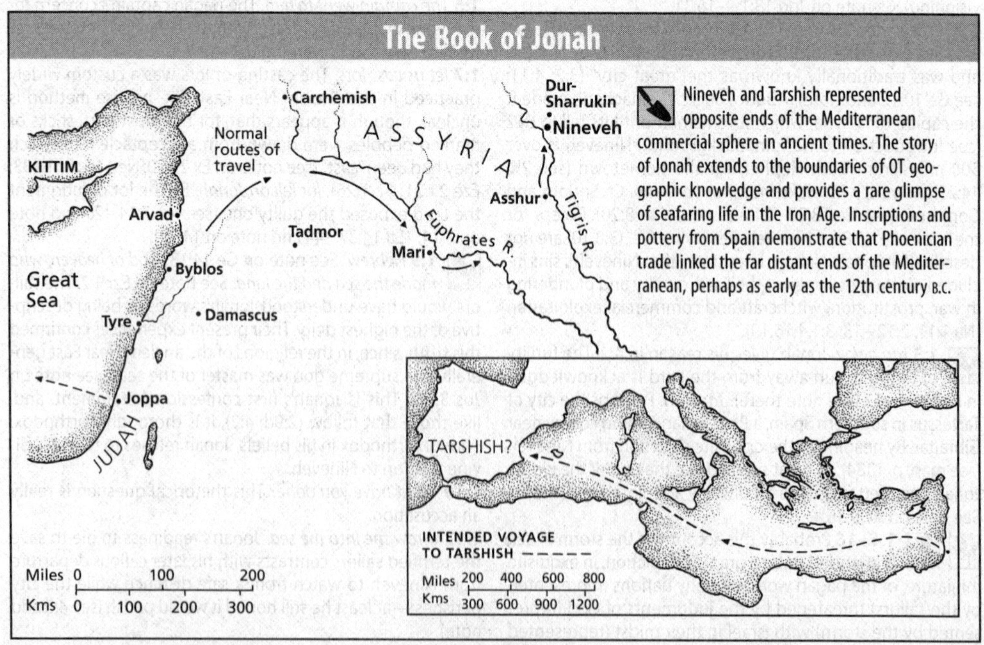

Nineveh and Tarshish represented opposite ends of the Mediterranean commercial sphere in ancient times. The story of Jonah extends to the boundaries of OT geographic knowledge and provides a rare glimpse of seafaring life in the Iron Age. Inscriptions and pottery from Spain demonstrate that Phoenician trade linked the far distant ends of the Mediterranean, perhaps as early as the 12th century B.C.

4 I said, 'I have been banished
from your sight;[g]
yet I will look again
toward your holy temple.'[h]
5 The engulfing waters threatened me,[a]
the deep surrounded me;
seaweed was wrapped around my
head.[i]
6 To the roots of the mountains[j] I sank
down;
the earth beneath barred me in
forever.
But you brought my life up from the
pit,[k]
O LORD my God.

7 "When my life was ebbing away,
I remembered[l] you, LORD,
and my prayer[m] rose to you,
to your holy temple.[n]

8 "Those who cling to worthless idols[o]
forfeit the grace that could be theirs.
9 But I, with a song of thanksgiving,[p]
will sacrifice[q] to you.
What I have vowed[r] I will make good.
Salvation[s] comes from the LORD."

10 And the LORD commanded the fish,
and it vomited Jonah onto dry land.

Jonah Goes to Nineveh

3 Then the word of the LORD came to Jonah[t] a second time: 2 "Go to the great
city of Nineveh and proclaim to it the message I give you."
3 Jonah obeyed the word of the LORD
and went to Nineveh. Now Nineveh was a
very important city—a visit required three
days. 4 On the first day, Jonah started into
the city. He proclaimed:[u] "Forty more days
and Nineveh will be overturned." 5 The
Ninevites believed God. They declared a
fast, and all of them, from the greatest to
the least, put on sackcloth.[v]
6 When the news reached the king of
Nineveh, he rose from his throne, took off
his royal robes, covered himself with sackcloth and sat down in the dust.[w] 7 Then he
issued a proclamation in Nineveh:

"By the decree of the king and his nobles:

Do not let any man or beast, herd
or flock, taste anything; do not let
them eat or drink.[x] 8 But let man and
beast be covered with sackcloth. Let
everyone call[y] urgently on God. Let
them give up[z] their evil ways[a] and
their violence.[b] 9 Who knows?[c] God
may yet relent[d] and with compassion
turn[e] from his fierce anger[f] so that we
will not perish."

10 When God saw what they did and how
they turned from their evil ways, he had
compassion[g] and did not bring upon them
the destruction[h] he had threatened.[i]

Jonah's Anger at the LORD's Compassion

4 But Jonah was greatly displeased and
became angry.[j] 2 He prayed to the LORD,
"O LORD, is this not what I said when I
was still at home? That is why I was so

2:4 [g] Ps 31:22; Jer 7:15 [h] S 1Ki 8:48
2:5 [i] Ps 69:1-2
2:6 [j] Job 28:9 [k] S Job 17:16; S 33:18; S Ps 30:3
2:7 [l] Ps 77:11-12 [m] 2Ch 30:27 [n] S Ps 11:4; 18:6
2:8 [o] S Dt 32:21; S 1Sa 12:21
2:9 [p] S Ps 42:4 [q] Ps 50:14, 23; Heb 13:15 [r] S Nu 30:2; Ps 116:14; S Ecc 5:4-5 [s] S Ex 15:2; S Ps 3:8
3:1 [t] Jnh 1:1
3:4 [u] S Jer 18:7-10
3:5 [v] Da 9:3; Mt 11:21; 12:41; Lk 11:32
3:6 [w] Est 4:1-3; S Job 2:8, 13; S Eze 27:30-31
3:7 [x] S 2Ch 20:3; S Ezr 10:6
3:8 [y] Ps 130:1; Jnh 1:6 [z] Jer 25:5 [a] Jer 7:3 [b] S Job 16:17
3:9 [c] 2Sa 12:22 [d] S Jer 18:8 [e] S Joel 2:14 [f] S Ps 85:3
3:10 [g] S Am 7:6 [h] S Jer 18:8 [i] S Ex 32:14
4:1 [j] ver 4; Mt 20:11; Lk 15:28

[a] 5 Or *waters were at my throat*

2:4 *yet I will look again toward your holy temple.* The same note of hopeful expectation found in the prayers of the Psalms (e.g., Ps 5:7; 27:4–6). "Temple" here probably refers to the temple in Jerusalem, while "temple" in v. 7 refers to God's heavenly temple. The Israelites held these two residences of God in inseparable association (see 1Ki 8:38–39).
2:6 *pit.* The grave (see note on v. 2; see also Ps 28:1; 30:1–3 and note on 30:1).
2:7 *holy temple.* See v. 4 and note.
2:9 *sacrifice … vowed.* Cf. the "sacrifice" and "vows" of the sailors (1:16). *What I have vowed.* In the book of Psalms, prayers were commonly accompanied by vows, usually involving thank offerings (see, e.g., Ps 50:14 and note; 56:12; 61:8; 65:1; 66:13–15; 116:12–19). *make good.* See Ps 76:11; Ecc 5:1–7. *Salvation comes from the LORD.* The climax of Jonah's thanksgiving prayer and his second confessional statement (see note on 1:9). It stands aptly at the literary midpoint since it is the theological foundation of the whole book.
3:1 *word of the LORD.* See 1:1 and note.
3:2 *great city.* See 1:2 and note. *proclaim to it the message I give you.* A prophet was the bearer of a message from God, not primarily a foreteller of coming events.
3:3 *obeyed.* But reluctantly, still wanting the Ninevites to be destroyed (see 4:1–5 and notes). *very important city.* See 4:11, which says the city had more than 120,000 inhabitants. Archaeological excavations indicate that the later imperial city of Nineveh was about eight miles around. The fact, however, that "a visit required three days" may suggest a larger area, such as the four-city complex of Nineveh, Rehoboth Ir, Calah and Resen mentioned in Ge 10:11–12. Greater Nineveh covered an area of some 60 miles in circumference. On the other hand, "three days" may have been a conventional way of describing a medium-length distance (see Ge 30:36; Ex 3:18 and note; Jos 9:16–17).
3:5–6 *fast … sackcloth … dust.* Customary signs of humbling oneself in repentance (see 1Ki 21:27; Ne 9:1 and note).
3:5 *believed God.* This may mean that the Ninevites genuinely turned to the Lord (cf. Mt 12:41). On the other hand, their belief in God may have gone no deeper than had the sailors' fear of God (see note on 1:16). At least they took the prophet's warning seriously and acted accordingly—something Israel was not doing!
3:6 *king of Nineveh.* King of Assyria.
3:8 *beast.* Inclusion of the domestic animals (see 4:11) was unusual and expressed the urgency with which the Ninevites sought mercy.
3:9 God often responds in mercy to human repentance by canceling threatened punishment (v. 10). See note on Jer 18:7–10.
3:10 *did not bring upon them the destruction … threatened.* See 1Ki 21:28–29 and note on 21:29; see also Introduction to Nahum: Background; Na 3:19 and note.
4:1 *angry.* Jonah was angry that God would have compassion on an enemy of Israel. He wanted God's goodness to be shown only to Israelites, not to Gentiles.
4:2 *prayed to the LORD.* Now in anger, not in distress (see 2:1–2 and note on 2:2). *That is why … flee to Tarshish.* See 1:3 and note. *gracious … love.* See Ex 34:6–7 and note.

quick to flee to Tarshish. I knew[k] that you
are a gracious[l] and compassionate God,
slow to anger and abounding in love,[m] a
God who relents[n] from sending calamity.[o]
3Now, O LORD, take away my life,[p] for it is
better for me to die[q] than to live."[r]
4But the LORD replied, "Have you any
right to be angry?"[s]
5Jonah went out and sat down at a place
east of the city. There he made himself a
shelter, sat in its shade and waited to see
what would happen to the city. 6Then the
LORD God provided[t] a vine and made it
grow up over Jonah to give shade for his
head to ease his discomfort, and Jonah
was very happy about the vine. 7But at
dawn the next day God provided a worm,
which chewed the vine so that it withered.[u] 8When the sun rose, God provided
a scorching east wind, and the sun blazed
on Jonah's head so that he grew faint. He
wanted to die,[v] and said, "It would be better for me to die than to live."
9But God said to Jonah, "Do you have a
right to be angry about the vine?"[w]
"I do," he said. "I am angry enough to
die."
10But the LORD said, "You have been
concerned about this vine, though you did
not tend it or make it grow. It sprang up
overnight and died overnight. 11But Nineveh[x] has more than a hundred and twenty thousand people who cannot tell their
right hand from their left, and many cattle
as well. Should I not be concerned[y] about
that great city?"

4:2 [k] Jer 20:7-8 [l] S Dt 4:31; Ps 103:8 [m] S Ex 22:27; Ps 86:5, 15 [n] S Nu 14:18 [o] S Joel 2:13 **4:3** [p] S Nu 11:15 [q] S Job 7:15 [r] Jer 8:3 **4:4** [s] Ge 4:6; Mt 20:11-15 **4:6** [t] S Jnh 1:17 **4:7** [u] Joel 1:12 **4:8** [v] S 1Ki 19:4 **4:9** [w] ver 4 **4:11** [x] Jnh 1:2; 3:2 [y] Jnh 3:10

This is the third and last of Jonah's confessional statements (see notes on 1:9; 2:9). *slow to anger.* In contrast, Jonah became angry quickly (vv. 1,9).

4:3 *take away my life.* See 1Ki 19:4 and note (Elijah). To Jonah, God's mercy to the Ninevites meant an end to Israel's favored standing with him. Jonah shortly before had rejoiced in his deliverance from death (2:2 – 9), but now that Nineveh lives, he prefers to die.

4:5 *shelter.* Apparently this shelter did not provide enough shade since the next verse indicates that God provided a vine to give more shade. *waited to see.* Jonah still hoped that Nineveh would be destroyed.

4:6 *God provided.* This characteristic phrase occurs also in vv. 7 – 8; see also 1:17 and note. *vine.* Possibly a castor oil plant, a shrub growing over 12 feet high with large, shady leaves. God graciously increased the comfort of his stubbornly defiant prophet.

4:8 *better for me to die.* See note on v. 3.

4:10 *sprang up overnight and died overnight.* Indicative of fleeting value.

4:11 *cannot tell their right hand from their left.* Like small children (see Dt 1:39 and note), the Ninevites needed God's fatherly compassion. *many cattle as well.* God's concern extended even to domestic animals (cf. 3:8). *Should I not be concerned . . . ?* God had the first word (1:1 – 2), and he also has the last. The commission he gave Jonah displayed his mercy and compassion to the Ninevites, and his last word to Jonah emphatically proclaimed that concern for every creature, both people and animals. Not only does the "LORD . . . preserve both man and beast" (Ps 36:6; see Ne 9:6; Ps 145:16); he also takes "no pleasure in the death of the wicked, but [desires] rather that they turn from their ways and live" (Eze 33:11 [see note there]; see also Eze 16:6; 18:23 notes; cf. 2Pe 3:9 and note). Jonah and his fellow Israelites traditionally rejoiced in God's special mercies to Israel but wished only his wrath on their enemies. God here rebukes such hardness and proclaims his own gracious benevolence. *great city.* See 1:2 and note. The book begins and ends by referring to Nineveh, the unlikely and unexpected scene of a remarkable display of divine compassion.

Micah

INTRODUCTION

Author

Little is known about the prophet Micah beyond what can be learned from the book itself and from Jer 26:18. Micah was from the town of Moresheth (1:1), probably Moresheth Gath (1:14) in southern Judah. The prophecy attests to Micah's deep sensitivity to the social ills of his day, especially as they affected the small towns and villages of his homeland.

A Quick Look

Author:
Micah

Audience:
The people of Israel and Judah, especially the oppressive landgrabbers who supported Israel's corrupt political and religious leaders

Date:
Between 700 and 650 B.C.

Theme:
Micah's message alternates between prophecies of doom and prophecies of hope; the theme is divine judgment and deliverance.

Date

Micah prophesied sometime between 750 and 686 B.C. during the reigns of Jotham, Ahaz and Hezekiah, kings of Judah (1:1; Jer 26:18). He was therefore a contemporary of Isaiah (see Isa 1:1) and Hosea (see Hos 1:1). Micah predicted the fall of Samaria (1:6), which took place in 722–721. This would place his early ministry in the reigns of Jotham (750–732) and Ahaz (735–715). (The reigns of Jotham and Ahaz overlapped.) Micah's message reflects social conditions prior to the religious reforms under Hezekiah (715–686). Micah's ministry most likely fell within the period 735–700.

If Micah himself wrote out his messages, the date for the earliest written form of his work would be c. 700. If one of his disciples arranged his messages in their present form, the date would be the early seventh century B.C. If a later editor collected and arranged his messages, the date would still need to be early enough in the seventh century to allow time for his prophecy of Jerusalem's fall (3:12) to become familiar enough to be quoted in Jer 26:18 c. 608.

Historical Background

The background of the book is the same as that found in the earlier portions of Isaiah, though Micah does not exhibit the same knowledge of Jerusalem's political life as Isaiah does. Perhaps this is because he, like Amos, was from a village in Judah. The relevant Biblical texts covering this period (see Date above) are 2Ki 15:32—20:21; 2Ch 27–32; Isa 7; 20; 36–39.

Israel was in an apostate condition. Micah predicted the fall of her capital, Samaria (1:5–7), and also foretold the inevitable desolation of Judah (1:9–16).

Several significant historical events occurred during this period:

Micah stresses that God hates idolatry, injustice, rebellion and empty ritualism, but delights in pardoning the penitent.

1. In 734–732 B.C. Tiglath-Pileser III of Assyria led a military campaign against Aram (Syria), Philistia and parts of Israel and Judah. Ashkelon and Gaza were defeated. Judah, Ammon, Edom and Moab paid tribute to the Assyrian king, but Israel did not fare as well. According to 2Ki 15:29 the northern kingdom lost most of its territory, including all of Gilead and much of Galilee. Damascus fell in 732 and was annexed to the Assyrian empire.
2. In 722–721 Samaria fell, and the northern kingdom of Israel was conquered by Assyria.
3. In 712 King Sargon II of Assyria captured Ashdod (see Isa 20:1 and note).
4. In 701 Judah joined a revolt against Assyria and was overrun by King Sennacherib and his army, though Jerusalem was spared.

Literary Analysis

1. *Structure.* The book's collection of short prophetic messages is organized in a pattern of three cycles of judgment and salvation/deliverance messages (see Outline below).

2. *Forms.* The book contains at least seven different literary forms (divine covenant lawsuit, lament, disputation, deliverance message, indictment/judgment message, judgment and salvation mixed, and prophetic liturgy). These are identified in the notes on the 20 individual units.

3. *Style.* Micah's style is similar to that of Isaiah. Both prophets use vigorous language and many figures of speech (see, e.g., Mic 1:4–5,7; 2:4,6,11; 3:2–3; 4:3–4,12–13; 5:1); both show great tenderness in threatening punishment and in promising justice. Micah makes frequent use of plays on words, 1:10–15 (see NIV text notes there) being the classic example.

Theme and Message

As the Outline shows, Micah's message alternates between oracles of doom and oracles of hope—in terms of Ro 11:22, between God's "sternness" and his "kindness." The theme is divine judgment and deliverance. Micah also stresses that God hates idolatry, injustice, rebellion and empty ritualism (see 3:8 and note), but delights in pardoning the penitent (see 7:18–19 and notes). Finally, the prophet declares that Zion will have greater glory in the future than ever before (see, e.g., 4:1–2 and note on 4:1–5). The Davidic kingdom, though it will seem to come to an end, will reach greater heights through the coming Messianic deliverer (see note on 5:1–4). Key passages include 1:2; 3:8–12; 5:1–4; 6:2,6–8; 7:18–20.

Outline

I. Title (1:1)
II. First Cycle: Judgment and Restoration of Israel and Judah (1:2—2:13)
  A. Judgment on Israel and Judah (1:2—2:11)
    1. The predicted destruction (1:2–7)
    2. Lamentation over the destruction (1:8–16)
    3. Woe to oppressive land-grabbers (2:1–5)
    4. Condemnation of the wealthy wicked and their false prophets (2:6–11)
  B. Restoration of a Remnant (2:12–13)
III. Second Cycle: Indictment of Judah's Leaders, but Future Hope for God's People (chs. 3–5)
  A. Indictment of Judah's Leaders (ch. 3)
    1. Guilty civil leaders (3:1–4)
    2. False prophets of peace and Micah's response (3:5–8)

3. Corrupt leaders and Zion's fall (3:9 – 12)

B. Future Hope for God's People (chs. 4 – 5)
   1. The coming kingdom (4:1 – 5)
   2. Restoration of a remnant and Zion (4:6 – 8)
   3. From distress to deliverance (4:9 – 10)
   4. From siege to victory (4:11 – 13)
   5. From helpless ruler to ideal king (5:1 – 4)
   6. The ideal king delivers his people (5:5 – 6)
   7. The remnant among the nations (5:7 – 9)
   8. Obliteration of military might and pagan worship (5:10 – 15)

IV. Third Cycle: God's Charges against His People and the Ultimate Triumph of His Kingdom (chs. 6 – 7)
   A. God's Charges against His People (6:1 — 7:7)
      1. A divine covenant lawsuit (6:1 – 8)
      2. Further charges and the sentence (6:9 – 16)
      3. A lament over a decadent society (7:1 – 7)
   B. The Ultimate Triumph of God's Kingdom (7:8 – 20)
      1. An expression of trust (7:8 – 10)
      2. A promise of restoration (7:11 – 13)
      3. A prayer, the Lord's answer, and the response (7:14 – 17)
      4. A hymn of praise to God (7:18 – 20)

1 The word of the LORD that came to Mi-
cah of Moresheth[a] during the reigns of
Jotham,[b] Ahaz[c] and Hezekiah,[d] kings of
Judah[e]—the vision[f] he saw concerning
Samaria and Jerusalem.

[2]Hear,[g] O peoples, all of you,[h]
listen, O earth[i] and all who are in it,
that the Sovereign LORD may witness[j]
against you,
the Lord from his holy temple.[k]

Judgment Against Samaria and Jerusalem

[3]Look! The LORD is coming from his
dwelling[l] place;
he comes down[m] and treads the high
places of the earth.[n]
[4]The mountains melt[o] beneath him[p]
and the valleys split apart,[q]
like wax before the fire,
like water rushing down a slope.
[5]All this is because of Jacob's
transgression,
because of the sins of the house of
Israel.
What is Jacob's transgression?
Is it not Samaria?[r]
What is Judah's high place?
Is it not Jerusalem?

[6]"Therefore I will make Samaria a heap
of rubble,
a place for planting vineyards.[s]
I will pour her stones[t] into the valley
and lay bare her foundations.[u]
[7]All her idols[v] will be broken to pieces;[w]
all her temple gifts will be burned
with fire;
I will destroy all her images.[x]
Since she gathered her gifts from the
wages of prostitutes,[y]
as the wages of prostitutes they will
again be used."

Weeping and Mourning

[8]Because of this I will weep[z] and wail;
I will go about barefoot[a] and
naked.
I will howl like a jackal
and moan like an owl.
[9]For her wound[b] is incurable;[c]
it has come to Judah.[d]
It[a] has reached the very gate[e] of my
people,
even to Jerusalem itself.
[10]Tell it not in Gath[b];
weep not at all.[c]
In Beth Ophrah[d]
roll in the dust.

1:1 [a] ver 14; Jer 26:18 [b] S 1Ch 3:12 [c] S 1Ch 3:13 [d] S 1Ch 3:13 [e] Hos 1:1 [f] Isa 1:1 **1:2** [g] S Dt 32:1 [h] Ps 50:7 [i] S Jer 6:19 [j] S Ge 31:50; S Dt 4:26; S Isa 1:2 [k] S Ps 11:4 **1:3** [l] S Isa 18:4 [m] S Isa 64:1 [n] S Am 4:13 **1:4** [o] S Ps 46:2,6 [p] S Job 9:5 [q] S Nu 16:31; Na 1:5 **1:5** [r] Am 8:14 **1:6** [s] S Dt 20:6 [t] S Am 5:11 [u] Eze 13:14 **1:7** [v] S Eze 6:6 [w] S Ex 32:20 [x] S Dt 9:21 [y] Dt 23:17-18 **1:8** [z] S Isa 15:3 [a] S Isa 20:2 **1:9** [b] Jer 46:11 [c] S Jer 10:19 [d] S 2Ki 18:13 [e] Isa 3:26

[a] *9* Or *He* [b] *10* *Gath* sounds like the Hebrew for *tell.* [c] *10* Hebrew; Septuagint may suggest *not in Acco.* The Hebrew for *in Acco* sounds like the Hebrew for *weep.* [d] *10* *Beth Ophrah* means *house of dust.*

1:1 *Micah.* Means "Who is like the LORD?" (cf. 7:18 and note). *Moresheth.* See Introduction: Author. *Jotham, Ahaz and Hezekiah.* See Introduction: Date. For background on these kings and the book of Micah see Introduction: Historical Background. Isaiah, Hosea and Micah prophesied at roughly the same time (see Isa 1:1; Hos 1:1). *vision.* See Pr 29:18; Isa 1:1 and notes. *Samaria and Jerusalem.* The capitals of Israel and Judah respectively. The judgment predicted by Micah involved these nations and not just their capital cities.
1:2—2:13 The first cycle of judgment (1:2—2:11) and salvation/restoration (2:12–13; see Introduction: Outline).
1:2–7 A divine covenant lawsuit, including a theophany (appearance of God, vv. 3–4). The Divine Warrior comes to judge Samaria and Israel.
1:2 *Hear.* The Hebrew for this word introduces prophetic addresses also in 3:1 and 6:1, where it is translated "Listen" (see also 3:9; 6:2). *peoples ... earth.* All nations—an announcement that the day of the Lord is at hand (see Am 5:18 and note), when God will call the nations to account. In view of that day Micah speaks in his prophecy of the impending judgments on Israel and Judah. *holy temple.* Heaven (see v. 3), as in Ps 11:4; Jnh 2:7; Hab 2:20.
1:3 *The LORD is coming.* An OT expression describing the Lord's intervention in history (see Ps 18:9; 96:13 and note; 144:5; Isa 26:21; 31:4; 64:1–3). *high places of the earth.* May refer to mountains as well as to pagan shrines, since both are cited here (vv. 4–5). Cf. Am 4:13. See Dt 33:29.
1:4 *mountains melt ... like wax.* See Ps 18:6–7; 97:5; Na 1:5; Hab 3:3 and note.
1:5 *All this.* The Lord's coming in judgment (vv. 3–4). *Jacob's.* Jacob was an alternate name for Israel (see Ge 32:28 and note; 35:10). *Israel.* Here (and in v. 13) specifically the northern kingdom, but Micah uses the name also for the southern kingdom (see 3:1,8–9; 5:1,3; 6:2) or for the whole covenant people (see vv. 14–15; 2:12; 5:2). *high place.* Pagan center of idolatry (see note on 1Ki 3:2).
1:6–7 God is the speaker. This prophecy was fulfilled during Micah's lifetime when Assyria destroyed Samaria in 722–721 B.C. (see 2Ki 17:6 and note).
1:6 *into the valley.* Samaria was built on a hill (see 1Ki 16:24 and note).
1:7 *prostitutes.* Prostitution is often an OT symbol for idolatry or spiritual unfaithfulness (see Ex 34:15 and note; Jdg 2:17; Eze 23:29–30). *wages.* The wealth that Samaria had gained from her idolatry will be taken by the Assyrians and placed in their own temples to be used again in the worship of idols.
1:8–16 Micah laments not only the imminent destruction of Samaria but also the coming invasion of Judah, fulfilled by Sennacherib of Assyria in 701 B.C.
1:8 *this.* The coming destruction of Samaria. *barefoot.* A sign of mourning (see 2Sa 15:30 and note). It is possible that Micah actually walked stripped and barefoot through Jerusalem (cf. Isa 20:2). The concept of mourning frames this section (see v. 16). *naked.* Perhaps clothed only in a loincloth.
1:9 *wound.* The judgment about to overtake Samaria. *incurable.* See Isa 1:6; see also Isa 17:11; Jer 30:12 and notes. *gate.* The Assyrian destruction of the northern kingdom will spread like a malignant disease to the "gate of Jerusalem" (v. 12). The gate was where the process of town government was carried on (see Ge 19:1 and note; Ru 4:1–4 and note on 4:1).
1:10–15 Several plays on words are explained in the NIV text notes. The towns mentioned lie in the Shephelah, i.e., the foothills (500–1,500 feet high) between the Mediterranean coastal plain and the mountains of Judah.
1:10 *Tell it not in Gath.* These words introduce a funeral lament over Judah. Micah did not want the pagan people in Gath to gloat over the downfall of God's people (see 2Sa 1:20 and note). *roll in the dust.* As a sign of grief over the coming catastrophe. See Isa 47:1 and note.

11 Pass on in nakedness[f] and shame,
you who live in Shaphir.[a]
Those who live in Zaanan[b]
will not come out.
Beth Ezel is in mourning;
its protection is taken from you.
12 Those who live in Maroth[c] writhe in pain,
waiting for relief,[g]
because disaster[h] has come from the LORD,
even to the gate of Jerusalem.
13 You who live in Lachish,[d i]
harness the team to the chariot.
You were the beginning of sin
to the Daughter of Zion,[j]
for the transgressions of Israel
were found in you.
14 Therefore you will give parting gifts[k]
to Moresheth[l] Gath.
The town of Aczib[e m] will prove
deceptive[n]
to the kings of Israel.
15 I will bring a conqueror against you
who live in Mareshah.[f o]
He who is the glory of Israel
will come to Adullam.[p]
16 Shave[q] your heads in mourning
for the children in whom you
delight;
make yourselves as bald as the vulture,
for they will go from you into exile.[r]

Man's Plans and God's

2 Woe to those who plan iniquity,
to those who plot evil[s] on their
beds![t]
At morning's light they carry it out
because it is in their power to
do it.
2 They covet fields[u] and seize them,[v]
and houses, and take them.
They defraud[w] a man of his home,
a fellowman of his inheritance.[x]

3 Therefore, the LORD says:

"I am planning disaster[y] against this
people,
from which you cannot save
yourselves.
You will no longer walk proudly,[z]
for it will be a time of calamity.
4 In that day men will ridicule you;
they will taunt you with this
mournful song:
'We are utterly ruined;[a]
my people's possession is divided
up.[b]
He takes it from me!
He assigns our fields to traitors.' "
5 Therefore you will have no one in the
assembly of the LORD
to divide the land[c] by lot.[d]

False Prophets

6 "Do not prophesy," their prophets say.
"Do not prophesy about these
things;
disgrace[e] will not overtake us.[f]"

1:11 [f] Eze 23:29 1:12 [g] Jer 14:19 [h] Jer 40:2 1:13 [i] S Jos 10:3 [j] S Ps 9:14 1:14 [k] 2Ki 16:8 [l] S ver 1 [m] S Jos 15:44 [n] Jer 15:18 1:15 [o] Jos 15:44 [p] S Jos 12:15 1:16 [q] S Lev 13:40; S Job 1:20 [r] S Dt 4:27; S Am 5:27 2:1 [s] S Isa 29:20 [t] Ps 36:4 2:2 [u] Isa 5:8 [v] S Pr 30:14 [w] S Jer 22:17 [x] S 1Sa 8:14; S Isa 1:23; S Eze 46:18 2:3 [y] Jer 18:11; S Am 3:1-2 [z] Isa 2:12 2:4 [a] S Lev 26:31; S Jer 4:13 [b] S Jer 6:12 2:5 [c] Dt 32:13; Jos 18:4 [d] S Nu 34:13 2:6 [e] Ps 44:13; Jer 18:16; 19:8; 25:18; 29:18; Mic 6:16 [f] S Am 2:12

[a] 11 *Shaphir* means *pleasant.* [b] 11 *Zaanan* sounds like the Hebrew for *come out.* [c] 12 *Maroth* sounds like the Hebrew for *bitter.* [d] 13 *Lachish* sounds like the Hebrew for *team.* [e] 14 *Aczib* means *deception.* [f] 15 *Mareshah* sounds like the Hebrew for *conqueror.*

1:11 *nakedness and shame.* A reference to their future humiliation as prisoners (see Isa 20:4). *will not come out.* Because of the invasion, the people will not dare to go outside their houses.
1:12 *has come.* Micah foresees the future so clearly that to him it seems as though it has already come (see v. 3 and note).
1:13 *Lachish.* One of the largest towns in Judah (see Isa 36:2 and note). Later, Sennacherib was so proud of capturing it that he decorated his palace at Nineveh with a relief picturing his exploits. *harness the team.* In order to escape. *Daughter of Zion.* A personification of Jerusalem (see note on 2Ki 19:21). *Israel.* See note on v. 5.
1:14 *parting gifts.* The Hebrew for these words is translated "wedding gift" in 1Ki 9:16. Jerusalem must give up Moresheth Gath to Assyria, as a father gives a "wedding gift" to his daughter when she marries. *Aczib.* See NIV text note. The word "deceptive" is used in Jer 15:18 (see note there) to describe a brook that has dried up in summer. Like such a brook, the city of Aczib will cease to exist. *Israel.* See note on v. 5.
1:15 Micah again represents God as speaking, as in vv. 6–7. *He who is the glory of Israel.* Lit. "The glory of Israel"—either God himself, in which case the NIV would be correct in adding "He who is" (see 1Sa 15:29 and note), or, as seems more likely here, Israel's leaders (see Isa 5:13, "men of rank," lit. "glory"), in which case the translation should be simply "The glory of Israel," referring to such leaders. *will come to Adullam.* In judgment if referring to God; in flight if referring to Israel's leaders.
1:16 *Shave your heads in mourning.* See note on Jer 16:6. *exile.* Israel was taken into exile by the Assyrians in 722–721 B.C., and Judah by the Babylonians in 586.
2:1–5 A judgment woe is pronounced on wealthy and oppressive land-grabbers. Their slogan is "Might makes right."
2:1 *plot evil.* Cf. Pr 6:14,18; Zec 7:10. *power to do it.* The rich, oppressing classes continued to get rich at the expense of the poor because they controlled the power structures of their society.
2:2 *They covet.* In violation of the tenth commandment (see Ex 20:17 and note; Dt 5:21). *inheritance.* Land that was to be the permanent possession of a particular family. See notes on Lev 25:13 (Year of Jubilee); Nu 27:1–11; 36:1–12 (Zelophehad's daughters); 1Ki 21:3 (Naboth's vineyard).
2:3 *Therefore.* Because of the sins of Israel's influential classes, calamity will strike. *disaster.* The impending exile.
2:4 *We ... me.* The rich landowners, on whom God's judgment will fall. *He.* God. *traitors.* The treacherous Assyrians (see Isa 33:1 and note), who will capture the land.
2:5 *you.* The oppressing classes—the rich landowners. *no one ... to divide the land.* They will be cut off from all the promises of the covenant people.
2:6–11 A disputation: Micah and his God versus the wealthy wicked and their false prophets. The unit is framed by "prophesy" (vv. 6,11).
2:6 *their prophets.* The false prophets whose words were addressed to Micah.

[7]Should it be said, O house of Jacob:
"Is the Spirit of the LORD angry?
Does he do such things?"

"Do not my words do good[g]
to him whose ways are upright?[h]
[8]Lately my people have risen up
like an enemy.
You strip off the rich robe
from those who pass by without a care,
like men returning from battle.
[9]You drive the women of my people
from their pleasant homes.[i]
You take away my blessing
from their children forever.
[10]Get up, go away!
For this is not your resting place,[j]
because it is defiled,[k]
it is ruined, beyond all remedy.
[11]If a liar and deceiver[l] comes and says,
'I will prophesy for you plenty of wine and beer,'[m]
he would be just the prophet for this people![n]

Deliverance Promised

[12]"I will surely gather all of you,
O Jacob;
I will surely bring together the remnant[o] of Israel.
I will bring them together like sheep in a pen,
like a flock in its pasture;
the place will throng with people.[p]
[13]One who breaks open the way will go up before[q] them;
they will break through the gate[r]
and go out.
Their king will pass through before them,
the LORD at their head."

2:7 [g]S Ps 119:65 [h]Ps 15:2; 84:11 2:9 [i]Jer 10:20 2:10 [j]S Dt 12:9 [k]Lev 18:25-29; Ps 106:38-39; S La 4:15 2:11 [l]S 2Ch 36:16; Jer 5:31 [m]S Lev 10:9 [n]Isa 30:10 2:12 [o]Mic 4:7; 5:7; 7:18 [p]S Ne 1:9 2:13 [q]S Isa 52:12 [r]S Isa 60:11

Leaders and Prophets Rebuked

3 Then I said,

"Listen, you leaders[s] of Jacob,
you rulers of the house of Israel.
Should you not know justice,
[2] you who hate good and love evil;
who tear the skin from my people
and the flesh from their bones;[t]
[3]who eat my people's flesh,[u]
strip off their skin
and break their bones in pieces;[v]
who chop[w] them up like meat for the pan,
like flesh for the pot?[x]"

[4]Then they will cry out to the LORD,
but he will not answer them.[y]
At that time he will hide his face[z] from them
because of the evil they have done.[a]

[5]This is what the LORD says:

"As for the prophets
who lead my people astray,[b]
if one feeds them,
they proclaim 'peace';[c]
if he does not,
they prepare to wage war against him.
[6]Therefore night will come over you,
without visions,
and darkness, without divination.[d]
The sun will set for the prophets,[e]
and the day will go dark for them.[f]
[7]The seers will be ashamed[g]
and the diviners disgraced.[h]
They will all cover[i] their faces[j]
because there is no answer from God.[k]"
[8]But as for me, I am filled with power,
with the Spirit of the LORD,
and with justice and might,

3:1 [s]S Jer 5:5 3:2 [t]Ps 53:4; S Eze 22:27 3:3 [u]S Ps 14:4 [v]S Eze 34:4; Zep 3:3 [w]S Job 24:14 [x]S Eze 11:7; S 24:4-5 3:4 [y]S Dt 1:45; S 1Sa 8:18; S Isa 58:4; S Jer 11:11 [z]S Dt 31:17 [a]S Job 15:31; S Eze 8:18 3:5 [b]S Isa 3:12; S 9:16; S 53:6 [c]S Jer 4:10 3:6 [d]Isa 8:19-22; S Eze 12:24 [e]Isa 29:10 [f]S Eze 7:26; S Am 8:11 3:7 [g]S Jer 6:15; Mic 7:16 [h]S Isa 44:25 [i]S Est 6:12 [j]S Lev 13:45 [k]S Eze 20:3

2:7 Verses 6–7a are spoken by Micah; vv. 7b–13 are spoken by God.
2:10 *resting place.* A place that could be regarded as a people's secure possession, where they could settle undisturbed (see Dt 3:20 and note; Jos 21:43–44; 22:4).
2:11 Anyone who promised greater affluence would gain a hearing.
2:12–13 A salvation message of deliverance. Although Israel will be carried into exile, a remnant will return (see note on Isa 1:9).
2:12 *Jacob ... Israel.* Here perhaps the entire nation, north and south. Contrast 1:5 (see note there).
2:13 *One who breaks open ... Their king ... the LORD.* Rabbinic interpretation refers all three to the Messiah.
3:1—5:15 The second cycle of judgment (ch. 3) and salvation/restoration (chs. 4–5; see Introduction: Outline).
3:1–12 Verses 1–4 deal with the sins of the leaders of Israel, vv. 5–7 with the false prophets and vv. 9–12 with the leaders, priests and prophets.
3:1–4 Probably another divine covenant lawsuit (see 1:2–7), in which God charges the civil leaders with acting like cannibals.
3:1 *Listen.* See note on 1:2; see also 6:1. *Jacob ... Israel.* Both names refer to Judah here (see vv. 9–10; 1:5 and note).
3:2–3 *tear the skin ... like flesh for the pot.* A series of figures of speech describing the cruel way the leaders treat the people.
3:2 *hate good and love evil.* Contrast Am 5:15; Ro 12:9.
3:4 *they.* The leaders. *he will not answer.* See v. 7. *hide his face.* See Dt 31:17; Isa 1:15 and note. Disobedience leads to separation from God.
3:5–8 Another disputation (see note on 2:6–11): Micah and the false prophets of peace.
3:5 *proclaim 'peace.'* The false prophets predicted peace for Judah, while Micah predicted destruction and captivity (see v. 12; 4:10). See also Jer 6:13–14 and note on 6:14; 8:10–11.
3:6–7 *without visions ... no answer from God.* See Jer 18:18 and note; Am 8:11–12 and note on 8:11.
3:7 *seers.* An older term for "prophets" (see note on 1Sa 9:9). *cover their faces.* In shame and humiliation.
3:8 *filled ... with the Spirit.* The prophets were Spirit-filled messengers (see Isa 48:16; 61:1 and note). *to declare ... his sin.* One of the chief purposes of Micah was to declare to Israel its sin.

to declare to Jacob his transgression,
to Israel his sin.[l]
9 Hear this, you leaders of the house of Jacob,
you rulers of the house of Israel,
who despise justice
and distort all that is right;[m]
10 who build[n] Zion with bloodshed,[o]
and Jerusalem with wickedness.[p]
11 Her leaders judge for a bribe,[q]
her priests teach for a price,[r]
and her prophets tell fortunes for money.[s]
Yet they lean[t] upon the LORD and say,
"Is not the LORD among us?
No disaster will come upon us."[u]
12 Therefore because of you,
Zion will be plowed like a field,
Jerusalem will become a heap of rubble,[v]
the temple[w] hill a mound overgrown with thickets.[x]

The Mountain of the LORD

4:1-3pp — Isa 2:1-4

4 In the last days
the mountain[y] of the LORD's temple will be established
as chief among the mountains;
it will be raised above the hills,[z]
and peoples will stream to it.[a]
2 Many nations will come and say,
"Come, let us go up to the mountain of the LORD,[b]
to the house of the God of Jacob.[c]
He will teach us[d] his ways,[e]
so that we may walk in his paths."
The law[f] will go out from Zion,
the word of the LORD from Jerusalem.
3 He will judge between many peoples
and will settle disputes for strong nations far and wide.[g]
They will beat their swords into plowshares
and their spears into pruning hooks.[h]
Nation will not take up sword against nation,
nor will they train for war[i] anymore.[j]
4 Every man will sit under his own vine
and under his own fig tree,[k]
and no one will make them afraid,[l]
for the LORD Almighty has spoken.[m]
5 All the nations may walk
in the name of their gods;[n]
we will walk in the name of the LORD
our God for ever and ever.[o]

The LORD's Plan

6 "In that day," declares the LORD,
"I will gather the lame;[p]
I will assemble the exiles[q]
and those I have brought to grief.[r]
7 I will make the lame a remnant,[s]
those driven away a strong nation.[t]
The LORD will rule over them in Mount Zion[u]
from that day and forever.[v]
8 As for you, O watchtower of the flock,
O stronghold[a] of the Daughter of Zion,
the former dominion will be restored[w] to you;
kingship will come to the Daughter of Jerusalem.[x]"
9 Why do you now cry aloud—
have you no king?[y]
Has your counselor perished,
that pain seizes you like that of a woman in labor?[z]

[a] 8 Or *hill*

3:8 [l] S Isa 57:12; 61:2 **3:9** [m] Ps 58:1-2; S Isa 1:23 **3:10** [n] S Jer 22:13 [o] Isa 59:7; Mic 7:2; Na 3:1; Hab 2:12 [p] Jer 22:17; S Eze 22:27 **3:11** [q] S Ex 23:8; S Lev 19:15; Mal 2:9 [r] S Eze 13:19 [s] Isa 1:23; S 56:11; Jer 6:13; S La 4:13; S Hos 4:8, 18 [t] S Isa 10:20 [u] Jer 7:4; S Eze 34:2 **3:12** [v] S 2Ki 25:9; S Isa 6:11 [w] S Jer 52:13 [x] S Lev 26:31; S Jer 17:3; S 22:6; S La 5:18; S Eze 5:14 **4:1** [y] S Ps 48:1; Zec 8:3 [z] S Eze 17:22 [a] S Ps 22:27; 86:9; S Jer 3:17; S 31:12; S Da 2:35 **4:2** [b] S Jer 31:6; S Eze 20:40 [c] Zec 2:11; 14:16 [d] S Ps 119:171 [e] Ps 25:8-9; S Isa 54:13 [f] S Dt 18:18 **4:3** [g] S Isa 11:4 [h] Joel 3:10; Zec 9:10 [i] S Ps 46:9 [j] Zec 8:20-22 **4:4** [k] S 1Ki 4:25 [l] S Lev 26:6; S Eze 39:26 [m] S Isa 1:20 **4:5** [n] 2Ki 17:29; Ac 14:16 [o] Jos 24:14-15; Isa 26:8; Zec 10:12 **4:6** [p] S Jer 31:8 [q] S Ps 106:47 [r] S Eze 34:13, 16; S 37:21; Zep 3:19 **4:7** [s] S Joel 2:32; S Mic 2:12 [t] S Ge 12:2 [u] S Isa 2:2 [v] S Da 2:44; S 7:14; S Lk 1:33; Rev 11:15 **4:8** [w] S Isa 1:26 [x] Zec 9:9 **4:9** [y] Jer 8:19 [z] S Ge 3:16; Jer 30:6; 48:41

3:9 – 12 A message of indictment and of judgment on corrupt leaders, resulting in Zion's fall.
3:9 *Hear.* See note on 1:2. *Jacob ... Israel.* See v. 1 and note.
3:10 *who build Zion with bloodshed.* See Eze 7:23 and note.
3:11 *for a bribe.* See 1Sa 8:3 and note; Isa 1:23; 5:23.
3:12 The destruction of Jerusalem occurred in 586 B.C. This verse was quoted a century later in Jer 26:18 (see note there). Jer 26:19 indicates that Micah's preaching may have been instrumental in the reformation under King Hezekiah (see 2Ki 18:1 – 6; 2Ch 29 – 31). *Jerusalem ... heap of rubble.* Just like Samaria (see 1:6).
4:1 – 5 An eschatological ("In the last days," v. 1) salvation message: Zion's future exaltation. Although the temple will be destroyed (3:12), in the Zion of the future it will be restored in even grander style to become the worship and learning center for all nations.
4:1 – 3 See notes on Isa 2:2 – 4, a passage that is almost the same as these verses.
4:3 *plowshares.* See note on Isa 2:4.
4:4 *vine and ... fig tree.* A reference to the peaceful security of the kingdom of God. See 1Ki 4:25; 2Ki 18:31; Zec 3:10. *no one will make them afraid.* Quoted in Zep 3:13. Fear will be a thing of the past.
4:5 *walk in the name of the LORD.* Confess, love, obey and rely on the Lord. Cf. Zec 10:12.
4:6 – 8 Another eschatological ("In that day," v. 6) salvation message: restoration of a remnant and Zion.
4:6 *In that day.* The Messianic period (see v. 1; see also notes on Isa 2:11,17,20; Joel 1:15).
4:7 *remnant.* The people of God (see 2:12; see also note on Isa 1:9).
4:8 *watchtower of the flock.* Jerusalem, the capital city of David, the shepherd-king. *Daughter of Zion ... Daughter of Jerusalem.* See vv. 10,13; a personification of Jerusalem (see note on 2Ki 19:21). *former dominion.* The reign of the house of David will be restored under the Messiah.
4:9 – 13 In vv. 9 – 10 Micah foresees the collapse of the monarchy and the impending exile in 586 B.C. as well as the restoration beginning in 538. Verses 11 – 13 are a prophecy of judgment against the gloating enemies of Jerusalem.
4:9 – 10 A prophecy of both judgment and salvation. The next three units (vv. 9 – 10,11 – 13; 5:1 – 4) all begin

10 Writhe in agony, O Daughter of Zion,
like a woman in labor,
for now you must leave the city
to camp in the open field.
You will go to Babylon;[a]
there you will be rescued.
There the LORD will redeem[b] you
out of the hand of your enemies.

11 But now many nations
are gathered against you.
They say, "Let her be defiled,
let our eyes gloat[c] over Zion!"
12 But they do not know
the thoughts of the LORD;
they do not understand his plan,[d]
he who gathers them like sheaves to
the threshing floor.

13 "Rise and thresh,[e] O Daughter of
Zion,
for I will give you horns of iron;
I will give you hoofs of bronze
and you will break to pieces many
nations."[f]
You will devote their ill-gotten gains to
the LORD,[g]
their wealth to the Lord of all the
earth.

A Promised Ruler From Bethlehem

5 Marshal your troops, O city of
troops,[a]
for a siege is laid against us.
They will strike Israel's ruler
on the cheek[h] with a rod.

2 "But you, Bethlehem[i] Ephrathah,[j]
though you are small among the
clans[b] of Judah,
out of you will come for me
one who will be ruler[k] over Israel,
whose origins[c] are from of old,[l]
from ancient times.[d]"[m]

3 Therefore Israel will be abandoned[n]
until the time when she who is in
labor gives birth
and the rest of his brothers return
to join the Israelites.

4 He will stand and shepherd his flock[o]
in the strength of the LORD,
in the majesty of the name of the
LORD his God.
And they will live securely, for then his
greatness[p]
will reach to the ends of the earth.
5 And he will be their peace.[q]

Deliverance and Destruction

When the Assyrian invades[r] our land
and marches through our fortresses,
we will raise against him seven
shepherds,
even eight leaders of men.[s]
6 They will rule[e] the land of Assyria with
the sword,
the land of Nimrod[t] with drawn
sword.[f][u]
He will deliver us from the Assyrian
when he invades our land
and marches into our borders.[v]

7 The remnant[w] of Jacob will be
in the midst of many peoples
like dew[x] from the LORD,
like showers on the grass,[y]
which do not wait for man
or linger for mankind.
8 The remnant of Jacob will be among
the nations,
in the midst of many peoples,
like a lion among the beasts of the
forest,[z]
like a young lion among flocks of
sheep,

4:10 [a]S Dt 21:10; 2Ki 20:18; Isa 43:14 [b]S Isa 48:20 **4:11** [c]S La 2:16; S Ob 1:12; Mic 7:8 **4:12** [d]S Ge 50:20; S Isa 55:8; Ro 11:33-34 **4:13** [e]S Isa 21:10 [f]S Isa 45:1; S Da 2:44 [g]S Isa 23:18 **5:1** [h]La 3:30 **5:2** [i]S Jn 7:42 [j]S Ge 35:16; S 48:7 [k]S Nu 24:19; S 1Sa 13:14; S 2Sa 6:21; S 2Ch 7:18 [l]Ps 102:25 [m]Mt 2:6* **5:3** [n]S Jer 7:29 **5:4** [o]Isa 40:11; 49:9; S Eze 34:11-15, 23; Mic 7:14 [p]Isa 52:13; Lk 1:32 **5:5** [q]S Isa 9:6; S Lk 2:14; Col 1:19-20 [r]Isa 8:7 [s]Isa 10:24-27 **5:6** [t]Ge 10:8 [u]Zep 2:13 [v]Na 2:11-13 **5:7** [w]S Am 5:15; S Mic 2:12 [x]S Ps 133:3 [y]Isa 44:4 **5:8** [z]S Ge 49:9

[a] 1 Or *Strengthen your walls, O walled city* [b] 2 Or *rulers* [c] 2 Hebrew *goings out* [d] 2 Or *from days of eternity* [e] 6 Or *crush* [f] 6 Or *Nimrod in its gates*

with the Hebrew word for "now" and end with an assertion that the present or anticipated bad situation will be changed for the better (here: from distress to deliverance).

4:11–13 A prophecy of judgment and salvation: from siege to victory (see note on vv. 9–10).

5:1–4 A prophecy of judgment and salvation: from helpless ruler to ideal King (see note on 4:9–10), who will be born in Bethlehem and whose "greatness will reach to the ends of the earth" (v. 4).

5:1 Jerusalem will be besieged, and her kings will be seized and taken to Babylon (the last king, Zedekiah, was blinded; see 2Ki 25:7 and note).

5:2 Quoted in part in Mt 2:6. In contrast to the dire prediction of v. 1, Micah shifts to a positive note. *Ephrathah.* The region in which Bethlehem was located (see Ru 1:2 and note). *ruler.* Ultimately Christ, who will rule (see note on 4:8) for God the Father. *origins ... from of old.* His beginnings were much earlier than his human birth (see Jn 8:58). *from ancient times.* Within history (see 2Sa 7:12–16; Isa 9:6–7 and notes; Am 9:11), and even from eternity (see NIV text note).

5:3 *Israel will be abandoned.* Until the Messiah is born and begins his rule. *Israel.* See note on 1:5.

5:4 The Messiah will shepherd and rule in the "strength" and "majesty" of God the Father.

5:5–6 A salvation message of deliverance: The ideal King will "deliver" (v. 6) his people. One could analyze the structure of this entire unit as consisting of an *a-b-c-d/d-a-b-c* pattern (a "chiasmus"), with *d* representing two lines.

5:5 *their peace.* Jesus is "our peace" (Eph 2:14). In addition to freedom from war, the Hebrew word for "peace" also connotes prosperity in the OT. See notes on Isa 9:6 ("Prince of Peace"); Lk 2:14. *Assyrian.* Symbolic of all the enemies of God's people in every age. See Isa 11:11; Zec 10:10 and notes. *we.* The people of God. *seven ... eight.* A figurative way of saying "many" (see note on Job 5:19).

5:6 *land of Nimrod.* Assyria. See Ge 10:8–12. *He.* The ruler of v. 2. *he.* "The Assyrian."

5:7–9 A salvation message of deliverance: the remnant among the nations.

5:7–8 *remnant.* See note on 4:7.

5:7 *like dew from the LORD.* See Isa 26:19; Hos 14:5 and notes.

5:8 *lion.* Like the previous simile (v. 7) this pictures the inevitable progress of the people of God toward triumph over their enemies (v. 9). God's kingdom will be victorious.

which mauls and mangles[a] as it goes,
and no one can rescue.[b]
9 Your hand will be lifted up[c] in triumph
over your enemies,
and all your foes will be destroyed.

10 "In that day," declares the LORD,

"I will destroy your horses from among
you
and demolish your chariots.[d]
11 I will destroy the cities[e] of your land
and tear down all your strongholds.[f]
12 I will destroy your witchcraft
and you will no longer cast spells.[g]
13 I will destroy your carved images[h]
and your sacred stones from among
you;[i]
you will no longer bow down
to the work of your hands.[j]
14 I will uproot from among you your
Asherah poles[a][k]
and demolish your cities.
15 I will take vengeance[l] in anger and
wrath
upon the nations that have not
obeyed me."

The LORD's Case Against Israel

6 Listen to what the LORD says:

"Stand up, plead your case before the
mountains;[m]
let the hills hear what you have to
say.
2 Hear,[n] O mountains, the LORD's
accusation;[o]
listen, you everlasting foundations of
the earth.
For the LORD has a case[p] against his
people;
he is lodging a charge[q] against Israel.

3 "My people, what have I done to you?
How have I burdened[r] you?[s] Answer
me.
4 I brought you up out of Egypt[t]
and redeemed you from the land of
slavery.[u]
I sent Moses[v] to lead you,
also Aaron[w] and Miriam.[x]
5 My people, remember
what Balak[y] king of Moab counseled
and what Balaam son of Beor
answered.
Remember ⌞your journey⌟ from Shittim[z]
to Gilgal,[a]
that you may know the righteous
acts[b] of the LORD."

6 With what shall I come before[c] the
LORD
and bow down before the exalted
God?
Shall I come before him with burnt
offerings,
with calves a year old?[d]
7 Will the LORD be pleased with
thousands of rams,[e]
with ten thousand rivers of oil?[f]
Shall I offer my firstborn[g] for my
transgression,
the fruit of my body for the sin of
my soul?[h]
8 He has showed you, O man, what is
good.
And what does the LORD require of
you?
To act justly[i] and to love mercy
and to walk humbly[j] with your
God.[k]

5:8 [a]Mic 4:13; Zec 10:5 [b]S Ps 50:22; S Isa 5:29; S Hos 5:14 **5:9** [c]S Ps 10:12 **5:10** [d]Ex 15:4, 19; S Hos 14:3; Hag 2:22; Zec 9:10 **5:11** [e]S Dt 29:23; Isa 6:11 [f]S La 2:2; S Hos 10:14; Am 5:9 **5:12** [g]Dt 18:10-12; Isa 2:6; 8:19 **5:13** [h]Na 1:14 [i]Hos 10:2 [j]S Isa 2:18; S Eze 6:9; Zec 13:2 **5:14** [k]S Ex 34:13; S Jdg 3:7; S 2Ki 17:10 **5:15** [l]S Isa 65:12 **6:1** [m]S Ps 50:1; S Eze 6:2 **6:2** [n]Dt 32:1 [o]S Hos 12:2 [p]S Isa 3:13 [q]Ps 50:7; S Jer 2:9 **6:3** [r]Jer 2:5 [s]Jer 2:5 **6:4** [t]S Ex 3:10; S 6:6 [u]Dt 7:8 [v]S Ex 4:16 [w]S Nu 33:1; Ps 77:20 [x]S Ex 15:20 **6:5** [y]S Nu 22:2 [z]S Nu 25:1 [a]S Dt 11:30; Jos 5:9-10 [b]Jdg 5:11; 1Sa 12:7 **6:6** [c]S Ps 95:2 [d]Ps 40:6-8; 51:16-17 **6:7** [e]S Isa 1:11; S 40:16 [f]Ps 50:8-10 [g]S Lev 18:21; S 2Ki 3:27 [h]Hos 5:6; S Am 5:22 **6:8** [i]S Isa 1:17; S Jer 22:3 [j]S 2Ki 22:19; S Isa 57:15 [k]S Ge 5:22; Dt 10:12-13; 1Sa 15:22; Hos 6:6; Zec 7:9-10; Mt 9:13; 23:23; Mk 12:33; Lk 11:42

[a] *14* That is, symbols of the goddess Asherah

5:9 *Your.* The remnant's (vv. 7–8).
5:10–15 An eschatological ("In that day," v. 10) salvation message: obliteration of military power and pagan worship. In the Messianic era the people of God will not depend on weapons of war or pagan idols (cf. 4:3 and note on Isa 2:4). The successes of his people are always achieved by dependence on him.
5:10 *In that day.* See note on 4:6.
5:14 *Asherah poles.* See Ex 34:13 and note.
6:1—7:20 The third cycle of judgment (6:1—7:7) and salvation/restoration (7:8–20; see Introduction: Outline).
6:1–16 This chapter depicts a courtroom scene in which the Lord lodges a legal complaint against Israel.
6:1–8 A divine covenant lawsuit. In v. 1 the Lord instructs his prophet to present his (i.e., the Lord's; see v. 2) case; in v. 2 he summons the mountains to listen as witnesses to his accusation. Then the Lord speaks to his people in vv. 3–5, poignantly reminding them of his gracious acts in their behalf. In vv. 6–7 Israel speaks, and in v. 8 Micah responds directly to the nation, answering the questions of vv. 6–7.
6:1–2 *mountains ... foundations of the earth.* Inanimate objects were called on as third-party witnesses because of their enduring nature and because they were witnesses to his covenant (see Dt 32:1; Jos 24:27; Isa 1:2 and note).
6:1 *Listen.* See note on 1:2; see also 3:1. *your.* Rather, "my" (see note on vv. 1–8).
6:2 *Israel.* Primarily Judah here (see note on 1:5).
6:3,5 *My people.* Covenant language (see note on v. 8).
6:4 *brought you up out of Egypt.* See Ex 20:2 and note. *Moses ... Aaron and Miriam.* See Nu 12:1–2 and note on 12:2).
6:5 *Balak ... Balaam.* See Nu 22–24 and note on 22:8. *Shittim to Gilgal.* See Nu 25:1; Jos 2:1; 3:1—4:25; 4:19 and notes. *righteous acts of the LORD.* See 1Sa 12:7 and note.
6:6 The same thought is expressed in 1Sa 15:22; Ps 51:17; Isa 1:11–15; Hos 6:6 (see notes on these verses). Micah does not deny the desirability of sacrifices but shows that it does no good to offer them without obedience.
6:7 These rhetorical questions, charged with hyperbole, demand a resoundingly negative answer.
6:8 The most memorable statement in the OT defining a proper relationship to God (see Jer 22:16; Hos 6:6 and notes; cf. Jas 1:27). Micah here summarizes major themes found in the prophecies of his near contemporaries: Amos ("act justly"; cf. Am 5:24), Hosea ("love mercy"; cf. Hos 6:6) and Isaiah ("walk humbly with your God"; cf. Isa 29:19). Cf. also Mt 23:23. *man.* The use of the singular makes the accusation

Israel's Guilt and Punishment

[9]Listen! The LORD is calling to the city—
and to fear your name is wisdom—
"Heed the rod[l] and the One who
appointed it.[a]
[10]Am I still to forget, O wicked house,
your ill-gotten treasures
and the short ephah,[b] which is
accursed?[m]
[11]Shall I acquit a man with dishonest
scales,[n]
with a bag of false weights?[o]
[12]Her rich men are violent;[p]
her people are liars[q]
and their tongues speak deceitfully.[r]
[13]Therefore, I have begun to destroy[s]
you,
to ruin you because of your sins.
[14]You will eat but not be satisfied;[t]
your stomach will still be empty.[c]
You will store up but save nothing,[u]
because what you save I will give to
the sword.
[15]You will plant but not harvest;[v]
you will press olives but not use the
oil on yourselves,
you will crush grapes but not drink
the wine.[w]
[16]You have observed the statutes of
Omri[x]
and all the practices of Ahab's[y]
house,
and you have followed their
traditions.[z]
Therefore I will give you over to ruin[a]
and your people to derision;
you will bear the scorn[b] of the
nations.[d]"

Israel's Misery

7 What misery is mine!
I am like one who gathers summer fruit
at the gleaning of the vineyard;
there is no cluster of grapes to eat,
none of the early figs[c] that I crave.
[2]The godly have been swept from the
land;[d]
not one[e] upright man remains.
All men lie in wait[f] to shed blood;[g]
each hunts his brother[h] with a net.[i]
[3]Both hands are skilled in doing evil;[j]
the ruler demands gifts,
the judge accepts bribes,[k]
the powerful dictate what they
desire—
they all conspire together.
[4]The best of them is like a brier,[l]
the most upright worse than a
thorn[m] hedge.
The day of your watchmen has
come,
the day God visits you.
Now is the time of their confusion.[n]
[5]Do not trust a neighbor;
put no confidence in a friend.[o]
Even with her who lies in your
embrace
be careful of your words.
[6]For a son dishonors his father,
a daughter rises up against her
mother,[p]
a daughter-in-law against her mother-
in-law—
a man's enemies are the members of
his own household.[q]

[7]But as for me, I watch[r] in hope[s] for the
LORD,
I wait for God my Savior;
my God will hear[t] me.

Israel Will Rise

[8]Do not gloat over me,[u] my enemy!
Though I have fallen, I will rise.[v]
Though I sit in darkness,
the LORD will be my light.[w]

6:9 [l]S Ge 17:1; Isa 11:4 **6:10** [m]Eze 45:9-10; S Am 3:10; 8:4-6 **6:11** [n]S Lev 19:36 [o]S Dt 25:13 **6:12** [p]S Isa 1:23 [q]S Ps 116:11; Isa 3:8 [r]S Ps 35:20; S Jer 9:3 **6:13** [s]Isa 1:7; 6:11 **6:14** [t]S Isa 9:20; S Hos 4:10 [u]Isa 30:6 **6:15** [v]S Dt 28:38; Jer 12:13 [w]Job 24:11; S Am 5:11; Zep 1:13 **6:16** [x]S 1Ki 16:25 [y]1Ki 16:29-33 [z]Jer 7:24 [a]S Jer 25:9 [b]S Dt 28:37; S Jer 51:51; S Mic 2:6 **7:1** [c]S SS 2:13 **7:2** [d]S Ps 12:1 [e]S Jer 2:29; 8:6 [f]Ps 10:8 [g]S Pr 6:17; S Mic 3:10 [h]S Isa 3:5 [i]S Jer 5:26 **7:3** [j]S Pr 4:16 [k]S Ex 23:8; S Eze 22:12 **7:4** [l]S Nu 33:55; S Eze 2:6 [m]S 2Sa 23:6 [n]S Job 31:14; Isa 22:5; S Hos 9:7 **7:5** [o]Jer 9:4 **7:6** [p]S Eze 22:7 [q]Mt 10:35-36*; S Mk 13:12 **7:7** [r]S Isa 21:8 [s]Ps 130:5; Isa 25:9 [t]S Ps 4:3 **7:8** [u]S Ps 22:17; S Pr 24:17; S Mic 4:11 [v]Ps 20:8; 37:24; S Am 9:11 [w]S 2Sa 22:29; Isa 9:2

[a] *9* The meaning of the Hebrew for this line is uncertain. [b] *10* An ephah was a dry measure. [c] *14* The meaning of the Hebrew for this word is uncertain. [d] *16* Septuagint; Hebrew *scorn due my people*

personal, though Micah is speaking to all Israel (see also Dt 10:12–13). *act justly . . . love mercy.* The kind of obedience God expects from his covenant people. *humbly.* Or "carefully" or "wisely." *your God.* Covenant language in accordance with "My people" in vv. 3,5.
6:9–16 A divine covenant lawsuit containing further charges and the sentence (a life of futility, frustration, scorn and destruction, vv. 13–15). Its outline: (1) opening statement (v. 9), (2) a list of commercial and social sins (vv. 10–12), (3) announcement of divine punishment (vv. 13–15), (4) summary statement (v. 16).
6:9 *city.* Jerusalem.
6:10 *ephah.* About half a bushel.
6:11 See Lev 19:35; Pr 11:1 and notes; Hos 12:7; Am 8:5.
6:12 *Her.* Jerusalem's.
6:13 *Therefore.* See note on 2:3.
6:14–15 See Hag 1:6 and note.
6:16 *Omri . . . Ahab's.* 1Ki 16:25,30 says that they did more evil than all the kings who preceded them. *ruin.* Disobedience brings disaster.
7:1–20 The speakers in this chapter are Micah (vv. 1–7), Zion (vv. 8–10), Micah (vv. 11–13), either Micah or Zion (v. 14), God (v. 15), Micah (vv. 16–20). The chapter begins on a note of gloom but ends with a statement of hope.
7:1–7 Micah's lament over a decadent society.
7:1–2 Looking for the godly is like looking for summer fruit when the harvest has ended (see also Jer 5:1; 8:20 and notes).
7:3 Power often corrupts. *accepts bribes.* See 1Sa 8:3 and note; 12:3.
7:4 *day of your watchmen.* The day of judgment that the prophets warned about (see Eze 3:17–21 and note on 3:17). *visits you.* For punishment.
7:6 The family unit was disintegrating (cf. Mt 10:21,34–36).
7:7 Micah's complaint (vv. 1–6) is followed by his expression of confidence. Such a hopeful element is actually quite common in laments (see, e.g., Ps 55:16–17).
7:8–20 This completes the final salvation section in the three cycles of judgment and salvation. The unit is a prophetic liturgy made up of four subunits: (1) an expression

[9]Because I have sinned against him,
I will bear the LORD's wrath,[x]
until he pleads my case[y]
and establishes my right.
He will bring me out into the light;[z]
I will see his righteousness.[a]
[10]Then my enemy will see it
and will be covered with shame,[b]
she who said to me,
"Where is the LORD your God?"[c]
My eyes will see her downfall;[d]
even now she will be trampled[e]
underfoot
like mire in the streets.

[11]The day for building your walls[f] will
come,
the day for extending your
boundaries.
[12]In that day people will come to you
from Assyria[g] and the cities of Egypt,
even from Egypt to the Euphrates
and from sea to sea
and from mountain to mountain.[h]
[13]The earth will become desolate
because of its inhabitants,
as the result of their deeds.[i]

Prayer and Praise

[14]Shepherd[j] your people with your staff,[k]
the flock of your inheritance,
which lives by itself in a forest,
in fertile pasturelands.[a][l]
Let them feed in Bashan[m] and Gilead[n]
as in days long ago.[o]

[15]"As in the days when you came out of
Egypt,
I will show them my wonders.[p]"

[16]Nations will see and be ashamed,[q]
deprived of all their power.
They will lay their hands on their
mouths[r]
and their ears will become deaf.
[17]They will lick dust[s] like a snake,
like creatures that crawl on the
ground.
They will come trembling[t] out of their
dens;
they will turn in fear[u] to the LORD
our God
and will be afraid of you.
[18]Who is a God[v] like you,
who pardons sin[w] and forgives[x] the
transgression
of the remnant[y] of his inheritance?[z]
You do not stay angry[a] forever
but delight to show mercy.[b]
[19]You will again have compassion on us;
you will tread our sins underfoot
and hurl all our iniquities[c] into the
depths of the sea.[d]
[20]You will be true to Jacob,
and show mercy to Abraham,[e]
as you pledged on oath to our fathers[f]
in days long ago.[g]

7:9 [x]La 3:39-40 [y]S Ps 119:154 [z]S Ps 107:10 [a]Isa 46:13 **7:10** [b]S Ps 35:26 [c]S Ps 42:3 [d]S Isa 51:23 [e]S 2Sa 22:43; S Job 40:12; S Isa 5:5; Zec 10:5 **7:11** [f]Isa 54:11; S Am 9:11 **7:12** [g]S Isa 11:11 [h]Isa 19:23-25; 60:4 **7:13** [i]Isa 3:10-11; S Eze 12:19; S 33:28-29 **7:14** [j]S Ps 28:9; S Mic 5:4 [k]Ps 23:4 [l]Ps 95:7 [m]S Isa 33:9 [n]S SS 4:1; S Jer 50:19 [o]Eze 36:11 **7:15** [p]S Ex 3:20; Ps 78:12 **7:16** [q]Isa 26:11 [r]S Jdg 18:19 **7:17** [s]S Ge 3:14 [t]2Sa 22:46 [u]Isa 25:3; 59:19 **7:18** [v]S Ex 8:10; S 1Sa 2:2 [w]S Isa 43:25; S Jer 50:20; Zec 3:4 [x]S 2Ch 6:21; Ps 103:8-13 [y]S Joel 2:32; S Am 5:15; S Mic 2:12 [z]S Ex 34:9 [a]S Ps 103:9; S Isa 54:9 [b]S 2Ch 30:9; S Jer 31:20; 32:41; S Eze 18:23 **7:19** [c]S Isa 43:25 [d]S Jer 31:34 **7:20** [e]Gal 3:16 [f]Dt 7:8; Lk 1:72 [g]Ps 108:4

[a] *14* Or *in the middle of Carmel*

of trust (vv. 8–10), (2) a promise of restoration (vv. 11–13), (3) a prayer, the Lord's answer and the response (vv. 14–17), (4) a hymn of praise (vv. 18–20).

7:8 *me.* Zion. *my enemy.* Other nations (see v. 10). *Though I have fallen.* Micah foresees the destruction of Jerusalem in 586 B.C.

7:10 *Where is the LORD . . . ?* See notes on Ps 3:2; 10:11.

7:12 *In that day.* See Isa 2:11,17,20; 10:20,27; Joel 1:15 and notes. *people will come.* See 4:2.

7:14–17 It is possible that these verses constitute a prayer that God will show his wonders again as in the exodus, that the nations will see and be ashamed, and that they will turn to the Lord in fear.

7:14 *Shepherd.* Rule over (see 5:4; Ps 23:1; Jer 2:8; Eze 34:2 and notes). *inheritance.* The land and people of Israel (see v. 18; Ps 94:14; see also Ps 127:3; Jer 2:7 and notes). *Bashan and Gilead.* Fertile areas with rich pasturelands (see Ge 31:21; Ps 22:12; Eze 39:18; Am 4:1 and notes).

7:16 When the nations see the awesome display of God's power (v. 15), they will be amazed.

7:17 *lick dust like a snake.* A picture of defeat and death (see Ge 3:14 and note).

7:18–20 The conclusion to the whole book, not just to ch. 7.

7:18–19a See Ex 34:6–7a.

7:18 *Who is a God like you . . . ?* Perhaps a pun on Micah's name (see note on 1:1). See Ex 15:11 and note.

7:19 *tread . . . underfoot.* Or "subdue." When God takes away sin's guilt so that it does not condemn us (v. 18), he also takes away its power so that it does not rule over us (see Ps 19:13; cf. Ro 6:14). *iniquities into the depths of the sea.* See note on Isa 38:17; see also Jer 50:2.

7:20 *Jacob . . . Abraham.* God had sworn to Abraham (see Ge 13:16; 15:5; 22:17 and notes) and Jacob (Ge 28:14) that their descendants would be as numerous as the stars in the sky, the dust of the earth and the sand on the seashore, and he had promised Abraham that he would be the father of many nations (Ge 17:5; cf. Lk 1:54–55). All believers are ultimately included in this promise (Ro 4; Gal 3:6–29; Heb 11:12).

Nahum

INTRODUCTION

Author

The book contains the "vision of Nahum" (1:1), whose name means "comfort" and is related to the name Nehemiah, meaning "The LORD comforts" or "comfort of the LORD." (Nineveh's fall, which is Nahum's theme, would bring comfort to Judah.) Nothing is known about him except his hometown (Elkosh), and even its general location is uncertain.

Date

In 3:8–10 the author speaks of the fall of Thebes, which happened in 663 B.C., as already past. In all three chapters Nahum prophesied Nineveh's fall, which was fulfilled in 612. Nahum therefore uttered this prophecy between 663 and 612, perhaps near the end of this period since he represents the fall of Nineveh as imminent (2:1; 3:14,19). This would place him during the reign of Josiah and make him a contemporary of Zephaniah and the young Jeremiah.

A Quick Look

Author:
Nahum

Audience:
The people of Judah

Date:
Shortly before 612 B.C.

Theme:
Nahum prophesies the Lord's judgment on Nineveh for her oppression, cruelty, idolotry and wickedness.

Background

Assyria (represented by Nineveh, 1:1) had already destroyed Samaria (722–721 B.C.), resulting in the exile of the northern kingdom of Israel, and posed a present threat to Judah. The Assyrians were brutally cruel, their kings often being depicted as gloating over the gruesome punishments inflicted on conquered peoples. They conducted their wars with shocking ferocity, uprooted whole populations as state policy and deported them to other parts of their empire. The leaders of conquered cities were tortured and horribly mutilated before being executed (see note on 3:3). No wonder the dread of Assyria fell on all her neighbors!

About 700 B.C. King Sennacherib made Nineveh the capital of the Assyrian empire, and it remained the capital until it was destroyed in 612. Jonah had announced its destruction earlier (Jnh 3:4), but the people put on at least a show of repentance and the destruction was temporarily averted (see Jnh 3:10 and note). Not long after that, however, Nineveh reverted to its extreme wickedness, cruelty and pride. The brutality reached its peak under Ashurbanipal (669 – 627), the last great ruler of the Assyrian empire. After his death, Assyria's influence and power waned rapidly until 612, when Nineveh was overthrown (see notes on 1:14; 2:1). (Further historical information is given in notes throughout the book.)

Recipients

Some words are addressed to Judah (see 1:12 – 13,15), but most are addressed to Nineveh (see 1:11,14; 2:1,13; 3:5 – 17,19) or its king (3:18). The book, however, was meant for Israelite readers living in Judah.

Literary Style

The contents are primarily made up of judgment prophecies, with appropriate descriptions and vocabulary, expressing intense moods, sights and sounds. The language is poetic, with frequent use of metaphors and similes, vivid word pictures, repetition and many short — often staccato — phrases (see, e.g., 3:1 – 3). Rhetorical questions punctuate the flow of thought, which has a marked stress on moral indignation toward injustice.

God's righteous and just kingdom will ultimately triumph, for kingdoms built on wickedness and tyranny must eventually fall, as Assyria did.

Theological Themes

The focal point of the entire book is the Lord's judgment on Nineveh for her oppression, cruelty, idolatry and wickedness. The book ends with the destruction of the city.

According to Ro 11:22, God is not only kind but also stern. In Nahum, God is not only "slow to anger" (1:3) and "a refuge … for those who trust in him" (1:7), but also one who "will not leave the guilty unpunished" (1:3). God's righteous and just kingdom will ultimately triumph, for kingdoms built on wickedness and tyranny must eventually fall, as Assyria did.

In addition, Nahum declares the universal sovereignty of God. God is Lord of history and of all nations; as such, he controls their destinies.

Outline

- I. Title (1:1)
- II. Nineveh's Judge (1:2 – 15)
  - A. The Lord's Kindness and Sternness (1:2 – 8)
  - B. Nineveh's Overthrow and Judah's Joy (1:9 – 15)
- III. Nineveh's Judgment (ch. 2)
  - A. Nineveh Besieged (2:1 – 10)
  - B. Nineveh's Desolation Contrasted with Her Former Glory (2:11 – 13)
- IV. Nineveh's Total Destruction (ch. 3)
  - A. Nineveh's Sins (3:1 – 4)
  - B. Nineveh's Doom (3:5 – 19)

1 An oracle[a] concerning Nineveh.[b] The book of the vision[c] of Nahum the Elkoshite.

The LORD's Anger Against Nineveh

2 The LORD is a jealous[d] and avenging
God;
the LORD takes vengeance[e] and is
filled with wrath.
The LORD takes vengeance on his foes
and maintains his wrath against his
enemies.[f]
3 The LORD is slow to anger[g] and great in
power;
the LORD will not leave the guilty
unpunished.[h]
His way is in the whirlwind[i] and the
storm,[j]
and clouds[k] are the dust of his feet.
4 He rebukes[l] the sea and dries it up;[m]
he makes all the rivers run dry.
Bashan and Carmel[n] wither
and the blossoms of Lebanon fade.
5 The mountains quake[o] before him
and the hills melt away.[p]
The earth trembles[q] at his presence,
the world and all who live in it.[r]
6 Who can withstand[s] his indignation?
Who can endure[t] his fierce
anger?[u]
His wrath is poured out like fire;[v]
the rocks are shattered[w] before
him.
7 The LORD is good,[x]
a refuge in times of trouble.[y]
He cares for[z] those who trust in him,[a]
8 but with an overwhelming flood[b]
he will make an end of ⌞Nineveh⌟;
he will pursue his foes into
darkness.
9 Whatever they plot[c] against the LORD
he[a] will bring to an end;
trouble will not come a second time.
10 They will be entangled among thorns[d]
and drunk[e] from their wine;
they will be consumed like dry
stubble.[b][f]
11 From you, ⌞O Nineveh,⌟ has one come
forth
who plots evil against the LORD
and counsels wickedness.

12 This is what the LORD says:

"Although they have allies and are
numerous,
they will be cut off[g] and pass away.
Although I have afflicted you,
⌞O Judah,⌟
I will afflict you no more.[h]
13 Now I will break their yoke[i] from your
neck
and tear your shackles away."[j]

14 The LORD has given a command
concerning you, ⌞Nineveh⌟:
"You will have no descendants to
bear your name.[k]
I will destroy the carved images[l] and
cast idols
that are in the temple of your gods.

1:1 [a]S Isa 13:1; 19:1; Jer 23:33-34 [b]S Ge 10:11; S Jer 50:18; Na 2:8; 3:7 [c]S Isa 1:1
1:2 [d]S Ex 20:5 [e]S Ge 4:24; S Dt 32:41; Ps 94:1 [f]S Dt 7:10
1:3 [g]S Ne 9:17 [h]S Ex 34:7 [i]S Ex 14:21; S 2Ki 2:1 [j]S Ps 50:3 [k]S 2Sa 22:10; S Ps 104:3
1:4 [l]S 2Sa 22:16 [m]S Ex 14:22 [n]S Isa 33:9
1:5 [o]S Ex 19:18; S Job 9:6 [p]S Mic 1:4 [q]S Joel 2:10 [r]S Eze 38:20
1:6 [s]S Ps 130:3 [t]S Eze 22:14 [u]S Ps 76:7 [v]S Isa 5:24-25; S 42:25; S Jer 10:10 [w]1Ki 19:11
1:7 [x]S Jer 33:11 [y]S Jer 17:17 [z]S Ps 1:6 [a]S Ps 22:9
1:8 [b]S Isa 8:7; S Da 9:26
1:9 [c]S Hos 7:15
1:10 [d]S 2Sa 23:6 [e]S Isa 49:26 [f]S Isa 5:24; Mal 4:1
1:12 [g]S Isa 10:34 [h]Isa 54:6-8; S La 3:31-32
1:13 [i]S Isa 9:4 [j]S Job 12:18; S Ps 107:14
1:14 [k]S Isa 14:22 [l]Mic 5:13

[a] 9 Or *What do you foes plot against the LORD? / He*
[b] 10 The meaning of the Hebrew for this verse is uncertain.

1:1 The title of the book. *oracle.* See Isa 13:1; Hab 1:1 and notes. *Nineveh.* See Introduction: Background; see also notes on Jnh 1:2; 3:3. Here the capital city stands for the entire Assyrian empire. *vision.* See Pr 29:18; Isa 1:1; Ob 1 and notes. *Nahum the Elkoshite.* See Introduction: Author.
1:2–3 The covenant name Yahweh ("the LORD") is emphasized here (see notes on Ge 2:4; Ex 3:14–15; 6:6; Dt 28:58).
1:2 *jealous.* See note on Ex 20:5. *avenging … vengeance … vengeance.* God acts justly in judgment toward all who oppose him and his kingdom. The repetition is for emphasis. "It is mine to avenge; I will repay" (Dt 32:35; see note there), says the Lord. *wrath.* See notes on Ps 2:5; Ro 1:18.
1:3 *slow to anger … not leave the guilty unpunished.* See Ex 34:6–7 and note. *the guilty.* Such as Nineveh. *whirlwind … storm … clouds.* Awesome natural phenomena that display God's majesty and power. See notes on Job 38:1; Ps 18:7–15; 68:4; 77:16–19; 104:3–4.
1:4 *rebukes the sea and dries it up.* As at the crossing of the Red Sea (see Ex 14:1—15:12; see also Ps 18:15 and note). *makes all the rivers run dry.* As at the crossing of the Jordan (see Jos 3:1—4:24 and note). *Bashan … Carmel … Lebanon.* See notes on Ps 22:12; SS 7:5; Isa 2:13; 33:9; 35:2; Eze 39:18; Am 4:1. These three places were noted for their fertility, vineyards and trees, but at the Lord's word they wither.
1:5 *mountains … hills … earth … world.* Emblems of stability and permanence.
1:6 *Who can withstand … ? Who can endure … ?* Rhetorical questions. If mountains quake before the Lord (v. 5), what human beings can think that they are not vulnerable? Cf. Ro 2:3–5; Rev 6:17.
1:7 *those who trust in him.* Such as Judah.
1:8 *overwhelming flood.* Symbolic of an invading army (see Isa 8:7–8; 28:17–19). *end … darkness.* In 612 B.C. that end came for Nineveh, and the darkness enveloped her.
1:9 *they plot.* See note on v. 11. *trouble will not come a second time.* God never permitted the Assyrians a second victory over Judah; the first was the fall of Samaria (722–721 B.C.) and of the northern kingdom (Sennacherib's invasion in 701 was not a complete victory; see 2Ki 18:13—19:36).
1:10 *drunk from their wine.* See 3:11 and note; but perhaps the line here should read: "and drenched as with their wine,/yet they …" (see NIV text note).
1:11 *one … who plots evil.* Possibly the Assyrian king Ashurbanipal (669–627 B.C.), the last great Assyrian emperor, whose western expeditions succeeded in subduing Egypt and to whom King Manasseh had to submit as a vassal (see 2Ch 33:11–13 and notes on 33:11; Ezr 4:9–10). *plots evil against the LORD.* All such schemes end in futility and destruction (Ps 2:1–4).
1:12 *they.* The Assyrians. *I have afflicted you.* God had used Assyria as the rod of his anger against his covenant-breaking people in the days of Ahaz (Isa 10:5) and again in the time of Manasseh.
1:13 See Jer 27:2 and note. *I will break their yoke.* Judah was Assyria's vassal; that yoke would be broken.
1:14 *I will prepare your grave.* God used the Babylonians and

I will prepare your grave,[m]
for you are vile."

15 Look, there on the mountains,
the feet of one who brings good
news,[n]
who proclaims peace![o]
Celebrate your festivals,[p] O Judah,
and fulfill your vows.
No more will the wicked invade you;[q]
they will be completely destroyed.

Nineveh to Fall

2 An attacker[r] advances against you,
⌞Nineveh⌟.
Guard the fortress,
watch the road,
brace yourselves,
marshal all your strength!

2 The LORD will restore[s] the splendor[t] of
Jacob
like the splendor of Israel,
though destroyers have laid them
waste
and have ruined their vines.

3 The shields of his soldiers are red;
the warriors are clad in scarlet.[u]
The metal on the chariots flashes
on the day they are made ready;
the spears of pine are brandished.[a]
4 The chariots[v] storm through the
streets,
rushing back and forth through the
squares.
They look like flaming torches;
they dart about like lightning.

5 He summons his picked troops,
yet they stumble[w] on their way.
They dash to the city wall;
the protective shield is put in
place.
6 The river gates[x] are thrown open
and the palace collapses.
7 It is decreed[b] that ⌞the city⌟
be exiled and carried away.
Its slave girls moan[y] like doves
and beat upon their breasts.[z]
8 Nineveh is like a pool,
and its water is draining away.
"Stop! Stop!" they cry,
but no one turns back.
9 Plunder the silver!
Plunder the gold!
The supply is endless,
the wealth from all its treasures!
10 She is pillaged, plundered, stripped!
Hearts melt,[a] knees give way,
bodies tremble, every face grows
pale.[b]

11 Where now is the lions' den,[c]
the place where they fed their
young,
where the lion and lioness went,
and the cubs, with nothing to
fear?

1:14 [m] S Jer 28:8; Eze 32:22-23 **1:15** [n] Isa 40:9; Ro 10:15 [o] S Isa 52:7; Ac 10:36 [p] Lev 23:2-4 [q] S Isa 52:1 **2:1** [r] Jer 51:20 **2:2** [s] S Eze 37:23 [t] Isa 60:15 **2:3** [u] S Eze 23:14-15 **2:4** [v] S Jer 4:13; S Eze 23:24 **2:5** [w] Jer 46:12 **2:6** [x] Isa 45:1; Na 3:13 **2:7** [y] S Ge 8:8; S Isa 59:11 [z] Isa 32:12 **2:10** [a] S Jos 2:11; S 7:5 [b] S Isa 29:22 **2:11** [c] Isa 5:29

[a] 3 Hebrew; Septuagint and Syriac / *the horsemen rush to and fro* [b] 7 The meaning of the Hebrew for this word is uncertain.

Medes to dig Nineveh's grave in 612 B.C. For the fulfillment of this prophecy see Eze 32:22–23.

1:15 *mountains.* Of Judah. *feet of one who brings good news.* This verse sets forth a principle that is applicable in several contexts of deliverance. Here the reference is to the good news of deliverance from the Assyrian threat; in Isa 52:7, deliverance from Babylonian exile; in Ro 10:15, deliverance from sin through the gospel ("good news") of Christ. *Celebrate your festivals.* In the joy of your deliverance. *fulfill your vows.* Those you uttered in the time of distress (see notes on Ps 7:17; 50:14; Jnh 2:9). *No more will the wicked invade you.* The Assyrian invasion in the days of Manasseh was the last (see v. 12 and note). *wicked.* See note on Dt 13:13. *completely destroyed.* Fulfilled in 612 when Nineveh fell (see note on v. 14).

2:1 *attacker.* Refers to the alliance of the Medes under Cyaxares and the Babylonians under Nabopolassar. *Guard the fortress ... marshal all your strength!* Probably irony, touched with sarcasm. *road.* By which the enemies will come.

2:2 *restore the splendor of Jacob ... Israel.* The nation will be restored to its previous greatness.

2:3 *his soldiers.* Those of the attacker (v. 1), or perhaps those of Nineveh itself. *red.* Either (1) the color of the shields, or (2) a reference to blood on them, or (3) the result of the reflection of the sun shining on them. *brandished.* Ready to use.

2:4 *chariots ... rushing.* Refers to either (1) the Assyrian war chariots as the Assyrians take frantic but vain steps to defend themselves, or (2) the chariots of Nineveh's invaders.

2:5 *He.* Perhaps the king of Assyria, though Nabopolassar (see note on v. 1) is equally possible. *city wall.* A moat 150 feet wide had to be filled in before reaching Nineveh's wall, which was almost 8 miles long with 15 gates. Then battering rams were moved up. *protective shield.* A large defensive framework covered with hides to deflect stones and arrows.

2:6 *river gates.* Perhaps the dams on the Khoser River, which ran through the city to the Tigris River. They were either already in place, or quickly built, to back up the river water, then suddenly released so the flood would damage the walls. *palace collapses.* One ancient historian (the author of the *Babylonian Chronicles*) speaks of a flood that washed away some of the wall, making it easier for the invaders to enter the city.

2:7 *slave girls.* Even the lowest in the social order will not escape the judgment.

2:8 *like a pool ... water is draining away.* Some think that this refers to the Tigris and the smaller rivers encircling and running through parts of the city, and to a system of dams to make the city more impenetrable. Others take the language less literally as a reference to Nineveh's people fleeing, like water draining from a pool.

2:9 The cry of the invaders.

2:10 *pillaged, plundered, stripped.* The *Babylonian Chronicles* confirms the fact that a great quantity of plunder was carried off by the invaders. *Hearts melt.* The powerful, insolent Ninevites become helpless with fear.

2:11–13 Nahum ironically contrasts the devastated and desolate city of Nineveh with its former glory and power, expressed in figurative terms.

2:11 *lion and lioness.* See Isa 5:29; Jer 4:7. The lion is an appropriate image to apply to Assyria because of the rapacious ways of the Assyrian monarchs and because Nineveh contained numerous lion sculptures.

[12]The lion killed[d] enough for his cubs
and strangled the prey for his mate,
filling his lairs[e] with the kill
and his dens with the prey.[f]

[13]"I am against[g] you,"
declares the LORD Almighty.
"I will burn up your chariots in smoke,[h]
and the sword[i] will devour your young lions.
I will leave you no prey on the earth.
The voices of your messengers
will no longer be heard."[j]

Woe to Nineveh

3 Woe to the city of blood,[k]
full of lies,[l]
full of plunder,
never without victims!
[2]The crack of whips,
the clatter of wheels,
galloping horses
and jolting chariots!
[3]Charging cavalry,
flashing swords
and glittering spears!
Many casualties,
piles of dead,
bodies without number,
people stumbling over the corpses[m]—
[4]all because of the wanton lust of a harlot,
alluring, the mistress of sorceries,[n]
who enslaved nations by her prostitution[o]
and peoples by her witchcraft.

[5]"I am against[p] you," declares the LORD Almighty.
"I will lift your skirts[q] over your face.
I will show the nations your nakedness[r]
and the kingdoms your shame.
[6]I will pelt you with filth,[s]
I will treat you with contempt[t]
and make you a spectacle.[u]
[7]All who see you will flee[v] from you
and say,
'Nineveh[w] is in ruins[x]—who will mourn for her?'[y]
Where can I find anyone to comfort[z] you?"

[8]Are you better than[a] Thebes,[a b]
situated on the Nile,[c]
with water around her?
The river was her defense,
the waters her wall.
[9]Cush[b d] and Egypt were her boundless strength;
Put[e] and Libya[f] were among her allies.
[10]Yet she was taken captive[g]
and went into exile.
Her infants were dashed[h] to pieces
at the head of every street.
Lots[i] were cast for her nobles,
and all her great men were put in chains.[j]
[11]You too will become drunk;[k]
you will go into hiding[l]
and seek refuge from the enemy.
[12]All your fortresses are like fig trees
with their first ripe fruit;[m]
when they are shaken,
the figs[n] fall into the mouth of the eater.
[13]Look at your troops—
they are all women![o]

2:12 [d]S Jer 51:34 [e]S Jer 4:7 [f]S Isa 37:18 **2:13** [g]Isa 10:5-13; S Jer 21:13; Na 3:5 [h]Ps 46:9 [i]S 2Sa 2:26 [j]S Mic 5:6 **3:1** [k]S Eze 22:2; S Mic 3:10 [l]Ps 12:2 **3:3** [m]2Ki 19:35; Isa 34:3; Jer 47:3 **3:4** [n]S Isa 47:9 [o]S Isa 23:17; Eze 16:25-29 **3:5** [p]S Na 2:13 [q]S Isa 20:4; Jer 13:22 [r]S Isa 47:3 **3:6** [s]S Ex 29:14; S Job 9:31 [t]S 1Sa 2:30; S Jer 51:37 [u]Isa 14:16 **3:7** [v]S Isa 13:14; S 31:9 [w]S Na 1:1 [x]S Job 3:14 [y]S Jer 15:5 [z]S Isa 51:19 **3:8** [a]Am 6:2 [b]S Jer 46:25 [c]Isa 19:6-9 **3:9** [d]S Ge 10:6; S 2Ch 12:3 [e]S Eze 27:10 [f]Eze 30:5 **3:10** [g]S Isa 20:4 [h]S 2Ki 8:12; S Isa 13:16; Hos 13:16 [i]S Job 6:27; S Eze 24:6 [j]S Jer 40:1 **3:11** [k]S Isa 49:26 [l]S Isa 2:10 **3:12** [m]S SS 2:13 [n]S Isa 28:4 **3:13** [o]S Isa 19:16

[a] 8 Hebrew *No Amon* [b] 9 That is, the upper Nile region

2:12 *filling his lairs ... with the prey.* Nineveh was filled with the spoils of war from many conquered nations.
2:13 *I will burn up.* Nineveh's fall will be an act of divine judgment. Nineveh had been put on trial, found guilty and sentenced to destruction. *voices ... no longer be heard.* History has confirmed this prediction.
3:1–3 See note on Joel 2:3–11.
3:1 *city of blood.* Nineveh's bloody massacres of her conquered rivals were well known. *never without victims.* The Assyrians were noted for their ruthlessness, brutality and terrible atrocities. Many of their victims were beheaded, impaled or burned.
3:3 *piles of dead.* The Assyrian king Shalmaneser III boasted of erecting a pyramid of chopped-off heads in front of an enemy's city. Other Assyrian kings stacked corpses like cordwood by the gates of defeated cities. Nahum's description of the cruel Assyrians is apropos.
3:4 *harlot ... prostitution.* The lure of luxury and wealth brought multitudes to Nineveh, but like the allurements of a prostitute it did not yield life's true pleasures. *sorceries ... witchcraft.* Pagan practices (see Dt 18:10 and note on 18:9).
3:5 *lift your skirts over your face.* A common punishment of prostitutes and adulteresses (see notes on Isa 47:3; Jer 13:22; Hos 2:3,10).
3:7 *who ... ? Where ... ?* Rhetorical questions. Nineveh will receive no sympathy.
3:8 *Thebes.* See NIV text note. No Amon means "city of (the god) Amun." Thebes was the great capital of Upper (southern) Egypt. Its site is occupied today by the towns of Luxor and Karnak. It was destroyed by the Assyrians in 663 B.C.
3:9 *Put and Libya.* Perhaps better "Put (i.e., Libya)"; see notes on Ge 10:6; Eze 27:10; 30:5.
3:10 *Her infants were dashed to pieces.* See Ps 137:9; Isa 13:16; Hos 13:16 and notes. *her great men were put in chains.* Assyrian kings often did this; e.g., King Ashurbanipal gave this description of his treatment of a captured leader: "I ... put a dog chain on him and made him occupy a kennel at the eastern gate of Nineveh."
3:11 *will become drunk.* Probably from the cup of God's wrath (see Isa 51:17; Jer 25:15 and notes).
3:12 *like fig trees with their first ripe fruit.* A simile for the eagerness with which the victors gather the rich loot of Nineveh. *figs fall into the mouth of the eater.* Nineveh's fortresses will finally fall just as easily.
3:13 *your troops ... are all women!* They are weak and unable to stand against the invading armies. *their bars.* The bars of the city gates.

The gates[p] of your land
are wide open to your enemies;
fire has consumed their bars.[q]

14 Draw water for the siege,[r]
strengthen your defenses![s]
Work the clay,
tread the mortar,
repair the brickwork!
15 There the fire[t] will devour you;
the sword[u] will cut you down
and, like grasshoppers, consume
you.
Multiply like grasshoppers,
multiply like locusts![v]
16 You have increased the number of your
merchants
till they are more than the stars of
the sky,
but like locusts[w] they strip the land
and then fly away.

3:13 [p]S Na 2:6 [q]S Isa 45:2 **3:14** [r]S 2Ch 32:4 [s]Na 2:1 **3:15** [t]S Isa 27:1 [u]S 2Sa 2:26 [v]S Jer 51:14; S Joel 1:4 **3:16** [w]S Ex 10:13 **3:17** [x]Jer 51:27 **3:18** [y]Ps 76:5-6; S Jer 25:27 [z]Isa 56:10 [a]S 1Ki 22:17 **3:19** [b]S Jer 30:13; S Mic 1:9 [c]S Job 27:23; S La 2:15; Zep 2:15 [d]Isa 37:18

17 Your guards are like locusts,[x]
your officials like swarms of locusts
that settle in the walls on a cold
day—
but when the sun appears they fly away,
and no one knows where.

18 O king of Assyria, your shepherds[a]
slumber;[y]
your nobles lie down to rest.[z]
Your people are scattered[a] on the
mountains
with no one to gather them.
19 Nothing can heal your wound;[b]
your injury is fatal.
Everyone who hears the news about
you
claps his hands[c] at your fall,
for who has not felt
your endless cruelty?[d]

[a] *18* Or *rulers*

3:14 *Draw water.* A normal preparation for siege. *strengthen your defenses!* Irony, the point being that it will do no good (see 2:1 and note).

3:15 *There.* Inside your strong fortifications. *fire will devour you.* Confirmed by history and archaeology. Assyria's king died in the flames of his palace.

3:16 *your merchants ... are more than the stars.* Speaks of Assyria's vast trading and commercial enterprises.

3:17 *locusts.* Feared by the farmers of the ancient Near East, because they came in huge swarms and devoured everything in their path. Their activity provided an apt simile for the exploitative actions of Nineveh's officials during her destruction. *no one knows where.* Thus will Nineveh's officials disappear, without a trace. Interestingly, for centuries no one knew where Nineveh itself lay buried; in 1845 it was finally uncovered by archaeologists (see note on Zep 2:13).

3:18 *king.* The reigning king at the time of Nineveh's fall was Sin-Shar-Ishkun; so these words are prophetically addressed to him. *shepherds.* Leaders (see Jer 2:8 and note). *lie down to rest.* Die. *people are scattered.* The age-old scene of refugees fleeing a place of destruction is repeated at Nineveh.

3:19 *your injury is fatal.* Nineveh was so totally destroyed that it was never rebuilt, and within a few centuries it was covered with windblown sand. So that "great city" (Jnh 1:2; 3:2; 4:11; see note on Jnh 3:3) fell in 612 B.C., never to rise again—all in fulfillment of God's word through his prophet Nahum. *your endless cruelty.* But now you lie in endless ruin.

Habakkuk

I N T R O D U C T I O N

Author

Little is known about Habakkuk except that he was a contemporary of Jeremiah and a man of vigorous faith rooted deeply in the religious traditions of Israel. The account of his ministering to the needs of Daniel in the lions' den in the Apocryphal book *Bel and the Dragon* is legendary rather than historical.

Date

The prediction of the coming Babylonian invasion (1:6) indicates that Habakkuk lived in Judah toward the end of Josiah's reign (640 – 609 B.C.) or at the beginning of Jehoiakim's (609 – 598). The prophecy is generally dated a little before or after the battle of Carchemish (605), when Egyptian forces, which had earlier gone to the aid of the last Assyrian king, were routed by the Babylonians under Nabopolassar and Nebuchadnezzar and were pursued as far as the Egyptian border (Jer 46). Habakkuk, like Jeremiah, probably lived to see the initial fulfillment of his prophecy when Jerusalem was attacked by the Babylonians in 597.

Theological Message

Among the prophetic writings, Habakkuk is somewhat unique in that it includes no messages addressed to Israel. It contains, rather, a dialogue between the prophet and God (see Outline). (The book of Jonah, while narrative, presents an account of conflict between the Lord and one of his prophets.) In the first two chapters, Habakkuk argues with God over his ways that appear to him unfathomable, if not unjust. Having received replies, he responds with a beautiful confession of faith (ch. 3).

This account of wrestling with God is, however, not just a fragment from a private journal that has somehow entered the public domain. It was composed for Israel. No doubt it repre-

> **A Quick Look**
>
> **Author:**
> Habakkuk
>
> **Audience:**
> The people of Judah, struggling to comprehend the ways of God
>
> **Date:**
> About 605 B.C.
>
> **Theme:**
> The prophet Habakkuk argues with God over his ways that appear to him unfathomable, if not unjust; after receiving replies from God, Habakkuk responds with a beautiful confession of faith.

sented the voice of the godly in Judah, struggling to comprehend the ways of God. God's answers therefore spoke to all who shared Habakkuk's troubled doubts. And Habakkuk's confession became a public expression — as indicated by its liturgical notations (see note on 3:1).

Habakkuk expresses his perplexity that wickedness, strife and oppression are rampant in Judah but God seemingly does nothing. When told that the Lord was preparing to do something about it through the "ruthless" Babylonians (1:6), his perplexity only intensified: How could God, who is "too pure to look on evil" (1:13), appoint such a nation "to execute judgment" (1:12) on a people "more righteous than themselves" (1:13)?

Habakkuk expresses his perplexity that wickedness, strife and oppression are rampant in Judah but God seemingly does nothing.

God makes it clear, however, that eventually the corrupt destroyer will itself be destroyed. In the end, Habakkuk learns to rest in God's sovereign appointments and await his working in a spirit of worship. He learns to wait patiently in faith (2:3 – 4) for God's kingdom to be expressed universally (2:14). See note on 3:18 – 19.

Literary Features

The author wrote clearly and with great feeling, and he penned many memorable phrases (2:2,4,14,20; 3:2,17 – 19). The book was popular during the intertestamental period; a complete commentary on its first two chapters has been found among the Dead Sea Scrolls (see essay, pp. 1452 – 1453).

Outline

I. Title (1:1)
II. Habakkuk's First Complaint: Why does the evil in Judah go unpunished? (1:2 – 4)
III. God's Answer: The Babylonians will punish Judah (1:5 – 11)
IV. Habakkuk's Second Complaint: How can a just God use wicked Babylonia to punish a people more righteous than themselves? (1:12 — 2:1)
V. God's Answer: Babylonia also will be punished, and faith will be rewarded (2:2 – 20)
VI. Habakkuk's Prayer: After asking for manifestations of God's wrath and mercy (as he has seen in the past), he closes with a confession of trust and joy in God (ch. 3)

1 The oracle[a] that Habakkuk the prophet received.

Habakkuk's Complaint

2 How long,[b] O LORD, must I call for help,
but you do not listen?[c]
Or cry out to you, "Violence!"
but you do not save?[d]
3 Why do you make me look at injustice?
Why do you tolerate[e] wrong?[f]
Destruction and violence[g] are before me;
there is strife,[h] and conflict abounds.
4 Therefore the law[i] is paralyzed,
and justice never prevails.
The wicked hem in the righteous,
so that justice[j] is perverted.[k]

The LORD's Answer

5 "Look at the nations and watch —
and be utterly amazed.[l]
For I am going to do something in your days
that you would not believe,
even if you were told.[m]
6 I am raising up the Babylonians,[a][n]
that ruthless and impetuous people,
who sweep across the whole earth[o]
to seize dwelling places not their own.[p]
7 They are a feared and dreaded people;[q]
they are a law to themselves
and promote their own honor.
8 Their horses are swifter[r] than leopards,
fiercer than wolves[s] at dusk.
Their cavalry gallops headlong;
their horsemen come from afar.
They fly like a vulture swooping to devour;
9 they all come bent on violence.
Their hordes[b] advance like a desert wind
and gather prisoners[t] like sand.
10 They deride kings
and scoff at rulers.[u]
They laugh at all fortified cities;
they build earthen ramps[v] and capture them.
11 Then they sweep past like the wind[w]
and go on —
guilty men, whose own strength is their god."[x]

Habakkuk's Second Complaint

12 O LORD, are you not from everlasting?[y]
My God, my Holy One,[z] we will not die.[a]
O LORD, you have appointed[b] them to execute judgment;
O Rock,[c] you have ordained them to punish.
13 Your eyes are too pure[d] to look on evil;
you cannot tolerate wrong.[e]
Why then do you tolerate[f] the treacherous?[g]

[a] 6 Or *Chaldeans* [b] 9 The meaning of the Hebrew for this word is uncertain.

1:1 [a] S Na 1:1
1:2 [b] S Ps 6:3 [c] Ps 13:1-2; 22:1-2 [d] Jer 14:9; Zec 1:12
1:3 [e] ver 13 [f] S Job 9:23 [g] Jer 20:8 [h] S Ps 55:9
1:4 [i] Ps 119:126 [j] S Isa 29:21 [k] S Job 19:7; S Isa 1:23; 5:20; S Eze 9:9
1:5 [l] S Isa 29:9 [m] Ac 13:41*
1:6 [n] S Dt 28:49; S 2Ki 24:2 [o] Rev 20:9 [p] S Jer 13:20; S 21:7
1:7 [q] Isa 18:7; Jer 39:5-9
1:8 [r] S Jer 4:13 [s] S Ge 49:27
1:9 [t] Hab 2:5
1:10 [u] S 2Ch 36:6 [v] S Jer 33:4
1:11 [w] Jer 4:11-12 [x] S Da 4:30
1:12 [y] S Ge 21:33 [z] Isa 31:1; 37:23 [a] Ps 118:17 [b] Isa 10:6 [c] S Ge 49:24; S Ex 33:22
1:13 [d] Ps 18:26 [e] S La 3:34-36 [f] ver 3 [g] S Ps 25:3

1:1 *oracle.* Such as the two found here (vv. 5 – 11; 2:2 – 20). Oracles were frequently received in visions. The Hebrew word for "oracle" (possibly meaning "burden," but perhaps only "pronouncement") often refers to revelations containing warnings of impending doom (see Isa 13:1 and note; 15:1; 19:1; 22:1), but in Zec 9:1; 12:1; Mal 1:1 it refers to messages that also contain hope. *Habakkuk.* The name is probably Babylonian and refers to a kind of garden plant. *prophet.* Habakkuk is called a prophet also in 3:1, tying ch. 3 closely to chs. 1 – 2. See notes on Ex 3:4; 7:1 – 2; 1Ki 22:19; Jnh 3:2; Zec 1:1.

1:2 — 2:20 A dialogue between the prophet and God. The basic themes are age-old: Why does evil seem to go unpunished? Why does God not respond to prayer?

1:2 *How long . . . ?* See Ps 6:3 and note; 13:1 – 2; 22:1 – 2. *Violence!* At this time Judah was probably under King Jehoiakim, who was ambitious, cruel and corrupt. Habakkuk describes the social corruption and spiritual apostasy of Judah in the late seventh century B.C.

1:3 *you tolerate.* See v. 13. The prophet was amazed that God seemed to condone cruelty and violence. *Destruction and violence are before me.* Jeremiah complains to the Lord in a similar vein (Jer 20:8).

1:4 *law is paralyzed . . . justice is perverted.* Because wealthy landowners controlled the courts through bribery (see Mic 3:11; 7:3).

1:5 Paul concludes his sermon in Pisidian Antioch by quoting these words (Ac 13:41). *your . . . you . . . you.* Judah as a whole is addressed (the pronouns are plural). *would not believe.* To the people of Judah it was incredible that God would give them over to the arrogant Babylonians.

1:6 *I am raising up the Babylonians.* See Isa 10:5 – 6 and note on 10:5. The apostate nation of Judah is to be punished by an invasion of the Babylonians, a powerful people who regained their independence from Assyria in 626 B.C., destroyed Assyrian power completely in 612 – 605, and flourished until 539. In this context, the Chaldeans (see NIV text note) are synonymous with the newly resurgent Babylonians. *seize dwelling places.* See 2:6 – 8.

1:7 *promote their own honor.* A mark of arrogance.

1:8 The speed with which Babylonia conquered her enemies had become proverbial. *vulture.* The Hebrew for "vulture" may also refer to an eagle (see Dt 28:49 – 50 and note on 28:49).

1:9 *violence.* The rapacious cruelty of the Babylonians was more than a match for that of the people of Judah (see v. 2 and note; see also v. 3). *gather prisoners like sand.* Like their Assyrian predecessors, the Babylonians deported conquered peoples as a matter of deliberate national policy (see 2:5).

1:10 *build earthen ramps.* A siege method.

1:11 *whose own strength is their god.* The Babylonians were so proud and confident of their military might that it had virtually become their god (see v. 16).

1:12 Habakkuk cannot see the justice in Judah's being punished by an even more wicked nation, and he thinks that the Babylonians surely would not be allowed to conquer Judah completely. *from everlasting.* See Ps 90:2. *LORD, you have appointed them.* The prophet recognizes Babylonia as God's agent of judgment (cf. Isa 7:18 – 20; 44:28 — 45:1). *Rock.* See 1Sa 2:2 and note.

1:13 A classic statement of the problem of evil within the context of Israel's faith: Why does evil appear to flourish unchecked by a just and holy God? *you tolerate.* See v. 3 and note. *treacherous . . . wicked.* The Babylonians. *those more righteous.* Judah.

Why are you silent while the wicked
swallow up those more righteous
than themselves?[h]
14 You have made men like fish in the
sea,
like sea creatures that have no ruler.
15 The wicked[i] foe pulls all of them up
with hooks,[j]
he catches them in his net,[k]
he gathers them up in his dragnet;
and so he rejoices and is glad.
16 Therefore he sacrifices to his net
and burns incense[l] to his dragnet,
for by his net he lives in luxury
and enjoys the choicest food.
17 Is he to keep on emptying his net,
destroying nations without mercy?[m]

2 I will stand at my watch[n]
and station myself on the ramparts;[o]
I will look to see what he will say[p] to
me,
and what answer I am to give to this
complaint.[a][q]

The LORD's Answer

2 Then the LORD replied:

"Write[r] down the revelation
and make it plain on tablets
so that a herald[b] may run with it.
3 For the revelation awaits an appointed
time;[s]
it speaks of the end[t]
and will not prove false.
Though it linger, wait[u] for it;
it[c] will certainly come and will not
delay.[v]

4 "See, he is puffed up;
his desires are not upright—
but the righteous[w] will live by his
faith[d][x]—
5 indeed, wine[y] betrays him;
he is arrogant[z] and never at rest.
Because he is as greedy as the grave[e]
and like death is never satisfied,[a]
he gathers to himself all the nations
and takes captive[b] all the peoples.

6 "Will not all of them taunt[c] him with
ridicule and scorn, saying,

" 'Woe to him who piles up stolen
goods
and makes himself wealthy by
extortion![d]
How long must this go on?'
7 Will not your debtors[f] suddenly arise?
Will they not wake up and make you
tremble?
Then you will become their victim.[e]
8 Because you have plundered many
nations,
the peoples who are left will plunder
you.[f]
For you have shed man's blood;[g]
you have destroyed lands and cities
and everyone in them.[h]
9 "Woe to him who builds[i] his realm by
unjust gain[j]
to set his nest[k] on high,
to escape the clutches of ruin!

1:13 [h] S Job 21:7
1:15 [i] Jer 5:26
[j] S Isa 19:8
[k] S Job 18:8; Jer 16:16
1:16 [l] Jer 44:8
1:17 [m] S Isa 14:6; 19:8
2:1 [n] S Isa 21:8
[o] S Ps 48:13
[p] Ps 85:8
[q] S Ps 5:3; S Eze 3:17
2:2 [r] S Isa 30:8; S Jer 36:2; S Eze 24:2; S Ro 4:24; Rev 1:19
2:3 [s] Da 11:27
[t] Da 8:17
[u] S Ps 27:14
[v] S Eze 12:25
2:4 [w] S Eze 18:9
[x] Ro 1:17*; Gal 3:11*; Heb 10:37-38*
2:5 [y] S Pr 20:1
[z] S Isa 2:11
[a] S Pr 27:20; S 30:15-16
[b] Hab 1:9
2:6 [c] S Isa 14:4
[d] Am 2:8
2:7 [e] S Pr 29:1
2:8 [f] Isa 33:1; Jer 50:17-18; S Ob 1:15; Zec 2:8-9 [g] ver 17
[h] S Eze 39:10
2:9 [i] S Jer 22:13
[j] S Jer 51:13
[k] S Job 39:27; S Isa 10:14

[a] 1 Or *and what to answer when I am rebuked*
[b] 2 Or *so that whoever reads it*
[c] 3 Or *Though he linger, wait for him; / he*
[d] 4 Or *faithfulness*
[e] 5 Hebrew *Sheol*
[f] 7 Or *creditors*

1:15 *hooks.* See note on Am 4:2. *catches them in his net.* Babylonia's victims are as powerless as fish swimming into a net. Mesopotamian reliefs symbolically portray conquerors capturing their enemies in fishnets.
1:16 See note on v. 11.
2:1 See Eze 3:17 and note. *I will stand at my watch.* The figure of a guard looking out from a tower and expecting a response to his challenge. Any rebuke (see NIV text note) would be for questioning God's justice. *ramparts.* The walls of Jerusalem. *he.* God.
2:2–3 *revelation.* See 1Ch 17:15; Pr 29:18 and note. The Hebrew for this word refers specifically to a prophet's vision (see, e.g., Isa 1:1 and note).
2:2 *Write down.* See Isa 30:8; Jer 36:2 and note. *so that a herald may run with it.* Lit. "so that he who reads it may run," i.e., so that a messenger may run to deliver the message and read it to those to whom he has been sent.
2:3 *the end.* Of the Babylonians, though some refer it to the end times, when God's redemptive purposes would be completed. *wait for it.* The following message deals with the fall of Babylon in 539 B.C., about 66 years after Habakkuk's prophecy. The Lord tells Habakkuk (and Judah) that fulfillment of the prophecy may "linger," but that he and the people are to expect it (see 3:16).
2:4 *he.* Collective for the Babylonians, but with special reference to their king. *but.* In contrast to the Babylonians, whose "desires are not upright." *the righteous will live by his faith.* See NIV text note; Eze 18:9; see also Isa 26, especially vv. 1–6. In light of God's revelation about how (and when) he is working, his people are to wait patiently and live by faith—trusting in their sovereign God. The clause is quoted frequently in the NT to support the teaching that people are saved by grace through faith (Ro 1:17; Gal 3:11; cf. Eph 2:8 and note) and should live by faith (Heb 10:38–39; 11:7). Together with Ge 15:6 (see note there; see also Ro 4:3,9,22–23; Gal 3:6; Jas 2:23 and note on 2:21), it became the rallying cry of the Protestant Reformation in the 16th century. The same principle that was applicable in the realm of national deliverance is applicable in the area of spiritual deliverance (salvation).
2:5 *greedy as the grave.* "The grave ... never says, 'Enough!'" (Pr 30:16; see note there; see also notes on Ps 49:14; Isa 5:14).
2:6–20 This taunt, an extended commentary on v. 4a (see note on 3:1), falls into two halves of ten (Hebrew) lines each (vv. 6–14 and vv. 15–20), each half concluding with a significant theological statement (vv. 14,20). Together these two statements set the five "woes" pronounced against Babylon (vv. 6,9,12,15,19; cf. Isa 5:8–23; Mt 23:13–32; Lk 6:24–26; Rev 9:12; 11:14) in a larger frame of reference. In addition, the first and fourth "woes" echo each other (see vv. 8,17).
2:6 *all of them taunt him.* The threatened victims of the Babylonian onslaught, especially Judah, will taunt ruthless Babylon (see Isa 14:4). *Woe.* The Babylonians' greed for conquest is condemned.
2:8 *you have shed man's blood.* See v. 17. Therefore Babylon's blood would be shed (see Ge 9:6 and note).
2:9 *Woe.* The Babylonians' pride in building is condemned (see v. 12; cf. Jer 22:13). *nest on high.* Like the eagle building an inaccessible nest, the Babylonians thought

10 You have plotted the ruin[l] of many
peoples,
shaming[m] your own house and
forfeiting your life.
11 The stones[n] of the wall will cry out,
and the beams of the woodwork will
echo it.

12 "Woe to him who builds a city with
bloodshed[o]
and establishes a town by crime!
13 Has not the LORD Almighty determined
that the people's labor is only fuel
for the fire,[p]
that the nations exhaust themselves
for nothing?[q]
14 For the earth will be filled with the
knowledge of the glory[r] of the
LORD,
as the waters cover the sea.[s]

15 "Woe to him who gives drink[t] to his
neighbors,
pouring it from the wineskin till they
are drunk,
so that he can gaze on their naked
bodies.
16 You will be filled with shame[u] instead
of glory.[v]
Now it is your turn! Drink[w] and be
exposed[a]![x]
The cup[y] from the LORD's right hand is
coming around to you,
and disgrace will cover your glory.
17 The violence[z] you have done to
Lebanon will overwhelm you,
and your destruction of animals will
terrify you.[a]
For you have shed man's blood;[b]
you have destroyed lands and cities
and everyone in them.

18 "Of what value[c] is an idol,[d] since a
man has carved it?
Or an image[e] that teaches lies?
For he who makes it trusts in his own
creation;
he makes idols that cannot speak.[f]
19 Woe to him who says to wood, 'Come
to life!'
Or to lifeless stone, 'Wake up!'[g]
Can it give guidance?
It is covered with gold and silver;[h]
there is no breath in it.[i]
20 But the LORD is in his holy temple;[j]
let all the earth be silent[k] before
him."

2:10 [l] Jer 26:19 [m] ver 16; S Na 3:6 **2:11** [n] S Jos 24:27; Zec 5:4; Lk 19:40 **2:12** [o] S Eze 22:2; S Mic 3:10 **2:13** [p] Isa 50:11 [q] S Isa 47:13 **2:14** [r] S Ex 16:7; S Nu 14:21 [s] S Isa 11:9 **2:15** [t] S Pr 23:20 **2:16** [u] S ver 10 [v] S Eze 23:32-34; Hos 4:7 [w] S Lev 10:9 [x] S La 4:21 [y] S Ps 16:5; S Isa 51:22 **2:17** [z] S Jer 51:35 [a] S Jer 50:15 [b] ver 8 **2:18** [c] S 1Sa 12:21 [d] S Jdg 10:14; S Isa 40:19; S Jer 5:21; S 14:22 [e] S Lev 26:1 [f] Ps 115:4-5; Jer 10:14; 1Co 12:2 **2:19** [g] 1Ki 18:27 [h] S Jer 10:4 [i] S Da 5:4,23; S Hos 4:12 **2:20** [j] S Ps 11:4 [k] S Isa 41:1 **3:1** [l] Ps 7 Title **3:2** [m] S Job 26:14; Ps 44:1 [n] S Ps 119:120 [o] S Ps 90:16 [p] Ps 85:6 [q] Isa 54:8

Habakkuk's Prayer

3 A prayer of Habakkuk the prophet. On
shigionoth.[b][l]

2 LORD, I have heard[m] of your fame;
I stand in awe[n] of your deeds,
O LORD.[o]
Renew[p] them in our day,
in our time make them known;
in wrath remember mercy.[q]

[a] 16 Masoretic Text; Dead Sea Scrolls, Aquila, Vulgate and Syriac (see also Septuagint) *and stagger*
[b] 1 Probably a literary or musical term

their empire to be unconquerable (see Isa 14:4,13–15; cf. Ob 3–4).
2:11 *The stones ... will cry out, and the beams.* The stones and beams in Babylonian houses were purchased with plunder, and thus testified against the occupants. Cf. Lk 19:40.
2:12 *Woe.* Babylonian injustice is condemned. Cf. Mic 3:10.
2:13 *fuel for the fire.* The cities built by the labor of the Babylonians (v. 12) will be burned (see Jer 51:58 and note).
2:14 Habakkuk quotes Isa 11:9 and expands its language. The Lord's future destruction of proud Babylonia and all her worldly glory will cause his greater glory to be known throughout the world (cf. Ex 14:4,17–18; Rev 17:1—19:4).
2:15 Cf. Ge 9:20–22. *Woe.* Babylonian violence is condemned. Her rapacious treatment of her neighbors, which stripped them of all their wealth (cf. what she later did to Jerusalem, 2Ki 25:8–21), is compared to one who makes his neighbors drunk so he can take lewd pleasure from their nakedness.
2:16 *be filled with shame ... be exposed.* The Lord will do to Babylonia what she has done to others. *cup from the LORD's right hand.* A symbol of divine retribution (see Ps 16:5 and note; Isa 51:17,21–22; Jer 25:15–17; La 4:21; Rev 14:10 and note; 16:19).
2:17 *violence you have done to Lebanon.* The Babylonians apparently had ravaged the cedar forests of Lebanon to adorn their temples and palaces (see Isa 14:8 and note). *destruction of animals.* Assyrian inscriptions record hunting expeditions in the Lebanon range, and such sport may have been indulged in by the invading Babylonians as well. Babylonian violence was destructive of all forms of life, not only of lands and cities. *you have shed man's blood.* See v. 8 and note.
2:18 *idols.* The Hebrew for this word means "godlets" or "nonentities" (cf. Isa 41:29; 44:9; Jer 10:15 and the condemnation of idolatry in Ex 20:4–5; see Ps 115:4–7 and note).
2:19 *Woe.* Babylonian idolatry is condemned. *Wake up!* Cf. Elijah's taunt of Baal's prophets on Mount Carmel (1Ki 18:27).
2:20 *But the LORD is in his holy temple.* From his heavenly temple (cf. Jnh 2:7) he judges all people in accordance with his righteousness (see Ps 11:4–7 and note; Mic 1:2). *be silent before him.* The stone and wooden idols of the nations (v. 19) are to be silent in unprotecting submission to the awesome divine judgment (see Zep 1:7; Zec 2:13; cf. Am 6:10; 8:3 and note).
3:1 *prayer.* In the strict sense, petition is found in this prayer only in v. 2 but, as with many of the psalms, it is set in a larger context of recollection (vv. 3–15) and expression of confidence and trust (vv. 16–19). In fact, Habakkuk's prayer, an extended commentary on 2:4b (see note on 2:6–20), appears to have been used as a psalm; note the psalm-like heading (v. 1) and the musical and/or literary notations (vv. 1,3,9,13,19). *prophet.* See 1:1 and note. *shigionoth.* See Ps 7 title and note.
3:2 *heard of your fame.* See Ps 44:1; 78:3. In vv. 3–15 Habakkuk recites a poetic celebration of God's mighty saving acts of old—perhaps one he had heard at the temple (see v. 16).

[3]God came from Teman,[r]
the Holy One[s] from Mount Paran.[t]
Selah[a]
His glory covered the heavens[u]
and his praise filled the earth.[v]
[4]His splendor was like the sunrise;[w]
rays flashed from his hand,
where his power[x] was hidden.
[5]Plague[y] went before him;
pestilence followed his steps.
[6]He stood, and shook the earth;
he looked, and made the nations
tremble.
The ancient mountains crumbled[z]
and the age-old hills[a] collapsed.[b]
His ways are eternal.[c]
[7]I saw the tents of Cushan in
distress,
the dwellings of Midian[d] in
anguish.[e]

[8]Were you angry with the rivers,[f]
O LORD?
Was your wrath against the
streams?
Did you rage against the sea[g]
when you rode with your horses
and your victorious chariots?[h]
[9]You uncovered your bow,
you called for many arrows.[i] *Selah*
You split the earth with rivers;
[10]the mountains saw you and
writhed.[j]
Torrents of water swept by;
the deep roared[k]
and lifted its waves[l] on high.

[11]Sun and moon stood still[m] in the
heavens
at the glint of your flying arrows,[n]
at the lightning[o] of your flashing
spear.
[12]In wrath you strode through the
earth
and in anger you threshed[p] the
nations.
[13]You came out[q] to deliver[r] your
people,
to save your anointed[s] one.
You crushed[t] the leader of the land
of wickedness,
you stripped him from head to
foot. *Selah*
[14]With his own spear you pierced his
head
when his warriors stormed out to
scatter us,[u]
gloating as though about to devour
the wretched[v] who were in hiding.
[15]You trampled the sea[w] with your
horses,
churning the great waters.[x]

[16]I heard and my heart pounded,
my lips quivered at the sound;
decay crept into my bones,
and my legs trembled.[y]
Yet I will wait patiently[z] for the day
of calamity
to come on the nation invading
us.
[17]Though the fig tree does not bud
and there are no grapes on the
vines,

3:3 [r]S Ge 36:11,15 [s]Isa 31:1 [t]S Nu 10:12 [u]S Ps 8:1 [v]Ps 48:10 **3:4** [w]S Isa 18:4 [x]S Job 9:6 **3:5** [y]S Lev 26:25 **3:6** [z]S Ps 46:2 [a]Ge 49:26 [b]S Ex 19:18; Ps 18:7; 114:1-6 [c]S Ge 21:33 **3:7** [d]S Ge 25:2; S Nu 25:15; Jdg 7:24-25 [e]Ex 15:14 **3:8** [f]S Ex 7:20 [g]S Ps 77:16 [h]S 2Ki 2:11; S Ps 68:17 **3:9** [i]S Dt 32:23; Ps 7:12-13 **3:10** [j]S Ps 77:16 [k]Ps 98:7 [l]S Ps 93:3 **3:11** [m]Jos 10:13 [n]Ps 18:14 [o]S Ps 144:6; Zec 9:14 **3:12** [p]S Isa 41:15 **3:13** [q]S Ex 13:21 [r]S Ps 20:6; S 28:8 [s]S 2Sa 23:1 [t]Ps 68:21; 110:6 **3:14** [u]Jdg 7:22 [v]Ps 64:2-5 **3:15** [w]S Job 9:8 [x]Ex 15:8 **3:16** [y]S Job 4:14 [z]S Ps 37:7

[a] *3* A word of uncertain meaning; possibly a musical term; also in verses 9 and 13

3:3 *God came.* When celebrating the exodus, the OT poets (and poet-prophets) combined recollections of the mighty acts of God with conventional images of a fearsome manifestation of the Lord. He came down with his heavenly host and rode on the mighty thunderstorm as his chariot, with his arrows flying in all directions, a cloudburst of rain descending on the earth and the mountains quaking before him (see Jdg 5:4–5; Ps 18:7–15; 68:7–10; 77:16–19; Mic 1:3 and notes). Such figures characterize many of the references in the following verses. *Teman.* Means "southland." God is pictured as coming from the area south of Judah during the exodus. *Mount Paran.* See Dt 33:2 and note; probably northwest of the Gulf of Aqaba and south of Kadesh Barnea, between Edom and Sinai. *Selah.* See Introduction to Psalms: Authorship and Titles (or Superscriptions). *filled the earth.* See note on 2:14.
3:5 *Plague ... pestilence.* Means of divine punishment (cf. Ex 7:14—12:30; Lev 26:25; Ps 91:3,6).
3:6 God's presence was frequently marked by earthquakes (see Ex 19:18; Ps 18:7; Jer 4:24; 10:10; Na 1:5). Landslides may also be alluded to here.
3:7 *Cushan ... Midian.* Arab tribes living near Edom. *distress ... anguish.* When Israel was delivered from Egypt under Moses, neighboring peoples were filled with fear (see Ex 15:14–16; Jos 2:9–10).
3:8 Poetic allusions to the plague on the Nile (Ex 7:20–24) and/or the stopping of the Jordan (Jos 3:15–17), and to the parting of the Red Sea (Ex 14:15–31).
3:9 *arrows.* Probably lightning bolts unleashed by the heavenly archer (see Ps 18:14 and note; 144:6). *rivers.* Caused by the accompanying thunderstorms.
3:11 *Sun and moon stood still.* Probably an allusion to the victory at Gibeon (see Jos 10:12–13 and note on 10:13), indicating that God's triumph over his enemies would be just as complete as on that occasion.
3:12 *threshed.* See note on Am 1:3.
3:13 *deliver your people.* God fought against the nations of Canaan (v. 12) but delivered his people. *save.* By giving victory to. *anointed one.* The covenant nation ("your people"; see Ps 28:8), the "kingdom of priests" (Ex 19:6; see note there), which God came to deliver. He destroyed the enemy, and in this great act of wrath (v. 12) remembered mercy (v. 2). *leader of the land of wickedness.* The pharaoh (see Ex 14:5–9).
3:14–15 Another reference to the destruction of the Egyptians in the Red Sea. God will likewise vanquish present foes.
3:15 *horses.* See v. 8 and note.
3:16 The hymnic recollection of God's mighty deeds of old in Israel's behalf (vv. 3–15) fills the prophet with an awe so profound that he feels physically weak. Alternatively, it is possible that the message from the Lord that Babylonia would be sent against Judah (1:5–11) had so devastated him that he felt ill—until he heard the Lord's further word. *wait patiently.* See 2:3 and note; Ps 37:7. *nation invading us.* Babylonia.
3:17 Probably anticipates the awful results of the imminent Babylonian invasion and devastation.

though the olive crop fails
and the fields produce no food,[a]
though there are no sheep in the pen
and no cattle in the stalls,[b]
18 yet I will rejoice in the LORD,[c]
I will be joyful in God my Savior.[d]

3:17 [a]Joel 1:10-12,18 [b]Jer 5:17
3:18 [c]Ps 97:12; S Isa 61:10; Php 4:4 [d]S Ex 15:2; S Lk 1:47
3:19 [e]S Dt 33:29; Ps 46:1-5 [f]S Dt 32:13; Ps 18:33

19 The Sovereign LORD is my strength;[e]
he makes my feet like the feet of a deer,
he enables me to go on the heights.[f]

For the director of music. On my stringed instruments.

3:18–19 Habakkuk has learned the lesson of faith (2:4)—to trust in God's providence regardless of circumstances. He declares that even if God should send suffering and loss, he would still rejoice in God his Savior—one of the strongest affirmations of faith in all Scripture.
3:18 *rejoice in the LORD.* See Ps 32:11; Php 3:1; 4:4. *be joyful in God my Savior.* See Lk 1:47.

3:19 *makes my feet like the feet of a deer.* Gives me surefooted confidence (see Ps 18:33). *director.* Probably the conductor of the temple musicians. This chapter may have formed part of the temple prayers that were chanted with the accompaniment of instruments (see 1Ch 16:4–7). *stringed instruments.* Including harp and lyre (Ps 33:2; 92:3; 144:9).

Zephaniah

INTRODUCTION

Author

The prophet Zephaniah was evidently a person of considerable social standing in Judah and was probably related to the royal line. The prophecy opens with a statement of the author's ancestry (1:1), which in itself is an unusual feature of the Hebrew prophetic tradition. Zephaniah was a fourth-generation descendant of Hezekiah, a notable king of Judah from 715 to 686 B.C. Apart from this statement, nothing more is said about his background. Whereas the prophet Micah dealt carefully and sympathetically with the problems of the common people of Judah, Zephaniah's utterances show a much greater familiarity with court circles and current political issues. Zephaniah was probably familiar with the writings of such prominent eighth-century prophets as Isaiah and Amos, whose utterances he reflects, and he may also have been aware of the ministry of the young Jeremiah.

A Quick Look

Author:
Zephaniah

Audience:
The people of Judah

Date:
During the reign of King Josiah (640 – 609 B.C.)

Theme:
The prophet Zephaniah predicts the coming of the day of the Lord, when God will severely punish the nations, including apostate Judah, but will yet be merciful to his people.

Date

According to 1:1, Zephaniah prophesied during the reign of King Josiah (640 – 609 B.C.), making him a contemporary of Jeremiah, Nahum and perhaps Habakkuk. His prophecy is probably to be dated relatively early in Josiah's reign, before that king's attempt at reform (and while conditions brought about by the reigns of Manasseh and Amon still prevailed) and before the Assyrian king Ashurbanipal's death in 627 (while Assyria was still powerful, though threatened).

Background

See Introductions to Jeremiah and Nahum: Background; see also 2Ki 22:1 — 23:30; 2Ch 34:1 — 36:1 and notes.

Purpose and Theological Theme

The intent of the author was to announce to Judah God's approaching judgment. A Scythian incursion into Canaan may have provided the immediate occasion. This fierce, horse-mounted people originated in what is now southern Russia, but by the seventh century B.C. they had migrated across the Caucasus and settled in and along the northern territories of the Assyrian empire. Alternately the enemies and allies of Assyria, they seem to have thrust south along the Mediterranean sometime in the 620s, destroying Ashkelon and Ashdod and halting at the Egyptian border only because of a payoff by Pharaoh Psamtik (Psammetichus). Ultimately, however, the destruction prophesied by Zephaniah came at the hands of the Babylonians after they had overpowered Assyria and brought that ancient power to its end.

Like many other prophets, Zephaniah ends his pronouncements of doom on the positive note of Judah's restoration by Yahweh, the King of Israel.

Zephaniah's main theme is the coming of the day of the Lord (see notes on Isa 2:11,17,20; Joel 1:15; 2:2; Am 5:18; 8:9), when God will severely punish the nations, including apostate Judah. Zephaniah portrays the stark horror of that ordeal with the same graphic imagery found elsewhere in the prophets. But he also makes it clear that God will yet be merciful toward his people; like many other prophets, Zephaniah ends his pronouncements of doom on the positive note of Judah's restoration by Yahweh, the King of Israel (3:15; see note there).

Outline

I. Introduction (1:1 – 3)
  A. Title: The Prophet Identified (1:1)
  B. Prologue: Double Announcement of Total Judgment (1:2 – 3)
II. The Day of the Lord Coming on Judah and the Nations (1:4 – 18)
  A. Judgment on the Idolaters in Judah (1:4 – 9)
  B. Wailing throughout Jerusalem (1:10 – 13)
  C. The Inescapable Day of the Lord's Wrath (1:14 – 18)
III. God's Judgment on the Nations (2:1 — 3:8)
  A. Call to Judah to Repent (2:1 – 3)
  B. Judgment on Philistia (2:4 – 7)
  C. Judgment on Moab and Ammon (2:8 – 11)
  D. Judgment on Cush (2:12)
  E. Judgment on Assyria (2:13 – 15)
  F. Judgment on Jerusalem (3:1 – 5)
  G. Jerusalem's Refusal to Repent (3:6 – 8)
IV. Redemption of the Remnant (3:9 – 20)
  A. The Nations Purified, the Remnant Restored, Jerusalem Purged (3:9 – 13)
  B. Rejoicing in the City (3:14 – 17)
  C. The Nation Restored (3:18 – 20)

1 The word of the LORD that came to Zephaniah son of Cushi, the son of Gedaliah, the son of Amariah, the son of Hezekiah, during the reign of Josiah[a] son of Amon[b] king of Judah:

Warning of Coming Destruction

2 "I will sweep away everything
from the face of the earth,"[c]
declares the LORD.
3 "I will sweep away both men and
animals;[d]
I will sweep away the birds of the
air[e]
and the fish of the sea.
The wicked will have only heaps of
rubble[a]
when I cut off man from the face of
the earth,"[f]
declares the LORD.[g]

Against Judah

4 "I will stretch out my hand[h] against
Judah
and against all who live in
Jerusalem.
I will cut off from this place every
remnant of Baal,[i]
the names of the pagan and the
idolatrous priests[j]—
5 those who bow down on the roofs
to worship the starry host,[k]
those who bow down and swear by the
LORD
and who also swear by Molech,[b][l]
6 those who turn back from following[m]
the LORD
and neither seek[n] the LORD nor
inquire[o] of him.
7 Be silent[p] before the Sovereign LORD,
for the day of the LORD[q] is near.
The LORD has prepared a sacrifice;[r]
he has consecrated those he has
invited.
8 On the day of the LORD's sacrifice
I will punish[s] the princes
and the king's sons[t]
and all those clad
in foreign clothes.
9 On that day I will punish
all who avoid stepping on the
threshold,[c][u]
who fill the temple of their gods
with violence and deceit.[v]
10 "On that day,[w]" declares the LORD,
"a cry will go up from the Fish Gate,[x]
wailing[y] from the New Quarter,
and a loud crash from the hills.
11 Wail,[z] you who live in the market
district[d];
all your merchants will be wiped out,
all who trade with[e] silver will be
ruined.[a]
12 At that time I will search Jerusalem
with lamps
and punish those who are
complacent,[b]

1:1 [a] 2Ki 22:1; 2Ch 34:1-35:25 [b] S 1Ch 3:14
1:2 [c] S Ge 6:7
1:3 [d] Jer 50:3 [e] S Jer 4:25 [f] ver 18; S Hos 4:3 [g] S Eze 14:17
1:4 [h] S Jer 6:12 [i] Mic 5:13; Zep 2:11 [j] S Jer 15:6; S Hos 10:5
1:5 [k] S Jer 8:2 [l] S Lev 18:21; Jer 5:7
1:6 [m] Isa 1:4; Jer 2:13 [n] S Isa 9:13 [o] S Hos 7:7
1:7 [p] S Isa 41:1 [q] ver 14; Isa 13:6; S Eze 7:19; S Joel 3:14; S Am 5:18-20 [r] S Lev 3:9; S Jer 46:10
1:8 [s] Isa 24:21 [t] Jer 39:6
1:9 [u] 1Sa 5:5 [v] S Am 3:10
1:10 [w] Isa 22:5 [x] S 2Ch 33:14 [y] S Am 5:16
1:11 [z] Jas 5:1 [a] Hos 9:6
1:12 [b] Am 6:1

[a] 3 The meaning of the Hebrew for this line is uncertain. [b] 5 Hebrew *Malcam*, that is, Milcom [c] 9 See 1 Samuel 5:5. [d] 11 Or *the Mortar* [e] 11 Or *in*

1:1 *word of the LORD.* A common introductory phrase in the prophets (see Jer 1:2; Hos 1:1 and notes). *Zephaniah.* Means "The LORD hides" or "The LORD protects," perhaps implying a prayer for God's protection of the child Zephaniah during the infamous reign of Manasseh. *son of … Hezekiah.* Judging from the author's pedigree, it is likely that he was in his early 20s when he began to prophesy. He is more closely identified with the ruling class than was Isaiah, although Isaiah also moved regularly in court circles and was perhaps of noble birth.
1:2–3 *sweep away.* Zephaniah speaks of the coming catastrophe in language reminiscent of God's utterances prior to the flood (Ge 6:7). But this time it will be by God's fire (v. 18; 3:8).
1:3 *heaps of rubble.* See NIV text note. Alternatively, the sense may be that God will place formidable obstacles in the paths of the wicked and destroy them completely.
1:4–6 Seems to indicate that Zephaniah's main ministry took place before 621 B.C., since the practices condemned here were abolished in Josiah's reforms (see 2Ki 23:4–16 and notes). Perhaps Zephaniah's message was partly instrumental in motivating King Josiah to undertake his reforms (cf. 2Ch 34:1–7).
1:4 Judah is censured for its unrepentant participation in the gross idolatry of Baal worship. *this place.* Jerusalem, where Zephaniah probably lived. *Baal.* See note on Jdg 2:13.
1:5 *on the roofs.* See 2Ki 23:12; Jer 19:13 and notes. *worship the starry host.* See Dt 4:19; 2Ki 17:16 and note; 21:3; Isa 47:13. *swear by the LORD … also swear by Molech.* Syncretism (worship of one's own god along with other gods). See Dt 6:13 and note. *Molech.* Worshiped by the Ammonites, his rituals sometimes involved child sacrifice. Molech worship was forbidden to the Israelites (see Lev 18:21 and note; 20:1–5). Despite this, Solomon set up an altar to Molech on the Mount of Olives (1Ki 11:7). Manasseh established the rituals in the Valley of Ben Hinnom (see 2Ch 33:6; Jer 7:31 and note; 32:35).
1:7 *Be silent before the Sovereign LORD.* See Hab 2:20 and note. *day of the LORD.* Zephaniah's main theme (see Introduction: Purpose and Theological Theme); not of deliverance for Judah, but of divine vengeance on the idolatrous covenant nation. *sacrifice.* The victim is Judah. *consecrated.* Since the coming slaughter of judgment is called a sacrifice, God's preparation of his guests is called his consecration of them—in preparation for their feasting on the plunder. *those … invited.* The pagan conquerors (mainly Babylonia).
1:8 *foreign clothes.* Dress that indicated conformity to Babylonian, Egyptian or Assyrian ways.
1:9 *avoid stepping on the threshold.* Perhaps referring to a pagan custom that began in the time of Samuel (see 1Sa 5:5 and note).
1:10–13 Wailing throughout the city (contrast 3:14–17).
1:10 Merchants who had grown rich through corrupt business practices would be destroyed. *Fish Gate.* In the north wall of the city (see note on Ne 3:3). Jerusalem was the most vulnerable to attacks from the north. *New Quarter.* See note on 2Ki 22:14; see also map No. 10 at the end of this study Bible.
1:11 *market district.* May have been an area in the Tyropoeon Valley (see note on Ne 2:13 and map, p. 1527).
1:12 *search Jerusalem with lamps.* The Babylonians later dragged people from houses, streets, sewers and tombs,

who are like wine left on its dregs,[c]
who think, 'The LORD will do nothing,[d]
either good or bad.'[e]
13 Their wealth will be plundered,[f]
their houses demolished.
They will build houses
but not live in them;
they will plant vineyards
but not drink the wine.[g]

The Great Day of the LORD

14 "The great day of the LORD[h] is near[i]—
near and coming quickly.
Listen! The cry on the day of the LORD
will be bitter,
the shouting of the warrior there.
15 That day will be a day of wrath,
a day of distress and anguish,
a day of trouble and ruin,
a day of darkness[j] and gloom,
a day of clouds and blackness,[k]
16 a day of trumpet and battle cry[l]
against the fortified cities
and against the corner towers.[m]
17 I will bring distress[n] on the people
and they will walk like blind[o] men,
because they have sinned against the
LORD.
Their blood will be poured out[p] like
dust
and their entrails like filth.[q]
18 Neither their silver nor their gold
will be able to save them
on the day of the LORD's wrath.[r]
In the fire of his jealousy[s]
the whole world will be consumed,[t]
for he will make a sudden end
of all who live in the earth.[u]"

2 Gather together,[v] gather together,
O shameful[w] nation,
2 before the appointed time arrives
and that day sweeps on like chaff,[x]
before the fierce anger[y] of the LORD
comes upon you,
before the day of the LORD's wrath[z]
comes upon you.
3 Seek[a] the LORD, all you humble of the
land,
you who do what he commands.
Seek righteousness,[b] seek humility;[c]
perhaps you will be sheltered[d]
on the day of the LORD's anger.

Against Philistia

4 Gaza[e] will be abandoned
and Ashkelon[f] left in ruins.
At midday Ashdod will be emptied
and Ekron uprooted.
5 Woe to you who live by the sea,
O Kerethite[g] people;
the word of the LORD is against you,[h]
O Canaan, land of the Philistines.

"I will destroy you,
and none will be left."[i]

6 The land by the sea, where the
Kerethites[a] dwell,
will be a place for shepherds and
sheep pens.[j]
7 It will belong to the remnant[k] of the
house of Judah;
there they will find pasture.
In the evening they will lie down
in the houses of Ashkelon.
The LORD their God will care for them;
he will restore their fortunes.[b][l]

Against Moab and Ammon

8 "I have heard the insults[m] of Moab[n]
and the taunts of the Ammonites,[o]

[a] 6 The meaning of the Hebrew for this word is uncertain. [b] 7 Or *will bring back their captives*

1:12 [c] Jer 48:11 [d] S 2Ki 21:16; S Eze 8:12 [e] S Job 22:13 **1:13** [f] S 2Ki 24:13; Jer 15:13 [g] Dt 28:30,39; La 5:2; S Am 5:11 **1:14** [h] S ver 7; S Joel 1:15 [i] S Eze 7:7; S Da 7:13 **1:15** [j] S 1Sa 2:9 [k] S Isa 22:5; Joel 2:2; Mk 13:24-25 **1:16** [l] S Jer 4:19 [m] S Dt 28:52; S Isa 2:15; S Joel 2:1 **1:17** [n] S Dt 28:52 [o] S Isa 59:10 [p] Ps 79:3 [q] S Ps 83:10 **1:18** [r] S Job 20:20; S 40:11; S Jer 4:4; S Eze 7:19 [s] S Dt 29:20 [t] S ver 2-3; Zep 3:8 [u] S Ge 6:7; S Eze 7:11 **2:1** [v] 2Ch 20:4; Joel 1:14 [w] S Jer 3:3; 6:15 **2:2** [x] Isa 17:13; Hos 13:3 [y] S Jer 10:25; S La 4:11 [z] S Jer 4:4; S Eze 7:19 **2:3** [a] S Am 5:6 [b] S Isa 1:17 [c] Ps 45:4 [d] Ps 57:1 **2:4** [e] S Ge 10:19; S Am 1:6,7-8; Zec 9:5-7 [f] Jer 47:5 **2:5** [g] S 1Sa 30:14 [h] S Lev 26:31; Am 3:1 [i] S Isa 14:30 **2:6** [j] S Isa 5:17 **2:7** [k] S Ge 45:7 [l] S Dt 30:3; Ps 126:4; Jer 32:44; S Hos 6:11; S Joel 3:1; Am 1:6-8 **2:8** [m] S Jer 48:27 [n] S Ge 19:37; S Isa 16:6 [o] S Eze 21:28

where they had hidden. *like wine left on its dregs.* See Isa 25:6 and note. *The LORD will do nothing.* A typical depiction of the arrogance of the wicked (see note on Ps 10:11).

1:13 The assets of those who have become wealthy through dishonesty will be exposed and plundered (see Dt 28:30).

1:14–18 In a dramatic passage of great lyrical power, the Lord describes the destruction that will sweep the earth in the day of God's wrath.

1:15 *That day will be a day of wrath.* The inspiration for Thomas of Celano's great medieval hymn, *Dies Irae Dies Illa* (c. A.D. 1250). *darkness ... blackness.* See Am 5:18–20.

1:17 *like blind men.* See Dt 28:28–29.

1:18 *Neither ... silver nor ... gold will ... save them.* In the day of God's judgment, material wealth cannot buy deliverance from punishment. *fire of his jealousy.* See vv. 2–3 and note; 3:8.

2:1–3 The prophet's exhortation to Judah to repent. This call to repentance and the later indictment of Jerusalem for refusal to repent (see 3:6–8 and note) frame the series of judgments that illustratively detail God's acts in the coming day of the Lord (2:4—3:5).

2:2 *like chaff.* See Ps 1:4 and note; 35:5; Isa 17:13; 29:5; Hos 13:3.

2:3 *Seek the LORD.* Even though destruction is imminent, there is still time to be sheltered from the calamity if only the nation will repent (see Am 5:4 and note). *humble.* Those who abandon the arrogance of their idolatry and wickedness and "seek humility."

2:4—3:8 God's coming judgment on the nations—including Jerusalem (see Am 1:3—2:16 and note).

2:4 *Gaza ... Ashkelon ... Ashdod ... Ekron.* Philistine cities located west of Judah "by the sea" (vv. 5–6; see notes on Am 1:6,8; see also map, p. 331).

2:5 *Kerethite.* See note on 1Sa 30:14. *Canaan.* See note on Ge 10:6. *I ... left.* The Lord's announced purpose.

2:6 The once-populous Philistine cities will revert to pastureland. *Kerethites.* See NIV text note.

2:7 The faithful remnant of Judah will occupy this land and graze their flocks on it. *restore their fortunes.* See NIV text note. Here and in vv. 9,11 the prophet anticipates the ultimate outcome of the day of the Lord, which he spells out more fully in 3:9–20.

2:8 *Moab ... Ammonites.* Peoples living east of Judah (see

who insulted[p] my people
and made threats against their
land.[q]
9 Therefore, as surely as I live,"
declares the LORD Almighty, the God
of Israel,
"surely Moab[r] will become like
Sodom,[s]
the Ammonites[t] like Gomorrah —
a place of weeds and salt pits,
a wasteland forever.
The remnant of my people will
plunder[u] them;
the survivors[v] of my nation will
inherit their land.[w]"
10 This is what they will get in return for
their pride,[x]
for insulting[y] and mocking the
people of the LORD Almighty.[z]
11 The LORD will be awesome[a] to them
when he destroys all the gods[b] of the
land.[c]
The nations on every shore will
worship him,[d]
every one in its own land.

Against Cush

12 "You too, O Cushites,[a][e]
will be slain by my sword.[f]"

Against Assyria

13 He will stretch out his hand against the
north
and destroy Assyria,[g]
leaving Nineveh[h] utterly desolate
and dry as the desert.[i]
14 Flocks and herds[j] will lie down there,
creatures of every kind.
The desert owl[k] and the screech owl[l][m]
will roost on her columns.

2:8 [p]Eze 25:3 [q]S La 3:61 **2:9** [r]S Dt 23:6; Isa 15:1-16:14; Jer 48:1-47; Eze 25:8-11 [s]Dt 29:23; Isa 13:19; Jer 49:18 [t]Jer 49:1-6; Eze 25:1-7 [u]S Isa 11:14 [v]S 2Ki 19:31 [w]S Am 2:1-3 **2:10** [x]S Job 40:12; S Isa 16:6 [y]S Jer 48:27 [z]S Ps 9:6 **2:11** [a]S Joel 2:11 [b]S Zep 1:4 [c]S 1Ch 19:1; Eze 25:6-7 [d]Ps 86:9; S Isa 12:4; Zep 3:9 **2:12** [e]S Ge 10:6; S Isa 20:4 [f]S Jer 46:10 **2:13** [g]S Isa 10:5 [h]S Ge 10:11; S Na 1:1 [i]S Mic 5:6; Zec 10:11 **2:14** [j]S Isa 5:17 [k]S Isa 14:23 [l]Rev 18:2 [m]S Ps 102:6 **2:15** [n]S Isa 32:9 [o]Isa 47:8 [p]Eze 28:2 [q]Jer 49:33 [r]S Isa 28:22; S Na 3:19 [s]S Eze 27:36 **3:1** [t]S Jer 6:6 [u]S Dt 21:18 [v]S Eze 23:30 **3:2** [w]S Jer 22:21 [x]S Lev 26:23; S Jer 7:28 [y]S Dt 1:32 [z]S Ps 73:28 **3:3** [a]S Ps 22:13 [b]S Ge 49:27 [c]S Mic 3:3 **3:4** [d]S Ps 25:3; S Isa 48:8; Jer 3:20; 9:4; Mal 2:10 [e]S Jer 23:11; S Eze 22:26 **3:5** [f]S Ezr 9:15 [g]Dt 32:4 [h]S Ps 5:3 [i]S La 3:23 [j]S Jer 3:3; S Eze 18:25

Their calls will echo through the
windows,
rubble will be in the doorways,
the beams of cedar will be exposed.
15 This is the carefree[n] city
that lived in safety.[o]
She said to herself,
"I am, and there is none besides
me."[p]
What a ruin she has become,
a lair for wild beasts![q]
All who pass by her scoff[r]
and shake their fists.[s]

The Future of Jerusalem

3 Woe to the city of oppressors,[t]
rebellious[u] and defiled![v]
2 She obeys[w] no one,
she accepts no correction.[x]
She does not trust[y] in the LORD,
she does not draw near[z] to her God.
3 Her officials are roaring lions,[a]
her rulers are evening wolves,[b]
who leave nothing for the morning.[c]
4 Her prophets are arrogant;
they are treacherous[d] men.
Her priests profane the sanctuary
and do violence to the law.[e]
5 The LORD within her is righteous;[f]
he does no wrong.[g]
Morning by morning[h] he dispenses his
justice,
and every new day he does not fail,[i]
yet the unrighteous know no shame.[j]

6 "I have cut off nations;
their strongholds are demolished.

a 12 That is, people from the upper Nile region

notes on Ge 19:36–38; Am 1:13; 2:3). For the hostility of Ammon and Moab toward Israel see Am 1:13; 2:3. They had often threatened to occupy Israelite territory (see Jdg 11:13 and note; Eze 25:2–7).

2:9 *Sodom ... Gomorrah.* See Ge 19. They were used in the OT to typify complete destruction at the hands of God (see Am 4:11 and note), and their mention added ominous overtones to the prophet's description of the day of the Lord. *weeds.* A symbol of depopulation (cf. Isa 7:23–25). *remnant ... will inherit their land.* See note on v. 7.

2:10 *in return for their pride, for insulting and mocking.* In reprisal, the faithful remnant will occupy Ammonite and Moabite territory.

2:11 *nations ... will worship him.* See 3:9 and note.

2:12 *You too.* Without elaboration, the prophet simply announces God's purpose against Egypt, located southwest of Judah (see vv. 5,8 and notes). *Cushites.* See NIV text note. Egypt was ruled from 715 to 663 B.C. by a Cushite dynasty. *my sword.* Probably Babylonia (see Eze 21:9–13,19; see also notes on Ps 7:12–13; Isa 10:5).

2:13 *north.* Although Nineveh was east of Judah, Assyrian armies normally invaded Canaan from the north (see notes on v. 12; 1:10), having first marched west along the Euphrates instead of through the Arabian Desert. *Nineveh.* See the books of Jonah and Nahum. Since Nineveh was destroyed in 612 B.C., Zephaniah's ministry had to be before that date. *utterly desolate.* Even the site of Nineveh was later forgotten — until discovered through modern excavations (see Na 3:17 and note).

2:15 *I am ... none besides me.* See Isa 47:10. Assyria's boast belongs properly to God alone (see Isa 47:8,10 and note). *has become.* Anticipating Nineveh's impending destruction.

3:1 *city.* Apostate Jerusalem is condemned for its sins. *oppressors.* See Jer 22:3.

3:3–4 *officials ... rulers ... prophets ... priests.* All classes of Judah's leaders are castigated for indulging in conduct completely opposed to their vocations and responsibilities (see Jer 1:18 and note).

3:3 *roaring lions ... evening wolves.* Those in power are rapacious.

3:4 *arrogant ... treacherous men.* Claiming to be prophets of the Lord, they proclaimed only lies (see Jer 5:31 and note; 14:14; 23:16,32). *priests ... do violence to the law.* When they should have been teachers of the law (see Dt 31:9–13; 2Ch 17:8–9; 19:8; Ezr 7:6; Jer 2:8; 18:18; Mal 2:7).

3:5 *Morning by morning ... he does not fail.* Cf. La 3:22–23 and notes.

3:6–8 Jerusalem's refusal to repent (see 2:1–3 and note).

3:6 *I have cut off nations.* The destruction of other nations was

I have left their streets deserted,
with no one passing through.
Their cities are destroyed;[k]
no one will be left—no one at all.
7 I said to the city,
'Surely you will fear me
and accept correction!'[l]
Then her dwelling would not be cut
off,
nor all my punishments come upon
her.
But they were still eager
to act corruptly[m] in all they did.
8 Therefore wait[n] for me," declares the
LORD,
"for the day I will stand up to
testify.[a]
I have decided to assemble[o] the
nations,[p]
to gather the kingdoms
and to pour out my wrath[q] on them—
all my fierce anger.[r]
The whole world will be consumed[s]
by the fire of my jealous anger.

9 "Then will I purify the lips of the
peoples,
that all of them may call[t] on the
name of the LORD[u]
and serve[v] him shoulder to shoulder.
10 From beyond the rivers of Cush[b w]
my worshipers, my scattered people,
will bring me offerings.[x]
11 On that day you will not be put to
shame[y]
for all the wrongs you have done to
me,[z]
because I will remove from this city
those who rejoice in their pride.[a]
Never again will you be haughty
on my holy hill.[b]
12 But I will leave within you
the meek[c] and humble,
who trust[d] in the name of the LORD.
13 The remnant[e] of Israel will do no
wrong;[f]
they will speak no lies,[g]
nor will deceit be found in their
mouths.[h]
They will eat and lie down[i]
and no one will make them afraid.[j]"

14 Sing, O Daughter of Zion;[k]
shout aloud,[l] O Israel!
Be glad and rejoice[m] with all your
heart,
O Daughter of Jerusalem!
15 The LORD has taken away your
punishment,
he has turned back your enemy.
The LORD, the King of Israel, is with
you;[n]
never again will you fear[o] any
harm.[p]
16 On that day they will say to Jerusalem,
"Do not fear, O Zion;
do not let your hands hang limp.[q]
17 The LORD your God is with you,
he is mighty to save.[r]
He will take great delight[s] in you,
he will quiet you with his love,[t]
he will rejoice over you with
singing."[u]

18 "The sorrows for the appointed feasts
I will remove from you;
they are a burden and a reproach to
you.[c]

3:6 [k]S Lev 26:31 **3:7** [l]S Jer 7:28 [m]S Hos 9:9 **3:8** [n]S Ps 27:14 [o]S Joel 3:11 [p]S Isa 2:3 [q]Ps 79:6; Rev 16:1 [r]S Jer 10:25; S La 4:11 [s]S Zep 1:18 **3:9** [t]S Zep 2:11 [u]S Ge 4:26 [v]S Isa 19:18 **3:10** [w]S Ge 10:6; S Ps 68:31 [x]S 2Ch 32:23; S Isa 60:7 **3:11** [y]S Isa 29:22; S Joel 2:26-27 [z]S Ge 50:15 [a]S Ps 59:12 [b]S Ex 15:17; S Lev 26:19 **3:12** [c]Isa 14:32 [d]S Jer 29:12; Na 1:7 **3:13** [e]S Isa 10:21 [f]Ps 119:3; S Isa 4:3 [g]S Jer 33:16; Rev 14:5 [h]S Job 16:17 [i]Eze 34:15; Zep 2:7 [j]S Lev 26:6; S Eze 34:25-28 **3:14** [k]S Ps 9:14; Zec 2:10 [l]S Ps 95:1; Isa 12:6; Zec 2:10 [m]S Ps 9:2; S Isa 51:11 **3:15** [n]Eze 37:26-28 [o]S Isa 54:14 [p]Zec 9:9 **3:16** [q]S 2Ki 19:26; S Job 4:3; Isa 35:3-4; Heb 12:12 **3:17** [r]S Isa 63:1; S Joel 2:21 [s]S Dt 28:63; S Isa 62:4 [t]S Hos 14:4 [u]S Isa 40:1

[a] 8 Septuagint and Syriac; Hebrew *will rise up to plunder*
[b] 10 That is, the upper Nile region
[c] 18 Or *"I will gather you who mourn for the appointed feasts; / your reproach is a burden to you*

meant to serve as a warning to wanton Judah, but to no avail (see v. 7). *will be.* Or "is."

3:7 *eager to act corruptly.* See, e.g., Jer 7:13,25–26.

3:8 *wait.* A sarcastic statement to Judah to wait for the threatened catastrophe. *to testify.* To lodge accusations (see Ps 50:7)—and then proceed to execute judgments. *I have decided.* Or "For I have decided." The Lord concludes his announcement of judgment with a general declaration of his intent. *consumed by the fire of my jealous anger.* See 1:2–3 and note; 1:18; La 1:13 and note.

3:9–20 A three-stanza poetic unit (vv. 9–13,14–17, 18–20) announcing redemption that will follow God's judgment.

3:9–13 The Lord gives assurance that the nations will be purified, the scattered remnant restored and Jerusalem purged.

3:9 God's fearful judgment of the nations will effect (or be followed by) their purification so that they will call on his name and serve him. Israel's God will be acknowledged by the nations, and God's people will be held in honor by them (cf. vv. 19–20).

3:10 *Cush.* See NIV text note; the most distant area imaginable (see 2:12; Isa 18:1 and notes). The most widely dispersed will be restored. *bring me offerings.* Rather than to Baal and Molech (cf. 1:4–5).

3:11 *me,/because.* In the Hebrew, this new line begins the same as the first line of v. 9. Hence it may be better to read: "me./Then." Thus vv. 9–11a constitute a three-line unit (in Hebrew) and vv. 11b,c–12 a three-line unit. The latter speaks of a purified Jerusalem. Verse 13 is a summary conclusion. *my holy hill.* Mount Zion (see Ps 2:6 and note).

3:13 *remnant.* See 2:7; Isa 1:9 and notes. *no one will make them afraid.* Quoted verbatim from Mic 4:4 (see note there).

3:14–17 Joy in the restored city (in two parts: vv. 14–15 and vv. 16–17)—the prophet's reassurance (contrast 1:10–13).

3:14 *Daughter of Zion ... Daughter of Jerusalem.* A personification of Jerusalem (see note on 2Ki 19:21).

3:15 *your enemy.* All those arrayed against Israel. *The LORD, the King of Israel.* See Isa 44:6; see also Introduction to Psalms: Theology.

3:16 *do not let your hands hang limp.* Do not be discouraged (see Jer 47:3 and note).

3:18–20 Summary announcement of restoration—the Lord's final assurance.

3:18 *sorrows.* Israel's sorrow at not being able to celebrate their great religious festivals. *appointed feasts.* See Lev 23 and chart, pp. 178–179.

[19]At that time I will deal
with all who oppressed[v] you;
I will rescue the lame
and gather those who have been
scattered.[w]
I will give them praise[x] and honor
in every land where they were put to
shame.
[20]At that time I will gather you;
at that time I will bring[y] you
home.
I will give you honor[z] and praise[a]
among all the peoples of the earth
when I restore your fortunes[a b]
before your very eyes,"
says the LORD.

3:19 [v]S Isa 14:2 [w]S Eze 34:16; S Mic 4:6 [x]Isa 60:18
3:20 [y]S Jer 29:14; S Eze 37:12 [z]Isa 56:5; 66:22 [a]S Dt 26:19; S Isa 60:18 [b]S Joel 3:1

[a] 20 Or *I bring back your captives*

3:19–20 *gather those ... give them ... gather you ... give you.* The level of intimacy increases as the Lord concludes his words of assurance.

3:20 *give you honor and praise.* See v. 19; see also Ge 12:2–3 and note.

Haggai

INTRODUCTION

Author

Haggai (1:1) was a prophet who, along with Zechariah, encouraged the returned exiles to rebuild the temple (see Ezr 5:1 – 2; 6:14). Haggai means "festal," which may indicate that the prophet was born during one of the three pilgrimage feasts (Unleavened Bread, Pentecost or Weeks, and Tabernacles; cf. Dt 16:16). Based on 2:3 (see note there), Haggai may have witnessed the destruction of Solomon's temple. If so, he must have been in his 70s during his ministry.

Background

In 538 B.C. the conqueror of Babylon, Cyrus king of Persia, issued a decree allowing the Jews to return to Jerusalem and rebuild the temple (see Ezr 1:2 – 4; 6:3 – 5). Led by Zerubbabel (but see note on Ezr 1:8, "Sheshbazzar"), about 50,000 Jews journeyed home and began work on the temple. About two years later (536) they completed the foundation amid great rejoicing (Ezr 3:8 – 11). Their success aroused the Samaritans and other neighbors who feared the political and religious implications of a rebuilt temple in a thriving Jewish state. They therefore opposed the project vigorously and managed to halt work until 520, after Darius the Great became king of Persia in 522 (Ezr 4:1 – 5,24).

Darius was interested in the religions of his empire, and Haggai and Zechariah began to preach in his second year, 520 B.C. (see 1:1; Zec 1:1). The Jews were more to blame for their inactivity than their opponents, and Haggai tried to arouse them from their lethargy. When the governor of Trans-Euphrates and other officials tried to interfere with the rebuilding efforts, Darius fully supported the Jews (Ezr 5:3 – 6; 6:6 – 12). In 516 the temple was finished and dedicated (Ezr 6:15 – 18).

A Quick Look

Author:
Haggai

Audience:
The postexilic Jews living in Judah

Date:
520 B.C.

Theme:
The prophet Haggai calls the complacent people of Judah to resume the rebuilding of the temple and in this way give glory to God.

Date

Haggai's messages are among the most carefully and precisely dated in the entire OT. They were given during a four-month period in 520 B.C., the second year of King Darius. The first message was delivered on the first day of the sixth month (Aug. 29), the last on the 24th day of the ninth month (Dec. 18). See notes on 1:1; 2:1,10; see also Introduction to Zechariah: Dates.

Themes and Theological Teaching

Apart from Obadiah, Haggai is the shortest book in the OT, but its teachings are none the less significant. Haggai clearly shows the consequences of disobedience (1:6,11; 2:16–17) and obedience (2:7–9,19). When the people give priority to God and his house, they are blessed rather than cursed (cf. Lk 12:31 and note). Obedience brings the encouragement and strength of the Spirit of God (2:4–5).

In ch. 2 God gives great encouragement to those laboring under difficult conditions to rebuild his temple by assuring them that the future glory of the modest temple they will build will be greater than the temple Solomon had built. The Jews in Judah may now be a much reduced community and under the hegemony of a powerful world empire, but the Lord will shake up the present world order and assert his claim to all the world's wealth so that the glory of his future temple will be without rival. "The desired of all nations will come, and I will fill this house with glory" (see 2:6–7 and notes).

God gives great encouragement to those laboring under difficult conditions to rebuild his temple by assuring them that the future glory of the modest temple they will build will be greater than the temple Solomon had built.

Literary Features

Like Malachi, Haggai uses a number of questions to highlight key issues (see 1:4,9; 2:3,19). He also makes effective use of repetition: "Give careful thought" occurs in 1:5,7; 2:15,18, and "I am with you" in 1:13; 2:4. "I will shake the heavens and the earth" is found in 2:6,21. The major sections of the book are marked off by the date on which the word of the Lord came "through" (or "to") Haggai (1:1; 2:1,10,20).

Several times the prophet appears to reflect other passages of Scripture (compare 1:6 with Dt 28:38–39 and 2:17 with Dt 28:22). The threefold use of "Be strong" in 2:4 (see note there) echoes the encouragement given in Jos 1:6–7,9,18. (For chiasm see Outline below.)

Outline

- I. First Message: The Call to Rebuild the Temple (1:1–11)
  - A. The People's Lame Excuse (1:1–4)
  - B. The Poverty of the People (1:5–6)
  - C. The Reason God Has Cursed Them (1:7–11)
- II. The Response of Zerubbabel and the People (1:12–15)
  - A. The Leaders and Remnant Obey (1:12)
  - B. The Lord Strengthens the Workers (1:13–15)
- III. Second Message: The Temple to Be Filled with Glory (2:1–9)
  - A. The People Encouraged (2:1–5)
  - B. The Promise of Glory and Peace (2:6–9)
- IV. Third Message: A Defiled People Purified and Blessed (2:10–19)
  - A. The Rapid Spread of Sin (2:10–14)
  - B. Poor Harvests because of Disobedience (2:15–17)
  - C. Blessing to Come as the Temple Is Rebuilt (2:18–19)
- V. Fourth Message: The Promise to Zerubbabel (2:20–23)
  - A. The Judgment of the Nations (2:20–22)
  - B. The Significance of Zerubbabel (2:23)

It is also possible to outline the book in a chiastic *a-b / b-a* pattern:

- a Negative effects of the unbuilt house (1:1 – 11)
  - b The Lord's presence energizes the present work (1:12 – 15)
  - b′ The Lord's presence guarantees future glory (2:1 – 9)
- a′ Positive effects of the rebuilt house (2:10 – 23)

Similar chiastic patterns exist in the subunits within these larger units.

A Call to Build the House of the LORD

1 In the second year of King Darius,[a] on the first day of the sixth month, the word of the LORD came through the prophet Haggai[b] to Zerubbabel[c] son of Shealtiel, governor[d] of Judah, and to Joshua[a][e] son of Jehozadak,[f] the high priest:[g]

2This is what the LORD Almighty[h] says: "These people[i] say, 'The time has not yet come for the LORD's house to be built.[j]' "

3Then the word of the LORD came through the prophet Haggai:[k] 4"Is it a time for you yourselves to be living in your paneled houses,[l] while this house remains a ruin?[m]"

5Now this is what the LORD Almighty says: "Give careful thought[n] to your ways. 6You have planted much, but have harvested little.[o] You eat, but never have enough.[p] You drink, but never have your fill.[q] You put on clothes, but are not warm. You earn wages,[r] only to put them in a purse with holes in it."

7This is what the LORD Almighty says: "Give careful thought[s] to your ways. 8Go up into the mountains and bring down timber[t] and build the house, so that I may take pleasure[u] in it and be honored,[v]" says the LORD. 9"You expected much, but see, it turned out to be little.[w] What you brought home, I blew[x] away. Why?" declares the LORD Almighty. "Because of my house, which remains a ruin,[y] while each of you is busy with his own house. 10Therefore, because of you the heavens have withheld[z] their dew[a] and the earth its crops.[b] 11I called for a drought[c] on the fields and the mountains,[d] on the grain, the new wine,[e] the oil[f] and whatever the ground produces, on men and cattle, and on the labor of your hands.[g]"

12Then Zerubbabel[h] son of Shealtiel, Joshua son of Jehozadak, the high priest, and the whole remnant[i] of the people obeyed[j] the voice of the LORD their God and the message of the prophet Haggai, because the LORD their God had sent him. And the people feared[k] the LORD.

13Then Haggai,[l] the LORD's messenger,[m] gave this message of the LORD to the people: "I am with[n] you," declares the LORD. 14So the LORD stirred up[o] the spirit of Zerubbabel[p] son of Shealtiel, governor of Judah, and the spirit of Joshua son of Jehozadak,[q] the high priest, and the spirit of the whole remnant[r] of the people. They came and began to work on the house of the LORD Almighty, their God, 15on the twenty-fourth day of the sixth month[s] in the second year of King Darius.[t]

[a] *1* A variant of *Jeshua*; here and elsewhere in Haggai

1:1 [a]S Ezr 4:24 [b]S Ezr 5:1 [c]S 1Ch 3:19; Mt 1:12-13 [d]Ezr 5:3; S Ne 5:14 [e]S Ezr 2:2 [f]S 1Ch 6:15; S Ezr 3:2 [g]Zec 3:8 **1:2** [h]Isa 13:4 [i]S Isa 29:13 [j]Ezr 1:2 **1:3** [k]S Ezr 5:1 **1:4** [l]S 2Sa 7:2 [m]ver 9; Jer 33:12 **1:5** [n]ver 7; La 3:40; Hag 2:15, 18 **1:6** [o]S Lev 26:20; S Isa 5:10 [p]S Isa 9:20; S 55:2 [q]Am 4:8 [r]Hag 2:16; Zec 8:10 **1:7** [s]S ver 5 **1:8** [t]S 1Ch 14:1 [u]S Job 22:3; Ps 132:13-14 [v]S Ex 29:43; Jer 13:11 **1:9** [w]S Dt 28:38; S Isa 5:10 [x]S Ps 103:16; S Eze 22:21 [y]S ver 4; S Ne 13:11 **1:10** [z]S Dt 28:24 [a]S Ge 27:28; 1Ki 17:1 [b]Lev 26:19; Dt 28:23 **1:11** [c]S Dt 11:26; S 28:22; S Ru 1:1; S 1Ki 17:1; S Isa 5:6 [d]Isa 7:25 [e]S Dt 28:51; Ps 4:7 [f]S Nu 18:12 [g]Hag 2:17 **1:12** [h]ver 1 [i]ver 14; Isa 1:9; Hag 2:2 [j]S Job 36:11; S Isa 50:10; Mt 28:20 [k]S Dt 31:12; S Isa 1:2 **1:13** [l]ver 1 [m]S Nu 27:21; S 2Ch 36:15 [n]S Ge 26:3; S Nu 14:9; S Mt 28:20; Ro 8:31 **1:14** [o]S Ezr 1:5 [p]S Ezr 5:2 [q]S 1Ch 6:15 [r]S ver 12 **1:15** [s]ver 1; Hag 2:10, 20 [t]S Ezr 4:24

1:1 *second year ... first day ... sixth month.* Aug. 29, 520 B.C. *King Darius.* Darius Hystaspes ruled Persia from 522 to 486 B.C. (see chart, p. 472). It was he who prepared the trilingual inscription on the Behistun cliff wall (located in modern Iran), through which cuneiform inscriptions were deciphered and the culture and history of ancient Mesopotamia were brought to light. *first day.* The New Moon was the day on which prophets were sometimes consulted (see 2Ki 4:22–23 and note on 4:23; see also note on Isa 1:14). *word of the LORD.* See v. 3; 2:2; Hos 1:1 and note. *Zerubbabel.* See note on Ezr 1:8, "Sheshbazzar." *son of Shealtiel.* See 1Ch 3:17–19 and note on 3:19. *governor ... high priest.* The civil and religious leaders of the restored Jewish community. *Joshua.* See note on Ezr 2:2; mentioned with Zerubbabel also in vv. 12,14; 2:2,4. *Jehozadak.* Had been taken captive by Nebuchadnezzar (1Ch 6:15).

1:2 *LORD Almighty.* Used more than 90 times in Haggai, Zechariah and Malachi. See notes on 1Sa 1:3; Isa 13:4. *These people.* See 2:14. Because of their sin, the nation is not called "my people" (see Isa 6:9–10; 8:6,11–12; Jer 14:10–11; see also notes on Ex 17:4; Hos 1:9). *time has not yet come.* After the foundation of the temple had been laid in 536 B.C. (see Ezr 3:8–10), the people became discouraged and halted the work until 520 (see Ezr 4:1–5,24).

1:4 *paneled houses.* Usually connected with royal dwellings, which had cedar paneling (see 1Ki 7:3,7; Jer 22:14–15 and note on 22:14).

1:5 *Give careful thought.* Repeated in v. 7; 2:15,18.

1:6 *planted much ... harvested little.* A curse for disobedience (see Dt 28:38–39). Lev 26:20 also describes the unfruitfulness of a land judged by God. *drink ... fill.* Cf. Isa 55:1–2. The people experience futility in all their activities, legitimate or illegitimate (cf. Hos 4:10–11; Mic 6:13–15). *purse with holes.* Famine causes prices to rise sharply.

1:8 *mountains ... timber.* Perhaps wood from nearby hills was to supplement the cedar wood already purchased from Lebanon (see Ezr 3:7). *take pleasure in it.* And in the sacrifices offered there (contrast Isa 1:11). *be honored.* An obedient nation would bring praise and honor to God (see Jer 13:11).

1:9 *busy with.* Lit. "running to."

1:10 *dew.* Normally abundant in the growing season, and often as valuable as rain (see 2Sa 1:21; 1Ki 17:1).

1:11 *mountains.* The hills were cultivated, especially through terracing (see Ps 104:13–15; Isa 7:25; Joel 3:18). *the grain, the new wine, the oil.* The three basic crops of the land, often mentioned in a context of blessing or cursing (see Dt 7:13; Joel 1:10 and notes). Olive oil was used as food, ointment and medicine. *men and cattle.* The drought affected people and cattle and so could be said to be "on" them too.

1:12 *remnant.* See note on Isa 1:9. *feared the LORD.* Showing trust, reverence and obedience (see Ge 20:11 and note).

1:13 *messenger.* A title for prophets (see 2Ch 36:15–16; Isa 42:19 and note) or priests (see Mal 2:7 and note). *I am with you.* A sure indication of success (see 2:4; Ge 26:3; Nu 14:9 and notes).

1:14 *stirred up the spirit.* The Hebrew for this expression is translated "moved (the) heart" in Ezr 1:5, where God stirred up many of these same people to return home and rebuild the temple.

1:15 *twenty-fourth day of the sixth month.* Sept. 21, 520 B.C.

The Promised Glory of the New House

2 On the twenty-first day of the seventh
month,[u] the word of the LORD came
through the prophet Haggai:[v] 2“Speak to
Zerubbabel[w] son of Shealtiel, governor of
Judah, to Joshua son of Jehozadak,[x] the
high priest, and to the remnant[y] of the
people. Ask them, 3‘Who of you is left
who saw this house[z] in its former glory?
How does it look to you now? Does it not
seem to you like nothing?[a] 4But now be
strong, O Zerubbabel,’ declares the LORD.
‘Be strong,[b] O Joshua son of Jehozadak,[c]
the high priest. Be strong, all you people
of the land,’ declares the LORD, ‘and work.
For I am with[d] you,’ declares the LORD Almighty. 5‘This is what I covenanted[e] with
you when you came out of Egypt.[f] And
my Spirit[g] remains among you. Do not
fear.’[h]
6“This is what the LORD Almighty says:
‘In a little while[i] I will once more shake
the heavens and the earth,[j] the sea and the
dry land. 7I will shake all nations, and the
desired[k] of all nations will come, and I
will fill this house[l] with glory,[m]’ says the
LORD Almighty. 8‘The silver is mine and
the gold[n] is mine,’ declares the LORD Almighty. 9‘The glory[o] of this present house[p]
will be greater than the glory of the former house,’ says the LORD Almighty. ‘And
in this place I will grant peace,[q]’ declares
the LORD Almighty.”

Blessings for a Defiled People

10On the twenty-fourth day of the ninth
month,[r] in the second year of Darius, the
word of the LORD came to the prophet Haggai: 11“This is what the LORD Almighty says:
‘Ask the priests[s] what the law says: 12If a
person carries consecrated meat[t] in the
fold of his garment, and that fold touches
some bread or stew, some wine, oil or other food, does it become consecrated?[u]’”
The priests answered, “No.”
13Then Haggai said, “If a person defiled
by contact with a dead body touches one
of these things, does it become defiled?”
“Yes,” the priests replied, “it becomes
defiled.[v]”
14Then Haggai said, “‘So it is with this
people[w] and this nation in my sight,’ declares the LORD. ‘Whatever they do and
whatever they offer[x] there is defiled.
15“‘Now give careful thought[y] to this
from this day on[a]—consider how things
were before one stone was laid[z] on an-

[a] 15 Or *to the days past*

2:1 [u] ver 10,20; S Lev 23:34; Jn 7:37 [v] S Ezr 5:1 **2:2** [w] Hag 1:1 [x] S 1Ch 6:15 [y] S Hag 1:12 **2:3** [z] S Ezr 3:12; S Isa 60:7 [a] Zec 4:10 **2:4** [b] S 1Ch 28:20; Zec 8:9; S Eph 6:10 [c] S 1Ch 6:15 [d] S Ex 33:14; S Nu 14:9; S 2Sa 5:10; Ac 7:9 **2:5** [e] S Ge 6:18 [f] S Ex 29:46 [g] S Ne 9:20 [h] S Ge 15:1; 1Ch 28:20; S Ezr 5:2; Zec 8:13 **2:6** [i] S Isa 10:25 [j] S Ex 19:18; S Job 9:6; S Isa 14:16; S Eze 38:19; Heb 12:26* **2:7** [k] S 1Sa 9:20 [l] S Isa 60:7 [m] S Ex 16:7; S 29:43; Lk 2:32 **2:8** [n] S 1Ch 29:2 **2:9** [o] S Ps 85:9; S Isa 11:10 [p] S Ezr 3:12; S Isa 60:7 [q] S Lev 26:6; S Isa 60:17 **2:10** [r] S ver 1; S Hag 1:15 **2:11** [s] S Lev 10:10-11; Dt 17:8-11; 33:8; S Jer 18:18 **2:12** [t] Jer 11:15 [u] S Ge 7:2; S Lev 6:27; Mt 23:19 **2:13** [v] Lev 22:4-6; Nu 19:13 **2:14** [w] S Isa 29:13 [x] S Ps 51:17; S Isa 1:13 **2:15** [y] S Hag 1:5 [z] S Ezr 3:10

2:1 *twenty-first day of the seventh month.* Oct. 17, 520 B.C., the last day of the Feast of Tabernacles. It was a time to celebrate the summer harvest (see Lev 23:34–43), though the crops were meager (see 1:11; cf. Jn 7:37). Solomon had dedicated his temple during this feast (see 1Ki 8:2 and note).
2:3 *is left.* Some of the older exiles (perhaps including Haggai himself) had seen Solomon's magnificent temple, destroyed by the Babylonians 66 years earlier. *this house in its former glory.* See vv. 7,9. Zerubbabel's temple was considered a continuation of Solomon's. *seem ... like nothing.* Cf. the reaction when the foundation of the temple was finished (Ezr 3:12).
2:4 *be strong ... work.* David used these words in 1Ch 28:20 when he encouraged Solomon to build the temple. The Lord had exhorted Joshua son of Nun with similar words (Jos 1:6–7,9,18). *I am with you.* See 1:13 and note; 1Ch 28:20. The same God who helped Solomon will empower Zerubbabel and the people.
2:5 *my Spirit.* The Holy Spirit had rested on Moses and the 70 elders as they had led the people out of Egypt and through the desert (see Nu 11:16–17,25; Isa 63:11). See also Ps 51:11; Zec 4:6 and notes. *Do not fear.* See notes on v. 4; Jos 1:18; Isa 41:10.
2:6 An announcement of the coming day of God's judgment on the nations—which the fall of Persia to Alexander the Great (333–330 B.C.) would foreshadow. Heb 12:26–27 relates this verse to the judgment of the nations at the second coming of Christ. The background for the shaking of the nations here and in vv. 21–22 is the judgment on Egypt at the Red Sea. Cf. also Isa 14:16–17.
2:7 *desired ... will come.* "Desired" can refer to individuals, as in Da 9:23 (where the same Hebrew verb is translated "highly esteemed"); cf. 1Sa 9:20. Thus it may have Messianic significance (see Da 11:37 and note; Mal 3:1). The same Hebrew word can also refer to articles of value, however (see 2Ch 20:25; 32:27)—such as the contribution of King Darius to the temple (Ezr 6:8). If that is the intent here, the bringing of the "riches of the nations" to Zion in Isa 60:5 is a close parallel (see note there). *fill ... with glory.* "Glory" can refer to material splendor (see Isa 60:7,13 and notes) or to the presence of God (Ex 40:34–35; 1Ki 8:10–11; Eze 10:4). The latter references connect the glory of the Lord with the cloud that filled the sanctuary. When Christ came to the earthly temple, God's presence was evident as never before (see Lk 2:27,32).
2:8 *silver ... gold.* Provided for Solomon's temple (1Ch 29:2,7) and for Zerubbabel's (Ezr 6:5).
2:9 *glory ... greater.* Ultimately because the Messiah would be present there (see v. 7 and note). *former house.* Solomon's temple. *this place.* Perhaps Jerusalem (see Zep 1:4 and note). *I will grant peace.* Perhaps an allusion to the priestly benediction (see Nu 6:26 and note).
2:10 *twenty-fourth day ... ninth month.* Dec. 18, 520 B.C.—when winter crops were planted.
2:11 *priests.* They were consulted about the precise meaning of the law (see Dt 31:11; Jer 18:18; Mal 2:7–9 and notes).
2:12 *consecrated meat.* Meat from an animal set apart for a sacrifice. *does it become consecrated?* A question about transmitting holiness. Consecrated meat made the garment "holy" because it was in direct contact with that garment (see Lev 6:27), but the garment could not pass on that holiness to a third object.
2:13 *does it become defiled?* Ceremonial uncleanness is transmitted much more easily than holiness. Anything touched by an unclean person becomes unclean (see Nu 19:11–13,22).
2:14 *this people.* See 1:2 and note. *Whatever they do ... is defiled.* Even though the people were back in the holy land, that holiness did not make them pure. They needed to obey the Lord, particularly with regard to rebuilding the temple. See notes on vv. 12–13.
2:15 *before one stone was laid.* Before the 24th day of the sixth month (1:14–15).

other in the LORD's temple.[a] 16When anyone came to a heap[b] of twenty measures,
there were only ten. When anyone went to
a wine vat[c] to draw fifty measures, there
were only twenty.[d] 17I struck all the work
of your hands[e] with blight,[f] mildew and
hail,[g] yet you did not turn[h] to me,' declares
the LORD.[i] 18'From this day on, from this
twenty-fourth day of the ninth month,
give careful thought[j] to the day when the
foundation[k] of the LORD's temple was laid.
Give careful thought: 19Is there yet any
seed left in the barn? Until now, the vine
and the fig tree, the pomegranate[l] and the
olive tree have not borne fruit.[m]
"'From this day on I will bless[n] you.'"

Zerubbabel the LORD's Signet Ring

20The word of the LORD came to Haggai[o]
a second time on the twenty-fourth day of
the month:[p] 21"Tell Zerubbabel[q] governor
of Judah that I will shake[r] the heavens and
the earth. 22I will overturn[s] royal thrones
and shatter the power of the foreign kingdoms.[t] I will overthrow chariots[u] and their
drivers; horses and their riders[v] will fall,
each by the sword of his brother.[w]
23"'On that day,[x]' declares the LORD Almighty, 'I will take you, my servant[y] Zerubbabel[z] son of Shealtiel,' declares the
LORD, 'and I will make you like my signet
ring,[a] for I have chosen you,' declares the
LORD Almighty."

2:15 [a]Ezr 4:24 **2:16** [b]S Ru 3:7 [c]S Job 24:11; S Isa 5:2 [d]S Dt 28:38; S Isa 5:10; S Hag 1:6 **2:17** [e]Hag 1:11 [f]S Dt 28:22 [g]S Ex 9:18; Ps 78:48 [h]S Isa 9:13; S Jer 3:10 [i]S Am 4:6 **2:18** [j]S Hag 1:5 [k]S Ezr 3:11 **2:19** [l]S Ex 28:33 [m]S Joel 1:12 [n]S Ge 12:2; S Lev 25:21; Ps 128:1-6; S Joel 2:14 **2:20** [o]S Ezr 5:1 [p]S ver 1; S Hag 1:15

2:21 [q]S Ezr 5:2 [r]S Isa 14:16; Eze 38:19-20 **2:22** [s]S Ge 19:25; S Job 2:13 [t]S Da 2:44 [u]S Mic 5:10 [v]S Ex 15:21 [w]S Jdg 7:22; S Eze 38:21 **2:23** [x]Isa 2:11; 10:20; Zec 4:10 [y]S Isa 20:3; S Da 9:24-26 [z]Mt 1:12 [a]S Ge 38:18; S Ex 28:9; 2Co 1:22

2:16 *heap.* Probably of grain (see Jer 50:26). *only ten ... only twenty.* The poor harvests were related to the sin of the people (see 1:11; Isa 5:10 and note). *wine vat.* Usually a shallow pit cut into solid rock, into which grape juice flowed when the grapes were trodden and where it was retained until fermentation had begun. The juice was later transferred to jars or skins for further fermentation and storage.

2:17 *blight, mildew.* Mentioned as a curse for disobedience in Dt 28:22 (see also 1Ki 8:37; Am 4:9). The blight was probably caused by a scorching east wind (see Ge 41:6 and note). *hail.* Sent to destroy the fields and livestock of Egypt (see Ex 9:25; Ps 78:47–48). *you did not turn.* See Am 4:6,8–11.

2:18 *when the foundation ... was laid.* The same potential for blessing had existed at the time when the foundation of the temple was laid in 536 B.C. (Ezr 3:11). This is a warning not to fail again.

2:19 *vine ... fig tree ... pomegranate ... olive tree.* Grapes, figs and pomegranates ripened in August and September, and olives from September to November. These harvests, like the earlier grain crops, had produced little (see 1:11 and note). *I will bless you.* Because of their response to Haggai's message, future abundance is assured. Cf. Mal 3:10.

2:20 See note on v. 10.

2:21 *shake ... the earth.* See v. 6 and note.

2:22 *overturn ... overthrow.* The Hebrew for these words is used with reference to Sodom and Gomorrah (see Ge 19:25; Am 4:11). *chariots ... horses ... riders.* Cf. the destruction of the pharaoh's army at the Red Sea (Ex 15:1,4,19,21). *each by ... his brother.* The plight of the armies of Midian (see Jdg 7:22 and note), Gog (see Eze 38:21 and note) and the nations fighting against Jerusalem in the last days (Zec 14:13).

2:23 *On that day.* The day of the Lord (see Isa 2:11,17,20; 10:20,27; Joel 1:15; Zec 2:11 and notes). *my servant.* A term applied to prophets (see Isa 20:3 and note), political leaders (Isa 22:20) and the Messiah (see Isa 41:8–9; 42:1 and notes). *signet ring.* A kind of seal that functioned as a signature (see Est 8:8) and was worn on one's finger (Est 3:10). Like other seals (see Ge 38:18 and note) it could be used as a pledge or guarantee of full payment. Its mention here apparently reverses the curse placed on King Jehoiachin in Jer 22:24 (see also Jdg 17:2 and note). Zerubbabel would then be a guarantee that indeed the future glory of the temple will be realized (see vv. 6–7,9; Zec 4:6–7 and notes). *chosen you.* See Isa 41:8–9; 42:1 and notes.

Zechariah

INTRODUCTION

Background

Zechariah's prophetic ministry took place in the postexilic period, the time of the Jewish restoration from Babylonian captivity. For historical details see Introduction to Haggai: Background.

Author and Unity

Like Jeremiah (1:1) and Ezekiel (1:3), Zechariah was not only a prophet (1:1) but also a member of a priestly family. He was born in Babylonia and was among those who returned to Judah in 538/537 B.C. under the leadership of Zerubbabel and Joshua (his grandfather Iddo is named among the returnees in Ne 12:4). At a later time, when Joiakim was high priest (see note on Ne 12:12 – 21), Zechariah apparently succeeded Iddo (1:1,7) as head of that priestly family (Ne 12:10 – 16). Since the grandson succeeded the grandfather, it has been suggested that the father (Berekiah, 1:1,7) died at an early age.

Zechariah was a contemporary of Haggai (Ezr 5:1; 6:14) but continued his ministry long after him (compare 1:1 and 7:1 with Hag 1:1; see also Ne 12:1 – 16). His young age (see 2:4 and note) in the early period of his ministry makes it possible that he ministered even into the reign of Artaxerxes I (465 – 424 B.C.).

Most likely Zechariah wrote the entire book that bears his name. Some have questioned his authorship of chs. 9 – 14, citing differences in style and other compositional features, and giving historical and chronological references that allegedly require a different date and author from those of chs. 1 – 8. All these objections, however, can be explained in other satisfactory ways, so there is no compelling reason to question the unity of the book.

Dates

The dates of Zechariah's recorded messages are best correlated with those of Haggai and with other historical events as follows:

1.	Haggai's first message (Hag 1:1 – 11; Ezr 5:1)	Aug. 29, 520 B.C.
2.	Resumption of the building of the temple (Hag 1:12 – 15; Ezr 5:2) (The rebuilding seems to have been hindered from 536 to c. 530 [Ezr 4:1 – 5], and the work ceased altogether from c. 530 to 520 [Ezr 4:24].)	Sept. 21, 520

3.	Haggai's second message (Hag 2:1 – 9)	Oct. 17, 520
4.	Beginning of Zechariah's preaching (1:1 – 6)	Oct./Nov., 520
5.	Haggai's third message (Hag 2:10 – 19)	Dec. 18, 520
6.	Haggai's fourth message (Hag 2:20 – 23)	Dec. 18, 520
7.	Tattenai's letter to Darius concerning the rebuilding of the temple (Ezr 5:3 — 6:14) (There must have been a lapse of time between the resumption of the building and Tattenai's appearance.)	519 – 518
8.	Zechariah's eight night visions (1:7 — 6:8)	Feb. 15, 519
9.	Joshua crowned (6:9 – 15)	Feb. 16 (?), 519
10.	Repentance urged, blessings promised (chs. 7 – 8)	Dec. 7, 518
11.	Dedication of the temple (Ezr 6:15 – 18)	Mar. 12, 516
12.	Zechariah's final prophecies (chs. 9 – 14)	After 480 (?)

Occasion and Purpose

The occasion of chs. 1 – 8 is the same as that of the book of Haggai (see Background; Dates). The chief purpose of Zechariah (and Haggai) was to rebuke the people of Judah and to encourage and motivate them to complete the rebuilding of the temple (Zec 4:8 – 10; Hag 1 – 2), though both prophets were clearly interested in spiritual renewal as well. In addition, the purpose of the eight night visions (1:7 — 6:8) is explained in 1:3,5 – 6: The Lord said that if Judah would return to him, he would return to them. Furthermore, his word would continue to be fulfilled. The primary purpose of chs. 9 – 14 was to provide encouragement to the Israelites — whether living in Judah or in exile — because of the glorious future that awaits them (see Literary Forms and Themes below).

Theological Teaching

The theology of Zechariah's prophecy matches his name, which means "The Lord (Yahweh) remembers." "The Lord" is the personal, covenant name of God and is a perpetual testimony to his faithfulness to his promises (see notes on Ge 2:4; Ex 3:14 – 15; 6:6; Dt 28:58). He "remembers" his covenant promises and takes action to fulfill them. In the book of Zechariah, God's promised deliverance from Babylonian exile, including a restored kingdom community and a functioning temple (the earthly throne of the divine King; see Introduction to Psalms: Theology), leads into even grander pictures of the salvation and restoration to come through the Messiah (see notes on 3:8 – 9; 4:3,14; 6:9 – 15; 9:9 – 10; 10:2,4; 11:4 – 14; 12:10 — 13:1; 13:7; 14:4 – 9).

The book as a whole also teaches the sovereignty of God in history, over people and nations — past, present and future (see, e.g., 1:10 – 11; 2:13; 4:10,14 and note; 6:5,7; 8:20 – 23; 9:10,13 – 14; 10:11; 12:1 – 5; 14:9,16 – 19). See also Literary Forms and Themes below.

A Quick Look

Author:
Zechariah

Audience:
The postexilic Jews living in Judah

Date:
520 to 480 B.C.

Theme:
The prophet Zechariah rebukes and encourages the discouraged exiles who have returned to Jerusalem from Babylonia to complete the rebuilding of the temple.

Literary Forms and Themes

The book is primarily a mixture of exhortation (call to repentance, 1:2 – 6), prophetic visions (1:7 — 6:8), a prophetic message of instruction or exhortation involving a symbolic coronation scene (6:9 – 15), hortatory messages (mainly of rebuke and hope) prompted by a question about fasting (chs. 7 – 8), and judgment and salvation messages (chs. 9 – 14). The prophetic visions of 1:7 — 6:8 are called apocalyptic (revelatory) literature, which is essentially a literature of encouragement to God's people. When the apocalyptic section is read along with the salvation (or deliverance) messages in chs. 9 – 14, it becomes obvious that the dominant emphasis of the book is encouragement because of the glorious future that awaits the people of God.

In fact, encouragement is the book's central theme — initially encouragement to complete the rebuilding of the temple. Various means are used to accomplish this end, and these function as subthemes. For example, great stress is laid on the coming of the Messiah and the overthrow of all anti-kingdom forces by him so that God's rule can be finally and fully established on earth. The then-current local scene thus becomes the basis for contemplating the universal, eschatological picture.

The dominant emphasis of the book is encouragement because of the glorious future that awaits the people of God.

Several interpreters have arranged the eight visions of 1:7 — 6:8 in a chiastic (or concentric) pattern of *a-b-b-c / c′-b′-b′-a′*:

- *a* The Lord controls the events of history (1:7 – 17)
  - *b* Nations that devastated Israel will in turn be devastated (1:18 – 21)
  - *b* Israel will be fully restored (ch. 2)
    - *c* Israel will be restored as a priestly nation (ch. 3)
    - *c′* Israel will be restored under royal and priestly leadership (ch. 4)
  - *b′* Lawbreakers will be purged from Israel (5:1 – 4)
  - *b′* The whole sinful system will be removed from the land (5:5 – 11)
- *a′* The Lord controls the events of history (6:1 – 8)

Outline

Part I (chs. 1 – 8)

- I. Introduction (1:1 – 6)
  - A. The Date and the Author's Name (1:1)
  - B. A Call to Repentance (1:2 – 6)
- II. A Series of Eight Visions in One Night (1:7 — 6:8)
  - A. The Horseman among the Myrtle Trees (1:7 – 17)
  - B. The Four Horns and the Four Craftsmen (1:18 – 21)
  - C. A Man with a Measuring Line (ch. 2)
  - D. Clean Garments for the High Priest (ch. 3)
  - E. The Gold Lampstand and the Two Olive Trees (ch. 4)
  - F. The Flying Scroll (5:1 – 4)
  - G. The Woman in a Basket (5:5 – 11)
  - H. The Four Chariots (6:1 – 8)
- III. The Symbolic Crowning of Joshua the High Priest (6:9 – 15)
- IV. The Problem of Fasting and the Promise of the Future (chs. 7 – 8)
  - A. The Question by the Delegation from Bethel (7:1 – 3)
  - B. The Rebuke by the Lord (7:4 – 7)
  - C. The Command to Repent (7:8 – 14)
  - D. The Restoration of Israel to God's Favor (8:1 – 17)
  - E. Kingdom Joy and Jewish Favor (8:18 – 23)

Part II (chs. 9 – 14)

- V. Two Prophetic Messages: The Great Messianic Future and the Full Realization of God's Kingdom (chs. 9 – 14)
  - A. The First Message: The Coming and Rejection of the Messiah (chs. 9 – 11)
    - 1. The coming of the Messianic King (chs. 9 – 10)
      - a. The destruction of surrounding nations but the preservation of Zion (9:1 – 8)
      - b. The coming of Zion's King (9:9 – 10)
      - c. The deliverance and blessing of Zion's people (9:11 — 10:1)

- d. The leaders warned and the people encouraged (10:2 – 4)
- e. Israel's victory and restoration (10:5 – 12)

2. The rejection of the Messianic Shepherd-King (ch. 11)
   - a. The prologue (11:1 – 3)
   - b. The rejection of the Good Shepherd (11:4 – 14)
   - c. The rise and fall of the worthless shepherd (11:15 – 17)

B. The Second Message: The Coming and Reception of the Messiah (chs. 12 – 14)

1. The deliverance and conversion of Israel (chs. 12 – 13)
   - a. The siege of Jerusalem (12:1 – 3)
   - b. The divine deliverance (12:4 – 9)
   - c. Israel completely delivered from sin (12:10 — 13:9)
2. The Messiah's coming and his kingdom (ch. 14)
   - a. The siege of Jerusalem (14:1 – 2)
   - b. The Messiah's return and its effects (14:3 – 8)
   - c. The establishment of the Messianic kingdom (14:9 – 11)
   - d. The punishment of Israel's enemies (14:12 – 15)
   - e. The universal worship of the holy King (14:16 – 21)

A Call to Return to the LORD

1 In the eighth month of the second year of Darius,[a] the word of the LORD came to the prophet Zechariah[b] son of Berekiah,[c] the son of Iddo:[d]

2 "The LORD was very angry[e] with your forefathers. 3 Therefore tell the people: This is what the LORD Almighty says: 'Return[f] to me,' declares the LORD Almighty, 'and I will return to you,'[g] says the LORD Almighty. 4 Do not be like your forefathers,[h] to whom the earlier prophets[i] proclaimed: This is what the LORD Almighty says: 'Turn from your evil ways[j] and your evil practices.' But they would not listen or pay attention to me,[k] declares the LORD.[l] 5 Where are your forefathers now? And the prophets, do they live forever? 6 But did not my words[m] and my decrees, which I commanded my servants the prophets, overtake your forefathers?[n]

"Then they repented and said, 'The LORD Almighty has done to us what our ways and practices deserve,[o] just as he determined to do.'"[p]

The Man Among the Myrtle Trees

7 On the twenty-fourth day of the eleventh month, the month of Shebat, in the second year of Darius, the word of the LORD came to the prophet Zechariah son of Berekiah, the son of Iddo.[q]

8 During the night I had a vision—and there before me was a man riding a red[r] horse! He was standing among the myrtle trees in a ravine. Behind him were red, brown and white horses.[s]

9 I asked, "What are these, my lord?"

The angel[t] who was talking with me answered, "I will show you what they are."[u]

10 Then the man standing among the myrtle trees explained, "They are the ones the LORD has sent to go throughout the earth."[v]

11 And they reported to the angel of the LORD,[w] who was standing among the myrtle trees, "We have gone throughout the earth and found the whole world at rest and in peace."[x]

12 Then the angel of the LORD said, "LORD Almighty, how long[y] will you withhold mercy[z] from Jerusalem and from the towns of Judah,[a] which you have been angry with these seventy[b] years?" 13 So the LORD spoke[c] kind and comforting words[d] to the angel who talked with me.[e]

14 Then the angel who was speaking to me said, "Proclaim this word: This is what the LORD Almighty says: 'I am very jealous[f] for Jerusalem and Zion, 15 but I am very angry with the nations that feel secure.[g] I was only a little angry,[h] but they added to the calamity.'[i]

1:1 [a] S Ezr 4:24; S 6:15 [b] S Ezr 5:1 [c] Mt 23:35; Lk 11:51 [d] ver 7; S Ne 12:4 **1:2** [e] S 2Ch 36:16 **1:3** [f] S Job 22:23 [g] Mal 3:7; Jas 4:8 **1:4** [h] S 2Ch 36:15 [i] Zec 7:7 [j] S 2Ki 17:13; S 2Ch 7:14; Ps 106:6; S Jer 23:22 [k] S 2Ch 24:19; Ps 78:8; S Jer 6:17; 17:23 [l] S Eze 20:18; S 33:4 **1:6** [m] S Isa 44:26 [n] S Dt 28:2; S Da 9:12; S Hos 5:9 [o] Jer 12:14-17; La 2:17 [p] Jer 23:20; 39:16; S 44:17 **1:7** [q] S ver 1 **1:8** [r] Rev 6:4 [s] Zec 6:2-7 **1:9** [t] Zec 4:1, 4-5; 5:5 [u] S Da 7:16 **1:10** [v] Zec 6:5-8 **1:11** [w] Ge 16:7 [x] S Isa 14:7 **1:12** [y] S Ps 6:3 [z] Ps 40:11 [a] S Jer 40:5 [b] S 2Ch 36:21; S Da 9:2 **1:13** [c] S Isa 35:4 [d] S Job 15:11 [e] Zec 4:1 **1:14** [f] S Isa 26:11; S Joel 2:18 **1:15** [g] Jer 48:11 [h] S 2Ch 28:9 [i] S Ps 69:26; 123:3-4; S Am 1:11

1:1 *eighth month of the second year.* October-November, 520 B.C. Haggai also began his prophetic ministry in Darius's second year (see chart, p. 472), on the first day of the sixth month, i.e., on Aug. 29, 520 (Hag 1:1). *word of the LORD.* A technical phrase for the prophetic word of revelation (see v. 7; 9:1; 12:1; see also 4:8; Hos 1:1 and notes). *prophet.* One called by God to speak his word on his behalf (see note on Ex 7:1–2). *Iddo.* See v. 7; Ezr 5:1; 6:14; Ne 12:4,16; see also Introduction: Author and Unity.

1:2 *very angry with your forefathers.* The Lord was angry because of the covenant-breaking sins of the Jews' preexilic ancestors, resulting in the destruction of Jerusalem and the temple in 586 B.C., followed by exile to Babylonia (2Ch 36:15–21).

1:3 *the LORD Almighty.* See note on 1Sa 1:3. *Return to me ... and I will return to you.* Cf. 7:13; 8:3; Mal 3:7. If the people of Zechariah's day would change their course and go in the opposite direction from that of their ancestors (v. 4), the Lord would return to them with blessing instead of with a curse (see v. 16; see also Jer 18:7–10 and note).

1:4 *earlier prophets.* Such as Isaiah (see Isa 45:22 and note), Jeremiah (see Jer 18:11 and note) and Ezekiel (see Eze 33:11 and note). See also 7:7,12; Jer 25:4–5; 35:15.

1:5 *do they live forever?* No, but God's words through them live on to be fulfilled (see v. 6).

1:6 *did not my words ... overtake your forefathers?* Cf. Isa 40:6–8; 55:10–11. For the imagery of "overtake" see Dt 28:2 ("accompany" is lit. "overtake"), 15,45. *my servants the prophets.* See 2Ki 9:7; 17:13,23; 21:10; 24:2; Ezr 9:11; Jer 7:25 and note; 25:4; Eze 38:17; Da 9:6,10; Am 3:7. *they repented.* Apparently a reference to what happened to some of the preexilic ancestors and/or their offspring during the exile and immediately afterward (cf. Ezr 9:1—10:17; Da 9:3–19).

1:7—6:8 See Introduction: Literary Forms and Themes.

1:7–17 The first vision. Although God's covenant people are troubled while the oppressing nations are at ease, God is jealous (see note on Ex 20:5) for his people and will restore them and their towns and the temple. The imagery of the first vision is reflected in that of the eighth and final vision (6:1–8).

1:7 *twenty-fourth day of ... Shebat.* Feb. 15, 519 B.C., about three months after the date of v. 1.

1:8 *During the night.* Zechariah had all eight visions (1:7—6:8) in one night. *vision.* Not a dream (see 4:1; see also Pr 29:18; Isa 1:1; Ob 1 and notes). The visions were given to Zechariah while he was fully awake. *man riding.* Later identified as the angel of the Lord (v. 11). He must not be confused with the interpreting angel, who is mentioned in vv. 9,13–14,19; 2:3; 4:1,4–5; 5:5,10; 6:4–5.

1:9 *angel.* See note on v. 8.

1:11 *angel of the LORD.* See 3:1; see also note on Ge 16:7. *at rest.* Cf. 6:8. While the Persian empire as a whole was secure and at ease by this time (v. 15), the Jews in Judah were oppressed and still under foreign domination (v. 12).

1:12 *mercy.* Tender compassion (also in v. 16). *seventy years.* See 7:5; Ezr 1:1; Jer 25:11–12 and notes.

1:13 *comforting words.* Those of vv. 14–17.

1:14 *jealous.* See 8:2. Through the use of such language the Lord's love for Judah is shown (see note on Ex 20:5; cf. Jas 4:4). The key idea is that of God avenging Judah for the violations against her (v. 15; see Dt 32:35,41; Jer 50:15; 51:6,11).

1:15 *nations that feel secure.* A security that will be completely undone (see Isa 32:9–13; Hag 2:6–7 and notes). *added to the*

16“Therefore, this is what the LORD says:
‘I will return[j] to Jerusalem with mercy,
and there my house will be rebuilt. And
the measuring line[k] will be stretched out
over Jerusalem,’ declares the LORD Almighty.[l]
17“Proclaim further: This is what the
LORD Almighty says: ‘My towns will again
overflow with prosperity, and the LORD
will again comfort[m] Zion and choose[n] Jerusalem.’ ”[o]

Four Horns and Four Craftsmen

18Then I looked up — and there before
me were four horns! 19I asked the angel who was speaking to me, “What are
these?”
He answered me, “These are the horns[p]
that scattered Judah, Israel and Jerusalem.”
20Then the LORD showed me four craftsmen. 21I asked, “What are these coming
to do?”
He answered, “These are the horns that
scattered Judah so that no one could raise
his head, but the craftsmen have come to
terrify them and throw down these horns
of the nations who lifted up their horns[q]
against the land of Judah to scatter its people.”[r]

A Man With a Measuring Line

2 Then I looked up — and there before
me was a man with a measuring line
in his hand! 2I asked, “Where are you going?”
He answered me, “To measure Jerusalem, to find out how wide and how long
it is.”[s]
3Then the angel who was speaking to
me left, and another angel came to meet
him 4and said to him: “Run, tell that
young man, ‘Jerusalem will be a city without walls[t] because of the great number[u] of
men and livestock in it.[v] 5And I myself will
be a wall[w] of fire[x] around it,’ declares the
LORD, ‘and I will be its glory[y] within.’[z][a]
6“Come! Come! Flee from the land of
the north,” declares the LORD, “for I have
scattered[b] you to the four winds of heav-
en,”[c] declares the LORD.[d]
7“Come, O Zion! Escape,[e] you who live
in the Daughter of Babylon!”[f] 8For this is
what the LORD Almighty says: “After he
has honored me and has sent me against
the nations that have plundered you — for
whoever touches you touches the apple
of his eye[g] — 9I will surely raise my hand
against them so that their slaves will plunder them.[a][h] Then you will know that the
LORD Almighty has sent me.[i]
10“Shout[j] and be glad, O Daughter of
Zion.[k] For I am coming,[l] and I will live
among you,”[m] declares the LORD.[n] 11“Many
nations will be joined with the LORD in
that day and will become my people.[o] I
will live among you and you will know
that the LORD Almighty has sent me to
you.[p] 12The LORD will inherit[q] Judah[r] as
his portion in the holy land and will again

[a] 8,9 *Or says after . . . eye: 9“I . . . plunder them.”*

1:16 [j]Zec 8:3 [k]S Job 38:5; Zec 2:1-2 [l]S Ezr 1:1 **1:17** [m]S Isa 40:1 [n]S Isa 14:1 [o]S Ezr 9:9; S Ps 51:18; Isa 54:8-10; S 61:4 **1:19** [p]Am 6:13 **1:21** [q]S 1Ki 22:11; Ps 75:4 [r]S Ps 75:10; S Isa 54:16-17; Zec 12:9 **2:2** [s]S Eze 40:3; S Zec 1:16; Rev 21:15 **2:4** [t]S Eze 38:11 [u]S Isa 49:20; S Jer 30:19; S 33:22 [v]Zec 14:11 **2:5** [w]S Isa 26:1; Eze 42:20 [x]S Isa 10:17 [y]S Ps 85:9; S Isa 11:10; S 24:23; Rev 21:23 [z]S Ps 125:2 [a]S Ps 46:5; S Eze 38:14 **2:6** [b]S Ps 44:11 [c]S Eze 17:21; S 37:9 [d]Mt 24:31; Mk 13:27 **2:7** [e]S Isa 42:7 [f]S Isa 48:20; Jer 3:18 **2:8** [g]S Dt 32:10 **2:9** [h]S Isa 14:2; S Jer 12:14; S Hab 2:8 [i]S Isa 48:16; Zec 4:9; 6:15 **2:10** [j]S Zep 3:14 [k]S Isa 23:12; S Zep 3:14 [l]Zec 9:9 [m]S Ex 25:8; Lev 26:12; S Nu 23:21; Zec 8:3 [n]S Rev 21:3 **2:11** [o]S Jer 24:7; S Mic 4:2; Zec 8:8,20-22 [p]Zec 4:9; 6:15 **2:12** [q]S Ex 34:9; Ps 33:12; Jer 10:16 [r]Jer 40:5

calamity. God was angry with Israel and used the Assyrians (see Isa 10:5 and note) and Babylonians (see Isa 47:6; Jer 25:9 and notes) to punish her, but they went too far by trying to destroy Israel as a people.

1:16 *I will return.* See note on v. 3. *mercy.* See v. 12 and note. *my house will be rebuilt.* See Ezr 6:14–16; Hag 1:8; see also Introduction to Haggai: Background. *measuring line.* A symbol of restoration (see Jer 31:38–40 and note on 31:39).

1:17 *comfort.* See v. 13 and note. *choose Jerusalem.* See 2:12; 3:2.

1:18–21 The second vision. The nations that devastated Israel (v. 19) will in turn be destroyed by other nations.

1:18 *four.* If the number is to be taken literally, the reference is probably to Assyria, Egypt, Babylonia and Persia. *horns.* Probably metallic, either bronze or iron; symbolic of strength in general (Ps 18:2), or the strength of a country, i.e., its king (Ps 89:17; Da 7:7–8; 8:20–21; Rev 17:12), or, as here (see v. 21), the power of a nation in general.

1:20 *four.* If the number is to be understood literally, perhaps the reference is to Egypt, Babylonia, Persia and Greece. What is clear is that all Israel's enemies will ultimately be defeated (v. 21). *craftsmen.* Probably metalsmiths (see 1Ki 22:11).

1:21 *terrify them.* Contrast vv. 11 ("at rest and in peace"), 15 ("feel secure"; see note there).

2:1–13 The third vision. There will be full restoration and blessing for the covenant people, temple and city.

2:1 *measuring line.* See note on 1:16.

2:4 *young man.* Evidently Zechariah. *without walls.* The city's population will overflow to the point that it will be as though it had no walls (see 10:8,10; see also note on Isa 49:19–20).

2:5 *wall of fire.* Here symbolic of divine protection (see 9:8; see also Ex 13:21; Isa 4:5–6 and notes). *glory.* See Ex 40:34; Hag 2:9 and notes.

2:6 *land of the north.* Babylonia (v. 7) invaded Judah from the north (see Isa 41:25 and note; Jer 1:14; 4:6; 6:1,22; 10:22). *to the four winds.* In all directions. The exiles would return from north, south, east and west (Isa 43:5–6; 49:12).

2:7 *Zion.* Jerusalem's exiles in Babylon. *Escape . . . Babylon.* Cf. Rev 18:2–4. *Daughter of Babylon.* A personification of Babylon (see note on 2Ki 19:21).

2:8 *me.* See also v. 9; probably the angel of the Lord (see 1:8 and note). *apple of his eye.* See note on Dt 32:10.

2:10 See 9:9 and note. *Daughter of Zion.* A personification of Jerusalem (see v. 7 and note). *I will live among you.* See v. 11; 8:3; Lev 26:11–12; Eze 37:27; Jn 1:14; 2 Co 6:16; Rev 21:3.

2:11 *Many nations.* In fulfillment of the promise to Abraham (Ge 12:3; cf. Zec 8:20–23; 14:16; Ge 18:18; 22:18; Isa 2:2–4 and note; 19:24–25). *that day.* The day of the Lord (see 3:10; see also 12:3; Isa 2:11,17,20; Joel 1:15; Am 5:18 and notes).

2:12 *holy land.* See Ps 78:54. The land was rendered holy chiefly because it was the site of the earthly throne and sanctuary of the holy King, who dwelt there among his covenant people (see note on Ex 3:5). *choose Jerusalem.* See 1:17; 3:2.

choose[s] Jerusalem. 13Be still[t] before the
LORD, all mankind, because he has roused
himself from his holy dwelling.[u]"

Clean Garments for the High Priest

3 Then he showed me Joshua[a v] the
high priest standing before the angel
of the LORD, and Satan[b w] standing at his
right side to accuse him. 2The LORD said
to Satan, "The LORD rebuke you,[x] Satan!
The LORD, who has chosen[y] Jerusalem, rebuke you! Is not this man a burning stick[z]
snatched from the fire?"[a]

3Now Joshua was dressed in filthy
clothes as he stood before the angel. 4The
angel said to those who were standing before him, "Take off his filthy clothes."

Then he said to Joshua, "See, I have
taken away your sin,[b] and I will put rich
garments[c] on you."

5Then I said, "Put a clean turban[d] on his
head." So they put a clean turban on his
head and clothed him, while the angel of
the LORD stood by.

6The angel of the LORD gave this charge
to Joshua: 7"This is what the LORD Almighty says: 'If you will walk in my ways
and keep my requirements,[e] then you will
govern my house[f] and have charge[g] of my
courts, and I will give you a place among
these standing here.[h]

8" 'Listen, O high priest[i] Joshua and your
associates seated before you, who are men
symbolic[j] of things to come: I am going to
bring my servant, the Branch.[k] 9See, the
stone I have set in front of Joshua![l] There
are seven eyes[c m] on that one stone,[n] and I
will engrave an inscription on it,' says the
LORD Almighty, 'and I will remove the sin[o]
of this land in a single day.

10" 'In that day each of you will invite
his neighbor to sit[p] under his vine and fig
tree,[q]' declares the LORD Almighty."

The Gold Lampstand and the Two Olive Trees

4 Then the angel who talked with me returned and wakened[r] me, as a man is
wakened from his sleep.[s] 2He asked me,
"What do you see?"[t]

I answered, "I see a solid gold lampstand[u]
with a bowl at the top and seven lights[v]
on it, with seven channels to the lights.

2:12 [s]S Dt 12:5; S Isa 14:1 **2:13** [t]S Ex 14:14; S Isa 41:1 [u]S Dt 26:15 **3:1** [v]S Ezr 2:2; Zec 6:11 [w]S 2Sa 24:1; S 2Ch 18:21; S Ps 109:6; S Mt 4:10 **3:2** [x]Jude 1:9 [y]S Isa 14:1 [z]S Isa 7:4 [a]Jude 1:23 **3:4** [b]S 2Sa 12:13; S Eze 36:25; S Mic 7:18 [c]S Ge 41:42; S Ps 132:9; S Isa 52:1; Rev 19:8 **3:5** [d]S Ex 29:6 **3:7** [e]S Lev 8:35 [f]Dt 17:8-11; S Eze 44:15-16 [g]2Ch 23:6 [h]Jer 15:19; Zec 6:15 **3:8** [i]Hag 1:1 [j]S Dt 28:46; S Eze 12:11 [k]S Isa 4:2; S 49:3; S Eze 17:22 **3:9** [l]S Ezr 2:2 [m]S 2Ch 16:9 [n]Isa 28:16 [o]S 2Sa 12:13; S Jer 50:20

[a] *1* A variant of *Jeshua*; here and elsewhere in Zechariah
[b] *1* *Satan* means *accuser.* [c] *9* Or *facets*

3:10 [p]S Job 11:18 [q]S Nu 16:14; S 1Ki 4:25; Mic 4:4 **4:1** [r]S Da 8:18 [s]Jer 31:26 **4:2** [t]S Jer 1:13 [u]S Ex 25:31; Rev 1:12 [v]Rev 4:5

2:13 *Be still before the LORD.* See Hab 2:20 and note. *roused himself.* To judge (cf. v. 9).

3:1–10 The fourth vision. Israel will be cleansed and restored as a priestly nation (see Ex 19:6 and note).

3:1 *Joshua.* The same person's name is given its Aramaic equivalent (Jeshua) in Ezra and Nehemiah (see NIV text note; Ezr 2:2 and note; Ne 7:7; see also NIV text note on Hag 1:1). Here he represents the sinful nation of Israel (see vv. 8–9). The names Joshua and Jeshua were common in ancient times. The Greek equivalent is spelled "Jesus" in English, and all three forms of the name mean "The LORD saves" (see NIV text note on Mt 1:21). *standing before.* Ministering before—as priest (see Dt 10:8; 2Ch 29:11; Eze 44:15). *angel of the LORD.* See 1:11; see also note on Ge 16:7. *Satan.* See NIV text note; Job 1:6–12 and note on 1:6; 2:1–7; Rev 12:10 and note. *right side.* See Ps 109:6. *accuse.* The Hebrew for this word has the same root as the Hebrew for "Satan."

3:2 *rebuke … rebuke.* Repeated for emphasis (see 4:7; see also note on Isa 40:1). *chosen Jerusalem.* See 1:17; 2:12. *burning stick snatched from the fire.* The Jews were retrieved from the fire of Babylonian exile to carry out God's future purpose for them (see Am 4:11 and note; see also Zec 13:8–9; Dt 4:20 and note; 7:7–8; Jer 30:7; Rev 12:13–16; cf. 1Co 3:15; Jude 23 and notes).

3:4 *those who were standing before him.* Probably angels (see also v. 7). *Take off his filthy clothes.* Thus depriving him of his priestly office. The act is here symbolic also of the removal of sin (see note on v. 9; cf. Isa 64:6).

3:5 *Put a clean turban on his head.* Thus reinstating him into his high-priestly function so that Israel once again has a divinely authorized priestly mediator. On the front of the turban were the words: "HOLY TO THE LORD" (Ex 28:36–37; 39:30–31; see Zec 14:20 and note).

3:7 If Joshua and his priestly associates are faithful, they will be coworkers with the angels in carrying out God's purposes for Zion and Israel (cf. Jer 31:22 and note). *these standing here.* See note on v. 4.

3:8 *associates.* Fellow priests. *my servant.* See notes on Ex 14:31; Ps 18 title; Isa 41:8–9; 42:1–4; 42:1; Ro 1:1. *Branch.* A Messianic title (see 6:12; Isa 4:2 and notes; 11:1; Jer 23:5 and note; 33:15).

3:9 *stone.* Probably another figure of the Messiah (see Ps 118:22; Isa 8:14; 28:16 and notes; Da 2:35,45). *seven eyes.* Perhaps symbolic of infinite intelligence (omniscience). Cf. note on 4:10. *I will remove the sin of this land.* The symbolic act of v. 4 is now explained. "Land" stands for the people of Israel. For the cleansing spoken of here see also 12:10—13:1; cf. Ro 11:26–27 and notes. *in a single day.* Ultimately Good Friday, though some believe that the reference also includes Christ's second coming.

3:10 *that day.* See 2:11 and note. *sit under his vine and fig tree.* A proverbial picture of peace, security and contentment (see Mic 4:4 and note; cf. 2Ki 18:31).

4:1–14 The fifth vision. The Jews are encouraged to rebuild the temple by being reminded of their divine resources. The light from the lampstand in the tabernacle/temple represents the reflection of God's glory in the consecration and holy service of God's people (see note on Ex 25:37)—made possible only by the power of God's Spirit (see v. 6; symbolized by the oil, v. 12). This enabling power will equip and sustain Zerubbabel in the rebuilding of the temple (vv. 6–10). And in the performance of their offices, Zerubbabel and Joshua (as representatives of the royal and priestly mediatorial offices) will channel the Spirit's enablement to God's people (vv. 11–14).

4:1 *wakened me.* On the same night (see note on 1:8).

4:2 *What do you see?* See 5:2; see also Jer 1:11 and note. The vision here was probably of seven lamps arranged around a large bowl that served as a bountiful reservoir of oil. The "seven channels to the lights" conveyed the oil from the bowl to the lamps. But the text is also open to a different interpretation, namely, that the "channels" are lips or spouts that held the wicks of these oil lamps, and that each of these lamps had seven of them (thus a total of 49 flames; see note

3 Also there are two olive trees[w] by it, one
on the right of the bowl and the other on
its left."

4 I asked the angel who talked with me,
"What are these, my lord?"

5 He answered, "Do you not know what
these are?"

"No, my lord," I replied.[x]

6 So he said to me, "This is the word of
the LORD to Zerubbabel:[y] 'Not[z] by might
nor by power,[a] but by my Spirit,'[b] says the
LORD Almighty.

7 "What[a] are you, O mighty mountain?
Before Zerubbabel you will become level
ground.[c] Then he will bring out the capstone[d] to shouts[e] of 'God bless it! God
bless it!' "

8 Then the word of the LORD came to me:
9 "The hands of Zerubbabel have laid the
foundation[f] of this temple; his hands will
also complete it.[g] Then you will know that
the LORD Almighty has sent me[h] to you.

10 "Who despises the day[i] of small
things?[j] Men will rejoice when they see
the plumb line in the hand of Zerubbabel.[k]

"(These seven are the eyes[l] of the LORD,
which range throughout the earth.)"

11 Then I asked the angel, "What are
these two olive trees[m] on the right and the
left of the lampstand?"

12 Again I asked him, "What are these
two olive branches beside the two gold
pipes that pour out golden oil?"

13 He replied, "Do you not know what
these are?"

"No, my lord," I said.

14 So he said, "These are the two who
are anointed[n] to[b] serve the Lord of all the
earth."

The Flying Scroll

5 I looked again—and there before me
was a flying scroll![o]

2 He asked me, "What do you see?"[p]

I answered, "I see a flying scroll, thirty
feet long and fifteen feet wide.[c]"

3 And he said to me, "This is the curse[q]
that is going out over the whole land; for
according to what it says on one side, every thief[r] will be banished, and according

[a] 7 Or *Who* [b] 14 Or *two who bring oil and*
[c] 2 Hebrew *twenty cubits long and ten cubits wide* (about 9 meters long and 4.5 meters wide)

4:3 [w] ver 11; S Ps 1:3; S Rev 11:4 **4:5** [x] S Zec 1:9 **4:6** [y] S 1Ch 3:19; S Ezr 5:2 [z] S 1Sa 13:22; S 1Ki 19:12 [a] S 1Sa 2:9 [b] S Ne 9:20; Isa 11:2-4; S Da 2:34; Hos 1:7 **4:7** [c] S Ps 26:12; Jer 51:25 [d] S Ps 118:22 [e] S 1Ch 15:28 **4:9** [f] S Ezr 3:11 [g] Ezr 3:8; S 6:15; Zec 6:12 [h] S Zec 2:9 **4:10** [i] S Hag 2:23 [j] Hag 2:3 [k] S Ezr 5:1; S Ne 12:1; S Job 38:5 [l] S 2Ch 16:9; Rev 5:6 **4:11** [m] S ver 3; S Rev 11:4 **4:14** [n] Ex 29:7; 40:15; S Ps 45:7; S Isa 20:3; S Da 9:24-26 **5:1** [o] S Ps 40:7; S Jer 36:4; Rev 5:1 **5:2** [p] S Jer 1:13

5:3 [q] Isa 24:6; 34:2; 43:28; Mal 3:9; 4:6 [r] Ex 20:15; Mal 3:8

on Ex 25:37). In any event, the bowl represents an abundant supply of oil, symbolizing the fullness of God's power through his Spirit (v. 6), and the "seven ... seven" represents the abundant light shining from the lamps (seven being the number of fullness). Cf. Rev 1:4 and note.

4:3 *two olive trees.* Cf. Rev 11:4. The two olive trees stand for the priestly and royal offices and symbolize a continuing supply of oil. The two olive branches (v. 12) stand for Joshua the priest (ch. 3) and Zerubbabel from the royal house of David (ch. 4; cf. v. 14). These two leaders were to do God's work (e.g., on the temple and in the lives of the people) in the power of his Spirit (v. 6). The community that produced the Dead Sea Scrolls (see essay, p. 1452) looked forward to the coming of two Messiahs (the "Messiah of Aaron" and the "Messiah of Israel" [of the house of David]). But the embodiment of the priestly and royal lines and their functions in one individual points ultimately to the Messianic King-Priest and his offices and functions (see 6:13 and note).

4:4 *these.* The two olive trees of v. 3, as v. 11 makes clear. The answer to the question is postponed until v. 14.

4:6 *Not by might nor by power.* Zerubbabel does not possess the royal might and power that David and Solomon had enjoyed, and in any event such worldly power is inadequate for the purpose of rebuilding the Lord's temple. *by my Spirit.* Interprets the symbolism of the oil (v. 12). The angel encouraged Zerubbabel to complete the rebuilding of the temple (vv. 7–10) and assured him of the Spirit's enablement (see Hag 2:5 and note).

4:7 *mountain ... level ground.* Faith in the power of God's Spirit (v. 6) can overcome mountainous obstacles. The figurative mountain probably included opposition (Ezr 4:1–5,24) and the people's unwillingness to persevere (cf. Hag 1:14; 2:1–5). Cf. the same or similar imagery in Isa 40:4; 41:15; 49:11; Mt 17:20; 21:21; 1Co 13:2; 2Co 10:4. *capstone.* The final stone to be put in place (see Ps 118:22 and note), marking the completion of the temple's restoration by Zerubbabel (see v. 9). *God bless it! God bless it!* Repeated for emphasis (see 3:2; see also note on Isa 40:1).

4:8 Introduces a prophetic message (see 6:9; 7:4,8; 8:1,18; see also note on Hos 1:1).

4:9 *laid the foundation.* In 536 B.C. (Ezr 3:8–11; 5:16). *complete it.* In 516 (see Ezr 6:15 and note).

4:10 *day of small things.* Some thought the work on the temple was insignificant (see Ezr 3:12; Hag 2:3 and note), but God was in the rebuilding program and, by his Spirit (v. 6), would enable Zerubbabel to finish it. *plumb line.* The meaning of the Hebrew for this phrase is uncertain. If "plumb line" is correct, the meaning is that the people would rejoice when they saw this implement in Zerubbabel's hand to complete the task. But the Hebrew for these words may also be rendered "separated (i.e., chosen) stone," referring to the capstone of v. 7. *seven ... eyes.* See note on 3:9. God oversees the whole earth (2Ch 16:9) and is therefore in control of the situation in Judah.

4:14 The meaning of the vision is now explained. *two ... anointed.* Zerubbabel from the royal line of David and Joshua the priest. The oil (v. 12) used in anointing symbolizes the Holy Spirit (v. 6). The combination of ruler and priest points ultimately to the Messianic King-Priest (see 4:3; 6:13 and notes; cf. Ps 110; Heb 7). *Lord of all the earth.* See 6:5; the master of the circumstances in which Zerubbabel and the people found themselves.

5:1–4 The sixth vision. Lawbreakers are condemned by the law they have broken; sinners will be purged from the land.

5:1 *flying.* Unrolled and waving like a banner, for all to read. *scroll.* See note on Ex 17:14.

5:2 *He.* The interpreting angel (v. 5; 4:11). *What do you see?* See 4:2 and note. *thirty ... fifteen.* Unusually large (especially in its width), for all to see. Such a bold, clear message of judgment against sin should spur the people on to repentance and righteousness.

5:3 *curse.* See Dt 27:26 and note. *on one side ... on the other.* Like the two tablets of the law (Ex 32:15), the scroll is inscribed on both sides (see Eze 2:10 and note). *thief.* One who breaks the eighth commandment (Ex 20:15). *every-*

to what it says on the other, everyone who
swears falsely[s] will be banished. 4The LORD
Almighty declares, 'I will send it out, and
it will enter the house of the thief and the
house of him who swears falsely[t] by my
name. It will remain in his house and destroy it, both its timbers and its stones.[u]' "

The Woman in a Basket

5Then the angel who was speaking to
me came forward and said to me, "Look up
and see what this is that is appearing."
6I asked, "What is it?"
He replied, "It is a measuring basket.[a][v]"
And he added, "This is the iniquity[b] of the
people throughout the land."
7Then the cover of lead was raised, and
there in the basket sat a woman! 8He said,
"This is wickedness," and he pushed her
back into the basket and pushed the lead
cover down over its mouth.[w]
9Then I looked up—and there before
me were two women, with the wind in
their wings! They had wings like those of
a stork,[x] and they lifted up the basket between heaven and earth.
10"Where are they taking the basket?" I
asked the angel who was speaking to me.
11He replied, "To the country of Babylonia[c][y] to build a house[z] for it. When it is
ready, the basket will be set there in its
place."[a]

5:3 [s] Ex 20:7; Isa 48:1
5:4 [t] Zec 8:17 [u] Lev 14:34-45; S Pr 3:33; S Hab 2:9-11; Mal 3:5
5:6 [v] Mic 6:10
5:8 [w] Mic 6:11
5:9 [x] Lev 11:19
5:11 [y] S Ge 10:10 [z] Jer 29:5,28 [a] S Da 1:2
6:1 [b] ver 5; S 2Ki 2:11
6:2 [c] Rev 6:5
6:3 [d] Rev 6:2
6:5 [e] S Eze 37:9; Mt 24:31; Rev 7:1 [f] S Jos 3:11
6:7 [g] Isa 43:6; Zec 1:8
6:8 [h] S Eze 5:13; S 24:13 [i] S Zec 1:10

Four Chariots

6 I looked up again—and there before
me were four chariots[b] coming out from
between two mountains—mountains of
bronze! 2The first chariot had red horses,
the second black,[c] 3the third white,[d] and
the fourth dappled—all of them powerful.
4I asked the angel who was speaking to
me, "What are these, my lord?"
5The angel answered me, "These are the
four spirits[d][e] of heaven, going out from
standing in the presence of the Lord of
the whole world.[f] 6The one with the black
horses is going toward the north country,
the one with the white horses toward the
west,[e] and the one with the dappled horses toward the south."
7When the powerful horses went out,
they were straining to go throughout
the earth.[g] And he said, "Go throughout
the earth!" So they went throughout the
earth.
8Then he called to me, "Look, those going toward the north country have given
my Spirit[f] rest[h] in the land of the north."[i]

A Crown for Joshua

9The word of the LORD came to me:

[a] 6 Hebrew *an ephah*; also in verses 7-11 [b] 6 Or *appearance* [c] 11 Hebrew *Shinar* [d] 5 Or *winds* [e] 6 Or *horses after them* [f] 8 Or *spirit*

one who swears falsely. See 8:17. Such a person violates the third commandment (compare v. 4 with Ex 20:7). Although theft and perjury may have been the most common forms of lawbreaking at the time, they are probably intended as representative sins. The people of Judah had been guilty of infractions against the whole law (see Jas 2:10 and note).

5:4 *The LORD Almighty.* See note on 1Sa 1:3. *it will enter ... and destroy.* "It" refers to the curse (v. 3). God's word, whether promise (ch. 4) or warning (as here), always accomplishes its purpose (cf. Ps 147:15; Isa 55:10–11; see Heb 4:12–13 and notes).

5:5–11 The seventh vision. Not only must flagrant, persistent sinners be removed from the land (vv. 1–4), but the whole sinful system will be removed—apparently to a more fitting place (Babylonia).

5:6 *measuring basket.* See NIV text note. A normal ephah-sized container would not be large enough to hold a person. This one was undoubtedly enlarged (like the flying scroll of vv. 1–2) for the purpose of the vision. *iniquity.* See v. 8 ("wickedness") and note.

5:7 *woman.* Perhaps the reason the people's wickedness was personified as a woman (cf. Rev 17:1–6) is that the Hebrew word for "wickedness" (v. 8) is feminine in gender.

5:8 *wickedness.* A general word denoting moral, religious and civil evil—frequently used as an antonym of righteousness (e.g., Pr 13:6; Eze 33:12). The whole evil system was to be destroyed (cf. 2Th 2:6–8).

5:9 *two women.* Divinely chosen agents. *wind.* Also an instrument of God (see Ps 104:3–4 and note). The removal of wickedness would be the work of God alone.

5:11 *Babylonia.* See Ge 10:10 and NIV text note; 11:2 and NIV text note; Rev 17–18. Babylonia, a land of idolatry, was an appropriate locale for wickedness—but not Israel, where God chose to dwell with his people. Only after purging it of its evil would the promised land truly be the "holy land" (2:12).

6:1–8 The eighth and last vision. It corresponds to the first (1:7–17), though there are differences in details, such as in the order and colors of the horses. As in the first vision, the Lord is depicted as the one who controls the events of history (see Introduction: Literary Forms and Themes). He will conquer the nations that oppress Israel.

6:1 *four chariots.* Angelic spirits as agents of divine judgment (v. 5). *two mountains.* Possibly Mount Zion and the Mount of Olives, with the Kidron Valley between them (cf. Joel 3:2 and note). *bronze.* Perhaps symbolic of judgment (cf. Nu 21:9).

6:2–3 *red ... black ... white ... dappled.* The horses may signify various divine judgments on the earth (see note on v. 8; see also Rev 6:1–8 and note on 6:2).

6:4 *these.* The chariots, with the horses harnessed to them.

6:5 *four spirits.* See note on v. 1. *Lord of the whole world.* See note on 4:14.

6:8 *north country.* Primarily Babylonia, but also the direction from which most of Israel's foes invaded them (see note on 2:6). *my Spirit.* If the alternative translation in the NIV text note ("spirit") is taken, the meaning is that the angelic beings dispatched to the north have triumphed and thus have pacified or appeased God's spirit (i.e., his anger; cf. Ecc 10:4, where the same Hebrew word is translated "anger"). See 1:15, where God's displeasure was aroused against oppressive nations. In either case, since conquest was announced in the north, victory was assured over all enemies.

6:9–15 The two central visions (the fourth and fifth) were concerned with the high priest and the civil governor (in the Davidic line); see Introduction: Literary Forms and Themes. Zechariah now relates the message of those two visions to the Messianic King-Priest.

6:9 See note on 4:8.

10“Take ⌞silver and gold⌟ from the exiles
Heldai, Tobijah and Jedaiah, who have
arrived from Babylon.[j] Go the same day
to the house of Josiah son of Zephaniah. 11Take the silver and gold and make
a crown,[k] and set it on the head of the
high priest, Joshua[l] son of Jehozadak.[m]
12Tell him this is what the LORD Almighty
says: ‘Here is the man whose name is the
Branch,[n] and he will branch out from his
place and build the temple of the LORD.[o]
13It is he who will build the temple of the
LORD, and he will be clothed with majesty
and will sit and rule on his throne. And
he will be a priest[p] on his throne. And
there will be harmony between the two.’
14The crown will be given to Heldai,[a] Tobijah, Jedaiah and Hen[b] son of Zephaniah
as a memorial[q] in the temple of the LORD.
15Those who are far away will come and
help to build the temple of the LORD,[r] and
you will know that the LORD Almighty has
sent me to you.[s] This will happen if you
diligently obey[t] the LORD your God.”

Justice and Mercy, Not Fasting

7 In the fourth year of King Darius, the
word of the LORD came to Zechariah[u]
on the fourth day of the ninth month, the
month of Kislev.[v] 2The people of Bethel had
sent Sharezer and Regem-Melech, together with their men, to entreat[w] the LORD[x]
3by asking the priests of the house of the
LORD Almighty and the prophets, “Should
I mourn[y] and fast in the fifth[z] month, as I
have done for so many years?”
4Then the word of the LORD Almighty
came to me: 5“Ask all the people of the
land and the priests, ‘When you fasted[a]
and mourned in the fifth and seventh[b]
months for the past seventy years,[c] was it
really for me that you fasted? 6And when
you were eating and drinking, were you
not just feasting for yourselves?[d] 7Are
these not the words the LORD proclaimed
through the earlier prophets[e] when Jerusalem and its surrounding towns were at
rest[f] and prosperous, and the Negev and
the western foothills[g] were settled?’ ”[h]
8And the word of the LORD came again
to Zechariah: 9“This is what the LORD Almighty says: ‘Administer true justice;[i]
show mercy and compassion to one another.[j] 10Do not oppress the widow[k] or the
fatherless, the alien[l] or the poor.[m] In your
hearts do not think evil of each other.’[n]
11“But they refused to pay attention;
stubbornly[o] they turned their backs[p]
and stopped up their ears.[q] 12They made
their hearts as hard as flint[r] and would

[a] *14* Syriac; Hebrew *Helem* [b] *14* Or *and the gracious one, the*

6:10 [j]Ezr 7:14-16; Jer 28:6 **6:11** [k]Ps 21:3 [l]S Ezr 2:2; S Zec 3:1 [m]S 1Ch 6:15; S Ezr 3:2 **6:12** [n]S Isa 4:2; S Eze 17:22 [o]Ezr 3:8-10; Zec 4:6-9 **6:13** [p]S Ps 110:4 **6:14** [q]S Ex 28:12 **6:15** [r]Isa 60:10 [s]Zec 2:9-11 [t]Isa 58:12; Jer 7:23; S Zec 3:7 **7:1** [u]S Ezr 5:1 [v]Ne 1:1 **7:2** [w]Jer 26:19; Zec 8:21 [x]Hag 2:10-14 **7:3** [y]Zec 12:12-14 [z]2Ki 25:9; Jer 52:12-14 **7:5** [a]Isa 58:5 [b]2Ki 25:25 [c]S Da 9:2 **7:6** [d]S Isa 43:23 **7:7** [e]Isa 1:11-20; Zec 1:4 [f]Jer 22:21 [g]S Jer 17:26 [h]Jer 44:4-5 **7:9** [i]S Jer 22:3; 42:5; Zec 8:16 [j]S Dt 22:1 **7:10** [k]Jer 49:11 [l]S Ex 22:21 [m]S Lev 25:17; Isa 1:23 [n]S Ex 22:22; S Job 35:8; S Isa 1:17; S Eze 45:9; S Mic 6:8 **7:11** [o]S Isa 9:9 [p]S Jer 32:33 [q]S Jer 5:3; 8:5; 11:10; S 17:23; S Eze 5:6 **7:12** [r]S Jer 5:3; 17:1; S Eze 11:19

6:10 *⌞silver and gold⌟.* Gifts for the temple (cf. Ezr 6:5; Hag 2:8).

6:11 *crown.* The Hebrew for this word is not the same as that used for the high priest's turban, but one referring to an ornate crown (cf. Rev 19:12). The royal crowning of the high priest foreshadows the goal and consummation of prophecy—the crowning and reign of the Messianic King-Priest (see vv. 12–13; cf. Ps 110:4; Heb 7:1–3).

6:12 *Here is the man.* Cf. Pilate's introduction of Jesus in Jn 19:5. *Branch.* See note on 3:8. According to the Aramaic Targum (a paraphrase), the Jerusalem Talmud (a collection of religious instruction) and the Midrash (practical exposition), Jews early regarded this verse as Messianic. *branch out.* The NIV here reflects the wordplay in the Hebrew text. *temple.* Cf. Isa 2:2–3; Eze 40–43; Hag 2:6–9.

6:13 *clothed with.* See note on Ps 109:29. *his throne.* See 2Sa 7:11,16; Isa 9:7; Lk 1:32 and notes. *priest on his throne.* The coming Davidic King will also be a priest. *two.* Probably the royal and priestly offices. Such a combination was not normally possible in Israel. For this reason, the community of Qumran (see essay, p. 1452) expected two Messianic figures—a high-priestly Messiah and a Davidic one. But the two offices and functions would in fact be united in the one person of the Messiah (see 4:3 and note; cf. Ps 110; Heb 7).

6:14 *Hen.* Means “gracious one” (see NIV text note), perhaps another name for Josiah—to honor him for his hospitality (v. 10).

6:15 *Those who are far away will … help.* Cf. Isa 60:4–7.

7:1—8:23 See Introduction: Literary Forms and Themes.

7:3 *prophets.* Including Zechariah. *I.* The people of Bethel collectively. *fast in the fifth month.* See note on 8:19. *so many years.* “The past seventy years” (v. 5).

7:4–7 A rebuke for selfish and insincere fasting on the part of the people and the priests.

7:4,8 See note on 4:8.

7:5 *fasted … fifth and seventh.* See note on 8:19. *seventy years.* See 1:12 and note. Since these fasts commemorated events related to the destruction of Jerusalem and the temple (see note on 8:19), the 70 years here are to be reckoned from 586 B.C. Strictly speaking, 68 years had transpired; 70 is thus a round number.

7:6 *for yourselves.* Cf. Isa 1:11–17; 58:1–7,13–14.

7:7,12 *earlier prophets.* See note on 1:4.

7:7 *Negev.* See note on Ge 12:9. *western foothills.* Sloping toward the Mediterranean.

7:9–10 Four tests of faithful covenant living, consisting of a series of social, moral and ethical commands.

7:9 *justice.* The proper ordering of all society (see 8:16–17 and note on 8:16; Isa 42:1,4; Mic 6:8 and notes). *mercy.* Or “faithful love” (see Hos 10:12; 12:6 and notes). *compassion.* See note on 1:12.

7:10 *oppress.* Oppression is denounced frequently in the OT (see, e.g., Am 2:6–8 and notes; 4:1; 5:11–12,21–24; 8:4–6). *widow … fatherless … alien … poor.* For the Biblical concern for such people see, e.g., Dt 10:18; Isa 1:17 and note; Jer 5:28; Jas 1:27; 1Jn 3:16–18. In the ancient Near East, the ideal king was expected to protect the oppressed and needy members of society. *think evil of each other.* In 8:17 the almost identical Hebrew is translated “plot evil against your neighbor,” which is probably the sense here as well (cf. Mic 2:1–2 and note on 2:1).

7:11 *they.* The preexilic ancestors, as the reference to the “earlier prophets” in v. 12 shows. *stubbornly they turned their backs.* See Dt 9:6,13,27. *stopped up their ears.* See Ps 58:4; Isa 6:10 and notes; cf. Isa 33:15.

7:12 *hard as flint.* See Eze 3:8–9. *words … sent by his Spirit.* The words of the prophets were inspired by God's Spirit (see Ne 9:30; 2Pe 1:21 and note). *very angry.* See 1:2,15.

not listen to the law or to the words that
the LORD Almighty had sent by his Spirit
through the earlier prophets.[s] So the LORD
Almighty was very angry.[t]
13“‘When I called, they did not listen;[u]
so when they called, I would not listen,’[v]
says the LORD Almighty.[w] 14‘I scattered[x]
them with a whirlwind[y] among all the nations, where they were strangers. The land
was left so desolate behind them that no
one could come or go.[z] This is how they
made the pleasant land desolate.[a]’ ”

The LORD Promises to Bless Jerusalem

8 Again the word of the LORD Almighty
came to me. 2This is what the LORD Almighty says: “I am very jealous[b] for Zion;
I am burning with jealousy for her.”
3This is what the LORD says: “I will return[c] to Zion[d] and dwell in Jerusalem.[e]
Then Jerusalem will be called the City
of Truth,[f] and the mountain[g] of the LORD
Almighty will be called the Holy Mountain.[h]”
4This is what the LORD Almighty says:
“Once again men and women of ripe old
age will sit in the streets of Jerusalem,[i]
each with cane in hand because of his age.
5The city streets will be filled with boys
and girls playing there.[j]”
6This is what the LORD Almighty says:
“It may seem marvelous to the remnant of
this people at that time,[k] but will it seem
marvelous to me?[l]” declares the LORD Almighty.
7This is what the LORD Almighty says: “I
will save my people from the countries of
the east and the west.[m] 8I will bring them
back[n] to live[o] in Jerusalem; they will be
my people,[p] and I will be faithful and righteous to them as their God.[q]”
9This is what the LORD Almighty says:
“You who now hear these words spoken
by the prophets[r] who were there when the
foundation[s] was laid for the house of the
LORD Almighty, let your hands be strong[t]
so that the temple may be built. 10Before
that time there were no wages[u] for man
or beast. No one could go about his business safely[v] because of his enemy, for I
had turned every man against his neighbor. 11But now I will not deal with the remnant of this people as I did in the past,”[w]
declares the LORD Almighty.
12“The seed will grow well, the vine will
yield its fruit,[x] the ground will produce its
crops,[y] and the heavens will drop their
dew.[z] I will give all these things as an inheritance[a] to the remnant of this people.[b]
13As you have been an object of cursing[c]
among the nations, O Judah and Israel, so
will I save[d] you, and you will be a blessing.[e] Do not be afraid,[f] but let your hands
be strong.[g]”
14This is what the LORD Almighty says:
“Just as I had determined to bring disaster[h] upon you and showed no pity when
your fathers angered me,” says the LORD
Almighty, 15“so now I have determined to
do good[i] again to Jerusalem and Judah.[j]

7:12 [s]S Ne 9:29 [t]S Jer 42:21; S Da 9:12 **7:13** [u]S Jer 7:27 [v]Isa 1:15; S Jer 11:11; 14:12; S Mic 3:4 [w]S Pr 1:28; S La 3:44; S Eze 20:31 **7:14** [x]S Lev 26:33; Dt 4:27; 28:64-67; S Ps 44:11 [y]Jer 23:19 [z]S Isa 33:8 [a]S Jer 7:34; S 44:6; S Eze 12:19 **8:2** [b]S Joel 2:18 **8:3** [c]Zec 1:16 [d]S Isa 52:8; S Joel 3:21 [e]S Zec 2:10 [f]S Ps 15:2; S Isa 1:26; S 48:1; S Jer 33:16 [g]S Jer 26:18 [h]S Isa 1:26; S Mic 4:1 **8:4** [i]S Isa 65:20 **8:5** [j]S Jer 30:20; 31:13 **8:6** [k]Ps 118:23; 126:1-3 [l]Jer 32:17,27 **8:7** [m]Ps 107:3; S Isa 11:11; S 43:5 **8:8** [n]S Eze 37:12; Zec 10:10 [o]S Jer 31:24 [p]S Isa 51:16; S Eze 11:19-20; S 36:28; S Zec 2:11; Heb 8:10 [q]Jer 11:4; Zec 10:6 **8:9** [r]S Ezr 5:1 [s]S Ezr 3:11 [t]S Hag 2:4 **8:10** [u]S Isa 5:10; S Hag 1:6 [v]S 2Ch 15:5 **8:11** [w]Isa 12:1 **8:12** [x]S Ps 85:12; S Joel 2:22 [y]S Ps 67:6 [z]S Ge 27:28 [a]S Ps 65:13; S Isa 60:21; Ob 1:17 [b]S Hos 2:21 **8:13** [c]S Nu 5:27; S Dt 13:15; S Ps 102:8; Jer 42:18 [d]S Ps 48:8 [e]S Ge 12:2; S Joel 2:14 [f]S Hag 2:5 [g]ver 9 **8:14** [h]S Eze 24:14 **8:15** [i]ver 13; S Jer 29:11; Mic 7:18-20 [j]Jer 31:28; 32:42

7:13 See note on 1:3.
7:14 *scattered them.* One of the curses for covenant disobedience (see Dt 28:36–37,64–68 and note on 28:64). *whirlwind.* See Pr 1:27 and note; Isa 40:24; Hos 4:19. *land ... desolate.* See Dt 28:41–42,45–52. *This is how.* By their sins. *pleasant land.* See Ps 106:24 and note.
8:1–23 Ten promises of blessing, each beginning with “This is what the LORD (Almighty) says” (vv. 2,3,4, 6,7,9,14,19,20,23).
8:1,18 See note on 4:8.
8:2 *jealous.* See 1:14 and note.
8:3 *I will return.* See 1:3 and note; 1:16. *dwell.* See note on 2:10. *the City of Truth.* Cf. v. 16; see Isa 1:26 and note. *the Holy Mountain.* Cf. 14:20–21.
8:4–5 See Isa 11:6–9 and note; 65:20–25.
8:6,11–12 *remnant.* See notes on Isa 1:9; 10:20–22.
8:6 *will it seem marvelous to me?* See Jer 32:27 and note.
8:7 *save my people.* Deliver them from exile, bondage and dispersion (cf. Isa 11:11–12; 43:5–7; Jer 30:7–11; 31:7–8). *from the countries of the east and the west.* Lit. “from the land of the sunrise and from the land of the going in of the sun,” i.e., from everywhere—wherever the people are (cf. Ps 50:1; 113:3; Mal 1:11).
8:8 *they will be my people, and I will be ... their God.* Covenant terminology, pertaining to intimate fellowship in the covenant relationship between God and his people (see 13:9; Ge 17:7 and note; Ex 6:7; 29:45–46; Lev 11:45; 22:33; 25:38; 26:12,45; Nu 15:41; Dt 29:13; Jer 24:7 and note; Eze 34:30–31; 36:28; 37:27; Hos 1:9–10; 11:20; 2Co 6:16; Heb 8:10; Rev 21:3). *faithful and righteous.* Judah’s restoration to covenant favor and blessing rests on the faithfulness (dependability) and righteousness of God.
8:9 *prophets.* Including Haggai (1:1) and Zechariah (1:1; see Ezr 5:1–2). *hands be strong.* See v. 13. The Hebrew for this expression is translated “be encouraged” in Jdg 7:11.
8:10 *Before that time.* Before the temple foundation was laid (see v. 9). *no wages.* See Hag 1:6–11; 2:15–19. *enemy.* For example, the Samaritans (Ezr 4:1–5).
8:11 *But now.* The reasons for discouragement have passed; God will now provide the grounds for encouragement.
8:12 Contrast with Hag 1:10–11. In Hag 2:19 God had predicted just such a reversal as is depicted here. Fertility and bounty are part of the covenant blessings for obedience promised in Lev 26:3–10; Dt 28:11–12; cf. Eze 34:25–27; Hos 1:21–24.
8:13 *object of cursing among the nations.* Part of the covenant curses for disobedience threatened in Dt 28:15–68 (see Dt 28:37; Jer 24:9; 25:18). *Judah and Israel.* The whole nation will experience this deliverance and blessing (cf. Jer 31:1–31; Eze 37:15–28). *blessing.* See vv. 20–23; cf. Ge 12:2. *hands be strong.* See note on v. 9.
8:14–17 Verses 14–15 specify God’s part in the people’s restoration to favor and blessing; vv. 16–17 delineate their part.
8:14 *your fathers angered me.* See note on 1:2.
8:15 *do good.* See vv. 12–13.

Do not be afraid. 16These are the things
you are to do: Speak the truth[k] to each
other, and render true and sound judgment[l] in your courts;[m] 17do not plot evil[n]
against your neighbor, and do not love to
swear falsely.[o] I hate all this," declares the
LORD.

18Again the word of the LORD Almighty
came to me. 19This is what the LORD Almighty says: "The fasts of the fourth,[p]
fifth,[q] seventh[r] and tenth[s] months will
become joyful[t] and glad occasions and
happy festivals for Judah. Therefore love
truth[u] and peace."

20This is what the LORD Almighty says:
"Many peoples and the inhabitants of
many cities will yet come, 21and the inhabitants of one city will go to another and
say, 'Let us go at once to entreat[v] the LORD
and seek[w] the LORD Almighty. I myself am
going.' 22And many peoples and powerful
nations will come to Jerusalem to seek the
LORD Almighty and to entreat him."[x]

23This is what the LORD Almighty says:
"In those days ten men from all languages
and nations will take firm hold of one Jew
by the hem of his robe and say, 'Let us go
with you, because we have heard that God
is with you.'"[y]

8:16 [k]S Ps 15:2; S Jer 33:16; S Eph 4:25 [l]S Eze 18:8 [m]S Eze 45:9; S Am 5:15; S Zec 7:9 **8:17** [n]Pr 3:29 [o]S Pr 6:16-19; S Jer 7:9; Zec 5:4 **8:19** [p]S 2Ki 25:7; Jer 39:2 [q]S Jer 52:12 [r]2Ki 25:25 [s]Jer 52:4 [t]Ps 30:11 [u]ver 16 **8:21** [v]S Zec 7:2 [w]Jer 26:19 **8:22** [x]S Ps 86:9; 117:1; Isa 2:2-3; S 44:5; S 45:14; 49:6; S Zec 2:11 **8:23** [y]S Ps 102:22; S Isa 14:1; S 45:14; S 56:3; 1Co 14:25

9:1 [z]S Isa 13:1; Jer 23:33 [a]Isa 17:1; S Am 1:5 **9:2** [b]S Jer 49:23 [c]Eze 28:1-19 [d]S Ge 10:15 **9:3** [e]Job 27:16; S Eze 28:4 **9:4** [f]S Isa 23:11 [g]S Isa 23:1; Jer 25:22; Eze 26:3-5; 27:32-36; 28:18 **9:5** [h]Jer 47:5

Judgment on Israel's Enemies

An Oracle[z]

9 The word of the LORD is against the
land of Hadrach
and will rest upon Damascus[a]—
for the eyes of men and all the tribes of
Israel
are on the LORD— [a]
2and upon Hamath[b] too, which borders
on it,
and upon Tyre[c] and Sidon,[d] though
they are very skillful.
3Tyre has built herself a stronghold;
she has heaped up silver like dust,
and gold like the dirt of the streets.[e]
4But the Lord will take away her
possessions
and destroy[f] her power on the sea,
and she will be consumed by fire.[g]
5Ashkelon[h] will see it and fear;
Gaza will writhe in agony,
and Ekron too, for her hope will
wither.
Gaza will lose her king
and Ashkelon will be deserted.

[a] 1 Or *Damascus. / For the eye of the LORD is on all mankind, / as well as on the tribes of Israel,*

8:16–17 See 7:9–10. Such moral and ethical behavior sums up the character of those who are in covenant relationship with the Lord.

8:16 *Speak the truth to each other.* See Eph 4:25 and note. *render true and sound judgment in your courts.* Because God requires justice (see 7:9; Dt 24:17–18; Ps 33:5; 89:14; 99:4; Am 2:7; 5:24 and notes; see also Introduction to Amos: Theological Theme and Message) and hates injustice (see v. 17; 5:3; 2Ch 19:7; Pr 6:16–19; Hab 1:4 and notes). *courts.* Lit. "gates" (see Ge 19:1 and note; 2Sa 18:24).

8:17 *swear falsely.* Perjure oneself (see note on 5:3). *I hate all this.* Pr 6:16–19 lists seven things the Lord hates, three of which relate directly to vv. 16–17 here: "a lying tongue," "a heart that devises wicked schemes" and "a false witness who pours out lies."

8:19 See 7:2–6. *fourth.* The fast that lamented the breaching of the walls of Jerusalem by Nebuchadnezzar (2 Ki 25:3–4; Jer 39:2). *fifth.* Commemorated the burning of the temple and the other important buildings (2Ki 25:8–10). *seventh.* Marked the anniversary of Gedaliah's assassination (2Ki 25:22–25; Jer 41:1–3). *tenth.* Mourned the beginning of Nebuchadnezzar's siege of Jerusalem (2Ki 25:1; Jer 39:1; Eze 24:1–2). *happy festivals.* Cf. Isa 65:18–19; Jer 31:10–14.

8:20–23 For similar predictions about Gentiles seeking the Lord see 2:11 and note; Isa 19:23–25; 25:6–8; Mic 4:1–5.

8:22 *powerful.* Or "numerous" (as in Ex 1:9; see also NIV text note on Isa 53:12); anticipates a fulfillment of the promise of Gentile blessing in the Abrahamic covenant (Ge 12:3; Gal 3:8,26–29; see also Isa 55:5; 56:6–7; Mk 11:17 and note).

8:23 *ten.* One way of indicating a large or complete number in Hebrew (see Ge 31:7 and note; Lev 26:26; Nu 14:22 and note; 1Sa 1:8; Ne 4:12). *Jew.* The word is ordinarily used in the OT only of the people of Judah after the exile (see note on Jer 34:9). *we have heard that God is with you.* God's blessings on his people will attract others to turn to him (cf. Ge 21:22; 26:28; 30:27; see also notes on Ge 39:2–6; 1Co 14:24).

9:1–8 Probably a prophetic description of the Lord's march south to Jerusalem, destroying—as Divine Warrior—the traditional enemies of Israel. As history shows, the agent of his judgment was Alexander the Great (333–332 B.C.; see essay, p. 1451).

9:1 *An Oracle/The word of the LORD.* The Hebrew for this phrase occurs only two other times in the OT (12:1; Mal 1:1), making it likely that Zec 9–14 and Malachi were written during the same general period. *word of the LORD.* See 1:1; 12:1; Hos 1:1 and note. *Hadrach.* Hatarikka, north of Hamath on the Orontes River (see v. 2). *Damascus.* The leading city-state of the Arameans (see notes on Dt 26:5; Isa 17:1). *eyes … on the LORD.* The thought may be that the eyes of people, especially all the tribes of Israel, are turned toward the Lord (for deliverance). But see NIV text note.

9:2 *upon Hamath too.* Judgment will rest upon Hamath, just as upon Hadrach and Damascus. Hamath is modern Hama (see Isa 10:9 and note). *it.* Damascus. *Tyre and Sidon.* Phoenician (modern Lebanese) coastal cities (see notes on Isa 23:1; 23:2,4,12). Their judgment (vv. 3–4) is also foretold in Isa 23; Eze 26:3–14; 28:20–24; Am 1:9–10.

9:3 *stronghold.* The Hebrew for this word is a pun on the Hebrew for "Tyre" (meaning "rock"). The stronghold was Tyre's island fortress (Isa 23:4; Eze 26:5). It fell (v. 4) to Alexander in July, 332 B.C., after a siege of seven months (see note on Eze 26:1—28:19). *silver like dust … gold like the dirt.* Cf. 1Ki 10:21,27. Tyre was a center of trade and commerce, and her wealth was proverbial (see Isa 23:2–3,8,18; Eze 26:12; 27:3–27,33; 28:4–5,7,12–14,16–18).

9:4 *her power on the sea.* Tyre's exploitation of commercial sea lanes in the Mediterranean was the source of much of her wealth.

9:5–7 The Philistine cities were greatly alarmed at Alexander's steady advance.

9:5 *Ashkelon … Gaza … Ekron.* Three of the five major Philistine cities (see map, p. 331). *her hope will wither.* As the northernmost city of Philistia, Ekron would be the first to suffer.

6 Foreigners will occupy Ashdod,
and I will cut off[i] the pride of the
Philistines.
7 I will take the blood from their
mouths,
the forbidden food from between
their teeth.
Those who are left will belong to our
God[j]
and become leaders in Judah,
and Ekron will be like the Jebusites.[k]
8 But I will defend[l] my house
against marauding forces.[m]
Never again will an oppressor overrun
my people,
for now I am keeping watch.[n]

The Coming of Zion's King

9 Rejoice greatly, O Daughter of Zion![o]
Shout,[p] Daughter of Jerusalem!
See, your king[a] comes to you,[q]
righteous and having salvation,[r]
gentle and riding on a donkey,[s]
on a colt, the foal of a donkey.[t]
10 I will take away the chariots from
Ephraim
and the war-horses from Jerusalem,
and the battle bow will be broken.[u]
He will proclaim peace[v] to the nations.
His rule will extend from sea to sea
and from the River[b] to the ends of
the earth.[c][w]
11 As for you, because of the blood of my
covenant[x] with you,
I will free your prisoners[y] from the
waterless pit.[z]
12 Return to your fortress,[a] O prisoners of
hope;
even now I announce that I will
restore twice[b] as much to you.
13 I will bend Judah as I bend my bow[c]
and fill it with Ephraim.[d]
I will rouse your sons, O Zion,
against your sons, O Greece,[e]
and make you like a warrior's sword.[f]

The LORD Will Appear

14 Then the LORD will appear over them;[g]
his arrow will flash like lightning.[h]
The Sovereign LORD will sound the
trumpet;[i]
he will march in the storms[j] of the
south,
15 and the LORD Almighty will shield[k]
them.

9:6 [i] S Isa 14:30 **9:7** [j] S Job 25:2 [k] S Jer 47:1; S Joel 3:4; S Zep 2:4 **9:8** [l] S Isa 26:1 [m] Zec 14:21 [n] S Isa 52:1; S 54:14; S Joel 3:17 **9:9** [o] S Isa 62:11 [p] S 1Ki 1:39 [q] S Ps 24:7; S 149:2; Mic 4:8 [r] Isa 9:6-7; 43:3-11; Jer 23:5-6; Zep 3:14-15; Zec 2:10 [s] S Ge 49:11; S 1Ki 1:33 [t] Mt 21:5*; Jn 12:15* **9:10** [u] Hos 1:7; 2:18; Mic 4:3; 5:10; Zec 10:4 [v] S Isa 2:4 [w] Ps 72:8 **9:11** [x] S Ex 24:8; S Mt 26:28; S Lk 22:20 [y] S Isa 10:4; S 42:7 [z] Jer 38:6 **9:12** [a] S Joel 3:16 [b] S Dt 21:17; S Isa 40:2 **9:13** [c] S 2Sa 22:35 [d] S Isa 49:2 [e] S Joel 3:6 [f] S Jer 51:20

[a] *9* Or *King* [b] *10* That is, the Euphrates [c] *10* Or *the end of the land*

9:14 [g] Isa 31:5 [h] Ps 18:14; S Hab 3:11 [i] S Lev 25:9; S Mt 24:31 [j] Isa 21:1; 66:15 **9:15** [k] Isa 31:5; 37:35; Zec 12:8

Her hope that Tyre would stem the tide would meet with disappointment.
9:6 *Foreigners.* People of mixed nationality; they characterized the postexilic period (Ne 13:23–24). *Ashdod.* The fourth remaining city in the Philistine group (see notes on v. 5; Am 1:8). *I.* God. *Philistines.* See note on Ge 10:14. At one time their control of Canaan was so extensive that the land was eventually named after them ("Palestine").
9:7 *blood.* Of idolatrous sacrifices. *forbidden food.* Ceremonially unclean food. *Jebusites.* These ancient inhabitants of Jerusalem (see notes on Ge 10:16; 2Sa 5:6) were absorbed into Judah (e.g., Araunah in 2Sa 24:16–24). So would it be with a remnant of the Philistines.
9:8 *defend my house against marauding forces.* See 2:5. Alexander spared the temple and the city of Jerusalem. *oppressor.* The Hebrew for this word is translated "slave driver" in Ex 3:7; 5:6,10 and elsewhere; thus it echoes the Egyptian bondage motif. *keeping watch.* See Ex 3:7; Ps 32:8; 121.
9:9 Quoted in the NT as Messianic and as referring ultimately to the "triumphal entry" of Jesus into Jerusalem as King (Mt 21:5; Jn 12:15). *Daughter of Zion ... Daughter of Jerusalem.* A personification of Jerusalem (see note on 2Ki 19:21). *your king.* The Davidic ("your") Messianic King. *righteous.* Conforming to the divine standard of morality and ethics, particularly as revealed in the Mosaic legislation; a characteristic of the ideal king (see 2Sa 23:3–4 and note on 23:3; Ps 4:1 and note; 72:1–3; Isa 9:7 and note; 53:11; Jer 23:6 and note). *gentle.* Or "humble" (cf. Isa 53:2–3,7; Mt 11:29). *riding on a donkey.* A suitable choice, since the donkey was a lowly animal of peace (contrast the war-horse of v. 10) as well as a princely mount (Jdg 10:4; 12:14; 2Sa 16:2) before the horse came into common use. The royal mount used by David and his sons was the mule (see 2Sa 13:29 and note).
9:10 *take away the chariots ... war-horses ... battle bow.* A similar era of disarmament is foreseen in Isa 2:4; 9:5–7; 11:1–10; Mic 5:10–11. *Ephraim.* See note on v. 13. *peace to the nations.* In sharp contrast to Alexander's empire, which was founded on bloodshed, the Messianic King will establish a universal kingdom of peace as the ultimate fulfillment of the Abrahamic covenant (cf. 14:16; see Ge 12:2–3 and note, but cf. Rev 19:11 and note). *from sea to sea.* Variously explained as "from the Nile to the Euphrates," "from the Mediterranean to the Red Sea" and "from the Mediterranean to the Dead Sea." The question is not important because the phrase is used to indicate totality or universality, as is true also of "from the River to the ends of the earth." The point is that the Davidic Messiah's rule will be universal (see Ps 22:27–28 and notes; 72:8–11 and note on 72:8; Isa 45:22; 52:10; 66:18).
9:11 *blood of my covenant with you.* Probably the Sinaitic covenant (Ex 24:3–8). *prisoners.* Perhaps those still in Babylonia, the land of exile. *waterless pit.* Cf. Ge 37:24; Jer 38:6.
9:12 *fortress.* Either (1) Jerusalem (Zion) and environs or (2) God himself (cf. 2:5). *hope.* In the future delivering King (vv. 9–10). *twice as much.* Full or complete restoration (see Isa 61:7 and note).
9:13 See note on 10:4. The Lord compares himself to a warrior who uses Judah as his bow and Ephraim (the northern kingdom) as his arrow. *your sons, O Zion.* The Maccabees (see note on Da 11:34; see also essay, p. 1451). *your sons, O Greece.* The Seleucids of Syria (after the breakup of Alexander's empire).
9:14 See Hab 3:3–15 and note on 3:3. *trumpet.* Probably a reference to thunder (see Ex 19:16–19 and note on 19:16). *south.* In the region of Mount Sinai, where the Sinaitic covenant was given (see v. 11 and note) and where the Lord's presence had frequently been manifested (see Jdg 5:4–5; Ps 68:8; Hab 3:3 and note; cf. Ex 3:1–2; 1Ki 19:8 and note).
9:15 The Apocryphal book 1 Maccabees (3:16–24; 4:6–16; 7:40–50) records a partial fulfillment of this verse. *slingstones.* Hurled at defenders on the city wall and onto the inhabitants inside. *bowl used for sprinkling.* See Ex 27:1–3 and note on 27:3; Lev 4:6–7.

They will destroy
and overcome with slingstones.[l]
They will drink and roar as with
wine;[m]
they will be full like a bowl[n]
used for sprinkling[a] the corners[o] of
the altar.
16 The LORD their God will save them on
that day[p]
as the flock of his people.
They will sparkle in his land
like jewels in a crown.[q]
17 How attractive and beautiful they will
be!
Grain will make the young men
thrive,
and new wine the young women.

The LORD Will Care for Judah

10 Ask the LORD for rain in the
springtime;
it is the LORD who makes the storm
clouds.
He gives showers of rain[r] to men,
and plants of the field[s] to everyone.
2 The idols[t] speak deceit,
diviners[u] see visions that lie;
they tell dreams[v] that are false,
they give comfort in vain.[w]
Therefore the people wander like
sheep
oppressed for lack of a shepherd.[x]

3 "My anger burns against the
shepherds,
and I will punish the leaders;[y]
for the LORD Almighty will care
for his flock, the house of Judah,
and make them like a proud horse
in battle.[z]
4 From Judah will come the
cornerstone,[a]
from him the tent peg,[b]
from him the battle bow,[c]
from him every ruler.
5 Together they[b] will be like mighty men
trampling the muddy streets in
battle.[d]
Because the LORD is with them,
they will fight and overthrow the
horsemen.[e]

6 "I will strengthen[f] the house of Judah
and save the house of Joseph.
I will restore them
because I have compassion[g] on
them.[h]
They will be as though
I had not rejected them,
for I am the LORD their God
and I will answer[i] them.
7 The Ephraimites will become like
mighty men,
and their hearts will be glad as with
wine.[j]
Their children will see it and be joyful;
their hearts will rejoice[k] in the LORD.
8 I will signal[l] for them
and gather them in.
Surely I will redeem them;
they will be as numerous[m] as
before.
9 Though I scatter them among the
peoples,
yet in distant lands they will
remember me.[n]
They and their children will survive,
and they will return.

[a] *15* Or *bowl, / like* [b] *4,5* Or *ruler, all of them together. / [5] They*

9:15 [l] Zec 14:3 [m] Zec 10:7 [n] Zec 14:20 [o] S Ex 27:2 **9:16** [p] S Isa 10:20 [q] S Jer 31:11 **10:1** [r] S Lev 26:4; S 1Ki 8:36; S Ps 104:13; S 135:7 [s] S Job 14:9 **10:2** [t] Eze 21:21 [u] S Isa 44:25 [v] Jer 23:16 [w] S Isa 40:19 [x] S Nu 27:17; S Jer 23:1; S Hos 3:4; S Mt 9:36 **10:3** [y] Isa 14:9; S Jer 25:34 [z] S Eze 34:8-10 **10:4** [a] S Ps 118:22; S Ac 4:11 [b] S Isa 22:23 [c] S Zec 9:10 **10:5** [d] S 2Sa 22:43; S Mic 7:10 [e] S Am 2:15; S Mic 5:8; Hag 2:22; Zec 12:4 **10:6** [f] S Eze 30:24 [g] S Ps 102:13; S Isa 14:1 [h] S Eze 36:37; 37:19; S Zec 8:7-8 [i] Ps 34:17; Isa 58:9; 65:24; Zec 13:9 **10:7** [j] Zec 9:15 [k] S 1Sa 2:1; S Isa 60:5; S Joel 2:23 **10:8** [l] Isa 5:26 [m] S Jer 33:22; S Eze 36:11 **10:9** [n] S Isa 44:21; S Eze 6:9

9:16 *that day.* See note on 2:11.

10:1 *it is the LORD who ... gives showers ... plants.* The Lord, not the Canaanite god Baal, is the one who controls the weather and the rain, giving life and fertility to the land (see Jer 14:22; Hos 2:8 and note; 6:3; Joel 2:21 – 27; Am 5:8; Mt 5:45). Therefore God's people are to pray to and trust in him.

10:2 *idols.* Household gods (see Ge 31:19 and note). They were used for divination during the period of the judges (see Jdg 17:5 and note; 18:14 – 20). *diviners.* Included among false prophets, they were the occult counterpart to true prophets. See Jer 27:9 – 10 and note on 27:9. Resorting to such sources for information and guidance is expressly forbidden in Dt 18:9 – 14 because God provided true prophets (and ultimately the Messianic Prophet) for that purpose (see Dt 13:1 – 5 and notes; 18:15 – 22 and note on 18:15; Isa 8:19 – 20 and notes; Jn 4:25; 6:14 and note; Ac 3:22 – 26 and note; see also note on Ge 30:27). *they give comfort in vain.* For example, when they wrongly promise rain, fruitful seasons, fertility, prosperity, peace and blessing. *people wander like sheep.* See Isa 53:6 and note. *lack of a shepherd.* Spiritual leadership is missing (cf. Mk 6:34). "Shepherd" is primarily a royal motif, whether referring to human kings (see Isa 44:28; Jer 2:8 and notes) or to God as King (see Ps 23:1 and note) or to the Messianic, Davidic King (Eze 34:23 – 24; Jn 10:11 – 16; Heb 13:20; 1Pe 5:4; Rev 7:17).

10:3 *I will punish the leaders.* Cf. Eze 34:1 – 10. *like a proud horse.* Triumphant.

10:4 Probably Messianic (as recognized in the Aramaic Targum). *From Judah.* See Ge 49:10; Jer 30:21 and note; Mic 5:2. *cornerstone.* See 3:9; Eph 2:20 and notes. *tent peg.* The ruler as the support of the state (see note on Isa 22:23; see also Isa 22:24). *battle bow.* Part of the Divine Warrior terminology (cf. 9:13; Ps 7:12; 45:5; La 2:4; 3:12; Hab 3:9).

10:5 *they.* Judah (v. 4), i.e., its people. *the LORD is with them.* See Jos 1:5; Jer 1:8 and note. *overthrow.* Partly fulfilled in the Maccabean victories (during the period between the OT and the NT).

10:6 *Judah ... Joseph.* The people of the southern and northern kingdoms will be reunited (see note on 8:13).

10:7 *Ephraimites.* See note on 9:13. *glad as with wine.* See Ps 104:15.

10:8 *signal.* Lit. "whistle," a continuation of the shepherd metaphor (vv. 2 – 3; see Jdg 5:16). *redeem.* The Hebrew for this word is often used of delivering from slavery or captivity (see Isa 35:10; Mic 6:4; cf. 1Pe 1:18 – 19). *as numerous as before.* See Ex 1:6 – 20 and note on 1:7.

10:9 *they will remember me.* According to the meaning of Zechariah's name, "the LORD remembers" (his covenant people and promises). Now they will remember him.

[10]I will bring them back from Egypt
and gather them from Assyria.[o]
I will bring them to Gilead[p] and
Lebanon,
and there will not be room[q] enough
for them.
[11]They will pass through the sea of
trouble;
the surging sea will be subdued
and all the depths of the Nile will
dry up.[r]
Assyria's pride[s] will be brought down
and Egypt's scepter[t] will pass away.[u]
[12]I will strengthen[v] them in the LORD
and in his name they will walk,[w]"
declares the LORD.

11 Open your doors, O Lebanon,[x]
so that fire[y] may devour your cedars!
[2]Wail, O pine tree, for the cedar has
fallen;
the stately trees are ruined!
Wail, oaks[z] of Bashan;
the dense forest[a] has been cut
down![b]
[3]Listen to the wail of the shepherds;
their rich pastures are destroyed!
Listen to the roar of the lions;[c]
the lush thicket of the Jordan is
ruined![d]

10:10 [o]S Isa 11:11; S Zec 8:8 [p]S Jer 50:19 [q]S Isa 49:19 **10:11** [r]Isa 19:5-7; S 51:10 [s]Zep 2:13 [t]Eze 30:13 [u]Eze 29:15 **10:12** [v]S Eze 30:24 [w]S Mic 4:5 **11:1** [x]S Eze 31:3 [y]S 2Ch 36:19; Zec 12:6 **11:2** [z]S Isa 2:13 [a]Isa 32:19 [b]S Isa 10:34 **11:3** [c]S Isa 5:29 [d]Jer 2:15; 50:44; Eze 19:9

11:4 [e]S Jer 25:34 **11:5** [f]Jer 50:7; S Eze 34:2-3 **11:6** [g]Zec 14:13 [h]Isa 9:19-21; S Jer 13:14; S La 2:21; 5:8; S Mic 5:8; 7:2-6 **11:7** [i]S Jer 25:34 **11:8** [j]S Eze 14:5 **11:9** [k]S Jer 43:11 [l]S Isa 9:20 **11:10** [m]ver 7 [n]S Ps 89:39; Jer 14:21

Two Shepherds

[4]This is what the LORD my God says:
"Pasture the flock marked for slaughter.[e]
[5]Their buyers slaughter them and go unpunished. Those who sell them say, 'Praise
the LORD, I am rich!' Their own shepherds
do not spare them.[f] [6]For I will no longer
have pity on the people of the land," declares the LORD. "I will hand everyone over
to his neighbor[g] and his king. They will
oppress the land, and I will not rescue
them from their hands."[h]

[7]So I pastured the flock marked for
slaughter,[i] particularly the oppressed of
the flock. Then I took two staffs and called
one Favor and the other Union, and I pastured the flock. [8]In one month I got rid of
the three shepherds.

The flock detested[j] me, and I grew weary
of them [9]and said, "I will not be your
shepherd. Let the dying die, and the perishing perish.[k] Let those who are left eat[l]
one another's flesh."

[10]Then I took my staff called Favor[m]
and broke it, revoking[n] the covenant I
had made with all the nations. [11]It was revoked on that day, and so the afflicted of
the flock who were watching me knew it
was the word of the LORD.

10:10 *Egypt ... Assyria.* See v. 11; Hos 7:16 and note. Probably representing all the countries where the Israelites are dispersed, these two evoke memories of slavery and exile. *gather them.* See Isa 11:11–16; Eze 39:27–29. *Gilead.* See Ge 31:21 and note; SS 6:5; Jer 50:19; Mic 7:14 and note. *Lebanon.* See 2Ki 19:23; see also Isa 33:9; 35:2; Jer 22:6 and notes. *not be room enough.* See v. 8; 2:4 and note; see also note on Isa 49:19–20.

10:11 *pass through the sea of trouble.* As at the Red Sea (see Ex 14:22 and note).

11:1–3 Some interpret this brief poem as a taunt song related to the lament that will be sung over the destruction of the nations' power and arrogance (ch. 10), represented by the cedar, the pine and the oak (vv. 1–2). Their kings are represented by the shepherds and the lions (v. 3). Understood in this way, vv. 1–3 would provide the conclusion to the preceding section. Other interpreters, however, without denying the presence of figurative language, see the piece more literally as a description of the devastation of Syro-Palestine due to the rejection of the Messianic Good Shepherd (vv. 4–14). Verses 1–3 would then furnish the introduction to the next section. The geography of the text—Lebanon, Bashan and Jordan—would seem to favor this interpretation. Part of the fulfillment would be the destruction and further subjugation of the area by the Romans, including the fall of Jerusalem in A.D. 70 and of Masada in 73. Understood in this way, the passage is in sharp contrast with ch. 10 and its prediction of Israel's full deliverance and restoration to the covenant land. Now the scene is one of desolation for the land (vv. 1–3), followed by the threat of judgment and disaster for both land and people (vv. 4–6).

11:1 *Lebanon.* See 10:10 and note.

11:2 *Bashan.* See note on Isa 2:13. The Israelites took this region from the Amorite king, Og, at the time of the conquest of Canaan (Nu 21:33–35). It was allotted to the half-tribe of Manasseh (Jos 13:29–30; 17:5). *dense forest.* Of Lebanon.

11:3 If the language is figurative, the shepherds and lions represent the rulers or leaders of the Jews (see v. 5; 10:3; cf. Jer 25:34–36). *lush thicket of the Jordan.* Where the lions had their lairs.

11:4–14 The reason for the judgment on Israel in vv. 1–3 is now given, namely, the people's rejection of the Messianic Shepherd-King. Just as the Servant in the "servant songs" (see note on Isa 42:1–4) is rejected, so here the Good Shepherd (a royal figure) is rejected. The same Messianic King is in view in both instances.

11:4 *says.* To Zechariah. *flock.* Israel.

11:5 *buyers.* The sheep (the Jews) are bought as slaves by outsiders. Part of the fulfillment came in A.D. 70 and the following years. *Those who sell them.* "Their own shepherds (rulers or leaders)."

11:6 *land.* Israel. *king.* Perhaps the Roman emperor (cf. Jn 19:15). *They.* Includes the Romans prophetically.

11:7 *I.* Zechariah, as a type (foreshadowing) of the Messianic Shepherd-King. *called one Favor.* To ensure divine favor on the flock. *Union.* See Eze 37:15–28 and note on 37:16. Such unity would be the result of the gracious leadership of the Good Shepherd. (For the significance of the subsequent breaking of the two staffs see vv. 10,14 and notes.)

11:8 *got rid of the three shepherds.* Although the three cannot be specifically identified, the Good Shepherd will dispose of all such unfit leaders. *I grew weary of them.* Cf. Isa 1:13–14.

11:9 *Let the dying die.* The Good Shepherd terminates his providential care of the sheep. *eat one another's flesh.* According to Josephus, this actually happened during the Roman siege of Jerusalem in A.D. 70 (see Jer 19:9 and note).

11:10 *covenant.* Apparently a covenant of security and restraint, by which the Shepherd had been keeping the nations from attacking his people (cf. Eze 34:25; Hos 2:18). Now, however, the nations (e.g., the Romans) will be permitted to overrun them.

11:11 *the afflicted of the flock.* Probably the faithful few, who recognize the authoritative word of the Lord

12I told them, "If you think it best, give
me my pay; but if not, keep it." So they
paid me thirty pieces of silver.[o]
13And the LORD said to me, "Throw it to
the potter" — the handsome price at which
they priced me! So I took the thirty pieces
of silver[p] and threw them into the house of
the LORD to the potter.[q]
14Then I broke my second staff called
Union, breaking the brotherhood between
Judah and Israel.
15Then the LORD said to me, "Take again
the equipment of a foolish shepherd. 16For
I am going to raise up a shepherd over the
land who will not care for the lost, or seek
the young, or heal the injured, or feed the
healthy, but will eat the meat of the choice
sheep, tearing off their hoofs.

17"Woe to the worthless shepherd,[r]
who deserts the flock!
May the sword strike his arm[s] and his
right eye!
May his arm be completely withered,
his right eye totally blinded!"[t]

Jerusalem's Enemies to Be Destroyed

An Oracle[u]

12 This is the word of the LORD concerning Israel. The LORD, who stretches
out the heavens,[v] who lays the foundation
of the earth,[w] and who forms the spirit of
man[x] within him, declares: 2"I am going
to make Jerusalem a cup[y] that sends all
the surrounding peoples reeling.[z] Judah[a]
will be besieged as well as Jerusalem. 3On
that day, when all the nations[b] of the earth
are gathered against her, I will make Jerusalem an immovable rock[c] for all the
nations. All who try to move it will injure[d] themselves. 4On that day I will strike
every horse with panic and its rider with
madness," declares the LORD. "I will keep
a watchful eye over the house of Judah,
but I will blind all the horses of the nations.[e] 5Then the leaders of Judah will say
in their hearts, 'The people of Jerusalem
are strong,[f] because the LORD Almighty is
their God.'
6"On that day I will make the leaders of
Judah like a firepot[g] in a woodpile, like a
flaming torch among sheaves. They will
consume[h] right and left all the surrounding peoples, but Jerusalem will remain intact[i] in her place.
7"The LORD will save the dwellings of
Judah first, so that the honor of the house
of David and of Jerusalem's inhabitants
may not be greater than that of Judah.[j]
8On that day the LORD will shield[k] those
who live in Jerusalem, so that the feeblest[l]
among them will be like David, and the
house of David will be like God,[m] like the
Angel of the LORD going before[n] them. 9On

11:12 [o]S Ge 23:16; Mt 26:15 **11:13** [p]S Ex 21:32 [q]Mt 27:9-10*; Ac 1:18-19 **11:17** [r]Jer 23:1 [s]S Eze 30:21-22 [t]S Jer 23:1 **12:1** [u]S Isa 13:1 [v]S Ge 1:8; S Ps 104:2; S Jer 51:15 [w]Ps 102:25; Heb 1:10 [x]S Isa 57:16 **12:2** [y]S Ps 75:8 [z]S Ps 60:3; S Isa 51:23 [a]Zec 14:14 **12:3** [b]Isa 66:18; Zec 14:2 [c]S Isa 28:16; Da 2:34-35 [d]S Isa 29:8 **12:4** [e]Ps 76:6; S Zec 10:5 **12:5** [f]S Eze 30:24 **12:6** [g]Isa 10:17-18; S Zec 11:1 [h]Ob 1:18 [i]Zec 14:10 **12:7** [j]Jer 30:18; S Am 9:11 **12:8** [k]S Ps 91:4; S Joel 3:16; S Zec 9:15 [l]Joel 3:10 [m]Ps 82:6 [n]Mic 7:8

(see also v. 7, where the same Hebrew phrase is rendered "the oppressed of the flock"). *it was the word of the LORD.* The faithful discern that what happens (e.g., the judgment on Jerusalem and the temple in A.D. 70) is a fulfillment of God's prophetic word — as a result of such actions as those denounced in Mt 23, which led to the rejection of the Good Shepherd.

11:12 *give me my pay.* Refers to the severance of the relationship. *keep it.* A more emphatic way of ending the relationship. *thirty pieces of silver.* The price of a slave among the Israelites in ancient times (see notes on Ex 21:32; Mt 26:15).

11:13 *handsome price.* Irony and sarcasm. *threw them into the house of the LORD to the potter.* For the NT use of vv. 12 – 13 see Mt 26:14 – 15; 27:3 – 10 and note on 27:9.

11:14 *broke my second staff called Union.* Signifying the dissolution of the covenant nation, particularly of the unity between the south and the north. The breaking up of the nation into parties hostile to each other was characteristic of later Jewish history; it greatly hindered the popular cause in the war against Rome (cf. Jn 11:48).

11:15 *again.* See v. 7. *foolish shepherd.* With the Shepherd of the Lord's choice removed from the scene, a foolish and worthless (v. 17) shepherd replaces him. A selfish, greedy, corrupt leader will arise and afflict the flock (the people of Israel).

11:16 *seek the young.* Cf. Ge 33:13; Isa 40:11. *tearing off their hoofs.* Apparently in a greedy search for the last edible piece.

11:17 *worthless shepherd.* See note on v. 15. This counterfeit shepherd may have found a partial historical fulfillment in such leaders as Simeon bar Kosiba or Kokhba (who led the Jewish revolt against the Romans in A.D. 132 – 135 and who was hailed as the Messiah by Rabbi Akiba). But it would seem that the final stage of the progressive fulfillment of this prophecy awaits the rise of the final antichrist (cf. Eze 34:2 – 4; Da 11:36 – 39; Jn 5:43; 2Th 2:3 – 10; Rev 13:1 – 8). *deserts the flock.* Contrast the Good Shepherd of Jn 10:11 – 16. *May his arm be completely withered.* May his power be paralyzed. *his right eye totally blinded.* May his intelligence be nullified. Thus this leader will be powerless to fight.

12:1 — 14:21 This second prophetic message in Part II of the book revolves around two scenes: the final siege of Jerusalem, and the Messiah's return to defeat Israel's enemies and establish his kingdom.

12:1 *An Oracle.* See note on 9:1. *Israel.* The whole nation, not just the northern kingdom. Judah and Jerusalem, however, are the main focus of attention (see v. 2). *The LORD, who stretches … lays … forms.* This description of the Lord's creative power shows that he is able to perform what he predicts; it also strengthens the royal and sovereign authority of the message.

12:2 *cup that sends all … reeling.* See notes on Ps 16:5; Isa 51:17; Jer 25:15; Ob 16; Hab 2:16.

12:3 *that day.* See note on 2:11. The phrase is used often in chs. 12 – 14 (12:4,6,8 – 9,11; 13:1 – 2,4; 14:4,6,8 – 9,13,20 – 21). *all the nations … gathered against her.* See 14:2,12; Joel 3:9 – 16; cf. Rev 16:16 – 21.

12:4 *panic … madness … blind.* Listed in Dt 28:28 among the covenant curses for disobeying the stipulations of the covenant. Now these curses are turned against Israel's enemies. *watchful eye.* See Ps 32:8; 33:18; 121.

12:5 *the LORD Almighty.* See note on 1Sa 1:3.

12:6 Like a fire destroying wood and sheaves of grain, Judah's discerning leaders (see v. 5) will consume their enemies (cf. Jdg 15:3 – 5; Mic 5:5 – 6; see note on Isa 1:31).

12:8 *like David.* Like a great warrior. *like God.* Cf. Ex 4:16; 7:1. *like the Angel of the LORD.* See Ge 48:16 and note; Ex 14:19; 23:20; 32:34; 33:2; Hos 12:3 – 4; see also Ge 16:7 and note.

that day I will set out to destroy all the nations[o] that attack Jerusalem.[p]

Mourning for the One They Pierced

10"And I will pour out on the house of David and the inhabitants of Jerusalem a spirit[a][q] of grace and supplication.[r] They will
look on[b] me, the one they have pierced,[s]
and they will mourn for him as one mourns
for an only child,[t] and grieve bitterly for
him as one grieves for a firstborn son.[u]
11On that day the weeping[v] in Jerusalem
will be great, like the weeping of Hadad
Rimmon in the plain of Megiddo.[w] 12The
land will mourn,[x] each clan by itself, with
their wives by themselves: the clan of the
house of David and their wives, the clan of
the house of Nathan and their wives, 13the
clan of the house of Levi and their wives,
the clan of Shimei and their wives, 14and all
the rest of the clans and their wives.[y]

Cleansing From Sin

13 "On that day a fountain[z] will be
opened to the house of David and
the inhabitants of Jerusalem, to cleanse[a]
them from sin and impurity.
2"On that day, I will banish the names of
the idols[b] from the land, and they will be
remembered no more,"[c] declares the LORD
Almighty. "I will remove both the prophets[d] and the spirit of impurity from the
land. 3And if anyone still prophesies, his
father and mother, to whom he was born,
will say to him, 'You must die, because
you have told lies[e] in the LORD's name.'
When he prophesies, his own parents will
stab him.[f]
4"On that day every prophet will be
ashamed[g] of his prophetic vision. He will
not put on a prophet's garment[h] of hair[i] in
order to deceive.[j] 5He will say, 'I am not a
prophet. I am a farmer; the land has been
my livelihood since my youth.[c]'[k] 6If someone asks him, 'What are these wounds on
your body[d]?' he will answer, 'The wounds
I was given at the house of my friends.'

The Shepherd Struck, the Sheep Scattered

7"Awake, O sword,[l] against my
shepherd,[m]
against the man who is close to me!"
declares the LORD Almighty.
"Strike the shepherd,
and the sheep will be scattered,[n]
and I will turn my hand against the
little ones.
8In the whole land," declares the LORD,
"two-thirds will be struck down and
perish;
yet one-third will be left in it.[o]

[a] 10 Or *the Spirit* [b] 10 Or *to* [c] 5 Or *farmer; a man sold me in my youth* [d] 6 Or *wounds between your hands*

12:9 [o] S Isa 29:7 [p] S Zec 1:21; 14:2-3 **12:10** [q] S Eze 37:9 [r] Isa 44:3; S Eze 39:29; Joel 2:28-29 [s] S Ps 22:16; Jn 19:34,37* [t] Jdg 11:34 [u] S Ge 21:16; Jer 31:19 **12:11** [v] Jer 50:4 [w] 2Ki 23:29 **12:12** [x] Mt 24:30; Rev 1:7 **12:14** [y] Zec 7:3 **13:1** [z] Jer 17:13 [a] S Lev 16:30; S Ps 51:2; Heb 9:14 **13:2** [b] S Jer 43:12; S Eze 6:6; S 36:25; S Hos 2:17 [c] S Mic 5:13 [d] 1Ki 22:22; Jer 23:14-15 **13:3** [e] S Jer 28:16 [f] Dt 13:6-11; 18:20; S Ne 6:14; Jer 23:34; S Eze 14:9 **13:4** [g] S Jer 6:15 [h] Mt 3:4 [i] S 1Ki 18:7; S Isa 20:2 [j] S Eze 12:24 **13:5** [k] S Am 7:14 **13:7** [l] S Isa 34:5; Jer 47:6 [m] Isa 40:11; S 53:4; Eze 37:24 [n] S 2Sa 17:2; Mt 26:31*; Mk 14:27* **13:8** [o] S Eze 5:2-4, 12; Zec 14:2

12:10 *a spirit.* See NIV text note; Isa 32:15; Eze 36:26–27 and notes; see also Isa 44:3; 59:20–21; Eze 39:29; Joel 2:28–29. *look on.* See NIV text note. The emphasis seems to be on looking "to" the Messiah in faith (cf. Nu 21:9; Isa 45:22; Jn 3:14–15). *me ... him ... him.* Same person. *pierced.* See Ps 22:16 and note; Jn 19:37. *mourns for an only child.* See Jer 6:26 and note. *grieves for a firstborn son.* Cf. Ex 11:5; Jer 6:26 and notes.

12:11 *Hadad Rimmon.* The name of either (1) a place near Megiddo, where the people mourned the death of King Josiah (2Ch 35:20–27; see v. 22 there for the plain of Megiddo and vv. 24–25 for the mourning), or (2) a Semitic storm god (see 2Ki 5:18 and note), whose name means "Hadad the thunderer" in Babylonian (as in the *Epic of Gilgamesh,* 11.98; see chart, p. xxii; see also Eze 8:14 for an example of the practice of weeping for a Babylonian deity).

12:12 *Nathan.* David's son (2Sa 5:14; Lk 3:31).

12:13 *Shimei.* Son of Gershon, the son of Levi (Nu 3:17–18,21). The repentance and mourning are led, then, by the civil (royal) and religious leaders.

13:1 *cleanse them from sin.* See 3:4–9 and note on 3:9; one of the provisions of the new covenant (Jer 31:34; Eze 36:25).

13:2 *names of the idols.* The influence and fame, and even the very existence, of the idols. *prophets.* False prophecy was still a problem in the postexilic period (see Ne 6:12–14) and would again be a problem in the future (see Mt 24:4–5,11,23–24; 2Th 2:2–4).

13:3 *lies.* False prophecies. *parents will stab him.* See Dt 13:5–10. The Hebrew for "stab" is the same as the verb for "pierced" in 12:10, perhaps indicating that the feelings and actions exhibited in piercing the Messiah will now be directed toward the false prophets.

13:4–6 Because of the stern measures just mentioned, a false prophet will be reluctant to identify himself as such and will be evasive in his responses to interrogation. To help conceal his true identity, he will not wear a "prophet's garment of hair" (v. 4), such as Elijah wore (see 2Ki 1:8 and note). Instead, to avoid the death penalty (v. 3), he will deny being a prophet and will claim to have been a farmer since his youth (v. 5). And if a suspicious person notices marks on his body and inquires about them (v. 6), he will claim he received them in a scuffle with friends (or perhaps as discipline from his parents during childhood). Apparently the accuser suspects that the false prophet's wounds were self-inflicted to arouse his prophetic ecstasy in idolatrous rites (as in 1Ki 18:28; see Jer 16:6 and note; 48:37).

13:5 *the land ... my youth.* If the alternative translation in the NIV text note is taken, the meaning is that someone sold him as a slave while still young.

13:6 Some take this verse as Messianic, but the interpretation given above seems preferable in this context (e.g., v. 5).

13:7 *my shepherd.* The royal (Messianic) Good Shepherd (cf. the true Shepherd of 11:4–14; contrast the foolish and worthless shepherd of 11:15–17). *Strike the shepherd.* In 11:17 it was the worthless shepherd who was to be struck; now it is the Good Shepherd (cf. also 12:10). *sheep will be scattered.* In partial fulfillment of the curses for covenant disobedience (see Dt 28:64 and note; 29:24–25). These two clauses are quoted by Jesus not long before his arrest (Mt 26:31; Mk 14:27) and applied to the scattering of the apostles (Mt 26:56; Mk 14:49–50), who in turn are probably typological of the dispersion of the Jews in A.D. 70 and subsequent years.

13:8–9 These verses depict a refining process for Israel (see note on Isa 48:10).

13:8 *one-third.* A remnant, thus revealing God's mercy in the midst of judgment.

9This third I will bring into the fire;[p]
I will refine them like silver[q]
and test them like gold.[r]
They will call[s] on my name[t]
and I will answer[u] them;
I will say, 'They are my people,'[v]
and they will say, 'The LORD is our
God.[w]' "

The LORD Comes and Reigns

14 A day of the LORD[x] is coming when
your plunder[y] will be divided among
you.
2I will gather all the nations[z] to Jerusalem to fight against it;[a] the city will be
captured, the houses ransacked, and the
women raped.[b] Half of the city will go into
exile, but the rest of the people will not be
taken from the city.[c]
3Then the LORD will go out and fight[d]
against those nations, as he fights in the
day of battle.[e] 4On that day his feet will
stand on the Mount of Olives,[f] east of Jerusalem, and the Mount of Olives will be split[g]
in two from east to west, forming a great
valley, with half of the mountain moving
north and half moving south. 5You will flee
by my mountain valley, for it will extend
to Azel. You will flee as you fled from the
earthquake[a][h] in the days of Uzziah king of
Judah. Then the LORD my God will come,[i]
and all the holy ones with him.[j]
6On that day there will be no light,[k] no
cold or frost. 7It will be a unique[l] day,
without daytime or nighttime[m]—a day
known to the LORD. When evening comes,
there will be light.[n]
8On that day living water[o] will flow[p] out
from Jerusalem, half to the eastern[q] sea[b]
and half to the western sea,[c] in summer
and in winter.[r]
9The LORD will be king[s] over the whole
earth.[t] On that day there will be one LORD,
and his name the only name.[u]
10The whole land, from Geba[v] to Rimmon,[w] south of Jerusalem, will become like
the Arabah. But Jerusalem will be raised
up[x] and remain in its place,[y] from the Benjamin Gate[z] to the site of the First Gate,
to the Corner Gate,[a] and from the Tower
of Hananel[b] to the royal winepresses. 11It
will be inhabited;[c] never again will it be
destroyed. Jerusalem will be secure.[d]
12This is the plague with which the
LORD will strike[e] all the nations that
fought against Jerusalem: Their flesh will
rot while they are still standing on their
feet, their eyes will rot in their sockets,
and their tongues will rot in their mouths.[f]
13On that day men will be stricken by the
LORD with great panic.[g] Each man will
seize the hand of another, and they will
attack each other.[h] 14Judah[i] too will fight
at Jerusalem. The wealth of all the surrounding nations will be collected[j]—great
quantities of gold and silver and clothing.
15A similar plague[k] will strike the horses
and mules, the camels and donkeys, and
all the animals in those camps.

[a] 5 Or *5My mountain valley will be blocked and will extend to Azel. It will be blocked as it was blocked because of the earthquake* [b] 8 That is, the Dead Sea [c] 8 That is, the Mediterranean

13:9 [p]S Isa 4:4; 33:14; Mal 3:2 [q]S Ps 12:6; S Da 11:35; 1Pe 1:6-7 [r]S Job 6:29; S Jer 6:27 [s]S Ps 50:15 [t]Ps 105:1 [u]S Ps 86:7; S Isa 30:19; S Zec 10:6 [v]S Lev 26:12; S Jer 30:22 [w]S Isa 44:5; S Jer 29:12; S Eze 20:38 **14:1** [x]Isa 13:6; S Joel 1:15; Mal 4:1 [y]S Isa 23:18 **14:2** [z]S Isa 2:3; S Zec 12:3 [a]S Eze 5:8 [b]S Ge 34:29; S La 5:11 [c]Isa 13:6; S Zec 13:8 **14:3** [d]Zec 9:14-15 [e]S Isa 8:9; S Zec 12:9 **14:4** [f]Eze 11:23 [g]S Nu 16:31 **14:5** [h]Am 1:1 [i]Isa 29:6; 66:15-16 [j]S Dt 33:2; Mt 16:27; 25:31; Jude 14 **14:6** [k]S Isa 13:10; S Jer 4:23 **14:7** [l]Jer 30:7 [m]Rev 21:23-25; 22:5 [n]S Isa 13:10; S 30:26 **14:8** [o]Eze 47:1-12; Jn 7:38; Rev 22:1-2 [p]S Isa 30:25 [q]Joel 2:20 [r]S Ge 8:22

14:9 [s]S Ps 22:28; S Ob 1:21 [t]S Dt 6:4; Ps 47:7; Isa 45:24; Rev 11:15 [u]Hab 2:14; Eph 4:5-6 **14:10** [v]1Ki 15:22 [w]S Jos 15:32 [x]Isa 2:2; Jer 30:18; S Am 9:11 [y]Zec 12:6 [z]S Jer 20:2 [a]S 2Ki 14:13 [b]S Ne 3:1 **14:11** [c]Zec 2:4 [d]S Ps 48:8; S Eze 34:25-28 **14:12** [e]S Isa 11:4 [f]ver 18; S Lev 26:16; S Dt 28:22; Job 18:13 **14:13** [g]S Ge 35:5 [h]S Jdg 7:22; S Zec 11:6 **14:14** [i]Zec 12:2 [j]S Isa 23:18 **14:15** [k]ver 12

13:9 *I will refine them.* See Ps 12:6 and note. *my people ... our God.* See note on 8:8. They will be restored to proper covenant relationship with the Lord (see also Eze 20:30–44).
14:1 *A day of the LORD.* Cf. Isa 2:12; Eze 30:3; Joel 1:15 and note. *your ... you.* Jerusalem (v. 2) is the object of the plunder.
14:2 *all the nations ... fight against it.* See v. 12; see also note on 12:3.
14:3 *day of battle.* Any occasion when the Lord supernaturally intervenes to deliver his people, such as at the Red Sea (see Ex 14:14 and note).
14:4 *Mount of Olives.* Called by this name elsewhere in the OT only in 2Sa 15:30. It faced the temple mount and, being about 2,700 feet high, rose about 200 feet above it. Cf. Eze 11:23. This prophecy is probably referred to in Ac 1:11–12.
14:5 *Azel.* The name of a place east of Jerusalem, marking the eastern end of the newly formed valley. *earthquake in the days of Uzziah.* Amos dates his prophecy by referring to it (see Am 1:1 and note). *holy ones.* May include both believers and angels. They will accompany our Lord when he comes (cf. Mt 25:31; 1Th 3:13; Jude 14; Rev 19:14).
14:7 *unique day.* Due to the topographical, cosmic and cataclysmic changes. See also Isa 60:19–20 and notes.
14:8 *living water will flow.* Perhaps both literal and symbolic (see Isa 8:6; Joel 3:18 and note; Jn 7:38).
14:9 *The LORD will be king over the whole earth.* A pervasive theological theme in Scripture (see Introduction to Psalms: Theology). *one LORD.* See Dt 6:4; Isa 43:11 and notes.
14:10 *Geba.* About six miles north-northeast of Jerusalem at the northern boundary of Judah (see 2Ki 23:8 and note). *Rimmon.* Also called En Rimmon (see Ne 11:29 and note), it was about 35 miles south-southwest of Jerusalem, where the hill country of Judah slopes away into the Negev. *Arabah.* See note on Dt 1:1. All the land around Jerusalem is to be leveled. *Jerusalem will be raised up.* See Isa 2:2–4 and note. The elevation may be both physical and in prominence. *Benjamin Gate ... First Gate ... Tower of Hananel.* All were probably at the northeastern part of the city wall (cf. Jer 31:38; 37:12–13; 38:7). *Corner Gate.* At the northwest corner (cf. Jer 31:38). *royal winepresses.* Just south of the city. Thus the whole city is included.
14:11 *inhabited.* See 2:4 and note. *never again ... destroyed.* As at the time of the exile to Babylonia (see Isa 43:28 and note). *Jerusalem will be secure.* See Jer 31:40.
14:12 *plague.* See Isa 37:36 and note. *nations that fought against Jerusalem.* See v. 2; see also note on 12:3.
14:13 *great panic ... attack each other.* See Jdg 7:22 and note.
14:14 *gold and silver and clothing.* The plunder of battle, thus reversing the situation in v. 1.
14:15 A similar plague will strike the beasts of burden, preventing the people from using them to escape.

[16]Then the survivors[l] from all the nations that have attacked Jerusalem will go
up year after year to worship[m] the King,[n]
the LORD Almighty, and to celebrate the
Feast of Tabernacles.[o] [17]If any of the peoples of the earth do not go up to Jerusalem to worship[p] the King, the LORD Almighty, they will have no rain.[q] [18]If the
Egyptian people do not go up and take
part, they will have no rain. The LORD[a]
will bring on them the plague[r] he inflicts
on the nations that do not go up to celebrate the Feast of Tabernacles.[s] [19]This will
be the punishment of Egypt and the punishment of all the nations that do not go
up to celebrate the Feast of Tabernacles.[t]

[20]On that day HOLY TO THE LORD[u] will be
inscribed on the bells of the horses, and
the cooking pots[v] in the LORD's house
will be like the sacred bowls[w] in front of
the altar. [21]Every pot in Jerusalem and
Judah will be holy[x] to the LORD Almighty,
and all who come to sacrifice will take
some of the pots and cook in them. And
on that day[y] there will no longer be a
Canaanite[b][z] in the house[a] of the LORD Almighty.[b]

[a] 18 Or *part, then the LORD* [b] 21 Or *merchant*

14:16 [l]S 2Ki 19:31 [m]S Ps 22:29; S 86:9; S Isa 19:21 [n]S Ob 1:21 [o]S Ex 23:16; Isa 60:6-9; S Mic 4:2 **14:17** [p]S 2Ch 32:23 [q]S Jer 14:4; S Am 4:7 **14:18** [r]S Ge 27:29 [s]S ver 12 **14:19** [t]S Ezr 3:4 **14:20** [u]S Ex 39:30 [v]S Eze 46:20 [w]Zec 9:15 **14:21** [x]S Jer 31:40; Ro 14:6-7; 1Co 10:31 [y]Ne 8:10 [z]Zec 9:8 [a]S Ne 11:1 [b]S Eze 44:9

14:16 See Isa 2:2–4 and note. *Feast of Tabernacles.* See notes on Ex 23:16; Ps 81:3. Of the three great pilgrimage festivals (see Ex 23:14–17), perhaps Tabernacles was selected as the one for representatives of the various Gentile nations because it was the last and greatest festival of the Hebrew calendar, gathering up into itself the year's worship (see note on Eze 45:25). It was to be a time of grateful rejoicing (see Lev 23:40; Dt 16:13–15; Ne 8:17 and note). Beginning with the period of Ezra and Nehemiah, the reading and teaching of "the Book of the Law of God" became an integral part of the festivities (Ne 8:18; cf. Isa 2:3). The festival seems to speak of the final, joyful regathering and restoration of Israel, as well as of the ingathering of the nations. See chart, pp. 178–179.

14:17 *no rain.* One of the curses for covenant disobedience (Dt 28:22–24; cf. Zec 9:11—10:1).

14:18 *Egyptian people … will have no rain.* See NIV text note. With either reading, the withholding of rain may still be included, for drought (v. 17) in the upper reaches of the Nile would cause the annual flooding of the Nile to fail.

14:20 *HOLY TO THE LORD.* Engraved on the gold plate worn on the high priest's turban (Ex 28:36–38) as a reminder of his consecration to the Lord's service (see note on 3:5). God's original purpose for Israel (see Ex 19:6 and note) will be realized.

14:21 *Every pot in Jerusalem … holy.* See Joel 3:17 and note. Even common things become holy when they are used for God's service. *cook.* Portions from the sacrifices. *Canaanite.* Represents anyone who is morally or spiritually unclean—anyone who is not included among the chosen people of God (cf. Isa 35:8; Eze 43:7; 44:9; Rev 21:27).

Malachi

I N T R O D U C T I O N

Author

The book is ascribed to Malachi, whose name means "my messenger." Since the term occurs in 3:1, and since both prophets and priests were called messengers of the Lord (see 2:7; Hag 1:13), some have thought "Malachi" to be only a title that tradition has given the author. The view has been supported by appeal to the pre-Christian Greek translation of the OT (the Septuagint), which translates the term in 1:1 "his messenger" rather than as a proper noun. The matter, however, remains uncertain, and it is still very likely that Malachi was in fact the author's name.

Background

Spurred on by the prophetic activity of Haggai and Zechariah, the returned exiles under the leadership of their governor Zerubbabel finished the temple in 516 B.C. In 458 the community was strengthened by the coming of the priest Ezra and several thousand more Jews. Artaxerxes, king of Persia, encouraged Ezra to reconstitute the temple worship (Ezr 7:17) and to make sure the law of Moses was being obeyed (Ezr 7:25 – 26).

Fourteen years later (444) the same Persian king permitted his cupbearer Nehemiah to return to Jerusalem and rebuild its walls (Ne 6:15). As newly appointed governor, Nehemiah also spearheaded reforms to help the poor (Ne 5:2 – 13), and he convinced the people to shun mixed marriages (Ne 10:30), to keep the Sabbath (Ne 10: 31) and to bring their tithes and offerings faithfully (Ne 10:37 – 39).

In 433 B.C. Nehemiah returned to the service of the Persian king, and during his absence the Jews fell into sin once more. Later, however, Nehemiah came back to Jerusalem to discover that the tithes were ignored, the Sabbath was broken, the people had intermarried with foreigners, and the priests had become corrupt (Ne 13:7 – 31). Several of these same sins are condemned by Malachi (see 1:6 – 14; 2:14 – 16; 3:8 – 11).

A Quick Look

Author:
Malachi

Audience:
The postexilic Jews living in Judah

Date:
430 B.C.

Theme:
The prophet Malachi assures the postexilic Jewish community that the Messianic King will come not only to judge his people but also to bless and restore them.

Date

The similarity between the sins denounced in Nehemiah and those denounced in Malachi suggests that the two leaders were contemporaries. Malachi may have been written after Nehemiah returned to Persia in 433 B.C. or during his second period as governor. Since the governor mentioned in 1:8 (see note there) probably was not Nehemiah, the first alternative may be more likely. Malachi was most likely the last prophet of the OT era (though some place Joel later).

Themes and Theology

The theological message of the book can be summed up in one sentence: The Great King (1:14) will come not only to judge his people (3:1 – 5; 4:1) but also to bless and restore them (3:6 – 12; 4:2).

Although the Jews had been allowed to return from exile and rebuild the temple, several discouraging factors brought about a general religious malaise: (1) Their land remained but a small province in the backwaters of the Persian empire, (2) the glorious future announced by the prophets (including the other postexilic prophets, Haggai and Zechariah) had not (yet) been realized, and (3) their God had not (yet) come to his temple (3:1) with majesty and power (as celebrated in Ps 68) to exalt his kingdom in the sight of the nations. Doubting God's covenant love (1:2) and no longer trusting his justice (2:17; 3:14 – 15), the Jews of the restored community began to lose hope. So their worship degenerated into a listless perpetuation of mere forms, and they no longer took the law seriously.

Doubting God's covenant love and no longer trusting his justice, the Jews of the restored community began to lose hope.

Malachi rebukes their doubt of God's love (1:2 – 5) and the faithlessness of both priests (1:6 — 2:9) and people (2:10 – 16). To their charge that God is unjust (2:17) because he has failed to come in judgment to exalt his people, Malachi answers with an announcement and a warning. The Lord they seek will come — but he will come "like a refiner's fire" (3:1 – 4). He will come to judge — but he will judge his people first (3:5).

Because the Lord does not change in his commitments and purpose, Israel has not been completely destroyed for her persistent unfaithfulness (3:6). But only through repentance and reformation will she again experience God's blessing (3:6 – 12). Those who honor the Lord will be spared when he comes to judge (3:16 – 18).

In conclusion, Malachi once more reassures and warns his readers that "the day ['that great and dreadful day of the LORD,' 4:5] is coming" and that "it will burn like a furnace" (4:1). In that day the righteous will rejoice, and "you will trample down the wicked" (4:2 – 3). So "remember the law of my servant Moses" (4:4). To prepare his people for that day the Lord will send "the prophet Elijah" to call them back to the godly ways of their forefathers (4:5 – 6).

Literary Features

The book of Malachi is called an "oracle" (1:1) and is written in what might be called lofty prose. The text features a series of questions asked by both God and the people. Frequently the Lord's statements are followed by sarcastic questions introduced by "(But/Yet) you ask" (1:2,6 – 7; 2:14,17; 3:7 – 8,13; cf. 1:13). In each case the Lord's response is given.

Repetition is a key element in the book. The name "LORD Almighty" occurs 20 times (see note on 1Sa 1:3). The book begins with a description of the wasteland of Edom (1:3 – 4) and ends with a warning of Israel's destruction (4:6).

Several vivid figures are employed within the book of Malachi. The priests sniff contemptuously at the altar of the Lord (1:13), and the Lord spreads on their faces the offal from their sacrifices (see 2:3 and note). As Judge, "he will be like a refiner's fire or a launderer's soap" (3:2), but for the righteous "the sun of righteousness will rise with healing in its wings. And you will go out and leap like calves released from the stall" (4:2).

Outline

I. Title (1:1)
II. Introduction: God's Faithful Covenant Love for Israel Affirmed (1:2 – 5)
III. Israel's Unfaithfulness Rebuked (1:6 — 2:16)
   A. The Unfaithfulness of the Priests (1:6 — 2:9)
      1. They dishonor God in their sacrifices (1:6 – 14)
      2. They do not faithfully teach the law (2:1 – 9)
   B. The Unfaithfulness of the People (2:10 – 16)
IV. The Lord's Coming Announced (2:17 — 4:6)
   A. The Lord Will Come to Purify the Priests and Judge the People (2:17 — 3:5)
   B. A Call to Repentance in View of the Lord's Coming (3:6 – 18)
      1. An exhortation to faithful giving (3:6 – 12)
      2. An exhortation to faithful service (3:13 – 18)
   C. The Day of the Lord Announced (ch. 4)

1 An oracle:[a] The word[b] of the LORD to
Israel through Malachi.[a]

Jacob Loved, Esau Hated

2 "I have loved[c] you," says the LORD.
"But you ask,[d] 'How have you
loved us?'
"Was not Esau Jacob's brother?" the
LORD says. "Yet I have loved Jacob,[e] 3 but
Esau I have hated,[f] and I have turned his
mountains into a wasteland[g] and left his
inheritance to the desert jackals.[h]"
4 Edom[i] may say, "Though we have been
crushed, we will rebuild[j] the ruins."
But this is what the LORD Almighty
says: "They may build, but I will demolish.[k] They will be called the Wicked Land,
a people always under the wrath of the
LORD.[l] 5 You will see it with your own eyes
and say, 'Great[m] is the LORD—even beyond the borders of Israel!'[n]

Blemished Sacrifices

6 "A son honors his father,[o] and a servant
his master.[p] If I am a father, where is the
honor due me? If I am a master, where is
the respect[q] due me?" says the LORD Almighty.[r] "It is you, O priests, who show
contempt for my name.
"But you ask,[s] 'How have we shown
contempt for your name?'
7 "You place defiled food[t] on my altar.
"But you ask,[u] 'How have we defiled
you?'
"By saying that the LORD's table[v] is contemptible. 8 When you bring blind animals
for sacrifice, is that not wrong? When you
sacrifice crippled or diseased animals,[w] is
that not wrong? Try offering them to your
governor! Would he be pleased[x] with you?
Would he accept you?" says the LORD Almighty.[y]
9 "Now implore God to be gracious to
us. With such offerings[z] from your hands,
will he accept[a] you?"—says the LORD Almighty.
10 "Oh, that one of you would shut the
temple doors,[b] so that you would not light
useless fires on my altar! I am not pleased[c]
with you," says the LORD Almighty, "and I
will accept[d] no offering[e] from your hands.
11 My name will be great[f] among the nations,[g] from the rising to the setting of the
sun.[h] In every place incense[i] and pure offerings[j] will be brought to my name, because my name will be great among the
nations," says the LORD Almighty.
12 "But you profane it by saying of the
Lord's table,[k] 'It is defiled,' and of its food,[l]
'It is contemptible.' 13 And you say, 'What
a burden!'[m] and you sniff at it contemptuously,[n]" says the LORD Almighty.
"When you bring injured, crippled or
diseased animals and offer them as sacrifices,[o] should I accept them from your
hands?"[p] says the LORD. 14 "Cursed is the
cheat who has an acceptable male in his
flock and vows to give it, but then sac-

1:1 [a] S Na 1:1 [b] Ac 7:38; Ro 3:1-2; 1Pe 4:11 **1:2** [c] S Dt 4:37 [d] ver 6,7; Mal 2:14,17; 3:7,13 [e] S Jer 46:27; Ro 9:13* **1:3** [f] Lk 14:26 [g] S Isa 34:10 [h] S Isa 13:22 **1:4** [i] S Isa 11:14; S 34:11 [j] Isa 9:10 [k] S Isa 34:5 [l] S La 4:22; S Eze 25:12-14; S 26:14 **1:5** [m] Ps 35:27; 48:1; Mic 5:4 [n] Isa 45:22; 52:10; S Am 1:11-12 **1:6** [o] S Lev 20:9; Mt 15:4; 23:9 [p] Lk 6:46 [q] S Dt 31:12; S Isa 1:2 [r] Job 5:17 [s] S ver 2 **1:7** [t] ver 12; Lev 21:6 [u] S ver 2 [v] S Eze 23:41 **1:8** [w] S Lev 1:3; S Dt 15:21 [x] S Ge 32:20 [y] S Isa 43:23 **1:9** [z] Lev 23:33-44; Ps 51:17; Mic 6:6-8; Ro 12:1; Heb 13:16 [a] S Jer 6:20 **1:10** [b] 2Ch 28:24 [c] S Hos 5:6 [d] Lev 22:20 [e] ver 13; Isa 1:11-14; Jer 14:12; Mal 2:12 **1:11** [f] S Isa 24:15; 56:6 [g] S Isa 6:3; S 12:4 [h] S Ps 113:3; S Mt 8:11 [i] Isa 60:6-7; Rev 5:8; 8:3 [j] S Isa 19:21; Heb 13:15 **1:12** [k] S Eze 41:22 [l] S ver 7 **1:13** [m] Isa 43:22-24 [n] S Nu 14:11 [o] S ver 10 [p] S Dt 15:21

[a] 1 *Malachi* means *my messenger.*

1:1 *oracle.* See Zec 9:1 and note; 12:1; see also Hab 1:1 and note. *word of the LORD.* See Hos 1:1 and note.

1:2 *loved you.* The Lord's reassuring word to his disheartened people.

1:3 *Esau I have hated.* If Israel doubts God's covenant love, they should consider the contrast between God's ways with them and his ways with Jacob's (Israel's) brother Esau (Edom). Paul explains God's love for Jacob and hatred for Esau on the basis of election (see Ro 9:10–13 and note on 9:13). God chose Jacob, not Esau. For the intended sense of "loved" and "hated" here, see Ge 29:31–33; Lk 14:26 and note. *wasteland.* Malachi's words about Edom echo those of the earlier prophets (see Am 1:11–12; Isa 34:5–15; Jer 49:7–22; Eze 25:12–14; 35:1–15; Obadiah). Between c. 550 and 400 B.C. the Nabatean Arabs gradually forced the Edomites from their homeland.

1:4 *Edom may say.* Her proud self-reliance has not assured her security and will not secure her future (cf. Jer 49:16).

1:5 *Great … Israel.* When she sees the ultimate fate of Edom, doubting Israel will acknowledge that the Lord is the great Ruler over all the nations.

1:6—2:9 The Lord rebukes the priests for unacceptable worship.

1:6 *son honors his father.* Cf. Isa 1:2–3. *priests, who show contempt for my name.* Contrast 2:5; cf. Isa 1:4.

1:7 *food.* The animal offerings (see v. 12; Lev 21:8,21). *defiled you.* By offering defiled sacrifices they defile the Lord himself. *the LORD's table.* The altar (see v. 12; see also v. 8; Eze 44:16 and notes). Since the priests ate from the sacrifices, the altar was also the table from which they got their food. *contemptible.* As the priests considered the Lord's altar and its sacrifices (v. 12) contemptible, so the Lord would cause the priests to be considered contemptible by the people (see 2:9 and note).

1:8 *blind … crippled.* Animals with defects or serious flaws were unacceptable as sacrifices (see Lev 1:3 and note; Dt 15:21). God deserves and will accept only the best. *governor.* Probably the Persian governor.

1:10 *shut the temple doors.* Better no sacrifices at all than sacrifices offered with contempt (see Isa 1:11–15 and note).

1:11 *great among the nations.* Cf. v. 14. God's judgment on Edom (v. 5) and other nations demonstrates his superiority over their gods, and it ultimately will evoke their recognition of him (see Zep 2:11; 3:9 and note). *incense and pure offerings.* Cf. the acceptable offerings presented by foreigners in Isa 56:6–7; 60:7. Some interpreters understand "incense" to refer to prayer (cf. Rev 5:8) and "offerings" to refer to praise (cf. Heb 13:15 and note).

1:12 *defiled … contemptible.* See v. 7 and note.

1:13 *sniff at it contemptuously.* Cf. the behavior of Eli's sons in 1Sa 2:15–17. *injured … diseased.* See v. 8 and note.

1:14 *vows … a blemished animal.* An animal sacrificed in fulfillment of a vow had to be a male without defect or blemish (see Lev 22:18–23). *great king.* See Zec 14:9 and note. *my name … feared.* More than the governor of v. 8 (see v. 11 and note).

rifices a blemished animal[q] to the Lord.
For I am a great king,[r]" says the LORD Almighty,[s] "and my name is to be feared[t]
among the nations.[u]

Admonition for the Priests

2 "And now this admonition is for you,
O priests.[v] 2 If you do not listen,[w] and
if you do not set your heart to honor[x] my
name," says the LORD Almighty, "I will
send a curse[y] upon you, and I will curse
your blessings.[z] Yes, I have already cursed
them, because you have not set your heart
to honor me.

3 "Because of you I will rebuke[a] your descendants[b]; I will spread on your faces the
offal[a] from your festival sacrifices, and you
will be carried off with it.[b] 4 And you will
know that I have sent you this admonition so that my covenant with Levi[c] may
continue," says the LORD Almighty. 5 "My
covenant was with him, a covenant[d] of life
and peace,[e] and I gave them to him; this
called for reverence[f] and he revered me
and stood in awe of my name. 6 True instruction[g] was in his mouth and nothing
false was found on his lips. He walked[h]
with me in peace[i] and uprightness,[j] and
turned many from sin.[k]

7 "For the lips of a priest[l] ought to preserve knowledge, and from his mouth
men should seek instruction[m]—because
he is the messenger[n] of the LORD Almighty.
8 But you have turned from the way[o] and
by your teaching have caused many to
stumble;[p] you have violated the covenant[q]
with Levi,"[r] says the LORD Almighty. 9 "So
I have caused you to be despised[s] and humiliated[t] before all the people, because
you have not followed my ways but have
shown partiality[u] in matters of the law."[v]

Judah Unfaithful

10 Have we not all one Father[c]?[w] Did not
one God create us?[x] Why do we profane
the covenant[y] of our fathers by breaking
faith[z] with one another?

11 Judah has broken faith. A detestable[a]
thing has been committed in Israel and
in Jerusalem: Judah has desecrated the
sanctuary the LORD loves,[b] by marrying[c]
the daughter of a foreign god.[d] 12 As for the
man who does this, whoever he may be,
may the LORD cut him off[e] from the tents
of Jacob[d][f]—even though he brings offerings[g] to the LORD Almighty.

13 Another thing you do: You flood the
LORD's altar with tears.[h] You weep and
wail[i] because he no longer pays attention[j]
to your offerings or accepts them with
pleasure from your hands.[k] 14 You ask,[l]
"Why?" It is because the LORD is acting
as the witness[m] between you and the wife
of your youth,[n] because you have broken

[a] 3 Or *cut off* (see Septuagint) [b] 3 Or *will blight your grain* [c] 10 Or *father* [d] 12 Or *12May the LORD cut off from the tents of Jacob anyone who gives testimony in behalf of the man who does this*

1:14 [q] Ex 12:5; S Lev 22:18-21 [r] Ps 95:3; S Ob 1:21; 1Ti 6:15 [s] Jer 46:18 [t] S Dt 28:58 [u] Ps 72:8-11 **2:1** [v] ver 7 **2:2** [w] Jer 13:17 [x] Mt 15:7-9; Jn 5:23; 1Ti 6:16; Rev 5:12-13 [y] S Dt 11:26; S 28:20 [z] Nu 6:23-27 **2:3** [a] S Ex 29:14; S Lev 4:11; S Job 9:31 [b] 1Ki 14:10 **2:4** [c] S Nu 3:12 **2:5** [d] Dt 33:9; Ps 25:10; 103:18; S Mt 26:28; S Lk 22:20; Heb 7:22 [e] S Nu 25:12 [f] S Dt 14:23; S 28:58; Ps 119:161; Heb 12:28 **2:6** [g] S Dt 33:10 [h] S Ge 5:22 [i] Lk 2:14; S Jn 14:27; Gal 5:22 [j] S Ps 25:21 [k] S Ro 11:14; Jas 5:19-20 **2:7** [l] S Jer 18:18 [m] S Lev 10:11; S 2Ch 17:7 [n] S Nu 27:21; S 2Ch 36:15; Mt 11:10; Mk 1:2 **2:8** [o] S Ex 32:8; Jer 2:8 [p] S Jer 18:15 [q] Jer 33:21; S Eze 22:26 [r] S Hos 4:6 **2:9** [s] S 1Sa 2:30; S Ps 22:6; S Jer 51:37 [t] S Ps 35:4; Jer 3:25; Ac 8:32-33 [u] S Ex 18:16; S Lev 19:15; Ac 10:34; Ro 2:11 [v] S 1Sa 2:17 **2:10** [w] S Ex 4:22; Mt 5:16; 6:4, 18; Lk 11:2; 1Co 8:6 [x] S Job 4:17; Isa 43:1 [y] Ex 19:5; S 2Ki 17:15; Jer 31:32 [z] S Zep 3:3-4 **2:11** [a] S Isa 1:13; S 48:8 [b] S Dt 4:37 [c] S Ne 13:23 [d] S Ex 34:16; Jer 3:7-9 **2:12** [e] S 1Sa 2:30-33; S Eze 24:21 [f] S Nu 24:5; 2Sa 20:1 [g] S Mal 1:10 **2:13** [h] S Jer 11:11 [i] Ps 39:12 [j] Ps 66:18; Jer 14:12 [k] Isa 58:2 **2:14** [l] S Mal 1:2 [m] S Ge 21:30; S Jos 24:22 [n] S Pr 5:18

2:2 *curse your blessings.* It was the function of the priests to pronounce God's blessing on the people (see Nu 6:23–27), but their blessings will become curses so that their uniquely priestly function will be worse than useless.

2:3 *Because of you.* Because of what you have done. *spread on your faces.* To disgrace you (see Na 3:6). *offal.* The contents of the intestines of a sacrificed animal (see Ex 29:14; Lev 8:17; 16:27).

2:4 *Levi.* The priests were chosen from the tribe of Levi (see Dt 21:5 and note).

2:5 *covenant of life and peace.* An allusion to the covenant with Phinehas, Aaron's grandson, in Nu 25:10–13 (see note on Nu 25:11). Phinehas defended God's honor by killing two offenders involved in the idolatry and immorality connected with the Baal of Peor (Nu 25:1–7). *he revered me.* Phinehas showed this by his zeal for God (see Nu 25:13; cf. Ps 106:30–31 and note on 106:31).

2:6–7 *instruction.* Priests were responsible to teach the law of Moses (see Lev 10:11; see also notes on Zep 3:4; Hag 2:11).

2:7 *messenger.* As teacher of the law and as one through whom people could inquire of God (see notes on 3:1; Hag 1:13).

2:8 *violated the covenant.* By unfaithful teaching, but also, it seems, by intermarriage with pagan foreigners (see Ezr 9:1 and note; 10:18–22; Ne 13:27–29). *with Levi.* See v. 4 and note on v. 5.

2:9 *despised.* In Hebrew the same word that is translated "contemptible" in 1:7,12 (see note on 1:7). *shown partiality.* Forbidden in Lev 19:15. The priests were to be like God in this respect (see Dt 10:17).

2:10–16 Malachi rebukes the people—in a passage in which references to breaking faith are thematic (vv. 10–11,14–16). Two examples of their sin are specifically mentioned: marrying pagan women and divorce.

2:10 *one Father.* See Isa 63:16. *create us.* As his special people (see Isa 43:1 and note). *covenant of our fathers.* The covenant that God made with their ancestors at Mount Sinai. *breaking faith.* The people could not even trust their own fellow Israelites or the national leaders—like the priests.

2:11 *daughter of a foreign god.* A pagan woman. Such marriages were strictly forbidden in the covenant law, not for ethnic or cultural reasons, but because they would lead to apostasy (see Ex 34:15–16; Dt 7:1–6 and notes; Jos 23:12–13 and note on 23:12). Ezra and Nehemiah both wrestled with this problem (see note on v. 8).

2:12 The alternative given in the NIV text note (particularly "gives testimony") is supported, e.g., by the use of the same Hebrew verb in Ge 30:33; Dt 5:20; 1Sa 12:3; 2Sa 1:16; Isa 3:9; Jer 14:7. On this reading, the one to be cut off is the one who speaks in defense of the wrongdoer. *tents of Jacob.* A figurative expression for the community (see Jer 30:18).

2:13 *weep and wail.* Because the Lord does not respond to their sacrifices with blessing, they add wailing to their prayers.

2:14 *witness ... marriage covenant.* Marriage involved making a covenant (see Pr 2:17; Eze 16:8 and notes), and covenants were affirmed before witnesses (see notes on Dt 30:19; 1Sa 20:23; Isa 8:1–2).

faith with her, though she is your partner,
the wife of your marriage covenant.[o]
15Has not ⌞the LORD⌟ made them one?[p]
In flesh and spirit they are his. And why
one? Because he was seeking godly offspring.[a][q] So guard yourself[r] in your spirit,
and do not break faith[s] with the wife of
your youth.
16"I hate divorce,[t]" says the LORD God of
Israel, "and I hate a man's covering himself[b] with violence[u] as well as with his
garment," says the LORD Almighty.
So guard yourself in your spirit,[v] and do
not break faith.

The Day of Judgment

17You have wearied[w] the LORD with your
words.
"How have we wearied him?" you ask.[x]
By saying, "All who do evil are good in
the eyes of the LORD, and he is pleased[y] with
them" or "Where is the God of justice?[z]"

3 "See, I will send my messenger,[a] who
will prepare the way before me.[b] Then
suddenly the Lord[c] you are seeking will
come to his temple; the messenger of the
covenant,[d] whom you desire,[e] will come,"
says the LORD Almighty.
2But who can endure[f] the day of his
coming?[g] Who can stand[h] when he appears? For he will be like a refiner's fire[i]
or a launderer's soap.[j] 3He will sit as a refiner and purifier of silver;[k] he will purify[l]
the Levites and refine them like gold and
silver.[m] Then the LORD will have men who
will bring offerings in righteousness,[n] 4and
the offerings[o] of Judah and Jerusalem will
be acceptable to the LORD, as in days gone
by, as in former years.[p]
5"So I will come near to you for judgment. I will be quick to testify against sorcerers,[q] adulterers[r] and perjurers,[s] against
those who defraud laborers of their wages,[t] who oppress the widows[u] and the fatherless, and deprive aliens[v] of justice, but
do not fear[w] me," says the LORD Almighty.

Robbing God

6"I the LORD do not change.[x] So you,
O descendants of Jacob, are not destroyed.[y] 7Ever since the time of your forefathers you have turned away[z] from my
decrees and have not kept them. Return[a]
to me, and I will return to you,"[b] says the
LORD Almighty.
"But you ask,[c] 'How are we to return?'
8"Will a man rob[d] God? Yet you rob me.
"But you ask, 'How do we rob you?'
"In tithes[e] and offerings. 9You are under
a curse[f]—the whole nation of you—because you are robbing me. 10Bring the
whole tithe[g] into the storehouse,[h] that
there may be food in my house. Test me
in this," says the LORD Almighty, "and see

[a] 15 Or *15But the one ⌞who is our father⌟ did not do this, not as long as life remained in him. And what was he seeking? An offspring from God* [b] 16 Or *his wife*

2:14 [o]S Eze 16:8; Heb 13:4 **2:15** [p]S Ge 2:24; Mt 19:4-6 [q]S Dt 14:2; 1Co 7:14 [r]S Dt 4:15 [s]S Isa 54:6; 1Co 7:10; Heb 13:4 **2:16** [t]S Dt 24:1; Mt 5:31-32; 19:4-9; Mk 10:4-5 [u]S Ge 6:11; 34:25; S Pr 4:17; S Isa 58:4 [v]Ps 51:10 **2:17** [w]S Isa 1:14 [x]S Mal 1:2 [y]Ps 5:4 [z]S Ge 18:25; S Job 8:3; S Eze 18:25 **3:1** [a]S Nu 27:21; S 2Ch 36:15 [b]S Isa 40:3; S Mt 3:3; 11:10*; Mk 1:2*; Lk 7:27* [c]Mic 5:2 [d]S Isa 42:6 [e]S 1Sa 9:20 **3:2** [f]S Eze 22:14; Rev 6:17 [g]S Eze 7:7; S Da 7:13; S Joel 2:31; S Mt 16:27; Jas 5:8; 2Pe 3:4; S Rev 1:7 [h]S 1Sa 6:20 [i]S Isa 1:31; S 30:30; S Zec 13:9; Mt 3:10-12 [j]S Job 9:30 **3:3** [k]S Da 12:10; S 1Co 3:13 [l]S 1Ch 23:28; S Isa 1:25 [m]S Job 28:1; S Ps 12:6; 1Pe 1:7; Rev 3:18 [n]S Ps 132:9 **3:4** [o]2Ch 7:12; Ps 51:19; Mal 1:11 [p]S 2Ch 7:3; S Eze 20:40 **3:5** [q]S Ex 7:11; S Isa 47:9 [r]Ex 20:14; Jas 2:11; 2Pe 2:12-14 [s]Lev 19:11-12; S Jer 7:9 [t]S Lev 19:13; Jas 5:4 [u]S Ex 22:22 [v]S Ex 22:21; S Dt 24:19; S Eze 22:7 [w]S Dt 31:12; S Isa 1:2 **3:6** [x]S Nu 23:19; S Heb 7:21; Jas 1:17 [y]S Job 34:15; S Hos 11:9 **3:7** [z]S Ex 32:8; S Jer 7:26; Ac 7:51 [a]S Isa 44:22; S Eze 18:32 [b]S Zec 1:3; Jas 4:8 [c]S Mal 1:2 **3:8** [d]S Zec 5:3 [e]S Lev 27:30; Nu 18:21; S Ne 13:10-12; Lk 18:12 **3:9** [f]S Dt 11:26; 28:15-68; S Zec 5:3 **3:10** [g]S Ex 22:29 [h]S Ne 13:12

2:15 *one.* See Ge 2:24 and note. *godly offspring.* Marriage "sanctifies" the children (see 1Co 7:14 and note). If the alternative translation in the NIV text note is accepted, this verse refers to Abraham, who "married" the foreigner Hagar in order to have a son (Ge 16:1–4). But Abraham did not divorce Sarah, who had suggested the union with Hagar in the first place.

2:16 *I hate divorce.* See Isa 50:1 and note. *violence.* See 3:5.

2:17—4:6 The second half of Malachi's prophecy speaks of God's coming to his people. They had given up on God (2:17) and had grown religiously cynical and morally corrupt. So God's coming will mean judgment and purification as well as redemption.

2:17 *wearied the LORD with your words.* In Isa 43:24 Israel's sins had wearied God. *All who do evil are good.* Such was the depth of their cynicism. *Where is ... justice?* Cf. the sarcastic taunts of Isa 5:19.

3:1 *my messenger.* The Hebrew for these words is *mal'aki* (see NIV text note on 1:1); it is normally used of a priest or prophet (see Hag 1:13 and note). These words are fulfilled in John the Baptist (see Mt 11:7–10; Mk 1:2–4; Lk 1:76). *who will prepare the way.* When the Lord comes, it will be to purify (v. 3) and judge (v. 5), but he will mercifully send one before him to prepare his people (see 4:5–6; Isa 40:3 and notes). *the Lord you are seeking ... whom you desire, will come.* See Hag 2:7 and note. *messenger of the covenant.* The Messiah, who as the Lord's representative will confirm and establish the covenant (see note on Isa 42:6).

3:2 *day of his coming.* The day of the Lord (see 4:1; see also Isa 2:11,17,20; Joel 1:15 and notes). Malachi announces the Lord's coming to complete God's work in history. *Who can stand ...?* Those who desire the Lord's coming must know that clean hands and a pure heart are required (see Ps 24:3–4 and note on 24:4; Isa 33:14–15). *refiner's fire.* See Isa 1:25; Zec 13:8–9 and notes. *launderer's soap.* See Isa 7:3 and note. White clothes signified purity (cf. Mk 9:3; Rev 3:5).

3:3 *sit as a refiner and purifier.* See Ps 12:6 and note. *purify the Levites.* Those who are supposed to be messengers of the Lord and who serve at the altar will be purged of their sins and unfaithfulness—such as those the Lord has rebuked in 1:6—2:9.

3:4 *be acceptable.* See 1:8 and note. *days gone by.* Probably the time of Moses and Phinehas (see note on 2:5).

3:5 When he comes, the Lord will both purify the Levites (vv. 3–4) and judge the people. *sorcerers.* Common in the ancient Near East (see Ex 7:11; Dt 18:10 and note on 18:9).

3:6 *do not change.* See Jas 1:17. Contrary to what many in Malachi's day were thinking, God remains faithful to his covenant. *not destroyed.* In contrast to Edom (1:3–5) and in spite of Israel's history of unfaithfulness.

3:7 *Return ... and I will return.* If the Lord is to come for Israel's redemption, she must repent (see Zec 1:3 and note).

3:9–10 *curse ... blessing.* See Dt 11:26–28.

3:10 *storehouse.* The treasury rooms of the sanctuary (see 1Ki 7:51; 2Ch 31:11–12; Ne 13:12). *floodgates of heaven.* Elsewhere the idiom refers to abundant provision of food (see 2Ki 7:2,19; Ps 78:23–24 and note on 78:23). *pour out ... blessing.* The promised covenant blessing (see Dt 28:12; cf. Isa 44:3).

if I will not throw open the floodgates[i] of heaven and pour out[j] so much blessing[k] that you will not have room enough for it.[l] 11I will prevent pests from devouring[m] your crops, and the vines in your fields will not cast their fruit,[n]" says the LORD Almighty. 12"Then all the nations will call you blessed,[o] for yours will be a delightful land,"[p] says the LORD Almighty.[q]

13"You have said harsh things[r] against me," says the LORD.

"Yet you ask,[s] 'What have we said against you?'

14"You have said, 'It is futile[t] to serve[u] God. What did we gain by carrying out his requirements[v] and going about like mourners[w] before the LORD Almighty? 15But now we call the arrogant[x] blessed. Certainly the evildoers[y] prosper,[z] and even those who challenge God escape.' "

16Then those who feared the LORD talked with each other, and the LORD listened and heard.[a] A scroll[b] of remembrance was written in his presence concerning those who feared[c] the LORD and honored his name.

17"They will be mine,[d]" says the LORD Almighty, "in the day when I make up my treasured possession.[a][e] I will spare[f] them, just as in compassion a man spares his son[g] who serves him. 18And you will again see the distinction between the righteous[h] and the wicked, between those who serve God and those who do not.[i]

3:10 [i]S 2Ki 7:2 [j]Isa 44:3 [k]S Lev 25:21; S Joel 2:14; 2Co 9:8-11 [l]S Joel 2:24 **3:11** [m]S Ex 10:15; S Dt 28:39 [n]S Ex 23:26 **3:12** [o]S Dt 28:3-12; Isa 61:9 [p]S Isa 62:4; S Eze 20:6 [q]S 2Ch 31:10 **3:13** [r]Mal 2:17 [s]S Mal 1:2 **3:14** [t]Ps 73:13; S Isa 57:10 [u]Ps 100:2; Jn 12:26; Ro 12:11 [v]S Jos 22:5; S Isa 1:14 [w]Isa 58:3 **3:15** [x]S Ps 119:21 [y]Ps 14:1; 36:1-2; Jer 7:10 [z]S Job 21:7 **3:16** [a]S Ps 34:15 [b]S Ex 32:32; S Ps 56:8; S 87:6; S Lk 10:20 [c]S Dt 28:58; S 31:12; Ps 33:18; S Pr 1:7; Rev 11:18 **3:17** [d]Isa 43:21 [e]S Ex 8:22; S Dt 7:6; S Ro 8:14; S Tit 2:14 [f]Ne 13:22; Ps 103:13; Isa 26:20; Lk 15:1-32 [g]Ro 8:32 **3:18** [h]S Ge 18:25 [i]Dt 32:4; Mt 25:32-33,41

The Day of the LORD

4 "Surely the day is coming;[j] it will burn like a furnace.[k] All the arrogant[l] and every evildoer will be stubble,[m] and that day that is coming will set them on fire,[n]" says the LORD Almighty. "Not a root or a branch[o] will be left to them. 2But for you who revere my name,[p] the sun of righteousness[q] will rise with healing[r] in its wings. And you will go out and leap[s] like calves released from the stall. 3Then you will trample[t] down the wicked; they will be ashes[u] under the soles of your feet on the day when I do these things," says the LORD Almighty.

4"Remember the law[v] of my servant Moses, the decrees and laws I gave him at Horeb[w] for all Israel.[x]

5"See, I will send you the prophet Elijah[y] before that great and dreadful day of the LORD comes.[z] 6He will turn the hearts of the fathers to their children,[a] and the hearts of the children to their fathers; or else I will come and strike[b] the land with a curse."[c]

[a] 17 Or *Almighty, "my treasured possession, in the day when I act*

4:1 [j]S Da 7:13; S Joel 2:31; Mt 11:14; Ac 2:20 [k]S Isa 31:9 [l]S Isa 2:12 [m]S Isa 5:24; S Na 1:10 [n]S Isa 1:31 [o]S 2Ki 10:11; S Eze 17:8; S Mt 3:10 **4:2** [p]S Dt 28:58; Ps 61:5; 111:9; Rev 14:1 [q]S Ps 118:27; S Isa 9:2; S 45:8; Lk 1:78; Eph 5:14 [r]S 2Ch 7:14; S Isa 30:26; S Mt 4:23; Rev 22:2 [s]S Isa 35:6 **4:3** [t]S Job 40:12; Ps 18:40-42 [u]Eze 28:18 **4:4** [v]S Dt 28:61; S Ps 147:19; Mt 5:17; 7:12; Ro 2:13; 4:15; Gal 3:24 [w]S Ex 3:1 [x]S Ex 20:1 **4:5** [y]S 1Ki 17:1; S Mt 11:14; 16:14 [z]S Joel 2:31 **4:6** [a]Lk 1:17 [b]S Isa 11:4; Rev 19:15 [c]S Dt 11:26; S 13:15; S Jos 6:17; S 23:15; S Zec 5:3

3:11 *pests ... cast their fruit.* Examples of the threatened covenant curses (see Dt 28:39–40).

3:12 *call you blessed.* In fulfillment of the promise to Abraham (see Ge 12:2–3; Isa 61:9 and notes).

3:14 *It is futile to serve God.* Because the redemption they longed for had not yet been realized. *like mourners.* In sackcloth and ashes.

3:15 *arrogant.* Evildoers—those who challenge God (see note on Ps 10:11). *blessed.* In their unbelief, the Jews call blessed those whom the godly know to be cursed (see Ps 119:21 and note)—but it is they who will be called blessed if they repent (v. 12). *evildoers prosper ... escape.* The psalmist struggled with the prosperity of the wicked in Ps 73:3,9–12 (see also Hab 1:2–4 and notes).

3:16 *those who feared the LORD.* Those who had not given way to doubts and cynicism. *talked with each other.* In the face of the widespread complaining against God (vv. 14–15), they sought mutual encouragement in fellowship. *scroll of remembrance.* Analogous to the records of notable deeds kept by earthly rulers (see Est 6:1–3; Isa 4:3; Da 7:10; 12:1). *honored his name.* Contrast the priests (1:12) and many among the people (vv. 14–15; 2:17).

3:17 *my treasured possession.* See note on Ex 19:5. *spare them.* In the day of judgment (see 4:1–2). *who serves him.* Cf. 1:6.

3:18 *you will again see.* As they apparently do not now see—hence their cynicism. *the righteous and the wicked.* See 2:17 and note.

4:1 *the day.* The day of the Lord (see v. 5; 3:2 and note). *burn like a furnace.* See 3:2–3; Isa 1:31; 66:15–16 and notes. *arrogant.* See 3:15 and note. *stubble ... fire.* See Isa 47:14 and note; see also John the Baptist's prophecy about the work of Christ in Mt 3:12. *Not a root or a branch.* Nothing of them will be left (see Eze 17:8–9).

4:2 *you who revere my name.* Or "you who fear my name," i.e., you who reverentially trust in the Lord and are committed to his will as revealed in his word (see notes on Ge 20:11; Ps 34:8–14; Pr 1:7). *sun of righteousness.* God and his glory are compared with the sun in Isa 60:19 (see note there). Christ is the "rising sun" from heaven (see Lk 1:78–79 and note on 1:78; see also Isa 9:2 and note). *righteousness ... healing.* Salvation and renewal are intended (see Isa 45:8; 46:13; 53:5; Jer 30:17 and notes). *its wings.* The sun's rays (cf. Ps 139:9). *like calves released from the stall.* Frisky young calves often frolic about when released from confinement.

4:3 *trample ... the wicked.* As one treads the winepress (see Isa 63:2–3 and notes).

4:4 *Remember the law.* A final exhortation to those who impatiently wait for the Lord's coming. *my servant Moses.* See Ex 14:31; Dt 34:5 and notes. *Horeb.* Mount Sinai (see Ex 3:1 and note).

4:5 See 3:1 and note. *Elijah.* As Elijah (whose ministry was one of judgment and redemption) came before Elisha, so "Elijah" will be sent to prepare God's people for the Lord's coming—in the person of Jesus, whose name (Joshua) was but a different form of the name Elisha. John the Baptist ministered "in the spirit and power of Elijah" (see Lk 1:17 and note; see also Mt 11:13–14; 17:12–13; Mk 9:11–13 and note on 9:13). And some feel that Elijah may also be one of the two witnesses in Rev 11:3 (see note there). *great and dreadful day.* See v. 1; see also 3:2; Joel 2:11 and note.

4:6 *turn the hearts of ... fathers to ... children, and ... children to ... fathers.* That is, unite the generations in loyal and obedient service to God (cf. Ge 18:19). According to Lk 1:17 John the Baptist sought to accomplish this. *curse.* Total destruction. If Israel does not repent, she will be dealt with as God had dealt with Edom (see 1:3–4; Isa 34:5).

From Malachi to Christ

THE PERSIAN PERIOD
450–330 B.C.

For about 200 years after Nehemiah's time the Persians controlled Judah, but the Jews were allowed to carry on their religious observances and were not interfered with. During this time Judah was ruled by high priests who were responsible to the Jewish governor appointed by the Persian emperor.

Rule of Alexander the Great

THE HELLENISTIC PERIOD
330–166 B.C.

In 333 B.C. the Persian armies stationed in Macedonia were defeated by Alexander the Great. He was convinced that Greek culture was the one force that could unify the world. Alexander permitted the Jews to observe their laws and even granted them exemption from tribute or tax during their sabbath years. When he built Alexandria in Egypt, he encouraged Jews to live there and gave them some of the same privileges he gave his Greek subjects.The Greek conquest prepared the way for the pre-Christian translation of the Hebrew OT into Greek (Septuagint version) beginning c. 250 B.C.

Rule of the Ptolemies of Egypt

Rule of the Seleucids of Syria

THE HASMONEAN PERIOD
166–63 B.C.

When this historical period began, the Jews were being greatly oppressed. The Ptolemies had been tolerant of the Jews and their religious practices, but the Seleucid rulers were determined to force Hellenism on them. Copies of the Scriptures were ordered destroyed and laws were enforced with extreme cruelty. The oppressed Jews revolted, led by Judas Maccabeus.

Hasmonean Dynasty

THE ROMAN PERIOD
63 B.C.

In the year 63 B.C. Pompey, the Roman general, captured Jerusalem, and the provinces in the Holy Land became subject to Rome. The local government was entrusted part of the time to princes and the rest of the time to Roman governors who were appointed by the emperors. Herod the Great was ruler of that whole region at the time of Christ's birth.

Herod the Great rules as king; subject to Rome

Timeline: 410 · **400 B.C.** · 390 · 380 · 370 · 360 · 350 · 340 · 330 · 320 · 310 · **300** · 290 · 280 · 270 · 260 · 250 · 240 · 230 · 220 · 210 · **200** · 190 · 180 · 170 · 160 · 150 · 140 · 130 · 120 · 110 · **100** · 90 · 80 · 70 · 60 · 50 · 40 · 30 · 20 · 10 · 10 · 20 · A.D. 30

- Malachi c. 430 B.C.
- 334–323 Alexander the Great conquers the East
- 330–328 Alexander's years of power
- 320 Ptolemy (I) Soter conquers Jerusalem
- 311 Seleucus conquers Babylon; Seleucid dynasty begins
- 226 Antiochus (III) of Syria conquers the Holy Land
- 223–187 Antiochus becomes Seleucid ruler of Syria
- 198 Antiochus defeats Egypt and gains control of the Holy Land
- 175–164 Antiochus (IV) Epiphanes rules Syria; Judaism is prohibited
- 167 Mattathias and his sons rebel against Antiochus; Maccabean revolt begins
- 166–160 Judas Maccabeus's leadership
- 160–143 Jonathan is high priest
- 142–134 Simon becomes high priest; establishes Hasmonean dynasty (see essay, pp. 1451–1454)
- 134–104 John Hyrcanus enlarges the independent Jewish state
- 103 Aristobulus's rule
- 102–76 Alexander Janneus's rule
- 75–67 Rule of Salome Alexandra with Hyrcanus II as high priest
- 66–63 Battle between Aristobulus II and Hyrcanus II
- 63 Pompey invades the Holy Land; Roman rule begins
- 63–40 Hyrcanus II governs but is subject to Rome
- 40–37 Parthians conquer Jerusalem
- 37 Herod becomes ruler of the Holy Land
- 19 Herod's temple begun
- 4 Herod dies; Archelaus succeeds him

The Time Between the Testaments

The time between the Testaments was one of ferment and change — a time of the realignment of traditional power blocs and the passing of a Near Eastern cultural tradition that had been dominant for almost 3,000 years.

In Biblical history, the approximately 400 years that separate the time of Nehemiah from the birth of Christ are known as the intertestamental period (c. 433 – 5 B.C.). Sometimes called the "silent" years, they were anything but silent. The events, literature and social forces of these years would shape the world of the NT.

History

With the Babylonian exile, Israel ceased to be an independent nation and became a minor territory in a succession of larger empires. Very little is known about the latter years of Persian domination because the Jewish historian Josephus (c. A.D. 37 – 100), our primary source for the intertestamental period, all but ignores them.

With Alexander the Great's acquisition of the Holy Land (332 B.C.), a new and more insidious threat to Israel emerged. Alexander was committed to the creation of a world united by Greek language and culture, a policy followed by his successors. This policy, called Hellenization, had a dramatic impact on the Jews.

At Alexander's death (323 B.C.) the empire he won was divided among his generals. Two of them founded dynasties — the Ptolemies of Egypt and the Seleucids in Syria and Mesopotamia — that would contend for control of the Holy Land for over a century.

The rule of the Ptolemies was considerate of Jewish religious sensitivities, but in 198 B.C. the Seleucids took control and paved the way for one of the most heroic periods in Jewish history.

The early Seleucid years were largely a continuation of the tolerant rule of the Ptolemies, but Antiochus IV Epiphanes (whose title means "God made manifest" and who ruled 175 – 164 B.C.) changed that when he attempted to consolidate his fading empire through a policy of radical Hellenization. While a segment of the Jewish aristocracy had already adopted Greek ways, the majority of Jews were outraged.

Antiochus's atrocities were aimed at the eradication of Jewish religion. He prohibited some of the central elements of Jewish practice, attempted to destroy all copies of the Torah (the Pentateuch) and required offerings to the Greek god Zeus. His crowning outrage was the erection of a statue of Zeus and the sacrificing of a pig in the Jerusalem temple itself.

Opposition to Antiochus was led by Mattathias, an elderly villager from a priestly family, and his five sons: Judas (Maccabeus — probably meaning "hammerer"), Jonathan, Simon, John and Eleazar. Mattathias destroyed a Greek altar established in his village, Modein, and killed Antiochus's emissary. This triggered the Maccabean revolt, a 24-year war (166 – 142 B.C.) that resulted in the independence of Judah until the Romans took control in 63 B.C.

The victory of Mattathias's family was a hollow one, however. With the death of his last son, Simon, the Hasmonean dynasty that they founded soon evolved into an aristocratic, Hellenistic regime sometimes hard to distinguish from that of the Seleucids. During the reign of Simon's son, John Hyrcanus, the orthodox Jews who had supported the Maccabees fell out of favor. With only a few exceptions, the rest of the Hasmoneans supported the Jewish Hellenizers. The Pharisees were actually persecuted by Alexander Janneus (102 – 76 B.C.).

The Hasmonean dynasty ended when, in 63 B.C., an expanding Roman empire intervened in a dynastic clash between the two sons of Janneus, Aristobulus II and Hyrcanus II. Pompey, the general who subdued the East for Rome, took Jerusalem after a three-month siege of the temple area, massacring priests in the performance of their duties and entering the Most Holy Place. This sacrilege began Roman rule in a way that Jews could neither forgive nor forget.

Literature

During these unhappy years of oppression and internal strife, the Jewish people produced a sizable body of literature that both recorded and addressed their era. Three of the more significant works are the Septuagint, the Apocrypha and the Dead Sea Scrolls.

Septuagint. Jewish legend says that 72 scholars, under the sponsorship of Ptolemy Philadelphus (c. 250 B.C.), were brought together on the island of Pharos, near Alexandria, where they produced a Greek translation of the OT in 72 days. From this tradition the Latin word for 70, "Septuagint," became the name attached to the translation. The Roman numeral for 70, LXX, is used as an abbreviation for it.

Behind the legend lies the probability that at least the Torah (the five books of Moses) was translated into Greek c. 250 B.C. for the use of the Greek-speaking Jews of Alexandria. The rest of the OT and some noncanonical books were also included in the LXX before the dawning of the Christian era, though it is difficult to be certain when.

The Septuagint quickly became the Bible of the Jews outside the Holy Land who, like the Alexandrians, no longer spoke Hebrew. It would be difficult to overestimate its influence. It made the Scriptures available both to the Jews who no longer spoke their ancestral language and to the entire Greek-speaking world. It later became the Bible of the early church, frequently quoted by the NT writers. Also, its widespread popularity and use contributed to the retention of the Apocrypha by some branches of Christendom.

Apocrypha. Derived from a Greek word that means "hidden," Apocrypha has acquired the meaning "false," but in a technical sense it describes a specific body of writings. This collection consists of a variety of books and additions to canonical books that, with the exception of 2 Esdras (c. A.D. 90), were written during the intertestamental period. Their recognition as authoritative in Roman and Eastern Christianity is the result of a complex historical process.

The limits of the Hebrew canon of the OT, also accepted by most Protestants today, were very likely established for most Jews by the dawn of the Christian era. In spite of disagreements among some of the church fathers as to which books were canonical and which were not, the Apocryphal books (which were included in the Septuagint) continued in common use by most Christians until the Reformation. During this period most Protestants decided to follow the Hebrew canon while Rome, at the Council of Trent (1546) and more recently at the First Vatican Council (1869–70), affirmed the larger Alexandrian canon that includes the Apocrypha.

The Apocryphal books have retained their place primarily through the weight of ecclesiastical authority, without which they would not commend themselves as canonical literature. There is no clear evidence that Jesus or the apostles ever quoted any Apocryphal works as inspired Scripture. The Jewish community that produced them repudiated them, and the historical surveys in the apostolic sermons recorded in Acts completely ignore the period they cover. Even the sober, historical account of 1 Maccabees is tarnished by numerous errors and anachronisms.

There is nothing of theological value in the Apocryphal books that cannot be duplicated in canonical Scripture, and they contain much that runs counter to its teachings. Nonetheless, this body of literature does provide a valuable source of information for the study of the intertestamental period.

Dead Sea Scrolls. In the spring of 1947 an Arab shepherd chanced upon a cave in the hills overlooking the southwestern shore of the Dead Sea that contained what has been called "the greatest manuscript discovery of modern times." The documents and fragments of documents found in those caves, dubbed the "Dead Sea Scrolls," included OT books, a few books of the Apocrypha, apocalyptic works, pseudepigrapha (books that purport to be the work of ancient heroes of the faith), and a number of books peculiar to the sect that produced them.

Approximately a third of the documents are Biblical, with Psalms, Deuteronomy and Isaiah — the books quoted most often in the NT — occurring most frequently. One of the most remarkable finds was a complete 24-foot-long scroll of Isaiah.

The Scrolls have made a significant contribution to the quest for a form of the OT texts most accurately reflecting the original manuscripts; they provide copies 1,000 years closer to the originals than were previously known. The understanding of Biblical Hebrew and Aramaic and knowledge of the development of Judaism between the Testaments have been increased significantly. Of great importance to readers of the Bible is the demonstration of the care with which OT texts were copied, thus providing objective evidence for the general reliability of those texts.

Social Developments

The Judaism of Jesus' day is, to a large extent, the result of changes that came about in response to the pressures of the intertestamental period.

Diaspora. The Diaspora (dispersion) of Israel begun in the exile accelerated during these years until a writer of the day could say that Jews filled "every land and sea."

Jews outside the Holy Land, cut off from the temple, concentrated their religious life in the study of the Torah as the chief guide for their daily living within the Gentile world and in the activities centered in the synagogue (see below). The missionaries of the early church began their Gentile ministries among the Diaspora, using their Greek translation of the OT (the Septuagint).

Sadducees. In the Holy Land, the Greek world made its greatest impact through the party of the Sadducees. Made up of aristocrats, it became the temple party. Because of their position, the Sadducees had a vested interest in the status quo.

Relatively few in number, they wielded disproportionate political power and controlled the high priesthood. They rejected all religious writings except the Torah, as well as any doctrine (such as resurrection from the dead) not found in those five books.

Synagogue. During the Babylonian exile, Israel was cut off from the temple, divested of nationhood and surrounded by pagan religious practices. The nation's faith was threatened with extinction. Under these circumstances, the exiles turned their religious focus from what they had lost to what they retained — the Torah and the belief that they were God's people. They concentrated on the law rather than nationhood, on personal piety rather than sacramental rectitude, and on prayer as an acceptable replacement for the sacrifices denied to them.

When they returned from the exile, they brought with them this new form of religious expression, as well as the synagogue (its center), and Judaism became a faith that could be practiced wherever the Torah could be carried. The emphases on personal piety and a relationship with God, which characterized synagogue worship, not only helped preserve Judaism but also prepared the way for the Christian gospel.

Pharisees. As the party of the synagogue, the Pharisees strove to reinterpret the law. They built a "hedge" around it to enable Jews to live righteously before God in a world that had changed drastically since the days of Moses. Although they were comparatively few in number, the Pharisees enjoyed the support of the people and influenced popular opinion if not national policy. They were the only party to survive the destruction of the temple in A.D. 70 and were the spiritual progenitors of modern Judaism.

Essenes. An almost forgotten Jewish sect until the discovery of the Dead Sea Scrolls, the Essenes were a small, separatist group that grew out of the conflicts of the Maccabean age. Like the Pharisees, they stressed strict legal observance, but they considered the temple priesthood corrupt and rejected much of the temple ritual and sacrificial system. Mentioned by several ancient writers (including Josephus and Pliny), the precise nature of the Essenes is still not certain, though it is generally agreed that the Qumran community that produced the Dead Sea Scrolls was probably an Essene group.

Because they were convinced that they were the true remnant, these Qumran Essenes had separated themselves from Judaism at large and devoted themselves to personal purity and preparation for the final war between the "Sons of Light and the Sons of Darkness." They practiced an apocalyptic faith, looking back to the contributions of their "Teacher of Righteousness" and forward to the coming of two, and possibly three, Messiahs. The destruction of the temple in A.D. 70, however, seems to have delivered a death blow to their apocalyptic expectations.

Attempts have been made to equate aspects of the beliefs of the Qumran community with the origins of Christianity. Some have seen a prototype of Jesus in their "Teacher of Righteousness," and both John the Baptist and Jesus have been assigned membership in the sect. There is, however, only a superficial, speculative base for these conjectures.

The New Testament

The Synoptic Gospels

A careful comparison of the four Gospels reveals that Matthew, Mark and Luke are noticeably similar, while John is quite different. The first three Gospels agree extensively in language, in the material they include, and in the order in which events and sayings from the life of Christ are narrated. (Chronological order does not appear to have been rigidly followed in any of the Gospels, however.) Because of this agreement, these three books are called the Synoptic Gospels (*syn*, "together with"; *optic*, "seeing"; thus "seeing together"). For an example of agreement in content see Mt 9:2–8; Mk 2:3–12; Lk 5:18–26. An instance of verbatim agreement is found in Mt 10:22a; Mk 13:13a; Lk 12:17. A mathematical comparison shows that 91 percent of Mark's gospel is contained in Matthew, while 53 percent of Mark is found in Luke. Such agreement raises questions as to the origin of the Synoptic Gospels. Did the authors rely on a common source? Were they interdependent? Questions such as these constitute what is known as the Synoptic Problem. Several suggested solutions have been advanced:

1. *The use of oral tradition.* Some have thought that oral tradition had become so stereotyped that it provided a common source from which all the Synoptic writers drew.

2. *The use of an early Gospel.* Some have postulated that the Synoptic authors all had access to an earlier Gospel, now lost.

3. *The use of written fragments.* Some have assumed that written fragments had been composed concerning various events from the life of Christ and that these were used by the Synoptic authors.

4. *Mutual dependence.* Some have suggested that the Synoptic writers drew from each other with the result that what they wrote was often very similar.

5. *The use of two major sources.* The most widely held view among Biblical scholars is that the Gospel of Mark and a hypothetical document, called *Quelle* (German for "source") or *Q*, were used by Matthew and Luke as sources for most of the materials included in their Gospels (see diagram [two-source theory] below).

6. *The priority and use of Matthew.* Another view suggests that the other two Synoptics drew from Matthew as their main source (see diagram [Matthean priority] below).

7. *The priority and use of Luke.* A similar view suggests that the other two Synoptics drew from Luke as their main source.

8. *A combination of the above.* This theory assumes that the authors of the Synoptic Gospels made use of oral tradition, written fragments, mutual dependence on other Synoptic writers or on their Gospels, and the testimony of eyewitnesses.

9. *Complete independence.* Some hold that the Synoptic writers worked independently of each other. According to this view, the similar — sometimes even verbatim — choice and order of words and events are best explained by the infallible guidance of the Holy Spirit on the authors.

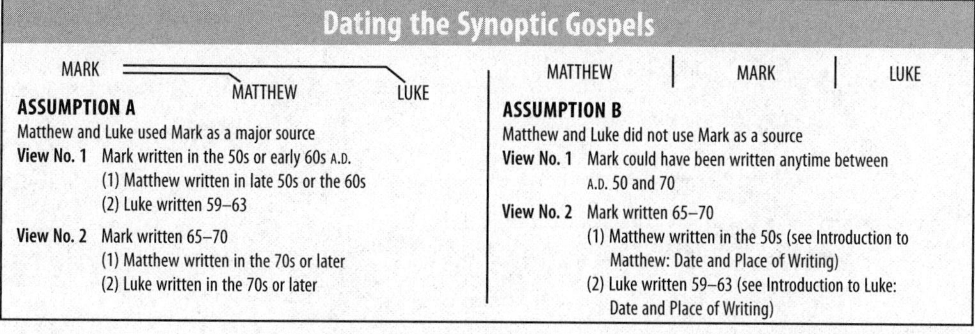
Dating the Synoptic Gospels

MARK — MATTHEW — LUKE

ASSUMPTION A

Matthew and Luke used Mark as a major source

View No. 1 Mark written in the 50s or early 60s A.D.
(1) Matthew written in late 50s or the 60s
(2) Luke written 59–63

View No. 2 Mark written 65–70
(1) Matthew written in the 70s or later
(2) Luke written in the 70s or later

MATTHEW | MARK | LUKE

ASSUMPTION B

Matthew and Luke did not use Mark as a source

View No. 1 Mark could have been written anytime between A.D. 50 and 70

View No. 2 Mark written 65–70
(1) Matthew written in the 50s (see Introduction to Matthew: Date and Place of Writing)
(2) Luke written 59–63 (see Introduction to Luke: Date and Place of Writing)

Matthew

INTRODUCTION

Author

Although the first Gospel is anonymous, the early church fathers were unanimous in holding that Matthew, one of the 12 apostles, was its author. However, the results of modern critical studies — in particular those that stress Matthew's alleged dependence on Mark for a substantial part of his Gospel — have caused some Biblical scholars to abandon Matthean authorship. Why, they ask, would Matthew, an eyewitness to the events of our Lord's life, depend so heavily on Mark's account? The best answer seems to be that he agreed with it and wanted to show that the apostolic testimony to Christ was not divided.

Matthew, whose name means "gift of the LORD," was a tax collector who left his work to follow Jesus (9:9 – 13). In Mark and Luke he is called by his other name, Levi.

A Quick Look

Author:

Matthew, also called Levi

Audience:

Greek-speaking Jewish Christians

Date:

Between A.D. 50 and 70

Theme:

Matthew presents Jesus as the Jewish Messiah sent by God to fulfill Old Testament prophecy.

Date and Place of Writing

Some have argued on the basis of its Jewish characteristics that Matthew's Gospel was written in the early church period, possibly the early part of A.D. 50, when the church was largely Jewish and the gospel was preached to Jews only (Ac 11:19). However, those who have concluded that both Matthew and Luke drew extensively from Mark's Gospel date it later — after the Gospel of Mark had been in circulation for a period of time. See essay and chart, p. 1457. Accordingly, some feel that Matthew would have been written in the late 50s or in the 60s. Others, who assume that Mark was written between 65 and 70, place Matthew in the 70s or even later. However, there is insufficient evidence to be dogmatic about either view.

The Jewish nature of Matthew's Gospel may suggest that it was written in the Holy Land, though many think it may have originated in Syrian Antioch.

Recipients

Since his Gospel was written in Greek, Matthew's readers were obviously Greek-speaking. They also seem to have been Jews. Many elements point to Jewish readership: Matthew's concern with fulfillment of the OT (he has more quotations from and allusions to the OT than any other NT author); his tracing of Jesus' descent from Abraham (1:1 – 17); his lack of explanation of Jewish customs (especially in contrast to Mark); his use of Jewish terminology (e.g., "kingdom of heaven," where "heaven" reveals the Jewish reverential reluctance to use the name of God; see note on 3:2); his emphasis on Jesus' role as "Son of David" (1:1; 9:27; 12:23; 15:22; 20:30 – 31; 21:9,15; 22:41 – 45). This does not mean, however, that Matthew restricts his Gospel to Jews. He records the coming of the Magi (non-Jews) to worship the infant Jesus (2:1 – 12), as well as Jesus' statement that the "field is the world" (13:38). He also gives a full statement of the Great Commission (28:18 – 20). These passages show that, although Matthew's Gospel is Jewish, it has a universal outlook.

Matthew includes many proof texts to drive home his basic theme: Jesus is the fulfillment of the OT predictions of the Messiah.

Purpose

Matthew's main purpose is to confirm for his Jewish Christian readers that Jesus is their Messiah. Although all the Gospel writers quote the OT, Matthew includes many proof texts (1:22 – 23; 2:15; 2:17 – 18; 2:23; 4:14 – 16; 8:17; 12:17 – 21; 13:35; 27:9 – 10) to drive home his basic theme: Jesus is the fulfillment of the OT predictions of the Messiah. Matthew even finds the history of God's people in the OT recapitulated in some aspects of Jesus' life (see, e.g., his quotation of Hos 11:1 in 2:15). To accomplish his purpose Matthew also emphasizes Jesus' Davidic lineage (see Recipients, p. 1459).

Structure

The way the material is arranged reveals an artistic touch. The whole Gospel is woven around five great discourses: (1) chs. 5 – 7; (2) ch. 10; (3) ch. 13; (4) ch. 18; (5) chs. 24 – 25. That this is deliberate is clear from the refrain that concludes each discourse: "When Jesus had finished saying these things," or similar words (7:28; 11:1; 13:53; 19:1; 26:1). The narrative sections, in each case, appropriately lead up to the discourses. The Gospel has a fitting prologue (chs. 1 – 2) and a challenging epilogue (28:16 – 20).

The fivefold division may suggest that Matthew has modeled his book on the structure of the Pentateuch (the first five books of the OT). He may also be presenting the gospel as a new Torah and Jesus as a new and greater Moses.

Outline

- I. The Birth and Early Years of Jesus (chs. 1 – 2)
  - A. His Genealogy (1:1 – 17)
  - B. His Birth (1:18 — 2:12)
  - C. His Sojourn in Egypt (2:13 – 23)
- II. The Beginnings of Jesus' Ministry (3:1 — 4:11)
  - A. His Forerunner (3:1 – 12)
  - B. His Baptism (3:13 – 17)
  - C. His Temptation (4:1 – 11)
- III. Jesus' Ministry in Galilee (4:12 — 14:12)
  - A. The Beginning of the Galilean Campaign (4:12 – 25)
  - B. The Sermon on the Mount (chs. 5 – 7)
  - C. A Collection of Miracles (chs. 8 – 9)
  - D. The Commissioning of the 12 Apostles (ch. 10)
  - E. Ministry throughout Galilee (chs. 11 – 12)
  - F. The Parables of the Kingdom (ch. 13)
  - G. Herod's Reaction to Jesus' Ministry (14:1 – 12)
- IV. Jesus' Withdrawals from Galilee (14:13 — 17:20 [21])
  - A. To the Eastern Shore of the Sea of Galilee (14:13 — 15:20)
  - B. To Phoenicia (15:21 – 28)

C. To the Decapolis (15:29—16:12)
D. To Caesarea Philippi (16:13—17:20 [21])

V. Jesus' Last Ministry in Galilee (17:22—18:35)
A. Prediction of Jesus' Death (17:22–23)
B. Temple Tax (17:24–27)
C. Discourse on Life in the Kingdom (ch. 18)

VI. Jesus' Ministry in Judea and Perea (chs. 19–20)
A. Teaching concerning Divorce (19:1–12)
B. Teaching concerning Little Children (19:13–15)
C. The Rich Young Man (19:16–30)
D. The Parable of the Workers in the Vineyard (20:1–16)
E. Prediction of Jesus' Death (20:17–19)
F. A Mother's Request (20:20–28)
G. Restoration of Sight at Jericho (20:29–34)

VII. Passion Week (chs. 21–27)
A. The Entry of Jesus into Jerusalem as King (21:1–11)
B. The Clearing of the Temple (21:12–17)
C. The Last Controversies with the Jewish Leaders (21:18—23:39)
D. The Olivet Discourse (chs. 24–25)
E. The Anointing of Jesus' Feet (26:1–13)
F. The Arrest, Trials and Death of Jesus (26:14—27:66)

VIII. The Resurrection (ch. 28)
A. The Earthquake and the Angel's Announcement (28:1–7)
B. Jesus' Encounter with the Women (28:8–10)
C. The Guards' Report and the Jewish Elders' Bribe (28:11–15)
D. The Great Commission (28:16–20)

The Genealogy of Jesus

1:1-17pp — Lk 3:23-38
1:3-6pp — Ru 4:18-22
1:7-11pp — 1Ch 3:10-17

1 A record of the genealogy of Jesus Christ the son of David,[a] the son of Abraham:[b]

[2]Abraham was the father of Isaac,[c]
Isaac the father of Jacob,[d]
Jacob the father of Judah and his brothers,[e]
[3]Judah the father of Perez and Zerah, whose mother was Tamar,[f]
Perez the father of Hezron,
Hezron the father of Ram,
[4]Ram the father of Amminadab,
Amminadab the father of Nahshon,
Nahshon the father of Salmon,
[5]Salmon the father of Boaz, whose mother was Rahab,[g]
Boaz the father of Obed, whose mother was Ruth,
Obed the father of Jesse,
[6]and Jesse the father of King David.[h]

David was the father of Solomon, whose mother had been Uriah's wife,[i]
[7]Solomon the father of Rehoboam,
Rehoboam the father of Abijah,
Abijah the father of Asa,
[8]Asa the father of Jehoshaphat,
Jehoshaphat the father of Jehoram,
Jehoram the father of Uzziah,
[9]Uzziah the father of Jotham,
Jotham the father of Ahaz,
Ahaz the father of Hezekiah,
[10]Hezekiah the father of Manasseh,[j]
Manasseh the father of Amon,
Amon the father of Josiah,
[11]and Josiah the father of Jeconiah[a] and his brothers at the time of the exile to Babylon.[k]

[12]After the exile to Babylon:
Jeconiah was the father of Shealtiel,[l]
Shealtiel the father of Zerubbabel,[m]
[13]Zerubbabel the father of Abiud,
Abiud the father of Eliakim,
Eliakim the father of Azor,
[14]Azor the father of Zadok,
Zadok the father of Akim,
Akim the father of Eliud,
[15]Eliud the father of Eleazar,
Eleazar the father of Matthan,
Matthan the father of Jacob,
[16]and Jacob the father of Joseph, the husband of Mary,[n] of whom was born Jesus, who is called Christ.[o]

[17]Thus there were fourteen generations in all from Abraham to David, fourteen from David to the exile to Babylon, and fourteen from the exile to the Christ.[b]

1:1 [a]2Sa 7:12-16; Isa 9:6,7; 11:1; Jer 23:5,6; S Mt 9:27; Lk 1:32,69; Rev 22:16 [b]Ge 22:18; S Gal 3:16 **1:2** [c]Ge 21:3,12 [d]Ge 25:26 [e]Ge 29:35; 49:10 **1:3** [f]Ge 38:27-30 **1:5** [g]S Heb 11:31 **1:6** [h]1Sa 16:1; 17:12 [i]2Sa 12:24 **1:10** [j]2Ki 20:21 **1:11** [k]2Ki 24:14-16; Jer 27:20; 40:1; Da 1:1,2 **1:12** [l]1Ch 3:17 [m]1Ch 3:19; Ezr 3:2 **1:16** [n]Lk 1:27 [o]Mt 27:17

[a] *11* That is, Jehoiachin; also in verse 12 [b] *17* Or *Messiah.* "The Christ" (Greek) and "the Messiah" (Hebrew) both mean "the Anointed One."

1:1–16 For a comparison of Matthew's genealogy with Luke's see note on Lk 3:23–38. The types of people mentioned in this genealogy reveal the broad scope of those who make up the people of God as well as the genealogy of Jesus.
1:1 *son of David.* A Messianic title (see Introduction: Recipients; Purpose; see also note on 9:27) found several times in this Gospel (in 1:20 it is not a Messianic title). In Jesus the Davidic covenant is fulfilled (see 2Sa 7:5–16 and note on 7:11). *son of Abraham.* Because Matthew was writing to Jews, it was important to identify Jesus in this way. In Jesus the Abrahamic covenant is fulfilled (see Ge 12:2–3; 15:9–21; 17; Zec 9:10 and note).
1:3 *Tamar.* In Matthew's genealogy five women are named: Tamar (here), Rahab (v. 5), Ruth (v. 5), Bathsheba (not by name but by description—"Solomon, whose mother had been Uriah's wife," v. 6) and, of course, Mary (v. 16). At least three of these women were Gentiles (Tamar, Rahab and Ruth). Bathsheba was probably an Israelite (1Ch 3:5) but was closely associated with the Hittites because of Uriah, her Hittite husband. By including these women (contrary to custom) in his genealogy, Matthew indicates at the very outset of his Gospel that God's saving activity is not limited to the people of Israel.
1:4 *Amminadab.* Father-in-law of Aaron (Ex 6:23).
1:5 *Rahab.* See Jos 2. Since quite a long time had elapsed between Rahab and David and because of Matthew's desire for systematic organization (see note on v. 17), a number of the generations between these two ancestors were not listed by Matthew (see Luke's list: David, Jesse, Obed, Boaz [Lk 3:31–32]; cf. note on Ge 4:17–18).
1:8 *Jehoram the father.* Matthew calls Jehoram the father of Uzziah, but from 2Ch 21:4—26:23 it is clear that, again, several generations were assumed (Ahaziah, Joash and Amaziah) and that "father" is used in the sense of "forefather" (see NIV text notes on 1Ch 1:5,10).
1:11 *Josiah the father.* Similarly (see note on v. 8), Josiah is called the father of Jeconiah (i.e., Jehoiachin; see NIV text note), whereas he was actually the father of Jehoiakim and the grandfather of Jehoiachin (2Ch 36:1–9).
1:12 *Shealtiel the father.* See note on 1Ch 3:19.
1:16 Matthew does not say that Joseph was the father of Jesus but only that he was the husband of Mary and that Jesus was born of her. In this genealogy Matthew shows that, although Jesus is not the physical son of Joseph, he is the legal son and therefore a descendant of David (see Lk 2:33; Jn 1:45 and notes).
1:17 *fourteen generations ... fourteen ... fourteen.* These divisions reflect two characteristics of Matthew's Gospel: (1) an apparent fondness for numbers and (2) concern for systematic arrangement. The number 14 may have been chosen because it is twice seven (the number of completeness) and/or because it is the numerical value of the name David (see notes on Pr 10:1; Rev 13:17). For the practice of telescoping genealogies to achieve the desired number of names see Introduction to 1 Chronicles: Genealogies.

The Birth of Jesus Christ

18This is how the birth of Jesus Christ
came about: His mother Mary was pledged
to be married to Joseph, but before they
came together, she was found to be with
child through the Holy Spirit.[p] 19Because
Joseph her husband was a righteous man
and did not want to expose her to public
disgrace, he had in mind to divorce[q] her
quietly.
20But after he had considered this, an
angel[r] of the Lord appeared to him in a
dream[s] and said, "Joseph son of David, do
not be afraid to take Mary home as your
wife, because what is conceived in her is
from the Holy Spirit. 21She will give birth
to a son, and you are to give him the name
Jesus,[a][t] because he will save his people
from their sins."[u]
22All this took place to fulfill[v] what the
Lord had said through the prophet: 23"The
virgin will be with child and will give birth
to a son, and they will call him Immanuel"[b][w]—which means, "God with us."
24When Joseph woke up, he did what
the angel[x] of the Lord had commanded him and took Mary home as his wife.
25But he had no union with her until she
gave birth to a son. And he gave him the
name Jesus.[y]

The Visit of the Magi

2 After Jesus was born in Bethlehem in
Judea,[z] during the time of King Herod,[a]
Magi[c] from the east came to Jerusalem
2and asked, "Where is the one who has
been born king of the Jews?[b] We saw his
star[c] in the east[d] and have come to worship him."
3When King Herod heard this he was
disturbed, and all Jerusalem with him.
4When he had called together all the people's chief priests and teachers of the law,
he asked them where the Christ[e] was to

1:18 [p]Lk 1:35 **1:19** [q]Dt 24:1 **1:20** [r]S Ac 5:19 [s]S Mt 27:19 **1:21** [t]S Lk 1:31 [u]Ps 130:8; S Lk 2:11; S Jn 3:17; Ac 5:31; S Ro 11:14; Tit 2:14 **1:22** [v]Mt 2:15,17,23; 4:14; 8:17; 12:17; 21:4; 26:54,56; 27:9; Lk 4:21; 21:22; 24:44; Jn 13:18; 19:24,28,36 **1:23** [w]Isa 7:14; 8:8,10 **1:24** [x]S Ac 5:19 **1:25** [y]ver 21; S Lk 1:31 **2:1** [z]Lk 2:4-7 [a]Lk 1:5 **2:2** [b]Jer 23:5; Mt 27:11; Mk 15:2; Lk 23:38; Jn 1:49; 18:33-37 [c]Nu 24:17

[a] 21 *Jesus* is the Greek form of *Joshua,* which means *the LORD saves.* [b] 23 Isaiah 7:14 [c] 1 Traditionally *Wise Men* [d] 2 Or *star when it rose* [e] 4 Or *Messiah*

1:18 *pledged to be married.* There were no sexual relations during a Jewish betrothal period, but it was a much more binding relationship than a modern engagement and could be broken only by divorce (see v. 19). In Dt 22:24 a betrothed woman is called a "wife," though the preceding verse speaks of her as being "pledged to be married." Matthew uses the terms "husband" (v. 19) and "wife" (v. 24) of Joseph and Mary before their marriage was consummated (see note on Joel 1:8). *the Holy Spirit.* The common NT way of referring to the divine Spirit, who in the OT was almost always called "the Spirit of God" or "the Spirit of the LORD." See Ps 51:11 and note. Christian reflection on the Biblical word about him (see 3:16–17; 28:19; 2Co 13:14 and notes) led to the understanding that he is one of the three persons of the Trinity.

1:19 *righteous.* To Jews this meant being zealous in keeping the law. *divorce her quietly.* He would sign the necessary legal papers but not have her judged publicly and put to death by stoning (see Dt 22:23–24).

1:20 *in a dream.* The phrase occurs five times in the first two chapters of Matthew (here; 2:12–13,19,22) and indicates the means the Lord used for speaking to Joseph. *Joseph son of David.* See notes on 1:1,16; perhaps a hint that the message of the angel related to the expected Messiah. *take Mary home as your wife.* They were legally bound to each other, but not yet living together as husband and wife. *what is conceived in her is from the Holy Spirit.* This agrees perfectly with the announcement to Mary (Lk 1:35), except that the latter is more specific (see note on Lk 1:26–35).

1:21 *the name Jesus.* See NIV text note; the meaning is more specifically explained in the rest of the verse. *save.* See Lk 2:11 and note.

1:22 *fulfill.* Twelve times (here; 2:15,23; 3:15; 4:14; 5:17; 8:17; 12:17; 13:14,35; 21:4; 27:9) Matthew speaks of the OT being fulfilled, i.e., of events in NT times that were prophesied in the OT—a powerful testimony to the divine origin of Scripture and its accuracy even in small details. In the fulfillments we also see the writer's concern for linking the gospel with the OT.

1:23 See note on Isa 7:14. This is the first of at least 47 quotations, most of them Messianic, that Matthew takes from the OT (see NIV text notes throughout Matthew).

1:24 *angel of the Lord.* See Lk 2:9 and note.

1:25 *he had no union with her until she gave birth.* Both Matthew and Luke (1:26–35) make it clear that Jesus was born of a virgin. *gave birth to . . . Jesus.* In 6 or 5 B.C. (see chart, p. 1508; see also note on 2:15).

2:1 *Bethlehem in Judea.* A village about five miles south of Jerusalem. Matthew says nothing of the events in Nazareth (cf. Lk 1:26–56). Possibly wanting to emphasize Jesus' Davidic background, he begins with the events that happened in David's city. It is called "Bethlehem in Judea," not only to distinguish it from the town of the same name about seven miles northwest of Nazareth, but also to emphasize that Jesus came from the tribe (Judah) and territory that produced the line of Davidic kings. That Jews expected the Messiah to be born in Bethlehem and to be from David's family is clear from Jn 7:42 (cf. Mic 5:2). *King Herod.* Herod the Great (37–4 B.C.), to be distinguished from the other Herods in the Bible (see chart, p. 1465). Herod was a non-Jew, an Idumean, who was appointed king of Judea by the Roman Senate in 40 B.C. and gained control in 37. Like many rulers of the day, he was ruthless, murdering one of his wives, three of his sons, his mother-in-law, a brother-in-law, an uncle and many others whom he suspected of threatening his royal power—not to mention the babies in Bethlehem (v. 16). His reign was also noted for splendor, as seen in the many theaters, amphitheaters, monuments, pagan altars, fortresses (see, e.g., note on v. 15) and other buildings he erected or refurbished—including the greatest work of all, the rebuilding of the temple in Jerusalem, begun in 20 B.C. and finished 68 years after his death. *Magi.* Probably astrologers, perhaps from Persia or southern Arabia, both of which are east of the Holy Land. *Jerusalem.* Since they were looking for the "king of the Jews" (v. 2), they naturally came to the Jewish capital city (see map No. 10 at the end of this study Bible).

2:2 *born king.* The Magi realized that Jesus was born a king, not that he would become one later on. *king of the Jews.* Indicates the Magi were Gentiles. Matthew wants to show that people of all nations acknowledged Jesus as "king of the Jews" and came to worship him as Lord. *star.* Probably not an ordinary star, planet or comet, though some interpreters have identified it with the conjunction of Jupiter and Saturn in 7 B.C. or with other astronomical phenomena (cf. Nu 24:17 and note).

2:4 *chief priests.* See note on Mk 8:31; Sadducees (see note on 3:7) who were in charge of worship at the temple in

be born. [5]"In Bethlehem[d] in Judea," they replied, "for this is what the prophet has written:

[6]" 'But you, Bethlehem, in the land of Judah,
are by no means least among the rulers of Judah;
for out of you will come a ruler
who will be the shepherd of my people Israel.'[a]"[e]

[7]Then Herod called the Magi secretly and found out from them the exact time the star had appeared. [8]He sent them to Bethlehem and said, "Go and make a careful search for the child. As soon as you find him, report to me, so that I too may go and worship him."

[9]After they had heard the king, they went on their way, and the star they had seen in the east[b] went ahead of them until it stopped over the place where the child was. [10]When they saw the star, they were overjoyed. [11]On coming to the house, they saw the child with his mother Mary, and they bowed down and worshiped him.[f] Then they opened their treasures and presented him with gifts[g] of gold and of incense and of myrrh. [12]And having been warned[h] in a dream[i] not to go back to Herod, they returned to their country by another route.

The Escape to Egypt

[13]When they had gone, an angel[j] of the Lord appeared to Joseph in a dream.[k] "Get up," he said, "take the child and his mother and escape to Egypt. Stay there until I tell you, for Herod is going to search for the child to kill him."[l]

2:5 [d]Jn 7:42
2:6 [e]2Sa 5:2; Mic 5:2
2:11 [f]Isa 60:3 [g]Ps 72:10
2:12 [h]Heb 11:7 [i]ver 13,19,22; S Mt 27:19
2:13 [j]S Ac 5:19 [k]ver 12,19,22; S Mt 27:19 [l]Rev 12:4

[14]So he got up, took the child and his mother during the night and left for Egypt, [15]where he stayed until the death of Herod. And so was fulfilled[m] what the Lord had said through the prophet: "Out of Egypt I called my son."[c n]

[16]When Herod realized that he had been outwitted by the Magi, he was furious, and he gave orders to kill all the boys in Bethlehem and its vicinity who were two years old and under, in accordance with the time he had learned from the Magi. [17]Then what was said through the prophet Jeremiah was fulfilled:[o]

[18]"A voice is heard in Ramah,
weeping and great mourning,
Rachel[p] weeping for her children
and refusing to be comforted,
because they are no more."[d q]

The Return to Nazareth

[19]After Herod died, an angel[r] of the Lord appeared in a dream[s] to Joseph in Egypt [20]and said, "Get up, take the child and his mother and go to the land of Israel, for those who were trying to take the child's life are dead."[t]

[21]So he got up, took the child and his mother and went to the land of Israel. [22]But when he heard that Archelaus was reigning in Judea in place of his father Herod, he was afraid to go there. Having been warned in a dream,[u] he withdrew to the district of Galilee,[v] [23]and he went and lived in a town called Nazareth.[w] So was fulfilled[x] what was said through the prophets: "He will be called a Nazarene."[y]

2:15 [m]ver 17,23; S Mt 1:22 [n]Ex 4:22,23; Hos 11:1
2:17 [o]ver 15,23; S Mt 1:22
2:18 [p]Ge 35:19 [q]Jer 31:15
2:19 [r]S Ac 5:19 [s]ver 12,13,22; S Mt 27:19
2:20 [t]Ex 4:19
2:22 [u]ver 12,13,19; S Mt 27:19 [v]Lk 2:39
2:23 [w]Mk 1:9; 6:1; S 1:24; Lk 1:26; 2:39,51; 4:16,23; Jn 1:45,46 [x]ver 15,17; S Mt 1:22 [y]S Mk 1:24

[a] 6 Micah 5:2 [b] 9 Or *seen when it rose* [c] 15 Hosea 11:1 [d] 18 Jer. 31:15

Jerusalem. *teachers of the law.* The Jewish scholars of the day, professionally trained in the development, teaching and application of OT law. Their authority was not official but arose merely from their training in the traditions of Scripture interpretation (see note on Lk 5:17).

2:6 See Mic 5:2 and note.

2:11 *house.* The Magi did not visit Jesus at the manger on the night of his birth as did the shepherds. They came some months later and visited him as a "child" in his "house." *the child with his mother Mary.* Every time the child Jesus and his mother are mentioned together, he is mentioned first (vv. 11,13–14,20–21). *gold... incense... myrrh.* The three gifts perhaps gave rise to the legend that there were three "wise men" (cf. NIV text note on v. 1). But the Bible does not indicate the number of the Magi, and they were almost certainly not kings. *incense.* Frankincense (see note on Ex 30:34). *myrrh.* See note on Ge 37:25.

2:13 *angel of the Lord.* See note on Lk 2:9.

2:15 *the death of Herod.* In 4 B.C. During the time of the Roman empire, a mistake was made in using the Roman calendar to calculate the year of Herod the Great's death, and the mistake found its way into the (Julian/Gregorian) calendar we use today. So, as odd as it may seem, King Herod died in 4 B.C., and since Christ was born one to two years before Herod's death, he (Christ) was born in 6 or 5 B.C. The ornate sarcophagus (coffin) in which Herod was buried was discovered by archaeologists in 2007 in the hilltop fortress of Herodium eight miles south of Jerusalem (see map, p. 1570). *Out of Egypt I called my son.* This quotation from Hos 11:1 originally referred to God's calling the nation of Israel out of Egypt in the time of Moses. But Matthew applies it also to Jesus. He sees the history of Israel (God's "son") recapitulated in the life of Jesus (God's unique Son; see Jn 3:16 and note). Just as Israel as an infant nation went down into Egypt, so the child Jesus went there. And as Israel was led by God out of Egypt, so also was Jesus. How long Jesus and his parents were in Egypt is not known.

2:16 *kill all the boys ... two years old and under.* The number killed has often been exaggerated as being in the thousands. In so small a village as Bethlehem, however (even with the surrounding area included), the number was probably not large—though the act, of course, was no less brutal.

2:18 See note on Jer 31:15.

2:22 *Archelaus.* This son of Herod the Great ruled over Judea and Samaria for only ten years (4 B.C.–A.D. 6). He was unusually cruel and tyrannical and so was deposed. Judea then became a Roman province, administered by governors appointed by the emperor (see chart, p. 1465). *Galilee.* The northern part of the Holy Land in Jesus' day (see map, p. 1467, and map No. 12 at the end of this study Bible).

2:23 *Nazareth.* A rather obscure town, nowhere mentioned in the OT. It was Jesus' hometown (21:11; 26:71;

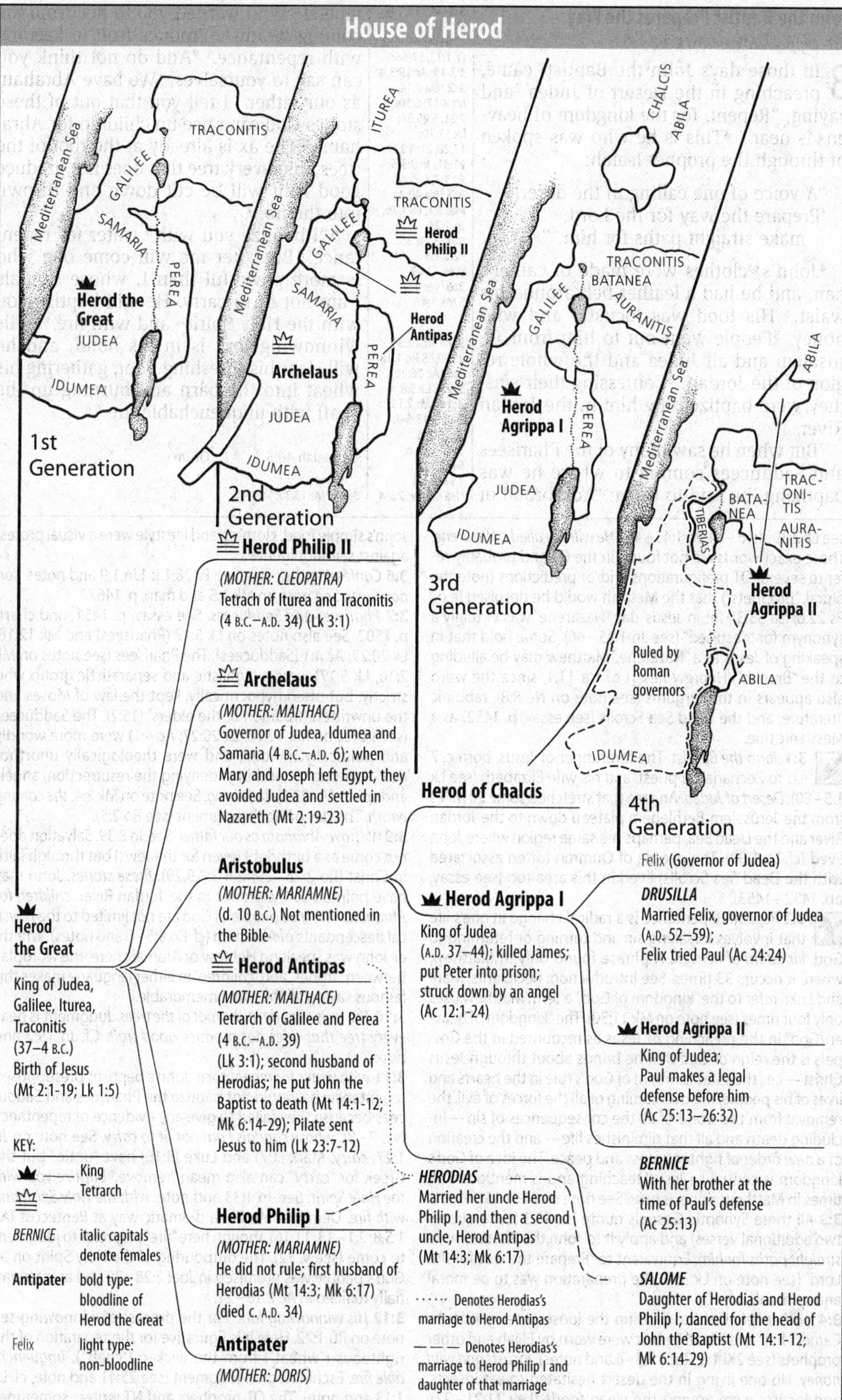
House of Herod
Mediterranean Sea
TRACONITIS
GALILEE
SAMARIA
PEREA
Herod the Great
JUDEA
IDUMEA
1st Generation
Mediterranean Sea
ITUREA
TRACONITIS
Herod Philip II
GALILEE
SAMARIA
Herod Antipas
PEREA
Archelaus
JUDEA
IDUMEA
2nd Generation
CHALCIS
ABILA
Mediterranean Sea
TRACONITIS
BATANEA
GALILEE
AURANITIS
Herod Agrippa I
PEREA
JUDEA
IDUMEA
3rd Generation
Mediterranean Sea
ABILA
TRACONITIS
BATANEA
TIBERIAS
AURANITIS
Herod Agrippa II
Ruled by Roman governors
ABILA
IDUMEA
4th Generation
Herod the Great
King of Judea, Galilee, Iturea, Traconitis (37–4 B.C.)
Birth of Jesus (Mt 2:1-19; Lk 1:5)
Herod Philip II
(MOTHER: CLEOPATRA)
Tetrach of Iturea and Traconitis (4 B.C.–A.D. 34) (Lk 3:1)
Archelaus
(MOTHER: MALTHACE)
Governor of Judea, Idumea and Samaria (4 B.C.–A.D. 6); when Mary and Joseph left Egypt, they avoided Judea and settled in Nazareth (Mt 2:19-23)
Aristobulus
(MOTHER: MARIAMNE)
(d. 10 B.C.) Not mentioned in the Bible
Herod Antipas
(MOTHER: MALTHACE)
Tetrarch of Galilee and Perea (4 B.C.–A.D. 39) (Lk 3:1); second husband of Herodias; he put John the Baptist to death (Mt 14:1-12; Mk 6:14-29); Pilate sent Jesus to him (Lk 23:7-12)
Herod Philip I
(MOTHER: MARIAMNE)
He did not rule; first husband of Herodias (Mt 14:3; Mk 6:17) (died c. A.D. 34)
Antipater
(MOTHER: DORIS)
Herod of Chalcis
Herod Agrippa I
King of Judea (A.D. 37–44); killed James; put Peter into prison; struck down by an angel (Ac 12:1-24)
HERODIAS
Married her uncle Herod Philip I, and then a second uncle, Herod Antipas (Mt 14:3; Mk 6:17)
Felix (Governor of Judea)
DRUSILLA
Married Felix, governor of Judea (A.D. 52–59); Felix tried Paul (Ac 24:24)
Herod Agrippa II
King of Judea; Paul makes a legal defense before him (Ac 25:13–26:32)
BERNICE
With her brother at the time of Paul's defense (Ac 25:13)
SALOME
Daughter of Herodias and Herod Philip I; danced for the head of John the Baptist (Mt 14:1-12; Mk 6:14-29)
KEY:
King
Tetrarch
BERNICE italic capitals denote females
Antipater bold type: bloodline of Herod the Great
Felix light type: non-bloodline
Denotes Herodias's marriage to Herod Antipas
Denotes Herodias's marriage to Herod Philip I and daughter of that marriage

John the Baptist Prepares the Way

3:1-12pp — Mk 1:3-8; Lk 3:2-17

3 In those days John the Baptist[z] came,
preaching in the Desert of Judea 2and
saying, "Repent, for the kingdom of heav-
en[a] is near." 3This is he who was spoken
of through the prophet Isaiah:

> "A voice of one calling in the desert,
> 'Prepare the way for the Lord,
> make straight paths for him.' "[a][b]

4John's[c] clothes were made of camel's
hair, and he had a leather belt around his
waist.[d] His food was locusts[e] and wild
honey. 5People went out to him from Jerusalem and all Judea and the whole region of the Jordan. 6Confessing their sins,
they were baptized[f] by him in the Jordan
River.
7But when he saw many of the Pharisees
and Sadducees coming to where he was
baptizing, he said to them: "You brood of
vipers![g] Who warned you to flee from the
coming wrath?[h] 8Produce fruit in keeping
with repentance.[i] 9And do not think you
can say to yourselves, 'We have Abraham
as our father.'[j] I tell you that out of these
stones God can raise up children for Abraham. 10The ax is already at the root of the
trees, and every tree that does not produce
good fruit will be cut down and thrown
into the fire.[k]
11"I baptize you with[b] water for repentance.[l] But after me will come one who
is more powerful than I, whose sandals
I am not fit to carry. He will baptize you
with the Holy Spirit[m] and with fire.[n] 12His
winnowing fork is in his hand, and he
will clear his threshing floor, gathering his
wheat into the barn and burning up the
chaff with unquenchable fire."[o]

[a] 3 Isaiah 40:3 [b] 11 Or *in*

3:1 [z] ver 13,14; Mt 9:14; 11:2-14; 14:1-12; Lk 1:13,57-66; 3:2-19; Ac 19:3,4 **3:2** [a] Da 7:14; Mt 4:17; 6:10; 7:21; S 25:34; Lk 11:20; 17:20,21; 19:11; 21:31; Jn 3:3,5; Ac 1:3,6 **3:3** [b] Isa 40:3; Mal 3:1; Lk 1:76; Jn 1:23 **3:4** [c] S Mt 3:1 [d] 2Ki 1:8 [e] Lev 11:22 **3:6** [f] ver 11; S Mk 1:4 **3:7** [g] Mt 12:34; 23:33 [h] S Ro 1:18 **3:8** [i] Ac 26:20 **3:9** [j] S Lk 3:8 **3:10** [k] Mt 7:19; Lk 3:9; 13:6-9; Jn 15:2,6 **3:11** [l] ver 6; S Mk 1:4 [m] S Mk 1:8 [n] Isa 4:4; Ac 2:3,4 **3:12** [o] Mt 13:30; S 25:41

see Lk 2:39; 4:16 – 24; Jn 1:45 – 46). *He will be called a Nazarene.* These exact words are not found in the OT and probably refer to several OT prefigurations and/or predictions (note the plural, "prophets") that the Messiah would be despised (e.g., Ps 22:6; Isa 53:3), for in Jesus' day "Nazarene" was virtually a synonym for "despised" (see Jn 1:45 – 46). Some hold that in speaking of Jesus as a "Nazarene," Matthew may be alluding to the "Branch" (Hebrew *neser*) of Isa 11:1, since the word also appears in the Targums (see note on Ne 8:8), rabbinic literature, and the Dead Sea Scrolls (see essay, p. 1452) as a Messianic title.

3:1 *John the Baptist.* The forerunner of Jesus, born c. 7 B.C. to Zechariah, a priest, and his wife Elizabeth (see Lk 1:5 – 80). *Desert of Judea.* An area that stretched some 20 miles from the Jerusalem-Bethlehem plateau down to the Jordan River and the Dead Sea, perhaps the same region where John lived (cf. Lk 1:80). The people of Qumran (often associated with the Dead Sea Scrolls) lived in this area too (see essay, pp. 1452 – 1453).

3:2 *Repent.* Repentance is a radical change in one's life that involves forsaking sin and turning or returning to God. *kingdom of heaven.* A phrase found only in Matthew, where it occurs 33 times. See Introduction: Recipients. Mark and Luke refer to the "kingdom of God," a term Matthew uses only four times (see note on Mk 11:30). The "kingdom of heaven/God" in the preaching of Jesus as recounted in the Gospels is the reign of God that he brings about through Jesus Christ — i.e., the establishment of God's rule in the hearts and lives of his people, the overcoming of all the forces of evil, the removal from the world of all the consequences of sin — including death and all that diminishes life — and the creation of a new order of righteousness and peace. The idea of God's kingdom is central to Jesus' teaching and is mentioned 50 times in Matthew alone. *is near.* See note on Mk 1:15.

3:3 All three Synoptic Gospels quote Isa 40:3 (Luke quotes two additional verses) and apply it to John the Baptist. *make straight paths for him.* Equivalent to "Prepare the way for the Lord" (see note on Lk 3:4). The preparation was to be moral and spiritual.

3:4 *leather belt.* Used to bind up the loose outer garments. Camel's hair and a leather belt were worn by Elijah and other prophets (see 2Ki 1:8; Zec 13:4 – 6 and notes). *locusts and wild honey.* No one living in the desert hesitated to eat insects, and locusts were among the clean foods (Lev 11:21 – 22). John's simple food, clothing and lifestyle were a visual protest against self-indulgence.

3:6 *Confessing their sins.* See Pr 28:13; 1Jn 1:9 and notes. *Jordan River.* See note on Mk 1:5 and map, p. 1467.

3:7 *Pharisees and Sadducees.* See essay, p. 1451, and chart, p. 1502. See also notes on Lk 5:17 (Pharisees) and Mk 12:18; Lk 20:27; Ac 4:1 (Sadducees). The Pharisees (see notes on Mk 2:16; Lk 5:17) were a legalistic and separatistic group who strictly, but often hypocritically, kept the law of Moses and the unwritten "tradition of the elders" (15:2). The Sadducees (see notes on Mk 12:18; Lk 20:27; Ac 4:1) were more worldly and politically minded, and were theologically unorthodox — among other things denying the resurrection, angels and spirits (Ac 23:8). *baptizing.* See note on Mk 1:4. *the coming wrath.* The day of God's judgment (see Ro 2:5).

3:9 *We have Abraham as our father.* See Jn 8:39. Salvation does not come as a birthright (even for the Jews) but through faith in Christ (Ro 2:28 – 29; Gal 3:7,9,29). *these stones.* John may have pointed to the stones in the Jordan River. *children for Abraham.* The true people of God are not limited to the physical descendants of Abraham (cf. Ro 9:6 – 8 and notes). Whether John was speaking Hebrew or Aramaic here, the wordplay between "stones" and "children" in either language makes this famous saying all the more memorable.

3:10 *The ax is already at the root of the trees.* Judgment is near. *every tree that does not produce good fruit.* Cf. Jn 15:2 and note.

3:11 *with water for repentance.* John's baptism presupposed repentance; he would not baptize the Pharisees and Sadducees because they failed to give any evidence of repentance (vv. 7 – 8). *whose sandals I am not fit to carry.* See note on Jn 1:27. *carry.* Mark (1:7) and Luke (3:16) have "untie," but the Greek for "carry" can also mean "remove." *baptize you with the Holy Spirit.* See Jn 1:33 and note. *with the Holy Spirit and with fire.* Demonstrated in a dramatic way at Pentecost (Ac 1:5,8; 2:1 – 13; 11:16), though here "fire" may refer to judgment to come (see v. 12). The outpouring of the Holy Spirit on all God's people was promised in Joel 2:28 – 29 and at least partially fulfilled in Ac 2:16 – 21.

3:12 *His winnowing fork.* For the process of winnowing see note on Ru 1:22. Here it is figurative for the separation of the righteous ("wheat") from the wicked ("chaff"). *unquenchable fire.* Eschatological judgment (see 25:41 and note; cf. La 1:13 and note). The OT prophets and NT writers sometimes

The Baptism of Jesus

3:13-17pp — Mk 1:9-11; Lk 3:21,22; Jn 1:31-34

[13]Then Jesus came from Galilee to the
Jordan to be baptized by John.[p] [14]But John
tried to deter him, saying, "I need to be baptized by you, and do you come to me?"
[15]Jesus replied, "Let it be so now; it is
proper for us to do this to fulfill all righteousness." Then John consented.

[16]As soon as Jesus was baptized, he
went up out of the water. At that moment
heaven was opened,[q] and he saw the Spirit of God[r] descending like a dove and light-
ing on him. [17]And a voice from heaven[s]
said, "This is my Son,[t] whom I love; with
him I am well pleased."[u]

3:13 [p] S Mt 3:1; S Mk 1:4 **3:16** [q] Eze 1:1; Jn 1:51; Ac 7:56; 10:11; Rev 4:1; 19:11 [r] Isa 11:2; 42:1 **3:17** [s] Dt 4:12; Mt 17:5; Jn 12:28 [t] Ps 2:7; Ac 13:33; Heb 1:1-5; 5:5; 2Pe 1:17,18 [u] Isa 42:1; Mt 12:18; 17:5; Mk 1:11; 9:7; Lk 3:22; 9:35; 2Pe 1:17

compress the first and second comings of Christ so that they seem to be one event (see, e.g., Isa 61:2 and note).

3:13 *Jesus ... baptized by John.* See map and accompanying text, p. 1468.

3:15 Jesus' baptism marked the beginning of his Messianic ministry. There were several reasons for his baptism: (1) The first, mentioned here, was "to fulfill all righteousness." His baptism indicated that he was consecrated to God and officially approved by him, as especially shown in the descent of the Holy Spirit (v. 16) and the words of the Father (v. 17; cf. Ps 2:7; Isa 42:1). All God's righteous requirements for the Messiah were fully met in Jesus. (2) At Jesus' baptism John publicly announced the arrival of the Messiah and the inception of his ministry (Jn 1:31–34). (3) By his baptism Jesus completely identified himself with humanity's sin and failure (though he himself needed no repentance or cleansing from sin; see Heb 4:15 and note), becoming our substitute (2Co 5:21). (4) His baptism was an example to his followers.

3:16–17 All three persons of the Trinity are clearly referred to here (see 1:18; 28:19 and notes).

3:16 *Spirit of God.* The Holy Spirit came upon Jesus not to overcome sin (for he was sinless), but to equip him (see note on Jdg 3:10) for his work as the divine-human Messiah. *like a dove.* That is, appearing in the form of a dove (see also note on Mk 1:10).

3:17 *voice from heaven.* The voice (1) authenticated Jesus' unique sonship and echoes Ps 2:7 ("This is my Son"), (2) identified Jesus with the suffering servant of Isa 42:1 ("whom I love"), and (3) offered the Father's support of Jesus in his mission ("with him I am well pleased"). This word from the Father must have greatly encouraged Jesus at the very outset of his earthly ministry. *my Son.* See notes on 14:33; Jn 3:16. *I am well pleased.* The tense of the Greek verb used here is timeless. God has always been and always will be "well pleased" with his Son.

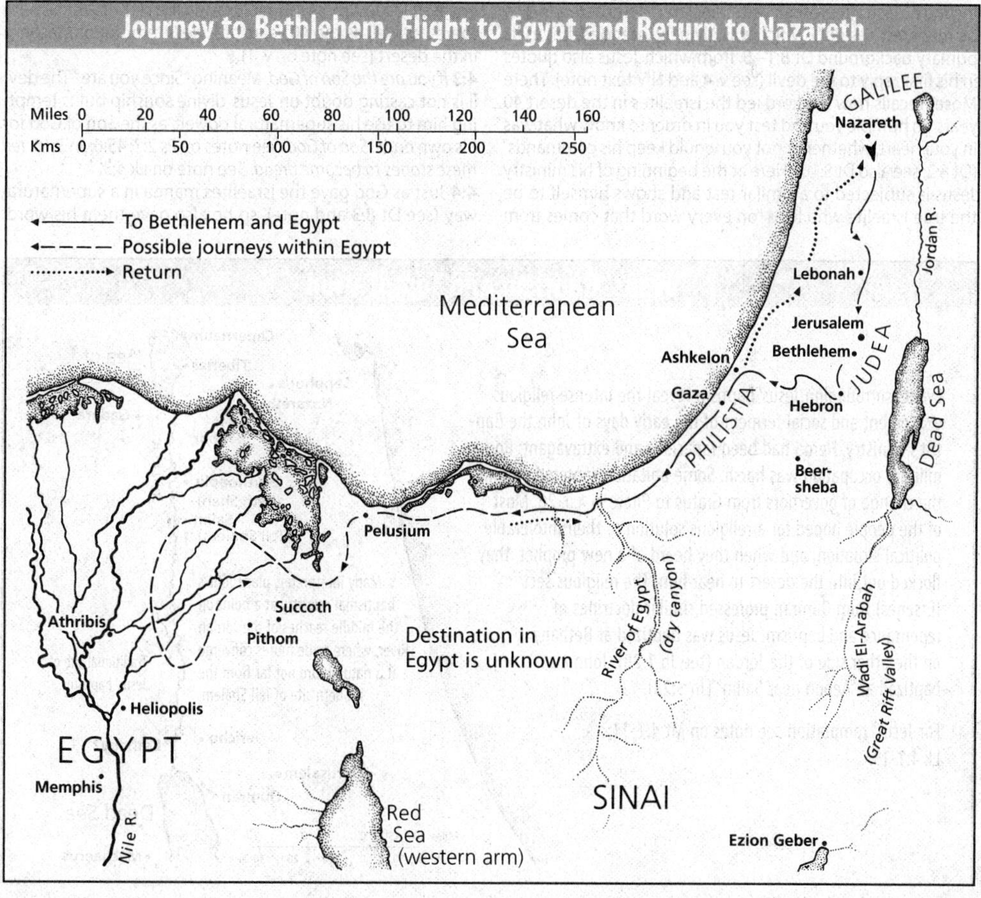

The Temptation of Jesus

4:1-11pp — Mk 1:12,13; Lk 4:1-13

4 Then Jesus was led by the Spirit into the desert to be tempted[v] by the devil.[w]
2After fasting forty days and forty nights,[x]
he was hungry. 3The tempter[y] came to
him and said, "If you are the Son of God,[z]
tell these stones to become bread."
4Jesus answered, "It is written: 'Man
does not live on bread alone, but on every word that comes from the mouth of
God.'[a]"[a]

[a] 4 Deut. 8:3

4:1 [v] Heb 4:15 [w] Ge 3:1-7 **4:2** [x] Ex 34:28; 1Ki 19:8 **4:3** [y] 1Th 3:5 [z] S Mt 3:17; 14:33; 16:16; 27:54; Mk 3:11; Lk 1:35; 22:70; Jn 1:34,49; 5:25; 11:27; 20:31; Ac 9:20; Ro 1:4; 1Jn 5:10-13,20; Rev 2:18 **4:4** [a] Dt 8:3; Jn 4:34

4:1–11 The significance of Jesus' temptations, especially because they occurred at the outset of his public ministry, seems best understood in terms of the kind of Messiah he was to be. He would not accomplish his mission by using his supernatural power for his own needs (first temptation), by using his power to win a large following by miracles or magic (second temptation) or by compromising with Satan (third temptation). Jesus had no inward desire or inclination to sin, for these in themselves are sin (Mt 5:28). Because he was God he did not sin in any way, whether by actions or word or inner desire (see 2Co 5:21; Heb 7:26; 1Pe 2:22 and note; 1Jn 3:5). Yet Jesus' temptation was real, not merely symbolic. He was "tempted in every way, just as we are — yet was without sin" (see Heb 4:15 and note). He was confronted by the tempter with a real opportunity to sin. Although Jesus was the Son of God, he defeated Satan by using a weapon that everyone has at their disposal: "the sword of the Spirit, which is the word of God" (Eph 6:17). He met all three temptations with Scriptural truth (vv. 4,7,10) from Deuteronomy.

4:1 *Jesus . . . tempted by the devil.* See map and accompanying text below. *led by the Spirit . . . to be tempted.* This testing of Jesus (the Greek verb translated "tempted" can also be rendered "tested"), which was divinely intended, has as its primary background Dt 8:1–5, from which Jesus also quotes in his first reply to the devil (see v. 4 and NIV text note). There Moses recalls how the Lord led the Israelites in the desert 40 years "to humble you and test you in order to know what was in your heart, whether or not you would keep his commands" (Dt 8:2; see also Dt 8:16). Here at the beginning of his ministry Jesus is subjected to a similar test and shows himself to be the true Israelite who lives "on every word that comes from the mouth of the LORD" (Dt 8:3). And whereas Adam failed the great test and plunged the whole race into sin (Ge 3), Jesus was faithful and thus demonstrated his qualification to become the Savior of all who receive him. It was, moreover, important that Jesus be tested/tempted as Israel and we are, so that he could become our "merciful and faithful high priest" (Heb 2:17; see note there) and thus be "able to help those who are being tempted" (Heb 2:18; see Heb 4:15–16). Finally, as the one who remained faithful in temptation he became the model for all believers when they are tempted. *desert.* Probably somewhere in the desert or wilderness area stretching from the central hill country of Judea to the lower Jordan Valley and to the Dead Sea, but still west of both. *by the devil.* God surely tests his people, but it is the devil who tempts to evil (see notes on Ge 22:1; Jas 1:13; see also 1Jn 3:8; Rev 2:9–10 and notes; Rev 12:9–10). Like the Hebrew for "Satan," the Greek for "devil" means "accuser" or "slanderer." The devil is a personal being, not a mere force or influence. He is the great archenemy of God and the leader of the hosts of darkness.

4:2 *forty days and forty nights.* The number recalls the experiences of Moses (Ex 24:18; 34:28) and Elijah (1Ki 19:8; see note there), as well as the 40 years of Israel's temptation (testing) in the desert (see note on v. 1).

4:3 *If you are the Son of God.* Meaning "Since you are." The devil is not casting doubt on Jesus' divine sonship but is tempting him to use his supernatural powers as the Son of God for his own ends. *Son of God.* See notes on Ps 2:7; 45:6; Jn 3:16. *tell these stones to become bread.* See note on Lk 4:3.

4:4 Just as God gave the Israelites manna in a supernatural way (see Dt 8:3 and note), so he also gave them his word,

Jesus' Baptism and Temptation

Events surrounding Jesus' baptism reveal the intense religious excitement and social ferment of the early days of John the Baptist's ministry. Herod had been rapacious and extravagant; Roman military occupation was harsh. Some agitation centered around the change of governors from Gratus to Pilate in A.D. 26. Most of the people hoped for a religious solution to their intolerable political situation, and when they heard of a new prophet, they flocked out into the desert to hear him. The religious sect (Essenes) from Qumran professed similar doctrines of repentance and baptism. Jesus was baptized at Bethany on the other side of the Jordan (see Jn 1:28). John also baptized at "Aenon near Salim" (Jn 3:23).

For Jesus' temptation see notes on Mt 4:1-11; Lk 4:1-13.

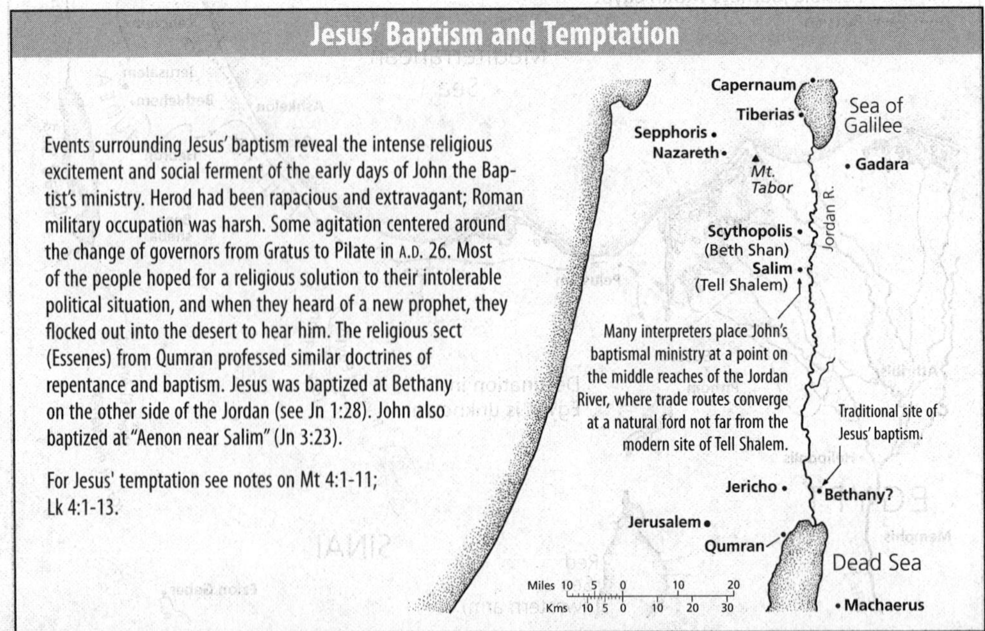

5Then the devil took him to the holy
city[b] and had him stand on the highest
point of the temple. 6"If you are the Son
of God,"[c] he said, "throw yourself down.
For it is written:

"'He will command his angels
concerning you,
and they will lift you up in their
hands,
so that you will not strike your foot
against a stone.'[a]"[d]

7Jesus answered him, "It is also written: 'Do not put the Lord your God to the
test.'[b]"[e]
8Again, the devil took him to a very
high mountain and showed him all the
kingdoms of the world and their splendor.
9"All this I will give you," he said, "if you
will bow down and worship me."
10Jesus said to him, "Away from me, Satan![f] For it is written: 'Worship the Lord
your God, and serve him only.'[c]"[g]
11Then the devil left him,[h] and angels
came and attended him.[i]

Jesus Begins to Preach

12When Jesus heard that John had been
put in prison,[j] he returned to Galilee.[k]
13Leaving Nazareth, he went and lived in
Capernaum,[l] which was by the lake in the
area of Zebulun and Naphtali— 14to fulfill[m] what was said through the prophet
Isaiah:

15"Land of Zebulun and land of
Naphtali,
the way to the sea, along the
Jordan,
Galilee of the Gentiles—
16the people living in darkness
have seen a great light;
on those living in the land of the
shadow of death
a light has dawned."[d][n]

17From that time on Jesus began to
preach, "Repent, for the kingdom of heav-
en[o] is near."

The Calling of the First Disciples

4:18-22pp — Mk 1:16-20; Lk 5:2-11; Jn 1:35-42

18As Jesus was walking beside the Sea
of Galilee,[p] he saw two brothers, Simon
called Peter[q] and his brother Andrew. They
were casting a net into the lake, for they
were fishermen. 19"Come, follow me,"[r]
Jesus said, "and I will make you fishers
of men." 20At once they left their nets and
followed him.[s]
21Going on from there, he saw two other brothers, James son of Zebedee and his
brother John.[t] They were in a boat with
their father Zebedee, preparing their nets.
Jesus called them, 22and immediately they
left the boat and their father and followed
him.[u]

4:5 [b]Ne 11:1; Da 9:24; Mt 27:53 **4:6** [c]S ver 3 [d]Ps 91:11,12 **4:7** [e]Dt 6:16 **4:10** [f]1Ch 21:1; Job 1:6-9; Mt 16:23; Mk 4:15; Lk 10:18; 13:16; 22:3,31; Ro 16:20; 2Co 2:11; 11:14; 2Th 2:9; Rev 12:9 [g]Dt 6:13 **4:11** [h]Jas 4:7 [i]Mt 26:53; Lk 22:43; Heb 1:14 **4:12** [j]Mt 14:3 [k]Mk 1:14 **4:13** [l]Mk 1:21; 9:33; Lk 4:23,31; Jn 2:12; 4:46,47 **4:14** [m]S Mt 1:22 **4:16** [n]Isa 9:1,2; Lk 2:32; Jn 1:4,5,9 **4:17** [o]S Mt 3:2 **4:18** [p]Mt 15:29; Mk 7:31; Jn 6:1 [q]Mt 16:17,18 **4:19** [r]ver 20,22; Mt 8:22; Mk 10:21,28,52; Lk 5:28; Jn 1:43; 21:19,22 **4:20** [s]S ver 19 **4:21** [t]Mt 17:1; 20:20; 26:37; Mk 3:17; 13:3; Lk 8:51; Jn 21:2 **4:22** [u]S ver 19

[a] 6 Psalm 91:11,12 [b] 7 Deut. 6:16 [c] 10 Deut. 6:13 [d] 16 Isaiah 9:1,2

which would give them life (see Dt 6:2; 30:19–20; 32:46–47; cf. Jn 4:32–34 and note on 4:34; 6:27).

4:5 See note on Lk 4:2. *highest point of the temple.* See note on Lk 4:9. *temple.* The temple, including the entire temple area, had been rebuilt by Herod the Great (see notes on 2:1; Jn 2:20). The courtyard had been greatly enlarged, to about 330 by 500 yards. To accomplish this a huge platform had been erected to compensate for the sharp falling off of the land to the southeast. An enormous retaining wall made of massive stones was built to support the platform. On the platform stood the temple building, porches and courtyards flanked by beautiful colonnades (see diagram, p. 1470).

4:6 *throw yourself down.* See note on Lk 4:9. *it is written.* See note on Lk 4:10.

4:9 *worship me.* See note on Lk 4:7.

4:10 *Satan.* See note on v. 1.

4:11 *the devil left him.* See note on Lk 4:13.

4:12 See map No. 11 at the end of this study Bible. *John had been put in prison.* See Mk 1:14 and note on Lk 3:20. The reason for John's imprisonment is given in 14:3–4.

4:13 *Capernaum.* Although not mentioned in the OT, it was evidently a sizable town in Jesus' day. Peter's house there became Jesus' base of operations during his extended ministry in Galilee (see Mk 2:1; 9:33). A fifth-century church now stands over the supposed site of Peter's house, and a fourth-century synagogue is located a short distance from it (see diagram, p. 1572).

4:15–16 Another Messianic prophecy from Isaiah. Jesus spent most of his public ministry "in the area of Zebulun and Naphtali" (v. 13), which is north and west of the Sea of Galilee.

4:15 *Galilee of the Gentiles.* A region that, from the Jewish perspective in Jesus' day, was "in darkness" and "the land of the shadow of death" (v. 16), probably because it was far removed from the religious influences of Jerusalem and because large numbers of Gentiles lived there. Matthew may have chosen this text (Isa 9:1–2) because of his interest in the universal intent of the gospel (see 2:1–12; 13:38; 28:19; see also Introduction: Recipients).

4:17 *From that time on.* These words indicate an important turning point in the life of Jesus and occur three times in Matthew's Gospel (see also 16:21; 26:16, NIV "From then on"). Some think these words mark the three main sections of the book. *Repent.* See note on Mk 1:4. Jesus began his public ministry with the same message as that of John the Baptist (see 3:2 and note). The people must repent because God's reign was drawing near in the person and ministry of Jesus Christ. *kingdom of heaven.* See note on 3:2. *is near.* See note on Mk 1:15.

4:18 *Sea of Galilee.* See note on Mk 1:16. *net.* A circular casting net used either from a boat or while standing in shallow water.

4:19 *fishers of men.* Evangelism was at the heart of Jesus' call to his disciples.

4:20 See note on Mk 1:17.

4:21 *boat.* In 1986 the remains of a 2,000-year-old typical fisherman's boat were found off the northwest shore of the Sea of Galilee. Its discoverers named it the Jesus Boat. *preparing their nets.* Washing, mending and hanging the nets up to dry in preparation for the next day's work.

Jesus Heals the Sick

[23]Jesus went throughout Galilee,[v] teaching in their synagogues,[w] preaching the good news[x] of the kingdom,[y] and healing every disease and sickness among the people.[z] [24]News about him spread all over Syria,[a] and people brought to him all who were ill with various diseases, those suffering severe pain, the demon-possessed,[b] those having seizures,[c] and the paralyzed,[d] and he healed them. [25]Large crowds from Galilee, the Decapolis,[a] Jerusalem, Judea and the region across the Jordan followed him.[e]

4:23 [v]Mk 1:39; Lk 4:15,44 [w]Mt 9:35; 13:54; Mk 1:21; Lk 4:15; Jn 6:59; 18:20 [x]Mk 1:14 [y]S Mt 3:2; Ac 20:25; 28:23,31 [z]Mt 8:16; 14:14; 15:30; Mk 3:10; Lk 7:22; Ac 10:38 **4:24** [a]S Lk 2:2 [b]Mt 8:16,28; 9:32; 12:22; 15:22; Mk 1:32; 5:15,16,18 [c]Mt 17:15 [d]Mt 8:6; 9:2; Mk 2:3 **4:25** [e]Mk 3:7,8; Lk 6:17

The Beatitudes

5:3-12pp — Lk 6:20-23

5 Now when he saw the crowds, he went up on a mountainside and sat down. His disciples came to him, [2]and he began to teach them, saying:

[a] *25* That is, the Ten Cities

4:23 *teaching ... preaching ... healing.* Jesus' threefold ministry. The synagogues (see note on Mk 1:21) provided a place for him to teach on the Sabbath. During the week he preached to larger crowds in the open air. *good news.* See note on Mk 1:1.
4:24 *Syria.* A Roman province of somewhat shifting boundaries, lying generally north of Galilee and extending to the Taurus Mountains. Antioch and Damascus were its two leading cities. *those having seizures.* The Greek word for this expression originally meant "moonstruck" and reflects the ancient superstition that seizures were caused by changes of the moon.
4:25 *Large crowds.* Jesus' influence spread quickly over a large geographical area. *the Decapolis.* A loose league of free (relatively independent from Roman administration) cities (see NIV text note and map, p. 1530) characterized by high Greek culture. All but one, Scythopolis (Beth Shan), were east of the Sea of Galilee and the Jordan River. The league stretched from a point northeast of the Sea of Galilee southward to Philadelphia (modern Amman). *followed him.* Not all who followed were true disciples; many were curious onlookers, as subsequent events revealed only too clearly.
5:1—7:29 The Sermon on the Mount is in effect King Jesus' inaugural address, explaining what he expects of members of his kingdom. It is the first of five great discourses in Matthew (chs. 5–7; 10; 13; 18; 24–25; see Introduction: Structure). It contains three types of material: (1) beatitudes, i.e., declarations of blessedness (5:1–12), (2) ethical admoni-

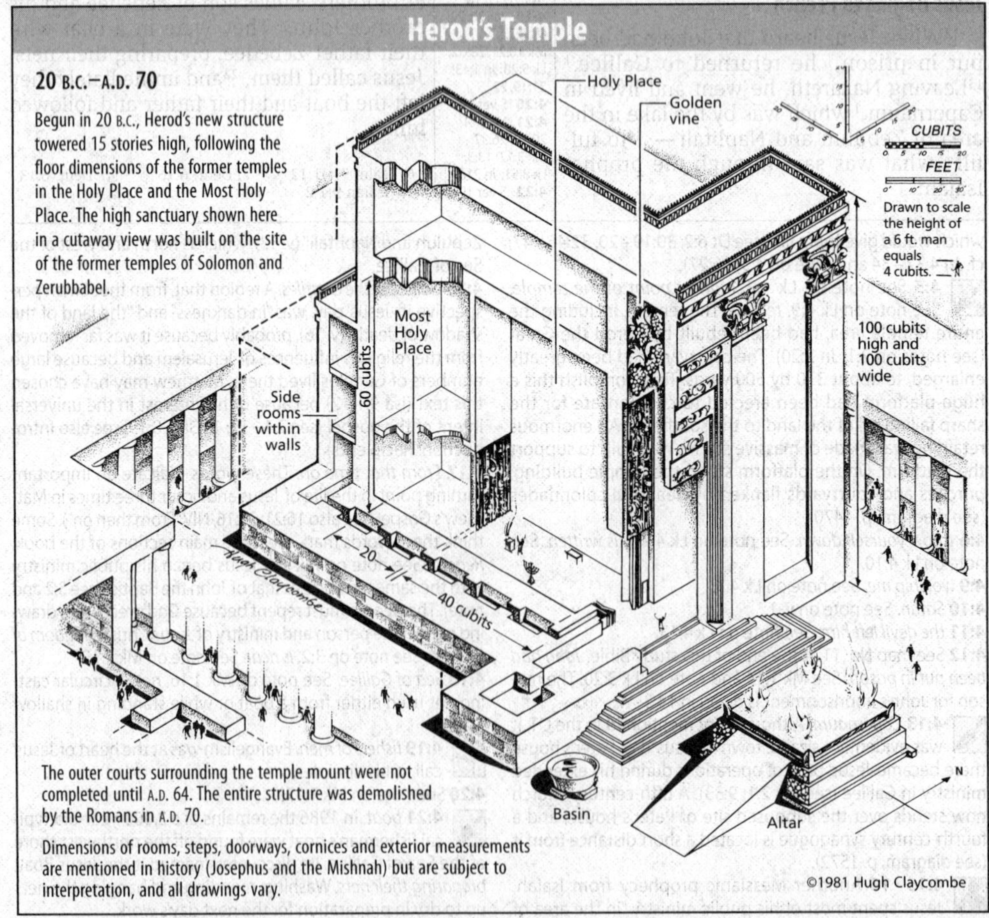

Begun in 20 B.C., Herod's new structure towered 15 stories high, following the floor dimensions of the former temples in the Holy Place and the Most Holy Place. The high sanctuary shown here in a cutaway view was built on the site of the former temples of Solomon and Zerubbabel.

The outer courts surrounding the temple mount were not completed until A.D. 64. The entire structure was demolished by the Romans in A.D. 70.

Dimensions of rooms, steps, doorways, cornices and exterior measurements are mentioned in history (Josephus and the Mishnah) but are subject to interpretation, and all drawings vary.

3 "Blessed are the poor in spirit,
for theirs is the kingdom of heaven.[f]
4 Blessed are those who mourn,
for they will be comforted.[g]
5 Blessed are the meek,
for they will inherit the earth.[h]
6 Blessed are those who hunger and
thirst for righteousness,
for they will be filled.[i]
7 Blessed are the merciful,
for they will be shown mercy.[j]
8 Blessed are the pure in heart,[k]
for they will see God.[l]
9 Blessed are the peacemakers,[m]
for they will be called sons of God.[n]
10 Blessed are those who are persecuted
because of righteousness,[o]
for theirs is the kingdom of
heaven.[p]

11 "Blessed are you when people insult
you,[q] persecute you and falsely say all
kinds of evil against you because of me.[r]
12 Rejoice and be glad,[s] because great is
your reward in heaven, for in the same
way they persecuted the prophets who
were before you.[t]

Salt and Light

13 "You are the salt of the earth. But if
the salt loses its saltiness, how can it be
made salty again? It is no longer good for
anything, except to be thrown out and
trampled by men.[u]
14 "You are the light of the world.[v] A
city on a hill cannot be hidden. 15 Neither
do people light a lamp and put it under a
bowl. Instead they put it on its stand, and
it gives light to everyone in the house.[w]
16 In the same way, let your light shine before men,[x] that they may see your good
deeds[y] and praise[z] your Father in heaven.

The Fulfillment of the Law

17 "Do not think that I have come to
abolish the Law or the Prophets; I have
not come to abolish them but to fulfill

5:3 [f] ver 10,19; S Mt 25:34 **5:4** [g] Isa 61:2,3; Rev 7:17 **5:5** [h] Ps 37:11; Ro 4:13 **5:6** [i] Isa 55:1,2 **5:7** [j] S Jas 2:13 **5:8** [k] Ps 24:3,4; 73:1 [l] Ps 17:15; 42:2; Heb 12:14; Rev 22:4 **5:9** [m] Jas 3:18; S Ro 14:19 [n] ver 44,45; S Ro 8:14 **5:10** [o] S 1Pe 3:14 [p] ver 3,19; S Mt 25:34 **5:11** [q] Isa 51:7 [r] S Jn 15:21 **5:12** [s] Ps 9:2; Ac 5:41; S 2Co 6:10; 12:10; Col 1:24; Jas 1:2; 1Pe 1:6; 4:13,16 [t] 2Ch 36:16; Mt 23:31,37; Ac 7:52; 1Th 2:15; Heb 11:32-38 **5:13** [u] Mk 9:50; Lk 14:34,35 **5:14** [v] Jn 8:12 **5:15** [w] Mk 4:21; Lk 8:16; 11:33 **5:16** [x] 1Co 10:31; Php 1:11 [y] S Tit 2:14 [z] S Mt 9:8

tions (5:13–20; 6:1—7:23) and (3) contrasts between Jesus' ethical teaching and Jewish legalistic traditions (5:21–48). The Sermon ends with a short parable stressing the importance of practicing what has just been taught (7:24–27) and an expression of amazement by the crowds at the authority with which Jesus spoke (7:28–29).

Opinion differs as to whether the Sermon is a summary of what Jesus taught on one occasion or a compilation of teachings presented on numerous occasions. Matthew possibly took a single sermon and expanded it with other relevant teachings of Jesus. Thirty-four of the verses in Matthew's Sermon occur in different contexts in Luke than the apparently parallel Sermon on the Plain (see Lk 6:20–49 and note).

The moral and ethical standard called for in the Sermon on the Mount is so high that some have dismissed the Sermon as being completely unrealistic or have projected its fulfillment to the future kingdom. There is no doubt, however, that Jesus (and Matthew) gave the Sermon as a standard for all Christians, realizing that its demands cannot be met in our own power. It is also true that Jesus occasionally used hyperbole to make his point (see, e.g., note on 5:29–30).

5:1 *mountainside.* The exact location is uncertain. It may have been the gently sloping hillside at the northwest corner of the Sea of Galilee, not far from Capernaum (see note on Lk 6:20–49). The new law, like the old (Ex 19:3), was given from a mountain. *sat down.* It was the custom for Jewish rabbis to be seated while teaching (see Mk 4:1 and note; 9:35; Lk 4:20 and note; 5:3; Jn 8:2; cf. Eze 8:1 and note). *disciples.* Lit. "learners." Since at the end of the Sermon the "crowds" expressed amazement at Jesus' teaching (7:28), "disciples" may here be used in a broader sense than the Twelve. Or perhaps the Sermon is addressed to the Twelve with the crowds also listening.

5:3 *Blessed.* The word means more than "happy," because happiness is an emotion often dependent on outward circumstances. "Blessed" here refers to the ultimate well-being and distinctive spiritual joy of those who share in the salvation of the kingdom of God. See notes on Ps 1:1; Rev 1:3. *poor in spirit.* In contrast to the spiritually proud and self-sufficient. *theirs is the kingdom of heaven.* The kingdom is not something earned. It is more a gift than a reward.

5:4 *those who mourn.* Over both personal and corporate sins (see Ezr 9:4; Ps 119:36).

5:5 *meek.* This beatitude is taken from Ps 37:11 (see note there) and refers not so much to an attitude toward people as to a disposition before God, namely, humility. *the earth.* The new promised land (see Rev 21:1; cf. note on Ps 37:9).

5:6 *hunger and thirst for righteousness.* Have a deep longing for both personal righteousness and justice for the oppressed.

5:8 *heart.* The center of one's being, including mind, will and emotions (see note on Ps 4:7).

5:9 *peacemakers.* Those who promote peace, as far as it depends on them (Ro 12:18). In so doing, they reflect the character of their heavenly Father and so are called "sons of God" (see Jas 3:17–18).

5:10 *Blessed.* Because persecution provides an opportunity for believers to prove their fitness for the kingdom (see Heb 12:4–11 and notes). *persecuted.* Righteous living is often offensive to unbelievers (cf. v. 11). *theirs is the kingdom of heaven.* For the blessings of God's kingdom see 3:2 and note.

5:13 *salt.* Used for flavoring and preserving (cf. Mk 9:50 and note). *loses its saltiness.* Most of the salt used in Israel came from the Dead Sea and was full of impurities. This caused it to lose some of its flavor.

5:14 *light of the world.* Although Jesus himself fulfilled the mission of the Lord's servant to be "a light for the Gentiles" (Isa 9:2; 42:6; see also Lk 2:32 and notes on Isa 49:6; Lk 2:31), he expected his followers to carry on the work (see vv. 15–16; cf. Jn 8:12; Php 2:15 and notes).

5:15 *lamp.* In Jesus' day people used small clay lamps that burned olive oil drawn up by a wick (see note on Ex 25:37). *bowl.* A bowl that held about eight quarts of ground meal or flour.

5:16 *praise your Father.* Good deeds are not to be done in a public way for one's own honor ("before men, to be seen by them," 6:1) but for the glory of God (see 1Co 10:31; Php 1:11; 1Pe 2:12 and notes). *Father in heaven.* Matthew uses the phrase "Father in heaven" or "heavenly Father" 17 times, Mark and Luke only once each, and John not at all.

5:17 *the Law.* The first five books of the OT. *the Prophets.* Not only the Latter Prophets—Isaiah, Jeremiah and Ezekiel, which we call Major Prophets, and the 12 Minor Prophets (lumped together by the Jews as "the Book of the Twelve")—but also the Former Prophets (Joshua, Judges, Samuel and Kings).

them.[a] 18I tell you the truth, until heav-
en and earth disappear, not the smallest
letter, not the least stroke of a pen, will
by any means disappear from the Law until everything is accomplished.[b] 19Anyone
who breaks one of the least of these commandments[c] and teaches others to do the
same will be called least in the kingdom of
heaven, but whoever practices and teaches these commands will be called great
in the kingdom of heaven. 20For I tell you
that unless your righteousness surpasses
that of the Pharisees and the teachers of
the law, you will certainly not enter the
kingdom of heaven.[d]

Murder

5:25,26pp — Lk 12:58,59

21"You have heard that it was said to the
people long ago, 'Do not murder,[a][e] and
anyone who murders will be subject to
judgment.' 22But I tell you that anyone who
is angry[f] with his brother[b] will be subject
to judgment.[g] Again, anyone who says to
his brother, 'Raca,[c]' is answerable to the
Sanhedrin.[h] But anyone who says, 'You
fool!' will be in danger of the fire of hell.[i]
23"Therefore, if you are offering your gift
at the altar and there remember that your
brother has something against you, 24leave
your gift there in front of the altar. First
go and be reconciled to your brother; then
come and offer your gift.
25"Settle matters quickly with your adversary who is taking you to court. Do it
while you are still with him on the way, or
he may hand you over to the judge, and
the judge may hand you over to the officer, and you may be thrown into prison.
26I tell you the truth, you will not get out
until you have paid the last penny.[d]

Adultery

27"You have heard that it was said, 'Do
not commit adultery.'[e][j] 28But I tell you
that anyone who looks at a woman lustfully has already committed adultery with
her in his heart.[k] 29If your right eye causes you to sin,[l] gouge it out and throw it
away. It is better for you to lose one part of
your body than for your whole body to be
thrown into hell. 30And if your right hand
causes you to sin,[m] cut it off and throw it
away. It is better for you to lose one part
of your body than for your whole body to
go into hell.

Divorce

31"It has been said, 'Anyone who divorces his wife must give her a certificate
of divorce.'[f][n] 32But I tell you that anyone
who divorces his wife, except for marital

5:17 [a]Jn 10:34,35; Ro 3:31
5:18 [b]Ps 119:89; Isa 40:8; 55:11; Mt 24:35; Mk 13:31; Lk 16:17; 21:33
5:19 [c]Jas 2:10
5:20 [d]Isa 26:2; Mt 18:3; Jn 3:5
5:21 [e]Ex 20:13; 21:12; Dt 5:17
5:22 [f]Ecc 7:9; 1Co 13:5; Eph 4:26; Jas 1:19,20 [g]1Jn 3:15 [h]Mt 26:59; Jn 11:47; Ac 5:21,27,34, 41; 6:12 [i]Mt 18:9; Mk 9:43,48; Lk 16:24; Jas 3:6
5:27 [j]Ex 20:14; Dt 5:18
5:28 [k]Pr 6:25; 2Pe 2:14
5:29 [l]ver 30; Mt 18:6,8,9; Mk 9:42-47; Lk 17:2; Ro 14:21; 1Co 8:13; S 2Co 6:3; 11:29
5:30 [m]S ver 29
5:31 [n]Dt 24:1-4

[a] *21* Exodus 20:13 [b] *22* Some manuscripts *brother without cause* [c] *22* An Aramaic term of contempt [d] *26* Greek *kodrantes* [e] *27* Exodus 20:14 [f] *31* Deut. 24:1

Taken together, "the Law" and "the Prophets" designated the entire OT (see Lk 24:27 and note), including the Writings, the third section of the Hebrew Bible. See 13:35, where Matthew introduces a quotation from the Writings (Ps 78:2) with "what was spoken through the prophet." *fulfill.* Jesus fulfilled the Law in the sense that he gave it its full meaning. He emphasized its deep, underlying principles and total commitment to it rather than mere external acknowledgment and obedience.

5:18–20 Jesus is not speaking against observing all the requirements of the Law but against hypocritical, Pharisaical legalism. Such legalism was not the keeping of all details of the Law but the hollow sham of keeping laws externally to gain merit before God while breaking them inwardly. It was following the letter of the Law while ignoring its spirit. Jesus repudiates the Pharisees' interpretation of the Law and their view of righteousness by works. He preaches a righteousness that comes only through faith in him and his work. In the rest of the chapter, he gives six examples of Pharisaical externalism.

5:18 *smallest letter.* In Greek *iota,* which we use when we say, "It doesn't make one iota of difference." It is the nearest Greek equivalent to the Hebrew *yodh,* the smallest letter of the Hebrew alphabet (see Ps 119:73 title). *least stroke of a pen.* The Greek word for this phrase means "horn" and was used to designate the slight extension of a pen stroke that distinguished one Hebrew letter from another similar letter (somewhat like the bottom of a "j" that distinguishes it from an "i").

5:20 *Pharisees.* See note on 3:7. *teachers of the law.* See note on 2:4. *kingdom of heaven.* See note on 3:2.

5:21–22 *it was said . . . But I tell you.* The contrast that Jesus sets up (vv. 21,27,31,33,38,43) is not between the OT and his teaching (he has just established the validity of the OT Law). Rather, it is between the externalistic interpretations of the Law present in the rabbinic tradition on the one hand and Jesus' correct interpretation of the Law on the other. *murder.* Several Hebrew and Greek verbs mean "kill." The ones used here and in Ex 20:13 mean specifically "murder."

5:22–24 *brother.* That is, brother or sister; the Greek word was commonly used to refer to both (see note on Ro 1:13).

5:22 *Raca.* May be related to the Aramaic word for "empty" and mean "Empty-head!" *Sanhedrin.* See note on Mk 14:55. *hell.* The Greek word is *ge(h)enna,* which derives its name from a deep ravine south of Jerusalem, the "Valley of (the Sons of) Hinnom" (Hebrew *ge' hinnom*). During the reigns of the wicked Ahaz and Manasseh, human sacrifices to the Ammonite god Molech were offered there. Josiah desecrated the valley because of the pagan worship there (2Ki 23:10; see Jer 7:31–32 and note on 7:31; 19:6). It became a sort of perpetually burning city dump and later a figure for the place of final punishment (see notes on Isa 66:24; Jer 7:31).

5:23–26 Two illustrations of dealing with anger by means of reconciliation.

5:25 Cf. Lk 12:57–59.

5:26 *penny.* The smallest Roman copper coin (see note on Lk 12:59).

5:28 *looks at a woman lustfully.* Not a passing glance but a willful, calculated stare that arouses sexual desire. According to Jesus this is a form of adultery even if it is only "in his heart" (see Job 31:1 and note).

5:29–30 Jesus is not teaching self-mutilation, for even a blind man can lust. What he is saying is that we should deal as drastically as necessary with sin, a point Jesus repeated on at least one other occasion (see 18:8–9; Mk 9:43–48).

5:30 *hell.* See note on v. 22.

5:32 *except for marital unfaithfulness.* See note on 19:3. Neither Mk 10:11–12 nor Lk 16:18 mentions this exception.

unfaithfulness, causes her to become an adulteress, and anyone who marries the divorced woman commits adultery.[o]

Oaths

33 "Again, you have heard that it was said to the people long ago, 'Do not break your oath,[p] but keep the oaths you have made to the Lord.'[q] 34 But I tell you, Do not swear at all:[r] either by heaven, for it is God's throne;[s] 35 or by the earth, for it is his footstool; or by Jerusalem, for it is the city of the Great King.[t] 36 And do not swear by your head, for you cannot make even one hair white or black. 37 Simply let your 'Yes' be 'Yes,' and your 'No,' 'No';[u] anything beyond this comes from the evil one.[v]

An Eye for an Eye

38 "You have heard that it was said, 'Eye for eye, and tooth for tooth.'[a w] 39 But I tell you, Do not resist an evil person. If someone strikes you on the right cheek, turn to him the other also.[x] 40 And if someone wants to sue you and take your tunic, let him have your cloak as well. 41 If someone forces you to go one mile, go with him two miles. 42 Give to the one who asks you, and do not turn away from the one who wants to borrow from you.[y]

Love for Enemies

43 "You have heard that it was said, 'Love your neighbor[b z] and hate your enemy.'[a] 44 But I tell you: Love your enemies[c] and pray for those who persecute you,[b] 45 that you may be sons[c] of your Father in heaven. He causes his sun to rise on the evil and the good, and sends rain on the righteous and the unrighteous.[d] 46 If you love those who love you, what reward will you get?[e] Are not even the tax collectors doing that? 47 And if you greet only your brothers, what are you doing more than others? Do not even pagans do that? 48 Be perfect, therefore, as your heavenly Father is perfect.[f]

Giving to the Needy

6 "Be careful not to do your 'acts of righteousness' before men, to be seen by them.[g] If you do, you will have no reward from your Father in heaven.

2 "So when you give to the needy, do not announce it with trumpets, as the hypocrites do in the synagogues and on the streets, to be honored by men. I tell you the truth, they have received their reward in full. 3 But when you give to the needy, do not let your left hand know what your right hand is doing, 4 so that your giving may be in secret. Then your Father, who sees what is done in secret, will reward you.[h]

[a] 38 Exodus 21:24; Lev. 24:20; Deut. 19:21
[b] 43 Lev. 19:18 [c] 44 Some late manuscripts *enemies, bless those who curse you, do good to those who hate you*

5:32 [o] S Lk 16:18 **5:33** [p] Lev 19:12 [q] Nu 30:2; Dt 23:21; Mt 23:16-22 **5:34** [r] Jas 5:12 [s] Isa 66:1; Mt 23:22 **5:35** [t] Ps 48:2 **5:37** [u] Jas 5:12 [v] Mt 6:13; 13:19,38; Jn 17:15; Eph 6:16; 2Th 3:3; 1Jn 2:13,14; 3:12; 5:18,19 **5:38** [w] Ex 21:24; Lev 24:20; Dt 19:21 **5:39** [x] Lk 6:29; Ro 12:17,19; 1Pe 3:9 **5:42** [y] Dt 15:8; Lk 6:30 **5:43** [z] Lev 19:18; Mt 19:19; 22:39; Mk 12:31; Lk 10:27; Ro 13:9; Gal 5:14; Jas 2:8 [a] Dt 23:6; Ps 139:21,22 **5:44** [b] Lk 6:27,28; 23:34; Jn 15:20; Ac 7:60; Ro 8:35; 12:14; 1Co 4:12; 1Pe 2:23 **5:45** [c] ver 9; Lk 6:35; S Ro 8:14 [d] Job 25:3 **5:46** [e] Lk 6:32 **5:48** [f] Lev 19:2; 1Pe 1:16 **6:1** [g] Mt 5:16; 23:5 **6:4** [h] ver 6,18; Col 3:23,24

5:33–37 The OT recognized the useful role of swearing oaths in certain situations (even God swore oaths: see, e.g., Ge 22:16; Jos 5:6; Ps 89:3–4,35; Isa 45:22; Jer 22:5; Eze 26:7; see also notes on Ge 9:13; 15:17; Dt 6:13; Jer 22:5; Heb 6:13)—common profanity is not in view. Jesus urged such honesty and integrity in all human speech that swearing oaths in support of assertions or commitments would not be necessary.
5:38 See notes on Ex 21:23–25; Lev 24:20.
5:39 *resist.* Here it probably means in a court of law. *strikes.* The Greek verb used here means "slaps you with the back of the hand." It was more an insult (cf. 26:67) than an act of violence. The point is that it is better to be insulted even twice than to take the matter to court. Ancient Near Eastern society had become very litigious.
5:40 *tunic ... cloak.* The first was an undergarment, the second a loose outer one. Since the outer garment was used to sleep in, OT law prohibited anyone from taking it even as a pledge overnight (see Ex 22:26–27; Dt 24:12–13).
5:42 Probably not a general requirement to give to everyone who asks but a reference to the poor (cf. Dt 15:7–11; Ps 112:5,9).
5:43 *hate your enemy.* Words not found anywhere in the OT. However, hatred for one's enemies was an accepted part of the Jewish ethic at that time in some circles (cf., e.g., the Dead Sea Scrolls work, *The Rule of the Community* 1.4,10). See note on Lev 19:18.
5:44 *Love your enemies.* See note on Ex 23:4–5. *pray.* Prayer is one of the practical ways love expresses itself (cf. Job 42:10; Ps 35:13–14 and notes).
5:45 *that you may be sons of your Father in heaven.* That is, be truly like him by loving "your enemies" and praying "for those who persecute you" (v. 44; see v. 48 and note). *the evil and the good.* God shows his love to people without distinction.
5:46 *tax collectors.* Traditionally known as "publicans," these were local men employed by Roman tax contractors to collect taxes for them. Because they worked for Rome and often demanded unreasonable payments, the tax collectors gained a bad reputation and were generally hated and considered traitors (see notes on Mk 2:14–15; Lk 3:12).
5:48 *Be perfect.* Christ sets up the high ideal of perfect love (see vv. 43–47)—not that we can fully attain it in this life. That, however, is God's high standard for us.
6:1 *acts of righteousness.* The language comes from Jewish tradition. This verse introduces the discussion of three acts of righteousness: (1) giving (vv. 2–4), (2) praying (vv. 5–15) and (3) fasting (vv. 16–18). Jesus' concern here is with the motives behind such acts. *reward from your Father.* Spiritual growth and maturity or perhaps a heavenly reward of some kind—or both.
6:2 *when you give.* Not "if you give." Jesus presupposes the disciples' giving to the poor. *announce it with trumpets.* Perhaps a reference to the noise made by coins as they were thrown into the temple treasury (see note on Mk 12:41). Or the phrase may be used figuratively to mean "make a big show of it." *hypocrites.* The Greek word means "play-actor." Matthew uses the word 13 times (Mark, twice; Luke, three times). Here it refers to those who fake being pious. *their reward in full.* The honor they receive from people is all the reward they get.
6:3 *do not let your left hand know what your right hand is doing.* Not to be taken literally but as a way of emphasizing that one should not call attention to one's giving. Self-glorification is always a present danger.

Prayer

6:9-13pp — Lk 11:2-4

5“And when you pray, do not be like
the hypocrites, for they love to pray standing[i] in the synagogues and on the street
corners to be seen by men. I tell you the
truth, they have received their reward in
full. 6But when you pray, go into your
room, close the door and pray to your Father,[j] who is unseen. Then your Father,
who sees what is done in secret, will reward you. 7And when you pray, do not
keep on babbling[k] like pagans, for they
think they will be heard because of their
many words.[l] 8Do not be like them, for
your Father knows what you need[m] before
you ask him.
9“This, then, is how you should pray:

“ ‘Our Father[n] in heaven,
hallowed be your name,
10your kingdom[o] come,
your will be done[p]
on earth as it is in heaven.
11Give us today our daily bread.[q]
12Forgive us our debts,
as we also have forgiven our
debtors.[r]
13And lead us not into temptation,[s]
but deliver us from the evil one.[a] ’[t]

14For if you forgive men when they sin
against you, your heavenly Father will also
forgive you.[u] 15But if you do not forgive
men their sins, your Father will not forgive
your sins.[v]

Fasting

16“When you fast,[w] do not look somber[x]
as the hypocrites do, for they disfigure
their faces to show men they are fasting. I
tell you the truth, they have received their
reward in full. 17But when you fast, put
oil on your head and wash your face, 18so
that it will not be obvious to men that you
are fasting, but only to your Father, who is
unseen; and your Father, who sees what is
done in secret, will reward you.[y]

Treasures in Heaven

6:22,23pp — Lk 11:34-36

19“Do not store up for yourselves treasures on earth,[z] where moth and rust destroy,[a] and where thieves break in and
steal. 20But store up for yourselves treasures in heaven,[b] where moth and rust
do not destroy, and where thieves do not
break in and steal.[c] 21For where your treasure is, there your heart will be also.[d]
22“The eye is the lamp of the body. If
your eyes are good, your whole body will

[a] 13 Or *from evil*; some late manuscripts *one, / for yours is the kingdom and the power and the glory forever. Amen.*

6:5 [i] Mk 11:25; Lk 18:10-14 **6:6** [j] 2Ki 4:33 **6:7** [k] Ecc 5:2 [l] 1Ki 18:26-29 **6:8** [m] ver 32 **6:9** [n] Jer 3:19; Mal 2:10; 1Pe 1:17 **6:10** [o] S Mt 3:2 [p] S Mt 26:39 **6:11** [q] Pr 30:8 **6:12** [r] Mt 18:21-35 **6:13** [s] Jas 1:13 [t] S Mt 5:37 **6:14** [u] Mt 18:21-35; Mk 11:25,26; Eph 4:32; Col 3:13 **6:15** [v] Mt 18:35 **6:16** [w] Lev 16:29,31; 23:27-32; Nu 29:7 [x] Isa 58:5; Zec 7:5; 8:19 **6:18** [y] ver 4,6 **6:19** [z] Pr 23:4; Lk 12:16-21; Heb 13:5 [a] S Jas 5:2,3 **6:20** [b] Mt 19:21; Lk 12:33; 16:9; 18:22; 1Ti 6:19 [c] Lk 12:33 **6:21** [d] Lk 12:34

6:6 Jesus' followers are not to make a show of their praying, in contrast to "the hypocrites" (v. 5). It does not mean that all prayer should be private, as the plurals "our" and "us" in vv. 9 – 13 indicate. *room.* The Greek word here probably means "storeroom," because unlike most of the rooms in the house, it had a door that could be shut.

6:7 *babbling like pagans.* They used long lists of the names of their gods in their prayers, hoping that by constantly repeating them they would call on the name of the god that could help them. Jesus is not necessarily condemning all long prayers, but meaningless verbiage in praying.

6:9 – 13 Commonly known as "The Lord's Prayer," it is really "The Disciples' Prayer," since it was meant as a model for them. The prayer nestles at the literary center of the Sermon on the Mount, and the surrounding texts in the Sermon echo the prayer's concerns. It contains six petitions, three relating more directly to God (vv. 9 – 10) and three to us (vv. 11 – 13). The order of these petitions is significant and intentional. A similar prayer in Lk 11:2 – 4 occurs in a different historical setting.

6:9 *Our Father.* Never used by Jesus to refer to his and the disciples' Father together (see note on vv. 9 – 13; see also Jn 20:17 and note). *hallowed.* God is already holy (see Lev 11:44 and note; 1Pe 1:15), so the prayer is not that God be made holy but that he be regarded as holy. By his saving and judging acts in history he shows himself holy (see Lev 10:3; Eze 36:23 and notes). This petition is that he so achieve his saving purposes in the world that his holiness is displayed before the eyes of the world's people and acknowledged by them — which will happen only as his kingdom comes. *name.* See notes on Ps 5:11; Eze 20:9.

6:10 *your kingdom come.* Not in the sense of to "come" into existence — after all, it is already here (see 3:2; Lk 17:21 and notes) — but to "come" more and more completely until its full and final consummation. *your will be done on earth.* Logically follows "your kingdom come." *on earth as it is in heaven.* Probably to be read with each of the three preceding petitions.

6:11 That is, meet our needs "each day" (Lk 11:3; see Ex 16:4 and note).

6:12 *debts.* Moral debts, i.e., sins (see note on Lk 11:4).

6:13 *lead us not into temptation.* That is, do not lead us through trials so deep that they would tempt us to be unfaithful to you (see 1Co 10:13 and note). God does not tempt (in the sense of enticing to sin; see Jas 1:13 and note). *the evil one.* Satan. Others think the reference is to "evil," i.e., evil circumstances (see the first part of the NIV text note). For the second part of the NIV text note cf. 1Ch 29:10 – 11.

6:15 *forgive … forgive.* See Eph 4:32 and note.

6:16 *fast.* See notes on Mk 2:18; Lk 18:12. Jesus does not condemn fasting as such but ostentation in fasting. *hypocrites.* See note on v. 2. *their reward in full.* See note on v. 2.

6:17 *put oil on your head and wash your face.* That is, maintain your regular appearance. Jews put ashes on their heads when fasting.

6:19 – 21 The dangers of riches are often mentioned in the NT (e.g., v. 24; 13:22; 19:22; Mk 10:17 – 30; Lk 12:16 – 21; 1Ti 6:9 – 10,17 – 19; Heb 13:5; Jas 5:2 – 3), but nowhere are they condemned in and of themselves. What Jesus condemns here is greed and the hoarding of wealth.

6:19 *Do not store up.* Or "Stop storing up." They may have already started to do it. *moth and rust.* Representative of all agents and processes that destroy worldly possessions. *break in and steal.* Most houses in the Holy Land had walls made of mud bricks and could be broken into easily.

6:20 *treasures in heaven.* Anything done in this life that has eternal value will be rewarded. Cf. "rich toward God" (Lk 12:21).

6:21 See Lk 12:34. *heart.* See note on 5:8.

6:22 *The eye is the lamp of the body.* It lets light in to illumine the body. *your eyes are good.* You recognize the folly of storing

be full of light. 23But if your eyes are bad,
your whole body will be full of darkness.
If then the light within you is darkness,
how great is that darkness!
24"No one can serve two masters. Either
he will hate the one and love the other, or
he will be devoted to the one and despise
the other. You cannot serve both God and
Money.[e]

Do Not Worry

6:25-33pp — Lk 12:22-31

25"Therefore I tell you, do not worry[f]
about your life, what you will eat or drink;
or about your body, what you will wear. Is
not life more important than food, and the
body more important than clothes? 26Look
at the birds of the air; they do not sow or
reap or store away in barns, and yet your
heavenly Father feeds them.[g] Are you not
much more valuable than they?[h] 27Who of
you by worrying can add a single hour to
his life[a]?[i]
28"And why do you worry about clothes?
See how the lilies of the field grow. They
do not labor or spin. 29Yet I tell you that
not even Solomon in all his splendor[j] was
dressed like one of these. 30If that is how
God clothes the grass of the field, which
is here today and tomorrow is thrown into
the fire, will he not much more clothe
you, O you of little faith?[k] 31So do not worry, saying, 'What shall we eat?' or 'What
shall we drink?' or 'What shall we wear?'
32For the pagans run after all these things,
and your heavenly Father knows that you
need them.[l] 33But seek first his kingdom[m]
and his righteousness, and all these things
will be given to you as well.[n] 34Therefore
do not worry about tomorrow, for tomorrow will worry about itself. Each day has
enough trouble of its own.

6:24 [e] Lk 16:13 **6:25** [f] ver 27,28, 31,34; Lk 10:41; 12:11,22 **6:26** [g] Job 38:41; Ps 104:21; 136:25; 145:15; 147:9 [h] Mt 10:29-31 **6:27** [i] Ps 39:5 **6:29** [j] 1Ki 10:4-7 **6:30** [k] Mt 8:26; 14:31; 16:8; Lk 12:28 **6:32** [l] ver 8 **6:33** [m] S Mt 3:2 [n] Ps 37:4; Mt 19:29

7:1 [o] Lk 6:37; Ro 14:4,10,13; 1Co 4:5; 5:12; Jas 4:11,12 **7:2** [p] Eze 35:11; Mk 4:24; Lk 6:38; Ro 2:1 **7:7** [q] 1Ki 3:5; Mt 18:19; 21:22; Jn 14:13,14; 15:7,16; 16:23,24; Jas 1:5-8; 4:2,3; 5:16; 1Jn 3:22; 5:14,15 **7:8** [r] Pr 8:17; Jer 29:12,13 **7:11** [s] Jas 1:17 **7:12** [t] Lk 6:31 [u] Ro 13:8-10; Gal 5:14

Judging Others

7:3-5pp — Lk 6:41,42

7 "Do not judge, or you too will be
judged.[o] 2For in the same way you
judge others, you will be judged, and with
the measure you use, it will be measured
to you.[p]
3"Why do you look at the speck of sawdust in your brother's eye and pay no
attention to the plank in your own eye?
4How can you say to your brother, 'Let me
take the speck out of your eye,' when all
the time there is a plank in your own eye?
5You hypocrite, first take the plank out of
your own eye, and then you will see clearly to remove the speck from your brother's
eye.
6"Do not give dogs what is sacred; do
not throw your pearls to pigs. If you do,
they may trample them under their feet,
and then turn and tear you to pieces.

Ask, Seek, Knock

7:7-11pp — Lk 11:9-13

7"Ask and it will be given to you;[q] seek
and you will find; knock and the door will
be opened to you. 8For everyone who asks
receives; he who seeks finds;[r] and to him
who knocks, the door will be opened.
9"Which of you, if his son asks for
bread, will give him a stone? 10Or if he
asks for a fish, will give him a snake? 11If
you, then, though you are evil, know how
to give good gifts to your children, how
much more will your Father in heaven give
good gifts[s] to those who ask him! 12So in
everything, do to others what you would
have them do to you,[t] for this sums up the
Law and the Prophets.[u]

[a] 27 Or *single cubit to his height*

up wealth (v. 19). The Greek term for "good," however, may also be rendered "healthy," here implying "generous." *whole body.* Entire person.

6:23 *your eyes are bad.* They are blind to the deceitfulness of wealth. The Greek term for "bad," however, may also be rendered "unhealthy," here implying "stingy."

6:24 See Lk 16:13; Jas 4:4.

6:25 *do not worry.* See Php 4:6 and note. *worry.* Undue anxiety — rather than a legitimate concern to provide for one's daily needs (cf. Lk 10:41 – 42; 2Th 3:6 – 12).

6:27 *add a single hour.* But anxiety may very well shorten one's life span, as modern medicine has shown.

6:28 *lilies.* Here represents flowers generally.

6:30 *thrown into the fire.* Grass was commonly used to heat clay ovens in the Holy Land. *you of little faith.* See 8:26; 14:31; 16:8; 17:20; Lk 12:28.

6:33 The heart of the matter. *kingdom.* See note on 3:2. *his righteousness.* The righteous life that God requires, as the content of the Sermon emphasizes (see, e.g., 5:6,10,20; 6:1).

7:1 The Christian is not to judge hypocritically or self-righteously, as can be seen from the context (v. 5). The same thought is expressed in 23:13 – 39 (cf. Ro 2:1). Obeying Christ's commands in this chapter does not preclude assessing another person's basic character — whether one is a dog (v. 6) or a false prophet (v. 15), or whether one's life shows fruit (v. 16). Scripture repeatedly exhorts believers to evaluate carefully (see Jn 7:24) and choose between good and bad people and things ("sexually immoral," 1Co 5:9; those who masquerade as angels of light, 2Co 11:14; "dogs," Php 3:2; "false prophets," 1Jn 4:1). The Christian is to "test everything" (1Th 5:21).

7:3 – 5 Jesus rebukes hypocritical judging.

7:3 *speck of sawdust ... plank.* An example of hyperbole in the teachings of Jesus (cf. 19:24). Its purpose is to drive home a point (see Lk 6:41 and note).

7:5 *hypocrite.* See note on 6:2.

7:6 Teaching about the kingdom should be given in accordance with the spiritual capacity of the learners. *dogs.* The unclean dogs of the street were held in low esteem.

7:7 – 11 See note on Lk 11:5 – 13.

7:8 *Asks ... seeks ... knocks.* Greek present imperatives are used here, indicating constant asking, seeking and knocking. Persistent prayer is being emphasized (cf. Jas 4:2 – 3; cf. also Ge 32:26 and note).

7:11 *good gifts.* See Lk 11:13 and note.

7:12 The so-called Golden Rule is found in negative form in

The Narrow and Wide Gates

13"Enter through the narrow gate.[v] For
wide is the gate and broad is the road
that leads to destruction, and many enter
through it. 14But small is the gate and narrow the road that leads to life, and only a
few find it.

A Tree and Its Fruit

15"Watch out for false prophets.[w] They
come to you in sheep's clothing, but inwardly they are ferocious wolves.[x] 16By
their fruit you will recognize them.[y] Do
people pick grapes from thornbushes, or
figs from thistles?[z] 17Likewise every good
tree bears good fruit, but a bad tree bears
bad fruit. 18A good tree cannot bear bad
fruit, and a bad tree cannot bear good
fruit.[a] 19Every tree that does not bear good
fruit is cut down and thrown into the fire.[b]
20Thus, by their fruit you will recognize
them.

21"Not everyone who says to me, 'Lord,
Lord,'[c] will enter the kingdom of heaven,[d]
but only he who does the will of my Father who is in heaven.[e] 22Many will say to
me on that day,[f] 'Lord, Lord, did we not
prophesy in your name, and in your name
drive out demons and perform many miracles?'[g] 23Then I will tell them plainly, 'I
never knew you. Away from me, you evildoers!'[h]

The Wise and Foolish Builders

7:24-27pp — Lk 6:47-49

24"Therefore everyone who hears these
words of mine and puts them into practice[i] is like a wise man who built his
house on the rock. 25The rain came down,
the streams rose, and the winds blew and
beat against that house; yet it did not fall,
because it had its foundation on the rock.
26But everyone who hears these words of
mine and does not put them into practice is like a foolish man who built his
house on sand. 27The rain came down,
the streams rose, and the winds blew and
beat against that house, and it fell with a
great crash."

28When Jesus had finished saying these
things,[j] the crowds were amazed at his
teaching,[k] 29because he taught as one who
had authority, and not as their teachers of
the law.

The Man With Leprosy

8:2-4pp — Mk 1:40-44; Lk 5:12-14

8 When he came down from the mountainside, large crowds followed him. 2A
man with leprosy[a] [l] came and knelt before
him[m] and said, "Lord, if you are willing,
you can make me clean."

3Jesus reached out his hand and touched
the man. "I am willing," he said. "Be
clean!" Immediately he was cured[b] of his
leprosy. 4Then Jesus said to him, "See that
you don't tell anyone.[n] But go, show yourself to the priest[o] and offer the gift Moses
commanded,[p] as a testimony to them."

7:13 [v] Lk 13:24; Jn 10:7,9 **7:15** [w] Jer 23:16; Mt 24:24; Lk 6:26; 2Pe 2:1; 1Jn 4:1; Rev 16:13 [x] Eze 22:27; Ac 20:29 **7:16** [y] Mt 12:33; Lk 6:44 [z] Jas 3:12 **7:18** [a] Lk 6:43 **7:19** [b] S Mt 3:10 **7:21** [c] Hos 8:2; Mt 25:11; S Jn 13:13; 1Co 12:3 [d] S Mt 3:2 [e] Mt 12:50; Ro 2:13; Jas 1:22; 1Jn 3:18 **7:22** [f] S Mt 10:15 [g] Lk 10:20; Ac 19:13; 1Co 13:1-3 **7:23** [h] Ps 6:8; Mt 25:12,41; Lk 13:25-27 **7:24** [i] ver 21; Jas 1:22-25 **7:28** [j] Mt 11:1; 13:53; 19:1; 26:1 [k] Mt 13:54; 22:33; Mk 1:22; 6:2; 11:18; Lk 4:32; Jn 7:46 **8:2** [l] Lev 13:45; Mt 10:8; 11:5; 26:6; Lk 5:12; 17:12 [m] Mt 9:18; 15:25; 18:26; 20:20 **8:4** [n] Mt 9:30; 12:16; Mk 5:43; 7:36; S 8:30; Lk 4:41 [o] Lk 17:14 [p] Lev 14:2-32

[a] 2 The Greek word was used for various diseases affecting the skin — not necessarily leprosy. [b] 3 Greek *made clean*

rabbinic Judaism and also in Hinduism, Buddhism and Confucianism. It occurred in various forms in Greek and Roman ethical teaching. Jesus stated it in positive form. *in everything.* Probably refers to the teaching of the entire Sermon up to this point. *sums up.* Cf. 22:36–40; Ro 13:8–10 and relevant notes. *the Law and the Prophets.* See note on 5:17.

7:13 *narrow gate.* The gate that leads into the kingdom of heaven is synonymous with "life" (v. 14). *destruction.* Separation from God in hell.

7:15 *false prophets.* People who have not been sent by God but who claim that they have been (see 24:24; Jer 23:16 and note).

7:19 See Jn 15:6 and note; cf. Mt 3:10.

7:20 Cf. Jn 15:7 and note.

7:21 *Lord.* Here seems to mean more than merely "sir" or "master" in view of the fact that Jesus is the one who makes the final decision about a person's eternal destiny. See Lk 6:46; Col 2:6; cf. Ro 10:9 and note; 14:9; 1Co 12:3; Php 2:11 and note on 2:10–11. *kingdom of heaven.* See note on 3:2. *does the will of my Father.* The deciding factor as to who enters the kingdom (see Mk 3:35; Ro 10:9–10 and notes).

7:22 *that day.* The day of judgment (cf. Mal 3:17–18). *prophesy.* In the Bible this verb primarily means to give a message from God, not necessarily to predict. *demons.* See note on Mk 1:23.

7:24–27 This parable ends the Sermon on the Mount — and it also ends the so-called Sermon on the Plain ("level place") found in Lk 6:17–49.

7:24 *rock.* The Bible often speaks metaphorically of God or Christ as a "rock" (see Ge 49:24; Ps 18:2; 1Co 10:4 and notes). Jesus' reference here to a rock foundation may involve a subtle allusion to this metaphor.

7:25 *rain came down.* The Holy Land is known for its torrential rains that often cause disastrous floods.

7:28 *were amazed.* A common reaction by Jesus' listeners to his teaching — both its presentation and its authority (see note on Mk 1:22).

7:29 *authority.* The teachers of the law quoted other rabbis to support their own teaching (see note on 2:4), but Jesus spoke with divine authority (see 9:6,8; cf. Jn 7:46).

8:1 *mountainside.* See 5:1 and note.

8:2 *leprosy.* See NIV text note; see also note on Lev 13:2. *Lord.* See note on 7:21. *make me clean.* Leprosy made a person ceremonially unclean (see Lev 13:3,8,11,20) and socially an outcast (see Lev 13:45–46).

8:3 *touched the man.* See note on Mk 1:41.

8:4 *don't tell anyone.* Jesus did not wish to stir up the popular, but mistaken, expectations that a wonder-working Messiah would soon arise as king of the Jews and deliver them from the Roman yoke. For similar instructions see 9:30; 12:16; 16:20; 17:9. In Mark see 1:34,44 and note on 1:34; 3:12; 5:43 and note; 7:36; 8:30; 9:9 and note. In Luke see 4:41; 8:56; 9:21 and note; 24:21 and note. In John see 6:15 and note. *show yourself to the priest.* See note on Lk 5:14. *a testimony to them.* See note on Mk 1:44. *them.* The priests and the people.

The Faith of the Centurion

8:5-13pp — Lk 7:1-10

5 When Jesus had entered Capernaum,
a centurion came to him, asking for help.
6 "Lord," he said, "my servant lies at home
paralyzed[q] and in terrible suffering."
7 Jesus said to him, "I will go and heal
him."
8 The centurion replied, "Lord, I do not
deserve to have you come under my roof.
But just say the word, and my servant will
be healed.[r] 9 For I myself am a man under
authority, with soldiers under me. I tell
this one, 'Go,' and he goes; and that one,
'Come,' and he comes. I say to my servant, 'Do this,' and he does it."
10 When Jesus heard this, he was astonished and said to those following him,
"I tell you the truth, I have not found
anyone in Israel with such great faith.[s]
11 I say to you that many will come from
the east and the west,[t] and will take their
places at the feast with Abraham, Isaac
and Jacob in the kingdom of heaven.[u]
12 But the subjects of the kingdom[v] will be
thrown outside, into the darkness, where
there will be weeping and gnashing of
teeth."[w]
13 Then Jesus said to the centurion,
"Go! It will be done just as you believed
it would."[x] And his servant was healed at
that very hour.

Jesus Heals Many

8:14-16pp — Mk 1:29-34; Lk 4:38-41

14 When Jesus came into Peter's house,
he saw Peter's mother-in-law lying in bed
with a fever. 15 He touched her hand and
the fever left her, and she got up and began to wait on him.
16 When evening came, many who were
demon-possessed were brought to him,
and he drove out the spirits with a word
and healed all the sick.[y] 17 This was to fulfill[z] what was spoken through the prophet
Isaiah:

"He took up our infirmities
and carried our diseases."[a a]

The Cost of Following Jesus

8:19-22pp — Lk 9:57-60

18 When Jesus saw the crowd around
him, he gave orders to cross to the other
side of the lake.[b] 19 Then a teacher of the
law came to him and said, "Teacher, I will
follow you wherever you go."
20 Jesus replied, "Foxes have holes and
birds of the air have nests, but the Son of
Man[c] has no place to lay his head."
21 Another disciple said to him, "Lord,
first let me go and bury my father."
22 But Jesus told him, "Follow me,[d] and
let the dead bury their own dead."

Jesus Calms the Storm

8:23-27pp — Mk 4:36-41; Lk 8:22-25
8:23-27Ref — Mt 14:22-33

23 Then he got into the boat and his disciples followed him. 24 Without warning, a
furious storm came up on the lake, so that
the waves swept over the boat. But Jesus
was sleeping. 25 The disciples went and
woke him, saying, "Lord, save us! We're
going to drown!"
26 He replied, "You of little faith,[e] why
are you so afraid?" Then he got up and
rebuked the winds and the waves, and it
was completely calm.[f]

[a] 17 Isaiah 53:4

8:6 [q] S Mt 4:24
8:8 [r] Ps 107:20
8:10 [s] Mt 15:28
8:11 [t] Ps 107:3; Isa 49:12; 59:19; Mal 1:11 [u] Lk 13:29
8:12 [v] Mt 13:38 [w] Mt 13:42,50; 22:13; 24:51; 25:30; Lk 13:28
8:13 [x] S Mt 9:22
8:16 [y] S Mt 4:23,24
8:17 [z] S Mt 1:22 [a] Isa 53:4
8:18 [b] Mk 4:35
8:20 [c] Da 7:13; Mt 12:8,32,40; 16:13,27,28; 17:9; 19:28; Mk 2:10; 8:31
8:22 [d] S Mt 4:19
8:26 [e] S Mt 6:30 [f] Ps 65:7; 89:9; 107:29

8:5 *Capernaum.* See note on 4:13. *centurion.* A Roman military officer in charge of 100 soldiers. In Luke's account (Lk 7:1–5) Jewish elders and friends of the centurion came to Jesus on his behalf, but Matthew does not mention these intermediaries.
8:8 *I do not deserve to have you come under my roof.* In Greek the words "I do not deserve" are the same as those used by John the Baptist in 3:11 ("I am not fit"). The entire statement reveals how highly the centurion regarded Jesus and also reveals his own sense of unworthiness to ask this Jewish wonder-worker to enter his house and heal his son.
8:10 *he was astonished.* See note on Lk 7:9. In his incarnate state Jesus experienced every human emotion. *such great faith.* See note on Lk 7:9.
8:11 The universality of the gospel is one of Matthew's themes (see Introduction: Recipients). *feast ... in the kingdom of heaven.* The eschatological Messianic banquet that symbolizes the blessings of an intimate relationship with God (see Isa 25:6–9 and note on 25:6).
8:12 *subjects of the kingdom.* Jews who thought their Judaism was an inherited passport for entrance into the kingdom (see 3:9–10 and note on 3:9). *outside, into the darkness.* Hell. *weeping and gnashing of teeth.* A phrase used only in Matthew's Gospel (here; 13:42,50; 22:13; 24:51; 25:30)—though an almost identical phrase occurs in Lk 13:28—to describe the horrible suffering experienced in hell.
8:14 *Peter's mother-in-law.* See notes on Mk 1:30; Lk 4:38.
8:15 *him.* Jesus. Mk 1:31 and Lk 4:39 have "them." She began to serve not only Jesus but also her guests, probably by preparing a meal for them.
8:16 *evening.* See Lk 4:40 and note. *demon-possessed.* See notes on Mk 1:23; Lk 4:33.
8:17 *carried.* Bore the burden of. The diseases were not transferred to Jesus in the sense of making him ill.
8:18 *the other side.* The east side.
8:19 *teacher of the law.* See note on 2:4.
8:20 *Son of Man.* See note on Mk 8:31.
8:21 *bury my father.* See note on Lk 9:59.
8:22 *let the dead bury their own dead.* Let the spiritually dead bury the physically dead. The time of Jesus' ministry was short and demanded full attention and commitment. This statement stresses the radical demands of Jesus' discipleship, since Jews placed great importance on the duty of children to bury their parents.
8:23–27 See note on Mk 4:35–41.
8:24 *furious storm.* See note on Mk 4:37. *But Jesus was sleeping.* See note on Mk 4:38; cf. Jnh 1:4–5.
8:26 *little faith.* See 6:30 and note.

27 The men were amazed and asked,
"What kind of man is this? Even the winds
and the waves obey him!"

The Healing of Two Demon-possessed Men

8:28-34pp — Mk 5:1-17; Lk 8:26-37

28 When he arrived at the other side in
the region of the Gadarenes,[a] two demon-
possessed[g] men coming from the tombs
met him. They were so violent that no
one could pass that way. 29 "What do you
want with us,[h] Son of God?" they shouted.
"Have you come here to torture us before
the appointed time?"[i]
30 Some distance from them a large herd
of pigs was feeding. 31 The demons begged
Jesus, "If you drive us out, send us into
the herd of pigs."
32 He said to them, "Go!" So they came
out and went into the pigs, and the whole
herd rushed down the steep bank into the
lake and died in the water. 33 Those tending the pigs ran off, went into the town
and reported all this, including what had
happened to the demon-possessed men.
34 Then the whole town went out to meet
Jesus. And when they saw him, they
pleaded with him to leave their region.[j]

Jesus Heals a Paralytic

9:2-8pp — Mk 2:3-12; Lk 5:18-26

9 Jesus stepped into a boat, crossed over
and came to his own town.[k] 2 Some
men brought to him a paralytic,[l] lying on a
mat. When Jesus saw their faith,[m] he said
to the paralytic, "Take heart,[n] son; your
sins are forgiven."[o]
3 At this, some of the teachers of the law
said to themselves, "This fellow is blaspheming!"[p]
4 Knowing their thoughts,[q] Jesus said,
"Why do you entertain evil thoughts in
your hearts? 5 Which is easier: to say, 'Your
sins are forgiven,' or to say, 'Get up and
walk'? 6 But so that you may know that the
Son of Man[r] has authority on earth to forgive sins . . . ." Then he said to the paralytic, "Get up, take your mat and go home."
7 And the man got up and went home.
8 When the crowd saw this, they were filled
with awe; and they praised God,[s] who had
given such authority to men.

The Calling of Matthew

9:9-13pp — Mk 2:14-17; Lk 5:27-32

9 As Jesus went on from there, he saw a
man named Matthew sitting at the tax collector's booth. "Follow me,"[t] he told him,
and Matthew got up and followed him.
10 While Jesus was having dinner at Matthew's house, many tax collectors and "sinners" came and ate with him and his disciples. 11 When the Pharisees saw this, they
asked his disciples, "Why does your teacher eat with tax collectors and 'sinners'?"[u]
12 On hearing this, Jesus said, "It is not
the healthy who need a doctor, but the
sick. 13 But go and learn what this means: 'I
desire mercy, not sacrifice.'[b][v] For I have not
come to call the righteous, but sinners."[w]

Jesus Questioned About Fasting

9:14-17pp — Mk 2:18-22; Lk 5:33-39

14 Then John's[x] disciples came and asked
him, "How is it that we and the Pharisees
fast,[y] but your disciples do not fast?"
15 Jesus answered, "How can the guests
of the bridegroom mourn while he is with
them?[z] The time will come when the
bridegroom will be taken from them; then
they will fast.[a]
16 "No one sews a patch of unshrunk
cloth on an old garment, for the patch will

8:28 [g] S Mt 4:24 **8:29** [h] Jdg 11:12; 2Sa 16:10; 1Ki 17:18; Mk 1:24; Lk 4:34; Jn 2:4 [i] 2Pe 2:4 **8:34** [j] Lk 5:8; Ac 16:39 **9:1** [k] Mt 4:13 **9:2** [l] S Mt 4:24 [m] S ver 22 [n] Jn 16:33 [o] Lk 7:48 **9:3** [p] Mt 26:65; Jn 10:33 **9:4** [q] Ps 94:11; Mt 12:25; Lk 6:8; 9:47; 11:17; Jn 2:25 **9:6** [r] S Mt 8:20 **9:8** [s] Mt 5:16; 15:31; Lk 7:16; 13:13; 17:15; 23:47; Jn 15:8; Ac 4:21; 11:18; 21:20 **9:9** [t] S Mt 4:19 **9:11** [u] Mt 11:19; Lk 5:30; 15:2; 19:7; Gal 2:15 **9:13** [v] Hos 6:6; Mic 6:6-8; Mt 12:7 [w] Lk 19:10; 1Ti 1:15 **9:14** [x] S Mt 3:1 [y] Mt 11:18, 19; Lk 18:12 **9:15** [z] Jn 3:29 [a] Ac 13:2, 3; 14:23

[a] 28 Some manuscripts *Gergesenes*; others *Gerasenes*
[b] 13 Hosea 6:6

8:27 *What kind of man is this?* See note on Mk 4:41.
8:28 *region of the Gadarenes.* The region around the city of Gadara, six miles southeast of the Sea of Galilee. Mark and Luke identify the region by the capital city Gerasa, located about 35 miles southeast of the Sea (see note on Lk 8:26). *two.* Mk 5:2 and Lk 8:27 (see note there) mention only one Gadarene demoniac. *demon-possessed.* See note on v. 16.
8:29 *Son of God.* See note on Lk 8:28. *appointed time.* The time of their judgment (see notes on Mk 5:10; Lk 8:31).
8:30 *herd of pigs.* Large numbers of Gentiles lived in the territory of the Decapolis (see map, p. 1530). Normally Jews did not raise pigs, since they were considered the most ceremonially unclean of all animals.
8:32 Though Jesus seemingly consented to the demons' request, the pigs carried the demons into the depths of the sea—perhaps symbolic of the Abyss (see Lk 8:31 and note).
8:34 *pleaded with him to leave.* They were probably more concerned about their financial loss than about the deliverance of the miserable demon-possessed man (see note on Mk 5:17).
9:1 *crossed over.* The northern end of the Sea of Galilee. *his own town.* Capernaum (see note on 4:13).
9:2 *their faith.* The faith of the men who carried him as well as the faith of the paralyzed man. *your sins are forgiven.* See note on Mk 2:5. In this case, perhaps there was a relationship between the man's sin and his paralysis (cf. Jn 9:1–3). Very likely Jesus is evoking Ps 103:3.
9:3 *blaspheming.* Here the term includes usurping God's prerogative to forgive sins (see notes on Mk 2:7; Lk 5:21).
9:5–6 See notes on Mk 2:9–10; 14:64.
9:6 *Son of Man.* See note on Mk 8:31.
9:9 *Matthew.* Mark and Luke call this disciple Levi in the parallel accounts (but see also Mk 3:18; Lk 6:15; Ac 1:13). *tax collector's booth.* See note on Mk 2:14. *got up and followed him.* See note on Lk 5:28.
9:10 *tax collectors.* See notes on 5:46; Mk 2:16. *"sinners."* See note on Mk 2:15.
9:11 *Pharisees.* See note on Mk 2:16.
9:12 *not the healthy who need a doctor, but the sick.* See note on Lk 5:31.
9:13 *I have not come to call the righteous, but sinners.* See note on Mk 2:17.
9:14 See notes on Mk 2:18; Lk 5:33.
9:15 See notes on Mk 2:19–20.

pull away from the garment, making the
tear worse. 17 Neither do men pour new
wine into old wineskins. If they do, the
skins will burst, the wine will run out and
the wineskins will be ruined. No, they
pour new wine into new wineskins, and
both are preserved."

A Dead Girl and a Sick Woman

9:18-26pp — Mk 5:22-43; Lk 8:41-56

18 While he was saying this, a ruler
came and knelt before him[b] and said,
"My daughter has just died. But come and
put your hand on her,[c] and she will live."
19 Jesus got up and went with him, and so
did his disciples.
20 Just then a woman who had been
subject to bleeding for twelve years came
up behind him and touched the edge of
his cloak.[d] 21 She said to herself, "If I only
touch his cloak, I will be healed."
22 Jesus turned and saw her. "Take
heart,[e] daughter," he said, "your faith has
healed you."[f] And the woman was healed
from that moment.[g]
23 When Jesus entered the ruler's house
and saw the flute players and the noisy
crowd,[h] 24 he said, "Go away. The girl is
not dead[i] but asleep."[j] But they laughed
at him. 25 After the crowd had been put
outside, he went in and took the girl by
the hand, and she got up.[k] 26 News of this
spread through all that region.[l]

Jesus Heals the Blind and Mute

27 As Jesus went on from there, two blind
men followed him, calling out, "Have mercy on us, Son of David!"[m]
28 When he had gone indoors, the blind
men came to him, and he asked them, "Do
you believe that I am able to do this?"
"Yes, Lord," they replied.[n]
29 Then he touched their eyes and said,
"According to your faith will it be done
to you";[o] 30 and their sight was restored.
Jesus warned them sternly, "See that no
one knows about this."[p] 31 But they went
out and spread the news about him all
over that region.[q]
32 While they were going out, a man who
was demon-possessed[r] and could not talk[s]
was brought to Jesus. 33 And when the demon was driven out, the man who had
been mute spoke. The crowd was amazed
and said, "Nothing like this has ever been
seen in Israel."[t]
34 But the Pharisees said, "It is by the
prince of demons that he drives out demons."[u]

The Workers Are Few

35 Jesus went through all the towns and
villages, teaching in their synagogues,
preaching the good news of the kingdom
and healing every disease and sickness.[v]
36 When he saw the crowds, he had compassion on them,[w] because they were harassed and helpless, like sheep without a
shepherd.[x] 37 Then he said to his disciples,
"The harvest[y] is plentiful but the workers
are few.[z] 38 Ask the Lord of the harvest,
therefore, to send out workers into his harvest field."

Jesus Sends Out the Twelve

10:2-4pp — Mk 3:16-19; Lk 6:14-16; Ac 1:13
10:9-15pp — Mk 6:8-11; Lk 9:3-5; 10:4-12
10:19-22pp — Mk 13:11-13; Lk 21:12-17
10:26-33pp — Lk 12:2-9
10:34,35pp — Lk 12:51-53

10 He called his twelve disciples to him
and gave them authority to drive out
evil[a] spirits[a] and to heal every disease and
sickness.[b]

[a] 1 Greek *unclean*

9:18 [b] S Mt 8:2 [c] S Mk 5:23 **9:20** [d] Mt 14:36; Mk 3:10; 6:56; Lk 6:19 **9:22** [e] ver 2; Jn 16:33 [f] ver 29; Mt 8:13; Mk 10:52; Lk 7:50; 17:19; 18:42 [g] Mt 15:28 **9:23** [h] 2Ch 35:25; Jer 9:17,18 **9:24** [i] Ac 20:10 [j] Da 12:2; Ps 76:5; Jn 11:11-14; Ac 7:60; 13:36; 1Co 11:30; 15:6,18,20; 1Th 4:13-16 **9:25** [k] S Lk 7:14 **9:26** [l] ver 31; Mt 4:24; 14:1; Mk 1:28,45; Lk 4:14,37; 5:15; 7:17 **9:27** [m] S Mt 1:1; 12:23; 15:22; 20:30,31; 21:9,15; 22:42; Mk 10:47 **9:28** [n] Ac 14:9

9:29 [o] S ver 22 **9:30** [p] S Mt 8:4 **9:31** [q] S ver 26; Mk 7:36 **9:32** [r] S Mt 4:24 [s] Mt 12:22-24 **9:33** [t] Mk 2:12 **9:34** [u] Mt 12:24 **9:35** [v] S Mt 4:23 **9:36** [w] Mt 14:14; 15:32; Mk 8:2 [x] Nu 27:17; 1Ki 22:17; Eze 34:5,6; Zec 10:2 **9:37** [y] Jn 4:35 [z] Lk 10:2 **10:1** [a] Mk 3:13-15; 6:7; Lk 4:36; 9:1 [b] S Mt 4:23

9:17 *new wineskins.* In ancient times goatskins were used to hold wine. As the fresh grape juice fermented, the wine would expand, and the new wineskin would stretch. But a used skin, already stretched, would break (see note on Job 32:19). Jesus brings a newness that cannot be confined within the old forms.

9:18 *ruler.* From Mark and Luke we know that he was a synagogue ruler named Jairus (see notes on Mk 5:22; Lk 8:41). *has just died.* Mk 5:23 has "is dying," but Matthew omits reference to the later messengers (Mk 5:35) and condenses (see notes on 21:12–17; 21:18–22) by presenting at the outset what was actually true before Jesus reached the house.

9:20 *subject to bleeding for twelve years.* See notes on Mk 5:25; Lk 8:43.

9:21 See notes on Mk 5:28; Lk 8:45.

9:22 *daughter.* See note on Lk 8:48. *healed.* See note on Mk 5:34.

9:23 *flute players.* Musicians hired to play in mourning ceremonies. *noisy crowd.* Mourners hired to wail and lament (see note on Mk 5:38).

9:24 *not dead but asleep.* See note on Lk 8:52.

9:25 *took the girl by the hand.* Touching a dead body ordinarily resulted in ceremonial uncleanness (see Lev 11:31; 21:1 and note,11; 22:4; Nu 19:14 and note), but Jesus' action brought life, not defilement.

9:27 *blind men.* Isaiah predicted the healing of the blind in the Messianic age (Isa 35:5). *Son of David.* A popular Jewish title for the coming Messiah (e.g., 12:23; 20:30; 21:9; 22:41–45; see note on 1:1).

9:29 *According to your faith.* That is, "Because you have faith," not "In proportion to your faith." Jesus did not provide healing according to the amount of faith the blind men had (see 17:20 and note). Cf. 8:13; Mk 9:23 and note; 11:23; Jn 11:40.

9:30 See notes on 8:4; 16:20.

9:32 *could not talk.* Isaiah also (see note on v. 27) predicted that the mute would talk in the Messianic age (Isa 35:6).

9:33 *amazed.* See 8:27; 13:54; 15:31; 21:20; 22:22; cf. Mk 1:22 and note.

9:34 *prince of demons.* See note on 10:25.

9:35 *synagogues.* See note on Mk 1:21. *good news.* See note on Mk 1:1.

9:36 *compassion.* Jesus' compassion for people is often noted in the Gospels (see 14:14; 15:22; 20:34; Mk 1:41; 6:34; 8:2). *like sheep without a shepherd.* See Eze 34:5; Zec 10:2; 13:7 and notes; Mk 6:34.

2These are the names of the twelve
apostles: first, Simon (who is called Peter) and his brother Andrew; James son
of Zebedee, and his brother John; 3Philip
and Bartholomew; Thomas and Matthew
the tax collector; James son of Alphaeus,
and Thaddaeus; 4Simon the Zealot and
Judas Iscariot, who betrayed him.[c]
5These twelve Jesus sent out with the
following instructions: "Do not go among
the Gentiles or enter any town of the Samaritans.[d] 6Go rather to the lost sheep of
Israel.[e] 7As you go, preach this message:
'The kingdom of heaven[f] is near.' 8Heal
the sick, raise the dead, cleanse those
who have leprosy,[a] drive out demons.
Freely you have received, freely give. 9Do
not take along any gold or silver or copper
in your belts;[g] 10take no bag for the journey, or extra tunic, or sandals or a staff;
for the worker is worth his keep.[h]
11"Whatever town or village you enter,
search for some worthy person there and
stay at his house until you leave. 12As
you enter the home, give it your greeting.[i] 13If the home is deserving, let your
peace rest on it; if it is not, let your peace
return to you. 14If anyone will not welcome you or listen to your words, shake
the dust off your feet[j] when you leave
that home or town. 15I tell you the truth,
it will be more bearable for Sodom and
Gomorrah[k] on the day of judgment[l] than
for that town.[m] 16I am sending you out
like sheep among wolves.[n] Therefore be
as shrewd as snakes and as innocent as
doves.[o]
17"Be on your guard against men; they
will hand you over to the local councils[p]
and flog you in their synagogues.[q] 18On
my account you will be brought before
governors and kings[r] as witnesses to them
and to the Gentiles. 19But when they arrest you, do not worry about what to say
or how to say it.[s] At that time you will be
given what to say, 20for it will not be you
speaking, but the Spirit of your Father[t]
speaking through you.
21"Brother will betray brother to death,
and a father his child; children will rebel
against their parents[u] and have them put
to death.[v] 22All men will hate you because
of me,[w] but he who stands firm to the end
will be saved.[x] 23When you are persecuted
in one place, flee to another. I tell you the
truth, you will not finish going through
the cities of Israel before the Son of Man
comes.[y]
24"A student is not above his teacher, nor a servant above his master.[z] 25It
is enough for the student to be like his
teacher, and the servant like his master. If
the head of the house has been called Beelzebub,[b][a] how much more the members
of his household!

[a] *8* The Greek word was used for various diseases affecting the skin—not necessarily leprosy.
[b] *25* Greek *Beezeboul* or *Beelzeboul*

10:4 [c]Mt 26:14-16,25,47; 27:3; Mk 14:10; Jn 6:71; 12:4; 13:2,26,27; Ac 1:16 **10:5** [d]1Ki 16:24; 2Ki 17:24; Lk 9:52; 10:33; 17:16; Jn 4:4-26,39,40; 8:48; Ac 8:5,25 **10:6** [e]Jer 50:6; Mt 15:24 **10:7** [f]S Mt 3:2 **10:9** [g]Lk 22:35 **10:10** [h]S 1Ti 5:18 **10:12** [i]1Sa 25:6 **10:14** [j]Ne 5:13; Mk 6:11; Lk 9:5; 10:11; Ac 13:51; 18:6 **10:15** [k]Ge 18:20; 19:24; 2Pe 2:6; Jude 7 [l]Mt 12:36; Ac 17:31; 2Pe 2:9; 3:7; 1Jn 4:17; Jude 6 [m]Mt 11:22,24 **10:16** [n]Lk 10:3; Ac 20:29 [o]S 1Co 14:20 **10:17** [p]S Mt 5:22 [q]Mt 23:34; Mk 13:9; Ac 5:40; 22:19; 26:11 **10:18** [r]Ac 25:24-26 **10:19** [s]Ex 4:12 **10:20** [t]Lk 12:11,12; Ac 4:8 **10:21** [u]ver 35,36; Mic 7:6 [v]Mk 13:12 **10:22** [w]S Jn 15:21 [x]Mt 24:13; Mk 13:13; Lk 21:19; Rev 2:10 **10:23** [y]S Lk 17:30 **10:24** [z]S Jn 13:16 **10:25** [a]S Mk 3:22

10:2–4 See notes on Lk 6:14–16.
10:2 *apostles.* The only occurrence of this word in Matthew's Gospel. See note on Mk 6:30.
10:3 *Thaddaeus.* Also called Judas (not Iscariot [Jn 14:22]); see Mk 3:18; Lk 6:16; Ac 1:13 and note.
10:4 *the Zealot.* Either a description of Simon's religious zeal or a reference to his membership in the party of the Zealots, a Jewish revolutionary group violently opposed to Roman rule over the Holy Land.
10:5 *Do not go.* The good news about the kingdom was to be proclaimed first to Jews only. After his death and resurrection, Jesus commanded the message to be taken to all nations (28:19; cf. 21:43). *Samaritans.* A mixed-blood race resulting from the intermarriage of Israelites left behind when the people of the northern kingdom were exiled and Gentiles brought into the land by the Assyrians (2Ki 17:24). Bitter hostility existed between Jews and Samaritans in Jesus' day (see Jn 4:9 and note).
10:7 *kingdom of heaven.* See note on 3:2.
10:8 *leprosy.* See NIV text note and note on Lev 13:2.
10:9–10 See notes on Mk 6:8–9.
10:10 *the worker is worth his keep.* Cf. 1Co 9:4–14; 1Ti 5:17–18 and note on 5:18.
10:11 *stay at his house.* See note on Lk 9:4.
10:12 *your greeting.* The Jews' greeting was *shalom,* "peace" (see Lk 10:5).
10:13 *If the home is deserving.* That is, "If a man of peace is there" (Lk 10:6). *let your peace return to you.* Either (1) retract your blessing, or (2) leave the house.
10:14 *shake the dust off your feet.* A symbolic act practiced by the Pharisees when they left a ceremonially unclean Gentile area. Here it represented an act of solemn warning to those who rejected God's message (see notes on Lk 9:5; Ac 13:51; cf. Ac 18:6).
10:15 *I tell you the truth.* See note on Mk 3:28. *Sodom and Gomorrah.* See Ge 19:23–29; Lk 10:12 and note.
10:16 Cf. 7:15; cf. also Paul's statement in Ro 16:19: "I want you to be wise about what is good, and innocent about what is evil."
10:17 *local councils.* The lower courts, connected with local synagogues, that tried less serious cases and flogged those found guilty. *synagogues.* See notes on Mk 1:21; Lk 21:12.
10:18 Anticipates the mission to the Gentiles. Matthew's Gospel emphasizes the universality of the gospel (see note on 8:11; see also Introduction: Recipients).
10:19 *do not worry about what to say.* Namely, to defend yourselves (Lk 21:14–15). *you will be given what to say.* "Words and wisdom" that cannot be resisted (Lk 21:15; see note there).
10:20 *the Spirit of your Father speaking.* See Mk 13:11; Lk 12:11–12; cf. Lk 21:14–15.
10:21 The allusion is to Mic 7:6, which is quoted in vv. 35–36.
10:22 *All.* Hyperbole. *he who stands firm to the end will be saved.* See note on Mk 13:13.
10:23 Some take Jesus' saying here as a reference to his second coming at the end of the age (see 24:30), but it is hard to reconcile this with the failure of the disciples to "finish going through" (evangelize) the cities of Israel before this happens. It is therefore probably best understood as referring to his coming in judgment on the Jews when Jerusalem and the temple were destroyed in A.D. 70.
10:25 *Beelzebub.* The prince of demons (12:24); the Greek form of the Hebrew name Baal-Zebub ("lord of the flies"),

26“So do not be afraid of them. There is nothing concealed that will not be disclosed, or hidden that will not be made known.[b] 27What I tell you in the dark, speak in the daylight; what is whispered in your ear, proclaim from the roofs. 28Do not be afraid of those who kill the body but cannot kill the soul. Rather, be afraid of the One[c] who can destroy both soul and body in hell. 29Are not two sparrows sold for a penny[a]? Yet not one of them will fall to the ground apart from the will of your Father. 30And even the very hairs of your head are all numbered.[d] 31So don’t be afraid; you are worth more than many sparrows.[e]

32“Whoever acknowledges me before men,[f] I will also acknowledge him before my Father in heaven. 33But whoever disowns me before men, I will disown him before my Father in heaven.[g]

34“Do not suppose that I have come to bring peace to the earth. I did not come to bring peace, but a sword. 35For I have come to turn

“ ‘a man against his father,
a daughter against her mother,
a daughter-in-law against her mother-in-law[h]—
36 a man’s enemies will be the members of his own household.’[b][i]

37“Anyone who loves his father or mother more than me is not worthy of me; anyone who loves his son or daughter more than me is not worthy of me;[j] 38and anyone who does not take his cross and follow me is not worthy of me.[k] 39Whoever finds his life will lose it, and whoever loses his life for my sake will find it.[l]

40“He who receives you receives me,[m] and he who receives me receives the one who sent me.[n] 41Anyone who receives a prophet because he is a prophet will receive a prophet’s reward, and anyone who receives a righteous man because he is a righteous man will receive a righteous man’s reward. 42And if anyone gives even a cup of cold water to one of these little ones because he is my disciple, I tell you the truth, he will certainly not lose his reward.”[o]

Jesus and John the Baptist

11:2-19pp — Lk 7:18-35

11 After Jesus had finished instructing his twelve disciples,[p] he went on from there to teach and preach in the towns of Galilee.[c]

2When John[q] heard in prison[r] what Christ was doing, he sent his disciples 3to ask him, “Are you the one who was to come,[s] or should we expect someone else?”

4Jesus replied, “Go back and report to John what you hear and see: 5The blind receive sight, the lame walk, those who have leprosy[d] are cured, the deaf hear, the dead are raised, and the good news is preached to the poor.[t] 6Blessed is the man who does not fall away on account of me.”[u]

7As John’s[v] disciples were leaving, Jesus began to speak to the crowd about John: “What did you go out into the desert[w] to see? A reed swayed by the wind? 8If not,

10:26 [b]Mk 4:22; Lk 8:17 **10:28** [c]Isa 8:12, 13; Heb 10:31 **10:30** [d]1Sa 14:45; 2Sa 14:11; 1Ki 1:52; Lk 21:18; Ac 27:34 **10:31** [e]Mt 6:26; 12:12 **10:32** [f]Ro 10:9 **10:33** [g]Mk 8:38; 2Ti 2:12 **10:35** [h]ver 21 **10:36** [i]Mic 7:6 **10:37** [j]Lk 14:26 **10:38** [k]Mt 16:24; Lk 14:27 **10:39** [l]S Jn 12:25 **10:40** [m]Ex 16:8; Mt 18:5; Gal 4:14 [n]Lk 9:48; 10:16; Jn 12:44; 13:20 **10:42** [o]Pr 14:31; 19:17; Mt 25:40; Mk 9:41; Ac 10:4; Heb 6:10 **11:1** [p]S Mt 7:28 **11:2** [q]S Mt 3:1 [r]Mt 14:3 **11:3** [s]Ps 118:26; Jn 11:27; Heb 10:37 **11:5** [t]Isa 35:4-6; 61:1; Mt 15:31; Lk 4:18, 19 **11:6** [u]Mt 13:21; 26:31 **11:7** [v]S Mt 3:1 [w]Mt 3:1

[a] 29 Greek *an assarion* [b] 36 Micah 7:6 [c] 1 Greek *in their towns* [d] 5 The Greek word was used for various diseases affecting the skin—not necessarily leprosy.

which is a parody on and mockery of the actual epithet, Baal-Zebul (“Exalted Baal” or “Baal the Prince”; see NIV text note here and note on Jdg 10:6). The name came to be used of Satan.

10:26–33 See Lk 12:2–9 and notes.

10:26 *them.* The persecutors (vv. 21–25).

10:28 *cannot kill the soul.* See Lk 12:4 and note. *soul.* The true self (see note on Ps 6:3). Body and soul are closely related in this life but are separated at death and then reunited at the resurrection (cf. 2Co 5:1–10 and notes; Php 1:23–24). *the One.* God. He alone determines the final destiny of us all. *destroy both soul and body in hell.* See Lk 12:5 and note. *hell.* See note on 5:22.

10:29 *two sparrows sold for a penny.* Cf. Lk 12:6 and note.

10:31 *worth more than many sparrows.* See 6:26.

10:32–33 See Lk 12:8–9 and notes.

10:34 At first glance this saying sounds like a contradiction of Isa 9:6 (“Prince of Peace”), Lk 2:14 (“on earth peace to men”) and Jn 14:27 (“Peace I leave with you”). It is true that Christ came to bring peace—peace between the believer and God, and peace among humans. Yet the inevitable result of Christ’s coming is conflict—between Christ and the antichrist, between light and darkness, between Christ’s children and the devil’s children. This conflict can occur even between members of the same family (vv. 35–36; Mk 10:29–30).

10:37 See Lk 14:26 and note.

10:38 *take his cross.* The first mention of the cross in Matthew’s Gospel. The cross was an instrument of death and here symbolizes the necessity of total commitment—even to the point of death—on the part of Jesus’ disciples (see note on Mk 8:34).

10:39 See note on Lk 9:24.

10:40–42 During times of persecution, hospitality was especially important and could be dangerous. So Jesus indicates that those who provide it and show kindness to God’s people will receive a reward.

10:42 *cup of cold water.* See note on Mk 9:41.

11:1 While the 12 apostles were carrying out their first mission, Jesus continued his ministry in Galilee. *Galilee.* See note on 2:2.

11:2 *John.* The Baptist (see note on 3:1). *in prison.* See note on Lk 7:19.

11:3 *the one who was to come.* The Messiah. *expect someone else.* See note on Lk 7:19.

11:4 *report to John what you hear and see.* See note on Lk 7:22.

11:5 *leprosy.* See NIV text note; see also note on Lev 13:2. *the good news is preached to the poor.* See note on Lk 7:22.

11:6 *man who does not fall away.* See note on Lk 7:23.

11:7–10 See Lk 7:24–28 and notes.

what did you go out to see? A man dressed
in fine clothes? No, those who wear fine
clothes are in kings' palaces. 9 Then what
did you go out to see? A prophet?[x] Yes, I
tell you, and more than a prophet. 10 This is
the one about whom it is written:

"'I will send my messenger ahead of
you,[y]
who will prepare your way before
you.'[a z]

11 I tell you the truth: Among those born of
women there has not risen anyone greater
than John the Baptist; yet he who is least
in the kingdom of heaven is greater than
he. 12 From the days of John the Baptist until now, the kingdom of heaven has been
forcefully advancing, and forceful men lay
hold of it. 13 For all the Prophets and the
Law prophesied until John.[a] 14 And if you
are willing to accept it, he is the Elijah
who was to come.[b] 15 He who has ears, let
him hear.[c]

16 "To what can I compare this generation? They are like children sitting in the
marketplaces and calling out to others:

17 "'We played the flute for you,
and you did not dance;
we sang a dirge,
and you did not mourn.'

18 For John came neither eating[d] nor drinking,[e] and they say, 'He has a demon.' 19 The
Son of Man came eating and drinking, and
they say, 'Here is a glutton and a drunkard, a friend of tax collectors and "sinners." '[f] But wisdom is proved right by
her actions."

Woe on Unrepentant Cities

11:21-23pp — Lk 10:13-15

20 Then Jesus began to denounce the cities in which most of his miracles had been
performed, because they did not repent.
21 "Woe to you, Korazin! Woe to you, Bethsaida![g] If the miracles that were performed
in you had been performed in Tyre and Sidon,[h] they would have repented long ago
in sackcloth and ashes.[i] 22 But I tell you,
it will be more bearable for Tyre and Sidon on the day of judgment than for you.[j]
23 And you, Capernaum,[k] will you be lifted
up to the skies? No, you will go down to
the depths.[b l] If the miracles that were performed in you had been performed in Sodom, it would have remained to this day.
24 But I tell you that it will be more bearable for Sodom on the day of judgment
than for you."[m]

Rest for the Weary

11:25-27pp — Lk 10:21,22

25 At that time Jesus said, "I praise you,
Father,[n] Lord of heaven and earth, because
you have hidden these things from the
wise and learned, and revealed them to
little children.[o] 26 Yes, Father, for this was
your good pleasure.

11:9 [x] Mt 14:5; 21:26; Lk 1:76; 7:26 **11:10** [y] Jn 3:28 [z] Mal 3:1; Mk 1:2; Lk 7:27 **11:13** [a] Lk 16:16 **11:14** [b] Mal 4:5; Mt 17:10-13; Mk 9:11-13; Lk 1:17; Jn 1:21 **11:15** [c] Mt 13:9,43; Mk 4:23; Lk 14:35; S Rev 2:7 **11:18** [d] Mt 3:4 [e] S Lk 1:15 **11:19** [f] S Mt 9:11 **11:21** [g] Mk 6:45; 8:22; Lk 9:10; Jn 1:44; 12:21 [h] Joel 3:4; Am 1:9; Mt 15:21; Mk 3:8; Lk 6:17; Ac 12:20 [i] Jnh 3:5-9 **11:22** [j] ver 24; Mt 10:15 **11:23** [k] S Mt 4:13 [l] Isa 14:13-15 **11:24** [m] S Mt 10:15 **11:25** [n] Mt 16:17; Lk 22:42; 23:34; Jn 11:41; 12:27,28 [o] S Mt 13:11; 1Co 1:26-29

[a] *10* Mal. 3:1 [b] *23* Greek *Hades*

11:10 See Mal 3:1 and note.
11:11 *greater than he.* John belonged to the age of the old covenant, which was preparatory to Christ. The least NT believer has a higher privilege in Christ as a part of his bride (the church, Eph 5:25–27,32) than John the Baptist, who was only a friend of the bridegroom (Jn 3:29). Another view, however, stresses the expression "he who is least," holding that the key to its meaning is found in 18:4—"whoever humbles himself like this child." Such a person, though "least," is regarded by God as even greater than John the Baptist.
11:12 *From the days of John the Baptist.* From the beginning of Jesus' ministry. *kingdom of heaven.* See note on 3:2. *forcefully advancing.* The Greek here can be taken in either an active (NIV) or a passive sense. In this context its passive meaning would be "suffering violent attacks." The term "forceful men," then, would be understood in a negative sense, "violent people." The verse would then emphasize the ongoing persecution of the people of the kingdom.
11:13 *Prophets and the Law.* The entire OT (see 5:17 and note) prophesied the coming of the kingdom. John represented the end of the old covenant era.
11:14 *he is the Elijah who was to come.* A reference to Mal 4:5, which prophesied the reappearance of Elijah before the day of the Lord. Some of the people remembered the prophecy and asked John the Baptist, "Are you Elijah?" He answered, "I am not" (Jn 1:21). John was not literally the reincarnation of Elijah, but he did fulfill the function and role of the prophet (see Mt 17:10–13 and note on Lk 1:17).
11:16 *like children sitting in the marketplaces.* See note on Lk 7:32.
11:17 *played the flute.* As at a wedding. *sang a dirge.* As at a funeral. The latter symbolized the ministry of John, the former that of Jesus. The people of Jesus' "generation" (v. 16) were like children who refused to respond on either occasion.
11:19 *Son of Man.* See note on Mk 8:31. *friend of tax collectors and "sinners."* See note on Lk 7:34. *wisdom is proved right by her actions.* Apparently means that God (wisdom) had sent both John and Jesus in specific roles, and that this would be vindicated by the lasting works of both Jesus and John (see note on Lk 7:35).
11:20 *repent.* See note on 3:2.
11:21 *Korazin.* Mentioned in the Bible only twice (here and in Lk 10:13), it was near the Sea of Galilee, probably about two miles north of Capernaum. *Bethsaida.* On the northeast shore of the Sea of Galilee. Philip the tetrarch rebuilt Bethsaida and named it Julias, after Julia, daughter of Caesar Augustus. *Tyre and Sidon.* Cities on the Phoenician coast north of the Holy Land (see note on Mk 7:31). *sackcloth.* Here a sign of repentance (see note on Ge 37:34). Cf. Rev 6:12. *ashes.* Also a sign of repentance.
11:23 *Capernaum.* See note on Lk 10:15. *Sodom.* See notes on 10:15; Ge 13:10; Lk 10:12.
11:25 *Lord of heaven and earth.* A title for God emphasizing his sovereignty and found only three times in the Bible (here; Lk 10:21; Ac 17:24). *these things.* Either the significance of Jesus' miracles (see vv. 20–24) or of his entire mission. *wise.* According to the standards of this age (see 1Co 1:26–29; cf. 1Co 3:18 and note). *little children.* The disciples or, more generally, the humble followers of Jesus.
11:26 *your good pleasure.* Since God is "Lord of heaven and earth" (v. 25), he sovereignly reveals and conceals.

27“All things have been committed to
me[p] by my Father.[q] No one knows the Son
except the Father, and no one knows the
Father except the Son and those to whom
the Son chooses to reveal him.[r]
28“Come to me,[s] all you who are weary
and burdened, and I will give you rest.[t]
29Take my yoke upon you and learn from
me,[u] for I am gentle and humble in heart,
and you will find rest for your souls.[v]
30For my yoke is easy and my burden is
light.”[w]

Lord of the Sabbath

12:1-8pp — Mk 2:23-28; Lk 6:1-5
12:9-14pp — Mk 3:1-6; Lk 6:6-11

12 At that time Jesus went through
the grainfields on the Sabbath. His
disciples were hungry and began to pick
some heads of grain[x] and eat them. 2When
the Pharisees saw this, they said to him,
“Look! Your disciples are doing what is
unlawful on the Sabbath.”[y]
3He answered, “Haven’t you read what
David did when he and his companions
were hungry?[z] 4He entered the house of
God, and he and his companions ate the
consecrated bread—which was not lawful
for them to do, but only for the priests.[a]
5Or haven’t you read in the Law that on
the Sabbath the priests in the temple desecrate the day[b] and yet are innocent? 6I
tell you that one[a] greater than the temple is here.[c] 7If you had known what these
words mean, ‘I desire mercy, not sacrifice,’[b][d] you would not have condemned
the innocent. 8For the Son of Man[e] is Lord
of the Sabbath.”
9Going on from that place, he went into
their synagogue, 10and a man with a shriveled hand was there. Looking for a reason
to accuse Jesus,[f] they asked him, “Is it
lawful to heal on the Sabbath?”[g]
11He said to them, “If any of you has a
sheep and it falls into a pit on the Sabbath,
will you not take hold of it and lift it out?[h]
12How much more valuable is a man than
a sheep![i] Therefore it is lawful to do good
on the Sabbath.”
13Then he said to the man, “Stretch out
your hand.” So he stretched it out and it
was completely restored, just as sound as
the other. 14But the Pharisees went out and
plotted how they might kill Jesus.[j]

God’s Chosen Servant

15Aware of this, Jesus withdrew from
that place. Many followed him, and he
healed all their sick,[k] 16warning them not
to tell who he was.[l] 17This was to fulfill[m]
what was spoken through the prophet Isaiah:

18“Here is my servant whom I have
chosen,
the one I love, in whom I delight;[n]
I will put my Spirit on him,[o]
and he will proclaim justice to the
nations.
19He will not quarrel or cry out;
no one will hear his voice in the
streets.
20A bruised reed he will not break,
and a smoldering wick he will not
snuff out,
till he leads justice to victory.
21 In his name the nations will put
their hope.”[c][p]

11:27 [p]S Mt 28:18 [q]S Jn 3:35 [r]Jn 10:15; 17:25,26 **11:28** [s]Jn 7:37 [t]Ex 33:14 **11:29** [u]Jn 13:15; Php 2:5; 1Pe 2:21; 1Jn 2:6 [v]Ps 116:7; Jer 6:16 **11:30** [w]1Jn 5:3 **12:1** [x]Dt 23:25 **12:2** [y]ver 10; Ex 20:10; 23:12; Dt 5:14; Lk 13:14; 14:3; Jn 5:10; 7:23; 9:16 **12:3** [z]1Sa 21:6 **12:4** [a]Lev 24:5,9 **12:5** [b]Nu 28:9,10; Jn 7:22,23 **12:6** [c]ver 41,42 **12:7** [d]Hos 6:6; Mic 6:6-8; Mt 9:13 **12:8** [e]S Mt 8:20 **12:10** [f]Mk 3:2; 12:13; Lk 11:54; 14:1; 20:20 [g]S ver 2 **12:11** [h]Lk 14:5 **12:12** [i]Mt 6:26; 10:31 **12:14** [j]Ge 37:18; Ps 71:10; Mt 26:4; 27:1; Mk 3:6; Lk 6:11; Jn 5:18; 7:1,19; 11:53 **12:15** [k]S Mt 4:23 **12:16** [l]S Mt 8:4 **12:17** [m]S Mt 1:22 **12:18** [n]S Mt 3:17 [o]S Jn 3:34 **12:21** [p]Isa 42:1-4

[a] 6 Or *something*; also in verses 41 and 42
[b] 7 Hosea 6:6 [c] 21 Isaiah 42:1-4

11:27 *All things.* The full revelation of God (see v. 25). *No one knows the Son.* Total knowledge of the Son belongs only to the Father. Believers can “know” the Son for salvation (1Jn 5:20) and in a deep and satisfying way, but not completely (see Jn 10:14 and note; cf. Php 3:7–11 and notes). *except … those to whom the Son chooses to reveal him.* Christ sovereignly chooses those to whom he reveals a saving knowledge of God (see Jn 14:6 and note).
11:28 *weary and burdened.* Probably a reference to the “heavy loads” the Pharisees placed “on men’s shoulders” by insisting on a legalistic interpretation of the law (23:4).
11:29 *yoke.* Cf. v. 30 and note. *find rest for your souls.* See Jer 6:16 and note.
11:30 *my burden is light.* Cf. Ps 55:22; 1Jn 5:3 and notes.
12:1 *grainfields.* Of wheat or barley, the latter eaten by poorer people. *pick some heads of grain.* See note on Mk 2:23.
12:2 *Pharisees.* See note on 3:7. *what is unlawful on the Sabbath.* See note on Mk 2:24.
12:3 *what David did.* See note on Mk 2:25.
12:4 *consecrated bread.* Each Sabbath, 12 fresh loaves of bread were to be set on a table in the Holy Place (Ex 25:30; Lev 24:5–9). The old loaves were eaten by the priests.
12:5 *desecrate the day.* By doing required work associated with the sacrifices (see Nu 28:9; cf. Jn 7:22–23 and note on 7:22).
12:8 *the Son of Man is Lord of the Sabbath.* See note on Lk 6:5.
12:9 *synagogue.* See note on Mk 1:21.
12:10 *heal on the Sabbath.* The rabbis prohibited healing on the Sabbath, unless it was feared the victim would die before the next day. Obviously the man with the shriveled hand was in no danger of this.
12:11–12 Jesus contrasts the worth of an animal with that of a human being (cf. Lk 13:15–16; 14:5 and notes).
12:12 *lawful to do good on the Sabbath.* See Mk 3:4; Lk 6:9 and notes.
12:13 *“Stretch out your hand.” So he stretched it out.* The fact that the man stretched out his shriveled hand shows there is a connection between faith and Jesus’ healing power.
12:14 See notes on Mk 3:6; Lk 6:11.
12:16 *not to tell who he was.* See note on 8:4.
12:18–21 Another fulfillment passage (see note on 1:22). This one is from Isaiah’s first servant song (see Isa 42:1–4 and note) and is the longest OT quotation in Matthew’s Gospel. It summarizes the quiet ministry of the Lord’s servant, who will bring justice and hope to the nations.
12:18 *my servant.* Jesus is called God’s servant only here and in Ac 3:13 (see note there), 26; 4:27,30. *the one I love, in whom I delight.* See note on 3:17. *put my Spirit on him.* See Isa 11:2; 61:1 and notes.
12:20 Jesus mends broken lives (see v. 15; Jn 4:4–42; 8:3–11).

Jesus and Beelzebub

12:25-29pp — Mk 3:23-27; Lk 11:17-22

22Then they brought him a demon-possessed man who was blind and mute, and
Jesus healed him, so that he could both
talk and see.[q] 23All the people were astonished and said, "Could this be the Son of
David?"[r]

24But when the Pharisees heard this,
they said, "It is only by Beelzebub,[a][s] the
prince of demons, that this fellow drives
out demons."[t]

25Jesus knew their thoughts[u] and said
to them, "Every kingdom divided against
itself will be ruined, and every city or
household divided against itself will not
stand. 26If Satan[v] drives out Satan, he is
divided against himself. How then can his
kingdom stand? 27And if I drive out demons by Beelzebub,[w] by whom do your
people[x] drive them out? So then, they will
be your judges. 28But if I drive out demons
by the Spirit of God, then the kingdom of
God[y] has come upon you.

29"Or again, how can anyone enter a
strong man's house and carry off his possessions unless he first ties up the strong
man? Then he can rob his house.

30"He who is not with me is against me,
and he who does not gather with me scatters.[z] 31And so I tell you, every sin and
blasphemy will be forgiven men, but the
blasphemy against the Spirit will not be
forgiven.[a] 32Anyone who speaks a word
against the Son of Man will be forgiven,
but anyone who speaks against the Holy
Spirit will not be forgiven, either in this
age[b] or in the age to come.[c]

33"Make a tree good and its fruit will
be good, or make a tree bad and its fruit
will be bad, for a tree is recognized by its
fruit.[d] 34You brood of vipers,[e] how can you
who are evil say anything good? For out
of the overflow of the heart the mouth
speaks.[f] 35The good man brings good
things out of the good stored up in him,
and the evil man brings evil things out of
the evil stored up in him. 36But I tell you
that men will have to give account on the
day of judgment for every careless word
they have spoken. 37For by your words you
will be acquitted, and by your words you
will be condemned."[g]

The Sign of Jonah

12:39-42pp — Lk 11:29-32
12:43-45pp — Lk 11:24-26

38Then some of the Pharisees and
teachers of the law said to him, "Teacher,
we want to see a miraculous sign[h] from
you."[i]

39He answered, "A wicked and adulterous generation asks for a miraculous sign!
But none will be given it except the sign
of the prophet Jonah.[j] 40For as Jonah was
three days and three nights in the belly of
a huge fish,[k] so the Son of Man[l] will be
three days and three nights in the heart
of the earth.[m] 41The men of Nineveh[n] will
stand up at the judgment with this generation and condemn it; for they repented
at the preaching of Jonah,[o] and now one[b]
greater than Jonah is here. 42The Queen of
the South will rise at the judgment with
this generation and condemn it; for she
came[p] from the ends of the earth to listen
to Solomon's wisdom, and now one greater than Solomon is here.

43"When an evil[c] spirit comes out of a
man, it goes through arid places seeking
rest and does not find it. 44Then it says, 'I
will return to the house I left.' When it arrives, it finds the house unoccupied, swept

12:22 [q]S Mt 4:24 **12:23** [r]S Mt 9:27 **12:24** [s]S Mk 3:22 [t]Mt 9:34 **12:25** [u]S Mt 9:4 **12:26** [v]S Mt 4:10 **12:27** [w]ver 24 [x]Ac 19:13 **12:28** [y]S Mt 3:2 **12:30** [z]Mk 9:40; Lk 11:23 **12:31** [a]Mk 3:28,29; Lk 12:10 **12:32** [b]Tit 2:12 [c]Mk 10:30; Lk 20:34,35; Eph 1:21; Heb 6:5 **12:33** [d]Mt 7:16,17; Lk 6:43,44 **12:34** [e]Mt 3:7; 23:33 [f]Mt 15:18; Lk 6:45 **12:37** [g]Job 15:6; Pr 10:14; 18:21; Jas 3:2 **12:38** [h]S Jn 2:11; S 4:48 [i]Mt 16:1; Mk 8:11,12; Lk 11:16; Jn 2:18; 6:30; 1Co 1:22 **12:39** [j]Mt 16:4; Lk 11:29 **12:40** [k]Jnh 1:17 [l]S Mt 8:20 [m]S Mt 16:21 **12:41** [n]Jnh 1:2 [o]Jnh 3:5 **12:42** [p]1Ki 10:1; 2Ch 9:1

[a] 24 Greek *Beezeboul* or *Beelzeboul*; also in verse 27
[b] 41 Or *something*; also in verse 42
[c] 43 Greek *unclean*

12:22 *demon-possessed.* See notes on Mk 1:23; Lk 4:33.
12:23 *Son of David.* See note on 9:27.
12:24 See 10:25; Lk 11:19 and notes.
12:25 *kingdom divided against itself.* See note on Lk 11:17.
12:26 *Satan.* See notes on 4:1; 16:23.
12:28 *kingdom of God.* See note on 3:2. *has come upon you.* See note on Mk 1:15.
12:30 There can be no double-mindedness in our relationship to Jesus (see note on Lk 11:23; cf. Ps 119:113; Mk 9:40; Lk 9:50 and note; Jas 1:8; 4:8).
12:31 *blasphemy against the Spirit will not be forgiven.* The context (vv. 24,28,32) suggests that the unpardonable sin was attributing to Satan Christ's authenticating miracles done in the power of the Holy Spirit (see note on Mk 3:29).
12:32 *Son of Man.* See note on Mk 8:31. *this age ... the age to come.* See Eph 1:21 and note.
12:33 See 3:16; cf. Jas 3:11–12.
12:34 *brood of vipers.* In the NT an expression used only by John the Baptist (3:7; Lk 3:7) and Jesus (here; 23:33). In this context it refers to the Pharisees (v. 24). *out of the overflow of the heart the mouth speaks.* See 15:18–19. *heart.* See note on Ps 4:7.
12:36 *day of judgment.* At Christ's second coming; sometimes referred to as "that day" (7:22; 2Ti 1:12,18), "the day of slaughter" (Jas 5:5; see note there).
12:38 *miraculous sign.* The Pharisees wanted to see a spectacular miracle, preferably in the sky (see Lk 11:16), as the sign that Jesus was the Messiah. Instead, he cites them a "sign" from history. See note on Lk 11:29.
12:39 *adulterous.* Referring to spiritual, not physical, adultery, in the sense that their generation had become unfaithful to its spiritual husband (God; see Ex 34:15; Hos 1:2 and notes). *sign of the prophet Jonah.* See note on Lk 11:30.
12:40 *three days and three nights.* Including at least part of the first day and part of the third day, a common Jewish reckoning of time. See note on Lk 24:46. *huge fish.* The Greek word does not mean "whale" but rather "sea creature," i.e., a huge fish (see note on Jnh 1:17). *Son of man.* See note on Mk 8:31.
12:41–42 *one greater than Jonah ... one greater than Solomon.* See note on Lk 11:31–32.
12:42 *Queen of the South.* In 1Ki 10:1 she is called the queen of Sheba, a country in southwest Arabia, now called Yemen.
12:43–45 See notes on Lk 11:24–25.

clean and put in order. 45Then it goes and
takes with it seven other spirits more
wicked than itself, and they go in and live
there. And the final condition of that man
is worse than the first.[q] That is how it will
be with this wicked generation."

Jesus' Mother and Brothers

12:46-50pp — Mk 3:31-35; Lk 8:19-21

46While Jesus was still talking to the
crowd, his mother[r] and brothers[s] stood
outside, wanting to speak to him. 47Some-
one told him, "Your mother and brothers
are standing outside, wanting to speak to
you."[a]

48He replied to him, "Who is my mother,
and who are my brothers?" 49Pointing to
his disciples, he said, "Here are my mother
and my brothers. 50For whoever does the
will of my Father in heaven[t] is my brother
and sister and mother."

The Parable of the Sower

13:1-15pp — Mk 4:1-12; Lk 8:4-10
13:16,17pp — Lk 10:23,24
13:18-23pp — Mk 4:13-20; Lk 8:11-15

13 That same day Jesus went out of the
house[u] and sat by the lake. 2Such
large crowds gathered around him that
he got into a boat[v] and sat in it, while all
the people stood on the shore. 3Then he
told them many things in parables, saying: "A farmer went out to sow his seed.
4As he was scattering the seed, some fell
along the path, and the birds came and ate
it up. 5Some fell on rocky places, where
it did not have much soil. It sprang up
quickly, because the soil was shallow.
6But when the sun came up, the plants
were scorched, and they withered because
they had no root. 7Other seed fell among
thorns, which grew up and choked the
plants. 8Still other seed fell on good soil,
where it produced a crop — a hundred,[w]
sixty or thirty times what was sown. 9He
who has ears, let him hear."[x]

12:45 [q] 2Pe 2:20
12:46 [r] Mt 1:18; 2:11,13,14,20; Lk 1:43; 2:33,34,48,51; Jn 2:1,5; 19:25,26 [s] Mt 13:55; Jn 2:12; 7:3,5; Ac 1:14; 1Co 9:5; Gal 1:19
12:50 [t] Mt 6:10; Jn 15:14
13:1 [u] ver 36; Mt 9:28
13:2 [v] Lk 5:3
13:8 [w] Ge 26:12
13:9 [x] S Mt 11:15
13:11 [y] S Mt 3:2 [z] Mt 11:25; 16:17; 19:11; Jn 6:65; 1Co 2:10,14; Col 1:27; 1Jn 2:20,27
13:12 [a] S Mt 25:29
13:13 [b] Dt 29:4; Jer 5:21; Eze 12:2
13:14 [c] ver 35; S Mt 1:22
13:15 [d] Isa 6:9,10; Jn 12:40; Ac 28:26,27; Ro 11:8
13:16 [e] Mt 16:17
13:17 [f] Jn 8:56; Heb 11:13; 1Pe 1:10-12
13:19 [g] Mt 4:23 [h] S Mt 5:37

10The disciples came to him and asked,
"Why do you speak to the people in parables?"

11He replied, "The knowledge of the secrets of the kingdom of heaven[y] has been
given to you,[z] but not to them. 12Whoever
has will be given more, and he will have
an abundance. Whoever does not have,
even what he has will be taken from him.[a]
13This is why I speak to them in parables:

"Though seeing, they do not see;
though hearing, they do not hear or
understand.[b]

14In them is fulfilled[c] the prophecy of Isaiah:

" 'You will be ever hearing but never
understanding;
you will be ever seeing but never
perceiving.
15For this people's heart has become
calloused;
they hardly hear with their ears,
and they have closed their eyes.
Otherwise they might see with their
eyes,
hear with their ears,
understand with their hearts
and turn, and I would heal them.'[b][d]

16But blessed are your eyes because they
see, and your ears because they hear.[e]
17For I tell you the truth, many prophets
and righteous men longed to see what you
see[f] but did not see it, and to hear what
you hear but did not hear it.

18"Listen then to what the parable of
the sower means: 19When anyone hears
the message about the kingdom[g] and does
not understand it, the evil one[h] comes
and snatches away what was sown in his
heart. This is the seed sown along the
path. 20The one who received the seed
that fell on rocky places is the man who
hears the word and at once receives it

[a] *47* Some manuscripts do not have verse 47.
[b] *15* Isaiah 6:9,10

12:46 *mother and brothers.* See note on Lk 8:19.
12:50 *whoever does the will of my Father.* See notes on Mk 3:35; Lk 8:21.
13:1 *went out of the house.* See "went into the house" (v. 36). These two phrases determine the setting of Jesus' teaching in vv. 1 – 35.
13:2 *sat in it.* See note on Mk 4:1.
13:3 – 9 See vv. 18 – 23 for the interpretation of this first parable.
13:3 *parables.* Our word "parable" comes from the Greek *parabole,* which means "a placing beside" — and thus a comparison or an illustration. Its most common use in the NT is for the illustrative stories that Jesus drew from nature and human life. The Synoptic Gospels contain about 30 of these stories. John's Gospel contains no parables but uses other figures of speech (see notes on Mk 4:2; Lk 8:4). *to sow his seed.* See note on Lk 8:5. According to Mk 4:14; Lk 8:11 (see notes there), the seed is the word of God.
13:4 – 6 See note on Mk 4:3 – 8.
13:4 *birds.* Satan, "the evil one" (v. 19).
13:5 *rocky places.* Not ground covered with small stones, but shallow soil on top of solid rock. See note on Lk 8:6.
13:8 *a hundred.* See notes on Mk 4:8; Lk 8:8.
13:9 *let him hear.* See note on Lk 8:8.
13:10 See note on Lk 8:9.
13:11 *secrets of the kingdom of heaven.* See notes on Mk 4:11; Lk 8:10.
13:13 – 14 Jesus speaks in parables because of the spiritual dullness of the people (see note on Lk 8:4).
13:13 *Though seeing, they do not see.* See notes on Mk 4:12; Lk 8:10.
13:14 – 15 See Isa 6:9 – 10 and notes.
13:18 *what the parable of the sower means.* Jesus seldom interpreted his parables, but here he does.
13:19 *message.* Cf. Luke's "word of God" (8:11). *evil one.* Satan (the devil; see Mk 4:15; Lk 8:12 and note).

with joy. 21But since he has no root, he
lasts only a short time. When trouble or
persecution comes because of the word,
he quickly falls away.[i] 22The one who received the seed that fell among the thorns
is the man who hears the word, but the
worries of this life and the deceitfulness
of wealth[j] choke it, making it unfruitful.
23But the one who received the seed that
fell on good soil is the man who hears the
word and understands it. He produces a
crop, yielding a hundred, sixty or thirty
times what was sown."[k]

The Parable of the Weeds

24Jesus told them another parable: "The
kingdom of heaven is like[l] a man who
sowed good seed in his field. 25But while
everyone was sleeping, his enemy came
and sowed weeds among the wheat, and
went away. 26When the wheat sprouted
and formed heads, then the weeds also
appeared.
27"The owner's servants came to him
and said, 'Sir, didn't you sow good seed
in your field? Where then did the weeds
come from?'
28" 'An enemy did this,' he replied.
"The servants asked him, 'Do you want
us to go and pull them up?'
29" 'No,' he answered, 'because while
you are pulling the weeds, you may root
up the wheat with them. 30Let both grow
together until the harvest. At that time I
will tell the harvesters: First collect the
weeds and tie them in bundles to be
burned; then gather the wheat and bring
it into my barn.' "[m]

The Parables of the Mustard Seed and the Yeast

13:31,32pp — Mk 4:30-32
13:31-33pp — Lk 13:18-21

31He told them another parable: "The
kingdom of heaven is like[n] a mustard
seed,[o] which a man took and planted in
his field. 32Though it is the smallest of all
your seeds, yet when it grows, it is the
largest of garden plants and becomes a
tree, so that the birds of the air come and
perch in its branches."[p]
33He told them still another parable:
"The kingdom of heaven is like[q] yeast
that a woman took and mixed into a
large amount[a] of flour[r] until it worked all
through the dough."[s]
34Jesus spoke all these things to the
crowd in parables; he did not say anything
to them without using a parable.[t] 35So was
fulfilled[u] what was spoken through the
prophet:

> "I will open my mouth in parables,
> I will utter things hidden since the
> creation of the world."[b][v]

The Parable of the Weeds Explained

36Then he left the crowd and went into
the house. His disciples came to him and
said, "Explain to us the parable[w] of the
weeds in the field."
37He answered, "The one who sowed the
good seed is the Son of Man.[x] 38The field
is the world, and the good seed stands for
the sons of the kingdom. The weeds are
the sons of the evil one,[y] 39and the enemy
who sows them is the devil. The harvest[z]
is the end of the age,[a] and the harvesters
are angels.[b]
40"As the weeds are pulled up and
burned in the fire, so it will be at the end
of the age. 41The Son of Man[c] will send out
his angels,[d] and they will weed out of his
kingdom everything that causes sin and
all who do evil. 42They will throw them
into the fiery furnace, where there will be

[a] *33* Greek *three satas* (probably about 1/2 bushel or 22 liters) [b] *35* Psalm 78:2

13:21 [i] Mt 11:6; 26:31 **13:22** [j] Mt 19:23; 1Ti 6:9,10,17 **13:23** [k] ver 8 **13:24** [l] ver 31,33,45,47; Mt 18:23; 20:1; 22:2; 25:1; Mk 4:26,30 **13:30** [m] Mt 3:12 **13:31** [n] S ver 24 [o] Mt 17:20; Lk 17:6 **13:32** [p] Ps 104:12; Eze 17:23; 31:6; Da 4:12 **13:33** [q] S ver 24 [r] Ge 18:6 [s] Gal 5:9 **13:34** [t] S Jn 16:25 **13:35** [u] ver 14; S Mt 1:22 [v] Ps 78:2; Ro 16:25,26; 1Co 2:7; Eph 3:9; Col 1:26 **13:36** [w] Mt 15:15 **13:37** [x] S Mt 8:20 **13:38** [y] Jn 8:44,45; 1Jn 3:10 **13:39** [z] Joel 3:13 [a] Mt 24:3; 28:20 [b] Rev 14:15 **13:41** [c] S Mt 8:20 [d] Mt 24:31

13:21 Cf. 24:10–12; see note on Lk 8:13.

13:22 *the worries of this life and the deceitfulness of wealth.* Lk 8:14 adds life's "pleasures" to these two phrases. *deceitfulness of wealth.* See note on Mk 4:19.

13:23 *understands.* Cf. the Isaiah quotation in vv. 14–15. Matthew uses this word six times in this chapter (here and in vv. 13–15,19,51). *hundred ... times.* See note on Lk 8:8.

13:24–30 See vv. 36–43 for the interpretation.

13:24 *The kingdom of heaven is like.* This phrase introduces six of the seven parables in this chapter (all but the parable of the sower).

13:25 *weeds.* Probably darnel, which looks very much like wheat while it is young, but can later be distinguished. This parable does not refer to unbelievers in the professing church. The field is the world (v. 38). Thus in this world the people of the kingdom live side by side with the people of the evil one.

13:30 *harvest.* The final judgment (see notes on Joel 3:13; Mk 4:29; Rev 14:15).

13:31–32 Although the kingdom will seem to have an insignificant beginning, it will eventually spread throughout the world (see note on Mk 4:30–34).

13:32 *the smallest ... the largest.* The mustard seed is not the smallest seed known today, but it was the smallest seed used by farmers and gardeners there and at that time, and under favorable conditions the plant could reach about ten feet in height. *a tree ... its branches.* Likely an allusion to Da 4:21, suggesting that the kingdom of heaven will expand to world dominion and that people from all nations will find rest in it (cf. Da 2:35,44–45; 7:27; Rev 11:15).

13:33 In the Bible, yeast usually symbolizes that which is evil or unclean (see note on Mk 8:15). Here, however, it is a symbol of growth. As yeast permeates a batch of dough, so the kingdom of heaven spreads through a person's life. Or it may signify the growth of the kingdom by the inner working of the Holy Spirit (using God's word). See note on Lk 13:21.

13:35 *spoken through the prophet.* The quotation is from Ps 78 (see note on 78:2), a psalm ascribed to Asaph, who according to 2Ch 29:30 was a "seer" (prophet). For another possible understanding of this phrase see 5:17 and note.

13:37,41 *Son of Man.* See note on Mk 8:31.

13:42 *fiery furnace.* Often mentioned in connection with the final judgment in apocalyptic literature (see Rev 19:20; 20:14).

weeping and gnashing of teeth.[e] 43Then the righteous will shine like the sun[f] in the kingdom of their Father. He who has ears, let him hear.[g]

The Parables of the Hidden Treasure and the Pearl

44"The kingdom of heaven is like[h] treasure hidden in a field. When a man found it, he hid it again, and then in his joy went and sold all he had and bought that field.[i]

45"Again, the kingdom of heaven is like[j] a merchant looking for fine pearls. 46When he found one of great value, he went away and sold everything he had and bought it.

The Parable of the Net

47"Once again, the kingdom of heaven is like[k] a net that was let down into the lake and caught all kinds[l] of fish. 48When it was full, the fishermen pulled it up on the shore. Then they sat down and collected the good fish in baskets, but threw the bad away. 49This is how it will be at the end of the age. The angels will come and separate the wicked from the righteous[m] 50and throw them into the fiery furnace, where there will be weeping and gnashing of teeth.[n]

51"Have you understood all these things?" Jesus asked.

"Yes," they replied.

52He said to them, "Therefore every teacher of the law who has been instructed about the kingdom of heaven is like the owner of a house who brings out of his storeroom new treasures as well as old."

A Prophet Without Honor

13:54-58pp — Mk 6:1-6

53When Jesus had finished these parables,[o] he moved on from there. 54Coming to his hometown, he began teaching the people in their synagogue,[p] and they were amazed.[q] "Where did this man get this wisdom and these miraculous powers?" they asked. 55"Isn't this the carpenter's son?[r] Isn't his mother's[s] name Mary, and aren't his brothers[t] James, Joseph, Simon and Judas? 56Aren't all his sisters with us? Where then did this man get all these things?" 57And they took offense[u] at him.

But Jesus said to them, "Only in his hometown and in his own house is a prophet without honor."[v]

58And he did not do many miracles there because of their lack of faith.

John the Baptist Beheaded

14:1-12pp — Mk 6:14-29

14 At that time Herod[w] the tetrarch heard the reports about Jesus,[x] 2and he said to his attendants, "This is John the Baptist;[y] he has risen from the dead! That is why miraculous powers are at work in him."

3Now Herod had arrested John and bound him and put him in prison[z] because of Herodias, his brother Philip's wife,[a] 4for John had been saying to him: "It is not lawful for you to have her."[b] 5Herod wanted to kill John, but he was afraid of the

13:42 [e]S Mt 8:12
13:43 [f]Da 12:3 [g]S Mt 11:15
13:44 [h]S ver 24 [i]Isa 55:1; Mt 19:21; Php 3:7,8
13:45 [j]S ver 24
13:47 [k]S ver 24 [l]Mt 22:10
13:49 [m]Mt 25:32
13:50 [n]S Mt 8:12
13:53 [o]S Mt 7:28
13:54 [p]S Mt 4:23 [q]S Mt 7:28
13:55 [r]Lk 3:23; Jn 6:42 [s]S Mt 12:46 [t]S Mt 12:46
13:57 [u]Jn 6:61 [v]Lk 4:24; Jn 4:44
14:1 [w]Mk 8:15; Lk 3:1,19; 13:31; 23:7,8; Ac 4:27; 12:1 [x]Lk 9:7-9
14:2 [y]S Mt 3:1
14:3 [z]Mt 4:12; 11:2 [a]Lk 3:19,20
14:4 [b]Lev 18:16; 20:21

---

weeping and gnashing of teeth. Occurs six times in Matthew's Gospel (here; v. 50; 8:12; 22:13; 24:51; 25:30) and nowhere else in the NT (but see note on 8:12).

13:43 *the righteous will shine like the sun.* See Da 12:3. *let him hear.* See note on Lk 8:8.

13:44–46 These two parables teach the same truth: The kingdom is of such great value that one should be willing to give up all one has in order to gain it. Jesus did not imply that one can purchase the kingdom with money or good deeds.

13:44 *treasure hidden in a field.* In ancient times it was common to hide treasure in the ground since there were no banks—though there were "bankers" (25:27; see note there).

13:47–51 The parable of the net teaches the same general lesson as the parable of the weeds: There will be a final separation of the righteous and the wicked. The parable of the weeds also emphasizes that we are not to try to make such a separation now. That is entirely the Lord's business (vv. 28–30,41–42). Cf. note on Eze 26:5.

13:50 See note on v. 42.

13:51 *Yes.* Probably an overstatement by the disciples, especially in view of Jesus' words in 15:16.

13:53 Concludes a teaching section and introduces a narrative section (cf. 7:28–29).

13:54 *his hometown.* Nazareth (see note on 2:23). *teaching the people in their synagogue.* See note on Mk 1:21. *amazed.* See note on 7:28.

13:55 *carpenter's son.* See note on Mk 6:3. Apparently Joseph was no longer living at the time of this incident. *brothers.* Sons born to Joseph and Mary after the virgin birth of Jesus (see note on Lk 8:19).

13:58 *lack of faith.* The close relationship between faith and miracles is stressed in Matthew's Gospel (cf. 8:10,13; 9:2,22,28–29).

14:1 *tetrarch.* The ruler of a fourth part of a region. "Herod the tetrarch" (Herod Antipas) was one of several sons of Herod the Great. When Herod the Great died, his kingdom was divided among three of his sons (see chart, p. 1465; see also map, p. 1570). Herod Antipas ruled over Galilee and Perea (4 B.C.–A.D. 39). Matthew correctly refers to him as tetrarch here, as Luke regularly does (Lk 3:19; 9:7; Ac 13:1). But in v. 9 Matthew calls him "king"—as Mk 6:14 also does—because that was his popular title among the Galileans, as well as in Rome.

14:2 *John … risen from the dead.* See note on Mk 6:16.

14:3 *Herod had arrested John.* See note on Mk 6:17. *Herodias.* A granddaughter of Herod the Great (see chart, p. 1465). First she married her uncle, Herod Philip (Herod the Great also had another son named Philip), who lived in Rome. While a guest in their home, Herod Antipas persuaded Herodias to leave her husband for him. Marriage to one's brother's wife, while the brother was still living, was forbidden by the Mosaic law (Lev 18:16). *Philip.* The son of Herod the Great and Mariamne, the daughter of Simon the high priest, and thus a half brother of Herod Antipas, born to Malthace (see chart, p. 1465).

people, because they considered him a prophet.[c]

⁶On Herod's birthday the daughter of Herodias danced for them and pleased Herod so much ⁷that he promised with an oath to give her whatever she asked. ⁸Prompted by her mother, she said, "Give me here on a platter the head of John the Baptist." ⁹The king was distressed, but because of his oaths and his dinner guests, he ordered that her request be granted ¹⁰and had John beheaded[d] in the prison. ¹¹His head was brought in on a platter and given to the girl, who carried it to her mother. ¹²John's disciples came and took his body and buried it.[e] Then they went and told Jesus.

Jesus Feeds the Five Thousand

14:13-21pp — Mk 6:32-44; Lk 9:10-17; Jn 6:1-13
14:13-21Ref — Mt 15:32-38

¹³When Jesus heard what had happened, he withdrew by boat privately to a solitary place. Hearing of this, the crowds followed him on foot from the towns. ¹⁴When Jesus landed and saw a large crowd, he had compassion on them[f] and healed their sick.[g]

¹⁵As evening approached, the disciples came to him and said, "This is a remote place, and it's already getting late. Send the crowds away, so they can go to the villages and buy themselves some food."

¹⁶Jesus replied, "They do not need to go away. You give them something to eat."

¹⁷"We have here only five loaves[h] of bread and two fish," they answered.

¹⁸"Bring them here to me," he said. ¹⁹And he directed the people to sit down on the grass. Taking the five loaves and the two fish and looking up to heaven, he gave thanks and broke the loaves.[i] Then he gave them to the disciples, and the disciples gave them to the people. ²⁰They all ate and were satisfied, and the disciples picked up twelve basketfuls of broken pieces that were left over. ²¹The number of those who ate was about five thousand men, besides women and children.

Jesus Walks on the Water

14:22-33pp — Mk 6:45-51; Jn 6:16-21
14:34-36pp — Mk 6:53-56

²²Immediately Jesus made the disciples get into the boat and go on ahead of him to the other side, while he dismissed the crowd. ²³After he had dismissed them, he went up on a mountainside by himself to pray.[j] When evening came, he was there alone, ²⁴but the boat was already a considerable distance[a] from land, buffeted by the waves because the wind was against it.

²⁵During the fourth watch of the night Jesus went out to them, walking on the lake. ²⁶When the disciples saw him walking on the lake, they were terrified. "It's a ghost,"[k] they said, and cried out in fear.

²⁷But Jesus immediately said to them: "Take courage![l] It is I. Don't be afraid."[m]

²⁸"Lord, if it's you," Peter replied, "tell me to come to you on the water."

²⁹"Come," he said.

Then Peter got down out of the boat, walked on the water and came toward Jesus. ³⁰But when he saw the wind, he was afraid and, beginning to sink, cried out, "Lord, save me!"

³¹Immediately Jesus reached out his hand and caught him. "You of little faith,"[n] he said, "why did you doubt?"

14:5 [c]S Mt 11:9 **14:10** [d]Mt 17:12 **14:12** [e]Ac 8:2 **14:14** [f]S Mt 9:36 [g]S Mt 4:23 **14:17** [h]Mt 16:9 **14:19** [i]1Sa 9:13; Mt 26:26; Mk 8:6; Lk 9:16; 24:30; Ac 2:42; 20:7, 11; 27:35; 1Co 10:16; 1Ti 4:4 **14:23** [j]S Lk 3:21 **14:26** [k]Lk 24:37 **14:27** [l]Mt 9:2; Ac 23:11 [m]Da 10:12; Mt 17:7; 28:10; Lk 1:13, 30; 2:10; Ac 18:9; 23:11; Rev 1:17 **14:31** [n]S Mt 6:30

[a] 24 Greek *many stadia*

14:6 *daughter of Herodias.* Salome, according to Josephus. She later married her granduncle, the other Philip (son of Herod the Great), who ruled the northern territories (Lk 3:1). At this time Salome was a young woman of marriageable age. Her dance was doubtless lascivious, and the performance pleased both Herod and his guests.
14:7 *whatever she asked.* See Mk 6:22 and note.
14:8 *platter.* A flat wooden dish on which meat was served.
14:13 – 21 See 15:37; Mk 6:32 – 44; Lk 9:10 – 17; Jn 6:1 – 13 and notes.
14:13 *what had happened.* Probably refers to vv. 1 – 2, namely, Herod's response to reports about Jesus. *withdrew ... to a solitary place.* To avoid the threat of Herod and the pressing of the crowds. Jesus' time had not yet come (see Jn 2:4 and note; cf. Jn 6:15).
14:14 *compassion.* See note on 9:36.
14:20 *twelve basketfuls.* See note on Jn 6:13.
14:21 *besides women and children.* Matthew alone notes this. He was writing to the Jews, who did not permit women and children to eat with men in public. So they were in a place by themselves.
14:22 *made.* The Greek word used here means "to compel" and suggests a crisis. John records that after the miracle of the loaves and fish the crowds "intended to ... make him [Jesus] king by force" (6:15). This involved a complete misunderstanding of the mission of Jesus. The disciples may have been caught up in the enthusiasm and needed to be removed from the area quickly.
14:23 *pray.* Matthew speaks of Jesus praying only here and in Gethsemane (cf. 26:36 – 46).
14:24 *considerable distance from land.* See Jn 6:19 and note.
14:25 *fourth watch.* 3:00 – 6:00 A.M. According to Roman reckoning the night was divided into four watches: (1) 6:00 – 9:00 P.M., (2) 9:00 P.M. – midnight, (3) midnight – 3:00 A.M. and (4) 3:00 – 6:00 A.M. (see note on Mk 13:35). The Jews had only three watches during the night: (1) sunset – 10:00 P.M., (2) 10:00 P.M. – 2:00 A.M. and (3) 2:00 A.M. – sunrise (see Jdg 7:19 and note; 1Sa 11:11). *walking on the lake.* See note on Mk 6:48. *lake.* The Sea of Galilee (see note on Mk 1:16).
14:26 *ghost.* See note on Mk 6:49.
14:27 *It is I.* Lit. "I am" (cf. Ex 3:14; Isa 43:10; 51:12; Jn 8:58 and note).
14:28 *if it's you.* A condition assumed to be true. Peter knew it was Jesus, and that is why he stepped out of the boat onto the water in the first place.
14:31 *You of little faith.* See note on 6:30. *why did you doubt?* See Jas 1:5 – 8.

32And when they climbed into the boat,
the wind died down. 33Then those who
were in the boat worshiped him, saying,
"Truly you are the Son of God."[o]
34When they had crossed over, they
landed at Gennesaret. 35And when the
men of that place recognized Jesus, they
sent word to all the surrounding country.
People brought all their sick to him 36and
begged him to let the sick just touch the
edge of his cloak,[p] and all who touched
him were healed.

Clean and Unclean

15:1-20pp — Mk 7:1-23

15 Then some Pharisees and teachers of
the law came to Jesus from Jerusalem and asked, 2"Why do your disciples
break the tradition of the elders? They
don't wash their hands before they eat!"[q]
3Jesus replied, "And why do you break
the command of God for the sake of your
tradition? 4For God said, 'Honor your father and mother'[a][r] and 'Anyone who curses his father or mother must be put to
death.'[b][s] 5But you say that if a man says to
his father or mother, 'Whatever help you
might otherwise have received from me is
a gift devoted to God,' 6he is not to 'honor
his father[c]' with it. Thus you nullify the
word of God for the sake of your tradition.
7You hypocrites! Isaiah was right when he
prophesied about you:

8" 'These people honor me with their
lips,
but their hearts are far from me.
9They worship me in vain;
their teachings are but rules taught
by men.'[t][d][u]"

10Jesus called the crowd to him and said,
"Listen and understand. 11What goes into
a man's mouth does not make him 'unclean,'[v] but what comes out of his mouth,
that is what makes him 'unclean.' "[w]
12Then the disciples came to him and
asked, "Do you know that the Pharisees
were offended when they heard this?"
13He replied, "Every plant that my heavenly Father has not planted[x] will be pulled
up by the roots. 14Leave them; they are
blind guides.[e][y] If a blind man leads a blind
man, both will fall into a pit."[z]
15Peter said, "Explain the parable
to us."[a]
16"Are you still so dull?"[b] Jesus asked
them. 17"Don't you see that whatever enters the mouth goes into the stomach and
then out of the body? 18But the things that
come out of the mouth come from the
heart,[c] and these make a man 'unclean.'
19For out of the heart come evil thoughts,
murder, adultery, sexual immorality, theft,
false testimony, slander.[d] 20These are what
make a man 'unclean';[e] but eating with
unwashed hands does not make him 'unclean.' "

The Faith of the Canaanite Woman

15:21-28pp — Mk 7:24-30

21Leaving that place, Jesus withdrew to
the region of Tyre and Sidon.[f] 22A Canaanite woman from that vicinity came to him,
crying out, "Lord, Son of David,[g] have
mercy on me! My daughter is suffering terribly from demon-possession."[h]
23Jesus did not answer a word. So his
disciples came to him and urged him,
"Send her away, for she keeps crying out
after us."
24He answered, "I was sent only to the
lost sheep of Israel."[i]
25The woman came and knelt before
him.[j] "Lord, help me!" she said.
26He replied, "It is not right to take
the children's bread and toss it to their
dogs."

[a] 4 Exodus 20:12; Deut. 5:16 [b] 4 Exodus 21:17; Lev. 20:9 [c] 6 Some manuscripts *father or his mother* [d] 9 Isaiah 29:13 [e] 14 Some manuscripts *guides of the blind*

14:33 [o]Ps 2:7; S Mt 4:3
14:36 [p]S Mt 9:20
15:2 [q]Lk 11:38
15:4 [r]Ex 20:12; Dt 5:16; Eph 6:2 [s]Ex 21:17; Lev 20:9
15:9 [t]Col 2:20-22 [u]Isa 29:13; Mal 2:2
15:11 [v]S Ac 10:14,15 [w]ver 18
15:13 [x]Isa 60:21; 61:3
15:14 [y]Mt 23:16,24; Ro 2:19 [z]Lk 6:39
15:15 [a]Mt 13:36
15:16 [b]Mt 16:9
15:18 [c]Mt 12:34; Lk 6:45; Jas 3:6
15:19 [d]Gal 5:19-21
15:20 [e]Ro 14:14
15:21 [f]S Mt 11:21
15:22 [g]S Mt 9:27 [h]S Mt 4:24
15:24 [i]Mt 10:6,23; Ro 15:8
15:25 [j]S Mt 8:2

14:33 *Son of God.* This is the first time the disciples use the full title in addressing Jesus (cf. 3:17, where God called him "my Son"; see also Jn 3:16 and note).
14:34 *Gennesaret.* Either the narrow plain (about four miles long and less than two miles wide) on the west side of the Sea of Galilee near the north end (north of Magdala), or a town in the plain. The plain was considered a garden spot, fertile and well watered.
14:36 *just touch the edge of his cloak.* See note on Mk 5:28.
15:2 *tradition of the elders.* After the Babylonian exile, the Jewish rabbis began to make meticulous rules and regulations governing the daily life of the people. These were interpretations and applications of the law of Moses, handed down from generation to generation. In Jesus' day this "tradition of the elders" was in oral form. It was not until c. A.D. 200 that it was put into writing in the Mishnah. *wash.* See note on Mk 7:3.
15:5–6 See notes on Mk 7:11,13.
15:7–20 See Mk 7:6–23 and notes.
15:7 *hypocrites.* See note on 6:2.
15:8–9 See Isa 29:13 and note.
15:13 *Every plant that my heavenly Father has not planted.* Probably refers to the Pharisees and teachers of the law who were in Jesus' audience (vv. 1,12).
15:15 *parable.* See note on Mk 13:3. The parable Peter refers to is found in v. 11.
15:21 *Tyre.* See note on Mk 7:24. *Sidon.* About 25 miles north of Tyre.
15:22 *Canaanite.* A term found many times in the OT but only here in the NT. In NT times there was no country known as Canaan. Some think this was the Semitic way of referring to the people of Phoenicia at this time. Mark says the woman was "a Greek, born in Syrian Phoenicia" (7:26; see note there). *Son of David.* See note on 9:27; shows that this pagan woman had some recognition of Jesus' Messianic claims. *demon-possession.* See Mk 1:23; Lk 4:33 and notes.
15:26 *children's.* "The lost sheep of Israel" (v. 24). *bread.* God's covenanted blessings. *dogs.* Gentiles. Jesus' point was that

27“Yes, Lord,” she said, “but even the
dogs eat the crumbs that fall from their
masters’ table.”
28Then Jesus answered, “Woman, you
have great faith![k] Your request is granted.”
And her daughter was healed from that
very hour.

Jesus Feeds the Four Thousand

15:29-31pp — Mk 7:31-37
15:32-39pp — Mk 8:1-10
15:32-39Ref — Mt 14:13-21

29Jesus left there and went along the Sea
of Galilee. Then he went up on a mountainside and sat down. 30Great crowds
came to him, bringing the lame, the blind,
the crippled, the mute and many others,
and laid them at his feet; and he healed
them.[l] 31The people were amazed when
they saw the mute speaking, the crippled made well, the lame walking and the
blind seeing. And they praised the God of
Israel.[m]
32Jesus called his disciples to him and
said, “I have compassion for these people;[n] they have already been with me three
days and have nothing to eat. I do not
want to send them away hungry, or they
may collapse on the way.”
33His disciples answered, “Where could
we get enough bread in this remote place
to feed such a crowd?”
34“How many loaves do you have?”
Jesus asked.
“Seven,” they replied, “and a few small
fish.”
35He told the crowd to sit down on the
ground. 36Then he took the seven loaves
and the fish, and when he had given
thanks, he broke them[o] and gave them
to the disciples, and they in turn to the
people. 37They all ate and were satisfied.
Afterward the disciples picked up seven
basketfuls of broken pieces that were left
over.[p] 38The number of those who ate was
four thousand, besides women and children. 39After Jesus had sent the crowd
away, he got into the boat and went to the
vicinity of Magadan.

15:28 [k]S Mt 9:22
15:30 [l]S Mt 4:23
15:31 [m]S Mt 9:8
15:32 [n]S Mt 9:36
15:36 [o]S Mt 14:19
15:37 [p]Mt 16:10

The Demand for a Sign

16:1-12pp — Mk 8:11-21

16 The Pharisees and Sadducees[q] came
to Jesus and tested him by asking
him to show them a sign from heaven.[r]
2He replied,[a] “When evening comes,
you say, ‘It will be fair weather, for the sky
is red,’ 3and in the morning, ‘Today it will
be stormy, for the sky is red and overcast.’
You know how to interpret the appearance
of the sky, but you cannot interpret the
signs of the times.[s] 4A wicked and adulterous generation looks for a miraculous
sign, but none will be given it except the
sign of Jonah.”[t] Jesus then left them and
went away.

The Yeast of the Pharisees and Sadducees

5When they went across the lake, the
disciples forgot to take bread. 6“Be careful,” Jesus said to them. “Be on your
guard against the yeast of the Pharisees
and Sadducees.”[u]
7They discussed this among themselves
and said, “It is because we didn’t bring
any bread.”
8Aware of their discussion, Jesus asked,
“You of little faith,[v] why are you talking
among yourselves about having no bread?
9Do you still not understand? Don’t you
remember the five loaves for the five thousand, and how many basketfuls you gathered?[w] 10Or the seven loaves for the four
thousand, and how many basketfuls you
gathered?[x] 11How is it you don’t understand that I was not talking to you about
bread? But be on your guard against the
yeast of the Pharisees and Sadducees.”

16:1 [q]S Ac 4:1 [r]S Mt 12:38
16:3 [s]Lk 12:54-56
16:4 [t]Mt 12:39
16:6 [u]Lk 12:1
16:8 [v]S Mt 6:30
16:9 [w]Mt 14:17-21
16:10 [x]Mt 15:34-38

[a] 2 Some early manuscripts do not have the rest of verse 2 and all of verse 3.

the gospel was to be given first to Jews. The woman understood Jesus’ implication and was willing to settle for “crumbs” (v. 27). Jesus rewarded her “great faith” (v. 28).
15:28 Jesus was pleased with the woman’s reply (v. 27). It revealed not only her wit but also her faith and humility. *Woman.* See note on Jn 2:4.
15:29 *there.* The “region of Tyre and Sidon” (v. 21; see note on Mk 7:31).
15:31 *amazed.* Cf. Mk 1:22 and note.
15:32 – 39 See notes on Mk 8:1 – 10.
15:32 *compassion.* See note on 9:36.
15:36 *when he had given thanks.* The Jewish practice at meals (see 1Ti 4:3 – 5).
15:37 The feeding of the 5,000 is recorded in all four Gospels, but the feeding of the 4,000 is only in Matthew and Mark. The 12 baskets mentioned in the accounts of the feeding of the 5,000 were possibly the lunch baskets of the 12 apostles. The 12 baskets of leftovers may also suggest a sufficient abundance to feed all 12 tribes of Israel (cf. note on Ex 25:30). The seven baskets mentioned here were probably larger.
15:39 *Magadan.* Also called Magdala, the home of Mary Magdalene. Mk 8:10 has “Dalmanutha.”
16:1 *Pharisees and Sadducees.* See note on 3:7. Normally these two groups were opponents, but they had a common enemy in Jesus. *sign from heaven.* See note on Mk 8:11.
16:4 *sign of Jonah.* See 12:39 – 40 and note on Lk 11:30.
16:6 *yeast of the Pharisees and Sadducees.* See v. 12; see also note on Mk 8:15.
16:7 *because we didn’t bring any bread.* Apparently the disciples took Jesus’ statement about “yeast” (v. 6) to somehow relate to their being short of bread. Perhaps they thought they would be required to bake bread when they arrived at the other side of the lake and were being warned by Jesus not to use any yeast provided by the spiritually contaminated religious leaders.
16:8 *little faith.* See note on 6:30.

12Then they understood that he was not
telling them to guard against the yeast
used in bread, but against the teaching of
the Pharisees and Sadducees.[y]

Peter's Confession of Christ

16:13-16pp — Mk 8:27-29; Lk 9:18-20

13When Jesus came to the region of
Caesarea Philippi, he asked his disciples,
"Who do people say the Son of Man is?"
14They replied, "Some say John the Baptist;[z] others say Elijah; and still others, Jeremiah or one of the prophets."[a]
15"But what about you?" he asked.
"Who do you say I am?"
16Simon Peter answered, "You are the
Christ,[a] the Son of the living God."[b]
17Jesus replied, "Blessed are you, Simon
son of Jonah, for this was not revealed to
you by man,[c] but by my Father in heaven.[d]
18And I tell you that you are Peter,[b][e] and
on this rock I will build my church,[f] and
the gates of Hades[c] will not overcome it.[d]
19I will give you the keys[g] of the kingdom
of heaven; whatever you bind on earth will
be[e] bound in heaven, and whatever you
loose on earth will be[e] loosed in heaven."[h]

16:12 [y]S Ac 4:1 **16:14** [z]S Mt 3:1 [a]Mk 6:15; Jn 1:21 **16:16** [b]S Mt 4:3; Ps 42:2; Jer 10:10; Ac 14:15; 2Co 6:16; 1Th 1:9; 1Ti 3:15; Heb 10:31; 12:22 **16:17** [c]1Co 15:50; Eph 6:12; Heb 2:14 [d]S Mt 13:11 **16:18** [e]Jn 1:42 [f]S Eph 2:20 **16:19** [g]Isa 22:22; Rev 3:7 [h]Mt 18:18; Jn 20:23

16:20 [i]S Mk 8:30 **16:21** [j]S Lk 9:51 [k]Ps 22:6; Isa 53:3; Mt 26:67,68; Mk 10:34; Lk 17:25; Jn 18:22,23; 19:3 [l]Mt 27:1,2 [m]Ac 2:23; 3:13 [n]Hos 6:2; Mt 12:40; Lk 24:21,46; Jn 2:19; 1Co 15:3,4 [o]Mt 17:22,23; 27:63; Mk 9:31; Lk 9:22; 18:31-33; 24:6,7 **16:23** [p]S Mt 4:10

20Then he warned his disciples not to tell
anyone[i] that he was the Christ.

Jesus Predicts His Death

16:21-28pp — Mk 8:31–9:1; Lk 9:22-27

21From that time on Jesus began to explain to his disciples that he must go to
Jerusalem[j] and suffer many things[k] at the
hands of the elders, chief priests and teachers of the law,[l] and that he must be killed[m]
and on the third day[n] be raised to life.[o]
22Peter took him aside and began to rebuke him. "Never, Lord!" he said. "This
shall never happen to you!"
23Jesus turned and said to Peter, "Get
behind me, Satan![p] You are a stumbling
block to me; you do not have in mind the
things of God, but the things of men."
24Then Jesus said to his disciples, "If
anyone would come after me, he must
deny himself and take up his cross and

[a] *16* Or *Messiah*; also in verse 20 [b] *18* *Peter* means *rock.* [c] *18* Or *hell* [d] *18* Or *not prove stronger than it* [e] *19* Or *have been*

16:12 Matthew often explains the meaning of Jesus' words (cf. 17:13).

16:13 *Caesarea Philippi.* To be distinguished from the magnificent city of Caesarea, which Herod the Great had built on the Mediterranean coast. Caesarea Philippi, rebuilt by Herod's son Philip (who named it after Tiberius Caesar and himself), was north of the Sea of Galilee near the slopes of Mount Hermon on what is today the Golan Heights. Originally it was called Paneas (the ancient name survives today as Banias) in honor of the Greek god Pan, whose shrine was located there. The region was especially pagan. *Who do people say the Son of Man is?* See note on Lk 9:18. *Son of Man.* See note on Mk 8:31.

16:14 *John the Baptist.* See Mk 6:16 and note. *Elijah.* See Mk 6:15 and note.

16:16 *Peter answered.* See note on Lk 9:20. *Christ.* See NIV text note on 1:17; see also note on Jn 1:25. The OT equivalent (*Messiah*) is used of anyone who was anointed with the holy oil, such as the priests and kings of Israel (e.g., Ex 29:7,21; 1Sa 10;1,6; 16:13; 2Sa 1:14,16). The word carries the idea of being chosen by God, consecrated to his service, and endowed with his power to accomplish the assigned task. Toward the end of the OT period the word assumed a special meaning. It denoted the ideal king anointed and empowered by God to rescue his people from their enemies and establish his righteous kingdom (Da 9:25–26). The ideas that clustered around the title *Messiah* tended to be political and national in nature. Probably for that reason Jesus seldom used the term. When he did accept it as applied to himself, he did so with reservations (cf. Mk 8:27–30; 14:61–63).

16:17 *Simon son of Jonah.* In Jn 1:42 Jesus identifies Peter as "Simon son of John." Probably Simon Peter was the son of Johanan (the Hebrew form of the name), and Jonah is an Aramaic abbreviation of Johanan while John is from the Greek form of the name. *man.* Lit. "flesh and blood" (see notes on 1Co 15:50; Gal 1:16).

16:18 *Peter … rock … church.* In the Greek "Peter" is *petros* ("detached stone") and "rock" is *petra* ("bedrock"). Several interpretations have been given to these words: The bedrock on which the church is built is (1) Christ; (2) Peter's confession of faith in Jesus as the Messiah (v. 16); (3) Christ's teachings—one of the great emphases of Matthew's Gospel; (4) Peter himself, understood in terms of his role on the day of Pentecost (Ac 2), the Cornelius incident (Ac 10) and his leadership among the apostles. Eph 2:20 indicates that the church is "built on the foundation of the apostles and prophets" (see note on Jn 1:42). *church.* In the Gospels this word is used only by Matthew (here and twice in 18:17). In the Septuagint (the pre-Christian Greek translation of the OT) the underlying Greek word is used for the congregation of Israel. In Greek circles of Jesus' day it indicated the assembly of free, voting citizens in a city (cf. Ac 19:32,39,41). *Hades.* The Greek name for the place of departed spirits, generally equivalent to the Hebrew *Sheol* (see note on Ge 37:35). The "gates of Hades" may mean the "powers of death," i.e., all forces opposed to Christ and his kingdom (but see note on Job 17:16).

16:19 *keys.* Perhaps Peter used these keys on the day of Pentecost (Ac 2) when he announced that the door of the kingdom was unlocked to Jews and proselytes and later when he acknowledged that it was also opened to Gentiles (Ac 10; cf. Isa 22:22; Rev 3:7 and notes). *bind … loose.* Not authority to determine, but to announce, guilt or innocence (see 18:18 and context; cf. Jn 20:23 and note; Ac 5:3,9).

16:20 *not to tell.* Because of the false concepts of the Jews, who looked for an exclusively national and political Messiah, Jesus didn't want to precipitate a revolution against Rome (see notes on 8:4; Lk 9:21).

16:21 *began.* The beginning of a new emphasis in Jesus' ministry. Instead of teaching the crowds in parables, he concentrated on preparing the disciples for his coming suffering and death.

16:22 *Peter … began to rebuke him.* See note on Mk 8:32.

16:23 *Satan.* A loanword from Hebrew, meaning "adversary" or "accuser" (see NIV text note on Job 1:6; see also notes on Mk 8:33; Rev 2:9).

16:24 See note on Mk 8:34. *take up his cross.* See note on 10:38 (Lk 9:23 adds "daily"; see also note there).

follow me.[q] [25]For whoever wants to save
his life[a] will lose it, but whoever loses his
life for me will find it.[r] [26]What good will it
be for a man if he gains the whole world,
yet forfeits his soul? Or what can a man
give in exchange for his soul? [27]For the
Son of Man[s] is going to come[t] in his Father's glory with his angels, and then he
will reward each person according to what
he has done.[u] [28]I tell you the truth, some
who are standing here will not taste death
before they see the Son of Man coming in
his kingdom."

The Transfiguration

17:1-8pp — Lk 9:28-36
17:1-13pp — Mk 9:2-13

17 After six days Jesus took with him
Peter, James and John[v] the brother
of James, and led them up a high mountain by themselves. [2]There he was transfigured before them. His face shone like
the sun, and his clothes became as white
as the light. [3]Just then there appeared before them Moses and Elijah, talking with
Jesus.

[4]Peter said to Jesus, "Lord, it is good for
us to be here. If you wish, I will put up
three shelters—one for you, one for Moses and one for Elijah."

[5]While he was still speaking, a bright
cloud enveloped them, and a voice from
the cloud said, "This is my Son, whom I
love; with him I am well pleased.[w] Listen
to him!"[x]

16:24 [q]Mt 10:38; Lk 14:27
16:25 [r]S Jn 12:25
16:27 [s]S Mt 8:20 [t]S Lk 17:30; Jn 14:3; Ac 1:11; S 1Co 1:7; S 1Th 2:19; 4:16; S Rev 1:7; 22:7, 12, 20 [u]2Ch 6:23; Job 34:11; Ps 62:12; Jer 17:10; Eze 18:20; 1Co 3:12-15; 2Co 5:10; Rev 22:12
17:1 [v]S Mt 4:21
17:5 [w]S Mt 3:17 [x]Ac 3:22, 23
17:7 [y]S Mt 14:27
17:9 [z]S Mk 8:30 [a]S Mt 8:20 [b]S Mt 16:21
17:11 [c]Mal 4:6; Lk 1:16, 17
17:12 [d]S Mt 11:14 [e]Mt 14:3, 10 [f]S Mt 16:21
17:13 [g]S Mt 3:1
17:15 [h]Mt 4:24

[6]When the disciples heard this, they fell
facedown to the ground, terrified. [7]But
Jesus came and touched them. "Get up,"
he said. "Don't be afraid."[y] [8]When they
looked up, they saw no one except Jesus.

[9]As they were coming down the mountain, Jesus instructed them, "Don't tell
anyone[z] what you have seen, until the Son
of Man[a] has been raised from the dead."[b]

[10]The disciples asked him, "Why then
do the teachers of the law say that Elijah
must come first?"

[11]Jesus replied, "To be sure, Elijah comes
and will restore all things.[c] [12]But I tell you,
Elijah has already come,[d] and they did not
recognize him, but have done to him everything they wished.[e] In the same way
the Son of Man is going to suffer[f] at their
hands." [13]Then the disciples understood
that he was talking to them about John
the Baptist.[g]

The Healing of a Boy With a Demon

17:14-19pp — Mk 9:14-28; Lk 9:37-42

[14]When they came to the crowd, a man
approached Jesus and knelt before him.
[15]"Lord, have mercy on my son," he said.
"He has seizures[h] and is suffering greatly.
He often falls into the fire or into the water. [16]I brought him to your disciples, but
they could not heal him."

[17]"O unbelieving and perverse generation," Jesus replied, "how long shall I stay

[a] *25* The Greek word means either *life* or *soul*; also in verse 26.

16:25 *save his life.* See note on Mk 8:35. *whoever loses his life.* See note on Lk 9:24.
16:26 *whole world.* See note on Mk 8:36. *soul.* See note on 10:28.
16:27 *Son of Man.* See note on Mk 8:31. *is going to come.* The second coming of Christ. *in his Father's glory.* See note on Mk 8:38; cf. Jn 17:1–5. *according to what he has done.* See Ps 62:12 and note; see also notes on Ro 2:1–16; 2:6–8.
16:28 There are two main interpretations of this verse: (1) It is a prediction of the transfiguration, which happened a week later (17:1) and which demonstrated that Jesus will return "in his Father's glory" (16:27). (2) It refers to the Son of Man's authority and kingly reign in his post-resurrection church. Some of his disciples will witness—even participate in—this as described in the book of Acts. The context seems to favor the first view. See note on 2Pe 1:16.
17:1–9 The transfiguration was: (1) a revelation of the glory of the Son of God, a glory hidden now but to be fully revealed when he returns (see 2Th 1:10); (2) a confirmation of the difficult teaching given to the disciples at Caesarea Philippi (16:13–20); and (3) a beneficial experience for the disciples, who were discouraged after having been reminded so recently of Jesus' impending suffering and death (16:21). See notes on Mk 9:2–7; Lk 9:28–35.
17:1 *six days.* Mark also says "six days" (Mk 9:2), counting just the days between Peter's confession and the transfiguration, whereas Luke, counting all the days involved, says, "About eight days" (Lk 9:28). *Peter, James and John.* See 26:37; Mk 5:37 and note. *high mountain.* See note on Lk 9:28. *by themselves.* Luke adds "to pray" (Lk 9:28).
17:2 *he was transfigured.* His appearance changed. The three disciples saw Jesus in his glorified state (see Jn 17:5; 2Pe 1:17).
17:3 *Moses and Elijah.* Moses appears as the representative of the old covenant and the promise of salvation, which was soon to be fulfilled in the death of Jesus. Elijah appears as the appointed restorer of all things (Mal 4:5–6; Mk 9:11–13). Lk 9:31 says that they talked about Christ's death. See note on Lk 9:30.
17:4 *three shelters.* See notes on Mk 9:5; Lk 9:33.
17:5 *bright cloud.* Signifying the presence of God (see Ex 13:21; 19:16 and notes; 24:15–16; 34:5; 40:34–38; see also note on Mk 9:7). *them.* Jesus, Moses and Elijah. *This is my Son, whom I love; with him I am well pleased.* The same words spoken from heaven at Jesus' baptism (see 3:17 and note). No mere man, but the very Son of God, was transfigured. *Listen to him.* See note on Mk 9:7.
17:6 *terrified.* Primarily with a sense of awe at the presence and majesty of God.
17:9 *Don't tell anyone.* See note on Mk 9:9; cf. Lk 9:36.
17:10 Traditional Jewish eschatology, based on Mal 4:5–6, held that Elijah must appear before the coming of the Messiah. The disciples reasoned that if Jesus really was the Messiah, as the transfiguration proved him to be, why had not Elijah appeared?
17:12 *In the same way.* As John the Baptist was not recognized and was killed, so Jesus would be rejected and killed (see 14:1–12).
17:13 See note on 16:12.
17:15 *seizures.* See note on 4:24.
17:17 *unbelieving.* See v. 20 and note.

with you? How long shall I put up with
you? Bring the boy here to me." 18Jesus
rebuked the demon, and it came out of
the boy, and he was healed from that moment.
19Then the disciples came to Jesus in
private and asked, "Why couldn't we drive
it out?"
20He replied, "Because you have so little
faith. I tell you the truth, if you have faith[i]
as small as a mustard seed,[j] you can say to
this mountain, 'Move from here to there'
and it will move.[k] Nothing will be impossible for you.[a]"
22When they came together in Galilee,
he said to them, "The Son of Man[l] is going to be betrayed into the hands of men.
23They will kill him,[m] and on the third
day[n] he will be raised to life."[o] And the
disciples were filled with grief.

The Temple Tax

24After Jesus and his disciples arrived
in Capernaum, the collectors of the two-
drachma tax[p] came to Peter and asked,
"Doesn't your teacher pay the temple
tax[b]?"
25"Yes, he does," he replied.
When Peter came into the house, Jesus
was the first to speak. "What do you
think, Simon?" he asked. "From whom
do the kings of the earth collect duty and
taxes[q]—from their own sons or from others?"
26"From others," Peter answered.
"Then the sons are exempt," Jesus said
to him. 27"But so that we may not offend[r]
them, go to the lake and throw out your
line. Take the first fish you catch; open its
mouth and you will find a four-drachma
coin. Take it and give it to them for my tax
and yours."

17:20 [i]S Mt 21:21 [j]Mt 13:31; Lk 17:6 [k]1Co 13:2 **17:22** [l]S Mt 8:20 **17:23** [m]Ac 2:23; 3:13 [n]S Mt 16:21 [o]S Mt 16:21 **17:24** [p]Ex 30:13 **17:25** [q]Mt 22:17-21; Ro 13:7 **17:27** [r]Jn 6:61

The Greatest in the Kingdom of Heaven

18:1-5pp — Mk 9:33-37; Lk 9:46-48

18 At that time the disciples came to
Jesus and asked, "Who is the greatest in the kingdom of heaven?"
2He called a little child and had him
stand among them. 3And he said: "I tell
you the truth, unless you change and become like little children,[s] you will never
enter the kingdom of heaven.[t] 4Therefore,
whoever humbles himself like this child is
the greatest in the kingdom of heaven.[u]
5"And whoever welcomes a little child
like this in my name welcomes me.[v] 6But
if anyone causes one of these little ones
who believe in me to sin,[w] it would be better for him to have a large millstone hung
around his neck and to be drowned in the
depths of the sea.[x]
7"Woe to the world because of the things
that cause people to sin! Such things must
come, but woe to the man through whom
they come![y] 8If your hand or your foot causes you to sin,[z] cut it off and throw it away.
It is better for you to enter life maimed or
crippled than to have two hands or two
feet and be thrown into eternal fire. 9And
if your eye causes you to sin,[a] gouge it out
and throw it away. It is better for you to
enter life with one eye than to have two
eyes and be thrown into the fire of hell.[b]

The Parable of the Lost Sheep

18:12-14pp — Lk 15:4-7

10"See that you do not look down on
one of these little ones. For I tell you that
their angels[c] in heaven always see the face
of my Father in heaven.[c]

18:3 [s]Mt 19:14; 1Pe 2:2 [t]S Mt 3:2 **18:4** [u]S Mk 9:35 **18:5** [v]Mt 10:40 **18:6** [w]S Mt 5:29 [x]Mk 9:42; Lk 17:2 **18:7** [y]Lk 17:1 **18:8** [z]S Mt 5:29 **18:9** [a]S Mt 5:29 [b]S Mt 5:22 **18:10** [c]Ge 48:16; Ps 34:7; Ac 12:11,15; Heb 1:14

[a] 20 Some manuscripts *you.* 21*But this kind does not go out except by prayer and fasting.* [b] 24 Greek *the two drachmas* [c] 10 Some manuscripts *heaven.* 11*The Son of Man came to save what was lost.*

17:20 *little faith.* Not so much the quantity of their faith as its quality—a faith that is bathed in prayer (see Mk 9:29). *mustard seed.* See 13:31–32 and notes. *say to this mountain, 'Move from here to there.'* A proverbial statement meaning to remove great difficulties (cf. Isa 54:10; Zec 4:7 and note; 1Co 13:2). In this context it probably refers to removing the problems associated with the work of the kingdom.

17:21 See NIV text note on v. 20.

17:22 The second prediction of Christ's death, the first being in 16:21. *Galilee.* See note on Mk 9:30. *Son of Man.* See note on Mk 8:31.

17:24 *Capernaum.* See note on Mk 4:13. *two-drachma tax.* The annual temple tax required of every male 20 years of age and older (Ex 30:13; 2Ch 24:9; Ne 10:32). It was worth half a shekel (approximately two days' wages) and was used for the upkeep of the temple.

17:25 *What do you think . . . ?* Jesus frequently asks this question in Matthew's Gospel (18:12; 21:28; 22:17,42).

17:26 *the sons are exempt.* The implication is that Peter and the rest of the disciples belonged to God's royal household, but unbelieving Jews did not (see 21:43).

17:27 *not offend.* Elsewhere the Greek verb used here means "to cause to sin" (18:6,8–9), "to fall away" (11:6; 26:31,33), "to put an obstacle in the way (of faith)" (Ro 14:13; 16:17). Here it would appear that Jesus does not want an inconsequential matter to create an obstacle for faith in him on the part of the Jews.

18:1 *Who is the greatest . . . ?* See v. 4 and note on Lk 9:46.

18:3 *like little children.* Trusting and unpretentious.

18:4 *greatest.* See note on Lk 9:48.

18:6,10,14 *little ones.* All believers, regardless of age (see Mk 9:42 and note; Lk 17:2).

18:6 *large millstone.* Lit. "millstone of a donkey," i.e., a millstone turned by a donkey—far larger and heavier than the small millstones (24:41) used by women each morning.

18:8–9 Hyperbole: Deal as drastically as necessary with sin in order to remove it from your life. This calls for self-discipline. See note on 5:29–30.

18:8 *thrown into eternal fire.* See Rev 19:20 and note; 20:15.

18:9 *hell.* See note on 5:22.

18:10 *their angels.* Guardian angels not exclusively for children, but for God's people in general (Ps 34:7; 91:11; Heb 1:14). *always see the face of.* Have constant access to.

18:11 See NIV text note on v. 10.

12"What do you think? If a man owns a
hundred sheep, and one of them wanders
away, will he not leave the ninety-nine on
the hills and go to look for the one that
wandered off? 13And if he finds it, I tell
you the truth, he is happier about that one
sheep than about the ninety-nine that did
not wander off. 14In the same way your
Father in heaven is not willing that any of
these little ones should be lost.

A Brother Who Sins Against You

15"If your brother sins against you,[a] go
and show him his fault,[d] just between the
two of you. If he listens to you, you have
won your brother over. 16But if he will
not listen, take one or two others along,
so that 'every matter may be established
by the testimony of two or three witnesses.'[b][e] 17If he refuses to listen to them, tell
it to the church;[f] and if he refuses to listen even to the church, treat him as you
would a pagan or a tax collector.[g]
18"I tell you the truth, whatever you
bind on earth will be[c] bound in heaven,
and whatever you loose on earth will be[c]
loosed in heaven.[h]
19"Again, I tell you that if two of you on
earth agree about anything you ask for, it
will be done for you[i] by my Father in heav-
en. 20For where two or three come together in my name, there am I with them."[j]

The Parable of the Unmerciful Servant

21Then Peter came to Jesus and asked,
"Lord, how many times shall I forgive my
brother when he sins against me?[k] Up to
seven times?"[l]
22Jesus answered, "I tell you, not seven
times, but seventy-seven times.[d][m]
23"Therefore, the kingdom of heaven
is like[n] a king who wanted to settle accounts[o] with his servants. 24As he began
the settlement, a man who owed him ten
thousand talents[e] was brought to him.
25Since he was not able to pay,[p] the master ordered that he and his wife and his
children and all that he had be sold[q] to
repay the debt.
26"The servant fell on his knees before
him.[r] 'Be patient with me,' he begged, 'and
I will pay back everything.' 27The servant's
master took pity on him, canceled the debt
and let him go.
28"But when that servant went out, he
found one of his fellow servants who owed
him a hundred denarii.[f] He grabbed him
and began to choke him. 'Pay back what
you owe me!' he demanded.
29"His fellow servant fell to his knees
and begged him, 'Be patient with me, and
I will pay you back.'
30"But he refused. Instead, he went
off and had the man thrown into prison
until he could pay the debt. 31When the
other servants saw what had happened,
they were greatly distressed and went and
told their master everything that had happened.
32"Then the master called the servant
in. 'You wicked servant,' he said, 'I canceled all that debt of yours because you
begged me to. 33Shouldn't you have had
mercy on your fellow servant just as I had
on you?' 34In anger his master turned him
over to the jailers to be tortured, until he
should pay back all he owed.
35"This is how my heavenly Father will
treat each of you unless you forgive your
brother from your heart."[s]

Divorce

19:1-9pp — Mk 10:1-12

19 When Jesus had finished saying these
things,[t] he left Galilee and went into
the region of Judea to the other side of the
Jordan. 2Large crowds followed him, and
he healed them[u] there.

18:15 [d] Lev 19:17; Lk 17:3; Gal 6:1; Jas 5:19, 20 **18:16** [e] Nu 35:30; Dt 17:6; 19:15; Jn 8:17; 2Co 13:1; 1Ti 5:19; Heb 10:28 **18:17** [f] 1Co 6:1-6 [g] S Ro 16:17 **18:18** [h] Mt 16:19; Jn 20:23 **18:19** [i] S Mt 7:7 **18:20** [j] S Mt 28:20 **18:21** [k] S Mt 6:14 [l] Lk 17:4 **18:22** [m] Ge 4:24 **18:23** [n] S Mt 13:24 [o] Mt 25:19 **18:25** [p] Lk 7:42 [q] Lev 25:39; 2Ki 4:1; Ne 5:5, 8 **18:26** [r] S Mt 8:2 **18:35** [s] S Mt 6:14; S Jas 2:13 **19:1** [t] S Mt 7:28 **19:2** [u] S Mt 4:23

[a] *15* Some manuscripts do not have *against you.*
[b] *16* Deut. 19:15
[c] *18* Or *have been*
[d] *22* Or *seventy times seven*
[e] *24* That is, millions of dollars
[f] *28* That is, a few dollars

18:12–14 The parable of the lost/wandering (see vv. 12–13) sheep is also found in Lk 15:3–7. There it applies to unbelievers, here to believers. Jesus used the same parable to teach different truths in different situations.
18:12 *sheep.* See note on Lk 15:4.
18:13 Cf. the "father" in the parable of the lost son (Lk 15:31–32).
18:14 *not willing that any … should be lost.* See 1Ti 2:4; 2Pe 3:9 and notes.
18:15 *brother.* Fellow believer. *just between the two of you.* To protect the brother from the harm caused by gossip.
18:17 *church.* Local congregation. Here and 16:18 are the only two places where the Gospels use the word "church." *pagan.* For the Jews this meant any Gentile. *tax collector.* See note on 5:46. This verse establishes one basis for excommunication (when people refuse to respond to church discipline; see 2Th 3:14 and note; cf. Ro 16:17).
18:18 See note on 16:19.
18:19 *anything.* Probably not a reference to prayer generally but to disciplinary decisions, especially in the context of vv. 15–18.
18:20 Christ promises his presence with those involved in the proper disciplinary function of the church.
18:22 *seventy-seven times.* Times without number (see NIV text note).
18:23 *kingdom of heaven.* See note on 3:2.
18:24 *ten thousand talents.* See NIV text note.
18:25 For this practice of selling into slavery see Ex 21:2; Lev 25:39; 2Ki 4:1; Ne 5:5; Isa 50:1.
18:28 *hundred denarii.* See 20:2 and note.
18:35 God is very forgiving, but he also judges those who refuse to forgive (v. 34; cf. 6:12, 14–15).
19:1 *Judea.* See note on Mk 10:1. *other side of the Jordan.* The east side, known later as Transjordan or Perea and today simply as Jordan. Jesus now began ministering there (see note on Lk 13:22). *Jordan.* See note on Mk 1:5.

3 Some Pharisees came to him to test
him. They asked, "Is it lawful for a man
to divorce his wife[v] for any and every reason?"
4 "Haven't you read," he replied, "that
at the beginning the Creator 'made them
male and female,'[a][w] 5 and said, 'For this
reason a man will leave his father and
mother and be united to his wife, and the
two will become one flesh'[b]?[x] 6 So they are
no longer two, but one. Therefore what
God has joined together, let man not separate."
7 "Why then," they asked, "did Moses
command that a man give his wife a certificate of divorce and send her away?"[y]
8 Jesus replied, "Moses permitted you to
divorce your wives because your hearts
were hard. But it was not this way from
the beginning. 9 I tell you that anyone who
divorces his wife, except for marital unfaithfulness, and marries another woman
commits adultery."[z]
10 The disciples said to him, "If this is the
situation between a husband and wife, it
is better not to marry."
11 Jesus replied, "Not everyone can accept this word, but only those to whom it
has been given.[a] 12 For some are eunuchs
because they were born that way; others
were made that way by men; and others
have renounced marriage[c] because of the
kingdom of heaven. The one who can accept this should accept it."

The Little Children and Jesus

19:13-15pp — Mk 10:13-16; Lk 18:15-17

13 Then little children were brought to
Jesus for him to place his hands on them[b]
and pray for them. But the disciples rebuked those who brought them.
14 Jesus said, "Let the little children
come to me, and do not hinder them, for
the kingdom of heaven belongs[c] to such as
these."[d] 15 When he had placed his hands
on them, he went on from there.

The Rich Young Man

19:16-29pp — Mk 10:17-30; Lk 18:18-30

16 Now a man came up to Jesus and asked,
"Teacher, what good thing must I do to get
eternal life[e]?"[f]
17 "Why do you ask me about what is
good?" Jesus replied. "There is only One
who is good. If you want to enter life, obey
the commandments."[g]
18 "Which ones?" the man inquired.
Jesus replied, " 'Do not murder, do not
commit adultery,[h] do not steal, do not
give false testimony, 19 honor your father
and mother,'[d][i] and 'love your neighbor as
yourself.'[e]"[j]
20 "All these I have kept," the young man
said. "What do I still lack?"
21 Jesus answered, "If you want to be
perfect,[k] go, sell your possessions and give

19:3 [v] Mt 5:31 **19:4** [w] Ge 1:27; 5:2 **19:5** [x] Ge 2:24; 1Co 6:16; Eph 5:31 **19:7** [y] Dt 24:1-4; Mt 5:31 **19:9** [z] S Lk 16:18 **19:11** [a] S Mt 13:11; 1Co 7:7-9, 17 **19:13** [b] S Mk 5:23 **19:14** [c] S Mt 25:34 [d] Mt 18:3; 1Pe 2:2 **19:16** [e] S Mt 25:46 [f] Lk 10:25 **19:17** [g] Lev 18:5 **19:18** [h] Jas 2:11 **19:19** [i] Ex 20:12-16; Dt 5:16-20 [j] Lev 19:18; S Mt 5:43 **19:21** [k] Mt 5:48

[a] *4* Gen. 1:27 [b] *5* Gen. 2:24 [c] *12* Or *have made themselves eunuchs* [d] *19* Exodus 20:12-16; Deut. 5:16-20 [e] *19* Lev. 19:18

19:3 *Pharisees.* See note on Mk 2:16. *for any and every reason.* This last part of the question is not in the parallel passage in Mark (10:2). Matthew possibly included it because he was writing to Jews, who were aware of the dispute between the schools of Shammai and Hillel over the interpretation of Dt 24:1 – 4. Shammai held that "something indecent" (Dt 24:1) meant "marital unfaithfulness" (Mt 19:9) — to him the only allowable cause for divorce in that passage. Hillel emphasized the preceding clause, "who becomes displeasing to him" (Dt 24:1). He would allow a man to divorce his wife if she did anything he disliked — even if she burned his food while cooking it. Jesus clearly took the side of Shammai (see v. 9), but only after first pointing back to God's original ideal for marriage in Ge 1:27; 2:24.

19:10 – 12 See 1Co 7:7 – 8,26,32 – 35.

19:11 *this word.* The disciples' conclusion in v. 10: "it is better not to marry." This teaching is not meant for everyone. Jesus then gives three examples of persons for whom it is meant in v. 12.

19:12 *born that way.* Impotent. *made that way.* By castration. *have renounced marriage because of the kingdom of heaven.* Those who have voluntarily adopted a celibate lifestyle in order to give themselves more completely to God's work. Under certain circumstances celibacy is recommended in Scripture (cf. 1Co 7:25 – 38), but it is never presented as superior to marriage.

19:14 *kingdom of heaven.* See note on 3:2. *belongs to such as these.* See note on Mk 10:14.

19:15 *placed his hands on them.* Mk 10:16 adds "and blessed them."

19:16 *a man.* See note on Mk 10:17. *what good thing must I do . . . ?* The rich man was thinking in terms of righteousness by works. Jesus had to correct this misunderstanding first before answering the question more fully. *eternal life.* The first use of this term in Matthew's Gospel (see v. 29; 25:46). In John it occurs much more frequently, often taking the place of the term "kingdom of God (or heaven)" used in the Synoptics, which treat the following three expressions as synonymous: (1) eternal life (v. 16; Mk 10:17; Lk 18:18), (2) entering the kingdom of heaven (v. 23; cf. Mk 10:24; Lk 18:24) and (3) being saved (vv. 25 – 26; Mk 10:26 – 27; Lk 18:26 – 27).

19:17 *Why do you ask me about what is good?* Jesus wanted the man to think seriously about what is good, especially since Jesus' concept of it differed widely from that of the religious leaders (cf. Mk 10:18). *There is only One who is good.* The good is not something to be done as meritorious in itself. God alone is good, and all other goodness derives from him — even the keeping of the commandments, which Jesus proceeded to enumerate (vv. 18 – 20). *If you want to enter life, obey the commandments.* "To enter life" is the same as "to get eternal life" (v. 16). The requirement to "obey the commandments" is not to establish one's merit before God but is to be an expression of true faith. The Bible always teaches that salvation is a gift of God's grace received through faith (see Eph 2:8 – 9 and notes).

19:19 *love your neighbor as yourself.* See Lev 19:18 and note.

19:20 *All these I have kept.* See note on Mk 10:20.

19:21 *perfect.* The Greek word means "goal, end" (cf. note on Ro 10:4). His goal was eternal life, but wealth and lack of commitment stood in his way. *go, sell your possessions.* In his listing of the commandments, Jesus omitted "Do not covet." This was the rich man's main problem and was preventing him from entering life (see note on Mk 10:21).

to the poor,[l] and you will have treasure in
heaven.[m] Then come, follow me."
22When the young man heard this, he
went away sad, because he had great
wealth.
23Then Jesus said to his disciples, "I tell
you the truth, it is hard for a rich man[n] to
enter the kingdom of heaven. 24Again I tell
you, it is easier for a camel to go through
the eye of a needle than for a rich man to
enter the kingdom of God."
25When the disciples heard this, they
were greatly astonished and asked, "Who
then can be saved?"
26Jesus looked at them and said, "With
man this is impossible, but with God all
things are possible."[o]
27Peter answered him, "We have left everything to follow you![p] What then will
there be for us?"
28Jesus said to them, "I tell you the truth,
at the renewal of all things, when the Son
of Man sits on his glorious throne,[q] you
who have followed me will also sit on
twelve thrones, judging the twelve tribes
of Israel.[r] 29And everyone who has left
houses or brothers or sisters or father or
mother[a] or children or fields for my sake
will receive a hundred times as much and
will inherit eternal life.[s] 30But many who
are first will be last, and many who are
last will be first.[t]

The Parable of the Workers in the Vineyard

20 "For the kingdom of heaven is like[u]
a landowner who went out early in
the morning to hire men to work in his
vineyard.[v] 2He agreed to pay them a denarius for the day and sent them into his
vineyard.
3"About the third hour he went out and
saw others standing in the marketplace
doing nothing. 4He told them, 'You also go
and work in my vineyard, and I will pay
you whatever is right.' 5So they went.
"He went out again about the sixth hour
and the ninth hour and did the same thing.
6About the eleventh hour he went out and
found still others standing around. He
asked them, 'Why have you been standing here all day long doing nothing?'
7"'Because no one has hired us,' they
answered.
"He said to them, 'You also go and work
in my vineyard.'
8"When evening came,[w] the owner of
the vineyard said to his foreman, 'Call the
workers and pay them their wages, beginning with the last ones hired and going on
to the first.'
9"The workers who were hired about
the eleventh hour came and each received
a denarius. 10So when those came who
were hired first, they expected to receive
more. But each one of them also received
a denarius. 11When they received it, they
began to grumble[x] against the landowner.
12'These men who were hired last worked
only one hour,' they said, 'and you have
made them equal to us who have borne
the burden of the work and the heat[y] of
the day.'
13"But he answered one of them,
'Friend,[z] I am not being unfair to you.
Didn't you agree to work for a denarius?
14Take your pay and go. I want to give the
man who was hired last the same as I gave
you. 15Don't I have the right to do what I
want with my own money? Or are you envious because I am generous?'[a]
16"So the last will be first, and the first
will be last."[b]

Jesus Again Predicts His Death

20:17-19pp — Mk 10:32-34; Lk 18:31-33

17Now as Jesus was going up to Jerusalem, he took the twelve disciples aside and
said to them, 18"We are going up to Jerusa-

[a] 29 Some manuscripts *mother or wife*

19:21 [l] S Ac 2:45 [m] S Mt 6:20
19:23 [n] Mt 13:22; 1Ti 6:9, 10
19:26 [o] Ge 18:14; Job 42:2; Jer 32:17; Lk 1:37; 18:27; Ro 4:21
19:27 [p] S Mt 4:19
19:28 [q] Mt 20:21; 25:31 [r] Lk 22:28-30; Rev 3:21; 4:4; 20:4
19:29 [s] Mt 6:33; S 25:46
19:30 [t] Mt 20:16; Mk 10:31; Lk 13:30
20:1 [u] S Mt 13:24 [v] Mt 21:28, 33
20:8 [w] Lev 19:13; Dt 24:15
20:11 [x] Jnh 4:1
20:12 [y] Jnh 4:8; Lk 12:55; Jas 1:11
20:13 [z] Mt 22:12; 26:50
20:15 [a] Dt 15:9; Mk 7:22
20:16 [b] S Mt 19:30

19:22 *went away sad.* See note on Mk 10:22.
19:23 *kingdom of heaven.* See note on 3:2.
19:24 *camel to go through the eye of a needle.* See note on Mk 10:25.
19:26 See note on Mk 10:27.
19:28 *I tell you the truth.* See note on Mk 3:28. *Son of Man.* See note on Mk 8:31. *judging.* Governing or ruling (cf. OT "judge"; see Introduction to Judges: Title).
19:29 *receive a hundred times as much.* Mark adds, "and with them, persecutions" (see note on Mk 10:30). *inherit eternal life.* Eternal life is not earned; it is a gift. The word "inherit" often occurs in eschatological contexts in the NT (see 5:5; Mk 10:17; 1Co 6:9–10; 15:50; Gal 5:21; Heb 1:14; 6:12; Rev 21:7).
19:30 This saying of Jesus also appears in other contexts (see 20:16; Mk 10:31 and note; Lk 13:30). In the kingdom of heaven there are many reversals, and the day of judgment will bring many surprises.
20:1–16 This parable occurs only in Matthew's Gospel. In its original setting, its main point seems to be the sovereign graciousness and generosity of God extended to latecomers (the poor and the outcasts of society) into God's kingdom. It is addressed to the grumblers (v. 11) who just cannot handle this amazing expression of God's grace. They almost certainly represent the religious leaders who opposed Jesus.
20:2 *denarius.* The usual daily wage. A Roman soldier also received one denarius a day.
20:3 *third hour.* 9:00 A.M.
20:5 *sixth hour ... ninth hour.* Noon and 3:00 P.M. respectively.
20:6 *eleventh hour.* 5:00 P.M.
20:8 *When evening came.* Because farm workers were poor, the law of Moses required that they be paid at the end of each day (cf. Lev 19:13; Dt 24:14–15).
20:13 *Friend.* A term of mild rebuke (see 22:12; 26:50).
20:15 *are you envious ... ?* Lit. "is your eye evil ... ?" Apparently the evil eye was associated with jealousy and envy (cf. 1Sa 18:9). *because I am generous.* It was not a matter of justice but of generosity.
20:16 See note on 19:30.
20:17–19 See Mk 10:32–34; Lk 18:31–33 and notes.

lem,[c] and the Son of Man[d] will be betrayed
to the chief priests and the teachers of the
law.[e] They will condemn him to death
19and will turn him over to the Gentiles to
be mocked and flogged[f] and crucified.[g] On
the third day[h] he will be raised to life!"[i]

A Mother's Request

20:20-28pp — Mk 10:35-45

20Then the mother of Zebedee's sons[j]
came to Jesus with her sons and, kneeling
down,[k] asked a favor of him.
21"What is it you want?" he asked.
She said, "Grant that one of these two
sons of mine may sit at your right and the
other at your left in your kingdom."[l]
22"You don't know what you are asking," Jesus said to them. "Can you drink
the cup[m] I am going to drink?"
"We can," they answered.
23Jesus said to them, "You will indeed
drink from my cup,[n] but to sit at my right
or left is not for me to grant. These places
belong to those for whom they have been
prepared by my Father."
24When the ten heard about this, they
were indignant[o] with the two brothers.
25Jesus called them together and said, "You
know that the rulers of the Gentiles lord it
over them, and their high officials exercise
authority over them. 26Not so with you.
Instead, whoever wants to become great
among you must be your servant,[p] 27and
whoever wants to be first must be your
slave— 28just as the Son of Man[q] did not
come to be served, but to serve,[r] and to
give his life as a ransom[s] for many."

Two Blind Men Receive Sight

20:29-34pp — Mk 10:46-52; Lk 18:35-43

29As Jesus and his disciples were leaving Jericho, a large crowd followed him.
30Two blind men were sitting by the roadside, and when they heard that Jesus was
going by, they shouted, "Lord, Son of David,[t] have mercy on us!"
31The crowd rebuked them and told
them to be quiet, but they shouted all the
louder, "Lord, Son of David, have mercy
on us!"
32Jesus stopped and called them.
"What do you want me to do for you?"
he asked.
33"Lord," they answered, "we want our
sight."
34Jesus had compassion on them and
touched their eyes. Immediately they received their sight and followed him.

The Triumphal Entry

21:1-9pp — Mk 11:1-10; Lk 19:29-38
21:4-9pp — Jn 12:12-15

21 As they approached Jerusalem and
came to Bethphage on the Mount of
Olives,[u] Jesus sent two disciples, 2saying
to them, "Go to the village ahead of you,
and at once you will find a donkey tied
there, with her colt by her. Untie them
and bring them to me. 3If anyone says
anything to you, tell him that the Lord
needs them, and he will send them right
away."
4This took place to fulfill[v] what was spoken through the prophet:

5"Say to the Daughter of Zion,
'See, your king comes to you,
gentle and riding on a donkey,
on a colt, the foal of a donkey.'"[a][w]

6The disciples went and did as Jesus
had instructed them. 7They brought the
donkey and the colt, placed their cloaks

20:18 [c]S Lk 9:51 [d]S Mt 8:20 [e]Mt 27:1,2 **20:19** [f]S Mt 16:21 [g]S Ac 2:23 [h]S Mt 16:21 [i]S Mt 16:21 **20:20** [j]S Mt 4:21 [k]S Mt 8:2 **20:21** [l]Mt 19:28 **20:22** [m]Isa 51:17,22; Jer 49:12; Mt 26:39,42; Mk 14:36; Lk 22:42; Jn 18:11 **20:23** [n]Ac 12:2; Rev 1:9 **20:24** [o]Lk 22:24,25 **20:26** [p]S Mk 9:35 **20:28** [q]S Mt 8:20 [r]Isa 42:1; Lk 12:37; 22:27; Jn 13:13-16; 2Co 8:9; Php 2:7 [s]Ex 30:12; Isa 44:22; 53:10; Mt 26:28; 1Ti 2:6; Tit 2:14; Heb 9:28; 1Pe 1:18,19 **20:30** [t]S Mt 9:27 **21:1** [u]Mt 24:3; 26:30; Mk 14:26; Lk 19:37; 21:37; 22:39; Jn 8:1; Ac 1:12 **21:4** [v]S Mt 1:22 **21:5** [w]Isa 62:11; Zec 9:9

[a] 5 Zech. 9:9

20:19 *will turn him over to the Gentiles to be mocked and flogged and crucified.* An additional statement in this third prediction of the passion. Jesus would not be killed by the Jews, which would have been by stoning, but would be crucified by the Romans. All three predictions include his resurrection on the third day (16:21; 17:23).
20:20 *mother of Zebedee's sons.* Mark has "James and John, the sons of Zebedee," asking the question (Mk 10:35–37), yet there is no contradiction. The three joined in making the petition.
20:21 *want.* See note on Mk 10:35–36. *sit at your right and the other at your left.* See note on Mk 10:37.
20:22 *drink the cup.* A figure of speech meaning to "undergo" or "experience." Here the reference is to suffering (cf. 26:39). The same figure of speech is used in Jer 25:15; Eze 23:31–32; Hab 2:16; Rev 14:10; 16:19; 18:6 for divine wrath or judgment. See note on Mk 10:38.
20:23 *drink from my cup.* James was martyred (see Ac 12:2 and note); John was exiled (see Rev 1:9 and note). *is not for me to grant.* See note on Mk 10:40; see also Mt 11:27; 24:36; Jn 14:28.
20:24 See note on Mk 10:41.
20:26 *Not so with you.* See note on Mk 10:43.
20:28 *Son of Man.* See note on Mk 8:31. *ransom.* The Greek word was used most commonly for the price paid to redeem a slave. Similarly, Christ paid the ransom price of his own life to free us from the slavery of sin. *for.* Emphasizes the substitutionary nature of Christ's death. *many.* Christ "gave himself as a ransom for all men" (1Ti 2:6). Salvation is offered to "all," but only the "many" (i.e., the elect) receive it. See note on Mk 10:45.
20:29 *Jericho.* See note on Mk 10:46.
20:30 *Two blind men.* The other Synoptics mention only one (see note on Lk 18:35). *Son of David.* A Messianic title (see note on 9:27).
20:34 *compassion.* See note on 9:36.
21:1 *Jerusalem.* See map No. 10 at the end of this study Bible. *Bethphage.* Means "house of figs." It is mentioned in the Bible only in connection with the Triumphal Entry. See map, p. 1552. *Mount of Olives.* See note on Mk 11:1.
21:2 *donkey.* An animal symbolic of humility, peace and Davidic royalty (see notes on Zec 9:9; Lk 19:30). See also note on Mk 11:2. *colt.* See notes on Mk 11:2; Lk 19:30.
21:3 *Lord.* See note on Lk 19:31.
21:5 See note on Zec 9:9.
21:7 *Jesus sat on them.* He sat on the cloaks. We know from

on them, and Jesus sat on them. 8 A very
large crowd spread their cloaks[x] on the
road, while others cut branches from the
trees and spread them on the road. 9 The
crowds that went ahead of him and those
that followed shouted,

"Hosanna[a] to the Son of David!"[y]

"Blessed is he who comes in the name
of the Lord!"[b][z]

"Hosanna[a] in the highest!"[a]

10 When Jesus entered Jerusalem, the
whole city was stirred and asked, "Who
is this?"
11 The crowds answered, "This is Jesus,
the prophet[b] from Nazareth in Galilee."

Jesus at the Temple

21:12-16pp — Mk 11:15-18; Lk 19:45-47

12 Jesus entered the temple area and
drove out all who were buying[c] and selling there. He overturned the tables of the
money changers[d] and the benches of those
selling doves.[e] 13 "It is written," he said to
them, "'My house will be called a house
of prayer,'[c][f] but you are making it a 'den
of robbers.'[d]"[g]
14 The blind and the lame came to him
at the temple, and he healed them.[h] 15 But
when the chief priests and the teachers of
the law saw the wonderful things he did
and the children shouting in the temple
area, "Hosanna to the Son of David,"[i] they
were indignant.[j]
16 "Do you hear what these children are
saying?" they asked him.

"Yes," replied Jesus, "have you never
read,

"'From the lips of children and infants
you have ordained praise'[e]?"[k]

17 And he left them and went out of
the city to Bethany,[l] where he spent the
night.

The Fig Tree Withers

21:18-22pp — Mk 11:12-14,20-24

18 Early in the morning, as he was on his
way back to the city, he was hungry. 19 Seeing a fig tree by the road, he went up to
it but found nothing on it except leaves.
Then he said to it, "May you never bear
fruit again!" Immediately the tree withered.[m]
20 When the disciples saw this, they were
amazed. "How did the fig tree wither so
quickly?" they asked.
21 Jesus replied, "I tell you the truth, if
you have faith and do not doubt,[n] not only
can you do what was done to the fig tree,
but also you can say to this mountain,
'Go, throw yourself into the sea,' and it
will be done. 22 If you believe, you will receive whatever you ask for[o] in prayer."

The Authority of Jesus Questioned

21:23-27pp — Mk 11:27-33; Lk 20:1-8

23 Jesus entered the temple courts, and,
while he was teaching, the chief priests

21:8 [x] 2Ki 9:13 **21:9** [y] ver 15; S Mt 9:27 [z] Ps 118:26; Mt 23:39 [a] Lk 2:14 **21:11** [b] Dt 18:15; Lk 7:16,39; 24:19; Jn 1:21,25; 6:14; 7:40 **21:12** [c] Dt 14:26 [d] Ex 30:13 [e] Lev 1:14 **21:13** [f] Isa 56:7 [g] Jer 7:11 **21:14** [h] S Mt 4:23 **21:15** [i] ver 9; S Mt 9:27 [j] Lk 19:39 **21:16** [k] Ps 8:2 **21:17** [l] Mt 26:6; Mk 11:1; Lk 24:50; Jn 11:1,18; 12:1 **21:19** [m] Isa 34:4; Jer 8:13 **21:21** [n] Mt 17:20; Lk 17:6; 1Co 13:2; Jas 1:6 **21:22** [o] S Mt 7:7

[a] 9 A Hebrew expression meaning "Save!" which became an exclamation of praise; also in verse 15
[b] 9 Psalm 118:26 [c] 13 Isaiah 56:7 [d] 13 Jer. 7:11
[e] 16 Psalm 8:2

Mark (11:2) and Luke (19:30; see note there) that he rode the colt.

21:8 *spread their cloaks on the road.* An act of royal homage (see 2Ki 9:13). *branches.* See note on Mk 11:8.

21:9 These are three separate quotations, not necessarily spoken at the same time. *Hosanna.* See Ps 118:25–26 and notes; Jer 31:7 and notes; expresses both prayer and praise (see NIV text note). *Son of David.* See note on 9:27. *in the highest.* That is, may those in heaven sing "Hosanna" (see Ps 148:1–2; Lk 2:14).

21:10 *Who is this?* Because of Jesus' dramatic entry into the city, the people were wondering who he really was.

21:11 *the prophet.* Refers either to a prophet in general (see 13:57) or to the prophet predicted in Dt 18:15–18 (see note on 18:15; see also Dt 34:10–12 and note on 34:12).

21:12–17 In the Synoptics the clearing of the temple occurs during the last week of Jesus' ministry; in John it takes place during the first few months (Jn 2:12–16). Two explanations are possible: (1) There were two clearings, one at the beginning and the other at the end of Jesus' public ministry. (2) There was only one clearing, which took place during Passion Week but which John placed at the beginning of his account for theological reasons—to show that God's judgment was operative through the Messiah from the outset of Jesus' ministry. However, different details are present in the two accounts (the selling of cattle and sheep in Jn 2:14, the whip in Jn 2:15, and the statements of Jesus in Mt 21:13; Jn 2:16). From Matthew's and Luke's accounts we might assume that the clearing of the temple took place on Sunday, following the so-called Triumphal Entry (21:1–11). But Mark (11:15–19) clearly indicates that it was on Monday. Matthew often compressed narratives.

21:12 *temple area.* The "buying and selling" took place in the large outer court of the Gentiles, which covered several acres (see notes on Mk 11:15; Lk 19:45; Jn 2:14).

21:13 *house of prayer.* Mark adds "for all nations" (11:17; see note there). *den of robbers.* See Jer 7:11 and note.

21:16 See Ps 8:1b–2 and note.

21:17 *Bethany.* See note on Mk 11:1; a village on the eastern slope of the Mount of Olives, about two miles from Jerusalem and the final station on the road from Jericho to Jerusalem. It was the home of Mary, Martha and Lazarus (Jn 12:1–3).

21:18–22 See note on vv. 12–17; another example of compressing narratives. Mark (11:12–14,20–25) places the cursing of the fig tree on Monday morning and the disciples' finding it withered on Tuesday morning. In Matthew's account the tree withered as soon as Jesus cursed it, emphasizing the immediacy of judgment. For the theological meaning of this event see note on Mk 11:14.

21:18 *city.* Jerusalem.

21:21 *have faith and do not doubt.* See 17:20 and note; Jas 1:5–8. *Go, throw yourself into the sea.* A proverbial hyperbolic statement (cf. 17:20 and note).

21:22 See 1Jn 5:14–15 and note on 5:14.

21:23 *temple courts.* See note on Mk 11:27. *chief priests and the elders.* See notes on 2:4; Mk 8:31; Lk 19:47. *By what authority ...?* See notes on Mk 11:28; Lk 20:2.

and the elders of the people came to him.
"By what authority[p] are you doing these
things?" they asked. "And who gave you
this authority?"
24Jesus replied, "I will also ask you one
question. If you answer me, I will tell
you by what authority I am doing these
things. 25John's baptism—where did it
come from? Was it from heaven, or from
men?"
They discussed it among themselves
and said, "If we say, 'From heaven,' he
will ask, 'Then why didn't you believe
him?' 26But if we say, 'From men'—we are
afraid of the people, for they all hold that
John was a prophet."[q]
27So they answered Jesus, "We don't
know."
Then he said, "Neither will I tell you by
what authority I am doing these things.

The Parable of the Two Sons

28"What do you think? There was a man
who had two sons. He went to the first
and said, 'Son, go and work today in the
vineyard.'[r]
29" 'I will not,' he answered, but later he
changed his mind and went.
30"Then the father went to the other son
and said the same thing. He answered, 'I
will, sir,' but he did not go.
31"Which of the two did what his father
wanted?"
"The first," they answered.
Jesus said to them, "I tell you the truth,
the tax collectors[s] and the prostitutes[t] are
entering the kingdom of God ahead of
you. 32For John came to you to show you
the way of righteousness,[u] and you did not
believe him, but the tax collectors[v] and the
prostitutes[w] did. And even after you saw
this, you did not repent[x] and believe him.

The Parable of the Tenants

21:33-46pp — Mk 12:1-12; Lk 20:9-19

33"Listen to another parable: There was
a landowner who planted[y] a vineyard. He
put a wall around it, dug a winepress in
it and built a watchtower.[z] Then he rented the vineyard to some farmers and went

21:23 [p] Ac 4:7; 7:27
21:26 [q] S Mt 11:9
21:28 [r] ver 33; Mt 20:1
21:31 [s] Lk 7:29 [t] Lk 7:50
21:32 [u] Mt 3:1-12 [v] Lk 3:12, 13; 7:29 [w] Lk 7:36-50 [x] Lk 7:30
21:33 [y] Ps 80:8 [z] Isa 5:1-7

[a] Mt 25:14, 15
21:34 [b] Mt 22:3
21:35 [c] 2Ch 24:21; Mt 23:34, 37; Heb 11:36, 37
21:36 [d] Mt 22:4
21:38 [e] Heb 1:2 [f] S Mt 12:14 [g] Ps 2:8
21:41 [h] Mt 8:11, 12 [i] S Ac 13:46
21:42 [j] Ps 118:22, 23; S Ac 4:11
21:43 [k] Mt 8:12
21:44 [l] S Lk 2:34
21:46 [m] S ver 11, 26
22:2 [n] S Mt 13:24

away on a journey.[a] 34When the harvest
time approached, he sent his servants[b] to
the tenants to collect his fruit.
35"The tenants seized his servants; they
beat one, killed another, and stoned a
third.[c] 36Then he sent other servants[d] to
them, more than the first time, and the
tenants treated them the same way. 37Last
of all, he sent his son to them. 'They will
respect my son,' he said.
38"But when the tenants saw the son,
they said to each other, 'This is the heir.[e]
Come, let's kill him[f] and take his inheritance.'[g] 39So they took him and threw him
out of the vineyard and killed him.
40"Therefore, when the owner of the
vineyard comes, what will he do to those
tenants?"
41"He will bring those wretches to a
wretched end,"[h] they replied, "and he will
rent the vineyard to other tenants,[i] who
will give him his share of the crop at harvest time."
42Jesus said to them, "Have you never
read in the Scriptures:

" 'The stone the builders rejected
has become the capstone[a];
the Lord has done this,
and it is marvelous in our eyes'[b]?[j]

43"Therefore I tell you that the kingdom
of God will be taken away from you[k] and
given to a people who will produce its
fruit. 44He who falls on this stone will be
broken to pieces, but he on whom it falls
will be crushed."[c][l]
45When the chief priests and the Pharisees heard Jesus' parables, they knew he
was talking about them. 46They looked for
a way to arrest him, but they were afraid
of the crowd because the people held that
he was a prophet.[m]

The Parable of the Wedding Banquet

22:2-14Ref — Lk 14:16-24

22 Jesus spoke to them again in parables, saying: 2"The kingdom of heav-
en is like[n] a king who prepared a wedding

[a] 42 Or *cornerstone* [b] 42 Psalm 118:22,23
[c] 44 Some manuscripts do not have verse 44.

21:25 *from heaven, or from men?* See notes on Mk 11:30; Lk 20:4.
21:31 *tax collectors.* See note on 5:46. *kingdom of God.* See notes on 3:2; Lk 4:43; 1Co 4:20.
21:32 *way of righteousness.* Doing what is right and obeying God's will, which included believing what Jesus was teaching about how one is to enter "the kingdom of God" (v. 31).
21:33–46 See notes on Mk 12:1–12; Lk 20:9–19.
21:33 *winepress.* See notes on Isa 5:2; Rev 14:19. *watchtower.* For guarding the vineyard, especially when the grapes ripened, and for shelter (see Isa 5:2 and note).
21:35–37 The tenants are the Jews, or their leaders. The servants represent the OT prophets, many of whom were killed. The son represents Christ, who was condemned to death by the religious leaders.
21:41 *other tenants.* Gentiles, to whom Paul turned when Jews, for the most part, rejected the gospel (Ac 13:46; 18:6). By the second century the church was composed mainly of Gentiles.
21:42 See note on Ps 118:22. *Have you never read ...?* See v. 16; 12:3; 19:4; Mk 12:10.
21:44 *will be broken to pieces.* See note on Lk 20:18.
21:45 *chief priests.* See notes on 2:4; Mk 8:31; Lk 19:47. *Pharisees.* See notes on 3:7; Mk 2:16; Lk 5:17. *parables.* See notes on 13:3; Mk 4:2; Lk 8:4.
22:1–14 In Luke's Gospel this parable is spoken by Jesus at a banquet in response to a remark made by one of the guests

banquet for his son. 3He sent his servants[o]
to those who had been invited to the banquet to tell them to come, but they refused
to come.
4"Then he sent some more servants[p]
and said, 'Tell those who have been invited that I have prepared my dinner: My
oxen and fattened cattle have been butchered, and everything is ready. Come to the
wedding banquet.'
5"But they paid no attention and went
off—one to his field, another to his business. 6The rest seized his servants, mistreated them and killed them. 7The king
was enraged. He sent his army and destroyed those murderers[q] and burned their
city.
8"Then he said to his servants, 'The
wedding banquet is ready, but those I invited did not deserve to come. 9Go to the
street corners[r] and invite to the banquet
anyone you find.' 10So the servants went
out into the streets and gathered all the
people they could find, both good and
bad,[s] and the wedding hall was filled with
guests.
11"But when the king came in to see the
guests, he noticed a man there who was
not wearing wedding clothes. 12'Friend,'[t]
he asked, 'how did you get in here without
wedding clothes?' The man was speechless.
13"Then the king told the attendants,
'Tie him hand and foot, and throw him
outside, into the darkness, where there
will be weeping and gnashing of teeth.'[u]
14"For many are invited, but few are
chosen."[v]

22:3 [o] Mt 21:34 **22:4** [p] Mt 21:36 **22:7** [q] Lk 19:27 **22:9** [r] Eze 21:21 **22:10** [s] Mt 13:47,48 **22:12** [t] Mt 20:13; 26:50 **22:13** [u] S Mt 8:12 **22:14** [v] Rev 17:14

Paying Taxes to Caesar

22:15-22pp — Mk 12:13-17; Lk 20:20-26

15Then the Pharisees went out and laid
plans to trap him in his words. 16They sent
their disciples to him along with the Herodians.[w] "Teacher," they said, "we know
you are a man of integrity and that you
teach the way of God in accordance with
the truth. You aren't swayed by men, because you pay no attention to who they
are. 17Tell us then, what is your opinion? Is
it right to pay taxes[x] to Caesar or not?"
18But Jesus, knowing their evil intent,
said, "You hypocrites, why are you trying
to trap me? 19Show me the coin used for
paying the tax." They brought him a denarius, 20and he asked them, "Whose portrait is this? And whose inscription?"
21"Caesar's," they replied.
Then he said to them, "Give to Caesar what is Caesar's,[y] and to God what is
God's."
22When they heard this, they were
amazed. So they left him and went away.[z]

Marriage at the Resurrection

22:23-33pp — Mk 12:18-27; Lk 20:27-40

23That same day the Sadducees,[a] who
say there is no resurrection,[b] came to him
with a question. 24"Teacher," they said,
"Moses told us that if a man dies without
having children, his brother must marry
the widow and have children for him.[c]
25Now there were seven brothers among
us. The first one married and died, and
since he had no children, he left his wife
to his brother. 26The same thing happened

22:16 [w] Mk 3:6 **22:17** [x] Mt 17:25 **22:21** [y] Ro 13:7 **22:22** [z] Mk 12:12 **22:23** [a] S Ac 4:1 [b] Ac 23:8; 1Co 15:12 **22:24** [c] Dt 25:5,6

about "the feast in the kingdom of God" (Lk 14:15; see note there).

22:7 *burned their city.* A common military practice; here possibly an allusion to the coming destruction of Jerusalem in A.D. 70.

22:11 *not wearing wedding clothes.* It may have been the custom for a host to provide guests with wedding garments. This would have been necessary for the guests at this banquet in particular, for they were brought in directly from the streets (vv. 9–10). The failure of the man in question to avail himself of a wedding garment was therefore an insult to the host, who had made the garments available.

22:12 *Friend.* See note on 20:13.

22:13 *gnashing of teeth.* See note on 13:42.

22:14 A proverb-like summary of the meaning of the parable. God invites "many" (perhaps "all" in view of the Semitic usage of "many"; cf. 20:28; 26:28; Ro 5:15,19) to be part of his kingdom, but only some (a comparative "few") are chosen by him (Jesus appears to echo 2 Esdras 8:3: "Many have been created, but few will be saved"). This does not mean that God chooses arbitrarily. The invitation must be accepted, followed by appropriate conduct. Proper behavior is evidence of being chosen.

22:15–17 The Pharisees were ardent nationalists, opposed to Roman rule, while the hated Herodians, as their name indicates, supported Roman rule represented by the Herods. Now, however, the Pharisees enlisted the help of the Herodians to trap Jesus in his words (cf. note on Mk 3:6). After trying to put him off guard with flattery, they sprang their question: "Is it right to pay taxes to Caesar or not?" (v. 17). If he said "No," the Herodians would report him to the Roman governor and he would be executed for treason. If he said "Yes," the Pharisees would denounce him to the people as disloyal to his nation.

22:17 *pay taxes to Caesar.* See note on Mk 12:14.

22:18 *hypocrites.* See note on 6:2.

22:19 *denarius.* The common Roman coin of that day (see note on 20:2). On one side was the portrait of Emperor Tiberius and on the other the inscription in Latin: "Tiberius Caesar Augustus, son of the divine Augustus." The coin was issued by Tiberius and was used for paying tax to him.

22:21 *to God what is God's.* In distinguishing clearly between Caesar and God, Jesus also protested against the false and idolatrous claims made on the coins (see previous note; see also note on Mk 12:17).

22:22 *amazed.* See Mk 1:22 and note.

22:23 *Sadducees.* See notes on 3:7; Ezr 7:2; Mk 12:18; Lk 20:27; Ac 4:1; see also chart, p. 1502, and essay, p. 1453.

22:23–40 See Mk 12:18–31; Lk 20:27–40 and notes.

22:24 *Moses told us.* Jesus quoted from the Pentateuch when arguing with the Sadducees, since those books had special authority for them (see note on Mk 12:18). The reference (Dt 25:5–10) is to the levirate law (from Latin *levir,* "brother-in-law"), which was given to protect the widow and guarantee continuance of the family line.

to the second and third brother, right on
down to the seventh. 27Finally, the woman died. 28Now then, at the resurrection,
whose wife will she be of the seven, since
all of them were married to her?"
29Jesus replied, "You are in error because you do not know the Scriptures[d] or
the power of God. 30At the resurrection
people will neither marry nor be given in
marriage;[e] they will be like the angels in
heaven. 31But about the resurrection of the
dead—have you not read what God said
to you, 32'I am the God of Abraham, the
God of Isaac, and the God of Jacob'[a]?[f] He
is not the God of the dead but of the living."
33When the crowds heard this, they
were astonished at his teaching.[g]

The Greatest Commandment

22:34-40pp — Mk 12:28-31

34Hearing that Jesus had silenced the
Sadducees,[h] the Pharisees got together. 35One of them, an expert in the law,[i]
tested him with this question: 36"Teacher,
which is the greatest commandment in the
Law?"
37Jesus replied: "'Love the Lord your
God with all your heart and with all your
soul and with all your mind.'[b j] 38This is the
first and greatest commandment. 39And
the second is like it: 'Love your neighbor
as yourself.'[c k] 40All the Law and the Prophets hang on these two commandments."[l]

Whose Son Is the Christ?

22:41-46pp — Mk 12:35-37; Lk 20:41-44

41While the Pharisees were gathered
together, Jesus asked them, 42"What do
you think about the Christ[d]? Whose son
is he?"
"The son of David,"[m] they replied.
43He said to them, "How is it then that
David, speaking by the Spirit, calls him
'Lord'? For he says,

44"'The Lord said to my Lord:
"Sit at my right hand
until I put your enemies
under your feet."'[e n]

45If then David calls him 'Lord,' how can
he be his son?" 46No one could say a word
in reply, and from that day on no one
dared to ask him any more questions.[o]

Seven Woes

23:1-7pp — Mk 12:38,39; Lk 20:45,46
23:37-39pp — Lk 13:34,35

23 Then Jesus said to the crowds and to
his disciples: 2"The teachers of the
law[p] and the Pharisees sit in Moses' seat.
3So you must obey them and do everything
they tell you. But do not do what they do,
for they do not practice what they preach.
4They tie up heavy loads and put them on
men's shoulders, but they themselves are
not willing to lift a finger to move them.[q]
5"Everything they do is done for men to
see:[r] They make their phylacteries[f s] wide
and the tassels on their garments[t] long;
6they love the place of honor at banquets
and the most important seats in the synagogues;[u] 7they love to be greeted in the
marketplaces and to have men call them
'Rabbi.'[v]
8"But you are not to be called 'Rabbi,'
for you have only one Master and you are
all brothers. 9And do not call anyone on
earth 'father,' for you have one Father,[w]
and he is in heaven. 10Nor are you to be
called 'teacher,' for you have one Teacher, the Christ.[g] 11The greatest among you
will be your servant.[x] 12For whoever exalts himself will be humbled, and whoever
humbles himself will be exalted.[y]
13"Woe to you, teachers of the law and
Pharisees, you hypocrites![z] You shut the

22:29 [d] Jn 20:9
22:30 [e] Mt 24:38
22:32 [f] Ex 3:6; Ac 7:32
22:33 [g] S Mt 7:28
22:34 [h] S Ac 4:1
22:35 [i] Lk 7:30; 10:25; 11:45; 14:3
22:37 [j] Dt 6:5
22:39 [k] Lev 19:18; S Mt 5:43
22:40 [l] Mt 7:12; Lk 10:25-28
22:42 [m] S Mt 9:27
22:44 [n] Ps 110:1; 1Ki 5:3; Ac 2:34,35; 1Co 15:25; Heb 1:13; 10:13
22:46 [o] Mk 12:34; Lk 20:40
23:2 [p] Ezr 7:6,25
23:4 [q] Lk 11:46; Ac 15:10; Gal 6:13
23:5 [r] Mt 6:1,2,5,16 [s] Ex 13:9; Dt 6:8 [t] Nu 15:38; Dt 22:12
23:6 [u] Lk 11:43; 14:7; 20:46
23:7 [v] ver 8; Mt 26:25,49; Mk 9:5; 10:51; Jn 1:38,49; 3:2,26; 20:16
23:9 [w] Mal 1:6; Mt 6:9; 7:11
23:11 [x] S Mk 9:35
23:12 [y] 1Sa 2:8; Ps 18:27; Pr 3:34; Isa 57:15; Eze 21:26; Lk 1:52; 14:11
23:13 [z] ver 15,23,25,27,29

[a] 32 Exodus 3:6 [b] 37 Deut. 6:5 [c] 39 Lev. 19:18 [d] 42 Or *Messiah* [e] 44 Psalm 110:1 [f] 5 That is, boxes containing Scripture verses, worn on forehead and arm [g] 10 Or *Messiah*

22:37 *with all your heart ... soul ... mind.* With your whole being. The Hebrew of Dt 6:5 (see note there) has "heart ... soul ... strength," but some manuscripts of the Septuagint (the pre-Christian Greek translation of the OT) add "mind." Jesus combined all four terms in Mk 12:30. *soul.* See note on 10:28.
22:39 See note on Lev 19:18.
22:40 *the Law and the Prophets.* The entire OT (see note on 5:17).
22:41-46 See notes on Mk 12:35-40; Lk 20:44-47.
22:44 See note on Ps 110:1. Jesus bases his argument on Ps 110, the most frequently quoted OT passage in the NT (see introduction to Ps 110). He assumes the traditional Davidic authorship of the psalm and uses it in support of his argument.
23:2 *teachers of the law.* See note on 2:4. *Pharisees.* See notes on 3:7; Lk 5:17. *sit in Moses' seat.* A position of authority. They considered themselves to be the authorized successors of Moses as teachers of the law.
23:3 *not practice what they preach.* See Jas 1:22-25.
23:4 *tie up heavy loads and put them on men's shoulders.* Cf. Jesus' words in 11:28-30 and see note on 11:28; see also note on Lk 11:46.
23:5 *phylacteries.* These miniature boxes (see NIV text note) contained four passages (Ex 13:1-10; 13:11-16; Dt 6:4-9; 11:13-21). *tassels.* See note on Nu 15:38.
23:6 *most important seats in the synagogues.* See note on Mk 12:39.
23:7 *Rabbi.* A Hebrew word meaning "(my) teacher."
23:8-10 The warning is against seeking titles of honor to foster pride.
23:12 See Jas 4:6,10; 1Pe 5:5.
23:13-32 Seven woes pronounced by Jesus on the religious leaders (see the six woes in Lk 11:42-44,46-52; cf. the six woes in Isa 5:8-25 and in 28:1—35:10 [see note there]; and the five woes in Hab 2:6-19).
23:13 *hypocrites.* See vv. 15,23,25,27,29; see also note on 6:2. *shut the kingdom ... in men's faces.* See Lk 11:52 and note.

kingdom of heaven in men's faces. You
yourselves do not enter, nor will you let
those enter who are trying to.[a][a]
15"Woe to you, teachers of the law and
Pharisees, you hypocrites! You travel over
land and sea to win a single convert,[b] and
when he becomes one, you make him
twice as much a son of hell[c] as you are.
16"Woe to you, blind guides![d] You say,
'If anyone swears by the temple, it means
nothing; but if anyone swears by the gold
of the temple, he is bound by his oath.'[e]
17You blind fools! Which is greater: the
gold, or the temple that makes the gold
sacred?[f] 18You also say, 'If anyone swears
by the altar, it means nothing; but if anyone swears by the gift on it, he is bound
by his oath.' 19You blind men! Which is
greater: the gift, or the altar that makes the
gift sacred?[g] 20Therefore, he who swears
by the altar swears by it and by everything
on it. 21And he who swears by the temple
swears by it and by the one who dwells[h] in
it. 22And he who swears by heaven swears

23:13 [a]Lk 11:52
23:15 [b]Ac 2:11; 6:5; 13:43 [c]S Mt 5:22
23:16 [d]ver 24; Isa 9:16; Mt 15:14 [e]Mt 5:33-35
23:17 [f]Ex 30:29
23:19 [g]Ex 29:37
23:21 [h]1Ki 8:13; Ps 26:8

[a] 13 Some manuscripts *to.* [14]*Woe to you, teachers of the law and Pharisees, you hypocrites! You devour widows' houses and for a show make lengthy prayers. Therefore you will be punished more severely.*

23:14 See NIV text note on v. 13.
23:15 Jesus does not criticize the Pharisees for their evangelistic zeal. He objects to its results. The converts became even more sons of hell (i.e., bound for hell) than their teachers. *convert.* The Greek for this word is found in the NT only here and in Ac 2:11 (see note there); 6:5 (see note there); 13:43. *hell.* See notes on 5:22; Lk 12:5.
23:16–22 When the teachers of the law and the Pharisees took an oath, they differentiated between what was binding and what was not. This allowed for evasive oath-taking. Jesus rejected all such subtleties by showing how foolish they were and by insisting that people simply tell the truth (see 5:33–37 and note).

Jewish Sects

PHARISEES Their roots can be traced to Hasidim of the second century B.C. (see note on Mk 2:16).	1. Along with the Torah, they accepted as equally inspired and authoritative all the prescriptions set forth in the oral traditions preserved by the rabbis. 2. On free will and determination, they held to a mediating view that did not allow either human free will or the sovereignty of God to cancel out the other. 3. They accepted a rather developed hierarchy of angels and demons. 4. They believed in the immortality of the soul and in reward and retribution after death. 5. They believed in the resurrection of the dead. 6. They were champions of human equality. 7. The main emphasis of their teaching was ethical rather than theological.
SADDUCEES They probably had their beginning during the Hasmonean period (166–63 B.C.). Their demise occurred c. A.D. 70 with the fall of Jerusalem and the destruction of the temple.	1. They considered only the books of Moses to be canonical Scripture, denying that the oral law was authoritative and binding. 2. They interpreted the Mosaic law more literally than did the Pharisees. 3. They were very exacting in Levitical purity. 4. They attributed everything to free will. 5. They argued that there is neither resurrection of the dead nor a future life. 6. They rejected the idea of a spiritual world. 7. They rejected belief in angels and demons.
ESSENES They probably originated among the Hasidim, along with the Pharisees, from whom they later separated (1 Maccabees 2:42; 7:13). They were a group of very strict and zealous Jews who took part with the Maccabeans in a revolt against the Syrians, c. 165–155 B.C., and may have been the group who moved to Qumran c. 150 B.C., where they copied scrolls and deposited them in nearby caves (see essay, pp. 1452–1453).	1. They strictly observed the purity laws of the Torah. 2. They practiced communal ownership of property. 3. They had a strong sense of mutual responsibility. 4. Daily worship was an important feature along with daily study of their sacred scriptures. 5. Solemn oaths of piety and obedience had to be taken. 6. Sacrifices were offered on holy days and during their sacred seasons, but not at the temple. 7. Marriage was avoided but was not condemned in principle. 8. They attributed to fate everything that happened.
ZEALOTS They originated during the reign of Herod the Great c. 6 B.C. and were exterminated at Masada in A.D. 73.	1. They opposed payment of taxes to a pagan emperor because they believed that allegiance was due to God alone. 2. They were fiercely loyal to Jewish tradition. 3. They endorsed the use of violence as long as it accomplished a good end. 4. They were opposed to the use of the Greek language in the Holy Land.

by God’s throne and by the one who sits
on it.[i]
23“Woe to you, teachers of the law and
Pharisees, you hypocrites! You give a
tenth[j] of your spices — mint, dill and cummin. But you have neglected the more important matters of the law — justice, mercy
and faithfulness.[k] You should have practiced the latter, without neglecting the former. 24You blind guides![l] You strain out a
gnat but swallow a camel.
25“Woe to you, teachers of the law and
Pharisees, you hypocrites! You clean the
outside of the cup and dish,[m] but inside
they are full of greed and self-indulgence.[n]
26Blind Pharisee! First clean the inside of
the cup and dish, and then the outside
also will be clean.
27“Woe to you, teachers of the law and
Pharisees, you hypocrites! You are like
whitewashed tombs,[o] which look beautiful on the outside but on the inside are
full of dead men’s bones and everything
unclean. 28In the same way, on the outside
you appear to people as righteous but on
the inside you are full of hypocrisy and
wickedness.
29“Woe to you, teachers of the law and
Pharisees, you hypocrites! You build tombs
for the prophets[p] and decorate the graves
of the righteous. 30And you say, ‘If we had
lived in the days of our forefathers, we
would not have taken part with them in
shedding the blood of the prophets.’ 31So
you testify against yourselves that you are
the descendants of those who murdered
the prophets.[q] 32Fill up, then, the measure[r]
of the sin of your forefathers![s]

33“You snakes! You brood of vipers![t]
How will you escape being condemned to
hell?[u] 34Therefore I am sending you prophets and wise men and teachers. Some of
them you will kill and crucify;[v] others you
will flog in your synagogues[w] and pursue
from town to town.[x] 35And so upon you
will come all the righteous blood that has
been shed on earth, from the blood of
righteous Abel[y] to the blood of Zechariah son of Berekiah,[z] whom you murdered
between the temple and the altar.[a] 36I tell
you the truth, all this will come upon this
generation.[b]
37“O Jerusalem, Jerusalem, you who
kill the prophets and stone those sent to
you,[c] how often I have longed to gather
your children together, as a hen gathers
her chicks under her wings,[d] but you were
not willing. 38Look, your house is left to
you desolate.[e] 39For I tell you, you will not
see me again until you say, ‘Blessed is he
who comes in the name of the Lord.’[a]”[f]

Signs of the End of the Age

24:1-51pp — Mk 13:1-37; Lk 21:5-36

24 Jesus left the temple and was walking away when his disciples came up
to him to call his attention to its buildings.
2“Do you see all these things?” he asked.
“I tell you the truth, not one stone here
will be left on another;[g] every one will be
thrown down.”
3As Jesus was sitting on the Mount of
Olives,[h] the disciples came to him privately. “Tell us,” they said, “when will this

[a] *39* Psalm 118:26

23:22 [i] Ps 11:4; Mt 5:34 **23:23** [j] Lev 27:30 [k] Mic 6:8; Lk 11:42 **23:24** [l] ver 16 **23:25** [m] Mk 7:4 [n] Lk 11:39 **23:27** [o] Lk 11:44; Ac 23:3 **23:29** [p] Lk 11:47,48 **23:31** [q] S Mt 5:12 **23:32** [r] 1Th 2:16 [s] Eze 20:4 **23:33** [t] Mt 3:7; 12:34 [u] S Mt 5:22 **23:34** [v] 2Ch 36:15,16; Lk 11:49 [w] S Mt 10:17 [x] Mt 10:23 **23:35** [y] Ge 4:8; Heb 11:4 [z] Zec 1:1 [a] 2Ch 24:21 **23:36** [b] Mt 10:23; 24:34; Lk 11:50,51 **23:37** [c] 2Ch 24:21; S Mt 5:12 [d] Ps 57:1; 61:4; Isa 31:5 **23:38** [e] 1Ki 9:7,8; Jer 22:5 **23:39** [f] Ps 118:26; Mt 21:9 **24:2** [g] Lk 19:44 **24:3** [h] S Mt 21:1

23:23 Jesus does not criticize the observance of the minutiae of the law (he says, “without neglecting” them — including the tithe), but he does criticize the hypocrisy often involved (see notes on 5:18 – 20; Lk 11:42). *cummin.* A spice indigenous to western Asia and resembling the caraway in taste and appearance. *justice, mercy and faithfulness.* See Mic 6:6,8 and notes.

23:24 *strain out.* The strict Pharisee would carefully strain his drinking water through a cloth to be sure he did not swallow a gnat, the smallest of ceremonially unclean animals. But, figuratively, he would swallow a camel — one of the largest. *swallow a camel.* Hyperbole (see 7:3 and note; 19:24; Mk 10:25 and note).

23:26 *clean the inside.* A total moral renewal that will manifest itself in righteous living (see v. 23).

23:27 *whitewashed tombs.* A person who stepped on a grave became ceremonially unclean (see Nu 19:16), so graves were whitewashed to make them easily visible, especially at night. They appeared clean and beautiful on the outside, but the inside contained the bones of the dead and related matters that defiled persons, making them unclean.

23:29 *tombs for the prophets.* See note on Lk 11:47.

23:31 *descendants.* In the sense that they imitate the actions of their murderous ancestors.

23:32 Cf. Ge 15:16; 1Th 2:14 – 16; spoken ironically. They would bring the sin of their ancestors to completion with the crucifixion of the Son of God (cf. 21:38 – 39 and note on 21:35 – 37).

23:33 *hell.* See notes on 5:22; Lk 12:5.

23:34 *prophets and wise men and teachers.* Cf. Jer 18:18; Eze 7:26 and notes. *synagogues.* See note on Mk 1:21.

23:35 *Abel to . . . Zechariah.* The murder of Abel is recorded in Ge 4:8 and that of Zechariah, son (perhaps grandson, since he is here called “son of Berekiah”; see NIV text note on 1Ch 1:5; see also note on Da 5:1) of Jehoiada, in 2Ch 24:20 – 22 (Chronicles comes at the close of the OT according to the Hebrew arrangement). The expression was somewhat like our “from Genesis to Revelation.” Jesus was summing up the history of martyrdom in the OT.

23:36 *all this.* All the righteous blood of the martyrs (see v. 30). *will come upon this generation.* Jesus’ contemporaries; a prophecy fulfilled, at least in part, in the destruction of Jerusalem and the temple in A.D. 70 (see vv. 37 – 38).

23:37 – 39 See notes on Lk 13:34 – 35.

24:1 — 25:46 The Olivet discourse, the fifth and last of the great discourses in Matthew’s Gospel (see notes on 5:1 — 7:29; Mk 13:1 – 37; Lk 21:5 – 37; see also Introduction: Structure).

24:2 *not one stone . . . left.* Fulfilled literally in A.D. 70, when the Romans under Titus completely destroyed Jerusalem and the temple buildings. Stones were even pried apart to collect the gold leaf that melted from the roof when the temple was set on fire. *stone.* See note on Mk 13:1. *thrown down.* Excavations in 1968 uncovered large numbers of these stones, toppled from the walls by the invaders.

24:3 *Mount of Olives.* A ridge a little more than a mile long, beyond the Kidron Valley east of Jerusalem and

happen, and what will be the sign of your
coming[i] and of the end of the age?"[j]
4 Jesus answered: "Watch out that no
one deceives you.[k] 5 For many will come
in my name, claiming, 'I am the Christ,[a]'
and will deceive many.[l] 6 You will hear of
wars and rumors of wars, but see to it that
you are not alarmed. Such things must
happen, but the end is still to come. 7 Nation will rise against nation, and kingdom
against kingdom.[m] There will be famines[n]
and earthquakes in various places. 8 All
these are the beginning of birth pains.
9 "Then you will be handed over to be
persecuted[o] and put to death,[p] and you
will be hated by all nations because of
me.[q] 10 At that time many will turn away
from the faith and will betray and hate
each other, 11 and many false prophets[r]
will appear and deceive many people.[s]
12 Because of the increase of wickedness,
the love of most will grow cold, 13 but he
who stands firm to the end will be saved.[t]
14 And this gospel of the kingdom[u] will be
preached in the whole world[v] as a testimony to all nations, and then the end will
come.
15 "So when you see standing in the holy
place[w] 'the abomination that causes desolation,'[b][x] spoken of through the prophet Daniel—let the reader understand—
16 then let those who are in Judea flee to
the mountains. 17 Let no one on the roof
of his house[y] go down to take anything
out of the house. 18 Let no one in the field
go back to get his cloak. 19 How dreadful it will be in those days for pregnant
women and nursing mothers![z] 20 Pray that
your flight will not take place in winter or
on the Sabbath. 21 For then there will be
great distress, unequaled from the beginning of the world until now—and never
to be equaled again.[a] 22 If those days had
not been cut short, no one would survive,
but for the sake of the elect[b] those days
will be shortened. 23 At that time if anyone
says to you, 'Look, here is the Christ!' or,
'There he is!' do not believe it.[c] 24 For false
Christs and false prophets will appear and
perform great signs and miracles[d] to deceive even the elect—if that were possible. 25 See, I have told you ahead of time.
26 "So if anyone tells you, 'There he is,
out in the desert,' do not go out; or, 'Here
he is, in the inner rooms,' do not believe
it. 27 For as lightning[e] that comes from the
east is visible even in the west, so will be
the coming[f] of the Son of Man.[g] 28 Wherever there is a carcass, there the vultures
will gather.[h]

24:3 [i]S Lk 17:30 [j]Mt 13:39; 28:20 **24:4** [k]S Mk 13:5 **24:5** [l]ver 11,23, 24; 1Jn 2:18 **24:7** [m]Isa 19:2 [n]Ac 11:28 **24:9** [o]Mt 10:17 [p]Jn 16:2 [q]S Jn 15:21 **24:11** [r]S Mt 7:15 [s]S Mk 13:5 **24:13** [t]S Mt 10:22 **24:14** [u]S Mt 4:23 [v]Lk 2:1; 4:5; Ac 11:28; 17:6; S Ro 10:18 **24:15** [w]S Ac 6:13 [x]Da 9:27; 11:31; 12:11 **24:17** [y]1Sa 9:25; Mt 10:27; Lk 12:3; Ac 10:9 **24:19** [z]Lk 23:29 **24:21** [a]Eze 5:9; Da 12:1; Joel 2:2 **24:22** [b]ver 24,31 **24:23** [c]Lk 17:23; 21:8 **24:24** [d]Ex 7:11,22; 2Th 2:9-11; Rev 13:13; 16:14; 19:20 **24:27** [e]Lk 17:24 [f]S Lk 17:30 [g]S Mt 8:20 **24:28** [h]Lk 17:37

[a] *5* Or *Messiah*; also in verse 23 [b] *15* Daniel 9:27; 11:31; 12:11

rising about 200 feet above the city (see map, pp. 1552–1553). *when will this happen, and what will be the sign of your coming and of the end of the age?* Jesus deals with these questions but does not distinguish them sharply. However, it appears that the description of the last days (which begin with Jesus' incarnation and end with his second coming) is presented in vv. 4–14, the destruction of Jerusalem in vv. 15–22 (see Lk 21:20) and Christ's coming in vv. 23–31. The rest of the discourse is largely taken up with warnings and exhortations to live responsibly and courageously despite trials, persecutions and uncertainty about the exact time of his coming (24:32—25:46). This last section contains several eschatological parables (25:1–13,14–30,31–46).

24:4 *Watch out.* See note on Mk 13:5.

24:5–14 See Lk 21:8–18 and note on 21:9.

24:5 *in my name.* Claiming to be the Messiah (see Mk 13:6 and note). *Christ.* See NIV text note on 1:17. *will deceive many.* See 1Jn 2:18 and note.

24:8 *birth pains.* The rabbis spoke of "birth pains," i.e., sufferings, that would precede the coming of the Messiah (see Isa 13:8 and note).

24:13 See note on Mk 13:13; cf. 2Ti 2:10–13; Heb 10:36; 11:27; Jas 1:12; 5:11.

24:14 *preached in the whole world.* Despite his Jewish interests, Matthew has a universal outlook (see Introduction: Recipients). *testimony to all nations.* This missionary mandate (see 28:18–20 and notes) must be fulfilled before the end comes.

24:15 *the abomination that causes desolation.* The detestable thing causing the desolation of the holy place. The primary reference in Daniel (see NIV text note for references) was to 168 B.C., when Antiochus IV Epiphanes erected a pagan altar to Zeus in the temple of Jerusalem. According to some, there were still two more stages in the progressive fulfillment of the predictions in Daniel and Matthew: (1) the Roman destruction of the temple in A.D. 70, and (2) the setting up of an image of the antichrist in Jerusalem (see 2Th 2:4; Rev 13:14–15; see also notes on Da 9:25–27; 11:31). *let the reader understand.* These are Jesus' words, not Matthew's. He exhorts the readers of Daniel's prophecy to understand what they read.

24:16 *mountains.* The Transjordan mountains, where Pella was located. Christians in Jerusalem fled to that area during the Roman siege shortly before A.D. 70. Some believe a similar fleeing will occur in a future tribulation period (identified with the 70th "seven" in Da 9:27).

24:17 *roof of his house.* See notes on Mk 2:4; Lk 17:31.

24:19 See note on Mk 13:17.

24:20 *in winter.* See note on Mk 13:18. *or on the Sabbath.* Matthew alone includes this phrase because he was writing to Jews, who were forbidden to travel more than about three quarters of a mile on the Sabbath ("a Sabbath day's walk," Ac 1:12; see note there).

24:21 *great distress, unequaled.* Josephus, the Jewish historian who was there, describes the destruction of Jerusalem in almost identical language. Some believe the reference is also to a future period of great distress (see note on v. 16; see also Da 12:1 and note; cf. Rev 6–18).

24:22 *days . . . cut short.* Some hold that this statement means that the distress will be of such intensity that, if allowed to continue, it would destroy everyone. Others believe that Christ is referring to the cutting short of a previously determined time period (such as the 70th "seven" of Da 9:27 or the 42 months of Rev 11:2; 13:5). *the elect.* The people of God.

24:24 *false Christs.* See 1Jn 2:18 and note.

24:26 *inner rooms.* See Lk 12:3 and note.

24:27 Christ's second coming will not be in secret, witnessed by only a favored few; it will be visible to all (see v. 30). *as lightning.* See note on Lk 17:24.

24:28 *there the vultures will gather.* The gathering of vultures obviously indicates the presence of carrion; the coming of

29“Immediately after the distress of
those days

“ ‘the sun will be darkened,
and the moon will not give its light;
the stars will fall from the sky,
and the heavenly bodies will be
shaken.’[a][i]

30“At that time the sign of the Son of
Man will appear in the sky, and all the nations of the earth will mourn.[j] They will
see the Son of Man coming on the clouds
of the sky,[k] with power and great glory.
31And he will send his angels[l] with a loud
trumpet call,[m] and they will gather his
elect from the four winds, from one end
of the heavens to the other.

32“Now learn this lesson from the fig
tree: As soon as its twigs get tender and its
leaves come out, you know that summer
is near. 33Even so, when you see all these
things, you know that it[b] is near, right at
the door.[n] 34I tell you the truth, this generation[c] will certainly not pass away until
all these things have happened.[o] 35Heaven
and earth will pass away, but my words
will never pass away.[p]

The Day and Hour Unknown

24:37-39pp — Lk 17:26,27
24:45-51pp — Lk 12:42-46

36“No one knows about that day or
hour, not even the angels in heaven, nor
the Son,[d] but only the Father.[q] 37As it was
in the days of Noah,[r] so it will be at the
coming of the Son of Man. 38For in the
days before the flood, people were eating and drinking, marrying and giving in
marriage,[s] up to the day Noah entered the
ark; 39and they knew nothing about what
would happen until the flood came and
took them all away. That is how it will be
at the coming of the Son of Man.[t] 40Two
men will be in the field; one will be taken
and the other left.[u] 41Two women will be
grinding with a hand mill; one will be tak-
en and the other left.[v]

42“Therefore keep watch, because you
do not know on what day your Lord will
come.[w] 43But understand this: If the owner of the house had known at what time
of night the thief was coming,[x] he would
have kept watch and would not have let
his house be broken into. 44So you also
must be ready,[y] because the Son of Man
will come at an hour when you do not expect him.

45“Who then is the faithful and wise servant,[z] whom the master has put in charge
of the servants in his household to give
them their food at the proper time? 46It
will be good for that servant whose master
finds him doing so when he returns.[a] 47I
tell you the truth, he will put him in charge
of all his possessions.[b] 48But suppose that
servant is wicked and says to himself, ‘My
master is staying away a long time,’ 49and
he then begins to beat his fellow servants
and to eat and drink with drunkards.[c]
50The master of that servant will come on
a day when he does not expect him and at
an hour he is not aware of. 51He will cut
him to pieces and assign him a place with
the hypocrites, where there will be weeping and gnashing of teeth.[d]

The Parable of the Ten Virgins

25 “At that time the kingdom of heav-
en will be like[e] ten virgins who took
their lamps[f] and went out to meet the
bridegroom.[g] 2Five of them were foolish
and five were wise.[h] 3The foolish ones took
their lamps but did not take any oil with
them. 4The wise, however, took oil in jars
along with their lamps. 5The bridegroom
was a long time in coming, and they all
became drowsy and fell asleep.[i]
6“At midnight the cry rang out: ‘Here's
the bridegroom! Come out to meet him!’

24:29 [i]Isa 13:10; 34:4; Eze 32:7; Joel 2:10,31; Zep 1:15; Rev 6:12,13; 8:12 **24:30** [j]Rev 1:7 [k]S Rev 1:7 **24:31** [l]Mt 13:41 [m]Isa 27:13; Zec 9:14; 1Co 15:52; 1Th 4:16; Rev 8:2; 10:7; 11:15 **24:33** [n]Jas 5:9 **24:34** [o]Mt 16:28; S 23:36 **24:35** [p]S Mt 5:18 **24:36** [q]Ac 1:7 **24:37** [r]Ge 6:5; 7:6-23 **24:38** [s]Mt 22:30 **24:39** [t]S Lk 17:30 **24:40** [u]Lk 17:34 **24:41** [v]Lk 17:35 **24:42** [w]Mt 25:13; Lk 12:40 **24:43** [x]S Lk 12:39 **24:44** [y]1Th 5:6 **24:45** [z]Mt 25:21,23 **24:46** [a]Rev 16:15 **24:47** [b]Mt 25:21,23 **24:49** [c]Lk 21:34 **24:51** [d]S Mt 8:12 **25:1** [e]S Mt 13:24 [f]Lk 12:35-38; Ac 20:8; Rev 4:5 [g]Rev 19:7; 21:2 **25:2** [h]Mt 24:45 **25:5** [i]1Th 5:6

[a] 29 Isaiah 13:10; 34:4 [b] 33 Or *he* [c] 34 Or *race*
[d] 36 Some manuscripts do not have *nor the Son.*

Christ will likewise be obvious. See note on Lk 17:37, where the saying is used in a slightly different sense.

24:29 See note on Mk 13:25.

24:30 *sign.* Here probably means "banner" or "standard" (see Isa 11:12; 18:3; 49:22; Jer 4:21; 51:27). *Son of Man.* See note on Mk 8:31. *all the nations … will mourn.* Because they now face judgment (see Rev 1:7; cf. Zec 12:10–12). *the Son of Man coming on the clouds.* Alludes to Da 7:13 and refers to Christ's second coming (see 2Th 1:7–10; Rev 19:11–16). *on the clouds.* After the manner in which God came down on Mount Sinai (see 17:5 and note). *with power and great glory.* Cf. 1Ch 29:11; Ps 63:2; 66:2–3; Hab 3:3–4.

24:31 *gather his elect.* See note on Mk 13:27.

24:33 *it.* The kingdom of God (see Lk 21:31 and note on 21:29).

24:34 *I tell you the truth.* See note on Mk 3:28. *this generation.* See note on Lk 21:32.

24:35 Jesus' words are more certain than the existence of the universe.

24:36 *that day.* See note on Lk 21:34. *nor the Son.* See note on Mk 13:32.

24:40–41 *taken.* See note on Lk 17:35.

24:42 *keep watch.* Vigilance is the order of the day, because the time of Christ's coming is unknown (see notes on Mk 13:32,37).

24:44 *be ready.* See 25:10,29; 1Th 5:6 and notes; cf. 1Jn 2:28.

24:51 *weeping and gnashing of teeth.* See note on 13:42.

25:1–12 The parable emphasizes the need for watchfulness in the event of a long delay in Christ's coming (see v. 13 and note).

25:1 *At that time.* The time of Christ's coming. *kingdom of heaven.* See note on 3:2. *ten virgins.* Perhaps the bridesmaids, who were responsible for preparing the bride to meet the bridegroom. *lamps.* The Greek noun can refer to lamps or torches (as in Rev 8:10), which is probably its meaning here.

25:3 *oil.* Olive oil.

7“Then all the virgins woke up and
trimmed their lamps. 8The foolish ones
said to the wise, ‘Give us some of your oil;
our lamps are going out.’[j]
9“ ‘No,’ they replied, ‘there may not be
enough for both us and you. Instead, go to
those who sell oil and buy some for yourselves.’
10“But while they were on their way to
buy the oil, the bridegroom arrived. The
virgins who were ready went in with him
to the wedding banquet.[k] And the door
was shut.
11“Later the others also came. ‘Sir! Sir!’
they said. ‘Open the door for us!’
12“But he replied, ‘I tell you the truth, I
don’t know you.’[l]
13“Therefore keep watch, because you
do not know the day or the hour.[m]

The Parable of the Talents

25:14-30Ref — Lk 19:12-27

14“Again, it will be like a man going on a
journey,[n] who called his servants and entrusted his property to them. 15To one he
gave five talents[a] of money, to another two
talents, and to another one talent, each according to his ability.[o] Then he went on
his journey. 16The man who had received
the five talents went at once and put his
money to work and gained five more. 17So
also, the one with the two talents gained
two more. 18But the man who had received
the one talent went off, dug a hole in the
ground and hid his master’s money.
19“After a long time the master of those
servants returned and settled accounts
with them.[p] 20The man who had received
the five talents brought the other five.
‘Master,’ he said, ‘you entrusted me with
five talents. See, I have gained five more.’
21“His master replied, ‘Well done, good
and faithful servant! You have been faithful with a few things; I will put you in
charge of many things.[q] Come and share
your master’s happiness!’
22“The man with the two talents also
came. ‘Master,’ he said, ‘you entrusted me
with two talents; see, I have gained two
more.’
23“His master replied, ‘Well done, good
and faithful servant! You have been faithful with a few things; I will put you in
charge of many things.[r] Come and share
your master’s happiness!’
24“Then the man who had received the
one talent came. ‘Master,’ he said, ‘I knew
that you are a hard man, harvesting where
you have not sown and gathering where
you have not scattered seed. 25So I was
afraid and went out and hid your talent
in the ground. See, here is what belongs
to you.’
26“His master replied, ‘You wicked, lazy
servant! So you knew that I harvest where
I have not sown and gather where I have
not scattered seed? 27Well then, you should
have put my money on deposit with the
bankers, so that when I returned I would
have received it back with interest.
28“ ‘Take the talent from him and give it
to the one who has the ten talents. 29For
everyone who has will be given more, and
he will have an abundance. Whoever does
not have, even what he has will be tak-
en from him.[s] 30And throw that worthless
servant outside, into the darkness, where
there will be weeping and gnashing of
teeth.’[t]

The Sheep and the Goats

31“When the Son of Man comes[u] in his
glory, and all the angels with him, he
will sit on his throne[v] in heavenly glory.

25:8 [j]Lk 12:35 **25:10** [k]Rev 19:9 **25:12** [l]ver 41; S Mt 7:23 **25:13** [m]Mt 24:42,44; Mk 13:35; Lk 12:40 **25:14** [n]Mt 21:33; Lk 19:12 **25:15** [o]Mt 18:24,25 **25:19** [p]Mt 18:23 **25:21** [q]ver 23; Mt 24:45,47; Lk 16:10 **25:23** [r]ver 21 **25:29** [s]Mt 13:12; Mk 4:25; Lk 8:18; 19:26 **25:30** [t]S Mt 8:12 **25:31** [u]S Lk 17:30 [v]Mt 19:28

[a] *15* A talent was worth more than a thousand dollars.

25:7 *trimmed.* The charred ends of the rags were cut off and oil was added.

25:9 *No.* When Christ returns, preparedness cannot be shared or transferred. Personal responsibility is emphasized (see v. 12). *there may not be enough.* Torches required large amounts of oil in order to keep burning, and the oil had to be replenished about every 15 minutes.

25:13 *keep watch.* The main point of the parable. *the day or the hour.* Of the coming of Christ (see 24:36 and note).

25:14–30 For a similar parable see Lk 19:12–27.

25:15 *talent.* The term was first used for a unit of weight (about 75 pounds), then for a unit of coinage. The present-day use of "talent" to indicate an ability or gift is derived from this parable and often leads to a misunderstanding of the parable.

25:21 *faithful with a few ... in charge of many.* Cf. 13:12; see notes on v. 29; Mk 4:25; Lk 19:26.

25:26 See note on Lk 19:22.

25:27 *bankers.* Sat at small tables and changed money (cf. 21:12).

25:29 The main point of the parable. Being ready for Christ's coming involves more than playing it safe and doing little or nothing. It demands the kind of devoted service in Christ's kingdom that produces results (see note on Lk 19:26).

25:30 *weeping and gnashing of teeth.* See note on 13:42.

25:31–46 The two most widely accepted interpretations of this judgment are: (1) It will occur at the beginning of an earthly millennial kingdom (vv. 31,34; see Rev 20:4 and note on 20:2). Its purpose will be to determine who will be allowed to enter the kingdom (v. 34). The basis for judgment will be the kind of treatment shown to the Jewish people ("these brothers of mine," v. 40) during the preceding great tribulation period (vv. 35–40,42–45). Ultimately, how one treats them will reveal whether or not one is saved (vv. 41,46). (2) The judgment referred to occurs at the great white throne at the end of the age (Rev 20:11–15). Its purpose will be to determine who will be allowed to enter the eternal kingdom of the saved and who will be consigned to eternal punishment in hell (vv. 34,46). The basis for judgment will be whether love is shown to God's people (see 1Jn 3:14–15). See note on v. 40.

25:31 *Son of Man.* See note on Mk 8:31. *in his glory.* See 16:27; 24:30. *angels.* See 13:41–42; 2Th 1:7; Rev 14:17–20. *sit on his throne.* Not only as judge but also as king (vv. 34,40).

32 All the nations will be gathered before him,
and he will separate[w] the people one from
another as a shepherd separates the sheep
from the goats.[x] 33 He will put the sheep on
his right and the goats on his left.
34 "Then the King will say to those on
his right, 'Come, you who are blessed by
my Father; take your inheritance, the kingdom[y] prepared for you since the creation
of the world.[z] 35 For I was hungry and you
gave me something to eat, I was thirsty
and you gave me something to drink, I
was a stranger and you invited me in,[a] 36 I
needed clothes and you clothed me,[b] I was
sick and you looked after me,[c] I was in
prison and you came to visit me.'[d]
37 "Then the righteous will answer him,
'Lord, when did we see you hungry and
feed you, or thirsty and give you something to drink? 38 When did we see you
a stranger and invite you in, or needing
clothes and clothe you? 39 When did we see
you sick or in prison and go to visit you?'
40 "The King will reply, 'I tell you the
truth, whatever you did for one of the least
of these brothers of mine, you did for me.'[e]
41 "Then he will say to those on his left,
'Depart from me,[f] you who are cursed,
into the eternal fire[g] prepared for the devil
and his angels.[h] 42 For I was hungry and
you gave me nothing to eat, I was thirsty
and you gave me nothing to drink, 43 I was
a stranger and you did not invite me in, I
needed clothes and you did not clothe me,
I was sick and in prison and you did not
look after me.'
44 "They also will answer, 'Lord, when
did we see you hungry or thirsty or a
stranger or needing clothes or sick or in
prison, and did not help you?'
45 "He will reply, 'I tell you the truth,
whatever you did not do for one of the
least of these, you did not do for me.'[i]
46 "Then they will go away to eternal
punishment, but the righteous to eternal
life."[j][k]

The Plot Against Jesus

26:2-5pp — Mk 14:1,2; Lk 22:1,2

26 When Jesus had finished saying all
these things,[l] he said to his disciples,
2 "As you know, the Passover[m] is two days
away—and the Son of Man will be handed over to be crucified."
3 Then the chief priests and the elders of
the people assembled[n] in the palace of the
high priest, whose name was Caiaphas,[o]
4 and they plotted to arrest Jesus in some
sly way and kill him.[p] 5 "But not during the
Feast," they said, "or there may be a riot[q]
among the people."

Jesus Anointed at Bethany

26:6-13pp — Mk 14:3-9
26:6-13Ref — Lk 7:37,38; Jn 12:1-8

6 While Jesus was in Bethany[r] in the
home of a man known as Simon the Leper,
7 a woman came to him with an alabaster
jar of very expensive perfume, which she
poured on his head as he was reclining at
the table.
8 When the disciples saw this, they were
indignant. "Why this waste?" they asked.
9 "This perfume could have been sold at
a high price and the money given to the
poor."
10 Aware of this, Jesus said to them,
"Why are you bothering this woman? She
has done a beautiful thing to me. 11 The
poor you will always have with you,[s] but

25:32 [w] Mal 3:18 [x] Eze 34:17,20 **25:34** [y] S Mt 3:2; 5:3,10,19; 19:14; S Ac 20:32; 1Co 15:50; Gal 5:21; Jas 2:5 [z] Heb 4:3; 9:26; Rev 13:8; 17:8 **25:35** [a] Job 31:32; Heb 13:2 **25:36** [b] Isa 58:7; Eze 18:7; Jas 2:15,16 [c] Jas 1:27 [d] 2Ti 1:16 **25:40** [e] S Mt 10:40,42; Heb 13:2 **25:41** [f] S Mt 7:23 [g] Isa 66:24; Mt 3:12; S 5:22; Mk 9:43,48; Lk 3:17; Jude 7 [h] 2Pe 2:4 **25:45** [i] Pr 14:31; 17:5 **25:46** [j] Mt 19:29; Jn 3:15,16,36; 17:2,3; Ro 2:7; Gal 6:8; 1Jn 1:2; 5:11,13,20 [k] Da 12:2; Jn 5:29; Ac 24:15; Ro 2:7,8; Gal 6:8 **26:1** [l] S Mt 7:28 **26:2** [m] S Jn 11:55 **26:3** [n] Ps 2:2 [o] ver 57; Lk 3:2; Jn 11:47-53; 18:13,14,24,28; Ac 4:6 **26:4** [p] S Mt 12:14 **26:5** [q] Mt 27:24 **26:6** [r] S Mt 21:17 **26:11** [s] Dt 15:11

25:32 *All the nations.* Both Jews and Gentiles (see 28:19 and note). *separates the sheep from the goats.* Cf. 7:21–23; 13:40–43.
25:33 *on his right.* See Mk 10:37 and note.
25:34–40 Rewards in the kingdom of heaven are given to those who serve without thought of reward. There is no hint of merit here, for God gives out of grace, not debt.
25:34 *inheritance.* See Ac 20:32; Eph 1:14,18; 5:5; Col 1:12; 3:24; Heb 9:15; 1Pe 1:4. *kingdom.* See note on 3:2. *since the creation of the world.* Cf. Eph 1:4 and note.
25:40 *least of these brothers of mine.* To whom does Jesus refer? The principal views are: (1) all who are hungry, thirsty, poor, needy or otherwise distressed—but this seems too comprehensive; (2) apostles and other Christian missionaries—but this seems too restrictive; (3) the Jews mentioned in the first interpretation in the note on vv. 31–46; (4) Jesus' disciples (12:46–50; 28:8–10); (5) "God's people" mentioned in the second interpretation in the note on vv. 31–46.
25:41 *eternal fire prepared for the devil.* See Rev 20:10. *fire.* See Jude 7; Rev 19:20 and notes; 20:15.
25:46 *eternal punishment … eternal life.* See Da 12:2; Jn 5:28–29; see also Jn 5:29; Ro 2:6–8; Gal 6:8 and notes. The parallelism between these two phrases prevents any weakening of the former.
26:2 *Passover.* See notes on Mk 14:1; Jn 2:13. *Son of Man.* See note on Mk 8:31.
26:3 *chief priests and the elders of the people.* The priestly and lay leadership of the Sanhedrin (see note on 2:4). *Caiaphas.* High priest A.D. 18–36 and the son-in-law of Annas (see Jn 18:13 and note), a former high priest, who served A.D. 6–15. In 1991 an ossuary (a limestone chest made for preserving the bones of the dead) was found in Jerusalem inscribed with the name Caiaphas (see chart, p. 1667).
26:5 *there may be a riot.* Hundreds of thousands of Jewish pilgrims came to Jerusalem for Passover (see note on Mk 14:2), and riots were not unknown. The religious leaders (v. 3) knew that many people admired Jesus.
26:6–13 See note on Jn 12:1–11.
26:6 *Bethany.* See note on 21:17. *Simon the Leper.* Mentioned elsewhere only in Mk 14:3. He was probably a well-known victim of leprosy who had been healed by Jesus.
26:7 *a woman.* Mary, sister of Martha and Lazarus (see Jn 12:3 and note). *alabaster jar.* See note on Mk 14:3. Most "alabaster" jars of that time were made from a form of marble.
26:9 *given to the poor.* See note on Mk 14:5.
26:10 *beautiful.* The Greek word has an aesthetic as well as an ethical meaning.
26:11 *The poor you will always have with you.* See note on Mk 14:7.

The Life of Christ

CHILDHOOD

Birth of Jesus, BETHLEHEM, 6/5 B.C., Mt 1:18-25; Lk 2:1-7
Visit by shepherds, BETHLEHEM, Lk 2:8-20
Presentation in the temple, JERUSALEM, Lk 2:21-40

Visit by the Magi, BETHLEHEM, Mt 2:1-12
Escape to Egypt, NILE DELTA, Mt 2:13-18

Return to Nazareth, LOWER GALILEE, Mt 2:19-23

Visit to temple as a boy, JERUSALEM, A.D. 7/8, Lk 2:41-52

YEAR OF INAUGURATION

YEAR OF POPULARITY

YEAR OF OPPOSITION
Begins less than full year of ministry

10 5 B.C. | A.D. 5 10 15 20 30 35

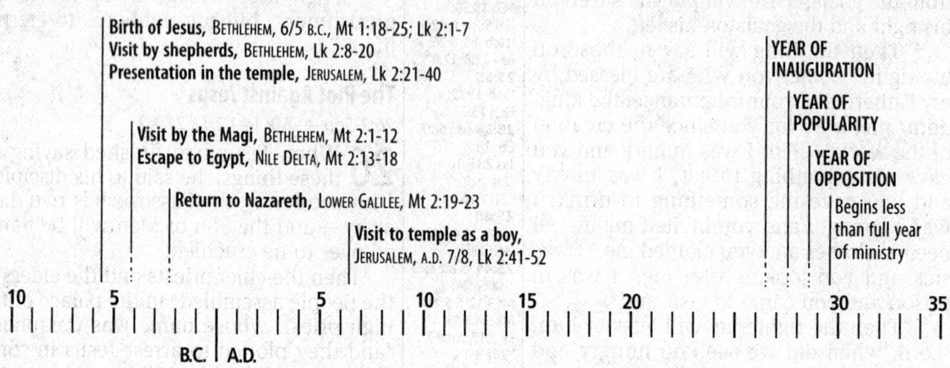

Jesus baptized
JORDAN RIVER
A.D. 26
Mt 3:13-17; Mk 1:9-11; Lk 3:21-23; Jn 1:29-39

Jesus tempted by Satan
DESERT OF JUDEA
Mt 4:1-11; Mk 1:12-13; Lk 4:1-13

Jesus' first miracle
CANA
Jn 2:1-11

4 fishermen become Jesus' followers
SEA OF GALILEE AT CAPERNAUM
A.D. 27
Mt 4:18-22; Mk 1:16-20; Lk 5:1-11

Jesus heals Peter's mother-in-law
CAPERNAUM
Mt 8:14-17; Mk 1:29-34; Lk 4:38-41

YEAR OF INAUGURATION — **YEAR OF POPULARITY**

A.D. 27: FALL | WINTER | SPRING | SUMMER | FALL | 28 WINTER

Jesus clears the temple
A.D. 27
Jn 2:14-22

Jesus and Nicodemus
JERUSALEM
A.D. 27
Jn 3:1-21

Jesus talks to the Samaritan woman
SAMARIA
Jn 4:5-42

Jesus heals a nobleman's son
CANA
Jn 4:46-54

The people of Jesus' hometown try to kill him
NAZARETH
Lk 4:16-31

Jesus begins his first preaching trip through Galilee
Mt 4:23-25; Mk 1:35-39; Lk 4:42-44

Matthew decides to follow Jesus
CAPERNAUM
Mt 9:9-13; Mk 2:13-17; Lk 5:27-32

Jesus chooses the 12 disciples
A.D. 28
Mk 3:13-19; Lk 6:12-15

Jesus preaches the Sermon on the Mount
Mt 5:1–7:29; Lk 6:20-49

[Dotted lines leading to the timeline are meant to define sequence of events only. All dates are approximate.]

A sinful woman anoints Jesus
CAPERNAUM
Lk 7:36-50

Jesus ministers again in Galilee
Lk 8:1-3

Jesus tells parables about the kingdom
Mt 13:1-52; Mk 4:1-34; Lk 8:4-18

Jesus calms the storm
SEA OF GALILEE
Mt 8:23-27; Mk 4:35-41; Lk 8:22-25

Jesus feeds the 5,000
NEAR BETHSAIDA
Spring, A.D. 29
Mt 14:13-21; Mk 6:30-44; Lk 9:10-17; Jn 6:1-14

Jesus walks on water
Mt 14:22-33; Mk 6:45-52; Jn 6:16-21

Jesus withdraws to Tyre and Sidon
Mt 15:21-28; Mk 7:24-30

Jesus feeds the 4,000
Mt 15:32-39; Mk 8:1-9

Peter says that Jesus is the Son of God
Mt 16:13-20; Mk 8:27-30; Lk 9:18-21

Jesus tells his disciples he is going to die soon
CAESAREA PHILIPPI
Mt 16:21-26; Mk 8:31-37; Lk 9:22-25

Jesus is transfigured
Mt 17:1-13; Mk 9:2-13; Lk 9:28-36

Jesus pays his temple tax
CAPERNAUM
Later in that year
Mt 17:24-27

YEAR OF OPPOSITION

SPRING | SUMMER | FALL *Oct. 29* | **29** WINTER | SPRING | SUMMER | FALL

Jairus's daughter is brought back to life by Jesus
CAPERNAUM
Mt 9:18-26; Mk 5:21-43; Lk 8:40-56

Jesus sends the Twelve out to preach and heal
Mt 9:35–11:1; Mk 6:6-13; Lk 9:1-6

John the Baptist is killed by Herod
MACHAERUS
A.D. 28
Mt 14:1-12; Mk 6:14-29; Lk 9:7-9

Jesus attends the Feast of Tabernacles
JERUSALEM
October, A.D. 29
Jn 7:11-52

Jesus heals a man who was born blind
JERUSALEM
Jn 9:1-41

Jesus visits Mary and Martha
BETHANY
Lk 10:38-42

[This is a tentative reconstruction only, since some sequences and dates are debatable.]

The Life of Christ—*continued*

Jesus begins his last trip to Jerusalem
A.D. 30
Lk 17:11

Jesus blesses the little children
ACROSS THE JORDAN
Mt 19:13-15; Mk 10:13-16; Lk 18:15-17

Jesus talks to the rich young man
ACROSS THE JORDAN
Mt 19:16-30; Mk 10:17-31; Lk 18:18-30

Jesus again predicts his death and resurrection
NEAR THE JORDAN
Mt 20:17-19; Mk 10:32-34; Lk 18:31-34

Jesus heals blind Bartimaeus
JERICHO
Mt 20:29-34; Mk 10:46-52; Lk 18:35-43

Jesus talks to Zacchaeus
JERICHO
Lk 19:1-10

Jesus returns to Bethany to visit Mary and Martha
BETHANY
Jn 11:55–12:1

THE LAST WEEK

The Triumphal Entry, JERUSALEM, Sunday
Mt 21:1-11; Mk 11:1-10; Lk 19:29-44; Jn 12:12-19

Jesus curses the fig tree, Monday
Mt 21:18-19; Mk 11:12-14

Jesus clears the temple, Monday
Mt 21:12-13; Mk 11:15-18

The authority of Jesus questioned, Tuesday
Mt 21:23-27; Mk 11:27-33; Lk 20:1-8

Jesus teaches in the temple, Tuesday
Mt 21:28–23:39; Mk 12:1-44; Lk 20:9–21:4

Jesus anointed, BETHANY, Tuesday
Mt 26:6-13; Mk 14:3-9; Jn 12:2-11

The plot against Jesus, Wednesday
Mt 26:14-16; Mk 14:10-11; Lk 22:3-6

The Last Supper, Thursday
Mt 26:17-29; Mk 14:12-25; Lk 22:7-20; Jn 13:1-38

Jesus comforts the disciples, Thursday
Jn 14:1–16:33

Gethsemane, Thursday
Mt 26:36-46; Mk 14:32-42; Lk 22:40-46

Jesus' arrest and trial, Thursday night and Friday
Mt 26:47–27:26; Mk 14:43–15:15;
Lk 22:47–23:25; Jn 18:2–19:16

Jesus' crucifixion and death, GOLGOTHA, Friday
Mt 27:27-56; Mk 15:16-41;
Lk 23:26-49; Jn 19:17-30

The burial of Jesus, JOSEPH'S TOMB, Friday
Mt 27:57-66; Mk 15:42-47;
Lk 23:50-56; Jn 19:31-42

30 WINTER | SPRING | SUMMER | FALL | A.D. **31** WINTER | SPRING | SUMMER

AFTER THE RESURRECTION

The empty tomb, JERUSALEM, Sunday
Mt 28:1-10; Mk 16:1-8; Lk 24:1-12; Jn 20:1-10

Mary Magdalene sees Jesus in the garden
JERUSALEM, Sunday
Mt 16:9-11; Jn 20:11-18

Jesus appears to the two going to Emmaus
Sunday
Mk 16:12-13; Lk 24:13-35

Jesus appears to 10 disciples
JERUSALEM, Sunday
Mk 16:14; Lk 24:36-43; Jn 20:19-25

Jesus appears to the 11 disciples
JERUSALEM, One week later
Jn 20:26-31

Jesus talks with some of his disciples
SEA OF GALILEE, One week later
Jn 21:1-25

Jesus ascends to his Father in Heaven
MT OF OLIVES, 40 days later
Mt 28:16-20; Mk 16:19-20; Lk 24:44-53

Jesus raises Lazarus from the dead
BETHANY
Winter, A.D. 30
Jn 11:1-44

you will not always have me. 12When she
poured this perfume on my body, she did
it to prepare me for burial.[t] 13I tell you the
truth, wherever this gospel is preached
throughout the world, what she has done
will also be told, in memory of her."

Judas Agrees to Betray Jesus

26:14-16pp — Mk 14:10,11; Lk 22:3-6

14Then one of the Twelve—the one
called Judas Iscariot[u]—went to the chief
priests 15and asked, "What are you willing to give me if I hand him over to you?"
So they counted out for him thirty silver
coins.[v] 16From then on Judas watched for
an opportunity to hand him over.

The Lord's Supper

26:17-19pp — Mk 14:12-16; Lk 22:7-13
26:20-24pp — Mk 14:17-21
26:26-29pp — Mk 14:22-25; Lk 22:17-20; 1Co 11:23-25

17On the first day of the Feast of Unleavened Bread,[w] the disciples came to Jesus
and asked, "Where do you want us to make
preparations for you to eat the Passover?"[x]
18He replied, "Go into the city to a certain man and tell him, 'The Teacher says:
My appointed time[y] is near. I am going to
celebrate the Passover with my disciples
at your house.'" 19So the disciples did as
Jesus had directed them and prepared the
Passover.
20When evening came, Jesus was reclining at the table with the Twelve. 21And
while they were eating, he said, "I tell you
the truth, one of you will betray me."[z]
22They were very sad and began to say
to him one after the other, "Surely not I,
Lord?"
23Jesus replied, "The one who has
dipped his hand into the bowl with me
will betray me.[a] 24The Son of Man will go
just as it is written about him.[b] But woe
to that man who betrays the Son of Man!
It would be better for him if he had not
been born."
25Then Judas, the one who would betray him,[c] said, "Surely not I, Rabbi?"[d]
Jesus answered, "Yes, it is you."[a]
26While they were eating, Jesus took
bread, gave thanks and broke it,[e] and gave
it to his disciples, saying, "Take and eat;
this is my body."
27Then he took the cup,[f] gave thanks
and offered it to them, saying, "Drink from
it, all of you. 28This is my blood of the[b]
covenant,[g] which is poured out for many
for the forgiveness of sins.[h] 29I tell you,
I will not drink of this fruit of the vine
from now on until that day when I drink it
anew with you[i] in my Father's kingdom."
30When they had sung a hymn, they
went out to the Mount of Olives.[j]

Jesus Predicts Peter's Denial

26:31-35pp — Mk 14:27-31; Lk 22:31-34

31Then Jesus told them, "This very night
you will all fall away on account of me,[k]
for it is written:

> "'I will strike the shepherd,
> and the sheep of the flock will be
> scattered.'[c][l]

32But after I have risen, I will go ahead of
you into Galilee."[m]

26:12 [t] Jn 19:40 **26:14** [u] ver 25,47; S Mt 10:4 **26:15** [v] Ex 21:32; Zec 11:12 **26:17** [w] Ex 12:18-20 [x] Dt 16:5-8 **26:18** [y] Mk 14:35,41; Jn 7:6,8,30; 8:20; 12:23; 13:1; 17:1 **26:21** [z] Lk 22:21-23; Jn 13:21 **26:23** [a] Ps 41:9; Jn 13:18 **26:24** [b] ver 31,54,56; Isa 53; Da 9:26; Mk 9:12; Lk 24:25-27,46; Ac 17:2,3; 26:22,23; 1Pe 1:10,11 **26:25** [c] S Mt 10:4 [d] S Mt 23:7 **26:26** [e] S Mt 14:19 **26:27** [f] 1Co 10:16 **26:28** [g] Ex 24:6-8; Zec 9:11; Mal 2:5; Heb 9:20; 10:29; S 13:20 [h] S Mt 20:28; Mk 1:4 **26:29** [i] Ac 10:41 **26:30** [j] S Mt 21:1 **26:31** [k] Mt 11:6; 13:21 [l] Zec 13:7; Jn 16:32 **26:32** [m] Mt 28:7,10,16

[a] *25* Or *"You yourself have said it"* [b] *28* Some manuscripts *the new* [c] *31* Zech. 13:7

26:12 *prepare me for burial.* See note on Mk 14:8.
26:14 *Iscariot.* See note on Mk 3:19. *chief priests.* See note on 2:4.
26:15 *thirty silver coins.* Equivalent to 120 denarii. Laborers customarily received one denarius for a day's work (20:1–16). See notes on 20:2; Zec 11:12.
26:17 *first day of the Feast of Unleavened Bread.* The 14th of Nisan (March-April), it was also called the preparation of the Passover. The Passover meal was eaten the evening of the 14th after sunset—and therefore technically on the 15th, since the Jewish day ended at sunset. The Feast of Unleavened Bread lasted seven days, from the 15th to the 21st of Nisan (see Lev 23:5–6), but in the time of Christ the entire period, Nisan 14–21, was referred to under that name (see note on Mk 14:12).
26:18–30 These verses indicate that Jesus ate the Passover meal with his disciples the night before his crucifixion. For more information on the Lord's Supper see notes on Mk 14:22,24.
26:18 *The Teacher says.* See note on Lk 22:11. *My appointed time.* Jesus' crucifixion.
26:19 *as Jesus had directed them.* See note on Lk 22:13. *prepared the Passover.* See note on Mk 14:15.
26:20 *When evening came.* See note on Mk 14:17. *reclining at the table.* See note on Mk 14:18.
26:21 *I tell you the truth.* See note on Mk 3:28.
26:23 *dipped his hand into the bowl with me.* It was the custom—still practiced by some in the Middle East—to take a piece of bread, or a piece of meat wrapped in bread, and dip it into a bowl of sauce (made of stewed fruit) on the table. *will betray me.* In that culture, as among Arabs today, to eat with a person was tantamount to saying, "I am your friend and will not hurt you." This fact made Judas's deed all the more despicable (cf. Ps 41:9 and note).
26:24 *as it is written about him.* See note on Mk 14:21. *Son of Man.* See note on Mk 8:31.
26:26–28 See notes on Mk 14:22–24.
26:27 *took the cup.* See note on Lk 22:17.
26:28 *blood of the covenant … poured out for many.* See note on Mk 14:24.
26:29 *drink it anew … in my Father's kingdom.* At the Messianic banquet (see Lk 22:16 and note).
26:30 *hymn.* The Passover fellowship was concluded with the second half of the Egyptian Hallel Psalms (Ps 115–118). Ps 113–114 were sung before the meal. *Mount of Olives.* See note on Mk 11:1.
26:31 *all fall away.* Not Peter only, but all the eleven (Judas had previously withdrawn, Jn 13:30). The meaning of the words "fall away" is seen in Peter's denial (vv. 69–75) and in the terrified flight of the other disciples (v. 56). *I will strike the shepherd.* See note on Zec 13:7.
26:32 *into Galilee.* Cf. 28:10,16–20; Mk 16:7; Jn 21:1–23.

33 Peter replied, "Even if all fall away on account of you, I never will."

34 "I tell you the truth," Jesus answered, "this very night, before the rooster crows, you will disown me three times."[n]

35 But Peter declared, "Even if I have to die with you,[o] I will never disown you." And all the other disciples said the same.

Gethsemane

26:36-46pp — Mk 14:32-42; Lk 22:40-46

36 Then Jesus went with his disciples to a place called Gethsemane, and he said to them, "Sit here while I go over there and pray." 37 He took Peter and the two sons of Zebedee[p] along with him, and he began to be sorrowful and troubled. 38 Then he said to them, "My soul is overwhelmed with sorrow[q] to the point of death. Stay here and keep watch with me."[r]

39 Going a little farther, he fell with his face to the ground and prayed, "My Father, if it is possible, may this cup[s] be taken from me. Yet not as I will, but as you will."[t]

40 Then he returned to his disciples and found them sleeping. "Could you men not keep watch with me[u] for one hour?" he asked Peter. 41 "Watch and pray so that you will not fall into temptation.[v] The spirit is willing, but the body is weak."

42 He went away a second time and prayed, "My Father, if it is not possible for this cup to be taken away unless I drink it, may your will be done."[w]

43 When he came back, he again found them sleeping, because their eyes were heavy. 44 So he left them and went away once more and prayed the third time, saying the same thing.

45 Then he returned to the disciples and said to them, "Are you still sleeping and resting? Look, the hour[x] is near, and the Son of Man is betrayed into the hands of sinners. 46 Rise, let us go! Here comes my betrayer!"

Jesus Arrested

26:47-56pp — Mk 14:43-50; Lk 22:47-53

47 While he was still speaking, Judas,[y] one of the Twelve, arrived. With him was a large crowd armed with swords and clubs, sent from the chief priests and the elders of the people. 48 Now the betrayer had arranged a signal with them: "The one I kiss is the man; arrest him." 49 Going at once to Jesus, Judas said, "Greetings, Rabbi!"[z] and kissed him.

50 Jesus replied, "Friend,[a] do what you came for."[a]

Then the men stepped forward, seized Jesus and arrested him. 51 With that, one of Jesus' companions reached for his sword,[b] drew it out and struck the servant of the high priest, cutting off his ear.[c]

52 "Put your sword back in its place," Jesus said to him, "for all who draw the sword will die by the sword.[d] 53 Do you think I cannot call on my Father, and he will at once put at my disposal more than twelve legions of angels?[e] 54 But how then would the Scriptures be fulfilled[f] that say it must happen in this way?"

55 At that time Jesus said to the crowd, "Am I leading a rebellion, that you have come out with swords and clubs to capture me? Every day I sat in the temple courts teaching,[g] and you did not arrest me. 56 But this has all taken place that the writings of the prophets might be fulfilled."[h] Then all the disciples deserted him and fled.

26:34 [n] ver 75; Jn 13:38
26:35 [o] Jn 13:37
26:37 [p] S Mt 4:21
26:38 [q] S Jn 12:27 [r] ver 40, 41
26:39 [s] S Mt 20:22 [t] ver 42; Ps 40:6-8; Isa 50:5; Mt 6:10; Jn 4:34; 5:30; 6:38
26:40 [u] ver 38
26:41 [v] Mt 6:13
26:42 [w] S ver 39
26:45 [x] S ver 18
26:47 [y] S Mt 10:4
26:49 [z] ver 25; S Mt 23:7
26:50 [a] Mt 20:13; 22:12
26:51 [b] Lk 22:36, 38 [c] Jn 18:10
26:52 [d] Ge 9:6; Ex 21:12; Rev 13:10
26:53 [e] 2Ki 6:17; Da 7:10; Mt 4:11
26:54 [f] S ver 24; S Mt 1:22
26:55 [g] Mk 12:35; Lk 21:37; Jn 7:14, 28; 18:20
26:56 [h] S ver 24; S Mt 1:22

[a] 50 Or *"Friend, why have you come?"*

26:34 *before the rooster crows.* The reference may be to the third of the Roman watches into which the night was divided (see note on 14:25; see also Mk 13:35 and note). Or it may simply refer to early morning when the rooster crows.
26:36 *Gethsemane.* The name means "oil press," a place for squeezing the oil from olives (see note on Mk 14:32).
26:37 *Peter and the two sons of Zebedee.* The latter were James and John. These three disciples seem to have been especially close to Jesus (see note on Mk 5:37).
26:38 – 39 Jesus did not die serenely as many martyrs have. He was no mere martyr; he was the Lamb of God bearing the penalty of the sins of the entire human race. The wrath of God was turned loose on him. Only this can adequately explain what took place at Gethsemane.
26:38 *soul.* See 10:28 and note. *overwhelmed with sorrow.* See Isa 53:3 and note.
26:39 *cup.* A symbol of deep sorrow and suffering. Here it refers to his Father's face being turned away from him when he who had no sin was made sin (perhaps a sin offering) for us (see 27:46; 2Co 5:21 and note).
26:41 See note on Mk 14:38.
26:45 *the hour.* See note on Lk 22:53. *Son of Man.* see note on Mk 8:31.
26:47 *Judas.* See notes on Jn 6:70; 17:12. *large crowd armed with swords and clubs.* See note on Mk 14:43. *chief priests and the elders.* See notes on v. 3; 2:4.
26:48 *the one I kiss.* See note on Lk 22:47.
26:49 *Rabbi.* Hebrew word for "(my) teacher." *kissed him.* See notes on Mk 14:45; Lk 22:47.
26:50 *Friend.* See note on 20:13.
26:51 *one of Jesus' companions.* Peter (see Jn 18:10 and note). *servant of the high priest.* Malchus (see Jn 18:10 and note). *cutting off his ear.* Perhaps Peter intended a more fatal blow but missed and only succeeded in "cutting off his ear."
26:53 *legions.* A Roman legion had 6,000 soldiers.
26:54 *Scriptures be fulfilled.* In view of v. 56 probably a reference to Zec 13:7 (see note on Mk 14:49).
26:55 Jesus protested the manner of his arrest. The crowd sent by the Sanhedrin (see note on Mk 14:55) had come after him as if he were a dangerous criminal or insurrectionist.
26:56 *disciples deserted him.* Contrast v. 35.

Before the Sanhedrin

26:57-68pp — Mk 14:53-65; Jn 18:12,13,19-24

57Those who had arrested Jesus took
him to Caiaphas,[i] the high priest, where
the teachers of the law and the elders
had assembled. 58But Peter followed him
at a distance, right up to the courtyard
of the high priest.[j] He entered and sat
down with the guards[k] to see the outcome.
59The chief priests and the whole Sanhedrin[l] were looking for false evidence
against Jesus so that they could put him
to death. 60But they did not find any,
though many false witnesses[m] came forward.
Finally two[n] came forward 61and declared, "This fellow said, 'I am able to destroy the temple of God and rebuild it in
three days.'"[o]
62Then the high priest stood up and said
to Jesus, "Are you not going to answer?
What is this testimony that these men
are bringing against you?" 63But Jesus remained silent.[p]
The high priest said to him, "I charge
you under oath[q] by the living God:[r] Tell us
if you are the Christ,[a][s] the Son of God."[t]
64"Yes, it is as you say,"[u] Jesus replied.
"But I say to all of you: In the future you
will see the Son of Man sitting at the right
hand of the Mighty One[v] and coming on
the clouds of heaven."[w]
65Then the high priest tore his clothes[x]
and said, "He has spoken blasphemy!
Why do we need any more witnesses?
Look, now you have heard the blasphemy. 66What do you think?"
"He is worthy of death,"[y] they answered.
67Then they spit in his face and struck
him with their fists.[z] Others slapped him
68and said, "Prophesy to us, Christ. Who
hit you?"[a]

26:57 [i]S ver 3 **26:58** [j]ver 69; Mk 14:66; Lk 22:55; Jn 18:15 [k]Mk 15:16; Lk 11:21; Jn 7:32,45,46 **26:59** [l]S Mt 5:22 **26:60** [m]Ps 27:12; 35:11; Ac 6:13 [n]Dt 19:15 **26:61** [o]S Jn 2:19 **26:63** [p]S Mk 14:61 [q]Lev 5:1 [r]S Mt 16:16 [s]Lk 22:67 [t]S Mt 4:3 **26:64** [u]Mt 27:11; Lk 22:70 [v]S Mk 16:19 [w]S Rev 1:7 **26:65** [x]S Mk 14:63 **26:66** [y]Lev 24:16; Jn 19:7 **26:67** [z]S Mt 16:21 **26:68** [a]Lk 22:63-65

26:75 [b]ver 34; Jn 13:38 **27:1** [c]S Mt 12:14; Mk 15:1; Lk 22:66 **27:2** [d]Mt 20:19 [e]Mk 15:1; Lk 13:1; Ac 3:13; 1Ti 6:13 **27:3** [f]S Mt 10:4 [g]Mt 26:14,15 **27:4** [h]ver 24

Peter Disowns Jesus

26:69-75pp — Mk 14:66-72; Lk 22:55-62; Jn 18:16-18,25-27

69Now Peter was sitting out in the courtyard, and a servant girl came to him. "You
also were with Jesus of Galilee," she said.
70But he denied it before them all. "I
don't know what you're talking about,"
he said.
71Then he went out to the gateway,
where another girl saw him and said to
the people there, "This fellow was with
Jesus of Nazareth."
72He denied it again, with an oath: "I
don't know the man!"
73After a little while, those standing
there went up to Peter and said, "Surely
you are one of them, for your accent gives
you away."
74Then he began to call down curses on
himself and he swore to them, "I don't
know the man!"
Immediately a rooster crowed. 75Then
Peter remembered the word Jesus had
spoken: "Before the rooster crows, you
will disown me three times."[b] And he
went outside and wept bitterly.

Judas Hangs Himself

27 Early in the morning, all the chief
priests and the elders of the people
came to the decision to put Jesus to death.[c]
2They bound him, led him away and handed him over[d] to Pilate, the governor.[e]
3When Judas, who had betrayed him,[f]
saw that Jesus was condemned, he was
seized with remorse and returned the thirty silver coins[g] to the chief priests and the
elders. 4"I have sinned," he said, "for I
have betrayed innocent blood."
"What is that to us?" they replied.
"That's your responsibility."[h]

[a] 63 Or *Messiah*; also in verse 68

26:57—27:26 For a summary of the two stages (religious and civil) of the trial of Jesus see note on Mk 14:53—15:15.

26:57 *Caiaphas.* See v. 3; Jn 11:49 and notes. *teachers of the law.* See note on 2:4. *elders.* See notes on Ex 3:16; 2Sa 3:17.

26:59 *Sanhedrin.* See note on Mk 14:55.

26:61 *I am able to destroy the temple of God.* Possibly an intentional distortion of Jesus' words (see Mk 14:58; Jn 2:19 and notes).

26:63 *I charge you under oath.* Jesus refused to answer the question of v. 62 (see v. 63a). But when the high priest used this form, Jesus was legally obliged to reply. *Christ.* See note on 16:16.

26:64 This Son of Man saying brings together Ps 110:1 and Da 7:13. See Mt 17:5; 24:30 and notes.

26:65 *tore his clothes.* Something that ordinarily the high priest was forbidden by law to do (Lev 10:6; 21:10), but this was considered a highly unusual circumstance. The high priest interpreted Jesus' answer in v. 64 as blasphemy (see note on Mk 14:64).

26:67-68 Mark (14:65) and Luke (22:64) report that they blindfolded Jesus, which explains the mocking command: "Prophesy ... Who hit you?"

26:73 *After a little while.* Lk 22:59 says "About an hour later." *your accent gives you away.* Peter had a Galilean accent that was conspicuous in Jerusalem. Cf. Jdg 12:6 and note.

27:1 *Early in the morning.* Continues the narrative from 26:68. The Sanhedrin could not have a legal session at night, so at daybreak they held a special meeting to make the death sentence (see 26:66) official. See notes on Mk 14:53—15:15; 15:1; Lk 22:66; Jn 18:28.

27:2 *handed him over to Pilate.* The Sanhedrin had been deprived by the Roman government of the right to carry out capital punishment, except in the case of a foreigner who entered the sacred precincts of the temple. So Jesus had to be handed over to Pilate for execution (see Jn 18:31 and note). For additional information about Pilate see note on Lk 3:1.

27:3-10 See Ac 1:16-19.

27:3 *thirty silver coins.* See 26:15 and note.

5 So Judas threw the money into the
temple[i] and left. Then he went away and
hanged himself.[j]
6 The chief priests picked up the coins
and said, "It is against the law to put this
into the treasury, since it is blood money." 7 So they decided to use the money to
buy the potter's field as a burial place for
foreigners. 8 That is why it has been called
the Field of Blood[k] to this day. 9 Then
what was spoken by Jeremiah the prophet
was fulfilled:[l] "They took the thirty silver
coins, the price set on him by the people
of Israel, 10 and they used them to buy the
potter's field, as the Lord commanded
me."[a m]

Jesus Before Pilate

27:11-26pp — Mk 15:2-15; Lk 23:2,3,18-25; Jn 18:29-19:16

11 Meanwhile Jesus stood before the governor, and the governor asked him, "Are
you the king of the Jews?"[n]
"Yes, it is as you say," Jesus replied.
12 When he was accused by the chief
priests and the elders, he gave no answer.[o] 13 Then Pilate asked him, "Don't
you hear the testimony they are bringing
against you?"[p] 14 But Jesus made no reply,[q]
not even to a single charge—to the great
amazement of the governor.
15 Now it was the governor's custom at
the Feast to release a prisoner[r] chosen by
the crowd. 16 At that time they had a notorious prisoner, called Barabbas. 17 So when
the crowd had gathered, Pilate asked
them, "Which one do you want me to release to you: Barabbas, or Jesus who is
called Christ?"[s] 18 For he knew it was out
of envy that they had handed Jesus over
to him.
19 While Pilate was sitting on the judge's
seat,[t] his wife sent him this message:
"Don't have anything to do with that innocent[u] man, for I have suffered a great deal
today in a dream[v] because of him."
20 But the chief priests and the elders
persuaded the crowd to ask for Barabbas
and to have Jesus executed.[w]
21 "Which of the two do you want me to
release to you?" asked the governor.
"Barabbas," they answered.
22 "What shall I do, then, with Jesus who
is called Christ?"[x] Pilate asked.
They all answered, "Crucify him!"
23 "Why? What crime has he committed?" asked Pilate.
But they shouted all the louder, "Crucify him!"
24 When Pilate saw that he was getting
nowhere, but that instead an uproar[y] was
starting, he took water and washed his
hands[z] in front of the crowd. "I am innocent of this man's blood,"[a] he said. "It is
your responsibility!"[b]
25 All the people answered, "Let his
blood be on us and on our children!"[c]
26 Then he released Barabbas to them.
But he had Jesus flogged,[d] and handed
him over to be crucified.

The Soldiers Mock Jesus

27:27-31pp — Mk 15:16-20

27 Then the governor's soldiers took
Jesus into the Praetorium[e] and gathered
the whole company of soldiers around
him. 28 They stripped him and put a scarlet robe on him,[f] 29 and then twisted together a crown of thorns and set it on his
head. They put a staff in his right hand
and knelt in front of him and mocked
him. "Hail, king of the Jews!" they said.[g]

[a] *10* See Zech. 11:12,13; Jer. 19:1-13; 32:6-9.

27:5 [i]Lk 1:9,21 [j]Ac 1:18 **27:8** [k]Ac 1:19 **27:9** [l]S Mt 1:22 **27:10** [m]Zec 11:12,13; Jer 32:6-9 **27:11** [n]S Mt 2:2 **27:12** [o]S Mk 14:61 **27:13** [p]Mt 26:62 **27:14** [q]S Mk 14:61 **27:15** [r]Jn 18:39 **27:17** [s]ver 22; Mt 1:16 **27:19** [t]Jn 19:13 [u]ver 24 [v]Ge 20:6; Nu 12:6; 1Ki 3:5; Job 33:14-16; Mt 1:20; 2:12,13,19,22 **27:20** [w]Ac 3:14 **27:22** [x]Mt 1:16 **27:24** [y]Mt 26:5 [z]Ps 26:6 [a]Dt 21:6-8 [b]ver 4 **27:25** [c]Jos 2:19; S Ac 5:28 **27:26** [d]Isa 53:5; Jn 19:1 **27:27** [e]Jn 18:28,33; 19:9 **27:28** [f]Jn 19:2 **27:29** [g]Isa 53:3; Jn 19:2,3

27:5 *temple.* Probably the treasury room of the temple (see v. 6). *hanged himself.* See note on Ac 1:18.

27:8 *Field of Blood.* Cf. "Valley of Slaughter" in Jer 19:6.

27:9 *Jeremiah.* The quotation that follows seems to combine Zec 11:12–13 and Jer 19:1–13 (or perhaps Jer 18:2–12 or 32:6–9). But Matthew attributes it to the better-known prophet Jeremiah, just as Mark (1:2–3) quotes Mal 3:1 and Isa 40:3 but attributes them both to the better-known prophet Isaiah (see note on Mk 1:2).

27:11 *governor.* Pontius Pilate (see note on v. 2). *king of the Jews.* See note on Jn 18:33.

27:14 *Jesus made no reply.* See 26:63; Mk 15:4; Isa 53:7 and notes. *amazement of the governor.* Probably because he had never seen such behavior before. He had no idea that Jesus was carrying out his Father's plan for the redemption of the world (see note on Mk 15:4).

27:15 *governor's custom.* Of which nothing is known outside the Gospels.

27:16 *notorious.* Barabbas had taken part in a rebellion (Lk 23:19; Jn 18:40), presumably against the Romans. So he would have been a folk hero among the Jews. See notes on Mk 15:7; Lk 23:18; Jn 18:40. Some manuscripts use Barabbas's full name, Jesus Barabbas, in vv. 16–17. If that is the correct reading, it sharpens the point of Pilate's question in v. 17.

27:19 Matthew is the only writer who records this incident. *dream.* Dreams play an important role in Matthew's account of Jesus' life and ministry, especially in his accounts of Jesus' infancy (see 1:20; 2:12,13,19,22) and of his death (here).

27:24 *washed his hands.* See Dt 21:6; Ps 26:6 and notes; 73:13.

27:25 A chilling response by a bloodthirsty crowd. It has often been used to justify the persecution of the Jewish people. It should be noted, however, that it was not God but the people themselves who uttered these words. There is no evidence here that God granted their request. If there was a fulfillment, it was most likely in the destruction of Jerusalem in A.D. 70.

27:26 *flogged.* Roman floggings were so brutal that sometimes the victim died before crucifixion (see note on Mk 15:15).

27:27 *Praetorium.* The governor's official residence in Jerusalem (see notes on Mk 15:16; Ac 23:25).

27:28 *scarlet robe.* The outer cloak of a Roman soldier. Mk 15:17,20; Jn 19:2,5 describe it as purple.

27:29 *crown of thorns.* See note on Mk 15:17. *staff.* A mock scepter. *Hail, king of the Jews.* See note on Mk 15:18.

30They spit on him, and took the staff and
struck him on the head again and again.[h]
31After they had mocked him, they took
off the robe and put his own clothes on
him. Then they led him away to crucify
him.[i]

The Crucifixion

27:33-44pp — Mk 15:22-32; Lk 23:33-43; Jn 19:17-24

32As they were going out,[j] they met a
man from Cyrene,[k] named Simon, and
they forced him to carry the cross.[l] 33They
came to a place called Golgotha (which
means The Place of the Skull).[m] 34There
they offered Jesus wine to drink, mixed
with gall;[n] but after tasting it, he refused
to drink it. 35When they had crucified
him, they divided up his clothes by casting lots.[a][o] 36And sitting down, they kept
watch[p] over him there. 37Above his head
they placed the written charge against
him: THIS IS JESUS, THE KING OF THE JEWS.
38Two robbers were crucified with him,[q]
one on his right and one on his left.
39Those who passed by hurled insults at
him, shaking their heads[r] 40and saying,
"You who are going to destroy the temple
and build it in three days,[s] save yourself![t]
Come down from the cross, if you are the
Son of God!"[u]
41In the same way the chief priests, the
teachers of the law and the elders mocked
him. 42"He saved others," they said, "but
he can't save himself! He's the King of
Israel![v] Let him come down now from the
cross, and we will believe[w] in him. 43He
trusts in God. Let God rescue him[x] now if
he wants him, for he said, 'I am the Son
of God.'" 44In the same way the robbers
who were crucified with him also heaped
insults on him.

The Death of Jesus

27:45-56pp — Mk 15:33-41; Lk 23:44-49; Jn 19:29-30

45From the sixth hour until the ninth
hour darkness[y] came over all the land.
46About the ninth hour Jesus cried out in
a loud voice, *"Eloi, Eloi,[b] lama sabachthani?"*—which means, "My God, my God,
why have you forsaken me?"[c][z]
47When some of those standing there
heard this, they said, "He's calling Elijah."
48Immediately one of them ran and got
a sponge. He filled it with wine vinegar,[a]
put it on a stick, and offered it to Jesus
to drink. 49The rest said, "Now leave him
alone. Let's see if Elijah comes to save
him."
50And when Jesus had cried out again in
a loud voice, he gave up his spirit.[b]
51At that moment the curtain of the temple[c] was torn in two from top to bottom.
The earth shook and the rocks split.[d] 52The
tombs broke open and the bodies of many
holy people who had died were raised to
life. 53They came out of the tombs, and after Jesus' resurrection they went into the
holy city[e] and appeared to many people.
54When the centurion and those with
him who were guarding[f] Jesus saw the
earthquake and all that had happened,
they were terrified, and exclaimed, "Surely he was the Son[d] of God!"[g]
55Many women were there, watching from a distance. They had followed
Jesus from Galilee to care for his needs.[h]
56Among them were Mary Magdalene,
Mary the mother of James and Joses, and
the mother of Zebedee's sons.[i]

27:30 [h] S Mt 16:21 **27:31** [i] Isa 53:7 **27:32** [j] Heb 13:12 [k] Ac 2:10; 6:9; 11:20; 13:1 [l] Mk 15:21; Lk 23:26 **27:33** [m] Jn 19:17 **27:34** [n] ver 48; Ps 69:21 **27:35** [o] Ps 22:18 **27:36** [p] ver 54 **27:38** [q] Isa 53:12 **27:39** [r] Ps 22:7; 109:25; La 2:15 **27:40** [s] S Jn 2:19 [t] ver 42 [u] Mt 4:3,6 **27:42** [v] Jn 1:49; 12:13 [w] S Jn 3:15 **27:43** [x] Ps 22:8

27:45 [y] Am 8:9 **27:46** [z] Ps 22:1 **27:48** [a] ver 34; Ps 69:21 **27:50** [b] Jn 19:30 **27:51** [c] Ex 26:31-33; Heb 9:3,8; 10:19,20 [d] ver 54 **27:53** [e] S Mt 4:5 **27:54** [f] ver 36 [g] S Mt 4:3; 17:5 **27:55** [h] Lk 8:2,3 **27:56** [i] Mk 15:47; Lk 24:10; Jn 19:25

[a] 35 A few late manuscripts *lots that the word spoken by the prophet might be fulfilled: "They divided my garments among themselves and cast lots for my clothing"* (Psalm 22:18) [b] 46 Some manuscripts *Eli, Eli* [c] 46 Psalm 22:1 [d] 54 *Or a son*

27:30–31 See Isa 50:6 and note.
27:30 *spit on him.* See note on Mk 15:19.
27:32 *they.* See v. 27. *Cyrene.* See note on Mk 15:21. *Simon ... to carry the cross.* See note on Mk 15:21.
27:33 *Golgotha.* See note on Mk 15:22.
27:34 *mixed with gall.* Tradition says that the women of Jerusalem customarily furnished this pain-killing narcotic to prisoners who were crucified. Matthew may intend an allusion to Ps 69:21. Jesus refused to drink it, probably because he wanted to be fully conscious until his death (v. 50).
27:35 *crucified.* See note on Mk 15:24. *casting lots.* Explained more precisely in Jn 19:23–24 (see notes there; see also NIV text note here).
27:37 See notes on Mk 15:26; Lk 23:38; Jn 19:19.
27:38 *Two robbers.* See note on Mk 15:27.
27:39 *shaking their heads.* See Ps 22:7 and note.
27:41 *chief priests, the teachers of the law and the elders.* The Sanhedrin (see note on v. 1).
27:43 See Ps 22:8 and note.
27:45 *From the sixth hour until the ninth hour.* From noon until 3:00 P.M.
27:46 *Eloi, Eloi, lama sabachthani?* Here Jesus spoke a dialect of Aramaic, which Matthew translates for his readers (see note on Mk 15:34).
27:47 *Elijah.* See note on Mk 15:35.
27:48 *sponge.* See note on Jn 19:29. *wine vinegar.* See notes on Mk 15:36; Lk 23:36; Jn 19:29.
27:49 See note on Mk 15:35.
27:50 *loud voice.* See note on Jn 19:30.
27:51 *curtain.* The curtain that separated the Holy Place from the Most Holy Place. The tearing of the curtain signified Christ's making it possible for believers to go directly into God's presence (see Mk 15:38; Lk 23:45; Heb 9:1–14; 10:14–22 and notes).
27:51b–53a *The earth shook ... they went.* Or "The earth shook, the rocks split 52and the tombs broke open. The bodies of many holy people who had died were raised to life. 53They came out of the tombs after Jesus' resurrection and went ..."
27:54 *centurion.* See note on 8:5. *Son of God.* See note on Lk 23:47.
27:55 *women ... to care for his needs.* Women played a significant role in the ministry of Jesus (see Mk 15:41; Lk 23:49) and his disciples (see Lk 8:3 and note).
27:56 See notes on Mk 15:40; Lk 24:10.

The Burial of Jesus

27:57-61pp — Mk 15:42-47; Lk 23:50-56; Jn 19:38-42

57As evening approached, there came a
rich man from Arimathea, named Joseph,
who had himself become a disciple of
Jesus. 58Going to Pilate, he asked for Jesus'
body, and Pilate ordered that it be given
to him. 59Joseph took the body, wrapped
it in a clean linen cloth, 60and placed it in
his own new tomb[j] that he had cut out of
the rock. He rolled a big stone in front of
the entrance to the tomb and went away.
61Mary Magdalene and the other Mary
were sitting there opposite the tomb.

The Guard at the Tomb

62The next day, the one after Preparation Day, the chief priests and the Pharisees went to Pilate. 63"Sir," they said, "we
remember that while he was still alive that
deceiver said, 'After three days I will rise
again.'[k] 64So give the order for the tomb to
be made secure until the third day. Otherwise, his disciples may come and steal the
body[l] and tell the people that he has been
raised from the dead. This last deception
will be worse than the first."

65"Take a guard,"[m] Pilate answered. "Go,
make the tomb as secure as you know
how." 66So they went and made the tomb
secure by putting a seal[n] on the stone[o] and
posting the guard.[p]

The Resurrection

28:1-8pp — Mk 16:1-8; Lk 24:1-10; Jn 20:1-8

28 After the Sabbath, at dawn on the
first day of the week, Mary Magdalene[q] and the other Mary[r] went to look at
the tomb.

2There was a violent earthquake,[s] for an
angel[t] of the Lord came down from heav-
en and, going to the tomb, rolled back the
stone[u] and sat on it. 3His appearance was
like lightning, and his clothes were white
as snow.[v] 4The guards were so afraid of
him that they shook and became like dead
men.

5The angel said to the women, "Do not
be afraid,[w] for I know that you are looking
for Jesus, who was crucified. 6He is not
here; he has risen, just as he said.[x] Come
and see the place where he lay. 7Then go
quickly and tell his disciples: 'He has risen
from the dead and is going ahead of you
into Galilee.[y] There you will see him.' Now
I have told you."

8So the women hurried away from the
tomb, afraid yet filled with joy, and ran
to tell his disciples. 9Suddenly Jesus met
them.[z] "Greetings," he said. They came to
him, clasped his feet and worshiped him.
10Then Jesus said to them, "Do not be
afraid. Go and tell my brothers[a] to go to
Galilee; there they will see me."

The Guards' Report

11While the women were on their way,
some of the guards[b] went into the city and
reported to the chief priests everything that
had happened. 12When the chief priests
had met with the elders and devised a
plan, they gave the soldiers a large sum
of money, 13telling them, "You are to say,
'His disciples came during the night and
stole him away[c] while we were asleep.' 14If
this report gets to the governor,[d] we will
satisfy him and keep you out of trouble."
15So the soldiers took the money and did
as they were instructed. And this story has
been widely circulated among the Jews to
this very day.

The Great Commission

16Then the eleven disciples went to Galilee, to the mountain where Jesus had

27:60 [j] Mt 27:66; 28:2; Mk 16:4; Ac 13:29
27:63 [k] S Mt 16:21
27:64 [l] Mt 28:13
27:65 [m] ver 66; Mt 28:11
27:66 [n] Da 6:17 [o] ver 60; Mt 28:2 [p] Mt 28:11
28:1 [q] Lk 8:2 [r] Mt 27:56
28:2 [s] Mt 27:51 [t] Jn 20:12; S Ac 5:19
[u] Mt 27:60
28:3 [v] Da 7:9; 10:6; Mk 9:3; S Jn 20:12
28:5 [w] ver 10; S Mt 14:27
28:6 [x] S Mt 16:21
28:7 [y] ver 10, 16; Mt 26:32
28:9 [z] Jn 20:14-18
28:10 [a] Mt 12:50; 25:40; Mk 3:34; Jn 20:17; Ro 8:29; Heb 2:11-13, 17
28:11 [b] Mt 27:65, 66
28:13 [c] Mt 27:64
28:14 [d] S Mt 27:2

27:57 *Arimathea.* A village about 20 miles northwest of Jerusalem; perhaps to be identified with Ramathaim, the birthplace of the prophet Samuel (see 1Sa 1:1 and note). *Joseph.* See notes on Lk 23:50; Jn 19:38.
27:58 *asked for Jesus' body.* See note on Lk 23:52.
27:60 *new tomb.* See note on Mk 15:46.
27:61 *the other Mary.* Presumably the mother of James and Joses (v. 56).
27:62 *The next day, the one after Preparation Day.* Saturday, the Sabbath. Friday was the preparation day for the Sabbath (sunset Friday to sunset Saturday).
27:64 *This last deception will be worse than the first.* The first would be that Jesus was the Messiah, the second that he had risen as the Son of God.
27:65 *Take a guard.* Either of Roman soldiers or of their own temple police; 28:14 implies that they were answerable to Pilate ("the governor"), which may favor Roman soldiers. On the other hand, the fact that in 28:11 they "reported to the chief priests" (instead of to Pilate) may favor temple police, who would have been under the authority of the religious leaders. ("Take a guard" may also be rendered "You have a guard.")
28:1 *first day of the week.* See note on Lk 24:1. *the other Mary.* See note on 27:61. Mk 16:1 adds Salome, and Lk 24:10 adds Joanna.
28:2 *There was.* The sense is "Now there had been." The parallel accounts (Mk 16:2–6; Lk 24:1–7; Jn 20:1) make it clear that the events of vv. 2–4 occurred before the women actually arrived at the tomb. *violent earthquake.* Only Matthew mentions this earthquake and the one at Jesus' death (27:51,54).
28:6 *just as he said.* See 16:21 and note.
28:7 *going ahead of you into Galilee.* See 26:32 and note.
28:10 *my brothers.* His "disciples" (v. 16).
28:11–15 Only Matthew tells of the posting of the guard (27:62–66), and he follows up by telling about their report.
28:11 *reported to the chief priests.* See note on 27:65.
28:13 *His disciples ... stole him away.* One of many human attempts to explain away Christ's resurrection. *while we were asleep.* It is more likely that Jewish temple police would be willing to admit to such dereliction of duty than Roman soldiers would.
28:14 See note on 27:65.
28:16 *eleven.* Judas had committed suicide (see 27:5 and note). *mountain.* Cf. note on 5:1. *had told them.* See v. 10.

told them to go.[e] 17When they saw him,
they worshiped him; but some doubted.
18Then Jesus came to them and said, "All
authority in heaven and on earth has been
given to me.[f] 19Therefore go and make disciples of all nations,[g] baptizing them in[a]
the name of the Father and of the Son and
of the Holy Spirit,[h] 20and teaching[i] them to
obey everything I have commanded you.
And surely I am with you[j] always, to the
very end of the age."[k]

28:16 [e] ver 7,10; Mt 26:32 **28:18** [f] Da 7:13,14; Lk 10:22; Jn 3:35; S 13:13; 17:2; 1Co 15:27; Eph 1:20-22; Php 2:9,10 **28:19** [g] Isa 49:6; Mk 16:15,16; Lk 24:47; Ac 1:8; 14:21 [h] Ac 1:8; 2:38; 8:16; Ro 6:3,4; Gal 3:27; Col 2:12 **28:20** [i] Jn 14:26; Ac 2:42 [j] Dt 31:6; 1Ki 8:57; Hag 1:13; Mt 18:20; Ac 18:10 [k] Mt 13:39; 24:3

[a] *19* Or *into*; see Acts 8:16; 19:5; Romans 6:3; 1 Cor. 1:13; 10:2 and Gal. 3:27.

28:17 *some.* Probably of the 11 disciples, though it may include others as well. *doubted.* Full recognition of Jesus' resurrection did not come to them immediately. After the traumatic experience of the crucifixion, it took time for the disciples to come to that full awareness (see Lk 24:10–11,25–26,36–47).

28:18 *authority.* See 10:1; see also 7:29; 16:28; Jn 17:2 and notes. *in heaven and on earth.* The scope of Christ's authority is the entire universe.

28:19–20 Christ's program of missions: "make disciples of all nations." It involves three steps: (1) "go," (2) "baptizing them" and (3) "teaching them to obey everything" Christ has commanded.

28:19 *disciples.* See 5:1 and note. *all nations.* Cf. Rev 5:9. Contrast 10:5–6 and note. *baptizing them.* As a sign of their union with and commitment to Christ (see notes on Ac 2:38; Ro 6:3–4). *Father ... Son ... Holy Spirit.* The Trinitarian formula (see 3:16–17 and note; 1Co 12:4–6; 2Co 13:14 and note; Eph 1:2–13; 4:4–6; 2Th 2:13 and note; Tit 3:4–6; 1Pe 1:2 and note; 1Jn 4:13–14; Rev 1:4–6 and NIV text note on 1:4).

28:20 *with you.* Matthew ends with the reassuring and empowering words of him who came to earth to be "God with us" (1:23). See note on 2Co 13:14.

Mark

I N T R O D U C T I O N

Author

Although there is no direct internal evidence of authorship, it was the unanimous testimony of the early church that this Gospel was written by John Mark ("John, also called Mark," Ac 12:12,25; 15:37). The most important evidence comes from Papias (c. A.D. 140), who quotes an even earlier source as saying: (1) Mark was a close associate of Peter, from whom he received the tradition of the things said and done by the Lord; (2) this tradition did not come to Mark as a finished, sequential account of the life of our Lord, but as the preaching of Peter — preaching directed to the needs of the early Christian communities; (3) Mark accurately preserved this material. The conclusion drawn from this tradition is that the Gospel of Mark largely consists of the preaching of Peter arranged and shaped by Mark (see Place of Writing, p. 1519; see also note on Ac 10:37). The actual shaping of "the gospel about Jesus Christ" (1:1) as presented in this Gospel traditionally ascribed to Mark may, however, have been more complex than Papias's testimony suggests.

John Mark in the NT

It is generally agreed that the Mark who is associated with Peter in the early non-Biblical tradition is also the John Mark of the NT. The first mention of him is in connection with his mother, Mary, who had a house in Jerusalem that served as a meeting place for believers (Ac 12:12). When Paul and Barnabas returned to Antioch from Jerusalem after the famine visit, Mark accompanied them (Ac 12:25). Mark next appears as a "helper" to Paul and Barnabas on their first missionary journey (Ac 13:5), but he left them at Perga in Pamphylia (see map, p. 1704) to return to Jerusalem (Ac 13:13). Paul must have been deeply disappointed with Mark's actions on this occasion, because when Barnabas proposed taking Mark on the second journey, Paul flatly refused, a refusal that broke up their working relationship (Ac 15:36 – 39). Barnabas took Mark, who was his cousin (Col 4:10), and departed for Cyprus. No further mention is made of either of them in the book of Acts. Mark reappears in Paul's

A Quick Look

Author:
John Mark

Audience:
Mostly Gentile Christians, probably in the church at Rome

Date:
Between the mid-fifties and late sixties A.D.

Theme:
To encourage his readers to persevere through suffering and persecution, Mark presents Jesus as the Servant-Messiah and Son of God who died as a ransom for sinners.

letter to the Colossians written from Rome. Paul sends a greeting from Mark and adds: "You have received instructions about him; if he comes to you, welcome him" (Col 4:10; see Phm 24, written about the same time). At this point Mark was apparently beginning to win his way back into Paul's confidence. By the end of Paul's life, Mark had fully regained Paul's favor (see 2Ti 4:11 and note).

Date of Composition

Some, who hold that Matthew and Luke used Mark as a major source (see essay and chart, p. 1457), have suggested that Mark may have been composed in the 50s or early 60s. Others have felt that the content of the Gospel and statements made about Mark by the early church fathers indicate that the book was written shortly before the destruction of Jerusalem in A.D. 70.

Mark's Gospel emphasizes more what Jesus did than what he said. Mark moves quickly from one episode in Jesus' life and ministry to another.

Place of Writing

According to early church tradition, Mark was written "in the regions of Italy" (Anti-Marcionite Prologue, a work possibly dating as early as the second century A.D. directed against the heretical view of Marcion) or, more specifically, in Rome (Irenaeus; Clement of Alexandria). These same authors closely associate Mark's writing of the Gospel with the apostle Peter. The above evidence is consistent with (1) the historical probability that Peter was in Rome during the last days of his life and was martyred there, and (2) the Biblical evidence that Mark also was in Rome about the same time and was closely associated with Peter (see 2Ti 4:11; cf. 1Pe 5:13, where the word "Babylon" may be a cryptogram for Rome; see also Introduction to 1 Peter: Place of Writing).

Recipients

The evidence points to the church at Rome, or at least to Gentile readers. Mark explains Jewish customs (7:2–4; 15:42), translates Aramaic words (3:17; 5:41; 7:11,34; 15:22,34) and seems to have a special interest in persecution and martyrdom (8:34–38; 13:9–13)—subjects of special concern to Roman believers (and to Peter as well; cf. 1 Peter). A Roman destination would explain the almost immediate acceptance of this Gospel and its rapid dissemination.

Occasion and Purpose

Since Mark's Gospel is traditionally associated with Rome, it may have been occasioned by the persecutions of the Roman church in the period c. A.D. 64–67. The famous burning of Rome in 64—probably done by Nero himself but blamed on Christians—resulted in widespread persecution. Even martyrdom was not unknown among Roman believers. Mark may be writing to prepare his readers for such suffering by placing before them the life of our Lord. There are many references, both explicit and veiled, to suffering and discipleship throughout his Gospel (see 1:12–13; 3:22,30; 8:34–38; 10:30,33–34,45; 13:8–13).

Emphases

1. *The cross.* Both the human cause (12:12; 14:1–2; 15:10) and the divine necessity (8:31; 9:31; 10:33–34) of the cross are emphasized by Mark.

2. *Discipleship.* Special instructions concerning discipleship accompany Jesus' predictions of his passion (8:34—9:1; 9:35—10:31; 10:42–45).

3. *The teachings of Jesus.* Although Mark records far fewer actual teachings of Jesus than the other Gospel writers, there is a remarkable emphasis on Jesus as teacher. The words "teacher," "teach" or "teaching," and "Rabbi" are applied to Jesus in Mark 39 times.

4. *The Messianic secret.* On several occasions Jesus warns his disciples or others to keep silent about who he is or what he has done (see 1:34,44 and notes; 3:12; 5:43; 7:36; 8:30; 9:9).

5. *Son of God.* This title is prominent in Mark's Gospel, emphasizing Jesus' Messiahship and his unique relationship with the Father (see 1:1,11; 3:11; 5:7; 9:7; 12:1–11; 13:32; 15:39). See note on Jn 3:16.

Special Characteristics

Mark's Gospel is a simple, succinct, unadorned, yet vivid account of Jesus' ministry, emphasizing more what Jesus did than what he said. Mark moves quickly from one episode in Jesus' life and ministry to another, often using the adverb "immediately" (see note on 1:12). The book as a whole may be characterized as "The beginning of the gospel" (1:1). The life, death and resurrection of Christ comprise the "beginning," of which the apostolic preaching in Acts is the continuation.

Outline

- I. The Beginnings of Jesus' Ministry (1:1 – 13)
  - A. His Forerunner (1:1 – 8)
  - B. His Baptism (1:9 – 11)
  - C. His Temptation (1:12 – 13)
- II. Jesus' Ministry in Galilee (1:14 — 6:29)
  - A. Early Galilean Ministry (1:14 — 3:12)
    1. Call of the first disciples (1:14 – 20)
    2. Miracles in Capernaum (1:21 – 34)
    3. Preaching and healing in Galilee (1:35 – 45)
    4. Ministry in Capernaum (2:1 – 22)
    5. Sabbath controversy (2:23 — 3:12)
  - B. Later Galilean Ministry (3:13 — 6:29)
    1. Choosing the 12 apostles (3:13 – 19)
    2. Teachings in Capernaum (3:20 – 35)
    3. Parables of the kingdom (4:1 – 34)
    4. Calming the Sea of Galilee (4:35 – 41)
    5. Healing a demon-possessed man (5:1 – 20)
    6. More Galilean miracles (5:21 – 43)
    7. Unbelief in Jesus' hometown (6:1 – 6)
    8. Six apostolic teams preach and heal in Galilee (6:7 – 13)
    9. King Herod's reaction to Jesus' ministry (6:14 – 29)
- III. Strategic Withdrawals from Galilee (6:30 — 9:29)
  - A. To the Eastern Shore of the Sea of Galilee (6:30 – 52)
  - B. To the Western Shore of the Sea (6:53 — 7:23)
  - C. To Syrian Phoenicia (7:24 – 30)
  - D. To the Region of the Decapolis (7:31 — 8:10)
  - E. To the Vicinity of Caesarea Philippi (8:11 – 30)
  - F. To the Mount of Transfiguration (8:31 — 9:29)
- IV. Final Ministry in Galilee (9:30 – 50)
- V. Jesus' Ministry in Judea and Perea (ch. 10)
  - A. Teaching Concerning Divorce (10:1 – 12)
  - B. Teaching Concerning Children (10:13 – 16)
  - C. The Rich Young Man (10:17 – 31)
  - D. A Request of Two Brothers (10:32 – 45)
  - E. Restoration of Bartimaeus's Sight (10:46 – 52)
- VI. The Passion of Jesus (chs. 11 – 15)
  - A. The Triumphal Entry (11:1 – 11)
  - B. The Clearing of the Temple (11:12 – 19)
  - C. Concluding Controversies with Jewish Leaders (11:20 — 12:44)
  - D. Signs of the End of the Age (ch. 13)
  - E. The Anointing of Jesus (14:1 – 11)
  - F. The Lord's Supper (14:12 – 26)
  - G. The Arrest, Trial and Death of Jesus (14:27 — 15:47)
- VII. The Resurrection of Jesus (ch. 16)

John the Baptist Prepares the Way

1:2-8pp — Mt 3:1-11; Lk 3:2-16

1 The beginning of the gospel about
Jesus Christ, the Son of God.[a][a]

[2]It is written in Isaiah the prophet:

"I will send my messenger ahead of
you,
who will prepare your way"[b][b]—
[3]"a voice of one calling in the desert,
'Prepare the way for the Lord,
make straight paths for him.'"[c][c]

[4]And so John[d] came, baptizing in the desert region and preaching a baptism of repentance[e] for the forgiveness of sins.[f] [5]The
whole Judean countryside and all the people of Jerusalem went out to him. Confessing their sins, they were baptized by him
in the Jordan River. [6]John wore clothing
made of camel's hair, with a leather belt
around his waist,[g] and he ate locusts[h] and
wild honey. [7]And this was his message:
"After me will come one more powerful
than I, the thongs of whose sandals I am
not worthy to stoop down and untie.[i] [8]I
baptize you with[d] water, but he will baptize you with the Holy Spirit."[j]

The Baptism and Temptation of Jesus

1:9-11pp — Mt 3:13-17; Lk 3:21,22
1:12,13pp — Mt 4:1-11; Lk 4:1-13

[9]At that time Jesus came from Nazareth[k] in Galilee and was baptized by John[l]
in the Jordan. [10]As Jesus was coming up
out of the water, he saw heaven being torn
open and the Spirit descending on him like
a dove.[m] [11]And a voice came from heaven:
"You are my Son,[n] whom I love; with you
I am well pleased."[o]
[12]At once the Spirit sent him out into
the desert, [13]and he was in the desert forty days,[p] being tempted by Satan.[q] He was
with the wild animals, and angels attended him.

1:1 [a]S Mt 4:3 **1:2** [b]Mal 3:1; Mt 11:10; Lk 7:27 **1:3** [c]Isa 40:3; Jn 1:23 **1:4** [d]S Mt 3:1 [e]ver 8; Jn 1:26,33; Ac 1:5,22; 11:36; 13:24; 18:25; 19:3,4 [f]Lk 1:77 **1:6** [g]2Ki 1:8 [h]Lev 11:22 **1:7** [i]Ac 13:25 **1:8** [j]Isa 44:3; Joel 2:28; Jn 1:33; Ac 1:5; 2:4; 11:16; 19:4-6 **1:9** [k]S Mt 2:23 [l]S Mt 3:1 **1:10** [m]Jn 1:32 **1:11** [n]S Mt 3:17 [o]S Mt 3:17 **1:13** [p]Ex 24:18; 1Ki 19:8 [q]S Mt 4:10; Heb 4:15

[a] *1* Some manuscripts do not have *the Son of God.*
[b] *2* Mal. 3:1 [c] *3* Isaiah 40:3 [d] *8* Or *in*

1:1 A summary of the main subject matter of Mark's Gospel (see Introduction: Special Characteristics). *The beginning.* Suggests the opening verse of Genesis (see Jn 1:1). *gospel.* From the Old English *godspel,* "good story" or "good news," which accurately translates the Greek. The good news is that God has provided salvation through the life, death and resurrection of Jesus Christ. *Jesus.* See NIV text note on Mt 1:21. *Christ.* See 8:29 and note. *Son of God.* See note on Jn 3:16.

1:2 *in Isaiah the prophet.* The quotation that immediately follows (see first two poetry lines) comes from Mal 3:1 (see note there) but is followed (v. 3) by one from Isa 40:3 (see note there). Isaiah here receives pride of place because he stands at the head of the prophetic canon, the division of the Hebrew Bible known as the Latter Prophets (see Introduction to Isaiah: Position in the Canon; cf. Introduction to Joshua: Title and Theme). See also note on Mt 27:9. Understanding the ministry of Jesus must begin with the OT. What Isaiah says about God applies to Jesus, his Son (v. 1). The passages cited speak of the messenger, the desert and the Lord, each of which is stressed in vv. 4–8.

1:4 *John came.* Mark, like John, has no nativity narrative, but begins with the ministry of John the Baptist. This is also where Peter begins in his proclamation of the gospel in Ac 10:37 (see note there; see also Introduction: Place of Writing). The name John means "The LORD is gracious." *baptizing.* John's practice of baptizing those who came to him in repentance was so characteristic of his ministry that he became known as "the Baptist" or "the Baptizer." *desert region.* The arid region west of the Dead Sea. *baptism.* John was preaching repentance-baptism, i.e., baptism that was preceded or accompanied by repentance. Baptism was not new to John's audience. They knew of baptism for Gentile converts, but had not heard that the descendants of Abraham (Jews) needed to repent and be baptized. *repentance.* Involves deliberate turning from sin to righteousness, and John's emphasis on repentance recalls the preaching of the prophets (e.g., Hos 3:4–5). God always grants forgiveness when there is repentance.

1:5 *whole ... all.* Hyperbole, indicating the high interest created by John's preaching. For centuries Israel had had no prophet. *people of Jerusalem.* See note on Jn 7:25. *Jordan River.* The principal river in the Holy Land, beginning in the snows of Mount Hermon and ending in the Dead Sea. Its closest point to Jerusalem is about 20 miles.

1:6 *camel's hair ... leather belt.* Worn by Elijah and other prophets (see 2Ki 1:8 and note; cf. Zec 13:4). *locusts and wild honey.* See note on Mt 3:4.

1:7 *message.* Mark's account of John's message is brief (cf. Mt 3:7–12; Lk 3:7–17) and focuses on the coming of the powerful One. *sandals I am not worthy to ... untie.* See note on Jn 1:27.

1:8 *baptize you with the Holy Spirit.* See note on Mt 3:11.

1:9 *At that time.* Jesus began his public ministry c. A.D. 27 (see chart, p. 1508), when he was approximately 30 years old (Lk 3:23). As far as we know, he had spent most of his previous life in Nazareth. *Nazareth.* See notes on Mt 2:23; Lk 4:23. *baptized by John.* For the significance of Jesus' baptism see Mt 3:15 and note.

1:10–11 All three persons of the Trinity are involved in Jesus' baptism: (1) the Father speaks, (2) the Son is baptized, and (3) the Holy Spirit descends on the Son (see note on Mt 28:19).

1:10 *Spirit descending on him.* Jesus' anointing for ministry—an anointing he claimed in the synagogue at Nazareth (see Lk 4:18 and note). *like a dove.* Symbolizing the gentleness, purity and guilelessness of the Holy Spirit (see Mt 10:16; Lk 3:22 and note).

1:11 An allusion to Ps 2:7; Isa 42:1. *voice.* God sometimes spoke directly from heaven (see 9:7; Lk 3:22 and note; Jn 12:28–29; cf. Ex 19:3). *You are my Son.* In v. 1 Mark proclaims Jesus as the Son of God; here God the Father himself proclaims Jesus as his Son.

1:12 *At once.* A distinctive characteristic of Mark's style is his use (some 47 times) of a Greek word that has been variously translated "at once," "without delay," "immediately," "quickly," "just then" (see, e.g., vv. 18,20,23,28,42–43).

1:13 *forty.* See Mt 4:2 and note. *tempted.* See notes on Mt 4:1–11. *Satan.* See Ge 3:1; Job 1:6,9; Zec 3:1; Rev 2:9–10; 12:9–10 and notes. *wild animals.* In Jesus' day there were many more wild animals in Israel than today. Only Mark reports their presence in this connection; he emphasizes that God kept Jesus safe in the desert. *angels attended him.* As they had attended Israel in the desert (see Ex 23:20,23; 32:34).

The Calling of the First Disciples

1:16-20pp — Mt 4:18-22; Lk 5:2-11; Jn 1:35-42

14 After John[r] was put in prison, Jesus
went into Galilee,[s] proclaiming the good
news of God.[t] 15 "The time has come,"[u] he
said. "The kingdom of God is near. Repent
and believe[v] the good news!"[w]
16 As Jesus walked beside the Sea of Galilee, he saw Simon and his brother Andrew casting a net into the lake, for they
were fishermen. 17 "Come, follow me,"
Jesus said, "and I will make you fishers
of men." 18 At once they left their nets and
followed him.[x]
19 When he had gone a little farther, he
saw James son of Zebedee and his brother John in a boat, preparing their nets.
20 Without delay he called them, and they
left their father Zebedee in the boat with
the hired men and followed him.

Jesus Drives Out an Evil Spirit

1:21-28pp — Lk 4:31-37

21 They went to Capernaum, and when
the Sabbath came, Jesus went into the
synagogue and began to teach.[y] 22 The people were amazed at his teaching, because
he taught them as one who had authority,
not as the teachers of the law.[z] 23 Just then
a man in their synagogue who was possessed by an evil[a] spirit cried out, 24 "What
do you want with us,[a] Jesus of Nazareth?[b]
Have you come to destroy us? I know who
you are—the Holy One of God!"[c]
25 "Be quiet!" said Jesus sternly. "Come
out of him!"[d] 26 The evil spirit shook the
man violently and came out of him with
a shriek.[e]
27 The people were all so amazed[f] that
they asked each other, "What is this? A
new teaching—and with authority! He
even gives orders to evil spirits and they
obey him." 28 News about him spread
quickly over the whole region[g] of Galilee.

Jesus Heals Many

1:29-31pp — Mt 8:14,15; Lk 4:38,39
1:32-34pp — Mt 8:16,17; Lk 4:40,41

29 As soon as they left the synagogue,[h]
they went with James and John to the
home of Simon and Andrew. 30 Simon's
mother-in-law was in bed with a fever,
and they told Jesus about her. 31 So he
went to her, took her hand and helped her
up.[i] The fever left her and she began to
wait on them.
32 That evening after sunset the people
brought to Jesus all the sick and demon-
possessed.[j] 33 The whole town gathered at
the door, 34 and Jesus healed many who
had various diseases.[k] He also drove out

1:14 [r]S Mt 3:1 [s]Mt 4:12 [t]Mt 4:23 **1:15** [u]Ro 5:6; Gal 4:4; Eph 1:10 [v]S Jn 3:15 [w]Ac 20:21 **1:18** [x]S Mt 4:19 **1:21** [y]ver 39; S Mt 4:23; S Mk 10:1 **1:22** [z]S Mt 7:28,29
1:24 [a]S Mt 8:29 [b]Mt 2:23; Lk 24:19; Jn 1:45,46; Ac 4:10; 24:5 [c]Ps 16:10; Isa 41:14,16,20; Lk 1:35; Jn 6:69; Ac 3:14; 1Jn 2:20 **1:25** [d]ver 34 **1:26** [e]Mk 9:20 **1:27** [f]Mk 10:24,32 **1:28** [g]S Mt 9:26 **1:29** [h]ver 21,23 **1:31** [i]S Lk 7:14 **1:32** [j]S Mt 4:24 **1:34** [k]S Mt 4:23

[a] 23 Greek *unclean*; also in verses 26 and 27

1:14 *After John was put in prison.* See Mt 4:12; Lk 3:20 and notes. *good news of God.* The good news from, as well as about, God (see 1:1 and note).

1:15 *The time has come.* Not simply chronological time, but the decisive time for God's action. With the coming of the kingdom, God was doing something special. *kingdom of God.* See note on Mt 3:2. *is near.* The coming of Christ (the King) brings the kingdom near to the people (see Lk 17:21 and note).

1:16 *Sea of Galilee.* A beautiful lake, almost 700 feet below sea level, 14 miles long and 6 miles wide, fed by the waters of the upper Jordan River. It was also called the Lake of Gennesaret (Lk 5:1) and the Sea of Tiberias (Jn 6:1; 21:1). In OT times it was known as the Sea of Kinnereth (e.g., Nu 34:11) because it is shaped like a harp (see note on Dt 3:17). *Simon.* Probably a contraction of the OT name Simeon (see NIV text note on Ac 15:14). Jesus gave Simon the name Peter (see 3:16; see also Mt 16:18; Jn 1:42 and notes). *net.* See note on Mt 4:18.

1:17 *Come, follow me.* The call to discipleship is definite and demands a response of total commitment. This was not Jesus' first encounter with Simon and Andrew (see Jn 1:35–42). *fishers of men.* Evangelists (see Lk 5:10).

1:21 *Capernaum.* See Mt 4:13; Lk 10:15 and notes. *Sabbath.* The seventh day of the week, the day of rest from life's normal labors (see 2:27; Ge 2:3; Ex 16:23; Isa 58:13 and notes), which the Jews came to use as a day for gathering at their synagogues. *synagogue.* A very important religious institution among the Jews of that day. Originating during the exile, it provided a place where Jews could gather to study the Scriptures and worship God. A synagogue could be established in any town where there were at least ten married Jewish men. See note on Ac 13:14; see also essay, p. 1453, and diagram, p. 1572. *began to teach.* Jesus, like Paul (see Ac 13:14–15 and notes; 14:1; 17:2; 18:4), took advantage of the custom that allowed visiting teachers to contribute to the worship service by invitation of the synagogue leaders (see Lk 4:16–17 and notes).

1:22 *amazed.* Mark frequently reported the amazement that Jesus' teaching and actions produced (see 2:12; 5:20,42; 6:2,51; 7:37; 10:26,32; 11:18; 12:17; 15:5). In these instances it was Christ's inherent authority that amazed. He did not quote human authorities, as did the teachers of the law, because his authority was directly from God (cf. Lk 2:46–48). *teachers of the law.* See note on Mt 2:4.

1:23 *man in their synagogue ... cried out.* It was actually the demon who cried out (see 5:7 and note). *possessed by an evil spirit.* Demonic possession intended to torment and destroy those who are created in God's image, but the demon recognized that Jesus was a powerful adversary, capable of destroying the forces of Satan.

1:24 *us.* The man was possessed by more than one demon (cf. 5:9), but only one spoke. *Holy One of God.* Apart from the parallel in Lk 4:34, the title is used elsewhere only in Jn 6:69 and points to Christ's divine origin rather than his Messiahship (see Lk 1:35). The name was perhaps used by the demons in accordance with the occult belief that the precise use of a person's name gave certain control over him (see 5:7).

1:25 *Be quiet!* Lit. "Be muzzled!" Jesus' superior power silences the shrieks of the demon-possessed man.

1:27 *with authority.* Jesus' authority in how he taught (v. 22) and in what he did (here) impressed the people.

1:29 *home of Simon and Andrew.* Jesus and the disciples probably went there for a meal, since the main Sabbath meal was served immediately following the synagogue service.

1:30 *Simon's mother-in-law.* 1Co 9:5 speaks of Peter's being married.

1:32 *evening.* See Lk 4:40 and note. *people brought.* They waited until the Sabbath was over ("after sunset") before carrying anything (see Jer 17:21–22).

1:34 *not let the demons speak.* See Introduction: Emphases. *because they knew who he was.* Luke says, "because they knew he was the Christ" (Lk 4:41). Jesus probably wanted first to

many demons, but he would not let the demons speak because they knew who he was.[l]

Jesus Prays in a Solitary Place

1:35-38pp — Lk 4:42,43

[35]Very early in the morning, while it was still dark, Jesus got up, left the house and went off to a solitary place, where he prayed.[m] [36]Simon and his companions went to look for him, [37]and when they found him, they exclaimed: "Everyone is looking for you!"

[38]Jesus replied, "Let us go somewhere else—to the nearby villages—so I can preach there also. That is why I have come."[n] [39]So he traveled throughout Galilee, preaching in their synagogues[o] and driving out demons.[p]

A Man With Leprosy

1:40-44pp — Mt 8:2-4; Lk 5:12-14

[40]A man with leprosy[a] came to him and begged him on his knees,[q] "If you are willing, you can make me clean."

[41]Filled with compassion, Jesus reached out his hand and touched the man. "I am willing," he said. "Be clean!" [42]Immediately the leprosy left him and he was cured.

[43]Jesus sent him away at once with a strong warning: [44]"See that you don't tell this to anyone.[r] But go, show yourself to the priest[s] and offer the sacrifices that Moses commanded for your cleansing,[t] as a testimony to them." [45]Instead he went out and began to talk freely, spreading the news. As a result, Jesus could no longer enter a town openly but stayed outside in lonely places.[u] Yet the people still came to him from everywhere.[v]

Jesus Heals a Paralytic

2:3-12pp — Mt 9:2-8; Lk 5:18-26

2 A few days later, when Jesus again entered Capernaum, the people heard that he had come home. [2]So many[w] gathered that there was no room left, not even outside the door, and he preached the word to them. [3]Some men came, bringing to him a paralytic,[x] carried by four of them. [4]Since they could not get him to Jesus because of the crowd, they made an opening in the roof above Jesus and, after digging through it, lowered the mat the paralyzed man was lying on. [5]When Jesus saw their faith, he said to the paralytic, "Son, your sins are forgiven."[y]

[6]Now some teachers of the law were sitting there, thinking to themselves, [7]"Why does this fellow talk like that? He's blaspheming! Who can forgive sins but God alone?"[z]

[8]Immediately Jesus knew in his spirit that this was what they were thinking in their hearts, and he said to them, "Why are you thinking these things? [9]Which is easier: to say to the paralytic, 'Your sins are forgiven,' or to say, 'Get up, take your mat and walk'? [10]But that you may know that the Son of Man[a] has authority on earth to forgive sins . . ." He said to the paralytic, [11]"I tell you, get up, take your mat and go home."

1:34 [l] Mk 3:12; Ac 16:17,18 **1:35** [m] S Lk 3:21 **1:38** [n] Isa 61:1 **1:39** [o] S Mt 4:23 [p] S Mt 4:24 **1:40** [q] Mk 10:17 **1:44** [r] S Mt 8:4 [s] Lev 13:49 [t] Lev 14:1-32 **1:45** [u] Lk 5:15,16 [v] Mk 2:13; Lk 5:17; Jn 6:2 **2:2** [w] ver 13; Mk 1:45 **2:3** [x] S Mt 4:24 **2:5** [y] Lk 7:48 **2:7** [z] Isa 43:25 **2:10** [a] S Mt 8:20

[a] *40* The Greek word was used for various diseases affecting the skin—not necessarily leprosy.

---

show by word and deed the kind of Messiah he was (in contrast to popular notions) before he clearly declared himself, and he would not let the demons frustrate this intent.

1:36 *companions.* Andrew, James and John (vv. 16,19,29), and perhaps also Philip and Nathanael (cf. Jn 1:43–45).

1:39 *throughout Galilee.* The first of what seem to be three preaching and healing tours of Galilee (second tour, Lk 8:1; third tour, Mk 6:6 and Mt 11:1).

1:40 *leprosy.* See NIV text note and Lev 13–14; see also note on Lev 13:2. *make me clean.* See notes on Lev 4:12; Mt 8:2.

1:41 *touched the man.* An act that, according to Mosaic law, brought defilement (see Lev 13, especially vv. 45–46; see also Lev 5:2). Jesus' compassion for the man superseded ceremonial considerations.

1:44 *don't tell this to anyone.* See Introduction: Emphases; see also notes on Mt 8:4; 16:20. *go, show yourself to the priest.* Who would then pronounce him ceremonially clean (see, e.g., Lev 13:6,13,17,23; see also note on Lk 5:14). *testimony to them.* The sacrifices were to be evidence to the priests and the people that the cure was real and that Jesus respected the law. The healing was also a testimony to Jesus' divine power, since Jews believed that only God could cure leprosy (see 2Ki 5:1–14 and notes).

1:45 *no longer enter a town openly.* Jesus' growing popularity with the people (see v. 28; 3:7–8; Lk 7:17) and the increasing opposition from Jewish leaders (see 2:6–7,16,24; 3:2,6,22) sometimes made it necessary for him to withdraw from the more populous areas.

2:1 *home.* When in Capernaum, Jesus probably made his home at Peter's house (see 1:21,29).

2:2 *So many gathered.* The same enthusiasm that greeted Jesus earlier (1:32–33,37) was evident at his return.

2:4 *made an opening in the roof.* A typical house in the Middle East had a flat roof accessible by means of an outside staircase. The roof was often made of a mat of branches laid across wood beams and covered with a layer of clay tamped down with a stone roller.

2:5 *Jesus saw their faith.* Jesus recognized that the bold action of the paralyzed man and his friends gave evidence of faith. *Son, your sins are forgiven.* Jesus first met the man's deepest need: forgiveness. By his action here Jesus may have deliberately evoked memory of Ps 103:3.

2:7 *He's blaspheming! Who can forgive sins but God alone?* In Jewish theology even the Messiah could not forgive sins, and Jesus' forgiveness of sin was a claim to deity—which they considered to be blasphemous (see note on 14:64).

2:9 *Which is easier . . . ?* Jesus' point probably was that neither forgiving sins nor healing was easier. Both are equally impossible for people and equally easy for God.

2:10 *But that you may know.* See note on Lk 5:24; probably spoken to the teachers of the law. The words "He said to the paralytic" are parenthetical to explain a change in the persons addressed. It is clear that one purpose of miracles was to give evidence of Jesus' deity. For the use of miraculous signs in John's Gospel see Jn 2:11; 20:30–31 and notes. *Son of Man.* See note on 8:31.

12He got up, took his mat and walked out in
full view of them all. This amazed everyone
and they praised God,[b] saying, "We have
never seen anything like this!"[c]

The Calling of Levi

2:14-17pp — Mt 9:9-13; Lk 5:27-32

13Once again Jesus went out beside the
lake. A large crowd came to him,[d] and
he began to teach them. 14As he walked
along, he saw Levi son of Alphaeus sitting at the tax collector's booth. "Follow
me,"[e] Jesus told him, and Levi got up and
followed him.

15While Jesus was having dinner at Levi's house, many tax collectors and "sinners" were eating with him and his disciples, for there were many who followed
him. 16When the teachers of the law who
were Pharisees[f] saw him eating with the
"sinners" and tax collectors, they asked
his disciples: "Why does he eat with tax
collectors and 'sinners'?"[g]

17On hearing this, Jesus said to them, "It
is not the healthy who need a doctor, but
the sick. I have not come to call the righteous, but sinners."[h]

Jesus Questioned About Fasting

2:18-22pp — Mt 9:14-17; Lk 5:33-38

18Now John's disciples and the Pharisees were fasting.[i] Some people came and
asked Jesus, "How is it that John's disciples and the disciples of the Pharisees are
fasting, but yours are not?"

19Jesus answered, "How can the guests
of the bridegroom fast while he is with
them? They cannot, so long as they have
him with them. 20But the time will come
when the bridegroom will be taken from
them,[j] and on that day they will fast.

21"No one sews a patch of unshrunk
cloth on an old garment. If he does, the
new piece will pull away from the old,
making the tear worse. 22And no one
pours new wine into old wineskins. If he
does, the wine will burst the skins, and
both the wine and the wineskins will be
ruined. No, he pours new wine into new
wineskins."

Lord of the Sabbath

2:23-28pp — Mt 12:1-8; Lk 6:1-5
3:1-6pp — Mt 12:9-14; Lk 6:6-11

23One Sabbath Jesus was going through
the grainfields, and as his disciples walked
along, they began to pick some heads of
grain.[k] 24The Pharisees said to him, "Look,
why are they doing what is unlawful on
the Sabbath?"[l]

25He answered, "Have you never read
what David did when he and his com-

2:12 [b]S Mt 9:8 [c]Mt 9:33
2:13 [d]Mk 1:45; Lk 5:15; Jn 6:2
2:14 [e]S Mt 4:19
2:16 [f]Ac 23:9 [g]S Mt 9:11
2:17 [h]Lk 19:10; 1Ti 1:15
2:18 [i]S Mt 6:16-18; Ac 13:2
2:20 [j]Lk 17:22
2:23 [k]Dt 23:25
2:24 [l]S Mt 12:2

2:12 *This amazed everyone.* See note on 1:22.

2:14 *Levi son of Alphaeus.* Matthew (see Mt 9:9; 10:3). His given name was probably Levi (for the possible meaning of this name see NIV text note on Ge 29:34), and Matthew ("gift of the LORD") his apostolic name. *tax collector's booth.* Levi was a tax collector (see note on Lk 3:12) under Herod Antipas, tetrarch of Galilee. The tax collector's booth where Jesus found Levi was probably a toll booth on the major international road that went west from Damascus through Capernaum to the Mediterranean coast and then south to Egypt (see Isa 9:1 and note). *Levi got up and followed.* See note on Lk 5:28.

2:15 *tax collectors.* Jews who contracted to collect Roman taxes were regarded as traitors and outcasts. They could not serve as witnesses or as judges in Jewish courts and were expelled from the synagogue. In the eyes of the Jewish community their disgrace extended to their families. See note on Mt 5:46. *"sinners."* Notoriously evil people as well as those who refused to follow the Mosaic law as interpreted by the teachers of the law. The term was commonly used of tax collectors, adulterers, robbers and the like. *were eating.* To eat with a person was a sign of friendship.

2:16 *teachers of the law who were Pharisees.* Not all teachers of the law were Pharisees—successors of the Hasidim, pious Jews who joined forces with the Maccabees during the struggle for freedom from Syrian oppression (166–142 B.C.). They were first called Pharisees during the reign of John Hyrcanus (135–105). Although some, no doubt, were godly, most of those who came into conflict with Jesus were hypocritical, envious, rigid and formalistic. According to Pharisaism, God's grace extended only to those who kept his law. See notes on Mt 2:4; 3:7.

2:17 *I have not come to call the righteous, but sinners.* Those who are self-righteous do not realize their need for salvation, but admitted sinners do.

2:18 *John's disciples.* John the Baptist's disciples may have been fasting because he was in prison (see 1:14), or this may have been a practice among them as an expression of repentance, intended to hasten the coming of redemption announced by John. *disciples of the Pharisees.* Pharisees as such were not teachers, but some were also "scribes" (teachers of the law), who often had disciples. Or perhaps the phrase is used in a nontechnical way to refer to people influenced by the Pharisees. *fasting.* In the Mosaic law only the fast of the Day of Atonement was required (see Lev 16:29,31 and note; 23:27–32; Nu 29:7). After the Babylonian exile four other yearly fasts were observed by the Jews (see Zec 7:5; 8:19 and notes). In Jesus' time the Pharisees fasted twice a week (see Lk 18:12 and note).

2:19 *How can the guests of the bridegroom fast while he is with them?* Jesus compared his disciples with the guests of a bridegroom. A Jewish wedding was a particularly joyous occasion, and the celebration associated with it often lasted a week. It was unthinkable to fast during such festivities, because fasting was associated with sorrow.

2:20 *bridegroom will be taken from them.* Jesus is the bridegroom, who would be taken from them by death, and then fasting would be in order.

2:22 *new wineskins.* See note on Mt 9:17.

2:23 *pick some heads of grain.* There was nothing inherently wrong in the action itself, which comes under the provision of Dt 23:25.

2:24 *what is unlawful on the Sabbath.* According to Jewish tradition (in the Mishnah), harvesting (which is what Jesus' disciples technically were doing) was forbidden on the Sabbath. See Ex 34:21.

2:25 *what David did.* See 1Sa 21:1–6. The relationship between the OT incident and the apparent infringement of the Sabbath by the disciples lies in the fact that on

panions were hungry and in need? 26In
the days of Abiathar the high priest,[m] he
entered the house of God and ate the consecrated bread, which is lawful only for
priests to eat.[n] And he also gave some to
his companions."[o]

27Then he said to them, "The Sabbath
was made for man,[p] not man for the Sabbath.[q] 28So the Son of Man[r] is Lord even
of the Sabbath."

3 Another time he went into the synagogue,[s] and a man with a shriveled
hand was there. 2Some of them were looking for a reason to accuse Jesus, so they
watched him closely[t] to see if he would
heal him on the Sabbath.[u] 3Jesus said to
the man with the shriveled hand, "Stand
up in front of everyone."

4Then Jesus asked them, "Which is lawful on the Sabbath: to do good or to do
evil, to save life or to kill?" But they remained silent.

5He looked around at them in anger and,
deeply distressed at their stubborn hearts,
said to the man, "Stretch out your hand."
He stretched it out, and his hand was completely restored. 6Then the Pharisees went
out and began to plot with the Herodians[v]
how they might kill Jesus.[w]

2:26 [m] 1Ch 24:6; 2Sa 8:17 [n] Lev 24:5-9 [o] 1Sa 21:1-6 **2:27** [p] Ex 23:12; Dt 5:14 [q] Col 2:16 **2:28** [r] S Mt 8:20 **3:1** [s] S Mt 4:23; Mk 1:21 **3:2** [t] S Mt 12:10 [u] Lk 14:1 **3:6** [v] Mt 22:16; Mk 12:13 [w] S Mt 12:14

3:7 [x] Mt 4:25 **3:8** [y] S Mt 11:21 **3:10** [z] S Mt 4:23 [a] S Mt 9:20 **3:11** [b] S Mt 4:3; Mk 1:23,24 **3:12** [c] S Mt 8:4; Mk 1:24,25,34; Ac 16:17,18 **3:13** [d] Mt 5:1 **3:14** [e] S Mk 6:30

Crowds Follow Jesus

3:7-12pp — Mt 12:15,16; Lk 6:17-19

7Jesus withdrew with his disciples to
the lake, and a large crowd from Galilee
followed.[x] 8When they heard all he was
doing, many people came to him from Judea, Jerusalem, Idumea, and the regions
across the Jordan and around Tyre and Sidon.[y] 9Because of the crowd he told his
disciples to have a small boat ready for
him, to keep the people from crowding
him. 10For he had healed many,[z] so that
those with diseases were pushing forward
to touch him.[a] 11Whenever the evil[a] spirits
saw him, they fell down before him and
cried out, "You are the Son of God."[b] 12But
he gave them strict orders not to tell who
he was.[c]

The Appointing of the Twelve Apostles

3:16-19pp — Mt 10:2-4; Lk 6:14-16; Ac 1:13

13Jesus went up on a mountainside and
called to him those he wanted, and they
came to him.[d] 14He appointed twelve—designating them apostles[b] [e]—that they might
be with him and that he might send them

[a] *11* Greek *unclean*; also in verse 30 [b] *14* Some manuscripts do not have *designating them apostles.*

both occasions godly men did something forbidden. Since, however, it is always "lawful to do good" (Mt 12:12) and to "save life" (Lk 6:9)—even on the Sabbath—both David and the disciples were within the spirit of the law (see 3:4; 1Sa 21:4 and notes; Isa 58:6–7; Lk 13:10–17; 14:1–6).

2:26 *In the days of Abiathar the high priest.* According to 1Sa 21:1, Ahimelech, Abiathar's father (1Sa 22:20), was then high priest (see note on 2Sa 8:17). *house of God.* The tabernacle (see 1Sa 1:9 and note; 21:1). *consecrated bread.* See note on Mt 12:4.

2:27 *The Sabbath was made for man, not man for the Sabbath.* Jewish tradition had so multiplied the requirements and restrictions for keeping the Sabbath that the burden had become intolerable. Jesus cut across these traditions and emphasized the God-given purpose of the Sabbath—a day intended for the benefit of people (for rest from daily labors, allowing spiritual, mental and physical restoration; see Ex 20:8–11).

2:28 See note on Lk 6:5.

3:1–6 A demonstration that Jesus is Lord of the Sabbath (see 2:28).

3:2 *Some of them.* The Pharisees (v. 6; cf. Lk 6:7). *to accuse Jesus.* Jesus' presence demanded a decision about his preaching, his acts and his person. The hostility, first seen in 2:6–7, continues to spread. See note on v. 6. *to see if he would heal him on the Sabbath.* An indication that the Pharisees believed in Jesus' power to perform miracles. The question was not "Could he?" but "Would he?" Jewish tradition prescribed that aid could be given the sick on the Sabbath only when the person's life was threatened, which obviously was not the case here. See notes on 2:25; Lk 13:14.

3:4 *to do good or to do evil, to save life or to kill?* Jesus asks: Which is better, to preserve life by healing or to destroy life by refusing to heal? The question is ironic since, whereas Jesus was ready to heal, the Pharisees were plotting to put him to death. It is obvious who was guilty of breaking the Sabbath. *they remained silent.* See 12:34.

3:5 *He looked around at them.* See note on Lk 6:10.

3:6 *the Pharisees ... began to plot.* The decision to seek Jesus' death was not the result of this incident alone, but was the response to a series of incidents (see 2:6–7,16–17,24). The plotting of the Pharisees and the Herodians is seen again on Tuesday of Passion Week (see 12:13 and note). *Herodians.* Evidently influential Jews who favored the Herodian dynasty, meaning they were supporters of Rome, from which the Herods received their authority. They joined the Pharisees in opposing Jesus because they feared he might have an unsettling political influence on the people. See Mt 22:15–17 and note.

3:8 Impressive evidence of Jesus' rapidly growing popularity among the people. This geographical list indicates that the crowds came not only from the areas in the vicinity of Capernaum but also from considerable distances. The regions mentioned included virtually all of Israel and its surrounding neighbors. Mark tells of Jesus' work in all these regions except Idumea (see 1:14, Galilee; 5:1 and 10:1, the region across the Jordan; 7:24,31, Tyre and Sidon; 10:1, Judea; 11:11, Jerusalem). *Idumea.* The Greek form of Hebrew Edom, but here referring to an area south of Judea, not to earlier Edomite territory. (See map, p. 1570.)

3:11 *evil spirits.* See note on 1:23. *You are the Son of God.* The evil spirits recognized who Jesus was, but they did not believe in him (see 1:24 and note).

3:12 *not to tell who he was.* See Introduction: Emphases. The time for revealing Jesus' identity had not yet come (see 1:34 and note; see also notes on Mt 8:4; 16:20), and demons were hardly the proper channel for such disclosure.

3:13 *mountainside.* Probably the hill country of Galilee around the lake.

3:14 *designating them apostles.* See note on 6:30. *that they might be with him.* The training of the Twelve included not only instruction and practice in various forms of ministry but also—first and foremost—continuous association and intimate fellowship with Jesus himself.

out to preach 15and to have authority to drive out demons.[f] 16These are the twelve he appointed: Simon (to whom he gave the name Peter);[g] 17James son of Zebedee and his brother John (to them he gave the name Boanerges, which means Sons of Thunder); 18Andrew, Philip, Bartholomew, Matthew, Thomas, James son of Alphaeus, Thaddaeus, Simon the Zealot 19and Judas Iscariot, who betrayed him.

Jesus and Beelzebub

3:23-27pp — Mt 12:25-29; Lk 11:17-22

20Then Jesus entered a house, and again a crowd gathered,[h] so that he and his disciples were not even able to eat.[i] 21When his family heard about this, they went to take charge of him, for they said, "He is out of his mind."[j]

22And the teachers of the law who came down from Jerusalem[k] said, "He is possessed by Beelzebub[a]![l] By the prince of demons he is driving out demons."[m]

23So Jesus called them and spoke to them in parables:[n] "How can Satan[o] drive out Satan? 24If a kingdom is divided against itself, that kingdom cannot stand. 25If a house is divided against itself, that house cannot stand. 26And if Satan opposes himself and is divided, he cannot stand; his end has come. 27In fact, no one can enter a strong man's house and carry off his possessions unless he first ties up the strong man. Then he can rob his house.[p] 28I tell you the truth, all the sins and blasphemies of men will be forgiven them. 29But whoever blasphemes against the Holy Spirit will never be forgiven; he is guilty of an eternal sin."[q]

3:15 [f] S Mt 10:1
3:16 [g] Jn 1:42
3:20 [h] ver 7 [i] Mk 6:31
3:21 [j] Jn 10:20; Ac 26:24
3:22 [k] Mt 15:1 [l] Mt 10:25; 11:18; 12:24; Jn 7:20; 8:48,52; 10:20 [m] Mt 9:34
3:23 [n] Mk 4:2 [o] S Mt 4:10
3:27 [p] Isa 49:24,25
3:29 [q] Mt 12:31,32; Lk 12:10

30He said this because they were saying, "He has an evil spirit."

Jesus' Mother and Brothers

3:31-35pp — Mt 12:46-50; Lk 8:19-21

31Then Jesus' mother and brothers arrived.[r] Standing outside, they sent someone in to call him. 32A crowd was sitting around him, and they told him, "Your mother and brothers are outside looking for you."

33"Who are my mother and my brothers?" he asked.

34Then he looked at those seated in a circle around him and said, "Here are my mother and my brothers! 35Whoever does God's will is my brother and sister and mother."

The Parable of the Sower

4:1-12pp — Mt 13:1-15; Lk 8:4-10
4:13-20pp — Mt 13:18-23; Lk 8:11-15

4 Again Jesus began to teach by the lake.[s] The crowd that gathered around him was so large that he got into a boat and sat in it out on the lake, while all the people were along the shore at the water's edge. 2He taught them many things by parables,[t] and in his teaching said: 3"Listen! A farmer went out to sow his seed.[u] 4As he was scattering the seed, some fell along the path, and the birds came and ate it up. 5Some fell on rocky places, where it did not have much soil. It sprang up quickly, because the soil was shallow. 6But when the sun came up, the plants were scorched, and they withered because they had no root.

3:31 [r] ver 21
4:1 [s] Mk 2:13; 3:7
4:2 [t] ver 11; Mk 3:23
4:3 [u] ver 26

[a] 22 Greek *Beezeboul* or *Beelzeboul*

3:16–19 See notes on Lk 6:14–16.

3:16 *Simon (to whom he gave the name Peter).* See note on 1:16.

3:17 *Boanerges.* One of many Aramaic words translated by Mark (see Introduction: Recipients). *Sons of Thunder.* Probably descriptive of their dispositions (see notes on 10:37; Lk 9:54).

3:18 *Thaddaeus.* Apparently the same as "Judas son of James" (see Lk 6:16; Ac 1:13). *the Zealot.* See note on Mt 10:4.

3:19 *Iscariot.* Probably means "the man from Kerioth," perhaps the town of Kerioth Hezron (Jos 15:25), 12 miles south of Hebron. For Judas's betrayal of Jesus see 14:10–11,43–46.

3:20 *house.* Perhaps the home of Peter and Andrew (see 1:29; 2:1 and notes; see also diagram, p. 1572).

3:21 *his family … went to take charge of him.* They may have come to Capernaum from Nazareth, about 30 miles away (see v. 31).

3:22 *who came down from Jerusalem.* See 7:1 and note. *Beelzebub.* See note on Mt 10:25.

3:23 *parables.* In this context the word is used in the general sense of comparisons (see note on 4:2).

3:24 *kingdom is divided against itself.* See note on Lk 11:17.

3:27 *enter a strong man's house and carry off his possessions.* Jesus was doing this very thing when he freed people from Satan's control.

3:28 *I tell you the truth.* A solemn affirmation used by Jesus to strengthen his assertions (see 8:12; 9:1,41; 10:15,29; 11:23; 12:43; 13:30; 14:9,18,25,30; see also note on Jn 1:51).

3:29 *whoever blasphemes against the Holy Spirit will never be forgiven.* Jesus identifies this sin in v. 30 (cf. v. 22)—the teachers of the law attributed Jesus' healing to Satan's power rather than to the Holy Spirit (see note on Mt 12:31).

3:31 *Jesus' mother and brothers.* See note on Lk 8:19.

3:35 *Whoever does God's will.* Membership in God's spiritual family, evidenced by obedience to him, is more important than membership in our human families (see 10:30 and note).

4:1 *sat in it.* Sitting was the usual position for Jewish teachers (see 9:35; see also Mt 5:1; Lk 4:20 and notes).

4:2 *parables.* Usually stories out of ordinary life used to illustrate spiritual or moral truth, sometimes in the form of brief similes, comparisons (see note on 3:23), analogies or proverbial sayings. They tended to have a single main point, and not every detail was meant to have significance. See notes on Mt 13:3; Lk 8:4.

4:3–8 In that day seed was broadcast by hand—which scattered some seed on unproductive ground (see note on Lk 8:5).

4:3 *Listen!* This parable begins and ends (v. 9) with a call for careful attention, which suggests that its meaning is not self-evident. *sow his seed.* See note on Lk 8:5.

Jerusalem During the Ministry of Jesus

Herod the Great (reigned 37–4 B.C.) rebuilt the temple and its surrounding walls, built a palace, a fortress, a theater and a hippodrome (stadium) for horse and chariot races. He brought the city to the zenith of its architectural beauty and Roman cultural expression. This became Jerusalem in the time of Jesus.

The **"THIRD WALL"** (shown with dotted line) was begun by Herod Agrippa I between A.D. 41 and 44 to enclose the growing northern suburbs, but the work was apparently stopped. Its construction was resumed, in haste, only after the First Jewish Revolt broke out in A.D. 66.

The **"SECOND WALL"** was built by Herod I or by earlier Hasmonean kings. Precise location is difficult to determine. This wall was put up around a market area in a valley, protecting it from raiding and looting, but was of questionable military value. At its eastern end, however, Herod built a military barracks (Antonia Fortress).

The **"FIRST WALL,"** so named by Josephus, encircled the city during the Hasmonean period, which began in 167 B.C. After the revolt led by Judas Maccabeus in 167, Jerusalem expanded steadily in a period of independence under its own Jewish kings.

Archaeological excavations have revealed a monumental stairway and the continuation of Tyropoeon Street,*** which lies along the valley called "Way of the Cheesemongers" by Josephus.

The Siloam aqueduct-tunnel,*** 1,749 ft. long, was cut through solid bedrock, was 5'11" high (average) and followed an "S" shaped course made necessary by engineering difficulties. It was dug by King Hezekiah and provided water during King Sennacherib's threat to lay siege to the city in 701 B.C. (2Ch 32:30). Water flows through it to this very day.

Buildings, streets and roads shown here are artist's concept only unless otherwise named and located. Wall heights remain generally unknown, except for those surrounding the Temple Mount.

Deep valleys on the east, south and west permitted urban expansion only to the north.

* Location generally known, but style of architecture is unknown; artist's concept only, and Roman architecture is assumed.

** Location and architecture unknown, but referred to in written history; shown here for illustrative purposes.

*** Ancient feature has remained, or appearance has been determined from evidence.

7Other seed fell among thorns, which grew
up and choked the plants, so that they did
not bear grain. 8Still other seed fell on
good soil. It came up, grew and produced
a crop, multiplying thirty, sixty, or even a
hundred times."[v]
9Then Jesus said, "He who has ears to
hear, let him hear."[w]
10When he was alone, the Twelve and
the others around him asked him about
the parables. 11He told them, "The secret
of the kingdom of God[x] has been given to
you. But to those on the outside[y] everything is said in parables 12so that,

"'they may be ever seeing but never
perceiving,
and ever hearing but never
understanding;
otherwise they might turn and be
forgiven!'[a]"[z]

13Then Jesus said to them, "Don't you
understand this parable? How then will
you understand any parable? 14The farmer sows the word.[a] 15Some people are
like seed along the path, where the word
is sown. As soon as they hear it, Satan[b]
comes and takes away the word that was
sown in them. 16Others, like seed sown on
rocky places, hear the word and at once
receive it with joy. 17But since they have
no root, they last only a short time. When
trouble or persecution comes because of
the word, they quickly fall away. 18Still
others, like seed sown among thorns, hear
the word; 19but the worries of this life, the
deceitfulness of wealth[c] and the desires for
other things come in and choke the word,
making it unfruitful. 20Others, like seed
sown on good soil, hear the word, accept
it, and produce a crop—thirty, sixty or
even a hundred times what was sown."

A Lamp on a Stand

21He said to them, "Do you bring in a
lamp to put it under a bowl or a bed? Instead, don't you put it on its stand?[d] 22For
whatever is hidden is meant to be disclosed, and whatever is concealed is meant
to be brought out into the open.[e] 23If anyone has ears to hear, let him hear."[f]
24"Consider carefully what you hear,"
he continued. "With the measure you use,
it will be measured to you—and even
more.[g] 25Whoever has will be given more;
whoever does not have, even what he has
will be taken from him."[h]

The Parable of the Growing Seed

26He also said, "This is what the kingdom of God is like.[i] A man scatters seed
on the ground. 27Night and day, whether
he sleeps or gets up, the seed sprouts and
grows, though he does not know how. 28All
by itself the soil produces grain—first the
stalk, then the head, then the full kernel in
the head. 29As soon as the grain is ripe, he
puts the sickle to it, because the harvest
has come."[j]

The Parable of the Mustard Seed

4:30-32pp — Mt 13:31,32; Lk 13:18,19

30Again he said, "What shall we say the
kingdom of God is like,[k] or what parable
shall we use to describe it? 31It is like a
mustard seed, which is the smallest seed

4:8 [v] Jn 15:5; Col 1:6
4:9 [w] ver 23; S Mt 11:15
4:11 [x] S Mt 3:2 [y] 1Co 5:12,13; Col 4:5; 1Th 4:12; 1Ti 3:7
4:12 [z] Isa 6:9,10; S Mt 13:13-15
4:14 [a] Mk 16:20; Lk 1:2; Ac 4:31; 8:4; 16:6; 17:11; Php 1:14
4:15 [b] S Mt 4:10
4:19 [c] Mt 19:23; 1Ti 6:9,10,17; 1Jn 2:15-17
4:21 [d] S Mt 5:15
4:22 [e] Jer 16:17; Mt 10:26; Lk 8:17; 12:2
4:23 [f] ver 9; S Mt 11:15
4:24 [g] S Mt 7:2
4:25 [h] S Mt 25:29
4:26 [i] S Mt 13:24
4:29 [j] Rev 14:15
4:30 [k] S Mt 13:24

[a] *12* Isaiah 6:9,10

4:8 *multiplying ... a hundred times.* A hundredfold yield was an unusually productive harvest (see Ge 26:12–13). Harvest was a common figure for the consummation of God's kingdom (see Joel 3:13; Rev 14:15 and notes).
4:9 See note on Lk 8:8.
4:11 *secret of the kingdom of God.* In the NT "secret" refers to something unknown until revealed by God. The secret is proclaimed to all, but only those who have faith understand. In this context the secret seems to be that the kingdom of God had drawn near (see v. 26; see also notes on 1:15; Mt 3:2) in the coming of Jesus Christ, the King.
4:12 *so that.* Jesus likens his preaching in parables to the ministry of Isaiah, which, while it gained some disciples (Isa 8:16), was also intended to expose the hardhearted resistance of many to God's warning and appeal.
4:14 *the word.* The interpretation calls attention to the response to the word of God that Jesus has been preaching. In spite of many obstacles, God's word will accomplish his purpose (cf. Isa 55:11 and note).
4:17 *trouble or persecution.* See Introduction: Occasion and Purpose; see also 8:34–38; 10:30 and notes; 13:9–13.
4:19 *deceitfulness of wealth.* Prosperity tends to give a false sense of self-sufficiency, security and well-being (see 10:17–25 and notes; Dt 8:17–18; 32:15; Ecc 2:4–11; see also Jas 5:1–6 and notes).
4:20 *hundred times.* See v. 8 and note.
4:21 *Do you bring in a lamp ...?* A lamp is placed to give light, not to hide it; so Jesus, "the light of the world" (Jn 8:12; see note there), is destined to be revealed. *lamp.* See Mt 5:15 and note.
4:22 See note on Lk 8:17.
4:23 See note on Lk 8:8.
4:24 See note on Lk 8:18.
4:25 Those who have begun to understand and appropriate the truth of what Jesus was teaching will be granted fuller understanding in the future, but those who have failed to appropriate it will experience no benefit from it.
4:26–29 Only Mark records this parable. Whereas the parable of the sower stresses the importance of proper soil for the growth of seed and the success of the harvest, here the mysterious power of the seed itself is emphasized. The gospel message contains its own power.
4:26 *kingdom of God.* See note on v. 11.
4:29 *he puts the sickle to it, because the harvest has come.* A possible allusion to Joel 3:13 (see note there), where harvest is a figure for the consummation of God's kingdom.
4:30–34 The main point of this parable is that the kingdom of God seemingly had insignificant beginnings. It was introduced by the despised and rejected Jesus and his 12 unimpressive disciples. But a day will come when its true greatness and power will be seen by the whole world.
4:31 See notes on Mt 13:31–32.

you plant in the ground. 32Yet when planted, it grows and becomes the largest of
all garden plants, with such big branches
that the birds of the air can perch in its
shade."
33With many similar parables Jesus
spoke the word to them, as much as they
could understand.[l] 34He did not say anything to them without using a parable.[m]
But when he was alone with his own disciples, he explained everything.

Jesus Calms the Storm

4:35-41pp — Mt 8:18,23-27; Lk 8:22-25

35That day when evening came, he said
to his disciples, "Let us go over to the
other side." 36Leaving the crowd behind,
they took him along, just as he was, in the
boat.[n] There were also other boats with
him. 37A furious squall came up, and the
waves broke over the boat, so that it was
nearly swamped. 38Jesus was in the stern,
sleeping on a cushion. The disciples woke
him and said to him, "Teacher, don't you
care if we drown?"
39He got up, rebuked the wind and said
to the waves, "Quiet! Be still!" Then the
wind died down and it was completely
calm.
40He said to his disciples, "Why are you
so afraid? Do you still have no faith?"[o]
41They were terrified and asked each
other, "Who is this? Even the wind and the
waves obey him!"

The Healing of a Demon-possessed Man

5:1-17pp — Mt 8:28-34; Lk 8:26-37
5:18-20pp — Lk 8:38,39

5 They went across the lake to the region of the Gerasenes.[a] 2When Jesus
got out of the boat,[p] a man with an evil[b]
spirit[q] came from the tombs to meet him.
3This man lived in the tombs, and no one
could bind him any more, not even with
a chain. 4For he had often been chained
hand and foot, but he tore the chains apart
and broke the irons on his feet. No one
was strong enough to subdue him. 5Night
and day among the tombs and in the hills
he would cry out and cut himself with
stones.
6When he saw Jesus from a distance,
he ran and fell on his knees in front of
him. 7He shouted at the top of his voice,
"What do you want with me,[r] Jesus, Son
of the Most High God?[s] Swear to God that
you won't torture me!" 8For Jesus had said
to him, "Come out of this man, you evil
spirit!"
9Then Jesus asked him, "What is your
name?"
"My name is Legion,"[t] he replied, "for

4:33 [l] Jn 16:12
4:34 [m] S Jn 16:25
4:36 [n] ver 1; Mk 3:9; 5:2,21; 6:32,45
4:40 [o] Mt 14:31; Mk 16:14
5:2 [p] Mk 4:1 [q] Mk 1:23
5:7 [r] S Mt 8:29 [s] S Mt 4:3; Lk 1:32; 6:35; Ac 16:17; Heb 7:1
5:9 [t] ver 15

[a] *1* Some manuscripts *Gadarenes;* other manuscripts *Gergesenes* [b] *2* Greek *unclean;* also in verses 8 and 13

4:34 *He did not say anything to them without using a parable.* Jesus used parables to illustrate truths, stimulate thinking and awaken spiritual perception. The people in general were not ready for the full truth of the gospel. When alone with his disciples Jesus taught more specifically, but even they usually needed to have things explained.

4:35 – 41 Although miracles are hard for people to accept today, the NT makes it clear that Jesus is Lord not only over his church but also over all creation.

4:35 *other side.* Jesus left the territory of Galilee to go to the "region of the Gerasenes" (5:1).

4:37 *furious squall came up.* Situated in a basin surrounded by mountains, the Sea of Galilee is particularly susceptible to sudden, violent storms. Cool air from the Mediterranean is drawn down through the narrow mountain passes and clashes with the hot, humid air lying over the lake.

4:38 *sleeping on a cushion.* The picture of Jesus, exhausted and asleep, is characteristic of Mark's human touch.

4:41 *Who is this?* In view of what Jesus had just done, the only answer to this rhetorical question was: He is the very Son of God! God's presence, as well as his power, was demonstrated (see Ps 65:6 – 7; 107:25 – 30 and notes; Pr 30:4). Mark indicates his answer to this question in the opening line of his Gospel (1:1). By such miracles Jesus sought to establish and increase the disciples' faith in his deity.

5:1 – 43 The stories of the healing of the demon-possessed man, Jairus's daughter, and the woman with the hemorrhage all have to do with ceremonial uncleanness.

5:1 *across the lake.* The east side of the lake, a territory largely inhabited by Gentiles, as indicated by the presence of the large herd of pigs — animals Jews considered ceremonially unclean and therefore unfit to eat (see Isa 65:4 and note). *region of the Gerasenes.* Gerasa, located about 35 miles southeast of the Sea of Galilee, may have had holdings on the eastern shore of the Sea, giving its name to a small village there now known as Khersa. About one mile south is a fairly steep slope within 40 yards of the shore, and about two miles from there are cavern tombs that appear to have been used as dwellings. See note on Lk 8:26.

5:2 *a man.* Mt 8:28 says there were two demon-possessed men (see note on Lk 8:27).

5:3 *lived in the tombs.* It was not unusual for the same cave to provide burial for the dead and shelter for the living. Very poor people often lived in such caves.

5:4 *often been chained.* Though the villagers no doubt chained him partly for their own protection, this harsh treatment added to his humiliation.

5:5 *cry out and cut himself with stones.* Every word in the story emphasizes the man's pathetic condition as well as the purpose of demonic possession — to torment and destroy the divine likeness in which human beings are created (see Ge 1:26 and note).

5:6 *fell on his knees.* An act of homage rather than worship. The demon showed respect because he recognized that he was confronted by one greatly superior to him.

5:7 *What do you want with me . . . ?* A way of saying, "What do we have in common?" Similar expressions are found in the OT (e.g., 2Sa 16:10; 19:22), where they mean, "Mind your own business!" The demon was speaking, using the voice of the possessed man (see 1:23 and note). *Son of the Most High God.* See note on 1:24. *Swear to God that you won't torture me!* The demon sensed that he was to be punished and used the strongest basis for an oath that he knew, though his appeal to God was strangely ironic.

5:9 *My name is Legion . . . for we are many.* A Roman legion was made up of 6,000 men. Here the term suggests that the man

we are many." 10And he begged Jesus
again and again not to send them out of
the area.
11A large herd of pigs was feeding on
the nearby hillside. 12The demons begged
Jesus, "Send us among the pigs; allow us to
go into them." 13He gave them permission,
and the evil spirits came out and went into
the pigs. The herd, about two thousand in
number, rushed down the steep bank into
the lake and were drowned.
14Those tending the pigs ran off and reported this in the town and countryside,
and the people went out to see what had
happened. 15When they came to Jesus,
they saw the man who had been possessed by the legion[u] of demons,[v] sitting
there, dressed and in his right mind; and
they were afraid. 16Those who had seen it
told the people what had happened to the
demon-possessed man—and told about
the pigs as well. 17Then the people began
to plead with Jesus to leave their region.
18As Jesus was getting into the boat,
the man who had been demon-possessed
begged to go with him. 19Jesus did not let
him, but said, "Go home to your family
and tell them[w] how much the Lord has

5:15 [u] ver 9 [v] ver 16,18; S Mt 4:24 **5:19** [w] S Mt 8:4

was possessed by numerous demons and perhaps also represents the many powers opposed to Jesus, who embodies the power of God (see 1:23–24 and notes).
5:10 *not to send them out of the area.* The demons were fearful of being sent into eternal punishment, i.e., "into the Abyss" (Lk 8:31; see note there).
5:11 *pigs.* See note on Lk 8:32.
5:13 *gave them permission.* See note on Mt 8:32.
5:16 *told about the pigs as well.* In addition to the remarkable change in the demon-possessed man, the drowning of the pigs seemed to be a major concern, no doubt because it was so dramatic and brought considerable financial loss to the owners.
5:17 *plead with Jesus to leave their region.* Fear of further loss may have motivated this response, but also the fact that a powerful force was at work in their midst that they could not comprehend.
5:19 *tell them how much the Lord has done for you.* This is in marked contrast to Jesus' exhortation to silence in the case of the man cleansed of leprosy (1:44; see 1:34; 3:12; Mt 8:4 and notes), perhaps because the healing of the demoniac was in Gentile territory, where there was little danger that Messianic ideas about Jesus might be circulated (see Introduction: Emphases).

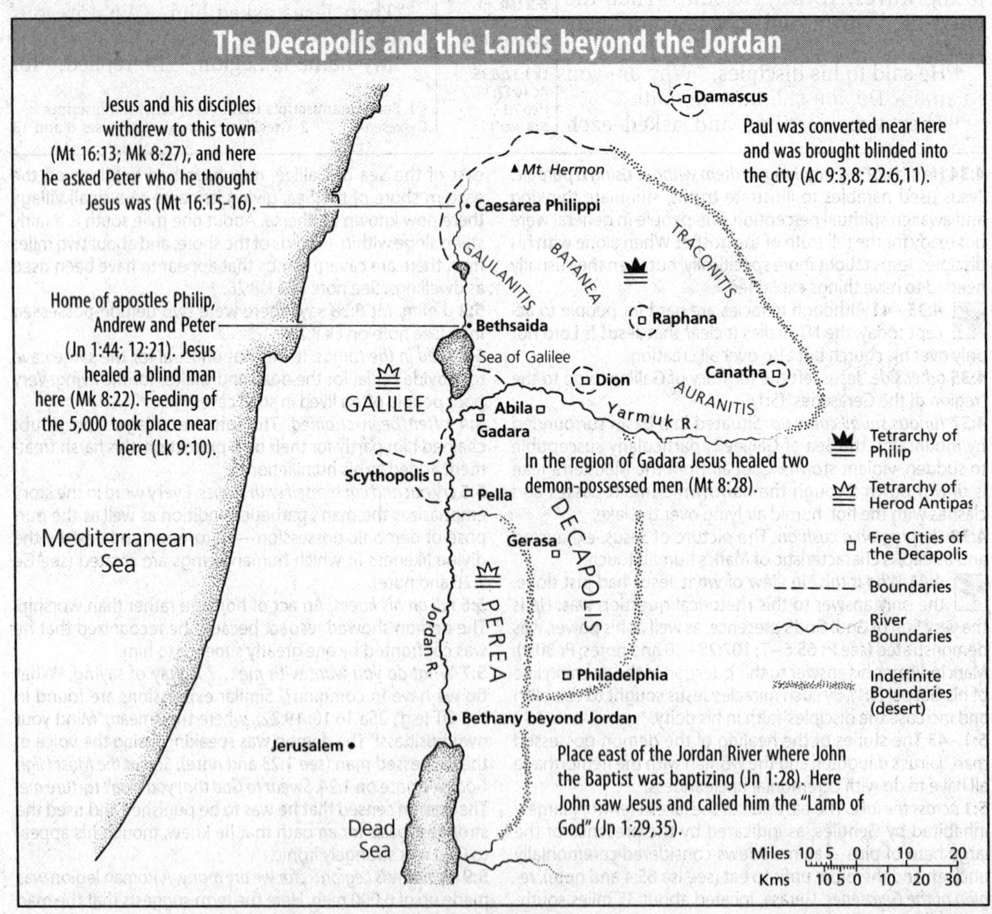
The Decapolis and the Lands beyond the Jordan
Jesus and his disciples withdrew to this town (Mt 16:13; Mk 8:27), and here he asked Peter who he thought Jesus was (Mt 16:15-16).
Damascus
Paul was converted near here and was brought blinded into the city (Ac 9:3,8; 22:6,11).
Mt. Hermon
Caesarea Philippi
GAULANITIS
BATANEA
TRACONITIS
Home of apostles Philip, Andrew and Peter (Jn 1:44; 12:21). Jesus healed a blind man here (Mk 8:22). Feeding of the 5,000 took place near here (Lk 9:10).
Bethsaida
Raphana
Sea of Galilee
Canatha
Dion
AURANITIS
GALILEE
Abila
Yarmuk R.
Gadara
In the region of Gadara Jesus healed two demon-possessed men (Mt 8:28).
Scythopolis
Pella
DECAPOLIS
Mediterranean Sea
Gerasa
Jordan R.
PEREA
Philadelphia
Bethany beyond Jordan
Jerusalem
Place east of the Jordan River where John the Baptist was baptizing (Jn 1:28). Here John saw Jesus and called him the "Lamb of God" (Jn 1:29,35).
Dead Sea
Tetrarchy of Philip
Tetrarchy of Herod Antipas
Free Cities of the Decapolis
Boundaries
River Boundaries
Indefinite Boundaries (desert)
Miles 10 5 0 10 20
Kms 10 5 0 10 20 30

done for you, and how he has had mercy on you." 20So the man went away and
began to tell in the Decapolis[a][x] how much
Jesus had done for him. And all the people
were amazed.

A Dead Girl and a Sick Woman

5:22-43pp — Mt 9:18-26; Lk 8:41-56

21When Jesus had again crossed over by
boat to the other side of the lake,[y] a large
crowd gathered around him while he was
by the lake.[z] 22Then one of the synagogue
rulers,[a] named Jairus, came there. Seeing
Jesus, he fell at his feet 23and pleaded earnestly with him, "My little daughter is dying. Please come and put your hands on[b]
her so that she will be healed and live."
24So Jesus went with him.

A large crowd followed and pressed
around him. 25And a woman was there
who had been subject to bleeding[c] for
twelve years. 26She had suffered a great
deal under the care of many doctors and
had spent all she had, yet instead of getting
better she grew worse. 27When she heard
about Jesus, she came up behind him in
the crowd and touched his cloak, 28because
she thought, "If I just touch his clothes,[d] I
will be healed." 29Immediately her bleeding stopped and she felt in her body that
she was freed from her suffering.[e]

30At once Jesus realized that power[f] had
gone out from him. He turned around in
the crowd and asked, "Who touched my
clothes?"

31"You see the people crowding against
you," his disciples answered, "and yet you
can ask, 'Who touched me?' "

32But Jesus kept looking around to see
who had done it. 33Then the woman,
knowing what had happened to her, came
and fell at his feet and, trembling with
fear, told him the whole truth. 34He said
to her, "Daughter, your faith has healed
you.[g] Go in peace[h] and be freed from your
suffering."

35While Jesus was still speaking, some
men came from the house of Jairus, the
synagogue ruler.[i] "Your daughter is dead,"
they said. "Why bother the teacher any
more?"

36Ignoring what they said, Jesus told the
synagogue ruler, "Don't be afraid; just believe."

37He did not let anyone follow him except Peter, James and John the brother of
James.[j] 38When they came to the home of
the synagogue ruler,[k] Jesus saw a commotion, with people crying and wailing loudly. 39He went in and said to them, "Why all
this commotion and wailing? The child is
not dead but asleep."[l] 40But they laughed
at him.

After he put them all out, he took the
child's father and mother and the disciples who were with him, and went in
where the child was. 41He took her by the
hand[m] and said to her, *"Talitha koum!"*
(which means, "Little girl, I say to you,
get up!").[n] 42Immediately the girl stood up
and walked around (she was twelve years
old). At this they were completely astonished. 43He gave strict orders not to let
anyone know about this,[o] and told them
to give her something to eat.

[a] *20* That is, the Ten Cities

5:20 [x] Mt 4:25; Mk 7:31 **5:21** [y] Mt 9:1 [z] Mk 4:1 **5:22** [a] ver 35, 36, 38; Lk 13:14; Ac 13:15; 18:8, 17 **5:23** [b] Mt 19:13; Mk 6:5; 7:32; 8:23; 16:18; Lk 4:40; 13:13; S Ac 6:6 **5:25** [c] Lev 15:25-30 **5:28** [d] S Mt 9:20 **5:29** [e] ver 34 **5:30** [f] Lk 5:17; 6:19 **5:34** [g] S Mt 9:22 [h] S Ac 15:33 **5:35** [i] S ver 22 **5:37** [j] S Mt 4:21 **5:38** [k] S ver 22 **5:39** [l] S Mt 9:24 **5:41** [m] Mk 1:31 [n] S Lk 7:14 **5:43** [o] S Mt 8:4

5:20 *Decapolis.* See note on Mt 4:25; see also map, p. 1530. *amazed.* See 1:22 and note.

5:21 *other side of the lake.* Jesus returned to the west side of the lake, perhaps to Capernaum.

5:22 *synagogue rulers.* A ruler of the synagogue was a layman whose responsibilities were administrative and included such things as looking after the building and supervising the worship. Though there were exceptions (see Ac 13:14–15), most synagogues had only one ruler. Sometimes the title was honorary, with no administrative responsibilities assigned.

5:23 *is dying.* See note on Mt 9:18. *put your hands on her.* See note on Ac 6:6.

5:25 *bleeding for twelve years.* The precise nature of the woman's problem is not known. Her existence was wretched because she was shunned by people generally, since anyone having contact with her was made ceremonially unclean (Lev 15:25–33).

5:26 *suffered a great deal under the care of many doctors.* The Jewish Talmud preserves a record of medicines and treatments prescribed for illnesses of this sort.

5:28 *If I just touch his clothes.* Although it needed to be bolstered by physical contact, her faith was rewarded (v. 34; cf. Ac 19:12).

5:30 *power had gone out from him.* The woman was healed because God graciously determined to heal her through the power then active in Jesus.

5:32 *kept looking around to see who had done it.* Jesus would not allow the woman to recede into the crowd without publicly commending her faith and assuring her that she was permanently healed.

5:34 *healed.* The Greek for "healed" actually means "saved." Here both physical healing ("be freed from your suffering") and spiritual salvation ("Go in peace") are meant. The two also appear together in 2:1–12 (see note on 2:9); 3:1–6.

5:37 *Peter, James and John.* These three disciples had an especially close relationship to Jesus (see note on Ac 3:1).

5:38 *people crying and wailing loudly.* It was customary for professional mourners to be brought in at the time of death. In this case, however, it is not certain that enough time had elapsed for mourners to have been secured.

5:39 *not dead but asleep.* See note on Lk 8:52.

5:41 *Talitha koum!* Mark is the only Gospel writer who here preserves the original Aramaic — one of the languages of the Holy Land in the first century A.D. and probably the language Jesus and his disciples ordinarily spoke (they may also have spoken Hebrew and Greek).

5:42 *astonished.* See 1:22 and note.

5:43 *not to let anyone know.* In the vicinity of Galilee Jesus often cautioned people whom he healed not to spread the story of the miracle. His great popularity with the people, coupled with the growing opposition from the religious leaders, could have precipitated a crisis before Jesus' ministry was completed (see v. 19 and note; 7:36; 8:26).

A Prophet Without Honor

6:1-6pp — Mt 13:54-58

6 Jesus left there and went to his hometown,[p] accompanied by his disciples.
2When the Sabbath came,[q] he began to
teach in the synagogue,[r] and many who
heard him were amazed.[s]
"Where did this man get these things?"
they asked. "What's this wisdom that has
been given him, that he even does miracles! 3Isn't this the carpenter? Isn't this
Mary's son and the brother of James, Joseph,[a] Judas and Simon?[t] Aren't his sisters here with us?" And they took offense
at him.[u]
4Jesus said to them, "Only in his hometown, among his relatives and in his own
house is a prophet without honor."[v] 5He
could not do any miracles there, except lay
his hands on[w] a few sick people and heal
them. 6And he was amazed at their lack
of faith.

Jesus Sends Out the Twelve

6:7-11pp — Mt 10:1,9-14; Lk 9:1,3-5

Then Jesus went around teaching from
village to village.[x] 7Calling the Twelve to
him,[y] he sent them out two by two[z] and
gave them authority over evil[b] spirits.[a]
8These were his instructions: "Take
nothing for the journey except a staff—no
bread, no bag, no money in your belts.
9Wear sandals but not an extra tunic.
10Whenever you enter a house, stay there
until you leave that town. 11And if any
place will not welcome you or listen to
you, shake the dust off your feet[b] when
you leave, as a testimony against them."
12They went out and preached that people should repent.[c] 13They drove out many
demons and anointed many sick people
with oil[d] and healed them.

John the Baptist Beheaded

6:14-29pp — Mt 14:1-12
6:14-16pp — Lk 9:7-9

14King Herod heard about this, for Jesus'
name had become well known. Some were
saying,[c] "John the Baptist[e] has been raised
from the dead, and that is why miraculous
powers are at work in him."
15Others said, "He is Elijah."[f]
And still others claimed, "He is a
prophet,[g] like one of the prophets of long
ago."[h]
16But when Herod heard this, he said,
"John, the man I beheaded, has been
raised from the dead!"
17For Herod himself had given orders to
have John arrested, and he had him bound
and put in prison.[i] He did this because of
Herodias, his brother Philip's wife, whom
he had married. 18For John had been saying to Herod, "It is not lawful for you to
have your brother's wife."[j] 19So Herodias
nursed a grudge against John and wanted to kill him. But she was not able to,
20because Herod feared John and protected him, knowing him to be a righteous
and holy man.[k] When Herod heard John,
he was greatly puzzled[d]; yet he liked to
listen to him.
21Finally the opportune time came. On
his birthday Herod gave a banquet[l] for his
high officials and military commanders

6:1 [p] S Mt 2:23 **6:2** [q] Mk 1:21 [r] S Mt 4:23 [s] S Mt 7:28 **6:3** [t] S Mt 12:46 [u] Mt 11:6; Jn 6:61 **6:4** [v] Lk 4:24; Jn 4:44 **6:5** [w] S Mk 5:23 **6:6** [x] Mt 9:35; Mk 1:39; Lk 13:22 **6:7** [y] Mk 3:13 [z] Dt 17:6; Lk 10:1 [a] S Mt 10:1 **6:11** [b] S Mt 10:14
6:12 [c] Lk 9:6 **6:13** [d] S Jas 5:14 **6:14** [e] S Mt 3:1 **6:15** [f] Mal 4:5 [g] S Mt 21:11 [h] Mt 16:14; Mk 8:28 **6:17** [i] Mt 4:12; 11:2; Lk 3:19,20 **6:18** [j] Lev 18:16; 20:21 **6:20** [k] S Mt 11:9 **6:21** [l] Est 1:3; 2:18

[a] 3 Greek *Joses,* a variant of *Joseph* [b] 7 Greek *unclean* [c] 14 Some early manuscripts *He was saying* [d] 20 Some early manuscripts *he did many things*

6:1 *his hometown.* Nazareth (see notes on Mt 2:23; Lk 4:23).
6:2 *teach in the synagogue.* See 1:21 and note. *amazed.* See 1:22 and note.
6:3 *carpenter.* Matthew reports that Jesus was called "the carpenter's son" (Mt 13:55); only in Mark is Jesus himself referred to as a carpenter. The Greek word can also apply to a mason, smith, or builder in general. The question is derogatory, meaning, "Isn't he a common worker with his hands like the rest of us?" *brother of James, Joseph, Judas and Simon.* See note on Lk 8:19. *they took offense at him.* They saw no reason to believe that he was different from them, much less that he was specially anointed by God.
6:5 *He could not do any miracles there.* It was not that Jesus did not have power to perform miracles at Nazareth, but that he chose not to in such a climate of unbelief (v. 6).
6:6 *he was amazed.* See note on Lk 7:9.
6:7–13 See note on Lk 9:1–6.
6:7 *the Twelve.* See notes on Ac 1:11; 1Co 15:5. *two by two.* The purpose of going in pairs may have been to bolster credibility by having the testimony of more than one witness (cf. Dt 17:6), as well as to provide mutual support during their training period.
6:8 *no bread, no bag, no money in your belts.* They were to depend entirely on the hospitality of those to whom they testified (see vv. 10–11; see also notes on Lk 9:3; 10:4).
6:9 *not an extra tunic.* At night an extra tunic was helpful as a covering to protect from the cold night air, and the implication here is that the disciples were to trust in God to provide lodging each night.
6:10 *stay there.* See note on Lk 9:4.
6:11 *shake the dust off your feet.* See note on Mt 10:14.
6:12–13 *preached ..... drove out many demons.* This mission marks the beginning of the disciples' own ministry in Jesus' name (see 3:14–15), and their message was precisely the same as his (1:15).
6:12 *repent.* See 1:4 and note.
6:13 *anointed many sick people with oil.* In the ancient world olive oil was widely used as a medicine (see Jas 5:14 and note).
6:14 *King Herod.* See note on Mt 14:1. Mark may here have used the title "king" sarcastically (since this Herod was actually a tetrarch; see chart, p. 1465), or perhaps he simply used Herod's popular title.
6:15 *He is Elijah.* See Mal 4:5 and note.
6:16 *John ... has been raised from the dead!* Herod, disturbed by an uneasy conscience and disposed to superstition, feared that John had come back to haunt him.
6:17 *John arrested ... and put in prison.* See 1:14 and note. Josephus says that John was imprisoned at Machaerus, a fortress in Perea on the eastern side of the Dead Sea (see map, p. 1570). *Herodias.* See note on Mt 14:3. *Philip.* See note on Mt 14:3.

and the leading men of Galilee.[m] 22When
the daughter of Herodias came in and
danced, she pleased Herod and his dinner guests.
The king said to the girl, "Ask me for
anything you want, and I'll give it to you."
23And he promised her with an oath,
"Whatever you ask I will give you, up to
half my kingdom."[n]
24She went out and said to her mother,
"What shall I ask for?"
"The head of John the Baptist," she answered.
25At once the girl hurried in to the king
with the request: "I want you to give me
right now the head of John the Baptist on
a platter."
26The king was greatly distressed, but
because of his oaths and his dinner guests,
he did not want to refuse her. 27So he immediately sent an executioner with orders
to bring John's head. The man went, beheaded John in the prison, 28and brought
back his head on a platter. He presented it
to the girl, and she gave it to her mother.
29On hearing of this, John's disciples came
and took his body and laid it in a tomb.

Jesus Feeds the Five Thousand

6:32-44pp — Mt 14:13-21; Lk 9:10-17; Jn 6:5-13
6:32-44Ref — Mk 8:2-9

30The apostles[o] gathered around Jesus
and reported to him all they had done and
taught.[p] 31Then, because so many people were coming and going that they did
not even have a chance to eat,[q] he said to
them, "Come with me by yourselves to a
quiet place and get some rest."
32So they went away by themselves in
a boat[r] to a solitary place. 33But many
who saw them leaving recognized them
and ran on foot from all the towns and got
there ahead of them. 34When Jesus landed and saw a large crowd, he had compassion on them, because they were like
sheep without a shepherd.[s] So he began
teaching them many things.
35By this time it was late in the day, so
his disciples came to him. "This is a remote place," they said, "and it's already
very late. 36Send the people away so they
can go to the surrounding countryside and
villages and buy themselves something to
eat."
37But he answered, "You give them
something to eat."[t]
They said to him, "That would take
eight months of a man's wages[a]! Are we
to go and spend that much on bread and
give it to them to eat?"
38"How many loaves do you have?" he
asked. "Go and see."
When they found out, they said,
"Five—and two fish."[u]
39Then Jesus directed them to have all
the people sit down in groups on the green
grass. 40So they sat down in groups of hundreds and fifties. 41Taking the five loaves
and the two fish and looking up to heav-
en, he gave thanks and broke the loaves.[v]
Then he gave them to his disciples to set
before the people. He also divided the two
fish among them all. 42They all ate and

6:21 [m]Lk 3:1
6:23 [n]Est 5:3,6; 7:2
6:30 [o]Mt 10:2; Lk 9:10; 17:5; 22:14; 24:10; Ac 1:2,26 [p]Lk 9:10
6:31 [q]Mk 3:20
6:32 [r]ver 45; S Mk 4:36
6:34 [s]S Mt 9:36
6:37 [t]2Ki 4:42-44
6:38 [u]Mt 15:34; Mk 8:5
6:41 [v]S Mt 14:19

[a] 37 Greek *take two hundred denarii*

6:22 *daughter of Herodias.* See note on Mt 14:6.
6:23 *up to half my kingdom.* A proverbial reference to generosity, not to be taken literally (see Est 5:3,6). Generosity suited the occasion and would win the approval of the guests.
6:25 *platter.* See note on Mt 14:8.
6:26 *greatly distressed.* The Greek for this phrase is also used to describe Jesus' agony in Gethsemane (14:34, "overwhelmed with sorrow").
6:30–44 The feeding of the 5,000 in Mark's Gospel begins with an elaborate introduction (vv. 30–38), is looked back to on two different occasions (v. 52; 8:17–19) and has a sequel in the feeding of the 4,000 (8:1–10).
6:30 *apostles.* In Mark's Gospel the word occurs only here and in 3:14 (in some manuscripts). The apostles were Jesus' authorized agents or representatives (see Heb 3:1 and note). In the NT the word is sometimes used quite generally (see Jn 13:16, where the Greek *apostolos* is translated "messenger"). In the technical sense it is used (1) of the Twelve (3:14)—in which sense it is also applied to Paul (Ro 1:1)—and (2) of a larger group including Barnabas (Ac 14:14), James the Lord's brother (Gal 1:19), and possibly Andronicus and Junias (Ro 16:7; see note there). *reported to him all they had done and taught.* Because he had commissioned them as his representatives. They were returning from what may have been a third preaching tour in Galilee (see vv. 12–13; 1:39 and notes).
6:32 *went away by themselves in a boat.* John reports that they went to the other side of the Sea of Galilee (Jn 6:1). Luke, more specifically, says they went to Bethsaida (Lk 9:10), which locates the feeding of the 5,000 on the northeast shore (see note on 7:24).
6:33 *ran on foot … and got there ahead of them.* Perhaps a strong headwind slowed the boat down so that the people had time to go on foot around the lake and arrive before the boat.
6:37 *eight months of a man's wages.* See NIV text note. The usual pay for a day's work was one denarius (see Mt 20:2 and note).
6:38 *loaves.* Barley loaves. Unlike our modern loaves, these were small and flat. One could easily eat several at a single meal (see note on Jn 6:9).
6:39 *green grass.* Grass is green around the Sea of Galilee after the late winter or early spring rains.
6:40 *groups of hundreds and fifties.* Recalls the order of the Mosaic camp in the desert (e.g., Ex 18:21).
6:42 *all ate and were satisfied.* Attempts to explain away this miracle (e.g., by suggesting that Jesus and his disciples shared their lunch and the crowd followed their good example) are inadequate. If Jesus was, as he claimed to be, God incarnate, the miracle presents no difficulties. God had promised that when the true Shepherd came, the desert would become rich pasture where the sheep would be gathered and fed (Eze 34:23–31). Jesus is the Shepherd who provides for all our needs so that we lack nothing (cf. Ps 23:1).

were satisfied, 43and the disciples picked
up twelve basketfuls of broken pieces of
bread and fish. 44The number of the men
who had eaten was five thousand.

Jesus Walks on the Water

6:45-51pp — Mt 14:22-32; Jn 6:15-21
6:53-56pp — Mt 14:34-36

45Immediately Jesus made his disciples get into the boat[w] and go on ahead of
him to Bethsaida,[x] while he dismissed the
crowd. 46After leaving them, he went up
on a mountainside to pray.[y]
47When evening came, the boat was in
the middle of the lake, and he was alone
on land. 48He saw the disciples straining
at the oars, because the wind was against
them. About the fourth watch of the
night he went out to them, walking on
the lake. He was about to pass by them,
49but when they saw him walking on the
lake, they thought he was a ghost.[z] They
cried out, 50because they all saw him and
were terrified.
Immediately he spoke to them and said,
"Take courage! It is I. Don't be afraid."[a]
51Then he climbed into the boat[b] with
them, and the wind died down.[c] They
were completely amazed, 52for they had
not understood about the loaves; their
hearts were hardened.[d]
53When they had crossed over, they
landed at Gennesaret and anchored there.[e]
54As soon as they got out of the boat, people recognized Jesus. 55They ran throughout that whole region and carried the sick
on mats to wherever they heard he was.

6:45 [w] ver 32 [x] S Mt 11:21 **6:46** [y] S Lk 3:21 **6:49** [z] Lk 24:37 **6:50** [a] S Mt 14:27 **6:51** [b] ver 32 [c] Mk 4:39 **6:52** [d] Mk 8:17-21 **6:53** [e] Jn 6:24,25 **6:56** [f] S Mt 9:20 **7:2** [g] Ac 10:14,28; 11:8; Ro 14:14 **7:3** [h] ver 5,8,9,13; Lk 11:38 **7:4** [i] Mt 23:25; Lk 11:39 **7:5** [j] S ver 3; Gal 1:14; Col 2:8 **7:7** [k] Isa 29:13

56And wherever he went—into villages,
towns or countryside—they placed the
sick in the marketplaces. They begged
him to let them touch even the edge of
his cloak,[f] and all who touched him were
healed.

Clean and Unclean

7:1-23pp — Mt 15:1-20

7 The Pharisees and some of the teachers
of the law who had come from Jerusalem gathered around Jesus and 2saw some
of his disciples eating food with hands that
were "unclean,"[g] that is, unwashed. 3(The
Pharisees and all the Jews do not eat unless
they give their hands a ceremonial washing, holding to the tradition of the elders.[h]
4When they come from the marketplace
they do not eat unless they wash. And they
observe many other traditions, such as the
washing of cups, pitchers and kettles.[a])[i]
5So the Pharisees and teachers of the
law asked Jesus, "Why don't your disciples live according to the tradition of the
elders[j] instead of eating their food with
'unclean' hands?"
6He replied, "Isaiah was right when he
prophesied about you hypocrites; as it is
written:

" 'These people honor me with their
lips,
but their hearts are far from me.
7They worship me in vain;
their teachings are but rules taught
by men.'[b][k]

[a] 4 Some early manuscripts *pitchers, kettles and dining couches* [b] 6,7 Isaiah 29:13

6:43 *twelve basketfuls of broken pieces of bread and fish.* Bread was regarded by Jews as a gift of God, and it was required that scraps that fell on the ground during a meal be picked up. The fragments were collected in small wicker baskets that were carried as a part of daily attire. Each of the disciples returned with his basket full (see note on Mt 15:37).
6:44 *men.* Lit. "males," as in all four Gospels. Matthew further emphasizes the point by adding "besides women and children" (Mt 14:21; see note there). *five thousand.* A number that could easily be calculated because of the division of the crowd into "groups of hundreds and fifties" (v. 40). The size of the crowd is amazing in light of the fact that the neighboring towns of Capernaum and Bethsaida probably had a population of only 2,000–3,000 each.
6:45 *go on ahead of him.* John indicates that the people were ready to take Jesus by force and make him king (see Jn 6:14–15 and note on 6:15), and Jesus therefore sent his disciples across the lake while he slipped away into the hills to pray (v. 46).
6:46 *pray.* Mark's mention of Jesus' praying is further evidence of a crisis situation. On only three occasions in this Gospel (here; 1:35; 14:32–36) does Jesus withdraw to pray; each time a crisis is involved.
6:48 *fourth watch.* 3:00–6:00 A.M. (see 13:35; Mt 14:25 and notes). *walking on the lake.* A special display of the majestic presence and power of the transcendent Lord, who rules over the sea (see Ps 89:9; Isa 51:10,15; Jer 31:35).
6:49 *a ghost.* Popular Jewish superstition held that the appearance of spirits during the night brought disaster. The disciples' terror was prompted by what they may have thought was a water spirit.
6:51 *amazed.* See 1:22 and note.
6:52 *they had not understood about the loaves.* If they had understood the feeding of the 5,000, they would not have been amazed at Jesus' walking on the water or his calming the waves. *hearts were hardened.* They were showing themselves to be similar to Jesus' opponents, who also exhibited hardness of heart (see 3:5; 8:17–21 and note on 8:16; Ex 4:21 and note).
6:53 *Gennesaret.* See note on Mt 14:34.
6:55 *carried the sick on mats.* See 2:3–4.
6:56 *touch even the edge of his cloak.* See note on 5:28.
7:1 *Pharisees … had come from Jerusalem.* Another delegation of fact-finding religious leaders from Jerusalem (see 3:22) sent to investigate the Galilean activities of Jesus (see 2:16; Mt 2:4 and notes).
7:3 *ceremonial washing.* See note on Jn 2:6. *tradition of the elders.* Considered to be binding (see v. 5 and note on Mt 15:2).
7:4 *marketplace.* Where Jews would come into contact with Gentiles, or with Jews who did not observe the ceremonial law, and thus become ceremonially unclean.
7:6 *Isaiah … prophesied.* Isaiah roundly denounced the religious leaders of his day (Isa 29:13), and Jesus quotes him to describe the tradition of the elders as "rules taught by men" (v. 7). *hypocrites.* See Mt 6:2 and note.

8You have let go of the commands of God and are holding on to the traditions of men."[l]

9And he said to them: "You have a fine way of setting aside the commands of God in order to observe[a] your own traditions![m] 10For Moses said, 'Honor your father and your mother,'[b][n] and, 'Anyone who curses his father or mother must be put to death.'[c][o] 11But you say[p] that if a man says to his father or mother: 'Whatever help you might otherwise have received from me is Corban' (that is, a gift devoted to God), 12then you no longer let him do anything for his father or mother. 13Thus you nullify the word of God[q] by your tradition[r] that you have handed down. And you do many things like that."

14Again Jesus called the crowd to him and said, "Listen to me, everyone, and understand this. 15Nothing outside a man can make him 'unclean' by going into him. Rather, it is what comes out of a man that makes him 'unclean.'[d]"

17After he had left the crowd and entered the house, his disciples asked him[s] about this parable. 18"Are you so dull?" he asked. "Don't you see that nothing that enters a man from the outside can make him 'unclean'? 19For it doesn't go into his heart but into his stomach, and then out of his body." (In saying this, Jesus declared all foods[t] "clean.")[u]

20He went on: "What comes out of a man is what makes him 'unclean.' 21For from within, out of men's hearts, come evil thoughts, sexual immorality, theft, murder, adultery, 22greed,[v] malice, deceit, lewdness, envy, slander, arrogance and folly. 23All these evils come from inside and make a man 'unclean.'"

7:8 [l]S ver 3 **7:9** [m]S ver 3 **7:10** [n]Ex 20:12; Dt 5:16 [o]Ex 21:17; Lev 20:9 **7:11** [p]Mt 23:16, 18 **7:13** [q]S Heb 4:12 [r]S ver 3 **7:17** [s]Mk 9:28 **7:19** [t]Ro 14:1-12; Col 2:16; 1Ti 4:3-5 [u]S Ac 10:15 **7:22** [v]Mt 20:15 **7:24** [w]S Mt 11:21 **7:25** [x]S Mt 4:24

The Faith of a Syrophoenician Woman

7:24-30pp — Mt 15:21-28

24Jesus left that place and went to the vicinity of Tyre.[e][w] He entered a house and did not want anyone to know it; yet he could not keep his presence secret. 25In fact, as soon as she heard about him, a woman whose little daughter was possessed by an evil[f] spirit[x] came and fell at his feet. 26The woman was a Greek, born in Syrian Phoenicia. She begged Jesus to drive the demon out of her daughter.

27"First let the children eat all they want," he told her, "for it is not right to take the children's bread and toss it to their dogs."

28"Yes, Lord," she replied, "but even the dogs under the table eat the children's crumbs."

29Then he told her, "For such a reply, you may go; the demon has left your daughter."

30She went home and found her child lying on the bed, and the demon gone.

[a] *9* Some manuscripts *set up* [b] *10* Exodus 20:12; Deut. 5:16 [c] *10* Exodus 21:17; Lev. 20:9 [d] *15* Some early manuscripts *'unclean.' 16If anyone has ears to hear, let him hear.* [e] *24* Many early manuscripts *Tyre and Sidon* [f] *25* Greek *unclean*

7:8 *commands of God ... traditions of men.* Jesus clearly contrasts the two. God's commands are found in Scripture and are binding; the "tradition of the elders" (v. 3) is not Biblical and therefore not authoritative or binding.

7:10 The fifth commandment is cited in both its positive and negative forms.

7:11 *Corban.* A Hebrew/Aramaic word meaning "offering" (see note on Lev 1:2). By using this word in a religious vow an irresponsible Jewish son could formally dedicate to God (i.e., to the temple) his earnings that otherwise would have gone for the support of his parents. The money, however, did not necessarily have to go for religious purposes. The Corban formula was simply a means of circumventing the clear responsibility of children toward their parents as prescribed in the law. The teachers of the law held that the Corban oath was binding, even when uttered rashly. The practice was one of many traditions that adhered to the letter of the law while ignoring its spirit. *(that is, a gift devoted to God).* By explaining this word, Mark reveals that he is addressing Gentile readers, probably Romans primarily (see Introduction: Recipients).

7:13 *you nullify the word of God by your tradition.* The teachers of the law appealed to Nu 30:1 – 2 in support of the Corban vow, but Jesus categorically rejects the practice of using one Biblical teaching to nullify another. The scribal interpretation of Nu 30:1 – 2 satisfied the letter of the passage but missed the meaning of the law as a whole. *nullify.* Cf. 2Co 4:2 and note.

7:16 See NIV text note on v. 15. Verse 16 appears to be a scribal addition derived from either 4:9 or 4:23.

7:19 *(In saying this, Jesus declared all foods "clean.").* Mark adds this parenthetical comment to help his readers see the significance of Jesus' pronouncement for them (see Ac 10:9 – 16 and note on 10:14).

7:20 *'unclean.'* Jesus replaced the normal Jewish understandings of defilement with the truth that defilement comes from an impure heart, not the violation of external rules. Fellowship with God is not interrupted by unclean hands or food, but by sin (see vv. 21 – 23).

7:24 *Tyre.* A Gentile city located in Phoenicia (modern Lebanon), which bordered Galilee to the northwest (see map, p. 1537). A journey of about 30 miles from Capernaum would have brought Jesus "to the vicinity of Tyre." *did not want anyone to know.* Ever since the feeding of the 5,000 (6:30 – 44) Jesus and his disciples had been, for the most part, skirting the region of Galilee. His purpose was to avoid the opposition in Galilee and to secure opportunity to teach his disciples privately (9:30 – 31). The regions to which he withdrew were: (1) the northeast shore of the Sea of Galilee (6:30 – 53), (2) Phoenicia (7:24 – 30), (3) the Decapolis (7:31 — 8:10) and (4) Caesarea Philippi (8:27 — 9:32).

7:26 *Greek.* Here probably equivalent to "Gentile." *Syrian Phoenicia.* At that time Phoenicia belonged administratively to Syria. Mark possibly used the term to distinguish this woman from the Libyan Phoenicians of North Africa.

7:27 *take the children's bread and toss it to their dogs.* See note on Mt 15:26.

7:28 *Yes, Lord.* The only time in Mark's Gospel that Jesus is addressed as "Lord" — and this by a Syrian Phoenician woman.

The Healing of a Deaf and Mute Man

7:31-37pp — Mt 15:29-31

31Then Jesus left the vicinity of Tyre[y]
and went through Sidon, down to the Sea
of Galilee[z] and into the region of the Decapolis.[a a] 32There some people brought to
him a man who was deaf and could hardly talk,[b] and they begged him to place his
hand on[c] the man.
33After he took him aside, away from
the crowd, Jesus put his fingers into the
man's ears. Then he spit[d] and touched the
man's tongue. 34He looked up to heaven[e]
and with a deep sigh[f] said to him, *"Ephphatha!"* (which means, "Be opened!").
35At this, the man's ears were opened,
his tongue was loosened and he began to
speak plainly.[g]
36Jesus commanded them not to tell
anyone.[h] But the more he did so, the more
they kept talking about it. 37People were
overwhelmed with amazement. "He has
done everything well," they said. "He
even makes the deaf hear and the mute
speak."

Jesus Feeds the Four Thousand

8:1-9pp — Mt 15:32-39
8:1-9Ref — Mk 6:32-44
8:11-21pp — Mt 16:1-12

8 During those days another large crowd
gathered. Since they had nothing to
eat, Jesus called his disciples to him and
said, 2"I have compassion for these people;[i] they have already been with me three
days and have nothing to eat. 3If I send
them home hungry, they will collapse on
the way, because some of them have come
a long distance."
4His disciples answered, "But where in
this remote place can anyone get enough
bread to feed them?"
5"How many loaves do you have?" Jesus
asked.
"Seven," they replied.
6He told the crowd to sit down on the
ground. When he had taken the seven
loaves and given thanks, he broke them
and gave them to his disciples to set before the people, and they did so. 7They had
a few small fish as well; he gave thanks
for them also and told the disciples to distribute them.[j] 8The people ate and were
satisfied. Afterward the disciples picked
up seven basketfuls of broken pieces that
were left over.[k] 9About four thousand men
were present. And having sent them away,
10he got into the boat with his disciples
and went to the region of Dalmanutha.
11The Pharisees came and began to question Jesus. To test him, they asked him for
a sign from heaven.[l] 12He sighed deeply[m]
and said, "Why does this generation ask
for a miraculous sign? I tell you the truth,
no sign will be given to it." 13Then he left
them, got back into the boat and crossed
to the other side.

The Yeast of the Pharisees and Herod

14The disciples had forgotten to bring
bread, except for one loaf they had with

7:31 [y] ver 24; S Mt 11:21 [z] S Mt 4:18 [a] Mt 4:25; Mk 5:20 **7:32** [b] Mt 9:32; Lk 11:14 [c] S Mk 5:23 **7:33** [d] Mk 8:23 **7:34** [e] Mk 6:41; Jn 11:41 [f] Mk 8:12 **7:35** [g] Isa 35:5,6 **7:36** [h] S Mt 8:4 **8:2** [i] S Mt 9:36 **8:7** [j] Mt 14:19 **8:8** [k] ver 20 **8:11** [l] S Mt 12:38 **8:12** [m] Mk 7:34

[a] *31* That is, the Ten Cities

7:31 *left the vicinity of Tyre and went through Sidon, down to the Sea of Galilee.* Apparently Jesus went north from Tyre to Sidon (about 25 miles) and then southeast through the territory of Herod Philip to the east side of the Sea of Galilee (see map, p. 1537). The route was circuitous—possibly to avoid entering Galilee, where Herod Antipas was in power (see 6:14–29) and where many people wanted to take Jesus by force and make him king (see Jn 6:14–15 and note on 6:15). Herod had intimated a hostile interest in Jesus (6:14–16). *Decapolis.* See notes on v. 24; Mt 4:25; see also map, p. 1530.
7:32 *place his hand on the man.* In order to heal him (see 1:41; 5:23; Ac 6:6 and note).
7:33 *spit.* See 8:23; Jn 9:6 and note.
7:34 *Ephphatha!* An Aramaic word that Mark translates for his Gentile readers (see Introduction: Recipients).
7:35 *man's ears were opened . . . he began to speak plainly.* Jesus was doing what God had promised to do when he came to redeem his people (see Isa 35:5–6 and notes).
7:36 *not to tell anyone.* See 5:19,43; Mt 8:4; 16:20 and notes.
7:37 *overwhelmed with amazement.* See 1:22 and note.
8:1–10 Although there are striking similarities between this account and 6:34–44, they are two distinct incidents, as indicated by the fact that Jesus himself refers to two feedings (see vv. 18–20).
8:1 *another large crowd gathered.* Since this incident took place in the region of the Decapolis (see 7:31), the crowd may have been made up of both Jews and Gentiles.
8:2 *compassion for these people.* As Jesus had compassion because the people were "like sheep without a shepherd" (6:34), he now has compassion because they have been so long without food.
8:4 *where . . . can anyone get enough bread to feed them?* The disciples' question reflects their inadequacy and acknowledges that Jesus alone could feed the people. They had not forgotten his feeding of the 5,000 (6:34–44) and were probably simply giving back to him the task of procuring bread. Alternatively, their question may reveal their spiritual dullness—they were slow learners (see note on v. 16).
8:8 *seven basketfuls.* See note on Mt 15:37.
8:9 *four thousand men.* See note on 6:44.
8:10 *Dalmanutha.* South of the Plain of Gennesaret (see note on Mt 14:34) a cave has been found bearing the name "Talmanutha," perhaps the spot where Jesus landed. Matthew says Jesus "went to the vicinity of Magadan" (Mt 15:39; see note there). Dalmanutha and Magadan (or Magdala), located on the western shore of the Sea of Galilee, may be names for the same place or for two places located close to each other.
8:11 *Pharisees.* See note on Mt 3:7. *sign from heaven.* The Pharisees wanted more compelling proof of Jesus' divine authority than his miracles, but he refused to perform such a sign because the request came from unbelief.
8:12 *I tell you the truth.* See note on 3:28.
8:13 *other side.* The eastern shore of the Sea of Galilee.

them in the boat. [15]"Be careful," Jesus
warned them. "Watch out for the yeast[n] of
the Pharisees[o] and that of Herod."[p]
[16]They discussed this with one another and said, "It is because we have no
bread."
[17]Aware of their discussion, Jesus asked
them: "Why are you talking about having
no bread? Do you still not see or understand? Are your hearts hardened?[q] [18]Do
you have eyes but fail to see, and ears but
fail to hear? And don't you remember?
[19]When I broke the five loaves for the five
thousand, how many basketfuls of pieces
did you pick up?"
"Twelve,"[r] they replied.
[20]"And when I broke the seven loaves
for the four thousand, how many basketfuls of pieces did you pick up?"
They answered, "Seven."[s]

8:15 [n] 1Co 5:6-8 [o] Lk 12:1 [p] S Mt 14:1; Mk 12:13
8:17 [q] Isa 6:9, 10; Mk 6:52
8:19 [r] Mt 14:20; Mk 6:41-44; Lk 9:17; Jn 6:13
8:20 [s] ver 6-9; Mt 15:37
8:21 [t] Mk 6:52
8:22 [u] S Mt 11:21 [v] Mk 10:46; Jn 9:1
8:23 [w] Mk 7:33 [x] S Mk 5:23

[21]He said to them, "Do you still not understand?"[t]

The Healing of a Blind Man at Bethsaida

[22]They came to Bethsaida,[u] and some
people brought a blind man[v] and begged
Jesus to touch him. [23]He took the blind
man by the hand and led him outside the
village. When he had spit[w] on the man's
eyes and put his hands on[x] him, Jesus
asked, "Do you see anything?"
[24]He looked up and said, "I see people;
they look like trees walking around."
[25]Once more Jesus put his hands on the
man's eyes. Then his eyes were opened,
his sight was restored, and he saw everything clearly. [26]Jesus sent him home, saying, "Don't go into the village.[a]"

[a] 26 Some manuscripts *Don't go and tell anyone in the village*

8:15 *yeast.* Here, as generally in the NT (Mt 16:6,11; Lk 12:1; see 1Co 5:6–8; Gal 5:9 and notes, but Mt 13:33 seems to be an exception — see note there), yeast is a symbol of evil or corruption. The metaphor includes the idea of a tiny amount of yeast being able to ferment a large amount of dough. In this context "the yeast of the Pharisees" may be either their teaching (see Mt 16:12) or their hypocrisy (see Lk 12:1) or both. But more likely Mark understood Jesus' words as referring to the failure on the part of both Herod (see 6:16) and the Pharisees (see vv. 11–12 and note on v. 11) to recognize that he is God's promised Messiah.

8:16 Another possible reading of the Greek text could be: "They discussed with one another why they had no bread." According to this rendering the disciples were so concerned to find out who was to blame for not bringing more bread that they completely ignored Jesus' warning about the yeast of the Pharisees and of Herod. Such an understanding heightens Mark's depiction of the disciples as slow learners (see 4:13; 5:51–52; 7:18; 8:4 and note, 17–21; 9:32; 10:13–14,35–40).

8:17 *hearts hardened.* See v. 4 and note; 6:52 and note.

8:18–20 See note on vv. 1–10.

8:22 *Bethsaida.* See note on Mt 11:21.

8:23 *spit.* See 7:33 and note. *put his hands on him.* See 1:41; Ac 6:6 and note.

8:24 *like trees walking around.* The man had no doubt bumped into trees in his blindness; now he dimly sees something like tree trunks moving about.

8:25 *Once more Jesus put his hands on the man's eyes.* This second laying on of hands is unique in the Gospel accounts of Jesus' healing ministry. In Mark's narrative it seems to underscore the condition of the disciples, whose "seeing" was still imperfect (v. 18) and in need of Jesus' further "healing." *saw everything clearly.* Giving sight to the blind was another indication that Jesus was doing what God had promised to do when he came to bring salvation (see 7:35 and note).

8:26 *Don't go into the village.* So as not to broadcast what

The Territories of Tyre and Sidon

In a unique excursion into pagan and semipagan areas, Jesus visited the districts of Tyre and Sidon and the confederation of free cities called the Decapolis. He was called to minister to "the lost sheep of Israel" (Mt 15:24) but the phenomenal public attention in Galilee was intense. Even here his fame had spread, and he could not keep his presence secret. The commercially magnificent cities of Tyre and Sidon had been a source of cultural seductiveness and religious heterodoxy since the time of Jezebel. The cities had been heavily influenced by Hellenism; the sophistication of Greek culture was apparent in their coinage and architecture. Each was also a proud, historic center of Canaanite paganism, with tombs of ancient kings and temples to Melqart/Heracles, Astarte and various other deities.

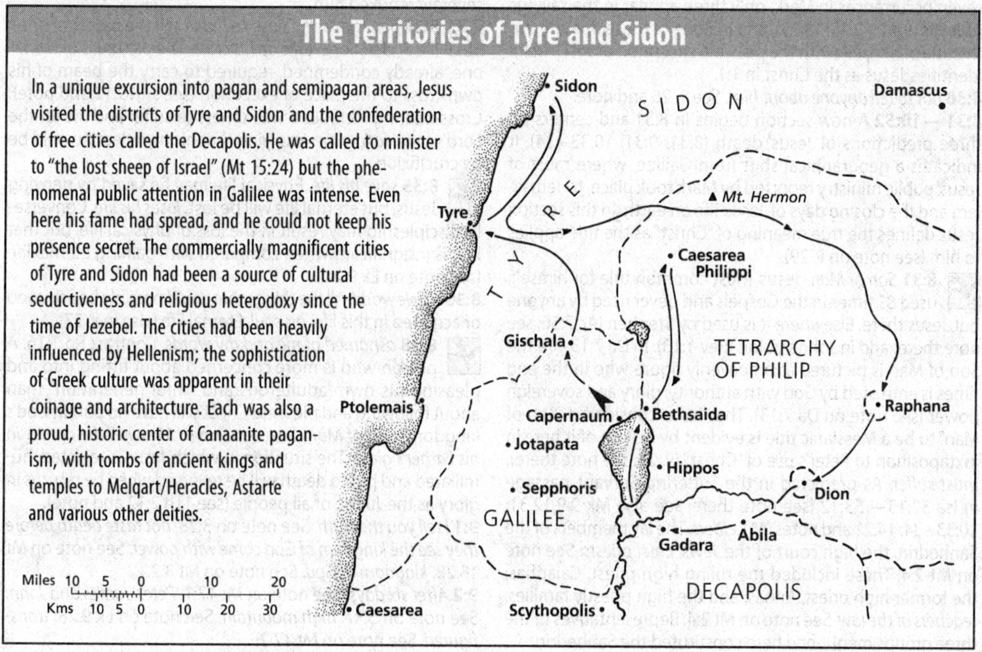

Peter's Confession of Christ

8:27-29pp — Mt 16:13-16; Lk 9:18-20

27 Jesus and his disciples went on to the
villages around Caesarea Philippi. On the
way he asked them, "Who do people say
I am?"
28 They replied, "Some say John the Baptist;[y] others say Elijah;[z] and still others,
one of the prophets."
29 "But what about you?" he asked.
"Who do you say I am?"
Peter answered, "You are the Christ.[a]"[a]
30 Jesus warned them not to tell anyone
about him.[b]

Jesus Predicts His Death

8:31–9:1pp — Mt 16:21-28; Lk 9:22-27

31 He then began to teach them that the
Son of Man[c] must suffer many things[d] and
be rejected by the elders, chief priests and
teachers of the law,[e] and that he must be
killed[f] and after three days[g] rise again.[h]
32 He spoke plainly[i] about this, and Peter
took him aside and began to rebuke him.
33 But when Jesus turned and looked at
his disciples, he rebuked Peter. "Get behind me, Satan!"[j] he said. "You do not
have in mind the things of God, but the
things of men."

34 Then he called the crowd to him
along with his disciples and said: "If anyone would come after me, he must deny
himself and take up his cross and follow
me.[k] 35 For whoever wants to save his life[b]
will lose it, but whoever loses his life for
me and for the gospel will save it.[l] 36 What
good is it for a man to gain the whole
world, yet forfeit his soul? 37 Or what can
a man give in exchange for his soul? 38 If
anyone is ashamed of me and my words
in this adulterous and sinful generation,
the Son of Man[m] will be ashamed of him[n]
when he comes[o] in his Father's glory with
the holy angels."
9 And he said to them, "I tell you the
truth, some who are standing here will
not taste death before they see the kingdom of God come[p] with power."[q]

The Transfiguration

9:2-8pp — Lk 9:28-36
9:2-13pp — Mt 17:1-13

2 After six days Jesus took Peter, James
and John[r] with him and led them up a
high mountain, where they were all alone.

8:28 [y] S Mt 3:1 [z] Mal 4:5 **8:29** [a] Jn 6:69; 11:27 **8:30** [b] S Mt 8:4; 16:20; 17:9; Mk 9:9; Lk 9:21 **8:31** [c] S Mt 8:20 [d] S Mt 16:21 [e] Mt 27:1,2 [f] Ac 2:23; 3:13 [g] S Mt 16:21 [h] S Mt 16:21 **8:32** [i] Jn 18:20 **8:33** [j] S Mt 4:10 **8:34** [k] Mt 10:38; Lk 14:27 **8:35** [l] S Jn 12:25 **8:38** [m] S Mt 8:20 [n] Mt 10:33; Lk 12:9 [o] S 1Th 2:19 **9:1** [p] Mk 13:30; Lk 22:18 [q] Mt 24:30; 25:31 **9:2** [r] S Mt 4:21

[a] *29* Or *Messiah.* "The Christ" (Greek) and "the Messiah" (Hebrew) both mean "the Anointed One."
[b] *35* The Greek word means either *life* or *soul*; also in verse 36.

Jesus had done for him and precipitate a crisis before Jesus had completed his ministry (see 5:19,43; Mt 8:4; 16:20 and notes).

8:27 *Caesarea Philippi.* See notes on 7:24; Mt 16:13.

8:29 *Christ.* See NIV text note; see also note on Mt 16:16. Because popular Jewish ideas associated with the term "Christ" were largely political and national, Jesus seldom used it. Of its seven occurrences in Mark, only three appear in the sayings of Jesus (9:41; 12:35; 13:21), and in none of these does he use the title of himself (with the possible exception of 9:41). Mark identifies Jesus as the Christ in 1:1.

8:30 *not to tell anyone about him.* See v. 26 and note.

8:31—10:52 A new section begins in 8:31 and centers on three predictions of Jesus' death (8:31; 9:31; 10:33-34). It indicates a geographical shift from Galilee, where most of Jesus' public ministry reported by Mark took place, to Jerusalem and the closing days of Jesus' life on earth. In this section Jesus defines the true meaning of "Christ" as the title applies to him (see note on v. 29).

8:31 *Son of Man.* Jesus' most common title for himself, used 81 times in the Gospels and never used by anyone but Jesus there. Elsewhere it is used by Stephen (Ac 7:56; see note there) and in John's vision (Rev 1:13). In Da 7:13-14 the Son of Man is pictured as a heavenly figure who in the end times is entrusted by God with authority, glory and sovereign power (see note on Da 7:13). That Jesus considered "Son of Man" to be a Messianic title is evident by his use of it here in juxtaposition to Peter's use of "Christ" (v. 29; see note there). *must suffer.* As predicted in the Suffering Servant passage in Isa 52:13—53:12 (see note there; see also Mk 9:9,12,31; 10:33-34; 14:21 and notes, 41). *elders.* The lay members of the Sanhedrin, the high court of the Jews. *chief priests.* See note on Mt 2:4. These included the ruling high priest, Caiaphas; the former high priest, Annas; and the high priestly families. *teachers of the law.* See note on Mt 2:4. Representatives of the three groups mentioned here constituted the Sanhedrin.

8:32 *Peter ... began to rebuke him.* Suffering and rejection had no place in Peter's conception of the Messiah, and he rebuked Jesus for teaching what to him seemed not only inconceivable but also terribly wrong.

8:33 *Satan.* Peter's attempt to dissuade Jesus from going to the cross contained the same temptation Satan gave at the outset of Jesus' ministry (see Mt 4:8-10), so Jesus severely rebuked him.

8:34 *deny himself.* Cease to make self the object of one's life and actions. *take up his cross.* The picture is of someone, already condemned, required to carry the beam of his own cross to the place of execution (see Jn 19:17 and note). Cross-bearing includes a willingness to suffer and die for the Lord's sake. *follow me.* Implying that his own death would be by crucifixion.

8:35 *save his life.* Physical life may be saved by denying Jesus, but eternal life will be lost. *loses his life.* Conversely, discipleship may result in the loss of physical life, but that loss is insignificant when compared with gaining eternal life (see note on Lk 9:24).

8:36 *whole world.* All the things that could possibly be achieved or acquired in this life. *his soul.* Eternal life (also in v. 37).

8:38 *ashamed of me and my words.* Contrast Ro 1:16. A person who is more concerned about fitting into and pleasing his own "adulterous and sinful generation" than about following and pleasing Christ will have no part in God's kingdom. *Son of Man.* See note on v. 31. *when he comes in his Father's glory.* The situation in which Jesus is rejected, humiliated and put to death will be reversed when he returns in glory as the Judge of all people (see 1Th 2:12 and note).

9:1 *I tell you the truth.* See note on 3:28. *not taste death before they see the kingdom of God come with power.* See note on Mt 16:28. *kingdom of God.* See note on Mt 3:2.

9:2 *After six days.* See note on Mt 17:1. *Peter, James and John.* See note on 5:37. *high mountain.* See note on Lk 9:28. *transfigured.* See note on Mt 17:2.

There he was transfigured before them.
3His clothes became dazzling white,[s] whiter than anyone in the world could bleach
them. 4And there appeared before them
Elijah and Moses, who were talking with
Jesus.

5Peter said to Jesus, "Rabbi,[t] it is good
for us to be here. Let us put up three shelters — one for you, one for Moses and one
for Elijah." 6(He did not know what to say,
they were so frightened.)

7Then a cloud appeared and enveloped
them, and a voice came from the cloud:[u]
"This is my Son, whom I love. Listen to
him!"[v]

8Suddenly, when they looked around,
they no longer saw anyone with them except Jesus.

9As they were coming down the mountain, Jesus gave them orders not to tell
anyone[w] what they had seen until the Son
of Man[x] had risen from the dead. 10They
kept the matter to themselves, discussing
what "rising from the dead" meant.

11And they asked him, "Why do the
teachers of the law say that Elijah must
come first?"

12Jesus replied, "To be sure, Elijah does
come first, and restores all things. Why
then is it written that the Son of Man[y]
must suffer much[z] and be rejected?[a] 13But
I tell you, Elijah has come,[b] and they have
done to him everything they wished, just
as it is written about him."

9:3 [s] S Mt 28:3
9:5 [t] S Mt 23:7
9:7 [u] Ex 24:16 [v] S Mt 3:17
9:9 [w] S Mk 8:30 [x] S Mt 8:20
9:12 [y] S Mt 8:20 [z] S Mt 16:21 [a] Lk 23:11
9:13 [b] S Mt 11:14

The Healing of a Boy With an Evil Spirit

9:14-28; 30-32pp — Mt 17:14-19; 22,23; Lk 9:37-45

14When they came to the other disciples,
they saw a large crowd around them and
the teachers of the law arguing with them.
15As soon as all the people saw Jesus, they
were overwhelmed with wonder and ran
to greet him.

16"What are you arguing with them
about?" he asked.

17A man in the crowd answered, "Teacher, I brought you my son, who is possessed
by a spirit that has robbed him of speech.
18Whenever it seizes him, it throws him
to the ground. He foams at the mouth,
gnashes his teeth and becomes rigid. I
asked your disciples to drive out the spirit, but they could not."

19"O unbelieving generation," Jesus replied, "how long shall I stay with you?
How long shall I put up with you? Bring
the boy to me."

20So they brought him. When the spirit
saw Jesus, it immediately threw the boy
into a convulsion. He fell to the ground and
rolled around, foaming at the mouth.[c]

21Jesus asked the boy's father, "How
long has he been like this?"

"From childhood," he answered. 22"It
has often thrown him into fire or water to
kill him. But if you can do anything, take
pity on us and help us."

23" 'If you can'?" said Jesus. "Everything
is possible for him who believes."[d]

9:20 [c] Mk 1:26
9:23 [d] S Mt 21:21; Mk 11:23; Jn 11:40

9:4 *Elijah and Moses.* See notes on Mt 17:3; Lk 9:30.

9:5 *Rabbi.* Hebrew for "(my) teacher." *three shelters.* Peter may have desired to erect new tents of meeting where God could again communicate with his people (see Ex 29:42). Or he may have been thinking of the booths used at the Feast of Tabernacles (see Lev 23:42 and note). In any case, he seemed eager to find fulfillment of the promised glory at that moment, prior to the sufferings that Jesus had announced as necessary.

9:7 *voice came from the cloud.* A cloud is frequently a symbol of God's presence to protect and guide (see note on Mt 17:5). *This is my Son, whom I love.* An allusion to Ps 2:7; Isa 42:1. *Listen to him!* The full sense includes obeying him. When God is involved, the only true hearing is obedient hearing (see Jas 1:22–25 and note on 1:25).

9:9 *not to tell anyone … until.* See 5:19,43; Mt 8:4; 16:20 and notes. After Jesus' resurrection the disciples were to tell everyone what they had experienced, for Jesus' finished work would have demonstrated his true and full character as the Messiah. *Son of Man.* See note on 8:31.

9:10 *what "rising from the dead" meant.* As Jews they were familiar with the doctrine of the resurrection; it was the resurrection of the Son of Man that baffled them, because their theology had no place for a suffering and dying Messiah.

9:11 *Elijah must come first.* See note on Mt 17:10.

9:12 *Elijah does come first, and restores all things.* A reference to the coming of Elijah, or one like him, in preparation for the coming of the Messiah (see note on Mt 17:10). *Son of Man.* See note on 8:31. *must suffer much and be rejected.* Just as "Elijah" (John the Baptist; see note on v. 13) has been rejected (see note on Mt 17:12).

9:13 *Elijah has come.* A reference to John the Baptist (see Mt 17:13). *they.* Herod and Herodias (see 6:17–29; Mt 14:3 and note). As Elijah was opposed by Ahab and Jezebel, so also John was opposed by a weak ruler and his wicked consort. *as it is written about him.* What Scripture says about Elijah in his relationship to Ahab and Jezebel (see 1Ki 19:1–10 and note on 19:3). There is no prediction of suffering associated with Elijah's ministry in the end times. However, what happened to Elijah under the threats of Jezebel foreshadowed what would happen to John the Baptist. The order of events suggested in vv. 11–13 is as follows: (1) Elijah ministered and suffered in the days of wicked Jezebel; (2) Elijah was a type of John the Baptist, who in turn suffered at the hands of Herodias; (3) the Son of Man suffered and was rejected a short time after John was beheaded.

9:14 *other disciples.* The nine besides Peter, James and John (see v. 2). *teachers of the law.* See note on Mt 2:4. If the transfiguration took place on Mount Hermon (see v. 2 and note), the presence of the teachers of the law so far north in the Holy Land would indicate their concern in monitoring the activities of Jesus.

9:17–18 See Mt 17:15,18 and notes.

9:18 Demonic possession was responsible for the boy's condition (see vv. 20,25–26).

9:19 *unbelieving generation.* Probably the referent should be restricted to the disciples. This cry of Jesus reveals his great disappointment with them (see note on 8:16).

9:22 *to kill him.* See note on 5:5.

9:23 *If you can?… Everything is possible for him who believes.* The question was not whether Jesus had the power to heal the boy but whether the father had faith to believe it. A person who truly believes will set no limits on what God can do.

24Immediately the boy's father exclaimed, "I do believe; help me overcome
my unbelief!"
25When Jesus saw that a crowd was
running to the scene,[e] he rebuked the evil[a]
spirit. "You deaf and mute spirit," he said,
"I command you, come out of him and
never enter him again."
26The spirit shrieked, convulsed him
violently and came out. The boy looked
so much like a corpse that many said,
"He's dead." 27But Jesus took him by the
hand and lifted him to his feet, and he
stood up.
28After Jesus had gone indoors, his disciples asked him privately,[f] "Why couldn't
we drive it out?"
29He replied, "This kind can come out
only by prayer.[b]"
30They left that place and passed through
Galilee. Jesus did not want anyone to
know where they were, 31because he was
teaching his disciples. He said to them,
"The Son of Man[g] is going to be betrayed
into the hands of men. They will kill him,[h]
and after three days[i] he will rise."[j] 32But
they did not understand what he meant[k]
and were afraid to ask him about it.

Who Is the Greatest?

9:33-37pp — Mt 18:1-5; Lk 9:46-48

33They came to Capernaum.[l] When he
was in the house,[m] he asked them, "What
were you arguing about on the road?" 34But
they kept quiet because on the way they
had argued about who was the greatest.[n]
35Sitting down, Jesus called the Twelve
and said, "If anyone wants to be first, he
must be the very last, and the servant of
all."[o]
36He took a little child and had him stand
among them. Taking him in his arms,[p] he
said to them, 37"Whoever welcomes one of
these little children in my name welcomes
me; and whoever welcomes me does not
welcome me but the one who sent me."[q]

Whoever Is Not Against Us Is for Us

9:38-40pp — Lk 9:49,50

38"Teacher," said John, "we saw a man
driving out demons in your name and we
told him to stop, because he was not one
of us."[r]
39"Do not stop him," Jesus said. "No one
who does a miracle in my name can in the
next moment say anything bad about me,
40for whoever is not against us is for us.[s]
41I tell you the truth, anyone who gives
you a cup of water in my name because
you belong to Christ will certainly not lose
his reward.[t]

Causing to Sin

42"And if anyone causes one of these
little ones who believe in me to sin,[u] it
would be better for him to be thrown into
the sea with a large millstone tied around
his neck.[v] 43If your hand causes you to
sin,[w] cut it off. It is better for you to enter life maimed than with two hands to go
into hell,[x] where the fire never goes out.[c][y]

9:25 [e]ver 15
9:28 [f]Mk 7:17
9:31 [g]S Mt 8:20 [h]ver 12; Ac 2:23; 3:13 [i]S Mt 16:21 [j]S Mt 16:21
9:32 [k]Lk 2:50; 9:45; 18:34; Jn 12:16
9:33 [l]S Mt 4:13 [m]Mk 1:29
9:34 [n]Lk 22:24
9:35 [o]Mt 18:4; Mk 10:43; Lk 22:26
9:36 [p]Mk 10:16
9:37 [q]S Mt 10:40
9:38 [r]Nu 11:27-29
9:40 [s]Mt 12:30; Lk 11:23
9:41 [t]S Mt 10:42
9:42 [u]S Mt 5:29 [v]Mt 18:6; Lk 17:2
9:43 [w]S Mt 5:29 [x]Mt 5:30; 18:8 [y]S Mt 25:41

[a] 25 Greek *unclean* [b] 29 Some manuscripts *prayer and fasting* [c] 43 Some manuscripts *out,* [44]*where / "'their worm does not die, / and the fire is not quenched.'*

9:24 *I do believe; help me overcome my unbelief!* Since human faith is never perfect, belief and unbelief are often mixed.

9:25 *When Jesus saw that a crowd was running to the scene, he rebuked the evil spirit.* As much as possible, Jesus wanted to avoid further publicity.

9:29 *This kind.* Seems to suggest that there are different kinds of demons. *only by prayer.* The disciples apparently had taken for granted the power given to them or had come to believe that it was inherent in them. Lack of prayer indicated they had forgotten that their power over the demonic spirits came from Jesus (see 3:15; 6:7,13; see also note on 6:12–13).

9:30 *passed through Galilee.* Jesus' public ministry in and around Galilee was now completed (see note on 7:24), and he was on his way to Jerusalem to suffer and die (see 10:32–34). As he had been doing for several months, Jesus continued to focus his teaching ministry on the Twelve (v. 31).

9:31 The second prediction of Jesus' death (see note on 8:31—10:52). *Son of Man.* See note on 8:31.

9:32 *they did not understand.* See v. 10; 8:32–33 and notes.

9:33–37 Parallel to 10:35–45 (see note there).

9:33 *Capernaum.* See Mt 4:13; Lk 10:15 and notes. *house.* Probably the one belonging to Peter and Andrew (see 1:29).

9:34 *they kept quiet.* No doubt due to embarrassment. *who was the greatest.* Questions of rank and status are normal and played an important role in the life of Jewish groups at this time, but they had no place in Jesus' value system (see v. 35; 10:42–44 and note on 10:43).

9:35 See note on Lk 9:48. *Sitting down.* See 4:1 and note.

9:38 *not one of us.* The man apparently was a believer, but he was not a member of the exclusive company of the Twelve. Nevertheless he acted in Jesus' name and had done what the disciples, on at least one occasion, had not been able to do (see vv. 14,28).

9:39 *Do not stop him.* Jesus' view of discipleship was far more inclusive than the narrow view held by the Twelve.

9:40 At first glance, this saying appears to contradict the one in Mt 12:30. There, however, reference is to those who vehemently opposed Jesus, whereas here it is to one who was in sympathy with Jesus and his ministry.

9:41 *I tell you the truth.* See note on 3:28. *gives you a cup of water.* God remembers even small acts of kindness extended to believers because they are believers (see note on Lk 9:50). *Christ.* See 8:29 and note. *his reward.* Including God's approval.

9:42 *little ones.* See Mt 18:6,10,14 and note; Lk 17:2. To cause believers to sin will bring serious judgment. *millstone.* A heavy stone slab used in grinding grain.

9:43 *cut it off.* Hyperbole, a figure of speech that exaggerates to make its point, is used here to emphasize the need for drastic action. Often sin can be conquered only by radical spiritual surgery. *life.* Eternal life in the presence of God. *hell.* See Mt 5:22 and note.

9:44,46 See NIV text notes on vv. 43,45. Verses 44,46 are identical with v. 48.

45And if your foot causes you to sin,[z] cut
it off. It is better for you to enter life crippled than to have two feet and be thrown
into hell.[a][a] 47And if your eye causes you
to sin,[b] pluck it out. It is better for you to
enter the kingdom of God with one eye
than to have two eyes and be thrown into
hell,[c] 48where

"'their worm does not die,
and the fire is not quenched.'[b][d]

49Everyone will be salted[e] with fire.
50"Salt is good, but if it loses its saltiness, how can you make it salty again?[f]
Have salt in yourselves,[g] and be at peace
with each other."[h]

Divorce

10:1-12pp — Mt 19:1-9

10 Jesus then left that place and went
into the region of Judea and across
the Jordan.[i] Again crowds of people came
to him, and as was his custom, he taught
them.[j]
2Some Pharisees[k] came and tested him
by asking, "Is it lawful for a man to divorce his wife?"
3"What did Moses command you?" he
replied.
4They said, "Moses permitted a man to
write a certificate of divorce and send her
away."[l]

9:45 [z]S Mt 5:29 [a]Mt 18:8 **9:47** [b]S Mt 5:29 [c]Mt 5:29; 18:9 **9:48** [d]Isa 66:24; S Mt 25:41 **9:49** [e]Lev 2:13 **9:50** [f]Mt 5:13; Lk 14:34,35 [g]Col 4:6 [h]Ro 12:18; 2Co 13:11; 1Th 5:13 **10:1** [i]Mk 1:5; Jn 10:40; 11:7 [j]S Mt 4:23; Mk 2:13; 4:2; 6:6,34 **10:2** [k]Mk 2:16 **10:4** [l]Dt 24:1-4; Mt 5:31

10:5 [m]Ps 95:8; Heb 3:15 **10:6** [n]Ge 1:27; 5:2 **10:8** [o]Ge 2:24; 1Co 6:16 **10:11** [p]S Lk 16:18 **10:12** [q]Ro 7:3; 1Co 7:10,11 **10:14** [r]S Mt 25:34

5"It was because your hearts were hard[m]
that Moses wrote you this law," Jesus replied. 6"But at the beginning of creation
God 'made them male and female.'[c][n] 7'For
this reason a man will leave his father and
mother and be united to his wife,[d] 8and
the two will become one flesh.'[e][o] So they
are no longer two, but one. 9Therefore
what God has joined together, let man not
separate."
10When they were in the house again,
the disciples asked Jesus about this. 11He
answered, "Anyone who divorces his wife
and marries another woman commits
adultery against her.[p] 12And if she divorces her husband and marries another man,
she commits adultery."[q]

The Little Children and Jesus

10:13-16pp — Mt 19:13-15; Lk 18:15-17

13People were bringing little children to
Jesus to have him touch them, but the
disciples rebuked them. 14When Jesus
saw this, he was indignant. He said to
them, "Let the little children come to me,
and do not hinder them, for the kingdom of God belongs to such as these.[r]

[a] 45 Some manuscripts *hell, 46where / "'their worm does not die, / and the fire is not quenched.'* [b] 48 Isaiah 66:24 [c] 6 Gen. 1:27 [d] 7 Some early manuscripts do not have *and be united to his wife.* [e] 8 Gen. 2:24

9:47 *kingdom of God.* See note on Mt 3:2.
9:48 Isa 66:24 (see note there) speaks of the punishment for rebellion against God. As the final word of Isaiah's message, the passage became familiar as a picture of endless destruction. *worm does not die.* Worms were always present in the rubbish dump (see Mt 5:22 and note).
9:49 The saying may mean that everyone who enters hell will suffer its fire, or (if only loosely connected with the preceding) it may mean that every Christian in this life can expect to undergo the fire of suffering and purification.
9:50 *Salt is good.* The distinctive mark of discipleship typified by salt is allegiance to Jesus and the gospel (see 8:35,38; Mt 5:13 and notes). *be at peace with each other.* Strife is resolved and peace restored when we recognize in one another a common commitment to Jesus and the gospel.
10:1 *region of Judea.* The Greek and Roman equivalent to the OT land of Judah, essentially the southern part of the Holy Land (exclusive of Idumea), which formerly had been the southern kingdom. For Jesus' ministry in Judea see note on Lk 9:51. *Jordan.* See note on 1:5. Jesus' journey took him south from Capernaum, over the mountains of Samaria into Judea and then east across the Jordan into Perea, where Herod Antipas ruled (see note on Mt 14:1). For Jesus' ministry in Perea see note on Lk 13:22.
10:2 *Pharisees.* See note on 2:16. *came and tested him.* The question of the Pharisees was hostile. It was for unlawful divorce and remarriage that John the Baptist denounced Herod Antipas and Herodias (see 6:17–18), and this rebuke cost him imprisonment and then his life. Jesus was now within Herod's jurisdiction, and the Pharisees may have hoped that Jesus' reply would cause the tetrarch to seize him as he had John. *Is it lawful ... to divorce his wife?* Jews of that day generally agreed that divorce was lawful, the only debated issue being the proper grounds for it (see note on Mt 19:3).
10:5 *because your hearts were hard.* See 6:52 and note. Divorce was an accommodation to human weakness and was used to bring order in a society that had disregarded God's will, but it was not the standard God had originally intended, as vv. 6–9 clearly indicate. The purpose of Dt 24:1–4 (see note there) was not to make divorce acceptable, but to reduce the hardship of its consequences.
10:6 *at the beginning of creation.* Jesus goes back to the time before human sin to show God's original intention. God instituted marriage as a great unifying blessing, bonding the male and female in his creation.
10:8 *no longer two, but one.* The deduction drawn by Jesus affirms the ideal of the permanence of marriage.
10:9 *Therefore what God has joined together.* Jesus grounds the sanctity of marriage in the authority of God himself, and his "No" to divorce safeguards against human selfishness, which always threatens to destroy marriage.
10:11 *Anyone who divorces his wife.* In Jewish practice divorce was effected by the husband himself, not by a judicial authority or court. *commits adultery against her.* A simple declaration of divorce on the part of a husband could not release him from the divine law of marriage and its moral obligations. This enduring force of the marriage bond was unrecognized in Rabbinic courts. But see Mt 19:3 and note; see also Mt 19:9, where an exception is mentioned. 1Co 7:15 may contain another exception (see notes on 1Co 7:12,15).
10:12 *she commits adultery.* In this historical and geographical context, Jesus' pronouncements confirm the bold denunciation by John the Baptist and equally condemn Herod Antipas and Herodias.
10:14 *kingdom of God.* See note on Mt 3:2. *belongs to such as these.* The kingdom of God belongs to those who, like children, are prepared to receive the kingdom as a gift of God (see note on v. 15).

15 I tell you the truth, anyone who will not
receive the kingdom of God like a little
child will never enter it."[s] 16 And he took
the children in his arms,[t] put his hands
on them and blessed them.

The Rich Young Man

10:17-31pp — Mt 19:16-30; Lk 18:18-30

17 As Jesus started on his way, a man ran
up to him and fell on his knees[u] before
him. "Good teacher," he asked, "what
must I do to inherit eternal life?"[v]
18 "Why do you call me good?" Jesus
answered. "No one is good—except God
alone. 19 You know the commandments:
'Do not murder, do not commit adultery,
do not steal, do not give false testimony,
do not defraud, honor your father and
mother.'[a]"[w]
20 "Teacher," he declared, "all these I
have kept since I was a boy."
21 Jesus looked at him and loved him.
"One thing you lack," he said. "Go, sell
everything you have and give to the poor,[x]
and you will have treasure in heaven.[y]
Then come, follow me."[z]
22 At this the man's face fell. He went
away sad, because he had great wealth.

10:15 [s]Mt 18:3
10:16 [t]Mk 9:36
10:17 [u]Mk 1:40
[v]Lk 10:25; S Ac 20:32
10:19 [w]Ex 20:12-16; Dt 5:16-20
10:21 [x]S Ac 2:45
[y]Mt 6:20; Lk 12:33
[z]S Mt 4:19
10:23 [a]Ps 52:7; 62:10; Mk 4:19; 1Ti 6:9, 10, 17
10:24 [b]Mt 7:13, 14; Jn 3:5
10:25 [c]Lk 12:16-20; 16:19-31
10:27 [d]S Mt 19:26
10:28 [e]S Mt 4:19
10:30 [f]Mt 6:33

23 Jesus looked around and said to his
disciples, "How hard it is for the rich[a] to
enter the kingdom of God!"
24 The disciples were amazed at his
words. But Jesus said again, "Children,
how hard it is[b] to enter the kingdom
of God![b] 25 It is easier for a camel to go
through the eye of a needle than for a rich
man to enter the kingdom of God."[c]
26 The disciples were even more amazed,
and said to each other, "Who then can be
saved?"
27 Jesus looked at them and said, "With
man this is impossible, but not with God;
all things are possible with God."[d]
28 Peter said to him, "We have left everything to follow you!"[e]
29 "I tell you the truth," Jesus replied,
"no one who has left home or brothers
or sisters or mother or father or children
or fields for me and the gospel 30 will fail
to receive a hundred times as much[f] in
this present age (homes, brothers, sisters, mothers, children and fields—and
with them, persecutions) and in the age

[a] 19 Exodus 20:12-16; Deut. 5:16-20 [b] 24 Some manuscripts *is for those who trust in riches*

10:15 *I tell you the truth.* See note on 3:28. *like a little child.* The point of comparison is the usual openness and receptivity of children. The kingdom of God must be received as a gift; it cannot be achieved by human effort. It may be entered only by those who know they are helpless, without claim or merit (see Mt 18:3; Lk 18:17 and notes).

10:16 *put his hands on them and blessed them.* See note on Ac 6:6. Jesus visually demonstrated that the blessings of the kingdom are freely given.

10:17 *man.* Lk 18:18 calls him a "ruler," meaning he was probably a member of an official council or court, and Mt 19:20 says he was "young." *what must I do ...?* Cf. Ac 16:30–31 and notes. The rich man was thinking in terms of earning righteousness to merit eternal life, but Jesus taught that it was a gift to be received (see v. 15 and note). *eternal life.* See note on Mt 19:16.

10:18 *Why do you call me good?* Jesus was not denying his own goodness but was forcing the man to recognize that his only hope was in total reliance on God, who alone can give eternal life. He may also have been encouraging the young man to consider the full identity and nature of the One he was addressing.

10:19 *do not defraud.* The prohibition of fraud may have represented the tenth commandment (against covetousness). If so, Jesus here mentions all six commandments that prohibit wrong actions and attitudes against others (see Ex 20:12–17; Dt 5:16–21).

10:20 *all these I have kept.* The man spoke sincerely, because for him keeping the law was a matter of external conformity. That the law also required inner obedience, which no one can fully satisfy, apparently escaped him completely. Paul speaks of having had a similar outlook before his conversion (see Php 3:6 and note). *since I was a boy.* Probably a reference to the age of 13, when a Jewish boy assumed personal responsibility for obeying the commandments and thus became a "son of the commandment(s)" (Aramaic *bar mitzvah*).

10:21 *Jesus ... loved him.* Jesus recognized the man's earnestness. Jesus' response was not intended to shame the man by exposing failure to understand the spiritual depth of the commandments but was an expression of genuine love. *One thing you lack ... Go, sell everything.* The young man's primary problem was his attachment to his wealth (see v. 22 and note), and therefore Jesus' prescription was to rid him of it. There is no indication that Jesus' command to him was meant for all Christians. It applies only to those who have the same spiritual problem. *treasure in heaven.* The gift of eternal life, or salvation. This treasure is not to be earned by self-denial or giving of one's material goods but is to be received by following Jesus. In giving away his wealth, the young man would have removed the obstacle that kept him from trusting in Jesus. *come, follow me.* See note on 1:17.

10:22 *He went away sad, because he had great wealth.* The tragic decision to turn away reflected a greater love for his possessions than for eternal life (see 4:19 and note).

10:25 *eye of a needle.* The camel was the largest animal found in the Holy Land. The vivid contrast between the largest animal and the smallest opening represents what, humanly speaking, is impossible. The oft-repeated suggestion that one of Jerusalem's gates was called the Needle's Eye is unsubstantiated.

10:26 *amazed.* See 1:22 and note.

10:27 *With man this is impossible, but not with God.* Salvation is totally the work of God. Every attempt to enter the kingdom on the basis of human achievement or merit is futile. Apart from the grace of God, no one can be saved (cf. Eph 2:8–9; Tit 3:5 and notes).

10:28 See 1:18.

10:29 *I tell you the truth.* See note on 3:28. *gospel.* See 1:1 and note.

10:30 *hundred times as much.* See 4:8 and note. *present age ... age to come.* These two terms take in all of time from the fall of Adam and Eve to the eternal state. The present age is evil (see Gal 1:4 and note), but the coming righteous age will begin with the second advent of Christ and continue forever. *and with them persecutions.* The life of discipleship is a combination of promise and persecution, blessing and

to come,[g] eternal life.[h] 31But many who are
first will be last, and the last first."[i]

Jesus Again Predicts His Death

10:32-34pp — Mt 20:17-19; Lk 18:31-33

32They were on their way up to Jerusalem, with Jesus leading the way, and
the disciples were astonished, while those
who followed were afraid. Again he took
the Twelve[j] aside and told them what was
going to happen to him. 33"We are going up to Jerusalem,"[k] he said, "and the
Son of Man[l] will be betrayed to the chief
priests and teachers of the law.[m] They will
condemn him to death and will hand him
over to the Gentiles, 34who will mock him
and spit on him, flog him[n] and kill him.[o]
Three days later[p] he will rise."[q]

The Request of James and John

10:35-45pp — Mt 20:20-28

35Then James and John, the sons of
Zebedee, came to him. "Teacher," they
said, "we want you to do for us whatever
we ask."
36"What do you want me to do for you?"
he asked.
37They replied, "Let one of us sit at your
right and the other at your left in your
glory."[r]
38"You don't know what you are asking,"[s]
Jesus said. "Can you drink the cup[t] I drink
or be baptized with the baptism I am baptized with?"[u]
39"We can," they answered.
Jesus said to them, "You will drink the
cup I drink and be baptized with the baptism I am baptized with,[v] 40but to sit at my
right or left is not for me to grant. These
places belong to those for whom they have
been prepared."
41When the ten heard about this, they
became indignant with James and John.
42Jesus called them together and said, "You
know that those who are regarded as rulers of the Gentiles lord it over them, and
their high officials exercise authority over
them. 43Not so with you. Instead, whoever
wants to become great among you must
be your servant,[w] 44and whoever wants to
be first must be slave of all. 45For even the
Son of Man did not come to be served, but
to serve,[x] and to give his life as a ransom
for many."[y]

Blind Bartimaeus Receives His Sight

10:46-52pp — Mt 20:29-34; Lk 18:35-43

46Then they came to Jericho. As Jesus
and his disciples, together with a large
crowd, were leaving the city, a blind man,
Bartimaeus (that is, the Son of Timae-
us), was sitting by the roadside begging.

10:30 [g] S Mt 12:32 [h] S Mt 25:46
10:31 [i] S Mt 19:30
10:32 [j] Mk 3:16-19
10:33 [k] S Lk 9:51 [l] S Mt 8:20 [m] Mt 27:1,2
10:34 [n] S Mt 16:21 [o] Ac 2:23; 3:13 [p] S Mt 16:21 [q] S Mt 16:21
10:37 [r] Mt 19:28
10:38 [s] Job 38:2 [t] S Mt 20:22 [u] Lk 12:50
10:39 [v] Ac 12:2; Rev 1:9
10:43 [w] S Mk 9:35
10:45 [x] S Mt 20:28 [y] S Mt 20:28

suffering. God takes nothing from a Christian without making multiplied restoration in a new and glorious form. Paradoxically, fellowship with other believers develops most deeply in persecution. *eternal life.* Beyond the conflicts of history is the triumph assured to those who belong to God (see Mt 19:16 and note).

10:31 *first will be last.* A warning against pride in sacrificial accomplishments such as Peter had manifested (v. 28; see vv. 42–44 and note on v. 43).

10:32 *on their way up to Jerusalem.* This last journey to Jerusalem began in a city called Ephraim (see Jn 11:54 and note) and took Jesus into Galilee (Lk 17:11), south through Perea to Jericho (Lk 18:35), then to Bethany (Lk 19:29) and finally to Jerusalem (Lk 19:41). See notes on Lk 9:51; 13:22. *astonished.* See 1:22 and note. Perhaps the disciples' astonishment was due to the determination with which Jesus proceeded to his goal (see Isa 50:7 and note). *those who followed.* Perhaps pilgrims on their way to the Passover in Jerusalem.

10:33–34 The third prediction of Jesus' death (see note on 8:31—10:52). *Gentiles, who will ... kill him.* The word "crucify" does not occur in any of the passion predictions in Mark's Gospel, but the statement that Jesus would be handed over to Gentiles to be killed by them suggests crucifixion, since this was the usual means of Roman execution of non-Romans.

10:33 *Son of Man ... chief priests ... teachers of the law.* See notes on 8:31; Mt 2:4.

10:35–45 Parallel to 9:33–37. Both passages deal with true greatness and both follow a prediction of Jesus' suffering and death. Both also show how spiritually undiscerning the disciples were (see note on 8:16).

10:35–36 *want ... want.* James's and John's desire for position and power would be realized only if they willingly submitted to servanthood (see "wants ... wants" in vv. 43–44).

10:35 *James and John, the sons of Zebedee.* See 1:19; 3:17.

10:37 *sit at your right and the other at your left.* Positions of prestige and power.

10:38 *drink the cup I drink.* A Jewish expression that meant to share someone's fate. In the OT the cup of wine was a common metaphor for God's wrath against human sin and rebellion (see Jer 25:15–16 and notes; 49:12). Accordingly, the cup Jesus had to drink refers to divine punishment on sin that he bore for the redemption of the human race (see v. 45; 14:36 and notes). *be baptized with the baptism I am baptized with.* The image of baptism is parallel to that of the cup, referring to his suffering and death as a baptism (see Lk 12:50 and note; cf. Ro 6:3–4 for the figure).

10:40 *is not for me to grant.* Jesus would not usurp his Father's authority.

10:41 *the ten.* The other disciples. *indignant.* Possibly because they desired the positions of prestige and power for themselves.

10:43 *Not so with you.* Jesus overturns the value structure of the world. The life of discipleship is to be characterized by humble and loving service.

10:45 A key verse in Mark's Gospel. Jesus came to this world as a servant—indeed, the Servant—who would suffer and die for our redemption, as Isaiah clearly predicted (Isa 52:13—53:12). *Son of Man.* See note on 8:31. *did not come to be served, but to serve, and to give his life.* See note on Jn 13:5. *ransom.* Means "the price paid for release (from bondage)." Jesus gave his life to release us from bondage to sin and death. *for.* That is, "in place of," pointing to Christ's substitutionary death. *many.* In contrast to the one life given for our ransom. See note on Mt 20:28.

10:46 *Jericho.* A very ancient city located five miles west of the Jordan and about 15 miles northeast of Jerusalem. In Jesus' time OT Jericho was largely abandoned, but a new city, south of the old one, had been built by Herod the Great. *leaving*

47When he heard that it was Jesus of Nazareth,[z] he began to shout, "Jesus, Son of
David,[a] have mercy on me!"
48Many rebuked him and told him to be
quiet, but he shouted all the more, "Son of
David, have mercy on me!"
49Jesus stopped and said, "Call him."
So they called to the blind man, "Cheer
up! On your feet! He's calling you."
50Throwing his cloak aside, he jumped to
his feet and came to Jesus.
51"What do you want me to do for you?"
Jesus asked him.
The blind man said, "Rabbi,[b] I want to
see."
52"Go," said Jesus, "your faith has
healed you."[c] Immediately he received his
sight and followed[d] Jesus along the road.

The Triumphal Entry

11:1-10pp — Mt 21:1-9; Lk 19:29-38
11:7-10pp — Jn 12:12-15

11 As they approached Jerusalem and
came to Bethphage and Bethany[e] at
the Mount of Olives,[f] Jesus sent two of his
disciples, 2saying to them, "Go to the village ahead of you, and just as you enter
it, you will find a colt tied there, which no
one has ever ridden.[g] Untie it and bring it
here. 3If anyone asks you, 'Why are you
doing this?' tell him, 'The Lord needs it
and will send it back here shortly.'"
4They went and found a colt outside in
the street, tied at a doorway.[h] As they untied it, 5some people standing there asked,
"What are you doing, untying that colt?"
6They answered as Jesus had told them to,
and the people let them go. 7When they
brought the colt to Jesus and threw their
cloaks over it, he sat on it. 8Many people
spread their cloaks on the road, while others spread branches they had cut in the
fields. 9Those who went ahead and those
who followed shouted,

"Hosanna![a]"

"Blessed is he who comes in the name
of the Lord!"[b][i]

10"Blessed is the coming kingdom of our
father David!"

"Hosanna in the highest!"[j]

11Jesus entered Jerusalem and went to
the temple. He looked around at everything, but since it was already late, he
went out to Bethany with the Twelve.[k]

Jesus Clears the Temple

11:12-14pp — Mt 21:18-22
11:15-18pp — Mt 21:12-16; Lk 19:45-47; Jn 2:13-16

12The next day as they were leaving
Bethany, Jesus was hungry. 13Seeing in the
distance a fig tree in leaf, he went to find
out if it had any fruit. When he reached
it, he found nothing but leaves, because
it was not the season for figs.[l] 14Then he
said to the tree, "May no one ever eat fruit
from you again." And his disciples heard
him say it.

[a] *9* A Hebrew expression meaning "Save!" which became an exclamation of praise; also in verse 10
[b] *9* Psalm 118:25,26

10:47 [z]S Mk 1:24 [a]S Mt 9:27 **10:51** [b]S Mt 23:7 **10:52** [c]S Mt 9:22 [d]S Mt 4:19 **11:1** [e]S Mt 21:17 [f]S Mt 21:1 **11:2** [g]Nu 19:2; Dt 21:3; 1Sa 6:7 **11:4** [h]Mk 14:16 **11:9** [i]Ps 118:25,26; Mt 23:39 **11:10** [j]Lk 2:14 **11:11** [k]Mt 21:12,17 **11:13** [l]Lk 13:6-9

the city. Luke says Jesus "approached Jericho" (Lk 18:35). He may have been referring to the new Jericho, while Matthew (20:29) and Mark may have meant the old city. *blind man.* See Lk 18:35 and note. *begging.* The presence of a blind beggar just outside the city gates, on a road pilgrims followed on the way to Jerusalem, was a common sight in that day.

10:47 *Nazareth.* See note on Mt 2:23. *Son of David.* A Messianic title (see Isa 11:1–2; Jer 23:5–6; Eze 34:23–24; Mt 1:1; 9:27 and notes). Verses 47–48 are the only places in Mark where it is used to address Jesus. Its only other occurrence in Mark is in 12:35.

10:51 *Rabbi.* See note on Jn 20:16.

10:52 *your faith has healed you.* See 5:28 and note.

11:1–11 At this point a new section in the Gospel of Mark begins. Jesus arrives in Jerusalem, and the rest of his ministry takes place within the confines of the Holy City. The Triumphal Entry, which inaugurates Passion Week, is a deliberate Messianic action, and the clue to its understanding is found in Zec 9:9 (quoted in Mt 21:5; Jn 12:15). Jesus purposefully offers himself as the Messiah, knowing that this will provoke Jewish leaders to take action against him.

11:1 *Bethphage.* See note on Mt 21:1 and map, p. 1553. *Bethany.* See note on Mt 21:17. *Mount of Olives.* Directly east of Jerusalem, it rises to a height of about 2,700 feet, some 200 feet higher than Mount Zion. Its summit commands a magnificent view of the city and especially of the temple (now the Dome of the Rock).

11:2 *the village ahead.* Probably Bethphage. *colt.* The Greek word can mean the young of any animal, but here it means the colt of a donkey (see Mt 21:2 and note; Jn 12:15). *which no one has ever ridden.* Unused animals were regarded as especially suitable for religious purposes (see Nu 19:2; Dt 21:3; 1Sa 6:7).

11:3 *If anyone asks you.* The message concerning the colt is not directed specifically to the owner but to anyone who might question the disciples' action. *Lord.* See note on Lk 19:31.

11:8 *branches.* The word means "leaves" or "leafy branches," which were readily available in nearby fields. Only John mentions "palm branches" (Jn 12:13; see note there), which may have come from Jericho, since they are not native to Jerusalem.

11:9 *Hosanna.* See NIV text note; see also note on Ps 118:25. *Blessed is he who comes.* A quotation of Ps 118:26 (see note there), one of the Hallel ("Praise") Psalms sung at Passover and especially fitting for this occasion.

11:10 *the coming kingdom of our father David.* The Messianic kingdom promised to David's son (see 2Sa 7:11–16 and notes).

11:11 *temple.* See note on Mt 4:5. *went out to Bethany.* Apparently Jesus spent each night through Thursday of Passion Week in Bethany (see note on Mt 21:17) at the home of his friends Mary, Martha and Lazarus (see v. 19; Jn 12:1–3).

11:12 *next day.* Monday of Passion Week.

11:13 *if it had any fruit.* The fig tree sometimes bore an early (minor) crop of figs—as has been documented. *not the season for figs.* Since it was not the season for the main crop of figs, Jesus went to find out if the tree had any early fruit.

11:14 *May no one ever eat fruit from you again.* Perhaps the incident was a parable of judgment, with the fig tree rep-

15On reaching Jerusalem, Jesus entered
the temple area and began driving out
those who were buying and selling there.
He overturned the tables of the money
changers and the benches of those selling doves, 16and would not allow anyone
to carry merchandise through the temple
courts. 17And as he taught them, he said,
"Is it not written:

"'My house will be called
a house of prayer for all nations'[a]?[m]

But you have made it 'a den of robbers.'[b]"[n]

18The chief priests and the teachers of
the law heard this and began looking for
a way to kill him, for they feared him,[o]
because the whole crowd was amazed at
his teaching.[p]

19When evening came, they[c] went out
of the city.[q]

The Withered Fig Tree

11:20-24pp — Mt 21:19-22

20In the morning, as they went along,
they saw the fig tree withered from the
roots. 21Peter remembered and said to
Jesus, "Rabbi,[r] look! The fig tree you
cursed has withered!"

22"Have[d] faith in God," Jesus answered.
23"I tell you the truth, if anyone says to
this mountain, 'Go, throw yourself into the
sea,' and does not doubt in his heart but
believes that what he says will happen,
it will be done for him.[s] 24Therefore I tell
you, whatever you ask for in prayer, believe that you have received it, and it will
be yours.[t] 25And when you stand praying,
if you hold anything against anyone, forgive him, so that your Father in heaven
may forgive you your sins.[e]"[u]

The Authority of Jesus Questioned

11:27-33pp — Mt 21:23-27; Lk 20:1-8

27They arrived again in Jerusalem,
and while Jesus was walking in the temple courts, the chief priests, the teachers
of the law and the elders came to him.
28"By what authority are you doing these
things?" they asked. "And who gave you
authority to do this?"

29Jesus replied, "I will ask you one
question. Answer me, and I will tell you
by what authority I am doing these things.
30John's baptism—was it from heaven, or
from men? Tell me!"

31They discussed it among themselves

11:17 [m]Isa 56:7 [n]Jer 7:11
11:18 [o]Mt 21:46; Mk 12:12; Lk 20:19 [p]S Mt 7:28
11:19 [q]Lk 21:37
11:21 [r]S Mt 23:7
11:23 [s]S Mt 21:21
11:24 [t]S Mt 7:7
11:25 [u]S Mt 6:14

[a] 17 Isaiah 56:7 [b] 17 Jer. 7:11 [c] 19 Some early manuscripts *he* [d] 22 Some early manuscripts *If you have* [e] 25 Some manuscripts *sins.* 26*But if you do not forgive, neither will your Father who is in heaven forgive your sins.*

resenting Israel (see Jer 24:1; Hos 9:10 and notes; Na 3:12). A tree full of leaves normally should have fruit, but this one was cursed because it had none. The fact that the clearing of the temple (vv. 15–19) is sandwiched between the two parts of the account of the fig tree (vv. 12–14,20–25) may underscore the theme of judgment (see v. 21 and note). The only application Jesus makes, however, is as an illustration of believing prayer (vv. 21–25).

11:15–19 All three Synoptic writers mention a clearing of the temple at the end of Jesus' ministry. Only John has one at the beginning. See notes on Mt 21:12–17; Jn 2:14–17.

11:15 *temple area.* The court of the Gentiles, the only part of the temple in which Gentiles could worship God and gather for prayer (see v. 17 and note). *buying and selling.* Pilgrims coming to the Passover Feast needed animals that met the ritual requirements for sacrifice, and the vendors set up their animal pens and money tables in the court of the Gentiles. *tables of the money changers.* Pilgrims needed their money changed into the local currency because the annual temple tax had to be paid in that currency. Also, according to the Mishnah (see note on Mt 15:2) currency from Tyre was required for some offerings. *those selling doves.* Doves were required for the ceremonial purification of women (Lev 12:6; Lk 2:22–24), the ceremonial cleansing of those with certain skin diseases (Lev 14:22–23), and other purposes (Lev 15:13–14,28–29). They were also the usual offering of the poor (Lev 5:7).

11:16 *to carry merchandise through the temple courts.* A detail found only in Mark. See note on v. 27.

11:17 *house of prayer for all nations.* Isa 56:7 assured godly Gentiles that they would be allowed to worship God in the temple. By allowing the court of the Gentiles to become a noisy, smelly marketplace, the Jewish religious leaders were interfering with God's provision. *den.* The place in which they found their security (see note on Jer 7:11). *of robbers.* Aptly so called, not only because they took financial advantage of the people but also because they robbed the temple of its sanctity.

11:18 *chief priests … teachers of the law.* See note on Mt 2:4. *began looking for a way to kill him.* See note on 3:6. They regarded Jesus as a dangerous threat to their whole way of life. *amazed.* See 1:22 and note.

11:19 *went out of the city.* To Bethany (see note on v. 11).

11:20 *In the morning.* Tuesday morning of Passion Week. *withered from the roots.* This detail indicates that the destruction was total (cf. Job 18:16) and that no one in the future would eat fruit from the tree. It served as a vivid warning of the judgment to come in A.D. 70 (see 13:2; Mt 24:2 and note).

11:21 *Rabbi.* Hebrew for "(my) teacher." *fig tree you cursed.* See note on v. 14. *has withered.* Perhaps prophetic of the fate of the Jewish authorities who were now about to reject their Messiah.

11:23 *I tell you the truth.* See note on 3:28. *this mountain … into the sea.* The Mount of Olives, from which the Dead Sea is visible. Cf. Mt 17:20 and note.

11:25 See Mt 18:35 and note; cf. Eph 4:32 and note.

11:26 This verse is not found in the earliest and best manuscripts of the NT (see NIV text note on v. 25), probably having been inserted from Mt 6:15 by a copyist.

11:27 *temple courts.* Several courts surrounded the main temple buildings, including the court of the women, the court of the men (Israelite), and the court of the Gentiles (see vv. 16–17 and notes). *chief priests … teachers of the law … elders.* See notes on 8:31; Mt 2:4.

11:28 *authority.* The Sanhedrin was asking why Jesus performed what appeared to be an official act if he possessed no official status (see note on Lk 20:2).

11:30 *from heaven, or from men?* "Heaven" was a common Jewish substitute for the divine name to avoid a possible misuse of God's name (see Ex 20:7 and note; see

and said, "If we say, 'From heaven,' he will
ask, 'Then why didn't you believe him?'
32But if we say, 'From men' . . . ." (They
feared the people, for everyone held that
John really was a prophet.)[v]
33So they answered Jesus, "We don't
know."
Jesus said, "Neither will I tell you by
what authority I am doing these things."

The Parable of the Tenants

12:1-12pp — Mt 21:33-46; Lk 20:9-19

12 He then began to speak to them in
parables: "A man planted a vineyard.[w] He put a wall around it, dug a pit
for the winepress and built a watchtower. Then he rented the vineyard to some
farmers and went away on a journey.
2At harvest time he sent a servant to the
tenants to collect from them some of the
fruit of the vineyard. 3But they seized
him, beat him and sent him away empty-handed. 4Then he sent another servant
to them; they struck this man on the head
and treated him shamefully. 5He sent still
another, and that one they killed. He sent
many others; some of them they beat, others they killed.
6"He had one left to send, a son, whom
he loved. He sent him last of all,[x] saying,
'They will respect my son.'
7"But the tenants said to one another,
'This is the heir. Come, let's kill him, and
the inheritance will be ours.' 8So they took
him and killed him, and threw him out of
the vineyard.
9"What then will the owner of the
vineyard do? He will come and kill those
tenants and give the vineyard to others.
10Haven't you read this scripture:

11:32 [v]S Mt 11:9
12:1 [w]Isa 5:1-7
12:6 [x]Heb 1:1-3
12:10 [y]S Ac 4:11
12:11 [z]Ps 118:22,23
12:12 [a]S Mk 11:18 [b]Mt 22:22
12:13 [c]Mt 22:16; Mk 3:6 [d]S Mt 12:10
12:17 [e]Ro 13:7
12:18 [f]S Ac 4:1 [g]Ac 23:8; 1Co 15:12

"'The stone the builders rejected
has become the capstone[a];[y]
11the Lord has done this,
and it is marvelous in our eyes'[b]?"[z]

12Then they looked for a way to arrest
him because they knew he had spoken the
parable against them. But they were afraid
of the crowd;[a] so they left him and went
away.[b]

Paying Taxes to Caesar

12:13-17pp — Mt 22:15-22; Lk 20:20-26

13Later they sent some of the Pharisees
and Herodians[c] to Jesus to catch him[d] in
his words. 14They came to him and said,
"Teacher, we know you are a man of integrity. You aren't swayed by men, because you pay no attention to who they
are; but you teach the way of God in accordance with the truth. Is it right to pay
taxes to Caesar or not? 15Should we pay or
shouldn't we?"
But Jesus knew their hypocrisy. "Why
are you trying to trap me?" he asked.
"Bring me a denarius and let me look at
it." 16They brought the coin, and he asked
them, "Whose portrait is this? And whose
inscription?"
"Caesar's," they replied.
17Then Jesus said to them, "Give to Caesar what is Caesar's and to God what is
God's."[e]
And they were amazed at him.

Marriage at the Resurrection

12:18-27pp — Mt 22:23-33; Lk 20:27-38

18Then the Sadducees,[f] who say there
is no resurrection,[g] came to him with a

[a] 10 Or *cornerstone* [b] 11 Psalm 118:22,23

also Introduction to Matthew: Recipients). Jesus' question implied that his authority, like that of John's baptism, came from God.

12:1–12 Many of Jesus' parables make one main point. This parable is rather complex, and the details fit the social situation in Jewish Galilee in the first century. Large estates, owned by absentee landlords, were put in the hands of local peasants who cultivated the land as tenant farmers. The parable exposed the planned attempt on Jesus' life, and God's judgment on the planners. See notes on Mt 21:35–37,41.

12:1 *them.* The representatives of the Sanhedrin mentioned in 11:27 (see note there). *parables.* See note on 4:2. *A man planted a vineyard.* The description reflects the language of Isa 5:1–2, where the vineyard clearly symbolizes Israel (see Isa 5:7). *watchtower.* See notes on Mt 21:33; Isa 5:2.

12:2 See note on Lk 20:10.

12:6 *son, whom he loved.* See 9:7 and note.

12:7 *inheritance will be ours.* Jewish law provided that a piece of property unclaimed by an heir would be declared ownerless, and could then be claimed by others. The tenants assumed that the son came as heir to claim his property and that if he were slain they could claim the land.

12:10 *capstone.* See note on Ps 118:22.

12:12 *them.* See note on v. 1.

12:13–17 This incident probably took place on Tuesday of Passion Week in one of the temple courts (see chart, p. 1510).

12:13 *they.* See note on v. 1. *Pharisees.* See note on Mt 3:7. *Herodians.* See notes on 3:6; Mt 22:15–17. The plan to destroy Jesus, which had originated early in his Galilean ministry, had now matured and was gaining momentum in Jerusalem.

12:14 *pay taxes to Caesar.* Subject peoples were required to pay a poll tax to the Roman emperor. The tax was highly unpopular, and some Jews flatly refused to pay it, believing that payment was an admission of Roman right to rule. See note on Mt 22:15–17.

12:15 *hypocrisy.* See 7:6; Mt 5:18–20 and note; 6:2 and note; 23:13–36. *denarius.* See notes on 6:37; Mt 22:19.

12:17 *Give to Caesar what is Caesar's.* See Mt 22:21 and note. There are obligations to the state that do not conflict with our obligations to God (see Ro 13:1–7; 1Ti 2:1–3; Tit 3:1–2; 1Pe 2:13–17 and notes). That a denarius belonged to Caesar was plainly marked in that on one side it bore a portrait of the emperor and on the other side an inscription that identified him. *to God what is God's.* Humans, who bear the image of God, owe to him their whole lives. *amazed.* See 1:22 and note.

12:18 *Sadducees.* A Jewish party that represented the wealthy and sophisticated classes. They were located largely in Jerusalem and made the temple and its administration their pri-

question. 19“Teacher,” they said, “Moses wrote for us that if a man’s brother dies and leaves a wife but no children, the man must marry the widow and have children for his brother.[h] 20Now there were seven brothers. The first one married and died without leaving any children. 21The second one married the widow, but he also died, leaving no child. It was the same with the third. 22In fact, none of the seven left any children. Last of all, the woman died too. 23At the resurrection[a] whose wife will she be, since the seven were married to her?”

24Jesus replied, “Are you not in error because you do not know the Scriptures[i] or the power of God? 25When the dead rise, they will neither marry nor be given in marriage; they will be like the angels in heaven.[j] 26Now about the dead rising—have you not read in the book of Moses, in the account of the bush, how God said to him, ‘I am the God of Abraham, the God of Isaac, and the God of Jacob’[b]?[k] 27He is not the God of the dead, but of the living. You are badly mistaken!”

The Greatest Commandment

12:28-34pp — Mt 22:34-40

28One of the teachers of the law[l] came and heard them debating. Noticing that Jesus had given them a good answer, he asked him, “Of all the commandments, which is the most important?”

29“The most important one,” answered Jesus, “is this: ‘Hear, O Israel, the Lord our God, the Lord is one.[c] 30Love the Lord your God with all your heart and with all your soul and with all your mind and with all your strength.’[d][m] 31The second is this: ‘Love your neighbor as yourself.’[e][n] There is no commandment greater than these.”

32“Well said, teacher,” the man replied. “You are right in saying that God is one and there is no other but him.[o] 33To love him with all your heart, with all your understanding and with all your strength, and to love your neighbor as yourself is more important than all burnt offerings and sacrifices.”[p]

34When Jesus saw that he had answered wisely, he said to him, “You are not far from the kingdom of God.”[q] And from then on no one dared ask him any more questions.[r]

Whose Son Is the Christ?

12:35-37pp — Mt 22:41-46; Lk 20:41-44
12:38-40pp — Mt 23:1-7; Lk 20:45-47

35While Jesus was teaching in the temple courts,[s] he asked, “How is it that the teachers of the law say that the Christ[f] is the son of David?[t] 36David himself, speaking by the Holy Spirit,[u] declared:

“ ‘The Lord said to my Lord:
“Sit at my right hand
until I put your enemies
under your feet.” ’[g][v]

37David himself calls him ‘Lord.’ How then can he be his son?”

The large crowd[w] listened to him with delight.

38As he taught, Jesus said, “Watch out for the teachers of the law. They like to walk around in flowing robes and be greeted in the marketplaces, 39and have the most important seats in the synagogues and the places of honor at banquets.[x]

12:19 [h]Dt 25:5 **12:24** [i]2Ti 3:15-17 **12:25** [j]1Co 15:42,49,52 **12:26** [k]Ex 3:6 **12:28** [l]Lk 10:25-28; 20:39 **12:30** [m]Dt 6:4,5 **12:31** [n]Lev 19:18; S Mt 5:43 **12:32** [o]Dt 4:35,39; Isa 45:6,14; 46:9 **12:33** [p]1Sa 15:22; Hos 6:6; Mic 6:6-8; Heb 10:8 **12:34** [q]S Mt 3:2 [r]Mt 22:46; Lk 20:40 **12:35** [s]S Mt 26:55 [t]S Mt 9:27 **12:36** [u]2Sa 23:2 [v]Ps 110:1; S Mt 22:44 **12:37** [w]Jn 12:9 **12:39** [x]Lk 11:43

[a] 23 Some manuscripts *resurrection, when men rise from the dead,* [b] 26 Exodus 3:6 [c] 29 Or *the Lord our God is one Lord* [d] 30 Deut. 6:4,5 [e] 31 Lev. 19:18 [f] 35 Or *Messiah* [g] 36 Psalm 110:1

mary interest. Though they were small in number, in Jesus’ time they exerted powerful political and religious influence. *say there is no resurrection.* See notes on Mt 3:7; Lk 20:27; Ac 4:1; see also chart, p. 1502.

12:19 See note on Mt 22:24.

12:24 *you do not know the Scriptures.* Cf. v. 10; 2:25.

12:25 See note on Lk 20:36. In the resurrection there will be a new order of existence brought about by “the power of God” (v. 24; see 1Co 15:42–44 and note). *like the angels.* The basic characteristics of resurrection life will be fellowship with and service for God (see note on Heb 1:14).

12:26 *book of Moses.* Exodus, one of the books of the Pentateuch (the first five books of the OT, all of which tradition ascribed to Moses). *account of the bush.* A common way of referring to Ex 3:1–6 (cf. Ro 11:2, where “the passage about Elijah” refers to 1Ki 19:1–18).

12:28 *which is the most important?* Jewish rabbis counted 613 individual statutes in the law and attempted to differentiate between “heavy” (or “great”) and “light” (or “little”) commands.

12:29 The OT citation came to be known as the Shema, named after the first word of Dt 6:4 in Hebrew, which means “Hear.” The Shema became the Jewish confession of faith, which was recited by pious Jews every morning and evening. To this day its recitation begins every synagogue service.

12:30 See notes on Dt 6:5; Mt 22:37; Lk 10:27.

12:31 According to Jesus, the second most important commandment (Lev 19:18) states that love for neighbor is the essential complement of love for God (see Jn 13:34; 1Jn 4:19–21 and notes). *neighbor.* See Lk 10:25–37.

12:32 *Well said, teacher.* Cf. Lk 20:39 and note.

12:33 *all burnt offerings and sacrifices.* See 1Sa 15:22; Isa 1:11–15; Hos 6:6; Mic 6:8 and notes.

12:34 *kingdom of God.* See note on Mt 3:2.

12:35 *Christ.* See 8:29 and note. *son of David.* See note on 10:47. Most of the people knew that the Messiah was to be from the family of David.

12:36 *The Lord said to my Lord.* God said to David’s Lord, i.e., David’s superior—ultimately the Messiah (see note on Ps 110:1). The purpose of the quotation was to show that the Messiah was more than a descendant of David—he was David’s Lord (see note on Lk 20:44).

12:37 See note on Lk 20:44.

12:38 *flowing robes.* The teachers of the law wore long robes that were fringed and almost reached to the ground.

12:39 *most important seats in the synagogues.* A reference to the bench that was in front of the “ark” containing the sacred scrolls. Those who sat there could be seen by all the worshipers in the synagogue.

40They devour widows' houses and for
a show make lengthy prayers. Such men
will be punished most severely."

The Widow's Offering

12:41-44pp — Lk 21:1-4

41Jesus sat down opposite the place
where the offerings were put[y] and
watched the crowd putting their money
into the temple treasury. Many rich people threw in large amounts. 42But a poor
widow came and put in two very small
copper coins,[a] worth only a fraction of a
penny.[b]
43Calling his disciples to him, Jesus
said, "I tell you the truth, this poor widow
has put more into the treasury than all the
others. 44They all gave out of their wealth;
but she, out of her poverty, put in everything—all she had to live on."[z]

Signs of the End of the Age

13:1-37pp — Mt 24:1-51; Lk 21:5-36

13 As he was leaving the temple, one
of his disciples said to him, "Look,
Teacher! What massive stones! What magnificent buildings!"
2"Do you see all these great buildings?"
replied Jesus. "Not one stone here will be
left on another; every one will be thrown
down."[a]
3As Jesus was sitting on the Mount of
Olives[b] opposite the temple, Peter, James,
John[c] and Andrew asked him privately,
4"Tell us, when will these things happen?
And what will be the sign that they are all
about to be fulfilled?"
5Jesus said to them: "Watch out that no
one deceives you.[d] 6Many will come in my
name, claiming, 'I am he,' and will deceive
many. 7When you hear of wars and rumors
of wars, do not be alarmed. Such things
must happen, but the end is still to come.
8Nation will rise against nation, and kingdom against kingdom. There will be earthquakes in various places, and famines.
These are the beginning of birth pains.
9"You must be on your guard. You will
be handed over to the local councils and
flogged in the synagogues.[e] On account of
me you will stand before governors and
kings as witnesses to them. 10And the gospel must first be preached to all nations.
11Whenever you are arrested and brought
to trial, do not worry beforehand about
what to say. Just say whatever is given
you at the time, for it is not you speaking,
but the Holy Spirit.[f]
12"Brother will betray brother to death,
and a father his child. Children will rebel
against their parents and have them put
to death.[g] 13All men will hate you because
of me,[h] but he who stands firm to the end
will be saved.[i]
14"When you see 'the abomination that
causes desolation'[c][j] standing where it[d]
does not belong—let the reader understand—then let those who are in Judea

12:41 [y] 2Ki 12:9; Jn 8:20 **12:44** [z] 2Co 8:12 **13:2** [a] Lk 19:44 **13:3** [b] S Mt 21:1 [c] S Mt 4:21

13:5 [d] ver 22; Jer 29:8; Eph 5:6; 2Th 2:3,10-12; 1Ti 4:1; 2Ti 3:13; 1Jn 4:6 **13:9** [e] S Mt 10:17 **13:11** [f] Mt 10:19,20; Lk 12:11,12 **13:12** [g] Mic 7:6; Mt 10:21; Lk 12:51-53 **13:13** [h] S Jn 15:21 [i] S Mt 10:22 **13:14** [j] Da 9:27; 11:31; 12:11

[a] *42* Greek *two lepta* [b] *42* Greek *kodrantes* [c] *14* Daniel 9:27; 11:31; 12:11 [d] *14* Or *he*; also in verse 29

12:40 *devour widows' houses.* Since the teachers of the law were not paid a regular wage, they were dependent on the generosity of patrons for their livelihood. Such a system was open to abuses, and widows were especially vulnerable to exploitation. *for a show make lengthy prayers.* See Mt 6:5-7. *punished most severely.* See note on Lk 20:47.

12:41 *temple treasury.* Located in the court of the women. Both men and women were allowed in this court, but women could go no farther into the temple buildings. It contained 13 trumpet-shaped receptacles for contributions brought by worshipers (see note on Lk 21:1).

12:42 *very small copper coins.* The smallest coins then in circulation in the Holy Land. Though her offering was meager, the widow brought "all she had" (v. 44; see 2Co 8:12 and note).

12:43 *I tell you the truth.* See note on 3:28.

13:1-37 Mark's version of the Olivet discourse (see note on Mt 24:1—25:46). It is the longest connected discourse in Mark's Gospel. The chapter falls into five sections: (1) Jesus' prophecy of the destruction of the temple, which gives rise to the disciples' questions (vv. 1-4); (2) warnings against deceivers, and false signs of the end (vv. 5-23); (3) the coming of the Son of Man (vv. 24-27); (4) the lesson of the fig tree (vv. 28-31); (5) exhortation to watchfulness (vv. 32-37).

13:1 *massive stones.* According to Josephus (*Antiquities,* 15.11.3), they were white, and some of them were 37 feet long, 12 feet high and 18 feet wide. *magnificent buildings.* See note on Lk 21:5.

13:2 See note on Mt 24:2.

13:3 *Mount of Olives.* See note on 11:1; see also map, p. 1553. *Peter, James, John and Andrew.* See 1:16-20; 5:37 and note.

13:4 The disciples thought that the destruction of the temple would be one of the events that ushered in the end times (see Mt 24:3 and note). *sign.* The way by which the disciples might know that the destruction of the temple was about to take place and that the end of the age was approaching.

13:5-13 See Lk 21:8-19 and note on 21:9.

13:5 *Watch out.* It is clear from such commands as "Watch out" (see also vv. 35,37) and "You must be on your guard" (v. 9; see also vv. 23,33) that one of the main purposes of the Olivet discourse was to alert the disciples to the danger of deception.

13:6 *he.* That is, the Messiah.

13:7 *the end.* Not the destruction of Jerusalem but the end of the age (see Mt 24:3).

13:8 *birth pains.* See note on Mt 24:8.

13:9 *local councils.* See Mt 10:17 and note. *flogged.* Infraction of Jewish regulations was punishable by flogging, the maximum penalty being 39 strokes with a whip (see 2Co 11:23-24). *synagogues.* See note on 1:21.

13:10 *gospel.* See 1:1 and note. *first.* Before the end of the age (see Mt 24:14).

13:13 *firm to the end.* Such perseverance is a sure indication of salvation (cf. Heb 3:6,14 and notes; 6:11-12; 10:36).

13:14 *abomination that causes desolation.* See note on Mt 24:15. *standing where it does not belong.* Cf. 2Th 2:4 and note. *flee to the mountains.* See note on Mt 24:16.

flee to the mountains. 15Let no one on
the roof of his house go down or enter
the house to take anything out. 16Let no
one in the field go back to get his cloak.
17How dreadful it will be in those days for
pregnant women and nursing mothers![k]
18Pray that this will not take place in winter, 19because those will be days of distress
unequaled from the beginning, when God
created the world,[l] until now—and never to be equaled again.[m] 20If the Lord had
not cut short those days, no one would
survive. But for the sake of the elect,
whom he has chosen, he has shortened
them. 21At that time if anyone says to you,
'Look, here is the Christ[a]!' or, 'Look, there
he is!' do not believe it.[n] 22For false Christs
and false prophets[o] will appear and perform signs and miracles[p] to deceive the
elect—if that were possible. 23So be on
your guard;[q] I have told you everything
ahead of time.

24"But in those days, following that distress,

"'the sun will be darkened,
and the moon will not give its light;
25the stars will fall from the sky,
and the heavenly bodies will be
shaken.'[b r]

26"At that time men will see the Son of
Man coming in clouds[s] with great power
and glory. 27And he will send his angels
and gather his elect from the four winds,
from the ends of the earth to the ends of
the heavens.[t]

28"Now learn this lesson from the fig
tree: As soon as its twigs get tender and its
leaves come out, you know that summer is
near. 29Even so, when you see these things
happening, you know that it is near, right
at the door. 30I tell you the truth, this generation[c u] will certainly not pass away until
all these things have happened.[v] 31Heaven
and earth will pass away, but my words
will never pass away.[w]

13:17 [k]Lk 23:29 13:19 [l]Mk 10:6 [m]Da 9:26; 12:1; Joel 2:2 13:21 [n]Lk 17:23; 21:8 13:22 [o]S Mt 7:15 [p]S Jn 4:48; 2Th 2:9,10 13:23 [q]2Pe 3:17 13:25 [r]Isa 13:10; 34:4; S Mt 24:29 13:26 [s]S Rev 1:7 13:27 [t]Zec 2:6 13:30 [u]Lk 17:25 [v]Mk 9:1 13:31 [w]S Mt 5:18 13:32 [x]Ac 1:7; 1Th 5:1,2 13:33 [y]1Th 5:6 13:34 [z]Mt 25:14 13:37 [a]Lk 12:35-40 14:1 [b]S Jn 11:55

The Day and Hour Unknown

32"No one knows about that day or
hour, not even the angels in heaven, nor
the Son, but only the Father.[x] 33Be on
guard! Be alert[d]![y] You do not know when
that time will come. 34It's like a man going
away: He leaves his house and puts his
servants[z] in charge, each with his assigned
task, and tells the one at the door to keep
watch.

35"Therefore keep watch because you do
not know when the owner of the house
will come back—whether in the evening,
or at midnight, or when the rooster crows,
or at dawn. 36If he comes suddenly, do not
let him find you sleeping. 37What I say to
you, I say to everyone: 'Watch!'"[a]

Jesus Anointed at Bethany

14:1-11pp — Mt 26:2-16
14:1,2,10,11pp — Lk 22:1-6
14:3-8Ref — Jn 12:1-8

14 Now the Passover[b] and the Feast of
Unleavened Bread were only two
days away, and the chief priests and the
teachers of the law were looking for some

[a] 21 Or *Messiah* [b] 25 Isaiah 13:10; 34:4 [c] 30 Or *race* [d] 33 Some manuscripts *alert and pray*

13:15 *roof of his house.* See notes on 2:4; Lk 17:31.
13:16 *cloak.* See note on Mt 5:40.
13:17 *pregnant women and nursing mothers.* Representative of anyone forced to flee under especially difficult circumstances. Jesus is very likely evoking the fearsome words of OT prophets describing the terrible events accompanying judgments to come (see 2Ki 8:12; Isa 13:16; Hos 13:16 and notes).
13:18 *winter.* The time when heavy rains caused streams to become swollen and impossible to cross, preventing many from reaching a place of refuge.
13:19 *days of distress unequaled.* See note on Mt 24:21.
13:20 *cut short those days.* See note on Mt 24:22. *elect.* People of God.
13:21 *Christ.* See 8:29 and note.
13:24–25 Imagery depicting the undoing of creation was commonly used by the OT prophets to describe God's awful judgment on a fallen world (see Isa 13:10; 24:21–23; 34:4; Jer 4:23–26; Eze 32:7; Joel 2:10,30–31; Am 8:9 and notes).
13:24 *in those days.* A common OT expression having to do with the Messianic age, the time of Israel's final redemption (see Jer 3:16,18; 31:29; 33:15–16; Joel 3:1; Zec 8:23; Heb 9:26 and note). *distress.* See v. 19 and note on Mt 24:21.
13:26 See Mt 24:30 and note. *Son of Man.* See note on 8:31. *coming in clouds with great power and glory.* A reference to Christ's second coming (see 8:38; Da 7:13; 2Th 1:6–10; Rev 19:11–16 and notes; cf. Ac 1:9–11 and note on 1:9).
13:27 *angels.* Cf. Rev 14:14–16. *gather his elect.* In the OT God is spoken of as gathering his scattered people (Dt 30:3–4; Isa 43:6; Jer 32:37; Eze 34:13; 36:24).
13:28 *fig tree.* See notes on 11:13; Lk 21:29.
13:29 *these things.* The signs listed in vv. 5–23 precede the destruction of Jerusalem and/or the end of the age. *it.* Probably a reference to the kingdom of God (see Lk 21:31) coming in the person of King Jesus (see NIV text note on Mt 24:33).
13:30 *I tell you the truth.* See note on 3:28. *generation.* See note on Lk 21:32.
13:32 *No one knows.* A specific outline of the future would be a hindrance, not a help, to faith. Certain signs have been given, but not for the purpose of making detailed, sequential predictions (see Ac 1:7; 1Th 5:1 and notes). *that day.* An OT expression (Am 9:11; Mic 4:6; 5:10). *nor the Son.* While on earth, even Jesus lived by faith—as his servants must—and obedience was the hallmark of his ministry (see Heb 10:5–7 and note on 10:5).
13:35 *in the evening, or at midnight, or when the rooster crows, or at dawn.* The four watches of the night used by the Romans (see note on Mt 14:25).
13:37 *Watch!* See note on v. 5.
14:1–9 See note on Jn 12:1–11.
14:1 *Passover.* The festival commemorating the time when the angel of the Lord passed over the homes of the Hebrews rather than killing their firstborn sons as he did in the Egyptian homes (see Ex 12:11 and note). The lambs or kids used

sly way to arrest Jesus and kill him.[c] 2“But
not during the Feast,” they said, “or the
people may riot.”
3While he was in Bethany,[d] reclining at
the table in the home of a man known as
Simon the Leper, a woman came with an
alabaster jar of very expensive perfume,
made of pure nard. She broke the jar and
poured the perfume on his head.[e]
4Some of those present were saying in-
dignantly to one another, “Why this waste
of perfume? 5It could have been sold for
more than a year’s wages[a] and the money
given to the poor.” And they rebuked her
harshly.
6“Leave her alone,” said Jesus. “Why
are you bothering her? She has done a
beautiful thing to me. 7The poor you will
always have with you, and you can help
them any time you want.[f] But you will not
always have me. 8She did what she could.
She poured perfume on my body beforehand to prepare for my burial.[g] 9I tell you
the truth, wherever the gospel is preached
throughout the world,[h] what she has done
will also be told, in memory of her.”
10Then Judas Iscariot, one of the Twelve,[i]
went to the chief priests to betray Jesus to
them.[j] 11They were delighted to hear this
and promised to give him money. So he
watched for an opportunity to hand him
over.

The Lord’s Supper

14:12-26pp — Mt 26:17-30; Lk 22:7-23
14:22-25pp — 1Co 11:23-25

12On the first day of the Feast of Unleavened Bread, when it was customary to sacrifice the Passover lamb,[k] Jesus’ disciples
asked him, “Where do you want us to go
and make preparations for you to eat the
Passover?”
13So he sent two of his disciples, telling
them, “Go into the city, and a man carrying a jar of water will meet you. Follow
him. 14Say to the owner of the house he
enters, ‘The Teacher asks: Where is my
guest room, where I may eat the Passover
with my disciples?’ 15He will show you a
large upper room,[l] furnished and ready.
Make preparations for us there.”
16The disciples left, went into the city
and found things just as Jesus had told
them. So they prepared the Passover.
17When evening came, Jesus arrived
with the Twelve. 18While they were reclining at the table eating, he said, “I tell you
the truth, one of you will betray me—one
who is eating with me.”

14:1 [c] S Mt 12:14
14:3 [d] S Mt 21:17 [e] Lk 7:37-39
14:7 [f] Dt 15:11
14:8 [g] Jn 19:40
14:9 [h] S Mt 24:14; Mk 16:15
14:10 [i] Mk 3:16-19 [j] S Mt 10:4
14:12 [k] Ex 12:1-11; Dt 16:1-4; 1Co 5:7
14:15 [l] Ac 1:13

[a] 5 Greek *than three hundred denarii*

in the feast were killed on the 14th of Nisan (March-April), and the meal was eaten the same evening between sundown and midnight. Since the Jewish day began at sundown, the Passover Feast took place on the 15th of Nisan (see note on Jn 2:13). *Feast of Unleavened Bread.* This feast followed Passover and lasted seven days (see Ex 12:17; 23:15 and notes). *chief priests.* See note on 8:31. *teachers of the law.* See note on Mt 2:4.

14:2 *not during the Feast.* During Passover and the week-long Feast of Unleavened Bread the population of Jerusalem increased from about 50,000 to several hundred thousand. It would have been too risky to apprehend Jesus with so large and excitable a crowd present.

14:3–9 In John’s Gospel this incident is placed before the beginning of Passion Week (see Jn 12:1–11 and note). Matthew and Mark may have placed it here to contrast the hatred of the religious leaders and the betrayal by Judas with the love and devotion of the woman who anointed Jesus.

14:3 *Bethany.* See note on Mt 21:17. *reclining at the table.* The usual posture for eating at a banquet. *Simon the Leper.* See note on Mt 26:6. *woman.* We know from Jn 12:3 that she was Mary, the sister of Martha and Lazarus. *alabaster jar.* A sealed flask with a long neck that was broken off when the contents were used and that contained enough ointment for one application. *nard.* See notes on SS 1:12; Jn 12:3. *poured the perfume on his head.* Anointing was a common custom at feasts (see Ps 23:5 and note). The woman’s action expressed her deep devotion to Jesus.

14:4 *Some of those present.* Mt 26:8 identifies them as the disciples, while Jn 12:4–5 singles out Judas Iscariot.

14:5 *given to the poor.* It was a Jewish custom to give gifts to the poor on the evening of Passover (see Jn 13:29).

14:7 *The poor you will always have with you.* See Dt 15:11 and note. Jesus’ statement did not express lack of concern for the poor, for their needs lay close to his heart (see Mt 6:2–4; Lk 4:18; 6:20; 14:13,21; 18:22; Jn 13:29). He was simply stating the truth.

14:8 *prepare for my burial.* It was a normal Jewish custom to anoint a dead body with aromatic oils in preparing it for burial (see 16:1 and note). Jesus seems to anticipate suffering a criminal’s death, for only in that circumstance was there no anointing of the body.

14:9 *I tell you the truth.* See note on 3:28. *gospel.* See note on 1:1.

14:10 *Judas Iscariot.* See note on 3:19. *chief priests.* See note on 8:31. This was an unexpected opportunity that they seized, even though they had intended not to apprehend Jesus during the Feast (see v. 2 and note).

14:11 *money.* Thirty silver coins (see Mt 26:15 and note).

14:12 *first day of the Feast of Unleavened Bread.* Here the 14th of Nisan is meant because Passover lambs were killed on that day (Ex 12:6). The entire eight-day celebration was sometimes referred to as the Feast of Unleavened Bread. *make preparations.* These preparations would have included obtaining food for the meal, such as unleavened bread, wine, bitter herbs and a lamb.

14:13 *two of his disciples.* Peter and John (Lk 22:8). *man carrying a jar.* See note on Lk 22:10.

14:14 *The Teacher asks.* See note on Lk 22:11. *Where is my guest room …?* It was a Jewish custom that anyone in Jerusalem who had a room available would give it upon request to a pilgrim to celebrate the Passover. Apparently, Jesus had made previous arrangements with the owner of the house (cf. note on Ac 12:12).

14:16 *as Jesus had told them.* See note on Lk 22:13.

14:17 *evening.* Thursday of Passion Week.

14:18 *reclining at the table eating.* Originally the Passover meal was eaten standing (see Ex 12:11), but in Jesus’ time it was customary to eat it while reclining (cf. v. 3 and note). *I tell you the truth.* See note on 3:28.

19They were saddened, and one by one they said to him, "Surely not I?"

20"It is one of the Twelve," he replied, "one who dips bread into the bowl with me.[m] 21The Son of Man[n] will go just as it is written about him. But woe to that man who betrays the Son of Man! It would be better for him if he had not been born."

22While they were eating, Jesus took bread, gave thanks and broke it,[o] and gave it to his disciples, saying, "Take it; this is my body."

23Then he took the cup, gave thanks and offered it to them, and they all drank from it.[p]

24"This is my blood of the[a] covenant,[q] which is poured out for many," he said to them. 25"I tell you the truth, I will not drink again of the fruit of the vine until that day when I drink it anew in the kingdom of God."[r]

26When they had sung a hymn, they went out to the Mount of Olives.[s]

Jesus Predicts Peter's Denial

14:27-31pp — Mt 26:31-35

27"You will all fall away," Jesus told them, "for it is written:

"'I will strike the shepherd,
and the sheep will be scattered.'[b][t]

28But after I have risen, I will go ahead of you into Galilee."[u]

29Peter declared, "Even if all fall away, I will not."

30"I tell you the truth," Jesus answered, "today—yes, tonight—before the rooster crows twice[c] you yourself will disown me three times."[v]

31But Peter insisted emphatically, "Even if I have to die with you,[w] I will never disown you." And all the others said the same.

Gethsemane

14:32-42pp — Mt 26:36-46; Lk 22:40-46

32They went to a place called Gethsemane, and Jesus said to his disciples, "Sit here while I pray." 33He took Peter, James and John[x] along with him, and he began to be deeply distressed and troubled. 34"My soul is overwhelmed with sorrow to the point of death,"[y] he said to them. "Stay here and keep watch."

35Going a little farther, he fell to the ground and prayed that if possible the hour[z] might pass from him. 36"*Abba*,[d] Father,"[a] he said, "everything is possible for you. Take this cup[b] from me. Yet not what I will, but what you will."[c]

37Then he returned to his disciples and found them sleeping. "Simon," he said to Peter, "are you asleep? Could you not keep watch for one hour? 38Watch and pray so that you will not fall into temptation.[d] The spirit is willing, but the body is weak."[e]

39Once more he went away and prayed the same thing. 40When he came back, he again found them sleeping, because their eyes were heavy. They did not know what to say to him.

14:20 [m] Jn 13:18-27
14:21 [n] S Mt 8:20
14:22 [o] S Mt 14:19
14:23 [p] 1Co 10:16
14:24 [q] S Mt 26:28
14:25 [r] S Mt 3:2
14:26 [s] S Mt 21:1
14:27 [t] Zec 13:7
14:28 [u] Mk 16:7
14:30 [v] ver 66-72; Lk 22:34; Jn 13:38
14:31 [w] Lk 22:33; Jn 13:37
14:33 [x] S Mt 4:21
14:34 [y] Jn 12:27
14:35 [z] ver 41; S Mt 26:18
14:36 [a] Ro 8:15; Gal 4:6 [b] S Mt 20:22 [c] S Mt 26:39
14:38 [d] Mt 6:13 [e] Ro 7:22,23

[a] 24 Some manuscripts *the new*
[b] 27 Zech. 13:7
[c] 30 Some early manuscripts do not have *twice.*
[d] 36 Aramaic for *Father*

14:20 *dips bread into the bowl with me.* See note on Mt 26:23.

14:21 *Son of Man.* See note on 8:31. *as it is written about him.* Jesus may have had the "suffering servant" passage of Isa 53 in mind.

14:22 The NT gives four accounts of the Lord's Supper (here; Mt 26:26–28; Lk 22:19–20; 1Co 11:23–25). Matthew's account is very much like Mark's, and Luke's and Paul's have similarities. All the accounts include the taking of the bread; the thanksgiving or blessing; the breaking of the bread; the saying, "This is my body"; the taking of the cup; and the explanation of the relation of blood to the covenant. Only Luke and Paul record Jesus' command to continue to celebrate the Supper. *this is my body.* The bread represented his body, given for them (see 1Co 11:24 and note).

14:23 *gave thanks.* The word "Eucharist," often used to refer to the Lord's Supper, is derived from the Greek term used here.

14:24 *my blood of the covenant.* The cup represents the blood of Jesus, which, in turn, represents his poured-out life (i.e., his death). God's commitments to his people in the new covenant are possible only through Christ's atoning death (see Ex 24:6,8; Jer 31:31–34; Lk 22:20; Heb 8:8–12 and notes). *for many.* See Ro 5:15 and note.

14:25 *I tell you the truth.* See note on 3:28. *kingdom of God.* See note on Mt 3:2.

14:26 *hymn.* See note on Mt 26:30. *Mount of Olives.* See note on 11:1.

14:27 *You will all fall away.* Not that the disciples will lose their faith in Jesus, but that their courage will fail and they will forsake him (see note on Mt 26:31).

14:28 *I will go ahead of you into Galilee.* See 16:7.

14:30 *I tell you the truth.* See note on 3:28. *crows twice.* See NIV text note here and on v. 72.

14:32 *Gethsemane.* An "olive grove" (Jn 18:1) on the lower slopes of the Mount of Olives, one of Jesus' favorite places (see Lk 22:39 and note; Jn 18:2). The name is Hebrew and means "oil press," i.e., a place for squeezing the oil from olives.

14:33 *Peter, James and John.* See note on 5:37.

14:36 *Abba, Father.* Expressive of an especially close relationship to God (see also NIV text note). *this cup.* The chalice of death and of God's wrath that Jesus took from the Father's hand in fulfillment of his mission. What Jesus dreaded was not death as such, but the manner of his death as the one who was taking "the sin of the world" (Jn 1:29) upon himself. See 10:38; Mt 26:39 and notes.

14:37 *Simon.* See note on 1:16. Perhaps he is singled out because of his bold assertion that he would not fail Jesus (see vv. 29–31).

14:38 *fall into temptation.* Be attacked by temptation. Here the temptation is to be unfaithful in the face of the threatening circumstances confronting them. *The spirit is willing.* The expression is taken from Ps 51:12 (see note on 51:10–12). When one's spirit is under God's control, it strives against human weakness.

Passion Week

Bethany, the Mount of Olives and Jerusalem

4. Clearing of the temple
MONDAY
Mt 21:12-17;
Mk 11:15-18;
Lk 19:45-48

Jesus returned to the temple and found the court of the Gentiles full of traders and money changers making a large profit. Jesus drove them out and overturned their benches and tables.

Alternate "Gordon's Calvary"

NORTH

Present Damascus Gate

Traditional crucifixion and tomb site

Jerusalem

Meters 0 100 200 300

Feet 0 500 1,000

KIDRON VALLEY

SOUTH

7. Passover, Last Supper
THURSDAY
Mt 26:17-30;
Mk 14:12-26; Lk 22:7-23

In an upper room Jesus prepared both himself and his disciples for his death. He gave the Passover meal a new meaning. The loaf of bread and cup of wine represented his body soon to be sacrificed and his blood soon to be shed. And so he instituted the "Lord's Supper." After singing a hymn they went to the Garden of Gethsemane, where Jesus prayed in agony, knowing what lay ahead for him.

8. Crucifixion
FRIDAY
Mt 27; Mk 15; Lk 22:66–23:56; Jn 18:28–19:37

Following betrayal, arrest, desertion, false trials, denial, condemnation, beatings and mockery, Jesus was required to carry his cross to The Place of the Skull, where he was crucified with two other prisoners.

9. In the tomb

Jesus' body was placed in the tomb before 6:00 P.M. Friday night, when the Sabbath began and all work stopped, and it lay in the tomb throughout the Sabbath.

10. Resurrection
SUNDAY
Mt 28:1-10; Mk 16:1-8; Lk 24:1-49; Jn 20

Early in the morning, women went to the tomb and found that the stone closing the tomb's entrance had been rolled back. An angel told them Jesus was alive and gave them a message. Jesus appeared to Mary Magdalene in the garden, to Peter, to two disciples on the road to Emmaus, and later that day to all the disciples but Thomas.

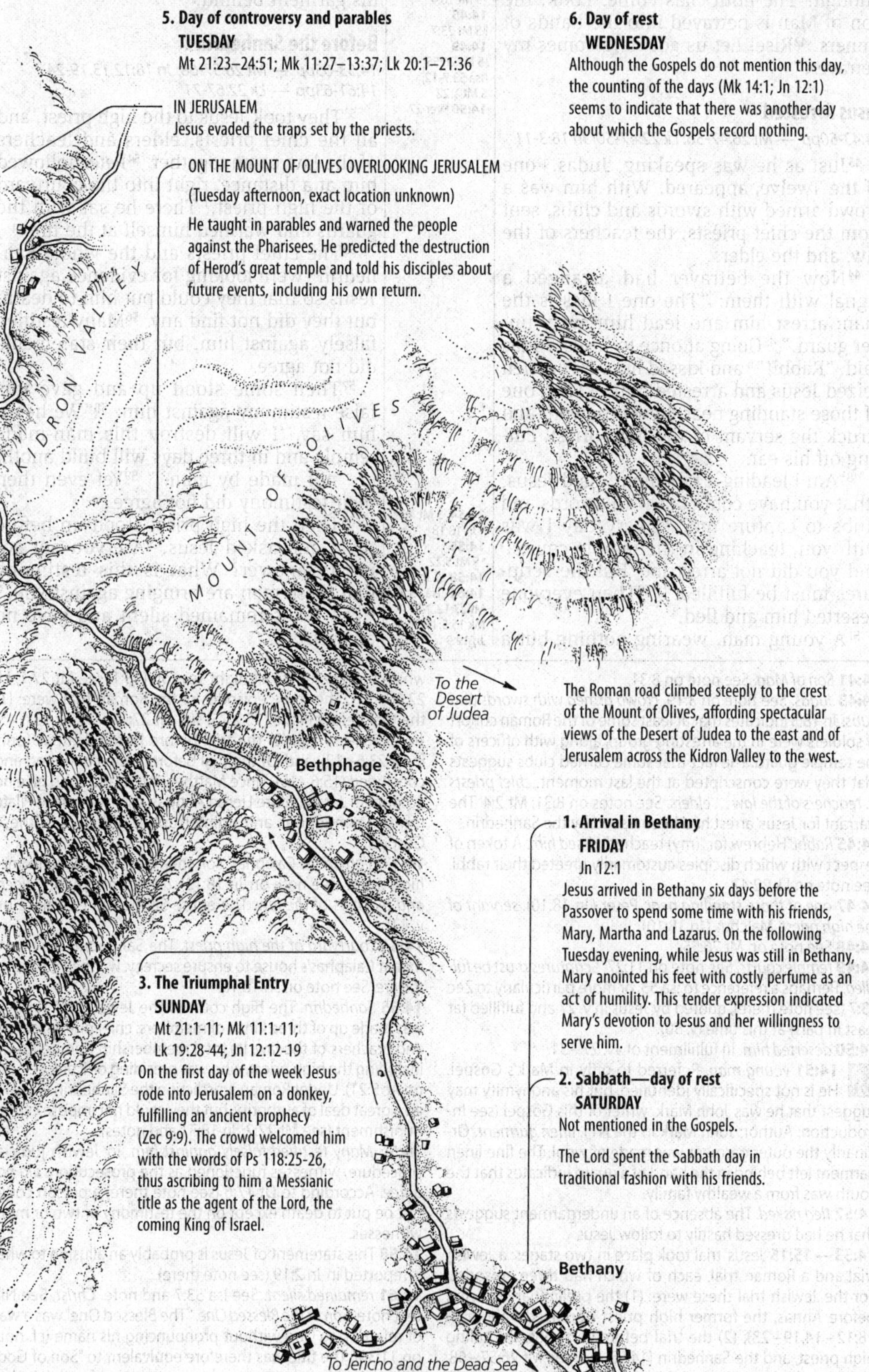
5. Day of controversy and parables
TUESDAY
Mt 21:23–24:51; Mk 11:27–13:37; Lk 20:1–21:36
IN JERUSALEM
Jesus evaded the traps set by the priests.
ON THE MOUNT OF OLIVES OVERLOOKING JERUSALEM
(Tuesday afternoon, exact location unknown)
He taught in parables and warned the people against the Pharisees. He predicted the destruction of Herod's great temple and told his disciples about future events, including his own return.
6. Day of rest
WEDNESDAY
Although the Gospels do not mention this day, the counting of the days (Mk 14:1; Jn 12:1) seems to indicate that there was another day about which the Gospels record nothing.
KIDRON VALLEY
MOUNT OF OLIVES
To the Desert of Judea
The Roman road climbed steeply to the crest of the Mount of Olives, affording spectacular views of the Desert of Judea to the east and of Jerusalem across the Kidron Valley to the west.
Bethphage
1. Arrival in Bethany
FRIDAY
Jn 12:1
Jesus arrived in Bethany six days before the Passover to spend some time with his friends, Mary, Martha and Lazarus. On the following Tuesday evening, while Jesus was still in Bethany, Mary anointed his feet with costly perfume as an act of humility. This tender expression indicated Mary's devotion to Jesus and her willingness to serve him.
3. The Triumphal Entry
SUNDAY
Mt 21:1-11; Mk 11:1-11; Lk 19:28-44; Jn 12:12-19
On the first day of the week Jesus rode into Jerusalem on a donkey, fulfilling an ancient prophecy (Zec 9:9). The crowd welcomed him with the words of Ps 118:25-26, thus ascribing to him a Messianic title as the agent of the Lord, the coming King of Israel.
2. Sabbath—day of rest
SATURDAY
Not mentioned in the Gospels.
The Lord spent the Sabbath day in traditional fashion with his friends.
Bethany
To Jericho and the Dead Sea

41Returning the third time, he said to
them, "Are you still sleeping and resting?
Enough! The hour[f] has come. Look, the
Son of Man is betrayed into the hands of
sinners. 42Rise! Let us go! Here comes my
betrayer!"

Jesus Arrested

14:43-50pp — Mt 26:47-56; Lk 22:47-50; Jn 18:3-11

43Just as he was speaking, Judas,[g] one
of the Twelve, appeared. With him was a
crowd armed with swords and clubs, sent
from the chief priests, the teachers of the
law, and the elders.

44Now the betrayer had arranged a
signal with them: "The one I kiss is the
man; arrest him and lead him away under guard." 45Going at once to Jesus, Judas
said, "Rabbi!"[h] and kissed him. 46The men
seized Jesus and arrested him. 47Then one
of those standing near drew his sword and
struck the servant of the high priest, cutting off his ear.

48"Am I leading a rebellion," said Jesus,
"that you have come out with swords and
clubs to capture me? 49Every day I was
with you, teaching in the temple courts,[i]
and you did not arrest me. But the Scriptures must be fulfilled."[j] 50Then everyone
deserted him and fled.[k]

51A young man, wearing nothing but a
linen garment, was following Jesus. When
they seized him, 52he fled naked, leaving
his garment behind.

Before the Sanhedrin

14:53-65pp — Mt 26:57-68; Jn 18:12,13,19-24
14:61-63pp — Lk 22:67-71

53They took Jesus to the high priest, and
all the chief priests, elders and teachers
of the law came together. 54Peter followed
him at a distance, right into the courtyard
of the high priest.[l] There he sat with the
guards and warmed himself at the fire.[m]

55The chief priests and the whole Sanhedrin[n] were looking for evidence against
Jesus so that they could put him to death,
but they did not find any. 56Many testified
falsely against him, but their statements
did not agree.

57Then some stood up and gave this
false testimony against him: 58"We heard
him say, 'I will destroy this man-made
temple and in three days will build another,[o] not made by man.'" 59Yet even then
their testimony did not agree.

60Then the high priest stood up before
them and asked Jesus, "Are you not going to answer? What is this testimony
that these men are bringing against you?"
61But Jesus remained silent and gave no
answer.[p]

14:41 [f] ver 35; S Mt 26:18 **14:43** [g] S Mt 10:4 **14:45** [h] S Mt 23:7 **14:49** [i] S Mt 26:55 [j] Isa 53:7-12; S Mt 1:22 **14:50** [k] ver 27 **14:54** [l] S Mt 26:3 [m] Jn 18:18 **14:55** [n] S Mt 5:22 **14:58** [o] S Jn 2:19 **14:61** [p] Isa 53:7; Mt 27:12,14; Mk 15:5; Lk 23:9; Jn 19:9

14:41 *Son of Man.* See note on 8:31.
14:43 *Judas.* See note on 3:19. *crowd armed with swords and clubs.* Jn 18:3 indicates that at least some of the Roman cohort of soldiers were in the arresting group, along with officers of the temple guard. The fact that some carried clubs suggests that they were conscripted at the last moment. *chief priests … teachers of the law … elders.* See notes on 8:31; Mt 2:4. The warrant for Jesus' arrest had been issued by the Sanhedrin.
14:45 *Rabbi.* Hebrew for "(my) teacher." *kissed him.* A token of respect with which disciples customarily greeted their rabbi. See note on Lk 22:47.
14:47 *one of those standing near.* Peter (Jn 18:10). *servant of the high priest.* Malchus (Jn 18:10).
14:48 See note on Mt 26:55.
14:49 *temple courts.* See note on 11:27. *Scriptures must be fulfilled.* Perhaps a reference to Isa 53, or more particularly to Zec 13:7 (see note there), quoted by Jesus in v. 27 and fulfilled (at least in part) at this time (v. 50).
14:50 *deserted him.* In fulfillment of vv. 27–31.
14:51 *young man.* Referred to only in Mark's Gospel. He is not specifically identified, but his anonymity may suggest that he was John Mark, writer of this Gospel (see Introduction: Author; John Mark in the NT). *linen garment.* Ordinarily the outer garment was made of wool. The fine linen garment left behind in the hand of a guard indicates that the youth was from a wealthy family.
14:52 *fled naked.* The absence of an undergarment suggests that he had dressed hastily to follow Jesus.
14:53—15:15 Jesus' trial took place in two stages: a Jewish trial and a Roman trial, each of which had three episodes. For the Jewish trial these were: (1) the preliminary hearing before Annas, the former high priest (reported only in Jn 18:12–14,19–23); (2) the trial before Caiaphas, the ruling high priest, and the Sanhedrin (14:53–65; see Mt 26:57–68; Lk 22:54–65; Jn 18:24); and (3) the final action of the council, which terminated its all-night session (15:1; see Mt 27:1; Lk 22:66–71). The three episodes of the Roman trial were: (1) the trial before Pilate (15:2–5; see Mt 27:11–26; Lk 23:1–5; Jn 18:28—19:16); (2) the trial before Herod Antipas (only in Lk 23:6–12); and (3) the trial before Pilate continued and concluded (15:6–15). Since Matthew, Mark and John give no account of Jesus before Herod Antipas, the trial before Pilate forms a continuous and uninterrupted narrative in these Gospels.
14:53 *high priest.* Caiaphas, son-in-law of Annas, the former high priest (see note on Jn 18:13). *all the chief priests, elders and teachers of the law.* The entire Sanhedrin (see note on v. 43).
14:54 *courtyard of the high priest.* The Sanhedrin may have met at Caiaphas's house to ensure secrecy. *warmed himself at the fire.* See note on Jn 18:18.
14:55 *Sanhedrin.* The high court of the Jews. In NT times it was made up of three kinds of members: chief priests, elders, and teachers of the law. Its total membership numbered 71, including the high priest, who was presiding officer (see note on Ac 5:21). Under Roman jurisdiction the Sanhedrin was given a great deal of authority, but they could not impose capital punishment (see Mt 27:2; Jn 18:31 and notes).
14:56 *Many testified falsely against him.* In Jewish judicial procedure, witnesses functioned as the prosecution. *did not agree.* According to Dt 17:6 (see note there) a person could not be put to death except on the testimony of two or more witnesses.
14:58 This statement of Jesus is probably an allusion to what is reported in Jn 2:19 (see note there).
14:61 *remained silent.* See Isa 53:7 and note. *Christ.* See NIV text note. *Son of the Blessed One.* "The Blessed One" was a way of referring to God without pronouncing his name (cf. note on 11:30). The title was therefore equivalent to "Son of God," though in this context it would seem not to refer to deity but

Again the high priest asked him, "Are
you the Christ,[a] the Son of the Blessed
One?"[q]
62"I am," said Jesus. "And you will see
the Son of Man sitting at the right hand of
the Mighty One and coming on the clouds
of heaven."[r]
63The high priest tore his clothes.[s] "Why
do we need any more witnesses?" he
asked. 64"You have heard the blasphemy.
What do you think?"
They all condemned him as worthy of
death.[t] 65Then some began to spit at him;
they blindfolded him, struck him with
their fists, and said, "Prophesy!" And the
guards took him and beat him.[u]

Peter Disowns Jesus

14:66-72pp — Mt 26:69-75; Lk 22:56-62; Jn 18:16-18,25-27

66While Peter was below in the courtyard,[v] one of the servant girls of the high
priest came by. 67When she saw Peter
warming himself,[w] she looked closely at
him.
"You also were with that Nazarene,
Jesus,"[x] she said.
68But he denied it. "I don't know or understand what you're talking about,"[y] he
said, and went out into the entryway.[b]
69When the servant girl saw him there,
she said again to those standing around,
"This fellow is one of them." 70Again he
denied it.[z]
After a little while, those standing near
said to Peter, "Surely you are one of them,
for you are a Galilean."[a]
71He began to call down curses on himself, and he swore to them, "I don't know
this man you're talking about."[b]
72Immediately the rooster crowed the
second time.[c] Then Peter remembered the
word Jesus had spoken to him: "Before
the rooster crows twice[d] you will disown
me three times."[c] And he broke down and
wept.

Jesus Before Pilate

15:2-15pp — Mt 27:11-26; Lk 23:2,3,18-25; Jn 18:29-19:16

15 Very early in the morning, the chief
priests, with the elders, the teachers of the law[d] and the whole Sanhedrin,[e]
reached a decision. They bound Jesus,
led him away and handed him over to Pilate.[f]
2"Are you the king of the Jews?"[g] asked
Pilate.
"Yes, it is as you say," Jesus replied.
3The chief priests accused him of many
things. 4So again Pilate asked him, "Aren't
you going to answer? See how many things
they are accusing you of."
5But Jesus still made no reply,[h] and Pilate was amazed.
6Now it was the custom at the Feast to
release a prisoner whom the people requested. 7A man called Barabbas was in
prison with the insurrectionists who had
committed murder in the uprising. 8The

14:61 [q]Mt 16:16; Jn 4:25,26 **14:62** [r]S Rev 1:7 **14:63** [s]Lev 10:6; 21:10; Nu 14:6; Ac 14:14 **14:64** [t]Lev 24:16 **14:65** [u]S Mt 16:21 **14:66** [v]ver 54 **14:67** [w]ver 54 [x]S Mk 1:24 **14:68** [y]ver 30,72 **14:70** [z]ver 30,68,72 [a]Ac 2:7 **14:71** [b]ver 30,72 **14:72** [c]ver 30,68 **15:1** [d]Mt 27:1; Lk 22:66 [e]S Mt 5:22 [f]S Mt 27:2 **15:2** [g]ver 9,12,18,26; S Mt 2:2 **15:5** [h]S Mk 14:61

[a] 61 Or *Messiah* [b] 68 Some early manuscripts *entryway and the rooster crowed* [c] 72 Some early manuscripts do not have *the second time.* [d] 72 Some early manuscripts do not have *twice.*

to royal Messiahship, since in popular Jewish belief the Messiah was to be a man, not God.

14:62 See Mt 26:64 and note. *I am.* See Ex 3:14 and note; Jn 8:58 – 59 and note on 8:58. *Son of Man.* See note on 8:31. This Son of Man saying brings together Da 7:13 (see note there) and Ps 110:1 (see note there).

14:63 *tore his clothes.* A sign of great grief or shock (see Ge 37:29; 2Ki 18:37 and note; 19:1). In the case of the high priest it was a form of judicial act expressing the fact that he regarded Jesus' answer as blasphemous (see note on Mt 26:65).

14:64 *blasphemy.* Not only involved reviling the name of God (see Lev 24:10 – 16) but also included any affront to his majesty or authority (see Mk 2:7 and note; 3:28 – 29; Jn 5:18 and note; 10:33). Jesus' claim to be the Messiah and, in fact, to have majesty and authority belonging only to God was therefore regarded by Caiaphas as blasphemy, for which the Mosaic law prescribed death by stoning (Lev 24:16).

14:65 *began to spit at him ... struck him with their fists.* Conventional gestures of rejection and condemnation (see Nu 12:14; Dt 25:9; Job 30:10; Isa 50:6 and note). *blindfolded him.* A Rabbinic interpretation of Isa 11:2 – 4 held that the Messiah could judge by smell without the aid of sight. *Prophesy!* Say who it was who struck you!

14:66 *below.* While Jesus was being beaten in an upstairs room of Caiaphas's house, Peter was below in the courtyard. *one of the servant girls.* The doorkeeper (see Jn 18:16; cf. Ac 12:3).

14:67 *Nazarene.* See note on Mt 2:23.

14:68 *I don't know or understand what you're talking about.* An expression used in Jewish law courts for a formal, legal denial.

14:70 *Galilean.* Peter's Galilean dialect showed him to be from Galilee, and his presence among the Judeans in the courtyard suggested he was a follower of Jesus.

14:72 *Before ... times.* See v. 30.

15:1 *Very early in the morning.* The working day of a Roman official began at daylight. *morning.* Friday of Passion Week. *Sanhedrin.* See note on 14:55. *reached a decision.* Apparently to accuse Jesus before the civil authority for treason rather than blasphemy (see Lk 23:1 – 14 and note on 23:2). *Pilate.* See note on Lk 3:1.

15:2 *king of the Jews.* See Jn 18:33 – 37 and notes on 18:33,36. *asked Pilate.* Judgment in a Roman court was the sole responsibility of the imperial magistrate.

15:3 *many things.* See Lk 23:2 and note. Multiple charges were common in criminal cases.

15:4 *Aren't you going to answer?* If Jesus made no defense, according to Roman law Pilate would have to pronounce against him.

15:5 *made no reply.* See 14:61; Isa 53:7 and note.

15:6 *custom.* See note on Jn 18:39. *Feast.* Passover (see 14:1 – 2 and notes).

15:7 *Barabbas.* Probably a member of the Zealots, a Jewish revolutionary group (see Mt 10:4; Jn 18:40; Ac 5:37 and note; see also chart, p. 1502). *uprising.* Nothing from other sources is known about this insurrection, though Mark speaks of it as if it were well known. Under the Roman governors such revolts were common (see Lk 13:1).

crowd came up and asked Pilate to do for
them what he usually did.
9“Do you want me to release to you the
king of the Jews?”[i] asked Pilate, 10knowing
it was out of envy that the chief priests
had handed Jesus over to him. 11But the
chief priests stirred up the crowd to have
Pilate release Barabbas[j] instead.
12“What shall I do, then, with the one
you call the king of the Jews?” Pilate asked
them.
13“Crucify him!” they shouted.
14“Why? What crime has he committed?” asked Pilate.
But they shouted all the louder, “Crucify him!”
15Wanting to satisfy the crowd, Pilate
released Barabbas to them. He had Jesus
flogged,[k] and handed him over to be crucified.

The Soldiers Mock Jesus

15:16-20pp — Mt 27:27-31

16The soldiers led Jesus away into the
palace[l] (that is, the Praetorium) and
called together the whole company of soldiers. 17They put a purple robe on him,
then twisted together a crown of thorns
and set it on him. 18And they began to
call out to him, “Hail, king of the Jews!”[m]
19Again and again they struck him on the
head with a staff and spit on him. Falling
on their knees, they paid homage to him.
20And when they had mocked him, they
took off the purple robe and put his own
clothes on him. Then they led him out[n] to
crucify him.

The Crucifixion

15:22-32pp — Mt 27:33-44; Lk 23:33-43; Jn 19:17-24

21A certain man from Cyrene,[o] Simon,
the father of Alexander and Rufus,[p] was
passing by on his way in from the country,
and they forced him to carry the cross.[q]
22They brought Jesus to the place called
Golgotha (which means The Place of
the Skull). 23Then they offered him wine
mixed with myrrh,[r] but he did not take it.
24And they crucified him. Dividing up his
clothes, they cast lots[s] to see what each
would get.
25It was the third hour when they crucified him. 26The written notice of the charge
against him read: THE KING OF THE JEWS.[t]

15:9 [i] S ver 2
15:11 [j] Ac 3:14
15:15 [k] Isa 53:6
15:16 [l] Jn 18:28,33; 19:9
15:18 [m] S ver 2
15:20 [n] Heb 13:12
15:21 [o] S Mt 27:32 [p] Ro 16:13 [q] Mt 27:32; Lk 23:26
15:23 [r] ver 36; Ps 69:21; Pr 31:6
15:24 [s] Ps 22:18
15:26 [t] S ver 2

15:13 – 14 *Crucify.* See note on v. 24.

15:15 *flogged.* The Romans used a whip made of several strips of leather into which were embedded (near the ends) pieces of bone and lead. The Jews limited the number of stripes to a maximum of 40 (in practice to 39 in case of a miscount; see Dt 25:3 and note), but no such limitation was recognized by the Romans, and victims of Roman floggings often did not survive (cf. Ac 22:24 and note). *crucified.* Tacitus (*Annals*, 15.44) indicates that "Christus … suffered the extreme penalty … at the hands of … Pontius Pilate." See note on v. 24.

15:16 *Praetorium.* The word was used originally of a general's tent, or of the headquarters in a military camp (see note on v. 1). *whole company.* The soldiers quartered in the Praetorium were recruited from non-Jewish inhabitants of the Holy Land and assigned to the military governor.

15:17 *purple robe.* Probably an old military cloak, whose color suggested royalty (see Ex 25:4; Mt 27:28; Ac 16:14 and notes). *crown of thorns.* Made from the branches of a thorny tree, of which there were many in the Holy Land. Both robe and crown were parts of the mock royal attire placed on Jesus.

15:18 *Hail, king of the Jews!* A mocking salutation that corresponded to "Hail, Caesar!"

15:19 *spit on him.* Probably a parody on the kiss of homage that was customary when greeting royalty (see note on 14:65).

15:20 *mocked him.* Cf. Ps 22:6 – 7; Isa 50:6 and note.

15:21 *Cyrene.* See Ac 6:9 and note. *Simon, the father of Alexander.* A first-century A.D. ossuary ("bone box"; see note on Mt 26:3) bearing the inscription "Alexander (son) of Simon" was found recently in Jerusalem. *Simon.* Probably a Jew who was in Jerusalem to celebrate the Passover. *Alexander and Rufus.* Only mentioned by Mark, but referred to in such a way as to suggest that they were known by those to whom he wrote (cf. Ro 16:13). *carry the cross.* Men condemned to death were usually forced to carry a beam of the cross, often weighing 30 or 40 pounds, to the place of crucifixion. Jesus started out by carrying his (see Jn 19:17 and note), but he had been so weakened by flogging that Simon was pressed into service.

15:22 *The Place of the Skull.* It may have been a small hill that looked like a skull, or it may have been so named because of the many executions that took place there.

15:23 *wine mixed with myrrh.* The Talmud gives evidence that incense was mixed with wine to deaden pain (cf. Pr 31:6). Myrrh is a spice derived from plants native to the Arabian deserts and parts of Africa (see note on Ge 37:25).

15:24 *crucified.* A Roman means of execution in which the prisoner was nailed to a cross (see note on Jn 19:17). Heavy, wrought-iron nails were driven through the wrists and the heel bones. If the victims lingered too long, death was hastened by breaking their legs (see Jn 19:31 and note). Archaeologists have discovered the bones of a crucified man, near Jerusalem, dating between A.D. 7 and 66, which shed light on the position of a person when nailed to a cross. Only slaves, the basest of criminals, and offenders who were not Roman citizens were executed in this manner. First-century authors vividly describe the agony and disgrace of being crucified (see note on v. 15; see also Php 2:8 and note). *Dividing up his clothes.* It was the accepted right of the executioner's squad to claim the minor possessions of the victim. Jesus' clothing probably consisted of an under and an outer garment, a belt, sandals and possibly a head covering (see note on Jn 19:18). *cast lots.* See Ps 22:18 and introduction to that psalm; see also Jn 19:23 – 24 and notes.

15:25 *third hour.* See Lk 23:44; Jn 19:14 and notes.

15:26 *charge against him.* It was customary to write the charge on a wooden board that was carried before the victim as he walked to the place of execution, and then the board was affixed to the cross above his head. *THE KING OF THE JEWS.* The wording of the charge differs slightly in the Gospels, but all agree that Jesus was crucified for claiming to be the king of the Jews. One possible reconstruction of the original is THIS IS JESUS OF NAZARETH, THE KING OF THE JEWS (cf. Mt 27:37; Lk 23:38; Jn 19:19).

27 They crucified two robbers with him,
one on his right and one on his left.[a]
29 Those who passed by hurled insults at
him, shaking their heads[u] and saying, "So!
You who are going to destroy the temple
and build it in three days,[v] 30 come down
from the cross and save yourself!"
31 In the same way the chief priests and
the teachers of the law mocked him[w]
among themselves. "He saved others,"
they said, "but he can't save himself! 32 Let
this Christ,[b][x] this King of Israel,[y] come
down now from the cross, that we may
see and believe." Those crucified with him
also heaped insults on him.

The Death of Jesus

15:33-41pp — Mt 27:45-56; Lk 23:44-49; Jn 19:29-30

33 At the sixth hour darkness came over
the whole land until the ninth hour.[z]
34 And at the ninth hour Jesus cried out in
a loud voice, *"Eloi, Eloi, lama sabachthani?"*—which means, "My God, my God,
why have you forsaken me?"[c][a]
35 When some of those standing near
heard this, they said, "Listen, he's calling
Elijah."
36 One man ran, filled a sponge with
wine vinegar,[b] put it on a stick, and offered it to Jesus to drink. "Now leave him
alone. Let's see if Elijah comes to take him
down," he said.
37 With a loud cry, Jesus breathed his
last.[c]
38 The curtain of the temple was torn in
two from top to bottom.[d] 39 And when
the centurion,[e] who stood there in front
of Jesus, heard his cry and[d] saw how he
died, he said, "Surely this man was the
Son[e] of God!"[f]
40 Some women were watching from a
distance.[g] Among them were Mary Magdalene, Mary the mother of James the younger
and of Joses, and Salome.[h] 41 In Galilee these
women had followed him and cared for his
needs. Many other women who had come
up with him to Jerusalem were also there.[i]

The Burial of Jesus

15:42-47pp — Mt 27:57-61; Lk 23:50-56; Jn 19:38-42

42 It was Preparation Day (that is, the
day before the Sabbath).[j] So as evening
approached, 43 Joseph of Arimathea, a
prominent member of the Council,[k] who
was himself waiting for the kingdom of
God,[l] went boldly to Pilate and asked for
Jesus' body. 44 Pilate was surprised to hear
that he was already dead. Summoning the
centurion, he asked him if Jesus had already died. 45 When he learned from the
centurion[m] that it was so, he gave the
body to Joseph. 46 So Joseph bought some
linen cloth, took down the body, wrapped
it in the linen, and placed it in a tomb cut
out of rock. Then he rolled a stone against

15:29 [u] Ps 22:7; 109:25 [v] S Jn 2:19
15:31 [w] Ps 22:7
15:32 [x] S Mk 14:61 [y] S ver 2
15:33 [z] Am 8:9
15:34 [a] Ps 22:1
15:36 [b] ver 23; Ps 69:21
15:37 [c] Jn 19:30
15:38 [d] Heb 10:19,20
15:39 [e] ver 45 [f] Mk 1:1,11; 9:7; S Mt 4:3
15:40 [g] Ps 38:11 [h] Mk 16:1; Lk 24:10; Jn 19:25
15:41 [i] Mt 27:55,56; Lk 8:2,3
15:42 [j] Mt 27:62; Jn 19:31
15:43 [k] S Mt 5:22 [l] S Mt 3:2; Lk 2:25,38
15:45 [m] ver 39

[a] 27 Some manuscripts *left,* [28] *and the scripture was fulfilled which says, "He was counted with the lawless ones"* (Isaiah 53:12) [b] 32 Or *Messiah* [c] 34 Psalm 22:1 [d] 39 Some manuscripts do not have *heard his cry and* [e] 39 Or *a son*

15:27 *two robbers.* According to Roman law, robbery was not a capital offense. Mark's term must signify men guilty of insurrection, who were crucified for high treason. If so, their crime was similar to that for which Jesus was crucified.
15:28 The earlier and more reliable Greek manuscripts do not have this verse (see NIV text note on v. 27). It was probably added from Lk 22:37 (quoting Isa 53:12). Mark does not include many OT quotations.
15:29 See 14:58 and note.
15:32 *Christ.* See NIV text note on Mt 1:17. *Those crucified with him.* One of the criminals later repented and asked to be included in Jesus' kingdom (Lk 23:39–43).
15:33 *sixth hour.* 12:00 noon. *ninth hour.* 3:00 P.M.
15:34 The words were spoken in a dialect of Aramaic, one of the languages commonly spoken in the Holy Land in Jesus' day. They reveal how deeply Jesus felt his abandonment by God as he bore "the sin of the world" (Jn 1:29; but see introduction to Ps 22 and note on Ps 22:1).
15:35 *Elijah.* The bystanders mistook the first words of Jesus' cry ("Eloi, Eloi") to be a cry for Elijah. It was commonly believed that Elijah would come in times of critical need to protect the innocent and rescue the righteous (v. 36).
15:36 *wine vinegar.* A sour wine, the drink of laborers and common soldiers (see note on Lk 23:36).
15:37 *With a loud cry.* See note on Jn 19:30. The strength of the cry indicates that Jesus did not die the ordinary death of those crucified, who normally suffered long periods of complete agony, exhaustion and then unconsciousness before dying (see note on v. 24).
15:38 *curtain of the temple.* The curtain that separated the Holy Place from the Most Holy Place (see Ex 26:31–35; 26:31 and notes). The tearing of the curtain indicated that Christ had entered heaven itself for us so that we too may now enter God's presence (see Heb 9:8–10,12; 10:19–20 and notes).
15:39 *centurion.* A commander of 100 men in the Roman army (see note on Ac 10:1). *saw how he died.* See note on v. 37. *Son of God.* See note on Mt 27:54.
15:40 *Mary Magdalene.* From Lk 8:2 we learn that Jesus had driven seven demons out of her. *Mary the mother of James the younger and of Joses.* See v. 47; 16:1. *Salome.* Probably the wife of Zebedee and the mother of James and John (see Mt 27:56).
15:41 *women had ... cared for his needs.* See notes on Mt 27:55; Lk 8:3.
15:42 *Preparation Day.* Friday. Since it was now late in the afternoon, there was an urgency to get Jesus' body down from the cross before sundown, when the Sabbath began.
15:43 *Joseph.* See note on Lk 23:50. *Arimathea.* See note on Mt 27:57. *Council.* The Sanhedrin (see note on 14:55). *kingdom of God.* See note on Mt 3:2. *Pilate.* See note on v. 1. *asked for Jesus' body.* See note on Lk 23:52.
15:44 *surprised.* Crucified men often lived two or three days before dying, and the early death of Jesus was therefore extraordinary.
15:45 *gave the body to Joseph.* The release of the body of one condemned for high treason, and especially to one who was not an immediate relative, was quite unusual.
15:46 *tomb cut out of rock.* Mt 27:60 states that the tomb belonged to Joseph and that it was new, i.e., it had not been used before. Its location was in a garden very near the site of the crucifixion (see Jn 19:41). There is archaeological

the entrance of the tomb.[n] 47Mary Magdalene and Mary the mother of Joses[o] saw
where he was laid.

The Resurrection

16:1-8pp — Mt 28:1-8; Lk 24:1-10

16 When the Sabbath was over, Mary
Magdalene, Mary the mother of
James, and Salome bought spices[p] so that
they might go to anoint Jesus' body. 2Very
early on the first day of the week, just after sunrise, they were on their way to the
tomb 3and they asked each other, "Who
will roll the stone away from the entrance
of the tomb?"[q]

4But when they looked up, they saw
that the stone, which was very large, had
been rolled away. 5As they entered the
tomb, they saw a young man dressed in a
white robe[r] sitting on the right side, and
they were alarmed.

6"Don't be alarmed," he said. "You are
looking for Jesus the Nazarene,[s] who was
crucified. He has risen! He is not here. See
the place where they laid him. 7But go,
tell his disciples and Peter, 'He is going
ahead of you into Galilee. There you will
see him,[t] just as he told you.' "[u]

8Trembling and bewildered, the women
went out and fled from the tomb. They
said nothing to anyone, because they
were afraid.

[The earliest manuscripts and some other ancient witnesses do not have Mark 16:9–20.]

9When Jesus rose early on the first
day of the week, he appeared first to
Mary Magdalene,[v] out of whom he
had driven seven demons. 10She went
and told those who had been with him
and who were mourning and weeping.
11When they heard that Jesus was alive
and that she had seen him, they did not
believe it.[w]

12Afterward Jesus appeared in a different form to two of them while they were
walking in the country.[x] 13These returned
and reported it to the rest; but they did
not believe them either.

14Later Jesus appeared to the Eleven
as they were eating; he rebuked them for
their lack of faith and their stubborn refusal to believe those who had seen him
after he had risen.[y]

15He said to them, "Go into all the
world and preach the good news to all
creation.[z] 16Whoever believes and is baptized will be saved, but whoever does not
believe will be condemned.[a] 17And these
signs[b] will accompany those who believe:
In my name they will drive out demons;[c]
they will speak in new tongues;[d] 18they
will pick up snakes[e] with their hands;
and when they drink deadly poison, it
will not hurt them at all; they will place
their hands on[f] sick people, and they will
get well."

19After the Lord Jesus had spoken to
them, he was taken up into heaven[g] and
he sat at the right hand of God.[h] 20Then
the disciples went out and preached everywhere, and the Lord worked with them
and confirmed his word by the signs[i] that
accompanied it.

15:46 [n] Mk 16:3
15:47 [o] ver 40
16:1 [p] Lk 23:56; Jn 19:39,40
16:3 [q] Mk 15:46
16:5 [r] S Jn 20:12
16:6 [s] S Mk 1:24
16:7 [t] Jn 21:1-23 [u] Mk 14:28
16:9 [v] Mk 15:47; Jn 20:11-18
16:11 [w] ver 13,14; Lk 24:11
16:12 [x] Lk 24:13-32
16:14 [y] Lk 24:36-43
16:15 [z] Mt 28:18-20; Lk 24:47,48; Ac 1:8
16:16 [a] Jn 3:16,18,36; Ac 16:31
16:17 [b] S Jn 4:48 [c] Mk 9:38; Lk 10:17; Ac 5:16; 8:7; 16:18; 19:13-16 [d] Ac 2:4; 10:46; 19:6; 1Co 12:10,28,30; 13:1; 14:2-39
16:18 [e] Lk 10:19; Ac 28:3-5 [f] S Ac 6:6
16:19 [g] Lk 24:50,51; Jn 6:62; Ac 1:9-11; 1Ti 3:16 [h] Ps 110:1; Mt 26:64; Ac 2:33; 5:31; Ro 8:34; Col 3:1; Heb 1:3; 12:2
16:20 [i] S Jn 4:48

---

evidence that the traditional site of the burial of Jesus (the Church of the Holy Sepulchre in Jerusalem) was a cemetery during the first century A.D. *stone.* A "large" (16:4), disc-shaped stone that rolled in a sloped channel.

16:1 *Sabbath was over.* About 6:00 P.M. Saturday evening. No purchases were possible on the Sabbath. *Mary Magdalene, Mary the mother of James, and Salome.* See note on 15:40. *spices.* Embalming was not practiced by the Jews. These spices were brought as an act of devotion and love (see note on Lk 23:56). *anoint Jesus' body.* The women had no expectation of Jesus' resurrection.

16:3 *Who will roll the stone away . . . ?* Setting the large stone in place was a relatively easy task, but once it had slipped into the groove cut in bedrock in front of the entrance it was very difficult to remove.

16:5 *As they entered the tomb.* Inside the large opening of the facade of the tomb was a forechamber, at the back of which a low rectangular opening led to the burial chamber. *young man dressed in a white robe.* Mt 28:2 identifies him as an angel. See Lk 24:4 and note.

16:6 *Nazarene.* See note on Mt 2:23. *crucified.* See note on 15:24. *He has risen!* The climax of Mark's Gospel is the resurrection, without which Jesus' death, though noble, would be indescribably tragic. But in the resurrection he "was declared with power to be the Son of God" (Ro 1:4).

16:7 *and Peter.* Jesus showed special concern for Peter, in view of his confident boasting and subsequent denials (14:29–31,66–72). *just as he told you.* See 14:28.

16:9–20 Serious doubt exists as to whether these verses belong to the Gospel of Mark. They are absent from important early manuscripts and display certain peculiarities of vocabulary, style and theological content that are unlike the rest of Mark. His Gospel probably ended at 16:8, or its original ending has been lost.

16:9 *Mary Magdalene.* See note on 15:40.

16:11,13 *did not believe.* See vv. 14,16; cf. Jn 20:24–29 and notes on 20:25,29.

16:12–13 A shortened account of the two men going to Emmaus (see Lk 24:13–35).

16:14 *the Eleven.* Judas Iscariot had committed suicide (see Mt 27:5 and note).

16:15–16 See the Great Commission in Mt 28:18–20 (see also note on Mt 28:19–20; cf. Lk 24:46–49; Jn 20:21–23; Ac 1:8.

16:16 *believes and is baptized.* See notes on 1:4; Ro 6:3–4.

16:18 *pick up snakes.* Cf. Paul in Ac 28:1–6. *drink deadly poison.* No other occurrence of drinking deadly poison without harm is found in the NT.

16:19 *taken up into heaven.* The ascension was witnessed by the apostles (see Lk 24:51; Ac 1:9; cf. 1Ti 3:16 and note). *right hand of God.* See 14:62; Ps 110:1 and note.

Luke

INTRODUCTION

Author

The author's name does not appear in the book, but much unmistakable evidence points to Luke. This Gospel is a companion volume to the book of Acts, and the language and structure of these two books indicate that both were written by the same person. They are addressed to the same individual, Theophilus, and the second volume refers to the first (Ac 1:1). Certain sections in Acts use the pronoun "we" (Ac 16:10 – 17; 20:5 – 15; 21:1 – 18; 27:1 — 28:16), indicating that the author was with Paul when the events described in these passages took place. By process of elimination, Paul's "dear friend Luke, the doctor" (Col 4:14) and "fellow worker" (Phm 24), becomes the most likely candidate. His authorship is supported by the uniform testimony of early Christian writings (e.g., the Muratorian Canon, A.D. 170, and the works of Irenaeus, c. 180).

Luke was probably a Gentile by birth, well educated in Greek culture, a physician by profession, a companion of Paul at various times from his second missionary journey to his final imprisonment in Rome, and a loyal friend who remained with the apostle after others had deserted him (2Ti 4:11).

Antioch (of Syria) and Philippi are among the places suggested as his hometown.

Recipient and Purpose

The Gospel is specifically directed to Theophilus (1:3), whose name means "one who loves God" and almost certainly refers to a particular person rather than to lovers of God in general. The use of "most excellent" with the name further indicates an individual and supports the idea that he was a Roman official or at least of high position and wealth. He was possibly Luke's patron, responsible for seeing that the writings were copied and distributed. Such a dedication to the publisher was common at that time.

Theophilus, however, was more than a publisher. The message of this Gospel was intended for his own instruction (1:4)

A Quick Look

Author:
Luke, a Gentile physician and missionary companion of Paul

Audience:
Addressed to Theophilus, but intended for all believers

Date:
Between the sixties and the eighties A.D.

Theme:
Luke presents Jesus as the Messiah and Lord whose life, death and resurrection make salvation available to all people everywhere.

as well as the instruction of those among whom the book would be circulated. The fact that the Gospel was initially directed to Theophilus does not narrow or limit its purpose. It was written to strengthen the faith of all believers and to answer the attacks of unbelievers. It was presented to displace some disconnected and ill-founded reports about Jesus (see 1:1–4 and note). Luke wanted to show that the place of the Gentile Christian in God's kingdom is based on the teaching of Jesus. He wanted to commend the preaching of the gospel to the whole world (24:47).

Luke's writing is characterized by literary excellence, historical detail, and warm, sensitive understanding of Jesus and those around him.

Date and Place of Writing

The two most commonly suggested periods for dating the Gospel of Luke are: (1) A.D. 59–63, and (2) the 70s or the 80s (see essay and chart, p. 1457).

The place of writing was possibly Rome, though Achaia, Ephesus and Caesarea have also been suggested. The place to which it was sent would, of course, depend on the residence of Theophilus. By its detailed designations of places in the Holy Land, the Gospel seems to be intended for readers who were unfamiliar with that land. Antioch, Achaia and Ephesus are possible destinations.

Style

Luke had an outstanding command of the Greek language. His vocabulary is extensive and rich, and his style at times approaches that of classical Greek (as in the preface, 1:1–4), while at other times it is quite Semitic (1:5—2:52)—often like the Septuagint (the pre-Christian Greek translation of the OT).

Characteristics

The third Gospel presents the works and teachings of Jesus that are especially important for understanding the way of salvation. Its scope is complete from the birth of Christ to his ascension, its arrangement is orderly, and it appeals to both Jews and Gentiles. Luke's writing is characterized by literary excellence, historical detail, and warm, sensitive understanding of Jesus and those around him.

Since the Synoptic Gospels (Matthew, Mark and Luke) report many of the same episodes in Jesus' life, one would expect much similarity in their accounts. The dissimilarities reveal the distinctive emphases of the separate writers. Luke's characteristic themes include: (1) universality, recognition of Gentiles as well as Jews in God's plan (see, e.g., 2:30–32 and notes on 2:31; 3:6); (2) emphasis on prayer, especially Jesus' praying before important occasions (see note on 3:21); (3) joy at the announcement of the gospel or "good news" (see note on 1:14); (4) special concern for the role of women (see, e.g., 8:1–3 and notes); (5) special interest in the poor (some of the rich were included among Jesus' followers, but he seemed closest to the poor; see note on 12:33); (6) concern for sinners (Jesus was a friend to those deep in sin); (7) stress on the family circle (Jesus' activity included men, women and children, with the setting frequently in the home); (8) repeated use of the Messianic title "Son of Man" (used 25 times; see 19:10; Da 7:13 and notes); (9) emphasis on the Holy Spirit (see note on 4:1); (10) inclusion of more parables than any other Gospel (see chart, p. 1598); (11) emphasis on praising God (see 1:64; 24:53 and notes).

Sources

Although Luke acknowledges that many others had written about Jesus' life (1:1), he does not indicate that he relied solely on these reports for his own writing. He used personal investigation and arrangement, based on testimony from "eyewitnesses and servants of the word" (1:2)—including the preaching and oral accounts of the apostles. His language differences from the other Synoptics and his blocks of distinctive material (e.g., 10:1—18:14; 19:1–28) indicate independent work, though he obviously used some of the same sources (see essay, p. 1457).

Plan

Luke's account of Jesus' ministry can be divided into three major parts: (1) the events that occurred in and around Galilee (4:14—9:50), (2) those that took place in Judea and Perea (9:51—19:27), and (3) those of the final week in Jerusalem (19:28—24:53). Luke's uniqueness is especially seen in the amount of material devoted to Jesus' closing ministry in Judea and Perea. This material is predominantly made up of accounts of Jesus' discourses. Twenty-one of the 28 parables that occur in Luke are found in 10:30—19:27. Of the 20 miracles recorded in Luke, only 5 appear in 9:51—19:27. Already in the ninth chapter (see note on 9:51), Jesus is seen anticipating his final appearance in Jerusalem and his crucifixion (see note on 13:22).

The main theme of the Gospel is the nature of Jesus' Messiahship and mission, and a key verse is 19:10.

Outline

- I. The Preface (1:1–4)
- II. The Births of John the Baptist and Jesus (1:5—2:52)
  - A. The Annunciations (1:5–56)
  - B. The Birth of John the Baptist (1:57–80)
  - C. The Birth and Childhood of Jesus (ch. 2)
- III. The Preparation of Jesus for His Public Ministry (3:1—4:13)
  - A. His Forerunner (3:1–20)
  - B. His Baptism (3:21–22)
  - C. His Genealogy (3:23–38)
  - D. His Temptation (4:1–13)
- IV. His Ministry in Galilee (4:14—9:9)
  - A. The Beginning of the Ministry in Galilee (4:14–41)
  - B. The First Tour of Galilee (4:42—5:39)
  - C. A Sabbath Controversy (6:1–11)
  - D. The Choice of the 12 Apostles (6:12–16)
  - E. The Sermon on the Plain (6:17–49)
  - F. Miracles in Capernaum and Nain (7:1–18)
  - G. The Inquiry of John the Baptist (7:19–29)
  - H. Jesus and the Pharisees (7:30–50)
  - I. The Second Tour of Galilee (8:1–3)
  - J. The Parables of the Kingdom (8:4–21)
  - K. The Trip across the Sea of Galilee (8:22–39)
  - L. The Third Tour of Galilee (8:40—9:9)
- V. His Withdrawal to Regions around Galilee (9:10–50)
  - A. To the Eastern Shore of the Sea of Galilee (9:10–17)
  - B. To Caesarea Philippi (9:18–50)
- VI. His Ministry in Judea (9:51—13:21)
  - A. Journey through Samaria to Judea (9:51–62)
  - B. The Mission of the 72 (10:1–24)
  - C. The Lawyer and the Parable of the Good Samaritan (10:25–37)
  - D. Jesus at Bethany with Mary and Martha (10:38–42)
  - E. Teachings in Judea (11:1—13:21)
- VII. His Ministry in and around Perea (13:22—19:27)
  - A. The Narrow Door (13:22–30)
  - B. Warning concerning Herod (13:31–35)
  - C. At a Pharisee's House (14:1–23)
  - D. The Cost of Discipleship (14:24–35)
  - E. The Parables of the Lost Sheep, the Lost Coin and the Lost Son (ch. 15)
  - F. The Parable of the Shrewd Manager (16:1–18)

G. The Rich Man and Lazarus (16:19–31)
H. Miscellaneous Teachings (17:1–10)
I. Ten Healed of Leprosy (17:11–19)
J. The Coming of the Kingdom (17:20–37)
K. The Persistent Widow (18:1–8)
L. The Pharisee and the Tax Collector (18:9–14)
M. Jesus and the Children (18:15–17)
N. The Rich Young Ruler (18:18–30)
O. Christ Foretells His Death (18:31–34)
P. A Blind Beggar Given His Sight (18:35–43)
Q. Jesus and Zacchaeus (19:1–10)
R. The Parable of the Ten Minas (19:11–27)

VIII. His Last Days: Sacrifice and Triumph (19:28—24:53)
A. The Triumphal Entry (19:28–44)
B. The Clearing of the Temple (19:45–48)
C. The Last Controversies with the Jewish Leaders (ch. 20)
D. The Olivet Discourse (ch. 21)
E. The Last Supper (22:1–38)
F. Jesus Praying in Gethsemane (22:39–46)
G. Jesus' Arrest (22:47–65)
H. Jesus on Trial (22:66—23:25)
I. The Crucifixion (23:26–56)
J. The Resurrection (24:1–12)
K. The Post-Resurrection Ministry (24:13–49)
L. The Ascension (24:50–53)

Introduction

1:1-4Ref — Ac 1:1

1 Many have undertaken to draw up an
account of the things that have been
fulfilled[a] among us, 2just as they were
handed down to us by those who from the
first[a] were eyewitnesses[b] and servants of
the word.[c] 3Therefore, since I myself have
carefully investigated everything from the
beginning, it seemed good also to me to
write an orderly account[d] for you, most
excellent[e] Theophilus,[f] 4so that you may
know the certainty of the things you have
been taught.[g]

The Birth of John the Baptist Foretold

5In the time of Herod king of Judea[h]
there was a priest named Zechariah, who
belonged to the priestly division of Abijah;[i]
his wife Elizabeth was also a descendant
of Aaron. 6Both of them were upright in
the sight of God, observing all the Lord's
commandments and regulations blamelessly.[j] 7But they had no children, because
Elizabeth was barren; and they were both
well along in years.
8Once when Zechariah's division was on
duty and he was serving as priest before
God,[k] 9he was chosen by lot,[l] according to
the custom of the priesthood, to go into
the temple of the Lord and burn incense.[m]
10And when the time for the burning of incense came, all the assembled worshipers
were praying outside.[n]
11Then an angel[o] of the Lord appeared
to him, standing at the right side of the
altar of incense.[p] 12When Zechariah saw
him, he was startled and was gripped with
fear.[q] 13But the angel said to him: "Do not
be afraid,[r] Zechariah; your prayer has been
heard. Your wife Elizabeth will bear you a
son, and you are to give him the name
John.[s] 14He will be a joy and delight to
you, and many will rejoice because of his
birth,[t] 15for he will be great in the sight of
the Lord. He is never to take wine or other
fermented drink,[u] and he will be filled with
the Holy Spirit[v] even from birth.[b][w] 16Many
of the people of Israel will he bring back
to the Lord their God. 17And he will go on
before the Lord,[x] in the spirit and power of
Elijah,[y] to turn the hearts of the fathers to
their children[z] and the disobedient to the
wisdom of the righteous — to make ready
a people prepared for the Lord."[a]

1:2 [a] Mk 1:1; Jn 15:27; Ac 1:21,22 [b] Heb 2:3; 1Pe 5:1; 2Pe 1:16; 1Jn 1:1 [c] S Mk 4:14 **1:3** [d] Ac 11:4 [e] Ac 24:3; 26:25 [f] Ac 1:1 **1:4** [g] Jn 20:31; Ac 2:42 **1:5** [h] Mt 2:1 [i] 1Ch 24:10 **1:6** [j] Ge 6:9; Dt 5:33; 1Ki 9:4; Lk 2:25 **1:8** [k] 1Ch 24:19; 2Ch 8:14 **1:9** [l] Ac 1:26 [m] Ex 30:7,8; 1Ch 23:13; 2Ch 29:11; Ps 141:2 **1:10** [n] Lev 16:17 **1:11** [o] S Ac 5:19 [p] Ex 30:1-10 **1:12** [q] Jdg 6:22,23; 13:22 **1:13** [r] ver 30; S Mt 14:27 [s] ver 60,63; S Mt 3:1 **1:14** [t] ver 58 **1:15** [u] Nu 6:3; Lev 10:9; Jdg 13:4; Lk 7:33 [v] ver 41,67; Ac 2:4; 4:8,31; 6:3,5; 9:17; 11:24; Eph 5:18; S Ac 10:44 [w] Jer 1:5; Gal 1:15 **1:17** [x] ver 76 [y] S Mt 11:14 [z] Mal 4:5,6 [a] S Mt 3:3

[a] 1 Or *been surely believed* [b] 15 Or *from his mother's womb*

1:1 – 4 Using language similar to classical Greek, Luke begins with a formal preface, common to historical works of that time, in which he states his purpose for writing and identifies the recipient. He acknowledges other reports on the subject, shows the need for this new work and states his method of approach and sources of information.

1:1 *things ... fulfilled among us.* Things prophesied in the OT and now fully accomplished.

1:2 *handed down.* A technical term for passing on information as authoritative tradition (see 1Co 15:3 and note). *eyewitnesses and servants of the word.* Luke, though not an eyewitness himself, received testimony from those who were eyewitnesses and were dedicated to spreading the gospel. Apostolic preaching and interviews with other individuals associated with Jesus' ministry were available to him.

1:3 *carefully investigated.* Luke's account was exact in historical detail, having been checked in every way. Inspiration by the Holy Spirit did not rule out human effort. The account is complete, extending back to the very beginning of Jesus' earthly life. It has an orderly, meaningful arrangement that is generally chronological. *most excellent.* Paul used this respectful term for governors Felix (Ac 24:3) and Festus (Ac 26:25). *Theophilus.* See Introduction: Recipient and Purpose.

1:4 *so that you may know.* Cf. John's purpose for writing (Jn 20:31; see note there).

1:5 *Herod king of Judea.* Herod the Great reigned 37 – 4 B.C. (see note on Mt 2:15), and his kingdom also included Samaria, Galilee, Perea and Traconitis (see chart, p. 1465; see also note on Mt 2:1). The "time" referred to here is probably c. 7 – 6 B.C. *Zechariah ... Elizabeth.* Both were of priestly descent from the line of Aaron. *priestly division of Abijah.* From the time of David the priests were organized into 24 divisions, and Abijah was one of the "heads of the priestly families" (Ne 12:12,17; see 1Ch 24:10 and note).

1:6 *upright ... blamelessly.* They were not sinless, but were faithful and sincere in keeping God's commandments. Simeon (2:25) and Joseph (Mt 1:19) are given similar praise.

1:7 *no children.* See note on v. 25.

1:9 It was one of the priest's duties to keep the incense burning on the altar in front of the Most Holy Place. He supplied it with fresh incense before the morning sacrifice and again after the evening sacrifice (Ex 30:6 – 8). Ordinarily a priest would have this privilege very infrequently, and sometimes never, since duty assignments were determined by lot. *chosen by lot.* See notes on Ne 11:1; Pr 16:33; Jnh 1:7; Ac 1:26.

1:11 *angel of the Lord.* See v. 19; see also Ge 16:7 and note.

1:12 *fear.* A common reaction, as with Gideon (Jdg 6:22 – 23) and Manoah (Jdg 13:22).

1:13 *Do not be afraid.* This word of reassurance is given many times in both OT and NT (see, e.g., v. 30; 2:10 and note; 5:10; 8:50; 12:7,32; Ge 15:1; 21:17; 26:24; Dt 1:21 and note; Jos 1:9; 8:1 and note). *John.* The name (derived from Hebrew) means "The LORD is gracious."

1:14 *joy.* A keynote of these opening chapters (vv. 44,47,58; 2:10).

1:15 *wine or other fermented drink.* It appears likely that John was to be subject to the Nazirite vow of abstinence from alcoholic drinks (see Nu 6:2 – 12 and notes). If so, he was a lifelong Nazirite, as were Samson (Jdg 13:4 – 7) and Samuel (1Sa 1:11). *filled with the Holy Spirit.* Consistent with his emphasis in his Gospel and in Acts (see note on 4:1), Luke's birth narratives stress the activity of the Holy Spirit (see vv. 35,41,67; 2:25 – 27). *from birth.* In the OT the Holy Spirit came upon individuals temporarily for some special task (see, e.g., Jdg 3:10 and note), but John was to be filled with the Spirit his entire life.

1:17 *in the spirit and power of Elijah.* John was not Elijah returning in the flesh (see Jn 1:21 and note), but he functioned like that OT preacher of repentance and was therefore a fulfillment of Mal 4:5 – 6 (see notes on Mal 4:5; Mt 11:14; 17:10).

18 Zechariah asked the angel, "How can
I be sure of this?[b] I am an old man and my
wife is well along in years."[c]
19 The angel answered, "I am Gabriel.[d] I
stand in the presence of God, and I have
been sent to speak to you and to tell you
this good news. 20 And now you will be silent and not able to speak[e] until the day
this happens, because you did not believe
my words, which will come true at their
proper time."
21 Meanwhile, the people were waiting for Zechariah and wondering why he
stayed so long in the temple. 22 When he
came out, he could not speak to them.
They realized he had seen a vision in the
temple, for he kept making signs[f] to them
but remained unable to speak.
23 When his time of service was completed, he returned home. 24 After this his
wife Elizabeth became pregnant and for
five months remained in seclusion. 25 "The
Lord has done this for me," she said. "In
these days he has shown his favor and
taken away my disgrace[g] among the people."

The Birth of Jesus Foretold

26 In the sixth month, God sent the angel
Gabriel[h] to Nazareth,[i] a town in Galilee,
27 to a virgin pledged to be married to a
man named Joseph,[j] a descendant of David. The virgin's name was Mary. 28 The
angel went to her and said, "Greetings,
you who are highly favored! The Lord is
with you."

29 Mary was greatly troubled at his words
and wondered what kind of greeting this
might be. 30 But the angel said to her, "Do
not be afraid,[k] Mary, you have found favor with God.[l] 31 You will be with child and
give birth to a son, and you are to give him
the name Jesus.[m] 32 He will be great and
will be called the Son of the Most High.[n]
The Lord God will give him the throne of
his father David,[o] 33 and he will reign over
the house of Jacob forever; his kingdom[p]
will never end."[q]
34 "How will this be," Mary asked the angel, "since I am a virgin?"
35 The angel answered, "The Holy Spirit
will come upon you,[r] and the power of the
Most High[s] will overshadow you. So the
holy one[t] to be born will be called[a] the
Son of God.[u] 36 Even Elizabeth your relative is going to have a child[v] in her old
age, and she who was said to be barren is
in her sixth month. 37 For nothing is impossible with God."[w]
38 "I am the Lord's servant," Mary answered. "May it be to me as you have
said." Then the angel left her.

Mary Visits Elizabeth

39 At that time Mary got ready and hurried to a town in the hill country of Judea,[x]
40 where she entered Zechariah's home
and greeted Elizabeth. 41 When Elizabeth
heard Mary's greeting, the baby leaped in
her womb, and Elizabeth was filled with
the Holy Spirit.[y] 42 In a loud voice she ex-

1:18 [b] Ge 15:8 [c] ver 34; Ge 17:17 **1:19** [d] ver 26; Da 8:16; 9:21 **1:20** [e] Ex 4:11; Eze 3:26 **1:22** [f] ver 62 **1:25** [g] Ge 30:23; Isa 4:1 **1:26** [h] S ver 19 [i] S Mt 2:23 **1:27** [j] Mt 1:16,18,20; Lk 2:4 **1:30** [k] ver 13; S Mt 14:27 [l] Ge 6:8 **1:31** [m] Isa 7:14; Mt 1:21,25; Lk 2:21 **1:32** [n] ver 35,76; S Mk 5:7 [o] S Mt 1:1 **1:33** [p] Mt 28:18 [q] 2Sa 7:16; Ps 89:3,4; Isa 9:7; Jer 33:17; Da 2:44; 7:14,27; Mic 4:7; Heb 1:8 **1:35** [r] Mt 1:18 [s] ver 32,76; S Mk 5:7 [t] S Mk 1:24 [u] S Mt 4:3 **1:36** [v] ver 24 **1:37** [w] S Mt 19:26 **1:39** [x] ver 65 **1:41** [y] S ver 15

[a] 35 Or *So the child to be born will be called holy,*

to turn the hearts of the fathers to their children. See Mal 4:6 and note. *people prepared for the Lord.* John helped fulfill Isaiah's prophecy (see Isa 40:3–5 and notes), as Luke shows in 3:4–6.

1:18 *How can I be sure ...?* Like Abraham (see Ge 15:8 and note), Gideon (see Jdg 6:17 and note) and Hezekiah (2Ki 20:8), Zechariah asked for a sign (cf. 1Co 1:22).

1:19 *Gabriel.* The name can mean "God is my hero" or "mighty man of God." Only two angels are identified by name in Scripture: Gabriel (Da 8:16; 9:21) and Michael (see Da 10:13 and note, 21; Jude 9; Rev 12:7 and note).

1:21 *the people were waiting for Zechariah.* To come out of the Holy Place and pronounce the Aaronic blessing (see Nu 6:24–26 and notes).

1:23 *his time of service.* Each priest was responsible for a week's service at the temple once every six months. *home.* See v. 39.

1:24 *remained in seclusion.* In joy, devotion and gratitude that the Lord had taken away her childlessness.

1:25 *The Lord ... has shown his favor and taken away my disgrace.* Not only did lack of children deprive the parents of personal happiness, but it was generally considered to indicate divine disfavor and often brought social reproach (see Ge 16:2, Sarai; 25:21, Rebekah; 30:23, Rachel; 1Sa 1:1–18, Hannah; see also Lev 20:20–21; Ps 128:3; Jer 22:30).

1:26–35 This section speaks clearly of the virginal conception of Jesus (vv. 27,34–35; see Mt 1:18–25 and notes). The conception was the work of the Holy Spirit; the eternal Second Person of the Trinity, while remaining God, also "became flesh" (Jn 1:14; see note there). From conception he was fully divine and fully human.

1:26 *In the sixth month.* That is, from the time of John's conception. *Nazareth.* See note on Mt 2:23.

1:27 *pledged to be married.* See note on Mt 1:18.

1:28 *Greetings. Ave* in the Latin Vulgate version of the Bible (from which comes "Ave Maria").

1:31 *Jesus.* See NIV text note on Mt 1:21 for the meaning of this name.

1:32 *the Son of the Most High.* This title has two senses: (1) the divine Son of God and (2) the Messiah born in time. His Messiahship is clearly referred to in the following context (vv. 32b–33). *Most High.* A title frequently used of God in both the OT and NT (see vv. 35,76; 6:35; 8:28; Ge 14:19 and note; 2Sa 22:14; Ps 7:10,17). *throne.* Promised in the OT to the Messiah descended from David (see 2Sa 7:13,16; Ps 2:6–7; 89:25–27; Isa 9:6–7 and notes). *his father David.* Mary was a descendant of David, as was Joseph (see Mt 1:16 and note); so Jesus could rightly be called a "son" of David (Mt 1:1).

1:33 *forever.* See Ps 45:6 and note; Rev 11:15. *his kingdom will never end.* Although Christ's role as mediator will one day be finished (see 1Co 15:24–28 and notes), the kingdom of the Father and Son, as one, will never end.

1:34 *How will this be ...?* Mary did not ask in disbelief, as Zechariah did (v. 20). See v. 45.

1:35 *holy one.* Jesus never sinned (see 2Co 5:21; Heb 4:15; 7:26 and notes; see also 1Pe 2:22; 1Jn 3:5).

1:36 *Elizabeth your relative.* It is not known whether she was a cousin, aunt or other relation.

claimed: "Blessed are you among wom-
en,[z] and blessed is the child you will bear!
43But why am I so favored, that the mother
of my Lord[a] should come to me? 44As soon
as the sound of your greeting reached my
ears, the baby in my womb leaped for joy.
45Blessed is she who has believed that
what the Lord has said to her will be accomplished!"

Mary's Song

1:46-53pp — 1Sa 2:1-10

46And Mary said:

"My soul glorifies the Lord[b]
47 and my spirit rejoices in God my
 Savior,[c]
48for he has been mindful
 of the humble state of his servant.[d]
From now on all generations will call
 me blessed,[e]
49 for the Mighty One has done great
 things[f] for me—
 holy is his name.[g]
50His mercy extends to those who fear
 him,
 from generation to generation.[h]
51He has performed mighty deeds with
 his arm;[i]
 he has scattered those who are
 proud in their inmost thoughts.[j]
52He has brought down rulers from their
 thrones
 but has lifted up the humble.[k]
53He has filled the hungry with good
 things[l]
 but has sent the rich away empty.
54He has helped his servant Israel,
 remembering to be merciful[m]
55to Abraham and his descendants[n]
 forever,
 even as he said to our fathers."

56Mary stayed with Elizabeth for about
three months and then returned home.

The Birth of John the Baptist

57When it was time for Elizabeth to have
her baby, she gave birth to a son. 58Her
neighbors and relatives heard that the
Lord had shown her great mercy, and they
shared her joy.
59On the eighth day they came to circumcise[o] the child, and they were going to
name him after his father Zechariah, 60but
his mother spoke up and said, "No! He is
to be called John."[p]
61They said to her, "There is no one
among your relatives who has that name."
62Then they made signs[q] to his father, to
find out what he would like to name the
child. 63He asked for a writing tablet, and
to everyone's astonishment he wrote, "His
name is John."[r] 64Immediately his mouth
was opened and his tongue was loosed,
and he began to speak,[s] praising God.
65The neighbors were all filled with awe,
and throughout the hill country of Judea[t]
people were talking about all these things.
66Everyone who heard this wondered about
it, asking, "What then is this child going to
be?" For the Lord's hand was with him.[u]

Zechariah's Song

67His father Zechariah was filled with
the Holy Spirit[v] and prophesied:[w]

68"Praise be to the Lord, the God of
 Israel,[x]
 because he has come and has
 redeemed his people.[y]
69He has raised up a horn[a][z] of salvation
 for us
 in the house of his servant David[a]

[a] *69 Horn* here symbolizes strength.

1:42 [z] Jdg 5:24 **1:43** [a] S Jn 13:13 **1:46** [b] Ps 34:2,3 **1:47** [c] Ps 18:46; Isa 17:10; 61:10; Hab 3:18; 1Ti 1:1; 2:3; 4:10 **1:48** [d] ver 38; Ps 138:6 [e] Lk 11:27 **1:49** [f] Ps 71:19 [g] Ps 111:9 **1:50** [h] Ex 20:6; Ps 103:17 **1:51** [i] Ps 98:1; Isa 40:10 [j] Ge 11:8; Ex 18:11; 2Sa 22:28; Jer 13:9; 49:16 **1:52** [k] S Mt 23:12 **1:53** [l] Ps 107:9 **1:54** [m] Ps 98:3 **1:55** [n] S Gal 3:16 **1:59** [o] Ge 17:12; Lev 12:3; Lk 2:21; Php 3:5 **1:60** [p] ver 13,63; S Mt 3:1 **1:62** [q] ver 22 **1:63** [r] ver 13,60; S Mt 3:1 **1:64** [s] ver 20; Eze 24:27 **1:65** [t] ver 39 **1:66** [u] Ge 39:2; Ac 11:21 **1:67** [v] S ver 15 [w] Joel 2:28 **1:68** [x] Ge 24:27; 1Ki 8:15; Ps 72:18 [y] Ps 111:9; Lk 7:16 **1:69** [z] 1Sa 2:1,10; 2Sa 22:3; Ps 18:2; 89:17; 132:17; Eze 29:21 [a] S Mt 1:1

1:44 *for joy.* In some mysterious way the Holy Spirit produced this remarkable response in the unborn baby.

1:46–55 One of four hymns preserved in Lk 1–2 (see vv. 68–79; 2:14; 2:29–32 and notes). This hymn of praise is known as the Magnificat because in the Latin Vulgate the opening word is *Magnificat,* which means "glorifies." This song is like a psalm, and should also be compared with the song of Hannah (1Sa 2:1–10; see note on 1Sa 2:1).

1:50 *those who fear him.* Those who revere God and live in harmony with his will (see notes on Ge 20:11; Pr 1:7).

1:51 *his arm.* A metaphor for God's powerful acts. God does not have a body; he is spirit (see Jn 4:24 and note).

1:53 *hungry.* Both physically and spiritually (Mt 5:6; Jn 6:35). The coming of God's kingdom will bring changes affecting every area of life.

1:54 *remembering to be merciful.* The song ends with an assurance that God will be true to his promises to his people (see Ge 22:16–18 and notes).

1:56 *three months.* Mary evidently remained with Elizabeth until John's birth and then returned to her home in Nazareth (see v. 36).

1:57–66 The birth of John the Baptist marks the fulfillment of the prophecy in vv. 5–25.

1:59 *name him after his father.* An accepted practice in that day, as seen in Josephus (*Life,* 1).

1:62 *they made signs to his father.* Apparently assuming that since he was mute he was also deaf.

1:63 *a writing tablet.* Probably a small wooden board covered with wax.

1:64 *praising God.* A common theme in Luke (2:13,20,28; 5:25–26; 7:16; 13:13; 17:15,18; 18:43; 19:37; 23:47; 24:53).

1:67 *filled with the Holy Spirit . . . prophesied.* Prophecy not only predicts but also proclaims God's word. Both Zechariah and Elizabeth (vv. 41–45) were enabled by the Holy Spirit to express what otherwise they could not have formulated.

1:68–79 This hymn is called the Benedictus ("Praise be") because the opening word in the Latin Vulgate translation is *Benedictus.* Whereas the Magnificat (see note on 1:46–55) is similar to a psalm, the Benedictus is more like a prophecy.

1:68 *redeemed his people.* Not limited to national security (v. 71), but including moral and spiritual salvation (vv. 75,77).

1:69 *horn.* Indicates strength (see NIV text note), as in the horn of an animal (Dt 33:17; Ps 22:21; Mic 4:13). Jesus, the Messiah from the house of David, has the power to save.

70 (as he said through his holy prophets
of long ago),[b]
71 salvation from our enemies
and from the hand of all who hate
us—
72 to show mercy to our fathers[c]
and to remember his holy
covenant,[d]
73 the oath he swore to our father
Abraham:[e]
74 to rescue us from the hand of our
enemies,
and to enable us to serve him[f]
without fear[g]
75 in holiness and righteousness[h]
before him all our days.

76 And you, my child, will be called a
prophet[i] of the Most High;[j]
for you will go on before the Lord to
prepare the way for him,[k]
77 to give his people the knowledge of
salvation
through the forgiveness of their
sins,[l]
78 because of the tender mercy of our
God,
by which the rising sun[m] will come
to us from heaven
79 to shine on those living in darkness
and in the shadow of death,[n]
to guide our feet into the path of
peace."[o]

80 And the child grew and became strong
in spirit;[p] and he lived in the desert until
he appeared publicly to Israel.

The Birth of Jesus

2 In those days Caesar Augustus[q] issued
a decree that a census should be taken
of the entire Roman world.[r] 2 (This was the
first census that took place while Quirinius was governor of Syria.)[s] 3 And everyone
went to his own town to register.

4 So Joseph also went up from the town
of Nazareth in Galilee to Judea, to Bethlehem[t] the town of David, because he belonged to the house and line of David. 5 He
went there to register with Mary, who was
pledged to be married to him[u] and was
expecting a child. 6 While they were there,
the time came for the baby to be born,
7 and she gave birth to her firstborn, a son.
She wrapped him in cloths and placed him
in a manger, because there was no room
for them in the inn.

The Shepherds and the Angels

8 And there were shepherds living out in
the fields nearby, keeping watch over their
flocks at night. 9 An angel[v] of the Lord appeared to them, and the glory of the Lord
shone around them, and they were terrified. 10 But the angel said to them, "Do
not be afraid.[w] I bring you good news of
great joy that will be for all the people.

1:70 [b] Jer 23:5; Ac 3:21; Ro 1:2 **1:72** [c] Mic 7:20 [d] Ps 105:8,9; 106:45; Eze 16:60 **1:73** [e] Ge 22:16-18 **1:74** [f] Heb 9:14 [g] 1Jn 4:18 **1:75** [h] Eph 4:24 **1:76** [i] S Mt 11:9 [j] ver 32,35; S Mk 5:7 [k] ver 17; S Mt 3:3 **1:77** [l] Jer 31:34; Mt 1:21; Mk 1:4 **1:78** [m] Mal 4:2 **1:79** [n] Ps 107:14; Isa 9:2; 59:9; Mt 4:16; S Ac 26:18 [o] S Lk 2:14 **1:80** [p] Lk 2:40,52 **2:1** [q] Mt 22:17; Lk 3:1 [r] S Mt 24:14 **2:2** [s] Mt 4:24; Ac 15:23,41; 21:3; Gal 1:21 **2:4** [t] S Jn 7:42 **2:5** [u] Lk 1:27 **2:9** [v] S Ac 5:19 **2:10** [w] S Mt 14:27

1:74 *to rescue us.* No doubt including liberation from all kinds of oppression and bondage as well as deliverance from sin.

1:76 *called a prophet of the Most High.* But Jesus will be called "the Son of the Most High" (see v. 32 and note). *prepare the way.* See note on 3:4.

1:78 *the rising sun.* A reference to the coming of the Messiah (see also similar figures in Nu 24:17; Isa 9:2; 60:1; Mal 4:2 and notes). Zechariah not only praised his own son, the "prophet of the Most High" (vv. 76–77), but also gave honor to the coming Messiah (vv. 78–79).

1:79 *those living in darkness.* The lost, separated from God (see Isa 9:1–2; Mt 4:15–16 and notes). *peace.* See note on 2:14.

1:80 *lived in the desert.* John's parents, old at his birth, probably died while he was young, and he apparently grew up in the Desert of Judea, which lies between Jerusalem and the Dead Sea. *until he appeared publicly.* John's preaching and announcing the coming of the Messiah marked his public appearance. He was about 30 years old when he began his ministry (see note on 3:23).

2:1–7 Jesus' birth marks the fulfillment of the prophecy in 1:26–38.

2:1 Luke is the only Gospel writer who relates his narrative to dates of world history. *Caesar Augustus.* The first and (according to many) greatest Roman emperor (31 B.C.–A.D. 14). Having replaced the republic with an imperial form of government, he expanded the empire to include the entire Mediterranean world, established the famed *Pax Romana* ("Roman Peace") and ushered in the golden age of Roman literature and architecture. Augustus (which means "exalted") was a title voted to him by the Roman senate in 27 B.C. *census.* Used for military service and taxation. Jews, however, were exempt from Roman military service. God used the decree of a pagan emperor to fulfill the prophecy of Mic 5:2 (see note there; see also Mt 2:3–6). *Roman world.* See map No. 14 at the end of this study Bible.

2:2 *Quirinius.* This official was possibly in office for two terms, first 6–4 B.C. and then A.D. 6–9. A census is associated with each term. This is the first; Ac 5:37 refers to the second.

2:3 *own town.* Probably the town of their ancestral origin.

2:4 *Nazareth … Bethlehem.* Bethlehem, the town where David was born (1Sa 17:12; 20:6), was at least a three-day trip from Nazareth. *Judea.* The Roman designation for the southern part of the Holy Land, earlier included in the kingdom of Judah.

2:5 *with Mary.* Mary too was of the house of David and probably was required to enroll. In Syria, the Roman province in which the Holy Land was located, women 12 years of age and older were required to pay a poll tax and therefore to register. *pledged to be married.* See Mt 1:18 and note.

2:7 *cloths.* Strips of cloth were regularly used to wrap a newborn infant. *manger.* The feeding trough of the animals. This is the only indication that Christ was born in a stable. Very early tradition suggests that it was a cave, perhaps used as a stable.

2:8 *living out in the fields.* Does not necessarily mean it was summer, the dry season. The flocks reserved for temple sacrifice were kept in the fields near Bethlehem throughout the year. *keeping watch.* Against thieves and predatory animals.

2:9 *An angel of the Lord.* A designation used throughout the birth narratives (see 1:11 and note; Mt 1:20,24; 2:13,19). The angel in 1:11 is identified as Gabriel (1:19; see 1:26). Cf. Ge 16:7 and note.

2:10 *Do not be afraid.* Fear was the common reaction to angelic appearances (see note on 1:13), and encouragement was needed. *joy.* See note on 1:14.

11 Today in the town of David a Savior[x] has
been born to you; he is Christ[a][y] the Lord.[z]
12 This will be a sign[a] to you: You will find
a baby wrapped in cloths and lying in a
manger."
13 Suddenly a great company of the heavenly host appeared with the angel, praising God and saying,

14 "Glory to God in the highest,
and on earth peace[b] to men on
whom his favor rests."

15 When the angels had left them and
gone into heaven, the shepherds said to
one another, "Let's go to Bethlehem and
see this thing that has happened, which
the Lord has told us about."
16 So they hurried off and found Mary
and Joseph, and the baby, who was lying
in the manger.[c] 17 When they had seen him,
they spread the word concerning what had
been told them about this child, 18 and all
who heard it were amazed at what the
shepherds said to them. 19 But Mary treasured up all these things and pondered
them in her heart.[d] 20 The shepherds returned, glorifying and praising God[e] for all
the things they had heard and seen, which
were just as they had been told.

Jesus Presented in the Temple

21 On the eighth day, when it was time to
circumcise him,[f] he was named Jesus, the
name the angel had given him before he
had been conceived.[g]
22 When the time of their purification according to the Law of Moses[h] had been
completed, Joseph and Mary took him to
Jerusalem to present him to the Lord 23 (as
it is written in the Law of the Lord, "Every firstborn male is to be consecrated to
the Lord"[b]),[i] 24 and to offer a sacrifice in
keeping with what is said in the Law of
the Lord: "a pair of doves or two young
pigeons."[c][j]
25 Now there was a man in Jerusalem
called Simeon, who was righteous and devout.[k] He was waiting for the consolation
of Israel,[l] and the Holy Spirit was upon
him. 26 It had been revealed to him by the
Holy Spirit that he would not die before
he had seen the Lord's Christ. 27 Moved by
the Spirit, he went into the temple courts.
When the parents brought in the child
Jesus to do for him what the custom of
the Law required,[m] 28 Simeon took him in
his arms and praised God, saying:

29 "Sovereign Lord, as you have
promised,[n]
you now dismiss[d] your servant in
peace.[o]
30 For my eyes have seen your salvation,[p]
31 which you have prepared in the
sight of all people,
32 a light for revelation to the Gentiles
and for glory to your people
Israel."[q]

2:11 [x] S Mt 1:21; S Jn 3:17; 4:42; Ac 5:31; 13:23; S Ro 11:14; 1Ti 4:10; 1Jn 4:14 [y] Mt 1:16; 16:16,20; Jn 11:27; Ac 2:36; 3:20; S 9:22 [z] S Jn 13:13 **2:12** [a] 1Sa 2:34; 10:7; 2Ki 19:29; Ps 86:17; Isa 7:14 **2:14** [b] Isa 9:6; 52:7; 53:5; Mic 5:5; Lk 1:79; S Jn 14:27; Ro 5:1; Eph 2:14,17 **2:16** [c] ver 7 **2:19** [d] ver 51 **2:20** [e] S Mt 9:8 **2:21** [f] S Lk 1:59 [g] S Lk 1:31 **2:22** [h] Lev 12:2-8 **2:23** [i] Ex 13:2,12,15; Nu 3:13 **2:24** [j] Lev 12:8 **2:25** [k] Lk 1:6 [l] ver 38; Isa 52:9; Lk 23:51 **2:27** [m] ver 22 **2:29** [n] ver 26 [o] Ac 2:24 **2:30** [p] Isa 40:5; 52:10; Lk 3:6 **2:32** [q] Isa 42:6; 49:6; Ac 13:47; 26:23

[a] *11* Or *Messiah.* "The Christ" (Greek) and "the Messiah" (Hebrew) both mean "the Anointed One"; also in verse 26. [b] *23* Exodus 13:2,12 [c] *24* Lev. 12:8 [d] *29* Or *promised, / now dismiss*

2:11 *town of David.* Bethlehem (v. 4). *Savior.* Many Jews were looking for a political leader to deliver them from Roman rule, while others were hoping for a savior to deliver them from sickness and physical hardship. But this announcement concerns the Savior who would deliver from sin and death (see Mt 1:21; Jn 4:42 and note). *Christ.* See NIV text note. *the Lord.* A designation used of God and his "Anointed" (the Messiah) (see Ac 2:36; Php 2:11).
2:13,20 *praising God.* See 1:64 and note.
2:14 See note on 1:46–55. This brief hymn is called the Gloria in Excelsis Deo, from the first words of the Latin Vulgate translation (meaning "Glory to God in the Highest"). The angels recognized the glory and majesty of God by giving praise to him. *in the highest.* A reference to heaven, where God dwells (cf. Mt 6:9). *peace to men on whom his favor rests.* Peace is not assured to all, but only to those pleasing to God—the objects of his good pleasure (see Luke's use of the words "pleased" and "pleasure" elsewhere: 3:22; 10:21; 12:32). The Roman world was experiencing the *Pax Romana* ("Roman Peace"), marked by external tranquillity. But the angels proclaimed a deeper, more lasting peace than that—a peace of mind and soul made possible by the Savior (v. 11). Peace with God is received by faith in Christ (see Ro 5:1 and note), and it is on believers that "his favor rests." The Davidic Messiah was called "Prince of Peace" (Isa 9:6; see note there), and Christ promised peace to his disciples (see Jn 14:27; Php 4:7 and notes). But Christ also brought conflict (the "sword"; see Mt 10:34 and note; cf. Lk 12:49), for peace with God involves opposition to Satan and his work (see Jas 4:7 and note).
2:19 *treasured up all these things … in her heart.* Cf. v. 51.
2:21 *circumcise.* See Ge 17:10; Jn 7:22 and notes.
2:22 *their purification.* Following the birth of a son, the mother had to wait 40 days before going to the temple to offer sacrifice for her purification. If she could not afford a lamb and a pigeon (or dove), then two pigeons (or doves) would be acceptable (see Lev 12:2–8 and notes; cf. Lev 5:11). *to Jerusalem.* The distance from Bethlehem to Jerusalem was only about five or six miles. *present him to the Lord.* The firstborn of both people and animals were to be dedicated to the Lord (see v. 23; see also Ex 13:2–13 and notes). The animals were sacrificed, but the human beings were to serve God throughout their lives. The Levites actually served in the place of all the firstborn males in Israel (see Nu 3:11–13; 8:17–18).
2:25 *the consolation of Israel.* The comfort the Messiah would bring to his people at his coming (see vv. 26,38; 23:51; 24:21; Isa 40:1–2 and notes; Mt 5:4). *the Holy Spirit was upon him.* Not in the way common to all believers after Pentecost. Simeon was given a special insight by the Spirit so that he would recognize the "Christ," i.e., the Messiah (v. 26; cf. 1:15 and note).
2:28 *praised God.* See 1:64 and note.
2:29–32 See note on 1:46–55. This hymn of Simeon has been called the Nunc Dimittis, from the first words of the Latin Vulgate translation, meaning "[You] now dismiss."
2:31 *all people.* As a Gentile himself, Luke was careful to emphasize the truth that salvation was offered to Gentiles (v. 32) as well as to Jews.

33The child's father and mother marveled at what was said about him. 34Then
Simeon blessed them and said to Mary, his
mother:[r] "This child is destined to cause
the falling[s] and rising of many in Israel, and to be a sign that will be spoken
against, 35so that the thoughts of many
hearts will be revealed. And a sword will
pierce your own soul too."
36There was also a prophetess,[t] Anna, the
daughter of Phanuel, of the tribe of Asher.
She was very old; she had lived with her
husband seven years after her marriage,
37and then was a widow until she was
eighty-four.[a u] She never left the temple but
worshiped night and day, fasting and praying.[v] 38Coming up to them at that very moment, she gave thanks to God and spoke
about the child to all who were looking forward to the redemption of Jerusalem.[w]
39When Joseph and Mary had done everything required by the Law of the Lord,
they returned to Galilee to their own town
of Nazareth.[x] 40And the child grew and became strong; he was filled with wisdom,
and the grace of God was upon him.[y]

The Boy Jesus at the Temple

41Every year his parents went to Jerusalem for the Feast of the Passover.[z] 42When
he was twelve years old, they went up to
the Feast, according to the custom. 43After
the Feast was over, while his parents were
returning home, the boy Jesus stayed behind in Jerusalem, but they were unaware
of it. 44Thinking he was in their company,
they traveled on for a day. Then they began looking for him among their relatives
and friends. 45When they did not find him,
they went back to Jerusalem to look for
him. 46After three days they found him in
the temple courts, sitting among the teachers, listening to them and asking them
questions. 47Everyone who heard him was
amazed[a] at his understanding and his answers. 48When his parents saw him, they
were astonished. His mother[b] said to him,
"Son, why have you treated us like this?
Your father[c] and I have been anxiously
searching for you."
49"Why were you searching for me?" he
asked. "Didn't you know I had to be in my
Father's house?"[d] 50But they did not understand what he was saying to them.[e]
51Then he went down to Nazareth with
them[f] and was obedient to them. But his
mother treasured all these things in her
heart.[g] 52And Jesus grew in wisdom and
stature, and in favor with God and men.[h]

John the Baptist Prepares the Way

3:2-10pp — Mt 3:1-10; Mk 1:3-5
3:16,17pp — Mt 3:11,12; Mk 1:7,8

3 In the fifteenth year of the reign of Tiberius Caesar—when Pontius Pilate[i]
was governor of Judea, Herod[j] tetrarch of
Galilee, his brother Philip tetrarch of Iturea and Traconitis, and Lysanias tetrarch

2:34 [r] S Mt 12:46 [s] Isa 8:14; Mt 21:44; 1Co 1:23; 2Co 2:16; Gal 5:11; 1Pe 2:7,8 **2:36** [t] S Ac 21:9 **2:37** [u] 1Ti 5:9 [v] Ac 13:3; 14:23; 1Ti 5:5 **2:38** [w] ver 25; Isa 40:2; 52:9; Lk 1:68; 24:21 **2:39** [x] ver 51; S Mt 2:23 **2:40** [y] ver 52; Lk 1:80 **2:41** [z] Ex 23:15; Dt 16:1-8; Lk 22:8 **2:47** [a] S Mt 7:28 **2:48** [b] S Mt 12:46 [c] Lk 3:23; 4:22 **2:49** [d] Jn 2:16 **2:50** [e] S Mk 9:32 **2:51** [f] ver 39; S Mt 2:23 [g] ver 19 **2:52** [h] ver 40; 1Sa 2:26; Pr 3:4; Lk 1:80 **3:1** [i] S Mt 27:2 [j] S Mt 14:1

[a] 37 Or *widow for eighty-four years*

2:33 *child's father.* Luke, aware of the virgin birth of Jesus (1:26–35), is referring to Joseph as Jesus' legal father (see v. 41; Jn 1:45 and note).
2:34 *falling and rising of many in Israel.* Christ raises up those who believe in him, but is a stumbling block for those who disbelieve (see 20:17–18 and note on 20:18; 1Co 1:23; 1Pe 2:6–8 and notes). *sign ... spoken against.* This somewhat enigmatic statement may mean that Jesus would be a sign from God (v. 12; 11:30) who would precipitate division, opposition and rejection.
2:35 *sword will pierce your own soul too.* The word "too" indicates that Mary, as well as Jesus, would suffer deep anguish—the first reference in this Gospel to Christ's suffering and death.
2:36 *prophetess.* Other female prophets were Miriam (Ex 15:20), Deborah (Jdg 4:4), Huldah (2Ki 22:14) and the daughters of Philip (Ac 21:9). *Anna.* Same name as OT Hannah (1Sa 1:2), which means "gracious." Anna praised God for the child Jesus as Hannah had praised God for the child Samuel (1Sa 2:1–10).
2:37 *never left the temple.* Herod's temple was quite large and included rooms for various uses, and Anna may have been allowed to live in one of them. This statement, however, probably means that she spent her waking hours attending and worshiping in the temple.
2:38 *Jerusalem.* The holy city of God's chosen people; here it stands for Israel as a whole. See Introduction to Psalms: Theology: Major Themes, 7, p. 784.
2:39 *they returned to Galilee.* Luke does not mention the coming of the Magi, the danger from Herod, or the flight to and return from Egypt (cf. Mt 2:1–23).
2:41 *Feast of the Passover.* Annual attendance at three feasts by all adult males (normally accompanied by their families) was commanded in the law: Passover, Pentecost and Tabernacles (see notes on Ex 23:14–17; Dt 16:16). Distance prevented many from attending all three, but most Jews tried to be at Passover.
2:42 *twelve years old.* At age 12 boys began preparing to take their place in the religious community the following year.
2:46 *the teachers.* The rabbis, experts in Judaism.
2:49 *in my Father's house.* Jesus pointed to his personal duty to his Father in heaven. He contrasted his "my Father" with Mary's "Your father" (v. 48). At 12 years of age he was aware of his unique relationship to God. But he was also "obedient" to his earthly parents (v. 51).
2:52 Luke says of Jesus what is said of Samuel in 1Sa 2:26 (see note there). *Jesus grew.* Although Jesus was God, there is no indication that he had all knowledge and wisdom from birth. He seems to have matured like any other boy.
3:1–2 Ancient historians frequently dated an event by giving the year of the ruler's reign in which the event happened.
3:1 *fifteenth year.* Several possible dates could be indicated by this description, but the date A.D. 25–26 (Tiberius had authority in the provinces beginning in A.D. 11) best fits the chronology of the life of Christ. The other rulers named do not help pinpoint the beginning of John's ministry, but only serve to indicate the general historical period. *Pontius Pilate.* The Roman governor of Judea from A.D. 26 to 36, whose official residence was in Caesarea on the Mediterranean coast. (In 1961 archaeologists unearthed a stone step in the Roman amphitheater in Caesarea contemporary with

of Abilene— 2during the high priesthood
of Annas and Caiaphas,[k] the word of
God came to John[l] son of Zechariah[m] in
the desert. 3He went into all the country
around the Jordan, preaching a baptism
of repentance for the forgiveness of sins.[n]
4As is written in the book of the words of
Isaiah the prophet:

"A voice of one calling in the desert,
'Prepare the way for the Lord,
make straight paths for him.
5Every valley shall be filled in,
every mountain and hill made low.
The crooked roads shall become
straight,
the rough ways smooth.
6And all mankind will see God's
salvation.' "[a][o]

7John said to the crowds coming out to
be baptized by him, "You brood of vipers![p]
Who warned you to flee from the coming
wrath?[q] 8Produce fruit in keeping with repentance. And do not begin to say to yourselves, 'We have Abraham as our father.'[r]
For I tell you that out of these stones God
can raise up children for Abraham. 9The ax
is already at the root of the trees, and every
tree that does not produce good fruit will
be cut down and thrown into the fire."[s]

10"What should we do then?"[t] the crowd
asked.
11John answered, "The man with two
tunics should share with him who has
none, and the one who has food should
do the same."[u]
12Tax collectors also came to be baptized.[v] "Teacher," they asked, "what
should we do?"
13"Don't collect any more than you are
required to,"[w] he told them.
14Then some soldiers asked him, "And
what should we do?"
He replied, "Don't extort money and
don't accuse people falsely[x]—be content
with your pay."
15The people were waiting expectantly and were all wondering in their hearts
if John[y] might possibly be the Christ.[b][z]
16John answered them all, "I baptize you
with[c] water.[a] But one more powerful than
I will come, the thongs of whose sandals I
am not worthy to untie. He will baptize you
with the Holy Spirit and with fire.[b] 17His
winnowing fork[c] is in his hand to clear his
threshing floor and to gather the wheat
into his barn, but he will burn up the chaff
with unquenchable fire."[d] 18And with many

3:2 [k]S Mt 26:3 [l]S Mt 3:1 [m]Lk 1:13
3:3 [n]ver 16; S Mk 1:4
3:6 [o]Ps 98:2; Isa 40:3-5; 42:16; 52:10; Lk 2:30
3:7 [p]Mt 12:34; 23:33 [q]S Ro 1:18
3:8 [r]Isa 51:2; Lk 19:9; Jn 8:33,39; Ac 13:26; Ro 4:1,11,12, 16,17; 9:7,8; Gal 3:7
3:9 [s]S Mt 3:10
3:10 [t]ver 12,14; Ac 2:37; 16:30
3:11 [u]Isa 58:7; Eze 18:7
3:12 [v]Lk 7:29
3:13 [w]Lk 19:8
3:14 [x]Ex 23:1; Lev 19:11
3:15 [y]S Mt 3:1 [z]Jn 1:19,20; Ac 13:25
3:16 [a]ver 3; S Mk 1:4 [b]Jn 1:26,33; Ac 1:5; 2:3; 11:16; 19:4
3:17 [c]Isa 30:24 [d]Mt 13:30; S 25:41

[a] 6 Isaiah 40:3-5 [b] *15* Or *Messiah* [c] *16* Or *in*

Pilate and bearing a Latin inscription that included these words: "Pontius Pilate, Prefect [Governor] of Judea"; see chart, p. 1667.) When he came to Jerusalem, he stayed in the magnificent palace built by Herod the Great, located southwest of the temple area. Mark calls this palace "the Praetorium" (Mk 15:16; see note there), and it was here that the Roman trial of Jesus took place (see note on Mk 14:53—15:15). *Herod tetrarch of Galilee.* At the death of Herod the Great (4 B.C.), his sons—Archelaus, Herod Antipas and Herod Philip—were given jurisdiction over his divided kingdom. Herod Antipas became the tetrarch of Galilee and Perea (see note on Mt 14:1). *Lysanias tetrarch of Abilene.* Nothing more is known of this Lysanias than that his name has been found in certain inscriptions (see map, p. 1570).

3:2 *the high priesthood of Annas and Caiaphas.* Annas was high priest from A.D. 6 until he was deposed by the Roman official Gratus in 15. He was followed by his son Eleazar, his son-in-law Caiaphas and then four more sons. Even though Rome had replaced Annas, the Jews continued to recognize his authority (see Jn 18:13; Ac 4:6 and notes); so Luke included his name as well as that of the Roman appointee, Caiaphas. *word of God.* The source of John's preaching and authority for his baptizing. God's message came to John as it came to the OT prophets (see Jer 1:2; Hos 1:1; Joel 1:1 and notes; see also Eze 1:3). *desert.* Refers to a desolate, uninhabited area, not necessarily a sandy, waterless place.

3:3 *baptism of repentance.* See note on Mt 3:11. John's baptism represented a change of heart, which includes sorrow for sin and a determination to lead a holy life. *forgiveness of sins.* Christ would deliver the repentant person from sin's penalty by dying on the cross.

3:4 *Prepare the way.* Before a king made a journey to a distant country, the roads he would travel were improved. Similarly, preparation for the Messiah was made in a moral and spiritual way by the ministry of John, which focused on repentance and forgiveness of sin and the need for a Savior.

3:6 *all mankind.* God's salvation was to be made known to both Jews and Gentiles—a major theme of Luke's Gospel (see note on 2:31).

3:7 *the coming wrath.* A reference to both the destruction of Jerusalem (21:20–23), which occurred in A.D. 70, and the final judgment (Jn 3:36). But see notes on 1Th 1:10; 5:9.

3:9 *ax ... at the root.* A symbolic way of saying that judgment is near for those who give no evidence of repentance. *fire.* A symbol of divine judgment (see Mt 7:19; 13:42 and note; see also La 1:13 and note).

3:11 *two tunics.* A tunic was something like a long undershirt. Since two such garments were not needed, the second should be given to a person in need of one (see 9:3 and note on Mk 6:9).

3:12 *Tax collectors.* Taxes were collected for the Roman government by Jewish agents, who were especially detested for helping the pagan conqueror and for frequently defrauding their own people (see notes on Mt 5:46; Mk 2:16).

3:14 *soldiers.* Limited military forces were allowed for certain Jewish leaders and institutions (such as those of Herod Antipas, the police guard of the temple, and escorts for tax collectors). The professions of tax collector and soldier as such were not condemned, but the common unethical practices associated with them were.

3:16 *baptize you with the Holy Spirit.* Fulfilled at Pentecost (see Ac 1:5; 2:4,38 and notes). *and with fire.* Here fire is associated with judgment (v. 17; see La 1:13 and note). See also the fire of Pentecost (see Ac 2:3 and note) and the fire of testing (see 1Co 3:13 and note).

3:17 *His winnowing fork.* See note on Ru 1:22. The chaff represents the unrepentant and the wheat the righteous. Many Jews thought that only pagans would be judged and punished when the Messiah came, but John declared that judgment would come to all who did not repent—including Jews.

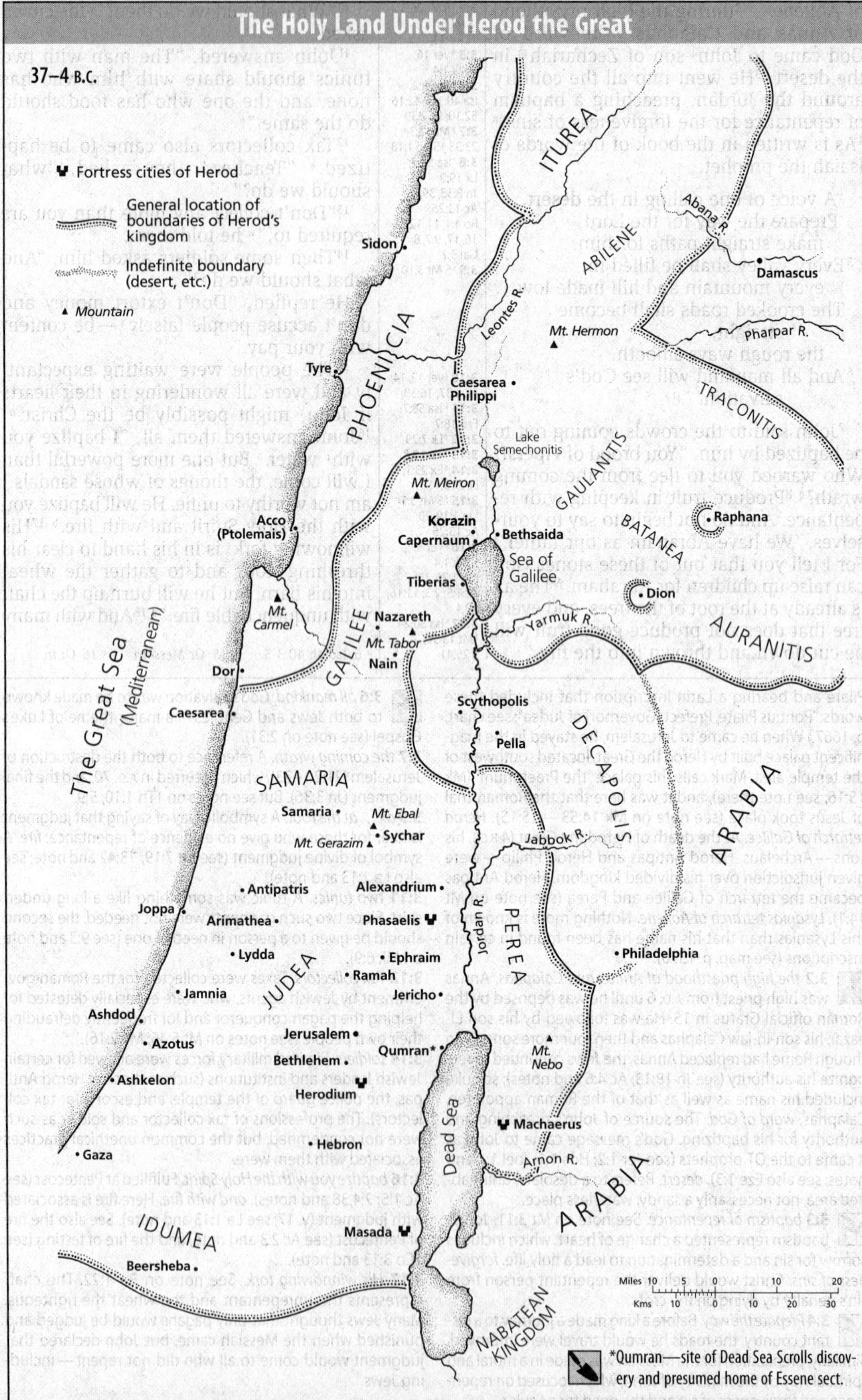
The Holy Land Under Herod the Great
37–4 B.C.
Fortress cities of Herod
General location of boundaries of Herod's kingdom
Indefinite boundary (desert, etc.)
Mountain
Sidon
Damascus
ITUREA
ABILENE
Abana R.
Leontes R.
Mt. Hermon
Pharpar R.
PHOENICIA
Tyre
Caesarea Philippi
TRACONITIS
Lake Semechonitis
GAULANITIS
Mt. Meiron
BATANEA
Raphana
Acco (Ptolemais)
Korazin
Bethsaida
Capernaum
Sea of Galilee
Tiberias
Dion
Mt. Carmel
Nazareth
Yarmuk R.
AURANITIS
Mt. Tabor
GALILEE
Nain
The Great Sea (Mediterranean)
Dor
Caesarea
Scythopolis
Pella
DECAPOLIS
SAMARIA
ARABIA
Samaria
Mt. Ebal
Sychar
Mt. Gerazim
Jabbok R.
Antipatris
Alexandrium
Joppa
Arimathea
Phasaelis
PEREA
Jordan R.
Lydda
Ephraim
Philadelphia
Ramah
JUDEA
Jamnia
Jericho
Ashdod
Azotus
Jerusalem
Qumran*
Mt. Nebo
Bethlehem
Ashkelon
Herodium
Machaerus
Dead Sea
Hebron
Gaza
Arnon R.
ARABIA
IDUMEA
Masada
Beersheba
Miles 10 5 0 10 20
Kms 10 10 0 10 20 30
NABATEAN KINGDOM
*Qumran—site of Dead Sea Scrolls discovery and presumed home of Essene sect.

other words John exhorted the people and
preached the good news to them.
19But when John rebuked Herod[e] the tetrarch because of Herodias, his brother's
wife, and all the other evil things he had
done, 20Herod added this to them all: He
locked John up in prison.[f]

The Baptism and Genealogy of Jesus

3:21,22pp — Mt 3:13-17; Mk 1:9-11
3:23-38pp — Mt 1:1-17

21When all the people were being baptized, Jesus was baptized too. And as he
was praying,[g] heaven was opened 22and
the Holy Spirit descended on him[h] in bodily form like a dove. And a voice came from
heaven: "You are my Son,[i] whom I love;
with you I am well pleased."[j]
23Now Jesus himself was about thirty
years old when he began his ministry.[k] He
was the son, so it was thought, of Joseph,[l]

the son of Heli, 24the son of Matthat,
the son of Levi, the son of Melki,
the son of Jannai, the son of Joseph,
25the son of Mattathias, the son of Amos,
the son of Nahum, the son of Esli,
the son of Naggai, 26the son of Maath,
the son of Mattathias, the son of Semein,
the son of Josech, the son of Joda,
27the son of Joanan, the son of Rhesa,
the son of Zerubbabel,[m] the son of Shealtiel,
the son of Neri, 28the son of Melki,
the son of Addi, the son of Cosam,
the son of Elmadam, the son of Er,
29the son of Joshua, the son of Eliezer,
the son of Jorim, the son of Matthat,
the son of Levi, 30the son of Simeon,
the son of Judah, the son of Joseph,
the son of Jonam, the son of Eliakim,
31the son of Melea, the son of Menna,
the son of Mattatha, the son of Nathan,[n]
the son of David, 32the son of Jesse,
the son of Obed, the son of Boaz,
the son of Salmon,[a] the son of Nahshon,
33the son of Amminadab, the son of Ram,[b]
the son of Hezron, the son of Perez,[o]
the son of Judah, 34the son of Jacob,
the son of Isaac, the son of Abraham,
the son of Terah, the son of Nahor,[p]
35the son of Serug, the son of Reu,
the son of Peleg, the son of Eber,
the son of Shelah, 36the son of Cainan,
the son of Arphaxad,[q] the son of Shem,
the son of Noah, the son of Lamech,[r]
37the son of Methuselah, the son of Enoch,
the son of Jared, the son of Mahalalel,
the son of Kenan,[s] 38the son of Enosh,
the son of Seth, the son of Adam,
the son of God.[t]

3:19 [e] ver 1; S Mt 14:1
3:20 [f] S Mt 14:3,4
3:21 [g] Mt 14:23; Mk 1:35; 6:46; Lk 5:16; 6:12; 9:18,28; 11:1
3:22 [h] Isa 42:1; Jn 1:32,33; Ac 10:38 [i] S Mt 3:17 [j] S Mt 3:17
3:23 [k] Mt 4:17; Ac 1:1 [l] Lk 1:27
3:27 [m] Mt 1:12
3:31 [n] 2Sa 5:14; 1Ch 3:5
3:33 [o] Ru 4:18-22; 1Ch 2:10-12
3:34 [p] Ge 11:24,26
3:36 [q] Ge 11:12 [r] Ge 5:28-32
3:37 [s] Ge 5:12-25
3:38 [t] Ge 5:1,2,6-9

[a] 32 Some early manuscripts *Sala* [b] 33 Some manuscripts *Amminadab, the son of Admin, the son of Arni*; other manuscripts vary widely.

3:19 *rebuked Herod … because of Herodias.* Herod Antipas had married the daughter of Aretas IV of Arabia, but divorced her to marry his own niece, Herodias, who was already his brother's (Herod Philip's) wife (see Mt 14:3 and note; Mk 6:17).

3:20 *locked John up in prison.* According to Josephus, John was imprisoned in Machaerus, east of the Dead Sea (*Antiquities*, 18.5.2). This did not occur until sometime after the beginning of Jesus' ministry (see Jn 3:22 – 24), but Luke mentions it here in order to conclude this section on John's ministry before commencing his account of the beginning of Jesus' ministry (see also Mt 4:12; Mk 1:14). He later briefly alludes to John's death (9:7 – 9).

3:21 *baptized.* See note on Mt 3:15. *as he was praying.* Only Luke notes Jesus' praying at the time of his baptism. Jesus in prayer is one of the special themes of Luke (see 5:16; 6:12; 9:18,28 – 29; 11:1; 22:32,41; 23:34,46).

3:22 *Holy Spirit descended.* Luke specifies "in bodily form." To John, it was a sign (see Jn 1:32 – 34; see also note on Mk 1:10). *my Son, whom I love.* See Ps 2:7 and note on 2:7 – 9; Isa 42:1; Heb 1:5 and note. Two other times the Gospel writers record the declarations of a voice from heaven addressing Jesus: (1) on the Mount of Transfiguration (9:35), and (2) in the temple area during Jesus' final week (Jn 12:28).

3:23 – 38 There are several differences between Luke's genealogy and Matthew's (1:2 – 16). Matthew begins with Abraham (the father of the Jewish people), while Luke traces the line in the reverse order and goes back to Adam, showing Jesus' relationship to the whole human race (see note on 2:31). From Abraham to David, the genealogies of Matthew and Luke are almost the same, but from David on they are different. Many interpreters suggest that this is because Matthew traces the legal descent of the house of David using only heirs to the throne, while Luke traces the direct bloodline of Joseph to David (see Introduction to 1 Chronicles: Genealogies). Another common explanation is that Matthew follows the line of Joseph (Jesus' legal father through Solomon; see Mt 1:6 – 7,16), while Luke emphasizes that of Mary (Jesus' blood relative through Nathan, v. 31). Although tracing a genealogy through the mother's side was unusual, so was the virgin birth. Luke's explanation here that Jesus was the son of Joseph, "so it was thought" (v. 23), brings to mind his explicit virgin birth statement (1:34 – 35) and suggests the importance of the role of Mary in Jesus' genealogy. However, this view is less likely since Luke here so explicitly names Joseph (v. 23), without any reference at all to Mary.

3:23 *about thirty years old.* Luke, a historian, relates the beginning of Jesus' public ministry both to world history (see vv. 1 – 2) and to the rest of Jesus' life. Thirty was the age when a Levite undertook his service (Nu 4:47) and when a man was considered mature. *so it was thought.* Luke had already affirmed the virgin birth (1:34 – 35) and here makes it clear again that Joseph was not Jesus' physical father.

The Temptation of Jesus

4:1-13pp — Mt 4:1-11; Mk 1:12,13

4 Jesus, full of the Holy Spirit,[u] returned
from the Jordan[v] and was led by the
Spirit[w] in the desert, 2where for forty days[x]
he was tempted by the devil.[y] He ate nothing during those days, and at the end of
them he was hungry.
3The devil said to him, "If you are the
Son of God,[z] tell this stone to become
bread."
4Jesus answered, "It is written: 'Man
does not live on bread alone.'[a]"[a]
5The devil led him up to a high place
and showed him in an instant all the
kingdoms of the world.[b] 6And he said
to him, "I will give you all their authority and splendor, for it has been given to
me,[c] and I can give it to anyone I want
to. 7So if you worship me, it will all be
yours."

4:1 [u] ver 14,18; S Lk 1:15,35; 3:16,22; 10:21 [v] Lk 3:3,21 [w] Eze 37:1; Lk 2:27 **4:2** [x] Ex 34:28; 1Ki 19:8 [y] Heb 4:15 **4:3** [z] S Mt 4:3 **4:4** [a] Dt 8:3 **4:5** [b] S Mt 24:14 **4:6** [c] Jn 12:31; 14:30; 1Jn 5:19

[a] 4 Deut. 8:3

4:1 *full of the Holy Spirit.* Luke emphasizes the Holy Spirit not only in his Gospel (1:35,41,67; 2:25–27; 3:16,22; 4:14,18; 10:21; 11:13; 12:10,12) but also in Acts, where the Spirit is mentioned 57 times. *in the desert.* The Desert of Judea (see notes on 1:80; Mt 3:1).

4:2 *he was tempted.* See notes on Mt 4:1–11; 4:1; Heb 2:18; 4:15. Luke states that Jesus was tempted for the 40 days he was fasting, and the three specific temptations recounted in Matthew and Luke seem to have occurred at the close of this period—when Jesus' hunger was greatest and his resistance lowest. The sequence of the second and third temptations differs in Matthew and Luke. Matthew probably followed the chronological order, since at the end of the mountain temptation (Matthew's third) Jesus told Satan to leave (Mt 4:10). To emphasize a certain point the Gospel writers often bring various events together, not intending to give chronological sequence. Perhaps Luke's focus here is geographical, as he concludes with Jesus in Jerusalem.

4:3 *If you are.* See note on Mt 4:3. *tell this stone to become bread.* The devil always makes his temptations seem attractive.

4:6 *their authority ... has been given to me.* Satan is elsewhere called "the prince of this world" (Jn 12:31), "the god of this age" (2Co 4:4) and "the ruler of the kingdom of the air" (Eph 2:2)—but remains under God's sovereign power and control (cf. notes on 2Sa 24:1; Job 1:12; 2Co 4:4).

4:7 *worship me.* The devil was tempting Jesus to avoid the sufferings of the cross, which he came specifically to

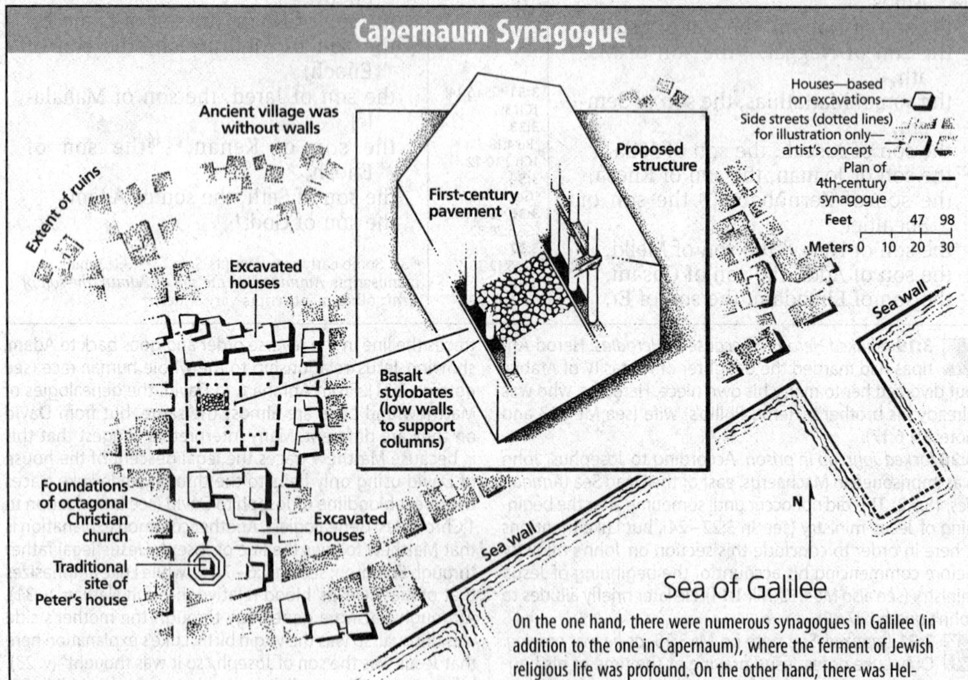

Capernaum was more than a seaside fishing village in the days of Jesus. It was the place that Christ chose to be the center of his ministry to the entire region of Galilee, and it possessed ideal characteristics as a point of dissemination for the gospel.

There were good reasons for this. The town itself was named *Kephar Nahum*, "village of (perhaps the prophet) Nahum," and was the centerpiece of a densely populated region having a bicultural flavor.

On the one hand, there were numerous synagogues in Galilee (in addition to the one in Capernaum), where the ferment of Jewish religious life was profound. On the other hand, there was Hellenism, a pervasive culture already centuries old and potent in its paganism—a lifestyle that influenced manners, dress, architecture and political institutions as well.

Recent archaeological work at Capernaum has revealed a section of the pavement of a first-century synagogue below the still-existing ruins of the fourth-century one on the site. A private house later made into a church and a place of pilgrimage has yielded some evidence that may link it to the site of Simon Peter's house (Lk 4:38).

8 Jesus answered, "It is written: 'Worship the Lord your God and serve him
only.'[a]"[d]
9 The devil led him to Jerusalem and had
him stand on the highest point of the temple. "If you are the Son of God," he said,
"throw yourself down from here. 10 For it
is written:

" 'He will command his angels
concerning you
to guard you carefully;
11 they will lift you up in their hands,
so that you will not strike your foot
against a stone.'[b]"[e]

12 Jesus answered, "It says: 'Do not put
the Lord your God to the test.'[c]"[f]
13 When the devil had finished all this
tempting,[g] he left him[h] until an opportune
time.

Jesus Rejected at Nazareth

14 Jesus returned to Galilee[i] in the power
of the Spirit, and news about him spread
through the whole countryside.[j] 15 He
taught in their synagogues,[k] and everyone
praised him.
16 He went to Nazareth,[l] where he had
been brought up, and on the Sabbath day
he went into the synagogue,[m] as was his
custom. And he stood up to read.[n] 17 The
scroll of the prophet Isaiah was handed
to him. Unrolling it, he found the place
where it is written:

18 "The Spirit of the Lord is on me,[o]
because he has anointed me
to preach good news[p] to the poor.
He has sent me to proclaim freedom
for the prisoners
and recovery of sight for the blind,
to release the oppressed,
19 to proclaim the year of the Lord's
favor."[d][q]

20 Then he rolled up the scroll, gave it
back to the attendant and sat down.[r] The
eyes of everyone in the synagogue were
fastened on him, 21 and he began by saying
to them, "Today this scripture is fulfilled[s]
in your hearing."
22 All spoke well of him and were
amazed at the gracious words that came
from his lips. "Isn't this Joseph's son?"
they asked.[t]
23 Jesus said to them, "Surely you will
quote this proverb to me: 'Physician, heal
yourself! Do here in your hometown[u]
what we have heard that you did in Capernaum.' "[v]
24 "I tell you the truth," he continued,
"no prophet is accepted in his hometown.[w] 25 I assure you that there were
many widows in Israel in Elijah's time,
when the sky was shut for three and a
half years and there was a severe famine
throughout the land.[x] 26 Yet Elijah was not

4:8 [d]Dt 6:13
4:11 [e]Ps 91:11,12
4:12 [f]Dt 6:16
4:13 [g]Heb 4:15 [h]Jn 14:30
4:14 [i]Mt 4:12 [j]S Mt 9:26
4:15 [k]S Mt 4:23
4:16 [l]S Mt 2:23 [m]Mt 13:54 [n]S 1Ti 4:13
4:18 [o]S Jn 3:34 [p]Mk 16:15
4:19 [q]Lev 25:10; Isa 61:1,2; Ps 102:20; 103:6; Isa 42:7; 49:8,9; 58:6
4:20 [r]ver 17; S Mt 26:55
4:21 [s]S Mt 1:22
4:22 [t]Mt 13:54,55; Jn 6:42; 7:15
4:23 [u]ver 16; S Mt 2:23 [v]Mk 1:21-28; 2:1-12
4:24 [w]Mt 13:57; Jn 4:44
4:25 [x]1Ki 17:1; 18:1; Jas 5:17,18; Rev 11:6

[a] *8* Deut. 6:13 [b] *11* Psalm 91:11,12 [c] *12* Deut. 6:16 [d] *19* Isaiah 61:1,2

endure (see Mk 10:45 and note). The temptation offered an easy shortcut to world dominion.
4:9 *the highest point of the temple.* Either the southeast corner of the temple colonnade, from which there was a drop of some 100 feet to the Kidron Valley below, or the pinnacle of the temple proper. *temple.* See note on Mt 4:5. *If you are.* See note on Mt 4:3. *throw yourself down.* Satan was tempting Jesus to test God's faithfulness and to attract public attention dramatically.
4:10 *For it is written.* This time Satan also quoted Scripture, though he misused Ps 91:11–12.
4:12 Jesus answered with Scripture, as he had on each of the other two occasions, quoting from Deuteronomy (see NIV text notes here and on vv. 4,8).
4:13 *he left him until an opportune time.* Satan continued his testing throughout Jesus' ministry (see Mk 8:33 and note), culminating in the supreme test at Gethsemane.
4:14 *in the power of the Spirit.* See note on v. 1.
4:15 *taught in their synagogues.* See note on Mk 1:21.
4:16 *He went to Nazareth.* Not at the start of his ministry but perhaps almost a year later (v. 23 presupposes that Jesus had already been ministering). Probably all the events of Jn 1:19—4:42 occurred between Lk 4:13 and 4:14. *as was his custom.* Jesus' custom of regular worship sets an example for all his followers. *to read.* Jesus probably read from Isaiah in Hebrew, and then he or someone else paraphrased it in Aramaic, one of the other common languages of the day.
4:17 *The scroll of the prophet Isaiah.* The books of the OT were written on scrolls, kept in a special place in the synagogue and handed to the reader by a special attendant. The passage Jesus read about the Messiah (Isa 61:1–2; see notes there) may have been one he chose to read, or it may have been the assigned passage for the day.
4:18 This verse tells of the Messiah's ministry of preaching and healing—to meet every human need. *he has anointed me.* Not with literal oil (see Ex 30:22–31), but with the Holy Spirit.
4:19 *the year of the Lord's favor.* Not a calendar year, but the period when salvation would be proclaimed—the Messianic age. This quotation from Isa 61:1–2 alludes to the Year of Jubilee (Lev 25:8–55), when once every 50 years slaves were freed, debts were canceled and ancestral property was returned to the original family. Isaiah predicted primarily the liberation of Israel from the future Babylonian exile, but Jesus proclaimed liberation from sin and all its consequences.
4:20 *sat down.* It was customary to stand while reading Scripture (v. 16; see Ne 8:3,5 and notes) but to sit while teaching (see 5:3; Mt 5:1 and note; 26:55; Mk 4:1; 9:35; Jn 8:2; Ac 16:13).
4:23 *hometown.* Nazareth. Although Jesus was born in Bethlehem, he was brought up in Nazareth, in Galilee (see 1:26; 2:39,51; Mt 2:23 and note). *Capernaum.* See note on Mt 4:13.
4:26–27 Mention of Jesus' reference to God's helping two non-Israelites (see 1Ki 17:7–24; 2Ki 5:1–19a and notes) reflects Luke's special concern for the Gentiles. Jesus' point was that when Israel was in rebellion and rejected God's messengers of redemption (Elijah and Elisha), God caused non-Israelites to receive the covenant blessings that were properly Israel's—in accordance with a word of Moses: "I will make them envious by those who are not a people ..." (Dt 32:21). See Paul's references to this word in Ro 10:19–21 (see notes on 10:19,21); 11:11,14.
4:26 *Sidon.* One of the oldest Phoenician cities, about 25 miles north of Tyre. Jesus later healed a Gentile woman's daughter in this region (Mt 15:21–28).

sent to any of them, but to a widow in
Zarephath in the region of Sidon.[y] 27 And
there were many in Israel with leprosy[a]
in the time of Elisha the prophet, yet not
one of them was cleansed—only Naaman
the Syrian."[z]

28 All the people in the synagogue were
furious when they heard this. 29 They got
up, drove him out of the town,[a] and took
him to the brow of the hill on which the
town was built, in order to throw him
down the cliff. 30 But he walked right
through the crowd and went on his
way.[b]

Jesus Drives Out an Evil Spirit

4:31-37pp — Mk 1:21-28

31 Then he went down to Capernaum,[c] a
town in Galilee, and on the Sabbath began
to teach the people. 32 They were amazed
at his teaching,[d] because his message had
authority.[e]

33 In the synagogue there was a man possessed by a demon, an evil[b] spirit. He cried
out at the top of his voice, 34 "Ha! What
do you want with us,[f] Jesus of Nazareth?[g]
Have you come to destroy us? I know who
you are[h]—the Holy One of God!"[i]

35 "Be quiet!" Jesus said sternly.[j] "Come
out of him!" Then the demon threw the
man down before them all and came out
without injuring him.

36 All the people were amazed[k] and said
to each other, "What is this teaching?
With authority[l] and power he gives orders
to evil spirits and they come out!" 37 And
the news about him spread throughout the
surrounding area.[m]

Jesus Heals Many

4:38-41pp — Mt 8:14-17
4:38-43pp — Mk 1:29-38

38 Jesus left the synagogue and went to
the home of Simon. Now Simon's mother-in-law was suffering from a high fever,
and they asked Jesus to help her. 39 So he
bent over her and rebuked[n] the fever, and
it left her. She got up at once and began to
wait on them.

40 When the sun was setting, the people brought to Jesus all who had various
kinds of sickness, and laying his hands on
each one,[o] he healed them.[p] 41 Moreover,
demons came out of many people, shouting, "You are the Son of God!"[q] But he
rebuked[r] them and would not allow them
to speak,[s] because they knew he was the
Christ.[c]

42 At daybreak Jesus went out to a solitary place. The people were looking for
him and when they came to where he
was, they tried to keep him from leaving
them. 43 But he said, "I must preach the
good news of the kingdom of God[t] to the
other towns also, because that is why I
was sent." 44 And he kept on preaching in
the synagogues of Judea.[d][u]

The Calling of the First Disciples

5:1-11pp — Mt 4:18-22; Mk 1:16-20; Jn 1:40-42

5 One day as Jesus was standing by the
Lake of Gennesaret,[e] with the people
crowding around him and listening to the

4:26 [y] 1Ki 17:8-16; S Mt 11:21
4:27 [z] 2Ki 5:1-14
4:29 [a] Nu 15:35; Ac 7:58; Heb 13:12
4:30 [b] Jn 8:59; 10:39
4:31 [c] ver 23; S Mt 4:13
4:32 [d] S Mt 7:28 [e] ver 36; Mt 7:29
4:34 [f] S Mt 8:29 [g] S Mk 1:24 [h] Jas 2:19 [i] ver 41; S Mk 1:24
4:35 [j] ver 39,41; Mt 8:26; Lk 8:24
4:36 [k] S Mt 7:28 [l] ver 32; Mt 7:29; S Mt 10:1
4:37 [m] ver 14; S Mt 9:26
4:39 [n] ver 35,41
4:40 [o] S Mk 5:23 [p] S Mt 4:23
4:41 [q] S Mt 4:3 [r] S ver 35 [s] S Mt 8:4
4:43 [t] S Mt 3:2
4:44 [u] S Mt 4:23

[a] 27 The Greek word was used for various diseases affecting the skin—not necessarily leprosy.
[b] 33 Greek *unclean*; also in verse 36
[c] 41 Or *Messiah*
[d] 44 Or *the land of the Jews*; some manuscripts *Galilee*
[e] 1 That is, Sea of Galilee

4:28 *furious.* Because of Jesus' inclusion of Gentiles as recipients of God's blessings.

4:30 *walked right through the crowd.* Luke does not explain whether the escape was miraculous or simply the result of Jesus' commanding presence. In any case, his time (to die) had not yet come (see Jn 7:30 and note).

4:32 See note on Mk 1:22.

4:33 *possessed by a demon.* To pagans, "demon" meant a supernatural being, whether good or bad, but Luke makes it clear that this was an evil spirit. Such a demon could cause mental disorder (Jn 10:20), violent action (Lk 8:26–29), bodily disease (13:11,16) and rebellion against God (Rev 16:14).

4:34 *Holy One of God.* See note on Mk 1:24.

4:36 *amazed.* See v. 32 and note on Mk 1:22.

4:38 *synagogue.* See notes on Mt 4:13; Mk 1:21. *home of Simon.* See diagram, p. 1572. *Simon's mother-in-law.* Cf. 1Co 9:5 and note. *high fever.* All three Synoptics tell of this miracle (Mt 8:14–15; Mk 1:29–31), but only Luke, the doctor, uses the more specific phrase "high fever."

4:40 *When the sun was setting.* The Sabbath (v. 31) was over at sundown (about 6:00 P.M.). According to the tradition of the elders, Jews could not carry a burden or travel more than about two-thirds of a mile on the Sabbath. Only after sundown could they carry the sick to Jesus, and their eagerness is seen in the fact that they came to him while the sun was still setting.

4:41 *because they knew he was the Christ.* See note on Mk 1:34.

4:42 *solitary place.* Mark includes the words "where he prayed" (Mk 1:35).

4:43 *kingdom of God.* Luke's first use of this phrase; it occurs over 30 times in his Gospel. Some of its different meanings in the Bible are: the eternal kingship of God; the presence of the kingdom in the person of Jesus, the King; the approaching spiritual form of the kingdom; the future kingdom. See note on Mt 3:2.

4:44 This summary statement includes not only what has just been described (from v. 14 on) but also what lay ahead in Jesus' ministry. No express mention is made in the Synoptics of the early Judean ministry recorded in John (2:13—4:3), though it may be reflected in 13:34 (see note there) and Mt 23:37. *Judea.* Some manuscripts, as well as the parallel accounts (Mt 4:23; Mk 1:39), mention Galilee instead of Judea (see NIV text note). In writing to a Gentile (see Introduction: Recipient and Purpose), Luke possibly used "Judea" to refer to the whole land of the Jews (see 23:5 and note; Ac 10:37; 11:1,29; 26:20).

5:1 *Lake of Gennesaret.* Luke is the only one who calls it this (cf. Mt 14:34 and note; Mk 6:53). The other Gospel writers call it the Sea of Galilee (see Mk 1:16 and note), and John twice calls it the Sea of Tiberias (see Jn 6:1 and note; 21:1).

word of God,[v] 2he saw at the water's edge two boats, left there by the fishermen, who were washing their nets. 3He got into one of the boats, the one belonging to Simon, and asked him to put out a little from shore. Then he sat down and taught the people from the boat.[w]

4When he had finished speaking, he said to Simon, "Put out into deep water, and let down[a] the nets for a catch."[x]

5Simon answered, "Master,[y] we've worked hard all night and haven't caught anything.[z] But because you say so, I will let down the nets."

6When they had done so, they caught such a large number of fish that their nets began to break.[a] 7So they signaled their partners in the other boat to come and help them, and they came and filled both boats so full that they began to sink.

8When Simon Peter saw this, he fell at Jesus' knees and said, "Go away from me, Lord; I am a sinful man!"[b] 9For he and all his companions were astonished at the catch of fish they had taken, 10and so were James and John, the sons of Zebedee, Simon's partners.

Then Jesus said to Simon, "Don't be afraid;[c] from now on you will catch men."
11So they pulled their boats up on shore, left everything and followed him.[d]

5:1 [v] S Mk 4:14; S Heb 4:12
5:3 [w] Mt 13:2
5:4 [x] Jn 21:6
5:5 [y] Lk 8:24, 45; 9:33, 49; 17:13 [z] Jn 21:3
5:6 [a] Jn 21:11
5:8 [b] Ge 18:27; Job 42:6; Isa 6:5
5:10 [c] S Mt 14:27
5:11 [d] ver 28; S Mt 4:19
5:12 [e] S Mt 8:2

The Man With Leprosy

5:12-14pp — Mt 8:2-4; Mk 1:40-44

12While Jesus was in one of the towns, a man came along who was covered with leprosy.[b][e] When he saw Jesus, he fell with his face to the ground and begged him, "Lord, if you are willing, you can make me clean."

13Jesus reached out his hand and touched the man. "I am willing," he said. "Be clean!" And immediately the leprosy left him.

14Then Jesus ordered him, "Don't tell anyone,[f] but go, show yourself to the priest and offer the sacrifices that Moses commanded[g] for your cleansing, as a testimony to them."

15Yet the news about him spread all the more,[h] so that crowds of people came to hear him and to be healed of their sicknesses. 16But Jesus often withdrew to lonely places and prayed.[i]

Jesus Heals a Paralytic

5:18-26pp — Mt 9:2-8; Mk 2:3-12

17One day as he was teaching, Pharisees and teachers of the law,[j] who had come from every village of Galilee and from Judea and Jerusalem, were sitting there. And the power of the Lord was present for him to heal the sick.[k] 18Some men came carrying a paralytic on a mat and tried to take him into the house to lay him before Jesus. 19When they could not find a way to do this because of the crowd, they went up on the roof and lowered him on his mat through the tiles into the middle of the crowd, right in front of Jesus.

20When Jesus saw their faith, he said, "Friend, your sins are forgiven."[l]

21The Pharisees and the teachers of the law began thinking to themselves, "Who is this fellow who speaks blasphemy? Who can forgive sins but God alone?"[m]

22Jesus knew what they were thinking and asked, "Why are you thinking these

5:14 [f] S Mt 8:4 [g] Lev 14:2-32
5:15 [h] S Mt 9:26
5:16 [i] S Lk 3:21
5:17 [j] Mt 15:1; Lk 2:46 [k] Mk 5:30; Lk 6:19
5:20 [l] Lk 7:48, 49
5:21 [m] Isa 43:25

[a] *4* The Greek verb is plural. [b] *12* The Greek word was used for various diseases affecting the skin—not necessarily leprosy.

5:2 *washing their nets.* After each period of fishing, the nets were washed, stretched and prepared for use again.
5:3 *sat down.* The usual position for teaching (see note on 4:20). The boat provided an ideal arrangement, removed from the press of the crowd but near enough to be seen and heard.
5:7 *their partners.* See v. 10.
5:8 *Go away from me, Lord.* The nearer people come to God, the more they feel their own sinfulness and unworthiness—as did Abraham (see Ge 18:27 and note), Job (see 42:6 and note) and Isaiah (6:5).
5:11 *left everything and followed him.* This was not the first time these men had been with Jesus (see Mk 1:17 and note; Jn 1:40–42; 2:1–2). Their periodic and loose association now became a closely knit fellowship as they followed the Master. The scene is the same as Mt 4:18–22 and Mk 1:16–20, but Luke expands his account of the event.
5:12 *covered with leprosy.* See NIV text note; see also note on Lev 13:2. Luke alone notes the extent of his disease.
5:14 *Don't tell anyone.* See notes on Mt 8:4; 16:20. *but go, show yourself to the priest.* By this command Jesus urged the man to keep the law, to provide further proof for the actual healing, to testify to the authorities concerning his ministry and to supply ritual certification of cleansing so the man could be reinstated into society. *a testimony to them.* See note on Mk 1:44.
5:17 *Pharisees and teachers of the law.* See notes on Mt 2:4; 3:7; Mk 2:16. Opposition was rising in Galilee from these religious leaders. *Pharisees.* Mentioned here for the first time in Luke (see essay, p. 1453, and chart, p. 1502). Their name means "separated ones"; they numbered about 6,000 and were spread over the whole of the Holy Land. They were teachers in the synagogues, religious examples in the eyes of the people and self-appointed guardians of the law and its proper observance. They considered the interpretations and regulations handed down by tradition to be virtually as authoritative as Scripture (Mk 7:8–13). Already Jesus had run counter to the Jewish leaders in Jerusalem (Jn 5:16–18). Now they came to a home in Capernaum (Mk 2:1–6) to hear and watch him. *teachers of the law.* "Scribes," who studied, interpreted and taught the law (both written and oral); see note on Ezr 7:6. The majority of these teachers belonged to the party of the Pharisees.
5:19 *roof.* See note on Mk 2:4. *tiles.* Probably ceiling tiles.
5:20 *sins are forgiven.* Very likely Jesus is evoking Ps 103:3.
5:21 *this fellow... speaks blasphemy.* See note on Mk 2:7. The Pharisees considered blasphemy to be the most serious sin anyone could commit (see note on Mk 14:64).

things in your hearts? 23Which is easier:
to say, 'Your sins are forgiven,' or to say,
'Get up and walk'? 24But that you may
know that the Son of Man[n] has authority on earth to forgive sins . . . ." He said
to the paralyzed man, "I tell you, get up,
take your mat and go home." 25Immedi-
ately he stood up in front of them, took
what he had been lying on and went home
praising God. 26Everyone was amazed and
gave praise to God.[o] They were filled with
awe and said, "We have seen remarkable
things today."

The Calling of Levi

5:27-32pp — Mt 9:9-13; Mk 2:14-17

27After this, Jesus went out and saw a
tax collector by the name of Levi sitting at
his tax booth. "Follow me,"[p] Jesus said to
him, 28and Levi got up, left everything and
followed him.[q]

29Then Levi held a great banquet for
Jesus at his house, and a large crowd of
tax collectors[r] and others were eating with
them. 30But the Pharisees and the teachers of the law who belonged to their sect[s]
complained to his disciples, "Why do you
eat and drink with tax collectors and 'sinners'?"[t]

31Jesus answered them, "It is not the
healthy who need a doctor, but the sick.
32I have not come to call the righteous, but
sinners to repentance."[u]

Jesus Questioned About Fasting

5:33-39pp — Mt 9:14-17; Mk 2:18-22

33They said to him, "John's disciples[v]
often fast and pray, and so do the disciples
of the Pharisees, but yours go on eating
and drinking."

5:24 [n] S Mt 8:20
5:26 [o] S Mt 9:8
5:27 [p] S Mt 4:19
5:28 [q] ver 11; S Mt 4:19
5:29 [r] Lk 15:1
5:30 [s] Ac 23:9 [t] S Mt 9:11
5:32 [u] S Jn 3:17
5:33 [v] Lk 7:18; Jn 1:35; 3:25,26

34Jesus answered, "Can you make the
guests of the bridegroom[w] fast while he is
with them? 35But the time will come when
the bridegroom will be taken from them;[x]
in those days they will fast."

36He told them this parable: "No one
tears a patch from a new garment and sews
it on an old one. If he does, he will have
torn the new garment, and the patch from
the new will not match the old. 37And no
one pours new wine into old wineskins. If
he does, the new wine will burst the skins,
the wine will run out and the wineskins
will be ruined. 38No, new wine must be
poured into new wineskins. 39And no one
after drinking old wine wants the new, for
he says, 'The old is better.' "

Lord of the Sabbath

6:1-11pp — Mt 12:1-14; Mk 2:23–3:6

6 One Sabbath Jesus was going through
the grainfields, and his disciples began
to pick some heads of grain, rub them in
their hands and eat the kernels.[y] 2Some of
the Pharisees asked, "Why are you doing
what is unlawful on the Sabbath?"[z]

3Jesus answered them, "Have you never read what David did when he and his
companions were hungry?[a] 4He entered
the house of God, and taking the consecrated bread, he ate what is lawful only
for priests to eat.[b] And he also gave some
to his companions." 5Then Jesus said to
them, "The Son of Man[c] is Lord of the
Sabbath."

6On another Sabbath[d] he went into the
synagogue and was teaching, and a man
was there whose right hand was shriveled.
7The Pharisees and the teachers of the law
were looking for a reason to accuse Jesus,
so they watched him closely[e] to see if he

5:34 [w] Jn 3:29
5:35 [x] Lk 9:22; 17:22; Jn 16:5-7
6:1 [y] Dt 23:25
6:2 [z] S Mt 12:2
6:3 [a] 1Sa 21:6
6:4 [b] Lev 24:5,9
6:5 [c] S Mt 8:20
6:6 [d] ver 1
6:7 [e] S Mt 12:10

5:23 *Which is easier: to say . . . ?* See notes on Mk 2:9 – 10.
5:24 *that you may know.* Jesus' power to heal was a visible affirmation of his power to forgive sins. *Son of Man.* See note on Mk 8:31.
5:25 *praising God.* See v. 26; see also 1:64 and note.
5:27 *tax collector.* See note on 3:12. *Levi.* Another name for Matthew (6:15). *tax booth.* The place where customs were collected (see note on Mk 2:14).
5:28 *left everything and followed him.* Since Jesus had been ministering in Capernaum for some time, Levi probably had known him previously (see note on v. 11).
5:29 *great banquet.* When Levi began to follow Jesus, he did not do it secretly (cf. Jn 19:38 and note).
5:30 *Pharisees . . . complained.* They probably stood outside and registered their complaints from a distance. *eat . . . with tax collectors and 'sinners.'* See note on Mk 2:15.
5:31 *not the healthy who need a doctor, but the sick.* Not to imply that the Pharisees were "the healthy," but that people must recognize themselves as sinners before they can be spiritually healed (see note on Mk 2:17).
5:33 *John's disciples . . . fast and pray.* John the Baptist had grown up in the desert and learned to subsist on an austere diet of locusts and wild honey. His ministry was characterized by a sober message and a strenuous schedule. For a contrast between Jesus' ministry and John the Baptist's see 7:24 – 28; Mt 11:1 – 19. The Pharisees also had rigorous lifestyles (see note on 18:12). But Jesus went to banquets, and his disciples enjoyed a freedom not known by the Pharisees. *fast.* See notes on 18:12; Mk 2:18. While Jesus rejected fasting legalistically for display (cf. Isa 58:3 – 11), he himself fasted privately and permitted its voluntary use for spiritual benefit (Mt 4:2; 6:16 – 18).
5:35 See notes on Mk 2:19 – 20.
5:36 *parable.* See notes on Mt 13:3; Mk 4:2.
5:38 *new wineskins.* See note on Mt 9:17.
5:39 *The old is better.* Jesus was indicating the reluctance of some people to change from their traditional religious ways and try the gospel.
6:1 *going through the grainfields.* See note on Mk 2:23.
6:3 *what David did.* See note on Mk 2:25.
6:4 *consecrated bread.* See note on Mt 12:4.
6:5 *Son of Man.* See note on Mk 8:31. *Lord of the Sabbath.* Jesus has the authority to overrule human regulations concerning the Sabbath, such as those reflecting the interpretations of the Pharisees (see Mt 12:8; Mk 2:27 and note).
6:7 *to see if he would heal on the Sabbath.* See note on Mk 3:2.

would heal on the Sabbath.[f] 8But Jesus
knew what they were thinking[g] and said
to the man with the shriveled hand, "Get
up and stand in front of everyone." So he
got up and stood there.
9Then Jesus said to them, "I ask you,
which is lawful on the Sabbath: to do good
or to do evil, to save life or to destroy it?"
10He looked around at them all, and then
said to the man, "Stretch out your hand."
He did so, and his hand was completely
restored. 11But they were furious[h] and began to discuss with one another what they
might do to Jesus.

The Twelve Apostles

6:13-16pp — Mt 10:2-4; Mk 3:16-19; Ac 1:13

12One of those days Jesus went out to a
mountainside to pray, and spent the night
praying to God.[i] 13When morning came,
he called his disciples to him and chose
twelve of them, whom he also designated apostles:[j] 14Simon (whom he named
Peter), his brother Andrew, James, John,
Philip, Bartholomew, 15Matthew,[k] Thomas,
James son of Alphaeus, Simon who was
called the Zealot, 16Judas son of James,
and Judas Iscariot, who became a traitor.

Blessings and Woes

6:20-23pp — Mt 5:3-12

17He went down with them and stood on
a level place. A large crowd of his disciples
was there and a great number of people
from all over Judea, from Jerusalem, and
from the coast of Tyre and Sidon,[l] 18who
had come to hear him and to be healed
of their diseases. Those troubled by evil[a]
spirits were cured, 19and the people all
tried to touch him,[m] because power was
coming from him and healing them all.[n]
20Looking at his disciples, he said:

"Blessed are you who are poor,
for yours is the kingdom of God.[o]
21 Blessed are you who hunger now,
for you will be satisfied.[p]
Blessed are you who weep now,
for you will laugh.[q]
22 Blessed are you when men hate you,
when they exclude you[r] and insult
you[s]
and reject your name as evil,
because of the Son of Man.[t]

23"Rejoice in that day and leap for joy,[u]
because great is your reward in heaven.
For that is how their fathers treated the
prophets.[v]

24 "But woe to you who are rich,[w]
for you have already received your
comfort.[x]
25 Woe to you who are well fed now,
for you will go hungry.[y]
Woe to you who laugh now,
for you will mourn and weep.[z]
26 Woe to you when all men speak well
of you,
for that is how their fathers treated
the false prophets.[a]

6:7 [f] S Mt 12:2 **6:8** [g] S Mt 9:4 **6:11** [h] Jn 5:18 **6:12** [i] S Lk 3:21 **6:13** [j] S Mk 6:30 **6:15** [k] Mt 9:9 **6:17** [l] Mt 4:25; S 11:21; Mk 3:7,8 **6:19** [m] S Mt 9:20 [n] Mk 5:30; Lk 5:17 **6:20** [o] S Mt 25:34 **6:21** [p] Isa 55:1,2; Mt 5:6 [q] Isa 61:2,3; Mt 5:4; Rev 7:17 **6:22** [r] Jn 9:22; 16:2 [s] Isa 51:7 [t] S Jn 15:21 **6:23** [u] S Mt 5:12 [v] S Mt 5:12 **6:24** [w] Jas 5:1 [x] Lk 16:25 **6:25** [y] Isa 65:13 [z] Pr 14:13 **6:26** [a] S Mt 7:15

[a] 18 Greek *unclean*

6:8 *stand in front of everyone.* So there would be no question about the healing.
6:9 *which is lawful on the Sabbath ...?* Jesus had been enduring questions and attacks from the Pharisees and now took the initiative by putting the questions to everyone in the synagogue (see notes on Mk 2:25; 3:4).
6:10 *He looked around at them.* Jesus wanted to see whether anyone objected to his question or the implied answer, but no one was bold enough to do so.
6:11 *they were furious.* Because they could not withstand Jesus' reasoning. Already they were plotting to take his life (see Jn 5:18). See note on Mk 3:6.
6:12 Before the important work of selecting his 12 apostles, Jesus characteristically (see 5:16) spent time in prayer.
6:13 *he called his disciples.* Among those who came to hear Jesus was a group who regularly followed him and were committed to his teachings. At least 72 men were included, since this many disciples were sent out on an evangelistic campaign (10:1,17). Later, 120 believers waited and worshiped in Jerusalem following the ascension (Ac 1:15). From such disciples Jesus at this time chose 12 to be his apostles, a title meaning "ones sent with a special commission" (see notes on Mk 6:30; 1Co 1:1; Heb 3:1).
6:14-16 Lists of the apostles appear also in Mt 10:2-4; Mk 3:16-19; Ac 1:13. Although the order of the names varies, Peter is always first and Judas Iscariot last.
6:14 *Bartholomew.* Seems to be (in the Synoptics) the same as Nathanael (in John). Nathanael is associated with Philip in Jn 1:45.
6:15 *Matthew.* Another name for Levi (5:27). *James son of Alphaeus.* Probably the same as James the younger (Mk 15:40). *the Zealot.* See note on Mt 10:4.
6:16 *Judas son of James.* Another name for Thaddaeus (see Mt 10:3; Mk 3:18 and note). *Judas Iscariot.* Probably the only one from Judea, the rest coming from Galilee (see note on Mk 3:19).
6:17 *stood on a level place.* Perhaps a plateau, which would satisfy both this context and that in Mt 5:1 (see note on Mt 5:1—7:29). *Tyre and Sidon.* In Phoenicia (modern Lebanon); see notes on 4:26; 10:14; Mk 7:24,31; see also maps, pp. 1537, 1570.
6:20-49 Luke's Sermon on the Plain, apparently parallel to Matthew's Sermon on the Mount (Mt 5-7). Although this sermon is much shorter than the one in Matthew, they both begin with the Beatitudes and end with the lesson of the builders. Some of Matthew's Sermon is found in other portions of Luke (e.g., 11:2-4; 12:22-31,33-34), suggesting that the material may have been given on various occasions in Jesus' preaching.
6:20-23 See Mt 5:3-12 and notes. The Beatitudes go deeper than material poverty (v. 20) and physical hunger (v. 21). Matthew's account indicates that Jesus spoke of poverty "in spirit" (Mt 5:3) and hunger "for righteousness" (Mt 5:6).
6:20 *poor.* Those who are aware of their need of God's grace and provisions (cf. Mt 5:3 and note).
6:24-26 This section is a point-by-point negative counterpart of vv. 20-22.

Love for Enemies

6:29,30pp — Mt 5:39-42

27“But I tell you who hear me: Love
your enemies, do good to those who hate
you,[b] 28bless those who curse you, pray
for those who mistreat you.[c] 29If someone
strikes you on one cheek, turn to him the
other also. If someone takes your cloak,
do not stop him from taking your tunic.
30Give to everyone who asks you, and if
anyone takes what belongs to you, do not
demand it back.[d] 31Do to others as you
would have them do to you.[e]

32“If you love those who love you, what
credit is that to you?[f] Even ‘sinners’ love
those who love them. 33And if you do good
to those who are good to you, what credit is that to you? Even ‘sinners’ do that.
34And if you lend to those from whom you
expect repayment, what credit is that to
you?[g] Even ‘sinners’ lend to ‘sinners,’ expecting to be repaid in full. 35But love your
enemies, do good to them,[h] and lend to
them without expecting to get anything
back. Then your reward will be great,
and you will be sons[i] of the Most High,[j]
because he is kind to the ungrateful and
wicked. 36Be merciful,[k] just as your Father[l]
is merciful.

Judging Others

6:37-42pp — Mt 7:1-5

37“Do not judge, and you will not be
judged.[m] Do not condemn, and you will
not be condemned. Forgive, and you will
be forgiven.[n] 38Give, and it will be given
to you. A good measure, pressed down,
shaken together and running over, will
be poured into your lap.[o] For with the
measure you use, it will be measured to
you.”[p]

39He also told them this parable: “Can
a blind man lead a blind man? Will they
not both fall into a pit?[q] 40A student is not
above his teacher, but everyone who is fully trained will be like his teacher.[r]

41“Why do you look at the speck of
sawdust in your brother’s eye and pay no
attention to the plank in your own eye?
42How can you say to your brother, ‘Brother, let me take the speck out of your eye,’
when you yourself fail to see the plank in
your own eye? You hypocrite, first take the
plank out of your eye, and then you will
see clearly to remove the speck from your
brother’s eye.

A Tree and Its Fruit

6:43,44pp — Mt 7:16,18,20

43“No good tree bears bad fruit, nor does
a bad tree bear good fruit. 44Each tree is
recognized by its own fruit.[s] People do not
pick figs from thornbushes, or grapes from
briers. 45The good man brings good things
out of the good stored up in his heart, and
the evil man brings evil things out of the
evil stored up in his heart. For out of the
overflow of his heart his mouth speaks.[t]

The Wise and Foolish Builders

6:47-49pp — Mt 7:24-27

46“Why do you call me, ‘Lord, Lord,’[u]
and do not do what I say?[v] 47I will show
you what he is like who comes to me and
hears my words and puts them into practice.[w] 48He is like a man building a house,
who dug down deep and laid the foundation on rock. When a flood came, the torrent struck that house but could not shake
it, because it was well built. 49But the one
who hears my words and does not put
them into practice is like a man who built
a house on the ground without a foundation. The moment the torrent struck that
house, it collapsed and its destruction was
complete.”

The Faith of the Centurion

7:1-10pp — Mt 8:5-13

7 When Jesus had finished saying all this[x]
in the hearing of the people, he entered
Capernaum. 2There a centurion’s servant,

6:27 [b]Ver 35; Mt 5:44; Ro 12:20
6:28 [c]S Mt 5:44
6:30 [d]Dt 15:7,8,10; Pr 21:26
6:31 [e]Mt 7:12
6:32 [f]Mt 5:46
6:34 [g]Mt 5:42
6:35 [h]ver 27 [i]S Ro 8:14 [j]S Mk 5:7
6:36 [k]Jas 2:13 [l]Mt 5:48; 6:1; Lk 11:2; 12:32; Ro 8:15; Eph 4:6; 1Pe 1:17; 1Jn 1:3; 3:1
6:37 [m]S Mt 7:1 [n]Mt 6:14
6:38 [o]Ps 79:12; Isa 65:6,7 [p]S Mt 7:2
6:39 [q]Mt 15:14
6:40 [r]S Jn 13:16
6:44 [s]Mt 12:33
6:45 [t]Pr 4:23; Mt 12:34,35; Mk 7:20
6:46 [u]S Jn 13:13 [v]Mal 1:6; Mt 7:21
6:47 [w]Lk 8:21; 11:28; Jas 1:22-25
7:1 [x]Mt 7:28

6:27 *Love your enemies, do good.* The heart of Jesus’ teaching is love. While the Golden Rule (v. 31) is sometimes expressed in negative form outside the Bible (see note on Mt 7:12), Jesus not only forbids treating others spitefully but also commands that we love everyone—even our enemies (see Mt 5:44 and note).

6:29 *turn to him the other.* We are not to have a retaliatory attitude. *cloak ... tunic.* The cloak was the outer coat, under which the tunic was worn (see note on 2Ti 4:13).

6:35 *Most High.* God (see Dt 32:8 and note).

6:36 *just as your Father is merciful.* God’s perfection should be our example and goal (see Mt 5:48 and note).

6:37 *Do not judge.* Jesus did not relieve his followers of the need for discerning right and wrong (cf. vv. 43–45), but he condemned unjust and hypocritical judging of others (see note on Mt 7:1). *Forgive, and you will be forgiven.* See 11:4 and note.

6:38 *poured into your lap.* Probably refers to the way the outer garment was worn, leaving a fold over the belt that could be used as a large pocket to hold a measure of wheat.

6:41 *speck ... plank.* Jesus used hyperbole (a figure of speech that overstates for emphasis) to sharpen the contrast and to emphasize how foolish and hypocritical it is for us to criticize someone for a fault while remaining blind to our own considerable faults (see Mt 7:3–4 and note on 7:3).

6:42 *hypocrite.* See notes on 13:15; Mt 23:23; Ac 5:9.

6:43–45 Cf. Jas 3:11–12 and note.

6:46–49 See Mt 7:24–27 and notes.

6:47,49 *hears my words and puts them into practice ... does not put them into practice.* See Jas 1:22–25.

7:1 *Capernaum.* See note on Mt 4:13.

7:2 *centurion’s servant.* The centurion was probably a member of Herod Antipas’s forces, which were organized in Roman fashion, ordinarily in companies of 100 men (see note on Mt 8:5). Roman centurions referred to in the NT showed characteristics to be admired (see e.g., Ac 10:2

whom his master valued highly, was sick
and about to die. 3The centurion heard of
Jesus and sent some elders of the Jews
to him, asking him to come and heal his
servant. 4When they came to Jesus, they
pleaded earnestly with him, "This man deserves to have you do this, 5because he
loves our nation and has built our synagogue." 6So Jesus went with them.

He was not far from the house when the
centurion sent friends to say to him: "Lord,
don't trouble yourself, for I do not deserve
to have you come under my roof. 7That is
why I did not even consider myself worthy
to come to you. But say the word, and my
servant will be healed.[y] 8For I myself am a
man under authority, with soldiers under
me. I tell this one, 'Go,' and he goes; and
that one, 'Come,' and he comes. I say to
my servant, 'Do this,' and he does it."

9When Jesus heard this, he was amazed
at him, and turning to the crowd following
him, he said, "I tell you, I have not found
such great faith even in Israel." 10Then the
men who had been sent returned to the
house and found the servant well.

Jesus Raises a Widow's Son

7:11-16Ref — 1Ki 17:17-24; 2Ki 4:32-37; Mk 5:21-24,35-43; Jn 11:1-44

11Soon afterward, Jesus went to a town
called Nain, and his disciples and a large
crowd went along with him. 12As he approached the town gate, a dead person
was being carried out—the only son of
his mother, and she was a widow. And a
large crowd from the town was with her.
13When the Lord[z] saw her, his heart went
out to her and he said, "Don't cry."
14Then he went up and touched the coffin, and those carrying it stood still. He
said, "Young man, I say to you, get up!"[a]
15The dead man sat up and began to talk,
and Jesus gave him back to his mother.
16They were all filled with awe[b] and
praised God.[c] "A great prophet[d] has appeared among us," they said. "God has
come to help his people."[e] 17This news
about Jesus spread throughout Judea[a] and
the surrounding country.[f]

Jesus and John the Baptist

7:18-35pp — Mt 11:2-19

18John's[g] disciples[h] told him about all
these things. Calling two of them, 19he
sent them to the Lord to ask, "Are you the
one who was to come, or should we expect someone else?"
20When the men came to Jesus, they
said, "John the Baptist sent us to you to
ask, 'Are you the one who was to come, or
should we expect someone else?'"
21At that very time Jesus cured many
who had diseases, sicknesses[i] and evil
spirits, and gave sight to many who were
blind. 22So he replied to the messengers,
"Go back and report to John what you
have seen and heard: The blind receive
sight, the lame walk, those who have leprosy[b] are cured, the deaf hear, the dead are
raised, and the good news is preached to
the poor.[j] 23Blessed is the man who does
not fall away on account of me."
24After John's messengers left, Jesus
began to speak to the crowd about John:

7:7 [y]Ps 107:20
7:13 [z]ver 19; Lk 10:1; 13:15; 17:5; 22:61; 24:34; Jn 11:2
7:14 [a]Mt 9:25; Mk 1:31; Lk 8:54; Jn 11:43; Ac 9:40
7:16 [b]Lk 1:65 [c]S Mt 9:8 [d]ver 39; S Mt 21:11 [e]Lk 1:68
7:17 [f]S Mt 9:26
7:18 [g]S Mt 3:1 [h]S Lk 5:33
7:21 [i]S Mt 4:23
7:22 [j]Isa 29:18, 19; 35:5,6; 61:1,2; Lk 4:18

[a] 17 Or *the land of the Jews* [b] 22 The Greek word was used for various diseases affecting the skin—not necessarily leprosy.

---

and note; 23:17–18; 27:43). This centurion showed genuine concern for his slave, and he was admired by the Jews, who spoke favorably of him even though he was a Gentile (see vv. 5,9).

7:3 *elders of the Jews.* Highly respected Jews of the community, though not necessarily rulers of the synagogue. They were willing to come and plead for the centurion. In Matthew's account (Mt 8:5–13) the centurion speaks with Jesus himself, while in Luke's account he speaks with Jesus through his friends (see note on Mt 8:5).

7:6 *I do not deserve to have you come under my roof.* See note on Mt 8:8.

7:9 Cf. note on Mt 8:11. *he was amazed.* The amazement of Jesus is only mentioned twice, here because of belief and at Nazareth because of unbelief (Mk 6:6; see note on Mk 6:5).

7:11 *Nain.* Mentioned only here. A small village located a few miles south of Nazareth still bears this name. It is generally accepted as the site where this incident took place.

7:14 *touched the coffin.* By so doing Jesus risked ritual uncleanness (cf. Nu 19:16). *coffin.* The man was probably carried in an open coffin, suggested by Jewish custom and the fact that he sat up in response to Jesus' command. This is the first of three instances of Jesus' raising someone from the dead, the others being Jairus's daughter (8:40–56) and Lazarus (Jn 11:38–44).

7:15 *gave him back to his mother.* Cf. 1Ki 17:23; 2Ki 4:36–37.

7:16 *praised God.* See 1:64 and note.

7:18 *John's disciples.* See note on 5:33; see also Mk 2:18. Despite John the Baptist's imprisonment, his disciples kept in contact with him and continued his ministry.

7:19 *should we expect someone else?* John had announced the coming of the Messiah, but now he himself had been languishing in prison for months, and the work of Jesus had not brought the results John apparently expected. His disappointment was natural. He wanted reassurance—and perhaps also wanted to urge Jesus to further action.

7:22 *report to John what you have seen and heard.* In answer, Jesus pointed to his healing and life-restoring miracles. He did not give promises but clearly observable evidence—evidence that reflected the predicted ministry of the Messiah. *the good news is preached to the poor.* In Jesus' review of his works, he used an ascending scale of impressive deeds, ending with the dead raised and the good news preached to the poor. In this way, Jesus reminded John that these were the things predicted of the Messiah in the Scriptures (see Isa 29:18–21; 35:5–6 and notes; 61:1; Lk 4:18 and note).

7:23 *the man who does not fall away.* Jesus did not want discouragement and doubt to ensnare John.

7:24 *What did you go ... to see?* John was not a weak messenger, swayed by the pressures of human opinion. On the contrary, he was a true prophet.

"What did you go out into the desert to see? A reed swayed by the wind? 25If not, what did you go out to see? A man dressed in fine clothes? No, those who wear expensive clothes and indulge in luxury are in palaces. 26But what did you go out to see? A prophet?[k] Yes, I tell you, and more than a prophet. 27This is the one about whom it is written:

> " 'I will send my messenger ahead of
> you,
> who will prepare your way before
> you.'[a][l]

28I tell you, among those born of women there is no one greater than John; yet the one who is least in the kingdom of God[m] is greater than he."

29(All the people, even the tax collectors, when they heard Jesus' words, acknowledged that God's way was right, because they had been baptized by John.[n] 30But the Pharisees and experts in the law[o] rejected God's purpose for themselves, because they had not been baptized by John.)

31"To what, then, can I compare the people of this generation? What are they like? 32They are like children sitting in the marketplace and calling out to each other:

> " 'We played the flute for you,
> and you did not dance;
> we sang a dirge,
> and you did not cry.'

33For John the Baptist came neither eating bread nor drinking wine,[p] and you say, 'He has a demon.' 34The Son of Man came eating and drinking, and you say, 'Here is a glutton and a drunkard, a friend of tax collectors and "sinners." '[q] 35But wisdom is proved right by all her children."

7:26 [k]S Mt 11:9 **7:27** [l]Mal 3:1; Mt 11:10; Mk 1:2 **7:28** [m]S Mt 3:2 **7:29** [n]Mt 21:32; Mk 1:5; Lk 3:12 **7:30** [o]S Mt 22:35 **7:33** [p]Lk 1:15 **7:34** [q]Lk 5:29,30; 15:1,2

Jesus Anointed by a Sinful Woman

7:37-39Ref — Mt 26:6-13; Mk 14:3-9; Jn 12:1-8
7:41,42Ref — Mt 18:23-34

36Now one of the Pharisees invited Jesus to have dinner with him, so he went to the Pharisee's house and reclined at the table. 37When a woman who had lived a sinful life in that town learned that Jesus was eating at the Pharisee's house, she brought an alabaster jar of perfume, 38and as she stood behind him at his feet weeping, she began to wet his feet with her tears. Then she wiped them with her hair, kissed them and poured perfume on them.

39When the Pharisee who had invited him saw this, he said to himself, "If this man were a prophet,[r] he would know who is touching him and what kind of woman she is—that she is a sinner."

40Jesus answered him, "Simon, I have something to tell you."

"Tell me, teacher," he said.

41"Two men owed money to a certain moneylender. One owed him five hundred denarii,[b] and the other fifty. 42Neither of them had the money to pay him back, so he canceled the debts of both. Now which of them will love him more?"

43Simon replied, "I suppose the one who had the bigger debt canceled."

"You have judged correctly," Jesus said.

44Then he turned toward the woman and said to Simon, "Do you see this woman? I came into your house. You did not give me any water for my feet,[s] but she wet my feet with her tears and wiped them with her hair. 45You did not give me a kiss,[t] but this woman, from the time I entered, has

7:39 [r]ver 16; S Mt 21:11 **7:44** [s]Ge 18:4; 19:2; 43:24; Jdg 19:21; Jn 13:4-14; 1Ti 5:10 **7:45** [t]Lk 22:47, 48; S Ro 16:16

[a] *27* Mal. 3:1 [b] *41* A denarius was a coin worth about a day's wages.

7:26 *more than a prophet.* John was the unique prophet sent to prepare the way for the Messiah (v. 27).

7:28 *one who is least in the kingdom of God.* See note on Mt 11:11.

7:29 *tax collectors.* See note on Mt 5:46.

7:30 *experts in the law.* A designation used by Luke (see 10:25,37; 11:45–46,52; 14:3; see also Mt 22:35) for the "scribes" (the teachers of the law), most of whom were Pharisees (see note on 5:17). *rejected God's purpose.* Tax collectors had shown their willingness to repent by accepting John's baptism, whereas the Pharisees showed their rejection of God's message by refusing to be baptized.

7:32 *like children sitting in the marketplace.* People had rejected both John and Jesus, but for different reasons—like children who refuse to play either a joyful game or a mournful one. They would not associate with John when he followed the strictest of rules or with Jesus when he freely associated with all kinds of people. *We played the flute.* See note on Mt 11:17.

7:34 *Son of Man.* See note on Mk 8:31. *friend of tax collectors and "sinners."* Jesus openly ate and talked with those who were considered social and religious outcasts. He even called a tax collector to be an apostle (5:27–32).

7:35 *wisdom is proved right by all her children.* In contrast to the rejection by foolish critics, spiritually wise persons could see that the ministries of both John and Jesus embodied God's wisdom, despite their differences. See note on Mt 11:19.

7:36–50 See note on Jn 12:1–11.

7:36 *one of the Pharisees.* See note on 5:17. His motive may have been to entrap Jesus rather than to learn from him.

7:37 *a woman who had lived a sinful life.* She must have heard Jesus preach, and in repentance she determined to lead a new life. She came out of love and gratitude, in the understanding that she could be forgiven. *alabaster jar.* A long-necked, globular bottle (see note on Mk 14:3). *perfume.* A perfumed ointment.

7:38 *stood behind him at his feet.* Jesus reclined on a couch with his feet extended away from the table, which made it possible for the woman to wipe his feet with her hair and still not disturb him. *poured perfume on them.* The anointing, perhaps originally intended for Jesus' head, was instead applied to his feet. A similar act was performed by Mary of Bethany just over a week before the crucifixion (see Jn 12:3 and note).

7:41 *five hundred denarii.* See NIV text note.

7:44 *water for my feet.* The minimal gesture of hospitality.

not stopped kissing my feet. 46You did not
put oil on my head,[u] but she has poured
perfume on my feet. 47Therefore, I tell you,
her many sins have been forgiven—for
she loved much. But he who has been forgiven little loves little."

48Then Jesus said to her, "Your sins are
forgiven."[v]

49The other guests began to say among
themselves, "Who is this who even forgives sins?"

50Jesus said to the woman, "Your faith
has saved you;[w] go in peace."[x]

The Parable of the Sower

8:4-15pp — Mt 13:2-23; Mk 4:1-20

8 After this, Jesus traveled about from
one town and village to another, proclaiming the good news of the kingdom
of God.[y] The Twelve were with him, 2and
also some women who had been cured
of evil spirits and diseases: Mary (called
Magdalene)[z] from whom seven demons
had come out; 3Joanna the wife of Cuza,
the manager of Herod's[a] household; Susanna; and many others. These women
were helping to support them out of their
own means.

4While a large crowd was gathering and
people were coming to Jesus from town
after town, he told this parable: 5"A farmer
went out to sow his seed. As he was scattering the seed, some fell along the path;
it was trampled on, and the birds of the air
ate it up. 6Some fell on rock, and when it
came up, the plants withered because they
had no moisture. 7Other seed fell among
thorns, which grew up with it and choked
the plants. 8Still other seed fell on good
soil. It came up and yielded a crop, a hundred times more than was sown."

When he said this, he called out, "He
who has ears to hear, let him hear."[b]

9His disciples asked him what this parable meant. 10He said, "The knowledge
of the secrets of the kingdom of God has
been given to you,[c] but to others I speak
in parables, so that,

" 'though seeing, they may not see;
though hearing, they may not
understand.'[a][d]

11"This is the meaning of the parable:
The seed is the word of God.[e] 12Those
along the path are the ones who hear, and
then the devil comes and takes away the
word from their hearts, so that they may
not believe and be saved. 13Those on the
rock are the ones who receive the word
with joy when they hear it, but they have
no root. They believe for a while, but in
the time of testing they fall away.[f] 14The
seed that fell among thorns stands for
those who hear, but as they go on their

7:46 [u]Ps 23:5; Ecc 9:8 **7:48** [v]Mt 9:2 **7:50** [w]S Mt 9:22 [x]S Ac 15:33 **8:1** [y]S Mt 4:23 **8:2** [z]Mt 27:55,56 **8:3** [a]S Mt 14:1 **8:8** [b]S Mt 11:15 **8:10** [c]S Mt 13:11 [d]Isa 6:9; S Mt 13:13,14 **8:11** [e]S Heb 4:12 **8:13** [f]Mt 11:6

[a] *10* Isaiah 6:9

7:47 *for she loved much.* Her love was evidence of her forgiveness, but not the basis for it. Verse 50 clearly states that she was saved by faith. See Eph 2:8 and note.

7:50 *Your faith has saved you.* Her sins were forgiven and she could experience God's peace (see 1:79 and note on 2:14).

8:1 *Jesus traveled about.* Jesus' ministry had been centered in Capernaum, and much of his preaching was in synagogues, but now he traveled again from town to town on a second tour of the Galilean countryside. For the first tour see 4:43–44; Mt 4:23–25; Mk 1:38–39. For the third tour see note on 9:1–6. *kingdom of God.* See note on 4:43.

8:2 *Mary (called Magdalene).* Her hometown was Magdala (see note on Mk 8:10). She is not to be confused with the sinful woman of ch. 7 or Mary of Bethany (Jn 11:1).

8:3 *Susanna.* Nothing more is known about her. *helping to support them.* Jesus and his disciples did not provide for themselves by miracles, but were supported by the service and means of such grateful people as these women.

8:4 *parable.* From this point on in Luke's Gospel Jesus used parables (see notes on Mt 13:3; Mk 4:2; see also Introduction: Characteristics) more extensively as a means of teaching. They were particularly effective and easy to remember because he used familiar scenes. Although parables clarified Jesus' teaching, they also included hidden meanings needing further explanation. These hidden meanings challenged the sincerely interested to further inquiry, and taught truths that Jesus wanted to conceal from unbelievers (see v. 10 and note). From parables Jesus' enemies could find no direct statements to use against him. The parable of the sower is one of three parables recorded in each of the Synoptic Gospels (Mt 13:1–23; Mk 4:1–20). The others are those of the mustard seed (13:19; Mt 13:31–32; Mk 4:30–32) and of the vineyard (20:9–19; Mt 21:33–46; Mk 12:1–12).

8:5 *sow his seed.* In Eastern practice the seed was sometimes sown first and the field plowed afterward. Roads and pathways went directly through many fields, and the traffic made much of the surface too hard for seed to take root.

8:6 *on rock.* On a thin layer of soil that covered solid rock. Any moisture that fell there soon evaporated, and the germinating seed withered and died (see Mt 13:5–6).

8:8 *a hundred times more.* Luke's version is more abbreviated than Matthew's (13:8) and Mark's (4:8), but the point is the same: The quantity of increase depends on the quality of soil. *let him hear.* A challenge for listeners to understand the message and appropriate it for themselves.

8:9 *His disciples.* They included "the Twelve and the others" (Mk 4:10).

8:10 *secrets of the kingdom of God.* Truths that can be known only by revelation from God (cf. Eph 3:3 and note; 1Pe 1:10–12). See note on Mk 4:11. *though seeing, they may not see.* This quotation from Isaiah (6:9) does not express a desire that some would not understand, but simply states the sad truth that those who are not willing to receive Jesus' message will find the truth hidden from them. Their ultimate fate is implied in the fuller quotation in Mt 13:14–15 (see note on Mk 4:12).

8:11 *the word of God.* The message that comes from God.

8:12 *may not believe.* The devil's purpose is that people will not hear with understanding and therefore will not appropriate the message and be saved.

8:13 *They believe for a while.* This kind of belief is superficial and does not save. It is similar to what James calls "dead" (Jas 2:17,26) or "useless" faith (Jas 2:20; see notes on Jas 2:14–26).

way they are choked by life's worries, riches[g] and pleasures, and they do not mature. 15But the seed on good soil stands for those with a noble and good heart, who hear the word, retain it, and by persevering produce a crop.

A Lamp on a Stand

16"No one lights a lamp and hides it in a jar or puts it under a bed. Instead, he puts it on a stand, so that those who come in can see the light.[h] 17For there is nothing hidden that will not be disclosed, and nothing concealed that will not be known or brought out into the open.[i] 18Therefore consider carefully how you listen. Whoever has will be given more; whoever does not have, even what he thinks he has will be taken from him."[j]

Jesus' Mother and Brothers

8:19-21pp — Mt 12:46-50; Mk 3:31-35

19Now Jesus' mother and brothers came to see him, but they were not able to get near him because of the crowd. 20Someone told him, "Your mother and brothers[k] are standing outside, wanting to see you."

21He replied, "My mother and brothers are those who hear God's word and put it into practice."[l]

Jesus Calms the Storm

8:22-25pp — Mt 8:23-27; Mk 4:36-41
8:22-25Ref — Mk 6:47-52; Jn 6:16-21

22One day Jesus said to his disciples, "Let's go over to the other side of the lake." So they got into a boat and set out. 23As they sailed, he fell asleep. A squall came down on the lake, so that the boat was being swamped, and they were in great danger.

24The disciples went and woke him, saying, "Master, Master,[m] we're going to drown!"

He got up and rebuked[n] the wind and the raging waters; the storm subsided, and all was calm.[o] 25"Where is your faith?" he asked his disciples.

In fear and amazement they asked one another, "Who is this? He commands even the winds and the water, and they obey him."

The Healing of a Demon-possessed Man

8:26-37pp — Mt 8:28-34
8:26-39pp — Mk 5:1-20

26They sailed to the region of the Gerasenes,[a] which is across the lake from Galilee. 27When Jesus stepped ashore, he was met by a demon-possessed man from the town. For a long time this man had not worn clothes or lived in a house, but had lived in the tombs. 28When he saw Jesus, he cried out and fell at his feet, shouting at the top of his voice, "What do you want with me,[p] Jesus, Son of the Most High God?[q] I beg you, don't torture me!" 29For Jesus had commanded the evil[b] spirit to come out of the man. Many times it had seized him, and though he was chained hand and foot and kept under guard, he had broken his chains and had been driven by the demon into solitary places.

30Jesus asked him, "What is your name?"

8:14 [g]Mt 19:23; 1Ti 6:9,10,17
8:16 [h]S Mt 5:15
8:17 [i]Mt 10:26; Mk 4:22; Lk 12:2
8:18 [j]S Mt 25:29
8:20 [k]Jn 7:5
8:21 [l]Lk 6:47; 11:28; Jn 14:21
8:24 [m]S Lk 5:5 [n]Lk 4:35,39,41 [o]Ps 107:29; Jnh 1:15
8:28 [p]S Mt 8:29 [q]S Mk 5:7

[a] 26 Some manuscripts *Gadarenes*; other manuscripts *Gergesenes*; also in verse 37 [b] 29 Greek *unclean*

8:16 *lights a lamp.* Although Jesus couched much of his message in parables, he intended that the disciples make the truths known as widely as possible (see note on 11:33). *puts it on a stand.* See note on Mt 5:15.

8:17 This verse explains v. 16. It is the destiny of the truth to be made known (cf. 12:2 and note). The disciples were to begin a proclamation that would become universal.

8:18 *consider carefully how you listen.* The disciples heard not only for themselves but also for those to whom they would minister (see Mk 4:24; cf. Jas 1:19–22). Truth that is not understood and appropriated will be lost (see 19:26; Php 3:16 and notes), but truth that is used will be multiplied.

8:19 *Jesus' mother and brothers came.* See note on Mk 3:21. More is known about their motive from Mk 3:21,31–32. The family, thinking he was "out of his mind" (Mk 3:21), probably wanted to get him away from his heavy schedule. *brothers.* Did not believe in Jesus at this time (Jn 7:5; see note on Jn 7:4). Various interpretations concerning their relationship to Jesus arose in the early church: They were sons of Joseph by a previous marriage (according to Epiphanius) or were cousins (said Jerome). The most natural conclusion (suggested by Helvidius) is that they were the sons of Joseph and Mary, younger half brothers of Jesus. Four of these brothers are named in Mk 6:3, where sisters are also mentioned. Since Joseph is not mentioned here, it is likely that he had died.

8:21 Jesus' reply was not meant to reject his natural family but to emphasize the higher priority of his spiritual relationship to those who believed in him (see 11:28 and note).

8:22 *lake.* See 5:1 and note.

8:23 *squall.* See note on Mk 4:37.

8:26 *region of the Gerasenes.* The Gospels describe the location of this event in two ways: (1) the region of the Gerasenes (see note on Mk 5:1); (2) the region of the Gadarenes (see note on Mt 8:28). Some manuscripts of Matthew, Mark and Luke read "Gergesenes" (see NIV text note here), but this spelling may have been introduced in an attempt to resolve the differences.

8:27 *demon-possessed man.* See note on 4:33. Matthew (8:28) refers to two demon-possessed men, but Mark (5:2) and Luke mention only one. *tombs.* An isolated burial ground avoided by most people (but see note on Mk 5:3).

8:28 *Son of the Most High God.* Cf. 1:32 and note; 4:34. The title "Most High God" was commonly used by Gentiles (see Ge 14:19 and note; Ac 16:17); its use here perhaps indicates that this man was not a Jew (but see note on Mk 1:24). *don't torture me!* See Mk 1:24 and note.

8:30 *What is your name?* Jesus asked the man his name, but it was the demons who replied, thus showing they were in control of the man. *Legion.* See note on Mk 5:9.

"Legion," he replied, because many
demons had gone into him. 31And they
begged him repeatedly not to order them
to go into the Abyss.[r]
32A large herd of pigs was feeding there
on the hillside. The demons begged Jesus
to let them go into them, and he gave them
permission. 33When the demons came out
of the man, they went into the pigs, and
the herd rushed down the steep bank into
the lake[s] and was drowned.
34When those tending the pigs saw
what had happened, they ran off and reported this in the town and countryside,
35and the people went out to see what
had happened. When they came to Jesus,
they found the man from whom the demons had gone out, sitting at Jesus' feet,[t]
dressed and in his right mind; and they
were afraid. 36Those who had seen it told
the people how the demon-possessed[u]
man had been cured. 37Then all the people
of the region of the Gerasenes asked Jesus
to leave them,[v] because they were overcome with fear. So he got into the boat
and left.
38The man from whom the demons had
gone out begged to go with him, but Jesus
sent him away, saying, 39"Return home
and tell how much God has done for you."
So the man went away and told all over
town how much Jesus had done for him.

A Dead Girl and a Sick Woman

8:40-56pp — Mt 9:18-26; Mk 5:22-43

40Now when Jesus returned, a crowd
welcomed him, for they were all expecting him. 41Then a man named Jairus, a
ruler of the synagogue,[w] came and fell at
Jesus' feet, pleading with him to come to
his house 42because his only daughter, a
girl of about twelve, was dying.
As Jesus was on his way, the crowds
almost crushed him. 43And a woman was
there who had been subject to bleeding[x] for twelve years,[a] but no one could
heal her. 44She came up behind him and
touched the edge of his cloak,[y] and immediately her bleeding stopped.
45"Who touched me?" Jesus asked.
When they all denied it, Peter said,
"Master,[z] the people are crowding and
pressing against you."
46But Jesus said, "Someone touched
me;[a] I know that power has gone out
from me."[b]
47Then the woman, seeing that she could
not go unnoticed, came trembling and fell
at his feet. In the presence of all the people, she told why she had touched him and
how she had been instantly healed. 48Then
he said to her, "Daughter, your faith has
healed you.[c] Go in peace."[d]
49While Jesus was still speaking, someone came from the house of Jairus, the
synagogue ruler.[e] "Your daughter is dead,"
he said. "Don't bother the teacher any
more."
50Hearing this, Jesus said to Jairus,
"Don't be afraid; just believe, and she will
be healed."
51When he arrived at the house of Jairus, he did not let anyone go in with him
except Peter, John and James,[f] and the
child's father and mother. 52Meanwhile,
all the people were wailing and mourning[g]
for her. "Stop wailing," Jesus said. "She is
not dead but asleep."[h]
53They laughed at him, knowing that she
was dead. 54But he took her by the hand
and said, "My child, get up!"[i] 55Her spirit
returned, and at once she stood up. Then
Jesus told them to give her something to
eat. 56Her parents were astonished, but he
ordered them not to tell anyone what had
happened.[j]

Jesus Sends Out the Twelve

9:3-5pp — Mt 10:9-15; Mk 6:8-11
9:7-9pp — Mt 14:1,2; Mk 6:14-16

9 When Jesus had called the Twelve
together, he gave them power and

8:31 [r] Rev 9:1,2, 11; 11:7; 17:8; 20:1,3
8:33 [s] ver 22,23
8:35 [t] Lk 10:39
8:36 [u] S Mt 4:24
8:37 [v] Ac 16:39
8:41 [w] ver 49; S Mk 5:22
8:43 [x] Lev 15:25-30
8:44 [y] S Mt 9:20
8:45 [z] S Lk 5:5
8:46 [a] Mt 14:36; Mk 3:10 [b] Lk 5:17; 6:19
8:48 [c] S Mt 9:22 [d] S Ac 15:33
8:49 [e] ver 41
8:51 [f] S Mt 4:21
8:52 [g] Lk 23:27 [h] S Mt 9:24
8:54 [i] S Lk 7:14
8:56 [j] S Mt 8:4

[a] 43 Many manuscripts *years, and she had spent all she had on doctors*

8:31 *Abyss.* A place of confinement for evil spirits and for Satan (see note on Rev 9:1).
8:32 *pigs.* Pigs were unclean to Jews, and eating them was forbidden (Lev 11:7 – 8), but this was the Decapolis, a predominantly Gentile territory. *he gave them permission.* See note on Mt 8:32.
8:39 *Return home and tell how much God has done for you.* Although the man wanted to follow Jesus, he was directed to make the miracle known in his own native territory. There was no danger here of interference with Jesus' ministry (see note on Mk 5:19).
8:41 *ruler of the synagogue.* The ruler was responsible for conducting services, selecting participants and maintaining order (see note on Mk 5:22).
8:43 *bleeding.* The hemorrhage had made her ceremonially unclean for 12 years (see Lev 15:19 – 30 and note on 15:25).
8:45 *Who touched me?* For the woman's good and for a testimony to the crowd, Jesus insisted that the miracle be made known.
8:46 *power has gone out.* See note on Mk 5:30.
8:48 *Daughter.* Jesus addressed the woman with a tender term (cf. 13:16; 23:28). *Go in peace.* Cf. 7:50 and note.
8:50 *will be healed.* See note on Mk 5:34.
8:52 *wailing and mourning.* See note on Mk 5:38. *not dead but asleep.* Jesus meant that she was not permanently dead (see Jn 11:11 – 14 for a similar statement about Lazarus).
8:56 *ordered them not to tell.* See notes on Mt 8:4; Mk 5:43. Further publicity at this time concerning a raising from the dead would have been counterproductive to Jesus' ministry.
9:1 – 6 A new phase of Jesus' ministry began when he sent out the apostles to do the type of preaching, teaching and healing they had observed him doing (Mt 9:35). This was the third tour of Galilee by Jesus and his disciples (see note on 8:1). On the first tour Jesus traveled with the four fishermen;

authority to drive out all demons[k] and
to cure diseases,[l] 2and he sent them out
to preach the kingdom of God[m] and to
heal the sick. 3He told them: "Take nothing for the journey — no staff, no bag, no
bread, no money, no extra tunic.[n] 4What-
ever house you enter, stay there until you
leave that town. 5If people do not welcome
you, shake the dust off your feet when you
leave their town, as a testimony against
them."[o] 6So they set out and went from
village to village, preaching the gospel and
healing people everywhere.

7Now Herod[p] the tetrarch heard about all
that was going on. And he was perplexed,
because some were saying that John[q] had
been raised from the dead,[r] 8others that
Elijah had appeared,[s] and still others that
one of the prophets of long ago had come
back to life.[t] 9But Herod said, "I beheaded
John. Who, then, is this I hear such things
about?" And he tried to see him.[u]

Jesus Feeds the Five Thousand

9:10-17pp — Mt 14:13-21; Mk 6:32-44; Jn 6:5-13
9:13-17Ref — 2Ki 4:42-44

10When the apostles[v] returned, they reported to Jesus what they had done. Then
he took them with him and they withdrew
by themselves to a town called Bethsaida,[w]
11but the crowds learned about it and followed him. He welcomed them and spoke
to them about the kingdom of God,[x] and
healed those who needed healing.

12Late in the afternoon the Twelve came
to him and said, "Send the crowd away so
they can go to the surrounding villages and
countryside and find food and lodging, because we are in a remote place here."

13He replied, "You give them something
to eat."

They answered, "We have only five
loaves of bread and two fish — unless
we go and buy food for all this crowd."
14(About five thousand men were there.)

But he said to his disciples, "Have them
sit down in groups of about fifty each."
15The disciples did so, and everybody sat
down. 16Taking the five loaves and the two
fish and looking up to heaven, he gave
thanks and broke them.[y] Then he gave
them to the disciples to set before the people. 17They all ate and were satisfied, and
the disciples picked up twelve basketfuls
of broken pieces that were left over.

Peter's Confession of Christ

9:18-20pp — Mt 16:13-16; Mk 8:27-29
9:22-27pp — Mt 16:21-28; Mk 8:31 – 9:1

18Once when Jesus was praying[z] in
private and his disciples were with him,
he asked them, "Who do the crowds say
I am?"

19They replied, "Some say John the Baptist;[a] others say Elijah; and still others, that
one of the prophets of long ago has come
back to life."[b]

20"But what about you?" he asked. "Who
do you say I am?"

Peter answered, "The Christ[a] of God."[c]

21Jesus strictly warned them not to tell

9:1 [k] S Mt 10:1 [l] S Mt 4:23; Lk 5:17 **9:2** [m] S Mt 3:2 **9:3** [n] Lk 10:4; 22:35 **9:5** [o] S Mt 10:14 **9:7** [p] S Mt 14:1 [q] S Mt 3:1 [r] ver 19 **9:8** [s] S Mt 11:14 [t] ver 19; Jn 1:21 **9:9** [u] Lk 23:8 **9:10** [v] S Mk 6:30 [w] S Mt 11:21 **9:11** [x] ver 2; S Mt 3:2

9:16 [y] S Mt 14:19 **9:18** [z] S Lk 3:21 **9:19** [a] S Mt 3:1 [b] ver 7,8 **9:20** [c] Jn 1:49; 6:66-69; 11:27

[a] 20 Or *Messiah*

on the second all 12 were with him; on the third Jesus traveled alone after sending out the Twelve two by two.

9:1 *the Twelve.* The apostles (see 6:13 and note on Mk 6:30). *power and authority.* Special power to heal (see 5:17; 8:46; Mk 5:30 and note) and authority in teaching and control over evil spirits. *demons.* Evil spirits (see note on 4:33).

9:2 *sent them out to preach.* Compare Jesus' accompanying instructions to the 12 with those he gave to the 72 he sent later (10:1 – 12).

9:3 *Take nothing.* No excess baggage that would encumber travel, not even the usual provisions. They were to be entirely dependent on the people with whom they were staying (see note on Mk 6:8).

9:4 *stay there.* They were not to move from house to house, seeking better lodging, but use only one home as headquarters while preaching in a community.

9:5 *shake the dust off your feet.* A sign of repudiation for their rejection of God's message and a gesture showing separation from everything associated with the place (see 10:11; see also notes on Mt 10:14; Ac 13:51).

9:7 *Herod the tetrarch.* See note on Mt 14:1. *John had been raised from the dead.* See note on Mk 6:16. Luke does not give details about John's death (see Mt 14:1 – 12; Mk 6:17 – 29), which occurred about this time, but simply notes that it had taken place (v. 9).

9:8 *Elijah had appeared.* See notes on 1:17; Mk 9:12.

9:9 *he tried to see him.* Herod's desire to see Jesus was not fulfilled until Jesus' trial (23:8 – 12).

9:10 – 17 The feeding of the 5,000 is the only miracle besides Jesus' resurrection that is reported in all four Gospels (see notes on Mk 6:30 – 44; Jn 6:1 – 14).

9:10 *Bethsaida.* See note on Mt 11:21. Jesus must have retired to a remote area near the town (v. 12).

9:12 *Late in the afternoon.* After the preaching and healing, the question was raised about food and lodging because they were in an isolated place. Jesus may have introduced the question (see Jn 6:5), but the Synoptics indicate that the disciples were also concerned.

9:14 *sit down in groups of about fifty.* See note on Mk 6:40.

9:17 *picked up twelve basketfuls of broken pieces.* This act served as an example of avoiding wastefulness and as a demonstration that everyone had been adequately fed (see notes on Mt 15:37; Mk 6:43).

9:18 *Who do the crowds say I am?* The report brought by the disciples was the same as the one that reached Herod (see vv. 7 – 8). This event occurred to the north, outside Herod's territory, in the vicinity of Caesarea Philippi (see Mt 16:13 and note; see also note on Mk 7:24).

9:20 *Peter answered.* He was the spokesman for the disciples. *The Christ of God.* See NIV text note on 2:11. This predicted Deliverer (the Messiah) had been desired for centuries (see notes on Mt 16:18; Mk 8:29; Jn 4:25).

9:21 *warned them not to tell.* The people had false notions about the Messiah and needed to be taught further before Jesus identified himself explicitly to the public. He had a crucial schedule to keep and could not be interrupted by premature reactions (see notes on Mt 8:4; 16:20; Mk 1:34).

this to anyone.[d] 22And he said, "The Son of Man[e] must suffer many things[f] and be rejected by the elders, chief priests and teachers of the law,[g] and he must be killed[h] and on the third day[i] be raised to life."[j]

23Then he said to them all: "If anyone would come after me, he must deny himself and take up his cross daily and follow me.[k] 24For whoever wants to save his life will lose it, but whoever loses his life for me will save it.[l] 25What good is it for a man to gain the whole world, and yet lose or forfeit his very self? 26If anyone is ashamed of me and my words, the Son of Man will be ashamed of him[m] when he comes in his glory and in the glory of the Father and of the holy angels.[n] 27I tell you the truth, some who are standing here will not taste death before they see the kingdom of God."

The Transfiguration

9:28-36pp — Mt 17:1-8; Mk 9:2-8

28About eight days after Jesus said this, he took Peter, John and James[o] with him and went up onto a mountain to pray.[p] 29As he was praying, the appearance of his face changed, and his clothes became as bright as a flash of lightning. 30Two men, Moses and Elijah, 31appeared in glorious splendor, talking with Jesus. They spoke about his departure,[q] which he was about to bring to fulfillment at Jerusalem. 32Peter and his companions were very sleepy,[r] but when they became fully awake, they saw his glory and the two men standing with him. 33As the men were leaving Jesus, Peter said to him, "Master,[s] it is good for us to be here. Let us put up three shelters — one for you, one for Moses and one for Elijah." (He did not know what he was saying.)

34While he was speaking, a cloud appeared and enveloped them, and they were afraid as they entered the cloud. 35A voice came from the cloud, saying, "This is my Son, whom I have chosen;[t] listen to him."[u] 36When the voice had spoken, they found that Jesus was alone. The disciples kept this to themselves, and told no one at that time what they had seen.[v]

The Healing of a Boy With an Evil Spirit

9:37-42,43-45pp — Mt 17:14-18,22,23; Mk 9:14-27,30-32

37The next day, when they came down from the mountain, a large crowd met him. 38A man in the crowd called out, "Teacher, I beg you to look at my son, for he is my only child. 39A spirit seizes him and he suddenly screams; it throws him into convulsions so that he foams at the mouth. It scarcely ever leaves him and is destroying him. 40I begged your disciples to drive it out, but they could not."

41"O unbelieving and perverse generation,"[w] Jesus replied, "how long shall I stay with you and put up with you? Bring your son here."

9:21 [d]S Mk 8:30
9:22 [e]S Mt 8:20 [f]S Mt 16:21 [g]Mt 27:1,2 [h]Ac 2:23; 3:13 [i]S Mt 16:21 [j]S Mt 16:21
9:23 [k]Mt 10:38; Lk 14:27
9:24 [l]S Jn 12:25
9:26 [m]Mt 10:33; Lk 12:9; 2Ti 2:12 [n]S Mt 16:27
9:28 [o]S Mt 4:21 [p]S Lk 3:21
9:31 [q]2Pe 1:15
9:32 [r]Mt 26:43
9:33 [s]S Lk 5:5
9:35 [t]Isa 42:1 [u]S Mt 3:17
9:36 [v]Mt 17:9
9:41 [w]Dt 32:5

9:22 *Son of Man.* See note on Mk 8:31. *must suffer.* Jesus' first explicit prediction of his death (for later references see v. 44; 12:50; 17:25; 18:31–33; cf. 24:7,25–27).

9:23 *take up his cross daily.* To follow Jesus requires self-denial, complete dedication and willing obedience. Luke emphasizes continued action, and "daily" is not mentioned explicitly in the parallel accounts (Mt 16:24–26; Mk 8:34). Disciples from Galilee knew what the cross meant, for hundreds of men had been executed by this means in their region.

9:24 *whoever loses his life for me.* A saying of Jesus found in all four Gospels and in two Gospels more than once (see 14:26–27; 17:33; Mt 10:38–39; 16:24–25; Mk 8:34–35; Jn 12:25 and note). No other saying of Jesus is given such emphasis.

9:26 *If anyone is ashamed.* See 12:9; see also note on Mk 8:38.

9:27 See note on Mt 16:28. *kingdom of God.* See note on Mt 3:2.

9:28 *About eight days.* Frequently used to indicate a week (e.g., Jn 20:26 in the Greek; see note on Mt 17:1). *Peter, John and James.* These three were also with Jesus at the healing of Jairus's daughter (8:51) and in his last visit to Gethsemane (Mk 14:33). *onto a mountain.* Although Mount Tabor is the traditional site of the Mount of Transfiguration, its distance from Caesarea Philippi (the vicinity of the last scene), its height (about 1,800 feet) and its occupation by a fortress make it unlikely. Mount Hermon fits the context much better by being both closer and higher (over 9,000 feet; see Mk 9:2). *pray.* Again Luke points out the place of prayer in an important event.

9:30 *Moses and Elijah.* Moses, the great OT deliverer and lawgiver, and Elijah, the representative of the prophets. Moses' work had been finished by Joshua, Elijah's by Elisha (another form of the name Joshua). They now spoke with Jesus (whose Hebrew name was Joshua) concerning the "exodus" (see note on v. 31) he was about to accomplish, by which he would deliver his people from the bondage of sin and bring to fulfillment the work of both Moses and Elijah (see notes on 1Ki 19:16; Mt 17:3).

9:31 *departure.* Greek *exodos,* a word that links Jesus' saving death, resurrection (v. 22) and ascension (v. 51) with God's saving of his people Israel out of Egypt.

9:32 *sleepy.* Likely the event took place at night when the "glorious splendor" (v. 31) would have pierced the darkness in a most striking manner (cf. v. 37, "The next day"). *saw his glory.* See note on Ex 33:18.

9:33 *three shelters.* Temporary structures to prolong the visit of the three important persons: lawgiver, prophet and Messiah. The idea was not appropriate, however, because Jesus had a work to finish in his few remaining days on earth (see note on Mk 9:5).

9:34–35 *cloud.* See Mt 17:5 and note.

9:35 *whom I have chosen.* Or "the Chosen One," related to a Jewish title found in Dead Sea Scrolls literature and possibly echoing Isa 42:1. See also 23:35. *have chosen.* Parallel to "love" (Mt 17:5; see Mt 3:17 and note; 2Pe 1:17).

9:39 *A spirit seizes him.* This evil spirit was causing seizures (Mt 17:15; see note on Mt 4:24) and a speechless condition (Mk 9:17). Evil spirits were responsible for many kinds of affliction (see note on 4:33).

42Even while the boy was coming, the
demon threw him to the ground in a convulsion. But Jesus rebuked the evil[a] spirit,
healed the boy and gave him back to his
father. 43And they were all amazed at the
greatness of God.
While everyone was marveling at all
that Jesus did, he said to his disciples,
44"Listen carefully to what I am about to
tell you: The Son of Man is going to be
betrayed into the hands of men."[x] 45But
they did not understand what this meant.
It was hidden from them, so that they did
not grasp it,[y] and they were afraid to ask
him about it.

Who Will Be the Greatest?

9:46-48pp — Mt 18:1-5
9:46-50pp — Mk 9:33-40

46An argument started among the disciples as to which of them would be the
greatest.[z] 47Jesus, knowing their thoughts,[a]
took a little child and had him stand beside him. 48Then he said to them, "Whoever welcomes this little child in my name
welcomes me; and whoever welcomes
me welcomes the one who sent me.[b] For
he who is least among you all—he is the
greatest."[c]
49"Master,"[d] said John, "we saw a man
driving out demons in your name and we
tried to stop him, because he is not one
of us."
50"Do not stop him," Jesus said, "for
whoever is not against you is for you."[e]

Samaritan Opposition

51As the time approached for him to be
taken up to heaven,[f] Jesus resolutely set
out for Jerusalem.[g] 52And he sent messengers on ahead, who went into a Samaritan[h] village to get things ready for him;
53but the people there did not welcome
him, because he was heading for Jerusalem. 54When the disciples James and John[i]
saw this, they asked, "Lord, do you want
us to call fire down from heaven to destroy them[b]?"[j] 55But Jesus turned and rebuked them, 56and[c] they went to another
village.

The Cost of Following Jesus

9:57-60pp — Mt 8:19-22

57As they were walking along the road,[k]
a man said to him, "I will follow you
wherever you go."
58Jesus replied, "Foxes have holes and
birds of the air have nests, but the Son of
Man[l] has no place to lay his head."
59He said to another man, "Follow
me."[m]
But the man replied, "Lord, first let me
go and bury my father."
60Jesus said to him, "Let the dead bury
their own dead, but you go and proclaim
the kingdom of God."[n]
61Still another said, "I will follow you,
Lord; but first let me go back and say
good-by to my family."[o]
62Jesus replied, "No one who puts his
hand to the plow and looks back is fit for
service in the kingdom of God."

9:44 [x]S ver 22
9:45 [y]S Mk 9:32
9:46 [z]Lk 22:24
9:47 [a]S Mt 9:4
9:48 [b]S Mt 10:40 [c]S Mk 9:35
9:49 [d]S Lk 5:5
9:50 [e]Mt 12:30; Lk 11:23
9:51 [f]S Mk 16:19 [g]Lk 13:22; 17:11; 18:31; 19:28
9:52 [h]S Mt 10:5
9:54 [i]S Mt 4:21 [j]2Ki 1:10,12
9:57 [k]ver 51
9:58 [l]S Mt 8:20
9:59 [m]S Mt 4:19
9:60 [n]S Mt 3:2
9:61 [o]1Ki 19:20

[a] 42 Greek *unclean* [b] 54 Some manuscripts *them, even as Elijah did* [c] 55,56 Some manuscripts *them. And he said, "You do not know what kind of spirit you are of, for the Son of Man did not come to destroy men's lives, but to save them."* 56*And*

9:44 Another prediction of Jesus' coming death (see note on v. 22), an indication of how it will be brought about (see 22:21).
9:45 *hidden from them.* Not yet disclosed to them by God (see 18:34; 19:42; 24:16).
9:46 *which … would be the greatest.* A subject that arose on a number of occasions (see 22:24; see also Mk 10:35 – 45 and note on Mk 9:34).
9:48 *he who is least … is the greatest.* People become great in God's sight as they sincerely and unpretentiously look away from self to revere him (see Mk 10:43 and note).
9:49 *not one of us.* Jesus shifts the pronoun to "you" in v. 50, which may mean that the man had a relationship to Jesus of which the disciples were unaware (see note on Mk 9:38).
9:50 *whoever is not against you is for you.* Spoken in the context of opposition to the disciples' work (cf. 11:23, set in a different context; see note there).
9:51 *taken up to heaven.* See 24:51; Ac 1:9. *set out for Jerusalem.* Lit. "set his face to go to Jerusalem" (cf. Isa 50:7). Luke emphasizes Jesus' determination to complete his mission (see note on 13:22). This journey to Jerusalem, however, is not the one that led to his crucifixion but marks the beginning of a period of ministry in Judea, of which Jerusalem was the central city. Mk 10:1 notes this departure for Judea, which John more specifically describes as a journey to Jerusalem during the Feast of Tabernacles (Jn 7:1 – 10). The Judean ministry (see Introduction: Outline) is recounted in 9:51 — 13:21 and Jn 7:10 — 10:39. Cf. note on Mk 10:32.
9:52 *a Samaritan village.* Samaritans were particularly hostile to Jews who were on their way to observe religious festivals in Jerusalem. It was at least a three-day journey from Galilee to Jerusalem through Samaria, and Samaritans refused overnight shelter for the pilgrims. Because of this antipathy, Jews traveling between Galilee and Jerusalem frequently went on the east side of the Jordan River.
9:54 *call fire down.* As Elijah had (2Ki 1:9 – 16). James and John were known as "Sons of Thunder" (Mk 3:17; see note there).
9:55 *rebuked them.* See note on 2Ki 1:10.
9:57 – 62 The cost of being a true follower of Jesus. Neither hardships (vv. 57 – 58) nor bereavement (vv. 59 – 60) nor family ties (v. 61) should keep anyone from following him (v. 62).
9:57 *As they were walking.* Continuing their journey through Samaria to Jerusalem.
9:59 *bury my father.* If his father had already died, the man would have been occupied with the burial. But evidently he wanted to wait until after his father's death, which might have been years away. Jesus told him that the spiritually dead could bury the physically dead, and that the spiritually alive should be busy proclaiming the kingdom of God (see Mt 8:21 – 22 and note on 8:22).
9:62 *looks back.* Cf. Jn 6:66; Php 3:13 and notes.

Jesus Sends Out the Seventy-two

10:4-12pp — Lk 9:3-5
10:13-15,21,22pp — Mt 11:21-23,25-27
10:23,24pp — Mt 13:16,17

10 After this the Lord[p] appointed seventy-two[a] others[q] and sent them two
by two[r] ahead of him to every town and
place where he was about to go.[s] 2He told
them, "The harvest is plentiful, but the
workers are few. Ask the Lord of the harvest, therefore, to send out workers into
his harvest field.[t] 3Go! I am sending you
out like lambs among wolves.[u] 4Do not
take a purse or bag or sandals; and do not
greet anyone on the road.
5"When you enter a house, first say,
'Peace to this house.' 6If a man of peace
is there, your peace will rest on him; if
not, it will return to you. 7Stay in that
house, eating and drinking whatever they
give you, for the worker deserves his wages.[v] Do not move around from house to
house.
8"When you enter a town and are welcomed, eat what is set before you.[w] 9Heal
the sick who are there and tell them, 'The
kingdom of God[x] is near you.' 10But when
you enter a town and are not welcomed,
go into its streets and say, 11'Even the dust
of your town that sticks to our feet we
wipe off against you.[y] Yet be sure of this:
The kingdom of God is near.'[z] 12I tell you,
it will be more bearable on that day for
Sodom[a] than for that town.[b]
13"Woe to you,[c] Korazin! Woe to you,
Bethsaida! For if the miracles that were
performed in you had been performed in
Tyre and Sidon, they would have repented long ago, sitting in sackcloth[d] and ashes. 14But it will be more bearable for Tyre
and Sidon at the judgment than for you.
15And you, Capernaum,[e] will you be lifted
up to the skies? No, you will go down to
the depths.[b]
16"He who listens to you listens to me;
he who rejects you rejects me; but he who
rejects me rejects him who sent me."[f]
17The seventy-two[g] returned with joy
and said, "Lord, even the demons submit
to us in your name."[h]
18He replied, "I saw Satan[i] fall like lightning from heaven.[j] 19I have given you authority to trample on snakes[k] and scorpions and to overcome all the power of the
enemy; nothing will harm you. 20However,
do not rejoice that the spirits submit to
you, but rejoice that your names are written in heaven."[l]
21At that time Jesus, full of joy through
the Holy Spirit, said, "I praise you, Father,
Lord of heaven and earth, because you
have hidden these things from the wise
and learned, and revealed them to little
children.[m] Yes, Father, for this was your
good pleasure.
22"All things have been committed to
me by my Father.[n] No one knows who
the Son is except the Father, and no one
knows who the Father is except the Son
and those to whom the Son chooses to reveal him."[o]
23Then he turned to his disciples and
said privately, "Blessed are the eyes
that see what you see. 24For I tell you
that many prophets and kings wanted
to see what you see but did not see it,
and to hear what you hear but did not
hear it."[p]

10:1 [p]S Lk 7:13 [q]Lk 9:1,2,51,52 [r]Mk 6:7 [s]Mt 10:1 **10:2** [t]Mt 9:37,38; Jn 4:35 **10:3** [u]Mt 10:16 **10:7** [v]S 1Ti 5:18 **10:8** [w]1Co 10:27 **10:9** [x]S Mt 3:2 **10:11** [y]S Mt 10:14 [z]ver 9 **10:12** [a]S Mt 10:15 [b]Mt 11:24 **10:13** [c]Lk 6:24-26 [d]S Rev 11:3 **10:15** [e]S Mt 4:13 **10:16** [f]S Mt 10:40 **10:17** [g]ver 1 [h]S Mk 16:17 **10:18** [i]S Mt 4:10 [j]Isa 14:12; Rev 9:1; 12:8,9 **10:19** [k]Mk 16:18; Ac 28:3-5 **10:20** [l]S Rev 20:12 **10:21** [m]1Co 1:26-29 **10:22** [n]S Mt 28:18 [o]Jn 1:18 **10:24** [p]1Pe 1:10-12

[a] *1* Some manuscripts *seventy*; also in verse 17
[b] *15* Greek *Hades*

10:1 *appointed seventy-two.* Recorded only in Luke, though similar instructions were given to the Twelve (Mt 9:37–38; 10:7–16; Mk 6:7–11; cf. Lk 9:3–5). Certain differences in early manuscripts make it unclear as to whether the number was 72 or 70 (see NIV text note). Jesus covered Judea with his message (see note on 9:51) as thoroughly as he had Galilee. *two by two.* During his ministry in Galilee, Jesus had also sent out the Twelve two by two (see 9:1–6; Mk 6:7 and notes), a practice continued in the early church (Ac 13:2; 15:27,39–40; 17:14; 19:22).

10:3 *lambs among wolves.* Cf. Mt 7:15; 10:16; Ac 20:29.

10:4 *Do not take a purse or bag or sandals.* They were to travel light, without moneybag, luggage or extra sandals (see note on 9:3). *do not greet anyone.* They were not to stop along the way to visit and exchange customary lengthy greetings. The mission was urgent.

10:7 *worker deserves … wages.* Cf. 1Co 9:3–12; 1Ti 5:18 and note. *Do not move around.* See note on 9:4.

10:9 *The kingdom of God is near.* The heart of Jesus' message (see notes on 4:43; Mt 3:2).

10:11 *dust … we wipe off.* See note on 9:5.

10:12 *more bearable … for Sodom.* Although Sodom was so sinful that God destroyed it (see Ge 18:20 and note; 19:24–28; Jude 7 and note), the people who heard the message of Jesus and his disciples were even more accountable, because they had the full gospel of the kingdom preached to them. *that day.* Judgment day.

10:13 *Korazin … Bethsaida.* See note on Mt 11:21. *sackcloth and ashes.* See Mt 11:21; Rev 11:3 and notes.

10:14 *Tyre and Sidon.* Gentile cities in Phoenicia (see note on 6:17), north of Galilee, which had not had opportunity to witness Jesus' miracles and hear his preaching as the people had in most of Galilee (see note on v. 12).

10:15 *Capernaum.* Jesus' headquarters on the north shore of the Sea of Galilee (see Mt 4:13 and note), whose inhabitants had many opportunities to see and hear Jesus. Therefore the condemnation for their rejection was the greater.

10:18 *Satan fall.* Even the demons were driven out by the disciples (v. 17), which meant that Satan was suffering defeat (may echo the language of Isa 14:12; see note on Isa 14:12–15). *Satan.* See notes on Mk 1:13; 1Th 3:5.

10:19 *snakes and scorpions … power of the enemy.* The snakes and scorpions may represent evil spirits; the enemy is Satan himself.

10:20 One's salvation is more important than power to overcome the evil one or escape his harm. *your names are written.* Salvation is recorded in heaven (see Ps 69:28 and note; Da 12:1).

10:21–22 See Mt 11:25–27 and notes.

10:23 *see what you see.* The Messiah and his saving work, for which they longed so much.

The Parable of the Good Samaritan

10:25-28pp — Mt 22:34-40; Mk 12:28-31

25 On one occasion an expert in the law
stood up to test Jesus. "Teacher," he asked,
"what must I do to inherit eternal life?"[q]
26 "What is written in the Law?" he replied. "How do you read it?"
27 He answered: " 'Love the Lord your
God with all your heart and with all your
soul and with all your strength and with
all your mind'[a];[r] and, 'Love your neighbor
as yourself.'[b]"[s]
28 "You have answered correctly," Jesus
replied. "Do this and you will live."[t]
29 But he wanted to justify himself,[u] so
he asked Jesus, "And who is my neighbor?"
30 In reply Jesus said: "A man was going down from Jerusalem to Jericho,
when he fell into the hands of robbers.
They stripped him of his clothes, beat him
and went away, leaving him half dead.
31 A priest happened to be going down the
same road, and when he saw the man, he
passed by on the other side.[v] 32 So too, a
Levite, when he came to the place and saw
him, passed by on the other side. 33 But a
Samaritan,[w] as he traveled, came where
the man was; and when he saw him, he
took pity on him. 34 He went to him and
bandaged his wounds, pouring on oil and
wine. Then he put the man on his own
donkey, took him to an inn and took care
of him. 35 The next day he took out two silver coins[c] and gave them to the innkeeper. 'Look after him,' he said, 'and when I
return, I will reimburse you for any extra
expense you may have.'
36 "Which of these three do you think
was a neighbor to the man who fell into
the hands of robbers?"
37 The expert in the law replied, "The
one who had mercy on him."
Jesus told him, "Go and do likewise."

At the Home of Martha and Mary

38 As Jesus and his disciples were on their
way, he came to a village where a woman named Martha[x] opened her home to
him. 39 She had a sister called Mary,[y] who
sat at the Lord's feet[z] listening to what he
said. 40 But Martha was distracted by all
the preparations that had to be made. She
came to him and asked, "Lord, don't you
care[a] that my sister has left me to do the
work by myself? Tell her to help me!"
41 "Martha, Martha," the Lord answered,
"you are worried[b] and upset about many
things, 42 but only one thing is needed.[d][c]
Mary has chosen what is better, and it will
not be taken away from her."

Jesus' Teaching on Prayer

11:2-4pp — Mt 6:9-13
11:9-13pp — Mt 7:7-11

11 One day Jesus was praying[d] in a certain place. When he finished, one of
his disciples said to him, "Lord,[e] teach us
to pray, just as John taught his disciples."
2 He said to them, "When you pray,
say:

" 'Father,[e]
hallowed be your name,
your kingdom[f] come.[f]

10:25 [q]Mt 19:16; Lk 18:18 **10:27** [r]Dt 6:5 [s]Lev 19:18; S Mt 5:43 **10:28** [t]S Ro 7:10 **10:29** [u]Lk 16:15 **10:31** [v]Lev 21:1-3 **10:33** [w]S Mt 10:5 **10:38** [x]Jn 11:1; 12:2 **10:39** [y]Jn 11:1; 12:3 [z]Lk 8:35 **10:40** [a]Mk 4:38 **10:41** [b]Mt 6:25-34; Lk 12:11,22 **10:42** [c]Ps 27:4 **11:1** [d]S Lk 3:21 [e]S Jn 13:13 **11:2** [f]S Mt 3:2

[a] 27 Deut. 6:5 [b] 27 Lev. 19:18 [c] 35 Greek *two denarii* [d] 42 Some manuscripts *but few things are needed—or only one* [e] 2 Some manuscripts *Our Father in heaven* [f] 2 Some manuscripts *come. May your will be done on earth as it is in heaven.*

10:25 *expert in the law.* A scholar well versed in Scripture asked a common question (18:18; cf. Mt 22:35), either to take issue with Jesus or simply to see what kind of teacher he was. See note on 7:30.

10:27 *Love ... God ... Love your neighbor.* Elsewhere Jesus uses these words in reply to another question (see Mt 22:35-40; Mk 12:28-31 and notes), putting the same two Scriptures together (Lev 19:18; Dt 6:5). Whether a fourfold love (heart, soul, strength and mind, as here and in Mk 12:30) or threefold (Dt 6:5; Mt 22:37; Mk 12:33), the significance is that total devotion is demanded.

10:28 *will live.* Will have eternal life (v. 25).

10:29 *to justify himself.* The answer to his first question was obviously one he knew, so to gain credibility he asked for an interpretation. In effect he said, "But the real question is: Who is my neighbor?" See note on Lev 19:18.

10:30 *Jerusalem to Jericho.* A distance of 17 miles and a descent from about 2,500 feet above sea level to about 800 feet below sea level. The road ran through rocky, desert country, which provided places for robbers to waylay defenseless travelers.

10:31-33 *priest ... Levite ... Samaritan.* It is significant that the person Jesus commended was neither the religious leader nor the lay associate, but a hated foreigner. Jews viewed Samaritans as half-breeds, both physically (see note on Mt 10:5) and spiritually (see notes on Jn 4:20,22). Samaritans and Jews practiced open hostility (see note on 9:52), but Jesus asserted that love of the neighbor knows no national boundaries.

10:34 A demonstration of "Love your neighbor" (v. 27). *oil and wine.* For their healing effects (cf. Isa 1:6 and note; Mk 6:13; Jas 5:14 and note).

10:35 *two silver coins.* Two days' wages, which would keep the man for up to two months in an inn.

10:36 *Which ... was a neighbor to the man ... ?* The question now became: Which one proves he is the good neighbor by his actions?

10:38 *village.* Bethany, about two miles from Jerusalem, was the home of Mary and Martha (Jn 12:1-3; see note on Mt 21:17).

11:1 *Jesus was praying.* Not only on special occasions (e.g., baptism, 3:21 [see note there]; choosing the Twelve, 6:12; Gethsemane, 22:41) but also as a regular practice (5:16; Mt 14:23; Mk 1:35; see Introduction: Characteristics). *teach us to pray.* The Lord's model prayer was given here in answer to a request, and is similar to Mt 6:9-13, where it is part of the Sermon on the Mount. Six petitions are included in the prayer as given in the Sermon on the Mount by Matthew, whereas five appear in the prayer in Luke.

3Give us each day our daily bread.
4Forgive us our sins,
for we also forgive everyone who
sins against us.[a g]
And lead us not into temptation.[b]' "[h]

5Then he said to them, "Suppose one
of you has a friend, and he goes to him at
midnight and says, 'Friend, lend me three
loaves of bread, 6because a friend of mine
on a journey has come to me, and I have
nothing to set before him.'
7"Then the one inside answers, 'Don't
bother me. The door is already locked, and
my children are with me in bed. I can't
get up and give you anything.' 8I tell you,
though he will not get up and give him the
bread because he is his friend, yet because
of the man's boldness[c] he will get up and
give him as much as he needs.[i]
9"So I say to you: Ask and it will be giv-
en to you;[j] seek and you will find; knock
and the door will be opened to you. 10For
everyone who asks receives; he who seeks
finds; and to him who knocks, the door
will be opened.
11"Which of you fathers, if your son asks
for[d] a fish, will give him a snake instead?
12Or if he asks for an egg, will give him
a scorpion? 13If you then, though you are
evil, know how to give good gifts to your
children, how much more will your Father
in heaven give the Holy Spirit to those
who ask him!"

Jesus and Beelzebub

11:14,15,17-22,24-26pp — Mt 12:22,24-29,43-45
11:17-22pp — Mk 3:23-27

14Jesus was driving out a demon that was
mute. When the demon left, the man who
had been mute spoke, and the crowd was
amazed.[k] 15But some of them said, "By
Beelzebub,[e l] the prince of demons, he is
driving out demons."[m] 16Others tested him
by asking for a sign from heaven.[n]
17Jesus knew their thoughts[o] and said
to them: "Any kingdom divided against itself will be ruined, and a house divided
against itself will fall. 18If Satan[p] is divided against himself, how can his kingdom
stand? I say this because you claim that I
drive out demons by Beelzebub. 19Now if I
drive out demons by Beelzebub, by whom
do your followers drive them out? So then,
they will be your judges. 20But if I drive
out demons by the finger of God,[q] then the
kingdom of God[r] has come to you.
21"When a strong man, fully armed,
guards his own house, his possessions are
safe. 22But when someone stronger attacks
and overpowers him, he takes away the
armor in which the man trusted and divides up the spoils.
23"He who is not with me is against me,
and he who does not gather with me, scatters.[s]
24"When an evil[f] spirit comes out of a
man, it goes through arid places seeking
rest and does not find it. Then it says, 'I
will return to the house I left.' 25When it
arrives, it finds the house swept clean and
put in order. 26Then it goes and takes sev-
en other spirits more wicked than itself,

11:4 [g]Mt 18:35; Mk 11:25 [h]Mt 26:41; Jas 1:13
11:8 [i]Lk 18:1-6
11:9 [j]S Mt 7:7
11:14 [k]Mt 9:32,33
11:15 [l]S Mk 3:22 [m]Mt 9:34
11:16 [n]S Mt 12:38
11:17 [o]S Mt 9:4
11:18 [p]S Mt 4:10
11:20 [q]Ex 8:19 [r]S Mt 3:2
11:23 [s]Mt 12:30; Mk 9:40; Lk 9:50

[a] 4 Greek *everyone who is indebted to us* [b] 4 Some manuscripts *temptation but deliver us from the evil one* [c] 8 Or *persistence* [d] 11 Some manuscripts *for bread, will give him a stone; or if he asks for* [e] 15 Greek *Beezeboul* or *Beelzeboul*; also in verses 18 and 19 [f] 24 Greek *unclean*

11:4 *Forgive us our sins.* Mt 6:12 has "debts," but the meaning is the same as "sins." Jesus taught this truth on other occasions as well (see Mt 18:35 and note; Mk 11:25; cf. Eph 4:32 and note).

11:5–13 Jesus now urged boldness (or persistence; see NIV text note on v. 8) in prayer (vv. 5–8) and gave assurance that God answers prayer (vv. 9–13). The argument is from the lesser to the greater (see v. 13).

11:13 *give the Holy Spirit.* Mt 7:11 has "give good gifts," meaning spiritual gifts. Luke emphasizes the work of the Spirit, who is one of the greatest of God's gifts.

11:14 *demon that was mute.* See note on 4:33. This evil spirit caused muteness. The probable parallel passage in Matthew (12:22–30; see also Mk 3:20–27) indicates that the man was also blind.

11:15 *Beelzebub, the prince of demons.* Satan (v. 18). See note on Mt 10:25.

11:16 *sign from heaven.* Jesus had just healed a mute. Here was their sign, and they would not recognize it (see Mk 8:11 and note).

11:17 *kingdom divided against itself.* If Satan gave power to Jesus, who opposed him in every way, he would be supporting an attack upon himself.

11:19 *by whom do your followers . . . ?* Jesus did not say whether the followers of the Pharisees (see Mt 12:24) actually drove out demons (see note on v. 24); but they claimed to drive them out by the power of God, and Jesus claimed the same. So to accuse Jesus of using Satanic power was implicitly to condemn their own followers as well. *your judges.* They will condemn you for your accusation against them.

11:20 *the kingdom of God has come.* In the sense that the King was present in the person of Jesus (see notes on 4:43; 17:21) and that the powers of evil were being overthrown.

11:22 *someone stronger attacks.* Jesus was stronger than Beelzebub, and by his exorcism of demons he demonstrated that he had overpowered Satan and disarmed him. It was therefore foolish to suggest that Jesus had cast out demons by Satan's power.

11:23 The one who does not support Jesus opposes him, making neutrality impossible (see note on Mt 12:30). Even the worker in 9:50, whom the disciples described as "not one of us" (9:49), was apparently a believer, acting in Jesus' name (see note on Mk 9:38), and Jesus did not condemn him.

11:24 *evil spirit comes out.* Jesus is perhaps referring to the work of Jewish exorcists, who claimed to cast out demons (cf. v. 19 and note) but who rejected the kingdom of God as represented by Jesus and whose exorcisms were therefore ineffective. See Mt 12:43–45, where Jesus makes a similar comment about the Jewish nation of that day.

11:25 *finds the house swept clean.* The place had been cleaned up but left unoccupied. A life reformed but lacking God's presence and power is open to reoccupancy by evil.

and they go in and live there. And the final
condition of that man is worse than the
first."[t]
27As Jesus was saying these things, a
woman in the crowd called out, "Blessed
is the mother who gave you birth and
nursed you."[u]
28He replied, "Blessed rather are those
who hear the word of God[v] and obey it."[w]

The Sign of Jonah

11:29-32pp — Mt 12:39-42

29As the crowds increased, Jesus said,
"This is a wicked generation. It asks for a
miraculous sign,[x] but none will be given
it except the sign of Jonah.[y] 30For as Jonah was a sign to the Ninevites, so also
will the Son of Man be to this generation.
31The Queen of the South will rise at the
judgment with the men of this generation
and condemn them; for she came from the
ends of the earth to listen to Solomon's
wisdom,[z] and now one[a] greater than Solomon is here. 32The men of Nineveh will
stand up at the judgment with this generation and condemn it; for they repented
at the preaching of Jonah,[a] and now one
greater than Jonah is here.

The Lamp of the Body

11:34,35pp — Mt 6:22,23

33"No one lights a lamp and puts it in
a place where it will be hidden, or under
a bowl. Instead he puts it on its stand, so
that those who come in may see the light.[b]
34Your eye is the lamp of your body. When
your eyes are good, your whole body also
is full of light. But when they are bad,
your body also is full of darkness. 35See
to it, then, that the light within you is not
darkness. 36Therefore, if your whole body
is full of light, and no part of it dark, it will
be completely lighted, as when the light of
a lamp shines on you."

Six Woes

37When Jesus had finished speaking,
a Pharisee invited him to eat with him;
so he went in and reclined at the table.[c]
38But the Pharisee, noticing that Jesus did
not first wash before the meal,[d] was surprised.
39Then the Lord[e] said to him, "Now then,
you Pharisees clean the outside of the cup
and dish, but inside you are full of greed
and wickedness.[f] 40You foolish people![g]
Did not the one who made the outside
make the inside also? 41But give what is
inside ⌞the dish⌟[b] to the poor,[h] and everything will be clean for you.[i]
42"Woe to you Pharisees, because you
give God a tenth[j] of your mint, rue and
all other kinds of garden herbs, but you
neglect justice and the love of God.[k] You
should have practiced the latter without
leaving the former undone.[l]
43"Woe to you Pharisees, because you
love the most important seats in the synagogues and greetings in the marketplaces.[m]
44"Woe to you, because you are like
unmarked graves,[n] which men walk over
without knowing it."

11:26 t 2Pe 2:20
11:27 u Lk 23:29
11:28 v S Heb 4:12 w Pr 8:32; Lk 6:47; 8:21; Jn 14:21
11:29 x ver 16; S Mt 12:38 y Jnh 1:17; Mt 16:4
11:31 z 1Ki 10:1; 2Ch 9:1
11:32 a Jnh 3:5
11:33 b S Mt 5:15
11:37 c Lk 7:36; 14:1
11:38 d Mk 7:3,4
11:39 e S Lk 7:13 f Mt 23:25,26; Mk 7:20-23
11:40 g Lk 12:20; 1Co 15:36
11:41 h Lk 12:33 i S Ac 10:15
11:42 j Lk 18:12 k Dt 6:5; Mic 6:8 l Mt 23:23
11:43 m Mt 23:6,7; Lk 14:7; 20:46
11:44 n Mt 23:27

[a] 31 Or *something*; also in verse 32 [b] 41 Or *what you have*

11:28 *Blessed rather.* Jesus is not denying the blessedness of Mary. He is stressing that it is even more blessed to be his obedient follower.

11:29 *asks for a miraculous sign.* On several occasions Jews asked for miraculous signs (see v. 16; Mt 12:38; Mk 8:11 and notes), but Jesus rejected their requests because they had wrong motives.

11:30 *as Jonah was a sign.* Jonah spent three days (see note on Mt 12:40) "buried" in the huge fish, just as Jesus would be buried for three days before his resurrection.

11:31–32 *one greater than Solomon … one greater than Jonah.* Jesus argued from the lesser to the greater. If the queen of Sheba responded positively to the wisdom of Solomon, and the people of Nineveh to the preaching of Jonah, how much more should the people of Jesus' day have responded to the ministry of Jesus, who is infinitely greater than Solomon or Jonah!

11:31 *The Queen of the South.* The queen of Sheba (see 1Ki 10:1–10 and notes).

11:33 *a bowl.* A container holding about one peck. *may see the light.* A lamp is meant to give light to those who are near it (see v. 36). Jesus had publicly exhibited the light of the gospel for all to see, but "a wicked generation" (v. 29) requested more spectacular signs. The problem was not with any failure on Jesus' part in giving light; it was with the faulty vision of his audience.

11:34 *lamp of your body.* See note on Mt 6:22. *eyes are good … bad.* Those asking for a sign do not need more light; they need good eyes to allow the light to enter. See notes on Mt 6:22–23.

11:38 *did not first wash.* Especially for ceremonial cleansing—not a practice commanded in the law but added in the tradition of the Pharisees (cf. Mt 15:9 and note on Jn 2:6).

11:39 *clean the outside.* Engage in ceremonial washings of the body. *greed and wickedness.* These Pharisees were more concerned about keeping ceremonies than about being moral (cf. Mk 7:20 and note).

11:40 *make the inside also.* The inside of a person (the heart and inner righteousness) is more important than the outside (ceremonial cleansing).

11:41 *⌞the dish⌟.* Supplied from the figures of speech used in v. 39. *everything will be clean.* Giving from the heart makes everything else right. If one gives to the poor, one's heart is no longer in the grip of "greed and wickedness" (v. 39).

11:42–52 Six woes pronounced by Jesus on the religious leaders (see note on Mt 23:13–32).

11:42 *tenth.* A tithe of all agricultural produce was required by OT law (see Dt 14:22–29 and note). *rue.* Strongly scented herbs with bitter leaves.

11:43 *most important seats in the synagogues.* See Mk 12:39 and note.

11:44 *unmarked graves.* The Jews whitewashed their tombs so that no one would accidentally touch them and be defiled (cf. Nu 19:16; Mt 23:27 and note). Just as touching a grave resulted in ceremonial uncleanness, so also being influenced

45One of the experts in the law[o] answered him, "Teacher, when you say these
things, you insult us also."
46Jesus replied, "And you experts in the
law, woe to you, because you load people
down with burdens they can hardly carry,
and you yourselves will not lift one finger
to help them.[p]
47"Woe to you, because you build
tombs for the prophets, and it was your
forefathers who killed them. 48So you
testify that you approve of what your
forefathers did; they killed the prophets,
and you build their tombs.[q] 49Because
of this, God in his wisdom[r] said, 'I will
send them prophets and apostles, some
of whom they will kill and others they
will persecute.'[s] 50Therefore this generation will be held responsible for the
blood of all the prophets that has been
shed since the beginning of the world,
51from the blood of Abel[t] to the blood of
Zechariah,[u] who was killed between the
altar and the sanctuary. Yes, I tell you,
this generation will be held responsible
for it all.[v]
52"Woe to you experts in the law, because you have taken away the key to
knowledge. You yourselves have not entered, and you have hindered those who
were entering."[w]
53When Jesus left there, the Pharisees
and the teachers of the law began to oppose him fiercely and to besiege him with
questions, 54waiting to catch him in something he might say.[x]

11:45 [o]S Mt 22:35 **11:46** [p]S Mt 23:4 **11:48** [q]Mt 23:29-32; Ac 7:51-53 **11:49** [r]1Co 1:24,30; Col 2:3 [s]Mt 23:34 **11:51** [t]Ge 4:8 [u]2Ch 24:20,21 [v]Mt 23:35,36 **11:52** [w]Mt 23:13 **11:54** [x]S Mt 12:10

Warnings and Encouragements

12:2-9pp — Mt 10:26-33

12 Meanwhile, when a crowd of many
thousands had gathered, so that they
were trampling on one another, Jesus began to speak first to his disciples, saying:
"Be on your guard against the yeast of the
Pharisees, which is hypocrisy.[y] 2There is
nothing concealed that will not be disclosed, or hidden that will not be made
known.[z] 3What you have said in the dark
will be heard in the daylight, and what
you have whispered in the ear in the inner
rooms will be proclaimed from the roofs.
4"I tell you, my friends,[a] do not be afraid
of those who kill the body and after that
can do no more. 5But I will show you
whom you should fear: Fear him who, after
the killing of the body, has power to throw
you into hell. Yes, I tell you, fear him.[b]
6Are not five sparrows sold for two pennies[a]? Yet not one of them is forgotten by
God. 7Indeed, the very hairs of your head
are all numbered.[c] Don't be afraid; you are
worth more than many sparrows.[d]
8"I tell you, whoever acknowledges me
before men, the Son of Man will also acknowledge him before the angels of God.[e]
9But he who disowns me before men
will be disowned[f] before the angels of
God. 10And everyone who speaks a word
against the Son of Man[g] will be forgiven,
but anyone who blasphemes against the
Holy Spirit will not be forgiven.[h]

12:1 [y]Mt 16:6, 11,12 **12:2** [z]S Mk 4:22 **12:4** [a]Jn 15:14,15 **12:5** [b]Heb 10:31 **12:7** [c]S Mt 10:30 [d]Mt 12:12 **12:8** [e]Lk 15:10 **12:9** [f]Mk 8:38; 2Ti 2:12 **12:10** [g]S Mt 8:20 [h]Mt 12:31,32; S 1Jn 5:16

[a] 6 Greek *two assaria*

by these misguided religious leaders could lead to moral uncleanness.

11:45 *experts in the law.* See note on 7:30.

11:46 *load people down.* By adding rules and regulations to the authentic law of Moses (see note on Mt 15:2) and doing nothing to help others keep them (Mt 23:4), while inventing ways for themselves to circumvent them (cf. Mt 11:28 and note).

11:47 *tombs for the prophets.* Outwardly these "experts in the law" (v. 46) appeared to honor the prophets in building or rebuilding memorials, but inwardly they rejected the Messiah the prophets announced. They lived in opposition to the teachings of the prophets, just as their ancestors had done.

11:49 *God in his wisdom said.* Not a quotation from the OT or any other known book. It may refer to God speaking through Jesus, or it may be referring in quotation form to God's decision to send prophets and apostles even though he knew they would be rejected.

11:51 *blood of Abel ... Zechariah.* See note on Mt 23:35.

11:52 *key to knowledge.* The very persons who should have opened the people's minds concerning the law obscured their understanding by faulty interpretation and an erroneous system of theology. They kept themselves and the people in ignorance of the way of salvation, or, as Matthew's account puts it, they "shut the kingdom of heaven in men's faces" (Mt 23:13).

11:54 *waiting to catch him.* The determination of the religious leaders to trap Jesus is evident throughout Luke (see 6:11 and note; 19:47–48; 20:19–20; 22:2).

12:1 *yeast of the Pharisees.* See note on Mk 8:15.

12:2 *nothing concealed that will not be disclosed.* In this context the meaning is that nothing hidden through hypocrisy will fail to be made known (cf. note on 8:17).

12:3 *inner rooms.* Storerooms were surrounded by other rooms so that no one could dig in from outside.

12:4 *after that can do no more.* Encouragement in the face of persecution (see Mt 10:28 and note).

12:5 *power to throw you into hell.* God alone has this power. The Greek word for "hell" is *ge(h)enna* (see note on Mt 5:22), not to be confused with Hades, the general name for the place of the dead. *fear him.* Respect his authority, stand in awe of his majesty and trust in him. Verses 6–7 give the basis for trust.

12:6 *five sparrows sold for two pennies.* God even cares for little birds, sold cheaply for food.

12:8 *acknowledges me.* When a person acknowledges that Jesus is the Messiah, the Son of God (see Mt 16:16; 1Jn 2:22 and notes), Jesus acknowledges that the individual is his loyal follower (cf. Mt 7:21).

12:9 *will be disowned.* See Mk 8:38; 2Ti 2:12 and notes; cf. Mt 7:21; 25:41–46. The same word is used in Peter's denial (22:34, "deny"; 22:61, "disown").

12:10 *blasphemes against the Holy Spirit.* See notes on Mt 12:31; Mk 3:29.

11 "When you are brought before synagogues, rulers and authorities, do not
worry about how you will defend yourselves or what you will say,[i] 12 for the Holy
Spirit will teach you at that time what you
should say."[j]

The Parable of the Rich Fool

13 Someone in the crowd said to him,
"Teacher, tell my brother to divide the inheritance with me."
14 Jesus replied, "Man, who appointed
me a judge or an arbiter between you?"
15 Then he said to them, "Watch out! Be
on your guard against all kinds of greed;
a man's life does not consist in the abundance of his possessions."[k]
16 And he told them this parable: "The
ground of a certain rich man produced a
good crop. 17 He thought to himself, 'What
shall I do? I have no place to store my
crops.'
18 "Then he said, 'This is what I'll do. I
will tear down my barns and build bigger
ones, and there I will store all my grain
and my goods. 19 And I'll say to myself,
"You have plenty of good things laid up
for many years. Take life easy; eat, drink
and be merry." '
20 "But God said to him, 'You fool![l] This
very night your life will be demanded
from you.[m] Then who will get what you
have prepared for yourself?'[n]
21 "This is how it will be with anyone
who stores up things for himself but is not
rich toward God."[o]

Do Not Worry

12:22-31pp — Mt 6:25-33

22 Then Jesus said to his disciples:
"Therefore I tell you, do not worry about
your life, what you will eat; or about
your body, what you will wear. 23 Life is
more than food, and the body more than
clothes. 24 Consider the ravens: They do
not sow or reap, they have no storeroom
or barn; yet God feeds them.[p] And how
much more valuable you are than birds!
25 Who of you by worrying can add a single hour to his life[a]? 26 Since you cannot
do this very little thing, why do you worry
about the rest?
27 "Consider how the lilies grow. They do
not labor or spin. Yet I tell you, not even
Solomon in all his splendor[q] was dressed
like one of these. 28 If that is how God
clothes the grass of the field, which is here
today, and tomorrow is thrown into the
fire, how much more will he clothe you,
O you of little faith![r] 29 And do not set your
heart on what you will eat or drink; do
not worry about it. 30 For the pagan world
runs after all such things, and your Father[s]
knows that you need them.[t] 31 But seek his
kingdom,[u] and these things will be given
to you as well.[v]
32 "Do not be afraid,[w] little flock, for your
Father has been pleased to give you the
kingdom.[x] 33 Sell your possessions and give
to the poor.[y] Provide purses for yourselves
that will not wear out, a treasure in heav-
en[z] that will not be exhausted, where no
thief comes near and no moth destroys.[a]
34 For where your treasure is, there your
heart will be also.[b]

Watchfulness

12:35,36pp — Mt 25:1-13; Mk 13:33-37
12:39,40; 42-46pp — Mt 24:43-51

35 "Be dressed ready for service and
keep your lamps burning, 36 like men waiting for their master to return from a wedding banquet, so that when he comes and
knocks they can immediately open the
door for him. 37 It will be good for those
servants whose master finds them watching when he comes.[c] I tell you the truth,
he will dress himself to serve, will have
them recline at the table and will come
and wait on them.[d] 38 It will be good for
those servants whose master finds them
ready, even if he comes in the second or

12:11 [i] Mt 10:17,19; Lk 21:12,14 **12:12** [j] Ex 4:12; Mt 10:20; Mk 13:11; Lk 21:15 **12:15** [k] Job 20:20; 31:24; Ps 62:10 **12:20** [l] Jer 17:11; Lk 11:40 [m] Job 27:8 [n] Ps 39:6; 49:10 **12:21** [o] ver 33 **12:24** [p] Job 38:41; Ps 147:9 **12:27** [q] 1Ki 10:4-7 **12:28** [r] S Mt 6:30 **12:30** [s] S Lk 6:36 [t] Mt 6:8 **12:31** [u] S Mt 3:2 [v] Mt 19:29 **12:32** [w] S Mt 14:27 [x] S Mt 25:34 **12:33** [y] S Ac 2:45 [z] S Mt 6:20 [a] S Jas 5:2 **12:34** [b] Mt 6:21 **12:37** [c] Mt 24:42,46; 25:13 [d] S Mt 20:28

[a] 25 Or *single cubit to his height*

12:12 *Holy Spirit will teach you ... what you should say.* See Mt 10:19 and note.
12:13 *divide the inheritance.* Dt 21:17 (see note there) gave the general rule that an elder son received double a younger one's portion. Disputes over such matters were normally settled by rabbis. This man's request of Jesus was selfish and materialistic. There is no indication that the man had been listening seriously to what Jesus had been saying (cf. vv. 1–11). Jesus replied with a parable about the consequences of greed.
12:16 *parable.* See note on 8:4.
12:19 *eat ... be merry.* See Isa 22:13 and note.
12:21 *rich toward God.* Cf. "treasures in heaven" (Mt 6:20; see note there; cf. Lk 12:34).
12:22 *do not worry.* See v. 29; see also Php 4:6–7 and notes.
12:27 *lilies.* See note on Mt 6:28.
12:28 See Mt 6:30 and note.
12:31 *seek his kingdom.* Since v. 32 suggests that Jesus is speaking to believers, who already possess the kingdom, this command probably means that Christians should seek the spiritual benefits of the kingdom rather than the material goods of the world (see Mt 6:33, which says, "seek first his kingdom").
12:33 *Sell your possessions.* Jesus does not instruct his disciples to sell all their possessions (see note on Mk 10:21). What is emphasized throughout this Gospel is that wealth is to be generously shared with the poor (see vv. 21–26). *give to the poor.* The danger of riches and the need for giving are characteristic themes in Luke (see 3:11; 6:30; 11:41 and note; 14:13–14; 16:9 and note; 18:22; 19:8). *treasure in heaven.* See v. 21 and note.
12:37 *dress himself to serve.* The master reverses the normal roles and serves the servants (cf. 22:27 and note on 22:26; Mk 10:45; Jn 13:5–14 and notes).
12:38 *second or third watch.* Night was divided into four watches by the Romans (Mk 13:35) and three by the Jews (see Jdg 7:19 and note); see note on Mt 14:25. These were prob-

third watch of the night. 39But understand
this: If the owner of the house had known
at what hour the thief[e] was coming, he
would not have let his house be broken
into. 40You also must be ready,[f] because
the Son of Man will come at an hour when
you do not expect him."
41Peter asked, "Lord, are you telling this
parable to us, or to everyone?"
42The Lord[g] answered, "Who then is the
faithful and wise manager, whom the master puts in charge of his servants to give
them their food allowance at the proper
time? 43It will be good for that servant
whom the master finds doing so when he
returns. 44I tell you the truth, he will put
him in charge of all his possessions. 45But
suppose the servant says to himself, 'My
master is taking a long time in coming,'
and he then begins to beat the menservants and maidservants and to eat and
drink and get drunk. 46The master of that
servant will come on a day when he does
not expect him and at an hour he is not
aware of.[h] He will cut him to pieces and
assign him a place with the unbelievers.
47"That servant who knows his master's
will and does not get ready or does not
do what his master wants will be beaten
with many blows.[i] 48But the one who does
not know and does things deserving punishment will be beaten with few blows.[j]
From everyone who has been given much,
much will be demanded; and from the one
who has been entrusted with much, much
more will be asked.

Not Peace but Division

12:51-53pp — Mt 10:34-36

49"I have come to bring fire on the earth,
and how I wish it were already kindled!
50But I have a baptism[k] to undergo, and
how distressed I am until it is completed![l]
51Do you think I came to bring peace on
earth? No, I tell you, but division. 52From
now on there will be five in one family
divided against each other, three against
two and two against three. 53They will
be divided, father against son and son
against father, mother against daughter
and daughter against mother, mother-in-
law against daughter-in-law and daughter-
in-law against mother-in-law."[m]

Interpreting the Times

54He said to the crowd: "When you see a
cloud rising in the west, immediately you
say, 'It's going to rain,' and it does.[n] 55And
when the south wind blows, you say, 'It's
going to be hot,' and it is. 56Hypocrites!
You know how to interpret the appearance
of the earth and the sky. How is it that you
don't know how to interpret this present
time?[o]
57"Why don't you judge for yourselves
what is right? 58As you are going with your
adversary to the magistrate, try hard to be
reconciled to him on the way, or he may
drag you off to the judge, and the judge
turn you over to the officer, and the officer
throw you into prison.[p] 59I tell you, you
will not get out until you have paid the
last penny.[a]"[q]

Repent or Perish

13 Now there were some present at that
time who told Jesus about the Galileans whose blood Pilate[r] had mixed with
their sacrifices. 2Jesus answered, "Do you
think that these Galileans were worse sinners than all the other Galileans because
they suffered this way?[s] 3I tell you, no! But

12:39 [e] Mt 6:19; 1Th 5:2; 2Pe 3:10; Rev 3:3; 16:15
12:40 [f] Mk 13:33; Lk 21:36
12:42 [g] S Lk 7:13
12:46 [h] ver 40
12:47 [i] Dt 25:2
12:48 [j] Lev 5:17; Nu 15:27-30
12:50 [k] Mk 10:38; [l] S Jn 19:30
12:53 [m] Mic 7:6; Mt 10:21
12:54 [n] Mt 16:2
12:56 [o] Mt 16:3
12:58 [p] Mt 5:25
12:59 [q] Mt 5:26; Mk 12:42
13:1 [r] S Mt 27:2
13:2 [s] Jn 9:2,3

[a] 59 Greek *lepton*

ably the last two of the Jewish watches. The banquet would have begun during the first watch.

12:40 Christ's return is certain, but the time is not known (see Mt 24:36; Mk 13:32 and note).

12:41 Jesus taught the people in parables but used a more direct approach with the disciples. However, he did not intend these warnings of watchfulness just for the disciples (see Mk 13:37). In the following verses he emphasizes the duty to fulfill responsibilities.

12:42 *wise manager.* An outstanding slave (v. 43) was sometimes left in charge of an estate (see 16:1 and note).

12:46–48 *cut him to pieces ... beaten with many blows ... beaten with few blows.* Three grades of punishment that the judge will mete out in proportion to both the privileges each person has enjoyed and one's response to those privileges (see Ro 2:12–16 and notes).

12:49 *fire.* Applied figuratively in different ways in the NT (see note on 3:16). Here it is associated with judgment (v. 49) and division (v. 51). Judgment falls on the wicked, who are separated from the righteous.

12:50 *baptism.* The suffering that Jesus was to endure on the cross (see note on Mk 10:38). *until it is completed.* The words from the cross would pronounce the completion (see Jn 19:30 and note). Jesus wished that the hour of suffering were already past.

12:54–56 Wind from the west was from the Mediterranean Sea; from the south it was from the desert. Although people could use such indicators to forecast the weather, they could not recognize the signs of spiritual crisis, the coming of the Messiah, the threat of his death, the coming confrontation with Rome, and the eternal consequences these events would have for their own lives.

12:57 *judge for yourselves.* Despite the insistence of the Pharisees, despite the Roman system, and even despite the pressure of family, a person must accept God on his terms. The signs of the times called for immediate decision—before judgment came on the Jewish nation.

12:58 *be reconciled ... or.* Settle accounts before it is too late.

13:1 *Galileans whose blood Pilate had mixed with their sacrifices.* Having people killed while offering sacrifices in the temple fits Pilate's reputation.

13:2,4 *worse sinners ... more guilty.* In ancient times it was often assumed that a calamity would befall only those who were extremely sinful (see Jn 9:2 and note; see also Job 4:7; 22:5, where Eliphaz falsely accused Job; see note on Job

unless you repent, you too will all perish. 4Or those eighteen who died when the tower in Siloam[t] fell on them — do you think they were more guilty than all the others living in Jerusalem? 5I tell you, no! But unless you repent,[u] you too will all perish."

6Then he told this parable: "A man had a fig tree, planted in his vineyard, and he went to look for fruit on it, but did not find any.[v] 7So he said to the man who took care of the vineyard, 'For three years now I've been coming to look for fruit on this fig tree and haven't found any. Cut it down![w] Why should it use up the soil?'

8"'Sir,' the man replied, 'leave it alone for one more year, and I'll dig around it and fertilize it. 9If it bears fruit next year, fine! If not, then cut it down.'"

A Crippled Woman Healed on the Sabbath

10On a Sabbath Jesus was teaching in one of the synagogues,[x] 11and a woman was there who had been crippled by a spirit for eighteen years.[y] She was bent over and could not straighten up at all. 12When Jesus saw her, he called her forward and said to her, "Woman, you are set free from your infirmity." 13Then he put his hands on her,[z] and immediately she straightened up and praised God.

14Indignant because Jesus had healed on the Sabbath,[a] the synagogue ruler[b] said to the people, "There are six days for work.[c] So come and be healed on those days, not on the Sabbath."

15The Lord answered him, "You hypocrites! Doesn't each of you on the Sabbath untie his ox or donkey from the stall and lead it out to give it water?[d] 16Then should not this woman, a daughter of Abraham,[e] whom Satan[f] has kept bound for eighteen long years, be set free on the Sabbath day from what bound her?"

17When he said this, all his opponents were humiliated,[g] but the people were delighted with all the wonderful things he was doing.

The Parables of the Mustard Seed and the Yeast

13:18,19pp — Mk 4:30-32
13:18-21pp — Mt 13:31-33

18Then Jesus asked, "What is the kingdom of God[h] like?[i] What shall I compare it to? 19It is like a mustard seed, which a man took and planted in his garden. It grew and became a tree,[j] and the birds of the air perched in its branches."[k]

20Again he asked, "What shall I compare the kingdom of God to? 21It is like yeast that a woman took and mixed into a large amount[a] of flour until it worked all through the dough."[l]

The Narrow Door

22Then Jesus went through the towns and villages, teaching as he made his way to Jerusalem.[m] 23Someone asked him, "Lord, are only a few people going to be saved?"

He said to them, 24"Make every effort to enter through the narrow door,[n] because many, I tell you, will try to enter and will not be able to. 25Once the owner of the house gets up and closes the door, you

[a] *21* Greek *three satas* (probably about 1/2 bushel or 20 liters)

13:4 [t] Jn 9:7,11 **13:5** [u] Mt 3:2; Ac 2:38 **13:6** [v] Isa 5:2; Jer 8:13; Mt 21:19 **13:7** [w] S Mt 3:10 **13:10** [x] S Mt 4:23 **13:11** [y] ver 16 **13:13** [z] S Mk 5:23 **13:14** [a] S Mt 12:2 [b] S Mk 5:22 [c] Ex 20:9 **13:15** [d] Lk 14:5 **13:16** [e] S Lk 3:8 [f] S Mt 4:10 **13:17** [g] Isa 66:5 **13:18** [h] S Mt 3:2 [i] S Mt 13:24 **13:19** [j] Lk 17:6 [k] S Mt 13:32 **13:21** [l] 1Co 5:6 **13:22** [m] S Lk 9:51 **13:24** [n] Mt 7:13

22:5 – 11). But Jesus pointed out that all are sinners who must repent or face a fearful end.

13:4 *tower in Siloam.* Built into the southeast section of Jerusalem's wall (cf. note on Jn 9:7).

13:6 *fig tree.* Probably refers to the Jewish nation (see note on Mk 11:14), but it may also apply to an individual.

13:7 *For three years.* A period of ample opportunity.

13:11 *crippled by a spirit.* Various disorders were caused by evil spirits (see note on 4:33). The description of this woman's infirmity suggests that the bones of her spine were rigidly fused together.

13:12 *Woman.* Cf. note on Jn 2:4. *set free.* The spirit had been cast out, and the woman was freed from her physical handicap.

13:13 *praised God.* See 1:64 and note.

13:14 *healed on the Sabbath.* A focal point of attack against Jesus was his conduct on the Sabbath (see 6:5; 14:5 and notes; Mt 12:1 – 8,11 – 12; Jn 5:10 and note; see also Ex 20:9 – 10). *synagogue ruler.* See note on 8:41.

13:15 *hypocrites.* See note on Mt 6:2. *untie his ox.* They had more regard for the needs of an animal than for the far greater need of a human being. Jesus called his critics "hypocrites" because they pretended zeal for the law, but their motive was to attack him and his healing.

13:19 *mustard seed.* See notes on Mt 13:31 – 32; Mk 4:31. Elsewhere in Scripture trees are sometimes used to symbolize great political powers (see Eze 17:23; 31:6; Da 4:11 and note).

13:21 *yeast.* See note on Mt 13:33. Its permeating quality is emphasized here as it works from the inside to affect all the dough. This parable speaks of the powerful influence of God's kingdom. *large amount.* See NIV text note; same amount as used by Sarah in Ge 18:6 (see NIV text note there).

13:22 *through the towns and villages.* See chart, p. 1508. Somewhere between the events of 11:1 and 13:21 Jesus left Judea and began his work in and around Perea, which is recorded in 13:22 — 19:27; Mt 19:1 — 20:28; Mk 10 (see note on 10:32); Jn 10:40 – 42. It appears that Jesus went north to Galilee during the last part of the Perean ministry and then traveled south again through Perea to Jericho and to Jerusalem. Some of Jesus' sayings that Luke attributes to the period of ministry in Perea are found in different settings in Matthew (7:13 – 14,22 – 23). Perhaps he repeated various sayings on different occasions. *Jerusalem.* Where he would die. Although Jesus was ministering throughout Perea, his eyes were constantly set on the Holy City and his ultimate destiny.

13:23 *only a few ... saved?* Perhaps the questioner had observed that in spite of the very large crowds that came to hear Jesus' preaching and be healed, there were only a few followers who were loyal. Jesus did not answer directly, but warned that many would try to enter after it was too late.

will stand outside knocking and pleading, 'Sir, open the door for us.'

"But he will answer, 'I don't know you or where you come from.'[o]

[26]"Then you will say, 'We ate and drank with you, and you taught in our streets.'

[27]"But he will reply, 'I don't know you or where you come from. Away from me, all you evildoers!'[p]

[28]"There will be weeping there, and gnashing of teeth,[q] when you see Abraham, Isaac and Jacob and all the prophets in the kingdom of God, but you yourselves thrown out. [29]People will come from east and west[r] and north and south, and will take their places at the feast in the kingdom of God. [30]Indeed there are those who are last who will be first, and first who will be last."[s]

Jesus' Sorrow for Jerusalem

13:34,35pp — Mt 23:37-39
13:34,35Ref — Lk 19:41

[31]At that time some Pharisees came to Jesus and said to him, "Leave this place and go somewhere else. Herod[t] wants to kill you."

[32]He replied, "Go tell that fox, 'I will drive out demons and heal people today and tomorrow, and on the third day I will reach my goal.'[u] [33]In any case, I must keep going today and tomorrow and the next day—for surely no prophet[v] can die outside Jerusalem!

[34]"O Jerusalem, Jerusalem, you who kill the prophets and stone those sent to you, how often I have longed to gather your children together, as a hen gathers her chicks under her wings,[w] but you were not willing! [35]Look, your house is left to you desolate.[x] I tell you, you will not see me again until you say, 'Blessed is he who comes in the name of the Lord.'[a]"[y]

Jesus at a Pharisee's House

14:8-10Ref — Pr 25:6,7

14 One Sabbath, when Jesus went to eat in the house of a prominent Pharisee,[z] he was being carefully watched.[a] [2]There in front of him was a man suffering from dropsy. [3]Jesus asked the Pharisees and experts in the law,[b] "Is it lawful to heal on the Sabbath or not?"[c] [4]But they remained silent. So taking hold of the man, he healed him and sent him away.

[5]Then he asked them, "If one of you has a son[b] or an ox that falls into a well on the Sabbath day, will you not immediately pull him out?"[d] [6]And they had nothing to say.

[7]When he noticed how the guests picked the places of honor at the table,[e] he told them this parable: [8]"When someone invites you to a wedding feast, do not take the place of honor, for a person more distinguished than you may have been invited. [9]If so, the host who invited both of you will come and say to you, 'Give this man your seat.' Then, humiliated, you will have to take the least important place. [10]But when you are invited, take the lowest place, so that when your host comes, he will say to you, 'Friend, move up to a better place.' Then you will be honored in the presence of all your fellow guests. [11]For everyone who exalts himself will be humbled, and he who humbles himself will be exalted."[f]

13:25 [o]Mt 7:23; 25:10-12 **13:27** [p]S Mt 7:23 **13:28** [q]S Mt 8:12 **13:29** [r]S Mt 8:11 **13:30** [s]S Mt 19:30 **13:31** [t]S Mt 14:1 **13:32** [u]S Heb 2:10 **13:33** [v]S Mt 21:11 **13:34** [w]S Mt 23:37 **13:35** [x]Jer 12:17; 22:5 [y]Ps 118:26; Lk 19:38 **14:1** [z]Lk 7:36; 11:37 [a]S Mt 12:10 **14:3** [b]S Mt 22:35 [c]S Mt 12:2 **14:5** [d]Lk 13:15 **14:7** [e]S Lk 11:43 **14:11** [f]S Mt 23:12

[a] 35 Psalm 118:26 [b] 5 Some manuscripts *donkey*

13:27 *I don't know you.* See Mt 7:23; 25:12.
13:29 *People ... from east and west and north and south.* From the four corners of the world (Ps 107:3) and from among all peoples, including Gentiles. *feast in the kingdom of God.* See 14:15; Mt 8:11 and notes.
13:30 See Mt 19:30 and note.
13:31 *Herod wants to kill you.* See note on Mt 14:1. Jesus was probably in Perea, which was under Herod's jurisdiction (see note on 3:1). The Pharisees wanted to frighten Jesus into leaving this area and going to Judea.
13:32 *fox.* A crafty animal. *today and tomorrow.* In Semitic usage this phrase could refer to an indefinite but limited period of time. *reach my goal.* Jesus' life had a predetermined plan that would be carried out, and no harm could come to him until his purpose was accomplished (cf. 4:43; 9:22).
13:33 *outside Jerusalem.* Jesus' hour had not yet come (see 2:38; Jn 2:4 and note; cf. Jn 8:59; 10:39; 11:54). He would die in Jerusalem as had numerous prophets before him.
13:34 *how often ...!* This lament over Jerusalem may suggest that Jesus was in Jerusalem more often than the Synoptics indicate (cf. Jn 2:13; 4:45; 5:1; 7:10; 10:22). However, the statement in vv. 34 – 35 may have been uttered some distance from Jerusalem, i.e., in Perea. According to Mt 23:37 – 38, the same utterance was spoken on Tuesday of Passion Week. Jesus almost certainly repeated many of his teachings and sayings at different times and in various places.
13:35 *house is left ... desolate.* God will abandon his temple and his city (see 21:20,24; Jer 12:7; 22:5 and notes). *not see me again until.* See Zec 12:10 and note; Rev 1:7; cf. Isa 45:23; Ro 14:11; Php 2:10 – 11.
14:1 Of seven recorded miracles on the Sabbath, Luke includes five (4:31,38; 6:6; 13:14; here); the other two are Jn 5:10 (see note there); 9:14. Concerning the vigil of the Pharisees see note on 13:14. Sabbath meals were prepared the day before.
14:2 *dropsy.* An excessive accumulation of fluid in the tissues and cavities of the body that indicates illness. The Greek for this word is a medical term found only here in the NT (see Introduction: Author).
14:3 *experts in the law.* See notes on 5:17; 7:30. By questioning them before the miracle, Jesus made it difficult for them to protest afterward.
14:5 *son.* See NIV text note. The reading "donkey" matches well with the "ox that falls into a well." But in Dt 5:14 the law is specified for both humans and animals; one category opens with "son" and another with "ox." Jesus' action was unlawful only according to rabbinic interpretations, not according to the Mosaic law itself (cf. note on Mk 2:25).
14:7 *places of honor.* Maneuvering for better seats may also have caused trouble at the Last Supper (22:24; see also 20:46; Mk 12:39 and note).
14:11 *humbles himself will be exalted.* A basic principle repeated often in the Bible (see 11:43; 18:14; 20:46; 2Ch 7:14 – 15; Pr 3:34; 25:6 – 7; Mt 18:4; 23:12; Jas 4:10; 1Pe 5:6).

12Then Jesus said to his host, "When
you give a luncheon or dinner, do not
invite your friends, your brothers or relatives, or your rich neighbors; if you do,
they may invite you back and so you will
be repaid. 13But when you give a banquet,
invite the poor, the crippled, the lame, the
blind,[g] 14and you will be blessed. Although
they cannot repay you, you will be repaid
at the resurrection of the righteous."[h]

The Parable of the Great Banquet

14:16-24Ref — Mt 22:2-14

15When one of those at the table with
him heard this, he said to Jesus, "Blessed
is the man who will eat at the feast[i] in the
kingdom of God."[j]
16Jesus replied: "A certain man was preparing a great banquet and invited many
guests. 17At the time of the banquet he
sent his servant to tell those who had
been invited, 'Come, for everything is now
ready.'
18"But they all alike began to make excuses. The first said, 'I have just bought
a field, and I must go and see it. Please
excuse me.'
19"Another said, 'I have just bought five
yoke of oxen, and I'm on my way to try
them out. Please excuse me.'
20"Still another said, 'I just got married,
so I can't come.'
21"The servant came back and reported
this to his master. Then the owner of the
house became angry and ordered his servant, 'Go out quickly into the streets and
alleys of the town and bring in the poor,
the crippled, the blind and the lame.'[k]
22" 'Sir,' the servant said, 'what you
ordered has been done, but there is still
room.'
23"Then the master told his servant, 'Go
out to the roads and country lanes and
make them come in, so that my house will
be full. 24I tell you, not one of those men
who were invited will get a taste of my
banquet.' "[l]

The Cost of Being a Disciple

25Large crowds were traveling with
Jesus, and turning to them he said: 26"If
anyone comes to me and does not hate
his father and mother, his wife and children, his brothers and sisters—yes, even
his own life—he cannot be my disciple.[m]
27And anyone who does not carry his cross
and follow me cannot be my disciple.[n]
28"Suppose one of you wants to build
a tower. Will he not first sit down and estimate the cost to see if he has enough
money to complete it? 29For if he lays the
foundation and is not able to finish it, everyone who sees it will ridicule him, 30say-
ing, 'This fellow began to build and was
not able to finish.'
31"Or suppose a king is about to go to
war against another king. Will he not first
sit down and consider whether he is able
with ten thousand men to oppose the one
coming against him with twenty thousand? 32If he is not able, he will send a
delegation while the other is still a long
way off and will ask for terms of peace.
33In the same way, any of you who does
not give up everything he has cannot be
my disciple.[o]
34"Salt is good, but if it loses its saltiness, how can it be made salty again?[p] 35It
is fit neither for the soil nor for the manure
pile; it is thrown out.[q]
"He who has ears to hear, let him
hear."[r]

The Parable of the Lost Sheep

15:4-7pp — Mt 18:12-14

15 Now the tax collectors[s] and "sinners"
were all gathering around to hear
him. 2But the Pharisees and the teachers
of the law muttered, "This man welcomes
sinners and eats with them."[t]

14:13 [g] ver 21 **14:14** [h] Ac 24:15 **14:15** [i] Isa 25:6; Mt 26:29; Lk 13:29; Rev 19:9 [j] S Mt 3:2 **14:21** [k] ver 13 **14:24** [l] Mt 21:43; Ac 13:46 **14:26** [m] Mt 10:37; S Jn 12:25 **14:27** [n] Mt 10:38; Lk 9:23 **14:33** [o] Php 3:7,8 **14:34** [p] Mk 9:50 **14:35** [q] Mt 5:13 [r] S Mt 11:15 **15:1** [s] Lk 5:29 **15:2** [t] S Mt 9:11

14:14 *resurrection of the righteous.* All will be resurrected (see Da 12:2; Jn 5:28–29 and notes; Ac 24:15). Some hold that the resurrection of the righteous (1Co 15:23; 1Th 4:16; Rev 20:4–6) is distinct from the general resurrection (1Co 15:12,21; Heb 6:2; Rev 20:11–15). *the righteous.* Those who have been pronounced so by God on the basis of Christ's atonement (see Ro 1:17 and note) and who have evidenced their faith by their actions (cf. Mt 25:34–40).

14:15 *feast in the kingdom.* The great Messianic banquet to come. Association of the future kingdom with a feast was common (see 13:29; Isa 25:6 and note; Mt 8:11 and note; 25:1–10; 26:29 and note; Rev 19:9).

14:16 *Jesus replied.* Jesus used the man's remark as the occasion for a parable warning that not everyone would enter the kingdom.

14:18 *bought a field.* The initial invitation must have been accepted, but when the final invitation came (by Jewish custom the announcement that came when the feast was ready), other interests took priority.

14:24 *those men who were invited.* Without explicitly mentioning them, Jesus warned the Jewish religious leaders that those who refuse the invitation to his Messianic banquet would not get one taste of it, but others would (see 20:9–19; see also note on Mt 21:41).

14:26 *hate his father.* A vivid hyperbole, meaning that one must love Jesus even more than one's immediate family (see Mal 1:2–3 for another use of the figure). See Mt 10:37 and note on Mal 1:3.

14:27 *carry his cross.* See 9:23; Mt 10:38 and notes.

14:28 *estimate the cost.* Jesus did not want a blind, naive commitment that expected only blessings. As a builder estimates costs or a king evaluates military strength (v. 31), so people must consider what Jesus expects of his followers before they commit their lives to him.

14:33 *give up everything he has.* The cost, Jesus warned, is complete surrender to him (see Php 3:7–8 and notes).

14:34 *Salt is good.* See note on Mk 9:50.

15:1 *tax collectors and "sinners."* See notes on 3:12; Mk 2:15.

15:2 *muttered.* Complained among themselves, but not open-

3Then Jesus told them this parable:[u]
4"Suppose one of you has a hundred sheep
and loses one of them. Does he not leave
the ninety-nine in the open country and
go after the lost sheep until he finds it?[v]
5And when he finds it, he joyfully puts it
on his shoulders 6and goes home. Then
he calls his friends and neighbors together
and says, 'Rejoice with me; I have found
my lost sheep.'[w] 7I tell you that in the same
way there will be more rejoicing in heav-
en over one sinner who repents than over
ninety-nine righteous persons who do not
need to repent.[x]

The Parable of the Lost Coin

8"Or suppose a woman has ten silver
coins[a] and loses one. Does she not light a
lamp, sweep the house and search carefully
until she finds it? 9And when she finds it,
she calls her friends and neighbors together and says, 'Rejoice with me; I have found
my lost coin.'[y] 10In the same way, I tell you,
there is rejoicing in the presence of the angels of God over one sinner who repents."[z]

The Parable of the Lost Son

11Jesus continued: "There was a man
who had two sons.[a] 12The younger one
said to his father, 'Father, give me my
share of the estate.'[b] So he divided his
property[c] between them.

13"Not long after that, the younger son
got together all he had, set off for a distant
country and there squandered his wealth[d]
in wild living. 14After he had spent everything, there was a severe famine in that
whole country, and he began to be in need.
15So he went and hired himself out to a citizen of that country, who sent him to his
fields to feed pigs.[e] 16He longed to fill his
stomach with the pods that the pigs were
eating, but no one gave him anything.

17"When he came to his senses, he
said, 'How many of my father's hired men
have food to spare, and here I am starving
to death! 18I will set out and go back to
my father and say to him: Father, I have
sinned[f] against heaven and against you.
19I am no longer worthy to be called your
son; make me like one of your hired men.'
20So he got up and went to his father.

"But while he was still a long way off,
his father saw him and was filled with compassion for him; he ran to his son, threw
his arms around him and kissed him.[g]

21"The son said to him, 'Father, I have
sinned against heaven and against you.[h]
I am no longer worthy to be called your
son.[b]'

22"But the father said to his servants,
'Quick! Bring the best robe[i] and put it on
him. Put a ring on his finger[j] and sandals
on his feet. 23Bring the fattened calf and
kill it. Let's have a feast and celebrate.
24For this son of mine was dead and is
alive again;[k] he was lost and is found.' So
they began to celebrate.[l]

25"Meanwhile, the older son was in the
field. When he came near the house, he
heard music and dancing. 26So he called
one of the servants and asked him what
was going on. 27'Your brother has come,'
he replied, 'and your father has killed the
fattened calf because he has him back safe
and sound.'

28"The older brother became angry[m] and
refused to go in. So his father went out
and pleaded with him. 29But he answered
his father, 'Look! All these years I've been
slaving for you and never disobeyed your
orders. Yet you never gave me even a
young goat so I could celebrate with my

15:3 [u]Mt 13:3
15:4 [v]Ps 23; 119:176; Jer 31:10; Eze 34:11-16; Lk 5:32; 19:10
15:6 [w]ver 9
15:7 [x]ver 10
15:9 [y]ver 6
15:10 [z]ver 7
15:11 [a]Mt 21:28
15:12 [b]Dt 21:17 [c]ver 30
15:13 [d]ver 30; Lk 16:1
15:15 [e]Lev 11:7
15:18 [f]Lev 26:40; Mt 3:2
15:20 [g]Ge 45:14,15; 46:29; Ac 20:37
15:21 [h]Ps 51:4
15:22 [i]Zec 3:4; Rev 6:11 [j]Ge 41:42
15:24 [k]Eph 2:1,5; 5:14; 1Ti 5:6 [l]ver 32
15:28 [m]Jnh 4:1

[a] *8* Greek *ten drachmas,* each worth about a day's wages
[b] *21* Some early manuscripts *son. Make me like one of your hired men.*

ly. *eats with them.* More than simple association, eating with a person indicated acceptance and recognition (cf. Ps 41:9; Jn 13:18 and notes; Ac 11:3; 1Co 5:11 and note; Gal 2:12).

15:3 *this parable.* Jesus responded with a story that contrasted God's love with the exclusiveness of the Pharisees.

15:4 *lost sheep.* The shepherd theme was familiar (see Ps 23; Isa 40:11; Eze 34:11 – 16 and notes).

15:6 *I have found my lost sheep.* Cf. 19:10 and note.

15:7 *rejoicing in heaven.* On the part of God and the angels — in sharp contrast to the attitude of the Pharisees and the teachers of the law (v. 2). *righteous … do not need to repent.* Probably irony: those who think they are righteous (such as the Pharisees and the teachers of the law) and feel no need to repent.

15:8 *ten silver coins.* See NIV text note. A *drachma* was a Greek coin approximately equivalent to the Roman *denarius,* worth about an average day's wages (Mt 20:2). *search carefully.* Near Eastern houses frequently had no windows and only earthen floors, making the search for a single coin difficult.

15:12 *share of the estate.* The father might divide the inheritance (double to the older son; see 12:13; Dt 21:17 and notes) but retain the income from it until his death. But to give a younger son his portion of the inheritance upon request was highly unusual. Cf. Pr 20:21 and note.

15:13 *got together all he had.* The son's motive becomes apparent when he departs, taking with him all his possessions and leaving nothing behind to come back to. He wants to be free of parental restraint and to spend his share of the family wealth as he pleases. *wild living.* More specific in v. 30, though the older brother may have exaggerated because of his bitter attitude.

15:15 *feed pigs.* The ultimate indignity for a Jew; the work was abhorrent to Jews because pigs were ceremonially unclean animals (Lev 11:7).

15:16 *pods.* Seeds of the carob tree.

15:22 – 23 *best robe … ring … sandals … feast.* Each was a sign of position and acceptance (cf. Ge 41:42 and note; Zec 3:4): a long robe of distinction, a signet ring of authority, sandals like a son (slaves went barefoot), and the fattened calf for a special occasion.

15:28 *older brother.* The forgiving love of the father symbolizes the divine mercy of God, and the older brother's resentment is like the attitude of the Pharisees and teachers of the law who opposed Jesus (v. 2).

15:29 *young goat.* Cheaper food than a fattened calf.

Parables of Jesus

PARABLE	MATTHEW	MARK	LUKE
Lamp under a bowl	5:14-15	4:21-22	8:16; 11:33
Wise and foolish builders	7:24-27		6:47-49
New cloth on an old coat	9:16	2:21	5:36
New wine in old wineskins	9:17	2:22	5:37-38
Sower and the soils	13:3-8,18-23	4:3-8,14-20	8:5-8,11-15
Weeds	13:24-30,36-43		
Mustard seed	13:31-32	4:30-32	13:18-19
Yeast	13:33		13:20-21
Hidden treasure	13:44		
Valuable pearl	13:45-46		
Net	13:47-50		
Owner of a house	13:52		
Lost sheep	18:12-14		15:4-7
Unmerciful servant	18:23-34		
Workers in the vineyard	20:1-16		
Two sons	21:28-32		
Tenants	21:33-44	12:1-11	20:9-18
Wedding banquet	22:2-14		
Fig tree	24:32-35	13:28-29	21:29-31
Faithful and wise servant	24:45-51		12:42-48
Ten virgins	25:1-13		
Talents (minas)	25:14-30		19:12-27
Sheep and goats	25:31-46		
Growing seed		4:26-29	
Watchful servants		13:35-37	12:35-40
Moneylender			7:41-43
Good Samaritan			10:30-37
Friend in need			11:5-8
Rich fool			12:16-21
Unfruitful fig tree			13:6-9
Lowest seat at the feast			14:7-14
Great banquet			14:16-24
Cost of discipleship			14:28-33
Lost coin			15:8-10
Lost (prodigal) son			15:11-32
Shrewd manager			16:1-8
Rich man and Lazarus			16:19-31
Master and his servant			17:7-10
Persistent widow			18:2-8
Pharisee and tax collector			18:10-14

friends. 30But when this son of yours who
has squandered your property[n] with prostitutes[o] comes home, you kill the fattened
calf for him!'
31" 'My son,' the father said, 'you are always with me, and everything I have is
yours. 32But we had to celebrate and be
glad, because this brother of yours was
dead and is alive again; he was lost and
is found.' "[p]

The Parable of the Shrewd Manager

16 Jesus told his disciples: "There was
a rich man whose manager was accused of wasting his possessions.[q] 2So he
called him in and asked him, 'What is
this I hear about you? Give an account of
your management, because you cannot be
manager any longer.'
3"The manager said to himself, 'What
shall I do now? My master is taking away
my job. I'm not strong enough to dig, and
I'm ashamed to beg— 4I know what I'll
do so that, when I lose my job here, people will welcome me into their houses.'
5"So he called in each one of his master's debtors. He asked the first, 'How
much do you owe my master?'
6" 'Eight hundred gallons[a] of olive oil,'
he replied.
"The manager told him, 'Take your bill,
sit down quickly, and make it four hundred.'
7"Then he asked the second, 'And how
much do you owe?'
" 'A thousand bushels[b] of wheat,' he replied.
"He told him, 'Take your bill and make
it eight hundred.'
8"The master commended the dishonest manager because he had acted shrewdly. For the people of this world[r] are more
shrewd[s] in dealing with their own kind
than are the people of the light.[t] 9I tell
you, use worldly wealth[u] to gain friends
for yourselves, so that when it is gone, you
will be welcomed into eternal dwellings.[v]
10"Whoever can be trusted with very
little can also be trusted with much,[w] and
whoever is dishonest with very little will
also be dishonest with much. 11So if you
have not been trustworthy in handling
worldly wealth,[x] who will trust you with
true riches? 12And if you have not been
trustworthy with someone else's property, who will give you property of your
own?
13"No servant can serve two masters.
Either he will hate the one and love the
other, or he will be devoted to the one and
despise the other. You cannot serve both
God and Money."[y]
14The Pharisees, who loved money,[z]
heard all this and were sneering at Jesus.[a]
15He said to them, "You are the ones who
justify yourselves[b] in the eyes of men, but
God knows your hearts.[c] What is highly
valued among men is detestable in God's
sight.

Additional Teachings

16"The Law and the Prophets were proclaimed until John.[d] Since that time, the
good news of the kingdom of God is being
preached,[e] and everyone is forcing his way

15:30 [n]ver 12, 13 [o]Pr 29:3
15:32 [p]ver 24; Mal 3:17
16:1 [q]Lk 15:13,30
16:8 [r]Ps 17:14 [s]Ps 18:26 [t]Jn 12:36; Eph 5:8; 1Th 5:5
16:9 [u]ver 11,13 [v]Mt 19:21; Lk 12:33
16:10 [w]Mt 25:21,23; Lk 19:17
16:11 [x]ver 9,13
16:13 [y]ver 9,11; Mt 6:24
16:14 [z]S 1Ti 3:3 [a]Lk 23:35
16:15 [b]Lk 10:29 [c]S Rev 2:23
16:16 [d]Mt 5:17; 11:12,13 [e]S Mt 4:23

[a] 6 Greek *one hundred batous* (probably about 3 kiloliters) [b] 7 Greek *one hundred korous* (probably about 35 kiloliters)

15:30 *this son of yours.* The older brother would not even recognize him as his brother, so bitter was his hatred.

15:31 *everything I have is yours.* The father loved both brothers. The parable shows a contrast between the self-centered exclusiveness of the Pharisees, who failed to understand God's love, and his joy over the repentance of sinners.

15:32 *dead and is alive.* A beautiful picture of the return of the younger son, which also pictures Christian conversion (see Ro 6:12–13 and note; Eph 2:1,5). The phrase "lost and is found" is often used to mean "perished and is saved" (see 19:10 and note; Mt 10:6; 18:12–14 and note).

16:1 *disciples.* Perhaps more than just the Twelve (see 6:13 and note; 10:1). *manager.* A steward who handled all the business affairs of the owner (cf. 1Co 4:1–2 and note on 4:1). *wasting.* He had squandered his master's possessions, just as the prodigal (wasteful) son (15:13).

16:3 *What shall I do now?* The "dishonest manager" (v. 8) had no scruples against using his position for his own benefit, even if it meant cheating his master. Knowing he would lose his job, the manager planned for his future by discounting the debts owed to his master in order to obligate the debtors to himself. Interpreters disagree as to whether his procedure of discounting was in itself dishonest. Was he giving away what really belonged to his master, or was he forgoing interest payments his master did not have a right to charge? Originally the manager may have overcharged the debtors, a common way of circumventing the Mosaic law that prohibited taking interest from fellow Jews (see Ex 22:25–27; Lev 25:36 and notes; Dt 23:19–20). So, to reduce the debts, he may have returned the figures to their initial amounts, which would both satisfy his master and gain the good favor of the debtors. In any event, the point remains the same: He was shrewd enough to use the means at his disposal to plan for his future well-being.

16:8 *people of the light.* God's people (see Jn 12:35–36; Eph 5:8; 1Th 5:5 and notes).

16:9 *worldly wealth.* That is, wealth that is corruptible; the Greek for "worldly" is the same as for "dishonest" (v. 8) when describing the corrupt manager (see also vv. 10–11). *to gain friends.* By helping those in need, who in the future will show their gratitude when they welcome their benefactors into heaven ("eternal dwellings"). In this way worldly (corruptible) wealth may be wisely used to gain eternal benefit.

16:10 *trusted with much.* Cf. 19:17; Mt 25:21. Faithfulness is not determined by the amount entrusted but by the character of the person who uses it.

16:11 *true riches.* The things that belong to God's kingdom, in contrast to "worldly wealth."

16:13 *two masters.* See Mt 6:24; cf. Jas 4:4 and note.

16:16 *until John.* The ministry of John the Baptist, which prepared the way for Jesus the Messiah, was the divid-

into it. 17It is easier for heaven and earth to
disappear than for the least stroke of a pen
to drop out of the Law.[f]
18"Anyone who divorces his wife and
marries another woman commits adultery, and the man who marries a divorced
woman commits adultery.[g]

The Rich Man and Lazarus

19"There was a rich man who was
dressed in purple and fine linen and lived
in luxury every day.[h] 20At his gate was laid
a beggar[i] named Lazarus, covered with
sores 21and longing to eat what fell from
the rich man's table.[j] Even the dogs came
and licked his sores.
22"The time came when the beggar died
and the angels carried him to Abraham's
side. The rich man also died and was buried. 23In hell,[a] where he was in torment,
he looked up and saw Abraham far away,
with Lazarus by his side. 24So he called to
him, 'Father Abraham,[k] have pity on me
and send Lazarus to dip the tip of his finger in water and cool my tongue, because
I am in agony in this fire.'[l]
25"But Abraham replied, 'Son, remember that in your lifetime you received your
good things, while Lazarus received bad
things,[m] but now he is comforted here and
you are in agony.[n] 26And besides all this,
between us and you a great chasm has
been fixed, so that those who want to go
from here to you cannot, nor can anyone
cross over from there to us.'
27"He answered, 'Then I beg you, father,
send Lazarus to my father's house, 28for I
have five brothers. Let him warn them,[o] so
that they will not also come to this place
of torment.'
29"Abraham replied, 'They have Mo-
ses[p] and the Prophets;[q] let them listen to
them.'
30" 'No, father Abraham,'[r] he said, 'but
if someone from the dead goes to them,
they will repent.'
31"He said to him, 'If they do not listen
to Moses and the Prophets, they will not
be convinced even if someone rises from
the dead.' "

Sin, Faith, Duty

17 Jesus said to his disciples: "Things
that cause people to sin[s] are bound
to come, but woe to that person through
whom they come.[t] 2It would be better for
him to be thrown into the sea with a millstone tied around his neck than for him to
cause one of these little ones[u] to sin.[v] 3So
watch yourselves.
"If your brother sins, rebuke him,[w] and
if he repents, forgive him.[x] 4If he sins
against you seven times in a day, and sev-
en times comes back to you and says, 'I
repent,' forgive him."[y]
5The apostles[z] said to the Lord,[a] "Increase our faith!"
6He replied, "If you have faith as small
as a mustard seed,[b] you can say to this
mulberry tree, 'Be uprooted and planted
in the sea,' and it will obey you.[c]

[a] 23 Greek *Hades*

16:17 [f] S Mt 5:18 **16:18** [g] Mt 5:31,32; 19:9; Mk 10:11; Ro 7:2,3; 1Co 7:10,11 **16:19** [h] Eze 16:49 **16:20** [i] Ac 3:2 **16:21** [j] Mt 15:27; Lk 15:16 **16:24** [k] ver 30; S Lk 3:8 [l] S Mt 5:22 **16:25** [m] Ps 17:14 [n] Lk 6:21,24,25 **16:28** [o] Ac 2:40; 20:23; 1Th 4:6 **16:29** [p] S Lk 24:27,44; Jn 1:45; 5:45-47; Ac 15:21 [q] Lk 4:17; 24:27,44; Jn 1:45 **16:30** [r] ver 24; S Lk 3:8 **17:1** [s] S Mt 5:29 [t] Mt 18:7 **17:2** [u] Mk 10:24; Lk 10:21 [v] S Mt 5:29 **17:3** [w] S Mt 18:15 [x] Eph 4:32; Col 3:13 **17:4** [y] Mt 18:21,22 **17:5** [z] S Mk 6:30 [a] S Lk 7:13 **17:6** [b] Mt 13:31; 17:20; Lk 13:19 [c] S Mt 21:21; Mk 9:23

ing line between the OT (the "Law and the Prophets") and the NT (see notes on Jer 31:31 – 34; Heb 8:6 – 12). *forcing his way.* The meaning is disputed, but it probably speaks of the fierce earnestness with which people were responding to the gospel of the kingdom. Multitudes were coming to hear Jesus and to receive his message.

16:17 The ministry of Jesus (introducing the new covenant era) was a fulfillment of the law (defining the old covenant era) in the most minute detail (cf. 21:33). *heaven and earth to disappear.* See Mk 13:24 – 25; 2Pe 3:7 and notes. *least stroke of a pen.* See Mt 5:17 – 18 and notes.

16:18 *divorces his wife.* See Mt 5:32; 19:3; Mk 10:11 – 12; 1Co 7:10 – 11 and notes. Jesus affirms the continuing authority of the law: For example, adultery was still adultery, still unlawful and still sinful. Matthew's treatment is fuller in that (1) it shows that this law was given because of hardened hearts in regard to divorce, and (2) it includes one exception as permissible grounds for divorce — marital unfaithfulness (Mt 19:9).

16:19 *rich man.* Sometimes given the name Dives (from the Latin for "rich man"). *purple and fine linen.* Characteristic of costly garments.

16:20 *Lazarus.* Not the Lazarus Jesus raised from the dead (Jn 11:43 – 44). If this is a parable, it is the only one in which Jesus gave a name to one of the characters. *covered with sores.* The Greek for this phrase is a medical term used commonly in Greek inscriptions but found only here in the NT (see Introduction: Author).

16:22 The Jewish Talmud mentions both paradise (see 23:43 and note) and Abraham's side as the final home of the righteous. "Abraham's side" refers to the place of blessedness to which the righteous dead go. Its bliss is the quality of blessedness reserved for people like Abraham.

16:23 *hell.* See NIV text note. Hades is here depicted as the place to which the wicked dead go and suffer torment.

16:28 *I have five brothers.* For the first time the rich man showed concern for others.

16:29 *Moses and the Prophets.* A way of designating the whole OT. The rich man had failed to pay attention to Scripture and its teaching, and feared his brothers would do the same. *listen to.* Hear and obey.

16:30 *someone from the dead.* The story may suggest that Lazarus was intended, but Luke's account seems to imply that Jesus was speaking also of his own resurrection (cf. v. 31; 9:22). If people's minds are closed and Scripture is rejected, no evidence — not even a resurrection — will change them.

17:2 *millstone.* A heavy stone for grinding grain. *little ones.* See Mt 18:6,10,14; Mk 9:42 and notes.

17:3 *your brother.* See Mt 18:15,17; Mk 3:35 and notes.

17:4 *seven times.* That is, forgiveness is to be unlimited (see notes on Ps 119:164; Mt 18:22; Eph 4:32).

17:5 *Increase our faith!* They felt incapable of measuring up to the standards set forth in vv. 1 – 4. They wanted greater faith to lay hold of the power to live up to Jesus' standards.

17:6 See Mt 17:20 and note; Mk 11:23; see also notes on Mt 13:31 – 32; Mk 4:31.

7“Suppose one of you had a servant
plowing or looking after the sheep. Would
he say to the servant when he comes in
from the field, ‘Come along now and sit
down to eat’? 8Would he not rather say,
‘Prepare my supper, get yourself ready and
wait on me[d] while I eat and drink; after
that you may eat and drink’? 9Would he
thank the servant because he did what he
was told to do? 10So you also, when you
have done everything you were told to do,
should say, ‘We are unworthy servants; we
have only done our duty.’ ”[e]

Ten Healed of Leprosy

11Now on his way to Jerusalem,[f] Jesus
traveled along the border between Samaria and Galilee.[g] 12As he was going into a
village, ten men who had leprosy[a h] met
him. They stood at a distance[i] 13and called
out in a loud voice, “Jesus, Master,[j] have
pity on us!”
14When he saw them, he said, “Go,
show yourselves to the priests.”[k] And as
they went, they were cleansed.
15One of them, when he saw he was
healed, came back, praising God[l] in a loud
voice. 16He threw himself at Jesus’ feet and
thanked him — and he was a Samaritan.[m]
17Jesus asked, “Were not all ten
cleansed? Where are the other nine? 18Was
no one found to return and give praise to
God except this foreigner?” 19Then he said
to him, “Rise and go; your faith has made
you well.”[n]

The Coming of the Kingdom of God

17:26,27pp — Mt 24:37-39

20Once, having been asked by the Pharisees when the kingdom of God would
come,[o] Jesus replied, “The kingdom of
God does not come with your careful observation, 21nor will people say, ‘Here it
is,’ or ‘There it is,’[p] because the kingdom
of God is within[b] you.”
22Then he said to his disciples, “The
time is coming when you will long to see
one of the days of the Son of Man,[q] but
you will not see it.[r] 23Men will tell you,
‘There he is!’ or ‘Here he is!’ Do not go
running off after them.[s] 24For the Son of
Man in his day[c] will be like the lightning,[t]
which flashes and lights up the sky from
one end to the other. 25But first he must
suffer many things[u] and be rejected[v] by
this generation.[w]
26“Just as it was in the days of Noah,[x]
so also will it be in the days of the Son of
Man. 27People were eating, drinking, marrying and being given in marriage up to
the day Noah entered the ark. Then the
flood came and destroyed them all.
28“It was the same in the days of Lot.[y]
People were eating and drinking, buying
and selling, planting and building. 29But
the day Lot left Sodom, fire and sulfur
rained down from heaven and destroyed
them all.
30“It will be just like this on the day the
Son of Man is revealed.[z] 31On that day no
one who is on the roof of his house, with
his goods inside, should go down to get
them. Likewise, no one in the field should
go back for anything.[a] 32Remember Lot’s

17:8 [d] Lk 12:37 **17:10** [e] 1Co 9:16 **17:11** [f] S Lk 9:51 [g] Lk 9:51,52; Jn 4:3,4 **17:12** [h] S Mt 8:2 [i] Lev 13:45,46 **17:13** [j] S Lk 5:5 **17:14** [k] Lev 14:2; Mt 8:4 **17:15** [l] S Mt 9:8 **17:16** [m] S Mt 10:5 **17:19** [n] S Mt 9:22 **17:20** [o] S Mt 3:2 **17:21** [p] ver 23 **17:22** [q] S Mt 8:20 [r] S Lk 5:35 **17:23** [s] Mt 24:23; Lk 21:8 **17:24** [t] Mt 24:27 **17:25** [u] S Mt 16:21 [v] Lk 9:22; 18:32 [w] Mk 13:30; Lk 21:32 **17:26** [x] Ge 6:5-8; 7:6-24 **17:28** [y] Ge 19:1-28 **17:30** [z] Mt 10:23; S 16:27; 24:3,27,37,39; 25:31; S 1Co 1:7; S 1Th 2:19; 2Th 1:7; 2:8; 2Pe 3:4; S Rev 1:7 **17:31** [a] Mt 24:17,18

[a] *12* The Greek word was used for various diseases affecting the skin — not necessarily leprosy. [b] *21* Or *among* [c] *24* Some manuscripts do not have *in his day.*

17:7 *a servant.* A slave, used to illustrate performance of duty (cf. 12:37 and note).

17:11 *border between Samaria and Galilee.* From this point Jesus seems to have journeyed to Perea, where he ministered on his way south to Jerusalem (see notes on 9:51; 13:22).

17:14 *show yourselves to the priests.* Normal procedure after being cured of leprosy (see Lev 13:2 – 3; 14:2 – 32).

17:15 *praising God.* See v. 18; see also 1:64 and note.

17:16 *Samaritan.* See note on 10:31 – 33. Normally Jews did not associate with Samaritans (see Jn 4:9 and note), but leprosy broke down social barriers while erecting others (see notes on Lev 13:2,4,45 – 46).

17:19 *your faith has made you well.* See Mt 9:22. The phrase may also be rendered “your faith has saved you” (7:50; see note on Mk 5:34). The fact that the Samaritan returned to thank Jesus may indicate that he had received salvation in addition to the physical healing all ten had received (cf. 7:50; 8:48,50 and notes).

17:20 *Pharisees.* See note on 5:17.

17:21 *the kingdom of God is within you.* Probably indicating that the kingdom is spiritual and internal (see Mt 23:26 and note), rather than physical and external (cf. Jn 18:36 and note). But see NIV text note (cf. 19:11; 21:7; Ac 1:6 and notes), meaning that the kingdom is present in the person of King Jesus (see also note on 4:43). However, the immediate context (v. 20) may favor the former interpretation, namely, that the kingdom is spiritual and so not visible. If this is the correct view, the pronoun “you” in the phrase “within you” is to be taken in a general sense rather than as referring to the unbelieving Pharisees personally. The kingdom certainly was not within them.

17:22 *long to see.* In time of trouble, believers will desire to experience the day when Jesus returns in his glory and delivers his people from their distress.

17:23 *Do not go running off after them.* Do not leave your work in order to pursue predictions of Christ’s second advent (see note on 1Th 4:11).

17:24 *like the lightning.* His coming will be sudden, unexpected and public (cf. 12:40 and note).

17:25 *he must suffer.* Jesus repeatedly foretold his coming death (see 5:35; 9:22,43 – 45 and note on 9:22; 12:50; 13:32 – 33; 18:32; 24:7; Mt 16:21; Mk 2:20 and note), which had to occur before his glorious return (see 1Pe 1:11 and note).

17:28 *in the days of Lot.* See Ge 18:16 — 19:28.

17:30 *Son of Man is revealed.* At Jesus’ second coming he will be plainly visible to all (see 1Co 1:7; 2Th 1:7 and note; 1Pe 1:7,13; 4:13; Rev 1:7).

17:31 *on the roof of his house.* It was customary to relax on the flat rooftop. When the final hour comes, however, the individual there should not be thinking of going into the house to retrieve some material objects. Matthew and Mark refer similarly to flight at the fall of Jerusalem, and indirectly to the

wife![b] 33Whoever tries to keep his life will
lose it, and whoever loses his life will preserve it.[c] 34I tell you, on that night two
people will be in one bed; one will be tak-
en and the other left. 35Two women will be
grinding grain together; one will be taken
and the other left.[a]"[d]
37"Where, Lord?" they asked.
He replied, "Where there is a dead body,
there the vultures will gather."[e]

The Parable of the Persistent Widow

18 Then Jesus told his disciples a parable to show them that they should
always pray and not give up.[f] 2He said:
"In a certain town there was a judge who
neither feared God nor cared about men.
3And there was a widow in that town who
kept coming to him with the plea, 'Grant
me justice[g] against my adversary.'
4"For some time he refused. But finally
he said to himself, 'Even though I don't
fear God or care about men, 5yet because
this widow keeps bothering me, I will see
that she gets justice, so that she won't
eventually wear me out with her coming!' "[h]
6And the Lord[i] said, "Listen to what the
unjust judge says. 7And will not God bring
about justice for his chosen ones, who cry
out[j] to him day and night? Will he keep
putting them off? 8I tell you, he will see
that they get justice, and quickly. However, when the Son of Man[k] comes,[l] will he
find faith on the earth?"

17:32 [b]Ge 19:26
17:33 [c]S Jn 12:25
17:35 [d]Mt 24:41
17:37 [e]Mt 24:28
18:1 [f]Isa 40:31; Lk 11:5-8; S Ac 1:14; S Ro 1:10; 12:12; Eph 6:18; Col 4:2; 1Th 5:17
18:3 [g]Isa 1:17
18:5 [h]Lk 11:8
18:6 [i]S Lk 7:13
18:7 [j]Ex 22:23; Ps 88:1; Rev 6:10
18:8 [k]S Mt 8:20 [l]S Mt 16:27
18:9 [m]Lk 16:15 [n]Isa 65:5
18:10 [o]Ac 3:1
18:11 [p]Mt 6:5; Mk 11:25
18:12 [q]Isa 58:3; Mt 9:14 [r]Mal 3:8; Lk 11:42
18:13 [s]Isa 66:2; Jer 31:19; Lk 23:48 [t]Lk 5:32; 1Ti 1:15
18:14 [u]S Mt 23:12

The Parable of the Pharisee and the Tax Collector

9To some who were confident of their
own righteousness[m] and looked down
on everybody else,[n] Jesus told this parable: 10"Two men went up to the temple
to pray,[o] one a Pharisee and the other a
tax collector. 11The Pharisee stood up[p] and
prayed about[b] himself: 'God, I thank you
that I am not like other men—robbers,
evildoers, adulterers—or even like this tax
collector. 12I fast[q] twice a week and give a
tenth[r] of all I get.'
13"But the tax collector stood at a distance. He would not even look up to heav-
en, but beat his breast[s] and said, 'God,
have mercy on me, a sinner.'[t]
14"I tell you that this man, rather than
the other, went home justified before God.
For everyone who exalts himself will be
humbled, and he who humbles himself
will be exalted."[u]

The Little Children and Jesus

18:15-17pp — Mt 19:13-15; Mk 10:13-16

15People were also bringing babies to
Jesus to have him touch them. When the
disciples saw this, they rebuked them.
16But Jesus called the children to him and
said, "Let the little children come to me,
and do not hinder them, for the kingdom
of God belongs to such as these. 17I tell
you the truth, anyone who will not receive

[a] 35 Some manuscripts *left.* 36*Two men will be in the field; one will be taken and the other left.* [b] 11 Or *to*

end time (Mt 24:17–18; Mk 13:15), but here the reference is explicitly to Jesus' return (see v. 30; cf. 21:21).

17:33 *whoever loses his life will preserve it.* See note on 9:24 (cf. Mt 10:39).

17:35 *taken.* Could refer to being "taken to/from destruction" or "taken into the kingdom." What is clear is that no matter how close two people may be in life, they have no guarantee of the same eternal destiny. One may go to judgment and condemnation, the other to salvation, reward and blessing.

17:36 See NIV text note on v. 35. A copyist probably inserted v. 36 here from Mt 24:40.

17:37 *Where ... there the vultures will gather.* A proverb. See note on Mt 24:28. In response to the disciples' question, Jesus explains that these things will take place wherever there are people to whom the event pertains.

18:2 *nor cared about men.* The judge was unconcerned about the needs of others or about their opinion of him.

18:3 *widow.* Particularly helpless and vulnerable because she had no family to uphold her cause. Only justice and her own persistence were in her favor (cf. 1Ti 5:3 and note).

18:7 *will not God bring about justice ...?* If an unworthy judge who feels no constraint of right or wrong is compelled by persistence to deal justly with a helpless individual, how much more will God answer prayer! *keep putting them off.* God will not delay his support of the chosen ones when they are right. He is not like the unjust judge, who had to be badgered until he wearied and gave in.

18:8 *will he find faith ...?* Particularly faith that perseveres in prayer and loyalty (see Mt 24:12–13). Christ makes a second application that looks forward to the time of his second coming. A period of spiritual decline and persecution is assumed—a time that will require perseverance such as the widow demonstrated.

18:10 *to pray.* Periods for prayer were scheduled daily in connection with the morning and evening sacrifices. People could also go to the temple at any time for private prayer. *tax collector.* See note on Mt 5:46.

18:12 *fast twice a week.* Fasting was not commanded in the Mosaic law except for the fast on the annual Day of Atonement (see Mk 2:18 and note). However, the Pharisees also fasted on Mondays and Thursdays of each week (see 5:33 and note; Mt 6:16; 9:14; Ac 27:9 and note). *a tenth of all I get.* As a typical first-century Pharisee, he tithed all that he acquired, not merely what he gained from agriculture and/or business.

18:13 *beat his breast.* Cf. 23:48 and note. *have mercy on me.* The verb used here means "to be appeased/reconciled" (see note on 1Jn 2:2). The tax collector does not plead his good works but the mercy of God in forgiving his sin.

18:14 *justified before God.* God reckoned him to be righteous, i.e., his sins were forgiven and he was accepted by God. *exalts ... humbled ... humbles ... exalted.* See Pr 3:34; Da 4:37; Jas 4:6; 1Pe 5:5.

18:17 *like a little child.* With total dependence, full trust, frank openness and complete sincerity (see Mt 18:3; 19:14; Mk 10:14–15 and notes; cf. 1Pe 2:2).

the kingdom of God like a little child[v] will
never enter it."

The Rich Ruler

18:18-30pp — Mt 19:16-29; Mk 10:17-30

18 A certain ruler asked him, "Good
teacher, what must I do to inherit eternal
life?"[w]
19 "Why do you call me good?" Jesus
answered. "No one is good—except God
alone. 20 You know the commandments:
'Do not commit adultery, do not murder,
do not steal, do not give false testimony,
honor your father and mother.'[a]"[x]
21 "All these I have kept since I was a
boy," he said.
22 When Jesus heard this, he said to him,
"You still lack one thing. Sell everything
you have and give to the poor,[y] and you
will have treasure in heaven.[z] Then come,
follow me."
23 When he heard this, he became very
sad, because he was a man of great wealth.
24 Jesus looked at him and said, "How hard
it is for the rich to enter the kingdom of
God![a] 25 Indeed, it is easier for a camel to
go through the eye of a needle than for a
rich man to enter the kingdom of God."
26 Those who heard this asked, "Who
then can be saved?"
27 Jesus replied, "What is impossible
with men is possible with God."[b]
28 Peter said to him, "We have left all we
had to follow you!"[c]
29 "I tell you the truth," Jesus said to
them, "no one who has left home or wife
or brothers or parents or children for the
sake of the kingdom of God 30 will fail to
receive many times as much in this age
and, in the age to come,[d] eternal life."[e]

Jesus Again Predicts His Death

18:31-33pp — Mt 20:17-19; Mk 10:32-34

31 Jesus took the Twelve aside and told
them, "We are going up to Jerusalem,[f] and
everything that is written by the prophets[g]
about the Son of Man[h] will be fulfilled.
32 He will be handed over to the Gentiles.[i]
They will mock him, insult him, spit on
him, flog him[j] and kill him.[k] 33 On the third
day[l] he will rise again."[m]
34 The disciples did not understand any
of this. Its meaning was hidden from
them, and they did not know what he was
talking about.[n]

A Blind Beggar Receives His Sight

18:35-43pp — Mt 20:29-34; Mk 10:46-52

35 As Jesus approached Jericho,[o] a blind
man was sitting by the roadside begging.
36 When he heard the crowd going by, he
asked what was happening. 37 They told
him, "Jesus of Nazareth is passing by."[p]
38 He called out, "Jesus, Son of David,[q]
have mercy[r] on me!"
39 Those who led the way rebuked him
and told him to be quiet, but he shouted
all the more, "Son of David, have mercy
on me!"[s]
40 Jesus stopped and ordered the man to
be brought to him. When he came near,
Jesus asked him, 41 "What do you want me
to do for you?"
"Lord, I want to see," he replied.
42 Jesus said to him, "Receive your sight;
your faith has healed you."[t] 43 Immediately
he received his sight and followed Jesus,
praising God. When all the people saw it,
they also praised God.[u]

Zacchaeus the Tax Collector

19 Jesus entered Jericho[v] and was passing through. 2 A man was there by
the name of Zacchaeus; he was a chief tax
collector and was wealthy. 3 He wanted to
see who Jesus was, but being a short man
he could not, because of the crowd. 4 So
he ran ahead and climbed a sycamore-fig[w]
tree to see him, since Jesus was coming
that way.[x]

[a] *20* Exodus 20:12-16; Deut. 5:16-20

18:17 [v]Mt 11:25; 18:3 **18:18** [w]Lk 10:25 **18:20** [x]Ex 20:12-16; Dt 5:16-20; Ro 13:9 **18:22** [y]S Ac 2:45 [z]S Mt 6:20 **18:24** [a]Pr 11:28 **18:27** [b]S Mt 19:26 **18:28** [c]S Mt 4:19 **18:30** [d]S Mt 12:32 [e]S Mt 25:46 **18:31** [f]S Lk 9:51 [g]Ps 22; Isa 53 [h]S Mt 8:20 **18:32** [i]Lk 23:1 [j]S Mt 16:21 [k]S Ac 2:23 **18:33** [l]S Mt 16:21 [m]S Mt 16:21 **18:34** [n]S Mk 9:32 **18:35** [o]Lk 19:1 **18:37** [p]Lk 19:4 **18:38** [q]ver 39; S Mt 9:27 [r]Mt 17:15; Lk 18:13 **18:39** [s]ver 38 **18:42** [t]S Mt 9:22 **18:43** [u]S Mt 9:8; Lk 13:17 **19:1** [v]Lk 18:35 **19:4** [w]1Ki 10:27; 1Ch 27:28; Isa 9:10 [x]Lk 18:37

18:18–27 For this event see notes on Mk 10:17–27.
18:18 *eternal life.* See note on Mt 19:16.
18:20 *You know the commandments.* See Ex 20:1–17; 20:2 and notes.
18:24 *kingdom of God.* See note on Mt 3:2.
18:30 *this age ... the age to come.* The present age of sin and misery and the future age to be inaugurated by the return of the Messiah (see Mk 10:30 and note).
18:31 *everything that is written by the prophets.* Sometimes referred to as the third prediction of Jesus' death, though the total number is more than three (see note on 17:25). The first distinct prediction is in 9:22 (see note there) and the second in 9:44 (see note there). The Messiah's death had been predicted and/or prefigured centuries before (see, e.g., 24:25–27; introduction to Ps 22; see also note on Isa 52:13—53:12; Zec 13:7 and note; Mt 26:24,31,54). *Son of Man.* See note on Mk 8:31.
18:34 *hidden from them.* See 9:45 and note.
18:35 *approached Jericho.* See note on Mk 10:46. *blind man.* Bartimaeus (Mk 10:46). Matthew reports that two blind men were healed (see note on Mt 20:30). Mark and Luke did not record the presence of the other.
18:38–39 *Son of David.* A Messianic title (see Mt 1:1 and note; 22:41–45; Mk 10:47 and note; 12:35; Jn 7:42; see also 2Sa 7:12–13; Ps 89:3–4; Am 9:11; Mt 12:23 and notes).
18:42 *your faith.* See note on 17:19.
18:43 *praising God ... praised God.* See 1:64 and note.
19:1 *entered Jericho.* See note on Mk 10:46.
19:2 *chief tax collector.* A position referred to only here in the Bible, probably designating one in charge of a district, with other tax collectors under him. The region was prosperous at this time, so it is no wonder that Zacchaeus had grown rich. See notes on 3:12; Mt 5:46; Mk 2:14–16.
19:4 *sycamore-fig tree.* A sturdy tree from 30 to 40 feet high, with a short trunk and spreading branches, capable of holding a grown man. See note on Am 7:14.

5When Jesus reached the spot, he
looked up and said to him, "Zacchaeus,
come down immediately. I must stay at
your house today." 6So he came down at
once and welcomed him gladly.
7All the people saw this and began to
mutter, "He has gone to be the guest of a
'sinner.'"[y]
8But Zacchaeus stood up and said to the
Lord,[z] "Look, Lord! Here and now I give
half of my possessions to the poor, and if I
have cheated anybody out of anything,[a] I
will pay back four times the amount."[b]
9Jesus said to him, "Today salvation
has come to this house, because this man,
too, is a son of Abraham.[c] 10For the Son of
Man came to seek and to save what was
lost."[d]

The Parable of the Ten Minas

19:12-27Ref — Mt 25:14-30

11While they were listening to this, he
went on to tell them a parable, because
he was near Jerusalem and the people
thought that the kingdom of God[e] was going to appear at once.[f] 12He said: "A man
of noble birth went to a distant country to
have himself appointed king and then to
return. 13So he called ten of his servants[g]
and gave them ten minas.[*a*] 'Put this money to work,' he said, 'until I come back.'
14"But his subjects hated him and sent
a delegation after him to say, 'We don't
want this man to be our king.'
15"He was made king, however, and
returned home. Then he sent for the servants to whom he had given the money,
in order to find out what they had gained
with it.
16"The first one came and said, 'Sir, your
mina has earned ten more.'
17" 'Well done, my good servant!'[h] his
master replied. 'Because you have been
trustworthy in a very small matter, take
charge of ten cities.'[i]
18"The second came and said, 'Sir, your
mina has earned five more.'
19"His master answered, 'You take
charge of five cities.'
20"Then another servant came and said,
'Sir, here is your mina; I have kept it laid
away in a piece of cloth. 21I was afraid of
you, because you are a hard man. You take
out what you did not put in and reap what
you did not sow.'[j]
22"His master replied, 'I will judge you
by your own words,[k] you wicked servant!
You knew, did you, that I am a hard man,
taking out what I did not put in, and reaping what I did not sow?[l] 23Why then didn't
you put my money on deposit, so that
when I came back, I could have collected
it with interest?'
24"Then he said to those standing by,
'Take his mina away from him and give it
to the one who has ten minas.'
25" 'Sir,' they said, 'he already has ten!'
26"He replied, 'I tell you that to everyone
who has, more will be given, but as for the
one who has nothing, even what he has
will be taken away.[m] 27But those enemies
of mine who did not want me to be king
over them—bring them here and kill them
in front of me.' "

The Triumphal Entry

19:29-38pp — Mt 21:1-9; Mk 11:1-10
19:35-38pp — Jn 12:12-15

28After Jesus had said this, he went on
ahead, going up to Jerusalem.[n] 29As he approached Bethphage and Bethany[o] at the
hill called the Mount of Olives,[p] he sent

19:7 [y]S Mt 9:11 **19:8** [z]S Lk 7:13 [a]Lk 3:12,13 [b]Ex 22:1; Lev 6:4,5; Nu 5:7; 2Sa 12:6; Eze 33:14,15 **19:9** [c]S Lk 3:8 **19:10** [d]Eze 34:12,16; S Jn 3:17 **19:11** [e]S Mt 3:2 [f]Lk 17:20; Ac 1:6 **19:13** [g]Mk 13:34 **19:17** [h]Pr 27:18 [i]Lk 16:10 **19:21** [j]Mt 25:24 **19:22** [k]2Sa 1:16; Job 15:6 [l]Mt 25:26 **19:26** [m]S Mt 25:29 **19:28** [n]Mk 10:32; S Lk 9:51 **19:29** [o]S Mt 21:17 [p]S Mt 21:1

a 13 A mina was about three months' wages.

19:5 *I must stay at your house.* Implies a divine necessity.
19:8 *four times.* The full repayment required under the law in case of theft (see Ex 22:1; 2Sa 12:6 and note).
19:9 *son of Abraham.* A true Jew—not only of the lineage of Abraham but one who also walks "in the footsteps" of Abraham's faith (Ro 4:12). Jesus recognized the tax collector as such, though Jewish society excluded him.
19:10 A key verse in Luke's Gospel. *Son of Man.* A Messianic title (see Introduction: Plan; see also note on Mk 8:31). *to seek and to save.* An important summary of Jesus' purpose—to bring salvation, meaning eternal life (18:18), and the kingdom of God (18:25). See note on 15:32.
19:11 *kingdom ... was going to appear.* They expected the Messiah to appear in power and glory and to set up his earthly kingdom, defeating all their political and military enemies.
19:12 *have himself appointed king.* A rather unusual procedure, but the Herods (see chart, p. 1465) did just that when they went to Rome to be appointed rulers over the Jews. Similarly, Jesus was soon to depart and in the future is to return as King. During his absence, his servants are entrusted with their master's affairs (for a similar parable see Mt 25:14–30).
19:13 *ten minas.* See NIV text note.
19:14 *sent a delegation.* Such an incident had occurred over 30 years earlier in the case of Archelaus (Josephus, *Wars*, 2.6.1; *Antiquities*, 17.9.3), as well as in a number of other instances. This aspect of the story may have been included to warn the Jews against rejecting Jesus as King.
19:22 *You knew ... that I am a hard man ...?* The master did not admit to the statement of the servant, but repeated it in a question. If this was the opinion of the servant, he should have acted accordingly.
19:26 *more will be given ... what he has will be taken away.* See 8:18; 17:33 and notes; Mt 13:12. Those who seek spiritual gain in the gospel, for themselves and others, will become richer, and those who neglect or squander what is given them will become impoverished, losing even what they have.
19:27 *those enemies of mine ... kill them.* Perhaps a reference to Jerusalem's destruction in A.D. 70. The punishment of those who rebelled and actively opposed the king (see v. 14 and note) was much more severe than that of the negligent servant.
19:28–44 The Triumphal Entry occurred on Sunday of Passion Week (see chart, p. 1510, and map, p. 1552; see also notes on Mt 21:1–9; Mk 11:1–10; Jn 12:12–15).
19:29 *Bethphage.* A village near the road going from Jericho to Jerusalem. *Bethany.* Another village about two miles

two of his disciples, saying to them, 30"Go
to the village ahead of you, and as you enter it, you will find a colt tied there, which
no one has ever ridden. Untie it and bring
it here. 31If anyone asks you, 'Why are you
untying it?' tell him, 'The Lord needs it.' "
32Those who were sent ahead went and
found it just as he had told them.[q] 33As they
were untying the colt, its owners asked
them, "Why are you untying the colt?"
34They replied, "The Lord needs it."
35They brought it to Jesus, threw their
cloaks on the colt and put Jesus on it. 36As
he went along, people spread their cloaks[r]
on the road.
37When he came near the place where
the road goes down the Mount of Olives,[s]
the whole crowd of disciples began joyfully to praise God in loud voices for all the
miracles they had seen:

38"Blessed is the king who comes in the
name of the Lord!"[a t]

"Peace in heaven and glory in the
highest!"[u]

39Some of the Pharisees in the crowd
said to Jesus, "Teacher, rebuke your disciples!"[v]
40"I tell you," he replied, "if they keep
quiet, the stones will cry out."[w]
41As he approached Jerusalem and saw
the city, he wept over it[x] 42and said, "If
you, even you, had only known on this
day what would bring you peace—but
now it is hidden from your eyes. 43The
days will come upon you when your enemies will build an embankment against
you and encircle you and hem you in on
every side.[y] 44They will dash you to the
ground, you and the children within your
walls.[z] They will not leave one stone on
another,[a] because you did not recognize
the time of God's coming[b] to you."

Jesus at the Temple

19:45,46pp — Mt 21:12-16; Mk 11:15-18; Jn 2:13-16

45Then he entered the temple area and
began driving out those who were selling.
46"It is written," he said to them, " 'My
house will be a house of prayer'[b];[c] but you
have made it 'a den of robbers.'[c]"[d]
47Every day he was teaching at the temple.[e] But the chief priests, the teachers of
the law and the leaders among the people
were trying to kill him.[f] 48Yet they could
not find any way to do it, because all the
people hung on his words.

The Authority of Jesus Questioned

20:1-8pp — Mt 21:23-27; Mk 11:27-33

20 One day as he was teaching the people in the temple courts[g] and preaching the gospel,[h] the chief priests and the
teachers of the law, together with the elders, came up to him. 2"Tell us by what
authority you are doing these things," they
said. "Who gave you this authority?"[i]

[a] *38* Psalm 118:26 [b] *46* Isaiah 56:7 [c] *46* Jer. 7:11

19:32 [q]Lk 22:13
19:36 [r]2Ki 9:13
19:37 [s]S Mt 21:1
19:38 [t]Ps 118:26; Lk 13:35 [u]S Lk 2:14
19:39 [v]Mt 21:15, 16
19:40 [w]Hab 2:11
19:41 [x]Isa 22:4; Lk 13:34, 35
19:43 [y]Isa 29:3; Jer 6:6; Eze 4:2; 26:8; Lk 21:20
19:44 [z]Ps 137:9 [a]Lk 21:6 [b]1Pe 2:12
19:46 [c]Isa 56:7 [d]Jer 7:11
19:47 [e]S Mt 26:55 [f]S Mt 12:14; Mk 11:18
20:1 [g]S Mt 26:55 [h]Lk 8:1
20:2 [i]Jn 2:18; Ac 4:7; 7:27

southeast of Jerusalem (Jn 11:18), and the home of Mary, Martha and Lazarus. *Mount of Olives.* A ridge a little more than a mile long (see note on Mk 11:1). For the Mount of Olives, Bethany and Bethphage in relationship to Jerusalem see map, pp. 1552–1553. *two of his disciples.* Not named here or in the parallel passages (Mt 21:1; Mk 11:1; cf. Jn 12:14).

19:30 *village.* Probably Bethphage. *colt.* In other accounts a donkey colt (Jn 12:15) is specified and the mother of the colt (Mt 21:7; see note there) with him. Luke uses a Greek word that the Septuagint (the pre-Christian Greek translation of the OT) frequently employed to translate the Hebrew for "donkey." Jesus chooses to enter Jerusalem this time mounted on a donkey to claim publicly that he was the chosen Son of David to sit on David's throne (see note on 1Ki 1:33), the one about whom the prophets had spoken (Zec 9:9; see note there). *which no one has ever ridden.* And thus available for sacred use (see note on Mk 11:2).

19:31 *The Lord.* Either God or, more likely, Jesus himself, here claiming his own unique status as Israel's Lord.

19:37 *praise God.* See 1:64 and note. *all the miracles.* The raising of Lazarus and the healing of blind Bartimaeus were recent examples, but included also would be the works recorded in John on various occasions in Jerusalem, as well as the whole of his ministry in Galilee (cf. Mt 21:14; Jn 12:17).

19:40 Perhaps an echo of Hab 2:11.

19:41 *he wept.* One of only two occasions when Jesus is said to have wept (see also Jn 11:35).

19:42 *peace.* That the Messiah would bring. *hidden from your eyes.* See 9:45 and note.

19:43 *your enemies will build an embankment.* See 21:20 and note; fulfilled when the Romans took Jerusalem in A.D. 70, using an embankment to besiege the city. The description is reminiscent of OT predictions of an earlier destruction of Jerusalem (Isa 29:3; 37:33; Eze 4:1–3).

19:44 *the time of God's coming to you.* God came to the Jews in the person of Jesus the Messiah, but they failed to recognize him and rejected him (see Jn 1:10–11; cf. Lk 20:13–16).

19:45 Mark (11:11–17) makes clear that this clearing of the temple occurred the day after the Triumphal Entry, i.e., on Monday of Passion Week. *temple area.* The outer court (of the Gentiles), where animals for sacrifice were sold at unfair prices (see note on Mk 11:15). John records a clearing of the temple at the beginning of Jesus' ministry (Jn 2:13–25), but the Synoptics (see Mt 21:12–13; Mk 11:15–17) speak only of a clearing of the temple at the close of Jesus' ministry (see notes on Mt 21:12–17; Jn 2:14–17).

19:47 *chief priests.* See 3:2; 22:52; 23:4; 24:20; see also note on Mt 2:4. They were part of the Sanhedrin, the ruling Jewish council (see note on Mk 14:55). *were trying to kill him.* See 20:19–20 (cf. Jn 7:1; 11:53–57).

20:1 The events of 20:1—21:36 all occurred on Tuesday of Passion Week—a long day of controversy. *One day.* Not specified, but Mark's parallel accounts (Mk 11:19–20,27–33) indicate that this day (Tuesday) followed the clearing of the temple (Monday), which followed the Triumphal Entry (Sunday). See map, pp. 1556–1557. *chief priests.* See 19:47 and note. *teachers of the law.* See 5:30 and note on 5:17. *elders.* See note on Mt 15:2. Each of these groups was represented in the Jewish council, the Sanhedrin (see 22:66).

20:2 *Who gave you this authority?* They had asked this of John the Baptist (Jn 1:19–25) and of Jesus early in his ministry

3He replied, "I will also ask you a question. Tell me, 4John's baptism[j]—was it
from heaven, or from men?"
5They discussed it among themselves
and said, "If we say, 'From heaven,' he
will ask, 'Why didn't you believe him?'
6But if we say, 'From men,' all the people[k]
will stone us, because they are persuaded
that John was a prophet."[l]
7So they answered, "We don't know
where it was from."
8Jesus said, "Neither will I tell you by
what authority I am doing these things."

The Parable of the Tenants

20:9-19pp — Mt 21:33-46; Mk 12:1-12

9He went on to tell the people this parable: "A man planted a vineyard,[m] rented
it to some farmers and went away for a
long time.[n] 10At harvest time he sent a servant to the tenants so they would give him
some of the fruit of the vineyard. But the
tenants beat him and sent him away empty-handed. 11He sent another servant, but
that one also they beat and treated shamefully and sent away empty-handed. 12He
sent still a third, and they wounded him
and threw him out.
13"Then the owner of the vineyard said,
'What shall I do? I will send my son, whom
I love;[o] perhaps they will respect him.'
14"But when the tenants saw him, they
talked the matter over. 'This is the heir,'
they said. 'Let's kill him, and the inheritance will be ours.' 15So they threw him
out of the vineyard and killed him.
"What then will the owner of the vineyard do to them? 16He will come and kill
those tenants[p] and give the vineyard to
others."

When the people heard this, they said,
"May this never be!"
17Jesus looked directly at them and
asked, "Then what is the meaning of that
which is written:

" 'The stone the builders rejected
has become the capstone[a]'[b]?[q]

18Everyone who falls on that stone will be
broken to pieces, but he on whom it falls
will be crushed."[r]
19The teachers of the law and the chief
priests looked for a way to arrest him[s] immediately, because they knew he had spoken this parable against them. But they
were afraid of the people.[t]

Paying Taxes to Caesar

20:20-26pp — Mt 22:15-22; Mk 12:13-17

20Keeping a close watch on him, they
sent spies, who pretended to be honest.
They hoped to catch Jesus in something he
said[u] so that they might hand him over to
the power and authority of the governor.[v]
21So the spies questioned him: "Teacher,
we know that you speak and teach what is
right, and that you do not show partiality
but teach the way of God in accordance
with the truth.[w] 22Is it right for us to pay
taxes to Caesar or not?"
23He saw through their duplicity and
said to them, 24"Show me a denarius.
Whose portrait and inscription are on it?"
25"Caesar's," they replied.
He said to them, "Then give to Caesar what is Caesar's,[x] and to God what is
God's."
26They were unable to trap him in what
he had said there in public. And astonished by his answer, they became silent.

[a] *17* Or *cornerstone* [b] *17* Psalm 118:22

20:4 [j] S Mk 1:4
20:6 [k] Lk 7:29 [l] S Mt 11:9
20:9 [m] Isa 5:1-7 [n] Mt 25:14
20:13 [o] S Mt 3:17
20:16 [p] Lk 19:27
20:17 [q] Ps 118:22; S Ac 4:11
20:18 [r] Isa 8:14, 15
20:19 [s] Lk 19:47 [t] S Mk 11:18
20:20 [u] S Mt 12:10 [v] Mt 27:2
20:21 [w] Jn 3:2
20:25 [x] Lk 23:2; Ro 13:7

(Jn 2:18–22). Here the reference is to the clearing of the temple, which not only defied the authority of the Jewish leaders but also hurt their monetary profits. The leaders may also have been looking for a way to discredit Jesus in the eyes of the people or raise suspicion of him as a threat to the authority of Rome.

20:4 *John's baptism ... from heaven, or from men?* By replying with a question, Jesus put the burden on his opponents—indicating only two alternatives: The work of John was either divinely inspired or humanly devised. By refusing to answer, they placed themselves in an awkward position. *from heaven.* See note on Mk 11:30.

20:10 *he sent a servant.* This parable (v. 9) is reminiscent of Isa 5:1–7 (see note on Isa 5:1). The servants who were sent to the tenants represent the prophets God sent in former times who were rejected (see Ne 9:26; Jer 7:25 and note; 25:4–7; Mt 23:34; Ac 7:52; Heb 11:36–38). *give him some of the fruit.* In accordance with a kind of sharecropping agreement, a fixed amount was due the landowner. At the proper time he would expect to receive his share.

20:13 *my son, whom I love.* The specific reference to the beloved son makes clearer the intended application of the son in the parable to the Son, Jesus Christ (see 3:22; Mt 17:5 and notes).

20:14 *inheritance will be ours.* See note on Mk 12:7.

20:16 *give the vineyard to others.* See note on Mt 21:41.

20:17 *capstone.* See Ac 4:11; Ro 9:33; 1Pe 2:7; see also note on Ps 118:22.

20:18 *will be broken to pieces.* As a pot dashed against a stone is broken, and as one lying beneath a falling stone is crushed, so those who reject Jesus the Messiah will be doomed (see Isa 8:14 and note; cf. Da 2:34–35,44; Lk 2:34).

20:19 *teachers of the law.* See note on Mt 2:4. For their opposition to Jesus see 5:17 and note, 30; 9:22; 19:47; 22:2; 23:10.

20:20 *authority of the governor.* Fearing to take action themselves, the Jewish religious leaders hoped to draw from Jesus a statement that would bring action from the Roman officials and remove him from his contact with the people.

20:22 *pay taxes to Caesar.* See note on Mk 12:14. To agree to the taxes demanded by Caesar would disappoint the people, but to advise no payment would disturb the Roman officials. The questioners hoped to trap Jesus with this dilemma (see note on Mt 22:15–17).

20:24 *denarius.* A Roman coin worth about a day's wages (see note on Mt 22:19).

20:25 *to God what is God's.* See notes on Mt 22:21; Mk 12:17.

The Resurrection and Marriage

20:27-40pp — Mt 22:23-33; Mk 12:18-27

27 Some of the Sadducees,[y] who say there is no resurrection,[z] came to Jesus with a question. 28 "Teacher," they said, "Moses wrote for us that if a man's brother dies and leaves a wife but no children, the man must marry the widow and have children for his brother.[a] 29 Now there were seven brothers. The first one married a woman and died childless. 30 The second 31 and then the third married her, and in the same way the seven died, leaving no children. 32 Finally, the woman died too. 33 Now then, at the resurrection whose wife will she be, since the seven were married to her?"

34 Jesus replied, "The people of this age marry and are given in marriage. 35 But those who are considered worthy of taking part in that age[b] and in the resurrection from the dead will neither marry nor be given in marriage, 36 and they can no longer die; for they are like the angels. They are God's children,[c] since they are children of the resurrection. 37 But in the account of the bush, even Moses showed that the dead rise, for he calls the Lord 'the God of Abraham, and the God of Isaac, and the God of Jacob.'[a][d] 38 He is not the God of the dead, but of the living, for to him all are alive."

39 Some of the teachers of the law responded, "Well said, teacher!" 40 And no one dared to ask him any more questions.[e]

Whose Son Is the Christ?

20:41-47pp — Mt 22:41–23:7; Mk 12:35-40

41 Then Jesus said to them, "How is it that they say the Christ[b] is the Son of David?[f] 42 David himself declares in the Book of Psalms:

"'The Lord said to my Lord:
"Sit at my right hand
43 until I make your enemies
a footstool for your feet."'[c][g]

44 David calls him 'Lord.' How then can he be his son?"

45 While all the people were listening, Jesus said to his disciples, 46 "Beware of the teachers of the law. They like to walk around in flowing robes and love to be greeted in the marketplaces and have the most important seats in the synagogues and the places of honor at banquets.[h] 47 They devour widows' houses and for a show make lengthy prayers. Such men will be punished most severely."

The Widow's Offering

21:1-4pp — Mk 12:41-44

21 As he looked up, Jesus saw the rich putting their gifts into the temple treasury.[i] 2 He also saw a poor widow put in two very small copper coins.[d] 3 "I tell you the truth," he said, "this poor widow has put in more than all the others. 4 All these people gave their gifts out of their wealth; but she out of her poverty put in all she had to live on."[j]

Signs of the End of the Age

21:5-36pp — Mt 24; Mk 13
21:12-17pp — Mt 10:17-22

5 Some of his disciples were remarking about how the temple was adorned with

20:27 [y] S Ac 4:1 [z] Ac 23:8; 1Co 15:12 **20:28** [a] Dt 25:5 **20:35** [b] S Mt 12:32 **20:36** [c] S Jn 1:12 **20:37** [d] Ex 3:6 **20:40** [e] Mt 22:46; Mk 12:34 **20:41** [f] S Mt 1:1 **20:43** [g] Ps 110:1; S Mt 22:44 **20:46** [h] S Lk 11:43 **21:1** [i] Mt 27:6; Jn 8:20 **21:4** [j] 2Co 8:12

[a] 37 Exodus 3:6 [b] 41 Or *Messiah* [c] 43 Psalm 110:1
[d] 2 Greek *two lepta*

20:27 *Saddusees.* An aristocratic, politically minded group, willing to compromise with secular and pagan leaders. They controlled the high priesthood at this time and held the majority of the seats in the Sanhedrin. They did not believe in the resurrection or an afterlife, and they rejected the oral tradition taught by the Pharisees (Josephus, *Antiquities*, 13.10.6). See notes on Ezr 7:2; Mt 2:4; 3:7; 22:23; Mk 12:18; Ac 4:1; see also essay, p. 1453, and chart, p. 1502.
20:28 *the man must marry the widow.* The levirate law (see note on Mt 22:24; cf. Ge 38:8 and note).
20:34–35 *this age ... that age.* See note on 18:30.
20:36 *like the angels.* The resurrection order cannot be assumed to follow present earthly lines. In the new age there will be no marriage, no procreation and no death (see note on Mk 12:25). *children of the resurrection.* Those who are to take part in the resurrection of the righteous (cf. Mk 12:18; Ac 4:1; 23:6 and notes).
20:37 *account of the bush.* Since the Biblical texts did not have the grid of numbered chapters and verses imposed on them until the Middle Ages, the passage of Scripture was identified by Jesus in this way, referring to Moses' experience with the burning bush (see Ex 3:2–6; Mk 12:26 and notes).
20:39 *Well said, teacher!* Even though there was great animosity against Jesus, the teachers of the law (who were Pharisees) sided with Jesus against the Sadducees on the matter of resurrection.

20:44 *David calls him 'Lord.'* Jesus' argument with the Jewish religious leaders is that since the Messiah is a descendant of David, how can this honored king refer to his offspring as Lord? Unless Jesus' opponents were ready to admit that the Messiah was also the divine Son of God, they could not answer his question. See notes on Ps 110:1; Mt 22:44; Mk 12:36.
20:46 *flowing robes ... important seats.* See notes on Mk 12:38–39.
20:47 *devour widows' houses.* They take advantage of this defenseless group by fraud and schemes for selfish gain. *punished most severely.* Cf. 12:46–48 and note. The higher the esteem received from others, the more severe the demands of true justice; and the more hypocrisy (Mt 23:1–36), the greater the condemnation.
21:1 *temple treasury.* In the court of women, east of Herod's temple, there were 13 boxes, shaped like inverted megaphones and positioned to receive the donations of the worshipers (see note on Mk 12:41).
21:2 *very small copper coins.* See note on Mk 12:42.
21:3–4 See note on 2Co 8:12.
21:3 *I tell you the truth.* See note on Mk 3:28.
21:5–36 See note on Mk 13:1–37.
21:5 *how the temple was adorned.* "Whatever was not overlaid with gold was purest white" (Josephus, *Wars*, 5.5.6.). Herod gave a golden vine for one of its decorations.

beautiful stones and with gifts dedicated
to God. But Jesus said, 6“As for what you
see here, the time will come when not one
stone will be left on another;[k] every one of
them will be thrown down.”
7“Teacher,” they asked, “when will these
things happen? And what will be the sign
that they are about to take place?”
8He replied: “Watch out that you are not
deceived. For many will come in my name,
claiming, ‘I am he,’ and, ‘The time is near.’
Do not follow them.[l] 9When you hear of
wars and revolutions, do not be frightened. These things must happen first, but
the end will not come right away.”
10Then he said to them: “Nation will rise
against nation, and kingdom against kingdom.[m] 11There will be great earthquakes,
famines and pestilences in various places, and fearful events and great signs from
heaven.[n]
12“But before all this, they will lay hands
on you and persecute you. They will deliver you to synagogues and prisons, and
you will be brought before kings and governors, and all on account of my name.
13This will result in your being witnesses
to them.[o] 14But make up your mind not
to worry beforehand how you will defend
yourselves.[p] 15For I will give you[q] words
and wisdom that none of your adversaries
will be able to resist or contradict. 16You
will be betrayed even by parents, brothers, relatives and friends,[r] and they will
put some of you to death. 17All men will
hate you because of me.[s] 18But not a hair
of your head will perish.[t] 19By standing
firm you will gain life.[u]
20“When you see Jerusalem being surrounded by armies,[v] you will know that
its desolation is near. 21Then let those who
are in Judea flee to the mountains, let
those in the city get out, and let those in
the country not enter the city.[w] 22For this is
the time of punishment[x] in fulfillment[y] of
all that has been written. 23How dreadful it
will be in those days for pregnant women
and nursing mothers! There will be great
distress in the land and wrath against this
people. 24They will fall by the sword and
will be taken as prisoners to all the nations. Jerusalem will be trampled[z] on by
the Gentiles until the times of the Gentiles
are fulfilled.
25“There will be signs in the sun, moon
and stars. On the earth, nations will be in
anguish and perplexity at the roaring and
tossing of the sea.[a] 26Men will faint from
terror, apprehensive of what is coming on
the world, for the heavenly bodies will be
shaken.[b] 27At that time they will see the
Son of Man[c] coming in a cloud[d] with power and great glory. 28When these things
begin to take place, stand up and lift up
your heads, because your redemption is
drawing near.”[e]
29He told them this parable: “Look at
the fig tree and all the trees. 30When they
sprout leaves, you can see for yourselves
and know that summer is near. 31Even so,
when you see these things happening, you
know that the kingdom of God[f] is near.

21:6 [k] Lk 19:44 **21:8** [l] Lk 17:23 **21:10** [m] 2Ch 15:6; Isa 19:2 **21:11** [n] Isa 29:6; Joel 2:30 **21:13** [o] Php 1:12 **21:14** [p] Lk 12:11 **21:15** [q] S Lk 12:12 **21:16** [r] Lk 12:52,53 **21:17** [s] S Jn 15:21 **21:18** [t] S Mt 10:30 **21:19** [u] S Mt 10:22 **21:20** [v] S Lk 19:43 **21:21** [w] Lk 17:31 **21:22** [x] Isa 63:4; Da 9:24-27; Hos 9:7 [y] S Mt 1:22 **21:24** [z] Isa 5:5; 63:18; Da 8:13; Rev 11:2 **21:25** [a] 2Pe 3:10,12 **21:26** [b] S Mt 24:29 **21:27** [c] S Mt 8:20 [d] S Rev 1:7 **21:28** [e] Lk 18:7 **21:31** [f] S Mt 3:2

Its grape clusters were as tall as a man. The full magnificence of the temple as elaborated and adorned by Herod has only recently come to light through archaeological investigations on the temple hill.

21:6 *not one stone . . . left.* Fulfilled in A.D. 70 when the Romans took Jerusalem and burned the temple (Mt 24:2; see note there).

21:7 *when . . . ?* Mark reports that this question was asked by four disciples: Peter, James, John and Andrew (Mk 13:3). Matthew gives the question in a fuller form, including an inquiry for the sign of Jesus' coming and the end of the age (Mt 24:3; see note there). *what will be the sign . . . ?* What would be the indication that these things are about to happen?

21:8 *I am he.* I am Jesus the Messiah (having come a second time). *The time.* The end time.

21:9 *the end will not come right away.* Refers to the end of the age (see Mt 24:3,6). All the events listed in vv. 8–18 are characteristic of the entire present age, not just signs of the end of the age.

21:11 *signs from heaven.* See v. 25. For prophetic descriptions of celestial signs accompanying the day of the Lord see note on Mk 13:24–25.

21:12 *deliver you to synagogues.* Synagogues were used not only for worship and school but also for community administration and for confinement of Jews who were awaiting trial before a Jewish court (see note on Mk 13:9; cf. Mt 23:34).

21:15 *none . . . will be able to resist.* See Ac 6:9–10.

21:18 Although persecution and death may come, God is in control, and the ultimate outcome will be eternal victory. *not a hair of your head will perish.* In view of v. 16 this cannot refer to physical safety. The figure indicates that there will be no real—i.e., spiritual and eternal—loss (see v. 19).

21:19 See note on Mk 13:13.

21:20 *surrounded by armies.* See 19:43 and note. The sign that the end was near (cf. v. 7 and note) would be the surrounding of Jerusalem with armies. Associated with this event would be the "abomination that causes desolation" (Mt 24:15; see note there).

21:21 *flee to the mountains.* When an army surrounds a city, it is natural to seek protection inside the walls, but Jesus directs his followers to seek the safety of the mountains because the city was doomed to destruction (see note on Mt 24:16).

21:22 *time of punishment.* God's retributive justice as the consequence of faithlessness (cf. Isa 63:4; Jer 5:29; Hos 9:7).

21:24 *times of the Gentiles.* The Gentiles would have both spiritual opportunities (see Mt 24:14 and note; Mk 13:10; cf. Lk 20:16; Ro 11:25 and note) and domination of Jerusalem, but these times will end when God's purpose for the Gentiles has been fulfilled.

21:27 See Mt 24:30 and note.

21:28 *lift up your heads.* Do not be downcast at the appearance of these signs, but look up in joy, hope and trust (cf. Ps 24:7). *redemption.* Final, completed redemption (see Ro 8:23; Heb 9:28 and notes).

21:29 *Look at the fig tree.* The coming of spring is announced by the greening of the trees (cf. Mt 24:32–35; Mk 11:13 and note; 13:28–31). In a similar way, one can anticipate the coming of the kingdom when its signs are seen. But "kingdom" is used in different ways (see note on 4:43). The reference in v. 31 is to the future kingdom.

32 "I tell you the truth, this generation[a][g] will certainly not pass away until all these things have happened. 33 Heaven and earth will pass away, but my words will never pass away.[h]

34 "Be careful, or your hearts will be weighed down with dissipation, drunkenness and the anxieties of life,[i] and that day will close on you unexpectedly[j] like a trap. 35 For it will come upon all those who live on the face of the whole earth. 36 Be always on the watch, and pray[k] that you may be able to escape all that is about to happen, and that you may be able to stand before the Son of Man."

37 Each day Jesus was teaching at the temple,[l] and each evening he went out[m] to spend the night on the hill called the Mount of Olives,[n] 38 and all the people came early in the morning to hear him at the temple.[o]

Judas Agrees to Betray Jesus

22:1,2pp — Mt 26:2-5; Mk 14:1,2,10,11

22 Now the Feast of Unleavened Bread, called the Passover, was approaching,[p] 2 and the chief priests and the teachers of the law were looking for some way to get rid of Jesus,[q] for they were afraid of the people. 3 Then Satan[r] entered Judas, called Iscariot,[s] one of the Twelve. 4 And Judas went to the chief priests and the officers of the temple guard[t] and discussed with them how he might betray Jesus. 5 They were delighted and agreed to give him money.[u] 6 He consented, and watched for an opportunity to hand Jesus over to them when no crowd was present.

The Last Supper

22:7-13pp — Mt 26:17-19; Mk 14:12-16
22:17-20pp — Mt 26:26-29; Mk 14:22-25; 1Co 11:23-25
22:21-23pp — Mt 26:21-24; Mk 14:18-21; Jn 13:21-30
22:25-27pp — Mt 20:25-28; Mk 10:42-45
22:33,34pp — Mt 26:33-35; Mk 14:29-31; Jn 13:37,38

7 Then came the day of Unleavened Bread on which the Passover lamb had to be sacrificed.[v] 8 Jesus sent Peter and John,[w] saying, "Go and make preparations for us to eat the Passover."

9 "Where do you want us to prepare for it?" they asked.

10 He replied, "As you enter the city, a man carrying a jar of water will meet you. Follow him to the house that he enters, 11 and say to the owner of the house, 'The Teacher asks: Where is the guest room, where I may eat the Passover with my disciples?' 12 He will show you a large upper room, all furnished. Make preparations there."

13 They left and found things just as Jesus had told them.[x] So they prepared the Passover.

14 When the hour came, Jesus and his apostles[y] reclined at the table.[z] 15 And he said to them, "I have eagerly desired to

21:32 [g] Lk 11:50; 17:25 **21:33** [h] S Mt 5:18 **21:34** [i] Mk 4:19 [j] Lk 12:40,46; 1Th 5:2-7 **21:36** [k] Mt 26:41 **21:37** [l] S Mt 26:55 [m] Mk 11:19 [n] S Mt 21:1 **21:38** [o] Jn 8:2 **22:1** [p] S Jn 11:55 **22:2** [q] S Mt 12:14 **22:3** [r] S Mt 4:10 [s] S Mt 10:4 **22:4** [t] ver 52; Ac 4:1; 5:24 **22:5** [u] Zec 11:12 **22:7** [v] Ex 12:18-20; Dt 16:5-8; S Mk 14:12 **22:8** [w] Ac 3:1,11; 4:13,19; 8:14 **22:13** [x] Lk 19:32 **22:14** [y] S Mk 6:30 [z] Mt 26:20; Mk 14:17,18

[a] 32 Or *race*

21:32 *this generation.* If reference here is to the destruction of Jerusalem that occurred about 40 years after Jesus spoke these words, "generation" is used in its ordinary sense of a normal life span. "All these things" would then have been fulfilled in the A.D. 70 destruction of Jerusalem. On the other hand, if reference here is to the second coming of Christ, "generation" might refer to a future generation alive at the beginning of "these things." It does not mean that Jesus had a mistaken notion he was going to return immediately.
21:34 *that day.* When Christ returns and the future aspect of God's kingdom is inaugurated (cf. v. 31). *close on you unexpectedly.* Does not mean that Christ's second coming will be completely unannounced, since there will be introductory signs (vv. 28,31; cf. 1Th 5:1–3).
21:35 *whole earth.* The second coming of Christ will involve the whole of humankind, whereas the fall of Jerusalem did not.
21:37 *Each day.* Each day during the final week of his life, from his Triumphal Entry to the time of the Passover (Sunday-Thursday). *Mount of Olives.* See notes on 19:29; Mt 21:17.
22:1 *Feast of Unleavened Bread ... Passover.* "Passover" was used in two different ways: (1) a specific meal begun at twilight on the 14th of Nisan (Lev 23:4–5), and (2) the week following the Passover meal (Eze 45:21), otherwise known as the Feast of Unleavened Bread, a week in which no leaven was allowed (see Ex 12:15 and note; 13:3–7; see also notes on Mk 14:1; Jn 2:13). By NT times the two names for the week-long festival were virtually interchangeable.
22:2 *the chief priests and the teachers of the law.* See 20:1 and note.
22:3 *Satan entered Judas.* In the Gospels this expression is used on two separate occasions: (1) before Judas went to the chief priests and offered to betray Jesus (here), and (2) during the Last Supper (Jn 13:27; see note there). Thus the Gospel writers depict Satan's control over Judas, who had never displayed strong commitment to Jesus (see Jn 13:2; see also notes on Jn 17:12; 1Co 15:2). *called Iscariot.* See Jn 6:71 and note.
22:4 *officers of the temple guard.* Jews, selected mostly from the Levites.
22:7 *Passover lamb had to be sacrificed.* On the 14th of Nisan between 2:30 and 5:30 P.M. in the court of the priests—Thursday of Passion Week.
22:10 *man carrying a jar.* It was extraordinary to see a man carrying a jar of water, since this was normally women's work.
22:11 *The Teacher asks.* This form of address may have been chosen because the owner was a follower already known to Jesus.
22:13 *as Jesus had told them.* It may be that Jesus had made previous arrangements with the man in order to make sure that the Passover meal would not be interrupted. Since Jesus did not identify ahead of time just where he would observe Passover, Judas was unable to inform the enemy, who might have interrupted this important occasion.
22:14–30 It appears that Luke does not attempt to be strictly chronological in his account of the Last Supper. He records the most important part of the occasion first—the sharing of the bread and the cup. Then he tells of Jesus' comments about his betrayer and about the argument over who would be greatest, though both of these subjects seem to have been introduced earlier. John's Gospel (13:26–30), e.g., indicates that Judas had already left the room before the bread and cup of the Lord's Supper were shared, but Luke does not tell when he left.
22:14 *reclined at the table.* See note on Mk 14:18.

eat this Passover with you before I suffer.[a]
16For I tell you, I will not eat it again until it finds fulfillment in the kingdom of
God."[b]
17After taking the cup, he gave thanks
and said, "Take this and divide it among
you. 18For I tell you I will not drink again
of the fruit of the vine until the kingdom
of God comes."
19And he took bread, gave thanks and
broke it,[c] and gave it to them, saying,
"This is my body given for you; do this in
remembrance of me."
20In the same way, after the supper he
took the cup, saying, "This cup is the new
covenant[d] in my blood, which is poured
out for you. 21But the hand of him who
is going to betray me is with mine on the
table.[e] 22The Son of Man[f] will go as it has
been decreed,[g] but woe to that man who
betrays him." 23They began to question
among themselves which of them it might
be who would do this.
24Also a dispute arose among them as
to which of them was considered to be
greatest.[h] 25Jesus said to them, "The kings
of the Gentiles lord it over them; and
those who exercise authority over them
call themselves Benefactors. 26But you are
not to be like that. Instead, the greatest
among you should be like the youngest,[i]
and the one who rules like the one who
serves.[j] 27For who is greater, the one who
is at the table or the one who serves? Is it
not the one who is at the table? But I am
among you as one who serves.[k] 28You are
those who have stood by me in my trials.
29And I confer on you a kingdom,[l] just as
my Father conferred one on me, 30so that
you may eat and drink at my table in my
kingdom[m] and sit on thrones, judging the
twelve tribes of Israel.[n]
31"Simon, Simon, Satan has asked[o] to
sift you[a] as wheat.[p] 32But I have prayed
for you,[q] Simon, that your faith may not
fail. And when you have turned back,
strengthen your brothers."[r]
33But he replied, "Lord, I am ready to go
with you to prison and to death."[s]
34Jesus answered, "I tell you, Peter, before the rooster crows today, you will deny
three times that you know me."
35Then Jesus asked them, "When I sent
you without purse, bag or sandals,[t] did
you lack anything?"
"Nothing," they answered.
36He said to them, "But now if you have
a purse, take it, and also a bag; and if you
don't have a sword, sell your cloak and
buy one. 37It is written: 'And he was numbered with the transgressors'[b];[u] and I tell
you that this must be fulfilled in me. Yes,
what is written about me is reaching its
fulfillment."
38The disciples said, "See, Lord, here are
two swords."
"That is enough," he replied.

22:15 [a]S Mt 16:21 **22:16** [b]S Lk 14:15 **22:19** [c]S Mt 14:19 **22:20** [d]Ex 24:8; Isa 42:6; Jer 31:31-34; Zec 9:11; 2Co 3:6; Heb 8:6; 9:15 **22:21** [e]Ps 41:9 **22:22** [f]S Mt 8:20 [g]Ac 2:23; 4:28 **22:24** [h]Mk 9:34; Lk 9:46 **22:26** [i]1Pe 5:5 [j]S Mk 9:35 **22:27** [k]S Mt 20:28 **22:29** [l]S Mt 25:34; 2Ti 2:12 **22:30** [m]S Lk 14:15 [n]S Mt 19:28 **22:31** [o]Job 1:6-12 [p]Am 9:9 **22:32** [q]Jn 17:9,15; S Ro 8:34 [r]Jn 21:15-17 **22:33** [s]Jn 11:16 **22:35** [t]Mt 10:9,10; Lk 9:3; 10:4 **22:37** [u]Isa 53:12

[a] *31* The Greek is plural. [b] *37* Isaiah 53:12

22:16 *until it finds fulfillment.* Jesus yearned to keep this Passover with his disciples because it was the last occasion before he himself was to be slain as the perfect "Passover lamb" (1Co 5:7; see note there) and thus fulfill this sacrifice for all time. Jesus would eat no more Passover meals until the coming of the future kingdom. After this he will renew fellowship with those who through the ages have commemorated the Lord's Supper. Finally the fellowship will be consummated in the great Messianic "wedding supper of the Lamb" to come (Rev 19:9).

22:17 *After taking the cup.* Either the first of the four cups shared during regular observance of the Passover meal, or the third cup.

22:18 *until the kingdom of God comes.* See notes on v. 16; 4:43.

22:19 *is.* Represents or signifies. *given for you.* Anticipating his substitutionary sacrifice on the cross. *in remembrance of me.* Just as the Passover was a constant reminder and proclamation of God's redemption of Israel from bondage in Egypt, so the keeping of Christ's command would be a remembering and proclaiming of the deliverance of believers from the bondage of sin through Christ's atoning work on the cross.

22:20 *after the supper.* Mentioned only here and in 1Co 11:25; see note on 1Co 11:23 – 26. *took the cup.* See note on Mk 14:24. *new covenant.* Promised through the prophet Jeremiah (see 31:31 – 34 and notes) — the fuller administration of God's saving grace, founded on and sealed by the death of Jesus ("in my blood"). See note on 1Co 11:25.

22:22 *as it has been decreed.* See Mk 14:21 and note.

22:25 *Benefactors.* A title assumed by or voted for rulers in Egypt, Syria and Rome as a display of honor, but frequently not representing actual service rendered.

22:26 *like the one who serves.* Jesus urges and exemplifies servant leadership — a trait that was as uncommon then as it is now (see Mk 10:45; Php 2:5,7 and notes).

22:28 *in my trials.* Including temptations (cf. 4:13), hardships (9:58) and rejection (Jn 1:11).

22:29 *confer on you a kingdom.* The following context (v. 30) indicates that this kingdom is the future form of the kingdom (see notes on 4:43; Mt 3:2).

22:30 *sit on thrones.* As they shared in Jesus' trials, so they will share in his rule (see 2Ti 2:12 and note). *judging.* Leading or ruling (see NIV text note on Jdg 2:16). *twelve tribes of Israel.* See Mt 19:28.

22:31 *sift you.* See NIV text note. Satan wanted to test the disciples, hoping to bring them to spiritual ruin.

22:34 See Mt 26:34; Jn 13:38 and notes.

22:36 *a purse … a bag.* Cf. previous instructions (9:3; 10:4). Until now they had been dependent on generous hospitality, but future opposition would require them to be prepared to pay their own way. *buy one.* An extreme figure of speech used to warn them of the perilous times about to come. They would need defense and protection, as Paul did when he appealed to Caesar (Ac 25:11; see note there) as the one whom God authorized to "bear the sword" (Ro 13:4).

22:37 *numbered with the transgressors.* Jesus was soon to be arrested as a criminal, in fulfillment of prophetic Scripture, and his disciples would also be in danger for being his followers.

22:38 *"… two swords." "That is enough."* Sensing that the disciples had taken him too literally, Jesus ironically closes the

Jesus Prays on the Mount of Olives

22:40-46pp — Mt 26:36-46; Mk 14:32-42

39 Jesus went out as usual[v] to the Mount
of Olives,[w] and his disciples followed him.
40 On reaching the place, he said to them,
"Pray that you will not fall into temptation."[x] 41 He withdrew about a stone's
throw beyond them, knelt down[y] and
prayed, 42 "Father, if you are willing, take
this cup[z] from me; yet not my will, but
yours be done."[a] 43 An angel from heaven
appeared to him and strengthened him.[b]
44 And being in anguish, he prayed more
earnestly, and his sweat was like drops of
blood falling to the ground.[a]
45 When he rose from prayer and went
back to the disciples, he found them
asleep, exhausted from sorrow. 46 "Why
are you sleeping?" he asked them. "Get
up and pray so that you will not fall into
temptation."[c]

Jesus Arrested

22:47-53pp — Mt 26:47-56; Mk 14:43-50; Jn 18:3-11

47 While he was still speaking a crowd
came up, and the man who was called Judas, one of the Twelve, was leading them.
He approached Jesus to kiss him, 48 but
Jesus asked him, "Judas, are you betraying the Son of Man with a kiss?"
49 When Jesus' followers saw what was
going to happen, they said, "Lord, should
we strike with our swords?"[d] 50 And one of
them struck the servant of the high priest,
cutting off his right ear.
51 But Jesus answered, "No more of this!"
And he touched the man's ear and healed
him.
52 Then Jesus said to the chief priests,
the officers of the temple guard,[e] and
the elders, who had come for him, "Am I
leading a rebellion, that you have come
with swords and clubs? 53 Every day I was
with you in the temple courts,[f] and you
did not lay a hand on me. But this is your
hour[g]—when darkness reigns."[h]

Peter Disowns Jesus

22:55-62pp — Mt 26:69-75; Mk 14:66-72; Jn 18:16-18,25-27

54 Then seizing him, they led him away
and took him into the house of the high
priest.[i] Peter followed at a distance.[j] 55 But
when they had kindled a fire in the middle
of the courtyard and had sat down together, Peter sat down with them. 56 A servant
girl saw him seated there in the firelight.
She looked closely at him and said, "This
man was with him."
57 But he denied it. "Woman, I don't
know him," he said.
58 A little later someone else saw him
and said, "You also are one of them."
"Man, I am not!" Peter replied.
59 About an hour later another asserted,
"Certainly this fellow was with him, for he
is a Galilean."[k]
60 Peter replied, "Man, I don't know
what you're talking about!" Just as he
was speaking, the rooster crowed. 61 The
Lord[l] turned and looked straight at Peter. Then Peter remembered the word
the Lord had spoken to him: "Before the
rooster crows today, you will disown me
three times."[m] 62 And he went outside and
wept bitterly.

22:39 [v] Lk 21:37 [w] S Mt 21:1
22:40 [x] Mt 6:13
22:41 [y] Lk 18:11
22:42 [z] S Mt 20:22 [a] S Mt 26:39
22:43 [b] Mt 4:11; Mk 1:13
22:46 [c] ver 40
22:49 [d] ver 38
22:52 [e] ver 4
22:53 [f] S Mt 26:55 [g] Jn 12:27 [h] Mt 8:12; Jn 1:5; 3:20
22:54 [i] Mt 26:57; Mk 14:53 [j] Mt 26:58; Mk 14:54; Jn 18:15
22:59 [k] Lk 23:6
22:61 [l] S Lk 7:13 [m] ver 34

[a] 44 Some early manuscripts do not have verses 43 and 44.

discussion with a curt "That's plenty!" Not long after this, Peter was rebuked for using a sword (v. 50).

22:39 *Mount of Olives.* See 19:29 and note. Matthew specifies Gethsemane (Mt 26:36; see note there), and John, an olive grove (Jn 18:1). The place apparently was located on the lower slopes of the Mount of Olives.

22:40 *temptation.* Here refers to severe trial of the kind referred to in vv. 28–38, which might lead to a faltering of their faith.

22:42 *if you are willing.* Notably, not "if you can." *this cup.* The cup of suffering (see Mt 20:22; Mk 14:36 and notes; cf. Isa 51:17; Eze 23:31 and notes).

22:43 *angel.* Matthew and Mark tell of angels ministering to Jesus at the close of his fasting and temptations (Mt 4:11; Mk 1:13). *strengthened him.* Cf. 2Co 12:8–10 and notes on 12:9–10.

22:44 *drops of blood.* Probably perspiration in large drops like blood, or possibly hematidrosis, the actual mingling of blood and sweat as in cases of extreme anguish, strain or sensitivity. Only Luke the doctor records this.

22:47 *crowd came up.* They were sent by the chief priests, elders (Mt 26:47) and teachers of the law (Mk 14:43; see note there), and they carried swords and clubs. Included was a detachment of soldiers with officials of the Jews (v. 52; Jn 18:3). *to kiss him.* This signal had been prearranged to identify Jesus to the authorities (Mt 26:48). It was unnecessary because Jesus identified himself (Jn 18:5), but Judas acted out his plan anyway.

22:50 *servant of the high priest.* Malchus by name; Simon Peter struck the blow (see Jn 18:10 and note).

22:51 *healed him.* Found only in Luke. Jesus rectified the wrong done by his follower. No faith on the part of Malchus was involved, but for Jesus to allow Peter's violent act to stand uncountered would have been contrary to Jesus' own teaching.

22:52 See note on Mt 26:55.

22:53 *your hour.* The time when the forces of darkness (the powers of evil) would do their worst and show their true character.

22:54 *house of the high priest.* See notes on 3:2; Mk 14:53.

22:57 *Woman.* Cf. note on Jn 2:4.

22:59 *he is a Galilean.* Recognized by his speech (see Mt 26:73 and note) and identified by a relative of Malchus, the high priest's slave (see Jn 18:26 and note).

22:61 *The Lord … looked straight at Peter.* Peter was outside in the enclosed courtyard, and perhaps Jesus was being taken from the trial by Caiaphas to the Sanhedrin when Jesus caught Peter's eye. *the word the Lord had spoken to him.* See v. 34.

The Guards Mock Jesus

22:63-65pp — Mt 26:67,68; Mk 14:65; Jn 18:22,23

63 The men who were guarding Jesus
began mocking and beating him. 64 They
blindfolded him and demanded, "Prophesy! Who hit you?" 65 And they said many
other insulting things to him.[n]

Jesus Before Pilate and Herod

22:67-71pp — Mt 26:63-66; Mk 14:61-63; Jn 18:19-21
23:2,3pp — Mt 27:11-14; Mk 15:2-5; Jn 18:29-37
23:18-25pp — Mt 27:15-26; Mk 15:6-15;
Jn 18:39 – 19:16

66 At daybreak the council[o] of the elders
of the people, both the chief priests and
teachers of the law, met together,[p] and
Jesus was led before them. 67 "If you are
the Christ,[a]" they said, "tell us."
Jesus answered, "If I tell you, you will
not believe me, 68 and if I asked you, you
would not answer.[q] 69 But from now on,
the Son of Man will be seated at the right
hand of the mighty God."[r]
70 They all asked, "Are you then the Son
of God?"[s]
He replied, "You are right in saying
I am."[t]
71 Then they said, "Why do we need any
more testimony? We have heard it from
his own lips."

23 Then the whole assembly rose and
led him off to Pilate.[u] 2 And they
began to accuse him, saying, "We have
found this man subverting our nation.[v] He
opposes payment of taxes to Caesar[w] and
claims to be Christ,[b] a king."[x]
3 So Pilate asked Jesus, "Are you the king
of the Jews?"
"Yes, it is as you say," Jesus replied.
4 Then Pilate announced to the chief
priests and the crowd, "I find no basis for
a charge against this man."[y]
5 But they insisted, "He stirs up the people all over Judea[c] by his teaching. He
started in Galilee[z] and has come all the
way here."
6 On hearing this, Pilate asked if the man
was a Galilean.[a] 7 When he learned that
Jesus was under Herod's jurisdiction, he
sent him to Herod,[b] who was also in Jerusalem at that time.
8 When Herod saw Jesus, he was greatly
pleased, because for a long time he had
been wanting to see him.[c] From what he
had heard about him, he hoped to see him
perform some miracle. 9 He plied him with
many questions, but Jesus gave him no
answer.[d] 10 The chief priests and the teachers of the law were standing there, vehemently accusing him. 11 Then Herod and
his soldiers ridiculed and mocked him.
Dressing him in an elegant robe,[e] they sent
him back to Pilate. 12 That day Herod and
Pilate became friends[f]—before this they
had been enemies.
13 Pilate called together the chief priests,
the rulers and the people, 14 and said to
them, "You brought me this man as one
who was inciting the people to rebellion.
I have examined him in your presence
and have found no basis for your charges against him.[g] 15 Neither has Herod, for
he sent him back to us; as you can see,
he has done nothing to deserve death.
16 Therefore, I will punish him[h] and then
release him.[d]"

22:65 [n] S Mt 16:21 **22:66** [o] S Mt 5:22 [p] Mt 27:1; Mk 15:1 **22:68** [q] Lk 20:3-8 **22:69** [r] S Mk 16:19 **22:70** [s] S Mt 4:3 [t] Mt 27:11; Lk 23:3 **23:1** [u] S Mt 27:2 **23:2** [v] ver 14 [w] Lk 20:22 [x] Jn 19:12 **23:4** [y] ver 14,22, 41; Mt 27:23; Jn 18:38; 1Ti 6:13; S 2Co 5:21 **23:5** [z] Mk 1:14 **23:6** [a] Lk 22:59 **23:7** [b] S Mt 14:1 **23:8** [c] Lk 9:9 **23:9** [d] S Mk 14:61 **23:11** [e] Mk 15:17-19; Jn 19:2,3 **23:12** [f] Ac 4:27 **23:14** [g] S ver 4 **23:16** [h] ver 22; Mt 27:26; Jn 19:1; Ac 16:37; 2Co 11:23,24

[a] 67 Or *Messiah*   [b] 2 Or *Messiah*; also in verses 35 and 39   [c] 5 Or *over the land of the Jews*   [d] 16 Some manuscripts *him.*" 17*Now he was obliged to release one man to them at the Feast.*

22:64 *blindfolded him.* See note on Mk 14:65.
22:66 *At daybreak.* Only after daylight could a legal trial take place for the whole council (Sanhedrin) to pass the death sentence (see note on Mk 14:53 — 15:15).
22:67 *If you are the Christ.* This demand is related to a question asked later: "Are you then the Son of God?" (v. 70).
22:69 *Son of Man.* See note on Mk 8:31.
22:71 *We have heard it.* The reaction to Jesus' reply makes clear that his answer was a strong affirmative. Mark has simply, "I am" (Mk 14:62). It was blasphemy to claim to be the Messiah and the Son of God — unless, of course, the claim was true (see note on Mk 14:64).
23:1 *whole assembly.* The body of the Sanhedrin (see Mt 26:59; 27:1 and note; Mk 14:55 and note) who had met at the earliest hint of dawn (see 22:66 and note). *led him off to Pilate.* See note on Lk 3:1. *Pilate.* See note on Mk 15:1. The Roman governor had his main headquarters in Caesarea, but he was in Jerusalem during Passover to prevent trouble from the large number of Jews assembled for the occasion.
23:2 *subverting our nation.* Large crowds followed Jesus, but he was not misleading them or turning them against Rome. *opposes payment of taxes.* Another untrue charge (see 20:25 and note on Mt 22:21). *claims to be Christ, a king.* Jesus claimed to be the Messiah, but not a political or military king, the kind Rome would be anxious to eliminate.
23:3 *Yes . . . say.* For an expanded account of this exchange see Jn 18:33 – 38 and notes.
23:5 *Judea.* See NIV text note; may here refer to the whole of the land of the Jews (including Galilee) or to the southern section only, where the region of Judea proper was governed by Pilate (see note on 4:44).
23:7 *Herod's jurisdiction.* See note on 3:1. Although Pilate and Herod were rivals, Pilate did not want to handle this case; so he sent Jesus to Herod (cf. v. 12). *in Jerusalem.* Herod's main headquarters was in Tiberias on the Sea of Galilee; but, like Pilate, he had come to Jerusalem because of the crowds at Passover.
23:8 *wanting to see him.* Herod was worried about Jesus' identity (see 9:9 and note) and had desired to kill him (see 13:31 and note), though the two had never met. There is no record that Jesus ever preached in Tiberias, where Herod's residence was located.
23:11 *elegant robe.* See note on Mk 15:17.
23:16 *I will punish him.* Although Pilate found Jesus not guilty as charged, he was willing to have him illegally beaten in order to satisfy the chief priests and the people and to warn against any possible trouble in the future. Scourging, though not intended to kill, was sometimes fatal (see note on Mk 15:15).
23:17 See NIV text note on v. 16. Apparently v. 17 was added here in some manuscripts from Mt 27:15 or Mk 15:6.

18With one voice they cried out, "Away with this man! Release Barabbas to us!"[i] 19(Barabbas had been thrown into prison for an insurrection in the city, and for murder.)

20Wanting to release Jesus, Pilate appealed to them again. 21But they kept shouting, "Crucify him! Crucify him!"

22For the third time he spoke to them: "Why? What crime has this man committed? I have found in him no grounds for the death penalty. Therefore I will have him punished and then release him."[j]

23But with loud shouts they insistently demanded that he be crucified, and their shouts prevailed. 24So Pilate decided to grant their demand. 25He released the man who had been thrown into prison for insurrection and murder, the one they asked for, and surrendered Jesus to their will.

The Crucifixion

23:33-43pp — Mt 27:33-44; Mk 15:22-32; Jn 19:17-24

26As they led him away, they seized Simon from Cyrene,[k] who was on his way in from the country, and put the cross on him and made him carry it behind Jesus.[l] 27A large number of people followed him, including women who mourned and wailed[m] for him. 28Jesus turned and said to them, "Daughters of Jerusalem, do not weep for me; weep for yourselves and for your children.[n] 29For the time will come when you will say, 'Blessed are the barren women, the wombs that never bore and the breasts that never nursed!'[o] 30Then

"'they will say to the mountains, "Fall on us!"
and to the hills, "Cover us!"'[a][p]

31For if men do these things when the tree is green, what will happen when it is dry?"[q]

32Two other men, both criminals, were also led out with him to be executed.[r] 33When they came to the place called the Skull, there they crucified him, along with the criminals—one on his right, the other on his left. 34Jesus said, "Father,[s] forgive them, for they do not know what they are doing."[b][t] And they divided up his clothes by casting lots.[u]

35The people stood watching, and the rulers even sneered at him.[v] They said, "He saved others; let him save himself if he is the Christ of God, the Chosen One."[w]

36The soldiers also came up and mocked him.[x] They offered him wine vinegar[y] 37and said, "If you are the king of the Jews,[z] save yourself."

38There was a written notice above him, which read: THIS IS THE KING OF THE JEWS.[a]

39One of the criminals who hung there hurled insults at him: "Aren't you the Christ? Save yourself and us!"[b]

40But the other criminal rebuked him. "Don't you fear God," he said, "since you are under the same sentence? 41We are punished justly, for we are getting what our deeds deserve. But this man has done nothing wrong."[c]

42Then he said, "Jesus, remember me when you come into your kingdom.[c]"[d]

23:18 [i]Ac 3:13,14
23:22 [j]ver 16
23:26 [k]S Mt 27:32 [l]Mk 15:21; Jn 19:17
23:27 [m]Lk 8:52
23:28 [n]Lk 19:41-44; 21:23,24
23:29 [o]Mt 24:19
23:30 [p]Isa 2:19; Hos 10:8; Rev 6:16
23:31 [q]Eze 20:47
23:32 [r]Isa 53:12; Mt 27:38; Mk 15:27; Jn 19:18
23:34 [s]S Mt 11:25 [t]S Mt 5:44 [u]Ps 22:18
23:35 [v]Ps 22:17 [w]Isa 42:1
23:36 [x]Ps 22:7 [y]Ps 69:21; Mt 27:48
23:37 [z]Lk 4:3,9
23:38 [a]S Mt 2:2
23:39 [b]ver 35,37
23:41 [c]S ver 4
23:42 [d]S Mt 16:27

[a] 30 Hosea 10:8 [b] 34 Some early manuscripts do not have this sentence. [c] 42 Some manuscripts *come with your kingly power*

23:18 *Barabbas.* Means "son of Abba" (see Mt 27:16 and note). Pilate offered a choice between Jesus and an obviously evil, dangerous criminal.
23:19 *insurrection … murder.* This particular uprising is otherwise unknown but, coupled with murder, it shows the gravity of his deeds (see Jn 18:40 and note).
23:22 *third time.* See vv. 4,14.
23:25 *surrendered Jesus.* Pilate had already handed Jesus over to the soldiers for scourging before he was convicted (Jn 19:1–5). He now handed him over for crucifixion.
23:26 *Simon.* His sons, Rufus and Alexander (see Mk 15:21 and note), must have been known in Christian circles at a later time, and perhaps were associated with the church at Rome (Ro 16:13). *Cyrene.* A leading city of Libya, west of Egypt (see note on Ac 6:9). *put the cross on him.* See note on Mk 15:21.
23:27–28 Found only in this Gospel. Luke emphasizes the role of women in the gospel story (see Introduction: Characteristics).
23:28 *weep for yourselves and for your children.* Because of the terrible suffering to befall Jerusalem about 40 years later when the Romans would besiege the city and utterly destroy the temple.
23:29 *Blessed are the barren.* It would be better not to have children than to have them experience such suffering. Cf. Jer 16:1–4; 1Co 7:25–35.
23:30 *Fall on us!* People would seek escape through destruction in death rather than endure continuing suffering and judgment (cf. Hos 10:8; Rev 6:16 and notes).
23:31 *tree is green … dry.* If they treat the Messiah this way when the "tree" is well-watered and green, what will their plight be when he is withdrawn from them and they suffer for their rejection in the dry period?
23:33 *the Skull.* Latin *Calvaria,* hence the name "Calvary" (see note on Mk 15:22). *crucified.* See note on Mk 15:24.
23:34 *forgive them.* Cf. Ac 7:60 (Stephen). *they do not know what they are doing.* Cf. Ac 3:17 and note. *divided up his clothes.* Any possessions an executed person had with him were taken by the executioners. Unwittingly the soldiers (cf. Jn 19:23–24) were fulfilling the words of Ps 22:18 (but see introduction to Ps 22 and notes on Ps 22:17,20–21).
23:35 *the Chosen One.* See note on 9:35.
23:36 *wine vinegar.* A sour wine, the drink of laborers and common soldiers. Jesus refused a sedative drink (see Mt 27:34; Mk 15:23 and notes) but later was given the vinegar drink when he cried out in thirst (see Jn 19:28–30 and notes). Luke shows that it was offered in mockery.
23:38 *written notice.* Indicated the crime for which a person was dying. This was Pilate's way of mocking the Jewish leaders as well as announcing what Jesus had been accused of. *KING OF THE JEWS.* See note on Mk 15:26.
23:39 *One of the criminals.* See note on Mk 15:32.

43 Jesus answered him, "I tell you the truth, today you will be with me in paradise."[e]

Jesus' Death

23:44-49pp — Mt 27:45-56; Mk 15:33-41; Jn 19:29-30

44 It was now about the sixth hour, and darkness came over the whole land until the ninth hour,[f] 45 for the sun stopped shining. And the curtain of the temple[g] was torn in two.[h] 46 Jesus called out with a loud voice,[i] "Father, into your hands I commit my spirit."[j] When he had said this, he breathed his last.[k]

47 The centurion, seeing what had happened, praised God[l] and said, "Surely this was a righteous man." 48 When all the people who had gathered to witness this sight saw what took place, they beat their breasts[m] and went away. 49 But all those who knew him, including the women who had followed him from Galilee,[n] stood at a distance,[o] watching these things.

Jesus' Burial

23:50-56pp — Mt 27:57-61; Mk 15:42-47; Jn 19:38-42

50 Now there was a man named Joseph, a member of the Council, a good and upright man, 51 who had not consented to their decision and action. He came from the Judean town of Arimathea and he was waiting for the kingdom of God.[p] 52 Going to Pilate, he asked for Jesus' body. 53 Then he took it down, wrapped it in linen cloth and placed it in a tomb cut in the rock, one in which no one had yet been laid. 54 It was Preparation Day,[q] and the Sabbath was about to begin.

55 The women who had come with Jesus from Galilee[r] followed Joseph and saw the tomb and how his body was laid in it. 56 Then they went home and prepared spices and perfumes.[s] But they rested on the Sabbath in obedience to the commandment.[t]

The Resurrection

24:1-10pp — Mt 28:1-8; Mk 16:1-8; Jn 20:1-8

24 On the first day of the week, very early in the morning, the women took the spices they had prepared[u] and went to the tomb. 2 They found the stone rolled away from the tomb, 3 but when they entered, they did not find the body of the Lord Jesus.[v] 4 While they were wondering about this, suddenly two men in clothes

23:43 [e] 2Co 12:3,4; Rev 2:7
23:44 [f] Am 8:9
23:45 [g] Ex 26:31-33; Heb 9:3,8 [h] Heb 10:19,20
23:46 [i] Mt 27:50 [j] Ps 31:5; 1Pe 2:23 [k] Jn 19:30
23:47 [l] S Mt 9:8
23:48 [m] Lk 18:13
23:49 [n] Lk 8:2 [o] Ps 38:11
23:51 [p] Lk 2:25,38
23:54 [q] Mt 27:62
23:55 [r] ver 49
23:56 [s] Mk 16:1; Lk 24:1 [t] Ex 12:16; 20:10
24:1 [u] Lk 23:56
24:3 [v] ver 23,24

23:43 *paradise.* In the Septuagint (the pre-Christian Greek translation of the OT) the word designated a garden (Ge 2:8–10; cf. note on 2:8) or forest (see Ne 2:8 and note), but in the NT (used only here and in 2Co 12:4; Rev 2:7 [see note there]) it refers to the place of bliss and rest between death and resurrection (cf. Lk 16:22; 2Co 12:2).
23:44 *about the sixth hour … the ninth hour.* From noon to three in the afternoon, by the Jewish method of designating time. Jesus had been put on the cross at the third hour (9:00 A.M., Mk 15:25). The "sixth hour" of John (Jn 19:14) may be Roman time (6:00 A.M.), when Pilate gave his decision (but see note on Jn 19:14).
23:45 *curtain of the temple.* The curtain between the Holy Place and the Most Holy Place. Its tearing symbolized Christ's opening the way directly to God (see Heb 9:3,8; 10:19–22 and notes on 10:19–20).
23:47 *praised God.* See 1:64 and note; either for having seen God publicly vindicate Jesus by mighty signs from heaven, or out of fear (see Mt 27:54) to appease the heavenly Judge and thus ward off a divine penalty for having carried out an unjust judgment. *this was a righteous man.* Or "this man was the Righteous One." Matthew and Mark report the centurion's words as "this man was the Son (or son) of God." "The Righteous One" and "the Son of God" would have been essentially equivalent terms. Similarly, "the son of God" and "a righteous man" would have been virtual equivalents. Which one the centurion intended is difficult to determine (see note on Mt 27:54). It seems clear, however, that the Gospel writers saw in his declaration a vindication of Jesus, and since the centurion was the Roman official in charge of the crucifixion, his testimony was viewed as significant (see also the declarations of Pilate: vv. 4,14–15,22; Mt 27:23–24).
23:48 *beat their breasts.* A sign of anguish, grief or contrition (cf. 18:13).
23:49 *women … from Galilee.* See Mk 15:40; Jn 19:25 and notes; cf. Lk 24:10 and note.
23:50 *Joseph, a member of the Council.* Either Joseph was not present at the meeting of the Sanhedrin (22:66), or he did not support the vote to have Jesus killed (see v. 51). Mk 14:64 suggests he was not present, for the decision was supported by "all."
23:51 *Arimathea.* See note on Mt 27:57. *waiting for the kingdom of God.* See 2:25 and note.
23:52 The remains of an executed criminal often were left unburied or at best put in a dishonored place in a pauper's field. A near relative, such as a mother, might ask for the body, but it was a courageous gesture for Joseph, a member of the Sanhedrin, to ask for Jesus' body.
23:53 *in which no one had yet been laid.* Rock-hewn tombs of that day (of which many are known) were usually made to accommodate several bodies. This one, though finished, had not yet been used. See notes on 19:30; Mk 15:46.
23:54 *Preparation Day.* Friday, the day before the Sabbath, when preparation was made for keeping the Sabbath. It could be used for Passover preparation, but since in this instance it is followed by the Sabbath, it indicates Friday (see note on Mt 27:62).
23:55 *women.* See v. 49 and note; cf. 8:2–3 and notes. They saw where Jesus was buried and would not mistake the location when they returned.
23:56 *spices and perfumes.* Yards of cloth and large quantities of spices were used in preparing a body for burial. Seventy-five pounds of myrrh and aloes were already used on that first evening (see Jn 19:39 and note). More was purchased for the return of the women after the Sabbath (see note on Mk 16:1).
24:1 *first day of the week.* By Jewish time, Sunday began at sundown on Saturday. The women bought spices after sunset on Saturday (see Mk 16:1 and note) and were ready to set out early the next day. When they started out, it was dark (see Jn 20:1 and note), and by the time they arrived at the tomb, it was still early dawn (see Mt 28:1; Mk 16:2).
24:2 *the stone rolled away.* A tomb's entrance was ordinarily closed to keep vandals and animals from disturbing the bodies. This stone, however, had been sealed by Roman authority for a different reason (see Mt 27:62–66).
24:4 *two men.* They looked like men, but their clothes were remarkable (see 9:29; Ac 1:10 and note; 10:30 and note).

that gleamed like lightning[w] stood beside
them. 5In their fright the women bowed
down with their faces to the ground, but
the men said to them, "Why do you look
for the living among the dead? 6He is not
here; he has risen! Remember how he told
you, while he was still with you in Galilee:[x] 7'The Son of Man[y] must be delivered
into the hands of sinful men, be crucified
and on the third day be raised again.' "[z]
8Then they remembered his words.[a]
9When they came back from the tomb,
they told all these things to the Eleven and
to all the others. 10It was Mary Magdalene,
Joanna, Mary the mother of James, and
the others with them[b] who told this to
the apostles.[c] 11But they did not believe[d]
the women, because their words seemed

24:4 [w]S Jn 20:12 **24:6** [x]Mt 17:22, 23; Lk 9:22; 24:44 **24:7** [y]S Mt 8:20 [z]S Mt 16:21 **24:8** [a]Jn 2:22 **24:10** [b]Lk 8:1-3 [c]S Mk 6:30 **24:11** [d]Mk 16:11

Other reports referring to them call them angels (v. 23; see also Jn 20:12 and note). Matthew speaks of one angel (Mt 28:2) and Mark of a young man in white (Mk 16:5). Words and posture (seated, Jn 20:12; standing, Lk 24:4) often change in the course of events, so these variations are not necessarily contradictory. They are merely evidence of independent accounts.

24:6 *while ... in Galilee.* Jesus had predicted his death and resurrection on a number of occasions (see 9:22 and note), but the disciples failed to comprehend or accept what he was saying.

24:7 See 9:22; 17:25 and notes.

24:9 *to the Eleven and to all the others.* "Eleven" is sometimes used to refer to the group of apostles (Ac 1:26; 2:14) after the betrayal by Judas. Judas was dead at the time the apostles first met the risen Christ, but the group was still called the Twelve (Jn 20:24). The "others" included disciples who, for the most part, came from Galilee.

24:10 *Mary Magdalene.* See note on 8:2. She is named first in most of the lists of women (see Mt 27:56; Mk 15:40 and note; but cf. Jn 19:25) and was the first to see the risen Christ (Jn 20:13–18; see chart below). *Joanna.* See 8:3. She is named by only Luke at this point (Mark is the only one who adds Salome in this context, Mk 16:1; see note on Mk 15:40). *Mary the mother of James.* See Mk 16:1. She is the "other Mary" of Mt 28:1 (see note there). The absence of the mother of Jesus is noteworthy. She was probably with John (cf. Jn 19:27 and note).

Resurrection Appearances

APPEARANCE	PLACE	TIME	MATTHEW	MARK	LUKE	JOHN	ACTS	1 CO
The empty tomb	Jerusalem	Resurrection Sunday	28:1-10	16:1-8	24:1-12	20:1-9		
To Mary Magdalene in the garden	Jerusalem	Resurrection Sunday		16:9-11		20:11-18 in the garden		
To other women	Jerusalem	Resurrection Sunday	28:9-10					
To two people going to Emmaus	Road to Emmaus	Resurrection Sunday		16:12-13	24:13-32			
To Peter	Jerusalem	Resurrection Sunday			24:34			15:5
To the ten disciples in the upper room	Jerusalem	Resurrection Sunday			24:36-43	20:19-25		
To the 11 disciples in the upper room	Jerusalem	Following Sunday		16:14		20:26-31		15:5
To seven disciples fishing	Sea of Galilee	Some time later				21:1-23		
To the 11 disciples on a mountain	Galilee	Some time later	28:16-20	16:15-18				
To more than 500	Unknown	Some time later						15:6
To James	Unknown	Some time later						15:7
To his disciples at his ascension	Mount of Olives	40 days after Jesus' resurrection			24:44-49		1:3-8	
To Paul	Damascus	Several years later					9:1-19 22:3-16 26:9-18	9:1

to them like nonsense. 12Peter, however,
got up and ran to the tomb. Bending over,
he saw the strips of linen lying by themselves,[e] and he went away,[f] wondering to
himself what had happened.

On the Road to Emmaus

13Now that same day two of them were
going to a village called Emmaus, about
seven miles[a] from Jerusalem.[g] 14They were
talking with each other about everything
that had happened. 15As they talked and
discussed these things with each other,
Jesus himself came up and walked along
with them;[h] 16but they were kept from recognizing him.[i]

17He asked them, "What are you discussing together as you walk along?"

They stood still, their faces downcast.
18One of them, named Cleopas,[j] asked
him, "Are you only a visitor to Jerusalem
and do not know the things that have happened there in these days?"

19"What things?" he asked.

"About Jesus of Nazareth,"[k] they replied.
"He was a prophet,[l] powerful in word and
deed before God and all the people. 20The
chief priests and our rulers[m] handed him
over to be sentenced to death, and they crucified him; 21but we had hoped that he was
the one who was going to redeem Israel.[n]
And what is more, it is the third day[o] since
all this took place. 22In addition, some of
our women amazed us.[p] They went to the
tomb early this morning 23but didn't find his
body. They came and told us that they had
seen a vision of angels, who said he was
alive. 24Then some of our companions went
to the tomb and found it just as the women
had said, but him they did not see."[q]

25He said to them, "How foolish you
are, and how slow of heart to believe all
that the prophets have spoken! 26Did not
the Christ[b] have to suffer these things and
then enter his glory?"[r] 27And beginning
with Moses[s] and all the Prophets,[t] he explained to them what was said in all the
Scriptures concerning himself.[u]

28As they approached the village to
which they were going, Jesus acted as if
he were going farther. 29But they urged
him strongly, "Stay with us, for it is nearly evening; the day is almost over." So he
went in to stay with them.

30When he was at the table with them,
he took bread, gave thanks, broke it[v] and
began to give it to them. 31Then their eyes
were opened and they recognized him,[w]
and he disappeared from their sight.
32They asked each other, "Were not our
hearts burning within us[x] while he talked
with us on the road and opened the Scriptures[y] to us?"

33They got up and returned at once to
Jerusalem. There they found the Eleven
and those with them, assembled together
34and saying, "It is true! The Lord[z] has ris-
en and has appeared to Simon."[a] 35Then
the two told what had happened on the
way, and how Jesus was recognized by
them when he broke the bread.[b]

Jesus Appears to the Disciples

36While they were still talking about
this, Jesus himself stood among them and
said to them, "Peace be with you."[c]

37They were startled and frightened,
thinking they saw a ghost.[d] 38He said to
them, "Why are you troubled, and why do
doubts rise in your minds? 39Look at my
hands and my feet. It is I myself! Touch
me and see;[e] a ghost does not have flesh
and bones, as you see I have."

40When he had said this, he showed
them his hands and feet. 41And while they
still did not believe it because of joy and
amazement, he asked them, "Do you have
anything here to eat?" 42They gave him a
piece of broiled fish, 43and he took it and
ate it in their presence.[f]

24:12 [e] Jn 20:3-7 [f] Jn 20:10 **24:13** [g] Mk 16:12 **24:15** [h] ver 36 **24:16** [i] Jn 20:14; 21:4 **24:18** [j] Jn 19:25 **24:19** [k] S Mk 1:24 [l] S Mt 21:11 **24:20** [m] Lk 23:13 **24:21** [n] Lk 1:68; 2:38; 21:28 [o] S Mt 16:21 **24:22** [p] ver 1-10 **24:24** [q] ver 12 **24:26** [r] Heb 2:10; 1Pe 1:11 **24:27** [s] Ge 3:15; Nu 21:9; Dt 18:15 [t] Isa 7:14; 9:6; 40:10,11; 53; Eze 34:23; Da 9:24; Mic 7:20; Mal 3:1 [u] Jn 1:45 **24:30** [v] S Mt 14:19 **24:31** [w] ver 16 **24:32** [x] Ps 39:3 [y] ver 27,45 **24:34** [z] S Lk 7:13 [a] 1Co 15:5 **24:35** [b] ver 30,31 **24:36** [c] Jn 20:19,21,26; S 14:27 **24:37** [d] Mk 6:49 **24:39** [e] Jn 20:27; 1Jn 1:1 **24:43** [f] Ac 10:41

[a] 13 Greek *sixty stadia* (about 11 kilometers) [b] 26 Or *Messiah*; also in verse 46

24:12 *Peter ... ran.* John's Gospel (20:3–9) includes another disciple, John himself.
24:13 *two of them.* One was named Cleopas (v. 18).
24:15 *Jesus ... came up and walked ... with them.* See chart, p. 1615.
24:16 *kept from recognizing him.* By special divine intervention (see 9:45 and note).
24:19 *prophet.* They had respect for Jesus as a man of God, but after his death they apparently were reluctant to call him the Messiah.
24:21 *to redeem Israel.* What they probably meant by this was: "to set the Jewish nation free from bondage to Rome and so usher in the kingdom of God" (see 1:68; 2:38; 21:28 and note, 31; cf. Tit 2:14; 1Pe 1:18 and notes). *the third day.* A reference either to the Jewish belief that after the third day the soul left the body or to Jesus' remark that he would be resurrected on the third day (9:22).
24:23 *vision of angels.* See note on v. 4.
24:24 *some of our companions.* See v. 12 and note.
24:26 *suffer ... enter his glory.* See 1Pe 1:11 and note.
24:27 *Moses and all the Prophets.* A way of designating the whole of the OT Scriptures (see v. 44 and note; 16:16,29).
24:28 *as if he were going farther.* Jesus awaited their invitation to remain with them.
24:31 *their eyes were opened.* Cf. v. 16; more than a matter of simple recognition.
24:33 *the Eleven and those with them.* See note on v. 9.
24:34 *appeared to Simon.* See chart, p. 1615.
24:36 *Jesus himself stood among them.* Behind locked doors (Jn 20:19; see chart, p. 1615), indicating that his body was of a different order. It was his glorified resurrection body. *Peace be with you.* The traditional greeting, now given new significance by the resurrection.
24:39 *my hands and my feet.* Indicating that Jesus' feet as well as his hands were nailed to the cross (see note on Mk 15:24; cf. Jn 20:20 and note, 27).
24:42 *a piece of broiled fish.* Demonstrating that he had a physical body that could consume food.

44He said to them, "This is what I told
you while I was still with you:[g] Everything
must be fulfilled[h] that is written about me
in the Law of Moses,[i] the Prophets[j] and
the Psalms."[k]
45Then he opened their minds so they
could understand the Scriptures. 46He told
them, "This is what is written: The Christ
will suffer[l] and rise from the dead on the
third day,[m] 47and repentance and forgiveness of sins will be preached in his name[n]
to all nations,[o] beginning at Jerusalem.[p]
48You are witnesses[q] of these things. 49I
am going to send you what my Father has
promised;[r] but stay in the city until you
have been clothed with power from on
high."

24:44 [g]Lk 9:45; 18:34 [h]S Mt 1:22; 16:21; Lk 9:22,44; 18:31-33; 22:37 [i]S ver 27 [j]S ver 27 [k]Ps 2; 16; 22; 69; 72; 110; 118 **24:46** [l]S Mt 16:21 [m]S Mt 16:21 **24:47** [n]Ac 5:31; 10:43; 13:38 [o]Mt 28:19; Mk 13:10 [p]Isa 2:3 **24:48** [q]S Jn 15:27; Ac 1:8; 2:32; 4:20; 5:32; 13:31; 1Pe 5:1

The Ascension

50When he had led them out to the vicinity of Bethany,[s] he lifted up his hands
and blessed them. 51While he was blessing them, he left them and was taken up
into heaven.[t] 52Then they worshiped him
and returned to Jerusalem with great joy.
53And they stayed continually at the temple,[u] praising God.

24:49 [r]S Jn 14:16; Ac 1:4 **24:50** [s]S Mt 21:17 **24:51** [t]2Ki 2:11 **24:53** [u]S Ac 2:46

24:44 *Law of Moses, the Prophets and the Psalms.* The three parts of the Hebrew OT (Psalms was the most prominent book of the third section, called the Writings), indicating that Christ (the Messiah) was foretold in the whole OT.
24:45 *opened their minds.* By explaining the OT Scriptures (cf. v. 27).

24:46 *suffer ... rise from the dead ... third day.* See 1Co 15:3–4. The OT depicts the Messiah as one who would suffer (see introduction to Ps 22; see also Isa 53) and rise from the dead on the third day (compare Ps 16:8–11 with Ac 2:23–33 and notes; see Isa 53:10–11 and notes; compare Jnh 1:17 with Mt 12:40 and note).

24:47 *repentance and forgiveness of sins.* See Ac 5:31; 10:43; 13:38; 26:18. The prediction of Christ's death and resurrection (v. 46) is joined with the necessary human response (repentance) and the resulting benefit (forgiveness; cf. Isa 49:6; Ac 13:47; 26:22–23). *to all nations.* Prophesied also in Mk 13:10; cf. Mt 28:19–20 and note; Ac 10:34–35; 15:16–17; Ro 1:13–14; 4:16–17; 15:7–12. *beginning at Jerusalem.* See Ac 1:8 and note.

24:49 *what my Father has promised.* See Joel 2:28–32 and notes. The reference is to the coming power of the Spirit, fulfilled in Ac 2:4 (see also Ac 2:17–22 and notes).
24:50 *Bethany.* A village on the Mount of Olives (see notes on 19:29; Mt 21:17; see also map, p. 1553).
24:51 *taken up into heaven.* Different from his previous disappearances (4:30; 24:3; Jn 8:59). They saw him ascend into a cloud (see Ac 1:9; see also Ac 1:11–12 and notes).
24:53 *at the temple.* During the period of time immediately following Christ's ascension the believers met continually at the temple (Ac 2:46; 3:1; 5:21,42), where many rooms were available for meetings (see note on 2:37). *praising God.* The Gospel of Luke begins (1:64; see note there) and ends (here) with praise to God in his temple. This Gospel also begins with the aged Zechariah's doubt (1:18) and unbelief (1:20); it ends with the disciples' worship of the risen and ascended Lord "with great joy" (v. 52). Luke has fittingly prepared the way for what follows in his second volume (see Ac 1:1 and note).

John

I N T R O D U C T I O N

Author

The author is the apostle John, "the disciple whom Jesus loved" (13:23 [see note there]; 19:26; 20:2; 21:7,20; see also 21:24). He was prominent in the early church but is not mentioned by name in this Gospel — which would be natural if he wrote it, but hard to explain otherwise. The author knew Jewish life well, as seen from references to popular Messianic speculations (see, e.g., 1:21 and note; 7:40 – 42), to the hostility between Jews and Samaritans (see 4:9 and note), and to Jewish customs, such as the duty of circumcision on the eighth day taking precedence over the prohibition of working on the Sabbath (see note on 7:22). He knew the geography of the Holy Land, locating Bethany about 15 stadia (about two miles) from Jerusalem (11:18) and mentioning Cana, a village not referred to in any earlier writing known to us (2:1 [see note there]; 21:2). The Gospel of John has many touches that appear to reflect the recollections of an eyewitness — such as the house at Bethany being filled with the fragrance of the broken perfume jar (see 12:3 and note). Early writers such as Irenaeus and Tertullian say that John wrote this Gospel, and all other evidence agrees (see Introduction to 1 John: Author).

> **A Quick Look**
>
> **Author:**
> The apostle John
>
> **Audience:**
> Primarily non-Jewish believers and seeking unbelievers
>
> **Date:**
> Between A.D. 50 and 85
>
> **Theme:**
> John presents Jesus as the Word, the Messiah and the incarnate Son of God, who has come to reveal the Father and to bring eternal life to all who believe in him.

Date

In general, two views of the dating of this Gospel have been advocated:

1. The traditional view places it toward the end of the first century, c. A.D. 85 or later (see Introduction to 1 John: Date).

2. More recently, some interpreters have suggested an earlier date, perhaps as early as the 50s and no later than 70.

The first view may be supported by reference to the statement of Clement of Alexandria (died between 211 and 216) that John wrote to supplement the accounts found in the other Gospels (Eusebius, *Ecclesiastical History*, 6.14.7), and thus his Gospel is later than the first three. It has also been argued that the seemingly more developed theology of the fourth Gospel indicates that it originated later.

The second view has found favor because it has been felt more recently that John wrote independently of the other Gospels (see essay and chart, p. 1457). This does not contradict the statement of Clement referred to above. Also, those who hold this view point out that developed theology does not necessarily argue for a late origin. The theology of Romans (written c. 57) is every bit as developed as that in John. Further, the statement in 5:2 that there "is" (rather than "was") a pool "near the Sheep Gate" may suggest a time before 70, when Jerusalem was destroyed. Others, however, observe that John elsewhere sometimes used the present tense when speaking of the past.

The literary style of this witness of Jesus is unique among the Gospels; here focus is on the "signs" of Jesus' identity and mission and on lengthy, theologically rich discourses.

Purpose and Emphases

John's Gospel is rather different from the other three. Whether or not he knew them (or any one of them) continues to be debated. In any event, his witness to Jesus goes its own way, highlighting matters that in the other Gospels remain implicit and underdeveloped. The literary style of this witness of Jesus is also unique among the Gospels; here focus is on the "signs" of Jesus' identity and mission and on lengthy, theologically rich discourses.

John begins with the profound announcement that Jesus is God — his divine "Word" of self-revelation — who existed with God from the beginning and through whom God created all things. Jesus the "Word" became embodied (incarnated) as a human being to be the light of life for the world. After this comes the proclamation that this Jesus is the Son of God sent from the Father to finish the Father's work in the world (see 4:34 and note). God's own glory is made visible in him ("Anyone who has seen me has seen the Father," 14:9), and what he does glorifies the Father. In him the full grace and truth of God has shown itself. Strikingly, a series of "I am" claims on Jesus' lips echoes God's naming of himself in Ex 3:14, further strengthening the link between the Father and the Son (see 6:35; 8:12; 9:5; 10:7,9,11,14; 11:25; 14:6; 15:1,5; see especially 6:35; 8:58 and notes).

Jesus' words to Nicodemus nicely summarize this Gospel's central theme: "For God so loved the world that he gave his one and only Son, that whoever believes in him shall not perish but have eternal life" (3:16). Although a variety of motivations for the composition of John's Gospel have been posited by interpreters (such as to supplement the other Gospels, to combat some form of heresy, to oppose the continuing followers of John the Baptist), the author himself states his main purpose clearly in 20:31: "that you may believe that Jesus is the Christ, the Son of God, and that by believing you may have life in his name."

For the main emphases of the book see notes on 1:4,7,9,14,19,49; 2:4,11; 3:27; 4:34; 6:35; 13:1 — 17:26; 13:31; 17:1 – 2,5; 20:31.

Outline

I. Prologue: The Word Became Flesh (1:1 – 18)
II. The Beginning of Jesus' Ministry (1:19 – 51)
  A. John the Baptist's Initial Testimony about Jesus (1:19 – 34)
  B. John's Disciples Follow Jesus (1:35 – 42)
  C. Jesus Calls Philip and Nathanael (1:43 – 51)
III. Jesus' Public Ministry: Signs and Discourses (chs. 2 – 11)
  A. Changing Water into Wine (2:1 – 11)
  B. Clearing the Temple (2:12 – 25)
  C. Jesus Teaches Nicodemus (3:1 – 21)
  D. John the Baptist's Final Testimony about Jesus (3:22 – 36)
  E. Jesus and the Samaritans (4:1 – 42)
  F. Healing of the Official's Son (4:43 – 54)

- G. Jesus' Visit to Jerusalem at an Annual Feast (ch. 5)
- H. Feeding the 5,000 and Jesus' Claim to Be the Bread of Life (ch. 6)
- I. Jesus at the Feast of Tabernacles and Disputes over Who He Is (chs. 7–8)
- J. Healing of the Man Born Blind (ch. 9)
- K. Jesus, the Good Shepherd (10:1–21)
- L. Conflict at the Feast of Dedication over Jesus' Identity (10:22–42)
- M. The Raising of Lazarus (ch. 11)

IV. The Passion Week (chs. 12–19)
- A. The Anointing of Jesus' Feet (12:1–11)
- B. Jesus' Entry into Jerusalem as King (12:12–19)
- C. Jesus Predicts His Death (12:20–36)
- D. Belief and Unbelief among the Jews (12:37–50)
- E. Jesus' Farewell Discourses and Prayer (chs. 13–17)
  1. At the Last Supper (chs. 13–14)
     - a. Jesus washes the disciples' feet (13:1–17)
     - b. Jesus predicts his betrayal (13:18–30)
     - c. Jesus predicts Peter's denial (13:31–38)
     - d. Jesus comforts his disciples (14:1–4)
     - e. Jesus is the way to the Father (14:5–14)
     - f. Jesus promises the Holy Spirit (14:15–30)
  2. On the way to Gethsemane (chs. 15–16)
     - a. The vine and the branches (15:1–17)
     - b. The world hates the disciples (15:18–25)
     - c. The work of the Holy Spirit (15:26—16:15)
     - d. The disciples' grief will turn to joy (16:16–33)
  3. Jesus' prayer (ch. 17)
     - a. For himself—that he be glorified (17:1–5)
     - b. For his disciples (17:6–19)
     - c. For all believers (17:20–26)
- F. Jesus' Betrayal and Arrest (18:1–11)
- G. Jesus' Trials before Jewish and Roman Officials (18:12–40)
- H. Jesus' Crucifixion (19:1–27)
- I. Jesus' Death and Burial (19:28–42)

V. Jesus' Resurrection (20:1–29)

VI. Statement of the Gospel's Purpose (20:30–31)

VII. Epilogue: Jesus' Recommissioning of the Disciples (ch. 21)

The Word Became Flesh

1 In the beginning was the Word,[a] and
the Word was with God,[b] and the Word
was God.[c] 2He was with God in the beginning.[d]
3Through him all things were made;
without him nothing was made that has
been made.[e] 4In him was life,[f] and that life
was the light[g] of men. 5The light shines in
the darkness,[h] but the darkness has not
understood[a] it.[i]
6There came a man who was sent from
God; his name was John.[j] 7He came as a
witness to testify[k] concerning that light, so
that through him all men might believe.[l]
8He himself was not the light; he came
only as a witness to the light. 9The true
light[m] that gives light to every man[n] was
coming into the world.[b]
10He was in the world, and though the
world was made through him,[o] the world
did not recognize him. 11He came to that
which was his own, but his own did not
receive him.[p] 12Yet to all who received
him, to those who believed[q] in his name,[r]
he gave the right to become children of
God[s]— 13children born not of natural descent,[c] nor of human decision or a husband's will, but born of God.[t]
14The Word became flesh[u] and made his
dwelling among us. We have seen his glory,[v] the glory of the One and Only,[d] who
came from the Father, full of grace[w] and
truth.[x]
15John testifies[y] concerning him. He
cries out, saying, "This was he of whom
I said, 'He who comes after me has sur-

1:1 [a]Isa 55:11; Rev 19:13 [b]Jn 17:5; 1Jn 1:2 [c]Php 2:6 **1:2** [d]Ge 1:1; Jn 8:58; 17:5,24; 1Jn 1:1; Rev 1:8 **1:3** [e]ver 10; 1Co 8:6; Col 1:16; Heb 1:2 **1:4** [f]S Jn 5:26; 6:57; 11:25; 14:6; Ac 3:15; Heb 7:16; 1Jn 1:1,2; 5:20; Rev 1:18 [g]Ps 36:9; Jn 3:19; 8:12; 9:5; 12:46 **1:5** [h]Ps 18:28 [i]Jn 3:19 **1:6** [j]S Mt 3:1 **1:7** [k]ver 15,19, 32; Jn 3:26; 5:33 [l]ver 12; S Jn 3:15 **1:9** [m]1Jn 2:8 [n]Isa 49:6 **1:10** [o]S ver 3 **1:11** [p]Isa 53:3 **1:12** [q]ver 7; S Jn 3:15 [r]S 1Jn 3:23 [s]Dt 14:1; S Ro 8:14; 8:16,21; Eph 5:1; 1Jn 3:1,2 **1:13** [t]Jn 3:6; Tit 3:5; Jas 1:18; 1Pe 1:23; 1Jn 3:9; 4:7; 5:1,4 **1:14** [u]Gal 4:4; Php 2:7,8; 1Ti 3:16; Heb 2:14; 1Jn 1:1,2; 4:2 [v]Ex 33:18; 40:34 [w]S Ro 3:24 [x]Jn 14:6 **1:15** [y]ver 7

[a] 5 Or *darkness, and the darkness has not overcome*
[b] 9 Or *This was the true light that gives light to every man who comes into the world*
[c] 13 Greek *of bloods*
[d] 14 Or *the Only Begotten*

1:1 *In the beginning.* A deliberate echo of Ge 1:1 (see note there) to link God's action in behalf of the world through Jesus Christ (cf. 3:16) with his first work, the creation of the world. *Word.* Greek *logos*, a term Greeks used not only of the spoken word but also of the unspoken word, the word still in the mind—the reason. When they applied it to the universe, they meant the rational principle that governs all things. The Jews, however, used it to refer to the "word" of God by which he created the world and governs it (see the Septuagint [the pre-Christian Greek translation of the OT] rendering of Ps 33:6; 119:89; 147:15,18) and to refer to the law of God that he gave Israel to be their life (see Dt 32:47 and note on 30:20). Of the law the rabbis said that it was "created before the world," that it "lay on God's bosom while God sat on the throne of glory," that it was divine, that it was God's "firstborn" through whom he "created the heaven and the earth," that it is "light" and "life" for the world and that it "is truth." This Jewish use of *logos* as that which comes from God to fulfill his purpose in and for the world appears to lie behind the heavily freighted affirmation with which John begins his Gospel. *with God.* The Word was distinct from the Father. *was God.* Jesus was God in the fullest sense (see note on Ro 9:5). The prologue (vv. 1–18) begins and ends with a ringing affirmation of his deity (see note on v. 18).

1:4 *life.* One of the great concepts of this Gospel. The Greek word for "life" is found 36 times in John, while no other NT book uses it more than 17 times. Life is Christ's gift (10:28), and he, in fact, is "the life" (14:6). *light of men.* This Gospel also links light with Christ, from whom comes all spiritual illumination. He is the "light of the world," who holds out wonderful hope for humanity (cf. 8:12 and note) and for the creation (see 3:16 and note). For an OT link between life and light see Ps 36:9 and note.

1:5 *darkness.* The stark contrast between light and darkness is a striking theme in this Gospel (see, e.g., 12:35).

1:6 *John.* In this Gospel the name John always refers to John the Baptist.

1:7 *as a witness to testify.* John the Baptist's singular ministry was to testify to Jesus (10:41). "Witness" is another important concept in this Gospel. The Greek noun for "witness" or "testimony" is used 14 times (in Matthew not at all, in Mark three times, in Luke once) and the verb ("testify") 33 times (found once each in Matthew and Luke, not at all in Mark)—in both cases more often than anywhere else in the NT. John (the author) thereby emphasizes that the facts about Jesus are amply attested. *that through him all men might believe.* People were not to believe "in" John the Baptist but "through" him. Similarly, the writer's purpose was to draw them to belief in Christ (20:31); he uses the Greek verb for "believe" 98 times.

1:8 *He himself was not the light.* The greatness of John the Baptist caused some of his followers to have exaggerated ideas about him (see v. 21), but while Jesus affirms John's greatness (see Mt 11:11 and note), he also makes clear his limitations: John is "a lamp" (5:35) but not "the light."

1:9 John is referring to the incarnation of Christ. *world.* Another common word in John's writings, the Greek noun for "world" is found 78 times in this Gospel and 24 times in his letters (only 47 times in all of Paul's writings). It can mean the universe, the earth, the people on earth, most people, people opposed to God, or the human system opposed to God's purposes. John emphasizes the word by repetition, and moves without explanation from one meaning to another (see, e.g., 17:5,14–15 and notes).

1:12 *believed.* See v. 7; 20:31 and notes. *he gave the right.* Membership in God's family is by grace alone—the gift of God (see Eph 2:8–9 and notes). It is never a human achievement, as v. 13 emphasizes; yet the imparting of the gift is dependent on human reception of it, as the words "received" and "believed" make clear.

1:13 *born of God.* The "children of God" (v. 12) have been given a new openness to and relationship with God that was not theirs as a result of their natural birth (see 3:3,5; 2Co 5:17; Gal 6:15; Tit 3:5 and notes).

1:14 *flesh.* A strong, almost crude, word that stresses the reality of Christ's humanity. *made his dwelling among us. We have seen his glory.* The Greek for "made his dwelling" is connected with the Hebrew word for "tent/tabernacle"; the verse would have reminded John's Jewish readers of the Tent of Meeting, which was filled with the glory of God (Ex 40:34–35). Christ revealed his glory to his disciples by the miracles he performed (see 2:11 and note) and by his death and resurrection. *grace and truth.* The corresponding Hebrew terms are often translated "(unfailing) love and faithfulness" (see notes on Ps 26:3; Pr 16:6). *grace.* A significant Christian concept (see notes on Jnh 4:2; Gal 1:3; Eph 1:2), though John never uses the word after the prologue (vv. 1–18). *truth.* John uses the Greek word for "truth" 25 times and links it closely with Jesus, who is the truth (see 14:6 and note).

1:15 *he was before me.* In ancient times the older person was given respect and regarded as greater than the

passed me because he was before me.' "[z]
16From the fullness[a] of his grace[b] we have
all received one blessing after another. 17For the law was given through Moses;[c] grace and truth came through Jesus
Christ.[d] 18No one has ever seen God,[e] but
God the One and Only,[a,b f] who is at the
Father's side, has made him known.

John the Baptist Denies Being the Christ

19Now this was John's[g] testimony when
the Jews[h] of Jerusalem sent priests and Levites to ask him who he was. 20He did not
fail to confess, but confessed freely, "I am
not the Christ.[c]"[i]

21They asked him, "Then who are you?
Are you Elijah?"[j]

He said, "I am not."

"Are you the Prophet?"[k]

He answered, "No."

22Finally they said, "Who are you? Give
us an answer to take back to those who
sent us. What do you say about yourself?"

23John replied in the words of Isaiah the
prophet, "I am the voice of one calling in
the desert,[l] 'Make straight the way for the
Lord.' "[d m]

24Now some Pharisees who had been
sent 25questioned him, "Why then do you
baptize if you are not the Christ, nor Elijah, nor the Prophet?"

26"I baptize with[e] water,"[n] John replied,
"but among you stands one you do not
know. 27He is the one who comes after
me,[o] the thongs of whose sandals I am not
worthy to untie."[p]

28This all happened at Bethany on the
other side of the Jordan,[q] where John was
baptizing.

Jesus the Lamb of God

29The next day John saw Jesus coming
toward him and said, "Look, the Lamb
of God,[r] who takes away the sin of the
world![s] 30This is the one I meant when I
said, 'A man who comes after me has sur-

1:15 [z]ver 30; Mt 3:11
1:16 [a]Eph 1:23; Col 1:19; 2:9 [b]S Ro 3:24
1:17 [c]Dt 32:46; Jn 7:19 [d]ver 14
1:18 [e]Ex 33:20; Jn 6:46; Col 1:15; 1Ti 6:16; 1Jn 4:12 [f]Jn 3:16,18; 1Jn 4:9
1:19 [g]S Mt 3:1 [h]Jn 2:18; 5:10,16; 6:41,52; 7:1; 10:24
1:20 [i]Jn 3:28; Lk 3:15,16
1:21 [j]S Mt 11:14 [k]Dt 18:15
1:23 [l]Mt 3:1 [m]Isa 40:3
1:26 [n]S Mk 1:4
1:27 [o]ver 15,30 [p]Mk 1:7
1:28 [q]Jn 3:26; 10:40
1:29 [r]ver 36; Ge 22:8; Isa 53:7; 1Pe 1:19; Rev 5:6; 13:8 [s]S Jn 3:17

[a] 18 Or *the Only Begotten* [b] 18 Some manuscripts *but the only* (or *only begotten*) *Son* [c] 20 Or *Messiah.* "The Christ" (Greek) and "the Messiah" (Hebrew) both mean "the Anointed One"; also in verse 25. [d] 23 Isaiah 40:3 [e] 26 Or *in*; also in verses 31 and 33

younger. People would normally have ranked Jesus lower in respect than John, who was older. John the Baptist explains that this is only apparent, since Jesus, as the Word, existed before he was born on earth.

1:16 *one blessing after another.* To the "blessing" that came through Moses has been added the greater "blessing" that has come through Jesus (see v. 17; see also Heb 1:1–4 and notes).

1:18 *God the One and Only.* An explicit declaration of Christ's deity (see vv. 1,14 and notes; 3:16; see also note on Ro 9:5). *has made him known.* Sometimes in the OT people are said to have seen God (see, e.g., Ex 24:10 and note). But we are also told that no one can see God and live (Ex 33:20). Therefore, since no human being can see God as he really is, those who saw God saw him in a form he took on himself temporarily for the occasion. Now, however, Christ "has made him known." (see 2Co 4:4; Col 1:15,19; 2:9 and notes).

1:19 *the Jews.* The phrase occurs about 70 times in this Gospel. It is used in a favorable sense (e.g., 4:22) and in a neutral sense (e.g., 2:6). But generally John used it of the Jewish leaders who were hostile to Jesus (e.g., 8:48). Here it refers to the delegation sent by the Sanhedrin to look into the activities of an unauthorized teacher. *Levites.* Descendants of the tribe of Levi, who were assigned to specific duties in connection with the tabernacle (Nu 3:17–37) and temple. They also had teaching responsibilities (2Ch 35:3; Ne 8:7–9), and it was probably in this role that they were sent with the priests to John the Baptist.

1:20 *I.* Emphatic, contrasting John the Baptist with someone else. Throughout the following verses this emphatic "I" occurs frequently, and almost invariably there is an implied contrast with Jesus, who is always given the higher place.

1:21 *Are you Elijah?... I am not.* The Jews remembered that Elijah had not died (2Ki 2:11) and believed that he would come back to earth to announce the end time. In this sense, John properly denied that he was Elijah. When Jesus later said the Baptist was Elijah (see Mt 11:14; 17:10 and notes), he meant it in the sense that John was a fulfillment of the prophecy of Mal 4:5 (see note there). *the Prophet.* The prophet of Dt 18:15 (see note there). The Jewish people expected a variety of persons to be associated with the coming of the Messiah. John the Baptist emphatically denies being "the Prophet." He had come to testify about Jesus, yet they kept asking him about himself. His answers became progressively more terse.

1:23 The Baptist applied the prophecy of Isa 40:3 (see note there) to his own ministry of calling people to repent in preparation for the coming of the Messiah. The men of Qumran (the community that produced the Dead Sea Scrolls; see essay, p. 1452) applied the same words to themselves, but they prepared for the Lord's coming by isolating themselves from the world to secure their own salvation. John concentrated on helping people come to the Messiah (the Christ).

1:24 *Pharisees.* The conservative religious party, who probed deeper than the rest of the delegation (v. 19). See notes on Mt 3:7; Mk 2:16; Lk 5:17; see also essay, p. 1453, and chart, p. 1502.

1:25 *the Christ.* Means "the Anointed One" (see NIV text note on v. 20). In OT times anointing signified being set apart for service, particularly as king (cf. 1Sa 16:1,13) or priest (Ex 28:41; 29:7; 30:30; 40:13,15). But people were looking for not just *an* anointed one but *the* Anointed One, the Messiah (cf. Mt 16:16 and note).

1:27 *whose sandals I am not worthy to untie.* A menial task, fit for a slave. Disciples would perform all sorts of service for their rabbis (teachers), but loosing sandal thongs was expressly excluded.

1:28 *Bethany.* The Bethany mentioned elsewhere in the Gospels was only about two miles from Jerusalem (see note on Mt 21:17). The site of this other Bethany is not known, except that it was located on the east side of the Jordan.

1:29 *Lamb of God.* An expression found in the Bible only here and in v. 36. Many suggestions have been made as to which "lamb" John had in mind (e.g., the lamb offered at Passover, or the lamb of Isa 53:7, of Jer 11:19, of Ge 22:8 or of Rev 5:6 [see note there]). It may be that John chose this unique way of referring to Jesus' mission to point both to the sacrificial offering that Jesus would become and to his subsequent conquest of all evil powers—the two ways by which he "takes away the sin of the whole world." (see 1Jn 2:2 and note).

passed me because he was before me.'[t] 31 I myself did not know him, but the reason I came baptizing with water was that he might be revealed to Israel."

32 Then John gave this testimony: "I saw the Spirit come down from heaven as a dove and remain on him.[u] 33 I would not have known him, except that the one who sent me to baptize with water[v] told me, 'The man on whom you see the Spirit come down and remain is he who will baptize with the Holy Spirit.'[w] 34 I have seen and I testify that this is the Son of God."[x]

Jesus' First Disciples

1:40-42pp — Mt 4:18-22; Mk 1:16-20; Lk 5:2-11

35 The next day John[y] was there again with two of his disciples. 36 When he saw Jesus passing by, he said, "Look, the Lamb of God!"[z]

37 When the two disciples heard him say this, they followed Jesus. 38 Turning around, Jesus saw them following and asked, "What do you want?"

They said, "Rabbi"[a] (which means Teacher), "where are you staying?"

39 "Come," he replied, "and you will see."

So they went and saw where he was staying, and spent that day with him. It was about the tenth hour.

40 Andrew, Simon Peter's brother, was one of the two who heard what John had said and who had followed Jesus. 41 The first thing Andrew did was to find his brother Simon and tell him, "We have found the Messiah" (that is, the Christ).[b] 42 And he brought him to Jesus.

Jesus looked at him and said, "You are Simon son of John. You will be called[c] Cephas" (which, when translated, is Peter[a]).[d]

Jesus Calls Philip and Nathanael

43 The next day Jesus decided to leave for Galilee. Finding Philip,[e] he said to him, "Follow me."[f]

44 Philip, like Andrew and Peter, was from the town of Bethsaida.[g] 45 Philip found Nathanael[h] and told him, "We have found the one Moses wrote about in the Law,[i] and about whom the prophets also wrote[j]—Jesus of Nazareth,[k] the son of Joseph."[l]

46 "Nazareth! Can anything good come from there?"[m] Nathanael asked.

"Come and see," said Philip.

47 When Jesus saw Nathanael approaching, he said of him, "Here is a true Israelite,[n] in whom there is nothing false."[o]

48 "How do you know me?" Nathanael asked.

Jesus answered, "I saw you while you were still under the fig tree before Philip called you."

49 Then Nathanael declared, "Rabbi,[p] you are the Son of God;[q] you are the King of Israel."[r]

50 Jesus said, "You believe[b] because I told you I saw you under the fig tree. You shall see greater things than that." 51 He then added, "I tell you[c] the truth, you[c] shall see heaven open,[s] and the angels of God ascending and descending[t] on the Son of Man."[u]

1:30 [t] ver 15,27 **1:32** [u] Mt 3:16 **1:33** [v] S Mk 1:4 [w] S Mk 1:8 **1:34** [x] ver 49; S Mt 4:3 **1:35** [y] S Mt 3:1 **1:36** [z] S ver 29 **1:38** [a] ver 49; S Mt 23:7 **1:41** [b] Jn 4:25 **1:42** [c] Ge 17:5, 15; 32:28; 35:10 [d] Mt 16:18 **1:43** [e] Mt 10:3; Jn 6:5-7; 12:21,22; 14:8,9 [f] S Mt 4:19 **1:44** [g] S Mt 11:21 **1:45** [h] Jn 21:2 [i] S Lk 24:27 [j] S Lk 24:27 [k] S Mk 1:24 [l] Lk 3:23 **1:46** [m] Jn 7:41,42,52 **1:47** [n] Ro 9:4,6 [o] Ps 32:2 **1:49** [p] ver 38; S Mt 23:7 [q] ver 34; S Mt 4:3 [r] S Mt 2:2; 27:42; Jn 12:13 **1:51** [s] S Mt 3:16 [t] Ge 28:12 [u] S Mt 8:20

[a] 42 Both *Cephas* (Aramaic) and *Peter* (Greek) mean *rock.* [b] 50 Or *Do you believe . . . ?* [c] 51 The Greek is plural.

1:31 *I ... did not know him.* John the Baptist, who "lived in the desert until he appeared publicly to Israel" (Lk 1:80), may not have known Jesus at all. But the words probably mean only that he did not know that Jesus was the Messiah until he saw the sign mentioned in vv. 32–33.

1:32 See note on Mt 3:15 for Jesus' baptism.

1:33 *baptize with the Holy Spirit.* John baptized with water, but Jesus would baptize with the Spirit—by which he would cause those who believe in him to participate in the powers and graces of the new life he came to give (see 20:22; Ac 1:5; 2:4; 11:15–16; 19:4–6; 1Co 12–14; Gal 3:5,14; 4:6; 5:16–25; Eph 1:13; 3:16; 5:18; Php 3:3; 1Th 4:8). *Holy Spirit.* His normal title in the NT, though only here and in 14:26; 20:22 in this Gospel—emphasizing his holiness rather than his power or greatness.

1:34 *Son of God.* See vv. 14,18; 3:16 and note; 20:31.

1:35 *two.* One was Andrew (v. 40). The other is not named, but from early times it has been thought that he was the author of this Gospel. *his disciples.* In the sense that they had been baptized by John and looked to him as their religious teacher.

1:36 *Lamb of God.* See note on v. 29.

1:39 *tenth hour.* 4:00 P.M.

1:40 *Andrew.* One of the 12 apostles (Mt 10:2). He was from Bethsaida (v. 44), but later lived with Peter at Capernaum (Mk 1:29), where they fished for a living (Mt 4:18).

1:41 *the Messiah.* See note on v. 25.

1:42 *Simon son of John.* See note on Mt 16:17. *Cephas ... Peter.* See NIV text note. In the Gospels, Peter was anything but a rock; he was impulsive and unstable. In Acts, he was a pillar of the early church. Jesus named him not for what he was but for what, by God's grace, he would become (see Mt 16:18 and note).

1:44 *Bethsaida.* See note on Mt 11:21.

1:45 *son of Joseph.* Not a denial of the virgin birth of Christ (see Mt 1:18,20,23,25 and note; Lk 1:26–35 and note). Joseph was Jesus' legal, though not his natural, father.

1:46 *Nazareth.* See 7:52; see also note on Mt 2:23.

1:47 *a true Israelite.* See 2:24–25.

1:48 *fig tree.* Its shade was a favorite place for study and prayer in hot weather.

1:49 *Rabbi.* Hebrew word for "(my) teacher." *the Son of God.* See vv. 14,18,34; 3:16 and note; 20:31. At the beginning of Jesus' ministry Nathanael acknowledged Jesus with this meaningful title; later it was used in mockery (Mt 27:40; cf. Jn 19:7). Andrew's "the Messiah" (v. 41) and Nathanael's "the Son of God" together match Peter's "You are the Christ, the Son of the living God" (Mt 16:16). *King of Israel.* See 12:13 and note. In Mk 15:32 "Christ" and "King of Israel" are equated.

1:51 *I tell you the truth.* See note on Mk 3:28; occurs more in this Gospel than in any other Gospel—and nowhere else in the NT. *heaven open.* In Jesus' ministry the disciples will see

Jesus Changes Water to Wine

2 On the third day a wedding took place
at Cana in Galilee.[v] Jesus' mother[w] was
there, 2and Jesus and his disciples had
also been invited to the wedding. 3When
the wine was gone, Jesus' mother said to
him, "They have no more wine."
4"Dear woman,[x] why do you involve
me?"[y] Jesus replied. "My time[z] has not yet
come."
5His mother said to the servants, "Do
whatever he tells you."[a]
6Nearby stood six stone water jars,
the kind used by the Jews for ceremonial washing,[b] each holding from twenty to
thirty gallons.[a]
7Jesus said to the servants, "Fill the jars
with water"; so they filled them to the
brim.
8Then he told them, "Now draw some
out and take it to the master of the banquet."
They did so, 9and the master of the banquet tasted the water that had been turned
into wine.[c] He did not realize where it had
come from, though the servants who had
drawn the water knew. Then he called the
bridegroom aside 10and said, "Everyone
brings out the choice wine first and then
the cheaper wine after the guests have had
too much to drink; but you have saved the
best till now."
11This, the first of his miraculous signs,[d]
Jesus performed at Cana in Galilee. He
thus revealed his glory,[e] and his disciples
put their faith in him.[f]

Jesus Clears the Temple

2:14-16pp — Mt 21:12,13; Mk 11:15-17; Lk 19:45,46

12After this he went down to Capernaum[g]
with his mother[h] and brothers[i] and his disciples. There they stayed for a few days.
13When it was almost time for the Jewish Passover,[j] Jesus went up to Jerusalem.[k]
14In the temple courts he found men selling cattle, sheep and doves,[l] and others
sitting at tables exchanging money.[m] 15So
he made a whip out of cords, and drove
all from the temple area, both sheep and
cattle; he scattered the coins of the money changers and overturned their tables.
16To those who sold doves he said, "Get
these out of here! How dare you turn my
Father's house[n] into a market!"

2:1 [v] Jn 4:46; 21:2 [w] S Mt 12:46 **2:4** [x] Jn 19:26 [y] S Mt 8:29 [z] S Mt 26:18 **2:5** [a] Ge 41:55 **2:6** [b] Mk 7:3,4; Jn 3:25 **2:9** [c] Jn 4:46 **2:11** [d] ver 23; Mt 12:38; Jn 3:2; S 4:48; 6:2,14,26,30; 12:37; 20:30 [e] Jn 1:14 [f] Ex 14:31 **2:12** [g] S Mt 4:13 [h] S Mt 12:46 [i] S Mt 12:46 **2:13** [j] S Jn 11:55 [k] Dt 16:1-6; Lk 2:41 **2:14** [l] Lev 1:14; Dt 14:26 [m] Dt 14:25 **2:16** [n] Lk 2:49

[a] 6 Greek *two to three metretes* (probably about 75 to 115 liters)

heaven's (God's) testimony to Jesus as plainly as if they heard an announcement from heaven concerning him. *the angels of God ascending and descending.* As in Jacob's dream (see Ge 28:12 and note), thus marking Jesus as God's elect one through whom redemption comes to the world — perhaps identifying Jesus as *the* "true Israelite" (v. 47). *Son of Man.* Jesus' favorite self-designation (see note on Mk 8:31).

2:1 *third day.* Cf. Ge 22:4 and note. *wedding.* Little is known of how a wedding was performed in the Holy Land in the first century, but clearly the feast was very important and might go on for a week. To fail in proper hospitality was a serious offense. *Cana.* Mentioned only in John's Gospel (v. 11; 4:46; 21:2). It was west of the Sea of Galilee, but the exact location is unknown.

2:3 *When the wine was gone.* More than a minor social embarrassment, since the family had an obligation to provide a feast of the socially required standard. There was no great variety in beverages, and people normally drank water or wine.

2:4 *Dear woman.* The Greek does not have the adjective "Dear," but it is necessary to convey the correct sense, since the potentially abrupt "Woman" could be understood as a harsh form of address. *My time has not yet come.* Several similar expressions scattered through this Gospel (see 7:6,8,30; 8:20 and notes) picture Jesus moving inevitably toward the destiny for which he had come: the time of his sacrificial death on the cross. At the crucifixion and resurrection Jesus' time had truly come (see 12:23,27 and notes; 13:1; 16:32; 17:1).

2:6 *ceremonial washing.* Jews became ceremonially defiled during the normal circumstances of daily life, and were cleansed by pouring water over the hands. For a lengthy feast with many guests a large amount of water was required for this purpose. *holding.* Refers to capacity, not actual content.

2:8 – 9 *master of the banquet.* A function mentioned only here in the NT. Apparently he was one of the guests charged with serving as master of ceremonies.

2:10 *too much to drink ... you have saved the best.* Ordinarily, after the guests' taste buds were dulled, the "cheaper wine" was served.

2:11 *signs.* See chart, p. 1625. John always refers to Jesus' miracles as "signs," a word emphasizing the significance of the action rather than the marvel (see, e.g., 4:54; 6:14; 9:16; 11:47 and notes). There are seven (the number of completeness and perfection) such "signs" in the main body of this Gospel; the large catch of fish in 21:1 – 11 is in the epilogue (see Introduction: Outline; cf. note on 6:35). They revealed Jesus' glory (see 1:14 and note). They likely also pointed to the fullness of the salvation he came to effect. In his account of Jesus' first display of "his glory" by providing an abundance of wine so that a wedding feast of common folk could be fully celebrated, John probably was testifying that Christ's saving mission would culminate in the redemption of the creation from all its distresses so that the wine of joy would flow fully, as the prophets had announced (see Isa 35:1 – 2; Joel 3:18; Am 9:13 and notes; cf. Ge 49:11 and note). *his disciples put their faith in him.* See 1:7; 20:31 and notes.

2:12 *went down.* Situated on the shore of the Sea of Galilee, Capernaum was at a lower level than Cana. *Capernaum.* See notes on Mt 4:13; Lk 10:15; see also diagram, p. 1572. *brothers.* See note on Lk 8:19.

2:13 *Passover.* See Ex 12 and notes on Ex 12:11 – 23; see also notes on Mt 26:17,18 – 30; Mk 14:1,12; Lk 22:1 and chart, pp. 178 – 179. Passover was one of the annual feasts that all Jewish men were required to celebrate in Jerusalem. See notes on 5:1; Dt 16:16.

2:14 – 17 Matthew, Mark and Luke record a clearing of the temple toward the end of Jesus' ministry (see note on Mt 21:12 – 17).

2:14 *cattle, sheep and doves.* Required for sacrifices. Jews who came great distances had to be able to buy sacrificial animals near the temple. The merchants, however, were selling them in the outer court of the temple itself, the one place where Gentiles could come to pray. *exchanging money.* Many coins had to be changed into currency acceptable to the temple authorities, which made money changers necessary (see note on Mk 11:15). They should not, however, have been working in the temple itself.

Miracles of Jesus

HEALING MIRACLES	MATTHEW	MARK	LUKE	JOHN
Man with leprosy	8:2-4	1:40-42	5:12-13	
Roman centurion's servant	8:5-13		7:1-10	
Peter's mother-in-law	8:14-15	1:30-31	4:38-39	
Two men from Gadara	8:28-34	5:1-15	8:27-35	
Paralyzed man	9:2-7	2:3-12	5:18-25	
Woman with bleeding	9:20-22	5:25-29	8:43-48	
Two blind men	9:27-31			
Mute, demon-possessed man	9:32-33			
Man with a shriveled hand	12:10-13	3:1-5	6:6-10	
Blind, mute, demon-possessed man	12:22		11:14	
Canaanite woman's daughter	15:21-28	7:24-30		
Boy with a demon	17:14-18	9:17-29	9:38-43	
Two blind men (including Bartimaeus)	20:29-34	10:46-52	18:35-43	
Deaf mute		7:31-37		
Possessed man in synagogue		1:23-26	4:33-35	
Blind man at Bethsaida		8:22-26		
Crippled woman			13:11-13	
Man with dropsy			14:1-4	
Ten men with leprosy			17:11-19	
The high priest's servant			22:50-51	
Official's son at Capernaum				4:46-54
Sick man at pool of Bethesda				5:1-9
Man born blind				9:1-7
MIRACLES SHOWING POWER OVER NATURE				
Calming the storm	8:23-27	4:37-41	8:22-25	
Walking on water	14:25	6:48-51		6:19-21
Feeding of the 5,000	14:15-21	6:35-44	9:12-17	6:6-13
Feeding of the 4,000	15:32-38	8:1-9		
Coin in fish's mouth	17:24-27			
Fig tree withered	21:18-22	11:12-14,20-25		
Large catch of fish			5:4-11	
Water turned into wine				2:1-11
Another large catch of fish				21:1-11
MIRACLES OF RAISING THE DEAD				
Jairus's daughter	9:18-19,23-25	5:22-24,38-42	8:41-42,49-56	
Widow's son at Nain			7:11-15	
Lazarus				11:1-44

17His disciples remembered that it is
written: "Zeal for your house will consume me."[a][o]
18Then the Jews[p] demanded of him,
"What miraculous sign[q] can you show us
to prove your authority to do all this?"[r]
19Jesus answered them, "Destroy this
temple, and I will raise it again in three
days."[s]
20The Jews replied, "It has taken forty-
six years to build this temple, and you are
going to raise it in three days?" 21But the
temple he had spoken of was his body.[t]
22After he was raised from the dead, his
disciples recalled what he had said.[u] Then
they believed the Scripture[v] and the words
that Jesus had spoken.
23Now while he was in Jerusalem at
the Passover Feast,[w] many people saw the
miraculous signs[x] he was doing and believed[y] in his name.[b] 24But Jesus would
not entrust himself to them, for he knew
all men. 25He did not need man's testimony about man,[z] for he knew what was in
a man.[a]

Jesus Teaches Nicodemus

3 Now there was a man of the Pharisees
named Nicodemus,[b] a member of the
Jewish ruling council.[c] 2He came to Jesus
at night and said, "Rabbi,[d] we know[e] you
are a teacher who has come from God. For
no one could perform the miraculous signs[f]
you are doing if God were not with him."[g]
3In reply Jesus declared, "I tell you the
truth, no one can see the kingdom of God
unless he is born again.[c]"[h][i]
4"How can a man be born when he is
old?" Nicodemus asked. "Surely he cannot enter a second time into his mother's
womb to be born!"
5Jesus answered, "I tell you the truth,
no one can enter the kingdom of God unless he is born of water and the Spirit.[j][k]
6Flesh gives birth to flesh, but the Spirit[d]
gives birth to spirit.[l] 7You should not be
surprised at my saying, 'You[e] must be born
again.' 8The wind blows wherever it pleases. You hear its sound, but you cannot tell
where it comes from or where it is going.
So it is with everyone born of the Spirit."[m]
9"How can this be?"[n] Nicodemus asked.
10"You are Israel's teacher,"[o] said Jesus,
"and do you not understand these things?
11I tell you the truth, we speak of what
we know,[p] and we testify to what we have
seen, but still you people do not accept
our testimony.[q] 12I have spoken to you of
earthly things and you do not believe; how
then will you believe if I speak of heavenly things? 13No one has ever gone into
heaven[r] except the one who came from
heaven[s]—the Son of Man.[f][t] 14Just as Moses lifted up the snake in the desert,[u] so
the Son of Man must be lifted up,[v] 15that
everyone who believes[w] in him may have
eternal life.[g][x]
16"For God so loved[y] the world that he
gave[z] his one and only Son,[h][a] that who-

[a] 17 Psalm 69:9 [b] 23 Or *and believed in him* [c] 3 Or *born from above*; also in verse 7 [d] 6 Or *but spirit* [e] 7 The Greek is plural. [f] 13 Some manuscripts *Man, who is in heaven* [g] 15 Or *believes may have eternal life in him* [h] 16 Or *his only begotten Son*

2:17 [o]Ps 69:9
2:18 [p]S Jn 1:19 [q]S ver 11 [r]S Mt 12:38
2:19 [s]S Mt 16:21; 26:61; 27:40; Mk 14:58; 15:29; Ac 6:14
2:21 [t]1Co 6:19
2:22 [u]Lk 24:5-8; Jn 12:16; 14:26 [v]Ps 16:10; S Lk 24:27
2:23 [w]ver 13 [x]S ver 11 [y]S Jn 3:15
2:25 [z]Isa 11:3 [a]Dt 31:21; 1Ki 8:39; S Mt 9:4; Jn 6:61,64; 13:11
3:1 [b]Jn 7:50; 19:39 [c]Lk 23:13
3:2 [d]S Mt 23:7 [e]ver 11 [f]S Jn 2:11 [g]Jn 10:38; 14:10,11; Ac 2:22; 10:38
3:3 [h]S Jn 1:13 [i]S Mt 3:2
3:5 [j]S Ac 22:16 [k]Tit 3:5
3:6 [l]S Jn 1:13; 1Co 15:50
3:8 [m]1Co 2:14-16
3:9 [n]Jn 6:52,60
3:10 [o]Lk 2:46
3:11 [p]Jn 1:18; 7:16,17 [q]ver 32
3:13 [r]Pr 30:4; Ac 2:34; Eph 4:8-10 [s]ver 31; Jn 6:38,42; Heb 4:14; 9:24 [t]S Mt 8:20
3:14 [u]Nu 21:8,9 [v]S Jn 12:32
3:15 [w]ver 16,36; Ge 15:6; Nu 14:11; Mt 27:42; Mk 1:15; Jn 1:7,12; 2:23; 5:24; 7:38; 20:29; Ac 13:39; 16:31; Ro 3:22; 10:9,10; 1Jn 5:1,5,10 [x]ver 16,36; S Mt 25:46; Jn 20:31
3:16 [y]Ro 5:8; Eph 2:4; 1Jn 4:9,10 [z]Isa 9:6; Ro 8:32 [a]Ge 22:12; Jn 1:18

2:17 *His disciples remembered.* Probably after Jesus' crucifixion (see v. 22)—when Ps 69 came to them like a prophecy of his suffering at the hands of those his "zeal" for the true worship of God had deeply antagonized (see introduction to Ps 69).
2:19 The Jews thought Jesus was referring to the literal temple, but John tells us he was not (v. 21). Just a few years later, Jesus was accused of saying that he would destroy the temple and raise it again (see Mt 26:61; Mk 14:58 and notes), and mockers repeated the charge as he hung on the cross (Mt 27:40; Mk 15:29). The same misunderstanding may have been behind the charge against Stephen (see Ac 6:13 and note).
2:20 *forty-six years.* The temple was not finally completed until A.D. 64. The meaning is that work had been going on for 46 years. Since it had begun c. 19 or 20 B.C., the year of the event recorded here is c. A.D. 27 (see chart, p. 1508).
2:22 *recalled what he had said.* See 14:26 and note. *Then they believed the Scripture.* See 20:9 and note. It is not clear whether reference here is to a particular word from the OT (see, e.g., Ps 16:10; 17:15 and notes) or to the OT in general (cf. 1Co 15:4).
2:23 *Passover Feast.* See note on v. 13. *name.* See notes on Ps 5:11; Eze 20:9.
3:1 *man of the Pharisees.* See notes on Mt 3:7; Mk 2:16; Lk 5:17.
3:2 *at night.* Perhaps Nicodemus was afraid to come by day. Or he may have wanted a long talk, which would have been difficult in the daytime with the crowds around Jesus. For later references to Nicodemus in this Gospel see 7:45–52; 19:38–42.
3:3,7 *born again.* The Greek also may mean "born from above" (see NIV text note). Both meanings are consistent with Jesus' redeeming work (see 1:13 and note).
3:5 *kingdom of God.* See note on Mt 3:2. *born of water and the Spirit.* A phrase understood in various ways: (1) It means much the same as "born of the Spirit" (v. 8; cf. Tit 3:5 and note). (2) Water here refers to purification. (3) Water refers to baptism—that of John (1:31) or that of Jesus and his disciples (see v. 22; 4:2 and notes). (4) Water refers to physical birth, specifically to the water of the amniotic sac (cf. v. 6).
3:7 *You.* See NIV text note. This assertion applies to everyone, not just Nicodemus. *must.* There are no exceptions. *born again.* See note on v. 3.
3:8 The Holy Spirit is sovereign. He works as he pleases in his renewal of human hearts.
3:11 *testimony.* See note on 1:7.
3:13 *Son of Man.* Jesus' favorite self-designation (see notes on Mk 8:31; Lk 19:10).
3:14 *Moses lifted up the snake.* See notes on Nu 21:8–9; 2Ki 18:4. *the Son of Man must be lifted up.* See 8:28; 12:32 and note.

3:15–16 *believes.* See note on 1:7. *eternal life.* Life in living fellowship with God—both now and forever.
3:16 *God so loved the world.* The great truth that motivated God's plan of salvation (cf. 1Jn 4:9–10). *world.*

ever believes[b] in him shall not perish but have eternal life.[c] 17For God did not send his Son into the world[d] to condemn the world, but to save the world through him.[e] 18Whoever believes in him is not condemned,[f] but whoever does not believe stands condemned already because he has not believed in the name of God's one and only Son.[a][g] 19This is the verdict: Light[h] has come into the world, but men loved darkness instead of light because their deeds were evil.[i] 20Everyone who does evil hates the light, and will not come into the light for fear that his deeds will be exposed.[j] 21But whoever lives by the truth comes into the light, so that it may be seen plainly that what he has done has been done through God."[b]

John the Baptist's Testimony About Jesus

22After this, Jesus and his disciples went out into the Judean countryside, where he spent some time with them, and baptized.[k] 23Now John[l] also was baptizing at Aenon near Salim, because there was plenty of water, and people were constantly coming to be baptized. 24(This was before John was put in prison.)[m] 25An argument developed between some of John's disciples and a certain Jew[c] over the matter of ceremonial washing.[n] 26They came to John and said to him, "Rabbi,[o] that man who was with you on the other side of the Jordan—the one you testified[p] about—well, he is baptizing, and everyone is going to him."

27To this John replied, "A man can receive only what is given him from heaven. 28You yourselves can testify that I said, 'I am not the Christ[d] but am sent ahead of him.'[q] 29The bride belongs to the bridegroom.[r] The friend who attends the bridegroom waits and listens for him, and is full of joy when he hears the bridegroom's voice. That joy is mine, and it is now complete.[s] 30He must become greater; I must become less.

31"The one who comes from above[t] is above all; the one who is from the earth belongs to the earth, and speaks as one from the earth.[u] The one who comes from heaven is above all. 32He testifies to what he has seen and heard,[v] but no one accepts his testimony.[w] 33The man who has accepted it has certified that God is truthful. 34For the one whom God has sent[x] speaks the words of God, for God[e] gives the Spirit[y] without limit. 35The Father loves the Son and has placed everything in his hands.[z] 36Whoever believes in the Son has eternal life,[a] but whoever rejects the Son will not see life, for God's wrath remains on him."[f]

Jesus Talks With a Samaritan Woman

4 The Pharisees heard that Jesus was gaining and baptizing more disciples

3:16 [b] S ver 15 [c] ver 36; Jn 6:29,40; 11:25,26 **3:17** [d] Jn 6:29,57; 10:36; 11:42; 17:8,21; 20:21 [e] Isa 53:11; S Mt 1:21; S Lk 2:11; 19:10; Jn 1:29; 12:47; S Ro 11:14; 1Ti 1:15; 2:5,6; 1Jn 2:2; 3:5 **3:18** [f] Jn 5:24 [g] Jn 1:18; 1Jn 4:9 **3:19** [h] S Jn 1:4 [i] Ps 52:3; Jn 7:7 **3:20** [j] Eph 5:11,13 **3:22** [k] Jn 4:2 **3:23** [l] S Mt 3:1 **3:24** [m] Mt 4:12; 14:3 **3:25** [n] Jn 2:6 **3:26** [o] S Mt 23:7 [p] Jn 1:7 **3:28** [q] Jn 1:20,23 **3:29** [r] Mt 9:15 [s] Jn 16:24; 17:13; Php 2:2; 1Jn 1:4; 2Jn 12 **3:31** [t] ver 13 [u] Jn 8:23; 1Jn 4:5 **3:32** [v] Jn 8:26; 15:15 [w] ver 11 **3:34** [x] S ver 17 [y] Isa 42:1; Mt 12:18; Lk 4:18; Ac 10:38 **3:35** [z] S Mt 28:18 **3:36** [a] S ver 15; Jn 5:24; 6:47

[a] *18* Or *God's only begotten Son* [b] *21* Some interpreters end the quotation after verse 15. [c] *25* Some manuscripts *and certain Jews* [d] *28* Or *Messiah* [e] *34* Greek *he* [f] *36* Some interpreters end the quotation after verse 30.

All people on earth—or perhaps all creation (see notes on 1:4,9). *gave his one and only Son.* Cf. Isa 9:6 ("a son is given," referring to the Messianic Son of David—who is also God's Son [see 2Sa 7:14 and note]). See also 1:14,18 and notes; cf. Ge 22:2,16; Ro 8:32 and notes. Although believers are also called "sons" of God (2Co 6:18; Gal 4:5–6), Jesus is God's Son in a unique sense (see 20:31 and note).

3:18 *believes ... does not believe.* John is not speaking of momentary beliefs and doubts but of continuing, settled convictions. *name.* See 2:23 and note.

3:22 *baptized.* According to 4:2 only the disciples actually baptized.

3:23 *Aenon.* Possibly about eight miles south of Scythopolis (Beth Shan), west of the Jordan.

3:24 See note on Lk 3:20.

3:25 *argument ... over ... ceremonial washing.* See 2:6 and note. The Dead Sea (Qumran) Scrolls (see essay, pp. 1452–1453) show that some Jews were deeply interested in the right way to achieve ceremonial purification.

3:26 *testified.* See note on 1:7. John's disciples knew that he had testified about Jesus, but they loved their master and were apparently envious of Jesus' success.

3:27 The words are true of both Jesus and John (and of everyone). Both had what God had given them, so there was no place for envy. *given.* The Greek verb is used 76 times in this Gospel, especially of the things the Father gives the Son.

3:29 *bridegroom.* The most important man at a wedding, referring here to Jesus. "The friend who attends the bridegroom" is there only to help him, which describes the role of John the Baptist. *full of joy.* Not because he was on center stage, but because the bridegroom was there. John's joy was to hear of Jesus' success.

3:30 John the Baptist's pointed way of reaffirming his subordinate position.

3:31 *The one who comes from above.* Jesus, whose heavenly origin (see v. 13; 1Co 15:47) meant much to John. *the one who is from the earth.* A general expression that could apply to anyone, but here it particularly refers to John the Baptist.

3:32 *what he has seen and heard.* Jesus taught from divine experience. *no one.* Does not mean that no person accepted what he said (see v. 33) but that people in general refused his teaching.

3:33 *certified.* When people accept Christ's testimony, they accept the truth that Jesus came from heaven and that God was acting in him for the world's salvation. They thereby testify that God is truthful.

3:34 *the one whom God has sent.* Jesus. *without limit.* Some hold that it is only to Jesus that the Spirit is given without limit. Others take the "he" (see NIV text note) as a reference to Christ's giving the Spirit without limit to believers.

3:36 *has.* Eternal life is a present possession, not something the believer will only obtain later (see note on v. 15). *God's wrath.* A strong expression, meaning that God is actively opposed to everything evil. The word "wrath" occurs only here in John's Gospel (see note on Ro 1:18). *remains.* No one who persists in rejecting the Son of God as Savior and Lord can expect God's wrath eventually to fade away. God's opposition to evil is both total and permanent.

4:1 *Pharisees.* These religious leaders took a close interest in John the Baptist (see 1:24 and note) and then also in Jesus.

than John,[b] 2although in fact it was not
Jesus who baptized, but his disciples.
3When the Lord[c] learned of this, he left Judea[d] and went back once more to Galilee.
4Now he had to go through Samaria.[e]
5So he came to a town in Samaria called
Sychar, near the plot of ground Jacob had
given to his son Joseph.[f] 6Jacob's well
was there, and Jesus, tired as he was from
the journey, sat down by the well. It was
about the sixth hour.
7When a Samaritan woman came to
draw water, Jesus said to her, "Will you
give me a drink?"[g] 8(His disciples had
gone into the town[h] to buy food.)
9The Samaritan woman said to him,
"You are a Jew and I am a Samaritan[i]
woman. How can you ask me for a drink?"
(For Jews do not associate with Samaritans.[a])
10Jesus answered her, "If you knew the
gift of God and who it is that asks you for
a drink, you would have asked him and he
would have given you living water."[j]
11"Sir," the woman said, "you have
nothing to draw with and the well is deep.
Where can you get this living water? 12Are
you greater than our father Jacob, who
gave us the well[k] and drank from it himself, as did also his sons and his flocks
and herds?"
13Jesus answered, "Everyone who drinks
this water will be thirsty again, 14but whoever drinks the water I give him will never
thirst.[l] Indeed, the water I give him will
become in him a spring of water[m] welling
up to eternal life."[n]
15The woman said to him, "Sir, give me
this water so that I won't get thirsty[o] and
have to keep coming here to draw water."
16He told her, "Go, call your husband
and come back."
17"I have no husband," she replied.
Jesus said to her, "You are right when
you say you have no husband. 18The fact
is, you have had five husbands, and the
man you now have is not your husband.
What you have just said is quite true."
19"Sir," the woman said, "I can see that
you are a prophet.[p] 20Our fathers worshiped on this mountain,[q] but you Jews
claim that the place where we must worship is in Jerusalem."[r]
21Jesus declared, "Believe me, woman, a
time is coming[s] when you will worship the
Father neither on this mountain nor in Jerusalem.[t] 22You Samaritans worship what
you do not know;[u] we worship what we
do know, for salvation is from the Jews.[v]
23Yet a time is coming and has now come[w]
when the true worshipers will worship
the Father in spirit[x] and truth, for they are
the kind of worshipers the Father seeks.

4:1 [b]Jn 3:22,26 **4:3** [c]S Lk 7:13 [d]Jn 3:22 **4:4** [e]S Mt 10:5 **4:5** [f]Ge 33:19; Jos 24:32 **4:7** [g]Ge 24:17; 1Ki 17:10 **4:8** [h]ver 5,39 **4:9** [i]S Mt 10:5 **4:10** [j]Isa 44:3; 55:1; Jer 2:13; 17:13; Zec 14:8; Jn 7:37,38; Rev 7:17; 21:6; 22:1,17 **4:12** [k]ver 6 **4:14** [l]Jn 6:35 [m]Isa 12:3; 58:11; Jn 7:38 [n]S Mt 25:46 **4:15** [o]Jn 6:34 **4:19** [p]S Mt 21:11 **4:20** [q]Dt 11:29; Jos 8:33 [r]Lk 9:53 **4:21** [s]Jn 5:28; 16:2 [t]Mal 1:11; 1Ti 2:8 **4:22** [u]2Ki 17:28-41 [v]Isa 2:3; Ro 3:1,2; 9:4,5; 15:8,9 **4:23** [w]Jn 5:25; 16:32 [x]Php 3:3

[a] 9 Or *do not use dishes Samaritans have used*

4:2 The disciples did not baptize without Jesus' approval (see 3:2 and note).

4:3 *left Judea.* Success (which aroused opposition; see note on 7:1—8:59), not failure, led Jesus to leave Judea.

4:4 *had to go.* Perhaps the necessity lay in Jesus' mission rather than in geography. *Samaria.* Here the whole region, not simply the city. Jews often avoided Samaria by crossing the Jordan and traveling on the east side (see notes on Mt 10:5; Lk 9:52).

4:5 *Sychar.* A small village near Shechem. Jacob bought some land in the vicinity of Shechem (Ge 33:18–19), and it was apparently this land that he gave to Joseph (Ge 48:21–22). See map, p. 1629.

4:6 *Jacob's well.* Mentioned nowhere else in Scripture. *sixth hour.* 12:00 noon.

4:7 *to draw water.* People normally drew water at the end of the day rather than in the heat of midday (see v. 6; Ge 24:11 and notes). But the practice is attested by Josephus, who says that the young ladies whom Moses helped (Ex 2:15–17) came to draw water at noon.

4:9 *do not associate with.* The point of the NIV text note (and probably of the text) is that Jews would become ceremonially unclean if they used a drinking vessel handled by a Samaritan, since they held that all Samaritans were ceremonially unclean.

4:10 *gift.* The Greek for this word is used only here in this Gospel and emphasizes God's grace through Christ. Jesus gave life and gave it freely. *living water.* Not stagnant cistern water but fresh, flowing water, as of a spring or mountain stream, that revives and refreshes life. In 7:38–39 the term is explained as referring to the Holy Spirit, but here it refers to that which produces eternal life (see v. 14).

4:11 *deep.* Christian pilgrim sources as early as the fourth century mention a well in this area that was about 100 feet deep. When the present well was cleaned out in 1935, it was found to be 138 feet deep.

4:12 *our father Jacob.* Deep regard for the past prevented her from seeing the great opportunity of the present.

4:14 *welling up.* The expression is a vigorous one, with a meaning like "leaping up." Jesus was speaking of vigorous, abundant life (cf. 10:10).

4:15 Cf. the misunderstanding of Nicodemus (3:4). In both cases the way was opened for further instruction.

4:18 *five husbands.* The Jews held that a woman might be divorced twice or at the most three times. If the Samaritans had the same standard, the woman's life had been exceedingly immoral. Apparently she had not married her present partner.

4:19 *you are a prophet.* Because of his special insight.

4:20 *this mountain.* Perhaps the woman did not like the way the conversation was going and so began to argue. The proper place of worship had long been a source of debate between Jews and Samaritans. Samaritans held that "this mountain" (Mount Gerizim) was especially sacred. Abraham and Jacob had built altars in the general vicinity (Ge 12:6–7; 33:18–20), and the people had been blessed from this mountain (Dt 11:29; 27:12). In the Samaritan Scriptures, Mount Gerizim (rather than Mount Ebal) was the mountain on which Moses had commanded an altar to be built (Dt 27:4–6). The Samaritans had built a temple on Mount Gerizim c. 400 B.C., which the Jews destroyed c. 128. Both actions, of course, increased hostility between the two groups. See map, p. 1629.

4:22 *worship what you do not know.* The Samaritan Bible contained only the Pentateuch. They worshiped the true God, but their failure to accept much of his revelation meant that they knew little about him. *salvation is from the Jews.* The Messiah would come from God's historic people (see notes on Ro 1:16; 11:18).

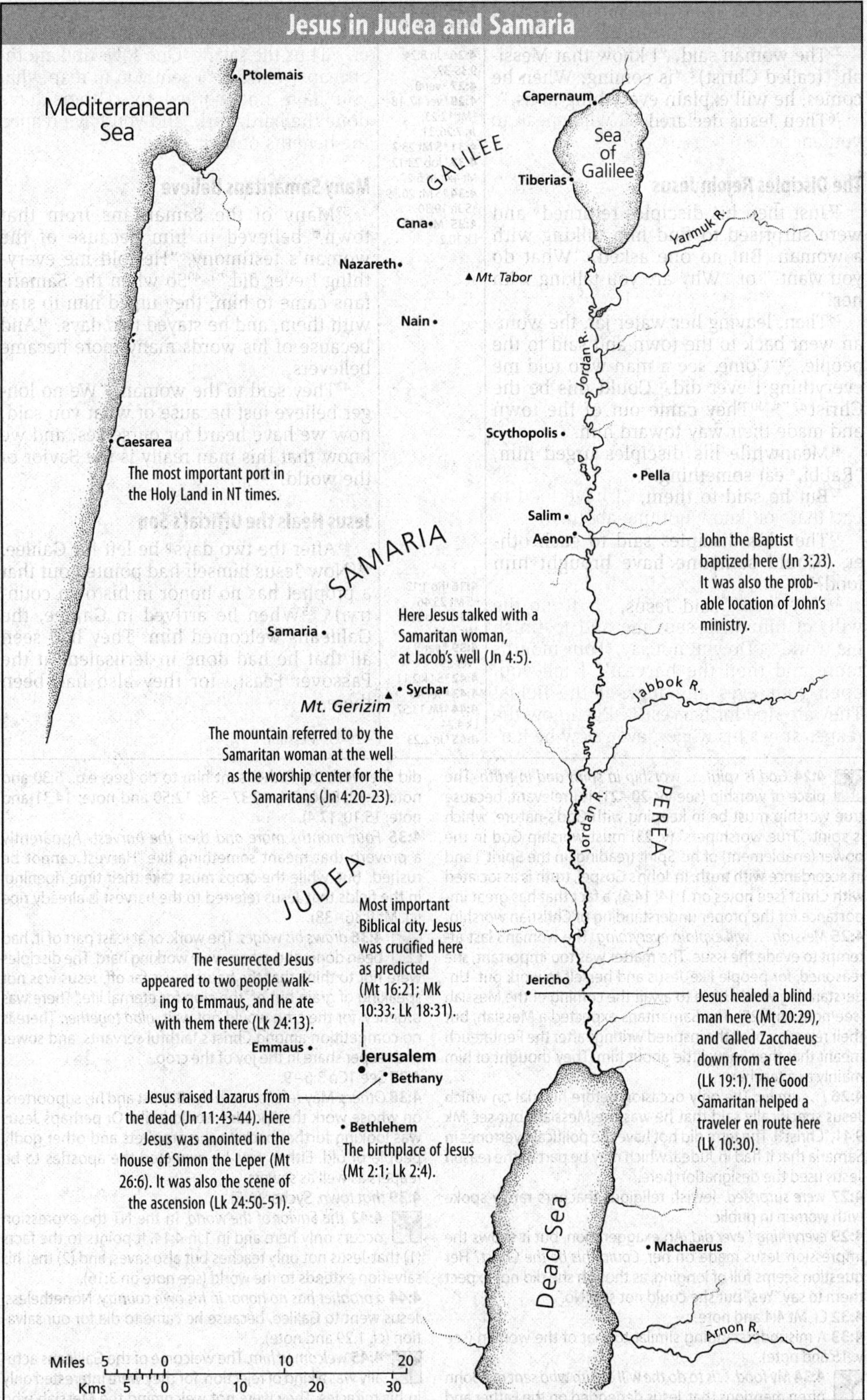
Jesus in Judea and Samaria
Ptolemais
Mediterranean Sea
Capernaum
Sea of Galilee
GALILEE
Tiberias
Yarmuk R.
Cana
Nazareth
Mt. Tabor
Nain
Jordan R.
Scythopolis
Caesarea
The most important port in the Holy Land in NT times.
Pella
Salim
Aenon
John the Baptist baptized here (Jn 3:23). It was also the probable location of John's ministry.
SAMARIA
Samaria
Here Jesus talked with a Samaritan woman, at Jacob's well (Jn 4:5).
Jabbok R.
Sychar
Mt. Gerizim
The mountain referred to by the Samaritan woman at the well as the worship center for the Samaritans (Jn 4:20-23).
Jordan R.
PEREA
JUDEA
Most important Biblical city. Jesus was crucified here as predicted (Mt 16:21; Mk 10:33; Lk 18:31).
The resurrected Jesus appeared to two people walking to Emmaus, and he ate with them there (Lk 24:13).
Jericho
Jesus healed a blind man here (Mt 20:29), and called Zacchaeus down from a tree (Lk 19:1). The Good Samaritan helped a traveler en route here (Lk 10:30).
Emmaus
Jerusalem
Bethany
Jesus raised Lazarus from the dead (Jn 11:43-44). Here Jesus was anointed in the house of Simon the Leper (Mt 26:6). It was also the scene of the ascension (Lk 24:50-51).
Bethlehem
The birthplace of Jesus (Mt 2:1; Lk 2:4).
Dead Sea
Machaerus
Arnon R.
Miles 5 0 10 20
Kms 5 0 10 20 30

[24]God is spirit,[y] and his worshipers must
worship in spirit and in truth."
[25]The woman said, "I know that Messiah" (called Christ)[z] "is coming. When he
comes, he will explain everything to us."
[26]Then Jesus declared, "I who speak to
you am he."[a]

The Disciples Rejoin Jesus

[27]Just then his disciples returned[b] and
were surprised to find him talking with
a woman. But no one asked, "What do
you want?" or "Why are you talking with
her?"
[28]Then, leaving her water jar, the woman went back to the town and said to the
people, [29]"Come, see a man who told me
everything I ever did.[c] Could this be the
Christ[a]?"[d] [30]They came out of the town
and made their way toward him.
[31]Meanwhile his disciples urged him,
"Rabbi,[e] eat something."
[32]But he said to them, "I have food to
eat[f] that you know nothing about."
[33]Then his disciples said to each other, "Could someone have brought him
food?"
[34]"My food," said Jesus, "is to do the
will[g] of him who sent me and to finish
his work.[h] [35]Do you not say, 'Four months
more and then the harvest'? I tell you,
open your eyes and look at the fields!
They are ripe for harvest.[i] [36]Even now the
reaper draws his wages, even now he harvests[j] the crop for eternal life,[k] so that the
sower and the reaper may be glad together. [37]Thus the saying 'One sows and another reaps'[l] is true. [38]I sent you to reap what
you have not worked for. Others have
done the hard work, and you have reaped
the benefits of their labor."

Many Samaritans Believe

[39]Many of the Samaritans from that
town[m] believed in him because of the
woman's testimony, "He told me everything I ever did."[n] [40]So when the Samaritans came to him, they urged him to stay
with them, and he stayed two days. [41]And
because of his words many more became
believers.
[42]They said to the woman, "We no longer believe just because of what you said;
now we have heard for ourselves, and we
know that this man really is the Savior of
the world."[o]

Jesus Heals the Official's Son

[43]After the two days[p] he left for Galilee.
[44](Now Jesus himself had pointed out that
a prophet has no honor in his own country.)[q] [45]When he arrived in Galilee, the
Galileans welcomed him. They had seen
all that he had done in Jerusalem at the
Passover Feast,[r] for they also had been
there.

[a] 29 Or *Messiah*

4:24 [y]Php 3:3 **4:25** [z]Mt 1:16; Jn 1:41 **4:26** [a]Jn 8:24; 9:35-37 **4:27** [b]ver 8 **4:29** [c]ver 17,18 [d]Mt 12:23; Jn 7:26,31 **4:31** [e]S Mt 23:7 **4:32** [f]Job 23:12; Mt 4:4; Jn 6:27 **4:34** [g]S Mt 26:39 [h]S Jn 19:30 **4:35** [i]Mt 9:37; Lk 10:2 **4:36** [j]Ro 1:13 [k]S Mt 25:46 **4:37** [l]Job 31:8; Mic 6:15 **4:39** [m]ver 5 [n]ver 29 **4:42** [o]S Lk 2:11 **4:43** [p]ver 40 **4:44** [q]Mt 13:57; Lk 4:24 **4:45** [r]Jn 2:23

4:24 *God is spirit … worship in spirit and in truth.* The place of worship (see vv. 20–21) is irrelevant, because true worship must be in keeping with God's nature, which is spirit. "True worshipers" (v. 23) must worship God in the power (enablement) of his Spirit (reading "in the Spirit") and in accordance with truth. In John's Gospel, truth is associated with Christ (see notes on 1:14; 14:6), a fact that has great importance for the proper understanding of Christian worship.
4:25 *Messiah … will explain everything.* The woman's last attempt to evade the issue. The matter was too important, she reasoned, for people like Jesus and herself to work out. Understanding would have to await the coming of the Messiah (see note on 1:25). The Samaritans expected a Messiah, but their rejection of all the inspired writings after the Pentateuch meant that they knew little about him. They thought of him mainly as a teacher.
4:26 *I … am he.* The only occasion before his trial on which Jesus specifically said that he was the Messiah (but see Mk 9:41, "Christ"). The term did not have the political overtones in Samaria that it had in Judea, which may be part of the reason Jesus used the designation here.
4:27 *were surprised.* Jewish religious teachers rarely spoke with women in public.
4:29 *everything I ever did.* An exaggeration, but it shows the impression Jesus made on her. *Could this be the Christ?* Her question seems full of longing, as though she did not expect them to say "Yes," but she could not say "No."
4:32 Cf. Mt 4:4 and note.
4:33 A misunderstanding similar to that of the woman (see v. 15 and note).
4:34 *My food … is to do the will of him who sent me.* John often mentions that Jesus depended on the Father and did the work the Father sent him to do (see, e.g., 5:30 and note; 6:38; 8:26; 9:4; 10:37–38; 12:50 and note; 14:31 and note; 15:10; 17:4).
4:35 *Four months more and then the harvest.* Apparently a proverb that meant something like "Harvest cannot be rushed." But, while the crops must take their time ripening, in the fields that Jesus referred to the harvest is already ripe (cf. Mt 9:36–38).
4:36 *draws his wages.* The work, or at least part of it, had been done, and others were working hard. The disciples were not to think that the harvest was far off. Jesus was not speaking of grain but of "the crop for eternal life." There was urgency, for the crop would not wait. *glad together.* There is no competition among Christ's faithful servants, and sower and reaper share in the joy of the crop.
4:37 See 1Co 3:6–9.
4:38 *Others.* May refer to John the Baptist and his supporters, on whose work the apostles would build. Or perhaps Jesus was looking further back, to the prophets and other godly people of old. Either way, he expected the apostles to be reapers as well as sowers.
4:39 *that town.* Sychar (v. 5).
4:42 *the Savior of the world.* In the NT the expression occurs only here and in 1Jn 4:14. It points to the facts (1) that Jesus not only teaches but also saves, and (2) that his salvation extends to the world (see note on 3:16).
4:44 *a prophet has no honor in his own country.* Nonetheless, Jesus went to Galilee, because he came to die for our salvation (cf. 1:29 and note).
4:45 *welcomed him.* The welcome of the Galileans actually was a kind of rejection, for they were interested only in his miracles. They were not welcoming the Messiah who

46Once more he visited Cana in Galilee, where he had turned the water into
wine.[s] And there was a certain royal official whose son lay sick at Capernaum.
47When this man heard that Jesus had arrived in Galilee from Judea,[t] he went to
him and begged him to come and heal his
son, who was close to death.
48"Unless you people see miraculous
signs and wonders,"[u] Jesus told him, "you
will never believe."
49The royal official said, "Sir, come
down before my child dies."
50Jesus replied, "You may go. Your son
will live."

The man took Jesus at his word and departed. 51While he was still on the way,
his servants met him with the news that
his boy was living. 52When he inquired as
to the time when his son got better, they
said to him, "The fever left him yesterday
at the seventh hour."
53Then the father realized that this was
the exact time at which Jesus had said to
him, "Your son will live." So he and all his
household[v] believed.
54This was the second miraculous sign[w]
that Jesus performed, having come from
Judea to Galilee.

The Healing at the Pool

5 Some time later, Jesus went up to Jerusalem for a feast of the Jews. 2Now there
is in Jerusalem near the Sheep Gate[x] a pool,
which in Aramaic[y] is called Bethesda[a]
and which is surrounded by five covered
colonnades. 3Here a great number of disabled people used to lie — the blind, the
lame, the paralyzed.[b] 5One who was there
had been an invalid for thirty-eight years.
6When Jesus saw him lying there and
learned that he had been in this condition
for a long time, he asked him, "Do you
want to get well?"
7"Sir," the invalid replied, "I have no
one to help me into the pool when the water is stirred. While I am trying to get in,
someone else goes down ahead of me."
8Then Jesus said to him, "Get up! Pick
up your mat and walk."[z] 9At once the
man was cured; he picked up his mat and
walked.
The day on which this took place was
a Sabbath,[a] 10and so the Jews[b] said to the
man who had been healed, "It is the Sabbath; the law forbids you to carry your
mat."[c]
11But he replied, "The man who made
me well said to me, 'Pick up your mat and
walk.' "
12So they asked him, "Who is this fellow
who told you to pick it up and walk?"
13The man who was healed had no idea
who it was, for Jesus had slipped away
into the crowd that was there.

4:46 [s]Jn 2:1-11 **4:47** [t]ver 3,54 **4:48** [u]Da 4:2,3; S Jn 2:11; Ac 2:43; 14:3; Ro 15:19; 2Co 12:12; Heb 2:4 **4:53** [v]S Ac 11:14 **4:54** [w]S ver 48; S Jn 2:11 **5:2** [x]Ne 3:1; 12:39 [y]Jn 19:13,17,20; 20:16; Ac 21:40; 22:2; 26:14 **5:8** [z]Mt 9:5,6 **5:9** [a]Mt 12:1-14; Jn 9:14 **5:10** [b]ver 16 [c]Ne 13:15-22; Jer 17:21; S Mt 12:2

[a] 2 Some manuscripts *Bethzatha*; other manuscripts *Bethsaida* [b] 3 Some manuscripts *paralyzed — and they waited for the moving of the waters. 4From time to time an angel of the Lord would come down and stir up the waters. The first one into the pool after each such disturbance would be cured of whatever disease he had.*

could save them, but only a miracle worker who could amaze them. *all that he had done.* See 20:30 and note. *Passover Feast.* The one narrated in 2:13 – 25.

4:46 *royal official.* Evidently an officer in Herod's service.

4:48 *Unless you … see … signs and wonders … you will never believe.* The general attitude of Galileans, not that of the official.

4:50 *Your son will live.* Not simply a prophecy, but words of power. Jesus was healing, not forecasting a happy ending (see vv. 51,53).

4:52 *seventh hour.* 1:00 P.M.

4:53 *believed.* Cf. the aim of this Gospel (see 20:31 and note; see also Introduction: Purpose and Emphases).

4:54 *second miraculous sign.* This was the second time Jesus performed a sign after coming from Judea to Galilee (see 2:11 and note; see also chart, p. 1625).

5:1 *feast of the Jews.* Probably Passover, Pentecost, Tabernacles, or even Purim (see chart, pp. 178 – 179). The identity of this feast is significant for the attempt to ascertain the number of Passovers included in Jesus' ministry, and thus the number of years his ministry lasted. John explicitly mentions at least three different Passovers: the first in 2:13,23 (see note on 2:13), the second in 6:4 and the third several times (e.g., in 11:55; 12:1), suggesting a public ministry lasting between two and three years. However, if the feast of 5:1 was a fourth Passover or assumes that a fourth Passover had come and gone, Jesus' ministry would have lasted between three and four years.

5:2 *there is.* Use of the present tense may mean that the pool was still in existence and that John wrote his Gospel before the destruction of Jerusalem. However, see Introduction: Date. *Bethesda.* The manuscripts have a variety of names (see NIV text note), but one of the Dead Sea Scrolls seems to show that Bethesda is the right name. The site is generally identified with the twin pools near the present-day Saint Anne's Church. There would have been a colonnade on each of the four sides and another between the two pools.

5:6 *Do you want to get well?* The man had not asked Jesus for help.

5:7 *when the water is stirred.* The man did not see Jesus as a potential healer, and his mind was set on the supposed curative powers of the water.

5:9 *the man was cured.* Ordinarily, faith in Jesus was essential to the cure (e.g., Mk 5:34), but here the man did not even know who Jesus was (v. 13). So while Jesus usually healed in response to faith, he was not limited by a person's lack of it.

5:10 *the law forbids you to carry your mat.* It was not the law of Moses itself but their traditional interpretation of it that prohibited carrying loads of any kind on the Sabbath. The Jews had very strict regulations on keeping the Sabbath, but also had many curious loopholes that their lawyers made full use of (cf. Mt 23:4). It is always lawful to do good and to save life — including on the Sabbath (see v. 17; 7:23; Mk 2:25; Lk 6:9; 13:15; 14:5 and notes).

5:12 *this fellow.* The Jews were contrasting the authority of the law of God, which in their view prohibited the action, and that of a mere man (as they considered Jesus to be) who permitted it.

14 Later Jesus found him at the temple and said to him, "See, you are well again. Stop sinning[d] or something worse may happen to you." 15 The man went away and told the Jews[e] that it was Jesus who had made him well.

Life Through the Son

16 So, because Jesus was doing these things on the Sabbath, the Jews persecuted him. 17 Jesus said to them, "My Father[f] is always at his work[g] to this very day, and I, too, am working." 18 For this reason the Jews tried all the harder to kill him;[h] not only was he breaking the Sabbath, but he was even calling God his own Father, making himself equal with God.[i]

19 Jesus gave them this answer: "I tell you the truth, the Son can do nothing by himself;[j] he can do only what he sees his Father doing, because whatever the Father does the Son also does. 20 For the Father loves the Son[k] and shows him all he does. Yes, to your amazement he will show him even greater things than these.[l] 21 For just as the Father raises the dead and gives them life,[m] even so the Son gives life[n] to whom he is pleased to give it. 22 Moreover, the Father judges no one, but has entrusted all judgment to the Son,[o] 23 that all may honor the Son just as they honor the Father. He who does not honor the Son does not honor the Father, who sent him.[p]

24 "I tell you the truth, whoever hears my word and believes him who sent me[q] has eternal life[r] and will not be condemned;[s] he has crossed over from death to life.[t] 25 I tell you the truth, a time is coming and has now come[u] when the dead will hear[v] the voice of the Son of God and those who hear will live. 26 For as the Father has life in himself, so he has granted the Son to have life[w] in himself. 27 And he has given him authority to judge[x] because he is the Son of Man.

28 "Do not be amazed at this, for a time is coming[y] when all who are in their graves will hear his voice 29 and come out—those who have done good will rise to live, and those who have done evil will rise to be condemned.[z] 30 By myself I can do nothing;[a] I judge only as I hear, and my judgment is just,[b] for I seek not to please myself but him who sent me.[c]

5:14 [d] Mk 2:5; Jn 8:11 **5:15** [e] S Jn 1:19 **5:17** [f] Lk 2:49 [g] Jn 9:4; 14:10 **5:18** [h] S Mt 12:14 [i] Jn 10:30,33; 19:7 **5:19** [j] ver 30; S Jn 14:24 **5:20** [k] Jn 3:35 [l] Jn 14:12 **5:21** [m] Ro 4:17; 8:11; 2Co 1:9; Heb 11:19 [n] Jn 11:25 **5:22** [o] ver 27; Ge 18:25; Jdg 11:27; Jn 9:39; S Ac 10:42 **5:23** [p] Lk 10:16; S 1Jn 2:23 **5:24** [q] S Mt 10:40; S Jn 3:15; S 3:17 [r] S Mt 25:46 [s] Jn 3:18 [t] 1Jn 3:14 **5:25** [u] Jn 4:23; 16:32 [v] Jn 8:43,47 **5:26** [w] Dt 30:20; Job 10:12; 33:4; Ps 36:9; S Jn 1:4 **5:27** [x] S ver 22 **5:28** [y] Jn 4:21; 16:2 **5:29** [z] S Mt 25:46 **5:30** [a] ver 19 [b] Isa 28:6; Jn 8:16 [c] S Mt 26:39

5:14 *Stop sinning.* Implies that the man's sins had caused his disability. In 9:1 Jesus repudiates the idea that disabilities (such as blindness there) are inevitably caused by sin, but he does not say they are never caused by sin. *something worse.* The eternal consequences of sin are more serious than any physical ailment.

5:16 *was doing.* The continuous action points to more than one incident, and the Jews (see note on 1:19) apparently discerned a pattern. *persecuted.* John does not tell us what form the persecution took.

5:17 *My Father is always at his work.* Jesus' justification for his action was his close relation to his Father. The Jews did not refer to God as "My Father," regarding the term as too intimate—though they might have used "Our Father" or, in prayer, "My Father in heaven." (But see the many OT names that begin with Abi-["my Father"], such as Abijah ["Yahweh is my Father"], Abiram ["The Exalted One is my Father"], Abinadab ["my Father is noble"], etc. See also Dt 32:6; Isa 63:16; 64:8; Jer 3:4,19; Mal 2:10; cf. 2Sa 7:14; Ps 89:21; Jer 3:4 and note.) Jesus also exemplified the way the Sabbath should be observed. God does not stop his deeds of compassion on that day and neither did Jesus.

5:18 *his own Father.* Referring to a special relationship. The Jews did not object to the idea that God is the Father of all, but they strongly objected to Jesus' claim that he stood in a special relationship to the Father—a relationship so close as to make himself equal with God.

5:19 *can do nothing by himself.* Because of who and what he was, it was not possible for Jesus to act except in dependence on the Father (see 4:34 and note).

5:20 *the Father loves the Son.* Therefore the Father revealed to the Son his plans and purposes, and the Son obediently carried them out (see 17:4). *greater things.* The Son's activities in raising the dead and judging (see following verses).

5:21 *the Father raises the dead.* A firm belief among the Jews (except the Sadducees; see p. 1453). They also held that he did not give this privilege to anyone else. Jesus claimed a prerogative that, according to his opponents, belonged only to God. *the Son gives life.* Probably refers to Christ's gift of abundant life here and now (10:10), though possibly also to the future resurrection (see 11:25 and note).

5:22 *entrusted all judgment to the Son.* The Jews believed that the Father is Judge of the world, so this teaching seemed heretical to them. For other NT assertions that Jesus will be the eschatological Judge, see Mt 25:31–33; Ac 10:42; 17:31; 2Co 5:10; 2Ti 4:1; 1Pe 4:5 and note.

5:24 *believes him … has eternal life.* Faith and life are connected (see 20:31 and note). *has eternal life.* A present possession (see notes on 3:15,36). *has crossed.* The decisive action has taken place, and the believer no longer belongs to the realm where death reigns supreme but to the realm of life.

5:25 *is coming and has now come.* A reference not only to the future resurrection but also to the fact that Christ gives life now. The spiritually dead who hear him receive life from him.

5:26 *has life in himself.* Must be understood against the background of the OT, where life is spoken of as belonging to God and as being his gift (see Dt 30:20 and note; Job 10:12; 33:4; Ps 16:11; 27:1; 36:9 and note). The Son has been given the same kind of life the Father possesses.

5:27 *authority to judge.* Granted to the Son by the Father (see v. 22 and note). *Son of Man.* See note on 1:51.

5:28–29 See Da 12:2 and note.

5:29 *done good … live … done evil … condemned.* As always in Scripture, judgment is based on what people have done in their lives (see Ro 2:6–8; Rev 20:12 and notes). Salvation, of course, is a gift from God in response to faith (see v. 24 and note), but true faith in Christ results in changed lives, lived in obedience to Christ as Lord (see Ro 10:9–10; Jas 2:14–26 and notes).

5:30 *By myself I can do nothing.* Jesus stresses his dependence on the Father (see note on v. 19). He judges only as he hears from the Father, which makes his judgment fair.

Testimonies About Jesus

31"If I testify about myself, my testimony is not valid.[d] 32There is another who testifies in my favor,[e] and I know that his testimony about me is valid.

33"You have sent to John and he has testified[f] to the truth. 34Not that I accept human testimony;[g] but I mention it that you may be saved.[h] 35John was a lamp that burned and gave light,[i] and you chose for a time to enjoy his light.

36"I have testimony weightier than that of John.[j] For the very work that the Father has given me to finish, and which I am doing,[k] testifies that the Father has sent me.[l] 37And the Father who sent me has himself testified concerning me.[m] You have never heard his voice nor seen his form,[n] 38nor does his word dwell in you,[o] for you do not believe[p] the one he sent.[q] 39You diligently study[a] the Scriptures[r] because you think that by them you possess eternal life.[s] These are the Scriptures that testify about me,[t] 40yet you refuse to come to me[u] to have life.

41"I do not accept praise from men,[v] 42but I know you. I know that you do not have the love of God in your hearts. 43I have come in my Father's name, and you do not accept me; but if someone else comes in his own name, you will accept him. 44How can you believe if you accept praise from one another, yet make no effort to obtain the praise that comes from the only God[b]?[w]

45"But do not think I will accuse you before the Father. Your accuser is Moses,[x] on whom your hopes are set.[y] 46If you believed Moses, you would believe me, for he wrote about me.[z] 47But since you do not believe what he wrote, how are you going to believe what I say?"[a]

Jesus Feeds the Five Thousand

6:1-13pp — Mt 14:13-21; Mk 6:32-44; Lk 9:10-17

6 Some time after this, Jesus crossed to the far shore of the Sea of Galilee (that is, the Sea of Tiberias), 2and a great crowd of people followed him because they saw the miraculous signs[b] he had performed on the sick. 3Then Jesus went up on a mountainside[c] and sat down with his disciples. 4The Jewish Passover Feast[d] was near.

5:31 [d]Jn 8:14
5:32 [e]ver 37; Jn 8:18
5:33 [f]S Jn 1:7
5:34 [g]1Jn 5:9 [h]Ac 16:30,31; Eph 2:8; Tit 3:5
5:35 [i]Da 12:3; 2Pe 1:19
5:36 [j]1Jn 5:9 [k]Jn 14:11; 15:24 [l]S Jn 3:17
5:37 [m]Jn 8:18 [n]Dt 4:12; 1Ti 1:17; S Jn 1:18
5:38 [o]1Jn 1:10; 2:14 [p]Isa 26:10 [q]S Jn 3:17
5:39 [r]Ro 2:17,18 [s]S Mt 25:46 [t]S Lk 24:27,44; Ac 13:27
5:40 [u]Jn 6:44
5:41 [v]ver 44
5:44 [w]S Ro 2:29
5:45 [x]Jn 9:28 [y]Ro 2:17
5:46 [z]Ge 3:15; S Lk 24:27,44; Ac 26:22
5:47 [a]Lk 16:29,31
6:2 [b]S Jn 2:11
6:3 [c]ver 15
6:4 [d]S Jn 11:55

[a] 39 Or *Study diligently* (the imperative) [b] 44 Some early manuscripts *the Only One*

5:31–47 This section stresses the testimonies (see note on 1:7) of John the Baptist (v. 33), of the works of Jesus (v. 36), of God the Father (v. 37), of the Scriptures (v. 39) and of Moses (v. 46).

5:31 Jesus' testimony about himself required the support of all God's revelation. Otherwise, it would have been unacceptable.

5:32 *another.* The Father testifies concerning the Son. The Jews might not accept this testimony, but it was the testimony that mattered most.

5:33 *You have sent to John.* A reference to the delegation from the Jewish leaders to John the Baptist (see 1:19 and note). *he has testified.* The testimony of John was important, though not, of course, equal to the testimony of the Father. But if the Jews had believed John, they would have believed Christ and would have been saved.

5:34 *Not that I accept human testimony.* Probably meaning that he does not rely on human testimony—which is always fallible and often fickle (1Jn 5:9).

5:35 *John was.* The past tense may indicate that John was dead or at least imprisoned. In any case, his work was done. *burned and gave light.* John's giving light was costly to him. *for a time.* The Jewish leaders never came to grips with John's message, and their responses to him were always at best tentative and superficial.

5:36 *work.* The miracles of Jesus, which testified to what he is and to his divine mission (see 10:25 and note).

5:37 *the Father … has himself testified … his voice.* Probably a reference to God's voice in the Scriptures (see vv. 38–39). God had also given his voice of approval at Jesus' baptism (see Mt 3:17 and note). *nor seen his form.* Probably refers to their lack of spiritual perception of who Jesus really is.

5:38 *you do not believe.* The Jews did not recognize what God was saying, as their failure to believe Jesus shows.

5:39 *You diligently study.* The Jewish leaders studied Scripture in minute detail. Despite their reverence for the very letter of Scripture (see notes on Mt 5:18–21), they did not recognize the one to whom Scripture bears supreme testimony.

5:41 *praise from men.* Jesus did not accept the kind of human praise that his opponents prized (v. 44).

5:42 *love of God.* May mean God's love for them or theirs for God. Probably it is the latter.

5:43–44 The Jews whom Jesus was addressing had their attention firmly fixed on people. Their emphasis on self-seeking and on human praise showed that they did not accept the one who came from God, and therefore they missed the praise that comes from God.

5:43 *if someone else … you will accept him.* See note on Zec 11:17.

5:45–47 The revelation God gave Moses is inseparable from the revelation God was giving through Jesus (see Lk 16:31; Ro 10:4 and note). Those who refused to believe the witness to Jesus in the earlier revelation would also reject the later revelation coming through Jesus. To their surprise, he declared that his listeners had refused to believe both and should therefore be accused before God by Moses.

5:46 *he wrote about me.* The authors of the NT books sometimes expressly stressed and everywhere assumed that the OT, rightly read, pervasively points to Christ (see Lk 24:25–27,44 and note). Here Jesus applies this truth specifically to the writings traditionally ascribed to Moses. He may have had Dt 18:15,18 especially in mind but probably was thinking more broadly of the whole scope of what the Pentateuch disclosed concerning God's saving program in history, which Jesus the Messiah came to complete.

6:1–15 The feeding of the 5,000 is the one miracle, apart from the resurrection, found in all four Gospels. It shows Jesus as the supplier of human need and also sets the stage for his testimony that he is the bread of life (v. 35).

6:1 *far shore.* The northeast shore, probably near Bethsaida (see Lk 9:10 and map, p. 1635). *Sea of Tiberias.* Probably the official Roman name of the Sea of Galilee (see note on Mk 1:16). The name came from the town of Tiberias (named after the emperor Tiberius), founded c. A.D. 20 (see map, p. 1635).

6:2 *miraculous signs.* See note on 2:11.

6:4 *Passover.* See notes on 2:13; 5:1.

5When Jesus looked up and saw a great crowd coming toward him, he said to Philip,[e] "Where shall we buy bread for these people to eat?" 6He asked this only to test him, for he already had in mind what he was going to do.

7Philip answered him, "Eight months' wages[a] would not buy enough bread for each one to have a bite!"

8Another of his disciples, Andrew, Simon Peter's brother,[f] spoke up, 9"Here is a boy with five small barley loaves and two small fish, but how far will they go among so many?"[g]

10Jesus said, "Have the people sit down." There was plenty of grass in that place, and the men sat down, about five thousand of them. 11Jesus then took the loaves, gave thanks,[h] and distributed to those who were seated as much as they wanted. He did the same with the fish.

12When they had all had enough to eat, he said to his disciples, "Gather the pieces that are left over. Let nothing be wasted." 13So they gathered them and filled twelve baskets with the pieces of the five barley loaves left over by those who had eaten.

14After the people saw the miraculous sign[i] that Jesus did, they began to say, "Surely this is the Prophet who is to come into the world."[j] 15Jesus, knowing that they intended to come and make him king[k] by force, withdrew again to a mountain by himself.[l]

Jesus Walks on the Water

6:16-21pp — Mt 14:22-33; Mk 6:47-51

16When evening came, his disciples went down to the lake, 17where they got into a boat and set off across the lake for Capernaum. By now it was dark, and Jesus had not yet joined them. 18A strong wind was blowing and the waters grew rough. 19When they had rowed three or three and a half miles,[b] they saw Jesus approaching the boat, walking on the water;[m] and they were terrified. 20But he said to them, "It is I; don't be afraid."[n] 21Then they were willing to take him into the boat, and immediately the boat reached the shore where they were heading.

22The next day the crowd that had stayed on the opposite shore of the lake[o] realized that only one boat had been there, and that Jesus had not entered it with his disciples, but that they had gone away alone.[p] 23Then some boats from Tiberias[q] landed near the place where the people had eaten the bread after the Lord had given thanks.[r] 24Once the crowd realized that neither Jesus nor his disciples were there, they got into the boats and went to Capernaum in search of Jesus.

Jesus the Bread of Life

25When they found him on the other side of the lake, they asked him, "Rabbi,[s] when did you get here?"

26Jesus answered, "I tell you the truth, you are looking for me,[t] not because you saw miraculous signs[u] but because you ate the loaves and had your fill. 27Do not work for food that spoils, but for food that endures[v] to eternal life,[w] which the Son of Man[x] will give you. On him God the Father has placed his seal[y] of approval."

28Then they asked him, "What must we do to do the works God requires?"

29Jesus answered, "The work of God is this: to believe[z] in the one he has sent."[a]

30So they asked him, "What miraculous sign[b] then will you give that we may see it and believe you?[c] What will you do? 31Our forefathers ate the manna[d] in the desert;

6:5 [e] S Jn 1:43 **6:8** [f] Jn 1:40 **6:9** [g] 2Ki 4:43 **6:11** [h] ver 23; S Mt 14:19 **6:14** [i] S Jn 2:11 [j] Dt 18:15,18; Mt 11:3; S 21:11 **6:15** [k] Jn 18:36 [l] Mt 14:23; Mk 6:46

6:19 [m] Job 9:8 **6:20** [n] S Mt 14:27 **6:22** [o] ver 2 [p] ver 15-21 **6:23** [q] ver 1 [r] ver 11 **6:25** [s] S Mt 23:7 **6:26** [t] ver 24 [u] ver 30; S Jn 2:11 **6:27** [v] Isa 55:2 [w] ver 54; S Mt 25:46 [x] S Mt 8:20 [y] Ro 4:11; 1Co 9:2; 2Co 1:22; Eph 1:13; 4:30; 2Ti 2:19; Rev 7:3 **6:29** [z] 1Jn 3:23 [a] S Jn 3:17 **6:30** [b] S Jn 2:11 [c] S Mt 12:38 **6:31** [d] Nu 11:7-9

[a] 7 Greek *two hundred denarii* [b] 19 Greek *rowed twenty-five or thirty stadia* (about 5 or 6 kilometers)

6:5 *Philip.* Since he came from nearby Bethsaida (see 1:44 and note), it was appropriate to ask him.

6:9 *barley loaves.* Cheap bread, the food of the poor.

6:10 *about five thousand.* The number of men; women and children were not included (see Mt 14:21 and note).

6:12 *Gather the pieces.* See note on Mk 6:43.

6:13 *twelve baskets … left over.* There was abundant supply (see note on Mk 6:43).

6:14 *sign … Prophet.* It pointed people to the Son of Man and the food for eternal life that he gives (see v. 27 and note), but they thought only of the Prophet, i.e., the prophet of Dt 18:15,18 who would be like Moses (see 1:21 and note). Through Moses, God had provided food and water for the people in the desert, and they expected the Prophet to do more than this.

6:15 *make him king by force.* Jesus rejected the widely held Jewish view of the Messiah's kingship (cf. notes on 18:36; Lk 24:21).

6:19 *three or three and a half miles.* Mark says they were "in the middle of the lake" (Mk 6:47). *terrified.* They thought they were seeing a ghost (Mt 14:26).

6:21 *immediately the boat reached the shore.* Some think that this was another miracle. In any event, the boat's safe arrival is implicitly credited to Jesus.

6:22–24 The crowd could not figure out what had happened to Jesus. But they wanted to see him again, so they looked for him in the most likely place, Capernaum (see map, p. 1635 and note on 2:12).

6:27 *eternal life.* Not something to be achieved but to be received by faith in Christ (see vv. 28–29; 3:15 and notes). *Son of Man.* See note on Mk 8:31. Submission of the Son to the Father is one of John's major themes (see note on 4:34).

6:28 *What must we do …?* They missed the point that eternal life is Christ's gift and were thinking in terms of achieving it by pious works (see Eph 2:8–9; Tit 3:5 and notes).

6:29 *work of God.* Believing in Jesus Christ is the indispensable "work" God calls for—the one that leads to eternal life (see 9:4 and note).

6:30 *What will you do?* They seek from Jesus a sign greater than the gift of manna that had accompanied Moses' ministry.

6:31 *manna.* A popular Jewish expectation was that when the Messiah came he would renew the sending of manna.

as it is written: 'He gave them bread from
heaven to eat.'[a]"[e]
32Jesus said to them, "I tell you the
truth, it is not Moses who has given you
the bread from heaven, but it is my Father who gives you the true bread from
heaven. 33For the bread of God is he who
comes down from heaven[f] and gives life
to the world."
34"Sir," they said, "from now on give us
this bread."[g]
35Then Jesus declared, "I am[h] the bread
of life.[i] He who comes to me will never go
hungry, and he who believes[j] in me will
never be thirsty.[k] 36But as I told you, you
have seen me and still you do not believe.
37All that the Father gives me[l] will come
to me, and whoever comes to me I will
never drive away. 38For I have come down
from heaven[m] not to do my will but to do

6:31 [e]Ex 16:4, 15; Ne 9:15; Ps 78:24; 105:40
6:33 [f]ver 50; Jn 3:13,31
6:34 [g]Jn 4:15
6:35 [h]Ex 3:14; Jn 8:12; 10:7,11; 11:25; 14:6; 15:1 [i]ver 48,51 [j]S Jn 3:15 [k]Jn 4:14
6:37 [l]ver 39; Jn 17:2,6,9,24
6:38 [m]Jn 3:13,31

[a] *31* Exodus 16:4; Neh. 9:15; Psalm 78:24,25

The crowd probably reasoned that Jesus had done little compared to Moses. He had fed 5,000; Moses had fed a nation. He did it once; Moses did it for 40 years. He gave ordinary bread (see note on vv. 1–15; see also note on v. 14); Moses gave "bread from heaven" (see notes on Ex 16:4; Nu 11:7).

6:32 Jesus corrected them, pointing out that the manna in the desert did not come from Moses but from God, and that the Father still "gives" (the present tense is important) the true bread from heaven (life through the Son).

6:33 *bread of God.* Jesus moved the discussion to something (and Someone) much more important than manna. *he who comes down from heaven.* This affirmation is repeated six times in this context (here and in vv. 38,41,50–51,58), emphasizing Jesus' divine origin.

6:34 *this bread.* Probably another misunderstanding, like that by the woman at the well (see 4:15 and note; cf. also Nicodemus, 3:4). Their minds ran along materialistic lines.

6:35 *I am.* The first of seven self-descriptions of Jesus introduced by "I am" (see 8:12; [9:5;] 10:7,9; 10:11,14; 11:25; 14:6; 15:1,5). In the Greek the words are solemnly emphatic and echo Ex 3:14 (see notes on Ex 3:12–15). *the bread of life.* May mean "the bread that is living" and/or "the bread that gives life." What is implied in v. 33 is now made explicit and repeated with minor variations in vv. 41,48,51.

6:36 Contrast 20:29.

6:37 God's action (see v. 44; 10:29; 17:6; 18:9 and notes), not ours (see v. 28 and note), is primary in salvation, and Christ's mercy is unfailing (see vv. 31–40; 10:28; 17:9,12 and note, 15,19 and note; 18:9).

6:38 *to do the will of him who sent me.* See note on 4:34.

Jesus in Galilee

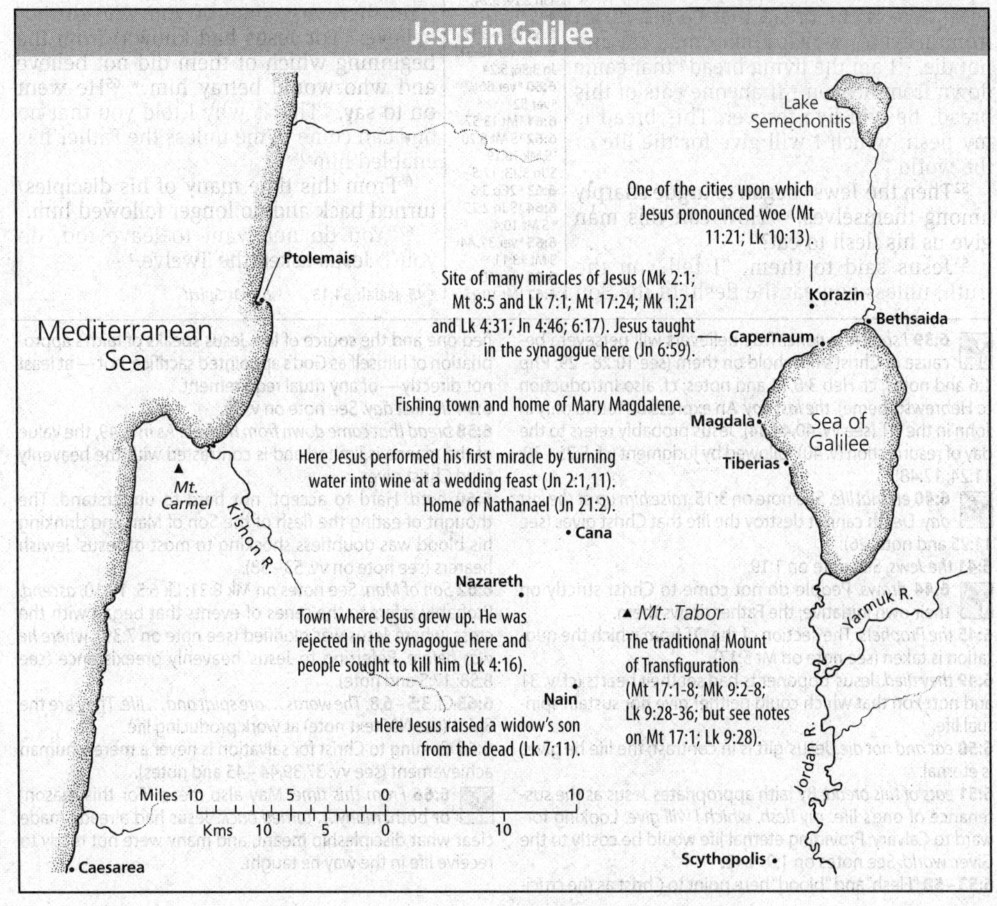

Lake Semechonitis
One of the cities upon which Jesus pronounced woe (Mt 11:21; Lk 10:13).
Ptolemais
Site of many miracles of Jesus (Mk 2:1; Mt 8:5 and Lk 7:1; Mt 17:24; Mk 1:21 and Lk 4:31; Jn 4:46; 6:17). Jesus taught in the synagogue here (Jn 6:59).
Korazin
Bethsaida
Capernaum
Mediterranean Sea
Fishing town and home of Mary Magdalene.
Magdala
Sea of Galilee
Tiberias
Here Jesus performed his first miracle by turning water into wine at a wedding feast (Jn 2:1,11). Home of Nathanael (Jn 21:2).
Mt. Carmel
Kishon R.
Cana
Nazareth
Town where Jesus grew up. He was rejected in the synagogue here and people sought to kill him (Lk 4:16).
Mt. Tabor
The traditional Mount of Transfiguration (Mt 17:1-8; Mk 9:2-8; Lk 9:28-36; but see notes on Mt 17:1; Lk 9:28).
Yarmuk R.
Nain
Here Jesus raised a widow's son from the dead (Lk 7:11).
Jordan R.
Miles 10 5 0 10
Kms 10 5 0 10
Caesarea
Scythopolis

the will[n] of him who sent me.[o] 39And this
is the will of him who sent me, that I shall
lose none of all that he has given me,[p] but
raise them up at the last day.[q] 40For my
Father's will is that everyone who looks
to the Son[r] and believes in him shall have
eternal life,[s] and I will raise him up at the
last day."

41At this the Jews began to grumble
about him because he said, "I am the
bread that came down from heaven."
42They said, "Is this not Jesus, the son
of Joseph,[t] whose father and mother we
know?[u] How can he now say, 'I came
down from heaven'?"[v]

43"Stop grumbling among yourselves,"
Jesus answered. 44"No one can come to
me unless the Father who sent me draws
him,[w] and I will raise him up at the last
day. 45It is written in the Prophets: 'They
will all be taught by God.'[a][x] Everyone who
listens to the Father and learns from him
comes to me. 46No one has seen the Father
except the one who is from God;[y] only he
has seen the Father. 47I tell you the truth,
he who believes has everlasting life.[z] 48I
am the bread of life.[a] 49Your forefathers ate
the manna in the desert, yet they died.[b]
50But here is the bread that comes down
from heaven,[c] which a man may eat and
not die. 51I am the living bread[d] that came
down from heaven.[e] If anyone eats of this
bread, he will live forever. This bread is
my flesh, which I will give for the life of
the world."[f]

52Then the Jews[g] began to argue sharply
among themselves,[h] "How can this man
give us his flesh to eat?"

53Jesus said to them, "I tell you the
truth, unless you eat the flesh[i] of the Son
of Man[j] and drink his blood,[k] you have
no life in you. 54Whoever eats my flesh
and drinks my blood has eternal life, and
I will raise him up at the last day.[l] 55For
my flesh is real food and my blood is
real drink. 56Whoever eats my flesh and
drinks my blood remains in me, and I in
him.[m] 57Just as the living Father sent me[n]
and I live because of the Father, so the
one who feeds on me will live because of
me. 58This is the bread that came down
from heaven. Your forefathers ate manna and died, but he who feeds on this
bread will live forever."[o] 59He said this
while teaching in the synagogue in Capernaum.

Many Disciples Desert Jesus

60On hearing it, many of his disciples[p]
said, "This is a hard teaching. Who can
accept it?"[q]

61Aware that his disciples were grumbling about this, Jesus said to them,
"Does this offend you?[r] 62What if you see
the Son of Man[s] ascend to where he was
before![t] 63The Spirit gives life;[u] the flesh
counts for nothing. The words I have spoken to you are spirit[b] and they are life.
64Yet there are some of you who do not
believe." For Jesus had known[v] from the
beginning which of them did not believe
and who would betray him.[w] 65He went
on to say, "This is why I told you that no
one can come to me unless the Father has
enabled him."[x]

66From this time many of his disciples[y]
turned back and no longer followed him.

67"You do not want to leave too, do
you?" Jesus asked the Twelve.[z]

6:38 [n]S Mt 26:39 [o]S Jn 3:17 **6:39** [p]Isa 27:3; Jer 23:4; Jn 10:28; 17:12; 18:9 [q]ver 40,44,54 **6:40** [r]Jn 12:45 [s]S Mt 25:46 **6:42** [t]Lk 4:22 [u]Jn 7:27,28 [v]ver 38,62 **6:44** [w]ver 65; Jer 31:3; Jn 12:32 **6:45** [x]Isa 54:13; Jer 31:33,34; 1Co 2:13; 1Th 4:9; Heb 8:10,11; 10:16; 1Jn 2:27 **6:46** [y]S Jn 1:18; 5:37; 7:29 **6:47** [z]S Mt 25:46 **6:48** [a]ver 35,51 **6:49** [b]ver 31,58 **6:50** [c]ver 33 **6:51** [d]ver 35,48 [e]ver 41,58 [f]Heb 10:10 **6:52** [g]S Jn 1:19 [h]Jn 7:43; 9:16; 10:19 **6:53** [i]Mt 26:26 [j]S Mt 8:20 [k]Mt 26:28 **6:54** [l]ver 39 **6:56** [m]Jn 15:4-7; 1Jn 2:24; 3:24; 4:15 **6:57** [n]S Jn 3:17 **6:58** [o]ver 49-51; Jn 3:36; 5:24 **6:60** [p]ver 66 [q]ver 52 **6:61** [r]Mt 13:57 **6:62** [s]S Mt 8:20 [t]S Mk 16:19; S Jn 3:13; 17:5 **6:63** [u]2Co 3:6 **6:64** [v]S Jn 2:25 [w]S Mt 10:4 **6:65** [x]ver 37,44; S Mt 13:11 **6:66** [y]ver 60 **6:67** [z]Mt 10:2

[a] *45* Isaiah 54:13 [b] *63* Or *Spirit*

6:39 *I shall lose none.* True believers will persevere because of Christ's firm hold on them (see 10:28–29; Php 1:6 and notes; cf. Heb 3:6,14 and notes; cf. also Introduction to Hebrews: Theme). *the last day.* An expression found only in John in the NT (see vv. 40,44,54). Jesus probably refers to the day of resurrection (v. 40) followed by judgment (cf. 5:25–30; 11:24; 12:48).

6:40 *eternal life.* See note on 3:15. *raise him up at the last day.* Death cannot destroy the life that Christ gives (see 11:25 and note, 26).

6:41 *the Jews.* See note on 1:19.

6:44 *draws.* People do not come to Christ strictly on their own initiative; the Father draws them.

6:45 *the Prophets.* The section of the OT from which the quotation is taken (see note on Mt 5:17).

6:49 *they died.* Jesus' opponents had set their hearts (cf. v. 31 and note) on that which could neither give nor sustain spiritual life.

6:50 *eat and not die.* Jesus' gift is in contrast; the life he gives is eternal.

6:51 *eats of this bread.* By faith appropriates Jesus as the sustenance of one's life. *my flesh, which I will give.* Looking forward to Calvary. Providing eternal life would be costly to the Giver. *world.* See notes on 1:9; 4:42.

6:53–58 "Flesh" and "blood" here point to Christ as the crucified one and the source of life. Jesus speaks of faith's appropriation of himself as God's appointed sacrifice, not—at least not directly—of any ritual requirement.

6:54 *the last day.* See note on v. 39.

6:58 *bread that came down from heaven.* As in v. 49, the value of the manna is limited and is contrasted with the heavenly food Christ gives.

6:60 *hard.* Hard to accept, not hard to understand. The thought of eating the flesh of the Son of Man and drinking his blood was doubtless shocking to most of Jesus' Jewish hearers (see note on vv. 53–58).

6:62 *Son of Man.* See notes on Mk 8:31; Lk 6:5; 19:10. *ascend.* Probably refers to the series of events that began with the cross, where Jesus was glorified (see note on 7:39). *where he was before.* Referring to Jesus' heavenly preexistence (see 8:58; 17:5 and note).

6:63 Cf. 3:5–6,8. *The words ... are spirit and ... life.* They are the Spirit (see NIV text note) at work producing life.

6:65 Coming to Christ for salvation is never a merely human achievement (see vv. 37,39,44–45 and notes).

6:66 *From this time.* May also mean "For this reason" or both. *many ... turned back.* Jesus had already made clear what discipleship meant, and many were not ready to receive life in the way he taught.

68 Simon Peter answered him,[a] "Lord, to whom shall we go? You have the words of eternal life.[b] 69 We believe and know that you are the Holy One of God."[c]

70 Then Jesus replied, "Have I not chosen you,[d] the Twelve? Yet one of you is a devil!"[e] 71 (He meant Judas, the son of Simon Iscariot,[f] who, though one of the Twelve, was later to betray him.)[g]

Jesus Goes to the Feast of Tabernacles

7 After this, Jesus went around in Galilee, purposely staying away from Judea because the Jews[h] there were waiting to take his life.[i] 2 But when the Jewish Feast of Tabernacles[j] was near, 3 Jesus' brothers[k] said to him, "You ought to leave here and go to Judea, so that your disciples may see the miracles you do. 4 No one who wants to become a public figure acts in secret. Since you are doing these things, show yourself to the world." 5 For even his own brothers did not believe in him.[l]

6 Therefore Jesus told them, "The right time[m] for me has not yet come; for you any time is right. 7 The world cannot hate you, but it hates me[n] because I testify that what it does is evil.[o] 8 You go to the Feast. I am not yet[a] going up to this Feast, because for me the right time[p] has not yet come." 9 Having said this, he stayed in Galilee.

10 However, after his brothers had left for the Feast, he went also, not publicly, but in secret. 11 Now at the Feast the Jews were watching for him[q] and asking, "Where is that man?"

12 Among the crowds there was widespread whispering about him. Some said, "He is a good man."

Others replied, "No, he deceives the people."[r] 13 But no one would say anything publicly about him for fear of the Jews.[s]

Jesus Teaches at the Feast

14 Not until halfway through the Feast did Jesus go up to the temple courts and begin to teach.[t] 15 The Jews[u] were amazed and asked, "How did this man get such learning[v] without having studied?"[w]

16 Jesus answered, "My teaching is not my own. It comes from him who sent me.[x] 17 If anyone chooses to do God's will, he will find out[y] whether my teaching comes from God or whether I speak on my own. 18 He who speaks on his own does so to gain honor for himself,[z] but he who works for the honor of the one who sent him is a man of truth; there is nothing false about him.

[a] 8 Some early manuscripts do not have *yet*.

6:68 [a] Mt 16:16 [b] ver 63; S Mt 25:46 **6:69** [c] S Mk 1:24; 8:29; Lk 9:20 **6:70** [d] Jn 15:16,19 [e] Jn 13:27; 17:12 **6:71** [f] S Mt 26:14 [g] S Mt 10:4 **7:1** [h] S Jn 1:19 [i] ver 19,25; S Mt 12:14 **7:2** [j] Lev 23:34; Dt 16:16 **7:3** [k] S Mt 12:46 **7:5** [l] Ps 69:8; Mk 3:21 **7:6** [m] S Mt 26:18 **7:7** [n] Jn 15:18,19 [o] Jn 3:19,20 **7:8** [p] ver 6; S Mt 26:18 **7:11** [q] Jn 11:56 **7:12** [r] ver 40,43 **7:13** [s] Jn 9:22; 12:42; 19:38; 20:19 **7:14** [t] ver 28; S Mt 26:55 **7:15** [u] S Jn 1:19 [v] Ac 26:24 [w] Mt 13:54 **7:16** [x] S Jn 14:24 **7:17** [y] Ps 25:14 **7:18** [z] Jn 5:41; 8:50,54

6:68 As in the other Gospels, Peter acts as spokesman. *words of eternal life.* The expression is general. Peter was not speaking of a formula but of the thrust of Jesus' teaching. He perceived the truth of v. 63 (see note there).

6:69 *We believe and know.* Since the Greek verbs are in the perfect tense, they mean, "We have entered a state of belief and knowledge that has continued until the present time." *Holy One of God.* Applied to Jesus in Mk 1:24 (see note there); Lk 4:34 (cf. Ac 2:27).

6:70 *a devil.* Judas (v. 71) would oppose Christ in the spirit of Satan.

6:71 *Iscariot.* Means "man from Kerioth" (in Judea; see Jos 15:25) and would apply equally to the father and the son (cf. 12:4). Judas seems to have been the only non-Galilean among the Twelve. *one of the Twelve.* Therefore one of the last persons likely to betray Jesus.

7:1—8:59 In chs. 7–8 John records strong opposition to Jesus, including repeated references to threats on his life (7:1,13,19,25,30,32,44; 8:37,40,59). The apostle seems to have gathered the major arguments against the Messiahship of Jesus and here answers them.

7:1 *After this.* Since 6:4 refers to the Passover Feast and 7:2 to the Feast of Tabernacles, the interval was about six months.

7:2 *Feast of Tabernacles.* The great feast in the Jewish year, celebrating the completion of harvest and commemorating God's goodness to the people during the desert wanderings (see Lev 23:33–43; Dt 16:13–15; Zec 14:16 and note). The name came from the leafy shelters in which people lived throughout the seven days of the Feast.

7:3 *brothers.* See note on Lk 8:19.

7:4 It is not clear whether the brothers claimed some knowledge of Jesus' miracles that other people did not have or were suggesting that any claim to Messiahship must be decided in Jerusalem. Their advice was not given sincerely, for they did not yet believe in Jesus (v. 5).

7:6 *right time.* Jesus moved in accordance with the will of God (see notes on 2:4; Ro 5:6).

7:7 *The world.* Either (1) people opposed to God or (2) the human system opposed to God's purposes (see note on 1Jn 2:15). The brothers belonged to the world and therefore could not be the objects of its hatred. Jesus, however, rebuked the world and was hated accordingly.

7:8 *not yet.* See NIV text note. Jesus was not refusing to go to the Feast, but refusing to go in the way the brothers suggested—as a pilgrim. When he went, it would be to deliver a prophetic message from God, for which he awaited the "right time" (v. 6).

7:10 *not publicly.* Rejecting the brothers' suggestion to show himself (v. 4).

7:12 *whispering.* Because it was not safe to speak openly (cf. v. 13).

7:14 *halfway through the Feast.* When the crowds would be at their maximum. Teaching in the temple courts at such a time would reach many.

7:15 *The Jews.* Distinct from "the crowds" (v. 12), who were also Jews (see note on 1:19). *without having studied.* Under a rabbi. Jesus had never been the disciple of a recognized Jewish teacher (see Ac 4:13 and note).

7:16 *not my own.* The Father, from whom he came, had been his "rabbi" (see note on 4:34; "rabbi" means "[my] teacher").

7:17 *chooses to do God's will.* Reflecting a whole attitude of life. A person sincerely set on doing God's will welcomes Jesus' teaching and believes in him (see 6:29 and note). *he will find out.* Augustine commented, "Understanding is the reward of faith … What is 'If any man be willing to do his will'? It is the same thing as to believe."

7:18 *is a man of truth.* Or "is truthful." They should recognize that Jesus was not self-seeking. In this Gospel, no one is spoken of as being "truthful" except God the Father (see 3:33 and note; 7:28; 8:26 ["reliable"]; see 1:14 and note) and Jesus (here). Once more John ranks Jesus with God.

19Has not Moses given you the law?[a] Yet
not one of you keeps the law. Why are you
trying to kill me?"[b]
20"You are demon-possessed,"[c] the
crowd answered. "Who is trying to kill
you?"
21Jesus said to them, "I did one miracle,[d]
and you are all astonished. 22Yet, because
Moses gave you circumcision[e] (though
actually it did not come from Moses, but
from the patriarchs),[f] you circumcise a
child on the Sabbath. 23Now if a child can
be circumcised on the Sabbath so that the
law of Moses may not be broken, why are
you angry with me for healing the whole
man on the Sabbath? 24Stop judging by
mere appearances, and make a right judgment."[g]

Is Jesus the Christ?

25At that point some of the people of
Jerusalem began to ask, "Isn't this the
man they are trying to kill?[h] 26Here he is,
speaking publicly, and they are not saying
a word to him. Have the authorities[i] really
concluded that he is the Christ[a]?[j] 27But we
know where this man is from;[k] when the
Christ comes, no one will know where he
is from."
28Then Jesus, still teaching in the temple
courts,[l] cried out, "Yes, you know me, and
you know where I am from.[m] I am not here
on my own, but he who sent me is true.[n]
You do not know him, 29but I know him[o]
because I am from him and he sent me."[p]
30At this they tried to seize him, but
no one laid a hand on him,[q] because his
time had not yet come.[r] 31Still, many in the
crowd put their faith in him.[s] They said,
"When the Christ comes, will he do more
miraculous signs[t] than this man?"
32The Pharisees heard the crowd whispering such things about him. Then the
chief priests and the Pharisees sent temple
guards to arrest him.
33Jesus said, "I am with you for only a
short time,[u] and then I go to the one who
sent me.[v] 34You will look for me, but you
will not find me; and where I am, you cannot come."[w]
35The Jews said to one another, "Where
does this man intend to go that we cannot
find him? Will he go where our people live
scattered[x] among the Greeks,[y] and teach
the Greeks? 36What did he mean when he
said, 'You will look for me, but you will
not find me,' and 'Where I am, you cannot
come'?"[z]
37On the last and greatest day of the
Feast,[a] Jesus stood and said in a loud
voice, "If anyone is thirsty, let him come
to me and drink.[b] 38Whoever believes[c] in
me, as[b] the Scripture has said,[d] streams of
living water[e] will flow from within him."[f]

7:19 [a]Dt 32:46; Jn 1:17 [b]ver 1; S Mt 12:14
7:20 [c]S Mk 3:22
7:21 [d]ver 23; Jn 5:2-9
7:22 [e]Lev 12:3 [f]Ge 17:10-14
7:24 [g]1Sa 16:7; Isa 11:3,4; Jn 8:15; 2Co 10:7
7:25 [h]ver 1; S Mt 12:14
7:26 [i]ver 48 [j]Jn 4:29
7:27 [k]Mt 13:55; Lk 4:22; Jn 6:42
7:28 [l]ver 14 [m]Jn 8:14 [n]Jn 8:26,42
7:29 [o]S Mt 11:27 [p]S Jn 3:17
7:30 [q]ver 32,44; Jn 10:39 [r]S Mt 26:18
7:31 [s]Jn 8:30; 10:42; 11:45; 12:11,42 [t]S Jn 2:11
7:33 [u]Jn 12:35; 13:33; 16:16 [v]Jn 16:5,10, 17,28
7:34 [w]ver 36; Jn 8:21; 13:33
7:35 [x]S Jas 1:1 [y]Jn 12:20; Ac 17:4; 18:4
7:36 [z]ver 34
7:37 [a]Lev 23:36 [b]Isa 55:1; Rev 22:17
7:38 [c]S Jn 3:15 [d]Isa 58:11 [e]S Jn 4:10 [f]S Jn 4:14

[a] 26 Or *Messiah*; also in verses 27, 31, 41 and 42
[b] 37,38 Or / *If anyone is thirsty, let him come to me.* / *And let him drink,* 38*who believes in me.* / As

7:19 *the law.* The Jews congratulated themselves on being the chosen recipients of the law, but Jesus told them that they all broke the law of which they were so proud (cf. Ro 2:17–29).
7:20 *You are demon-possessed.* The accusation of demon possession is made elsewhere in John (e.g., 8:48–52; 10:20–21; cf. Mt 12:24–32; Mk 3:22–30). *crowd.* Probably the pilgrims who had come up to Jerusalem for the Feast—different from "the Jews" who were trying to kill Jesus (v. 1) and the Jerusalem mob that knew of the plot (see v. 25 and note).
7:21 *one miracle.* Evidently that of healing the lame man (5:1–9), as the discussion about the Sabbath shows.
7:22 *circumcision.* The requirement of circumcision was included in the law Moses gave (see Ex 12:44,48 and note; Lev 12:3), yet it did not originate with Moses but went back to Abraham (see Ge 17:10–12 and notes). The Jews took such regulations as that in Lev 12:3 to mean that circumcision must be performed on the eighth day even if it was the Sabbath. This exception is of critical importance in understanding the controversy (v. 23). Jesus was not saying that the Sabbath should not be observed or that the Jewish regulations were too harsh. He was saying that his opponents did not understand what the Sabbath meant. The command to circumcise showed that sometimes work not only *might* be done on the Sabbath but *must* be done then. Deeds of mercy were in this category (see notes on 5:10; Mk 2:25; 3:2).
7:25 *people of Jerusalem.* An expression found only here and in Mk 1:5 in the NT, probably referring to the Jerusalem mob (see note on v. 20). They did not originate the plot against Jesus, but they knew about it.
7:26 *the Christ.* See note on 1:25.
7:27 *no one will know where he is from.* Some Jews held that the OT gave the origin of the Messiah (cf. v. 42; Mt 2:4–6), but others believed that it did not.
7:28 *you know me.* Irony, because in a sense they knew Jesus and that he came from Nazareth, but in a deeper sense they did not know Jesus or the Father (see 8:19 and note). Jesus mentioned again his dependence on the Father (see 4:34 and note) and went on to declare that he had real knowledge of God and that they did not. Both his origin and mission were from God.
7:30 *they tried to seize him.* Jesus' enemies were powerless against him until his time came (see note on 2:4).
7:31 *crowd.* Of pilgrims (see note on v. 20). Many of them believed on the basis of the miraculous signs (cf. 6:26).
7:32 *Pharisees.* See note on Mt 3:7; see also essay, p. 1453, and chart, p. 1502. *chief priests.* See notes on Mt 2:4; Mk 8:31. There was only one ruling chief priest, but the Romans had deposed a number of chief priests, and these retained the title by courtesy.
7:33 *then I go.* Jesus changed the topic from his miracles to his death, to which he referred enigmatically (v. 34).
7:35 *scattered among the Greeks.* From the time of the exile, many Jews lived outside the Holy Land and were found in most cities throughout the Roman empire.
7:37 *last … day of the Feast.* Either the seventh or the eighth day: The Feast of Tabernacles lasted seven days (Lev 23:34; Dt 16:13,15) but had a "closing assembly" on the eighth day (Lev 23:36). See note on Mk 14:12. *stood and said in a loud voice.* Teachers usually sat, so Jesus drew special attention to his message.
7:38 *living water.* See note on 4:10.

39By this he meant the Spirit,[g] whom those
who believed in him were later to receive.[h]
Up to that time the Spirit had not been
given, since Jesus had not yet been glorified.[i]
40On hearing his words, some of the
people said, "Surely this man is the Prophet."[j]
41Others said, "He is the Christ."
Still others asked, "How can the Christ
come from Galilee?[k] 42Does not the Scripture say that the Christ will come from
David's family[a][l] and from Bethlehem,[m]
the town where David lived?" 43Thus the
people were divided[n] because of Jesus.
44Some wanted to seize him, but no one
laid a hand on him.[o]

Unbelief of the Jewish Leaders

45Finally the temple guards went back to
the chief priests and Pharisees, who asked
them, "Why didn't you bring him in?"
46"No one ever spoke the way this man
does,"[p] the guards declared.
47"You mean he has deceived you also?"[q]
the Pharisees retorted. 48"Has any of the
rulers or of the Pharisees believed in him?[r]
49No! But this mob that knows nothing of
the law—there is a curse on them."
50Nicodemus,[s] who had gone to Jesus
earlier and who was one of their own
number, asked, 51"Does our law condemn
anyone without first hearing him to find
out what he is doing?"
52They replied, "Are you from Galilee,
too? Look into it, and you will find that a
prophet[b] does not come out of Galilee."[t]

[The earliest manuscripts and many other ancient witnesses do not have John 7:53—8:11.]

53Then each went to his own home.
8 But Jesus went to the Mount of Olives.[u] 2At dawn he appeared again in
the temple courts, where all the people
gathered around him, and he sat down to
teach them.[v] 3The teachers of the law and
the Pharisees brought in a woman caught
in adultery. They made her stand before
the group 4and said to Jesus, "Teacher,
this woman was caught in the act of adultery. 5In the Law Moses commanded us
to stone such women.[w] Now what do you
say?" 6They were using this question as a
trap,[x] in order to have a basis for accusing him.[y]

[a] 42 Greek *seed* [b] 52 Two early manuscripts *the Prophet*

7:39 [g] Joel 2:28; Jn 1:33; Ac 2:17,33 [h] S Jn 20:22 [i] Jn 12:23; 13:31,32 **7:40** [j] S Mt 21:11 **7:41** [k] ver 52; Jn 1:46 **7:42** [l] S Mt 1:1 [m] Mic 5:2; Mt 2:5,6; Lk 2:4 **7:43** [n] Jn 6:52; 9:16; 10:19 **7:44** [o] ver 30 **7:46** [p] S Mt 7:28 **7:47** [q] ver 12 **7:48** [r] Jn 12:42 **7:50** [s] Jn 3:1; 19:39 **7:52** [t] ver 41 **8:1** [u] S Mt 21:1 **8:2** [v] ver 20; S Mt 26:55 **8:5** [w] Lev 20:10; Dt 22:22; Job 31:11 **8:6** [x] Mt 22:15,18 [y] S Mt 12:10

7:39 *the Spirit.* Explaining the "living water" (v. 38). *had not been given.* In the manner in which he would be given at Pentecost (see Ac 2:1–2,4 and notes). *glorified.* Here probably refers to Jesus' crucifixion, resurrection and exaltation (see note on 13:31). The fullness of the Spirit's work depends on Jesus' prior work of salvation.
7:40 *people.* The "crowd" of v. 20 (see note there). *the Prophet.* See 1:21 and note.
7:42 *the Christ will come from David's family and from Bethlehem.* See 1Sa 20:6; 2Sa 7:12–16 and notes; Ps 89:3–4; Mic 5:2. *from Bethlehem.* There were different ideas about the Messiah's place of origin (see v. 27 and note).
7:46 *guards.* They knew they would be in trouble for failing to make the arrest, but did not mention the hostility of part of the crowd, which would have given them something of an excuse before the Pharisees. They were favorably impressed by the teaching of Jesus and were not inclined to cause him trouble.
7:47 *Pharisees retorted.* They must have been greatly irritated. Ordinarily the chief priests would have rebuked the temple guards.
7:49 *this mob.* The pilgrim crowd again (see note on v. 20). *knows nothing.* The Pharisees exaggerated the people's ignorance of Scripture (cf. v. 42). But the average Jew paid little attention to the minutiae that mattered so much to the Pharisees. The "tradition of the elders" (Mt 15:2; see note there) was too great a burden for people who earned their living by hard physical work, and consequently these regulations were widely disregarded.
7:50–51 There is irony here. The Pharisees implied that no leader believed in Jesus, yet Nicodemus, "a member of the Jewish ruling council" (3:1), spoke up. They called for people to observe the law, but Nicodemus pointed to their own disregard for the law in this instance.
7:52 *a prophet does not come out of Galilee.* See 1:46; see also note on Mt 2:23. They were angry—and wrong. Jonah came from Galilee, and perhaps other prophets as well. Moreover, the Pharisees overlooked the right of God to raise up prophets from wherever he chooses.
7:53—8:11 This story may not have belonged originally to the Gospel of John. It is absent from almost all the early manuscripts, and those that have it sometimes place it elsewhere (e.g., after Lk 21:38). But the story may well be authentic.
7:53 This verse (along with 8:1) shows that the story was originally attached to another narrative, since Jesus was not present at the meeting of the Sanhedrin described in vv. 45–52.
8:1 *Mount of Olives.* See notes on Zec 14:4; Mk 11:1; Lk 19:29; Ac 1:12.
8:3 *teachers of the law.* See notes on Mt 2:4; Mk 2:16; Lk 5:17. *a woman caught in adultery.* This sin cannot be committed alone, so the question arises as to why only one offender was brought. The incident was staged to trap Jesus (see v. 6 and note), and provision had been made for the man to escape. The woman's accusers must have been especially eager to humiliate her, since they could have kept her in private custody while they spoke to Jesus.
8:4 *caught in the act.* Mere compromising circumstances were not sufficient evidence; Jewish law required witnesses who had seen the act.
8:5 *to stone such women.* They altered the law a little. The manner of execution was not prescribed unless the woman was a betrothed virgin (Dt 22:23–24). And the law required the execution of both parties (Lev 20:10; Dt 22:22), not just the woman.
8:6 *using this question as a trap.* The Romans did not allow the Jews to carry out death sentences (see 18:31 and note), so if Jesus had said to stone her, he could have been in conflict with the Romans. If he had said not to stone her, he could have been accused of being unsupportive of the law. *write on the ground with his finger.* This would seem to recall that the tablets of the law were inscribed in stone "by the finger of

But Jesus bent down and started to write
on the ground with his finger. 7When they
kept on questioning him, he straightened
up and said to them, "If any one of you is
without sin, let him be the first to throw
a stone[z] at her."[a] 8Again he stooped down
and wrote on the ground.
9At this, those who heard began to go
away one at a time, the older ones first,
until only Jesus was left, with the woman
still standing there. 10Jesus straightened up
and asked her, "Woman, where are they?
Has no one condemned you?"
11"No one, sir," she said.
"Then neither do I condemn you,"[b]
Jesus declared. "Go now and leave your
life of sin."[c]

The Validity of Jesus' Testimony

12When Jesus spoke again to the
people, he said, "I am[d] the light of the
world.[e] Whoever follows me will never
walk in darkness, but will have the light
of life."[f]
13The Pharisees challenged him, "Here
you are, appearing as your own witness;
your testimony is not valid."[g]
14Jesus answered, "Even if I testify on
my own behalf, my testimony is valid, for
I know where I came from and where I am
going.[h] But you have no idea where I come
from[i] or where I am going. 15You judge by
human standards;[j] I pass judgment on no
one.[k] 16But if I do judge, my decisions are
right, because I am not alone. I stand with
the Father, who sent me.[l] 17In your own
Law it is written that the testimony of two
men is valid.[m] 18I am one who testifies for
myself; my other witness is the Father,
who sent me."[n]
19Then they asked him, "Where is your
father?"
"You do not know me or my Father,"[o]
Jesus replied. "If you knew me, you would
know my Father also."[p] 20He spoke these
words while teaching[q] in the temple area
near the place where the offerings were
put.[r] Yet no one seized him, because his
time had not yet come.[s]
21Once more Jesus said to them, "I am
going away, and you will look for me, and
you will die[t] in your sin. Where I go, you
cannot come."[u]
22This made the Jews ask, "Will he kill
himself? Is that why he says, 'Where I go,
you cannot come'?"
23But he continued, "You are from below; I am from above. You are of this
world; I am not of this world.[v] 24I told you
that you would die in your sins; if you do
not believe that I am ⌞the one I claim to
be⌟,[a][w] you will indeed die in your sins."
25"Who are you?" they asked.
"Just what I have been claiming all
along," Jesus replied. 26"I have much to
say in judgment of you. But he who sent
me is reliable,[x] and what I have heard
from him I tell the world."[y]
27They did not understand that he was
telling them about his Father. 28So Jesus
said, "When you have lifted up the Son of
Man,[z] then you will know that I am ⌞the
one I claim to be⌟ and that I do nothing on
my own but speak just what the Father

8:7 [z] Dt 17:7; Eze 16:40 [a] Ro 2:1,22
8:11 [b] Jn 3:17 [c] Jn 5:14
8:12 [d] S Jn 6:35 [e] S Jn 1:4 [f] Pr 4:18; Mt 5:14
8:13 [g] Jn 5:31
8:14 [h] Jn 13:3; 16:28 [i] Jn 7:28; 9:29
8:15 [j] S Jn 7:24 [k] Jn 3:17
8:16 [l] Jn 5:30
8:17 [m] S Mt 18:16
8:18 [n] Jn 5:37
8:19 [o] Jn 16:3 [p] S 1Jn 2:23
8:20 [q] S Mt 26:55 [r] Mk 12:41 [s] S Mt 26:18
8:21 [t] Eze 3:18 [u] Jn 7:34; 13:33
8:23 [v] Jn 3:31; 17:14
8:24 [w] Jn 4:26; 13:19
8:26 [x] Jn 7:28 [y] Jn 3:32; 15:15
8:28 [z] S Jn 12:32

[a] 24 Or *I am he*; also in verse 28

God" (Ex 31:18) and may suggest that the accusation against the woman is, by contrast, as ephemeral as something written in the dust by Jesus' finger.

8:7 *without sin.* The phrase is quite general and means "without any sin," not "without this sin." *let him be the first.* Jesus' answer disarmed them. Since he spoke of throwing a stone, he could not be accused of failure to uphold the law. But the qualification for throwing it prevented anyone from acting.

8:9 *began to go away.* Because they were not "without sin" (v. 7). *older ones.* They were the first to realize what was involved. But all the men were either conscience-stricken or afraid, and in the end only Jesus and the woman remained.

8:10 *Woman.* See note on 2:4.

8:11 *Go now and leave your life of sin.* Jesus did not condone what the woman had done.

8:12 *I am.* See note on 6:35. *the light.* See 1:4 and note; 9:5; 12:46. It is also true that "God is light" (1Jn 1:5). And as Jesus' followers reflect the light that comes from him, they too are "the light of the world" (Mt 5:14; cf. Php 2:15). *darkness.* Both the darkness of this world and that of Satan. *light of life.* "God is light" (1Jn 1:5); but Jesus is also the light from God that lights the way for life—as the pillar of fire lighted the way for the Israelites (see Ex 13:21 and note; Ne 9:12).

8:13 *Pharisees.* See note on 7:32.

8:14 Jesus made two points: First, he was qualified to bear testimony, whereas the Pharisees were not; and he knew both his origin and his destination, whereas they knew neither. (See note on vv. 16–18 for the second point.)

8:15 The judgment of the Pharisees was limited and worldly. In the sense they meant, Jesus made it clear that he did not judge at all. In the proper sense, of course, he did judge (v. 26).

8:16–18 Jesus' second point was that his testimony was not unsupported: The Father was with him, so he and the Father were the two witnesses required by the law (see Dt 17:6 and note; 19:15).

8:16 *the Father who sent me.* Jesus was always aware of his mission (see note on 4:34).

8:19 *If you knew me.* John makes it clear that the Word (Jesus) was with God and was God (see 1:1 and note) and reveals God (see 1:18 and note). Jesus here stresses that the Father is known through the Son and that to know the one is to know the other (see 14:7,10–11 and notes).

8:20 *his time.* See note on 2:4.

8:23 Things other than death divide people (cf., e.g., v. 47; 3:31; 15:19 and note; 1Jn 3:10). *of.* Here denotes origin. Jesus was certainly in the world, but he was not of the world. They belonged to "this world"—Satan's domain (1Jn 5:19; cf. Jn 12:31; 14:30; 16:11).

8:24 *believe.* See note on 1:7. *I am.* Jesus echoes God's great affirmation about himself (see v. 58; 6:35; Ex 3:14 and notes).

8:26 *reliable.* Or "truthful" (see 3:33; 7:18 and notes).

8:28 *lifted up.* Normally used in the NT in the sense of "exalt," but John uses it of the crucifixion (see 3:14; 12:32 and

has taught me.[a] 29The one who sent me is
with me; he has not left me alone,[b] for I
always do what pleases him."[c] 30Even as
he spoke, many put their faith in him.[d]

The Children of Abraham

31To the Jews who had believed him,
Jesus said, "If you hold to my teaching,[e]
you are really my disciples. 32Then you
will know the truth, and the truth will set
you free."[f]

33They answered him, "We are Abraham's descendants[a][g] and have never been
slaves of anyone. How can you say that we
shall be set free?"

34Jesus replied, "I tell you the truth, everyone who sins is a slave to sin.[h] 35Now a
slave has no permanent place in the family, but a son belongs to it forever.[i] 36So
if the Son sets you free,[j] you will be free
indeed. 37I know you are Abraham's descendants. Yet you are ready to kill me,[k]
because you have no room for my word.
38I am telling you what I have seen in the
Father's presence,[l] and you do what you
have heard from your father.[b]"[m]

39"Abraham is our father," they answered.

"If you were Abraham's children,"[n] said
Jesus, "then you would[c] do the things
Abraham did. 40As it is, you are determined to kill me,[o] a man who has told you
the truth that I heard from God.[p] Abraham
did not do such things. 41You are doing the
things your own father does."[q]

"We are not illegitimate children," they
protested. "The only Father we have is
God himself."[r]

8:28 [a]S Jn 14:24
8:29 [b]ver 16; Jn 16:32 [c]Isa 50:5; Jn 4:34; 5:30; 6:38
8:30 [d]S Jn 7:31
8:31 [e]Jn 15:7; 2Jn 9
8:32 [f]ver 36; Ro 8:2; 2Co 3:17; Gal 5:1,13
8:33 [g]ver 37,39; S Lk 3:8
8:34 [h]S Ro 6:16
8:35 [i]Gal 4:30
8:36 [j]ver 32
8:37 [k]ver 39,40
8:38 [l]Jn 5:19,30; 14:10,24 [m]ver 41,44
8:39 [n]ver 37; S Lk 3:8
8:40 [o]S Mt 12:14 [p]ver 26
8:41 [q]ver 38,44 [r]Isa 63:16; 64:8

The Children of the Devil

42Jesus said to them, "If God were your
Father, you would love me,[s] for I came
from God[t] and now am here. I have not
come on my own;[u] but he sent me.[v] 43Why
is my language not clear to you? Because
you are unable to hear what I say. 44You
belong to your father, the devil,[w] and you
want to carry out your father's desire.[x] He
was a murderer from the beginning, not
holding to the truth, for there is no truth
in him. When he lies, he speaks his native
language, for he is a liar and the father of
lies.[y] 45Yet because I tell the truth,[z] you do
not believe me! 46Can any of you prove me
guilty of sin? If I am telling the truth, why
don't you believe me? 47He who belongs
to God hears what God says.[a] The reason
you do not hear is that you do not belong
to God."

The Claims of Jesus About Himself

48The Jews answered him, "Aren't we
right in saying that you are a Samaritan[b]
and demon-possessed?"[c]

49"I am not possessed by a demon," said
Jesus, "but I honor my Father and you dishonor me. 50I am not seeking glory for myself;[d] but there is one who seeks it, and
he is the judge. 51I tell you the truth, if
anyone keeps my word, he will never see
death."[e]

52At this the Jews exclaimed, "Now we
know that you are demon-possessed![f]

8:42 [s]1Jn 5:1 [t]S Jn 13:3 [u]Jn 7:28 [v]S Jn 3:17
8:44 [w]1Jn 3:8 [x]ver 38,41 [y]Ge 3:4; 4:9; 2Ch 18:21; Ps 5:6; 12:2
8:45 [z]Jn 18:37
8:47 [a]Jn 18:37; 1Jn 4:6
8:48 [b]S Mt 10:5 [c]ver 52; S Mk 3:22
8:50 [d]ver 54; Jn 5:41
8:51 [e]Jn 11:26
8:52 [f]ver 48; S Mk 3:22

[a] 33 Greek *seed*; also in verse 37 [b] 38 Or *presence. Therefore do what you have heard from the Father.* [c] 39 Some early manuscripts *"If you are Abraham's children," said Jesus, "then*

notes). *Son of Man.* See note on Mk 8:31. *I am.* See notes on vv. 24,58.

8:30 *faith.* See 1:7; 20:31 and notes.

8:31 *believed.* Here seems to mean "made a formal profession of faith." Their words show that they were not true believers (see vv. 33,37).

8:32 *truth.* Closely connected with Jesus (see v. 36; 14:6 and note), it is not philosophical truth but the truth that leads to salvation. *free.* Freedom from sin, not from ignorance (see v. 36).

8:33 *have never been slaves.* Appears to be an amazing disregard of their Roman overlords—and their Egyptian, Assyrian, Babylonian, Persian and Syrian overlords as well. Perhaps they meant that they have always viewed themselves as the descendants of Abraham and heirs of the promises God made to him and so have never accepted servitude to others as their proper status.

8:34 *slave to sin.* Because sinners cannot break free by their own strength (see Ro 6:18 and note).

8:37 *you are ready to kill me.* See note on 7:1—8:59.

8:38 Note the contrasts: "I ... you"; "seen ... heard" (cf. Job 42:5 and note); "the Father ... your father." Not until later (see v. 44 and note) did Jesus say who their father was, but it is clear even at this point that it was neither God nor Abraham as they claimed.

8:39–41 Their deeds revealed their parentage.

8:41 *illegitimate.* May have been a slander aimed at Jesus.

8:43 *my language.* The form of expression—the actual words. *what I say.* The content. These descendants of Abraham (v. 33) were so convinced of their own preconceptions that they did not really hear and understand what Jesus was saying (cf. v. 47).

8:44 *You belong to your father, the devil.* Jesus warned his Jewish opponents of the reality of Satan's murderous and deceitful influence. Since "salvation is from the Jews" (4:22; see note there), Jesus' words do not apply to the Jewish people as a whole. His warning should caution both Gentiles and Jews to follow Abraham's example (vv. 39–40; cf. Ro 4:16). *you want.* Points to determination of will. Their problem was basically spiritual, not intellectual. Being oriented toward Satan, they were bent on murder (v. 37) and eventually would succeed (v. 28). *truth.* Foreign to Satan and those who are his (see 14:6 and note).

8:46 *Can ... you prove me guilty of sin?* The asking of the question was more significant than the opponents' failure to answer, in that it showed Jesus had a perfectly clear conscience.

8:47 *hears what God says.* See 10:3–4 and notes; 1Jn 4:6.

8:48 *The Jews.* See note on 1:19. *Samaritan.* Possibly to suggest that he was lax in Jewish observances—"no better than a Samaritan"—or that he was a Samaritan by birth. *demon-possessed.* See 10:20 and note on 7:20.

8:51 *my word.* The whole of Jesus' message, which when accepted brings deliverance from death.

Abraham died and so did the prophets, yet
you say that if anyone keeps your word,
he will never taste death. 53Are you greater
than our father Abraham?[g] He died, and
so did the prophets. Who do you think
you are?"
54Jesus replied, "If I glorify myself,[h] my
glory means nothing. My Father, whom
you claim as your God, is the one who
glorifies me.[i] 55Though you do not know
him,[j] I know him.[k] If I said I did not, I
would be a liar like you, but I do know
him and keep his word.[l] 56Your father
Abraham[m] rejoiced at the thought of seeing my day; he saw it[n] and was glad."
57"You are not yet fifty years old," the
Jews said to him, "and you have seen
Abraham!"
58"I tell you the truth," Jesus answered,
"before Abraham was born,[o] I am!"[p] 59At
this, they picked up stones to stone him,[q]
but Jesus hid himself,[r] slipping away from
the temple grounds.

Jesus Heals a Man Born Blind

9 As he went along, he saw a man blind
from birth. 2His disciples asked him,
"Rabbi,[s] who sinned,[t] this man[u] or his
parents,[v] that he was born blind?"
3"Neither this man nor his parents
sinned," said Jesus, "but this happened so
that the work of God might be displayed
in his life.[w] 4As long as it is day,[x] we must
do the work of him who sent me. Night is
coming, when no one can work. 5While
I am in the world, I am the light of the
world."[y]
6Having said this, he spit[z] on the
ground, made some mud with the saliva,
and put it on the man's eyes. 7"Go," he
told him, "wash in the Pool of Siloam"[a]
(this word means Sent). So the man went
and washed, and came home seeing.[b]
8His neighbors and those who had formerly seen him begging asked, "Isn't this
the same man who used to sit and beg?"[c]
9Some claimed that he was.
Others said, "No, he only looks like
him."
But he himself insisted, "I am the man."
10"How then were your eyes opened?"
they demanded.
11He replied, "The man they call Jesus
made some mud and put it on my eyes.
He told me to go to Siloam and wash. So I
went and washed, and then I could see."[d]
12"Where is this man?" they asked him.
"I don't know," he said.

The Pharisees Investigate the Healing

13They brought to the Pharisees the
man who had been blind. 14Now the day
on which Jesus had made the mud and
opened the man's eyes was a Sabbath.[e]
15Therefore the Pharisees also asked him
how he had received his sight.[f] "He put
mud on my eyes," the man replied, "and I
washed, and now I see."
16Some of the Pharisees said, "This man
is not from God, for he does not keep the
Sabbath."[g]

8:53 [g] ver 39; Jn 4:12
8:54 [h] ver 50 [i] Jn 16:14; 17:1,5
8:55 [j] ver 19 [k] Jn 7:28,29 [l] Jn 15:10
8:56 [m] ver 37,39; Ge 18:18 [n] S Mt 13:17
8:58 [o] S Jn 1:2 [p] Ex 3:14; 6:3
8:59 [q] Ex 17:4; Lev 24:16; 1Sa 30:6; Jn 10:31; 11:8 [r] Jn 12:36
9:2 [s] S Mt 23:7 [t] ver 34; Lk 13:2; Ac 28:4 [u] Eze 18:20 [v] Ex 20:5; Job 21:19
9:3 [w] Jn 11:4
9:4 [x] Jn 11:9; 12:35
9:5 [y] S Jn 1:4
9:6 [z] Mk 7:33; 8:23
9:7 [a] ver 11; 2Ki 5:10; Lk 13:4 [b] Isa 35:5; Jn 11:37
9:8 [c] Ac 3:2,10
9:11 [d] ver 7
9:14 [e] Mt 12:1-14; Jn 5:9
9:15 [f] ver 10
9:16 [g] S Mt 12:2

8:53 *Are you greater . . . ?* The question was framed to expect the answer "No." This is ironic, since Jesus was indeed far greater than Abraham, even as he was greater than Moses (see 6:30–35 and notes).

8:56 *my day.* All that was involved in the incarnation. Jesus probably was not referring to any one occasion but to Abraham's general joy in the fulfilling of the purposes of God in the Messiah, by which all nations on earth would receive blessing (see note on Ge 12:2–3). *he saw it.* In faith, from afar.

8:57 *not yet fifty years old.* A generous allowance for Jesus' maximum possible age. Jesus was "about" 30 when he began his ministry (see Lk 3:23 and note).

8:58 *I tell you the truth.* See note on Mk 3:28. *I am!* A solemnly emphatic declaration echoing God's great affirmation in Ex 3:14 (see vv. 24,28; see also note on 6:35). Jesus did not say "I was" but "I am," expressing the eternity of his being and his oneness with the Father (see 1:1). With this climactic statement Jesus concludes his speech that began with the related claim, "I am the light of the world" (v. 12; see note there).

8:59 *to stone him.* Those who heard Jesus could not interpret his claim as other than blasphemy, for which stoning was the proper penalty (Lev 24:16).

9:1–12 Jesus performed more miracles of this kind than of any other. Giving sight to the blind was predicted as a Messianic activity (see Isa 29:18; 35:5 and notes; 42:7). Thus these miracles were additional evidence that Jesus was the Messiah (see 20:31 and note).

9:2 *who sinned . . . ?* The rabbis had developed the principle that "There is no death without sin, and there is no suffering without iniquity" (cf. Introduction to Job: Theme and Message). They were even capable of thinking that a child could sin in the womb or that its soul might have sinned in a preexistent state. They also held that terrible punishments came on certain people because of the sin of their parents. As the next verse shows, Jesus plainly contradicted these beliefs.

9:3 *work of God might be displayed.* Cf. 11:4 and note, 40.

9:4 *we.* Not Jesus only; his disciples share with him the responsibility of doing what God wants done. *Night is coming.* When Jesus, "the light of the world" (v. 5), will be taken away in death.

9:5 *the light of the world.* See note on 8:12.

9:6 Jesus used variety in his cures. He could turn even the dirt of the earth into a medium of restoration (cf. Mk 8:22–25).

9:7 *Pool of Siloam.* Until recent years the general site of the pool on the southern end of the main ridge on which Jerusalem was built was marked by a structure from the Byzantine period. In 2004, however, archaeologists identified nearby remains that proved to be the original Pool of Siloam of Jesus' day. The aqueduct leading into the pool served as part of the major water system developed by King Hezekiah (see notes on 2Ki 20:20; Ne 2:14; Job 28:10; Isa 8:6). *Sent.* Or "one who has been sent."

9:8 *begging.* About the only way blind people of that day could support themselves.

9:13 *Pharisees.* See note on 7:32.

9:14 *Sabbath.* Cf. 5:16 and the discussion that follows (see note on 5:10).

9:16 *Some . . . others.* The first group started from their entrenched position and ruled out the possibility of

But others asked, "How can a sinner do
such miraculous signs?"[h] So they were divided.[i]
17Finally they turned again to the blind
man, "What have you to say about him? It
was your eyes he opened."
The man replied, "He is a prophet."[j]
18The Jews[k] still did not believe that
he had been blind and had received his
sight until they sent for the man's parents.
19"Is this your son?" they asked. "Is this
the one you say was born blind? How is it
that now he can see?"
20"We know he is our son," the parents
answered, "and we know he was born
blind. 21But how he can see now, or who
opened his eyes, we don't know. Ask him.
He is of age; he will speak for himself."
22His parents said this because they were
afraid of the Jews,[l] for already the Jews
had decided that anyone who acknowledged that Jesus was the Christ[a] would
be put out[m] of the synagogue.[n] 23That was
why his parents said, "He is of age; ask
him."[o]
24A second time they summoned the
man who had been blind. "Give glory to
God,[b]"[p] they said. "We know this man is
a sinner."[q]
25He replied, "Whether he is a sinner or
not, I don't know. One thing I do know. I
was blind but now I see!"
26Then they asked him, "What did he do
to you? How did he open your eyes?"
27He answered, "I have told you already[r]
and you did not listen. Why do you want
to hear it again? Do you want to become
his disciples, too?"
28Then they hurled insults at him and
said, "You are this fellow's disciple! We
are disciples of Moses![s] 29We know that
God spoke to Moses, but as for this fellow, we don't even know where he comes
from."[t]
30The man answered, "Now that is remarkable! You don't know where he
comes from, yet he opened my eyes. 31We
know that God does not listen to sinners.
He listens to the godly man who does his
will.[u] 32Nobody has ever heard of opening
the eyes of a man born blind. 33If this man
were not from God,[v] he could do nothing."
34To this they replied, "You were steeped
in sin at birth;[w] how dare you lecture us!"
And they threw him out.[x]

Spiritual Blindness

35Jesus heard that they had thrown him
out, and when he found him, he said, "Do
you believe[y] in the Son of Man?"[z]
36"Who is he, sir?" the man asked. "Tell
me so that I may believe in him."[a]
37Jesus said, "You have now seen him; in
fact, he is the one speaking with you."[b]
38Then the man said, "Lord, I believe,"
and he worshiped him.[c]
39Jesus said, "For judgment[d] I have
come into this world,[e] so that the blind
will see[f] and those who see will become
blind."[g]
40Some Pharisees who were with him
heard him say this and asked, "What? Are
we blind too?"[h]
41Jesus said, "If you were blind, you
would not be guilty of sin; but now that you
claim you can see, your guilt remains.[i]

a 22 Or *Messiah* *b* 24 A solemn charge to tell the truth (see Joshua 7:19)

9:16 [h]S Jn 2:11 [i]S Jn 6:52 **9:17** [j]S Mt 21:11 **9:18** [k]S Jn 1:19 **9:22** [l]S Jn 7:13 [m]ver 34; Lk 6:22 [n]Jn 12:42; 16:2 **9:23** [o]ver 21 **9:24** [p]Jos 7:19 [q]ver 16 **9:27** [r]ver 15 **9:28** [s]Jn 5:45 **9:29** [t]Jn 8:14 **9:31** [u]Ge 18:23-32; Ps 34:15, 16; 66:18; 145:19, 20; Pr 15:29; Isa 1:15; 59:1, 2; Jn 15:7; Jas 5:16-18; 1Jn 5:14, 15 **9:33** [v]ver 16; Jn 3:2 **9:34** [w]ver 2 [x]ver 22, 35; Isa 66:5 **9:35** [y]S Jn 3:15 [z]S Mt 8:20 **9:36** [a]Ro 10:14 **9:37** [b]Jn 4:26 **9:38** [c]Mt 28:9 **9:39** [d]S Jn 5:22 [e]Jn 3:19; 12:47 [f]Lk 4:18 [g]Mt 13:13 **9:40** [h]Ro 2:19 **9:41** [i]Jn 15:22, 24

Jesus being from God. The second started from the fact of the "miraculous signs" and ruled out the possibility of his being a sinner (cf. vv. 30–33 and notes).

9:17 *What have you to say about him?* It is curious that they put such a question to such a person; their doing so reflected their perplexity. *prophet.* Probably the highest designation the man could think of. He progressed in his thinking about Jesus: from a man (v. 11), to a prophet (v. 17) who might be followed by disciples (v. 27), to one "from God" (v. 33), to one who was properly to be worshiped (v. 38).

9:18 *The Jews.* See note on 1:19. In their prejudice they did not learn from the sign but tried to discredit the miracle.

9:21 *He is of age.* There was much to which the parents could not testify, but their emphasis on the son's responsibility showed their fear of getting involved.

9:22 *put out of the synagogue.* Excommunication is reported as early as the time of Ezra (10:8), but there is practically no information about the way it was practiced in NT times. The synagogue was the center of Jewish community life (see note on 6:59), so excommunication cut a person off from many social relationships (though in some of its forms, at least in later times, not from worship).

9:24 *We.* Emphatic in the Greek.

9:27 *his disciples, too.* The man already counted himself a disciple.

9:30–33 Good reasoning from an unschooled man.

9:31 *God does not listen to sinners.* Cf. the remark of some of the Pharisees in v. 16.

9:34 *threw him out.* May mean "expelled him from their assembly" or, more probably, "excommunicated him" (see note on v. 22; cf. note on 1Co 5:5).

9:35 *when he found him.* Jesus obviously had been looking for the man. *Son of Man.* See note on Mk 8:31.

9:36 The man was ready to follow any suggestion from his benefactor.

9:38 *I believe.* See notes on 1:7; 20:31. *Lord ... he worshiped him.* The man was giving Jesus the reverence due to God.

9:39 It is unlikely that the conversation of vv. 35–38 took place in the presence of the Pharisees. The incident of vv. 39–41, therefore, probably occurred a little later. *For judgment.* In a sense Jesus did not come for judgment (see 3:17; 12:47 and note), but his coming divides people, and this always brings a type of judgment. Those who reject his gift end up "blind."

9:40 *Pharisees.* They found it incredible that anyone would consider them spiritually blind. See note on v. 13.

9:41 The Pharisees' claim to sight showed their complete unawareness of their spiritual blindness and need. And, though they claimed to have sight, their actions were evidence of their blindness.

The Shepherd and His Flock

10 “I tell you the truth, the man who
does not enter the sheep pen by the
gate, but climbs in by some other way, is a
thief and a robber.[j] 2The man who enters
by the gate is the shepherd of his sheep.[k]
3The watchman opens the gate for him, and
the sheep listen to his voice.[l] He calls his
own sheep by name and leads them out.[m]
4When he has brought out all his own, he
goes on ahead of them, and his sheep follow him because they know his voice.[n] 5But
they will never follow a stranger; in fact,
they will run away from him because they
do not recognize a stranger’s voice.” 6Jesus
used this figure of speech,[o] but they did not
understand what he was telling them.[p]
7Therefore Jesus said again, “I tell you
the truth, I am[q] the gate[r] for the sheep. 8All
who ever came before me[s] were thieves
and robbers,[t] but the sheep did not listen
to them. 9I am the gate; whoever enters
through me will be saved.[a] He will come
in and go out, and find pasture. 10The thief
comes only to steal and kill and destroy;
I have come that they may have life,[u] and
have it to the full.[v]
11“I am[w] the good shepherd.[x] The good
shepherd lays down his life for the sheep.[y]
12The hired hand is not the shepherd who
owns the sheep. So when he sees the wolf
coming, he abandons the sheep and runs
away.[z] Then the wolf attacks the flock and
scatters it. 13The man runs away because
he is a hired hand and cares nothing for
the sheep.
14“I am the good shepherd;[a] I know my
sheep[b] and my sheep know me— 15just
as the Father knows me and I know the
Father[c]—and I lay down my life for the
sheep.[d] 16I have other sheep[e] that are not
of this sheep pen. I must bring them also.
They too will listen to my voice, and there
shall be one flock[f] and one shepherd.[g]
17The reason my Father loves me is that
I lay down my life[h]—only to take it up
again. 18No one takes it from me, but I lay
it down of my own accord.[i] I have authority to lay it down and authority to take it
up again. This command I received from
my Father.”[j]
19At these words the Jews were again
divided.[k] 20Many of them said, “He is demon-possessed[l] and raving mad.[m] Why
listen to him?”
21But others said, “These are not the sayings of a man possessed by a demon.[n] Can
a demon open the eyes of the blind?”[o]

The Unbelief of the Jews

22Then came the Feast of Dedication[b] at
Jerusalem. It was winter, 23and Jesus was
in the temple area walking in Solomon’s

[a] 9 Or *kept safe* [b] 22 That is, Hanukkah

10:1 [j] ver 8, 10 **10:2** [k] ver 11, 14; Mk 6:34 **10:3** [l] ver 4, 5, 14, 16, 27 [m] ver 4, 5, 14, 16, 27 **10:4** [n] S ver 3 **10:6** [o] S Jn 16:25 [p] S Mk 9:32 **10:7** [q] S Jn 6:35 [r] ver 9 **10:8** [s] Jer 23:1, 2; Eze 34:2 [t] ver 1 **10:10** [u] S Jn 1:4; 3:15, 16; 5:40; 20:31 [v] Ps 65:11; Ro 5:17 **10:11** [w] S Jn 6:35 [x] ver 14; Ps 23:1; Isa 40:11; Eze 34:11-16, 23; Mt 2:6; Lk 12:32; Heb 13:20; 1Pe 2:25; 5:4; Rev 7:17 [y] ver 15, 17, 18; Jn 15:13; 1Jn 3:16 **10:12** [z] Zec 11:16, 17 **10:14** [a] S ver 11 [b] ver 27; Ex 33:12 **10:15** [c] Mt 11:27 [d] ver 11, 17, 18 **10:16** [e] Isa 56:8; Ac 10:34, 35 [f] Jn 11:52; 17:20, 21; Eph 2:11-19 [g] Eze 34:23; 37:24 **10:17** [h] ver 11, 15, 18 **10:18** [i] Mt 26:53 [j] Jn 15:10; Php 2:8; Heb 5:8 **10:19** [k] S Jn 6:52 **10:20** [l] S Mk 3:22 [m] 2Ki 9:11; Jer 29:26; Mk 3:21 **10:21** [n] S Mt 4:24 [o] Ex 4:11; Jn 9:32, 33

10:1 – 30 Should be understood in light of the OT (and ancient Near Eastern) concept of “shepherd,” symbolizing a royal caretaker of God’s people. God himself was called the “Shepherd of Israel” (Ps 80:1; see Ps 23:1 and note; Isa 40:10 – 11; Eze 34:11 – 16 and note on 34:2; Zec 10:2 and note), and he had given great responsibility to the leaders (“shepherds”) of Israel, which they failed to respect. God denounced these false shepherds (see Isa 56:9 – 12; Eze 34) and promised to provide the true Shepherd, the Messiah, to care for the sheep (Eze 34:23).

10:1 *I tell you the truth.* See note on Mk 3:28. *sheep pen.* An enclosure with only one entrance. Its walls kept the sheep from wandering away.

10:3 *watchman.* Apparently in charge of a large sheep pen, where several flocks were kept. *his voice.* The sheep responded only to the voice of their own shepherd. *his own sheep.* Shepherds did not call sheep randomly, but only those that belonged to them.

10:4 *he goes on ahead.* Palestinian shepherds led their sheep (they did not drive them), and the sheep followed because they knew their own shepherd’s voice.

10:6 *did not understand.* See 8:27; 12:16; Mk 8:16 and note; Lk 2:50; 9:45; 18:34.

10:7 *I am.* See note on 6:35.

10:8 *All … before me.* False shepherds like the Pharisees and the chief priests, not the true OT prophets (see note on vv. 1 – 30; cf. Zec 11:5,8 and notes).

10:9 *the gate.* The one way into salvation. Inside there is safety, and one is able to go out and find pasture, i.e., the supply of all needs.

10:10 *thief.* His interest is in himself. Christ’s interest is in his sheep, whom he enables to have life to the full (see note on 1:4).

10:11 *I am.* See note on 6:35. *lays down his life.* Palestinian shepherds might risk danger for their sheep (see Ge 31:39; 1Sa 17:34 – 37), but they expected to come through alive. Jesus said that the good shepherd will die for his sheep (cf. 15:13).

10:12 *hired hand.* Interested in wages, not in the sheep (v. 13).

10:14 *I know … my sheep know.* A deep mutual knowledge, like that of the Father and the Son.

10:15 *I lay down my life.* See v. 11 and note; the fact of central importance.

10:16 *other sheep.* These already belonged to Christ, though they had not yet been brought to him. *not of this sheep pen.* Those outside Judaism. Here is a glimpse of the future worldwide scope of the church. *one flock.* All God’s people have the same Shepherd (see 17:20 – 23).

10:17 – 18 That Christ would die for his people runs through this section of John’s Gospel. Both the love and the plan of the Father are involved, as well as the authority he gave to the Son. Christ obediently chose to die; otherwise, no one would have had the power to kill him (cf. Lk 23:46).

10:19 *divided.* See 7:43; 9:16.

10:20 *demon-possessed.* See note on 7:20.

10:21 See 9:16.

10:22 *Feast of Dedication.* The commemoration of the dedication (see NIV text note) of the temple by Judas Maccabeus in December 165 B.C., after it had been profaned by Antiochus IV Epiphanes. This was the last great deliverance the Jews had experienced. *It was winter.* A reference for those unfamiliar with the Jewish calendar (see bottom of chart, p. 178).

10:23 *Solomon’s Colonnade.* See Ac 3:11 and note; 5:12. It was a roofed structure — somewhat similar to a Greek stoa — commonly but erroneously thought to date back to Solomon’s time.

Colonnade.[p] 24The Jews[q] gathered around him, saying, "How long will you keep us in suspense? If you are the Christ,[a] tell us plainly."[r]

25Jesus answered, "I did tell you,[s] but you do not believe. The miracles I do in my Father's name speak for me,[t] 26but you do not believe because you are not my sheep.[u] 27My sheep listen to my voice; I know them,[v] and they follow me.[w] 28I give them eternal life,[x] and they shall never perish;[y] no one can snatch them out of my hand.[z] 29My Father, who has given them to me,[a] is greater than all[b];[b] no one can snatch them out of my Father's hand. 30I and the Father are one."[c]

31Again the Jews picked up stones to stone him,[d] 32but Jesus said to them, "I have shown you many great miracles from the Father. For which of these do you stone me?"

33"We are not stoning you for any of these," replied the Jews, "but for blasphemy, because you, a mere man, claim to be God."[e]

34Jesus answered them, "Is it not written in your Law,[f] 'I have said you are gods'[c]?[g] 35If he called them 'gods,' to whom the word of God[h] came—and the Scripture cannot be broken[i]— 36what about the one whom the Father set apart[j] as his very own[k] and sent into the world?[l] Why then do you accuse me of blasphemy because I said, 'I am God's Son'?[m] 37Do not believe me unless I do what my Father does.[n] 38But if I do it, even though you do not believe me, believe the miracles, that you may know and understand that the Father is in me, and I in the Father."[o] 39Again they tried to seize him,[p] but he escaped their grasp.[q]

40Then Jesus went back across the Jordan[r] to the place where John had been baptizing in the early days. Here he stayed 41and many people came to him. They said, "Though John never performed a miraculous sign,[s] all that John said about this man was true."[t] 42And in that place many believed in Jesus.[u]

The Death of Lazarus

11 Now a man named Lazarus was sick. He was from Bethany,[v] the village of Mary and her sister Martha.[w] 2This Mary, whose brother Lazarus now lay sick, was the same one who poured perfume on the

[a] 24 Or *Messiah* [b] 29 Many early manuscripts *What my Father has given me is greater than all* [c] 34 Psalm 82:6

10:23 [p] Ac 3:11; 5:12 **10:24** [q] S Jn 1:19 [r] Lk 22:67; Jn 16:25,29 **10:25** [s] Jn 4:26; 8:58 [t] Jn 5:36; 14:11 **10:26** [u] Jn 8:47 **10:27** [v] ver 14 [w] ver 4 **10:28** [x] S Mt 25:46 [y] Isa 66:22 [z] S Jn 6:39 **10:29** [a] Jn 17:2,6,24 [b] Jn 14:28 **10:30** [c] Dt 6:4; Jn 17:21-23 **10:31** [d] S Jn 8:59 **10:33** [e] Lev 24:16; Mt 26:63-66; Jn 5:18 **10:34** [f] Jn 8:17; 12:34; 15:25; Ro 3:19; 1Co 14:21 [g] Ps 82:6 **10:35** [h] S Heb 4:12 [i] S Mt 5:18 **10:36** [j] Jer 1:5 [k] Jn 6:69 [l] S Jn 3:17 [m] Jn 5:17,18 **10:37** [n] ver 25 **10:38** [o] Jn 14:10,11,20; 17:21 **10:39** [p] Jn 7:30 [q] Lk 4:30; Jn 8:59 **10:40** [r] Jn 1:28 **10:41** [s] S Jn 2:11 [t] Jn 1:26,27,30,34 **10:42** [u] S Jn 7:31 **11:1** [v] S Mt 21:17 [w] Lk 10:38

10:24 *If you are the Christ.* Because of the different ideas about Messiahship then in vogue, it was not easy for Jews to resolve this critical issue. See notes on 1:25; 20:31.

10:25 *I did tell you.* Jesus had not specifically affirmed his Messiahship except to the Samaritan woman (see 4:26 and note). He may have meant here that the general thrust of his teaching made his claim clear or that such statements as that in 8:58 (see note there) were sufficient. Or he may have been referring to the evidence of his whole manner of life (including the miracles)—all he had done in the Father's name (for the name see note on 2:23).

10:26 *not my sheep.* Their failure to believe arose from what they were.

10:27 *voice.* See v. 3 and note. *I know them.* See v. 14 and note. *they follow.* See v. 4 and note.

10:28 *eternal life.* Christ's gift (see note on 3:15). *never perish.* The Greek construction here is a strong denial that the sheep will ever perish. The sheep's security is in the power of the shepherd, who will let no one take them from him (see 3:16).

10:29 *My Father.* See note on 5:17. *no one can snatch them.* The Father's power ("hand") is greater than that of any enemy, making the sheep completely secure (cf. 17:11–12 and notes).

10:30 *one.* The Greek is neuter—"one thing," not "one person." The two are one in essence or nature, but they are not identical persons. This great truth is what warrants Jesus' "I am" declarations (see 6:35; 8:24,58; 17:21–22 and notes).

10:31 *the Jews.* See note on 1:19. *to stone him.* They took Jesus' words as blasphemy, and therefore prepared to carry out the law (Lev 24:16), though without due process.

10:32 *great miracles.* Or "good deeds" (as, e.g., in Mt 5:16; 1Ti 5:10,25; 6:18). Although the reference here includes Jesus' miracles, the underlying Greek words refer to works in general that are fine and noble in character first of all (see note on v. 38).

10:33 *blasphemy.* The Jewish leaders correctly understood the thrust of Jesus' words, but their preconceptions and unbelief prevented them from accepting his claim as true.

10:34 *your Law.* In its strictest sense the term meant the Pentateuch, but was often used, as here, of the whole OT. *you are gods.* The words Jesus quotes from Ps 82:6 (see note on 82:1) refer to the judges (or other leaders or rulers), whose tasks were divinely appointed (see Ex 22:28 and NIV text note; Dt 1:17; 16:18; 2Ch 19:6).

10:35 *Scripture cannot be broken.* Jesus testified to the complete authority and reliability of the OT.

10:36 If there is any sense in which humans can be spoken of as "gods" (as Ps 82:6 speaks of human rulers or judges), how much more may the term be used of him whom the Father set apart and sent!

10:37 *what my Father does.* The kind of works of compassion that the Father himself does.

10:38 *miracles.* Lit. "works." The miracles were a part of Jesus' works. It was Jesus' quality of life, not people's inability to explain his marvels, that he primarily spoke of here (see note on v. 32).

10:39 *they tried to seize him.* It is not clear if this was to arrest him for trial or to take him out for stoning. *he escaped.* John does not say why they failed, but he often makes it clear that Jesus could not be killed before the appointed time (see note on 2:4; see also Lk 4:30 and note).

10:40 *where John had been baptizing.* See 1:28 and note.

10:41 *all that John said.* For John the Baptist as a witness see 1:7 and note.

11:1 *Lazarus.* Mentioned only in chs. 11–12 of John's Gospel (the name is found also in the parable of Lk 16:19–31). The sisters are mentioned in Lk 10:38–42.

11:2 *poured perfume.* See 12:3 and note.

Lord and wiped his feet with her hair.[x] [3]So the sisters sent word to Jesus, "Lord, the one you love[y] is sick."

[4]When he heard this, Jesus said, "This sickness will not end in death. No, it is for God's glory[z] so that God's Son may be glorified through it." [5]Jesus loved Martha and her sister and Lazarus. [6]Yet when he heard that Lazarus was sick, he stayed where he was two more days.

[7]Then he said to his disciples, "Let us go back to Judea."[a]

[8]"But Rabbi,"[b] they said, "a short while ago the Jews tried to stone you,[c] and yet you are going back there?"

[9]Jesus answered, "Are there not twelve hours of daylight? A man who walks by day will not stumble, for he sees by this world's light.[d] [10]It is when he walks by night that he stumbles, for he has no light."

[11]After he had said this, he went on to tell them, "Our friend[e] Lazarus has fallen asleep;[f] but I am going there to wake him up."

[12]His disciples replied, "Lord, if he sleeps, he will get better." [13]Jesus had been speaking of his death, but his disciples thought he meant natural sleep.[g]

[14]So then he told them plainly, "Lazarus is dead, [15]and for your sake I am glad I was not there, so that you may believe. But let us go to him."

[16]Then Thomas[h] (called Didymus) said to the rest of the disciples, "Let us also go, that we may die with him."

Jesus Comforts the Sisters

[17]On his arrival, Jesus found that Lazarus had already been in the tomb for four days.[i] [18]Bethany[j] was less than two miles[a] from Jerusalem, [19]and many Jews had come to Martha and Mary to comfort them in the loss of their brother.[k] [20]When Martha heard that Jesus was coming, she went out to meet him, but Mary stayed at home.[l]

[21]"Lord," Martha said to Jesus, "if you had been here, my brother would not have died.[m] [22]But I know that even now God will give you whatever you ask."[n]

[23]Jesus said to her, "Your brother will rise again."

[24]Martha answered, "I know he will rise again in the resurrection[o] at the last day."[p]

[25]Jesus said to her, "I am[q] the resurrection and the life.[r] He who believes[s] in me will live, even though he dies; [26]and whoever lives and believes[t] in me will never die.[u] Do you believe this?"

[27]"Yes, Lord," she told him, "I believe that you are the Christ,[b][v] the Son of God,[w] who was to come into the world."[x]

11:2 [x] Mk 14:3; Lk 7:38; Jn 12:3
11:3 [y] ver 5,36
11:4 [z] ver 40
11:7 [a] Jn 10:40
11:8 [b] S Mt 23:7 [c] Jn 8:59; 10:31
11:9 [d] Jn 9:4; 12:35
11:11 [e] ver 3 [f] S Mt 9:24
11:13 [g] Mt 9:24
11:16 [h] Mt 10:3; Jn 14:5; 20:24-28; 21:2; Ac 1:13
11:17 [i] ver 6,39
11:18 [j] ver 1; S Mt 21:17
11:19 [k] ver 31; Job 2:11
11:20 [l] Lk 10:38-42
11:21 [m] ver 32,37
11:22 [n] ver 41,42
11:24 [o] Da 12:2; Jn 5:28,29; Ac 24:15 [p] Jn 6:39,40
11:25 [q] S Jn 6:35 [r] S Jn 1:4 [s] S Jn 3:15
11:26 [t] S Jn 3:15 [u] S Mt 25:46
11:27 [v] S Lk 2:11 [w] S Mt 4:3 [x] Jn 6:14

[a] *18* Greek *fifteen stadia* (about 3 kilometers)
[b] *27* Or *Messiah*

11:3 *the one you love.* The relationship must have been exceptionally close.

11:4 Cf. 9:3 and note on 9:2. *This sickness will not end in death.* Thus predicting the raising of Lazarus (v. 44), since Jesus already knew of his death (v. 14). In fact, Lazarus must have died shortly after the messengers left Bethany, accounting for the "four days" of vv. 17,39: one day for the journey of the messengers, the two days when Jesus remained where he was (see v. 6 and note), and a day for Jesus' journey to Bethany. But see note on v. 17. *glory.* See notes on 7:39; 12:41; 13:31. Here God's Son would be glorified through what happened to Lazarus, partly because the miracle displays the glory of God (who alone can raise the dead; see 5:21 and note) in Jesus (v. 40) and partly because it would help initiate events leading to the cross (vv. 46–53).

11:6 *he stayed.* Jesus moved as the Father directed, not as people (here Mary and Martha) wished (cf. 2:4 and note). *where he was.* In Perea, east of the Jordan River (10:40).

11:8 *the Jews.* See note on 1:19. *tried to stone you.* See note on 10:31. There was clear danger in going into Judea.

11:9 *twelve hours.* Enough time for what must be done, but no time for waste.

11:11 *fallen asleep.* A euphemism for death, used by the unbelieving world as well as by Christians.

11:15 *believe.* See 1:7; 20:31 and notes.

11:16 *Thomas … Didymus.* The Hebrew word from which we get "Thomas" and the Greek word *Didymus* both mean "twin." Usually remembered for his doubting (see 20:24–25), he was also capable of devotion and courage, as here.

11:17 *four days.* See note on v. 4. Many Jews believed that the soul remained near the body for three days after death in the hope of returning to it. If this idea was in the minds of these people, they obviously thought all hope was gone — Lazarus was irrevocably dead.

11:18 *Bethany.* See note on Mt 21:17; see also map, p. 1553.

11:19 *to comfort them.* Jewish custom provided for three days of very heavy mourning, then four of heavy mourning, followed by lighter mourning for the remainder of 30 days. It was usual for friends to visit the family to comfort them.

11:20 *she went out to meet him.* Perhaps because as the older sister she was hostess.

11:21 Repeated by Mary in v. 32. Perhaps the sisters had said this to one another often as they awaited Jesus' arrival.

11:22 *whatever you ask.* This comment seems to mean that Martha hoped for an immediate resurrection in spite of the fact that Lazarus's body had already begun to decay. Nothing is too difficult for God to do (see Ge 18:14; Jer 32:17,27 and notes).

11:25 *I am.* See note on 6:35. *life.* See note on 1:4. Jesus was saying more than that he gives resurrection and life. In some way these are identified with him, and his nature is such that final death is impossible for him. He is life (see 14:6 and note; Ac 3:15; Heb 7:16 and note). *He who believes … will live.* See note on 1:7. Jesus not only is life but conveys life to believers so that death will never triumph over them (cf. 1Co 15:57 and note).

11:26 *never die.* Believers may die physically but, as those who have eternal life, their physical death is not their ultimate end (v. 25). Death cannot destroy the life Christ gives.

11:27 *I believe.* Martha is often remembered for her shortcoming recorded in Lk 10:40–41. But she was a woman of faith, as this magnificent declaration shows.

[28]And after she had said this, she went back and called her sister Mary aside. "The Teacher[y] is here," she said, "and is asking for you." [29]When Mary heard this, she got up quickly and went to him. [30]Now Jesus had not yet entered the village, but was still at the place where Martha had met him.[z] [31]When the Jews who had been with Mary in the house, comforting her,[a] noticed how quickly she got up and went out, they followed her, supposing she was going to the tomb to mourn there.

[32]When Mary reached the place where Jesus was and saw him, she fell at his feet and said, "Lord, if you had been here, my brother would not have died."[b]

[33]When Jesus saw her weeping, and the Jews who had come along with her also weeping, he was deeply moved[c] in spirit and troubled.[d] [34]"Where have you laid him?" he asked.

"Come and see, Lord," they replied.

[35]Jesus wept.[e]

[36]Then the Jews said, "See how he loved him!"[f]

[37]But some of them said, "Could not he who opened the eyes of the blind man[g] have kept this man from dying?"[h]

Jesus Raises Lazarus From the Dead

[38]Jesus, once more deeply moved,[i] came to the tomb. It was a cave with a stone laid across the entrance.[j] [39]"Take away the stone," he said.

"But, Lord," said Martha, the sister of the dead man, "by this time there is a bad odor, for he has been there four days."[k]

[40]Then Jesus said, "Did I not tell you that if you believed,[l] you would see the glory of God?"[m]

[41]So they took away the stone. Then Jesus looked up[n] and said, "Father,[o] I thank you that you have heard me. [42]I knew that you always hear me, but I said this for the benefit of the people standing here,[p] that they may believe that you sent me."[q]

[43]When he had said this, Jesus called in a loud voice, "Lazarus, come out!"[r] [44]The dead man came out, his hands and feet wrapped with strips of linen,[s] and a cloth around his face.[t]

Jesus said to them, "Take off the grave clothes and let him go."

The Plot to Kill Jesus

[45]Therefore many of the Jews who had come to visit Mary,[u] and had seen what Jesus did,[v] put their faith in him.[w] [46]But some of them went to the Pharisees and told them what Jesus had done. [47]Then the chief priests and the Pharisees[x] called a meeting[y] of the Sanhedrin.[z]

"What are we accomplishing?" they asked. "Here is this man performing many miraculous signs.[a] [48]If we let him go on like this, everyone will believe in him, and then the Romans will come and take away both our place[a] and our nation."

[49]Then one of them, named Caiaphas,[b] who was high priest that year,[c] spoke up, "You know nothing at all! [50]You do not realize that it is better for you that one man die for the people than that the whole nation perish."[d]

11:28 [y] Mt 26:18; Jn 13:13
11:30 [z] ver 20
11:31 [a] ver 19
11:32 [b] ver 21
11:33 [c] ver 38 [d] S Jn 12:27
11:35 [e] Lk 19:41
11:36 [f] ver 3
11:37 [g] Jn 9:6,7 [h] ver 21,32
11:38 [i] ver 33 [j] Mt 27:60; Lk 24:2; Jn 20:1
11:39 [k] ver 17
11:40 [l] ver 23-25 [m] ver 4
11:41 [n] Jn 17:1 [o] S Mt 11:25
11:42 [p] Jn 12:30 [q] S Jn 3:17
11:43 [r] S Lk 7:14
11:44 [s] Jn 19:40 [t] Jn 20:7
11:45 [u] ver 19 [v] Jn 2:23 [w] Ex 14:31; S Jn 7:31
11:47 [x] ver 57 [y] Mt 26:3 [z] S Mt 5:22 [a] S Jn 2:11
11:49 [b] S Mt 26:3 [c] ver 51; Jn 18:13,14
11:50 [d] Jn 18:14

[a] 48 Or *temple*

11:28 *The Teacher.* A significant description to be given by a woman. The rabbis would not teach women (see 4:27 and note), but Jesus taught them frequently (see, e.g., Lk 10:38–42).
11:31 *to mourn there.* Wailing at a tomb was common, and the Jews immediately thought this was in Mary's mind. Because they followed her, Jesus got maximum publicity.
11:32 Cf. v. 21.
11:33 *weeping.* Both times the word denotes a loud expression of grief, i.e., "wailing." *troubled.* See notes on 12:27; 13:21.
11:35 *wept.* The Greek for this word is not the one for loud grief, as in v. 33, but one that denotes quiet weeping, i.e., "shed tears."
11:36 Cf. v. 5.
11:37 Their position was like that of Martha (v. 21) and Mary (v. 32), but they based it on Jesus' ability to give sight to the blind (cf. ch. 9).
11:38 *cave with a stone laid across the entrance.* This type of burial place was not uncommon in the Holy Land at this time, especially for the wealthy (cf. 20:1 and notes on Mk 15:46; Lk 24:2).
11:39 *four days.* See notes on vv. 4,17.
11:40 *glory.* See note on v. 4.
11:44 *strips of linen.* Narrow strips, like bandages. Sometimes a shroud was used (see note on 19:40). *a cloth.* A separate item.
11:45 *many of the Jews … put their faith in him.* Perhaps some who had been opposed to Jesus now came to believe (see notes on 1:7,19; 20:31).
11:46 *Pharisees.* See note on 7:32.
11:47 *the chief priests and the Pharisees.* In all four Gospels the Pharisees appear as Jesus' principal opponents throughout his public ministry. But they lacked political power, and it is the chief priests (see note on Mt 2:4) who were prominent in the events that led to Jesus' crucifixion. Here both groups are associated in a meeting of the Sanhedrin (see note on Mk 14:55). They did not deny the reality of the miraculous signs (see note on 2:11), but they did not understand their meaning, for they failed to believe.
11:48 *place.* Probably the temple (see NIV text note and Ac 6:13 and note; 21:28), though sometimes the Jews used the expression to denote Jerusalem.
11:49 *Caiaphas.* High priest c. A.D. 18–36. He was the son-in-law of Annas (see 18:13 and note), who had been deposed from the high priesthood by the Romans in A.D. 15. *high priest that year.* Probably means simply that he was high priest at that time. *You know nothing at all!* A remark typical of Sadducean rudeness (Caiaphas, as high priest, was a Sadducee). Josephus says that Sadducees "in their intercourse with their peers are as rude as to aliens." For Sadducees see note on Mt 3:7.
11:50 *better.* Caiaphas was concerned with political expediency, not with guilt and innocence. He believed that one man, no matter how innocent, should perish rather

51He did not say this on his own, but as
high priest that year he prophesied that
Jesus would die for the Jewish nation,
52and not only for that nation but also
for the scattered children of God, to bring
them together and make them one.[e] 53So
from that day on they plotted to take his
life.[f]

54Therefore Jesus no longer moved
about publicly among the Jews.[g] Instead
he withdrew to a region near the desert, to
a village called Ephraim, where he stayed
with his disciples.

55When it was almost time for the Jewish Passover,[h] many went up from the
country to Jerusalem for their ceremonial
cleansing[i] before the Passover. 56They kept
looking for Jesus,[j] and as they stood in
the temple area they asked one another,
"What do you think? Isn't he coming to
the Feast at all?" 57But the chief priests and
Pharisees had given orders that if anyone
found out where Jesus was, he should report it so that they might arrest him.

Jesus Anointed at Bethany

12:1-8Ref — Mt 26:6-13; Mk 14:3-9; Lk 7:37-39

12 Six days before the Passover,[k] Jesus
arrived at Bethany,[l] where Lazarus
lived, whom Jesus had raised from the
dead. 2Here a dinner was given in Jesus'
honor. Martha served,[m] while Lazarus
was among those reclining at the table
with him. 3Then Mary took about a pint[a]
of pure nard, an expensive perfume;[n] she
poured it on Jesus' feet and wiped his feet
with her hair.[o] And the house was filled
with the fragrance of the perfume.

4But one of his disciples, Judas Iscariot,
who was later to betray him,[p] objected,
5"Why wasn't this perfume sold and the
money given to the poor? It was worth a
year's wages.[b]" 6He did not say this because he cared about the poor but because
he was a thief; as keeper of the money
bag,[q] he used to help himself to what was
put into it.

7"Leave her alone," Jesus replied. "⌊It
was intended⌋ that she should save this
perfume for the day of my burial.[r] 8You
will always have the poor among you,[s] but
you will not always have me."

9Meanwhile a large crowd of Jews found
out that Jesus was there and came, not
only because of him but also to see Lazarus, whom he had raised from the dead.[t]
10So the chief priests made plans to kill
Lazarus as well, 11for on account of him[u]
many of the Jews were going over to Jesus
and putting their faith in him.[v]

The Triumphal Entry

12:12-15pp — Mt 21:4-9; Mk 11:7-10; Lk 19:35-38

12The next day the great crowd that had
come for the Feast heard that Jesus was
on his way to Jerusalem. 13They took palm
branches[w] and went out to meet him,
shouting,

[a] 3 Greek *a litra* (probably about 0.5 liter) [b] 5 Greek *three hundred denarii*

11:52 [e]Isa 49:6; Jn 10:16 **11:53** [f]S Mt 12:14 **11:54** [g]Jn 7:1 **11:55** [h]Ex 12:13,23,27; Mt 26:1,2; Mk 14:1; Jn 13:1 [i]2Ch 30:17,18 **11:56** [j]Jn 7:11 **12:1** [k]S Jn 11:55 [l]S Mt 21:17 **12:2** [m]Lk 10:38-42 **12:3** [n]Mk 14:3 [o]Jn 11:2 **12:4** [p]S Mt 10:4 **12:6** [q]Jn 13:29 **12:7** [r]Jn 19:40 **12:8** [s]Dt 15:11 **12:9** [t]Jn 11:43,44 **12:11** [u]ver 17,18; Jn 11:45 [v]S Jn 7:31 **12:13** [w]Lev 23:40

than that the nation be put in jeopardy. Ironically in A.D. 70 the nation still perished.

11:51 *as high priest.* Caiaphas was not a private citizen but God's high priest, and God overruled in what he said. *that year.* See note on v. 49. *prophesied.* His words were true in a way he could not imagine. Prophecy in Scripture is the impartation of divinely revealed truth. In reality Caiaphas's words meant that Jesus' death would be for the nation, not by way of removing political trouble, but by taking away the sins of those who believed in him.

11:52 *for the scattered children of God.* Jesus' death would have effects far beyond the nation (cf. 1:29; 3:16; 4:42; 10:16 and notes).

11:54 *he withdrew.* Jesus was not to die before his "time" (2:4; see note there), but he would not act imprudently. Knowing the attitude of his opponents, he withdrew. He would die for others, but in his own time, not that of his enemies.

11:55 *Passover.* See notes on 2:13; 5:1. *ceremonial cleansing.* Especially important at a time like Passover, because without it, it would not be possible to keep the Feast (see notes on 2:6; 18:28).

11:56 *Isn't he coming ...?* The question expected the answer "No."

12:1-11 All four Gospels have an account of a woman anointing Jesus. John's account seems to tell of the same incident recorded in Mt 26:6-13 and Mk 14:3-9, while that in Lk 7:36-50 is probably a different event (see notes on all these passages).

12:1 *Bethany.* See note on Mt 21:17.

12:3 *nard.* The name of both a plant and the fragrant oil it yielded. Since it was very expensive, Mary's act of devotion was costly. It was also an unusual act, both because she poured the oil on Jesus' feet (normally it was poured on the head) and because she used her hair to wipe them (a respectable woman did not unbind her hair in public). Further, it showed her humility, for it was a servant's work to attend to the feet (see notes on 1:27; 13:5).

12:4 *Judas Iscariot.* See notes on 6:71; 17:12.

12:5 *money given to the poor.* See note on Mk 14:5.

12:6 *thief.* The one passage from which we learn that Judas was dishonest. Yet he must have been thought to be a man of some reliability, for he was keeper of the money bag.

12:7 *save.* Probably the meaning is "save for this purpose." Perfume was normally associated with festivity, but it was also used in burials (see 19:39-40), and Jesus links it with his burial, which Mary's act unwittingly anticipates.

12:8 *You will always have the poor among you.* See note on Mk 14:7.

12:9 *Jews.* See note on 1:19.

12:10 The Jewish leaders previously had spoken of the death of one man (see 11:50 and note), but now they wanted another death. Sin grows (cf. Jas 1:15).

12:12 *great crowd.* Pilgrims who had gathered for the Passover Feast. Many of the pilgrims had doubtless seen and heard Jesus in Galilee, and they welcomed the opportunity to proclaim him as the Messiah.

12:13 *palm branches.* See note on Mk 11:8. They were used in celebration of victory. John saw a multitude with palm branches in heaven (Rev 7:9). *Hosanna!* See NIV text note; see also note on Mt 21:9. *name.* See note on 2:23. *Blessed is*

"Hosanna![a]"
"Blessed is he who comes in the name
of the Lord!"[b][x]
"Blessed is the King of Israel!"[y]
14 Jesus found a young donkey and sat
upon it, as it is written,
15 "Do not be afraid, O Daughter of Zion;
see, your king is coming,
seated on a donkey's colt."[c][z]
16 At first his disciples did not understand all this.[a] Only after Jesus was glorified[b] did they realize that these things had
been written about him and that they had
done these things to him.
17 Now the crowd that was with him[c]
when he called Lazarus from the tomb
and raised him from the dead continued to
spread the word. 18 Many people, because
they had heard that he had given this miraculous sign,[d] went out to meet him. 19 So
the Pharisees said to one another, "See,
this is getting us nowhere. Look how the
whole world has gone after him!"[e]

Jesus Predicts His Death

20 Now there were some Greeks[f] among
those who went up to worship at the Feast.
21 They came to Philip, who was from Bethsaida[g] in Galilee, with a request. "Sir,"
they said, "we would like to see Jesus."
22 Philip went to tell Andrew; Andrew and
Philip in turn told Jesus.

12:13 [x]Ps 118:25,26 [y]S Jn 1:49 **12:15** [z]Zec 9:9 **12:16** [a]S Mk 9:32 [b]ver 23; Jn 2:22; 7:39 **12:17** [c]Jn 11:42 **12:18** [d]ver 11; Lk 19:37 **12:19** [e]Jn 11:47,48 **12:20** [f]Jn 7:35; Ac 11:20 **12:21** [g]S Mt 11:21 **12:23** [h]S Mt 26:18 [i]Jn 13:32; 17:1 **12:24** [j]1Co 15:36 **12:25** [k]Mt 10:39; Mk 8:35; Lk 14:26; 17:33 [l]S Mt 25:46 **12:26** [m]Jn 14:3; 17:24; 2Co 5:8; Php 1:23; 1Th 4:17 **12:27** [n]Mt 26:38,39; Jn 11:33,38; 13:21 [o]S Mt 11:25 [p]ver 23 **12:28** [q]S Mt 3:17 **12:30** [r]Ex 19:9; Jn 11:42 **12:31** [s]Jn 16:11 [t]Jn 14:30; 16:11; 2Co 4:4; Eph 2:2; 1Jn 4:4; 5:19 **12:32** [u]ver 34; Isa 11:10; Jn 3:14; 8:28 [v]Jn 6:44 **12:33** [w]Jn 18:32; 21:19

23 Jesus replied, "The hour[h] has come for
the Son of Man to be glorified.[i] 24 I tell you
the truth, unless a kernel of wheat falls
to the ground and dies,[j] it remains only a
single seed. But if it dies, it produces many
seeds. 25 The man who loves his life will
lose it, while the man who hates his life
in this world will keep it[k] for eternal life.[l]
26 Whoever serves me must follow me; and
where I am, my servant also will be.[m] My
Father will honor the one who serves me.
27 "Now my heart is troubled,[n] and what
shall I say? 'Father,[o] save me from this
hour'?[p] No, it was for this very reason I
came to this hour. 28 Father, glorify your
name!"
Then a voice came from heaven,[q] "I
have glorified it, and will glorify it again."
29 The crowd that was there and heard it
said it had thundered; others said an angel
had spoken to him.
30 Jesus said, "This voice was for your
benefit,[r] not mine. 31 Now is the time for
judgment on this world;[s] now the prince
of this world[t] will be driven out. 32 But I,
when I am lifted up from the earth,[u] will
draw all men to myself."[v] 33 He said this
to show the kind of death he was going
to die.[w]

[a] *13* A Hebrew expression meaning "Save!" which became an exclamation of praise [b] *13* Psalm 118:25,26 [c] *15* Zech. 9:9

the King of Israel! The people's addition to the words of the psalm, which John alone records. It reflects his special interest in Jesus' royalty, which he brings out throughout the passion narrative.

12:14 *donkey.* See notes on Zec 9:9; Mt 21:2,7; Mk 11:2; Lk 19:30.

12:15 *Daughter of Zion.* A personification of Jerusalem (see note on 2Ki 19:21).

12:16 An example of the meaning of 16:13. *glorified.* See notes on v. 41; 11:4; 13:31. Only after the crucifixion and the coming of the Holy Spirit did the disciples appreciate the meaning of the prophecy and its fulfillment.

12:19 *Pharisees.* See note on 7:32. *whole world has gone out after him!* A good example of hyperbole in the Bible.

12:20 *Greeks.* Probably "God-fearers" (see Ac 13:14 and note), people attracted to Judaism by its monotheism and morality, but repelled by its nationalism and requirements such as circumcision. They worshiped in the synagogues but did not become proselytes (cf. note on Ac 16:14).

12:21 *Philip.* A Greek name, which may be why they came to this disciple (though he was not the only one of the Twelve to have a Greek name). *to see.* Means "to have an interview with." After v. 22 John records no more about these Greeks (yet see note on v. 32). He regarded their coming as important but not their conversation with Jesus. Jesus came to die for the world, and the coming of these Gentiles indicates the scope of the effectiveness of his approaching crucifixion. *Bethsaida.* See note on Mt 11:21.

12:22 *Andrew.* See note on 1:40.

12:23 *The hour has come.* The hour to which everything else led (see note on 2:4). *glorified.* Jesus was speaking about his death on the cross and his subsequent resurrection and exaltation (see notes on v. 41; 11:4; 13:31).

12:24 *if it dies, it produces.* The principle of life through death is seen in the plant world. The kernel must perish as a kernel if there is to be a plant.

12:25 *the man who hates his life ... will keep it.* To love one's life here and now—to concentrate on one's own success—is to lose what matters (cf. Mk 8:34–35; Lk 9:23–24 and notes). Supremely, of course, the principle is seen in the cross of Jesus. *hates.* Love for God must be such that all other loves are, by comparison, hatred (see notes on Mal 1:3; Lk 14:26). *eternal life.* See note on 3:15.

12:27 *troubled.* John's equivalent to the agony in Gethsemane described in the other Gospels (see Mt 26:38–39 and notes; Mk 14:34–36; Lk 22:42 and note). *this hour.* Jesus faced the prospect of becoming sin (or a sin offering) for sinful people (see 2Co 5:21 and note). He considered praying for God to save him from this death, but refused to pray it, because the very reason he had come was to die.

12:28 *Father, glorify your name!* His prayer was not for deliverance but for the Father to be glorified (cf. Mt 6:9 and note). The voice from heaven gave the answer. *name.* See note on 2:23.

12:31 *judgment on this world.* The cross was God's judgment on the world. *prince of this world.* Satan (see 16:11). The cross would seem to be his triumph; in fact, it was his defeat. Out of it would flow the greatest good ever to come to the world.

12:32 *lifted up.* Jesus refers here first of all to his crucifixion (see v. 33), but he most likely refers also to his resurrection and ascension into heaven to reign at God's right

[34]The crowd spoke up, "We have heard
from the Law[x] that the Christ[a] will remain
forever,[y] so how can you say, 'The Son of
Man[z] must be lifted up'?[a] Who is this 'Son
of Man'?"
[35]Then Jesus told them, "You are going
to have the light[b] just a little while longer. Walk while you have the light,[c] before
darkness overtakes you.[d] The man who
walks in the dark does not know where he
is going. [36]Put your trust in the light while
you have it, so that you may become sons
of light."[e] When he had finished speaking,
Jesus left and hid himself from them.[f]

The Jews Continue in Their Unbelief

[37]Even after Jesus had done all these miraculous signs[g] in their presence, they still
would not believe in him. [38]This was to
fulfill the word of Isaiah the prophet:

"Lord, who has believed our message
and to whom has the arm of the
Lord been revealed?"[b h]

[39]For this reason they could not believe,
because, as Isaiah says elsewhere:

[40]"He has blinded their eyes
and deadened their hearts,
so they can neither see with their eyes,
nor understand with their hearts,
nor turn—and I would heal them."[c i]

12:34 [x]S Jn 10:34 [y]Ps 110:4; Isa 9:7; Eze 37:25; Da 7:14 [z]S Mt 8:20 [a]Jn 3:14
12:35 [b]ver 46 [c]Eph 5:8 [d]1Jn 1:6; 2:11
12:36 [e]ver 46; S Lk 16:8 [f]Jn 8:59
12:37 [g]S Jn 2:11
12:38 [h]Isa 53:1; Ro 10:16
12:40 [i]Isa 6:10; S Mt 13:13,15
12:41 [j]Isa 6:1-4 [k]Lk 24:27
12:42 [l]ver 11; Jn 7:48 [m]S Jn 7:13 [n]Jn 9:22
12:43 [o]1Sa 15:30 [p]S Ro 2:29
12:44 [q]S Mt 10:40; Jn 5:24
12:45 [r]S Jn 14:9
12:46 [s]S Jn 1:4
12:47 [t]S Jn 3:17
12:48 [u]Jn 5:45
12:49 [v]Jn 14:31
12:50 [w]S Mt 25:46 [x]S Jn 14:24

[41]Isaiah said this because he saw Jesus'
glory[j] and spoke about him.[k]
[42]Yet at the same time many even
among the leaders believed in him.[l] But
because of the Pharisees[m] they would not
confess their faith for fear they would
be put out of the synagogue;[n] [43]for they
loved praise from men[o] more than praise
from God.[p]
[44]Then Jesus cried out, "When a man
believes in me, he does not believe in me
only, but in the one who sent me.[q] [45]When
he looks at me, he sees the one who sent
me.[r] [46]I have come into the world as a
light,[s] so that no one who believes in me
should stay in darkness.
[47]"As for the person who hears my
words but does not keep them, I do not
judge him. For I did not come to judge the
world, but to save it.[t] [48]There is a judge
for the one who rejects me and does not
accept my words; that very word which I
spoke will condemn him[u] at the last day.
[49]For I did not speak of my own accord,
but the Father who sent me commanded me[v] what to say and how to say it. [50]I
know that his command leads to eternal
life.[w] So whatever I say is just what the
Father has told me to say."[x]

[a] *34* Or *Messiah* [b] *38* Isaiah 53:1 [c] *40* Isaiah 6:10

hand (see v. 41; 3:14 and notes; see also 8:28; cf. Ac 2:33; 5:31, where "exalted" renders the same Greek word). *all men.* Christ will draw people to himself without regard for nationality, ethnic affiliation or status. It is significant that Greek Gentiles were present on this occasion (see v. 20 and note).

12:34 *the Law.* Here seems to mean OT Scripture in general (see note on 10:34), the reference being to passages such as Ps 89:30–37; 110:4; Isa 9:7 (see notes there). *the Christ.* See NIV text note; see also note on 1:25. *Son of Man.* The only place in the Gospels where anyone other than Jesus used the expression, and even here Jesus is being quoted (see note on Mk 8:31).

12:35–36 *light.* Closely identified with Jesus, as seen from the call to believe in the light (see notes on 1:4; 8:12).

12:37 *they still would not believe.* God's ancient people should have responded when God sent his Messiah. They should have seen the significance of the signs he did.

12:39 *could not believe.* Does not mean that the people in question had no choice. They purposely rejected God and chose evil, and v. 40 explains that God in turn brought on them a judicial blinding of eyes and hardening of hearts. Yet many Jewish leaders did believe in Jesus as the Messiah (see v. 42 and note).

12:40 These words from Isa 6:10 (see note there) are quoted by Jesus (see Mt 13:13–14; Mk 4:12; Lk 8:10) and by Paul (Ac 28:26–27). See notes on Mk 4:12; Lk 8:11.

12:41 *saw Jesus' glory.* Isaiah spoke primarily of the glory of God (Isa 6:3). John spoke of the glory of Jesus and made no basic distinction between the two, attesting Jesus' oneness with God (cf. Heb 1:6,10 and notes). The thought of glory here is complex. There is the idea of majesty, and there is also the idea (which meant so much to John) that Jesus' death on the cross and his subsequent resurrection and exaltation show his real glory. Isaiah foresaw the rejection of Christ, as the passages quoted (Isa 53:1; 6:10) show. He spoke of the Messiah both in the words about blind eyes and hard hearts, on the one hand, and about healing, on the other. This is the cross and this is glory, for the cross and resurrection and exaltation portray both suffering and healing, rejection and triumph, humiliation and glory.

12:42 *many ... leaders believed.* John does not give a picture of unrelieved gloom. Many Jewish leaders believed (see note on 1:7), though they remained secret believers for fear of excommunication (see note on 9:22). Two such cases in this Gospel are Nicodemus and Joseph of Arimathea (see 3:1–2; 19:38–39 and notes).

12:44 *cried out.* The words are given special emphasis by being spoken in a loud voice. *believe in me.* John ends his story of the public ministry of Jesus with an appeal for belief (see notes on 1:7; 20:31; see also Introduction: Purpose and Emphases). He does not say when Jesus spoke these words (they may have been uttered earlier), but they are a fitting close to this part of his account. *the one who sent me.* Jesus' mission as well as the inseparability of the Father and the Son are stressed throughout this Gospel (see note on 4:34).

12:46 *I have come into the world.* Points to both Jesus' preexistence and his mission. *light.* See vv. 35–36 and note.

12:47 *to judge.* Not the purpose of Jesus' coming (3:17–18), but judgment is the other side of salvation. It is not the purpose of the sun's shining to cast shadows, but when the sun shines, shadows are inevitable.

12:49 *the Father ... commanded me what to say.* Jesus' hearers have a great responsibility. His "word" (v. 48) is that which the Father commanded him to say. To reject it, therefore, is to reject God.

12:50 *eternal life.* See note on 3:15. *So.* Jesus said what he did in order to fulfill the will of the Father—a wonderful note on which to end the account of Jesus' public ministry (see v. 44 and note).

Jesus Washes His Disciples' Feet

13 It was just before the Passover Feast.[y] Jesus knew that the time had come[z] for him to leave this world and go to the Father.[a] Having loved his own who were in the world, he now showed them the full extent of his love.[a]

[2]The evening meal was being served, and the devil had already prompted Judas Iscariot, son of Simon, to betray Jesus.[b] [3]Jesus knew that the Father had put all things under his power,[c] and that he had come from God[d] and was returning to God; [4]so he got up from the meal, took off his outer clothing, and wrapped a towel around his waist.[e] [5]After that, he poured water into a basin and began to wash his disciples' feet,[f] drying them with the towel that was wrapped around him.

[6]He came to Simon Peter, who said to him, "Lord, are you going to wash my feet?"

[7]Jesus replied, "You do not realize now what I am doing, but later you will understand."[g]

[8]"No," said Peter, "you shall never wash my feet."

Jesus answered, "Unless I wash you, you have no part with me."

[9]"Then, Lord," Simon Peter replied, "not just my feet but my hands and my head as well!"

[10]Jesus answered, "A person who has had a bath needs only to wash his feet; his whole body is clean. And you are clean,[h] though not every one of you."[i] [11]For he knew who was going to betray him,[j] and that was why he said not every one was clean.

[12]When he had finished washing their feet, he put on his clothes and returned to his place. "Do you understand what I have done for you?" he asked them. [13]"You call me 'Teacher'[k] and 'Lord,'[l] and rightly so, for that is what I am. [14]Now that I, your Lord and Teacher, have washed your feet, you also should wash one another's feet.[m] [15]I have set you an example that you should do as I have done for you.[n] [16]I tell you the truth, no servant is greater than his master,[o] nor is a messenger greater than the one who sent him. [17]Now that you know these things, you will be blessed if you do them.[p]

Jesus Predicts His Betrayal

[18]"I am not referring to all of you;[q] I know those I have chosen.[r] But this is to fulfill the scripture:[s] 'He who shares my bread[t] has lifted up his heel[u] against me.'[b][v]

[19]"I am telling you now before it happens, so that when it does happen you

13:1 [y]S Jn 11:55 [z]S Mt 26:18 [a]Jn 16:28
13:2 [b]S Mt 10:4
13:3 [c]S Mt 28:18 [d]Jn 8:42; 16:27,28,30; 17:8
13:4 [e]S Mt 20:28
13:5 [f]S Lk 7:44
13:7 [g]ver 12
13:10 [h]Jn 15:3 [i]ver 18
13:11 [j]S Mt 10:4
13:13 [k]Mt 26:18; Jn 11:28 [l]S Mt 28:18; Lk 1:43; 2:11; 6:46; 11:1; Ac 10:36; Ro 10:9,12; 14:9; 1Co 12:3; Php 2:11; Col 2:6
13:14 [m]1Pe 5:5
13:15 [n]S Mt 11:29; S 1Ti 4:12
13:16 [o]Mt 10:24; Lk 6:40; Jn 15:20
13:17 [p]Mt 7:24,25; Lk 11:28; Jas 1:25
13:18 [q]ver 10 [r]Jn 15:16,19 [s]S Mt 1:22 [t]Mt 26:23 [u]Jn 6:70 [v]Ps 41:9

[a] *1* Or *he loved them to the last* [b] *18* Psalm 41:9

13:1—17:26 John has by far the longest account of the upper room, though curiously he says nothing about the institution of the Lord's Supper. Still we owe to him most of our information about what our Lord said to his disciples on that night. One feature of the discourse is Jesus' emphasis on love. The Greek noun *agape* ("love") and the verb *agapao* ("love") occur only eight times in chs. 1–12 but 31 times in chs. 13–17.

13:1 *Passover Feast.* See notes on 2:13; 5:1. *the time.* See note on 2:4.

13:2 *evening meal.* Some believe that this feast was a fellowship meal eaten sometime before the Passover Feast. This would mean that the Last Supper could not have been the Passover meal as the Synoptic Gospels clearly indicate. However, this meal may have been the Passover Feast itself, in which case the accounts of the Synoptics and John would agree. *the devil.* See v. 27. *Judas Iscariot.* See note on 6:71.

13:3 *the Father had put all things under his power.* John again emphasizes the fulfillment of God's plan and Jesus' control of the situation. *was returning to God.* See 20:17 and note.

13:5 *began to wash his disciples' feet.* A menial task (see note on 1:27), normally performed by a servant. On this occasion there was no servant and no one else volunteered. Jesus' action was during the meal, not upon arrival, done deliberately to emphasize a point. It was a lesson in humility, but it also set forth the principle of selfless service that was so soon to be exemplified in the cross. John alone tells of this incident, but Luke says that in rebuking the disciples over a quarrel concerning who would be the greatest, Jesus said, "I am among you as one who serves" (Lk 22:27). Jesus' life of service would culminate on the cross (see Php 2:5–8 and notes).

13:8 *No.* Characteristically, Peter objected, though apparently no one else did. He was a mixture of humility (he did not want Jesus to perform this lowly service for him) and pride (he tried to dictate to Jesus; see also Mt 16:21–23). *Unless I wash you.* Jesus' reply looks beyond the incident to what it symbolizes: Peter needed a spiritual cleansing. The external washing was a picture of cleansing from sin.

13:9 *my hands and my head.* Peter's response was wholehearted, but he was still dictating to Jesus.

13:10 *only to wash his feet.* A man would bathe himself before going to a feast. When he arrived, he only needed to wash his feet to be entirely clean again.

13:11 *he knew.* Again John emphasizes Jesus' command of the situation.

13:13 *'Teacher' ... 'Lord.'* An instructor would normally be called "Teacher," but "Lord" referred to one occupying the supreme place. Jesus accepted both titles.

13:14–15 Some Christians believe that Christ intended to institute a foot-washing ordinance to be practiced regularly. Most Christians, however, interpret Christ's action here as providing an example of humble service.

13:14 *wash one another's feet.* Christians should be willing to perform the most menial services for one another.

13:16 With minor variations this saying, which Jesus used often, is found in 15:20; Mt 10:24; Lk 6:40 (cf. Lk 22:27).

13:18 *not referring to all of you.* Jesus was leading up to his prediction of the betrayal (see v. 21 and note). *shares my bread.* To eat bread together was a mark of close fellowship (see note on Ps 41:9). *lifted up his heel.* May be derived from a horse's preparing to kick, or perhaps something like shaking off the dust from one's feet (see Lk 9:5 and note).

13:19 *so that ... you will believe.* See note on 12:44. Jesus' concern was for the disciples, not himself. *I am He.* An emphatic form of speech, such as that in 8:58 (see note there).

will believe[w] that I am He.[x] 20 I tell you the
truth, whoever accepts anyone I send accepts me; and whoever accepts me accepts
the one who sent me."[y]
21 After he had said this, Jesus was troubled in spirit[z] and testified, "I tell you the
truth, one of you is going to betray me."[a]
22 His disciples stared at one another, at
a loss to know which of them he meant.
23 One of them, the disciple whom Jesus
loved,[b] was reclining next to him. 24 Simon
Peter motioned to this disciple and said,
"Ask him which one he means."
25 Leaning back against Jesus, he asked
him, "Lord, who is it?"[c]
26 Jesus answered, "It is the one to whom
I will give this piece of bread when I have
dipped it in the dish." Then, dipping the
piece of bread, he gave it to Judas Iscariot,[d] son of Simon. 27 As soon as Judas took
the bread, Satan entered into him.[e]
"What you are about to do, do quickly,"
Jesus told him, 28 but no one at the meal
understood why Jesus said this to him.
29 Since Judas had charge of the money,[f]
some thought Jesus was telling him to buy
what was needed for the Feast,[g] or to give
something to the poor.[h] 30 As soon as Judas
had taken the bread, he went out. And it
was night.[i]

Jesus Predicts Peter's Denial

13:37,38pp — Mt 26:33-35; Mk 14:29-31; Lk 22:33,34

31 When he was gone, Jesus said, "Now
is the Son of Man[j] glorified[k] and God is
glorified in him.[l] 32 If God is glorified in
him,[a] God will glorify the Son in himself,[m]
and will glorify him at once.
33 "My children, I will be with you only a
little longer. You will look for me, and just
as I told the Jews, so I tell you now: Where
I am going, you cannot come.[n]
34 "A new command[o] I give you: Love
one another.[p] As I have loved you, so you
must love one another.[q] 35 By this all men
will know that you are my disciples, if you
love one another."[r]
36 Simon Peter asked him, "Lord, where
are you going?"[s]
Jesus replied, "Where I am going, you
cannot follow now,[t] but you will follow
later."[u]
37 Peter asked, "Lord, why can't I follow you now? I will lay down my life for
you."
38 Then Jesus answered, "Will you really
lay down your life for me? I tell you the
truth, before the rooster crows, you will
disown me three times![v]

Jesus Comforts His Disciples

14 "Do not let your hearts be troubled.[w]
Trust[x] in God[b];[y] trust also in me. 2 In
my Father's house are many rooms; if it
were not so, I would have told you. I am

[a] 32 Many early manuscripts do not have *If God is glorified in him.* [b] 1 Or *You trust in God*

13:19 [w] Jn 14:29; 16:4 [x] Jn 4:26; 8:24
13:20 [y] S Mt 10:40
13:21 [z] S Jn 12:27 [a] Mt 26:21
13:23 [b] Jn 19:26; 20:2; 21:7,20
13:25 [c] Mt 26:22; Jn 21:20
13:26 [d] S Mt 10:4
13:27 [e] Lk 22:3
13:29 [f] Jn 12:6 [g] ver 1 [h] Jn 12:5
13:30 [i] Lk 22:53
13:31 [j] S Mt 8:20 [k] Jn 7:39; 12:23 [l] Jn 14:13; 17:4; 1Pe 4:11
13:32 [m] Jn 17:1
13:33 [n] S Jn 7:33,34
13:34 [o] Jn 15:12; 1Jn 2:7-11; 3:11 [p] Lev 19:18; 1Th 4:9; 1Pe 1:22 [q] Jn 15:12; Eph 5:2; 1Jn 4:10,11
13:35 [r] 1Jn 3:14; 4:20
13:36 [s] Jn 16:5 [t] ver 33; Jn 14:2 [u] Jn 21:18,19; 2Pe 1:14
13:38 [v] Jn 18:27
14:1 [w] ver 27 [x] S Jn 3:15 [y] Ps 4:5

13:20 *anyone I send ... the one who sent me.* Jesus' mission is a common theme in this Gospel (see notes on 4:34; 12:44; 17:3–4,18), and now the mission of his followers is linked with it (cf. 20:21).

13:21 *troubled.* See 11:33 and note. Though he knew of it long before it happened, Jesus was grieved by the betrayal of a friend.

13:22 *at a loss.* The disciples' astonishment shows that Judas had concealed his contacts with the high priests. No one suspected him (see v. 28), but all seem to have thought that the betrayal would be involuntary (see Mk 14:19).

13:23 *the disciple whom Jesus loved.* Usually thought to be John, the author of this Gospel (see Introduction: Author). The expression does not, of course, mean that Jesus did not love the others, but that there was a special bond with this man. *reclining.* At a dinner, guests reclined on couches, leaning on the left elbow with the head toward the table (cf. note on Mk 14:18).

13:26 *the one to whom I ... give ... bread ... dipped ... in the dish.* Evidently Judas was near Jesus, possibly in the seat of honor. John used Judas's full name (see note on 6:71) in recording this solemn moment.

13:27 *As soon as Judas took the bread.* Evidently the critical moment. If the giving of the bread to Judas was a mark of honor, it also seems to have been a final appeal—which Judas did not accept. *Satan.* The name is used only here in John (cf. v. 2; see notes on Job 1:6; Zec 3:1; Rev 12:9–10). *do quickly.* Jesus' words once more indicate his control. He would die as he directed, not as his opponents determined.

13:29 *the Feast.* See v. 1 and note on v. 2. *the poor.* See 12:5 and note on Mk 14:5.

13:30 *night.* In light of John's emphasis on the conflict between light and darkness, this may have been more than a time note (cf. Lk 22:53 and note)—picturing also the darkness of Judas's soul (cf. notes on 1:4; 8:12; Isa 60:2).

13:31 *Son of Man.* See note on Mk 8:31. *glorified.* See v. 32 and note on 7:39. Here the idea of glory includes a reference to Jesus' sacrificial death on the cross and the glorious salvation that would result. *God is glorified in him.* The glory of the Father is closely bound to that of the Son.

13:34 *A new command.* In a sense it was an old one (see Lev 19:18 and note), but for Christ's disciples it was new, because it was the mark of their special bond, created by Christ's great love for them (cf. Mt 22:37,39; Mk 12:31; Lk 10:27 and notes). *As I have loved you.* Our standard is Christ's love for us.

13:35 *love.* The distinguishing mark of Christ's followers (cf. 1Jn 3:23; 4:7–8,11–12,19–21).

13:36 *where are you going?* Peter seems to have ignored Jesus' words about love and was more concerned about his Master's departure. In Jesus' reply "you" is singular and thus personal to Peter, whereas in v. 33 the word is plural.

13:37 *I will lay down my life.* Words similar to those of the good shepherd in 10:11. Peter was characteristically sure of himself, when in fact he would not at this time lay down his life for Jesus (though later he would; see 21:18–19 and notes). Exactly the opposite would be true.

13:38 *you will disown me three times.* Peter's denial is prophesied in all four Gospels (Mt 26:33–35; Mk 14:29–31; Lk 22:31–34).

14:1 *Do not ... be troubled.* The apostles had just received disturbing news (13:33,36). *Trust in God ... in me.* Jesus' antidote for a troubled heart (cf. Ps 56:3–4; Isa 26:3–4).

14:2 *my Father's house.* Heaven. *many rooms.* Lit. "many dwelling places," implying permanence and plenty of room.

going there[z] to prepare a place for you.
3And if I go and prepare a place for you, I
will come back[a] and take you to be with
me that you also may be where I am.[b]
4You know the way to the place where I
am going."

Jesus the Way to the Father

5Thomas[c] said to him, "Lord, we don't
know where you are going, so how can we
know the way?"
6Jesus answered, "I am[d] the way[e] and
the truth[f] and the life.[g] No one comes to
the Father except through me.[h] 7If you
really knew me, you would know[a] my Father as well.[i] From now on, you do know
him and have seen him."
8Philip[j] said, "Lord, show us the Father
and that will be enough for us."
9Jesus answered: "Don't you know me,
Philip, even after I have been among you
such a long time? Anyone who has seen
me has seen the Father.[k] How can you say,
'Show us the Father'? 10Don't you believe
that I am in the Father, and that the Father
is in me?[l] The words I say to you are not
just my own.[m] Rather, it is the Father, living in me, who is doing his work. 11Believe
me when I say that I am in the Father and
the Father is in me; or at least believe on
the evidence of the miracles themselves.[n]
12I tell you the truth, anyone who has
faith[o] in me will do what I have been doing.[p] He will do even greater things than
these, because I am going to the Father.
13And I will do whatever you ask[q] in my
name, so that the Son may bring glory to
the Father. 14You may ask me for anything
in my name, and I will do it.

Jesus Promises the Holy Spirit

15"If you love me, you will obey what I
command.[r] 16And I will ask the Father, and
he will give you another Counselor[s] to be
with you forever— 17the Spirit of truth.[t]
The world cannot accept him,[u] because it
neither sees him nor knows him. But you
know him, for he lives with you and will
be[b] in you. 18I will not leave you as orphans;[v] I will come to you.[w] 19Before long,
the world will not see me anymore, but
you will see me.[x] Because I live, you also
will live.[y] 20On that day[z] you will realize
that I am in my Father,[a] and you are in me,
and I am in you.[b] 21Whoever has my commands and obeys them, he is the one who
loves me.[c] He who loves me will be loved
by my Father,[d] and I too will love him and
show myself to him."

[a] 7 Some early manuscripts *If you really have known me, you will know* [b] 17 Some early manuscripts *and is*

14:2 [z] Jn 13:33, 36; 16:5 **14:3** [a] ver 18, 28; S Mt 16:27 [b] S Jn 12:26 **14:5** [c] S Jn 11:16 **14:6** [d] S Jn 6:35 [e] Jn 10:9; Eph 2:18; Heb 10:20 [f] Jn 1:14 [g] S Jn 1:4 [h] Ac 4:12 **14:7** [i] Jn 1:18; S 1Jn 2:23 **14:8** [j] S Jn 1:43 **14:9** [k] Isa 9:6; Jn 1:14; 12:45; 2Co 4:4; Php 2:6; Col 1:15; Heb 1:3 **14:10** [l] ver 11, 20; Jn 10:38; 17:21 [m] S ver 24 **14:11** [n] Jn 5:36; 10:38 **14:12** [o] Mt 21:21 [p] Lk 10:17 **14:13** [q] S Mt 7:7 **14:15** [r] ver 21, 23; Ps 103:18; Jn 15:10; 1Jn 2:3-5; 3:22, 24; 5:3; 2Jn 6; Rev 12:17; 14:12 **14:16** [s] ver 26; Jn 15:26; 16:7 **14:17** [t] Jn 15:26; 16:13; 1Jn 4:6; 5:6 [u] 1Co 2:14 **14:18** [v] 1Ki 6:13 [w] ver 3, 28; S Mt 16:27 **14:19** [x] Jn 7:33, 34; 16:16 [y] Jn 6:57 **14:20** [z] Jn 16:23, 26 [a] ver 10, 11; Jn 10:38; 17:21 [b] S Ro 8:10 **14:21** [c] S ver 15 [d] Dt 7:13; Jn 16:27; 1Jn 2:5

14:3 *I will come back.* Jesus comes in many ways, but the primary reference here is to his second advent (cf. Rev 22:7,12,20).
14:4 *way.* See v. 6 and note.
14:5 *Thomas.* He was honest, and plainly told the Lord he did not understand (see note on 11:16).
14:6 *I am.* See note on 6:35. *the way.* To God. Jesus is not one way among many, but the only way (see Ac 4:12; Heb 10:19–20 and notes). In the early church, Christianity was sometimes called "the Way" (see, e.g., Ac 9:2 and note). *the truth.* A key emphasis in this Gospel (see note on 1:14). *the life.* See note on 1:4. Very likely the statement means "I am the way (to the Father) in that I am the truth and the life."
14:7 *me … my Father.* Once more Jesus stresses the intimate connection between the Father and himself. Jesus brought a full revelation of the Father (see 1:18 and note), so that the apostles had real knowledge of him.
14:10 *not just my own.* Jesus' teaching was not of human origin, and there was an inseparable connection between his words and his work.
14:11 *Believe … that I am in the Father and the Father is in me.* Saving faith is trust in a person, but it must also have factual content. Faith includes believing that Jesus is one with the Father (see 10:30; 17:21–22 and notes).
14:12 *I tell you the truth.* See note on Mk 3:28. *greater things.* Miracles (see v. 11). These depended on Jesus' going to the Father, because they are works done in the strength of the Holy Spirit, whom Jesus would send from the Father (see vv. 16–17; 15:26 and notes).
14:13 *in my name.* Not simply prayer that mentions Jesus' name but prayer in accordance with all that the person who bears the name is (see note on 2:23). It is prayer aimed at carrying forward the work Jesus did—prayer that he himself will answer (see also v. 14).
14:15 *love … obey.* Love, like faith (see Jas 2:14–26 and notes), cannot be separated from obedience.
14:16 *the Father … will give you.* The first of a series of important passages about the Holy Spirit (see v. 26; 15:26; 16:7–15 and notes), the gift of the Father. *another.* Besides Jesus. *Counselor.* Or "Helper" or "Advocate." It is a legal term, but with a broader meaning than "counsel for the defense" (see 1Jn 2:1 and note). It referred to any person who helped someone in trouble with the law. The Spirit will always stand by Christ's people.
14:17 *Spirit of truth.* In essence and in action the Spirit is characterized by truth. He brings people to the truth of God. All three persons of the Trinity are linked with truth. See also the Father (see 4:24 and note; cf. Ps 31:5; Isa 65:16 and note) and the Son (see v. 6 and note). *The world.* Which takes no notice of the Spirit of God (see notes on 1:9; 1Co 2:14). But the Spirit was "with" Jesus' disciples and would be "in" them. Some believe the latter relationship (indwelling) specifically anticipates the coming of the Holy Spirit on the day of Pentecost (see Ac 1:2; 2:4,17,38 and notes; cf. Ro 8:9).
14:18 *I will come to you.* The words relate to the coming of the Spirit, but Jesus also speaks of his own appearances after the resurrection and at his second coming (see vv. 3 and note, 19, 28; 16:22 and note).
14:19 *world … but you.* The cross separated the world (who would not see Jesus thereafter) from the disciples (who would). *Because I live, you also will live.* The life of the Christian always depends on the life of Christ (see 1:4; 3:15; 10:10; Php 1:21 and notes).
14:20 *On that day you will realize.* The resurrection would radically change their thinking.
14:21 *obeys … loves.* Love for Christ and keeping his commands cannot be separated (see note on v. 15).

22Then Judas[e] (not Judas Iscariot) said,
"But, Lord, why do you intend to show
yourself to us and not to the world?"[f]
23Jesus replied, "If anyone loves me,
he will obey my teaching.[g] My Father
will love him, and we will come to him
and make our home with him.[h] 24He
who does not love me will not obey my
teaching. These words you hear are not
my own; they belong to the Father who
sent me.[i]
25"All this I have spoken while still with
you. 26But the Counselor,[j] the Holy Spirit,
whom the Father will send in my name,[k]
will teach you all things[l] and will remind
you of everything I have said to you.[m]
27Peace I leave with you; my peace I give
you.[n] I do not give to you as the world
gives. Do not let your hearts be troubled[o]
and do not be afraid.
28"You heard me say, 'I am going away
and I am coming back to you.'[p] If you
loved me, you would be glad that I am going to the Father,[q] for the Father is greater
than I.[r] 29I have told you now before it
happens, so that when it does happen you
will believe.[s] 30I will not speak with you
much longer, for the prince of this world[t]
is coming. He has no hold on me, 31but
the world must learn that I love the Father
and that I do exactly what my Father has
commanded me.[u]
"Come now; let us leave.

14:22 [e]Lk 6:16; Ac 1:13 [f]Ac 10:41 **14:23** [g]S ver 15 [h]S Ro 8:10 **14:24** [i]ver 10; Dt 18:18; Jn 5:19; 7:16; 8:28; 12:49,50 **14:26** [j]ver 16; Jn 15:26; 16:7 [k]Ac 2:33 [l]Jn 16:13; 1Jn 2:20,27 [m]Jn 2:22 **14:27** [n]Nu 6:26; Ps 85:8; Mal 2:6; S Lk 2:14; 24:36; Jn 16:33; Php 4:7; Col 3:15 [o]ver 1 **14:28** [p]ver 2-4, 18; S Mt 16:27 [q]Jn 5:18 [r]Jn 10:29 **14:29** [s]Jn 13:19; 16:4 **14:30** [t]S Jn 12:31 **14:31** [u]Jn 10:18; 12:49 **15:1** [v]S Jn 6:35 [w]Ps 80:8-11; Isa 5:1-7 **15:2** [x]ver 6; S Mt 3:10 [y]Ps 92:14; Mt 3:8; 7:20; Gal 5:22; Eph 5:9; Php 1:11 **15:3** [z]Jn 13:10; 17:17; Eph 5:26 **15:4** [a]S Jn 6:56 **15:5** [b]ver 16 **15:6** [c]ver 2; Eze 15:4; S Mt 3:10 **15:7** [d]ver 4; S Jn 6:56 [e]S Mt 7:7 **15:8** [f]S Mt 9:8

The Vine and the Branches

15 "I am[v] the true vine,[w] and my Father is the gardener. 2He cuts off
every branch in me that bears no fruit,[x]
while every branch that does bear fruit[y] he
prunes[a] so that it will be even more fruitful. 3You are already clean because of the
word I have spoken to you.[z] 4Remain in
me, and I will remain in you.[a] No branch
can bear fruit by itself; it must remain in
the vine. Neither can you bear fruit unless
you remain in me.
5"I am the vine; you are the branches. If
a man remains in me and I in him, he will
bear much fruit;[b] apart from me you can
do nothing. 6If anyone does not remain in
me, he is like a branch that is thrown away
and withers; such branches are picked up,
thrown into the fire and burned.[c] 7If you
remain in me[d] and my words remain in
you, ask whatever you wish, and it will be
given you.[e] 8This is to my Father's glory,[f]

[a] 2 The Greek for *prunes* also means *cleans*.

loved by my Father . . . I too will love him. The love of the Father cannot be separated from that of the Son.

14:22 *why . . . ?* Judas (and, for that matter, the other apostles) probably looked for Jesus to fulfill popular Messianic expectations. It was not easy, therefore, to understand how that would mean showing himself to the disciples but not to the world.

14:23 *loves . . . obey . . . love.* Again love and obedience are linked (see vv. 15,21; 15:10 and notes).

14:24 Once more the close relationship between Jesus' words and the Father's is stressed (see v. 10; 7:16).

14:26 *Counselor.* See note on v. 16. *Holy Spirit.* See 1:33 and note. *whom the Father will send.* Both the Father and the Son are involved in the sending (see 15:26 and note). *name.* See notes on v. 13; 2:23. *remind you of everything I have said to you.* Crucial for the life of the church—and for the writing of the NT.

14:27 *Peace . . . my peace.* A common Hebrew greeting (see 20:19 and note, 21,26), which Jesus uses here in an unusual way. The term speaks, in effect, of the salvation that Christ's redemptive work will achieve for his disciples—total well-being and inner rest of spirit, in fellowship with God. All true peace is his gift, which the repetition emphasizes. *I do not give . . . as the world gives.* In its greetings of peace the world can only express a longing or wish. But Jesus' peace is real and present (see 16:33 and note). *troubled.* See note on v. 1.

14:28 *heard me say.* Cf. v. 3. *the Father is greater than I.* Revealing the subordinate role Jesus accepted as a necessary part of the incarnation. The statement must be understood in the light of the unity between the Father and the Son (see 10:30 and note).

14:30 *prince of this world.* See note on 12:31. *has no hold on me.* Satan has a hold on people because of their fallen state. Since Christ was sinless, Satan could have no hold on him.

14:31 *I do exactly what my Father has commanded me.* Jesus had stressed the importance of his followers being obedient (see vv. 15,21,23 and notes), and he set the example. With these words he goes to fulfill his mission (chs. 18–19).

15:1 *I am.* See note on 6:35. *the true vine.* The vine is frequently used in the OT as a symbol of Israel (see, e.g., Ps 80:8–16; Isa 5:1–7; Jer 2:21 and notes). When this imagery is used, Israel is often shown as lacking in some way. Jesus, however, is "the true vine."

15:2 *cuts off.* A reference to judgment (see note on v. 6). *prunes.* Pruning produces fruitfulness. In the NT the figure of good fruit represents the product of a godly life (see Mt 3:8; 7:16–20) or virtues of character (see Gal 5:22–23; Eph 5:9; Php 1:11 and notes).

15:3 *clean.* See NIV text note on v. 2. *the word.* Sums up the message of Jesus.

15:4 *Remain in me.* The believer has no fruitfulness apart from union and fellowship with Christ. A branch out of contact with the vine is lifeless.

15:5 *I am the vine.* See note on v. 1. The repetition gives emphasis. *remains in me and I in him.* A living union with Christ is absolutely necessary; without it there is nothing (cf. Php 4:13 and note).

15:6 *thrown into the fire and burned.* Judged (see note on v. 2). In light of such passages as 6:39; 10:27–29 (see notes there), these branches probably do not represent true believers. Genuine salvation is evidenced by a life of fruitfulness (see notes on vv. 2,4,10; see also Heb 6:9, "things that accompany salvation," and note there; cf. Mt 7:19–23).

15:7 *my words remain in you.* It is impossible to pray correctly apart from knowing and believing the teachings of Christ. *ask whatever you wish.* See 14:13; 1Jn 5:14 and notes.

15:8 *to my Father's glory.* The Father is glorified in the work of the Son (see 13:31 and note), and he is also glorified in the fruit-bearing of disciples (see Mt 7:20; Lk 6:43–45).

that you bear much fruit, showing yourselves to be my disciples.[g]
9"As the Father has loved me,[h] so have
I loved you. Now remain in my love. 10If
you obey my commands,[i] you will remain
in my love, just as I have obeyed my Father's commands and remain in his love.
11I have told you this so that my joy may
be in you and that your joy may be complete.[j] 12My command is this: Love each
other as I have loved you.[k] 13Greater love
has no one than this, that he lay down his
life for his friends.[l] 14You are my friends[m]
if you do what I command.[n] 15I no longer
call you servants, because a servant does
not know his master's business. Instead,
I have called you friends, for everything
that I learned from my Father I have made
known to you.[o] 16You did not choose me,
but I chose you and appointed you[p] to go
and bear fruit[q]—fruit that will last. Then
the Father will give you whatever you ask
in my name.[r] 17This is my command: Love
each other.[s]

The World Hates the Disciples

18"If the world hates you,[t] keep in mind
that it hated me first. 19If you belonged to
the world, it would love you as its own. As
it is, you do not belong to the world, but I
have chosen you[u] out of the world. That is
why the world hates you.[v] 20Remember the
words I spoke to you: 'No servant is greater
than his master.'[a][w] If they persecuted
me, they will persecute you also.[x] If they
obeyed my teaching, they will obey yours
also. 21They will treat you this way because
of my name,[y] for they do not know the
One who sent me.[z] 22If I had not come and
spoken to them,[a] they would not be guilty
of sin. Now, however, they have no excuse
for their sin.[b] 23He who hates me hates my
Father as well. 24If I had not done among
them what no one else did,[c] they would
not be guilty of sin.[d] But now they have
seen these miracles, and yet they have hated both me and my Father. 25But this is to
fulfill what is written in their Law:[e] 'They
hated me without reason.'[b][f]
26"When the Counselor[g] comes, whom I
will send to you from the Father,[h] the Spirit of truth[i] who goes out from the Father,
he will testify about me.[j] 27And you also
must testify,[k] for you have been with me
from the beginning.[l]
16 "All this[m] I have told you so that
you will not go astray.[n] 2They will
put you out of the synagogue;[o] in fact,
a time is coming when anyone who kills
you will think he is offering a service to
God.[p] 3They will do such things because
they have not known the Father or me.[q]

[a] *20* John 13:16 [b] *25* Psalms 35:19; 69:4

15:8 [g] Jn 8:31 **15:9** [h] Jn 17:23,26 **15:10** [i] S Jn 14:15 **15:11** [j] S Jn 3:29 **15:12** [k] ver 17; S Jn 13:34 **15:13** [l] Ge 44:33; Jn 10:11; Ro 5:7,8 **15:14** [m] Job 16:20; Pr 18:24; Lk 12:4 [n] Mt 12:50 **15:15** [o] Jn 8:26 **15:16** [p] ver 19; Jn 13:18 [q] ver 5 [r] S Mt 7:7 **15:17** [s] ver 12 **15:18** [t] Isa 66:5; Jn 7:7; 1Jn 3:13 **15:19** [u] ver 16 [v] Jn 17:14 **15:20** [w] S Jn 13:16 [x] 2Ti 3:12 **15:21** [y] Isa 66:5; Mt 5:10,11; 10:22; Lk 6:22; Ac 5:41; 1Pe 4:14; Rev 2:3 [z] Jn 16:3 **15:22** [a] Eze 2:5; 3:7 [b] Jn 9:41; Ro 1:20; 2:1 **15:24** [c] Jn 5:36 [d] Jn 9:41 **15:25** [e] S Jn 10:34 [f] Ps 35:19; 69:4; 109:3 **15:26** [g] Jn 14:16 [h] Jn 14:26; 16:7 [i] S Jn 14:17 [j] 1Jn 5:7 **15:27** [k] S Lk 24:48; Jn 21:24; 1Jn 1:2; 4:14 [l] S Lk 1:2 **16:1** [m] Jn 15:18-27 [n] Mt 11:6 **16:2** [o] Jn 9:22; 12:42 [p] Isa 66:5; Ac 26:9,10; Rev 6:9 **16:3** [q] Jn 15:21; 17:25; 1Jn 3:1

15:10 *obey ... as I have obeyed.* Again the importance of obedience (cf. 14:15,21,23), and again the example of Christ (see 14:31 and note). *my love ... his love.* See vv. 12,14. Obedience and love go together (see 14:15,21,23; 1Jn 2:5 and notes; 5:2–3).

15:11 *joy.* Mentioned previously in this Gospel only in 3:29, but one of the characteristic notes of the upper room discourse (see 16:22,24 and note on 16:22; 17:13). The Christian way is never dreary, for Jesus desires his disciples' joy to be complete (see also Introduction to Philippians: Characteristics, 4; see also Php 4:4; 1Th 5:16; 1Jn 1:4 and notes).

15:13 Christ's love was not only in words but also in his sacrificial death (see Eph 5:25 and note).

15:15 *servants ... friends.* Servants are simply agents, doing what their master commands and often not understanding their master's purpose. But Jesus takes his friends into his confidence. *everything ... I have made known to you.* From 16:12 we learn that though Jesus had let his disciples know as much as they were able to absorb of the Father's plan, the revelation was not yet complete. The Spirit would make other things known in due course (see 16:12–13 and notes).

15:16 *I chose you ... bear fruit ... ask.* Disciples normally chose the particular rabbi to whom they wanted to be attached, but it was not so with Jesus' disciples. He chose them, and for a purpose—the bearing of fruit (see v. 2 and note). We usually desire a strong prayer life in order that we may be fruitful, but here it is the other way around. Jesus enables us to bear fruit, and then the Father will hear our prayers. *in my name.* See notes on 2:23; 14:13.

15:18–19 *world.* Here refers to the human system that opposes God's purpose (see note on 1:9).

15:21 *They will treat you this way.* Because Christians do not belong to the world, persecution from the world is inevitable. The basic reason is the world's ignorance and rejection of the Father (cf. 16:3). *name.* See note on 2:23.

15:22 *no excuse.* Privilege and responsibility go together. The Jews had had the great privilege of having the Son of God among them—in addition to having received God's special revelation in the OT. Those who rejected him were totally guilty and without excuse. If he had not come to them, they would still have been sinners, but they would not have been guilty of rejecting him directly (see v. 24).

15:23 Contrast 13:20.

15:25 *to fulfill what is written.* See note on Ps 35:19. In the end God's purpose is always accomplished, despite the belief of those who reject Jesus that they have successfully opposed it. *Law.* See notes on 10:34; 12:34.

15:26 *Counselor.* See note on 14:16. *I will send.* See notes on 14:16,26. *Spirit of truth.* See note on 14:17. *goes out from the Father.* Probably refers to the Spirit's being sent to do the Father's work on earth rather than to his eternal relationship with the Father. *testify.* See note on 1:7.

15:27 *you also.* Emphatic. Believers bear their testimony to Christ in the power of the Spirit (see Ac 1:8 and note). But it is their testimony, and they are responsible for bearing it. *from the beginning.* The apostles bore the definitive testimony, for they were uniquely chosen and taught by Christ and were eyewitnesses of his glory (see Lk 24:48; Ac 10:39,41).

16:2 *put you out of the synagogue.* See note on 9:22. *a service to God.* Religious people have often persecuted others in the strong conviction that they were doing God's will (see Ac 26:9–11; Gal 1:13–14).

16:3 *the Father.* See note on 5:17. *or me.* Again the Father and the Son are linked. Not to know Christ is to be ignorant of the Father (see 14:7,10–11; 17:6–7,22–23,26 and notes).

4I have told you this, so that when the time
comes you will remember[r] that I warned
you. I did not tell you this at first because
I was with you.[s]

The Work of the Holy Spirit

5"Now I am going to him who sent me,[t]
yet none of you asks me, 'Where are you
going?'[u] 6Because I have said these things,
you are filled with grief.[v] 7But I tell you the
truth: It is for your good that I am going
away. Unless I go away, the Counselor[w]
will not come to you; but if I go, I will
send him to you.[x] 8When he comes, he
will convict the world of guilt[a] in regard
to sin and righteousness and judgment:
9in regard to sin,[y] because men do not believe in me; 10in regard to righteousness,[z]
because I am going to the Father,[a] where
you can see me no longer; 11and in regard
to judgment, because the prince of this
world[b] now stands condemned.

12"I have much more to say to you,
more than you can now bear.[c] 13But
when he, the Spirit of truth,[d] comes, he
will guide you into all truth.[e] He will not
speak on his own; he will speak only what
he hears, and he will tell you what is yet
to come. 14He will bring glory to me by
taking from what is mine and making it
known to you. 15All that belongs to the Father is mine.[f] That is why I said the Spirit
will take from what is mine and make it
known to you.

16"In a little while[g] you will see me no
more, and then after a little while you will
see me."[h]

The Disciples' Grief Will Turn to Joy

17Some of his disciples said to one another, "What does he mean by saying, 'In
a little while you will see me no more, and
then after a little while you will see me,'[i]
and 'Because I am going to the Father'?"[j]
18They kept asking, "What does he mean
by 'a little while'? We don't understand
what he is saying."

19Jesus saw that they wanted to ask him
about this, so he said to them, "Are you
asking one another what I meant when
I said, 'In a little while you will see me
no more, and then after a little while you
will see me'? 20I tell you the truth, you will
weep and mourn[k] while the world rejoices. You will grieve, but your grief will turn
to joy.[l] 21A woman giving birth to a child
has pain[m] because her time has come; but
when her baby is born she forgets the anguish because of her joy that a child is
born into the world. 22So with you: Now
is your time of grief,[n] but I will see you
again[o] and you will rejoice, and no one

16:4 [r] Jn 13:19; 14:29 [s] Jn 15:27
16:5 [t] ver 10, 17, 28; Jn 7:33 [u] Jn 13:36; 14:5
16:6 [v] ver 22
16:7 [w] Jn 14:16, 26; 15:26 [x] Jn 7:39; 14:26
16:9 [y] Jn 15:22
16:10 [z] Ac 3:14; 7:52; Ro 1:17; 3:21, 22; 1Pe 3:18 [a] S ver 5
16:11 [b] S Jn 12:31
16:12 [c] Mk 4:33; 1Co 3:2
16:13 [d] S Jn 14:17 [e] Ps 25:5; Jn 14:26
16:15 [f] Jn 17:10
16:16 [g] S Jn 7:33 [h] ver 22; Jn 14:18-24
16:17 [i] ver 16 [j] ver 5
16:20 [k] Mk 16:10; Lk 23:27 [l] Jn 20:20
16:21 [m] Isa 13:8; 21:3; 26:17; Mic 4:9; 1Th 5:3
16:22 [n] ver 6 [o] ver 16

[a] 8 Or *will expose the guilt of the world*

16:5 *none of you asks me, 'Where are you going?'* Peter had asked such a question (13:36), but quickly turned his attention to another subject. His concern had been about what would happen to himself and the others and not about where Jesus was going.
16:6 *you are filled with grief.* Because of his announced departure.
16:7 *Unless I go away.* Jesus did not say why the Spirit would not come until he went away, but clearly taught that his saving work on the cross was necessary before the sending of the Spirit. *Counselor.* See note on 14:16. *I will send him.* See note on 14:26.
16:8 *he will convict the world.* The work the Spirit does in the world (see NIV text note). The NT normally speaks of his work in believers.
16:9 *in regard to sin.* Apart from the Spirit's convicting work, people can never see themselves as sinners. *because men do not believe.* May mean that their sin is their failure to believe, or that their unbelief is a classic example of sin. Typically, John may have had both of these in mind.
16:10 *in regard to righteousness.* The righteousness brought about by Christ's sacrificial death (see Ro 1:17; 3:21–24 and notes). No one but the Holy Spirit can reveal to a person that a righteous status before God does not depend on good works but on Christ's death on the cross. *because I am going to the Father.* The ascension, which as part of Christ's exaltation placed God's seal of approval on Christ's redemptive act.
16:11 *in regard to judgment.* Jesus was speaking of the defeat of Satan, which was a form of judgment, not simply a victory. More than power is in question. God acts with justice. *prince of this world.* See note on 12:31.
16:12 *more than you can now bear.* This may mean "more than you can understand now," or "more than you can perform without the Spirit's help" (to live out Christ's teaching requires the enabling presence of the Spirit).
16:13 *Spirit of truth.* See note on 14:17. *only what he hears.* We are not told whether he hears from the Father or the Son, but it obviously does not matter, for the verse stresses the close relationship among the three. *what is yet to come.* Probably means the whole Christian way or revelation (presented and preserved in the apostolic writings), still future at the time Jesus spoke.
16:14 *glory to me.* See note on 1:14. The Spirit draws no attention to himself but promotes the glory of Christ.
16:15 *All that belongs to the Father is mine.* Cf. 17:10. The three Persons are closely related.
16:16 *a little while ... a little while.* Few doubt that the first phrase refers to the interval before the crucifixion. But interpretations differ as to whether the second refers to the interval preceding the resurrection or the coming of the Spirit or the second coming of Christ. It seems that the language here best fits the resurrection (see v. 22 and note).
16:17 *going to the Father.* See v. 10 and note. Jesus had not linked this with "a little while," but the apostles saw them as connected.
16:20 *weep.* The same verb for loud wailing as in 11:33 (see note there), which carries the idea of deep sorrow and its outward expression.
16:21 *A woman giving birth.* Giving birth usually causes both pain and joy (cf. Isa 26:17–19; 66:7–14; Hos 13:13–14).
16:22 *I will see you again.* As in v. 16, probably a reference to Jesus' appearances after his resurrection. *no one will take away your joy.* The resurrection would change things permanently, bringing a joy that cannot be removed by the world's assaults (see note on 15:11).

will take away your joy.[p] 23 In that day[q] you
will no longer ask me anything. I tell you
the truth, my Father will give you whatever you ask in my name.[r] 24 Until now you
have not asked for anything in my name.
Ask and you will receive,[s] and your joy
will be complete.[t]
25 "Though I have been speaking figuratively,[u] a time is coming[v] when I will no
longer use this kind of language but will
tell you plainly about my Father. 26 In that
day you will ask in my name.[w] I am not
saying that I will ask the Father on your
behalf. 27 No, the Father himself loves you
because you have loved me[x] and have
believed that I came from God.[y] 28 I came
from the Father and entered the world;
now I am leaving the world and going
back to the Father."[z]
29 Then Jesus' disciples said, "Now you
are speaking clearly and without figures of
speech.[a] 30 Now we can see that you know
all things and that you do not even need
to have anyone ask you questions. This
makes us believe[b] that you came from
God."[c]
31 "You believe at last!"[a] Jesus answered.
32 "But a time is coming,[d] and has come,
when you will be scattered,[e] each to his
own home. You will leave me all alone.[f]
Yet I am not alone, for my Father is
with me.[g]
33 "I have told you these things, so that
in me you may have peace.[h] In this world
you will have trouble.[i] But take heart! I
have overcome[j] the world."

Jesus Prays for Himself

17 After Jesus said this, he looked toward heaven[k] and prayed:
"Father, the time has come.[l] Glorify
your Son, that your Son may glorify
you.[m] 2 For you granted him authority over all people[n] that he might give
eternal life[o] to all those you have giv-
en him.[p] 3 Now this is eternal life: that
they may know you,[q] the only true
God, and Jesus Christ, whom you
have sent.[r] 4 I have brought you glory[s] on earth by completing the work
you gave me to do.[t] 5 And now, Father,
glorify me[u] in your presence with the
glory I had with you[v] before the world
began.[w]

Jesus Prays for His Disciples

6 "I have revealed you[b][x] to those
whom you gave me[y] out of the world.
They were yours; you gave them to
me and they have obeyed your word.

[a] 31 Or *"Do you now believe?"* [b] 6 Greek *your name*; also in verse 26

16:22 [p] ver 20; Jer 31:12 **16:23** [q] ver 26; Jn 14:20 [r] S Mt 7:7 **16:24** [s] S Mt 7:7 [t] S Jn 3:29 **16:25** [u] ver 29; Ps 78:2; Eze 20:49; Mt 13:34; Mk 4:33,34; Jn 10:6 [v] ver 2 **16:26** [w] ver 23,24 **16:27** [x] Jn 14:21,23 [y] ver 30; S Jn 13:3 **16:28** [z] ver 5,10,17; Jn 13:3 **16:29** [a] S ver 25 **16:30** [b] 1Ki 17:24 [c] ver 27; S Jn 13:3 **16:32** [d] ver 2,25 [e] Mt 26:31 [f] Mt 26:56 [g] Jn 8:16,29 **16:33** [h] S Jn 14:27 [i] Jn 15:18-21 [j] Ro 8:37; 1Jn 4:4; 5:4; Rev 2:7,11,17,26; 3:5,12,21; 21:7 **17:1** [k] Jn 11:41 [l] S Mt 26:18 [m] Jn 12:23; 13:31,32 **17:2** [n] S Mt 28:18 [o] S Mt 25:46 [p] ver 6,9,24; Da 7:14; Jn 6:37,39 **17:3** [q] S Php 3:8 [r] ver 8,18,21,23,25; S Jn 3:17 **17:4** [s] Jn 13:31 [t] S Jn 19:30 **17:5** [u] ver 1 [v] Php 2:6 [w] S Jn 1:2 **17:6** [x] ver 26; Jn 1:18 [y] S ver 2

16:23 *you will no longer ask me anything.* Seems to mean asking for information (rather than asking in prayer), which would not be necessary after the resurrection. Jesus then moved on to the subject of prayer. However, Jesus may have been saying that his disciples previously had been praying to Christ, but after his death and resurrection they were to go directly to the Father and pray in Christ's name (see vv. 24,26–27 and notes). *name.* See notes on 2:23; 14:13.

16:24 *Until now.* Previously they had asked the Father or Christ, but they had not asked the Father in Christ's name. *your joy.* See note on 15:11.

16:25 *I have been speaking figuratively.* Throughout the discourse, not just in the immediately preceding words. *a time is coming.* After the resurrection.

16:26 *in my name.* See notes on 2:23; 14:13. *I am not saying that I will ask.* Not a contradiction of Ro 8:34; Heb 7:25; 1Jn 2:1 (see notes there). Those passages mean that Christ's presence in heaven as the crucified and risen Lord is itself an intercession. Here the teaching is that there will be no need for him to make petitions in our behalf.

16:27 *the Father himself loves you.* Christ is explaining why the disciples can come directly to the Father in prayer. It is because the disciples have loved and trusted in Jesus, and in love God will hear their requests in Jesus' name.

16:29 *without figures of speech.* See v. 25 and note.

16:30 *believe that you came from God.* Two recurring themes of this Gospel: believing (see note on 1:7) and Jesus' coming from God (see notes on 4:34; 17:3,8).

16:32 *you will be scattered.* The disciples had faith, but not enough to stand firm in the face of disaster. Jesus knew they would fail (see Mt 26:31 and note; cf. Zec 13:7 and note); however, his church is not built on people's strength but on God's ability to use people even after they have failed.

16:33 Notice the contrasts: between "in me" and "in this world" (see note on 1:9) and between "peace" and "trouble." *I have overcome.* Just before his death Jesus affirms his final victory.

17:1–26 Jesus' longest recorded prayer.

17:1 *he looked toward heaven.* The customary attitude in prayer (11:41; Ps 123:1; Mk 7:34), though sometimes Jesus prostrated himself (see Mt 26:39). *Father.* Used of God in John's Gospel about 120 times. *the time.* See note on 2:4. *Glorify ... glorify.* See notes on 1:14; 7:39; 13:31. The glory of the Father and that of the Son are closely connected, and the death by which Jesus would glorify God would lead to eternal life for believers (v. 2).

17:2 *granted.* The act of giving is stressed in this chapter (vv. 4,6–9,11–12,14,22,24); see note on 3:27. *eternal life.* See note on 3:15. *those you have given him.* Again God's initiative in salvation is stressed (see vv. 6,12; 6:37,39,44 and notes).

17:3 *sent.* Again the mission of Jesus is mentioned (see 13:20 and note).

17:4 *I have brought you glory.* Christ's mission was not self-centered. *the work you gave me.* Jesus emphasized the supreme place of the Father (see note on 4:34).

17:5 *glorify me ... with the glory I had with you.* Jesus asks the Father to return him to his previous position of glory, to exchange humiliation for glorification. This occurred at Christ's resurrection and exaltation to God's right hand. *world.* The universe (see notes on v. 14; 1:9). The Greek word for "world" occurs 18 times in this prayer.

17:6 *I have revealed you.* See NIV text note and notes on 2:23; 14:13; cf. 1:18. *those whom you gave me.* Again the divine initiative (see note on v. 2).

7Now they know that everything you
have given me comes from you. 8For
I gave them the words you gave me[z]
and they accepted them. They knew
with certainty that I came from you,[a]
and they believed that you sent me.[b]
9I pray for them.[c] I am not praying
for the world, but for those you have
given me,[d] for they are yours. 10All
I have is yours, and all you have is
mine.[e] And glory has come to me
through them. 11I will remain in the
world no longer, but they are still in
the world,[f] and I am coming to you.[g]
Holy Father, protect them by the power of your name — the name you gave
me — so that they may be one[h] as we
are one.[i] 12While I was with them, I
protected them and kept them safe
by that name you gave me. None has
been lost[j] except the one doomed to
destruction[k] so that Scripture would
be fulfilled.[l]
13"I am coming to you now,[m] but
I say these things while I am still in
the world, so that they may have the
full measure of my joy[n] within them.
14I have given them your word and

17:8 [z]ver 14,26; S Jn 14:24 [a]S Jn 13:3 [b]ver 3,18,21,23, 25; S Jn 3:17
17:9 [c]Lk 22:32 [d]S ver 2
17:10 [e]Jn 16:15
17:11 [f]Jn 13:1 [g]ver 13; Jn 7:33 [h]ver 21-23; Ps 133:1 [i]Jn 10:30
17:12 [j]S Jn 6:39 [k]Jn 6:70 [l]S Mt 1:22
17:13 [m]ver 11 [n]S Jn 3:29
17:14 [o]Jn 15:19 [p]ver 16; Jn 8:23
17:15 [q]S Mt 5:37
17:16 [r]ver 14
17:17 [s]S Jn 15:3; 2Sa 7:28; 1Ki 17:24
17:18 [t]ver 3,8,21,23, 25; S Jn 3:17 [u]Jn 20:21
17:19 [v]ver 17
17:21 [w]Jer 32:39 [x]ver 11; Jn 10:38 [y]ver 3,8,18,23, 25; S Jn 3:17
17:22 [z]Jn 1:14 [a]S Jn 14:20

the world has hated them,[o] for they
are not of the world any more than I
am of the world.[p] 15My prayer is not
that you take them out of the world
but that you protect them from the
evil one.[q] 16They are not of the world,
even as I am not of it.[r] 17Sanctify[a]
them by the truth; your word is truth.[s]
18As you sent me into the world,[t] I
have sent them into the world.[u] 19For
them I sanctify myself, that they too
may be truly sanctified.[v]

Jesus Prays for All Believers

20"My prayer is not for them alone.
I pray also for those who will believe
in me through their message, 21that all
of them may be one,[w] Father, just as
you are in me and I am in you.[x] May
they also be in us so that the world
may believe that you have sent me.[y]
22I have given them the glory that you
gave me,[z] that they may be one as we
are one:[a] 23I in them and you in me.
May they be brought to complete unity to let the world know that you sent

[a] 17 Greek *hagiazo* (*set apart for sacred use* or *make holy*); also in verse 19

17:7 *everything ... comes from you.* Only as people see the Father at work in Jesus do they have a proper concept of God. The disciples had at last reached this understanding. Cf. Jas 1:17.

17:8 Three things about the disciples are mentioned: (1) They accepted the teaching (unlike the Pharisees and others who heard it but did not receive it). (2) They knew with certainty Jesus' divine origin. Acceptance of that revelation led them further into truth. (3) They believed (see notes on 1:7,12; 20:31).

17:9 *not ... for the world.* The only prayer Jesus could pray for the world was that it cease to be worldly (i.e., opposed to God), and this he did pray (vv. 21,23).

17:11 *Holy Father.* A form of address found only here in the NT (but cf. 1Pe 1:16; Rev 4:8 and notes). The name suggests both remoteness and nearness; God is both awe-inspiring (see Lev 11:44 and note) and loving. *that they may be one.* The latter part of the prayer strongly emphasizes unity. Here the unity is already given, not something to be achieved. The meaning is "that they continually be one" rather than "that they become one." The unity is to be like that between the Father and the Son. It is much more than unity of organization, but the church's present divisions are the result of the failures of Christians.

17:12 *I protected them.* Christ's power is adequate for every need (cf. 1Pe 1:5 and note). *the one doomed to destruction.* Lit. "the son of destruction" (see 2Th 2:3 and note), i.e., one belonging to the sphere of damnation and destined for destruction (but predestination is not in view here). Reference is to Judas Iscariot.

17:13 *my joy.* See note on 15:11.

17:14 *the world.* The world that is hostile to God and God's people (see notes on v. 5; 1:9). *not of the world.* They do not have the mind-set of the world, i.e., hostility to God, for they have been "born of the Spirit" (3:8) and are "children of God" (1:12).

17:15 *not that you take them out of the world.* The world is where Jesus' disciples are to do their work; Jesus does not wish them to be taken from it until that work is done (see v. 18). *the evil one.* Especially active in the world (Mt 6:13; 1Jn 5:19), making God's protection indispensable.

17:17 *Sanctify.* See NIV text note; see also v. 19 and note. *the truth; your word.* Sanctification and revelation (as recorded in God's word) go together (cf. 1Pe 2:2 and note). For the relationship between Christ's teaching and truth see 8:31 – 32 and note on 8:32.

17:18 *As you sent me ... I have sent them.* Jesus' mission is one of the dominant themes of this Gospel and is given as the pattern for his followers (see v. 3 and note). *into the world.* We may long for heaven, but it is on earth that our work is done.

17:19 *I sanctify myself.* This statement appears to be unparalleled. In the Septuagint (the pre-Christian Greek translation of the OT) the verb is used of consecrating priests (Ex 28:41) and sacrifices (Ex 28:38; Nu 18:9). Jesus solemnly sets himself apart to do God's will, which at this point meant his death. *that they too may be ... sanctified.* Jesus died on the cross not only to save us but also to consecrate us to God's service (see NIV text note on v. 17).

17:20 *those who will believe in me.* Jesus had just spoken of the mission and the sanctification of his followers (vv. 18 – 19). He was confident that they would spread the gospel, and he prayed for those who would believe as a result. All future believers are included in this prayer.

17:21 *that all of them may be one.* See note on v. 11. *Father.* See note on v. 1. *that the world may believe.* The unity of believers should have an effect on outsiders, to convince them of the mission of Christ. Jesus' prayer is a rebuke of the groundless and often bitter divisions among believers.

17:22 *glory.* See note on v. 1. Believers are to be characterized by humility and service, just as Christ was, and it is on them that God's glory rests. *that they may be one as we are one.* Again the Lord emphasized the importance of unity among his followers, and again the standard is the unity of the Father and the Son.

17:23 *I in them and you in me.* There are two indwellings here: that of the Son in believers, and that of the

me[b] and have loved them[c] even as
you have loved me.
24"Father, I want those you have
given me[d] to be with me where I am,[e]
and to see my glory,[f] the glory you
have given me because you loved me
before the creation of the world.[g]
25"Righteous Father, though the
world does not know you,[h] I know
you, and they know that you have
sent me.[i] 26I have made you known
to them,[j] and will continue to make
you known in order that the love you
have for me may be in them[k] and that
I myself may be in them."

Jesus Arrested

18:3-11pp — Mt 26:47-56; Mk 14:43-50; Lk 22:47-53

18 When he had finished praying, Jesus
left with his disciples and crossed the
Kidron Valley.[l] On the other side there was
an olive grove,[m] and he and his disciples
went into it.[n]
2Now Judas, who betrayed him, knew
the place, because Jesus had often met
there with his disciples.[o] 3So Judas came
to the grove, guiding[p] a detachment of
soldiers and some officials from the chief
priests and Pharisees.[q] They were carrying
torches, lanterns and weapons.
4Jesus, knowing all that was going to
happen to him,[r] went out and asked them,
"Who is it you want?"[s]
5"Jesus of Nazareth,"[t] they replied.
"I am he," Jesus said. (And Judas the
traitor was standing there with them.)
6When Jesus said, "I am he," they drew
back and fell to the ground.
7Again he asked them, "Who is it you
want?"[u]
And they said, "Jesus of Nazareth."
8"I told you that I am he," Jesus answered. "If you are looking for me, then let
these men go." 9This happened so that the
words he had spoken would be fulfilled: "I
have not lost one of those you gave me."[a][v]
10Then Simon Peter, who had a sword,
drew it and struck the high priest's servant, cutting off his right ear. (The servant's name was Malchus.)
11Jesus commanded Peter, "Put your
sword away! Shall I not drink the cup[w] the
Father has given me?"

Jesus Taken to Annas

18:12,13pp — Mt 26:57

12Then the detachment of soldiers with
its commander and the Jewish officials[x]
arrested Jesus. They bound him 13and
brought him first to Annas, who was the
father-in-law of Caiaphas,[y] the high priest
that year. 14Caiaphas was the one who had
advised the Jews that it would be good if
one man died for the people.[z]

17:23 [b] ver 3,8, 18,21,25; S Jn 3:17 [c] Jn 16:27 **17:24** [d] S ver 2 [e] S Jn 12:26 [f] Jn 1:14 [g] ver 5; S Mt 25:34; S Jn 1:2 **17:25** [h] Jn 15:21; 16:3 [i] ver 3,8,18,21, 23; S Jn 3:17; 16:27 **17:26** [j] ver 6 [k] Jn 15:9 **18:1** [l] 2Sa 15:23 [m] ver 26; S Mt 21:1 [n] Mt 26:36 **18:2** [o] Lk 21:37; 22:39 **18:3** [p] Ac 1:16 [q] ver 12 **18:4** [r] Jn 6:64; 13:1,11 [s] ver 7 **18:5** [t] S Mk 1:24 **18:7** [u] ver 4 **18:9** [v] S Jn 6:39 **18:11** [w] S Mt 20:22 **18:12** [x] ver 3 **18:13** [y] ver 24; S Mt 26:3 **18:14** [z] Jn 11:49-51

[a] 9 John 6:39

Father in the Son. It is because the latter is a reality that the former can take place. *complete unity.* Again the emphasis on unity has an evangelistic aim. This time it is connected not only with the mission of Jesus but also with God's love for people and for Christ.

17:24 *Father.* See note on v. 1. *I want.* Means "I will that." Jesus said, "I will"—his last will and testament for his followers. Where he himself was concerned, he prayed, "not what I will, but what you will" (Mk 14:36). *to be with me.* The Christian's greatest blessing (see 14:3; 1Th 4:17 and note). *my glory.* Perhaps used here to refer to Jesus' eternal splendor (see 1Jn 3:2). Or Jesus' prayer may have been that in the life to come they might fully appreciate the glory of his lowly service (cf. Eph 2:7).

17:25 *Righteous Father.* A form of address found only here in the NT (cf. note on "Holy Father" in v. 11). *they know.* They did not know God directly and personally, but they knew that God had sent Christ. To recognize God in Christ's mission is a great advance over anything the world can know.

17:26 *made you known to them.* See 16:3 and note.

18:1 *crossed the Kidron Valley.* East of Jerusalem and dry except during the rainy season (see map, pp. 1552–1553).

18:3 *Judas.* See note on 6:71. *officials from the chief priests and Pharisees.* Equivalent to the temple guard sent by the Sanhedrin (see notes on Mt 2:4; 3:7; Mk 14:55). *torches.* Resinous pieces of wood fastened together. *lanterns.* Terra-cotta holders into which household lamps could be inserted.

18:4 *knowing all that was going to happen to him.* Jesus was not taken by surprise.

18:5 *I am.* See 6:35; 8:58 and notes. *with them.* John does not let us forget where Judas belonged.

18:6 *fell to the ground.* They came to arrest a meek peasant and instead were met in the dim light by a majestic and powerful person.

18:8 *I am.* The threefold repetition (vv. 5,6,8) emphasizes the solemn words. *let these men go.* Jesus cared for the disciples even as he was going to his death. Twice he had made the arresting party say plainly that he was the one they wanted (vv. 4–5,7).

18:9 *would be fulfilled.* Words normally used in quoting Scripture, and Jesus' words are on the same level (see 6:39; 17:12 and notes).

18:10 *Simon Peter.* It is to John that we owe the information that the man with the sword (the Greek for this word refers to a short sword) was Peter, and that the man he wounded was named Malchus.

18:11 *the cup.* Often points to suffering (see Ps 75:8; Eze 23:31 and note) and the wrath of God (see notes on Ps 16:5; Isa 51:17; Jer 25:15; Ro 1:18; Rev 14:10). *the Father has given me.* The Synoptic Gospels also speak of the cup at the time of Jesus' prayer at Gethsemane (see Mt 26:39; Mk 14:36; Lk 22:42 and notes), and John says it came from the Father. God was in control.

18:12 *bound him.* The reason for the bonds is not clear. Perhaps their use was standard procedure, much like the modern use of handcuffs.

18:13 *Annas.* Had been deposed from the high priesthood by the Romans in A.D. 15 but was probably still regarded by many as the true high priest (see note on Lk 3:2). In Jewish law no one could be sentenced on the day their trial was held. The two examinations—this one (mentioned only by John; see note on Mk 14:53—15:15) and that before Caiaphas—may have been conducted to give some form of legitimacy to what was done. *high priest that year.* See note on 11:49.

18:14 *Caiaphas ... had advised the Jews.* A reference to 11:49–50 (see notes there). For John it was this unconscious

Peter's First Denial

18:16-18pp — Mt 26:69,70; Mk 14:66-68; Lk 22:55-57

15Simon Peter and another disciple
were following Jesus. Because this disciple was known to the high priest,[a] he
went with Jesus into the high priest's
courtyard,[b] 16but Peter had to wait outside at the door. The other disciple, who
was known to the high priest, came
back, spoke to the girl on duty there and
brought Peter in.

17"You are not one of his disciples, are
you?" the girl at the door asked Peter.

He replied, "I am not."[c]

18It was cold, and the servants and officials stood around a fire[d] they had made to
keep warm. Peter also was standing with
them, warming himself.[e]

The High Priest Questions Jesus

18:19-24pp — Mt 26:59-68; Mk 14:55-65; Lk 22:63-71

19Meanwhile, the high priest questioned
Jesus about his disciples and his teaching.

20"I have spoken openly to the world,"
Jesus replied. "I always taught in synagogues[f] or at the temple,[g] where all the
Jews come together. I said nothing in secret.[h] 21Why question me? Ask those who
heard me. Surely they know what I said."

22When Jesus said this, one of the officials[i] nearby struck him in the face.[j] "Is
this the way you answer the high priest?"
he demanded.

23"If I said something wrong," Jesus replied, "testify as to what is wrong. But if I
spoke the truth, why did you strike me?"[k]
24Then Annas sent him, still bound, to Caiaphas[l] the high priest.[a]

Peter's Second and Third Denials

18:25-27pp — Mt 26:71-75; Mk 14:69-72; Lk 22:58-62

25As Simon Peter stood warming himself,[m] he was asked, "You are not one of
his disciples, are you?"

He denied it, saying, "I am not."[n]

26One of the high priest's servants, a
relative of the man whose ear Peter had
cut off,[o] challenged him, "Didn't I see you
with him in the olive grove?"[p] 27Again Peter denied it, and at that moment a rooster
began to crow.[q]

Jesus Before Pilate

18:29-40pp — Mt 27:11-18,20-23; Mk 15:2-15; Lk 23:2,3,18-25

28Then the Jews led Jesus from Caiaphas to the palace of the Roman governor.[r]
By now it was early morning, and to avoid
ceremonial uncleanness the Jews did not
enter the palace;[s] they wanted to be able

18:15 [a] S Mt 26:3 [b] Mt 26:58; Mk 14:54; Lk 22:54 **18:17** [c] ver 25 **18:18** [d] Jn 21:9 [e] Mk 14:54,67 **18:20** [f] S Mt 4:23 [g] Mt 26:55 [h] Jn 7:26 **18:22** [i] ver 3 [j] Mt 16:21; Jn 19:3 **18:23** [k] Mt 5:39; Ac 23:2-5 **18:24** [l] ver 13; S Mt 26:3 **18:25** [m] ver 18 [n] ver 17 **18:26** [o] ver 10 [p] ver 1 **18:27** [q] Jn 13:38 **18:28** [r] S Mt 27:2 [s] ver 33; Jn 19:9

[a] 24 Or *(Now Annas had sent him, still bound, to Caiaphas the high priest.)*

prophecy that mattered most about Caiaphas. John may also have been hinting that a fair trial could not be expected from a man who had already said that putting Jesus to death was expedient.

18:15 *another disciple.* Perhaps John himself. *known to the high priest.* Refers to more than casual acquaintance; he had entrée into the high priest's house and could bring Peter in.

18:17 *the girl at the door.* All four Gospels tell us that Peter's first challenge came from a slave girl, the most unimportant person imaginable. The form of the girl's question implied a negative answer, and Peter capitalized on that by saying, "I am not." The other Gospels seem to indicate that the other denials followed immediately, but it is likely that there were intervals during which other things happened (see Lk 22:58–59).

18:18 *Peter also was standing with them.* On a cold night he would have been conspicuous if he had stayed away from the fire.

18:19 *questioned.* Not legal, since witnesses were supposed to be brought in first to establish guilt. The accused were not required to prove their innocence. Perhaps Annas regarded this as a preliminary inquiry, not a trial.

18:20 *I have spoken openly.* It should not have been difficult to find witnesses (v. 21). *nothing in secret.* Not a denial that he taught the disciples privately, but a denial that he had secretly taught them subversive teaching different from his public message.

18:22 *struck.* Another illegality. The word apparently means a blow with the open hand—a slap.

18:23 *testify.* A legal term, indicating an invitation to act in proper legal form. John stresses the importance of testimony throughout his Gospel (see note on 1:7).

18:25 *he was asked.* Lit. "they asked him." Some find a difficulty in that Mt 26:71 says another girl asked this question, whereas Mk 14:69 says it was the same girl, and Lk 22:58 that it was a man. But with a group of servants talking around a fire, several would doubtless take up and repeat such a question, which could be the meaning of John's "they." As on the first occasion (v. 17) the question anticipated the answer "No." The servants probably did not really expect to find a follower of Jesus in the high priest's courtyard, but the question seemed worth asking.

18:26 *a relative.* Another piece of information we owe to John. A relative would have a deeper interest in the swordsman than other people had. But the light in the garden would have been dim, as in the courtyard (a charcoal fire glows, but does not have flames). *Didn't I see you . . . ?* Expected the answer "Yes."

18:27 *a rooster began to crow.* The fulfillment of the prophecy in 13:38 (see note there).

18:28 *Roman governor.* John says little about the Jewish phase of Jesus' trial but much about the Roman trial (see note on Mk 14:53—15:15). It is possible that John was in the Praetorium, the governor's official residence, for this trial. *early morning.* The chief priests evidently held a second session of the Sanhedrin after daybreak to give some appearance of legality to what they did (Mk 15:1). This occasion would have been immediately after that, perhaps between 6:00 A.M. and 7:00 A.M. *ceremonial uncleanness.* A result of entering a Gentile residence. *to eat the Passover.* Does not mean that the time of the Passover meal had not yet come, for this would contradict the Synoptic Gospels, which have Jesus eating the Passover meal the night before. The term "Passover" was used to refer to the whole festival of Passover and Unleavened Bread, which lasted seven days and included a number of meals.

to eat the Passover.[t] 29So Pilate came out
to them and asked, "What charges are you
bringing against this man?"
30"If he were not a criminal," they replied, "we would not have handed him
over to you."
31Pilate said, "Take him yourselves and
judge him by your own law."
"But we have no right to execute anyone," the Jews objected. 32This happened
so that the words Jesus had spoken indicating the kind of death he was going to
die[u] would be fulfilled.
33Pilate then went back inside the palace,[v] summoned Jesus and asked him,
"Are you the king of the Jews?"[w]
34"Is that your own idea," Jesus asked,
"or did others talk to you about me?"
35"Am I a Jew?" Pilate replied. "It was
your people and your chief priests who
handed you over to me. What is it you
have done?"
36Jesus said, "My kingdom[x] is not of this
world. If it were, my servants would fight
to prevent my arrest by the Jews.[y] But now
my kingdom is from another place."[z]
37"You are a king, then!" said Pilate.
Jesus answered, "You are right in saying
I am a king. In fact, for this reason I was
born, and for this I came into the world, to
testify to the truth.[a] Everyone on the side
of truth listens to me."[b]
38"What is truth?" Pilate asked. With
this he went out again to the Jews and
said, "I find no basis for a charge against
him.[c] 39But it is your custom for me to release to you one prisoner at the time of the
Passover. Do you want me to release 'the
king of the Jews'?"
40They shouted back, "No, not him!
Give us Barabbas!" Now Barabbas had
taken part in a rebellion.[d]

Jesus Sentenced to Be Crucified

19:1-16pp — Mt 27:27-31; Mk 15:16-20

19 Then Pilate took Jesus and had him
flogged.[e] 2The soldiers twisted together a crown of thorns and put it on his
head. They clothed him in a purple robe
3and went up to him again and again, saying, "Hail, king of the Jews!"[f] And they
struck him in the face.[g]
4Once more Pilate came out and said to
the Jews, "Look, I am bringing him out[h] to
you to let you know that I find no basis for
a charge against him."[i] 5When Jesus came
out wearing the crown of thorns and the
purple robe,[j] Pilate said to them, "Here is
the man!"
6As soon as the chief priests and their
officials saw him, they shouted, "Crucify!
Crucify!"
But Pilate answered, "You take him and
crucify him.[k] As for me, I find no basis for
a charge against him."[l]
7The Jews insisted, "We have a law, and
according to that law he must die,[m] because he claimed to be the Son of God."[n]
8When Pilate heard this, he was even
more afraid, 9and he went back inside the

18:28 [t]Jn 11:55 **18:32** [u]Mt 20:19; 26:2; Jn 3:14; 8:28; 12:32,33 **18:33** [v]ver 28,29; Jn 19:9 [w]Lk 23:3; S Mt 2:2 **18:36** [x]S Mt 3:2 [y]Mt 26:53 [z]Lk 17:21; Jn 6:15 **18:37** [a]Jn 3:32 [b]Jn 8:47; 1Jn 4:6 **18:38** [c]S Lk 23:4 **18:40** [d]Ac 3:14 **19:1** [e]Dt 25:3; Isa 50:6; 53:5; Mt 27:26 **19:3** [f]Mt 27:29 [g]Jn 18:22 **19:4** [h]Jn 18:38 [i]ver 6; S Lk 23:4 **19:5** [j]ver 2 **19:6** [k]Ac 3:13 [l]ver 4; S Lk 23:4 **19:7** [m]Lev 24:16 [n]Mt 26:63-66; Jn 5:18; 10:33

18:29 *Pilate.* The Roman governor (see note on Mk 15:1). He showed himself tolerant of Jewish ways. *What charges ...?* A normal question at the beginning of a trial, but it was difficult to answer, because the Jews had no charge that would stand up in a Roman court of law.
18:31 *Take him yourselves.* In other words, no Roman charge, no Roman trial. *no right to execute anyone.* They were looking for an execution, not a fair trial. The restriction was important, for otherwise Rome's supporters could be quietly removed by local legal executions. Sometimes the Romans seem to have tolerated local executions (e.g., of Stephen, Ac 7), but normally they retained the right to inflict the death penalty.
18:32 *the kind of death he was going to die.* Cf. 12:32–33 and "must" in 12:34. Jewish execution was by stoning, but Jesus' death was to be by crucifixion, whereby he would bear the curse (see Dt 21:22–23 and notes). The Romans, not the Jews, had to put Jesus to death. God was overruling in the whole process.
18:33 *Are you the king of the Jews?* Pilate's first words to Jesus, identical in all four Gospels. One glance was enough to show him that a dangerous rebel existed only in the imaginations of Jesus' enemies.
18:34 *Is that your own idea ...?* If so, Pilate's question (v. 33) had meant, "Are you a rebel?" If the question had originated with the Jews, it meant, "Are you the Messianic King?"
18:36 *My kingdom.* Jesus agrees that he has a kingdom, but asserts that it is not the kind of kingdom that has soldiers to fight for it. It was not built, nor is it maintained, by military might.
18:37 *to testify to the truth.* Two of this Gospel's important ideas (see 1:7; 1:14; 14:6 and notes).
18:38 *What is truth?* Pilate may have been jesting and meant, "What does truth matter?" Or he may have been serious and meant, "It is not easy to find truth. What is it?" Either way, it was clear to him that Jesus was no rebel. *I find no basis for a charge against him.* Repeated in 19:4,6 (see note on 19:6). Teaching the truth was not a criminal offense.
18:39 *your custom.* Prisoners are known to have been released on special occasions in other places. *king of the Jews.* John keeps his emphasis on the note of royalty. Pilate may have hoped that the use of the title would influence the people toward the way he wanted them to decide.
18:40 *Barabbas.* A rebel and a murderer (see Lk 23:19 and note on 23:18). The name is Aramaic and means "son of Abba," i.e., "son of the father"; in place of this man, the "Son of the Father" died (see note on Mt 27:16).
19:1 Pilate hoped a flogging would satisfy the Jews and enable him to release Jesus (see note on Mk 15:15).
19:2 *thorns.* A general term relating to any thorny plant (see note on Mk 15:17). *purple.* A color used by royalty.
19:6 *You ... crucify him.* The petulant utterance of an exasperated man, for the Jews could not carry out this form of execution. *I find no basis for a charge against him.* For the third time Pilate proclaimed Jesus' innocence (see 18:38 and note; 19:4). Luke also records this threefold proclamation (Lk 23:4,14,22).
19:7 *he must die.* Apparently referring to the penalty for blasphemy (Lev 24:16).
19:8 *even more afraid.* Pilate was evidently superstitious, and this charge frightened him.
19:9 *Jesus gave him no answer.* The reason is not clear since Jesus had answered other questions readily. Perhaps Pilate

palace.[o] "Where do you come from?" he
asked Jesus, but Jesus gave him no answer.[p] 10"Do you refuse to speak to me?"
Pilate said. "Don't you realize I have power either to free you or to crucify you?"
11Jesus answered, "You would have no
power over me if it were not given to you
from above.[q] Therefore the one who handed me over to you[r] is guilty of a greater
sin."
12From then on, Pilate tried to set Jesus
free, but the Jews kept shouting, "If you
let this man go, you are no friend of Caesar. Anyone who claims to be a king[s] opposes Caesar."
13When Pilate heard this, he brought
Jesus out and sat down on the judge's
seat[t] at a place known as the Stone Pavement (which in Aramaic[u] is Gabbatha).
14It was the day of Preparation[v] of Passover Week, about the sixth hour.[w]
"Here is your king,"[x] Pilate said to the
Jews.
15But they shouted, "Take him away!
Take him away! Crucify him!"
"Shall I crucify your king?" Pilate
asked.
"We have no king but Caesar," the chief
priests answered.
16Finally Pilate handed him over to them
to be crucified.[y]

19:9 [o] Jn 18:33 [p] S Mk 14:61 **19:11** [q] S Ro 13:1 [r] Jn 18:28-30; Ac 3:13 **19:12** [s] Lk 23:2 **19:13** [t] Mt 27:19 [u] S Jn 5:2 **19:14** [v] Mt 27:62 [w] Mk 15:25 [x] ver 19,21 **19:16** [y] Mt 27:26; Mk 15:15; Lk 23:25

The Crucifixion

19:17-24pp — Mt 27:33-44; Mk 15:22-32; Lk 23:33-43

So the soldiers took charge of Jesus.
17Carrying his own cross,[z] he went out to
the place of the Skull[a] (which in Aramaic[b]
is called Golgotha). 18Here they crucified
him, and with him two others[c]—one on
each side and Jesus in the middle.
19Pilate had a notice prepared and fastened to the cross. It read: JESUS OF NAZA-
RETH,[d] THE KING OF THE JEWS.[e] 20Many of the
Jews read this sign, for the place where
Jesus was crucified was near the city,[f] and
the sign was written in Aramaic, Latin and
Greek. 21The chief priests of the Jews protested to Pilate, "Do not write 'The King of
the Jews,' but that this man claimed to be
king of the Jews."[g]
22Pilate answered, "What I have written,
I have written."
23When the soldiers crucified Jesus, they
took his clothes, dividing them into four
shares, one for each of them, with the undergarment remaining. This garment was
seamless, woven in one piece from top to
bottom.
24"Let's not tear it," they said to one another. "Let's decide by lot who will get it."
This happened that the scripture might
be fulfilled[h] which said,

19:17 [z] Ge 22:6; Lk 14:27; 23:26 [a] Lk 23:33 [b] S Jn 5:2 **19:18** [c] Lk 23:32 **19:19** [d] S Mk 1:24 [e] ver 14,21 **19:20** [f] Heb 13:12 **19:21** [g] ver 14 **19:24** [h] ver 28,36,37; S Mt 1:22

would not have understood the answer or would not have believed it.

19:10 *I have power.* Pilate was incredulous and very conscious of his authority. His second question indicates his personal responsibility for crucifying Jesus.

19:11 Jesus' last words to Pilate. *from above.* All earthly authority comes ultimately from God (cf. Ro 13:14 and note). *greater sin.* That of Caiaphas (not Judas, who was only a means). But "greater" implies that there was a lesser sin, so Pilate's sin was also real.

19:12 *no friend of Caesar.* Some people had official status as "Friends of Caesar," but the term seems to be used here in the general sense. There was an implied threat that if he released Jesus, Pilate would be accused before Caesar. His record was such that he could not face such a prospect without concern.

19:13 *the Stone Pavement.* Not a translation of *Gabbatha,* which seems to mean "the hill of the house," but a different name for the same place.

19:14 *day of Preparation.* Normally Friday was the day people prepared for the Sabbath. Here the meaning is Friday of Passover week. *about the sixth hour.* About noon. Mk 15:25 says that Jesus was crucified at "the third hour" (= 9:00 A.M.). It is possible that Mark's Gospel contains a copyist's error, for the Greek numerals for three and six could be confused. Or it may be that John was using Roman time, in which case the appearance before Pilate would have been at 6:00 A.M. and the crucifixion at 9:00 A.M. (the third hour according to Jewish reckoning; see Mk 15:33). In any event, "about" indicates that John is giving only an approximation. For other time references see Mt 27:45–46; Mk 15:33–34; Lk 23:44 and note. *Here is your king.* John does not let us forget the sovereignty of Jesus. Pilate did not mean the expression seriously, but John did. *the Jews.* See note on 1:19.

19:15 *We have no king but Caesar.* More irony. They rejected any suggestion that they were rebels against Rome, but expressed the truth of their spiritual condition.

19:17 *Carrying his own cross.* A cross might be shaped like a *T,* an *X,* a *Y,* or an *I,* as well as like the traditional form. A condemned man would normally carry a beam of it to the place of execution. Somewhere along the way Simon of Cyrene took Jesus' cross (see Mk 15:21 and note), probably because Jesus was weakened by the flogging. *Golgotha.* "Calvary" comes from a Latin word that has the same meaning (see Mk 15:22 and note).

19:18 *they crucified him.* See note on Mk 15:24. As with the scourging, John describes this horror with one Greek word. None of the Gospel writers dwells on the physical sufferings of Jesus. *one on each side.* Perhaps meant as a final insult, but it brings out the important truth that in his death Jesus was identified with sinners (see note on Mk 15:27).

19:19 *a notice.* A placard stating the crime for which someone was executed was often fastened to his cross. *THE KING OF THE JEWS.* Again the royalty theme.

19:20 *Aramaic.* One of the languages of the Jewish people at that time (along with Hebrew). *Latin.* The official language of Rome. *Greek.* The common language of communication throughout the empire. The threefold inscription may account for the slight differences in wording in the four Gospels (but see note on Mk 15:26).

19:22 Pilate must have a sufficient reason for the execution, and he was not above mocking the Jews, but for John his insistence may also have served to underscore that Jesus' kingship is final and unalterable.

19:23 *undergarment.* A type of shirt, reaching from the neck to the knees or ankles. *seamless.* Therefore too valuable to be cut up.

19:24 See introduction to Ps 22 and notes on Ps 22:17, 20–21.

> “They divided my garments among
> them
> and cast lots for my clothing.”[a][i]

So this is what the soldiers did.

25 Near the cross[j] of Jesus stood his mother,[k] his mother’s sister, Mary the wife of Clopas, and Mary Magdalene.[l] 26 When Jesus saw his mother[m] there, and the disciple whom he loved[n] standing nearby, he said to his mother, “Dear woman, here is your son,” 27 and to the disciple, “Here is your mother.” From that time on, this disciple took her into his home.

The Death of Jesus

19:29,30pp — Mt 27:48,50; Mk 15:36,37; Lk 23:36

28 Later, knowing that all was now completed,[o] and so that the Scripture would be fulfilled,[p] Jesus said, “I am thirsty.” 29 A jar of wine vinegar[q] was there, so they soaked a sponge in it, put the sponge on a stalk of the hyssop plant, and lifted it to Jesus’ lips. 30 When he had received the drink, Jesus said, “It is finished.”[r] With that, he bowed his head and gave up his spirit.

31 Now it was the day of Preparation,[s] and the next day was to be a special Sabbath. Because the Jews did not want the bodies left on the crosses[t] during the Sabbath, they asked Pilate to have the legs broken and the bodies taken down. 32 The soldiers therefore came and broke the legs of the first man who had been crucified with Jesus, and then those of the other.[u] 33 But when they came to Jesus and found that he was already dead, they did not break his legs. 34 Instead, one of the soldiers pierced[v] Jesus’ side with a spear, bringing a sudden flow of blood and water.[w] 35 The man who saw it[x] has given testimony, and his testimony is true.[y] He knows that he tells the truth, and he testifies so that you also may believe. 36 These things happened so that the scripture would be fulfilled:[z] “Not one of his bones will be broken,”[b][a] 37 and, as another scripture says, “They will look on the one they have pierced.”[c][b]

The Burial of Jesus

19:38-42pp — Mt 27:57-61; Mk 15:42-47; Lk 23:50-56

38 Later, Joseph of Arimathea asked Pilate for the body of Jesus. Now Joseph was a disciple of Jesus, but secretly because he feared the Jews.[c] With Pilate’s permission, he came and took the body away. 39 He was accompanied by Nicodemus,[d] the man who earlier had visited Jesus at night. Nicodemus brought a mixture of myrrh and aloes, about seventy-five pounds.[d] 40 Taking Jesus’ body, the two of them wrapped it, with the spices, in strips of linen.[e] This was in accordance with Jewish burial customs.[f] 41 At the place where Jesus was crucified, there was a garden, and in the garden a new tomb, in which no one had ever been laid. 42 Because it was the Jewish day of Preparation[g] and since the tomb was nearby,[h] they laid Jesus there.

[a] *24* Psalm 22:18 [b] *36* Exodus 12:46; Num. 9:12; Psalm 34:20 [c] *37* Zech. 12:10 [d] *39* Greek *a hundred litrai* (about 34 kilograms)

19:24 [i] Ps 22:18
19:25 [j] Mt 27:55, 56 [k] S Mt 12:46 [l] Lk 24:18
19:26 [m] S Mt 12:46 [n] S Jn 13:23
19:28 [o] S ver 30; Jn 13:1 [p] ver 24,36,37; S Mt 1:22
19:29 [q] Ps 69:21
19:30 [r] Lk 12:50; Jn 4:34; 17:4
19:31 [s] ver 14,42 [t] Dt 21:23; Jos 8:29; 10:26,27
19:32 [u] ver 18
19:34 [v] Zec 12:10; Rev 1:7 [w] 1Jn 5:6,8
19:35 [x] S Lk 24:48 [y] Jn 15:27; 21:24
19:36 [z] ver 24,28,37; S Mt 1:22 [a] Ex 12:46; Nu 9:12; Ps 34:20
19:37 [b] Zec 12:10; Rev 1:7
19:38 [c] S Jn 7:13
19:39 [d] Jn 3:1; 7:50
19:40 [e] Lk 24:12; Jn 11:44; 20:5,7 [f] Mt 26:12
19:42 [g] ver 14,31 [h] ver 20,41

19:25 *Clopas.* Mentioned only here in the NT. *Mary Magdalene.* Appears in the crucifixion and resurrection story in all four Gospels, but apart from that we read of her only in Lk 8:2–3 (see note on 8:2).

19:26 *disciple whom he loved.* John (see note on 13:23). *Dear woman.* See note on 2:4.

19:27 *took her into his home.* And so took responsibility for her. It may be that Jesus’ brothers still did not believe in him (see 7:5).

19:28 *I am thirsty.* May refer to Ps 69:21 (see note there; cf. Ps 22:15).

19:29 *wine vinegar.* Equivalent to cheap wine, the drink of ordinary people (see notes on Mk 15:36; Lk 23:36). *hyssop.* The name given to a number of plants (see note on Ex 12:22).

19:30 *It is finished.* Apparently the loud cry of Mt 27:50; Mk 15:37. Jesus died as a victor and had “completed” (v. 28; the Greek verb is the same as that for “finished”) what he came to do (cf. 17:4). *gave up his spirit.* An unusual way of describing death, perhaps suggesting an act of will (cf. 10:17–18 and note).

19:31 *Preparation.* See note on v. 14. *a special Sabbath.* The Sabbath that fell at Passover time. The Passover meal had been eaten on Thursday evening, the day of Preparation was Friday, and the Sabbath came on Saturday. *the Jews.* See note on 1:19. *to have the legs broken.* To hasten death, because the victim then could not put any weight on his legs and breathing would be difficult.

19:34 *pierced Jesus’ side.* Probably to make doubly sure that Jesus was dead, but perhaps simply an act of brutality (see v. 37; Isa 53:5; Zec 12:10; cf. Ps 22:16). *blood and water.* The result of the spear piercing the pericardium (the sac that surrounds the heart) and the heart itself.

19:35 *The man who saw it.* Either John himself or someone he regarded as reliable. Obviously he considered the incident important, and comments that it was well attested. *testifies … believe.* See note on 1:7.

19:36–37 *scripture.* Again John observes God’s overruling in the fulfillment of Scripture. It was extraordinary that Jesus was the only one of the three whose legs were not broken and that he suffered an unusual spear thrust that did not break a bone.

19:38 See note on Lk 23:52. *Joseph.* A rich disciple (Mt 27:57), and a member of the Sanhedrin who had not agreed to Jesus’ condemnation (Lk 23:51; see note on 23:50). *Arimathea.* See note on Mt 27:57. *secretly.* It would have been hard for a member of the Sanhedrin to support Jesus’ cause openly. Jesus’ closest followers all ran away (see Mk 14:50 and note), and it was left to Joseph and Nicodemus to provide for his burial. *With Pilate’s permission.* Otherwise people could take away their crucified friends before they died and revive them.

19:39 *Nicodemus.* John alone tells us that he joined Joseph in the burial. *seventy-five pounds.* A very large amount, such as was used in royal burials (cf. 2Ch 16:14).

19:40 *strips of linen.* Thin strips like bandages. There was also a shroud, a large sheet (Mt 27:59; Mk 15:46; Lk 23:53).

19:41 *new tomb.* Joseph’s own tomb (Mt 27:60).

19:42 *Preparation.* See note on v. 14. *nearby.* Haste was neces-

The Empty Tomb

20:1-8pp — Mt 28:1-8; Mk 16:1-8; Lk 24:1-10

20 Early on the first day of the week, while it was still dark, Mary Magdalene[i] went to the tomb and saw that the stone had been removed from the entrance.[j] 2So she came running to Simon Peter and the other disciple, the one Jesus loved,[k] and said, "They have taken the Lord out of the tomb, and we don't know where they have put him!"[l]

3So Peter and the other disciple started for the tomb.[m] 4Both were running, but the other disciple outran Peter and reached the tomb first. 5He bent over and looked in[n] at the strips of linen[o] lying there but did not go in. 6Then Simon Peter, who was behind him, arrived and went into the tomb. He saw the strips of linen lying there, 7as well as the burial cloth that had been around Jesus' head.[p] The cloth was folded up by itself, separate from the linen. 8Finally the other disciple, who had reached the tomb first,[q] also went inside. He saw and believed. 9(They still did not understand from Scripture[r] that Jesus had to rise from the dead.)[s]

Jesus Appears to Mary Magdalene

10Then the disciples went back to their homes, 11but Mary stood outside the tomb crying. As she wept, she bent over to look into the tomb[t] 12and saw two angels in white,[u] seated where Jesus' body had been, one at the head and the other at the foot.

13They asked her, "Woman, why are you crying?"[v]

"They have taken my Lord away," she said, "and I don't know where they have put him."[w] 14At this, she turned around and saw Jesus standing there,[x] but she did not realize that it was Jesus.[y]

15"Woman," he said, "why are you crying?[z] Who is it you are looking for?"

Thinking he was the gardener, she said, "Sir, if you have carried him away, tell me where you have put him, and I will get him."

16Jesus said to her, "Mary."

She turned toward him and cried out in Aramaic,[a] "Rabboni!"[b] (which means Teacher).

17Jesus said, "Do not hold on to me, for I have not yet returned to the Father. Go instead to my brothers[c] and tell them, 'I am returning to my Father[d] and your Father, to my God and your God.'"

18Mary Magdalene[e] went to the disciples[f] with the news: "I have seen the Lord!" And she told them that he had said these things to her.

Jesus Appears to His Disciples

19On the evening of that first day of the week, when the disciples were together, with the doors locked for fear of the Jews,[g] Jesus came and stood among them

20:1 [i] ver 18; Lk 8:2; Jn 19:25 [j] Mt 27:60,66
20:2 [k] S Jn 13:23 [l] ver 13
20:3 [m] Lk 24:12
20:5 [n] ver 11 [o] S Jn 19:40
20:7 [p] Jn 11:44
20:8 [q] ver 4
20:9 [r] Mt 22:29; Jn 2:22 [s] Lk 24:26,46; Ac 2:24
20:11 [t] ver 5
20:12 [u] Mt 28:2,3; Mk 16:5; Lk 24:4; Ac 1:10; S 5:19; 10:30
20:13 [v] ver 15 [w] ver 2
20:14 [x] Mk 16:9 [y] Lk 24:16; Jn 21:4
20:15 [z] ver 13
20:16 [a] S Jn 5:2 [b] S Mt 23:7
20:17 [c] S Mt 28:10 [d] Jn 7:33
20:18 [e] S ver 1 [f] Lk 24:10,22,23
20:19 [g] S Jn 7:13

---

sary, since it was near sunset, when the Sabbath would start and no work could be done.

20:1 *while it was still dark.* Mark says it was "just after sunrise" (Mk 16:2). Perhaps the women came in groups, with Mary Magdalene coming very early. Or John may refer to the time of leaving home, Mark to that of arrival at the tomb. *Mary Magdalene.* See note on 19:25; cf. Mk 16:9.

20:2 *Simon Peter.* Despite his denials, he was still the leading figure among the disciples. *the one Jesus loved.* John (see note on 13:23). *we.* Indicates that there were others with Mary (see Mt 28:1; Mk 16:1; Lk 24:10), though John does not identify them. *have put him.* Mary had no thought of resurrection.

20:7 *folded up.* An orderly arrangement, not in disarray, as would have resulted from a grave robbery.

20:8 *He saw and believed.* Cf. v. 29. John did not say what he believed, but it must have been that Jesus was resurrected.

20:9 *Scripture.* First they came to know of the resurrection through what they saw in the tomb; only later did they see it in Scripture. It is obvious they did not make up a story of resurrection to fit a preconceived understanding of Scriptural prophecy. *had to rise.* It was in Scripture and thus the will of God.

20:11 *Mary.* Perhaps Jesus appeared first to Mary because she needed him most at that time. *crying.* As in 11:33 (see note there), it means "wailing," a loud expression of grief.

20:12 *two angels.* Matthew has one angel (Mt 28:2), Mark a young man (Mk 16:5) and Luke two men who were angels (Lk 24:4,23). See note on Lk 24:4.

20:13 *Woman.* See v. 15; see also note on 2:4.

20:14 *did not realize that it was Jesus.* A number of times the risen Jesus was not recognized (21:4; Mt 28:17; Lk 24:16,37). He may have looked different, or he may intentionally have prevented recognition (see Lk 24:16 and note on Lk 9:45).

20:16 *Mary.* Cf. 10:3–4. *Rabboni.* A strengthened form of *Rabbi,* and in the NT found elsewhere only in Mk 10:51 (in the Greek). Although the word means "(my) teacher," there are few if any examples of its use in ancient Judaism as a form of address other than in calling on God in prayer. However, John's explanation casts doubt on any thought that Mary intended to address Jesus as God here.

20:17 *I have not yet returned.* See 13:3. The meaning appears to be that the ascension was still some time off. Mary would have opportunity to see Jesus again, so she need not cling to him. Alternatively, Jesus may be reminding Mary that after his crucifixion she cannot have him with her except through the Holy Spirit (see 16:5–16). *my brothers.* Probably the disciples (see v. 18; Mk 3:35 and note). The members of his family did not believe in him (see 7:5 and note on 7:4), though they became disciples not long after this (see Ac 1:14 and note). *my Father and your Father.* God is Father both of Christ and of believers, but in different senses (see 1:12,14,18,34; 3:16 and note; Mt 6:9 and note).

20:18 *have seen the Lord.* Although Mary was the first to see the risen Lord, others would soon follow (see vv. 20,25,29; see also chart, p. 1615).

20:19 See Lk 24:36 and note. *disciples.* Probably includes others besides the apostles, "the Twelve" (v. 24). *the Jews.* See note on 1:19. *Peace be with you!* The normal Hebrew greeting (cf. Da 10:19). Because of their behavior the previous Friday, they may have expected rebuke and censure; but Jesus calmed their fears (see note on 14:27).

and said, "Peace[h] be with you!"[i] 20After he
said this, he showed them his hands and
side.[j] The disciples were overjoyed[k] when
they saw the Lord.
21Again Jesus said, "Peace be with you![l]
As the Father has sent me,[m] I am sending you."[n] 22And with that he breathed on
them and said, "Receive the Holy Spirit.[o]
23If you forgive anyone his sins, they are
forgiven; if you do not forgive them, they
are not forgiven."[p]

Jesus Appears to Thomas

24Now Thomas[q] (called Didymus), one
of the Twelve, was not with the disciples
when Jesus came. 25So the other disciples
told him, "We have seen the Lord!"
But he said to them, "Unless I see the
nail marks in his hands and put my finger
where the nails were, and put my hand
into his side,[r] I will not believe it."[s]
26A week later his disciples were in the
house again, and Thomas was with them.
Though the doors were locked, Jesus came
and stood among them and said, "Peace[t]
be with you!"[u] 27Then he said to Thomas, "Put your finger here; see my hands.
Reach out your hand and put it into my
side. Stop doubting and believe."[v]
28Thomas said to him, "My Lord and my
God!"
29Then Jesus told him, "Because you
have seen me, you have believed;[w] blessed
are those who have not seen and yet have
believed."[x]
30Jesus did many other miraculous signs[y]
in the presence of his disciples, which are
not recorded in this book.[z] 31But these are
written that you may[a] believe[a] that Jesus
is the Christ, the Son of God,[b] and that by
believing you may have life in his name.[c]

Jesus and the Miraculous Catch of Fish

21 Afterward Jesus appeared again to
his disciples,[d] by the Sea of Tiberias.[b][e] It happened this way: 2Simon Peter,
Thomas[f] (called Didymus), Nathanael[g]
from Cana in Galilee,[h] the sons of Zebedee,[i] and two other disciples were together. 3"I'm going out to fish," Simon Peter
told them, and they said, "We'll go with
you." So they went out and got into the
boat, but that night they caught nothing.[j]
4Early in the morning, Jesus stood on
the shore, but the disciples did not realize
that it was Jesus.[k]
5He called out to them, "Friends, haven't
you any fish?"
"No," they answered.
6He said, "Throw your net on the right
side of the boat and you will find some."
When they did, they were unable to haul
the net in because of the large number of
fish.[l]
7Then the disciple whom Jesus loved[m]
said to Peter, "It is the Lord!" As soon as
Simon Peter heard him say, "It is the Lord,"
he wrapped his outer garment around him
(for he had taken it off) and jumped into

20:19 [h] S Jn 14:27 [i] ver 21,26; Lk 24:36-39
20:20 [j] Lk 24:39,40; Jn 19:34 [k] Jn 16:20,22
20:21 [l] ver 19 [m] S Jn 3:17 [n] Mt 28:19; Jn 17:18
20:22 [o] Jn 7:39; Ac 2:38; 8:15-17; 19:2; Gal 3:2
20:23 [p] Mt 16:19; 18:18
20:24 [q] S Jn 11:16
20:25 [r] ver 20 [s] Mk 16:11
20:26 [t] S Jn 14:27 [u] ver 21
20:27 [v] ver 25; Lk 24:40
20:29 [w] S Jn 3:15 [x] 1Pe 1:8
20:30 [y] S Jn 2:11
[z] Jn 21:25
20:31 [a] S Jn 3:15; 19:35 [b] S Mt 4:3 [c] S Mt 25:46
21:1 [d] ver 14; Jn 20:19,26 [e] Jn 6:1
21:2 [f] S Jn 11:16 [g] Jn 1:45 [h] Jn 2:1 [i] S Mt 4:21
21:3 [j] Lk 5:5
21:4 [k] Lk 24:16; Jn 20:14
21:6 [l] Lk 5:4-7
21:7 [m] S Jn 13:23

[a] *31* Some manuscripts *may continue to* [b] *1* That is, Sea of Galilee

20:20 *his hands and side.* Where the wounds were (John does not refer to the wounds in the feet). According to Lk 24:37 they thought they were seeing a ghost. Jesus was clearly identifying himself.

20:21 *Peace be with you!* See note on v. 19. *I am sending you.* See note on 17:18.

20:22 *Receive the Holy Spirit.* Thus anticipating what happened 50 days later on the day of Pentecost (see Ac 2:2,4,14,17,33,38 and notes). The disciples needed God's help to carry out the commission they had just been given.

20:23 Lit. "If you forgive anyone their sins, they have (already) been forgiven; if you do not forgive, they have not been forgiven." The intent of this word of Jesus has been much debated, but it seems right to say that God does not forgive people's sins because the apostles (or we) do so, nor does he withhold forgiveness because the apostles (or we) do. However, through the Holy Spirit (v. 22) the apostles and all believers do participate in Christ's saving mission, which has as one of its crucial effects God's forgiveness of the sins of all who repent and believe in Jesus as God's Son and the Savior of the world (cf. Mt 16:19 and note and NIV text note; 18:18 and NIV text note).

20:24 *Thomas.* See note on 11:16.

20:25 *Unless I see ... and put ... I will not believe.* Hard-headed skepticism can scarcely go further than this.

20:26 *Peace.* See vv. 19,21 and note on 14:27.

20:28 *My Lord and my God!* To acknowledge Jesus as one's Lord and God is the high point of faith (see note on 1:1).

20:29 *those who have not seen and yet have believed.* Would have been very few at this time (see v. 8 and note). All whom John mentions had seen in some sense. The words, of course, apply to future believers as well.

20:30 *miraculous signs.* See note on 2:11. John had selected from among many. *in the presence of his disciples.* Those who could testify to what he had done. John again stresses testimony (see note on 1:7).

20:31 *that you may believe.* Expresses John's evangelistic purpose. *believe.* See note on 1:7. *Jesus is the Christ, the Son of God.* Faith has content. *the Christ.* See note on 1:25. This whole Gospel is written to show the truth of Jesus' Messiahship and to present him as the Son of God, so that the readers may believe in him. *Son of God.* See 3:16 and note. *that by believing you may have life.* Another expression of purpose—to bring about faith that leads to life (see notes on 1:4; 3:15–16). *name.* Represents all that he is and stands for (see note on 2:23).

21:1 *Sea of Tiberias.* See note on 6:1.

21:2 *Simon Peter.* See note on Mk 1:16. *Thomas.* See note on 11:16. *sons of Zebedee.* Not named in this Gospel (see Mt 4:21).

21:3 *that night.* Nighttime was favored by fishermen in ancient times (as Aristotle, e.g., informs us).

21:4 *did not realize that it was Jesus.* Cf. Mary Magdalene (see 20:14 and note).

21:7 *disciple whom Jesus loved.* See note on 13:23. *his outer garment.* It is curious that he put on this garment (the word appears only here in the NT) preparatory to jumping into the

the water. 8 The other disciples followed in the boat, towing the net full of fish, for they were not far from shore, about a hundred yards.[a] 9 When they landed, they saw a fire[n] of burning coals there with fish on it,[o] and some bread.

10 Jesus said to them, "Bring some of the fish you have just caught."

11 Simon Peter climbed aboard and dragged the net ashore. It was full of large fish, 153, but even with so many the net was not torn. 12 Jesus said to them, "Come and have breakfast." None of the disciples dared ask him, "Who are you?" They knew it was the Lord. 13 Jesus came, took the bread and gave it to them, and did the same with the fish.[p] 14 This was now the third time Jesus appeared to his disciples[q] after he was raised from the dead.

Jesus Reinstates Peter

15 When they had finished eating, Jesus said to Simon Peter, "Simon son of John, do you truly love me more than these?"

"Yes, Lord," he said, "you know that I love you."[r]

Jesus said, "Feed my lambs."[s]

16 Again Jesus said, "Simon son of John, do you truly love me?"

He answered, "Yes, Lord, you know that I love you."

Jesus said, "Take care of my sheep."[t]

17 The third time he said to him, "Simon son of John, do you love me?"

Peter was hurt because Jesus asked him the third time, "Do you love me?"[u] He said, "Lord, you know all things;[v] you know that I love you."

Jesus said, "Feed my sheep.[w] 18 I tell you the truth, when you were younger you dressed yourself and went where you wanted; but when you are old you will stretch out your hands, and someone else will dress you and lead you where you do not want to go." 19 Jesus said this to indicate the kind of death[x] by which Peter would glorify God.[y] Then he said to him, "Follow me!"[z]

20 Peter turned and saw that the disciple whom Jesus loved[a] was following them. (This was the one who had leaned back against Jesus at the supper and had said, "Lord, who is going to betray you?")[b] 21 When Peter saw him, he asked, "Lord, what about him?"

22 Jesus answered, "If I want him to remain alive until I return,[c] what is that to you? You must follow me."[d] 23 Because of this, the rumor spread among the brothers[e] that this disciple would not die. But Jesus did not say that he would not die; he only said, "If I want him to remain alive until I return, what is that to you?"

24 This is the disciple who testifies to these things[f] and who wrote them down. We know that his testimony is true.[g]

25 Jesus did many other things as well.[h] If every one of them were written down, I suppose that even the whole world would not have room for the books that would be written.

21:9 [n] Jn 18:18 [o] ver 10,13 **21:13** [p] ver 9 **21:14** [q] Jn 20:19,26 **21:15** [r] Mt 26:33,35; Jn 13:37 [s] Lk 12:32 **21:16** [t] 2Sa 5:2; Eze 34:2; Mt 2:6; S Jn 10:11; Ac 20:28; 1Pe 5:2,3 **21:17** [u] Jn 13:38 [v] Jn 16:30 [w] S ver 16 **21:19** [x] Jn 12:33; 18:32 [y] Jn 13:36; 2Pe 1:14 [z] S Mt 4:19 **21:20** [a] ver 7; S Jn 13:23 [b] Jn 13:25 **21:22** [c] S Mt 16:27 [d] ver 19; S Mt 4:19 **21:23** [e] S Ac 1:16 **21:24** [f] S Jn 15:27 [g] Jn 19:35 **21:25** [h] Jn 20:30

[a] 8 Greek *about two hundred cubits* (about 90 meters)

---

water. But Jews regarded a greeting as a religious act that could be done only when one was clothed. Peter may have been preparing himself to greet the Lord.

21:9 *burning coals.* Lit. "charcoal," as in 18:18 ("fire"; see note on 18:26).

21:11 *the net was not torn.* In contrast to the nets mentioned in Lk 5:6.

21:14 *third time.* The third appearance to a group of disciples (20:19–23,24–29), though there had been other appearances to individuals.

21:15–17 *love.* The Greek word for "love" in Jesus' first two questions is different from that in his third question and in all Peter's answers. It is uncertain whether a distinction in meaning is intended since John often made slight word variations, apparently for stylistic reasons. Also, no distinction is made between these two words elsewhere in this Gospel. The more important point is that Peter's threefold denial of Jesus (18:16–18,25–27) is now reversed with Peter's threefold affirmation of his love for Jesus.

21:15 *more than these.* May mean "more than you love these men" or "more than these men love me" or "more than you love these things" (i.e., the fishing gear). Perhaps the second is best, for Peter had claimed a devotion above that of the others (Mt 26:33; Mk 14:29; cf. Jn 13:37). Peter did not take up the comparison, and Jesus did not explain it. *Feed my lambs.* Cf. "Take care of my sheep" (v. 16) and "Feed my sheep" (v. 17).

21:17 *you know all things.* Peter's replies stress Christ's knowledge, not his own grasp of the situation.

21:18 *I tell you the truth.* See note on Mk 3:28. *stretch out your hands.* The early church understood this as a prophecy of crucifixion.

21:19 *the kind of death.* Peter would be a martyr. Tradition indicates that he was crucified upside down.

21:20 *disciple whom Jesus loved.* See note on 13:23. *was following.* He was doing what Peter was twice told to do (vv. 19,22). *at the supper.* See 13:23–25.

21:22 *until I return.* A clear declaration of the second coming (see 14:3 and note).

21:24 *disciple who testifies.* Testimony is important throughout this Gospel (see note on 1:7). We now learn that it was the beloved disciple who was the witness behind the account. *these things.* Must refer to the whole book. *who wrote them down.* The beloved disciple was not only the witness but also the actual author. *We know.* Evidently written by contemporaries in a position to know the truth.

21:25 *many other things.* As in 20:30 (see note there) we are assured that the author has been selective. *even the whole world would not have room.* Hyperbole (for another example of this figure of speech see Lk 14:26 and note). Our historical knowledge of Jesus is at best partial, but we have been given all we need to know.

Major Archaeological Finds Relating to the NT		
SITE OR ARTIFACT	**LOCATION**	**RELATING SCRIPTURE**
	ISRAEL	
Caiaphas ossuary	Jerusalem	Mt 26:3
Herod's temple	Jerusalem	Lk 1:9
Herod's winter palace	Jericho	Mt 2:4
The Herodium (site of Herod's tomb)	Near Bethlehem	Mt 2:19
Masada	Near western shore of Dead Sea	Cf. Lk 21:20
Early synagogue	Capernaum	Mt 4:13; Mk 1:21
Pool of Siloam	Jerusalem	Jn 9:7
Pool of Bethesda	Jerusalem	Jn 5:2
Pilate inscription	Caesarea	Lk 3:1
Inscription: Gentile entrance of temple sanctuary	Jerusalem	Ac 21:27-29
Skeletal remains of crucified man	Jerusalem	Mk 15:24
Alexander (son) of Simon ossuary	Jerusalem	Mk 15:21
Peter's house	Capernaum	Mt 4:13; Lk 4:38
Jacob's well	Nablus	Jn 4:5-6
	ASIA MINOR	
Derbe inscription	Kerti Hüyük	Ac 14:20
Sergius Paulus inscription	Kythraia, Cyprus	Ac 13:6-7
Zeus altar (Satan's throne?)	Pergamum	Rev 2:13
Fourth-century B.C. walls	Assos	Ac 20:13-14
Artemis temple and altar	Ephesus	Ac 19:27-28
Ephesian theater	Ephesus	Ac 19:29
Silversmith shops	Ephesus	Ac 19:24
Artemis statues	Ephesus	Ac 19:35
	GREECE	
Erastus inscription	Corinth	Ro 16:23
Synagogue inscription	Corinth	Ac 18:4
Meat market inscription	Corinth	1Co 10:25
Cult dining rooms (in Asclepius and Demeter temples)	Corinth	1Co 8:10; 10:14
Court (bema)	Corinth	Ac 18:12
Marketplace (bema)	Philippi	Ac 16:19
Starting gate for races	Isthmia	1Co 9:24,26
Gallio inscription	Delphi	Ac 18:12
Egnatian Way	Neapolis (Kavalla), Philippi, Amphipolis, Apollonia, Thessalonica	Cf. Ac 16:11-12; 17:1
Politarch inscription	Thessalonica	Ac 17:6
	ITALY	
Tomb of Augustus	Rome	Lk 2:1
Mamertine Prison	Rome	2Ti 1:16-17; 2:9; 4:6-8
Appian Way	Puteoli to Rome	Ac 28:13-16
Golden House of Nero	Rome	Cf. Ac 25:10; 1Pe 2:13
Arch of Titus	Rome	Cf. Lk 19:43-44; 21:6,20

A Harmony of the Gospels

	MATTHEW	MARK	LUKE	JOHN
A PREVIEW OF WHO JESUS IS				
Luke's purpose in writing a gospel			1:1-4	
John's prologue: Jesus Christ, the preexistent Word incarnate				1:1-18
Genealogies of Jesus	1:1-17		3:23b-38	
THE EARLY YEARS OF JOHN THE BAPTIST				
John's birth foretold to Zechariah			1:5-25	
Jesus' birth foretold to Mary			1:26-38	
Mary's visit to Elizabeth, and Elizabeth's song			1:39-45	
Mary's song of joy			1:46-56	
John's birth			1:57-66	
Zechariah's prophetic song			1:67-79	
John's growth and early life			1:80	
THE EARLY YEARS OF JESUS CHRIST				
Circumstances of Jesus' birth explained to Joseph	1:18-25			
Birth of Jesus			2:1-7	
Praise of the angels, and witness of the shepherds			2:8-20	
Circumcision of Jesus			2:21	
Jesus presented in the temple with the homage of Simeon and Anna			2:22-38	
Visit of the Magi	2:1-12			
Escape into Egypt, and murder of boys in Bethlehem	2:13-18			
Return to Nazareth	2:19-23		2:39	
Growth and early life of Jesus			2:40	
Jesus' first Passover in Jerusalem			2:41-50	
Jesus' growth to adulthood			2:51-52	
THE PUBLIC MINISTRY OF JOHN THE BAPTIST				
His ministry launched		1:1	3:1-2	
His person, proclamation and baptism	3:1-6	1:2-6	3:3-6	
His messages to the Pharisees, Sadducees, crowds, tax collectors and soldiers	3:7-10		3:7-14	
His description of Christ	3:11-12	1:7-8	3:15-18	
THE END OF JOHN'S MINISTRY AND THE BEGINNING OF CHRIST'S PUBLIC MINISTRY				
Jesus' baptism by John	3:13-17	1:9-11	3:21-23a	
Jesus' temptation in the desert	4:1-11	1:12-13	4:1-13	
John's testimony about himself to the priests and Levites				1:19-28
John's testimony to Jesus as the Son of God				1:29-34
Jesus' first followers				1:35-51
Jesus' first miracle: water becomes wine				2:1-11
Jesus' first stay in Capernaum with his relatives and early disciples				2:12
First clearing of the temple at the Passover				2:13-22
Early response to Jesus' miracles				2:23-25
Nicodemus's interview with Jesus				3:1-21
John superseded by Jesus				3:22-36
Jesus' departure from Judea	4:12	1:14a	3:19-20; 4:14a	4:1-4
Discussion with a Samaritan woman				4:5-26
Challenge of a spiritual harvest				4:27-38
Evangelization of Sychar				4:39-42
Arrival in Galilee				4:43-45
THE MINISTRY OF CHRIST IN GALILEE				
Opposition at Home and a New Headquarters				
Nature of the Galilean ministry	4:17	1:14b-15	4:14b-15	
Child at Capernaum healed by Jesus while at Cana				4:46-54
Ministry and rejection at Nazareth			4:16-31a	
Move to Capernaum	4:13-16			

[This is a tentative harmony only, since some sequences are debatable.]

	MATTHEW	MARK	LUKE	JOHN
Disciples Called and Ministry Throughout Galilee				
Call of the four	4:18-22	1:16-20	5:1-11	
Teaching in the synagogue of Capernaum authenticated by healing a demoniac		1:21-28	4:31b-37	
Peter's mother-in-law and others healed	8:14-17	1:29-34	4:38-41	
Tour of Galilee with Simon and others	4:23-25	1:35-39	4:42-44	
Healing of a man with leprosy, followed by much publicity	8:2-4	1:40-45	5:12-16	
Forgiving and healing of a paralyzed man	9:1-8	2:1-12	5:17-26	
Call of Matthew	9:9	2:13-14	5:27-28	
Banquet at Matthew's house	9:10-13	2:15-17	5:29-32	
With three parables Jesus defends his disciples for feasting instead of fasting	9:14-17	2:18-22	5:33-39	
Sabbath Controversies and Withdrawals				
Jesus heals an invalid on the Sabbath				5:1-9
Effort to kill Jesus for breaking the Sabbath and saying he was equal with God				5:10-18
Discourse demonstrating the Son's equality with the Father				5:19-47
Controversy over disciples' picking grain on the Sabbath	12:1-8	2:23-28	6:1-5	
Healing of a man's shriveled hand on the Sabbath	12:9-14	3:1-6	6:6-11	
Withdrawal to the Sea of Galilee with large crowds from many places	12:15-21	3:7-12		
Appointment of the Twelve and Sermon on the Mount				
Twelve apostles chosen		3:13-19	6:12-16	
Setting of the Sermon	5:1-2		6:17-19	
Blessings of those who inherit the kingdom and woes to those who do not	5:3-12		6:20-26	
Responsibility while awaiting the kingdom	5:13-16			
Law, righteousness and the kingdom	5:17-20			
Six contrasts in interpreting the law	5:21-48		6:27-30,32-36	
Three hypocritical "acts of righteousness" to be avoided	6:1-18			
Three prohibitions against avarice, harsh judgment, and unwise exposure of sacred things	6:19–7:6		6:37-42	
Application and conclusion	7:7-27		6:31,43-49	
Reaction of the crowds	7:28–8:1			
Growing Fame and Emphasis on Repentance				
A centurion's faith and the healing of his servant	8:5-13		7:1-10	
A widow's son raised at Nain			7:11-17	
John the Baptist's relationship to the kingdom	11:2-19		7:18-35	
Woes upon Korazin and Bethsaida for failure to repent	11:20-30			
Christ's feet anointed by a sinful but contrite woman			7:36-50	
First Public Rejection by Jewish Leaders				
A tour with the Twelve and other followers			8:1-3	
Blasphemous accusation by the teachers of the law and Pharisees	12:22-37	3:20-30		
Request for a sign refused	12:38-45			
Announcement of new spiritual kinship	12:46-50	3:31-35	8:19-21	
Secrets About the Kingdom Given in Parables				
TO THE CROWDS BY THE SEA				
The setting of the parables	13:1-3a	4:1-2	8:4	
The parable of the soils	13:3b-23	4:3-25	8:5-18	
The parable of the seed's spontaneous growth		4:26-29		
The parable of the weeds	13:24-30			
The parable of the mustard seed	13:31-32	4:30-32		
The parable of the leavened loaf	13:33-35	4:33-34		
TO THE DISCIPLES IN THE HOUSE				
The parable of the weeds explained	13:36-43			
The parable of the hidden treasure	13:44			
The parable of the valuable pearl	13:45-46			
The parable of the net	13:47-50			
The parable of the house owner	13:51-53			

A Harmony of the Gospels—*continued*

	MATTHEW	MARK	LUKE	JOHN
Continuing Opposition				
Crossing the lake and calming the storm	8:18,23-27	4:35-41	8:22-25	
Healing the Gerasene demoniacs and resultant opposition	8:28-34	5:1-20	8:26-39	
Return to Galilee, healing of a woman who touched Jesus' garment, and raising of Jairus's daughter	9:18-26	5:21-43	8:40-56	
Three miracles of healing, and another blasphemous accusation	9:27-34			
Final visit to unbelieving Nazareth	13:54-58	6:1-6a		
Final Galilean Campaign				
Shortage of workers	9:35-38	6:6b		
Commissioning of the Twelve	10:1-42	6:7-11	9:1-5	
Workers sent out	11:1	6:12-13	9:6	
Antipas's mistaken identification of Jesus	14:1-2	6:14-16	9:7-9	
Earlier imprisonment and beheading of John the Baptist	14:3-12	6:17-29		
THE MINISTRY OF CHRIST AROUND GALILEE				
Lesson on the Bread of Life				
Return of the workers		6:30	9:10a	
Withdrawal from Galilee	14:13-14	6:31-34	9:10b-11	6:1-3
Feeding the five thousand	14:15-21	6:35-44	9:12-17	6:4-13
A premature attempt to make Jesus king blocked	14:22-23	6:45-46		6:14-15
Walking on the water during a storm on the lake	14:24-33	6:47-52		6:16-21
Healings at Gennesaret	14:34-36	6:53-56		
Discourse on the true bread of life				6:22-59
Defection among the disciples				6:60-71
Lesson on the Leaven of the Pharisees, Sadducees, and Herodians				
Conflict over the tradition of ceremonial uncleanness	15:1-3a,7-9b, 3b-6,10-20	7:1-23		7:1
Ministry to a believing Greek woman in Tyre and Sidon	15:21-28	7:24-30		
Healings in the Decapolis	15:29-31	7:31-37		
Feeding the four thousand in the Decapolis	15:32-38	8:1-9a		
Return to Galilee and encounter with the Pharisees and Sadducees	15:39–16:4	8:9b-12		
Warning about the error of the Pharisees, Sadducees and Herodians	16:5-12	8:13-21		
Healing a blind man at Bethsaida		8:22-26		
Lesson of Messiahship Learned and Confirmed				
Peter's identification of Jesus as the Christ, and first prophecy of the church	16:13-20	8:27-30	9:18-21	
First direct prediction of the rejection, crucifixion and resurrection	16:21-26	8:31-37	9:22-25	
Coming of the Son of Man and judgment	16:27-28	8:38–9:1	9:26-27	
Transfiguration of Jesus	17:1-8	9:2-8	9:28-36a	
Discussion of resurrection, Elijah and John the Baptist	17:9-13	9:9-13	9:36b	
Lessons on Responsibility to Others				
Healing of demoniac boy and unbelief rebuked	17:14-20	9:14-29	9:37-43a	
Second prediction of Jesus' death and resurrection	17:22-23	9:30-32	9:43b-45	
Payment of temple tax	17:24-27			
Rivalry over greatness in the kingdom	18:1-5	9:33-37	9:46-48	
Warning against causing believers to sin	18:6-14	9:38-50	9:49-50	
Treatment and forgiveness of a sinning brother	18:15-35			
Journey to Jerusalem for the Feast of Tabernacles				
Complete commitment required of followers	8:19-22		9:57-62	
Ridicule by Jesus' half-brothers				7:2-9
Journey through Samaria			9:51-56	7:10
THE LATER JUDEAN MINISTRY OF CHRIST				
Ministry Beginning at the Feast of Tabernacles				
Mixed reaction to Jesus' teaching and miracles				7:11-31
Frustrated attempt to arrest Jesus				7:32-52

	MATTHEW	MARK	LUKE	JOHN
Jesus' forgiveness of a woman caught in adultery				[7:53–8:11]
Conflict over Jesus' claim to be the light of the world				8:12-20
Jesus' relationship to God the Father				8:21-30
Jesus' relationship to Abraham, and attempted stoning				8:31-59
Healing of a man born blind				9:1-7
Response of the blind man's neighbors				9:8-12
Examination and excommunication of the blind man by the Pharisees				9:13-34
Jesus' identification of himself to the blind man				9:35-38
Spiritual blindness of the Pharisees				9:39-41
Allegory of the good shepherd and the thief				10:1-18
Further division among the Jews				10:19-21
Private Lessons on Loving Service and Prayer				
Commissioning of the seventy			10:1-16	
Return of the seventy			10:17-24	
Story of the good Samaritan			10:25-37	
Jesus' visit with Mary and Martha			10:38-42	
Lesson on how to pray, and parable of the bold friend			11:1-13	
Second Debate with the Teachers of the Law and the Pharisees				
A third blasphemous accusation and a second debate			11:14-36	
Woes to the Pharisees and the teachers of the law while eating with a Pharisee			11:37-54	
Warning the disciples about hypocrisy			12:1-12	
Warning about greed and trust in wealth			12:13-34	
Warning against being unprepared for the Son of Man's coming			12:35-48	
Warning about the coming division			12:49-53	
Warning against failing to discern the present time			12:54-59	
Two alternatives: repent or perish			13:1-9	
Opposition from a synagogue ruler for healing a woman on the Sabbath			13:10-21	
Another attempt to stone or arrest Jesus for blasphemy at the Feast of Dedication				10:22-39
THE MINISTRY OF CHRIST IN AND AROUND PEREA				
Principles of Discipleship				
From Jerusalem to Perea				10:40-42
Question about salvation and entering the kingdom			13:22-30	
Anticipation of Jesus' coming death, and his sorrow over Jerusalem			13:31-35	
Healing of a man with dropsy while eating with a prominent Pharisee on the Sabbath, and three parables suggested by the occasion			14:1-24	
Cost of discipleship			14:25-35	
Parables in defense of association with sinners			15:1-32	
Parable to teach the proper use of money			16:1-13	
Story to teach the danger of wealth			16:14-31	
Four lessons on discipleship			17:1-10	
Sickness and death of Lazarus				11:1-16
Lazarus raised from the dead				11:17-44
Decision of the Sanhedrin to put Jesus to death				11:45-54
Teaching While on Final Journey to Jerusalem				
Healing of ten lepers while passing through Samaria and Galilee			17:11-21	
Instructions regarding the Son of Man's coming			17:22-37	
Two parables on prayer: the persistent widow, and the Pharisee and the tax collector			18:1-14	
Conflict with Pharisaic teaching on divorce	19:1-12	10:1-12		
Example of little children in relation to the kingdom	19:13-15	10:13-16	18:15-17	
Riches and the kingdom	19:16-30	10:17-31	18:18-30	
Parable of the landowner's sovereignty	20:1-16			
Third prediction of Jesus' death and resurrection	20:17-19	10:32-34	18:31-34	
Warning against ambitious pride	20:20-28	10:35-45		
Healing of blind Bartimaeus and his companion	20:29-34	10:46-52	18:35-43	

A Harmony of the Gospels—*continued*	MATTHEW	MARK	LUKE	JOHN
Salvation of Zacchaeus			19:1-10	
Parable to teach responsibility while the kingdom is delayed			19:11-28	
THE FORMAL PRESENTATION OF CHRIST TO ISRAEL AND THE RESULTING CONFLICT				
Triumphal Entry and the Fig Tree				
Arrival at Bethany				11:55–12:1,9-11
Triumphal entry into Jerusalem	21:1-3,6-7, 4-5,8-11, 14-17	11:1-11	19:29-44	12:12-19
Cursing of the fig tree having leaves but no figs	21:18-19a	11:12-14		
Second clearing of the temple	21:12-13	11:15-18	19:45-48	
Request of some Greeks to see Jesus, and necessity of the Son of Man's being lifted up				12:20-36a
Different responses to Jesus, and Jesus' response to the crowds				12:36b-50
Withered fig tree and the lesson on faith	21:19b-22	11:19-25	21:37-38	
Official Challenge to Christ's Authority				
Questioning of Jesus' authority by the chief priests, teachers of the law, and elders	21:23-27	11:27-33	20:1-8	
Jesus' response with his own question and three parables	21:28–22:14	12:1-12	20:9-19	
Attempts by Pharisees and Herodians to trap Jesus with a question about paying taxes to Caesar	22:15-22	12:13-17	20:20-26	
Sadducees' puzzling question about the resurrection	22:23-33	12:18-27	20:27-40	
A Pharisee's legal question	22:34-40	12:28-34		
Christ's Response to His Enemies' Challenges				
Christ's relationship to David as son and Lord	22:41-46	12:35-37	20:41-44	
Seven woes against the teachers of the law and Pharisees	23:1-36	12:38-40	20:45-47	
Jesus' sorrow over Jerusalem	23:37-39			
A poor widow's gift of all she had		12:41-44	21:1-4	
PROPHECIES IN PREPARATION FOR THE DEATH OF CHRIST				
The Olivet Discourse: Jesus Speaks Prophetically About the Temple and His Own Second Coming				
Setting of the discourse	24:1-3	13:1-4	21:5-7	
Beginning of birth pains	24:4-14	13:5-13	21:8-19	
Abomination of desolation, and subsequent distress	24:15-28	13:14-23	21:20-24	
Coming of the Son of Man	24:29-31	13:24-27	21:25-27	
Signs of nearness but unknown time	24:32-41	13:28-32	21:28-33	
Five parables to teach watchfulness and faithfulness	24:42–25:30	13:33-37	21:34-36	
Judgment at the Son of Man's coming	25:31-46			
Arrangements for Betrayal				
Plot by the Sanhedrin to arrest and kill Jesus	26:1-5	14:1-2	22:1-2	
Mary's anointing of Jesus for burial	26:6-13	14:3-9		12:2-8
Judas's agreement to betray Jesus	26:14-16	14:10-11	22:3-6	
The Last Supper				
Preparation for the Passover meal	26:17-19	14:12-16	22:7-13	
Beginning of the Passover meal, and dissension among the disciples over greatness	26:20	14:17	22:14-16, 24-30	
Washing the disciples' feet				13:1-20
Identification of the betrayer	26:21-25	14:18-21	22:21-23	13:21-30
Prediction of Peter's denial	26:31-35	14:27-31	22:31-38	13:31-38
Conclusion of the meal, and the Lord's Supper instituted (1Co 11:23-26)	26:26-29	14:22-25	22:17-20	
Discourse and Prayers from the Upper Room to Gethsemane				
Questions about his destination, the Father, and the Holy Spirit answered				14:1-31

	MATTHEW	MARK	LUKE	JOHN
The vine and the branches				15:1-17
Opposition from the world				15:18–16:4
Coming and ministry of the Spirit				16:5-15
Prediction of joy over his resurrection				16:16-22
Promise of answered prayer and peace				16:23-33
Jesus' prayer for himself, his disciples and all who believe				17:1-26
Jesus' three agonizing prayers in Gethsemane	26:30,36-46	14:26,32-42	22:39-46	18:1
THE DEATH OF CHRIST				
Betrayal and Arrest				
Jesus betrayed, arrested and forsaken	26:47-56	14:43-52	22:47-53	18:2-12
Trial				
First Jewish phase, before Annas				18:13-14, 19-23
Second Jewish phase, before Caiaphas and the Sanhedrin	26:57,59-68	14:53,55-65	22:54a,63-65	18:24
Peter's denials	26:58,69-75	14:54,66-72	22:54b-62	18:15-18, 25-27
Third Jewish phase, before the Sanhedrin	27:1	15:1a	22:66-71	
Remorse and suicide of Judas Iscariot (Ac 1:18-19)	27:3-10			
First Roman phase, before Pilate	27:2,11-14	15:1b-5	23:1-5	18:28-38
Second Roman phase, before Herod Antipas			23:6-12	
Third Roman phase, before Pilate	27:15-26	15:6-15	23:13-25	18:39–19:16a
Crucifixion				
Mockery by the Roman soldiers	27:27-30	15:16-19		
Journey to Golgotha	27:31-34	15:20-23	23:26-33a	19:16b-17
First three hours of crucifixion	27:35-44	15:24-32	23:33b-43	19:18,23-24, 19-22,25-27
Last three hours of crucifixion	27:45-50	15:33-37	23:44-45a,46	19:28-30
Witness of Jesus' death	27:51-56	15:38-41	23:45b,47-49	
Burial				
Certification of Jesus' death, and procurement of his body	27:57-58	15:42-45	23:50-52	19:31-38
Jesus' body placed in a tomb	27:59-60	15:46	23:53-54	19:39-42
The tomb watched by the women and guarded by the soldiers	27:61-66	15:47	23:55-56	
THE RESURRECTION AND ASCENSION OF CHRIST				
The Empty Tomb				
The tomb visited by the women	28:1	16:1		
The stone rolled away	28:2-4			
The tomb found to be empty by the women	28:5-8	16:2-8	24:1-8	20:1
The tomb found to be empty by Peter and John			24:9-12	20:2-10
The Resurrection Appearances				
Appearance to Mary Magdalene		[16:9-11]		20:11-18
Appearance to the other women	28:9-10			
Report of the soldiers to the Jewish authorities	28:11-15			
Appearance to the two disciples traveling to Emmaus		[16:12-13]	24:13-32	
Report of the two disciples to the rest (1Co 15:5a)			24:33-35	
Appearance to the ten assembled disciples		[16:14]	24:36-43	20:19-25
Appearance to the eleven assembled disciples (1Co 15:5b)				20:26-31
Appearance to the seven disciples while fishing				21:1-25
Appearance to the Eleven in Galilee (1Co 15:6)	28:16-20	[16:15-18]		
Appearance to James, Jesus' brother (1Co 15:7)				
Appearance to the disciples in Jerusalem (Ac 1:3-8)			24:44-49	
The Ascension				
Christ's parting blessing and departure (Ac 1:9-12)		[16:19-20]	24:50-53	

Acts

INTRODUCTION

Author

Although the author does not name himself, evidence outside the Scriptures and inferences from the book itself lead to the conclusion that the author was Luke.

The earliest of the external testimonies appears in the Muratorian Canon (c. A.D. 170), where the explicit statement is made that Luke was the author of both the third Gospel and the "Acts of All the Apostles." Eusebius (c. 325) lists information from numerous sources to identify the author of these books as Luke (*Ecclesiastical History*, 3.4).

Within the writing itself are some clues as to who the author was:

1. *Luke, the companion of Paul.* In the description of the happenings in Acts, certain passages make use of the pronoun "we." At these points the author includes himself as a companion of Paul in his travels (16:10 – 17; 20:5 — 21:18; 27:1 — 28:16; see notes on 16:10,17; 27:1). A historian as careful with details as this author proves to be would have good reason for choosing to use "we" in some places and "they" elsewhere. The author was therefore probably present with Paul at the particular events described in the "we" sections.

These "we" passages include the period of Paul's two-year imprisonment at Rome (ch. 28). During this time Paul wrote, among other letters, Philemon and Colossians. In them he sends greetings from his companions, and Luke is included among them (see Col 4:9 – 17 and notes; Phm 23 – 24). In fact, after eliminating those who, for one reason or another, would not fit the requirements for the author of Acts, Luke is left as the most likely candidate.

2. *Luke, the physician.* Although it cannot be proved that the author of Acts was a physician simply from his vocabulary, the words he uses and the traits and education reflected in his writings fit well his role as a physician (see, e.g., note on 28:6). It is true that the doctor of the first century did not have as specialized a vocabulary as that of doctors today, but there are some usages in Luke–Acts that seem to suggest that a medical man was the author of these books. And it should be remembered that Paul uses the term "doctor" in describing Luke (see Col 4:14 and note).

Date

Two dates are possible for the writing of this book: (1) c. A.D. 63, soon after the last event recorded in the book, and (2) c. 70 or even later.

The earlier date is supported by:

1. *Silence about later events.* While arguments from silence are not conclusive, it is perhaps significant that the book contains no allusion to events that happened after the close of Paul's two-

year imprisonment in Rome: e.g., the burning of Rome and the persecution of the Christians there (A.D. 64), the martyrdom of Peter and Paul (possibly 67) and the destruction of Jerusalem (70).

2. *No outcome of Paul's trial.* If Luke knew the outcome of the trial Paul was waiting for (see 28:30 and note), why did he not record it at the close of Acts? Perhaps it was because he had brought the history up to date.

Those who prefer the later date hold that 1:8 (see note there) reveals one of the purposes Luke had in writing his history, and that this purpose influenced the way the book ended. Luke wanted to show how the church penetrated the world of his day in ever-widening circles (Jerusalem, Judea, Samaria, the ends of the earth) until it reached Rome, the world's political and cultural center. On this understanding, mention of the martyrdom of Paul (c. A.D. 67) and of the destruction of Jerusalem (70) was not pertinent. This would allow for the writing of Acts c. 70 or even later.

Recipient

The addressee of the book, Theophilus, is the same person named in the first volume, the Gospel of Luke (see Introduction to Luke: Recipient and Purpose), but the book was no doubt intended to be read by a larger Christian audience.

Importance

The book of Acts provides a bridge for the writings of the NT. As a second volume to Luke's Gospel, it joins what Jesus "began to do and to teach" (1:1; see note there) as told in the Gospels with what he continued to do and teach through the apostles' preaching and the establishment of the church. Besides linking the Gospel narratives on the one hand and the apostolic letters on the other, it supplies an account of the life of Paul from which we can learn the setting for his letters. Geographically its story spans the lands between Jerusalem, where the church began, and Rome, the political center of the empire. Historically it provides a highly selective account of the first 30 years of the church. It is also a bridge that ties the church in its beginning with each succeeding age. This book reveals the potential of the church when it is guided and empowered by the Holy Spirit.

A Quick Look

Author:

Luke, a Gentile physician and missionary companion of Paul

Audience:

Addressed to Theophilus, but intended for all believers

Date:

About A.D. 63 or later

Theme:

Luke shows how the gospel rapidly spread from Jerusalem to the whole Roman empire and from its Jewish roots to the Gentile world.

Theme and Purpose

The theme of the work is best summarized in 1:8 (see note there). It was ordinary procedure for a historian at this time to begin a second volume by summarizing the first volume and indicating the contents anticipated in his second volume. Luke summarized his first volume in 1:1 – 3; the theme of his second volume is presented in the words of Jesus: "You will be my witnesses in Jerusalem, and in all Judea and Samaria, and to the ends of the earth" (1:8). This is, in effect, an outline of the book of Acts (see Plan and Outline below).

The main purposes of the book appear to be:

1. *To present a history.* The significance of Acts as a historical account of Christian origins cannot be overestimated. It tells of the founding of the church, the spread of the gospel, the beginnings of congregations, and evangelistic efforts in the apostolic pattern. One of the unique aspects of Christianity is its firm historical foundation. The life and teachings of Jesus Christ are established in the four Gospel narratives, and the book of Acts provides a coordinated account of the beginning and spread of the church as the result of the work of the risen Lord and the Holy Spirit through the apostles.

2. *To give a defense.* One finds embedded in Acts a record of Christian defenses made to both Jews (e.g., 4:8 – 12) and Gentiles (e.g., 25:8 – 11), with the underlying purpose of conversion. It shows how the early church coped with pagan and Jewish thought, the Roman government and Hellenistic society.

Luke may have written this work as Paul awaited trial in Rome. If his case came to court, what better court brief could Paul have had than a life of Jesus, a history of the beginnings of the church (including the activity of Paul) and an early collection of Paul's letters?

3. *To provide a guide.* Luke had no way of knowing how long the church would continue on this earth, but as long as it pursues its course, the book of Acts will be one of its major guides. In Acts we see basic principles being applied to specific situations in the context of problems and persecutions. These same principles continue to be applicable until Christ returns.

4. *To depict the triumph of Christianity in the face of bitter persecution.* The success of the church in carrying the gospel from Jerusalem to Rome and in planting local churches across the Roman empire demonstrated that Christianity was not a merely human work. It triumphed under the rule of the exalted Christ and through the power of the Holy Spirit.

Characteristics

1. *Accurate historical detail.* Every page of Acts abounds with sharp, precise details, to the delight of the historian. The account covers a period of about 30 years and reaches across the lands from Jerusalem to Rome. Luke's description of these times and places is filled with all kinds of people and cultures, a variety of governmental administrations, court scenes in Caesarea, and dramatic events involving such centers as Antioch, Ephesus, Athens, Corinth and Rome. Barbarian country districts and Jewish centers are included as well. Yet in each instance archaeological findings reveal that Luke uses the proper terms for the time and place being described. Hostile criticism has not succeeded in disproving the detailed accuracy of Luke's political and geographical designations (see chart, p. 1667, and maps and archaeological notes scattered throughout the book).

As a second volume to Luke's Gospel, the book of Acts joins what Jesus "began to do and to teach" as told in the Gospels with what he continued to do and teach through the apostles' preaching and the establishment of the church.

2. *Literary excellence.* Not only does Luke have a large vocabulary compared with other NT writers, but he also uses these words in literary styles that fit the cultural settings of the events he is recording. At times he employs good, classical Greek; at other times the Palestinian Aramaic of the first century shows through his expressions. This is an indication of Luke's careful practice of using language appropriate to the time and place being described. Aramaisms are used when Luke is describing happenings that took place in the Holy Land (chs. 1 – 12).

3. *Dramatic description.* Luke's skillful use of speeches contributes to the drama of his narrative. Not only are they carefully spaced and well balanced between Peter and Paul, but the speeches of a number of other individuals add variety and vividness to the account (see 5 below). Luke's use of details brings the action to life. Nowhere in ancient literature is there an account of a shipwreck superior to Luke's with its nautical details (ch. 27). The book is vivid and fast-moving throughout.

4. *Historical Reliability.* Luke's careful arrangement of material need not detract from the accuracy of his record. He demonstrates the veracity of his account by recording the failures as well as the successes, the bad as well as the good, in the early church. Not only is the discontent between the Hellenistic Jews and the Hebraic Jews recorded (see 6:1 and note) but also the discord between Paul and Barnabas (see 15:39 and note). Divisions and differences are recognized (15:2; 21:20 – 21).

5. *Effective use of speeches.* One of the distinguishing features of the book of Acts is its speeches. They may be classified as follows: (1) evangelistic — two types: to Jews and God-fearers (2:14 – 40; 3:12 – 26; 4:8 – 12; 5:29 – 32; 10:34 – 43; 13:16 – 41), to pagans (17:22 – 31); (2) deliberative — using persuasive arguments (1:16 – 17,20 – 22; 15:7 – 11,13 – 21); (3) apologetic — defending the gospel (7:2 – 52; 22:1 – 21; 23:1 – 6; 24:10 – 21; 25:8,10; 26:2 – 23; 28:17 – 20,21 – 22,25 – 28); (4) hortatory — urging behavioral change (20:18 – 35).

The speeches are obviously not verbatim reports; any of them can be read in a few minutes. We know, e.g., that Paul at times preached very long sermons (see 20:7,9; 28:23). However, studies of these speeches (speakers, audiences, circumstances, language and style of writing) give us reason to believe that they are accurate summaries of what was actually said.

Plan and Outline

Luke weaves together different interests and emphases as he relates the beginnings and expansion of the church. The design of his book revolves around (1) key players in the expansion of the gospel: Peter, Stephen, Philip, Paul, etc.; (2) important topics and events: the role of the Holy Spirit, pioneer missionary outreach to new fields, conversions, the growth of the church, and life in the Christian community; (3) significant problems: conflict between Jews and Gentiles, persecution of the church by some Jewish elements, trials before Jews and Romans, confrontations with Gentiles, and other hardships in the ministry; (4) geographical advances: five significant stages (see the quotations in the outline; see also map, p. 1702; cf. note on 1:8).

I. Peter and the Beginnings of the Church in the Holy Land (chs. 1 – 12)
  A. "Throughout Judea, Galilee and Samaria" (1:1 — 9:31; see 9:31 and note)
    1. Introduction (1:1 – 2)
    2. Christ's resurrection ministry (1:3 – 11)
    3. The period of waiting for the Holy Spirit (1:12 – 26)
    4. The filling with the Spirit (ch. 2)
    5. The healing of the lame man and the resultant arrest of Peter and John (3:1 — 4:31)
    6. The community of goods (4:32 — 5:11)
    7. The arrest of the 12 apostles (5:12 – 42)
    8. The choice of the Seven (6:1 – 7)
    9. Stephen's arrest and martyrdom (6:8 — 7:60)
    10. The scattering of the Jerusalem believers (8:1 – 4)
    11. Philip's ministry (8:5 – 40)
      a. In Samaria (8:5 – 25)
      b. To the Ethiopian eunuch (8:26 – 40)
    12. Saul's conversion (9:1 – 31)
  B. "As far as Phoenicia, Cyprus and Antioch" (9:32 — 12:25; see 11:19 and note)
    1. Peter's ministry on the Mediterranean coast (9:32 — 11:18)
      a. To Aeneas and Dorcas (9:32 – 43)
      b. To Cornelius (10:1 — 11:18)
    2. The new Gentile church in Antioch (11:19 – 30)
    3. Herod's persecution of the church and his subsequent death (ch. 12)
II. Paul and the Expansion of the Church from Antioch to Rome (chs. 13 – 28)
  A. "Throughout the region of Phrygia and Galatia" (13:1 — 15:35; see 16:6 and note)
    1. Paul's first missionary journey (chs. 13 – 14)
    2. The Jerusalem conference (15:1 – 35)
  B. "Over to Macedonia" (15:36 — 21:16; see 16:9 and note)
    1. Paul's second missionary journey (15:36 — 18:22)
    2. Paul's third missionary journey (18:23 — 21:16)
  C. "To Rome" (21:17 — 28:31; see 28:14 and note)
    1. Paul's imprisonment in Jerusalem (21:17 — 23:35)
      a. Arrest (21:17 — 22:29)
      b. Trial before the Sanhedrin (22:30 — 23:11)
      c. Transfer to Caesarea (23:12 – 35)
    2. Paul's imprisonment in Caesarea (chs. 24 – 26)
      a. Trial before Felix (ch. 24)
      b. Trial before Festus (25:1 – 12)
      c. Hearing before Festus and Agrippa (25:13 — 26:32)
    3. Voyage to Rome (27:1 — 28:15)
    4. Two years under house arrest in Rome (28:16 – 31)

Jesus Taken Up Into Heaven

1 In my former book,[a] Theophilus, I wrote about all that Jesus began to do and to teach[b] 2 until the day he was taken up to heaven,[c] after giving instructions[d] through the Holy Spirit to the apostles[e] he had chosen.[f] 3 After his suffering, he showed himself to these men and gave many convincing proofs that he was alive. He appeared to them[g] over a period of forty days and spoke about the kingdom of God.[h] 4 On one occasion, while he was eating with them, he gave them this command: "Do not leave Jerusalem, but wait[i] for the gift my Father promised, which you have heard me speak about.[j] 5 For John baptized with[a] water,[k] but in a few days you will be baptized with the Holy Spirit."[l]

6 So when they met together, they asked him, "Lord, are you at this time going to restore[m] the kingdom to Israel?"

7 He said to them: "It is not for you to know the times or dates the Father has set by his own authority.[n] 8 But you will receive power when the Holy Spirit comes on you;[o] and you will be my witnesses[p] in Jerusalem, and in all Judea and Samaria,[q] and to the ends of the earth."[r]

9 After he said this, he was taken up[s] before their very eyes, and a cloud hid him from their sight.

10 They were looking intently up into the sky as he was going, when suddenly two men dressed in white[t] stood beside them. 11 "Men of Galilee,"[u] they said, "why do you stand here looking into the sky? This same Jesus, who has been taken from you into heaven, will come back[v] in the same way you have seen him go into heaven."

Matthias Chosen to Replace Judas

12 Then they returned to Jerusalem[w] from the hill called the Mount of Olives,[x] a Sabbath day's walk[b] from the city. 13 When they arrived, they went upstairs to the room[y] where they were staying. Those present were Peter, John, James and Andrew; Philip and Thomas, Bartholomew and Matthew; James son of Alphaeus and Simon the Zealot, and Judas son of James.[z] 14 They all joined together constantly in prayer,[a] along with the women[b] and Mary the mother of Jesus, and with his brothers.[c]

15 In those days Peter stood up among

[a] 5 Or *in* [b] 12 That is, about 3/4 mile (about 1,100 meters)

1:1 [a] Lk 1:1-4 [b] Lk 3:23 **1:2** [c] ver 9,11; S Mk 16:19 [d] Mt 28:19,20 [e] S Mk 6:30 [f] Jn 13:18; 15:16,19 **1:3** [g] Mt 28:17; Lk 24:34,36; Jn 20:19,26; 21:1,14; 1Co 15:5-7 [h] S Mt 3:2 **1:4** [i] Ps 27:14 [j] Lk 24:49; Jn 14:16; Ac 2:33 **1:5** [k] S Mk 1:4 [l] S Mk 1:8 **1:6** [m] Mt 17:11; Ac 3:21 **1:7** [n] Dt 29:29; Ps 102:13; Mt 24:36 **1:8** [o] Ac 2:1-4 [p] S Lk 24:48 [q] Ac 8:1-25 [r] S Mt 28:19 **1:9** [s] ver 2; S Mk 16:19 **1:10** [t] S Jn 20:12 **1:11** [u] Ac 2:7 [v] S Mt 16:27 **1:12** [w] Lk 24:52 [x] S Mt 21:1 **1:13** [y] Ac 9:37; 20:8 [z] Mt 10:2-4; Mk 3:16-19; Lk 6:14-16 **1:14** [a] Ac 2:42; 4:24; 6:4; S Lk 18:1; S Ro 1:10 [b] Lk 23:49,55 [c] S Mt 12:46

1:1 *my former book.* The Gospel of Luke. Acts was addressed to the same patron, Theophilus (see Introduction to Luke: Recipient and Purpose). *began to do and to teach.* An apt summation of Luke's Gospel, implying that Jesus' work continues in Acts through his own personal interventions and the ministry of the Holy Spirit (see note on Lk 24:53).

1:2 *taken up to heaven.* The last scene of Luke's Gospel (24:50–52) and the opening scene of this second volume (vv. 6–11). The ascension occurred 40 days after the resurrection (v. 3). *through the Holy Spirit.* Jesus' postresurrection instruction of his apostles was carried on through the Holy Spirit, and succeeding statements make it clear that what the apostles were to accomplish was likewise to be done through the Spirit (vv. 4–5,8; see Lk 24:49 and note; Jn 20:22; see also Introduction to Judges: Themes and Theology). Luke characteristically stresses the Holy Spirit's work and enabling power (e.g., v. 8; 2:4,17; 4:8,31; 5:3; 6:3,5; 7:55; 8:16; 9:17,31; 10:44; 13:2,4; 15:28; 16:6; 19:2,6; see note on Lk 4:1).

1:3 *many convincing proofs.* See the resurrection appearances (Mt 28:1–20; Lk 24:1–53; Jn 20:1–29; 1Co 15:3–8). *kingdom of God.* The heart of Jesus' preaching (see notes on Mt 3:2; Lk 4:43).

1:4 *the gift my Father promised.* The Holy Spirit (see Lk 24:49 and note; Jn 14:26; 15:26–27; 16:12–13).

1:5 *John baptized with water.* See Lk 3:16 and note. *in a few days.* The day of Pentecost came ten days later, when the baptism with the Holy Spirit occurred (2:1–4).

1:6 *restore the kingdom to Israel?* Like their fellow countrymen, they were looking for the deliverance of the people of Israel from foreign domination and for the establishment of an earthly kingdom. The reference to the coming of the Spirit had caused them to wonder if the new age was about to dawn.

1:7 *the times or dates.* The elapsing time or the character of coming events (see Mk 13:32; 1Th 5:1 and notes).

1:8 A virtual outline of Acts: The apostles were to be witnesses in Jerusalem (chs. 1–7), Judea and Samaria (chs. 8–9) and the ends of the earth—including Caesarea, Antioch, Asia Minor, Greece and Rome (chs. 10–28). However, they were not to begin this staggering task until they had been equipped with the power of the Spirit (vv. 4–5). *my witnesses.* An important theme throughout Acts (2:32; 3:15; 5:32; 10:39; 13:31; 22:15). *Judea.* The region in which Jerusalem was located. *Samaria.* The adjoining region to the north.

1:9 *taken up.* See note on v. 2. *a cloud hid him.* See Mt 17:5 and note.

1:10 *two men dressed in white.* Cf. Lk 24:4; Jn 20:12.

1:11 *Men of Galilee.* All the Twelve were from Galilee except Judas, and he was no longer present. *in the same way.* In the same resurrection body and in clouds and with "great glory" (Mt 24:30).

1:12 *Mount of Olives.* The ascension occurred on the eastern slope of the mount between Jerusalem and Bethany (Lk 19:28–29,37; see notes on Zec 14:4; Mk 11:1; Lk 19:29; 24:50). *Sabbath day's walk.* See NIV text note. This distance was drawn from Rabbinical reasoning based on several OT passages (Ex 16:29; Nu 35:5; Jos 3:4). A faithful Jew was to travel no farther on the Sabbath.

1:13 *room.* Probably an upper room of a large house, such as the one where the Last Supper was held (Mk 14:15) or that of Mary, mother of Mark (see note on 12:12). *Bartholomew.* Apparently John calls him Nathanael (see Jn 1:45–49; 21:2). *James son of Alphaeus.* The same as James the younger (Mk 15:40). *Zealot.* See note on Mt 10:4. *Judas son of James.* Not Judas Iscariot, but the same as Thaddaeus (see note on Mt 10:3).

1:14 *with the women.* Possibly wives of the apostles (cf. 1Co 9:5 and note) and those listed as ministering to Jesus (Mt 27:55; Lk 8:2–3; 24:22). *Mary the mother of Jesus.* Last mentioned here in Scripture. *brothers.* See note on Lk 8:19. These brothers would include James, who later became a leader in the Jerusalem church (12:17; 15:13; 21:18; Gal 1:19; 2:9; see Introduction to James: Author).

the believers[a] (a group numbering about
a hundred and twenty) 16and said, "Brothers,[d] the Scripture had to be fulfilled[e]
which the Holy Spirit spoke long ago
through the mouth of David concerning
Judas,[f] who served as guide for those who
arrested Jesus— 17he was one of our number[g] and shared in this ministry."[h]
18(With the reward[i] he got for his wickedness, Judas bought a field;[j] there he fell
headlong, his body burst open and all his
intestines spilled out. 19Everyone in Jerusalem heard about this, so they called that
field in their language[k] Akeldama, that is,
Field of Blood.)
20"For," said Peter, "it is written in the
book of Psalms,

"'May his place be deserted;
let there be no one to dwell in it,'[b][l]

and,

"'May another take his place of
leadership.'[c][m]

21Therefore it is necessary to choose one
of the men who have been with us the
whole time the Lord Jesus went in and out
among us, 22beginning from John's baptism[n] to the time when Jesus was taken
up from us. For one of these must become
a witness[o] with us of his resurrection."
23So they proposed two men: Joseph
called Barsabbas (also known as Justus)
and Matthias. 24Then they prayed,[p] "Lord,
you know everyone's heart.[q] Show us[r]
which of these two you have chosen 25to
take over this apostolic ministry, which
Judas left to go where he belongs." 26Then
they cast lots, and the lot fell to Matthias;
so he was added to the eleven apostles.[s]

1:16 [d] Ac 6:3; 11:1,12,29; 14:2; 18:18,27; 21:7; S 22:5; S Ro 7:1 [e] ver 20; S Mt 1:22 [f] S Mt 10:4 **1:17** [g] Jn 6:70,71 [h] ver 25 **1:18** [i] Mt 26:14,15 [j] Mt 27:3-10 **1:19** [k] S Jn 5:2 **1:20** [l] Ps 69:25 [m] Ps 109:8 **1:22** [n] S Mk 1:4 [o] ver 8; S Lk 24:48 **1:24** [p] Ac 6:6; 13:3; 14:23 [q] Ac 15:8; S Rev 2:23 [r] 1Sa 14:41 **1:26** [s] Ac 2:14 **2:1** [t] Lev 23:15,16; Ac 20:16; 1Co 16:8 [u] Ac 1:14 **2:2** [v] Ac 4:31 **2:4** [w] S Lk 1:15 [x] S Mk 16:17 **2:5** [y] Lk 2:25; Ac 8:2

The Holy Spirit Comes at Pentecost

2 When the day of Pentecost[t] came, they
were all together[u] in one place. 2Sud-
denly a sound like the blowing of a violent wind came from heaven and filled
the whole house where they were sitting.[v]
3They saw what seemed to be tongues of
fire that separated and came to rest on
each of them. 4All of them were filled with
the Holy Spirit[w] and began to speak in other tongues[d][x] as the Spirit enabled them.
5Now there were staying in Jerusalem
God-fearing[y] Jews from every nation under

[a] *15* Greek *brothers* [b] *20* Psalm 69:25 [c] *20* Psalm 109:8 [d] *4* Or *languages*; also in verse 11

1:16 *the Scripture had to be fulfilled.* For the Scripture referred to see NIV text notes on v. 20. Both before and after Christ came, numerous psalms were viewed as Messianic. What happened in the psalmist's experience was typical of the experiences of the Messiah. No doubt Jesus' instruction in Lk 24:27,45–47 included these Scriptures.

1:18 *Judas bought a field.* Judas bought the field indirectly: The money he returned to the priests (Mt 27:3) was used to purchase the potter's field (Mt 27:7). *fell headlong.* Mt 27:5 reports that Judas hanged himself. It appears that when the body finally fell, either because of decay or because someone cut it down, it was in a decomposed condition and so broke open in the middle.

1:20 *it is written.* Two passages of Scripture (see NIV text notes) were put together to suggest that Judas had left a vacancy that had to be filled (see notes on Ps 69:25; 109:8).

1:21 *went in and out among us.* Ministered publicly (cf. 9:28).

1:22 *a witness with us of his resurrection.* Apparently several met this requirement. On this occasion, however, the believers were selecting someone to become an official witness to the resurrection—thus, a 12th apostle (v. 25).

1:23 *Barsabbas.* Means "son of (the) Sabbath." This patronymic was used for two early Jewish Christians, possibly brothers. One was Joseph (here); the other was Judas, a prophet in Jerusalem who was sent to Antioch with Silas (15:22,32). *Justus.* Joseph's Hellenistic name. Nothing more is known of him.

1:26 *cast lots.* See Pr 16:33 and note. By casting lots they submitted the decision to the ascended Lord. The use of rocks or sticks to designate the choice was common (see 1Ch 26:13–16; see also notes on Ne 11:1; Jnh 1:7). This is the Bible's last mention of casting lots, perhaps because from that time on guidance from God would be mediated through the Holy Spirit's ministry in the lives of believers (see ch. 2; cf. 13:2; Ro 8:14 and notes).

2:1 *day of Pentecost.* The 50th day after the Sabbath of Passover week (Lev 23:15–16), thus the first day of the week. Pentecost is also called the Feast of Weeks (Dt 16:10), the Feast of Harvest (Ex 23:16) and the day of firstfruits (Nu 28:26). See chart, pp. 178–179. *they were all together.* The nearest antecedent of "they" is the 11 apostles (plus Matthias), but the reference is probably to all those mentioned in 1:13–15. *in one place.* Evidently not the upstairs room where they were staying (1:13) but perhaps some place in the temple precincts, for the apostles were "continually at the temple" when it was open (Lk 24:53; see note there).

2:2 *violent wind.* Breath or wind is a symbol of the Spirit of God (see Eze 37:9,14; Jn 3:8). The coming of the Spirit is marked by audible (wind) and visible (fire) signs. *whole house.* May refer to the temple (cf. 7:47).

2:3 *tongues.* A descriptive metaphor appropriate to the context, in which several languages are about to be spoken. *fire.* A symbol of the divine presence (see Ex 3:2 and note), it was also associated with judgment (see Mt 3:12 and note).

2:4 *All of them.* Could refer either to the apostles or to the 120. Those holding that the 120 are meant point to the fulfillment of Joel's prophecy (vv. 17–18) as involving more than the 12 apostles. The nearest reference, however, is to the apostles (see note on v. 1), and the narrative continues with Peter and the 11 standing to address the crowd (v. 14). *filled with the Holy Spirit.* A fulfillment of 1:4–5,8; see also Jesus' promise in Lk 24:49 and note there (cf. Jn 14:16–18; 20:22 and note). Their spirits were completely under the control of the Holy Spirit; their words were his words. *in other tongues.* The Spirit enabled them to speak in languages they had not previously learned (see NIV text note). Two other examples of speaking in tongues are found in Acts (see 10:46; 19:6 and note). One extended NT passage deals with this spiritual gift (1Co 12–14). Not all agree, however, that these other passages refer to speaking in known languages. The gift had particular relevance here, where people of different nationalities and languages were gathered.

2:5 *God-fearing Jews.* Devout Jews from different parts of the world but assembled now in Jerusalem either as pilgrims attending the Feast of Pentecost or as current residents (cf. Lk 2:25).

heaven. 6When they heard this sound, a
crowd came together in bewilderment, because each one heard them speaking in
his own language. 7Utterly amazed,[z] they
asked: "Are not all these men who are
speaking Galileans?[a] 8Then how is it that
each of us hears them in his own native
language? 9Parthians, Medes and Elamites; residents of Mesopotamia, Judea and
Cappadocia,[b] Pontus[c] and Asia,[d] 10Phryg-
ia[e] and Pamphylia,[f] Egypt and the parts
of Libya near Cyrene;[g] visitors from Rome
11(both Jews and converts to Judaism); Cretans and Arabs — we hear them declaring
the wonders of God in our own tongues!"
12Amazed and perplexed, they asked one
another, "What does this mean?"
13Some, however, made fun of them and
said, "They have had too much wine.[a]"[h]

Peter Addresses the Crowd

14Then Peter stood up with the Eleven,

2:7 [z] ver 12 [a] Ac 1:11 **2:9** [b] 1Pe 1:1 [c] Ac 18:2; 1Pe 1:1 [d] Ac 16:6; 19:10; Ro 16:5; 1Co 16:19; 2Co 1:8; Rev 1:4 **2:10** [e] Ac 16:6; 18:23 [f] Ac 13:13; 14:24; 15:38 [g] S Mt 27:32 **2:13** [h] 1Co 14:23; Eph 5:18

[a] *13* Or *sweet wine*

2:6 *speaking in his own language.* These Jews heard the apostles speak in languages native to the different places they came from (see map, below).
2:9 *Parthians.* Inhabitants of the territory from the Tigris River to India. *Medes.* Media lay east of Mesopotamia, northwest of Persia and south-southwest of the Caspian Sea. *Elamites.* Elam was north of the Persian Gulf, bounded on the west by the Tigris. *Mesopotamia.* Between the Euphrates and Tigris rivers. *Judea.* The homeland of the Jews, perhaps used here in the OT sense "from the river of Egypt to . . . the Euphrates" (Ge 15:18), including Galilee. *Cappadocia, Pontus and Asia.* Districts in Asia Minor. *Asia.* See note on 2Co 1:8.
2:10 *Phrygia and Pamphylia.* Districts in Asia Minor. *Egypt.* Jews had lived in Egypt since the sixth century B.C. Two out of the five districts of Alexandria were Jewish. *Libya.* A region west of Egypt. *Cyrene.* The capital of a district of Libya called Cyrenaica. See 6:9 and note. *Rome.* Thousands of Jews lived in Rome (see map, p. 1735).
2:11 *converts to Judaism.* Gentiles who undertook the full observance of the Mosaic law were received into full fellowship with the Jews. *Cretans.* Represented an island lying south-southeast of Greece. *Arabs.* From a region to the east. The kingdom of the Nabatean Arabs lay between the Red Sea and the Euphrates, with Petra as its capital. *we hear them declaring.* Not a miracle of hearing but of speaking. The believers were declaring God's wonders in the native languages of the various visiting Jews (see map, below).
2:14 – 40 The pattern and themes of the message that follows became common in the early church: (1) an explanation of events (vv. 14 – 21); (2) the gospel of Jesus Christ — his death, resurrection and exaltation (vv. 22 – 36);

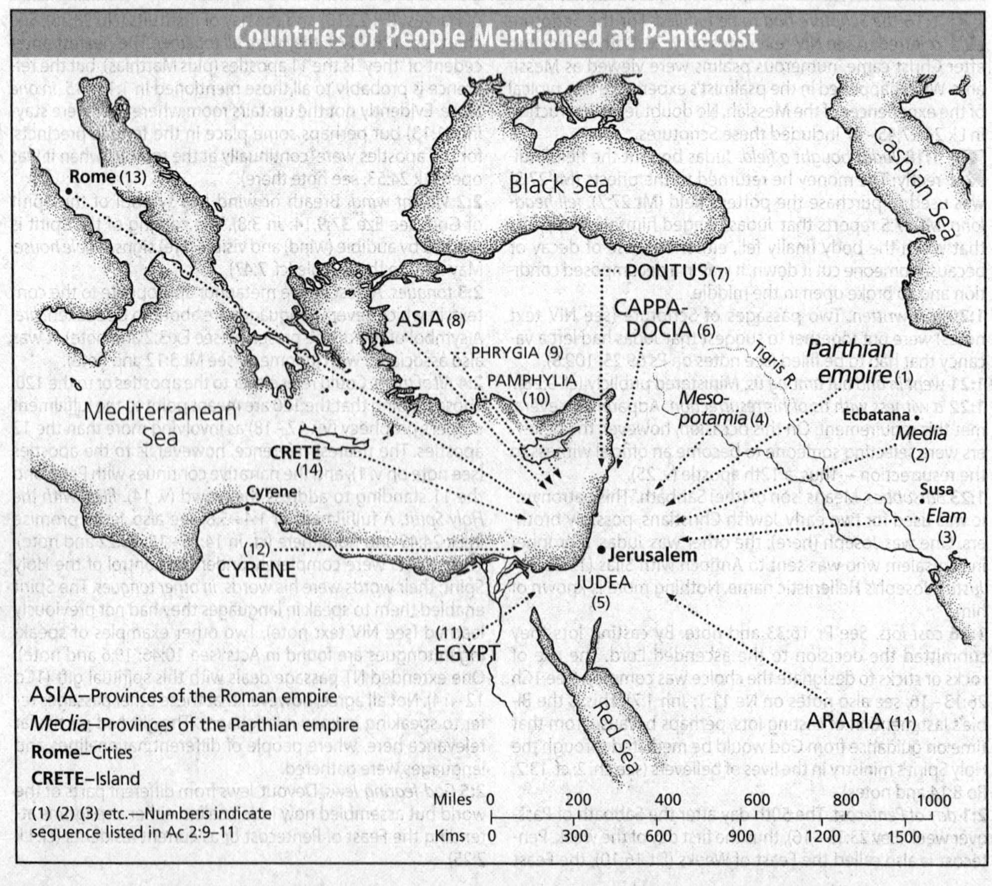

raised his voice and addressed the crowd:
"Fellow Jews and all of you who live in
Jerusalem, let me explain this to you; listen carefully to what I say. 15These men
are not drunk, as you suppose. It's only
nine in the morning![i] 16No, this is what
was spoken by the prophet Joel:

17" 'In the last days, God says,
I will pour out my Spirit on all
people.[j]
Your sons and daughters will
prophesy,[k]
your young men will see visions,
your old men will dream dreams.
18Even on my servants, both men and
women,
I will pour out my Spirit in those
days,
and they will prophesy.[l]
19I will show wonders in the heaven
above
and signs on the earth below,[m]
blood and fire and billows of
smoke.
20The sun will be turned to darkness
and the moon to blood[n]
before the coming of the great and
glorious day of the Lord.
21And everyone who calls
on the name of the Lord[o] will be
saved.'[a][p]

22"Men of Israel, listen to this: Jesus of
Nazareth[q] was a man accredited by God
to you by miracles, wonders and signs,[r]
which God did among you through him,[s]
as you yourselves know. 23This man was
handed over to you by God's set purpose
and foreknowledge;[t] and you, with the
help of wicked men,[b] put him to death by
nailing him to the cross.[u] 24But God raised
him from the dead,[v] freeing him from the
agony of death, because it was impossible
for death to keep its hold on him.[w] 25David
said about him:

" 'I saw the Lord always before me.
Because he is at my right hand,
I will not be shaken.
26Therefore my heart is glad and my
tongue rejoices;
my body also will live in hope,
27because you will not abandon me to
the grave,
nor will you let your Holy One see
decay.[x]
28You have made known to me the paths
of life;
you will fill me with joy in your
presence.'[c][y]

29"Brothers,[z] I can tell you confidently
that the patriarch[a] David died and was
buried,[b] and his tomb is here[c] to this day.
30But he was a prophet and knew that
God had promised him on oath that he
would place one of his descendants on
his throne.[d] 31Seeing what was ahead, he
spoke of the resurrection of the Christ,[d]
that he was not abandoned to the grave,
nor did his body see decay.[e] 32God has
raised this Jesus to life,[f] and we are all witnesses[g] of the fact. 33Exalted[h] to the right
hand of God,[i] he has received from the
Father[j] the promised Holy Spirit[k] and has
poured out[l] what you now see and hear.
34For David did not ascend to heaven, and
yet he said,

" 'The Lord said to my Lord:
"Sit at my right hand

2:15 [i]1Th 5:7 **2:17** [j]Nu 11:25; Isa 44:3; Eze 39:29; Jn 7:37-39; Ac 10:45 [k]S Ac 21:9 **2:18** [l]Ac 21:9-12 **2:19** [m]Lk 21:11 **2:20** [n]S Mt 24:29 **2:21** [o]Ge 4:26; 26:25; Ps 105:1; Ac 9:14; 1Co 1:2; 2Ti 2:22 [p]Joel 2:28-32; Ro 10:13 **2:22** [q]S Mk 1:24 [r]S Jn 4:48 [s]S Jn 3:2 **2:23** [t]Isa 53:10; Ac 3:18; 4:28 [u]Mt 16:21; Lk 24:20; Ac 3:13 **2:24** [v]ver 32; Ac 13:30, 33, 34, 37; 17:31; Ro 6:4; 8:11; 10:9; 1Co 6:14; 15:15; Eph 1:20; Col 2:12; Heb 13:20; 1Pe 1:21 [w]Jn 20:9 **2:27** [x]ver 31; Ac 13:35 **2:28** [y]Ps 16:8-11 **2:29** [z]S Ac 22:5 [a]Ac 7:8, 9 [b]1Ki 2:10; Ac 13:36 [c]Ne 3:16 **2:30** [d]S Mt 1:1 **2:31** [e]Ps 16:10 **2:32** [f]S ver 24 [g]S Lk 24:48 **2:33** [h]S Php 2:9 [i]S Mk 16:19 [j]Ac 1:4 [k]Jn 7:39; 14:26; 15:26 [l]Ac 10:45

[a] *21* Joel 2:28-32 [b] *23* Or *of those not having the law* (that is, Gentiles) [c] *28* Psalm 16:8-11 [d] *31* Or *Messiah.* "The Christ" (Greek) and "the Messiah" (Hebrew) both mean "the Anointed One"; also in verse 36.

(3) an exhortation to repentance and baptism (vv. 37 – 40). The outline of this sermon is similar to those in chs. 3; 10; 13.
2:14 *with the Eleven.* The apostles had been baptized with the Holy Spirit and had spoken in other languages to various groups. Now they stood with Peter, who served as their spokesman.
2:15 *only nine in the morning!* On a festival day such as Pentecost, a Jew would not break his fast until at least 10:00 A.M. So it was extremely unlikely that a group of men would be drunk at such an early hour.
2:17 – 18 *all people ... sons ... daughters ... young men ... old men ... men ... women.* The Spirit is bestowed on all, irrespective of gender, age and rank.
2:17 *last days.* See Isa 2:2 and note; Hos 3:5; Mic 4:1; see also notes on 1Ti 4:1; 2Ti 3:1; Heb 1:2; 1Pe 1:20; 1Jn 2:18. In the passage quoted from Joel the Hebrew has "afterward" and the Septuagint (the pre-Christian Greek translation of the OT) "after these things." Peter interprets Joel 2:28 – 32 as referring specifically to the latter days of the new covenant (see Jer 31:33 – 34; Eze 36:26 – 27; 39:29) in contrast to the former days of the old covenant. The age of Messianic fulfillment has arrived. *my Spirit.* See note on 1:2.
2:18 *they will prophesy.* See 1Co 12:10 and note.
2:19 – 20 See notes on Joel 2:30 – 31; Mk 13:24 – 25.
2:21 *everyone who calls.* Cf. v. 39; includes faith and response rather than merely using words (Mt 7:21).
2:22 *accredited ... by miracles, wonders and signs.* The mighty works done by Jesus were signs that the Messiah had come (cf. Jn 2:11; 20:31 and notes).
2:23 *God's set purpose and foreknowledge.* God's purpose revealed through the prophets was that the Messiah must suffer and die (see 17:2 – 3; 26:22 – 23; Lk 24:25 – 26,45 – 46; cf. 1Pe 1:11 and note). *wicked men.* See NIV text note; here, however, the Gentiles were acting in an evil way.
2:27 *not abandon me to the grave.* Peter understood that David's words applied ultimately to the Messiah (v. 31). God would not allow his physical body to decompose. See note on Ps 16:9 – 11.
2:29 *his tomb is here.* The tomb of David could be seen in Jerusalem. The words of Ps 16:8 – 11 did not fully apply to him.
2:33 *Exalted to the right hand of God.* See note on Heb 1:2 – 3. *promised Holy Spirit.* See note on 1:4. *has poured out.* See v. 17; Joel 2:28.
2:34 *The Lord said to my Lord.* The Lord (God) said to my Lord (the Son of David, the Messiah). According to Peter,

35 until I make your enemies
a footstool for your feet.' "[a][m]

36 "Therefore let all Israel be assured of
this: God has made this Jesus, whom you
crucified, both Lord[n] and Christ."[o]
37 When the people heard this, they
were cut to the heart and said to Peter and
the other apostles, "Brothers, what shall
we do?"[p]
38 Peter replied, "Repent and be baptized,[q]
every one of you, in the name of Jesus
Christ for the forgiveness of your sins.[r] And
you will receive the gift of the Holy Spirit.[s]
39 The promise is for you and your children[t]
and for all who are far off[u] — for all whom
the Lord our God will call."
40 With many other words he warned
them; and he pleaded with them, "Save
yourselves from this corrupt generation."[v]
41 Those who accepted his message were
baptized, and about three thousand were
added to their number[w] that day.

The Fellowship of the Believers

42 They devoted themselves to the apostles' teaching[x] and to the fellowship, to the
breaking of bread[y] and to prayer.[z] 43 Everyone was filled with awe, and many wonders and miraculous signs were done by
the apostles.[a] 44 All the believers were together and had everything in common.[b]
45 Selling their possessions and goods, they
gave to anyone as he had need.[c] 46 Every
day they continued to meet together in the
temple courts.[d] They broke bread[e] in their
homes and ate together with glad and sincere hearts, 47 praising God and enjoying
the favor of all the people.[f] And the Lord
added to their number[g] daily those who
were being saved.

Peter Heals the Crippled Beggar

3 One day Peter and John[h] were going up
to the temple[i] at the time of prayer — at
three in the afternoon.[j] 2 Now a man crippled from birth[k] was being carried to the
temple gate[l] called Beautiful, where he
was put every day to beg[m] from those going into the temple courts. 3 When he saw
Peter and John about to enter, he asked
them for money. 4 Peter looked straight at
him, as did John. Then Peter said, "Look at
us!" 5 So the man gave them his attention,
expecting to get something from them.
6 Then Peter said, "Silver or gold I do not
have, but what I have I give you. In the
name of Jesus Christ of Nazareth,[n] walk."

[a] *35* Psalm 110:1

2:35 [m] Ps 110:1; S Mt 22:44 **2:36** [n] S Mt 28:18 [o] S Lk 2:11 **2:37** [p] Lk 3:10,12,14; Ac 16:30 **2:38** [q] ver 41; Ac 8:12,16,36,38; 9:18; 10:48; 16:15,33; 19:5; 22:16; Col 2:12 [r] Jer 36:3; Mk 1:4; S Lk 24:47; Ac 3:19 [s] S Jn 20:22 **2:39** [t] Isa 44:3; 65:23 [u] Isa 57:19; Ac 10:45; Eph 2:13 **2:40** [v] Dt 32:5; Php 2:15 **2:41** [w] ver 47; Ac 4:4; 5:14; 6:1,7; 9:31,35,42; 11:21,24; 14:1,21; 16:5; 17:12 **2:42** [x] Mt 28:20 [y] S Mt 14:19 [z] S Ac 1:14 **2:43** [a] Ac 5:12 **2:44** [b] Ac 4:32 **2:45** [c] Mt 19:21; Lk 12:33; 18:22; Ac 4:34,35; 6:1 **2:46** [d] Lk 24:53; Ac 3:1; 5:21,42 [e] ver 42; S Mt 14:19

2:47 [f] S Ro 14:18 [g] S ver 41 **3:1** [h] S Lk 22:8 [i] Ac 2:46 [j] Ps 55:17; Ac 10:30 **3:2** [k] Ac 14:8 [l] Lk 16:20 [m] Jn 9:8 **3:6** [n] ver 16; S Mk 1:24

David referred to his descendant with uncommon respect because he, through the inspiration of the Spirit, recognized how great and divine he would be (Mt 22:41 – 45). He was not only to be resurrected (vv. 31 – 32) but also to be exalted to God's right hand (vv. 33 – 35). And his presence there was now being demonstrated by the sending of the Holy Spirit (v. 33; Jn 16:7). See note on Ps 110:1; see also introduction to that psalm.

2:37 *cut to the heart.* Because they now realized the enormity of their guilt.

2:38 *Repent and be baptized.* Repentance was important in the message of the forerunner, John the Baptist (Mk 1:4; Lk 3:3), in the preaching of Jesus (Mk 1:15; Lk 13:3) and in the directions Jesus left just before his ascension (Lk 24:47). So also baptism was important to John the Baptist (Mk 1:4), in the instructions of Jesus (Mt 28:18 – 19) and in the preaching recorded in Acts — where it was associated with belief (8:12; 18:8), acceptance of the word (v. 41) and repentance (here). *in the name of Jesus Christ.* Not a contradiction to the fuller formula given in Mt 28:19. In Acts the abbreviated form emphasizes the distinctive quality of this baptism, for Jesus is now included in a way that he was not in John's baptism (19:4 – 5). *for the forgiveness of your sins.* Not that baptism effects forgiveness. Rather, forgiveness comes through that which is symbolized by baptism (see Ro 6:3 – 4 and note). *Holy Spirit.* Two gifts are now given: the forgiveness of sins (see also 22:16) and the Holy Spirit. The promise of the indwelling gift of the Holy Spirit is given to all Christians (cf. Ro 8:9 – 11 and note on 8:9; 1Co 12:13 and note).

2:41 *their number.* The number of believers.

2:42 *apostles' teaching.* Included all that Jesus himself taught (Mt 28:20), especially the gospel, which was centered in his death, burial and resurrection (see vv. 23 – 24; 3:15; 4:10; 1Co 15:1 – 4). It was a unique teaching in that it came from God and was clothed with the authority conferred on the apostles (2Co 13:10; 1Th 4:2). Today it is available in the books of the NT. *the fellowship.* The corporate fellowship of believers in worship. *breaking of bread.* Although this phrase is used of an ordinary meal in v. 46 (see Lk 24:30,35), the Lord's Supper seems to be indicated here (see note on 20:7; cf. 1Co 10:16; 11:20). *prayer.* Acts emphasizes the importance of prayer in the Christian life — private as well as public (1:14; 3:1; 6:4; 10:4,31; 12:5; 16:13,16).

2:44 *believers were together.* The unity of the early church (see 4:32; Jn 17:11,21 – 23; Ro 15:5; Eph 4:1 – 16; Php 2:1 – 4 and notes). *everything in common.* See 4:34 – 35. This was a voluntary sharing to provide for those who did not have enough for the essentials of living (see good and bad examples of sharing, 4:36 — 5:9).

2:46 *temple courts.* Probably Solomon's Colonnade (see 3:11 and note; 5:12). *broke bread in their homes.* Here the daily life of Christians is described, distinguishing their activity in the temple from that in their homes, where they ate their meals — not the Lord's Supper (see note on v. 42) — with gladness and generosity. *glad and sincere hearts.* The fellowship, oneness and sharing enjoyed in the early church are fruits of the Spirit. Joy is to be the mood of the believer (see note on 16:34).

3:1 *Peter and John.* Among the foremost apostles (Gal 2:9). Along with John's brother, James, they had been especially close to Jesus (Mk 9:2; 13:3; 14:33; Lk 22:8). Arrested together (4:3), they were also together in Samaria (8:14). *time of prayer.* The three stated times of prayer for later Judaism were mid-morning (the third hour, 9:00 A.M.), the time of the evening sacrifice (the ninth hour, 3:00 P.M.) and sunset.

3:2 *gate called Beautiful.* The favorite entrance to the temple court, it was probably the bronze-sheathed gate that is elsewhere called the Nicanor Gate. Apparently it led from the court of the Gentiles to the court of women, east of the temple.

3:6 *In the name of Jesus Christ.* Not by power of their own, but by the authority of the Messiah.

7 Taking him by the right hand, he helped
him up, and instantly the man's feet and
ankles became strong. 8 He jumped to his
feet and began to walk. Then he went with
them into the temple courts, walking and
jumping,[o] and praising God. 9 When all
the people[p] saw him walking and praising
God, 10 they recognized him as the same
man who used to sit begging at the temple
gate called Beautiful,[q] and they were filled
with wonder and amazement at what had
happened to him.

Peter Speaks to the Onlookers

11 While the beggar held on to Peter and
John,[r] all the people were astonished and
came running to them in the place called
Solomon's Colonnade.[s] 12 When Peter saw
this, he said to them: "Men of Israel, why
does this surprise you? Why do you stare
at us as if by our own power or godliness
we had made this man walk? 13 The God of
Abraham, Isaac and Jacob,[t] the God of our
fathers,[u] has glorified his servant Jesus.
You handed him over[v] to be killed, and
you disowned him before Pilate,[w] though
he had decided to let him go.[x] 14 You disowned the Holy[y] and Righteous One[z] and
asked that a murderer be released to you.[a]
15 You killed the author of life, but God
raised him from the dead.[b] We are witnesses[c] of this. 16 By faith in the name of
Jesus,[d] this man whom you see and know
was made strong. It is Jesus' name and
the faith that comes through him that has
given this complete healing to him, as you
can all see.

17 "Now, brothers,[e] I know that you acted
in ignorance,[f] as did your leaders.[g] 18 But
this is how God fulfilled[h] what he had
foretold[i] through all the prophets,[j] saying
that his Christ[a] would suffer.[k] 19 Repent,
then, and turn to God, so that your sins
may be wiped out,[l] that times of refreshing may come from the Lord, 20 and that
he may send the Christ,[m] who has been
appointed for you — even Jesus. 21 He must
remain in heaven[n] until the time comes for
God to restore everything,[o] as he promised
long ago through his holy prophets.[p] 22 For
Moses said, 'The Lord your God will raise
up for you a prophet like me from among
your own people; you must listen to everything he tells you.[q] 23 Anyone who does
not listen to him will be completely cut off
from among his people.'[b][r]
24 "Indeed, all the prophets[s] from Samuel on, as many as have spoken, have
foretold these days. 25 And you are heirs[t]
of the prophets and of the covenant[u] God
made with your fathers. He said to Abraham, 'Through your offspring all peoples
on earth will be blessed.'[c][v] 26 When God
raised up[w] his servant, he sent him first[x]
to you to bless you by turning each of you
from your wicked ways."

Peter and John Before the Sanhedrin

4 The priests and the captain of the temple guard[y] and the Sadducees[z] came up
to Peter and John while they were speak-

3:8 [o] Isa 35:6; Ac 14:10
3:9 [p] Ac 4:16,21
3:10 [q] ver 2
3:11 [r] S Lk 22:8 [s] Jn 10:23; Ac 5:12
3:13 [t] Ex 3:6 [u] Ac 5:30; 7:32; 22:14 [v] Ac 2:23 [w] S Mt 27:2 [x] S Lk 23:4
3:14 [y] S Mk 1:24; Ac 4:27 [z] Ac 7:52 [a] Mk 15:11; Lk 23:18-25
3:15 [b] S Ac 2:24 [c] S Lk 24:48
3:16 [d] ver 6
3:17 [e] S Ac 22:5 [f] Lk 23:34 [g] Ac 13:27
3:18 [h] S Mt 1:22 [i] Ac 2:23 [j] S Lk 24:27 [k] Ac 17:2,3; 26:22,23
3:19 [l] Ps 51:1; Isa 43:25; 44:22; S Ac 2:38
3:20 [m] S Lk 2:11
3:21 [n] Ac 1:11 [o] Mt 17:11; Ac 1:6 [p] Lk 1:70
3:22 [q] Dt 18:15,18; Ac 7:37
3:23 [r] Dt 18:19
3:24 [s] S Lk 24:27
3:25 [t] Ac 2:39 [u] Ro 9:4,5 [v] Ge 12:3; 22:18; 26:4; 28:14
3:26 [w] ver 22; S Ac 2:24 [x] Ac 13:46; Ro 1:16
4:1 [y] Lk 22:4 [z] Mt 3:7; 16:1,6; 22:23,34; Ac 5:17; 23:6-8

[a] *18* Or *Messiah*; also in verse 20
[b] *23* Deut. 18:15,18,19 [c] *25* Gen. 22:18; 26:4

3:7 *he helped him up.* But he had faith to be healed (v. 16).
3:8 *into the temple courts.* From the outer court (for Gentiles also) into the court of women, containing the treasury (Mk 12:41 – 44), and then into the court of Israel (see map No. 10 at the end of this study Bible). From the outer court, nine gates led into the inner courts.
3:11 *Solomon's Colonnade.* A porch along the inner side of the wall enclosing the outer court, with rows of 27-foot-high stone columns and a roof of cedar (see note on Jn 10:23).
3:12 – 26 See note on 2:14 – 40.
3:13 *his servant Jesus.* A reminder of the suffering servant prophesied in Isa 52:13 — 53:12 (see Mt 12:18; Ac 4:27,30). *disowned him.* Voted against Jesus, spurned him, denied him and refused to acknowledge him as the true Messiah. *Pilate … had decided to let him go.* See Jn 19:12.
3:14 *Holy … One.* Cf. note on Lev 11:44. *Righteous One.* For this description of the Messiah elsewhere see 7:52; 22:14; cf. 1Jn 2:1. *murderer.* Barabbas (see Lk 23:18 and note).
3:15 *You killed … God raised … We are witnesses.* A recurring theme in the speeches of Acts (see 2:23 – 24; 4:10; 5:30 – 32; 10:39 – 41; 13:28 – 29; cf. 1Co 15:1 – 4).
3:17 *brothers.* "Men of Israel" (v. 12). *you acted in ignorance.* They did not know that Jesus was the true Messiah (see Lk 23:34). Nevertheless, God will be generous in his mercy if they only repent and turn to him (see v. 19 and note).
3:18 *foretold through all the prophets.* Echoes what Jesus had said (Lk 24:26 – 27). The suffering was prophesied (compare Isa 53:7 – 8 with Ac 8:32 – 33; Ps 2:1 – 2 with Ac 4:25 – 26; Ps 22:1 with Mt 27:46; see also 1Pe 1:11).
3:19 *Repent.* Repentance is a change of mind and will that arises from sorrow for sin and leads to transformation of life (see notes on 2:38; Lk 3:3). *turn to God.* Subsequent to repentance and not completely identical with it. See 11:21 ("believed and turned") and 26:20 ("repent and turn"; see also 9:35; 14:15; 15:19; 26:18; 28:27). In the strictest sense, repentance is turning from sin, and faith is turning to God. However, the word "turn" is not always used with such precision. *your sins … wiped out.* Your sins will be forgiven as a result of repentance.
3:22,26 *raise up … raised up.* Christ is the fulfillment of prophecies made relative to Moses, David and Abraham. He was to be a prophet like Moses (vv. 22 – 23), he was foretold in Samuel's declarations concerning David (v. 24; see note there), and he was to bring blessing to all people as promised to Abraham (vv. 25 – 26).
3:24 *prophets from Samuel on.* Samuel anointed David to be king and spoke of the establishment of his kingdom (1Sa 16:13; cf. 13:14; 15:28; 28:17). Nathan's prophecy (2Sa 7:12 – 16) was ultimately Messianic (see Ac 13:22 – 23,34; Heb 1:5).
3:25 *offspring.* The word is singular, ultimately signifying Christ (see Gal 3:16).
4:1 *priests.* Those who were serving that week in the temple precincts (see note on Lk 1:23). *captain of the temple guard.* A member of one of the leading priestly families; next in rank to

ing to the people. 2They were greatly disturbed because the apostles were teaching
the people and proclaiming in Jesus the
resurrection of the dead.[a] 3They seized
Peter and John, and because it was evening, they put them in jail[b] until the next
day. 4But many who heard the message
believed, and the number of men grew[c] to
about five thousand.
5The next day the rulers,[d] elders and
teachers of the law met in Jerusalem. 6An-
nas the high priest was there, and so were
Caiaphas,[e] John, Alexander and the other
men of the high priest's family. 7They had
Peter and John brought before them and
began to question them: "By what power
or what name did you do this?"
8Then Peter, filled with the Holy Spirit,[f] said to them: "Rulers and elders of the
people![g] 9If we are being called to account
today for an act of kindness shown to a
cripple[h] and are asked how he was healed,
10then know this, you and all the people of
Israel: It is by the name of Jesus Christ of
Nazareth,[i] whom you crucified but whom
God raised from the dead,[j] that this man
stands before you healed. 11He is

" 'the stone you builders rejected,
which has become the capstone.[a]' [b][k]

12Salvation is found in no one else, for
there is no other name under heaven given
to men by which we must be saved."[l]
13When they saw the courage of Peter
and John[m] and realized that they were unschooled, ordinary men,[n] they were astonished and they took note that these men
had been with Jesus.[o] 14But since they

4:2 [a]Ac 17:18
4:3 [b]Ac 5:18
4:4 [c]S Ac 2:41
4:5 [d]Lk 23:13
4:6 [e]S Mt 26:3
4:8 [f]S Lk 1:15
[g]ver 5; Lk 23:13
4:9 [h]Ac 3:6
4:10 [i]S Mk 1:24
[j]S Ac 2:24
4:11 [k]Ps 118:22; Isa 28:16; Zec 10:4; Mt 21:42; Eph 2:20; 1Pe 2:7
4:12 [l]S Mt 1:21; Jn 14:6; Ac 10:43; S Ro 11:14; 1Ti 2:5
4:13 [m]S Lk 22:8
[n]Mt 11:25
[o]Mk 3:14
4:15 [p]S Mt 5:22
4:16 [q]Jn 11:47
[r]Ac 3:6-10
4:18 [s]Am 7:13; Ac 5:40
4:19 [t]Ac 5:29
4:20 [u]Job 32:18; Jer 20:9; Am 3:8
[v]S Lk 24:48
4:21 [w]Ac 5:26
[x]S Mt 9:8
4:24 [y]S Ac 1:14
[z]Ne 9:6; Job 41:11; Isa 37:16

could see the man who had been healed
standing there with them, there was nothing they could say. 15So they ordered them
to withdraw from the Sanhedrin[p] and then
conferred together. 16"What are we going
to do with these men?"[q] they asked. "Everybody living in Jerusalem knows they
have done an outstanding miracle,[r] and
we cannot deny it. 17But to stop this thing
from spreading any further among the
people, we must warn these men to speak
no longer to anyone in this name."
18Then they called them in again and
commanded them not to speak or teach
at all in the name of Jesus.[s] 19But Peter
and John replied, "Judge for yourselves
whether it is right in God's sight to obey
you rather than God.[t] 20For we cannot help
speaking[u] about what we have seen and
heard."[v]
21After further threats they let them
go. They could not decide how to punish
them, because all the people[w] were praising God[x] for what had happened. 22For the
man who was miraculously healed was
over forty years old.

The Believers' Prayer

23On their release, Peter and John went
back to their own people and reported all
that the chief priests and elders had said to
them. 24When they heard this, they raised
their voices together in prayer to God.[y]
"Sovereign Lord," they said, "you made
the heaven and the earth and the sea, and
everything in them.[z] 25You spoke by the

[a] *11* Or *cornerstone* [b] *11* Psalm 118:22

---

the high priest (see 5:24,26; Lk 22:4,52). *Sadducees.* A Jewish sect whose members came from the priestly line and controlled the temple. They did not believe in the resurrection or a personal Messiah, but held that the Messianic age—an ideal time—was then present and must be preserved. The high priest, one of their number, presided over the Sanhedrin (see 5:17; 23:6-8; Mt 22:23-33). See notes on Ezr 7:2; Mt 3:7; Mk 12:18; Lk 20:27; see also essay, p. 1453, and chart, p. 1502.

4:2 *in Jesus.* On the basis of Jesus' resurrection.

4:3 *evening.* The evening sacrifices ended about 4:00 P.M., and the temple gates would be closed at that time. Any judgments involving life and death must be begun and concluded in daylight hours.

4:4 *men.* Lit. "males." *five thousand.* A growth from the 3,000 at Pentecost (2:41); see later growth (5:14; 6:7).

4:5 *rulers, elders and teachers of the law.* The three groups making up the Sanhedrin, Israel's supreme court (see Lk 22:66; see also notes on Mt 2:4; 15:2; Mk 2:16; 14:55; Lk 5:17).

4:6 *Annas.* High priest A.D. 6-15, but deposed by the Romans and succeeded by his son, Eleazar, then by his son-in-law, Caiaphas (18-36), who was also called Joseph. However, Annas was still recognized by the Jews as high priest (Lk 3:2; cf. Jn 18:13,24). *John.* May be Jonathan son of Annas, who was appointed high priest in A.D. 36. Others suggest it was Johanan ben Zaccai, who became the president of the Great Synagogue after the fall of Jerusalem. *Alexander.* Not further identified.

4:8 *filled with the Holy Spirit.* See note on 2:4.

4:10 *Jesus Christ of Nazareth.* See Mt 2:23 and note.

4:11 *the stone ... rejected.* Fulfillment of prophecy was an important element in early Christian sermons and defenses. Jesus had also used Ps 118:22 (Mt 21:42; see 1Pe 2:7 and cf. Ro 9:33; Isa 28:16).

4:12 *no other name.* See 10:43; Jn 14:6; 1Ti 2:5; see also NIV text note on Mt 1:21.

4:13 *courage.* A certain boldness characterized by the assurance, authority and forthrightness of the apostles (2:29; 4:29; 28:31), and shared by the believers (4:31). *unschooled, ordinary men.* Peter and John had not been trained in the Rabbinic schools, nor did they hold official positions in recognized religious circles. *took note that these men had been with Jesus.* Probably because they were displaying some of his power and authority (cf. Mk 1:22 and note; 3:14).

4:15 *Sanhedrin.* See notes on v. 5; 5:21; Mk 14:55.

4:19 See note on Ro 13:3.

4:20 *cannot help speaking.* See 5:29; cf. Jer 20:9.

4:22 *forty years old.* Normally healing at such an advanced age (for that time) did not take place.

4:23 *went back.* Probably to the same upper room where the apostles had met before (1:13) and where the congregation may have continued to meet (12:12).

4:24 *Sovereign Lord.* See Lk 2:29.

Holy Spirit through the mouth of your servant, our father David:[a]

"'Why do the nations rage
and the peoples plot in vain?
26The kings of the earth take their stand
and the rulers gather together
against the Lord
and against his Anointed One.[a'][b][b]

27Indeed Herod[c] and Pontius Pilate[d] met
together with the Gentiles and the people[c]
of Israel in this city to conspire against
your holy servant Jesus,[e] whom you
anointed. 28They did what your power and
will had decided beforehand should happen.[f] 29Now, Lord, consider their threats
and enable your servants to speak your
word with great boldness.[g] 30Stretch out
your hand to heal and perform miraculous
signs and wonders[h] through the name of
your holy servant Jesus."[i]

31After they prayed, the place where
they were meeting was shaken.[j] And they
were all filled with the Holy Spirit[k] and
spoke the word of God[l] boldly.[m]

The Believers Share Their Possessions

32All the believers were one in heart
and mind. No one claimed that any of his
possessions was his own, but they shared
everything they had.[n] 33With great power the apostles continued to testify[o] to the
resurrection[p] of the Lord Jesus, and much
grace[q] was upon them all. 34There were
no needy persons among them. For from
time to time those who owned lands or
houses sold them,[r] brought the money
from the sales 35and put it at the apostles'
feet,[s] and it was distributed to anyone as
he had need.[t]

36Joseph, a Levite from Cyprus, whom
the apostles called Barnabas[u] (which
means Son of Encouragement), 37sold a
field he owned and brought the money
and put it at the apostles' feet.[v]

Ananias and Sapphira

5 Now a man named Ananias, together with his wife Sapphira, also sold
a piece of property. 2With his wife's full
knowledge he kept back part of the money
for himself,[w] but brought the rest and put
it at the apostles' feet.[x]

3Then Peter said, "Ananias, how is it
that Satan[y] has so filled your heart[z] that
you have lied to the Holy Spirit[a] and have
kept for yourself some of the money you
received for the land?[b] 4Didn't it belong to
you before it was sold? And after it was
sold, wasn't the money at your disposal?[c] What made you think of doing such
a thing? You have not lied to men but to
God."[d]

5When Ananias heard this, he fell down
and died.[e] And great fear[f] seized all who
heard what had happened. 6Then the
young men came forward, wrapped up
his body,[g] and carried him out and buried him.

7About three hours later his wife came

4:25 [a]Ac 1:16 **4:26** [b]Ps 2:1,2; Da 9:25; Lk 4:18; Ac 10:38; Heb 1:9 **4:27** [c]S Mt 14:1 [d]S Mt 27:2; Lk 23:12 [e]ver 30; Ac 3:13,14 **4:28** [f]Ac 2:23 **4:29** [g]ver 13,31; Ps 138:3; Ac 9:27; 13:46; 14:3; 28:31; Eph 6:19; Php 1:14 **4:30** [h]S Jn 4:48 [i]ver 27 **4:31** [j]Ac 2:2 [k]S Lk 1:15 [l]S Heb 4:12 [m]S ver 29 **4:32** [n]Ac 2:44 **4:33** [o]S Lk 24:48 [p]Ac 1:22 [q]S Ro 3:24 **4:34** [r]Mt 19:21; Ac 2:45 **4:35** [s]ver 37; Ac 5:2 [t]Ac 2:45; 6:1 **4:36** [u]Ac 9:27; 11:22,30; 13:2; 1Co 9:6; Gal 2:1,9,13 **4:37** [v]ver 35; Ac 5:2 **5:2** [w]Jos 7:11 [x]Ac 4:35,37 **5:3** [y]S Mt 4:10 [z]Jn 13:2,27 [a]ver 9 [b]Dt 23:21 **5:4** [c]Dt 23:22 [d]Lev 6:2 **5:5** [e]ver 10; Ps 5:6 [f]ver 11 **5:6** [g]Jn 19:40

[a] *26* That is, Christ or Messiah [b] *26* Psalm 2:1,2
[c] *27* The Greek is plural.

4:27 *Herod.* Herod Antipas, tetrarch of Galilee and Perea (Lk 23:7–15; see chart, p. 1465). *Pontius Pilate.* Roman governor of Judea (see Lk 3:1 and note).

4:28 *decided beforehand.* Not that God had compelled them to act as they did, but he willed to use them and their freely chosen acts to accomplish his saving purpose (see 2:23).

4:30 *holy servant.* See note on 3:13.

4:31 *was shaken.* An immediate sign that the prayers had been heard (see 16:26). *filled with the Holy Spirit.* See note on 2:4. *spoke the word of God.* They continued preaching the gospel despite the warnings of the council (see vv. 18–22 and note on v. 13). Note that the gospel is here called "the word of God."

4:32 *one in heart and mind.* In complete accord, extending to their attitude toward personal possessions (see 2:44 and note).

4:33 *testify to the resurrection.* As significant as the death of Christ was, the most decisive event was the resurrection—an event about which the disciples could not keep silent.

4:34 *those who owned lands or houses sold them.* See note on 2:44.

4:35 See 2:44–45.

4:36 *Levite.* Although Levites were assigned no regional inheritance like the other tribes in the promised land, they were assigned towns to live in and their surrounding pasturelands for their flocks and herds (see Nu 35:1–5; Jos 14:4; 21:2–3). These properties could be bought and sold, within certain restrictions (see Lev 25:32–34; cf. Jer 32:6–15; 37:12). Furthermore, there appear to have been no restrictions on a Levite purchasing property from other Israelites—to be held until the Year of Jubilee. However, just how closely these original arrangements and regulations were still observed after the Babylonian exile is uncertain. *Cyprus.* An island in the eastern part of the Mediterranean Sea. Jews had settled there from Maccabean times. *Barnabas.* Used here as a good example of giving. In this way Luke introduces the one who will become an important companion of Paul (see 13:1–4). For other significant contributions of this great-hearted leader to the life and ministry of the early church see 9:27; 11:22,25; 15:37–39.

5:1 *Ananias … Sapphira.* Given as bad examples of sharing (Barnabas was the good example; see note on 4:36). Their love of praise for (pretended) generosity and love for money served as a warning to the readers that "God cannot be mocked" (Gal 6:7). Compare this divine judgment at the beginning of the church era with God's judgments on Nadab and Abihu (Lev 10:2; see note there), on Achan (Jos 7:25) and on Uzzah (2Sa 6:7; see note there)—all at the beginning of new eras in the history of redemption.

5:2 *kept back part.* They had a right to keep back whatever they chose, but to make it appear that they had given all when they had not was sinful.

5:3 *Satan has so filled your heart.* The continuing activity of Satan is noted (see Lk 22:3; Jn 13:2,27; 1Pe 5:8). *lied to the Holy Spirit.* A comparison with v. 4 shows that the Holy Spirit is regarded as God himself present with his people.

in, not knowing what had happened. 8Pe-
ter asked her, "Tell me, is this the price
you and Ananias got for the land?"
"Yes," she said, "that is the price."[h]
9Peter said to her, "How could you agree
to test the Spirit of the Lord?[i] Look! The
feet of the men who buried your husband
are at the door, and they will carry you
out also."
10At that moment she fell down at his
feet and died.[j] Then the young men came
in and, finding her dead, carried her out
and buried her beside her husband.[k]
11Great fear[l] seized the whole church and
all who heard about these events.

The Apostles Heal Many

12The apostles performed many miraculous signs and wonders[m] among the
people. And all the believers used to meet
together[n] in Solomon's Colonnade.[o] 13No
one else dared join them, even though
they were highly regarded by the people.[p]
14Nevertheless, more and more men and
women believed in the Lord and were added to their number.[q] 15As a result, people
brought the sick into the streets and laid
them on beds and mats so that at least Peter's shadow might fall on some of them
as he passed by.[r] 16Crowds gathered also
from the towns around Jerusalem, bringing their sick and those tormented by evil[a]
spirits, and all of them were healed.[s]

The Apostles Persecuted

17Then the high priest and all his associates, who were members of the party[t] of
the Sadducees,[u] were filled with jealousy.

5:8 [h] ver 2
5:9 [i] ver 3
5:10 [j] ver 5 [k] ver 6
5:11 [l] ver 5; Ac 19:17
5:12 [m] S Jn 4:48; Ac 2:43 [n] Ac 4:32 [o] Jn 10:23; Ac 3:11
5:13 [p] Ac 2:47; 4:21
5:14 [q] S Ac 2:41
5:15 [r] Ac 19:12
5:16 [s] Mt 8:16; S Mk 16:17
5:17 [t] Ac 15:5 [u] S Ac 4:1
5:18 [v] Ac 4:3
5:19 [w] Ge 16:7; Ex 3:2; Mt 1:20; 2:13,19; 28:2; Lk 1:11; 2:9; S Jn 20:12; Ac 8:26; 10:3; 12:7,23; 27:23 [x] Ac 16:26 [y] Ps 34:7
5:20 [z] Jn 6:63,68
5:21 [a] Ac 4:5,6 [b] ver 27,34,41; S Mt 5:22
5:22 [c] Ac 12:18,19
5:24 [d] Ac 4:1
5:26 [e] Ac 4:21
5:27 [f] S Mt 5:22
5:28 [g] Ac 4:18 [h] Mt 23:35; 27:25; Ac 2:23,36; 3:14,15; 7:52

18They arrested the apostles and put them
in the public jail.[v] 19But during the night an
angel[w] of the Lord opened the doors of the
jail[x] and brought them out.[y] 20"Go, stand
in the temple courts," he said, "and tell the
people the full message of this new life."[z]
21At daybreak they entered the temple
courts, as they had been told, and began
to teach the people.
When the high priest and his associates[a] arrived, they called together the Sanhedrin[b]—the full assembly of the elders
of Israel—and sent to the jail for the apostles. 22But on arriving at the jail, the officers did not find them there.[c] So they went
back and reported, 23"We found the jail securely locked, with the guards standing at
the doors; but when we opened them, we
found no one inside." 24On hearing this report, the captain of the temple guard and
the chief priests[d] were puzzled, wondering
what would come of this.
25Then someone came and said, "Look!
The men you put in jail are standing in
the temple courts teaching the people."
26At that, the captain went with his officers and brought the apostles. They did
not use force, because they feared that the
people[e] would stone them.
27Having brought the apostles, they
made them appear before the Sanhedrin[f]
to be questioned by the high priest. 28"We
gave you strict orders not to teach in this
name,"[g] he said. "Yet you have filled Jerusalem with your teaching and are determined to make us guilty of this man's
blood."[h]

[a] 16 Greek *unclean*

5:9 *to test the Spirit of the Lord.* If no dire consequences had followed this act of sin, the results among the believers would have been serious when the deceit became known. Not only would dishonesty appear profitable, but the conclusion that the Spirit could be deceived would follow. It was important to set the course properly at the outset in order to leave no doubt that God will not tolerate such hypocrisy and deceit.

5:11 *church.* The first use of the term in Acts. It can denote either the local congregation (8:1; 11:22; 13:1) or the universal church (see 20:28). The Greek word for "church" (*ekklesia*) was already being used for political and other assemblies (see 19:32,41) and, in the Septuagint (the pre-Christian Greek translation of the OT), for Israel when gathered in religious assembly.

5:12 *Solomon's Colonnade.* See note on 3:11.

5:13 *No one else dared join them.* Because of the fate of Ananias and his wife, no pretenders or halfhearted followers risked identification with the believers. Luke cannot mean that no one joined the Christian community, since v. 14 indicates that many were coming to Christ.

5:14 *more men and women believed.* See 4:4. This is the first explicit mention in Acts of women believing (cf. 8:3,12; 9:2; 13:50; 16:1,13–14; 17:4,12,34; 18:2; 21:5; but cf. also 1:14).

5:15 *Peter's shadow.* Parallels such items as Paul's handkerchiefs (19:12) and the edge of Jesus' cloak (Mt 9:20)—not that any of these material objects had magical qualities, but the least article or shadow represented a direct means of contact with Jesus or his apostles.

5:17 *high priest.* The official high priest recognized by Rome was Caiaphas, but the Jews considered Annas, Caiaphas's father-in-law, to be the actual high priest since the high priesthood was to be held for life (see note on 4:6). *his associates.* His family members. *party of the Sadducees.* See note on 4:1.

5:18 *in the public jail.* To await trial the next day.

5:19 *an angel of the Lord.* This phrase is used three other times in Acts: (1) "an angel of the Lord" is said to have guided Philip (8:26); (2) we are told that "an angel of the Lord" liberated Peter from prison (12:7–10); (3) Luke reports that "an angel of the Lord" struck down Herod (12:23). See also Mt 1:20–24; 2:13,19; 28:2; Lk 1:11–38; 2:9.

5:20 *full message of this new life.* The good news of eternal life in all its fullness (see Jn 6:68; Ro 6:4; 2Co 5:17; Php 1:21 and notes).

5:21 *Sanhedrin.* The supreme Jewish court, consisting of 70 to 100 men (71 being the proper number). They sat in a semicircle, backed by three rows of disciples of the learned men, with the clerks of the court standing in front. See note on Mk 14:55.

5:24 *captain of the temple guard.* See note on 4:1.

5:28 *make us guilty of this man's blood.* Probably a reference to the apostles' repeated declaration that some of the Jews and some of their leaders had killed Jesus (2:23; 3:13–15; 4:10–11; cf. Mt 27:25).

29 Peter and the other apostles replied:
"We must obey God rather than men![i]
30 The God of our fathers[j] raised Jesus from
the dead[k]—whom you had killed by hanging him on a tree.[l] 31 God exalted him to
his own right hand[m] as Prince and Savior[n]
that he might give repentance and forgiveness of sins to Israel.[o] 32 We are witnesses
of these things,[p] and so is the Holy Spirit,[q]
whom God has given to those who obey
him."
33 When they heard this, they were furious[r] and wanted to put them to death.
34 But a Pharisee named Gamaliel,[s] a teacher of the law,[t] who was honored by all the
people, stood up in the Sanhedrin and
ordered that the men be put outside for
a little while. 35 Then he addressed them:
"Men of Israel, consider carefully what
you intend to do to these men. 36 Some
time ago Theudas appeared, claiming to
be somebody, and about four hundred
men rallied to him. He was killed, all his
followers were dispersed, and it all came
to nothing. 37 After him, Judas the Galilean
appeared in the days of the census[u] and
led a band of people in revolt. He too was
killed, and all his followers were scattered.
38 Therefore, in the present case I advise
you: Leave these men alone! Let them go!
For if their purpose or activity is of human origin, it will fail.[v] 39 But if it is from
God, you will not be able to stop these
men; you will only find yourselves fighting against God."[w]
40 His speech persuaded them. They called
the apostles in and had them flogged.[x]
Then they ordered them not to speak in
the name of Jesus, and let them go.
41 The apostles left the Sanhedrin, rejoicing[y] because they had been counted worthy of suffering disgrace for the Name.[z]
42 Day after day, in the temple courts[a] and
from house to house, they never stopped
teaching and proclaiming the good news[b]
that Jesus is the Christ.[a][c]

The Choosing of the Seven

6 In those days when the number of
disciples was increasing,[d] the Grecian
Jews[e] among them complained against the
Hebraic Jews because their widows[f] were
being overlooked in the daily distribution
of food.[g] 2 So the Twelve gathered all the
disciples[h] together and said, "It would not
be right for us to neglect the ministry of
the word of God[i] in order to wait on tables. 3 Brothers,[j] choose seven men from
among you who are known to be full of
the Spirit[k] and wisdom. We will turn this
responsibility over to them[l] 4 and will give
our attention to prayer[m] and the ministry
of the word."
5 This proposal pleased the whole group.
They chose Stephen,[n] a man full of faith
and of the Holy Spirit;[o] also Philip,[p] Proc-
orus, Nicanor, Timon, Parmenas, and Nicolas from Antioch, a convert to Judaism.

[a] 42 Or *Messiah*

5:29 [i] Ex 1:17; Ac 4:19 **5:30** [j] S Ac 3:13 [k] S Ac 2:24 [l] Ac 10:39; 13:29; Gal 3:13 **5:31** [m] S Mk 16:19 [n] S Lk 2:11 [o] S Mt 1:21; Mk 1:4; Lk 24:47; Ac 2:38; 3:19; 10:43 **5:32** [p] S Lk 24:48 [q] Jn 15:26 **5:33** [r] Ac 2:37; 7:54 **5:34** [s] Ac 22:3 [t] Lk 2:46; 5:17 **5:37** [u] Lk 2:1, 2 **5:38** [v] Mt 15:13 **5:39** [w] 2Ch 13:12; Pr 21:30; Isa 46:10; Ac 7:51; 11:17 **5:40** [x] S Mt 10:17 **5:41** [y] S Mt 5:12 [z] S Jn 15:21 **5:42** [a] S Ac 2:46 [b] S Ac 13:32 [c] S Ac 9:22 **6:1** [d] S Ac 2:41 [e] Ac 9:29 [f] Ac 9:39, 41; 1Ti 5:3 [g] Ac 4:35 **6:2** [h] S Ac 11:26 [i] S Heb 4:12 **6:3** [j] S Ac 1:16 [k] S Lk 1:15 [l] Ex 18:21; Ne 13:13 **6:4** [m] S Ac 1:14 **6:5** [n] ver 8; Ac 7:55-60; 11:19; 22:20 [o] S Lk 1:15 [p] Ac 8:5-40; 21:8

5:29 See 4:19 and note.

5:30 *tree.* Used to describe the cross (see 1Pe 2:24 and note; see also Dt 21:22–23). Like its Hebrew counterpart, the Greek for this word could refer to a tree, a pole, a wooden beam or a similar object.

5:32 *so is the Holy Spirit ... given to those who obey him.* See Jn 15:26–27. The disciples' testimony was directed and confirmed by the Holy Spirit, who convicts the world through the word (Jn 16:8–11) and is given to those who respond to God with "the obedience that comes from faith" (Ro 1:5; see note on 6:7).

5:34 *a Pharisee named Gamaliel.* The most famous Jewish teacher of his time and traditionally listed among the heads of the schools. Possibly he was the grandson of Hillel. Like Hillel (see note on Mt 19:3), he was moderate in his views, a characteristic that is apparent in his cautious recommendation on this occasion. Saul (Paul) was one of his students (22:3).

5:36 *Theudas.* We know of him from no other historical source.

5:37 *Judas the Galilean.* The Jewish historian Josephus refers to him as a man from Gamala in Gaulanitis who refused to give tribute to Caesar. His revolt was crushed, but a movement, started in his time, may have lived on in the party of the Zealots (see 1:13 and note on Mt 10:4). *days of the census.* Not the first census of Quirinius, noted by Luke in his Gospel (see 2:2 and note), but the one in A.D. 6.

5:40 *flogged.* Beaten with the Jewish penalty of "the forty lashes minus one" (2Co 11:24).

6:1 *the number of disciples was increasing.* A considerable length of time may have transpired since the end of ch. 5. The church continued to grow (see 5:14), but this gave rise to inevitable problems, both from within (6:1–7) and from without (6:8—7:60). At this stage of its development, the church was entirely Jewish in its composition. However, there were two groups of Jews within the fellowship: (1) *Grecian Jews.* Hellenists—those born in lands other than the Holy Land who spoke the Greek language and were more Grecian than Hebraic in their attitudes and outlook. (2) *Hebraic Jews.* Those who spoke Palestinian Aramaic and/or Hebrew and preserved Jewish culture and customs. *daily distribution of food.* Help was needed by widows who had no one to care for them and so became the church's responsibility (cf. 4:35; 11:28–29; see also 1Ti 5:3–16).

6:2 *the Twelve.* At this early stage, the apostles were responsible for church life in general, including the ministry of the word of God and the care of the needy. *to wait on tables.* To preside over the distribution of charitable gifts. The early church was concerned not only about a spiritual ministry ("word of God" and "prayer"; see v. 4) but also about a material ministry.

6:3 *choose seven men.* The church elected them (v. 5), and the apostles ordained them (v. 6). In this way they were appointed to their work. *full of the Spirit.* See note on 2:4.

6:5 *They chose Stephen ... Nicolas.* It is significant that all seven of the men chosen had Greek names. The murmuring had come from the Greek-speaking segment of the church; so those elected to care for the work came from their number so as to represent their interests fairly. Only Stephen and Philip of the Seven receive further notice (Stephen, 6:8—7:60; Philip, 8:5–40; 21:8–9). *from Antioch, a convert to Judaism.* It is significant that a proselyte (as they were called)

6They presented these men to the apostles, who prayed[q] and laid their hands on
them.[r]
7So the word of God spread.[s] The number of disciples in Jerusalem increased
rapidly,[t] and a large number of priests became obedient to the faith.

Stephen Seized

8Now Stephen, a man full of God's grace
and power, did great wonders and miraculous signs[u] among the people. 9Oppo-
sition arose, however, from members of
the Synagogue of the Freedmen (as it was
called) — Jews of Cyrene[v] and Alexandria as
well as the provinces of Cilicia[w] and Asia.[x]
These men began to argue with Stephen,
10but they could not stand up against his
wisdom or the Spirit by whom he spoke.[y]
11Then they secretly[z] persuaded some
men to say, "We have heard Stephen
speak words of blasphemy against Moses
and against God."[a]

6:6 [q] S Ac 1:24 [r] Nu 8:10; 27:18; Ac 9:17; 19:6; 28:8; 1Ti 4:14; S Mk 5:23 **6:7** [s] Ac 12:24; 19:20 [t] S Ac 2:41 **6:8** [u] S Jn 4:48 **6:9** [v] S Mt 27:32 [w] Ac 15:23,41; 22:3; 23:34 [x] S Ac 2:9 **6:10** [y] Lk 21:15 **6:11** [z] 1Ki 21:10 [a] Mt 26:59-61 **6:12** [b] S Mt 5:22 **6:13** [c] Ex 23:1; Ps 27:12 [d] Mt 24:15; Ac 7:48; 21:28 **6:14** [e] S Jn 2:19 [f] Ac 15:1; 21:21; 26:3; 28:17 **6:15** [g] S Mt 5:22 **7:2** [h] Ac 22:1 [i] Ps 29:3 [j] Ge 11:31; 15:7

12So they stirred up the people and the
elders and the teachers of the law. They
seized Stephen and brought him before
the Sanhedrin.[b] 13They produced false witnesses,[c] who testified, "This fellow never
stops speaking against this holy place[d] and
against the law. 14For we have heard him
say that this Jesus of Nazareth will destroy
this place[e] and change the customs Moses
handed down to us."[f]
15All who were sitting in the Sanhedrin[g] looked intently at Stephen, and they
saw that his face was like the face of an
angel.

Stephen's Speech to the Sanhedrin

7 Then the high priest asked him, "Are
these charges true?"
2To this he replied: "Brothers and fathers,[h] listen to me! The God of glory[i]
appeared to our father Abraham while he
was still in Mesopotamia, before he lived
in Haran.[j] 3'Leave your country and your

was included in the number and that Luke points out his place of origin as Antioch, the city to which the gospel was soon to be taken and which was to become the headquarters for the forthcoming Gentile missionary effort.

6:6 *prayed and laid their hands on them.* Laying on of hands was used in the OT period to confer blessing (Ge 48:13 – 20), to transfer guilt from sinner to sacrifice (Lev 1:4) and to commission a person for a new responsibility (Nu 27:23). In the NT period, laying on of hands was observed in healing (28:8; Mk 1:41), blessing (Mk 10:16), ordaining or commissioning (here; 13:3; 1Ti 5:22) and imparting of spiritual gifts (Ac 8:17; 19:6; 1Ti 4:14; 2Ti 1:6). These seven men were appointed to responsibilities turned over to them by the Twelve. The Greek word used to describe their responsibility ("wait on," v. 2) is the verb from which the noun "deacon" comes. Later one reads of deacons in Php 1:1; 1Ti 3:8 – 13. The Greek noun for "deacon" can also be translated "minister" or "servant." The men appointed on this occasion were simply called the Seven (21:8), just as the apostles were called the Twelve. It is disputed whether the Seven were the first deacons or were later replaced by deacons (see note on 1Ti 3:8).

6:7 One of a series of progress reports given periodically throughout the book of Acts (1:15; 2:41; 4:4; 5:14; 6:7; 9:31; 12:24; 16:5; 19:20; 28:31). *a large number of priests.* Though involved by lineage and life service in the priestly observances of the old covenant, they accepted the preaching of the apostles, which proclaimed a sacrifice that made the old sacrifices unnecessary (see Heb 8:13 and note; 10:1 – 4,11 – 14). *became obedient to the faith.* Responded to the commands of the gospel. To believe is to obey God. Faith itself is obedience, but faith also produces obedience (Ro 1:5; Eph 2:8 – 10; Jas 2:14 – 26).

6:8 *great wonders and miraculous signs.* Until now, Acts told of only the apostles working miracles (2:43; 3:4 – 8; 5:12). But now, after the laying on of the apostles' hands, Stephen too is reported as working miraculous signs. Philip also will soon do the same (8:6).

6:9 *Freedmen.* Persons who had been freed from slavery. They came from different Hellenistic areas. *Cyrene.* The chief city in Libya and north Africa (see notes on 2:10; Mk 15:21), halfway between Alexandria and Carthage. One of its population groups was Jewish (see 11:19 – 21). *Alexandria.* Capital of Egypt and second only to Rome in the empire. Two out of five districts in Alexandria were Jewish. *Cilicia.* A Roman province in the southeast corner of Asia Minor adjoining Syria. Tarsus, the birthplace of Paul, was one of its principal towns. *Asia.* A Roman province in the western part of Asia Minor. Ephesus, where Paul later ministered for a few years, was its capital. *These men began to argue.* Since Saul was from Tarsus, this may have been the synagogue he attended, and he may have been among those who argued with Stephen. He was present when Stephen was stoned (7:58).

6:11 *blasphemy against Moses and against God.* Since Stephen declared that the worship of God was no longer to be restricted to the temple (7:48 – 49), his opponents twisted these words to trump up an accusation that Stephen was attacking the temple, the law, Moses and, ultimately, God.

6:12 *the elders and the teachers of the law.* See notes on Mt 2:4; 15:2; Mk 2:16; Lk 5:17. *Sanhedrin.* See note on Mk 14:55.

6:13 *speaking against this holy place and against the law.* Similar to the charges brought against Christ (see Mt 26:61). Stephen may have referred to Jesus' words as recorded in Jn 2:19 (see note there), and the words may have been misunderstood or purposely misinterpreted (v. 14), as at the trial of Jesus. *holy place.* The temple in Jerusalem.

7:1 *high priest.* Probably Caiaphas (see Mt 26:57 – 66), but see note on 4:6; cf. Jn 18:19, 24. *Are these charges true?* See notes on 6:11,13.

7:2 – 53 See Introduction: Characteristics, 5. *Effective use of speeches.* Since the author of Acts gives more space to Stephen's speech than to any other, it is safe to assume that he considered it particularly important. Broadly speaking, it is not meant to be a personal defense with the hope of conciliating Stephen's accusers (see vv. 51 – 52) but an attack on the foundations of Judaism by citing the history of its failures. It deals with the three great pillars of Jewish piety: (1) the land (vv. 2 – 36), (2) the law (vv. 37 – 43) and (3) the temple (vv. 44 – 50), and ends with a resounding denunciation of Stephen's accusers (vv. 51 – 52). The speech marks a decisive break between Judaism and Christianity and points forward to the vigorous explanations of the differences between the old faith and the new faith found in the writings of Paul and the author of Hebrews.

7:2 *Abraham ... in Mesopotamia, before he lived in Haran.* Abraham's call came in Ur, not Haran (cf. Ge 12:1 and note; 15:7; Ne 9:7). Or perhaps he was called first in Ur, and then later his call was renewed in Haran (see note on Jer 15:19 – 21).

people,' God said, 'and go to the land I will
show you.'[a][k]
4"So he left the land of the Chaldeans
and settled in Haran. After the death of
his father, God sent him to this land where
you are now living.[l] 5He gave him no inheritance here,[m] not even a foot of ground.
But God promised him that he and his descendants after him would possess the
land,[n] even though at that time Abraham
had no child. 6God spoke to him in this
way: 'Your descendants will be strangers
in a country not their own, and they will
be enslaved and mistreated four hundred
years.[o] 7But I will punish the nation they
serve as slaves,' God said, 'and afterward
they will come out of that country and
worship me in this place.'[b][p] 8Then he gave
Abraham the covenant of circumcision.[q]
And Abraham became the father of Isaac
and circumcised him eight days after his
birth.[r] Later Isaac became the father of Jacob,[s] and Jacob became the father of the
twelve patriarchs.[t]
9"Because the patriarchs were jealous
of Joseph,[u] they sold him as a slave into
Egypt.[v] But God was with him[w] 10and rescued him from all his troubles. He gave
Joseph wisdom and enabled him to gain
the goodwill of Pharaoh king of Egypt; so
he made him ruler over Egypt and all his
palace.[x]
11"Then a famine struck all Egypt and
Canaan, bringing great suffering, and our
fathers could not find food.[y] 12When Jacob
heard that there was grain in Egypt, he
sent our fathers on their first visit.[z] 13On
their second visit, Joseph told his brothers
who he was,[a] and Pharaoh learned about
Joseph's family.[b] 14After this, Joseph sent
for his father Jacob and his whole family,[c] seventy-five in all.[d] 15Then Jacob went
down to Egypt, where he and our fathers
died.[e] 16Their bodies were brought back
to Shechem and placed in the tomb that
Abraham had bought from the sons of
Hamor at Shechem for a certain sum of
money.[f]
17"As the time drew near for God to fulfill his promise to Abraham, the number
of our people in Egypt greatly increased.[g]
18Then another king, who knew nothing
about Joseph, became ruler of Egypt.[h]
19He dealt treacherously with our people
and oppressed our forefathers by forcing
them to throw out their newborn babies
so that they would die.[i]
20"At that time Moses was born, and he
was no ordinary child.[c] For three months
he was cared for in his father's house.[j]
21When he was placed outside, Pharaoh's
daughter took him and brought him up as
her own son.[k] 22Moses was educated in
all the wisdom of the Egyptians[l] and was
powerful in speech and action.
23"When Moses was forty years old, he
decided to visit his fellow Israelites. 24He
saw one of them being mistreated by an
Egyptian, so he went to his defense and

[a] 3 Gen. 12:1 [b] 7 Gen. 15:13,14 [c] 20 Or *was fair in the sight of God*

7:3 [k]Ge 12:1 **7:4** [l]Ge 12:5 **7:5** [m]Heb 11:13 [n]Ge 12:7; 17:8; 26:3 **7:6** [o]Ex 1:8-11; 12:40 **7:7** [p]Ge 15:13, 14; Ex 3:12 **7:8** [q]Ge 17:9-14 [r]Ge 21:2-4 [s]Ge 25:26 [t]Ge 29:31-35; 30:5-13, 17-24; 35:16-18, 22-26 **7:9** [u]Ge 37:4, 11 [v]Ge 37:28; Ps 105:17 [w]Ge 39:2, 21, 23; Hag 2:4 **7:10** [x]Ge 41:37-43; Ps 105:20-22 **7:11** [y]Ge 41:54 **7:12** [z]Ge 42:1, 2 **7:13** [a]Ge 45:1-4 [b]Ge 45:16 **7:14** [c]Ge 45:9, 10 [d]Ge 46:26, 27; Ex 1:5; Dt 10:22 **7:15** [e]Ge 46:5-7; 49:33; Ex 1:6 **7:16** [f]Ge 23:16-20; 33:18, 19; 50:13; Jos 24:32 **7:17** [g]Ex 1:7; Ps 105:24 **7:18** [h]Ex 1:8 **7:19** [i]Ex 1:10-22 **7:20** [j]Ex 2:2; Heb 11:23 **7:21** [k]Ex 2:3-10 **7:22** [l]1Ki 4:30; Isa 19:11

7:4 *land of the Chaldeans.* A district in southern Babylonia, the name was later applied to a region that included all Babylonia (see map No. 1 at the end of this study Bible). *After the death of his father.* Ge 11:26 does not mean that all three sons — Abraham, Nahor and Haran — were born to Terah in the same year when he was 70 years old. See Ge 11:26 — 12:1. It may be that Haran was Terah's firstborn and that Abraham was born 60 years later. Thus the death of Terah at 205 years of age could have occurred just before Abraham, at 75, left Haran.
7:6 *four hundred years.* A round number for the length of Israel's stay in Egypt (Ex 12:40 – 41 has 430 years). That four generations would represent considerably less than 400 years is not a necessary conclusion (see note on Ge 15:16). Ex 6:16 – 20 makes Moses the great-grandson of Levi, son of Jacob and brother of Joseph. This would make four generations from Levi to Moses. But in 1Ch 7:22 – 27 a list of ten names represents the generations between Ephraim, the son of Joseph, and Joshua. The ten generations at 40 years each would equal 400 years, the same period of time noted as four generations. But one list is abbreviated and the other gives a fuller genealogy.
7:8 *covenant of circumcision.* See notes on Ge 17:10 – 11. The essential conditions for the religion of Israel were already fulfilled long before the temple was built and their present religious customs began. *twelve patriarchs.* See Ge 35:23 – 26.
7:9 *they sold him.* Israel consistently rejected God's favored individuals. In building his case concerning the Jewish rejection of Jesus, Stephen recalls Joseph's rejection (out of jealousy; cf. Mt 27:18; Mk 15:10 ["envy"]) by his brothers (Ge 37:12 – 36).
7:13 *second visit.* See Ge 43.
7:14 *Jacob and his whole family, seventy-five in all.* Although the Hebrew Bible uses the number 70 (see Ge 46:26 – 27 and note on 46:27; see also Ex 1:5 and NIV text note there; Dt 10:22), the pre-Christian Greek translation of the OT (the Septuagint) adds at Ge 46:20 the names of one son of Manasseh, two of Ephraim, and one grandson of each. This makes the number 75 and is the number that Stephen uses.
7:16 Stephen brings together OT accounts of two land purchases (by Abraham and Jacob) and two burial places (at Hebron and Shechem). According to the OT, Abraham purchased land at Hebron (Ge 23:17 – 18), where he (Ge 25:9 – 11), Isaac (Ge 35:29) and Jacob (Ge 50:13) were buried. Jacob bought land at Shechem (Ge 33:19), where Joseph was later buried (Jos 24:32). Josephus preserves a tradition that Joseph's brothers were buried at Hebron. Stephen's rhetorical device (by which he recalls that Jacob and the 12 patriarchs were not buried in Egypt but in Canaan) is strange to modern ears but would have been well understood by his hearers.
7:18 *another king, who knew nothing about Joseph.* See note on Ex 1:8.
7:22 *Moses was educated in all the wisdom of the Egyptians.* Not explicitly stated in the OT but to be expected if he grew up in the household of the pharaoh's daughter. Both Philo and Josephus speak of Moses' great learning. *was powerful in speech.* See Ex 4:10 and note.
7:23 *Moses was forty.* Moses was 80 years old when sent to speak before the pharaoh (Ex 7:7) and 120 years old when he died (Dt 34:7). Stephen's words agree with a tradition that at Moses' first departure from Egypt he was 40 years of age.

avenged him by killing the Egyptian. 25Mo-
ses thought that his own people would realize that God was using him to rescue
them, but they did not. 26The next day
Moses came upon two Israelites who were
fighting. He tried to reconcile them by saying, 'Men, you are brothers; why do you
want to hurt each other?'
27"But the man who was mistreating the
other pushed Moses aside and said, 'Who
made you ruler and judge over us?[m] 28Do
you want to kill me as you killed the Egyptian yesterday?'[a] 29When Moses heard
this, he fled to Midian, where he settled
as a foreigner and had two sons.[n]
30"After forty years had passed, an angel appeared to Moses in the flames of a
burning bush in the desert near Mount Sinai. 31When he saw this, he was amazed
at the sight. As he went over to look more
closely, he heard the Lord's voice:[o] 32'I am
the God of your fathers,[p] the God of Abraham, Isaac and Jacob.'[b] Moses trembled
with fear and did not dare to look.[q]
33"Then the Lord said to him, 'Take off
your sandals; the place where you are
standing is holy ground.[r] 34I have indeed
seen the oppression of my people in Egypt.
I have heard their groaning and have come
down to set them free. Now come, I will
send you back to Egypt.'[c s]
35"This is the same Moses whom they
had rejected with the words, 'Who made
you ruler and judge?'[t] He was sent to be
their ruler and deliverer by God himself,
through the angel who appeared to him
in the bush. 36He led them out of Egypt[u]
and did wonders and miraculous signs[v] in
Egypt, at the Red Sea[d w] and for forty years
in the desert.[x]
37"This is that Moses who told the Israelites, 'God will send you a prophet like
me from your own people.'[e y] 38He was in
the assembly in the desert, with the angel[z]
who spoke to him on Mount Sinai, and
with our fathers;[a] and he received living
words[b] to pass on to us.[c]
39"But our fathers refused to obey him.
Instead, they rejected him and in their
hearts turned back to Egypt.[d] 40They told
Aaron, 'Make us gods who will go before
us. As for this fellow Moses who led us out
of Egypt—we don't know what has happened to him!'[f e] 41That was the time they
made an idol in the form of a calf. They
brought sacrifices to it and held a celebration in honor of what their hands had
made.[f] 42But God turned away[g] and gave
them over to the worship of the heavenly
bodies.[h] This agrees with what is written
in the book of the prophets:

" 'Did you bring me sacrifices and
offerings
forty years in the desert, O house of
Israel?
43You have lifted up the shrine of Molech
and the star of your god Rephan,
the idols you made to worship.
Therefore I will send you into exile'[g i]
beyond Babylon.

44"Our forefathers had the tabernacle of
the Testimony[j] with them in the desert. It
had been made as God directed Moses, according to the pattern he had seen.[k] 45Hav-
ing received the tabernacle, our fathers
under Joshua brought it with them when
they took the land from the nations God
drove out before them.[l] It remained in the

7:27 m Ge 19:9; Nu 16:13 **7:29** n Ex 2:11-15 **7:31** o Ex 3:1-4 **7:32** p S Ac 3:13 q Ex 3:6 **7:33** r Ex 3:5; Jos 5:15 **7:34** s Ex 3:7-10 **7:35** t ver 27 **7:36** u Ex 12:41; 33:1 v Ex 11:10; S Jn 4:48 w Ex 14:21 x Ex 15:25; 17:5,6
7:37 y Dt 18:15,18; Ac 3:22 **7:38** z ver 53 a Ex 19:17; Lev 27:34 b Dt 32:45-47; Heb 4:12 c Ro 3:2 **7:39** d Nu 14:3,4 **7:40** e Ex 32:1,23 **7:41** f Ex 32:4-6; Ps 106:19,20; Rev 9:20 **7:42** g Jos 24:20; Isa 63:10 h Jer 19:13 **7:43** i Am 5:25-27 **7:44** j Ex 38:21; Nu 1:50; 17:7 k Ex 25:8,9,40 **7:45** l Jos 3:14-17; 18:1; 23:9; 24:18; Ps 44:2

a *28* Exodus 2:14 b *32* Exodus 3:6 c *34* Exodus 3:5,7,8,10 d *36* That is, Sea of Reeds e *37* Deut. 18:15 f *40* Exodus 32:1 g *43* Amos 5:25-27

7:29 *fled to Midian.* Rejected by his own people, Moses feared that they would inform the Egyptians, and this led to his flight to Midian, the land flanking the Gulf of Aqaba on both sides (see Ex 2:15 and note). *had two sons.* Gershom and Eliezer (Ex 2:22; 18:3–4; 1Ch 23:15).

7:30 *After forty years.* Plus the 40 years of v. 23, making the 80 years of Ex 7:7. *Mount Sinai.* Called Horeb in Ex 3:1 (see note there).

7:35 *the same Moses ... sent to be their ruler and deliverer.* Israel rejected Moses, their deliverer, just as the Jews of Stephen's day were rejecting Jesus, their deliverer. Yet both were sent by God. *angel who appeared to him in the bush.* See Ex 3:2.

7:37 *prophet like me.* See 3:22–23; see also notes on Dt 18:15; 34:10,12.

7:38 *assembly.* The assembled Israelites. *angel who spoke to him.* According to Jewish interpretation at that time, the law was given to Moses by angel mediation—after the manner of the original call of Moses (see Ex 3:2; see also v. 53; Gal 3:19; Heb 2:2). *he received living words to pass on to us.* Moses was the mediator between God and Israel on Mount Sinai.

7:39 *refused to obey him.* Another rejection of God's representative and his commands.

7:40 *Make us gods.* While Moses was on Sinai receiving the law, the people made the golden calf, rejecting God and his representative (Ex 32:1). The people had not traveled far from the idolatry of Egypt.

7:42 *God ... gave them over.* See note on Ro 1:24. *heavenly bodies.* See note on Jer 19:13.

7:43 Stephen quotes Am 5:25–27 as translated in the Septuagint, except that he replaces Damascus with Babylon in view of the fact that the final exile of Israel from the promised land was carried out by the Babylonians (Amos was speaking first of the Assyrian exile of the northern kingdom). *Molech ... Rephan.* See note on Am 5:26. *Molech.* See note on Lev 18:21.

7:44–50 Because he had been accused of "speaking against the holy place" (6:13), Stephen concludes his recital with a word about the sanctuary. Presumably, he had been preaching that the risen Christ had now replaced the temple as the mediation of God's saving presence among his people and as the one through whom they (and "all nations," Mk 11:17) could come to God in prayer (see note on 6:13).

7:44 *tabernacle of the Testimony.* So called by Stephen because the primary contents of the desert tabernacle were the ark of the covenant and the two covenant tablets it contained, which were called "the Testimony" (see Ex 25:16,21 and notes).

land until the time of David,[m] 46 who enjoyed God's favor and asked that he might
provide a dwelling place for the God of
Jacob.[a][n] 47 But it was Solomon who built
the house for him.[o]
48 "However, the Most High[p] does not
live in houses made by men.[q] As the
prophet says:

49 " 'Heaven is my throne,
and the earth is my footstool.[r]
What kind of house will you build
for me?
says the Lord.
Or where will my resting place be?
50 Has not my hand made all these
things?'[b][s]

51 "You stiff-necked people,[t] with uncircumcised hearts[u] and ears! You are just
like your fathers: You always resist the Holy
Spirit! 52 Was there ever a prophet your fathers did not persecute?[v] They even killed
those who predicted the coming of the Righteous One. And now you have betrayed and
murdered him[w]— 53 you who have received
the law that was put into effect through angels[x] but have not obeyed it."

The Stoning of Stephen

54 When they heard this, they were furious[y] and gnashed their teeth at him. 55 But
Stephen, full of the Holy Spirit,[z] looked up
to heaven and saw the glory of God, and
Jesus standing at the right hand of God.[a]
56 "Look," he said, "I see heaven open[b] and
the Son of Man[c] standing at the right hand
of God."
57 At this they covered their ears and,
yelling at the top of their voices, they all
rushed at him, 58 dragged him out of the
city[d] and began to stone him.[e] Meanwhile,
the witnesses[f] laid their clothes[g] at the feet
of a young man named Saul.[h]
59 While they were stoning him, Stephen
prayed, "Lord Jesus, receive my spirit."[i]
60 Then he fell on his knees[j] and cried out,
"Lord, do not hold this sin against them."[k]
When he had said this, he fell asleep.[l]
8 And Saul[m] was there, giving approval
to his death.

The Church Persecuted and Scattered

On that day a great persecution broke
out against the church at Jerusalem, and
all except the apostles were scattered[n]
throughout Judea and Samaria.[o] 2 Godly
men buried Stephen and mourned deeply
for him. 3 But Saul[p] began to destroy the
church.[q] Going from house to house, he
dragged off men and women and put them
in prison.

Philip in Samaria

4 Those who had been scattered[r]
preached the word wherever they went.[s]
5 Philip[t] went down to a city in Samaria
and proclaimed the Christ[c] there. 6 When
the crowds heard Philip and saw the miraculous signs he did, they all paid close
attention to what he said. 7 With shrieks,
evil[d] spirits came out of many,[u] and many
paralytics and cripples were healed.[v] 8 So
there was great joy in that city.

Simon the Sorcerer

9 Now for some time a man named Simon had practiced sorcery[w] in the city

7:45 [m] 2Sa 7:2,6 **7:46** [n] 2Sa 7:8-16; 1Ki 8:17; Ps 132:1-5 **7:47** [o] 1Ki 6:1-38 **7:48** [p] S Mk 5:7 [q] 1Ki 8:27; 2Ch 2:6 **7:49** [r] Mt 5:34,35 **7:50** [s] Isa 66:1,2 **7:51** [t] Ex 32:9; 33:3,5 [u] Lev 26:41; Dt 10:16; Jer 4:4; 9:26 **7:52** [v] S Mt 5:12 [w] Ac 3:14; 1Th 2:15 **7:53** [x] ver 38; Gal 3:19; Heb 2:2 **7:54** [y] Ac 5:33 **7:55** [z] S Lk 1:15 [a] S Mk 16:19 **7:56** [b] S Mt 3:16 [c] S Mt 8:20 **7:58** [d] Lk 4:29 [e] Lev 24:14,16 [f] Dt 17:7 [g] Ac 22:20 [h] Ac 8:1 **7:59** [i] Ps 31:5; Lk 23:46 **7:60** [j] Lk 22:41; Ac 9:40 [k] S Mt 5:44 [l] S Mt 9:24 **8:1** [m] Ac 7:58 [n] ver 4; Ac 11:19 [o] Ac 9:31 **8:3** [p] Ac 7:58 [q] Ac 9:1,13,21; 22:4,19; 26:10,11; 1Co 15:9; Gal 1:13,23; Php 3:6; 1Ti 1:13 **8:4** [r] ver 1 [s] Ac 15:35 **8:5** [t] Ac 6:5; 21:8 **8:7** [u] S Mk 16:17 [v] S Mt 4:24 **8:9** [w] Ac 13:6

[a] 46 Some early manuscripts *the house of Jacob*
[b] 50 Isaiah 66:1,2 [c] 5 Or *Messiah* [d] 7 Greek *unclean*

7:49 Isa 66:1–2 reminded Israel that all creation is the temple that God himself had made. Stephen recalls that word to remind his hearers that ultimately God builds his own temple.

7:51 *uncircumcised hearts and ears.* Though physically circumcised, they were acting like the uncircumcised pagan nations around them. They were not truly consecrated to the Lord.

7:52 *Righteous One.* See 3:14 and note.

7:53 *law that was put into effect through angels.* See note on v. 38.

7:55 *full of the Holy Spirit.* See note on 2:4; see also 6:5. *glory of God.* See note on Lk 2:9.

7:56 *Son of Man.* See note on Mk 8:31. *standing at the right hand of God.* Cf. Ps 110:1 and note; Mk 14:62; Lk 22:69; Heb 1:2–3 and note. The significance of Jesus' "standing" is debated, but it may reflect the common OT idiom that used "stand before" as indicative of one in the service of Yahweh or a king (see, e.g., 1Ki 10:8; 17:1 [see note there]; Jer 15:19 [see note there]; 33:18; Eze 44:15).

7:58 *laid their clothes at the feet of … Saul.* Some have thought that this marked Saul as being in charge of the execution. In any case, it is Luke's way of introducing the main character of the second section of the book (chs. 13–28).

7:60 *do not hold this sin against them.* Cf. Jesus' words in Lk 23:34. *fell asleep.* See note on Jn 11:11.

8:1 *giving approval.* See 22:20 and note. *all except the apostles.* For the apostles to stay in Jerusalem would be an encouragement to those in prison and a center of appeal to those scattered. The church now went underground. *scattered throughout Judea and Samaria.* The beginning of the fulfillment of the commission in 1:8—not by the church's plan, but by events beyond the believers' control. See map, p. 1702.

8:3 *began to destroy.* See 22:4. The Greek underlying this phrase sometimes describes the ravages of wild animals.

8:4 *preached the word.* Many witnesses to the gospel went everywhere proclaiming the good news. The number of witnesses multiplied, and the territory covered was expanded greatly (cf. 11:19–20).

8:5 *Philip.* One of the Seven in the Jerusalem church (6:3,5; see note on 6:6), who now becomes an evangelist, proclaiming the Christ (Messiah); see also 21:8. Philip is an example of one of those who were scattered. *a city in Samaria.* Some manuscripts have "the city of Samaria," a reference to the old capital Samaria, renamed Sebaste or Neapolis (modern Nablus).

8:9 *Simon.* In early Christian literature the "sorcerer" (Simon Magus) is described as the arch-heretic of the church and the "father" of Gnostic teaching. *sorcery.* See note on 2Ki 17:17.

and amazed all the people of Samaria.
He boasted that he was someone great,[x]
10and all the people, both high and low,
gave him their attention and exclaimed,
"This man is the divine power known as
the Great Power."[y] 11They followed him because he had amazed them for a long time
with his magic. 12But when they believed
Philip as he preached the good news of the
kingdom of God[z] and the name of Jesus
Christ, they were baptized,[a] both men and
women. 13Simon himself believed and was
baptized. And he followed Philip everywhere, astonished by the great signs and
miracles[b] he saw.

14When the apostles in Jerusalem heard
that Samaria[c] had accepted the word of
God,[d] they sent Peter and John[e] to them.
15When they arrived, they prayed for them
that they might receive the Holy Spirit,[f]
16because the Holy Spirit had not yet
come upon any of them;[g] they had simply been baptized into[a] the name of the
Lord Jesus.[h] 17Then Peter and John placed
their hands on them,[i] and they received
the Holy Spirit.[j]

18When Simon saw that the Spirit was
given at the laying on of the apostles'
hands, he offered them money 19and said,
"Give me also this ability so that everyone

8:9 [x]Ac 5:36 8:10 [y]Ac 14:11; 28:6 8:12 [z]S Mt 3:2 [a]S Ac 2:38 8:13 [b]ver 6; Ac 19:11 8:14 [c]ver 1 [d]S Heb 4:12 [e]S Lk 22:8 8:15 [f]S Jn 20:22 8:16 [g]S Ac 10:44; 19:2 [h]Mt 28:19; S Ac 2:38 8:17 [i]S Ac 6:6 [j]S Jn 20:22

[a] 16 Or *in*

8:10 *the Great Power.* Simon claimed to be either God himself or, more likely, his chief representative.
8:13 *Simon himself believed and was baptized.* It is difficult to know whether Simon's faith was genuine. Even though Luke says Simon believed, Peter's statement that Simon had no part in the apostles' ministry because his heart was not "right before God" (v. 21) casts some doubt.
8:14 *Samaria.* That is, some of its citizens. Cf. 1:8. *had accepted the word of God.* Were obedient to the gospel proclaimed by Philip. *sent Peter and John.* The Jerusalem church assumed the responsibility of inspecting new evangelistic efforts and the communities of believers they produced (see 11:22).
8:16 *not yet come upon any of them.* Since the day of Pentecost, those who "belong to Christ" (Ro 8:9) also have the Holy Spirit. But the Spirit had not yet been made manifest to the Christians in Samaria by the usual signs. This deficiency was now graciously supplied (v. 17).
8:17 *placed their hands on them.* See v. 18; 19:1–7; cf. 2Ti 1:6; see also note on 6:6.
8:18 *he offered them money.* Simon had boasted of having great powers before (see v. 10 and note), and now he tried to buy this magical power he believed the apostles possessed.

Philip's and Peter's Missionary Journeys

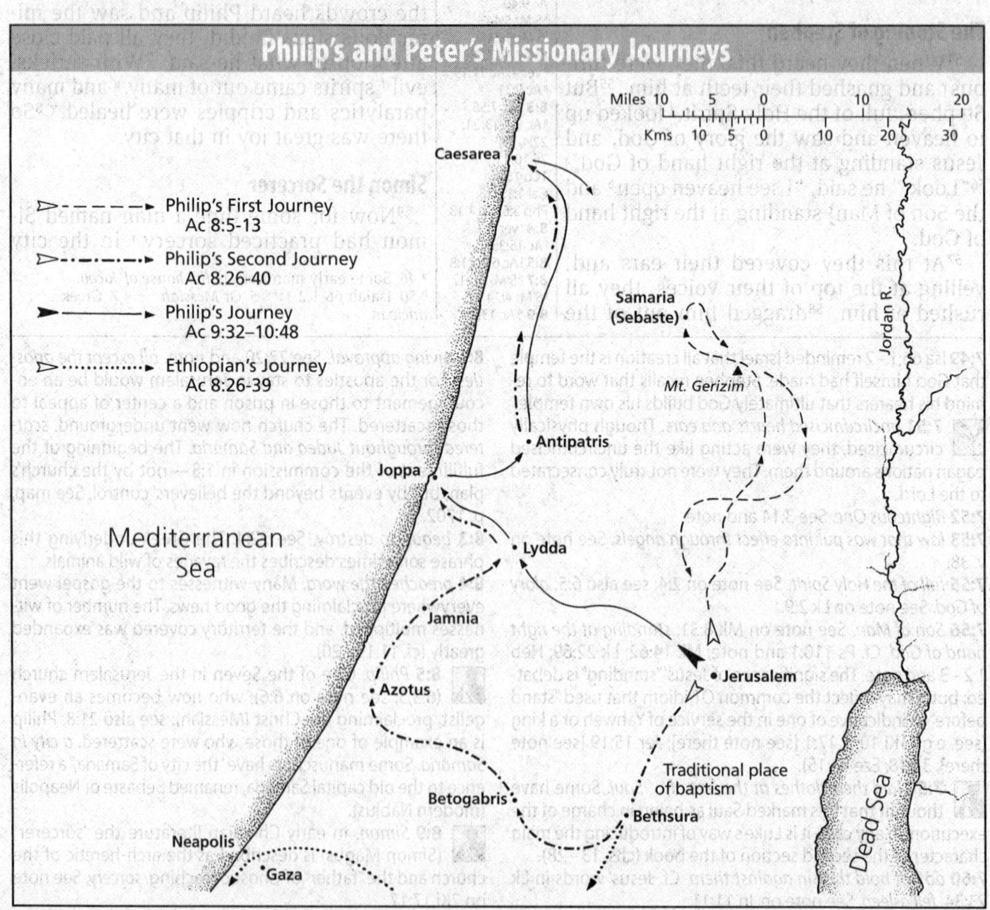

on whom I lay my hands may receive the
Holy Spirit."
20Peter answered: "May your money
perish with you, because you thought
you could buy the gift of God with money![k] 21You have no part or share[l] in this
ministry, because your heart is not right[m]
before God. 22Repent[n] of this wickedness
and pray to the Lord. Perhaps he will forgive you for having such a thought in your
heart. 23For I see that you are full of bitterness and captive to sin."
24Then Simon answered, "Pray to the
Lord for me[o] so that nothing you have said
may happen to me."
25When they had testified and proclaimed the word of the Lord,[p] Peter and
John returned to Jerusalem, preaching the
gospel in many Samaritan villages.[q]

Philip and the Ethiopian

26Now an angel[r] of the Lord said to
Philip,[s] "Go south to the road—the desert road—that goes down from Jerusalem
to Gaza." 27So he started out, and on his
way he met an Ethiopian[a][t] eunuch,[u] an
important official in charge of all the treasury of Candace, queen of the Ethiopians.
This man had gone to Jerusalem to worship,[v] 28and on his way home was sitting
in his chariot reading the book of Isaiah
the prophet. 29The Spirit told[w] Philip, "Go
to that chariot and stay near it."
30Then Philip ran up to the chariot and
heard the man reading Isaiah the prophet.
"Do you understand what you are reading?" Philip asked.
31"How can I," he said, "unless someone explains it to me?" So he invited Philip to come up and sit with him.
32The eunuch was reading this passage
of Scripture:

"He was led like a sheep to the
slaughter,
and as a lamb before the shearer is
silent,
so he did not open his mouth.
33In his humiliation he was deprived of
justice.
Who can speak of his descendants?
For his life was taken from the
earth."[b][x]

34The eunuch asked Philip, "Tell me,
please, who is the prophet talking about,
himself or someone else?" 35Then Philip
began[y] with that very passage of Scripture[z]
and told him the good news[a] about Jesus.
36As they traveled along the road, they
came to some water and the eunuch said,
"Look, here is water. Why shouldn't I be
baptized?"[c][b] 38And he gave orders to stop
the chariot. Then both Philip and the eunuch went down into the water and Philip
baptized him. 39When they came up out
of the water, the Spirit of the Lord suddenly took Philip away,[c] and the eunuch did
not see him again, but went on his way
rejoicing. 40Philip, however, appeared at
Azotus and traveled about, preaching the
gospel in all the towns[d] until he reached
Caesarea.[e]

Saul's Conversion

9:1-19pp — Ac 22:3-16; 26:9-18

9 Meanwhile, Saul was still breathing out
murderous threats against the Lord's
disciples.[f] He went to the high priest 2and
asked him for letters to the synagogues in
Damascus,[g] so that if he found any there

8:20 [k] 2Ki 5:16; Da 5:17; Mt 10:8; Ac 2:38
8:21 [l] Ne 2:20 [m] Ps 78:37
8:22 [n] Ac 2:38
8:24 [o] Ex 8:8; Nu 21:7; 1Ki 13:6; Jer 42:2
8:25 [p] S Ac 13:48 [q] ver 40
8:26 [r] S Ac 5:19 [s] Ac 6:5
8:27 [t] Ps 68:31; 87:4; Zep 3:10 [u] Isa 56:3-5 [v] 1Ki 8:41-43; Jn 12:20
8:29 [w] Ac 10:19; 11:12; 13:2; 20:23; 21:11
8:33 [x] Isa 53:7,8
8:35 [y] Mt 5:2 [z] Lk 24:27; Ac 17:2; 18:28; 28:23 [a] S Ac 13:32
8:36 [b] S Ac 2:38; 10:47
8:39 [c] 1Ki 18:12; 2Ki 2:16; Eze 3:12,14; 8:3; 11:1,24; 43:5; 2Co 12:2; 1Th 4:17; Rev 12:5
8:40 [d] ver 25 [e] Ac 10:1,24; 12:19; 21:8,16; 23:23,33; 25:1,4,6,13
9:1 [f] S Ac 8:3
9:2 [g] Isa 17:1; Jer 49:23

[a] *27* That is, from the upper Nile region
[b] *33* Isaiah 53:7,8
[c] *36* Some late manuscripts *baptized?" 37Philip said, "If you believe with all your heart, you may." The eunuch answered, "I believe that Jesus Christ is the Son of God."*

8:23 *full of bitterness.* See Dt 29:18. *captive to sin.* See Ro 6:20.
8:26 *an angel of the Lord.* Cf. v. 29; see note on 5:19. *from Jerusalem to Gaza.* A distance of about 50 miles (see map, p. 1692).
8:27 *an Ethiopian.* Ethiopia corresponded in this period to Nubia, from the upper Nile region at the first cataract (Aswan) to Khartoum. *Candace.* The traditional title of the queen mother, responsible for performing the secular duties of the reigning king—who was thought to be too sacred for such activities. *gone to Jerusalem to worship.* If not a full-fledged convert to Judaism (Dt 23:1), the Ethiopian was a Gentile God-fearer (see note on 10:2).
8:30 *heard the man reading.* It was customary practice to read aloud.
8:34 *who is the prophet talking about ...?* Beginning with Isa 53 (see v. 35), Philip may have identified the suffering servant with the Davidic Messiah of Isa 11 or with the Son of Man (Da 7:13).
8:35 *good news.* The way of salvation through Jesus Christ (see note on Mk 1:1).
8:36 *they came to some water.* There were several possibilities: a brook in the Valley of Elah (which David crossed to meet Goliath, 1Sa 17:40); the Wadi el-Hasi just north of Gaza; water from a spring or one of the many pools in the area.
8:37 See NIV text note on v. 36.
8:39 *rejoicing.* Joy is associated with salvation in Acts (see note on 16:34).
8:40 *Azotus.* OT Ashdod (see 1Sa 5:1), one of the five Philistine cities (see map, p. 331). It was about 19 miles from Gaza and 60 miles from Caesarea (see map, p. 1692). *Caesarea.* Rebuilt by Herod, and with an excellent harbor it served as the headquarters of the Roman governors. The account leaves Philip in Caesarea at this time; his next appearance is 20 years later, and he is still located in the same place (21:8).
9:1 *Saul.* Introduced at the stoning of Stephen (7:58), he was born in Tarsus and trained under Gamaliel (22:3). See notes on Ro 1:1; Php 3:4-14. *murderous threats.* We do not know that Saul was directly involved in the death of anyone other than Stephen (8:1), but there appear to have been similar cases (22:4; 26:10). *high priest.* Probably Caiaphas (see note on 4:6) and the members of the Sanhedrin, who had authority over Jews both in Judea and elsewhere.
9:2 *Damascus.* See map, p. 1695. Located in the Roman province of Syria, it was the nearest important city outside the Holy Land. It also had a large Jewish population. The

who belonged to the Way,[h] whether men
or women, he might take them as prisoners to Jerusalem. 3As he neared Damascus on his journey, suddenly a light from
heaven flashed around him.[i] 4He fell to
the ground and heard a voice[j] say to him,
"Saul, Saul, why do you persecute me?"
5"Who are you, Lord?" Saul asked.
"I am Jesus, whom you are persecuting," he replied. 6"Now get up and go into
the city, and you will be told what you
must do."[k]
7The men traveling with Saul stood
there speechless; they heard the sound[l]
but did not see anyone.[m] 8Saul got up from
the ground, but when he opened his eyes
he could see nothing.[n] So they led him by
the hand into Damascus. 9For three days
he was blind, and did not eat or drink anything.
10In Damascus there was a disciple
named Ananias. The Lord called to him in
a vision,[o] "Ananias!"
"Yes, Lord," he answered.
11The Lord told him, "Go to the house
of Judas on Straight Street and ask for a
man from Tarsus[p] named Saul, for he is
praying. 12In a vision he has seen a man
named Ananias come and place his hands
on[q] him to restore his sight."
13"Lord," Ananias answered, "I have
heard many reports about this man and
all the harm he has done to your saints[r] in
Jerusalem.[s] 14And he has come here with
authority from the chief priests[t] to arrest
all who call on your name."[u]
15But the Lord said to Ananias, "Go!
This man is my chosen instrument[v] to carry my name before the Gentiles[w] and their
kings[x] and before the people of Israel. 16I
will show him how much he must suffer
for my name."[y]
17Then Ananias went to the house and
entered it. Placing his hands on[z] Saul, he
said, "Brother Saul, the Lord—Jesus, who
appeared to you on the road as you were
coming here—has sent me so that you
may see again and be filled with the Holy
Spirit."[a] 18Immediately, something like
scales fell from Saul's eyes, and he could
see again. He got up and was baptized,[b]
19and after taking some food, he regained
his strength.

Saul in Damascus and Jerusalem

Saul spent several days with the disciples[c] in Damascus.[d] 20At once he began
to preach in the synagogues[e] that Jesus
is the Son of God.[f] 21All those who heard
him were astonished and asked, "Isn't
he the man who raised havoc in Jerusalem among those who call on this name?[g]
And hasn't he come here to take them as
prisoners to the chief priests?"[h] 22Yet Saul
grew more and more powerful and baffled
the Jews living in Damascus by proving
that Jesus is the Christ.[a][i]
23After many days had gone by, the Jews
conspired to kill him,[j] 24but Saul learned
of their plan.[k] Day and night they kept
close watch on the city gates in order to
kill him. 25But his followers took him by
night and lowered him in a basket through
an opening in the wall.[l]
26When he came to Jerusalem,[m] he
tried to join the disciples, but they were

9:2 [h] Ac 19:9,23; 22:4; 24:14,22 **9:3** [i] 1Co 15:8 **9:4** [j] Isa 6:8 **9:6** [k] ver 16; Eze 3:22 **9:7** [l] Jn 12:29 [m] Da 10:7 **9:8** [n] ver 18 **9:10** [o] Ac 10:3, 17,19; 12:9; 16:9,10; 18:9 **9:11** [p] ver 30; Ac 11:25; 21:39; 22:3 **9:12** [q] S Mk 5:23 **9:13** [r] ver 32; Ac 26:10; Ro 1:7; 15:25,26,31; 16:2,15; Eph 1:1; Php 1:1 [s] S Ac 8:3 **9:14** [t] ver 2,21 [u] S Ac 2:21 **9:15** [v] Ac 13:2; Ro 1:1; Gal 1:15; 1Ti 1:12 [w] Ro 11:13; 15:15,16; Gal 1:16; 2:7,8 [x] Ac 25:22,23; 26:1 **9:16** [y] Ac 20:23; 21:11; 2Co 6:4-10; 11:23-27; 2Ti 1:8; 2:3,9 **9:17** [z] S Ac 6:6 [a] S Lk 1:15 **9:18** [b] S Ac 2:38 **9:19** [c] S Ac 11:26 [d] Ac 26:20 **9:20** [e] Ac 13:5, 14; 14:1; 17:2, 10,17; 18:4,19; 19:8 [f] S Mt 4:3 **9:21** [g] S Ac 8:3 [h] ver 14 **9:22** [i] S Lk 2:11; Ac 5:42; 17:3; 18:5,28 **9:23** [j] S Ac 20:3 **9:24** [k] Ac 20:3,19; 23:16,30 **9:25** [l] 1Sa 19:12; 2Co 11:32,33 **9:26** [m] Ac 22:17; 26:20; Gal 1:17,18

[a] 22 Or *Messiah*

distance from Jerusalem to Damascus was about 150 miles, four to six days' travel. *the Way.* A name for Christianity occurring a number of times in Acts (16:17; 18:25–26; 19:9,23; 22:4; 24:14,22; see 2Pe 2:2). Jesus called himself "the way" (Jn 14:6). *prisoners to Jerusalem.* Where the full authority of the Sanhedrin could be exercised in trial for either acquittal or death.

9:3 *a light from heaven.* "About noon" (26:13).

9:4 *why do you persecute me?* To persecute the church is to persecute Christ, for the church is his body (see 1Co 12:27; Eph 1:22–23).

9:5 *Who are you, Lord?* In Rabbinic tradition such a voice from heaven would have been understood as the voice of God himself. The solemn repetition of Saul's name and the bright light suggested to him that he was in the presence of deity.

9:7 *heard the sound.* Those with Saul "heard the sound" but "did not understand" what the voice was saying (22:9; cf. Da 10:7).

9:10 *Ananias.* This Ananias is mentioned elsewhere only in 22:12. His was a common name (5:1; 23:2). The Greek form is derived from the Hebrew name Hananiah, meaning "The LORD is gracious/shows grace" (see Da 1:6 and note).

9:11 *Straight Street.* Probably followed the same route of the long, straight street that today runs through the city from east to west. It is a decided contrast to the numerous crooked streets of the city (see map, p. 1695). *Tarsus.* See note on 22:3. *praying.* Prayer is often associated with visions in Luke and Acts (see 10:9–11; Lk 1:10; 3:21; 9:28).

9:13,32 *saints.* See notes on Ro 1:7; Php 1:1.

9:15 *before the Gentiles.* See Ro 1:13–14. *their kings.* Agrippa (26:1) and Caesar at Rome (25:11–12; 28:19).

9:16 *how much he must suffer.* See 2Co 11:23–28 and notes.

9:17 *Jesus, who appeared to you.* The Damascus road experience was not merely a vision. The resurrected Christ actually appeared to Saul, and on this fact Saul based his qualification to be an apostle (see 1Co 9:1 and note; 15:8).

9:20 *At once.* Following his baptism (v. 18). *synagogues.* It became Saul's regular practice to preach at every opportunity in the synagogues (13:5; 14:1; 17:1–2,10; 18:4,19; 19:8). *Jesus is the Son of God.* Saul's message was a declaration of what he himself had become convinced of on the Damascus road: Christ's deity and Messiahship (see NIV text note on v. 22).

9:23 *After many days.* Three years (Gal 1:17–18). It is probable that the major part of this period was spent in Arabia, away from Damascus, though the borders of Arabia extended to the environs of Damascus. *the Jews conspired to kill him.* Upon Saul's return to Damascus, the governor under Aretas IV gave orders for his arrest (2Co 11:32; see note there).

9:25 *lowered him in a basket.* See 2Co 11:33 (cf. Jos 2:15; 1Sa 19:12).

9:26 *he came to Jerusalem.* From Gal 1:19 we learn that all the apostles were away except Peter and James, the Lord's brother. James was not one of the Twelve, but he held a position in Jerusalem comparable to that of an apostle (see Gal 2:9).

all afraid of him, not believing that he
really was a disciple. 27But Barnabas[n] took
him and brought him to the apostles. He
told them how Saul on his journey had
seen the Lord and that the Lord had spoken to him,[o] and how in Damascus he had
preached fearlessly in the name of Jesus.[p]
28So Saul stayed with them and moved
about freely in Jerusalem, speaking boldly in the name of the Lord. 29He talked
and debated with the Grecian Jews,[q] but
they tried to kill him.[r] 30When the brothers[s] learned of this, they took him down to
Caesarea[t] and sent him off to Tarsus.[u]
31Then the church throughout Judea,
Galilee and Samaria[v] enjoyed a time of
peace. It was strengthened; and encouraged by the Holy Spirit, it grew in numbers,[w] living in the fear of the Lord.

Aeneas and Dorcas

32As Peter traveled about the country, he
went to visit the saints[x] in Lydda. 33There
he found a man named Aeneas, a paralytic
who had been bedridden for eight years.
34"Aeneas," Peter said to him, "Jesus
Christ heals you.[y] Get up and take care
of your mat." Immediately Aeneas got up.
35All those who lived in Lydda and Sharon[z] saw him and turned to the Lord.[a]

9:27 [n] S Ac 4:36 [o] ver 3-6 [p] ver 20,22 **9:29** [q] Ac 6:1 [r] 2Co 11:26 **9:30** [s] S Ac 1:16 [t] S Ac 8:40 [u] S ver 11 **9:31** [v] Ac 8:1 [w] S Ac 2:41 **9:32** [x] S ver 13 **9:34** [y] Ac 3:6, 16; 4:10 **9:35** [z] 1Ch 5:16; 27:29; SS 2:1; Isa 33:9; 35:2; 65:10 [a] S Ac 2:41

9:27 *Barnabas.* See note on 4:36.
9:29 *He talked and debated.* Formerly Saul was arguing against Christ; now he is forcefully presenting Jesus as the Messiah.
9:30 *Caesarea.* See note on 8:40. *Tarsus.* Saul's birthplace (see note on 22:3).
9:31 *church.* The whole Christian body, including Christians in the districts of Judea, Galilee and Samaria. The singular thus does not here refer to the various congregations but to the church as a whole (see note on 5:11). *encouraged by the Holy Spirit.* The work of the Spirit is particularly noted throughout the book of Acts (see 13:2 and note on 1:2). This is why the book is sometimes called the Acts of the Holy Spirit.
9:32 *Lydda.* A town two or three miles north of the road connecting Joppa and Jerusalem. Lydda is about 12 miles from Joppa.
9:33 *Aeneas.* Since Peter was there to visit the believers, Aeneas was probably one of the Christians.
9:35 *Sharon.* The fertile plain of Sharon runs about 50 miles along the Mediterranean coast, roughly from Joppa to Caesarea. The reference here, however, may be to a village in the neighborhood of Lydda instead of to a district (an Egyptian papyrus refers to a town by that name in the Holy Land).

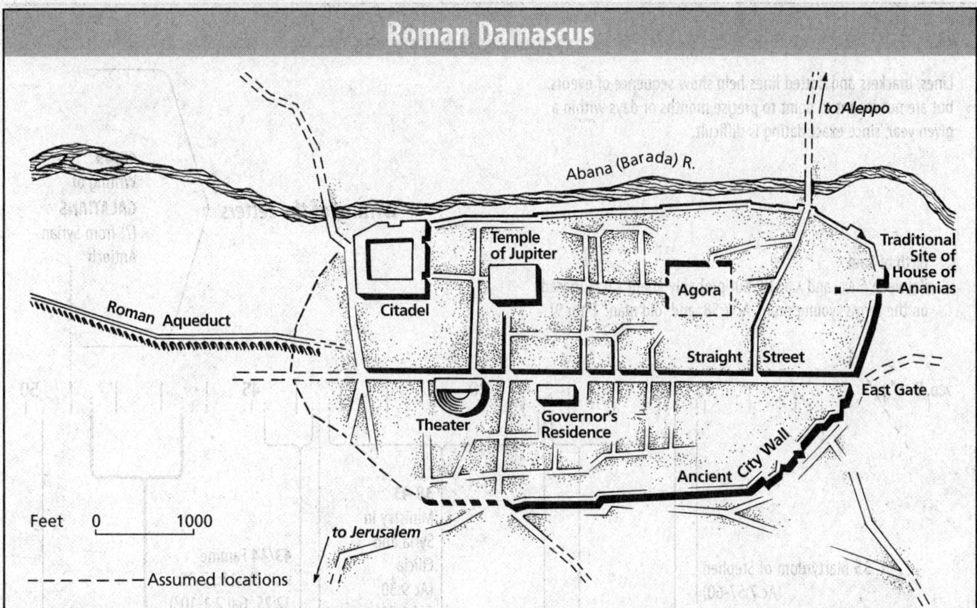

Damascus represented much more to Saul, the strict Pharisee, than any other stop on his campaign of repression. It was the hub of a vast commercial network with far-flung lines of caravan trade reaching into north Syria, Mesopotamia, Anatolia, Persia and Arabia. If the new "Way" of Christianity flourished in Damascus, it would quickly reach all these places. From the viewpoint of the Sanhedrin and of Saul, the arch-persecutor, it had to be stopped in Damascus.

The city itself was a veritable oasis, situated in a plain watered by the Biblical rivers Abana and Pharpar (see note on 2Ki 5:12; see also map, p. 1570). Roman architecture overlaid the Hellenistic town plan with a great temple to Jupiter and a mile-long colonnaded street, the "Straight Street" of Ac 9:11. The city gates and a section of the town wall may still be seen today, as well as the lengthy bazaar that runs along the line of the ancient street.

The dominant political figure at the time of Paul's escape from Damascus (2Co 11:32-33) was Aretas IV, king of the Nabateans (9 B.C.–A.D. 40), though normally the Decapolis cities were attached to the province of Syria and were thus under the influence of Rome.

[36]In Joppa[b] there was a disciple named
Tabitha (which, when translated, is Dorcas[a]), who was always doing good[c] and helping the poor. [37]About that time she became sick and died, and her body was washed and placed in an upstairs room.[d]
[38]Lydda was near Joppa; so when the disciples[e] heard that Peter was in Lydda, they sent two men to him and urged him, "Please come at once!"
[39]Peter went with them, and when he arrived he was taken upstairs to the room. All the widows[f] stood around him, crying and showing him the robes and other clothing that Dorcas had made while she was still with them.
[40]Peter sent them all out of the room;[g] then he got down on his knees[h] and prayed. Turning toward the dead woman, he said, "Tabitha, get up."[i] She opened her eyes, and seeing Peter she sat up. [41]He took her by the hand and helped her to her feet. Then he called the believers and the widows and presented her to them alive. [42]This became known all over Joppa, and many people believed in the Lord.[j] [43]Peter stayed in Joppa for some time with a tanner named Simon.[k]

9:36 [b] Jos 19:46; 2Ch 2:16; Ezr 3:7; Jnh 1:3; Ac 10:5 [c] 1Ti 2:10; Tit 3:8 **9:37** [d] Ac 1:13; 20:8 **9:38** [e] S Ac 11:26 **9:39** [f] Ac 6:1; 1Ti 5:3 **9:40** [g] Mt 9:25 [h] Lk 22:41; Ac 7:60 [i] S Lk 7:14 **9:42** [j] S Ac 2:41 **9:43** [k] Ac 10:6

[a] 36 Both *Tabitha* (Aramaic) and *Dorcas* (Greek) mean *gazelle*.

9:36 *Joppa.* About 38 miles from Jerusalem, the main seaport of Judea. Today it is known as Jaffa and is a suburb of Tel Aviv.
9:37 *body was washed.* In preparation for burial, a custom common to both Jews ("Purification of the Dead," Mishna, *Shabboth* 23.5) and Greeks. *upstairs room.* If burial was delayed, it was customary to lay the body in an upper room. In Jerusalem the body had to be buried the day the person died, but outside Jerusalem up to three days might be allowed for burial.
9:38 *near Joppa.* See note on v. 32. *come at once!* Whether for consolation or for a miracle, Peter was urged to hurry in order to arrive before the burial.
9:40 *sent them all out.* Cf. 1Ki 17:23; 2Ki 4:33. Peter had been present on all three occasions recorded in Scripture when Jesus raised individuals from the dead (Mt 9:25; Lk 7:11–17; Jn 11:1–44). As when Jesus raised Jairus's daughter, the crowd in the room was told to leave. Unlike Jesus, however, Peter knelt and prayed.
9:42 *many people believed.* Cf. Jn 12:11.
9:43 *a tanner.* Occupations were frequently used with personal names to identify individuals further (see 16:14; 18:3;

Timeline of Paul's Life

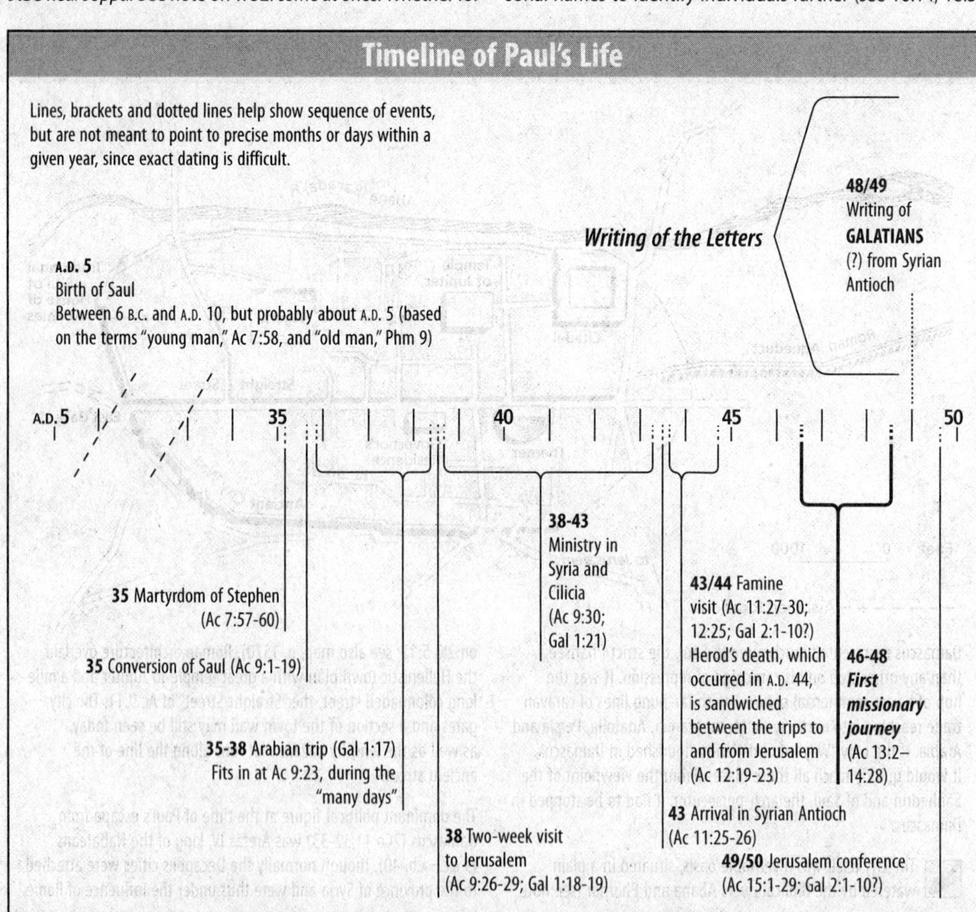

Cornelius Calls for Peter

10 At Caesarea[l] there was a man named
Cornelius, a centurion in what was
known as the Italian Regiment. 2He and all
his family were devout and God-fearing;[m]
he gave generously to those in need and
prayed to God regularly. 3One day at about
three in the afternoon[n] he had a vision.[o]
He distinctly saw an angel[p] of God, who
came to him and said, "Cornelius!"
4Cornelius stared at him in fear. "What
is it, Lord?" he asked.
The angel answered, "Your prayers and
gifts to the poor have come up as a memorial offering[q] before God.[r] 5Now send
men to Joppa[s] to bring back a man named

10:1 [l] S Ac 8:40 **10:2** [m] ver 22,35; Ac 13:16,26 **10:3** [n] Ps 55:17; Ac 3:1 [o] S Ac 9:10 [p] S Ac 5:19 **10:4** [q] Ps 20:3; S Mt 10:42; 26:13 [r] Rev 8:4 **10:5** [s] S Ac 9:36

19:24; 2Ti 4:14), but in this case it is especially significant. A tanner was involved in treating the skins of dead animals, thus contacting the unclean according to Jewish law; so he was despised by many. Peter's decision to stay with him shows already a willingness to reject Jewish prejudice and helps to prepare the way for his coming vision and the mission to the Gentiles.

10:1 *Caesarea.* Located 30 miles north of Joppa and named in honor of Augustus Caesar, it was the headquarters for the Roman forces of occupation (see also note on 8:40). *Cornelius.* A Latin name made popular when Cornelius Sulla liberated some 10,000 slaves over 100 years earlier. These had all taken his family name, Cornelius. *centurion.* Commanded a military unit that normally numbered at least 100 men (see note on Mt 8:5). The Roman legion (about 6,000 men) was divided into ten regiments, each of which had a designation. This was the "Italian" (another was the "Imperial," or "Augustan," 27:1). A centurion commanded about a sixth of a regiment. Centurions were carefully selected; all of them mentioned in the NT appear to have had noble qualities (e.g., Lk 7:5). The Roman centurions provided necessary stability to the entire Roman system.

10:2 *devout.* In spite of all his good deeds, Cornelius needed to hear the way of salvation from a human messenger. The role of the angel (v. 3) was to bring Cornelius and Peter together (cf. 8:26; 9:10). *God-fearing.* The term used of one who was not a full-fledged convert to Judaism but who believed in one God and respected the moral and ethical teachings of the Jews.

10:3 *about three in the afternoon.* Another indication that Cornelius followed Jewish religious practices. Three in the afternoon was a Jewish hour of prayer (see 3:1 and note)—the hour of the evening incense. *a vision.* Not a dream or trance but a revelation through an angel to Cornelius while at prayer (see v. 30; see also note on 9:11).

10:4 *have come up.* Like the smoke of a sacrifice (see Ps 141:2; Php 4:18 and note; Heb 13:15–16). *memorial offering.* A portion of the grain offering burned on the altar was called a "memorial" (Lev 2:2; see note on Lev 2:2,9,16).

10:5–6 *Joppa ... Simon the tanner.* See notes on 9:36,43.

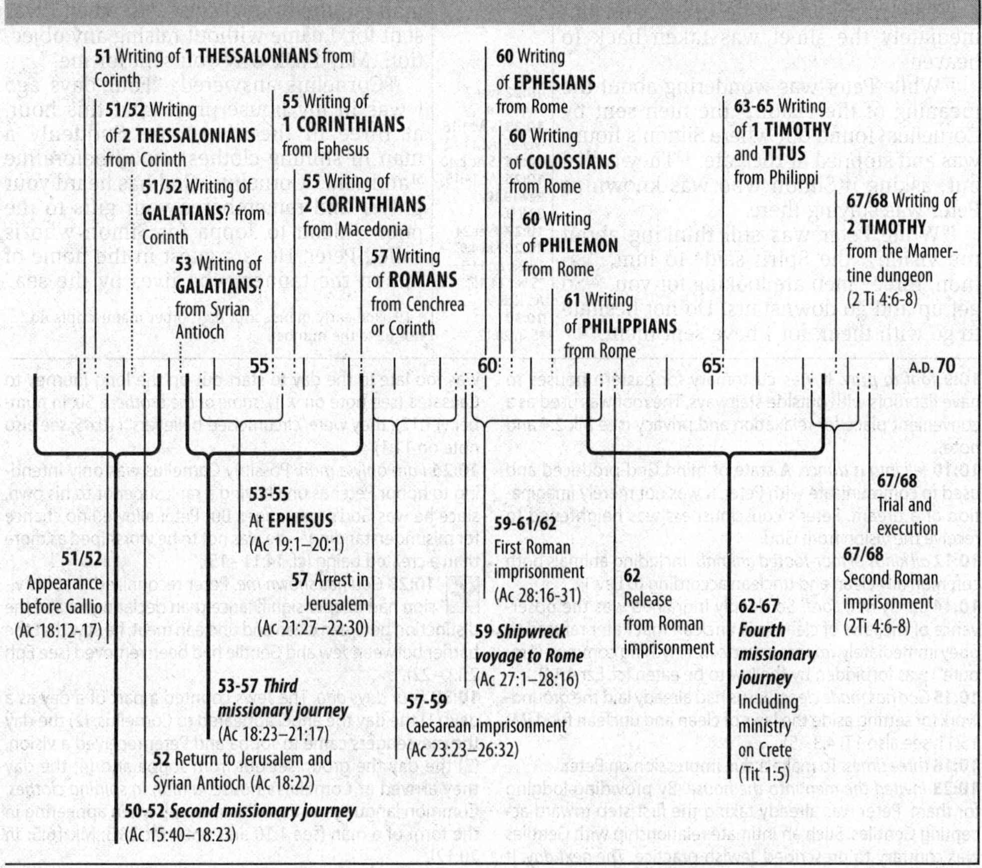

Simon who is called Peter. 6He is staying with Simon the tanner,[t] whose house is by the sea."

7When the angel who spoke to him had gone, Cornelius called two of his servants and a devout soldier who was one of his attendants. 8He told them everything that had happened and sent them to Joppa.[u]

Peter's Vision

10:9-32Ref — Ac 11:5-14

9About noon the following day as they were on their journey and approaching the city, Peter went up on the roof[v] to pray. 10He became hungry and wanted something to eat, and while the meal was being prepared, he fell into a trance.[w] 11He saw heaven opened[x] and something like a large sheet being let down to earth by its four corners. 12It contained all kinds of four-footed animals, as well as reptiles of the earth and birds of the air. 13Then a voice told him, "Get up, Peter. Kill and eat."

14"Surely not, Lord!"[y] Peter replied. "I have never eaten anything impure or unclean."[z]

15The voice spoke to him a second time, "Do not call anything impure that God has made clean."[a]

16This happened three times, and immediately the sheet was taken back to heaven.

17While Peter was wondering about the meaning of the vision,[b] the men sent by Cornelius[c] found out where Simon's house was and stopped at the gate. 18They called out, asking if Simon who was known as Peter was staying there.

19While Peter was still thinking about the vision,[d] the Spirit said[e] to him, "Simon, three[a] men are looking for you. 20So get up and go downstairs. Do not hesitate to go with them, for I have sent them."[f]

21Peter went down and said to the men, "I'm the one you're looking for. Why have you come?"

22The men replied, "We have come from Cornelius the centurion. He is a righteous and God-fearing man,[g] who is respected by all the Jewish people. A holy angel told him to have you come to his house so that he could hear what you have to say."[h] 23Then Peter invited the men into the house to be his guests.

Peter at Cornelius's House

The next day Peter started out with them, and some of the brothers[i] from Joppa went along.[j] 24The following day he arrived in Caesarea.[k] Cornelius was expecting them and had called together his relatives and close friends. 25As Peter entered the house, Cornelius met him and fell at his feet in reverence. 26But Peter made him get up. "Stand up," he said, "I am only a man myself."[l]

27Talking with him, Peter went inside and found a large gathering of people.[m] 28He said to them: "You are well aware that it is against our law for a Jew to associate with a Gentile or visit him.[n] But God has shown me that I should not call any man impure or unclean.[o] 29So when I was sent for, I came without raising any objection. May I ask why you sent for me?"

30Cornelius answered: "Four days ago I was in my house praying at this hour, at three in the afternoon. Suddenly a man in shining clothes[p] stand before me 31and said, 'Cornelius, God has heard your prayer and remembered your gifts to the poor. 32Send to Joppa for Simon who is called Peter. He is a guest in the home of Simon the tanner, who lives by the sea.'

[a] *19* One early manuscript *two*; other manuscripts do not have the number.

10:6 [t] Ac 9:43
10:8 [u] S Ac 9:36
10:9 [v] S Mt 24:17
10:10 [w] Ac 22:17
10:11 [x] S Mt 3:16
10:14 [y] Ac 9:5 [z] Lev 11:4-8, 13-20; 20:25; Dt 14:3-20; Eze 4:14
10:15 [a] ver 28; Ge 9:3; Mt 15:11; Lk 11:41; Ac 11:9; Ro 14:14, 17, 20; 1Co 10:25; 1Ti 4:3, 4; Tit 1:15
10:17 [b] S Ac 9:10 [c] ver 7, 8
10:19 [d] S Ac 9:10 [e] S Ac 8:29
10:20 [f] Ac 15:7-9
10:22 [g] ver 2 [h] Ac 11:14
10:23 [i] S Ac 1:16 [j] ver 45; Ac 11:12
10:24 [k] S Ac 8:40
10:26 [l] Ac 14:15; Rev 19:10; 22:8, 9
10:27 [m] ver 24
10:28 [n] Jn 4:9; 18:28; Ac 11:3 [o] S ver 14, 15; Ac 15:8, 9
10:30 [p] S Jn 20:12

10:9 *roof to pray.* It was customary for eastern houses to have flat roofs with outside stairways. The roof was used as a convenient place for relaxation and privacy (see Mk 2:4 and note).

10:10 *fell into a trance.* A state of mind God produced and used to communicate with Peter. It was not merely imagination or a dream. Peter's consciousness was heightened to receive the vision from God.

10:12 *all kinds of four-footed animals.* Including animals both ceremonially clean and unclean according to Lev 11.

10:14 *Surely not, Lord!* So deeply ingrained was the observance of the laws of clean and unclean that Peter refused to obey immediately. *impure or unclean.* Anything common ("impure") was forbidden by the law to be eaten (cf. Ezr 4:14).

10:15 *God has made clean.* Jesus had already laid the groundwork for setting aside the laws of clean and unclean food (Mt 15:11; see also 1Ti 4:3–5).

10:16 *three times.* To make a due impression on Peter.

10:23 *invited the men into the house.* By providing lodging for them, Peter was already taking the first step toward accepting Gentiles. Such an intimate relationship with Gentiles was contrary to prescribed Jewish practice. *The next day.* It was too late in the day to start out on the long journey to Caesarea (see note on v. 1). *some of the brothers.* Six in number (11:12), they were "circumcised believers" (10:45; see also note on 11:1).

10:26 *I am only a man.* Possibly Cornelius was only intending to honor Peter as one having a rank superior to his own, since he was God's messenger. But Peter allowed no chance for misunderstanding — he was not to be worshiped as more than a created being (cf. 14:11–15).

10:28 *God has shown me.* Peter recognized that his vision had deeper significance than declaring invalid the distinction between clean and unclean meat; he saw that the barrier between Jew and Gentile had been removed (see Eph 2:11–22).

10:30 *Four days ago.* The Jews counted a part of a day as a day: (1) the day the angel appeared to Cornelius, (2) the day the messengers came to Joppa and Peter received a vision, (3) the day the group set out from Joppa and (4) the day they arrived at Cornelius's house. *a man in shining clothes.* Common language to describe an angel when appearing in the form of a man (see 1:10 and note; Mt 28:3; Mk 16:5; Jn 20:12).

33So I sent for you immediately, and it
was good of you to come. Now we are all
here in the presence of God to listen to
everything the Lord has commanded you
to tell us."
34Then Peter began to speak: "I now realize how true it is that God does not show
favoritism[q] 35but accepts men from every
nation who fear him and do what is right.[r]
36You know the message[s] God sent to the
people of Israel, telling the good news[t] of
peace[u] through Jesus Christ, who is Lord
of all.[v] 37You know what has happened
throughout Judea, beginning in Galilee
after the baptism that John preached—
38how God anointed[w] Jesus of Nazareth
with the Holy Spirit and power, and how
he went around doing good and healing[x]
all who were under the power of the devil,
because God was with him.[y]
39"We are witnesses[z] of everything he did
in the country of the Jews and in Jerusalem.
They killed him by hanging him on a tree,[a]
40but God raised him from the dead[b] on the
third day and caused him to be seen. 41He
was not seen by all the people,[c] but by witnesses whom God had already chosen—by
us who ate[d] and drank with him after he
rose from the dead. 42He commanded us to
preach to the people[e] and to testify that he
is the one whom God appointed as judge
of the living and the dead.[f] 43All the prophets testify about him[g] that everyone[h] who
believes[i] in him receives forgiveness of sins
through his name."[j]
44While Peter was still speaking these
words, the Holy Spirit came on[k] all who
heard the message. 45The circumcised believers who had come with Peter[l] were
astonished that the gift of the Holy Spirit
had been poured out[m] even on the Gentiles.[n] 46For they heard them speaking in
tongues[a][o] and praising God.
Then Peter said, 47"Can anyone keep
these people from being baptized with
water?[p] They have received the Holy Spirit just as we have."[q] 48So he ordered that
they be baptized in the name of Jesus
Christ.[r] Then they asked Peter to stay with
them for a few days.

Peter Explains His Actions

11 The apostles and the brothers[s]
throughout Judea heard that the Gentiles also had received the word of God.[t]
2So when Peter went up to Jerusalem, the
circumcised believers[u] criticized him 3and
said, "You went into the house of uncircumcised men and ate with them."[v]
4Peter began and explained everything to
them precisely as it had happened: 5"I was
in the city of Joppa praying, and in a trance
I saw a vision.[w] I saw something like a
large sheet being let down from heaven by
its four corners, and it came down to where
I was. 6I looked into it and saw four-footed
animals of the earth, wild beasts, reptiles,
and birds of the air. 7Then I heard a voice
telling me, 'Get up, Peter. Kill and eat.'
8"I replied, 'Surely not, Lord! Nothing
impure or unclean has ever entered my
mouth.'

a 46 *Or other languages*

10:34 q Dt 10:17; 2Ch 19:7; Job 34:19; Mk 12:14; Ro 2:11; Gal 2:6; Eph 6:9; Col 3:25; Jas 2:1; 1Pe 1:17 **10:35** r Ac 15:9 **10:36** s 1Jn 1:5 t S Ac 13:32 u S Lk 2:14 v S Mt 28:18 **10:38** w S Ac 4:26 x S Mt 4:23 y S Jn 3:2 **10:39** z ver 41; S Lk 24:48 a S Ac 5:30 **10:40** b S Ac 2:24 **10:41** c Jn 14:17,22 d Lk 24:43; Jn 21:13; Ac 1:4 **10:42** e Mt 28:19,20 f S Jn 5:22; Ac 17:31; Ro 14:9; 2Co 5:10; 2Ti 4:1; 1Pe 4:5 **10:43** g Isa 53:11; Ac 26:22 h Ac 15:9 i S Jn 3:15 j S Lk 24:27 **10:44** k Ac 8:15,16; 11:15; 15:8; 19:6; S Lk 1:15 **10:45** l ver 23 m Ac 2:33,38 n Ac 11:18; 15:8 **10:46** o S Mk 16:17 **10:47** p Ac 8:36 q S Jn 20:22; Ac 11:17 **10:48** r S Ac 2:38 **11:1** s S Ac 1:16 t S Heb 4:12 **11:2** u Ac 10:45 **11:3** v Ac 10:25,28; Gal 2:12 **11:5** w S Ac 9:10; 10:9-32

10:34 *God does not show favoritism.* God does not favor individuals because of their station in life, their nationality or their material possessions (see Ro 2:11; Jas 2:1 and notes; see also Dt 10:17–19; 2Co 19:17; Job 34:19; Eph 6:9; Col 3:25; 1Pe 1:17). He does, however, respect their character and judge their work. This is evident because God "accepts men from every nation who fear him and do what is right" (v. 35). Cornelius already worshiped the true God, but this was not enough: He lacked faith in Christ (v. 36).
10:36 *people of Israel.* The first recipients of the "message" but not restricted to them, as the phrase "Lord of all" indicates (see Jn 3:16; Ro 1:16). *peace.* Between God and humans (see Ro 5:1 and note). *Lord of all.* Lord of both Jew and Gentile (see vv. 34–35).
10:37 *after the baptism that John preached.* Similar to the outline of Mark's Gospel, Peter's sermon begins with John's baptism and continues to the resurrection of Jesus. This is significant since the early church fathers viewed Mark as the interpreter of Peter (see Introduction to Mark: Author). See previous summaries of Peter's preaching (2:14–41; 3:12–26; 4:8–12; 5:29–32); see also note on 2:14–40.
10:38 *how God anointed Jesus.* See Isa 61:1–3; Lk 4:18–21.
10:39 *hanging him on a tree.* See note on 5:30.
10:41 *who ate and drank.* Those who ate with Jesus after he rose from the dead received unmistakable evidence of his bodily resurrection (see Lk 24:42–43; Jn 21:12–15).
10:44 *the Holy Spirit came on.* See 8:16 and note.
10:45 *astonished . . . even on the Gentiles.* Apparently the early Jewish Christians failed to understand that the gospel was for the Gentiles as well as for the Jews, and that they would share alike in the benefits of redemption. Gentile converts to Judaism, however, were accepted (see 6:5).
10:46 *speaking in tongues.* The same experience the disciples had at Pentecost (2:4,11) and "some disciples" at Ephesus (19:1,6).
10:47 *Can anyone keep these people from being baptized with water?* The Gentiles had received the same gift (11:17) as the Jewish believers; they spoke in tongues as did the Jewish Christians on the day of Pentecost. This was unmistakable evidence that the invitation to the kingdom was open to Gentiles as well as to Jews.
11:1 *The apostles and the brothers.* At times "brothers" is used to refer to those of common Jewish lineage (2:29; 7:2), but in Christian contexts it denotes those united in Christ (6:3; 10:23; see note on Ro 1:13). In matters of deep concern, the apostles did not act alone. The divine will gave guidance, and the apostles interpreted and exhorted, but the consent of the whole church was sought ("the whole group," 6:5; "the apostles and the brothers," 11:1; "the church," 11:22; "the church and the apostles and elders," 15:4; cf. 15:22).
11:2 *circumcised believers.* Jewish Christians.
11:3 *uncircumcised men.* The Gentiles who would not observe the laws of clean and unclean food and would violate Jewish regulations concerning food preparation. *ate with them.* See Lk 15:2 and note.
11:4–17 See notes on 10:1–23,28–33.

9“The voice spoke from heaven a second
time, ‘Do not call anything impure that
God has made clean.’[x] 10This happened
three times, and then it was all pulled up
to heaven again.
11“Right then three men who had been
sent to me from Caesarea[y] stopped at the
house where I was staying. 12The Spirit
told[z] me to have no hesitation about going with them.[a] These six brothers[b] also
went with me, and we entered the man’s
house. 13He told us how he had seen an
angel[c] appear in his house and say, ‘Send
to Joppa for Simon who is called Peter.
14He will bring you a message[d] through
which you and all your household[e] will
be saved.’
15“As I began to speak, the Holy Spirit
came on[f] them as he had come on us at
the beginning.[g] 16Then I remembered what
the Lord had said: ‘John baptized with[a]
water,[h] but you will be baptized with the
Holy Spirit.’[i] 17So if God gave them the
same gift[j] as he gave us,[k] who believed in
the Lord Jesus Christ, who was I to think
that I could oppose God?”
18When they heard this, they had no further objections and praised God, saying,
“So then, God has granted even the Gentiles repentance unto life.”[l]

The Church in Antioch

19Now those who had been scattered by
the persecution in connection with Stephen[m] traveled as far as Phoenicia, Cyprus
and Antioch,[n] telling the message only to
Jews. 20Some of them, however, men from
Cyprus[o] and Cyrene,[p] went to Antioch[q]
and began to speak to Greeks also, telling them the good news[r] about the Lord
Jesus. 21The Lord’s hand was with them,[s]
and a great number of people believed and
turned to the Lord.[t]
22News of this reached the ears of the
church at Jerusalem, and they sent Barnabas[u] to Antioch. 23When he arrived and
saw the evidence of the grace of God,[v]
he was glad and encouraged them all
to remain true to the Lord with all their
hearts.[w] 24He was a good man, full of the
Holy Spirit[x] and faith, and a great number
of people were brought to the Lord.[y]
25Then Barnabas went to Tarsus[z] to
look for Saul, 26and when he found him,
he brought him to Antioch. So for a whole
year Barnabas and Saul met with the
church and taught great numbers of people. The disciples[a] were called Christians
first[b] at Antioch.
27During this time some prophets[c] came
down from Jerusalem to Antioch. 28One
of them, named Agabus,[d] stood up and
through the Spirit predicted that a severe
famine would spread over the entire Roman world.[e] (This happened during the
reign of Claudius.)[f] 29The disciples,[g] each
according to his ability, decided to provide help[h] for the brothers[i] living in Judea.
30This they did, sending their gift to the
elders[j] by Barnabas[k] and Saul.[l]

[a] 16 Or *in*

11:9 [x]S Ac 10:15 **11:11** [y]S Ac 8:40 **11:12** [z]S Ac 8:29 [a]Ac 15:9; Ro 3:22 [b]ver 1,29; S Ac 1:16 **11:13** [c]S Ac 5:19 **11:14** [d]Ac 10:36 [e]Jn 4:53; Ac 16:15,31-34; 18:8; 1Co 1:11,16 **11:15** [f]S Ac 10:44 [g]Ac 2:4 **11:16** [h]S Mk 1:4 [i]S Mk 1:8 **11:17** [j]Ac 2:38 [k]Ac 10:45,47 **11:18** [l]Ro 10:12,13; 2Co 7:10 **11:19** [m]Ac 8:1,4 [n]ver 26,27; Ac 13:1; 14:26; 18:22; Gal 2:11 **11:20** [o]Ac 4:36 [p]S Mt 27:32 [q]S ver 19 [r]S Ac 13:32 **11:21** [s]Lk 1:66 [t]S Ac 2:41 **11:22** [u]S Ac 4:36 **11:23** [v]Ac 13:43; 14:26; 15:40; 20:24 [w]Ac 14:22 **11:24** [x]S Lk 1:15 [y]S Ac 2:41 **11:25** [z]S Ac 9:11 **11:26** [a]ver 29; Ac 6:1,2; 9:19,26,38; 13:52 [b]Ac 26:28; 1Pe 4:16 **11:27** [c]Ac 13:1; 15:32; 1Co 11:4; 12:28,29; 14:29,32,37; S Eph 4:11 **11:28** [d]Ac 21:10 [e]S Mt 24:14 [f]Ac 18:2 **11:29** [g]S ver 26 [h]Ro 15:26; 2Co 8:1-4; 9:2 [i]ver 1,12; S Ac 1:16 **11:30** [j]Ac 14:23; 15:2,22; 20:17; 1Ti 5:17; Tit 1:5; Jas 5:14; 1Pe 5:1; 2Jn 1 [k]S Ac 4:36 [l]Ac 12:25

11:14 *you and all your household.* Not only the family but also slaves and employed individuals under Cornelius’s authority (see note on Ge 6:18).

11:17 *oppose God.* Peter could not deny the Gentiles the invitation to be baptized (10:47) and to enjoy full fellowship in Christ with all believers. The Jewish believers were compelled to recognize that God was going to save Gentiles on equal terms with Jews. By divine action rather than by human choice, the door was being opened to Gentiles.

11:18 *repentance unto life.* A change of one’s attitude toward sin, which leads to a turning from sin to God and results in eternal life (see note on 2:38).

11:19 *persecution in connection with Stephen.* See 8:1–4 and notes. *Phoenicia.* A country about 15 miles wide and 120 miles long stretching along the northeastern Mediterranean coast (modern Lebanon). Its important cities were Tyre and Sidon. *Cyprus.* An island in the northeastern Mediterranean; the home of Barnabas (4:36). *Antioch.* The third city of the Roman empire (after Rome and Alexandria). It was 15 miles inland from the northeast corner of the Mediterranean. The first largely Gentile local church was located here, and it was from this church that Paul’s three missionary journeys were launched (13:1–4; 15:40; 18:23).

11:20 *Cyrene.* See note on 2:10. *Greeks.* Not Greek-speaking Jews, but Gentiles.

11:21 *Lord’s hand.* Indicates the presence of the Lord’s power to assist and bless (see 4:30; Lk 1:16; but see also Ac 13:11), sometimes evidenced by signs and wonders (cf. Ex 8:19).

11:22 *Barnabas.* See notes on 4:36; 9:27. *Antioch.* See note on v. 19. The sending of Barnabas was apparently in keeping with the Jerusalem church’s policy of sending leaders to check on new ministries that came to their attention (see 8:14).

11:23 *he … encouraged them.* His name means “Son of Encouragement” (4:36; see note there).

11:24 *full of the Holy Spirit and faith.* See the description of Stephen (6:5).

11:25 *Tarsus.* See 9:11,30 and note on 22:3.

11:26 *whole year.* Luke notes definite periods of time (18:11; 19:8,10; 24:27; 28:30). *Christians.* Whether adopted by believers or invented by enemies as a term of reproach, it is an apt title for those “belonging to Christ” (the meaning of the term). It occurs elsewhere in Scripture only in 26:28; 1Pe 4:16.

11:27 *prophets.* The first mention of the gift of prophecy in Acts. Prophets preach, exhort, explain or, as in this case, foretell (see 13:1; 15:32; 19:6; 21:9–10; Ro 12:6; 1Co 12:10; 13:2,8; 14:3,6,29–37; see also notes on Jnh 3:2; Zec 1:1; Eph 4:11).

11:28 *Agabus.* Later foretells Paul’s imprisonment (21:10). In Acts, prophets are engaged in foretelling (v. 27; 21:9–10) at least as often as in forthtelling (15:32). *Claudius.* Emperor of Rome (A.D. 41–54).

11:29 *each according to his ability.* Cf. 2Co 8:3.

11:30 *elders.* First reference to them in Acts (see notes on 1Ti 3:1; 5:17). Since the apostles are not mentioned, they may have been absent from Jerusalem at this time.

Peter's Miraculous Escape From Prison

12 It was about this time that King Herod[m] arrested some who belonged to
the church, intending to persecute them.
2He had James, the brother of John,[n] put
to death with the sword.[o] 3When he saw
that this pleased the Jews,[p] he proceeded
to seize Peter also. This happened during
the Feast of Unleavened Bread.[q] 4After arresting him, he put him in prison, handing him over to be guarded by four squads
of four soldiers each. Herod intended to
bring him out for public trial after the
Passover.[r]
5So Peter was kept in prison, but the
church was earnestly praying to God for
him.[s]
6The night before Herod was to bring
him to trial, Peter was sleeping between
two soldiers, bound with two chains,[t] and
sentries stood guard at the entrance. 7Sud-
denly an angel[u] of the Lord appeared and
a light shone in the cell. He struck Peter
on the side and woke him up. "Quick, get
up!" he said, and the chains fell off Peter's
wrists.[v]
8Then the angel said to him, "Put on
your clothes and sandals." And Peter did
so. "Wrap your cloak around you and follow me," the angel told him. 9Peter followed him out of the prison, but he had
no idea that what the angel was doing was
really happening; he thought he was seeing a vision.[w] 10They passed the first and
second guards and came to the iron gate
leading to the city. It opened for them by
itself,[x] and they went through it. When
they had walked the length of one street,
suddenly the angel left him.
11Then Peter came to himself[y] and said,
"Now I know without a doubt that the
Lord sent his angel and rescued me[z] from
Herod's clutches and from everything the
Jewish people were anticipating."
12When this had dawned on him, he
went to the house of Mary the mother of
John, also called Mark,[a] where many people had gathered and were praying.[b] 13Pe-
ter knocked at the outer entrance, and a
servant girl named Rhoda came to answer
the door.[c] 14When she recognized Peter's
voice, she was so overjoyed[d] she ran back
without opening it and exclaimed, "Peter
is at the door!"
15"You're out of your mind," they told
her. When she kept insisting that it was
so, they said, "It must be his angel."[e]
16But Peter kept on knocking, and when
they opened the door and saw him, they
were astonished. 17Peter motioned with his
hand[f] for them to be quiet and described
how the Lord had brought him out of prison. "Tell James[g] and the brothers[h] about
this," he said, and then he left for another
place.
18In the morning, there was no small
commotion among the soldiers as to what
had become of Peter. 19After Herod had a
thorough search made for him and did not
find him, he cross-examined the guards
and ordered that they be executed.[i]

Herod's Death

Then Herod went from Judea to Caes-

12:1 [m] S Mt 14:1 **12:2** [n] S Mt 4:21 [o] Mk 10:39 **12:3** [p] Ac 24:27; 25:9 [q] Ex 12:15; 23:15; Ac 20:6 **12:4** [r] S Jn 11:55 **12:5** [s] S Ac 1:14; Ro 15:30,31; Eph 6:18 **12:6** [t] Ac 21:33 **12:7** [u] S Ac 5:19 [v] Ps 107:14; Ac 16:26 **12:9** [w] S Ac 9:10 **12:10** [x] Ac 5:19; 16:26 **12:11** [y] Lk 15:17 [z] Ps 34:7; Da 3:28; 6:22; 2Co 1:10; 2Pe 2:9 **12:12** [a] ver 25; Ac 13:5,13; 15:37,39; Col 4:10; 2Ti 4:11; Phm 24; 1Pe 5:13 [b] ver 5 **12:13** [c] Jn 18:16,17 **12:14** [d] Lk 24:41 **12:15** [e] S Mt 18:10 **12:17** [f] Ac 13:16; 19:33; 21:40 [g] S Ac 15:13 [h] S Ac 1:16 **12:19** [i] Ac 16:27

12:1 *about this time.* Some hold that the events recorded in ch. 12 group together matters concerning Herod Agrippa I (see below; see also chart, p. 1465) and may not be in strict chronological order. For example, the arrival of Barnabas and Saul in Jerusalem (11:30) may have followed Herod's persecution and Peter's release from prison. Since the date of Herod's death was A.D. 44, these events would probably have occurred in 43. According to this view, the famine of 11:28 occurred c. 46, following Herod's death (v. 23). Others hold that such juggling of events is not necessary. Thus the relief gift of 11:30 came before Herod's death in 44, and the return of Barnabas and Saul (v. 25) followed Herod's death. According to the former view, the Jerusalem visit of Gal 2:1–10 was the famine visit of v. 25; 11:30. According to the latter view, the Gal 2:1 visit was the Jerusalem council visit of 15:1–29 (see chart, pp. 1696–1697). *King Herod.* Agrippa I, grandson of Herod the Great (see notes on Mt 2:1; 14:1) and son of Aristobulus. He was a nephew of Herod Antipas, who had beheaded John the Baptist (Mt 14:3–12) and had tried Jesus (Lk 23:8–12). When Antipas was exiled, Agrippa received his tetrarchy as well as those of Philip and Lysanias (see Lk 3:1 and note). In A.D. 41 Judea and Samaria were added to his realm.

12:2 *James.* Brother of John the apostle and son of Zebedee (Mt 4:21). This event took place about ten years after Jesus' death and resurrection. Jesus had warned of their coming suffering (Mt 20:20–23). *death with the sword.* Beheaded, like John the Baptist.

12:3 *Feast of Unleavened Bread.* See notes on Mk 14:1; Lk 22:1.

12:4 *four squads.* One company of four soldiers for each of the four watches of the night (see note on Mt 14:25). *Passover.* Another way of referring to the whole week of the festival (see note on Lk 22:1).

12:7 *angel of the Lord.* See note on 5:19. *a light shone.* Reflecting the glory of the Lord (see 7:55 and note).

12:9 *prison.* Probably the tower of Antonia, located at the northwest corner of the temple—the "barracks" where Paul was later held (see 21:34).

12:12 *Mary.* The aunt of Barnabas (see Col 4:10). Apparently her home was a gathering place for Christians. It may have been the location of the upper room where the Last Supper was held (see Mk 14:13–15; see also Ac 1:13) and the place of prayer in 4:31. *John ... Mark.* See note on v. 25.

12:13 *Rhoda.* A hired servant, but in sympathy with the family and the church.

12:15 *his angel.* Reflects the belief that everyone has a personal angel who ministers to them (cf. Mt 18:10 and note; Heb 1:14).

12:16 *they were astonished.* Though they had been "earnestly praying to God for him" (v. 5).

12:17 *James.* The Lord's brother, a leader in the Jerusalem church (see Gal 1:19 and note). James, the brother of John, had been killed (see v. 2). *brothers.* See note on 11:1.

12:19 *Caesarea.* Not only a headquarters for Roman governors, but Agrippa used it as his capital when no governors were assigned to Judea (see notes on 8:40; 10:1).

The Spread of the Gospel

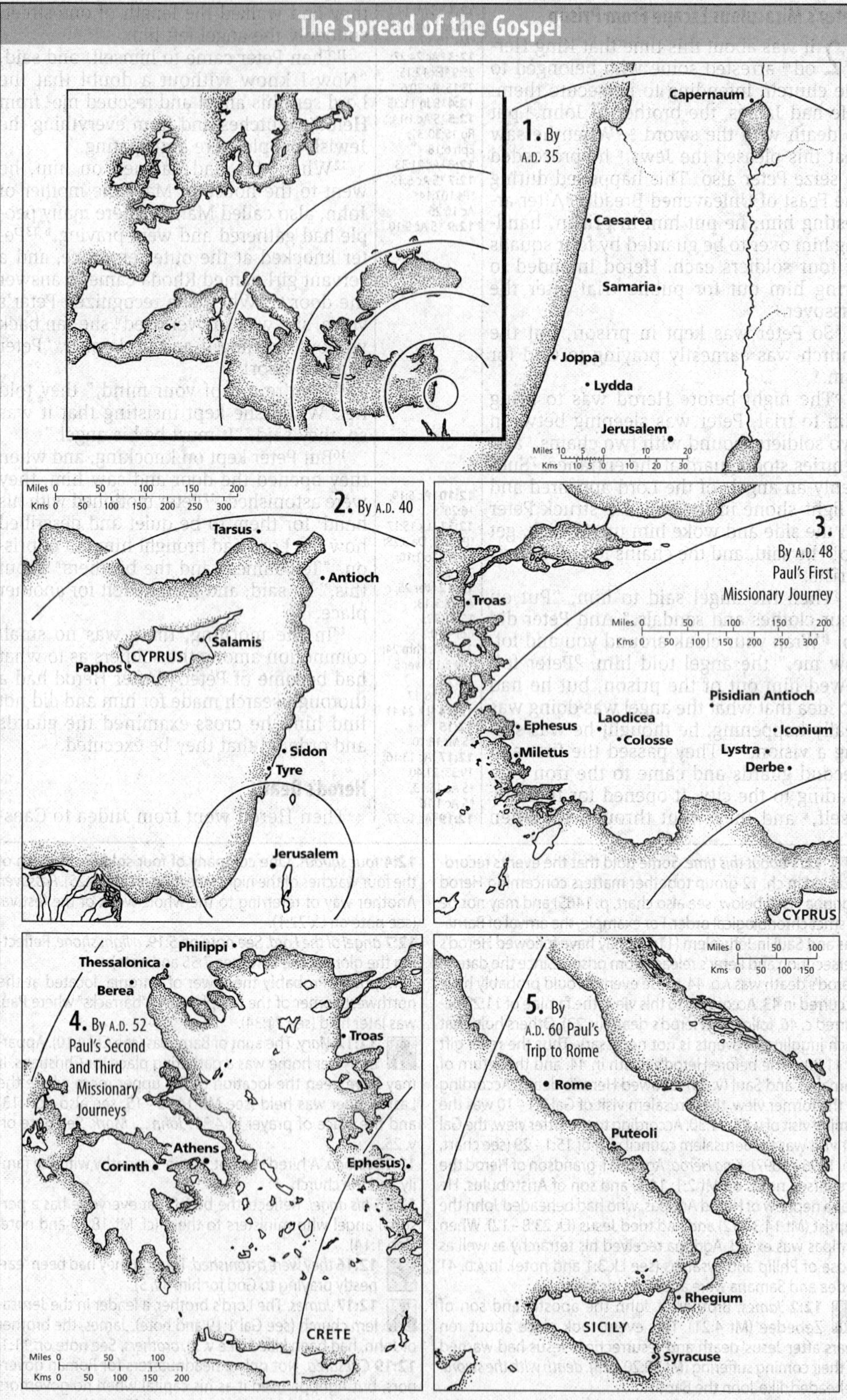
1. By A.D. 35
Capernaum
Caesarea
Samaria
Joppa
Lydda
Jerusalem
Miles 10 5 0 10 20
Kms 10 5 0 10 20 30
2. By A.D. 40
Miles 0 50 100 150 200
Kms 0 50 100 150 200 250 300
Tarsus
Antioch
CYPRUS
Salamis
Paphos
Sidon
Tyre
Jerusalem
3. By A.D. 48
Paul's First
Missionary Journey
Miles 0 50 100 150 200
Kms 0 50 100 150 200 250 300
Troas
Pisidian Antioch
Ephesus
Laodicea
Iconium
Colosse
Miletus
Lystra
Derbe
CYPRUS
4. By A.D. 52
Paul's Second
and Third
Missionary
Journeys
Philippi
Thessalonica
Berea
Troas
Athens
Corinth
Ephesus
CRETE
Miles 0 50 100
Kms 0 50 100 150 200
5. By
A.D. 60 Paul's
Trip to Rome
Miles 0 50 100
Kms 0 50 100 150
Rome
Puteoli
Rhegium
SICILY
Syracuse

area[j] and stayed there a while. 20He had
been quarreling with the people of Tyre
and Sidon;[k] they now joined together and sought an audience with him.
Having secured the support of Blastus,
a trusted personal servant of the king,
they asked for peace, because they depended on the king's country for their
food supply.[l]
21On the appointed day Herod, wearing his royal robes, sat on his throne and
delivered a public address to the people.
22They shouted, "This is the voice of a
god, not of a man." 23Immediately, because Herod did not give praise to God,
an angel[m] of the Lord struck him down,[n]
and he was eaten by worms and died.
24But the word of God[o] continued to increase and spread.[p]
25When Barnabas[q] and Saul had finished their mission,[r] they returned from[a]
Jerusalem, taking with them John, also
called Mark.[s]

Barnabas and Saul Sent Off

13 In the church at Antioch[t] there were
prophets[u] and teachers:[v] Barnabas,[w]
Simeon called Niger, Lucius of Cyrene,[x]
Manaen (who had been brought up with
Herod[y] the tetrarch) and Saul. 2While
they were worshiping the Lord and fasting, the Holy Spirit said,[z] "Set apart for
me Barnabas and Saul for the work[a] to
which I have called them."[b] 3So after they
had fasted and prayed, they placed their
hands on them[c] and sent them off.[d]

On Cyprus

4The two of them, sent on their way by
the Holy Spirit,[e] went down to Seleucia
and sailed from there to Cyprus.[f] 5When
they arrived at Salamis, they proclaimed
the word of God[g] in the Jewish synagogues.[h] John[i] was with them as their
helper.
6They traveled through the whole island until they came to Paphos. There
they met a Jewish sorcerer[j] and false
prophet[k] named Bar-Jesus, 7who was an
attendant of the proconsul,[l] Sergius Paulus. The proconsul, an intelligent man,
sent for Barnabas and Saul because he
wanted to hear the word of God. 8But Elymas the sorcerer[m] (for that is what his
name means) opposed them and tried
to turn the proconsul[n] from the faith.[o]

12:19 [j] S Ac 8:40
12:20 [k] S Mt 11:21 [l] 1Ki 5:9,11; Eze 27:17
12:23 [m] S Ac 5:19 [n] 1Sa 25:38; 2Sa 24:16,17; 2Ki 19:35
12:24 [o] S Heb 4:12 [p] Ac 6:7; 19:20
12:25 [q] S Ac 4:36 [r] Ac 11:30 [s] S ver 12
13:1 [t] S Ac 11:19 [u] S Ac 11:27 [v] S Eph 4:11 [w] S Ac 4:36 [x] S Mt 27:32 [y] S Mt 14:1
13:2 [z] S Ac 8:29 [a] Ac 14:26 [b] Ac 9:15; 22:21
13:3 [c] S Ac 6:6 [d] Ac 14:26
13:4 [e] ver 2,3 [f] Ac 4:36
13:5 [g] S Heb 4:12 [h] S Ac 9:20 [i] S Ac 12:12
13:6 [j] Ac 8:9 [k] S Mt 7:15
13:7 [l] ver 8,12; Ac 18:12; 19:38
13:8 [m] Ac 8:9 [n] S ver 7 [o] Isa 30:11; Ac 6:7

[a] 25 Some manuscripts *to*

12:20 *Tyre and Sidon.* The leading cities of Phoenicia (Lebanon today). They were dependent on the grainfields of Galilee for their food. *Blastus.* The treasurer; not otherwise known.

12:21 *On the appointed day.* A festival Herod was celebrating in honor of Claudius Caesar (Josephus, *Antiquities*, 19.8.2). *wearing his royal robes.* The historian Josephus describes a silver robe, dazzling bright, that Herod wore that day. When people acclaimed him a god, he did not deny it. He was seized with violent pains, was carried out and died five days later (Josephus, *Antiquities*, 19.8.2).

12:23 *angel of the Lord.* See note on v. 7. *eaten by worms.* A miserable death associated with Herod's acceptance of acclaim to be divine, but may also be seen as divine retribution for his persecution of the church.

12:24 *the word of God ... spread.* Third summary report of progress (see 6:7; 9:31). Three more follow (16:5; 19:20; 28:31).

12:25 *John ... Mark.* See v. 12. He was perhaps the young man who fled on the night of Jesus' arrest (Mk 14:51–52). He wrote the second Gospel (see Introduction to Mark: Author; John Mark in the NT) and accompanied Barnabas and Saul on the first part of their first missionary journey (see notes on 15:38–39).

13:1 *prophets.* See note on 11:27. The special gift of inspiration experienced by OT prophets (Dt 18:18–20; 2Pe 1:21) was known in the NT as well (2:17–18; 1Co 14:29–32; Eph 3:5). The prophets are second to the apostles in Paul's lists (1Co 12:28–29; Eph 2:20; 4:11; but cf. Lk 11:49; Ro 12:6; 1Co 12:10). *teachers.* See 11:26; 15:35; 18:11; 20:20; 28:31; 1Co 12:28–29; Eph 4:11. *Barnabas ... Saul.* The church leaders at Antioch, perhaps listed in the order of their importance. *Barnabas.* See note on 4:36. He was sent originally to Antioch by the church in Jerusalem (11:22), had recently returned from taking alms to Jerusalem (12:25) and was a recognized leader in the church at Antioch. *Simeon called Niger.* "Simeon" suggests Jewish background; in that case, Niger (Latin for "black") may indicate his dark complexion. *Lucius of Cyrene.* Lucius is a Latin name. In the second group of preachers coming to Antioch, some were from Cyrene (11:20), capital of Libya (see 6:9 and note). *Manaen.* In Hebrew, Menahem. He was the foster brother or intimate friend of Herod Antipas.

13:2 *worshiping the Lord and fasting.* Paul's first missionary journey did not result from a planning session but from the Spirit's initiative as the leaders worshiped (see v. 4). The communication from the Holy Spirit may have come through the prophets.

13:3 *placed their hands on them.* For the purpose of separating the two for the designated work (see 14:26 for the completion of the mission). Fasting and prayer accompany this appointment (see 14:23; cf. Lk 2:37).

13:4—14:28 Paul's first missionary journey (see map, p. 1704).

13:4 See map No. 13 at the end of this study Bible. *Seleucia.* The seaport of Antioch (16 miles to the west, and 5 miles upstream from the mouth of the Orontes River). *Cyprus.* Many Jews lived there, and the gospel had already been preached there (11:19–20; see note on 11:19).

13:5 *Salamis.* A town on the east coast of the central plain of Cyprus, near modern Famagusta. *John.* John Mark, a cousin of Barnabas (see 12:25; Col 4:10 and note). *helper.* In what way we are not told. Some hold that he served as a catechist for new converts, but Luke seems to use the term in a broader sense (see 26:16; Lk 1:2 ["servants"]).

13:6 *Paphos.* At the western end of Cyprus, nearly 100 miles from Salamis. It was the headquarters for Roman rule. *Bar-Jesus.* "Bar" is Aramaic for "son of"; "Jesus" is derived from the Greek for "Joshua" (see NIV text note on Mt 1:21).

13:7 *proconsul.* Since Cyprus was a Roman senatorial province, a proconsul was assigned to it. *Sergius Paulus.* See chart, p. 1667.

13:8 *Elymas.* A Semitic name meaning "sorcerer" or "magician" or "wise man" (probably a self-assumed designation).

9 Then Saul, who was also called Paul,
filled with the Holy Spirit,[p] looked straight
at Elymas and said, 10 "You are a child of
the devil[q] and an enemy of everything that
is right! You are full of all kinds of deceit
and trickery. Will you never stop perverting the right ways of the Lord?[r] 11 Now the
hand of the Lord is against you.[s] You are
going to be blind, and for a time you will
be unable to see the light of the sun."[t]
Immediately mist and darkness came
over him, and he groped about, seeking
someone to lead him by the hand. 12 When
the proconsul[u] saw what had happened,
he believed, for he was amazed at the
teaching about the Lord.

In Pisidian Antioch

13 From Paphos,[v] Paul and his companions sailed to Perga in Pamphylia,[w] where
John[x] left them to return to Jerusalem.
14 From Perga they went on to Pisidian
Antioch.[y] On the Sabbath[z] they entered
the synagogue[a] and sat down. 15 After the
reading from the Law[b] and the Prophets,
the synagogue rulers sent word to them,

13:9 [p] S Lk 1:15 **13:10** [q] Mt 13:38; Jn 8:44 [r] Hos 14:9 **13:11** [s] Ex 9:3; 1Sa 5:6, 7; Ps 32:4 [t] Ge 19:10, 11; 2Ki 6:18 **13:12** [u] S ver 7 **13:13** [v] ver 6 [w] S Ac 2:10 [x] S Ac 12:12 **13:14** [y] Ac 14:19, 21 [z] ver 27, 42, 44; Ac 16:13; 18:4 [a] S Ac 9:20 **13:15** [b] Ac 15:21

13:9 *Saul ... called Paul.* The names mean "asked [of God]" and "little" respectively. It was customary to have a given name, in this case Saul (Hebrew, Jewish background), and a later name, in this case Paul (Roman, Hellenistic background). From now on Saul is called Paul in Acts. This may be due to Saul's success in preaching to "Paulus" (v. 7) or to the fact that he is now entering the Gentile phase of his ministry. The order in which they are mentioned now changes from "Barnabas and Saul" (v. 7) to "Paul and Barnabas" for the most part (e.g., v. 42).

13:11 *hand of the Lord.* See note on 11:21. *You are going to be blind.* Cf. Paul's experience in 9:8–18.

13:12 *he believed.* He was convinced by the miracle and the message.

13:13 *Perga in Pamphylia.* Perga was the capital of Pamphylia, a coastal province of Asia Minor between the provinces of Lycia and Cilicia, and was 5 miles inland and 12 miles east of the important seaport Attalia (see map, below). *John left them.* See 12:25 and note. Homesickness to get back to Jerusalem, an illness of Paul necessitating a change in plans and a trip to Galatia, and a change in leadership from Barnabas to Paul have all been suggested as reasons for John Mark's return. Paul's dissatisfaction with his departure is noted later (15:37–39).

13:14–41 Paul and Barnabas in the synagogue of Pisidian Antioch. For another account of a synagogue service see Lk 4:16–21.

13:14 *Pisidian.* See note on 14:24. *Antioch.* Named after Antiochus, king of Syria after the death of Alexander the Great. It was 110 miles from Perga, 3,600 feet above sea level, and was at the hub of good roads and trade. The city had a large Jewish population. It was a Roman colony, which meant that a contingent of retired military men was settled there. They were given free land and were made citizens of the city of Rome, with all the accompanying privileges. *synagogue.* Paul's regular practice was to begin his preaching in the synagogue as long as the Jews would allow it (see v. 5; 14:1; 17:1,10,17; 18:4,19; 19:8). His reason for doing so was grounded in his understanding of God's redemptive plan (see v. 46; Ro 1:16 and note; 2:9–10 and note on 2:9; see also Ro 9–11). He was not neglecting his Gentile mission, for the God-fearers ("Gentiles who worship God," v. 16; see note on 10:2) were part of the audience. Moreover, the synagogue provided a ready-made preaching situation with a building, regularly scheduled meetings and a people who knew the OT Scriptures. It was customary to invite visitors, and especially visiting rabbis (such as Paul), to address the gathering.

13:15 *the Law and the Prophets.* Sections from the OT were read, followed by exposition and exhortation. *synagogue*

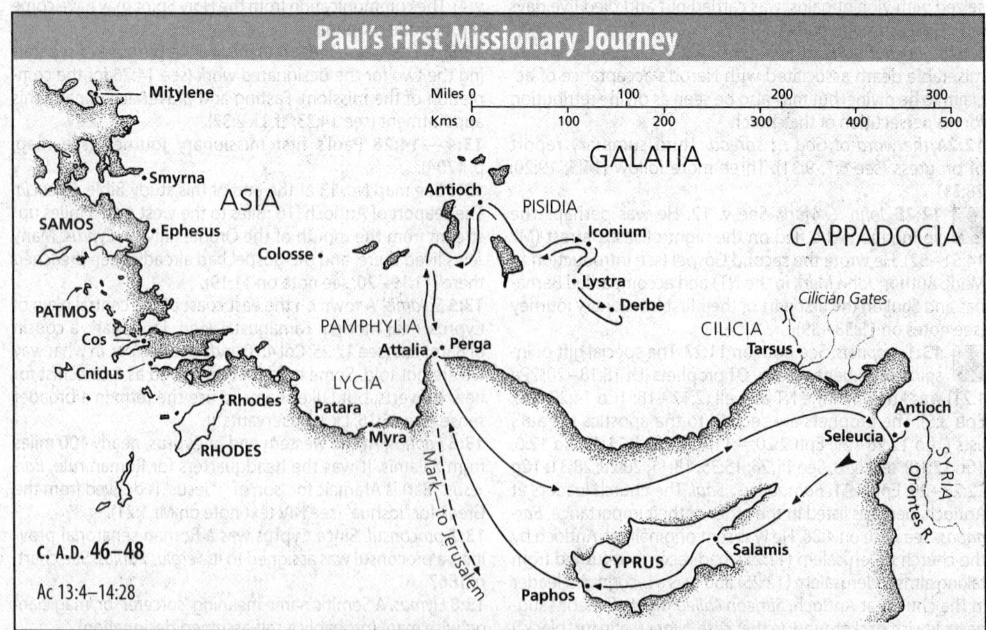

saying, "Brothers, if you have a message
of encouragement for the people, please
speak."
16Standing up, Paul motioned with his
hand[c] and said: "Men of Israel and you
Gentiles who worship God, listen to me!
17The God of the people of Israel chose our
fathers; he made the people prosper during their stay in Egypt, with mighty power he led them out of that country,[d] 18he
endured their conduct[a][e] for about forty
years in the desert,[f] 19he overthrew seven
nations in Canaan[g] and gave their land to
his people[h] as their inheritance.[i] 20All this
took about 450 years.
"After this, God gave them judges[j] until
the time of Samuel the prophet.[k] 21Then
the people asked for a king,[l] and he gave
them Saul[m] son of Kish, of the tribe of
Benjamin,[n] who ruled forty years. 22Af-
ter removing Saul,[o] he made David their
king.[p] He testified concerning him: 'I have
found David son of Jesse a man after my
own heart;[q] he will do everything I want
him to do.'[r]
23"From this man's descendants[s] God
has brought to Israel the Savior[t] Jesus,[u]
as he promised.[v] 24Before the coming of
Jesus, John preached repentance and baptism to all the people of Israel.[w] 25As John
was completing his work,[x] he said: 'Who
do you think I am? I am not that one.[y] No,
but he is coming after me, whose sandals
I am not worthy to untie.'[z]
26"Brothers,[a] children of Abraham,[b] and
you God-fearing Gentiles, it is to us that
this message of salvation[c] has been sent.
27The people of Jerusalem and their rulers did not recognize Jesus,[d] yet in condemning him they fulfilled the words of
the prophets[e] that are read every Sabbath.
28Though they found no proper ground for
a death sentence, they asked Pilate to have
him executed.[f] 29When they had carried
out all that was written about him,[g] they
took him down from the tree[h] and laid him
in a tomb.[i] 30But God raised him from the
dead,[j] 31and for many days he was seen
by those who had traveled with him from
Galilee to Jerusalem.[k] They are now his
witnesses[l] to our people.
32"We tell you the good news:[m] What
God promised our fathers[n] 33he has fulfilled for us, their children, by raising
up Jesus.[o] As it is written in the second
Psalm:

"'You are my Son;
today I have become your Father.[b]'[c][p]

34The fact that God raised him from the
dead, never to decay, is stated in these
words:

"'I will give you the holy and sure
blessings promised to David.'[d][q]

35So it is stated elsewhere:

"'You will not let your Holy One see
decay.'[e][r]

36"For when David had served God's
purpose in his own generation, he fell
asleep;[s] he was buried with his fathers[t]
and his body decayed. 37But the one
whom God raised from the dead[u] did not
see decay.
38"Therefore, my brothers, I want you to
know that through Jesus the forgiveness
of sins is proclaimed to you.[v] 39Through
him everyone who believes[w] is justified
from everything you could not be justified
from by the law of Moses.[x] 40Take care that
what the prophets have said does not happen to you:

41"'Look, you scoffers,
wonder and perish,
for I am going to do something in your
days
that you would never believe,
even if someone told you.'[f]"[y]

42As Paul and Barnabas were leaving
the synagogue,[z] the people invited them
to speak further about these things on the
next Sabbath. 43When the congregation
was dismissed, many of the Jews and devout converts to Judaism followed Paul and
Barnabas, who talked with them and urged
them to continue in the grace of God.[a]

a 18 Some manuscripts *and cared for them* *b 33* Or *have begotten you* *c 33* Psalm 2:7 *d 34* Isaiah 55:3 *e 35* Psalm 16:10 *f 41* Hab. 1:5

13:16 cS Ac 12:17 **13:17** dEx 6:6,7; Dt 7:6-8 **13:18** eDt 1:31 fNu 14:33; Ps 95:10; Ac 7:36 **13:19** gDt 7:1 hJos 19:51; Ac 7:45 iPs 78:55 **13:20** jJdg 2:16 k1Sa 3:19,20; Ac 3:24 **13:21** l1Sa 8:5,19 m1Sa 10:1 n1Sa 9:1,2 **13:22** o1Sa 15:23,26 p1Sa 16:13; Ps 89:20 q1Sa 13:14; Jer 3:15 rIsa 44:28 **13:23** sS Mt 1:1 tS Lk 2:11 uMt 1:21 vver 32; 2Sa 7:11; 22:51; Jer 30:9 **13:24** wS Mk 1:4 **13:25** xAc 20:24 yJn 1:20 zMt 3:11; Jn 1:27 **13:26** aS Ac 22:5 bS Lk 3:8 cAc 4:12; 28:28 **13:27** dAc 3:17 eS Lk 24:27; S Mt 1:22 **13:28** fMt 27:20-25; Ac 3:14 **13:29** gS Mt 1:22; Lk 18:31 hS Ac 5:30 iLk 23:53 **13:30** jS Mt 16:21; 28:6; S Ac 2:24 **13:31** kMt 28:16 lS Lk 24:48 **13:32** mIsa 40:9; 52:7; Ac 5:42; 8:35; 10:36; 14:7,15,21; 17:18 nAc 26:6; Ro 1:2; 4:13; 9:4 **13:33** oS Ac 2:24 pPs 2:7; S Mt 3:17 **13:34** qIsa 55:3 **13:35** rPs 16:10; Ac 2:27 **13:36** sS Mt 9:24 t2Sa 7:12; 1Ki 2:10; 2Ch 29:28; Ac 2:29 **13:37** uS Ac 2:24 **13:38** vS Lk 24:47; Ac 2:38 **13:39** wS Jn 3:15 xS Ro 3:28 **13:41** yHab 1:5 **13:42** zver 14 **13:43** aS Ac 11:23; 14:22; S Ro 3:24

rulers. See note on Mk 5:22. *message of encouragement.* See Introduction to Hebrews: Literary Form.

13:20 *about 450 years.* The 400 years of the "stay in Egypt" (v. 17; see note on 7:6) plus the 40 years in the desert and the time between the crossing of the Jordan and the distribution of the land (see Jos 14–19).

13:23 *as he promised.* See, e.g., Isa 11:1–16.

13:25 *John ... said.* See Mt 3:11; Mk 1:7; Lk 3:16; Jn 1:20,27.

13:26 *God-fearing Gentiles.* See note on v. 14.

13:28 *no proper ground for a death sentence.* Cf. Jn 19:4 and note.

13:29–31 *tree ... tomb ... God raised ... witnesses.* See note on 3:15.

13:31 *many days.* Forty days (see 1:3).

13:33 *today I have become your Father.* Here refers to the resurrection of Jesus (see NIV text note here and note on Ps 2:7–9; cf. Ro 1:4).

13:35 *not let your Holy One see decay.* Quoted also in Peter's sermon at Pentecost (see notes on 2:27; Ps 16:10).

13:39 *justified from.* Justification combines two aspects: (1) the forgiveness of sins (here); (2) the gift of righteousness (see Ro 3:21–22 and note on 3:24).

13:43 *continue in the grace of God.* See Tit 2:11–12 and note on 2:12.

44On the next Sabbath almost the whole
city gathered to hear the word of the Lord.
45When the Jews saw the crowds, they
were filled with jealousy and talked abusively[b] against what Paul was saying.[c]
46Then Paul and Barnabas answered
them boldly: "We had to speak the word
of God to you first.[d] Since you reject it and
do not consider yourselves worthy of eternal life, we now turn to the Gentiles.[e] 47For
this is what the Lord has commanded us:

" 'I have made you[a] a light for the
Gentiles,[f]
that you[a] may bring salvation to the
ends of the earth.'[b]"[g]

48When the Gentiles heard this, they
were glad and honored the word of the
Lord;[h] and all who were appointed for
eternal life believed.
49The word of the Lord[i] spread through
the whole region. 50But the Jews incited the
God-fearing women of high standing and
the leading men of the city. They stirred
up persecution against Paul and Barnabas,
and expelled them from their region.[j] 51So
they shook the dust from their feet[k] in protest against them and went to Iconium.[l]
52And the disciples[m] were filled with joy
and with the Holy Spirit.[n]

In Iconium

14 At Iconium[o] Paul and Barnabas
went as usual into the Jewish synagogue.[p] There they spoke so effectively
that a great number[q] of Jews and Gentiles
believed. 2But the Jews who refused to
believe stirred up the Gentiles and poisoned their minds against the brothers.[r]
3So Paul and Barnabas spent considerable
time there, speaking boldly[s] for the Lord,
who confirmed the message of his grace
by enabling them to do miraculous signs
and wonders.[t] 4The people of the city were
divided; some sided with the Jews, others
with the apostles.[u] 5There was a plot afoot
among the Gentiles and Jews,[v] together
with their leaders, to mistreat them and
stone them.[w] 6But they found out about it
and fled[x] to the Lycaonian cities of Lystra
and Derbe and to the surrounding country, 7where they continued to preach[y] the
good news.[z]

In Lystra and Derbe

8In Lystra there sat a man crippled in
his feet, who was lame from birth[a] and
had never walked. 9He listened to Paul as
he was speaking. Paul looked directly at
him, saw that he had faith to be healed[b]
10and called out, "Stand up on your feet!"[c]
At that, the man jumped up and began to
walk.[d]
11When the crowd saw what Paul had
done, they shouted in the Lycaonian language, "The gods have come down to us
in human form!"[e] 12Barnabas they called
Zeus, and Paul they called Hermes because
he was the chief speaker.[f] 13The priest of
Zeus, whose temple was just outside the
city, brought bulls and wreaths to the city
gates because he and the crowd wanted to
offer sacrifices to them.

[a] 47 The Greek is singular. [b] 47 Isaiah 49:6

13:45 [b] Ac 18:6; 1Pe 4:4; Jude 10 [c] S 1Th 2:16
13:46 [d] ver 26; Ac 3:26 [e] Mt 21:41; Ac 18:6; 22:21; 26:20; 28:28; Ro 11:11
13:47 [f] S Lk 2:32 [g] Isa 49:6
13:48 [h] ver 49; Ac 8:25; 15:35,36; 19:10,20
13:49 [i] S ver 48
13:50 [j] S 1Th 2:16
13:51 [k] S Mt 10:14 [l] Ac 14:1,19,21; 16:2; 2Ti 3:11
13:52 [m] S Ac 11:26 [n] S Lk 1:15
14:1 [o] S Ac 13:51 [p] S Ac 9:20 [q] S Ac 2:41
14:2 [r] S Ac 1:16
14:3 [s] S Ac 4:29 [t] S Jn 4:48
14:4 [u] Ac 17:4,5; 28:24
14:5 [v] S Ac 20:3 [w] ver 19
14:6 [x] Mt 10:23
14:7 [y] Ac 16:10 [z] ver 15,21; S Ac 13:32
14:8 [a] Ac 3:2
14:9 [b] Mt 9:28,29; 13:58
14:10 [c] Eze 2:1 [d] Ac 3:8
14:11 [e] Ac 8:10; 28:6
14:12 [f] Ex 7:1

13:46 *had to speak ... to you first.* Since the gospel came from and was for the Jews first and since Paul was himself a Jew with great compassion for his people (Ro 1:16; 9:1–5; 10:1–3). See note on v. 14.

13:47 *you.* See NIV text note; see also 9:15–16; 22:14–15,21; 26:15–18. Paul extends the prophetic word concerning the Messianic "servant" (Isa 49:6) to those who continue that servant's mission (cf. Isa 54:17 and note).

13:48 *all who were appointed for eternal life believed.* Possession of eternal life involves both human faith and divine appointment.

13:51 *shook the dust.* To show the severance of responsibility and the repudiation of those who had rejected their message and had brought suffering to the servants of the Lord (see note on Lk 9:5). *Iconium.* Modern Konya; it was an important crossroads and agricultural center in the central plain of the province of Galatia.

13:52 *filled ... with the Holy Spirit.* See note on 2:4.

14:1 *went as usual into the ... synagogue.* See note on 13:14. *great number.* At first there was good success, then bitter opposition from the Jews (v. 2). But these evidently failed in their initial attempt, for Paul and Barnabas remained there a considerable time (v. 3). A second wave of persecution was planned, involving violence (v. 5).

14:3 *confirmed ... by ... miraculous signs.* A major purpose of miracles was to confirm the truth of the words and the approval of God (cf. 2:22 and note).

14:4 *apostles.* Both Paul and Barnabas are called apostles (see v. 14; see also note on Mk 6:30). The term is used here not of the Twelve but in the broader sense to refer to persons sent on a mission, i.e., missionaries (see 13:2–3).

14:5 *stone them.* A Jewish mode of execution for blasphemy (see note on Jn 10:31). Probably mob action was planned here.

14:6 *Lycaonian cities.* Lycaonia was a district east of Pisidia, north of the Taurus Mountains. It was part of the Roman province of Galatia. *Lystra.* A Roman colony (see note on 13:14) and probable home of Timothy (see 16:1 and note—though he was known in Iconium as well [see 16:2]), it was about 20 miles from Iconium and 130 miles from Antioch. *Derbe.* About 60 miles from Lystra; home of Gaius (see 20:4 and note on 14:20).

14:12 *Zeus ... Hermes.* Zeus was the patron god of Lystra, and his temple was there. People who came to bring sacrifices to Zeus apparently decided to make an offering to Paul and Barnabas instead. The identification of Zeus with Barnabas may indicate that his appearance was more imposing, and Paul was identified as the god Hermes (the Roman Mercury) because he was the spokesman (see 28:6). This incident may have been occasioned by an ancient legend that told of a supposed visit to the same general area by Zeus and Hermes. They were, however, not recognized by anyone except an old couple. So the people of Lystra were determined not to allow such an oversight to happen again.

14:13 *city gates.* The Greek for this expression can refer to the temple gates, the city gates or house gates.

14But when the apostles Barnabas and
Paul heard of this, they tore their clothes[g]
and rushed out into the crowd, shouting:
15"Men, why are you doing this? We too
are only men,[h] human like you. We are
bringing you good news,[i] telling you to
turn from these worthless things[j] to the
living God,[k] who made heaven and earth[l]
and sea and everything in them.[m] 16In the
past, he let[n] all nations go their own way.[o]
17Yet he has not left himself without testimony:[p] He has shown kindness by giving
you rain from heaven and crops in their
seasons;[q] he provides you with plenty
of food and fills your hearts with joy."[r]
18Even with these words, they had difficulty keeping the crowd from sacrificing
to them.

19Then some Jews[s] came from Antioch
and Iconium[t] and won the crowd over.
They stoned Paul[u] and dragged him outside the city, thinking he was dead. 20But
after the disciples[v] had gathered around
him, he got up and went back into the
city. The next day he and Barnabas left
for Derbe.

The Return to Antioch in Syria

21They preached the good news[w] in that
city and won a large number[x] of disciples.
Then they returned to Lystra, Iconium[y]
and Antioch, 22strengthening the disciples and encouraging them to remain true
to the faith.[z] "We must go through many
hardships[a] to enter the kingdom of God,"
they said. 23Paul and Barnabas appointed elders[a][b] for them in each church and,
with prayer and fasting,[c] committed them
to the Lord,[d] in whom they had put their
trust. 24After going through Pisidia, they
came into Pamphylia,[e] 25and when they
had preached the word in Perga, they went
down to Attalia.

26From Attalia they sailed back to Antioch,[f] where they had been committed to
the grace of God[g] for the work they had
now completed.[h] 27On arriving there, they
gathered the church together and reported all that God had done through them[i]
and how he had opened the door[j] of faith
to the Gentiles. 28And they stayed there a
long time with the disciples.[k]

The Council at Jerusalem

15 Some men[l] came down from Judea
to Antioch and were teaching the
brothers:[m] "Unless you are circumcised,[n]
according to the custom taught by Moses,[o] you cannot be saved." 2This brought
Paul and Barnabas into sharp dispute and
debate with them. So Paul and Barnabas
were appointed, along with some other
believers, to go up to Jerusalem[p] to see
the apostles and elders[q] about this question. 3The church sent them on their way,
and as they traveled through Phoenicia[r]
and Samaria, they told how the Gentiles

14:14 [g]S Mk 14:63 **14:15** [h]S Ac 10:26 [i]ver 7,21; S Ac 13:32 [j]1Sa 12:21; 1Th 1:9 [k]S Mt 16:16 [l]Ge 1:1 [m]Ps 146:6; Rev 14:7 **14:16** [n]Ac 17:30 [o]Ps 81:12; Mic 4:5 **14:17** [p]Ro 1:20 [q]Dt 11:14; Job 5:10; Ps 65:10 [r]Ps 4:7 **14:19** [s]Ac 13:45 [t]S Ac 13:51 [u]2Co 11:25; 2Ti 3:11 **14:20** [v]ver 22,28; S Ac 11:26 **14:21** [w]S Ac 13:32 [x]S Ac 2:41 [y]S Ac 13:51 **14:22** [z]Ac 11:23; 13:43 [a]Jn 16:33; 1Th 3:3; 2Ti 3:12 **14:23** [b]S Ac 11:30 [c]Ac 13:3 [d]Ac 20:32 **14:24** [e]S Ac 2:10 **14:26** [f]S Ac 11:19 [g]S Ac 11:23 [h]Ac 13:1,3 **14:27** [i]Ac 15:4,12; 21:19 [j]1Co 16:9; 2Co 2:12; Col 4:3; Rev 3:8 **14:28** [k]S Ac 11:26

[a] *23* Or *Barnabas ordained elders*; or *Barnabas had elders elected*

15:1 [l]ver 24; Gal 2:12 [m]S Ac 1:16 [n]ver 5; Gal 5:2,3 [o]S Ac 6:14 **15:2** [p]Gal 2:2 [q]S Ac 11:30 **15:3** [r]Ac 11:19

14:14 *tore their clothes.* A Jewish way of expressing great anguish (see Ge 37:29,34 and note on 37:34).

14:15 *worthless things.* Used in the OT to denote false gods (see 1Sa 12:21).

14:16 See 17:30 and note.

14:19 *They stoned Paul.* Inside the city rather than at the usual place of execution outside the walls (7:58; see Gal 6:17 and note).

14:20 *disciples had gathered around him.* Young Timothy may have been present (see 2Ti 3:10–11 and note on 3:11). *got up ... next day ... left.* Luke's description of Paul's quick recovery from stoning suggests a miracle (cf. 28:5–6). *Derbe.* A border town in the southeastern part of the Lycaonian region of Galatia (see note on v. 6). An inscription naming the city has been discovered about 30 miles east of what was previously thought to be the city site.

14:21 *they returned.* Not by the shorter route through the Taurus Mountains but to the cities where they had established churches (see v. 22).

14:22 *many hardships.* See Php 1:29 and note.

14:23 *appointed.* The Greek for this word (used also in 2Co 8:19) can mean (1) to stretch out the hand, (2) to appoint by show of hands or (3) to appoint or elect without regard to the method. In 6:6 the appointment of the Seven included selection by the church and presentation to the apostles, who prayed and laid their hands on them. Because these were new churches, at least partly pagan in background, Paul and Barnabas may have both selected and appointed the elders.

14:24 *Pisidia.* A district about 120 miles long and 50 miles wide, north of Pamphylia (13:13–14). Bandits frequented the region (see perhaps 2Co 11:26). *Pamphylia.* A district 80 miles long and 20 miles at the widest part, on the southern coast of Asia Minor. After A.D. 74 Pisidia was included in the Roman province of Pamphylia (see 13:13).

14:25 *Perga.* See note on 13:13. *Attalia.* The best harbor on the coast of Pamphylia (see 13:13).

14:26 *Antioch.* See 11:20; see also note on 11:19.

14:27 *opened the door of faith.* God had brought Gentiles to faith—had, as it were, opened the door for them to believe (cf. 11:18).

14:28 *long time.* Probably more than a year.

15:1 *Some men.* Probably from "the party of the Pharisees" (v. 5). These were believers who insisted that before anyone could become a true Christian they must keep the law of Moses, and the test of such compliance was circumcision. *from Judea.* Meant that these Judaizers (or legalists) were given a hearing, not that they correctly represented the apostles and elders of Jerusalem (cf. v. 24).

15:2 *go up to Jerusalem.* See notes on 12:1; Gal 2:1. Those who hold that Gal 2:1–10 refers to the famine visit of 11:27–30; 12:25 argue that since Gal 2:2 says that the visit mentioned there was occasioned by a revelation, it must refer to Agabus's prediction of the coming famine (11:27–28). Those who believe that Gal 2:1–10 refers to the Jerusalem council visit of 15:1–22 assert that the famine visit occurred at the time of Herod Agrippa's death in A.D. 44 (11:27–30; 12:25). Thus Saul's conversion, which was 14 years earlier (Gal 2:1), would have occurred in 30, the probable year of Christ's crucifixion—which obviously seems too early.

had been converted.[s] This news made all
the brothers very glad. 4When they came
to Jerusalem, they were welcomed by the
church and the apostles and elders, to
whom they reported everything God had
done through them.[t]
5Then some of the believers who belonged to the party[u] of the Pharisees[v]
stood up and said, "The Gentiles must be
circumcised and required to obey the law
of Moses."[w]
6The apostles and elders met to consider
this question. 7After much discussion, Peter got up and addressed them: "Brothers,
you know that some time ago God made
a choice among you that the Gentiles
might hear from my lips the message of
the gospel and believe.[x] 8God, who knows
the heart,[y] showed that he accepted them
by giving the Holy Spirit to them,[z] just as
he did to us. 9He made no distinction between us and them,[a] for he purified their
hearts by faith.[b] 10Now then, why do you
try to test God[c] by putting on the necks of
the disciples a yoke[d] that neither we nor
our fathers have been able to bear? 11No!
We believe it is through the grace[e] of our
Lord Jesus that we are saved, just as they
are."
12The whole assembly became silent as
they listened to Barnabas and Paul telling
about the miraculous signs and wonders[f]
God had done among the Gentiles through
them.[g] 13When they finished, James[h] spoke
up: "Brothers, listen to me. 14Simon[a] has
described to us how God at first showed
his concern by taking from the Gentiles
a people for himself.[i] 15The words of the
prophets are in agreement with this, as it
is written:

16" 'After this I will return
and rebuild David's fallen tent.
Its ruins I will rebuild,
and I will restore it,
17that the remnant of men may seek the Lord,
and all the Gentiles who bear my name,
says the Lord, who does these things'[b][j]
18 that have been known for ages.[c][k]

19"It is my judgment, therefore, that we
should not make it difficult for the Gentiles who are turning to God. 20Instead we
should write to them, telling them to abstain from food polluted by idols,[l] from
sexual immorality,[m] from the meat of
strangled animals and from blood.[n] 21For
Moses has been preached in every city

15:3 [s]Ac 14:27 **15:4** [t]ver 12; Ac 14:27; 21:19 **15:5** [u]Ac 5:17 [v]Mt 3:7 [w]ver 1 **15:7** [x]Ac 10:1-48 **15:8** [y]S Rev 2:23 [z]S Ac 10:44, 47 **15:9** [a]Ac 10:28, 34; 11:12 [b]Ac 10:43 **15:10** [c]Ac 5:9 [d]S Mt 23:4; Gal 5:1 **15:11** [e]S Ro 3:24; Gal 2:16; Eph 2:5-8 **15:12** [f]S Jn 4:48 [g]ver 4; Ac 14:27; 21:19 **15:13** [h]Ac 12:17; 21:18; 1Co 15:7; Gal 1:19; 2:9, 12 **15:14** [i]2Pe 1:1 **15:17** [j]Am 9:11, 12 **15:18** [k]Isa 45:21 **15:20** [l]1Co 8:7-13; 10:14-28; Rev 2:14, 20 [m]1Co 10:7, 8; Rev 2:14, 20 [n]ver 29; Ge 9:4; Lev 3:17; 7:26; 17:10-13; 19:26; Dt 12:16, 23

[a] 14 Greek *Simeon,* a variant of *Simon*; that is, Peter [b] 17 Amos 9:11,12 [c] 17,18 Some manuscripts *things'— / 18known to the Lord for ages is his work*

15:4–22 The sequence of meetings described in vv. 4–22 is: (1) a general meeting of welcome and report (vv. 4–5); (2) a meeting of the leaders (perhaps to one side) while the church was still assembled (vv. 6–11); (3) a meeting of the apostles, the elders and the whole assembly (vv. 12–22).
15:4 The first meeting was a report, cordially received, about the work done among the Gentiles.
15:5 *believers who belonged to the party of the Pharisees.* Some Pharisees became Christians and brought their Judaic beliefs with them. They believed that Gentiles must first become converts to Judaism and be circumcised (see v. 1), and then they would be eligible to be saved by faith. Perhaps some of them had gone to Antioch and now returned to present their case.
15:7 *Peter got up.* After a period of considerable discussion by the apostles and elders, Peter addressed them. *Gentiles might hear.* Peter's argument was his own experience: God had sent him to preach to the Gentiles (see 10:28–29 and note on 10:28).
15:8 *giving the Holy Spirit to them.* The irrefutable proof of God's acceptance (see 10:44,47 and note; 11:17–18).
15:9 *purified their hearts by faith.* Peter's way of saying what Paul affirmed (Ro 5:1; cf. Gal 2:15–16).
15:10 *yoke.* The law (see Gal 5:1 and note; cf. Mt 11:28–29 and notes).
15:11 *through the grace of our Lord.* No circumcision was required. *we are saved, just as they are.* See Ro 3:9.
15:12 *assembly became silent.* See note on vv. 4–22. Apparently the people had remained in place while the apostles and elders met. The assembly had not remained quiet during that time, but now they became silent to listen to the leaders. *Barnabas and Paul.* The order here (see also 13:7; 14:12,14) puts Barnabas first (perhaps reflecting his importance in Jerusalem), whereas in the account of the missionary journey the order was usually "Paul and Barnabas" after the events on the island of Cyprus (13:42–43,46,50; 14:1,3,20,23). *miraculous signs and wonders.* See 8:19–20; 14:3.
15:13 *James.* The Lord's brother (see note on 12:17; see also Introduction to James: Author). His argument added proof from Scripture.
15:14 *Simon.* Peter (see v. 7). James uses Peter's Hebrew name in its Hebrew form (Simeon; see NIV text note). *a people for himself.* A new community largely made up of Gentiles but including Jews as well (see Jn 10:16 and note; cf. 1Pe 2:9–10).
15:15 *prophets.* Specifically Am 9:11–12 (see NIV text note on Am 9:12).
15:16 *After this I will return.* Some have taken this quotation from Amos as setting forth a sequence of the end times, including (1) the church age (taking out "a people for himself," v. 14), (2) the restoration of Israel as a nation (v. 16) and (3) the final salvation of the Gentiles (vv. 17–18). Others declare that the quotation merely confirms God's intent to save Gentiles.
15:18 *for ages.* Since OT times (see Ro 15:9 and note).
15:19 *not make it difficult.* Circumcision was not required, but four other stipulations were laid down (see note on v. 20). These were in areas where the Gentiles had particular weaknesses and where the Jews were particularly repulsed by Gentile violations. It would help both the individual and the relationship between Gentile and Jew if these requirements were observed. They involved divine directives that the Jews believed were given before the Mosaic laws.
15:20 *food polluted by idols.* See v. 29; 1Co 8:7–13; Rev 2:14, 20. *sexual immorality.* A sin taken too lightly by the Greeks and also associated with certain pagan religious festivals. *meat of strangled animals.* Thus retaining the blood that was forbidden to be eaten (see Ge 9:4). *blood.* Expressly forbidden in Jewish law (see Lev 17:10–12). Reference here may be to consuming blood apart from meat.

from the earliest times and is read in the synagogues on every Sabbath."[o]

The Council's Letter to Gentile Believers

22Then the apostles and elders,[p] with the whole church, decided to choose some of their own men and send them to Antioch[q] with Paul and Barnabas. They chose Judas (called Barsabbas) and Silas,[r] two men who were leaders among the brothers. 23With them they sent the following letter:

The apostles and elders, your brothers,

To the Gentile believers in Antioch,[s] Syria[t] and Cilicia:[u]

Greetings.[v]

24We have heard that some went out from us without our authorization and disturbed you, troubling your minds by what they said.[w] 25So we all agreed to choose some men and send them to you with our dear friends Barnabas and Paul— 26men who have risked their lives[x] for the name of our Lord Jesus Christ. 27Therefore we are sending Judas and Silas[y] to confirm by word of mouth what we are writing. 28It seemed good to the Holy Spirit[z] and to us not to burden you with anything beyond the following requirements: 29You are to abstain from food sacrificed to idols, from blood, from the meat of strangled animals and from sexual immorality.[a] You will do well to avoid these things.

Farewell.

30The men were sent off and went down to Antioch, where they gathered the church together and delivered the letter. 31The people read it and were glad for its encouraging message. 32Judas and Silas,[b] who themselves were prophets,[c] said much to encourage and strengthen the brothers. 33After spending some time there, they were sent off by the brothers with the blessing of peace[d] to return to those who had sent them.[a] 35But Paul and Barnabas remained in Antioch, where they and many others taught and preached[e] the word of the Lord.[f]

Disagreement Between Paul and Barnabas

36Some time later Paul said to Barnabas, "Let us go back and visit the brothers in all the towns[g] where we preached the word of the Lord[h] and see how they are doing." 37Barnabas wanted to take John, also called Mark,[i] with them, 38but Paul did not think it wise to take him, because he had deserted them[j] in Pamphylia and had not continued with them in the work. 39They had such a sharp disagreement that they parted company. Barnabas took Mark and sailed for Cyprus, 40but Paul chose Silas[k] and left, commended by the brothers to the grace of the Lord.[l] 41He went through Syria[m] and Cilicia,[n] strengthening the churches.[o]

Timothy Joins Paul and Silas

16 He came to Derbe and then to Lystra,[p] where a disciple named Timothy[q] lived, whose mother was a Jewess

[a] 33 Some manuscripts *them,* [34]*but Silas decided to remain there*

15:21 [o]Ac 13:15; 2Co 3:14,15
15:22 [p]S Ac 11:30 [q]S Ac 11:19 [r]ver 27,32,40; Ac 16:19,25,29; 2Co 1:19; 1Th 1:1; 2Th 1:1; 1Pe 5:12
15:23 [s]ver 1; S Ac 11:19 [t]S Lk 2:2 [u]ver 41; S Ac 6:9 [v]Ac 23:25,26; Jas 1:1
15:24 [w]ver 1; Gal 1:7; 5:10
15:26 [x]Ac 9:23-25; 14:19; 1Co 15:30
15:27 [y]S ver 22
15:28 [z]Ac 5:32
15:29 [a]ver 20; Ac 21:25
15:32 [b]S ver 22 [c]S Ac 11:27
15:33 [d]1Sa 1:17; Mk 5:34; Lk 7:50; Ac 16:36; 1Co 16:11
15:35 [e]Ac 8:4 [f]S Ac 13:48
15:36 [g]Ac 13:4,13,14,51; 14:1,6,24,25 [h]S Ac 13:48
15:37 [i]S Ac 12:12
15:38 [j]Ac 13:13
15:40 [k]S ver 22 [l]S Ac 11:23
15:41 [m]ver 23; S Lk 2:2 [n]S Ac 6:9 [o]Ac 16:5
16:1 [p]Ac 14:6 [q]Ac 17:14; 18:5; 19:22; 20:4; Ro 16:21; 1Co 4:17; 16:10; 2Co 1:1,19; Php 1:1; 2:19; Col 1:1; 1Th 1:1; 3:2,6; 2Th 1:1; 1Ti 1:2,18; 2Ti 1:2,5,6; Phm 1

15:22 *apostles and elders, with the whole church.* Apparently there was unanimous agreement with the choice of messengers and with the contents of the letter (vv. 23–29). *Judas (called Barsabbas).* The same surname as that of Joseph Barsabbas (see 1:23 and note). The two may have been brothers. *Silas.* A leader in the Jerusalem church, a prophet (v. 32), a Roman citizen (16:37–38) and Paul's companion on his second missionary journey (15:40).
15:23 *in Antioch, Syria and Cilicia.* Antioch was the leading city of the combined provinces of Syria and Cilicia.
15:26 *risked their lives.* See 13:15; 14:2,5,19.
15:28 *seemed good to the Holy Spirit and to us.* Prior authority is given to the Spirit (whose working in the assembly is thus claimed), but there was also agreement among the apostles, elders and brothers (vv. 22–23).
15:29 *abstain from food … sexual immorality.* See note on v. 20.
15:32 *prophets.* One of the primary functions of prophets in the early church was, as here indicated, to encourage and strengthen believers (see notes on 11:27; 1Co 14:3).
15:33 *those who had sent them.* The Jerusalem church (see v. 22).
15:34 See NIV text note on v. 33.
15:36 *towns where we preached the word.* Towns of the first missionary journey (see 13:4—14:26).
15:38 *he had deserted them.* Mark had turned back at Perga and did not go to Antioch, Iconium, Lystra and Derbe (see note on 13:13).
15:39—18:22 Paul's second missionary journey (see map No. 13 at the end of this study Bible; see also map, p. 1711).
15:39 *they parted company.* Barnabas and Mark do not appear again in Acts. However, in 1Co 9:6 Paul names Barnabas as setting a noble example in working to support himself. Also in Gal 2:11–13 another scene is described in Antioch that includes Barnabas. Mark evidently returned from his work with Barnabas and became associated with Peter (see 1Pe 5:13 and note). During Paul's first imprisonment, Mark was included in Paul's group (see Col 4:10; Phm 24). By the end of Paul's life he came to admire Mark so much that he requested him to come to be with him during his final days (see 2Ti 4:11 and note; see also Introduction to Mark: John Mark in the NT). *Cyprus.* The island of Barnabas's birthplace (4:36).
15:40 *Silas.* Had returned to Jerusalem with Judas after delivering the Jerusalem letter (vv. 32–33). His presence in Antioch now indicates that, after reporting to those who had sent him, he came back to Antioch to participate in the church's work there.
16:1 *Derbe.* See notes on 14:6,20. Paul had approached Derbe on the first trip from the opposite direction, so

and a believer,[r] but whose father was a
Greek. 2The brothers[s] at Lystra and Iconium[t] spoke well of him. 3Paul wanted to
take him along on the journey, so he circumcised him because of the Jews who
lived in that area, for they all knew that
his father was a Greek.[u] 4As they traveled
from town to town, they delivered the decisions reached by the apostles and elders[v]
in Jerusalem[w] for the people to obey.[x] 5So
the churches were strengthened[y] in the
faith and grew daily in numbers.[z]

Paul's Vision of the Man of Macedonia

6Paul and his companions traveled
throughout the region of Phrygia[a] and Galatia,[b] having been kept by the Holy Spirit
from preaching the word in the province
of Asia.[c] 7When they came to the border of
Mysia, they tried to enter Bithynia, but the
Spirit of Jesus[d] would not allow them to.
8So they passed by Mysia and went down
to Troas.[e] 9During the night Paul had a
vision[f] of a man of Macedonia[g] standing
and begging him, "Come over to Macedonia and help us." 10After Paul had seen
the vision, we[h] got ready at once to leave
for Macedonia, concluding that God had
called us to preach the gospel[i] to them.

Lydia's Conversion in Philippi

11From Troas[j] we put out to sea and
sailed straight for Samothrace, and the
next day on to Neapolis. 12From there we
traveled to Philippi,[k] a Roman colony and
the leading city of that district of Macedonia.[l] And we stayed there several days.
13On the Sabbath[m] we went outside the
city gate to the river, where we expected to
find a place of prayer. We sat down and began to speak to the women who had gathered there. 14One of those listening was
a woman named Lydia, a dealer in purple cloth from the city of Thyatira,[n] who
was a worshiper of God. The Lord opened
her heart[o] to respond to Paul's message.

16:1 [r]2Ti 1:5 **16:2** [s]ver 40; S Ac 1:16 [t]S Ac 13:51 **16:3** [u]Gal 2:3 **16:4** [v]S Ac 11:30 [w]Ac 15:2 [x]Ac 15:28,29 **16:5** [y]Ac 9:31; 15:41 [z]S Ac 2:41 **16:6** [a]Ac 2:10; 18:23 [b]Ac 18:23; Gal 1:2; 3:1 [c]S Ac 2:9 **16:7** [d]Ro 8:9; Gal 4:6; Php 1:19; 1Pe 1:11 **16:8** [e]ver 11; Ac 20:5; 2Co 2:12; 2Ti 4:13 **16:9** [f]S Ac 9:10 [g]Ac 19:21,29; 20:1,3; Ro 15:26; 1Co 16:5; 1Th 1:7,8 **16:10** [h]ver 10-17; Ac 20:5-15; 21:1-18; 27:1-28:16 [i]Ac 14:7 **16:11** [j]S ver 8 **16:12** [k]Ac 20:6; Php 1:1; 1Th 2:2 [l]S ver 9 **16:13** [m]S Ac 13:14 **16:14** [n]Rev 1:11; 2:18,24 [o]Lk 24:45

the order of towns is reversed here. *Lystra.* See note on 14:6. *Timothy.* See Introduction to 1 Timothy: Recipient. Since Paul addressed him as a young man some 15 years later (see 1Ti 4:12), he must have been in his teens at this time. *father was a Greek.* Statements concerning his mother's faith (here and in 2Ti 1:5) and silence concerning any faith on his father's part suggest that the father was neither a convert to Judaism nor a believer in Christ.

16:3 *he circumcised him.* As a matter of expediency so that his work among the Jews might be more effective. This was different from Titus's case (see Gal 2:3), where circumcision was refused because some were demanding it as necessary for salvation.

16:6 *his companions.* Silas and Timothy. *Phrygia.* The district was formerly the Hellenistic territory of Phrygia, but it had more recently been divided between the Roman provinces of Asia and Galatia. Iconium and Antioch were in Galatian Phrygia. *Galatia.* The name had been used to denote the Hellenistic kingdom, but in 25 B.C. it had been expanded considerably to become the Roman province of that name. *Asia.* This, too, had been a smaller area formerly but now was a Roman province including the Hellenistic districts of Mysia, Lydia, Caria and parts of Phrygia.

16:7 *Mysia.* In the northwest part of the province of Asia. Luke uses these old Hellenistic names, but Paul preferred the provincial (Roman) names. *Bithynia.* A senatorial province formed after 74 B.C., it was east of Mysia. *Spirit of Jesus.* As the "Holy Spirit" was used at times interchangeably with "God" (5:3–4), so here "Holy Spirit" (v. 6) is used interchangeably with "Spirit of Jesus." *not allow.* The Spirit may have led in any of a number of ways: vision, circumstances, good sense or use of the prophetic gift.

16:8 *Troas.* Located ten miles from ancient Troy. Alexandria Troas (its full name) was a Roman colony and an important seaport for connections between Macedonia and Greece on the one hand and Asia Minor on the other. Paul returned to Troas following his work in Ephesus on his third journey (see 2Co 2:12). At some time—on Paul's second journey or on his third—a church was started there, for Paul ministered to believers in Troas when he returned from his third journey on his way to Jerusalem (20:5–12).

16:9 *vision.* One of the ways God gave direction (cf. 10:3). *man of Macedonia.* Macedonia had become a Roman province in 148 B.C. There is no indication that the man of the vision is Luke, as some have suggested, but he does join the group at this point.

16:10 *we got ready.* This is where the "we" passages of Acts begin (see Introduction: Author). The conclusion is that Luke is informing the reader that he had joined the party at Troas.

16:11 *Samothrace.* An island in the northeastern Aegean Sea. It was a convenient place for boats to anchor rather than risk sailing at night. *Neapolis.* The seaport for Philippi, ten miles away; modern Kavalla.

16:12 *Philippi.* A city in eastern Macedonia named after Philip II, father of Alexander the Great (see map, p. 1836). Since it was a Roman colony, it was independent of provincial administration and had a governmental organization modeled after that of Rome (see note on 13:14). Many retired legionnaires from the Roman army settled there, but few Jews. See Introduction to Philippians: Recipients. *leading city.* Thessalonica was the capital of Macedonia. But Macedonia had four districts, and Philippi was in the first of these. Amphipolis, however, was the first city of that district. Luke may have intended to say that Philippi was "a" leading city (there is no article in the Greek), or that it was the first city reached from the border, or that its fame and significance made it truly the leading city of the area.

16:13 *place of prayer.* There were so few Jews in Philippi that there was no synagogue (ten married men were required), so the Jews who were there met for prayer along the banks of the Gangites River (see map, p. 1836). It was customary for such places of prayer to be located outdoors near running water.

16:14 *Lydia.* A businesswoman. Her name may be associated with her place of origin, the Hellenistic district of Lydia. *Thyatira.* In the Roman province of Asia, 20 miles southeast of Pergamum (in the Hellenistic kingdom of Lydia; see map, p. 1967; see also map No. 13 at the end of this study Bible). It was famous for its dyeing works, especially royal purple (crimson). See Rev 1:11 and note on Rev 2:18. *worshiper of God.* Lydia was a Gentile who, like Cornelius (see 10:2), believed in the true God and followed the moral teachings of Scripture. She had not, however, become a full convert to Judaism. *opened her heart.* After the resurrection the minds of

[15]When she and the members of her household[p] were baptized,[q] she invited us to her home. "If you consider me a believer in the Lord," she said, "come and stay at my house." And she persuaded us.

Paul and Silas in Prison

[16]Once when we were going to the place of prayer,[r] we were met by a slave girl who had a spirit[s] by which she predicted the future. She earned a great deal of money for her owners by fortune-telling. [17]This girl followed Paul and the rest of us, shouting, "These men are servants of the Most High God,[t] who are telling you the way to be saved." [18]She kept this up for many days. Finally Paul became so troubled that he turned around and said to the spirit, "In the name of Jesus Christ I command you to come out of her!" At that moment the spirit left her.[u]

[19]When the owners of the slave girl realized that their hope of making money[v] was gone, they seized Paul and Silas[w] and dragged[x] them into the marketplace to face the authorities. [20]They brought them before the magistrates and said, "These men are Jews, and are throwing our city into an uproar[y] [21]by advocating customs unlawful for us Romans[z] to accept or practice."[a]

16:15 [p]S Ac 11:14 [q]S Ac 2:38
16:16 [r]ver 13 [s]Dt 18:11; 1Sa 28:3,7
16:17 [t]S Mk 5:7
16:18 [u]S Mk 16:17
16:19 [v]ver 16; Ac 19:25,26 [w]S Ac 15:22 [x]Ac 8:3; 17:6; 21:30; Jas 2:6
16:20 [y]Ac 17:6
16:21 [z]ver 12 [a]Est 3:8

the disciples were opened to understand the Scriptures (Lk 24:45); similarly, Lydia's heart was opened to respond to the gospel message of Paul.

16:15 *come and stay at my house.* Cf. Lk 19:5.

16:16 *spirit by which she predicted the future.* A demonic python spirit. The python was a mythical snake worshiped at Delphi and associated with the Delphic oracle. The term "python" came to be used of the persons through whom the python spirit supposedly spoke. Since such persons spoke involuntarily, the term "ventriloquist" was used to describe them. To what extent she actually predicted the future is not known.

16:17 *rest of us.* The "we" section (see note on v. 10) ends here and begins again in 20:5. *Most High God.* A title used by the man possessed by an evil spirit (Mk 5:7). It was a common title among both Jews (see Nu 24:16; Isa 14:14; Da 3:26) and Greeks (found in inscriptions). But the title is not used of God in the NT by Christians or Jews (though cf. Ac 7:48).

16:20 *magistrates.* The Greek term *strategos* (Latin *praetor*), not the usual word but a term of courtesy used in some Roman colonies, such as Philippi.

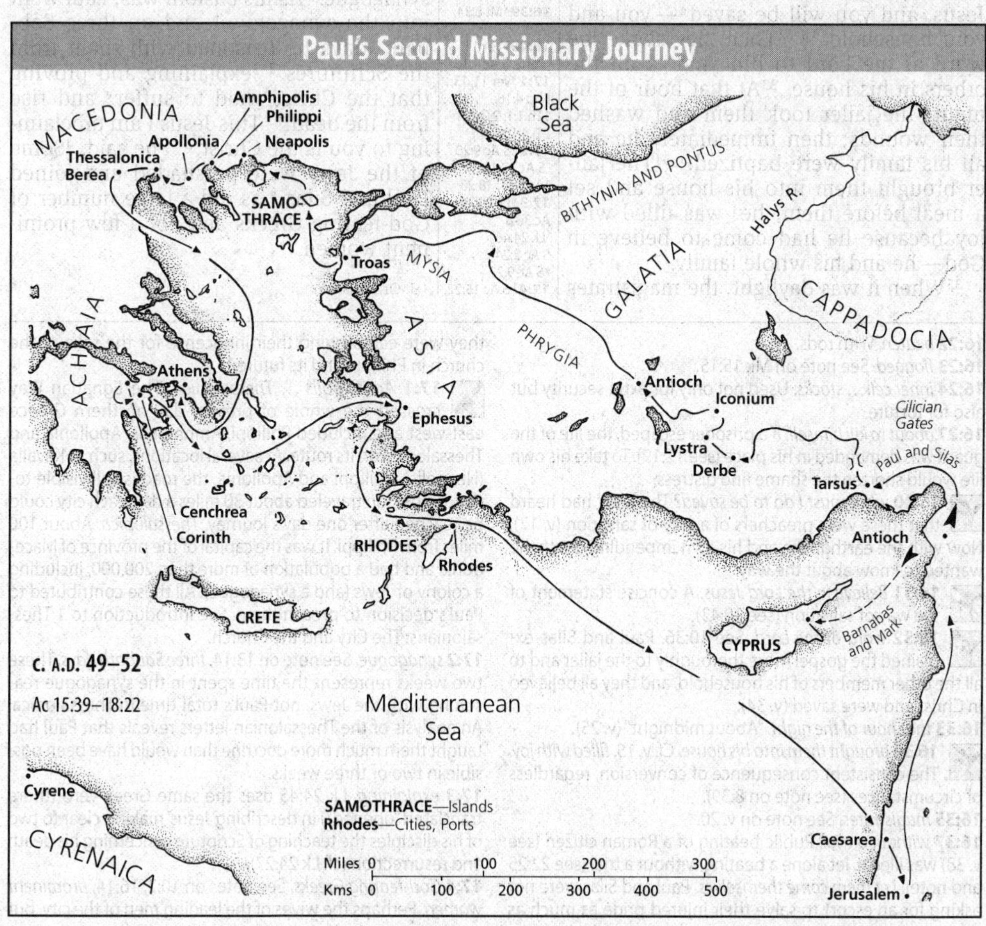

22The crowd joined in the attack against
Paul and Silas, and the magistrates ordered
them to be stripped and beaten.[b] 23Af-
ter they had been severely flogged, they
were thrown into prison, and the jailer[c]
was commanded to guard them carefully.
24Upon receiving such orders, he put them
in the inner cell and fastened their feet in
the stocks.[d]
25About midnight[e] Paul and Silas[f] were
praying and singing hymns[g] to God, and
the other prisoners were listening to them.
26Suddenly there was such a violent earthquake that the foundations of the prison
were shaken.[h] At once all the prison doors
flew open,[i] and everybody's chains came
loose.[j] 27The jailer woke up, and when he
saw the prison doors open, he drew his
sword and was about to kill himself because he thought the prisoners had escaped.[k] 28But Paul shouted, "Don't harm
yourself! We are all here!"
29The jailer called for lights, rushed in
and fell trembling before Paul and Silas.[l]
30He then brought them out and asked,
"Sirs, what must I do to be saved?"[m]
31They replied, "Believe[n] in the Lord
Jesus, and you will be saved[o]—you and
your household."[p] 32Then they spoke the
word of the Lord to him and to all the
others in his house. 33At that hour of the
night[q] the jailer took them and washed
their wounds; then immediately he and
all his family were baptized.[r] 34The jailer brought them into his house and set
a meal before them; he[s] was filled with
joy because he had come to believe in
God—he and his whole family.
35When it was daylight, the magistrates
sent their officers to the jailer with the order: "Release those men." 36The jailer[t] told
Paul, "The magistrates have ordered that
you and Silas be released. Now you can
leave. Go in peace."[u]
37But Paul said to the officers: "They
beat us publicly without a trial, even
though we are Roman citizens,[v] and threw
us into prison. And now do they want to
get rid of us quietly? No! Let them come
themselves and escort us out."
38The officers reported this to the magistrates, and when they heard that Paul
and Silas were Roman citizens, they were
alarmed.[w] 39They came to appease them
and escorted them from the prison, requesting them to leave the city.[x] 40After
Paul and Silas came out of the prison, they
went to Lydia's house,[y] where they met
with the brothers[z] and encouraged them.
Then they left.

In Thessalonica

17 When they had passed through Amphipolis and Apollonia, they came to
Thessalonica,[a] where there was a Jewish
synagogue. 2As his custom was, Paul went
into the synagogue,[b] and on three Sabbath[c] days he reasoned with them from
the Scriptures,[d] 3explaining and proving
that the Christ[a] had to suffer[e] and rise
from the dead.[f] "This Jesus I am proclaiming to you is the Christ,[a]"[g] he said. 4Some
of the Jews were persuaded and joined
Paul and Silas,[h] as did a large number of
God-fearing Greeks and not a few prominent women.

16:22 [b]2Co 11:25; 1Th 2:2
16:23 [c]ver 27,36
16:24 [d]Job 13:27; 33:11; Jer 20:2,3; 29:26
16:25 [e]Ps 119:55,62 [f]S Ac 15:22 [g]S Eph 5:19
16:26 [h]Ac 4:31 [i]Ac 5:19; 12:10 [j]Ac 12:7
16:27 [k]Ac 12:19
16:29 [l]S Ac 15:22
16:30 [m]Ac 2:37
16:31 [n]S Jn 3:15 [o]S Ro 11:14 [p]S Ac 11:14
16:33 [q]ver 25 [r]S Ac 2:38
16:34 [s]S Ac 11:14
16:36 [t]ver 23,27 [u]S Ac 15:33
16:37 [v]Ac 22:25-29
16:38 [w]Ac 22:29
16:39 [x]Mt 8:34; Lk 8:37
16:40 [y]ver 14 [z]ver 2; S Ac 1:16
17:1 [a]ver 11,13; Php 4:16; 1Th 1:1; 2Th 1:1; 2Ti 4:10
17:2 [b]S Ac 9:20 [c]S Ac 13:14 [d]Ac 8:35; 18:28
17:3 [e]Lk 24:26; Ac 3:18 [f]Lk 24:46; S Ac 2:24 [g]S Ac 9:22
17:4 [h]S Ac 15:22

[a] 3 Or *Messiah*

16:22 *beaten.* With rods.
16:23 *flogged.* See note on Mk 15:15.
16:24 *inner cell ... stocks.* Used not only for extra security but also for torture.
16:27 *about to kill himself.* If a prisoner escaped, the life of the guard was demanded in his place (see 12:19). To take his own life would shorten the shame and distress.
16:30 *what must I do to be saved?* The jailer had heard that these were preachers of a way of salvation (v. 17). Now with the earthquake and his own impending death, he wanted to know about the way.
16:31 *Believe in the Lord Jesus.* A concise statement of the way of salvation (see 10:43).
16:32 *word of the Lord.* See 10:36. Paul and Silas explained the gospel more thoroughly to the jailer and to all the other members of his household, and they all believed in Christ and were saved (v. 34).
16:33 *that hour of the night.* "About midnight" (v. 25).
16:34 *brought them into his house.* Cf. v. 15. *filled with joy.* The consistent consequence of conversion, regardless of circumstances (see note on 8:39).
16:35 *magistrates.* See note on v. 20.
16:37 *without a trial.* Public beating of a Roman citizen (see v. 38) was illegal, let alone a beating without a trial (see 22:25 and note). *Let them come themselves.* Paul and Silas were not asking for an escort to salve their injured pride as much as they were establishing their innocence for the sake of the church in Philippi and its future.
17:1 *Amphipolis ... Thessalonica.* The Egnatian Way crossed the whole of present-day northern Greece east-west and included Philippi, Amphipolis, Apollonia and Thessalonica on its route. At several locations, such as Kavalla (Neapolis), Philippi and Apollonia, the road is still visible today. If a person traveled about 30 miles a day, each city could be reached after one day's journey. *Thessalonica.* About 100 miles from Philippi. It was the capital of the province of Macedonia and had a population of more than 200,000, including a colony of Jews (and a synagogue). All these contributed to Paul's decision to preach there. See Introduction to 1 Thessalonians: The City and the Church.
17:2 *synagogue.* See note on 13:14. *three Sabbath days.* These two weeks represent the time spent in the synagogue reasoning with the Jews, not Paul's total time in Thessalonica. An analysis of the Thessalonian letters reveals that Paul had taught them much more doctrine than would have been possible in two or three weeks.
17:3 *explaining.* Lk 24:45 uses the same Greek verb (there translated "opened") in describing Jesus' making clear to two of his disciples the teaching of Scripture concerning his death and resurrection (cf. Lk 24:27).
17:4 *God-fearing Greeks.* See notes on 10:2; 16:14. *prominent women.* Perhaps the wives of the leading men of the city, but

5But the Jews were jealous; so they
rounded up some bad characters from
the marketplace, formed a mob and started a riot in the city.[i] They rushed to Jason's[j] house in search of Paul and Silas
in order to bring them out to the crowd.[a]
6But when they did not find them, they
dragged[k] Jason and some other brothers[l]
before the city officials, shouting: "These
men who have caused trouble all over the
world[m] have now come here,[n] 7and Jason has welcomed them into his house.
They are all defying Caesar's decrees, saying that there is another king, one called
Jesus."[o] 8When they heard this, the crowd
and the city officials were thrown into turmoil. 9Then they made Jason[p] and the others post bond and let them go.

In Berea

10As soon as it was night, the brothers
sent Paul and Silas[q] away to Berea.[r] On arriving there, they went to the Jewish synagogue.[s] 11Now the Bereans were of more
noble character than the Thessalonians,[t]
for they received the message with great
eagerness and examined the Scriptures[u]
every day to see if what Paul said was
true.[v] 12Many of the Jews believed, as did
also a number of prominent Greek women
and many Greek men.[w]
13When the Jews in Thessalonica
learned that Paul was preaching the word
of God at Berea,[x] they went there too, ag-
itating the crowds and stirring them up.
14The brothers[y] immediately sent Paul to
the coast, but Silas[z] and Timothy[a] stayed
at Berea. 15The men who escorted Paul
brought him to Athens[b] and then left with
instructions for Silas and Timothy to join
him as soon as possible.[c]

In Athens

16While Paul was waiting for them in
Athens, he was greatly distressed to see
that the city was full of idols. 17So he reasoned in the synagogue[d] with the Jews
and the God-fearing Greeks, as well as in
the marketplace day by day with those
who happened to be there. 18A group of
Epicurean and Stoic philosophers began
to dispute with him. Some of them asked,
"What is this babbler trying to say?" Others remarked, "He seems to be advocating
foreign gods." They said this because Paul
was preaching the good news[e] about Jesus
and the resurrection.[f] 19Then they took him
and brought him to a meeting of the Areopagus,[g] where they said to him, "May we
know what this new teaching[h] is that you
are presenting? 20You are bringing some
strange ideas to our ears, and we want to

17:5 [i]ver 13; S 1Th 2:16 [j]Ro 16:21 **17:6** [k]S Ac 16:19 [l]S Ac 1:16 [m]S Mt 24:14 [n]Ac 16:20 **17:7** [o]Lk 23:2; Jn 19:12 **17:9** [p]ver 5 **17:10** [q]S Ac 15:22 [r]ver 13; Ac 20:4 [s]S Ac 9:20 **17:11** [t]S ver 1 [u]Lk 16:29; Jn 5:39 [v]Dt 29:29 **17:12** [w]S Ac 2:41 **17:13** [x]S Heb 4:12 **17:14** [y]S Ac 9:30 [z]S Ac 15:22 [a]S Ac 16:1 **17:15** [b]ver 16,21,22; Ac 18:1; 1Th 3:1 [c]Ac 18:5 **17:17** [d]S Ac 9:20 **17:18** [e]S Ac 13:32 [f]ver 31,32; Ac 4:2 **17:19** [g]ver 22 [h]Mk 1:27

[a] 5 Or *the assembly of the people*

women who deserve notice and position in their own right (see also v. 12).

17:5 *were jealous.* Because of the large number of people (including some Jews, many God-fearing Gentiles and many prominent women) who responded to Paul's ministry (cf. 13:45). *Jason's house.* Paul had probably been staying there.

17:6 *city officials.* The Greek term *politarch* (lit. "city ruler"), used here and in v. 8, is found nowhere else in Greek literature, but it was discovered in 1835 in a Greek inscription on an arch that had spanned the Egnatian Way on the west side of Thessalonica. (The arch was destroyed in 1867, but the block with the inscription was rescued and is now in the British Museum in London.) The term has since been found in 16 other inscriptions in surrounding towns of Macedonia, and elsewhere.

17:7 *defying Caesar's decrees.* Blasphemy was the gravest accusation for a Jew, but treason—to support a rival king above Caesar—was the worst accusation for a Roman. Cf. the charge against Jesus that he claimed to be king (see Jn 18:12).

17:9 *post bond.* Jason was forced to guarantee a peaceful, quiet community, or he would face the confiscation of his properties and perhaps even death.

17:10 *Paul and Silas.* Timothy was probably left at Philippi, later rejoining Paul and Silas at Berea (compare v. 10 with v. 14). *Berea.* Modern Verria, located 50 miles from Thessalonica in another district of Macedonia. *synagogue.* See note on 13:14.

17:11 *Bereans.* Luke includes a Berean, Sopater son of Pyrrhus, in the list of delegates who accompanied Paul to Jerusalem to deliver the contributions for the poor (see 20:4 and note).

17:14 *coast.* One might conclude that Paul went by boat to Athens. But the road to Athens is also a coast road, and Paul may have walked the distance after having been escorted to the coast (some 20 miles). In any event, Christian companions stayed with him until reaching Athens.

17:15 *Athens.* Five centuries before Paul, Athens had been at the height of its glory in art, philosophy and literature. She had retained her reputation in philosophy through the years and still maintained a leading university in Paul's day.

17:17 *synagogue.* See note on 13:14. *God-fearing Greeks.* See note on 10:2.

17:18 *Epicurean … philosophers.* Originally they taught that the supreme good is happiness—but not mere momentary pleasure or temporary gratification. By Paul's time, however, this philosophy had degenerated into a more sensual system of thought. *Stoic philosophers.* They taught that people should live in accord with nature, recognize their own self-sufficiency and independence, and suppress their desires. At its best, Stoicism had some admirable qualities, but, like Epicureanism, by Paul's time it had degenerated into a system of pride. *babbler.* The Greek word meant "seed picker," a bird picking up seeds here and there. Then it came to refer to the loafer in the marketplace who picked up whatever scraps of learning he could find and paraded them without digesting them himself.

17:19 *Areopagus.* Means "hill of Ares." Ares was the Greek god of thunder and war (the Roman equivalent was Mars). The Areopagus was located just west of the acropolis and south of the Agora and had once been the site of the meeting of the Court or Council of the Areopagus. Earlier the Council governed a Greek city-state, but by NT times the Areopagus retained authority only in the areas of religion and morals and met in the Royal Portico at the northwest corner of the Agora. They considered themselves the custodians of teachings that introduced new religions and foreign gods.

know what they mean." 21(All the Athenians[i] and the foreigners who lived there
spent their time doing nothing but talking
about and listening to the latest ideas.)
22Paul then stood up in the meeting of
the Areopagus[j] and said: "Men of Athens! I see that in every way you are very
religious.[k] 23For as I walked around and
looked carefully at your objects of worship, I even found an altar with this inscription: TO AN UNKNOWN GOD. Now what
you worship as something unknown[l] I am
going to proclaim to you.
24"The God who made the world and
everything in it[m] is the Lord of heaven
and earth[n] and does not live in temples
built by hands.[o] 25And he is not served by
human hands, as if he needed anything,
because he himself gives all men life and
breath and everything else.[p] 26From one
man he made every nation of men, that
they should inhabit the whole earth; and
he determined the times set for them and
the exact places where they should live.[q]
27God did this so that men would seek him
and perhaps reach out for him and find
him, though he is not far from each one
of us.[r] 28'For in him we live and move and
have our being.'[s] As some of your own poets have said, 'We are his offspring.'
29"Therefore since we are God's offspring, we should not think that the divine
being is like gold or silver or stone—an
image made by man's design and skill.[t]
30In the past God overlooked[u] such ignorance,[v] but now he commands all people
everywhere to repent.[w] 31For he has set a
day when he will judge[x] the world with
justice[y] by the man he has appointed.[z] He
has given proof of this to all men by raising him from the dead."[a]
32When they heard about the resurrection of the dead,[b] some of them sneered,
but others said, "We want to hear you
again on this subject." 33At that, Paul left
the Council. 34A few men became followers of Paul and believed. Among them
was Dionysius, a member of the Areopagus,[c] also a woman named Damaris, and a
number of others.

In Corinth

18 After this, Paul left Athens[d] and
went to Corinth.[e] 2There he met a
Jew named Aquila, a native of Pontus,
who had recently come from Italy with
his wife Priscilla,[f] because Claudius[g] had
ordered all the Jews to leave Rome. Paul
went to see them, 3and because he was
a tentmaker as they were, he stayed and

17:21 [i]S ver 15 **17:22** [j]ver 19 [k]ver 16 **17:23** [l]Jn 4:22 **17:24** [m]Isa 42:5; Ac 14:15 [n]Dt 10:14; Isa 66:1,2; Mt 11:25 [o]1Ki 8:27; Ac 7:48 **17:25** [p]Ps 50:10-12; Isa 42:5 **17:26** [q]Dt 32:8; Job 12:23 **17:27** [r]Dt 4:7; Isa 55:6; Jer 23:23,24 **17:28** [s]Dt 30:20; Job 12:10; Da 5:23 **17:29** [t]Isa 40:18-20; Ro 1:23 **17:30** [u]Ac 14:16; Ro 3:25 [v]ver 23; 1Pe 1:14 [w]Lk 24:47; Tit 2:11,12 **17:31** [x]S Mt 10:15 [y]Ps 9:8; 96:13; 98:9 [z]S Ac 10:42 [a]S Ac 2:24 **17:32** [b]ver 18,31 **17:34** [c]ver 19,22 **18:1** [d]S Ac 17:15 [e]Ac 19:1; 1Co 1:2; 2Co 1:1,23; 2Ti 4:20 **18:2** [f]ver 19,26; Ro 16:3; 1Co 16:19; 2Ti 4:19 [g]Ac 11:28

17:22 *religious.* Or "superstitious." The Greek for this word could be used to congratulate people or to criticize them, depending on whether those using it included themselves in the circle of individuals they were describing. The Athenians would not know which meaning to take until Paul continued. In this context it is clear that Paul wanted to be complimentary in order to gain a hearing.

17:23 *TO AN UNKNOWN GOD.* The Greeks were fearful of offending any god by failing to give him attention; so they felt they could cover any omissions by the label "unknown god." Other Greek writers confirm that such altars could be seen in Athens—a striking point of contact for Paul.

17:24 *The God who made the world.* Thus a personal Creator, in contrast with the views of pantheistic Stoicism. *does not live in temples built by hands.* Cf. Stephen's similar declaration in his famous speech (7:28); cf. also 1Ki 8:27.

17:26 *From one man he made every nation.* All people are of one family (whether Athenians or Romans, Greeks or barbarians, Jews or Gentiles). *determined the times.* He planned the exact times when nations should emerge and decline. *places where they should live.* He also planned the specific area to be occupied by each nation. He is God, the Designer (things were not left to Chance, as the Epicureans thought).

17:28 *some of your own poets.* There are two quotations here: (1) "In him we live and move and have our being," from the Cretan poet Epimenides (c. 600 B.C.) in his *Cretica,* and (2) "We are his offspring," from the Cilician poet Aratus (c. 315–240) in his *Phaenomena,* as well as from Cleanthes (331–233) in his *Hymn to Zeus.* Paul quotes Greek poets elsewhere as well (see 1Co 15:33; Tit 1:12 and notes).

17:30 *overlooked such ignorance.* God had not judged them for worshiping false gods in their ignorance, but now the situation has changed (see v. 31).

17:31 *the man he has appointed.* Jesus, the Son of Man (see Da 7:13; cf. Mt 25:31–46; Ac 10:42).

17:32–34 Three responses to Paul's sermon: (1) Some rejected ("sneered"), (2) some procrastinated ("We want to hear you again"), (3) some accepted ("became followers of Paul and believed").

17:32 *resurrection of the dead.* Immortality of the soul was accepted by the Greeks, but not resurrection of a dead body.

17:33 *the Council.* The meeting of the Areopagites.

17:34 *Dionysius.* Later tradition states, though it cannot be proved, that he became bishop of Athens. *Damaris.* Some have suggested that she must have been a foreign, educated woman to have been present at a public meeting such as the Areopagus. It is also possible that she was a God-fearing Gentile who had heard Paul at the synagogue (v. 17).

18:1 *went to Corinth.* Either by land along the isthmus (a distance of about 50 miles) or by sea from Piraeus, the port of Athens, to Cenchrea, on the eastern shore of the isthmus of Corinth. See Introduction to 1 Corinthians: The City of Corinth; see also map, p. 1766.

18:2 *Pontus.* In the northeastern region of Asia Minor, a province lying along the Black Sea between Bithynia and Armenia (see 2:9). *Aquila . . . Priscilla.* Since no mention is made of a conversion and since a partnership is established in work (see v. 3), it is likely that they were already Christians. They may have been converted in Rome by those returning from Pentecost or by others at a later time (see vv. 18–19; 1Co 16:9; Ro 16:3–4). *Claudius.* Emperor of Rome (A.D. 41–54). *ordered all the Jews to leave Rome.* Recorded in Suetonius (*Claudius,* 25). The expulsion order was given, Suetonius writes, because of "their [the Jews'] continual tumults instigated by Chrestus" (a common misspelling of "Christ"). If "Chrestus" refers to Christ, the riots obviously were "about" him rather than led "by" him.

18:3 *tentmaker.* Paul would have been taught this trade as a youth. It was the Jewish custom to provide manual training for sons, whether rich or poor.

worked with them.[h] 4Every Sabbath[i] he
reasoned in the synagogue,[j] trying to persuade Jews and Greeks.
5When Silas[k] and Timothy[l] came from
Macedonia,[m] Paul devoted himself exclusively to preaching, testifying to the Jews
that Jesus was the Christ.[a][n] 6But when the
Jews opposed Paul and became abusive,[o]
he shook out his clothes in protest[p] and
said to them, "Your blood be on your own
heads![q] I am clear of my responsibility.[r]
From now on I will go to the Gentiles."[s]
7Then Paul left the synagogue and went
next door to the house of Titius Justus,
a worshiper of God.[t] 8Crispus,[u] the synagogue ruler,[v] and his entire household[w]
believed in the Lord; and many of the
Corinthians who heard him believed and
were baptized.
9One night the Lord spoke to Paul in a
vision:[x] "Do not be afraid;[y] keep on speaking, do not be silent. 10For I am with you,[z]
and no one is going to attack and harm
you, because I have many people in this
city." 11So Paul stayed for a year and a half,
teaching them the word of God.[a]
12While Gallio was proconsul[b] of Achaia,[c] the Jews made a united attack on Paul
and brought him into court. 13"This man,"
they charged, "is persuading the people
to worship God in ways contrary to the
law."
14Just as Paul was about to speak, Gallio
said to the Jews, "If you Jews were making a complaint about some misdemeanor
or serious crime, it would be reasonable
for me to listen to you. 15But since it involves questions about words and names
and your own law[d]—settle the matter
yourselves. I will not be a judge of such
things." 16So he had them ejected from the
court. 17Then they all turned on Sosthenes[e] the synagogue ruler[f] and beat him in
front of the court. But Gallio showed no
concern whatever.

Priscilla, Aquila and Apollos

18Paul stayed on in Corinth for some
time. Then he left the brothers[g] and sailed
for Syria,[h] accompanied by Priscilla and
Aquila.[i] Before he sailed, he had his hair
cut off at Cenchrea[j] because of a vow he
had taken.[k] 19They arrived at Ephesus,[l]
where Paul left Priscilla and Aquila. He
himself went into the synagogue and reasoned with the Jews. 20When they asked
him to spend more time with them, he
declined. 21But as he left, he promised,
"I will come back if it is God's will."[m]
Then he set sail from Ephesus. 22When
he landed at Caesarea,[n] he went up and
greeted the church and then went down
to Antioch.[o]

[a] 5 Or *Messiah;* also in verse 28

18:3 [h] Ac 20:34; 1Co 4:12; 1Th 2:9; 2Th 3:8 **18:4** [i] S Ac 13:14 [j] S Ac 9:20 **18:5** [k] S Ac 15:22 [l] S Ac 16:1 [m] S Ac 16:9; 17:14,15 [n] S Ac 9:22 **18:6** [o] S Ac 13:45 [p] S Mt 10:14 [q] 2Sa 1:16; Eze 33:4 [r] Eze 3:17-19; Ac 20:26 [s] S Ac 13:46 **18:7** [t] Ac 16:14 **18:8** [u] 1Co 1:14 [v] S Mk 5:22 [w] S Ac 11:14 **18:9** [x] S Ac 9:10 [y] S Mt 14:27 **18:10** [z] S Mt 28:20 **18:11** [a] S Heb 4:12 **18:12** [b] Ac 13:7,8,12; 19:38 [c] ver 27; Ro 15:26; 1Co 16:15; 2Co 9:2; 1Th 1:7,8 **18:15** [d] Ac 23:29; 25:11,19 **18:17** [e] 1Co 1:1 [f] ver 8 **18:18** [g] ver 27; S Ac 1:16 [h] S Lk 2:2 [i] S ver 2 [j] Ro 16:1 [k] Nu 6:2,5,18; Ac 21:24 **18:19** [l] ver 21,24; Ac 19:1,17,26; 1Co 15:32; 16:8; Eph 1:1; 1Ti 1:3; Rev 1:11; 2:1 **18:21** [m] Ro 1:10; 15:32; 1Co 4:19; Jas 4:15 **18:22** [n] S Ac 8:40 [o] S Ac 11:19

18:4 *synagogue.* See note on 13:14.

18:5 *Silas and Timothy came from Macedonia.* Paul instructed these two to come to him at Athens (17:15). Evidently they did (see 1Th 3:1–2), but they may have been sent back to Macedonia almost immediately to check on the churches—perhaps Silas to Philippi and Timothy to Thessalonica.

18:7 *Titius Justus.* Titius was a common Roman name. Justus is used to distinguish him from the Titus of 2Co 2:13; 7:13–14; 8:16,23. *worshiper of God.* Like Titus (see Gal 2:3), an uncircumcised Gentile, but attending the synagogue.

18:8 *Crispus.* Paul baptized him (1Co 1:14). *synagogue ruler.* See note on 13:15.

18:9 *in a vision.* Paul had seen the Lord in a resurrection body at his conversion (9:4–6; 1Co 15:8) and in the temple at Jerusalem in a trance (22:17–18). Now he sees him in a vision (see 23:11).

18:10 *I have many people.* Corinth was a large, strategic, political, commercial and religious center. It was important that a strong church be established there (see note on v. 1).

18:11 *a year and a half.* During this time he may also have taken the gospel to the neighboring districts of Achaia (see 2Co 1:1 and note).

18:12 *Gallio.* The brother of Seneca, the philosopher, who was the tutor of Nero. Gallio was admired as a man of exceptional fairness and calmness. From an inscription found at Delphi, it is known that Gallio was proconsul of Achaia in A.D. 51–52. This information enables us to date Paul's visit to Corinth on his second journey as well as his writing of the Thessalonian letters (see Introduction to 1 Thessalonians: Author, Date and Place of Writing).

18:13 *contrary to the law.* The Jews were claiming that Paul was advocating a religion not recognized by Roman law as Judaism was. If he had been given the opportunity to speak, he could have argued that the gospel he was preaching was the faith of his fathers (see 24:14–15; 26:6–7) and thus authorized by Roman law.

18:17 *they all turned on Sosthenes.* It is not clear whether the Greeks beat Sosthenes, seeing the occasion as an opportunity to vent their feelings against the Jews, or the Jews beat their own synagogue ruler because he was unsuccessful in presenting their case—probably the former. A Sosthenes is included with Paul in the writing of 1 Corinthians (1:1). Perhaps he was the second ruler of the synagogue at Corinth to become a Christian in response to Paul's preaching (see v. 8).

18:18 *Priscilla and Aquila.* The order of the names used here (but cf. v. 2) may indicate the prominent role of Priscilla or her higher social position (see Ro 16:3; 2Ti 4:19). *vow he had taken.* Grammatically this could refer to Aquila, but the emphasis on Paul and his activity makes Paul more probable. It was probably a temporary Nazirite vow (see Nu 6:1–21). Different vows were frequently taken to express thanks for deliverance from grave dangers. Shaving the head marked the end of a vow.

18:19 *Ephesus.* Leading commercial city of Asia Minor, the capital of provincial Asia and the warden of the temple of Artemis (Diana). See Introduction to Ephesians: The City of Ephesus; see also map, p. 1823. *synagogue.* See note on 13:14.

18:22 *greeted the church.* Could refer to a congregation in Caesarea, but the explanation that "he went up" makes it more likely that it was the church in Jerusalem, some 2,500 feet above sea level (see, e.g., 15:2; 25:9).

23After spending some time in Antioch,
Paul set out from there and traveled from
place to place throughout the region of Galatia[p] and Phrygia,[q] strengthening all the
disciples.[r]
24Meanwhile a Jew named Apollos,[s] a
native of Alexandria, came to Ephesus.[t]
He was a learned man, with a thorough
knowledge of the Scriptures. 25He had
been instructed in the way of the Lord, and
he spoke with great fervor[a][u] and taught
about Jesus accurately, though he knew
only the baptism of John.[v] 26He began to
speak boldly in the synagogue. When Priscilla and Aquila[w] heard him, they invited
him to their home and explained to him
the way of God more adequately.
27When Apollos wanted to go to Achaia,[x] the brothers[y] encouraged him and
wrote to the disciples there to welcome
him. On arriving, he was a great help to
those who by grace had believed. 28For
he vigorously refuted the Jews in public
debate, proving from the Scriptures[z] that
Jesus was the Christ.[a]

Paul in Ephesus

19 While Apollos[b] was at Corinth,[c] Paul
took the road through the interior
and arrived at Ephesus.[d] There he found
some disciples 2and asked them, "Did you
receive the Holy Spirit[e] when[b] you believed?"
They answered, "No, we have not even
heard that there is a Holy Spirit."
3So Paul asked, "Then what baptism did
you receive?"
"John's baptism," they replied.
4Paul said, "John's baptism[f] was a baptism of repentance. He told the people
to believe in the one coming after him,
that is, in Jesus."[g] 5On hearing this, they
were baptized into[c] the name of the Lord
Jesus.[h] 6When Paul placed his hands on
them,[i] the Holy Spirit came on them,[j] and
they spoke in tongues[d][k] and prophesied.
7There were about twelve men in all.
8Paul entered the synagogue[l] and spoke
boldly there for three months, arguing persuasively about the kingdom of God.[m] 9But
some of them[n] became obstinate; they refused to believe and publicly maligned the
Way.[o] So Paul left them. He took the disciples[p] with him and had discussions daily
in the lecture hall of Tyrannus. 10This went
on for two years,[q] so that all the Jews and
Greeks who lived in the province of Asia[r]
heard the word of the Lord.[s]

[a] 25 Or *with fervor in the Spirit* [b] 2 Or *after* [c] 5 Or *in* [d] 6 Or *other languages*

18:23 [p] S Ac 16:6 [q] Ac 2:10; 16:6 [r] Ac 14:22; 15:32,41 **18:24** [s] Ac 19:1; 1Co 1:12; 3:5,6,22; 4:6; 16:12; Tit 3:13 [t] S ver 19 **18:25** [u] Ro 12:11 [v] S Mk 1:4 **18:26** [w] S ver 2 **18:27** [x] S ver 12 [y] ver 18; S Ac 1:16 **18:28** [z] Ac 8:35; 17:2 [a] ver 5; S Ac 9:22 **19:1** [b] S Ac 18:24 [c] S Ac 18:1 [d] S Ac 18:19 **19:2** [e] S Jn 20:22 **19:4** [f] S Mk 1:4 [g] Jn 1:7 **19:5** [h] S Ac 2:38 **19:6** [i] S Ac 6:6 [j] S Ac 10:44 [k] S Mk 16:17 **19:8** [l] S Ac 9:20 [m] S Mt 3:2; Ac 28:23 **19:9** [n] Ac 14:4 [o] ver 23; S Ac 9:2 [p] ver 30; S Ac 11:26 **19:10** [q] Ac 20:31 [r] ver 22,26,27; S Ac 2:9 [s] S Ac 13:48

18:23—21:17 Paul's third missionary journey (see map No. 13 at the end of this study Bible; see also map, p. 1718; cf. maps, pp. 1704, 1711).
18:23 *region of Galatia and Phrygia.* The use of the phrase may indicate the southern part of Galatia in the Phrygian area (see note on 16:6).
18:24 *Alexandria.* In Egypt—where the OT had been translated into Greek (see essay, p. 1452 [Septuagint]). It was the second most important city in the Roman empire and had a large Jewish population. *the Scriptures.* The pre-Christian Greek translation of the OT.
18:25 *baptism of John.* It was not in the name of Jesus (see also 19:2–4). Apollos knew something about Jesus, but basically he, like John, was still looking forward to the coming of the Messiah. His baptism was based on repentance rather than on faith in the finished work of Christ.
18:27 *Achaia.* The Roman province with Corinth as its capital.
18:28 *the Scriptures.* The Greek OT that was read and known in Corinth (see note on v. 24). Apollos's Christian exposition of the Greek Scriptures put him above both Paul and Peter in the eyes of some in the Corinthian church (see 1Co 1:12 and note).
19:1 *Apollos was at Corinth.* Apollos was introduced at Ephesus (18:24) in the absence of Paul; he moved to Corinth before Paul returned to Ephesus. But later Apollos came back to Ephesus during Paul's ministry there (see 1Co 16:12). *through the interior.* Not the lower direct route down the Lycus and Meander valleys but the upper Phrygian route approaching Ephesus from a more northerly direction. If Paul got to northern Galatia, which is unlikely, it must have been on one of these trips through the interior (see 16:6; 18:23 and notes). *Ephesus.* See note on 18:19. *some disciples.* These 12 (v. 7) seem to have been followers of Jesus, but indirectly through John the Baptist or some of his followers. Or perhaps they had received their teaching from Apollos himself in his earlier state of partial understanding (see 18:26 and note on 18:25). Like Apollos, they had a limited understanding of the gospel.
19:2 *receive the Holy Spirit.* Paul finds that they were not informed about the Holy Spirit at all (vv. 3–6).
19:4 *John's baptism.* See notes on Mt 3:11,15. *baptism of repentance.* A summation of John's teaching. It was preparatory and provisional, stressing human sinfulness and thus creating a sense of need for the gospel. John's baptism looked forward to Jesus, who by his death would make possible the forgiveness of sins (see note on Mk 1:4).
19:6 *placed his hands on them.* See note on 6:6. *Holy Spirit came on them ... spoke in tongues and prophesied.* The same experience the disciples had at Pentecost (2:4,11) and the Gentiles had in Caesarea (10:46).
19:8 *three months.* Much longer than the three Sabbaths in Thessalonica (17:2), but the same approach: Jews first, then Greeks (see note on 13:14). *kingdom of God.* See notes on Mt 3:2; Lk 4:43.
19:9 *the Way.* See note on 9:2. *lecture hall of Tyrannus.* See map, p. 1823; probably a school used regularly by Tyrannus, a philosopher or rhetorician. Instruction was probably given in the cooler, morning hours. One Greek manuscript adds that Paul did his instructing from 11:00 A.M. to 4:00 P.M. This would have been the hot time of the day, but the hall was available and the people were not at their regular work.
19:10 *two years.* Two years and three months (see v. 8) was the longest stay in one missionary location that Luke records. By Jewish reckoning, any part of a year is considered a year; so this period can be spoken of as three years (20:31). *all ... in the province of Asia heard.* One of the elements of Paul's missionary strategy is seen here. Many of the cities where Paul planted churches were strategic centers that, when evangelized, served as focal points from which the gospel radiated out to the surrounding areas. Other examples are Antioch in Pisidia (see 13:14 and note), Thessalonica (see 17:1 and note), Athens (see 17:15 and note) and Corinth (see 18:1).

11God did extraordinary miracles[t]
through Paul, 12so that even handkerchiefs
and aprons that had touched him were
taken to the sick, and their illnesses were
cured[u] and the evil spirits left them.
13Some Jews who went around driving
out evil spirits[v] tried to invoke the name
of the Lord Jesus over those who were demon-possessed. They would say, "In the
name of Jesus,[w] whom Paul preaches, I
command you to come out." 14Seven sons
of Sceva, a Jewish chief priest, were doing
this. 15⌞One day⌟ the evil spirit answered
them, "Jesus I know, and I know about
Paul, but who are you?" 16Then the man
who had the evil spirit jumped on them
and overpowered them all. He gave them
such a beating that they ran out of the
house naked and bleeding.
17When this became known to the Jews
and Greeks living in Ephesus,[x] they were
all seized with fear,[y] and the name of the
Lord Jesus was held in high honor. 18Many
of those who believed now came and openly confessed their evil deeds. 19A number
who had practiced sorcery brought their
scrolls together and burned them publicly. When they calculated the value of the
scrolls, the total came to fifty thousand
drachmas.[a] 20In this way the word of the
Lord[z] spread widely and grew in power.[a]
21After all this had happened, Paul decided to go to Jerusalem,[b] passing through
Macedonia[c] and Achaia.[d] "After I have
been there," he said, "I must visit Rome
also."[e] 22He sent two of his helpers,[f] Timothy[g] and Erastus,[h] to Macedonia, while
he stayed in the province of Asia[i] a little
longer.

19:11 [t]Ac 8:13
19:12 [u]Ac 5:15
19:13 [v]Mt 12:27 [w]Mk 9:38
19:17 [x]S Ac 18:19 [y]Ac 5:5,11
19:20 [z]S Ac 13:48 [a]Ac 6:7; 12:24
19:21 [b]Ac 20:16,22; 21:4,12,15; Ro 15:25 [c]S Ac 16:9 [d]S Ac 18:12 [e]Ro 15:24,28
19:22 [f]Ac 13:5 [g]S Ac 16:1 [h]Ro 16:23; 2Ti 4:20 [i]ver 10,26,27; S Ac 2:9
19:23 [j]S Ac 9:2
19:25 [k]Ac 16:16,19,20
19:26 [l]S Ac 18:19 [m]S Ac 2:9 [n]Dt 4:28; Ps 115:4; Isa 44:10-20; Jer 10:3-5; Ac 17:29; 1Co 8:4; Rev 9:20
19:28 [o]S Ac 18:19
19:29 [p]Ac 20:4; Ro 16:23; 1Co 1:14 [q]Ac 20:4; 27:2; Col 4:10; Phm 24 [r]S Ac 16:9
19:30 [s]S Ac 11:26
19:32 [t]Ac 21:34

The Riot in Ephesus

23About that time there arose a great
disturbance about the Way.[j] 24A silversmith named Demetrius, who made silver shrines of Artemis, brought in no little business for the craftsmen. 25He called
them together, along with the workmen in
related trades, and said: "Men, you know
we receive a good income from this business.[k] 26And you see and hear how this
fellow Paul has convinced and led astray
large numbers of people here in Ephesus[l]
and in practically the whole province of
Asia.[m] He says that man-made gods are
no gods at all.[n] 27There is danger not only
that our trade will lose its good name, but
also that the temple of the great goddess
Artemis will be discredited, and the goddess herself, who is worshiped throughout
the province of Asia and the world, will be
robbed of her divine majesty."
28When they heard this, they were furious and began shouting: "Great is Artemis of the Ephesians!"[o] 29Soon the whole
city was in an uproar. The people seized
Gaius[p] and Aristarchus,[q] Paul's traveling
companions from Macedonia,[r] and rushed
as one man into the theater. 30Paul wanted
to appear before the crowd, but the disciples[s] would not let him. 31Even some
of the officials of the province, friends of
Paul, sent him a message begging him not
to venture into the theater.
32The assembly was in confusion: Some
were shouting one thing, some another.[t]
Most of the people did not even know

[a] *19* A drachma was a silver coin worth about a day's wages.

19:12 *handkerchiefs.* Probably used by Paul in his trade of leatherworking: one for tying around his head, the other around his waist. Cf. 5:15 and note.

19:14 *Sceva, a Jewish chief priest.* May have been related to the high priestly family of Jerusalem. But more likely he took this title himself to make further impression with his magical wiles. Drawn by Paul's ability to drive out evil spirits, Jewish exorcists wanted to copy his work (cf. 8:9–24; 13:6).

19:19 *scrolls.* Such documents bearing alleged magical formulas and secret information have been unearthed. Ephesus was a center for magical incantations. *fifty thousand drachmas.* The high price (see NIV text note) was not due to the quality of the books but to the supposed power gained by their secret rigmarole of words and names.

19:21 *Macedonia and Achaia.* See notes on 1Th 1:7–8; see also map, p. 1711.

19:22 *Erastus.* An important figure at Corinth, "the city's director of public works" at one time (see note on Ro 16:23). He is located later at Corinth also (2Ti 4:20). Just now he returns to Corinth by way of Macedonia with Timothy.

19:23 *the Way.* See 9:2 and note.

19:24 *silversmith named Demetrius.* Each trade had its guild, and Demetrius was probably a responsible leader of the guild for the manufacture of silver shrines and images. *Artemis.* The Greek name for the Roman goddess Diana. The Ephesian Artemis, however, was very different from the Greco-Roman goddess. She had taken on the characteristics of Cybele, the mother goddess of fertility worshiped in Asia Minor and served by many prostitute priestesses. A meteorite may be the basis of the many-breasted image of heavenly workmanship claimed for Artemis (v. 35). (Some have identified the objects that cover the torso of the image as ostrich eggs.) Reproductions of the original image from the time of the emperor Domitian (A.D. 81–96) have been found in Ephesus.

19:25 *good income.* Since the temple of Artemis was one of the seven wonders of the ancient world, people came from far and wide to view it. Their purchase of silver shrines and images produced a lucrative business for the craftsmen.

19:27 *temple of the great goddess.* See map, p. 1823. The temple was the glory of Ephesus: 425 feet long and 220 feet wide, having 127 white marble columns 62 feet high and less than 4 feet apart. In the inner sanctuary was the many-breasted image supposedly dropped from heaven.

19:29 *Gaius.* See note on 20:4. *Aristarchus.* Traveled later with Paul from Corinth to Jerusalem (20:3–4), and also accompanied Paul on the voyage from Jerusalem to Rome (27:1–2; see Col 4:10 and note).

19:31 *officials of the province.* Greek *Asiarchon* (lit. "chief rulers of Asia"), members of a council of men of wealth and influence elected to promote the worship of the emperor. Paul had friends in this highest circle.

why they were there. 33 The Jews pushed
Alexander to the front, and some of the
crowd shouted instructions to him. He
motioned[u] for silence in order to make
a defense before the people. 34 But when
they realized he was a Jew, they all shouted in unison for about two hours: "Great
is Artemis of the Ephesians!"[v]
35 The city clerk quieted the crowd and
said: "Men of Ephesus,[w] doesn't all the
world know that the city of Ephesus is
the guardian of the temple of the great
Artemis and of her image, which fell
from heaven? 36 Therefore, since these
facts are undeniable, you ought to be
quiet and not do anything rash. 37 You
have brought these men here, though
they have neither robbed temples[x] nor
blasphemed our goddess. 38 If, then, Demetrius and his fellow craftsmen[y] have
a grievance against anybody, the courts
are open and there are proconsuls.[z] They
can press charges. 39 If there is anything
further you want to bring up, it must be
settled in a legal assembly. 40 As it is, we
are in danger of being charged with ri-
oting because of today's events. In that
case we would not be able to account for
this commotion, since there is no reason
for it." 41 After he had said this, he dismissed the assembly.

Through Macedonia and Greece

20 When the uproar had ended, Paul
sent for the disciples[a] and, after encouraging them, said good-by and set out

19:33 [u] S Ac 12:17 **19:34** [v] ver 28 **19:35** [w] S Ac 18:19 **19:37** [x] Ro 2:22 **19:38** [y] ver 24 [z] Ac 13:7,8,12; 18:12 **20:1** [a] S Ac 11:26

19:33 *Alexander.* Pushed forward by the Jews either to make clear the disassociation of the Jews from the Christians and/or to accuse the Christians further of an offense against the Greeks. The crowd recognized that the Jews were not worshipers of Artemis any more than the Christians were.
19:35 *city clerk.* The secretary of the city who published the decisions of the civic assembly. He was the most important local official and the chief executive officer of the assembly, acting as go-between for Ephesus and the Roman authorities. *fell from heaven.* See note on v.24.
19:38 *courts ... proconsuls.* Probably general terms, not intended to refer to more than one court or one proconsul. As capital city of the province of Asia, Ephesus was the headquarters for the proconsul.
19:39 *legal assembly.* The regular civil meeting ordinarily held three times a month.
20:1 *said good-by and set out.* Paul wanted to: (1) leave Ephesus, (2) preach in Troas on his way to Macedonia, (3) meet

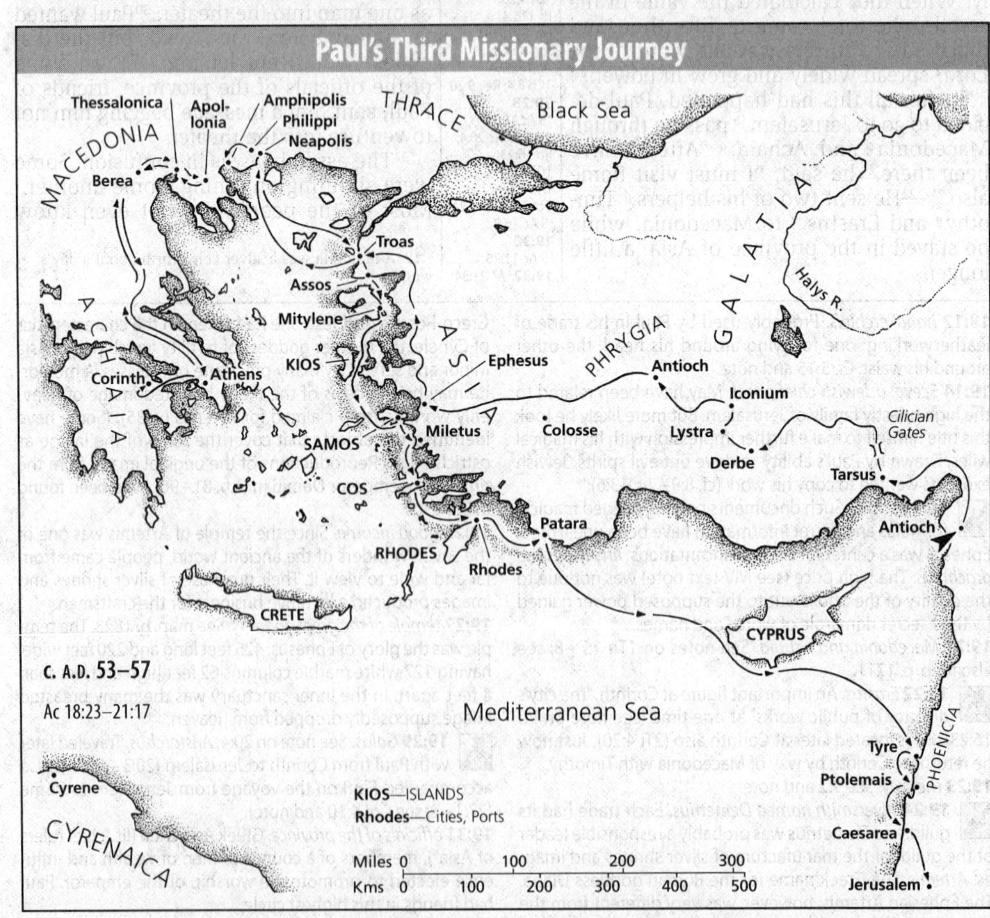

for Macedonia.[b] 2He traveled through that
area, speaking many words of encouragement to the people, and finally arrived in
Greece, 3where he stayed three months.
Because the Jews made a plot against
him[c] just as he was about to sail for Syria,[d] he decided to go back through Macedonia.[e] 4He was accompanied by Sopater
son of Pyrrhus from Berea, Aristarchus[f]
and Secundus from Thessalonica,[g] Gaius[h] from Derbe, Timothy[i] also, and Tychicus[j] and Trophimus[k] from the province
of Asia.[l] 5These men went on ahead and
waited for us[m] at Troas.[n] 6But we sailed
from Philippi[o] after the Feast of Unleavened Bread, and five days later joined the
others at Troas,[p] where we stayed seven
days.

Eutychus Raised From the Dead at Troas

7On the first day of the week[q] we came
together to break bread.[r] Paul spoke to
the people and, because he intended to
leave the next day, kept on talking until
midnight. 8There were many lamps in the
upstairs room[s] where we were meeting.
9Seated in a window was a young man
named Eutychus, who was sinking into a
deep sleep as Paul talked on and on. When
he was sound asleep, he fell to the ground
from the third story and was picked up
dead. 10Paul went down, threw himself on
the young man[t] and put his arms around
him. "Don't be alarmed," he said. "He's
alive!"[u] 11Then he went upstairs again and
broke bread[v] and ate. After talking until
daylight, he left. 12The people took the
young man home alive and were greatly
comforted.

Paul's Farewell to the Ephesian Elders

13We went on ahead to the ship and
sailed for Assos, where we were going to
take Paul aboard. He had made this arrangement because he was going there on
foot. 14When he met us at Assos, we took
him aboard and went on to Mitylene. 15The
next day we set sail from there and arrived
off Kios. The day after that we crossed
over to Samos, and on the following day

20:1 [b] S Ac 16:9 **20:3** [c] ver 19; Ac 9:23,24; 14:5; 23:12,15,30; 25:3; 2Co 11:26; S 1Th 2:16 [d] S Lk 2:2 [e] S Ac 16:9 **20:4** [f] S Ac 19:29 [g] S Ac 17:1 [h] S Ac 19:29 [i] S Ac 16:1 [j] Eph 6:21; Col 4:7; Tit 3:12 [k] Ac 21:29; 2Ti 4:20 [l] S Ac 2:9 **20:5** [m] S Ac 16:10 [n] S Ac 16:8 **20:6** [o] S Ac 16:12 [p] S Ac 16:8 **20:7** [q] 1Co 16:2; Rev 1:10 [r] S Mt 14:19 **20:8** [s] Ac 1:13; 9:37 **20:10** [t] 1Ki 17:21; 2Ki 4:34 [u] Mt 9:23,24 **20:11** [v] ver 7; S Mt 14:19

Titus at Troas with a report from Corinth (see 2Co 2:12–13 and note on 2:12) and (4) continue collecting the offering for Judea (see 1Co 16:1–4; 2Co 8:1—9:15; Ro 15:25–28). *Macedonia.* Where Paul probably wrote 2 Corinthians (see 2Co 7:5; 8:1; 9:4; see also chart, p. 1697).

20:2 *He traveled through that area.* May cover a considerable period. He may have gone to Illyricum (see Ro 15:19 and note) at this time.

20:3 *three months.* Probably a reference to the stay in Corinth, the capital of Achaia. These would be the winter months when ships did not sail regularly. Paul probably wrote Romans at this time (see Introduction to Romans: Occasion). *a plot against him.* The Jews were determined to take Paul's life; also, at this time he was carrying the offering for the Christians in Judea, so there would have been a temptation for theft as well. The port at Cenchrea would have provided a convenient place for Paul's enemies to detect him as he entered a ship to embark for Syria.

20:4 These men seem to be the delegates appointed to accompany Paul and the money given for the needy in Judea (see note on 2Co 8:23). Three were from Macedonia, two from Galatia and two from Asia. Luke may have joined them at Philippi ("we sailed," v. 6; see note on 16:10). *Sopater.* May be the same as Sosipater (Ro 16:21). *Aristarchus.* See note on 19:29. *Secundus.* Not mentioned elsewhere. His name means "second," as Tertius (see Ro 16:22) means "third" and Quartus (see Ro 16:23) means "fourth." *Gaius from Derbe.* A Gaius from Macedonia was associated with Aristarchus (see 19:29), but the grouping of the names in pairs (after the reference to Sopater) indicates that this Gaius was associated with Roman Galatia and is different from the Macedonian Gaius. *Timothy.* May have represented more than one particular church. He was from Lystra but had been responsible for working in other churches (1Co 16:10–11; Php 2:19–23). He had been sent to Macedonia before Paul left Ephesus (19:22). *Tychicus.* A constant help to Paul, especially in association with the churches of Asia (Eph 6:21–22; Col 4:7–9; 2Ti 4:12; Tit 3:12). *Trophimus.* Appears again in 21:29 (see 2Ti 4:20). He was an Ephesian, and it is implied that he was a Gentile.

20:5 *Troas.* Was to be the rendezvous for Paul and those who went on ahead by sea from Neapolis, the seaport of Philippi (16:11). Paul and his immediate companions stayed in Philippi before sailing a week later.

20:6 *from Philippi.* From the seaport, Neapolis, about ten miles away. *Feast of Unleavened Bread.* Began with Passover and lasted a week. Paul spent the period in Philippi. Formerly he had hoped to reach Jerusalem sooner (see 19:21), but now he hoped to arrive there for Pentecost (see 20:16). *five days later.* The voyage from Neapolis to Troas took five days. It had taken about two days the other direction (16:11). *seven days.* Although Paul was in a hurry to arrive at Jerusalem by Pentecost, he remained seven days at Troas. This might have been because of a ship schedule, but more likely the delay was in order to meet with the believers on the first day of the week to break bread.

20:7 *first day of the week.* Sunday. Although some maintain that they met on Saturday evening since the Jewish day began at six o'clock the previous evening, there is no indication that Luke is using the Jewish method of reporting time to tell of happenings in this Hellenistic city. *break bread.* Here indicates the Lord's Supper, since breaking bread was the express purpose for this formal gathering. The Lord's Supper had been commanded (Lk 22:19), and it was observed regularly (see 2:42 and note). *kept on talking until midnight.* All the speeches of Paul as recorded in Acts are short, indicating that they are summaries (see Introduction: Characteristics).

20:9 *Eutychus.* A name common among the Freedmen class (see note on 6:9).

20:10 *He's alive!* As Peter had raised Tabitha (9:40), so Paul raised Eutychus.

20:13 *Assos.* On the opposite side of the peninsula from Troas—about 20 miles away by land. The coastline, however, was about 40 miles. Thus Paul was not far behind the ship that sailed around the peninsula.

20:14 *Mitylene.* After the first day of sailing, they put into this harbor on the southeast shore of the island of Lesbos.

20:15 *Kios.* The second night they spent off the shore of this larger island, which lay along the west coast of Asia Minor (see map, p. 1718). *Samos.* Crossing the mouth of the bay that leads to Ephesus, they came on the third day to Samos, one of the most important islands in the Aegean. *Miletus.* About 35 miles south of Ephesus, the destination of the ship Paul

arrived at Miletus.[w] 16Paul had decided to
sail past Ephesus[x] to avoid spending time
in the province of Asia,[y] for he was in a
hurry to reach Jerusalem,[z] if possible, by
the day of Pentecost.[a]
17From Miletus,[b] Paul sent to Ephesus
for the elders[c] of the church. 18When they
arrived, he said to them: "You know how
I lived the whole time I was with you,[d]
from the first day I came into the province
of Asia.[e] 19I served the Lord with great
humility and with tears,[f] although I was
severely tested by the plots of the Jews.[g]
20You know that I have not hesitated to
preach anything[h] that would be helpful to
you but have taught you publicly and from
house to house. 21I have declared to both
Jews[i] and Greeks that they must turn to
God in repentance[j] and have faith in our
Lord Jesus.[k]
22"And now, compelled by the Spirit, I
am going to Jerusalem,[l] not knowing what
will happen to me there. 23I only know that
in every city the Holy Spirit warns me[m]
that prison and hardships are facing me.[n]
24However, I consider my life worth nothing to me,[o] if only I may finish the race[p]
and complete the task[q] the Lord Jesus has
given me[r]—the task of testifying to the
gospel of God's grace.[s]
25"Now I know that none of you among
whom I have gone about preaching the
kingdom[t] will ever see me again.[u] 26There-
fore, I declare to you today that I am innocent of the blood of all men.[v] 27For I have
not hesitated to proclaim to you the whole
will of God.[w] 28Keep watch over yourselves
and all the flock[x] of which the Holy Spirit
has made you overseers.[a][y] Be shepherds
of the church of God,[b][z] which he bought[a]
with his own blood.[b] 29I know that after I
leave, savage wolves[c] will come in among
you and will not spare the flock.[d] 30Even
from your own number men will arise and
distort the truth in order to draw away disciples[e] after them. 31So be on your guard!
Remember that for three years[f] I never
stopped warning each of you night and
day with tears.[g]
32"Now I commit you to God[h] and to the
word of his grace, which can build you
up and give you an inheritance[i] among all
those who are sanctified.[j] 33I have not coveted anyone's silver or gold or clothing.[k]
34You yourselves know that these hands
of mine have supplied my own needs and
the needs of my companions.[l] 35In everything I did, I showed you that by this kind
of hard work we must help the weak, remembering the words the Lord Jesus himself said: 'It is more blessed to give than
to receive.' "
36When he had said this, he knelt down
with all of them and prayed.[m] 37They all
wept as they embraced him and kissed
him.[n] 38What grieved them most was his
statement that they would never see his
face again.[o] Then they accompanied him
to the ship.[p]

20:15 [w]ver 17; 2Ti 4:20 **20:16** [x]S Ac 18:19 [y]S Ac 2:9 [z]S Ac 19:21 [a]S Ac 2:1 **20:17** [b]ver 15 [c]S Ac 11:30 **20:18** [d]Ac 18:19-21; 19:1-41 [e]S Ac 2:9 **20:19** [f]Ps 6:6 [g]S ver 3 **20:20** [h]ver 27; Ps 40:10; Jer 26:2; 42:4 **20:21** [i]Ac 18:5 [j]S Ac 2:38 [k]Ac 24:24; 26:18; Eph 1:15; Col 2:5; Phm 5 **20:22** [l]ver 16 **20:23** [m]S Ac 8:29; 21:4 [n]S Ac 9:16 **20:24** [o]Ac 21:13 [p]2Ti 4:7 [q]2Co 4:1 [r]Gal 1:1; Tit 1:3 [s]S Ac 11:23 **20:25** [t]S Mt 4:23 [u]ver 38 **20:26** [v]Eze 3:17-19; Ac 18:6 **20:27** [w]S ver 20 **20:28** [x]ver 29; S Jn 21:16 [y]S 1Ti 3:1 [z]S 1Co 10:32 [a]S 1Co 6:20 [b]S Ro 3:25 **20:29** [c]Eze 34:5; Mt 7:15 [d]ver 28 **20:30** [e]S Ac 11:26 **20:31** [f]Ac 19:10 [g]ver 19 **20:32** [h]Ac 14:23 [i]S Eph 1:14; S Mt 25:34; Col 1:12; 3:24; Heb 9:15; 1Pe 1:4 [j]Ac 26:18 **20:33** [k]1Sa 12:3; 1Co 9:12; 2Co 2:17; 7:2; 11:9; 12:14-17; 1Th 2:5 **20:34** [l]S Ac 18:3 **20:36** [m]Lk 22:41; Ac 9:40; 21:5 **20:37** [n]S Lk 15:20 **20:38** [o]ver 25 [p]Ac 21:5

[a] *28* Traditionally *bishops* [b] *28* Many manuscripts *of the Lord*

---

was on. He would have had to change ships to put into Ephesus, which would have lost time (see v. 16). If he had come to Ephesus, he would have had to visit a number of families, which would have taken more time. If trouble should arise, such as the riot of a year ago (19:23–41), even more time would be lost. It could not be risked.

20:16 *by the day of Pentecost.* Fifty days from Passover. Five days plus seven days (v. 6) plus four days (vv. 13–15) had already gone by, leaving only about two-thirds of the time for the remainder of the trip. *Pentecost.* See note on 2:1.

20:17 *elders of the church.* The importance of the leadership of elders has been evident throughout Paul's ministry. He had delivered the famine gift from the church at Antioch to the elders of the Jerusalem church (11:30). He had appointed elders on his first missionary journey (see 14:23) and had addressed the holders of this office later in Philippi (Php 1:1, "overseers"). He requested the Ephesian elders to meet with him on this solemn occasion (see v. 28). Some years later he wrote down instructions about the elders' qualifications (1Ti 3; Tit 1).

20:19 *with tears.* See v. 31. Paul's ministry at Ephesus was conducted with emotional fervency and a sense of urgency.

20:22 *compelled by the Spirit.* Paul did not go to Jerusalem against the direction of the Spirit, as some have suggested, but because of the guidance of the Spirit. People pleaded with him not to go (21:4,12), not because the Spirit prohibited his going but because the Spirit revealed the capture that awaited him there (21:11–12).

20:24 *finish the race.* See 2Ti 4:7 and note.

20:25 *none of you … will ever see me again.* Not a message from God but what Paul anticipated. He had been mistaken before in his plans: He had intended to stay in Ephesus until Pentecost, but he had to leave earlier (see v. 1; 1Co 16:8–9). His prophetic power was not used to foresee his own future, just as his healing power was not used to heal his own disease (see 2Co 12:7–9). As it turned out, it seems that Paul did revisit Ephesus (see 1Ti 1:3). *kingdom.* See notes on Mt 3:2; Lk 4:43.

20:28 *overseers. Be shepherds.* The "elders" (v. 17) were called "overseers" and told to pastor ("shepherd") the flock—demonstrating that the same men could be called "elders," "overseers" or "pastors." *his own blood.* Lit. "the blood of his own one," a term of endearment (connoting "the blood of his own dear one," referring to his own Son).

20:29 *wolves.* See Lk 10:3 and note.

20:31 *three years.* See note on 19:10.

20:32 *inheritance.* See 1Pe 1:4 and note. *sanctified.* See note on 1Co 1:2.

20:34 *supplied my own needs.* Paul had worked in Thessalonica (1Th 2:9) and Corinth (Ac 18:3).

20:35 *remembering the words the Lord Jesus himself said.* A formula regularly used in the early church to introduce a quotation from Jesus (1 Clement 46:7). This is a rare instance of a saying of Jesus not found in the canonical Gospels.

20:38 *never see his face again.* See v. 25 and note.

On to Jerusalem

21 After we[q] had torn ourselves away
from them, we put out to sea and
sailed straight to Cos. The next day we
went to Rhodes and from there to Patara.
2We found a ship crossing over to Phoenicia,[r] went on board and set sail. 3After
sighting Cyprus and passing to the south
of it, we sailed on to Syria.[s] We landed at
Tyre, where our ship was to unload its cargo. 4Finding the disciples[t] there, we stayed
with them seven days. Through the Spirit[u]
they urged Paul not to go on to Jerusalem.
5But when our time was up, we left and
continued on our way. All the disciples
and their wives and children accompanied
us out of the city, and there on the beach
we knelt to pray.[v] 6After saying good-by to
each other, we went aboard the ship, and
they returned home.

7We continued our voyage from Tyre[w] and
landed at Ptolemais, where we greeted the
brothers[x] and stayed with them for a day.
8Leaving the next day, we reached Caesarea[y] and stayed at the house of Philip[z] the
evangelist,[a] one of the Seven. 9He had four
unmarried daughters who prophesied.[b]

10After we had been there a number
of days, a prophet named Agabus[c] came
down from Judea. 11Coming over to us,
he took Paul's belt, tied his own hands
and feet with it and said, "The Holy Spirit
says,[d] 'In this way the Jews of Jerusalem
will bind[e] the owner of this belt and will
hand him over to the Gentiles.'"[f]

12When we heard this, we and the people there pleaded with Paul not to go up to
Jerusalem. 13Then Paul answered, "Why
are you weeping and breaking my heart? I
am ready not only to be bound, but also to
die[g] in Jerusalem for the name of the Lord
Jesus."[h] 14When he would not be dissuad-
ed, we gave up[i] and said, "The Lord's will
be done."[j]

15After this, we got ready and went up
to Jerusalem.[k] 16Some of the disciples from
Caesarea[l] accompanied us and brought us
to the home of Mnason, where we were to
stay. He was a man from Cyprus[m] and one
of the early disciples.

Paul's Arrival at Jerusalem

17When we arrived at Jerusalem, the
brothers[n] received us warmly.[o] 18The next
day Paul and the rest of us went to see
James,[p] and all the elders[q] were present.
19Paul greeted them and reported in detail
what God had done among the Gentiles[r]
through his ministry.[s]

20When they heard this, they praised
God. Then they said to Paul: "You see,
brother, how many thousands of Jews
have believed, and all of them are zealous[t] for the law.[u] 21They have been informed that you teach all the Jews who
live among the Gentiles to turn away from
Moses,[v] telling them not to circumcise
their children[w] or live according to our
customs.[x] 22What shall we do? They will
certainly hear that you have come, 23so do
what we tell you. There are four men with
us who have made a vow.[y] 24Take these
men, join in their purification rites[z] and

21:1 [q]S Ac 16:10 **21:2** [r]Ac 11:19 **21:3** [s]S Lk 2:2 **21:4** [t]S Ac 11:26 [u]ver 11; Ac 20:23 **21:5** [v]Lk 22:41; Ac 9:40; 20:36 **21:7** [w]Ac 12:20 [x]S Ac 1:16 **21:8** [y]S Ac 8:40 [z]Ac 6:5; 8:5-40 [a]Eph 4:11; 2Ti 4:5 **21:9** [b]Ex 15:20; Jdg 4:4; Ne 6:14; Lk 2:36; Ac 2:17; 1Co 11:5 **21:10** [c]Ac 11:28 **21:11** [d]S Ac 8:29 [e]ver 33 [f]1Ki 22:11; Isa 20:2-4; Jer 13:1-11; Mt 20:19 **21:13** [g]Ac 20:24 [h]S Jn 15:21; S Ac 9:16 **21:14** [i]Ru 1:18 [j]S Mt 26:39 **21:15** [k]S Ac 19:21 **21:16** [l]S Ac 8:40 [m]ver 3, 4 **21:17** [n]S Ac 9:30 [o]Ac 15:4 **21:18** [p]S Ac 15:13 [q]S Ac 11:30 **21:19** [r]Ac 14:27; 15:4, 12 [s]Ac 1:17 **21:20** [t]Ac 22:3; Ro 10:2; Gal 1:14; Php 3:6 [u]Ac 15:1, 5 **21:21** [v]ver 28 [w]Ac 15:19-21; 1Co 7:18, 19 [x]S Ac 6:14 **21:23** [y]Nu 6:2, 5, 18; Ac 18:18 **21:24** [z]ver 26; Ac 24:18

21:1 *sailed straight to Cos.* Favorable winds took them to a stopping place for the night at this island. *Rhodes.* The leading city on the island of Rhodes, once noted for its harbor colossus, one of the seven wonders of the ancient world (but demolished over two centuries before Paul arrived there). It took them a day to get to Rhodes. *Patara.* On the southern coast of Lycia. Paul changed ships from a vessel that hugged the shore of Asia Minor to one going directly to Tyre and Phoenicia.
21:3 *Cyprus.* See 13:4 and note. *Tyre.* Paul had passed through this Phoenician area at least once before (15:3; cf. Mk 7:24).
21:4 *seven days.* These, added to the 29 days since the Passover in Philippi, would leave only two weeks until Pentecost. *urged Paul not to go.* The Spirit warned of the coming trials in store for Paul at Jerusalem (20:23). Because of these warnings, Paul's Christian friends urged him not to go on, knowing that trials lay ahead. But Paul felt "compelled by the Spirit" to go (20:22; see note there).
21:7 *Ptolemais.* The modern city of Acco, north of and across the bay from Mount Carmel. It was one day's journey from Tyre on the north and another 35 miles to Caesarea on the south.
21:8 *Caesarea.* A Gentile city, the capital of Roman Judea (see note on 10:1). *Philip the evangelist.* Philip's evangelistic work may have focused on Caesarea for almost 25 years (see note on 8:40). "Evangelist" is a title used only here and in Eph 4:11; 2Ti 4:5.
21:9 *unmarried daughters.* They may have been dedicated in a special way to serving the Lord (cf. 1Co 7:34). *prophesied.* See 1Co 11:5; 12:8–10; cf. Lk 2:36. For OT prophetesses see Ex 15:20; Jdg 4:4; 2Ki 22:14; Ne 6:14.
21:10 *prophet named Agabus.* Evidently he held the office of prophet, as Philip held the office of evangelist (v. 8). This is the same prophet who had been in Antioch prophesying the coming famine in Jerusalem some 15 years earlier (11:27–29).
21:12 *we and the people there.* Now Luke, in the company of travelers with Paul, joins in urging Paul not to go to Jerusalem.
21:13 *to die.* Cf. Php 1:21 and note.
21:14 *Lord's will be done.* May mean that they finally recognized that it was the Lord's will for Paul to go to Jerusalem.
21:16 *Mnason.* Must have been a disciple of some means to be able to accommodate Paul and a group of about nine men traveling with him.
21:17 *arrived at Jerusalem.* No more than a day or two before Pentecost. *the brothers received us warmly.* May indicate the grateful reception of the offering as well.
21:18 *James.* The brother of the Lord, author of the letter of James and leader of the church in Jerusalem (see Gal 1:19 and note; 2:9). He is called an apostle but was not one of the Twelve.
21:23 *made a vow.* They were evidently under the temporary Nazirite vow and became unclean before the completion time of the vow (perhaps from contact with a dead body); cf. Nu 6:2–12.
21:24 *purification rites.* In some instances the rites included the offering of sacrifices. Such rites were observed by choice

pay their expenses, so that they can have
their heads shaved.[a] Then everybody will
know there is no truth in these reports
about you, but that you yourself are living in obedience to the law. 25 As for the
Gentile believers, we have written to them
our decision that they should abstain from
food sacrificed to idols, from blood, from
the meat of strangled animals and from
sexual immorality."[b]
26 The next day Paul took the men and
purified himself along with them. Then he
went to the temple to give notice of the
date when the days of purification would
end and the offering would be made for
each of them.[c]

Paul Arrested

27 When the seven days were nearly
over, some Jews from the province of Asia
saw Paul at the temple. They stirred up the
whole crowd and seized him,[d] 28 shouting,
"Men of Israel, help us! This is the man
who teaches all men everywhere against
our people and our law and this place. And
besides, he has brought Greeks into the
temple area and defiled this holy place."[e]
29 (They had previously seen Trophimus[f]
the Ephesian[g] in the city with Paul and
assumed that Paul had brought him into
the temple area.)
30 The whole city was aroused, and the
people came running from all directions.
Seizing Paul,[h] they dragged him[i] from the
temple, and immediately the gates were
shut. 31 While they were trying to kill him,
news reached the commander of the Roman troops that the whole city of Jerusalem was in an uproar. 32 He at once took
some officers and soldiers and ran down
to the crowd. When the rioters saw the
commander and his soldiers, they stopped
beating Paul.[j]
33 The commander came up and arrested
him and ordered him to be bound[k] with
two[l] chains.[m] Then he asked who he was
and what he had done. 34 Some in the crowd
shouted one thing and some another,[n] and
since the commander could not get at the
truth because of the uproar, he ordered that
Paul be taken into the barracks.[o] 35 When
Paul reached the steps,[p] the violence of
the mob was so great he had to be carried
by the soldiers. 36 The crowd that followed
kept shouting, "Away with him!"[q]

Paul Speaks to the Crowd

22:3-16pp — Ac 9:1-22; 26:9-18

37 As the soldiers were about to take Paul
into the barracks,[r] he asked the commander, "May I say something to you?"
"Do you speak Greek?" he replied.
38 "Aren't you the Egyptian who started a
revolt and led four thousand terrorists out
into the desert[s] some time ago?"[t]
39 Paul answered, "I am a Jew, from Tarsus[u] in Cilicia,[v] a citizen of no ordinary
city. Please let me speak to the people."
40 Having received the commander's
permission, Paul stood on the steps and
motioned[w] to the crowd. When they were
all silent, he said to them in Aramaic[a]:[x]

[a] 40 Or possibly *Hebrew*; also in 22:2

21:24 [a] Ac 18:18
21:25 [b] Ac 15:20,29
21:26 [c] Nu 6:13-20; Ac 24:18
21:27 [d] Jer 26:8; Ac 24:18; 26:21; S 1Th 2:16
21:28 [e] Mt 24:15; Ac 6:13; 24:5,6
21:29 [f] Ac 20:4; 2Ti 4:20 [g] S Ac 18:19
21:30 [h] Ac 26:21 [i] S Ac 16:19
21:32 [j] Ac 23:27
21:33 [k] ver 11 [l] Ac 12:6 [m] Ac 20:23; 22:29; Eph 6:20; 2Ti 2:9
21:34 [n] Ac 19:32 [o] ver 37; Ac 22:24; 23:10,16,32
21:35 [p] ver 40
21:36 [q] Lk 23:18; Jn 19:15; Ac 22:22
21:37 [r] S ver 34
21:38 [s] Mt 24:26 [t] Ac 5:36
21:39 [u] S Ac 9:11 [v] S Ac 6:9
21:40 [w] S Ac 12:17 [x] S Jn 5:2

by some Jewish Christians but were not required of Christians, whether Jew or Gentile. *pay their expenses.* Paul's part in sponsoring these men would include (1) paying part or all of the expenses of the sacrificial victims (in this case eight pigeons and four lambs, Nu 6:9–12) and (2) going to the temple to notify the priest when their days of purification would be fulfilled so the priests would be prepared to sacrifice their offerings (v. 26). *living in obedience to the law.* Paul had earlier taken a vow himself (see 18:18 and note), he had been a Jew to the Jews (see 1Co 9:20–21), and Timothy had been circumcised (see 16:3 and note). However, Paul was very careful not to sacrifice Christian principle in any act of obedience to the law (he would not have Titus circumcised, Gal 2:3).

21:25 See 15:23–29 and notes.

21:27 *seven days.* Cf. Nu 6:9. These were the days required for purification, shaving their heads at the altar, the sacrifice of a sin offering and burnt offering for each, and announcing the completion to the priests. *Jews from the province of Asia.* Paul had suffered already from the hands of Asian Jews (20:19).

21:28 *teaches ... against our people and our law and this place.* Cf. the accusations brought against Stephen in 6:13. *brought Greeks into the temple area.* Explicitly forbidden according to inscribed stone markers (still in existence; see chart, p. 1667). Any Gentiles found within the bounds of the court of Israel would be killed. But there is no evidence that Paul had brought anyone other than Jews into the area.

21:29 *Trophimus.* See 20:4 and note. Paul probably did not take him into the forbidden area. If he had, they should have attacked Trophimus rather than Paul.

21:30 *gates were shut.* By order of the temple officer to prevent further trouble inside the sacred precincts.

21:31 *commander.* Greek *chiliarch*, a commander of 1,000 (a regiment), Claudius Lysias by name (23:26), who was stationed at the Fortress of Antonia (see note on v. 37).

21:32 *some officers.* Centurions. Since the plural is used, it is likely that at least two centurions and 200 soldiers were involved.

21:33 *two chains.* Probably his hands were chained to a soldier on either side.

21:34 *barracks.* See note on 12:9.

21:37 *barracks.* The Fortress of Antonia was connected to the northern end of the temple area by two flights of steps. The tower overlooked the temple area.

21:38 *the Egyptian who started a revolt.* Josephus tells of an Egyptian false prophet who some years earlier had led 4,000 (Josephus, through a misreading of a Greek capital letter, says "30,000") out to the Mount of Olives. Roman soldiers killed hundreds, but the leader escaped. *terrorists.* The Greek here is a loanword from Latin *sicarii*, meaning "dagger-men," who were violent assassins.

21:39 *Tarsus.* See note on 22:3.

21:40 *Aramaic.* More likely Aramaic than Hebrew (see NIV text note), since Aramaic was the most commonly used language among Palestinian Jews.

22 1“Brothers and fathers,[y] listen now to
my defense.”
2When they heard him speak to them in
Aramaic,[z] they became very quiet.
Then Paul said: 3“I am a Jew,[a] born in
Tarsus[b] of Cilicia,[c] but brought up in this
city. Under[d] Gamaliel[e] I was thoroughly trained in the law of our fathers[f] and
was just as zealous[g] for God as any of you
are today. 4I persecuted[h] the followers of
this Way[i] to their death, arresting both
men and women and throwing them into
prison,[j] 5as also the high priest and all the
Council[k] can testify. I even obtained letters from them to their brothers[l] in Damascus,[m] and went there to bring these people
as prisoners to Jerusalem to be punished.
6“About noon as I came near Damascus, suddenly a bright light from heaven
flashed around me.[n] 7I fell to the ground
and heard a voice say to me, ‘Saul! Saul!
Why do you persecute me?’
8“ ‘Who are you, Lord?’ I asked.
“ ‘I am Jesus of Nazareth,[o] whom you
are persecuting,’ he replied. 9My companions saw the light,[p] but they did not
understand the voice[q] of him who was
speaking to me.
10“ ‘What shall I do, Lord?’ I asked.
“ ‘Get up,’ the Lord said, ‘and go into
Damascus. There you will be told all that
you have been assigned to do.’[r] 11My companions led me by the hand into Damascus, because the brilliance of the light had
blinded me.[s]
12“A man named Ananias came to see
me.[t] He was a devout observer of the law
and highly respected by all the Jews living there.[u] 13He stood beside me and said,
‘Brother Saul, receive your sight!’ And at
that very moment I was able to see him.
14“Then he said: ‘The God of our fathers[v] has chosen you to know his will
and to see[w] the Righteous One[x] and to
hear words from his mouth. 15You will be
his witness[y] to all men of what you have
seen[z] and heard. 16And now what are you
waiting for? Get up, be baptized[a] and wash
your sins away,[b] calling on his name.’[c]
17“When I returned to Jerusalem[d] and
was praying at the temple, I fell into a
trance[e] 18and saw the Lord speaking.
‘Quick!’ he said to me. ‘Leave Jerusalem
immediately, because they will not accept
your testimony about me.’
19“ ‘Lord,’ I replied, ‘these men know
that I went from one synagogue to another
to imprison[f] and beat[g] those who believe
in you. 20And when the blood of your martyr[a] Stephen was shed, I stood there giving my approval and guarding the clothes
of those who were killing him.’[h]
21“Then the Lord said to me, ‘Go; I will
send you far away to the Gentiles.’ ”[i]

Paul the Roman Citizen

22The crowd listened to Paul until he
said this. Then they raised their voices and
shouted, “Rid the earth of him![j] He’s not
fit to live!”[k]
23As they were shouting and throwing off
their cloaks[l] and flinging dust into the air,[m]

a 20 Or *witness*

22:1 [y]Ac 7:2 **22:2** [z]Ac 21:40; S Jn 5:2 **22:3** [a]Ac 21:39 [b]S Ac 9:11 [c]S Ac 6:9 [d]Lk 10:39 [e]Ac 5:34 [f]Ac 26:5 [g]1Ki 19:10; S Ac 21:20 **22:4** [h]S Ac 8:3 [i]S Ac 9:2 [j]ver 19,20 **22:5** [k]Lk 22:66 [l]S Ac 1:16; 2:29; 13:26; 23:1; 28:17,21; S Ro 7:1; 9:3 [m]Ac 9:2 **22:6** [n]Ac 9:3 **22:8** [o]S Mk 1:24 **22:9** [p]Ac 26:13 [q]Ac 9:7 **22:10** [r]Ac 16:30 **22:11** [s]Ac 9:8 **22:12** [t]Ac 9:17 [u]Ac 10:22 **22:14** [v]S Ac 3:13 [w]S 1Co 15:8 [x]Ac 7:52 **22:15** [y]Ac 23:11; 26:16 [z]ver 14 **22:16** [a]S Ac 2:38 [b]Lev 8:6; Ps 51:2; Eze 36:25; Jn 3:5; 1Co 6:11; Eph 5:26; Tit 3:5; Heb 10:22; 1Pe 3:21 [c]Ro 10:13 **22:17** [d]Ac 9:26 [e]Ac 10:10 **22:19** [f]ver 4; S Ac 8:3 [g]S Mt 10:17 **22:20** [h]Ac 7:57-60; 8:1 **22:21** [i]S Ac 9:15; S 13:46 **22:22** [j]Ac 21:36 [k]Ac 25:24 **22:23** [l]Ac 7:58 [m]2Sa 16:13

22:1 *Brothers.* See note on 11:1.

22:2 *Aramaic.* See note on 21:40. Actually, if he had spoken in Hebrew, they would have become even quieter in order not to miss a single word, because it would have been more difficult for them to understand.

22:3 *born in Tarsus.* Paul had citizenship in Tarsus (21:39) as well as being a Roman citizen. “No ordinary city” (21:39) was used by Euripides to describe Athens. Tarsus was 10 miles inland on the Cydnus River and 30 miles from the mountains, which were cut by a deep, narrow gorge called the Cilician Gates (see map, p. 1704). It was an important commercial center, university city and crossroads of travel. *brought up in this city.* Paul must have come to Jerusalem at an early age. Another translation (“brought up in this city at the feet of Gamaliel, being thoroughly trained according to the law of our fathers”) would suggest that Paul came to Jerusalem when he was old enough to begin training under Gamaliel. *Gamaliel.* The most honored rabbi of the first century. Possibly he was the grandson of Hillel (see also 5:34–40).

22:4 *I persecuted the followers.* See 9:1–4. *this Way.* See 9:2 and note.

22:5 *high priest.* Caiaphas, the high priest over 20 years earlier, was now dead, and Ananias was high priest (see 23:2 and note); but the records of the high priest would show Paul’s testimony to be true. *Council.* The Sanhedrin (see Mk 14:55 and note).

22:6 *About noon.* A detail not included in the earlier account (9:1–22).

22:8 *Who are you, Lord?* See note on 9:5. *persecuting.* See note on 9:4.

22:9 *did not understand the voice.* They heard the sound (9:7) but did not understand what was said.

22:12 *Ananias . . . devout observer of the law.* Important to this audience (see note on Lk 1:6).

22:14 *to see the Righteous One.* Cf. 3:14; Lk 23:47 and notes. To see the resurrected Jesus was all-important to Paul (see 26:16; 1Co 9:1; 15:8). It was that experience that had convinced him of the truth of the gospel and that became the foundation of his theology.

22:16 *wash your sins away.* Baptism is the outward sign of an inward work of grace. The reality and the symbol are closely associated in the NT (see 2:38; Tit 3:5; 1Pe 3:21 and notes). The outward rite, however, does not produce the inward grace (cf. Ro 2:28–29; Eph 2:8–9; Php 3:4–9). See note on Ro 6:3–4.

22:17 *When I returned to Jerusalem.* Refers to the visit described in 9:26; Gal 1:17–18. *at the temple, I fell into a trance.* See Peter’s trance (10:10; 11:5; cf. 2Co 12:3). Paul was not a blasphemer of the temple but continued to hold it in high honor.

22:20 *giving my approval.* Does not necessarily mean that Paul had to be a member of the Sanhedrin, though some have thought so (see note on 26:10). He could show his approval by allowing them to put their cloaks at his feet.

24the commander ordered Paul to be tak-
en into the barracks.[n] He directed[o] that he
be flogged and questioned in order to find
out why the people were shouting at him
like this. 25As they stretched him out to
flog him, Paul said to the centurion standing there, "Is it legal for you to flog a Roman citizen who hasn't even been found
guilty?"[p]
26When the centurion heard this, he
went to the commander and reported it.
"What are you going to do?" he asked.
"This man is a Roman citizen."
27The commander went to Paul and
asked, "Tell me, are you a Roman citizen?"
"Yes, I am," he answered.
28Then the commander said, "I had to
pay a big price for my citizenship."
"But I was born a citizen," Paul replied.
29Those who were about to question
him[q] withdrew immediately. The commander himself was alarmed when he
realized that he had put Paul, a Roman
citizen,[r] in chains.[s]

Before the Sanhedrin

30The next day, since the commander
wanted to find out exactly why Paul was being accused by the Jews,[t] he released him[u]
and ordered the chief priests and all the
Sanhedrin[v] to assemble. Then he brought
Paul and had him stand before them.
23 Paul looked straight at the Sanhedrin[w] and said, "My brothers,[x] I have
fulfilled my duty to God in all good conscience[y] to this day." 2At this the high
priest Ananias[z] ordered those standing
near Paul to strike him on the mouth.[a]
3Then Paul said to him, "God will strike
you, you whitewashed wall![b] You sit there
to judge me according to the law, yet you
yourself violate the law by commanding
that I be struck!"[c]
4Those who were standing near Paul
said, "You dare to insult God's high
priest?"
5Paul replied, "Brothers, I did not realize
that he was the high priest; for it is written: 'Do not speak evil about the ruler of
your people.'[a]"[d]
6Then Paul, knowing that some of them
were Sadducees[e] and the others Pharisees,
called out in the Sanhedrin, "My brothers,[f] I am a Pharisee,[g] the son of a Pharisee. I stand on trial because of my hope
in the resurrection of the dead."[h] 7When
he said this, a dispute broke out between
the Pharisees and the Sadducees, and the
assembly was divided. 8(The Sadducees
say that there is no resurrection,[i] and that
there are neither angels nor spirits, but the
Pharisees acknowledge them all.)
9There was a great uproar, and some of
the teachers of the law who were Pharisees[j] stood up and argued vigorously. "We
find nothing wrong with this man,"[k] they
said. "What if a spirit or an angel has spoken to him?"[l] 10The dispute became so violent that the commander was afraid Paul
would be torn to pieces by them. He ordered the troops to go down and take him

22:24 [n]S Ac 21:34 [o]ver 29 **22:25** [p]Ac 16:37 **22:29** [q]ver 24 [r]ver 24,25; Ac 16:38 [s]S Ac 21:33 **22:30** [t]Ac 23:28 [u]Ac 21:33 [v]S Mt 5:22 **23:1** [w]Ac 22:30 [x]S Ac 22:5 [y]Ac 24:16; 1Co 4:4; 2Co 1:12; 1Ti 1:5,19; 3:9; 2Ti 1:3; Heb 9:14; 10:22; 13:18; 1Pe 3:16,21 **23:2** [z]Ac 24:1 [a]Jn 18:22 **23:3** [b]Mt 23:27 [c]Lev 19:15; Dt 25:1,2; Jn 7:51 **23:5** [d]Ex 22:28 **23:6** [e]ver 7,8; S Ac 4:1 [f]S Ac 22:5 [g]Ac 26:5; Php 3:5 [h]Ac 24:15,21; 26:8 **23:8** [i]Mt 22:23; 1Co 15:12 **23:9** [j]Mk 2:16 [k]ver 29; Jer 26:16; S Lk 23:4; Ac 25:25; 26:31; 28:18 [l]Ac 22:7,17,18

[a] 5 Exodus 22:28

22:24 *commander.* See note on 21:31. *barracks.* See note on 21:37. *that he be flogged.* Not with the rod, as at Philippi (16:22–24), but with the scourge, a merciless instrument of torture. It was legal to use it to force a confession from a slave or alien but never from a Roman citizen. The scourge consisted of a whip of leather thongs with pieces of bone or metal attached to the ends (cf. Mk 15:15 and note).

22:25 *they stretched him out.* The Greek word used for tying a person to a post for whipping. *centurion.* See note on 10:1. *Roman citizen.* According to Roman law, all Roman citizens were assured exclusion from all degrading forms of punishment: beating with rods, scourging, crucifixion.

22:28 *pay a big price.* There were three ways to obtain Roman citizenship: (1) receive it as a reward for some outstanding service to Rome; (2) buy it at a considerable price; (3) be born into a family of Roman citizens. How Paul's father or an earlier ancestor had gained citizenship, no one knows. By 171 B.C. a large number of Jews were citizens of Tarsus, and in the time of Pompey (106–48) some of these could have received Roman citizenship as well.

22:29 *alarmed.* Cf. the same reaction of the magistrates in Philippi (16:38).

22:30 *he released him.* Paul was no longer bound, and presumably he would have been free completely if the Sanhedrin had not wished to detain him. *chief priests.* Those of the high priestly line of descent (mainly Sadducees; see note on Mt 2:4), but the Sanhedrin now included a considerable number of Pharisees. These men constituted the ruling body of the Jews. The Jewish court was respected by the Roman governor, whose approval had to be obtained before sentencing to capital punishment.

23:1 *Sanhedrin.* See notes on 5:21; 22:30. *brothers.* Fellow Jews (see note on 11:1). *good conscience.* A consistent claim of Paul (see 24:16; Ro 9:1; 1Co 4:4; 2Co 1:12; 2Ti 1:3).

23:2 *Ananias.* High priest A.D. 47–59, son of Nebedaeus. He is not to be confused with the high priest Annas (A.D. 6–15; see note on Lk 3:2). Ananias was noted for cruelty and violence. When the revolt against Rome broke out, he was assassinated by his own people.

23:3 *whitewashed wall!* Having an attractive exterior but filled with unclean contents, such as tombs holding dead bodies (see Mt 23:27); or walls that look substantial but fall before the winds (see Eze 13:10–12). It is a metaphor for a hypocrite.

23:5 *I did not realize that he was the high priest.* Explained in different ways: (1) Paul had poor eyesight (suggested by such passages as Gal 4:15; 6:11 [see note there]) and failed to see that the one who presided was the high priest. (2) He failed to discern that the one who presided was the high priest because on some occasions others had sat in his place. (3) He was using pure irony: A true high priest would not give such an order. (4) He refused to acknowledge that Ananias was the high priest under these circumstances.

23:6 *Sadducees.* See note on 4:1. They denied the resurrection and angels and spirits (v. 8). *Pharisees.* See notes on Mt 3:7; Mk 2:16; Lk 5:17.

23:10 *commander.* See note on 21:31. *barracks.* See note on 21:37.

away from them by force and bring him
into the barracks.[m]
11 The following night the Lord stood
near Paul and said, "Take courage![n] As
you have testified about me in Jerusalem,
so you must also testify in Rome."[o]

The Plot to Kill Paul

12 The next morning the Jews formed a
conspiracy[p] and bound themselves with
an oath not to eat or drink until they had
killed Paul.[q] 13 More than forty men were
involved in this plot. 14 They went to the
chief priests and elders and said, "We
have taken a solemn oath not to eat anything until we have killed Paul.[r] 15 Now
then, you and the Sanhedrin[s] petition the
commander to bring him before you on
the pretext of wanting more accurate information about his case. We are ready to
kill him before he gets here."
16 But when the son of Paul's sister heard
of this plot, he went into the barracks[t] and
told Paul.
17 Then Paul called one of the centurions and said, "Take this young man to
the commander; he has something to
tell him." 18 So he took him to the commander.
The centurion said, "Paul, the prisoner,[u] sent for me and asked me to bring this
young man to you because he has something to tell you."
19 The commander took the young man
by the hand, drew him aside and asked,
"What is it you want to tell me?"
20 He said: "The Jews have agreed to ask
you to bring Paul before the Sanhedrin[v]
tomorrow on the pretext of wanting more
accurate information about him.[w] 21 Don't
give in to them, because more than forty[x] of them are waiting in ambush for
him. They have taken an oath not to eat
or drink until they have killed him.[y] They
are ready now, waiting for your consent to
their request."
22 The commander dismissed the young
man and cautioned him, "Don't tell anyone that you have reported this to me."

Paul Transferred to Caesarea

23 Then he called two of his centurions
and ordered them, "Get ready a detachment of two hundred soldiers, seventy
horsemen and two hundred spearmen[a] to
go to Caesarea[z] at nine tonight.[a] 24 Provide
mounts for Paul so that he may be taken
safely to Governor Felix."[b]
25 He wrote a letter as follows:

26 Claudius Lysias,

To His Excellency,[c] Governor Felix:

Greetings.[d]

27 This man was seized by the Jews
and they were about to kill him,[e] but
I came with my troops and rescued
him,[f] for I had learned that he is a Roman citizen.[g] 28 I wanted to know why
they were accusing him, so I brought
him to their Sanhedrin.[h] 29 I found that
the accusation had to do with questions about their law,[i] but there was
no charge against him[j] that deserved
death or imprisonment. 30 When I was
informed[k] of a plot[l] to be carried out
against the man, I sent him to you
at once. I also ordered his accusers[m]
to present to you their case against
him.

31 So the soldiers, carrying out their orders, took Paul with them during the night
and brought him as far as Antipatris. 32 The
next day they let the cavalry[n] go on with
him, while they returned to the barracks.[o]
33 When the cavalry[p] arrived in Caesarea,[q]
they delivered the letter to the governor[r]
and handed Paul over to him. 34 The governor read the letter and asked what province he was from. Learning that he was

a 23 The meaning of the Greek for this word is uncertain.

23:10 [m] S Ac 21:34
23:11 [n] S Mt 14:27 [o] Ac 19:21; 28:23
23:12 [p] S Ac 20:3 [q] ver 14, 21, 30; Ac 25:3
23:14 [r] ver 12
23:15 [s] ver 1; Ac 22:30
23:16 [t] ver 10; S Ac 21:34
23:18 [u] S Eph 3:1
23:20 [v] ver 1 [w] ver 14, 15
23:21 [x] ver 13 [y] ver 12, 14
23:23 [z] S Ac 8:40 [a] ver 33
23:24 [b] ver 26, 33; Ac 24:1-3, 10; 25:14
23:26 [c] Lk 1:3; Ac 24:3; 26:25 [d] Ac 15:23
23:27 [e] Ac 21:32 [f] Ac 21:33 [g] Ac 22:25-29
23:28 [h] Ac 22:30
23:29 [i] Ac 18:15; 25:19 [j] S ver 9
23:30 [k] ver 20, 21 [l] S Ac 20:3 [m] ver 35; Ac 24:19; 25:16
23:32 [n] ver 23 [o] S Ac 21:34
23:33 [p] ver 23, 24 [q] S Ac 8:40 [r] ver 26

23:11 *the Lord stood near.* In times of crisis and need for strength, Paul was given help (see 18:9; 22:18; 27:23; cf. 2Co 12:7–10 and notes).
23:12 *bound themselves with an oath.* Probably these were from the Zealots or the "terrorists" (see note on 21:38) later responsible for revolt against Rome.
23:17 *centurions.* See note on 10:1.
23:22 *Don't tell anyone.* For the boy's own safety and because of the commander's plans to transfer Paul under cover of night (see v. 23).
23:23 *soldiers … horsemen … spearmen.* Heavily armed infantry, cavalry and lightly armed soldiers. The commander assigned 470 men to protect Paul, the Roman citizen (cf. 22:25–29)—but the Greek for "spearmen" is an obscure word and could perhaps be translated "additional mounts and pack animals" (see NIV text note).
23:24 *Governor Felix.* See note on v. 34.
23:27 *for I had learned that he is a Roman citizen.* Inserted to gain the commander's favor with Rome, but not a true statement, because the commander did not learn of Paul's citizenship until he was about to scourge him to gain information.
23:29 Cf. the false charge made against Paul before Gallio in Corinth (18:13–16).
23:30 *ordered his accusers to present to you their case.* He anticipated that the order would be given by the time the letter was delivered.
23:31 *Antipatris.* Rebuilt by Herod the Great and named for his father (Antipater). It was a military post between Samaria and Judea—30 miles from Jerusalem.
23:33 *Caesarea.* The headquarters of Roman rule for Samaria and Judea—28 miles from Antipatris (see note on 8:40).
23:34 *The governor.* Antonius Felix. The emperor Claudius had appointed him governor of Judea c. A.D. 52, a time when Felix's brother was the emperor's favorite minister.

from Cilicia,[s] 35he said, "I will hear your case when your accusers[t] get here." Then he ordered that Paul be kept under guard[u] in Herod's palace.

The Trial Before Felix

24 Five days later the high priest Ananias[v] went down to Caesarea with some of the elders and a lawyer named Tertullus, and they brought their charges[w] against Paul before the governor.[x] 2When Paul was called in, Tertullus presented his case before Felix: "We have enjoyed a long period of peace under you, and your foresight has brought about reforms in this nation. 3Everywhere and in every way, most excellent[y] Felix, we acknowledge this with profound gratitude. 4But in order not to weary you further, I would request that you be kind enough to hear us briefly.

5"We have found this man to be a troublemaker, stirring up riots[z] among the Jews[a] all over the world. He is a ringleader of the Nazarene[b] sect[c] 6and even tried to desecrate the temple;[d] so we seized him. 8By[a] examining him yourself you will be able to learn the truth about all these charges we are bringing against him."

9The Jews joined in the accusation,[e] asserting that these things were true.

10When the governor[f] motioned for him to speak, Paul replied: "I know that for a number of years you have been a judge over this nation; so I gladly make my defense. 11You can easily verify that no more than twelve days[g] ago I went up to Jerusalem to worship. 12My accusers did not find me arguing with anyone at the temple,[h] or stirring up a crowd[i] in the synagogues or anywhere else in the city. 13And they cannot prove to you the charges they are now making against me.[j] 14However, I admit that I worship the God of our fathers[k] as a follower of the Way,[l] which they call a sect.[m] I believe everything that agrees with the Law and that is written in the Prophets,[n] 15and I have the same hope in God as these men, that there will be a resurrection[o] of both the righteous and the wicked.[p] 16So I strive always to keep my conscience clear[q] before God and man.

17"After an absence of several years, I came to Jerusalem to bring my people gifts for the poor[r] and to present offerings. 18I was ceremonially clean[s] when they found me in the temple courts doing this. There was no crowd with me, nor was I involved in any disturbance.[t] 19But there are some Jews from the province of Asia,[u] who ought to be here before you and bring charges if they have anything against me.[v] 20Or these who are here should state what crime they found in me when I stood be-

[a] 6-8 Some manuscripts *him and wanted to judge him according to our law. 7But the commander, Lysias, came and with the use of much force snatched him from our hands 8and ordered his accusers to come before you. By*

23:34 [s] S Ac 6:9; 21:39
23:35 [t] ver 30; Ac 24:19; 25:16 [u] Ac 24:27
24:1 [v] Ac 23:2 [w] Ac 23:30,35 [x] S Ac 23:24
24:3 [y] Lk 1:3; Ac 23:26; 26:25
24:5 [z] Ac 16:20; 17:6 [a] Ac 21:28 [b] S Mk 1:24 [c] ver 14; Ac 26:5; 28:22
24:6 [d] Ac 21:28
24:9 [e] S 1Th 2:16
24:10 [f] S Ac 23:24
24:11 [g] Ac 21:27; ver 1
24:12 [h] Ac 25:8; 28:17 [i] ver 18
24:13 [j] Ac 25:7
24:14 [k] S Ac 3:13 [l] S Ac 9:2 [m] S ver 5 [n] Ac 26:6,22; 28:23
24:15 [o] Ac 23:6; 28:20 [p] S Mt 25:46
24:16 [q] S Ac 23:1
24:17 [r] Ac 11:29,30; Ro 15:25-28,31; 1Co 16:1-4,15; 2Co 8:1-4; Gal 2:10
24:18 [s] Ac 21:26 [t] ver 12
24:19 [u] S Ac 2:9 [v] Ac 23:30

The brothers had formerly been slaves, then Freedmen, then high officials in government. The historian Tacitus said of Felix, "He held the power of a tyrant with the disposition of a slave." He married three queens in succession, one of whom was Drusilla (see note on 24:24). *from Cilicia.* If Paul had come from a province nearby, Felix might have turned him over for trial under another's jurisdiction.

23:35 *Herod's palace.* Erected as a royal residence by Herod the Great but now used as a Roman praetorium—the headquarters of the local Roman governor. Praetoria were located in Rome (Php 1:13), Ephesus, Jerusalem (Jn 18:28; see note there), Caesarea and other parts of the empire.

24:1 *Five days later.* After the departure from Jerusalem. This would allow just enough time for a messenger to go from Caesarea to Jerusalem, the Sanhedrin to appoint their representatives, and the appointees to make the return journey to Caesarea. *Ananias.* See note on 23:2. The high priest himself made the 60-mile journey to supervise the case personally. *elders.* The Sanhedrin was made up of 71 elders. The designation was used of both the religious and the political councils. See notes on Ex 3:16; 2Sa 3:17; Joel 1:2; Mt 15:2. *lawyer.* Lit. "orator." In a court trial one trained in forensic rhetoric would serve as an attorney at law. *Tertullus.* A common variant of the name Tertius. Possibly he was a Roman but more likely a Hellenistic Jew familiar with the procedures of the Roman court.

24:2–3 *long period of peace ... with profound gratitude.* The expected eulogy with which to introduce a speech before a judge. In his six years in office Felix had eliminated bands of robbers, thwarted organized assassins and crushed a movement led by an Egyptian (see note on 21:38). But in general his record was not good. He was recalled by Rome two years later because of misrule. His reforms and improvements are hard to identify historically.

24:5 *troublemaker ... ringleader of the Nazarene sect.* To excite dissension in the empire was treason against Caesar. To be a leader of a religious sect without Roman approval was contrary to law. *Nazarene sect.* Christianity.

24:6 *tried to desecrate the temple.* The charge is now qualified by an attempt, rather than the former claim (see 21:28 and note).

24:7 See NIV text note on vv. 6–8.

24:10 Paul's reserved introduction lacks the flattery employed by Tertullus (vv. 2–4).

24:11 *twelve days ago.* Paul answers each accusation. He was not a troublemaker, and he had not been involved in disturbances. He had but recently arrived in Jerusalem. He had spent five days in Caesarea and nearly seven in Jerusalem.

24:14 *worship ... God ... as a follower of the Way.* Paul admits to his part in the Way, but he still believes the Law and the Prophets. He shares the same hope as the Jews—resurrection and judgment (v. 15).

24:16 *conscience clear.* See note on 23:1.

24:17 *to bring my people gifts for the poor.* The only explicit reference in Acts to the collection that was so important to Paul (see note on 20:4). *to present offerings.* May refer to Paul's help in sponsoring those who were fulfilling their vows (see 21:24 and note). He also may have intended to present offerings for himself.

24:19 *Jews from the province of Asia.* See 21:27–29. The absence of these Asian Jews would seem to suggest that they could not substantiate their accusations.

fore the Sanhedrin— 21 unless it was this
one thing I shouted as I stood in their presence: 'It is concerning the resurrection of
the dead that I am on trial before you today.' "[w]
22 Then Felix, who was well acquainted
with the Way,[x] adjourned the proceedings.
"When Lysias the commander comes," he
said, "I will decide your case." 23 He ordered the centurion to keep Paul under
guard[y] but to give him some freedom[z]
and permit his friends to take care of his
needs.[a]
24 Several days later Felix came with his
wife Drusilla, who was a Jewess. He sent
for Paul and listened to him as he spoke
about faith in Christ Jesus.[b] 25 As Paul discoursed on righteousness, self-control[c]
and the judgment[d] to come, Felix was
afraid[e] and said, "That's enough for now!
You may leave. When I find it convenient,
I will send for you." 26 At the same time
he was hoping that Paul would offer him
a bribe, so he sent for him frequently and
talked with him.
27 When two years had passed, Felix was
succeeded by Porcius Festus,[f] but because
Felix wanted to grant a favor to the Jews,[g]
he left Paul in prison.[h]

The Trial Before Festus

25 Three days after arriving in the province, Festus[i] went up from Caesarea[j]
to Jerusalem, 2 where the chief priests and
Jewish leaders appeared before him and
presented the charges against Paul.[k] 3 They
urgently requested Festus, as a favor to
them, to have Paul transferred to Jerusalem, for they were preparing an ambush to
kill him along the way.[l] 4 Festus answered,
"Paul is being held[m] at Caesarea,[n] and I
myself am going there soon. 5 Let some
of your leaders come with me and press
charges against the man there, if he has
done anything wrong."
6 After spending eight or ten days with
them, he went down to Caesarea, and the
next day he convened the court[o] and ordered that Paul be brought before him.[p]
7 When Paul appeared, the Jews who
had come down from Jerusalem stood
around him, bringing many serious charges against him,[q] which they could not
prove.[r]
8 Then Paul made his defense: "I have
done nothing wrong against the law of the
Jews or against the temple[s] or against Caesar."
9 Festus, wishing to do the Jews a favor,[t]
said to Paul, "Are you willing to go up to
Jerusalem and stand trial before me there
on these charges?"[u]
10 Paul answered: "I am now standing
before Caesar's court, where I ought to be
tried. I have not done any wrong to the
Jews,[v] as you yourself know very well.

24:21 [w] Ac 23:6
24:22 [x] S Ac 9:2
24:23 [y] Ac 23:35 [z] Ac 28:16 [a] Ac 23:16; 27:3
24:24 [b] S Ac 20:21
24:25 [c] Gal 5:23; 1Th 5:6; 1Pe 4:7; 5:8; 2Pe 1:6 [d] Ac 10:42 [e] Jer 36:16
24:27 [f] Ac 25:1,4,9,14 [g] Ac 12:3; 25:9 [h] Ac 23:35; 25:14
25:1 [i] S Ac 24:27 [j] S Ac 8:40
25:2 [k] ver 15; Ac 24:1
25:3 [l] S Ac 20:3
25:4 [m] Ac 24:23 [n] S Ac 8:40
25:6 [o] ver 17 [p] ver 10
25:7 [q] Mk 15:3; Lk 23:2,10; Ac 24:5,6 [r] Ac 24:13
25:8 [s] Ac 6:13; 24:12; 28:17
25:9 [t] Ac 24:27; 12:3 [u] ver 20
25:10 [v] ver 8

24:21 *concerning the resurrection.* Paul again introduces the point of contention between the Pharisees and Sadducees (see 23:6–8; see also chart, p. 1502).

24:22 *well acquainted with the Way.* Felix could not have governed Judea and Samaria for six years without becoming familiar with the place and activities of the Christians.

24:23 *to give him some freedom.* Perhaps Paul was under house arrest similar to what he experienced while awaiting trial in Rome (28:30–31)—in recognition of the fact that he was a Roman citizen who had not been found guilty of any crime.

24:24 *Drusilla.* Felix's third wife, daughter of Herod Agrippa I. At age 15 she married Azizus, king of Emesa, but deserted him for Felix a year later. Her son, also named Agrippa, died in the eruption of Vesuvius (A.D. 79).

24:25 *Felix was afraid.* Hearing of "righteousness, self-control and ... judgment," Felix looked at his past life and was filled with fear. He had a spark of sincerity and concern. *When I find it convenient.* Lust, pride, greed and selfish ambition made it continually inconvenient to change.

24:26 *offer him a bribe.* Felix supposed that Paul had access to considerable funds. He had heard of his bringing an offering to the Jewish Christians in Jerusalem (see v. 17 and note). So he wanted Paul to give him money in order to secure his release. Paul no longer had the money, nor would he offer a bribe if he had it.

24:27 *Felix was succeeded by ... Festus.* Felix was recalled to Rome in A.D. 59/60 to answer for disturbances and irregularities in his rule, such as his handling of riots between Jewish and Syrian inhabitants. Festus is not mentioned in existing historical records before his arrival in Judea. He died in office after two years, but his record for that time shows wisdom and honesty superior to both his predecessor, Felix, and his successor, Albinus. *to grant a favor to the Jews.* Felix did not want to incite more anger among the Jews, whom he would be facing in Roman court shortly. To release Paul from prison would do just that.

25:1 *from Caesarea to Jerusalem.* Sixty miles, a two-day trip. Festus was anxious to go immediately to the center of Jewish rule and worship.

25:2 *chief priests and Jewish leaders.* The Sanhedrin (see note on Mk 14:55).

25:3 *ambush.* Probably the same group that had earlier made a vow to take Paul's life (see 23:12 and note).

25:6 *convened the court.* To make his decision binding as a formal ruling.

25:7 *which they could not prove.* Again, as in the first hearing, Paul's adversaries produced no witnesses or evidence of any kind (see 24:2–9).

25:8 *nothing ... against the law.* Paul had respect for the law (see Ro 7:12; 8:3–4; 1Co 9:20 and note). *against the temple.* See notes on 21:28–29. Paul had not defied its customs by taking Trophimus into forbidden areas (21:29). Jesus had prophesied its destruction, but he was not responsible for its plight (Lk 21:5–6). *against Caesar.* Paul proclaimed the kingdom of God but not as a political rival of Rome (cf. 17:6–7). He advocated respect for law and order (see Ro 13:1–7) and prayer for civil rulers (see 1Ti 2:1–2).

25:9 *Are you willing to go up to Jerusalem ...?* Obviously not. Festus had said that the trial would be before him; so Paul insisted that he was then standing in the Roman civil court (v. 10). He wanted to keep his trial there rather than suffer at the hands of a Jewish religious court. As a Roman citizen, he could refuse to go to a local provincial court; instead, he looked to a higher Roman court.

11If, however, I am guilty of doing anything
deserving death, I do not refuse to die. But
if the charges brought against me by these
Jews are not true, no one has the right to
hand me over to them. I appeal to Caesar!"[w]
12After Festus had conferred with his
council, he declared: "You have appealed
to Caesar. To Caesar you will go!"

Festus Consults King Agrippa

13A few days later King Agrippa and Bernice arrived at Caesarea[x] to pay their respects to Festus. 14Since they were spending many days there, Festus discussed
Paul's case with the king. He said: "There
is a man here whom Felix left as a prisoner.[y] 15When I went to Jerusalem, the chief
priests and elders of the Jews brought
charges against him[z] and asked that he be
condemned.
16"I told them that it is not the Roman
custom to hand over any man before he
has faced his accusers and has had an opportunity to defend himself against their
charges.[a] 17When they came here with me,
I did not delay the case, but convened the
court the next day and ordered the man to
be brought in.[b] 18When his accusers got
up to speak, they did not charge him with
any of the crimes I had expected. 19In-
stead, they had some points of dispute[c]
with him about their own religion[d] and
about a dead man named Jesus who Paul
claimed was alive. 20I was at a loss how to
investigate such matters; so I asked if he
would be willing to go to Jerusalem and
stand trial there on these charges.[e] 21When
Paul made his appeal to be held over for
the Emperor's decision, I ordered him held
until I could send him to Caesar."[f]
22Then Agrippa said to Festus, "I would
like to hear this man myself."
He replied, "Tomorrow you will hear
him."[g]

Paul Before Agrippa

26:12-18pp — Ac 9:3-8; 22:6-11

23The next day Agrippa and Bernice[h]
came with great pomp and entered the
audience room with the high ranking officers and the leading men of the city. At the
command of Festus, Paul was brought in.
24Festus said: "King Agrippa, and all who
are present with us, you see this man! The
whole Jewish community[i] has petitioned
me about him in Jerusalem and here in
Caesarea, shouting that he ought not to
live any longer.[j] 25I found he had done
nothing deserving of death,[k] but because
he made his appeal to the Emperor[l] I decided to send him to Rome. 26But I have
nothing definite to write to His Majesty
about him. Therefore I have brought him
before all of you, and especially before
you, King Agrippa, so that as a result of
this investigation I may have something
to write. 27For I think it is unreasonable to
send on a prisoner without specifying the
charges against him."

26 Then Agrippa said to Paul, "You have
permission to speak for yourself."[m]
So Paul motioned with his hand[n] and
began his defense: 2"King Agrippa, I consider myself fortunate to stand before you[o]
today as I make my defense against all the

25:11 [w] ver 21, 25; Ac 26:32; 28:19
25:13 [x] S Ac 8:40
25:14 [y] Ac 24:27
25:15 [z] ver 2; Ac 24:1
25:16 [a] ver 4, 5; Ac 23:30
25:17 [b] ver 6, 10
25:19 [c] Ac 18:15; 23:29 [d] Ac 17:22
25:20 [e] ver 9
25:21 [f] ver 11, 12
25:22 [g] Ac 9:15
25:23 [h] ver 13; Ac 26:30
25:24 [i] ver 2, 3, 7 [j] Ac 22:22
25:25 [k] S Ac 23:9 [l] S ver 11
26:1 [m] Ac 9:15; 25:22 [n] S Ac 12:17
26:2 [o] Ps 119:46

25:11 *I appeal to Caesar!* Nero had become the emperor by this time. It was the right of every Roman citizen to have his case heard before Caesar himself (or his representative) in Rome. This was the highest court of appeal, and winning such a case could have led to more than just Paul's acquittal. It could have resulted in official recognition of Christianity as distinct from Judaism.
25:12 *his council.* The officials and legal experts who made up the advisory council for the Roman governor.
25:13 *King Agrippa.* Herod Agrippa II. He was 17 years old at the death of his father in A.D. 44 (12:23). Being too young to succeed his father, he was replaced by Roman governors. Eight years later, however, a gradual extension of territorial authority began. Ultimately he ruled over territory north and northeast of the Sea of Galilee, over several Galilean cities and over some cities in Perea. At the Jewish revolt, when Jerusalem fell, he was on the side of the Romans. He died c. A.D. 100 — the last of the Herods (see chart, p. 1465). *Bernice.* The oldest daughter of Agrippa I, she was 16 years old at his death. When only 13, she married her uncle, Herod of Chalcis, and had two sons. When Herod died, she lived with her brother, Agrippa II. To silence rumors that she was living in incest with her brother, she married Polemon, king of Cilicia, but left him soon to return to Agrippa. She became the mistress of the emperor Vespasian's son Titus but was later ignored by him. *to pay their respects.* It was customary for rulers to pay a complimentary visit to a new ruler at the time of his assignment. It was advantageous to each that they get along (cf. Herod Antipas and Pilate, Lk 23:6 – 12).
25:19 *religion.* Or "superstition," the same word used by Paul in 17:22 (see note there).
25:22 *I would like to hear.* Agrippa had been wishing to hear Paul (cf. Antipas wanting to see Jesus, Lk 9:9; 23:8).
25:23 *audience room.* Not the judgment hall, for this was not a court trial. It was in an auditorium appropriate for the pomp of the occasion, with a king, his sister, the Roman governor and the outstanding leaders of both the Jews and the Roman government present. *high ranking officers.* Five regiments were stationed at Caesarea, so their five commanders would be in attendance (see note on 21:31).
25:26 *I have nothing definite.* Festus was required to send Caesar an explicit report on the case when an appeal was made. He hoped for some help from Agrippa in this matter. This was not an official trial but a special hearing to satisfy the curiosity of Agrippa and provide an assessment for Festus. *especially before you, King Agrippa.* He would be sensitive to differences between Pharisees and Sadducees, expectations of the Messiah, differences between Jews and Christians, and Jewish customs pertinent to these problems (see 26:2 – 3 and note on 26:3).
26:1 *permission to speak.* Agrippa gave the permission because Festus allowed him to have charge of the hearing.

accusations of the Jews,[p] 3and especially
so because you are well acquainted with
all the Jewish customs[q] and controversies.[r] Therefore, I beg you to listen to me
patiently.
4"The Jews all know the way I have
lived ever since I was a child,[s] from the
beginning of my life in my own country,
and also in Jerusalem. 5They have known
me for a long time[t] and can testify, if they
are willing, that according to the strictest
sect[u] of our religion, I lived as a Pharisee.[v]
6And now it is because of my hope[w] in
what God has promised our fathers[x] that I
am on trial today. 7This is the promise our
twelve tribes[y] are hoping to see fulfilled as
they earnestly serve God day and night.[z]
O king, it is because of this hope that the
Jews are accusing me.[a] 8Why should any
of you consider it incredible that God raises the dead?[b]
9"I too was convinced[c] that I ought to
do all that was possible to oppose[d] the
name of Jesus of Nazareth.[e] 10And that is
just what I did in Jerusalem. On the authority of the chief priests I put many of
the saints[f] in prison,[g] and when they were
put to death, I cast my vote against them.[h]
11Many a time I went from one synagogue
to another to have them punished,[i] and I
tried to force them to blaspheme. In my
obsession against them, I even went to
foreign cities to persecute them.
12"On one of these journeys I was going
to Damascus with the authority and commission of the chief priests. 13About noon,
O king, as I was on the road, I saw a light
from heaven, brighter than the sun, blazing around me and my companions. 14We
all fell to the ground, and I heard a voice[j]
saying to me in Aramaic,[a][k] 'Saul, Saul,
why do you persecute me? It is hard for
you to kick against the goads.'
15"Then I asked, 'Who are you, Lord?'
"'I am Jesus, whom you are persecuting,' the Lord replied. 16'Now get up
and stand on your feet.[l] I have appeared
to you to appoint you as a servant and
as a witness of what you have seen of
me and what I will show you.[m] 17I will
rescue you[n] from your own people and
from the Gentiles.[o] I am sending you to
them 18to open their eyes[p] and turn them
from darkness to light,[q] and from the
power of Satan to God, so that they may
receive forgiveness of sins[r] and a place
among those who are sanctified by faith
in me.'[s]
19"So then, King Agrippa, I was not
disobedient[t] to the vision from heaven.
20First to those in Damascus,[u] then to
those in Jerusalem[v] and in all Judea, and
to the Gentiles[w] also, I preached that they
should repent[x] and turn to God and prove
their repentance by their deeds.[y] 21That is
why the Jews seized me[z] in the temple
courts and tried to kill me.[a] 22But I have
had God's help to this very day, and so I
stand here and testify to small and great
alike. I am saying nothing beyond what
the prophets and Moses said would happen[b]— 23that the Christ[b] would suffer[c]
and, as the first to rise from the dead,[d]
would proclaim light to his own people
and to the Gentiles."[e]
24At this point Festus interrupted Paul's
defense. "You are out of your mind,[f]
Paul!" he shouted. "Your great learning[g]
is driving you insane."
25"I am not insane, most excellent[h] Festus," Paul replied. "What I am saying is

[a] 14 Or *Hebrew* [b] 23 Or *Messiah*

26:2 p Ac 24:1,5; 25:2,7,11 **26:3** q ver 7; S Ac 6:14 r Ac 25:19 **26:4** s Gal 1:13,14; Php 3:5 **26:5** t Ac 22:3 u S Ac 24:5 v Ac 23:6; Php 3:5 **26:6** w Ac 23:6; 24:15; 28:20 x S Ac 13:32; Ro 15:8 **26:7** y Jas 1:1 z 1Th 3:10; 1Ti 5:5 a ver 2 **26:8** b Ac 23:6 **26:9** c 1Ti 1:13 d Jn 16:2 e S Jn 15:21 **26:10** f S Ac 9:13 g S Ac 8:3; 9:2,14,21 h Ac 22:20 **26:11** i S Mt 10:17 **26:14** j Ac 9:7 k S Jn 5:2 **26:16** l Eze 2:1; Da 10:11 m Ac 22:14,15 **26:17** n Jer 1:8,19 o S Ac 9:15; S 13:46 **26:18** p Isa 35:5 q Ps 18:28; Isa 42:7,16; Eph 5:8; Col 1:13; 1Pe 2:9 r Lk 24:47; Ac 2:38 s S Ac 20:21,32 **26:19** t Isa 50:5 **26:20** u Ac 9:19-25 v Ac 9:26-29; 22:17-20 w S Ac 9:15; S 13:46 x Ac 3:19 y Jer 18:11; 35:15; Mt 3:8; Lk 3:8 **26:21** z Ac 21:27,30 a Ac 21:31 **26:22** b S Lk 24:27,44; Ac 10:43; 24:14 **26:23** c S Mt 16:21 d 1Co 15:20,23; Col 1:18; Rev 1:5 e S Lk 2:32 **26:24** f S Jn 10:20; S 1Co 4:10 g Jn 7:15 **26:25** h S Ac 23:26

26:3 *well acquainted with all the Jewish customs.* Agrippa as king controlled the temple treasury and the investments of the high priest, and could appoint the high priest. He was consulted by the Romans on religious matters. This is one of the reasons Festus wanted him to assess Paul (see note on 25:26).

26:5 *I lived as a Pharisee.* Cf. Gal 1:14; Php 3:4–6.

26:6 *my hope in what God has promised.* Including God's kingdom, the Messiah and the resurrection (see v. 8).

26:8 Paul had been speaking to Agrippa but at this point must have addressed others as well, such as Festus and the commanders (see note on 21:31), who did not believe in the resurrection. Agrippa was also allied with the Sadducees, whom he appointed high priests, and probably rejected both the resurrection of Christ and resurrection in general.

26:10 *I cast my vote against them.* Does not necessarily mean that Paul was a member of the Sanhedrin (see note on 22:20). He may have been appointed to a commission to carry out the prosecution (see v. 12).

26:11 *force them to blaspheme.* He tried to force them either to curse Jesus or to confess publicly that Jesus is the Son of God, in which case they could be condemned for blasphemy, a sufficient cause for death (see Mt 26:63–66).

26:12 *I was going to Damascus.* Again Paul gives an account of his conversion (see 9:1–19; 22:4–21 and notes).

26:14 *I heard a voice.* See notes on 9:7; 22:9. *to kick against the goads.* A Greek proverb for useless resistance—the ox succeeds only in hurting itself.

26:17 *to them.* Not only to the Jews but also to the Gentiles (see 22:21; Gal 1:15–16). His mission was from God (Gal 1:1).

26:18 *from darkness to light.* A figure especially characteristic of Paul (see Ro 13:12; 2Co 4:6; Eph 5:8–14; Col 1:13; 1Th 5:5). *Satan.* See Mt 16:23; 1Jn 3:8 and notes. *sanctified.* See note on 1Co 1:2.

26:20 *prove … repentance by … deeds.* Works do not secure salvation either before or after conversion, but they are a sign of the reality of repentance (cf. 3:19 and note).

26:22 *the prophets and Moses.* The OT Scriptures (Lk 24:27,44).

26:23 *the first to rise from the dead.* The firstfruits of the dead—to die no more (see 1Co 15:20; Col 1:18 and notes). *to the Gentiles.* Cf. Isa 49:6.

26:24 *You are out of your mind.* See Jn 10:20; cf. 1Co 14:23. The governor felt that Paul's education and reading of the sacred Scriptures had led him to a mania about prophecy and resurrection.

true and reasonable. 26The king is familiar
with these things,[i] and I can speak freely
to him. I am convinced that none of this
has escaped his notice, because it was not
done in a corner. 27King Agrippa, do you
believe the prophets? I know you do."
28Then Agrippa said to Paul, "Do you
think that in such a short time you can
persuade me to be a Christian?"[j]
29Paul replied, "Short time or long—I
pray God that not only you but all who are
listening to me today may become what I
am, except for these chains."[k]
30The king rose, and with him the governor and Bernice[l] and those sitting with
them. 31They left the room, and while talking with one another, they said, "This man
is not doing anything that deserves death
or imprisonment."[m]
32Agrippa said to Festus, "This man
could have been set free[n] if he had not appealed to Caesar."[o]

Paul Sails for Rome

27 When it was decided that we[p] would
sail for Italy,[q] Paul and some other
prisoners were handed over to a centurion
named Julius, who belonged to the Imperial
Regiment.[r] 2We boarded a ship from Adramyttium about to sail for ports along the
coast of the province of Asia,[s] and we put
out to sea. Aristarchus,[t] a Macedonian[u]
from Thessalonica,[v] was with us.
3The next day we landed at Sidon;[w] and
Julius, in kindness to Paul,[x] allowed him to
go to his friends so they might provide for
his needs.[y] 4From there we put out to sea
again and passed to the lee of Cyprus because the winds were against us.[z] 5When
we had sailed across the open sea off the
coast of Cilicia[a] and Pamphylia,[b] we landed at Myra in Lycia. 6There the centurion
found an Alexandrian ship[c] sailing for Italy[d] and put us on board. 7We made slow
headway for many days and had difficulty
arriving off Cnidus. When the wind did
not allow us to hold our course,[e] we sailed
to the lee of Crete,[f] opposite Salmone. 8We
moved along the coast with difficulty and
came to a place called Fair Havens, near
the town of Lasea.
9Much time had been lost, and sailing
had already become dangerous because
by now it was after the Fast.[a][g] So Paul
warned them, 10"Men, I can see that our

26:26 [i]ver 3
26:28 [j]Ac 11:26
26:29 [k]S Ac 21:33
26:30 [l]Ac 25:23
26:31 [m]S Ac 23:9
26:32 [n]Ac 28:18 [o]S Ac 25:11
27:1 [p]S Ac 16:10 [q]Ac 18:2; 25:12,25 [r]Ac 10:1
27:2 [s]S Ac 2:9 [t]S Ac 19:29 [u]S Ac 16:9 [v]S Ac 17:1
27:3 [w]Mt 11:21 [x]ver 43 [y]Ac 24:23; 28:16
27:4 [z]ver 7
27:5 [a]S Ac 6:9 [b]S Ac 2:10
27:6 [c]Ac 28:11 [d]ver 1; Ac 18:2; 25:12,25
27:7 [e]ver 4 [f]ver 12,13,21; Tit 1:5
27:9 [g]Lev 16:29-31; 23:27-29; Nu 29:7

[a] *9* That is, the Day of Atonement (Yom Kippur)

26:26 *not done in a corner.* This gospel is based on actual events, lived out in historical times and places. The king must himself attest to the truth of what Paul has affirmed.
26:27 *do you believe the prophets?* King Agrippa was faced with a dilemma. If he said "Yes," Paul would press him to recognize their fulfillment in Jesus; if he said "No," he would be in trouble with the devout Jews, who accepted the message of the prophets as the very word of God.
26:28 *in such a short time you can persuade me to be a Christian?* His question is an evasion of Paul's question and an answer to what he anticipates Paul's next question would be. His point is that he will not be persuaded by such a brief statement. *Christian.* See note on 11:26.
26:29 *these chains.* Paul was still bound as a prisoner.
26:31 *not doing anything that deserves death or imprisonment.* Luke calls attention to the officials' agreement on Paul's innocence (cf. Herod's and Pilate's agreement on Jesus' innocence in Lk 23:13–15).
27:1 See map No. 13 at the end of this study Bible; see also map, p. 1731. *we would sail.* The "we" narrative (see note on 16:10) begins again (the last such reference appeared in 21:18). Probably Luke had spent the two years of Paul's Caesarean imprisonment nearby, and now he joins those ready to sail. *centurion named Julius.* Otherwise unknown. Perhaps he was given the specific duties of an imperial courier, which included delivering prisoners for trial. *Imperial Regiment.* The Roman legions were designated by number, and each of the regiments also had designations. The identification "Augustan," or "Imperial" (belonging to the empire), was common (see note on 10:1).
27:2 *Adramyttium.* A harbor on the west coast of the province of Asia, southeast of Troas, east of Assos. *ports along the coast.* At one of these stops, Julius would plan to transfer to a ship going to Rome. *Aristarchus.* See 19:29 and note; see also Phm 24, which indicates that he was in Rome with Paul later.
27:3 *Sidon.* About 70 miles north of Caesarea.
27:4 *the lee of Cyprus.* They sought the protecting shelter of the island by sailing north on the eastern side of the island, then west along the northern side. *winds were against us.* Prevailing winds in summer were westerly.
27:5 *Cilicia and Pamphylia.* Adjoining provinces on the southern shore of Asia Minor. From Sidon to Myra along this coast would normally be a voyage of 10 to 15 days. *Myra in Lycia.* The growing importance of the city of Myra was associated with the development of navigation. Instead of hugging the coast from point to point, more ships were daring to run directly from Alexandria in Egypt to harbors like Myra on the southern coast of Asia Minor. It was considerably out of the way on the trip to Rome from Egypt, but the prevailing westerly wind would not allow a direct voyage toward the west. Myra became an important grain-storage city as well.
27:6 *Alexandrian ship.* A ship from Egypt (with grain cargo, v. 38) bound for Rome. Paul and the others could have remained on the first ship and continued up the coast to Macedonia, then taken the land route over the Egnatian Way across Greece and on to Rome, entering Italy at the port of Brundisium. But Julius chose to change ships here, accepting the opportunity of a voyage direct to Rome. Some suggest that Aristarchus from Macedonia stayed with the first ship and went to his home area to tell of Paul's coming imprisonment in Rome. If so, he later joined Paul in Rome (see note on v. 2).
27:7 *Cnidus.* From Myra to Cnidus at the southwest point of Asia Minor was about 170 miles. The trip probably took another 10 to 15 days. *Crete.* An island 160 miles long. Rather than cross the open sea to Greece, the ship was forced to bear south, seeking to sail west with the protection of the island of Crete on the north ("to the lee of Crete"). *Salmone.* A promontory on the northeast point of Crete.
27:8 *Fair Havens ... Lasea.* The former was a port about midway on the southern coast of Crete, and the latter was a city about five miles away (see inset map, p. 1731).
27:9 *the Fast.* The Jewish Day of Atonement fell in the latter part of September or in October. The usual sailing season by Jewish calculation lasted from Pentecost (May-June) to Tabernacles, which was five days after the Fast. The Romans

voyage is going to be disastrous and bring
great loss to ship and cargo, and to our
own lives also."[h] 11But the centurion, instead of listening to what Paul said, followed the advice of the pilot and of the
owner of the ship. 12Since the harbor was
unsuitable to winter in, the majority decided that we should sail on, hoping to
reach Phoenix and winter there. This was
a harbor in Crete,[i] facing both southwest
and northwest.

The Storm

13When a gentle south wind began to
blow, they thought they had obtained
what they wanted; so they weighed anchor
and sailed along the shore of Crete. 14Be-
fore very long, a wind of hurricane force,[j]
called the "northeaster," swept down from
the island. 15The ship was caught by the
storm and could not head into the wind; so
we gave way to it and were driven along.
16As we passed to the lee of a small island
called Cauda, we were hardly able to make
the lifeboat[k] secure. 17When the men had
hoisted it aboard, they passed ropes under the ship itself to hold it together. Fearing that they would run aground[l] on the
sandbars of Syrtis, they lowered the sea
anchor and let the ship be driven along.
18We took such a violent battering from
the storm that the next day they began to
throw the cargo overboard.[m] 19On the third
day, they threw the ship's tackle overboard

27:10 [h] ver 21
27:12 [i] S ver 7
27:14 [j] Mk 4:37
27:16 [k] ver 30
27:17 [l] ver 26,39
27:18 [m] ver 19,38; Jnh 1:5

considered sailing after Sept. 15 doubtful and after Nov. 11, suicidal.

27:12 *Phoenix.* A major city that served as a wintering place, having a harbor with protection against the storms.

27:13–44 Luke's magnificent account of the storm at sea is possibly intended to be more than just an interesting story well told. Here at the climax of his account of the spread of the gospel from Jerusalem to Rome, especially through the labors of the apostle Paul, he provides in cameo an exquisite depiction of the state of the world seen from the perspective of Paul's gospel: The peoples of the world (represented by the ship's passengers) stand under the threat of God's judgment (represented by the terrible storm), with Paul and what he represents being their only hope. On board are representatives of the world's economic, military and political powers and those skilled in navigating the sea, but none of these can master the raging storm to save themselves or their possessions. They escape only as they follow Paul's instructions. Cf. note on Jnh 1:4–16.

27:14 *"northeaster."* A typhoon-like, east-northeast wind (the Euroquilo), which drove the ship away from its destination (see inset map, below).

27:16 *Cauda.* About 23 miles from Crete. This provided enough shelter to make preparation against the storm. *to make the lifeboat secure.* A small boat was being towed behind the ship. It was interfering with the progress of the ship and with the steering. It may also have been in danger of being crushed against the ship in the wind and the waves. It had to be taken aboard (v. 17).

27:17 *passed ropes under the ship.* Probably crosswise, in order to keep the ship from being broken apart by the storm. *Syrtis.* A long stretch of desolate banks of quicksand along northern Africa off the coast of Tunis and Tripoli—still far away, but in such a storm the ship could be driven a great distance. *sea anchor.* Lowered apparently to keep the ship from running onto the sandbars of Syrtis, but the Greek for this expression should perhaps be rendered "mainsail."

27:18 *throw the cargo overboard.* To lighten the ship. They kept some bags of grain, however (see v. 38).

27:19 *ship's tackle.* Spars, planks and perhaps the yardarm with the mainsail attached. At times these were dragged behind, serving as a brake.

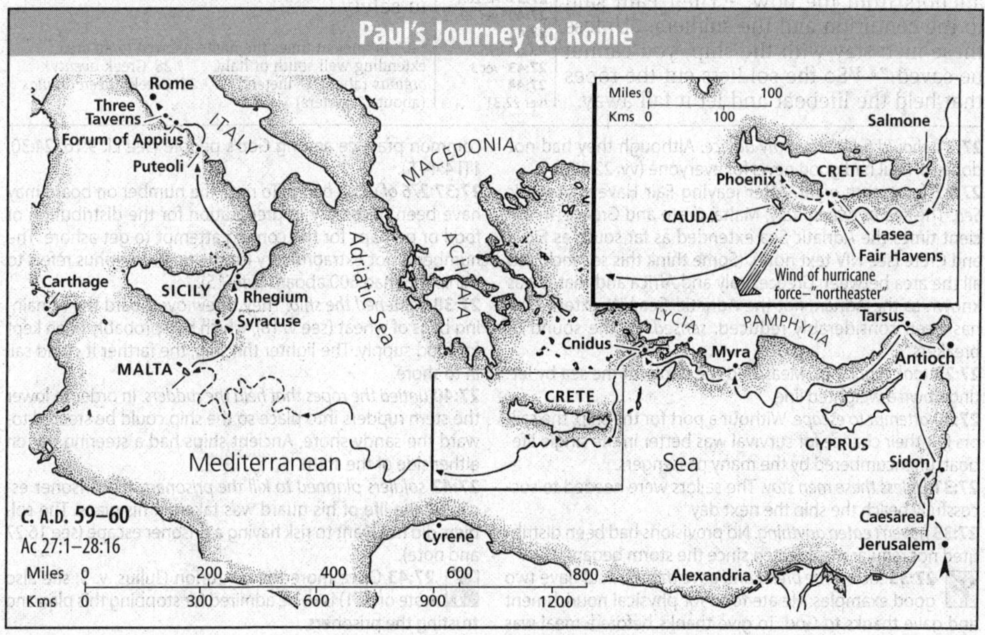

with their own hands. [20]When neither sun nor stars appeared for many days and the storm continued raging, we finally gave up all hope of being saved.

[21]After the men had gone a long time without food, Paul stood up before them and said: "Men, you should have taken my advice[n] not to sail from Crete;[o] then you would have spared yourselves this damage and loss. [22]But now I urge you to keep up your courage,[p] because not one of you will be lost; only the ship will be destroyed. [23]Last night an angel[q] of the God whose I am and whom I serve[r] stood beside me[s] [24]and said, 'Do not be afraid, Paul. You must stand trial before Caesar;[t] and God has graciously given you the lives of all who sail with you.'[u] [25]So keep up your courage,[v] men, for I have faith in God that it will happen just as he told me.[w] [26]Nevertheless, we must run aground[x] on some island."[y]

The Shipwreck

[27]On the fourteenth night we were still being driven across the Adriatic[a] Sea, when about midnight the sailors sensed they were approaching land. [28]They took soundings and found that the water was a hundred and twenty feet[b] deep. A short time later they took soundings again and found it was ninety feet[c] deep. [29]Fearing that we would be dashed against the rocks, they dropped four anchors from the stern and prayed for daylight. [30]In an attempt to escape from the ship, the sailors let the lifeboat[z] down into the sea, pretending they were going to lower some anchors from the bow. [31]Then Paul said to the centurion and the soldiers, "Unless these men stay with the ship, you cannot be saved."[a] [32]So the soldiers cut the ropes that held the lifeboat and let it fall away.

[33]Just before dawn Paul urged them all to eat. "For the last fourteen days," he said, "you have been in constant suspense and have gone without food—you haven't eaten anything. [34]Now I urge you to take some food. You need it to survive. Not one of you will lose a single hair from his head."[b] [35]After he said this, he took some bread and gave thanks to God in front of them all. Then he broke it[c] and began to eat. [36]They were all encouraged[d] and ate some food themselves. [37]Altogether there were 276 of us on board. [38]When they had eaten as much as they wanted, they lightened the ship by throwing the grain into the sea.[e]

[39]When daylight came, they did not recognize the land, but they saw a bay with a sandy beach,[f] where they decided to run the ship aground if they could. [40]Cutting loose the anchors,[g] they left them in the sea and at the same time untied the ropes that held the rudders. Then they hoisted the foresail to the wind and made for the beach. [41]But the ship struck a sandbar and ran aground. The bow stuck fast and would not move, and the stern was broken to pieces by the pounding of the surf.[h]

[42]The soldiers planned to kill the prisoners to prevent any of them from swimming away and escaping. [43]But the centurion wanted to spare Paul's life[i] and kept them from carrying out their plan. He ordered those who could swim to jump overboard first and get to land. [44]The rest were to get there on planks or on pieces of the ship. In this way everyone reached land in safety.[j]

27:21 [n]ver 10 [o]S ver 7 **27:22** [p]ver 25,36 **27:23** [q]S Ac 5:19 [r]Ro 1:9 [s]Ac 18:9; 23:11; 2Ti 4:17 **27:24** [t]Ac 23:11 [u]ver 44 **27:25** [v]ver 22,36 [w]Ro 4:20,21 **27:26** [x]ver 17,39 [y]Ac 28:1 **27:30** [z]ver 16 **27:31** [a]ver 24 **27:34** [b]S Mt 10:30 **27:35** [c]S Mt 14:19 **27:36** [d]ver 22,25 **27:38** [e]ver 18; Jnh 1:5 **27:39** [f]Ac 28:1 **27:40** [g]ver 29 **27:41** [h]2Co 11:25 **27:43** [i]ver 3 **27:44** [j]ver 22,31

[a] *27* In ancient times the name referred to an area extending well south of Italy. [b] *28* Greek *twenty orguias* (about 37 meters) [c] *28* Greek *fifteen orguias* (about 27 meters)

27:21 *should have taken my advice.* Although they had not done so, Paul had good news for everyone (vv. 22–26).

27:27 *fourteenth night.* After leaving Fair Havens. *Adriatic Sea.* The sea between Italy, Malta, Crete and Greece. In ancient times the Adriatic Sea extended as far south as Sicily and Crete (see NIV text note). (Some think this sea included all the area between Greece, Italy and Africa and that it was known as the Adrian, not the Adriatic, Sea.) Its extent now has been considerably reduced. *sensed.* By the sound of breakers.

27:28 *took soundings.* Measured the depth of the sea by letting down a weighted line.

27:30 *attempt to escape.* Without a port for the ship, the sailors felt their chance for survival was better in the single lifeboat, unencumbered by the many passengers.

27:31 *Unless these men stay.* The sailors were needed to successfully beach the ship the next day.

27:33 *haven't eaten anything.* No provisions had been distributed nor regular meals eaten since the storm began.

27:35 *took some bread and gave thanks.* Paul gave two good examples: He ate food for physical nourishment and gave thanks to God. To give thanks before a meal was common practice among God's people (see Lk 9:16; 24:30; 1Ti 4:4–5).

27:37 *276 of us on board.* To note the number on board may have been necessary in preparation for the distribution of food or perhaps for the coming attempt to get ashore. The number is not extraordinary for the time. Josephus refers to a ship that had 600 aboard (*Life,* 15).

27:38 *lightened the ship.* They threw overboard the remaining bags of wheat (see v. 18), which had probably been kept for food supply. The lighter the ship, the farther it could sail in to shore.

27:40 *untied the ropes that held the rudders.* In order to lower the stern rudders into place so the ship could be steered toward the sandy shore. Ancient ships had a steering oar on either side of the stern.

27:42 *soldiers planned to kill the prisoners.* If a prisoner escaped, the life of his guard was taken in his place. The soldiers did not want to risk having a prisoner escape (see 16:27 and note).

27:43 Once more the centurion (Julius, v. 3; see also note on v. 1) is to be admired for stopping this plan and trusting the prisoners.

Ashore on Malta

28 Once safely on shore, we[k] found out
that the island[l] was called Malta.
2 The islanders showed us unusual kindness. They built a fire and welcomed us
all because it was raining and cold. 3 Paul
gathered a pile of brushwood and, as he
put it on the fire, a viper, driven out by the
heat, fastened itself on his hand. 4 When
the islanders saw the snake hanging from
his hand,[m] they said to each other, "This
man must be a murderer; for though he
escaped from the sea, Justice has not allowed him to live."[n] 5 But Paul shook the
snake off into the fire and suffered no ill
effects.[o] 6 The people expected him to swell
up or suddenly fall dead, but after waiting
a long time and seeing nothing unusual
happen to him, they changed their minds
and said he was a god.[p]
7 There was an estate nearby that belonged to Publius, the chief official of the
island. He welcomed us to his home and
for three days entertained us hospitably.
8 His father was sick in bed, suffering from
fever and dysentery. Paul went in to see
him and, after prayer,[q] placed his hands
on him[r] and healed him.[s] 9 When this had
happened, the rest of the sick on the island came and were cured. 10 They honored us[t] in many ways and when we were
ready to sail, they furnished us with the
supplies we needed.

28:1 [k] S Ac 16:10 [l] Ac 27:26,39 **28:4** [m] Mk 16:18 [n] Lk 13:2,4 **28:5** [o] Lk 10:19 **28:6** [p] Ac 14:11 **28:8** [q] Jas 5:14,15 [r] S Ac 6:6 [s] Ac 9:40 **28:10** [t] Ps 15:4

Arrival at Rome

11 After three months we put out to sea
in a ship that had wintered in the island.
It was an Alexandrian ship[u] with the figurehead of the twin gods Castor and Pollux. 12 We put in at Syracuse and stayed
there three days. 13 From there we set sail
and arrived at Rhegium. The next day the
south wind came up, and on the following day we reached Puteoli. 14 There we
found some brothers[v] who invited us to
spend a week with them. And so we came
to Rome. 15 The brothers[w] there had heard
that we were coming, and they traveled as
far as the Forum of Appius and the Three
Taverns to meet us. At the sight of these
men Paul thanked God and was encouraged. 16 When we got to Rome, Paul was
allowed to live by himself, with a soldier
to guard him.[x]

Paul Preaches at Rome Under Guard

17 Three days later he called together the
leaders of the Jews.[y] When they had assembled, Paul said to them: "My brothers,[z]
although I have done nothing against our
people[a] or against the customs of our ancestors,[b] I was arrested in Jerusalem and
handed over to the Romans. 18 They examined me[c] and wanted to release me,[d] because I was not guilty of any crime deserving death.[e] 19 But when the Jews objected,
I was compelled to appeal to Caesar[f]—

28:11 [u] Ac 27:6 **28:14** [v] S Ac 1:16 **28:15** [w] S Ac 1:16 **28:16** [x] Ac 24:23; 27:3 **28:17** [y] Ac 25:2 [z] S Ac 22:5 [a] S Ac 25:8 [b] S Ac 6:14 **28:18** [c] Ac 22:24 [d] Ac 26:31,32 [e] S Ac 23:9 **28:19** [f] S Ac 25:11

28:1 *Malta.* Known as Melita by the Greeks and Romans. It was included in the province of Sicily and is located 58 miles south of that large island.
28:2 *islanders.* Lit. "barbarians"; all non-Greek-speaking people were called this by Greeks. Far from being uncivilized tribesmen, they were Phoenician in ancestry and used a Phoenician dialect but were thoroughly Romanized. *raining and cold.* It was the end of October or the beginning of November.
28:3 *a viper.* Must have been known to the islanders to be poisonous.
28:6 *to swell up.* The usual medical term for inflammation; it is used only by Luke in the NT (see Introduction to Luke: Author). *said he was a god.* Parallel to the Lystrans' attempt to worship Paul and Barnabas (14:11–18).
28:7 *Publius.* A Roman name, but the first name and not the family name. It must have been what the islanders called him. *chief official.* A technical term for the top authority. Luke's designation is accurate here, as elsewhere, even though the Greek term used is not a common one. Cf. also "proconsul" (Greek *anthypatos*, 13:7), "magistrates" (Greek *strategoi*, 16:20), "city officials" (Greek *politarchas*, 17:6), "officials of the province" (Greek *Asiarchon*, 19:31; see note there). *for three days.* Probably until they could find more permanent housing for the winter (see v. 11).
28:11 *After three months.* They had to remain here until the sailing season opened in late February or early March. *figurehead.* A carving mounted at the prow of the ship. *Castor and Pollux.* The two "sons of Zeus" (Greek *Dioscuroi*), the guardian deities of sailors.
28:12 *Syracuse.* The leading city on the island of Sicily, situated on the east coast.
28:13 *Rhegium.* A town on the coast of Italy, near the southwestern tip and close to the narrowest point of the strait separating that country from Sicily, opposite Messina. Around the promontory north of the town was the whirlpool of Charybdis and the rock of Scylla. Coming from his triumph in Judea, the general Titus landed here on his way to Rome. *Puteoli.* Modern Pozzuoli, almost 200 miles from Rhegium. It was situated in the northern part of the Bay of Naples and was the chief port of Rome, though 75 miles away. The population included Jews as well as Christians.
28:14 *spend a week.* Either the centurion had business to care for or he was free to delay the journey at Paul's request (see 27:42–43; see also 27:3). *Rome.* See map, p. 1735.
28:15 *Forum of Appius.* A small town 43 miles from Rome, noted for its wickedness. Some Roman Christians came this far to meet Paul. Beyond this they would not be certain of the way he would come. *Three Taverns.* A town 33 miles from Rome. Other Roman believers met Paul here. The term "tavern" was used to designate any kind of shop.
28:16 *live by himself.* "In his own rented house" (v. 30). He had committed no flagrant crime and was not politically dangerous. So he was allowed to have his own living quarters, but a guard was with him at all times, perhaps chained to him (Eph 6:20; Php 1:13–14,17; Col 4:3,18; Phm 10,13).
28:17 *leaders of the Jews.* The decree of the emperor Claudius (see 18:2 and note) had been allowed to lapse, and Jews had returned to Rome with their leaders. *My brothers.* An epithet that recognized the common Jewish blood he shared with them. Cf. the usage in v. 15, referring to brothers in Christ (see note on 11:1).

not that I had any charge to bring against
my own people. 20For this reason I have
asked to see you and talk with you. It is
because of the hope of Israel[g] that I am
bound with this chain."[h]

21They replied, "We have not received
any letters from Judea concerning you,
and none of the brothers[i] who have come
from there has reported or said anything
bad about you. 22But we want to hear
what your views are, for we know that
people everywhere are talking against this
sect."[j]

23They arranged to meet Paul on a certain day, and came in even larger numbers
to the place where he was staying. From
morning till evening he explained and declared to them the kingdom of God[k] and
tried to convince them about Jesus[l] from
the Law of Moses and from the Prophets.[m]
24Some were convinced by what he said,
but others would not believe.[n] 25They disagreed among themselves and began to
leave after Paul had made this final statement: "The Holy Spirit spoke the truth to
your forefathers when he said[o] through
Isaiah the prophet:

26" 'Go to this people and say,
"You will be ever hearing but never
understanding;
you will be ever seeing but never
perceiving."
27For this people's heart has become
calloused;[p]
they hardly hear with their ears,
and they have closed their eyes.
Otherwise they might see with their
eyes,
hear with their ears,
understand with their hearts
and turn, and I would heal them.'[a][q]

28"Therefore I want you to know that
God's salvation[r] has been sent to the Gentiles,[s] and they will listen!"[b]
30For two whole years Paul stayed there
in his own rented house and welcomed all
who came to see him. 31Boldly[t] and without hindrance he preached the kingdom
of God[u] and taught about the Lord Jesus
Christ.

28:20 [g] Ac 26:6,7 [h] S Ac 21:33 **28:21** [i] S Ac 22:5 **28:22** [j] S Ac 24:5,14 **28:23** [k] S Mt 3:2; Ac 19:8 [l] Ac 17:3 [m] S Ac 8:35 **28:24** [n] Ac 14:4; 17:4,5 **28:25** [o] S Heb 3:7 **28:27** [p] Ps 119:70 [q] Isa 6:9,10; S Mt 13:15 **28:28** [r] Lk 2:30 [s] S Ac 13:46 **28:31** [t] S Ac 4:29 [u] ver 23; S Mt 4:23

[a] *27* Isaiah 6:9,10 [b] *28* Some manuscripts *listen!"* [29] *After he said this, the Jews left, arguing vigorously among themselves.*

28:20 *hope of Israel.* See note on 26:6.

28:22 *we want to hear ... your views.* The Jews in Rome were well aware of the dispute over whether Jesus was the Messiah. They wanted to hear Paul's presentation, and he was eager to present it before the arrival of adverse opinions from the Jewish leaders of Jerusalem.

28:23 *Law of Moses ... Prophets.* The OT Scriptures (see Lk 24:27,44).

28:26–27 This OT passage (Isa 6:9–10; see notes there) was quoted by Jesus (see Mt 13:14–15; Mk 4:12; Lk 8:10; Jn 12:39–40 and notes) to make a similar point. Paul, too, had alluded to it in his letter to the Romans (Ro 11:8).

28:28 *God's salvation has been sent to the Gentiles.* The main thought of the book of Acts. The gospel is meant for all. And Paul was a chosen vessel to carry the message to Gentiles as well as to Jews (see 9:15 and note; Ro 1:13; 11:13 and note).

28:29 See NIV text note on v. 28.

28:30 *two whole years.* Paul served the Lord (v. 31) during the full period of waiting for his accusers to press the trial in Rome. There are a number of indications that he was released from this imprisonment: (1) Acts stops abruptly at this time. (2) Paul wrote to churches expecting to visit them soon; so he must have anticipated a release (see Php 2:24; Phm 22). (3) A number of the details in the Pastoral Letters do not fit into the historical setting given in the book of Acts. These details indicate a return to Asia Minor, Crete and Greece after the events at the close of Acts. (4) Tradition indicates that Paul went to Spain. Even if he did not go, the very fact that a tradition arose suggests a time when he could have taken that journey. See map, pp. 1872–1873.

28:31 Acts ends on a triumphant note (just as Luke's Gospel does; see Lk 24:50–53). Despite being under house arrest, Paul is "boldly and without hindrance" preaching and teaching in Rome, the capital city of the Roman empire (see 1:8 and note).

Rome in the Time of Paul

The Neronian persecution in A.D. 64 was a transparent attempt by the emperor to throw the blame on Christians for the great fire that destroyed large parts of the city. The populace, however, blamed Nero and felt sorry for those unjustly tortured in the arena (cf. Tacitus, *Annals*, 15.44).

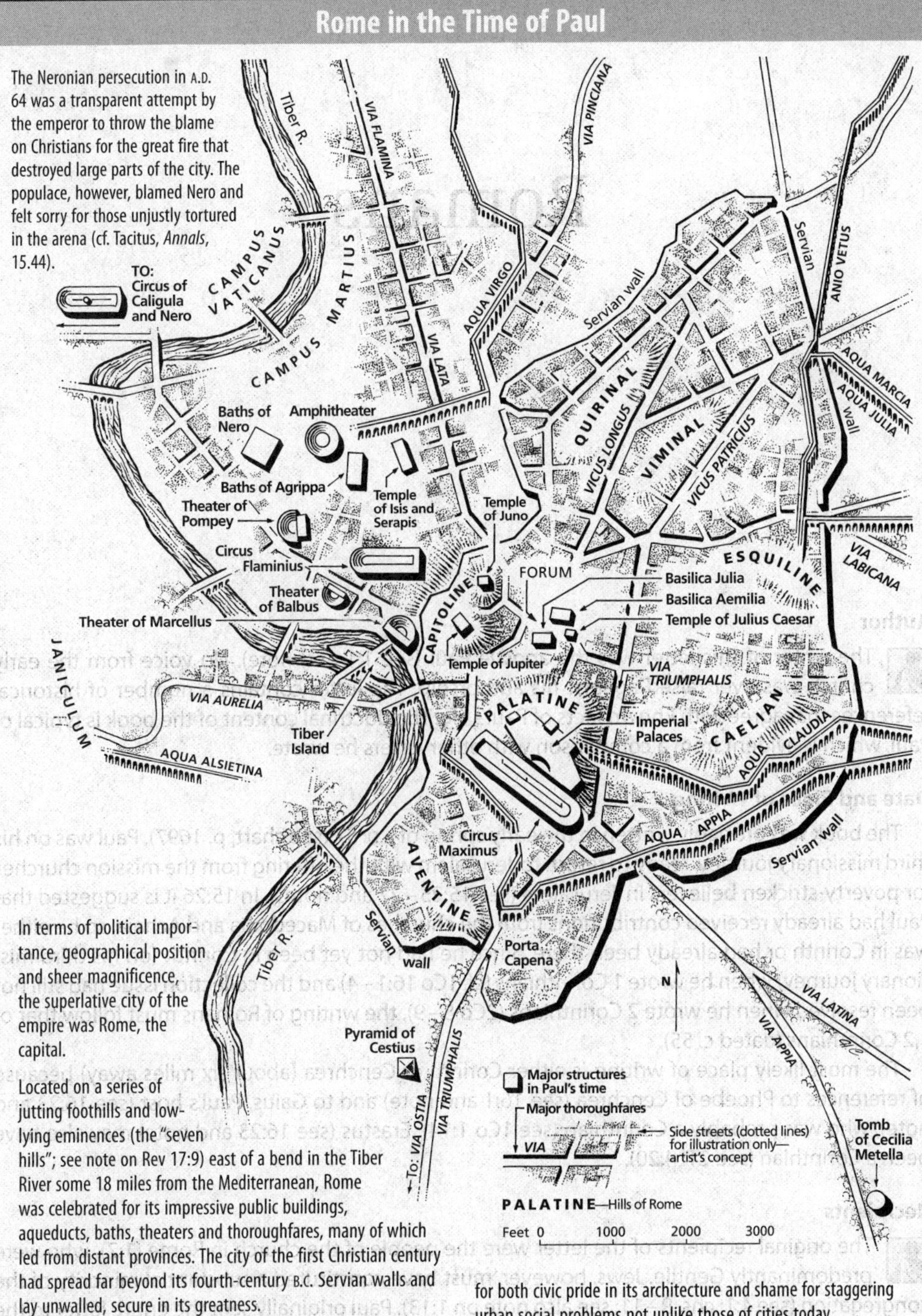

In terms of political importance, geographical position and sheer magnificence, the superlative city of the empire was Rome, the capital.

Located on a series of jutting foothills and low-lying eminences (the "seven hills"; see note on Rev 17:9) east of a bend in the Tiber River some 18 miles from the Mediterranean, Rome was celebrated for its impressive public buildings, aqueducts, baths, theaters and thoroughfares, many of which led from distant provinces. The city of the first Christian century had spread far beyond its fourth-century B.C. Servian walls and lay unwalled, secure in its greatness.

The most prominent features were the Capitoline hill, with temples to Jupiter and Juno, and the nearby Palatine, adorned with imperial palaces, including Nero's "Golden House". Both hills overlooked the Roman Forum, the hub of the entire empire.

Alternatively described as the glorious crowning achievement of humankind and as the sewer of the universe where all the scum from every corner of the empire gathered, Rome had reasons for both civic pride in its architecture and shame for staggering urban social problems not unlike those of cities today.

The apostle Paul entered the city from the south on the Appian Way. He first lived under house arrest and then, after a period of freedom, as a condemned prisoner in the Mamertine dungeon near the Forum. Remarkably, Paul was able to proclaim the gospel among all classes of people, from the palace to the prison. According to tradition, he was executed at a spot on the Ostian Way outside Rome in A.D. 68.

Romans

INTRODUCTION

Author

The writer of this letter was the apostle Paul (see 1:1 and note). No voice from the early church was ever raised against his authorship. The letter contains a number of historical references that agree with known facts of Paul's life. The doctrinal content of the book is typical of Paul, which is evident from a comparison with other letters he wrote.

Date and Place of Writing

The book was probably written in the early spring of A.D. 57 (see chart, p. 1697). Paul was on his third missionary journey, ready to return to Jerusalem with the offering from the mission churches for poverty-stricken believers in Jerusalem (see 15:25 – 27 and notes). In 15:26 it is suggested that Paul had already received contributions from the churches of Macedonia and Achaia, so he either was in Corinth or had already been there. Since he had not yet been in Corinth (on his third missionary journey) when he wrote 1 Corinthians (cf. 1Co 16:1 – 4) and the collection issue had still not been resolved when he wrote 2 Corinthians (2Co 8 – 9), the writing of Romans must follow that of 1,2 Corinthians (dated c. 55).

The most likely place of writing is either Corinth or Cenchrea (about six miles away) because of references to Phoebe of Cenchrea (see 16:1 and note) and to Gaius, Paul's host (see 16:23 and note), who was probably a Corinthian (see 1Co 1:14). Erastus (see 16:23 and note) may also have been a Corinthian (see 2Ti 4:20).

Recipients

The original recipients of the letter were the people of the church in Rome (1:7), who were predominantly Gentile. Jews, however, must have constituted a substantial minority of the congregation (see 4:1; chs. 9 – 11; see also note on 1:13). Paul originally sent the entire letter to the Roman church, but later he or someone else may have used a shorter form (chs. 1 – 14 or 1 – 15) for more general distribution. See note on 2Pe 3:15; see also map, p. 1735.

Major Theme

Paul's primary theme in Romans is the basic gospel, God's plan of salvation for all peoples, Jew and Gentile alike (see 1:16 – 17 and notes). Although justification by faith has been suggested by some as the theme, it would seem that a broader theme states the message of the book more adequately. Paul's emphasis on "righteousness from God" (1:17) includes justification by faith, but it also embraces such related ideas as guilt, sanctification and security.

Purpose

Paul's purposes for writing this letter were varied:

1. He wrote to prepare the way for his coming visit to Rome and to enlist support for his proposed mission to Spain (1:10–15; 15:22–29).

2. He wrote to present the basics of the Christian gospel of salvation to confirm to the church at Rome that they shared the same gospel.

3. He sought to explain the relationship between Jew and Gentile in God's overall plan of redemption. The Jewish Christians may have been rejected by the larger Gentile group in the church (see 14:1 and note) because the Jewish believers still felt constrained to observe dietary laws and sacred days (14:2–6).

Occasion

When Paul wrote this letter, he was probably in Corinth (see Ac 20:2–3 and notes) on his third missionary journey. His work in the eastern Mediterranean was almost finished (see 15:18–23), and he greatly desired to visit the Roman church (see 1:11–12; 15:23–24). At this time, however, he could not go to Rome because he felt he must personally deliver the collection taken among the Gentile churches for the poverty-stricken Christians of Jerusalem (see 15:25–28 and notes). So instead of going to Rome, he sent a letter to prepare the Christians there for his intended visit in connection with a mission to Spain (see 15:23–24 and note on 15:24). For many years Paul had wanted to visit Rome to minister there (see 1:13–15), and this letter served as a careful and systematic theological introduction to that hoped-for personal ministry. Since he was not acquainted directly with the Roman church, he says little about its problems (but see 14:1—15:13; cf. also 13:1–7; 16:17–18).

A Quick Look

Author:
The apostle Paul

Audience:
The church in Rome, predominatly Gentile but including a minority of Jews

Date:
About A.D. 57

Theme:
Paul writes to the church in Rome to present his basic gospel, God's plan of salvation for all peoples, Jew and Gentile alike.

Content

Paul begins by surveying the spiritual condition of all people. He finds Jews and Gentiles alike to be sinners and in need of salvation. That salvation has been provided by God through Jesus Christ and his redemptive work on the cross. It is a provision, however, that must be received by faith—a principle by which God has always dealt with humankind, as the example of Abraham shows. Since salvation is only the beginning of Christian experience, Paul moves on to show how believers are freed from sin, law and death—a provision made possible by their union with Christ in both death and resurrection and by the indwelling presence and power of the Holy Spirit. Paul then shows that Israel too, though presently in a state of unbelief, has a place in God's sovereign redemptive plan. Now she consists of only a remnant, allowing for the conversion of the Gentiles, but the time will come when "all Israel will be saved" (11:26; see note there). The letter concludes with an appeal to the readers to work out their Christian faith in practical ways, both in the church and in the world. None of Paul's other letters states so thoroughly the content of the gospel and its implications for both the present and the future.

Special Characteristics

1. *The most systematic of Paul's letters.* It reads more like an elaborate theological essay than a letter.

Paul shows that Israel . . . has a place in God's sovereign redemptive plan. Now she consists of only a remnant, allowing for the conversion of the Gentiles, but the time will come when "all Israel will be saved."

2. *Emphasis on Christian doctrine.* The number and importance of the theological themes touched upon are impressive: sin and death, salvation, grace, faith, righteousness, justification, sanctification, redemption, resurrection and glorification.

3. *Widespread use of OT quotations.* Although Paul regularly quotes from the OT in his letters, in Romans the argument is sometimes carried along by such quotations (see especially chs. 9 – 11).

4. *Deep concern for Israel.* Paul writes about her present status, her relationship to the Gentiles and her final salvation (chs. 9 – 11).

Outline

- I. Introduction (1:1 – 15)
- II. Theme: Righteousness from God (1:16 – 17)
- III. The Unrighteousness of All People (1:18 — 3:20)
  - A. Gentiles (1:18 – 32)
  - B. Jews (2:1 — 3:8)
  - C. Summary: All People (3:9 – 20)
- IV. Righteousness Imputed: Justification (3:21 — 5:21)
  - A. Through Christ (3:21 – 26)
  - B. Received by Faith (3:27 — 4:25)
    - 1. The principle established (3:27 – 31)
    - 2. The principle illustrated (ch. 4)
  - C. The Fruits of Righteousness (5:1 – 11)
  - D. Summary: Humanity's Unrighteousness Contrasted with God's Gift of Righteousness (5:12 – 21)
- V. Righteousness Imparted: Sanctification (chs. 6 – 8)
  - A. Freedom from Sin's Tyranny (ch. 6)
  - B. Freedom from the Law's Condemnation (ch. 7)
  - C. Life in the Power of the Holy Spirit (ch. 8)
- VI. God's Righteousness Vindicated: The Justice of His Way with Israel (chs. 9 – 11)
  - A. The Justice of God's Rejection of Israel (9:1 – 29)
  - B. The Cause of That Rejection (9:30 — 10:21)
  - C. The Rejection Is Neither Complete nor Final (ch. 11)
    - 1. There is even now a remnant (11:1 – 10)
    - 2. The rejection is only temporary (11:11 – 24)
    - 3. God's ultimate purpose is mercy (11:25 – 36)
- VII. Righteousness Practiced (12:1 — 15:13)
  - A. In the Body — the Church (ch. 12)
  - B. In the World (ch. 13)
  - C. Among Weak and Strong Christians (14:1 — 15:13)
- VIII. Conclusion (15:14 – 33)
- IX. Commendation, Greetings and Doxology (ch. 16)

1 Paul, a servant of Christ Jesus, called
to be an apostle[a] and set apart[b] for the
gospel of God[c]— 2the gospel he promised
beforehand[d] through his prophets[e] in the
Holy Scriptures[f] 3regarding his Son, who
as to his human nature[g] was a descendant
of David,[h] 4and who through the Spirit[a]
of holiness was declared with power to be
the Son of God[b][i] by his resurrection from
the dead:[j] Jesus Christ our Lord.[k] 5Through
him and for his name's sake, we received
grace[l] and apostleship to call people from
among all the Gentiles[m] to the obedience
that comes from faith.[n] 6And you also are
among those who are called to belong to
Jesus Christ.[o]

7To all in Rome who are loved by God[p]
and called to be saints:[q]

Grace and peace to you from God our
Father and from the Lord Jesus Christ.[r]

Paul's Longing to Visit Rome

8First, I thank my God through Jesus
Christ for all of you,[s] because your faith is
being reported all over the world.[t] 9God,
whom I serve[u] with my whole heart in
preaching the gospel of his Son, is my witness[v] how constantly I remember you 10in
my prayers at all times;[w] and I pray that
now at last by God's will[x] the way may be
opened for me to come to you.[y]

11I long to see you[z] so that I may impart
to you some spiritual gift[a] to make you
strong— 12that is, that you and I may be
mutually encouraged by each other's faith.
13I do not want you to be unaware,[b] brothers,[c] that I planned many times to come to
you (but have been prevented from doing
so until now)[d] in order that I might have
a harvest among you, just as I have had
among the other Gentiles.

14I am obligated[e] both to Greeks and
non-Greeks, both to the wise and the foolish. 15That is why I am so eager to preach
the gospel also to you who are at Rome.[f]

16I am not ashamed of the gospel,[g] because it is the power of God[h] for the salvation of everyone who believes:[i] first for the

[a] 4 Or *who as to his spirit* [b] 4 Or *was appointed to be the Son of God with power*

1:1 [a]S 1Co 1:1 [b]S Ac 9:15 [c]Ro 15:16; S 2Co 2:12; 11:7; 1Th 2:8, 9; 1Pe 4:17 **1:2** [d]S Ac 13:32; Tit 1:2 [e]Lk 1:70; Ro 3:21 [f]Gal 3:8 **1:3** [g]S Jn 1:14; Ro 9:5 [h]S Mt 1:1 **1:4** [i]S Mt 4:3 [j]S Ac 2:24 [k]1Co 1:2 **1:5** [l]1Ti 1:14 [m]S Ac 9:15 [n]Ac 6:7; Ro 16:26 **1:6** [o]Jude 1; Rev 17:14 **1:7** [p]Ro 8:39; 1Th 1:4 [q]S Ac 9:13 [r]1Co 1:3; Eph 1:2; 1Ti 1:2; Tit 1:4; 1Pe 1:2 **1:8** [s]1Co 1:4; Eph 1:16; 1Th 2:13; 2Th 1:3; 2Ti 1:3 [t]S Ro 10:18; 16:19 **1:9** [u]2Ti 1:3 [v]Job 16:19; Jer 42:5; 2Co 1:23; Gal 1:20; Php 1:8; 1Th 2:5, 10

1:10 [w]1Sa 12:23; S Lk 18:1; S Ac 1:14; Eph 1:16; Php 1:4; Col 1:9; 2Th 1:11; 2Ti 1:3; Phm 4 [x]S Ac 18:21 [y]ver 13; Ro 15:32 **1:11** [z]Ro 15:23 [a]1Co 1:7; 12:1-31 **1:13** [b]S Ro 11:25 [c]S Ro 7:1 [d]Ro 15:22, 23 **1:14** [e]1Co 9:16 **1:15** [f]Ro 15:20 **1:16** [g]2Ti 1:8 [h]1Co 1:18 [i]S Jn 3:15

1:1 *Paul.* In ancient times writers put their names at the beginning of letters. For the story of Paul's ministry see Ac 9:1–30 and note on 9:1; 13:1—28:31; for his autobiographical accounts see 2Co 6:3–10; 11:21—12:10; Gal 1:13–24; Php 3:4–14; 1Ti 1:12–16. *servant.* The Greek for this word means (1) a "slave," who completely belongs to his owner and has no freedom to leave, and (2) a "servant," who willingly chooses to serve his master. See notes on Ex 14:31; Ps 18 title; Isa 41:8–9; 42:1. *apostle.* One specially commissioned by Christ (see notes on Mk 6:30; 1Co 1:1; Heb 3:1). *set apart.* See Gal 1:15 and note. *gospel.* See note on Mk 1:1.
1:2 *prophets.* Not just the writers of the prophetic books, for the whole OT prophesied about Jesus (see Lk 24:27,44–47 and notes). *Holy Scriptures.* The OT.
1:3 *regarding his Son.* The central figure of the gospel is Jesus, in and through whom the history and the promises of the OT are fulfilled (see Lk 24:27,44–47 and notes; cf. 2Co 1:20 and note).
1:4 *Son of God.* See Jn 3:16 and note. *his resurrection.* The authentication of Jesus' divine nature, the climax of his earthly ministry and the focal point of the apostolic proclamation (see Ac 2:14–40; 4:33 and notes).
1:7 *saints.* The basic idea of the Greek for this word is "holiness." All Christians are saints in that they stand in a special relationship with God as his people and are being made increasingly "holy" by the Holy Spirit (see note on 1Co 1:2). *Grace and peace.* The initial greeting used by both Paul and Peter in their letters. It combines the traditional Greek ("grace") and Hebrew ("peace") greetings but links them expressly with the only true source of "grace" (in the sense of God's unmerited favor, especially that which comes to sinful humanity through the saving work of Christ) and "peace" (the total well-being and security that only God can provide and that he does provide fully only to those who are at peace with him; see 5:1; Php 4:7 and notes; Gal 1:3; Eph 1:2; see also Jn 14:27; 20:19 and notes). This greeting is echoed in the conclusions of Paul's and Peter's letters, so that these letters stand framed in what amounts to an apostolic benediction on those who are addressed. Cf. Ex 34:6–7 and note. *Lord Jesus Christ.* See note on 1Th 1:1.
1:8 *thank.* Paul often began his letters with thanks (see 1Co 1:4; Eph 1:16; Php 1:3–4 and note; Col 1:3 and note; 1Th 1:2; 2Th 1:3; 2Ti 1:3; Phm 4). *through Jesus Christ.* All access to God, whether in prayer (Jn 15:16) or in giving thanks (see Eph 5:20; Col 3:17), is through Christ, just as all distinctively Christian acts are to be done "in the name of the Lord Jesus" (Col 3:17). *all over the world.* Every place where the gospel has been preached.
1:9 *gospel of his Son.* The same as the "gospel of God" (v. 1).
1:10 *way may be opened.* See 15:23–29.
1:12 *mutually.* Paul's genuine humility is seen in his desire to be ministered to by the believers at Rome as well as to minister to them.
1:13 *brothers.* Here, as elsewhere, Paul employs a word that was commonly used in his day to address a crowd or community that included men and women (see Ac 1:14–16). *harvest.* New converts as well as spiritual growth by those already converted. *among you … among the other Gentiles.* Suggests that the church at Rome was predominantly Gentile.
1:14 *Greeks.* Those Gentiles who spoke Greek or followed the Greek way of life, even though they may have been Latin-speaking citizens of the Roman empire. *non-Greeks.* Lit. "barbarians," a word that probably imitated the unintelligible sound of their languages to Greek ears. They were the other Gentiles to whom Paul ministered.
1:16–17 The theme of the entire book.
1:16 *not ashamed.* Not even in the capital city of the Roman empire (see v. 15). *gospel.* See note on Mk 1:1. *first.* Not only in time but also in privilege. "Salvation is from the Jews" (Jn 4:22), and the Messiah was a Jew. The "very words of God" (3:2), the covenants, law, temple worship, revelation of the divine glory, and Messianic prophecies came to them (9:3–5; see notes there). These privileges, however, were not extended to the Jews because of their superior merit or because of God's partiality toward them. It was necessary that the invasion of this world by the gospel begin at a particular point with a particular people, who in turn were responsible to carry that gospel to the other nations.

Jew,[j] then for the Gentile.[k] 17For in the gospel a righteousness from God is revealed,[l]
a righteousness that is by faith[m] from first
to last,[a] just as it is written: "The righteous will live by faith."[b n]

God's Wrath Against Mankind

18The wrath of God[o] is being revealed
from heaven against all the godlessness
and wickedness of men who suppress the
truth by their wickedness, 19since what
may be known about God is plain to them,
because God has made it plain to them.[p]
20For since the creation of the world God's
invisible qualities—his eternal power and
divine nature—have been clearly seen,
being understood from what has been
made,[q] so that men are without excuse.[r]
21For although they knew God, they neither glorified him as God nor gave thanks
to him, but their thinking became futile
and their foolish hearts were darkened.[s]
22Although they claimed to be wise, they
became fools[t] 23and exchanged the glory
of the immortal God for images[u] made to
look like mortal man and birds and animals and reptiles.
24Therefore God gave them over[v] in the
sinful desires of their hearts to sexual impurity for the degrading of their bodies
with one another.[w] 25They exchanged the
truth of God for a lie,[x] and worshiped and
served created things[y] rather than the Creator—who is forever praised.[z] Amen.[a]
26Because of this, God gave them over[b]
to shameful lusts.[c] Even their women exchanged natural relations for unnatural
ones.[d] 27In the same way the men also
abandoned natural relations with women
and were inflamed with lust for one another. Men committed indecent acts with
other men, and received in themselves the
due penalty for their perversion.[e]
28Furthermore, since they did not think
it worthwhile to retain the knowledge of
God, he gave them over[f] to a depraved
mind, to do what ought not to be done.
29They have become filled with every kind
of wickedness, evil, greed and depravity.
They are full of envy, murder, strife, deceit and malice. They are gossips,[g] 30slan-
derers, God-haters, insolent, arrogant and
boastful; they invent ways of doing evil;
they disobey their parents;[h] 31they are
senseless, faithless, heartless,[i] ruthless.
32Although they know God's righteous decree that those who do such things deserve
death,[j] they not only continue to do these
very things but also approve[k] of those who
practice them.

God's Righteous Judgment

2 You, therefore, have no excuse,[l] you
who pass judgment on someone else,
for at whatever point you judge the other,
you are condemning yourself, because you
who pass judgment do the same things.[m]

1:16 [j]Ac 3:26; 13:46 [k]S Ac 13:46; Ro 2:9,10 **1:17** [l]Ro 3:21; Php 3:9 [m]S Ro 9:30 [n]Hab 2:4; Gal 3:11; Heb 10:38 **1:18** [o]Jn 3:36; Ro 5:9; Eph 5:6; Col 3:6; 1Th 1:10; Rev 19:15 **1:19** [p]Ac 14:17 **1:20** [q]Ps 19:1-6 [r]Ro 2:1 **1:21** [s]Ge 8:21; Jer 2:5; 17:9; Eph 4:17,18 **1:22** [t]1Co 1:20,27; 3:18,19 **1:23** [u]Dt 4:16,17; Ps 106:20; Jer 2:11; Ac 17:29 **1:24** [v]ver 26,28; Ps 81:12; Eph 4:19 [w]1Pe 4:3 **1:25** [x]Isa 44:20 [y]Jer 10:14; 13:25; 16:19,20 [z]Ro 9:5; 2Co 11:31 [a]S Ro 11:36 **1:26** [b]ver 24,28 [c]Eph 4:19; 1Th 4:5 [d]Lev 18:22,23 **1:27** [e]Lev 18:22; 20:13; 1Co 6:18 **1:28** [f]ver 24,26 **1:29** [g]2Co 12:20; 1Ti 5:13; Jas 3:2; 3Jn 10 **1:30** [h]2Ti 3:2 **1:31** [i]2Ti 3:3 **1:32** [j]S Ro 6:23 [k]Ps 50:18; Lk 11:48; Ac 8:1; 22:20 **2:1** [l]Ro 1:20 [m]2Sa 12:5-7; S Mt 7:1,2

[a] *17* Or *is from faith to faith* [b] *17* Hab. 2:4

1:17 *righteousness.* The state of being in the right in relation to God (see notes on 2:13; 3:21,24).

1:18—3:20 In developing the theme of righteousness from God (1:17; 3:21—5:21), Paul sets the stage by showing that all have sinned and therefore need the righteousness that only God can provide. He shows the sin of the Gentiles (1:18-32) and the sin of the Jews (2:1—3:8) and then summarizes the sin of all—Gentile and Jew alike (3:9-20).

1:18-20 No one—not even one who has not heard of the Bible or of Christ—has an excuse for not honoring God, because the whole creation reveals the Creator (cf. Ps 19:1-4; 29:3-9; 104:1-30).

1:18 *wrath of God.* Not a petulant, irrational burst of anger, such as humans often exhibit, but a holy, just revulsion against what is contrary to and opposes his holy nature and will. *is being revealed.* God's wrath is not limited to the end-time judgment of the wicked (1Th 1:10; Rev 19:15; 20:11-15). Here the wrath of God is his abandonment of the wicked to their sins (vv. 24-32). *the truth.* The truth about God revealed in the creation order.

1:21 *knew God.* From seeing his revelation in creation (vv. 19-20). The fact that these people were idolaters (v. 23) and knew God only through the creation order indicates that they were Gentiles. *gave thanks.* For earthly blessings, such as sun, rain and crops (see Mt 5:45 and note; Ac 14:17).

1:23 *glory.* God's unique majesty (see Isa 40:5 and note; 48:11), which fallen humankind has lost sight of and for which they have substituted deities of their own devising, patterned after various creatures (see Ps 106:20).

1:24,26,28 *God gave them over.* God allowed sin to run its course as an act of judgment.

1:25 *Amen.* A Hebrew word that can mean either "Yes indeed, it is so" or "So be it" (see 9:5; 11:36; 15:33; 16:27; see also Dt 27:15 and note; 1Ki 1:36).

1:26 *their women.* Not necessarily their wives.

1:27 Homosexual practice is sinful in God's eyes. The OT also condemns the practice (see Lev 18:22; 20:13).

1:28 *knowledge of God.* See vv. 19,21. *depraved mind.* The intent precedes the act (see v. 21; Mk 7:20-23).

1:29-31 A list of vices similar to those found in 13:13; 1Co 5:10-11; 6:9-10; 2Co 12:20-21; Gal 5:19-21; Eph 4:31; 5:3-5; Col 3:5,8; 1Ti 1:9-10; 2Ti 3:2-5; Rev 21:8; 22:15.

1:32 *they know.* Their outrageous conduct was not due to total ignorance of what God required but to self-will and rebellion. *approve.* The extreme of sin is applauding, rather than regretting, the sins of others.

2:1-16 In this section Paul sets forth principles that govern God's judgment. God judges (1) according to truth (v. 2), (2) according to deeds (vv. 6-11) and (3) according to the light a person has (vv. 12-15). These principles lay the groundwork for Paul's discussion of the guilt of the Jews (vv. 17-29).

2:1 *no excuse.* Paul's teaching about judging agrees with that of Jesus (see note on Mt 7:1), who did not condemn judging as such, but hypocritical judging. *you who pass judgment.* A warning that had special relevance for Jews, who were inclined to look down on Gentiles because of their ignorance of God's revelation in the OT and because of their immoral lives.

2 Now we know that God's judgment against those who do such things is based on truth. 3 So when you, a mere man, pass judgment on them and yet do the same things, do you think you will escape God's judgment? 4 Or do you show contempt for the riches[n] of his kindness,[o] tolerance[p] and patience,[q] not realizing that God's kindness leads you toward repentance?[r]

5 But because of your stubbornness and your unrepentant heart, you are storing up wrath against yourself for the day of God's wrath[s], when his righteous judgment[t] will be revealed. 6 God "will give to each person according to what he has done."[a][u] 7 To those who by persistence in doing good seek glory, honor[v] and immortality,[w] he will give eternal life.[x] 8 But for those who are self-seeking and who reject the truth and follow evil,[y] there will be wrath and anger.[z] 9 There will be trouble and distress for every human being who does evil:[a] first for the Jew, then for the Gentile;[b] 10 but glory, honor and peace for everyone who does good: first for the Jew, then for the Gentile.[c] 11 For God does not show favoritism.[d]

12 All who sin apart from the law will also perish apart from the law, and all who sin under the law[e] will be judged by the law. 13 For it is not those who hear the law who are righteous in God's sight, but it is those who obey[f] the law who will be declared righteous. 14 (Indeed, when Gentiles, who do not have the law, do by nature things required by the law,[g] they are a law for themselves, even though they do not have the law, 15 since they show that the requirements of the law are written on their hearts, their consciences also bearing witness, and their thoughts now accusing, now even defending them.) 16 This will take place on the day when God will judge men's secrets[h] through Jesus Christ,[i] as my gospel[j] declares.

The Jews and the Law

17 Now you, if you call yourself a Jew; if you rely on the law and brag about your relationship to God;[k] 18 if you know his will and approve of what is superior because you are instructed by the law; 19 if you are convinced that you are a guide for the blind, a light for those who are in the dark, 20 an instructor of the foolish, a teacher of infants, because you have in the law the embodiment of knowledge and truth— 21 you, then, who teach others, do you not teach yourself? You who preach against stealing, do you steal?[l] 22 You who say that people should not commit adultery, do you commit adultery? You who abhor idols, do you rob temples?[m] 23 You who brag about the law,[n] do you dishonor God by breaking the law? 24 As it is written: "God's name is blasphemed among the Gentiles because of you."[b][o]

25 Circumcision has value if you observe the law,[p] but if you break the law, you have become as though you had not been circumcised.[q] 26 If those who are not circumcised keep the law's requirements,[r] will they not be regarded as though they were circumcised?[s] 27 The one who is not circumcised physically and yet obeys the

2:4 [n]Ro 9:23; 11:33; Eph 1:7, 18; 2:7; 3:8, 16; Col 2:2 [o]Ro 11:22 [p]Ro 3:25 [q]Ex 34:6; Ro 9:22; 1Ti 1:16; 1Pe 3:20; 2Pe 3:15 [r]2Pe 3:9 **2:5** [s]Ps 110:5; Rev 6:17 [t]Jude 6 **2:6** [u]Ps 62:12; S Mt 16:27 **2:7** [v]ver 10 [w]1Co 15:53, 54; 2Ti 1:10 [x]S Mt 25:46 **2:8** [y]2Th 2:12 [z]Eze 22:31 **2:9** [a]Ps 32:10 [b]ver 10; Ro 1:16 **2:10** [c]ver 9; Ro 1:16 **2:11** [d]S Ac 10:34 **2:12** [e]Ro 3:19; 6:14; 1Co 9:20, 21; Gal 4:21; 5:18; S Ro 7:4 **2:13** [f]Jas 1:22, 23, 25 **2:14** [g]Ac 10:35 **2:16** [h]Ecc 12:14; 1Co 4:5 [i]Ac 10:42 [j]Ro 16:25; 2Ti 2:8 **2:17** [k]ver 23; Jer 8:8; Mic 3:11; Jn 5:45; Ro 9:4 **2:21** [l]Mt 23:3, 4 **2:22** [m]Ac 19:37 **2:23** [n]S ver 17 **2:24** [o]Isa 52:5; Eze 36:22; 2Pe 2:2 **2:25** [p]ver 13, 27; Gal 5:3 [q]Jer 4:4; 9:25, 26 **2:26** [r]Ro 8:4 [s]S 1Co 7:19

[a] 6 Psalm 62:12; Prov. 24:12 [b] 24 Isaiah 52:5; Ezek. 36:22

2:2 *we know.* An expression Paul frequently used that assumed the persons addressed agreed with the statement that followed (see 3:19; 6:6,9; 7:14; 8:22,28; 1Co 8:1,4; 2Co 5:1; 1Ti 1:8).

2:3 Jesus also condemned such judgmental acts (see Mt 7:3 and note; cf. Lk 18:9).

2:4 The purpose of God's kindness is to give opportunity for repentance (see 2Pe 3:9 and note). The Jews had misconstrued his patience to be a lack of intent to judge.

2:5 *day of God's wrath.* See v. 8; judgment in the end times in contrast to the judgment discussed in 1:18–32.

2:6–7 Paul is not contradicting his continual emphasis in all his writings, including Romans, that people are saved not by what they do but by faith in what Christ has done for them. Paul is referring to "persistence in doing good" as the proof of genuine faith (see Gal 5:6; Jas 2:14–26 and notes).

2:8 *wrath and anger.* On the day of final judgment.

2:9 *first for the Jew.* With spiritual privilege comes spiritual responsibility (see Am 3:2 and note; Lk 12:48).

2:11 A basic teaching of both the OT and the NT.

2:12 *law.* The Mosaic law. "All who sin apart from the law" refers to Gentiles. God judges according to the light available to people. Gentiles will not be condemned for not obeying a law they did not possess. Their judgment will be on other grounds (see v. 15 and note on vv. 1–16; 1:18–20 and note; cf. Am 1:3—2:3).

2:13 *will be declared righteous.* At God's pronouncement of acquittal on judgment day (see note on 3:24).

2:14 *by nature.* By natural impulse without the external constraint of the Mosaic law. *things required by the law.* Does not mean that pagans fulfilled the requirements of the Mosaic law but refers to practices in pagan society that agreed with the law, such as caring for the sick and elderly, honoring parents and condemning adultery. *law for themselves.* The moral nature of pagans, enlightened by conscience (v. 15), functioned for them as the Mosaic law did for the Jews.

2:16 This verse should be read with v. 13, as the parentheses around vv. 14–15 indicate. *my gospel.* See 16:25 and note.

2:17–24 The presentation takes the form of a dialogue. Paul knew how a self-righteous Jew thought, for he had been one himself. He cites one advantage after another that Jews regarded as unqualified assets. But those assets became liabilities when there was no correspondence between profession and practice. Paul applied to the Jew the principles of judgment set forth in vv. 1–16 (see note on those verses).

2:19–20 *the blind ... infants.* Gentiles, to whom Jews regarded themselves as vastly superior because they (the Jews) possessed the Mosaic law.

2:22 *do you rob temples?* See Ac 19:37. Large amounts of wealth were often stored in pagan temples.

2:25 *Circumcision.* A sign of the covenant (see Ge 17:10–12 and notes) that God made with Israel. The Jews had come to regard circumcision as a guarantee of God's favor.

2:27 If a Gentile's deeds excelled those of a Jew in righteousness, that very fact condemned the Jew, who had an immeasurably better set of standards in the law of Moses.

law will condemn you[t] who, even though
you have the[a] written code and circumcision, are a lawbreaker.
28 A man is not a Jew if he is only one
outwardly,[u] nor is circumcision merely
outward and physical.[v] 29 No, a man is a
Jew if he is one inwardly; and circumcision is circumcision of the heart,[w] by the
Spirit,[x] not by the written code.[y] Such a
man's praise is not from men, but from
God.[z]

God's Faithfulness

3 What advantage, then, is there in being a Jew, or what value is there in circumcision? 2 Much in every way![a] First of
all, they have been entrusted with the very
words of God.[b]
3 What if some did not have faith?[c] Will
their lack of faith nullify God's faithfulness?[d] 4 Not at all! Let God be true,[e] and
every man a liar.[f] As it is written:

"So that you may be proved right when
you speak
and prevail when you judge."[b g]

5 But if our unrighteousness brings out
God's righteousness more clearly,[h] what
shall we say? That God is unjust in bringing his wrath on us? (I am using a human
argument.)[i] 6 Certainly not! If that were so,
how could God judge the world?[j] 7 Someone might argue, "If my falsehood enhances God's truthfulness and so increases
his glory,[k] why am I still condemned as
a sinner?"[l] 8 Why not say—as we are being slanderously reported as saying and as
some claim that we say—"Let us do evil
that good may result"?[m] Their condemnation is deserved.

2:27 [t] Mt 12:41,42
2:28 [u] Mt 3:9; Jn 8:39; Ro 9:6,7 [v] Gal 6:15
2:29 [w] Dt 30:6 [x] Php 3:3; Col 2:11 [y] Ro 7:6; 2Co 3:6 [z] Jn 5:44; 12:43; 1Co 4:5; 2Co 10:18; Gal 1:10; 1Th 2:4; 1Pe 3:4
3:2 [a] Ro 9:4,5 [b] Dt 4:8; Ps 147:19; Ac 7:38
3:3 [c] Ro 10:16; Heb 4:2 [d] 2Ti 2:13
3:4 [e] Jn 3:33 [f] Ps 116:11 [g] Ps 51:4
3:5 [h] Ro 5:8 [i] Ro 6:19; Gal 3:15
3:6 [j] Ge 18:25; Ro 2:16
3:7 [k] ver 4 [l] Ro 9:19
3:8 [m] Ro 6:1
3:9 [n] ver 1 [o] ver 19,23; 1Ki 8:46; 2Ch 6:36; Ps 106:6; Ro 5:12; 11:32; Gal 3:22
3:12 [p] Ps 14:1-3; 53:1-3; Ecc 7:20
3:13 [q] Ps 5:9 [r] Ps 140:3
3:14 [s] Ps 10:7
3:17 [t] Isa 59:7,8
3:18 [u] Ps 36:1
3:19 [v] S Jn 10:34 [w] S Ro 2:12 [x] Ps 63:11; 107:42; Eze 16:63 [y] ver 9
3:20 [z] Ac 13:39; Gal 2:16 [a] S Ro 4:15

No One Is Righteous

9 What shall we conclude then? Are we
any better[c]?[n] Not at all! We have already
made the charge that Jews and Gentiles
alike are all under sin.[o] 10 As it is written:

"There is no one righteous, not even
one;
11 there is no one who understands,
no one who seeks God.
12 All have turned away,
they have together become
worthless;
there is no one who does good,
not even one."[d p]
13 "Their throats are open graves;
their tongues practice deceit."[e q]
"The poison of vipers is on their
lips."[f r]
14 "Their mouths are full of cursing
and bitterness."[g s]
15 "Their feet are swift to shed blood;
16 ruin and misery mark their ways,
17 and the way of peace they do not
know."[h t]
18 "There is no fear of God before their
eyes."[i u]

19 Now we know that whatever the law
says,[v] it says to those who are under the
law,[w] so that every mouth may be silenced[x]
and the whole world held accountable to
God.[y] 20 Therefore no one will be declared
righteous in his sight by observing the
law;[z] rather, through the law we become
conscious of sin.[a]

[a] 27 Or *who, by means of a* [b] 4 Psalm 51:4
[c] 9 Or *worse* [d] 12 Psalms 14:1-3; 53:1-3; Eccles. 7:20
[e] 13 Psalm 5:9 [f] 13 Psalm 140:3 [g] 14 Psalm 10:7
[h] 17 Isaiah 59:7,8 [i] 18 Psalm 36:1

2:29 *by the Spirit.* The true sign of belonging to God is not an outward mark on the physical body, but the regenerating power of the Holy Spirit within (see Tit 3:5 and note)—what Paul meant by "circumcision of the heart" (see Dt 30:6 and notes on Ge 17:10; Jer 4:4). *praise is not from men, but from God.* Cf. Jn 5:41,44; 12:43; 1Co 4:3–5 and notes on 4:3,5.

3:2 *First of all.* Paul does not discuss the other advantages of being a Jew until 9:4–5 (see notes there). *entrusted.* The advantage of having the very words of God involves a duty. *very words of God.* The OT.

3:3 *God's faithfulness.* God is faithful to his promises and would punish Israel for its unbelief (v. 5; see 2Ti 2:13).

3:4 God's punishment of sin exhibits his faithfulness to his righteous character.

3:5 *brings out God's righteousness.* By contrast, in showing it up against the dark background of human sin. *human argument.* "Human" in the sense of its weakness and absurdity.

3:6 *judge.* On judgment day. *world.* All moral creatures (also in v. 19)—a more limited reference than in 1:20.

3:8 *Let us do evil that good may result.* Paul deals with this issue more fully in ch. 6.

3:9 *Are we any better?* Are Jews better than Gentiles in the sight of God? *all.* Nine times in four verses (vv. 9–12) Paul mentions the universality of sin ("all," two times; "no one," four times; "not even one," two times; "together," once). *under sin.* Under its power and condemnation.

3:10–18 A collection of OT quotations that underscores Paul's charge that both Jews and Gentiles are under the power of sin. Several factors explain why the citations are not always verbatim: (1) NT quotations sometimes gave the general sense and were not meant to be word-for-word. (2) Quotation marks were not used in Greek. (3) The quotations were often taken from the pre-Christian Greek translation (the Septuagint) of the Hebrew OT, because Greek readers were not familiar with the Hebrew Bible. (4) Sometimes the NT writer, in order to drive home his point, would purposely (under the inspiration of the Holy Spirit) enlarge, abbreviate or adapt an OT passage or combine two or more passages.

3:11 *understands.* About God and what is right.

3:13 *open graves.* Expressive of the evil intents of their hearts (see Ps 5:9 and note).

3:18 *fear of God.* Awesome reverence for God; the source of all godliness (see notes on Ge 20:11; Pr 1:7).

3:19 *we know.* See note on 2:2. *law.* The OT (as in Jn 10:34; 15:25; 1Co 14:21). *those who are under the law.* The Jews. *every mouth ... whole world.* Jews as well as Gentiles are guilty.

3:20 *declared righteous.* See notes on vv. 24; 2:13. *we become conscious of sin.* According to Paul, this is one of the primary purposes of the law (see 7:7 and note).

Righteousness Through Faith

21But now a righteousness from God,[b]
apart from law, has been made known,
to which the Law and the Prophets testify.[c] 22This righteousness from God[d] comes
through faith[e] in Jesus Christ[f] to all who
believe.[g] There is no difference,[h] 23for all
have sinned[i] and fall short of the glory
of God, 24and are justified[j] freely by his
grace[k] through the redemption[l] that came
by Christ Jesus. 25God presented him as
a sacrifice of atonement,[a m] through faith
in his blood.[n] He did this to demonstrate
his justice, because in his forbearance he
had left the sins committed beforehand
unpunished[o]— 26he did it to demonstrate
his justice at the present time, so as to be
just and the one who justifies those who
have faith in Jesus.

27Where, then, is boasting?[p] It is excluded. On what principle? On that of observing the law? No, but on that of faith. 28For
we maintain that a man is justified by faith
apart from observing the law.[q] 29Is God the
God of Jews only? Is he not the God of
Gentiles too? Yes, of Gentiles too,[r] 30since
there is only one God, who will justify the
circumcised by faith and the uncircumcised through that same faith.[s] 31Do we,
then, nullify the law by this faith? Not at
all! Rather, we uphold the law.

Abraham Justified by Faith

4 What then shall we say[t] that Abraham, our forefather,[u] discovered in this
matter? 2If, in fact, Abraham was justified by works, he had something to boast
about—but not before God.[v] 3What does
the Scripture say? "Abraham believed God,
and it was credited to him as righteousness."[b w]

[a] 25 Or *as the one who would turn aside his wrath, taking away sin* [b] 3 Gen. 15:6; also in verse 22

3:21 [b]Isa 46:13; Jer 23:6; Ro 1:17; 9:30 [c]Ac 10:43; Ro 1:2 **3:22** [d]Ro 1:17 [e]S Ro 9:30 [f]Gal 2:16; 3:22 [g]S Jn 3:15; Ro 4:11; 10:4 [h]Ro 10:12; Gal 3:28; Col 3:11 **3:23** [i]S ver 9 **3:24** [j]S Ro 4:25 [k]Jn 1:14, 16, 17; Ro 4:16; 5:21; 6:14; 11:5; 2Co 12:9; Eph 2:8; 4:7; Tit 2:11; Heb 4:16 [l]Ps 130:7; 1Co 1:30; Gal 4:5; Eph 1:7, 14; Col 1:14; Heb 9:12 **3:25** [m]Ex 25:17; Lev 16:10; Ps 65:3; Heb 2:17; 9:28; 1Jn 4:10 [n]Ac 20:28; Ro 5:9; Eph 1:7; Heb 9:12, 14; 13:12; 1Pe 1:19; Rev 1:5 [o]Ac 14:16; 17:30 **3:27** [p]Ro 2:17, 23; 4:2; 1Co 1:29-31; Eph 2:9 **3:28** [q]ver 20, 21; Ac 13:39; Gal 2:16; 3:11; Eph 2:9; Jas 2:20, 24, 26 **3:29** [r]Ac 10:34, 35; Ro 9:24; 10:12; 15:9; Gal 3:28 **3:30** [s]Ro 4:11, 12; Gal 3:8 **4:1** [t]S Ro 8:31 [u]S Lk 3:8 **4:2** [v]1Co 1:31 **4:3** [w]ver 5, 9, 22; Ge 15:6; Gal 3:6; Jas 2:23

3:21—5:21 Having shown that all people (both Gentiles and Jews) are unrighteous (1:18—3:20), Paul now shows that God has provided a righteousness for them.

3:21 *But now.* There are two possible meanings: (1) temporal—all of time is divided into two periods, and in the "now" period the righteousness from God has been made known; (2) logical—the contrast is between the righteousness gained by observing the law (which is impossible, v. 20) and the righteousness provided by God. *apart from law.* Quite independently of the law. *the Law and the Prophets testify.* See Ge 15:6; Ps 32:1–2; Hab 2:4 and notes.

3:22 *no difference.* Between Jews and Gentiles (see 10:12 and note).

3:23 *glory of God.* What God intended humans to be. The glory they had before the fall (see Ge 1:26–28; Ps 8:4–8 and notes; cf. Eph 4:24; Col 3:10) believers will again have through Christ (see Heb 2:5–9 and notes).

3:24 *justified.* Paul uses the Greek verb for "justified" 27 times, mostly in Romans and Galatians. It is translated "justify" in all cases except two (2:13; 3:20, where it is translated "declared righteous"). The term describes what happens when people believe in Christ as their Savior: From the negative viewpoint, God declares them to be not guilty; from the positive viewpoint, he declares them to be righteous. He cancels the guilt of their sin and credits righteousness to them. Paul emphasizes two points in this regard: (1) No one lives a perfectly good, holy, righteous life. On the contrary, "there is no one righteous" (v. 10), and "all have sinned and fall short of the glory of God" (v. 23). "Therefore no one will be declared righteous in his [God's] sight by observing the law" (v. 20). (2) But even though all are sinners, God will declare those who put their trust in Jesus not guilty but righteous. This legal declaration is valid because Christ died to pay the penalty for our sin and lived a life of perfect righteousness that can in turn be imputed to us. This is the central theme of Romans and is stated in the theme verse, 1:17 ("a righteousness from God"). Christ's righteousness (his obedience to God's law and his sacrificial death) will be credited to believers as their own. Paul uses the Greek for "credited" ten times in ch. 4 alone. *freely by his grace.* The central thought in justification is that, although people clearly and totally deserve to be declared guilty (vv. 9–19), God declares them righteous because of their trust in Christ. This is stated in several ways here: (1) "freely" (as a gift, for nothing), (2) "by his grace," (3) "through the redemption that came by Christ Jesus" and (4) "through faith" (v. 25). *redemption.* A word taken from the slave market—the basic idea is that of obtaining release by payment of a ransom. Paul uses this word to refer to release from guilt, with its liability for judgment, and to deliverance from slavery to sin, because Christ in his death paid the ransom to set us free (cf. Ex 13:13; 21:30; Mt 20:28; Mk 10:45; 1Co 7:23; Eph 1:7; 1Pe 1:18 and notes).

3:25 *sacrifice of atonement.* The Greek for this phrase speaks of a sacrifice that turns away the righteous wrath of God. Without this appeasement all people are justly condemned to suffer eternal punishment. See NIV text note here; see also note on 1Jn 2:2. *faith in his blood.* Saving faith looks to Jesus Christ in his sacrificial death for us.

3:25b–26 The sins of God's people, punished symbolically in the animal sacrifices of the OT period, would be totally punished in the once-for-all sacrifice of Christ on the cross.

3:28 *by faith.* When Luther translated this passage, he added the word "alone," which, though not in the Greek, accurately reflects the meaning (see note on Jas 2:14–26).

3:30 *only one God.* By appealing to the first article of Jewish faith ("the LORD is one," Dt 6:4; see note there), Paul argues that there is only one way of salvation for both Jew ("circumcised") and Gentile ("uncircumcised"), namely, faith in Christ.

3:31 Paul anticipated being charged with antinomianism (against law): If justification comes by faith alone, then is not the law rejected? He gives a more complete answer in chs. 6–7 and reasserts the validity of the law in 13:8–10.

4:1 *Abraham, our forefather.* The great patriarch of the Jewish nation, the true example of a justified person (see Jas 2:21–23 and notes). The Jews of Jesus' time used Abraham as an example of justification by works, but Paul holds him up as a shining example of righteousness by faith (see Gal 3:7–9 and notes).

4:2 *If … Abraham was justified by works.* Many of Paul's Jewish contemporaries held that Abraham was justified by works (acts done in obedience to God's laws—in the Apocrypha see Ecclesiasticus 44:21), but the fact is that he was not (see v. 3), and therefore all boasting on his part is excluded.

4:3 The reference is to Ge 15:6, where nothing is mentioned about works (see note on 3:21). *credited.* Abra-

4 Now when a man works, his wages are
not credited to him as a gift,[x] but as an obligation. 5 However, to the man who does
not work but trusts God who justifies the
wicked, his faith is credited as righteousness.[y] 6 David says the same thing when
he speaks of the blessedness of the man
to whom God credits righteousness apart
from works:

7 "Blessed are they
whose transgressions are forgiven,
whose sins are covered.
8 Blessed is the man
whose sin the Lord will never count
against him."[a][z]

9 Is this blessedness only for the circumcised, or also for the uncircumcised?[a] We
have been saying that Abraham's faith
was credited to him as righteousness.[b]
10 Under what circumstances was it credited? Was it after he was circumcised, or
before? It was not after, but before! 11 And
he received the sign of circumcision, a
seal of the righteousness that he had by
faith while he was still uncircumcised.[c] So
then, he is the father[d] of all who believe[e]
but have not been circumcised, in order
that righteousness might be credited to
them. 12 And he is also the father of the
circumcised who not only are circumcised
but who also walk in the footsteps of the
faith that our father Abraham had before
he was circumcised.

13 It was not through law that Abraham
and his offspring received the promise[f]
that he would be heir of the world,[g] but
through the righteousness that comes by
faith.[h] 14 For if those who live by law are
heirs, faith has no value and the promise
is worthless,[i] 15 because law brings wrath.[j]
And where there is no law there is no
transgression.[k]

16 Therefore, the promise comes by
faith, so that it may be by grace[l] and
may be guaranteed[m] to all Abraham's offspring—not only to those who are of the
law but also to those who are of the faith
of Abraham. He is the father of us all.[n] 17 As
it is written: "I have made you a father of
many nations."[b][o] He is our father in the
sight of God, in whom he believed—the
God who gives life[p] to the dead and calls[q]
things that are not[r] as though they were.

18 Against all hope, Abraham in hope believed and so became the father of many
nations,[s] just as it had been said to him,
"So shall your offspring be."[c][t] 19 Without
weakening in his faith, he faced the fact

4:4 [x] Ro 11:6 **4:5** [y] ver 3,9,22; S Ro 9:30 **4:8** [z] Ps 32:1,2; 103:12; 2Co 5:19 **4:9** [a] Ro 3:30 [b] S ver 3 **4:11** [c] Ge 17:10,11 [d] ver 16,17; S Lk 3:8 [e] S Ro 3:22 **4:13** [f] S Ac 13:32; Gal 3:16,29 [g] Ge 17:4-6 [h] S Ro 9:30 **4:14** [i] Gal 3:18 **4:15** [j] Ro 7:7-25; 1Co 15:56; 2Co 3:7; Gal 3:10; S Ro 7:12 [k] Ro 3:20; 5:13; 7:7 **4:16** [l] S Ro 3:24 [m] Ro 15:8 [n] ver 11; S Lk 3:8; S Gal 3:16 **4:17** [o] Ge 17:5 [p] S Jn 5:21 [q] Isa 48:13 [r] 1Co 1:28 **4:18** [s] ver 17 [t] Ge 15:5

[a] *8* Psalm 32:1,2 [b] *17* Gen. 17:5 [c] *18* Gen. 15:5

ham had kept no law, rendered no service and performed no ritual that earned credit to his account before God. His belief in God, who had made promises to him, was credited to him as righteousness.

4:6–8 God does not continue to credit unrighteousness to sinners who repent, but forgives them when they confess (see Ps 32:3–5 and notes; Eze 18:23 and note,27–28,32 and note; 33:14–16).

4:9 See 3:30 and note.

4:10 *not after, but before!* Abraham was declared righteous (Ge 15:6) some 14 years before he was circumcised (Ge 17:24, 26). See Gal 3:17 for a similar statement.

4:11 *sign.* Circumcision was, among other things, the outward sign of the righteousness that God had credited to Abraham for his faith (see Ge 17:11 and note). *So then.* Abraham is the "father" of believing Gentiles (the uncircumcised), because he believed and was justified before the rite of circumcision (the mark of Jews) was instituted.

4:12 *father of the circumcised.* Abraham is also the father of believing Jews. Thus his story shows that for Jew and Gentile alike there is only one way of justification—the way of faith.

4:13 *not through law.* Not on the condition that the promise be merited by acts done in accordance with the law. *his offspring.* All those of whom Abraham is said to be father (vv. 11–12). *heir of the world.* "World" here refers to the creation, as in 1:20. No express mention of this broad an inheritance is made in the Genesis account of Abraham. He is promised "offspring like the dust of the earth" (Ge 13:16) and possession of the land of Canaan (Ge 12:7; 13:14–15; 15:7,18–21; 17:8), and that all the peoples on earth will be blessed through him (see Ge 12:2–3 and note; 18:18) or his offspring (Ge 22:18). But since, as Genesis already makes clear, God purposed through Abraham and his offspring to work out the destiny of the whole world, it was implicit in the promises to Abraham that he and his offspring would "inherit the land/earth" (see Ps 37:9 and note,11,22,29,34; Mt 5:5). The full realization of this awaits the consummation of the Messianic kingdom at Christ's return.

4:14 *those who live by law.* Those whose claim to the inheritance is based on their obedience to the law. *promise.* See note on v. 13.

4:15 *law brings wrath.* The law, because it reveals sin and even stimulates it (see 7:7–11), provokes God's wrath and does not lead to the fulfillment of God's promises. *transgression.* Overstepping a clearly defined line. Where there is no law there is still sin, but it does not have the character of transgression.

4:16 A summary of the thought of vv. 11–12. For the close correlation between faith and grace see 3:24–25; Eph 2:8–9 and notes. *those who are of the law.* Jewish Christians. *those who are of the faith of Abraham.* Gentile Christians who share Abraham's faith but who, like Abraham, do not possess the law.

4:17 *in the sight of God.* God considers Abraham the father of Jews and believing Gentiles alike, no matter how others (especially the Jews) may see him. *the God who gives life to the dead.* The main reference is to the birth of Isaac through Abraham and Sarah, both of whom were far past the age of childbearing (see Ge 18:11). Secondarily Paul alludes also to the resurrection of Christ (see vv. 24–25 and notes). *calls things that are not.* God has the ability to create out of nothing, as he demonstrated in the birth of Isaac.

4:18 *Against all hope ... in hope believed.* When all hope, as a human possibility, failed, Abraham placed his hope in God.

4:19 *Without weakening in his faith.* Abraham had some anxious moments (see Ge 17:17–18), but God did not count these against him. *faced the fact.* Faith does not refuse to face reality but looks beyond all difficulties to God and his promises. *Sarah's womb was also dead.* Sarah was ten years younger than Abraham (see Ge 17:17) but well past the age of bearing children.

that his body was as good as dead[u]—since he was about a hundred years old[v]—and that Sarah's womb was also dead.[w] 20 Yet he did not waver through unbelief regarding the promise of God, but was strengthened[x] in his faith and gave glory to God,[y] 21 being fully persuaded that God had power to do what he had promised.[z] 22 This is why "it was credited to him as righteousness."[a] 23 The words "it was credited to him" were written not for him alone, 24 but also for us,[b] to whom God will credit righteousness—for us who believe in him[c] who raised Jesus our Lord from the dead.[d] 25 He was delivered over to death for our sins[e] and was raised to life for our justification.[f]

Peace and Joy

5 Therefore, since we have been justified[g] through faith,[h] we[a] have peace[i] with God through our Lord Jesus Christ,[j] 2 through whom we have gained access[k] by faith into this grace in which we now stand.[l] And we[a] rejoice in the hope[m] of the glory of God. 3 Not only so, but we[a] also rejoice in our sufferings,[n] because we know that suffering produces perseverance;[o] 4 perseverance, character; and character, hope. 5 And hope[p] does not disappoint us, because God has poured out his love[q] into our hearts by the Holy Spirit,[r] whom he has given us.

6 You see, at just the right time,[s] when we were still powerless,[t] Christ died for the ungodly.[u] 7 Very rarely will anyone die for a righteous man, though for a good man someone might possibly dare to die. 8 But God demonstrates his own love for us in this: While we were still sinners, Christ died for us.[v]

9 Since we have now been justified[w] by his blood,[x] how much more shall we be saved from God's wrath[y] through him! 10 For if, when we were God's enemies,[z] we were reconciled[a] to him through the death of his Son, how much more, having been reconciled, shall we be saved through his life![b] 11 Not only is this so, but we also rejoice in God through our Lord Jesus Christ, through whom we have now received reconciliation.[c]

[a] *1,2,3* Or *let us*

4:19 [u]Heb 11:11,12 [v]Ge 17:17 [w]Ge 18:11 **4:20** [x]1Sa 30:6 [y]S Mt 9:8 **4:21** [z]Ge 18:14; S Mt 19:26 **4:22** [a]S ver 3 **4:24** [b]Ps 102:18; Hab 2:2; Ro 15:4; 1Co 9:10; 10:11; 2Ti 3:16,17 [c]Ro 10:9; 1Pe 1:21 [d]S Ac 2:24 **4:25** [e]Isa 53:5,6; Ro 5:6,8; 8:32; 2Co 5:21 [f]Isa 53:11; Ro 3:24; 5:1,9,16,18; 8:30; 1Co 6:11; 2Co 5:15 **5:1** [g]S Ro 4:25 [h]S Ro 3:28 [i]S Lk 2:14 [j]ver 10 **5:2** [k]Eph 2:18; 3:12 [l]1Co 15:1 [m]S Heb 3:6 **5:3** [n]S Mt 5:12 [o]S Heb 10:36 **5:5** [p]Php 1:20; S Heb 3:6; 1Jn 3:2,3 [q]ver 8; Jn 3:16; Ro 8:39 [r]Ac 2:33; 10:45; Tit 3:5,6 **5:6** [s]Mk 1:15; Gal 4:4; Eph 1:10 [t]ver 8,10 [u]Ro 4:25 **5:8** [v]Jn 3:16; 15:13; 1Pe 3:18; 1Jn 3:16; 4:10 **5:9** [w]S Ro 4:25 [x]S Ro 3:25 [y]S Ro 1:18 **5:10** [z]Ro 11:28; Col 1:21 [a]ver 11; Ro 11:15; 2Co 5:18,19; Col 1:20,22 [b]Ro 8:34; Heb 7:25 **5:11** [c]S ver 10

4:20 *gave glory to God.* Because Abraham had faith to believe that God would do what he promised. Whereas works are human attempts to establish a claim on God, faith brings glory to him.

4:22 *This is why.* Abraham's faith was "credited to him as righteousness" because it was true faith, i.e., complete confidence in God's promise.

4:24 *but also for us.* As Abraham was justified because he believed in a God who brought life from the dead, so we will be justified by believing "in him who raised Jesus our Lord from the dead" (see 10:9 and note).

4:25 These words, which reflect the Septuagint (Greek) translation of Isa 53:12, are probably quoted from an early Christian confessional formula. *justification.* See 3:24 and note.

5:1 *peace with God.* Not merely a subjective feeling (peace of mind) but primarily an objective status, a new relationship with God: Once we were his enemies, but now we are his friends (see v. 10 and note; Eph 2:16; Col 1:21–22).

5:2 *access.* Jesus ushers us into the presence of God. The heavy curtain (of the temple) that separated us from God and God from us has been removed (see notes on Mt 27:51; Heb 10:19–22). *hope of the glory of God.* Our confidence that the purpose for which God created us will be ultimately realized (see note on 3:23).

5:3 *rejoice in our sufferings.* Not "because of" but "in." Paul does not advocate a morbid view of life but a joyous and triumphant one (see Jas 1:2 and note).

5:4 Christians can rejoice in suffering because they know that it is not meaningless. Part of God's purpose is to produce character in his children (see Jas 1:3).

5:5 *hope does not disappoint us.* The believer's hope is not to be equated with unfounded optimism. On the contrary, it is the blessed assurance of our future destiny and is based on God's love, which is revealed to us by the Holy Spirit and objectively demonstrated to us in the death of Christ. Paul has moved from faith (v. 1) to hope (vv. 2,4–5) to love (here; see 1Co 13:13; 1Th 1:3 and notes). *has poured out.* The verb indicates a present status resulting from a past action. When we first believed in Christ, the Holy Spirit poured out his love in our hearts, and his love for us continues to dwell in us. *whom he has given us.* All true believers have the gift of the Spirit (see 8:9 and note).

5:6 *the right time.* The appointed moment in God's redemptive plan (see Mk 1:15 and note). *Christ died for the ungodly.* Christ's love is grounded in God's free grace and is not the result of any inherent worthiness found in its objects (human beings). In fact, it is lavished on us in spite of our undesirable character.

5:7 *righteous ... good.* We were neither righteous nor good, but sinners, when Christ died for us (see v. 8; 3:10–12).

5:9 *by his blood.* By laying down his life as a sacrifice—a reference to Christ's death for our sins (see 3:25 and note). *God's wrath.* The final judgment, as the verb "shall ... be saved" makes clear (see note on 1:18; cf. 1Th 1:9–10 and notes).

5:10 *God's enemies.* Humans are enemies of God, not the reverse. Thus the hostility must be removed from humans if reconciliation is to be accomplished. God took the initiative in bringing this about through the death of his Son (see v. 11; Col 1:21–22 and note on 1:20). *reconciled.* To reconcile is "to put an end to hostility," and is closely related to the term "justified," as the parallelism in vv. 9–10 indicates:

v. 9	v. 10
justified	reconciled
by his blood	through the death of his Son
shall we be saved	shall we be saved

saved through his life. A reference to the unending life and ministry of the resurrected Christ for his people (see Heb 7:25 and note). Since we were reconciled when we were God's enemies, we will be saved because Christ lives to keep us.

5:11 *we have now received reconciliation.* Reconciliation, like justification (v. 1), is a present reality for Christians and is something to rejoice about (see Col 1:20 and note).

Death Through Adam, Life Through Christ

12Therefore, just as sin entered the world
through one man,[d] and death through sin,[e]
and in this way death came to all men, because all sinned[f]— 13for before the law
was given, sin was in the world. But sin
is not taken into account when there is no
law.[g] 14Nevertheless, death reigned from
the time of Adam to the time of Moses,
even over those who did not sin by breaking a command, as did Adam,[h] who was a
pattern of the one to come.[i]
15But the gift is not like the trespass.
For if the many died by the trespass of
the one man,[j] how much more did God's
grace and the gift that came by the grace
of the one man, Jesus Christ,[k] overflow to
the many! 16Again, the gift of God is not
like the result of the one man's sin: The
judgment followed one sin and brought
condemnation, but the gift followed many
trespasses and brought justification. 17For
if, by the trespass of the one man, death[l]
reigned through that one man, how much
more will those who receive God's abundant provision of grace and of the gift of
righteousness reign in life[m] through the
one man, Jesus Christ.
18Consequently, just as the result of one
trespass was condemnation for all men,[n]
so also the result of one act of righteousness was justification[o] that brings life[p] for
all men. 19For just as through the disobedience of the one man[q] the many were made
sinners,[r] so also through the obedience[s]
of the one man the many will be made
righteous.
20The law was added so that the trespass
might increase.[t] But where sin increased,
grace increased all the more,[u] 21so that,
just as sin reigned in death,[v] so also grace[w]
might reign through righteousness to bring
eternal life[x] through Jesus Christ our Lord.

Dead to Sin, Alive in Christ

6 What shall we say, then?[y] Shall we go
on sinning so that grace may increase?[z]
2By no means! We died to sin;[a] how can
we live in it any longer? 3Or don't you
know that all of us who were baptized[b]
into Christ Jesus were baptized into his
death? 4We were therefore buried with
him through baptism into death[c] in order
that, just as Christ was raised from the
dead[d] through the glory of the Father, we
too may live a new life.[e]

5:12 [d]ver 15,16, 17; Ge 3:1-7; 1Co 15:21,22 [e]ver 14,18; Ge 2:17; 3:19; S Ro 6:23 [f]S Ro 3:9 **5:13** [g]S Ro 4:15 **5:14** [h]Ge 3:11,12 [i]1Co 15:22,45 **5:15** [j]ver 12,18,19 [k]Ac 15:11 **5:17** [l]S ver 12 [m]Jn 10:10 **5:18** [n]S ver 12 [o]S Ro 4:25 [p]Isa 53:11 **5:19** [q]ver 12 [r]S Ro 3:9 [s]S Php 2:8 **5:20** [t]Ro 3:20; 7:7,8; Gal 3:19 [u]Ro 6:1; 1Ti 1:13,14 **5:21** [v]ver 12,14; S Ro 6:16 [w]S Ro 3:24 [x]S Mt 25:46 **6:1** [y]S Ro 8:31 [z]ver 15; Ro 3:5,8 **6:2** [a]S ver 6; ver 10,11; S ver 18; Ro 8:13; Col 3:3,5; 1Pe 2:24 **6:3** [b]S Mt 28:19 **6:4** [c]S ver 6 [d]S Ac 2:24 [e]Ro 7:6; S 2Co 5:17; Eph 4:22-24; Col 3:10

5:12–21 A contrast between Adam and Christ. Adam introduced sin and death into the world; Christ brought righteousness and life. The comparison begun in v. 12 is completed in v. 18; these two verses summarize the whole passage. These two men also sum up the message of the book up to this point. Adam stands for humanity's condemnation (1:18—3:20); Christ stands for the believer's justification (3:21—5:11).

5:12 *death.* Physical death is the penalty for sin. It is also the symbol of spiritual death—ultimate separation from God (Rev 20:15; 21:8). *because all sinned.* Not a repetition of 3:23. The context shows that Adam's sin involved the rest of humankind in condemnation (vv. 18–19) and death (v. 15). We do not start life with even the possibility of living it sinlessly; we begin it with a sinful nature (see Ge 8:21; Ps 51:5; 58:3 and notes; Eph 2:3).

5:13 *sin is not taken into account.* In the period when there was no (Mosaic) law, people were not charged with sin in the sense of "breaking a command" (v. 14).

5:14 *pattern.* Adam by his sin brought universal ruin on the human race. In this act he is the prototype of Christ, who through one righteous act (v. 18) brought universal blessing. The analogy is one of contrast.

5:15 *the many.* The same as "all men" in v. 12 (see Isa 53:11; Mk 10:45). *how much more.* A theme that runs through this section. God's grace is infinitely greater for good than is Adam's sin for evil.

5:16 *gift of God.* Salvation. *many trespasses.* The sins of the succeeding generations.

5:17 *will ... reign in life.* The future reign of believers with Jesus Christ (see 2Ti 2:12 and note; Rev 20:4,6; 22:5).

5:18 *life for all.* Contrast v. 12. Does not mean that everyone eventually will be saved, but that salvation is available to all (see 1Jn 2:2 and note). To be effective, God's gracious gift must be received (see v. 17).

5:19 *made righteous.* A reference to a person's status before God (see v. 17; 2Co 5:21 and note), not to a change in character. The latter (the doctrine of sanctification) is developed in chs. 6–8.

5:20 *law was added.* Not to bring about redemption but to point up the need for it. The law made sin even more sinful by revealing what sin is in stark contrast to God's holiness.

6:1—8:39 In 3:21—5:21 Paul explains how God has provided for our redemption and justification. He next explains the doctrine of sanctification—the process by which believers grow to maturity in Christ. He treats this subject in three parts: (1) freedom from sin's tyranny (ch. 6), (2) freedom from the law's condemnation (ch. 7) and (3) life in the power of the Holy Spirit (ch. 8).

6:1 *Shall we go on sinning so that grace may increase?* This question arose out of what Paul had just said in 5:20: "Where sin increased, grace increased all the more."

6:2 *died to sin.* The reference is to an event in the past and is explained in v. 3 (see note on vv. 3–4).

6:3–4 The when and how of the Christian's death to sin. In NT times baptism so closely followed conversion that the two were considered part of one event (see Ac 2:38 and note). So although baptism is not a means by which we enter into a vital faith relationship with Jesus Christ, it is closely associated with faith. Baptism depicts graphically what happens as a result of the Christian's union with Christ, which comes with faith—through faith we are united with Christ, just as through our natural birth we are united with Adam. As we fell into sin and became subject to death in father Adam, so we now have died and been raised again with Christ—which baptism symbolizes.

6:3 *know.* Three key words in this chapter are "know" (here and in vv. 6,9), "offer" (vv. 13,16,19) and "obey" (vv. 12,16–17).

6:4 *buried with him through baptism into death.* Amplified in vv. 5–7. *through the glory of the Father.* By the power of God. God's glory is his divine excellence, his perfection. Any one of his attributes is a manifestation of his excellence. Thus his power is a manifestation of his glory, as is his

5If we have been united with him like
this in his death, we will certainly also be
united with him in his resurrection.[f] 6For
we know that our old self[g] was crucified
with him[h] so that the body of sin[i] might be
done away with,[a] that we should no longer be slaves to sin[j]— 7because anyone
who has died has been freed from sin.[k]
8Now if we died with Christ, we believe
that we will also live with him.[l] 9For we
know that since Christ was raised from the
dead,[m] he cannot die again; death no longer has mastery over him.[n] 10The death he
died, he died to sin[o] once for all;[p] but the
life he lives, he lives to God.
11In the same way, count yourselves dead
to sin[q] but alive to God in Christ Jesus.
12Therefore do not let sin reign[r] in your
mortal body so that you obey its evil desires. 13Do not offer the parts of your body
to sin, as instruments of wickedness,[s] but
rather offer yourselves to God, as those
who have been brought from death to life;
and offer the parts of your body to him
as instruments of righteousness.[t] 14For sin
shall not be your master,[u] because you are
not under law,[v] but under grace.[w]

Slaves to Righteousness

15What then? Shall we sin because we
are not under law but under grace?[x] By
no means! 16Don't you know that when
you offer yourselves to someone to obey
him as slaves, you are slaves to the one
whom you obey[y]—whether you are slaves
to sin,[z] which leads to death,[a] or to obedience, which leads to righteousness? 17But
thanks be to God[b] that, though you used
to be slaves to sin,[c] you wholeheartedly
obeyed the form of teaching[d] to which you
were entrusted. 18You have been set free
from sin[e] and have become slaves to righteousness.[f]
19I put this in human terms[g] because
you are weak in your natural selves. Just
as you used to offer the parts of your body
in slavery to impurity and to ever-increasing wickedness, so now offer them in slavery to righteousness[h] leading to holiness.
20When you were slaves to sin,[i] you were
free from the control of righteousness.[j]
21What benefit did you reap at that time
from the things you are now ashamed of?
Those things result in death![k] 22But now
that you have been set free from sin[l] and

[a] 6 Or *be rendered powerless*

6:5 [f]ver 4,8; Ro 8:11; 2Co 4:10; Eph 2:6; Php 3:10,11; Col 2:12; 3:1; 2Ti 2:11 **6:6** [g]S Gal 5:24; Eph 4:22; Col 3:9 [h]S ver 2; ver 3-8; 2Co 4:10; Gal 2:20; 5:24; 6:14; Php 3:10; Col 2:12,20; 3:3 [i]Ro 7:24 [j]S ver 16 **6:7** [k]S ver 18 **6:8** [l]S ver 5 **6:9** [m]ver 4; S Ac 2:24 [n]Rev 1:18 **6:10** [o]S ver 2 [p]S Heb 7:27 **6:11** [q]S ver 2 **6:12** [r]ver 16 **6:13** [s]ver 16,19; Ro 7:5 [t]Ro 12:1; 2Co 5:14,15; 1Pe 2:24 **6:14** [u]S ver 16 [v]S Ro 2:12 [w]S Ro 3:24 **6:15** [x]ver 1,14 **6:16** [y]2Pe 2:19 [z]ver 6,12,14, 17,20; Ge 4:7; Ps 51:5; 119:133; Jn 8:34; Ro 5:21; 7:14,23,25; 8:2; 2Pe 2:19 [a]S ver 23 **6:17** [b]Ro 1:8; S 2Co 2:14 [c]S ver 16 [d]2Ti 1:13 **6:18** [e]S ver 2; ver 7,22; Ro 8:2; 1Pe 4:1; S ver 16 [f]S ver 22 **6:19** [g]Ro 3:5; Gal 3:15 [h]S ver 13; S ver 22 **6:20** [i]S ver 16 [j]ver 16 **6:21** [k]S ver 23 **6:22** [l]S ver 18

righteousness (see 3:23 and note). Glory and power are often closely related in the Bible (see Ps 145:11; Col 1:11; 1Pe 4:11; Rev 1:6; 4:11; 5:12–13; 7:12; 19:1). *live a new life.* Amplified in vv. 8–10.

6:6 *our old self.* Our unregenerate self; what we once were. *body of sin.* The self in its pre-Christian state, dominated by sin. This is a figurative expression in which the old self is personified. It is a "body" that can be put to death. For the believer, this old self has been "rendered powerless" (see NIV text note) so that it can no longer enslave us to sin—whatever lingering vitality it may yet exert in its death throes.

6:7 *has died.* The believer's death with Christ to sin's ruling power (see v. 3). *freed from sin.* Not sinless, but free from sin's shackles and power.

6:8 As resurrection followed death in the experience of Christ, so the believer who dies with Christ is raised to a new quality of life here and now. Resurrection in the sense of a new birth is already a fact, and it increasingly exerts itself in the believer's life.

6:10 *he died to sin once for all.* In his death Christ (for the sake of sinners) submitted to the "reign" of sin (5:21); but his death broke the judicial link between sin and death, and he passed forever from the sphere of sin's "reign." Having been raised from the dead, he now lives forever to glorify God. *to God.* For the glory of God.

6:11 *count yourselves.* The first step toward victory over sin in the life of believers (for the succeeding steps see note on vv. 12–13). They are dead to sin and alive to God, and by faith they are to live out this reality. *in Christ.* The first occurrence in Romans of this phrase, which is found often in Paul's writings. True believers are "in Christ" because they have died with Christ and have been raised to new life in union with him. See note on Eph 1:1.

6:12–13 A call for Christians to become in practice what they already are in their status before God—dead to sin (see vv. 5–7) and alive to God (see vv. 8–10). The second step toward victory over sin is refusal to let sin control one's life (v. 12). The third step is to offer oneself to God (v. 13).

6:13 *offer.* Put yourselves in the service of, perhaps also echoing the language of sacrifice. *parts of your body.* All the separate capacities of your being (also in v. 19).

6:14 *sin shall not be your master.* Paul conceived of sin as a power that enslaves, and so personified it (see Ps 19:13). *not under law.* The meaning is not that Christians have been freed from all moral authority. They have, however, been freed from the law in the manner in which God's people were under law in the OT era. Law provides no enablement to resist the power of sin; it only condemns the sinner. But grace enables. *under grace.* For the disciplinary aspect of grace see Tit 2:11–12 and notes.

6:15–23 The question raised here seems to come from those who are afraid that the doctrine of justification by faith alone will remove all moral restraint. Paul rejects such a suggestion and shows that Christians do not throw morality to the winds. To the contrary, they exchange sin for righteousness as their master.

6:16 The contrast between sin and obedience suggests that sin is by nature disobedience to God.

6:17 *wholeheartedly obeyed.* Christian obedience is not forced or legalistic, but willing. *form of teaching.* May refer to a summary of the moral and ethical teachings of Christ that was given to new converts in the early church.

6:18 *slaves to righteousness.* Christians have changed masters. Whereas they were formerly slaves to sin (vv. 16–17), now they become slaves (willing servants) to righteousness.

6:19 *I put this in human terms.* Paul apologizes for using an imperfect analogy. The word "slave" when applied to Christians, who are free in Christ, naturally presents problems.

6:22 *set free from sin.* See note on v. 6. *holiness.* Slavery to God produces holiness, and the end of the process is eternal life (viewed not in its present sense but in its final,

have become slaves to God,[m] the benefit
you reap leads to holiness, and the result
is eternal life.[n] 23For the wages of sin is
death,[o] but the gift of God is eternal life[p]
in[a] Christ Jesus our Lord.

An Illustration From Marriage

7 Do you not know, brothers[q]—for I
am speaking to men who know the
law—that the law has authority over a
man only as long as he lives? 2For example, by law a married woman is bound to
her husband as long as he is alive, but if
her husband dies, she is released from the
law of marriage.[r] 3So then, if she marries
another man while her husband is still
alive, she is called an adulteress.[s] But if
her husband dies, she is released from that
law and is not an adulteress, even though
she marries another man.
4So, my brothers, you also died to the
law[t] through the body of Christ,[u] that you
might belong to another,[v] to him who
was raised from the dead, in order that
we might bear fruit to God. 5For when we
were controlled by the sinful nature,[b w]
the sinful passions aroused by the law[x]
were at work in our bodies,[y] so that we
bore fruit for death.[z] 6But now, by dying
to what once bound us, we have been released from the law[a] so that we serve in
the new way of the Spirit, and not in the
old way of the written code.[b]

Struggling With Sin

7What shall we say, then?[c] Is the law
sin? Certainly not![d] Indeed I would not
have known what sin was except through
the law.[e] For I would not have known
what coveting really was if the law had
not said, "Do not covet."[c f] 8But sin, seizing the opportunity afforded by the commandment,[g] produced in me every kind
of covetous desire. For apart from law,
sin is dead.[h] 9Once I was alive apart from
law; but when the commandment came,
sin sprang to life and I died. 10I found that
the very commandment that was intended to bring life[i] actually brought death.
11For sin, seizing the opportunity afforded by the commandment,[j] deceived me,[k]
and through the commandment put me
to death. 12So then, the law is holy, and
the commandment is holy, righteous and
good.[l]
13Did that which is good, then, become
death to me? By no means! But in order
that sin might be recognized as sin, it pro-

[a] 23 Or *through* [b] 5 Or *the flesh*; also in verse 25
[c] 7 Exodus 20:17; Deut. 5:21

6:22 [m] ver 18,19; Ro 7:25; 1Co 7:22; Eph 6:6; 1Pe 2:16 [n] S Mt 25:46 **6:23** [o] ver 16,21; Ge 2:17; Pr 10:16; Eze 18:4; Ro 1:32; S 5:12; 7:5,13; 8:6,13; Gal 6:7,8; Jas 1:15 [p] S Mt 25:46 **7:1** [q] S Ac 1:16; S 22:5; Ro 1:13; 1Co 1:10; 5:11; 6:6; 14:20,26; Gal 3:15; 6:18 **7:2** [r] 1Co 7:39 **7:3** [s] S Lk 16:18 **7:4** [t] ver 6; S Ro 6:6; 8:2; Gal 2:19; 3:23-25; 4:31; 5:1 [u] Col 1:22 [v] Gal 2:19,20 **7:5** [w] S Gal 5:24 [x] Ro 7:7-11 [y] Ro 6:13 [z] S Ro 6:23 **7:6** [a] S ver 4 [b] Ro 2:29; 2Co 3:6 **7:7** [c] S Ro 8:31 [d] S ver 12 [e] S Ro 4:15 [f] Ex 20:17; Dt 5:21 **7:8** [g] ver 11 [h] S Ro 4:15 **7:10** [i] Lev 18:5; Lk 10:26-28; S Ro 10:5; Gal 3:12 **7:11** [j] ver 8 [k] Ge 3:13 **7:12** [l] ver 7,13,14,16; Ro 8:4; Gal 3:21; 1Ti 1:8; S Ro 4:15

future sense). There is no eternal life without holiness (see Heb 12:14). Those who have been justified will surely give evidence of that fact by the presence of holiness in their lives. For other occurrences of the words "holiness" and "holy" see v. 19; Lev 11:44 and note; 1Co 1:30 and note on 1:2; 1Th 4:4,7; 1Ti 2:15; Heb 12:14.

6:23 Two kinds of servitude are contrasted here. One brings death as its wages; the other results in eternal life, not as wages earned or merited, but as a gift of God (cf. Eph 2:8–9 and notes). For the contrast between wages and gift see 4:4. *eternal life.* See Jn 17:3.

7:1 *law.* Perhaps Paul has in mind the Mosaic law, but his concern here is with the fundamental character of law as such.

7:2–3 These verses illustrate the principle set down in v. 1. Death decisively changes a person's relationship to the law.

7:4 *So.* Paul now draws the conclusion from the principle stated in v. 1 and illustrated in vv. 2–3. *died to the law.* The law's power to condemn no longer threatens believers, whose death here is to be understood in terms of 6:2–7. There, however, they die to sin; here they die to the law. The result is that the law has no more hold on them. *through the body of Christ.* His physical body (self) crucified. *belong to another.* The resurrected Christ (see 6:5; cf. Tit 2:14; 1Pe 2:9 and note). The purpose of this union is to produce the fruit of holiness.

7:5 *controlled by the sinful nature.* A condition, so far as Christians are concerned, that belongs to the past—the unregenerate state (cf. 1Co 6:11; Gal 5:19–23 and notes). *aroused by the law.* The law not only reveals sin; it also stimulates it. The natural human tendency is to desire the forbidden thing. *death.* Physical death and, beyond that, spiritual death—final separation from God (see note on 5:12)—were the fruit of our union with the law (cf. note on v. 4).

7:6 *what once bound us.* The law (see later in this verse, as well as v. 4). *released from the law.* In the sense of its condemnation (see note on v. 4). *new way of the Spirit.* See note on 8:4. *old way of the written code.* Life under the OT law.

7:7 *Is the law sin?* This question was occasioned by the remarks about the law in vv. 4–6. *I.* Paul seems to be using the first person pronoun of himself, but also as representative of people in general (vv. 7–12) and of Christians in particular (vv. 13–25). *I would not have known what sin was.* The law fulfilled the important function of revealing the presence and fact of sin.

7:8 *opportunity afforded by the commandment.* See note on v. 5. *sin is dead.* Not nonexistent but not fully perceived (see 5:13 and note).

7:9 *Once I was alive.* Paul reviews his own experience from the vantage point of his present understanding. Before he realized that the law condemned him to death, he was alive. Reference is to the time either before his *bar mitzvah* (see below) or before his conversion, when the true rigor of the law became clear to him (cf. Lk 18:20–21; see Php 3:6 and note). *when the commandment came.* When Paul came to the realization that he stood guilty before the law—a reference either to his *bar mitzvah,* when he, at age 13, assumed full responsibility for the law, or to the time when he became aware of the full force of the law (at his conversion). *I died.* Paul came to realize he was condemned to death, because law reveals sin, and sin's wages is death (see 6:23 and note).

7:10 *was intended to bring life.* See Lev 18:5 and note. As it worked out in Paul's experience, the law became the avenue through which sin entered generally. Instead of giving life, the law brought condemnation; instead of producing holiness, it stimulated sin.

7:12 *the law is holy.* Despite the despicable use that sin made of the law, the law was not to blame. The law is God's and as such is "holy, righteous and good."

7:13–25 Whether Paul is describing a Christian or non-Christian experience has been hotly debated through

duced death in me[m] through what was
good,[n] so that through the commandment
sin might become utterly sinful.
14We know that the law is spiritual; but
I am unspiritual,[o] sold[p] as a slave to sin.[q]
15I do not understand what I do. For what
I want to do I do not do, but what I hate I
do.[r] 16And if I do what I do not want to do,
I agree that the law is good.[s] 17As it is, it is
no longer I myself who do it, but it is sin
living in me.[t] 18I know that nothing good
lives in me, that is, in my sinful nature.[a u]
For I have the desire to do what is good,
but I cannot carry it out. 19For what I do
is not the good I want to do; no, the evil I
do not want to do—this I keep on doing.[v]
20Now if I do what I do not want to do, it
is no longer I who do it, but it is sin living
in me that does it.[w]
21So I find this law at work:[x] When I
want to do good, evil is right there with
me. 22For in my inner being[y] I delight in
God's law;[z] 23but I see another law at work
in the members of my body, waging war[a]
against the law of my mind and making me
a prisoner of the law of sin[b] at work within my members. 24What a wretched man
I am! Who will rescue me from this body
of death?[c] 25Thanks be to God—through
Jesus Christ our Lord![d]
So then, I myself in my mind am a slave
to God's law,[e] but in the sinful nature a
slave to the law of sin.[f]

7:13 [m]S Ro 6:23 [n]S ver 12 **7:14** [o]1Co 3:1 [p]1Ki 21:20,25; 2Ki 17:17 [q]S Ro 6:16 **7:15** [r]ver 19; Gal 5:17 **7:16** [s]S ver 12 **7:17** [t]ver 20 **7:18** [u]ver 25; S Gal 5:24 **7:19** [v]ver 15 **7:20** [w]ver 17 **7:21** [x]ver 23,25 **7:22** [y]Eph 3:16 [z]Ps 1:2; 40:8 **7:23** [a]Gal 5:17; Jas 4:1; 1Pe 2:11 [b]S Ro 6:16 **7:24** [c]Ro 6:6; 8:2 **7:25** [d]S 2Co 2:14 [e]S Ro 6:22 [f]S Ro 6:16 **8:1** [g]ver 34 [h]ver 39; S Ro 16:3 **8:2** [i]Ro 7:25 [j]1Co 15:45 [k]Jn 8:32,36; S Ro 6:18 [l]S Ro 6:16; S 7:4 **8:3** [m]Heb 7:18; 10:1-4 [n]Ro 7:18, 19; S Gal 5:24 [o]S Php 2:7 [p]Heb 2:14,17 **8:4** [q]Ro 2:26 [r]S Gal 5:16

Life Through the Spirit

8 Therefore, there is now no condemnation[g] for those who are in Christ
Jesus,[b h] 2because through Christ Jesus[i]
the law of the Spirit of life[j] set me free[k]
from the law of sin[l] and death. 3For what
the law was powerless[m] to do in that it
was weakened by the sinful nature,[c n] God
did by sending his own Son in the likeness
of sinful man[o] to be a sin offering.[d p] And
so he condemned sin in sinful man,[e] 4in
order that the righteous requirements[q] of
the law might be fully met in us, who do
not live according to the sinful nature but
according to the Spirit.[r]

[a] 18 Or *my flesh* [b] 1 Some later manuscripts *Jesus, who do not live according to the sinful nature but according to the Spirit,* [c] 3 Or *the flesh*; also in verses 4, 5, 8, 9, 12 and 13 [d] 3 Or *man, for sin* [e] 3 Or *in the flesh*

the centuries. That he is speaking of the non-Christian life is suggested by: (1) the use of phrases such as "sold as a slave to sin" (v. 14), "I know that nothing good lives in me" (v. 18) and "What a wretched man I am!" (v. 24)—which do not seem to describe Christian experience; (2) the contrast between ch. 7 and ch. 8, making it difficult for the other view to be credible; (3) the problem of the value of conversion if one ends up in spiritual misery. In favor of the view that Paul is describing Christian experience are: (1) the use of the present tense throughout the passage; (2) Paul's humble opinion of himself (v. 18); (3) his high regard for God's law (vv. 14,16); (4) the location of this passage in the section of Romans where Paul is dealing with sanctification—the growth of the Christian in holiness.

7:13 Sin used a holy thing (law) for an unholy end (death). By this fact the contemptible nature of sin is revealed.

7:14 *spiritual.* The law had its origin in God. *I am.* The personal pronoun and the verb, taken together, suggest that Paul is describing his present (Christian) experience. *unspiritual.* Even believers have the seeds of rebellion in their hearts. *sold as a slave to sin.* A phrase so strong that many refuse to accept it as descriptive of a Christian. However, it may graphically point out the failure even of Christians to meet the radical ethical and moral demands of the gospel (see note on Mt 5:1—7:29). It also points up the persistent nature of sin. Cf. Paul's statement in 1Ti 1:15: "sinners—of whom I am the worst" (see note there).

7:15 *I do not understand.* The struggle within creates tension, ambivalence and confusion (cf. Gal 5:16–17 and notes).

7:16 *I agree that the law is good.* Even when Paul is rebellious and disobedient, the Holy Spirit reveals to him the essential goodness of the law.

7:17 *no longer I myself who do it.* Not an attempt to escape moral responsibility but a statement of the great control sin can have over a Christian's life.

7:18 *nothing good lives in me.* A reference to Paul's fallen nature, as the last phrase of the sentence indicates.

7:20 *sin . . . does it.* See note on v. 17.

7:21 *law.* Here means "principle."

7:22 *I delight in God's law.* The Mosaic law or God's law generally. It is difficult to see how a non-Christian could say this.

7:23 *another law.* A principle or force at work in Paul preventing him from giving obedience to God's law. *law of my mind.* His desire to obey God's law. *law of sin.* Essentially the same as "another law," mentioned above.

7:24 *body of death.* Figurative for the body of sin (see 6:6; 8:10 and notes) that hung on him like a corpse and from which he could not gain freedom.

7:25 The first half of this verse is the answer to the question raised in v. 24—deliverance comes, not through legalistic effort, but through Christ (see 8:2 and note). The last half is a summary of vv. 13–24. *I myself.* The real self—the inner being that delights in God's law (see v. 22 and note). *slave to the law of sin.* Christians must reckon with the enslaving power of their sinful nature (see note on v. 23) as long as they live—until "the redemption of our bodies" (8:23).

8:1 *condemnation.* The law brings condemnation because it points out, stimulates and condemns sin. But the Christian is no longer "under law" (6:14; see note there). *in Christ Jesus.* United with him, as explained in 6:1–10 (see note on 6:11; see also Php 2:1 and note).

8:2 *law of the Spirit of life.* The controlling power of the Holy Spirit, who is life-giving. Paul uses the word "law" in several different ways in Romans—to mean, e.g., a controlling power (here); God's law (2:17–20; 9:31; 10:3–5); the Pentateuch (3:21b); the OT as a whole (see 3:19 and note); a principle (3:27). *law of sin and death.* The controlling power of sin, which ultimately produces death (see 7:24 and note).

8:3 *powerless to do.* The law was not able to overcome sin (cf. Heb 7:18 and note). It could point out, condemn and even stimulate sin, but it could not remove it. *in the likeness of sinful man.* Christ in his incarnation became truly human, but, unlike all other humans, was sinless (see note on Mt 4:1–11). *in sinful man.* See NIV text note; when Paul says "in the flesh," he is probably referring to Christ's human body (on the cross).

8:4 *righteous requirements of the law.* The law still plays a role in the life of a believer—not, however, as a means of

5Those who live according to the sinful
nature have their minds set on what that
nature desires;[s] but those who live in accordance with the Spirit have their minds
set on what the Spirit desires.[t] 6The mind
of sinful man[a] is death,[u] but the mind controlled by the Spirit is life[v] and peace; 7the
sinful mind[b] is hostile to God.[w] It does
not submit to God's law, nor can it do so.
8Those controlled by the sinful nature[x]
cannot please God.

9You, however, are controlled not by
the sinful nature[y] but by the Spirit, if the
Spirit of God lives in you.[z] And if anyone
does not have the Spirit of Christ,[a] he does
not belong to Christ. 10But if Christ is in
you,[b] your body is dead because of sin, yet
your spirit is alive because of righteousness. 11And if the Spirit of him who raised
Jesus from the dead[c] is living in you, he
who raised Christ from the dead will also
give life to your mortal bodies[d] through
his Spirit, who lives in you.

12Therefore, brothers, we have an obligation—but it is not to the sinful nature, to live according to it.[e] 13For if you
live according to the sinful nature, you
will die;[f] but if by the Spirit you put to
death the misdeeds of the body,[g] you will
live,[h] 14because those who are led by the
Spirit of God[i] are sons of God.[j] 15For you
did not receive a spirit[k] that makes you a
slave again to fear,[l] but you received the
Spirit of sonship.[c] And by him we cry,
"*Abba*,[d] Father."[m] 16The Spirit himself testifies with our spirit[n] that we are God's
children.[o] 17Now if we are children, then
we are heirs[p]—heirs of God and co-heirs
with Christ, if indeed we share in his sufferings[q] in order that we may also share
in his glory.[r]

Future Glory

18I consider that our present sufferings
are not worth comparing with the glory
that will be revealed in us.[s] 19The creation
waits in eager expectation for the sons of
God[t] to be revealed. 20For the creation was
subjected to frustration, not by its own
choice, but by the will of the one who
subjected it,[u] in hope 21that[e] the creation
itself will be liberated from its bondage to
decay[v] and brought into the glorious freedom of the children of God.[w]

22We know that the whole creation has
been groaning[x] as in the pains of child-

8:5 [s]Gal 5:19-21 [t]Gal 5:22-25 **8:6** [u]S Ro 6:23 [v]ver 13; Gal 6:8 **8:7** [w]Jas 4:4 **8:8** [x]S Gal 5:24 **8:9** [y]S Gal 5:24 [z]ver 11; 1Co 6:19; 2Ti 1:14 [a]Jn 14:17; S Ac 16:7; 1Jn 4:13 **8:10** [b]ver 9; Ex 29:45; Jn 14:20,23; 2Co 13:5; Gal 2:20; Eph 3:17; Col 1:27; Rev 3:20 **8:11** [c]S Ac 2:24 [d]Jn 5:21; S Ro 6:5 **8:12** [e]ver 4; S Gal 5:24 **8:13** [f]S Ro 6:23 [g]S Ro 6:2 [h]ver 6; Gal 6:8 **8:14** [i]S Gal 5:18 [j]ver 19; Hos 1:10; Mal 3:17; Mt 5:9; S Jn 1:12; Gal 3:26; 4:5; Eph 1:5; Rev 21:7 **8:15** [k]S Jn 20:22 [l]S 2Ti 1:7 [m]Mk 14:36; Gal 4:5,6 **8:16** [n]2Co 1:22; Eph 1:13 [o]S ver 14; S Jn 1:12 **8:17** [p]S Ac 20:32; Gal 3:29; 4:7; Eph 3:6; Tit 3:7 [q]S 2Co 1:5 [r]2Ti 2:12; 1Pe 4:13 **8:18** [s]2Co 4:17; 1Pe 4:13; 5:1 **8:19** [t]S ver 14 **8:20** [u]Ge 3:17-19; 5:29 **8:21** [v]Ac 3:21; 2Pe 3:13; Rev 21:1 [w]S Jn 1:12 **8:22** [x]Jer 12:4

[a] 6 Or *mind set on the flesh* [b] 7 Or *the mind set on the flesh* [c] 15 Or *adoption* [d] 15 Aramaic for *Father* [e] 20,21 Or *subjected it in hope.* 21*For*

salvation but as a moral and ethical guide, obeyed out of love for God and by the power that the Spirit provides. This is the fulfillment of Jer 31:31–34 (a prophecy of the new covenant; see notes there). *fully met.* Lit. "fulfilled." God's aim in sending his Son was that believers might be enabled to embody the true and full intentions of the law. *according to the Spirit.* How the law's righteous requirements can be fully met—by no longer letting the sinful nature hold sway but by yielding to the directing and empowering ministry of the Holy Spirit.

8:5–8 Two mind-sets are described here: that of the sinful nature and that of the Spirit. The former leads to death, the latter to life and peace. The sinful nature is bound up with death (v. 6), hostility to God (v. 7), insubordination (v. 7) and unacceptability to God (v. 8).

8:9 Paul makes it unmistakably clear that "the Spirit of God lives in" every believer.

8:10 *your body is dead because of sin.* Even a Christian's body is subject to physical death, the consequence of sin. *your spirit is alive.* Or "the Spirit is life" (see v. 2 and note). On this reading, "body" is understood as in 7:24. *because of righteousness.* Christians are indwelt by the life-giving Spirit as a result of their justification.

8:11 For the close connection between the resurrection of Christ and that of believers see 1Co 6:14; 15:20,23; 2Co 4:14; Php 3:21; 1Th 4:14 and notes. *give life to your mortal bodies.* The resurrection of our bodies, guaranteed to believers by the indwelling presence of the Holy Spirit—whose presence is evidenced by a Spirit-controlled life (vv. 4–9), which in turn provides assurance that our resurrection is certain.

8:14 *sons of God.* God is the Father of all in the sense that he created all and his love and providential care are extended to all (see Mt 5:45 and note). But not all are his children. Jesus said to the unbelieving Jews of his day, "You belong to your father, the devil" (Jn 8:44; see note there). People become children of God through faith in God's unique Son (see Jn 1:12 and note), and being led by God's Spirit is the hallmark of this relationship.

8:15 *sonship.* The underlying word here is "adoption" (see NIV text note). It occurs four other times in the NT (v. 23; 9:4; Gal 4:5 [see note there]; Eph 1:5). Adoption was common among the Greeks and Romans, who granted the adopted son all the privileges of a natural son, including inheritance rights. Christians are adopted sons by grace; Christ, however, is God's Son by nature. *Abba, Father.* Expressive of an especially close relationship to God (see also NIV text note).

8:16 *testifies with our spirit.* The inner testimony of the Holy Spirit to our relationship to Christ. *God's children.* The same as "sons of God" (v. 14), terms that in the NT are synonymous.

8:17 *heirs.* Those who have already entered, at least partially, into the possession of their inheritance. *co-heirs with Christ.* Everything really belongs to Christ, but by grace we share in what is his. *if indeed we share in his sufferings.* The meaning is not that there is some doubt about sharing Christ's glory. Rather, despite the fact that Christians presently suffer, they are assured a future entrance into their inheritance (see v. 18).

8:19 *creation.* Both animate and inanimate, but exclusive of human beings (see vv. 22–23, where "whole creation" and "we ourselves" are contrasted). *sons of God to be revealed.* Christians are already sons of God, but the full manifestation of all that this means will not come until the end (see 1Jn 3:1–2).

8:20 *was subjected to frustration.* A reference to Ge 3:17–19. *in hope.* A possible allusion to the promise of Ge 3:15 (see note there).

8:21 *will be liberated from its bondage to decay.* The physical universe is not destined for destruction (annihilation) but for renewal (see 2Pe 3:13 and note; Rev 21:1). And living things will no longer be subject to death and decay, as they are today.

8:22 *has been groaning.* Creation is personified as a woman in labor waiting for the birth of her child.

birth right up to the present time. 23Not
only so, but we ourselves, who have the
firstfruits of the Spirit,[y] groan[z] inwardly
as we wait eagerly[a] for our adoption as
sons, the redemption of our bodies.[b] 24For
in this hope we were saved.[c] But hope that
is seen is no hope at all.[d] Who hopes for
what he already has? 25But if we hope for
what we do not yet have, we wait for it
patiently.[e]

26In the same way, the Spirit helps us in
our weakness. We do not know what we
ought to pray for, but the Spirit[f] himself
intercedes for us[g] with groans that words
cannot express. 27And he who searches
our hearts[h] knows the mind of the Spirit,
because the Spirit intercedes[i] for the saints
in accordance with God's will.

More Than Conquerors

28And we know that in all things God
works for the good[j] of those who love
him,[a] who[b] have been called[k] according
to his purpose.[l] 29For those God foreknew[m]
he also predestined[n] to be conformed to
the likeness of his Son,[o] that he might be
the firstborn[p] among many brothers. 30And
those he predestined,[q] he also called;[r]
those he called, he also justified;[s] those
he justified, he also glorified.[t]

31What, then, shall we say in response to
this?[u] If God is for us,[v] who can be against
us?[w] 32He who did not spare his own Son,[x]
but gave him up for us all—how will he
not also, along with him, graciously give
us all things? 33Who will bring any charge[y]
against those whom God has chosen? It is
God who justifies. 34Who is he that condemns?[z] Christ Jesus, who died[a]—more
than that, who was raised to life[b]—is at
the right hand of God[c] and is also interceding for us.[d] 35Who shall separate us from
the love of Christ?[e] Shall trouble or hardship or persecution or famine or nakedness
or danger or sword?[f] 36As it is written:

> "For your sake we face death all day
> long;
> we are considered as sheep to be
> slaughtered."[c][g]

37No, in all these things we are more than
conquerors[h] through him who loved us.[i]
38For I am convinced that neither death
nor life, neither angels nor demons,[d] neither the present nor the future,[j] nor any

[a] 28 Some manuscripts *And we know that all things work together for good to those who love God* [b] 28 Or *works together with those who love him to bring about what is good—with those who* [c] 36 Psalm 44:22 [d] 38 Or *nor heavenly rulers*

8:23 [y] S 2Co 5:5 [z] 2Co 5:2,4 [a] ver 19; Gal 5:5 [b] ver 11; Php 3:21 **8:24** [c] 1Th 5:8; Tit 3:7 [d] S 2Co 4:18 **8:25** [e] Ps 37:7 **8:26** [f] ver 15,16 [g] Eph 6:18 **8:27** [h] S Rev 2:23 [i] S ver 34 **8:28** [j] Ge 50:20; Isa 38:17; Jer 29:11 [k] ver 30; Ro 11:29; 1Co 1:9; Gal 1:6,15; Eph 4:1,4; 1Th 2:12; 2Ti 1:9; Heb 9:15; 1Pe 2:9; 2Pe 1:10 [l] Eph 1:11; 3:11; Heb 6:17 **8:29** [m] Ro 11:2; 1Pe 1:2 [n] Eph 1:5,11 [o] 1Co 15:49; 2Co 3:18; Php 3:21; 1Jn 3:2 [p] S Col 1:18 **8:30** [q] Eph 1:5,11 [r] S ver 28 [s] S Ro 4:25 [t] Ro 9:23 **8:31** [u] Ro 4:1; 6:1; 7:7; 9:14,30 [v] Ex 3:12; Isa 41:10; Hag 1:13 [w] Ps 56:9; 118:6; Isa 8:10; Jer 20:11; Heb 13:6

8:32 [x] Ge 22:13; Mal 3:17; Jn 3:16; Ro 5:8 **8:33** [y] Isa 50:8,9 **8:34** [z] ver 1 [a] Ro 5:6-8 [b] S Ac 2:24 [c] S Mk 16:19 [d] ver 27; Job 16:20; Isa 53:12; Heb 7:25; 9:24; 1Jn 2:1 **8:35** [e] ver 37-39 [f] 1Co 4:11; 2Co 11:26,27 **8:36** [g] Ps 44:22; 1Co 4:9; 15:30,31; 2Co 4:11; 6:9; 11:23 **8:37** [h] 1Co 15:57 [i] Ro 5:8; Gal 2:20; Eph 5:2; Rev 1:5; 3:9 **8:38** [j] 1Co 3:22

8:23 *firstfruits of the Spirit.* Believers' possession of the Holy Spirit is not only evidence of their present salvation (vv. 14,16) but also a pledge of their future inheritance—and not only a pledge but also the down payment on that inheritance (see 2Co 1:22; 5:5 and notes; Eph 1:14). *firstfruits.* See Ex 23:19 and note; cf. 1Co 15:20 and note. *adoption as sons.* See note on v. 15. Christians are already God's children, but this is a reference to the full realization of our inheritance in Christ. *redemption of our bodies.* The resurrection, as the final stage of our adoption. The first stage was God's predestination of our adoption (see Eph 1:5); the second is our present inclusion as children of God (see v. 14; Gal 3:25–26 and notes).

8:24 *in this hope.* We are saved by faith (see Eph 2:8 and note), not hope; but hope accompanies salvation.

8:26 *In the same way.* As hope sustains believers when they suffer, so the Holy Spirit helps them when they pray. *with groans that words cannot express.* In v. 23 it is the believer who groans; here it is the Holy Spirit. Whether Paul means words that are unspoken or words that cannot be expressed in human language is not clear—probably the former, though v. 27 seems to suggest the latter.

8:27 The relationship between the Holy Spirit and God the Father is so close that the Holy Spirit's prayers need not be audible. God knows his every thought.

8:28 *the good.* That which conforms us "to the likeness of his Son" (v. 29). *called.* Effectual calling: the call of God to which there is invariably a positive response.

8:29 *foreknew.* Some insist that the knowledge here is not abstract but is couched in love and mixed with purpose. They hold that God not only knew us before we had any knowledge of him but that he also knew us, in the sense of choosing us by his grace, before the foundation of the world (see Eph 1:4; 2Ti 1:9 and notes). Others believe that Paul here refers to the fact that in eternity past God knew those who by faith would become his people. *predestined.* Predestination here is to moral conformity to the likeness of his Son. *that he might be the firstborn among many brothers.* The reason God foreknew, predestined and conformed believers to Christ's likeness is that the Son might hold the position of highest honor in the great family of God.

8:30 *predestined ... glorified.* The sequence by which God carries out his predestination. *glorified.* Since this final stage is firmly grounded in God's set purpose, it is as certain as if it had already happened.

8:31 *If.* That is, "Since."

8:32 The argument (from the greater to the lesser) here is similar to that in 5:9–10. If God gave the supreme gift of his Son to save us, he will certainly also give whatever is necessary to bring to fulfillment the work begun at the cross. See note on Ge 22:16.

8:33–34 A court of law is in mind. No charge can be brought against the Christian because God has already pronounced a verdict of not guilty.

8:34 *Who ... condemns?* Echoes the language of Isa 50:9. Paul gives three reasons why no one can condemn God's elect: (1) Christ died for us; (2) Christ is alive and seated at the right hand of God, the position of power; (3) Christ is interceding for us (see Heb 7:25; 1Jn 2:1 and notes).

8:35–39 Paul wanted to show his readers that suffering does not separate believers from Christ but actually carries them along toward their ultimate goal.

8:36 Ps 44:22 (see note there) is quoted to show that suffering has always been part of the experience of God's people (see Php 1:29 and note).

8:37 *who loved us.* Referring especially to Christ's death on the cross (see note on Ge 22:16; see also Gal 2:20; Eph 5:25 and notes).

powers,[k] 39 neither height nor depth, nor
anything else in all creation, will be able
to separate us from the love of God[l] that is
in Christ Jesus our Lord.[m]

God's Sovereign Choice

9 I speak the truth in Christ—I am not
lying,[n] my conscience confirms[o] it in
the Holy Spirit— 2 I have great sorrow
and unceasing anguish in my heart. 3 For
I could wish that I myself[p] were cursed[q]
and cut off from Christ for the sake of
my brothers,[r] those of my own race,[s]
4 the people of Israel.[t] Theirs is the adoption as sons;[u] theirs the divine glory,[v] the
covenants,[w] the receiving of the law,[x]
the temple worship[y] and the promises.[z]
5 Theirs are the patriarchs,[a] and from them
is traced the human ancestry of Christ,[b]
who is God over all,[c] forever praised![a][d]
Amen.
6 It is not as though God's word[e] had
failed. For not all who are descended from
Israel are Israel.[f] 7 Nor because they are his
descendants are they all Abraham's children. On the contrary, "It is through Isaac
that your offspring will be reckoned."[b][g]
8 In other words, it is not the natural children who are God's children,[h] but it is the
children of the promise who are regarded as Abraham's offspring.[i] 9 For this was
how the promise was stated: "At the appointed time I will return, and Sarah will
have a son."[c][j]
10 Not only that, but Rebekah's children
had one and the same father, our father
Isaac.[k] 11 Yet, before the twins were born
or had done anything good or bad[l]—in
order that God's purpose[m] in election
might stand: 12 not by works but by him
who calls—she was told, "The older will
serve the younger."[d][n] 13 Just as it is written: "Jacob I loved, but Esau I hated."[e][o]
14 What then shall we say?[p] Is God unjust? Not at all![q] 15 For he says to Moses,

"I will have mercy on whom I have
mercy,
and I will have compassion on
whom I have compassion."[f][r]

[a] 5 Or *Christ, who is over all. God be forever praised!* Or *Christ. God who is over all be forever praised!*
[b] *7* Gen. 21:12 [c] *9* Gen. 18:10,14 [d] *12* Gen. 25:23
[e] *13* Mal. 1:2,3 [f] *15* Exodus 33:19

8:38 [k]Eph 1:21; Col 1:16; 1Pe 3:22 **8:39** [l]S Ro 5:8 [m]ver 1; S Ro 16:3 **9:1** [n]Ps 15:2; 2Co 11:10; Gal 1:20; 1Ti 2:7 [o]S Ro 1:9 **9:3** [p]Ex 32:32 [q]1Co 12:3; 16:22 [r]S Ac 22:5 [s]Ro 11:14 **9:4** [t]ver 6 [u]Ex 4:22; 6:7; Dt 7:6 [v]Heb 9:5 [w]Ge 17:2; Dt 4:13; Ac 3:25; Eph 2:12 [x]Ps 147:19 [y]Heb 9:1 [z]S Ac 13:32; S Gal 3:16 **9:5** [a]Ro 11:28 [b]Mt 1:1-16; Ro 1:3 [c]Jn 1:1; Col 2:9 [d]Ro 1:25; 2Co 11:31 **9:6** [e]S Heb 4:12 [f]Ro 2:28,29; Gal 6:16 **9:7** [g]Ge 21:12; Heb 11:18 **9:8** [h]S Ro 8:14 [i]S Gal 3:16 **9:9** [j]Ge 18:10,14 **9:10** [k]Ge 25:21 **9:11** [l]ver 16 [m]Ro 8:28 **9:12** [n]Ge 25:23 **9:13** [o]Mal 1:2,3 **9:14** [p]S Ro 8:31 [q]2Ch 19:7 **9:15** [r]Ex 33:19

8:39 *neither height nor depth.* It is impossible to get beyond God's loving reach (see Eph 3:17–19). *nor anything else in all creation.* Includes all created things. Only God is not included, and he is the one who has justified us (see note on vv. 33–34).

9:1—11:36 God's way with Israel. Among other matters, Paul addresses three urgent questions occasioned by the rejection of the gospel by many Jews in Paul's day: (1) Has the word of God to Israel concerning her salvation come to nothing? (2) Has God completely and finally rejected his people Israel? (3) Is the gospel incapable of saving the Jews? His answer to all three is an emphatic "No!" See Introduction: Content; Outline.

9:1 *in the Holy Spirit.* Conscience is a reliable guide only when enlightened by the Holy Spirit.

9:3 *cursed.* The Greek for this word is *anathema,* and it means delivered over to the wrath of God for eternal destruction (see 1Co 12:3; 16:22; Gal 1:8 and notes). Such was Paul's great love for his fellow Jews. For a similar expression of love see Ex 32:32.

9:4 *people of Israel.* The descendants of Jacob (who was renamed Israel by God; see Ge 32:28 and note). The name was used of the entire nation (see Ex 3:16), then of the northern kingdom after the nation was divided (see 1Ki 12), the southern kingdom being called Judah. During the intertestamental period and later in NT times, Palestinian Jews used the title to indicate that they were the chosen people of God. Its use here is especially relevant because Paul is about to show that, despite Israel's unbelief and disobedience, God's promises to her are still valid. *adoption.* Israel had been accepted as God's son (see Ex 4:22; Jer 31:9; Hos 11:1 and notes). *glory.* The evidence of the presence of God among his people (see Ex 16:7,10; Lev 9:6,23; Nu 16:19). *covenants.* For example, the Abrahamic (Ge 15:17–21; 17:1–8); the Mosaic (Ex 19:5; 24:1–4), renewed on the plains of Moab (Dt 29:1–15), at Mounts Ebal and Gerizim (Jos 8:30–35) and at Shechem (Jos 24); the Levitical (Nu 25:12–13; Jer 33:21; Mal 2:4–5); the Davidic (2Sa 7; 23:5; Ps 89:3–4,28–29; 132:11–12); and the new (prophesied in Jer 31:31–34). See chart, p. 19. *promises.* Especially those made to Abraham (see Ge 12:7; 13:14–17; see also 17:5–8; 22:16–18 and notes) but also including the many OT Messianic promises (see, e.g., 2Sa 7:12,16; Isa 9:6–7; Jer 23:5; 31:31–34; Eze 34:23–24; 37:24 and notes).

9:5 *patriarchs.* Abraham, Isaac, Jacob and his sons. *Christ, who is God.* One of the clearest statements of the deity of Jesus Christ found in the entire NT (but see NIV text note). See also 1:4; 10:9; Mt 1:23; 28:19; Lk 1:35; 5:20–21; Jn 1:1,3,10,14,18; 5:18; 20:28; 2Co 13:14; Php 2:6; Col 1:15–20; 2:9; Tit 2:13; Heb 1:2–3,6,8; 2Pe 1:1; Rev 1:13–18; 22:13 and related notes.

9:6 *God's word.* His clearly stated purpose, which has not failed, because "not all who are descended from Israel are Israel." Paul is not denying the election of all Israel (as a nation) but stating that within Israel there is a separation, that of unbelieving Israel and believing Israel. Physical descent is no guarantee of a place in God's spiritual family.

9:7 *descendants.* Physical descendants (e.g., Ishmael and his offspring).

9:8 *natural children.* Those merely biologically descended from Abraham. *God's children.* See v. 4. Not all Israelites were God's children (see Jn 8:44 and note). The reference is to the descendants of Abraham who shared his faith.

9:11 *done anything good or bad.* God's choice of Jacob was based on sovereign freedom, not on the fulfillment of any prior conditions. *God's purpose in election.* God's purpose embodied in his election (see note on Eph 1:4).

9:12 *not by works but by him who calls.* Before Rebekah's children were even born, God made a choice—a choice obviously not based on works. *calls.* See 8:28 and note.

9:13 *Jacob I loved, but Esau I hated.* Equivalent to "Jacob I chose, but Esau I rejected" (cf. Mal 1:3; Lk 14:26 and notes).

9:14 *Is God unjust?* Unjust to elect on the basis of his sovereign freedom, as with Jacob and Esau.

9:15 Paul denies injustice in God's dealing with Isaac and Ishmael, and Jacob and Esau, by appealing to God's sovereign right to dispense mercy as he chooses.

16It does not, therefore, depend on man's
desire or effort, but on God's mercy.[s] 17For
the Scripture says to Pharaoh: "I raised you
up for this very purpose, that I might display my power in you and that my name
might be proclaimed in all the earth."[a][t]
18Therefore God has mercy on whom he
wants to have mercy, and he hardens
whom he wants to harden.[u]
19One of you will say to me:[v] "Then why
does God still blame us?[w] For who resists
his will?"[x] 20But who are you, O man, to
talk back to God?[y] "Shall what is formed
say to him who formed it,[z] 'Why did you
make me like this?' "[b][a] 21Does not the potter have the right to make out of the same
lump of clay some pottery for noble purposes and some for common use?[b]
22What if God, choosing to show his
wrath and make his power known, bore
with great patience[c] the objects of his
wrath—prepared for destruction?[d] 23What
if he did this to make the riches of his glory[e] known to the objects of his mercy,
whom he prepared in advance for glory[f]—
24even us, whom he also called,[g] not only
from the Jews but also from the Gentiles?[h]
25As he says in Hosea:

"I will call them 'my people' who are
not my people;
and I will call her 'my loved one'
who is not my loved one,"[c][i]

26and,

"It will happen that in the very place
where it was said to them,
'You are not my people,'
they will be called 'sons of the living
God.' "[d][j]

27Isaiah cries out concerning Israel:

"Though the number of the Israelites
be like the sand by the sea,[k]
only the remnant will be saved.[l]
28For the Lord will carry out
his sentence on earth with speed
and finality."[e][m]

29It is just as Isaiah said previously:

"Unless the Lord Almighty[n]
had left us descendants,
we would have become like Sodom,
we would have been like
Gomorrah."[f][o]

Israel's Unbelief

30What then shall we say?[p] That the
Gentiles, who did not pursue righteousness, have obtained it, a righteousness
that is by faith;[q] 31but Israel, who pursued
a law of righteousness,[r] has not attained
it.[s] 32Why not? Because they pursued it not
by faith but as if it were by works. They

9:16 [s] Eph 2:8; Tit 3:5 **9:17** [t] Ex 9:16; 14:4; Ps 76:10 **9:18** [u] Ex 4:21; 7:3; 14:4,17; Dt 2:30; Jos 11:20; Ro 11:25 **9:19** [v] Ro 11:19; 1Co 15:35; Jas 2:18 [w] Ro 3:7 [x] 2Sa 16:10; 2Ch 20:6; Da 4:35 **9:20** [y] Job 1:22; 9:12; 40:2 [z] Isa 64:8; Jer 18:6 [a] Isa 29:16; 45:9; 10:15 **9:21** [b] 2Ti 2:20 **9:22** [c] S Ro 2:4 [d] Pr 16:4 **9:23** [e] S Ro 2:4 [f] Ro 8:30 **9:24** [g] S Ro 8:28 [h] S Ro 3:29 **9:25** [i] Hos 2:23; 1Pe 2:10 **9:26** [j] Hos 1:10; S Mt 16:16; S Ro 8:14 **9:27** [k] Ge 22:17; Hos 1:10 [l] 2Ki 19:4; Jer 44:14; 50:20; Joel 2:32; Ro 11:5 **9:28** [m] Isa 10:22,23 **9:29** [n] Jas 5:4 [o] Isa 1:9; Ge 19:24-29; Dt 29:23; Isa 13:19; Jer 50:40 **9:30** [p] S Ro 8:31 [q] Ro 1:17; 3:22; 4:5,13; 10:6; Gal 2:16; Php 3:9; Heb 11:7 **9:31** [r] Dt 6:25; Isa 51:1; Ro 10:2,3; 11:7 [s] Gal 5:4

[a] *17* Exodus 9:16 [b] *20* Isaiah 29:16; 45:9
[c] *25* Hosea 2:23 [d] *26* Hosea 1:10
[e] *28* Isaiah 10:22,23 [f] *29* Isaiah 1:9

9:16 *It.* God's choice, which is not controlled in any way by human beings. However, Paul makes it clear that the basis for Israel's rejection was her unbelief (see vv. 30–32 and notes).
9:17 *Pharaoh.* The pharaoh of the exodus. *raised you up.* Made you ruler of Egypt. *that my name might be proclaimed.* That is, that all the world might come to hear of me and what I have done for my people Israel (cf. Ex 15:13–18; Jos 2:10–11; 9:9; 1Sa 4:8).
9:18 The first part of this verse again echoes Ex 33:19 (see v. 15 and NIV text note there) and the last part such texts as Ex 7:3; 9:12; 14:4,17, in which God is said to harden the hearts of the pharaoh and the Egyptians. *on whom he wants to have mercy.* Cannot mean that God is arbitrary in his mercy, because Paul ultimately bases God's rejection of Israel on her unbelief (see vv. 30–32).
9:20 *who are you … to talk back to God?* Paul is not silencing all human questioning of God, but he is speaking to those with an impenitent, God-defying attitude who want to make God answerable to them for what he does and who, by their questions, defame the character of God.
9:21 The main point of the analogy between God and the potter is the sovereign freedom of God in dealing with people (cf. Jer 18:1–10 and notes).
9:22–23 An illustration of the principle stated in v. 21. The emphasis is on God's mercy, not his wrath.
9:22 No one can call God to account for what he does. But he does not exercise his freedom of choice arbitrarily, and he shows great patience even toward the objects of his wrath. In light of 2:4 (see note there), the purpose of such patience is to bring about repentance.
9:23 *glory.* See note on 3:23.
9:25–26 In the original context these passages from Hosea refer to the spiritual restoration of Israel. And Paul finds in them the principle that God is a saving, forgiving, restoring God, who delights to take those who are "not my people" and make them "my people." Paul then applies this principle to Gentiles, whom God makes his people by sovereignly grafting them into covenant relationship with him (see ch. 11).
9:27–29 Isa 10:22–23 and 1:9 (see NIV text notes here) indicate that only a small remnant will survive from the great multitude of Israelites. God's calling includes both Jews and Gentiles (see v. 24), but the vast majority are Gentiles, as v. 30 suggests.
9:30—10:21 The cause of the rejection of Israel.
9:30–32 A new step in Paul's argument: The reason for Israel's present (partial) rejection lay in the nature of her response to God's way with her and his word to her. She failed to live by faith in God and his gracious covenant promises and attempted to obtain God's favor by a meticulous observance of the law code he had given her.
9:31 *law of righteousness.* The law that prescribed the way to righteousness. Paul does not reject obedience to the law but righteousness by works, the attempt to use the law to put God in one's debt.
9:32 *not by faith.* The failure of Israel was not that she pursued the wrong thing (i.e., righteous standing before God), but that she pursued it by works in a futile effort to merit God's favor rather than pursuing it by faith. *"stumbling stone."* Jesus, the Messiah. God's rejection of Israel was not arbitrary but was based on Israel's rejection of God's way of gaining righteousness (faith).

stumbled over the "stumbling stone."[t]
33As it is written:

> "See, I lay in Zion a stone that causes
> men to stumble
> and a rock that makes them fall,
> and the one who trusts in him will
> never be put to shame."[a][u]

10 Brothers, my heart's desire[v] and
prayer to God for the Israelites is
that they may be saved. 2For I can testify
about them that they are zealous[w] for God,
but their zeal is not based on knowledge.
3Since they did not know the righteousness that comes from God and sought to
establish their own, they did not submit
to God's righteousness.[x] 4Christ is the end
of the law[y] so that there may be righteousness for everyone who believes.[z]

5Moses describes in this way the righteousness that is by the law: "The man
who does these things will live by them."[b][a]
6But the righteousness that is by faith[b]
says: "Do not say in your heart, 'Who will
ascend into heaven?'[c]"[c] (that is, to bring
Christ down) 7"or 'Who will descend into
the deep?'[d]"[d] (that is, to bring Christ up
from the dead).[e] 8But what does it say?
"The word is near you; it is in your mouth
and in your heart,"[e][f] that is, the word of
faith we are proclaiming: 9That if you confess[g] with your mouth, "Jesus is Lord,"[h]
and believe[i] in your heart that God raised
him from the dead,[j] you will be saved.[k]
10For it is with your heart that you believe
and are justified, and it is with your mouth
that you confess and are saved. 11As the
Scripture says, "Anyone who trusts in him
will never be put to shame."[f][l] 12For there
is no difference between Jew and Gentile[m]—the same Lord is Lord of all[n] and
richly blesses all who call on him, 13for,
"Everyone who calls on the name of the
Lord[o] will be saved."[g][p]

14How, then, can they call on the one
they have not believed in? And how can
they believe in the one of whom they have
not heard? And how can they hear without

9:32 [t]1Pe 2:8
9:33 [u]Isa 8:14; 28:16; Ro 10:11; 1Pe 2:6,8
10:1 [v]Ps 20:4
10:2 [w]S Ac 21:20
10:3 [x]Ro 1:17; S 9:31
10:4 [y]Gal 3:24; Ro 7:1-4 [z]S Ro 3:22
10:5 [a]Lev 18:5; Dt 4:1; 6:24; Ne 9:29; Pr 19:16; Isa 55:3; Eze 20:11,13,21; S Ro 7:10
10:6 [b]S Ro 9:30 [c]Dt 30:12
10:7 [d]Dt 30:13 [e]S Ac 2:24
10:8 [f]Dt 30:14
10:9 [g]Mt 10:32 [h]S Jn 13:13 [i]S Jn 3:15 [j]S Ac 2:24 [k]S Ro 11:14
10:11 [l]Isa 28:16; Ro 9:33
10:12 [m]S Ro 3:22,29 [n]S Mt 28:18
10:13 [o]S Ac 2:21 [p]Joel 2:32

[a] *33* Isaiah 8:14; 28:16 [b] *5* Lev. 18:5 [c] *6* Deut. 30:12 [d] *7* Deut. 30:13 [e] *8* Deut. 30:14 [f] *11* Isaiah 28:16 [g] *13* Joel 2:32

9:33 Isa 8:14 and 28:16 (see NIV text note), which are here combined, apparently were commonly used by early Christians in defense of Jesus' Messiahship (see 1Pe 2:4,6–8; see also Ps 118:22 and note; Lk 20:17–18).

10:1 *prayer to God for the Israelites.* Paul often prayed for the churches (see Eph 1:15–23; 3:14–21; Php 1:9–11; Col 1:3–14; 1Th 1:2–3; 2Th 1:3,11–12). Here he prays for the salvation of his fellow "Israelites."

10:2 *zealous for God.* The Jews' zeal for God (see Ac 21:20; 22:3; Gal 1:14) was commendable in that God was its object, but it was flawed because it was not based on right knowledge about God's way of salvation. Paul, before his conversion, was an example of such zeal (see Gal 1:14 and note).

10:3 *righteousness that comes from God.* Righteous standing based on faith (see 1:17 and note), which comes from God as a gift and cannot be earned by human works. *their own.* Righteous standing based on their own efforts.

10:4 *Christ is the end of the law.* Although the Greek for "end" (*telos*) can mean either (1) "termination," "cessation," or (2) "goal," "culmination," "fulfillment," it seems best here to understand it in the latter sense. Christ is the fulfillment of the law (see Mt 5:17 and note) in the sense that he brought it to completion by obeying perfectly its demands and by fulfilling its types and prophecies. Christians are no longer "under law" (6:14; see note there), since Christ has freed them from its condemnation, but the law still plays a role in their lives. They are liberated by the Holy Spirit to fulfill its moral demands (see 8:4 and note). *righteousness.* The righteous standing before God that Christ makes available to everyone who believes (see notes on 1:17; 3:24).

10:5 *The man who does these things will live by them.* Paul quotes Lev 18:5 (see note there; see also Dt 6:25 and note), which speaks of the righteousness to which Israel was called under the Sinai covenant.

10:6–7 The scripture here quoted by Paul (Dt 30:12–14) was frequently quoted (sometimes rather loosely) in Jewish circles for various purposes. Paul uses it to sharpen the contrast between "the righteousness that is by the law" (v. 5) and "the righteousness that is by faith." He takes a word that originally referred to the Mosaic law that was given as the way to life and applies it to the gospel of Christ as the way to life. In the case of Christ, just as in the case of the law, the way to life is accessible without any superhuman effort on the part of people. They do not have to bring the transcended Christ down from heaven, and they do not have to raise a dead Christ from the dead; he is accessible through the gospel proclaimed by the apostle.

10:8 *The word is near you.* In the OT passage (Dt 30:14; see note on 30:12,14) the "word" is God's word as found in the law. Paul takes the passage and applies it to the gospel, "the word of faith"—the main point being the accessibility of the gospel. Righteousness is gained by faith, not by deeds, and is readily available to anyone who will receive it freely from God through Christ.

10:9 *Jesus is Lord.* This affirmation, the earliest Christian confession of faith (see also 1Co 12:3 and note), served as the Christian equivalent to the Jewish *Shema* (see Dt 6:4–9; Mk 12:29; Jas 2:19 and notes). It was probably used at baptisms. In view of the fact that "Lord" is used over 6,000 times in the Septuagint (the pre-Christian Greek translation of the OT) to translate the name of Israel's God (Yahweh), it is clear that Paul, when using this title for Jesus, is affirming that in Jesus the God of Israel was himself present among his people. *in your heart.* In Biblical terms the heart is not merely the seat of the emotions and affections, but also of the intellect and will (see Ps 4:7 and note). *God raised him from the dead.* A bedrock truth of Christian doctrine (see 1Co 15:4,14,17) and the central thrust of apostolic preaching (see, e.g., note on Ac 2:14–40; see also Ac 3:15 and note; 4:10; 10:40). Christians believe not only that Jesus lived but also that he still lives. *will be saved.* This may include final salvation—salvation at the last day (see Heb 9:28 and note).

10:10 Salvation involves inward belief ("with your heart") as well as outward confession ("with your mouth").

10:12 *no difference between Jew and Gentile.* In the sense that both are on the same footing as far as salvation is concerned (see v. 13; 3:22).

10:13 Peter cited this same passage (Joel 2:32) on the day of Pentecost (see Ac 2:21 and note).

10:14–15 Since it might be argued that Jews had never had a fair opportunity to hear and respond to the gospel, Paul, by

someone preaching to them? 15And how
can they preach unless they are sent? As it
is written, "How beautiful are the feet of
those who bring good news!"[a][q]
16But not all the Israelites accepted the
good news.[r] For Isaiah says, "Lord, who
has believed our message?"[b][s] 17Conse-
quently, faith comes from hearing the message,[t] and the message is heard through
the word of Christ.[u] 18But I ask: Did they
not hear? Of course they did:

"Their voice has gone out into all the
earth,
their words to the ends of the
world."[c][v]

19Again I ask: Did Israel not understand?
First, Moses says,

"I will make you envious[w] by those
who are not a nation;
I will make you angry by a nation
that has no understanding."[d][x]

20And Isaiah boldly says,

"I was found by those who did not
seek me;
I revealed myself to those who did
not ask for me."[e][y]

21But concerning Israel he says,

"All day long I have held out my
hands
to a disobedient and obstinate
people."[f][z]

The Remnant of Israel

11 I ask then: Did God reject his people? By no means![a] I am an Israelite
myself, a descendant of Abraham,[b] from
the tribe of Benjamin.[c] 2God did not reject
his people,[d] whom he foreknew.[e] Don't
you know what the Scripture says in the
passage about Elijah—how he appealed
to God against Israel: 3"Lord, they have
killed your prophets and torn down your
altars; I am the only one left, and they are
trying to kill me"[g]?[f] 4And what was God's
answer to him? "I have reserved for myself seven thousand who have not bowed
the knee to Baal."[h][g] 5So too, at the present
time there is a remnant[h] chosen by grace.[i]
6And if by grace, then it is no longer by
works;[j] if it were, grace would no longer
be grace.[i]
7What then? What Israel sought so earnestly it did not obtain,[k] but the elect did.
The others were hardened,[l] 8as it is written:

"God gave them a spirit of stupor,
eyes so that they could not see
and ears so that they could not
hear,[m]
to this very day."[j][n]

9And David says:

"May their table become a snare and a
trap,
a stumbling block and a retribution
for them.
10May their eyes be darkened so they
cannot see,[o]
and their backs be bent forever."[k][p]

10:15 [q]Isa 52:7; Na 1:15 **10:16** [r]Heb 4:2 [s]Isa 53:1; Jn 12:38 **10:17** [t]Gal 3:2,5 [u]Col 3:16 **10:18** [v]Ps 19:4; S Mt 24:14; Ro 1:8; Col 1:6,23; 1Th 1:8 **10:19** [w]Ro 11:11,14 [x]Dt 32:21 **10:20** [y]Isa 65:1; Ro 9:30 **10:21** [z]Isa 65:2; Jer 35:17 **11:1** [a]Lev 26:44; 1Sa 12:22; Ps 94:14; Jer 31:37; 33:24-26 [b]2Co 11:22 [c]Php 3:5 **11:2** [d]S ver 1 [e]S Ro 8:29 **11:3** [f]1Ki 19:10,14 **11:4** [g]1Ki 19:18 **11:5** [h]S Ro 9:27 [i]S Ro 3:24 **11:6** [j]Ro 4:4 **11:7** [k]Ro 9:31 [l]ver 25; S Ro 9:18 **11:8** [m]S Mt 13:13-15 [n]Dt 29:4; Isa 29:10 **11:10** [o]ver 8 [p]Ps 69:22,23

[a] *15* Isaiah 52:7 [b] *16* Isaiah 53:1 [c] *18* Psalm 19:4 [d] *19* Deut. 32:21 [e] *20* Isaiah 65:1 [f] *21* Isaiah 65:2 [g] *3* 1 Kings 19:10,14 [h] *4* 1 Kings 19:18 [i] *6* Some manuscripts *be grace. But if by works, then it is no longer grace; if it were, work would no longer be work.* [j] *8* Deut. 29:4; Isaiah 29:10 [k] *10* Psalm 69:22,23

means of a series of rhetorical questions, states (in reverse order) the conditions necessary to call on Christ and be saved: (1) a preacher sent from God, (2) proclamation of the message, (3) hearing the message, (4) believing the message.

10:15 *How beautiful are the feet of those who bring good news!* The quotation is from Isa 52:7 (see note there), which refers to those who bring the exiles the good news of their imminent release from captivity in Babylonia. Here it is applied to gospel preachers, who bring the good news of release from captivity to sin.

10:17 *word of Christ.* Either (1) the gospel concerning Christ, or (2) Christ speaking his message through his messengers—probably the former.

10:18 *Their voice … world.* The quotation is from Ps 19:4 (see note there), which refers to the testimony of the heavens to the glory of God. Here "their voice" is applied to gospel preachers and is used to show that Israel cannot offer the excuse that she did not have opportunity to hear, since preachers went everywhere. These words (originally used to describe God's revelation in nature) aptly describe the widespread preaching of the gospel.

10:19 *Did Israel not understand?* The quotation that follows (from Dt 32:21; see note there) answers this question by suggesting that the Gentiles, whom the Jews considered to be spiritually unenlightened, understood. Surely if they understood the message, the Jews could have. *those who are not a nation.* The Gentiles, those who are not a nation of God's forming in the sense that Israel was.

10:21 The responsibility for Israel's rejection as a nation rested with Israel herself. She had failed to meet God's requirement, namely, faith. Yet, as Isa 65:2 stated, God continued to reach out in love to the people of Israel in spite of their disobedience.

11:1 *reject.* Totally reject. There has always been a faithful remnant among the Jewish people.

11:2 *whom he foreknew.* See note on 8:29.

11:5 *remnant.* As it was in Elijah's day, so it was in Paul's day. Despite widespread unbelief, a believing remnant of Jews remained. *chosen by grace.* The grounds for the existence of the remnant was not their good works but God's grace.

11:7 *What Israel sought so earnestly.* A righteous standing before God, which eluded the greater part of Israel. *the elect.* The faithful remnant among the Jews. *others were hardened.* Because they refused the way of faith (see 9:30–32 and notes), God made them impervious to spiritual truth (see notes on v. 25; Isa 6:8–10; Mk 4:12; Lk 8:10)—a judicial hardening of Israel.

11:8 *to this very day.* The spiritual dullness of the Jews had continued from Isaiah's day to Paul's day.

11:9–10 The passage from Ps 69:22–23 (see notes there) was probably originally spoken by David concerning his enemies; Paul uses it to describe the effects of the divine hardening.

Ingrafted Branches

11 Again I ask: Did they stumble so as to fall beyond recovery? Not at all![q] Rather, because of their transgression, salvation has come to the Gentiles[r] to make Israel envious.[s] 12 But if their transgression means riches for the world, and their loss means riches for the Gentiles,[t] how much greater riches will their fullness bring!

13 I am talking to you Gentiles. Inasmuch as I am the apostle to the Gentiles,[u] I make much of my ministry 14 in the hope that I may somehow arouse my own people to envy[v] and save[w] some of them. 15 For if their rejection is the reconciliation[x] of the world, what will their acceptance be but life from the dead?[y] 16 If the part of the dough offered as firstfruits[z] is holy, then the whole batch is holy; if the root is holy, so are the branches.

17 If some of the branches have been broken off,[a] and you, though a wild olive shoot, have been grafted in among the others[b] and now share in the nourishing sap from the olive root, 18 do not boast over those branches. If you do, consider this: You do not support the root, but the root supports you.[c] 19 You will say then, "Branches were broken off so that I could be grafted in." 20 Granted. But they were broken off because of unbelief, and you stand by faith.[d] Do not be arrogant,[e] but be afraid.[f] 21 For if God did not spare the natural branches, he will not spare you either.

22 Consider therefore the kindness[g] and sternness of God: sternness to those who fell, but kindness to you, provided that you continue[h] in his kindness. Otherwise, you also will be cut off.[i] 23 And if they do not persist in unbelief, they will be grafted in, for God is able to graft them in again.[j] 24 After all, if you were cut out of an olive tree that is wild by nature, and contrary to nature were grafted into a cultivated olive tree,[k] how much more readily will these, the natural branches, be grafted into their own olive tree!

All Israel Will Be Saved

25 I do not want you to be ignorant[l] of this mystery,[m] brothers, so that you may not be conceited:[n] Israel has experienced

11:11 [q] ver 1 [r] S Ac 13:46 [s] ver 14; Ro 10:19 **11:12** [t] ver 25 **11:13** [u] S Ac 9:15 **11:14** [v] ver 11; Ro 10:19; 1Co 10:33; 1Th 2:16 [w] S Mt 1:21; S Lk 2:11; S Jn 3:17; Ac 4:12; 16:31; 1Co 1:21; 1Ti 2:4; Tit 3:5 **11:15** [x] S Ro 5:10 [y] Lk 15:24,32 **11:16** [z] Lev 23:10,17; Nu 15:18-21 **11:17** [a] Jer 11:16; Jn 15:2 [b] Ac 2:39; Eph 2:11-13 **11:18** [c] Jn 4:22 **11:20** [d] 1Co 10:12; 2Co 1:24 [e] 1Ti 6:17 [f] 1Pe 1:17 **11:22** [g] Ro 2:4 [h] 1Co 15:2; Col 1:23; Heb 3:6 [i] Jn 15:2 **11:23** [j] 2Co 3:16 **11:24** [k] Jer 11:16 **11:25** [l] Ro 1:13; 1Co 10:1; 12:1; 2Co 1:8; 1Th 4:13 [m] S Ro 16:25 [n] Ro 12:16

11:11 *their transgression.* The Jews' rejection of the gospel. *make Israel envious.* See v. 14; 10:19 and note; see also notes on 1Ki 17:16; 2Ki 5:14.

11:12 *riches for the world.* Equivalent to "riches for the Gentiles," a reference to the abundant benefits of salvation already enjoyed by believing Gentiles, which had come about because of the rejection of the gospel by the Jews. That rejection caused the apostles to turn to the Gentiles (see Ac 13:46–48; 18:6). *their loss.* Equivalent to "their transgression" (see note on v. 11), but focusing on the loss that this transgression entailed. *greater riches.* See note on v. 15. *their fullness.* The salvation of Israel (see vv. 26–27 and notes; see also the "full number of the Gentiles," v. 25).

11:13 *apostle to the Gentiles.* See 1:5; 15:9,12,16 and notes; Ac 9:15; Gal 1:16; 2:7,9 and note on 2:7; see also Eph 2:11–22; 3:3,6,10 and notes.

11:15 *their rejection.* God's temporary and partial exclusion of the Jews (see v. 25 and note). *reconciliation of the world.* Somewhat equivalent to "riches for the world" (see note on v. 12). *life from the dead.* Equivalent to "greater riches" in v. 12. The sequence of redemptive events is: The "transgression" and "loss" (v. 12) of Israel leads to the salvation of the Gentiles, which leads to the jealousy or envy of Israel, which leads to the "fullness" (v. 12) of Israel when the hardening is removed, which leads to even more riches for the Gentiles. But what are the "greater riches" (v. 12) for the Gentiles, which Paul describes here as "life from the dead"? Three views may be suggested: (1) an unprecedented spiritual awakening in the world; (2) the consummation of redemption at the resurrection of the dead; (3) a figurative expression describing the conversion of the Jews as a joyful and glorious event (like resurrection)—which will result in even greater blessing for the world. Of these three views the first seems least likely, since, before Israel's spiritual rebirth, the fullness of the Gentiles will already have come in (see v. 25). Since the Gentile mission will then be complete, there seems to be no place for a period of unprecedented spiritual awakening. The second view also seems unlikely, since the context suggests nothing of bodily resurrection.

11:16 The first half of this verse is a reference to Nu 15:17–21. Part of the dough made from the first of the harvested grain (firstfruits) was offered to the Lord. This consecrated the whole batch. *firstfruits.* The patriarchs (cf. Ex 23:19 and note). *whole batch.* The Jewish people. *holy.* Not that all Jews are righteous (i.e., saved) but that God will be true to his promises concerning them (see 3:3–4 and notes). Paul foresaw a future for Israel, even though she was for a time set aside. *root.* The patriarchs. *branches.* The Jewish people.

11:17 *branches.* Individual Jews. *wild olive shoot.* Gentile Christians. *grafted in.* The usual procedure was to insert a shoot or slip of a cultivated tree into a common or wild one. In vv. 17–24, however, the metaphor is used, "contrary to nature" (v. 24), of grafting a wild olive branch (the Gentiles) into the cultivated olive tree. Such a procedure is unnatural, which is precisely the point. Normally, such a graft would be unfruitful. *olive root.* The patriarchs. The whole olive tree represents the people of God.

11:18 *the root supports you.* The salvation of Gentile Christians is dependent on the Jews, especially the patriarchs (e.g., the Abrahamic covenant). See Jn 4:22 and note.

11:19 *Branches.* Unbelieving Jews.

11:20 *be afraid.* On the fear of God see note on Ge 20:11; see also Pr 1:7 and note; 3:7; Php 2:12–13; Heb 4:1, "be careful"; 1Pe 1:17.

11:22 *kindness and sternness of God.* Any adequate doctrine of God must include these two elements. When we ignore his kindness, God seems a ruthless tyrant; when we ignore his sternness, he seems a doting Father.

11:23 *God is able to graft them in again.* Paul holds out hope for the Jews—God is able (see Mk 10:27 and note).

11:24 *contrary to nature.* Paul recognized that such grafting was not commonly practiced (see note on v. 17). The inclusion of Gentiles in the family of God is "contrary to nature" (see Eph 2:12 and note). Obviously, the reasoning in this verse is more theological than horticultural. It would be difficult horticulturally to graft broken branches back into the parent tree, but the Jews really belong (historically and theologically) to the parent tree. Thus they will "much more readily ... be grafted into their own olive tree."

11:25 *mystery.* The so-called mystery religions of Paul's day used the Greek word (*mysterion*) in the sense of

a hardening[o] in part until the full number
of the Gentiles has come in.[p] 26And so all
Israel will be saved,[q] as it is written:

"The deliverer will come from Zion;
he will turn godlessness away from
Jacob.
27And this is[a] my covenant with them
when I take away their sins."[b r]

28As far as the gospel is concerned, they
are enemies[s] on your account; but as far
as election is concerned, they are loved on
account of the patriarchs,[t] 29for God's gifts
and his call[u] are irrevocable.[v] 30Just as you
who were at one time disobedient[w] to God
have now received mercy as a result of
their disobedience, 31so they too have now
become disobedient in order that they too
may now[c] receive mercy as a result of
God's mercy to you. 32For God has bound
all men over to disobedience[x] so that he
may have mercy on them all.

Doxology

33Oh, the depth of the riches[y] of the
wisdom and[d] knowledge of
God![z]
How unsearchable his judgments,
and his paths beyond tracing out![a]
34"Who has known the mind of the
Lord?
Or who has been his counselor?"[e b]
35"Who has ever given to God,
that God should repay him?"[f c]
36For from him and through him and to
him are all things.[d]
To him be the glory forever! Amen.[e]

Living Sacrifices

12 Therefore, I urge you,[f] brothers, in
view of God's mercy, to offer your
bodies as living sacrifices,[g] holy and pleasing to God—this is your spiritual[g] act of
worship. 2Do not conform[h] any longer to
the pattern of this world,[i] but be transformed by the renewing of your mind.[j]
Then you will be able to test and approve

11:25 [o]ver 7; S Ro 9:18 [p]Lk 21:24 **11:26** [q]Isa 45:17; Jer 31:34 **11:27** [r]Isa 59:20, 21; 27:9; Heb 8:10, 12 **11:28** [s]Ro 5:10 [t]Dt 7:8; 10:15; Ro 9:5 **11:29** [u]S Ro 8:28 [v]S Heb 7:21 **11:30** [w]S Eph 2:2 **11:32** [x]S Ro 3:9 **11:33** [y]S Ro 2:4 [z]Ps 92:5; Eph 3:10; Col 2:3

[a]Job 5:9; 11:7; Ps 139:6; Ecc 8:17; Isa 40:28 **11:34** [b]Isa 40:13, 14; Job 15:8; 36:22; Jer 23:18; 1Co 2:16 **11:35** [c]Job 41:11; 35:7 **11:36** [d]1Co 8:6; 11:12; Col 1:16; Heb 2:10

[a] *27* Or *will be* [b] *27* Isaiah 59:20,21; 27:9; Jer. 31:33,34 [c] *31* Some manuscripts do not have *now.* [d] *33* Or *riches and the wisdom and the* [e] *34* Isaiah 40:13 [f] *35* Job 41:11 [g] *1* Or *reasonable*

[e]Ro 16:27; Eph 3:21; 1Ti 1:17; 1Pe 5:11; Jude 25; Rev 5:13; 7:12
12:1 [f]Eph 4:1; 1Pe 2:11 [g]Ro 6:13, 16, 19; 1Co 6:20; 1Pe 2:5
12:2 [h]1Pe 1:14 [i]1Co 1:20; 2Co 10:2; 1Jn 2:15 [j]Eph 4:23

something that was to be revealed only to the initiated. Paul himself, however, used it to refer to something formerly hidden or obscure but now revealed by God for all to know and understand (see 16:25; 1Co 2:7 and note; 4:1; 13:2; 14:2; 15:51 and note; Eph 1:9; 3:3 and note,9; 5:32 and note; 6:19; Col 1:26–27 and notes; 2:2; 4:3; 2Th 2:7 and note; 1Ti 3:9,16). The word is used of (1) the incarnation (1Ti 3:16; see note there), (2) the death of Christ (1Co 2:1, NIV text note; 2:7, "secret wisdom"), (3) God's purpose to sum up all things in Christ (Eph 1:9–10) and especially to include both Jews and Gentiles in the NT church (Eph 3:3–6), (4) the change that will take place at the resurrection (1Co 15:51), and (5) the plan of God by which both Jew and Gentile, after a period of disobedience by both, will by his mercy be included in his kingdom (here). *so that you may not be conceited.* God's merciful plan to include the Gentiles in his great salvation plan should humble them, not fill them with arrogance. *in part.* Israel's hardening is partial, not total. *until.* Israel's hardening is temporary, not permanent. *full number of the Gentiles.* The total number of the elect Gentiles.

11:26 *And so.* An emphatic statement that this is the way all Israel will be saved. *all Israel.* Three main interpretations of this phrase are: (1) the total number of elect Jews of every generation (equivalent to the "fullness" of Israel [v. 12; see note there], which is analogous to the "full number of the Gentiles" [v. 25; see note there]); (2) the total number of the elect, both Jews and Gentiles, of every generation; (3) the great majority of Jews of the final generation. *will be saved.* The salvation of the Jews will, of course, be on the same basis as anyone's salvation: personal faith in Jesus Christ, crucified and risen from the dead. *The deliverer will come from Zion.* The quotation is from Isa 59:20, where the deliverer ("Redeemer") seems to refer to God. The Talmud (a Jewish collection of religious instruction) understood the text to be a reference to the Messiah, and Paul appears to use it in this way. *Zion.* See notes on Gal 4:26; Heb 12:22.

11:27 *covenant.* The new covenant of Jer 31:31–34 (see notes there). *when I take away their sins.* See Jer 31:34; Zec 13:1 and note. Just as salvation for Gentiles involves forgiveness of sins, so the Jews, when they are saved, are forgiven by the mercy of God—his forgiveness based only on their repentance and faith (see v. 23; Zec 12:10—13:1 and notes).

11:28 *they are enemies.* Only temporarily. *on your account.* Explained in v. 11. *loved on account of the patriarchs.* Not because any merit was passed on from the patriarchs to the Jewish people as a whole, but because God in love chose Israel and that choice was irrevocable.

11:29 *God's gifts and his call are irrevocable.* God does not change his mind with reference to his call. Even though Israel is presently in a state of unbelief, God's purpose will be fulfilled in her.

11:32 *all men.* Both groups under discussion (Jews and Gentiles). There has been a period of disobedience for each in order that God may have mercy on them all. Paul is in no way teaching universal salvation.

11:33–36 The doxology that ends this section of Romans is the natural outpouring of Paul's praise to God, whose wisdom and knowledge brought about his great plan for the salvation of both Jews and Gentiles.

12:1—16:27 Paul now turns to the practical application of all he has said previously in the letter. This does not mean that he has not said anything about Christian living up to this point. Chs. 6–8 have touched on this already, but now Paul goes into detail to show that Jesus Christ is to be Lord of every area of life. These chapters are not a postscript to the great theological discussions in chs. 1–11. In a real sense the entire letter has been directed toward the goal of showing that God demands our action as well as our believing and thinking. Faith expresses itself in obedience (see notes on Jas 2:14–26).

12:1 *Therefore, I urge you.* Paul draws an important inference from the truth set forth in chs. 1–11. *God's mercy.* Much of the letter has been concerned with demonstrating this. *your bodies.* See 6:13 and note. *living sacrifices.* In contrast to dead animal sacrifices, or perhaps "living" in the sense of having the new life of the Holy Spirit (see 6:4; 8:2 and note). *spiritual act.* Not merely ritual activity but the involvement of heart, mind, will and life—the whole of what creatures such as human beings are and do. *worship.* Obedient service—the "liturgy" of life.

12:2 *this world.* With all its evil and corruption (see Gal 1:4; 1Jn 2:15 and notes). *be transformed.* Here a process, not

what God's will is[k]—his good, pleasing[l]
and perfect will.
3For by the grace given me[m] I say to every one of you: Do not think of yourself
more highly than you ought, but rather
think of yourself with sober judgment,
in accordance with the measure of faith
God has given you. 4Just as each of us has
one body with many members, and these
members do not all have the same function,[n] 5so in Christ we who are many form
one body,[o] and each member belongs to
all the others. 6We have different gifts,[p] according to the grace given us. If a man's
gift is prophesying,[q] let him use it in proportion to his[a] faith.[r] 7If it is serving, let
him serve; if it is teaching, let him teach;[s]
8if it is encouraging, let him encourage;[t]
if it is contributing to the needs of others,
let him give generously;[u] if it is leadership,
let him govern diligently; if it is showing
mercy, let him do it cheerfully.

Love

9Love must be sincere.[v] Hate what is
evil; cling to what is good.[w] 10Be devoted
to one another in brotherly love.[x] Honor
one another above yourselves.[y] 11Never
be lacking in zeal, but keep your spiritual fervor,[z] serving the Lord. 12Be joyful
in hope,[a] patient in affliction,[b] faithful in
prayer.[c] 13Share with God's people who are
in need.[d] Practice hospitality.[e]
14Bless those who persecute you;[f] bless
and do not curse. 15Rejoice with those who
rejoice; mourn with those who mourn.[g]
16Live in harmony with one another.[h] Do
not be proud, but be willing to associate
with people of low position.[b] Do not be
conceited.[i]
17Do not repay anyone evil for evil.[j] Be
careful to do what is right in the eyes of everybody.[k] 18If it is possible, as far as it depends on you, live at peace with everyone.[l]

12:2 [k]S Eph 5:17 [l]S 1Ti 5:4 **12:3** [m]Ro 15:15; 1Co 15:10; Gal 2:9; Eph 3:7; 4:7; 1Pe 4:10,11 **12:4** [n]1Co 12:12-14; Eph 4:16 **12:5** [o]1Co 6:15; 10:17; 12:12,20,27; Eph 2:16; 4:4,25; 5:30; Col 3:15 **12:6** [p]1Co 7:7; 12:4,8-10 [q]S Eph 4:11 [r]1Pe 4:10,11 **12:7** [s]S Eph 4:11 **12:8** [t]Ac 11:23; 13:15; 15:32 [u]2Co 8:2; 9:5-13 **12:9** [v]2Co 6:6; 1Ti 1:5 [w]Ps 97:10; Am 5:15; 1Th 5:21,22 **12:10** [x]Ps 133:1; 1Th 4:9; Heb 13:1; 1Pe 1:22 [y]Php 2:3 **12:11** [z]Ac 18:25 **12:12** [a]Ro 5:2 [b]Heb 10:32,36 [c]S Lk 18:1

[a] 6 Or *in agreement with the* [b] 16 Or *willing to do menial work*

12:13 [d]S Ac 24:17 [e]2Ki 4:10; Job 31:32; 1Ti 3:2; 5:10; Heb 13:2; 1Pe 4:9 **12:14** [f]S Mt 5:44 **12:15** [g]Job 30:25 **12:16** [h]S Ro 15:5 [i]ver 3; Ps 131:1; Isa 5:21; Jer 45:5; Ro 11:25 **12:17** [j]ver 19; Pr 20:22; 24:29 [k]2Co 8:21 **12:18** [l]S Mk 9:50; S Ro 14:19

a single event. The same Greek word is used in the transfiguration narratives (Mt 17:2–8; Mk 9:2–8) and in 2Co 3:18 (see note there). *mind.* Thought and will as they relate to morality (see 1:28). *Then.* After the spiritual transformation just described has taken place. *God's will.* What God wants from the believer here and now. *good.* That which leads to the spiritual and moral growth of the Christian. *pleasing.* To God, not necessarily to us. *perfect.* No improvement can be made on the will of God.

12:3 *measure of faith.* The power given by God to each believer to fulfill various ministries in the church (see vv. 4–8 and notes). *God has given.* Since the power comes from God, there can be no basis for a superior attitude or self-righteousness.

12:4–8 Paul likens Christians to members of a human body. There are many members and each has a different function, but all are needed for the health and full enablement of the body. The emphasis is on unity within diversity (see 1Co 12:12–31 and notes).

12:5 *in Christ.* The key to Paul's concept of Christian unity. It is only in Jesus Christ that any unity in the church is possible. True unity is spiritually based. See note on 6:11.

12:6 *gifts.* Greek *charismata,* referring to special gifts of grace—freely given by God to his people to meet the needs of the body (see notes on 1Co 1:7; 12:4). *prophesying.* See notes on 1Co 12:10; 14:1–5. *let him use it.* There is to be no false modesty that denies the existence of gifts or refuses to use them. *in proportion to his faith.* Probably means about the same thing as "measure of faith" in v. 3 (see note there).

12:7 *serving.* Any kind of service needed by the body of Christ or by any of its members. *teaching.* See notes on 1Co 12:28; Eph 4:11.

12:8 *encouraging.* Exhorting others with an uplifting, cheerful call to worthwhile accomplishment. The teacher often carried out this function. In teaching, believers are shown what they must do; in encouraging, they are helped to do it. *contributing.* Giving what is one's own, or possibly distributing what has been given by others. *let him govern.* Possibly a reference to an elder. The Ephesian church had elders by about this time (see Ac 20:17; 1Ti 5:17 and notes). *showing mercy.* Caring for the sick, the poor and the aged. *cheerfully.* Serving the needy should be a delight, not a chore.

12:9 *Love.* Believers' love for fellow Christians and perhaps also for other people. *sincere.* True love, not pretense. In view of the preceding paragraph, with its emphasis on social concern, the love Paul speaks of here is not mere emotion but love in action, as delineated in the rest of the chapter (cf. Jas 2:1–4,14–17; 1Jn 3:16–18; 4:19–21). *evil … good.* See Am 5:15. "Evil" and "good" frame vv. 9–21.

12:10 *brotherly love.* Love within the family of God. *Honor one another above yourselves.* Only a mind renewed by the Holy Spirit (see v. 2) could possibly do this (see Php 2:3 and note).

12:11 *spiritual fervor.* Lit. "fervent in spirit." If "spirit" means "Holy Spirit" here, the reference would be to the fervor the Holy Spirit provides.

12:12 *Be joyful in hope.* The certainty of the Christian's hope is a cause for joy (see 5:5 and note; see also 8:16–25; 1Pe 1:3–9). *patient.* Enduring triumphantly—necessary for Christians, because affliction is their inevitable experience (see Jn 16:33; 2Ti 3:12 and notes). *faithful in prayer.* One must not only pray in hard times, but also maintain communion with God through prayer at all times (see Lk 18:1; 1Th 5:17 and note).

12:13 *Share with God's people.* The Christian has social responsibility to all people, but especially to other believers (see Gal 6:10; 1Ti 5:8).

12:14 *Bless those who persecute you.* Paul is echoing Jesus' teaching (see Mt 5:44 and note; Lk 6:28 and note on 6:27).

12:15 Identification with others in their joys and in their sorrows is a Christian's privilege and responsibility.

12:17 *Do not repay anyone evil for evil.* See Mt 5:39–42,44–45; 1Th 5:15; 1Pe 3:9 and notes. *Be careful to do what is right in the eyes of everybody.* A possible reflection of Pr 3:4 in the Septuagint (the pre-Christian Greek translation of the OT). Christian conduct should never betray the high moral standards of the gospel, or it will provoke the disdain of unbelievers and bring the gospel into disrepute (see 2Co 8:21 and note; 1Ti 3:7).

12:18 *If it is possible … live at peace.* Jesus pronounced a blessing on peacemakers (see Mt 5:9 and note), and believers are to cultivate peace with everyone to the extent that it depends on them (see Jas 3:18 and note).

19Do not take revenge,[m] my friends, but
leave room for God's wrath, for it is written: "It is mine to avenge; I will repay,"[a][n]
says the Lord. 20On the contrary:

"If your enemy is hungry, feed him;
if he is thirsty, give him something
to drink.
In doing this, you will heap burning
coals on his head."[b][o]

21Do not be overcome by evil, but overcome evil with good.

Submission to the Authorities

13 Everyone must submit himself to
the governing authorities,[p] for there
is no authority except that which God
has established.[q] The authorities that exist have been established by God. 2Con-
sequently, he who rebels against the
authority is rebelling against what God
has instituted,[r] and those who do so will
bring judgment on themselves. 3For rulers
hold no terror for those who do right, but
for those who do wrong. Do you want to
be free from fear of the one in authority?
Then do what is right and he will commend you.[s] 4For he is God's servant to
do you good. But if you do wrong, be
afraid, for he does not bear the sword for
nothing. He is God's servant, an agent of
wrath to bring punishment on the wrongdoer.[t] 5Therefore, it is necessary to submit to the authorities, not only because
of possible punishment but also because
of conscience.[u]
6This is also why you pay taxes,[v] for the
authorities are God's servants, who give
their full time to governing. 7Give everyone what you owe him: If you owe taxes,
pay taxes;[w] if revenue, then revenue; if respect, then respect; if honor, then honor.

Love, for the Day Is Near

8Let no debt remain outstanding, except
the continuing debt to love one another,
for he who loves his fellowman has fulfilled the law.[x] 9The commandments, "Do
not commit adultery," "Do not murder,"
"Do not steal," "Do not covet,"[c][y] and
whatever other commandment there may
be, are summed up[z] in this one rule: "Love
your neighbor as yourself."[d][a] 10Love does
no harm to its neighbor. Therefore love is
the fulfillment of the law.[b]
11And do this, understanding the present time. The hour has come[c] for you to
wake up from your slumber,[d] because our
salvation is nearer now than when we first
believed. 12The night is nearly over; the
day is almost here.[e] So let us put aside the
deeds of darkness[f] and put on the armor[g]

12:19 [m]ver 17; Lev 19:18; Pr 20:22; 24:29 [n]Dt 32:35; Ge 50:19; 1Sa 26:10; Ps 94:1; Jer 51:36 **12:20** [o]Pr 25:21,22; Ex 23:4; Mt 5:44; Lk 6:27 **13:1** [p]Tit 3:1; 1Pe 2:13,14 [q]Da 2:21; 4:17; Jn 19:11 **13:2** [r]Ex 16:8 **13:3** [s]1Pe 2:14 **13:4** [t]1Th 4:6 **13:5** [u]Pr 24:21,22 **13:6** [v]Mt 22:17 **13:7** [w]Mt 17:25; 22:17,21; Lk 23:2 **13:8** [x]ver 10; S Mt 5:43; Jn 13:34; Col 3:14 **13:9** [y]Ex 20:13-15,17; Dt 5:17-19,21 [z]Mt 7:12 [a]Lev 19:18; S Mt 5:43 **13:10** [b]S ver 8; ver 9 **13:11** [c]1Co 7:29-31; 10:11; Jas 5:8; 1Pe 4:7; 1Jn 2:18; Rev 22:10 [d]Eph 5:14; 1Th 5:5,6 **13:12** [e]Heb 10:25; 1Jn 2:8 [f]Eph 5:11 [g]Eph 6:11,13; 1Th 5:8

[a] *19* Deut. 32:35 [b] *20* Prov. 25:21,22
[c] *9* Exodus 20:13-15,17; Deut. 5:17-19,21
[d] *9* Lev. 19:18

12:19 See note on Dt 32:35.

12:20 *heap burning coals on his head.* Doing good to one's enemy (v. 21), instead of trying to take revenge, may bring about his repentance (see note on Pr 25:22).

12:21 *evil ... good.* See note on v. 9.

13:1 *submit.* A significant word in vv. 1–7. *governing authorities.* The civil rulers, all of whom were probably pagans at the time Paul was writing. Christians may have been tempted not to submit to them and to claim allegiance only to Christ. *established by God.* Even the possibility of a persecuting state did not shake Paul's conviction that civil government is ordained by God (see 1Pe 2:13–17 and notes).

13:2 *judgment.* Either divine judgment or, more likely, punishment by the governing authorities, since v. 3 ("For") explains this verse; see also v. 4.

13:3 *do what is right and he will commend you.* Paul is not stating that this will always be true but is describing the proper, ideal function of rulers. When civil rulers overstep their proper function, the Christian is to obey God rather than human authorities (see Ac 4:19; 5:29).

13:4 *he is God's servant.* In the order of divine providence the ruler is God's servant (see Isa 45:1 and note). *good.* Rulers exist for the benefit of society—to protect the general public by maintaining good order. *sword.* The symbol of Roman authority on both the national and the international levels. Here we find the Biblical principle of using force for the maintenance of good order.

13:5 *because of conscience.* Civil authorities are ordained by God, and in order to maintain a good conscience Christians must duly honor them.

13:6 *you pay taxes.* Because rulers are God's agents, who function for the benefit of society in general.

13:8 *continuing debt.* To love is the one debt that is never paid off. No matter how much people have loved, they are under obligation to keep on loving. *one another.* Includes not only fellow Christians but all people, as the second half of the verse makes clear ("fellowman"). *who loves ... has fulfilled the law.* Provides a frame with "love is the fulfillment of the law" (v. 10). *the law.* The Mosaic law, which lays down both moral and social responsibilities.

13:9 Further explains the last statement of v. 8, namely, that love of neighbor encompasses all our social responsibilities. *your neighbor.* Jesus taught that our neighbor is anyone in need (see Lk 10:25–36 and notes), which is probably the idea Paul has in mind here. *as yourself.* Not a command to love ourselves but a recognition of the fact that we naturally do so (cf. Eph 5:33).

13:10 *love is the fulfillment of the law.* See v. 8 and note. This is true because love "does no harm to its neighbor." Cf. Mt 22:34–40; Jn 14:15 and note; Col 3:14; Jas 2:8 and note; 1Jn 4:8,16; 5:3.

13:11–14 In this section, as in other NT passages, the certain coming of the end of the present age is used to provide motivation for godly living (see, e.g., Mt 25:31–46; Mk 13:33–37; Lk 21:36; Php 4:5; 1Th 5:6,8; Tit 2:11–14; Jas 5:7–11; 2Pe 3:11–14; 1Jn 2:28; 3:2–3).

13:11 *present time.* The time of salvation, the closing period of the present age, before the consummation of the kingdom. *The hour.* The time for action. *our salvation.* The full realization of salvation at the second coming of Jesus Christ (see 8:23; Heb 9:28; 1Pe 1:5 and notes). *is nearer now.* Every day brings us closer to the second advent of Christ.

13:12 *The night.* The present evil age. *is nearly over; the day is almost here.* A clear example of the NT teaching of

of light. 13Let us behave decently, as in the
daytime, not in orgies and drunkenness,[h]
not in sexual immorality and debauchery,
not in dissension and jealousy.[i] 14Rath-
er, clothe yourselves with the Lord Jesus
Christ,[j] and do not think about how to
gratify the desires of the sinful nature.[a k]

The Weak and the Strong

14 Accept him whose faith is weak,[l]
without passing judgment on disputable matters. 2One man's faith allows him
to eat everything, but another man, whose
faith is weak, eats only vegetables.[m] 3The
man who eats everything must not look
down on[n] him who does not, and the man
who does not eat everything must not condemn[o] the man who does, for God has accepted him. 4Who are you to judge someone else's servant?[p] To his own master he
stands or falls. And he will stand, for the
Lord is able to make him stand.

5One man considers one day more sacred than another;[q] another man considers
every day alike. Each one should be fully
convinced in his own mind. 6He who regards one day as special, does so to the
Lord. He who eats meat, eats to the Lord,
for he gives thanks to God;[r] and he who
abstains, does so to the Lord and gives
thanks to God. 7For none of us lives to himself alone[s] and none of us dies to himself
alone. 8If we live, we live to the Lord; and
if we die, we die to the Lord. So, whether
we live or die, we belong to the Lord.[t]

9For this very reason, Christ died and returned to life[u] so that he might be the Lord
of both the dead and the living.[v] 10You,
then, why do you judge your brother? Or
why do you look down on[w] your brother?
For we will all stand before God's judgment seat.[x] 11It is written:

"'As surely as I live,'[y] says the Lord,
'every knee will bow before me;
every tongue will confess to God.'"[b z]

12So then, each of us will give an account
of himself to God.[a]

13Therefore let us stop passing judgment[b] on one another. Instead, make up
your mind not to put any stumbling block
or obstacle in your brother's way.[c] 14As one
who is in the Lord Jesus, I am fully convinced that no food[c] is unclean in itself.[d]

13:13 [h]S Eph 5:18 [i]Lk 21:34; Gal 5:20,21; Eph 5:18; 1Pe 4:3 **13:14** [j]Gal 3:27; Eph 4:24; Col 3:10,12 [k]S Gal 5:24 **14:1** [l]Ro 15:1; 1Co 8:9-12; 9:22 **14:2** [m]ver 14 **14:3** [n]ver 10; Lk 18:9 [o]ver 10,13; Col 2:16 **14:4** [p]S Mt 7:1 **14:5** [q]Gal 4:10; Col 2:16 **14:6** [r]S Mt 14:19; 1Co 10:30,31; 1Ti 4:3,4 **14:7** [s]2Co 5:15; Gal 2:20 **14:8** [t]Php 1:20 **14:9** [u]Rev 1:18; 2:8 [v]S Ac 10:42; 2Co 5:15 **14:10** [w]ver 3; S Mt 7:1 [x]S 2Co 5:10 **14:11** [y]Isa 49:18 [z]Isa 45:23; Php 2:10,11 **14:12** [a]Mt 12:36; 1Pe 4:5 **14:13** [b]ver 1; S Mt 7:1 [c]S 2Co 6:3 **14:14** [d]ver 20; S Ac 10:15

[a] *14 Or the flesh* [b] *11* Isaiah 45:23 [c] *14 Or that nothing*

the nearness of the end times (see 1Co 7:29–31; Php 4:5; Jas 5:9; 1Pe 4:7; 1Jn 2:18 and notes). These texts do not mean that the early Christians believed that Jesus would return within a few years (and thus were mistaken). Rather, they regarded the death and resurrection of Christ as the crucial events of history that began the last days (see Heb 1:1–2 and notes). Since the next great event in God's redemptive plan is the second coming of Jesus Christ, "the night," no matter how long chronologically it may last, is "nearly over." *the day.* The appearing of Jesus Christ, which ushers in the consummation of the kingdom.

13:13 See 1:29–31 and note.

13:14 *clothe yourselves with the Lord Jesus Christ.* See Gal 3:27. Paul exhorts believers to display outwardly what has already taken place inwardly (see Col 3:1–10 and notes)—including practicing all the virtues associated with Christ. *clothe … with.* See note on Ps 109:29.

14:1 *whose faith is weak.* Probably Jewish Christians at Rome who were unwilling to give up the observance of certain requirements of the law, such as dietary restrictions and the keeping of the Sabbath and other special days. Their concern was not quite the same as that of the Judaizers of Galatia. The Judaizers thought they could put God in their debt by works of righteousness and were trying to force this heretical teaching on the Galatian churches (see Introduction to Galatians: Occasion and Purpose), but the "weak" Roman Christians did neither. They were not yet clear as to the status of OT regulations under the new covenant inaugurated by the coming of Christ. *without passing judgment on disputable matters.* Fellowship among Christians is not to be based on everyone's agreement on disputable questions. Christians do not agree on all matters pertaining to the Christian life, nor do they need to.

14:2 *One man's faith.* In contrast, Paul now describes the strong Christian. Here faith is used in the sense of assurance or confidence. The strong Christians' understanding of the gospel allows them to recognize that one's dietary choices have no spiritual significance.

14:4 *someone else's.* God's. A Christian must not reject a fellow Christian, who is also a servant of God. *To his own master he stands or falls.* The weak Christian is not the master of the strong Christian, nor is the strong the master of the weak. God is Master, and to him alone are all believers responsible.

14:5 *one day more sacred than another.* Some feel that this refers primarily to the Sabbath, but it is probably a reference to all the special days of the OT ceremonial law. *considers every day alike.* All days are to be dedicated to God through holy living and godly service. *fully convinced in his own mind.* The importance of personal conviction in disputable matters of conduct runs through this passage (see vv. 14,16,22–23).

14:6 The motivation behind the actions of both the strong and the weak is to be the same: Both should want to serve the Lord and give thanks for his provision.

14:7 *none of us lives to himself alone.* The reference is to "us" Christians. We do not live to please ourselves but the Lord. *none of us dies to himself alone.* Even in death the important thing is one's relationship to the Lord. Paul repeats the truths of this verse in v. 8.

14:9 *Lord.* See note on 10:9. Christ's Lordship over both the dead and the living arises out of his death and resurrection.

14:10 *why do you judge your brother?* Addressed to weak Christians. *why do you look down on your brother?* Addressed to strong Christians. *we will all.* Refers to every Christian. *God's judgment seat.* All Christians will be judged, and the judgment will be based on works (see 2Co 5:10 and note; cf. 1Co 3:10–15 and notes).

14:13 *Instead.* The words that immediately follow are addressed to strong Christians. *obstacle.* Something that causes one to fall into sin.

14:14 *As one who is in the Lord Jesus, I am fully convinced.* Now that Paul was a Christian, the old food taboos no longer applied (see Mk 7:19–20; Ac 10:15,28 and notes). *no food is unclean in itself.* For Paul's teaching elsewhere on this

But if anyone regards something as unclean, then for him it is unclean.[e] 15If your
brother is distressed because of what you
eat, you are no longer acting in love.[f] Do
not by your eating destroy your brother for
whom Christ died.[g] 16Do not allow what
you consider good to be spoken of as evil.[h]
17For the kingdom of God is not a matter of
eating and drinking,[i] but of righteousness,
peace[j] and joy in the Holy Spirit,[k] 18because
anyone who serves Christ in this way is
pleasing to God and approved by men.[l]
19Let us therefore make every effort to
do what leads to peace[m] and to mutual edification.[n] 20Do not destroy the work of God
for the sake of food.[o] All food is clean,[p]
but it is wrong for a man to eat anything
that causes someone else to stumble.[q] 21It
is better not to eat meat or drink wine or
to do anything else that will cause your
brother to fall.[r]
22So whatever you believe about these
things keep between yourself and God.
Blessed is the man who does not condemn[s] himself by what he approves. 23But
the man who has doubts[t] is condemned
if he eats, because his eating is not from
faith; and everything that does not come
from faith is sin.

14:14 [e]1Co 8:7 **14:15** [f]Eph 5:2 [g]ver 20; 1Co 8:11 **14:16** [h]1Co 10:30 **14:17** [i]1Co 8:8 [j]Isa 32:17 [k]Ro 15:13; Gal 5:22 **14:18** [l]Lk 2:52; Ac 24:16; 2Co 8:21 **14:19** [m]Ps 34:14; Ro 12:18; 1Co 7:15; 2Ti 2:22; Heb 12:14 [n]Ro 15:2; 1Co 14:3-5, 12,17,26; 2Co 12:19; Eph 4:12,29 **14:20** [o]ver 15 [p]ver 14; S Ac 10:15 [q]ver 13; 1Co 8:9-12 **14:21** [r]S Mt 5:29 **14:22** [s]1Jn 3:21 **14:23** [t]ver 5

15:1 [u]Ro 14:1; 1Th 5:14 **15:2** [v]S 1Co 10:24 [w]S Ro 14:19 **15:3** [x]2Co 8:9 [y]Ps 69:9

15 We who are strong ought to bear
with the failings of the weak[u] and
not to please ourselves. 2Each of us should
please his neighbor for his good,[v] to build
him up.[w] 3For even Christ did not please
himself[x] but, as it is written: "The insults
of those who insult you have fallen on
me."[a][y] 4For everything that was written
in the past was written to teach us,[z] so
that through endurance and the encouragement of the Scriptures we might have
hope.
5May the God who gives endurance and
encouragement give you a spirit of unity[a]
among yourselves as you follow Christ
Jesus, 6so that with one heart and mouth
you may glorify[b] the God and Father[c] of
our Lord Jesus Christ.
7Accept one another,[d] then, just as Christ
accepted you, in order to bring praise to
God. 8For I tell you that Christ has become a servant of the Jews[b][e] on behalf
of God's truth, to confirm the promises[f]

[a] *3* Psalm 69:9 [b] *8* Greek *circumcision*

15:4 [z]S Ro 4:23,24 **15:5** [a]Ro 12:16; 1Co 1:10; 2Co 13:11; Eph 4:3; Php 2:2; Col 3:14; 1Pe 3:8 **15:6** [b]Ps 34:3 [c]Rev 1:6 **15:7** [d]Ro 14:1 **15:8** [e]Mt 15:24; Ac 3:25,26 [f]2Co 1:20

subject see 1Ti 4:4; Tit 1:15 and note. *if anyone regards something as unclean, then for him it is unclean.* Not to be generalized to mean that sin is only a matter of subjective opinion or conscience. Paul is not discussing conduct that in the light of Scripture is clearly sinful, but conduct concerning which Christians may legitimately differ (in this case, food regulations). With regard to such matters, decisions should be guided by conscience.

14:15 *love.* The key to proper settlement of disputes. *your brother for whom Christ died.* Christ so valued weak Christians that he died for them. Surely strong Christians ought to be willing to make adjustments in their own behavior for the sake of such fellow believers (see 1Co 8:11–13; 10:23,28–29,32–33 and notes).

14:16 *what you consider good.* From your own understanding of Christian liberty. *to be spoken of as evil.* To exercise freedom without responsibility can lead to evil results.

14:17 *kingdom of God.* See notes on Mt 3:2; Lk 4:43. *is not a matter of eating and drinking.* To be concerned with such trivial matters is to miss completely the essence of Christian living. *righteousness.* Righteous living. Paul's concern for the moral and ethical dimension of the Christian life stands out in all his letters. *peace.* See 5:1 and note. *joy in the Holy Spirit.* Joy given by the Holy Spirit.

14:19 *mutual edification.* The spiritual building up of individual Christians and of the church (see 1:11–12 and note on 1:12).

14:20 *work of God.* The weak Christian who as a redeemed person is God's work and in whom God continues to work (cf. Eph 2:10). *causes someone else to stumble.* Paul recognizes a strong Christian's right to certain freedoms, but qualifies it with the principle of regard for a weak Christian's scruples.

14:22 *keep between yourself and God.* Strong Christians are not required to go against their convictions or change their standards. Yet they are not to flaunt their Christian freedom but keep it a private matter. *what he approves.* Probably a reference to the eating of certain foods.

14:23 *everything.* The matters discussed above, namely, conduct about which there can be legitimate differences of opinion between Christians. *faith.* Here the conviction that one's action is in keeping with God's will.

15:1 *We who are strong.* Paul identifies himself with the strong Christians, those whose personal convictions allow them more freedom than the weak. *to bear.* Not merely to tolerate or put up with but to uphold lovingly. *failings.* Not sins, since in the matters under discussion there is no clear guidance in Scripture. *not to please ourselves.* Not that Christians should never please themselves, but that they should not insist on doing what they want without regard to the scruples of other Christians.

15:3 *Christ did not please himself.* He came to do the will of the Father, not his own will (see Jn 4:34 and note). This involved suffering and even death (see Mt 20:28; Mk 10:45; 2Co 8:9; Php 2:5–8 and notes). *The insults of those who insult you have fallen on me.* In the psalm quoted (69:9; see note there) "you" refers to God and "me" refers to the righteous sufferer, whom Paul identifies with Christ. The quotation serves to show how Christ did not please himself, but voluntarily bore human hostility toward God.

15:4 Here Paul defends his application of Ps 69:9 to Christ. In so doing, he states a great truth concerning the purpose of Scripture: It was written for our instruction, so that as we patiently endure we might be encouraged to hold fast our hope in Christ (see 1Co 10:6,11).

15:5 *a spirit of unity among yourselves.* Not that believers should all come to the same conclusions on the matters of conscience discussed above, but that they might agree to disagree in love.

15:7 *just as Christ accepted you.* See 14:3; see also 14:1,4,15 and notes.

15:8 *Christ has become a servant of the Jews.* Clearly revealed in his earthly ministry. He was sent to the Jewish people and largely limited his ministry to them (see Mt 15:24). God gave a special priority, so far as the gospel is concerned, to the Jews (see 1:16 and note; 3:1–8; see also 9:4–5 and notes). *promises*

made to the patriarchs [9]so that the Gentiles[g] may glorify God[h] for his mercy, as
it is written:

"Therefore I will praise you among the
Gentiles;
I will sing hymns to your name."[a i]

[10]Again, it says,

"Rejoice, O Gentiles, with his
people."[b j]

[11]And again,

"Praise the Lord, all you Gentiles,
and sing praises to him, all you
peoples."[c k]

[12]And again, Isaiah says,

"The Root of Jesse[l] will spring up,
one who will arise to rule over the
nations;
the Gentiles will hope in him."[d m]

[13]May the God of hope fill you with all
joy and peace[n] as you trust in him, so that
you may overflow with hope by the power
of the Holy Spirit.[o]

Paul the Minister to the Gentiles

[14]I myself am convinced, my brothers,
that you yourselves are full of goodness,[p]
complete in knowledge[q] and competent to
instruct one another. [15]I have written you
quite boldly on some points, as if to remind you of them again, because of the
grace God gave me[r] [16]to be a minister
of Christ Jesus to the Gentiles[s] with the
priestly duty of proclaiming the gospel of
God,[t] so that the Gentiles might become
an offering[u] acceptable to God, sanctified
by the Holy Spirit.

[17]Therefore I glory in Christ Jesus[v] in
my service to God.[w] [18]I will not venture to
speak of anything except what Christ has
accomplished through me in leading the
Gentiles[x] to obey God[y] by what I have said
and done— [19]by the power of signs and
miracles,[z] through the power of the Spirit.[a]
So from Jerusalem[b] all the way around to
Illyricum, I have fully proclaimed the gospel of Christ.[c] [20]It has always been my ambition to preach the gospel[d] where Christ
was not known, so that I would not be
building on someone else's foundation.[e]
[21]Rather, as it is written:

"Those who were not told about him
will see,
and those who have not heard will
understand."[e f]

[22]This is why I have often been hindered
from coming to you.[g]

Paul's Plan to Visit Rome

[23]But now that there is no more place
for me to work in these regions, and since
I have been longing for many years to
see you,[h] [24]I plan to do so when I go to
Spain.[i] I hope to visit you while passing
through and to have you assist[j] me on my
journey there, after I have enjoyed your

15:9 [g] S Ro 3:29 [h] S Mt 9:8 [i] 2Sa 22:50; Ps 18:49 **15:10** [j] Dt 32:43; Isa 66:10 **15:11** [k] Ps 117:1 **15:12** [l] S Rev 5:5 [m] Isa 11:10; Mt 12:21 **15:13** [n] Ro 14:17 [o] ver 19; 1Co 2:4; 4:20; 1Th 1:5 **15:14** [p] Eph 5:9 [q] S 2Co 8:7; 2Pe 1:12 **15:15** [r] S Ro 12:3 **15:16** [s] S Ac 9:15 [t] ver 19; S Ro 1:1 [u] Isa 66:20 **15:17** [v] Php 3:3 [w] Heb 2:17 **15:18** [x] Ac 15:12; 21:19; Ro 1:5 [y] Ro 16:26 **15:19** [z] S Jn 4:48; Ac 19:11 [a] S ver 13 [b] Ac 22:17-21 [c] S 2Co 2:12 **15:20** [d] Ro 1:15 [e] 2Co 10:15,16 **15:21** [f] Isa 52:15 **15:22** [g] Ro 1:13 **15:23** [h] Ac 19:21; Ro 1:10,11 **15:24** [i] ver 28 [j] 1Co 16:6; Tit 3:13

[a] *9* 2 Samuel 22:50; Psalm 18:49 [b] *10* Deut. 32:43 [c] *11* Psalm 117:1 [d] *12* Isaiah 11:10 [e] *21* Isaiah 52:15

made to the patriarchs. The covenant promises made to Abraham (Ge 12:1–3; 17:7; 18:19; 22:18), Isaac (Ge 26:3–4) and Jacob (Ge 28:13–15; 46:2–4; see chart, p. 19).

15:9 *so that the Gentiles may glorify God.* From the beginning, God's redemptive work in and for Israel had in view the redemption of the Gentiles (see Ge 12:2–3 and note). They would both see God's mighty and gracious acts for his people and hear the praises of God's people as they celebrated what God had done for them (a common theme in the Psalms; see Paul's quotations in vv. 9b–12 and note on Ps 9:1). Thus they would come to know the true God and glorify him for his mercy (see notes on Ps 46:10; 47:9). God's greatest and climactic act for Israel's salvation was the sending of the Messiah to fulfill the promises made to the patriarchs and so to gather in the great harvest of the Gentiles.

15:12 *Root of Jesse.* Jesse was the father of David (see 1Sa 16:5–13; Mt 1:6), and the Messiah was the "son of David" (see Mt 1:1 and note; 21:9; see also Isa 11:1; Rev 5:5 and notes). *Gentiles will hope in him.* The Gentile mission of the early church was a fulfillment of this prophecy (Isa 11:10; see note there), as is the continuing evangelization of the nations (cf. Isa 42:4 and note).

15:13 *God of hope.* Any hope the Christian has comes from God (see note on 5:5). *by the power of the Holy Spirit.* Hope cannot be conjured up by human effort; it is God's gift by his Spirit (see 8:24–25).

15:15 *as if to remind you of them again.* Since Paul had never preached or taught in Rome, he may be referring to Christian doctrine generally known in the church.

15:16 *minister of Christ Jesus to the Gentiles.* See note on 11:13. *priestly duty of proclaiming the gospel.* Paul's priestly function was different from that of the Levitical priests. They were involved with the rituals of the temple, whereas he preached the gospel. *an offering acceptable to God, sanctified by the Holy Spirit.* The offering Paul brought to God was the Gentile church. *sanctified.* See note on 1Co 1:2.

15:17 *I glory.* Paul was not boasting about his own achievements but about what Christ had accomplished through him (v. 18).

15:19 *signs and miracles.* See Ac 14:8–10; 16:16–18,25–26; 20:9–12; 28:8–9; 2Co 12:12 and note; Heb 2:4 and note. *from Jerusalem.* The home of the mother church, where the gospel originated and its dissemination began (see Ac 1:8 and note; see also maps, p. 1702, and Introduction to Acts: Plan and Outline). *Illyricum.* A Roman province north of Macedonia (present-day Albania and Yugoslavia). Acts mentions nothing of his ministry there, and perhaps all he means is that through his preaching at Corinth and elsewhere his converts in their travels had spread the message to faraway places. *I have fully proclaimed the gospel.* Not everyone had heard the gospel in the eastern Mediterranean, but Paul believed that his work there had been completed and it was time to move on to other places.

15:22 *hindered from coming to you.* Paul's great desire to complete the missionary task in the eastern Mediterranean had prevented him from making a trip to Rome.

15:23 *no more place for me to work.* Because of the principle stated in v. 20. *longing for many years to see you.* See 1:11–15.

15:24 *to have you assist me on my journey there.* Paul wanted to use the Roman church as a base of operations for a mis-

company for a while. 25Now, however, I
am on my way to Jerusalem[k] in the service[l] of the saints[m] there. 26For Macedonia[n] and Achaia[o] were pleased to make a
contribution for the poor among the saints
in Jerusalem.[p] 27They were pleased to do
it, and indeed they owe it to them. For if
the Gentiles have shared in the Jews' spiritual blessings, they owe it to the Jews to
share with them their material blessings.[q]
28So after I have completed this task and
have made sure that they have received
this fruit, I will go to Spain[r] and visit you
on the way. 29I know that when I come to
you,[s] I will come in the full measure of the
blessing of Christ.

30I urge you, brothers, by our Lord Jesus
Christ and by the love of the Spirit,[t] to join
me in my struggle by praying to God for
me.[u] 31Pray that I may be rescued[v] from
the unbelievers in Judea and that my service[w] in Jerusalem may be acceptable to
the saints[x] there, 32so that by God's will[y]
I may come to you[z] with joy and together with you be refreshed.[a] 33The God of
peace[b] be with you all. Amen.

Personal Greetings

16 I commend[c] to you our sister Phoebe, a servant[a] of the church in Cenchrea.[d] 2I ask you to receive her in the
Lord[e] in a way worthy of the saints[f] and
to give her any help she may need from
you, for she has been a great help to many
people, including me.

15:25 [k]S Ac 19:21 [l]S Ac 24:17 [m]S Ac 9:13 **15:26** [n]S Ac 16:9 [o]S Ac 18:12 [p]S Ac 24:17 **15:27** [q]1Co 9:11 **15:28** [r]ver 24 **15:29** [s]Ro 1:10, 11 **15:30** [t]Gal 5:22; Col 1:8 [u]2Co 1:11; Col 4:12 **15:31** [v]2Co 1:10; 2Th 3:2; 2Ti 3:11; 2Pe 2:9 [w]ver 25; S Ac 24:17 [x]S Ac 9:13 **15:32** [y]S Ac 18:21 [z]Ro 1:10, 13 [a]1Co 16:18; Phm 7 **15:33** [b]Ro 16:20; 2Co 13:11; Php 4:9; 1Th 5:23; 2Th 3:16; Heb 13:20 **16:1** [c]S 2Co 3:1 [d]Ac 18:18 **16:2** [e]Php 2:29 [f]S Ac 9:13 **16:3** [g]S Ac 18:2 [h]S Php 2:25 [i]ver 7, 9, 10; Ro 8:1, 39; 1Co 1:30; 2Co 5:17; Gal 1:22; 5:6; Eph 1:13 **16:5** [j]1Co 16:19; Col 4:15; Phm 2 [k]1Co 16:15 [l]S Ac 2:9

3Greet Priscilla[b] and Aquila,[g] my fellow workers[h] in Christ Jesus.[i] 4They
risked their lives for me. Not only I
but all the churches of the Gentiles
are grateful to them.
5Greet also the church that meets at their
house.[j]
Greet my dear friend Epenetus, who
was the first convert[k] to Christ in the
province of Asia.[l]
6Greet Mary, who worked very hard for
you.
7Greet Andronicus and Junias, my relatives[m] who have been in prison with
me.[n] They are outstanding among the
apostles, and they were in Christ[o] before I was.
8Greet Ampliatus, whom I love in the
Lord.
9Greet Urbanus, our fellow worker in
Christ,[p] and my dear friend Stachys.
10Greet Apelles, tested and approved in
Christ.[q]
Greet those who belong to the household[r] of Aristobulus.
11Greet Herodion, my relative.[s]
Greet those in the household[t] of Narcissus who are in the Lord.
12Greet Tryphena and Tryphosa, those
women who work hard in the Lord.
Greet my dear friend Persis, another

[a] *1* Or *deaconess* [b] *3* Greek *Prisca,* a variant of *Priscilla*

16:7 [m]ver 11, 21 [n]Col 4:10; Phm 23 [o]S ver 3 **16:9** [p]S ver 3 **16:10** [q]S ver 3 [r]S Ac 11:14 **16:11** [s]ver 7, 21 [t]S Ac 11:14

sion to Spain (see also v. 28). *enjoyed your company for a while.* More than a quick stop at Rome was contemplated (see 1:11–12).

15:25 *in the service of the saints there.* Paul wanted to present the gift (see v. 26) personally to the Jerusalem church. The gift needed interpretation. It was not merely money; it represented the love and concern of the Gentile churches for their Jewish brothers and sisters in Christ. *saints.* Refers generally to believers in Jesus Christ (see note on 1:7).

15:26 *Macedonia and Achaia.* See note on 1Th 1:7. *contribution.* See 1Co 16:1–4; 2Co 8:1—9:15 and notes.

15:27 *Jews' spiritual blessings.* Especially Christ and the gospel.

15:28 *this fruit.* The collection from the Gentile churches.

15:31 *Pray that I may be rescued from the unbelievers in Judea.* Paul wanted to go to Jerusalem. The delivery of the collection was important to him, but he had received warnings about what might happen to him there (see Ac 20:22–23 and note on 20:22). *may be acceptable.* Perhaps a reference to the way in which the money was to be distributed—often a delicate and difficult task.

15:32 *with you be refreshed.* See 1:11–12.

15:33 *God of peace.* See notes on 5:1; 1Th 5:23.

16:1 *our sister.* In the sense of being a fellow believer. *Phoebe.* Probably the carrier of the letter to Rome (cf. v. 2). *servant.* See NIV text note; one who serves or ministers in any way. When church related, as it is here, it probably refers to a specific office—woman deacon or deaconess. *Cenchrea.* A port located about six miles east of Corinth on the Saronic Gulf.

16:3 *Priscilla and Aquila.* Close friends of Paul who worked in the same trade of tentmaking (see Ac 18:2–3 and notes).

16:4 *risked their lives for me.* There is no other record of this in the NT or elsewhere, but it must have been widely known, as the last part of the verse indicates (cf. Php 2:25–30 and notes).

16:6 *Mary.* Six persons are known by this name in the NT. This one is unknown apart from this reference.

16:7 *Junias.* The preferred reading of the Greek text is Junia, a feminine name. Andronicus and Junia may have been husband and wife (cf. Priscilla and Aquila [v. 3] and probably Philologus and Julia [v. 15]). *among the apostles.* Two possible interpretations are: (1) "Apostles" is used in a wider sense than the Twelve—to include preachers of the gospel recognized by the churches (see Ac 14:4 and note, 14; 1Th 2:6). (2) "Apostles" is here preceded by the definite article; this may indicate that the Twelve are in view. If that is the case, the meaning would be that these two persons were outstanding "in the opinion of" the apostles.

16:8–10 *Ampliatus ... Urbanus ... Stachys ... Apelles.* All common slave names found in the imperial household.

16:10 *Aristobulus.* Perhaps refers to the grandson of Herod the Great and brother of Herod Agrippa I.

16:11 *my relative.* Perhaps a reference to his being a Jew. *Narcissus.* Sometimes identified with Tiberius Claudius Narcissus, a wealthy freedman of the Roman emperor Tiberius.

16:12 *Tryphena and Tryphosa.* Perhaps sisters, even twins, because it was common for such persons to be given names from the same root. *Persis.* Means "Persian woman."

woman who has worked very hard in
the Lord.
13 Greet Rufus,[u] chosen[v] in the Lord, and
his mother, who has been a mother
to me, too.
14 Greet Asyncritus, Phlegon, Hermes, Patrobas,
Hermas and the brothers with
them.
15 Greet Philologus, Julia, Nereus and his
sister, and Olympas and all the saints[w]
with them.[x]
16 Greet one another with a holy kiss.[y]
All the churches of Christ send greetings.

17 I urge you, brothers, to watch out for
those who cause divisions and put obstacles
in your way that are contrary to the
teaching you have learned.[z] Keep away
from them.[a] 18 For such people are not
serving our Lord Christ,[b] but their own appetites.[c]
By smooth talk and flattery they
deceive[d] the minds of naive people. 19 Everyone
has heard[e] about your obedience,
so I am full of joy over you; but I want you
to be wise about what is good, and innocent
about what is evil.[f]
20 The God of peace[g] will soon crush[h] Satan[i]
under your feet.

The grace of our Lord Jesus be with
you.[j]
21 Timothy,[k] my fellow worker, sends his
greetings to you, as do Lucius,[l] Jason[m] and
Sosipater, my relatives.[n]
22 I, Tertius, who wrote down this letter,
greet you in the Lord.
23 Gaius,[o] whose hospitality I and the
whole church here enjoy, sends you his
greetings.
Erastus,[p] who is the city's director of
public works, and our brother Quartus
send you their greetings.[a]
25 Now to him who is able[q] to establish
you by my gospel[r] and the proclamation
of Jesus Christ, according to the revelation
of the mystery[s] hidden for long ages
past, 26 but now revealed and made known
through the prophetic writings[t] by the
command of the eternal God, so that all
nations might believe and obey[u] him—
27 to the only wise God be glory forever
through Jesus Christ! Amen.[v]

[a] 23 Some manuscripts *their greetings.* [24] *May the grace of our Lord Jesus Christ be with all of you. Amen.*

16:13 [u] Mk 15:21 [v] S 2Jn 1 **16:15** [w] ver 2; S Ac 9:13 [x] ver 14 **16:16** [y] 1Co 16:20; 2Co 13:12; 1Th 5:26; 1Pe 5:14 **16:17** [z] Gal 1:8,9; 1Ti 1:3; 6:3 [a] Mt 18:15-17; 1Co 5:11; 2Th 3:6,14; 2Ti 3:5; Tit 3:10; 2Jn 10 **16:18** [b] Ro 14:18 [c] Php 3:19 [d] 2Sa 15:6; Ps 12:2; Isa 30:10; Col 2:4 **16:19** [e] Ro 1:8 [f] S 1Co 14:20 **16:20** [g] S Ro 15:33 [h] Ge 3:15 [i] S Mt 4:10 [j] 2Co 13:14; S Gal 6:18; 1Th 5:28; Rev 22:21 **16:21** [k] S Ac 16:1 [l] Ac 13:1 [m] Ac 17:5 [n] ver 7,11 **16:23** [o] S Ac 19:29 [p] Ac 19:22; 2Ti 4:20 **16:25** [q] 2Co 9:8; Eph 3:20; Jude 24 [r] Ro 2:16; 2Ti 2:8 [s] Isa 48:6; Eph 1:9; 3:3-6,9; Col 1:26,27; 2:2; 1Ti 3:16 **16:26** [t] Ro 1:2 [u] Ro 1:5 **16:27** [v] S Ro 11:36

16:14–15 None of these persons can be further identified, except that they were slaves or freedmen in the Roman church.
16:16 *holy kiss.* See 1Co 16:20; 2Co 13:12; 1Th 5:26 and notes; 1Pe 5:14. Justin Martyr (A.D. 150) tells us that the holy kiss was a regular part of the worship service in his day. It is still a practice in some churches.
16:17 *those who cause divisions and put obstacles in your way.* Who these people were we cannot tell, but some of their characteristics are mentioned in v. 18.
16:19 *wise about what is good.* Christians are to be experts in doing good.
16:20 *God of peace.* See 15:33 and note; cf. note on 1:7. *will soon crush Satan.* A reference to Satan's final doom. For "soon" see note on 13:12. *under your feet.* Believers will share in Christ's victory over Satan (see Ge 3:15 and note). *grace.* See note on 1:7. *with you.* See note on 2Co 13:14.
16:21 *Jason.* Possibly the Jason mentioned in Ac 17:5–9. *Sosipater.* Probably Sopater son of Pyrrhus from Berea (see Ac 20:4 and note).
16:22 *I, Tertius, who wrote down this letter.* He had functioned as Paul's secretary.
16:23 *Gaius.* Usually identified with Titius Justus, a God-fearer, in whose house Paul stayed while in Corinth (see Ac 18:7 and note; 1Co 1:14). His full name would be Gaius Titius Justus. *here.* In Corinth. *Erastus.* At Corinth archaeologists have discovered a reused block of stone in a paved square, with the Latin inscription: "Erastus, commissioner of public works, bore the expense of this pavement." This may refer to the Erastus mentioned here. If it does, it is the earliest reference to a Christian by name outside the NT. He may also be the same person referred to in Ac 19:22 and 2Ti 4:20 (see notes there), though it is difficult to be certain because the name was fairly common. *Quartus.* Means "fourth (son)."
16:24 See NIV text note on v. 23.
16:25 *my gospel.* Not a gospel different from that preached by others, but a gospel Paul received by direct revelation (see Gal 1:12 and note on 1:11). *proclamation of Jesus Christ.* A description of the gospel; it is about Jesus Christ, who is its content (see 1:3; 1Co 15:3–4 and notes). *mystery.* See note on 11:25. *for long ages.* From eternity past (see 1Co 2:7 and note).
16:26 *revealed and made known through the prophetic writings.* See 1:2 and note. *all nations.* The universality of the gospel (see Mt 28:19 and note).
16:27 *to … God be glory.* The ultimate purpose of all things (see 11:36; Ps 29:1–2; 86:9,12; 96:7–8; 115:1; Lk 2:14 and note; 1Co 10:31 and note; Eph 1:12,14; Rev 5:13; 7:12; 15:4; 19:1,7).

1 Corinthians

INTRODUCTION

Author and Date

Paul is acknowledged as the author both by the letter itself (1:1 – 2; 16:21) and by the early church fathers. His authorship was attested by Clement of Rome as early as A.D. 96, and today practically all NT interpreters concur. The letter was written c. A.D. 55 (see chart, p. 1697) toward the close of Paul's three-year residency in Ephesus (see 16:5 – 9; Ac 20:31). It is clear from his reference to staying at Ephesus until Pentecost (16:8) that he intended to remain there somewhat less than a year when he wrote 1 Corinthians.

The City of Corinth

Corinth was a thriving city; it was at the time the chief city of Greece both commercially and politically. See map and diagram, p. 1766.

1. *Its commerce.* Located just off the Corinthian isthmus (see map, p. 1718), it was a crossroads for travelers and traders. It had two harbors: (1) Cenchrea, six miles to the east on the Saronic Gulf, and (2) Lechaion, a mile and a half to the north on the Corinthian Gulf. Goods were transported across the isthmus on a *diolkos* (see map and accompanying text, p. 1766), a stone road by which smaller ships could be hauled fully loaded across the isthmus, and by which cargoes of larger ships could be transported by wagons from one side to the other. Trade flowed through the city from Italy and Spain to the west and from Asia Minor, Phoenicia and Egypt to the east.

2. *Its culture.* Although Corinth was not a university town like Athens, it was characterized nevertheless by typical Greek culture. Its people were interested in Greek philosophy and placed a high premium on wisdom.

3. *Its religion.* Corinth contained at least 12 temples. Whether they were all in use during Paul's time is not known for certain. One of the most infamous was the temple dedicated to Aphrodite, the goddess of love (located on the high acropolis that loomed over the city; see map, below),

A Quick Look

Author:
The apostle Paul

Audience:
Believers at Corinth, a church torn apart by factions and spiritual immaturity

Date:
A.D. 55

Theme:
Paul addresses problems in the church and answers questions from the church.

whose worshipers practiced religious prostitution. About a fourth of a mile north of the theater stood the temple of Asclepius, the god of healing, and in the middle of the city the sixth-century B.C. temple of Apollo was located. In addition, the Jews had established a synagogue; the inscribed lintel of it has been found and placed in the museum at old Corinth.

> *Paul reveals a true pastor's heart as he deals with problems of Christian conduct in the church at Corinth.*

4. *Its immorality.* Like any large commercial city (especially seaports), Corinth was a center for open and unbridled sexual immorality. The worship of Aphrodite fostered prostitution in the name of religion. At an earlier time 1,000 sacred (priestess) prostitutes served her temple. So widely known did the immorality of Corinth become that the Greek verb "to Corinthianize" came to mean "to practice sexual immorality." In a setting like this it is no wonder that the Corinthian church was plagued with numerous problems.

Occasion and Purpose

Paul had received information from several sources concerning the conditions existing in the church at Corinth. Some members of the household of Chloe had informed him of the factions that had developed in the church (1:11). There were three individuals—Stephanas, Fortunatus and Achaicus—who had come to Paul in Ephesus to make some contribution to his ministry (16:17), but whether these were the ones from Chloe's household we do not know.

Some of those who had come had brought disturbing information concerning moral irregularities in the church (chs. 5–6). Immorality had plagued the Corinthian assembly almost from the

Corinth in the Time of Paul

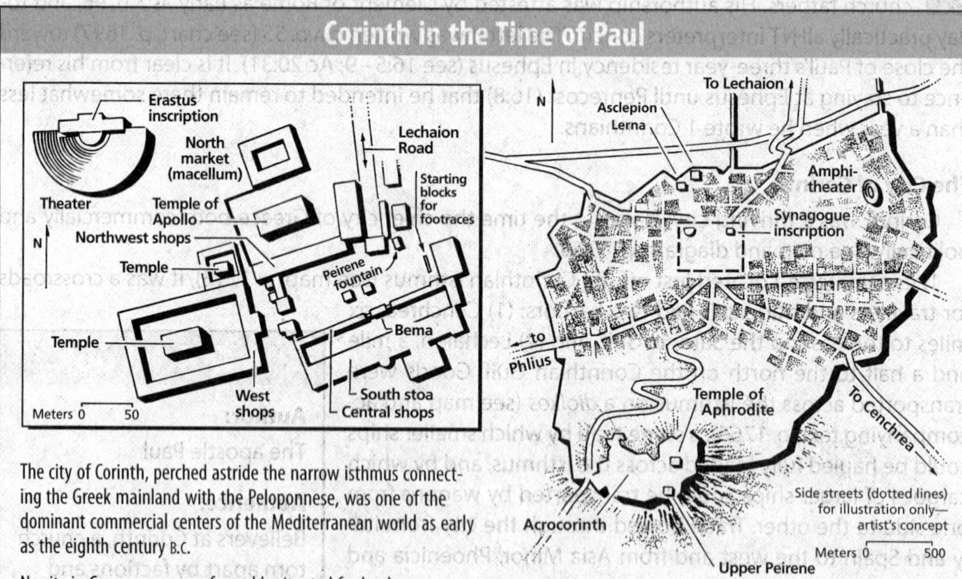

The city of Corinth, perched astride the narrow isthmus connecting the Greek mainland with the Peloponnese, was one of the dominant commercial centers of the Mediterranean world as early as the eighth century B.C.

No city in Greece was more favorably situated for land and sea trade. With a high, strong citadel at its back, it lay between the Saronic Gulf and the Ionian Sea, with ports at Lechaion and Cenchrea. A *diolkos*, or stone road for the overland transport of ships and/or offloaded cargo, linked the two seas. Crowning the Acrocorinth was the temple of Aphrodite, served at an earlier time, according to Strabo, by more than 1,000 pagan priestess-prostitutes.

By the time the gospel reached Corinth in the spring of A.D. 52, the city had a proud history of leadership in the Achaian League, and a spirit of revived Hellenism under Roman domination after 44 B.C., following the destruction of the city by Mummius in 146 B.C.

Paul's lengthy stay in Corinth brought him directly in contact with the major monuments of the *agora*, many of which still survive. The fountain-house of the spring *Peirene*, the temple of Apollo, the *macellum* or meat market (1Co 10:25) and the theater, the bema (Ac 18:12), and the unimpressive synagogue all played a part in the experience of the apostle. An inscription from the theater names the city official Erastus, probably the friend of Paul mentioned in Ro 16:23 (see note there).

beginning. From 5:9 – 10 it is apparent that Paul had written previously concerning moral laxness. He had urged believers "not to associate with sexually immoral people" (5:9). Because he had not been well understood, he now finds it necessary to clarify his instruction (5:10 – 11) and to urge immediate and drastic action (5:3 – 5,13).

Other Corinthian visitors had brought a letter from the church that requested counsel on several subjects (see 7:1 and note; cf. 8:1; 12:1; 16:1).

It is clear that, although the church was gifted (see 1:4 – 7), it was immature and unspiritual (3:1 – 4). Paul's purposes for writing were: (1) to instruct and restore the church in its areas of weakness, correcting erroneous practices such as divisions (1:10 — 4:21), immorality (ch. 5; 6:12 – 20), litigation in pagan courts (6:1 – 8) and abuse of the Lord's Supper (11:17 – 34); (2) to correct false teaching concerning the resurrection (ch. 15); and (3) to answer questions addressed to Paul in the letter that had been perhaps also brought to him (see previous paragraph); and (4) to call the church to obedience in the light of a growing challenge to Paul's authority, an issue that would provide the immediate context for 2 Corinthians.

Theme

The letter revolves around the theme of problems in Christian conduct in the church. It thus has to do with progressive sanctification, the continuing development of a holy character. Paul reveals a true pastor's heart as he deals with problems of Christian conduct in the church at Corinth.

Relevance

This letter continues to be timely for the church today, both to instruct and to inspire. Christians are still powerfully influenced by their cultural environment, and most of the questions and problems that confronted the church at Corinth are still very much with us — problems like immaturity, instability, divisions, jealousy and envy, lawsuits, marital difficulties, sexual immorality and misuse of spiritual gifts. Yet in spite of this concentration on problems, Paul's letter contains some of the most familiar and beloved chapters in the entire Bible — e.g., ch. 13 (on love) and ch. 15 (on resurrection).

Outline

- I. Introduction (1:1 – 9)
- II. Divisions in the Church (1:10 — 4:21)
  - A. The Fact of the Divisions (1:10 – 17)
  - B. The Causes of the Divisions (1:18 — 4:13)
    - 1. A wrong conception of the Christian message (1:18 — 3:4)
    - 2. A wrong conception of Christian ministry and ministers (3:5 — 4:5)
    - 3. A wrong conception of the Christian (4:6 – 13)
  - C. The Exhortation to End the Divisions (4:14 – 21)
- III. Moral and Ethical Disorders in the Life of the Church (chs. 5 – 6)
  - A. Laxity in Church Discipline (ch. 5)
  - B. Lawsuits before Non-Christian Judges (6:1 – 11)
  - C. Sexual Immorality (6:12 – 20)
- IV. Instruction on Marriage (ch. 7)
  - A. General Principles (7:1 – 7)
  - B. The Problems of the Married (7:8 – 24)
  - C. The Problems of the Unmarried (7:25 – 40)
- V. Instruction on Questionable Practices (8:1 — 11:1)
  - A. The Principles Involved (ch. 8)
  - B. The Principles Illustrated (ch. 9)
  - C. A Warning from the History of Israel (10:1 – 22)
  - D. The Principles Applied (10:23 — 11:1)

VI. Instruction on Public Worship (11:2 — 14:40)
   A. Propriety in Worship (11:2 – 16)
   B. The Lord's Supper (11:17 – 34)
   C. Spiritual Gifts (chs. 12 – 14)
      1. The test of the gifts (12:1 – 3)
      2. The unity of the gifts (12:4 – 11)
      3. The diversity of the gifts (12:12 – 31a)
      4. The necessity of exercising the gifts in love (12:31b — 13:13)
      5. The superiority of prophecy over tongues (14:1 – 25)
      6. Rules governing public worship (14:26 – 40)
VII. Instruction on the Resurrection (ch. 15)
   A. The Certainty of the Resurrection (15:1 – 34)
   B. The Consideration of Certain Objections (15:35 – 57)
   C. The Concluding Appeal (15:58)
VIII. Conclusion: Practical and Personal Matters (ch. 16)

1 Paul, called to be an apostle[a] of Christ
Jesus by the will of God,[b] and our
brother Sosthenes,[c]

2To the church of God[d] in Corinth,[e] to
those sanctified in Christ Jesus and called[f]
to be holy, together with all those everywhere who call on the name[g] of our Lord
Jesus Christ—their Lord and ours:

3Grace and peace to you from God our
Father and the Lord Jesus Christ.[h]

Thanksgiving

4I always thank God for you[i] because
of his grace given you in Christ Jesus.
5For in him you have been enriched[j] in
every way—in all your speaking and in
all your knowledge[k]— 6because our testimony[l] about Christ was confirmed in
you. 7Therefore you do not lack any spiritual gift[m] as you eagerly wait for our Lord
Jesus Christ to be revealed.[n] 8He will keep
you strong to the end, so that you will be
blameless[o] on the day of our Lord Jesus
Christ.[p] 9God, who has called you[q] into
fellowship with his Son Jesus Christ our
Lord,[r] is faithful.[s]

Divisions in the Church

10I appeal to you, brothers,[t] in the name
of our Lord Jesus Christ, that all of you
agree with one another so that there may
be no divisions among you[u] and that you
may be perfectly united[v] in mind and
thought. 11My brothers, some from Chloe's
household[w] have informed me that there
are quarrels among you. 12What I mean
is this: One of you says, "I follow Paul";[x]
another, "I follow Apollos";[y] another, "I
follow Cephas[a]";[z] still another, "I follow
Christ."

13Is Christ divided? Was Paul crucified for you? Were you baptized into[b] the
name of Paul?[a] 14I am thankful that I did
not baptize any of you except Crispus[b] and
Gaius,[c] 15so no one can say that you were
baptized into my name. 16(Yes, I also baptized the household[d] of Stephanas;[e] beyond that, I don't remember if I baptized
anyone else.) 17For Christ did not send me
to baptize,[f] but to preach the gospel—not
with words of human wisdom,[g] lest the
cross of Christ be emptied of its power.

Christ the Wisdom and Power of God

18For the message of the cross is foolishness[h] to those who are perishing,[i] but to

[a] *12* That is, Peter [b] *13* Or *in*; also in verse 15

1:1 [a]Ro 1:1; Eph 1:1; 2Ti 1:1 [b]S 2Co 1:1 [c]Ac 18:17 **1:2** [d]S 1Co 10:32 [e]S Ac 18:1 [f]Ro 1:7 [g]S Ac 2:21 **1:3** [h]S Ro 1:7 **1:4** [i]S Ro 1:8 **1:5** [j]2Co 9:11 [k]S 2Co 8:7 **1:6** [l]2Th 1:10; 1Ti 2:6; Rev 1:2 **1:7** [m]Ro 1:11; 1Co 12:1-31 [n]S Mt 16:27; S Lk 17:30; 1Th 1:10; S 2:19; Tit 2:13; Jas 5:7,8; 1Pe 1:13; 2Pe 3:12; S Rev 1:7 **1:8** [o]S 1Th 3:13 [p]Am 5:18; 1Co 5:5; Php 1:6,10; 2:16; 1Th 5:2 **1:9** [q]S Ro 8:28 [r]1Jn 1:3 [s]Dt 7:9; Isa 49:7; 1Co 10:13; 1Th 5:24; 2Th 3:3; 2Ti 2:13; Heb 10:23; 11:11 **1:10** [t]S Ro 7:1 [u]1Co 11:18 [v]S Ro 15:5 **1:11** [w]S Ac 11:14

1:12 [x]1Co 3:4,22 [y]S Ac 18:24 [z]Jn 1:42; 1Co 3:22; 9:5 **1:13** [a]S Mt 28:19 **1:14** [b]Ac 18:8 [c]S Ac 19:29 **1:16** [d]S Ac 11:14 [e]1Co 16:15 **1:17** [f]Jn 4:2; S Ac 2:38 [g]1Co 2:1,4,13 **1:18** [h]ver 21,23,25; 1Co 2:14 [i]2Co 2:15; 4:3; 2Th 2:10

1:1 *Paul.* See note on Ro 1:1. *apostle of Christ Jesus.* See notes on Mk 6:30; Heb 3:1. Paul uses this title in all his letters (except Philippians, 1,2 Thessalonians and Philemon) to establish his authority as Christ's messenger—an authority that had been challenged (see ch. 9; 2Co 11). He reinforces his authority by adding "by the will of God" (see 15:9–11; Ac 9:1–16; 13:2; 18:9–10; 22:6–21; 26:12–18). *Sosthenes.* Perhaps the synagogue ruler at Corinth who was assaulted by the Greeks (Ac 18:17). If so, he obviously became a Christian—possibly while Paul was preaching at Corinth (Ac 18:18) or during Apollos's ministry there (Ac 19:1).

1:2 *church of God.* Used only by Paul and only in Ac 20:28, here and 2Co 1:1. Its OT counterpart is the expression "assembly (or community) of the LORD" (Dt 23:1; see Nu 16:3; 20:4; 1Ch 28:8). *sanctified in Christ Jesus.* Consecrated to the service of God through Christ's saving action in their lives—as Jesus had "sanctified" himself (see Jn 17:19 and note; see also 17:17 and NIV text note). Such consecration to God's service marks them as "holy" (set apart for God; see Ex 3:5; 19:6; Ro 6:22 and notes) and requires that they be morally "holy" (see Lev 11:44 and note). *everywhere.* See note on 1Th 1:8.

1:3 *Grace and peace.* See Ro 1:7 and note. *Lord Jesus Christ.* See note on 1Th 1:1.

1:4 *thank.* See Ro 1:8 and note.

1:5 *speaking and . . . knowledge.* Gifts of the Spirit (see 12:8–10 and notes; see also 2Co 8:7).

1:6 *confirmed.* Paul's preaching about Christ had been accepted by the Corinthians, and their changed lives had proved it to be true.

1:7 *any spiritual gift.* Probably refers to the spiritual gifts of chs. 12–14. According to those chapters, a "spiritual" gift is a capability given through the Holy Spirit that enables one to minister to the needs of Christ's body, the church (see 12:7–11; 14:3,12,17). The Greek word used here stresses that it is a gift of grace.

1:8 *He.* God the Father (see v. 9). *end.* Of the age, when Christ comes again. *on the day of our Lord Jesus Christ.* When he returns (v. 7; see Php 1:6 and note).

1:9 *God . . . is faithful.* He may be trusted to do what he has promised (see 1Th 5:24 and note), namely, to keep believers "strong to the end" (v. 8; see note there).

1:10 *brothers.* See note on Ro 1:13.

1:11 *quarrels.* See Gal 5:20; 2Ti 2:23–24; Jas 4:1–2.

1:12 *Apollos.* He had carried on a fruitful ministry in Corinth (see Ac 18:24—19:1 and notes). *Cephas.* See NIV text notes here and on Jn 1:42. Those who followed Cephas in Corinth were probably Jewish Christians.

1:13 *Is Christ divided?* See 12:12–13 and notes. *baptized.* Cf. Ro 6:3–4 and note.

1:14 *Crispus.* Probably the synagogue ruler mentioned in Ac 18:8. *Gaius.* Probably the Gaius referred to in Ro 16:23.

1:16 *household.* Other examples of households being baptized are those of Cornelius (Ac 10:24,48), Lydia (Ac 16:15) and the Philippian jailer (Ac 16:33–34). The term may include family members, servants or any permanent resident in the house (cf. Ge 17:12–13,23). *household of Stephanas.* See 16:15 and note.

1:17 *not . . . to baptize.* Paul is not minimizing baptism; rather, he is asserting that his God-given task was primarily to preach. Jesus (Jn 4:2) and Peter (Ac 10:48) also had others baptize for them. *words of human wisdom.* Lit. "wisdom of speech." Paul's mission was not to couch the gospel in the language of a trained orator, who applied the special rhetorical techniques of persuasion that had been developed by the rabbis among the Jews and by the philosophers among the Greeks. *emptied of its power.* On the hearers. The heart of the gospel message would not be affected by such preaching.

us who are being saved[j] it is the power of
God.[k] 19For it is written:

> "I will destroy the wisdom of the wise;
> the intelligence of the intelligent I
> will frustrate."[a][l]

20Where is the wise man?[m] Where is the
scholar? Where is the philosopher of this
age?[n] Has not God made foolish[o] the wisdom of the world? 21For since in the wisdom
of God the world[p] through its wisdom did
not know him, God was pleased through
the foolishness of what was preached to
save[q] those who believe.[r] 22Jews demand
miraculous signs[s] and Greeks look for wisdom, 23but we preach Christ crucified:[t] a
stumbling block[u] to Jews and foolishness[v]
to Gentiles, 24but to those whom God has
called,[w] both Jews and Greeks, Christ the
power of God[x] and the wisdom of God.[y]
25For the foolishness[z] of God is wiser than
man's wisdom, and the weakness[a] of God
is stronger than man's strength.

26Brothers, think of what you were
when you were called.[b] Not many of you
were wise[c] by human standards; not many
were influential; not many were of noble
birth. 27But God chose[d] the foolish[e] things
of the world to shame the wise; God chose
the weak things of the world to shame the
strong. 28He chose the lowly things of this
world and the despised things—and the
things that are not[f]—to nullify the things
that are, 29so that no one may boast before
him.[g] 30It is because of him that you are
in Christ Jesus,[h] who has become for us
wisdom from God—that is, our righteousness,[i] holiness[j] and redemption.[k] 31There-
fore, as it is written: "Let him who boasts
boast in the Lord."[b][l]

2 When I came to you, brothers, I did
not come with eloquence or superior
wisdom[m] as I proclaimed to you the testimony about God.[c] 2For I resolved to know
nothing while I was with you except Jesus
Christ and him crucified.[n] 3I came to you[o]
in weakness[p] and fear, and with much
trembling.[q] 4My message and my preaching were not with wise and persuasive
words,[r] but with a demonstration of the
Spirit's power,[s] 5so that your faith might
not rest on men's wisdom, but on God's
power.[t]

Wisdom From the Spirit

6We do, however, speak a message of wisdom among the mature,[u] but not the wis-

1:18 [j]Ac 2:47 [k]ver 24; Ro 1:16 **1:19** [l]Isa 29:14 **1:20** [m]Isa 19:11, 12 [n]1Co 2:6, 8; 3:18; 2Co 4:4; Gal 1:4 [o]ver 27; Job 12:17; Isa 44:25; Jer 8:9; Ro 1:22; 1Co 3:18, 19 **1:21** [p]ver 27, 28; 1Co 6:2; 11:32 [q]S Ro 11:14 [r]S Ro 3:22 **1:22** [s]S Mt 12:38; S Jn 2:11; S 4:48 **1:23** [t]1Co 2:2; Gal 3:1 [u]S Lk 2:34 [v]S ver 18 **1:24** [w]S Ro 8:28 [x]ver 18; Ro 1:16 [y]ver 30; S Col 2:3 **1:25** [z]S ver 18 [a]2Co 13:4 **1:26** [b]S Ro 8:28 [c]ver 20 **1:27** [d]Jas 2:5 [e]ver 20; Ro 1:22; 1Co 3:18, 19 **1:28** [f]Ro 4:17 **1:29** [g]Eph 2:9 **1:30** [h]S Ro 16:3 [i]Jer 23:5, 6; 33:16; 2Co 5:21; Php 3:9 [j]1Co 1:2 [k]S Ro 3:24 **1:31** [l]Jer 9:23, 24; Ps 34:2; 44:8; 2Co 10:17 **2:1** [m]ver 4, 13; 1Co 1:17

[a] *19* Isaiah 29:14 [b] *31* Jer. 9:24 [c] *1* Some manuscripts *as I proclaimed to you God's mystery*

2:2 [n]Gal 6:14; 1Co 1:23 **2:3** [o]Ac 18:1-18 [p]1Co 4:10; 9:22; 2Co 11:29, 30; 12:5, 9, 10; 13:9 [q]S 2Co 7:15 **2:4** [r]ver 1 [s]S Ro 15:13 **2:5** [t]2Co 4:7; 6:7 **2:6** [u]Eph 4:13; Php 3:15; Col 4:12; Heb 5:14; 6:1; Jas 1:4

1:19 Paul loosely quotes the Septuagint (pre-Christian Greek) translation of God's word to Jerusalem in Isa 29:14, and has God speak these words again in a new context. *the wise.* Aristides said that on every street in Corinth one met a so-called wise man, who had his own solutions to humanity's problems.

1:20 *wise man.* Probably a reference to Gentile philosophers in general. *scholar.* Probably the Jewish teacher of the law (see note on Mt 2:4). *philosopher of this age.* Probably refers to the Greek sophists, who engaged in long and subtle disputes. *God made foolish the wisdom of the world.* All humanly devised philosophical and ideological systems end in meaninglessness because they have a wrong concept of God and his revelation.

1:21 *wisdom ... foolishness.* Jesus expresses a similar thought in Lk 10:21. It is God's intention that worldly wisdom should not be the means of knowing him. *foolishness of what was preached.* Not that preaching is foolish, but that the message being preached (Christ crucified) is viewed by "the world" (both Jews and Greeks) as foolish.

1:22 *Jews demand ... signs.* They want to see a display of divine power effecting their deliverance (see Mt 12:38; 16:1,4; Mk 8:11–12; Jn 2:18; 6:30). *Greeks look for wisdom.* Specifically they look for the kind of insight into the workings of the world that would relieve humanity of its woes.

1:23 *Christ crucified.* See 2:2. *stumbling block to Jews.* They expected a triumphant, political Messiah (see Ac 1:6 and note), not a crucified one. For use of the metaphor "stumbling block" in reference to the Jews see Ro 11:9; cf. Ro 9:32–33; 1Pe 2:8. *foolishness to Gentiles.* Greeks and Romans were sure that no reputable person would be crucified, so it was unthinkable that a crucified criminal could be the world's Savior.

1:24 *power.* See Ro 1:4,16. *wisdom.* See v. 30. The crucified Christ is the power and the wisdom of God that saves.

1:26–31 The Corinthian Christians were living proof that salvation does not depend on anything in themselves, so that those who are saved can only "boast in the Lord" (v. 31). Their salvation did not spring from the cleverness of human intellect or the centers of human power but from the free grace of God. Compare Paul's elaboration of this theme with the song of Hannah (1Sa 2:1–10) and the song of Mary (Lk 1:46–55).

1:30 *because of him ... you are in Christ.* It is God who has called you to union and communion with Christ. *righteousness.* It is by faith in Christ that we are justified (declared righteous); see Ro 5:19. *holiness.* See note on v. 2. *redemption.* See note on Ro 3:24.

1:31 See Jer 9:24 and note.

2:1 *When I came to you.* On his initial trip to Corinth c. A.D. 51 (Ac 18). *brothers.* See 1:10 and note. *with eloquence or superior wisdom.* See note on 1:17.

2:2 *know nothing ... except Jesus Christ.* Paul resolved to make Christ the sole subject of his teaching and preaching while he was with them. *Jesus Christ.* See 1:30. *him crucified.* See 1:17–18,23.

2:4 *not with wise and persuasive words.* This does not give preachers a license to neglect study and preparation. Paul's letters reveal a great deal of knowledge in many areas of learning, and his eloquence is apparent in his address before the Areopagus (see Ac 17:22–31 and notes). Paul's point is that unless the Holy Spirit works in a listener's heart, the wisdom and eloquence of a preacher are ineffective. Paul's confidence as a preacher did not rest on intellectual and oratorical ability, as did that of the Jewish rabbis and the Greek orators (see note on 1:17). *demonstration.* The Greek word is used of producing proofs in an argument in court. Paul's preaching was marked by the convincing demonstration of the power of the Holy Spirit.

2:6 *mature.* Wise, developed Christians; contrast the "infants" mentioned in 3:1 (see Heb 5:13—6:3).

dom of this age[v] or of the rulers of this age,
who are coming to nothing.[w] 7No, we speak
of God's secret wisdom, a wisdom[x] that has
been hidden[y] and that God destined for our
glory before time began. 8None of the rulers
of this age[z] understood it, for if they had,
they would not have crucified the Lord of
glory.[a] 9However, as it is written:

"No eye has seen,
no ear has heard,
no mind has conceived
what God has prepared for those
who love him"[a][b]—

10but God has revealed[c] it to us by his
Spirit.[d]

The Spirit searches all things, even the
deep things of God. 11For who among men
knows the thoughts of a man[e] except the
man's spirit[f] within him? In the same way
no one knows the thoughts of God except
the Spirit of God. 12We have not received
the spirit[g] of the world[h] but the Spirit who
is from God, that we may understand what
God has freely given us. 13This is what we
speak, not in words taught us by human
wisdom[i] but in words taught by the Spirit, expressing spiritual truths in spiritual
words.[b] 14The man without the Spirit does
not accept the things that come from the
Spirit of God,[j] for they are foolishness[k] to
him, and he cannot understand them, because they are spiritually discerned. 15The
spiritual[l] man makes judgments about all
things, but he himself is not subject to any
man's judgment:

16"For who has known the mind of the
Lord
that he may instruct him?"[c][m]

But we have the mind of Christ.[n]

On Divisions in the Church

3 Brothers, I could not address you as
spiritual[o] but as worldly[p]—mere infants[q] in Christ. 2I gave you milk, not solid food,[r] for you were not yet ready for
it.[s] Indeed, you are still not ready. 3You
are still worldly. For since there is jealousy and quarreling[t] among you, are you
not worldly? Are you not acting like mere
men? 4For when one says, "I follow Paul,"
and another, "I follow Apollos,"[u] are you
not mere men?

5What, after all, is Apollos?[v] And what
is Paul? Only servants,[w] through whom
you came to believe—as the Lord has
assigned to each his task. 6I planted the
seed,[x] Apollos watered it, but God made
it grow. 7So neither he who plants nor he
who waters is anything, but only God, who
makes things grow. 8The man who plants
and the man who waters have one purpose, and each will be rewarded according
to his own labor.[y] 9For we are God's fellow workers;[z] you are God's field,[a] God's
building.[b]

a 9 Isaiah 64:4 *b* 13 Or *Spirit, interpreting spiritual truths to spiritual men* *c* 16 Isaiah 40:13

2:6 [v]ver 8; S 1Co 1:20 [w]Ps 146:4 **2:7** [x]ver 1 [y]Ro 16:25 **2:8** [z]ver 6; S 1Co 1:20 [a]Ps 24:7; Ac 7:2; Jas 2:1 **2:9** [b]Isa 64:4; 65:17 **2:10** [c]S Mt 13:11; 2Co 12:1,7; Gal 1:12; 2:2; Eph 3:3,5 [d]Jn 14:26 **2:11** [e]Jer 17:9 [f]Pr 20:27 **2:12** [g]Ro 8:15 [h]1Co 1:20,27; Jas 2:5 **2:13** [i]ver 1,4; 1Co 1:17 **2:14** [j]Jn 14:17 [k]S 1Co 1:18 **2:15** [l]1Co 3:1; Gal 6:1 **2:16** [m]Isa 40:13; S Ro 11:34 [n]Jn 15:15 **3:1** [o]1Co 2:15 [p]Ro 7:14; 1Co 2:14 [q]1Co 14:20 **3:2** [r]Heb 5:12-14; 1Pe 2:2 [s]Jn 16:12 **3:3** [t]Ro 13:13; 1Co 1:11; Gal 5:20 **3:4** [u]1Co 1:12 **3:5** [v]S Ac 18:24 [w]1Co 4:1; 2Co 6:4; Eph 3:7; Col 1:23,25 **3:6** [x]Ac 18:4-11; 1Co 4:15; 9:1; 15:1 **3:8** [y]ver 14; Ps 18:20; 62:12; Mt 25:21; 1Co 9:17 **3:9** [z]Mk 16:20; 2Co 6:1; 1Th 3:2 [a]Isa 61:3 [b]Eph 2:20-22; 1Pe 2:5

2:7 *secret.* Cf. Ro 11:25; Eph 3:3; 1Ti 3:16 and notes. The secret, or mystery, was once hidden but is now known because God has revealed it to his people (v. 10). To unbelievers it is still hidden. *for our glory.* God's wisdom will cause every believer to share eventually in Christ's glory (see Ro 8:17 and note). *before time began.* See Ro 8:29–30; Eph 1:4; 2Ti 1:9 and notes; see also Jn 17:24.

2:8 *rulers of this age.* Such as the chief priests (Lk 24:20), Pilate and Herod Antipas (cf. Ac 4:27). *crucified the Lord of glory.* The cross is here contrasted with the majesty of the victim.

2:9 *what God has prepared.* Probably not to be limited to either present or future blessing; both are involved (cf. vv. 7,12).

2:10 *Spirit searches all things.* Not in order to know them, for he knows all things. Instead he comprehends the depth of God's nature and his plans of grace; so he is fully competent to make the revelation claimed here. *deep things of God.* See Ro 11:33–36 and note; cf. Rev 2:24.

2:12 *spirit of the world.* Cf. v. 6 ("wisdom of this age"); the spirit of human wisdom as alienated from God—the attitude of the sinful nature (see Ro 8:5–8 and note).

2:13 *words taught by the Spirit.* The message Paul proclaimed was expressed in words given by the Holy Spirit. Thus spiritual truth was aptly combined with Spirit-taught words (but see NIV text note).

2:14—3:4 This passage explains why many fail to apprehend true wisdom (2:9). It is because such wisdom is perceived only by the Spirit-enlightened (mature) Christian (2:14–16; cf. v. 6). The Corinthians, however, were still worldly (infant) believers (3:1–4), and the proof of their immaturity was their division over human leaders (3:3–4).

2:14 *man without the Spirit.* Described in Jude 19 as one who follows "mere natural instincts" (cf. Ro 8:9). The non-Christian is governed in thought and life by an unrenewed, worldly heart. Such persons are yet untouched by the Holy Spirit and are not equipped to receive appreciatively truth that comes from the Spirit. They need the new birth (see Jn 3:8; Tit 3:5 and notes). *foolishness.* See 1:18.

2:15 *spiritual.* Renewed by the Spirit (mature, v. 6). *not subject to any man's judgment.* One who does not have the Spirit is not qualified to judge anyone who has the Spirit. Thus believers are not rightfully subject to the opinions of unbelievers.

3:1 *Brothers.* See 1:10 and note. *spiritual.* See note on 2:15. *worldly.* See note on 2:14—3:4.

3:2 *milk, not solid food.* See Heb 5:12,14 and notes.

3:3 *like mere men.* Like people of the world instead of people of God. They were following merely human standards.

3:4 *I follow Paul ... Apollos.* See 1:12.

3:6 *I planted.* See Ac 18:4–11. Paul's work was of a pioneer nature, preaching where no one had ever preached before (see 2Co 10:13–16; Ro 15:20–21). *Apollos watered.* See Ac 18:24–28. Apollos worked in the established church, teaching and encouraging the converts Paul had won.

3:9 *God's field.* The people are God's farmland. *God's building.* They are also depicted as God's temple (vv. 16–17). Paul's choice of metaphors accords with the fact that in the ancient world planting the land and building a house (or city or temple) were traditionally the two basic focal points of human industry.

10By the grace God has given me,[c] I
laid a foundation[d] as an expert builder,
and someone else is building on it. But
each one should be careful how he builds.
11For no one can lay any foundation other
than the one already laid, which is Jesus
Christ.[e] 12If any man builds on this foundation using gold, silver, costly stones,
wood, hay or straw, 13his work will be
shown for what it is,[f] because the Day[g]
will bring it to light. It will be revealed
with fire, and the fire will test the quality of each man's work.[h] 14If what he has
built survives, he will receive his reward.[i]
15If it is burned up, he will suffer loss; he
himself will be saved, but only as one escaping through the flames.[j]
16Don't you know that you yourselves
are God's temple[k] and that God's Spirit
lives in you?[l] 17If anyone destroys God's
temple, God will destroy him; for God's
temple is sacred, and you are that temple.
18Do not deceive yourselves. If any one
of you thinks he is wise[m] by the standards
of this age,[n] he should become a "fool"
so that he may become wise. 19For the
wisdom of this world is foolishness[o] in
God's sight. As it is written: "He catches
the wise in their craftiness"[a];[p] 20and again,
"The Lord knows that the thoughts of the
wise are futile."[b][q] 21So then, no more
boasting about men![r] All things are yours,[s]
22whether Paul or Apollos[t] or Cephas[c][u] or
the world or life or death or the present or
the future[v]—all are yours, 23and you are
of Christ,[w] and Christ is of God.

Apostles of Christ

4 So then, men ought to regard us as servants[x] of Christ and as those entrusted[y]
with the secret things[z] of God. 2Now it is
required that those who have been given
a trust must prove faithful. 3I care very little if I am judged by you or by any human
court; indeed, I do not even judge myself.
4My conscience[a] is clear, but that does not
make me innocent.[b] It is the Lord who
judges me.[c] 5Therefore judge nothing[d] before the appointed time; wait till the Lord
comes.[e] He will bring to light[f] what is hidden in darkness and will expose the motives of men's hearts. At that time each
will receive his praise from God.[g]
6Now, brothers, I have applied these
things to myself and Apollos for your benefit, so that you may learn from us the
meaning of the saying, "Do not go beyond
what is written."[h] Then you will not take
pride in one man over against another.[i]
7For who makes you different from anyone
else? What do you have that you did not
receive?[j] And if you did receive it, why do
you boast as though you did not?
8Already you have all you want! Already
you have become rich![k] You have become

[a] *19* Job 5:13 [b] *20* Psalm 94:11 [c] *22* That is, Peter

3:10 [c]S Ro 12:3 [d]Ro 15:20; S Eph 2:20 **3:11** [e]Isa 28:16; Eph 2:20 **3:13** [f]1Co 4:5 [g]S 1Co 1:8; 2Th 1:7-10; 2Ti 1:12, 18; 4:8 [h]Nu 31:22, 23; Jer 23:28, 29; Mal 3:3; S 2Th 1:7 **3:14** [i]S ver 8 **3:15** [j]Jude 23 **3:16** [k]1Co 6:19; 2Co 6:16; Eph 2:21, 22; Heb 3:6 [l]S Ro 8:9 **3:18** [m]Isa 5:21; 1Co 8:2; Gal 6:3 [n]S 1Co 1:20 **3:19** [o]ver 18; Ro 1:22; 1Co 1:20, 27 [p]Job 5:13 **3:20** [q]Ps 94:11 **3:21** [r]1Co 4:6 [s]Ro 8:32 **3:22** [t]ver 5, 6 [u]S 1Co 1:12 [v]Ro 8:38 **3:23** [w]1Co 15:23; 2Co 10:7; Gal 3:29 **4:1** [x]S 1Co 3:5 [y]1Co 9:17; Tit 1:7 [z]S Ro 16:25 **4:4** [a]S Ac 23:1 [b]Ro 2:13 [c]2Co 10:18 **4:5** [d]S Mt 7:1, 2 [e]S 1Th 2:19 [f]Job 12:22; Ps 90:8; 1Co 3:13 [g]S Ro 2:29 **4:6** [h]1Co 1:19, 31; 3:19, 20 [i]1Co 1:12; 3:4 **4:7** [j]Jn 3:27; Ro 12:3, 6 **4:8** [k]Rev 3:17, 18

3:10 *I laid a foundation.* By preaching Christ and him crucified (2:2). *someone else.* Apollos—and possibly others.

3:12 *If any man builds.* Reference is to those whose position in the church is that of builders. *gold, silver, costly stones.* Precious, durable work that stands the test of divine judgment; symbolic of pure Christian doctrine and living. *wood, hay or straw.* Worthless work that will not stand the test; symbolic of someone's teaching and life that merely confuses or actually misleads believers.

3:13 Cf. 4:5; 2Co 5:10 and note. *the Day.* See 1:8 and note. *fire.* God's judgment. The work of some believers will stand the test while that of others will disappear—emphasizing the importance of teaching the pure word of God.

3:15 *loss.* Of reward (v. 14). *as one escaping through the flames.* Perhaps a Greek proverbial phrase, meaning "by a narrow escape," with one's work burned up by the fire of God's holy justice and judgment (cf. Zec 3:2 and note).

3:16 *God's temple.* The church (see Eph 2:21–22 and notes). Paul says, "You yourselves (plural) are God's temple (singular)," and the "you" of v. 17 is also plural. In 6:19 he speaks of each Christian as a temple of the Holy Spirit.

3:17 *God will destroy him.* Such a foolish laborer is not one of the Lord's true servants and suffers a worse end than the builder of v. 15. In the context of chs. 1–4 Paul here refers to people who tear the local church apart by factions and quarrels concerning their understanding of the gospel (1:11–12). *sacred.* Holy, set apart for God's use and glory (see note on 1:2); so do not desecrate the church by breaking it up into various factions.

3:18 *become a "fool."* Turn away from human wisdom (from being "wise by the standards of this age"). Cf. 1:18. *become wise.* Cf. 1:21,24 and notes.

3:21 *about men.* About being some particular builder's disciple (see 1:12 and note; 3:4; cf. 1:31; 4:6). *All things are yours.* Because of their relationship to God through Christ (v. 23), they are heirs of all things (see Ro 8:17 and note)—heirs of the ministries of all those who faithfully promote the gospel, and also of everything over which God and Christ hold sovereign rule, namely, all those things that the philosophers of this world claim to have mastered by their wisdom.

3:23 *you are of Christ.* You are united with and belong to Christ (see 1:30 and note). *Christ is of God.* Christ is in union with God the Father (see Jn 10:30 and note).

4:1 *those entrusted.* The Greek underlying this phrase means "house manager" or "steward." *secret things.* Things that human wisdom could not discover but that are now revealed by God to his people (see 2:7 and note).

4:5 *appointed time.* When God will judge believers (see 3:13 and note). *expose the motives.* Cf. 1Sa 16:7; 1Ki 8:39; 1Ch 28:9; Ps 139:23–24; Pr 16:2; 21:2; Lk 16:15; Heb 4:12–13.

4:6 *brothers.* See 1:10 and note. *these things.* See 3:5—4:5. *what is written.* The Corinthian believers should view even Paul and Apollos in light of what the OT has to say about human weakness and limitations. *pride.* One of the root causes of divisions.

4:8 Paul uses irony and sarcasm here to get the Corinthians to see how poor they really are because of their haughtiness and spiritual immaturity in comparison with apostles. *have become rich.* Cf. 1:5; 2Co 9:11. *have become kings.* They think they already participate fully in Christ's reign (see Ro 5:17 and note; 2Ti 2:12) and have no need of the apostle's ministry.

kings — and that without us! How I wish
that you really had become kings so that
we might be kings with you! 9For it seems
to me that God has put us apostles on display at the end of the procession, like men
condemned to die[l] in the arena. We have
been made a spectacle[m] to the whole universe, to angels as well as to men. 10We
are fools for Christ,[n] but you are so wise in
Christ![o] We are weak, but you are strong![p]
You are honored, we are dishonored! 11To
this very hour we go hungry and thirsty,
we are in rags, we are brutally treated,
we are homeless.[q] 12We work hard with
our own hands.[r] When we are cursed, we
bless;[s] when we are persecuted,[t] we endure it; 13when we are slandered, we answer kindly. Up to this moment we have
become the scum of the earth, the refuse[u]
of the world.

14I am not writing this to shame you,[v]
but to warn you, as my dear children.[w]
15Even though you have ten thousand
guardians in Christ, you do not have many
fathers, for in Christ Jesus I became your
father[x] through the gospel.[y] 16Therefore I
urge you to imitate me.[z] 17For this reason
I am sending to you[a] Timothy,[b] my son[c]
whom I love, who is faithful in the Lord.
He will remind you of my way of life in
Christ Jesus, which agrees with what I
teach everywhere in every church.[d]

18Some of you have become arrogant,[e]
as if I were not coming to you.[f] 19But I
will come to you very soon,[g] if the Lord is
willing,[h] and then I will find out not only
how these arrogant people are talking, but
what power they have. 20For the kingdom
of God is not a matter of[i] talk but of power.[j] 21What do you prefer? Shall I come to
you with a whip,[k] or in love and with a
gentle spirit?

Expel the Immoral Brother!

5 It is actually reported that there is sexual immorality among you, and of a
kind that does not occur even among pagans: A man has his father's wife.[l] 2And
you are proud! Shouldn't you rather have
been filled with grief[m] and have put out
of your fellowship[n] the man who did this?
3Even though I am not physically present,
I am with you in spirit.[o] And I have already passed judgment on the one who
did this, just as if I were present. 4When
you are assembled in the name of our Lord
Jesus[p] and I am with you in spirit, and the
power of our Lord Jesus is present, 5hand
this man over[q] to Satan,[r] so that the sinful
nature[a] may be destroyed and his spirit
saved on the day of the Lord.[s]

6Your boasting is not good.[t] Don't you
know that a little yeast[u] works through the

[a] 5 Or *that his body*; or *that the flesh*

4:9 [l] S Ro 8:36 [m] Ps 71:7; Heb 10:33 **4:10** [n] S 1Co 1:18; Ac 17:18; 26:24 [o] 1Co 3:18; 2Co 11:19 [p] S 1Co 2:3 **4:11** [q] Ro 8:35; 2Co 11:23-27 **4:12** [r] S Ac 18:3 [s] Ro 12:14; 1Pe 3:9 [t] S Mt 5:44 **4:13** [u] Jer 20:18; La 3:45 **4:14** [v] 1Co 6:5; 15:34; 2Th 3:14 [w] S 1Th 2:11 **4:15** [x] S ver 14 [y] 1Co 9:12, 14, 18, 23; 15:1 **4:16** [z] 1Co 11:1; Php 3:17; 4:9; 1Th 1:6; 2Th 3:7, 9 **4:17** [a] 1Co 16:10 [b] S Ac 16:1 [c] S 1Ti 1:2 [d] S 1Co 7:17 **4:18** [e] Jer 43:2 [f] ver 21 **4:19** [g] 1Co 16:5, 6; 2Co 1:15, 16 [h] S Ac 18:21 **4:20** [i] Ro 14:17 [j] S Ro 15:13 **4:21** [k] 2Co 1:23; 2:1; 13:2, 10 **5:1** [l] Lev 18:8; Dt 22:30; 27:20 **5:2** [m] 2Co 7:7-11 [n] ver 13 **5:3** [o] Col 2:5; 1Th 2:17

5:4 [p] 2Th 3:6 **5:5** [q] 1Ti 1:20 [r] S Mt 4:10 [s] S 1Co 1:8 **5:6** [t] Jas 4:16 [u] Mt 16:6, 12

4:9 *apostles.* See note on 1:1. *spectacle.* "Theater" is derived from the Greek word used here. Paul refers to the triumphal procession of a victorious Roman general with captives of war bringing up the rear — men condemned to die in the arena in mortal combat with gladiators or with ferocious beasts. He pictures all the world and even angels looking on while the apostles are brought in last to fight to the death.
4:10 More irony. *wise ... strong.* Paul uses different Greek words here from those in 1:24.
4:11 – 13 A graphic description of Paul's condition right up to the writing of this letter.
4:12 *We work hard with our own hands.* Paul was a tentmaker by trade (see Ac 18:3 and note; cf. Ac 20:34 – 35; 1Co 9:6,18). *we bless.* See Mt 5:44; Lk 6:28; Ro 12:14 and note. *endure it.* Instead of retaliating.
4:14 *my dear children.* See v. 15.
4:15 *guardians.* See Gal 3:24 and note. *your father.* Cf. 3:6,10.
4:16 *imitate me.* See 11:1 and note.
4:17 *I am sending to you Timothy.* Apparently Timothy had already begun his journey to Corinth by way of Macedonia (see 16:10 and note).
4:18 *Some of you.* Some of the Corinthians who were trying to undercut Paul's authority (see 9:1 – 3) were teaching that he was unstable (see 2Co 1:17 and note) and that his ministry was worthless (see 2Co 10:10 and note; cf. 12:11 – 12 and notes).
4:19 *arrogant.* See 5:2 and note.
4:20 *kingdom of God.* God's present reign in the lives of his people (cf. note on Mt 3:2) — that dynamic new life in Christ (see 2Co 5:17 and note), the power of the new birth (Jn 3:3 – 8), showing itself in a humble life, dedicated to Christ and his mission. *not ... of talk but of power.* Empty talk is contrasted with the genuine power of the Holy Spirit. *power.* Paul returns to the Greek word he used in 1:24.
4:21 *with a whip.* See 2Co 1:28; 2:1; 13:2,10 and notes.
5:1 *not ... even among pagans.* The Roman orator Cicero states that incest was practically unheard of in Roman society. *his father's wife.* That this expression was used rather than "his mother" suggests that the woman was his stepmother. The OT prohibited such sexual relations (see Lev 18:8; Dt 22:30 and notes).
5:2 *proud.* Evidently proud of their liberty — a distortion of grace (cf. Ro 6:1 – 2 and note on 6:1). *put out of your fellowship.* Excommunicated from the church (cf. Jn 9:22).
5:4 *assembled in the name of our Lord Jesus.* The Corinthians are to pass judgment on the man by the authority of the Lord Jesus. *the power of our Lord Jesus is present.* Jesus' power is present through his word and his Holy Spirit.
5:5 *hand this man over to Satan.* Abandon this sinful man to the devil that he may afflict him as he pleases. This abandonment to Satan was to be accomplished not by a magical incantation but by expelling the man from the church (see v. 13; see also vv. 2,7,11). To expel him was to put him out in the devil's territory, severed from any connection with God's people. *so that the sinful nature may be destroyed.* So that being officially ostracized from the church will cause the man such anguish that he will repent and forsake his wicked way. For an alternative interpretation see NIV text note. In the latter view, Satan is allowed to bring physical affliction on the man, which would bring him to repentance. *his spirit saved.* Cf. 3:15. *day of the Lord.* When Christ returns (see 1:7).
5:6 *a little yeast ... the whole batch of dough.* To illustrate Christian holiness and discipline, Paul alludes to the prohibition against the use of leaven (or yeast) in the bread

whole batch of dough?[v] 7Get rid of the old
yeast that you may be a new batch without yeast—as you really are. For Christ,
our Passover lamb, has been sacrificed.[w]
8Therefore let us keep the Festival, not
with the old yeast, the yeast of malice
and wickedness, but with bread without
yeast,[x] the bread of sincerity and truth.
9I have written you in my letter not to
associate[y] with sexually immoral people— 10not at all meaning the people of
this world[z] who are immoral, or the greedy
and swindlers, or idolaters. In that case you
would have to leave this world. 11But now I
am writing you that you must not associate
with anyone who calls himself a brother[a]
but is sexually immoral or greedy, an idolater[b] or a slanderer, a drunkard or a swindler. With such a man do not even eat.[c]
12What business is it of mine to judge
those outside[d] the church? Are you not to
judge those inside?[e] 13God will judge those
outside. "Expel the wicked man from
among you."[a f]

Lawsuits Among Believers

6 If any of you has a dispute with another, dare he take it before the ungodly for judgment instead of before the
saints?[g] 2Do you not know that the saints
will judge the world?[h] And if you are to
judge the world, are you not competent to
judge trivial cases? 3Do you not know that
we will judge angels? How much more the
things of this life! 4Therefore, if you have
disputes about such matters, appoint as
judges even men of little account in the
church![b] 5I say this to shame you.[i] Is it
possible that there is nobody among you
wise enough to judge a dispute between
believers?[j] 6But instead, one brother[k] goes
to law against another—and this in front
of unbelievers![l]
7The very fact that you have lawsuits
among you means you have been completely defeated already. Why not rather
be wronged? Why not rather be cheated?[m]
8Instead, you yourselves cheat and do
wrong, and you do this to your brothers.[n]
9Do you not know that the wicked will
not inherit the kingdom of God?[o] Do not
be deceived:[p] Neither the sexually immoral nor idolaters nor adulterers[q] nor male
prostitutes nor homosexual offenders[r]
10nor thieves nor the greedy nor drunkards

5:6 [v] Gal 5:9 **5:7** [w] Ex 12:3-6, 21; Mk 14:12; 1Pe 1:19 **5:8** [x] Ex 12:14,15; Dt 16:3 **5:9** [y] Eph 5:11; 2Th 3:6,14 **5:10** [z] 1Co 10:27 **5:11** [a] S Ro 7:1 [b] 1Co 10:7,14 [c] S Ro 16:17 **5:12** [d] S Mk 4:11 [e] ver 3-5; 1Co 6:1-4 **5:13** [f] Dt 13:5; 17:7; 19:19; 22:21,24; 24:7; Jdg 20:13
6:1 [g] Mt 18:17 **6:2** [h] Mt 19:28; Lk 22:30; 1Co 5:12 **6:5** [i] S 1Co 4:14 [j] Ac 1:15 **6:6** [k] S Ro 7:1 [l] 2Co 6:14,15; 1Ti 5:8 **6:7** [m] Mt 5:39,40 **6:8** [n] 1Th 4:6 **6:9** [o] S Mt 25:34 [p] Job 13:9; 1Co 15:33; Gal 6:7; Jas 1:16 [q] Lev 18:20; Dt 22:22 [r] Lev 18:22

[a] 13 Deut. 17:7; 19:19; 21:21; 22:21,24; 24:7
[b] 4 Or *matters, do you appoint as judges men of little account in the church?*

eaten in the Passover Feast (see Ex 12:15 and note). Leaven in Scripture usually symbolizes evil or sin (see Mk 8:15 and note), and the church here is called on to get rid of the yeast of sin (v. 8) because they are an unleavened batch of dough—new creations in Christ (see 2Co 5:17 and note).

5:7 *Get rid of the old yeast.* Perhaps refers to the Passover custom of sweeping all the (leavened) bread crumbs out of one's house before preparing the Passover meal. *without yeast—as you really are.* Already sanctified in God's sight (see 1:2 and note; 6:11), Paul calls on them to become holy in conduct. *Christ, our Passover lamb.* In his death on the cross, Christ fulfilled the true meaning of the Jewish sacrifice of the Passover lamb (cf. Jn 1:29 and note). Christ, the Lamb of God, was crucified on Passover day, a celebration that began the evening before when the Passover meal was eaten (cf. Ex 12:8).

5:8 *let us keep the Festival.* Keeping the Feast of Unleavened Bread (which followed Passover; see chart, pp. 178–179) symbolized living the Christian life in holy dedication to God and not getting involved in such sins as malice, wickedness and incestuous relations.

5:9 *I have written you in my letter.* Paul here clarifies a previous letter (one not preserved). Some in the Corinthian church mistook that letter to mean that, on separating from sin, they should disassociate themselves from all immoral persons, including non-Christian people. Instead, Paul meant that they should separate from immoral persons who were affiliated with the church (vv. 10–11).

5:10–11 See note on Ro 1:29–31.

5:11 *With such a man do not even eat.* Calling oneself a Christian while continuing to live an immoral life is reprehensible and degrading, and gives a false testimony to Christ. If the true Christian has intimate association with someone who does this, the non-Christian world may assume that the church approves such immoral, ungodly living and thus the name of Christ would be dishonored. Questions could arise concerning the true character of the Christian's own testimony (cf. Ro 16:17–18; see also 2Th 3:6,14–15 and notes).

5:12 *judge those inside.* The church is to exercise spiritual discipline over the professing believers in the church (cf. Mt 18:15–18), but it is not to attempt to judge those outside its membership. There are governing authorities in place to judge them (see Ro 13:1–5 and notes), and their ultimate judge is God (v. 13; cf. Rev 20:11–15).

6:1 *a dispute with another.* Paul seems to be talking about various kinds of civil court cases here (cf. "rather be cheated," v. 7), not criminal cases that should be handled by the state (Ro 13:3–4). *before the saints.* The Corinthians should take their civil cases before qualified Christians for settlement. In Paul's day the Romans allowed the Jews to apply their own law in such matters, and since the Romans did not yet consider Christians as a separate class from the Jews, Christians no doubt had the same rights.

6:2 *saints will judge the world.* As those who share in Christ's reign (cf. Mt 19:28; 2Ti 2:12; Rev 20:4). *competent to judge trivial cases.* Paul views believers as fully competent to judge cases where Christians have claims against each other, because they view matters from a godly vantage point. In comparison with their future role in the judgment of the world and of angels (v. 3), judgments concerning things of this life are insignificant.

6:3 *we will judge angels.* Cf. 2Pe 2:4,9; Jude 6.

6:4 *even men of little account.* See NIV text note. Either the verse suggests that the least in the church are capable of judging such small matters, or it asks ironically if believers should submit their cases to pagan judges, who really are not qualified to decide on cases between Christians.

6:7 *completely defeated already.* Most likely by greed, retaliation and hatred, instead of practicing unselfishness, forgiveness and love—even willingness to suffer loss.

6:9–10 See Ro 1:29–31 and note.

6:9 *not inherit the kingdom of God.* See Eph 5:5. *sexually immoral.* Paul here identifies three kinds of sexually immoral

nor slanderers nor swindlers[s] will inherit
the kingdom of God. 11And that is what
some of you were.[t] But you were washed,[u]
you were sanctified,[v] you were justified[w]
in the name of the Lord Jesus Christ and
by the Spirit of our God.

Sexual Immorality

12"Everything is permissible for
me"—but not everything is beneficial.[x]
"Everything is permissible for me"—but I
will not be mastered by anything. 13"Food
for the stomach and the stomach for
food"—but God will destroy them both.[y]
The body is not meant for sexual immorality, but for the Lord,[z] and the Lord for the
body. 14By his power God raised the Lord
from the dead,[a] and he will raise us also.[b]
15Do you not know that your bodies are
members of Christ himself?[c] Shall I then
take the members of Christ and unite them
with a prostitute? Never! 16Do you not
know that he who unites himself with a
prostitute is one with her in body? For it is
said, "The two will become one flesh."[a d]
17But he who unites himself with the Lord
is one with him in spirit.[e]
18Flee from sexual immorality.[f] All other
sins a man commits are outside his body,
but he who sins sexually sins against his
own body.[g] 19Do you not know that your
body is a temple[h] of the Holy Spirit, who
is in you, whom you have received from
God? You are not your own;[i] 20you were
bought at a price.[j] Therefore honor God
with your body.[k]

Marriage

7 Now for the matters you wrote about: It
is good for a man not to marry.[b l] 2But
since there is so much immorality, each
man should have his own wife, and each
woman her own husband. 3The husband
should fulfill his marital duty to his wife,[m]
and likewise the wife to her husband. 4The
wife's body does not belong to her alone

6:10 [s] 1Ti 1:10; Rev 21:8; 22:15 **6:11** [t] S Eph 2:2 [u] S Ac 22:16 [v] 1Co 1:2 [w] S Ro 4:25 **6:12** [x] 1Co 10:23 **6:13** [y] Col 2:22 [z] ver 15, 19; Ro 12:1 **6:14** [a] S Ac 2:24 [b] S Ro 6:5; Eph 1:19, 20; 1Th 4:16 **6:15** [c] S Ro 12:5 **6:16** [d] Ge 2:24; Mt 19:5; Eph 5:31 **6:17** [e] Jn 17:21-23; Ro 8:9-11; Gal 2:20 **6:18** [f] ver 9; 1Co 5:1; 2Co 12:21; Gal 5:19; Eph 5:3; 1Th 4:3, 4; Heb 13:4 [g] Ro 6:12 **6:19** [h] Jn 2:21 [i] Ro 14:7, 8 **6:20** [j] Ps 74:2; S Mt 20:28; Ac 20:28; 1Co 7:23; Rev 5:9; 14:4 [k] Php 1:20 **7:1** [l] ver 8, 26 **7:3** [m] Ex 21: 10; 1Pe 3:7

[a] *16* Gen. 2:24 [b] *1* Or *"It is good for a man not to have sexual relations with a woman."*

persons: adulterers, male prostitutes and males who practice homosexuality. In Ro 1:26 he adds the category of females who practice homosexuality. People who engage in such practices, as well as the other offenders listed in vv. 9–10, are explicitly excluded from God's kingdom (but see next note).

6:11 *some of you were. But.* God, however, does save and sanctify people like those described in vv. 9–10. *sanctified.* See 1:2 and note. *justified.* See Ro 3:24 and note.

6:12 *Everything is permissible for me.* Paul is quoting some in the Corinthian congregation who boasted that they had a right to do anything they pleased (see v. 13; 7:1; 10:23 and notes). The apostle counters by observing that such freedom of action may not benefit the Christian. *not be mastered by anything.* One may become enslaved by those actions in which one freely chooses to indulge.

6:13 *Food for the stomach and the stomach for food.* Paul quotes some Corinthians again who were claiming that as the physical acts of eating and digesting food have no bearing on one's inner spiritual life, so the physical act of promiscuous sexual activity does not affect one's spiritual life. *The body is not meant for sexual immorality, but for the Lord.* Paul here declares the dignity of the human body: It is intended for the Lord. Although granting that food and the stomach are transitory, Paul denies that what one does with one's body is unimportant. This is particularly true of the use of sex, which the Lord has appointed for use in the man-woman relationship in marriage (see 7:2–5; cf. Heb 13:4).

6:14 *God raised the Lord ... us also.* As an illustration of God's high regard for the body, Paul cites the resurrection of Christ's body and, eventually, the believer's body (see 15:51–53; 1Th 4:16–17). A body destined for resurrection should not be used for immorality.

6:15 *members of Christ.* See 12:27. It is not merely one's spirit that is a member of Christ's body; it is the whole person, consisting of spirit and body. This fact gives dignity to the human body.

6:16 *one with her in body.* In a sexual relationship the two bodies become one (cf. Ge 2:24; Mt 19:4–5), and a new human being may emerge from the sexual union. Sexual relations outside the marriage bond are a gross perversion of the divinely established marriage union.

6:17 *one with him in spirit.* There is a higher union than the marriage bond: the believer's spiritual union with Christ, which is the perfect model for the kind of unity that should mark the marriage relationship (cf. Eph 5:21–33 and notes on 5:23,32).

6:18 *Flee.* The Greek for this imperative may suggest that one must continually run away from sexual sinning (advice particularly needed in Corinth). *he who sins sexually sins against his own body.* The body is a temple of the Holy Spirit (v. 19); thus to use it in prostitution (see notes on Ge 20:9; Ex 34:15) disgraces God's temple. Furthermore, the prostitutes of Corinth were dedicated to the service of Aphrodite, the goddess of love and sex (see note on 7:2; see also Introduction: The City of Corinth).

6:19 *your body is a temple of the Holy Spirit.* It is therefore sacred and is to be treated as sacred (holy). Christians should also realize that by the Spirit's presence and power they can be helped against such sins as sexual immorality (Ro 8:9). *not your own.* Cf. 1Pe 2:9 and note.

6:20 *bought at a price.* See 7:23 and note. *honor God with your body.* Cf. 10:31; Ro 6:12–13 and notes.

7:1 *matters you wrote about.* The Corinthians had written Paul, asking him a number of vexing questions (see 8:1; 12:1; 16:1). *good for a man not to marry.* See vv. 26,28 and notes. Since elsewhere (Eph 5:22–33; Col 3:18–19; 1Ti 3:2,12; 5:14) Paul speaks approvingly of the married state and in 1Ti 4:1–3 teaches that forbidding to marry would be a sign of the end-time apostasy, the best understanding of this statement is that Paul is again (see notes on 6:12–13,18) quoting a slogan of the Corinthians (see NIV text note). He refutes this idea in v. 2 by stating that sexual relations have their proper expression in marriage.

7:2 *so much immorality.* Example: The temple to Aphrodite on the Acrocorinth, the rocky eminence above Corinth, at one time had in service 1,000 priestess prostitutes (see note on 6:18).

7:3 *fulfill ... marital duty.* Married couples should have regular sexual relations. Permanent abstention deprives the other partner of his or her natural right.

7:4 *In the same way.* Both husband and wife have conjugal rights and exclusive possession of the other in this area.

but also to her husband. In the same way,
the husband's body does not belong to
him alone but also to his wife. 5Do not deprive each other except by mutual consent
and for a time,[n] so that you may devote
yourselves to prayer. Then come together
again so that Satan[o] will not tempt you[p]
because of your lack of self-control. 6I say
this as a concession, not as a command.[q]
7I wish that all men were as I am.[r] But
each man has his own gift from God; one
has this gift, another has that.[s]
8Now to the unmarried and the widows
I say: It is good for them to stay unmarried, as I am.[t] 9But if they cannot control
themselves, they should marry,[u] for it is
better to marry than to burn with passion.
10To the married I give this command
(not I, but the Lord): A wife must not separate from her husband.[v] 11But if she does,
she must remain unmarried or else be reconciled to her husband.[w] And a husband
must not divorce his wife.
12To the rest I say this (I, not the Lord):[x]
If any brother has a wife who is not a believer and she is willing to live with him,
he must not divorce her. 13And if a woman
has a husband who is not a believer and
he is willing to live with her, she must
not divorce him. 14For the unbelieving
husband has been sanctified through his
wife, and the unbelieving wife has been
sanctified through her believing husband.
Otherwise your children would be unclean, but as it is, they are holy.[y]
15But if the unbeliever leaves, let him
do so. A believing man or woman is not
bound in such circumstances; God has
called us to live in peace.[z] 16How do you
know, wife, whether you will save[a] your
husband?[b] Or, how do you know, husband, whether you will save your wife?
17Nevertheless, each one should retain
the place in life that the Lord assigned to
him and to which God has called him.[c]
This is the rule I lay down in all the
churches.[d] 18Was a man already circumcised when he was called? He should not
become uncircumcised. Was a man uncircumcised when he was called? He should
not be circumcised.[e] 19Circumcision is
nothing and uncircumcision is nothing.[f]
Keeping God's commands is what counts.
20Each one should remain in the situation
which he was in when God called him.[g]
21Were you a slave when you were called?
Don't let it trouble you—although if you
can gain your freedom, do so. 22For he
who was a slave when he was called by
the Lord is the Lord's freedman;[h] similarly, he who was a free man when he was

7:5 [n]Ex 19:15; 1Sa 21:4,5 [o]S Mt 4:10 [p]1Th 3:5
7:6 [q]2Co 8:8
7:7 [r]ver 8; 1Co 9:5 [s]Mt 19:11,12; Ro 12:6; 1Co 12:4,11
7:8 [t]ver 1,26
7:9 [u]1Ti 5:14
7:10 [v]Mal 2:14-16; S Lk 16:18
7:11 [w]ver 39; Ro 7:2,3
7:12 [x]ver 6,10; 2Co 11:17
7:14 [y]Mal 2:15
7:15 [z]S Ro 14:19; 1Co 14:33
7:16 [a]S Ro 11:14 [b]1Pe 3:1
7:17 [c]Ro 12:3 [d]1Co 4:17; 14:33; 2Co 8:18; 11:28
7:18 [e]Ac 15:1,2
7:19 [f]Ro 2:25-27; Gal 5:6; 6:15; Col 3:11
7:20 [g]ver 24
7:22 [h]Jn 8:32,36

7:5 *Do not deprive each other.* Of sexual fulfillment. *Satan ... not tempt you because of your lack of self-control.* The Christian deprived of regular sexual activity with his or her marriage partner may be tempted by Satan to sexual immorality. The normal God-given sexual drive in the human being is strong.

7:6 *I say this.* See v. 2. *concession, not as a command.* Although marriage is desirable and according to God's plan, it is not mandatory under all circumstances (see vv. 25–38).

7:7 *as I am.* Unmarried. Paul views his celibate lifestyle as a "gift from God" that made it possible for him to accept his unmarried state and use it in the service of his Lord.

7:10 *I give this command (not I, but the Lord).* Paul is citing a command from the Lord Jesus during his earthly ministry that married couples must stay together (Mt 5:32; 19:3–9; Mk 10:2–12; Lk 16:18). Paul probably heard about such commands from other disciples (cf. Gal 1:18–19).

7:11 *But if she does, she must remain unmarried or else be reconciled.* Paul argues that in the light of Christ's command she (or he) is not to marry again. Rather, the separated or divorced couple are to be reconciled. Clearly the ideal is that marriage should not be permanently disrupted.

7:12 *I say this (I, not the Lord).* Paul is not quoting a direct command from Jesus here. *any brother has a wife ... not a believer.* The apostle is talking here (and in v. 13) about couples already married, when one of them becomes a Christian. If at all possible, they should remain together, unless the unbeliever, whether man or woman, refuses to remain (v. 15).

7:14 *sanctified through his wife ... sanctified through her believing husband.* These words of Paul are among those that are "hard to understand" (2Pe 3:16). Paul here affirms that, within the marriage relationship, unbelieving marriage partners in some sense participate with their believing spouse in the quality of being consecrated to God's service ("sanctified"; see 1:2 and note)—at least to the effect that the children born of their union are "holy" (consecrated to God's service). Some believe that such children are called holy because they are included with their parents in the new covenant in Christ, just as the children of Abraham were included in the covenant with their father (and so were circumcised).

7:15 *A believing man or woman is not bound in such circumstances.* The believer is not under obligation to try to continue living with the unbeliever. *live in peace.* If the unbeliever were forced to live with the believer, there would be no peace in the home.

7:17 *retain the place in life that the Lord assigned to him.* Christians are to live confidently for the Lord in whatever station in life God has placed them. See v. 18 for an example. No change of status that anyone brings about by their own action can advance their salvation.

7:18 *circumcised ... uncircumcised.* Jew ... Gentile. In the religious sphere, Christian Jews should not undo their circumcision, and Christian Gentiles should not yield to Jewish pressure for circumcision (cf. Ac 15:1–5; Gal 5:1–3).

7:19 See Gal 5:6 and note.

7:21 *Were you a slave ...?* In the social and economic sphere, Christian slaves should live contentedly in their situation, realizing that they have become free in Christ (v. 22; Jn 8:32,36). *if you can gain your freedom, do so.* If Christian slaves have an opportunity to get their freedom, they should take advantage of it. In the Roman empire slaves were sometimes freed by Roman patricians. There is nothing wrong with seeking to improve one's social condition, but this will have no bearing on one's standing with God.

7:22 *is the Lord's freedman.* Has been set free from bondage to sin (see Ro 6:18,22; Heb 9:15 and notes; cf. Jn 8:34,36; 1Pe 2:16) and is therefore free to serve Christ as his "slave"—just as Israel was set free from Egyptian bondage so that in freedom they could become the servant people of God (see Ex 6:6–7; 19:4–6).

called is Christ's slave.[i] 23You were bought
at a price;[j] do not become slaves of men.
24Brothers, each man, as responsible to
God, should remain in the situation God
called him to.[k]
25Now about virgins: I have no command from the Lord,[l] but I give a judgment as one who by the Lord's mercy[m]
is trustworthy. 26Because of the present
crisis, I think that it is good for you to remain as you are.[n] 27Are you married? Do
not seek a divorce. Are you unmarried? Do
not look for a wife.[o] 28But if you do marry,
you have not sinned;[p] and if a virgin marries, she has not sinned. But those who
marry will face many troubles in this life,
and I want to spare you this.
29What I mean, brothers, is that the time
is short.[q] From now on those who have
wives should live as if they had none;
30those who mourn, as if they did not;
those who are happy, as if they were not;
those who buy something, as if it were not
theirs to keep; 31those who use the things
of the world, as if not engrossed in them.
For this world in its present form is passing away.[r]
32I would like you to be free from concern. An unmarried man is concerned
about the Lord's affairs[s]—how he can
please the Lord. 33But a married man
is concerned about the affairs of this
world—how he can please his wife—
34and his interests are divided. An unmarried woman or virgin is concerned about
the Lord's affairs: Her aim is to be devoted
to the Lord in both body and spirit.[t] But
a married woman is concerned about the
affairs of this world—how she can please
her husband. 35I am saying this for your
own good, not to restrict you, but that you
may live in a right way in undivided[u] devotion to the Lord.
36If anyone thinks he is acting improperly toward the virgin he is engaged to, and
if she is getting along in years and he feels
he ought to marry, he should do as he
wants. He is not sinning.[v] They should get
married. 37But the man who has settled the
matter in his own mind, who is under no
compulsion but has control over his own
will, and who has made up his mind not
to marry the virgin—this man also does
the right thing. 38So then, he who marries
the virgin does right,[w] but he who does
not marry her does even better.[a]
39A woman is bound to her husband as
long as he lives.[x] But if her husband dies,
she is free to marry anyone she wishes,
but he must belong to the Lord.[y] 40In my
judgment,[z] she is happier if she stays as
she is—and I think that I too have the
Spirit of God.

Food Sacrificed to Idols

8 Now about food sacrificed to idols:[a] We
know that we all possess knowledge.[b][b]

[a] 36-38 Or *36If anyone thinks he is not treating his daughter properly, and if she is getting along in years, and he feels she ought to marry, he should do as he wants. He is not sinning. He should let her get married. 37But the man who has settled the matter in his own mind, who is under no compulsion but has control over his own will, and who has made up his mind to keep the virgin unmarried—this man also does the right thing. 38So then, he who gives his virgin in marriage does right, but he who does not give her in marriage does even better.* [b] 1 Or *"We all possess knowledge," as you say*

7:22 [i] S Ro 6:22
7:23 [j] S 1Co 6:20
7:24 [k] ver 20
7:25 [l] ver 6; 2Co 8:8 [m] 2Co 4:1; 1Ti 1:13, 16
7:26 [n] ver 1, 8
7:27 [o] ver 20, 21
7:28 [p] ver 36
7:29 [q] ver 31; S Ro 13:11, 12
7:31 [r] ver 29; S Heb 12:27
7:32 [s] 1Ti 5:5
7:34 [t] Lk 2:37
7:35 [u] Ps 86:11
7:36 [v] ver 28
7:38 [w] Heb 13:4
7:39 [x] Ro 7:2, 3 [y] 2Co 6:14
7:40 [z] ver 25
8:1 [a] ver 4, 7, 10; Ac 15:20 [b] Ro 15:14

7:23 *bought at a price ... not ... slaves of men.* Christians in all stations of life should realize that their ultimate allegiance is to Christ, who bought them with his blood (see 6:20; 1Pe 1:18–19 and note on 1:18).

7:25 *Now about virgins.* Paul answers another major question the Corinthians had asked (v. 1). *I give a judgment as one who ... is trustworthy.* Paul is not giving a direct command from Jesus here (as in v. 10; cf. Ac 20:35 and note). In this matter, which is not a question of right and wrong, Paul expresses his own judgment. Even though he put it this way, he is certainly not denying that he wrote under the influence of divine inspiration (see v. 40 and note). And since he writes under inspiration, what he recommends is clearly the better course of action.

7:26 *present crisis.* Probably a reference to the pressures of the Christian life in an immoral and particularly hostile environment (cf. vv. 2,28; 5:1; 2Ti 3:12). Paul's recommendation here does not apply to all times and all situations.

7:28 *many troubles.* Times of suffering and persecution for Christ, when being married would mean even greater hardship in taking care of one's family.

7:29–31 Christians already live under the foreshadowings of Christ's return, when the world in its present form will pass away. For this reason, believers should not treat present realities as having ultimate significance.

7:29 *brothers.* See note on Ro 1:13.

7:31 *this world ... is passing away.* Cf. 1Jn 2:17.

7:34 *his interests are divided.* He cannot give undistracted service to Christ (v. 35). This is particularly true in times of persecution.

7:36 *he is acting improperly toward the virgin he is engaged to ... getting along in years ... They should get married.* In the light of hostility toward believers in Corinth, a man might refrain from marrying his fiancée. But if he then realizes that his fiancée is getting beyond her prime marriageable age and the situation thus seems unfair to her, it is perfectly proper for them to get married.

7:37 *has control over his own will ... does the right thing.* The man who determines that there is no need for him to marry his fiancée under the circumstances has made a good decision too (v. 38). Paul may be referring to a man who has control of his passions, as in v. 7 (cf. v. 9).

7:39 *bound to her husband as long as he lives.* Marriage is a lifelong union (yet see the exception clause in Mt 19:9). *if her husband dies.* Death breaks the marriage bond, and a Christian is then free to marry another Christian ("he must belong to the Lord").

7:40 *as she is.* A widow. *I think that I too have the Spirit of God.* Paul writes as one convinced that he is guided by the Holy Spirit.

8:1 *Now about food.* Another matter the Corinthians had written about (see 7:1 and note). *sacrificed to idols.* Offered on pagan altars. Meat left over from a sacrifice might be eaten by the priests, eaten by the offerer and his

Knowledge puffs up, but love builds up.
2The man who thinks he knows something[c] does not yet know as he ought to
know.[d] 3But the man who loves God is
known by God.[e]

4So then, about eating food sacrificed to
idols:[f] We know that an idol is nothing at
all in the world[g] and that there is no God
but one.[h] 5For even if there are so-called
gods,[i] whether in heaven or on earth (as
indeed there are many "gods" and many
"lords"), 6yet for us there is but one God,[j]
the Father,[k] from whom all things came[l]
and for whom we live; and there is but
one Lord,[m] Jesus Christ, through whom all
things came[n] and through whom we live.

7But not everyone knows this.[o] Some
people are still so accustomed to idols
that when they eat such food they think
of it as having been sacrificed to an idol,
and since their conscience is weak,[p] it is
defiled. 8But food does not bring us near
to God;[q] we are no worse if we do not eat,
and no better if we do.

9Be careful, however, that the exercise of
your freedom does not become a stumbling
block[r] to the weak.[s] 10For if anyone with a
weak conscience sees you who have this
knowledge eating in an idol's temple, won't
he be emboldened to eat what has been
sacrificed to idols?[t] 11So this weak brother, for whom Christ died, is destroyed[u] by
your knowledge. 12When you sin against
your brothers[v] in this way and wound their
weak conscience, you sin against Christ.[w]
13Therefore, if what I eat causes my brother
to fall into sin, I will never eat meat again,
so that I will not cause him to fall.[x]

The Rights of an Apostle

9 Am I not free?[y] Am I not an apostle?[z]
Have I not seen Jesus our Lord?[a] Are
you not the result of my work in the Lord?[b]
2Even though I may not be an apostle to
others, surely I am to you! For you are the
seal[c] of my apostleship in the Lord.

3This is my defense to those who sit in
judgment on me. 4Don't we have the right
to food and drink?[d] 5Don't we have the
right to take a believing wife[e] along with
us, as do the other apostles and the Lord's
brothers[f] and Cephas[a]?[g] 6Or is it only I and
Barnabas[h] who must work for a living?

7Who serves as a soldier[i] at his own expense? Who plants a vineyard[j] and does
not eat of its grapes? Who tends a flock
and does not drink of the milk? 8Do I say
this merely from a human point of view?
Doesn't the Law say the same thing? 9For

[a] 5 That is, Peter

8:2 [c] 1Co 3:18 [d] 1Co 13:8,9,12; 1Ti 6:4 **8:3** [e] Jer 1:5; Ro 8:29; Gal 4:9 **8:4** [f] ver 1,7,10; Ex 34:15 [g] Ac 14:15; 1Co 10:19; Gal 4:8 [h] ver 6; Dt 6:4; Ps 86:10; Eph 4:6; 1Ti 2:5 **8:5** [i] 2Th 2:4 **8:6** [j] S ver 4 [k] Mal 2:10 [l] S Ro 11:36 [m] Eph 4:5 [n] S Jn 1:3 **8:7** [o] ver 1 [p] Ro 14:14; 1Co 10:28 **8:8** [q] Ro 14:17 **8:9** [r] S 2Co 6:3; Gal 5:13 [s] Ro 14:1 **8:10** [t] ver 1,4,7 **8:11** [u] Ro 14:15,20 **8:12** [v] Mt 18:6 [w] Mt 25:40,45 **8:13** [x] S Mt 5:29 **9:1** [y] ver 19 [z] S 1Co 1:1; 2Co 12:12 [a] S 1Co 15:8 [b] 1Co 3:6; 4:15 **9:2** [c] 2Co 3:2,3 **9:4** [d] ver 14; S Ac 18:3 **9:5** [e] 1Co 7:7,8 [f] S Mt 12:46 [g] S 1Co 1:12 **9:6** [h] S Ac 4:36 **9:7** [i] 2Ti 2:3,4 [j] Dt 20:6; Pr 27:18; 1Co 3:6,8

friends at a feast in the temple (see note on v. 10) or sold in the public meat market. Some Christians felt that if they ate such meat, they participated in pagan worship and thus compromised their testimony for Christ. Other Christians did not feel this way. *knowledge.* Explained in vv. 2–6. *Knowledge puffs up.* It fills one with false pride. *love builds up.* Explained in vv. 7–13.

8:2 *does not yet know.* Even the wisest and most knowledgeable among Christians have only limited knowledge. God is the only one who knows all (cf. Ro 11:33–36).

8:3 *the man who loves God is known by God.* Not their knowledge as such but their love for God is what counts; their love is a manifestation that God has accepted them and has dealt with them as among his own (see Gal 4:9). The background of Paul's assertion is very likely the OT use of Hebrew *yada'* ("to know") in such passages as Ge 18:19 ("have chosen"); 2Sa 7:20 ("to know"); Ps 1:6 ("watches over"); Am 3:2 ("have ... chosen"); Na 1:7 ("cares for").

8:4 *an idol is nothing.* It represents no real god and possesses no power (see Ps 115:4–7; 135:15–17; Isa 44:12–20). But there are demons behind them (10:20).

8:5 *so-called gods.* The gods of Greek and Roman mythology.

8:6 *one God.* See Dt 6:4 and note. *from whom all things came ... through whom all things came.* See Heb 2:10. God the Father is the ultimate source of all creation (Ac 4:24; Ro 11:36). God the Son is the dynamic one through whom, with the Father, all things came into existence (see Jn 1:3; Col 1:16 and note; Heb 1:2).

8:7 *knows this.* Knows that an idol is an empty symbol, representing no real divine being. *sacrificed to an idol.* Sacrificed to the god the idol represents. *since their conscience is weak, it is defiled.* They think that in eating meat sacrificed on pagan altars they have involved themselves in pagan worship and thus have sinned against Christ.

8:9 *your freedom.* To eat meat sacrificed to idols because you know that an idol is nothing (v. 4). *the weak.* Those Christians whose consciences are weak, who think it is wrong to eat meat sacrificed to idols.

8:10 *this knowledge.* See vv. 1,4,8. *eating in an idol's temple.* At the site of ancient Corinth, archaeologists have discovered two temples containing rooms apparently used for pagan feasts where meat offered to idols was eaten. To such feasts Christians may have been invited by pagan friends.

8:12 *wound their weak conscience.* Eating meat offered to idols when they feel it is wrong tends to blunt their consciences, so that doing what is wrong becomes much easier. The result may be moral tragedy. *you sin against Christ.* Cf. Mt 10:40; 18:5; Mk 9:37; Lk 9:48; Ro 14:15 and note; 14:19–20.

8:13 *I will never eat meat again.* Paul presents himself as an example for the church (cf. Ro 14:21).

9:1 *Am I not free?* Do I not have the rights that any Christian has? See note on v. 12. *Am I not an apostle?* Some at Corinth (2Co 12:11–12) questioned Paul's genuine apostleship. To certify his apostleship Paul gives this proof: that he has seen the Lord Jesus (Ac 9:1–9; 22:6–16; 26:12–18), as was true of the other apostles (Ac 1:21–22). Furthermore, he adds that his ministry has produced true spiritual fruit (the Corinthians) for the Lord, which should confirm to them that he is indeed an apostle.

9:4 *right to food and drink.* Paul and Barnabas, as God's workers, have a right to have their food and other physical needs supplied at the church's expense (cf. vv. 6,13–14).

9:5 *take a believing wife along with us.* Paul asserts his right to be married, if he wishes. This does not mean that he was married, as some have imagined (see 7:7 and note). Other apostles, including Peter (see Mk 1:30), had wives.

9:9 *Is it about oxen ...?* See 1Ti 5:18. In the Mosaic law that Paul quotes (Dt 25:4), God was indeed concerned about oxen

it is written in the Law of Moses: "Do not
muzzle an ox while it is treading out the
grain."[a][k] Is it about oxen that God is concerned?[l] 10Surely he says this for us, doesn't
he? Yes, this was written for us,[m] because
when the plowman plows and the thresher
threshes, they ought to do so in the hope of
sharing in the harvest.[n] 11If we have sown
spiritual seed among you, is it too much if
we reap a material harvest from you?[o] 12If
others have this right of support from you,
shouldn't we have it all the more?

But we did not use this right.[p] On the
contrary, we put up with anything rather
than hinder[q] the gospel of Christ. 13Don't
you know that those who work in the
temple get their food from the temple, and
those who serve at the altar share in what
is offered on the altar?[r] 14In the same way,
the Lord has commanded that those who
preach the gospel should receive their living from the gospel.[s]

15But I have not used any of these
rights.[t] And I am not writing this in the
hope that you will do such things for me. I
would rather die than have anyone deprive
me of this boast.[u] 16Yet when I preach the
gospel, I cannot boast, for I am compelled
to preach.[v] Woe to me if I do not preach
the gospel! 17If I preach voluntarily, I have
a reward;[w] if not voluntarily, I am simply
discharging the trust committed to me.[x]
18What then is my reward? Just this: that
in preaching the gospel I may offer it free
of charge,[y] and so not make use of my
rights[z] in preaching it.

19Though I am free[a] and belong to no
man, I make myself a slave to everyone,[b]
to win as many as possible.[c] 20To the Jews
I became like a Jew, to win the Jews.[d] To
those under the law I became like one under the law (though I myself am not under
the law),[e] so as to win those under the law.
21To those not having the law I became like
one not having the law[f] (though I am not
free from God's law but am under Christ's
law),[g] so as to win those not having the
law. 22To the weak I became weak, to win
the weak.[h] I have become all things to all
men[i] so that by all possible means I might
save some.[j] 23I do all this for the sake of the
gospel, that I may share in its blessings.

24Do you not know that in a race all the
runners run, but only one gets the prize?[k]
Run[l] in such a way as to get the prize.
25Everyone who competes in the games
goes into strict training. They do it to get a
crown[m] that will not last; but we do it to get
a crown that will last forever.[n] 26Therefore
I do not run like a man running aimlessly;[o]
I do not fight like a man beating the air.[p]
27No, I beat my body[q] and make it my slave
so that after I have preached to others, I myself will not be disqualified for the prize.[r]

a 9 Deut. 25:4

9:9 [k] Dt 25:4; 1Ti 5:18 [l] Dt 22:1-4; Pr 12:10 **9:10** [m] S Ro 4:23,24 [n] Pr 11:25; 2Ti 2:6 **9:11** [o] ver 14; Ro 15:27; Gal 6:6 **9:12** [p] ver 15,18; S Ac 18:3 [q] 2Co 6:3; 11:7-12 **9:13** [r] Lev 6:16,26; Dt 18:1 **9:14** [s] S 1Ti 5:18 **9:15** [t] ver 12,18; S Ac 18:3 [u] 2Co 11:9,10 **9:16** [v] Ro 1:14; Ac 9:15; 26:16-18 **9:17** [w] 1Co 3:8,14 [x] 1Co 4:1; Gal 2:7; Col 1:25

9:18 [y] 2Co 11:7; 12:13 [z] ver 12,15 **9:19** [a] ver 1 [b] 2Co 4:5; Gal 5:13 [c] Mt 18:15; 1Pe 3:1 **9:20** [d] Ac 16:3; 21:20-26; Ro 11:14 [e] S Ro 2:12 **9:21** [f] Ro 2:12,14 [g] Gal 6:2 **9:22** [h] S Ro 14:1; S 1Co 2:3 [i] 1Co 10:33 [j] S Ro 11:14 **9:24** [k] Php 3:14; Col 2:18 [l] ver 25,26; Gal 2:2; 5:7; Php 2:16; 2Ti 4:7; Heb 12:1

9:25 [m] 2Ti 2:5 [n] 2Ti 4:8; Jas 1:12; 1Pe 5:4; Rev 2:10; 3:11 **9:26** [o] S ver 24 [p] 1Ti 6:12 **9:27** [q] Ro 8:13 [r] ver 24

that labored for their owners (cf. Jnh 4:11 and note). But this law was also illustrative of a basic principle of justice that God was teaching Israel and "us" (v. 10), a principle with greater moral weight when persons are involved than when draft animals are involved.

9:11 *material harvest.* Food, lodging and pay supplied by the Corinthians (cf. Gal 6:6). Paul here sets forth the principle that those who serve the church should be supported by the church (cf. Php 4:14–19).

9:12 *did not use this right.* The point of Paul's discussion in ch. 9. He had numerous rights that he did not claim because of his love for the Corinthians. Thus ch. 9 is an extended personal illustration of the practice advocated in ch. 8. Because of love for others, believers should be ready to surrender their rights (see Ro 14:15 and note).

9:13 *those who work in the temple.* The Corinthian believers would understand this illustration not only from their knowledge of the OT (cf. Lev 7:28–36; Nu 18:8–20) but also from the practice in pagan temples in Greece and Rome.

9:15 *this boast.* That he had preached the gospel without charge, so that they could not say that they had paid him for it.

9:16 *I am compelled to preach.* The Lord had laid on Paul the necessity of preaching the gospel (Ac 9:1–16; 26:16–18; see also Jer 20:9 and note). *Woe to me.* Cf. v. 27 and note.

9:18 *my reward ... in preaching the gospel.* Paul's reward in preaching is not material things but the boasting that he has preached to the Corinthians without charge and has not taken advantage of the rights he deserves: food and drink, shelter and pay (vv. 3–12).

9:19 *I make myself a slave to everyone.* Not only did Paul not use his right to material support in preaching the gospel but he also deprived himself—curtailed his personal privileges and social and religious rights—in dealing with different kinds of people. *to win.* To bring to Christ.

9:20 *those under the law.* Those under the OT law and religious practices (the Jews). *I became like one under the law.* For the Jews' sake Paul conformed to the Jewish law (see Ac 16:3; 18:18 and notes; 21:20–26 and notes on 21:23–24).

9:21 *those not having the law.* Those who had not been raised under the OT law (the Gentiles). *I became like one not having the law.* Paul accommodated himself to Gentile culture when it did not violate his allegiance to Christ, though he still reckoned that he was under God's law and Christ's law. (By "Christ's law" Paul is probably referring to Christ's teachings, though the term is not necessarily restricted to them.)

9:22 *the weak.* Those whose consciences are weak (8:9–12). *I became weak.* Paul did not exercise his Christian freedom in such things as eating meat sacrificed to idols (8:9,13).

9:23 *share in its blessings.* Paul's hope concerning the manner of his own participation in the future glory of believers is linked with the faithfulness with which he carried out the apostolic mission Christ gave him (cf. v. 27 and note; see 2Co 3:1–3; 5:10; Php 2:16; 1Th 2:19–20 and notes).

9:24 *race ... runners.* The Corinthians were familiar with the foot races in their own Isthmian games, which occurred every other year and were second only to the Olympic games in importance. *prize.* In ancient times the prize was a perishable wreath (v. 25).

9:25 *crown that will last forever.* See 1Pe 5:4 and note; cf. 1Th 2:19 and note.

9:26 *not ... running aimlessly.* See Php 3:14 and note.

9:27 *I beat my body and make it my slave.* Here Paul uses the figure of boxing to represent the Christian life. He

Warnings From Israel's History

10 For I do not want you to be ignorant[s] of the fact, brothers, that our forefathers were all under the cloud[t] and that they all passed through the sea.[u] 2They were all baptized into[v] Moses in the cloud and in the sea. 3They all ate the same spiritual food[w] 4and drank the same spiritual drink; for they drank from the spiritual rock[x] that accompanied them, and that rock was Christ. 5Nevertheless, God was not pleased with most of them; their bodies were scattered over the desert.[y]

6Now these things occurred as examples[a][z] to keep us from setting our hearts on evil things as they did. 7Do not be idolaters,[a] as some of them were; as it is written: "The people sat down to eat and drink and got up to indulge in pagan revelry."[b][b] 8We should not commit sexual immorality, as some of them did—and in one day twenty-three thousand of them died.[c] 9We should not test the Lord,[d] as some of them did—and were killed by snakes.[e] 10And do not grumble, as some of them did[f]—and were killed[g] by the destroying angel.[h]

11These things happened to them as examples[i] and were written down as warnings for us,[j] on whom the fulfillment of the ages has come.[k] 12So, if you think you are standing firm,[l] be careful that you don't fall! 13No temptation has seized you except what is common to man. And God is faithful;[m] he will not let you be tempted beyond what you can bear.[n] But when you are tempted, he will also provide a way out so that you can stand up under it.

Idol Feasts and the Lord's Supper

14Therefore, my dear friends,[o] flee from idolatry.[p] 15I speak to sensible people; judge for yourselves what I say. 16Is not the cup of thanksgiving for which we give thanks a participation in the blood of Christ? And

10:1 [s]S Ro 11:25 [t]Ex 13:21; Ps 105:39 [u]Ex 14:22,29; Ps 66:6 **10:2** [v]Ro 6:3 **10:3** [w]S Jn 6:31 **10:4** [x]Ex 17:6; Nu 20:11; Ps 78:15; 105:41 **10:5** [y]Nu 14:29; Heb 3:17; Jude 5 **10:6** [z]ver 11 **10:7** [a]ver 14 [b]Ex 32:4,6,19 **10:8** [c]Nu 25:1-9 **10:9** [d]Ex 17:2; Ps 78:18; 95:9; 106:14 [e]Nu 21:5,6 **10:10** [f]Nu 16:41; 17:5, 10 [g]Nu 16:49 [h]Ex 12:23; 1Ch 21:15; Heb 11:28 **10:11** [i]ver 6 [j]S Ro 4:24 [k]S Ro 13:11 **10:12** [l]Ro 11:20; 2Co 1:24 **10:13** [m]S 1Co 1:9 [n]2Pe 2:9 **10:14** [o]Heb 6:9; 1Pe 2:11; 1Jn 2:7; Jude 3 [p]ver 7; 1Jn 5:21

[a] 6 Or *types*; also in verse 11 [b] 7 Exodus 32:6

does not aimlessly beat the air, but he severely disciplines his own body in serving Christ. *not be disqualified for the prize.* Paul realizes that he must with rigor serve the Lord and battle against sin. If he fails in this, he may be excluded from the reward (see 3:10–15).

10:1 *the cloud ... the sea.* These two watery entities had played a central role in God's deliverance of Israel out of Egypt through his servant Moses (the cloud signifying God's guidance [see Ex 13:21; 40:36–37; Nu 9:17,21; 10:11–12; 14:14; Ne 9:12,19; Ps 78:14] and the sea signifying God's climactic act of deliverance in which he brought his people safely through the sea but brought judgment on the Egyptians [see Ex 14:1—15:20; Dt 11:4; Jos 2:10; Ne 9:9,11; Ps 66:6; 77:16,19; 78:13,53; 106:9–11; 136:13–15; Isa 43:16–17; 51:10; 63:11–13]). The Israelites' journey guided by the cloud and their safe passage through the sea under the ministry of Moses united them with God's servant Moses in the working out of God's redemptive program (see v. 2 and note).

10:2 *baptized.* Figurative language Paul used to depict Israel's union with Moses in God's redemptive program is analogous in important ways to the Christian's union with Christ in his death and resurrection as signified by Christian baptism (see Ro 6:3–4 and note).

10:3–4 *spiritual food ... spiritual drink.* The manna and the water from the rock (Ex 16:2–36; 17:1–7; Nu 20:2–11; 21:16) are used as figures representing the spiritual sustenance that God continually provides for his people—as signified in the Lord's Supper.

10:4 *that rock was Christ.* The rock, from which the water came, and the manna are here viewed by Paul as symbolic of the spiritual sustenance God's people experienced already in the desert through Christ, the bread of life and the water of life (see Jn 4:14; 6:30–35 and notes). For Christ's presence with God's people already in the desert cf. 8:6 and note.

10:5 *God was not pleased with most of them.* In spite of the remarkable privileges given to Israel (vv. 1–4), they failed to obey God, thus incurring his displeasure. Of the adults who came out of Egypt, only Caleb and Joshua were allowed to enter Canaan (Nu 14:22–24,28–35; Dt 1:34–36; Jos 1:1–2; 14:6–14).

10:6 *as they did.* What Paul has in mind is described in vv. 7–10.

10:7 *idolaters.* Referring to the incident of the golden calf (Ex 32:1–6). The people ate a ritual meal sacrificed to an idol (cf. ch. 8).

10:8 Refers to Israel's participation in the worship of the Baal of Peor and the sexual practices associated with that worship (see Nu 25:1–9). *twenty-three thousand.* The Hebrew and Greek (Septuagint) texts of Nu 25:9 have 24,000. It is clear that Paul is not striving for exactness. He is only speaking approximately. First-century writers were not as concerned about being precise as 21st-century authors often are.

10:10 *do not grumble.* As in Nu 16:41. *destroying angel.* Paul links the angel who brought the plague of Nu 16:41–50—because of the grumbling of the Israelites against Moses and Aaron (Nu 16:41)—with the destroying angel of Ex 12:23.

10:11 *written down as warnings.* See Ro 15:4 and note. *fulfillment of the ages.* The period of time inaugurated by Christ's death and resurrection and continuing into the future until Christ's second coming and beyond. It is the period of fulfillment when all that God has been doing for his people throughout all previous ages comes to its fruition in the Messiah.

10:13 *temptation.* Temptation in itself is not sin. Jesus was tempted (Mt 4:1–11). Yielding to the temptation is sin. The Greek for "temptation" and "tempted" can also mean "testing" and "tested," so Paul may have been speaking of "testing" with its accompanying temptation (see Mt 6:13 and note). *stand up under it.* Through God's enablement to resist the temptation to sin or to endure the trial without falling.

10:14 *flee from idolatry.* Like that described in Ex 32:1–6. Corinthian Christians had come out of a background of paganism. Temples for the worship of Apollo, Asclepius, Demeter, Aphrodite and other pagan gods and goddesses were seen daily by the Corinthians as they engaged in the activities of everyday life. The worship of Aphrodite was a particularly strong temptation (see note on 6:18).

10:16 *cup of thanksgiving.* The cup of wine that Christians drink during the celebration of the Lord's Supper (see Mt 26:27–28; Mk 14:23–24 and note; Lk 22:20). Drinking the wine of the Lord's Supper as an act of faith is a claim of personal participation in the benefits of Christ's shed blood. *bread that we break.* The loaf of bread that is broken and eaten during the Lord's Supper (see Mt 26:26; Mk 14:22 and note; Lk

is not the bread that we break[q] a participation in the body of Christ?[r] 17Because there
is one loaf, we, who are many, are one
body,[s] for we all partake of the one loaf.
18Consider the people of Israel: Do not
those who eat the sacrifices[t] participate in
the altar? 19Do I mean then that a sacrifice
offered to an idol is anything, or that an
idol is anything?[u] 20No, but the sacrifices
of pagans are offered to demons,[v] not to
God, and I do not want you to be participants with demons. 21You cannot drink the
cup of the Lord and the cup of demons
too; you cannot have a part in both the
Lord's table and the table of demons.[w]
22Are we trying to arouse the Lord's jealousy?[x] Are we stronger than he?[y]

The Believer's Freedom

23"Everything is permissible" — but not
everything is beneficial.[z] "Everything is
permissible" — but not everything is constructive. 24Nobody should seek his own
good, but the good of others.[a]
25Eat anything sold in the meat market
without raising questions of conscience,[b]
26for, "The earth is the Lord's, and everything in it."[a c]
27If some unbeliever invites you to a
meal and you want to go, eat whatever is
put before you[d] without raising questions
of conscience. 28But if anyone says to you,
"This has been offered in sacrifice," then
do not eat it, both for the sake of the man
who told you and for conscience' sake[b e] —
29the other man's conscience, I mean, not
yours. For why should my freedom[f] be
judged by another's conscience? 30If I take
part in the meal with thankfulness, why
am I denounced because of something I
thank God for?[g]
31So whether you eat or drink or whatever you do, do it all for the glory of God.[h]
32Do not cause anyone to stumble,[i] whether Jews, Greeks or the church of God[j] —
33even as I try to please everybody in every
way.[k] For I am not seeking my own good
but the good of many,[l] so that they may
11 be saved.[m] 1Follow my example,[n] as I
follow the example of Christ.[o]

Propriety in Worship

2I praise you[p] for remembering me in
everything[q] and for holding to the teachings,[c] just as I passed them on to you.[r]
3Now I want you to realize that the head
of every man is Christ,[s] and the head of

10:16 [q] S Mt 14:19 [r] Mt 26:26-28; 1Co 11:23-25 **10:17** [s] S Ro 12:5 **10:18** [t] Lev 7:6,14,15 **10:19** [u] S 1Co 8:4 **10:20** [v] Lev 17:7; Dt 32:17; Ps 106:37; Rev 9:20 **10:21** [w] 2Co 6:15,16 **10:22** [x] Dt 32:16,21; 1Ki 14:22; Ps 78:58; Jer 44:8 [y] Ecc 6:10; Isa 45:9 **10:23** [z] 1Co 6:12 **10:24** [a] ver 33; S Ro 15:1,2; 1Co 13:5; Php 2:4,21 **10:25** [b] S Ac 10:15; 1Co 8:7 **10:26** [c] Ps 24:1; Ex 9:29; 19:5; Job 41:11; Ps 50:12; 1Ti 4:4 **10:27** [d] Lk 10:7 **10:28** [e] 1Co 8:7,10-12 **10:29** [f] 1Co 9:1,19 **10:30** [g] S Ro 14:6 **10:31** [h] Zec 14:21; Col 3:17; 1Pe 4:11

[a] *26* Psalm 24:1 [b] *28* Some manuscripts *conscience' sake, for "the earth is the Lord's and everything in it"*
[c] *2* Or *traditions*

10:32 [i] S Mt 5:29; Ac 24:16; S 2Co 6:3 [j] Ac 20:28; 1Co 1:2; 11:16,22; 15:9; 1Ti 3:5,15 **10:33** [k] Ro 15:2; 1Co 9:22 [l] S ver 24 [m] S Ro 11:14 **11:1** [n] S 1Co 4:16 [o] Ro 15:3; 1Pe 2:21 **11:2** [p] ver 17,22 [q] 1Co 4:17 [r] ver 23; 1Co 15:2,3; 2Th 2:15; 3:6 **11:3** [s] S Eph 1:22

22:19 and note). *participation in the body of Christ.* The sense is similar to Paul's statement concerning participation in the blood of Christ.

10:17 *one loaf.* The act of many believers partaking of one loaf of bread symbolizes the unity of the body of Christ, the church, which is nourished by the one bread of life (cf. Jn 6:33 – 58).

10:18 *those who eat the sacrifices participate in the altar.* When the people of Israel ate part of the sacrifice made at the altar (Lev 7:15; 8:31; Dt 12:17 – 18), they participated with the altar in consuming the sacrifices, and what was consumed on the altar (with fire) was Yahweh's portion.

10:19 *Do I mean ... that an idol is anything?* See 8:4 – 6 and notes.

10:20 *offered to demons.* In reality, demons (not gods) were the objects of idol worship. God's people are warned that if they do eat meat sacrificed to idols, they should not eat it with pagans in their temple feasts, for to do so is to become "participants with demons."

10:22 *arouse the Lord's jealousy.* By sharing in pagan idolatry and worship (cf. Ex 20:5 and note).

10:23 *not everything is constructive.* See 6:12 and note. Personal freedom and desire for one's rights are not the only considerations. One must also consider "the good of others" (v. 24; cf. 8:1; Gal 6:2).

10:25 *Eat anything sold in the meat market.* Even if it has been sacrificed to an idol, because out in the public market it has lost its pagan religious significance.

10:26 A quotation from Ps 24:1 used at Jewish mealtimes as a blessing (cf. Ps 50:12; 89:11).

10:27 *eat whatever is put before you.* Whether or not it might be meat sacrificed to idols, ask no questions. As long as the subject has not been brought up, you are free to eat the meat.

10:28 *for the sake of the man who told you.* If the meat has been identified as meat sacrificed to idols and you eat it, the informant might think you condone or even are willing to participate in the worship of idols. *for conscience' sake.* So as not to cause someone else (v. 29) to think it is all right to eat meat sacrificed to idols even though they have doubts about it.

10:29 *my freedom.* Cf. Ro 14:16 and note. The exercise of one's personal freedom is to be governed by whether it will bring glory to God, whether it will build up the church of God and whether it will encourage the unsaved to receive Christ as Savior and Lord (vv. 31 – 33).

10:30 *something I thank God for.* Paul could thank God for meat sacrificed to idols, for the idol is nothing and the meat is a part of God's created world.

10:31 *all for the glory of God.* The all-inclusive principle that governs the discussion in chs. 8 – 10 is that God should be glorified in everything the Christian does (see note on Ro 16:27).

10:32 *Do not cause anyone to stumble.* Living to glorify God will result in doing what is beneficial for others, whether Christians ("the church of God") or non-Christians ("Jews, Greeks").

10:33 *please everybody in every way.* Paul will do nothing that might hinder someone else from receiving the salvation proclaimed in his gospel. *that they may be saved.* See 9:22.

11:1 Notice the order: (1) Christ is the supreme example (cf. 1Pe 2:21); (2) Christ's apostle follows his example ("as I follow"); (3) we are to follow the apostle's example.

11:3 – 16 The subject of this section is propriety in public worship. Clearly Paul is concerned that the proper relationship between husbands and wives be reflected in public worship; however, much remains uncertain. As in the previous section, he desires that all be done to the glory of God (10:31).

11:3 Some understand the term "head" to refer primarily to

the woman is man,[t] and the head of Christ
is God.[u] [4]Every man who prays or prophesies[v] with his head covered dishonors his
head. [5]And every woman who prays or
prophesies[w] with her head uncovered dishonors her head—it is just as though her
head were shaved.[x] [6]If a woman does not
cover her head, she should have her hair
cut off; and if it is a disgrace for a woman to have her hair cut or shaved off, she
should cover her head. [7]A man ought not
to cover his head,[a] since he is the image[y]
and glory of God; but the woman is the
glory of man. [8]For man did not come from
woman, but woman from man;[z] [9]neither
was man created for woman, but woman
for man.[a] [10]For this reason, and because
of the angels, the woman ought to have a
sign of authority on her head.

[11]In the Lord, however, woman is not
independent of man, nor is man independent of woman. [12]For as woman came
from man, so also man is born of woman.
But everything comes from God.[b] [13]Judge
for yourselves: Is it proper for a woman to pray to God with her head uncovered? [14]Does not the very nature of things
teach you that if a man has long hair, it
is a disgrace to him, [15]but that if a woman has long hair, it is her glory? For long
hair is given to her as a covering. [16]If anyone wants to be contentious about this,
we have no other practice—nor do the
churches of God.[c]

11:3 [t]Ge 3:16; Eph 5:23 [u]1Co 3:23 **11:4** [v]S Ac 11:27 **11:5** [w]S Ac 21:9 [x]Dt 21:12 **11:7** [y]Ge 1:26; 5:1; 9:6; Jas 3:9 **11:8** [z]Ge 2:21-23; 1Ti 2:13 **11:9** [a]Ge 2:18 **11:12** [b]S Ro 11:36 **11:16** [c]S 1Co 7:17; S 10:32 **11:17** [d]ver 2, 22 **11:18** [e]1Co 1:10-12; 3:3 **11:19** [f]1Jn 2:19 **11:21** [g]2Pe 2:13; Jude 12

The Lord's Supper

11:23-25pp — Mt 26:26-28; Mk 14:22-24; Lk 22:17-20

[17]In the following directives I have no
praise for you,[d] for your meetings do
more harm than good. [18]In the first place,
I hear that when you come together as a
church, there are divisions[e] among you,
and to some extent I believe it. [19]No doubt
there have to be differences among you to
show which of you have God's approval.[f]
[20]When you come together, it is not the
Lord's Supper you eat, [21]for as you eat,
each of you goes ahead without waiting
for anybody else.[g] One remains hungry,

[a] 4-7 Or *[4]Every man who prays or prophesies with long hair dishonors his head. [5]And every woman who prays or prophesies with no covering ⌞of hair⌟ on her head dishonors her head—she is just like one of the "shorn women." [6]If a woman has no covering, let her be for now with short hair, but since it is a disgrace for a woman to have her hair shorn or shaved, she should grow it again. [7]A man ought not to have long hair*

the concept of honor, in that one's physical head is the seat of one's honor (cf. vv. 4–5). Thus as Christ honored God, each man is to honor Christ, and each woman is to honor her husband. Others see in the word "head" the idea of authority (which would also include the concept of honor). They point out that Paul clearly uses the term in the sense of authority in Eph 1:21–22 ("under his feet"; "head over everything"), in Eph 5:22–23 (where headship is seen in a context of submission) and in Col 1:18; 2:10. Thus as Christ has authority over "every man" and is therefore to be honored by them, so the husband holds a position of authority and is therefore to be honored by his wife. See note on 15:28.

11:4 The first use of "head" in this verse refers to a man's physical head; the second refers to his spiritual Head (Christ)—or perhaps is intended in a double sense. In the culture of Paul's day, men uncovered their heads in worship to signify their respect for and submission to deity. When a man prayed or prophesied with his head covered, he failed to show the proper attitude toward Christ. *prophesies.* See 12:10 and note.

11:5–6 Paul's message to women was: Show respect for and submission to your husband by covering your head during public worship. Some do not see in these verses a temporary cultural significance to the covering/uncovering of the head. They insist that, since Paul referred to the order of creation (vv. 7–9), his directive is not to be restricted to his time. Thus women of all times should wear a head covering.

Others find a lasting principle in the passage requiring wives, in all ways, to show respect for their husbands by submitting to their authority—not merely by a particular style of attire, but by godly lives. The man, who was created first, is to have authority over his wife (see 1Ti 2:12–14 and notes). The wife was made out of his body (Ge 2:21–24) to be his helper and companion (Ge 2:20). She is to honor her husband by submitting to him as her head (see v. 3).

Still others see these verses, not as a mandate for all marriages, but as reflecting marriage relationships at that time in Corinth and therefore giving a reason why the women there should have covered their heads (v. 10). They point to vv. 11–12 as a contrast, emphasizing equality and mutual dependence between men and women who are "in the Lord" (v. 11; see Gal 3:28; 1Pe 3:7).

11:10 Paul's meaning here is obscure. *angels.* Perhaps mentioned here because they are interested in all aspects of the Christian's salvation and are sensitive to decorum in worship (cf. Eph 3:10 and note). But see next entry ("sign of authority"). *sign of authority.* Understood by some to refer to the woman's authority as co-ruler with man in the creation (Ge 1:26–27). Others take the phrase to refer to the man's authority as properly recognized by the woman in her head covering. Yet others would render the phrase "have authority over her own head." And still others understand Paul as viewing the woman's head covering as a symbol of protection against the influence of fallen angels.

11:13–14 *proper ... the very nature of things.* Believers must be conscious of how their actions appear in their culture, in light of what is considered to be honorable behavior.

11:16 In worship services, Paul and the churches in general followed the common custom of the men wearing short hair and the women long hair. Paul was basing his remarks, particularly in vv. 13–16, on common custom in the churches.

11:17 *no praise.* Contrast v. 2.

11:18 *divisions.* Paul had already dealt with one aspect of these divisions (1:10–17).

11:19 *God's approval.* As deplorable as factions may be, they serve one good purpose: They distinguish those who are faithful and true in God's sight.

11:20 *not the Lord's Supper you eat.* Their intention was to eat the Lord's Supper, but it was profaned by their gluttony and discrimination.

11:21 *remains hungry ... gets drunk.* The early church held the *agape* ("love") feast in connection with the Lord's Supper (cf. 2Pe 2:13 and note; Jude 12). Perhaps the meal was something like a present-day potluck dinner. In good Greek style they brought food for all to share, the rich bringing more and the poor less, but because of their cliques the rich ate much and the poor were left hungry.

another gets drunk. 22 Don't you have
homes to eat and drink in? Or do you despise the church of God[h] and humiliate
those who have nothing?[i] What shall I say
to you? Shall I praise you[j] for this? Certainly not!
23 For I received from the Lord[k] what I
also passed on to you:[l] The Lord Jesus,
on the night he was betrayed, took bread,
24 and when he had given thanks, he broke
it and said, "This is my body,[m] which is
for you; do this in remembrance of me."
25 In the same way, after supper he took
the cup, saying, "This cup is the new covenant[n] in my blood;[o] do this, whenever
you drink it, in remembrance of me." 26 For
whenever you eat this bread and drink
this cup, you proclaim the Lord's death
until he comes.[p]
27 Therefore, whoever eats the bread or
drinks the cup of the Lord in an unworthy
manner will be guilty of sinning against
the body and blood of the Lord.[q] 28 A man
ought to examine himself[r] before he eats
of the bread and drinks of the cup. 29 For
anyone who eats and drinks without recognizing the body of the Lord eats and drinks
judgment on himself. 30 That is why many
among you are weak and sick, and a number of you have fallen asleep.[s] 31 But if we
judged ourselves, we would not come under judgment.[t] 32 When we are judged by the
Lord, we are being disciplined[u] so that we
will not be condemned with the world.[v]
33 So then, my brothers, when you
come together to eat, wait for each other.
34 If anyone is hungry,[w] he should eat at
home,[x] so that when you meet together it
may not result in judgment.
And when I come[y] I will give further
directions.

Spiritual Gifts

12 Now about spiritual gifts,[z] brothers,
I do not want you to be ignorant.[a]
2 You know that when you were pagans,[b]
somehow or other you were influenced
and led astray to mute idols.[c] 3 Therefore
I tell you that no one who is speaking by
the Spirit of God says, "Jesus be cursed,"[d]
and no one can say, "Jesus is Lord,"[e] except by the Holy Spirit.[f]
4 There are different kinds of gifts,
but the same Spirit.[g] 5 There are different kinds of service, but the same Lord.

11:22 [h]S 1Co 10:32 [i]Jas 2:6 [j]ver 2, 17 **11:23** [k]Gal 1:12 [l]S ver 2 **11:24** [m]1Co 10:16 **11:25** [n]S Lk 22:20 [o]1Co 10:16 **11:26** [p]S 1Co 1:7 **11:27** [q]Heb 10:29 **11:28** [r]2Co 13:5 **11:30** [s]S Mt 9:24 **11:31** [t]Ps 32:5; 1Jn 1:9 **11:32** [u]Ps 94:12; 118:18; Pr 3:11, 12; Heb 12:7-10; Rev 3:19 [v]Jn 15:18, 19 **11:34** [w]ver 21 [x]ver 22 [y]S 1Co 4:19 **12:1** [z]Ro 1:11; 1Co 1:7; 14:1, 37 [a]S Ro 11:25 **12:2** [b]S Eph 2:2 [c]Ps 115:5; Jer 10:5; Hab 2:18, 19 **12:3** [d]Ro 9:3; 1Co 16:22 [e]S Jn 13:13 [f]1Jn 4:2, 3 **12:4** [g]ver 8-11; Ro 12:4-8; Eph 4:11; Heb 2:4

11:22 *Shall I praise you for this?* See v. 17.

11:23–26 Observe the similarity of Paul's words here with Mt 26:26–29; Mk 14:22–25; and especially Lk 22:17–20.

11:23 *I received from the Lord.* Paul does not necessarily mean that he received the message about the Lord's Supper directly from Christ. The information probably was passed on to him by others who had heard it from Jesus (see 15:3 and note; cf. 7:10 and note).

11:24 *had given thanks.* The Jewish practice at meals. This makes it a true Eucharist ("thanksgiving"). *my body.* The broken bread is a symbol of Christ's body "given" for sinners (Lk 22:19; see note there). *in remembrance of me.* As the Feast of Passover was a commemorative meal (see Ex 12:14), so also the Lord's Supper is a memorial supper, recalling and portraying Christ's death for sinners.

11:25 *after supper.* After the Passover supper. The Lord's Supper was first celebrated by Jesus in connection with the Passover meal (cf. Mt 26:18–30 and parallels in Mark and Luke). *cup.* A symbol of the new covenant in Jesus' blood (see Mk 14:24 and note; Lk 22:20; cf. Jer 31:31–34). (The old covenant was the Mosaic or Sinaitic covenant; see Ex 24:3–8 and notes on 24:6,8.) By the use of this covenant sign God signifies his bestowal of salvation upon his people, sealed and paid for by the shedding of Jesus' blood.

11:26 *whenever you eat ... and drink.* The Lord's Supper should be held periodically, but there is no explicit instruction as to how often. *you proclaim the Lord's death.* The Lord's Supper is never celebrated apart from a proclamation of "Christ crucified" (1:23; cf. 2:2). *until he comes.* Cf. Mt 26:29 and note.

11:27 *in an unworthy manner.* In the unloving and self-centered manner that characterized some of the Corinthians at their unruly *agape* supper (vv. 20–22; see note on v. 21).

11:28 *examine himself.* Everyone should test the attitude of their own heart and actions and their awareness of the significance of the Supper, thus making the Supper, under God, a spiritual means of grace.

11:29 *without recognizing the body of the Lord.* The word "body" may refer to either the Lord's physical body or the church as the body of Christ (see 12:13,27 and notes). The first view means that the person partakes of the Lord's Supper without recognizing that it symbolizes Christ's crucified body. But in that case, why is the blood not mentioned? The second view means that the participant is not aware of the nature of the church as the body of Christ, resulting in the self-centered actions of vv. 20–21. *judgment.* Not God's eternal judgment, which is to come on the unbeliever, but such disciplinary judgment as physical sickness and death (v. 30).

11:30 *have fallen asleep.* See Jn 11:11 and note.

11:32 *disciplined.* As God's redeemed children we are disciplined—just as parents discipline their children (see Heb 12:5–11 and notes).

11:33 *come together to eat.* Another reference to the *agape* fellowship meal (see note on v. 21). Each person was to exercise restraint and wait to eat with the others. Those who are too hungry should satisfy their hunger at home and not bring selfish and discriminatory practices into the church (v. 34).

12:1 *Now about.* Suggests Paul is answering another question raised by the Corinthians in their letter (cf. 7:1; 8:1; 16:1). *spiritual gifts.* See 1:7 and note.

12:2 *led astray to mute idols.* At one time the Corinthians had been led by various influences to worship mute idols (see 8:4–6 and notes), but now they are to be led by the Holy Spirit.

12:3 *"Jesus be cursed" ... "Jesus is Lord."* Those who are regenerated by the Holy Spirit cannot pronounce a curse on Jesus; rather, they are the only ones who can confess from the heart, "Jesus is Lord" (cf. Jn 20:28; 1Jn 4:2–3). The Greek word for "Lord" here is used in the pre-Christian Greek translation of the OT (the Septuagint) to translate the Hebrew name *Yahweh* ("the LORD"). See note on Ro 10:9.

12:4–6 *same Spirit ... same Lord ... same God.* These verses, reflecting the Trinity, show the diversity and unity of spiritual gifts.

12:4 *gifts.* Gifts of grace produced by the indwelling Holy Spirit. See note on v. 1.

12:5 *service.* The Greek word in its various forms is used to indicate service to the Christian community, such as serving

6There are different kinds of working, but
the same God[h] works all of them in all
men.[i]
7Now to each one the manifestation of
the Spirit is given for the common good.[j]
8To one there is given through the Spirit the message of wisdom,[k] to another
the message of knowledge[l] by means of
the same Spirit, 9to another faith[m] by the
same Spirit, to another gifts of healing[n]
by that one Spirit, 10to another miraculous powers,[o] to another prophecy,[p] to
another distinguishing between spirits,[q]
to another speaking in different kinds of
tongues,[a r] and to still another the interpretation of tongues.[a] 11All these are the
work of one and the same Spirit,[s] and he
gives them to each one, just as he determines.

One Body, Many Parts

12The body is a unit, though it is made
up of many parts; and though all its parts
are many, they form one body.[t] So it is
with Christ.[u] 13For we were all baptized[v]
by[b] one Spirit[w] into one body—whether
Jews or Greeks, slave or free[x]—and we
were all given the one Spirit to drink.[y]
14Now the body is not made up of one
part but of many.[z] 15If the foot should
say, "Because I am not a hand, I do not
belong to the body," it would not for
that reason cease to be part of the body.
16And if the ear should say, "Because I
am not an eye, I do not belong to the
body," it would not for that reason cease
to be part of the body. 17If the whole
body were an eye, where would the
sense of hearing be? If the whole body
were an ear, where would the sense of
smell be? 18But in fact God has arranged[a]
the parts in the body, every one of them,
just as he wanted them to be.[b] 19If they
were all one part, where would the body
be? 20As it is, there are many parts, but
one body.[c]
21The eye cannot say to the hand, "I
don't need you!" And the head cannot say

[a] *10* Or *languages*; also in verse 28 [b] *13* Or *with*; or *in*

12:6 [h] Eph 4:6 [i] S Php 2:13 **12:7** [j] 1Co 14:12; Eph 4:12 **12:8** [k] 1Co 2:6 [l] S 2Co 8:7 **12:9** [m] Mt 17:19,20; 1Co 13:2 [n] ver 28,30; Mt 10:1 **12:10** [o] ver 28-30; Gal 3:5 [p] S Eph 4:11 [q] 1Jn 4:1 [r] S Mk 16:17 **12:11** [s] S ver 4 **12:12** [t] S Ro 12:5 [u] ver 27 **12:13** [v] S Mk 1:8 [w] Eph 2:18 [x] Gal 3:28; Col 3:11 [y] Jn 7:37-39 **12:14** [z] ver 12,20 **12:18** [a] ver 28 [b] ver 11 **12:20** [c] ver 12,14; S Ro 12:5

tables (Ac 6:2–3); it is also the word used in the early church for the office of deacon (Php 1:1).

12:6 *working.* The Greek word indicates power in operation that produces obvious results.

12:7 *to each one the manifestation ... given for the common good.* Every member of the body of Christ has been given some spiritual gift that is an evidence of the Spirit's working in their lives. All the gifts are intended to build up the members of the Christian community (see 1Pe 4:10–11). They are not to be used for selfish advantage, as some in the Corinthian community apparently were doing.

12:8 *To one ... to another.* Not everyone has the same gift or all the gifts. *message of wisdom ... knowledge.* Gifts that meet the need of the Christian community when knowledge or wisdom is required to make decisions or to choose proper courses of action.

12:9 *faith.* Not saving faith, which all Christians have, but faith to meet a specific need within the body of Christ. *gifts of healing.* Lit. "gifts of healings." The double plural may suggest different kinds of illnesses and the various ways God heals them.

12:10 *miraculous powers.* Lit. "deeds of power." In Scripture, miracles are events that in the eyes of those who experienced and/or witnessed them clearly evidenced God's power purposefully at work in a way beyond the usual or the expected. *prophecy.* A message imparted to a believer by the Holy Spirit. It may be a prediction (cf. Agabus, Ac 11:28 [see note there]; 21:10–11) or an indication of the will of God in a given situation (cf. 14:1–5,29–30 and notes; Ac 13:1–2 and note on 13:1). *distinguishing between spirits.* Since there can also be false prophecies that come from evil spirits, this gift is necessary in order for the church to distinguish the true from the false (cf. 1Jn 4:1–6). *different kinds of tongues.* Since the Greek word for "tongues" is elsewhere used to refer to "languages" or "dialects," some understand it to refer here to the ability to speak in human languages not learned by other means, as the apostles did on the day of Pentecost (see Ac 2:4,6,11 and notes; cf. also 1Co 14:9–10). Others believe that in chs. 12–14 the term "tongues" refers to both earthly and heavenly languages, including ecstatic languages of praise and prayer (see 13:1; 14:2,10 and notes). *interpretation of tongues.* The ability to make intelligible the sense of what is spoken in a tongue so that hearers can understand and be edified (cf. 14:5,13,27–28).

12:11 *as he determines.* The Holy Spirit sovereignly determines which gift or gifts each believer should have.

12:12 *a unit ... many parts.* This example illustrates the unity and diversity of the different spiritual gifts exercised by God's people, who are all members of the one body of Christ. *with Christ.* With Christ's body, the church, of which he is the head (Eph 1:22–23; cf. Ro 12:4–8 and notes).

12:13 Cf. Ro 6:3–4 and note. *all baptized by one Spirit into one body.* Regenerated by the Holy Spirit (Jn 3:3,5) and united with Christ as part of his body. *Jews or Greeks.* In Christ there is no ethnic or cultural distinction (see Gal 3:28 and note). *slave or free.* No social distinction. *all given the one Spirit to drink.* God has given all his people the Holy Spirit to indwell them (6:19) so that their lives may overflow with the fruit of the Spirit (Gal 5:22–23; cf. Jn 7:37–39).

12:14–20 Addressed mainly to those who feel that their gifts are inferior and unimportant. Apparently the more spectacular gifts (such as tongues) had been glorified in the Corinthian church, making those who did not have them feel inferior.

12:14 See Ro 12:4–8. As the human body must have diversity to work effectively as a whole, so the members of Christ's body have diverse gifts, the use of which can help bring about the accomplishment of Christ's united purpose.

12:18 Paul stresses the sovereign purpose of God in diversifying the parts of the body; by implication he is saying that God has arranged that different Christians in the body of Christ exercise different spiritual gifts, not the same gift. And this diversity is intended to accomplish God's unified purpose. God's method employs diversity to create unity.

12:21–26 Addressed mainly to those who feel that their gifts are superior and most important (see note on vv. 14–20). These verses provide another indication that some gifts, like tongues, had been magnified as being preeminent.

12:21 The principle here is the interdependence of the parts of the body in the one whole. Christians in the body of Christ are mutually dependent as they exercise their distinctive functions.

to the feet, "I don't need you!" 22On the
contrary, those parts of the body that seem
to be weaker are indispensable, 23and the
parts that we think are less honorable we
treat with special honor. And the parts
that are unpresentable are treated with
special modesty, 24while our presentable
parts need no special treatment. But God
has combined the members of the body
and has given greater honor to the parts
that lacked it, 25so that there should be
no division in the body, but that its parts
should have equal concern for each other. 26If one part suffers, every part suffers
with it; if one part is honored, every part
rejoices with it.

27Now you are the body of Christ,[d] and
each one of you is a part of it.[e] 28And in
the church[f] God has appointed first of all
apostles,[g] second prophets,[h] third teachers, then workers of miracles, also those
having gifts of healing,[i] those able to help
others, those with gifts of administration,[j]
and those speaking in different kinds of
tongues.[k] 29Are all apostles? Are all prophets? Are all teachers? Do all work miracles?
30Do all have gifts of healing? Do all speak
in tongues[a]?[l] Do all interpret? 31But eagerly desire[b][m] the greater gifts.

Love

And now I will show you the most excellent way.

13 If I speak in the tongues[c][n] of men
and of angels, but have not love, I
am only a resounding gong or a clanging
cymbal. 2If I have the gift of prophecy[o] and
can fathom all mysteries[p] and all knowledge,[q] and if I have a faith[r] that can move
mountains,[s] but have not love, I am nothing. 3If I give all I possess to the poor[t] and
surrender my body to the flames,[d][u] but
have not love, I gain nothing.

4Love is patient,[v] love is kind. It does not
envy, it does not boast, it is not proud.[w]
5It is not rude, it is not self-seeking,[x] it is
not easily angered,[y] it keeps no record of
wrongs.[z] 6Love does not delight in evil[a]
but rejoices with the truth.[b] 7It always protects, always trusts, always hopes, always
perseveres.[c]

12:27 [d]Eph 1:23; 4:12; Col 1:18,24 [e]S Ro 12:5 **12:28** [f]S 1Co 10:32 [g]S Eph 4:11 [h]S Eph 4:11 [i]ver 9 [j]Ro 12:6-8 [k]ver 10; S Mk 16:17 **12:30** [l]ver 10 **12:31** [m]1Co 14:1,39 **13:1** [n]ver 8; S Mk 16:17 **13:2** [o]ver 8; S Eph 4:11; S Ac 11:27 [p]1Co 14:2 [q]S 2Co 8:7 [r]1Co 12:9 [s]Mt 17:20; 21:21 **13:3** [t]Lk 19:8; S Ac 2:45 [u]Da 3:28 **13:4** [v]1Th 5:14 [w]1Co 5:2 **13:5** [x]S 1Co 10:24 [y]S Mt 5:22 [z]Job 14:16,17; Pr 10:12; 17:9; 1Pe 4:8 **13:6** [a]2Th 2:12 [b]2Jn 4; 3Jn 3,4 **13:7** [c]ver 8,13

[a] 30 Or *other languages* [b] 31 Or *But you are eagerly desiring* [c] 1 Or *languages* [d] 3 Some early manuscripts *body that I may boast*

12:22 *weaker are indispensable.* Christians who seem to have less important functions in the body of Christ are actually indispensable.

12:23 Christians should give "special honor" and support to those in the church who have ordinary gifts.

12:24 Persons with more spectacular gifts do not need to be given special honor.

12:25 *no division.* See 1:10–12.

12:26 *every part suffers.* In the body of Christ if one Christian suffers, all the Christians are affected (cf. Ac 12:1–5—the martyrdom of James and the imprisonment of Peter).

12:27 *you are the body of Christ.* Addressed to the local church at Corinth. Each local church is the body of Christ just as the universal church is Christ's body.

12:28 The list here differs somewhat from that in vv. 8–10 (see notes there). Paul notes three of the gifts of Eph 4:11 (see note there), then five of the spiritual gifts listed in vv. 8–10. The apostles and prophets were part of the foundation of the church (see Mt 16:18; Eph 2:20 and notes), and teaching was associated with the pastoral office (see Eph 4:11 and note; 1Ti 3:2). These three gifts are listed as "first," "second" and "third," indicating their importance in the church. The rest of the list is introduced with "then," indicating the variety that follows. Paul's lists of spiritual gifts seem to be largely random samples. Apart from v. 28a he does not rank them in importance since he has already insisted that all gifts are important (vv. 21–26). *apostles.* Those chosen by Christ during his earthly ministry to be with him and to go out and preach (Mk 3:14). They were also to be witnesses of the resurrection (Ac 1:21–22). The term was occasionally used in a broader sense (see Mk 6:30; Ac 14:4 and notes). *miracles... healing... tongues.* See notes on vv. 9–10. *to help others.* Any act of helping others may be the product of a spiritual gift (see Ro 12:6–8 and notes), though the primary reference here is probably to a ministry to the poor, needy, sick and distressed (cf. Ac 6:1–6). *administration.* Those with gifts of administration were enabled by the Holy Spirit to organize and project plans and spiritual programs in the church.

12:29–30 *Are all apostles...?* Christians have different gifts, and no one gift should be expected by everyone.

12:31 *eagerly desire the greater gifts.* See 14:1–5 and notes. If the alternative translation (see NIV text note) is correct, the Corinthians were apparently seeking status through the exercise of the gifts that seemed to them to be more important. *the most excellent way.* Paul now shows the right way to exercise all spiritual gifts—the way of love. He does not identify love as a gift; rather, it is a fruit of the Spirit (Gal 5:22).

13:1–3 *tongues... prophecy... faith... give.* Paul selects four gifts as examples. He declares that even their most spectacular manifestations mean nothing unless motivated by love.

13:1 *tongues of men and of angels.* Paul uses hyperbole. Even if he could speak not only the various languages that human beings speak but even the languages used by angels—if he did not speak in love, it would be nothing but noise. *love.* The Greek for this word indicates a selfless concern for the welfare of others. It is like Christ's love manifested on the cross (cf. Jn 3:16; 13:34–35; Eph 5:25; 1Jn 3:16).

13:2 *all mysteries and all knowledge.* Again Paul uses hyperbole to express the amount of understanding possessed. Even if he is gifted with unlimited knowledge—if he does not possess and exercise that knowledge in love, he is nothing. *faith that can move mountains.* A special capacity to trust God to remove or overcome overwhelming threats or insurmountable obstacles (cf. Zec 4:7; Mt 17:20 and notes). Again Paul uses hyperbole.

13:3 *surrender my body to the flames.* A reference to suffering martyrdom through burning at the stake, as many early Christians experienced. Even the supreme sacrifice, if not motivated by love, accomplishes nothing.

13:4–7 Love is now described both positively and negatively.

13:4 *not proud.* See 8:1 and note.

13:5 *not rude.* Perhaps an indirect reference to their unruly conduct in worship (11:18–22).

13:6 *does not delight in evil.* As they were doing in ch. 5.

8 Love never fails. But where there are
prophecies,[d] they will cease; where there
are tongues,[e] they will be stilled; where
there is knowledge, it will pass away. 9 For
we know in part[f] and we prophesy in part,
10 but when perfection comes,[g] the imperfect disappears. 11 When I was a child, I
talked like a child, I thought like a child,
I reasoned like a child. When I became
a man, I put childish ways[h] behind me.
12 Now we see but a poor reflection as in
a mirror;[i] then we shall see face to face.[j]
Now I know in part; then I shall know fully, even as I am fully known.[k]
13 And now these three remain: faith,
hope and love.[l] But the greatest of these
is love.[m]

Gifts of Prophecy and Tongues

14 Follow the way of love[n] and eagerly
desire[o] spiritual gifts,[p] especially the
gift of prophecy.[q] 2 For anyone who speaks
in a tongue[a r] does not speak to men but
to God. Indeed, no one understands him;[s]
he utters mysteries[t] with his spirit.[b] 3 But
everyone who prophesies speaks to men
for their strengthening,[u] encouragement[v]
and comfort. 4 He who speaks in a tongue[w]
edifies[x] himself, but he who prophesies[y]
edifies the church. 5 I would like every one
of you to speak in tongues,[c] but I would
rather have you prophesy.[z] He who prophesies is greater than one who speaks in
tongues,[c] unless he interprets, so that the
church may be edified.[a]
6 Now, brothers, if I come to you and
speak in tongues, what good will I be to
you, unless I bring you some revelation[b]
or knowledge[c] or prophecy or word of
instruction?[d] 7 Even in the case of lifeless
things that make sounds, such as the flute
or harp, how will anyone know what tune
is being played unless there is a distinction
in the notes? 8 Again, if the trumpet does
not sound a clear call, who will get ready
for battle?[e] 9 So it is with you. Unless you
speak intelligible words with your tongue,
how will anyone know what you are saying? You will just be speaking into the air.
10 Undoubtedly there are all sorts of languages in the world, yet none of them is

13:8 [d] ver 2 [e] ver 1 **13:9** [f] ver 12; S 1Co 8:2 **13:10** [g] Php 3:12 **13:11** [h] Ps 131:2 **13:12** [i] Job 26:14; 36:26 [j] Ge 32:30; Job 19:26; 1Jn 3:2 [k] 1Co 8:3; Gal 4:9 **13:13** [l] Ro 5:2-5; Gal 5:5,6; Eph 4:2-5; Col 1:4,5; 1Th 1:3; 5:8; Heb 6:10-12 [m] Mt 22:37-40; 1Co 16:14; Gal 5:6; 1Jn 4:7-12,16 **14:1** [n] 1Co 16:14 [o] ver 39; 1Co 12:31 [p] S 1Co 12:1 [q] ver 39; S Eph 4:11 **14:2** [r] S Mk 16:17 [s] ver 6-11,16 [t] 1Co 13:2 **14:3** [u] ver 4,5, 12,17,26; S Ro 14:19 [v] ver 31 **14:4** [w] S Mk 16:17 [x] S ver 3 [y] S 1Co 13:2 **14:5** [z] Nu 11:29 [a] S ver 3 **14:6** [b] ver 26; Eph 1:17 [c] S 2Co 8:7 [d] Ro 6:17 **14:8** [e] Nu 10:9; Jer 4:19

[a] 2 Or *another language*; also in verses 4, 13, 14, 19, 26 and 27 [b] 2 Or *by the Spirit* [c] 5 Or *other languages*; also in verses 6, 18, 22, 23 and 39

13:8 *never fails.* Never comes to an end, is never replaced by anything else (see v. 13 and note). *prophecies ... will cease; ... tongues ... will be stilled; ... knowledge ... will pass away.* These three will cease because they are limited in nature (v. 9) and will be unnecessary when what is complete has come (v. 10).

13:10 *perfection.* The Greek for this word can mean "end," "fulfillment," "completeness" or "maturity." In this context the contrast is between the partial and the complete. Verse 12 seems to indicate that Paul is here speaking of Christ's second coming.

13:12 *we see but a poor reflection as in a mirror.* The imagery is of a polished metal (probably bronze) mirror in which one could receive only an imperfect reflection (cf. Jas 1:23)—in contrast to seeing the Lord directly and clearly in the new creation. *know fully ... fully known.* The Christian will know the Lord to the fullest extent possible for a finite being, similar to the way the Lord knows the Christian fully and infinitely. This will not be true until the Lord returns.

13:13 *remain.* Now and forever. *faith, hope and love.* See 1Th 1:3 and note. *the greatest of these is love.* Because God is love (1Jn 4:8) and has communicated his love to us (1Jn 4:10) and commands us to love one another (Jn 13:34–35; cf. Ro 13:10; 1Co 8:1; Gal 5:6; Eph 4:16; 5:20; Php 1:9; Col 3:14; 1Pe 4:8). Love supersedes the gifts because it outlasts them all. Long after these sought-after gifts are no longer necessary, love will still be the governing principle that controls all that God and his redeemed people are and do.

14:1–5 The basic principle Paul insists on is that whatever is done in the church must contribute to the edification (building up) of the body. This is in keeping with the declaration in 12:7 that gifts are "given for the common good." It also is in agreement with the principle of love (ch. 13). What is spoken in the church, then, must be intelligible—it must be spoken in the vernacular language or at least be interpreted in the vernacular. Prophecy is therefore more desirable than tongues (unless an interpreter is present) because prophecy is spoken in the native language of the listeners.

14:1 *way of love ... spiritual gifts.* Love is the means by which spiritual gifts are made effective. *gift of prophecy.* See note on 12:10.

14:2 *tongue.* See NIV text note. The hearers cannot understand what those who speak in a tongue are saying. Therefore what they say is a mystery unless it is interpreted. Only God understands it. *with his spirit.* It is not spoken from one's mind (see vv. 14–17).

14:3 In prophesying the speaker can edify and encourage others (see 12:7 and note).

14:4 *edifies himself.* It is a personal edification in the area of the emotions, of deepening conviction, of fuller commitment and greater love.

14:5 *like ... you to speak in tongues.* Paul was not opposed to tongues-speaking if it was practiced properly. *He who prophesies is greater.* Because those who prophesy serve the common good more effectively since what they say can be understood and thus edifies the church. *unless he interprets.* If tongues-speakers also have the gift of interpretation, their speaking is as beneficial as prophecy, for then it can be understood (see v. 13).

14:6 *what good will I be ...?* It would be useless to speak in tongues unless, by interpretation, one brings the church something understandable and edifying.

14:7 *flute or harp.* Instruments that were well known in Greece. *distinction in the notes.* For a person to recognize the tune and to understand and appreciate it, there must be a variety of notes so arranged as to create a meaningful tune. One note repeated monotonously cannot accomplish this.

14:8 *trumpet ... ready for battle.* All Greeks would be acquainted with the use of the trumpet for battle signals (cf. Homer's *Iliad,* 18.219), and the Jews would be familiar with the use of the ram's horn (Nu 10:9; Jos 6:4,9). Again, the notes sounded must convey a message.

14:9 *speak intelligible words.* Speak in the vernacular language of the listeners rather than in a tongue (or else provide an interpretation).

14:10 *all sorts of languages.* Some see vv. 10–11 as an indica-

without meaning. 11 If then I do not grasp
the meaning of what someone is saying, I
am a foreigner to the speaker, and he is a
foreigner to me.[f] 12 So it is with you. Since
you are eager to have spiritual gifts,[g] try to
excel in gifts that build up[h] the church.

13 For this reason anyone who speaks
in a tongue should pray that he may interpret what he says.[i] 14 For if I pray in a
tongue, my spirit prays,[j] but my mind is
unfruitful. 15 So what shall I do? I will pray
with my spirit,[k] but I will also pray with
my mind; I will sing[l] with my spirit, but I
will also sing with my mind. 16 If you are
praising God with your spirit, how can
one who finds himself among those who
do not understand[a] say "Amen"[m] to your
thanksgiving,[n] since he does not know
what you are saying? 17 You may be giving
thanks well enough, but the other man is
not edified.[o]

18 I thank God that I speak in tongues
more than all of you. 19 But in the church I
would rather speak five intelligible words
to instruct others than ten thousand words
in a tongue.[p]

20 Brothers, stop thinking like children.[q]
In regard to evil be infants,[r] but in your
thinking be adults. 21 In the Law[s] it is written:

"Through men of strange tongues
and through the lips of foreigners
I will speak to this people,
but even then they will not listen
to me,"[b][t]
says the Lord.

22 Tongues, then, are a sign, not for believers but for unbelievers; prophecy,[u]
however, is for believers, not for unbelievers. 23 So if the whole church comes together and everyone speaks in tongues, and
some who do not understand[c] or some
unbelievers come in, will they not say that
you are out of your mind?[v] 24 But if an unbeliever or someone who does not understand[d] comes in while everybody is prophesying, he will be convinced by all that he
is a sinner and will be judged by all, 25 and
the secrets[w] of his heart will be laid bare.
So he will fall down and worship God, ex-
claiming, "God is really among you!"[x]

Orderly Worship

26 What then shall we say, brothers?[y]
When you come together, everyone[z] has a
hymn,[a] or a word of instruction,[b] a revelation, a tongue[c] or an interpretation.[d] All
of these must be done for the strengthening[e] of the church. 27 If anyone speaks in
a tongue, two—or at the most three—
should speak, one at a time, and someone

14:11 [f] Ge 11:7
14:12 [g] S 1Co 12:1 [h] S ver 3
14:13 [i] ver 5
14:14 [j] ver 2
14:15 [k] ver 2,14 [l] S Eph 5:19
14:16 [m] Dt 27:15-26; 1Ch 16:36; Ne 8:6; Ps 106:48; Rev 5:14; 7:12 [n] S Mt 14:19; 1Co 11:24
14:17 [o] S ver 3
14:19 [p] ver 6
14:20 [q] 1Co 3:11; Eph 4:14; Heb 5:12,13; 1Pe 2:2 [r] Jer 4:22; Mt 10:16; Ro 16:19
14:21 [s] ver 34; S Jn 10:34 [t] Dt 28:49; Isa 28:11,12
14:22 [u] ver 1
14:23 [v] Ac 2:13
14:25 [w] Ro 2:16 [x] Isa 45:14; Zec 8:23
14:26 [y] S Ro 7:1 [z] 1Co 12:7-10 [a] S Eph 5:19 [b] ver 6 [c] ver 2 [d] 1Co 12:10 [e] S Ro 14:19

[a] *16* Or *among the inquirers* [b] *21* Isaiah 28:11,12 [c] *23* Or *some inquirers* [d] *24* Or *or some inquirer*

tion that the tongues of chs. 12–14 were languages otherwise unknown to the speakers.

14:12 *excel in gifts that build up the church.* The basic principle of ch. 14.

14:14 *mind is unfruitful.* When a person speaks in tongues or prays in tongues, the human mind does not produce the language.

14:15–17 *pray ... sing ... praising God ... say "Amen" ... thanksgiving.* Elements employed in OT (1Ch 16:36; Ne 5:13; 8:6; Ps 104:33; 136:1; 148:1) and NT worship (Ro 11:36; Eph 5:18–20). "Amen," meaning "It is true" or "So be it," is the believer's confession of agreement with the words spoken (see Ro 1:25 and note). Thus it is important that a message in tongues be interpreted.

14:15 *pray with my spirit ... with my mind ... sing with my spirit ... with my mind.* May mean that Paul will sometimes pray or sing with his spirit in a tongue; at other times he will pray or sing with his mind in his own language. Others believe that Paul was declaring his intention to pray or sing with both mind and spirit at the same time.

14:19 *But in the church.* Some believe that an interpretation is unnecessary when the gift of tongues is being used as a private prayer language. They base such a distinction on v. 18 (see v. 14) when compared with the phrase "in the church."

14:20 *In regard to evil be infants.* Just as in the case of infants, have no evil desires or wrong motives in wanting to excel in spiritual gifts (such as speaking in tongues) as an end in itself.

14:21–22 The passage from Isa 28 (see NIV text note) indicates that the foreign language of the Assyrians was a sign to unbelieving Israel that judgment was coming on them. Paul deduced from this fact that tongues were intended to be a sign of judgment for unbelievers (cf. v. 22 and note), as, e.g., in Ac 2:4–12. Similarly, prophecy was for the benefit of believers (v. 22) since it communicated revealed truth to those disposed to receive it (cf. Mt 13:11–16).

14:21 *the Law.* See Jn 10:34; 12:34 and note; 15:25; Ro 3:19 and note.

14:22 *Tongues ... a sign, not for believers.* Because they do not need a sign of God's judgment as unbelievers do.

14:23 *some who do not understand.* Perhaps those who had become "inquirers" (see NIV text note) concerning the gospel but as yet did not really understand. *some unbelievers.* Those who have made no movement toward saving faith. The context is a meeting of the church in which everyone is speaking in tongues with the result that general confusion reigns. *out of your mind.* The visitors will be repulsed by the confusion, and the phenomenon meant to be an impressive sign will have a negative effect on the unsaved.

14:24 *everybody is prophesying.* Prophecy, spoken in the vernacular language and intended for believers, turns out to have a positive effect on unbelievers because they hear and understand and are convicted of their sins. (Yet see restrictions on prophesying in vv. 29–32 and notes there.)

14:26–27 *everyone ... anyone ... someone.* The stress here is again on the diversity and yet complementary nature of spiritual gifts. It is also apparent that every member could participate in worship, not just certain leaders or officers.

14:26 *a hymn, or a word of instruction, a revelation, a tongue or an interpretation.* Elements that made up the worship service at Corinth (see note on vv. 15–17). Some of these elements (the hymn and the word of instruction) came from OT and synagogue worship (see Lk 4:16–22). All parts of Christian worship should be edifying ("strengthening") to the church.

14:27–28 Three restrictions are placed on speaking in a tongue "in the church" (v. 28): (1) Only two or three should do so in a meeting. (2) They should do so one at a time. (3) There must be interpretation.

must interpret. 28If there is no interpreter, the speaker should keep quiet in the
church and speak to himself and God.
29Two or three prophets[f] should speak,
and the others should weigh carefully
what is said.[g] 30And if a revelation comes
to someone who is sitting down, the first
speaker should stop. 31For you can all
prophesy in turn so that everyone may be
instructed and encouraged. 32The spirits
of prophets are subject to the control of
prophets.[h] 33For God is not a God of disorder[i] but of peace.[j]
As in all the congregations[k] of the
saints,[l] 34women should remain silent in
the churches. They are not allowed to
speak,[m] but must be in submission,[n] as the
Law[o] says. 35If they want to inquire about
something, they should ask their own husbands at home; for it is disgraceful for a
woman to speak in the church.
36Did the word of God[p] originate with
you? Or are you the only people it has
reached? 37If anybody thinks he is a prophet[q] or spiritually gifted,[r] let him acknowledge that what I am writing to you is the
Lord's command.[s] 38If he ignores this, he
himself will be ignored.[a]
39Therefore, my brothers, be eager[t] to
prophesy,[u] and do not forbid speaking in
tongues. 40But everything should be done
in a fitting and orderly[v] way.

The Resurrection of Christ

15 Now, brothers, I want to remind you
of the gospel[w] I preached to you,[x]
which you received and on which you
have taken your stand. 2By this gospel you
are saved,[y] if you hold firmly[z] to the word
I preached to you. Otherwise, you have
believed in vain.

[a] *38* Some manuscripts *If he is ignorant of this, let him be ignorant*

14:29 [f] ver 32, 37; S 1Co 13:2 [g] 1Co 12:10 **14:32** [h] 1Jn 4:1 **14:33** [i] ver 40 [j] S Ro 15:33 [k] S 1Co 7:17; S 10:32 [l] S Ac 9:13 **14:34** [m] 1Co 11:5,13 [n] S Eph 5:22; 1Ti 2:11,12 [o] ver 21; Ge 3:16 **14:36** [p] S Heb 4:12 **14:37** [q] S Ac 11:27; 1Co 13:2; 2Co 10:7 [r] 1Co 2:15; S 12:1 [s] 1Jn 4:6 **14:39** [t] ver 1; 1Co 12:31 [u] ver 1; S Eph 4:11 **14:40** [v] ver 33; Col 2:5 **15:1** [w] Isa 40:9; Ro 2:16 [x] S 1Co 3:6; S Gal 1:8 **15:2** [y] Ro 1:16 [z] S Ro 11:22

14:28 *the speaker should keep quiet.* The implication seems to be that it was up to the one speaking in a tongue in the Corinthian church to make certain that there was in the audience someone to interpret his message.

14:29 *Two or three prophets should speak.* Apparently in turn (v. 31), as with the tongues-speakers (v. 27). *weigh carefully.* Judge. The prophets themselves were to decide whether the messages of their fellow prophets were valid (see note on v. 32).

14:30 *a revelation.* Prophecies referred to in chs. 12–14 could come through any member of the church (vv. 26,29–31) and were intended for particular persons in particular circumstances; the "revelation" they contained could be a prediction (Agabus, Ac 11:28; 21:10–11), a divine directive (Ac 13:1–2) or a message designed to strengthen, encourage or comfort (v. 3).

14:32 *control of prophets.* Prophecy (and tongues as well) was not an uncontrollable emotional ecstasy. Paul insists that these gifts should be controlled by the recipients themselves (vv. 15,26–32). See notes on vv. 27–29.

14:33 *God … of peace.* See 1Th 5:23 and note. *disorder.* Paul was concerned that disorderly and unregulated worship at Corinth would bring discredit on the name of the God who had called them in Christ to peace and unity. *in all the congregations of the saints.* A unique expression in the NT that stresses the universality and commonality of the whole visible church of God on earth. All congregations are to obey the directives that follow.

14:34–35 See note on 11:3–16. Some believe that in light of 11:3 there is a God-ordained order that is to be the basis for administration and authority. Women are to be in submission to their husbands both at home (see Eph 5:22) and in the church (see v. 34; 1Ti 2:11–12) regardless of their particular culture. According to this view, a timeless order was established at creation (see note on 11:5–6).

Others maintain that Paul's concern is that the church be strengthened (v. 26) by believers showing respect for others (see vv. 30–31) and for God (see v. 33) as they exercise their spiritual gifts. Such respect must necessarily take account of accepted social practices. If within a particular social order, it is disgraceful for a woman to speak in church—and it was in this case (v. 35)—then she shows disrespect by doing so and should remain silent. There were occasions, though—even in this culture—for women to speak in church. For example, in 11:5 Paul assumes that women pray and prophesy in public worship. Thus his purpose, according to this view, was not to define the role of women but to establish a fitting (vv. 34–35) and orderly (vv. 27–31) way of worship (v. 40).

Still others say that in this context Paul is discussing primarily the disruption of worship by women who become involved in noisy discussions surrounding tongues-speaking and prophecy. Instead of publicly clamoring for explanations, the wives were to discuss matters with their husbands at home (cf. v. 35). Paul does not altogether forbid women to speak in church (see 11:5). What he is forbidding is the disorderly speaking indicated in these verses.

14:34 *as the Law says.* Cf. Ge 3:16; 1Pe 3:6 and note.

14:36 Paul asks these rhetorical questions sarcastically, suggesting that the Corinthians were following their own practice in these matters rather than conforming to God's word.

14:37 *the Lord's command.* Paul's commands are the Lord's commands and are to be followed. In a situation where so much stress was being placed on gifts, Paul insists that any genuinely gifted person will recognize the apostle's God-given authority.

14:38 *he himself will be ignored.* By Paul and the churches, or by God.

14:39 *brothers.* See note on Ro 1:13. *do not forbid speaking in tongues.* Paul's solution to the tongues problem in the Corinthian church was not to forbid tongues, but to correct the improper use of the gift.

14:40 *a fitting and orderly way.* As spelled out in vv. 26–35.

15:1–58 When Paul began this letter to the Corinthians, he foregrounded the cross of Christ (1:17–18)—"we preach Christ crucified" (1:23); "I resolved to know nothing while I was with you except Jesus Christ and him crucified" (2:2; cf. 15:3–4). Now, as he nears the end of his letter, he develops at length the essential truth of Christ's resurrection, a reality assumed throughout the letter as a whole.

15:1,50 *brothers.* See note on Ro 1:13.

15:1 *gospel.* See note on Mk 1:1.

15:2 *if you hold firmly.* See Heb 3:14 and note. *believed in vain.* The gospel Paul preached is the good news of victory over sin through the saving effects of Christ's death by crucifixion and of his triumph over death in his resurrection. "Christ crucified" (1:23) and "raised from the dead" (15:20) is the only hope for sinful mortals to "inherit the kingdom of God" (v. 50; see vv. 53–57).

3 For what I received[a] I passed on to you[b]
as of first importance[a]: that Christ died for
our sins[c] according to the Scriptures,[d] 4 that
he was buried,[e] that he was raised[f] on the
third day[g] according to the Scriptures,[h]
5 and that he appeared to Peter,[b][i] and then
to the Twelve.[j] 6 After that, he appeared to
more than five hundred of the brothers
at the same time, most of whom are still
living, though some have fallen asleep.[k]
7 Then he appeared to James,[l] then to all
the apostles,[m] 8 and last of all he appeared
to me also,[n] as to one abnormally born.

9 For I am the least of the apostles[o] and
do not even deserve to be called an apostle, because I persecuted[p] the church of
God.[q] 10 But by the grace[r] of God I am what
I am, and his grace to me[s] was not without effect. No, I worked harder than all
of them[t]—yet not I, but the grace of God
that was with me.[u] 11 Whether, then, it was
I or they,[v] this is what we preach, and this
is what you believed.

The Resurrection of the Dead

12 But if it is preached that Christ has been
raised from the dead,[w] how can some of
you say that there is no resurrection[x] of
the dead?[y] 13 If there is no resurrection
of the dead, then not even Christ has
been raised. 14 And if Christ has not been
raised,[z] our preaching is useless and so is
your faith. 15 More than that, we are then
found to be false witnesses about God, for
we have testified about God that he raised
Christ from the dead.[a] But he did not raise
him if in fact the dead are not raised. 16 For
if the dead are not raised, then Christ has
not been raised either. 17 And if Christ has
not been raised, your faith is futile; you are
still in your sins.[b] 18 Then those also who
have fallen asleep[c] in Christ are lost. 19 If
only for this life we have hope in Christ,
we are to be pitied more than all men.[d]

20 But Christ has indeed been raised
from the dead,[e] the firstfruits[f] of those
who have fallen asleep.[g] 21 For since death
came through a man,[h] the resurrection
of the dead[i] comes also through a man.
22 For as in Adam all die, so in Christ all

[a] 3 Or *you at the first* [b] 5 Greek *Cephas*

15:3 [a]Gal 1:12 [b]S 1Co 11:2 [c]Isa 53:5; Jn 1:29; S Gal 1:4; 1Pe 2:24 [d]S Mt 26:24; S Lk 24:27; S 24:44; Ac 17:2; 26:22,23 **15:4** [e]Mt 27:59, 60 [f]S Ac 2:24 [g]S Mt 16:21 [h]Jn 2:21,22; Ac 2:25,30,31 **15:5** [i]Lk 24:34 [j]Mk 16:14; Lk 24:36-43 **15:6** [k]ver 18,20; S Mt 9:24 **15:7** [l]S Ac 15:13 [m]Lk 24:33,36,37; Ac 1:3,4 **15:8** [n]Ac 9:3-6, 17; 1Co 9:1; Gal 1:16 **15:9** [o]2Co 12:11; Eph 3:8; 1Ti 1:15 [p]S Ac 8:3 [q]S 1Co 10:32 **15:10** [r]S Ro 3:24 [s]S Ro 12:3 [t]2Co 11:23; Col 1:29 [u]S Php 2:13 **15:11** [v]Gal 2:6 **15:12** [w]ver 4 [x]S Jn 11:24 [y]Ac 17:32; 23:8; 2Ti 2:18 **15:14** [z]1Th 4:14 **15:15** [a]S Ac 2:24 **15:17** [b]S Ro 4:25 **15:18** [c]ver 6,20; S Mt 9:24 **15:19** [d]S 1Co 4:9 **15:20** [e]1Pe 1:3 [f]ver 23; S Ac 26:23 [g]ver 6,18; S Mt 9:24 **15:21** [h]S Ro 5:12 [i]ver 12

15:3 *what I received I passed on to you as of first importance.* Here Paul links himself with early Christian tradition. He was not its originator, nor did he receive it directly from the Lord. His source was other Christians. The verbs he uses are technical terms for receiving and transmitting tradition (see note on 11:23). What follows is the heart of the gospel: that Christ died for our sins (not for his own sins; cf. Heb 7:27), that he was buried (confirmation that he had really died) and that he was raised from the dead. *according to the Scriptures.* Paul probably had in mind Isa 53:5–6,11–12, but he may also have been thinking of the Passover sacrifice and other sin offerings of the OT sacrificial system (see chart, p. 153).

15:4 *on the third day.* Cf. Mt 12:40. The Jews counted parts of days as whole days. Thus the three days would include part of Friday afternoon, all of Saturday, and Sunday morning. A similar way of reckoning time is seen in Jn 20:26 ("A week later" lit. "After eight days"); two Sundays are implied, one at each end of the expression. *according to the Scriptures.* Here Paul may have had in mind Ps 16:8–11; Isa 53:10–12; cf. Hos 6:2; Jnh 1:17 and note.

15:5–8 Six resurrection appearances of Christ are listed here. The Gospels tell of others (see chart, p. 1615).

15:5 *Peter ... the Twelve.* The appearance to Peter is the one mentioned in Lk 24:34, which occurred on Easter Sunday. The appearance to the Twelve seems to have taken place on Sunday evening (see Lk 24:36–43; Jn 20:19–23). "The Twelve" seems to be a conventional way of referring to the group of original apostles, even though Judas was no longer with them.

15:6 *more than five hundred ... at the same time.* This appearance may be the one in Galilee recorded in Mt 28:10,16–20, where the Eleven and possibly more met the risen Lord. *some have fallen asleep.* See Jn 11:11 and note.

15:7 *James.* Since this James is listed in addition to the apostles, he is not James son of Zebedee or James son of Alphaeus (Mt 10:2–3). This is James, the half-brother of Jesus (Mt 13:55), who did not believe in Christ before the resurrection (Jn 7:5) but afterward joined the apostolic band (Ac 1:14) and later became prominent in the Jerusalem church (Ac 15:13). It is not clear in Scripture when and where this appearance to James occurred. *to all the apostles.* Probably the same as "the Twelve" in v. 5 (but see also Ac 1:6–11).

15:8 *last of all.* See Ac 9:1–8. This appearance to Paul came several years after the resurrection (perhaps c. A.D. 33). *one abnormally born.* Paul was not part of the original group of apostles. He had not lived with Christ as the others had. His entry into the apostolic office was not "normal." Furthermore, at his conversion he was abruptly snatched from his former way of life (Ac 9:3–6).

15:9 *I persecuted.* See 1Ti 1:13 and note. *church of God.* In persecuting the church, he was actually persecuting Christ (see Ac 9:4 and note).

15:12–19 Some at Corinth were saying that there was no resurrection of the body, and Paul draws out the implications of this false contention.

15:12 *Christ has been raised.* Paul uses the same verb form (that expresses the certainty of Christ's bodily resurrection) a total of seven times in this passage (vv. 4,12–14,16–17,20).

15:19 If faith in Christ brings benefits only for the present life and not deliverance from the ultimate "wages of sin" (Ro 6:23), then believers are worse off (because deluded) than those who live "without hope and without God in the world" (Eph 2:12).

15:20 *But Christ has indeed been raised.* Paul's categorical conclusion based on his evidence set forth in vv. 3–8. *firstfruits.* The first sheaf of the harvest given to the Lord as a token that all the harvest belonged to the Lord and would be dedicated to him through dedicated lives (see Ex 23:19; Lev 2:12 and notes). So Christ, who has been raised, is the guarantee of the resurrection of all of God's redeemed people (cf. 1Th 4:13–18 and notes).

15:21 *death came through a man.* Through Adam (see Ge 3:17–19; Ro 5:12 and note). *the resurrection of the dead comes also through a man.* Through Christ, the second Adam, "the last Adam" (v. 45; cf. Ro 5:12–21 and note).

15:22 *in Adam all die.* All who are "in Adam"—i.e., his descendants—suffer death. *in Christ all will be made alive.* All who

will be made alive.[j] 23But each in his own
turn: Christ, the firstfruits;[k] then, when he
comes,[l] those who belong to him.[m] 24Then
the end will come, when he hands over the
kingdom[n] to God the Father after he has
destroyed all dominion, authority and power.[o] 25For he must reign[p] until he has put
all his enemies under his feet.[q] 26The last
enemy to be destroyed is death.[r] 27For he
"has put everything under his feet."[a][s] Now
when it says that "everything" has been
put under him, it is clear that this does not
include God himself, who put everything
under Christ.[t] 28When he has done this,
then the Son himself will be made subject
to him who put everything under him,[u] so
that God may be all in all.[v]

29Now if there is no resurrection, what
will those do who are baptized for the
dead? If the dead are not raised at all,
why are people baptized for them? 30And
as for us, why do we endanger ourselves
every hour?[w] 31I die every day[x]—I mean
that, brothers—just as surely as I glory
over you in Christ Jesus our Lord. 32If I
fought wild beasts[y] in Ephesus[z] for merely
human reasons, what have I gained? If the
dead are not raised,

> "Let us eat and drink,
> for tomorrow we die."[b][a]

33Do not be misled:[b] "Bad company corrupts good character."[c] 34Come back to
your senses as you ought, and stop sinning; for there are some who are ignorant
of God[d]—I say this to your shame.[e]

The Resurrection Body

35But someone may ask,[f] "How are the
dead raised? With what kind of body will
they come?"[g] 36How foolish![h] What you
sow does not come to life unless it dies.[i]

[a] 27 Psalm 8:6 [b] 32 Isaiah 22:13

15:22 [j]Ro 5:14-18; S 1Co 6:14 **15:23** [k]ver 20 [l]ver 52; S 1Th 2:19 [m]S 1Co 3:23 **15:24** [n]Da 2:44; 7:14,27; 2Pe 1:11 [o]Ro 8:38 **15:25** [p]Isa 9:7; 52:7 [q]ver 27; S Mt 22:44 **15:26** [r]2Ti 1:10; Rev 20:14; 21:4 **15:27** [s]ver 25; Ps 8:6; S Mt 22:44 [t]S Mt 28:18 **15:28** [u]Php 3:21 [v]1Co 3:23 **15:30** [w]2Co 11:26 **15:31** [x]S Ro 8:36 **15:32** [y]2Co 1:8 [z]S Ac 18:19 [a]Isa 22:13; Lk 12:19 **15:33** [b]S 1Co 6:9 [c]Pr 22:24,25 **15:34** [d]S Gal 4:8 [e]S 1Co 4:14 **15:35** [f]Ro 9:19 [g]Eze 37:3 **15:36** [h]Lk 11:40; 12:20 [i]Jn 12:24

---

are "in Christ"—i.e., who are related to him by faith—will be made alive at the resurrection (cf. Jn 5:25; Ro 5:17–18; 1Th 4:16–17 and note; Rev 20:6).

15:23 *each in his own turn.* Christ, the firstfruits, was raised in his own time in history (c. A.D. 30), and those who are identified with Christ by faith will be raised at his second coming. His resurrection is the pledge that ours will follow.

15:24 *the end.* The second coming of Christ and all the events accompanying it. This includes his handing over the kingdom to the Father, following his destroying all dominion, authority and power of the persons and forces opposing him.

15:25 *For he must reign.* During this process of Christ's destroying all dominion and handing over the kingdom to the Father, Christ must reign (Rev 20:1–6). Some take this to mean that Christ will literally reign with his saints for 1,000 years on the earth (cf. Isa 2:2–4; Mic 4:1–5). Others believe that this refers to Christ's reign over the course of history and in the lives of his people, who are spiritually raised, or born again. This reign is viewed as continuing throughout the present age. *under his feet.* An OT figure for complete conquest. Verse 25 is an allusion to Ps 110:1 (cf. Mt 22:44; Ac 2:34; Heb 1:13 and notes).

15:26 *last enemy.* For death as enemy see Ps 49:14; Jer 9:21 and notes. The final destruction of death (cf. 2Ti 1:10) will occur as the climax of events when Christ returns (see Rev 20:14; 21:4).

15:27 *everything under his feet.* An allusion to Ps 8:6. For another reading of Ps 8 as ultimately a word about Jesus Christ see Heb 2:5–9 and notes.

15:28 *the Son himself will be made subject to him.* The Son will be made subject to the Father in the sense that administratively, after he subjects all things to his power, he will then turn it all over to God the Father, the administrative head. This is not to suggest that the Son is in any way inferior to the Father. All three persons of the Trinity are equal in deity and in dignity. The subordination referred to is one of function (see Jn 4:34; 5:19; 7:16 and notes). The Father is supreme in the Trinity; the Son carries out the Father's will; the Spirit is sent by the Father and the Son to vitalize life, communicate God's truth, apply his salvation to people and enable them to obey God's will. *so that God may be all in all.* The triune God will be shown to be supreme and sovereign in all things (cf. 3:21 and note).

15:29 *those … who are baptized for the dead.* The present tense suggests that at Corinth people were currently being baptized for the dead. But because Paul does not give any more information about the practice, many attempts have been made to interpret the concept. Three of these are: (1) Living believers were being baptized for believers who died before they were baptized, so that they too, in this way, would not miss out on baptism. (2) Christians were being baptized in anticipation of the resurrection of the dead. (3) New converts were being baptized to fill the ranks of Christians who had died. At any rate, Paul mentions this custom almost in passing, using it in his arguments substantiating the resurrection of the dead, but without necessarily approving the practice. The passage will likely remain obscure.

15:30 *why do we endanger ourselves every hour?* Cf. 2Co 11:23–29.

15:31 *I die every day.* Paul faced the reality of death daily (cf. 2Co 4:8–12; 11:23–26), and he wanted the Corinthians to know it. *glory over you.* Over their conversion and growth in grace—in spite of their failures (cf. 1Th 2:20).

15:32 *I fought wild beasts in Ephesus.* This statement can be taken literally or figuratively. But since Ac 19 makes no mention of Paul suffering imprisonment and having to face the lions in Ephesus, it is more likely that the expression means that the enemies in Ephesus were as ferocious as wild beasts. *Let us eat and drink, for tomorrow we die.* See Isa 22:13; an alternative philosophy of life if there is no resurrection.

15:33 A quotation from the Greek comedy *Thais* written by the Greek poet Menander, whose writings the Corinthians would know. The application of the quotation is that those who are teaching that there is no resurrection (v. 12) are the "bad company," and they are corrupting the "good character" of those who hold to the correct doctrine. Cf. Ps 1:1; Pr 22:24–25 and notes.

15:34 *stop sinning.* The sin of denying that there is a resurrection and thus doubting even the resurrection of Christ, all of which had a negative effect on the lives they were living. *some who are ignorant of God.* Even in the Corinthian church. This, Paul says, is a shameful situation.

15:35–49 In discussing the nature of the resurrection body, Paul compares it to plant life (vv. 36–38), to fleshly beings (v. 39) and to celestial and earthly physical bodies (vv. 40–41).

15:36–38 Plant organisms, though organized similarly in their own order, are different; the seed sown is related to the

37When you sow, you do not plant the
body that will be, but just a seed, perhaps
of wheat or of something else. 38But God
gives it a body as he has determined, and
to each kind of seed he gives its own body.[j]
39All flesh is not the same: Men have one
kind of flesh, animals have another, birds
another and fish another. 40There are also
heavenly bodies and there are earthly bodies; but the splendor of the heavenly bodies is one kind, and the splendor of the
earthly bodies is another. 41The sun has
one kind of splendor,[k] the moon another and the stars another;[l] and star differs
from star in splendor.
42So will it be[m] with the resurrection of
the dead.[n] The body that is sown is perishable, it is raised imperishable;[o] 43it is
sown in dishonor, it is raised in glory;[p] it
is sown in weakness, it is raised in power;
44it is sown a natural body, it is raised a
spiritual body.[q]
If there is a natural body, there is also
a spiritual body. 45So it is written: "The
first man Adam became a living being"[a];[r]
the last Adam,[s] a life-giving spirit.[t] 46The
spiritual did not come first, but the natural, and after that the spiritual.[u] 47The
first man was of the dust of the earth,[v]
the second man from heaven.[w] 48As was
the earthly man, so are those who are of
the earth; and as is the man from heav-
en, so also are those who are of heaven.[x]
49And just as we have borne the likeness
of the earthly man,[y] so shall we[b] bear the
likeness of the man from heaven.[z]
50I declare to you, brothers, that flesh
and blood[a] cannot inherit the kingdom
of God,[b] nor does the perishable inherit the imperishable.[c] 51Listen, I tell you a
mystery:[d] We will not all sleep,[e] but we
will all be changed[f]— 52in a flash, in the
twinkling of an eye, at the last trumpet.
For the trumpet will sound,[g] the dead[h]
will be raised imperishable, and we will
be changed. 53For the perishable[i] must
clothe itself with the imperishable,[j] and
the mortal with immortality. 54When the
perishable has been clothed with the imperishable, and the mortal with immortality, then the saying that is written will
come true: "Death has been swallowed up
in victory."[c][k]

55"Where, O death, is your victory?
Where, O death, is your sting?"[d][l]

56The sting of death is sin,[m] and the power
of sin is the law.[n] 57But thanks be to God![o]
He gives us the victory through our Lord
Jesus Christ.[p]
58Therefore, my dear brothers, stand
firm. Let nothing move you. Always give
yourselves fully to the work of the Lord,[q]
because you know that your labor in the
Lord is not in vain.[r]

The Collection for God's People

16 Now about the collection[s] for God's
people:[t] Do what I told the Galatian[u]

[a] *45* Gen. 2:7 [b] *49* Some early manuscripts *so let us* [c] *54* Isaiah 25:8 [d] *55* Hosea 13:14

15:38 [j]Ge 1:11 **15:41** [k]Ps 19:4-6 [l]Ps 8:1,3 **15:42** [m]Da 12:3; Mt 13:43 [n]ver 12 [o]ver 50,53,54 **15:43** [p]Php 3:21; Col 3:4 **15:44** [q]ver 50 **15:45** [r]Ge 2:7 [s]Ro 5:14 [t]Jn 5:21; 6:57,58; Ro 8:2 **15:46** [u]ver 44 **15:47** [v]Ge 2:7; 3:19; Ps 90:3 [w]Jn 3:13,31 **15:48** [x]Php 3:20,21 **15:49** [y]Ge 5:3 [z]S Ro 8:29 **15:50** [a]Eph 6:12; Heb 2:14 [b]S Mt 25:34 [c]ver 42,53,54 **15:51** [d]1Co 13:2; 14:2 [e]S Mt 9:24 [f]2Co 5:4; Php 3:21 **15:52** [g]S Mt 24:31 [h]Jn 5:25 **15:53** [i]ver 42,50,54 [j]2Co 5:2,4 **15:54** [k]Isa 25:8; Heb 2:14; Rev 20:14 **15:55** [l]Hos 13:14 **15:56** [m]S Ro 5:12 [n]S Ro 4:15 **15:57** [o]S 2Co 2:14 [p]Ro 8:37; Heb 2:14,15 **15:58** [q]1Co 16:10 [r]Isa 65:23 **16:1** [s]S Ac 24:17 [t]S Ac 9:13 [u]S Ac 16:6

new plant that sprouts, but the new sprout has a different and genuinely new body that God has given it.

15:39 *All flesh is not the same.* Although there is much that is similar in the organizational character of fleshly beings, each species is different: humans, animals, birds, fish.

15:40–41 Here the analogy involves inanimate objects of creation: the sun, moon and stars with their differing splendor, and the earthly bodies (possibly the great mountains, canyons and seas) with their splendor. In it all, God can take similar physical material and organize it differently to accomplish his purpose.

15:42–44 In applying these analogies, the apostle says that in the case of the resurrection of the dead, God will take a perishable, dishonorable, weak (and sinful) body—"a natural body" characterized by sin—and in the resurrection make it an imperishable, glorious, powerful body, fit to live eternally with God. There is continuity, but there is also change.

15:44–49 The contrast here between the natural body and the spiritual body again follows from their two representatives (see notes on vv. 21–22). One is the first Adam, who had a natural body made "from the dust of the ground" (Ge 2:7) and through whom a natural body is given to his descendants. The other is the last Adam, Christ, the life-giving spirit (cf. Jn 5:26) who through his death and resurrection will at the second coming give his redeemed people a spiritual body similar to Christ's resurrected, glorified body (cf. Lk 24:36–43; Php 3:21 and notes; 1Jn 3:2).

15:50 Paul's final argument about the resurrection of the body: God's redeemed people must have newly organized, imperishable bodies to live with him. "Flesh and blood" stands for the perishable, corrupt, weak, sinful state of human beings (see note on Gal 1:16).

15:51 *mystery.* Things about the resurrection body that were not understood but are now revealed (see note on Ro 11:25). *We will not all sleep.* Some believers will not experience death and the grave (see 1Th 4:15 and note).

15:52 *in a flash.* The change to an imperishable body will occur instantly at the great trumpet call that announces the consummation of redemption (see Mt 24:31; 1Th 4:16–17).

15:53–54 *clothe itself with … clothed with.* See note on Ps 109:29.

15:56 *The sting of death is sin.* It was sin that brought humanity under death's power (see Ro 5:12–21 and notes). *the power of sin is the law.* The law of God gives sin its power, for it reveals our sin and condemns us because of our sin (cf. Ro 7:7–12 and notes).

15:57 *victory through our Lord Jesus Christ.* Victory over the condemnation for sin that the law brought (v. 56) and over death and the grave (vv. 54–55), through the death and resurrection of Christ (cf. Ro 4:25).

15:58 *Therefore.* Because of Christ's resurrection and ours, we know that serving him is not empty, useless activity. *your labor in the Lord is not in vain.* All our efforts in service to Christ are invested in his winning cause. He will also reward us at his second coming (Mt 25:21; cf. Lk 19:17; 1Co 2:7 and note; 2Co 4:17 and note).

16:1 *Now about.* Again an answer to one of the questions of the Corinthians (cf. 7:1; 8:1; 12:1). *collection.* Cf. 2Co 8–9; Ro

churches to do. 2On the first day of every
week,[v] each one of you should set aside
a sum of money in keeping with his income, saving it up, so that when I come
no collections will have to be made.[w]
3Then, when I arrive, I will give letters of
introduction to the men you approve[x] and
send them with your gift to Jerusalem. 4If
it seems advisable for me to go also, they
will accompany me.

Personal Requests

5After I go through Macedonia, I will
come to you[y]—for I will be going through
Macedonia.[z] 6Perhaps I will stay with you
awhile, or even spend the winter, so that
you can help me on my journey,[a] wherever I go. 7I do not want to see you now and
make only a passing visit; I hope to spend
some time with you, if the Lord permits.[b]
8But I will stay on at Ephesus[c] until Pentecost,[d] 9because a great door for effective
work has opened to me,[e] and there are
many who oppose me.
10If Timothy[f] comes, see to it that he
has nothing to fear while he is with
you, for he is carrying on the work of
the Lord,[g] just as I am. 11No one, then,
should refuse to accept him.[h] Send him
on his way[i] in peace[j] so that he may return to me. I am expecting him along
with the brothers.
12Now about our brother Apollos:[k]
I strongly urged him to go to you with
the brothers. He was quite unwilling to
go now, but he will go when he has the
opportunity.
13Be on your guard; stand firm[l] in the
faith; be men of courage; be strong.[m] 14Do
everything in love.[n]
15You know that the household of
Stephanas[o] were the first converts[p] in
Achaia,[q] and they have devoted themselves to the service[r] of the saints.[s] I
urge you, brothers, 16to submit[t] to such
as these and to everyone who joins in
the work, and labors at it. 17I was glad
when Stephanas, Fortunatus and Achaicus arrived, because they have supplied
what was lacking from you.[u] 18For they
refreshed[v] my spirit and yours also. Such
men deserve recognition.[w]

Final Greetings

19The churches in the province of Asia[x]
send you greetings. Aquila and Priscilla[a][y]

[a] 19 Greek *Prisca*, a variant of *Priscilla*

16:2 [v] Ac 20:7 [w] 2Co 9:4,5
16:3 [x] 2Co 3:1; 8:18,19
16:5 [y] S 1Co 4:19 [z] S Ac 16:9
16:6 [a] Ro 15:24; Tit 3:13
16:7 [b] S Ac 18:21
16:8 [c] S Ac 18:19 [d] S Ac 2:1
16:9 [e] S Ac 14:27
16:10 [f] S Ac 16:1 [g] 1Co 15:58
16:11 [h] 1Ti 4:12; [i] 2Co 1:16; 3Jn 6 [j] S Ac 15:33
16:12 [k] S Ac 18:24
16:13 [l] 1Co 1:8; 2Co 1:21; Gal 5:1; Php 1:27; 1Th 3:8; S Tit 1:9 [m] S Eph 6:10
16:14 [n] 1Co 14:1
16:15 [o] 1Co 1:16 [p] Ro 16:5 [q] S Ac 18:12 [r] S Ac 24:17 [s] S Ac 9:13
16:16 [t] 1Th 5:12; Heb 13:17
16:17 [u] 2Co 11:9; Php 2:30
16:18 [v] Ro 15:32; Phm 7 [w] Php 2:29
16:19 [x] S Ac 2:9 [y] S Ac 18:2

15:25–28. *God's people.* His people at Jerusalem (cf. v. 3; Ro 15:26). *Galatian churches.* The fact that the Galatian and Macedonian churches (2Co 8:1; 9:1–4) are involved, along with the Corinthians, indicates that the collection of this offering was quite widespread. The Jerusalem believers may have become poverty-stricken because of the famine recorded in Ac 11:28 (c. A.D. 44 or 46), or because of the persecution of Jerusalem Christians (cf. Ac 8:1).

16:2 *On the first day of every week, each one of you should set aside.* Every Sunday believers were to bring what they had set aside for the Lord's work—an amount proportionate to their income. Since it was to be brought on Sunday, the day when Christians gathered for worship (see Ac 20:7; Rev 1:10 and notes), it was probably collected at the worship service rather than at home. Justin Martyr indicates (in his *Apology*, 1.67–68) that in his time (c. A.D. 150) offerings were brought to the church on Sundays.

16:3 For proper financial accountability and responsibility these approved men would act as auditors and guardians of the funds the Corinthians gave (cf. 2Co 8:16–21 and notes).

16:4 *If it seems advisable for me to go also.* Possibly to take care of important missionary business, or to be there to explain about the gift when it arrives.

16:5 *After I go through Macedonia.* After leaving Ephesus (v. 8), where he was when he wrote 1 Corinthians, Paul planned to go up to Macedonia, no doubt to visit the Philippians and others in northern Greece, and then to Corinth. He had originally planned to go to Corinth first and then to Macedonia but thought it best to change his plans (see 2Co 1:12—2:4).

16:6 *even spend the winter.* Probably the three-month stay in Greece mentioned in Ac 20:3 (see note there). *help me on my journey.* With supplies and equipment, and certainly with prayers and goodwill. However, Paul had indicated earlier in the letter (9:7–12) that he did not want to be a financial burden to them.

16:8 *until Pentecost.* The 50th day (Pentecost means "50") after Passover, when the Jews celebrated the Feast of Firstfruits (Lev 23:10–16)—late spring.

16:9 *many who oppose me.* Probably a reference to the pagan craftsmen who made the silver shrines of Artemis and to the general populace whom they had stirred up (Ac 19:23–34).

16:10 *If Timothy comes.* In Ac 19:22 Paul sends Timothy (and Erastus) into Macedonia, after which Timothy was to go on to Corinth (1Co 4:17). *see to it that he has nothing to fear.* Timothy seems to have been somewhat timid (see 1Ti 4:12; 2Ti 1:7 and notes), and Paul wants the Corinthians to treat him kindly.

16:11,23 *peace ... grace.* See note on Ro 1:7.

16:11 *brothers.* Possibly including Erastus (cf. Ac 19:22), who was a believer from Corinth and "the city's director of public works" (Ro 16:23; see note there).

16:12 *Now about ... Apollos.* The Corinthians had asked Paul about Apollos (cf. the similar words, "Now (for the matters you wrote) about," in 7:1; 8:1; 12:1; 16:1) and his coming to see them. For other words about Apollos see 1:12; 3:4–6,22; 4:6; cf. Ac 18:24,27; 19:1; Tit 3:13.

16:15 *household of Stephanas.* Some of the few people Paul baptized at Corinth (1:16). They were among the first converts in Achaia (Greece), along with the few individuals in Athens who had believed a short time earlier (Ac 17:34). *service.* The whole household of Stephanas was serving.

16:17 Probably the ones who had brought to the apostle the letter from the Corinthians referred to in 7:1. Their coming "supplied what was lacking" from the Corinthians, i.e., the affection of these three brothers supplied the affection Paul desired from the whole Corinthian church.

16:18 *refreshed my spirit and yours.* Perhaps through their willingness to come to get Paul's advice and to bring it back to Corinth. At least a new relationship between Paul and the Corinthians was in the making.

16:19 *province of Asia.* The Roman province (presently in western Turkey) in which Ephesus and the surrounding cities were located (see Ac 19:10 and note; see also map, p. 1967). During Paul's long ministry in Ephesus all in the province of

greet you warmly in the Lord, and so does
the church that meets at their house.[z] 20All
the brothers here send you greetings. Greet
one another with a holy kiss.[a]
21I, Paul, write this greeting in my own
hand.[b]
22If anyone does not love the Lord[c]—a
curse[d] be on him. Come, O Lord[a]![e]

23The grace of the Lord Jesus be with
you.[f]
24My love to all of you in Christ Jesus.
Amen.[b]

16:19 [z]S Ro 16:5 **16:20** [a]S Ro 16:16 **16:21** [b]Gal 6:11; Col 4:18; 2Th 3:17; Phm 19 **16:22** [c]Eph 6:24 [d]Ro 9:3 [e]Rev 22:20 **16:23** [f]S Ro 16:20

[a] 22 In Aramaic the expression *Come, O Lord* is *Marana tha.* [b] 24 Some manuscripts do not have *Amen.*

Asia heard the word. The churches of Colosse, Laodicea and Hierapolis (cf. Col 4:13–16; Rev 1:11), which were located on the border of the province of Asia, may be included in the greetings, along with the other churches of Rev 2–3 (see map, p. 1967). *Aquila and Priscilla.* They had helped Paul found the church at Corinth (Ac 18:1–4). *warmly in the Lord.* Enthusiastically as fellow believers. *the church that meets at their house.* Aquila and Priscilla had left Corinth with Paul and had gone to Ephesus (Ac 18:18–19). Evidently they were still there, and a church was meeting at their house; it now sends greetings. House churches were common in this early period (cf. Ro 16:3–5; Phm 2).

16:20 *holy kiss.* See notes on 2Co 13:12; Ro 16:16. The kiss of mutual respect and love in the Lord was evidently the public practice of early Christians—from a practice that was customary in the ancient East. Such a practice may have been used in the first-century A.D. synagogue—men kissing men, and women kissing women—and it would have been natural for the practice to have been continued in the early Jewish-Gentile churches.

16:21 *greeting in my own hand.* Paul now signs this letter, as was his habit (see Gal 6:11; Col 4:18; Phm 19), a mark of the authenticity of the letter (2Th 3:17). Someone else had been penning the letter for him up to this point (cf. Ro 16:22).

16:22 *a curse be on him.* May those who have not come to love the Lord Jesus Christ in response to the preaching of the gospel experience God's displeasure and wrath (see Jn 3:36 and note). Paul's curse is based on God as witness to the unbelievers' essential lack of love for the Lord Jesus and of obedience to God (cf. Gal 1:8–9; Ro 9:3 and note). *Come, O Lord!* Lit. "Our Lord, come!" See NIV text note; an expression used by the early church as an appeal for Christ to come again soon.

16:23 The apostle's usual benediction (see Gal 6:18; Eph 6:24; Php 4:23); a longer Trinitarian benediction is found in 2Co 13:14. *grace.* See note on vv. 11,23. *with you.* See note on 2Co 13:14.

16:24 Although he has been severe with the Corinthians, Paul wants them to know that he loves them as believers in Christ Jesus.

2 Corinthians

INTRODUCTION

Author

Paul is the author of this letter (see 1:1; 10:1). It is stamped with his style and contains more autobiographical material than any of his other writings.

Date

The available evidence indicates that the year A.D. 55 is a reasonable estimate for the writing of this letter. From 1Co 16:5–8 it may be concluded that 1 Corinthians was written from Ephesus before Pentecost (in the late spring) and that 2 Corinthians may have been written later that same year before the onset of winter. Second Corinthians 2:13; 7:5 indicate that it was probably written from Macedonia (see chart, p. 1697).

Recipients

The opening greeting of the letter states that it was addressed to the church in Corinth and to Christians throughout Achaia (the Roman province comprising all of Greece south of Macedonia; see map, p. 2266).

Occasion

It seems that Paul wrote at least four letters to the church at Corinth: (1) the letter referred to in 1Co 5:9 (see note there); (2) 1 Corinthians; (3) the severe letter (see 2Co 2:3–4; see also below); (4) 2 Corinthians. After writing 1 Corinthians Paul continued his ministry at Ephesus until he heard that his letter had not completely accomplished its purpose. A group of men had come to Corinth who presented themselves as apostles. They were false teachers who were challenging, among other things, Paul's personal integrity and his authority as an apostle (see 11:4; 12:11).

In the face of this serious situation, Paul decided to make a quick trip to Corinth (12:4; 13:1–2) to see whether he could remedy the situation. The visit turned out to be painful and did not ac-

A Quick Look

Author:
The apostle Paul

Audience:
The church in Corinth

Date:
A.D. 55

Theme:
Paul encourages the Corinthian believers to be reconciled with him and to reject false apostles who are challenging his authority and creating dissension in the church.

complish its purpose. So when Paul returned to Ephesus, he wrote the Corinthians a severe letter "out of great distress and anguish of heart and with many tears" (2:4), probably sending it by Titus (12:8). Some identify this letter with 2Co 10 – 13. Others think it has been lost.

After writing the severe letter, Paul had second thoughts. He was deeply concerned about how the Corinthians might react to it. So after the riot caused by Demetrius and his fellow silversmiths (see Ac 19:23 – 41), he left Ephesus and set out for Macedonia by way of Troas. He expected to meet Titus in Troas to get news of the effect of his severe letter on the Corinthian church, but Titus was not there (see 2Co 2:12 – 13). Still deeply concerned and despite the fact that the Lord had opened up an opportunity to preach the gospel at Troas, Paul said good-by to the believers there and moved on to Macedonia, where he met Titus. To his relief, the news from the Corinthian church was basically good. The severe letter had brought its intended results (7:5 – 16). The encouraging report of Titus of the improved situation at Corinth is the immediate occasion of the writing of 2 Corinthians.

Paul writes to explain to the Corinthian believers the true nature (its joys, sufferings and rewards) and high calling of Christian ministry.

How, then, does one explain the harsh tone of chs. 10 – 13, which is so different from the rest of the letter? Some think that when Paul had just completed writing the first nine chapters, a report came to him that a strong and vocal minority was still causing trouble at Corinth. So before sending off the letter he added the last four chapters to address this troublemaking group. Others hold that chs. 10 – 13 were written some time after Paul had sent the first nine chapters and that they constitute a separate letter. There is, however, no manuscript evidence that warrants splitting 2 Corinthians into two parts.

Purposes

Because of the occasion that prompted this letter, Paul had a number of purposes in mind:

1. To express the comfort and joy Paul felt because the Corinthians had responded favorably to his painful letter (1:3 – 4; 7:8 – 9,12 – 13).
2. To let them know about the trouble he went through in the province of Asia (1:8 – 11).
3. To explain why he had changed his travel plans (1:12 — 2:4).
4. To ask them to forgive the offending party (2:5 – 11).
5. To warn them not to be "yoked together with unbelievers" (6:14 — 7:1).
6. To explain to them the true nature (its joys, sufferings and rewards) and high calling of Christian ministry. This is the so-called great digression, but it turns out to be in some ways the most important section of the letter (2:14 — 7:4; see note on 2:14).
7. To teach the Corinthians about the grace of giving and to make sure that they complete the collection for the poor Christians at Jerusalem (chs. 8 – 9).
8. To deal with the minority opposition in the church (chs. 10 – 13).
9. To prepare the Corinthians for his upcoming visit (12:14; 13:1 – 3,10).

Structure

The structure of the letter relates primarily to Paul's impending third visit to Corinth. The letter falls naturally into three sections:

1. Paul explains the reason for the changes in his itinerary (chs. 1 – 7).
2. Paul encourages the Corinthians to complete their collection in preparation for his arrival (chs. 8 – 9).
3. Paul stresses the certainty of his coming, his authenticity as an apostle and his readiness to exercise discipline if necessary (chs. 10 – 13).

Unity

Some have questioned the unity of this letter (see above), but it forms a coherent whole, as the structure above shows. Tradition has been unanimous in affirming its unity (the early church fathers, e.g., knew the letter only in its present form). Furthermore, none of the early Greek manuscripts breaks up the book.

Outline

- I. Apologetic: Paul's Explanation of His Conduct and Apostolic Ministry (chs. 1 – 7)
  - A. Greetings (1:1 – 2)
  - B. Thanksgiving for Divine Comfort in Affliction (1:3 – 11)
  - C. The Integrity of Paul's Motives and Conduct (1:12 — 2:4)
  - D. Forgiving the Offending Party at Corinth (2:5 – 11)
  - E. God's Direction in Ministry (2:12 – 17)
  - F. The Corinthian Believers — a Letter from Christ (3:1 – 11)
  - G. Seeing the Glory of God with Unveiled Faces (3:12 — 4:6)
  - H. Treasure in Clay Jars (4:7 – 16a)
  - I. The Prospect of Death and What It Means for the Christian (4:16b — 5:10)
  - J. The Ministry of Reconciliation (5:11 — 6:10)
  - K. A Spiritual Father's Appeal to His Children (6:11 — 7:4)
  - L. The Meeting with Titus (7:5 – 16)
- II. Hortatory: The Collection for the Christians at Jerusalem (chs. 8 – 9)
  - A. Generosity Encouraged (8:1 – 15)
  - B. Titus and His Companions Sent to Corinth (8:16 — 9:5)
  - C. Results of Generous Giving (9:6 – 15)
- III. Polemical: Paul's Vindication of His Apostolic Authority (chs. 10 – 13)
  - A. Paul's Defense of His Apostolic Authority and the Area of His Mission (ch. 10)
  - B. Paul Forced into Foolish Boasting (chs. 11 – 12)
  - C. Final Warnings (13:1 – 10)
  - D. Conclusion, Final Greetings and Benediction (13:11 – 14)

1 Paul, an apostle[a] of Christ Jesus by the
will of God,[b] and Timothy[c] our brother,

To the church of God[d] in Corinth,[e] together with all the saints throughout
Achaia:[f]

2Grace and peace to you from God our
Father and the Lord Jesus Christ.[g]

The God of All Comfort

3Praise be to the God and Father of our
Lord Jesus Christ,[h] the Father of compassion and the God of all comfort, 4who
comforts us[i] in all our troubles, so that
we can comfort those in any trouble with
the comfort we ourselves have received
from God. 5For just as the sufferings of
Christ flow over into our lives,[j] so also
through Christ our comfort overflows. 6If
we are distressed, it is for your comfort
and salvation;[k] if we are comforted, it is
for your comfort, which produces in you
patient endurance of the same sufferings
we suffer. 7And our hope for you is firm,
because we know that just as you share
in our sufferings,[l] so also you share in our
comfort.

8We do not want you to be uninformed,[m]
brothers, about the hardships we suffered[n]
in the province of Asia.[o] We were under
great pressure, far beyond our ability to
endure, so that we despaired even of life.
9Indeed, in our hearts we felt the sentence
of death. But this happened that we might
not rely on ourselves but on God,[p] who
raises the dead.[q] 10He has delivered us
from such a deadly peril,[r] and he will deliver us. On him we have set our hope[s]
that he will continue to deliver us, 11as you
help us by your prayers.[t] Then many will
give thanks[u] on our[a] behalf for the gracious favor granted us in answer to the
prayers of many.

Paul's Change of Plans

12Now this is our boast: Our conscience[v]
testifies that we have conducted ourselves
in the world, and especially in our relations with you, in the holiness[w] and sincerity[x] that are from God. We have done
so not according to worldly wisdom[y] but
according to God's grace. 13For we do not
write you anything you cannot read or understand. And I hope that, 14as you have
understood us in part, you will come to
understand fully that you can boast of us
just as we will boast of you in the day of
the Lord Jesus.[z]

15Because I was confident of this, I
planned to visit you[a] first so that you
might benefit twice.[b] 16I planned to visit you on my way[c] to Macedonia[d] and to
come back to you from Macedonia, and
then to have you send me on my way[e] to
Judea.[f] 17When I planned this, did I do it
lightly? Or do I make my plans in a worldly manner[g] so that in the same breath I
say, "Yes, yes" and "No, no"?

1:1 [a]S 1Co 1:1 [b]1Co 1:1; Eph 1:1; Col 1:1; 2Ti 1:1 [c]S Ac 16:1 [d]S 1Co 10:32 [e]S Ac 18:1 [f]S Ac 18:12 **1:2** [g]S Ro 1:7 **1:3** [h]Eph 1:3; 1Pe 1:3 **1:4** [i]Isa 49:13; 51:12; 66:13; 2Co 7:6,7,13 **1:5** [j]Ro 8:17; 2Co 4:10; Gal 6:17; Php 3:10; Col 1:24; 1Pe 4:13 **1:6** [k]2Co 4:15 **1:7** [l]S ver 5 **1:8** [m]S Ro 11:25 [n]1Co 15:32 [o]S Ac 2:9 **1:9** [p]Jer 17:5,7 [q]S Jn 5:21 **1:10** [r]S Ro 15:31 [s]1Ti 4:10 **1:11** [t]Ro 15:30; Php 1:19 [u]2Co 4:15; 9:11 **1:12** [v]S Ac 23:1 [w]1Th 2:10 [x]2Co 2:17 [y]1Co 1:17; 2:1,4,13 **1:14** [z]S 1Co 1:8 **1:15** [a]S 1Co 4:19 [b]Ro 1:11,13; 15:29 **1:16** [c]1Co 16:5-7 [d]S Ac 16:9 [e]1Co 16:11; 3Jn 6 [f]Ac 19:21 **1:17** [g]2Co 10:2,3; 11:18

[a] *11* Many manuscripts *your*

1:1 *Paul.* See note on Ro 1:1. *apostle … by the will of God.* See 1Co 1:1 and note. *Timothy.* Evidently with Paul when this letter was written, but not necessarily a co-author. *our brother.* Our fellow believer, our brother in Christ (see Ac 9:17; Heb 2:11 and note). *church of God.* The community of believers, the local representatives of the universal church (see note on 1Co 1:2). *Corinth.* See Introduction to 1 Corinthians: The City of Corinth; see also map, p. 1766. *saints.* Another term for God's people (see note on Ro 1:7). *Achaia.* Greece, as distinct from Macedonia in the north (see map, p. 1718). Though the letter deals particularly with the situation in Corinth, it was also intended for Christians elsewhere in Greece. Presumably copies of the letter would be made in Corinth and circulated to them.

1:2 *Grace and peace.* See note on Ro 1:7. *Lord Jesus Christ.* See note on 1Th 1:1.

1:3 *God and Father of our Lord Jesus Christ.* See note on Eph 1:3. *comfort.* Consolation and encouragement. This comfort flows to believers when they suffer for Jesus' sake, and it equips them to comfort others who are in trouble (vv. 4–7).

1:8 *We.* Throughout this letter Paul uses the editorial plural (we, us, our, ourselves). Except where the context indicates otherwise, these plurals should be understood as referring to Paul alone. *brothers.* See note on Ro 1:13. *Asia.* A Roman province in western Asia Minor, now Turkish territory (see map, p. 1704).

1:9 Paul's hardships were so life-threatening that he regarded his survival and recovery as tantamount to being raised from the dead. *rely … on God.* A key principle of this letter. God's grace is all-sufficient; Christ strengthens us when we are weak (see 12:9–10; Php 4:13 and note).

1:10 *hope.* See note on Eph 1:18.

1:11 *you help us by your prayers.* Cf. Ro 15:31; Eph 6:19–20.

1:12 In defending his trustworthiness against the slanders being spread about him, Paul appeals to the witness of his own conscience and to the Corinthians' firsthand knowledge of his character. He had spent 18 months with them when he first came to Corinth (Ac 18:11), so they could not plead ignorance of his integrity.

1:14 *day of the Lord Jesus.* Time of his return (cf. 1Th 2:19–20).

1:15 *you might benefit twice.* Here and in v. 16 Paul refers to his change of itinerary. Originally he had planned to cross over by sea from Ephesus to Corinth, visiting the Corinthians before traveling north to Macedonia, and then, returning from Macedonia, to visit them a second time, thus giving them the benefit of two short visits. This was when he was on good terms with them. What probably occurred was that he paid them an additional quick visit directly from Ephesus, a visit he had not earlier contemplated and that proved to be "painful" (2:1; see note there). That visit then gave rise to his letter that caused them sorrow (see 7:8–9 and note).

1:16 *Macedonia.* See notes on v. 1; Php 4:15.

1:17 Paul's opponents in Corinth had been attempting to persuade the Christians there that this change of plan was evidence that his word was not to be trusted, that he was fickle and unreliable. The two rhetorical questions are in effect his denial that he acts lightly and that he says "Yes" and "No" at the same time so that it is impossible to know what he means. In any case, his plan to visit the Corinthians had not been abandoned; it had simply been modified.

18But as surely as God is faithful,[h] our message to you is not "Yes" and "No." 19For the Son of God,[i] Jesus Christ, who was preached among you by me and Silas[a][j] and Timothy,[k] was not "Yes" and "No," but in him it has always[l] been "Yes." 20For no matter how many promises[m] God has made, they are "Yes" in Christ. And so through him the "Amen"[n] is spoken by us to the glory of God.[o] 21Now it is God who makes both us and you stand firm[p] in Christ. He anointed[q] us, 22set his seal[r] of ownership on us, and put his Spirit in our hearts as a deposit, guaranteeing what is to come.[s]

23I call God as my witness[t] that it was in order to spare you[u] that I did not return to Corinth. 24Not that we lord it over[v] your faith, but we work with you for your joy, because it is by faith you stand firm.[w]

2 1So I made up my mind that I would not make another painful visit to you.[x] 2For if I grieve you,[y] who is left to make me glad but you whom I have grieved? 3I wrote as I did[z] so that when I came I should not be distressed[a] by those who ought to make me rejoice. I had confidence[b] in all of you, that you would all share my joy. 4For I wrote you[c] out of great distress and anguish of heart and with many tears, not to grieve you but to let you know the depth of my love for you.

Forgiveness for the Sinner

5If anyone has caused grief,[d] he has not so much grieved me as he has grieved all of you, to some extent—not to put it too severely. 6The punishment[e] inflicted on him by the majority is sufficient for him. 7Now instead, you ought to forgive and comfort him,[f] so that he will not be overwhelmed by excessive sorrow. 8I urge you, therefore, to reaffirm your love for him. 9The reason I wrote you[g] was to see if you would stand the test and be obedient in everything.[h] 10If you forgive anyone, I also forgive him. And what I have forgiven—if there was anything to forgive—I have forgiven in the sight of Christ for your sake, 11in order that Satan[i] might not outwit us. For we are not unaware of his schemes.[j]

Ministers of the New Covenant

12Now when I went to Troas[k] to preach the gospel of Christ[l] and found that the Lord had opened a door[m] for me, 13I still had no peace of mind,[n] because I did not find my brother Titus[o] there. So I said good-by to them and went on to Macedonia.[p]

[a] *19* Greek *Silvanus*, a variant of *Silas*

1:18 [h]S 1Co 1:9 **1:19** [i]S Mt 4:3 [j]S Ac 15:22 [k]S Ac 16:1 [l]Heb 13:8 **1:20** [m]Ro 15:8 [n]S 1Co 14:16 [o]Ro 15:9 **1:21** [p]S 1Co 16:13 [q]1Jn 2:20, 27 **1:22** [r]Ge 38:18; Eze 9:4; Hag 2:23 [s]S 2Co 5:5 **1:23** [t]S Ro 1:9 [u]1Co 4:21; 2Co 2:1, 3; 13:2, 10 **1:24** [v]1Pe 5:3 [w]Ro 11:20; 1Co 15:1 **2:1** [x]S 2Co 1:23 **2:2** [y]2Co 7:8 **2:3** [z]ver 4, 9; 2Co 7:8, 12 [a]2Co 12:21 [b]2Co 7:16; 8:22; Gal 5:10; 2Th 3:4; Phm 21 **2:4** [c]ver 3, 9; 2Co 7:8, 12 **2:5** [d]1Co 5:1, 2 **2:6** [e]1Co 5:4, 5; 2Co 7:11 **2:7** [f]Gal 6:1; Eph 4:32; Col 3:13 **2:9** [g]ver 3, 4; 2Co 7:8, 12 [h]2Co 7:15; 10:6 **2:11** [i]S Mt 4:10 [j]Lk 22:31; 2Co 4:4; 1Pe 5:8, 9 **2:12** [k]S Ac 16:8 [l]S Ro 1:1; 2Co 4:3, 4; 8:18; 9:13; 1Th 3:2 [m]S Ac 14:27 **2:13** [n]2Co 7:5 [o]2Co 7:6, 13; 8:6, 16, 23; 12:18; Gal 2:1, 3; Tit 1:4 [p]S Ac 16:9

1:18–19 *not "Yes" and "No."* Paul now appeals to the gospel message he had preached to them. Believing it, they had found it to be true and free from ambiguity, and by their experience of its dynamic power they had proved it to be one great affirmative in Christ.

1:19 *who was preached among you.* During Paul's first visit to Corinth (see Ac 18:5). *Silas.* See Ac 15:22 and note.

1:20 *"Amen."* The "Amen" uttered by the congregation at the end of an offering of prayer or praise (cf. 1Co 14:16 and note on 14:15–17).

1:21 *anointed us.* See Ex 29:7 and note; 1Sa 16:13; Isa 61:1.

1:22 *seal.* See notes on Hag 2:23; Eph 1:13; cf. Eph 4:30. *deposit.* A part given as a guarantee that the whole will be forthcoming (see Ro 8:23 and note). The first installment of a sum of money that has been inherited, e.g., assures the recipient that the whole will be received.

1:23 *to spare you.* Paul's change of plans for visiting the Corinthian Christians had been motivated, not by a fickle and insensitive attitude, but by love and concern for them.

2:1 *another painful visit.* Paul had already made one painful visit to Corinth, and he wanted to avoid another such visit, though he was ready to assert his authority if it should prove necessary (cf. 13:2). This former visit could not have been the one he made to Corinth at the time when the church there was founded in response to the preaching of the gospel (cf. Ac 18). Therefore he must have paid a second visit, which is confirmed by 12:14 and 13:1, where he states that the visit he is now about to make will be his third. The second visit probably took place between the writing of 1 and 2 Corinthians, though some hold that it occurred before 1 Corinthians was written.

2:3–4 See Introduction: Occasion.

2:5–11 Speaks of a particular person who has been the cause of serious offense in Corinth and upon whom church discipline has been imposed. Paul admonishes the Corinthians that because the offender has shown genuine sorrow and repentance for his sin the punishment should be discontinued and he should be lovingly restored to their fellowship. The offense in question probably took place during Paul's intermediate visit to Corinth (see note on v. 1) and may have been the occasion for his writing the severe letter demanding the punishment of the offender (see note on vv. 3–4). Another view is that Paul refers to the incident recorded in 1Co 5.

2:7 *comfort.* See 1:3–7 and note on 1:3.

2:11 *Satan.* See Mt 16:23; 1Jn 3:8 and notes. *his schemes.* See Ge 3:1; Lk 22:31; Jn 8:44 and notes; see also 1Pe 5:8.

2:12 *I went to Troas.* Paul had traveled up from Ephesus to Troas, a city on the Aegean coast (see Ac 16:8 and note; see also map, p. 1711), hoping to find Titus there and to receive news from him about the Corinthian church. But Titus, who presumably Paul knew would be following the same route in reverse, did not arrive in Troas; so Paul, anxious for news from Corinth, "went on to Macedonia" (v. 13), perhaps to the city of Philippi (see map, p. 1711). *opened a door.* See Ac 14:27; Rev 3:8 and notes; see also 1Co 16:9; Col 4:3.

2:13 *my brother.* Cf. 8:23. *Titus.* See Introduction to Titus: Recipient. Paul held Titus in high esteem; he entrusted Titus with the organization of the collection of funds in Corinth for the relief of the poverty-stricken Christians of Jerusalem (see 8:6 and note), and he chose him to carry this letter to the Corinthian Christians (see 8:16–17 and note on 8:16).

14But thanks be to God,[q] who always
leads us in triumphal procession in Christ
and through us spreads everywhere the
fragrance[r] of the knowledge[s] of him. 15For
we are to God the aroma[t] of Christ among
those who are being saved and those who
are perishing.[u] 16To the one we are the
smell of death;[v] to the other, the fragrance
of life. And who is equal to such a task?[w]
17Unlike so many, we do not peddle the
word of God for profit.[x] On the contrary,
in Christ we speak before God with sincerity,[y] like men sent from God.[z]

3 Are we beginning to commend ourselves[a] again? Or do we need, like some
people, letters of recommendation[b] to you
or from you? 2You yourselves are our letter, written on our hearts, known and read
by everybody.[c] 3You show that you are a
letter from Christ, the result of our ministry, written not with ink but with the Spirit
of the living God,[d] not on tablets of stone[e]
but on tablets of human hearts.[f]
4Such confidence[g] as this is ours through
Christ before God. 5Not that we are competent in ourselves[h] to claim anything
for ourselves, but our competence comes
from God.[i] 6He has made us competent as
ministers of a new covenant[j] — not of the
letter[k] but of the Spirit; for the letter kills,
but the Spirit gives life.[l]

The Glory of the New Covenant

7Now if the ministry that brought
death,[m] which was engraved in letters on
stone, came with glory, so that the Israelites could not look steadily at the face of
Moses because of its glory,[n] fading though

2:14 [q]Ro 6:17; 7:25; 1Co 15:57; 2Co 9:15 [r]Eze 20:41; Eph 5:2; Php 4:18 [s]S 2Co 8:7 **2:15** [t]S ver 14; Ge 8:21; Ex 29:18; Nu 15:3 [u]S 1Co 1:18 **2:16** [v]S Lk 2:34; Jn 3:36 [w]2Co 3:5,6 **2:17** [x]S Ac 20:33; 2Co 4:2; 1Th 2:5 [y]1Co 5:8 [z]2Co 1:12; 12:19 **3:1** [a]Ro 16:1; 2Co 5:12; 10:12,18; 12:11 [b]Ac 18:27; Ro 16:1; 1Co 16:3 **3:2** [c]1Co 9:2 **3:3** [d]S Mt 16:16 [e]ver 7; Ex 24:12; 31:18; 32:15,16 [f]Pr 3:3; 7:3; Jer 31:33; Eze 36:26 **3:4** [g]S Eph 3:12 **3:5** [h]2Co 2:16 [i]1Co 15:10 **3:6** [j]S Lk 22:20 [k]Ro 2:29; 7:6 [l]Jn 6:63 **3:7** [m]ver 9; S Ro 4:15 [n]ver 13; Ex 34:29-35; Isa 42:21

2:14 At this point Paul breaks off the narrative of his itinerary and in a characteristic manner begins a lengthy digression (the narrative is not resumed until 7:5; see note there). The digression, however, is relevant to the main tenor of this letter, for it is an outpouring of triumphant faith in praise of the adequacy of God's grace for every situation. *leads us in triumphal procession.* A victorious Roman general would lead his soldiers and their captives in festive procession, while the people watched and applauded and the air was filled with the sweet smell released by the burning of spices in the streets (cf. note on 1Co 4:9). *everywhere.* Cf. note on 1Th 1:8.

2:16 *smell of death ... fragrance of life.* As the gospel aroma is released in the world through Christian testimony, it is always sweet-smelling, even though it may be differently received. Ultimately there are two kinds of people: "those who are being saved and those who are perishing" (v. 15). To the latter, testifying Christians are the smell of death, not because the gospel message has become evil-smelling or death-dealing, but because in rejecting the life-giving grace of God unbelievers choose death for themselves. To those who welcome the gospel of God's grace, Christians with their testimony are the fragrance of life. *who is equal to such a task?* For the answer see 3:4 – 5.

2:17 *peddle the word of God for profit.* Paul is referring to false teachers who had infiltrated the Corinthian church. Such persons — themselves insincere, self-sufficient and boastful — artfully presented themselves in a persuasive manner, and their chief interest was to take money from gullible church members (cf. Mic 3:5,11). Paul, by contrast, had preached the gospel sincerely and free of charge, taking care not to be a financial burden to the Corinthian believers (see 11:7 – 9; 1Co 9:11 – 15 and notes).

3:1 *Are we beginning to commend ourselves again?* Paul realizes that virtually everything he wrote or said was liable to be twisted by the false teachers in Corinth. *letters of recommendation.* The appearance of vagrant impostors led to the need for letters of recommendation. Paul needed no such confirmation; but others, including the Corinthian intruders, did need authentication and often resorted to unscrupulous methods for obtaining or forging such letters.

3:2 *known and read by everybody.* Because of the power of the gospel demonstrated by their transformed lives.

3:3 *letter from Christ.* Paul is no more than an instrument in the hands of the Master. *written not with ink.* As a parchment or papyrus document would be — but ink fades and may easily be deleted or blocked out. *with the Spirit of the living God.* The Spirit is himself life and therefore life-giving (v. 6), and the life he gives is eternal and without defect. *not on tablets of stone.* As at Sinai (see note on v. 6). *on tablets of human hearts.* See Jer 31:33; Eze 11:19; 36:26 and notes. Paul explains the significance of this contrast between the old and the new covenants in vv. 7 – 18.

3:4 – 5 Answers the question raised in 2:16.

3:6 *ministers of.* Those who serve the cause of (see Ro 15:16; Col 1:7; 4:7; 1Ti 4:6). Paul will return to the theme of "this ministry" in 4:1. *new covenant.* Here Paul takes up the theme suggested by the mention of "tablets of human hearts" (v. 3; see note there). See Heb 8 – 10. Paul's reference to "ministers of a new covenant" in contrast to the "ministry that brought death" (v. 7) may have been occasioned by his opponents in Corinth who were Judaizers, perhaps those who claimed to be associated with Peter (see 1Co 1:12 and note) and who are referred to as Hebrews in 11:22 (see note there). *the letter.* The Ten Commandments originally written on the two tablets of stone (see Ex 24:12; 31:18 and note). *the Spirit.* The writing of the law "with the Spirit of the living God ... on tablets of human hearts" (v. 3; see note there), which was the promise of the new covenant as foretold by the prophets (see Jer 31:31 – 34 and notes). *the letter kills, but the Spirit gives life.* Does not mean that the external, literal sense of Scripture is deadly or unprofitable while the inner, spiritual sense is vital. "The letter" is synonymous with the law as an external standard before which all people, because they are lawbreakers, stand guilty and condemned to death. Therefore it is described as the "ministry that brought death" and the "ministry that condemns" (vv. 7,9). On the other hand, the Spirit who "gives life" writes that same law inwardly "on tablets of human hearts" (v. 3). He thus provides believers with love for God's law, which previously they had hated, and with power to keep it, which previously they had not possessed.

3:7 – 18 Paul is defending his ministry of the new covenant in Christ (cf. v. 6 and note) and here compares the experiences of Moses, who mediated the old covenant of Sinai, and his own as a minister of the new covenant. But he now applies the word "ministry" (v. 7) to the law that was "engraved in letters on stone" and to the Spirit, who writes "on tablets of human hearts" (v. 3; see note there). The point of comparison is the fading glory that shone on Moses' face and the "ever-increasing glory" (v. 18; see note there) reflected in the faces of those who minister the new covenant.

3:7 *came with glory.* The law of the old covenant given at Sinai was in no way bad or evil; on the contrary, Paul describes it

it was, 8will not the ministry of the Spirit be even more glorious? 9If the ministry that condemns men[o] is glorious, how much more glorious is the ministry that brings righteousness![p] 10For what was glorious has no glory now in comparison with the surpassing glory. 11And if what was fading away came with glory, how much greater is the glory of that which lasts!

12Therefore, since we have such a hope,[q] we are very bold.[r] 13We are not like Moses, who would put a veil over his face[s] to keep the Israelites from gazing at it while the radiance was fading away. 14But their minds were made dull,[t] for to this day the same veil remains when the old covenant[u] is read.[v] It has not been removed, because only in Christ is it taken away. 15Even to this day when Moses is read, a veil covers their hearts. 16But whenever anyone turns to the Lord,[w] the veil is taken away.[x] 17Now the Lord is the Spirit,[y] and where the Spirit of the Lord is, there is freedom.[z] 18And we, who with unveiled faces all reflect[a][a] the Lord's glory,[b] are being transformed into his likeness[c] with ever-increasing glory, which comes from the Lord, who is the Spirit.

3:9 [o]ver 7; Dt 27:26 [p]Ro 1:17; 3:21,22 **3:12** [q]Ro 5:4,5; 8:24,25 [r]S Ac 4:29 **3:13** [s]ver 7; Ex 34:33 **3:14** [t]Ro 11:7,8; 2Co 4:4 [u]Ac 13:15; 15:21 [v]ver 6 **3:16** [w]Ro 11:23 [x]Ex 34:34; Isa 25:7 **3:17** [y]Isa 61:1,2; Gal 4:6,7 [z]S Jn 8:32 **3:18** [a]1Co 13:12 [b]Jn 17:22,24; 2Co 4:4,6 [c]S Ro 8:29

4:1 [d]1Co 7:25; 1Ti 1:13,16 [e]ver 16; Ps 18:45; Isa 40:31 **4:2** [f]Ro 6:21; S 1Co 4:5 [g]2Co 2:17; S Heb 4:12 [h]2Co 5:11 **4:3** [i]S 2Co 2:12 [j]2Co 3:14 [k]S 1Co 1:18 **4:4** [l]S Jn 12:31 [m]S 1Co 1:20 [n]2Co 3:14 [o]ver 6 [p]S Jn 14:9

Treasures in Jars of Clay

4 Therefore, since through God's mercy[d] we have this ministry, we do not lose heart.[e] 2Rather, we have renounced secret and shameful ways;[f] we do not use deception, nor do we distort the word of God.[g] On the contrary, by setting forth the truth plainly we commend ourselves to every man's conscience[h] in the sight of God. 3And even if our gospel[i] is veiled,[j] it is veiled to those who are perishing.[k] 4The god[l] of this age[m] has blinded[n] the minds of unbelievers, so that they cannot see the light of the gospel of the glory of Christ,[o] who is the image of God.[p] 5For we do not preach ourselves,[q] but Jesus Christ as Lord,[r] and ourselves as your servants[s] for Jesus' sake. 6For God, who said, "Let light shine out of darkness,"[b][t] made his light shine in our hearts[u] to give us the light of the knowledge of the glory of God in the face of Christ.[v]

7But we have this treasure in jars of clay[w] to show that this all-surpassing power is

[a] 18 Or *contemplate* [b] 6 Gen. 1:3

4:5 [q]1Co 1:13 [r]1Co 1:23 [s]1Co 9:19 **4:6** [t]Ge 1:3; Ps 18:28 [u]2Pe 1:19 [v]ver 4 **4:7** [w]Job 4:19; Isa 64:8; 2Ti 2:20

elsewhere as holy, righteous, good and spiritual (Ro 7:12,14). The evil is in the hearts and deeds of people who, as lawbreakers, bring upon themselves the condemnation of the law and the penalty of death—and the law engraved on stone could not purge away that evil. *its glory.* The glory of God surrounded the giving of the law and was reflected on the face of Moses when he descended from the mountain (see Ex 34:29–30).

3:8–9 *ministry of the Spirit... brings righteousness.* Giving life instead of death (cf. Isa 46:13 and note).

3:11 *what was fading away.* The old covenant of Sinai, which was not to endure forever. In due course it was superseded by the unfading and much more glorious radiance belonging to the new covenant (see Heb 8 and notes on 8:7–13).

3:13 *Moses, who would put a veil over his face.* See Ex 34:33–35 and note on 34:33. The purpose of the veil was to prevent the Israelites from seeing the fading of the glory.

3:14 *to this day the same veil remains.* The veil that prevented the Israelites from seeing the fading of the glory on Moses' face kept them from recognizing the temporary and inadequate character of the old covenant—a "veil" that is removed only in Christ.

3:17 *the Lord is the Spirit.* This statement should be linked with what was said at the end of v. 6: "the Spirit gives life." Only by turning to the Lord Jesus Christ (v. 16) can the condemnation and the sentence of death pronounced by the law on the lawbreaker be annulled and replaced by the free life-giving grace of the new covenant. *where the Spirit of the Lord is, there is freedom.* See Jn 8:33,36 and note on 8:32.

3:18 *with unveiled faces.* In contrast to Moses. *transformed into his likeness with ever-increasing glory.* Christ himself is the glory of God in the fullness of its radiance (see Heb 1:2–3 and note); his is the eternal and unfading glory, which he had with the Father "before the world began" (Jn 17:5). Cf. Ro 8:29; 12:2 and notes.

4:1 *this ministry.* See 3:6 and note. *not lose heart.* When God through his mercy calls and commissions his servants, he also supplies the strength necessary for them to persevere in the face of hardship and persecution.

4:2 *renounced secret and shameful ways.* Paul is referring to the false teachers in Corinth. By contrast, he is able to appeal to the conscience of every one of them and also to his own integrity "in the sight of God," because his practice was always that of setting forth the truth plainly, i.e., without obscuring it or resorting to deception (cf. 1:12,18–24 and note on 1:12).

4:3 *gospel is veiled.* See 3:13–18 and notes.

4:4 *god of this age.* The devil, who is the archenemy of God and the unseen power behind all unbelief and ungodliness. Those who follow him have in effect made him their god. *this age.* Used in contrast to the future eternal age when God's creation will be forever purged of all that now mars and defiles it. Paul calls it the "present evil age" in Gal 1:4 (see note there). *blinded the minds of unbelievers.* Paul continues to use the imagery of the veil that covers the divine glory so that those who reject the gospel fail to see that glory (3:13–18). *image of God.* Christ, the incarnate Son, authentically displays God to us, for he is the very radiance of divine glory (Heb 1:3). He is the image of God in which humanity was originally created (see Ge 1:26 and note) and into which redeemed humanity is being gloriously transformed (3:18) until at last, when Christ comes again at the end of this age, we who believe will "be like him" (1Jn 3:2).

4:5 *we do not preach ourselves.* As did the false teachers, puffed up with self-importance (cf. 1Co 2:2 and note).

4:6 *Let light shine out of darkness.* God said this at the creation (see Ge 1:2–4 and notes), and God says it again in the new creation or new birth (see 5:17; Jn 3:3 and notes; 1Pe 1:3) as the darkness of sin is dispelled by the light of the gospel. *the light of the knowledge of the glory of God.* The light that now shines in Paul's heart (qualifying him to be a proclaimer of Christ) is the knowledge of God's glory as it was displayed in the face of Christ—who has come from the glorious presence of God in heaven (see Jn 1:14 and note).

4:7 *this treasure.* The gospel. *jars of clay.* Treasures were concealed in clay jars, which had little value or beauty and did not attract attention to themselves and their con-

from God[x] and not from us. 8We are hard pressed on every side,[y] but not crushed; perplexed,[z] but not in despair; 9persecuted,[a] but not abandoned;[b] struck down, but not destroyed.[c] 10We always carry around in our body the death of Jesus,[d] so that the life of Jesus may also be revealed in our body.[e] 11For we who are alive are always being given over to death for Jesus' sake,[f] so that his life may be revealed in our mortal body. 12So then, death is at work in us, but life is at work in you.[g]

13It is written: "I believed; therefore I have spoken."[a][h] With that same spirit of faith[i] we also believe and therefore speak, 14because we know that the one who raised the Lord Jesus from the dead[j] will also raise us with Jesus[k] and present us with you in his presence.[l] 15All this is for your benefit, so that the grace that is reaching more and more people may cause thanksgiving[m] to overflow to the glory of God.

16Therefore we do not lose heart.[n] Though outwardly we are wasting away, yet inwardly[o] we are being renewed[p] day by day. 17For our light and momentary troubles are achieving for us an eternal glory that far outweighs them all.[q] 18So we fix our eyes not on what is seen, but on what is unseen.[r] For what is seen is temporary, but what is unseen is eternal.

Our Heavenly Dwelling

5 Now we know that if the earthly[s] tent[t] we live in is destroyed, we have a building from God, an eternal house in heaven, not built by human hands. 2Meanwhile we groan,[u] longing to be clothed with our heavenly dwelling,[v] 3because when we are clothed, we will not be found naked. 4For while we are in this tent, we groan[w] and are burdened, because we do not wish to be unclothed but to be clothed with our heavenly dwelling,[x] so that what is mortal may be swallowed up by life. 5Now it is God who has made us for this very purpose and has given us the Spirit as a deposit, guaranteeing what is to come.[y]

6Therefore we are always confident and know that as long as we are at home in the body we are away from the Lord.

[a] *13* Psalm 116:10

4:7 [x]Jdg 7:2; 1Co 2:5; 2Co 6:7 **4:8** [y]2Co 7:5 [z]Gal 4:20 **4:9** [a]Jn 15:20; Ro 8:35 [b]Heb 13:5 [c]Ps 37:24; Pr 24:16 **4:10** [d]S Ro 6:6; S 2Co 1:5 [e]S Ro 6:5 **4:11** [f]Ro 8:36 **4:12** [g]2Co 13:9 **4:13** [h]Ps 116:10 [i]1Co 12:9 **4:14** [j]S Ac 2:24 [k]1Th 4:14 [l]Eph 5:27; Col 1:22; Jude 24 **4:15** [m]2Co 1:11; 9:11 **4:16** [n]ver 1; Ps 18:45 [o]Ro 7:22 [p]Ps 103:5; Isa 40:31; Col 3:10 **4:17** [q]Ps 30:5; Ro 8:18; 1Pe 1:6,7 **4:18** [r]2Co 5:7; Ro 8:24; Heb 11:1 **5:1** [s]1Co 15:47 [t]Isa 38:12; 2Pe 1:13,14 **5:2** [u]ver 4; Ro 8:23 [v]ver 4; 1Co 15:53,54 **5:4** [w]ver 2; Ro 8:23 [x]ver 2; 1Co 15:53,54 **5:5** [y]Ro 8:23; 2Co 1:22; Eph 1:13,14

tents. Here they represent Paul's human frailty and unworthiness. *all-surpassing power is from God and not from us.* The idea that the absolute insufficiency of human beings reveals the total sufficiency of God pervades this letter.

4:8–12 See 11:23–26 and notes.

4:10 *We always carry around in our body the death of Jesus.* The frailty of the clay jar of Paul's humanity (v. 7) is plainly seen in the constant hardships and persecutions with which he is buffeted for the sake of the gospel and through which he shares in Christ's suffering (see 1:5; see also Ro 8:17; Php 3:10; Col 1:24 and notes). *that the life of Jesus may also be revealed in our body.* Refers to Christ's resurrection life and power (see Php 3:10 and note). Once again (see v. 7 and note), human weakness provides the occasion for the triumph of divine power.

4:12 *death.* See 1Co 15:31 and note. *life.* See v. 10 and note.

4:13 *I believed; therefore I have spoken.* Faith leads to testimony. Paul therefore tirelessly labored and journeyed to bring the gospel message to others.

4:14 *one who raised the Lord Jesus.* God (Ac 2:24). *raise us with Jesus.* See Ro 8:11; 1Co 15:20 and notes.

4:16 *we do not lose heart.* Repeating the statement in v. 1. The intervening paragraphs explain why the apostle continues to have a cheerful heart, and the rest of the chapter summarizes the argument he has developed. *wasting away.* Because of the hardships to which he is subjected. *being renewed.* Because of the flame of resurrection life burning within.

4:17 *light and momentary troubles.* Seen from the perspective of eternity, the Christian's difficulties diminish in importance. *eternal glory that far outweighs them all.* By comparison, the eternal glory is far greater than all the suffering one may face in this life (see Ro 8:17–18 and note on 8:17).

4:18 *what is seen … what is unseen.* The experiences and circumstances of this present life are visible to the Christian; but these are merely temporary and fleeting. To fix our eyes on them would cause us to "lose heart" (vv. 1,16). By contrast the unseen realities, which are no less real for being invisible (cf. Heb 11:1,7,26–27), are eternal and imperishable. Accordingly, we look up and away from the impermanent appearances of this present world scene (see Php 3:20; Heb 12:2 and notes).

5:1 *earthly tent we live in.* Our present body (see Jn 1:14 and note; 2Pe 1:13). As a tent is a temporary and flimsy abode, so our bodies are frail, vulnerable and wasting away (see 4:10–12,16 and notes). *a building from God, an eternal house in heaven.* A solid structure—permanent, not temporary. This is one of the eternal realities that are as yet "unseen" (4:18). *not built by human hands.* The work of God, and therefore perfect and permanent (see Heb 9:11 and note).

5:2 *Meanwhile.* As we await the Lord's return. *we groan.* Because we long for the perfection that will be ours when we put on the glorious spiritual body (cf. 1Co 15:42–49 and notes). *clothed with our heavenly dwelling.* The eternal dwelling provided by God is pictured as a garment.

5:3 *naked.* Without the clothing of a body, which is the state of those whose earthly dwelling has been dismantled by death (see v. 8 and note).

5:4 *what is mortal.* Our present mortal body. *swallowed up by life.* By our participation in the resurrection life of Jesus (see 4:10 and note) our mortal being is "swallowed up by life," not by death. Paul reverses the age-old imagery of death and the grave being the great swallower (see Ps 49:14 and note), as did Isaiah (see Isa 25:8; see also 1Co 15:54).

5:5 *God … has given us the Spirit.* The Holy Spirit applies the benefits of Christ's redeeming work to the hearts of believers and makes his resurrection power a reality of their daily experience (cf. 4:10–16 and notes). This guarantees their eventual transformation into the likeness of Christ's glorified body (see Php 3:21 and note). *deposit.* See 1:22 and note.

5:6 *at home in the body … away from the Lord.* Still living here in our earthly dwelling (see v. 1 and note); it does not mean that we are deprived of the Lord's spiritual presence with us in our daily lives.

7We live by faith, not by sight.[z] 8We are
confident, I say, and would prefer to be
away from the body and at home with the
Lord.[a] 9So we make it our goal to please
him,[b] whether we are at home in the body
or away from it. 10For we must all appear
before the judgment seat of Christ, that
each one may receive what is due him[c] for
the things done while in the body, whether good or bad.

The Ministry of Reconciliation

11Since, then, we know what it is to fear
the Lord,[d] we try to persuade men. What
we are is plain to God, and I hope it is also
plain to your conscience.[e] 12We are not trying to commend ourselves to you again,[f]
but are giving you an opportunity to take
pride in us,[g] so that you can answer those
who take pride in what is seen rather than
in what is in the heart. 13If we are out
of our mind,[h] it is for the sake of God;
if we are in our right mind, it is for you.
14For Christ's love compels us, because we
are convinced that one died for all, and
therefore all died.[i] 15And he died for all,
that those who live should no longer live
for themselves[j] but for him who died for
them[k] and was raised again.
16So from now on we regard no one
from a worldly[l] point of view. Though
we once regarded Christ in this way, we
do so no longer. 17Therefore, if anyone is
in Christ,[m] he is a new creation;[n] the old
has gone, the new has come![o] 18All this is
from God,[p] who reconciled us to himself
through Christ[q] and gave us the ministry
of reconciliation: 19that God was reconciling the world to himself in Christ, not
counting men's sins against them.[r] And he
has committed to us the message of reconciliation. 20We are therefore Christ's ambassadors,[s] as though God were making
his appeal through us.[t] We implore you
on Christ's behalf: Be reconciled to God.[u]
21God made him who had no sin[v] to be
sin[a] for us, so that in him we might become the righteousness of God.[w]

6 As God's fellow workers[x] we urge you
not to receive God's grace in vain.[y] 2For
he says,

> "In the time of my favor I heard you,
> and in the day of salvation I helped
> you."[b][z]

I tell you, now is the time of God's favor,
now is the day of salvation.

[a] *21* Or *be a sin offering* [b] *2* Isaiah 49:8

5:7 [z] 1Co 13:12; S 2Co 4:18 **5:8** [a] S Jn 12:26 **5:9** [b] Ro 14:18; Eph 5:10; Col 1:10; 1Th 4:1 **5:10** [c] S Mt 16:27; Ac 10:42; Ro 2:16; 14:10; Eph 6:8 **5:11** [d] Job 23:15; Heb 10:31; 12:29; Jude 23 [e] 2Co 4:2 **5:12** [f] S 2Co 3:1 [g] 2Co 1:14 **5:13** [h] 2Co 11:1,16,17; 12:11 **5:14** [i] Ro 6:6,7; Gal 2:20; Col 3:3 **5:15** [j] Ro 14:7-9 [k] Ro 4:25 **5:16** [l] 2Co 10:4; 11:18 **5:17** [m] S Ro 16:3 [n] S Jn 1:13; S Ro 6:4; Gal 6:15 [o] Isa 65:17; Rev 21:4,5 **5:18** [p] S Ro 11:36 [q] S Ro 5:10 **5:19** [r] S Ro 4:8 **5:20** [s] 2Co 6:1; Eph 6:20 [t] ver 18 [u] Isa 27:5 **5:21** [v] Heb 4:15; 7:26; 1Pe 2:22,24; 1Jn 3:5 [w] S Ro 1:17; S 1Co 1:30 **6:1** [x] S 1Co 3:9; 2Co 5:20 [y] 1Co 15:2 **6:2** [z] Isa 49:8; Ps 69:13; Isa 55:6

5:7 *by faith, not by sight.* See 4:18 and note; cf. 1Co 13:12 and note.

5:8 *away from the body ... at home with the Lord.* The situation of believers after death, when they are no longer living in their mortal bodies (see Php 1:23 and note).

5:9 *whether we are at home in the body or away from it.* Whether we will still be alive or will already be with the Lord.

5:10 *appear before the judgment seat of Christ.* To give an accounting of what we have done with our lives as Christians (cf. 1Co 3:11–15 and note on 3:13). *things done while in the body.* Although the body is wasting away, we are responsible for our actions while in it.

5:11 *fear the Lord.* As the one to whom we are accountable (v. 10; see Ge 20:11; Pr 1:7 and notes). *we try to persuade.* Paul needs to persuade some members of the Corinthian church that he, not any of the false teachers who have invaded their ranks, is their authentic apostle.

5:12 *take pride in what is seen.* The pretension of the false apostles is a superficial front; their concern is not with spirituality that is true and deep, but with money, popularity and self-importance.

5:13 *out of our mind ... in our right mind.* Perhaps Paul's enemies were asserting that he was suffering from religious mania—what they regarded as his insane way of life. If this is what it means to be out of his mind, Paul does not deny it, for this whole letter shows how willingly and joyfully he endured affliction for the gospel (see 12:10). On the other hand, there was nothing that could be called eccentric about his manner of presenting the gospel to the Corinthians, for he had been sensible and sober-minded, avoiding flowery rhetoric and all forms of sensationalism (see 1Co 2:1–5 and notes).

5:14 *Christ's love.* As shown in his death for us, though some hold that the meaning here is "our love for Christ." *one.* The incarnate Son. *therefore all died.* Because Christ died for all, he involved all in his death. For some his death would confirm their own death, but for others (those who by faith would become united with him) his death was their death to sin and self, so that they now live in and with the resurrected Christ (v. 15; see Ro 6:1–11). However, some interpreters hold that Paul is not speaking specifically here about the scope of Christ's atonement but about the effect of Christ's death on the Christian life. Thus "all" would refer not to every human being but only to believers.

5:16 *we once regarded Christ in this way.* Paul admits that before his conversion he held views of Christ that were "worldly"—based on purely human considerations.

5:17 *in Christ.* United with Christ through faith in him and commitment to him (see Ro 6:11; Eph 1:1; Php 2:1 and notes). *new creation.* Redemption is the restoration and fulfillment of God's purposes in creation (see 4:6 and note), and this takes place in Christ, through whom all things were made (see Col 1:16 and note; Heb 1:2) and in whom all things are restored or created anew (cf. Ro 8:19–23; Eph 2:10).

5:18 *All this is from God.* God takes the initiative in redemption (see Jn 3:16; Ro 5:8; Eph 2:8–10 and notes), and he sustains it and brings it to completion (see Php 1:6 and note). *ministry of reconciliation.* We who are the recipients of divine reconciliation have the privilege and obligation of now being God's instruments to proclaim the "message of reconciliation" (v. 19) throughout the world. *reconciliation.* See Ro 5:10 and note.

5:21 A summary of the gospel. Christ, the only entirely righteous one, at Calvary took our sin upon himself and endured the punishment we deserved (see NIV text note), namely, death and separation from God. Thus, by a marvelous exchange, he made it possible for us to receive his righteousness and thereby be reconciled to God (cf. 1Co 1:30 and note).

6:1 *to receive God's grace in vain.* To live for oneself (see 5:15) is one way to do this.

6:2 *time of my favor ... day of salvation.* An affirmation that is true in a general sense of all God's saving acts in the his-

Paul's Hardships

3We put no stumbling block in anyone's path,[a] so that our ministry will not be discredited. 4Rather, as servants of God we commend ourselves in every way: in great endurance; in troubles, hardships and distresses; 5in beatings, imprisonments[b] and riots; in hard work, sleepless nights and hunger;[c] 6in purity, understanding, patience and kindness; in the Holy Spirit[d] and in sincere love;[e] 7in truthful speech[f] and in the power of God;[g] with weapons of righteousness[h] in the right hand and in the left; 8through glory and dishonor,[i] bad report[j] and good report; genuine, yet regarded as impostors;[k] 9known, yet regarded as unknown; dying,[l] and yet we live on;[m] beaten, and yet not killed; 10sorrowful, yet always rejoicing;[n] poor, yet making many rich;[o] having nothing,[p] and yet possessing everything.[q]

11We have spoken freely to you, Corinthians, and opened wide our hearts to you.[r] 12We are not withholding our affection from you, but you are withholding yours from us. 13As a fair exchange—I speak as to my children[s]—open wide your hearts[t] also.

Do Not Be Yoked With Unbelievers

14Do not be yoked together[u] with unbelievers.[v] For what do righteousness and wickedness have in common? Or what fellowship can light have with darkness?[w] 15What harmony is there between Christ and Belial[a]?[x] What does a believer[y] have in common with an unbeliever?[z] 16What agreement is there between the temple of God and idols?[a] For we are the temple[b] of the living God.[c] As God has said: "I will live with them and walk among them, and I will be their God, and they will be my people."[b][d]

17"Therefore come out from them[e]
and be separate,
says the Lord.
Touch no unclean thing,
and I will receive you."[c][f]
18"I will be a Father to you,
and you will be my sons and
daughters,[g]
says the Lord Almighty."[d][h]

7 Since we have these promises,[i] dear friends,[j] let us purify ourselves from everything that contaminates body and spirit, perfecting holiness[k] out of reverence for God.

Paul's Joy

2Make room for us in your hearts.[l] We have wronged no one, we have corrupted no one, we have exploited no one. 3I do not say this to condemn you; I have said before that you have such a place in our hearts[m] that we would live or die with you. 4I have great confidence in you; I take great pride in you.[n] I am greatly encouraged;[o] in all our troubles my joy knows no bounds.[p]

6:3 [a]S Mt 5:29; Ro 14:13,20; 1Co 8:9,13; 9:12; 10:32 **6:5** [b]Ac 16:23; 2Co 11:23-25 [c]1Co 4:11 **6:6** [d]1Co 2:4; 1Th 1:5 [e]Ro 12:9; 1Ti 1:5 **6:7** [f]2Co 4:2 [g]2Co 4:7 [h]Ro 13:12; 2Co 10:4; Eph 6:10-18 **6:8** [i]1Co 4:10 [j]1Co 4:13 [k]Mt 27:63 **6:9** [l]S Ro 8:36 [m]2Co 1:8-10; 4:10,11 **6:10** [n]S Mt 5:12; 2Co 7:4; Php 2:17; 4:4; Col 1:24; 1Th 1:6 [o]2Co 8:9 [p]Ac 3:6 [q]Ro 8:32; 1Co 3:21 **6:11** [r]2Co 7:3 **6:13** [s]S 1Th 2:11 [t]2Co 7:2 **6:14** [u]Ge 24:3; Dt 22:10; 1Co 5:9,10 [v]1Co 6:6 [w]Eph 5:7,11; 1Jn 1:6 **6:15** [x]1Co 10:21 [y]Ac 5:14 [z]1Co 6:6 **6:16** [a]1Co 10:21 [b]S 1Co 3:16 [c]S Mt 16:16 [d]Lev 26:12; Jer 32:38; Eze 37:27; Rev 21:3 **6:17** [e]Rev 18:4 [f]Isa 52:11; Eze 20:34,41 **6:18** [g]Ex 4:22; 2Sa 7:14; 1Ch 17:13; Isa 43:6; S Ro 8:14 [h]2Sa 7:8 **7:1** [i]2Co 6:17,18 [j]S 1Co 10:14 [k]1Th 4:7; 1Pe 1:15,16 **7:2** [l]2Co 6:12,13 **7:3** [m]2Co 6:11,12; Php 1:7 **7:4** [n]ver 14; 2Co 8:24 [o]ver 13 [p]S 2Co 6:10

[a] 15 Greek *Beliar,* a variant of *Belial* [b] 16 Lev. 26:12; Jer. 32:38; Ezek. 37:27 [c] 17 Isaiah 52:11; Ezek. 20:34,41 [d] 18 2 Samuel 7:14; 7:8

tory of his people, but that finds its particular fulfillment in this present age of grace between the two comings of Christ. *now.* Underscores the urgency of the divine invitation (see Ps 32:6 and note).

6:4–10 Cf. 4:8–12.

6:4 *as servants of God we commend ourselves.* Paul commends himself again inasmuch as the gospel he preached in Corinth is at stake; but, in contrast to the false apostles who were no better than self-servers, he does so as God's servant.

6:5 *imprisonments.* See, e.g., Ac 16:23; Eph 3:1; Php 1:13–14; Col 4:18; 2Ti 1:16; Phm 1.

6:7 *weapons of righteousness.* Cf. Eph 6:14–17 and notes.

6:10 *making many rich.* True wealth does not consist in worldly possessions but in being "rich toward God" (Lk 12:21). Believers, even if they have nothing of this world's goods, nevertheless have everything in him who is Lord of all (cf. 1Co 1:4–5; 3:21–23; Eph 2:7; 3:8; Php 4:19 and note; Col 2:3).

6:11–13 Paul has always been completely open and sincere in his relations with the Christians in Corinth (cf. 1:12–14; 4:2 and note), but the false apostles among them have been trying to persuade them that Paul does not really love them. Now the apostle tenderly appeals to these Corinthians, who are the beneficiaries of his love for them (cf. 11:11).

6:14 *Do not be yoked together with unbelievers.* Cf. Dt 22:10. For the Corinthian believers to cooperate with false teachers, who are in reality servants of Satan notwithstanding their charming and persuasive ways (see 11:13–14 and notes), is to become unequally yoked, destroying the harmony and fellowship that unite true believers in Christ. *what fellowship can light have with darkness?* See 4:6 and note.

6:15 *Belial.* Satan (see Dt 13:13 and note).

6:16 *agreement … between the temple of God and idols.* There can be no reversion to or compromise with the idolatry they have forsaken for the gospel (cf. 1Th 1:9). *temple of the living God.* Built of "living stones," namely, Christian believers (1Pe 2:5; see note there); therefore it is all the more important that they form no defiling and unholy alliances (cf. 1Co 6:19–20). *their God … my people.* The supreme OT affirmation of covenant relationship between God and his people (see Jer 7:23; Hos 1:9; Zec 8:8 and notes).

6:17 *come out from them.* See Rev 18:4 and note.

7:1 *holiness.* See 1Co 1:2; Ex 3:5; Lev 11:44; Ro 6:22; 1Th 4:7 and notes.

7:2 *Make room for us in your hearts.* Resumes the thought of 6:13 after a brief digression. *We have … exploited no one.* Implies that Paul had been accused by the false teachers of being unjust, destructive and fraudulent—the very things they themselves were guilty of. Cf. 1Sa 12:3 and note.

7:3 Again Paul declares the depth of his affection for the Corinthian believers and appeals to them to respond by displaying their love for him (cf. 6:11–13 and note).

7:4 *great confidence … my joy knows no bounds.* The long digression that started at 2:14 (see note there) concludes here

5For when we came into Macedonia,[q] this body of ours had no rest, but we were harassed at every turn[r]—conflicts on the outside, fears within.[s] 6But God, who comforts the downcast,[t] comforted us by the coming of Titus,[u] 7and not only by his coming but also by the comfort you had given him. He told us about your longing for me, your deep sorrow, your ardent concern for me, so that my joy was greater than ever.

8Even if I caused you sorrow by my letter,[v] I do not regret it. Though I did regret it—I see that my letter hurt you, but only for a little while— 9yet now I am happy, not because you were made sorry, but because your sorrow led you to repentance. For you became sorrowful as God intended and so were not harmed in any way by us. 10Godly sorrow brings repentance that leads to salvation[w] and leaves no regret, but worldly sorrow brings death. 11See what this godly sorrow has produced in you: what earnestness, what eagerness to clear yourselves, what indignation, what alarm, what longing, what concern,[x] what readiness to see justice done. At every point you have proved yourselves to be innocent in this matter. 12So even though I wrote to you,[y] it was not on account of the one who did the wrong[z] or of the injured party, but rather that before God you could see for yourselves how devoted to us you are. 13By all this we are encouraged.

In addition to our own encouragement, we were especially delighted to see how happy Titus[a] was, because his spirit has been refreshed by all of you. 14I had boasted to him about you,[b] and you have not embarrassed me. But just as everything we said to you was true, so our boasting about you to Titus[c] has proved to be true as well. 15And his affection for you is all the greater when he remembers that you were all obedient,[d] receiving him with fear and trembling.[e] 16I am glad I can have complete confidence in you.[f]

Generosity Encouraged

8 And now, brothers, we want you to know about the grace that God has given the Macedonian[g] churches. 2Out of the most severe trial, their overflowing joy and their extreme poverty welled up in rich generosity.[h] 3For I testify that they gave as much as they were able,[i] and even beyond their ability. Entirely on their own, 4they urgently pleaded with us for the privilege of sharing[j] in this service[k] to the saints.[l] 5And they did not do as we expected, but they gave themselves first to the Lord and then to us in keeping with God's will. 6So we urged[m] Titus,[n] since he had earlier made a beginning, to bring also to completion[o] this act of grace on your part. 7But just as you excel in everything[p]—in faith, in speech, in knowledge,[q] in complete earnestness and in your love for us[a]—see that you also excel in this grace of giving.

8I am not commanding you,[r] but I want to test the sincerity of your love by comparing it with the earnestness of others. 9For you know the grace[s] of our Lord Jesus Christ,[t] that though he was rich, yet for your sakes he became poor,[u] so that you through his poverty might become rich.[v]

7:5 [q]2Co 2:13; S Ac 16:9 [r]2Co 4:8 [s]Dt 32:25 **7:6** [t]2Co 1:3,4 [u]ver 13; S 2Co 2:13 **7:8** [v]2Co 2:2,4 **7:10** [w]Ac 11:18 **7:11** [x]ver 7 **7:12** [y]ver 8; 2Co 2:3,9 [z]1Co 5:1,2 **7:13** [a]ver 6; S 2Co 2:13 **7:14** [b]ver 4 [c]ver 6 **7:15** [d]2Co 2:9; 10:6 [e]Ps 55:5; 1Co 2:3; Php 2:12 **7:16** [f]S 2Co 2:3 **8:1** [g]S Ac 16:9 **8:2** [h]Ex 36:5; 2Co 9:11 **8:3** [i]1Co 16:2 **8:4** [j]ver 1 [k]S Ac 24:17 [l]S Ac 9:13 **8:6** [m]ver 17; 2Co 12:18 [n]ver 16,23; S 2Co 2:13 [o]ver 10,11 **8:7** [p]2Co 9:8 [q]Ro 15:14; 1Co 1:5; 12:8; 13:1,2; 14:6 **8:8** [r]1Co 7:6 **8:9** [s]S Ro 3:24 [t]2Co 13:14 [u]Mt 20:28; Php 2:6-8 [v]2Co 6:10

[a] 7 Some manuscripts *in our love for you*

on this note of exhilaration. The news he had been so anxiously awaiting from Corinth has turned out to be reassuring, and Paul is overjoyed to receive it.

7:5 *we.* Paul and Titus. Here Paul resumes the account he began in 2:12–13, where he described how his hopes of meeting Titus in Troas were disappointed and how, restless for news, he had decided to press on into Macedonia. He now explains that on reaching Macedonia, he was at last comforted by the arrival of Titus, who had been well received in Corinth and was able to assure Paul (see v. 7) of the "longing" and "ardent concern" of the Corinthian Christians for him and of the "deep sorrow" they had expressed because of the grief they had caused him. Consequently, his "joy was greater than ever." *Macedonia.* See notes on 1:1; Php 4:15.

7:6 *God … comforts the downcast.* See 1:3 and note; cf. Ps 42:5,11; 43:5. *Titus.* See Introduction to Titus: Recipient.

7:8 Paul regretted the necessity of writing a letter to the Corinthians that caused them sorrow. *my letter.* Some think Paul here refers either to 1 Corinthians or to 2Co 10–13 (see Introduction: Occasion), but more likely he refers to a letter now lost that he wrote shortly after his "painful visit" (2:1; see note there).

7:10 *Godly sorrow … worldly sorrow.* The former manifests itself by repentance and the experience of divine grace; the latter brings death because, instead of being God-centered sorrow over the wickedness of sin, it is self-centered sorrow over the painful consequences of sin.

7:15 *you were all obedient.* This seems to indicate that when Titus left Corinth to report to Paul, there was no strong opposition party (see note on 10:1).

8:1—9:15 Paul addresses the question of the collection of money for the distressed believers in Jerusalem, which the Corinthians had started but not completed.

8:1 *grace.* The "grace of giving" on the part of believers (v. 7) is more than matched by the self-giving "grace of our Lord Jesus Christ" (v. 9).

8:2 *overflowing joy.* In the blessings of the gospel.

8:5 *they gave themselves first to the Lord.* The true basis of all Christian giving. God's grace makes a difference in the lives and attitudes of his people—a central theme of this letter (cf. 12:9–10).

8:6 *we urged Titus.* The collection had been started in Corinth under the direction of Titus during the previous year (see v. 10; 9:2) but had slowed down or come to a standstill. Paul is now sending Titus back to them, bearing this present letter, for the purpose of completing this "act of grace."

8:7 *you excel in everything.* Cf. 1Co 1:4–7.

8:8 *I am not commanding you.* True charity and generosity cannot be commanded. *sincerity of your love.* They can prove this by giving selflessly and spontaneously. *earnestness of others.* The remarkable example of the Macedonian churches (vv. 1–5).

8:9 *though he was rich … he became poor.* The eternal Son, in his incarnation and atoning death, emptied himself of his riches (see Php 2:7 and note). *through his poverty*

10And here is my advice[w] about what is
best for you in this matter: Last year you
were the first not only to give but also to
have the desire to do so.[x] 11Now finish the
work, so that your eager willingness[y] to
do it may be matched by your completion
of it, according to your means. 12For if the
willingness is there, the gift is acceptable
according to what one has,[z] not according
to what he does not have.
13Our desire is not that others might
be relieved while you are hard pressed,
but that there might be equality. 14At the
present time your plenty will supply what
they need,[a] so that in turn their plenty will
supply what you need. Then there will be
equality, 15as it is written: "He who gathered much did not have too much, and
he who gathered little did not have too
little."[a][b]

Titus Sent to Corinth

16I thank God,[c] who put into the heart[d]
of Titus[e] the same concern I have for you.
17For Titus not only welcomed our appeal,
but he is coming to you with much enthusiasm and on his own initiative.[f] 18And we
are sending along with him the brother[g]
who is praised by all the churches[h] for his
service to the gospel.[i] 19What is more, he
was chosen by the churches to accompany us[j] as we carry the offering, which we
administer in order to honor the Lord himself and to show our eagerness to help.[k]
20We want to avoid any criticism of the
way we administer this liberal gift. 21For
we are taking pains to do what is right,
not only in the eyes of the Lord but also in
the eyes of men.[l]
22In addition, we are sending with them
our brother who has often proved to us in
many ways that he is zealous, and now
even more so because of his great confidence in you. 23As for Titus,[m] he is my
partner[n] and fellow worker[o] among you;
as for our brothers,[p] they are representatives of the churches and an honor to
Christ. 24Therefore show these men the
proof of your love and the reason for our
pride in you,[q] so that the churches can
see it.

9 There is no need[r] for me to write to you
about this service[s] to the saints.[t] 2For I
know your eagerness to help,[u] and I have
been boasting[v] about it to the Macedonians, telling them that since last year[w] you
in Achaia[x] were ready to give; and your
enthusiasm has stirred most of them to
action. 3But I am sending the brothers[y] in
order that our boasting about you in this
matter should not prove hollow, but that
you may be ready, as I said you would be.[z]
4For if any Macedonians[a] come with me
and find you unprepared, we — not to say
anything about you — would be ashamed
of having been so confident. 5So I thought
it necessary to urge the brothers[b] to visit you in advance and finish the arrangements for the generous gift you had promised. Then it will be ready as a generous
gift,[c] not as one grudgingly given.[d]

Sowing Generously

6Remember this: Whoever sows sparingly will also reap sparingly, and whoever sows generously will also reap generously.[e] 7Each man should give what he
has decided in his heart to give,[f] not reluctantly or under compulsion,[g] for God
loves a cheerful giver.[h] 8And God is able[i]
to make all grace abound to you, so that
in all things at all times, having all that

[a] 15 Exodus 16:18

8:10 [w] 1Co 7:25,40 [x] 1Co 16:2,3; 2Co 9:2
8:11 [y] ver 12,19; Ex 25:2; 2Co 9:2
8:12 [z] Mk 12:43,44; 2Co 9:7
8:14 [a] Ac 4:34; 2Co 9:12
8:15 [b] Ex 16:18
8:16 [c] S 2Co 2:14 [d] Rev 17:17 [e] S 2Co 2:13
8:17 [f] ver 6
8:18 [g] 2Co 12:18 [h] S 1Co 7:17 [i] S 2Co 2:12
8:19 [j] Ac 14:23; 1Co 16:3,4 [k] ver 11,12
8:21 [l] Ro 12:17; S 14:18; S Tit 2:14
8:23 [m] S 2Co 2:13 [n] Phm 17 [o] S Php 2:25 [p] ver 18,22
8:24 [q] 2Co 7:4,14; 9:2
9:1 [r] 1Th 4:9 [s] S Ac 24:17 [t] S Ac 9:13
9:2 [u] 2Co 8:11,12,19 [v] 2Co 7:4,14; 8:24 [w] 2Co 8:10 [x] S Ac 18:12
9:3 [y] 2Co 8:23 [z] 1Co 16:2
9:4 [a] Ro 15:26
9:5 [b] ver 3 [c] Php 4:17 [d] 2Co 12:17,18
9:6 [e] Pr 11:24,25; 22:9; Gal 6:7,9
9:7 [f] Ex 25:2; 2Co 8:12 [g] Dt 15:10 [h] Ro 12:8
9:8 [i] Eph 3:20

might become rich. The supreme and inescapable incentive of all genuine Christian generosity.

8:11 The work they had started "last year" with "desire" (v. 10) needs to be completed (see note on v. 6).

8:12 *according to what one has.* See v. 11. What matters is the willingness, no matter how small the amount that can be afforded (see Mk 12:41 – 44 and note on 12:42). The mechanics of the collection being made in Corinth had been proposed by Paul in his earlier letter (see 1Co 16:1 – 2 and notes).

8:13 – 15 Paul's desire is that believers throughout the whole Christian community share what they have with believers who are in need so that a measure of equality is maintained within the church — so that, as with Israel in the desert (see Ex 16:18 and note), there would be none who has "too much" and none who has "too little" (v. 15).

8:16 – 17 Titus had established a relationship of trust and affection with the Corinthians (see 7:6 – 7,13 – 15). He had organized the collection when it was started the previous year (see note on v. 6).

8:18 *brother.* Perhaps Luke or Barnabas.

8:19 Paul provides a good example of the care that church leaders should take in handling money (see 1Co 16:3 – 4 and note on 16:3).

8:20 It is important not only that God sees but also that people see (cf. vv. 19,21) that one is carrying on the Lord's work in an ethical way.

8:21 *taking pains to do what is right.* Paul is the victim of disgraceful slander (implied by 12:17 – 18; see note on 12:16; see also Introduction: Purposes), but the integrity of his representatives (see v. 23 and note) reflects well on his own integrity.

8:22 *our brother.* This second brother is also anonymous (cf. v. 18 and note).

8:23 *partner and fellow worker.* See 2:13 and note. *representatives of the churches.* Duly elected delegates of the churches at large (so that they could not be dismissed as cronies chosen by Paul alone); see note on Ac 20:4. *an honor to Christ.* By their outstanding faithfulness.

9:2 *Macedonians ... Achaia.* See 1:1 and note.

9:5 *generous gift, not ... grudgingly given.* See vv. 6 – 7,11.

9:6 Probably a well-known proverb. For a similar principle cf. Pr 11:24 – 25; 22:8 – 9; Lk 6:38; Gal 6:7.

9:8 *all grace ... all things ... all times ... all that you need.* Through his abounding grace, God can enable each Christian to abound in generous deeds (see v. 11).

you need,[j] you will abound in every good
work. 9As it is written:

> "He has scattered abroad his gifts[k] to
> the poor;
> his righteousness endures forever."[a][l]

10Now he who supplies seed to the sower
and bread for food[m] will also supply and
increase your store of seed and will enlarge the harvest of your righteousness.[n]
11You will be made rich[o] in every way so
that you can be generous[p] on every occasion, and through us your generosity will
result in thanksgiving to God.[q]
12This service that you perform is not
only supplying the needs[r] of God's people
but is also overflowing in many expressions of thanks to God.[s] 13Because of the
service[t] by which you have proved yourselves, men will praise God[u] for the obedience that accompanies your confession[v]
of the gospel of Christ,[w] and for your generosity[x] in sharing with them and with everyone else. 14And in their prayers for you
their hearts will go out to you, because of
the surpassing grace God has given you.
15Thanks be to God[y] for his indescribable
gift![z]

Paul's Defense of His Ministry

10 By the meekness and gentleness[a]
of Christ, I appeal to you—I, Paul,[b]
who am "timid" when face to face with
you, but "bold" when away! 2I beg you
that when I come I may not have to be as
bold[c] as I expect to be toward some people who think that we live by the standards of this world.[d] 3For though we live
in the world, we do not wage war as the
world does.[e] 4The weapons we fight with[f]
are not the weapons of the world. On the
contrary, they have divine power[g] to demolish strongholds.[h] 5We demolish arguments and every pretension that sets itself
up against the knowledge of God,[i] and
we take captive every thought to make it
obedient[j] to Christ. 6And we will be ready
to punish every act of disobedience, once
your obedience is complete.[k]
7You are looking only on the surface of
things.[b][l] If anyone is confident that he belongs to Christ,[m] he should consider again
that we belong to Christ just as much as
he.[n] 8For even if I boast somewhat freely
about the authority the Lord gave us[o] for
building you up rather than pulling you
down,[p] I will not be ashamed of it. 9I do
not want to seem to be trying to frighten
you with my letters. 10For some say, "His
letters are weighty and forceful, but in
person he is unimpressive[q] and his speaking amounts to nothing."[r] 11Such people
should realize that what we are in our letters when we are absent, we will be in our
actions when we are present.

9:8 [j]Php 4:19 **9:9** [k]Mal 3:10 [l]Ps 112:9 **9:10** [m]Isa 55:10 [n]Hos 10:12 **9:11** [o]1Co 1:5 [p]ver 5 [q]2Co 1:11; 4:15 **9:12** [r]2Co 8:14 [s]S 2Co 1:11 **9:13** [t]S 2Co 8:4 [u]S Mt 9:8 [v]S Heb 3:1 [w]S 2Co 2:12 [x]ver 5 **9:15** [y]S 2Co 2:14 [z]Ro 5:15,16 **10:1** [a]Mt 11:29 [b]Gal 5:2; Eph 3:1 **10:2** [c]S 1Co 4:21 [d]Ro 12:2 **10:3** [e]ver 2 **10:4** [f]S 2Co 6:7 [g]1Co 2:5 [h]ver 8; Jer 1:10; 23:29; 2Co 13:10 **10:5** [i]Isa 2:11,12; 1Co 1:19 [j]2Co 9:13 **10:6** [k]2Co 2:9; 7:15 **10:7** [l]S Jn 7:24; 2Co 5:12 [m]1Co 1:12; S 3:23; 14:37 [n]2Co 11:23 **10:8** [o]ver 13,15 [p]ver 4; Jer 1:10; 2Co 13:10 **10:10** [q]ver 1; 1Co 2:3; Gal 4:13,14 [r]1Co 1:17; 2Co 11:6

[a] 9 Psalm 112:9 [b] 7 Or *Look at the obvious facts*

9:9–10 *righteousness.* See note on Ps 1:5.

9:10 The God who is the ultimate source of the physical food that sustains all human life is the same God who supplies the spiritual nourishment that enables believers to flourish and serve.

9:12 *not only supplying the needs of God's people.* The effect of generous giving on the part of the Corinthians will extend beyond Jerusalem to the church as a whole, causing widespread prayer and praise to be offered (see vv. 11,13–14).

9:14 *the surpassing grace God has given you.* Displayed in this unselfish demonstration of their loving concern for fellow believers who are in desperate need.

9:15 *indescribable gift.* His own Son (see Jn 3:16 and note). God is the first giver; he selflessly gives himself to us in the person of his Son, and all true Christian giving is our grateful response (cf. 8:9 and note; 1Jn 4:9–11).

10:1—13:14 See Introduction: Occasion. From the mild tone of the first nine chapters of this letter, it appears that most of the Corinthian believers had been won over to Paul (cf. 7:6–16), after having been alienated by his opponents. In this final section, however, Paul deals firmly with the slanders that have been spread against him in Corinth by the remaining opposition. Those who wish to discredit him have been saying that he is bold at a distance, threatening in his letters to take severe disciplinary action (cf., e.g., his warning that, if necessary, he will come "with a whip" [1Co 4:21]). But they say that he will not dare to be anything but weak and indecisive if he is present with them in person—in short, that he does not have the apostolic authority he claims to have. Paul is ready to prove otherwise, should the occasion demand, when he comes to Corinth for the third time (see 10:6,10–11 and note on 10:10).

10:1 *meekness and gentleness of Christ.* An indication of his own affectionate desire to show these same qualities when present with them.

10:4 *weapons we fight with.* Paul is prepared for warfare; his weapons, however, are not the weapons prized by this fallen world and fashioned by human pride (cf. 1:17; 4:2). *strongholds.* Of "arguments and every pretension" (v. 5) defiantly raised "against the knowledge of God" (cf. Ro 1:18–23), among which are the faulty reasonings by which the false apostles have been trying to shake the faith of the Christians in Corinth (see 1Co 2:13–14).

10:6 *every act of disobedience.* On the part of the interlopers and those who sided with them.

10:7 *belongs to Christ.* Probably echoes the claim to superior spirituality by the Christ party (see 1Co 1:12) and the false teachers in Corinth. Paul, who had dramatically encountered and had been commissioned by the risen Lord (see Ac 9:3–9; 22:6–11; 26:12–18) and who had received the gospel he preached "by revelation from Jesus Christ" (Gal 1:12; cf. 2Co 12:2–7), asserts that he belongs to Christ "just as much."

10:8 *authority . . . for building you up.* The primary purpose of Paul's apostolic authority is constructive, not destructive (see 13:10).

10:9 *frighten you with my letters.* See 2:3–4 and note; 7:8–9; chs. 10–13; 1Co 4:14–21.

10:10 *His letters are weighty and forceful.* Paul had already written at least three letters to Corinth (see Introduction: Occasion). *his speaking amounts to nothing.* See note on 10:1—13:14. Paul's adversaries used a professional type of oratory designed to extract money from their gullible audiences. But Paul's manner of speaking was plain, straightforward and free from artificiality—and also "free of charge" (11:7; see note there), which meant, if his slanderous opponents were to be believed, that what he said was worthless.

12We do not dare to classify or compare
ourselves with some who commend themselves.[s] When they measure themselves by
themselves and compare themselves with
themselves, they are not wise. 13We, however, will not boast beyond proper limits,
but will confine our boasting to the field
God has assigned to us,[t] a field that reaches even to you. 14We are not going too far
in our boasting, as would be the case if we
had not come to you, for we did get as far
as you[u] with the gospel of Christ.[v] 15Neither
do we go beyond our limits[w] by boasting of
work done by others.[a][x] Our hope is that,
as your faith continues to grow,[y] our area
of activity among you will greatly expand,
16so that we can preach the gospel[z] in the
regions beyond you.[a] For we do not want to
boast about work already done in another
man's territory. 17But, "Let him who boasts
boast in the Lord."[b][b] 18For it is not the one
who commends himself[c] who is approved,
but the one whom the Lord commends.[d]

Paul and the False Apostles

11 I hope you will put up with[e] a little of
my foolishness;[f] but you are already
doing that. 2I am jealous for you with a
godly jealousy. I promised you to one husband,[g] to Christ, so that I might present
you[h] as a pure virgin to him. 3But I am
afraid that just as Eve was deceived by the
serpent's cunning,[i] your minds may somehow be led astray from your sincere and
pure devotion to Christ. 4For if someone
comes to you and preaches a Jesus other
than the Jesus we preached,[j] or if you receive a different spirit[k] from the one you
received, or a different gospel[l] from the
one you accepted, you put up with it[m] easily enough. 5But I do not think I am in the
least inferior to those "super-apostles."[n] 6I
may not be a trained speaker,[o] but I do
have knowledge.[p] We have made this perfectly clear to you in every way.

7Was it a sin[q] for me to lower myself in
order to elevate you by preaching the gospel of God[r] to you free of charge?[s] 8I robbed
other churches by receiving support from
them[t] so as to serve you. 9And when I was
with you and needed something, I was not
a burden to anyone, for the brothers who
came from Macedonia supplied what I
needed.[u] I have kept myself from being a
burden to you[v] in any way, and will continue to do so. 10As surely as the truth of
Christ is in me,[w] nobody in the regions of
Achaia[x] will stop this boasting[y] of mine.

10:12 [s]ver 18; S 2Co 3:1 **10:13** [t]ver 15,16; S Ro 12:3 **10:14** [u]S 1Co 3:6 [v]S 2Co 2:12 **10:15** [w]ver 13 [x]Ro 15:20 [y]2Th 1:3 **10:16** [z]S Ro 1:1; S 2Co 2:12 [a]S Ac 19:21 **10:17** [b]Jer 9:24; Ps 34:2; 44:8; 1Co 1:31 **10:18** [c]ver 12 [d]S Ro 2:29 **11:1** [e]ver 4,19,20; Mt 17:17 [f]ver 16,17,21; 2Co 5:13 **11:2** [g]Hos 2:19; Eph 5:26,27 [h]S 2Co 4:14 **11:3** [i]Ge 3:1-6,13; 1Ti 2:14; Rev 12:9 **11:4** [j]1Co 3:11 [k]Ro 8:15 [l]Gal 1:6-9 [m]S ver 1 **11:5** [n]2Co 12:11; Gal 2:6 **11:6** [o]S 1Co 1:17 [p]S 2Co 8:7; Eph 3:4 **11:7** [q]2Co 12:13 [r]S Ro 1:1 [s]1Co 9:18 **11:8** [t]Php 4:15,18 **11:9** [u]Php 4:15,18 [v]2Co 12:13,14,16 **11:10** [w]S Ro 9:1 [x]S Ac 18:12 [y]1Co 9:15

[a] 13-15 Or *13We, however, will not boast about things that cannot be measured, but we will boast according to the standard of measurement that the God of measure has assigned us—a measurement that relates even to you. 14 . . . 15Neither do we boast about things that cannot be measured in regard to the work done by others.*
[b] 17 Jer. 9:24

But Paul proclaimed the message of Christ crucified, and the transformed lives of the Corinthian believers testified to the divine power with which he spoke (cf. 1Co 2:1–5 and notes).

10:12 *they measure themselves by themselves.* The false teachers in Corinth behave as though there is no standard of comparison higher than themselves, but Paul boasts only "in the Lord" (v. 17; cf. 1Co 1:31 [see note there]).

10:13 *the field God has assigned to us.* The picture may be that of an athletic contest in which lanes are marked out for the different runners. In that case, "field" should be rendered "lane"—as should also "area of activity" (v. 15) and "territory" (v. 16). In intruding themselves into Corinth, the false apostles had crossed into Paul's "lane." Others understand the Greek word in question to refer to an assigned sphere of authority.

10:16 *regions beyond.* Perhaps Spain (see Ro 15:24,28).

10:17 See 1Co 1:31 and note. *boast in the Lord.* Boast in what Jesus Christ has done either for us (see Gal 6:14) or through us (see Ro 15:18; cf. Ac 14:27).

11:1 *my foolishness.* In order to compare his own ministry with that of the false apostles, Paul has to speak about himself, which inevitably seems like foolish boasting.

11:2 *godly jealousy.* Paul cannot bear the thought that there might be any rival to Christ and his gospel. *I promised you to one husband.* As their spiritual father (cf. 6:13), Paul has promised the Corinthian believers to Christ, who is frequently depicted in the NT as the bridegroom, with the church portrayed as his bride (see Mt 9:15; Jn 3:29 and note; Eph 5:23–32 and notes; Rev 19:7–9; 21:2). *pure virgin.* Undefiled by the doctrines of false teachers (see vv. 3–4).

11:3 *deceived by the serpent's cunning.* See Ge 3:1–7 and note on 3:1.

11:4 *a Jesus other than the Jesus we preached.* A Jesus cast in the mold of Judaistic teachings (Paul's opponents were Jews; see v. 22). *different spirit.* A spirit of bondage, fear and worldliness (cf. Ro 8:15; 1Co 2:12 and note; Gal 2:4; Col 2:20–23 and note on 2:23) instead of a spirit of freedom, love, joy, peace and power (cf. 3:17; Ro 14:17 and notes; Gal 2:4; 5:1,22; Eph 3:20; Col 1:11; 2Ti 1:7). *different gospel.* Cf. Gal 1:6–9. *you put up with it easily enough.* They have been undiscerningly tolerant of these deceivers in their midst.

11:5 *"super-apostles."* Paul's sarcastic way of referring to the false apostles who had infiltrated the Corinthian church and were in reality not apostles at all, except in their own arrogantly inflated opinion of themselves (cf. 10:12 and note).

11:6 *I may not be a trained speaker.* Using the skills, references and flourishes of professional rhetoric (see 10:10 and note). *I do have knowledge.* As the Corinthian believers well knew, Paul had knowledge of Christ that was true, powerful and God-given.

11:7 *free of charge.* Another slanderous criticism made by Paul's adversaries was that his refusal to accept payment for his instruction proved that it was worth nothing. This accusation at the same time helped to cloak their own grasping character, since their method of operation was to demand payment for their "professional" services. Paul, his enemies said, was lowering himself by breaking the rule that teachers should receive payment in proportion to the worth of their performance (cf. 1Co 9:3–14).

11:8 *robbed other churches.* Accepted freely given support from established congregations.

11:9 *burden.* A financial liability (see 2:17 and note). This reinforced his teaching that the gospel of Jesus Christ is a free gift (see Ro 6:23 and note). *brothers who came from Macedonia.* See note on 1:1. They brought gifts from the churches there (Ac 18:5), particularly from the church at Philippi (Php 4:15).

11:10 *Achaia.* See note on 1:1.

11Why? Because I do not love you? God knows[z] I do![a] 12And I will keep on doing what I am doing in order to cut the ground from under those who want an opportunity to be considered equal with us in the things they boast about.

13For such men are false apostles,[b] deceitful[c] workmen, masquerading as apostles of Christ.[d] 14And no wonder, for Satan[e] himself masquerades as an angel of light. 15It is not surprising, then, if his servants masquerade as servants of righteousness. Their end will be what their actions deserve.[f]

Paul Boasts About His Sufferings

16I repeat: Let no one take me for a fool.[g] But if you do, then receive me just as you would a fool, so that I may do a little boasting. 17In this self-confident boasting I am not talking as the Lord would,[h] but as a fool.[i] 18Since many are boasting in the way the world does,[j] I too will boast.[k] 19You gladly put up with[l] fools since you are so wise![m] 20In fact, you even put up with[n] anyone who enslaves you[o] or exploits you or takes advantage of you or pushes himself forward or slaps you in the face. 21To my shame I admit that we were too weak[p] for that!

What anyone else dares to boast about — I am speaking as a fool — I also dare to boast about.[q] 22Are they Hebrews? So am I.[r] Are they Israelites? So am I.[s] Are they Abraham's descendants? So am I.[t] 23Are they servants of Christ?[u] (I am out of my mind to talk like this.) I am more. I have worked much harder,[v] been in prison more frequently,[w] been flogged more severely,[x] and been exposed to death again and again.[y] 24Five times I received from the Jews the forty lashes[z] minus one. 25Three times I was beaten with rods,[a] once I was stoned,[b] three times I was shipwrecked,[c] I spent a night and a day in the open sea, 26I have been constantly on the move. I have been in danger from rivers, in danger from bandits, in danger from my own countrymen,[d] in danger from Gentiles; in danger in the city,[e] in danger in the country, in danger at sea; and in danger from false brothers.[f] 27I have labored and toiled[g] and have often gone without sleep; I have known hunger and thirst and have often gone without food;[h] I have been cold and naked. 28Besides everything else, I face daily the pressure of my concern for all the churches.[i] 29Who is weak, and I do not feel weak?[j] Who is led into sin,[k] and I do not inwardly burn?

30If I must boast, I will boast[l] of the things that show my weakness.[m] 31The God and Father of the Lord Jesus, who is to be praised forever,[n] knows[o] that I am not

11:11 [z] ver 31; S Ro 1:9 [a] 2Co 12:15 **11:13** [b] S Mt 7:15 [c] Tit 1:10 [d] Rev 2:2 **11:14** [e] S Mt 4:10 **11:15** [f] S Mt 16:27; Php 3:19 **11:16** [g] ver 1 **11:17** [h] 1Co 7:12,25 [i] ver 21 **11:18** [j] 2Co 5:16; 10:4 [k] ver 21; Php 3:3,4 **11:19** [l] S ver 1 [m] 1Co 4:10 **11:20** [n] S ver 1 [o] Gal 2:4; 4:9; 5:1 **11:21** [p] 2Co 10:1,10 [q] ver 17,18; Php 3:4 **11:22** [r] Php 3:5 [s] Ro 9:4; 11:1 [t] S Lk 3:8; Ro 11:1 **11:23** [u] S 1Co 3:5 [v] S 1Co 15:10 [w] Ac 16:23; 2Co 6:4,5 [x] Ac 16:23; 2Co 6:4,5 [y] S Ro 8:36 **11:24** [z] Dt 25:3 **11:25** [a] Ac 16:22 [b] Ac 14:19 [c] Ac 27:1-44 **11:26** [d] S Ac 20:3 [e] Ac 21:31 [f] Gal 2:4 **11:27** [g] S Ac 18:3; Col 1:29 [h] 1Co 4:11,12; 2Co 6:5 **11:28** [i] S 1Co 7:17 **11:29** [j] S Ro 14:1; S 1Co 2:3 [k] S Mt 5:29 **11:30** [l] ver 16; Gal 6:14; 2Co 12:5,9 [m] S 1Co 2:3 **11:31** [n] Ro 1:25; 9:5 [o] ver 11; S Ro 1:9

11:12 *I will keep on.* Paul will not be deterred from presenting the gospel without charge. *equal.* In financial matters.

11:13 *masquerading as apostles of Christ.* Now Paul exposes these would-be "super-apostles" (v. 5; see note there) as "false apostles" and servants of Satan (v. 14) who are covering up their true identity.

11:14 *as an angel of light.* Though in reality he is the prince of darkness.

11:16 *Let no one take me for a fool.* See note on v. 1.

11:18 *boast.* By speaking of the nature of his apostolic ministry.

11:19 *You gladly put up with fools.* Resumes the implied rebuke of v. 4 and has the same ironic tone. There it was a matter of their readiness to tolerate false teaching; here it is a matter of their willingness to put up with disgraceful treatment by these false teachers.

11:20 *enslaves you.* By imposing human rules (cf. Gal 5:1 and note). *exploits you.* See Mk 12:40 and note. *takes advantage of you.* Thanks to the Corinthians' lack of discernment and their readiness to be impressed by outward show and clever talk. *pushes himself forward.* For the purpose of lording it over the members of the church (cf. 1:24). *slaps you in the face.* Using physical violence to cow them into submission.

11:21 *too weak for that.* Compared with the self-seeking crudeness of the impostors, Paul's conduct may well be considered weak — but he is probably speaking ironically here.

11:22 *Hebrews ... Israelites ... Abraham's descendants.* The claims implied here on the part of the false apostles indicate that they were Jews who felt superior to Gentile Christians. Thus it is probable that they were Judaizers, wishing to impose distinctive Jewish practices on Gentile converts. This, of course, was not Paul's position (see Ro 2:28–29; 1Co 12:13; Gal 3:28–29; Eph 2:11–18; Col 3:11 and note). For Paul's claim see Ac 22:3–5; 26:4–5; Php 3:5–6.

11:23 *servants of Christ.* Paul is not granting their claim to be servants of Christ. Indeed, the consideration of the nature of his ministry and its cost to him in suffering will show that he is more Christ's servant than any or all of them. *exposed to death again and again.* Cf. 4:8–11.

11:24–25 *lashes ... rods.* Eight floggings are mentioned here, five at the hands of Jewish authorities (cf. Dt 25:3; Mk 15:15 and notes) and three at the hands of Roman authorities. On these occasions the Romans used rods (see Ac 16:22). The three beatings with rods took place despite the fact that Paul, a Roman citizen, was legally protected from such punishment (cf. Ac 16:37; 22:25 and notes).

11:25 *stoned.* A traditional manner of Jewish execution (cf. Jn 8:59; Ac 7:57–59; 14:19–20). *shipwrecked.* Only one shipwreck is recorded in Acts, but it took place after the writing of this letter (Ac 27:39–44). The three shipwrecks referred to here could have taken place during the voyages mentioned in Ac 9:30; 11:25–26; 13:4,13; 14:26; 16:11; 18:18–19,21–22.

11:26 *in danger from bandits.* See note on Ac 14:24.

11:28–29 Paul felt the weakness of any Corinthian believer who was weak. If any of them was led into sin, Paul burned with indignation against the person responsible but also experienced the shame of the offense and longed for the restoration of the one who had stumbled.

11:30 *I will boast of the things that show my weakness.* His weakness opens the way for him to boast about the strength of God's grace in his life.

lying. 32 In Damascus the governor under
King Aretas had the city of the Damascenes
guarded in order to arrest me.[p] 33 But I was
lowered in a basket from a window in the
wall and slipped through his hands.[q]

Paul's Vision and His Thorn

12 I must go on boasting.[r] Although
there is nothing to be gained, I will
go on to visions and revelations[s] from the
Lord. 2 I know a man in Christ[t] who fourteen years ago was caught up[u] to the third
heaven.[v] Whether it was in the body or out
of the body I do not know—God knows.[w]
3 And I know that this man—whether in
the body or apart from the body I do not
know, but God knows— 4 was caught
up[x] to paradise.[y] He heard inexpressible
things, things that man is not permitted to
tell. 5 I will boast about a man like that, but
I will not boast about myself, except about
my weaknesses.[z] 6 Even if I should choose
to boast,[a] I would not be a fool,[b] because I
would be speaking the truth. But I refrain,
so no one will think more of me than is
warranted by what I do or say.

7 To keep me from becoming conceited
because of these surpassingly great revelations,[c] there was given me a thorn in my
flesh,[d] a messenger of Satan,[e] to torment
me. 8 Three times I pleaded with the Lord
to take it away from me.[f] 9 But he said to
me, "My grace[g] is sufficient for you, for
my power[h] is made perfect in weakness.[i]"[j]
Therefore I will boast all the more gladly about my weaknesses, so that Christ's
power may rest on me. 10 That is why, for
Christ's sake, I delight[k] in weaknesses, in
insults, in hardships,[l] in persecutions,[m] in
difficulties. For when I am weak, then I
am strong.[n]

Paul's Concern for the Corinthians

11 I have made a fool of myself,[o] but you
drove me to it. I ought to have been commended by you, for I am not in the least
inferior to the "super-apostles,"[p] even
though I am nothing.[q] 12 The things that
mark an apostle—signs, wonders and
miracles[r]—were done among you with
great perseverance. 13 How were you inferior to the other churches, except that I
was never a burden to you?[s] Forgive me
this wrong![t]

14 Now I am ready to visit you for the
third time,[u] and I will not be a burden to
you, because what I want is not your possessions but you. After all, children should
not have to save up for their parents,[v] but
parents for their children.[w] 15 So I will very
gladly spend for you everything I have
and expend myself as well.[x] If I love you
more,[y] will you love me less? 16 Be that as
it may, I have not been a burden to you.[z]
Yet, crafty fellow that I am, I caught you
by trickery! 17 Did I exploit you through
any of the men I sent you? 18 I urged[a] Titus[b] to go to you and I sent our brother[c]
with him. Titus did not exploit you, did
he? Did we not act in the same spirit and
follow the same course?

19 Have you been thinking all along that
we have been defending ourselves to you?

11:32 [p] Ac 9:24
11:33 [q] Ac 9:25
12:1 [r] ver 5,9; 2Co 11:16,30 [s] ver 7; S 1Co 2:10
12:2 [t] S Ro 16:3 [u] ver 4; S Ac 8:39 [v] Eph 4:10 [w] 2Co 11:11
12:4 [x] ver 2 [y] Lk 23:43; Rev 2:7
12:5 [z] ver 9,10; S 1Co 2:3
12:6 [a] 2Co 10:8 [b] ver 11; 2Co 11:16
12:7 [c] ver 1; S 1Co 2:10 [d] Nu 33:55 [e] S Mt 4:10
12:8 [f] Mt 26:39,44
12:9 [g] S Ro 3:24 [h] S Php 4:13 [i] S 1Co 2:3 [j] 1Ki 19:12
12:10 [k] S Mt 5:12 [l] 2Co 6:4 [m] 2Th 1:4 [n] 2Co 13:4
12:11 [o] 2Co 11:1 [p] 2Co 11:5 [q] 1Co 15:9,10
12:12 [r] S Jn 4:48
12:13 [s] ver 14; 1Co 9:12,18 [t] 2Co 11:7
12:14 [u] 2Co 13:1 [v] 1Co 4:14,15 [w] Pr 19:14
12:15 [x] Php 2:17; 1Th 2:8 [y] 2Co 11:11
12:16 [z] 2Co 11:9
12:18 [a] 2Co 8:6,16 [b] S 2Co 2:13 [c] 2Co 8:18

11:32–33 Paul relates this incident here because it was another example of the humiliation ("weakness," v. 30) he suffered.

11:32 *Damascus.* See note on Ac 9:2; see also map, p. 1695. *King Aretas.* Aretas IV, father-in-law of Herod Antipas, ruled over the Nabatean Arabs from c. 9 B.C. to A.D. 40. The Roman emperor Caligula may have given Damascus back to Aretas since it was once part of his territory.

11:33 *from a window.* See Ac 9:25. For similar escapes see Jos 2:15; 1Sa 19:12.

12:2,4 *caught up to the third heaven … caught up to paradise.* Paul is unsure whether this remarkable experience included his body or took place in separation from it (cf. Eze 8:3 and note). The "third heaven" designates a place beyond the immediate heaven of the earth's atmosphere and beyond the further heaven of outer space into the presence of God himself. Thus the risen and glorified Lord Jesus is said to have passed "through the heavens" (Heb 4:14; see note there), and now, having "ascended higher than all the heavens" (Eph 4:10), to be "exalted above the heavens" (Heb 7:26). The term "paradise" (see Ne 2:8; Lk 23:43; Rev 2:7 and notes) is synonymous with the third heaven, where believers who have died are "at home with the Lord" (5:8 [see note there]; cf. "with Christ," Php 1:23).

12:2 *a man in Christ.* Paul himself. *fourteen years ago.* Early in his ministry, before his first missionary journey (Ac 13:4—14:28).

12:7 *revelations.* See v. 1. *thorn in my flesh.* The nature of this affliction is unknown. *messenger of Satan.* A further description of Paul's thorn (cf. Job 2:7 and note).

12:9 *My grace is sufficient for you.* A better solution than to remove Paul's thorn. Human weakness provides the ideal opportunity for the display of divine power.

12:10 Cf. Php 4:13 and note. The classic example of power in weakness is the cross of Christ (cf. 13:4).

12:11 *made a fool of myself.* See note on 11:1. *you drove me to it.* The Corinthian Christians have put Paul under pressure to write about himself as he did because they had accepted the claims of the "super-apostles" (see 11:5 and note) who had invaded their ranks, challenging Paul's apostolic authority.

12:12 *signs, wonders and miracles.* See Heb 2:4 and note. By implication, false teachers had come to Corinth without these apostolic signs.

12:13 *never a burden to you.* See 11:9 and note; see also notes on 11:7,12. *Forgive me this wrong!* Irony—resuming the line of discussion in 11:7–12.

12:14 *third time.* See 2:1 and note; 13:1. *children.* Cf. 6:13. Paul is their spiritual father.

12:16 *I caught you by trickery!* Sarcastically echoes another of the slanders being made against Paul by the false apostles: that he was exploiting them by the trick of organizing a collection for the poverty-stricken Christians in Jerusalem—contributions that would never reach their intended destination because they went into Paul's own pocket (v. 17).

12:18 *Titus … our brother.* See notes on 8:6,16–17, 18,23.

12:19 *speaking in the sight of God as those in Christ.* See 1Co

We have been speaking in the sight of God[d]
as those in Christ; and everything we do,
dear friends,[e] is for your strengthening.[f]
20For I am afraid that when I come[g] I may
not find you as I want you to be, and you
may not find me as you want me to be.[h] I
fear that there may be quarreling,[i] jealousy, outbursts of anger, factions,[j] slander,[k]
gossip,[l] arrogance[m] and disorder.[n] 21I am
afraid that when I come again my God
will humble me before you, and I will be
grieved[o] over many who have sinned earlier[p] and have not repented of the impurity,
sexual sin and debauchery[q] in which they
have indulged.

Final Warnings

13 This will be my third visit to you.[r]
"Every matter must be established by
the testimony of two or three witnesses."[a][s]
2I already gave you a warning when I was
with you the second time. I now repeat
it while absent:[t] On my return I will not
spare[u] those who sinned earlier[v] or any
of the others, 3since you are demanding
proof that Christ is speaking through me.[w]
He is not weak in dealing with you, but is
powerful among you. 4For to be sure, he
was crucified in weakness,[x] yet he lives by
God's power.[y] Likewise, we are weak[z] in
him, yet by God's power we will live with
him[a] to serve you.
5Examine yourselves[b] to see whether you are in the faith; test yourselves.[c]
Do you not realize that Christ Jesus is in
you[d]—unless, of course, you fail the test?
6And I trust that you will discover that we
have not failed the test. 7Now we pray to
God that you will not do anything wrong.
Not that people will see that we have
stood the test but that you will do what
is right even though we may seem to have
failed. 8For we cannot do anything against
the truth, but only for the truth. 9We are
glad whenever we are weak[e] but you are
strong;[f] and our prayer is for your perfection.[g] 10This is why I write these things
when I am absent, that when I come I may
not have to be harsh[h] in my use of authority—the authority the Lord gave me
for building you up, not for tearing you
down.[i]

Final Greetings

11Finally, brothers,[j] good-by. Aim for
perfection, listen to my appeal, be of one
mind, live in peace.[k] And the God of love[l]
and peace[m] will be with you.
12Greet one another with a holy kiss.[n]
13All the saints send their greetings.[o]
14May the grace of the Lord Jesus Christ,[p]
and the love of God,[q] and the fellowship of
the Holy Spirit[r] be with you all.

[a] 1 Deut. 19:15

12:19 [d]Ro 9:1 [e]S 1Co 10:14 [f]S Ro 14:19; 2Co 10:8 **12:20** [g]2Co 2:1-4 [h]1Co 4:21 [i]1Co 1:11; 3:3 [j]Gal 5:20 [k]Ro 1:30 [l]S Ro 1:29 [m]1Co 4:18 [n]1Co 14:33 **12:21** [o]2Co 2:1,4 [p]2Co 13:2 [q]S 1Co 6:18 **13:1** [r]2Co 12:14 [s]Dt 19:15; S Mt 18:16 **13:2** [t]ver 10 [u]2Co 1:23 [v]2Co 12:21 **13:3** [w]Mt 10:20; 1Co 5:4 **13:4** [x]1Co 1:25; Php 2:7,8; 1Pe 3:18 [y]Ro 1:4; 6:4; 1Co 6:14 [z]ver 9; S 1Co 2:3 [a]S Ro 6:5 **13:5** [b]1Co 11:28 [c]La 3:40; Jn 6:6 [d]S Ro 8:10 **13:9** [e]S 1Co 2:3 [f]2Co 4:12 [g]ver 11; Eph 4:13 **13:10** [h]S 2Co 1:23 [i]2Co 10:8 **13:11** [j]1Th 4:1; 2Th 3:1 [k]S Mk 9:50 [l]1Jn 4:16 [m]S Ro 15:33; Eph 6:23

13:12 [n]S Ro 16:16 **13:13** [o]Php 4:22 **13:14** [p]S Ro 16:20; 2Co 8:9 [q]Ro 5:5; Jude 21 [r]Php 2:1

4:3–4 and note on 4:3. *everything we do ... is for your strengthening.* See 10:8 and note.
12:20–21 See Ro 1:29–31 and note.
12:20 The church at Corinth was immature, unspiritual, disorganized and schismatic (see 1Co 3:1–4 and notes).
12:21 *sinned earlier ... sexual sin and debauchery.* See 1Co 5:1,11; 6:13,16,18–19 and notes.
13:1 *third visit.* See 2:1 and note; 12:14. *two or three witnesses.* Cf. Dt 17:6 and note.
13:2 *those who sinned earlier.* See 12:21 and note. *any of the others.* Probably the Corinthians who had sided with the false teachers.
13:3 *demanding proof that Christ is speaking through me.* See note on 10:10.
13:4 *crucified in weakness.* See 12:10 and note; cf. 8:9; Php 2:6–8.
13:5 *Examine yourselves ... test yourselves.* Cf. 2Pe 1:10–11 and notes.
13:7 *do what is right.* Then there will be no need for Paul to give evidence of his authority by taking disciplinary action when he comes to them.
13:8 *we cannot do anything against the truth.* Paul can exercise his apostolic authority only in a way that supports the truth.
13:9 *weak.* To have no need to give proof of his apostolic strength (cf. 12:9–10 and notes). *strong.* In the truth. *perfection.* Perhaps better "restoration," as indicated by the use of the verb form in Gal 6:1 (see note there).
13:10 *building you up, not ... tearing you down.* See 10:8 and note.
13:11–13 These concluding exhortations and greetings exhibit a note of confidence.
13:11,14 *peace ... grace.* See note on Ro 1:7.
13:11 *brothers.* See note on Ro 1:13. *perfection.* See v. 9 and note. *God of love.* See 1Jn 4:8 and note. *God of ... peace.* See 1Th 5:23 and note; Heb 13:20.
13:12 *holy kiss.* See 1Co 16:20; Ro 16:16 and notes.
13:13 *saints.* See note on Ro 1:7.
13:14 This benediction is Trinitarian in form and has ever since been a part of Christian worship tradition (cf. Mt 28:19 and note). *fellowship of the Holy Spirit.* See note on Php 2:1. *with you.* This phrase or its equivalent ("with your spirit" [Php 4:23; see note there; see also Gal 6:18; 2Ti 4:22; Phm 25]) occurs near the end of all of Paul's letters except Ephesians. Its OT counterpart is the Immanuel theme—"God with us"—and its equivalents (see Ge 26:3; Isa 7:14; Rev 21:3 and notes).

Galatians

INTRODUCTION

Author

The opening verse identifies the author of Galatians as the apostle Paul. Apart from a few 19th-century scholars, no one has seriously questioned his authorship.

Date and Destination

The date of Galatians depends to a great extent on the destination of the letter. There are two main views:

1. *The North Galatian theory.* This older view holds that the letter was addressed to churches located in north-central Asia Minor (Pessinus, Ancyra and Tavium), where the Gauls had settled when they invaded the area in the third century B.C. It is held that Paul visited this area on his second missionary journey, though Acts contains no reference to such a visit. Galatians, it is maintained, was written between A.D. 53 and 57 from Ephesus or Macedonia.

2. *The South Galatian theory.* According to this view, Galatians was written to churches in the southern area of the Roman province of Galatia (Antioch, Iconium, Lystra and Derbe) that Paul had founded on his first missionary journey (see note on 1:2). Some believe that Galatians was written from Syrian Antioch in 48–49 after Paul's first journey and before the Jerusalem council meeting (Ac 15). Others say that Galatians was written in Syrian Antioch or Corinth between 51 and 53 (see chart, pp. 1696–1697).

A Quick Look

Author:
The apostle Paul

Audience:
Churches in southern Galatia, and perhaps northern Galatia, founded by Paul during his missionary journey

Date:
A.D. 48, or in the fifties A.D.

Theme:
Paul writes to counter the claims of legalistic Judaizers who were telling the Galatian believers that they must be circumcised and keep the law of Moses in order to be saved.

Occasion and Purpose

Judaizers were Jewish Christians who believed, among other things, that a number of the ceremonial practices of the OT were still binding on the NT church. Following Paul's successful campaign in Galatia, they insisted that Gentile converts to Christianity abide by certain OT rites, especially circumcision. They may have been motivated by a desire to avoid persecution from Jews who objected to their fraternizing with Gentiles (see 6:12). The Judaizers argued that Paul was not an authentic apostle and that out of a desire to make the message more appealing to Gentiles he had removed from the gospel certain legal requirements.

Paul responded by clearly establishing his apostolic authority and thereby substantiating the gospel he preached. By introducing additional requirements for justification (e.g., works of the law) his adversaries had perverted the gospel of grace and, unless prevented, would bring Paul's converts into the bondage of legalism. It is by grace through faith alone that people are saved, and it is by faith alone that they are to live out their new life in the freedom of the Spirit.

The Judaizers argued that Paul was not an authentic apostle and that out of a desire to make the message more appealing to Gentiles he had removed from the gospel certain legal requirements.

Theological Teaching

Galatians stands as an eloquent and vigorous apologetic for the essential NT truth that people are justified by faith in Jesus Christ — by nothing less and nothing more — and that they are sanctified not by legalistic works but by the obedience that comes from faith in God's work for them, in them and through them by the grace and power of Christ and the Holy Spirit. It was the rediscovery of the basic message of Galatians (and Romans) that brought about the Protestant Reformation. Galatians is often referred to as "Luther's book," because Martin Luther relied so strongly on this letter in all his preaching, teaching and writing against the prevailing theology of his day. It is also referred to as the "Magna Carta of Christian Liberty." A key verse is 2:16 (see note there).

Outline

- I. Introduction (1:1 – 10)
  - A. Greetings (1:1 – 5)
  - B. Denunciation (1:6 – 10)
- II. Personal: Authentication of the Apostle of Liberty and Faith (1:11 — 2:21)
  - A. Paul's Gospel Was Received by Special Revelation (1:11 – 12)
  - B. Paul's Gospel Was Independent of the Jerusalem Apostles and the Judean Churches (1:13 — 2:21)
    - 1. Evidenced by his early activities as a Christian (1:13 – 17)
    - 2. Evidenced by his first postconversion visit to Jerusalem (1:18 – 24)
    - 3. Evidenced by his second postconversion visit to Jerusalem (2:1 – 10)
    - 4. Evidenced by his rebuke of Peter at Antioch (2:11 – 21)
- III. Doctrinal: Justification of the Doctrine of Liberty and Faith (chs. 3 – 4)
  - A. The Galatians' Experience of the Gospel (3:1 – 5)
  - B. The Experience of Abraham (3:6 – 9)
  - C. The Curse of the Law (3:10 – 14)
  - D. The Priority of the Promise (3:15 – 18)
  - E. The Purpose of the Law (3:19 – 25)
  - F. Sons, Not Slaves (3:26 — 4:7)
  - G. The Danger of Turning Back (4:8 – 11)
  - H. Appeal to Embrace the Freedom of God's Children (4:12 – 20)
  - I. God's Children Are Children of the Free Woman (4:21 – 31)
- IV. Practical: Practice of the Life of Liberty and Faith (5:1 — 6:10)
  - A. Exhortation to Freedom (5:1 – 12)
  - B. Life by the Spirit, Not by Humanity's Sinful Nature (5:13 – 26)
  - C. Call for Mutual Assistance (6:1 – 10)
- V. Conclusion and Benediction (6:11 – 18)

1 Paul, an apostle[a]—sent not from men
nor by man,[b] but by Jesus Christ[c] and
God the Father,[d] who raised him from the
dead[e]— 2 and all the brothers with me,[f]

To the churches in Galatia:[g]

3 Grace and peace to you from God our
Father and the Lord Jesus Christ,[h] 4 who
gave himself for our sins[i] to rescue us
from the present evil age,[j] according to the
will of our God and Father,[k] 5 to whom be
glory for ever and ever. Amen.[l]

No Other Gospel

6 I am astonished that you are so quickly
deserting the one who called[m] you by the
grace of Christ and are turning to a different gospel[n]— 7 which is really no gospel
at all. Evidently some people are throwing you into confusion[o] and are trying to
pervert[p] the gospel of Christ. 8 But even if
we or an angel from heaven should preach
a gospel other than the one we preached
to you,[q] let him be eternally condemned![r]
9 As we have already said, so now I say
again: If anybody is preaching to you a
gospel other than what you accepted,[s] let
him be eternally condemned!
10 Am I now trying to win the approval
of men, or of God? Or am I trying to please
men?[t] If I were still trying to please men, I
would not be a servant of Christ.

Paul Called by God

11 I want you to know, brothers,[u] that the
gospel I preached[v] is not something that
man made up. 12 I did not receive it from
any man,[w] nor was I taught it; rather, I received it by revelation[x] from Jesus Christ.[y]
13 For you have heard of my previous
way of life in Judaism,[z] how intensely I
persecuted the church of God[a] and tried
to destroy it.[b] 14 I was advancing in Judaism beyond many Jews of my own age and
was extremely zealous[c] for the traditions
of my fathers.[d] 15 But when God, who set
me apart from birth[a][e] and called me[f] by
his grace, was pleased 16 to reveal his Son
in me so that I might preach him among
the Gentiles,[g] I did not consult any man,[h]
17 nor did I go up to Jerusalem to see those
who were apostles before I was, but I went
immediately into Arabia and later returned
to Damascus.[i]
18 Then after three years,[j] I went up to
Jerusalem[k] to get acquainted with Peter[b]

[a] 15 Or *from my mother's womb* [b] 18 Greek *Cephas*

1:1 [a] S 1Co 1:1 [b] ver 11,12 [c] ver 15,16; S Ac 9:15; 20:24 [d] ver 15,16; S Ac 9:15; 20:24 [e] S Ac 2:24 **1:2** [f] Php 4:21 [g] S Ac 16:6 **1:3** [h] S Ro 1:7 **1:4** [i] S Mt 20:28; S Ro 4:25; S 1Co 15:3; Gal 2:20 [j] S 1Co 1:20 [k] S Php 4:20 **1:5** [l] S Ro 11:36 **1:6** [m] ver 15; S Ro 8:28 [n] 2Co 11:4 **1:7** [o] Ac 15:24; Gal 5:10 [p] Jer 23:16,36 **1:8** [q] ver 11,16; 1Co 15:1; 2Co 11:4; Gal 2:2 [r] Ro 9:3 **1:9** [s] Ro 16:17 **1:10** [t] S Ro 2:29 **1:11** [u] 1Co 15:1 [v] S ver 8 **1:12** [w] ver 1 [x] ver 16; S 1Co 2:10 [y] 1Co 11:23; 15:3 **1:13** [z] Ac 26:4,5 [a] S 1Co 10:32 [b] S Ac 8:3 **1:14** [c] S Ac 21:20 [d] Mt 15:2 **1:15** [e] Isa 49:1,5; Jer 1:5 [f] S Ac 9:15; S Ro 8:28 **1:16** [g] S Ac 9:15; Gal 2:9 [h] Mt 16:17 **1:17** [i] Ac 9:2,19-22 **1:18** [j] Ac 9:22,23 [k] Ac 9:26,27

1:1 *Paul.* See note on Ro 1:1. *apostle.* One sent on a mission with full authority of representation; an ambassador (see note on 1Co 1:1). *raised him from the dead.* The resurrection is the central affirmation of the Christian faith (see Ac 17:18; Ro 1:4; 1Co 15:20; 1Pe 1:3), and because Paul had seen the risen Christ he was qualified to be an apostle (see Ac 1:22 and note; 2:32; 1Co 15:8).

1:2 *brothers.* See note on Ro 1:13. *churches.* This was a circular letter to several congregations. *Galatia.* The term occurs three times in the NT (and "Galatian" once [1Co 16:1]). In 2Ti 4:10 the reference is uncertain. In 1Pe 1:1 it refers to the northern area of Asia Minor occupied by the Gauls. Here (and in 1Co 16:1) Paul probably uses the term to refer to the Roman province of Galatia and an additional area to the south, through which he traveled on his first missionary journey (Ac 13:14—14:23). See Introduction: Date and Destination.

1:3 *Grace and peace.* See note on Ro 1:7.

1:4 *for our sins.* See Mt 1:21; Jn 1:29; 1Co 15:3; 1Pe 2:24 and note. *present evil age.* The present period of the world's history (see note on 2Co 4:4). In contrast to the age to come (the climax of the Messianic age), this present age is characterized by wickedness (Eph 2:1–2; 6:12).

1:5 For other doxologies see, e.g., Ro 9:5; 11:36; 16:27; Eph 3:21; 1Ti 1:17.

1:6 *so quickly.* So soon after your conversion. *one who called you.* God. *grace of Christ.* The test of a pure, unadulterated gospel.

1:7 *no gospel at all.* Because it lacks the heart of the gospel—the good news of God's marvelous grace in Christ (see notes on Mk 1:1; 1Co 15:3). *some people.* The Judaizers (see Introduction: Occasion and Purpose).

1:8 *eternally condemned.* The Greek word (*anathema*) originally referred to a pagan temple offering in payment for a vow. Later it came to represent a curse (see v. 9; Ro 9:3 and note; 1Co 12:3; 16:22).

1:10 *servant of Christ.* Paul once wore the "yoke of slavery" (5:1) but, having been set free from sin by the redemption that is in Christ, he became a slave of righteousness, a slave of God (see Ro 6:18 and note, 22).

1:11 *I want you to know, brothers.* A similar phrase is found in 1Co 15:1, where Paul sets forth the gospel he received. *the gospel I preached.* Called "my gospel" in Ro 2:16; 16:25 (see note there).

1:12 *received it by revelation.* See Eph 3:2–6.

1:13 *Judaism.* The Jewish faith and way of life that developed during the period between the OT and the NT. The term is derived from Judah, the southern kingdom that came to an end in the sixth century B.C. with the exile into Babylonia (see essay, pp. 1451–1452). *church of God.* The NT counterpart of the OT assembly (see Nu 16:21) or community of the Lord (Nu 20:4).

1:14 *zealous.* See Php 3:6. *traditions of my fathers.* Traditions orally transmitted from previous generations and contrasted with the written law of Moses. Cf. the "tradition of the elders" (Mt 15:2; see note there).

1:15 *set me apart from birth.* See Isa 49:1; Jer 1:5; Ro 1:1.

1:16 *Gentiles.* Lit. "nations" or "peoples." The term commonly designated foreigners—hence pagans, or the non-Jewish world. *any man.* Lit. "flesh and blood"—in the NT usually with the implication of human weakness or ignorance (see Mt 16:17; 1Co 15:50 and note). Paul received his message from God.

1:17 *Jerusalem.* The religious center of Judaism and the birthplace of Christianity. *Arabia.* The Nabatean kingdom in Transjordan stretching southward from Damascus toward the Arabian peninsula. *Damascus.* The capital of ancient Syria (Aram in the OT). Paul had been converted en route from Jerusalem to Damascus (see Ac 9:1–9 and note on 9:2; see also map, p. 1695).

1:18 *after three years.* From the time of his departure into Arabia. The text does not say he spent the three years in Arabia. *I went up to Jerusalem.* Probably the visit referred to in Ac 9:26–30, though some equate it with the one in Ac 11:30.

and stayed with him fifteen days. 19I saw
none of the other apostles—only James,[l]
the Lord's brother. 20I assure you before
God[m] that what I am writing you is no lie.[n]
21Later I went to Syria[o] and Cilicia.[p] 22I was
personally unknown to the churches of Judea[q] that are in Christ.[r] 23They only heard
the report: "The man who formerly persecuted us is now preaching the faith[s] he
once tried to destroy."[t] 24And they praised
God[u] because of me.

Paul Accepted by the Apostles

2 Fourteen years later I went up again to
Jerusalem,[v] this time with Barnabas.[w] I
took Titus[x] along also. 2I went in response
to a revelation[y] and set before them the
gospel that I preach among the Gentiles.[z]
But I did this privately to those who
seemed to be leaders, for fear that I was
running or had run my race[a] in vain. 3Yet
not even Titus,[b] who was with me, was
compelled to be circumcised, even though
he was a Greek.[c] 4⌞This matter arose⌟ because some false brothers[d] had infiltrated
our ranks to spy on[e] the freedom[f] we have
in Christ Jesus and to make us slaves. 5We
did not give in to them for a moment, so
that the truth of the gospel[g] might remain
with you.
6As for those who seemed to be important[h]—whatever they were makes no
difference to me; God does not judge by
external appearance[i]—those men added nothing to my message.[j] 7On the contrary, they saw that I had been entrusted
with the task[k] of preaching the gospel to
the Gentiles,[a][l] just as Peter[m] had been to
the Jews.[b] 8For God, who was at work in
the ministry of Peter as an apostle[n] to the
Jews, was also at work in my ministry as
an apostle[o] to the Gentiles. 9James,[p] Peter[c][q] and John, those reputed to be pillars,[r] gave me and Barnabas[s] the right
hand of fellowship when they recognized
the grace given to me.[t] They agreed that
we should go to the Gentiles,[u] and they
to the Jews. 10All they asked was that we
should continue to remember the poor,[v]
the very thing I was eager to do.

Paul Opposes Peter

11When Peter[w] came to Antioch,[x] I opposed him to his face, because he was
clearly in the wrong. 12Before certain men
came from James,[y] he used to eat with
the Gentiles.[z] But when they arrived, he
began to draw back and separate himself
from the Gentiles because he was afraid
of those who belonged to the circumcision
group.[a] 13The other Jews joined him in his
hypocrisy, so that by their hypocrisy even
Barnabas[b] was led astray.

[a] 7 Greek *uncircumcised* [b] 7 Greek *circumcised*; also in verses 8 and 9 [c] 9 Greek *Cephas*; also in verses 11 and 14

1:19 [l] Mt 13:55; S Ac 15:13 **1:20** [m] S Ro 1:9 [n] S Ro 9:1 **1:21** [o] S Lk 2:2 [p] S Ac 6:9 **1:22** [q] 1Th 2:14 [r] S Ro 16:3 **1:23** [s] Ac 6:7 [t] S Ac 8:3 **1:24** [u] S Mt 9:8 **2:1** [v] Ac 15:2 [w] S Ac 4:36 [x] S 2Co 2:13 **2:2** [y] S 1Co 2:10 [z] Ac 15:4,12 [a] S 1Co 9:24 **2:3** [b] ver 1; S 2Co 2:13 [c] Ac 16:3; 1Co 9:21 **2:4** [d] S Ac 1:16; 2Co 11:26 [e] Jude 4 [f] Gal 5:1,13 **2:5** [g] ver 14 **2:6** [h] ver 2 [i] S Ac 10:34; S Rev 2:23 [j] 1Co 15:11 **2:7** [k] 1Th 2:4; 1Ti 1:11 [l] S Ac 9:15 [m] ver 9,11,14 **2:8** [n] Ac 1:25 [o] S 1Co 1:1 **2:9** [p] S Ac 15:13 [q] ver 7,11,14 [r] 1Ti 3:15; Rev 3:12 [s] ver 1; S Ac 4:36 [t] S Ro 12:3 [u] S Ac 9:15 **2:10** [v] S Ac 24:17 **2:11** [w] ver 7,9,14 [x] S Ac 11:19 **2:12** [y] S Ac 15:13 [z] Ac 11:3 [a] Ac 10:45; 11:2 **2:13** [b] ver 1; S Ac 4:36

Peter. Or *Cephas* (see NIV text note), from the Aramaic word for "stone" (see Mt 16:18 and note). The name highlights a like quality in the bearer (see note on Jn 1:42).

1:19 *James.* See Introduction to James: Author. In Ac 21:18 this James appears to be the leader of the elders in the Jerusalem church. *the Lord's brother.* See note on Lk 8:19.

1:21 *Syria and Cilicia.* Roman provinces in Asia Minor (see map, p. 1704). Specifically Paul went to Tarsus (see Ac 9:30 and note), his hometown.

2:1 *Fourteen years later.* Probably from the date of Paul's conversion. *I went up again to Jerusalem.* According to some, the visit mentioned in Ac 11:30; according to others, the one in Ac 15:1–4 (see notes on Ac 12:1; 15:2). *Barnabas.* Means "one who encourages." His given name was Joseph, and he was a Levite from the island of Cyprus (see Ac 4:36 and note). He was Paul's companion on the first missionary journey (Ac 13:1—14:28). *Titus.* A Gentile Christian who served as Paul's delegate to Corinth (see 2Co 2:13; 7:6–7; 8:6,16; 12:18) and later was left in Crete to oversee the church there (see Tit 1:5; see also Introduction to Titus: Recipient).

2:2 *those who seemed to be leaders.* Paul recognized their authority, and is probably referring to James, Peter and John (v. 9; cf. v. 6). *had run my race in vain.* Cf. 1Co 15:58; Php 2:16.

2:4 *false brothers.* Judaizers who held that Gentile converts should be circumcised and obey the law of Moses (cf. Ac 15:5; 2Co 11:26). *spy on.* Used in the Septuagint (the pre-Christian Greek translation of the OT) in 2Sa 10:3 and 1Ch 19:3 of spying out a territory. *freedom.* See 5:1,13; Ro 6:18,20,22; 8:2. "Free" and "freedom" are key words in Galatians, occurring 11 times (here; 3:28; 4:22–23,26,30–31; 5:1,13).

2:6 *those who seemed to be important.* See note on v. 2. *judge by external appearance.* Cf. Dt 10:17; 1Sa 16:7; Lk 20:21; Jas 2:1.

2:7 *to the Gentiles.* Paul's ministry was not exclusively to the Gentiles. In fact, he regularly went first to the synagogue when arriving in a new location (see note on Ac 13:14). He did, however, consider himself to be first and foremost an apostle to the Gentiles (see Ro 11:13 and note).

2:9 *James.* See note on 1:19. His name may have been mentioned first because he played a dominant role in the Jerusalem council (Ac 15:12–21). *pillars.* A common metaphor for those who represent and strongly support an institution. *right hand of fellowship.* A common practice among both Jews and Greeks, indicating a pledge of friendship. *grace.* The entrusting to Paul of the gospel to the Gentiles (see v. 7).

2:10 Paul already had been involved in a trip to Jerusalem to help the impoverished Christians there (see Ac 11:29–30). He would make another visit for the same purpose at the end of his third missionary journey (see Ac 24:17 and note; Ro 15:25–27; 1Co 16:3–4; 2Co 9).

2:11 *Antioch.* The leading city of Roman Syria and third leading city of the empire (after Rome and Alexandria; see map, p. 1731). From it Paul had been sent out on his missionary journeys (see Ac 13:1–3; 14:26). *in the wrong.* For yielding to the pressure of the circumcision party (the Judaizers), thus going against what he knew to be right.

2:12 *circumcision group.* Judaizers, who believed that circumcision was necessary for salvation (cf. Ac 10:45; 11:2; Ro 4:12).

2:13 *other Jews.* Jewish Christians not associated with the circumcision party but whom Peter's behavior had led astray. *hypocrisy.* See note on Mt 6:2.

14When I saw that they were not acting
in line with the truth of the gospel,[c] I said
to Peter[d] in front of them all, "You are a
Jew, yet you live like a Gentile and not
like a Jew.[e] How is it, then, that you force
Gentiles to follow Jewish customs?[f]

15"We who are Jews by birth[g] and not
'Gentile sinners'[h] 16know that a man is not
justified by observing the law,[i] but by faith
in Jesus Christ.[j] So we, too, have put our
faith in Christ Jesus that we may be justified by faith in Christ and not by observing the law, because by observing the law
no one will be justified.[k]

17"If, while we seek to be justified in
Christ, it becomes evident that we ourselves are sinners,[l] does that mean that
Christ promotes sin? Absolutely not![m] 18If I
rebuild what I destroyed, I prove that I am
a lawbreaker. 19For through the law I died
to the law[n] so that I might live for God.[o]
20I have been crucified with Christ[p] and
I no longer live, but Christ lives in me.[q]
The life I live in the body, I live by faith in
the Son of God,[r] who loved me[s] and gave
himself for me.[t] 21I do not set aside the
grace of God, for if righteousness could be
gained through the law,[u] Christ died for
nothing!"[a]

Faith or Observance of the Law

3 You foolish[v] Galatians![w] Who has be-
witched you?[x] Before your very eyes
Jesus Christ was clearly portrayed as crucified.[y] 2I would like to learn just one thing
from you: Did you receive the Spirit[z] by
observing the law,[a] or by believing what
you heard?[b] 3Are you so foolish? After beginning with the Spirit, are you now trying
to attain your goal by human effort? 4Have
you suffered so much for nothing—if it
really was for nothing? 5Does God give
you his Spirit and work miracles[c] among
you because you observe the law, or because you believe what you heard?[d]

6Consider Abraham: "He believed God,
and it was credited to him as righteousness."[b e] 7Understand, then, that those who
believe[f] are children of Abraham.[g] 8The
Scripture foresaw that God would justify
the Gentiles by faith, and announced the
gospel in advance to Abraham: "All nations will be blessed through you."[c h] 9So
those who have faith[i] are blessed along
with Abraham, the man of faith.[j]

10All who rely on observing the law[k] are
under a curse,[l] for it is written: "Cursed
is everyone who does not continue to
do everything written in the Book of the
Law."[d m] 11Clearly no one is justified before
God by the law,[n] because, "The righteous
will live by faith."[e o] 12The law is not based
on faith; on the contrary, "The man who
does these things will live by them."[f p]
13Christ redeemed us from the curse of
the law[q] by becoming a curse for us, for

2:14 [c]ver 5 [d]ver 7,9,11 [e]Ac 10:28 [f]ver 12 **2:15** [g]Php 3:4,5 [h]1Sa 15:18; Lk 24:7 **2:16** [i]S Ro 3:28 [j]S Ro 9:30 [k]S Ro 3:28; S 4:25 **2:17** [l]ver 15 [m]Gal 3:21 **2:19** [n]S Ro 7:4 [o]Ro 6:10,11,14; 2Co 5:15 **2:20** [p]S Ro 6:6 [q]S Ro 8:10; 1Pe 4:2 [r]S Mt 4:3 [s]S Ro 8:37 [t]S Gal 1:4 **2:21** [u]Gal 3:21 **3:1** [v]Lk 24:25 [w]S Ac 16:6 [x]Gal 5:7 [y]1Co 1:23 **3:2** [z]S Jn 20:22 [a]ver 5,10; Gal 2:16 [b]Ro 10:17; Heb 4:2 **3:5** [c]1Co 12:10 [d]ver 2,10; Gal 2:16 **3:6** [e]Ge 15:6; S Ro 4:3 **3:7** [f]ver 9 [g]S Lk 3:8 **3:8** [h]Ge 12:3; 18:18; 22:18; 26:4; Ac 3:25 **3:9** [i]ver 7; Ro 4:16 [j]Ro 4:18-22 **3:10** [k]ver 2,5; Gal 2:16 [l]ver 13; S Ro 4:15 [m]Dt 27:26; Jer 11:3 **3:11** [n]S Ro 3:28 [o]Hab 2:4; S Ro 9:30; Heb 10:38 **3:12** [p]Lev 18:5; S Ro 10:5 **3:13** [q]Gal 4:5

[a] *21* Some interpreters end the quotation after verse 14. [b] *6* Gen. 15:6 [c] *8* Gen. 12:3; 18:18; 22:18 [d] *10* Deut. 27:26 [e] *11* Hab. 2:4 [f] *12* Lev. 18:5

2:14 *you live like a Gentile.* You do not observe Jewish customs, especially dietary restrictions (see v. 12).

2:16 A key verse in Galatians (see Introduction: Theological Teaching). Three times it tells us that no one is justified by observing the law, and three times it underscores the indispensable requirement of placing one's faith in Christ. *not by observing the law.* Paul is not depreciating the law itself, for he clearly maintained that God's law is "holy, righteous and good" (Ro 7:12; see note there). He is arguing against an illegitimate use of the OT law that made the observance of that law the grounds of acceptance with God. *justified by faith.* The essence of the gospel message (see Ro 3:20,28; Php 3:9; see also notes on Ro 3:24,28). Faith is the means by which justification is received, not its basis (cf. notes on Eph 2:8–9; Jas 2:14–26).

2:17 See Ro 6:1 and note.

2:19 *I died to the law.* See v. 20; see also note on Ro 7:4.

2:20 *crucified with Christ.* See 5:24; Ro 6:8–10; 7:6; see also note on Ro 6:7. *gave himself for me.* See 1:4; 1Ti 2:6; Tit 2:14.

2:21 *Christ died for nothing.* To mingle legalism with grace distorts grace and makes a mockery of the cross.

3:1 *foolish.* They were not mentally deficient but simply failed to use their powers of perception (see Lk 24:25; Ro 1:14; 1Ti 6:9; Tit 3:3). *Who . . . ?* Obviously legalistic Judaizers. *portrayed as crucified.* See 1Co 1:23; 2:2. The verb means "to publicly portray or placard." Cf. the bronze snake that Moses displayed on a pole (Nu 21:9).

3:2 *the Spirit.* A major theme in Galatians from this point on (Paul refers to the Holy Spirit 16 times).

3:3 *beginning with the Spirit . . . attain your goal.* Both salvation and sanctification are the work of the Holy Spirit. *human effort.* Lit. "the flesh," a reference to human nature in its unregenerate weakness. Trying to achieve righteousness by works, including circumcision, was a part of life in the "flesh."

3:4 *if it really was for nothing.* Paul hopes that those who have been misled will return to the true gospel.

3:7 *children of Abraham.* Abraham was the physical and spiritual father of the Jewish race (see Jn 8:33,39,53; Ac 7:2; Ro 4:12). Here all believers (Jews and Gentiles) are called his spiritual children (see notes on Ro 4:11–12). They are also referred to as the "seed" or "descendants" of Abraham (v. 16; Heb 2:16).

3:8 *Scripture foresaw.* A personification of Scripture that calls attention to its divine origin (see 1Ti 5:18).

3:9 *Abraham, the man of faith.* Paul develops this theme at length in Ro 4; see also Heb 11:8–19.

3:10 *rely on observing the law.* The reference is to legalists—those who refuse God's offer of grace and insist on pursuing righteousness through works. *under a curse.* Because no one under the law ever perfectly kept the law. God's blessing has never been earned, but has always been freely given. *everything.* See Jas 2:10 and note.

3:11 *will live.* Means here (and in v. 12) almost the same thing as "will be justified."

3:12 See note on Lev 18:5.

3:13 *Christ redeemed us.* See 4:5; Eph 1:7 and note. *tree.* Used in classical Greek of stocks and poles on which bodies were impaled (cf. Est 2:23 and note), here of the cross (see Ac 5:30 and note; 1Pe 2:24).

it is written: "Cursed is everyone who is
hung on a tree."[a][r] 14He redeemed us in
order that the blessing given to Abraham
might come to the Gentiles through Christ
Jesus,[s] so that by faith we might receive
the promise of the Spirit.[t]

The Law and the Promise

15Brothers,[u] let me take an example from
everyday life. Just as no one can set aside
or add to a human covenant that has been
duly established, so it is in this case. 16The
promises were spoken to Abraham and to
his seed.[v] The Scripture does not say "and
to seeds," meaning many people, but "and
to your seed,"[b][w] meaning one person, who
is Christ. 17What I mean is this: The law,
introduced 430 years[x] later, does not set
aside the covenant previously established
by God and thus do away with the promise. 18For if the inheritance depends on the
law, then it no longer depends on a promise;[y] but God in his grace gave it to Abraham through a promise.
19What, then, was the purpose of the
law? It was added because of transgressions[z] until the Seed[a] to whom the promise referred had come. The law was put
into effect through angels[b] by a mediator.[c]
20A mediator,[d] however, does not represent
just one party; but God is one.
21Is the law, therefore, opposed to the
promises of God? Absolutely not![e] For if a
law had been given that could impart life,
then righteousness would certainly have
come by the law.[f] 22But the Scripture declares that the whole world is a prisoner
of sin,[g] so that what was promised, being
given through faith in Jesus Christ, might
be given to those who believe.
23Before this faith came, we were held
prisoners[h] by the law, locked up until faith
should be revealed.[i] 24So the law was put
in charge to lead us to Christ[c][j] that we
might be justified by faith.[k] 25Now that
faith has come, we are no longer under
the supervision of the law.[l]

Sons of God

26You are all sons of God[m] through faith
in Christ Jesus, 27for all of you who were
baptized into Christ[n] have clothed yourselves with Christ.[o] 28There is neither Jew
nor Greek, slave nor free,[p] male nor female,[q] for you are all one in Christ Jesus.[r]
29If you belong to Christ,[s] then you are
Abraham's seed,[t] and heirs[u] according to
the promise.[v]

4 What I am saying is that as long as the
heir is a child, he is no different from a
slave, although he owns the whole estate.
2He is subject to guardians and trustees
until the time set by his father. 3So also,
when we were children, we were in slavery[w] under the basic principles of the
world.[x] 4But when the time had fully come,[y]
God sent his Son,[z] born of a woman,[a]

3:13 [r]Dt 21:23; S Ac 5:30
3:14 [s]Ro 4:9,16 [t]ver 2; Joel 2:28; S Jn 20:22; S Ac 2:33
3:15 [u]S Ro 7:1
3:16 [v]Ge 17:19; Ps 132:11; Mic 7:20; Lk 1:55; Ro 4:13,16; 9:4,8; Gal 3:29; 4:28 [w]Ge 12:7; 13:15; 17:7,8,10; 24:7
3:17 [x]Ge 15:13,14; Ex 12:40; Ac 7:6
3:18 [y]Ro 4:14
3:19 [z]Ro 5:20 [a]ver 16 [b]Dt 33:2; Ac 7:53 [c]Ex 20:19; Dt 5:5
3:20 [d]1Ti 2:5; Heb 8:6; 9:15; 12:24
3:21 [e]Gal 2:17; S Ro 7:12 [f]Gal 2:21
3:22 [g]Ro 3:9-19; 11:32
3:23 [h]Ro 11:32 [i]ver 25
3:24 [j]ver 19; Ro 10:4; S 4:15 [k]Gal 2:16
3:25 [l]S Ro 7:4
3:26 [m]S Ro 8:14
3:27 [n]S Mt 28:19 [o]S Ro 13:14
3:28 [p]1Co 12:13; Col 3:11 [q]Ge 1:27; 5:2; Joel 2:29 [r]Jn 10:16; 17:11; Eph 2:14,15
3:29 [s]S 1Co 3:23 [t]ver 16; S Lk 3:8 [u]S Ro 8:17
[v]ver 16 **4:3** [w]ver 8,9,24,25; Gal 2:4 [x]Col 2:8,20 **4:4** [y]Mk 1:15; Ro 5:6; Eph 1:10 [z]S Jn 3:17 [a]S Jn 1:14

[a] *13* Deut. 21:23 [b] *16* Gen. 12:7; 13:15; 24:7
[c] *24* Or *charge until Christ came*

3:14 *blessing given to Abraham.* See v. 8; Ro 4:1–5. *promise of the Spirit.* See Eze 36:26; 37:14; 39:29; Jn 14:16–17; cf. Eph 1:13.
3:15 *Brothers.* See note on 1:2. *human covenant.* The Greek word normally indicates a last will or testament, which is probably the legal instrument Paul is referring to here. But in the Septuagint (the pre-Christian Greek translation of the OT) it had been widely used of God's covenant with his people (see also Mt 26:28; Lk 1:72; Ac 3:25; 7:8; 2Co 3:14; Heb 8:9), so Paul's choice of analogy was apt for his purpose.
3:16 *promises.* See notes on Ro 4:13; 9:4.
3:17 *430 years.* See Ex 12:40–41. The period in Egypt is designated in round numbers as "400 years" in Ge 15:13; Ac 7:6 (see note there).
3:19 *was added.* From the time of Abraham, the promise covenanted to him (Ge 12:2–3,7; 15:18–20; 17:4–8) had stood at the center of God's relationship with his people. After the exodus the law contained in the Sinaitic covenant (Ex 19–24) became an additional element in that relationship—what Jeremiah by implication called the "old covenant" when he brought God's promise of a "new covenant" (Jer 31:31–34). *because of transgressions.* To make them known, even to increase them (see Ro 4:15; 7:7–11 and notes). *the Seed.* Christ (v. 16). *through angels.* See Ac 7:38,53 and note. *mediator.* Moses (see note on v. 20).
3:20 The Sinaitic covenant was a formal arrangement of mutual commitments between God and Israel, with Moses as the mediator. But since the promise God covenanted with Abraham involved commitment only from God's side (and God is one; see note on Dt 6:4), no mediator was involved.
3:21 The reason the law is not opposed to the promise is that, although in itself it cannot save, it serves to reveal sin, which alienates God from humans, and to show the need for the salvation that the promise offers.
3:23 *this faith.* In Christ (v. 22). *held prisoners by the law.* To be a prisoner of sin (v. 22) and a prisoner of law amounts to much the same, because law reveals and stimulates sin (see v. 19 and note; cf. Col 2:20).
3:24 *was put in charge.* The expression translates the Greek *paidagogos* (from which "pedagogue" is derived). It refers to the personal slave-attendant who accompanied a freeborn boy wherever he went and exercised a certain amount of discipline over him. His function was more like that of a babysitter than a teacher (see 1Co 4:15, "guardians").
3:25–26 By adoption, the justified believer is a full adult and heir in God's family, with all the attendant rights and privileges (4:1–7; Ro 8:14–17).
3:27 *baptized into Christ.* See Ro 6:3–11; 1Co 12:13 and note. *clothed ... with.* See note on Ps 109:29.
3:28 Unity in Christ transcends ethnic, social and gender distinctions (see Ro 10:12; 1Co 12:13; Eph 2:15–16).
3:29 Christians are Abraham's true, spiritual descendants.
4:1 *child.* A minor. Contrast with "adults" in 1Co 14:20 ("mature" in Php 3:15).
4:2 *guardians.* A broader term than "[one] put in charge to lead us" in 3:24. See Mt 20:8 ("foreman"); Lk 8:3 ("manager").
4:3 *in slavery.* See note on 3:23. *basic principles.* See Col 2:8 and note.
4:4 *time had fully come.* The time "set" (v. 2) by God for his children to become adult sons and heirs. *God sent his Son.* See

born under law,[b] 5to redeem[c] those under
law, that we might receive the full rights[d]
of sons.[e] 6Because you are sons, God sent
the Spirit of his Son[f] into our hearts,[g] the
Spirit who calls out, *"Abba,*[a] Father."[h] 7So
you are no longer a slave, but a son; and
since you are a son, God has made you
also an heir.[i]

Paul's Concern for the Galatians

8Formerly, when you did not know
God,[j] you were slaves[k] to those who by
nature are not gods.[l] 9But now that you
know God—or rather are known by
God[m]—how is it that you are turning back
to those weak and miserable principles?
Do you wish to be enslaved[n] by them all
over again?[o] 10You are observing special
days and months and seasons and years![p]
11I fear for you, that somehow I have wasted my efforts on you.[q]

12I plead with you, brothers,[r] become
like me, for I became like you. You have
done me no wrong. 13As you know, it was
because of an illness[s] that I first preached
the gospel to you. 14Even though my illness was a trial to you, you did not treat
me with contempt or scorn. Instead, you
welcomed me as if I were an angel of God,
as if I were Christ Jesus himself.[t] 15What
has happened to all your joy? I can testify that, if you could have done so, you
would have torn out your eyes and given
them to me. 16Have I now become your
enemy by telling you the truth?[u]

17Those people are zealous to win you
over, but for no good. What they want
is to alienate you ⌞from us⌟, so that you
may be zealous for them.[v] 18It is fine to
be zealous, provided the purpose is good,
and to be so always and not just when I
am with you.[w] 19My dear children,[x] for
whom I am again in the pains of childbirth until Christ is formed in you,[y] 20how
I wish I could be with you now and
change my tone, because I am perplexed
about you!

Hagar and Sarah

21Tell me, you who want to be under the
law,[z] are you not aware of what the law
says? 22For it is written that Abraham had
two sons, one by the slave woman[a] and
the other by the free woman.[b] 23His son
by the slave woman was born in the ordinary way;[c] but his son by the free woman
was born as the result of a promise.[d]

24These things may be taken figuratively, for the women represent two covenants. One covenant is from Mount Sinai

[a] 6 Aramaic for *Father*

4:4 [b] Lk 2:27
4:5 [c] S Ro 3:24 [d] Jn 1:12 [e] S Ro 8:14
4:6 [f] S Ac 16:7 [g] Ro 5:5 [h] Ro 8:15,16
4:7 [i] S Ro 8:17
4:8 [j] Ro 1:28; 1Co 1:21; 15:34; 1Th 4:5; 2Th 1:8 [k] S ver 3 [l] 2Ch 13:9; Isa 37:19; Jer 2:11; 5:7; 16:20; 1Co 8:4,5
4:9 [m] 1Co 8:3 [n] S ver 3 [o] Col 2:20
4:10 [p] Ro 14:5; Col 2:16
4:11 [q] 1Th 3:5
4:12 [r] S Ro 7:1; Gal 6:18
4:13 [s] 1Co 2:3
4:14 [t] Mt 10:40
4:16 [u] Am 5:10
4:17 [v] Gal 2:4,12
4:18 [w] ver 13,14
4:19 [x] S 1Th 2:11 [y] Ro 8:29; Eph 4:13
4:21 [z] S Ro 2:12
4:22 [a] Ge 16:15 [b] Ge 21:2
4:23 [c] ver 28,29; Ro 9:7,8 [d] Ge 17:16-21; 18:10-14; 21:1; Heb 11:11

Jn 1:14; 3:16; Ro 1:1–6; 1Jn 4:14. *born of a woman.* Showing that Christ was truly human. *born under law.* Subject to the Jewish law.

4:5 *those under law.* Those under the authority of the law of Moses (cf. notes on 5:18; Ro 6:14; 1Co 9:20). *full rights of sons.* Lit. "adoption [of a son]." See Ro 8:15, where the "Spirit of sonship" is contrasted with "a spirit that makes you a slave" (cf. Eph 1:5 and note). God takes into his family as fully recognized sons and heirs both Jews (those who had been under the law) and Gentiles who believe in Christ.

4:6 *Spirit of his Son.* A new "guardian" (v. 2), identified as the "Spirit of God" and "Spirit of Christ" in Ro 8:9 (see Ro 8:2; Eph 1:13–14). *calls out.* The Greek for this phrase is a vivid verb expressing deep emotion, often used of an inarticulate cry. In Mt 27:50 it is used of Jesus' final cry on the cross. *Abba, Father.* Expressive of an especially close relationship to God (see also NIV text note).

4:8 *when you did not know God.* See 1Co 12:2; 1Th 4:5. *are not gods.* When the Galatians were pagans, they thought that the beings they worshiped were gods; but when they became Christians, they learned better (see 1Co 8:5 and note).

4:9 *turning back.* See 3:1–3. *weak and miserable principles.* See note on v. 3. *enslaved ... again.* Legalistic trust in rituals, in moral achievement, in the law, in good works, or even in cold, dead orthodoxy may indicate a relapse into second childhood on the part of those who should be knowing and enjoying the freedom of full-grown sons.

4:10 *special days.* Such as the Sabbath and the Day of Atonement (tenth day of Tishri; see Lev 16:29–34), which had never been, and can never be, in themselves means of salvation or sanctification. *months and seasons.* Such as New Moons (see Nu 28:11–15; Isa 1:13–14), Passover (Ex 12:18) and Firstfruits (Lev 23:10). *years.* Such as the sabbath year (see Lev 25:4). The Pharisees meticulously observed all these in an attempt to gain merit before God.

4:11 *wasted my efforts.* Due to their return to Pharisaic legalism.

4:12 *brothers.* See note on 1:2.

4:13 *illness.* On the basis of v. 15; 6:11 (see note there) some suggest it was eye trouble. Others have suggested malaria or epilepsy. *first preached.* When Paul visited Galatia on his first missionary journey (Ac 13:14—14:23; see map, p. 1704).

4:14 *you welcomed me.* He implies that under the influence of Judaizers they have changed their attitude toward him.

4:15 *What has happened to all your joy?* Because of the restraints of legalistic Judaism they had lost their blessing and joy. *torn out your eyes.* A hyperbole indicating their willingness, for his benefit, to part with that which was most precious to them (cf. Mt 5:29–30 and note).

4:16 *your enemy.* Telling the truth sometimes results in loss of friends. *the truth.* The good news about God's grace in Christ.

4:17 *Those people.* Judaizers (see 2:4,12).

4:19 *My dear children.* For Paul's affectionate relationship to his converts see Ac 20:37–38; Php 4:1; 1Th 2:7–8. The expression occurs only here in Paul's writings, but is common in John's (e.g., Jn 13:33; 1Jn 2:1; 3:7). *until Christ is formed in you.* The goal of Paul's ministry (see Ro 8:29; Eph 4:13,15; Col 1:27).

4:21 *under the law.* See note on v. 5.

4:22 *two sons.* Ishmael was born to the slave woman, Hagar (Ge 16:1–16), and Isaac to the free woman, Sarah (Ge 21:2–5).

4:23 *promise.* See Ge 17:19; 18:10–15 and note on 18:10; cf. Ro 9:6–9.

4:24 *may be taken figuratively.* The Sarah-Hagar account is not an allegory in the sense that it was nonhistorical, but in the sense that Paul uses the events to illustrate a theological truth. *covenant.* See note on 3:15. *Mount Sinai.* Where the old covenant was established, with its law governing Israel's life (see Ex 19:2; 20:1–17).

and bears children who are to be slaves: This is Hagar. 25Now Hagar stands for Mount Sinai in Arabia and corresponds to the present city of Jerusalem, because she is in slavery with her children. 26But the Jerusalem that is above[e] is free, and she is our mother. 27For it is written:

"Be glad, O barren woman,
who bears no children;
break forth and cry aloud,
you who have no labor pains;
because more are the children of the
desolate woman
than of her who has a husband."[a f]

28Now you, brothers, like Isaac, are children of promise.[g] 29At that time the son born in the ordinary way[h] persecuted the son born by the power of the Spirit.[i] It is the same now. 30But what does the Scripture say? "Get rid of the slave woman and her son, for the slave woman's son will never share in the inheritance with the free woman's son."[b j] 31Therefore, brothers, we are not children of the slave woman,[k] but of the free woman.[l]

Freedom in Christ

5 It is for freedom that Christ has set us free.[m] Stand firm,[n] then, and do not let yourselves be burdened again by a yoke of slavery.[o]

2Mark my words! I, Paul, tell you that if you let yourselves be circumcised,[p] Christ will be of no value to you at all. 3Again I declare to every man who lets himself be circumcised that he is obligated to obey the whole law.[q] 4You who are trying to be justified by law[r] have been alienated from Christ; you have fallen away from grace.[s] 5But by faith we eagerly await through the Spirit the righteousness for which we hope.[t] 6For in Christ Jesus[u] neither circumcision nor uncircumcision has any value.[v] The only thing that counts is faith expressing itself through love.[w]

7You were running a good race.[x] Who cut in on you[y] and kept you from obeying the truth? 8That kind of persuasion does not come from the one who calls you.[z] 9"A little yeast works through the whole batch of dough."[a] 10I am confident[b] in the Lord that you will take no other view.[c] The one who is throwing you into confusion[d] will pay the penalty, whoever he may be. 11Brothers, if I am still preaching circumcision, why am I still being persecuted?[e] In that case the offense[f] of the cross has been abolished. 12As for those agitators,[g] I wish they would go the whole way and emasculate themselves!

4:26 [e] Heb 12:22; Rev 3:12; 21:2,10
4:27 [f] Isa 54:1
4:28 [g] ver 23; S Gal 3:16
4:29 [h] ver 23 [i] Ge 21:9
4:30 [j] Ge 21:10
4:31 [k] S Ro 7:4 [l] ver 22
5:1 [m] ver 13; Jn 8:32; Gal 2:4; S Ro 7:4 [n] S 1Co 16:13 [o] S Mt 23:4; Gal 2:4
5:2 [p] ver 3,6,11,12; Ac 15:1
5:3 [q] Ro 2:25; Gal 3:10; Jas 2:10
5:4 [r] S Ro 3:28 [s] Heb 12:15; 2Pe 3:17
5:5 [t] Ro 8:23,24
5:6 [u] S Ro 16:3 [v] S 1Co 7:19 [w] 1Th 1:3; Jas 2:22
5:7 [x] S 1Co 9:24 [y] Gal 3:1
5:8 [z] S Ro 8:28
5:9 [a] 1Co 5:6
5:10 [b] S 2Co 2:3 [c] Php 3:15 [d] ver 12; Gal 1:7
5:11 [e] Gal 4:29; 6:12 [f] S Lk 2:34
5:12 [g] ver 10

[a] 27 Isaiah 54:1 [b] 30 Gen. 21:10

4:25 *corresponds to the present city of Jerusalem.* Jerusalem can be equated with Mount Sinai because it represents the center of Judaism.
4:26 *the Jerusalem that is above.* Rabbinical teaching held that the Jerusalem above was the heavenly archetype that in the Messianic period would be let down to earth (cf. Rev 21:2). Here it refers to the heavenly city of God, in which Christ reigns and of which Christians are citizens, in contrast to the "present city of Jerusalem" (v. 25). *our mother.* As citizens of the heavenly Jerusalem, Christians are her children.
4:27 Paul applies Isaiah's joyful promise (see Isa 54:1 and note) to exiled Jerusalem (in her exile "barren" of children) to the ingathering of believers through the gospel, by which "Jerusalem's" children have become many.
4:28 *children of promise.* Children by virtue of God's promise (see 3:29; Ro 9:8).
4:29 *persecuted the son born by the power of the Spirit.* Suggested by Ge 21:9 (see note there); cf. Ps 83:5–6. *the same now.* See Ac 13:50; 14:2–5,19; 1Th 2:14–16.
4:30 *Get rid of the slave woman.* Sarah's words in Ge 21:10 were used by Paul as the Scriptural basis for teaching the Galatians to put the Judaizers out of the church.
4:31 *we are not children of the slave woman.* The believer is not enslaved to the law but is a child of promise and lives by faith (cf. 3:7,29).
5:1 *freedom.* Emphasized by its position in the Greek sentence. The freedom spoken of here is freedom from the yoke of the law. *burdened.* Cf. Mt 11:28–30 and notes on 11:29–30. *yoke of slavery.* The burden of the rigorous demands of the law as the means for gaining God's favor—an intolerable burden for sinful humanity (see Ac 15:10–11 and notes).
5:2 As a condition for God's acceptance, circumcision impeded the development of the Christian life through trusting in Christ.
5:3 *obligated to obey the whole law.* The OT law is a unit; submission to it cannot be selective (see Jas 2:10 and note).
5:4 *fallen away from grace.* Placed yourself outside the scope of divine favor, because gaining God's favor by observing the law and receiving it by grace are mutually exclusive (see 2:2 and note; cf. 3:3 and note).
5:5 *righteousness for which we hope.* A reference to God's final verdict of "not guilty," assured presently to the believer by faith and by the sanctifying work of the Holy Spirit. This is one of the few eschatological statements in Galatians.
5:6 *neither circumcision nor uncircumcision has any value.* See v. 2; 2:21; 6:15; 1Co 7:19. *faith expressing itself through love.* Faith is not mere intellectual assent (see Jas 2:18–19) but a living trust in God's grace that expresses itself in acts of love (see 1Th 1:3).
5:7 *were running a good race.* Before the Judaizers hindered them. Paul was fond of depicting the Christian life as a race (see, e.g., 2:2; 1Co 9:24–27 and note on 9:27; Php 2:16; 2Ti 4:7).
5:8 *persuasion.* By the Judaizers.
5:9 A proverb used here to stress the pervasive effect of Judaism. When the word "yeast" in the Bible is used as a symbol, it indicates evil or the corrupting influence of false teaching (see note on Mk 8:15), except in Mt 13:33 (see note there).
5:11 *Brothers.* See note on 1:2. *why am I still being persecuted?* Because human pride refuses to acknowledge that it is incapable of doing anything to merit salvation. Paul's preaching excluded circumcision and obedience to the law as a means of justification and focused instead on Christ's finished work on the cross. This was an offense to the Judaizers, and continues to be so to many people in our own day (see Ro 9:32–33 and note on 9:32; 1Co 1:23 and note).
5:12 *emasculate themselves.* Paul's sarcasm is evident (cf. Php 3:2).

13You, my brothers, were called to be
free.[h] But do not use your freedom to indulge the sinful nature[a];[i] rather, serve
one another[j] in love. 14The entire law is
summed up in a single command: "Love
your neighbor as yourself."[b k] 15If you
keep on biting and devouring each other, watch out or you will be destroyed by
each other.

Life by the Spirit

16So I say, live by the Spirit,[l] and you
will not gratify the desires of the sinful nature.[m] 17For the sinful nature desires what
is contrary to the Spirit, and the Spirit what
is contrary to the sinful nature.[n] They are
in conflict with each other, so that you do
not do what you want.[o] 18But if you are led
by the Spirit,[p] you are not under law.[q]

19The acts of the sinful nature are obvious: sexual immorality,[r] impurity and
debauchery; 20idolatry and witchcraft;
hatred, discord, jealousy, fits of rage, selfish ambition, dissensions, factions 21and

5:13 [h]S ver 1 [i]S ver 24; 1Co 8:9; 1Pe 2:16 [j]1Co 9:19; 2Co 4:5; Eph 5:21 **5:14** [k]Lev 19:18; S Mt 5:43; Gal 6:2 **5:16** [l]ver 18,25; Ro 8:2,4-6,9,14; S 2Co 5:17 [m]S ver 24 **5:17** [n]Ro 8:5-8 [o]Ro 7:15-23 **5:18** [p]S ver 16 [q]S Ro 2:12; 1Ti 1:9 **5:19** [r]S 1Co 6:18

[a] 13 Or *the flesh*; also in verses 16, 17, 19 and 24
[b] 14 Lev. 19:18

5:13 *do not use your freedom to indulge the sinful nature.* See Ro 6:1 and note. True Christian liberty is not license to sin but freedom to serve God and one another in love (see 1Pe 2:16 and note).

5:14 *entire law is summed up.* Doing to others what you would have them do to you expresses the spirit and intention of "the Law and the Prophets" (Mt 7:12; cf. Mt 5:17 and note; Mk 12:31).

5:15 *biting and devouring each other.* The opposite of vv. 13–14. Seeking to attain status with God and human beings by mere observance of the law breeds a self-righteous, critical spirit.

5:16 *live.* Present tense—"go on living" (used of habitual conduct). Living by the promptings and power of the Spirit is the key to conquering sinful desires (see v. 25 and note; Ro 8:2–4).

5:17 *in conflict with each other.* Cf. Ro 7:13–25; 1Pe 2:11 and notes.

5:18 *led by the Spirit.* See Ro 8:14. *not under law.* Not under the bondage of trying to please God by minute observance of the law for salvation or sanctification (see Ro 6:14 and note).

5:19–21 See Ro 1:29–31 and note.

The Fruit of the Spirit

The aspects of the fruit of the Spirit advocated by Paul in Galatians 5:22–23 occur not only here but also elsewhere in the Scriptures. Most of the attributes are those by which God himself lives.

Aspect	GK number*	Definition	Attribute of God	Attribute for Christians
love	26	sacrificial, unmerited deeds to help a needy person	Ex 34:6; Jn 3:16; Ro 5:8; 1Jn 4:8,16	Jn 13:34–35; Ro 12:9,10; 1Pe 1:22; 1Jn 4:7,11–12,21
joy	5915	an inner happiness not dependent on outward circumstances	Ps 104:31; Isa 62:5; Lk 15:7,10	Dt 12:7,12,18; Ps 64:10; Isa 25:9; Php 4:4; 1Pe 1:8
peace	1645	harmony in all relationships	Isa 9:6–7; Eze 34:25; Jn 14:27; Heb 13:20	Isa 26:3; Ro 5:1; 12:18; 14:17; Eph 2:14–17
patience	3429	putting up with others, even when one is severely tried	Ro 9:22; 1Ti 1:16; 1Pe 3:20; 2Pe 3:9,15	Eph 4:2; Col 1:11; Heb 6:12; Jas 5:7–8,10
kindness	5983	doing thoughtful deeds for others	Ro 2:4; 11:22; Eph 2:7; Tit 3:4	1Co 13:4; Eph 4:32; Col 3:12
goodness	20	showing generosity to others	Ne 9:25,35; Ps 31:19; Mk 10:18	Ro 15:14; Eph 5:9; 2Th 1:11
faithfulness	4411	trustworthiness and reliability	Ps 33:4; 1Co 1:9; 10:13; Heb 10:23; 1Jn 1:9	Lk 16:10–12; 2Th 1:4; 2Ti 4:7; Tit 2:10
gentleness	4559	meekness and humility	Zec 9:9; Mt 11:29	Isa 66:2; Mt 5:5; Eph 4:2; Col 3:12
self-control	1602	victory over sinful desires		Pr 16:32; Tit 1:8; 2:12; 1Pe 5:8–9; 2Pe 1:6

 *The numbers refer to the Greek dictionary entry numbers in Goodrick & Kohlenberger, *The NIV Exhaustive Concordance*.

envy; drunkenness, orgies, and the like.[s] I
warn you, as I did before, that those who
live like this will not inherit the kingdom
of God.[t]
22But the fruit[u] of the Spirit is love,[v]
joy, peace,[w] patience, kindness, goodness,
faithfulness, 23gentleness and self-control.[x] Against such things there is no law.[y]
24Those who belong to Christ Jesus have
crucified the sinful nature[z] with its passions and desires.[a] 25Since we live by the
Spirit,[b] let us keep in step with the Spirit.
26Let us not become conceited,[c] provoking
and envying each other.

Doing Good to All

6 Brothers, if someone is caught in a
sin, you who are spiritual[d] should restore[e] him gently. But watch yourself, or
you also may be tempted. 2Carry each
other's burdens, and in this way you will
fulfill the law of Christ.[f] 3If anyone thinks
he is something[g] when he is nothing, he
deceives himself.[h] 4Each one should test
his own actions. Then he can take pride
in himself,[i] without comparing himself to
somebody else,[j] 5for each one should carry his own load.[k]
6Anyone who receives instruction in the
word must share all good things with his
instructor.[l]
7Do not be deceived:[m] God cannot be
mocked. A man reaps what he sows.[n] 8The
one who sows to please his sinful nature,[o]
from that nature[a] will reap destruction;[p]
the one who sows to please the Spirit,
from the Spirit will reap eternal life.[q] 9Let
us not become weary in doing good,[r] for
at the proper time we will reap a harvest
if we do not give up.[s] 10Therefore, as we
have opportunity, let us do good[t] to all
people, especially to those who belong to
the family[u] of believers.

Not Circumcision but a New Creation

11See what large letters I use as I write to
you with my own hand![v]
12Those who want to make a good impression outwardly[w] are trying to compel
you to be circumcised.[x] The only reason
they do this is to avoid being persecuted[y]
for the cross of Christ. 13Not even those
who are circumcised obey the law,[z] yet
they want you to be circumcised that they
may boast about your flesh.[a] 14May I never boast except in the cross of our Lord
Jesus Christ,[b] through which[b] the world
has been crucified to me, and I to the
world.[c] 15Neither circumcision nor uncircumcision means anything;[d] what counts
is a new creation.[e] 16Peace and mercy to

[a] 8 Or *his flesh, from the flesh* [b] 14 Or *whom*

5:21 [s] Mt 15:19; Ro 13:13 [t] S Mt 25:34 **5:22** [u] Mt 7:16-20; Eph 5:9 [v] Col 3:12-15 [w] Mal 2:6 **5:23** [x] S Ac 24:25 [y] ver 18 **5:24** [z] ver 13, 16-21; S Ro 6:6; 7:5, 18; 8:3-5, 8, 9, 12, 13; 13:14; Gal 6:8; Col 2:11 [a] ver 16, 17 **5:25** [b] S ver 16 **5:26** [c] Php 2:3 **6:1** [d] 1Co 2:15; 3:1 [e] S Mt 18:15; S 2Co 2:7 **6:2** [f] 1Co 9:21; Jas 2:8 **6:3** [g] Ro 12:3; 1Co 8:2 [h] 1Co 3:18 **6:4** [i] 2Co 13:5 [j] 2Co 10:12 **6:5** [k] ver 2; Jer 31:30 **6:6** [l] 1Co 9:11, 14; 1Ti 5:17, 18 **6:7** [m] S 1Co 6:9 [n] Pr 22:8; Jer 34:17; Hos 10:12, 13; 2Co 9:6 **6:8** [o] S Gal 5:24 [p] Job 4:8; Hos 8:7; S Ro 6:23 [q] Jas 3:18 **6:9** [r] 1Co 15:58; 2Co 4:1 [s] Job 42:12; Ps 126:5; Heb 12:3; Rev 2:10 **6:10** [t] Pr 3:27; S Tit 2:14 [u] Eph 2:19; 1Pe 4:17 **6:11** [v] S 1Co 16:21 **6:12** [w] Mt 23:25, 26 [x] Ac 15:1 [y] Gal 5:11 **6:13** [z] Ro 2:25 [a] Php 3:3 **6:14** [b] 1Co 2:2 [c] S Ro 6:2, 6 **6:15** [d] S 1Co 7:19 [e] S 2Co 5:17

5:22–23 For other lists of virtues see 2Co 6:6–10; Eph 4:2; 5:9; Php 4:8–9; Col 3:12–15. Christian character is produced by the Holy Spirit, not by the mere moral discipline of trying to live by the law. Paul makes it clear that justification by faith does not result in libertinism. The indwelling Holy Spirit produces Christian virtues in the believer's life.
5:22 *fruit of the Spirit.* Compare the singular "fruit" with the plural "acts" (v. 19).
5:23 *no law.* See 1Ti 1:9.
5:24 *crucified the sinful nature.* See 2:20; 6:14.
5:25 *keep in step with.* Or "walk in line with," a different Greek verb from "live by" (or "walk by") in v. 16.
6:1 *Brothers.* See note on 1:2. *you who are spiritual.* Contrast with 1Co 3:1–3. *restore.* See note on 2Co 13:9. The Greek for this verb is used elsewhere in the NT for mending nets (Mk 1:19) and bringing factions together (1Co 1:10).
6:2 *Carry each other's burdens.* The emphasis is on moral burdens or weaknesses (see v. 1; Ro 15:1–3). *law of Christ.* See 1Co 9:21 and note.
6:4 *Each one should test his own actions.* The emphasis here is on personal responsibility (see 1Co 11:28; 2Co 13:5).
6:5 *carry his own load.* The "for" at the beginning of the verse connects it with v. 4. Each of us is responsible before God. The reference may be to the future judgment (the Greek verb is in the future tense), when every Christian will give an account to God (see Ro 14:10,12 and note on 14:10; 2Co 5:10 and note).
6:6 *share all good things.* See Php 4:14–19; 1Ti 5:17 and note.
6:7 *reaps what he sows.* See 2Co 9:6. As vv. 8–9 show, the principle applies not only negatively but also positively.
6:8 See Ro 8:13. *destruction.* See 5:19–21. *eternal life.* In 5:21 Paul speaks of inheriting "the kingdom of God," here of reaping "eternal life." The first focuses on the realm (sphere, context) that will be inherited (as Israel inherited the promised land); the second focuses on the blessed life that will be enjoyed in that realm (see Jn 3:15 and note).
6:10 *especially to those who belong to the family of believers.* See 1Ti 5:8.
6:11 *large letters.* May have been for emphasis or, as some have suggested, because he had poor eyesight (see note on 4:13). *with my own hand.* The letter up to this point had probably been dictated to a scribe, after which Paul took the pen in his own hand and finished the letter (cf. Ro 16:22 and note).
6:12 *compel you to be circumcised.* Cf. 2:3. *to avoid being persecuted.* By advocating circumcision (see 5:11) the Judaizers were less apt to experience opposition from the Jewish opponents of Christianity. They were thinking only of themselves. See Introduction: Occasion and Purpose.
6:14 *boast except in the cross.* See 1Co 1:31; 2:2. *world.* All that is against God (see notes on Jn 1:9; 1Jn 2:15). *crucified to me, and I to the world.* See 2:19–20; 5:24.
6:15 *new creation.* In Christ the redeemed undergo a transformation that results in an entirely new being. Creation again takes place (see 2Co 5:17 and note).
6:16,18 *Peace ... grace.* See note on Ro 1:7.
6:16 *Peace and mercy.* Cf. Ps 125:5; 128:6. *this rule.* See vv. 14–15. *Israel of God.* In contrast to "Israel according to flesh" (a literal rendering of the Greek for "people of Israel" in 1Co 10:18), the NT church, made up of believing Jews and Gentiles, is the new seed of Abraham and the heir according to the promise (3:29; cf. Ro 9:6; Php 3:3) — though some limit the phrase here to Christian Jews (translating the conjunction as "and" instead of "even").

all who follow this rule, even to the Israel
of God.
17Finally, let no one cause me trouble, for
I bear on my body the marks[f] of Jesus.
18The grace of our Lord Jesus Christ[g] be
with your spirit,[h] brothers. Amen.

6:17 [f]Isa 44:5; S 2Co 1:5; 11:23 **6:18** [g]S Ro 16:20 [h]Php 4:23; 2Ti 4:22; Phm 25

6:17 *marks of Jesus.* In ancient times the Greek word for "marks" was used for the brand that identified slaves or animals. Paul's suffering (stoning, Ac 14:19; beatings, Ac 16:22; 2Co 11:25; illness, 2Co 12:7; Gal 4:13–14) marked him as a "servant of Christ" (1:10; cf. 2Co 4:10). **6:18** *be with your spirit.* Be with you (see 2Co 13:14 and note). *brothers.* See note on Ro 1:13. *Amen.* A word of confirmation often used at the close of a doxology or benediction.

Ephesians

I N T R O D U C T I O N

Author, Date and Place of Writing

The author identifies himself as Paul (1:1; 3:1; cf. 3:7,13; 4:1; 6:19 – 20). Some have taken the absence of the usual personal greetings and the verbal similarity of many parts to Colossians, among other reasons, as grounds for doubting authorship by the apostle Paul. However, this was probably a circular letter, intended for other churches in addition to the one in Ephesus (see notes on 1:1,15; 6:21 – 23). Paul may have written it about the same time as Colossians, c. A.D. 60, while he was in prison at Rome (see 3:1; 4:1; 6:20; see also chart, p. 1697).

The City of Ephesus

Ephesus was the most important city in western Asia Minor (now western Turkey). It had a harbor that at that time opened into the Cayster River (see map, p. 1823), which in turn emptied into the Aegean Sea (see map, p. 1967). Because it was also at an intersection of major trade routes, Ephesus became a commercial center. It boasted a pagan temple dedicated to the Roman goddess Diana (Greek *Artemis*); cf. Ac 19:23 – 31. Paul made Ephesus his base of operations for evangelism for about three years during which he and his disciples evangelized (see note on Ac 19:10), and the church there apparently flourished for some time, but later needed the warning of Rev 2:1 – 7.

A Quick Look

Author:
The apostle Paul

Audience:
Believers in the church at Ephesus and probably other Christians in western Asia Minor

Date:
A.D. 60

Theme:
Paul summarizes his gospel of salvation by grace through faith alone and describes the nature and role of the church in God's eternal plan.

Theological Message

Unlike several of the other letters Paul wrote, Ephesians does not address any particular error or heresy. Paul wrote to expand the horizons of his readers, so that they might understand better the dimensions of God's eternal purpose and grace and come to appreciate the high goals God has for the church.

The letter opens with a sequence of statements about God's blessings, which are interspersed with a remarkable variety of expressions drawing attention to God's wisdom, forethought and purpose. Paul emphasizes that we have been saved, not only for our personal benefit, but also to bring praise and glory to God. The climax of God's purpose, "when the times will have reached their fulfillment," is to bring all things in the universe together under Christ (1:10). It is crucially important that Christians realize this, so in 1:15 – 23 Paul prays for their understanding (a second prayer occurs in 3:14 – 21).

Paul wrote to expand the horizons of his readers, so that they might understand better the dimensions of God's eternal purpose and grace, and come to appreciate the high goals God has for the church.

Having explained God's great goals for the church, Paul proceeds to show the steps toward their fulfillment. First, God has reconciled individuals to himself as an act of grace (2:1 – 10). Second, God has reconciled these saved individuals to each other, Christ having broken down the barriers through his own death (2:11 – 22). But God has done something even beyond this: He has united these reconciled individuals in one body, the church. This is a "mystery" not fully known until it was revealed to Paul (3:1 – 6). Now Paul is able to state even more clearly what God has intended for the church, namely, that it be the means by which he displays his "manifold wisdom" to the "rulers and authorities in the heavenly realms" (3:7 – 13). It is clear through the repetition of "heavenly realms" (1:3,20; 2:6; 3:10; 6:12) that Christian existence is not merely on an earthly plane. It receives its meaning and significance from heaven, where Christ is exalted at the right hand of God (1:20).

Ephesus in the Time of Paul

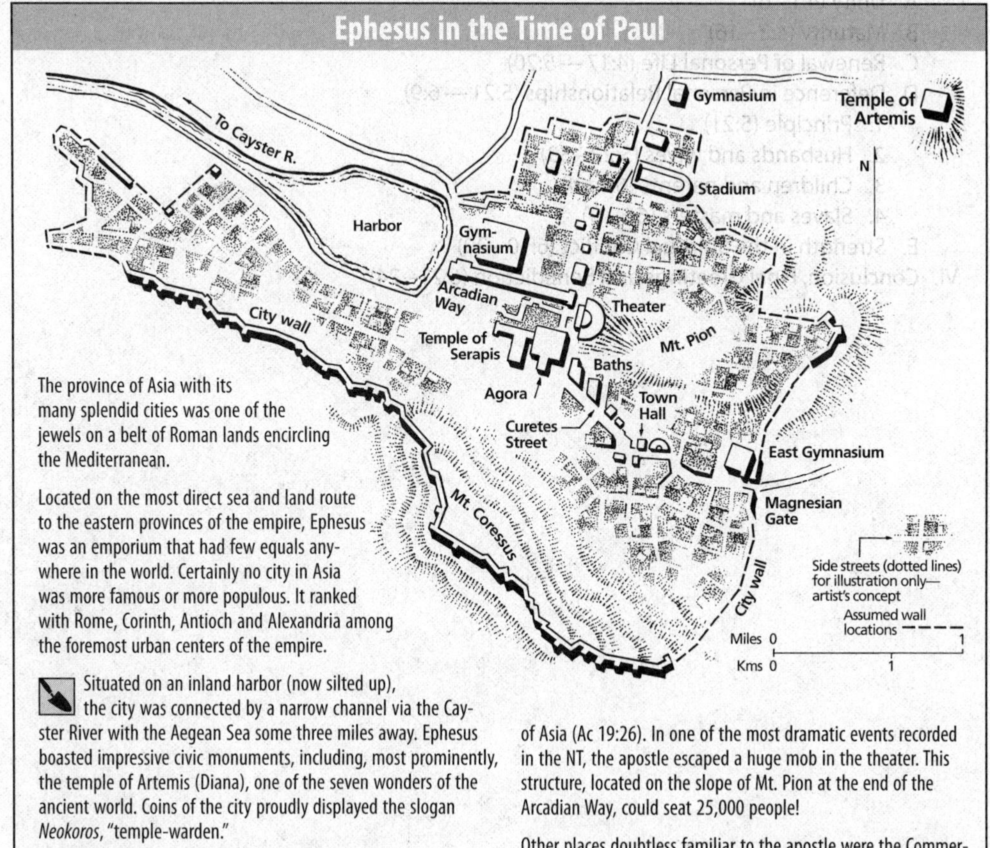

The province of Asia with its many splendid cities was one of the jewels on a belt of Roman lands encircling the Mediterranean.

Located on the most direct sea and land route to the eastern provinces of the empire, Ephesus was an emporium that had few equals anywhere in the world. Certainly no city in Asia was more famous or more populous. It ranked with Rome, Corinth, Antioch and Alexandria among the foremost urban centers of the empire.

Situated on an inland harbor (now silted up), the city was connected by a narrow channel via the Cayster River with the Aegean Sea some three miles away. Ephesus boasted impressive civic monuments, including, most prominently, the temple of Artemis (Diana), one of the seven wonders of the ancient world. Coins of the city proudly displayed the slogan *Neokoros*, "temple-warden."

Here in Ephesus Paul preached to large crowds of people. The silversmiths complained that he had influenced large numbers of people here in Ephesus and in practically the whole province of Asia (Ac 19:26). In one of the most dramatic events recorded in the NT, the apostle escaped a huge mob in the theater. This structure, located on the slope of Mt. Pion at the end of the Arcadian Way, could seat 25,000 people!

Other places doubtless familiar to the apostle were the Commercial Agora, the Magnesian Gate, the Town Hall or "Council House," and the Street of the Curetes. The location of the lecture hall of Tyrannus, where Paul taught, is unknown.

Nevertheless, that life is lived out on earth, where the practical daily life of the believer continues to work out the purposes of God. The ascended Lord gave "gifts" to the members of his church to enable them to minister to one another and so promote unity and maturity (4:1 – 16). The unity of the church under the headship of Christ foreshadows the uniting of "all things in heaven and on earth" under Christ (1:10). The new life of purity and mutual deference stands in contrast to the old way of life without Christ (4:17 — 6:9). Those who are "strong in the Lord" have victory over the evil one in the great spiritual conflict, especially through the power of prayer (6:10 – 20; see note on 1:3).

Outline

I. Greetings (1:1 – 2)
II. The Divine Purpose: The Glory and Headship of Christ (1:3 – 14)
III. Prayer That Christians May Realize God's Purpose and Power (1:15 – 23)
IV. Steps Toward the Fulfillment of God's Purpose (chs. 2 – 3)
   A. Salvation of Individuals by Grace (2:1 – 10)
   B. Reconciliation of Jew and Gentile through the Cross (2:11 – 18)
   C. Uniting of Jew and Gentile in One Household (2:19 – 22)
   D. Revelation of God's Wisdom through the Church (3:1 – 13)
   E. Prayer for Deeper Experience of God's Fullness (3:14 – 21)
V. Practical Ways to Fulfill God's Purpose in the Church (4:1 — 6:20)
   A. Unity (4:1 – 6)
   B. Maturity (4:7 – 16)
   C. Renewal of Personal Life (4:17 — 5:20)
   D. Deference in Personal Relationships (5:21 — 6:9)
      1. Principle (5:21)
      2. Husbands and wives (5:22 – 33)
      3. Children and parents (6:1 – 4)
      4. Slaves and masters (6:5 – 9)
   E. Strength in the Spiritual Conflict (6:10 – 20)
VI. Conclusion, Final Greetings and Benediction (6:21 – 24)

1 Paul, an apostle[a] of Christ Jesus by the
will of God,[b]
To the saints[c] in Ephesus,[ad] the faithful[be] in Christ Jesus:
[2]Grace and peace to you from God our
Father and the Lord Jesus Christ.[f]

Spiritual Blessings in Christ

[3]Praise be to the God and Father of our
Lord Jesus Christ,[g] who has blessed us in
the heavenly realms[h] with every spiritual
blessing in Christ. [4]For he chose us[i] in him
before the creation of the world[j] to be holy
and blameless[k] in his sight. In love[l] [5]he[c]
predestined[m] us to be adopted as his sons[n]
through Jesus Christ, in accordance with
his pleasure[o] and will— [6]to the praise of
his glorious grace,[p] which he has freely
given us in the One he loves.[q] [7]In him we
have redemption[r] through his blood,[s] the
forgiveness of sins, in accordance with
the riches[t] of God's grace [8]that he lavished on us with all wisdom and understanding. [9]And he[d] made known to us the
mystery[u] of his will according to his good
pleasure, which he purposed[v] in Christ,
[10]to be put into effect when the times will
have reached their fulfillment[w]—to bring
all things in heaven and on earth together
under one head, even Christ.[x]
[11]In him we were also chosen,[e] having
been predestined[y] according to the plan of
him who works out everything in conformity with the purpose[z] of his will, [12]in order that we, who were the first to hope in
Christ, might be for the praise of his glory.[a]

1:1 [a]S 1Co 1:1 [b]S 2Co 1:1 [c]S Ac 9:13 [d]S Ac 18:19 [e]Col 1:2 **1:2** [f]S Ro 1:7 **1:3** [g]2Co 1:3; 1Pe 1:3 [h]ver 20; Eph 2:6; 3:10; 6:12 **1:4** [i]2Th 2:13 [j]S Mt 25:34 [k]Lev 11:44; 20:7; 2Sa 22:24; Ps 15:2; Eph 5:27; Col 1:22 [l]Eph 4:2,15,16 **1:5** [m]ver 11; Ro 8:29,30 [n]S Ro 8:14,15 [o]Lk 12:32; 1Co 1:21; Col 1:19 **1:6** [p]ver 12,14 [q]Mt 3:17 **1:7** [r]ver 14; S Ro 3:24 [s]S Ro 3:25 [t]S Ro 2:4 **1:9** [u]S Ro 16:25 [v]S ver 11 **1:10** [w]Mk 1:15; Ro 5:6; Gal 4:4 [x]Col 1:20 **1:11** [y]ver 5; Ro 8:29,30 [z]ver 9; Ro 8:28; Eph 3:11; Heb 6:17 **1:12** [a]ver 6,14

[a] *1* Some early manuscripts do not have *in Ephesus.*
[b] *1* Or *believers who are*
[c] *4,5* Or *sight in love. [5]He*
[d] *8,9* Or *us. With all wisdom and understanding, [9]he*
[e] *11* Or *were made heirs*

1:1 *Paul.* See note on Ro 1:1. *apostle ... by the will of God.* See 1Co 1:1 and note. Paul not only stresses his authority under God, but also anticipates the strong emphasis he will make later in this chapter and book on God's sovereign plan and purpose. *saints.* Those God has called to be his own people, i.e., all Christians (see vv. 15,18). The word carried the idea of dedication to a deity (see note on Ro 1:7). *in Ephesus.* See NIV text note. The book may have been intended as a circular letter to several churches, including the one at Ephesus (see notes on v. 15; 6:21–23; Ac 19:10). *in Christ Jesus.* This phrase (or a similar one) occurs ten times in vv. 1–13. It refers to the spiritual union of Christ with believers, which Paul often symbolizes by the metaphor "body of Christ" (4:12; cf. 1:23; 2:16; 4:4,16; 5:23,30).

1:2 *Grace and peace.* See note on Ro 1:7. Paul uses the word "grace" 12 times and "peace" 8 times in Ephesians. *Lord Jesus Christ.* See note on 1Th 1:1.

1:3–14 All one sentence in Greek, this section is often called a doxology because it recites what God has done and is an expression of worship to honor him. Paul speaks first of the blessings we have through the Father (vv. 3–6), then of those that come through the Son (vv. 7–12) and finally of those through the Holy Spirit (vv. 13–14).

1:3 *Father of our Lord Jesus Christ.* Jesus' relation to God the Father is unique (see Jn 20:17 and note). *blessed ... blessing.* Jewish people used the word "bless" to express both God's kindness to us and our thanks or praise to him. *heavenly realms.* Occurs five times in Ephesians, emphasizing Paul's perception that in the exaltation of Christ (his resurrection and enthronement at God's right hand) and in the Christian's union with the exalted Christ ultimate issues are involved—issues that pertain to the divine realm and that in the final analysis are worked out in and from that realm. At stake are God's eternal eschatological purpose (3:11) and the titanic conflict between God and the powerful spiritual forces arrayed against him—a purpose and a conflict that come to focus in the history of redemption. Here (v. 3) Paul asserts that, through their union with the exalted Christ, Christians have already been made beneficiaries of every spiritual blessing that belongs to and comes from the heavenly realm. In vv. 20–22, he proclaims Christ's exaltation to that realm and his elevation over all other powers and titles so that he rules over all for the sake of his church. According to 2:6, those who have been made alive with Christ (2:5) share in Christ's exaltation and enthronement in heaven. Thus (3:10) by the gathering of Gentiles and Jews into one body of Christ (the church), God triumphantly displays his "manifold wisdom" to the "rulers and authorities" in the heavenly realm. As a result, the spiritual struggle of the saints here and now is not so much against "flesh and blood" as against the great spiritual forces that war against God in heaven (see 6:12 and note).

1:4 *chose.* Divine election is a frequent theme in Paul's letters (Ro 8:29–33; 9:6–26; 11:5,7,28; 16:13; Col 3:12; 1Th 1:4; 2Th 2:13; Tit 1:1). In this chapter it is emphasized in the following ways: (1) "he chose us" (here); (2) "he predestined us" (v. 5); (3) "we were also chosen" (v. 11); (4) "having been predestined" (v. 11). *before the creation of the world.* Cf. Jn 17:24. *holy and blameless.* See 5:27 for the same pair of words. Holiness is the result—not the basis—of God's choosing. It refers both to the holiness imparted to the believer because of Christ and to the believer's personal sanctification (see notes on Ex 3:5; Lev 11:44; 1Co 1:2). *In love.* See NIV text note on vv. 4–5; cf. 3:17; 4:2,15–16; 5:2.

1:5 *adopted.* See Ro 8:23 and note.

1:6 *to the praise.* See vv. 12,14. Election by grace is for God's glory.

1:7 *redemption.* See v. 14; 4:30; see also Ro 3:24; Tit 2:14 and notes. The Ephesians were familiar with the Greco-Roman practice of redemption: Slaves were freed by the payment of a ransom. Similarly, the ransom necessary to free sinners from the bondage of sin and the resulting curse imposed by the law (see Gal 3:13) was the death of Christ (called here "his blood"). *through his blood.* Cf. 2:13; 1Pe 1:18–19.

1:9 *mystery.* See notes on Ro 11:25; Col 1:26.

1:10 *to bring ... under one head.* Paul uses a significant term here that not only has the idea of leadership but also was often used of adding up a column of figures. A contemporary way of putting it might be to say that in a world of confusion, where things do not "add up" or make sense, we look forward to the time when everything will be brought into meaningful relationship under the headship of Christ.

1:11 *In him.* Christ is the center of God's plan. Whether the universe or the individual Christian is in view, only in relationship to Christ is there a meaningful future. Paul goes on to speak, not of the world as a whole, but of those who respond to God's call. *predestined.* See vv. 4–5; see also Ro 8:29–30 and notes.

1:12 *we, who were the first to hope in Christ.* Probably a reference to those Jews who, like Paul, had become believers before many Gentiles had.

13And you also were included in Christ[b]
when you heard the word of truth,[c] the
gospel of your salvation. Having believed,
you were marked in him with a seal,[d] the
promised Holy Spirit,[e] 14who is a deposit
guaranteeing our inheritance[f] until the redemption[g] of those who are God's possession—to the praise of his glory.[h]

Thanksgiving and Prayer

15For this reason, ever since I heard
about your faith in the Lord Jesus[i] and
your love for all the saints,[j] 16I have not
stopped giving thanks for you,[k] remembering you in my prayers.[l] 17I keep asking that
the God of our Lord Jesus Christ, the glorious Father,[m] may give you the Spirit[a] of
wisdom[n] and revelation, so that you may
know him better. 18I pray also that the eyes
of your heart may be enlightened[o] in order
that you may know the hope to which he
has called[p] you, the riches[q] of his glorious inheritance[r] in the saints,[s] 19and his
incomparably great power for us who believe. That power[t] is like the working of
his mighty strength,[u] 20which he exerted in
Christ when he raised him from the dead[v]
and seated him at his right hand[w] in the
heavenly realms,[x] 21far above all rule and
authority, power and dominion,[y] and every title[z] that can be given, not only in the
present age but also in the one to come.[a]

1:13 [b]S Ro 16:3 [c]Eph 4:21; Col 1:5 [d]Eph 4:30 [e]Jn 14:16,17 **1:14** [f]S Ac 20:32; S 2Co 5:5 [g]ver 7; S Ro 3:24 [h]ver 6,12 **1:15** [i]S Ac 20:21 [j]S Col 1:4 **1:16** [k]S Ro 1:8 [l]S Ro 1:10 **1:17** [m]Jn 20:17; Ro 15:6; Rev 1:6 [n]Ex 28:3; Isa 11:2; Php 1:9; Col 1:9 **1:18** [o]Job 42:5; 2Co 4:6; Heb 6:4 [p]S Ro 8:28 [q]ver 7; S Ro 2:4 [r]ver 11 [s]Col 1:12 **1:19** [t]Eph 3:7; Col 1:29 [u]Isa 40:26; Eph 6:10 **1:20** [v]S Ac 2:24 [w]S Mk 16:19 [x]S ver 3 **1:21** [y]Eph 3:10; Col 1:16 [z]Php 2:9,10 [a]S Mt 12:32 **1:22** [b]S Mt 22:44; S 28:18 [c]1Co 11:3; Eph 4:15; 5:23; Col 1:18; 2:19 **1:23** [d]S 1Co 12:27 [e]S Jn 1:16; Eph 3:19 [f]Eph 4:10

22And God placed all things under his feet[b]
and appointed him to be head[c] over everything for the church, 23which is his body,[d]
the fullness of him[e] who fills everything
in every way.[f]

Made Alive in Christ

2 As for you, you were dead in your transgressions and sins,[g] 2in which you used
to live[h] when you followed the ways of
this world[i] and of the ruler of the kingdom
of the air,[j] the spirit who is now at work
in those who are disobedient.[k] 3All of us
also lived among them at one time,[l] gratifying the cravings of our sinful nature[b][m]
and following its desires and thoughts.
Like the rest, we were by nature objects of
wrath. 4But because of his great love for
us,[n] God, who is rich in mercy, 5made us
alive with Christ even when we were dead
in transgressions[o]—it is by grace you have
been saved.[p] 6And God raised us up with
Christ[q] and seated us with him[r] in the
heavenly realms[s] in Christ Jesus, 7in order that in the coming ages he might show
the incomparable riches of his grace,[t] expressed in his kindness[u] to us in Christ

[a] *17* Or *a spirit* [b] *3* Or *our flesh*

2:1 [g]ver 5; Col 2:13 **2:2** [h]ver 3, 11-13; Ro 11:30; 1Co 6:11; 5:8; Col 3:7; Tit 3:3; 1Pe 4:3 [i]Ro 12:2 [j]S Jn 12:31 [k]Eph 5:6 **2:3** [l]S ver 2 [m]S Gal 5:24 **2:4** [n]S Jn 3:16 **2:5** [o]ver 1; Ps 103:12 [p]ver 8; Jn 5:24; S Ac 15:11 **2:6** [q]S Ro 6:5 [r]Eph 1:20 [s]S Eph 1:3 **2:7** [t]S Ro 2:4 [u]Tit 3:4

1:13 *And you also.* Probably refers to the majority of the Ephesians, who were Gentiles. *word of truth.* See 2Ti 2:15 and note. *marked ... with a seal.* In those days a seal denoted ownership and security.

1:14 *deposit.* See note on Ro 8:23. *inheritance.* See Col 1:12; see also Heb 9:15; 1Pe 1:4 and notes.

1:15 *ever since I heard.* This sounds strange from one who had spent a few years in Ephesus. He may be referring to a greatly enlarged church there, many of whom Paul did not know, or, if Ephesians was intended as a circular letter (see note on v. 1), he may be referring to news from the whole area, only a part of which he had visited.

1:17 *God of our Lord Jesus Christ.* See note on v. 3. *him.* God the Father.

1:18 *eyes of your heart.* Your mind or understanding or inner awareness. *hope.* Has an objective quality of certainty (see Ro 5:5 and note). It is the assurance of eternal life guaranteed by the present possession of the Holy Spirit (see v. 14). *called.* See Ro 8:28 and note; Php 3:14; 2Ti 1:9; Heb 3:1. *his glorious inheritance in the saints.* Either the inheritance we have from God (see v. 14; Col 1:12) or the inheritance God receives, i.e., the saints themselves (cf. Ps 2:8; Isa 53:10). *saints.* See note on v. 1.

1:19 In this verse Paul piles term upon term to emphasize that the extraordinary divine force by which Jesus Christ was raised (v. 20) is the same power at work in and through believers (see Php 3:10 and note).

1:20 *right hand.* The symbolic place of highest honor and authority.

1:21 *all rule ... every title that can be given.* Including whatever supernatural beings his contemporaries might conceive of, for in his day many people believed not only in the existence of angels and demons but also in that of other beings. Christ is above them all. *the present age ... the one to come.* See Mt 12:32. Like the Rabbinic teachers of his day, Paul distinguishes between the present age, which is evil, and the future age when the Messiah will consummate his kingdom and there will be a completely righteous society on earth.

1:22 *under his feet.* Ps 8:5–6 emphasizes the destiny of human beings, and Heb 2:6–9 shows that ultimately it is the Son of Man who rules over everything (cf. Heb 10:13). *head.* Christ is not only head of the church, but also head over everything (see note on v. 10).

1:23 *his body.* See 2:16; 4:4,12,16; 5:23,30. *fullness ... fills.* The church is the fullness of Christ probably in the sense that it is filled by him who fills all things.

2:1–10 In ch. 1 Paul wrote of the great purposes and plan of God, culminating in the universal headship of Christ (1:10,22), all of which is to be for "the praise of his glory" (1:14). He now proceeds to explain the steps by which God will accomplish his purposes, beginning with the salvation of individuals.

2:1 A description of their past moral and spiritual condition, separated from the life of God (cf. Col 1:21).

2:2 *ruler.* Satan (cf. Jn 14:30, "prince"). *air.* Satan is no mere earthbound enemy (cf. 6:12). *spirit.* Satan is a created, but not a human, being (cf. Job 1:6; Eze 28:15; see note on Isa 14:12–15).

2:3 *All of us.* Jews and Gentiles. *objects of wrath.* See Ro 1:18–20; 2:5; 9:22.

2:5 *made us alive with Christ.* This truth is expanded in Ro 6:1–10 (see notes there).

2:6 *heavenly realms.* See note on 1:3. *in Christ Jesus.* Through our union with Christ (see note on 1:1).

2:7 *coming ages.* Cf. 1:21; refers to the future of eternal blessing with Christ. *show.* Or "exhibit" or "prove."

Jesus. 8For it is by grace[v] you have been
saved,[w] through faith[x]—and this not from
yourselves, it is the gift of God— 9not by
works,[y] so that no one can boast.[z] 10For
we are God's workmanship,[a] created[b] in
Christ Jesus to do good works,[c] which God
prepared in advance for us to do.

One in Christ

11Therefore, remember that formerly[d]
you who are Gentiles by birth and called
"uncircumcised" by those who call themselves "the circumcision" (that done in the
body by the hands of men)[e]— 12remem-
ber that at that time you were separate
from Christ, excluded from citizenship in
Israel and foreigners[f] to the covenants of
the promise,[g] without hope[h] and without
God in the world. 13But now in Christ Jesus
you who once[i] were far away have been
brought near[j] through the blood of Christ.[k]
14For he himself is our peace,[l] who has
made the two one[m] and has destroyed the
barrier, the dividing wall of hostility, 15by
abolishing in his flesh[n] the law with its
commandments and regulations.[o] His purpose was to create in himself one[p] new
man out of the two, thus making peace,
16and in this one body to reconcile both of
them to God through the cross,[q] by which
he put to death their hostility. 17He came
and preached peace[r] to you who were far
away and peace to those who were near.[s]
18For through him we both have access[t] to
the Father[u] by one Spirit.[v]
19Consequently, you are no longer foreigners and aliens,[w] but fellow citizens[x]
with God's people and members of God's
household,[y] 20built[z] on the foundation[a] of
the apostles and prophets,[b] with Christ
Jesus himself[c] as the chief cornerstone.[d]
21In him the whole building is joined together and rises to become a holy temple[e]

2:8 [v] S Ro 3:24 [w] ver 5 [x] S Ro 9:30 **2:9** [y] Dt 9:5; Ro 4:2; 2Ti 1:9; Tit 3:5 [z] 1Co 1:29 **2:10** [a] Isa 29:23; 43:7; 60:21 [b] Eph 4:24 [c] S Tit 2:14 **2:11** [d] S ver 2 [e] Col 2:11 **2:12** [f] Isa 14:1; 65:1 [g] Gal 3:17 [h] 1Th 4:13 **2:13** [i] S ver 2 [j] ver 17 [k] Col 1:20 **2:14** [l] ver 15; S Jn 14:27 [m] 1Co 12:13; Eph 3:6 **2:15** [n] Col 1:21,22 [o] Col 2:14 [p] Gal 3:28 **2:16** [q] 2Co 5:18; Col 1:20,22 **2:17** [r] S Lk 2:14 [s] ver 13; Ps 148:14; Isa 57:19 **2:18** [t] Eph 3:12 [u] Col 1:12 [v] 1Co 12:13; Eph 4:4 **2:19** [w] ver 12 [x] Php 3:20 [y] Gal 6:10 **2:20** [z] 1Co 3:9 [a] Mt 16:18; 1Co 3:10; Rev 21:14 [b] S Eph 4:11 [c] 1Co 3:11 [d] S Ac 4:11; 1Pe 2:4-8 **2:21** [e] 1Co 3:16,17

2:8 A major passage for understanding God's grace, i.e., his kindness, unmerited favor and forgiving love. *you have been saved.* "Saved" has a wide range of meanings. It includes salvation from God's wrath, which we all had incurred by our sinfulness. The tense of the verb (also in v. 5) suggests a completed action with emphasis on its present effect. *through faith.* See Ro 3:21 – 31 (and notes on that passage), which establishes the necessity of faith in Christ as the only means of being made right with God. *not from yourselves.* No human effort can contribute to our salvation; it is the gift of God (see Tit 3:5 and note).

2:9 *not by works.* One cannot earn salvation by "observing the law" (Ro 3:20,28; cf. Jas 2:14 – 26 and notes). Such a legalistic approach to salvation (or sanctification) is consistently condemned in Scripture (see Gal 2:16 and note). *no one can boast.* No one can take credit for their salvation. Cf. 2Co 5:17 and note.

2:10 *workmanship.* The Greek for this word sometimes has the connotation of a "work of art." *prepared in advance.* Carries forward the theme of God's sovereign purpose and planning, seen in ch. 1 (see, e.g., 1:4 and note).

2:11 – 22 From the salvation of individuals, Paul moves to another aspect of salvation in which God reconciles Jews and Gentiles, previously hostile peoples, not only to himself but also to each other through Christ (vv. 11 – 16). Even more than that, God unites these now reconciled people in one body, a truth introduced in vv. 19 – 22 and explained in ch. 3.

2:11 – 12 Refers to the state of those without Christ, described in vv. 1 – 10.

2:11 *you who are Gentiles.* Most of the Ephesians (cf. 1:13, "And you also"). *"uncircumcised" ... "the circumcision."* The rite of circumcision was applied to all Jewish male babies; so this physical act ("done in the body by the hands of men") was a clear mark of distinction between Jew and Gentile, in which Jewish people naturally took pride.

2:12 *at that time.* Before salvation, in contrast to "But now" (v. 13). *separate from Christ ... without God.* All these expressions emphasize the distance of unbelieving Gentiles from Israel, as well as from Christ. *covenants.* God had promised blessings to and through the Jewish people (see note on Ro 9:4).

2:13 *But now.* Not only contrasts with "at that time" (v. 12) but also introduces the contrast between "from Christ" (v. 12) and "in Christ" (here). *blood of Christ.* Expresses the violent death of Christ as he poured out his lifeblood as a sacrifice for us (see 1:7; Heb 9:11 – 13 and notes).

2:14 *the two.* Believing Jews and believing Gentiles. *barrier ... dividing wall.* Possibly an allusion to the barricade in the Jerusalem temple area that marked the limit to which a Gentile might go. It is used here to describe the total religious isolation Jews and Gentiles experienced from each other. *hostility.* Between Jews and Gentiles.

2:15 *abolishing ... the law.* Since Mt 5:17 and Ro 3:31 teach that God's moral standard expressed in the OT law is not changed by the coming of Christ, what is abolished here is probably the effect of the specific "commandments and regulations" in separating Jews from Gentiles, whose nonobservance of the Jewish law renders them ritually unclean (cf. Col 2:13 – 14). *in his flesh.* Probably refers to the death of Christ (cf. note on Ro 8:3). *one new man.* The united body of believers, the church.

2:16 *this one body.* While this could possibly mean the body of Christ offered on the cross (cf. "in his flesh," v. 15), it probably refers to the "one new man" just mentioned, the body of believers.

2:17 *far away ... near.* Gentiles and Jews respectively.

2:19 *Consequently.* Paul indicates that the unity described in vv. 19 – 22 is based on what Christ did through his death, described in vv. 14 – 18. *you.* The Gentiles at Ephesus are particularly in mind here. *citizens ... household.* Familiar imagery. The household in ancient times was what we today might call an "extended family."

2:20 *foundation.* Further metaphorical language to convey the idea of a solid, integrated structure. *apostles and prophets.* Probably refers to the founding work of the early Christian apostles and prophets as they preached and taught God's word (cf. Mt 16:18 and note; 1Co 3:10 – 11). *cornerstone.* Isa 28:16, which uses the same term in its pre-Christian Greek translation (the Septuagint), refers to a foundation with a "tested" stone at the corner.

2:21 *joined together.* Cf. 4:16 for the same word. Both passages speak of the close relationship between believers. *rises.* This description of a building under construction conveys the sense of the dynamic growth of the church. *holy temple.* Paul now uses the metaphor of a temple, thereby indicating the purpose ("to become") for which God has established his church (see 1Co 3:16 and note).

in the Lord. 22 And in him you too are being built together to become a dwelling in
which God lives by his Spirit.[f]

Paul the Preacher to the Gentiles

3 For this reason I, Paul, the prisoner[g] of
Christ Jesus for the sake of you Gentiles—
2 Surely you have heard about the administration of God's grace that was given
to me[h] for you, 3 that is, the mystery[i] made
known to me by revelation,[j] as I have already written briefly. 4 In reading this,
then, you will be able to understand my
insight[k] into the mystery of Christ, 5 which
was not made known to men in other
generations as it has now been revealed
by the Spirit to God's holy apostles and
prophets.[l] 6 This mystery is that through
the gospel the Gentiles are heirs[m] together with Israel, members together of one
body,[n] and sharers together in the promise
in Christ Jesus.[o]
7 I became a servant of this gospel[p] by
the gift of God's grace given me[q] through
the working of his power.[r] 8 Although I
am less than the least of all God's people,[s] this grace was given me: to preach
to the Gentiles[t] the unsearchable riches of
Christ,[u] 9 and to make plain to everyone
the administration of this mystery,[v] which
for ages past was kept hidden in God, who
created all things. 10 His intent was that
now, through the church, the manifold
wisdom of God[w] should be made known[x]
to the rulers and authorities[y] in the heavenly realms,[z] 11 according to his eternal
purpose[a] which he accomplished in Christ
Jesus our Lord. 12 In him and through faith
in him we may approach God[b] with freedom and confidence.[c] 13 I ask you, therefore, not to be discouraged because of my
sufferings for you, which are your glory.

A Prayer for the Ephesians

14 For this reason I kneel[d] before the Fa-

2:22 [f] 1Co 3:16
3:1 [g] Ac 23:18; Eph 4:1; 2Ti 1:8; Phm 1,9
3:2 [h] Col 1:25
3:3 [i] S Ro 16:25 [j] S 1Co 2:10
3:4 [k] 2Co 11:6
3:5 [l] Ro 16:26; S Eph 4:11
3:6 [m] S Ro 8:17 [n] Eph 2:15,16 [o] Eze 47:22
3:7 [p] S 1Co 3:5 [q] S Ro 12:3 [r] Eph 1:19; Col 1:29
3:8 [s] S 1Co 15:9 [t] S Ac 9:15 [u] S Ro 2:4
3:9 [v] S Ro 16:25
3:10 [w] S Ro 11:33; 1Co 2:7 [x] 1Pe 1:12 [y] Eph 1:21; 6:12; Col 2:10,15 [z] S Eph 1:3
3:11 [a] S Eph 1:11
3:12 [b] Eph 2:18 [c] 2Co 3:4; Heb 3:14; 4:16; 10:19,35; 1Jn 2:28; 3:21; 4:17
3:14 [d] Php 2:10

2:22 *dwelling.* The church is to be a people or community in whom the Holy Spirit dwells (cf. 2Co 6:16 and note).

3:1–13 Having saved people individually by his grace (2:1–10), and having reconciled them to each other as well as to himself through the sacrificial death of Christ (2:11–22), God also now unites them on an equal basis in one body, the church. This step in God's eternal plan was not fully revealed in previous times. Paul calls it a "mystery."

3:1 *For this reason.* Because of all that God has done, explained in the preceding several verses. *prisoner.* Apparently Paul was under house arrest at this time (see Ac 28:16,30 and note on 28:16). *of Christ.* Paul's physical imprisonment was because he obeyed Christ in spite of opposition. After this verse Paul breaks his train of thought to explain the "mystery" (v. 4). He resumes his initial thought in v. 14.

3:2 *Surely you have heard.* Most of the Ephesians would have heard of Paul's ministry because of his long stay there earlier. However, if this was a circular letter (see note on 1:1), the other churches may not have known much about it. *administration.* Paul unfolds God's administrative plan for the church and for the universe in this letter (see especially 1:3–12). He has been given a significant responsibility in the execution of this plan.

3:3 *mystery.* A truth known only by divine revelation (v. 5; see Ro 16:25; see also notes on Ro 11:25; Col 1:26). Here the word "mystery" has the special meaning of the private, wise plan of God, which in Ephesians relates primarily to the unification of believing Jews and Gentiles in the new body, the church (see v. 6). It may be thought of as a secret that is temporarily hidden, but more than that, it is a plan God is actively working out and revealing stage by stage (cf. 1:9–10; Rev 10:7). *by revelation.* See Gal 1:12. *as I have already written briefly.* May refer to 1:9–10.

3:5 *not made known to men in other generations.* See note on v. 6. *holy.* Set apart for God's service. *apostles and prophets.* See note on 2:20. Although Paul was the chief recipient, others received this revelation also.

3:6 *together … together … together.* The repetition of this word indicates the unique aspect of the mystery that was not previously known: the equality and mutuality that Gentiles had with Jews in the church, the one body. That Gentiles would turn to the God of Israel and be saved was prophesied in the OT (see Ro 15:9–12); that they would come into an organic unity with believing Jews on an equal footing was unexpected. *heirs.* See note on 1:18; cf. Gal 3:26–29 and notes.

3:7 *God's grace given me.* See v. 2 and note.

3:8 *less than the least.* Cf. 1Ti 1:15 and note. Paul never ceased to be amazed that one so unworthy as he should have been chosen for so high a task. His modesty was genuine, even though we may disagree with his self-evaluation. *grace.* In this case, a special endowment that brings responsibility for service. *to preach.* Lit. "to gospelize"; parallels "to make plain" (v. 9). *unsearchable.* Far beyond what we can know, but not beyond our appreciation—at least in part (cf. Ro 11:33).

3:9 *administration of this mystery.* See v. 2 and note; cf. v. 3 and note.

3:10 *now.* In contrast to the "ages past" (v. 9). *through the church.* The fact that God had done the seemingly impossible—reconciling and organically uniting Jews and Gentiles in the church—makes the church the perfect means of displaying God's wisdom. *manifold.* Variegated or multifaceted (in the way that many facets of a diamond reflect and enhance its beauty). *rulers and authorities.* Christ had ascended over all these (1:20–21). It is a staggering thought that the church on earth is observed, so to speak, by these spiritual powers and that to the degree the church is spiritually united it portrays to them the wisdom of God. This thought may be essential in understanding the meaning of "calling" in 4:1. *heavenly realms.* See note on 1:3.

3:11 *eternal purpose.* The effective headship of Christ over a united church is in preparation for his ultimate assumption of headship over the universe (1:10).

3:12 See Heb 4:16; 10:19–22 and notes.

3:14–21 Paul now expresses a prayer that grows out of his awareness of all that God is doing in believers. God's key gifts are "power" (vv. 16,18,20) and "love" (vv. 17–19).

3:14 *For this reason.* Resumes the thought of v. 1. *I kneel.* Expresses deep emotion and reverence, as people in Paul's day usually stood to pray.

ther, 15from whom his whole family[a] in heaven and on earth derives its name. 16I pray that out of his glorious riches[e] he may strengthen you with power[f] through his Spirit in your inner being,[g] 17so that Christ may dwell in your hearts[h] through faith. And I pray that you, being rooted[i] and established in love, 18may have power, together with all the saints,[j] to grasp how wide and long and high and deep[k] is the love of Christ, 19and to know this love that surpasses knowledge[l]—that you may be filled[m] to the measure of all the fullness of God.[n]

20Now to him who is able[o] to do immeasurably more than all we ask[p] or imagine, according to his power[q] that is at work within us, 21to him be glory in the church and in Christ Jesus throughout all generations, for ever and ever! Amen.[r]

Unity in the Body of Christ

4 As a prisoner[s] for the Lord, then, I urge you to live a life worthy[t] of the calling[u] you have received. 2Be completely humble and gentle; be patient, bearing with one another[v] in love.[w] 3Make every effort to keep the unity[x] of the Spirit through the bond of peace.[y] 4There is one body[z] and one Spirit[a]—just as you were called to one hope when you were called[b]— 5one Lord,[c] one faith, one baptism; 6one God and Father of all,[d] who is over all and through all and in all.[e]

7But to each one of us[f] grace[g] has been given[h] as Christ apportioned it. 8This is why it[b] says:

> "When he ascended on high,
> he led captives[i] in his train
> and gave gifts to men."[c][j]

9(What does "he ascended" mean except that he also descended to the lower, earthly regions[d]? 10He who descended is the very one who ascended[k] higher than all the heavens, in order to fill the whole universe.)[l] 11It was he who gave[m] some to be apostles,[n] some to be prophets,[o] some to be evangelists,[p] and some to be pastors

3:16 [e]ver 8; S Ro 2:4 [f]S Php 4:13 [g]Ro 7:22 **3:17** [h]S Ro 8:10 [i]Col 2:7 **3:18** [j]Eph 1:15 [k]Job 11:8,9; Ps 103:11 **3:19** [l]Php 4:7 [m]Col 2:10 [n]Eph 1:23 **3:20** [o]Ro 16:25; 2Co 9:8 [p]1Ki 3:13 [q]ver 7 **3:21** [r]S Ro 11:36 **4:1** [s]S Eph 3:1 [t]Php 1:27; Col 1:10; 1Th 2:12 [u]S Ro 8:28 **4:2** [v]Col 3:12,13 [w]ver 15,16; Eph 1:4 **4:3** [x]S Ro 15:5 [y]Col 3:15 **4:4** [z]S Ro 12:5 [a]1Co 12:13; Eph 2:18 [b]S Ro 8:28 **4:5** [c]1Co 8:6 **4:6** [d]Dt 6:4; Zec 14:9 [e]S Ro 11:36 **4:7** [f]1Co 12:7,11 [g]S Ro 3:24 [h]S Ro 12:3 **4:8** [i]Col 2:15 [j]Ps 68:18 **4:10** [k]Pr 30:1-4 [l]Eph 1:23 **4:11** [m]ver 8 [n]1Co 12:28; Eph 2:20; 3:5; 2Pe 3:2; Jude 17 [o]S Ac 11:27; Ro 12:6; 1Co 12:10,28; 13:2,8; 14:1,39; Eph 2:20; 3:5; 2Pe 3:2 [p]Ac 21:8; 2Ti 4:5

[a] 15 Or *whom all fatherhood* [b] 8 Or *God*
[c] 8 Psalm 68:18 [d] 9 Or *the depths of the earth*

3:15 *family.* The word in Greek is similar to the word for "father" (see NIV text note), so it can be said that the "family" derives its name (and being) from the "father." God is our Father, and we can commit our prayers to him in confidence.
3:16 *inner being.* See v. 17; 2Co 4:16 and notes.
3:17 *dwell.* Be completely at home. Christ was already present in the Ephesian believers' lives (cf. Ro 8:9). *hearts.* The whole inner being.
3:18 Cf. Ro 8:35–39.
3:19 *surpasses knowledge.* Not unknowable, but so great that it cannot be completely known. *fullness.* God, who is infinite in all his attributes, allows us to draw on his resources—in this case, his love.
3:20 *immeasurably more.* Has specific reference to the matters presented in this section of Ephesians but is not limited to these. *his power.* See 1:19–21.
3:21 *to him be glory.* The ultimate goal of our existence (see 1:6 and note). *in the church and in Christ Jesus.* A remarkable parallel. God has called the church to an extraordinary position and vocation (cf. v. 10; 4:1).
4:1–32 The chapter begins (v. 2) and ends (v. 32) with exhortations to love and forgive one another.
4:1–16 So far Paul has taught that God brought Jew and Gentile into a new relationship to each other in the church and that he called the church to display his wisdom. Paul now shows how God made provision for those in the church to live and work together in unity and to grow together into maturity.
4:1 *prisoner.* See note on 3:1. *calling.* See 3:10,21 and notes.
4:3 *keep the unity.* Which God produced through the reconciling death of Christ (see 2:14–22). It is the heavy responsibility of Christians to keep that unity from being disturbed.
4:4 *one hope.* Has different aspects (e.g., 1:5,10; 2:7), but it is still one hope, tied to the glorious future of Christ, in which all believers share.
4:5 *one baptism.* Probably not the baptism of the Spirit (see 1Co 12:13), which was inward and therefore invisible, but water baptism (see note on Ro 6:3–4). Since Paul apparently has in mind that which identifies all believers as belonging together, he would naturally refer to that church ordinance in which every new convert participated publicly. At that time it was a more obvious common mark of identification of Christians than it is now, when it is celebrated in different ways and often only seen by those in the church.
4:7 *grace.* See 3:7–8.
4:8 Ps 68:18 (see note there) speaks of God's triumphant ascension to his throne in the temple at Jerusalem (symbol of his heavenly throne). Paul applies this to Christ's triumphal ascension into heaven. Where the psalm states further that God "received gifts from men," Paul apparently takes his cue from certain Rabbinic interpretations current in his day that read the Hebrew preposition for "from" in the sense of "to" (a meaning it often has) and the verb for "received" in the sense of "take and give" (a meaning it sometimes has—but with a different preposition; see Ge 15:9; 18:5; 27:13; Ex 25:2; 1Ki 17:10–11). *captives.* Paul probably applies this to the spiritual enemies Christ defeated at the cross.
4:9 *ascended ... descended.* Although Paul quoted from the psalm to introduce the idea of the "gifts to men," he takes the opportunity to remind his readers of Christ's coming to earth (his incarnation) and his subsequent resurrection and ascension. This passage probably does not teach, as some think and as some translations suggest, that Christ descended into hell.
4:11 *It was he who gave.* The quotation from Ps 68 has its ultimate meaning when applied to Christ as the ascended Lord, who himself has given gifts. *apostles.* Mentioned here because of their role in establishing the church (see 2:20). For qualifications of the initial group of apostles see Ac 1:21–22; see also notes on Mk 6:30; Ro 1:1; 1Co 1:1; Heb 3:1. In a broader sense, Paul was also an apostle (see 1:1). *prophets.* People to whom God made known a message for his people that was appropriate to their particular need or situation (see Ac 11:27; 1Co 12:10 and notes). *evangelists.* See Ac 21:8; 1Co 1:17. While the other gifted people helped the church grow through edification, the evangelists helped the church grow by augmentation. Since the objective mentioned in v. 12 is "to

and teachers,[q] 12to prepare God's people
for works of service, so that the body of
Christ[r] may be built up[s] 13until we all
reach unity[t] in the faith and in the knowledge of the Son of God[u] and become mature,[v] attaining to the whole measure of
the fullness of Christ.[w]
14Then we will no longer be infants,[x]
tossed back and forth by the waves,[y] and
blown here and there by every wind of
teaching and by the cunning and craftiness of men in their deceitful scheming.[z]
15Instead, speaking the truth in love,[a] we
will in all things grow up into him who
is the Head,[b] that is, Christ. 16From him
the whole body, joined and held together
by every supporting ligament, grows[c] and
builds itself up[d] in love,[e] as each part does
its work.

Living as Children of Light

17So I tell you this, and insist on it in the
Lord, that you must no longer[f] live as the
Gentiles do, in the futility of their thinking.[g] 18They are darkened in their understanding[h] and separated from the life of
God[i] because of the ignorance that is in
them due to the hardening of their hearts.[j]
19Having lost all sensitivity,[k] they have giv-
en themselves over[l] to sensuality[m] so as to
indulge in every kind of impurity, with a
continual lust for more.
20You, however, did not come to know
Christ that way. 21Surely you heard of him
and were taught in him in accordance
with the truth that is in Jesus. 22You were
taught, with regard to your former way
of life, to put off[n] your old self,[o] which is
being corrupted by its deceitful desires;[p]
23to be made new in the attitude of your
minds;[q] 24and to put on[r] the new self,[s] created to be like God in true righteousness
and holiness.[t]

4:11 [q] Ac 13:1; Ro 2:21; 12:7; 1Co 12:28; 14:26; 1Ti 1:7; Jas 3:1 **4:12** [r] S 1Co 12:27 [s] S Ro 14:19 **4:13** [t] ver 3,5 [u] S Php 3:8 [v] S 1Co 2:6; Col 1:28 [w] Jn 1:16; Eph 1:23; 3:19 **4:14** [x] S 1Co 14:20 [y] Isa 57:20; Jas 1:6 [z] Eph 6:11 **4:15** [a] ver 2,16; Eph 1:4 [b] S Eph 1:22 **4:16** [c] Col 2:19 [d] 1Co 12:7 [e] ver 2,15; Eph 1:4 **4:17** [f] Eph 2:2 [g] Ro 1:21 **4:18** [h] Dt 29:4; Ro 1:21 [i] Eph 2:12 [j] 2Co 3:14 **4:19** [k] 1Ti 4:2 [l] Ro 1:24 [m] Col 3:5; 1Pe 4:3 **4:22** [n] ver 25,31; Col 3:5,8,9; Jas 1:21; 1Pe 2:1 [o] S Ro 6:6 [p] Jer 17:9; Heb 3:13 **4:23** [q] Ro 12:2; Col 3:10 **4:24** [r] S Ro 13:14 [s] S Ro 6:4 [t] Eph 2:10

---

prepare God's people for works of service," we may assume that evangelists, among their various ministries, helped other Christians in their testimony. *pastors and teachers.* Because of the Greek grammatical construction (also, the word "some" introduces both words together), it is clear that these groups of gifted people are closely related. Those who have pastoral care for God's people (the image is that of shepherding) will naturally provide "solid food" (1Co 3:2; see Heb 5:12 and note) from the Scriptures (teaching). They will be especially gifted as teachers (cf. 1Ti 3:2).

4:12 *to prepare God's people for works of service.* Those mentioned in v. 11 were not to do all the work for the people, but were to train the people to do the work themselves. *so that the body of Christ may be built up.* See v. 16. Spiritual gifts are for the body, the church, and are not to be exercised individualistically. "Built up" reflects the imagery of 2:19 – 22. Both concepts — body and building — occurring together emphasize the key idea of growth.

4:13 *until.* Expresses not merely duration but also purpose. *unity.* Carries forward the ideal of vv. 1 – 6. *in the faith.* Here "faith" refers to the Christians' common conviction about Christ and the doctrines concerning him, as the following words make clear (cf. also "the apostles' teaching" in Ac 2:42). *knowledge of the Son of God.* Unity is not just a matter of a loving attitude or religious feeling, but of truth and a common understanding about God's Son. *mature … fullness of Christ.* Not the maturity of doctrinal conviction just mentioned, nor a personal maturity that includes the ability to relate well to other people (cf. vv. 2 – 3), but the maturity of the perfectly balanced character of Christ.

4:14 *infants.* Contrast the maturity of v. 13 (cf. 1Co 3:1). *tossed.* The nautical imagery pictures the instability of those who are not strong Christians (cf. Jas 1:6). *teaching.* Then, as now, there were many distorted teachings and heresies that would easily throw the immature off course. *cunning … craftiness … deceitful scheming.* Sometimes those who try to draw people away from the Christian faith are not innocently misguided but deliberately deceitful and evil (cf. 1Ti 4:1 – 2).

4:15 *speaking the truth in love.* A truthful and loving manner of life is implied. *grow up … Head.* A slightly different restatement of v. 13, based now on the imagery of Christ as the Head of the body, which is the church. Paul thus speaks primarily of corporate maturity. It is the "body of Christ" that is to be "built up" (v. 12). In v. 13 "we all" are to become "mature."

4:16 Further details of the imagery of the body growing under the direction of the Head. The parts of the body help each other in the growing process, picturing the mutual ministries of God's people spoken of in vv. 11 – 13 (cf. Ro 12:3 – 8). *love.* Maturity and unity are impossible without it (cf. vv. 2,15).

4:17 — 5:20 Paul has just discussed unity and maturity as twin goals for the church, which God has brought into existence through the death of Christ. He now goes on to show that purity is also essential among those who belong to him.

4:17 *futility of their thinking.* Life without God is intellectually frustrating, useless and meaningless (see, e.g., Ecc 1:2 and note; Ro 1:21).

4:18 *darkened in their understanding.* Continues the idea of a futile thought life. *hardening of their hearts.* Moral unresponsiveness.

4:19 *have given themselves over.* Just as the pharaoh's heart was hardened reciprocally by himself and by God (see Ex 7 – 11; see also note on Ex 4:21), so here the Gentiles have given themselves over to a sinful kind of life, while Ro 1:24,26,28 says that God gave them over to that life.

4:20 *You.* Emphatic.

4:21 *truth that is in Jesus.* The wording and the use of the name Jesus (rather than Christ) suggest that Paul is referring to the embodiment of truth in Jesus' earthly life.

4:22 *former way of life.* Described in 2:1 – 3. *old self.* Probably means the kind of person the Christian used to be (cf. 1Co 6:11 and note). The old lifestyle resulted from deceitful desires.

4:23 *minds.* Cf. the evil thoughts of unbelievers (vv. 17 – 18).

4:24 *new self, created to be like God.* Since the new self is created, it cannot refer to the indwelling Christ, but rather to the kind of person he produces in the new believer. Nor is it some kind of new essential nature the believer has, because that would have been brought into existence at his new birth. In contrast, this is a new way of life that one not only "puts on" positionally at conversion (note the past tense in the parallel in Col 3:9 – 10) but is also urged to "put on" experientially as a Christian (see note on Ro 6:12 – 13).

25Therefore each of you must put off falsehood and speak truthfully[u] to his neighbor,
for we are all members of one body.[v] 26"In
your anger do not sin"[a]:[w] Do not let the sun
go down while you are still angry, 27and
do not give the devil a foothold.[x] 28He who
has been stealing must steal no longer, but
must work,[y] doing something useful with
his own hands,[z] that he may have something to share with those in need.[a]

29Do not let any unwholesome talk
come out of your mouths,[b] but only what
is helpful for building others up[c] according to their needs, that it may benefit
those who listen. 30And do not grieve the
Holy Spirit of God,[d] with whom you were
sealed[e] for the day of redemption.[f] 31Get
rid of[g] all bitterness, rage and anger, brawling and slander, along with every form of
malice.[h] 32Be kind and compassionate to
one another,[i] forgiving each other, just as
in Christ God forgave you.[j]

5 Be imitators of God,[k] therefore, as
dearly loved children[l] 2and live a life
of love, just as Christ loved us[m] and gave
himself up for us[n] as a fragrant offering
and sacrifice to God.[o]

3But among you there must not be even
a hint of sexual immorality,[p] or of any kind
of impurity, or of greed,[q] because these
are improper for God's holy people. 4Nor
should there be obscenity, foolish talk[r] or
coarse joking, which are out of place, but
rather thanksgiving.[s] 5For of this you can
be sure: No immoral, impure or greedy
person—such a man is an idolater[t]—has
any inheritance[u] in the kingdom of Christ
and of God.[b][v] 6Let no one deceive you[w]
with empty words, for because of such
things God's wrath[x] comes on those who
are disobedient.[y] 7Therefore do not be
partners with them.

8For you were once[z] darkness, but now
you are light in the Lord. Live as children
of light[a] 9(for the fruit[b] of the light consists in all goodness,[c] righteousness and
truth) 10and find out what pleases the
Lord.[d] 11Have nothing to do with the fruitless deeds of darkness,[e] but rather expose

4:25 [u] Ps 15:2; Lev 19:11; Zec 8:16; Col 3:9 [v] S Ro 12:5 **4:26** [w] Ps 4:4; S Mt 5:22 **4:27** [x] 2Co 2:10,11 **4:28** [y] Ac 20:35 [z] 1Th 4:11 [a] Gal 6:10 **4:29** [b] Mt 12:36; Eph 5:4; Col 3:8 [c] S Ro 14:19 **4:30** [d] Isa 63:10; 1Th 5:19 [e] 2Co 1:22; 5:5; Eph 1:13 [f] Ro 8:23 **4:31** [g] S ver 22 [h] Col 3:8; 1Pe 2:1 **4:32** [i] 1Pe 3:8 [j] Mt 6:14,15; Col 3:12,13 **5:1** [k] Mt 5:48; Lk 6:36 [l] S Jn 1:12 **5:2** [m] S Jn 13:34 [n] ver 25; S Gal 1:4; 2:20 [o] Heb 7:27 **5:3** [p] S 1Co 6:18 [q] Col 3:5 **5:4** [r] Eph 4:29 [s] S ver 20 **5:5** [t] Col 3:5 [u] S Ac 20:32 [v] S Mt 25:34 **5:6** [w] S Mk 13:5 [x] S Ro 1:18 [y] Eph 2:2 **5:8** [z] S Eph 2:2 [a] Jn 8:12; S Lk 16:8; S Ac 26:18 **5:9** [b] Mt 7:16-20; Gal 5:22 [c] Ro 15:14 **5:10** [d] S 1Ti 5:4 **5:11** [e] Ro 13:12; 2Co 6:14

[a] *26* Psalm 4:4 [b] *5* Or *kingdom of the Christ and God*

4:25 *truthfully.* Cf. vv. 15,21. "Speak truthfully to his neighbor" echoes Zec 8:16. *neighbor.* Probably means fellow Christians in this context.

4:26 *In your anger.* Christians do not lose their emotions at conversion, but their emotions should be purified. Some anger is sinful, some is not (see Ps 4:4 and note). *Do not let the sun go down.* No anger is to outlast the day.

4:27 *devil.* Personal sin is usually due to our evil desires (see Jas 1:14) rather than to direct tempting by the devil. However, Satan can use our sins—especially those, like anger, that are against others—to bring about greater evil, such as divisions among Christians.

4:28 *steal no longer … work … have something to share.* It is not enough to cease from sin; one must do good. The former thief must now help those in need (cf. 1Th 4:11–12; 2Th 3:6–13).

4:29 *only what is helpful.* An exhortation parallel to the previous one. Christians not only stop saying unwholesome things; they also begin to say things that will help build others up (cf. 1Co 14:3).

4:30 *grieve.* By sin, such as "unwholesome talk" (v. 29) and the sins mentioned in v. 31. The verb also demonstrates that the Holy Spirit is a person, not just an influence, for only a person can be grieved. *sealed.* See note on 1:13. *day of redemption.* See 1:14; 1Pe 1:5 and notes.

4:31 *bitterness … malice.* Such things grieve the Holy Spirit. This continues the instruction concerning one's speech (v. 29). See note on Ro 1:29–31.

4:32 *kind and compassionate.* The opposite of the negative qualities of v. 31. *forgiving.* This basic Christian attitude, which is a result of being forgiven in Christ, along with being kind and compassionate, brings to others what we have received from God.

5:1 *Be imitators.* One way of imitating God is to have a forgiving spirit (4:32). The way we imitate our Lord is to act "just as" (v. 2; 4:32) he did. The sacrificial way Jesus expressed his love for us is not only the means of salvation (as seen in ch. 2) but also an example of the way we are to live for the sake of others.

5:2 *Christ loved us and gave himself up for us.* See v. 25 and note. *fragrant offering.* In the OT the offering of a sacrifice pleased the Lord so much that it was described as a "pleasing aroma" (Ge 8:21 [see note there]; Ex 29:18,25,41; Lev 1:9,13,17).

5:3–5 See note on Ro 1:29–31.

5:3 *not … even a hint.* See v. 12. *any kind of impurity, or of greed.* Paul moves from specifically sexual sins to more general sins, such as greed. These include sexual lust but refer to other kinds of excessive desire as well. *holy people.* See 2:21; 1Co 1:2 and note.

5:4 *foolish talk or coarse joking.* The context and the word "obscenity" indicate that it is not humor as such but off-color jokes and the like that are out of place. *thanksgiving.* See v. 20; 1Th 5:18. By being grateful for all that God has given us, we can displace evil thoughts and words.

5:5 *immoral, impure or greedy.* See v. 3. *idolater.* Cf. Col 3:5. The greedy want things more than they want God, and put things in place of God, thereby committing idolatry. *inheritance.* Those who persist in sexual and other kinds of greed have excluded God, who therefore excludes them from the kingdom (but see notes on 1Co 6:9,11).

5:6 *God's wrath.* See Zec 1:2; Ro 1:18 and notes.

5:7 *partners.* Although Christians live in normal social relationships with others, as did the Lord Jesus (Lk 5:30–32; 15:1–2), they are not to participate in the sinful lifestyle of unbelievers (cf. 2Co 6:14 and note).

5:8 *darkness … light.* This section emphasizes the contrast between light and darkness, showing that those who belong to him who is "light" (1Jn 1:5), i.e., pure and true, not only have their lives illumined by him but also are the means of introducing that light into the dark areas of human conduct (cf. Mt 5:14).

5:9 *fruit of the light.* A mixed metaphor, but the meaning is clear. Light is productive (consider the effect of light on plant growth), and those who live in God's light produce the fruit of moral and ethical character (cf. Gal 5:22–23), while those who live in darkness do not (see v. 11).

5:11 *Have nothing to do with.* See v. 7. *expose.* Light, by nature, exposes what is in darkness, and the contrast shows sin for what it really is.

them. 12For it is shameful even to mention
what the disobedient do in secret. 13But
everything exposed by the light[f] becomes
visible, 14for it is light that makes everything visible. This is why it is said:

"Wake up, O sleeper,[g]
rise from the dead,[h]
and Christ will shine on you."[i]

15Be very careful, then, how you live[j] —
not as unwise but as wise, 16making the
most of every opportunity,[k] because the
days are evil.[l] 17Therefore do not be foolish, but understand what the Lord's will
is.[m] 18Do not get drunk on wine,[n] which
leads to debauchery. Instead, be filled
with the Spirit.[o] 19Speak to one another
with psalms, hymns and spiritual songs.[p]
Sing and make music in your heart to the
Lord, 20always giving thanks[q] to God the
Father for everything, in the name of our
Lord Jesus Christ.

21Submit to one another[r] out of reverence for Christ.

Wives and Husbands

5:22-6:9pp — Col 3:18-4:1

22Wives, submit to your husbands[s] as
to the Lord.[t] 23For the husband is the head
of the wife as Christ is the head of the
church,[u] his body, of which he is the Savior. 24Now as the church submits to Christ,
so also wives should submit to their husbands[v] in everything.

25Husbands, love your wives,[w] just as
Christ loved the church and gave himself
up for her[x] 26to make her holy,[y] cleansing[a]
her by the washing[z] with water through

[a] 26 Or *having cleansed*

5:13 [f] Jn 3:20,21 **5:14** [g] Ro 13:11 [h] Isa 26:19; Jn 5:25 [i] Isa 60:1; Mal 4:2 **5:15** [j] ver 2 **5:16** [k] Col 4:5 [l] Eph 6:13 **5:17** [m] Ro 12:2; Col 1:9; 1Th 4:3 **5:18** [n] Lev 10:9; Pr 20:1; Isa 28:7; Ro 13:13 [o] S Lk 1:15 **5:19** [p] Ps 27:6; 95:2; Ac 16:25; 1Co 14:15,26; Col 3:16 **5:20** [q] ver 4; Job 1:21; Ps 34:1; Col 3:17; Heb 13:15 **5:21** [r] Gal 5:13; 1Pe 5:5 **5:22** [s] Ge 3:16; 1Co 14:34; Col 3:18; 1Ti 2:12; Tit 2:5; 1Pe 3:1,5,6 [t] Eph 6:5 **5:23** [u] S Eph 1:22 **5:24** [v] S ver 22 **5:25** [w] ver 28,33; Col 3:19 [x] S ver 2 **5:26** [y] Jn 17:19; Heb 2:11; 10:10,14; 13:12 [z] S Ac 22:16

5:12 *shameful ... to mention.* Christians should not dwell on the evils that their lives are exposing in others.

5:13–14 *everything ... visible.* By the repetition of these words, Paul seems to be stressing the all-pervasive nature of the light of God and its inevitable effect.

5:14 *it is said.* What follows may well be a hymn used by early Christians (see note on Col 3:16). *sleeper ... dead.* Two images that describe a sinner (cf. 2:1 and note). *Christ will shine on you.* With his life-giving light.

5:15 *unwise ... wise.* Cf. Jas 3:13–17. Having emphasized the contrast between light and darkness, Paul now turns to the contrast between wisdom and foolishness.

5:16 *opportunity.* The foolish person has no strategy for life and misses opportunities to live for God in an evil environment (see Col 4:5).

5:17 *foolish ... understand.* The contrast continues. The foolish not only miss opportunities to make wise use of time; they have a more fundamental problem: They do not understand what God's purposes are for humankind and for Christians. God's purposes are a basic theme in Ephesians (see ch. 1).

5:18 *Do not get drunk ... be filled with the Spirit.* The Greek present tense is used to indicate that the filling of the Spirit is not a once-for-all experience. Repeatedly, as the occasion requires, the Spirit empowers for worship, service and testimony. The contrast between being filled with wine and filled with the Spirit is obvious. But there is something in common that enables Paul to make the contrast, namely, that people can be under an influence that affects them, whether of wine or of the Spirit. Since Col 3:15—4:1 is very similar to Eph 5:18—6:9, we may assume that Paul intends to convey a basically similar thought in the introductory sentences to each passage. When he speaks here of being filled with the Spirit and when he speaks in Colossians of being under the rule of the peace of Christ and indwelt by the "word" of Christ, he means to be under God's control. The effect of this control is essentially the same in both passages: a happy, mutual encouragement to praise God and a healthy, mutual relationship with people. See note on v. 21.

5:19 *psalms ... songs.* Every kind of appropriate song — whether psalms like those of the OT, or hymns directed to God or to others that Christians were accustomed to singing — could provide a means for praising and thanking God (v. 20). Actually, however, all three terms may refer to different types of psalms (see note on Col 3:16). *spiritual songs.* Songs prompted by the Spirit.

5:20 *always giving thanks.* See Col 2:7; 3:15; 4:2; 1Th 5:18.

5:21—6:9 In chs. 2–4 Paul showed the way God brought believing Jews and Gentiles together into a new relationship in Christ. In 4:1–6 he stressed the importance of unity. Now he shows how believers, filled with the Spirit, can live together in a practical way in various human relationships. This list of mutual responsibilities is similar to the pattern found in Col 3:18—4:1; 1Pe 2:13—3:12; cf. Ro 13:1–10.

5:21 *Submit to one another.* Goes equally well with both the preceding and the following sections, but it is especially basic to the following paragraphs. Paul will show how, in each relationship, each partner can have a conciliatory attitude that will help that relationship. The Greek grammar indicates that this mutual submission is associated with the filling of the Spirit in v. 18. The command "be filled" (v. 18) is followed by a series of participles in the Greek: speaking (v. 19), singing (v. 19), making music (v. 19), giving thanks (v. 20) and submitting (v. 21).

5:22 *Wives, submit.* An aspect of the mutual submission taught in v. 21. The term could connote obedience (see 1Pe 3:5–6), but that meaning is not called for here. *as to the Lord.* Does not put a woman's husband in the place of the Lord, but shows rather that a woman ought to submit to her husband as an act of submission to the Lord.

5:23 *head of the wife.* See 1Co 11:3 and note. *as Christ.* The analogy between the relationship of Christ to the church and that of the husband to the wife is basic to the entire passage. *his body.* See 2:16; 4:4,12,16.

5:24 *submit ... in everything.* But only when such submission is clearly "as to the Lord" (v. 22).

5:25 *Husbands.* Paul now shows that this is not a one-sided submission, but a reciprocal relationship. *love.* Explained by what follows. *Christ loved the church and gave himself up for her.* Not only the expression of our Lord's love, but also an example of how the husband ought to devote himself to his wife's good. To give oneself up to death for the beloved is a more extreme expression of devotion than the wife is called on to make.

5:26 *washing with water through the word.* Many attempts have been made to see marriage customs or liturgical symbolism in these words. One thing is clear: The Lord Jesus died not only to bring forgiveness, but also to effect a new life of holiness in the church, which is "his bride" (Rev 19:7; see note there; see also Rev 21:9). A study of the concepts of washing,

the word, 27and to present her to himself[a] as a radiant church, without stain
or wrinkle or any other blemish, but holy
and blameless.[b] 28In this same way, husbands ought to love their wives[c] as their
own bodies. He who loves his wife loves
himself. 29After all, no one ever hated his
own body, but he feeds and cares for it,
just as Christ does the church— 30for we
are members of his body.[d] 31"For this reason a man will leave his father and mother
and be united to his wife, and the two will
become one flesh."[a][e] 32This is a profound
mystery—but I am talking about Christ
and the church. 33However, each one of
you also must love his wife[f] as he loves
himself, and the wife must respect her
husband.

Children and Parents

6 Children, obey your parents in the
Lord, for this is right.[g] 2"Honor your
father and mother"—which is the first
commandment with a promise— 3"that it
may go well with you and that you may
enjoy long life on the earth."[b][h]
4Fathers, do not exasperate your children;[i] instead, bring them up in the training and instruction of the Lord.[j]

Slaves and Masters

5Slaves, obey your earthly masters with
respect[k] and fear, and with sincerity of
heart,[l] just as you would obey Christ.[m]
6Obey them not only to win their favor
when their eye is on you, but like slaves
of Christ,[n] doing the will of God from your
heart. 7Serve wholeheartedly, as if you
were serving the Lord, not men,[o] 8because
you know that the Lord will reward everyone for whatever good he does,[p] whether
he is slave or free.
9And masters, treat your slaves in the
same way. Do not threaten them, since
you know that he who is both their Master and yours[q] is in heaven, and there is no
favoritism[r] with him.

The Armor of God

10Finally, be strong in the Lord[s] and in
his mighty power.[t] 11Put on the full armor
of God[u] so that you can take your stand
against the devil's schemes. 12For our
struggle is not against flesh and blood,[v] but
against the rulers, against the authorities,[w]
against the powers[x] of this dark world and
against the spiritual forces of evil in the
heavenly realms.[y] 13Therefore put on the
full armor of God,[z] so that when the day of
evil comes, you may be able to stand your
ground, and after you have done everything, to stand. 14Stand firm then, with the
belt of truth buckled around your waist,[a]
with the breastplate of righteousness in
place,[b] 15and with your feet fitted with the
readiness that comes from the gospel of

5:27 [a] S 2Co 4:14 [b] Eph 1:4
5:28 [c] ver 25
5:30 [d] S Ro 12:5; S 1Co 12:27
5:31 [e] Ge 2:24; Mt 19:5; 1Co 6:16
5:33 [f] ver 25
6:1 [g] Pr 6:20; Col 3:20
6:3 [h] Ex 20:12; Dt 5:16
6:4 [i] Col 3:21 [j] Ge 18:19; Dt 6:7; Pr 13:24; 22:6
6:5 [k] 1Ti 6:1; Tit 2:9; 1Pe 2:18 [l] Col 3:22 [m] Eph 5:22
6:6 [n] S Ro 6:22
6:7 [o] Col 3:23
6:8 [p] S Mt 16:27; Col 3:24
6:9 [q] Job 31:13, 14 [r] S Ac 10:34
6:10 [s] 2Sa 10:12; Ps 27:14; Hag 2:4; 1Co 16:13; 2Ti 2:1 [t] Eph 1:19
6:11 [u] ver 13; Ro 13:12; 1Th 5:8
6:12 [v] 1Co 15:50; Heb 2:14 [w] Eph 1:21; 3:10 [x] Ro 8:38 [y] S Eph 1:3
6:13 [z] ver 11; S 2Co 6:7
6:14 [a] Isa 11:5 [b] Ps 132:9; Isa 59:17; 1Th 5:8

[a] *31* Gen. 2:24 [b] *3* Deut. 5:16

of water and of the word should include reference to Jn 3:5 (see note there); 15:3; see also Tit 3:5; Heb 10:22; Jas 1:18; 1Pe 1:23; 3:21 and notes.

5:27 *holy and blameless.* See 1:4 and note.

5:28–29 *as their own bodies ... loves himself ... his own body.* The basis for such expressions and for the teaching of these verses is the quotation from Ge 2:24 in v. 31. If the husband and wife become "one flesh," then for the man to love his wife is to love one who has become part of himself.

5:32 *mystery.* See note on Ro 11:25. The profound truth of the union of Christ and his "bride," the church, is beyond unaided human understanding. It is not that the relationship of husband and wife provides an illustration of the union of Christ and the church, but that the basic reality is the latter, with marriage a human echo of that relationship.

5:33 *love ... respect.* A rephrasing and summary of the whole passage.

6:1 *obey your parents.* Cf. Pr 30:17; Col 3:20 and note; 2Ti 3:2. *in the Lord.* In fellowship with the Lord and in obedience to him.

6:3 *on the earth.* In Dt 5:16 (see Ex 20:12), where this commandment occurs, the "promise" (v. 2) was expressed in terms of the anticipated occupation of the "land," i.e., Canaan. That specific application was, of course, not appropriate to the Ephesians, so the more general application is made here.

6:4 *do not exasperate.* Fathers must surrender any right they may feel they have to act unreasonably toward their children.

6:5 *Slaves.* Both the OT and the NT included regulations for societal situations such as slavery and divorce (see Dt 24:1–4), which were the results of the hardness of hearts (Mt 19:8). Such regulations did not encourage or condone such situations but were divinely-given, practical ways of dealing with the realities of the day.

6:8 *the Lord will reward.* Probably a reference to the believer's final reward (see 1Co 3:10–15; 2Co 5:10 and notes).

6:9 *masters.* Once again Paul stresses reciprocal attitudes (cf. 5:21—6:4). See Tit 2:9 and note. *their Master and yours.* Cf. Ro 14:4 and note. *no favoritism with him.* See Ac 10:34 and note.

6:10–20 Paul's scope in Ephesians has been cosmic. From the very beginning he has drawn attention to the unseen world (see note on 1:3; see also 1:10,20–23; 2:6; 6:10), and now he describes the spiritual battle that takes place against evil "in the heavenly realms" (v. 12).

6:10 *strong ... power.* Implies that human effort is inadequate but God's power is invincible.

6:12 *not against flesh and blood.* A caution against lashing out against human opponents as though they were the real enemy and also against assuming that the battle can be fought using merely human resources. *rulers ... forces.* Cf. Paul's earlier allusions to powerful beings in the unseen world (see notes on 1:21; 3:10). *heavenly realms.* See note on 1:3.

6:13–14 *stand your ground ... Stand firm.* In this context the imagery is not that of a massive invasion of the domain of evil, but of individual soldiers withstanding assault.

6:14 *belt of truth.* Cf. the symbolic clothing of the Messiah in Isa 11:5. Character, not brute force, wins the battle, just as in the case of the Messiah. *breastplate of righteousness.* Here again, the warriors' character is their defense. God himself is symbolically described as putting on a breastplate of righteousness when he goes forth to bring about justice (see Isa 59:17 and note).

6:15 *feet fitted with the readiness.* Whereas the description of the messenger's feet in Isa 52:7 reflects the custom of running

peace.[c] 16In addition to all this, take up the
shield of faith,[d] with which you can extinguish all the flaming arrows of the evil
one.[e] 17Take the helmet of salvation[f] and
the sword of the Spirit,[g] which is the word
of God.[h] 18And pray in the Spirit[i] on all
occasions[j] with all kinds of prayers and
requests.[k] With this in mind, be alert and
always keep on praying[l] for all the saints.
19Pray also for me,[m] that whenever I
open my mouth, words may be given me
so that I will fearlessly[n] make known the
mystery[o] of the gospel, 20for which I am an
ambassador[p] in chains.[q] Pray that I may
declare it fearlessly, as I should.

6:15 [c]Isa 52:7; Ro 10:15 **6:16** [d]1Jn 5:4 [e]S Mt 5:37 **6:17** [f]Isa 59:17 [g]Isa 49:2 [h]S Heb 4:12 **6:18** [i]Ro 8:26,27 [j]S Lk 18:1 [k]Mt 26:41; Php 1:4; 4:6 [l]S Ac 1:14; Col 1:3 **6:19** [m]S 1Th 5:25 [n]S Ac 4:29 [o]S Ro 16:25 **6:20** [p]2Co 5:20 [q]S Ac 21:33 **6:21** [r]S Ac 20:4

Final Greetings

21Tychicus,[r] the dear brother and faithful
servant in the Lord, will tell you everything, so that you also may know how I
am and what I am doing. 22I am sending
him to you for this very purpose, that you
may know how we are,[s] and that he may
encourage you.[t]
23Peace[u] to the brothers, and love with
faith from God the Father and the Lord
Jesus Christ. 24Grace to all who love our
Lord Jesus Christ with an undying love.

6:22 [s]Col 4:7-9 [t]Col 2:2; 4:8 **6:23** [u]Gal 6:16; 2Th 3:16; 1Pe 5:14

barefooted, here the message of the gospel is picturesquely connected with the protective and supportive footgear of the Roman soldier. *gospel of peace.* An expression found only here in the Bible (cf. 2:14–16; Ro 5:1 and note).

6:16 *shield of faith ... extinguish ... flaming arrows.* Describes the large Roman shield covered with leather, which could be soaked in water and used to put out flame-tipped arrows.

6:17–18 *sword of the Spirit ... pray in the Spirit.* Reminders that the battle is spiritual and must be fought in God's strength, depending on the word and on God through prayer.

6:17 *helmet of salvation.* Isa 59:17 has similar language, along with the breastplate imagery (see note on v. 14). The helmet protected the soldier and, under certain circumstances, helmets provided a striking symbol of military victory.

6:18 *pray in the Spirit.* Pray with the help of the Spirit (cf. Ro 8:26 and note). *saints.* See note on 1:1.

6:19 *mystery.* See 3:3,9 and note on 3:3.

6:20 *in chains.* See Php 1:7,13 and note; Col 4:3; Phm 10,13.

6:21–23 Paul concludes with greetings that lack personal references such as are usually found in his letters. This is understandable if Ephesians is a circular letter (see note on 1:1).

6:21 *Tychicus.* An associate of Paul who traveled as his representative (cf. Col 4:7; 2Ti 4:12; Tit 3:12).

6:23–24 *Peace ... Grace.* See note on Ro 1:7.

6:23 *brothers.* See note on Ro 1:13.

6:24 *love our Lord Jesus.* Cf. Jn 14:15,21,23 and notes; 21:15–17 and note.

Philippians

INTRODUCTION

Author, Date and Place of Writing

The early church was unanimous in its testimony that Philippians was written by the apostle Paul (see 1:1). Internally the letter reveals the stamp of genuineness. The many personal references of the author fit what we know of Paul from other NT books.

It is evident that Paul wrote the letter from prison (see 1:13–14). Some have argued that this imprisonment took place in Ephesus, perhaps c. A.D. 53–55; others put it in Caesarea c. 57–59. The best evidence, however, favors Rome as the place of origin and the date as c. 61 (see chart, p. 1697). This fits well with the account of Paul's house arrest in Ac 28:14–31. When he wrote Philippians, he was not in the Mamertine dungeon as he was when he wrote 2 Timothy. He was in his own rented house, where for two years he was free to share the gospel with all who came to him (Ac 28:3–31).

A Quick Look

Author:
The apostle Paul

Audience:
The believers at Philippi, a prosperous Roman colony

Date:
About A.D 61

Theme:
Paul writes to encourage the Christians at Philippi to live joyfully in every circumstance.

Purpose

Paul's primary purpose in writing this letter was to thank the Philippians for the gift they had sent him upon learning of his detention at Rome (1:5; 4:10–19). However, he makes use of this occasion to fulfill several other desires: (1) to report on his own circumstances (1:12–26; 4:10–19); (2) to encourage the Philippians to stand firm in the face of persecution and rejoice regardless of circumstances (1:27–30; 4:4); (3) to exhort them to humility and unity (2:1–11; 4:2–5); (4) to commend Timothy and Epaphroditus to the Philippian church (2:19–30); and (5) to warn the Philippians against the Judaizers (legalists) and antinomians (libertines) among them (ch. 3).

Recipients

The city of Philippi (see map, p. 1836) was named after King Philip II of Macedon, father of Alexander the Great. It was a prosperous Roman colony, which meant that the citizens of Philippi were also citizens of the city of Rome itself. They prided themselves on being Romans (see Ac 16:21), dressed like Romans and often spoke Latin. No doubt this was the background for Paul's reference to the believer's heavenly citizenship (3:20 – 21). Many of the Philippians were retired military men who had been given land in the vicinity and who in turn served as a military presence in this frontier city. That Philippi was a Roman colony may explain why there were not enough Jews there to permit the establishment of a synagogue and why Paul does not quote the OT in the Philippian letter.

Paul wrote to thank the Philippians for the gift they had sent him and to encourage the Philippians to stand firm in the face of persecution and rejoice regardless of circumstances.

Characteristics

1. Philippians contains no OT quotations (but see note on Job 13:16).

2. It is a missionary thank-you letter in which the missionary reports on the progress of his work.

3. It manifests a particularly vigorous type of Christian living: (1) self-humbling (2:1 – 4); (2) pressing toward the goal (3:13 – 14); (3) lack of anxiety (4:6); (4) ability to do all things (4:13).

4. It is outstanding as the NT letter of joy; the word "joy" in its various forms occurs some 16 times.

5. It contains one of the most profound Christological passages in the NT (2:5 – 11). Yet, profound as it is, Paul includes it mainly for illustrative purposes: to call God's people to unity and humility in the light of Christ's incarnation.

Outline

I. Greetings (1:1 – 2)
II. Thanksgiving and Prayer for the Philippians (1:3 – 11)
III. Paul's Personal Circumstances (1:12 – 26)
IV. Exhortations (1:27 — 2:18)
  A. Living a Life Worthy of the Gospel (1:27 – 30)

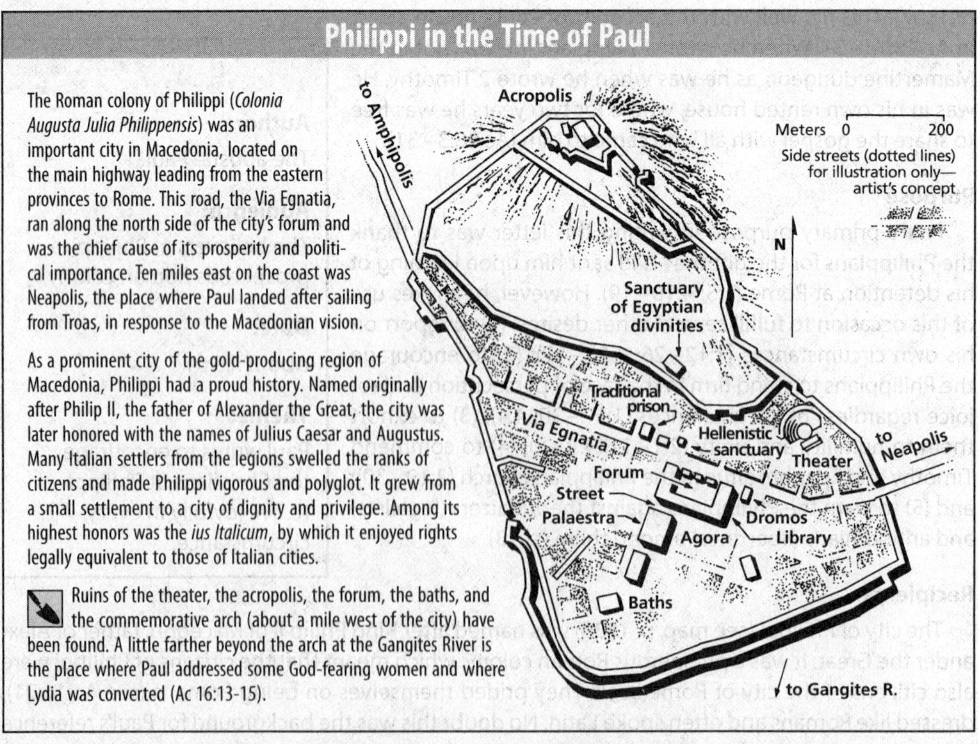

The Roman colony of Philippi (*Colonia Augusta Julia Philippensis*) was an important city in Macedonia, located on the main highway leading from the eastern provinces to Rome. This road, the Via Egnatia, ran along the north side of the city's forum and was the chief cause of its prosperity and political importance. Ten miles east on the coast was Neapolis, the place where Paul landed after sailing from Troas, in response to the Macedonian vision.

As a prominent city of the gold-producing region of Macedonia, Philippi had a proud history. Named originally after Philip II, the father of Alexander the Great, the city was later honored with the names of Julius Caesar and Augustus. Many Italian settlers from the legions swelled the ranks of citizens and made Philippi vigorous and polyglot. It grew from a small settlement to a city of dignity and privilege. Among its highest honors was the *ius Italicum*, by which it enjoyed rights legally equivalent to those of Italian cities.

Ruins of the theater, the acropolis, the forum, the baths, and the commemorative arch (about a mile west of the city) have been found. A little farther beyond the arch at the Gangites River is the place where Paul addressed some God-fearing women and where Lydia was converted (Ac 16:13-15).

- B. Following the Servant Attitude of Christ (2:1 – 18)

V. Paul's Associates in the Gospel (2:19 – 30)
- A. Timothy (2:19 – 24)
- B. Epaphroditus (2:25 – 30)

VI. Warnings against Judaizers and Antinomians (3:1 — 4:1)
- A. Against Judaizers or Legalists (3:1 – 16)
- B. Against Antinomians or Libertines (3:17 — 4:1)

VII. Final Exhortations, Thanks and Conclusion (4:2 – 23)
- A. Exhortations concerning Various Aspects of the Christian Life (4:2 – 9)
- B. Concluding Testimony and Repeated Thanks (4:10 – 20)
- C. Final Greetings and Benediction (4:21 – 23)

1 Paul and Timothy,[a] servants of Christ
Jesus,

To all the saints[b] in Christ Jesus at Philippi,[c] together with the overseers[a][d] and
deacons:[e]

2Grace and peace to you from God our
Father and the Lord Jesus Christ.[f]

Thanksgiving and Prayer

3I thank my God every time I remember you.[g] 4In all my prayers for all of you,
I always pray[h] with joy 5because of your
partnership[i] in the gospel from the first
day[j] until now, 6being confident of this,
that he who began a good work in you will
carry it on to completion[k] until the day of
Christ Jesus.[l]
7It is right[m] for me to feel this way about
all of you, since I have you in my heart;[n]
for whether I am in chains[o] or defending[p]
and confirming the gospel, all of you share
in God's grace with me. 8God can testify[q]
how I long for all of you with the affection
of Christ Jesus.

9And this is my prayer: that your love[r]
may abound more and more in knowledge
and depth of insight,[s] 10so that you may
be able to discern what is best and may
be pure and blameless until the day of
Christ,[t] 11filled with the fruit of righteousness[u] that comes through Jesus Christ — to
the glory and praise of God.

Paul's Chains Advance the Gospel

12Now I want you to know, brothers,
that what has happened to me has really
served to advance the gospel. 13As a result, it has become clear throughout the
whole palace guard[b] and to everyone else
that I am in chains[v] for Christ. 14Because
of my chains,[w] most of the brothers in the
Lord have been encouraged to speak the
word of God more courageously and fearlessly.[x]
15It is true that some preach Christ out
of envy and rivalry, but others out of goodwill. 16The latter do so in love, knowing
that I am put here for the defense of the

1:1 [a] S Ac 16:1; 2Co 1:1 [b] S Ac 9:13 [c] S Ac 16:12 [d] S 1Ti 3:1 [e] 1Ti 3:8 **1:2** [f] S Ro 1:7 **1:3** [g] S Ro 1:8 **1:4** [h] S Ro 1:10 **1:5** [i] Ac 2:42; Php 4:15 [j] Ac 16:12-40 **1:6** [k] Ps 138:8 [l] ver 10; S 1Co 1:8 **1:7** [m] 2Pe 1:13 [n] 2Co 7:3 [o] ver 13,14,17; S Ac 21:33 [p] ver 16 **1:8** [q] S Ro 1:9 **1:9** [r] 1Th 3:12 [s] S Eph 1:17 **1:10** [t] ver 6; S 1Co 1:8 **1:11** [u] S Jas 3:18 **1:13** [v] ver 7,14,17; S Ac 21:33 **1:14** [w] ver 7,13,17; S Ac 21:33 [x] S Ac 4:29

[a] *1* Traditionally *bishops* [b] *13* Or *whole palace*

1:1–2 As in all his letters, Paul follows the conventional letter format of his day, with its three elements: (1) identification of the sender, (2) identification of the recipients, (3) greeting.

1:1 *Paul.* See note on Ro 1:1. *Timothy.* See Introduction to 1 Timothy: Recipient. Timothy is identified with the contents of the letter as Paul's associate, but not as co-author. *servants.* See Ro 1:1 and note; Tit 1:1; Jas 1:1; 2Pe 1:1; Jude 1; Rev 1:1. In Paul's case, this designation brings out an essential aspect of the more usual identification of himself as "apostle." *saints.* See Ro 1:7 and note. *Philippi.* See Introduction: Recipients. *overseers and deacons.* The only place in Paul's writings where church officers as a group are singled out as recipients of a letter. *overseers.* See note on 1Ti 3:1. *deacons.* See note on 1Ti 3:8.

1:2 *Grace and peace.* See note on Ro 1:7. *Lord Jesus Christ.* See note on 1Th 1:1.

1:3–4 *I thank my God ... prayers for ... you ... with joy.* Prayers of joyful thanksgiving for his readers' response to the gospel are a hallmark of the opening sentences of Paul's letters (see Ro 1:8; 1Co 1:4; Col 1:3; 1Th 1:2; 2Th 1:3; 2Ti 1:3; Phm 4).

1:5 *your partnership in the gospel.* The basis of Paul's prayerful thanksgiving is not only their reception of the gospel but also their active support of his ministry (see 4:15 and note). *from the first day.* When Paul first came to Philippi (Ac 16:12). *now.* Toward the close (see 2:24 and note) of Paul's first Roman imprisonment (see Ac 28:16–31).

1:6 *work in you.* Paul is confident, not only of what God has done "for" the readers in forgiving their sins, but also of what he has done "in" them (see v. 11). "Work" refers to God's activity in saving them. *day of Christ Jesus.* His return, when their salvation will be brought to completion (see 1:10; 2:16; 1Co 1:8; 5:5; 2Co 1:14). It is God who initiates salvation, who continues it and who will one day bring it to its consummation.

1:7 *in chains.* See note on Eph 6:20. *share in God's grace.* Not even imprisonment and persecution can change such sharing. Even in Paul's imprisonment they willingly identified themselves with Paul by sending Epaphroditus and their financial gifts (2:25–30; 4:18). They had become one with Paul in his apostolic commission to preach the gospel (see v. 5).

1:8 *affection of Christ Jesus.* The deep yearning and intense, compassionate love exhibited by Jesus himself and now fostered in Paul by his union with Christ. This affection reaches out to all impartially and without exception.

1:9 *abound more and more.* Real love requires growth and maturation (see 1Th 3:12; 4:10; 2Th 1:3). *in knowledge.* The way love grows (cf. Col 1:9). *depth of insight.* Practical discernment and sensitivity. Christian love is not mere sentiment; it is rooted in knowledge and understanding.

1:10 *discern what is best.* Christians are to approve (and practice) what is morally and ethically superior. *pure and blameless.* The goal of Christians in this life is to be without any mixture of evil and not open to censure because of moral or spiritual failure. *until the day of Christ.* Then the goal will be perfectly realized (see note on v. 6), and then Christians must give an account (see 2Co 5:10 and note; Ro 14:10,12 and note on 14:10).

1:11 *filled with the fruit of righteousness.* What is expected of all Christians (cf. Mt 5:20–48; Heb 12:11; Jas 3:18; see also Am 6:12; Gal 5:22–23). *through Jesus Christ.* Produced by Christ (in union with him) through the work of the Holy Spirit (cf. Jn 15:5; Eph 2:10). *to the glory and praise of God.* The ultimate goal of all that God does in believers (see Eph 1:6,12,14).

1:12 *brothers.* See note on Ro 1:13. *what has happened to me.* Paul's detainment in prison. *advance the gospel.* Instead of hindering the gospel, Paul's imprisonment had served to make it known.

1:13 *clear ... chains for Christ.* It has become apparent to all who know of Paul's situation that he is imprisoned, not because he is guilty of a crime, but on account of his stand for the gospel. *whole palace guard.* A contingent of soldiers, numbering several thousand, many of whom would have had personal contact with Paul or would have been assigned individually to guard him during the course of his imprisonment (see Ac 28:16,30). *chains.* Either actual chains or a broader reference to his sufferings and imprisonment (see v. 14).

1:14 *in the Lord.* Probably best taken with "encouraged." *encouraged to speak.* The unexpected result of Paul's imprisonment.

1:16 *The latter do so in love.* Those who preach with a right motive recognize the true reason for Paul's imprisonment,

gospel.[y] 17The former preach Christ out of
selfish ambition,[z] not sincerely, supposing
that they can stir up trouble for me while I
am in chains.[a a] 18But what does it matter?
The important thing is that in every way,
whether from false motives or true, Christ
is preached. And because of this I rejoice.
Yes, and I will continue to rejoice, 19for
I know that through your prayers[b] and the
help given by the Spirit of Jesus Christ,[c]
what has happened to me will turn out for
my deliverance.[b d] 20I eagerly expect[e] and
hope that I will in no way be ashamed,
but will have sufficient courage[f] so that
now as always Christ will be exalted in my
body,[g] whether by life or by death.[h] 21For
to me, to live is Christ[i] and to die is gain.
22If I am to go on living in the body, this
will mean fruitful labor for me. Yet what
shall I choose? I do not know! 23I am torn
between the two: I desire to depart[j] and be
with Christ,[k] which is better by far; 24but
it is more necessary for you that I remain
in the body. 25Convinced of this, I know
that I will remain, and I will continue with
all of you for your progress and joy in the
faith, 26so that through my being with you
again your joy in Christ Jesus will overflow on account of me.
27Whatever happens, conduct yourselves in a manner worthy[l] of the gospel
of Christ. Then, whether I come and see
you or only hear about you in my absence,
I will know that you stand firm[m] in one
spirit, contending[n] as one man for the faith
of the gospel 28without being frightened in
any way by those who oppose you. This is
a sign to them that they will be destroyed,
but that you will be saved—and that by
God. 29For it has been granted to you[o] on
behalf of Christ not only to believe on him,
but also to suffer[p] for him, 30since you are
going through the same struggle[q] you saw[r]
I had, and now hear[s] that I still have.

Imitating Christ's Humility

2 If you have any encouragement from
being united with Christ, if any comfort
from his love, if any fellowship with the
Spirit,[t] if any tenderness and compassion,[u]

1:16 [y] ver 7,12
1:17 [z] Php 2:3
[a] ver 7,13,14; S Ac 21:33
1:19 [b] 2Co 1:11
[c] S Ac 16:7
[d] Phm 22
1:20 [e] Ro 8:19
[f] ver 14 [g] 1Co 6:20
[h] Ro 14:8
1:21 [i] Gal 2:20
1:23 [j] 2Ti 4:6
[k] S Jn 12:26
1:27 [l] S Eph 4:1
[m] S 1Co 16:13
[n] Jude 3
1:29 [o] Mt 5:11,12; Ac 5:41
[p] S Ac 14:22
1:30 [q] 1Th 2:2; Heb 10:32
[r] Ac 16:19-40
[s] ver 13
2:1 [t] 2Co 13:14
[u] Col 3:12

[a] *16,17* Some late manuscripts have verses 16 and 17 in reverse order. [b] *19* Or *salvation*

already expressed earlier in v. 13, and are encouraged to take the same bold stand that he has taken.

1:17 *The former preach Christ out of selfish ambition.* Those who preach with wrong, insincere motives do so out of a sense of competition with Paul and so think they are making his imprisonment more difficult to bear. *not sincerely.* Not from pure motives.

1:18 *whether from false motives or true, Christ is preached.* These preachers are not to be viewed as being heretical. Their message is true, even though their motives are not pure. The gospel has its objectivity and validity apart from those who proclaim it; the message is more than the medium. *I rejoice ... will continue to rejoice.* An example of the kind of vigorous Christian experience Paul expressed. He was under arrest, and fellow Christians sought, by their preaching, to add to his difficulties; yet he kept on rejoicing.

1:19 *Spirit of Jesus Christ.* The Holy Spirit is not only the Spirit of God the Father (Ro 8:9,14; 1Co 2:10–11,14) but also the Spirit of Christ, the second person of the Trinity (Ac 16:7; Ro 8:9; Gal 4:6). He is sent by the Father (Jn 14:16–17,26; Gal 4:6) and by the Son (Jn 15:26; 16:7). *turn out for my deliverance.* Either Paul's release from prison (see v. 25; 2:24) or, in view of the immediately following verses, the deliverance brought to the believer by death (cf. Ro 8:38–39). Verse 25, however, seems to point to the former interpretation (see note there). See Job 13:16 and note.

1:20 *ashamed ... sufficient courage.* The circumstances of imprisonment, with all its attendant suffering and oppression, constitute a real temptation for Paul to abandon the gospel and his resolute service for Christ. *my body.* Where the exalted Christ dwells by his Spirit and is at work (cf. Ro 8:9–10), and so is exalted by what Paul does. *whether by life or by death.* Whether his service for Christ continues or ends in death.

1:21 *to live is Christ.* Christ was the source and secret of Paul's continual joy (even in prison), for Paul's life found all its meaning in Christ (cf. 3:8–10 and notes). *gain.* Verse 23 specifies that the gain brought by death is to "be with Christ," so that here Paul is saying that his ultimate concern and most precious possession, both now and forever, is Christ and his relationship to him.

1:22 *fruitful labor.* The spread of the gospel and the upbuilding of the church.

1:23–24 *depart and be with Christ ... remain in the body.* Either alternative was a good one. While mysteries remain, this passage clearly teaches that when believers die they are with Christ (see 2Co 5:6,8–9 and notes).

1:23 *better by far.* Being with Christ after death must involve some kind of conscious presence and fellowship (cf. 2Co 5:6,8 and note on 5:8).

1:24 *necessary for you.* Paul puts the needs of those he ministers to ahead of his personal preference.

1:25 *I will remain.* Possibly Paul was later released from prison (see map, p. 1872). *progress ... in the faith.* The Christian life is to be one of joyful growth and advance (see note on v. 9).

1:26 *your joy in Christ Jesus ... on account of me.* Paul's conduct of his ministry among the Philippians will be a reason for their rejoicing in what Christ is doing among them.

1:27 *worthy of the gospel.* Appropriate to the standards and goals given with the gospel. *in one spirit.* Having a common disposition and purpose. *contending as one man.* Particularly where the gospel is under attack, Christians need each other and must stand together.

1:28 *sign.* Persistent opposition to the church and the gospel is a sure sign of eventual destruction, since it involves rejection of the only way of salvation. By the same token, when Christians are persecuted for their faith, this is a sign of the genuineness of their salvation (see 2Th 1:5 and note).

1:29 *granted ... to suffer.* Given as a gift or privilege. Christian suffering, as well as faith, is a blessing (cf. Mt 5:11–12; Ac 5:41; Jas 1:2; 1Pe 4:14). The Christian life is to be a "not only ... but also" proposition: not only believing but also suffering.

1:30 *same struggle.* Their common involvement with Paul in conflict with those who oppose the gospel. *you saw.* When Paul and Silas first visited Philippi and were imprisoned (see Ac 16:19–40).

2:1 *united with Christ.* Or "united in Christ." In Paul's teaching, this personal union is the basic reality of salvation. To be in Christ is to be saved. It is to be in intimate personal

[2]then make my joy complete[v] by being
like-minded,[w] having the same love, being one[x] in spirit and purpose. [3]Do nothing
out of selfish ambition or vain conceit,[y]
but in humility consider others better than
yourselves.[z] [4]Each of you should look not
only to your own interests, but also to the
interests of others.[a]
[5]Your attitude should be the same as
that of Christ Jesus:[b]

[6]Who, being in very nature[a] God,[c]
did not consider equality with God[d]
something to be grasped,
[7]but made himself nothing,[e]
taking the very nature[b] of a servant,[f]
being made in human likeness.[g]
[8]And being found in appearance as a
man,
he humbled himself
and became obedient to death[h]—
even death on a cross![i]

2:2 [v]S Jn 3:29 [w]Php 4:2 [x]S Ro 15:5 **2:3** [y]Gal 5:26 [z]Ro 12:10; 1Pe 5:5 **2:4** [a]S 1Co 10:24 **2:5** [b]S Mt 11:29 **2:6** [c]Jn 1:1; S 14:9 [d]Jn 5:18 **2:7** [e]2Co 8:9 [f]S Mt 20:28 [g]S Jn 1:14; Ro 8:3; Heb 2:17 **2:8** [h]S Mt 26:39; Jn 10:18; Ro 5:19; Heb 5:8 [i]S 1Co 1:23 **2:9** [j]Isa 52:13; 53:12; Da 7:14; Ac 2:33; Heb 2:9 [k]Eph 1:20,21 **2:10** [l]Ps 95:6; Isa 45:23; Ro 14:11 [m]Mt 28:18; Eph 1:10; Col 1:20

[9]Therefore God exalted him[j] to the
highest place
and gave him the name that is above
every name,[k]
[10]that at the name of Jesus every knee
should bow,[l]
in heaven and on earth and under
the earth,[m]
[11]and every tongue confess that Jesus
Christ is Lord,[n]
to the glory of God the Father.

Shining as Stars

[12]Therefore, my dear friends, as you
have always obeyed—not only in my
presence, but now much more in my absence—continue to work out your salva-

[a] 6 Or *in the form of* [b] 7 Or *the form*

2:11 [n]S Jn 13:13

relationship with Christ the Savior. From this relationship flow all the particular benefits and fruits of salvation, like encouragement (see, e.g., 3:8–10; Ro 8:1; 2Co 5:17; Gal 2:20). *comfort from his love.* The comforting knowledge and assurance that come from God's love in Christ, demonstrated especially in Christ's death for the forgiveness of sins and eternal life (see Jn 3:16; Ro 5:8; 8:38–39; 1Jn 3:16; 4:9–10,16). *fellowship with the Spirit.* The fellowship among believers produced by the Spirit, who indwells each of them (see 2Co 13:14). *tenderness and compassion.* Christians are to have intense care and deep sympathy for each other (see 1:8 and note; Col 3:12). All these benefits—encouragement, comfort, fellowship, tenderness, compassion—are viewed by Paul as present realities for the Philippians.

2:2 *like-minded ... same love ... one in spirit and purpose.* Emphasizes the unity that should exist among Christians. *like-minded.* Not uniformity in thought but the common disposition to work together and serve one another—the "attitude" of Christ (v. 5; see 4:2; Ro 12:16; 15:5 and note; 2Co 13:11).

2:3 *selfish ambition or vain conceit.* The mortal enemies of unity and harmony in the church (cf. 1:17; see Gal 5:19–20, where "selfish ambition" is listed among the "acts of the sinful nature"). *humility.* Required for Christian unity. This is the mind-set of those who are not conceited but who have a right attitude toward themselves and others. *consider others better than yourselves.* Not that everyone else is superior or more talented, but that Christian love sees others as worthy of preferential treatment (see Ro 12:10 and note; Gal 5:13; Eph 5:21; 1Pe 5:5 and note).

2:4 *your own interests.* These are proper, but only if there is equal concern for the interests of others (cf. Ro 15:1 and note).

2:5 *Your attitude ... the same as ... Christ.* In spite of all that is unique and radically different about the person and work of Christ (see vv. 6–11), Christians are to have his attitude of self-sacrificing humility and love for others (see vv. 2–4; Mt 11:29; Jn 13:12–17).

2:6–11 The poetic character of these verses is apparent. Many view them as an early Christian hymn (see note on Col 3:16), taken over and perhaps modified by Paul. If so, they nonetheless express his convictions. The passage treats Christ's humiliation (vv. 6–8) and exaltation (vv. 9–11).

2:6 *in very nature God.* Affirming that Jesus is fully God (see Ro 9:5 and note). *nature.* Essential form (see NIV text note), the sum of those qualities that make God specifically God. *equality with God.* The status and privileges that inevitably follow from being in very nature God. *something to be grasped.* Perhaps something to be forcibly retained—the glory Christ had with the Father before his incarnation. But he did not consider that high position to be something he could not give up. On the other hand, it may be something still to be attained, like a prize, as if he did not yet possess it.

2:7 *made himself nothing.* Lit. "emptied himself." He did this, not by giving up deity, but by laying aside his glory (see Jn 17:5) and submitting to the humiliation of becoming a man (see 2Co 8:9 and note). Jesus is truly God and truly human. Another view is that he emptied himself, not of deity itself, but of its prerogatives—the high position and glory of deity. *nature of a servant.* Emphasizes the full reality of his servant identity (see Mt 20:28). As a servant, he was always submissive to the will of the Father (see Lk 22:42; Jn 4:34 and note).

2:8 *appearance as a man.* Not only was Jesus "like" a human being (v. 7), but he also took on all the actual characteristics of a man (see Jn 1:14; Ro 8:3; Heb 2:17 and notes). *humbled himself.* See v. 7; 2Co 8:9. *obedient.* How Jesus humbled himself (cf. Heb 5:7–8). A "servant" (v. 7) obeys. *to death.* Stresses both the totality and the climax of Jesus' obedience. *on a cross.* Heightens Jesus' humiliation; he died as someone cursed (see Gal 3:13; Heb 12:2). Crucifixion was the most degrading kind of execution that could be inflicted on a person.

2:9 *exalted.* See Mt 28:18; Ac 2:33; cf. Isa 52:13. *the name ... above every name.* Reference doubtless is to the office or rank conferred on Jesus—his glorious position ("Lord," v. 11), not his proper name (cf. Eph 1:21; Heb 1:4–5 and notes).

2:10–11 *bow ... confess.* Cf. Isa 45:23. God's design is that all people everywhere should worship and serve Jesus as Lord. Ultimately all will acknowledge him as Lord (see Ro 14:9), whether willingly or not.

2:10 *at the name of Jesus.* In honor of his exalted position as "Lord" (v. 11; see v. 9 and note).

2:12 *Therefore.* Because of Christ's incomparable example (vv. 5–11). *obeyed.* The commands of God as passed on to the Philippians by Paul (see Ro 1:5; 15:18; 2Co 10:5–6). *my presence.* During the course of Paul's second (see Ac 16:12–40) and third (see Ac 20:1–3,6) missionary journeys. *work out your salvation.* Work it out to the finish; not a reference to the attempt to earn one's salvation by works, but to the expression of one's salvation in spiritual growth

tion with fear and trembling,[o] 13for it is
God who works in you[p] to will and to act
according to his good purpose.[q]
14Do everything without complaining[r] or
arguing, 15so that you may become blameless[s] and pure, children of God[t] without
fault in a crooked and depraved generation,[u] in which you shine like stars in the
universe 16as you hold out[a] the word of
life—in order that I may boast on the day
of Christ[v] that I did not run[w] or labor for
nothing.[x] 17But even if I am being poured
out like a drink offering[y] on the sacrifice[z]
and service coming from your faith, I am
glad and rejoice with all of you.[a] 18So you
too should be glad and rejoice with me.

Timothy and Epaphroditus

19I hope in the Lord Jesus to send Timothy[b] to you soon,[c] that I also may be
cheered when I receive news about you.
20I have no one else like him,[d] who takes
a genuine interest in your welfare. 21For
everyone looks out for his own interests,[e]
not those of Jesus Christ. 22But you know
that Timothy has proved himself, because
as a son with his father[f] he has served
with me in the work of the gospel. 23I
hope, therefore, to send him as soon as
I see how things go with me.[g] 24And I am
confident[h] in the Lord that I myself will
come soon.
25But I think it is necessary to send
back to you Epaphroditus, my brother,
fellow worker[i] and fellow soldier,[j] who is
also your messenger, whom you sent to
take care of my needs.[k] 26For he longs for
all of you[l] and is distressed because you
heard he was ill. 27Indeed he was ill, and
almost died. But God had mercy on him,
and not on him only but also on me, to
spare me sorrow upon sorrow. 28Therefore
I am all the more eager to send him,[m] so
that when you see him again you may be
glad and I may have less anxiety. 29Wel-
come him in the Lord with great joy, and
honor men like him,[n] 30because he almost
died for the work of Christ, risking his life
to make up for the help you could not
give me.[o]

No Confidence in the Flesh

3 Finally, my brothers, rejoice in the
Lord! It is no trouble for me to write
the same things to you again,[p] and it is a
safeguard for you.
2Watch out for those dogs,[q] those men
who do evil, those mutilators of the flesh.

[a] 16 Or *hold on to*

2:12 [o] S 2Co 7:15 **2:13** [p] Ezr 1:5; 1Co 12:6; 15:10; Gal 2:8; Heb 13:21 [q] Eph 1:5 **2:14** [r] 1Co 10:10; 1Pe 4:9 **2:15** [s] S 1Th 3:13 [t] Mt 5:45,48; Eph 5:1 [u] Ac 2:40 **2:16** [v] S 1Co 1:8 [w] S 1Co 9:24 [x] 1Th 2:19 **2:17** [y] 2Co 12:15; 2Ti 4:6 [z] Ro 15:16 [a] S 2Co 6:10 **2:19** [b] S Ac 16:1 [c] ver 23 **2:20** [d] 1Co 16:10 **2:21** [e] S 1Co 10:24 **2:22** [f] 1Co 4:17; 1Ti 1:2 **2:23** [g] ver 19 **2:24** [h] Php 1:25 **2:25** [i] Ro 16:3,9,21; 2Co 8:23; Php 4:3; Col 4:11; Phm 1 [j] Phm 2 [k] Php 4:18 **2:26** [l] Php 1:8 **2:28** [m] ver 25 **2:29** [n] 1Co 16:18; 1Ti 5:17 **2:30** [o] 1Co 16:17 **3:1** [p] Php 2:18 **3:2** [q] Ps 22:16,20; Rev 22:15

and development. Salvation is not merely a gift received once for all; it expresses itself in an ongoing process in which the believer is strenuously involved (cf. Mt 24:13; 1Co 9:24–27; Heb 3:14; 6:9–11; 2Pe 1:5–8)—the process of perseverance, humble service, spiritual growth and maturation. *fear and trembling.* Not because of doubt or anxiety; rather, the reference is to an active reverence and a singleness of purpose in response to God's grace.

2:13 *God ... works in you.* See Col 1:29 and note. *to will and to act.* Intention, or faith, and our obedience cannot be separated (cf. Gal 5:6 and note; Jas 2:18,20,22).

2:14–17 Some things involved in working out our salvation.

2:14 *complaining.* Being discontented with God's will is an expression of unbelief that prevents one from doing what pleases God (v. 13; cf. 1Co 10:10 and note). *arguing.* Over debatable points that do not need to be settled for the good of the church (see 2Ti 2:23; Tit 3:9).

2:15 *blameless and pure ... without fault.* Not absolute, sinless perfection, but wholehearted, unmixed devotion to doing God's will (see 1:10 and note). *crooked and depraved generation.* A description of the unbelieving world (see Ac 2:40; Eph 2:1–3; cf. Mt 17:17). *shine like stars.* The contrast, like light in darkness, that Christians are to be to the world around them (cf. Mt 5:15–16).

2:16 *boast.* Not out of pride or a sense of self-accomplishment, but because of what God has done through Paul (see 1Th 2:19). *day of Christ.* See note on 1:6. *for nothing.* Cf. 1Co 9:24–27.

2:17–18 *I ... rejoice ... you too should ... rejoice.* Christian joy ought always to be mutual.

2:17 *I am being poured out.* The reference may be to his entire ministry as one large thanksgiving sacrifice. However, it is more probable that Paul refers to his present imprisonment, which may end in a martyr's death. His life would then be poured out as a drink offering accompanying the sacrificial service of the Philippians. *like a drink offering.* The OT background is the daily sacrifices in Ex 29:38–41. *coming from your faith.* Genuine faith is active and working (see note on v. 13).

2:19–23 Paul plans to send Timothy, who is with him in Rome (see 1:1 and note), to discover and report on conditions in the Philippian church.

2:20 *I have no one else like him.* Timothy was a good example of the kind of person envisioned in the exhortation of v. 4.

2:21 A sharp contrast between Timothy and Paul's other associates—an outstanding commendation for one so young (see 1Ti 4:12 and note).

2:22 *as a son with his father.* This relationship between Timothy and Paul is developed at length in 1,2 Timothy. *served.* Like Jesus and Paul, Timothy had a servant attitude.

2:24 Paul anticipates his release in the near future (see 1:25).

2:25–30 Epaphroditus, after a close brush with death (vv. 27,30), is being sent home to Philippi.

2:25 *messenger.* A broader use of the Greek word often translated "apostle," applied here to Epaphroditus as a representative of the Philippian church (cf. 2Co 8:23).

2:27 Cf. 1:21–26.

2:28 *anxiety.* The legitimate cares and concerns that come with the Christian life and the gospel ministry (see note on 4:6; cf. 2Co 4:8; 11:28).

2:29 *in the Lord.* As a fellow believer (see Ro 16:2).

3:1 *Finally.* Marks a transition to a new section as Paul moves toward his conclusion; this does not mark the close of the letter, however (cf. 4:8). *rejoice in the Lord!* See 4:4 and note. *same things ... again.* Matters taken up in the verses that follow, which Paul had previously dealt with either orally when he was in Philippi or perhaps in an earlier letter. *safeguard.* Where serious error is present, there is safety in repetition.

3:2 *dogs.* A harsh word for Paul's opponents, showing their aggressive opposition to the gospel and the seriousness of their error and its destructive, "devouring" results (cf. Gal 5:15).

3 For it is we who are the circumcision,[r]
we who worship by the Spirit of God, who
glory in Christ Jesus,[s] and who put no
confidence in the flesh— 4 though I myself
have reasons for such confidence.[t]

If anyone else thinks he has reasons to
put confidence in the flesh, I have more:
5 circumcised[u] on the eighth day, of the
people of Israel,[v] of the tribe of Benjamin,[w]
a Hebrew of Hebrews; in regard to the law,
a Pharisee;[x] 6 as for zeal,[y] persecuting the
church;[z] as for legalistic righteousness,[a]
faultless.

7 But whatever was to my profit I now
consider loss[b] for the sake of Christ.
8 What is more, I consider everything a loss
compared to the surpassing greatness of
knowing[c] Christ Jesus my Lord, for whose
sake I have lost all things. I consider them
rubbish, that I may gain Christ[d] 9 and be
found in him, not having a righteousness
of my own that comes from the law,[e] but
that which is through faith in Christ—the
righteousness[f] that comes from God and
is by faith.[g] 10 I want to know[h] Christ and
the power of his resurrection and the fellowship of sharing in his sufferings,[i] becoming like him in his death,[j] 11 and so,
somehow, to attain to the resurrection[k]
from the dead.

Pressing on Toward the Goal

12 Not that I have already obtained all
this, or have already been made perfect,[l]
but I press on to take hold[m] of that for
which Christ Jesus took hold of me.[n]
13 Brothers, I do not consider myself yet
to have taken hold of it. But one thing I
do: Forgetting what is behind[o] and straining toward what is ahead, 14 I press on[p] toward the goal to win the prize[q] for which
God has called[r] me heavenward in Christ
Jesus.

15 All of us who are mature[s] should take
such a view of things.[t] And if on some

3:3 [r] Ro 2:28,29; Gal 6:15; Col 2:11 [s] Ro 15:17; Gal 6:14 **3:4** [t] 2Co 11:21 **3:5** [u] S Lk 1:59 [v] 2Co 11:22 [w] Ro 11:1 [x] Ac 23:6 **3:6** [y] S Ac 21:20 [z] S Ac 8:3 [a] ver 9; Ro 10:5 **3:7** [b] Mt 13:44; Lk 14:33 **3:8** [c] ver 10; Jer 9:23,24; Jn 17:3; Eph 4:13; S 2Pe 1:2 [d] Ps 73:25 **3:9** [e] ver 6; Ro 10:5 [f] Jer 33:16 [g] S Ro 9:30 **3:10** [h] S ver 8 [i] S 2Co 1:5 [j] S Ro 6:3-5 **3:11** [k] S Jn 11:24; S Ro 6:5; Rev 20:5,6 **3:12** [l] 1Co 13:10 [m] 1Ti 6:12 [n] Ac 9:5,6 **3:13** [o] Lk 9:62 **3:14** [p] Heb 6:1 [q] 1Co 9:24 [r] S Ro 8:28 **3:15** [s] S 1Co 2:6 [t] Gal 5:10

Their teaching was probably similar to what Paul had to oppose in the Galatian churches (see Introduction to Galatians: Occasion and Purpose). *mutilators.* Again a strong, painfully vivid term; the false teachers have so distorted the meaning of circumcision (cf. v. 3) that it has become nothing more than a useless cutting of the body.

3:3 *circumcision.* Its true, inner meaning is realized only in believers, who worship God with genuine spiritual worship and who glory in Christ as their Savior rather than trusting in their own human effort (cf. Ro 2:28–29 and note on 2:29; Col 2:11–13; see also Dt 30:6; Eze 36:26). *glory ... no confidence.* Everyone is a boaster, either in Christ or in themselves. *flesh.* Weak human nature (see Gal 3:3 and note).

3:4–14 Paul's personal testimony, a model for every believer; one of the most significant autobiographical sections in his letters (see note on Ro 1:1; cf. Ac 22:1–21; 26:1–23).

3:4–6 Paul's pre-Christian confidence, rooted in his Jewish heritage, privileges and attainments.

3:5 *eighth day.* See Ge 17:12 and note. *of the people of Israel.* Paul was born a Jew and was not a convert to Judaism. *tribe of Benjamin.* His Jewish roots are deep and unambiguous. Jerusalem, the Holy City, lay on the border of the tribal territory of Benjamin. *Hebrew of Hebrews.* In convictions, language, attitudes and lifestyle (see Ac 22:2–3; Gal 1:14). *Pharisee.* See note on Mt 3:7.

3:6 *legalistic righteousness.* Righteousness produced by using the law as an attempt to merit God's approval and blessing (cf. v. 9)—a use of the law strongly opposed by Paul as contrary to the gospel itself (see Ro 3:27–28; 4:1–5; Gal 2:16 and note; 3:10–12 and note on 3:10). *faultless.* In terms of legalistic standards of scrupulous external conformity to the law.

3:7–14 Paul's confidence in Christ.

3:7 *whatever.* The things mentioned in vv. 5–6. *profit ... loss.* The great reversal in Paul—begun on the road to Damascus (see Ac 9:3–16)—from being self-centered to being centered in Christ.

3:8 *knowing Christ Jesus.* Not only a knowledge of facts but a knowledge gained through experience that, in its surpassing greatness, transforms the entire person (see 2Co 5:17 and note). The following verses spell this out. *rubbish.* What Paul now has as a Christian is not merely preferable or a better alternative; in contrast, his former way of life was worthless and despicable (cf. Eph 2:3–7).

3:9 *be found in him.* Union with Christ (see note on 2:1; cf. 1Co 1:30)—not simply an experience in the past, but a present, continuing relationship. *righteousness ... from the law.* See note on v. 6. *righteousness ... by faith.* A principal benefit of union with Christ (see Ro 3:21–22; 1Co 1:30; Gal 2:16 and note).

3:10 *know Christ.* As in v. 8, this knowledge is not merely factual; it includes the experience of the "power of his resurrection" (see Eph 1:17–20), of "fellowship ... in his sufferings" (cf. Ac 9:16) and of being "like him in his death" (see 2Co 4:7–12; 12:9–10). Believers already share positionally in Christ's death and resurrection (cf. Ro 6:2–13; Gal 2:20; 5:24; 6:14; Eph 2:6; Col 2:12–13; 3:1). In v. 10, however, Paul speaks of the actual experience of Christ's resurrection power and of suffering with and for him, even to the point of death.

3:11 *somehow.* Not an indication of doubt or uncertainty, but of humility because Paul does not want to be guilty of presumption. *resurrection.* The great personal anticipation of every believer (see Da 12:2; Jn 5:29; Ac 24:15; 1Co 15:23; 1Th 4:16).

3:12–14 The Christian life is like a race; elsewhere Paul uses athletic imagery in a similar way (1Co 9:24–27; 1Ti 6:12; 2Ti 4:7–8; cf. Mt 24:13; Heb 12:1).

3:12 *take hold ... took hold of me.* Paul's goal is Christ's goal for him, and Christ supplies the resources for him to "press on toward the goal" (v. 14; cf. 2:12–13).

3:13 *Forgetting.* Not losing all memory of his sinful past (see vv. 4–6), but leaving it behind him as done with and settled.

3:14 *prize.* The winner of the Greek races received a wreath of leaves and sometimes a cash award (see 1Co 9:24 and note); the Christian receives an award of everlasting glory (see 2Co 4:17; 2Ti 2:10 and notes). *heavenward.* Paul's ultimate aspirations are found not in this life but in heaven, because Christ is there (see Col 3:1–2).

3:15 *mature.* Those who have made reasonable progress in spiritual growth and stability (see 1Co 2:6 and note; 3:1–3; Heb 5:14 and note). *such a view.* That expressed in vv. 12–14: There are heights yet to be scaled; do not become complacent. *think differently.* If the readers accept the view set forth in vv. 12–14 and yet fail to agree in some lesser point, God will clarify the matter for them.

point you think differently, that too God
will make clear to you.[u] 16Only let us live
up to what we have already attained.
17Join with others in following my example,[v] brothers, and take note of those
who live according to the pattern we gave
you.[w] 18For, as I have often told you before
and now say again even with tears,[x] many
live as enemies of the cross of Christ.[y]
19Their destiny[z] is destruction, their god is
their stomach,[a] and their glory is in their
shame.[b] Their mind is on earthly things.[c]
20But our citizenship[d] is in heaven.[e] And
we eagerly await a Savior from there, the
Lord Jesus Christ,[f] 21who, by the power[g]
that enables him to bring everything under his control, will transform our lowly
bodies[h] so that they will be like his glorious body.[i]

4 Therefore, my brothers, you whom I
love and long for,[j] my joy and crown,
that is how you should stand firm[k] in the
Lord, dear friends!

3:15 [u] Eph 1:17; 1Th 4:9
3:17 [v] S 1Co 4:16 [w] S 1Ti 4:12
3:18 [x] Ac 20:31 [y] Gal 6:12
3:19 [z] Ps 73:17 [a] Ro 16:18 [b] Ro 6:21; Jude 13 [c] Ro 8:5,6; Col 3:2
3:20 [d] Eph 2:19 [e] Col 3:1; Heb 12:22 [f] S 1Co 1:7
3:21 [g] Eph 1:19 [h] 1Co 15:43-53 [i] Ro 8:29; Col 3:4
4:1 [j] Php 1:8 [k] S 1Co 16:13
4:2 [l] Php 2:2
4:3 [m] S Php 2:25 [n] S Rev 20:12
4:4 [o] Ps 85:6; 97:12; Hab 3:18; S Mt 5:12; Ro 12:12; Php 3:1
4:5 [p] Ps 119:151; 145:18; Heb 10:37; Jas 5:8,9
4:6 [q] Mt 6:25-34 [r] Eph 6:18; 1Ti 2:1
4:7 [s] Isa 26:3; S Jn 14:27 [t] Eph 3:19

Exhortations

2I plead with Euodia and I plead with
Syntyche to agree with each other[l] in the
Lord. 3Yes, and I ask you, loyal yokefellow,[a] help these women who have contended at my side in the cause of the gospel, along with Clement and the rest of my
fellow workers,[m] whose names are in the
book of life.[n]
4Rejoice in the Lord always. I will say
it again: Rejoice![o] 5Let your gentleness be
evident to all. The Lord is near.[p] 6Do not
be anxious about anything,[q] but in everything, by prayer and petition, with thanksgiving, present your requests to God.[r]
7And the peace of God,[s] which transcends
all understanding,[t] will guard your hearts
and your minds in Christ Jesus.
8Finally, brothers, whatever is true,

[a] 3 Or *loyal Syzygus*

3:16 *live up to what ... already attained.* Put into practice the truth they have already comprehended. We are responsible for the truth we currently possess.

3:17 *following my example.* As Paul follows the example of Christ (see 1Co 11:1 and note). *take note of those who live.* The lifestyles Christians lead ought to be models worth following.

3:18 *told you before.* See v. 1. *with tears.* Cf. Ac 20:19,31. *live as enemies of the cross.* In glaring contrast to Paul's conduct (v. 10) and to the truth of the gospel.

3:19 *destruction.* The opposite of salvation. *god ... stomach.* A deep self-centeredness; their appetites and desires come first (see Ro 16:18). *earthly things.* They have set their minds on the things of this life (see Col 3:1 – 2 and note on 3:1); they are antinomians (libertines), the opposite of the legalists of v. 2.

3:20 *citizenship.* In this world Christians are aliens, fully involved in it, yet not of it (cf. Jn 17:14 – 15 and notes; 1Co 7:29 – 31 and note on 7:29; 1Pe 2:11 and note). *in heaven.* Where Christ is (see Gal 4:26 and note); contrast the "earthly things" of v. 19 (cf. Eph 2:6; Col 3:1 – 4). *eagerly await ... from there.* See Ro 8:19; 1Co 1:7; 1Th 1:9 – 10; 2Ti 4:8.

3:21 *power ... under his control.* Christ's present power, earned by his obedience to death (see 2:8) and received in his resurrection and ascension, is universal and absolute (see Mt 28:18; 1Co 15:27; Eph 1:20 – 22). *will transform.* By the Holy Spirit at the resurrection (see Ro 8:11 and note). *our lowly bodies.* Subject to weakness, decay and death, due to sin (see Ro 8:10,20 – 23; 1Co 15:42 – 44 and note). *like his glorious body.* See Ro 8:29; 1Jn 3:2. The resurrection body, received already by Christ, who is the "firstfruits," will be received by believers in the future resurrection harvest (see 1Co 15:20,49). It is "spiritual" (1Co 15:44,46), i.e., transformed by the power of the Holy Spirit.

4:1 *love and long for.* See notes on 1:8; 2:1. *my joy and crown.* True not only now, but especially when Christ returns (see 1Th 2:19 and note). *that is how.* Refers to the closing statements of ch. 3. In the face of libertine practices (3:18 – 19), the Philippians should follow Paul's example (3:17), having their minds set on heavenly things (3:20 – 21). *stand firm.* In the midst of present struggles for the sake of the gospel (cf. 1:27 – 30; 1Co 15:58).

4:2 – 3 The disagreement between Euodia and Syntyche is serious enough to be mentioned in a letter to be read publicly, but Paul seems confident that "these women" (v. 3) will be reconciled. His handling of the situation is a model of tact — he does not take sides but encourages others closer to the situation to promote reconciliation (see 2:2 and note).

4:3 *yokefellow.* See NIV text note. *at my side ... my fellow workers.* Those associated with the apostle in the cause of the gospel (women as well as men) are his equals, not subordinates (cf. 2:25; Ro 16:3,9,21; Phm 24). *Clement.* Not mentioned elsewhere in the NT. *the rest of my fellow workers.* Not mentioned individually because they are known to God and their names are entered in the book of life, the heavenly register of the elect (see note on Rev 3:5).

4:4 *Rejoice in the Lord.* See 3:1. *always.* Under all kinds of circumstances, including suffering (see Hab 3:17 – 18 and note; Jas 1:2; 1Pe 4:13).

4:5 *gentleness.* Christlike consideration for others (cf. 2Co 10:1). It is especially essential in church leaders (see 1Ti 3:3; Tit 3:2, "considerate"). *near.* See Ro 13:11 and note; cf. Jas 5:8 – 9 and note on 5:9; Rev 22:7,12,20. The next great event in God's prophetic schedule is Christ's return. The whole period from Christ's first coming to the consummation of the kingdom is viewed in the NT as the last time (see 1Jn 2:18 and note). From God's vantage point, "a thousand years are like a day" (2Pe 3:8; see note there). Thus there is a sense in which, for every generation, the Lord's coming is near.

4:6 *anxious.* Self-centered, counterproductive worry, not legitimate cares and concerns for the spread of the gospel (see 2:28 and note; 2Co 11:28; see also Mt 6:25 – 31; 1Pe 5:7). *in everything, by prayer.* Anxiety and prayer are two great opposing forces in Christian experience. *thanksgiving.* The antidote to worry (along with prayer and petition).

4:7 *peace of God.* Not merely a psychological state of mind, but an inner tranquillity based on peace with God — the peaceful state of those whose sins are forgiven (cf. Jn 14:27; Ro 5:1 and note). The opposite of anxiety, it is the tranquillity that comes when believers commit all their cares to God in prayer and worry about them no more. *transcends all understanding.* The full dimensions of God's love and care are beyond human comprehension (see Eph 3:18 – 20). *guard ... hearts ... minds.* A military concept depicting a sentry standing guard. God's protective custody of those who are in Christ Jesus extends to the core of their beings and to their deepest intentions (cf. 1Pe 1:5 and note).

4:8 *Finally.* See note on 3:1. *true ... praiseworthy.* Paul understood the influence of one's thoughts on one's

whatever is noble, whatever is right, whatever is pure, whatever is lovely, whatever
is admirable — if anything is excellent or
praiseworthy — think about such things.
[9]Whatever you have learned or received
or heard from me, or seen in me — put it
into practice.[u] And the God of peace[v] will
be with you.

Thanks for Their Gifts

[10]I rejoice greatly in the Lord that at last
you have renewed your concern for me.[w]
Indeed, you have been concerned, but
you had no opportunity to show it. [11]I am
not saying this because I am in need, for I
have learned to be content[x] whatever the
circumstances. [12]I know what it is to be in
need, and I know what it is to have plenty.
I have learned the secret of being content
in any and every situation, whether well
fed or hungry,[y] whether living in plenty
or in want.[z] [13]I can do everything through
him who gives me strength.[a]

[14]Yet it was good of you to share[b] in my
troubles. [15]Moreover, as you Philippians
know, in the early days[c] of your acquaintance with the gospel, when I set out from
Macedonia,[d] not one church shared with
me in the matter of giving and receiving,
except you only;[e] [16]for even when I was in
Thessalonica,[f] you sent me aid again and
again when I was in need.[g] [17]Not that I
am looking for a gift, but I am looking for
what may be credited to your account.[h] [18]I
have received full payment and even more;
I am amply supplied, now that I have received from Epaphroditus[i] the gifts you
sent. They are a fragrant[j] offering, an acceptable sacrifice, pleasing to God. [19]And
my God will meet all your needs[k] according to his glorious riches[l] in Christ Jesus.

[20]To our God and Father[m] be glory for
ever and ever. Amen.[n]

Final Greetings

[21]Greet all the saints in Christ Jesus. The
brothers who are with me[o] send greetings.
[22]All the saints[p] send you greetings, especially those who belong to Caesar's household.

[23]The grace of the Lord Jesus Christ[q] be
with your spirit.[r] Amen.[a]

[a] 23 Some manuscripts do not have *Amen*.

4:9 [u] S 1Co 4:16 [v] S Ro 15:33
4:10 [w] 2Co 11:9
4:11 [x] 1Ti 6:6,8; Heb 13:5
4:12 [y] S 1Co 4:11 [z] 2Co 11:9
4:13 [a] 2Co 12:9; Eph 3:16; Col 1:11; 1Ti 1:12; 2Ti 4:17
4:14 [b] Php 1:7
4:15 [c] Php 1:5 [d] S Ac 16:9 [e] 2Co 11:8,9
4:16 [f] S Ac 17:1 [g] 1Th 2:9
4:17 [h] 1Co 9:11,12
4:18 [i] Php 2:25 [j] S 2Co 2:14
4:19 [k] Ps 23:1; 2Co 9:8 [l] S Ro 2:4
4:20 [m] Gal 1:4; 1Th 1:3; 3:11,13 [n] S Ro 11:36
4:21 [o] Gal 1:2
4:22 [p] S Ac 9:13
4:23 [q] S Ro 16:20 [r] S Gal 6:18

life. What people allow to occupy their minds will sooner or later determine their speech and action. Paul's exhortation to "think about such things" is followed by a second exhortation, "put it into practice" (v. 9). The combination of virtues listed in vv. 8 – 9 is sure to produce wholesome thought patterns, which in turn will result in a life of moral and spiritual excellence (see note on Gal 5:22 – 23).

4:9 *seen in me.* See note on 3:17. *God of peace.* See note on 1Th 5:23; cf. the "peace of God" (v. 7).

4:10 *at last ... no opportunity.* The delay in sending gifts to Paul was not the fault of the Philippians, nor was it because they were lacking in concern for him (cf. 2Co 11:9). Perhaps Paul's uncertain itinerary prior to his arrival at Rome or the lack of an available messenger had prevented the Philippians from showing their concern.

4:11 *content whatever the circumstances.* Paul genuinely appreciates the gifts from Philippi (see vv. 14,18) but he is not ultimately dependent on them (cf. 1Ti 6:6 – 8).

4:12 *content ... whether well fed ... whether living in plenty.* Prosperity, too, can be a source of discontent.

4:13 *everything.* All those circumstances that Paul has just spoken of in vv. 11 – 12. *him who gives me strength.* Christ. Union with the living, exalted Christ is the secret of being content (v. 12) and the source of Paul's abiding strength (see especially 2Co 12:9 – 10; see also Jn 15:5; Eph 3:16 – 17; Col 1:11).

4:14 *share.* The Philippians' gifts are a means of involving them in Paul's troubles (cf. Heb 10:33).

4:15 *early days.* During Paul's second missionary journey, when he first preached in Philippi (see Ac 16:12 – 40). *set out.* For the south (Achaia), where Athens and Corinth were located (see Ac 17:14 – 16; 18:1 – 4). *Macedonia.* The northern part of modern-day Greece, where Berea and Thessalonica, as well as Philippi, were located (see map, p. 1711). *shared with me in the matter of.* Or "participated with me in an account of." Paul uses commercial language to describe "giving and receiving" (credit and debit) between the Philippians and himself (see "credited to your account," v. 17). Yet this commercial imagery is plainly transcended by the mutual concern and self-sacrifice of their relationship. *except you only.* The generosity of the Philippian church is unique and unmatched (cf. 2Co 8:1 – 5).

4:16 *when I was in Thessalonica.* While he was still in Macedonia (see Ac 17:1 – 9). *aid again and again.* The gifts sent to Rome through Epaphroditus are the latest in a long and consistent pattern of generosity (cf. 2Co 8:1 – 5).

4:17 *credited to your account.* See note on v. 15. The investment value of the Philippians' gift is not primarily what Paul received, but the spiritual dividends they received.

4:18 *a fragrant offering, an acceptable sacrifice.* The OT background is the sacrifice, not of atonement for sin, but of thanksgiving and praise (cf. Lev 7:12 – 15; Ro 12:1; Eph 5:2 and note; Heb 13:15 – 16 and note on 13:15). *acceptable ... pleasing to God.* Because of Christ's work for us (see 1Pe 2:5) and God's work in us (see Php 2:13).

4:19 *my.* A personal touch (cf. "my God" in 1:3). *will meet.* A promise given to a church that had sacrificially given to meet Paul's need. *your needs.* Paul is concerned not only about his own situation but also about that of the Philippians. *his glorious riches in Christ Jesus.* The true measure of God's blessings to the church (cf. Eph 1:18; 3:16 – 20).

4:20 Paul cannot hold back a doxology, especially as he considers the truth of v. 19.

4:21 – 22 Final greetings are a typical feature of Paul's letters (see, e.g., Ro 16:3 – 16,21 – 23; 1Co 16:19 – 20; 2Co 13:12 – 13; Col 4:10 – 12,14 – 15,18).

4:21 *saints.* See note on Ro 1:7. *brothers who are with me.* Paul's fellow workers at Rome, especially Timothy (see 1:1,14,16).

4:22 *Caesar's household.* Not necessarily blood relatives of the emperor, but those employed (slave or free) in or around the palace area (cf. "palace guard," 1:13).

4:23 A typical closing benediction of Paul. *grace.* See note on Ro 1:7. *be with your spirit.* See note on Gal 6:18.

Colossians

INTRODUCTION

Author, Date and Place of Writing

That Colossians is a genuine letter of Paul (1:1) is usually not disputed. In the early church, all who speak on the subject of authorship ascribe it to Paul. In the 19th century, however, some thought that the heresy refuted in ch. 2 was second-century Gnosticism. But a careful analysis of ch. 2 shows that the heresy referred to there is noticeably less developed than the Gnosticism of leading Gnostic teachers of the second and third centuries. Also, the seeds of what later became the full-blown Gnosticism of the second century were present in the first century and were already making inroads into the churches. Consequently, it is not necessary to date Colossians in the second century at a time too late for Paul to have written the letter.

Instead, it is to be dated during Paul's first imprisonment in Rome, where he spent at least two years under house arrest (see Ac 28:16–31). Some have argued that Paul wrote Colossians from Ephesus or Caesarea, but most of the evidence favors Rome as the place where he penned all the Prison Letters (Ephesians, Colossians, Philippians and Philemon). Colossians should be dated c. A.D. 60, in the same year as Ephesians and Philemon (see chart, p. 1697).

A Quick Look

Author:
The apostle Paul

Audience:
The believers at Colosse, a church perhaps planted by Paul's coworker

Date:
About A.D. 60

Theme:
Paul wries to demonstrate that Christ is supreme over every human philosophy and accomplishment.

Colosse: The Town and the Church

Several hundred years before Paul's day, Colosse had been a leading city in Asia Minor (present-day Turkey). It was located on the Lycus River and on the great east-west trade route leading from Ephesus on the Aegean Sea to the Euphrates River (see map, p. 1718). By the first century A.D. Colosse was diminished to a second-rate market town, which had been surpassed long before in power and importance by the neighboring towns of Laodicea and Hierapolis (see 4:13).

What gave Colosse NT importance, however, was the fact that, during Paul's three-year ministry in Ephesus, Epaphras had been converted and had carried the gospel to Colosse (cf. 1:7–8; Ac 19:10). The young church that resulted then became the target of heretical attack, which led to

Epaphras's visit to Paul in Rome and ultimately to the penning of the Colossian letter.

Perhaps as a result of the efforts of Epaphras or other converts of Paul, Christian churches had also been established in Laodicea and Hierapolis. Some of them were house churches (see 4:15; Phm 2). Most likely all of them were primarily Gentile.

The Colossian Heresy

Paul never explicitly describes the false teaching he opposes in the Colossian letter. The nature of the heresy (or heresies) must be inferred from statements he made in opposition to the false teachers. An analysis of his refutation suggests that such false teachings were diverse in nature. Some of the elements of its teachings were:

1. *Ceremonialism.* It held to strict rules about the kinds of food and drink that were permissible, about religious festivals (2:16–17) and about circumcision (2:11; 3:11).

2. *Asceticism.* "Do not handle! Do not taste! Do not touch!" (2:21; cf. 2:23).

3. *Angel worship.* See 2:18 and note.

4. *Failure to grasp the full significance of Christ.* This is implied in Paul's emphasis on the supremacy of Christ (1:15–20; 2:2–3,9).

5. *Secret knowledge.* The later Gnostics boasted of this (see 2:18 and Paul's emphasis in 2:2–3 on Christ, "in whom are hidden all the treasures of wisdom").

6. *Reliance on human wisdom and tradition.* See 2:4,8.

These elements seem to fall into two categories, Jewish and proto-Gnostic. It is likely, therefore, that the false teaching at Colosse was a mixture of an extreme form of Judaism and an early stage of Gnosticism (see Introduction to 1 John: Gnosticism; see also note on 2:23).

To refute the Colossian heresy, Paul exalts Christ as the very image of God the Creator, the head of the church, the first to be resurrected, the fullness of deity in bodily form, and the one who reconciles all things to God.

Purpose and Theme

Paul's purpose is to refute the Colossian heresy (or heresies). To accomplish this goal, he exalts Christ as the very image of God (1:15), the Creator (1:16), the preexistent sustainer of all things (1:17), the head of the church (1:18), the first to be resurrected (1:18), the fullness of deity in bodily form (1:19; 2:9) and the one who reconciles all through God (1:20–22). Thus Christ is completely adequate. We "have been given fullness in Christ" (2:10). At the same time, Paul exposes the Colossian view of Christ as altogether deficient. It was a hollow and deceptive philosophy (2:8), lacking any ability to overcome the old sinful nature (2:23).

The theme of Colossians is the complete adequacy of Christ as contrasted with the emptiness of mere human philosophy.

Outline

- I. Introduction (1:1–14)
  - A. Greetings (1:1–2)
  - B. Thanksgiving (1:3–8)
  - C. Prayer (1:9–14)
- II. The Supremacy of Christ (1:15–23)
- III. Paul's Labor for the Church (1:24—2:7)
  - A. His Ministry for the Sake of the Church (1:24–29)
  - B. His Concern for the Spiritual Welfare of His Readers (2:1–7)
- IV. Freedom from Human Regulations through Life with Christ (2:8–23)
  - A. Warning to Guard against the False Teachers (2:8–15)
  - B. Pleas to Reject the False Teachers (2:16–19)
  - C. An Analysis of the Heresy (2:20–23)

V. Rules for Holy Living (3:1 — 4:6)
   A. The Old Self and the New Self (3:1 – 17)
   B. Rules for Christian Households (3:18 — 4:1)
   C. Further Instructions (4:2 – 6)
VI. Final Greetings and Benediction (4:7 – 18)

1 Paul, an apostle[a] of Christ Jesus by the
will of God,[b] and Timothy[c] our brother,

2To the holy and faithful[a] brothers in
Christ at Colosse:

Grace[d] and peace to you from God our
Father.[b e]

Thanksgiving and Prayer

3We always thank God,[f] the Father of
our Lord Jesus Christ, when we pray for
you, 4because we have heard of your faith
in Christ Jesus and of the love[g] you have
for all the saints[h]— 5the faith and love
that spring from the hope[i] that is stored
up for you in heaven[j] and that you have
already heard about in the word of truth,[k]
the gospel 6that has come to you. All over
the world[l] this gospel is bearing fruit[m] and
growing, just as it has been doing among
you since the day you heard it and understood God's grace in all its truth. 7You
learned it from Epaphras,[n] our dear fellow servant, who is a faithful minister[o] of
Christ on our[c] behalf, 8and who also told
us of your love in the Spirit.[p]
9For this reason, since the day we heard
about you,[q] we have not stopped praying
for you[r] and asking God to fill you with the
knowledge of his will[s] through all spiritual wisdom and understanding.[t] 10And we
pray this in order that you may live a life
worthy[u] of the Lord and may please him[v]
in every way: bearing fruit in every good
work, growing in the knowledge of God,[w]
11being strengthened with all power[x] according to his glorious might so that you
may have great endurance and patience,[y]
and joyfully 12giving thanks to the Father,[z]
who has qualified you[d] to share in the inheritance[a] of the saints in the kingdom of
light.[b] 13For he has rescued us from the
dominion of darkness[c] and brought us
into the kingdom[d] of the Son he loves,[e]
14in whom we have redemption,[e f] the forgiveness of sins.[g]

The Supremacy of Christ

15He is the image[h] of the invisible God,[i]

1:1 [a] S 1Co 1:1 [b] S 2Co 1:1 [c] S Ac 16:1 1:2 [d] Col 4:18 [e] S Ro 1:7 1:3 [f] S Ro 1:8 1:4 [g] Gal 5:6 [h] S Ac 9:13; Eph 1:15; Phm 5 1:5 [i] ver 23; 1Th 5:8; Tit 1:2 [j] 1Pe 1:4 [k] S 2Ti 2:15 1:6 [l] ver 23; S Ro 10:18 [m] Jn 15:16 1:7 [n] Col 4:12; Phm 23 [o] Col 4:7 1:8 [p] Ro 15:30 1:9 [q] ver 4; Eph 1:15 [r] S Ro 1:10 [s] S Eph 5:17 [t] S Eph 1:17 1:10 [u] S Eph 4:1 [v] S 2Co 5:9 [w] ver 6 1:11 [x] S Php 4:13 [y] Eph 4:2 1:12 [z] Eph 5:20 [a] S Ac 20:32 [b] S Ac 26:18 1:13 [c] S Ac 26:18 [d] 2Pe 1:11 [e] Mt 3:17 1:14 [f] S Ro 3:24 [g] Eph 1:7 1:15 [h] S Jn 14:9 [i] S Jn 1:18; 1Ti 1:17; Heb 11:27

[a] 2 Or *believing* [b] 2 Some manuscripts *Father and the Lord Jesus Christ* [c] 7 Some manuscripts *your* [d] 12 Some manuscripts *us* [e] 14 A few late manuscripts *redemption through his blood*

1:1 *Paul.* It was customary to put the writer's name at the beginning of a letter. For more information on Paul see note on Ro 1:1. *apostle ... by the will of God.* See 1Co 1:1 and note. *Christ.* Paul is very Christ-centered, as seen by this short letter in which he uses the title "Christ" 29 times and the title "Lord" (alone) 9 times. *Timothy.* Paul also mentions Timothy in 2 Corinthians, Philippians, 1,2 Thessalonians and Philemon, but Paul is really the sole author, as seen by the constant use of the pronoun "I" (beginning in v. 23; see especially 4:18).

1:2 *holy.* Because of Christ's substitutionary death, the Colossian believers are declared holy in the sight of God, and because of the Holy Spirit's work, they are continuing to be made holy in their lives (see notes on Ro 1:7; 6:22; 1Co 1:2). *faithful.* See 1:7; 4:7,9. *brothers.* See note on Ro 1:13. *in Christ.* Paul mentions the spiritual union with Christ 12 times in Colossians (see note on Eph 1:1). *Grace and peace.* See note on Ro 1:7.

1:3 *We.* Paul and Timothy (v. 1). *thank God.* Every one of Paul's letters, except Galatians, begins with thanks or praise (see note on Php 1:3–4). In Colossians thanks is an important theme (see v. 12; 2:7; 3:15–17; 4:2). In the Bible humans are never thanked for their faith and love, but rather God, who is the source of these virtues.

1:4 *saints.* See note on Ro 1:7.

1:5 The three great Christian virtues of faith, love and hope appear also in Ro 5:2–5; 1Co 13:13; Gal 5:5–6; 1Th 1:3; 5:8; Heb 10:22–24. *hope.* Not wishful thinking but a firm assurance (see Ro 5:5 and note). For this unusual thought of faith and love coming from hope see Tit 1:2. *word of truth.* The "gospel" (see Eph 1:13; 2Ti 2:15).

1:6 *All over the world.* Hyperbole, to dramatize the rapid spread of the gospel into every quarter of the Roman empire within three decades of Pentecost (see v. 23; Ro 1:8 and note; 10:18; 16:19). In refutation of the charge of the false teachers, Paul insists that a believing response to the gospel is not a mere local or regional reality but is worldwide.

1:7 *Epaphras.* A native (4:12) and probably founder of the Colossian church, and an evangelist in nearby Laodicea and Hierapolis (4:13). Paul loved and admired him, calling him a "fellow prisoner" (Phm 23), his "dear fellow servant" and "a faithful minister of Christ." Epaphras was the one who told Paul at Rome about the Colossian church problem and thereby stimulated him to write this letter (vv. 4,8). His name, a shortened form of Epaphroditus (from "Aphrodite," the Greek goddess of love), suggests that he was a convert from paganism. He is not the Epaphroditus of Php 2:25; 4:18.

1:8 *your love in the Spirit.* The Holy Spirit is the source of all Christian love (see Ro 5:5; Gal 5:22–23 and notes).

1:9 *knowledge of his will.* Biblical "knowledge" is not merely the possession of facts. Rather, knowledge and wisdom in the Bible are practical, having to do with godly living. This is borne out by vv. 10–12, where knowledge, wisdom and understanding result in a life worthy of the Lord.

1:10 *live a life.* This phrase (lit. "walk") is linked to 2:7; 3:7; 4:5 ("act") by the same Greek verb, which thus appears as a connecting motif in all four chapters of the letter. *bearing fruit ... growing.* Cf. v. 6.

1:12 *inheritance.* See 1Pe 1:4 and note. *light.* Often symbolizes holiness (see 1Jn 1:5 and note), truth (Ps 119:105,130; 2Co 4:6), glory (Isa 60:1–3; 1Ti 6:16) or life (Jn 1:4). Accordingly, God (1Jn 1:5), Christ (Jn 8:12) and the Christian (Eph 5:8) are characterized by light. The "kingdom of light" is the opposite of the "dominion of darkness" (v. 13). See also note on Ps 27:1.

1:13 *kingdom.* Does not here refer to a territory but to the authority, rule or sovereign power of a king. Here it means that the Christian is no longer under the dominion of evil (darkness) but under the benevolent rule of God's Son.

1:14 *redemption.* Deliverance and freedom from the penalty of sin by the payment of a ransom—the substitutionary death (see notes on Ge 22:13; Lev 16:20–22) of Christ (see Ro 3:24 and note).

1:15–20 Perhaps an early Christian hymn (see note on 3:16) on the supremacy of Christ—used here by Paul to counteract the false teaching at Colosse. It is divided into two parts: (1) Christ's supremacy in creation (vv. 15–17); (2) Christ's supremacy in redemption (vv. 18–20).

the firstborn[j] over all creation. 16For by
him all things were created:[k] things in
heaven and on earth, visible and invisible,
whether thrones or powers or rulers or authorities;[l] all things were created by him
and for him.[m] 17He is before all things,[n]
and in him all things hold together. 18And
he is the head[o] of the body, the church;[p]
he is the beginning and the firstborn[q] from
among the dead,[r] so that in everything he
might have the supremacy. 19For God was
pleased[s] to have all his fullness[t] dwell in
him, 20and through him to reconcile[u] to
himself all things, whether things on earth
or things in heaven,[v] by making peace[w]
through his blood,[x] shed on the cross.

21Once you were alienated from God and
were enemies[y] in your minds[z] because of[a]
your evil behavior. 22But now he has reconciled[a] you by Christ's physical body[b]
through death to present you[c] holy in his
sight, without blemish and free from accusation[d]— 23if you continue[e] in your faith,
established[f] and firm, not moved from the
hope[g] held out in the gospel. This is the
gospel that you heard and that has been
proclaimed to every creature under heav-
en,[h] and of which I, Paul, have become a
servant.[i]

Paul's Labor for the Church

24Now I rejoice[j] in what was suffered for
you, and I fill up in my flesh what is still
lacking in regard to Christ's afflictions,[k] for
the sake of his body, which is the church.[l]
25I have become its servant[m] by the commission God gave me[n] to present to you
the word of God[o] in its fullness— 26the
mystery[p] that has been kept hidden for
ages and generations, but is now disclosed
to the saints. 27To them God has chosen
to make known[q] among the Gentiles the
glorious riches[r] of this mystery, which is
Christ in you,[s] the hope of glory.

28We proclaim him, admonishing[t] and
teaching everyone with all wisdom,[u] so

[a] 21 Or *minds, as shown by*

1:15 [j]S ver 18 **1:16** [k]S Jn 1:3 [l]Eph 1:20,21 [m]S Ro 11:36 **1:17** [n]S Jn 1:2 **1:18** [o]S Eph 1:22 [p]ver 24; S 1Co 12:27 [q]ver 15; Ps 89:27; Ro 8:29; Heb 1:6 [r]Ac 26:23; Rev 1:5 **1:19** [s]S Eph 1:5 [t]S Jn 1:16 **1:20** [u]S Ro 5:10 [v]Eph 1:10 [w]S Lk 2:14 [x]Eph 2:13 **1:21** [y]Ro 5:10 [z]Eph 2:3 **1:22** [a]ver 20; S Ro 5:10 [b]Ro 7:4 [c]S 2Co 4:14 [d]Eph 1:4; 5:27 **1:23** [e]S Ro 11:22 [f]Eph 3:17 [g]ver 5 [h]ver 6; S Ro 10:18 [i]ver 25; S 1Co 3:5 **1:24** [j]S 2Co 6:10 [k]S 2Co 1:5 [l]S 1Co 12:27 **1:25** [m]ver 23; S 1Co 3:5 [n]Eph 3:2 [o]S Heb 4:12 **1:26** [p]S Ro 16:25 **1:27** [q]S Mt 13:11 [r]S Ro 2:4 [s]S Ro 8:10 **1:28** [t]Col 3:16 [u]1Co 2:6,7

1:15 *image.* Christ is called the "image of ... God" here and in 2Co 4:4 (see note there). In Heb 1:3 he is described as "the radiance of God's glory and the exact representation of his being." This figure of the image suggests two truths: (1) God is invisible ("No one has ever seen God," Jn 1:18); (2) Christ, who is the eternal Son of God and who became the God-man, reflects and reveals him (see also Jn 1:18; 14:9). *firstborn over all creation.* Just as the firstborn son had certain privileges and rights in the Biblical world, so also Christ has certain rights in relation to all creation—priority, preeminence and sovereignty (vv. 16–18).

1:16 *by him all things were created.* See Jn 1:3. Seven times in vv. 15–20 Paul mentions "all creation," "all things" and "everything," thus stressing that Christ is supreme over all. *thrones or powers or rulers or authorities.* Angels. An angelic hierarchy figured prominently in the Colossian heresy (see Introduction: The Colossian Heresy).

1:17 *He is before all things.* Referring to time, as in Jn 1:1–2; 8:58.

1:18 *head.* Christ is supreme in the church as the one on whom it is dependent (see notes on 1Co 11:3; Eph 1:22). *beginning.* Of the new creation. *firstborn.* Christ was the first to rise from the dead with a resurrection body. Elsewhere Paul calls him the "firstfruits of those who have fallen asleep" (1Co 15:20). Others who were raised from the dead (2Ki 4:35; Lk 7:15; Jn 11:44; Ac 9:36–41; 20:7–12) were raised only to die again.

1:19 *fullness.* Part of the technical vocabulary of some Gnostic philosophies. In these systems it meant the sum of the supernatural forces controlling the fate of people. For Paul "fullness" meant the totality of God with all his powers and attributes (see 2:9 and note).

1:20 *reconcile to himself all things.* Does not mean that Christ by his death has saved all people. Scripture speaks of an eternal hell and makes clear that only believers are saved. When Adam and Eve sinned, not only was the harmony between God and human beings destroyed, but also disorder came into creation (Ro 8:19–22). So when Christ died on the cross, he made peace possible between God and humans, and he restored in principle the harmony in the physical world, though the full realization of the latter will come only when Christ returns (see Ro 8:21 and note).

1:22 *death.* Christ's death.

1:23 *every creature.* See note on v. 6.

1:24 *what was suffered.* By Paul. During his mission to the Gentiles, he experienced all kinds of affliction (see 2Co 11:23–27), but here he was probably referring especially to his imprisonment. *fill up ... what is still lacking.* Does not mean that there was a deficiency in the atoning sacrifice of Christ. Rather, it means that Paul suffered afflictions because he was preaching the good news of Christ's atonement. Christ suffered on the cross to atone for sin, and Paul filled up Christ's afflictions by experiencing the added sufferings necessary to carry this good news to a lost world.

1:25 *commission.* The task with which he was entrusted (see 1Co 9:17). *to present ... the word of God in its fullness.* The meaning seems to be that the word of God is brought to completion, i.e., to its intended purpose, only when it is proclaimed (cf. Isa 55:11). Paul's commission to bring the word to completion, therefore, required him to make the word of God heard in Colosse as well as elsewhere. See Ro 15:19 for a similar statement.

1:26 *mystery.* The purpose of God, unknown to humans except by revelation. This word was a popular, pagan religious term, used in the mystery religions to refer to secret information available only to an exclusive group of people. Paul changes that meaning radically by always combining it with words such as "disclosed" (here), "made known" (Eph 1:9), "make plain" (Eph 3:9) and "revelation" (Ro 16:25; see note there). The Christian mystery is not secret knowledge for a few. It is a revelation of divine truths—once hidden but now openly proclaimed.

1:27 *Gentiles ... Christ in you.* The mystery is the fact that Christ indwells Gentiles, for it had not been previously revealed that the Gentiles would be admitted to the church on equal terms with Israel (see note on Eph 3:6). *glory.* The glorious future prepared by God for his people (see 3:4; Ro 5:2 and note; 8:17–18; 1Co 2:7 and note; 15:42–44 and note; 2Co 4:17 and note; 1Th 2:12; 2Th 2:14; 2Ti 2:10; Heb 2:10; 1Pe 5:1 and note, 4).

1:28 *perfect.* Or "fully mature"; employed by the mystery religions and the Gnostics to describe those who had become possessors of the secrets or knowledge boasted of by the particular religion (see Introduction to 1 John: Gnosticism). But in Christ every believer is one of the "perfect" (or mature).

that we may present everyone perfect[v] in
Christ. 29To this end I labor,[w] struggling[x]
with all his energy, which so powerfully
works in me.[y]

2 I want you to know how much I am
struggling[z] for you and for those at
Laodicea,[a] and for all who have not met
me personally. 2My purpose is that they
may be encouraged in heart[b] and united in love, so that they may have the
full riches of complete understanding,
in order that they may know the mystery[c] of God, namely, Christ, 3in whom
are hidden all the treasures of wisdom
and knowledge.[d] 4I tell you this so that
no one may deceive you by fine-sounding arguments.[e] 5For though I am absent
from you in body, I am present with you
in spirit[f] and delight to see how orderly[g] you are and how firm[h] your faith in
Christ[i] is.

Freedom From Human Regulations Through Life With Christ

6So then, just as you received Christ
Jesus as Lord,[j] continue to live in him,
7rooted[k] and built up in him, strengthened
in the faith as you were taught,[l] and overflowing with thankfulness.
8See to it that no one takes you captive
through hollow and deceptive philosophy,[m] which depends on human tradition
and the basic principles of this world[n]
rather than on Christ.
9For in Christ all the fullness[o] of the Deity lives in bodily form, 10and you have
been given fullness in Christ, who is the
head[p] over every power and authority.[q]
11In him you were also circumcised,[r] in
the putting off of the sinful nature,[a][s] not
with a circumcision done by the hands of
men but with the circumcision done by
Christ, 12having been buried with him in
baptism[t] and raised with him[u] through
your faith in the power of God, who raised
him from the dead.[v]
13When you were dead in your sins[w]
and in the uncircumcision of your sinful nature,[b] God made you[c] alive[x] with
Christ. He forgave us all our sins,[y] 14hav-
ing canceled the written code, with its
regulations,[z] that was against us and that
stood opposed to us; he took it away, nailing it to the cross.[a] 15And having disarmed
the powers and authorities,[b] he made a
public spectacle of them, triumphing over
them[c] by the cross.[d]
16Therefore do not let anyone judge you[d]
by what you eat or drink,[e] or with regard
to a religious festival,[f] a New Moon cele-

[a] *11* Or *the flesh* [b] *13* Or *your flesh* [c] *13* Some manuscripts *us* [d] *15* Or *them in him*

1:28 [v] Mt 5:48; Eph 5:27 **1:29** [w] 1Co 15:10; 2Co 11:23 [x] Col 2:1 [y] Eph 1:19; 3:7 **2:1** [z] Col 1:29; 4:12 [a] Col 4:13,15,16; Rev 1:11; 3:14 **2:2** [b] Eph 6:22; Col 4:8 [c] S Ro 16:25 **2:3** [d] Isa 11:2; Jer 23:5; Ro 11:33; 1Co 1:24,30 **2:4** [e] S Ro 16:18 **2:5** [f] 1Co 5:4; 1Th 2:17 [g] 1Co 14:40 [h] 1Pe 5:9 [i] S Ac 20:21 **2:6** [j] S Jn 13:13; Col 1:10 **2:7** [k] Eph 3:17 [l] Eph 4:21 **2:8** [m] 1Ti 6:20 [n] ver 20; Gal 4:3 **2:9** [o] S Jn 1:16 **2:10** [p] S Eph 1:22 [q] S Mt 28:18 **2:11** [r] Ro 2:29; Php 3:3 [s] S Gal 5:24 **2:12** [t] S Mt 28:19 [u] S Ro 6:5 [v] S Ac 2:24 **2:13** [w] Eph 2:1,5 [x] Eph 2:5 [y] Eph 4:32 **2:14** [z] Eph 2:15 [a] 1Pe 2:24 **2:15** [b] ver 10; Eph 6:12 [c] Mt 12:29; Lk 10:18; Jn 12:31 **2:16** [d] Ro 14:3,4 [e] Mk 7:19; Ro 14:17 [f] Lev 23:2; Ro 14:5

1:29 An example of the combination of human effort and divine help (see Php 2:12–13).

2:1 *I am struggling.* Probably a reference to Paul's prayers and inner conflicts and concerns for the Colossians. *Laodicea.* This letter was to be read to the church there too (4:16). Laodicea (near modern Denizli) was only about 11 miles northwest of Colosse (see map 3, p. 1702).

2:2 *mystery.* See notes on 1:26; Ro 11:25.

2:3 *knowledge.* Paul stressed "understanding" and "knowledge" in this letter (v. 2; 1:9–10) because he was refuting a heresy that emphasized knowledge as the means of salvation (see Introduction to 1 John: Gnosticism). Paul insisted that the Christian, not the Gnostic, possessed genuine knowledge and understanding.

2:5 *absent ... in body, ... present ... in spirit.* Cf. 1Co 5:3.

2:6–7 Cf. Eph 3:16–19.

2:6 *live in him.* The believer's intimate, spiritual, living union with Christ is mentioned repeatedly in this letter (see, e.g., vv. 7,10–13,20; 1:2,27–28; 3:1,3). *live.* Lit. "walk" (see note on 1:10).

2:7 *overflowing with thankfulness.* See Eph 5:20 and note.

2:8 *basic principles of this world.* This term (which occurs also in v. 20; Gal 4:3,9) refers to false, worldly, religious, elementary teachings—or, as some believe, to elemental spiritual forces active in this present world. Paul was counteracting the Colossian heresy, which, in part, taught that for salvation one needed to combine faith in Christ with secret knowledge and with human regulations concerning such physical and external practices as circumcision, eating and drinking, and observance of religious festivals.

2:9 *fullness of the Deity.* See note on 1:19. The declaration that the very essence of deity was fully present in the human Jesus was a direct refutation of Gnostic teaching.

2:10–15 Here Paul declares that the Christian is complete in Christ, rather than being deficient as the Gnostics claimed. This completeness includes the putting off of the sinful nature (v. 11), resurrection from spiritual death (vv. 12–13), forgiveness of sins (v. 13) and deliverance from legalistic requirements (v. 14) as well as deliverance from evil spirit beings (v. 15).

2:10 *head.* Cf. 1:18 and note; see Eph 1:19–22 and notes.

2:11–12 *circumcision ... baptism.* In the OT, circumcision signified being consecrated (in covenant) to the service of God (see notes on Ge 17:10–12; Ro 2:25). Paul here declares that this consecration has now been fully accomplished by Christ, as signified in baptism (cf. Ac 2:38; Ro 6:3–4 and notes).

2:12 See Ro 6:3–4 and notes.

2:13 Cf. Eph 2:1–9 and notes.

2:14 *written code.* A business term, meaning a certificate of indebtedness in the debtor's handwriting. Paul uses it as a designation for the Mosaic law, with all its regulations, under which everyone is a debtor to God.

2:15 *having disarmed.* Not only did God cancel out the accusations of the law against the Christian, but he also conquered and disarmed the evil angels (powers and authorities, 1:16; Eph 6:12), who entice people to follow asceticism and false teachings about Christ. The picture is of conquered soldiers stripped of their clothes as well as their weapons to symbolize their total defeat. *triumphing over them.* Lit. "leading them in a triumphal procession." The metaphor recalls a Roman general leading his captives through the streets of his city for all the citizens to see as evidence of his complete victory (see 2Co 2:14 and note). That Christ triumphed over the devil and his cohorts is a pervasive NT theme.

2:16 Cf. Paul's exhortations to the Roman church (Ro 14:1—15:13).

bration[g] or a Sabbath day.[h] 17These are a shadow of the things that were to come;[i] the reality, however, is found in Christ. 18Do not let anyone who delights in false humility[j] and the worship of angels disqualify you for the prize.[k] Such a person goes into great detail about what he has seen, and his unspiritual mind puffs him up with idle notions. 19He has lost connection with the Head,[l] from whom the whole body,[m] supported and held together by its ligaments and sinews, grows as God causes it to grow.[n]

20Since you died with Christ[o] to the basic principles of this world,[p] why, as though you still belonged to it, do you submit to its rules:[q] 21"Do not handle! Do not taste! Do not touch!"? 22These are all destined to perish[r] with use, because they are based on human commands and teachings.[s] 23Such regulations indeed have an appearance of wisdom, with their self-imposed worship, their false humility[t] and their harsh treatment of the body, but they lack any value in restraining sensual indulgence.

Rules for Holy Living

3 Since, then, you have been raised with Christ,[u] set your hearts on things above, where Christ is seated at the right hand of God.[v] 2Set your minds on things above, not on earthly things.[w] 3For you died,[x] and your life is now hidden with Christ in God. 4When Christ, who is your[a] life,[y] appears,[z] then you also will appear with him in glory.[a]

5Put to death,[b] therefore, whatever belongs to your earthly nature:[c] sexual immorality,[d] impurity, lust, evil desires and greed,[e] which is idolatry.[f] 6Because of these, the wrath of God[g] is coming.[b] 7You used to walk in these ways, in the life you once lived.[h] 8But now you must rid yourselves[i] of all such things as these: anger, rage, malice, slander,[j] and filthy language from your lips.[k] 9Do not lie to each other,[l] since you have taken off your old self[m] with its practices 10and have put on the new self,[n] which is being renewed[o] in knowledge in the image of its Creator.[p] 11Here there is no Greek or Jew,[q] circumcised or uncircumcised,[r] barbarian, Scythian, slave or free,[s] but Christ is all,[t] and is in all.

[a] 4 Some manuscripts *our* [b] 6 Some early manuscripts *coming on those who are disobedient*

2:16 [g] 1Ch 23:31 [h] Mk 2:27,28; Gal 4:10
2:17 [i] Heb 8:5; 10:1
2:18 [j] ver 23 [k] 1Co 9:24; Php 3:14
2:19 [l] S Eph 1:22 [m] S 1Co 12:27 [n] Eph 4:16
2:20 [o] S Ro 6:6 [p] ver 8; Gal 4:3, 9 [q] ver 14, 16
2:22 [r] 1Co 6:13 [s] Isa 29:13; Mt 15:9; Tit 1:14
2:23 [t] ver 18
3:1 [u] S Ro 6:5 [v] S Mk 16:19
3:2 [w] Php 3:19, 20
3:3 [x] S Ro 6:2; 2Co 5:14
3:4 [y] Gal 2:20 [z] 1Co 1:7 [a] 1Pe 1:13; 1Jn 3:2
3:5 [b] S Ro 6:2; S Eph 4:22 [c] S Gal 5:24 [d] S 1Co 6:18 [e] Eph 5:3 [f] Gal 5:19-21; Eph 5:5
3:6 [g] S Ro 1:18
3:7 [h] S Eph 2:2
3:8 [i] S Eph 4:22 [j] Eph 4:31 [k] Eph 4:29
3:9 [l] S Eph 4:22, 25 [m] S Ro 6:6 **3:10** [n] S Ro 6:4; S 13:14 [o] Ro 12:2; S 2Co 4:16; Eph 4:23 [p] Eph 2:10 **3:11** [q] Ro 10:12; 1Co 12:13 [r] S 1Co 7:19 [s] Gal 3:28 [t] Eph 1:23

2:17 *shadow . . . reality.* The ceremonial laws of the OT are here referred to as shadows (cf. Heb 8:5; 10:1) because they symbolically depicted the coming of Christ; so any insistence on the observance of such ceremonies is a failure to recognize that their fulfillment has already taken place. This element of the Colossian heresy was combined with a rigid asceticism, as vv. 20 – 21 reveal.

2:18 *false humility.* Humility in which one delights is of necessity mock humility. Paul may be referring to a professed humility in view of the absolute God, who was believed to be so far above humans that he could only be worshiped indirectly through the worship of the angels he had created. Second-century Gnosticism conceived of a list of spirit beings who had emanated from God and through whom God may be approached. *disqualify.* This term pictures an umpire or referee who excludes from competition any athlete who fails to follow the rules. The Colossians were not to permit any false teacher to deny the reality of their salvation because they were not delighting in their "false humility" and in the worship of angelic beings. *what he has seen.* Probably refers to professed visions by the false teachers.

2:19 *lost connection with the Head.* The central error of the Colossian heresy is a defective view of Christ, in which he is believed to be less than deity (see v. 9; 1:19).

2:20 *basic principles.* See note on v. 8.

2:21 *Do not handle . . . taste . . . touch!* The strict ascetic nature of the heresy is seen here. These prohibitions seem to carry OT ceremonial laws to the extreme.

2:23 A rather detailed analysis of the Colossian heresy: (1) It appeared to set forth an impressive system of religious philosophy. (2) It was, however, a system created by the false teachers themselves ("self-imposed"), rather than being of divine origin. (3) The false teachers attempted to parade their humility. (4) This may have been done by a harsh asceticism that brutally misused the body. Paul's analysis is that such practices are worthless because they totally fail to control sinful desires. *self-imposed worship.* The false teachers themselves had created the regulations of their heretical system. They were not from God.

3:1 *then.* "Then" (or "therefore") links the doctrinal section of the letter with the practical section, just as it does in Ro 12:1; Eph 4:1; Php 4:1. *you have been raised.* Verses 1 – 10 set forth what has been described as the indicative and the imperative of the Christian. The indicative statements describe believers in Christ: They have "died" (v. 3); they have been raised with Christ (v. 1); they are with Christ in heaven ("hidden with Christ," v. 3); they have "taken off the old self" (v. 9); and they have "put on the new self" (v. 10). The imperative statements indicate what believers are to do as a result: set their hearts (or minds) on things above (vv. 1 – 2); put to death practices that belong to their earthly nature (v. 5); and rid themselves of practices that characterized the unregenerate self (v. 8). In summary, they are called upon to become in daily experience what they are in Christ (cf. Ro 6:1 – 13).

3:4 *appears.* Refers to Christ's second coming (see 1Jn 3:2).

3:5,8 See note on Ro 1:29 – 31.

3:6 *wrath of God.* See notes on Zec 1:2; Ro 1:18. God is unalterably opposed to sin and will invariably make sure that it is justly punished.

3:7 *walk.* See note on 1:10.

3:9 – 10 *taken off . . . put on.* As one takes off dirty clothes and puts on clean ones, so Christians are called upon to renounce their evil ways and live in accordance with the rules of Christ's kingdom (see vv. 12 – 14; cf. Ro 13:12; Gal 3:27; Eph 4:22 – 24).

3:10 *renewed.* See 2 Co 5:17. *knowledge.* See 1:10; 2:2 – 3 and note on 2:3. *image of its Creator.* See note on Ge 1:26.

3:11 *barbarian.* Someone who did not speak Greek and was therefore thought to be uncivilized. *Scythian.* Scythians were known especially for their brutality and were considered by others as little better than wild beasts. They came originally from what is today south Russia. *Christ is all, and is in all.* Christ transcends all barriers and unifies

12Therefore, as God's chosen people,
holy and dearly loved, clothe yourselves[u]
with compassion, kindness, humility,[v]
gentleness and patience.[w] 13Bear with each
other[x] and forgive whatever grievances
you may have against one another. Forgive as the Lord forgave you.[y] 14And over
all these virtues put on love,[z] which binds
them all together in perfect unity.[a]
15Let the peace of Christ[b] rule in your
hearts, since as members of one body[c] you
were called to peace.[d] And be thankful.
16Let the word of Christ[e] dwell in you richly as you teach and admonish one another
with all wisdom,[f] and as you sing psalms,[g]
hymns and spiritual songs with gratitude
in your hearts to God.[h] 17And whatever
you do,[i] whether in word or deed, do it
all in the name of the Lord Jesus, giving
thanks[j] to God the Father through him.

Rules for Christian Households

3:18–4:1pp — Eph 5:22–6:9

18Wives, submit to your husbands,[k] as is
fitting in the Lord.
19Husbands, love your wives and do not
be harsh with them.
20Children, obey your parents in everything, for this pleases the Lord.
21Fathers, do not embitter your children,
or they will become discouraged.
22Slaves, obey your earthly masters in
everything; and do it, not only when their
eye is on you and to win their favor, but
with sincerity of heart and reverence for
the Lord. 23Whatever you do, work at it
with all your heart, as working for the
Lord, not for men, 24since you know that
you will receive an inheritance[l] from the
Lord as a reward.[m] It is the Lord Christ you
are serving. 25Anyone who does wrong
will be repaid for his wrong, and there is
no favoritism.[n]

4 Masters, provide your slaves with what
is right and fair,[o] because you know
that you also have a Master in heaven.

Further Instructions

2Devote yourselves to prayer,[p] being
watchful and thankful. 3And pray for
us, too, that God may open a door[q] for
our message, so that we may proclaim
the mystery[r] of Christ, for which I am in
chains.[s] 4Pray that I may proclaim it clearly, as I should. 5Be wise[t] in the way you
act toward outsiders;[u] make the most of
every opportunity.[v] 6Let your conversation
be always full of grace,[w] seasoned with
salt,[x] so that you may know how to answer everyone.[y]

Final Greetings

7Tychicus[z] will tell you all the news
about me. He is a dear brother, a faithful
minister and fellow servant[a] in the Lord.
8I am sending him to you for the express
purpose that you may know about our[a]
circumstances and that he may encourage

3:12 [u]ver 10 [v]Php 2:3 [w]2Co 6:6; Gal 5:22,23; Eph 4:2 **3:13** [x]Eph 4:2 [y]Eph 4:32 **3:14** [z]1Co 13:1-13 [a]S Ro 15:5 **3:15** [b]S Jn 14:27 [c]S Ro 12:5 [d]S Ro 14:19 **3:16** [e]Ro 10:17 [f]Col 1:28 [g]Ps 47:7 [h]S Eph 5:19 **3:17** [i]1Co 10:31 [j]S Eph 5:20 **3:18** [k]S Eph 5:22 **3:24** [l]S Ac 20:32 [m]S Mt 16:27 **3:25** [n]S Ac 10:34 **4:1** [o]Lev 25:43,53 **4:2** [p]S Lk 18:1 **4:3** [q]S Ac 14:27 [r]S Ro 16:25 [s]S Ac 21:33 **4:5** [t]Eph 5:15 [u]S Mk 4:11 [v]Eph 5:16 **4:6** [w]Eph 4:29 [x]Mk 9:50 [y]1Pe 3:15 **4:7** [z]S Ac 20:4 [a]Eph 6:21,22; Col 1:7

[a] 8 Some manuscripts *that he may know about your*

people from all cultures, races and nations. Such distinctions are no longer significant. Christ alone matters (see Gal 3:28 and note).

3:12 *God's chosen people.* Israel was called this (Dt 4:37), and so is the Christian community (1Pe 2:9; see note there). Divine election is a constant theme in Paul's letters (see note on Eph 1:4), but the Bible never teaches that it dulls human responsibility. On the contrary, as this verse shows, it is precisely because Christians have been "chosen" for eternal salvation that they must put forth every effort to live the godly life. For Paul, divine sovereignty and human responsibility go hand in hand. *clothe ... with.* See note on Ps 109:29).

3:14 See 1Co 13:13 and note.

3:15 *peace of Christ.* The attitude of peace that Christ alone gives — in place of the attitude of bitterness and quarrelsomeness. This attitude is to "rule" (lit. "function as an umpire") in all human relationships (cf. Mt 10:34 and note). *be thankful.* See Eph 5:20 and note.

3:16 *word of Christ.* Refers especially to Christ's teaching, which in the time of the Colossians was transmitted orally. But by implication it includes the OT as well as the NT. *psalms, hymns and spiritual songs.* Some of the most important doctrines were expressed in Christian hymns preserved for us now only in Paul's letters (1:15–20; Eph 5:14; Php 2:6–11; 1Ti 3:16). "Psalms" refers to the OT psalms (see Lk 20:42; 24:44; Ac 1:20; 13:33), some of which may have been set to music by the church. "Psalm" could also describe a song newly composed for Christian worship (cf. 1Co 14:26, where "hymn" is lit. "psalm" in the Greek text). A "hymn" was a song of praise, especially used in a celebration (see Mt 26:30 and note; Heb 2:12), much like the OT psalms that praise God for all that he is and does in the present (see Ps 150:2 and note). A "song" recounted the acts of God and praised him for them (see Rev 5:9 and note; 15:3), much like the OT psalms that thanked God for all that he had done in the past. See Eph 5:19 and note.

3:18—4:1 See Eph 5:22—6:9 and notes.

3:20 *in everything.* In everything not sinful (see Ac 5:29).

3:22—4:1 Paul neither condones slavery nor sanctions revolt against masters. Rather, he calls on both slaves and masters to show Christian principles in their relationship and thus to attempt to change the institution from within. The reason Paul writes more about slaves and masters than about wives, husbands, children and fathers may be that the slave Onesimus (4:9) is going along with Tychicus (4:7) to deliver this Colossian letter and the letter to Philemon, Onesimus's master, who also lived in Colosse.

3:24 *inheritance.* See Heb 9:15; 1Pe 1:4 and notes.

3:25 *no favoritism.* See Ac 10:34 and note.

4:2 *Devote yourselves to prayer.* See notes on Lk 11:1; Ac 2:42; Ro 12:12; 1Th 5:17. *being watchful.* Being spiritually alert. *being ... thankful.* See Eph 5:20 and note.

4:3 *mystery.* See notes on 1:26–27; Ro 11:25.

4:5 *act.* Lit. "walk" in the sense of "live" (see note on 1:10). *outsiders.* Non-Christians (see 1Co 5:12–13; 1Th 4:12; 1Ti 3:7). *make the most of every opportunity.* See Eph 5:16 and note.

4:6 *seasoned with salt.* Salt is a preservative and is tasty (see Mt 5:13 and note). Similarly, the Christian's conversation is to be wholesome and helpful (see 3:8; Eph 4:29).

4:7 *Tychicus.* See note on Eph 6:21.

your hearts.[b] 9He is coming with Onesimus,[c] our faithful and dear brother, who is
one of you.[d] They will tell you everything
that is happening here.
10My fellow prisoner Aristarchus[e] sends
you his greetings, as does Mark,[f] the
cousin of Barnabas.[g] (You have received
instructions about him; if he comes to
you, welcome him.) 11Jesus, who is called
Justus, also sends greetings. These are the
only Jews among my fellow workers[h] for
the kingdom of God, and they have proved
a comfort to me. 12Epaphras,[i] who is one
of you[j] and a servant of Christ Jesus, sends
greetings. He is always wrestling in prayer
for you,[k] that you may stand firm in all the
will of God, mature[l] and fully assured. 13I
vouch for him that he is working hard for
you and for those at Laodicea[m] and Hierapolis. 14Our dear friend Luke,[n] the doctor, and Demas[o] send greetings. 15Give my
greetings to the brothers at Laodicea,[p] and
to Nympha and the church in her house.[q]
16After this letter has been read to you,
see that it is also read[r] in the church of the
Laodiceans and that you in turn read the
letter from Laodicea.
17Tell Archippus:[s] "See to it that you
complete the work you have received in
the Lord."[t]
18I, Paul, write this greeting in my own
hand.[u] Remember[v] my chains.[w] Grace be
with you.[x]

4:8 [b]Eph 6:21, 22; Col 2:2 **4:9** [c]Phm 10 [d]ver 12 **4:10** [e]S Ac 19:29 [f]S Ac 12:12 [g]S Ac 4:36 **4:11** [h]S Php 2:25 **4:12** [i]Col 1:7; Phm 23 [j]ver 9 [k]S Ro 15:30 [l]S 1Co 2:6 **4:13** [m]S Col 2:1 **4:14** [n]2Ti 4:11; Phm 24 [o]2Ti 4:10; Phm 24 **4:15** [p]S Col 2:1 [q]S Ro 16:5 **4:16** [r]2Th 3:14; S 1Ti 4:13 **4:17** [s]Phm 2 [t]2Ti 4:5

4:18 [u]S 1Co 16:21 [v]Heb 13:3 [w]S Ac 21:33 [x]1Ti 6:21; 2Ti 4:22; Tit 3:15; Heb 13:25

4:9–17 Onesimus (v. 9), Aristarchus (v. 10), Mark (v. 10), Epaphras (v. 12), Luke (v. 14), Demas (v. 14) and Archippus (v. 17) are mentioned in Philemon. This suggests that the letters to Colosse and Philemon were written at the same time and place.
4:9 *Onesimus.* See Introduction to Philemon: Recipient, Background and Purpose.
4:10 *Aristarchus.* A Macedonian, who is mentioned three times in Acts: (1) He was with Paul during the Ephesian riot (Ac 19:29) and therefore was known in Colosse. (2) Both he and Tychicus (Ac 20:4) were with Paul in Greece. (3) He accompanied Paul on his trip to Rome (Ac 27:2). *Mark.* The author of the second Gospel. Against Barnabas's advice, Paul refused to take Mark on the second missionary journey because Mark had "deserted" him in Pamphylia (see Ac 15:38 and note). But now—about 12 years later—the difficulties seem to have been ironed out, because Paul, both here and in Phm 24 (sent at the same time to Philemon, who was in Colosse), sends Mark's greetings. About five years later, Paul even writes that Mark "is helpful to me in my ministry" (2Ti 4:11). See note on Ac 15:39.
4:13 *Hierapolis.* A town in Asia Minor (present-day Turkey), about 6 miles from Laodicea (see map, p. 1967) and 14 miles from Colosse. Its church may have been founded during Paul's three-year stay in Ephesus (Ac 19), but probably not by Paul himself (cf. 2:1).
4:14 *Luke.* Wrote about Paul in the book of Acts, having often accompanied him on his travels (see note on Ac 16:10). He was with Paul in Rome during his imprisonment (Ac 28), where this letter was written. *Demas.* A Christian worker who would later desert Paul (2Ti 4:10).
4:15 *church in her house.* For the most part, the early church had no buildings, so it usually met for worship and instruction in homes. It often centered around one family, as, e.g., Priscilla and Aquila (Ro 16:5; 1Co 16:19), Philemon (Phm 2) and Mary the mother of John Mark (Ac 12:12).
4:16 *After this letter has been read to you.* The practice of the early church was to read Paul's letters aloud to the assembled congregation. *letter from Laodicea.* Probably not a letter by the Laodiceans. Rather, it was likely one that the Laodiceans were to lend to the Colossians—a letter that Paul had originally written to the Laodiceans. This may have been a fourth letter that Tychicus carried to this area in what is present-day Turkey, in addition to Ephesians, Colossians and Philemon. Or it could have been Paul's letter to the Ephesians—a circular letter making the rounds from Ephesus to Laodicea to Colosse (see Introduction to Ephesians: Author, Date and Place of Writing).
4:17 *Archippus.* Phm 2 calls him Paul's "fellow soldier."
4:18 Paul's custom was to dictate his letters (see Ro 16:22) and pen a few greetings himself (1Co 16:21; Gal 6:11; 2Th 3:17; Phm 19). His personal signature was the guarantee of the genuineness of the letter. *Grace.* See note on Ro 1:7. *with you.* See note on 2Co 13:14.

1 Thessalonians

INTRODUCTION

Background of the Thessalonian Letters

It is helpful to trace the locations of Paul and his companions that relate to the Thessalonian correspondence. The travels were as follows:

1. Paul, Silas and Timothy founded the church in Thessalonica on Paul's second missionary journey (see map, p. 1711).

2. When persecution broke out, Paul and Silas fled from Thessalonica to Berea. Since Timothy is not mentioned (see Ac 17:10 and note), it is possible that he stayed in Thessalonica or went back to Philippi and then rejoined Paul and Silas in Berea (Ac 17:14).

3. Paul fled to Athens from Berean persecution, leaving Silas and Timothy in Berea (see Ac 17:14).

4. Paul sent word back, instructing Silas and Timothy to come to him in Athens (see Ac 17:15; see also note on 1Th 3:1 – 2).

5. Timothy rejoined Paul at Athens and was sent back to Thessalonica (see 3:1 – 5). Since Silas is not mentioned, it has been conjectured that he went back to Philippi when Timothy went to Thessalonica (see note on 3:1 – 2).

6. Paul moved on to Corinth (see Ac 18:1).

7. Silas and Timothy came to Paul in Corinth (see 3:6; Ac 18:5).

8. Paul wrote 1 Thessalonians and sent it to the church.

9. Some time later (A.D. 51/52) he sent 2 Thessalonians in response to further information about the church there.

A Quick Look

Author:
The apostle Paul

Audience:
The largely Gentile church in Thessalonica, founded by Paul

Date:
About A.D. 51

Theme:
Paul praises the Thessalonian believers for their spiritual maturity and perseverance, and encourages them to further growth in view of Christ's imminent return.

Author, Date and Place of Writing

Both external and internal evidence (see 1:1; 2:18) support the view that Paul wrote 1 Thessalonians (from Corinth; see note on 3:1 – 2). Early church writers are agreed on the matter, with testimonies beginning as early as A.D. 140 (Marcion). Paul's known characteristics are apparent in the letter (3:1 – 2,8 – 11 compared with Ac 15:36; 2Co 11:28). Historical allusions in the book fit Paul's life as recounted in Acts and in his own letters (2:14 – 16 compared with Ac 17:5 – 10; 3:6 compared with Ac 17:16). In the face of such evidence, few have ever rejected authorship by Paul.

It is generally dated c. A.D. 51 (see chart, p. 1697). Weighty support for this date was found in an inscription discovered at Delphi, Greece (see map No. 13 at the end of this study Bible), that dates Gallio's proconsulship to c. 51 – 52 and thus places Paul at Corinth at the same time (see Ac 18:12 – 17 and note on 18:12; see also chart, p. 1667). Except for the possibility of an early date for Galatians (48 – 49?), 1 Thessalonians is Paul's earliest letter to be preserved in the canon of accepted Scripture.

Paul writes to encourage the new converts in their trials and to give assurance concerning the future of believers who die before Christ returns.

Thessalonica: The City and the Church

Thessalonica was a bustling seaport city at the head of the Thermaic Gulf (see map, p. 1711). It was an important communication and trade center, located at the junction of the great Egnatian Way and the road leading north to the Danube. It was the largest city in Macedonia and was also the capital of its province.

The background of the Thessalonian church is found in Ac 17:1 – 9. Since Paul began his ministry there in the Jewish synagogue, it is reasonable to assume that the new church included some Jews. However, 1:9 – 10; Ac 17:4 seem to indicate that the church was largely Gentile in membership.

Purpose

Paul had left Thessalonica abruptly (see Ac 17:5 – 10) after a rather brief stay. Recent converts from paganism (1:9) were thus left with little external support in the midst of persecution. Paul's purpose in writing this letter was to encourage the new converts in their trials (3:3 – 5), to give instruction concerning godly living (4:1 – 12) and to give assurance concerning the future of believers who die before Christ returns (4:13 – 18; see Theme below; see also notes on 4:13,15).

Themes

The central theme of the letter is Paul's encouragement for the church at Thessalonica, which is thriving despite persecution. A strong secondary theme in both Thessalonian letters, however, is eschatology (doctrine of last things). Every chapter of 1 Thessalonians ends with a reference to the second coming of Christ, with ch. 4 giving it major consideration (1:9 – 10; 2:19 – 20; 3:13; 4:13 – 18; 5:23 – 24). Thus the second coming permeates Thessalonians, and the two letters are often designated as the eschatological letters of Paul.

Outline

- I. Thanksgiving for the Thessalonians (ch. 1)
  - A. Grounds for the Thanksgiving (1:1 – 4)
  - B. Genuineness of the Grounds (1:5 – 10)
- II. Defense of the Apostolic Actions and Absence (chs. 2 – 3)
  - A. Defense of the Apostolic Actions (2:1 – 16)
  - B. Defense of the Apostolic Absence (2:17 — 3:10)
  - C. A Prayer (3:11 – 13)
- III. Exhortations to the Thessalonians (4:1 — 5:22)
  - A. Primarily concerning Personal Life (4:1 – 12)
  - B. Concerning the Coming of Christ (4:13 — 5:11)
  - C. Primarily concerning Church Life (5:12 – 22)
- IV. Concluding Prayer, Greetings and Benediction (5:23 – 28)

1 Paul, Silas[a a] and Timothy,[b]

To the church of the Thessalonians[c] in
God the Father and the Lord Jesus Christ:

Grace and peace to you.[b d]

Thanksgiving for the Thessalonians' Faith

2 We always thank God for all of you,[e]
mentioning you in our prayers.[f] 3 We continually remember before our God and Father[g] your work produced by faith,[h] your
labor prompted by love,[i] and your endurance inspired by hope[j] in our Lord Jesus
Christ.

4 For we know, brothers loved by God,[k]
that he has chosen you, 5 because our gospel[l] came to you not simply with words,
but also with power,[m] with the Holy Spirit
and with deep conviction. You know[n] how
we lived among you for your sake. 6 You
became imitators of us[o] and of the Lord; in
spite of severe suffering,[p] you welcomed
the message with the joy[q] given by the Holy
Spirit.[r] 7 And so you became a model[s] to
all the believers in Macedonia[t] and Achaia.[u] 8 The Lord's message[v] rang out from
you not only in Macedonia and Achaia—
your faith in God has become known everywhere.[w] Therefore we do not need to
say anything about it, 9 for they themselves
report what kind of reception you gave us.
They tell how you turned[x] to God from
idols[y] to serve the living and true God,[z]
10 and to wait for his Son from heaven,[a]
whom he raised from the dead[b]—Jesus,
who rescues us from the coming wrath.[c]

Paul's Ministry in Thessalonica

2 You know, brothers, that our visit to
you[d] was not a failure.[e] 2 We had previously suffered[f] and been insulted in Philippi,[g] as you know, but with the help of
our God we dared to tell you his gospel
in spite of strong opposition.[h] 3 For the appeal we make does not spring from error
or impure motives,[i] nor are we trying to
trick you.[j] 4 On the contrary, we speak as
men approved by God to be entrusted with
the gospel.[k] We are not trying to please

[a] 1 Greek *Silvanus,* a variant of *Silas* [b] 1 Some early manuscripts *you from God our Father and the Lord Jesus Christ*

1:1 [a] S Ac 15:22 [b] S Ac 16:1; 2Th 1:1 [c] S Ac 17:1 [d] S Ro 1:7 **1:2** [e] S Ro 1:8; Eph 5:20 [f] S Ro 1:10 **1:3** [g] S Php 4:20 [h] Gal 5:6; 2Th 1:11; Jas 2:14-26 [i] 1Th 3:6; 2Th 1:3; S 1Co 13:13 [j] Ro 8:25 **1:4** [k] Col 3:12; 2Th 2:13 **1:5** [l] S 2Co 2:12; 2Th 2:14 [m] Ro 1:16; S Ro 15:13 [n] 1Th 2:10 **1:6** [o] S 1Co 4:16 [p] Ac 17:5-10 [q] S 2Co 6:10 [r] Ac 13:52 **1:7** [s] S 1Ti 4:12 [t] S Ac 16:9 [u] S Ac 18:12 **1:8** [v] 2Th 3:1 [w] Ro 1:8 **1:9** [x] Ac 14:15 [y] 1Co 12:2; Gal 4:8 [z] S Mt 16:16 **1:10** [a] S 1Co 1:7 [b] S Ac 2:24 [c] S Ro 1:18 **2:1** [d] 1Th 1:5,9 [e] 2Th 1:10 **2:2** [f] Ac 14:19; 16:22; Php 1:30 [g] S Ac 16:12 [h] Ac 17:1-9 **2:3** [i] 2Co 2:17 [j] 2Co 4:2 **2:4** [k] Gal 2:7; 1Ti 1:11

1:1 *Paul.* See note on Ro 1:1. *Silas.* See note on Ac 15:22. He accompanied Paul on most of his second missionary journey. *Timothy.* See Introduction to 1 Timothy: Recipient. Both he and Silas helped Paul found the Thessalonian church (see Ac 17:1–14). *in.* Indicates the vital union and living relationship that Christians have with the Father and the Son (see Jn 14:23; 17:21). The close connection between the Father and the Son points to the Trinitarian relationship (see 3:11; 2Th 1:2,8,12; 2:16; 3:5). *Lord Jesus Christ.* Occurs also at the end of this letter (5:28). For the meanings of "Lord," "Jesus" and "Christ" see NIV text notes on Mt 1:17,21; see also notes on Lk 2:11; Ro 10:9; 1Co 12:3; Php 2:9–11. *Grace and peace.* See note on Ro 1:7.

1:2 *thank.* See note on Php 1:3–4.

1:3 The triad of faith, hope and love is found often in the NT (5:8; Ro 5:2–5; 1Co 13:13; Gal 5:5–6; Col 1:4–5; Heb 6:10–12; 10:22–24; 1Pe 1:3–8,21–22). *work produced by faith.* Faith produces action (see Ro 1:5; 16:26; Gal 5:6 and note; 2Th 1:11; Jas 2:14–26). *hope.* Not unfounded wishful thinking, but firm confidence in our Lord Jesus Christ and his return (v. 10). See Heb 6:18–20 and notes on Ro 5:5; Col 1:5.

1:4 *know.* The reasons for Paul's conviction regarding their election are stated in vv. 5–10. *brothers.* United to each other through union with Christ (see note on Ro 1:13). This term (including its singular form) is used 28 times in the two letters to the Thessalonians. *loved ... chosen.* Both words speak of God's electing love (see Col 3:12 and note; 2Th 2:13; see also note on Eph 1:4).

1:5 *our gospel.* The gospel preached by Paul, Silas and Timothy (see Ro 16:25 and note). It is first of all God the Father's (2:8) because he originated it, and Christ's (3:2) because it springs from his atoning death. *power.* The power that delivered them from spiritual bondage. That power comes from the Holy Spirit (see Ro 15:13,18–19; 1Co 2:4–5), but it also resides in the gospel itself (see Ro 1:16). *deep conviction.* Such conviction, on the part of both the preachers and the Thessalonians, also came from the Holy Spirit.

1:6 *imitators.* The order in Christian imitation: (1) Believers in Macedonia and Achaia imitated the Thessalonians (v. 7), just as the Thessalonians imitated the churches in Judea (2:14); (2) the Thessalonians imitated Paul, just as the Corinthians did (1Co 4:6; 11:1) and just as all believers were to imitate their leaders (2Th 3:7,9; 1Ti 4:12; Tit 2:7; 1Pe 5:3); (3) Paul imitated Christ (1Co 11:1) as did the Thessalonians (here); (4) all were to imitate God (Eph 5:1). *severe suffering.* Such as recorded in Ac 17:5–14 (see also 1Th 2:14).

1:7 *Macedonia and Achaia.* The two Roman provinces into which Greece was then divided (see Ac 19:21; Ro 15:26; see also map, p. 1873). *Macedonia.* See note on Php 4:15.

1:8 *everywhere.* In every place they visited or knew about (see Ro 1:8 and note; 1Co 1:2; 2Co 2:14; 1Ti 2:8). The news spread because of Thessalonica's strategic location (see Introduction: Thessalonica: The City and the Church).

1:9–10 Three marks of true conversion: (1) turning from idols, (2) serving God and (3) waiting for Christ to return. In his two short letters to the Thessalonians, Paul speaks much about the second coming of Christ (v. 10; 2:19; 3:13; 4:13—5:4; 2Th 1:7–10; 2:1–12).

1:10 *wrath.* See note on Ro 1:18. Some see a reference here to the final judgment (see 2:16; Ro 2:5 and notes), while others think it refers to a future period of tribulation (described, it is thought, in Rev 6–18; 1Th 5:9; Rev 6:16).

2:1–12 A manual for a minister: (1) His message is God's good news ("gospel," v. 2). (2) His motive is not impurity (v. 3), pleasing people (v. 4), greed (v. 5) or seeking praise from people (v. 6), but pleasing God (v. 4). (3) His manner is not one of trickery (v. 3), flattery (v. 5) or a cover-up (v. 5), but of courage (v. 2), gentleness (v. 7), love (vv. 8,11), toil (v. 9) and holiness (v. 10).

2:1 *You know.* The local church could refute the accusation of insincerity that evidently had been leveled against Paul (v. 3).

2:2 *insulted.* Paul was deeply hurt by the way he had been treated in the city of Philippi (see Ac 16:19–40).

2:3 *trick.* The Greek for this word was originally used of a lure for catching fish; it came to be used of any sort of cunning used for profit.

2:4 *our hearts.* Not simply our emotions, but also our intellects and wills (see note on Ps 4:7).

men[l] but God, who tests our hearts.[m] 5You
know we never used flattery, nor did we
put on a mask to cover up greed[n]—God
is our witness.[o] 6We were not looking for
praise from men,[p] not from you or anyone else.
As apostles[q] of Christ we could have
been a burden to you,[r] 7but we were gentle among you, like a mother caring for
her little children.[s] 8We loved you so much
that we were delighted to share with you
not only the gospel of God[t] but our lives
as well,[u] because you had become so dear
to us. 9Surely you remember, brothers, our
toil and hardship; we worked[v] night and
day in order not to be a burden to anyone[w] while we preached the gospel of God
to you.
10You are witnesses,[x] and so is God,[y] of
how holy,[z] righteous and blameless we
were among you who believed. 11For you
know that we dealt with each of you as a
father deals with his own children,[a] 12en-
couraging, comforting and urging you to
live lives worthy[b] of God, who calls[c] you
into his kingdom and glory.
13And we also thank God continually[d]
because, when you received the word of
God,[e] which you heard from us, you accepted it not as the word of men, but as it
actually is, the word of God, which is at
work in you who believe. 14For you, brothers, became imitators[f] of God's churches
in Judea,[g] which are in Christ Jesus: You
suffered from your own countrymen[h] the
same things those churches suffered from
the Jews, 15who killed the Lord Jesus[i] and
the prophets[j] and also drove us out. They
displease God and are hostile to all men
16in their effort to keep us from speaking
to the Gentiles[k] so that they may be saved.
In this way they always heap up their sins
to the limit.[l] The wrath of God has come
upon them at last.[a]

2:4 [l] S Ro 2:29 [m] S Rev 2:23 **2:5** [n] S Ac 20:33 [o] ver 10; S Ro 1:9 **2:6** [p] Jn 5:41,44 [q] 1Co 9:1,2 [r] 2Co 11:7-11 **2:7** [s] S ver 11 **2:8** [t] S Ro 1:1 [u] 2Co 12:15; 1Jn 3:16 **2:9** [v] S Ac 18:3 [w] S 2Co 11:9; 2Th 3:8 **2:10** [x] 1Th 1:5 [y] ver 5; S Ro 1:9 [z] 2Co 1:12 **2:11** [a] ver 7; 1Co 4:14; Gal 4:19; S 1Ti 1:2; Phm 10; S 1Jn 2:1 **2:12** [b] S Eph 4:1 [c] S Ro 8:28 **2:13** [d] 1Th 1:2; S Ro 1:8 [e] S Heb 4:12 **2:14** [f] 1Th 1:6 [g] Gal 1:22 [h] Ac 17:5; 2Th 1:4 **2:15** [i] Lk 24:20; Ac 2:23 [j] S Mt 5:12 **2:16** [k] Ac 13:45,50; 17:5; S 20:3; 21:27; 24:9 [l] Mt 23:32 **2:17** [m] 1Co 5:3; Col 2:5 [n] 1Th 3:10 **2:18** [o] S Mt 4:10 [p] Ro 1:13; 15:22 **2:19** [q] Isa 62:3; Php 4:1 [r] 2Co 1:14 [s] S Mt 16:27; S Lk 17:30; S 1Co 1:7; 4:5; 1Th 3:13; 2Th 1:8-10; 1Pe 1:7; 1Jn 2:28; S Rev 1:7 **2:20** [t] 2Co 1:14 **3:1** [u] ver 5 [v] S Ac 17:15 **3:2** [w] S Ac 16:1 [x] S 1Co 3:9 [y] S 2Co 2:12

Paul's Longing to See the Thessalonians

17But, brothers, when we were torn
away from you for a short time (in person, not in thought),[m] out of our intense
longing we made every effort to see you.[n]
18For we wanted to come to you—certainly I, Paul, did, again and again—but Satan[o] stopped us.[p] 19For what is our hope,
our joy, or the crown[q] in which we will
glory[r] in the presence of our Lord Jesus
when he comes?[s] Is it not you? 20Indeed,
you are our glory[t] and joy.

3 So when we could stand it no longer,[u] we thought it best to be left by
ourselves in Athens.[v] 2We sent Timothy,[w]
who is our brother and God's fellow worker[b][x] in spreading the gospel of Christ,[y] to
strengthen and encourage you in your

[a] 16 Or *them fully* [b] 2 Some manuscripts *brother and fellow worker*; other manuscripts *brother and God's servant*

2:5 *mask to cover up greed.* Personal profit was never Paul's aim (see Ac 20:33).

2:6 *apostles.* See note on Mk 6:30. *burden.* Apostles were entitled to be supported by the church (see 1Co 9:3–14; 2Co 11:7–11). Paul did not always take advantage of the right, but insisted that he had it.

2:7 *like a mother.* See v. 11, where Paul also applies the metaphor of a father to himself.

2:9 *toil and hardship.* Greeks despised manual labor and viewed it as fit only for slaves, but Paul was not ashamed of doing any sort of work that would help further the gospel. He did not want to be unduly dependent on others (see 2Th 3:8).

2:11 *as a father.* See note on v. 7.

2:12 *live lives worthy of God.* See Eph 4:1. *calls.* See notes on 1:4; Ro 8:28. *kingdom.* The chief subject of Jesus' teaching. Paul did not use this term often, but used it once to sum up the message of his preaching (see notes on Mt 3:2; Lk 4:43; Ac 20:25; cf. Ac 28:31). *glory.* God's splendor and majesty revealed to us at the consummation of his kingdom (see Mk 8:38; Ro 5:2; 8:18; cf. Eze 43:2 and note; 1Jn 3:2).

2:13 *not as the word of men.* Not tailored to fit the popular knowledge of the day.

2:14 *imitators.* See note on 1:6. *You suffered from your own countrymen.* At the time of Paul's initial visit to Thessalonica, persecution instigated by the Jews apparently was carried out by Gentiles (see Ac 17:5–9). *Jews.* Although Paul had great love and deep concern for the salvation of those of his own race (see Ro 9:1–3; 10:1), he did not fail to rebuke harshly Jews who persecuted the church.

2:15 *prophets.* Throughout OT history, Israelites had persecuted their prophets (cf. Ac 7:52). *drove us out.* See Ac 9:23–25,29–30; 13:50–51; 14:5–6,19; 17:10,13–14.

2:16 *wrath of God has come.* The eschatological wrath, the final outpouring of God's anger upon sinful humanity (see 1:10 and note). It is spoken of as already present, either because it had been partially experienced by the Jews or because of its absolute certainty.

2:17 *torn away.* Lit. "orphaned." Paul is like a mother (v. 7), a father (v. 11) and now an orphan.

2:18 *Satan stopped us.* Cf. Introduction to Job: Theme and Message; cf. also note on Eph 1:3.

2:19 *crown.* Not a royal crown, but a wreath used on festive occasions or as the prize in the Greek games (see 2Ti 4:8 and note; Jas 1:12; 1Pe 5:4; Rev 2:10 and note). *when he comes.* See 3:13; 4:15; 5:23; 2Th 2:1,8. The expression was used regarding the arrival of a great person, as on a royal visit.

2:20 *you are our glory and joy.* True both now (cf. Php 4:1) and when Christ returns.

3:1–2 Paul first went to Athens alone, then sent to Berea for Silas and Timothy (Ac 17:14–15). It is not clear whether Silas, as instructed (Ac 17:15), came to Athens with Timothy. However, when Timothy later returned from Thessalonica to Paul, who was now at Corinth, Silas came with him (Ac 18:5). See Introduction: Background of the Thessalonian Letters.

3:1 *we.* An editorial "we," referring to Paul alone.

3:2 *God's fellow worker.* A striking way of viewing Christian service, found also in 1Co 3:9. *gospel of Christ.* See notes on 1:5; Mk 1:1. *strengthen.* In Greek classical literature the word was generally used in the literal sense of putting a buttress on a building. In the NT it is mainly used figuratively, as here.

faith, 3so that no one would be unsettled by these trials.[z] You know quite well
that we were destined for them.[a] 4In fact,
when we were with you, we kept telling
you that we would be persecuted. And it
turned out that way, as you well know.[b]
5For this reason, when I could stand it
no longer,[c] I sent to find out about your
faith.[d] I was afraid that in some way the
tempter[e] might have tempted you and our
efforts might have been useless.[f]

Timothy's Encouraging Report

6But Timothy[g] has just now come to
us from you[h] and has brought good news
about your faith and love.[i] He has told us
that you always have pleasant memories
of us and that you long to see us, just as
we also long to see you.[j] 7Therefore, brothers, in all our distress and persecution we
were encouraged about you because of
your faith. 8For now we really live, since
you are standing firm[k] in the Lord. 9How
can we thank God enough for you[l] in return for all the joy we have in the presence
of our God because of you?[m] 10Night and
day we pray[n] most earnestly that we may
see you again[o] and supply what is lacking
in your faith.
11Now may our God and Father[p] himself
and our Lord Jesus clear the way for us to
come to you. 12May the Lord make your
love increase and overflow for each other[q]
and for everyone else, just as ours does
for you. 13May he strengthen your hearts
so that you will be blameless[r] and holy in
the presence of our God and Father[s] when
our Lord Jesus comes[t] with all his holy
ones.[u]

3:3 [z]Mk 4:17; Jn 16:33; Ro 5:3; 2Co 1:4; 4:17; 2Ti 3:12 [a]S Ac 9:16; 14:22 **3:4** [b]1Th 2:14 **3:5** [c]ver 1 [d]ver 2 [e]Mt 4:3 [f]Gal 2:2; Php 2:16 **3:6** [g]S Ac 16:1 [h]Ac 18:5 [i]1Th 1:3 [j]1Th 2:17, 18 **3:8** [k]S 1Co 16:13 **3:9** [l]1Th 1:2 [m]1Th 2:19, 20 **3:10** [n]2Ti 1:3 [o]1Th 2:17 **3:11** [p]ver 13; S Php 4:20 **3:12** [q]Php 1:9; 1Th 4:9, 10; 2Th 1:3 **3:13** [r]Ps 15:2; 1Co 1:8; Php 2:15; 1Th 5:23; 1Ti 6:14; 2Pe 3:14 [s]ver 11; S Php 4:20 [t]S 1Th 2:19 [u]Mt 25:31; 2Th 1:7 **4:1** [v]2Co 13:11; 2Th 3:1 [w]S Eph 4:1 [x]S 2Co 5:9 **4:3** [y]S Eph 5:17 [z]S 1Co 6:18 **4:4** [a]1Co 7:2, 9 **4:5** [b]Ro 1:26 [c]Eph 4:17 [d]S Gal 4:8

Living to Please God

4 Finally, brothers,[v] we instructed you
how to live[w] in order to please God,[x]
as in fact you are living. Now we ask you
and urge you in the Lord Jesus to do this
more and more. 2For you know what instructions we gave you by the authority of
the Lord Jesus.
3It is God's will[y] that you should be
sanctified: that you should avoid sexual immorality;[z] 4that each of you should
learn to control his own body[a][a] in a way
that is holy and honorable, 5not in passionate lust[b] like the heathen,[c] who do
not know God;[d] 6and that in this matter
no one should wrong his brother or take
advantage of him.[e] The Lord will punish
men[f] for all such sins,[g] as we have already

[a] 4 Or *learn to live with his own wife*; or *learn to acquire a wife*

4:6 [e]Lev 25:17; 1Co 6:8 [f]Dt 32:35; Ps 94:1; Ro 2:5-11; 12:19; Heb 10:30, 31 [g]Heb 13:4

3:3 *trials.* The opposition and persecution suffered by the Thessalonian converts. *we were destined for them.* Christians must expect troubles (see Mk 4:17; Jn 16:33; Ac 14:22; Php 1:29; 2Ti 3:12; cf. 1Pe 2:21 and note), but these are not disasters, for they advance God's purposes (see Ac 11:19; Ro 5:3; 2Co 1:4; 4:17 and note).

3:5 *I.* Paul uses the Greek emphatic pronoun (elsewhere used only in 2:18) to bring out his deep concern. *tempter.* Satan is spoken of in every major division of the NT. He is supreme among evil spirits (see Jn 12:31; 16:11; Eph 2:2). His activities can affect the physical (see 2Co 12:7) and the spiritual (see Mt 13:39; Mk 4:15; 2Co 4:4 and note). He tempted Jesus (Mt 4:1–11), and he continues to tempt Jesus' servants (see Lk 22:3; 1Co 7:5). He hinders missionary work (2:18). But he has already been defeated (see Mt 12:29; Col 2:15 and note), and Christians need not be overwhelmed by him (see Eph 6:16). His final overthrow is certain (see Rev 20:10).

3:6 *brought good news.* The only place where the Greek for this phrase is used by Paul for anything other than the gospel. Three things caused him joy: (1) "your faith"—a right attitude toward God; (2) "your ... love"—a right attitude toward others; (3) "you long to see us"—a right attitude toward Paul.

3:9 *thank God.* The preceding shows that Paul's work of evangelism had been effective. He might have congratulated himself on work well done, but instead he thanked God for the joy he had from what God had done.

3:10 *Night and day.* Not prayer at two set times, but frequent prayer (see 1:2–3). *most earnestly.* Translates a strong and unusual Greek compound word (found elsewhere in the NT only in 5:13; Eph 3:20) that brings out Paul's passionate longing. *what is lacking.* Some of the things lacking were of a practical nature, such as moral (4:1–12) and disciplinary matters (5:12–24). Others were doctrinal, such as confusion over Christ's return (4:13—5:11). *your faith.* The fifth time in the chapter that Paul speaks of their faith (see vv. 2,5–7).

3:11 In the middle of a letter Paul frequently breaks into prayer (e.g., Eph 1:15–23; 3:14–21; Php 1:9–11; Col 1:9–12). For the link between Father and Son see note on 1:1.

3:12 *Lord.* In Paul's writings this usually means Jesus rather than the Father.

3:13 *strengthen.* See note on v. 2. *holy.* The basic idea is "set apart [for God]" (see notes on Ex 3:5; Lev 11:44; Ro 6:22; Eph 1:1). Here it refers to the completed process of sanctification (see note on 1Co 1:2). *holy ones.* Used of the saints (Christians) in many NT passages (see note on Ro 1:7). Here it may mean the departed saints who will return with Jesus, or it may mean the angels (see Mk 8:38) or, probably, both.

4:1 *Finally.* The main section of the letter is finished, though much is yet to come (see Php 3:1 and note). *live.* Lit. "walk." Paul uses this metaphor often of the Christian way (see Ro 6:4; 2Co 5:7; Eph 4:1; 5:15; Col 1:10, "live a life"; 2:6; 4:5, "act"). It points to steady progress. *we ask you and urge you.* Paul is not arrogant, but he does speak with authority in the Lord Jesus. He has the "mind of Christ" (1Co 2:16).

4:2 *instructions.* Used of authoritative commands and has a military ring ("orders," Ac 5:28; 16:24).

4:3 *sanctified.* See note on 3:13. *sexual immorality.* In the first century moral standards were generally very low, and chastity was regarded as an unreasonable restriction. Paul, however, would not compromise God's clear and demanding standards. The warning was needed, for Christians were not immune to the temptation (see 1Co 5:1).

4:5 *like the heathen.* See Ro 1:24–27. The Christian is to be different. *who do not know God.* See 2Th 1:8 and note; Gal 4:8; cf. Ps 79:6–7 and note.

4:6 *wrong his brother.* Sexual sin harms others besides those who engage in it. In adultery, e.g., the spouse is

told you and warned you. 7For God did not call us to be impure, but to live a holy life.[h] 8Therefore, he who rejects this instruction does not reject man but God, who gives you his Holy Spirit.[i]

9Now about brotherly love[j] we do not need to write to you,[k] for you yourselves have been taught by God[l] to love each other.[m] 10And in fact, you do love all the brothers throughout Macedonia.[n] Yet we urge you, brothers, to do so more and more.[o]

11Make it your ambition to lead a quiet life, to mind your own business and to work with your hands,[p] just as we told you, 12so that your daily life may win the respect of outsiders[q] and so that you will not be dependent on anybody.

The Coming of the Lord

13Brothers, we do not want you to be ignorant[r] about those who fall asleep,[s] or to grieve like the rest of men, who have no hope.[t] 14We believe that Jesus died and rose again[u] and so we believe that God will bring with Jesus those who have fallen asleep in him.[v] 15According to the Lord's own word, we tell you that we who are still alive, who are left till the coming of the Lord,[w] will certainly not precede those who have fallen asleep.[x] 16For the Lord himself will come down from heaven,[y] with a loud command, with the voice of the archangel[z] and with the trumpet call of God,[a] and the dead in Christ will rise first.[b] 17After that, we who are still alive and are left[c] will be caught up together with them in the clouds[d] to meet the Lord in the air. And so we will be with the Lord[e] forever. 18Therefore encourage each other[f] with these words.

5 Now, brothers, about times and dates[g] we do not need to write to you,[h] 2for you know very well that the day of the Lord[i] will come like a thief in the night.[j]

4:7 [h] Lev 11:44; 1Pe 1:15 **4:8** [i] Eze 36:27; Ro 5:5; 2Co 1:22; Gal 4:6; 1Jn 3:24 **4:9** [j] S Ro 12:10 [k] 1Th 5:1 [l] S Jn 6:45 [m] S Jn 13:34 **4:10** [n] S Ac 16:9 [o] S 1Th 3:12 **4:11** [p] Eph 4:28; 2Th 3:10-12 **4:12** [q] S Mk 4:11 **4:13** [r] S Ro 11:25 [s] S Mt 9:24 [t] Eph 2:12 **4:14** [u] Ro 14:9; 1Co 15:3,4; 2Co 5:15 [v] 1Co 15:18 **4:15** [w] S 1Co 1:7 [x] 1Co 15:52 **4:16** [y] S Mt 16:27 [z] Jude 9 [a] S Mt 24:31 [b] 1Co 15:23; 2Th 2:1; Rev 14:13 **4:17** [c] 1Co 15:52 [d] Ac 1:9; S Ac 8:39; S Rev 1:7; 11:12 [e] S Jn 12:26 **4:18** [f] 1Th 5:11 **5:1** [g] Ac 1:7 [h] 1Th 4:9 **5:2** [i] S 1Co 1:8 [j] S Lk 12:39

---

always wronged. Premarital sex wrongs the future partner by robbing him or her of the virginity that ought to be brought to marriage. *The Lord will punish.* A motive for chastity.

4:7 Another reason for chastity is God's call to holiness.

4:8 *God, who gives you his Holy Spirit.* Still another reason for chastity is that sexual sin is against God (see Ge 39:9 and note), who gives the Holy Spirit to believers for their sanctification. To live in sexual immorality is to reject God, specifically in regard to the Spirit (see 1Co 6:12–20 and notes).

4:9 *brotherly love.* Translates *philadelphia,* a Greek word that outside the NT almost without exception denoted the mutual love of children of the same father. In the NT it always means love of fellow believers in Christ, all of whom have the same heavenly Father. *taught by God.* Cf. Isa 54:13; Jn 6:45; 1Co 2:13.

4:11 *to mind your own business.* Some Thessalonians, probably because of idleness, were taking undue interest in other people's affairs (see 2Th 3:11 and note). *work with your hands.* The Greeks in general thought manual labor degrading and fit only for slaves. Christians took seriously the need for earning their own living, but some of the Thessalonians, perhaps as a result of their belief in the imminent return of Christ (see 2Th 3:11), were neglecting work and relying on others to support them.

4:12 *not be dependent on anybody.* Or "have need of nothing." Both meanings are true and significant. Christians in need because of their idleness are not obedient Christians (cf. Tit 3:14).

4:13 *those who fall asleep.* For the Christian, sleep is a particularly apt metaphor for death, since death's finality and horror are removed by the assurance of resurrection. Some of the Thessalonians seem to have misunderstood Paul and thought all believers would live until Christ returns. When some died, the question arose, "Will those who have died have part in that great day?" See note on v. 15. *who have no hope.* Inscriptions on tombs and references in literature show that first-century pagans viewed death with horror, as the end of everything. The Christian attitude was in strong contrast (see 1Co 15:55–57; Php 1:21–23).

4:14 *died.* Paul does not say that Christ "slept," perhaps to underscore the fact that he bore the full horror of death so that those who believe in him would not have to. *rose again.* For the importance of the resurrection see 1Co 15, especially vv. 14,17–22. *those who have fallen asleep in him.* Believers who have died, trusting in Jesus.

4:15 *According to the Lord's own word.* The doctrine mentioned here is not recorded in the Gospels and was either a direct revelation to Paul or something Jesus said that Christians passed on orally. *we who are still alive.* Those believers who will be alive when Christ returns. "We" does not necessarily mean that Paul thought that he would be alive then. He often identified himself with those he wrote to or about. Elsewhere he says that God will raise "us" at that time (1Co 6:14; 2Co 4:14). *will certainly not precede.* The Thessalonians had evidently been concerned that those among them who died would miss their place in the great events when the Lord comes, and Paul assures them this will not be the case.

4:16 *the Lord himself.* See Ac 1:11. *archangel.* The only named archangel in the Bible is Michael (Jude 9; see Da 10:13). In Scripture, Gabriel is simply called an angel (Lk 1:19,26). *will rise first.* Before the ascension of believers mentioned in the next verse.

4:17 *we who are still alive.* See note on v. 15. *caught up.* The only place in the NT where a "rapture" (from the Latin Vulgate rendering) is clearly referred to. Some hold that this will be secret, but Paul seems to be describing something open and public, with loud voices and a trumpet blast. *in the clouds.* Cf. Ac 1:9 and note. *with the Lord.* The chief hope of the believer (see 5:10; Jn 14:3; 2Co 5:8; Php 1:23; Col 3:4).

4:18 *encourage each other.* The primary purpose of vv. 13–18 is not to give a chronology of future events, though that is involved, but to urge mutual encouragement, as shown here and in v. 13.

5:1 *times and dates.* See Ac 1:6–7. There have always been some Christians who try to fix the date of our Lord's return, but apparently the Thessalonians were not among them.

5:2 *day of the Lord.* See 1Co 5:5. The expression goes back to Am 5:18 (see note there). In the OT it is a time when God will come and intervene with judgment and/or blessing (see note on Joel 1:15). In the NT the thought of judgment continues (see Ro 2:5; 2Pe 2:9), but it is also the "day of redemption" (Eph 4:30); the "day of God" (2Pe 3:12),

3While people are saying, "Peace and safety,"[k] destruction will come on them suddenly,[l] as labor pains on a pregnant woman, and they will not escape.[m]
4But you, brothers, are not in darkness[n]
so that this day should surprise you like a
thief.[o] 5You are all sons of the light[p] and
sons of the day. We do not belong to the
night or to the darkness. 6So then, let us
not be like others, who are asleep,[q] but
let us be alert[r] and self-controlled.[s] 7For
those who sleep, sleep at night, and those
who get drunk, get drunk at night.[t] 8But
since we belong to the day,[u] let us be self-
controlled, putting on faith and love as a
breastplate,[v] and the hope of salvation[w]
as a helmet.[x] 9For God did not appoint us
to suffer wrath[y] but to receive salvation
through our Lord Jesus Christ.[z] 10He died
for us so that, whether we are awake or
asleep, we may live together with him.[a]
11Therefore encourage one another[b] and
build each other up,[c] just as in fact you
are doing.

5:3 [k] Jer 4:10; 6:14; Eze 13:10 [l] Job 15:21; Ps 35:8; 55:15; Isa 29:5; 47:9, 11 [m] 2Th 1:9 **5:4** [n] S Ac 26:18; 1Jn 2:8 [o] ver 2 **5:5** [p] S Lk 16:8 **5:6** [q] Ro 13:11 [r] S Mt 25:13 [s] S Ac 24:25 **5:7** [t] Ac 2:15; Ro 13:13; 2Pe 2:13 **5:8** [u] ver 5 [v] S Eph 6:14 [w] Ro 8:24 [x] Isa 59:17; Eph 6:17 **5:9** [y] 1Th 1:10 [z] 2Th 2:13, 14 **5:10** [a] Ro 14:9; 2Co 5:15 **5:11** [b] 1Th 4:18 [c] Eph 4:29 **5:12** [d] Ro 16:6, 12; 1Co 15:10 [e] 1Ti 5:17; Heb 13:17 **5:13** [f] S Mk 9:50

Final Instructions

12Now we ask you, brothers, to respect
those who work hard[d] among you, who
are over you in the Lord[e] and who admonish you. 13Hold them in the highest
regard in love because of their work. Live
in peace with each other.[f] 14And we urge
you, brothers, warn those who are idle,[g]
encourage the timid, help the weak,[h] be
patient with everyone. 15Make sure that
nobody pays back wrong for wrong,[i] but
always try to be kind to each other[j] and to
everyone else.
16Be joyful always;[k] 17pray continually;[l]
18give thanks in all circumstances,[m] for
this is God's will for you in Christ Jesus.
19Do not put out the Spirit's fire;[n] 20do
not treat prophecies[o] with contempt. 21Test
everything.[p] Hold on to the good.[q] 22Avoid
every kind of evil.

5:14 [g] 2Th 3:6, 7, 11 [h] Ro 14:1; 1Co 8:7-12 **5:15** [i] Ro 12:17; 1Pe 3:9 [j] Eph 4:32 **5:16** [k] Php 4:4 **5:17** [l] S Lk 18:1 **5:18** [m] S Eph 5:20 **5:19** [n] Eph 4:30 **5:20** [o] 1Co 14:1-40 **5:21** [p] 1Co 14:29; 1Jn 4:1 [q] Ro 12:9

or of Christ (1Co 1:8; Php 1:6); and the "last day" (Jn 6:39), the "great Day" (Jude 6) or simply "the day" (2Th 1:10). It is the consummation of all things. There will be some preliminary signs (e.g., 2Th 2:3), but for unbelievers the coming will be as unexpected as that of a thief in the night (cf. Mt 24:43–44; Lk 12:39–40; 2Pe 3:10; Rev 3:3; 16:15).

5:3 *destruction.* Not annihilation, but exclusion from the Lord's presence (see 2Th 1:9 and note); thus the ruin of life and all its proud accomplishments. *suddenly.* Paul stresses the surprise of unbelievers. He uses a word found elsewhere in the NT only in Lk 21:34 ("unexpectedly"). *labor pains.* Here the idea is not the pain of childbirth so much as the suddenness and inevitability of such pains. *not.* An emphatic double negative in the Greek, a construction Paul uses only four times in all his writings.

5:4 *darkness.* Believers no longer live in darkness, nor are they of the darkness (v. 5). See Ac 26:18; 2Co 6:14; see also 1Jn 1:5–7 and notes. *thief.* See note on v. 2.

5:5 *sons of . . . sons of.* Echoes Hebrew idiom, in which to be the "sons of" a quality meant to be characterized by that quality. Christians do not simply live in the light; they are characterized by light.

5:6 *asleep.* Unbelievers are spiritually insensitive, but this kind of sleep is not for "sons of the light." *be alert.* Lit. "watch," which is in keeping with the emphasis Paul is placing on Christ's coming (cf. Mt 24:42–43; 25:13; Mk 13:34–37). *self-controlled.* A contrast with the conduct mentioned in v. 7.

5:8 *the day.* A reference to the light that characterizes Christians; perhaps it refers also to the coming of Christ (see v. 2 and note). *breastplate . . . helmet.* Paul also uses the metaphor of armor in Ro 13:12; 2Co 6:7; 10:4; Eph 6:13–17 (see notes on Eph 6:14,17). He does not consistently attach a particular virtue to each piece of armor; it is the general idea of equipment for battle that is pictured. For the triad of faith, hope and love see 1:3 and note.

5:9 *appoint.* God's appointment, not human choice, is the significant thing. *wrath.* See note on 1:10. *salvation.* Our final, completed salvation.

5:10 *are awake or asleep.* That is, live or die; or, if the sense is moral, are alert or carnal (see v. 6). *with him.* To be Christ's is to have entered a relationship that nothing can destroy.

5:11 *build . . . up.* The verb basically applies to building houses, but Paul frequently used it for Christians being edified.

5:12 *those who work hard among you.* Not much is known about the organization and leadership of the church at this period, but the reference is possibly to elders (cf. Heb 13:7,17 and notes).

5:13 *because of their work.* Not merely because of personal attachment or respect for their high position, but in appreciation for their work. *Live in peace.* The words apply to Christian relationships in general, but here they probably refer especially to right relations between leaders and those under them (cf. Ro 14:17,19).

5:14 *those who are idle.* It seems that some Thessalonians were so sure the second coming was close that they had given up their jobs in order to prepare for it, but Paul says they should work (see 2Th 3:10–11 and notes). *the timid . . . the weak.* These are to be helped, not rejected, by the strong (cf. Ro 14:1–15; 1Co 8:13 and note).

5:15 *pays back.* Retaliation is never a Christian option (cf. Ro 12:17 and note). Christians are called to forgive (see Mt 5:38–42; 18:21–35).

5:16 See Php 4:4 and note.

5:17 For the practice of continual (or regular) prayer see 1:3; 2:13; Ro 1:9–10; Eph 6:18; Col 1:3; 2Ti 1:3.

5:18 *give thanks.* See Eph 5:20 and note.

5:19 *Spirit's fire.* There is a warmth, a glow, about the Spirit's presence that makes this language appropriate. The kind of conduct Paul is opposing may include loafing, immorality and the other sins he has denounced. On the other hand, he may be warning against a mechanical attitude toward worship that discourages the expression of the gifts of the Spirit in the local assembly (see v. 20).

5:20 *prophecies.* For the gift of prophecy see Ro 12:6; 1Co 12:10 and note, 28; 13:2; 14; Eph 4:11. For the function of prophecies see 1Co 14:3.

5:21 *Test everything.* The approval of prophecy (v. 20) does not mean that anyone who claims to speak in the name of the Lord is to be accepted without question. Paul does not say what specific tests are to be applied, but he is clear that every teaching must be tested—surely they must be in agreement with his gospel.

23May God himself, the God of peace,[r]
sanctify you through and through. May
your whole spirit, soul[s] and body be kept
blameless[t] at the coming of our Lord Jesus
Christ.[u] 24The one who calls[v] you is faithful[w] and he will do it.[x]

25Brothers, pray for us.[y] 26Greet all the
brothers with a holy kiss.[z] 27I charge you
before the Lord to have this letter read to
all the brothers.[a]

28The grace of our Lord Jesus Christ be
with you.[b]

5:23 [r]S Ro 15:33 [s]Heb 4:12 [t]S 1Th 3:13 [u]S 1Th 2:19 **5:24** [v]S Ro 8:28 [w]S 1Co 1:9 [x]Nu 23:19; Php 1:6 **5:25** [y]Eph 6:19; Col 4:3; 2Th 3:1; Heb 13:18 **5:26** [z]S Ro 16:16 **5:27** [a]2Th 3:14; S 1Ti 4:13 **5:28** [b]S Ro 16:20

5:23 A typical prayer. *God of peace.* A fitting reference to God in view of vv. 12–15. But Paul often refers to God in this way near the end of his letters (see Ro 1:7 and note; 15:33; 16:20; 1Co 14:33; 2Co 13:11; Php 4:9; cf. 2Th 3:16). See also Heb 13:20–21. *sanctify.* See 1Co 1:2 and note. *your whole spirit, soul and body.* Paul emphasizes the whole person without attempting to differentiate various parts (see Heb 4:12 and note).

5:24 Paul's confidence rests in the nature of God (cf. Ge 18:25 and note), who can be relied on to complete what he begins (see Nu 23:19; Php 1:6 and notes).

5:26 *all.* Paul sent a warm greeting to everyone, even those he had corrected. *holy kiss.* A kiss was a normal greeting of that day, similar to our modern handshake (see Ro 16:16; 1Co 16:20; 2Co 13:12 and notes; cf. "kiss of love," 1Pe 5:14).

5:27 *I charge you.* Surprisingly strong language, meaning "I put you on oath"—used only here in the NT. Paul clearly wanted every member of the church to read or hear his letter and to know of his concern and advice for them.

5:28 Paul always ended his letters with a benediction of grace for his readers, sometimes adding other blessings, as in 2Co 13:14. *grace.* See note on Ro 1:7. *Lord Jesus Christ.* See note on 1:1. *with you.* See note on 2Co 13:14.

2 Thessalonians

INTRODUCTION

Author, Date and Place of Writing

Paul's authorship of 2 Thessalonians has been questioned more often than that of 1 Thessalonians, in spite of the fact that it has more support from early Christian writers. Objections are based on internal factors rather than on the adequacy of the statements of the church fathers. It is thought that there are differences in the vocabulary (ten words not used elsewhere), in the style (it is said to be unexpectedly formal) and in the eschatology (the doctrine of the "man of lawlessness" is not taught elsewhere). However, such arguments have not convinced current interpreters. A majority still hold to Paul's authorship of 2 Thessalonians.

Because of its similarity to 1 Thessalonians, it was likely written not long after the first letter — perhaps about six months. The situation in the church seems to have been much the same. Paul probably penned it (see 1:1; 3:17) c. A.D. 51 or 52 in Corinth, after Silas and Timothy had returned from delivering 1 Thessalonians (see chart, p. 1697; see also Introduction to 1 Thessalonians).

A Quick Look

Author:
The apostle Paul

Audience:
The church at Thessalonica

Date:
A.D. 51 or 52

Theme:
Paul writes to correct a misunderstanding concerning the Lord's return and to exhort the Thessalonian believers to be steadfast and to work for a living.

Purpose

Inasmuch as the situation in the Thessalonian church has not changed substantially, Paul's purpose in writing is very much the same as in his first letter to them. He writes (1) to encourage persecuted believers (1:4 – 10), (2) to correct a misunderstanding concerning the Lord's return (2:1 – 12) and (3) to exhort the Thessalonians to be steadfast and to work for a living (2:13 — 3:15).

Theme

Like 1 Thessalonians, this letter deals extensively with eschatology (see Introduction to 1 Thessalonians: Theme). In fact, in 2 Thessalonians 18 out of 47 verses deal with this subject.

Outline

- I. Introduction (ch. 1)
  - A. Greetings (1:1 – 2)
  - B. Thanksgiving for Their Faith, Love and Perseverance (1:3 – 10)
  - C. Intercession for Their Spiritual Progress (1:11 – 12)
- II. Instruction (ch. 2)
  - A. Prophecy Regarding the Day of the Lord (2:1 – 12)
  - B. Thanksgiving for Their Election and Calling (Their Position) (2:13 – 15)
  - C. Prayer for Their Service and Testimony (Their Practice) (2:16 – 17)
- III. Injunctions (3:1 – 15)
  - A. Call to Prayer (3:1 – 5)
  - B. Charge to Discipline the Disorderly and Lazy (3:6 – 15)
- IV. Conclusion, Final Greetings and Benediction (3:16 – 18)

1 Paul, Silas[a][a] and Timothy,[b]

To the church of the Thessalonians[c] in
God our Father and the Lord Jesus Christ:

2 Grace and peace to you from God the
Father and the Lord Jesus Christ.[d]

Thanksgiving and Prayer

3 We ought always to thank God for
you,[e] brothers, and rightly so, because
your faith is growing more and more, and
the love every one of you has for each other is increasing.[f] 4 Therefore, among God's
churches we boast[g] about your perseverance and faith[h] in all the persecutions and
trials you are enduring.[i]
5 All this is evidence[j] that God's judgment is right, and as a result you will be
counted worthy[k] of the kingdom of God,
for which you are suffering. 6 God is just:[l]
He will pay back trouble to those who
trouble you[m] 7 and give relief to you who
are troubled, and to us as well. This will
happen when the Lord Jesus is revealed
from heaven[n] in blazing fire[o] with his
powerful angels.[p] 8 He will punish[q] those
who do not know God[r] and do not obey
the gospel of our Lord Jesus.[s] 9 They will
be punished with everlasting destruction[t]
and shut out from the presence of the
Lord[u] and from the majesty of his power[v] 10 on the day[w] he comes to be glorified[x]
in his holy people and to be marveled at
among all those who have believed. This
includes you, because you believed our
testimony to you.[y]
11 With this in mind, we constantly pray
for you,[z] that our God may count you worthy[a] of his calling,[b] and that by his power he may fulfill every good purpose[c] of
yours and every act prompted by your
faith.[d] 12 We pray this so that the name of
our Lord Jesus may be glorified in you,[e]
and you in him, according to the grace of
our God and the Lord Jesus Christ.[b]

The Man of Lawlessness

2 Concerning the coming of our Lord
Jesus Christ[f] and our being gathered
to him,[g] we ask you, brothers, 2 not to become easily unsettled or alarmed by some
prophecy, report or letter[h] supposed to
have come from us, saying that the day

[a] 1 Greek *Silvanus*, a variant of *Silas* [b] 12 Or *God and Lord, Jesus Christ*

1:1 [a]S Ac 15:22 [b]S Ac 16:1; 1Th 1:1 [c]S Ac 17:1 **1:2** [d]S Ro 1:7 **1:3** [e]S Ro 1:8; Eph 5:20 [f]S 1Th 3:12 **1:4** [g]2Co 7:14 [h]1Th 1:3 [i]1Th 1:6; 2:14; S 3:3 **1:5** [j]Php 1:28 [k]Lk 20:35 **1:6** [l]Lk 18:7,8 [m]Ro 12:19; Col 3:25; S Rev 6:10 **1:7** [n]S Lk 17:30 [o]Heb 10:27; S 12:29; 2Pe 3:7; S Rev 1:14 [p]Jude 14 **1:8** [q]Ps 79:6; Isa 66:15; Jer 10:25 [r]S Gal 4:8 [s]Ro 2:8; S 2Co 2:12 **1:9** [t]Php 3:19; 1Th 5:3; 2Pe 3:7 [u]2Ki 17:18 [v]Isa 2:10,19; 2Th 2:8 **1:10** [w]1Co 3:13 [x]Jn 17:10 [y]1Co 1:6 **1:11** [z]S Ro 1:10 [a]ver 5 [b]S Ro 8:28 [c]Ro 15:14 [d]1Th 1:3 **1:12** [e]Isa 24:15; Php 2:9-11 **2:1** [f]S 1Th 2:19 [g]Mk 13:27; 1Th 4:15-17 **2:2** [h]ver 15; 2Th 3:17

1:1–2 See note on 1Th 1:1.

1:1 *Paul.* See note on Ro 1:1. *Lord Jesus Christ.* Occurs also at the end of this letter (3:18). See note on 1Th 1:1.

1:2 *Grace and peace.* See note on Ro 1:7.

1:3 *ought.* Paul is obliged to give thanks where it is due (cf. 1Th 1:7–8; see note on Php 1:3–4). *brothers.* See note on Ro 1:13. *faith ... love.* Two virtues that Paul had been pleased to acknowledge in the Thessalonian church (see 1Th 3:6–7 and note on 3:6), but that were also somewhat lacking (see 1Th 3:10 and note, 12). *is increasing.* The same verb Paul had used in his prayer that their love might grow (1Th 3:12).

1:4 *we.* Emphatic, "we ourselves." Paul seems to imply that it was unusual for the founders of a church to boast about it, though others might do so (cf. 1Th 1:9). But the Thessalonians were so outstanding that Paul departed from normal practice. *persecutions and trials.* See 1Th 1:6; 2:14; 3:3.

1:5 *evidence that God's judgment is right.* The evidence was in the way the Thessalonians endured trials. The judgment on them was right because God did not leave them to their own resources. He provided strength to endure, and this in turn produced spiritual and moral character. It also proved that God was on their side and gave a warning to their persecutors (cf. Php 1:28 and note). *kingdom of God.* See notes on 1Th 2:12; Mt 3:2.

1:6 *God is just.* The justice of God brings punishment on unrepentant sinners (cf. Mk 9:47–48; Lk 13:3–5), and it may be in the here and now (see Ro 1:24,26,28 and note) as well as on judgment day.

1:7 *give relief.* God's judgment not only brings about punishment of the evil but also relief for those being wronged. *us as well.* Paul was no academic theologian writing in comfort from a distance; rather, he was suffering just as they were. *revealed.* Christ is now hidden, but at his second coming he will be seen by everyone in all his glory. *blazing fire.* He comes to punish wickedness (see Rev 19:12; cf. Isa 66:15; Rev 1:14). *his powerful angels.* Perhaps a class of angels (such a group is mentioned in apocalyptic writings) given special power to do God's will (cf. Rev 19:14 and note).

1:8 *do not know God.* Does not refer to those who have never heard of the true God but to those who refuse to recognize him (cf. 2:10 and note, 12; Ro 1:28). *do not obey.* The gospel invites acceptance, and rejection is disobedience to a royal invitation.

1:9 *destruction.* Since salvation implies resurrection of the body, annihilation cannot be in mind here (see 1Th 5:3 and note). The word means something like "complete ruin" (see Mt 7:13 and note). Here it means being shut out from Christ's presence. This eternal separation is the penalty of sin and the essence of hell (cf. Rev 20:14–15; 21:8,27).

1:10 *the day.* See note on 1Th 5:2. *glorified in his holy people.* Not simply "among" but "in" them. His glory is seen in what they are. *holy people.* See note on 1Th 3:13. *our testimony.* The preaching of the gospel is essentially bearing testimony to what God has done in Christ.

1:11 *constantly pray.* See notes on 1Th 5:17; Col 4:2. *good purpose.* God initiates every good purpose and every act prompted by faith; accordingly Paul prays that God will bring them both to fulfillment.

1:12 *name.* In ancient times one's name was often more than a personal label; it signified what a person was (see 1Sa 25:25 and note). *Lord Jesus may be glorified in you.* Paul looks for glory to be ascribed to Christ because of all he will do in the lives of the Thessalonian Christians (see v. 10 and note). *and you in him.* Christians will share in Christ's glory by virtue of their union with him (cf. Jn 15:4 and note; 17:21).

2:1 *coming.* See 1Th 2:19 and note. The second coming of Christ is the principal topic of 2 Thessalonians. What Paul wrote was supplemental to his oral teaching and the instructions contained in his earlier letter. *gathered to him.* See 1Th 4:17 and note.

2:2 *unsettled.* The Greek for this verb was often used of a ship adrift from its mooring, and suggests lack of stability.

of the Lord[i] has already come.[j] 3Don't let
anyone deceive you[k] in any way, for ⌞that
day will not come⌟ until the rebellion[l] occurs and the man of lawlessness[a] is revealed,[m] the man doomed to destruction.
4He will oppose and will exalt himself over
everything that is called God[n] or is worshiped, so that he sets himself up in God's
temple, proclaiming himself to be God.[o]
5Don't you remember that when I was
with you I used to tell you these things?[p]
6And now you know what is holding him
back,[q] so that he may be revealed at the
proper time. 7For the secret power of lawlessness is already at work; but the one
who now holds it back[r] will continue to
do so till he is taken out of the way. 8And
then the lawless one will be revealed,[s]
whom the Lord Jesus will overthrow with
the breath of his mouth[t] and destroy by
the splendor of his coming.[u] 9The coming
of the lawless one will be in accordance
with the work of Satan[v] displayed in all
kinds of counterfeit miracles, signs and
wonders,[w] 10and in every sort of evil that
deceives those who are perishing.[x] They
perish because they refused to love the
truth and so be saved.[y] 11For this reason
God sends them[z] a powerful delusion[a]
so that they will believe the lie[b] 12and so
that all will be condemned who have not
believed the truth but have delighted in
wickedness.[c]

Stand Firm

13But we ought always to thank God for
you,[d] brothers loved by the Lord, because
from the beginning God chose you[b][e] to
be saved[f] through the sanctifying work of
the Spirit[g] and through belief in the truth.
14He called you[h] to this through our gospel,[i] that you might share in the glory of
our Lord Jesus Christ. 15So then, brothers,
stand firm[j] and hold to the teachings[c] we
passed on to you,[k] whether by word of
mouth or by letter.

2:2 [i]S 1Co 1:8 [j]2Ti 2:18 **2:3** [k]S Mk 13:5 [l]Mt 24:10-12 [m]ver 8; Da 7:25; 8:25; 11:36; Rev 13:5,6 **2:4** [n]1Co 8:5 [o]Isa 14:13,14; Eze 28:2 **2:5** [p]1Th 3:4 **2:6** [q]ver 7 **2:7** [r]ver 6 **2:8** [s]S ver 3 [t]Isa 11:4; Rev 2:16; 19:15 [u]S Lk 17:30 **2:9** [v]S Mt 4:10 [w]Mt 24:24; Rev 13:13; S Jn 4:48 **2:10** [x]S 1Co 1:18 [y]Pr 4:6; Jn 3:17-19 **2:11** [z]Ro 1:28 [a]Mt 24:5; S Mk 13:5 [b]Ro 1:25 **2:12** [c]Ro 1:32; 2:8 **2:13** [d]S Ro 1:8 [e]Eph 1:4 [f]1Th 5:9 [g]1Pe 1:2 **2:14** [h]S Ro 8:28; S 11:29 [i]1Th 1:5 **2:15** [j]S 1Co 16:13 [k]S 1Co 11:2

[a] *3* Some manuscripts *sin* [b] *13* Some manuscripts *because God chose you as his firstfruits* [c] *15* Or *traditions*

alarmed. Jesus issued a similar instruction, using the same verb (Mk 13:7). *some.* Paul seems to be uncertain about what was disturbing them, so he uses a general expression. *prophecy.* Lit. "spirit," denoting a revelation inspired by either the Holy Spirit or some other spirit. *report.* Lit. "word," perhaps referring to a sermon or other oral communication. *letter supposed to have come from us.* A forgery. *day of the Lord.* See 1Th 5:2 and note. *has already come.* Obviously Christ's climactic return had not occurred, but Paul was combating the idea that the final days had begun and their completion would be imminent.

2:3 *the rebellion.* In the end times there will be a falling away from the faith (see Mt 24:10 – 12; 1Ti 4:1). But here Paul is speaking of a specific act of rebellion that embodies the supreme opposition of evil to the things of God. *the man of lawlessness.* The leader of the forces of evil in the end times. Only here is he called by this name. John tells us of many "antichrists" (1Jn 2:18), and this may be the worst of them — the antichrist of Rev 13 — though Paul's description of the man of lawlessness has some distinctive features. He is not Satan, because he is clearly distinguished from him in v. 9. *revealed.* Since the Greek for this word is from the same root as that used of Jesus Christ in 1:7, it may indicate something supernatural. *doomed to destruction.* For all his proud claims, his final overthrow is certain. The same expression is used of Judas Iscariot (see Jn 17:12).

2:4 *everything that is called God or is worshiped.* He is not merely a political or military man, but claims a place above every god and everything associated with worship. He even claims to be God. *God's temple.* Apparently refers to the temple in Jerusalem (cf. Da 11:36 – 37; Mt 24:15 and note; Rev 13:5 – 8).

2:6 *what is holding him back.* The expression is neuter, but the masculine equivalent is in v. 7. There have been many suggestions as to the identity of this restrainer: (1) the Roman state with its emperor, (2) Paul's missionary work, (3) the Jewish nation, (4) the principle of law and government embodied in the state, (5) the Holy Spirit or (6) the restraining ministry of the Holy Spirit through the church, and others.

2:7 *secret power.* Lit. "mystery" (see note on Ro 11:25). It is most often used in reference to the gospel or some aspect of it. The expression here, however, indicates that we know something about evil only as God reveals it. This evil is already at work and will continue until the restrainer is removed at the end time.

2:8 *the lawless one will be revealed.* Evidently refers to some supernatural aspects of his appearing (see v. 9). *overthrow with the breath of his mouth.* Despite his impressiveness (v. 4), the man of lawlessness will easily be destroyed by Christ (cf. Da 11:45; Rev 19:20). *splendor.* In 2Ti 1:10 ("appearing") the Greek for this word refers to Jesus' first coming, but everywhere else in the NT to his second coming.

2:9 *coming.* The same word used of Christ's coming in v. 8. Satan empowers him with miracles, signs and wonders (cf. Mt 24:24). *counterfeit.* Not "bogus," but "producing false impressions."

2:10 *deceives.* The aim of the miracles of v. 9. *refused.* Their unbelief was willful and intentional. *truth.* Often closely connected with Jesus (see Jn 14:6 and note; Eph 4:21) and with the gospel (see Gal 2:5; Eph 1:13).

2:11 *For this reason.* Because of their deliberate rejection of the truth (v. 10). *God sends them a powerful delusion.* God uses sin to punish the sinful (cf. Ro 1:24 – 28). *the lie.* Not just any lie, but the great lie that the man of lawlessness is God (v. 4).

2:13 *loved by the Lord ... God chose.* For the connection between God's love and election see Col 3:12; 1Th 1:4; see also note on Eph 1:4. *from the beginning.* Election is from eternity (see Eph 1:4). *sanctifying work.* A necessary aspect of salvation, not something reserved for special Christians (see 1Th 3:13; 4:3; 1Co 1:2 and notes). *truth.* See note on v. 10. All three persons of the Trinity are mentioned in this verse (see note on 1Th 1:1).

2:14 *called ... through our gospel.* The past tense refers to the time when the Thessalonians were converted; but the divine call is a present reality in 1Th 5:24. *our gospel.* See note on 1Th 1:5. *glory of our Lord Jesus Christ.* Cf. 1Th 2:12 and note. Ultimately there is no glory other than God's (cf. Heb 1:2 – 3 and note).

2:15 *teachings.* Lit. "traditions." Until the NT was written, essential Christian teaching was passed on in the "traditions," just as Rabbinic law was (see Mt 15:2 and note); it could be either oral or written. In 1Co 15:3 (see note there) Paul uses the technical words for receiving and handing on traditions.

16May our Lord Jesus Christ himself and
God our Father,[l] who loved us[m] and by his
grace gave us eternal encouragement and
good hope, 17encourage[n] your hearts and
strengthen[o] you in every good deed and
word.

Request for Prayer

3 Finally, brothers,[p] pray for us[q] that the
message of the Lord[r] may spread rapidly and be honored, just as it was with
you.[s] 2And pray that we may be delivered
from wicked and evil men,[t] for not everyone has faith. 3But the Lord is faithful,[u]
and he will strengthen and protect you
from the evil one.[v] 4We have confidence[w]
in the Lord that you are doing and will
continue to do the things we command.
5May the Lord direct your hearts[x] into
God's love and Christ's perseverance.

Warning Against Idleness

6In the name of the Lord Jesus Christ,[y]
we command you, brothers, to keep away
from[z] every brother who is idle[a] and does
not live according to the teaching[a] you received from us.[b] 7For you yourselves know
how you ought to follow our example.[c] We
were not idle when we were with you, 8nor
did we eat anyone's food without paying
for it. On the contrary, we worked[d] night
and day, laboring and toiling so that we
would not be a burden to any of you. 9We
did this, not because we do not have the
right to such help,[e] but in order to make
ourselves a model for you to follow.[f] 10For
even when we were with you,[g] we gave
you this rule: "If a man will not work,[h] he
shall not eat."

11We hear that some among you are
idle. They are not busy; they are busybodies.[i] 12Such people we command and urge
in the Lord Jesus Christ[j] to settle down
and earn the bread they eat.[k] 13And as for
you, brothers, never tire of doing what is
right.[l]

14If anyone does not obey our instruction in this letter, take special note of him.
Do not associate with him,[m] in order that
he may feel ashamed.[n] 15Yet do not regard him as an enemy, but warn him as
a brother.[o]

Final Greetings

16Now may the Lord of peace[p] himself
give you peace at all times and in every
way. The Lord be with all of you.[q]

17I, Paul, write this greeting in my own
hand,[r] which is the distinguishing mark in
all my letters. This is how I write.

18The grace of our Lord Jesus Christ be
with you all.[s]

[a] 6 Or *tradition*

2:16 [l] S Php 4:20 [m] S Jn 3:16 **2:17** [n] 1Th 3:2 [o] 2Th 3:3 **3:1** [p] 1Th 4:1 [q] S 1Th 5:25 [r] 1Th 1:8 [s] 1Th 2:13 **3:2** [t] S Ro 15:31 **3:3** [u] S 1Co 1:9 [v] S Mt 5:37 **3:4** [w] S 2Co 2:3 **3:5** [x] 1Ch 29:18 **3:6** [y] 1Co 5:4 [z] ver 14; S Ro 16:17 [a] ver 7,11 [b] S 1Co 11:2 **3:7** [c] ver 9; S 1Co 4:16 **3:8** [d] S Ac 18:3; Eph 4:28 **3:9** [e] 1Co 9:4-14 [f] ver 7; S 1Co 4:16 **3:10** [g] 1Th 3:4 [h] 1Th 4:11 **3:11** [i] ver 6,7; 1Ti 5:13 **3:12** [j] 1Th 4:1 [k] 1Th 4:11; Eph 4:28 **3:13** [l] Gal 6:9 **3:14** [m] ver 6; S Ro 16:17 [n] S 1Co 4:14 **3:15** [o] Gal 6:1; 1Th 5:14; Phm 16 **3:16** [p] S Ro 15:33 [q] Ru 2:4 **3:17** [r] S 1Co 16:21 **3:18** [s] S Ro 16:20

2:16–17 There is a similar prayer in the first letter (1Th 3:11–13).
2:17 *encourage ... strengthen.* Also used together in 1Th 3:2. The prayer is for inner strength that will produce results in both action and speech.
3:1 *Finally.* See 1Th 4:1 and note. In 1Th 5:25 Paul simply asked for prayer; here he mentions specifics. *just as it was with you.* Lit. "just as also with you." The expression is general enough to cover the present as well as the past (cf. 1Th 2:13).
3:2 For Paul's difficulties at Corinth (where he wrote this letter) see Ac 18:12–13.
3:3 *faithful.* In the Greek the word immediately follows "faith" (v. 2), putting the faithfulness of God in sharp contrast with the lack of faith in people (cf. 1Co 1:9 and note; 10:13; 2Co 1:18).
3:5 *hearts.* See note on 1Th 2:4. *God's love.* Paul is about to rebuke the idle, and is here reminding them of God's love. There should be no hard feelings among those who owe everything to the love of God. *Christ's perseverance.* The endurance he so marvelously displayed in his incarnate life on earth (see Heb 12:1–3 and notes).
3:6 *the name.* See 1:12 and note. *command.* An authoritative word with a military ring. *keep away.* Not withdrawal of all contact but withholding of close fellowship. Idleness is sinful and disruptive, but those guilty of it are still brothers and sisters in Christ (v. 15). *idle.* The problem was mentioned in the first letter (4:11–12; 5:14; see notes there), and evidently had worsened. Paul takes it seriously and gives more attention to it in this letter than to anything else but the second coming. *teaching.* See 2:15 and note.
3:7 *follow our example.* See 1Th 1:6 and note.
3:8 *eat ... food.* A Hebraism for "make a living" (see, e.g., Ge 3:19; Am 7:12). Paul is not saying that he never accepted hospitality but that he had not depended on other people for his living (see 1Th 2:9 and note).
3:9 *the right.* See note on 1Th 2:6.
3:10 Pagan parallels are in the form, "He who does not work does not eat." But Paul uses an imperative: lit. "let him not eat."
3:11 *busybodies.* Worse than idle, they were interfering with other people's affairs, a problem to which idleness often leads.
3:12 *settle down.* Not going about as useless "busybodies" (v. 11).
3:14 Paul realizes that some may not heed his letter. *associate with.* The Greek for this phrase is an unusual double compound, meaning "mix up together with" (used elsewhere in the NT only in 1Co 5:9,11—of a similar withdrawal of close fellowship). It indicates a disassociation that will bring the person back to a right attitude. *feel ashamed.* And repent. The aim is not punishment but restoration to fellowship.
3:15 Discipline in the church should be brotherly, never harsh. *warn.* See 1Th 5:12, where the Greek for this verb is translated "admonish." *brother.* See note on Ro 1:13.
3:16,18 *peace ... grace.* See note on Ro 1:7.
3:16 *Lord of peace.* The more usual phrase is "God of peace" (see note on 1Th 5:23). *all of you.* Even the disorderly.
3:17 Paul normally dictated his letters (cf. Ro 16:22), but toward the end of some of them he added a brief word in his own handwriting (see 1Co 16:21 and note; Gal 6:11; Col 4:18). Here he tells us that this practice was his distinguishing mark.
3:18 See 1Th 5:28 and note. Paul has criticized his offenders, but his last prayer is for everyone. *Lord Jesus Christ.* See note on 1:1. *with you.* See note on 2Co 13:14.

The Pastoral Letters

"Pastoral" characterizes the contents of 1,2 Timothy and Titus. These letters provide instruction concerning the care of the churches.

Biblical interpreters have raised more doubts about the authenticity of the Pastoral Letters than about any of the other letters of Paul. They have alleged that:

1. The events mentioned in the Pastorals cannot be fitted into the account of Paul's life and ministry in Acts.
2. The theological emphases are different from those found in the other letters of Paul, and the church organization is more advanced.
3. The vocabulary and style of writing are not characteristic of Paul.

Although some construe these as formidable objections to authorship by Paul, there are satisfactory answers:

1. Paul's death is not reported in Ac 28. In all probability he was released from prison and went on another mission (see map, pp. 1872–1873 and accompanying text), during which there was adequate time for the historical events mentioned in the Pastoral Letters to take place.
2. The theology is consistent with that found in other letters of Paul, and the church organization in the Pastorals is no more advanced than that found, e.g., in Philippians (see 1:1).
3. While the scope of these letters is too limited to draw any firm conclusions about authorship based on vocabulary and style, these features of the Pastorals can be satisfactorily accounted for by considering the different circumstances, addressees and subject matter Paul is dealing with.

Certain themes and phrases recur throughout the Pastoral Letters: (1) God the Savior (see note on Tit 1:3); (2) sound doctrine, faith and teaching (see note on Tit 1:9); (3) godliness (see note on 1Ti 2:2); (4) controversies (1Ti 1:4; 6:4; 2Ti 2:23; Tit 3:9); (5) trustworthy sayings (see note on 1Ti 1:15).

1 Timothy

INTRODUCTION

Author

Both early tradition and the salutations of the Pastoral Letters (1,2 Timothy; Titus) themselves claim Paul as their author (1:1; 2Ti 1:1; Tit 1:1). Some objections have been raised in recent years on the basis of an alleged uncharacteristic vocabulary and style (see, e.g., notes on 1:15; 2:2), but other evidence still convincingly supports Paul's authorship. See essay, p. 1867.

Background and Purpose

During his fourth missionary journey (see map, pp. 1872 – 1873), Paul had instructed Timothy to care for the church in Ephesus (1:3) while he went on to Macedonia. When he realized that he might not return to Ephesus in the near future (3:14 – 15), he wrote this first letter to Timothy to develop the charge he had given his young assistant (1:3,18), to refute false teachings (1:3 – 7; 4:1 – 8; 6:3 – 5,20 – 21) and to supervise the affairs of the growing Ephesian church (church worship, ch. 2; the appointment of qualified church leaders, 3:1 – 13; 5:17 – 25).

A major problem in the Ephesian church was a heresy that combined Gnosticism (see Introduction to 1 John: Gnosticism), decadent Judaism (1:3 – 7) and false asceticism (4:1 – 5).

A Quick Look

Author:
The apostle Paul

Audience:
Timothy, one of Paul's closest associates, but no doubt intended to be read to the whole church in Ephesus

Date:
About A.D. 64

Theme:
Paul writes to instruct Timothy concerning the care of the church at Ephesus.

Date

1 Timothy was written sometime after the events of Ac 28 (c. A.D. 63 – 65; see chart, p. 1697), at least eight years after Paul's three-year stay in Ephesus (see Ac 19:10 and note).

Recipient

As the salutation indicates (1:2), Paul is writing to Timothy, a native of Lystra (in modern Turkey). Timothy's father was Greek, while his mother was a Jewish Christian (Ac 16:1). From childhood he had been taught the OT (2Ti 1:5; 3:15). Paul called him "my true son in the faith" (1:2; see note there), perhaps having led him to faith in Christ during his first visit to Lystra. At the time of his second visit Paul invited Timothy to join him on his missionary travels, circumcising him so that his Greek ancestry would not be a liability in working with the Jews (Ac 16:3). Timothy helped Paul evangelize Macedonia and Achaia (Ac 17:14–15; 18:5) and was with him during much of his long preaching ministry in Ephesus (Ac 19:22). He traveled with him from Ephesus to Macedonia, to Corinth (see Ac 20:3 and note), back to Macedonia, and to Asia Minor (Ac 20:1–6). He may even have accompanied him all the way to Jerusalem. He was with Paul during the apostle's first Roman imprisonment (Php 1:1; Col 1:1; Phm 1).

Paul's admiration of Timothy is seen in the letter to the Philippians, where Paul speaks highly of his younger associates.

Following Paul's release (after Ac 28), Timothy again traveled with him but eventually stayed at Ephesus to deal with the problems there, while Paul went on to Macedonia. Paul's closeness to and admiration of Timothy are seen in Paul's naming him as the co-sender of six of his letters (2 Corinthians, Philippians, Colossians, 1,2 Thessalonians and Philemon) and in his speaking highly of him to the Philippians (Php 2:19–22). At the end of Paul's life he requested Timothy to join him in Rome (2Ti 4:9,21). According to Heb 13:23, Timothy himself was imprisoned and subsequently released—whether in Rome or elsewhere, we do not know.

Timothy was not an apostle. It may be best to regard him as an apostolic representative, delegated to carry out special work (cf. Tit 1:5).

Outline

- I. Greetings (1:1–2)
- II. Warning against False Teachers (1:3–11)
  - A. The Nature of the Heresy (1:3–7)
  - B. The Purpose of the Law (1:8–11)
- III. The Lord's Grace to Paul (1:12–17)
- IV. The Purpose of Paul's Instructions to Timothy (1:18–20)
- V. Instructions concerning Church Administration (chs. 2–3)
  - A. Public Worship (ch. 2)
    - 1. Prayer in public worship (2:1–8)
    - 2. Women in public worship (2:9–15)
  - B. Qualifications for Church Officers (3:1–13)
    - 1. Overseers (3:1–7)
    - 2. Deacons (3:8–13)
  - C. Purpose of These Instructions (3:14–16)
- VI. Instructions concerning False Teaching (ch. 4)
  - A. False Teaching Described (4:1–5)
  - B. Methods of Dealing with It Explained (4:6–16)
- VII. Instructions concerning Different Groups in the Church (5:1—6:2)
  - A. The Older and the Younger (5:1–2)
  - B. Widows (5:3–16)
  - C. Elders (5:17–25)
  - D. Slaves (6:1–2)
- VIII. Miscellaneous Matters (6:3–19)
  - A. False Teachers (6:3–5)
  - B. Love of Money (6:6–10)
  - C. Charge to Timothy (6:11–16)
  - D. The Rich (6:17–19)
- IX. Concluding Appeal and Benediction (6:20–21)

1 Paul, an apostle of Christ Jesus by the
command of God[a] our Savior[b] and of
Christ Jesus our hope,[c]

2 To Timothy[d] my true son[e] in the faith:

Grace, mercy and peace from God the
Father and Christ Jesus our Lord.[f]

Warning Against False Teachers of the Law

3 As I urged you when I went into Macedonia,[g] stay there in Ephesus[h] so that you
may command certain men not to teach
false doctrines[i] any longer 4 nor to devote
themselves to myths[j] and endless genealogies.[k] These promote controversies[l] rather
than God's work — which is by faith. 5 The
goal of this command is love, which comes
from a pure heart[m] and a good conscience[n]
and a sincere faith.[o] 6 Some have wandered
away from these and turned to meaningless talk. 7 They want to be teachers[p] of the
law, but they do not know what they are
talking about or what they so confidently
affirm.[q]

8 We know that the law is good[r] if one
uses it properly. 9 We also know that law[a]
is made not for the righteous[s] but for lawbreakers and rebels,[t] the ungodly and sinful, the unholy and irreligious; for those
who kill their fathers or mothers, for murderers, 10 for adulterers and perverts, for
slave traders and liars and perjurers — and
for whatever else is contrary to the sound
doctrine[u] 11 that conforms to the glorious
gospel of the blessed God, which he entrusted to me.[v]

The Lord's Grace to Paul

12 I thank Christ Jesus our Lord, who has
given me strength,[w] that he considered
me faithful, appointing me to his service.[x]
13 Even though I was once a blasphemer
and a persecutor[y] and a violent man, I
was shown mercy[z] because I acted in ignorance and unbelief.[a] 14 The grace of our
Lord was poured out on me abundantly,[b]
along with the faith and love that are in
Christ Jesus.[c]

15 Here is a trustworthy saying[d] that deserves full acceptance: Christ Jesus came
into the world to save sinners[e] — of whom
I am the worst. 16 But for that very reason I was shown mercy[f] so that in me,
the worst of sinners, Christ Jesus might
display his unlimited patience[g] as an example for those who would believe[h] on
him and receive eternal life.[i] 17 Now to the
King[j] eternal, immortal,[k] invisible,[l] the
only God,[m] be honor and glory for ever
and ever. Amen.[n]

18 Timothy, my son,[o] I give you this instruction in keeping with the prophecies
once made about you,[p] so that by following them you may fight the good fight,[q]

1:1 [a]S 2Co 1:1; Tit 1:3 [b]S Lk 1:47 [c]Col 1:27 **1:2** [d]S Ac 16:1 [e]ver 18; 1Co 4:17; S 1Th 2:11; 2Ti 1:2; Tit 1:4 [f]S Ro 1:7 **1:3** [g]S Ac 16:9 [h]S Ac 18:19 [i]Gal 1:6,7; 1Ti 6:3 **1:4** [j]1Ti 4:7; 2Ti 4:4; Tit 1:14 [k]Tit 3:9 [l]S 2Ti 2:14 **1:5** [m]2Ti 2:22 [n]S Ac 23:1; 1Ti 4:2 [o]Gal 5:6; 2Ti 1:5 **1:7** [p]S Eph 4:11 [q]Job 38:2 **1:8** [r]Ro 7:12 **1:9** [s]Gal 5:23 [t]Gal 3:19 **1:10** [u]1Ti 6:3; 2Ti 1:13; 4:3; Tit 1:9; 2:1 **1:11** [v]Gal 2:7; 1Th 2:4; Tit 1:3 **1:12** [w]S Php 4:13 [x]S Ac 9:15 **1:13** [y]S Ac 8:3 [z]ver 16 [a]Ac 26:9 **1:14** [b]2Co 4:15 [c]2Ti 1:13; S 1Th 1:3 **1:15** [d]1Ti 3:1; 4:9; 2Ti 2:11; Tit 3:8 [e]Mk 2:17; S Jn 3:17 **1:16** [f]ver 13 [g]S Ro 2:4 [h]S Jn 3:15 [i]S Mt 25:46 **1:17** [j]Rev 15:3 [k]1Ti 6:16 [l]S Col 1:15 [m]Jude 25 [n]S Ro 11:36 **1:18** [o]S ver 2 [p]1Ti 4:14 [q]1Ti 6:12; 2Ti 2:3; 4:7

[a] 9 Or *that the law*

1:1 *Paul.* See note on Ro 1:1. *apostle.* One specially commissioned by Christ (see 1Co 1:1 and note). *God our Savior.* See Tit 1:3 and note. *Christ Jesus our hope.* See Tit 2:13. *hope.* Expresses absolute certainty, not a mere wish (see note on Eph 1:18).

1:2 *true son in the faith.* Spiritual son (see 1:18; 1Co 4:17; 2Ti 1:2; 2:1; Phm 10). *Grace … peace.* See note on Ro 1:7. *mercy.* See Ro 9:22 – 23 and note; included only here and in 2Ti 1:2 in the greetings of Paul's letters.

1:3 – 11 In this section, along with 4:1 – 8; 6:3 – 5,20 – 21, Paul warns against heretical teachers in the Ephesian church. They are characterized by (1) teaching "false doctrines" (v. 3; 6:3); (2) building up endless, far-fetched, fictitious stories based on obscure genealogical points (v. 4; 4:7); (3) being argumentative (v. 4; 6:4); (4) using talk that was "meaningless" (v. 6); (5) wanting to be teachers of the OT law (v. 7); (6) being conceited (v. 7; 6:4); (7) not knowing what they were talking about (v. 7; 6:4); (8) teaching ascetic practices (4:3); and (9) using their positions of religious leadership for "financial gain" (6:5). These heretics probably were forerunners of the Gnostics (see 6:20 and note).

1:3 *I went into Macedonia.* Since this incident is not recorded in Acts, it probably occurred after Ac 28, between Paul's first and second Roman imprisonments (see Introduction: Recipient). *Macedonia.* See note on Php 4:15. *stay there in Ephesus.* And do the Lord's work in the Ephesian church — which was well established by this time. Paul had an extensive ministry there on his third missionary journey about eight years earlier (Ac 19:1 — 20:1). *Ephesus.* See Introduction to Ephesians: The City of Ephesus; see also map, p. 1823.

1:4 *myths.* Perhaps mythical stories built on OT history ("genealogies") that later developed into intricate Gnostic philosophical systems (see Introduction to 1 John: Gnosticism).

1:5 *pure heart.* See 2Ti 2:22; Ps 24:4 and note; 51:10; cf. Mt 5:8.

1:8 *the law is good.* See Ro 7:7 – 12 and note on 7:12.

1:9 – 10 See note on Ro 1:29 – 31.

1:10 *sound doctrine.* See Tit 1:9 and note.

1:11 *gospel.* See Mk 1:1 and note. *entrusted.* See 6:20; 1Co 9:17; Gal 2:7; 1Th 2:4; 2Ti 1:14.

1:12 *Christ … has given me strength.* See Php 4:13 and note. *appointing me to his service.* See v. 1 and note.

1:13 *a blasphemer and a persecutor and a violent man.* See Ac 9:1; 22:4 – 5,19; 26:10 – 11 and note on 26:11.

1:14 *faith and love … in Christ.* See 2Ti 1:13 and note.

1:15 *Here is a trustworthy saying.* A clause found nowhere else in the NT but used five times in the Pastorals (here; 3:1; 4:9; 2Ti 2:11; Tit 3:8) to identify a key teaching. *of whom I am the worst.* The closer one gets to a holy God, the more the magnitude of one's sin becomes evident (cf. Isa 6:5; see 1Co 15:9; Eph 3:8 and note).

1:16 *eternal life.* See Jn 3:15 and note.

1:17 *invisible.* See Col 1:15 and note.

1:18 *son.* See v. 2 and note. *prophecies once made about you.* In the early church God revealed his will in various matters through prophets (see Ac 13:1 – 3, where prophets had an active role in sending Paul and Barnabas on their mission to the Gentiles). In Timothy's case a prophecy may have occurred at the time of or before his ordination (4:14), perhaps about 12 years earlier on Paul's second missionary journey (see Ac 16:1 – 3). *fight the good fight.* See 6:12; 2Ti 2:3; 4:7 and note.

19holding on to faith and a good conscience.[r] Some have rejected these and so
have shipwrecked their faith.[s] 20Among
them are Hymenaeus[t] and Alexander,[u]
whom I have handed over to Satan[v] to be
taught not to blaspheme.

Instructions on Worship

2 I urge, then, first of all, that requests,
prayers,[w] intercession and thanksgiving be made for everyone— 2for kings and
all those in authority,[x] that we may live
peaceful and quiet lives in all godliness[y]
and holiness. 3This is good, and pleases[z]
God our Savior,[a] 4who wants[b] all men[c] to
be saved[d] and to come to a knowledge of
the truth.[e] 5For there is one God[f] and one
mediator[g] between God and men, the man
Christ Jesus,[h] 6who gave himself as a ransom[i] for all men—the testimony[j] given in
its proper time.[k] 7And for this purpose I
was appointed a herald and an apostle—I
am telling the truth, I am not lying[l]—and a
teacher[m] of the true faith to the Gentiles.[n]

8I want men everywhere to lift up holy
hands[o] in prayer, without anger or disputing.
9I also want women to dress modestly, with decency and propriety, not with
braided hair or gold or pearls or expensive
clothes,[p] 10but with good deeds,[q] appropriate for women who profess to worship
God.
11A woman should learn in quietness
and full submission.[r] 12I do not permit a
woman to teach or to have authority over
a man; she must be silent.[s] 13For Adam
was formed first, then Eve.[t] 14And Adam
was not the one deceived; it was the woman who was deceived and became a sinner.[u] 15But women[a] will be saved[b] through
childbearing—if they continue in faith,
love[v] and holiness with propriety.

[a] *15* Greek *she* [b] *15* Or *restored*

1:19 [r]ver 5; S Ac 23:1 [s]1Ti 6:21; 2Ti 2:18 **1:20** [t]2Ti 2:17 [u]2Ti 4:14 [v]1Co 5:5 **2:1** [w]Eph 6:18 **2:2** [x]Ezr 6:10; Ro 13:1 [y]1Ti 3:16; 4:7,8; 6:3,5,6,11; 2Ti 3:5; Tit 1:1 **2:3** [z]S 1Ti 5:4 [a]S Lk 1:47 **2:4** [b]Eze 18:23, 32; 33:11 [c]1Ti 4:10; Tit 2:11; 2Pe 3:9 [d]S Jn 3:17; S Ro 11:14 [e]2Ti 2:25; Tit 1:1; Heb 10:26 **2:5** [f]Dt 6:4; Ro 3:29,30; 10:12 [g]S Gal 3:20 [h]Ro 1:3 **2:6** [i]S Mt 20:28 [j]S 1Co 1:6 [k]1Ti 6:15; Tit 1:3 **2:7** [l]S Ro 9:1 [m]2Ti 1:11 [n]S Ac 9:15 **2:8** [o]Ps 24:4; 63:4; 134:2; 141:2; Lk 24:50 **2:9** [p]1Pe 3:3 **2:10** [q]Pr 31:13 **2:11** [r]1Pe 3:3,4 **2:12** [s]S Eph 5:22 **2:13** [t]Ge 2:7,22; 1Co 11:8 **2:14** [u]Ge 3:1-6,13; 2Co 11:3 **2:15** [v]1Ti 1:14

1:20 *Hymenaeus.* See 2Ti 2:17–18. *Alexander.* Perhaps the Alexander of 2Ti 4:14. *handed over to Satan.* The reference is to church discipline (see Mt 18:17 and note). Paul had excluded these two men from the church, which was considered a sanctuary from Satan's power. Out in the world, away from the fellowship and care of the church, they would be "taught" (the word means basically "to discipline") not to blaspheme. The purpose of such drastic action was more remedial than punitive. For a similar situation see 1Co 5:5,13 and note on 5:5.

2:1–2 *prayers ... for kings and all those in authority.* See Jer 29:7; 1Pe 2:13 and note. The notorious Roman emperor Nero (A.D. 54–68) was in power when Paul wrote these words. *godliness.* A key word (along with "godly") in the Pastorals, occurring ten times (here; 3:16; 4:7–8; 6:3,5–6,11; 2Ti 3:5; Tit 1:1), but nowhere else in the writings of Paul. It implies a good and holy life, with special emphasis on its source, a deep reverence for God.

2:3 *God our Savior.* See Tit 1:3 and note.

2:4 *wants all men to be saved.* God desires the salvation of all people. On the other hand, the Bible indicates that God chooses some (not all) people to be saved (see 4:10; Ro 8:29 and notes).

2:5 *there is one God.* The basic belief of Judaism (see Dt 6:4 and note), which every Jew confessed daily in the *Shema* (see Mk 12:29 and note). *mediator.* One who represents God to humans and humans to God—and who removes all alienation between them by offering himself as "a ransom for all" (v. 6). Cf. Jn 14:6; Heb 8:6 and notes.

2:6 *ransom.* See Mt 20:28 and note. *testimony.* The apostolic testimony that Christ gave himself as the ransom. *proper time.* See Gal 4:4 and note.

2:7 *for this purpose.* To testify that, through his death, Christ has bridged the gap between God and human beings and made salvation available to all. *herald.* See 2Ti 1:11; one who with authority makes a public proclamation. *apostle.* See 1Co 1:1 and note.

2:8 *men.* The Greek for this word does not refer to humankind (as in vv. 5–6) but to male as distinct from female. Women also prayed in public, however (see 1Co 11:5 and note).

2:9–14 Some maintain that Paul's teaching about women here is historically conditioned, not universal and timeless. Others view these verses as unaffected by the historical situation and therefore applicable to every age.

2:9 Not a total ban on the wearing of jewelry or braided hair. Rather, Paul was expressing caution in a society where such things were signs of extravagant luxury and proud personal display.

2:10 See 1Pe 3:3–5 and note on 3:3.

2:12 *not permit a woman to teach.* Some believe that Paul here prohibited teaching only by women not properly instructed, i.e., by the women at Ephesus. Such women tended to exercise authority over, i.e., to domineer, the men. Others maintain that Paul did not allow a woman to be an official teacher in the assembled church. This is indicated by the added restriction concerning exercising "authority over a man" (a male), i.e., functioning as an overseer (see note on 3:1).

2:13–14 Paul based the restrictions on Ge 2–3. Some argue that "For" does not express the reason for woman's silence and submission, but is used only as a connective word as in v. 5. The meaning, then, would be that Adam's priority in creation illustrates the present situation of male priority in teaching at Ephesus, and Eve's deception illustrates the deception of the untrained and aggressive Ephesian women involved in false teaching. Thus the prohibition is not universal and permanent but restricted to the church situation (see Introduction: Background and Purpose). Under different circumstances the restrictions would not apply (e.g., 1Co 11:1–5). Others believe that the appeal to the creation account makes the restrictions universal and permanent: (1) *Adam was formed first.* Paul appeals to the priority of Adam in creation, which predates the fall. Thus he views the man-woman relationship set forth in this passage as grounded in creation. (2) *the woman ... was deceived.* Paul appears to argue that since the woman was deceived (and then led Adam astray), she is not to be entrusted with the teaching function of an overseer (or elder) in the public worship services of the assembled church.

2:15 *saved through childbearing.* Three possible meanings are: (1) It speaks of the godly woman finding fulfillment in her role as wife and mother in the home; (2) it refers to women being saved spiritually through the most significant birth of all, the incarnation of Christ; or (3) it refers to women being kept physically safe in childbirth.

Overseers and Deacons

3 Here is a trustworthy saying:[w] If anyone
sets his heart on being an overseer,[a][x]
he desires a noble task. 2Now the overseer
must be above reproach,[y] the husband of
but one wife,[z] temperate,[a] self-controlled,
respectable, hospitable,[b] able to teach,[c]
3not given to drunkenness,[d] not violent
but gentle, not quarrelsome,[e] not a lover
of money.[f] 4He must manage his own family well and see that his children obey him
with proper respect.[g] 5(If anyone does not
know how to manage his own family, how
can he take care of God's church?)[h] 6He
must not be a recent convert, or he may
become conceited[i] and fall under the same
judgment[j] as the devil. 7He must also have
a good reputation with outsiders,[k] so that
he will not fall into disgrace and into the
devil's trap.[l]
8Deacons,[m] likewise, are to be men worthy of respect, sincere, not indulging in
much wine,[n] and not pursuing dishonest

[a] *1* Traditionally *bishop*; also in verse 2

3:1 [w]S 1Ti 1:15 [x]Ac 20:28; Php 1:1; Tit 1:7 **3:2** [y]Tit 1:6-8 [z]ver 12 [a]ver 11; Tit 2:2 [b]S Ro 12:13 [c]2Ti 2:24 **3:3** [d]Tit 1:7 [e]2Ti 2:24 [f]Lk 16:14; 1Ti 6:10; 2Ti 3:2; Heb 13:5; 1Pe 5:2 **3:4** [g]ver 12; Tit 1:6 **3:5** [h]S 1Co 10:32 **3:6** [i]1Ti 6:4; 2Ti 3:4 [j]S 2Pe 2:4 **3:7** [k]S Mk 4:11 [l]2Ti 2:26 **3:8** [m]Php 1:1 [n]1Ti 5:23; Tit 1:7; 2:3

3:1 *trustworthy saying.* See note on 1:15. *overseer.* In Greek culture the word was used of a presiding official in a civic or religious organization. Here it refers to a man who oversees a local congregation. The equivalent word from the Jewish background of Christianity is "elder." The terms "overseer" and "elder" are often used interchangeably (see Ac 20:17,28; Tit 1:5–7; 1Pe 5:1–2 and notes). The duties of an overseer were to teach and preach (3:2; 5:17), to direct the affairs of the church (3:5; 5:17), to shepherd ("pastor") the flock of God (Ac 20:28; see note there) and to guard the church from error (Ac 20:28–31).

3:2 *overseer must be.* See chart, p. 1874. *the husband of but one wife.* A general principle that applies to any violation of God's marriage law, whether in the form of polygamy or of marital unfaithfulness (see note on Tit 1:6). Or perhaps, as some believe, the phrase should be rendered "faithful to his wife."

3:5 *church.* See notes on Ac 9:31; 2Co 1:1.

3:7 *devil's trap.* See 2Ti 2:26; cf. 1Pe 5:8.

3:8 *Deacons.* In its nontechnical usage, the Greek for this word means simply "one who serves." The men chosen in Ac 6:1–6 were probably not only the first deacons mentioned in the NT but also the first to be appointed in the church (but see note on Ac 6:6). Generally, their service was meant to free the elders to give full attention to prayer and the ministry of the word (Ac 6:2,4). The only two local church offices mentioned in the NT are those of overseer (also called elder; see note on v. 1) and deacon (see Php 1:1, where the two offices are clearly distinguished).

Paul's Fourth Missionary Journey(?)

c. A.D. 62–68

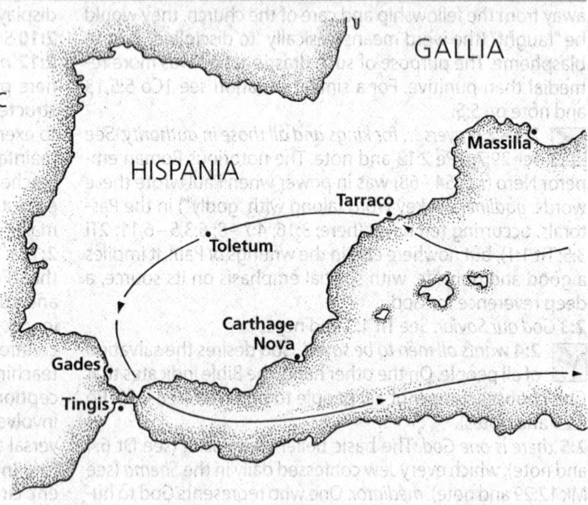

It is clear from Ac 13:1–21:17 that Paul went on three missionary journeys. There is also reason to believe that he made a fourth journey after his release from the Roman imprisonment recorded in Ac 28. The conclusion that such a journey did indeed take place is based on: (1) Paul's declared intention to go to Spain (Ro 15:24,28), (2) Eusebius's implication that Paul was released following his first Roman imprisonment (*Ecclesiastical History*, 2.22.2-3) and (3) statements in early Christian literature that he took the gospel as far as Spain (Clement of Rome, *Epistle to the Corinthians*, ch. 5; *Actus Petri Vercellenses*, chs. 1-3; Muratorian Canon, lines 34-39).

The places Paul may have visited after his release from prison are indicated by statements of intention in his earlier writings and by subsequent mention in the Pastoral Letters. The order of his travel cannot be determined with certainty, but the itinerary at the right seems likely.

1. **Rome**—released from prison in A.D. 62
2. **Spain**—62–64 (Ro 15:24,28)
3. **Crete**—64–65 (Tit 1:5)
4. **Miletus**—65 (2Ti 4:20)
5. **Colosse**—66 (Phm 22)
6. **Ephesus**—66 (1Ti 1:3)
7. **Philippi**—66 (Php 2:23-24; 1Ti 1:3)
8. **Nicopolis**—66–67 (Tit 3:12)
9. **Rome**—67 (2Ti 1:17)
10. Martyrdom—67/68 (2Ti 4:6)

gain. 9They must keep hold of the deep
truths of the faith with a clear conscience.[o]
10They must first be tested;[p] and then if
there is nothing against them, let them
serve as deacons.
11In the same way, their wives[a] are to be
women worthy of respect, not malicious
talkers[q] but temperate[r] and trustworthy in
everything.
12A deacon must be the husband of but
one wife[s] and must manage his children
and his household well.[t] 13Those who
have served well gain an excellent standing
and great assurance in their faith in
Christ Jesus.
14Although I hope to come to you soon,
I am writing you these instructions so that,
15if I am delayed, you will know how people
ought to conduct themselves in God's
household, which is the church[u] of the living
God,[v] the pillar and foundation of the
truth. 16Beyond all question, the mystery[w]
of godliness[x] is great:

He[b] appeared in a body,[c y]
was vindicated by the Spirit,
was seen by angels,
was preached among the nations,[z]
was believed on in the world,
was taken up in glory.[a]

3:9 [o] S Ac 23:1 3:10 [p] 1Ti 5:22 3:11 [q] 2Ti 3:3; Tit 2:3 [r] ver 2 3:12 [s] ver 2 [t] ver 4 3:15 [u] ver 5; S 1Co 10:32 [v] S Mt 16:16 3:16 [w] S Ro 16:25 [x] S 1Ti 2:2 [y] S Jn 1:14 [z] Ps 9:11; Col 1:23 [a] S Mk 16:19

[a] 11 Or *way, deaconesses* [b] 16 Some manuscripts *God* [c] 16 Or *in the flesh*

3:9 *the faith.* Apostolic teaching (see 4:1,6; 6:10,12,21; 2Ti 4:7 and note; Tit 1:13; cf. 1Co 15:3; 2Th 2:15 and notes).

3:11 *their wives.* The Greek for this phrase simply means "the women" and therefore could refer to (1) deacons' wives or (2) deaconesses (see NIV text note). However, the fact that deacons are referred to again in vv. 12–13 seems to rule out a separate office of deaconess—but many judge otherwise.

3:12 *husband of but one wife.* See v. 2 and note.

3:14 *I am writing ... so that.* Here, in brief, Paul states the purpose for writing the letter—to give instructions concerning church conduct (v. 15).

3:15 *God's household.* The family of God, made up of believers. *pillar and foundation of the truth.* See 2Ti 2:19 and note.

3:16 *mystery of godliness.* See Ro 11:25; Col 1:26 and notes. The phrase means the "revealed secret of true piety," i.e., the secret that produces piety in people. That secret, as the following words indicate, is none other than Jesus Christ. His incarnation, in all its aspects (particularly his saving work), is the source of genuine piety. The words are printed in poetic form and probably come from an early creedal hymn (see note on Col 3:16). *godliness.* See 2:2 and note on 2:1–2.

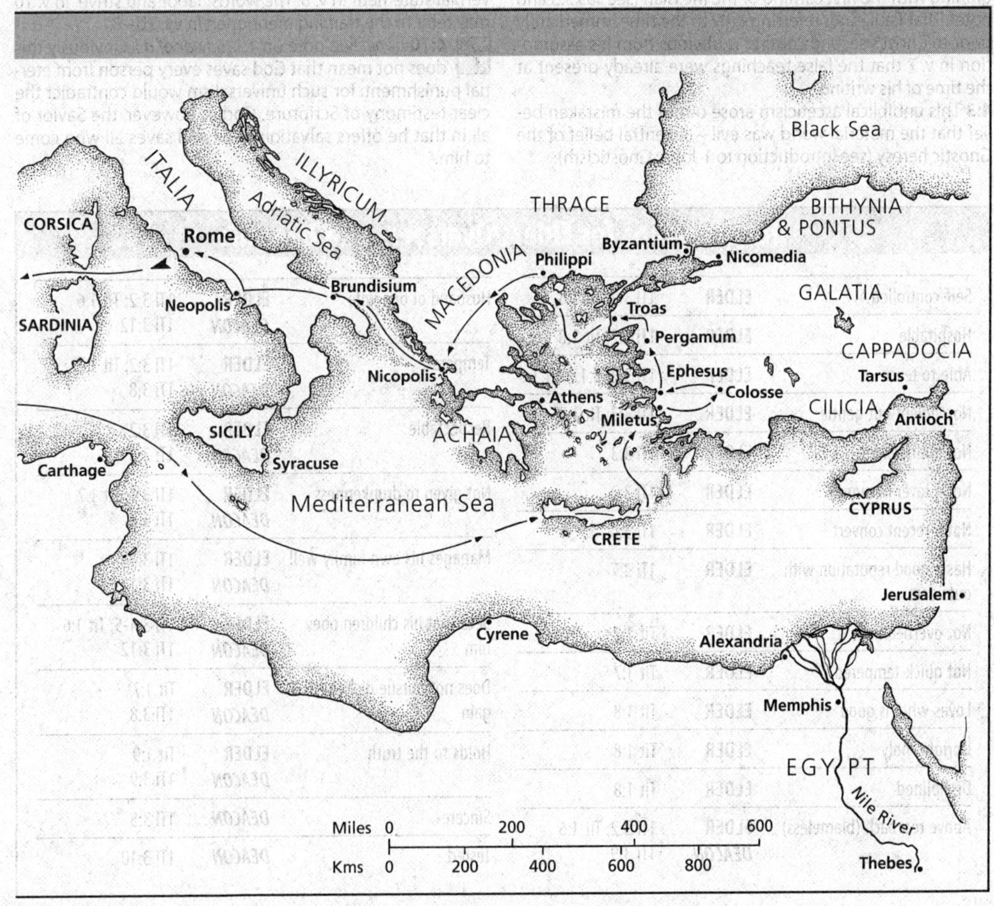

Instructions to Timothy

4 The Spirit[b] clearly says that in later
times[c] some will abandon the faith and
follow deceiving spirits[d] and things taught
by demons. 2Such teachings come through
hypocritical liars, whose consciences have
been seared as with a hot iron.[e] 3They forbid people to marry[f] and order them to abstain from certain foods,[g] which God created[h] to be received with thanksgiving[i] by
those who believe and who know the truth.
4For everything God created is good,[j] and
nothing is to be rejected[k] if it is received
with thanksgiving, 5because it is consecrated by the word of God[l] and prayer.
6If you point these things out to the
brothers, you will be a good minister of
Christ Jesus, brought up in the truths of
the faith[m] and of the good teaching that
you have followed.[n] 7Have nothing to do
with godless myths and old wives' tales;[o]
rather, train yourself to be godly.[p] 8For
physical training is of some value, but
godliness has value for all things,[q] holding promise for both the present life[r] and
the life to come.[s]
9This is a trustworthy saying[t] that deserves full acceptance 10(and for this we
labor and strive), that we have put our
hope in the living God,[u] who is the Savior
of all men,[v] and especially of those who
believe.

4:1 [b]Jn 16:13; S Ac 8:29; 1Co 2:10 [c]2Ti 3:1; 2Pe 3:3 [d]S Mk 13:5 **4:2** [e]Eph 4:19 **4:3** [f]Heb 13:4 [g]Col 2:16 [h]Ge 1:29; 9:3 [i]ver 4; Ro 14:6; 1Co 10:30 **4:4** [j]Ge 1:10,12, 18,21,25,31; Mk 7:18,19; Ro 14:14-18 [k]S Ac 10:15 **4:5** [l]S Heb 4:12 **4:6** [m]1Ti 1:10 [n]2Ti 3:15 **4:7** [o]1Ti 1:4; 2Ti 2:16 [p]S 1Ti 2:2 **4:8** [q]1Ti 6:6 [r]Ps 37:9,11; Pr 22:4; Mt 6:33; Mk 10:29,30 [s]Mk 10:29,30 **4:9** [t]S 1Ti 1:15 **4:10** [u]S Mt 16:16 [v]S Lk 1:47; S 2:11

vindicated by the Spirit. The Holy Spirit enabled Jesus to drive out demons (see Mt 12:28) and perform miracles. Most important, the Spirit raised Jesus from the dead (see Ro 1:4; cf. 1Pe 3:18 and note) and thereby vindicated him, showing that he was indeed the Son of God. *seen by angels.* At his resurrection (Mt 28:2) and ascension (Ac 1:10; see note there).

4:1,6 *the faith.* See note on 3:9.

4:1 *The Spirit clearly says.* As, e.g., in Mk 13:22; Ac 20:29–30; 2Th 2:3. Paul, however, is perhaps speaking here of a specific revelation made to him by the Spirit. *later times.* The time beginning with the first coming of the Messiah (see Jas 5:3 and note). That Paul is not referring only to the time immediately prior to Christ's second coming is obvious from his assumption in v. 7 that the false teachings were already present at the time of his writing.

4:3 This unbiblical asceticism arose out of the mistaken belief that the material world was evil—a central belief of the Gnostic heresy (see Introduction to 1 John: Gnosticism).

4:4 *everything God created is good.* See Ge 1:4 and note, 10,12,18,21,25,31; see also Tit 1:15 and note.

4:6 *good teaching that you have followed.* Even from early childhood (see 2Ti 3:15 and note).

4:7 *myths.* See 1:4 and note. *train yourself to be godly.* See 2:2 and note on 2:1–2. Godliness requires self-discipline.

4:9 *trustworthy saying.* See note on 1:15. Although the NIV understands the expression in this instance to refer to what follows, it is possible that it refers back to the seemingly proverbial statement in v. 8. The words "labor and strive" in v. 10 may refer to the training mentioned in vv. 7b–8.

4:10 *hope.* See note on 1:1. *Savior of all.* Obviously this does not mean that God saves every person from eternal punishment, for such universalism would contradict the clear testimony of Scripture. God is, however, the Savior of all in that he offers salvation to all and saves all who come to him.

Qualifications for Elders/Overseers and Deacons

Qualification	Office	Reference
Self-controlled	ELDER	1Ti 3:2; Tit 1:8
Hospitable	ELDER	1Ti 3:2; Tit 1:8
Able to teach	ELDER	1Ti 3:2; 5:17; Tit 1:9
Not violent but gentle	ELDER	1Ti 3:3; Tit 1:7
Not quarrelsome	ELDER	1Ti 3:3
Not a lover of money	ELDER	1Ti 3:3
Not a recent convert	ELDER	1Ti 3:6
Has a good reputation with outsiders	ELDER	1Ti 3:7
Not overbearing	ELDER	Tit 1:7
Not quick-tempered	ELDER	Tit 1:7
Loves what is good	ELDER	Tit 1:8
Upright, holy	ELDER	Tit 1:8
Disciplined	ELDER	Tit 1:8
Above reproach (blameless)	ELDER *DEACON*	1Ti 3:2; Tit 1:6 1Ti 3:9
Husband of one wife	ELDER *DEACON*	1Ti 3:2; Tit 1:6 1Ti 3:12
Temperate	ELDER *DEACON*	1Ti 3:2; Tit 1:7 1Ti 3:8
Respectable	ELDER *DEACON*	1Ti 3:2 1Ti 3:8
Not given to drunkenness	ELDER *DEACON*	1Ti 3:3; Tit 1:7 1Ti 3:8
Manages his own family well	ELDER *DEACON*	1Ti 3:4 1Ti 3:12
Sees that his children obey him	ELDER *DEACON*	1Ti 3:4-5; Tit 1:6 1Ti 3:12
Does not pursue dishonest gain	ELDER *DEACON*	Tit 1:7 1Ti 3:8
Holds to the truth	ELDER *DEACON*	Tit 1:9 1Ti 3:9
Sincere	*DEACON*	1Ti 3:8
Tested	*DEACON*	1Ti 3:10

11Command and teach these things.[w]
12Don't let anyone look down on you[x] because you are young, but set an example[y]
for the believers in speech, in life, in love,
in faith[z] and in purity. 13Until I come,[a]
devote yourself to the public reading of
Scripture,[b] to preaching and to teaching.
14Do not neglect your gift, which was
given you through a prophetic message[c]
when the body of elders[d] laid their hands
on you.[e]
15Be diligent in these matters; give yourself wholly to them, so that everyone may
see your progress. 16Watch your life and
doctrine closely. Persevere in them, because if you do, you will save[f] both yourself and your hearers.

Advice About Widows, Elders and Slaves

5 Do not rebuke an older man[g] harshly,[h]
but exhort him as if he were your father. Treat younger men[i] as brothers, 2old-
er women as mothers, and younger wom-
en as sisters, with absolute purity.
3Give proper recognition to those widows who are really in need.[j] 4But if a widow has children or grandchildren, these
should learn first of all to put their religion
into practice by caring for their own family
and so repaying their parents and grandparents,[k] for this is pleasing to God.[l] 5The
widow who is really in need[m] and left all
alone puts her hope in God[n] and continues
night and day to pray[o] and to ask God for
help. 6But the widow who lives for pleasure is dead even while she lives.[p] 7Give
the people these instructions,[q] too, so that
no one may be open to blame. 8If anyone
does not provide for his relatives, and especially for his immediate family, he has
denied[r] the faith and is worse than an unbeliever.
9No widow may be put on the list of
widows unless she is over sixty, has been
faithful to her husband,[a] 10and is well
known for her good deeds,[s] such as bringing up children, showing hospitality,[t]
washing the feet[u] of the saints, helping
those in trouble[v] and devoting herself to
all kinds of good deeds.
11As for younger widows, do not put
them on such a list. For when their sensual desires overcome their dedication to
Christ, they want to marry. 12Thus they
bring judgment on themselves, because
they have broken their first pledge. 13Be-
sides, they get into the habit of being idle
and going about from house to house. And
not only do they become idlers, but also
gossips[w] and busybodies,[x] saying things
they ought not to. 14So I counsel younger
widows to marry,[y] to have children, to
manage their homes and to give the enemy no opportunity for slander.[z] 15Some
have in fact already turned away to follow
Satan.[a]
16If any woman who is a believer has
widows in her family, she should help
them and not let the church be burdened
with them, so that the church can help
those widows who are really in need.[b]
17The elders[c] who direct the affairs of the
church well are worthy of double honor,[d]
especially those whose work is preaching
and teaching. 18For the Scripture says, "Do
not muzzle the ox while it is treading out

4:11 [w] 1Ti 5:7; 6:2 **4:12** [x] S 2Ti 1:7; Tit 2:15 [y] Php 3:17; 1Th 1:7; 2Th 3:9; Tit 2:7; 1Pe 5:3 [z] 1Ti 1:14 **4:13** [a] 1Ti 3:14 [b] Lk 4:16; Ac 13:14-16; Col 4:16; 1Th 5:27 **4:14** [c] 1Ti 1:18 [d] S Ac 11:30 [e] S Ac 6:6; 2Ti 1:6 **4:16** [f] S Ro 11:14 **5:1** [g] Tit 2:2 [h] Lev 19:32 [i] Tit 2:6 **5:3** [j] ver 5, 16 **5:4** [k] ver 8; Eph 6:1, 2 [l] Ro 12:2; Eph 5:10; 1Ti 2:3 **5:5** [m] ver 3, 16 [n] 1Co 7:34; 1Pe 3:5 [o] Lk 2:37; S Ro 1:10 **5:6** [p] S Lk 15:24 **5:7** [q] 1Ti 4:11; 6:2 **5:8** [r] 2Pe 2:1; Jude 4 **5:10** [s] Ac 9:36; 1Ti 6:18; 1Pe 2:12 [t] S Ro 12:13 [u] S Lk 7:44 [v] ver 16 **5:13** [w] S Ro 1:29 [x] 2Th 3:11 **5:14** [y] 1Co 7:9 [z] 1Ti 6:1 **5:15** [a] S Mt 4:10 **5:16** [b] ver 3-5 **5:17** [c] S Ac 11:30 [d] Php 2:29; 1Th 5:12

[a] 9 Or *has had but one husband*

4:12 *because you are young.* Timothy was probably in his mid–30s or younger, and in that day, such an influential position was not usually held by a man so young. For this reason, perhaps his leadership had been called into question. *example.* See Tit 2:7–8 and note.
4:13 *Until I come.* Paul's journey had taken him from Ephesus to Macedonia (see map, p. 1872), but he hoped to rejoin Timothy soon in Ephesus (3:14).
4:14 *prophetic message.* See 1:18 and note. *laid their hands on you.* As an act of commissioning to service (see Ac 6:6; Heb 6:1–2 and notes).
4:16 *you will save … your hearers.* God alone saves, but Christians can be God's instruments to bring about the salvation of others.
5:3 *Give proper recognition to those widows.* Probably means taking care of them, including the giving of material support. Widows were particularly vulnerable in ancient societies because pensions, government assistance, life insurance, and the like were not available to them.
5:4 *put their religion into practice.* See Jas 1:22–27; 2:14–26 and note.
5:5 For an example of such a widow see Lk 2:36–38.
5:6 *dead even while she lives.* Dead spiritually while living physically.
5:8 *the faith.* See note on 3:9. Apostolic teaching emphasized social responsibility. *worse than an unbeliever.* Even in the pagan world of that time, people generally took care of their family members.
5:9 The church in Ephesus seems to have maintained a "list of widows" supported by the church. While there is no evidence of an order of widows comparable to that of the overseers, it appears that those on the list were expected to devote themselves to prayer (v. 5) and good deeds (v. 10).
5:10 *washing the feet of the saints.* A menial task, but necessary in NT times because of dusty roads and the wearing of sandals (see Jn 13:14). *saints.* See notes on Ro 1:7; Eph 1:1.
5:12 *broken their first pledge.* Perhaps when a widow was added to the list she pledged special devotion to Christ, which would be diminished by remarriage. Or Paul may be referring to the believer's basic trust in Christ, which a widow would compromise by marrying outside the faith.
5:13 *busybodies.* See 2Th 3:11 and note.
5:15 *Satan.* See notes on Job 1:6; Mt 16:23; 1Th 3:5; 1Jn 3:8; Rev 12:9–10.
5:17 All elders were to exercise leadership (3:4–5) and to teach and preach (3:2), and all were to receive honor. But those who excelled in leadership were to be counted "worthy of double honor." This was especially true of those who labored at teaching and preaching. (The Greek word translated "work" refers to toil.) That such honor should include financial support is indicated by the two illustrations in v. 18.
5:18 *Scripture.* The use of this term for both an OT (Dt 25:4) and a NT (Lk 10:7) passage shows that by this time

the grain,"[a][e] and "The worker deserves his
wages."[b][f] 19Do not entertain an accusation
against an elder[g] unless it is brought by
two or three witnesses.[h] 20Those who sin
are to be rebuked[i] publicly, so that the
others may take warning.[j]
21I charge you, in the sight of God and
Christ Jesus[k] and the elect angels, to keep
these instructions without partiality, and
to do nothing out of favoritism.
22Do not be hasty in the laying on of
hands,[l] and do not share in the sins of others.[m] Keep yourself pure.[n]
23Stop drinking only water, and use a
little wine[o] because of your stomach and
your frequent illnesses.
24The sins of some men are obvious,
reaching the place of judgment ahead of
them; the sins of others trail behind them.
25In the same way, good deeds are obvious, and even those that are not cannot
be hidden.

6 All who are under the yoke of slavery
should consider their masters worthy of
full respect,[p] so that God's name and our
teaching may not be slandered.[q] 2Those
who have believing masters are not to
show less respect for them because they
are brothers.[r] Instead, they are to serve
them even better, because those who benefit from their service are believers, and
dear to them. These are the things you are
to teach and urge on them.[s]

Love of Money

3If anyone teaches false doctrines[t] and
does not agree to the sound instruction[u] of
our Lord Jesus Christ and to godly teaching, 4he is conceited[v] and understands
nothing. He has an unhealthy interest in
controversies and quarrels about words[w]
that result in envy, strife, malicious talk,
evil suspicions 5and constant friction between men of corrupt mind, who have
been robbed of the truth[x] and who think
that godliness is a means to financial
gain.
6But godliness with contentment[y] is
great gain.[z] 7For we brought nothing into
the world, and we can take nothing out
of it.[a] 8But if we have food and clothing,
we will be content with that.[b] 9People who
want to get rich[c] fall into temptation and
a trap[d] and into many foolish and harmful
desires that plunge men into ruin and destruction. 10For the love of money[e] is a root
of all kinds of evil. Some people, eager for
money, have wandered from the faith[f] and
pierced themselves with many griefs.[g]

Paul's Charge to Timothy

11But you, man of God,[h] flee from all
this, and pursue righteousness, godliness,[i]
faith, love,[j] endurance and gentleness.
12Fight the good fight[k] of the faith. Take
hold of[l] the eternal life[m] to which you were
called when you made your good confession[n] in the presence of many witnesses.
13In the sight of God, who gives life to everything, and of Christ Jesus, who while
testifying before Pontius Pilate[o] made the
good confession,[p] I charge you[q] 14to keep
this command without spot or blame[r] until the appearing of our Lord Jesus Christ,[s]

5:18 [e] Dt 25:4; 1Co 9:7-9 [f] Lk 10:7; Lev 19:13; Dt 24:14,15; Mt 10:10; 1Co 9:14 **5:19** [g] S Ac 11:30 [h] S Mt 18:16 **5:20** [i] 2Ti 4:2; Tit 1:13; 2:15 [j] Dt 13:11 **5:21** [k] 1Ti 6:13; 2Ti 4:1 **5:22** [l] S Ac 6:6 [m] Eph 5:11 [n] Ps 18:26 **5:23** [o] 1Ti 3:8 **6:1** [p] S Eph 6:5 [q] 1Ti 5:14; Tit 2:5,8 **6:2** [r] Phm 16 [s] 1Ti 4:11 **6:3** [t] 1Ti 1:3 [u] S 1Ti 1:10 **6:4** [v] 1Ti 3:6; 2Ti 3:4 [w] S 2Ti 2:14 **6:5** [x] 2Ti 3:8; Tit 1:15 **6:6** [y] Php 4:11; Heb 13:5 [z] 1Ti 4:8 **6:7** [a] Job 1:21; Ps 49:17; Ecc 5:15 **6:8** [b] Pr 30:8; Heb 13:5 **6:9** [c] Pr 15:27; 28:20 [d] 1Ti 3:7 **6:10** [e] S 1Ti 3:3 [f] ver 21; Jas 5:19 [g] Jos 7:21 **6:11** [h] 2Ti 3:17 [i] ver 3,5,6; S 1Ti 2:2 [j] 1Ti 1:14; 2Ti 2:22; 3:10 **6:12** [k] 1Co 9:25,26; S 1Ti 1:18 [l] ver 19; Php 3:12 [m] S Mt 25:46 [n] S Heb 3:1

a 18 Deut. 25:4 *b 18* Luke 10:7

6:13 [o] Jn 18:33-37 [p] ver 12 [q] 1Ti 5:21; 2Ti 4:1 **6:14** [r] S 1Th 3:13 [s] S 1Co 1:7; 2Ti 1:10; 4:1,8

portions of the NT (or what ultimately became a part of the NT) were considered to be equal in authority to the OT Scriptures (see 2Pe 3:16 and note). *Do not muzzle ... grain.* See 1Co 9:9–11 and notes on 9:9,11.

5:19 *two or three witnesses.* Cf. Dt 17:6 and note.

5:20 *Those who sin.* The context indicates that Paul is speaking of the discipline of elders.

5:21 *elect angels.* Chosen angels, in contrast to Satan and the other fallen angels. *do nothing out of favoritism.* See Ex 23:3; Lev 19:15; Dt 1:17; 16:19; Job 13:10; Pr 18:5; 24:23; 28:21; Mal 2:9; Jas 2:1,9; 3:7. Cf. note on Ac 10:34.

5:22 *Do not be hasty in the laying on of hands.* Paul is speaking about the ordination of elders (see 4:14 and note), which should not be done until candidates have had time to prove themselves. *do not share in the sins of others.* Do not ordain a person unworthy of the office of elder. *Keep yourself pure.* Probably here refers to refusal to become involved in the ordination of an unworthy man.

5:23 *Stop drinking only water.* A parenthetical comment in Paul's discussion of elders. In view of Timothy's physical ailments, and perhaps because safe drinking water was often difficult to find, Paul advised him to drink "a little wine."

5:24–25 *sins of some men ... good deeds.* Paul advises being alert to hidden sins as well as to good deeds in the lives of candidates for ordination.

6:1 *slavery.* See notes on Eph 6:5; Col 3:22—4:1; see also Phm 16.

6:2 *urge on them.* Refers to the instructions to slaves.

6:3–5 Paul returns to the subject of 1:3 (see note on 1:3–11).

6:3 *sound instruction ... godly.* See essay, p. 1867.

6:5 *robbed of the truth.* They had once known the truth but had been led into error. *who think that godliness is a means to financial gain.* See notes on 2Co 2:17; 11:7.

6:7 *take nothing out of it.* See Ps 49:17.

6:8 See Php 4:11–12 and notes.

6:9 See Lk 12:13–21 and note on 12:13.

6:10,12,21 *the faith.* See note on 3:9.

6:12 *Fight the good fight.* See 1:18 and note. *Take hold of the eternal life.* Timothy had possessed eternal life since he had first been saved, but Paul urges him to claim its benefits in greater fullness (see vv. 17–19 and note on 4:16). *when you made your good confession.* Perhaps a reference to Timothy's confession of faith at his baptism during Paul's first missionary journey.

6:13 *who while testifying before Pontius Pilate made the good confession.* Probably a reference to Jesus' statements recorded in Jn 18:34–37; 19:11.

6:14 *this command.* Perhaps the whole charge given to Timothy to preach the gospel and care for the church (see

15 which God will bring about in his own
time[t] — God, the blessed[u] and only Ruler,[v] the King of kings and Lord of lords,[w]
16 who alone is immortal[x] and who lives
in unapproachable light,[y] whom no one
has seen or can see.[z] To him be honor and
might forever. Amen.[a]

17 Command those who are rich[b] in this
present world not to be arrogant nor to put
their hope in wealth,[c] which is so uncertain, but to put their hope in God,[d] who
richly provides us with everything for our
enjoyment.[e] 18 Command them to do good,
to be rich in good deeds,[f] and to be generous and willing to share.[g] 19 In this way
they will lay up treasure for themselves[h]
as a firm foundation for the coming age,
so that they may take hold of[i] the life that
is truly life.

20 Timothy, guard what has been entrusted[j] to your care. Turn away from godless
chatter[k] and the opposing ideas of what
is falsely called knowledge, 21 which some
have professed and in so doing have wandered from the faith.[l]

Grace be with you.[m]

6:15 [t] 1Ti 2:6; Tit 1:3 [u] 1Ti 1:11 [v] 1Ti 1:17 [w] Dt 10:17; Ps 136:3; Da 2:47; Rev 1:5; 17:14; 19:16 **6:16** [x] 1Ti 1:17 [y] Ps 104:2; 1Jn 1:7 [z] S Jn 1:18 [a] S Ro 11:36 **6:17** [b] ver 9 [c] Ps 62:10; Jer 49:4; Lk 12:20, 21 [d] 1Ti 4:10 [e] Ac 14:17 **6:18** [f] S 1Ti 5:10 [g] Ro 12:8, 13; Eph 4:28 **6:19** [h] S Mt 6:20 [i] ver 12; Php 3:12 **6:20** [j] 2Ti 1:12, 14 [k] 2Ti 2:16 **6:21** [l] ver 10; 2Ti 2:18 [m] S Col 4:18

v. 20) — though the preceding context may indicate that Paul used the singular "command" to sum up the various commands listed in vv. 11 – 12.
6:15 *in his own time.* Just as Jesus' first coming occurred at the precise time God wanted (Gal 4:4), so also his second coming will be at God's appointed time. *King of kings and Lord of lords.* See Rev 17:14 and note; 19:16.
6:16 *whom no one has seen or can see.* See Jn 1:18 and note.
6:17 – 19 See note on v. 12.
6:19 *lay up treasure.* See Mt 6:19 – 21 and note; 19:21; Lk 12:33 and note.
6:20 *what has been entrusted to your care.* The gospel (see 2Ti 1:14). *what is falsely called knowledge.* Perhaps a reference to an early form of the heresy of Gnosticism, which taught that one may be saved by knowledge. (The term "Gnosticism" comes from the Greek word for knowledge; see Introduction to 1 John: Gnosticism.)
6:21 *Grace.* See note on Ro 1:7. *with you.* See note on 2Co 13:14. *you.* The Greek is plural, indicating that Paul expects his letter to Timothy to be read to the entire Ephesian congregation (see note on 2Ti 4:22).

2 Timothy

I N T R O D U C T I O N

Author, Date and Setting

See essay, p. 1867. After Paul's release from prison in Rome in A.D. 62 (Ac 28) and after his fourth missionary journey (see map, pp. 1872–1873), during which he wrote 1 Timothy and Titus, Paul was again imprisoned under Emperor Nero c. 66–67. It was during this time that he wrote 2 Timothy (see chart, p. 1697). In contrast to his first imprisonment, when he lived in a "rented house" (Ac 28:30; see note there), he now languished in a cold dungeon (see 4:13 and note), chained like a common criminal (1:16; 2:9). His friends even had a hard time finding out where he was being kept (1:17). Paul knew that his work was done and that his life was nearly at an end (4:6–8).

A Quick Look

Author:
The apostle Paul

Audience:
Paul's disciple Timothy, who was ministering in Ephesus

Date:
About A.D. 66–67

Theme:
Facing imminent death, Paul encourages Timothy to carry on the ministry and faithfully guard the gospel.

Reasons for Writing

Paul had three reasons for writing to Timothy at this time:

1. Paul was lonely. Phygelus and Hermogenes, "everyone in the province of Asia" (1:15), and Demas (4:10) had deserted him. Crescens, Titus and Tychicus were away (4:10–12), and only Luke was with him (4:11). Paul wanted very much for Timothy to join him also. Timothy was his "fellow worker" (Ro 16:21), who "as a son with his father" (Php 2:22 ; see note there) had served closely with Paul (see 1Co 4:17). Of him Paul could say, "I have no one else like him" (Php 2:20). Paul longed for Timothy (1:4) and twice asked him to come soon (4:9,21). For more information on Timothy see Introduction to 1 Timothy: Recipient.

2. Paul was concerned about the welfare of the churches during this time of persecution under Nero, and he admonishes Timothy to guard the gospel (1:14), to persevere in it (3:14), to keep on preaching it (4:2) and, if necessary, to suffer for it (1:8; 2:3).

3. Paul wanted to write to the Ephesian church through his letter to Timothy (see note on 4:22).

Outline

- I. Introduction (1:1–4)
- II. Paul's Concern for Timothy (1:5–14)
- III. Paul's Situation (1:15–18)
- IV. Special Instructions to Timothy (ch. 2)
  - A. Call for Endurance (2:1–13)
  - B. Warning about Foolish Controversies (2:14–26)
- V. Warning about the Last Days (ch. 3)
  - A. Terrible Times (3:1–9)
  - B. Means of Combating Them (3:10–17)
- VI. Paul's Departing Remarks (4:1–8)
  - A. Charge to Preach the Word (4:1–5)
  - B. Paul's Victorious Prospect (4:6–8)
- VII. Final Requests, Greetings and Benediction (4:9–22)

1 Paul, an apostle[a] of Christ Jesus by the
will of God,[b] according to the promise
of life that is in Christ Jesus,[c]

2To Timothy,[d] my dear son:[e]

Grace, mercy and peace from God the
Father and Christ Jesus our Lord.[f]

Encouragement to Be Faithful

3I thank God,[g] whom I serve, as my
forefathers did, with a clear conscience,[h]
as night and day I constantly remember
you in my prayers.[i] 4Recalling your tears,[j]
I long to see you,[k] so that I may be filled
with joy. 5I have been reminded of your
sincere faith,[l] which first lived in your
grandmother Lois and in your mother Eunice[m] and, I am persuaded, now lives in
you also. 6For this reason I remind you to
fan into flame the gift of God, which is in
you through the laying on of my hands.[n]
7For God did not give us a spirit of timidity,[o] but a spirit of power,[p] of love and of
self-discipline.

8So do not be ashamed[q] to testify about
our Lord, or ashamed of me his prisoner.[r] But join with me in suffering for
the gospel,[s] by the power of God, 9who
has saved[t] us and called[u] us to a holy
life—not because of anything we have
done[v] but because of his own purpose and
grace. This grace was given us in Christ
Jesus before the beginning of time, 10but
it has now been revealed[w] through the appearing of our Savior, Christ Jesus,[x] who
has destroyed death[y] and has brought life
and immortality to light through the gospel. 11And of this gospel[z] I was appointed[a]
a herald and an apostle and a teacher.[b]
12That is why I am suffering as I am. Yet I
am not ashamed,[c] because I know whom
I have believed, and am convinced that he
is able to guard[d] what I have entrusted to
him for that day.[e]

13What you heard from me,[f] keep[g] as the
pattern[h] of sound teaching,[i] with faith and
love in Christ Jesus.[j] 14Guard[k] the good deposit that was entrusted to you—guard it
with the help of the Holy Spirit who lives
in us.[l]

15You know that everyone in the province of Asia[m] has deserted me,[n] including
Phygelus and Hermogenes.

16May the Lord show mercy to the
household of Onesiphorus,[o] because he
often refreshed me and was not ashamed[p]
of my chains.[q] 17On the contrary, when he
was in Rome, he searched hard for me until he found me. 18May the Lord grant that
he will find mercy from the Lord on that
day![r] You know very well in how many
ways he helped me[s] in Ephesus.[t]

1:1 [a]S 1Co 1:1 [b]S 2Co 1:1 [c]Eph 3:6; Tit 1:2; 1Ti 6:19 **1:2** [d]S Ac 16:1 [e]S 1Ti 1:2 [f]S Ro 1:7 **1:3** [g]S Ro 1:8 [h]S Ac 23:1 [i]S Ro 1:10 **1:4** [j]Ac 20:37 [k]2Ti 4:9 **1:5** [l]1Ti 1:5 [m]Ac 16:1; 2Ti 3:15 **1:6** [n]S Ac 6:6; 1Ti 4:14 **1:7** [o]Jer 42:11; Ro 8:15; 1Co 16:10, 11; 1Ti 4:12; Heb 2:15 [p]Isa 11:2 **1:8** [q]ver 12, 16; Mk 8:38 [r]S Eph 3:1 [s]2Ti 2:3, 9; 4:5 **1:9** [t]S Ro 11:14 [u]S Ro 8:28 [v]S Eph 2:9 **1:10** [w]Eph 1:9 [x]S 1Ti 6:14 [y]1Co 15:26, 54 **1:11** [z]ver 8 [a]S Ac 9:15 [b]1Ti 2:7 **1:12** [c]ver 8, 16; Mk 8:38 [d]ver 14; 1Ti 6:20 [e]ver 18; S 1Co 1:8; 2Ti 4:8 **1:13** [f]2Ti 2:2 [g]S Tit 1:9 [h]Ro 6:17 [i]S 1Ti 1:10 [j]S 1Th 1:3; 1Ti 1:14 **1:14** [k]ver 12 [l]S Ro 8:9 **1:15** [m]S Ac 2:9 [n]2Ti 4:10, 11, 16 **1:16** [o]2Ti 4:19 [p]ver 8, 12; Mk 8:38 [q]S Ac 21:33 **1:18** [r]S ver 12 [s]Heb 6:10 [t]S Ac 18:19

1:1 *Paul.* See note on Ro 1:1. *apostle.* See note on 1Co 1:1. *according to the promise of life.* God's choice of Paul to be an apostle was in keeping with that promise, because apostles were appointed to preach and explain the good news that eternal life is available to all who will receive it through faith in Christ.

1:2 *Timothy, my dear son.* See note on 1Ti 1:2. *Grace ... peace.* See note on Ro 1:7. *mercy.* See 1Ti 1:2 and note.

1:3 *thank God ... in my prayers.* See note on Php 1:3–4.

1:4 *Recalling your tears.* Perhaps refers to Timothy's tears when Paul left for Macedonia (see 1Ti 1:3 and note). *long to see you.* See 4:9,21.

1:5 *your grandmother Lois ... your mother Eunice.* According to Ac 16:1, Timothy's mother was a Jewish Christian. Here we learn that his grandmother too was a Christian. Timothy's father, however, was a Greek and apparently an unbeliever (Ac 16:1).

1:6 *fan into flame the gift of God.* Gifts are not given in full bloom; they need to be developed through use. *through the laying on of my hands.* See 1Ti 4:14 and note. Paul was God's instrument, through whom the gift came from the Holy Spirit to Timothy (see note on 1Ti 1:18).

1:7 *spirit of timidity.* Apparently Timothy was not as bold and assertive as Paul wanted him to be (see 1Co 16:10–11 and note on 16:10; 1Ti 4:12).

1:8 *do not be ashamed.* Cf. v. 12; Ro 1:16 and note.

1:9 *called us to a holy life.* See Eph 1:4 and note; 1Th 4:7. *not because of anything we have done but because of his own purpose and grace.* Salvation is by grace alone and is based not on human effort but on God's saving plan and the gracious gift of his Son (see Ro 3:28; see also Eph 2:8–9; Tit 3:5 and notes). *before the beginning of time.* God's plan to save lost sinners was made in eternity past (see Eph 1:4; 1Pe 1:20 and notes; Rev 13:8).

1:10 *Christ ... has destroyed death.* See 1Co 15:26 and note, 54–57 and note on 15:57. *has brought life and immortality to light.* See Ro 2:7; 1Co 15:42–57 and note on 15:42–44. *gospel.* See note on Mk 1:1.

1:11 *a herald and an apostle.* See 1Ti 2:7 and note.

1:12 *I am not ashamed.* Cf. v. 8 and note. *what I have entrusted to him.* Lit. "my deposit" or "my trust," which can mean either "something entrusted to me" or "something I have entrusted to someone else." If the former, reference is probably to the gospel (see v. 14; 1Ti 6:20 and notes); if the latter, reference is most likely to Paul's very being, his (immortal) life (cf. 2:8–13; 4:8). *that day.* The day of judgment.

1:13 *sound teaching.* See Tit 1:9 and note. *faith and love in Christ.* See 1Ti 1:14; faith and love through union with Christ—another way of saying "Christian faith and love."

1:14 *good deposit ... entrusted to you.* The gospel (see note on v. 12). Paul gives the same command in 1Ti 6:20. *Holy Spirit who lives in us.* See Ro 5:5; 1Co 6:19 and notes; see also Ro 8:9.

1:15 *everyone.* Probably a deliberate exaggeration to express widespread desertion. *province of Asia.* Timothy was in Ephesus, the capital of the province of Asia (see Introduction to Ephesians: The City of Ephesus; see also map, p. 1823).

1:16 *Onesiphorus.* Probably he and his family lived in Ephesus (v. 18; 4:19).

1:17 *Rome.* See Introduction: Author, Date and Setting; cf. v. 8; 2:9.

1:18 *that day.* The day of judgment (see v. 12). *he helped me in Ephesus.* Either on Paul's third missionary journey (see map, p. 1718) or on his fourth (see map, p. 1873).

2 You then, my son,[u] be strong[v] in the
grace that is in Christ Jesus. 2And the
things you have heard me say[w] in the presence of many witnesses[x] entrust to reliable
men who will also be qualified to teach
others. 3Endure hardship with us[y] like a
good soldier[z] of Christ Jesus. 4No one serving as a soldier gets involved in civilian affairs — he wants to please his commanding
officer. 5Similarly, if anyone competes as
an athlete, he does not receive the victor's
crown[a] unless he competes according to
the rules. 6The hardworking farmer should
be the first to receive a share of the crops.[b]
7Reflect on what I am saying, for the Lord
will give you insight into all this.
8Remember Jesus Christ, raised from
the dead,[c] descended from David.[d] This
is my gospel,[e] 9for which I am suffering[f]
even to the point of being chained[g] like a
criminal. But God's word[h] is not chained.
10Therefore I endure everything[i] for the
sake of the elect,[j] that they too may obtain the salvation[k] that is in Christ Jesus,
with eternal glory.[l]
11Here is a trustworthy saying:[m]

If we died with him,
we will also live with him;[n]
12if we endure,
we will also reign with him.[o]
If we disown him,
he will also disown us;[p]

2:1 [u]S 1Ti 1:2 [v]S Eph 6:10 **2:2** [w]2Ti 1:13 [x]1Ti 6:12 **2:3** [y]ver 9; 2Ti 1:8; 4:5 [z]S 1Ti 1:18 **2:5** [a]S 1Co 9:25 **2:6** [b]1Co 9:10 **2:8** [c]S Ac 2:24 [d]S Mt 1:1 [e]Ro 2:16; 16:25 **2:9** [f]S Ac 9:16 [g]S Ac 21:33 [h]S Heb 4:12 **2:10** [i]Col 1:24 [j]Tit 1:1 [k]2Co 1:6 [l]2Co 4:17; 1Pe 5:10 **2:11** [m]S 1Ti 1:15 [n]Ro 6:2-11 **2:12** [o]Ro 8:17; 1Pe 4:13 [p]Mt 10:33 **2:13** [q]Ro 3:3; S 1Co 1:9 **2:14** [r]ver 23; 1Ti 1:4; 6:4; Tit 3:9 **2:15** [s]Eph 1:13; Col 1:5; Jas 1:18 **2:16** [t]Tit 3:9; 1Ti 6:20 **2:17** [u]1Ti 1:20 **2:18** [v]2Th 2:2 [w]1Ti 1:19; 6:21 **2:19** [x]Isa 28:16 [y]Ex 33:12; Nu 16:5; Jn 10:14; 1Co 8:3; Gal 4:9 [z]1Co 1:2 **2:20** [a]Ro 9:21

13if we are faithless,
he will remain faithful,[q]
for he cannot disown himself.

A Workman Approved by God

14Keep reminding them of these things.
Warn them before God against quarreling about words;[r] it is of no value, and
only ruins those who listen. 15Do your
best to present yourself to God as one approved, a workman who does not need to
be ashamed and who correctly handles
the word of truth.[s] 16Avoid godless chatter,[t] because those who indulge in it will
become more and more ungodly. 17Their
teaching will spread like gangrene. Among
them are Hymenaeus[u] and Philetus, 18who
have wandered away from the truth. They
say that the resurrection has already tak-
en place,[v] and they destroy the faith of
some.[w] 19Nevertheless, God's solid foundation stands firm,[x] sealed with this inscription: "The Lord knows those who are
his,"[a][y] and, "Everyone who confesses the
name of the Lord[z] must turn away from
wickedness."
20In a large house there are articles not
only of gold and silver, but also of wood
and clay; some are for noble purposes
and some for ignoble.[a] 21If a man cleanses
himself from the latter, he will be an in-

[a] *19* Num. 16:5 (see Septuagint)

2:1 *my son.* See 1Ti 1:2 and note. *strong in the grace ... in Christ.* Enabling power comes from a relationship to Christ (see 2Co 12:9 – 10; Eph 6:10 and notes).

2:2 *in the presence of many witnesses.* Refers to Paul's preaching and teaching, which Timothy had heard repeatedly on Paul's missionary journeys.

2:3 – 6 Paul gives three examples for Timothy to follow: (1) a soldier who wants to please his commander; (2) an athlete who follows the rules of the game; and (3) a farmer who works hard.

2:5 *victor's crown.* Cf. 1Co 9:25 and note.

2:6 *receive a share of the crops.* In this illustration, as in the previous two (soldier, vv. 3 – 4; athlete, v. 5), the main lesson is that dedicated effort will be rewarded (see 1Ti 5:17 and note).

2:8 *raised from the dead, descended from David.* Christ's resurrection proclaims his deity, and his descent from David shows his humanity; both truths are basic to the gospel. Since Christ is God, his death has infinite value; since he is human, he could rightfully become our substitute.

2:9 *chained like a criminal.* Apparently Paul was awaiting execution (see 4:6 and note).

2:10 *I endure everything for the sake of the elect.* No suffering is too great if it brings about the salvation of God's chosen ones who will yet believe. *in Christ.* See notes on 1:13; Eph 1:1. *eternal glory.* The final state of salvation.

2:11 – 13 Probably an early Christian hymn. The point to which Paul appeals is that suffering for Christ will be followed by glory (see Ro 8:17 – 18).

2:11 *trustworthy saying.* See note on 1Ti 1:15. *If we died with him, we will also live with him.* The Greek grammatical construction here assumes that we "died with" Christ in the past, when he died for us on the cross. We are therefore assured that we will also live with him eternally (cf. Ro 6:2 – 11).

2:12 *If we endure, we will also reign.* Faithfully bearing up under suffering and trial will result in reward when Christ returns (see Ro 8:17 and note). *If we disown him.* See Mt 10:33.

2:13 *he will remain faithful.* See Ro 3:3 – 4 and notes.

2:14 – 18 The wording of vv. 14 – 16 indicates that the heresy mentioned here is an early form of Gnosticism — the same as that dealt with in 1 Timothy and Titus (see note on 1Ti 1:3 – 11 and Introduction to 1 John: Gnosticism). Two leaders of this heresy, Hymenaeus (see 1Ti 1:20) and Philetus (v. 17), denied bodily resurrection (v. 18) and probably asserted that there is only spiritual resurrection (similar to the error mentioned in 1Co 15:12 – 19; see notes there). Gnosticism interpreted resurrection allegorically, not literally.

2:15 *ashamed.* See 1:8 and note. *word of truth.* The gospel (Eph 1:13; Col 1:5), whose truth Timothy was to believe and obey and whose contents he was therefore to preach (4:2).

2:16 *godless chatter.* See note on 1Ti 1:3 – 11.

2:19 *God's solid foundation.* The church, which upholds the truth (1Ti 3:15). In spite of the heresy of Hymenaeus and Philetus (v. 17), Timothy should be heartened to know that the church is God's solid foundation. There are two inscriptions on it: One stresses the security of the church ("The Lord knows those who are his"; here "know," as often in the Bible, means to be intimately acquainted with), while the other emphasizes human responsibility ("Everyone who confesses the name of the Lord must turn away from wickedness"). *sealed.* The church is owned and securely protected by God (see Eph 1:13 and note).

2:21 *made holy.* Set apart to God for his use (see 1Co 1:2; 1Pe 1:16 and notes).

strument for noble purposes, made holy,
useful to the Master and prepared to do
any good work.[b]
22Flee the evil desires of youth, and pursue righteousness, faith, love[c] and peace,
along with those who call on the Lord[d]
out of a pure heart.[e] 23Don't have anything
to do with foolish and stupid arguments,
because you know they produce quarrels.[f]
24And the Lord's servant must not quarrel;
instead, he must be kind to everyone, able
to teach, not resentful.[g] 25Those who oppose him he must gently instruct, in the
hope that God will grant them repentance
leading them to a knowledge of the truth,[h]
26and that they will come to their senses
and escape from the trap of the devil,[i] who
has taken them captive to do his will.

Godlessness in the Last Days

3 But mark this: There will be terrible
times in the last days.[j] 2People will be
lovers of themselves, lovers of money,[k]
boastful, proud,[l] abusive,[m] disobedient to
their parents,[n] ungrateful, unholy, 3with-
out love, unforgiving, slanderous, without
self-control, brutal, not lovers of the good,
4treacherous,[o] rash, conceited,[p] lovers of
pleasure rather than lovers of God— 5hav-
ing a form of godliness[q] but denying its
power. Have nothing to do with them.[r]
6They are the kind who worm their way[s]
into homes and gain control over weak-
willed women, who are loaded down with
sins and are swayed by all kinds of evil
desires, 7always learning but never able
to acknowledge the truth.[t] 8Just as Jannes
and Jambres opposed Moses,[u] so also
these men oppose[v] the truth—men of depraved minds,[w] who, as far as the faith
is concerned, are rejected. 9But they will
not get very far because, as in the case
of those men,[x] their folly will be clear to
everyone.

Paul's Charge to Timothy

10You, however, know all about my
teaching,[y] my way of life, my purpose,
faith, patience, love, endurance, 11per-
secutions, sufferings—what kinds of
things happened to me in Antioch,[z] Iconium[a] and Lystra,[b] the persecutions I endured.[c] Yet the Lord rescued[d] me from all
of them.[e] 12In fact, everyone who wants
to live a godly life in Christ Jesus will be
persecuted,[f] 13while evil men and impostors will go from bad to worse,[g] deceiving and being deceived.[h] 14But as for you,
continue in what you have learned and
have become convinced of, because you
know those from whom you learned it,[i]
15and how from infancy[j] you have known
the holy Scriptures,[k] which are able to
make you wise[l] for salvation through
faith in Christ Jesus. 16All Scripture is
God-breathed[m] and is useful for teaching,[n] rebuking, correcting and training in
righteousness,[o] 17so that the man of God[p]
may be thoroughly equipped for every
good work.[q]

4 In the presence of God and of Christ
Jesus, who will judge the living and
the dead,[r] and in view of his appearing[s]
and his kingdom, I give you this charge:[t]

2:21 [b]2Co 9:8; Eph 2:10; 2Ti 3:17
2:22 [c]1Ti 1:14; 6:11 [d]S Ac 2:21 [e]1Ti 1:5
2:23 [f]S ver 14
2:24 [g]1Ti 3:2,3
2:25 [h]S 1Ti 2:4
2:26 [i]1Ti 3:7
3:1 [j]1Ti 4:1; 2Pe 3:3
3:2 [k]S 1Ti 3:3 [l]Ro 1:30 [m]2Pe 2:10-12 [n]Ro 1:30
3:4 [o]Ps 25:3 [p]1Ti 3:6; 6:4
3:5 [q]S 1Ti 2:2 [r]S Ro 16:17
3:6 [s]Jude 4
3:7 [t]S 1Ti 2:4
3:8 [u]Ex 7:11 [v]Ac 13:8 [w]1Ti 6:5
3:9 [x]Ex 7:12; 8:18; 9:11
3:10 [y]1Ti 4:6
3:11 [z]Ac 13:14,50 [a]S Ac 13:51 [b]Ac 14:6 [c]2Co 11:23-27 [d]S Ro 15:31 [e]Ps 34:19
3:12 [f]Jn 15:20; S Ac 14:22
3:13 [g]2Ti 2:16 [h]S Mk 13:5
3:14 [i]2Ti 1:13
3:15 [j]2Ti 1:5 [k]Jn 5:39 [l]Dt 4:6; Ps 119:98,99
3:16 [m]2Pe 1:20,21 [n]S Ro 4:23,24 [o]Dt 29:29
3:17 [p]1Ti 6:11 [q]2Ti 2:21
4:1 [r]S Ac 10:42 [s]ver 8; S 1Ti 6:14 [t]1Ti 5:21; 6:13

2:22 *youth.* See 1Ti 4:12 and note. *peace.* See Ro 12:16. *pure heart.* See 1Ti 1:5 and note.

2:23 The Gnostic heresy is in view again (see note on vv. 14–18).

2:24 *Lord's servant.* Seems to refer primarily to a person who, like Timothy, is set aside for special service. *able to teach.* Cf. note on 1Ti 3:1.

2:25 *repentance.* See Mt 4:17 and note. *knowledge of the truth.* See 1Ti 2:4.

2:26 *trap of the devil.* See 1Ti 3:7; cf. Eph 6:11; 1Pe 5:8.

3:1 *last days.* The Messianic era, the time beginning with Christ's first coming (see 1Ti 4:1; Heb 1:1–2 and notes; 1Pe 1:20). That "the last days" in this passage does not refer only to the time just prior to Christ's return is apparent from Paul's command to Timothy to "have nothing to do" (v. 5) with the unbelieving and unfaithful people who characterize this time.

3:2–5 For similar lists of vices see note on Ro 1:29–31.

3:2 *lovers of money.* See 1Ti 6:9–10,17–18.

3:5 *godliness.* See 1Ti 2:2 and note on 2:1–2.

3:6 *weak-willed women.* Unstable women who are guilt-ridden because of their sins, torn by lust, and victims of various false teachers ("always learning," v. 7, but never coming to a saving knowledge of Christ).

3:8 *Jannes and Jambres.* According to Jewish tradition they were the Egyptian court magicians who opposed Moses (see Ex 7:11 and note).

3:11 *Antioch, Iconium and Lystra.* Three cities in the Roman province of Galatia (see map, p. 1711), which Paul visited on his first and second missionary journeys (see Ac 13:14,51; 14:6 and notes). Since Timothy was from Lystra (Ac 16:1), he would have known firsthand of Paul's sufferings in that region. *the Lord rescued me from all of them.* Even from execution by stoning (see Ac 14:19–20 and notes).

3:12 See Mt 10:22; Ac 14:22; Php 1:29 and note; 1Pe 4:12. *in Christ.* See notes on 1:13; Eph 1:1.

3:14 *those from whom you learned it.* Perhaps a reference to Paul as well as to Timothy's mother and grandmother (see 1:5 and note).

3:15 *from infancy you have known the holy Scriptures.* A Jewish boy formally began to study the OT when he was five years old. Timothy was taught at home by his mother and grandmother even before he reached this age.

3:16 *All Scripture.* The primary reference is to the OT, since some of the NT books had not even been written at this time. (See 1Ti 5:18 and note for indications that some NT books—or material ultimately included in the NT—were already considered equal in authority to the OT Scriptures.) *God-breathed.* Paul affirms God's active involvement in the writing of Scripture, an involvement so powerful and pervasive that what is written is the infallible and authoritative word of God (see 2Pe 1:20–21 and notes).

4:1 Paul states his charge to Timothy, aware that he does so in the presence of God the Father and of Christ, who will judge everyone. He is also keenly aware of the twin facts of Christ's

2Preach[u] the Word;[v] be prepared in season and out of season; correct, rebuke[w]
and encourage[x]—with great patience and
careful instruction. 3For the time will come
when men will not put up with sound doctrine.[y] Instead, to suit their own desires,
they will gather around them a great number of teachers to say what their itching
ears want to hear.[z] 4They will turn their
ears away from the truth and turn aside
to myths.[a] 5But you, keep your head in all
situations, endure hardship,[b] do the work
of an evangelist,[c] discharge all the duties
of your ministry.
6For I am already being poured out like
a drink offering,[d] and the time has come
for my departure.[e] 7I have fought the good
fight,[f] I have finished the race,[g] I have
kept the faith. 8Now there is in store for
me[h] the crown of righteousness,[i] which
the Lord, the righteous Judge, will award
to me on that day[j]—and not only to me,
but also to all who have longed for his
appearing.[k]

Personal Remarks

9Do your best to come to me quick-
ly,[l] 10for Demas,[m] because he loved this
world,[n] has deserted me and has gone
to Thessalonica.[o] Crescens has gone to
Galatia,[p] and Titus[q] to Dalmatia. 11Only
Luke[r] is with me.[s] Get Mark[t] and bring
him with you, because he is helpful to
me in my ministry. 12I sent Tychicus[u] to
Ephesus.[v] 13When you come, bring the
cloak that I left with Carpus at Troas,[w]
and my scrolls, especially the parchments.
14Alexander[x] the metalworker did me
a great deal of harm. The Lord will repay him for what he has done.[y] 15You too
should be on your guard against him, because he strongly opposed our message.
16At my first defense, no one came to
my support, but everyone deserted me.
May it not be held against them.[z] 17But
the Lord stood at my side[a] and gave me
strength,[b] so that through me the message might be fully proclaimed and all the
Gentiles might hear it.[c] And I was delivered from the lion's mouth.[d] 18The Lord
will rescue me from every evil attack[e] and
will bring me safely to his heavenly kingdom.[f] To him be glory for ever and ever.
Amen.[g]

4:2 [u] 1Ti 4:13 [v] Gal 6:6 [w] 1Ti 5:20; Tit 1:13; 2:15 [x] Tit 2:15 **4:3** [y] S 1Ti 1:10 [z] Isa 30:10 **4:4** [a] S 1Ti 1:4 **4:5** [b] 2Ti 1:8; 2:3,9 [c] Ac 21:8; Eph 4:11 **4:6** [d] Nu 15:1-12; 28:7,24; Php 2:17 [e] Php 1:23 **4:7** [f] S 1Ti 1:18 [g] S 1Co 9:24; Ac 20:24 **4:8** [h] Col 1:5; 1Pe 1:4 [i] S 1Co 9:25 [j] S 2Ti 1:12 [k] S 1Ti 6:14 **4:9** [l] ver 21; Tit 3:12 **4:10** [m] Col 4:14; Phm 24 [n] 1Jn 2:15 [o] S Ac 17:1 [p] S Ac 16:6 [q] S 2Co 2:13 **4:11** [r] Col 4:14; Phm 24 [s] 2Ti 1:15 [t] S Ac 12:12 **4:12** [u] S Ac 20:4 [v] S Ac 18:19 **4:13** [w] S Ac 16:8 **4:14** [x] Ac 19:33; 1Ti 1:20 [y] Ps 28:4; 109:20; Ro 2:6; 12:19 **4:16** [z] Ac 7:60 **4:17** [a] Ac 23:11 [b] S Php 4:13 [c] S Ac 9:15 [d] 1Sa 17:37; Ps 22:21; Da 6:22; 1Co 15:32 **4:18** [e] Ps 121:7; 2Pe 2:9 [f] ver 1 [g] S Ro 11:36

return ("his appearing") and the coming establishment of God's kingdom in its fullest expression. Timothy was to view a charge so given as of utmost importance. *Jesus, who will judge.* See Mt 25:31–33; see also Jn 5:22; Jas 5:9; 1Pe 4:5 and notes.

4:2 *be prepared.* Be ready in any situation to speak the needed word, whether of correction, of rebuke or of encouragement.

4:3 *sound doctrine.* See Tit 1:9 and note. *itching ears.* Ears that want to be "scratched" by words in keeping with one's evil desires.

4:4 *myths.* See 1Ti 1:4 and note.

4:6 *drink offering.* The offering of wine poured out to the Lord (see Nu 15:1–12; 28:7). Paul views his approaching death as the pouring out of his life as an offering to Christ (see Php 2:17 and note). *my departure.* His impending death in A.D. 67/68 (see chart, p. 1697; cf. Php 1:23).

4:7 Paul looks back over 30 years of labor as an apostle (c. A.D. 36–67/68). Like an athlete who had engaged successfully in a contest ("fought the good fight"; see note on 1Ti 1:18), he had "finished the race" and "kept the faith," i.e., had carefully preserved the deposit of Christian truth. *the faith.* See note on 1Ti 3:9.

4:8 *crown of righteousness.* Continuing with the same figure of speech, Paul uses the metaphor of the wreath given to the winner of a race (see 1Co 9:25 and note). He could be referring to (1) a crown given as a reward for a righteous life, (2) a crown consisting of righteousness or (3) a crown given righteously (justly) by the righteous Judge. *that day.* The day of Christ's second coming ("appearing"; see v. 1).

4:10 *Demas.* See Col 4:14 and note; Phm 24. *Thessalonica.* See Introduction to 1 Thessalonians: Thessalonica: The City and the Church; see also map, p. 1711. *Galatia.* Either the northern area of Asia Minor (Gaul) or a Roman province in what is now central Turkey (see note on Gal 1:2). *Titus.* See Introduction to Titus: Recipient. *Dalmatia.* Also known as Illyricum (Ro 15:19; see map No.13 at the end of this study Bible).

4:11 *Mark.* See Introduction to Mark: Mark in the NT. John Mark had deserted Paul and Barnabas on their first missionary journey (Ac 13:13). After Paul refused to take Mark on the second journey, Barnabas separated from Paul, taking Mark with him on a mission to Cyprus (Ac 15:36–41). Ultimately Mark proved himself to Paul, indicated by his presence with Paul during Paul's first Roman imprisonment (Col 4:10; Phm 24) and by Paul's request here for Timothy to bring Mark with him to Rome.

4:12 *Tychicus.* See Ac 20:4; Eph 6:21 and notes.

4:13 *cloak.* For protection against the cold dampness (see Introduction: Author, Date and Setting). It was probably a heavy, sleeveless, outer garment, circular in shape with a hole in the middle for one's head. *Troas.* See Ac 16:8 and note; see also map, p. 1873. *scrolls, especially the parchments.* The scrolls (see note on Ex 17:14) were made of leather or papyrus, and the parchments were made of the skins of animals. The latter may have been copies of parts of the OT.

4:14 *Alexander the metalworker.* Perhaps the Alexander mentioned in 1Ti 1:20.

4:16 *my first defense.* The first court hearing of Paul's present case, not his defense on the occasion of his first imprisonment (Ac 28).

4:17 *through me the message might be fully proclaimed.* Even in these dire circumstances Paul used the occasion to testify about Jesus Christ in the imperial court (cf. Ac 16:25; cf. also Php 1:12–14 and notes). *delivered from the lion's mouth.* Since, as a Roman citizen, Paul could not be thrown to the lions in the amphitheater, this must be a figurative way of saying that his first hearing did not result in an immediate guilty verdict.

4:18 *will rescue me from every evil attack.* Since Paul fully expected to die soon (see v. 6 and note), the rescue he speaks of here is spiritual, not physical. *heavenly kingdom.* Heaven itself.

Final Greetings

[19]Greet Priscilla[a] and Aquila[h] and the
household of Onesiphorus.[i] [20]Erastus[j]
stayed in Corinth, and I left Trophimus[k]
sick in Miletus.[l] [21]Do your best to get here
before winter.[m] Eubulus greets you, and
so do Pudens, Linus, Claudia and all the
brothers.

[22]The Lord be with your spirit.[n] Grace
be with you.[o]

4:19 [h] S Ac 18:2 [i] 2Ti 1:16 4:20 [j] Ac 19:22 [k] Ac 20:4; 21:29 [l] Ac 20:15, 17 4:21 [m] ver 9; Tit 3:12 4:22 [n] S Gal 6:18 [o] S Col 4:18

[a] *19* Greek *Prisca,* a variant of *Priscilla*

4:19 *Priscilla and Aquila.* See Ac 18:2,18; 1Co 16:19 and notes. *Onesiphorus.* See 1:16 and note.

4:20 *Erastus.* See Ro 16:23 and note. *Corinth.* See Introduction to 1 Corinthians: The City of Corinth; see also map, p. 1766. *Trophimus.* See note on Ac 20:4. *Miletus.* A seaport on the coast of Asia Minor about 35 miles south of Ephesus (see map, p. 1873). See Ac 20:15 and note.

4:21 *Linus.* Early tradition says he was bishop of Rome after the deaths of Peter and Paul. *brothers.* See note on Ro 1:13.

4:22 *be with your spirit.* See note on Gal 6:18. *Grace.* See note on Ro 1:7. *with you.* See note on 2Co 13:14. *you.* As at the end of 1 Timothy (see note on 1Ti 6:21), "you" here is plural, showing that the letter was intended for public use. The word "your" in the first part of the verse, however, is singular, indicating that it was addressed to Timothy alone.

Titus

INTRODUCTION

Author

See essay, p. 1867. The author is Paul (see 1:1 and note; see also Introduction to 1 Timothy: Author).

Recipient

The letter is addressed to Titus, one of Paul's converts (see 1:4 and note) and a considerable help to Paul in his ministry. When Paul left Antioch to discuss the gospel with the Jerusalem leaders, he took Titus with him (Gal 2:1 – 3); acceptance of Titus (a Gentile) as a Christian without circumcision vindicated Paul's stand there (Gal 2:3 – 5). Presumably Titus, who is not referred to in Acts (but is mentioned 13 times in the rest of the NT), worked with Paul in Ephesus during his third missionary journey (see map, p. 1718). It is likely that he was the bearer of Paul's severe letter to the Corinthian church (see Introduction to 2 Corinthians: Occasion). Paul was concerned about the possible negative reaction of the Corinthian church to his severe letter, so he arranged to meet Titus at Troas (2Co 2:12 – 13). When Titus did not appear, Paul traveled on to Macedonia. There he met Titus and with great relief heard the good news that the worst of the trouble was over in Corinth (2Co 7:6 – 7,13 – 14). Titus, accompanied by two Christian brothers, was the carrier of 2 Corinthians (2Co 8:23) and was given the responsibility for making final arrangements for the collection, begun a year earlier, in Corinth (see 2Co 8:6,16 – 17 and notes).

Following Paul's release from his first Roman imprisonment (Ac 28), he and Titus worked briefly in Crete (1:5), after which he commissioned Titus to remain there as his representative and complete some needed work (1:5; 2:15; 3:12 – 13). Paul asked Titus to meet him at Nicopolis (see map, p. 1873) when a replacement arrived (see 3:12 and note). Later, Titus went on a mission to Dalmatia (see 2Ti 4:10 and note), the last word we hear about him in the NT. Considering the assignments given him, he obviously was a capable and resourceful leader.

A Quick Look

Author:
The apostle Paul

Audience:
Titus, a trusted Gentile companion of Paul

Date:
About A.D. 63–65

Theme:
Paul writes to instruct Titus concerning the care of the church on the island of Crete.

Crete

The fourth largest island in the Mediterranean Sea, Crete lies directly south of the Aegean Sea (see map and inset, p. 1731; cf. note on 1Sa 30:14; cf. also Paul's experiences there in Ac 27:7 – 13). In NT times life in Crete had sunk to a deplorable moral level. The dishonesty, gluttony and laziness of its inhabitants were proverbial (1:12).

Occasion and Purpose

Apparently Paul introduced Christianity in Crete when he and Titus visited the island, after which he left Titus there to organize the converts. Paul sent the letter with Zenas and Apollos, who were on a journey that took them through Crete (3:13), to give Titus personal authorization and guidance in meeting opposition (1:5; 2:1,7 – 8,15; 3:9), instructions about faith and conduct, and warnings about false teachers. Paul also informed Titus of his future plans for him (3:12).

The letter is addressed to Titus, one of Paul's converts and a considerable help to Paul in his ministry. When Paul left Antioch to discuss the gospel with the Jerusalem leaders, he took Titus with him.

Place and Date of Writing

Paul possibly wrote from Macedonia, for he had not yet reached Nicopolis (see 3:12). The letter was written after he was released from his first Roman imprisonment (Ac 28), probably between A.D. 63 and 65 (see chart, p. 1697) — or possibly at a later date if he wrote after his planned (see Ro 15:24 and note) trip to Spain.

Distinctive Characteristics

Especially significant, considering the nature of the Cretan heresy, are the repeated emphases on loving and doing and teaching "what is good" (1:8,16; 2:3,7,14; 3:1,8,14) and the classic summaries of Christian doctrine (2:11 – 14; 3:4 – 7).

Outline

I. Greetings (1:1 – 4)
II. Concerning Elders (1:5 – 9)
  A. Reasons for Leaving Titus in Crete (1:5)
  B. Qualifications of Elders (1:6 – 9)
III. Concerning False Teachers (1:10 – 16)
IV. Concerning Various Groups in the Congregations (ch. 2)
  A. The Instructions to Different Groups (2:1 – 10)
  B. The Foundation for Christian Living (2:11 – 14)
  C. The Duty of Titus (2:15)
V. Concerning Believers in General (3:1 – 8)
  A. Obligations as Citizens (3:1 – 2)
  B. Motives for Godly Conduct (3:3 – 8)
VI. Concerning Response to Spiritual Error (3:9 – 11)
VII. Conclusion, Final Greetings and Benediction (3:12 – 15)

1 Paul, a servant of God[a] and an apostle[b]
of Jesus Christ for the faith of God's
elect and the knowledge of the truth[c] that
leads to godliness[d] — 2a faith and knowledge resting on the hope of eternal life,[e]
which God, who does not lie,[f] promised
before the beginning of time,[g] 3and at his
appointed season[h] he brought his word to
light[i] through the preaching entrusted to
me[j] by the command of God[k] our Savior,[l]

4To Titus,[m] my true son[n] in our common
faith:

Grace and peace from God the Father
and Christ Jesus our Savior.[o]

Titus's Task on Crete

1:6-8Ref — 1Ti 3:2-4

5The reason I left you in Crete[p] was
that you might straighten out what was
left unfinished and appoint[a] elders[q] in
every town, as I directed you. 6An elder
must be blameless,[r] the husband of but
one wife, a man whose children believe
and are not open to the charge of being
wild and disobedient. 7Since an overseer[b s] is entrusted with God's work,[t] he
must be blameless — not overbearing, not
quick-tempered, not given to drunkenness, not violent, not pursuing dishonest
gain.[u] 8Rather he must be hospitable,[v] one
who loves what is good,[w] who is self-controlled,[x] upright, holy and disciplined. 9He
must hold firmly[y] to the trustworthy message as it has been taught, so that he can
encourage others by sound doctrine[z] and
refute those who oppose it.

10For there are many rebellious people,
mere talkers[a] and deceivers, especially
those of the circumcision group.[b] 11They
must be silenced, because they are ruining
whole households[c] by teaching things they
ought not to teach — and that for the sake
of dishonest gain. 12Even one of their own
prophets[d] has said, "Cretans[e] are always
liars, evil brutes, lazy gluttons." 13This
testimony is true. Therefore, rebuke[f] them

1:1 [a]Ro 1:1; Jas 1:1 [b]S 1Co 1:1 [c]S 1Ti 2:4 [d]S 1Ti 2:2 **1:2** [e]Tit 3:7; 2Ti 1:1 [f]Nu 23:19; Heb 6:18 [g]2Ti 1:9 **1:3** [h]1Ti 2:6; 6:15 [i]2Ti 1:10 [j]S 1Ti 1:11 [k]S 2Co 1:1; 1Ti 1:1 [l]S Lk 1:47 **1:4** [m]S 2Co 2:13 [n]S 1Ti 1:2 [o]S Ro 1:7 **1:5** [p]Ac 27:7 [q]S Ac 11:30 **1:6** [r]S 1Th 3:13; 1Ti 3:2 **1:7** [s]S 1Ti 3:1 [t]1Co 4:1 [u]S 1Ti 3:3,8 **1:8** [v]S Ro 12:13 [w]2Ti 3:3 [x]Tit 2:2,5,6,12 **1:9** [y]S 1Co 16:13; 1Ti 1:19; 2Ti 1:13; 3:14 [z]S 1Ti 1:10 **1:10** [a]1Ti 1:6 [b]Ac 10:45; 11:2 **1:11** [c]1Ti 5:13 **1:12** [d]Ac 17:28 [e]Ac 2:11 **1:13** [f]S 1Ti 5:20

[a] 5 Or *ordain* [b] 7 Traditionally *bishop*

1:1 *Paul.* See note on Ro 1:1. *servant of God.* Only here does Paul call himself a servant of God; elsewhere he says "servant of Christ" (Ro 1:1; Gal 1:10; Php 1:1). James uses both terms of himself (Jas 1:1). *servant.* See note on Ro 1:1. *apostle.* See note on 1Co 1:1. *for the faith ... and the knowledge.* Paul's appointed mission as God's servant and Christ's apostle — further explained in v. 2 (see Ac 9:15; 22:15; 26:16 – 18). *godliness.* See 1Ti 2:2 and note on 2:1 – 2.

1:2 *hope.* See Col 1:5 and note. *eternal life.* See note on Jn 3:15. *does not lie.* In contrast to the Cretans (v. 12) — and the devil (Jn 8:44). *before the beginning of time.* See 2Ti 1:9 and note.

1:3 *appointed season.* Crucial events in God's program occur at his designated times in history (see 1Ti 2:6; 6:15 and notes). *his word.* The authoritative message that centers in Christ. *God our Savior.* Three times in the letter God the Father is called Savior (here; 2:10; 3:4; see also 1Ti 1:1; 2:3; 4:10), and three times Jesus is called Savior (v. 4; 2:13; 3:6; see also 2Ti 1:10).

1:4 *my true son.* Titus, like Timothy (1Ti 1:2), was a spiritual son, having been converted through Paul's ministry. Onesimus was also called a son by Paul (Phm 10). *true.* Genuine. *our common faith.* The faith shared by all true believers. *Grace and peace.* See note on Ro 1:7. *Savior.* In all of Paul's other greetings Jesus is called "Lord." Paul uses "Savior" 12 times in all his letters, half of the references being in Titus.

1:5 *left you in Crete.* Implies that Paul and Titus had been together in Crete, a ministry not mentioned in Acts. On his voyage to Rome, Paul visited Crete briefly as a prisoner (Ac 27:7 – 8), but now that he had been released from his first Roman imprisonment he was free to travel wherever he wished (see 3:12 and note). *appoint elders.* Though Paul and Titus perhaps had already preached in Crete, they had not had time to organize churches. The appointing of elders is consistent with Paul's usual practice (see Ac 14:23 and note).

1:6 – 9 1Ti 3:1 – 7 gives a parallel list of qualifications for elders, but the two lists reflect the different situations in which Timothy and Titus ministered. See chart, p. 1874.

1:6 *husband of but one wife.* Since elders, by definition, were chosen from among the older men of the congregation, Paul assumed they already would be married and have children. A qualified unmarried man was not necessarily barred. It is also improbable that the standard forbids an elder to remarry if his wife dies (cf. Ro 7:2 – 3; 1Co 7:39). The most likely meaning is simply that a faithful monogamous married life must be maintained. See note on 1Ti 3:2.

1:7 *overseer.* The use of "elder" in v. 5 and "overseer" (or "bishop") in v. 7 indicates that the terms were used interchangeably (cf. Ac 20:17,28; 1Pe 5:1 – 2 and notes). "Elder" indicates qualification (maturity and experience), while "overseer" indicates responsibility (watching over God's flock).

1:8 *self-controlled.* A virtue much needed in Crete (see vv. 10 – 14); Paul refers to it five times in two chapters (here; 2:2,5 – 6,12). *disciplined.* Possessing the inner strength to control one's desires and actions.

1:9 *sound doctrine.* Correct teaching, in keeping with that of the apostles (see 1Ti 1:10; 6:3; 2Ti 1:13; 4:3). The teaching is called "sound" not only because it builds up in the faith, but also because it protects against the corrupting influence of false teachers. Soundness of doctrine, faith and speech is a basic concern in all the Pastoral Letters (1,2 Timothy; Titus). In them, this use of "sound" occurs eight times (here; v. 13; 2:1 – 2; 1Ti 1:10; 6:3; 2Ti 1:13; 4:3) but is found nowhere else in Paul's writings.

1:10 *rebellious.* Against the word of God and against Paul and Titus as the Lord's authoritative ministers. These troublemakers had three main characteristics: (1) They belonged to the "circumcision group," like the people of Gal 2:12, believing that, for salvation or sanctification or both, it was necessary to be circumcised and to keep the Jewish ceremonial law (see Introduction to Galatians: Occasion and Purpose). (2) They held to unscriptural "Jewish myths" (v. 14) and "genealogies" (3:9; see 1Ti 1:4 and note). (3) They were ascetics (vv. 14 – 15), having scruples against things that God declared to be good. *mere talkers.* Paul used similar language in writing to Timothy about this kind of person (1Ti 1:6).

1:12 The quotation is from the poet Epimenides, a sixth-century B.C. native of Crete, who was held in high esteem by the Cretans. He was credited with several predictions that were fulfilled. For other uses of pagan sayings by Paul see Ac 17:28; 1Co 15:33 and notes. In Greek literature "to Cretanize" meant to lie.

1:13 *the faith.* See note on 1Ti 3:9.

sharply, so that they will be sound in the
faith[g] [14]and will pay no attention to Jewish
myths[h] or to the commands[i] of those who
reject the truth.[j] [15]To the pure, all things
are pure,[k] but to those who are corrupted and do not believe, nothing is pure.[l]
In fact, both their minds and consciences
are corrupted.[m] [16]They claim to know God,
but by their actions they deny him.[n] They
are detestable, disobedient and unfit for
doing anything good.[o]

What Must Be Taught to Various Groups

2 You must teach what is in accord with
sound doctrine.[p] [2]Teach the older men[q]
to be temperate,[r] worthy of respect, self-
controlled,[s] and sound in faith,[t] in love
and in endurance.
[3]Likewise, teach the older women to be
reverent in the way they live, not to be
slanderers[u] or addicted to much wine,[v]
but to teach what is good. [4]Then they can
train the younger women[w] to love their
husbands and children, [5]to be self-controlled[x] and pure, to be busy at home,[y] to
be kind, and to be subject to their husbands,[z] so that no one will malign the
word of God.[a]
[6]Similarly, encourage the young men[b] to
be self-controlled.[c] [7]In everything set them
an example[d] by doing what is good.[e] In
your teaching show integrity, seriousness
[8]and soundness of speech that cannot be
condemned, so that those who oppose
you may be ashamed because they have
nothing bad to say about us.[f]
[9]Teach slaves to be subject to their masters in everything,[g] to try to please them,
not to talk back to them, [10]and not to steal
from them, but to show that they can be
fully trusted, so that in every way they will
make the teaching about God our Savior[h]
attractive.[i]
[11]For the grace[j] of God that brings salvation has appeared[k] to all men.[l] [12]It teaches
us to say "No" to ungodliness and worldly
passions,[m] and to live self-controlled,[n] upright and godly lives[o] in this present age,
[13]while we wait for the blessed hope—the
glorious appearing[p] of our great God and

1:13 [g]Tit 2:2 **1:14** [h]S 1Ti 1:4 [i]S Col 2:22 [j]2Ti 4:4 **1:15** [k]Ps 18:26; Mt 15:10,11; Mk 7:14-19; Ac 10:9-16,28; Col 2:20-22 [l]Ro 14:14,23 [m]1Ti 6:5 **1:16** [n]Jer 5:2; 12:2; 1Jn 2:4 [o]Hos 8:2,3 **2:1** [p]S 1Ti 1:10 **2:2** [q]1Ti 5:1 [r]1Ti 3:2 [s]ver 5,6,12; Tit 1:8 [t]Tit 1:13 **2:3** [u]1Ti 3:11 [v]1Ti 3:8 **2:4** [w]1Ti 5:2 **2:5** [x]ver 2,6,12; Tit 1:8 [y]1Ti 5:14 [z]S Eph 5:22 [a]1Ti 6:1; S Heb 4:12 **2:6** [b]1Ti 5:1 [c]ver 2,5,12; Tit 1:8 **2:7** [d]S 1Ti 4:12 [e]S ver 14 **2:8** [f]S 1Pe 2:12 **2:9** [g]S Eph 6:5 **2:10** [h]S Lk 1:47 [i]Mt 5:16 **2:11** [j]S Ro 3:24 [k]2Ti 1:10 [l]S 1Ti 2:4 **2:12** [m]Tit 3:3 [n]ver 2,5,6; Tit 1:8 [o]2Ti 3:12 **2:13** [p]S 1Co 1:7; S 1Ti 6:14

1:14 *Jewish myths.* See note on v. 10.

1:15 *To the pure, all things are pure.* To Christians, who have been purified by the atoning death of Christ, "everything God created is good, and nothing is to be rejected if it is received with thanksgiving" (1Ti 4:4; see note there). *to those who are corrupted and do not believe, nothing is pure.* Unbelievers, especially ascetics with unbiblical scruples against certain foods, marriage and the like (cf. Col 2:21; 1Ti 4:3 and notes), do not enjoy the freedom of true Christians, who receive all God's creation with thanksgiving. Instead, they set up arbitrary, human prohibitions against what they consider to be impure (see Mt 15:10–11,16–20; Ac 10:9–16; Ro 14:20). The principle of this verse does not conflict with the many NT teachings against practices that are morally and spiritually wrong. *consciences.* See 1Ti 4:2–3.

1:16 *by their actions they deny him.* The false teachers stood condemned by the test of personal conduct. *good.* See Introduction: Distinctive Characteristics. Right knowledge is extremely important because it "leads to godliness" (v. 1). Paul maintained a balance between doctrine and practice.

2:1 *You.* Emphatic, contrasting the work of Titus with that of the false teachers just denounced (1:10–16). *sound doctrine.* See 1:9 and note.

2:2–10 Sound doctrine demands right conduct of all believers, regardless of age, gender or position.

2:2 Older men, as leaders, were to be moral and spiritual examples. *temperate.* Instead of being "lazy gluttons," as were Cretans in general (1:12), these older believers were to be responsible and sensible.

2:3 *Likewise.* The same moral standards applied to women as to men. *not to be slanderers.* Slanderous talk apparently was a common vice among Cretan women. *addicted to much wine.* Cf. 1:7; 1Ti 3:3,8.

2:4 *love their husbands.* Just as husbands are exhorted (Eph 5:25) to love their wives.

2:5 *subject to their husbands.* See Eph 5:22 and note; Col 3:18; 1Pe 3:1 and note. *no one will malign the word of God.* Indicating Paul's deep spiritual concern behind these ethical instructions. See also vv. 8,10, dealing with his concern that Christian living should help rather than hinder the spread of the gospel.

2:7–8 Perhaps Titus was still a young man and was not yet well respected by the Cretan churches. The demands on a leader are all-inclusive, involving not only his word but also his lifestyle (see Jas 3:1 and note).

2:7 *good.* See Introduction: Distinctive Characteristics.

2:9–10 Instructions for a distinct group in the churches. Slavery was a basic element of Roman society, and the impact of Christianity upon slaves was a vital concern. Guidance for the conduct of Christian slaves was essential (see Eph 6:5 and note; Phm 15–16).

2:9 *masters.* The Greek for this word, from which our English term "despot" is derived, indicates the owner's absolute authority over his slave. Roman slaves had no legal rights, their fates being entirely in their masters' hands (see note on Col 3:22—4:1).

2:10 *make the teaching ... attractive.* Christian slaves could give a unique and powerful testimony to the gospel by their willing faithfulness and obedience to their masters.

2:11–14 Briefly describes the effect grace should have on believers. It encourages rejection of ungodliness and leads to holier living—in keeping with Paul's repeated insistence that profession of Christ be accompanied by godly living (vv. 1–2,4–5,10; 3:8).

2:11 *For.* Introduces the doctrinal basis for the ethical demands just stressed. Right conduct must be founded on right doctrine. *grace of God.* The undeserved love God showed us in Christ while we were still sinners and his enemies (Ro 5:6–10) and by which we are saved apart from any moral achievements or religious acts on our part (see 3:5; Eph 2:8–9 and notes). But this same grace instructs us that our salvation should produce good works (see v. 14 and note; Eph 2:10).

2:12 *teaches us.* The word translated "teaches" refers to more than instruction; it includes the whole process of training a child—instruction, encouragement, correction and discipline. *this present age.* See 2Co 4:4 and note.

2:13 *the blessed hope—the glorious appearing.* The second coming (see 1Ti 6:14; 2Ti 4:1; see also note on

Savior, Jesus Christ,[q] 14who gave himself
for us[r] to redeem us from all wickedness[s]
and to purify[t] for himself a people that are
his very own,[u] eager to do what is good.[v]
15These, then, are the things you should
teach. Encourage and rebuke with all authority. Do not let anyone despise you.

Doing What Is Good

3 Remind the people to be subject to rulers
and authorities,[w] to be obedient, to be
ready to do whatever is good,[x] 2to slander
no one,[y] to be peaceable and considerate,
and to show true humility toward all men.
3At one time[z] we too were foolish, disobedient, deceived and enslaved by all
kinds of passions and pleasures. We lived
in malice and envy, being hated and hating one another. 4But when the kindness[a]
and love of God our Savior[b] appeared,[c]
5he saved us,[d] not because of righteous
things we had done,[e] but because of his
mercy.[f] He saved us through the washing[g] of rebirth and renewal[h] by the Holy
Spirit, 6whom he poured out on us[i] generously through Jesus Christ our Savior, 7so
that, having been justified by his grace,[j]
we might become heirs[k] having the hope[l]
of eternal life.[m] 8This is a trustworthy saying.[n] And I want you to stress these things,
so that those who have trusted in God may
be careful to devote themselves to doing
what is good.[o] These things are excellent
and profitable for everyone.
9But avoid[p] foolish controversies and
genealogies and arguments and quarrels[q]
about the law,[r] because these are unprofitable and useless.[s] 10Warn a divisive person once, and then warn him a second
time. After that, have nothing to do with
him.[t] 11You may be sure that such a man is
warped and sinful; he is self-condemned.

Final Remarks

12As soon as I send Artemas or Tychicus[u] to you, do your best to come to me at
Nicopolis, because I have decided to winter there.[v] 13Do everything you can to help
Zenas the lawyer and Apollos[w] on their
way and see that they have everything
they need. 14Our people must learn to devote themselves to doing what is good,[x] in
order that they may provide for daily necessities and not live unproductive lives.
15Everyone with me sends you greetings.
Greet those who love us in the faith.[y]
Grace be with you all.[z]

2:13 [q] 2Pe 1:1 **2:14** [r] S Mt 20:28 [s] S Mt 1:21 [t] Heb 1:3; 1Jn 1:7 [u] Ex 19:5; Dt 4:20; 14:2; Ps 135:4; Mal 3:17; 1Pe 2:9 [v] ver 7; Pr 16:7; Mt 5:16; 2Co 8:21; Eph 2:10; Tit 3:1,8,14; 1Pe 2:12,15; 3:13 **3:1** [w] Ro 13:1; 1Pe 2:13,14 [x] S 2Ti 2:21; S Tit 2:14 **3:2** [y] Eph 4:31 **3:3** [z] S Eph 2:2 **3:4** [a] Eph 2:7 [b] S Lk 1:47 [c] Tit 2:11 **3:5** [d] S Ro 11:14 [e] S Eph 2:9 [f] 1Pe 1:3 [g] S Ac 22:16 [h] Ro 12:2 **3:6** [i] S Ro 5:5 **3:7** [j] S Ro 3:24 [k] S Ro 8:17 [l] Ro 8:24 [m] S Mt 25:46; Tit 1:2 **3:8** [n] S 1Ti 1:15 [o] S Tit 2:14 **3:9** [p] 2Ti 2:16 [q] S 2Ti 2:14 [r] Tit 1:10-16 [s] 2Ti 2:14 **3:10** [t] S Ro 16:17 **3:12** [u] S Ac 20:4 [v] 2Ti 4:9,21 **3:13** [w] S Ac 18:24 **3:14** [x] S Tit 2:14 **3:15** [y] 1Ti 1:2 [z] S Col 4:18

2Ti 4:8). *our great God and Savior, Jesus Christ.* It is possible to translate this phrase "the great God and our Saviour, Jesus Christ" (KJV), but the NIV rendering better represents the Greek construction. It is an explicit testimony to the deity of Christ (see Ro 9:5 and note).

2:14 Salvation involves the double work of redeeming us from guilt and judgment (see Ro 3:24 and note) and of producing moral purity and helpful service to others (see Introduction: Distinctive Characteristics).

2:15 A summary of Titus's responsibility and authority. *things.* The content of the whole chapter.

3:1–2 NT teaching is not confined to the area of personal salvation but includes much instruction about practical living. Although believers are citizens of heaven (see Php 3:20 and note), they must also submit themselves to earthly government (see Ro 13:1–7; 1Pe 2:13–17 and notes) and help promote the well-being of the community.

3:1 *rulers and authorities.* The terms refer to all forms and levels of human government (cf. Eph 3:10; 6:12 for application to angels). *good.* See Introduction: Distinctive Characteristics.

3:3 Cf. Eph 2:1–3.

3:4 *kindness and love of God.* The reasons why God did not simply banish fallen human beings but acted to save them (cf. 2:11).

3:5 *saved us ... because of his mercy.* Salvation is not achieved by human effort or merit but comes through God's mercy alone (see Eph 2:8–9 and notes). *washing of rebirth.* A reference to new birth, of which baptism (among other things) is a sign. It cannot mean that baptism is necessary for regeneration, since the NT plainly teaches that the new birth is an act of God's Spirit (see, e.g., Jn 3:5) and is not effected or achieved by ceremony. *renewal by the Holy Spirit.* Also a reference to new birth.

3:6 *whom he poured out on us generously.* Cf. Ro 5:5.

3:7 *justified by his grace.* See Ro 3:24 and note. *heirs.* See Ro 8:17 and note. *hope.* See notes on Ro 5:5; Col 1:5.

3:8 *trustworthy saying.* See note on 1Ti 1:15. Here the phrase refers to the doctrinal summary in vv. 4–7. *good.* See Introduction: Distinctive Characteristics.

3:9 *genealogies.* See note on 1Ti 1:4. *about the law.* A reference to the situation described in 1:10–16. A similar problem existed in Ephesus (see 1Ti 1:3–7 and note on 1:3–11).

3:11 Stubborn refusal to listen to correction reveals inner perversion.

3:12 *Tychicus.* Paul's trusted coworker, who on various occasions traveled with or for Paul (see Ac 20:4; Eph 6:21 and notes). *Nicopolis.* Means "city of victory." Several cities had this name, but the reference here apparently is to the city in Epirus on the western shore of Greece (see map, p. 1873). *decided to winter there.* Indicates that Paul had not arrived there when he wrote and that he was still free to travel at will, not yet having been imprisoned in Rome for the second time.

3:13 *Zenas the lawyer.* If he was a Jewish convert, "lawyer" means that he was an expert in the Mosaic law; if he was a Gentile convert, that he was a Roman jurist. *Apollos.* A native of Alexandria and one of Paul's well-known coworkers (Ac 18:24–28; 19:1; 1Co 1:12; 3:4–6,22; 16:12). The two travelers apparently brought the letter from Paul.

3:14 *good.* See Introduction: Distinctive Characteristics. *provide for daily necessities.* See 1Ti 5:8; cf. 2Th 3:10–12.

3:15 *Grace.* See note on Ro 1:7. *with you.* See note on 2Co 13:14.

Philemon

INTRODUCTION

Author, Date and Place of Writing

Paul wrote this short letter (see vv. 1,9,19) probably at the same time as Colossians (c. A.D. 60; see Introduction to Colossians: Author, Date and Place of Writing) and sent it to Colosse with the same travelers, Onesimus and Tychicus. He apparently wrote both letters from prison in Rome, though possibly from Ephesus (see Introduction to Philippians: Author, Date and Place of Writing; see also chart, p. 1697).

Recipient, Background and Purpose

Paul wrote this letter to Philemon, a believer in Colosse who, along with others, was a slave owner (cf. Col 4:1; for slavery in the NT see note on Eph 6:5). One of his slaves, Onesimus, had apparently stolen from him (cf. v. 18) and then run away, which under Roman law was punishable by death. But Onesimus met Paul and through his ministry became a Christian (see v. 10). Now he was willing to return to his master, and Paul writes this personal appeal to ask that he be accepted as a Christian brother (see v. 16).

A Quick Look

Author:
The apostle Paul

Audience:
Philemon and the members of the church at Colosse

Date:
About A.D. 60

Theme:
Paul urges Philemon to show grace to his runaway slave, Onesimus.

Approach and Structure

To win Philemon's willing acceptance of Onesimus, Paul writes very tactfully and in a lighthearted tone, which he creates with a wordplay (see note on v. 11). The appeal (vv. 4–21) is organized in a way prescribed by ancient Greek and Roman teachers: to build rapport (vv. 4–10), to persuade the mind (vv. 11–19) and to move the emotions (vv. 20–21). The name Onesimus is not mentioned until the rapport has been built (v. 10), and the appeal itself is stated only near the end of the section to persuade the mind (v. 17).

Outline

I. Greetings (1–3)
II. Thanksgiving and Prayer (4–7)
III. Paul's Plea for Onesimus (8–21)
IV. Final Request, Greetings and Benediction (22–25)

1Paul, a prisoner[a] of Christ Jesus, and
Timothy[b] our brother,[c]

To Philemon our dear friend and fellow
worker,[d] 2to Apphia our sister, to Archippus[e] our fellow soldier[f] and to the church
that meets in your home:[g]

3Grace to you and peace from God our
Father and the Lord Jesus Christ.[h]

Thanksgiving and Prayer

4I always thank my God[i] as I remember you in my prayers,[j] 5because I hear
about your faith in the Lord Jesus[k] and
your love for all the saints.[l] 6I pray that
you may be active in sharing your faith,
so that you will have a full understanding of every good thing we have in Christ.
7Your love has given me great joy and encouragement,[m] because you, brother, have
refreshed[n] the hearts of the saints.

Paul's Plea for Onesimus

8Therefore, although in Christ I could be
bold and order you to do what you ought
to do, 9yet I appeal to you[o] on the basis of
love. I then, as Paul—an old man and now
also a prisoner[p] of Christ Jesus— 10I appeal to you for my son[q] Onesimus,[a][r] who
became my son while I was in chains.[s]
11Formerly he was useless to you, but now
he has become useful both to you and
to me.

12I am sending him—who is my very
heart—back to you. 13I would have liked
to keep him with me so that he could take
your place in helping me while I am in
chains[t] for the gospel. 14But I did not want
to do anything without your consent, so
that any favor you do will be spontaneous
and not forced.[u] 15Perhaps the reason he
was separated from you for a little while
was that you might have him back for
good— 16no longer as a slave,[v] but better
than a slave, as a dear brother.[w] He is very
dear to me but even dearer to you, both as
a man and as a brother in the Lord.

17So if you consider me a partner,[x] welcome him as you would welcome me. 18If
he has done you any wrong or owes you
anything, charge it to me.[y] 19I, Paul, am
writing this with my own hand.[z] I will pay
it back—not to mention that you owe me
your very self. 20I do wish, brother, that I
may have some benefit from you in the
Lord; refresh[a] my heart in Christ. 21Con-
fident[b] of your obedience, I write to you,
knowing that you will do even more than
I ask.

22And one thing more: Prepare a guest
room for me, because I hope to be[c] restored to you in answer to your prayers.[d]

23Epaphras,[e] my fellow prisoner[f] in
Christ Jesus, sends you greetings. 24And so
do Mark,[g] Aristarchus,[h] Demas[i] and Luke,
my fellow workers.[j]

25The grace of the Lord Jesus Christ be
with your spirit.[k]

1 [a] ver 9,23; S Eph 3:1 [b] S Ac 16:1 [c] 2Co 1:1 [d] S Php 2:25
2 [e] Col 4:17 [f] Php 2:25 [g] S Ro 16:5
3 [h] S Ro 1:7
4 [i] S Ro 1:8 [j] S Ro 1:10
5 [k] S Ac 20:21 [l] S Col 1:4; 1Th 3:6
7 [m] 2Co 7:4,13 [n] ver 20; Ro 15:32; 1Co 16:18
9 [o] 1Co 1:10 [p] ver 1,23; S Eph 3:1
10 [q] S 1Th 2:11 [r] Col 4:9 [s] S Ac 21:33
13 [t] ver 10; S Ac 21:33
14 [u] 2Co 9:7; 1Pe 5:2
16 [v] 1Co 7:22 [w] Mt 23:8; S Ac 1:16; 1Ti 6:2
17 [x] 2Co 8:23
18 [y] Ge 43:9
19 [z] S 1Co 16:21
20 [a] ver 7; 1Co 16:18
21 [b] S 2Co 2:3
22 [c] Php 1:25; 2:24; Heb 13:19 [d] 2Co 1:11; Php 1:19
23 [e] Col 1:7 [f] ver 1; Ro 16:7; Col 4:10
24 [g] S Ac 12:12 [h] S Ac 19:29 [i] Col 4:14; 2Ti 4:10 [j] ver 1
25 [k] S Gal 6:18

[a] 10 *Onesimus* means *useful.*

1–2 Although Paul writes together with Timothy and although he addresses the entire church in Colosse, in this very personal letter to Philemon he uses "I" rather than "we," and "you" (singular except in vv. 22,25).

1 *Paul.* See note on Ro 1:1. *prisoner.* See Eph 3:1; Php 1:13 and notes. *Timothy.* See note on Col 1:1; see also Introduction to 1 Timothy: Recipient. *Philemon.* A Christian living in Colosse or nearby and the owner of the slave Onesimus.

2 *Apphia.* Probably Philemon's wife. *Archippus.* See Col 4:17.

3 *Grace … peace.* See note on Ro 1:7.

4 *thank … remember you in my prayers.* See Php 1:3–4 and note.

5 See Col 1:4. *saints.* See notes on Ro 1:7; Eph 1:1.

7 *hearts.* Figurative for the emotions of pity and love (see vv. 12,20).

10 *Onesimus.* See NIV text note; see also Introduction: Recipient, Background and Purpose. *my son.* See note on 1Ti 1:2.

11 *useless … useful.* A play on the meaning of Onesimus's name (see NIV text note on v. 10).

13 *in chains for the gospel.* See v. 1 and note.

16 Cf. 1Ti 6:2.

17–19 Martin Luther said, "Even as Christ did for us with God the Father, thus Paul also does for Onesimus with Philemon."

19 *writing this with my own hand.* See 1Co 16:21 and note. *owe me your very self.* Paul probably led Philemon to faith in Christ.

20 *I … my.* Both pronouns are emphatic, making an obvious allusion to v. 7. *benefit.* The Greek for this word is another play on the name Onesimus.

21 *even more than I ask.* Perhaps suggesting that Philemon set Onesimus free.

22 *one thing more.* It was not unusual for an ancient letter, though occasioned by one matter, to also include another matter. Often, as here, the second matter had to do with how and when the author planned to meet the recipient again.

23 *Epaphras.* See Col 1:7 and note; 4:12.

24 *Mark, Aristarchus.* See note on Col 4:10. *Demas and Luke.* See note on Col 4:14.

25 *grace.* See note on Ro 1:7. *be with your spirit.* See note on Gal 6:18.

Hebrews

INTRODUCTION

Author

The writer of this letter does not identify himself, but he was obviously well known to the original recipients. Though for some 1,200 years (c. A.D. 400 – 1600) the book was commonly called "The Epistle of Paul to the Hebrews," there was no agreement in the earliest centuries regarding its authorship. Since the Reformation it has been widely recognized that Paul could not have been the writer. There is no disharmony between the teaching of Hebrews and that of Paul's letters, but the specific emphases and writing styles are markedly different. Contrary to Paul's usual practice, the author of Hebrews nowhere identifies himself in the letter — except to indicate that he was a man (see note on 11:32). Moreover, the statement "This salvation, which was first announced by the Lord, was confirmed to us by those who heard him" (2:3), indicates that the author had neither been with Jesus during his earthly ministry nor received special revelation directly from the risen Lord, as had Paul (Gal 1:11 – 12).

The earliest suggestion of authorship is found in Tertullian's *De Pudicitia*, 20 (c. A.D. 200), in which he quotes from "an epistle to the Hebrews under the name of Barnabas." From the letter itself it is clear that the writer must have had authority in the apostolic church and was an intellectual Hebrew Christian well versed in the OT. Barnabas meets these requirements. He was a Jew of the priestly tribe of Levi (Ac 4:36) who became a close friend of Paul after the latter's conversion. Under the guidance of the Holy Spirit, the church at Antioch commissioned Barnabas and Paul for the work of evangelism and sent them off on the first missionary journey (Ac 13:1 – 4).

The other leading candidate for authorship is Apollos, whose name was first suggested by Martin Luther and who is favored by many interpreters today. Apollos, an Alexandrian by birth, was also a Jewish Christian with notable intellectual and oratorical abilities. Luke tells us that "he was a learned man, with a thorough knowledge of the Scriptures" (Ac 18:24). We also

> **A Quick Look**
>
> **Author:**
> Unknown, possibly Apollos or Barnabas
>
> **Audience:**
> Primarily Jewish Christians
>
> **Date:**
> About A.D. 67–70
>
> **Theme:**
> The author demonstrates the absolute supremacy and sufficiency of Jesus Christ as revealer and mediator of God's grace.

know that Apollos was associated with Paul in the early years of the church in Corinth (1Co 1:12; 3:4–6,22).

One thing is evident: The author was a master of the Greek language of his day, and he was thoroughly acquainted with the pre-Christian Greek translation of the OT (the Septuagint), which he regularly quotes.

Date

Hebrews must have been written before the destruction of Jerusalem and the temple in A.D. 70 because: (1) If it had been written after this date, the author surely would have mentioned the temple's destruction and the end of the Jewish sacrificial system; and (2) the author consistently uses the Greek present tense when speaking of the temple and the priestly activities connected with it (see 5:1–3; 7:23,27; 8:3–5; 9:6–9,13,25; 10:1,3–4,8,11; 13:10–11).

From the OT itself, Christ is shown to be superior to the ancient prophets, to angels, to Moses (the mediator of the former covenant) and to Aaron and the priestly succession descended from him.

Recipients

The letter was addressed primarily to Jewish Christians who were familiar with the OT and who were being tempted to revert to Judaism or to Judaize the gospel (cf. Gal 2:14). It has been suggested that the recipients were from the "large number of priests [who] became obedient to the faith" (Ac 6:7).

Theme

The theme of Hebrews is the absolute supremacy and sufficiency of Jesus Christ as revealer and as mediator of God's grace. The prologue (1:1–4) presents Christ as God's full and final revelation, far surpassing the revelation given in the OT. The prophecies and promises of the OT are fulfilled in the "new covenant" (or "new testament"), of which Christ is the mediator (9:15; 12:24). From the OT itself, Christ is shown to be superior to the ancient prophets, to angels, to Moses (the mediator of the former covenant) and to Aaron and the priestly succession descended from him. Hebrews could be called "the book of better things" since the two Greek words for "better" and "superior" occur 15 times in the letter. A striking feature of this presentation of the gospel is the unique manner in which the author employs expositions of eight specific passages of the OT Scriptures:

1. 2:5–9: Exposition of Ps 8:4–6
2. 3:7—4:13: Exposition of Ps 95:7–11
3. 4:14—7:28: Exposition of Ps 110:4
4. 8:1—10:18: Exposition of Jer 31:31–34
5. 10:1–10: Exposition of Ps 40:6–8
6. 10:32—12:3: Exposition of Hab 2:3–4
7. 12:4–13: Exposition of Pr 3:11–12
8. 12:18–24: Exposition of Ex 19:10–23

Practical applications of this theme are given throughout the book. The readers are told that there can be no turning back to or continuation in the old Jewish system, which has been superseded by the unique priesthood of Christ. God's people must now look only to him, whose atoning death, resurrection and ascension have opened the way into the true, heavenly sanctuary of God's presence. To "ignore such a great salvation" (2:3) or to give up the pursuit of holiness (12:10,14) is to face the anger of the "living God" (10:31). Five times the author weaves into his presentation of the gospel stern warnings (see note on 2:1–4) and reminds his readers of the divine judgment that came to the rebellious generation of Israelites in the desert.

Literary Form

Hebrews is commonly referred to as a letter, though it does not have the typical form of a letter. It ends like a letter (13:22–25) but begins more like an essay or sermon (1:1–4). The author does not identify himself or those addressed, which letter writers normally did. And he offers no manner of greeting, such as is usually found at the beginning of ancient letters. Rather, he begins with a magnificent statement about Jesus Christ. He calls his work a "word of exhortation" (13:22), the conventional designation given a sermon in a synagogue service (see Ac 13:15, where "message of encouragement" translates the same Greek words as "word of exhortation"). Like a sermon, Hebrews is full of encouragement, exhortations and stern warnings. It is likely that the author used sermonic materials and sent them out in a modified letter form.

Outline

- I. Prologue: The Superiority of God's New Revelation (1:1–4)
- II. The Superiority of Christ to Leading Figures under the Old Covenant (1:5—7:28)
  - A. Christ Is Superior to the Angels (1:5—2:18)
    1. Scriptural proof of his superiority (1:5–14)
    2. Exhortation not to ignore the revelation of God in his Son (2:1–4)
    3. Jesus was made a little lower than the angels (2:5–9)
    4. Having been made like us, Jesus was enabled to save us (2:10–18)
  - B. Christ Is Superior to Moses (3:1—4:13)
    1. Demonstration of Christ's superiority (3:1–6)
    2. Exhortation to enter salvation-rest (3:7—4:13)
  - C. Christ Is Superior to the Aaronic Priests (4:14—7:28)
    1. Jesus is the great high priest (4:14–16)
    2. Qualifications of a priest (5:1–10)
    3. Exhortation to press on toward maturity (5:11—6:12)
    4. The certainty of God's promise (6:13–20)
    5. Christ's superior priestly order (ch. 7)
- III. The Superior Sacrificial Work of Our High Priest (8:1—10:18)
  - A. A New Sanctuary and a New Covenant (ch. 8)
  - B. The Old Sanctuary (9:1–10)
  - C. The Better Sacrifice (9:11—10:18)
- IV. A Call to Follow Jesus Faithfully and with Perseverance (10:19—12:29)
  - A. Having Confidence to Enter the Sanctuary (10:19–25)
  - B. A Warning against Persistence in Sin (10:26–31)
  - C. Persevering in Faith under Pressure (10:32—12:3)
    1. As in the past, so in the future (10:32–39)
    2. Faith and its many outstanding examples (ch. 11)
    3. Jesus, the supreme example (12:1–3)
  - D. Encouragement to Persevere in the Face of Hardship (12:4–13)
  - E. Exhortation to Holy Living (12:14–17)
  - F. Crowning Motivation and Warning (12:18–29)
- V. Conclusion (ch. 13)
  - A. Rules for Christian Living (13:1–17)
  - B. Request for Prayer (13:18–19)
  - C. Benediction (13:20–21)
  - D. Personal Remarks (13:22–23)
  - E. Greetings and Final Benediction (13:24–25)

The Son Superior to Angels

1 In the past God spoke[a] to our forefathers through the prophets[b] at many
times and in various ways,[c] 2 but in these
last days[d] he has spoken to us by his Son,[e]
whom he appointed heir[f] of all things, and
through whom[g] he made the universe.[h]
3 The Son is the radiance of God's glory[i]
and the exact representation of his being,[j] sustaining all things[k] by his powerful
word. After he had provided purification
for sins,[l] he sat down at the right hand of
the Majesty in heaven.[m] 4 So he became as
much superior to the angels as the name
he has inherited is superior to theirs.[n]
5 For to which of the angels did God ever
say,

"You are my Son;
today I have become your
Father[a]"[b]?[o]

Or again,

"I will be his Father,
and he will be my Son"[c]?[p]

6 And again, when God brings his firstborn[q] into the world,[r] he says,

"Let all God's angels worship
him."[d][s]

7 In speaking of the angels he says,

"He makes his angels winds,
his servants flames of fire."[e][t]

8 But about the Son he says,

"Your throne, O God, will last for ever
and ever,[u]
and righteousness will be the scepter
of your kingdom.
9 You have loved righteousness and
hated wickedness;
therefore God, your God, has set you
above your companions[v]
by anointing you with the oil[w] of
joy."[f][x]

10 He also says,

"In the beginning, O Lord, you laid the
foundations of the earth,
and the heavens are the work of
your hands.[y]

1:1 [a] Jn 9:29; Heb 2:2, 3; 4:8; 12:25 [b] Lk 1:70; Ac 2:30 [c] Nu 12:6, 8 **1:2** [d] Dt 4:30; Heb 9:26; 1Pe 1:20 [e] ver 5; S Mt 3:17; Heb 3:6; 5:8; 7:28 [f] Ps 2:8; Mt 11:27; S 28:18 [g] S Jn 1:3 [h] Heb 11:3 **1:3** [i] Jn 1:14 [j] S Jn 14:9 [k] Col 1:17 [l] Tit 2:14; Heb 7:27; 9:11-14 [m] S Mk 16:19 **1:4** [n] Eph 1:21; Php 2:9, 10; Heb 8:6 **1:5** [o] Ps 2:7; S Mt 3:17 [p] 2Sa 7:14 **1:6** [q] Jn 3:16; S Col 1:18 [r] Heb 10:5 [s] Dt 32:43 (LXX and DSS); Ps 97:7 **1:7** [t] Ps 104:4 **1:8** [u] S Lk 1:33 **1:9** [v] Php 2:9 [w] Isa 61:1, 3 [x] Ps 45:6, 7 **1:10** [y] Ps 8:6; Zec 12:1

[a] 5 Or *have begotten you* [b] 5 Psalm 2:7 [c] 5 2 Samuel 7:14; 1 Chron. 17:13 [d] 6 Deut. 32:43 (see Dead Sea Scrolls and Septuagint) [e] 7 Psalm 104:4 [f] 9 Psalm 45:6,7

1:1 *In the past.* In contrast to "in these last days" (v. 2), the Messianic era inaugurated by the incarnation (see Ac 2:17; 1Ti 4:1; 1Jn 2:18 and notes). *God spoke.* Cf. "he has spoken" (v. 2). God is the ultimate author of both the OT and the NT. *to our forefathers.* In contrast to "to us" (v. 2). *through the prophets.* All OT writers are here viewed as prophets in that their testimony was preparation for the coming of Christ; cf. "by his Son" (v. 2), a new and unique category of revelation in contrast to that of the prophets. *at many times and in various ways.* The OT revelation was occasional and lacking in finality.

1:2–3 The superiority of God's revelation through his Son is demonstrated by seven great descriptive statements about him: (1) *appointed heir of all things.* The incarnate Son, having performed the work of redemption, was gloriously exalted to the position of the firstborn heir of God, i.e., he received the inheritance of God's estate ("all things"). See Ro 8:17. (2) *through whom he made the universe.* See Jn 1:3; 1Co 8:6; Col 1:16 and note. (3) *radiance of God's glory.* As the brilliance of the sun is inseparable from the sun itself, so the Son's radiance is inseparable from deity, for he himself is God, the second person of the Trinity (see Jn 1:14,18 and notes). (4) *exact representation of his being.* Jesus is not merely an image or reflection of God. Because the Son himself is God (see note on Ro 9:5), he is the absolutely authentic representation of God's being (see Jn 14:9; Col 1:15 and note). (5) *sustaining all things.* Christ is not like Atlas, the mythical Greek god who held the world on his shoulders. The Son dynamically holds together all that has been created through him (Col 1:17). (6) *provided purification for sins.* Through his redeeming death on the cross (see 7:27; 9:12; Tit 2:14 and notes). (7) *sat down at the right hand of the Majesty in heaven.* Being seated at God's right hand indicates that Christ is actively ruling with God as Lord over all (see v. 13; 8:1; 10:12; 12:2; Mt 26:64; Ac 2:23; 5:34; Ro 8:34; Eph 1:20; Col 3:1; 1Pe 3:22).

1:2 *these last days.* The time when all that was promised and worked toward in the OT was coming to fulfillment (see v. 1; Jas 5:3; 2Pe 3:3 and notes; see also 1Pe 1:20; Jude 18).

1:4 *superior to the angels.* To most Jews angels were exalted beings, especially revered because they were involved in giving the law at Sinai (see 2:2) and to the Jews the law was God's supreme revelation. The Dead Sea Scrolls reflect the expectation that the archangel Michael would be the supreme figure in the Messianic kingdom. *name.* See Php 2:9 and note. What follows indicates that this name was "Son"—a name to which no angel could lay claim.

1:5–14 Christ's superiority to angels is documented by seven OT quotations (see NIV text notes), showing that he is God's Son, that he is worshiped by angels and that, though he is God, he is distinguished from the Father.

1:5 *You are my Son; today I have become your Father.* This passage (Ps 2:7) is quoted in Ac 13:33 as fulfilled in Christ's resurrection (cf. Ro 1:4). *I will be his Father, and he will be my Son.* Jews acknowledged 2Sa 7:14 (of which this passage is a quotation) and Ps 2 to be Messianic in their ultimate application (see Lk 1:32–33 and notes). This royal personage is neither an angel nor an archangel; he is God's Son.

1:6 *firstborn.* See Col 1:15 and note. *Let all God's angels worship him.* The author quotes a line that was in his Greek version of Deuteronomy (see NIV text note). This statement, which in the OT refers to the Lord God (Yahweh), is here applied to Christ, giving clear indication of his full deity. The very beings with whom Christ is being compared are commanded to proclaim his superiority by worshiping him.

1:7 *He makes his angels winds, his servants flames of fire.* Ps 104:4 speaks of the storm wind and the lightning as agents of God's purposes. The Septuagint (the pre-Christian Greek translation of the OT), which the author of Hebrews quotes as the version familiar to his readers, reflects the developing doctrine of angels during the period between the OT and the NT. *angels.* English "angel" comes from the Greek word *angelos,* which means "messenger" or "agent." The Hebrew word most often translated "angel" has essentially the same meaning.

1:8 *But about the Son he says, "Your throne, O God, will last for ever."* The author selects a passage that intimates the deity of the Messianic (and Davidic) King, further demonstrating the Son's superiority over angels (see Ps 45:6 and note).

1:10 *In the beginning, O Lord, you laid the foundations of the*

11 They will perish, but you remain;
they will all wear out like a garment.[z]
12 You will roll them up like a robe;
like a garment they will be changed.
But you remain the same,[a]
and your years will never end."[a][b]

13 To which of the angels did God ever say,

"Sit at my right hand[c]
until I make your enemies
a footstool[d] for your feet"[b]?[e]

14 Are not all angels ministering spirits[f] sent
to serve those who will inherit[g] salvation?[h]

Warning to Pay Attention

2 We must pay more careful attention,
therefore, to what we have heard, so
that we do not drift away.[i] 2 For if the message spoken[j] by angels[k] was binding, and
every violation and disobedience received
its just punishment,[l] 3 how shall we escape
if we ignore such a great salvation?[m] This
salvation, which was first announced by
the Lord,[n] was confirmed to us by those
who heard him.[o] 4 God also testified to it
by signs, wonders and various miracles,[p]
and gifts of the Holy Spirit[q] distributed according to his will.[r]

1:11 [z] Isa 34:4; 51:6; S Heb 12:27 **1:12** [a] Heb 13:8 [b] Ps 102:25-27 **1:13** [c] ver 3; S Mk 16:19 [d] Jos 10:24; Heb 10:13 [e] Ps 110:1; S Mt 22:44 **1:14** [f] Ps 91:11; 103:20; Da 7:10 [g] Mt 25:34; Mk 10:17; S Ac 20:32 [h] S Ro 11:14; Heb 2:3; 5:9; 9:28 **2:1** [i] S Ro 11:22 **2:2** [j] S Heb 1:1 [k] Dt 33:2; Ac 7:53; Gal 3:19 [l] Heb 10:28 **2:3** [m] Heb 10:29; 12:25 [n] Heb 1:2 [o] S Lk 1:2 **2:4** [p] Mk 16:20; S Jn 4:48 [q] S 1Co 12:4 [r] S Eph 1:5 **2:6** [s] Heb 4:4 [t] Job 7:17; Ps 144:3 **2:8** [u] Ps 8:4-6; S Mt 22:44 **2:9** [v] ver 7; Ac 3:13; S Php 2:9 [w] Php 2:7-9 [x] 2Co 5:15 **2:10** [y] S Ro 11:36

Jesus Made Like His Brothers

5 It is not to angels that he has subjected the world to come, about which we
are speaking. 6 But there is a place where
someone[s] has testified:

"What is man that you are mindful of him,
the son of man that you care for him?[t]
7 You made him a little[c] lower than the angels;
you crowned him with glory and honor
8 and put everything under his feet."[d][u]

In putting everything under him, God left
nothing that is not subject to him. Yet at
present we do not see everything subject to him. 9 But we see Jesus, who was
made a little lower than the angels, now
crowned with glory and honor[v] because
he suffered death,[w] so that by the grace of
God he might taste death for everyone.[x]
10 In bringing many sons to glory, it was
fitting that God, for whom and through
whom everything exists,[y] should make the
author of their salvation perfect through

[a] 12 Psalm 102:25-27 [b] 13 Psalm 110:1 [c] 7 Or *him for a little while*; also in verse 9 [d] 8 Psalm 8:4-6

earth. As in v. 6, a passage addressed to Yahweh ("O Lord") is applied to the Son.

1:13 *Sit at my right hand.* See note on vv. 2–3. Ps 110 is applied repeatedly to Jesus in Hebrews (vv. 3,13; 5:6,10; 6:20; 7:3,11,17,21; 8:1; 10:12–13; 12:2).

1:14 *ministering spirits.* Christ reigns; angels minister as those sent to serve.

2:1–4 The first of five warnings strategically positioned throughout the letter (see 3:7—4:13; 6:4–8; 10:26–31; 12:25–29).

2:1 *what we have heard.* The message of the gospel, including that of Christ's person as the God-man and his redemptive work on the cross. *drift away.* From the greater revelation given through the Son.

2:2 *the message spoken by angels.* The law given through Moses at Sinai (see Ac 7:38 and note).

2:3 *how shall we escape . . . ?* See 12:25. *such a great salvation.* The argument here is from the lesser to the greater, and assumes that the gospel is greater than the law. Thus, if disregard for the law brought certain punishment, disregard for the gospel will bring even greater punishment. *confirmed to us by those who heard him.* The eyewitnesses, chiefly the apostles (see Ac 1:21–22 and note on 1:22; 1Jn 1:1 and note; cf. 2Pe 1:16 and note), had vouched for the message first announced by Christ. The author himself apparently was neither an apostle nor an eyewitness (see Introduction: Author).

2:4 *signs, wonders and various miracles.* God added his confirmation to the gospel message through supernatural acts such as healing the sick (see Ac 3:7–9,11–12,16; 5:12–16; 9:32–41; 14:3,8–9; 19:11–12; 28:8–9). *gifts of the Holy Spirit.* Such as the gift of tongues (see Ac 2:4–12). *distributed according to his will.* See 1Co 12:4–11.

2:5–9 An exposition of Ps 8:4–6, which continues to show Christ's superiority over the angels—in him humanity's appointed role as ruler (under God) over God's other creatures (cf. Ge 1:26,28 and notes) comes to ultimate fulfillment (see note on Ps 8:4–6).

2:5 *It is not to angels that he has subjected the world to come.* Christ, as bearer of the new revelation (see 1:2–3 and note), is superior to angels who had participated in bringing the revelation at Sinai (see 2:2 and note).

2:6–8 Awed by the marvelous order and immensity of God's handiwork in the celestial universe, the psalmist marveled at the high dignity God had bestowed on puny mortals by entrusting them with dominion over the other creatures (see Ge 1:26–28 and notes).

2:7 *angels.* The author here quotes his Greek version of the Psalter, which renders the common Hebrew word for "God" or "gods" in this way in Ps 8:5 (see NIV text note there) as it does the Hebrew for "sons of God" in Job 1:6; 2:1 (see NIV text note there).

2:8 *everything.* God's purpose from the beginning was that humanity should be sovereign in the creaturely realm, subject only to God. Due to sin, that purpose of God has not yet been fully realized. Indeed, humans are themselves "in slavery" (v. 15).

2:9 *Jesus . . . now crowned with glory and honor.* See 10:13 and note. Ps 8 is here applied to Jesus in particular. As forerunner of humanity's restored dominion over the earth, he was made lower than the angels for a while (see NIV text note on v. 7) but is now crowned with glory and honor at God's right hand. By his perfect life, his death on the cross and his exaltation, he has made possible for redeemed humanity the ultimate fulfillment of Ps 8 in the future kingdom.

2:10 *many sons to glory.* Those who believe in Christ are made God's children through his only Son (cf. Jn 1:12–13; Ro 8:14–23 and notes on 8:14–15,17,23; Gal 3:26; 4:5 and note; Eph 4:5; 5:1; 1Jn 3:1–2). *author.* The Greek word often expresses the idea of "originator, founder." It was also applied to a leader, ruler or prince. In the present context, it

suffering.[z] 11Both the one who makes men
holy[a] and those who are made holy[b] are of
the same family. So Jesus is not ashamed
to call them brothers.[c] 12He says,

"I will declare your name to my
brothers;
in the presence of the congregation I
will sing your praises."[a][d]

13And again,

"I will put my trust in him."[b][e]

And again he says,

"Here am I, and the children God has
given me."[c][f]

14Since the children have flesh and
blood,[g] he too shared in their humanity[h] so that by his death he might destroy[i]
him who holds the power of death—that
is, the devil[j]— 15and free those who all
their lives were held in slavery by their
fear[k] of death. 16For surely it is not angels
he helps, but Abraham's descendants.[l]
17For this reason he had to be made like
his brothers[m] in every way, in order that
he might become a merciful[n] and faithful
high priest[o] in service to God,[p] and that

[a] *12* Psalm 22:22 [b] *13* Isaiah 8:17 [c] *13* Isaiah 8:18

2:10 [z] Lk 24:26; Heb 5:8, 9; 7:28 **2:11** [a] Heb 13:12 [b] S Eph 5:26 [c] S Mt 28:10 **2:12** [d] Ps 22:22; 68:26 **2:13** [e] Isa 8:17 [f] Isa 8:18; Jn 10:29 **2:14** [g] 1Co 15:50; Eph 6:12 [h] S Jn 1:14 [i] Ge 3:15; 1Co 15:54-57; 2Ti 1:10 [j] 1Jn 3:8 **2:15** [k] S 2Ti 1:7 **2:16** [l] S Lk 3:8 **2:17** [m] ver 14; S Php 2:7 [n] Heb 5:2 [o] Heb 3:1; 4:14, 15; 5:5, 10; 7:26, 28; 8:1, 3; 9:11 [p] Heb 5:1

perhaps has the sense of "champion"—the one who came to the aid of those enslaved to "him who holds the power of death" (v. 14; cf. v. 15; 12:2 and note; Ac 3:15; 5:31 ["Prince"]). *make ... perfect through suffering.* It was through Christ's suffering that God fully qualified him as the one sent to carry out his redemptive mission, specifically the priestly aspects of that mission (see v. 17 and note; see also 5:9; 7:28).

2:11 *who makes men holy ... who are made holy.* Christ became a human being to identify himself with humans and, by his substitutionary sacrifice on the cross, to restore their lost holiness. *holy.* See 1Co 1:2 and note.

2:12 *I will declare your name to my brothers.* A quotation from Ps 22:22, a psalm describing the sufferings and relief of God's righteous servant (see introduction to Ps 22). The key phrase is "my brothers," seen here as coming from the lips of the triumphant Messiah.

2:13 *I will put my trust in him.* An expression of true dependence on God perfectly exemplified in Christ. In him humanity is seen as it was intended to be. *Here am I, and the children God has given me.* Also seen ultimately as an utterance of the incarnate Son. The Father's children are given to the Son to be his brothers and sisters (see v. 11; cf. Mt 12:50).

2:14 *him who holds the power of death.* Satan wields the power of death only insofar as he induces people to sin and to come under sin's penalty, which is death (see Ro 5:12; 6:23 and notes).

2:15 *free.* See 1Co 15:54–57 and notes on 15:56–57; Rev 1:18.

2:16 *Abraham's descendants.* Christ came to redeem Abraham's descendants—those who have Abraham's faith (see Ge 12:2–3; Ro 4:11,16; 9:8; Gal 3:29 and notes).

2:17 *merciful and faithful high priest.* See v. 18; 5:2. *high priest.*

The "Greater-Thans" in Hebrews

One of the author's main points in Hebrews is that Jesus is greater than all those things associated with the Jewish religion and way of life. Sometimes he actually uses the words "greater than"; sometimes he does not. But in all cases the theme is clear.

Theme	Passage in Hebrews
Jesus is greater than the prophets	1:1–3
Jesus is greater than the angels	1:4–14; 2:5
Jesus is greater than Moses	3:1–6
Jesus is greater than Joshua	4:6–11
Jesus is greater than the high priest	5:1–10; 7:26—8:2
Jesus is greater than the Levitical priests	6:20—7:25
Jesus as the high priest after Melchizedek is greater than Abraham	7:1–10
Jesus' ministry is greater than the tabernacle ministry	8:3–6; 9:1–28
Jesus' new covenant is greater than the old covenant	8:7–13
Jesus' sacrifice is greater than OT sacrifices	10:1–14
Experiencing Jesus is greater than the experience on Mount Sinai	12:18–24

he might make atonement for[q] the sins of
the people.[a] 18 Because he himself suffered
when he was tempted, he is able to help
those who are being tempted.[r]

Jesus Greater Than Moses

3 Therefore, holy brothers,[s] who share in
the heavenly calling,[t] fix your thoughts
on Jesus, the apostle and high priest[u]
whom we confess.[v] 2 He was faithful to
the one who appointed him, just as Moses
was faithful in all God's house.[w] 3 Jesus has
been found worthy of greater honor than
Moses,[x] just as the builder of a house has
greater honor than the house itself. 4 For
every house is built by someone, but God
is the builder of everything.[y] 5 Moses was
faithful as a servant[z] in all God's house,[a]
testifying to what would be said in the future. 6 But Christ is faithful as a son[b] over
God's house. And we are his house,[c] if we
hold on[d] to our courage and the hope[e] of
which we boast.

Warning Against Unbelief

7 So, as the Holy Spirit says:[f]

"Today, if you hear his voice,
8 do not harden your hearts[g]
as you did in the rebellion,
during the time of testing in the
desert,
9 where your fathers tested and tried me
and for forty years saw what I did.[h]
10 That is why I was angry with that
generation,
and I said, 'Their hearts are always
going astray,
and they have not known my ways.'
11 So I declared on oath in my anger,[i]
'They shall never enter my rest.'[j]"[b][k]

12 See to it, brothers, that none of you has
a sinful, unbelieving heart that turns away
from the living God.[l] 13 But encourage one
another daily,[m] as long as it is called Today, so that none of you may be hardened
by sin's deceitfulness.[n] 14 We have come to
share in Christ if we hold firmly[o] till the
end the confidence[p] we had at first. 15 As
has just been said:

"Today, if you hear his voice,
do not harden your hearts
as you did in the rebellion."[c][q]

16 Who were they who heard and rebelled?
Were they not all those Moses led out of
Egypt?[r] 17 And with whom was he angry
for forty years? Was it not with those who
sinned, whose bodies fell in the desert?[s]

[a] 17 Or *and that he might turn aside God's wrath, taking away* [b] *11* Psalm 95:7-11 [c] *15* Psalm 95:7,8

2:17 [q] S Ro 3:25 **2:18** [r] Heb 4:15 **3:1** [s] Heb 2:11 [t] S Ro 8:28 [u] S Heb 2:17 [v] 1Ti 6:12; Heb 4:14; 10:23; 2Co 9:13 **3:2** [w] ver 5; Nu 12:7 **3:3** [x] Dt 34:12 **3:4** [y] Ge 1:1 **3:5** [z] Ex 14:31 [a] ver 2; Nu 12:7 **3:6** [b] S Heb 1:2 [c] S 1Co 3:16; 1Ti 3:15 [d] ver 14; S Ro 11:22; Heb 4:14 [e] Ro 5:2; Heb 6:11,18,19; 7:19; 11:1 **3:7** [f] Ac 28:25; Heb 9:8; 10:15 **3:8** [g] ver 15; Heb 4:7 **3:9** [h] Nu 14:33; Dt 1:3; Ac 7:36 **3:11** [i] Dt 1:34,35 [j] Heb 4:3,5 [k] Ps 95:7-11 **3:12** [l] S Mt 16:16 **3:13** [m] Heb 10:24,25 [n] Jer 17:9; Eph 4:22 **3:14** [o] ver 6 [p] S Eph 3:12 **3:15** [q] ver 7,8; Ps 95:7,8; Heb 4:7 **3:16** [r] Nu 14:2 **3:17** [s] Nu 14:29; Ps 106:26; 1Co 10:5

In Israel the head of the priestly order, the only one who could enter into the very presence of God in the Most Holy Place in the temple—to make atonement for the people of God (see 9:7 and note; 13:11; Lev 16:1–34 and note). *make atonement.* See NIV text note. In order for Christ to turn aside the wrath of God against guilty sinners, he had to become one with them and die as a substitute for them (see notes on Lev 16:20–22; 17:11; Ro 3:25; 1Jn 2:2).

2:18 *he was tempted.* See note on 4:15.

3:1–6 The faithful high priest who is worthy of our trust because he is greater than Moses.

3:1 *holy.* See note on 1Co 1:2. *brothers.* See note on Ro 1:13. *share in the heavenly calling.* That is, participate (see note on v. 14) in the invitation to enter into and enjoy the presence of God (see 11:16; 12:22 and notes). *apostle.* Means "one who is sent" (see note on Mk 6:30). Jesus repeatedly spoke of himself as having been sent into the world by the Father (e.g., Mt 10:40; 15:24; Mk 9:37; Lk 9:48; Jn 4:34; 5:24,30,36–38; 6:38). He is the supreme apostle, the one from whom all other apostleship flows. *high priest.* See note on 2:17.

3:2 A comparison of Christ and Moses, both of whom were sent by the Father to lead his people—the one to lead them from bondage under the pharaoh to the promised land, the other to lead them from bondage under the devil (2:14–15) to the Sabbath-rest promised to those who believe (4:3,9). The analogy focuses on faithful stewardship.

3:3 *the builder . . . has greater honor than the house.* Jesus is the actual builder of the house (or household), whereas Moses was simply a part of it.

3:4 *God is the builder of everything.* Jesus is here equated with God, making it beyond question that Christ is greater than Moses.

3:5–6 *a servant in all God's house . . . a son over God's house.* The superiority of Christ over Moses is shown in two comparisons: (1) Moses was a servant, whereas Christ is a son, and (2) Moses was in God's house, i.e., a part of it, whereas Christ is over God's house.

3:5 *faithful . . . in all God's house.* See Nu 12:7.

3:6 *we are his house.* The house is made up of God's people, his household (see Eph 2:19; 1Pe 2:5 and notes). *if we hold on to our courage.* Failure to persevere reveals that a person is actually not a child of God, whereas perseverance is the hallmark of his children (cf. 10:35–36). *hope.* Assurance of free access to God (see v. 1; 6:18–19 and notes; 11:1; Ro 5:2 and note). *boast.* Rejoice over (cf. Gal 6:14; cf. also 1Co 1:29,31; 2Co 10:17; Eph 2:9).

3:7—4:13 An exposition of Ps 95:7–11, stressing Christ's superiority over Moses, and a warning (the second; see note on 2:1–4) against disobedience and unbelief.

3:7–11 This quotation from Ps 95:7–11 summarizes the inglorious history of Israel under Moses' leadership in the desert. Three time periods are alluded to: that of the exodus, that of the psalmist and that of the writing of Hebrews. The example of Israel under Moses was used by the psalmist to warn the Israelites of his day against unbelief and disobedience. Similarly the author of Hebrews recalls the psalmist's words to warn the readers of this letter.

3:7 *Holy Spirit.* For the Holy Spirit as the speaker in (OT) Scripture see 9:8; 10:15; Mk 12:36; Ac 1:16; 4:25; 21:11; 28:25; 1Pe 1:12; see also 2Pe 1:20–21 and notes; cf. 2Ti 3:16 and note.

3:13 *as long as it is called Today.* See 4:7.

3:14 *to share in Christ.* To belong to him and participate in the blessings he gives (cf. v. 1). *hold firmly till the end.* Cf. 6:11; Mt 10:22; 24:13; Mk 13:13; Ro 2:26; cf. also 1Co 1:8. *confidence we had at first.* That is, our original conviction and the faith commitment we made on the basis of that conviction.

3:16–19 The argument is pursued with a series of rhetorical questions. The important truths are that the people who failed to enter Canaan were the ones who had heard God's promise concerning the land and that they refused to believe

18And to whom did God swear that they would never enter his rest[t] if not to those who disobeyed[a]?[u] 19So we see that they were not able to enter, because of their unbelief.[v]

A Sabbath-Rest for the People of God

4 Therefore, since the promise of entering his rest still stands, let us be careful that none of you be found to have fallen short of it.[w] 2For we also have had the gospel preached to us, just as they did; but the message they heard was of no value to them, because those who heard did not combine it with faith.[b x] 3Now we who have believed enter that rest, just as God has said,

> "So I declared on oath in my anger,
> 'They shall never enter my rest.' "[c y]

And yet his work has been finished since the creation of the world. 4For somewhere he has spoken about the seventh day in these words: "And on the seventh day God rested from all his work."[d z] 5And again in the passage above he says, "They shall never enter my rest."[a]

6It still remains that some will enter that rest, and those who formerly had the gospel preached to them did not go in, because of their disobedience.[b] 7Therefore God again set a certain day, calling it Today, when a long time later he spoke through David, as was said before:

> "Today, if you hear his voice,
> do not harden your hearts."[e c]

8For if Joshua had given them rest,[d] God would not have spoken[e] later about another day. 9There remains, then, a Sabbath-rest for the people of God; 10for anyone who enters God's rest also rests from his own work,[f] just as God did from his.[g] 11Let us, therefore, make every effort to enter that rest, so that no one will fall by following their example of disobedience.[h]

12For the word of God[i] is living[j] and active.[k] Sharper than any double-edged sword,[l] it penetrates even to dividing soul and spirit, joints and marrow; it judges the thoughts and attitudes of the heart.[m] 13Nothing in all creation is hidden from God's sight.[n] Everything is uncovered and laid bare before the eyes of him to whom we must give account.

Jesus the Great High Priest

14Therefore, since we have a great high priest[o] who has gone through the

[a] 18 Or *disbelieved* [b] 2 Many manuscripts *because they did not share in the faith of those who obeyed* [c] 3 Psalm 95:11; also in verse 5 [d] 4 Gen. 2:2 [e] 7 Psalm 95:7,8

3:18 [t]Nu 14:20-23; Dt 1:34,35 [u]Heb 4:6 **3:19** [v]Ps 78:22; 106:24; Jn 3:36 **4:1** [w]Heb 12:15 **4:2** [x]1Th 2:13 **4:3** [y]Ps 95:11; Dt 1:34,35; Heb 3:11 **4:4** [z]Ge 2:2,3; Ex 20:11 **4:5** [a]Ps 95:11; S ver 3 **4:6** [b]ver 11; Heb 3:18 **4:7** [c]Ps 95:7,8; Heb 3:7,8,15 **4:8** [d]Jos 22:4 [e]S Heb 1:1 **4:10** [f]Lev 23:3; Rev 14:13 [g]ver 4 **4:11** [h]ver 6; Heb 3:18 **4:12** [i]S Mk 4:14; Lk 5:1; 11:28; Jn 10:35; Ac 12:24; 1Th 2:13; 2Ti 2:9; 1Pe 1:23; 1Jn 2:14; Rev 1:2,9 [j]Ac 7:38; 1Pe 1:23 [k]Isa 55:11; Jer 23:29; 1Th 2:13 [l]Eph 6:17; S Rev 1:16 [m]1Co 14:24,25 **4:13** [n]Ps 33:13-15; Pr 5:21; Jer 16:17; 23:24; Da 2:22 **4:14** [o]S Heb 2:17

what God had promised (v. 19)—an action described as rebellion (v. 16), sin (v. 17) and disobedience (v. 18). Consequently, God in his anger closed the doors of Canaan in the face of that whole generation of Israelites (Nu 14:21–35).

4:1 *promise of entering his rest.* See Ex 33:14; Dt 3:20 and note. *still stands.* God's promise to bring his people into circumstances of "rest" in his creation, while conditional, was open-ended. It was grounded in God's covenanted promises to Abraham (see Ge 15:12–21; 17:1–8; 22:15–18), was later reinforced by God's covenant with David (see 2Sa 7:5–16 and notes; cf. 1Ki 5:4 and note) and eventually came to be focused on the Messiah (see Isa 11:1–9 and notes). Through the Messiah's reign, God's promise of rest will ultimately be fulfilled in the new creation (see Isa 65:17; 66:22; Rev 21:4).

4:3 *we who have believed enter that rest.* Just as entering into rest in Canaan demanded faith in God's promise, so the ultimate salvation-rest is entered only by faith in the person and work of Jesus Christ. *his work has been finished since the creation of the world.* God rested from his work on the seventh day of creation (see v. 4; Ge 2:2), and thus his rest is already a reality. The rest God calls us to enter (vv. 10–11) is not our rest but his rest, which he invites us to share.

4:6–8 Israel's going into Canaan under Joshua was a partial and temporary entering of God's rest. That, however, was not the end of entering, as shown in the continuing invitation of Ps 95:7–8.

4:7 *calling it Today.* See 3:13.

4:9 *There remains, then, a Sabbath-rest.* God's rest may still be entered by faith in his Son. Since the pre-Christian Greek translation of the OT (the Septuagint) that the author and his readers knew well made no verbal distinction between the Sabbath "rest" (Hebrew *shabbat* [see, e.g., Ge 2:2; Ex 20:11; 23:12]) and the condition of "rest" that Israel, if faithful, was to experience every day in the promised land (Hebrew *nuah/menuhah* [see, e.g., Ex 31:14; Dt 3:20]), the writer associates these two in a way that suggests he saw in the weekly Sabbath-rest a sign and pledge of the promised life of rest. The fact that neither the Hebrew nor the Septuagint made any verbal distinction between God's "rest" in Ps 95:11 and his "resting place" in Ps 132:14; Isa 66:1 (see note on Ps 132:8) may have reinforced this striking conceptual association.

4:10 *rests from his own work.* Believers cease their efforts to gain salvation by their own works and rest in the finished work of Christ on the cross. The believer's final rest may also be in view here (see Rev 14:13).

4:11 *make every effort.* Not a call to earn one's salvation by works, but an exhortation to enter salvation-rest by faith and not follow Israel's sad example in the desert.

4:12–13 The reasons for giving serious attention to the exhortation of v. 11.

4:12 *word of God.* God's truth was revealed by Jesus (the incarnate Word; see Jn 1:1,14), but it has also been given verbally, the word referred to here. This dynamic word of God is active in accomplishing God's purposes (see Ps 19:7–11; 107:20; 147:15,18; Isa 40:8; 55:11; Gal 3:8; Eph 5:26; Jas 1:18; 1Pe 1:23). The author of Hebrews describes it as a "living" power that judges as with an all-seeing eye, penetrating a person's innermost being. *soul and spirit, joints and marrow.* The totality and depth of one's being (see 1Th 5:23 and note).

4:13 *Nothing in all creation is hidden from God's sight.* The author associates the activity of the word with the activity of God as though they are one and the same—which in a sense they are.

4:14—7:28 An exposition of Ps 110:4, stressing Christ's superiority over Aaron because his is a better priesthood.

4:14 *great high priest.* See 2:17 and note; 3:1. *through the*

heavens,[a][p] Jesus the Son of God,[q] let us hold firmly to the faith we profess.[r] 15For we do not have a high priest[s] who is unable to sympathize with our weaknesses, but we have one who has been tempted in every way, just as we are[t]—yet was without sin.[u] 16Let us then approach[v] the throne of grace with confidence,[w] so that we may receive mercy and find grace to help us in our time of need.

5 Every high priest is selected from among men and is appointed to represent them in matters related to God,[x] to offer gifts and sacrifices[y] for sins.[z] 2He is able to deal gently with those who are ignorant and are going astray,[a] since he himself is subject to weakness.[b] 3This is why he has to offer sacrifices for his own sins, as well as for the sins of the people.[c]

4No one takes this honor upon himself; he must be called by God, just as Aaron was.[d] 5So Christ also did not take upon himself the glory[e] of becoming a high priest.[f] But God said[g] to him,

> "You are my Son;
> today I have become your
> Father.[b]"[c][h]

6And he says in another place,

> "You are a priest forever,
> in the order of Melchizedek.[i]"[d][j]

7During the days of Jesus' life on earth, he offered up prayers and petitions[k] with loud cries and tears[l] to the one who could save him from death, and he was heard[m] because of his reverent submission.[n] 8Although he was a son,[o] he learned obedience from what he suffered[p] 9and, once made perfect,[q] he became the source of eternal salvation for all who obey him 10and was designated by God to be high priest[r] in the order of Melchizedek.[s]

Warning Against Falling Away

6:4-6Ref — Heb 10:26-31

11We have much to say about this, but it is hard to explain because you are slow to learn. 12In fact, though by this time you ought to be teachers, you need someone to teach you the elementary truths[t] of God's word all over again. You need milk, not solid food![u] 13Anyone who lives on milk, being still an infant,[v] is not acquainted with the teaching about righteousness. 14But solid food is for the mature,[w] who by constant use have trained themselves to distinguish good from evil.[x]

[a] 14 Or *gone into heaven* [b] 5 Or *have begotten you* [c] 5 Psalm 2:7 [d] 6 Psalm 110:4

4:14 [p]Heb 6:20; 8:1; 9:24 [q]S Mt 4:3 [r]S Heb 3:1 **4:15** [s]S Heb 2:17 [t]Heb 2:18 [u]S 2Co 5:21 **4:16** [v]S Heb 7:19 [w]S Eph 3:12 **5:1** [x]Heb 2:17 [y]Heb 8:3; 9:9 [z]Heb 7:27 **5:2** [a]Isa 29:24; Heb 2:18; 4:15 [b]Heb 7:28 **5:3** [c]Lev 9:7; 16:6; Heb 7:27; 9:7 **5:4** [d]Ex 28:1; Nu 14:40; 18:7 **5:5** [e]Jn 8:54 [f]S Heb 2:17 [g]S Heb 1:1 [h]Ps 2:7; S Mt 3:17 **5:6** [i]ver 10; Ge 14:18; Heb 6:20; 7:1-22 [j]Ps 110:4; Heb 7:17,21 **5:7** [k]Lk 22:41-44 [l]Mt 27:46,50; Lk 23:46 [m]Ps 22:24 [n]Mk 14:36 **5:8** [o]S Heb 1:2 [p]S Php 2:8 **5:9** [q]S Heb 2:10 **5:10** [r]ver 5; S Heb 2:17 [s]S ver 6 **5:12** [t]Heb 6:1 [u]1Co 3:2; 1Pe 2:2 **5:13** [v]S 1Co 14:20 **5:14** [w]S 1Co 2:6 [x]Isa 7:15

heavens. As the Aaronic high priest on the Day of Atonement passed from the sight of the people into the Most Holy Place (see Lev 16:15,17), so Jesus passed from the sight of his watching disciples, ascending through the heavens into the heavenly sanctuary, his work of atonement accomplished (Ac 1:9–11). *hold firmly to the faith we profess.* Suggests that the readers were in danger of letting their faith slip (see similar admonitions in 2:1; 3:6,14).

4:15 *tempted in every way, just as we are.* See 2:18. The author stresses the parallel between Christ's temptations and ours. He did not have each temptation we have but experienced the whole range of our temptations. *yet was without sin.* The way in which Christ's temptations were different from ours was in the results—his temptations never led to sin (see Mt 4:1–11 and notes).

4:16 *Let us then approach.* Because Christ our high priest has experienced human temptation, he stands ready to give immediate and sympathetic help when we are tempted (see 2:10 and note).

5:1–4 The high-priestly office had two specific qualifications: (1) The high priest had to be "selected from among men" (v. 1) and thus be able to represent them before God; and (2) he had to "be called by God" (v. 4).

5:1 *high priest.* See note on 2:17. *gifts and sacrifices.* See 8:3; 9:9 and notes on Lev 1:2; 2:1; see also chart, p. 153.

5:2 *those who are ignorant and are going astray.* See Ps 119:176 and note. Contrast the unintentional sin (see Lev 4 and note on 4:2; Nu 15:22–29 and note on 15:22) with defiant rebellion against God (see Nu 15:30–31 and note on 15:30; cf. Heb 6:4–6; 10:26–31 and notes).

5:4 *No one takes this honor upon himself.* In Christ's day the high-priestly office was in the hands of a family that had bought control of it.

5:5 *Christ also did not take upon himself the glory of becoming a high priest.* The Son was appointed by the Father, as the two passages cited here show (Ps 2:7; 110:4). *today I have become your Father.* See 1:5; Ps 2:7–9 and notes; cf. Ro 1:4.

5:6 *in the order of Melchizedek.* See notes on 7:3; Ge 14:20; Ps 110:4.

5:7 *prayers . . . tears.* The principal reference here is to Christ's agony in Gethsemane and on Golgotha. *to the one who could save him from death.* To the Father. Jesus did not shrink from physical suffering and death but from the indescribable agony of taking humankind's sin on himself (cf. Mt 27:46). Although he asked that the cup of suffering might be taken from him, he did not waver in his determination to fulfill the Father's will (see Mt 26:36–46 and note on 26:38–39). *he was heard.* His prayer was granted by the Father, who saved him from death—through resurrection.

5:8 *he was a son.* Probably better "he was *God's* Son" (see 1:2–3). *learned obedience.* Learned experientially what his full obedience to God's will for humankind entailed for him. *from what he suffered.* Especially in the ordeal of his atoning death, by which "he became the source of eternal salvation for all who obey him" (v. 9).

5:9 *made perfect.* See 2:10 and note.

5:11 *much to say about this.* About Christ's eternal priesthood "in the order of Melchizedek" (v. 10). *slow to learn.* Instead of progressing in the Christian life, the readers had become spiritually sluggish and mentally lazy (6:12).

5:12 *by this time.* They were not recent converts. *elementary truths of God's word.* Such as those listed in 6:1–2 (see note there). Having taken the first steps toward becoming (mature) Christians, they had slipped back to where they started. *solid food.* Advanced teaching such as that given in ch. 7.

5:14 *mature.* Those who had progressed in spiritual life and had become Christians of sound judgment and discernment. *distinguish good from evil.* Something neither physical nor spiritual infants can do.

6 Therefore let us leave[y] the elementary teachings[z] about Christ and go on
to maturity, not laying again the foundation of repentance from acts that lead to
death,[a][a] and of faith in God, 2instruction
about baptisms,[b] the laying on of hands,[c]
the resurrection of the dead,[d] and eternal
judgment. 3And God permitting,[e] we will
do so.
4It is impossible for those who have
once been enlightened,[f] who have tasted
the heavenly gift,[g] who have shared in the
Holy Spirit,[h] 5who have tasted the goodness[i] of the word of God[j] and the powers
of the coming age, 6if they fall away, to be
brought back to repentance,[k] because[b] to
their loss they are crucifying the Son of
God[l] all over again and subjecting him to
public disgrace.
7Land that drinks in the rain often falling on it and that produces a crop useful
to those for whom it is farmed receives the
blessing of God. 8But land that produces
thorns and thistles is worthless and is in
danger of being cursed.[m] In the end it will
be burned.
9Even though we speak like this, dear
friends,[n] we are confident of better things
in your case — things that accompany salvation. 10God is not unjust; he will not
forget your work and the love you have
shown him as you have helped his people and continue to help them.[o] 11We want
each of you to show this same diligence to
the very end, in order to make your hope[p]
sure. 12We do not want you to become
lazy, but to imitate[q] those who through
faith and patience[r] inherit what has been
promised.[s]

The Certainty of God's Promise

13When God made his promise to Abraham, since there was no one greater for
him to swear by, he swore by himself,[t]
14saying, "I will surely bless you and give
you many descendants."[c][u] 15And so after
waiting patiently, Abraham received what
was promised.[v]
16Men swear by someone greater than
themselves, and the oath confirms what
is said and puts an end to all argument.[w]
17Because God wanted to make the unchanging[x] nature of his purpose very clear
to the heirs of what was promised,[y] he
confirmed it with an oath. 18God did this
so that, by two unchangeable things in

6:1 [y]Php 3:12-14 [z]Heb 5:12 [a]Heb 9:14 **6:2** [b]Jn 3:25 [c]S Ac 6:6 [d]S Ac 2:24; Ac 17:18,32 **6:3** [e]Ac 18:21 **6:4** [f]Heb 10:32 [g]Eph 2:8 [h]Gal 3:2 **6:5** [i]Ps 34:8 [j]S Heb 4:12 **6:6** [k]2Pe 2:21; 1Jn 5:16 [l]S Mt 4:3 **6:8** [m]Ge 3:17,18; Isa 5:6; 27:4 **6:9** [n]S 1Co 10:14 **6:10** [o]S Mt 10:40,42; 1Th 1:3 **6:11** [p]S Heb 3:6 **6:12** [q]Heb 13:7 [r]2Th 1:4; Jas 1:3; Rev 13:10; 14:12 [s]Heb 10:36 **6:13** [t]Ge 22:16; Lk 1:73 **6:14** [u]Ge 22:17 **6:15** [v]Ge 21:5 **6:16** [w]Ex 22:11 **6:17** [x]ver 18; Ps 110:4 [y]Ro 4:16; Heb 11:9

[a] *1* Or *from useless rituals* [b] *6* Or *repentance while* [c] *14* Gen. 22:17

6:1 – 2 *not laying again the foundation.* Six fundamental doctrines are mentioned: (1) *repentance.* The change of mind that causes one to turn away from sin (see note on Mt 4:17). (2) *faith in God.* The counterpart of repentance. As repentance is turning away from sin, faith is turning to God (cf. 1Th 1:9). (3) *instruction about baptisms.* Probably refers to different baptisms with which the readers were familiar, such as Jewish baptism of proselytes, John the Baptist's baptism, and the baptism commanded by Jesus (see Mt 28:19 and note). (4) *laying on of hands.* Sometimes followed baptism (Ac 8:17). Otherwise laying on of hands was practiced in connection with ordaining or commissioning (Ac 6:6; see note there), healing the sick (see Mk 6:5; Lk 4:40; Ac 28:8) and bestowal of blessing (see Mt 19:13 – 15). (5) *resurrection of the dead.* The resurrection of all people in the last days (see Jn 5:25 – 29; 11:25; 2Co 4:14). (6) *eternal judgment.* Either the fact of God's judgment or the verdict that determines the eternal condition of those judged.

6:1 *elementary teachings about Christ.* See note on 5:12. *acts that lead to death.* Lit. "dead works"; deeds or rituals that cannot impart life (see 9:14).

6:3 A common expression of dependence on the will of God (cf. 1Co 16:7). Only the Lord can open minds and hearts and bring spiritual maturity.

6:4 – 8 The third warning (see note on 2:1 – 4).

6:4 – 6 The most common interpretations of this difficult passage are: (1) It refers to Christians who actually lose their salvation. (2) It is a hypothetical argument to warn immature Hebrew Christians (5:11 – 14) that they must progress to maturity (see v. 1) or else experience divine discipline or judgment (see vv. 7 – 8). (3) It refers to professing Christians whose apostasy proves that their faith was not genuine (cf. 1Jn 2:19). This view sees chs. 3 – 4 as a warning based on the rebellion of the Israelites in the desert. As Israel could not enter the promised land after spying out the region and tasting its fruit, so the professing Hebrew Christians would not be able to repent if they adamantly turned against the light they had received. According to this interpretation, such expressions as "enlightened," "tasted the heavenly gift" and "shared in the Holy Spirit" indicate that such persons had come under the influence of God's covenant blessings and had professed to turn from darkness to light but were in danger of a public and final rejection of Christ, proving they had never been regenerated (see 10:26 – 31 and notes; cf. 2Pe 2:20 – 22 and notes; 1Jn 2:19).

6:5 *the coming age.* See Mk 10:30 and note; 1Ti 6:19.

6:7 – 8 A short parable graphically illustrating the warning just given (cf. Mt 13:3 – 23).

6:8 *be burned.* Cf. 10:27 and note.

6:9 *confident of better things … that accompany salvation.* Although the author has suggested the possibility that some of his readers may still be unsaved, he is confident that God has been at work among them. Their changed lives and works of love (v. 10) suggest that most of them were indeed regenerated.

6:11 *to the very end.* A call for perseverance in faith as an evidence of salvation. *make your hope sure.* See 3:6 and note; 11:1; 2Pe 1:10 and note.

6:12 *lazy.* See 5:11 and note. *those who through faith and patience inherit what has been promised.* For examples see ch. 11.

6:13 *God made his promise to Abraham.* The promise of many descendants was made with an oath to emphasize its unchanging character (see Ge 22:16 – 18). Ordinarily the swearing of an oath belongs to our fallen human situation, in which a person's word is not always trustworthy (cf. Mt 5:23 – 26 and note). God's swearing of an oath was a condescension to human frailty, thus making his word, which in itself is absolutely trustworthy, doubly dependable (see v. 18 and note).

6:15 *after waiting patiently.* For 25 years (see Ge 12:3 – 4; 21:5). *received what was promised.* The birth of his son Isaac (Ge 17:2; 18:10; 21:5).

6:18 *two unchangeable things.* God's promise, which in itself is absolutely trustworthy, and God's oath confirming that

which it is impossible for God to lie,[z] we
who have fled to take hold of the hope[a]
offered to us may be greatly encouraged.
19We have this hope as an anchor for the
soul, firm and secure. It enters the inner
sanctuary behind the curtain,[b] 20where
Jesus, who went before us, has entered on
our behalf.[c] He has become a high priest[d]
forever, in the order of Melchizedek.[e]

Melchizedek the Priest

7 This Melchizedek was king of Salem[f]
and priest of God Most High.[g] He met
Abraham returning from the defeat of the
kings and blessed him,[h] 2and Abraham
gave him a tenth of everything. First, his
name means "king of righteousness";
then also, "king of Salem" means "king of
peace." 3Without father or mother, without genealogy,[i] without beginning of days
or end of life, like the Son of God[j] he remains a priest forever.

4Just think how great he was: Even the
patriarch[k] Abraham gave him a tenth of
the plunder![l] 5Now the law requires the
descendants of Levi who become priests to
collect a tenth from the people[m]—that is,
their brothers—even though their brothers are descended from Abraham. 6This
man, however, did not trace his descent
from Levi, yet he collected a tenth from
Abraham and blessed[n] him who had the
promises.[o] 7And without doubt the lesser
person is blessed by the greater. 8In the
one case, the tenth is collected by men
who die; but in the other case, by him
who is declared to be living.[p] 9One might
even say that Levi, who collects the tenth,
paid the tenth through Abraham, 10be-
cause when Melchizedek met Abraham,
Levi was still in the body of his ancestor.

Jesus Like Melchizedek

11If perfection could have been attained
through the Levitical priesthood (for on
the basis of it the law was given to the
people),[q] why was there still need for another priest to come[r]—one in the order of
Melchizedek,[s] not in the order of Aaron?
12For when there is a change of the priesthood, there must also be a change of the
law. 13He of whom these things are said
belonged to a different tribe,[t] and no one
from that tribe has ever served at the altar.[u] 14For it is clear that our Lord descended from Judah,[v] and in regard to that tribe
Moses said nothing about priests. 15And
what we have said is even more clear if
another priest like Melchizedek appears,
16one who has become a priest not on the
basis of a regulation as to his ancestry but
on the basis of the power of an indestructible life. 17For it is declared:

"You are a priest forever,
in the order of Melchizedek."[a][w]

18The former regulation is set aside because it was weak and useless[x] 19(for the
law made nothing perfect),[y] and a better

6:18 [z]Nu 23:19; Tit 1:2 [a]S Heb 3:6 **6:19** [b]Lev 16:2; Heb 9:2,3,7 **6:20** [c]S Heb 4:14 [d]S Heb 2:17 [e]S Heb 5:6 **7:1** [f]Ps 76:2 [g]S Mk 5:7 [h]ver 6; Ge 14:18-20 **7:3** [i]ver 6 [j]S Mt 4:3 **7:4** [k]Ac 2:29 [l]Ge 14:20 **7:5** [m]Nu 18:21,26 **7:6** [n]Ge 14:19,20 [o]Ro 4:13 **7:8** [p]Heb 5:6; 6:20 **7:11** [q]ver 18,19; Heb 8:7 [r]Heb 10:1 [s]ver 17; S Heb 5:6 **7:13** [t]ver 11 [u]ver 14 **7:14** [v]Isa 11:1; Mt 1:3; 2:6; Lk 3:33; Rev 5:5 **7:17** [w]Ps 110:4; ver 21; S Heb 5:6 **7:18** [x]Ro 8:3 **7:19** [y]ver 11; Ro 3:20; 7:7,8; Gal 3:21; Heb 9:9; 10:1

[a] *17* Psalm 110:4

promise. *be greatly encouraged.* Since we look back on the fulfillment of the promise that Abraham saw only in anticipation (see 11:13; Jn 8:56 and notes).

6:19 *as an anchor for the soul, firm and secure.* Like an anchor holding a ship safely in position, our hope in Christ guarantees our safety. *inner sanctuary behind the curtain.* Whereas the ship's anchor goes down to the ocean bed, the Christian's anchor goes up into the true, heavenly sanctuary.

6:20 *a high priest forever, in the order of Melchizedek.* The grand theme that the author introduced briefly in 5:6–10 and now develops in ch. 7. *high priest.* See note on 2:17.

7:1 *Melchizedek.* See Ge 14:18–20 and notes; cf. Ps 110:4 and note. *king ... and priest.* Of particular significance is Melchizedek's holding both offices, one of the ways in which he is treated here as a prefiguration of Christ (see notes on Zec 4:14; 6:13). *Salem.* Jerusalem (see note on Ge 14:18).

7:2 *king of righteousness ... king of peace.* Messianic titles (see Isa 9:6–7; Jer 23:5–6 and notes).

7:3 *Without father ... or end of life.* Ge 14:18–20, contrary to the practice elsewhere in the early chapters of Genesis, does not mention Melchizedek's parentage and children, or his birth and death. That he was a real, historical figure is clear, but the author of Hebrews (in accordance with Jewish interpretation) uses the silence of Scripture about Melchizedek's genealogy to portray him as a prefiguration of Christ. Melchizedek's priesthood anticipates Christ's eternal existence and his unending priesthood. Some believe the appearance of Melchizedek to Abraham was a manifestation of Christ before his incarnation, but the comparison "like the Son of God" argues against such an interpretation.

7:4 *think how great he was.* The one who receives a tithe is greater than the one who pays it, and "the lesser person is blessed by the greater" (v. 7). In both ways Melchizedek was greater than Abraham.

7:11 *the law was given.* The law of Moses and the priesthood went together. All the people without exception were sinners, subject to the law's condemnation, and thus were in need of a priestly system to mediate between them and God. *in the order of Melchizedek, not in the order of Aaron.* Implies that the Aaronic (or Levitical) priesthood was imperfect but that Melchizedek's was perfect. The announcement of a coming one who would be a priest forever (Ps 110:4) was written midway in the history of the Levitical priesthood—which could be understood as a hint that the existing system was to give way to something better.

7:16 *become a priest not on the basis of a regulation as to his ancestry.* In the law of Moses the priestly function was restricted to the family of Aaron from the tribe of Levi (see Ex 28:1–4; 40:12–15; Nu 3:10), but Jesus came from the nonpriestly tribe of Judah (vv. 14–15). *power of an indestructible life.* According to Ps 110:4 the priest in the order of Melchizedek is "a priest forever." This is what Jesus became as a result of the act of God's power that raised him from the dead as the eternal victor over death.

7:18 *The former regulation ... was weak and useless.* The law is holy and good (Ro 7:12), but it could neither give the ability to fulfill its demands nor provide the atonement necessary for those who violated it (v. 19a; cf. Ro 8:2–4 and notes).

7:19 The law was only preparatory (see Gal 3:23–24 and notes) and brought nothing to fulfillment (see Mt 5:17 and note). *bet-*

hope[z] is introduced, by which we draw near to God.[a]

20And it was not without an oath! Others became priests without any oath, 21but he became a priest with an oath when God said to him:

"The Lord has sworn
and will not change his mind:[b]
'You are a priest forever.' "[a c]

22Because of this oath, Jesus has become the guarantee of a better covenant.[d]

23Now there have been many of those priests, since death prevented them from continuing in office; 24but because Jesus lives forever, he has a permanent priesthood.[e] 25Therefore he is able to save[f] completely[b] those who come to God[g] through him, because he always lives to intercede for them.[h]

26Such a high priest[i] meets our need—one who is holy, blameless, pure, set apart from sinners,[j] exalted above the heavens.[k] 27Unlike the other high priests, he does not need to offer sacrifices[l] day after day, first for his own sins,[m] and then for the sins of the people. He sacrificed for their sins once for all[n] when he offered himself.[o] 28For the law appoints as high priests men who are weak;[p] but the oath, which came after the law, appointed the Son,[q] who has been made perfect[r] forever.

7:19 [z]S Heb 3:6 [a]ver 25; Heb 4:16; 10:1,22; Jas 4:8 **7:21** [b]Nu 23:19; 1Sa 15:29; Mal 3:6; Ro 11:29 [c]Ps 110:4; S Heb 5:6 **7:22** [d]S Lk 22:20 **7:24** [e]ver 28 **7:25** [f]S Ro 11:14 [g]S ver 19 [h]S Ro 8:34 **7:26** [i]S Heb 2:17 [j]S 2Co 5:21 [k]S Heb 4:14 **7:27** [l]Heb 5:1 [m]S Heb 5:3 [n]Ro 6:10; Heb 9:12,26,28; 10:10; 1Pe 3:18 [o]Eph 5:2; Heb 9:14,28 **7:28** [p]Heb 5:2 [q]S Heb 1:2 [r]S Heb 2:10 **8:1** [s]S Heb 2:17 [t]S Mk 16:19; S Heb 4:14 **8:2** [u]Heb 9:11,24 **8:3** [v]S Heb 2:17 [w]Heb 5:1; 9:9 [x]Heb 9:14 **8:4** [y]Heb 5:1; 9:9 **8:5** [z]Heb 9:23 [a]Col 2:17; Heb 10:1 [b]Heb 11:7; 12:25 [c]Ex 25:40 **8:6** [d]ver 8,13; S Lk 22:20 [e]S Gal 3:20

The High Priest of a New Covenant

8 The point of what we are saying is this: We do have such a high priest,[s] who sat down at the right hand of the throne of the Majesty in heaven,[t] 2and who serves in the sanctuary, the true tabernacle[u] set up by the Lord, not by man.

3Every high priest[v] is appointed to offer both gifts and sacrifices,[w] and so it was necessary for this one also to have something to offer.[x] 4If he were on earth, he would not be a priest, for there are already men who offer the gifts prescribed by the law.[y] 5They serve at a sanctuary that is a copy[z] and shadow[a] of what is in heaven. This is why Moses was warned[b] when he was about to build the tabernacle: "See to it that you make everything according to the pattern shown you on the mountain."[c c] 6But the ministry Jesus has received is as superior to theirs as the covenant[d] of which he is mediator[e] is superior to the old one, and it is founded on better promises.

7For if there had been nothing wrong

[a] *21* Psalm 110:4 [b] *25* Or *forever* [c] *5* Exodus 25:40

ter hope. The new covenant is better because it assures us of complete redemption and brings us into the very presence of God. See 3:6 and note; see also Introduction: Theme.

7:20 No divine oath was associated with the establishment of the Levitical priesthood.

7:21 *with an oath.* For the significance of the oath see 6:17.

7:22 *better covenant.* See chs. 8–10.

7:23 *death prevented them from continuing in office.* Impermanence was further evidence of the imperfection of the Levitical order.

7:25 *completely.* May include the ideas of completeness and permanence (see NIV text note). *always lives to intercede.* His people will never be without a priest to represent them in the very presence of God, interceding on their behalf (see 1Jn 2:1–2 and notes; cf. Jn 17:6–26).

7:26 *high priest.* See note on 2:17. *meets our need.* Of salvation from sin and its consequences.

7:27 *day after day.* A reference to the endless repetition of sacrifices throughout the year (see Ex 29:36–42), evidence that these sacrifices never effectively and finally atoned for sin. *first for his own sins.* Christ's priesthood is superior because he has no personal sins for which sacrifice had to be made (see Lev 9:8 and note). *once for all.* A key phrase in Hebrews (see 9:12,26 and note on 9:12; 10:2,10). *offered himself.* Levitical priests offered up only animals; our high priest offered himself, the perfect substitute for us.

7:28 *men who are weak.* Because (1) they are mortal and therefore impermanent, v. 23; (2) they are sinful, v. 27; and (3) they could only offer animals, which could never provide a genuine substitute for human beings made in the image of God (see Ge 1:26–28 and notes). *made perfect forever.* In regard to his appointed mission (see 2:10; 5:9 and notes).

8:1—10:18 The argument of this section grows out of an exposition of Jer 31:31–34 and demonstrates that Christ is the mediator of a "better covenant" (7:22).

8:1 See note on 1:2–3. *high priest.* See note on 2:17.

8:2 *true tabernacle.* In contrast to the tabernacle erected by Moses, which was an imperfect and impermanent copy of the heavenly one. *set up by the Lord, not by man.* The heavenly sanctuary built by God corresponds to the Most Holy Place, the innermost sanctuary in Moses' tabernacle, into which the high priest briefly entered with the blood of atonement once a year (see Lev 16:13–15,34). In the heavenly sanctuary, however, our great high priest dwells eternally as our intercessor (7:25).

8:3 *gifts and sacrifices.* See 5:1 and note.

8:4 *men who offer the gifts.* The present tense of the verb "offer," here and elsewhere in the letter, indicates that the temple in Jerusalem was still standing. This letter, therefore, must have been written prior to the temple's destruction in A.D. 70 (see Introduction: Date).

8:5 *copy and shadow of what is in heaven.* An implication the author draws from the words of Ex 25:40. *make everything according to the pattern.* Because both the tabernacle and its ministry were intended to symbolize the only way sinners may approach a holy God and find forgiveness.

8:6 *mediator.* Cf. 1Ti 2:5 and note. In Hebrews "mediator" is always "of a new covenant" (9:15; 12:24). The role of "mediator" here appears to be not that of instituting the covenant but of guaranteeing that the covenant promises are fulfilled (cf. 7:22), that the promised deliverance is actually accomplished (cf. Moses' mediatorial acts in Ex 32:31–32; 33:12–23; 34:5–10; Nu 14:13–20).

8:7 *if there had been nothing wrong with that first covenant.* The line of argument here is similar to that in 7:11, where the Levitical priestly order is shown to be inferior because it was replaced by the order of Melchizedek represented by Jesus. Similarly, if the Sinaitic covenant were without defect, there would have been no need to replace it with a new covenant.

with that first covenant, no place would
have been sought for another.[f] 8But God
found fault with the people and said[a]:

"The time is coming, declares the
Lord,
when I will make a new covenant[g]
with the house of Israel
and with the house of Judah.
9It will not be like the covenant
I made with their forefathers[h]
when I took them by the hand
to lead them out of Egypt,
because they did not remain faithful to
my covenant,
and I turned away from them,
declares the Lord.
10This is the covenant[i] I will make with
the house of Israel
after that time, declares the Lord.
I will put my laws in their minds
and write them on their hearts.[j]
I will be their God,
and they will be my people.[k]
11No longer will a man teach his
neighbor,
or a man his brother, saying, 'Know
the Lord,'
because they will all know me,[l]
from the least of them to the
greatest.
12For I will forgive their wickedness
and will remember their sins no
more."[m][b][n]

13By calling this covenant "new,"[o] he
has made the first one obsolete;[p] and what
is obsolete and aging will soon disappear.

8:7 [f]Heb 7:11, 18; 10:1 **8:8** [g]ver 6, 13; S Lk 22:20 **8:9** [h]Ex 19:5, 6; 20:1-17 **8:10** [i]Ro 11:27 [j]2Co 3:3; Heb 10:16 [k]Eze 11:20; Zec 8:8 **8:11** [l]Isa 54:13; S Jn 6:45 **8:12** [m]Heb 10:17 [n]Ro 11:27 **8:13** [o]ver 6, 8; S Lk 22:20 [p]2Co 5:17

9:1 [q]Ex 25:8 **9:2** [r]Ex 25:8, 9 [s]Ex 25:31-39 [t]Ex 25:23-29 [u]Ex 25:30; Lev 24:5-8 [v]Ex 26:33, 34 **9:3** [w]Ex 26:31-33 **9:4** [x]Ex 30:1-5 [y]Ex 25:10-22 [z]Ex 16:32, 33 [a]Nu 17:10 [b]Ex 31:18; 32:15 **9:5** [c]Ex 25:17-19 [d]Ex 25:20-22; 26:34 **9:6** [e]Nu 28:3 **9:7** [f]Lev 16:11-19 [g]ver 2, 3 [h]Lev 16:34 [i]Lev 16:11, 14 [j]Lev 16:11; Heb 5:2, 3 [k]Heb 5:2, 3 **9:8** [l]S Heb 3:7 [m]Jn 14:6; Heb 10:19, 20 **9:9** [n]Heb 10:1 [o]Heb 5:1; 8:3 [p]S Heb 7:19 **9:10** [q]Lev 11:2-23

Worship in the Earthly Tabernacle

9 Now the first covenant had regulations
for worship and also an earthly sanctuary.[q] 2A tabernacle[r] was set up. In its first
room were the lampstand,[s] the table[t] and
the consecrated bread;[u] this was called the
Holy Place.[v] 3Behind the second curtain
was a room called the Most Holy Place,[w]
4which had the golden altar of incense[x]
and the gold-covered ark of the covenant.[y]
This ark contained the gold jar of manna,[z] Aaron's staff that had budded,[a] and
the stone tablets of the covenant.[b] 5Above
the ark were the cherubim of the Glory,[c]
overshadowing the atonement cover.[c][d]
But we cannot discuss these things in detail now.

6When everything had been arranged
like this, the priests entered regularly[e] into
the outer room to carry on their ministry.
7But only the high priest entered[f] the inner room,[g] and that only once a year,[h] and
never without blood,[i] which he offered for
himself[j] and for the sins the people had
committed in ignorance.[k] 8The Holy Spirit
was showing[l] by this that the way[m] into
the Most Holy Place had not yet been disclosed as long as the first tabernacle was
still standing. 9This is an illustration[n] for
the present time, indicating that the gifts
and sacrifices being offered[o] were not
able to clear the conscience[p] of the worshiper. 10They are only a matter of food[q]

[a] 8 Some manuscripts may be translated *fault and said to the people.* [b] 12 Jer. 31:31-34 [c] 5 Traditionally *the mercy seat*

8:8–12 A quotation from Jer 31:31–34 (see note there) containing a prophetic announcement and definition of the new covenant, which was to be different from the Sinaitic covenant (v. 9). Its superior benefits are: (1) God's laws will become inner principles (v. 10a) that enable his people to delight in doing his will (cf. Eze 36:26–27; Ro 8:2–4 and notes); (2) God and his people will have intimate fellowship (v. 10b); (3) sinful ignorance of God will be removed forever (v. 11); and (4) forgiveness of sins will be an everlasting reality (v. 12).

8:10 *their God ... my people.* See note on Zec 8:8.

8:13 *obsolete and aging.* The Sinaitic covenant—but not the Abrahamic covenant (cf. Ro 4:16–17; chs. 9–11; Gal 3:7–9,14,16–18; Eph 2:12).

9:1 *first covenant.* The covenant made at Sinai (see 8:13 and note).

9:2 *A tabernacle was set up.* The tabernacle built under Moses. *lampstand.* Made of hammered gold and placed at the south side of the Holy Place (Ex 40:24), it had seven lamps that were kept burning every night (Ex 25:31–40; 27:21). *the table and the consecrated bread.* Made of acacia wood overlaid with gold (Ex 25:23–30), it stood on the north side of the Holy Place (Ex 40:22). On it were twelve loaves, replaced every Sabbath and arranged in two rows of six (Lev 24:5–8).

9:4 *which had the golden altar of incense.* Although the altar of incense stood in the Holy Place, the author describes it as belonging to the Most Holy Place. His purpose was to show its close relationship to the inner sanctuary and the ark of the covenant (cf. Ex 30:1–6). On the Day of Atonement the high priest took incense from this altar, along with the blood of the sin offering, into the Most Holy Place (Lev 16:12–14). *ark of the covenant.* A chest made of acacia wood, overlaid inside and out with gold (Ex 25:10–16). See diagram, p. 127. *manna ... staff ... tablets.* See notes on Ex 16:33–34; see also Nu 17:8–10.

9:5 *cherubim of the Glory.* Two winged figures made of pure gold, of one piece with the atonement cover, or mercy seat, and stationed at either end of it. It was between them that the glory of God's presence appeared (Ex 25:17–22; Lev 16:2; Nu 7:89). *atonement cover.* Fitting exactly over the top of the ark of the covenant, it was a slab of pure gold on which the blood of the sin offering was sprinkled by the high priest on the Day of Atonement (Lev 16:14–15).

9:7 *only once a year.* On the Day of Atonement (*Yom Kippur*), the tenth day of the seventh month (Lev 16:29,34). For a description of its ritual see Lev 16 and notes. *sins ... committed in ignorance.* See 5:2 and note.

9:8 *Holy Spirit.* See 3:7 and note. *as long as the first tabernacle was still standing.* As long as the Mosaic system with its imperfect priesthood and sacrifice remained in effect (8:7–8,13).

9:9 *an illustration for the present time.* The Mosaic tabernacle and its temple replacement, though superseded, still provided instruction through their typical (symbolic) significance and were reminders that returning to the old order was useless, since it could not deal effectively with sin. *gifts and sacrifices.* See 5:1 and note.

9:10 *the new order.* The new covenant, with its new priesthood, new sanctuary and new sacrifice, all introduced by Christ.

and drink[r] and various ceremonial washings[s]—external regulations[t] applying until the time of the new order.

The Blood of Christ

11When Christ came as high priest[u] of the good things that are already here,[a][v] he went through the greater and more perfect tabernacle[w] that is not man-made,[x] that is to say, not a part of this creation. 12He did not enter by means of the blood of goats and calves;[y] but he entered the Most Holy Place[z] once for all[a] by his own blood,[b] having obtained eternal redemption. 13The blood of goats and bulls[c] and the ashes of a heifer[d] sprinkled on those who are ceremonially unclean sanctify them so that they are outwardly clean. 14How much more, then, will the blood of Christ, who through the eternal Spirit[e] offered himself[f] unblemished to God, cleanse our consciences[g] from acts that lead to death,[b][h] so that we may serve the living God![i]

15For this reason Christ is the mediator[j] of a new covenant,[k] that those who are called[l] may receive the promised[m] eternal inheritance[n]—now that he has died as a ransom to set them free from the sins committed under the first covenant.[o]

16In the case of a will,[c] it is necessary to prove the death of the one who made it, 17because a will is in force only when somebody has died; it never takes effect while the one who made it is living. 18This is why even the first covenant was not put into effect without blood.[p] 19When Moses had proclaimed[q] every commandment of the law to all the people, he took the blood of calves,[r] together with water, scarlet wool and branches of hyssop, and sprinkled the scroll and all the people.[s] 20He said, "This is the blood of the covenant, which God has commanded you to keep."[d][t] 21In the same way, he sprinkled with the blood both the tabernacle and everything used in its ceremonies. 22In fact, the law requires that nearly everything be cleansed with blood,[u] and without the shedding of blood there is no forgiveness.[v]

23It was necessary, then, for the copies[w] of the heavenly things to be purified with these sacrifices, but the heavenly things themselves with better sacrifices than these. 24For Christ did not enter a man-made sanctuary that was only a copy of the true one;[x] he entered heaven itself,[y] now to appear for us in God's presence.[z] 25Nor did he enter heaven to offer himself again and again, the way the high priest enters the Most Holy Place[a] every year with blood that is not his own.[b] 26Then Christ would have had to suffer many times since the creation of the world.[c] But now he has appeared[d] once for all[e] at the end of the ages to do away with sin by the sacrifice of himself.[f] 27Just as man is destined to die once,[g] and after that to face judgment,[h] 28so Christ was sacrificed once[i] to take away the sins of many people; and he will appear a second time,[j] not to bear sin,[k] but to bring salvation[l] to those who are waiting for him.[m]

[a] *11* Some early manuscripts *are to come* [b] *14* Or *from useless rituals* [c] *16* Same Greek word as *covenant*; also in verse 17 [d] *20* Exodus 24:8

9:10 [r] Nu 6:3; Col 2:16 [s] Lev 11:25,28,40 [t] Heb 7:16 **9:11** [u] S Heb 2:17 [v] Heb 10:1 [w] ver 24; Heb 8:2 [x] S Jn 2:19 **9:12** [y] ver 19; Lev 16:6,15; Heb 10:4 [z] ver 24 [a] ver 26,28; S Heb 7:27 [b] ver 14; S Ro 3:25 **9:13** [c] Heb 10:4 [d] Nu 19:9,17,18 **9:14** [e] 1Pe 3:18 [f] S Eph 5:2 [g] Ps 51:2; 65:3; Jer 33:8; Zec 13:1; S Tit 2:14; Heb 10:2,22 [h] Heb 6:1 [i] S Mt 16:16 **9:15** [j] S Gal 3:20 [k] S Lk 22:20 [l] S Ro 8:28; S 11:29 [m] Heb 6:15; 10:36 [n] S Ac 20:32 [o] Heb 7:22 **9:18** [p] Ex 24:6-8 **9:19** [q] Heb 1:1 [r] ver 12 [s] Ex 24:6-8 **9:20** [t] Ex 24:8; S Mt 26:28 **9:22** [u] Ex 29:21; Lev 8:15 [v] Lev 17:11 **9:23** [w] Heb 8:5 **9:24** [x] Heb 8:2 [y] ver 12; S Heb 4:14 [z] S Ro 8:34 **9:25** [a] Heb 10:19 [b] ver 7,8 **9:26** [c] Heb 4:3 [d] 1Jn 3:5 [e] ver 12,28; S Heb 7:27 [f] ver 12 **9:27** [g] Ge 3:19 [h] 2Co 5:10 **9:28** [i] ver 12,26; S Heb 7:27 [j] S Mt 16:27 [k] 1Pe 2:24 [l] Heb 5:9 [m] S 1Co 1:7

9:11 *not a part of this creation.* It was not an earthly tabernacle, but the heavenly sanctuary of God's presence (v. 24; 8:2).

9:12 *blood of goats and calves.* See note on Lev 17:11. *he entered ... once for all.* Not repeatedly year after year as did the Levitical high priests. Christ's sacrifice was perfect, because it was completely effective and did not need to be repeated. After he had obtained eternal redemption, Christ ascended into the true heavenly sanctuary.

9:13 *blood of goats and bulls.* As on the Day of Atonement. *ashes of a heifer.* As prescribed in Nu 19 for those who became ceremonially unclean as a result of contact with a corpse (see note on Nu 19:18). *outwardly clean.* Such sprinkling, since it was only external, could not cleanse a person from sin.

9:14 *through the eternal Spirit.* An unusual expression that is much debated but probably refers to the Holy Spirit, who empowered Jesus to fulfill his mission (see Mt 3:16 and note). *offered himself.* He was the one who offered the sacrifice, and he was the sacrifice itself. *unblemished.* See Lev 22:19–21. *cleanse our consciences.* Remove sin's defilement from the very core of our beings. *acts that lead to death.* See 6:1 and note.

9:15 *mediator.* See 8:6 and note. *new covenant.* See 7:22; 8:6,13. *the promised eternal inheritance.* Specified in Jer 31:31–34 (see note on 8:8–12). On the basis of Christ's atoning death, this inheritance has become real for those who are called by God (cf. Ro 8:28). *as a ransom.* See Mk 10:45 and note.

9:16 *will.* Translates the same Greek word as that for "covenant" (v. 15), but here and in v. 17 used in the sense of a last will and testament. (Verse 18 returns to the concept of covenant.) Beneficiaries have no claim on the benefits assigned to them in a will until the testator dies (v. 17). Since Christ's death has been duly attested, "the promised eternal inheritance" (v. 15) is available to his beneficiaries.

9:18–20 For the ceremony referred to here see Ex 24:4–8.

9:18 *without blood.* Without death—the death of the calves from which Moses took blood to seal the old covenant.

9:21 See, e.g., Lev 8:10,19,30.

9:22 See note on Lev 17:11.

9:23 *copies of the heavenly things.* See 8:5. Whereas it was necessary for the earthly sanctuary to be purified with animal sacrifices, it was necessary for the heavenly sanctuary to be purified with the better sacrifice of Christ himself.

9:24 *now to appear for us in God's presence.* See 7:25; 1Jn 2:1 and notes. Christ also "has appeared" (v. 26), and "he will appear" (v. 28).

9:26 *end of the ages.* His coming has ushered in the great Messianic era, toward which all history has moved (see notes on 1:1–2).

9:28 *appear a second time.* See, e.g., Mt 24:3–21; 25:31–46; Jn 14:3; 1Co 1:7; 15:23; 1Th 2:19; 4:13–18; 2Th 1:7; Tit 2:13; 2Pe 3:4; Rev 3:11; 19:11–16. *to bring salvation.* The consummation of the salvation purchased for us on the cross (see, e.g., Ro 8:29–30; Php 3:20–21; 1Jn 3:2). *waiting*

Christ's Sacrifice Once for All

10 The law is only a shadow[n] of the good things[o] that are coming—not the realities themselves.[p] For this reason it can never, by the same sacrifices repeated endlessly year after year, make perfect[q] those who draw near to worship.[r] 2If it could, would they not have stopped being offered? For the worshipers would have been cleansed once for all, and would no longer have felt guilty for their sins.[s] 3But those sacrifices are an annual reminder of sins,[t] 4because it is impossible for the blood of bulls and goats[u] to take away sins.[v]

5Therefore, when Christ came into the world,[w] he said:

"Sacrifice and offering you did not
desire,
but a body you prepared for me;[x]
6with burnt offerings and sin offerings
you were not pleased.
7Then I said, 'Here I am—it is written
about me in the scroll[y]—
I have come to do your will,
O God.'"[a][z]

8First he said, "Sacrifices and offerings, burnt offerings and sin offerings you did not desire, nor were you pleased with them"[a] (although the law required them to be made). 9Then he said, "Here I am, I have come to do your will."[b] He sets aside the first to establish the second. 10And by that will, we have been made holy[c] through the sacrifice of the body[d] of Jesus Christ once for all.[e]

11Day after day every priest stands and performs his religious duties; again and again he offers the same sacrifices,[f] which can never take away sins.[g] 12But when this priest had offered for all time one sacrifice for sins,[h] he sat down at the right hand of God.[i] 13Since that time he waits for his enemies to be made his footstool,[j] 14because by one sacrifice he has made perfect[k] forever those who are being made holy.[l]

15The Holy Spirit also testifies[m] to us about this. First he says:

16"This is the covenant I will make with
them
after that time, says the Lord.
I will put my laws in their hearts,
and I will write them on their
minds."[b][n]

17Then he adds:

"Their sins and lawless acts
I will remember no more."[c][o]

18And where these have been forgiven, there is no longer any sacrifice for sin.

A Call to Persevere

19Therefore, brothers, since we have confidence[p] to enter the Most Holy Place[q] by the blood of Jesus, 20by a new and living way[r] opened for us through the curtain,[s] that is, his body, 21and since we have a great priest[t] over the house of God,[u]

[a] 7 Psalm 40:6-8 (see Septuagint) [b] 16 Jer. 31:33 [c] 17 Jer. 31:34

10:1 [n]Col 2:17; Heb 8:5 [o]Heb 9:11 [p]Heb 9:23 [q]ver 4,11; S Heb 7:19 [r]S Heb 7:19 **10:2** [s]Heb 9:9 **10:3** [t]Lev 16:34; Heb 9:7 **10:4** [u]Heb 9:12,13 [v]ver 1,11 **10:5** [w]Heb 1:6 [x]Heb 2:14; 1Pe 2:24 **10:7** [y]Ezr 6:2; Jer 36:2 [z]Ps 40:6-8; S Mt 26:39 **10:8** [a]ver 5,6; S Mk 12:33 **10:9** [b]ver 7 **10:10** [c]ver 14; S Eph 5:26 [d]Heb 2:14; 1Pe 2:24 [e]S Heb 7:27 **10:11** [f]Heb 5:1 [g]ver 1,4 **10:12** [h]Heb 5:1 [i]S Mk 16:19 **10:13** [j]Jos 10:24; Heb 1:13 **10:14** [k]ver 1 [l]ver 10; S Eph 5:26 **10:15** [m]S Heb 3:7 **10:16** [n]Jer 31:33; Heb 8:10 **10:17** [o]Jer 31:34; Heb 8:12 **10:19** [p]S Eph 3:12 [q]Lev 16:2; Eph 2:18; Heb 9:8,12,25 **10:20** [r]Heb 9:8 [s]Heb 6:19; 9:3 **10:21** [t]S Heb 2:17 [u]S Heb 3:6

for him. As the Israelites on the Day of Atonement waited for the high priest to reappear after ministering in the Most Holy Place, bringing assurance that their sins had been atoned for (cf. 2Ti 4:8; Tit 2:13).

10:1–10 An exposition of Ps 40:6–8 (see notes there).

10:1 *The law.* Together with the Levitical priesthood to which it was closely linked under the Mosaic system (see note on 7:11). *only a shadow.* The sacrifices prescribed by the law prefigured Christ's ultimate sacrifice. Thus they were repeated year after year, the very repetition bearing testimony that the perfect, sin-removing sacrifice had not yet been offered. *make perfect.* See v. 14 and note.

10:4 *impossible for the blood of bulls and goats to take away sins.* An animal cannot possibly be a completely adequate substitute for a human being, who is made in God's image.

10:5–6 The different terms used for Levitical sacrifices represent four of the five types of offerings prescribed by the Mosaic Law (Lev 1–7), namely, fellowship, grain, burnt and sin (see chart, p. 153).

10:5 *when Christ came into the world, he said.* The words of this psalm of David (40:6–8) express Christ's obedient submission to the Father in coming to earth. The Mosaic sacrifices are replaced by submissive obedience to the will of God (v. 7).

10:6 *you were not pleased.* See 1Sa 15:22; Ps 40:6 and notes.

10:7 *to do your will.* The will of the Father was the Son's consuming concern (see Lk 22:42; Jn 4:34 and note).

10:9 *He sets aside the first to establish the second.* His perfect sacrifice, offered in complete submission to God's will, supersedes and therefore replaces all previous sacrifices as the means by which sinners are made holy.

10:10,14 *made holy.* Cleansed from all sin (forgiven and purified) and consecrated to God's service (see note on 1Co 1:2).

10:10 *once for all.* Contrast v. 1 (see note there; see also v. 12; 7:27 and note).

10:11–12 A contrast between standing and sitting. The Levitical priest always stood, because his work was never finished (see 7:27 and note).

10:12 *for all time.* See 7:27 and note. *sat down at the right hand of God.* See 1:13 and note.

10:13 Having offered, as priest, the all-sufficient sacrifice, Jesus now sits enthroned as king, looking forward to the ultimate triumph over all that opposes his rule (see 1:3 and note on 1:2–3; cf. Rev 5:6–14 and note on 5:6; cf. also Rev 7:10,17; 11:15; 19:11–21; 20:4).

10:14 *made perfect.* The one "made perfect" (5:9; see 7:28 and note; see also 2:10) has "made" sinners "perfect" in regard to God's will for their holiness.

10:15 *Holy Spirit.* See 3:7 and note.

10:16–18 The two quotations included here are from Jer 31:31–34 (already cited in 8:8–12). The new covenant guarantees that sins will be completely forgiven (v. 17), with the result that no additional sacrifice for sins is needed (v. 18).

10:19 *confidence to enter the Most Holy Place.* See vv. 13–14 and notes.

10:20 *the curtain, that is, his body.* Having sacrificed himself in his body on the cross, Jesus our high priest entered the

[22]let us draw near to God[v] with a sincere heart in full assurance of faith,[w] having our hearts sprinkled to cleanse us from a guilty conscience[x] and having our bodies washed with pure water.[y] [23]Let us hold unswervingly to the hope[z] we profess,[a] for he who promised is faithful.[b] [24]And let us consider how we may spur one another on toward love and good deeds.[c] [25]Let us not give up meeting together,[d] as some are in the habit of doing, but let us encourage one another[e]—and all the more as you see the Day approaching.[f]

[26]If we deliberately keep on sinning[g] after we have received the knowledge of the truth,[h] no sacrifice for sins is left, [27]but only a fearful expectation of judgment and of raging fire[i] that will consume the enemies of God. [28]Anyone who rejected the law of Moses died without mercy on the testimony of two or three witnesses.[j] [29]How much more severely do you think a man deserves to be punished who has trampled the Son of God[k] under foot,[l] who has treated as an unholy thing the blood of the covenant[m] that sanctified him,[n] and who has insulted the Spirit[o] of grace?[p] [30]For we know him who said, "It is mine to avenge; I will repay,"[a][q] and again, "The Lord will judge his people."[b][r] [31]It is a dreadful thing[s] to fall into the hands[t] of the living God.[u]

[32]Remember those earlier days after you had received the light,[v] when you stood your ground in a great contest in the face of suffering.[w] [33]Sometimes you were publicly exposed to insult and persecution;[x] at other times you stood side by side with those who were so treated.[y] [34]You sympathized with those in prison[z] and joyfully accepted the confiscation of your property, because you knew that you yourselves had better and lasting possessions.[a]

[35]So do not throw away your confidence;[b] it will be richly rewarded. [36]You need to persevere[c] so that when you have done the will of God, you will receive what he has promised.[d] [37]For in just a very little while,

"He who is coming[e] will come and will
not delay.[f]
[38] But my righteous one[c] will live by
faith.[g]
And if he shrinks back,
I will not be pleased with him."[d][h]

[39]But we are not of those who shrink back and are destroyed, but of those who believe and are saved.

By Faith

11 Now faith is being sure of what we hope for[i] and certain of what we do not see.[j] [2]This is what the ancients were commended for.[k]

[a] *30* Deut. 32:35 [b] *30* Deut. 32:36; Psalm 135:14
[c] *38* One early manuscript *But the righteous*
[d] *38* Hab. 2:3,4

10:22 [v] ver 1; S Heb 7:19 [w] Eph 3:12 [x] Eze 36:25; Heb 9:14; 12:24; 1Pe 1:2 [y] S Ac 22:16 **10:23** [z] S Heb 3:6 [a] S Heb 3:1 [b] S 1Co 1:9 **10:24** [c] S Tit 2:14 **10:25** [d] Ac 2:42 [e] Heb 3:13 [f] S 1Co 3:13 **10:26** [g] Ex 21:14; Nu 15:30; Heb 5:2; 6:4-8; 2Pe 2:20 [h] S 1Ti 2:4 **10:27** [i] Isa 26:11; 2Th 1:7; Heb 9:27; 12:29 **10:28** [j] Dt 17:6,7; S Mt 18:16; Heb 2:2 **10:29** [k] S Mt 4:3 [l] Heb 6:6 [m] S Mt 26:28 [n] 1Co 6:11; Rev 1:5 [o] Eph 4:30; Heb 6:4 [p] Heb 2:3; 12:25 **10:30** [q] Dt 32:35; Ro 12:19 [r] Dt 32:36; Ps 135:14 **10:31** [s] S 2Co 5:11 [t] Isa 19:16 [u] S Mt 16:16 **10:32** [v] Heb 6:4 [w] Php 1:29,30 **10:33** [x] 1Co 4:9 [y] Php 4:14; 1Th 2:14 **10:34** [z] Heb 13:3 [a] Heb 11:16; 1Pe 1:4,5 **10:35** [b] S Eph 3:12 **10:36** [c] Ro 5:3; Heb 12:1; Jas 1:3,4,12; 5:11; 2Pe 1:6 [d] Heb 6:15; 9:15 **10:37** [e] Mt 11:3 [f] Rev 22:20 **10:38** [g] Ro 1:17; Gal 3:11 [h] Hab 2:3,4 **11:1** [i] S Heb 3:6 [j] S 2Co 4:18 **11:2** [k] ver 4,39

Most Holy Place (see 6:19 and note; cf. 9:11 and note), and he made sinners "perfect" in holiness (see v. 14 and note) so that they too may enter through the curtain—his sacrificed and resurrected body being for us the "new and living way" (cf. Mt 27:51; Mk 15:38 and notes).

10:22–25 Five exhortations spring from Jesus' provision for our reconciliation to his Father: (1) "Let us draw near to God." (2) "Let us hold unswervingly to ... hope." (3) "Let us consider how we may spur one another on." (4) "Let us not give up meeting together." (5) "Let us encourage one another." For the triad of faith, hope and love in vv. 22–24 see note on 1Th 1:3.

10:22 Four conditions are given for drawing "near to God": (1) *a sincere heart.* Undivided allegiance in the inner being. (2) *full assurance of faith.* Faith that knows no hesitation in trusting in and following Christ. (3) *hearts sprinkled ... from a guilty conscience.* Total freedom from a sense of guilt, a freedom based on the once-for-all sacrifice of Christ. (4) *bodies washed with pure water.* Very likely both "hearts sprinkled" and "bodies washed" allude to Christian baptism (cf. Mt 28:19) and the cleansing from sin through the sacrificial death of Christ that it signifies (see Ro 6:3–11 and notes). For OT background see Eze 36:25 and note; see also Lev 14:9; 15:13; 16:4,24,26; Nu 19:19; cf. Zec 13:1.

10:23 *hope we profess.* See 3:6; 6:18–19 and notes. *he who promised is faithful.* Cf. 2Ti 2:13.

10:25 *not give up meeting together.* The Greek word translated "give up" speaks of desertion and abandonment (see Mt 27:46; 2Co 4:9; 2Ti 4:10,16). *the Day.* Of the Lord's return (see 1Th 5:2,4; 2Th 1:10; 2:2; 2Pe 3:10).

10:26–31 The fourth warning (see note on 2:1–4). This warning is especially to persons ("some," v. 25) deserting the Christian assembly. See 6:4–8, where the same spiritual condition is discussed (see also notes there).

10:26 *deliberately keep on sinning.* Committing the sin of apostasy (see v. 29; see also note on 5:2). The OT background is Nu 15:27–31. *no sacrifice for sins is left.* To reject Christ's sacrifice for sins is to reject the only sacrifice; there is no other.

10:27 *judgment and ... raging fire.* See 12:29; 2Th 1:6–9 and notes. For fire as the instrument of divine judgment see La 1:13 and note.

10:28 See Dt 17:6 and note.

10:29 *blood of the covenant.* See 9:20 and note on 9:18; 13:20; see also Mt 26:28; Mk 14:24 and note.

10:30 See notes on Dt 32:35–36 and 32:35.

10:31 See 12:29.

10:32—12:3 An exposition of Hab 2:3–4.

10:32 *those earlier days.* Presumably following their first enthusiastic response to the gospel, when they had unflinchingly suffered loss and persecution and were deeply concerned for one another.

10:34 *better and lasting possessions.* Such as salvation in Christ and future reward (see 11:10,16,35; 13:14 and notes).

10:38 *my righteous one will live by faith.* See note on Hab 2:4.

10:39 *shrink back and are destroyed.* The opposite of "believe and are saved." The author is confident that those to whom he is writing are, for the most part, among the saved (see 6:9 and note).

11:1—12:3 Encouragements to persevere in faith.

11:2 *the ancients.* Heroes of faith in the pre-Christian era, such

3By faith we understand that the universe was formed at God's command,[l]
so that what is seen was not made out of
what was visible.
4By faith Abel offered God a better sacrifice than Cain did. By faith he was commended[m] as a righteous man, when God
spoke well of his offerings.[n] And by faith
he still speaks, even though he is dead.[o]
5By faith Enoch was taken from this
life, so that he did not experience death;
he could not be found, because God had
taken him away.[p] For before he was taken,
he was commended as one who pleased
God. 6And without faith it is impossible to
please God, because anyone who comes to
him[q] must believe that he exists and that
he rewards those who earnestly seek him.
7By faith Noah, when warned about
things not yet seen,[r] in holy fear built an
ark[s] to save his family.[t] By his faith he
condemned the world and became heir of
the righteousness that comes by faith.[u]
8By faith Abraham, when called to go to
a place he would later receive as his inheritance,[v] obeyed and went,[w] even though
he did not know where he was going. 9By
faith he made his home in the promised
land[x] like a stranger in a foreign country;
he lived in tents,[y] as did Isaac and Jacob,
who were heirs with him of the same
promise.[z] 10For he was looking forward to
the city[a] with foundations,[b] whose architect and builder is God.[c]
11By faith Abraham, even though he
was past age—and Sarah herself was barren[d]—was enabled to become a father[e]
because he[a] considered him faithful[f] who
had made the promise. 12And so from this
one man, and he as good as dead,[g] came
descendants as numerous as the stars in
the sky and as countless as the sand on
the seashore.[h]
13All these people were still living by
faith when they died. They did not receive
the things promised;[i] they only saw them
and welcomed them from a distance.[j]
And they admitted that they were aliens
and strangers on earth.[k] 14People who say
such things show that they are looking for
a country of their own. 15If they had been
thinking of the country they had left, they
would have had opportunity to return.[l]
16Instead, they were longing for a better
country—a heavenly one.[m] Therefore God
is not ashamed[n] to be called their God,[o]
for he has prepared a city[p] for them.
17By faith Abraham, when God tested him, offered Isaac as a sacrifice.[q] He
who had received the promises was
about to sacrifice his one and only son,
18even though God had said to him, "It
is through Isaac that your offspring[b] will
be reckoned."[c][r] 19Abraham reasoned that
God could raise the dead,[s] and figuratively
speaking, he did receive Isaac back from
death.
20By faith Isaac blessed Jacob and Esau
in regard to their future.[t]
21By faith Jacob, when he was dying, blessed each of Joseph's sons,[u] and
worshiped as he leaned on the top of his
staff.

[a] 11 Or *By faith even Sarah, who was past age, was enabled to bear children because she* [b] 18 Greek *seed* [c] 18 Gen. 21:12

11:3 [l]Ge 1; Jn 1:3; Heb 1:2; 2Pe 3:5 **11:4** [m]ver 2,39 [n]Ge 4:4; 1Jn 3:12 [o]Heb 12:24 **11:5** [p]Ge 5:21-24 **11:6** [q]Heb 7:19 **11:7** [r]S ver 1 [s]Ge 6:13-22 [t]1Pe 3:20 [u]Ge 6:9; Eze 14:14,20; S Ro 9:30 **11:8** [v]Ge 12:7 [w]Ge 12:1-4; Ac 7:2-4 **11:9** [x]Ac 7:5 [y]Ge 12:8; 18:1,9 [z]Heb 6:17 **11:10** [a]Heb 12:22; 13:14 [b]Rev 21:2,14 [c]ver 16 **11:11** [d]Ge 17:17-19; 18:11-14 [e]Ge 21:2 [f]S 1Co 1:9 **11:12** [g]Ro 4:19 [h]Ge 22:17 **11:13** [i]ver 39 [j]S Mt 13:17 [k]Ge 23:4; Lev 25:23; Php 3:20; 1Pe 1:17; 2:11 **11:15** [l]Ge 24:6-8 **11:16** [m]2Ti 4:18 [n]Mk 8:38 [o]Ge 26:24; 28:13; Ex 3:6,15 [p]ver 10; Heb 13:14 **11:17** [q]Ge 22:1-10; Jas 2:21 **11:18** [r]Ge 21:12; Ro 9:7 **11:19** [s]Ro 4:21; S Jn 5:21 **11:20** [t]Ge 27:27-29,39,40 **11:21** [u]Ge 48:1,8-22

as those listed in this chapter. *were commended for.* Repeated in v. 39, thus framing the chapter with a key thematic emphasis.

11:4 See Ge 4:2–5. *commended as a righteous man.* The chief reason for the acceptance of Abel's sacrifice was that he offered it "by faith." It is implied that Cain's sacrifice was rejected because he offered it without faith, as a mere formality (see note on Ge 4:3–4; see also 1Jn 3:12).

11:5 *Enoch.* See Ge 5:18–24. *taken him away.* To God's presence (see note on Ge 5:24; cf. Ps 49:15; 73:24).

11:6 *without faith it is impossible to please God.* That Enoch pleased God is proof of his faith. *believe that he exists.* Faith must have an object, and the proper object of genuine faith is God. *who earnestly seek him.* Cf. Jer 29:13.

11:7 *Noah.* See Ge 5:28—9:29. *By his faith he condemned.* When the flood came, God's word was proved to be true, Noah's faith was vindicated, and the world's unbelief was judged. *righteousness that comes by faith.* Noah expressed complete trust in God and his word, even when it related to "things not yet seen" (cf. v. 1), namely, the coming flood. Thus Noah also fitted the description of God's righteous ones who "live by faith" (10:38).

11:8 *Abraham.* Presented in the NT as the outstanding example of those who live "by faith" and as the "father of all who believe" (Ro 4:11–12,16; see Gal 3:7,9,29). *called.* See Ge 12:1–3. His faith expressed itself in obedience (see note on Ge 12:4). *a place he would later receive.* Canaan.

11:10 *city with foundations.* Speaks of permanence in contrast to the tents in which the patriarch lived (v. 9). This city is "the heavenly Jerusalem" (12:22), "the city that is to come" (13:14) and "the new Jerusalem" (Rev 21:2). *builder.* See v. 16; cf. Eph 2:19–22; 1Pe 2:4–5 and notes; cf. also Ps 147:2 and note on Isa 62:5.

11:11 *Sarah … was barren.* See Ge 11:30; 18:11–12 and notes.

11:12 *as good as dead.* Because he was 100 years old (see Ge 21:5; Ro 4:19). *stars in the sky … sand on the seashore.* See Ge 13:16 and note; 15:5; 22:17; 26:4; 1Ki 4:20 and note.

11:13 *saw them and welcomed them from a distance.* By faith they saw—dimly—the realities to which the promises pointed and were sure that what they hoped for would ultimately be theirs (see v. 1). *aliens and strangers on earth.* As were the patriarchs in Canaan (see Ge 17:8; 23:4; 28:4). Their true home was the future city of God (see vv. 10,16).

11:14 *country of their own.* A country in which they would no longer be "aliens and strangers" (v. 13). "Country" and "city" were virtually interchangeable since a country was viewed as an extension of its royal city.

11:16 *prepared a city for them.* See v. 10 and note.

11:17 See Ge 22. *his one and only son.* See Ge 22:2,12,16 and notes.

11:19 Cf. Ge 22:13 and note.

11:20 See Ge 27:27–40.

11:21 See 48:9–20. *worshiped … staff.* See Ge 47:31 and note.

22By faith Joseph, when his end was near, spoke about the exodus of the Israelites from Egypt and gave instructions about his bones.[v]

23By faith Moses' parents hid him for three months after he was born,[w] because they saw he was no ordinary child, and they were not afraid of the king's edict.[x]

24By faith Moses, when he had grown up, refused to be known as the son of Pharaoh's daughter.[y] 25He chose to be mistreated[z] along with the people of God rather than to enjoy the pleasures of sin for a short time. 26He regarded disgrace[a] for the sake of Christ[b] as of greater value than the treasures of Egypt, because he was looking ahead to his reward.[c] 27By faith he left Egypt,[d] not fearing the king's anger; he persevered because he saw him who is invisible. 28By faith he kept the Passover and the sprinkling of blood, so that the destroyer[e] of the firstborn would not touch the firstborn of Israel.[f]

29By faith the people passed through the Red Sea[a] as on dry land; but when the Egyptians tried to do so, they were drowned.[g]

30By faith the walls of Jericho fell, after the people had marched around them for seven days.[h]

31By faith the prostitute Rahab, because she welcomed the spies, was not killed with those who were disobedient.[b][i]

32And what more shall I say? I do not have time to tell about Gideon,[j] Barak,[k] Samson,[l] Jephthah,[m] David,[n] Samuel[o] and the prophets, 33who through faith conquered kingdoms,[p] administered justice, and gained what was promised; who shut the mouths of lions,[q] 34quenched the fury of the flames,[r] and escaped the edge of the sword;[s] whose weakness was turned to strength;[t] and who became powerful in battle and routed foreign armies.[u] 35Women received back their dead, raised to life again.[v] Others were tortured and refused to be released, so that they might gain a better resurrection. 36Some faced jeers and flogging,[w] while still others were chained

[a] 29 That is, Sea of Reeds [b] 31 Or *unbelieving*

11:22 [v] Ge 50:24,25; Ex 13:19; Jos 24:32 **11:23** [w] Ex 2:2 [x] Ex 1:16,22 **11:24** [y] Ex 2:10,11 **11:25** [z] ver 37 **11:26** [a] Heb 13:13 [b] Lk 14:33 [c] Heb 10:35 **11:27** [d] Ex 12:50,51 **11:28** [e] 1Co 10:10 [f] Ex 12:21-23 **11:29** [g] Ex 14:21-31 **11:30** [h] Jos 6:12-20 **11:31** [i] Jos 2:1,9-14; 6:22-25; Jas 2:25 **11:32** [j] Jdg 6-8 [k] Jdg 4-5 [l] Jdg 13-16 [m] Jdg 11-12 [n] 1Sa 16:1,13 [o] 1Sa 1:20 **11:33** [p] 2Sa 8:1-3 [q] Da 6:22 **11:34** [r] Da 3:19-27 [s] Ex 18:4 [t] 2Ki 20:7 [u] Jdg 15:8 **11:35** [v] 1Ki 17:22,23; 2Ki 4:36,37 **11:36** [w] Jer 20:2; 37:15

11:22 See Ge 50:24–25. Jacob (v. 21) and Joseph are additional examples of those whose faith is no less strong at death than in life (v. 13).

11:23 See Ex 2:2–3; Ac 7:20–44. *Moses' parents.* See Ex 6:20; Nu 26:58–59. *no ordinary child.* See note on Ex 2:2. *were not afraid.* At least to the extent that they were ready to defy the king's edict. *king's edict.* To kill all Israelite males at birth (Ex 1:16,22).

11:24 *son of Pharaoh's daughter.* See Ex 2:10.

11:25 *pleasures of sin.* The luxury and prestige of Egypt's royal palace.

11:26 *for the sake of Christ.* Although Moses' understanding of the details of Israel's promised future was extremely limited, he chose to be associated with the people through whom that future was to be realized. The author of Hebrews here concretizes that future in the person of the Messiah he is proclaiming as the one through whom God has guaranteed the promised future. *treasures of Egypt.* The priceless treasures of King Tutankhamun's tomb alone included several thousand pounds of pure gold.

11:27 *By faith he left Egypt.* Probably referring to his flight to Midian when he was 40 years old (see Ex 2:11–15 and note; Ac 7:23–29). *not fearing the king's anger.* Exodus indicates that Moses was afraid (Ex 2:14) but does not expressly say of whom. And it tells us that he fled from the pharaoh when the pharaoh tried to kill him (Ex 2:15) but does not expressly say that he fled out of fear. The author of Hebrews capitalizes on these features of the account to highlight the fact that, in his fleeing from the pharaoh, Moses was sustained by his trust in God that the liberation of Israel would come and that he would have some part in it. *he persevered.* For 40 years in Midian (Ac 7:30). *saw him who is invisible.* See vv. 1,6; see also Ro 1:20; Col 1:15 and note; 1Ti 1:17.

11:28 See Ex 12:1–30.

11:29 See Ex 14–15. The third and final 40-year period of Moses' life was spent leading the Israelites through the desert. At the age of 120 years he died in Moab (Dt 34:1–7).

11:30–31 See Jos 2; 6.

11:30 *Jericho.* The first obstacle to Israel's conquest of the promised land under Joshua's leadership was captured by faith without a battle.

11:31 *By faith.* See Jos 6:9–11. *prostitute.* A designation of this Canaanite's way of life within Canaanite society. *welcomed the spies.* See Jas 2:25.

11:32–38 There were many more heroes of faith before the coming of Christ, and much more could be written about them. Only a small sampling is given, representing all types of men and women of faith. The great quality they had in common was that of overcoming "through faith" (v. 33).

11:32 *to tell.* Translates the masculine form of a Greek verb, indicating that the author of Hebrews was a man (see Introduction: Author). *Gideon, Barak, Samson, Jephthah.* See Jdg 4–8; 11–16; 1Sa 12:11 and NIV text note. *Samuel and the prophets.* For Samuel being counted as the first among the prophets see Ac 3:24; 13:20; cf. Ps 99:6; Jer 15:1 and notes.

11:33 *conquered kingdoms.* See, e.g., David's conquests (2Sa 5:6–25; 8:1–14; 10:1–19; 12:26–31). *administered justice.* See, e.g., Samuel (1Sa 12:3–5); David (2Sa 8:15); Solomon (1Ki 3:9,12,16–28). *gained what was promised.* May refer to Israel's circumstances of rest in the promised land to which Solomon refers in 1Ki 5:4 (see note there); see also Jos 23:14; 24:8–13; 2Ch 20:30 (see note there). *shut the mouths of lions.* See, e.g., Daniel in the lions' den (Da 6).

11:34 *quenched the fury of the flames.* See, e.g., Daniel's friends, Shadrach, Meshach and Abednego, in the "blazing furnace" (Da 3:6,11,15,17,20–21,23,26; see note on Da 3:17). *escaped the … sword.* See, e.g., David (1Sa 17:45–49); Elijah (2Ki 1); Elisha (2Ki 6:31); Jeremiah (Jer 26:7–24). *weakness was turned to strength.* See, e.g., Samson (Jdg 16:21–30); Hannah (1Sa 1); Jeremiah (Jer 1:6–10).

11:35 *Women received back their dead.* Cf. the widow of Zarephath (1Ki 17:17–24) and the Shunammite woman (2Ki 4:8–36). *were tortured and refused to be released, so that they might gain a better resurrection.* Strongly reminiscent of the heroic Maccabean Jewish patriots of the second century B.C. (in the Apocrypha see 2 Maccabees 7).

11:36 *jeers and flogging.* See, e.g., Jeremiah (Jer 20:2,7–8). *put in prison.* See, e.g., Jeremiah (Jer 37:15–16).

and put in prison.[x] 37They were stoned[a];[y]
they were sawed in two; they were put to
death by the sword.[z] They went about in
sheepskins and goatskins,[a] destitute, persecuted and mistreated— 38the world was
not worthy of them. They wandered in
deserts and mountains, and in caves[b] and
holes in the ground.

39These were all commended[c] for their
faith, yet none of them received what had
been promised.[d] 40God had planned something better for us so that only together
with us[e] would they be made perfect.[f]

God Disciplines His Sons

12 Therefore, since we are surrounded
by such a great cloud of witnesses,
let us throw off everything that hinders
and the sin that so easily entangles, and
let us run[g] with perseverance[h] the race
marked out for us. 2Let us fix our eyes
on Jesus,[i] the author[j] and perfecter of
our faith, who for the joy set before him
endured the cross,[k] scorning its shame,[l]
and sat down at the right hand of the
throne of God.[m] 3Consider him who endured such opposition from sinful men,
so that you will not grow weary[n] and lose
heart.

4In your struggle against sin, you have
not yet resisted to the point of shedding
your blood.[o] 5And you have forgotten that
word of encouragement that addresses
you as sons:

11:36 [x]Ge 39:20 **11:37** [y]2Ch 24:21 [z]1Ki 19:10; Jer 26:23 [a]2Ki 1:8 **11:38** [b]1Ki 18:4; 19:9 **11:39** [c]ver 2,4 [d]ver 13; Heb 10:36 **11:40** [e]Rev 6:11 [f]S Heb 2:10 **12:1** [g]S 1Co 9:24 [h]S Heb 10:36 **12:2** [i]Ps 25:15 [j]Heb 2:10 [k]Php 2:8,9; Heb 2:9 [l]Heb 13:13 [m]S Mk 16:19 **12:3** [n]Gal 6:9; Rev 2:3 **12:4** [o]Heb 10:32-34; 13:13 **12:5** [p]ver 3 **12:6** [q]Ps 94:12; 119:75; Rev 3:19 [r]Pr 3:11,12 **12:7** [s]Dt 8:5; 2Sa 7:14; Pr 13:24 **12:8** [t]1Pe 5:9 **12:9** [u]Nu 16:22; 27:16; Rev 22:6 [v]Isa 38:16 **12:10** [w]S 2Pe 1:4 **12:11** [x]Isa 32:17; Jas 3:17,18 **12:12** [y]Isa 35:3 **12:13** [z]Pr 4:26 [a]Gal 6:1

"My son, do not make light of the
Lord's discipline,
and do not lose heart[p] when he
rebukes you,
6because the Lord disciplines those he
loves,[q]
and he punishes everyone he accepts
as a son."[b][r]

7Endure hardship as discipline; God is
treating you as sons.[s] For what son is not
disciplined by his father? 8If you are not
disciplined (and everyone undergoes discipline),[t] then you are illegitimate children and not true sons. 9Moreover, we
have all had human fathers who disciplined us and we respected them for it.
How much more should we submit to the
Father of our spirits[u] and live![v] 10Our fathers disciplined us for a little while as
they thought best; but God disciplines us
for our good, that we may share in his
holiness.[w] 11No discipline seems pleasant
at the time, but painful. Later on, however, it produces a harvest of righteousness and peace[x] for those who have been
trained by it.

12Therefore, strengthen your feeble arms
and weak knees.[y] 13"Make level paths for
your feet,"[c][z] so that the lame may not be
disabled, but rather healed.[a]

[a] *37* Some early manuscripts *stoned; they were put to the test;* [b] *6* Prov. 3:11,12 [c] *13* Prov. 4:26

11:37 *They were stoned.* See, e.g., Zechariah, the son of Jehoiada the priest, who was stoned to death for declaring the truth (2Ch 24:21). *sawed in two.* Perhaps refers to Isaiah, who, according to tradition, met this kind of death under wicked King Manasseh (see Introduction to Isaiah: Author).

11:39 *all commended for their faith.* By the Holy Spirit in the Scriptural accounts (see v. 2; 3:7 and notes).

11:40 *God had planned something better.* The fulfillment for them, as for us, is in Christ who is "the resurrection and the life" (Jn 11:25). *only together with us would they be made perfect.* All persons of faith who had gone before focused their faith on God and his promises. The fulfillment of God's promises to them has now come in Jesus Christ, and their redemption too is now complete in him.

12:1 *surrounded by such a great cloud of witnesses.* The imagery suggests an athletic contest in a great amphitheater. The witnesses are the heroes of the past who have just been mentioned (ch. 11). They are not spectators but inspiring examples. The Greek word translated "witnesses" is the origin of the English word "martyr" and means "testifiers." They bear testimony to the power of faith and to God's faithfulness. *run with perseverance.* See Ac 20:24; 1Co 9:24–26; Gal 2:2; 5:7; Php 2:16; 2Ti 4:7. The Christian life is pictured as a long-distance race rather than a short sprint.

12:2 *author and perfecter of our faith.* That is, the beginner (cf. note on 2:10) and completer of faith—the One who went ahead of all believers in their faith and led on to its definitive goal, hence the perfect embodiment of faith and the supreme model for faith. *joy set before him.* His glorification at the Father's "right hand" (see note on 1:2–3, No. 7; cf. Isa 53:10–12 and notes). *endured the cross.* See Php 2:8 and note. *scorning its shame.* As with Christ, the humiliation of our present suffering for the gospel's sake is far outweighed by the prospect of future glory (see Mt 5:10–12; Ro 8:18; 2Co 4:17; 1Pe 4:13; 5:1,10).

12:3 *Consider him.* He suffered infinitely more than any of his disciples is asked to suffer—a great encouragement for us when we are weary and tempted to become discouraged. *not grow weary.* See Gal 6:9; Rev 2:3; cf. Isa 40:28–31.

12:4–13 Encouragement to persevere in the face of hardship: an exposition of Pr 3:11–12.

12:5 *the Lord's discipline.* Suffering and persecution should be seen as corrective and instructive training for our spiritual development as God's children.

12:6 *punishes.* The Greek for this verb means "to whip." God chastens us in order to correct our faults.

12:7 *treating you as sons.* God's discipline is evidence that we are his children. Far from being a reason for despair, discipline is a basis for encouragement and perseverance (v. 10).

12:11 *produces a harvest of righteousness.* When received submissively (see v. 9), discipline is wholesome and beneficial.

12:12 See Isa 35:3.

12:13 *Make level paths.* A call for upright conduct that will help, rather than hinder, the spiritual and moral welfare of others, especially the "lame" who waver in the Christian faith.

Warning Against Refusing God

14Make every effort to live in peace with
all men[b] and to be holy;[c] without holiness
no one will see the Lord.[d] 15See to it that
no one misses the grace of God[e] and that
no bitter root[f] grows up to cause trouble
and defile many. 16See that no one is sexually immoral,[g] or is godless like Esau,
who for a single meal sold his inheritance
rights as the oldest son.[h] 17Afterward, as
you know, when he wanted to inherit
this blessing, he was rejected. He could
bring about no change of mind, though he
sought the blessing with tears.[i]

18You have not come to a mountain that
can be touched and that is burning with
fire; to darkness, gloom and storm;[j] 19to
a trumpet blast[k] or to such a voice speaking words[l] that those who heard it begged
that no further word be spoken to them,[m]
20because they could not bear what was
commanded: "If even an animal touches
the mountain, it must be stoned."[a][n] 21The
sight was so terrifying that Moses said, "I
am trembling with fear."[b][o]

22But you have come to Mount Zion,[p] to
the heavenly Jerusalem,[q] the city[r] of the
living God.[s] You have come to thousands
upon thousands of angels in joyful assembly, 23to the church of the firstborn,[t] whose
names are written in heaven.[u] You have
come to God, the judge of all men,[v] to the
spirits of righteous men made perfect,[w]
24to Jesus the mediator[x] of a new covenant,
and to the sprinkled blood[y] that speaks a
better word than the blood of Abel.[z]

25See to it that you do not refuse[a] him
who speaks.[b] If they did not escape when
they refused him who warned[c] them on
earth, how much less will we, if we turn
away from him who warns us from heav-
en?[d] 26At that time his voice shook the
earth,[e] but now he has promised, "Once
more I will shake not only the earth but
also the heavens."[c][f] 27The words "once
more" indicate the removing of what can
be shaken[g]—that is, created things—so
that what cannot be shaken may remain.

28Therefore, since we are receiving a
kingdom that cannot be shaken,[h] let us be
thankful, and so worship God acceptably
with reverence and awe,[i] 29for our "God is
a consuming fire."[d][j]

a 20 Exodus 19:12,13 *b 21* Deut. 9:19
c 26 Haggai 2:6 *d 29* Deut. 4:24

12:14 [b]S Ro 14:19 [c]Ro 6:22 [d]S Mt 5:8 **12:15** [e]Gal 5:4; Heb 3:12; 4:1 [f]Dt 29:18 **12:16** [g]S 1Co 6:18 [h]Ge 25:29-34 **12:17** [i]Ge 27:30-40 **12:18** [j]Ex 19:12-22; 20:18; Dt 4:11 **12:19** [k]Ex 20:18 [l]Dt 4:12 [m]Ex 20:19; Dt 5:5,25; 18:16 **12:20** [n]Ex 19:12,13 **12:21** [o]Dt 9:19 **12:22** [p]Isa 24:23; 60:14; Rev 14:1 [q]S Gal 4:26 [r]Heb 11:10; 13:14 [s]S Mt 16:16 **12:23** [t]Ex 4:22 [u]S Rev 20:12 [v]Ge 18:25; Ps 94:2 [w]Php 3:12 **12:24** [x]S Gal 3:20 [y]Heb 9:19; 10:22; 1Pe 1:2 [z]Ge 4:10; Heb 11:4 **12:25** [a]Heb 3:12 [b]S Heb 1:1 [c]Heb 8:5; 11:7 [d]Dt 18:19; Heb 2:2,3; 10:29 **12:26** [e]Ex 19:18 [f]Hag 2:6 **12:27** [g]Isa 34:4; 54:10; 1Co 7:31; Heb 1:11,12; 2Pe 3:10; 1Jn 2:17 **12:28** [h]Ps 15:5; Da 2:44 [i]Mal 2:5; 4:2; Heb 13:15 **12:29** [j]Ex 24:17; Dt 4:24; 9:3; Ps 97:3; Isa 33:14; S 2Th 1:7

12:14–17 Exhortation to holy living (see 4:1; 6:4–8; Gal 5:4 and note).

12:14 *without holiness no one will see the Lord.* Cf. 1Pe 1:15–16 and note on 1:16; see also 1Co 1:2 and note; cf. 1Jn 3:2–3.

12:15 *misses the grace of God.* "Falls short of" or "fails to lay hold of" God's grace (see 6:4–8 and notes). *bitter root.* Pride, animosity, rivalry or anything else harmful to others.

12:16 *godless like Esau.* See Ge 25:29–34. He had no appreciation for true values (cf. Php 3:19). He "despised his birthright" (Ge 25:34) by valuing food for his stomach more highly than his birthright.

12:17 *he was rejected.* Because he only regretted his loss, and did not repent of his sin (Ge 27; cf. Ge 4:13 and note). His sorrow was not "godly sorrow" that "brings repentance that leads to salvation," but "worldly sorrow" that "brings death" (2Co 7:10). *could bring about no change of mind.* Could not undo what he had done (cf. 6:4–6 and note). *blessing.* Of the firstborn. The readers may have contemplated compromising their faith in order to gain relief from persecution. But to trade their spiritual birthright for temporary ease in this world would deprive them of Christ's blessing. *with tears.* Not tears of repentance. See Ge 27:34–38.

12:18–29 Crowning motivation and warning (the fifth; see note on 2:1–4—including an exposition of Ex 19:10–23 in vv. 18–24).

12:18–21 These verses recall the awesome occasion when the law was given at Mount Sinai (see Ex 19:10–25; Dt 4:11–12; 5:22–26).

12:22 *Mount Zion.* Not the literal Mount Zion (Jerusalem, or its southeast portion), but the heavenly city of God and those who dwell there with him (see 11:10,13–16; 13:14; Php 3:20). The circumstances under which the old covenant was given (vv. 18–21) and the features of the new covenant (vv. 22–24) point up the utter contrast between the two covenants, and lay the foundation for one more warning and exhortation to those still thinking of going back to Judaism. *thousands upon thousands of angels.* See Rev 5:11–12.

12:23 *church of the firstborn.* Believers in general who make up the church: (1) Reference cannot be to the angels since these have just been mentioned (v. 22). (2) "Firstborn" cannot refer to Christ (though he is called firstborn, 1:6; Ro 8:29; Col 1:15–18; Rev 1:5), since here the Greek word is plural. (3) The fact that the names of these "firstborn" are recorded in heaven reminds us of the redeemed (see Rev 3:5; 13:8; 17:8; 20:12; 21:27). The designation of them as "firstborn" suggests their privileged position as heirs together with Christ, the supreme firstborn and "heir of all things" (1:2). *God, the judge of all.* See 4:13; Ro 14:10–12; 1Co 3:10–15; 2Co 5:10; Rev 20:11–15. *spirits of righteous men made perfect.* For the most part, these were pre-Christian believers such as Abel (11:4) and Noah (11:7). They are referred to as "spirits" because they are waiting for the resurrection and as "righteous" because God credited their faith to them as righteousness, as he did to Abraham (see Ge 15:6; Ro 4:3 and notes). Actual justification was not accomplished, however, until Christ made it complete by his death on the cross (see 11:40; Ro 3:24–26 and notes; 4:23–25).

12:24 *mediator of a new covenant.* See 8:6 and note. *better word than the blood of Abel.* Abel's blood cried out for justice and retribution (see Ge 4:10 and note), whereas the blood of Jesus shed on the cross speaks of forgiveness and reconciliation (see 9:12 and note; 10:19; Col 1:20; 1Jn 1:7).

12:25–29 The fifth warning (see note on 2:1–4).

12:25 *him who speaks.* God. *warned them on earth.* At Sinai. *him who warns us from heaven.* Christ, who is both from and in heaven (1:1–3; 4:14; 6:20; 7:26; 9:24). Since we have greater revelation, we have greater responsibility and therefore greater danger (see 2:2–3 and notes).

12:26 *shook the earth.* See Ex 19:18; cf. Jdg 5:4–5; Ps 68:7–8.

12:27 *once more.* During the great end-time upheavals associated with the second advent of Christ (see Mt 24:29; Mk 13:24–25 and note; Lk 21:11,25; Ac 2:20). *what cannot be shaken.* The kingdom (v. 28).

12:28 *worship God acceptably.* See Jn 4:19–24; Ro 12:1.

12:29 See NIV text note; cf. 10:27 and note; Ex 24:17; Dt 9:3.

Concluding Exhortations

13 Keep on loving each other as brothers.[k] 2Do not forget to entertain
strangers,[l] for by so doing some people
have entertained angels without knowing
it.[m] 3Remember those in prison[n] as if you
were their fellow prisoners, and those who
are mistreated as if you yourselves were
suffering.
4Marriage should be honored by all,[o]
and the marriage bed kept pure, for God
will judge the adulterer and all the sexually immoral.[p] 5Keep your lives free from the
love of money[q] and be content with what
you have,[r] because God has said,

"Never will I leave you;
never will I forsake you."[a][s]

6So we say with confidence,

"The Lord is my helper; I will not be
afraid.
What can man do to me?"[b][t]

7Remember your leaders,[u] who spoke
the word of God[v] to you. Consider the outcome of their way of life and imitate[w] their
faith. 8Jesus Christ is the same yesterday
and today and forever.[x]
9Do not be carried away by all kinds of
strange teachings.[y] It is good for our hearts
to be strengthened[z] by grace, not by ceremonial foods,[a] which are of no value to
those who eat them.[b] 10We have an altar
from which those who minister at the tabernacle[c] have no right to eat.[d]
11The high priest carries the blood of animals into the Most Holy Place as a sin offering,[e] but the bodies are burned outside
the camp.[f] 12And so Jesus also suffered
outside the city gate[g] to make the people
holy[h] through his own blood.[i] 13Let us,
then, go to him[j] outside the camp, bearing
the disgrace he bore.[k] 14For here we do not
have an enduring city,[l] but we are looking
for the city that is to come.[m]
15Through Jesus, therefore, let us
continually offer to God a sacrifice[n] of
praise—the fruit of lips[o] that confess his
name. 16And do not forget to do good and
to share with others,[p] for with such sacrifices[q] God is pleased.
17Obey your leaders[r] and submit to their
authority. They keep watch over you[s] as
men who must give an account. Obey
them so that their work will be a joy, not
a burden, for that would be of no advantage to you.
18Pray for us.[t] We are sure that we have
a clear conscience[u] and desire to live honorably in every way. 19I particularly urge
you to pray so that I may be restored to
you soon.[v]

[a] 5 Deut. 31:6 [b] 6 Psalm 118:6,7

13:1 [k]S Ro 12:10
13:2 [l]Job 31:32; Mt 25:35; S Ro 12:13 [m]Ge 18:1-33; 19:1-3
13:3 [n]Mt 25:36; Col 4:18; Heb 10:34
13:4 [o]Mal 2:15; 1Co 7:38; 1Ti 4:3 [p]Dt 22:22; 1Co 6:9; Rev 22:15
13:5 [q]S 1Ti 3:3 [r]Php 4:11; 1Ti 6:6,8 [s]Dt 31:6,8; Jos 1:5
13:6 [t]Ps 118:6,7
13:7 [u]ver 17,24; 1Co 16:16 [v]S Heb 4:12 [w]Heb 6:12
13:8 [x]Ps 102:27; Heb 1:12
13:9 [y]Eph 4:14 [z]Col 2:7 [a]Col 2:16 [b]Heb 9:10
13:10 [c]Heb 8:5 [d]1Co 9:13; 10:18
13:11 [e]Lev 16:15 [f]Ex 29:14; Lev 4:12,21; 9:11; 16:27
13:12 [g]Jn 19:17 [h]S Eph 5:26 [i]S Ro 3:25
13:13 [j]Lk 9:23 [k]Heb 11:26
13:14 [l]Heb 12:27 [m]Php 3:20; Heb 11:10,27; 12:22
13:15 [n]1Pe 2:5 [o]Isa 57:19; Hos 14:2
13:16 [p]Ro 12:13 [q]Php 4:18
13:17 [r]ver 7,24 [s]Isa 62:6; Ac 20:28
13:18 [t]S 1Th 5:25 [u]S Ac 23:1
13:19 [v]Phm 22

13:2 *entertain strangers.* See Mt 25:35. *strangers.* Members of the Christian community not personally known. *entertained angels without knowing it.* As did Abraham (Ge 18), Gideon (Jdg 6) and Manoah (Jdg 13).

13:3 *Remember those in prison ... and those who are mistreated.* Especially fellow believers (see 10:32–34; Mt 25:36; 1Co 12:26).

13:4 See Ex 20:14 and note. *Marriage should be honored.* See 1Co 6:13–18; 7:1–15; Eph 5:26–31; 1Ti 4:3. *adulterer and ... sexually immoral.* See 1Co 6:9.

13:5 *love of money.* See Lk 12:15,21; Php 4:10–13; 1Ti 6:6–10,17–19. *be content.* See Php 4:11–12; 1Ti 6:8.

13:7–17 A unit framed by the exhortation to "Remember your [past] leaders ... and imitate their faith" and the exhortation to "Obey your [present] leaders and submit to their authority."

13:7 *leaders, who spoke the word of God.* See 2:3; 5:12. *Consider the outcome of their way of life.* Consider how they persevered in their faith and entered into the promised inheritance (see 6:12). *imitate their faith.* See 6:12; Eph 5:1; 1Th 1:6 and notes; cf. 1Co 4:16.

13:8 *Jesus Christ is the same.* A confession of the changelessness of Christ, no doubt related to the preceding verse. The substance of their former leaders' faith was the unchanging Christ. *yesterday.* Probably the days of Christ's life on earth, when the eyewitnesses observed him (2:3). *today.* The Christ whom the eyewitnesses saw was still the same, and what they had said about him was still true. *forever.* And it will always be true. To compromise his absolute supremacy by returning to the inferior Aaronic priesthood and sacrifices (see chs. 5–10) is to undermine the gospel.

13:9 *not by ceremonial foods.* As the legalistic Judaizers were teaching. The old Mosaic order was done away with at the cross and must not be revived.

13:10 *We have an altar.* Probably refers to the cross, which marked the end of the whole Aaronic priesthood and its replacement by the order of Melchizedek, of which Christ is the unique and only priest. *no right to eat.* The priests could not eat any part of the sacrifice on the Day of Atonement, but we can partake of our sacrifice, so to speak—through spiritual reception of Christ by faith (see Jn 6:48–58). We have a higher privilege than the priests under the old covenant had.

13:11 *burned outside the camp.* See Lev 4:12 and note; 16:27.

13:12 *Jesus also suffered outside the city gate.* Christ's death outside Jerusalem represented the removal of sin, as had the removal of the bodies of sacrificial animals outside the camp of Israel.

13:13 *go to him outside the camp.* Calls for separation from Judaism to Christ. As he died in disgrace outside the city, so the readers should be willing to be disgraced by turning unequivocally from Judaism to Christ (cf. Ac 5:41).

13:14 *city that is to come.* See notes on 11:10,14,16.

13:15 *sacrifice of praise.* Cf. Ro 12:1. For the OT background see notes on Lev 3:1; Ps 7:17; cf. Ps 51:17 and note.

13:16 *sacrifices.* See Php 4:18 and note.

13:17 *your leaders.* Their present leaders, as distinct from their first ones, now dead, mentioned in v. 7 (see note on vv. 7–17). *submit to their authority.* Dictatorial leadership is not condoned by this command (see 2Co 10:8 and note), but respect for authority, orderliness and discipline in the church are taught throughout the NT.

13:19 *restored to you soon.* The identity and whereabouts of the writer are not known to us, but "restored" suggests that somehow he had been delayed in visiting those to whom he was writing, perhaps by his current ministry. That he was not under arrest is clear from v. 23.

[20]May the God of peace,[w] who through
the blood of the eternal covenant[x] brought
back from the dead[y] our Lord Jesus, that
great Shepherd of the sheep,[z] [21]equip you
with everything good for doing his will,[a]
and may he work in us[b] what is pleasing
to him,[c] through Jesus Christ, to whom be
glory for ever and ever. Amen.[d]

[22]Brothers, I urge you to bear with my
word of exhortation, for I have written you
only a short letter.[e]
[23]I want you to know that our brother
Timothy[f] has been released. If he arrives
soon, I will come with him to see you.
[24]Greet all your leaders[g] and all God's
people. Those from Italy[h] send you their
greetings.
[25]Grace be with you all.[i]

13:20 [w]S Ro 15:33 [x]Ge 9:16; 17:7,13,19; Isa 55:3; 61:8; Eze 37:26; S Mt 26:28 [y]S Ac 2:24 [z]S Jn 10:11 **13:21** [a]2Co 9:8 [b]S Php 2:13 [c]1Jn 3:22 [d]S Ro 11:36 **13:22** [e]1Pe 5:12 **13:23** [f]S Ac 16:1 **13:24** [g]ver 7,17 [h]Ac 18:2 **13:25** [i]S Col 4:18

13:20,25 *peace ... Grace.* See note on Ro 1:7.
13:20–21 This benediction provides a fitting conclusion to the letter.
13:20 *God of peace.* A title for God used frequently in benedictions (see Ro 15:33; 16:20; Php 4:9; 1Th 5:23 and note). *blood of.* See 10:29 and note. *eternal covenant.* The new covenant (see note on 8:8–12). What Jeremiah designates as the new covenant in 31:31 he describes as everlasting in 32:40 (cf. Isa 55:3; 61:8 and notes). *great Shepherd.* See, e.g., Ps 23; Isa 40:11; Eze 34:11–16,23; 37:24; Jn 10:2–3,11,14,27; 1Pe 2:25; 5:4.
13:21 *everything good.* Such as faith, faithfulness, obedience and perseverance.
13:22–25 A postscript.
13:22 *Brothers.* See note on Ro 1:13. *word of exhortation.* See Introduction: Literary Form. The main thrust of the letter is to go on in Christian maturity and not fall away from Christ. *short.* Compared to the lengthy treatise that would be necessary to explain fully the superiority of Christ.
13:23 *Timothy.* See Introduction to 1 Timothy: Recipient.
13:24 *leaders.* Mentioned in v. 17. *Those from Italy.* From this brief greeting no firm conclusion can be drawn concerning the source or destination of this "letter." The writer may simply be passing on to his readers greetings from some Italian believers.
13:25 *with you.* Cf. note on 2Co 13:14.

The General Letters

The seven letters following Hebrews — James; 1,2 Peter; 1,2,3 John; Jude — have often been designated as the General Letters. This term goes back to the early church historian Eusebius (c. A.D. 265 – 340), who in his *Ecclesiastical History* (2:23 – 25) first referred to these seven letters as the Catholic Letters, using the word "catholic" to mean "universal."

The letters so designated may be said to be, for the most part, addressed to general audiences rather than to specific persons or localized groups. 2 and 3 John, the two letters that seem most obviously addressed to individuals, have long been viewed as appendages of 1 John, which is clearly general in its address. However, when compared with Paul's letters, all these letters except 3 John are clearly general in nature. By contrast, Paul addresses his letters to such recipients as the Christians at Philippi, or the churches of Galatia, or Timothy or Titus.

As Eusebius noted long ago, one interesting fact connected with the General Letters is that most of them were at one time among the books of the NT whose authorship was disputed. James, 2 Peter, 2 John, 3 John and Jude were all questioned extensively before being admitted to the canon of Scripture.

James

INTRODUCTION

Author

The author identifies himself as James (1:1); he was probably the brother of Jesus and leader of the Jerusalem council (Ac 15). Four men in the NT have this name. The author of this letter could not have been the apostle James, who died too early (A.D. 44) to have written it. The other two men named James had neither the stature nor the influence that the writer of this letter had.

James was one of several brothers of Christ, probably the oldest since he heads the list in Mt 13:55. At first he did not believe in Jesus and even challenged him and misunderstood his mission (Jn 7:2 – 5). Later he became very prominent in the church:

1. He was one of the select individuals Christ appeared to after his resurrection (see 1Co 15:7 and note).

2. Paul called him a "pillar" of the church (Gal 2:9).

3. Paul, on his first post-conversion visit to Jerusalem, saw James (Gal 1:19).

4. Paul did the same on his last visit (Ac 21:18).

5. When Peter was rescued from prison, he told his friends to tell James (Ac 12:17).

6. James was a leader in the important council of Jerusalem (Ac 15:13).

7. Jude could identify himself simply as "a brother of James" (Jude 1), so well known was James.

8. James was martyred c. A.D. 62.

Date

Some date the letter in the early 60s. There are indications, however, that it was written before A.D. 50:

1. Its distinctively Jewish nature suggests that it was composed when the church was still predominantly Jewish.

2. It reflects a simple church order — officers of the church are called "elders" (5:14) and "teachers" (3:1).

3. No reference is made to the controversy over Gentile circumcision.

A Quick Look

Author:
James, a leader of the Jerusalem church

Audience:
Jewish Christians, perhaps Jerusalem believers scattered after Stephen's death

Date:
Perhaps before A.D. 50

Theme:
James emphasises vital Christianity characterized by good deeds and faith that works.

4. The Greek term *synagoge* ("synagogue" or "meeting") is used to designate the meeting or meeting place of the church (2:2).

If this early dating is correct, this letter is the earliest of all the NT writings — with the possible exception of Galatians.

Recipients

The recipients are identified explicitly only in 1:1: "the twelve tribes scattered among the nations." Some hold that this expression refers to Christians in general, but the term "twelve tribes" would more naturally apply to Jewish Christians. Furthermore, a Jewish audience would be more in keeping with the obviously Jewish nature of the letter (e.g., the use of the Hebrew title for God, *kyrios sabaoth,* "Lord Almighty," 5:4). That the recipients were Christians is clear from 2:1; 5:7 – 8. It has been plausibly suggested that these were believers from the early Jerusalem church who, after Stephen's death, were scattered as far as Phoenicia, Cyprus and Syrian Antioch (see Ac 8:1; 11:19 and notes). This would account for James's references to trials and oppression, his intimate knowledge of the readers and the authoritative nature of the letter. As leader of the Jerusalem church, James writes as pastor to instruct and encourage his dispersed people in the face of their difficulties (see essay, p. 1914).

James writes as pastor to instruct and encourage his dispersed people in the face of their difficulties.

Distinctive Characteristics

Characteristics that make the letter distinctive are: (1) its unmistakably Jewish nature; (2) its emphasis on vital Christianity, characterized by good deeds and a faith that works (genuine faith must and will be accompanied by a consistent lifestyle); (3) its simple organization; (4) its familiarity with Jesus' teachings preserved in the Sermon on the Mount (compare 2:5 with Mt 5:3; 3:10 – 12 with Mt 7:15 – 20; 3:18 with Mt 5:9; 5:2 – 3 with Mt 6:19 – 20; 5:12 with Mt 5:33 – 37); (5) its similarity to OT wisdom writings such as Proverbs (see essay, p. 727); (6) its excellent Greek.

Outline

- I. Greetings (1:1)
- II. Trials and Temptations (1:2 – 18)
  - A. The Testing of Faith (1:2 – 12)
  - B. The Source of Temptation (1:13 – 18)
- III. Listening and Doing (1:19 – 27)
- IV. Favoritism Forbidden (2:1 – 13)
- V. Faith and Deeds (2:14 – 26)
- VI. Taming the Tongue (3:1 – 12)
- VII. Two Kinds of Wisdom (3:13 – 18)
- VIII. Warning against Worldliness (ch. 4)
  - A. Quarrelsomeness (4:1 – 3)
  - B. Spiritual Unfaithfulness (4:4)
  - C. Pride (4:5 – 10)
  - D. Slander (4:11 – 12)
  - E. Boasting (4:13 – 17)
- IX. Warning to Rich Oppressors (5:1 – 6)
- X. Miscellaneous Exhortations (5:7 – 20)
  - A. Concerning Patience in Suffering (5:7 – 11)
  - B. Concerning Oaths (5:12)
  - C. Concerning the Prayer of Faith (5:13 – 18)
  - D. Concerning Those Who Wander from the Truth (5:19 – 20)

1 James,[a] a servant of God[b] and of the
Lord Jesus Christ,

To the twelve tribes[c] scattered[d] among
the nations:

Greetings.[e]

Trials and Temptations

2Consider it pure joy, my brothers,
whenever you face trials of many kinds,[f]
3because you know that the testing of
your faith[g] develops perseverance.[h] 4Per-
severance must finish its work so that you
may be mature[i] and complete, not lacking
anything. 5If any of you lacks wisdom, he
should ask God,[j] who gives generously to
all without finding fault, and it will be giv-
en to him.[k] 6But when he asks, he must
believe and not doubt,[l] because he who
doubts is like a wave of the sea, blown
and tossed by the wind. 7That man should
not think he will receive anything from the
Lord; 8he is a double-minded man,[m] unstable[n] in all he does.
9The brother in humble circumstances
ought to take pride in his high position.[o]
10But the one who is rich should take pride
in his low position, because he will pass
away like a wild flower.[p] 11For the sun rises with scorching heat[q] and withers[r] the
plant; its blossom falls and its beauty is
destroyed.[s] In the same way, the rich man
will fade away even while he goes about
his business.

12Blessed is the man who perseveres
under trial,[t] because when he has stood
the test, he will receive the crown of life[u]
that God has promised to those who love
him.[v]
13When tempted, no one should say,
"God is tempting me." For God cannot be
tempted by evil, nor does he tempt anyone; 14but each one is tempted when, by
his own[w] evil desire, he is dragged away
and enticed. 15Then, after desire has conceived, it gives birth to sin;[x] and sin, when
it is full-grown, gives birth to death.[y]
16Don't be deceived,[z] my dear brothers.[a] 17Every good and perfect gift is from
above,[b] coming down from the Father of
the heavenly lights,[c] who does not change[d]
like shifting shadows. 18He chose to give
us birth[e] through the word of truth,[f] that
we might be a kind of firstfruits[g] of all he
created.

Listening and Doing

19My dear brothers,[h] take note of this:
Everyone should be quick to listen, slow
to speak[i] and slow to become angry, 20for
man's anger[j] does not bring about the righteous life that God desires. 21Therefore, get
rid of[k] all moral filth and the evil that is
so prevalent and humbly accept the word
planted in you,[l] which can save you.

1:1 [a]S Ac 15:13 [b]Ro 1:1; Tit 1:1 [c]Ac 26:7 [d]Dt 32:26; Jn 7:35; 1Pe 1:1 [e]Ac 15:23 **1:2** [f]ver 12; S Mt 5:12; Heb 10:34; 12:11 **1:3** [g]1Pe 1:7 [h]S Heb 10:36 **1:4** [i]S 1Co 2:6 **1:5** [j]1Ki 3:9,10; Pr 2:3-6 [k]Ps 51:6; Da 1:17; 2:21; S Mt 7:7 **1:6** [l]S Mt 21:21; Mk 11:24 **1:8** [m]Ps 119:113; Jas 4:8 [n]2Pe 2:14; 3:16 **1:9** [o]S Mt 23:12 **1:10** [p]Job 14:2; Ps 103:15,16; Isa 40:6,7; 1Co 7:31; 1Pe 1:24 **1:11** [q]Mt 20:12 [r]Ps 102:4,11 [s]Isa 40:6-8 **1:12** [t]ver 2; Ge 22:1; Jas 5:11; 1Pe 3:14 [u]S 1Co 9:25 [v]Ex 20:6; 1Co 2:9; 8:3; Jas 2:5 **1:14** [w]Pr 19:3 **1:15** [x]Ge 3:6; Job 15:35; Ps 7:14; Isa 59:4 [y]S Ro 6:23 **1:16** [z]S 1Co 6:9 [a]ver 19; Jas 2:5 **1:17** [b]Ps 85:12; Jn 3:27; Jas 3:15,17 [c]Ge 1:16; Ps 136:7; Da 2:22; 1Jn 1:5 [d]Nu 23:19; Ps 102:27; Mal 3:6 **1:18** [e]S Jn 1:13 [f]S 2Ti 2:15 [g]Jer 2:3; Rev 14:4 **1:19** [h]ver 16; Jas 2:5 [i]Pr 10:19; Jas 3:3-12 **1:20** [j]S Mt 5:22 **1:21** [k]S Eph 4:22 [l]Eph 1:13

1:1 *James.* See Introduction: Author. *servant.* See note on Ro 1:1. *twelve tribes.* See Introduction: Recipients.
1:2–3 *trials ... testing ... develops perseverance.* This, together with similar language in v. 12, forms a frame around James's word about trials.
1:2 *joy.* See Mt 5:11–12; Ac 5:41; Ro 5:3 and note; Php 4:4 and note; 1Pe 1:6. *brothers.* Cf. note on Ro 1:13. James addresses the readers as "brothers" 15 times in this short letter. He has many rebukes for them, but he chides them in brotherly love. *trials.* The same Greek root lies behind the word "trials" here and the word "tempted" in v. 13. In vv. 2–3 the emphasis is on difficulties that come from outside; in vv. 13–15 it is on inner moral trials such as temptation to sin.
1:5 *wisdom.* Enables one to face trials with "pure joy" (v. 2). Wisdom is not just acquired information but practical insight with spiritual implications (see 3:13–18; Pr 1:2–4 and note on 1:2; 2:10–15; 4:5–9; 9:10–12).
1:6 *wave of the sea.* See Eph 4:14 and note.
1:9–10 *brother in humble circumstances ... one who is rich.* Christians who experience poverty are to take pride in their high position (v. 9) as believers (see 2:5). Wealthy believers, on the other hand, should take pride not in their possessions but in the fact that God has humbled them and given them a godly value system, so that they now realize how transitory life and wealth are (v. 10).
1:10 *pass away like a wild flower.* See Job 14:2; Ps 103:15; Isa 40:6–7; 1Pe 1:24; cf. Lk 12:15,20–21; 1Ti 6:8–10,17–19.
1:11 *will fade away.* Cf. 4:14 and note.
1:12 *Blessed.* See vv. 2–3 and note; Jer 17:7–8; Mt 5:3–12; see also notes on Ps 1:1; Mt 5:3; Rev 1:3. *crown.* The Greek for this word was the usual term for the wreath placed on the head of a victorious athlete or military leader (see 2Ti 4:8; 1Pe 5:4; Rev 2:10 and notes). *life.* Eternal life, as the future tense of the verb ("will receive") indicates.
1:13 *tempted.* In vv. 13–14 the verb refers to temptations that test one's moral strength to resist sin (see note on Mt 4:1). *God cannot be tempted.* Because God in his very nature is holy, there is nothing in him for sin to appeal to. *nor does he tempt anyone.* See note on Ge 22:1.
1:14 *evil desire.* A person's innate tendency to sin (cf. Jer 17:9). *dragged away and enticed.* Words commonly used to describe hunting methods, used here metaphorically of how evil desire operates (cf. 2Pe 2:14 and note).
1:15 The three stages — desire, sin, death — are seen in the temptations of Eve (Ge 3:6–22) and David (2Sa 11:2–17).
1:17 *Every good and perfect gift is from above.* See v. 5; 3:17. *Father of ... lights.* God is the Creator of the heavenly bodies, which give light to the earth, but, unlike them, he does not change.
1:18 *birth.* Not a reference to creation but to regeneration (see Jn 3:3,5,7 and notes). *word of truth.* The proclamation of the gospel (see 1Pe 1:23–25 and note on 1:23). *firstfruits.* See Lev 23:9–14 and chart, pp. 178–179. Just as the first sheaf of the harvest was an indication that the whole harvest would eventually follow, so the early Christians were an indication that a great number of people would eventually be born again (cf. 1Co 15:20 and note).
1:19 *Everyone should be ... slow to speak.* See v. 26.
1:21 *word.* Of God (cf. 1Pe 1:23). *save you.* Here eschatological (future) salvation is primarily in view (cf. Heb 1:14; 9:28 and note).

[22]Do not merely listen to the word, and
so deceive yourselves. Do what it says.[m]
[23]Anyone who listens to the word but
does not do what it says is like a man who
looks at his face in a mirror [24]and, after
looking at himself, goes away and immediately forgets what he looks like. [25]But
the man who looks intently into the perfect law that gives freedom,[n] and continues to do this, not forgetting what he has
heard, but doing it—he will be blessed in
what he does.[o]

[26]If anyone considers himself religious
and yet does not keep a tight rein on his
tongue,[p] he deceives himself and his religion is worthless. [27]Religion that God
our Father accepts as pure and faultless is
this: to look after[q] orphans and widows[r]
in their distress and to keep oneself from
being polluted by the world.[s]

Favoritism Forbidden

2 My brothers, as believers in our glorious[t] Lord Jesus Christ, don't show
favoritism.[u] [2]Suppose a man comes into
your meeting wearing a gold ring and fine
clothes, and a poor man in shabby clothes
also comes in. [3]If you show special attention to the man wearing fine clothes and
say, "Here's a good seat for you," but say
to the poor man, "You stand there" or "Sit
on the floor by my feet," [4]have you not
discriminated among yourselves and become judges[v] with evil thoughts?

[5]Listen, my dear brothers:[w] Has not God
chosen those who are poor in the eyes of
the world[x] to be rich in faith[y] and to inherit
the kingdom[z] he promised those who love
him?[a] [6]But you have insulted the poor.[b] Is
it not the rich who are exploiting you? Are
they not the ones who are dragging you
into court?[c] [7]Are they not the ones who
are slandering the noble name of him to
whom you belong?

[8]If you really keep the royal law found
in Scripture, "Love your neighbor as yourself,"[a d] you are doing right. [9]But if you
show favoritism,[e] you sin and are convicted by the law as lawbreakers.[f] [10]For
whoever keeps the whole law and yet
stumbles[g] at just one point is guilty of
breaking all of it.[h] [11]For he who said, "Do
not commit adultery,"[b i] also said, "Do not
murder."[c j] If you do not commit adultery
but do commit murder, you have become
a lawbreaker.

[12]Speak and act as those who are going to be judged[k] by the law that gives
freedom,[l] [13]because judgment without
mercy will be shown to anyone who has
not been merciful.[m] Mercy triumphs over
judgment!

Faith and Deeds

[14]What good is it, my brothers, if a man
claims to have faith but has no deeds?[n]

[a] *8* Lev. 19:18 [b] *11* Exodus 20:14; Deut. 5:18
[c] *11* Exodus 20:13; Deut. 5:17

1:22 [m] S Mt 7:21; Jas 2:14-20 **1:25** [n] Ps 19:7; Jn 8:32; Gal 2:4; Jas 2:12 [o] S Jn 13:17 **1:26** [p] Ps 34:13; 39:1; 141:3; Jas 3:2-12; 1Pe 3:10 **1:27** [q] Mt 25:36 [r] Dt 14:29; Job 31:16,17,21; Ps 146:9; Isa 1:17,23 [s] Ro 12:2; Jas 4:4; 2Pe 1:4; 2:20 **2:1** [t] Ac 7:2; 1Co 2:8 [u] ver 9; Dt 1:17; Lev 19:15; Pr 24:23; S Ac 10:34 **2:4** [v] S Jn 7:24 **2:5** [w] Jas 1:16,19 [x] Job 34:19; 1Co 1:26-28 [y] Lk 12:21; Rev 2:9 [z] S Mt 25:34 [a] S Jas 1:12 **2:6** [b] 1Co 11:22 [c] Ac 8:3; 16:19 **2:8** [d] Lev 19:18; S Mt 5:43 **2:9** [e] ver 1 [f] Dt 1:17 **2:10** [g] Jas 3:2 [h] Mt 5:19; Gal 3:10; 5:3 **2:11** [i] Ex 20:14; Dt 5:18 [j] Ex 20:13; Dt 5:17 **2:12** [k] S Mt 16:27 [l] S Jas 1:25 **2:13** [m] Mt 5:7; 9:13; 12:7; 18:32-35; Lk 6:37 **2:14** [n] Mt 7:26; Jas 1:22-25

1:25 *perfect law.* The moral and ethical teaching of Christianity, which is based on the OT moral law, as embodied in the Ten Commandments (see Ps 19:7), but brought to completion (perfection) by Jesus Christ (see notes on Mt 5:17; Ro 10:4). *freedom.* In contrast to the sinner, who is a slave to sin (see Jn 8:34 and note), obeying the moral law gives Christians the joyous freedom to be what they were created to be.

1:26–27 An example of a person not doing the word and of one doing it.

1:26 *religious.* Refers to the outward acts of religion: e.g., giving to the needy, fasting and public acts of praying and worshiping (see Mt 6:1–18 and note on 6:1). *keep a tight rein on his tongue.* See 3:1–12.

1:27 See Jer 22:16 and note. *orphans and widows.* See notes on Ex 22:21–27; Isa 1:17. *world.* Not the world of nature but the world of people in their rebellion against and alienation from God (see 1Jn 2:15 and note).

2:1 *as believers … don't show favoritism.* God does not show favoritism (see note on Ac 10:34)—nor should believers (see vv. 5–13 and note; see also note on 1Ti 5:21). *glorious.* See Jn 1:14; Heb 1:3 and notes.

2:2 *meeting.* The Greek for this term is the origin of the English word "synagogue."

2:4 *judges with evil thoughts.* Cf. Lev 19:15.

2:5–13 James gives three arguments against showing favoritism to the rich: (1) The rich persecute the poor—the believers (vv. 5–7). (2) Favoritism violates the royal law of love and thus is sin (vv. 8–11). (3) Favoritism will be judged (vv. 12–13).

2:5 *Has not God chosen those who are poor …?* Cf. Lk 6:20 and note on 6:20–23; 1Co 1:26–31. *kingdom.* The kingdom that is entered by the new birth (see note on 1:18) and that will be consummated in the future (Mt 25:34,46; see note on Mt 3:2).

2:8 *royal law.* The law of love (see Lev 19:18 and note) is called "royal" because it is the supreme law that is the source of all other laws governing human relationships. It is the summation of all such laws (see Mk 12:28–31; Ro 13:8–10 and notes).

2:10 *guilty of breaking all.* The law is the expression of the character and will of God; therefore to violate one part of the law is to violate God's will and thus his whole law (cf. Mt 5:18–19; 23:23).

2:11 James may have chosen these two commandments because both violate the law of love to one's neighbor (v. 8).

2:12 *judged.* This judgment is not for determining eternal destiny, for James is speaking to believers (v. 1), whose destiny is already determined (see Jn 5:24 and note). Rather, it is for giving rewards to believers (see 1Co 3:12–15; 2Co 5:10; Rev 22:12 and notes). *law that gives freedom.* The royal law of love (v. 8).

2:13 *Mercy triumphs over judgment!* If people are merciful, God will be merciful to them on the Day of Judgment (see Pr 21:13; Mt 5:7; 6:14–15; 18:21–35).

2:14–26 In vv. 14–20,24,26 "faith" is not used in the sense of genuine, saving faith. Rather, it is demonic (v. 19), useless (v. 20) and dead (v. 26). It is a mere intellectual acceptance of certain truths without trust in Christ as Savior. James is also not saying that a person is saved by works

Can such faith save him? 15 Suppose a brother or sister is without clothes and daily food.[o] 16 If one of you says to him, "Go, I wish you well; keep warm and well fed," but does nothing about his physical needs, what good is it?[p] 17 In the same way, faith by itself, if it is not accompanied by action, is dead.[q]

18 But someone will say, "You have faith; I have deeds."

Show me your faith without deeds,[r] and I will show you my faith[s] by what I do.[t] 19 You believe that there is one God.[u] Good! Even the demons believe that[v]—and shudder.

20 You foolish man, do you want evidence that faith without deeds is useless[a]?[w] 21 Was not our ancestor Abraham considered righteous for what he did when he offered his son Isaac on the altar?[x] 22 You see that his faith and his actions were working together,[y] and his faith was made complete by what he did.[z] 23 And the scripture was fulfilled that says, "Abraham believed God, and it was credited to him as righteousness,"[b][a] and he was called God's friend.[b] 24 You see that a person is justified by what he does and not by faith alone.

25 In the same way, was not even Rahab the prostitute considered righteous for what she did when she gave lodging to the spies and sent them off in a different direction?[c] 26 As the body without the spirit is dead, so faith without deeds is dead.[d]

2:15 [o] Mt 25:35,36 **2:16** [p] Lk 3:11; 1Jn 3:17,18 **2:17** [q] ver 20,26; Gal 5:6 **2:18** [r] Ro 3:28 [s] Heb 11 [t] Mt 7:16,17; Jas 3:13 **2:19** [u] Dt 6:4; Mk 12:29; 1Co 8:4-6 [v] Mt 8:29; Lk 4:34 **2:20** [w] ver 17,26 **2:21** [x] Ge 22:9,12 **2:22** [y] Heb 11:17 [z] 1Th 1:3 **2:23** [a] Ge 15:6; S Ro 4:3 [b] 2Ch 20:7; Isa 41:8 **2:25** [c] S Heb 11:31 **2:26** [d] ver 17,20

3:1 [e] S Eph 4:11 [f] S Mt 7:1 [g] Ro 2:21 **3:2** [h] 1Ki 8:46; Ro 3:9-20; Jas 2:10; 1Jn 1:8 [i] Ps 39:1; Pr 10:19; 1Pe 3:10 [j] S Mt 12:37 [k] Jas 1:26 **3:3** [l] Ps 32:9 **3:5** [m] Ps 12:3,4; 73:8,9 **3:6** [n] Pr 16:27 [o] Mt 15:11,18,19 [p] S Mt 5:22 **3:8** [q] Ps 140:3; Ro 3:13 **3:9** [r] Ge 1:26,27; 1Co 11:7

Taming the Tongue

3 Not many of you should presume to be teachers,[e] my brothers, because you know that we who teach will be judged[f] more strictly.[g] 2 We all stumble[h] in many ways. If anyone is never at fault in what he says,[i] he is a perfect man,[j] able to keep his whole body in check.[k]

3 When we put bits into the mouths of horses to make them obey us, we can turn the whole animal.[l] 4 Or take ships as an example. Although they are so large and are driven by strong winds, they are steered by a very small rudder wherever the pilot wants to go. 5 Likewise the tongue is a small part of the body, but it makes great boasts.[m] Consider what a great forest is set on fire by a small spark. 6 The tongue also is a fire,[n] a world of evil among the parts of the body. It corrupts the whole person,[o] sets the whole course of his life on fire, and is itself set on fire by hell.[p]

7 All kinds of animals, birds, reptiles and creatures of the sea are being tamed and have been tamed by man, 8 but no man can tame the tongue. It is a restless evil, full of deadly poison.[q]

9 With the tongue we praise our Lord and Father, and with it we curse men, who have been made in God's likeness.[r] 10 Out of the same mouth come praise and cursing. My brothers, this should not be. 11 Can both fresh water and salt[c] water flow from

[a] 20 Some early manuscripts *dead* [b] 23 Gen. 15:6
[c] 11 Greek *bitter* (see also verse 14)

and not by genuine faith. Rather, he is saying, to use Martin Luther's words, that people are justified (declared righteous before God) by faith alone, but not by a faith that is alone. Genuine faith will produce good deeds, but only faith in Christ saves (see note on v. 21). (For more information on justification see note on Ro 3:24.)

2:15–16 This illustration of false faith is parallel to the illustration of false love found in 1Jn 3:17 (see note there). The latter passage calls for love in action; this one calls for faith in action.

2:18 *You have faith; I have deeds.* The false claim is that there are "faith" Christians and "deeds" Christians, i.e., that faith and deeds can exist independently of each other. *Show me your faith without deeds.* Irony; James denies the possibility of this.

2:19 *there is one God.* A declaration of monotheism that reflects the well-known Jewish creed called in Hebrew the *Shema,* "Hear" (Dt 6:4 [see notes on 6:4–9]; Mk 12:29 [see note there]).

2:21 Apart from its context, this verse might seem to contradict the Biblical teaching that people are saved by faith and not by good deeds (see Ro 3:28 and note; Gal 2:15–16 and note on 2:16). But James means only that righteous action is evidence of genuine faith—not that it saves, for the verse (Ge 15:6; see note there) that he cites (v. 23) to substantiate his point says, "Abram believed the LORD, and he credited it [i.e., faith, not works] to him as righteousness." Furthermore, Abraham's act of faith recorded in Ge 15:6 occurred before he offered up Isaac, which was only a proof of the genuineness of his faith. As Paul wrote, "The only thing that counts is faith expressing itself through love" (Gal 5:6; see note there). Faith that saves produces good deeds. See note on vv. 14–26.

2:23 *God's friend.* This designation (see 2Ch 20:7 and note on Ge 18:17) further describes Abraham's relationship to God as one of complete acceptance (cf. Jn 15:13–15).

2:24 *not by faith alone.* Not by an intellectual assent to certain truths (see note on 2:14–26).

2:25 *Rahab the prostitute.* James does not approve Rahab's occupation. He merely commends her for her faith (see also Heb 11:31 and note), which she demonstrated by helping the spies (Jos 2).

3:1 *judged more strictly.* Because teachers have great influence, they will be held more accountable (cf. Mt 23:1–33; Lk 20:46–47; Heb 13:17).

3:2 *perfect man.* Since the tongue is so difficult to control, those who control it perfectly gain control of themselves in all other areas of life as well.

3:6 *world of evil.* Like the world in its fallenness. *corrupts the whole person.* Because the tongue is the cause of so many sins (cf. Mk 7:20–23). *set on fire by hell.* A figurative way of saying that the source of the tongue's evil is the devil (see Jn 8:44 and note). *hell.* See notes on Mt 5:22; Lk 16:23.

3:9 *in God's likeness.* Since humans have been made like God (see Ge 1:26–27 and notes), to curse a human being is to show contempt for God (see Ge 9:6 and note).

3:11–12 Only a renewed heart can produce pure speech.

the same spring? 12My brothers, can a fig
tree bear olives, or a grapevine bear figs?[s]
Neither can a salt spring produce fresh
water.

Two Kinds of Wisdom

13Who is wise and understanding
among you? Let him show it[t] by his good
life, by deeds[u] done in the humility that
comes from wisdom. 14But if you harbor
bitter envy and selfish ambition[v] in your
hearts, do not boast about it or deny the
truth.[w] 15Such "wisdom" does not come
down from heaven[x] but is earthly, unspiritual, of the devil.[y] 16For where you have
envy and selfish ambition,[z] there you find
disorder and every evil practice.
17But the wisdom that comes from heav-
en[a] is first of all pure; then peace-loving,[b]
considerate, submissive, full of mercy[c] and
good fruit, impartial and sincere.[d] 18Peace-
makers[e] who sow in peace raise a harvest
of righteousness.[f]

Submit Yourselves to God

4 What causes fights and quarrels[g]
among you? Don't they come from
your desires that battle[h] within you? 2You
want something but don't get it. You kill[i]
and covet, but you cannot have what you
want. You quarrel and fight. You do not
have, because you do not ask God. 3When
you ask, you do not receive,[j] because you
ask with wrong motives,[k] that you may
spend what you get on your pleasures.
4You adulterous[l] people, don't you know
that friendship with the world[m] is hatred
toward God?[n] Anyone who chooses to be
a friend of the world becomes an enemy
of God.[o] 5Or do you think Scripture says
without reason that the spirit he caused
to live in us[p] envies intensely?[a] 6But he
gives us more grace. That is why Scripture says:

"God opposes the proud
but gives grace to the humble."[b q]

7Submit yourselves, then, to God. Resist the devil,[r] and he will flee from you.
8Come near to God and he will come near
to you.[s] Wash your hands,[t] you sinners,
and purify your hearts,[u] you double-minded.[v] 9Grieve, mourn and wail. Change
your laughter to mourning and your joy
to gloom.[w] 10Humble yourselves before the
Lord, and he will lift you up.[x]
11Brothers, do not slander one another.[y]
Anyone who speaks against his brother or
judges him[z] speaks against the law[a] and
judges it. When you judge the law, you
are not keeping it,[b] but sitting in judgment
on it. 12There is only one Lawgiver and
Judge,[c] the one who is able to save and
destroy.[d] But you—who are you to judge
your neighbor?[e]

Boasting About Tomorrow

13Now listen,[f] you who say, "Today or
tomorrow we will go to this or that city,
spend a year there, carry on business and
make money."[g] 14Why, you do not even
know what will happen tomorrow. What
is your life? You are a mist that appears for

[a] 5 Or *that God jealously longs for the spirit that he made to live in us*; or *that the Spirit he caused to live in us longs jealously* [b] 6 Prov. 3:34

3:12 [s] Mt 7:16 **3:13** [t] Jas 2:18 [u] S 1Pe 2:12 **3:14** [v] ver 16; 2Co 12:20 [w] Jas 5:19 **3:15** [x] ver 17; Jas 1:17 [y] 1Ti 4:1 **3:16** [z] ver 14; Gal 5:20,21 **3:17** [a] 1Co 2:6; Jas 1:17 [b] Heb 12:11 [c] Lk 6:36 [d] Ro 12:9 **3:18** [e] Mt 5:9; S Ro 14:19 [f] Pr 11:18; Isa 32:17; Hos 10:12; Php 1:11 **4:1** [g] Tit 3:9 [h] S Ro 7:23 **4:2** [i] Mt 5:21,22; Jas 5:6; 1Jn 3:15 **4:3** [j] Ps 18:41; S Mt 7:7 [k] Ps 66:18; 1Jn 3:22; 5:14 **4:4** [l] Isa 54:5; Jer 3:20; Hos 2:2-5; 3:1; 9:1 [m] S Jas 1:27 [n] Ro 8:7; 1Jn 2:15 [o] Jn 15:19 **4:5** [p] 1Co 6:19 **4:6** [q] Pr 3:34; S Mt 23:12 **4:7** [r] Eph 4:27; 6:11; 1Pe 5:6-9 **4:8** [s] Ps 73:28; Zec 1:3; Mal 3:7; Heb 7:19 [t] Isa 1:16 [u] Ps 24:4; Jer 4:14 [v] Ps 119:113; Jas 1:8 **4:9** [w] Lk 6:25 **4:10** [x] ver 6; Job 5:11; 1Pe 5:6 **4:11** [y] Ro 1:30; 2Co 12:20; 1Pe 2:1 [z] S Mt 7:1 [a] Jas 2:8 [b] Jas 1:22 **4:12** [c] Isa 33:22; S Jas 5:9 [d] Mt 10:28 [e] S Mt 7:1 **4:13** [f] Jas 5:1 [g] Pr 27:1; Lk 12:18-20

3:13 *wisdom.* See note on 1:5.
3:15 *from heaven.* From God (see 1:5; 1Co 2:6–16; see also Da 4:26 and note).
3:16 *disorder.* Cf. "God is not a God of disorder but of peace" (1Co 14:33; see note there).
3:17 *impartial.* See 2:1–13; see also note on 1Ti 5:21.
3:18 *Peacemakers.* Contrast v. 16. Discord cannot produce conduct pleasing to God.
4:2 *kill.* Some hold that this word is here used figuratively (cf. Mt 5:21–22) for "hate." Others hold that it should be understood straightforwardly to describe what can happen when covetous desire is sufficiently frustrated (see, e.g., Ahab's murder of Naboth, 1Ki 21:1–16; David's murder of Uriah, 2Sa 11).
4:4 *adulterous people.* Those who are spiritually unfaithful, who love the world rather than God. For spiritual adultery see Ex 34:15 and note. *world.* See note on 1:27.
4:5 *Scripture.* The passage James had in mind is not known. *the spirit ... envies intensely.* The words "the spirit he caused to live in us" allude to God's creation of Adam (see Ge 2:7 and note). Because of the fall, a person's spirit "envies intensely," but God's grace (v. 6) is able to overcome human envy. Regarding the two alternative translations (see NIV text note), the meaning of the first is that God jealously longs for our faithfulness and love (see v. 4). In this case the Scripture referred to may be Ex 20:5 (see note there). The second capitalizes "Spirit" and makes him the subject. It is the Holy Spirit who longs jealously for our full devotion. If this is the correct translation, it is the only clear reference to the Holy Spirit in the letter.
4:6 See 1Pe 5:5, which also quotes Pr 3:34.
4:7–10 These verses contain ten commands, each of which is so stated in Greek that it calls for immediate action in rooting out the sinful attitude of pride.
4:7 *Resist the devil.* See Eph 6:10–20 and note; 1Pe 5:8–9.
4:8 *Wash your hands.* Before the OT priests approached God at the tabernacle, they had to wash their hands and feet at the bronze basin as a symbol of spiritual cleansing (Ex 30:17–21). For the imagery of "clean hands and a pure heart" see Ps 24:4 and note.
4:9 *Grieve, mourn and wail.* Repent.
4:10 See Mt 23:12; Lk 14:11 and note; 1Pe 5:6.
4:11 *speaks against his brother ... speaks against the law.* See note on 2:8; see also Ex 20:16 and note; Ps 15:3; 50:19–20; Pr 6:16,19 and note. To speak against a Christian brother or sister is to scorn the law of love.
4:13—5:6 Jas 4:13–17 is addressed to traveling merchants and condemns arrogance; 5:1–6 is a warning to wealthy landowners about their improper use of wealth.
4:14 *mist.* Cf. "shadow" (1Ch 29:15); "breath" (Job 7:7); "cloud" (Job 7:9); "evening shadow" (Ps 102:11).

a little while and then vanishes.[h] 15Instead,
you ought to say, "If it is the Lord's will,[i]
we will live and do this or that." 16As it is,
you boast and brag. All such boasting is
evil.[j] 17Anyone, then, who knows the good
he ought to do and doesn't do it, sins.[k]

Warning to Rich Oppressors

5 Now listen,[l] you rich people,[m] weep
and wail[n] because of the misery that is
coming upon you. 2Your wealth has rotted,
and moths have eaten your clothes.[o] 3Your
gold and silver are corroded. Their corrosion will testify against you and eat your
flesh like fire. You have hoarded wealth
in the last days.[p] 4Look! The wages you
failed to pay the workmen[q] who mowed
your fields are crying out against you. The
cries[r] of the harvesters have reached the
ears of the Lord Almighty.[s] 5You have lived
on earth in luxury and self-indulgence.
You have fattened yourselves[t] in the day
of slaughter.[a][u] 6You have condemned and
murdered[v] innocent men,[w] who were not
opposing you.

Patience in Suffering

7Be patient, then, brothers, until the
Lord's coming.[x] See how the farmer waits
for the land to yield its valuable crop and
how patient he is[y] for the autumn and
spring rains.[z] 8You too, be patient and
stand firm, because the Lord's coming[a] is
near.[b] 9Don't grumble against each other, brothers,[c] or you will be judged. The
Judge[d] is standing at the door![e]
10Brothers, as an example of patience
in the face of suffering, take the prophets[f] who spoke in the name of the Lord.
11As you know, we consider blessed[g] those
who have persevered. You have heard of
Job's perseverance[h] and have seen what
the Lord finally brought about.[i] The Lord
is full of compassion and mercy.[j]
12Above all, my brothers, do not
swear — not by heaven or by earth or
by anything else. Let your "Yes" be yes,
and your "No," no, or you will be condemned.[k]

The Prayer of Faith

13Is any one of you in trouble? He should
pray.[l] Is anyone happy? Let him sing songs
of praise.[m] 14Is any one of you sick? He
should call the elders[n] of the church to
pray over him and anoint him with oil[o]
in the name of the Lord. 15And the prayer
offered in faith[p] will make the sick person
well; the Lord will raise him up. If he has
sinned, he will be forgiven. 16Therefore
confess your sins[q] to each other and pray
for each other so that you may be healed.[r]
The prayer of a righteous man is powerful
and effective.[s]

4:14 [h] Job 7:7; Ps 39:5; 102:3; 144:4; Isa 2:22 **4:15** [i] S Ac 18:21 **4:16** [j] 1Co 5:6 **4:17** [k] Lk 12:47; Jn 9:41 **5:1** [l] Jas 4:13 [m] Lk 6:24; 1Ti 6:9; Jas 2:2-6 [n] Isa 13:6; Eze 30:2 **5:2** [o] Job 13:28; Ps 39:11; Isa 50:9; Mt 6:19,20 **5:3** [p] ver 7,8 **5:4** [q] Lev 19:13; Jer 22:13; Mal 3:5 [r] Dt 24:15 [s] Ro 9:29 **5:5** [t] Eze 16:49; Am 6:1; Lk 16:19 [u] Jer 12:3; 25:34 **5:6** [v] Jas 4:2 [w] Heb 10:38 **5:7** [x] S 1Co 1:7 [y] Gal 6:9 [z] Dt 11:14; Jer 5:24; Joel 2:23 **5:8** [a] S 1Co 1:7 [b] S Ro 13:11 **5:9** [c] Jas 4:11 [d] Ps 94:2; 1Co 4:5; Jas 4:12; 1Pe 4:5 [e] Mt 24:33 **5:10** [f] S Mt 5:12 **5:11** [g] Mt 5:10 [h] Job 1:21,22; 2:10; S Heb 10:36 [i] Job 42:10,12-17 [j] Ex 34:6; Nu 14:18; Ps 103:8 **5:12** [k] Mt 5:34-37

[a] 5 Or *yourselves as in a day of feasting*

5:13 [l] Ps 50:15 [m] Col 3:16 **5:14** [n] S Ac 11:30 [o] Ps 23:5; Isa 1:6; Mk 6:13; 16:18; Lk 10:34 **5:15** [p] Jas 1:6 **5:16** [q] Mt 3:6; Ac 19:18 [r] Heb 12:13; 1Pe 2:24 [s] S Mt 7:7; S Jn 9:31

5:1 *rich.* These (as also in 2:2,6) are not Christians, for James warns them to repent and weep because of the coming misery. Verses 1–6 are similar to OT declarations of judgment against pagan nations, interspersed in books otherwise addressed to God's people (Isa 13–23; Jer 46–51; Eze 25–32; Am 1:3—2:16; Zep 2:4–15).

5:2 *clothes.* One of the forms of wealth in the ancient world (see Jdg 14:12–13 and note on 14:12; Ac 20:33).

5:3 *corrosion.* The result of hoarding. It will both testify against and judge the selfish rich. *last days.* See notes on Ac 2:17; 1Ti 4:1; 2Ti 3:1; Heb 1:1–2; 1Jn 2:18.

5:4 *the Lord Almighty.* See comments on "the LORD of hosts" in the Preface to the NIV; see also note on 1Sa 1:3.

5:5 *luxury and self-indulgence.* See Lk 16:19–31. *the day of slaughter.* The day of judgment. The wicked rich are like cattle that continue to fatten themselves on the very day they are to be slaughtered, totally unaware of coming destruction.

5:6 *condemned.* Probably through control of the courts by the rich and powerful.

5:7–8 *Be patient.* Resist resentment and retaliation (see v. 9).

5:7 *then.* Refers back to vv. 1–6. Since the believers are suffering at the hands of the wicked rich, they are to look forward patiently to the Lord's return. *autumn and spring rains.* In Israel the autumn rain comes in October and November soon after the grain is sown, and the spring rain comes in March and April just prior to harvest (Dt 11:14; Jer 5:24; Hos 6:3; Joel 2:23).

5:9 *Don't grumble.* James calls for patience toward believers as well as unbelievers (vv. 7–8). *The Judge is standing at the door!* A reference to Christ's second coming (see vv. 7–8) and the judgment associated with it. The NT insistence on imminence (see Ro 13:12 and note; Heb 10:25; 1Pe 4:7; Rev 22:20) arises from the teaching that the "last days" began with the incarnation. We have been living in the "last days" (v. 3) ever since (see notes on Heb 1:1–2). The next great event in redemptive history is Christ's second coming. The NT does not say when it will take place, but its certainty is never questioned and believers are consistently admonished to watch for it. It was in this light that James expected the imminent return of Christ.

5:10 *as an example of patience in … suffering, take the prophets.* Cf. Mt 5:12; 23:31; Ac 7:52.

5:11 *Job's perseverance.* Not "patience." Job was not patient (Job 3; 12:1–3; 16:1–3; 21:4), but he persevered (Job 1:20–22; 2:9–10; 13:15). This is the only place in the NT where Job is mentioned, though Job 5:13 is quoted in 1Co 3:19.

5:12 *do not swear.* James's words are very close to Christ's (Mt 5:33–37; see note there). James is not condemning the taking of solemn oaths, such as God's before Abraham (see Heb 6:13 and note) or Jesus' before Caiaphas (Mt 26:63–64) or Paul's (Ro 1:9; 9:1). Rather, he is condemning the flippant use of God's name or a sacred object to guarantee the truth of what is spoken.

5:14 *elders.* See notes on 1Ti 3:1; 5:17. *church.* See note on Mt 16:18. *oil.* One of the best-known ancient medicines (referred to by Philo, Pliny and the physician Galen; see also Isa 1:6 and note; Lk 10:34). Some believe that James may be using the term medicinally in this passage. Others, however, regard its use here as an aid to faith, an outward sign of the healing to be brought about by God in response to "prayer offered in faith" (v. 15; see Mk 6:13 and note).

17 Elijah was a man just like us.[t] He
prayed earnestly that it would not rain,
and it did not rain on the land for three
and a half years.[u] 18 Again he prayed, and
the heavens gave rain, and the earth produced its crops.[v]

19 My brothers, if one of you should wander from the truth[w] and someone should
bring him back,[x] 20 remember this: Whoever turns a sinner from the error of his way
will save[y] him from death and cover over
a multitude of sins.[z]

5:17 [t] Ac 14:15 [u] 1Ki 17:1; Lk 4:25 **5:18** [v] 1Ki 18:41-45 **5:19** [w] Jas 3:14 [x] S Mt 18:15 **5:20** [y] S Ro 11:14 [z] 1Pe 4:8

5:17 *Elijah ... prayed.* That Elijah prayed may be assumed from 1Ki 17:1; 18:41–46. The three and a half years (see also Lk 4:25) are probably a round number (half of seven), based on 1Ki 18:1 (see note there; cf. Rev 11:1–6 and notes).
5:19 *brothers.* See note on Ro 1:13. *wander from the truth.* The wanderer is either a professing Christian, whose faith is not genuine (cf. Heb 6:4–8 and note on 6:4–6; 2Pe 2:20–22 and notes), or a sinning Christian, who needs to be restored. For the former, the death spoken of in v. 20 is the "second death" (Rev 21:8); for the latter, it is physical death (cf. 1Co 11:29–32 and notes). See note on 1Jn 5:16.
5:20 *cover over ... sins.* The sins of the wanderer will be forgiven by God (see Pr 10:12 and note).

1 Peter

INTRODUCTION

Author and Date

The author identifies himself as the apostle Peter (1:1), and the contents and character of the letter support his authorship (see notes on 1:12; 4:13; 5:1–2,5,13). Moreover, the letter reflects the history and terminology of the Gospels and Acts (notably Peter's speeches). Its themes and concepts reflect Peter's experiences and his associations in the period of our Lord's earthly ministry and in the apostolic age. That he was acquainted, e.g., with Paul and his letters is made clear in 2Pe 3:15–16 (see notes there); Gal 1:18; 2:1–21 and elsewhere. Coincidences in thought and expression with Paul's writings are therefore not surprising.

From the beginning, 1 Peter was recognized as authoritative and as the work of the apostle Peter. The earliest reference to it may be 2Pe 3:1 (see note there), where Peter himself refers to a former letter he had written. 1 Clement (A.D. 95) seems to indicate acquaintance with 1 Peter. Polycarp, a disciple of the apostle John, makes use of 1 Peter in his letter to the Philippians. The author of the Gospel of Truth (140–150) was acquainted with 1 Peter. Eusebius (fourth century) indicated that it was universally received.

The letter was explicitly ascribed to Peter by that group of church fathers whose testimonies appear in the attestation of so many of the genuine NT writings, namely, Irenaeus (A.D. 140–203), Tertullian (150–222), Clement of Alexandria (155–215) and Origen (185–253). It is thus clear that Peter's authorship of the book has early and strong support.

Nevertheless some claim that the idiomatic Greek of this letter is beyond Peter's competence. But in his time Aramaic, Hebrew and Greek were used in the Holy Land, and he may well have been acquainted with more than one language. That he was not a professionally trained scribe (Ac 4:13) does not mean that he was unacquainted with Greek; in fact, as a Galilean fisherman he in all likelihood did use it. Even if he had not known it in the earliest days of the church, he may have acquired it as an important aid to his apostolic ministry in the decades that intervened between then and the writing of 1 Peter.

A Quick Look

Author:
The apostle Peter

Audience:
Gentile and Jewish believers in Pontus, Galatia, Cappadocia, western Asia Minor and Bithynia

Date:
About A.D. 60 to 64

Theme:
Peter gives instructions on holy living for those suffering persecution.

It is true, however, that the Greek of 1 Peter is good literary Greek, and even though Peter could no doubt speak Greek, as so many in the Mediterranean world could, it is unlikely that he would write such polished Greek. But it is at this point that Peter's remark in 5:12 (see note there) concerning Silas may be significant. Here the apostle claims that he wrote "with the help of" (more lit. "through" or "by means of") Silas. This phrase cannot refer merely to Silas as a letter carrier. Thus Silas was the intermediate agent in writing. Some have claimed that Silas's qualifications for recording Peter's letter in literary Greek are found in Ac 15:22–29. It is known that a secretary in those days often composed documents in good Greek for those who did not have the language facility to do so. Thus in 1 Peter Silas's Greek may be seen, while in 2 Peter it may be Peter's rough Greek that appears.

> *First Peter has been characterized as a letter of separation, of suffering and persecution, of suffering and glory, of hope, of pilgrimage, of courage, and as a letter dealing with the true grace of God.*

Some also maintain that the book reflects a situation that did not exist until after Peter's death, suggesting that the persecution referred to in 4:14–16; 5:8–9 is descriptive of Domitian's reign (A.D. 81–96). However, the situation that was developing in Nero's time (54–68) fits the description found in these verses just as well.

The book can be satisfactorily dated in the early 60s. It cannot be placed earlier than 60 since it shows familiarity with Paul's Prison Letters (e.g., Colossians and Ephesians, which are to be dated no earlier than 60): Compare 1:1–3 with Eph 1:1–3; 2:18 with Col 3:22; 3:1–6 with Eph 5:22–24. Furthermore, it cannot be dated later than 67/68, since Peter was martyred during Nero's reign.

Place of Writing

In 5:13 Peter indicates that he was "in Babylon" when he wrote 1 Peter. Although a number of other possibilities have been proposed (e.g., [1] an Egyptian "Babylon," which was then a Roman military post, [2] a Mesopotamian Babylon, still occupied, but not by many Jews, according to Josephus, [3] Jerusalem, symbolically called "Babylon"), the long-held tradition that Peter was referring to Rome (cf. Rev 14:8 and note) is still the most likely, and most widely held, view today.

Recipients

See note on 1:1.

Themes

Although 1 Peter is a short letter, it touches on various doctrines and has much to say about Christian life and duties. It is not surprising that different readers have found it to have different principal themes. For example, it has been characterized as a letter of separation, of suffering and persecution, of suffering and glory, of hope, of pilgrimage, of courage, and as a letter dealing with the true grace of God. Peter says that he has written "encouraging you and testifying that this is the true grace of God" (5:12). This is a definitive general description of the letter, but it does not exclude the recognition of numerous subordinate and contributory themes. The letter includes a series of exhortations (imperatives) that run from 1:13 to 5:11.

Outline

- I. Greetings (1:1–2)
- II. Praise to God for His Grace and Salvation (1:3–12)
- III. Exhortations to Holiness of Life (1:13—5:11)
    - A. The Requirement of Holiness (1:13—2:3)
    - B. The Status of Believers (2:4–12)
        1. A spiritual house (2:4–8)
        2. A chosen people (2:9–10)
        3. Aliens and strangers (2:11–12)

- C. Submission to Authority (2:13—3:7)
  1. Submission to rulers (2:13–17)
  2. Submission to masters (2:18–20)
  3. Christ's example of submission (2:21–25)
  4. Submission of wives to husbands (3:1–6)
  5. The corresponding duty of husbands (3:7)
- D. Duties of All (3:8–17)
- E. Christ's Example (3:18—4:6)
- F. Conduct in View of the End of All Things (4:7–11)
- G. Conduct of Those Who Suffer for Christ (4:12–19)
- H. Conduct of Elders (5:1–4)
- I. Conduct of the Young (5:5–11)

IV. The Purpose of the Letter (5:12)

V. Final Greetings and Benediction (5:13–14)

1 Peter, an apostle of Jesus Christ,[a]

To God's elect,[b] strangers in the world,[c]
scattered[d] throughout Pontus,[e] Galatia,[f]
Cappadocia, Asia and Bithynia,[g] 2who have
been chosen according to the foreknowledge[h] of God the Father, through the sanctifying work of the Spirit,[i] for obedience[j] to
Jesus Christ and sprinkling by his blood:[k]

Grace and peace be yours in abundance.[l]

Praise to God for a Living Hope

3Praise be to the God and Father of our
Lord Jesus Christ![m] In his great mercy[n]
he has given us new birth[o] into a living
hope[p] through the resurrection of Jesus
Christ from the dead,[q] 4and into an inheritance[r] that can never perish, spoil
or fade[s]—kept in heaven for you,[t] 5who
through faith are shielded by God's power[u] until the coming of the salvation[v] that
is ready to be revealed[w] in the last time.
6In this you greatly rejoice,[x] though now
for a little while[y] you may have had to suffer grief in all kinds of trials.[z] 7These have
come so that your faith—of greater worth
than gold, which perishes even though refined by fire[a]—may be proved genuine[b]
and may result in praise, glory and honor[c]
when Jesus Christ is revealed.[d] 8Though
you have not seen him, you love him; and
even though you do not see him now, you
believe in him[e] and are filled with an inexpressible and glorious joy, 9for you are
receiving the goal of your faith, the salvation of your souls.[f]

10Concerning this salvation, the prophets, who spoke[g] of the grace that was to
come to you,[h] searched intently and with
the greatest care,[i] 11trying to find out the
time and circumstances to which the Spirit of Christ[j] in them was pointing when
he predicted[k] the sufferings of Christ and
the glories that would follow. 12It was revealed to them that they were not serving

1:1 [a]2Pe 1:1 [b]Mt 24:22 [c]S Heb 11:13 [d]S Jas 1:1 [e]Ac 2:9; 18:2 [f]S Ac 16:6 [g]Ac 16:7 **1:2** [h]Ro 8:29 [i]2Th 2:13 [j]ver 14,22 [k]Heb 10:22; 12:24 [l]S Ro 1:7 **1:3** [m]2Co 1:3; Eph 1:3 [n]Tit 3:5 [o]ver 23; S Jn 1:13 [p]ver 13,21; S Heb 3:6 [q]1Co 15:20; 1Pe 3:21 **1:4** [r]S Ac 20:32; S Ro 8:17 [s]1Pe 5:4 [t]Col 1:5; 2Ti 4:8 **1:5** [u]1Sa 2:9; Jn 10:28 [v]S Ro 11:14 [w]S Ro 8:18 **1:6** [x]Ro 5:2 [y]1Pe 5:10 [z]Jas 1:2; 1Pe 4:12 **1:7** [a]Job 23:10; Ps 66:10; Pr 17:3; Isa 48:10 [b]Jas 1:3 [c]2Co 4:17 [d]ver 13; S 1Th 2:19; 1Pe 4:13 **1:8** [e]Jn 20:29 **1:9** [f]Ro 6:22 **1:10** [g]S Mt 26:24 [h]ver 13 [i]S Mt 13:17 **1:11** [j]S Ac 16:7; 2Pe 1:21 [k]S Mt 26:24

1:1 *Peter.* See Introduction: Author and Date; see also notes on Mt 16:18; Jn 1:42. *apostle.* See notes on Mk 6:30; 1Co 1:1; Heb 3:1. *elect.* See note on Eph 1:4. *strangers in the world.* People temporarily residing on earth but whose home is in heaven (see Gal 4:26; Heb 11:10,13–14 and notes; cf. 1Ch 29:15; Ps 39:12 and note; Heb 13:14). *scattered throughout Pontus … Bithynia.* Gentile and Jewish Christians scattered throughout much of Asia Minor (see map, p. 1711). People from this area were in Jerusalem on the day of Pentecost (see Ac 2:9–11 and map, p. 1680). Paul preached and taught in some of these provinces (see, e.g., Ac 16:6; 18:23 and notes; 19:10,26).

1:2 *chosen.* See note on Eph 1:4. *foreknowledge.* See note on Ro 8:29. *Father … Spirit … Jesus Christ.* All three persons of the Trinity (see note on Mt 28:19) are involved in the redemption of the elect. *sanctifying work.* See notes on 1Co 1:2; 2Th 2:13. The order of the terms employed suggests that the sanctifying work of the Spirit referred to here is the influence of the Spirit that draws one from sin toward holiness. Peter says it is "for" (or "to") obedience and sprinkling of Christ's blood, i.e., the Spirit's sanctifying leads to obedient saving faith and cleansing from sin (see note on 1Co 7:14). *obedience to Jesus Christ.* God's choice is designed to bring this about. *sprinkling by his blood.* The benefits of Christ's shed blood (of the new covenant) are applied to his people (cf. Ex 24:4–8; Isa 52:15; Heb 9:11–14,18–28). *Grace and peace.* See note on Ro 1:7.

1:3 *mercy.* See note on Ro 9:22–23. *new birth.* See Jn 3:3–8 and note on 3:3. *living hope.* In spite of the frequent suffering and persecution mentioned in this letter (v. 6; 2:12,18–25; 3:13–18; 4:1,4,12–19; 5:1,7–10), hope is such a key thought in it (the word itself is used here and in vv. 13,21; 3:5,15) that it may be called a letter of hope in the midst of suffering (see Introduction: Themes). In the Bible, hope is not wishful thinking but a firm conviction, much like faith that is directed toward the future (see note on Eph 1:18). *resurrection of Jesus Christ.* Secures for his people their new birth and the hope that they will be resurrected just as he was (see 1Co 15:20–23 and notes on 15:20,23).

1:4 *into an inheritance.* Believers are born again not only to a hope but also to the inheritance that is the substance of the hope. The inheritance is eternal—in its essence (it is not subject to decay) and in its preservation (it is divinely kept for us). See Heb 9:15 and note.

1:5 *through faith … by God's power.* There are two sides to the perseverance of Christians. They are shielded (1) by God's power and (2) by their own faith. Thus they are never kept contrary to their will nor apart from God's activity. *salvation.* See note on 2Ti 1:9. The Bible speaks of salvation as (1) past—when a person first believes (see, e.g., Tit 3:5), (2) present—the continuing process of salvation, or sanctification (see vv. 2 and note, 9; Lev 11:44 and note; 1Co 1:18), and (3) future—when Christ returns and salvation, or sanctification, is completed through glorification (here; see also Ro 8:23,30; 13:11; Heb 9:28; Jas 1:21 and notes).

1:7 *that your faith … may be proved genuine.* See Ro 5:3; Jas 1:2–4. Not only is the faith itself precious, but Peter's words indicate that the trial of faith is also valuable. Believers will share in the "praise, glory and honor" of God (see 5:4; 1Co 4:5).

1:8 *though you do not see him now, you believe.* Similar to Jesus' saying in Jn 20:29, on an occasion when Peter was present.

1:9 *souls.* Implies the whole person. Peter is not excluding the body from the inheritance (v. 4) that will be received.

1:10 *prophets … searched intently.* Inspiration (see 2Pe 1:21 and note) did not bestow omniscience. The prophets probably did not always understand the full significance of all the words they spoke (see v. 11). *grace that was to come to you.* The "salvation" they were already experiencing (see also v. 9). For the "grace" of ultimate redemption see v. 13 and note.

1:11 *Spirit of Christ.* The Holy Spirit is called this because Christ sent him (see Jn 16:7) and ministered through him (see Lk 4:14,18). *the sufferings of Christ and the glories.* A theme running through the Bible (see, e.g., Ps 22; Isa 52:13—53:12; Zec 9:9–10; 13:7; Mt 16:21–27; 17:22–23; 20:18–19; Lk 24:26,44,46; Jn 2:19; Ac 3:17–21; Php 2:5–11; 1Ti 3:16; cf. Lk 9:26; 21:27), and a basic concept in this letter (vv. 18–21; 3:17–22; 4:12–16; 5:1,4,9–10). Those who are united to Christ will also, after suffering, enter into glory. And they will benefit in the midst of their present sufferings from his having already entered into glory (3:21–22).

1:12 *Holy Spirit sent from heaven.* By Christ, on the day of Pentecost (see Ac 2:33), at which Peter was present. God the Father also sent the Spirit (see Jn 14:16,26).

themselves but you,[l] when they spoke of the things that have now been told you by those who have preached the gospel to you[m] by the Holy Spirit sent from heaven.[n] Even angels long to look into these things.

Be Holy

13 Therefore, prepare your minds for action; be self-controlled;[o] set your hope[p] fully on the grace to be given you[q] when Jesus Christ is revealed.[r] 14 As obedient[s] children, do not conform[t] to the evil desires you had when you lived in ignorance.[u] 15 But just as he who called you is holy, so be holy in all you do;[v] 16 for it is written: "Be holy, because I am holy."[a][w]

17 Since you call on a Father[x] who judges each man's work[y] impartially,[z] live your lives as strangers[a] here in reverent fear.[b] 18 For you know that it was not with perishable things such as silver or gold that you were redeemed[c] from the empty way of life[d] handed down to you from your forefathers, 19 but with the precious blood[e] of Christ, a lamb[f] without blemish or defect.[g] 20 He was chosen before the creation of the world,[h] but was revealed in these last times[i] for your sake. 21 Through him you believe in God,[j] who raised him from the dead[k] and glorified him,[l] and so your faith and hope[m] are in God.

22 Now that you have purified[n] yourselves by obeying[o] the truth so that you have sincere love for your brothers, love one another deeply,[p] from the heart.[b] 23 For you have been born again,[q] not of perishable seed, but of imperishable,[r] through the living and enduring word of God.[s] 24 For,

> "All men are like grass,
> and all their glory is like the flowers of the field;
> the grass withers and the flowers fall,
> 25 but the word of the Lord stands forever."[c][t]

And this is the word that was preached to you.

2 Therefore, rid yourselves[u] of all malice and all deceit, hypocrisy, envy, and

[a] *16* Lev. 11:44,45; 19:2 [b] *22* Some early manuscripts *from a pure heart* [c] *25* Isaiah 40:6-8

1:12 [l] S Ro 4:24 [m] ver 25 [n] S Lk 24:49 **1:13** [o] S Ac 24:25 [p] ver 3, 21; S Heb 3:6 [q] ver 10 [r] ver 7; S 1Co 1:7 **1:14** [s] ver 2, 22 [t] Ro 12:2 [u] Eph 4:18 **1:15** [v] Isa 35:8; 1Th 4:7; 1Jn 3:3 **1:16** [w] Lev 11:44, 45; 19:2; 20:7 **1:17** [x] S Mt 6:9 [y] S Mt 16:27 [z] S Ac 10:34 [a] S Heb 11:13 [b] Heb 12:28 **1:18** [c] S Mt 20:28; S 1Co 6:20 [d] Gal 4:3 **1:19** [e] S Ro 3:25 [f] S Jn 1:29 [g] Ex 12:5 **1:20** [h] Eph 1:4; S Mt 25:34 [i] Heb 9:26 **1:21** [j] Ro 4:24; 10:9 [k] S Ac 2:24 [l] Php 2:7-9; Heb 2:9 [m] ver 3, 13; S Heb 3:6 **1:22** [n] Jas 4:8 [o] ver 2, 14 [p] S Jn 13:34; S Ro 12:10 **1:23** [q] ver 3; S Jn 1:13 [r] Jn 1:13 [s] S Heb 4:12 **1:25** [t] Isa 40:6-8; S Jas 1:10, 11 **2:1** [u] S Eph 4:22

1:13 *prepare ... for action.* The first of a long series of exhortations that end at 5:11 (see Introduction: Themes). This one is a graphic call for action. In the language of the first century it meant that the readers should literally gather up their long, flowing garments and be ready for physical action (cf. Jer 1:17 and note). *grace to be given you.* The final state of complete blessedness and deliverance from sin. Peter later indicates that a major purpose of this letter is to encourage and testify regarding "the true grace of God" (5:12; cf. also 5:10).

1:14 *children.* Christians, born into the family of God (see v. 23), are children of their heavenly Father (v. 17) and can pray, "Our Father in heaven" (Mt 6:9). Believers are also described as being adopted into God's family (see Ro 8:15 and note).

1:16 *Be holy, because I am holy.* To be holy is to be set apart—separated from sin and impurity, and set apart to God (see notes on Ex 3:5; Lev 11:44; Ro 6:22; 1Co 1:2). The complete moral perfection of God, whose eyes are too pure to look on evil with favor (Hab 1:13), should move his people to strive for moral purity. 1 Peter is a letter of practical earnestness, filled with exhortations and encouragements.

1:17 *impartially.* See Ac 10:34 and note. *strangers.* See note on v. 1. *reverent fear.* Not terror, but wholesome reverence and respect for God, which is the basis for all godly living (cf. Pr 1:7 and note).

1:18 *redeemed.* In the Bible, to redeem someone usually means to rescue them from some bad situation (e.g., Israel from Egyptian bondage [Ex 6:6; 15:15], the psalmist from the threat of death [Ps 26:11] or from enemies [Ps 31:5]). Often this comes at a cost to the one who redeems. In the Greco-Roman world slaves could be redeemed by the payment of a price, either by someone else or by the slaves themselves. Jesus redeems believers (see Ro 3:24 and note; Tit 2:14) at the cost of his blood (see v. 19; Eph 1:7 and note; Rev 5:9), i.e., his death (see Mt 20:28; Heb 9:15 and notes; cf. Gal 3:13). The result is the "forgiveness of sins" (Col 1:14) and justification (see Ro 3:24 and note). *empty way of life ... from your forefathers.* Some maintain that the recipients must have been pagans because the NT stresses the emptiness of pagan life (see Ro 1:21; Eph 4:17 and note). Others think they were Jews since Jews were traditionalists who stressed the influence of the father as teacher in the home. In the light of the context of the whole letter, probably both Jews and Gentiles are addressed.

1:19 *lamb.* The OT sacrifices were types (foreshadowings) of Christ, depicting the ultimate and only effective sacrifice. Thus Christ is the Passover lamb (see 1Co 5:7 and note), who takes away the sin of the world (see Jn 1:29 and note). *without blemish or defect.* See Heb 9:14 and note; see also Introduction to Leviticus: Theological Themes.

1:20 *chosen.* Some think the Greek for this word means "foreknown," i.e., God knew before creation that it would be necessary for Christ to redeem human beings (cf. Rev 13:8), but he has revealed Christ in these last times. Others interpret the word as meaning that in eternity past God chose Christ as Redeemer. *these last times.* See note on Jas 5:3.

1:22 *sincere love.* See Ro 12:9 and note. *brothers.* See note on Ro 1:13. *love one another.* A command no doubt based on Jesus' teaching as recorded in Jn 13:34–35 (see notes there). See also 1Th 4:9–10 (and note on 4:9), where, like Peter, Paul commends his readers for their love of fellow believers and then urges them to love still more. *deeply.* Fervently.

1:23 *born again ... through the ... word of God.* The new birth comes about through the direct action of the Holy Spirit (see Tit 3:5 and note), but the word of God also plays an important role (see Jas 1:18), for it presents the gospel to sinners and calls on them to repent and believe in Christ (see v. 25). *perishable seed ... imperishable.* In this context the seed is doubtless the word of God, which is imperishable, living and enduring.

1:25 *the word ... stands forever.* The main point of the quotation here.

2:1 *Therefore.* Connects the exhortations that follow with 1:23–25; compare "born again" (1:23) with "newborn babies" (2:2).

slander[v] of every kind. 2Like newborn babies, crave pure spiritual milk,[w] so that
by it you may grow up[x] in your salvation,
3now that you have tasted that the Lord
is good.[y]

The Living Stone and a Chosen People

4As you come to him, the living Stone[z]—
rejected by men but chosen by God[a] and
precious to him— 5you also, like living
stones, are being built[b] into a spiritual
house[c] to be a holy priesthood,[d] offering spiritual sacrifices acceptable to God
through Jesus Christ.[e] 6For in Scripture it
says:

"See, I lay a stone in Zion,
a chosen and precious cornerstone,[f]
and the one who trusts in him
will never be put to shame."[a][g]

7Now to you who believe, this stone is precious. But to those who do not believe,[h]

"The stone the builders rejected[i]
has become the capstone,[b]"[c][j]

8and,

"A stone that causes men to stumble
and a rock that makes them fall."[d][k]

They stumble because they disobey the
message—which is also what they were
destined for.[l]
9But you are a chosen people,[m] a royal
priesthood,[n] a holy nation,[o] a people belonging to God,[p] that you may declare the
praises of him who called you out of darkness into his wonderful light.[q] 10Once you
were not a people, but now you are the
people of God;[r] once you had not received
mercy, but now you have received mercy.
11Dear friends,[s] I urge you, as aliens
and strangers in the world,[t] to abstain
from sinful desires,[u] which war against
your soul.[v] 12Live such good lives among
the pagans that, though they accuse you
of doing wrong, they may see your good
deeds[w] and glorify God[x] on the day he visits us.

[a] 6 Isaiah 28:16 [b] 7 Or *cornerstone*
[c] 7 Psalm 118:22 [d] 8 Isaiah 8:14

2:1 [v]S Jas 4:11 **2:2** [w]1Co 3:2; Heb 5:12,13 [x]Eph 4:15,16 **2:3** [y]Ps 34:8; Heb 6:5 **2:4** [z]ver 7 [a]Isa 42:1 **2:5** [b]Pr 9:1; 1Co 3:9; Eph 2:20-22 [c]1Ti 3:15 [d]ver 9; Ex 19:6; Isa 61:6; Rev 1:6; 5:10; 20:6 [e]Php 4:18; Heb 13:15 **2:6** [f]Eph 2:20 [g]Isa 28:16; Ro 9:32,33; 10:11 **2:7** [h]2Co 2:16 [i]ver 4 [j]Ps 118:22; S Ac 4:11 **2:8** [k]Isa 8:14; S Lk 2:34 [l]Ro 9:22 **2:9** [m]Dt 10:15; 1Sa 12:22 [n]ver 5 [o]Ex 19:6; Dt 7:6; Isa 62:12 [p]S Tit 2:14 [q]S Ac 26:18 **2:10** [r]Hos 1:9,10; 2:23; Ro 9:25,26 **2:11** [s]S 1Co 10:14 [t]S Heb 11:13 [u]Ro 13:14; Gal 5:16 [v]Jas 4:1 **2:12** [w]Php 2:15; Tit 2:8; S Tit 2:14; 1Pe 3:16 [x]S Mt 9:8

2:2 *crave.* The unrestrained hunger of a healthy baby provides an example of the kind of eager desire for spiritual food that ought to mark the believer. *spiritual milk.* Probably referring to God's word (1:23,25). The author is speaking figuratively. Milk is not to be understood here as in 1Co 3:2; Heb 5:12–14—in unfavorable contrast to solid food—but as an appropriate nourishment for babies. *grow up.* The Greek for this phrase is the standard term for the desirable growth of children (cf. 2Pe 3:18).
2:3 *have tasted.* The tense of the Greek verb used here suggests that an initial act of tasting is referred to. Since this taste has proved satisfactory, the believers are urged to long for additional spiritual food.
2:4 *living Stone.* Christ (see vv. 6–8 and NIV text notes; cf. Mt 21:42; Mk 12:10–11; Lk 20:17; Ac 4:11; Ro 9:33). The Stone is living in that it is personal. Furthermore he is a life-giving Stone. Christ as the Son of God has life in himself (see Jn 1:4; 5:26 and notes). See also "living water" (Jn 4:10–14 [see note on 4:10]; 7:38), "living bread" (Jn 6:51 [see note on 6:35]) and "living way" (Heb 10:20). *rejected by men but chosen by God.* Peter repeatedly makes a contrast in Acts between the hostility of unbelievers toward Jesus and God's exaltation of him (Ac 2:22–36; 3:13–15; 4:10–11; 10:39–42).
2:5 *living stones.* Believers derive their life from Christ, who is the original living Stone, the "life-giving spirit" (1Co 15:45) to whom they have come (v. 4). These references to stones may reflect Jesus' words to Peter in Mt 16:18 (see note there). *spiritual house.* The house is spiritual in a metaphorical sense, but also in that it is formed and indwelt by the Spirit of God. Every stone in the house has been made alive by the Holy Spirit, sent by the exalted living Stone, Jesus Christ (cf. Ac 2:33). The OT temple provides the background of this passage (cf. Jn 2:19; 1Co 3:16; Eph 2:19–22 and notes). *holy priesthood.* The whole body of believers. As priests, believers are to (1) reflect the holiness of God and that of their high priest (see 1:15; Heb 7:26; 10:10 and note on 10:10,14), (2) offer spiritual sacrifices (here), (3) intercede for others before God and (4) represent God before them. *spiritual sacrifices.* The NT refers to a variety of offerings: bodies offered to God (Ro 12:1), offerings of money or material goods (Php 4:18; Heb 13:16), sacrifices of praise to God (Heb 13:15) and sacrifices of doing good (Heb 13:16). *acceptable to God.* Through the work of our Mediator, Jesus Christ (cf. Jn 14:6). Believers are living stones that make up a spiritual temple in which, as a holy priesthood, they offer up spiritual sacrifices.
2:6 *precious cornerstone.* See Ps 118:22 and note; Mt 21:42; Mk 12:10; Lk 20:17; Ac 4:11 and note. This is an obvious reference to Christ, as vv. 6b–8 make clear. The cornerstone, which determined the design and orientation of the building, was the most significant stone in the structure. The picture that Peter creates is of a structure made up of believers (living stones, v. 5), the design and orientation of which are all in keeping with Christ, the cornerstone. *the one who trusts in him.* Two attitudes toward the cornerstone are evident: (1) Some trust in him; (2) others reject him (v. 7) and, as a result, stumble and fall (v. 8).
2:8 *what they were destined for.* Some see here an indication that some people are destined to fall and be lost. Others say that unbelievers are destined to be lost because God in his foreknowledge (cf. 1:2 and note) saw them as unbelievers. Still others hold that Peter means that unbelief is destined to result in eternal destruction.
2:9 *chosen people.* See Eph 1:4 and note; Isa 43:10,20; 44:1–2. As Israel was called God's chosen people in the OT, so in the NT believers are designated as chosen, or elect. *royal priesthood.* See notes on v. 5; Ex 19:6; cf. Isa 61:6. *holy nation.* Cf. Dt 28:9. *people belonging to God.* See Ex 19:5 and note. Though once not the people of God, they are now the recipients of God's mercy (cf. Hos 1:6–10 and note on 1:10; Ro 9:25–26 and note; 10:19). *declare the praises of him.* See Isa 43:21; Ac 2:11.
2:10 See notes on Hos 1:6,9; 2:1,22; Ro 9:25–26. In Hosea it is Israel who is not God's people; in Romans it is the Gentiles to whom Paul applies Hosea's words; in 1 Peter the words are applied to both.
2:11 *aliens and strangers.* See note on 1:1. As aliens and strangers on earth, whose citizenship is in heaven, they are to be separated from the corruption of the world, not yielding to its destructive sinful desires.
2:12 *see your good deeds.* Deeds that can be seen to be good

Submission to Rulers and Masters

[13]Submit yourselves for the Lord's sake to every authority[y] instituted among men: whether to the king, as the supreme authority, [14]or to governors, who are sent by him to punish those who do wrong[z] and to commend those who do right.[a] [15]For it is God's will[b] that by doing good you should silence the ignorant talk of foolish men.[c] [16]Live as free men,[d] but do not use your freedom as a cover-up for evil;[e] live as servants of God.[f] [17]Show proper respect to everyone: Love the brotherhood of believers,[g] fear God, honor the king.[h]

[18]Slaves, submit yourselves to your masters with all respect,[i] not only to those who are good and considerate,[j] but also to those who are harsh. [19]For it is commendable if a man bears up under the pain of unjust suffering because he is conscious of God.[k] [20]But how is it to your credit if you receive a beating for doing wrong and endure it? But if you suffer for doing good and you endure it, this is commendable before God.[l] [21]To this[m] you were called,[n] because Christ suffered for you,[o] leaving you an example,[p] that you should follow in his steps.

> [22]"He committed no sin,[q]
> and no deceit was found in his
> mouth."[a][r]

[23]When they hurled their insults at him,[s] he did not retaliate; when he suffered, he made no threats.[t] Instead, he entrusted himself[u] to him who judges justly.[v] [24]He himself bore our sins[w] in his body on the tree,[x] so that we might die to sins[y] and live for righteousness; by his wounds you have been healed.[z] [25]For you were like sheep going astray,[a] but now you have returned to the Shepherd[b] and Overseer of your souls.[c]

2:13 [y]Ro 13:1; Tit 3:1 **2:14** [z]Ro 13:4 [a]Ro 13:3 **2:15** [b]1Pe 3:17; 4:19 [c]S ver 12 **2:16** [d]S Jn 8:32 [e]Gal 5:13 [f]S Ro 6:22 **2:17** [g]S Ro 12:10 [h]Pr 24:21; Ro 13:7 **2:18** [i]S Eph 6:5 [j]Jas 3:17 **2:19** [k]1Pe 3:14, 17 **2:20** [l]1Pe 3:17 **2:21** [m]S Ac 14:22; Php 1:29; 1Pe 3:9 [n]S Ro 8:28 [o]1Pe 3:18; 4:1, 13 [p]S Mt 11:29; 16:24 **2:22** [q]S 2Co 5:21 [r]Isa 53:9 **2:23** [s]Heb 12:3; 1Pe 3:9 [t]Isa 53:7 [u]Lk 23:46 [v]Ps 9:4 **2:24** [w]Isa 53:4, 11; Heb 9:28 [x]S Ac 5:30 [y]S Ro 6:2 [z]Dt 32:39; Ps 103:3; Isa 53:5; Heb 12:13; Jas 5:16 **2:25** [a]Isa 53:6 [b]S Jn 10:11 [c]Job 10:12

[a] *22* Isaiah 53:9

(cf. Mt 5:16). The Greek word translated "see" refers to a careful watching, over a period of time. The pagans' evaluation is not a snap judgment. *the day he visits us.* Perhaps the day of judgment and ensuing punishment, or possibly the day when God visits a person with salvation. The believer's good life may then influence the unbeliever to repent and believe.

2:13—3:6 Peter urges that Christians submit to all legitimate authorities, whether or not the persons exercising authority are believers. The recognition of properly constituted authority is necessary for the greatest good of the largest number of people, and it is necessary to best fulfill the will of God in the world.

2:13 *every authority instituted among men.* Such authority depends on God for its existence (see Ro 13:1–2 and note on 13:1). Indirectly, when people disobey a human ruler they disobey God, who ordained the system of human government (cf. Ro 13:2). *king.* When Peter wrote, the emperor was the godless, brutal Nero, who ruled from A.D. 54 to 68 (see Introduction: Author and Date). Of course, obedience to the emperor must never be in violation of the law of God (to see this basic principle in action cf. Ac 4:19; 5:29).

2:15 *silence the ignorant talk.* Good citizenship counters false charges made against Christians and thus commends the gospel to unbelievers (cf. Tit 2:7–8).

2:16 *Live as free men.* Does not authorize rebellion against constituted authority, but urges believers freely to submit to God and to earthly authorities (as long as such submission does not conflict with the law of God). *as a cover-up for evil.* Genuine freedom is the freedom to serve God, a freedom exercised under law. Liberty is not license to do as we please.

2:17 *proper respect to everyone.* Because every human being bears the image of God. *fear God.* See note on 1:17.

2:18 *Slaves.* Household servants, whatever their particular training and functions. The context indicates that Peter is addressing Christian slaves. NT writers do not attack slavery as an institution (see note on Eph 6:5), but the NT contains the principles that ultimately uprooted slavery (see Phm 16). Peter's basic teachings on the subject may apply to employer-employee relations today (see Eph 6:5–8; Col 3:22–25; 1Ti 6:1–2; Tit 2:9–10).

2:19 *conscious of God.* As submission to duly constituted authority is "for the Lord's sake" (v. 13; cf. Eph 6:7–8), so one will submit to the point of suffering unjustly if it is God's will.

2:21 *To this you were called.* The patient endurance of injustice is part of God's plan for the Christian. It was an important feature of the true grace of God experienced by the readers (5:12). *Christ suffered for you.* Cf. Isa 52:13—53:12. Christ is the supreme example of suffering evil for doing good. His experience as the suffering Servant-Savior transforms the sufferings of his followers from misery into privilege (cf. Ac 5:41).

2:22 Scripture declares the sinlessness of Christ in the clearest of terms, allowing for no exception (see 1:19; Ac 3:14 and note; 2Co 5:21; Heb 4:15; 7:26; 1Jn 3:5). *no deceit.* Cf. v. 1; 3:10.

2:23 Prominent examples of our Lord's silent submission are found in Mt 27:12–14,34–44 (see also parallels in the other Gospels). *entrusted himself.* Cf. 4:19.

2:24 *bore our sins.* See Isa 53:12. Although dealing with the example set by Christ, Peter touches also on the redemptive work of Christ, which has significance far beyond that of setting an example. Peter here points to the substitutionary character of the atonement. Christ, like the sacrificial lamb of the OT, died for our sins, the innocent for the guilty (see Ro 5:6; 1Jn 2:2 and notes). *tree.* A figurative reference to the cross (see note on Ac 5:30; see also Ac 10:39; 13:29; Gal 3:13 and note). *that we might die to sins and live for righteousness.* Cf. Ro 6:3–14. Peter here highlights how the cross bears on our sanctification. As a result of Christ's death on the cross and believers' union with Christ in his death, they are "dead" to sin so that they may live new lives and present themselves to God as instruments of righteousness (see notes on Ro 6:11–13). *you have been healed.* See Isa 53:5 and note; not generally viewed as a reference to physical healing, though some believe that such healing was included in the atonement (cf. Isa 53:4 and note; Mt 8:16–17). Others see spiritual healing in this passage. It is another way of asserting that Christ's death brings salvation to those who trust in him.

2:25 *Shepherd.* A concept raised here in connection with the allusion to the wandering sheep of Isa 53. The sheep had wandered from their shepherd, and to their Shepherd (Christ) they have now returned. See note on Ps 23:1; see also Jn 10:11,14 and note on Heb 13:20. *Overseer.* Christ (cf. 5:2,4; Ac 20:28). Elders are to be both shepherds and overseers, i.e., they are to look out for the welfare of the flock. These are not two separate offices or functions; the second term is a further explanation of the first.

Wives and Husbands

3 Wives, in the same way be submissive[d] to your husbands[e] so that, if any
of them do not believe the word, they may
be won over[f] without words by the behavior of their wives, 2when they see the
purity and reverence of your lives. 3Your
beauty should not come from outward
adornment, such as braided hair and the
wearing of gold jewelry and fine clothes.[g]
4Instead, it should be that of your inner
self,[h] the unfading beauty of a gentle and
quiet spirit, which is of great worth in
God's sight.[i] 5For this is the way the holy
women of the past who put their hope in
God[j] used to make themselves beautiful.[k]
They were submissive to their own husbands, 6like Sarah, who obeyed Abraham
and called him her master.[l] You are her
daughters if you do what is right and do
not give way to fear.
7Husbands,[m] in the same way be considerate as you live with your wives, and
treat them with respect as the weaker partner and as heirs with you of the gracious
gift of life, so that nothing will hinder your
prayers.

Suffering for Doing Good

8Finally, all of you, live in harmony with
one another;[n] be sympathetic, love as
brothers,[o] be compassionate and humble.[p]
9Do not repay evil with evil[q] or insult with
insult,[r] but with blessing,[s] because to this[t]
you were called[u] so that you may inherit a
blessing.[v] 10For,

"Whoever would love life
and see good days
must keep his tongue from evil
and his lips from deceitful speech.
11He must turn from evil and do good;
he must seek peace and pursue it.
12For the eyes of the Lord are on the
righteous
and his ears are attentive to their
prayer,
but the face of the Lord is against
those who do evil."[a][w]

13Who is going to harm you if you
are eager to do good?[x] 14But even if you
should suffer for what is right, you are
blessed.[y] "Do not fear what they fear[b];
do not be frightened."[c][z] 15But in your
hearts set apart Christ as Lord. Always
be prepared to give an answer[a] to everyone who asks you to give the reason for
the hope[b] that you have. But do this with

3:1 [d] 1Pe 2:18 [e] S Eph 5:22 [f] 1Co 7:16; 9:19 3:3 [g] Isa 3:18-23; 1Ti 2:9 3:4 [h] Ro 7:22; Eph 3:16 [i] S Ro 2:29 3:5 [j] 1Ti 5:5 [k] Est 2:15 3:6 [l] Ge 18:12 3:7 [m] Eph 5:25-33; Col 3:19
3:8 [n] S Ro 15:5 [o] S Ro 12:10 [p] Eph 4:2; 1Pe 5:5 3:9 [q] Ro 12:17; 1Th 5:15 [r] 1Pe 2:23 [s] S Mt 5:44 [t] S 1Pe 2:21 [u] S Ro 8:28 [v] Heb 6:14 3:12 [w] Ps 34:12-16 3:13 [x] S Tit 2:14 3:14 [y] ver 17; 1Pe 2:19,20; 4:15,16 [z] Isa 8:12,13 3:15 [a] Col 4:6 [b] S Heb 3:6

[a] 12 Psalm 34:12-16 [b] 14 Or *not fear their threats* [c] 14 Isaiah 8:12

3:1–6 Instructions to wives (cf. Ge 3:16; 1Co 11:3 and notes; Eph 5:22–24 and note on 5:22; Col 3:18; 1Ti 2:9–10; Tit 2:5).

3:1 *in the same way.* As believers are to submit to government authorities (2:13–17), and as slaves are to submit to masters (2:18–25). *be submissive.* The same Greek verb as is used in 2:13,18, a term that calls for submission to a recognized authority. Inferiority is not implied by this passage. The submission is one of role or function necessary for the orderly operation of the home. *the word.* The gospel message. *without words.* Believing wives are not to rely on argumentation to win their unbelieving husbands, but on the quality of their lives. Actions speak louder than words.

3:2 *purity and reverence.* Their lives are to be marked by a moral purity that springs from reverence toward God.

3:3 *hair ... jewelry.* See 1Ti 2:9 and note; extreme coiffures and gaudy exhibits of jewelry. Christian women should not rely on such extremes of adornment for beauty. *clothes.* The Greek for this word simply means "garment," but in this context expensive garments are meant.

3:5 *holy women of the past.* The standards stated by Peter are not limited to any particular time or culture.

3:6 *called him her master.* An expression of the submission called for in v. 1 (see Ge 18:12). *her daughters ... fear.* Christian women become daughters of Sarah as they become like her in doing good and in not fearing any potential disaster, but trusting in God (cf. Pr 3:25–27; 31:10–31).

3:7 *weaker partner.* Not a reference to moral stamina, strength of character or mental capacity, but most likely to physical strength and social status. *heirs with you of the gracious gift of life.* Women experience the saving grace of God on equal terms with men (see Gal 3:28 and note). *hinder your prayers.* Spiritual fellowship, with God and with one another, may be hindered by disregarding God's instruction concerning husband-wife relationships.

3:8–12 In 2:11–17 Peter addressed all his readers, and in 2:18–25 he spoke directly to slaves; in 3:1–6 he addressed wives, and in 3:7 husbands. Now he encourages all his readers to develop virtues appropriate in their relations with others (see "all of you," v. 8).

3:8 *live in harmony.* See Ro 12:16; Php 2:2 and note. *be sympathetic.* See Ro 12:15; 1Co 12:26 and notes. *love as brothers.* See 1Th 4:9 and note; Heb 13:1. *be compassionate.* See Col 3:12. *humble.* See Php 2:6–8 and notes.

3:9 See 2:23; Ro 12:17–21 and notes.

3:10–12 Peter introduces this quotation from Ps 34 with the explanatory conjunction "For," showing that he views the quotation as giving reasons for obeying the exhortation of v. 9. According to the psalmist, (1) those who do such things will find life to be most gratifying (v. 10), (2) their days will be blessed with good things (v. 10), (3) God's eyes will ever be on them to bless them (v. 12), and (4) God's ears will be ready to hear their prayer (v. 12).

3:12 *face of the Lord.* See Ps 13:1 and note.

3:13 *Who ... harm you ... ?* As a general rule, people are not harmed for acts of kindness. This is especially true if one is an enthusiast ("eager") for doing good.

3:14 *even if you should suffer.* In the Greek, this conditional clause is the furthest removed from stating a reality. Suffering for righteousness is a remote possibility, but even if it does occur, it brings special blessing to the sufferer (see Mt 5:10–12). *what they fear.* See NIV text note. In Isaiah's context God's people are not to view things as unbelievers do. They are not to make worldly judgments or be afraid of the enemies of God. Instead, they are to fear God (see Isa 8:13).

3:15 *set apart Christ as Lord.* An exhortation to the readers to make an inner commitment to Christ (cf. Ro 10:9 and note). Then they need not be speechless when called on to defend their faith. Instead, there will be a readiness to answer. *Always be prepared to give an answer.* At the very least, this requires a knowledge of God's word. *hope.* See Ro 5:5 and

gentleness and respect, 16keeping a clear
conscience,[c] so that those who speak maliciously against your good behavior in
Christ may be ashamed of their slander.[d]
17It is better, if it is God's will,[e] to suffer
for doing good[f] than for doing evil. 18For
Christ died for sins[g] once for all,[h] the righteous for the unrighteous, to bring you to
God.[i] He was put to death in the body[j]
but made alive by the Spirit,[k] 19through
whom[a] also he went and preached to the
spirits in prison[l] 20who disobeyed long
ago when God waited patiently[m] in the
days of Noah while the ark was being
built.[n] In it only a few people, eight in
all,[o] were saved[p] through water, 21and this
water symbolizes baptism that now saves
you[q] also—not the removal of dirt from
the body but the pledge[b] of a good conscience[r] toward God. It saves you by the
resurrection of Jesus Christ,[s] 22who has
gone into heaven[t] and is at God's right
hand[u]—with angels, authorities and powers in submission to him.[v]

Living for God

4 Therefore, since Christ suffered in his
body,[w] arm yourselves also with the
same attitude, because he who has suffered in his body is done with sin.[x] 2As
a result, he does not live the rest of his
earthly life for evil human desires,[y] but
rather for the will of God. 3For you have
spent enough time in the past[z] doing what

[a] 18,19 Or *alive in the spirit, 19through which*
[b] 21 Or *response*

3:16 [c]ver 21; S Ac 23:1 [d]1Pe 2:12,15 **3:17** [e]1Pe 2:15; 4:19 [f]1Pe 2:20; 4:15,16 **3:18** [g]1Pe 2:21; 4:1,13 [h]S Heb 7:27 [i]S Ro 5:2 [j]Col 1:22; 1Pe 4:1 [k]1Pe 4:6 **3:19** [l]1Pe 4:6 **3:20** [m]S Ro 2:4 [n]Ge 6:3,5,13,14 [o]Ge 8:18 [p]Heb 11:7 **3:21** [q]S Ac 22:16 [r]ver 16; S Ac 23:1 [s]1Pe 1:3 **3:22** [t]S Heb 4:14 [u]S Mk 16:19 [v]S Mt 28:18; S Ro 8:38 **4:1** [w]S 1Pe 2:21 [x]S Ro 6:18 **4:2** [y]Ro 6:2; 1Pe 1:14 **4:3** [z]S Eph 2:2

note. *with gentleness and respect.* A Christian should always be gracious and considerate, even when opposed by unbelievers. Our apologetic ("answer") is always to be given with love, never in degrading terms.

3:16 *ashamed of their slander.* Because it is shown to be obviously untrue and because the believer's loving attitude puts the opponent's bitterness in a bad light.

3:18 *once for all.* See Heb 9:28. *the righteous for the unrighteous.* Peter, like Paul in Php 2:5–11, refers to Jesus as an example of the type of conduct that should characterize the Christian. We are to be ready to suffer for doing good (vv. 13–14,17). The thought of Christ's suffering and death, however, leads Peter to comment on what occurred after Christ's death—which leads to tangential remarks about preaching to the spirits in prison and about baptism (see vv. 19–21). *made alive by the Spirit.* Referring to the resurrection. Elsewhere the resurrection is attributed to the Father (Ac 2:32; Gal 1:1; Eph 1:20) and to the Son (Jn 10:17–18). If the NIV text note is correct, the reference would be to Christ's own spirit, through which also "he preached to the spirits in prison" (v. 19).

3:19–20a Three main interpretations of this passage have been suggested: (1) Some hold that in his preincarnate state Christ went and preached through Noah to the wicked generation of that time. (2) Others argue that between his death and resurrection Christ went to the prison where fallen angels are incarcerated and there preached to the angels who are said to have left their proper state and married human women during Noah's time (cf. Ge 6:1–4; 2Pe 2:4; Jude 6). The "sons of God" in Ge 6:2,4 are said to have been angels, as they are in Job 1:6; 2:1 (see NIV text note). The message he preached to these evil angels was probably a declaration of victory. (3) Still others say that between death and resurrection Christ went to the place of the dead and preached to the spirits of Noah's wicked contemporaries. What he proclaimed may have been the gospel, or it may have been a declaration of victory for Christ and doom for his hearers.

The weakness of the first view is that it does not relate the event to Christ's death and resurrection, as the context seems to do. The main problem with the second view is that it assumes sexual relations between angels and women, and such physical relations may not be possible for angels since they are spirits (see note on Ge 6:2). A major difficulty with the third view is that the term "spirits" is only used of human beings when qualifying terms are added. Otherwise the term seems restricted to supernatural beings.

Perhaps a more satisfactory view would be to translate: "And in that [resurrection] state, by means of (his) ascension [see v. 22, where the same verb form is used of Christ's ascension] he made proclamation to the spirits in prison." The latter phrase most likely refers to the disobedient spirits ("angels, authorities and powers," v. 22). Thus Christ's ascension "into heaven" (v. 22) was itself a victory proclamation to them (cf. Eph 3:10 and note).

3:21 *water symbolizes baptism.* There is a double figure here. The flood symbolizes baptism, and baptism symbolizes salvation. The flood was a figure of baptism in that in both instances the water that spoke of judgment (in the flood the death of the wicked, in baptism the death of Christ and the believer) is the water that saves. Baptism is a symbol of salvation in that it depicts Christ's death, burial and resurrection and our identification with him in these experiences (see Ro 6:4). *now saves you also.* In reality, believers are saved by what baptism symbolizes—Christ's death and resurrection. The symbol and the reality are so closely related that the symbol is sometimes used to refer to the reality (see note on Ro 6:3–4). *pledge of a good conscience toward God.* The act of baptism is a commitment on the part of believers in all good conscience to make sure that what baptism symbolizes will become a reality in their lives. *saves you by the resurrection of Jesus Christ.* In the final analysis people are saved not by any ritual, but by the supernatural power of the resurrection.

3:22 *gone into heaven.* See Ac 1:9–11. *at God's right hand.* See Heb 1:3 and note; 12:2. *angels, authorities and powers.* See vv. 19–20a; Eph 1:21; 6:12 and notes.

4:1 *Therefore.* Since 3:19–22 is parenthetical, 4:1 ties directly back to 3:18. The aspect of Christ's suffering that these passages stress is suffering unjustly because one has done good. Furthermore, it is physical suffering—"in his body." *arm yourselves also with the same attitude.* Believers are to be prepared also to suffer unjustly, and to face such abuse with Christ's attitude—with his willingness to suffer for doing good. (For a similar principle in Paul's writings see Php 2:5–11.) *because ... is done with sin.* Such suffering enables believers to straighten out their priorities. Sinful desires and practices that once seemed important now seem insignificant when one's life is in jeopardy. Serious suffering for Christ advances the progress of sanctification.

4:2 *for evil human desires ... for the will of God.* Now that Christ's attitude prevails, God's will is the determining factor in life.

4:3 *time in the past.* The time before conversion (see Eph 2:1–3 and note on 2:1). *pagans.* Lit. "the Gentiles." Along with the term "idolatry," this suggests that at least some of the readers were Gentiles (see note on 1:1) who had been converted from a pagan lifestyle.

pagans choose to do—living in debauchery, lust, drunkenness, orgies, carousing
and detestable idolatry.[a] 4They think it
strange that you do not plunge with them
into the same flood of dissipation, and
they heap abuse on you.[b] 5But they will
have to give account to him who is ready
to judge the living and the dead.[c] 6For this
is the reason the gospel was preached
even to those who are now dead,[d] so that
they might be judged according to men in
regard to the body, but live according to
God in regard to the spirit.
7The end of all things is near.[e] Therefore
be clear minded and self-controlled[f] so that
you can pray. 8Above all, love each other
deeply,[g] because love covers over a multitude of sins.[h] 9Offer hospitality[i] to one
another without grumbling.[j] 10Each one
should use whatever gift he has received
to serve others,[k] faithfully[l] administering
God's grace in its various forms. 11If anyone speaks, he should do it as one speaking the very words of God.[m] If anyone
serves, he should do it with the strength
God provides,[n] so that in all things God
may be praised[o] through Jesus Christ. To
him be the glory and the power for ever
and ever. Amen.[p]

4:3 [a]S Ro 13:13 **4:4** [b]1Pe 3:16 **4:5** [c]S Ac 10:42 **4:6** [d]1Pe 3:19 **4:7** [e]S Ro 13:11 [f]S Ac 24:25 **4:8** [g]S 1Pe 1:22 [h]Pr 10:12; Jas 5:20 **4:9** [i]S Ro 12:13 [j]Php 2:14 **4:10** [k]Ro 12:6,7 [l]1Co 4:2 **4:11** [m]1Th 2:4 [n]Eph 6:10 [o]1Co 10:31 [p]S Ro 11:36

Suffering for Being a Christian

12Dear friends, do not be surprised at the
painful trial you are suffering,[q] as though
something strange were happening to you.
13But rejoice[r] that you participate in the
sufferings of Christ,[s] so that you may be
overjoyed when his glory is revealed.[t] 14If
you are insulted because of the name of
Christ,[u] you are blessed,[v] for the Spirit of
glory and of God rests on you. 15If you suffer, it should not be as a murderer or thief
or any other kind of criminal, or even as
a meddler. 16However, if you suffer as a
Christian, do not be ashamed, but praise
God that you bear that name.[w] 17For it is
time for judgment to begin with the family
of God;[x] and if it begins with us, what will
the outcome be for those who do not obey
the gospel of God?[y] 18And,

"If it is hard for the righteous to be
saved,
what will become of the ungodly
and the sinner?"[a][z]

19So then, those who suffer according
to God's will[a] should commit themselves
to their faithful Creator and continue to
do good.

4:12 [q]1Pe 1:6,7 **4:13** [r]S Mt 5:12 [s]S 2Co 1:5 [t]Ro 8:17; 1Pe 1:7; 5:1 **4:14** [u]S Jn 15:21 [v]Mt 5:11 **4:16** [w]Ac 5:41 **4:17** [x]Jer 25:29; Eze 9:6; Am 3:2; 1Ti 3:15 [y]2Th 1:8 **4:18** [z]Pr 11:31; Lk 23:31 **4:19** [a]1Pe 2:15; 3:17

[a] *18* Prov. 11:31

4:4 *They think it strange ... and they heap abuse on you.* Godly living can bring persecution (see 2Ti 3:12 and note).

4:5 *have to give account.* See Mt 12:36; Ac 17:31; Ro 2:5 and note, 16. *him who is ready to judge.* In the NT both the Father and the Son are said to be judge on the great, final judgment day. The Father is the ultimate source of judgment, but he will delegate judgment to the Son (cf. Jn 5:27; Ac 17:31 and notes). *the living and the dead.* Those alive and those dead when the final judgment day dawns.

4:6 *For this is the reason.* The reason referred to is expressed in the latter part of the verse (in the "so that" clause), not in the preceding verse. *was preached even to those who are now dead.* This preaching was a past event. The word "now" does not occur in the Greek, but it is necessary to make it clear that the preaching was done not after these people had died, but while they were still alive. (There will be no opportunity for people to be saved after death; see Heb 9:27.) *that they might be judged according to men in regard to the body.* The first reason that the gospel was preached to those now dead. Some say that this judgment is that to which all people must submit, either in this life (see Jn 5:24) or in the life to come (see v. 5). The gospel is preached to people in this life so that in Christ's death they may receive judgment now and avoid judgment to come. Others hold that these people are judged according to human standards by the pagan world, which does not understand why God's people no longer follow its sinful way of life (see vv. 2–4). So also the world misunderstood Christ (see Ac 2:22–24,36; 3:13–15; 5:30–32; 7:51–53). *but live according to God in regard to the spirit.* The second reason that the gospel was preached to those now dead. Some believe this means that all gospel preaching has as its goal that the hearers may live as God lives—eternally—and that this life is given by the Holy Spirit. Others maintain that it means that the ultimate reason for the preaching of the gospel is that God's people, even though the wicked world may abuse them and put them to death, will have eternal life, which the Holy Spirit imparts.

4:7 *The end ... is near.* See note on Jas 5:9. *Therefore.* Anticipating the end times, particularly Christ's return, should influence believers' attitudes, actions and relationships (see 2Pe 3:11–14 and notes). *clear minded.* Christians are to be characterized by reason; are to make wise, mature decisions; and are to have a clearly defined, decisive purpose in life. *self-controlled.* See Gal 5:23. *so that you can pray.* Cf. 3:7 and note; 1Co 7:5.

4:8 *love each other deeply.* See 1Th 4:9; 2Pe 1:7 and notes; 1Jn 4:7–11. *love covers over ... sins.* See Jas 5:20 and note. Love forgives again and again (see Mt 18:21–22 and note on 18:22; 1Co 13:5; Eph 4:32 and note).

4:9 *Offer hospitality.* See Ro 12:13 and note; 1Ti 3:2; 5:10; Tit 1:8; Heb 13:2 and note; 3Jn 5–8.

4:10 *use whatever gift he has received.* See Ro 12:4–8; 1Co 12:7–11 and notes.

4:11 *very words.* The Greek for this phrase is used to refer to the Scriptures or to words God has spoken (see Ac 7:38; Ro 3:2 and note). *To him be the glory.* See 1Co 1:26–31 and note; Jude 24–25.

4:12 *do not be surprised at the painful trial.* See 1:6–7 and note on 1:7; 2:20–21 and note on 2:21.

4:13 *rejoice that you participate in the sufferings of Christ.* See Col 1:24 and note. Peter once rebelled against the idea that Christ would suffer (see Mt 16:21–23).

4:14 *insulted because of the name of Christ.* See Mt 5:11–12; Jn 15:18–20; Ac 5:41; 14:22; Ro 8:17 and note; 2Co 1:5; Php 3:10 and note; 2Ti 3:12 and note.

4:16 *Christian.* See note on Ac 11:26.

4:17 *judgment to begin with the family of God.* The persecutions that believers were undergoing were divinely sent judgment intended to purify God's people. *the outcome ... for those who do not obey the gospel.* If God brings judgment on his own people, how much more serious will the judgment be that he will bring on unbelievers!

To Elders and Young Men

5 To the elders among you, I appeal as
a fellow elder,[b] a witness[c] of Christ's
sufferings and one who also will share in
the glory to be revealed:[d] 2Be shepherds of
God's flock[e] that is under your care, serving as overseers — not because you must,
but because you are willing, as God wants
you to be;[f] not greedy for money,[g] but eager to serve; 3not lording it over[h] those entrusted to you, but being examples[i] to the
flock. 4And when the Chief Shepherd[j] appears, you will receive the crown of glory[k]
that will never fade away.[l]

5Young men, in the same way be submissive[m] to those who are older. All of
you, clothe yourselves with humility[n] toward one another, because,

"God opposes the proud
but gives grace to the humble."[a][o]

6Humble yourselves, therefore, under
God's mighty hand, that he may lift you
up in due time.[p] 7Cast all your anxiety on
him[q] because he cares for you.[r]

8Be self-controlled[s] and alert. Your enemy the devil prowls around[t] like a roaring lion[u] looking for someone to devour.
9Resist him,[v] standing firm in the faith,[w]
because you know that your brothers
throughout the world are undergoing the
same kind of sufferings.[x]

10And the God of all grace, who called
you[y] to his eternal glory[z] in Christ, after
you have suffered a little while,[a] will himself restore you and make you strong,[b]
firm and steadfast. 11To him be the power
for ever and ever. Amen.[c]

Final Greetings

12With the help of Silas,[b][d] whom I regard as a faithful brother, I have written
to you briefly,[e] encouraging you and testifying that this is the true grace of God.
Stand fast in it.[f]

13She who is in Babylon, chosen together with you, sends you her greetings, and
so does my son Mark.[g] 14Greet one another with a kiss of love.[h]

Peace[i] to all of you who are in Christ.

5:1 [b] S Ac 11:30 [c] S Lk 24:48 [d] 1Pe 1:5,7; 4:13; Rev 1:9 **5:2** [e] S Jn 21:16 [f] 2Co 9:7; Phm 14 [g] S 1Ti 3:3 **5:3** [h] Eze 34:4; Mt 20:25-28 [i] S 1Ti 4:12 **5:4** [j] S Jn 10:11 [k] S 1Co 9:25 [l] 1Pe 1:4 **5:5** [m] Eph 5:21 [n] 1Pe 3:8 [o] Pr 3:34; S Mt 23:12 **5:6** [p] Job 5:11; Jas 4:10 **5:7** [q] Ps 37:5; Mt 6:25 [r] Ps 55:22; Heb 13:5 **5:8** [s] S Ac 24:25 [t] Job 1:7 [u] 2Ti 4:17 **5:9** [v] S Jas 4:7 [w] Col 2:5 [x] S Ac 14:22 **5:10** [y] S Ro 8:28 [z] 2Co 4:17; 2Ti 2:10 [a] 1Pe 1:6 [b] Ps 18:32; 2Th 2:17 **5:11** [c] S Ro 11:36 **5:12** [d] S Ac 15:22 [e] Heb 13:22 [f] S 1Co 16:13 **5:13** [g] S Ac 12:12 **5:14** [h] S Ro 16:16 [i] S Eph 6:23

[a] 5 Prov. 3:34 [b] 12 Greek *Silvanus,* a variant of *Silas*

5:1 *fellow elder.* See notes on Ex 3:16; 2Sa 3:17; Ac 20:17; 1Ti 3:1; 5:17. Peter, who identified himself as an apostle at the beginning of his letter (1:1), chooses now to identify himself with the elders of the churches (cf. 2Jn 1; 3Jn 1). This would be heartening to them in light of their great responsibilities and the difficult situation faced by the churches. *witness of Christ's sufferings.* Peter had been with Jesus from the early days of his ministry and was a witness of all its phases and aspects, including the climactic events of his suffering (cf. Mt 26:58; Mk 14:54; Lk 22:60–62; Jn 18:10–11,15–16). In this letter he bears notable witness to Christ's sufferings (see 2:21–24) and obeys his command in Ac 1:8. *share in the glory to be revealed.* See Ro 8:18. Peter witnessed Christ's glory in his ministry in general (see Jn 1:14; 2:11), and, as one present at the transfiguration (see 2Pe 1:16 and note; Mt 16:27; 17:8), he had already seen the glory of Christ's coming kingdom. In God's appointed time, just as Christ suffered and entered into glory, so all his people, after their sufferings, will participate in his future glory (see vv. 4,10).

5:2 *Be shepherds of God's flock.* A metaphor that our Lord himself had employed (Jn 10:1–18; Lk 15:3–7) and that must have been etched on Peter's mind (see Jn 21:15–17; cf. 1Pe 2:25). Peter is fulfilling Christ's command to feed his sheep as he writes this letter. What he writes to the elders is reminiscent of Paul's farewell address to the Ephesian elders (especially Ac 20:28; see note there). The term "shepherd" is an OT metaphor as well (see Eze 34:1–10, where the Lord holds the leaders of Israel responsible for failing to care for the flock). *serving as overseers.* The same term is used in Ac 20:28; Php 1:1; 1Ti 3:2; Tit 1:7. See note on 1Ti 3:1. It is clear from this passage, as well as from Ac 20:17,28, that the three terms "elder," "overseer" and "shepherd" (pastor) all apply to one office (see note on Tit 1:7).

5:3 *not lording it over those entrusted to you.* Cf. Mt 16:24–27; Mk 10:42–45; Php 2:6–11; 2Th 3:9. Although Peter has full apostolic authority (see v. 1), he does not lord it over his readers in this letter, but exemplifies the virtues he recommends.

5:4 *Chief Shepherd.* Christ. When he returns, he will reward those who have served as shepherds under him. *never fade away.* See 1:4 and note.

5:5 *be submissive.* The theme that runs throughout 2:13—3:6. *those who are older.* Or "those who hold the office of elder" (see v. 1 and note). *clothe yourselves with humility toward one another.* Peter may have had in mind the footwashing scene that is reported in Jn 13, in which he figured prominently. Although he was at first rebellious, he writes now with understanding (see Jn 13:7). *clothe ... with.* See note on Ps 109:29.

5:6 See Lk 14:11 and note. *lift you up in due time.* His help will come at just the right time (cf. Heb 4:16 and note).

5:7 See Php 4:6–7 and notes; cf. Ps 55:22.

5:8 *Be self-controlled.* See Gal 5:23; 1Th 5:6,8. *alert.* Perhaps Peter remembered his own difficulty in keeping awake during our Lord's agony in Gethsemane (see Mt 26:36–46). *devil.* See 2Co 4:4; 1Jn 3:8 and notes.

5:9 *Resist him.* See Jas 4:7 and note. *your brothers.* See note on Ac 11:1. They are not isolated; they belong to a fellowship of suffering.

5:10,12,14 *grace ... grace ... Peace.* See note on Ro 1:7.

5:10 *God of all grace.* Cf. 1:10,13 and notes.

5:12 *With the help of Silas.* Silas may have been the bearer of the letter to its destination. He may also have been a scribe who recorded what Peter dictated or who aided, as an informed and intelligent secretary, in the phrasing of Peter's thoughts (see Introduction: Author and Date). *encouraging ... grace of God.* See Introduction: Themes.

5:13 *She.* Perhaps a Christian congregation (see 2Jn 1 and note. *Babylon.* See Introduction: Place of Writing. *chosen.* See note on Eph 1:4. *my son Mark.* Peter regards Mark with such warmth and affection that he calls him his son. It is possible that Peter had led Mark to Christ (cf. 1Ti 1:2 and note). Early Christian tradition closely associates Mark and Peter (see Introduction to Mark: Author).

5:14 *kiss.* See note on 1Co 16:20. *Peace to all ... in Christ.* Spiritual well-being and blessedness to all who are united to Christ. Peter thus ends with a reference to the union of believers with Christ (see note on Eph 1:1), a concept fundamental to the understanding of the whole letter.

2 Peter

INTRODUCTION

Author

The author identifies himself as Simon Peter (1:1). He uses the first person singular pronoun in a highly personal passage (1:12–15) and claims to be an eyewitness of the transfiguration (1:16–18 [see note on 1:16]; cf. Mt 17:1–5). He asserts that this is his second letter to the readers (3:1) and refers to Paul as "our dear brother" (3:15; see note there). In short, the letter claims to be Peter's, and its character is compatible with that claim.

Although 2 Peter was not as widely known and recognized in the early church as 1 Peter, some may have used and accepted it as authoritative as early as the second century and perhaps even in the latter part of the first century (1 Clement [A.D. 95] may allude to it). It was not ascribed to Peter until Origen's time (185–253), and he seems to reflect some doubt concerning it. Eusebius (265–340) placed it among the questioned books, though he admits that most accept it as from Peter. After Eusebius's time, it seems to have been quite generally accepted as canonical.

> **A Quick Look**
>
> **Author:**
> The apostle Peter
>
> **Audience:**
> Peter writes to Christians in western Asia Minor.
>
> **Date:**
> Between A.D. 65 and 68
>
> **Theme:**
> Peter teaches how to deal with false teachers and evildoers who have come into the church.

In recent centuries, however, its genuineness has been challenged by a considerable number of interpreters. One of the objections that has been raised is the difference in style from that of 1 Peter. But that difference is not great as some have claimed; there are noteworthy similarities in vocabulary and in other matters. In fact, no other known writing is as much like 1 Peter as 2 Peter. The differences that do exist may be accounted for by variations in subject matter, in the form and purpose of the letters, in the time and circumstances of writing, in sources used or models followed, and in scribes who may have been employed. Perhaps most significant is the statement in 1Pe 5:12 that Silas assisted in the writing of 1 Peter. No such statement is made concerning 2 Peter, which may explain its noticeable difference in style (see Introduction to 1 Peter: Author and Date).

Other objections arise from a secular reconstruction of early Christian history or misconstruals of the available data. For example, some argue that the reference to Paul's letters in 3:15–16 indicates an advanced date for this book—beyond Peter's lifetime. But it is quite possible that Paul's letters were gathered at an early date, since some of them had been in existence and perhaps in circulation for more than ten years (Thessalonians by as much as 15 years) prior to Peter's death. Besides, what Peter says may only indicate that he was acquainted with some of Paul's letters (communication in the Roman world and in the early church was good), not that there was a formal, ecclesiastical collection of them.

Date

2 Peter was written toward the end of Peter's life (cf. 1:12–15), after he had written a prior letter (3:1) to the same readers (probably 1 Peter). Since Peter was martyred during the reign of Nero, his death must have occurred prior to A.D. 68; so it is very likely that he wrote 2 Peter between 65 and 68.

Some have argued that this date is too early for the writing of 2 Peter, but nothing in the book requires a later date. The error combated is comparable to the kind of heresy present in the first century. To insist that the second chapter was directed against second-century Gnosticism is to assume more than the contents of the chapter warrant. While the heretics referred to in 2 Peter may well have been among the forerunners of second-century Gnostics, nothing is said of them that would not fit into the later years of Peter's life.

Peter's purpose is to stimulate Christian growth, to combat false teaching and to encourage watchfulness for the Lord's certain return.

Some have suggested a later date because they interpret the reference to the fathers in 3:4 to mean an earlier Christian generation. However, the word is most naturally interpreted as the OT patriarchs (cf. Jn 6:31, "forefathers"; Ac 3:13; Heb 1:1). Similarly, reference to Paul and his letters (3:15–16; see Author) does not require a date beyond Peter's lifetime.

2 Peter and Jude

There are conspicuous similarities between 2 Peter and Jude (compare 2Pe 2 with Jude 4–18), but there are also significant differences. It has been suggested that one borrowed from the other or that they both drew on a common source. If there is borrowing, it is not a slavish borrowing but one that adapts to suit the writer's purpose. While many have insisted that Jude used Peter, it is more reasonable to assume that the longer letter (2 Peter) incorporated much of the shorter (Jude). Such borrowing is fairly common in ancient writings. For example, many believe that Paul used parts of early hymns in Php 2:6–11 and 1Ti 3:16.

Purpose

In his first letter Peter feeds Christ's sheep by instructing them how to deal with persecution from outside the church (see 1Pe 4:12); in this second letter he teaches them how to deal with false teachers and evildoers who have come into the church (see 2:1; 3:3–4 and notes). While the particular situations naturally call for variations in content and emphasis, in both letters Peter, as a pastor ("shepherd") of Christ's sheep (Jn 21:15–17), seeks to commend to his readers a wholesome combination of Christian faith and practice. More specifically, his purpose is threefold: (1) to stimulate Christian growth (ch. 1), (2) to combat false teaching (ch. 2) and (3) to encourage watchfulness in view of the Lord's certain return (ch. 3).

Outline

- I. Greetings (1:1–2)
- II. Exhortation to Growth in Christian Virtues (1:3–11)
  - A. The Divine Enablement (1:3–4)
  - B. The Call for Growth (1:5–7)
  - C. The Value of Such Growth (1:8–11)
- III. The Purpose and Authentication of Peter's Message (1:12–21)
  - A. His Aim in Writing (1:12–15)

- B. The Basis of His Authority (1:16 – 21)
- IV. Warning against False Teachers (ch. 2)
  - A. Their Coming Predicted (2:1 – 3a)
  - B. Their Judgment Assured (2:3b – 9)
  - C. Their Characteristics Set Forth (2:10 – 22)
- V. The Fact of Christ's Return (3:1 – 16)
  - A. Peter's Purpose in Writing Restated (3:1 – 2)
  - B. The Coming of Scoffers (3:3 – 7)
  - C. The Certainty of Christ's Return (3:8 – 10)
  - D. Exhortations Based on the Fact of Christ's Return (3:11 – 16)
- VI. Conclusion and Doxology (3:17 – 18)

1 Simon Peter, a servant[a] and apostle of
Jesus Christ,[b]

To those who through the righteousness[c] of our God and Savior Jesus Christ[d]
have received a faith as precious as ours:

2 Grace and peace be yours in abundance[e] through the knowledge of God and
of Jesus our Lord.[f]

Making One's Calling and Election Sure

3 His divine power[g] has given us everything we need for life and godliness
through our knowledge of him[h] who
called us[i] by his own glory and goodness. 4 Through these he has given us his
very great and precious promises,[j] so that
through them you may participate in the
divine nature[k] and escape the corruption
in the world caused by evil desires.[l]

5 For this very reason, make every effort to add to your faith goodness; and
to goodness, knowledge;[m] 6 and to knowledge, self-control;[n] and to self-control,
perseverance;[o] and to perseverance, godliness;[p] 7 and to godliness, brotherly kindness; and to brotherly kindness, love.[q] 8 For
if you possess these qualities in increasing
measure, they will keep you from being ineffective and unproductive[r] in your knowledge of our Lord Jesus Christ.[s] 9 But if anyone does not have them, he is nearsighted
and blind,[t] and has forgotten that he has
been cleansed from his past sins.[u]

10 Therefore, my brothers, be all the more
eager to make your calling[v] and election
sure. For if you do these things, you will
never fall,[w] 11 and you will receive a rich
welcome into the eternal kingdom[x] of our
Lord and Savior Jesus Christ.[y]

Prophecy of Scripture

12 So I will always remind you of these
things,[z] even though you know them and
are firmly established in the truth[a] you
now have. 13 I think it is right to refresh
your memory[b] as long as I live in the tent
of this body,[c] 14 because I know that I will
soon put it aside,[d] as our Lord Jesus Christ

1:1 [a] Ro 1:1 [b] 1Pe 1:1 [c] Ro 3:21-26 [d] Tit 2:13 **1:2** [e] S Ro 1:7 [f] ver 3,8; 2Pe 2:20; 3:18; S Php 3:8 **1:3** [g] 1Pe 1:5 [h] S ver 2 [i] S Ro 8:28 **1:4** [j] 2Co 7:1 [k] Eph 4:24; Heb 12:10; 1Jn 3:2 [l] Jas 1:27; 2Pe 2:18-20 **1:5** [m] S ver 2; Col 2:3 **1:6** [n] S Ac 24:25 [o] S Heb 10:36 [p] ver 3 **1:7** [q] S Ro 12:10; 1Th 3:12 **1:8** [r] Jn 15:2; Col 1:10; Tit 3:14 [s] S ver 2 **1:9** [t] 1Jn 2:11 [u] Eph 5:26; S Mt 1:21 **1:10** [v] S Ro 8:28 [w] Ps 15:5; 2Pe 3:17; Jude 24 **1:11** [x] Ps 145:13; 2Ti 4:18 [y] 2Pe 2:20; 3:18 **1:12** [z] Php 3:1; 1Jn 2:21; Jude 5 [a] 2Jn 2 **1:13** [b] 2Pe 3:1 [c] Isa 38:12; 2Co 5:1,4 **1:14** [d] 2Ti 4:6

1:1 *Simon Peter.* See Introduction to 1 Peter: Author and Date; see also notes on Mt 16:18; Jn 1:42. *servant.* See note on Ro 1:1. *apostle.* See notes on Mk 6:30; 1Co 1:1; Heb 3:1. *To those.* Probably the same people as those in 1Pe 1:1. *God and Savior Jesus Christ.* Assumes that Jesus is both God and Savior. For other passages that ascribe deity to Christ see note on Ro 9:5. *have received.* God in his justice ("righteousness") imparts to people the ability to believe. *a faith.* Not here a body of truth to be believed — the faith — but the act of believing, or the God-given capacity to trust in Christ for salvation.
1:2 *Grace and peace.* See note on Ro 1:7. *knowledge of God and of Jesus.* The concept of Christian knowledge is prominent in 2 Peter (see vv. 3 and note, 5,8; 3:18 and note). Peter was combating heretical teaching, and one of the best antidotes for heresy is true knowledge.
1:3 *everything we need for life and godliness.* God has made available all that we need spiritually through our knowledge of him. If 2 Peter was written to combat an incipient Gnosticism, the apostle may be insisting that the knowledge possessed by those in apostolic circles was entirely adequate to meet their spiritual needs. No secret, esoteric knowledge is necessary for salvation (see Introduction to 1 John: Gnosticism). *godliness.* A genuine reverence toward God that governs one's attitude toward every aspect of life (see 1Ti 2:2 and note on 2:1 – 2). *glory and goodness.* The excellence of God: "Glory" expresses the excellence of his being — his attributes and essence; "goodness" depicts excellence expressed in deeds — virtue in action. God uses both to bring about our salvation.
1:4 *Through these.* Through God's excellence — internal and external — he has given us great promises. Their nature is suggested in the words that follow: participation in the divine nature and escape from worldly corruption. *participate in the divine nature.* Does not indicate that Christians become divine in any sense, but only that we are indwelt by God through his Holy Spirit (see Jn 14:16 – 17 and notes). Our humanity and his deity, as well as the human personality and the divine, remain distinct and separate. *world.* See note on Jn 1:9. *evil desires.* See 2:10 and note.
1:5 – 9 The virtues that will produce a well-rounded, fruitful Christian life (see Gal 5:22 – 23 and note).
1:5 *faith.* The root of the Christian life (see v. 1 and note). *goodness.* Cf. v. 3 and note. *knowledge.* See notes on vv. 2 – 3.
1:6 *self-control.* According to many of the false teachers, knowledge made self-control unnecessary; according to Peter, Christian knowledge leads to self-control (cf. Pr 25:28; Gal 5:23).
1:7 *brotherly kindness.* Warmhearted affection toward all in the family of faith. *love.* The kind of outgoing, selfless attitude that leads one to sacrifice for the good of others (see note on 1Pe 4:8).
1:8 *if you possess these qualities.* Peter does not mean to imply that the believer is to cultivate each listed quality in turn, one after the other until all have been perfected. Instead, they are all to be cultivated simultaneously. *increasing measure.* Peter has continuing spiritual growth in mind (cf. 3:18; 1Pe 2:2; Php 3:10; 1Th 3:12). *keep you from being ... unproductive in your knowledge.* Christians' knowledge should affect the way they live. It does not set them free from moral restraints, as the heretics taught (see Introduction to 1 John: Gnosticism). Rather, it produces holiness and all such virtues (cf. Col 1:9 – 12).
1:9 *nearsighted and blind.* Since one cannot be both at the same time, Peter may have in mind a possible alternative meaning for "nearsighted," namely, "to shut the eyes." Such people are blind because they have closed their eyes to the truth (see 1Jn 2:11).
1:10 *brothers.* See note on Ro 1:13. *make your calling and election sure.* By cultivating the qualities listed in vv. 5 – 7, they and others can be assured that God has chosen them and called them (cf. Mt 7:20; Gal 5:6; Jas 2:18 and notes). When God elects and calls, it is to obedience and holiness (see 1Pe 1:2; Eph 1:3 – 6 and notes), and these fruits confirm their divine source. *never fall.* Those who in this way give evidence of their faith will never cease to persevere.
1:11 *receive a rich welcome.* By producing the fruits Peter is commending to them (see vv. 5 – 10). *eternal kingdom.* Eternal life (cf. Mt 25:46).
1:12 See Ro 15:15; Php 3:1; 1Jn 2:21.
1:13 *tent of this body.* See Jn 1:14; 2Co 5:1 and notes.
1:14 *Christ has made clear to me.* Either the revelation recorded in Jn 21:18 – 19 (see notes there) or a subsequent one.

has made clear to me.[e] 15And I will make
every effort to see that after my departure[f]
you will always be able to remember these
things.
16We did not follow cleverly invented
stories when we told you about the power and coming of our Lord Jesus Christ,[g]
but we were eyewitnesses of his majesty.[h]
17For he received honor and glory from
God the Father when the voice came to
him from the Majestic Glory, saying, "This
is my Son, whom I love; with him I am
well pleased."[a][i] 18We ourselves heard this
voice that came from heaven when we
were with him on the sacred mountain.[j]
19And we have the word of the prophets
made more certain,[k] and you will do well
to pay attention to it, as to a light[l] shining
in a dark place, until the day dawns[m] and
the morning star[n] rises in your hearts.[o]
20Above all, you must understand[p] that no
prophecy of Scripture came about by the
prophet's own interpretation. 21For prophecy never had its origin in the will of man,
but men spoke from God[q] as they were
carried along by the Holy Spirit.[r]

False Teachers and Their Destruction

2 But there were also false prophets[s]
among the people, just as there will
be false teachers among you.[t] They will
secretly introduce destructive heresies,
even denying the sovereign Lord[u] who
bought them[v]—bringing swift destruction
on themselves. 2Many will follow their
shameful ways[w] and will bring the way of
truth into disrepute. 3In their greed[x] these
teachers will exploit you[y] with stories they
have made up. Their condemnation has
long been hanging over them, and their
destruction has not been sleeping.
4For if God did not spare angels when
they sinned,[z] but sent them to hell,[b] putting them into gloomy dungeons[c] to be

1:14 [e]Jn 13:36; 21:18,19
1:15 [f]Lk 9:31
1:16 [g]Mk 13:26; 14:62 [h]Mt 17:1-8
1:17 [i]S Mt 3:17
1:18 [j]Mt 17:6
1:19 [k]1Pe 1:10,11 [l]Ps 119:105 [m]Lk 1:78 [n]Rev 22:16 [o]2Co 4:6
1:20 [p]2Pe 3:3
1:21 [q]2Ti 3:16 [r]2Sa 23:2; Ac 1:16; 3:18; 1Pe 1:11
2:1 [s]Dt 13:1-3; Jer 6:13; S Mt 7:15 [t]1Ti 4:1 [u]Jude 4 [v]S 1Co 6:20
2:2 [w]Jude 4
2:3 [x]ver 14 [y]2Co 2:17; 1Th 2:5
2:4 [z]Ge 6:1-4

[a] *17* Matt. 17:5; Mark 9:7; Luke 9:35 [b] *4* Greek *Tartarus* [c] *4* Some manuscripts *into chains of darkness*

1:15 *always be able to remember these things.* An aim that was realized, whether intentionally or unintentionally, through the Gospel of Mark, which early tradition connected with Peter.

1:16 *cleverly invented stories.* Peter's message was based on his eyewitness account of the supernatural events that marked the life of Jesus. It was not made up of myths and imaginative stories as was the message of the heretics of 2:3 (see note there). *coming of our Lord Jesus Christ.* In Christ's transfiguration the disciples received a foretaste of what his coming will be like when he returns to establish his eternal kingdom (see Mt 16:28 and note). *eyewitnesses of his majesty.* A reference to Christ's transfiguration (see vv. 17–18; Mt 16:28—17:8).

1:18 *sacred mountain.* See note on Lk 9:28.

1:19–21 Peter's message rests on two solid foundations: (1) the voice from God at the transfiguration (vv. 16–18) and (2) the still more significant testimony of Scripture (vv. 19–21). An alternative, but less probable, view is that the apostles' testimony to the transfiguration fulfills and thus confirms the Scriptures that predicted such things.

1:19 *more certain.* Or "very certain." *morning star.* See Rev 22:16; cf. Nu 24:17 and note.

1:20 Two major views of this verse are: (1) No prophecy is to be privately or independently interpreted (cf. the false teachers in 3:16). The Holy Spirit, Scripture itself and the church should be included in the interpretative process. (2) No prophecy originated through the prophet's own interpretation (the sense of the NIV). The preceding and following contexts indicate that this view is probably to be preferred. In vv. 16–18 the subject discussed is the origin of the apostolic message. Did it come from human imaginings, or was it from God? In v. 21 again the subject is origin. No prophecy of Scripture arose from a merely human interpretation of things. This understanding of v. 20 is further supported by the explanatory "For" with which v. 21 begins. Verse 21 explains v. 20 by restating its content and then affirming God as the origin of prophecy.

1:21 *carried along by the Holy Spirit.* See 2Ti 3:16 and note. In the production of Scripture both God and humans were active participants. God was the source of the content of Scripture, so that what it says is what God has said. But the human authors also actively spoke; they were more than recorders. Yet what they said came from God. Although actively speaking, "they were carried along by the Holy Spirit."

2:1 *false prophets.* See 1Ki 18:19; Isa 9:13–17; Jer 5:31; 14:14; 23:30–32 and note on 23:31; Mic 3:5,7 and notes. *there will be false teachers among you.* Numerous NT passages warn of false teachers who are already present or yet to come (see Mt 24:4–5,11; Ac 20:29–30; Gal 1:6–9; Php 3:2; Col 2:4,8,18,20–23; 2Th 2:1–3; 1Ti 1:3–7; 4:1–3; 2Ti 3:1–8; 1Jn 2:18–19,22–23; 2Jn 7–11; Jude 3–4). *destructive heresies.* Divisive opinions or teachings that result in the moral and spiritual destruction of those who accept them. *sovereign Lord who bought them.* See Jude 4 and note; does not necessarily mean that the false teachers were believers. Christ's death paid the penalty for their sin, but it would not become effective for their salvation unless they trusted in Christ as Savior. (However, see vv. 20–22, where it is obvious that the heretics had at least professed knowing the Lord.) *swift destruction.* Not immediate physical calamity, but sudden doom, whether at death or at the Lord's second coming (cf. Mt 24:50–51; 2Th 1:9 and note).

2:2 *shameful ways.* Open, extreme immorality not held in check by any sense of shame. *way of truth.* See Ps 119:30. The Christian faith is not only correct doctrine but also correct living.

2:3 *In their greed.* They will be motivated by a desire for money and will commercialize the Christian faith to their own selfish advantage. *stories they have made up.* See note on 1:16. *long been hanging over them.* Long ago, in OT times, their condemnation was declared (see vv. 4–9 for OT examples of the fact that judgment is coming on the wicked). *destruction has not been sleeping.* Although delay makes it seem that they have escaped God's judgment, destruction is a reality that is sure to come upon them.

2:4–8 Three examples showing that God will rescue the godly and destroy the wicked.

2:4 *angels when they sinned.* Some believe this sin was the one referred to in Ge 6:2, where the sons of God are said to have intermarried with the daughters of men, meaning (according to this view) that angels married human women. The offspring of those marriages are said to have been the Nephilim (Ge 6:4; see notes on Ge 6:2,4). But since it appears impossible for angels, who are spirits, to have sexual relations with women, the sin referred to in this verse probably

held for judgment;[a] 5if he did not spare
the ancient world[b] when he brought the
flood on its ungodly people,[c] but protected Noah, a preacher of righteousness, and
seven others;[d] 6if he condemned the cities
of Sodom and Gomorrah by burning them
to ashes,[e] and made them an example[f] of
what is going to happen to the ungodly;[g]
7and if he rescued Lot,[h] a righteous man,
who was distressed by the filthy lives of
lawless men[i] 8(for that righteous man,[j]
living among them day after day, was tormented in his righteous soul by the lawless deeds he saw and heard)— 9if this
is so, then the Lord knows how to rescue
godly men from trials[k] and to hold the unrighteous for the day of judgment,[l] while
continuing their punishment.[a] 10This is
especially true of those who follow the
corrupt desire[m] of the sinful nature[b] and
despise authority.

Bold and arrogant, these men are not
afraid to slander celestial beings;[n] 11yet
even angels, although they are stronger
and more powerful, do not bring slanderous accusations against such beings
in the presence of the Lord.[o] 12But these
men blaspheme in matters they do not understand. They are like brute beasts, creatures of instinct, born only to be caught
and destroyed, and like beasts they too
will perish.[p]

13They will be paid back with harm for
the harm they have done. Their idea of
pleasure is to carouse in broad daylight.[q]
They are blots and blemishes, reveling in
their pleasures while they feast with you.[c r]
14With eyes full of adultery, they never
stop sinning; they seduce[s] the unstable;[t]
they are experts in greed[u]—an accursed
brood![v] 15They have left the straight way
and wandered off to follow the way of Balaam[w] son of Beor, who loved the wages of
wickedness. 16But he was rebuked for his
wrongdoing by a donkey—a beast without
speech—who spoke with a man's voice
and restrained the prophet's madness.[x]

17These men are springs without water[y] and mists driven by a storm. Blackest

2:4 [a] 1Ti 3:6; Jude 6; Rev 20:1,2 **2:5** [b] 2Pe 3:6 [c] Ge 6:5-8:19 [d] Heb 11:7; 1Pe 3:20 **2:6** [e] Ge 19:24, 25 [f] Nu 26:10; Jude 7 [g] Mt 10:15; 11:23,24; Ro 9:29 **2:7** [h] Ge 19:16 [i] 2Pe 3:17 **2:8** [j] Heb 11:4 **2:9** [k] Ps 37:33; S Ro 15:31; Rev 3:10 [l] S Mt 10:15 **2:10** [m] 2Pe 3:3; Jude 16,18 [n] Jude 8 **2:11** [o] Jude 9 **2:12** [p] Ps 49:12; Jude 10 **2:13** [q] S Ro 13:13; 1Th 5:7 [r] 1Co 11:20,21; Jude 12 **2:14** [s] ver 18 [t] Jas 1:8; 2Pe 3:16 [u] ver 3 [v] Eph 2:3 **2:15** [w] Nu 22:4-20; 31:16; Dt 23:4; Jude 11; Rev 2:14 **2:16** [x] Nu 22:21-30 **2:17** [y] Jude 12

[a] *9* Or *unrighteous for punishment until the day of judgment* [b] *10* Or *the flesh* [c] *13* Some manuscripts *in their love feasts*

occurred before the fall of Adam and Eve. The angels who fell became the devil and the evil angels (probably the demons and evil spirits referred to in the NT). *sent them to hell.* See NIV text note. *Tartarus* was the term used by the Greeks to designate the place where the most wicked spirits were sent to be punished. Why some evil angels are imprisoned and others are free to serve Satan as demons is not explained in Scripture. *judgment.* The final judgment, probably associated with the great white throne judgment of Rev 20:11–15.

2:5 *ungodly people.* See Ge 6:5,11–12. *preacher of righteousness.* A description of Noah found nowhere else in Scripture. However, similar descriptions are used of him in Josephus (*Antiquities*, 1.3.1), *1 Clement* (7.6; 9.4) and the *Sibylline Oracles* (1.128–29). *seven others.* Noah's wife, three sons and three daughters-in-law (Noah was the eighth; see 1Pe 3:20).

2:6 *condemned the cities of Sodom and Gomorrah.* See Ge 19.

2:7 *distressed by the filthy lives.* See Ge 19:4–9. How Lot could be so distressed, how he could be called a "righteous man," and yet offer to turn his two daughters over to the wicked townsmen to be sexually abused is difficult to understand apart from a knowledge of the code of honor characteristic of that day (see note on Ge 19:8).

2:9 States the point made in vv. 4–8—the wicked whose coming Peter predicts will surely be punished.

2:10 *This is especially true.* The heretics of Peter's day are certain to come under judgment for two main reasons: (1) They "follow the corrupt desire of the sinful nature," referring to inordinate sexual indulgence (see v. 18; 1:4; 3:3). (2) They "despise authority." *slander celestial beings.* A specific example of despising authority. This could refer to the slander of earthly dignitaries such as church leaders, which might well be expected from such shameless peddlers of error. On the other hand, it could refer to the blaspheming of angels, as the NIV text suggests. This view seems more likely since the parallel passage in Jude 8–10 is speaking of angels.

2:11 *angels ... do not bring slanderous accusations.* Even good angels, who might have more right to do so because of their greater power, do not bring such accusations against inferior evil angels.

2:12 *matters they do not understand.* The heresy to which Peter refers may have been an early form of second-century Gnosticism (see Introduction to 1 John: Gnosticism) that claimed to possess special, esoteric knowledge. If so, it is ironic that those who professed special knowledge acted out of abysmal ignorance, and the result was arrogant blasphemy. *like brute beasts.* A scathing denunciation. They are like irrational animals, whose lives are guided by mere instinct and who are born merely to be slaughtered. Destruction is their final lot.

2:13 *carouse in broad daylight.* See 1Th 5:7. Even the pagan world carried on their corrupt practices under cover of darkness, but these heretics were utterly shameless. *in their pleasures while they feast with you.* See NIV text note. Jude 12 without doubt reads "love feasts," which may well have been the intended reading here. These false teachers seem to have been involved in the sacred feasts of brotherly love that, in the early church, accompanied the Lord's Supper. In fact, it appears that they injected their carousing into these holy observances and delighted in their shameless acts (cf. 1Co 11:17–22,27–34 and notes on 11:20–22).

2:14 *eyes full of adultery.* Lit. "eyes full of an adulteress," which means that they desired every woman they saw, viewing her as a potential sex partner. *never stop sinning.* Their eyes serve as constant instruments of lust. *seduce the unstable.* For a parallel use of the Greek for "seduce" see Jas 1:14 and note. It depicts the fisherman who attempts to lure and catch fish with bait. *experts in greed.* The Greek text implies that they had exercised themselves like an athlete, not in physical activity but in greed.

2:15 *way of Balaam son of Beor.* See Nu 22–24. Balaam was bent on cursing Israel, though God had forbidden it. Balaam wanted the money Balak offered him. Similarly these false teachers apparently were guilty of attempting to extract money from naive listeners. For a donkey to rebuke the prophet's madness (v. 16) reflects not only on the foolishness of Balaam but also on that of the false teachers of Peter's day.

2:17 *springs without water.* A picture of cruel deception. The thirsty traveler comes to the spring expecting cool, refreshing water but finds it dry (see Jer 15:18 and note). So the false

darkness is reserved for them.[z] 18 For they mouth empty, boastful words[a] and, by appealing to the lustful desires of sinful human nature, they entice people who are just escaping[b] from those who live in error. 19 They promise them freedom, while they themselves are slaves of depravity—for a man is a slave to whatever has mastered him.[c] 20 If they have escaped the corruption of the world by knowing[d] our Lord and Savior Jesus Christ[e] and are again entangled in it and overcome, they are worse off at the end than they were at the beginning.[f] 21 It would have been better for them not to have known the way of righteousness, than to have known it and then to turn their backs on the sacred command that was passed on to them.[g] 22 Of them the proverbs are true: "A dog returns to its vomit,"[a][h] and, "A sow that is washed goes back to her wallowing in the mud."

2:17 [z] Jude 13
2:18 [a] Jude 16 [b] ver 20; 2Pe 1:4
2:19 [c] S Ro 6:16
2:20 [d] S 2Pe 1:2 [e] 2Pe 1:11; 3:18 [f] Mt 12:45
2:21 [g] Eze 18:24; Heb 6:4-6; 10:26,27
2:22 [h] Pr 26:11

The Day of the Lord

3 Dear friends,[i] this is now my second letter to you. I have written both of them as reminders[j] to stimulate you to wholesome thinking. 2 I want you to recall the words spoken in the past by the holy prophets[k] and the command given by our Lord and Savior through your apostles.[l]

3 First of all, you must understand that in the last days[m] scoffers will come, scoffing and following their own evil desires.[n] 4 They will say, "Where is this 'coming' he promised?[o] Ever since our fathers died, everything goes on as it has since the beginning of creation."[p] 5 But they deliberately forget that long ago by God's word[q] the heavens existed and the earth was formed out of water and by water.[r] 6 By these waters also the world of that time[s] was deluged and destroyed.[t] 7 By the same word

3:1 [i] S 1Co 10:14 [j] 2Pe 1:13
3:2 [k] Lk 1:70; Ac 3:21 [l] S Eph 4:11
3:3 [m] 1Ti 4:1; 2Ti 3:1 [n] 2Pe 2:10; Jude 18
3:4 [o] Isa 5:19; Eze 12:22; Mt 24:48; S Lk 17:30 [p] Mk 10:6
3:5 [q] Ge 1:6,9; Heb 11:3 [r] Ps 24:2
3:6 [s] 2Pe 2:5 [t] Ge 7:21,22

[a] 22 Prov. 26:11

teachers promise satisfying truth but in reality have nothing to offer. *mists driven by a storm.* Gone before a drop of moisture falls. *Blackest darkness.* Their destiny is hell.

2:18 *mouth empty, boastful words.* Words that sound impressive to the new convert but in reality have nothing to offer. *lustful desires.* See v. 10 and note. *entice.* See note on v. 14 ("seduce"). *people who are just escaping.* New converts who have just broken away from pagan friends. Thus the depraved false teachers prey on new converts, who have not yet had a chance to develop spiritual resistance.

2:19 *They promise them freedom.* Probably freedom from moral restraint (cf. 1Co 6:12–13; Gal 5:13 and notes). The very ones who promise freedom from bondage to rules and regulations are themselves slaves of depravity. Freedom from law resulted in bondage to sin, and liberty was turned into license.

2:20–22 Some point to this passage as clear proof that genuinely saved persons may lose their salvation. They know the Lord; they escape the world's corruption; they know the way of righteousness. Then they turn away from the message and go back to their old way of life. Their knowledge is said to have been genuine; their change of life was real; and their return to their old way of life was not superficial. Others insist that the knowledge of the Lord and of the way of righteousness could not have been genuine. If such people had been truly regenerated, they would have persevered in their faith. It is argued that the teaching of Jn 10:27–30 (especially v. 28) and Ro 8:28–39 makes it clear that no genuinely saved person can be lost. Thus, according to this view, the persons described here could not have been genuinely saved. See 1Jn 2:19.

2:20 *If they have escaped the corruption of the world.* A reference to false teachers who had once apparently been believers in Christ. Their professed knowledge of Christ had at least produced a change in lifestyle. *again entangled in it and overcome.* A complete return to the old sinful pattern of life.

2:21 *better … not to have known the way of righteousness.* Knowledge of the way increases people's responsibility and their hardness of heart if they then reject it. In its early days, Christianity was known as "the Way" (Ac 9:2 [see note there]). *sacred command.* The whole Christian message that people are commanded to receive (cf. note on Jude 3).

2:22 *A dog returns … A sow … goes back.* In both cases the nature of the animal is not changed. The sow returns to the mud because by nature it is still a sow. The change was merely cosmetic.

3:1 *second letter.* The first letter may have been 1 Peter, though there is some reason to doubt this identification. For example, 1 Peter cannot be very accurately described as a reminder. *reminders.* See 1:12–13,15.

3:2 *holy prophets.* OT personages. *command.* See note on 2:21. *your apostles.* Peter places the OT prophets and the NT apostles on an equal plane. Both are vehicles of God's sacred truth. Peter, being one of the apostles, can speak with knowledge and authority as a representative of the apostolic group.

3:3 *First of all.* The Greek for this expression is used in 1:20 ("Above all") to call attention to a matter of great importance. *last days.* An expression that refers to the whole period introduced by Christ's first coming. These days are last in comparison to OT days, which were preliminary and preparatory (see notes on Heb 1:1–2). Also, the Christian era is the time of the beginnings of prophetic fulfillment. *scoffers will come.* Perhaps the same false teachers described in ch. 2 (e.g., they follow their own evil desires; cf. 2:10,18–19). In ch. 3, however, the emphasis is on Christ's return. These people may have been early Gnostics who resisted the idea of a time of judgment and moral accountability. *evil desires.* See 2:10 and note.

3:4 *he.* Christ. *Ever since our fathers died.* Either the first Christians to die after Christ's death and resurrection (e.g., Stephen, James the brother of John, and other early Christian leaders who had died; cf. Heb 13:7 and note) or the OT patriarchs (see Introduction: Date). *everything goes on as it has.* Their argument against Christ's return was: Since it has not occurred up to this time, it will never occur. That nature is not subject to divine intervention, they say, has been proved by observation (1) of the period since the fathers died—perhaps 30 years—and (2) of the period since creation.

3:5 *they deliberately forget.* Ignoring the flood as a divine intervention was not an oversight; it was deliberate. They did not want to face up to the fallacy in their argument. *God's word.* Of command, such as "Let there be light" (Ge 1:3). *earth was formed out of water and by water.* See Ge 1:6–10 (see notes there), where the waters on earth were separated from the atmospheric waters of the heavens, and the mountains then appeared, causing the earthly waters to be gathered into oceans.

3:6 *By these waters also the world … was deluged and destroyed.* Peter points out the fallacy of the scoffers' argument. There has been a divine intervention since the time of creation, namely, the flood (see note on Ge 6:17).

3:7 *By the same word.* The word of God that brought the world into existence (v. 5) and that brought watery destruction on

the present heavens and earth are reserved
for fire,[u] being kept for the day of judgment[v] and destruction of ungodly men.
8But do not forget this one thing, dear
friends: With the Lord a day is like a thousand years, and a thousand years are like
a day.[w] 9The Lord is not slow in keeping
his promise,[x] as some understand slow-
ness. He is patient[y] with you, not wanting
anyone to perish, but everyone to come to
repentance.[z]
10But the day of the Lord will come like
a thief.[a] The heavens will disappear with
a roar;[b] the elements will be destroyed by
fire,[c] and the earth and everything in it
will be laid bare.[a][d]
11Since everything will be destroyed in
this way, what kind of people ought you
to be? You ought to live holy and godly
lives 12as you look forward[e] to the day of
God and speed its coming.[b][f] That day will
bring about the destruction of the heavens
by fire, and the elements will melt in the
heat.[g] 13But in keeping with his promise
we are looking forward to a new heaven
and a new earth,[h] the home of righteousness.
14So then, dear friends, since you are
looking forward to this, make every effort to be found spotless, blameless[i] and
at peace with him. 15Bear in mind that
our Lord's patience[j] means salvation,[k]
just as our dear brother Paul also wrote
you with the wisdom that God gave him.[l]
16He writes the same way in all his letters,
speaking in them of these matters. His letters contain some things that are hard to
understand, which ignorant and unstable[m]
people distort,[n] as they do the other Scriptures,[o] to their own destruction.
17Therefore, dear friends, since you already know this, be on your guard[p] so that
you may not be carried away by the error[q]
of lawless men[r] and fall from your secure
position.[s] 18But grow in the grace[t] and
knowledge[u] of our Lord and Savior Jesus
Christ.[v] To him be glory both now and forever! Amen.[w]

3:7 [u]ver 10,12; S 2Th 1:7 [v]S Mt 10:15 **3:8** [w]Ps 90:4 **3:9** [x]Hab 2:3; Heb 10:37 [y]S Ro 2:4 [z]S 1Ti 2:4; Rev 2:21 **3:10** [a]S Lk 12:39 [b]Isa 34:4 [c]ver 7,12; S 2Th 1:7 [d]Mt 24:35; S Heb 12:27; Rev 21:1 **3:12** [e]S 1Co 1:7 [f]Ps 50:3 [g]ver 10 **3:13** [h]Isa 65:17; 66:22; Rev 21:1 **3:14** [i]S 1Th 3:13 **3:15** [j]S Ro 2:4 [k]ver 9 [l]Eph 3:3 **3:16** [m]Jas 1:8; 2Pe 2:14 [n]Ps 56:5; Jer 23:36 [o]ver 2 **3:17** [p]1Co 10:12 [q]2Pe 2:18 [r]2Pe 2:7 [s]Rev 2:5 **3:18** [t]S Ro 3:24 [u]S 2Pe 1:2 [v]2Pe 1:11; 2:20 [w]S Ro 11:36

[a] 10 Some manuscripts *be burned up* [b] 12 Or *as you wait eagerly for the day of God to come*

the wicked of Noah's day will bring fiery destruction on the world that exists today and on its wicked people.

3:8 *a thousand years are like a day.* Cf. Ps 90:4–5 and note. God does not view time as humans do. He stands above time, with the result that when time is seen in the light of eternity, an age appears no longer than one short day, and a day seems no shorter than a long age. Since time is purely relative with God, he waits patiently while human beings stew with impatience.

3:9 God's seeming delay in bringing about the consummation of all things is a result not of indifference but of patience in waiting for all who will come to repentance. Thus the scoffers are wrong on two points: (1) They fail to recognize that all things have not continued without divine intervention since creation (the flood was an intervention, vv. 4–6). (2) They misunderstand the reason for apparent divine delay (God is a long-suffering God). *repentance.* See Mt 4:17; Mk 1:4 and note.

3:10 *day of the Lord.* See notes on Isa 2:11,17,20; Joel 1:15; Am 5:18; 1Th 5:2. *like a thief.* Suddenly and unexpectedly. *The heavens will disappear with a roar.* Apocalyptic language, common to books like Daniel and Revelation. Due to the figurative nature of such writings, we must not expect complete literalism but recognize it as an attempt to describe the indescribable, a task as impossible as it would have been for a first-century writer to describe the phenomena of our atomic age. What may be referred to is the destruction of the atmospheric heavens with a great rushing sound (see v. 12). *elements.* Refers either to the heavenly bodies or to the physical elements—in the first century, such things as earth, air, fire and water. *fire.* See vv. 7,12. *earth ... laid bare.* See NIV text note. Either the earth and its contents will disappear and not be seen anymore, or the earth and all human works will appear before God's judgment seat.

3:11 *Since everything will be destroyed.* The transitory nature of the material universe ought to make a difference in one's system of values and one's priorities. The result should be lives of holiness (separated from sin and to God) and godliness (devoted to the worship and service of God). Cf. 1:13–16; Mt 25:13; 1Th 5:6,8,11.

3:12 *the day of God.* Apparently synonymous with "the day of the Lord" (see v. 10 and note) since it is characterized by the same kind of events. Cf. Rev 16:14. *speed its coming.* That day may be hastened by God's people as they speed up the accomplishment of his purposes. Since he is waiting for all who will come to repentance (v. 9), the sooner believers bring others to the Savior the sooner that day will dawn (cf. Ac 3:19–20). Prayer also serves to hasten the day (Mt 6:10), as does holy living (v. 11). *destruction of the heavens.* See v. 10. *elements will melt in the heat.* See v. 10; Isa 34:4 and notes.

3:13 *his promise.* New heavens and a new earth are promised by Isaiah (65:17; 66:22). This promise is confirmed by Rev 21:1. *home of righteousness.* Righteousness will dwell there as a permanent resident. Cf. Isa 11:4–5; 45:8; Da 9:24 and notes.

3:14,18 *peace ... grace.* See note on Ro 1:7.

3:14 *spotless, blameless.* Cf. 1Pe 1:19, where the same two Greek words are applied to Christ. *at peace with him.* Believers have peace with God as a result of being justified by faith (see Ro 5:1 and note), but they may displease him by failing to live as he desires and thus not receive his commendation and his reward when he returns (cf. 1Co 3:10–15; 2Co 5:10 and notes).

3:15 *our Lord's patience means salvation.* See v. 9 and note. *our dear brother Paul.* Peter expresses warmth in his reference to Paul. The unity of teaching and purpose that governed their relationship, abundantly attested in Paul's letters and the book of Acts, is confirmed here by Peter. It has been suggested that what Paul wrote to the recipients of 2 Peter may have been a copy of Romans, which was sent to the churches as a circular letter (see Introduction to Romans: Recipients; see also note on 1Pe 1:1).

3:16 *writes the same way in all his letters.* Peter may be referring in general to the exhortations to holy living in vv. 11–14, which parallel many passages in Paul's writings. *ignorant and unstable people.* The ignorant are simply the unlearned who have not been taught basic apostolic teaching and thus may be easily led astray (cf. 2:14 and note). *other Scriptures.* Peter placed Paul's writings on the same level of authority as the God-breathed writings of the OT (see 1:21; 2Ti 3:16 and notes).

3:17 *already know this.* That false teachers are coming (cf. ch. 2).

3:18 *grow in ... knowledge.* Peter concludes by again stressing knowledge (see 1:2–3 and notes; see also 1:5), probably as an antidote to the false teachers who boasted in their esoteric knowledge.

1 John

INTRODUCTION

Author

The author is John son of Zebedee (see Mk 1:19 – 20) — the apostle and the author of the Gospel of John and Revelation (see Introductions to both books: Author). He was a fisherman, one of Jesus' inner circle (together with James and Peter), and "the disciple whom Jesus loved" (Jn 13:23; see note there). He may have been a first cousin of Jesus (his mother may have been Salome, possibly a sister of Mary; cf. Mt 27:56; Mk 15:40 and note; 16:1; Jn 19:25 — this view assumes that "his mother's sister" in Jn 19:25 refers to Salome; some further assume that "Mary the wife of Clopas" there stands in apposition to "his mother's sister," which would mean that this Mary and Salome were one and the same person).

Unlike most NT letters, 1 John does not tell us who its author is. The earliest identification of him comes from the church fathers: Irenaeus (c. A.D. 140 – 203), Clement of Alexandria (c. 150 – 215), Tertullian (c. 155 – 222) and Origen (c. 185 – 253) all designated the writer as the apostle John. As far as we know, no one else was suggested by the early church.

This traditional identification is confirmed by evidence in the letter itself:

1. The style of the Gospel of John is markedly similar to that of this letter. Both are written in simple Greek and use contrasting figures, such as light and darkness, life and death, truth and lies, love and hate.

2. Similar phrases and expressions, such as those found in the following passages, are striking:

1 John	Gospel of John
1:1	1:1,14
1:4	16:24
1:6 – 7	3:19 – 21
2:7	13:34 – 35
3:8	8:44
3:14	5:24
4:6	8:47
4:9	1:14,18; 3:16
5:9	5:32,37
5:12	3:36

3. The mention of eyewitness testimony (1:1 – 4) harmonizes with the fact that John was a follower of Christ from the earliest days of his ministry.

4. The authoritative manner that pervades the letter—seen in its commands (2:15,24,28; 4:1; 5:21), its firm assertions (2:6; 3:14; 4:12) and its pointed identification of error (1:6,8; 2:4,22)—is what would be expected from an apostle.

5. The suggestions of advanced age (addressing his readers as "children," 2:1,28; 3:7) agree with early church tradition concerning John's age when he wrote the books known to be his.

6. The description of the heretics as antichrists (2:18), liars (2:22) and children of the devil (3:10) is consistent with Jesus' characterization of John as a son of thunder (Mk 3:17).

7. The indications of a close relationship with the Lord (1:1; 2:5–6,24,27–28) fit the descriptions of "the disciple whom Jesus loved" and the one who reclined "next to him" (Jn 13:23).

A Quick Look

Author:

The apostle John

Audience:

Believers in western Asia Minor

Date:

Between A.D. 85 and 95

Theme:

John writes to assure believers of the certainty of their faith and to refute heretical doctrines that Jesus was not fully human and divine.

Date

The letter is difficult to date with precision, but factors such as (1) evidence from early Christian writers (Irenaeus and Clement of Alexandria), (2) the early form of Gnosticism reflected in the denunciations of the letter and (3) indications of the advanced age of John suggest the end of the first century. Since the author of 1 John seems to build on concepts and themes found in the fourth Gospel (see 1Jn 2:7–11), it is reasonable to date the letter somewhere between A.D. 85 and 95, after the writing of the Gospel, which may have been written c. 85 (see Introduction to John: Date), and before the writing of Revelation, which may have been written c. 95 (see Introduction to Revelation: Date).

Recipients

1Jn 2:12–14,19; 3:1; 5:13 make it clear that this letter was addressed to believers. But the letter itself does not indicate who they were or where they lived. The fact that it mentions no one by name suggests it was a circular letter sent to Christians in a number of places. Evidence from early Christian writers places the apostle John in Ephesus during most of his later years (c. A.D. 70–100). The earliest confirmed use of 1 John was in the Roman province of Asia (in modern Turkey), where Ephesus was located. Clement of Alexandria indicates that John ministered in the various churches scattered throughout that province. It may be assumed, therefore, that 1 John was sent to the churches of the Roman province of Asia (see map No. 13 at the end of this study Bible).

Gnosticism

One of the most dangerous heresies of the first two centuries of the church was Gnosticism. Its central teaching was that spirit is entirely good and matter is entirely evil. From this unbiblical dualism flowed five important errors:

1. The human body, which is matter, is therefore evil. It is to be contrasted with God, who is wholly spirit and therefore good.

2. Salvation is the escape from the body, achieved not by faith in Christ but by special knowledge (the Greek word for "knowledge" is *gnosis,* hence Gnosticism).

3. Christ's true humanity was denied in two ways: (1) Some said that Christ only seemed to have a body, a view called Docetism, from the Greek *dokeo* ("to seem"), and (2) others said that the divine Christ joined the man Jesus at baptism and left him before he died, a view called Cerinthianism, after its most prominent spokesman, Cerinthus. This view is the background of much of 1 John (see 1:1; 2:22; 4:2–3 and notes).

4. Since the body was considered evil, it was to be treated harshly. This ascetic form of Gnosticism is the background of part of the letter to the Colossians (see Col 2:21,23 and notes).

5. Paradoxically, this dualism also led to licentiousness. The reasoning was that, since matter — and not the breaking of God's law (1Jn 3:4) — was considered evil, breaking his law was of no moral consequence.

The Gnosticism addressed in the NT was an early form of the heresy, not the intricately developed system of the second and third centuries. In addition to that seen in Colossians and in John's letters, acquaintance with early Gnosticism is reflected in 1,2 Timothy, Titus, and 2 Peter and perhaps 1 Corinthians.

By giving eyewitness testimony to the incarnation, John sought to confirm his readers' belief in the incarnate Christ.

Occasion and Purpose

John's readers were confronted with an early form of Gnostic teaching of the Cerinthian variety (see Gnosticism above). This heresy was also libertine, throwing off all moral restraints.

Consequently, John wrote this letter with two basic purposes in mind: (1) to expose and refute false teachers (see 2:26 and note) and (2) to give believers assurance of salvation (see 5:13 and note). In keeping with his intention to combat Gnostic teachers, John specifically struck at their total lack of morality (3:8 – 10); and by giving eyewitness testimony to the incarnation, he sought to confirm his readers' belief in the incarnate Christ (1:3). John set forth several key tests of authentic Christian faith: (1) belief that Jesus is the Son of God (2:18 – 28; 3:23 — 4:6; 4:14 – 15; 5:1,5); (2) obedience to Christian commands (1:5 — 2:6; 2:29 — 3:10; 3:22 – 24; 5:4 – 21); (3) love for brothers and sisters in Christ (2:7 – 17; 3:10 – 24; 4:7 — 5:3). These are the indisputable hallmarks of true believers. Success in this would give the writer joy (1:4).

Outline*

I. Introduction: The Reality of the Incarnation (1:1 – 4)
II. The Christian Life as Fellowship with the Father and the Son (1:5 — 2:28)
  A. Ethical Tests of Fellowship (1:5 — 2:11)
    1. Moral likeness (1:5 – 7)
    2. Confession of sin (1:8 — 2:2)
    3. Obedience (2:3 – 6)
    4. Love for fellow believers (2:7 – 11)
  B. Two Digressions (2:12 – 17)
  C. Christological Test of Fellowship (2:18 – 28)
    1. Contrast: apostates versus believers (2:18 – 21)
    2. Person of Christ: the crux of the test (2:22 – 23)
    3. Persistent belief: key to continuing fellowship (2:24 – 28)
III. The Christian Life as Divine Sonship (2:29 — 4:6)
  A. Ethical Tests of Sonship (2:29 — 3:24)
    1. Righteousness (2:29 — 3:10a)
    2. Love (3:10b – 24)
  B. Christological Tests of Sonship (4:1 – 6)
IV. The Christian Life as an Integration of the Ethical and the Christological (4:7 — 5:12)
  A. The Ethical Test: Love (4:7 — 5:5)
    1. The source of love (4:7 – 16)
    2. The fruit of love (4:17 – 19)
    3. The relationship of love for God and love for one's fellow Christian (4:20 — 5:1)
    4. Obedience: the evidence of love for God's children (5:2 – 5)
  B. The Christological Test (5:6 – 12)
V. Conclusion: Great Christian Certainties (5:13 – 21)

The Word of Life

1 That which was from the beginning,[a]
which we have heard, which we have
seen with our eyes,[b] which we have looked
at and our hands have touched[c]—this we
proclaim concerning the Word of life. 2The
life appeared;[d] we have seen it and testify
to it,[e] and we proclaim to you the eternal
life,[f] which was with the Father and has
appeared to us. 3We proclaim to you what
we have seen and heard,[g] so that you also
may have fellowship with us. And our fellowship is with the Father and with his
Son, Jesus Christ.[h] 4We write this[i] to make
our[a] joy complete.[j]

Walking in the Light

5This is the message we have heard[k]
from him and declare to you: God is light;[l]
in him there is no darkness at all. 6If we
claim to have fellowship with him yet walk
in the darkness,[m] we lie and do not live by
the truth.[n] 7But if we walk in the light,[o] as
he is in the light, we have fellowship with
one another, and the blood of Jesus, his
Son, purifies us from all[b] sin.[p]
8If we claim to be without sin,[q] we deceive ourselves and the truth is not in us.[r]
9If we confess our sins, he is faithful and
just and will forgive us our sins[s] and purify us from all unrighteousness.[t] 10If we
claim we have not sinned,[u] we make him
out to be a liar[v] and his word has no place
in our lives.[w]

2 My dear children,[x] I write this to you
so that you will not sin. But if anybody
does sin, we have one who speaks to the
Father in our defense[y]—Jesus Christ, the
Righteous One. 2He is the atoning sacrifice
for our sins,[z] and not only for ours but
also for[c] the sins of the whole world.[a]
3We know[b] that we have come to know
him[c] if we obey his commands.[d] 4The man
who says, "I know him,"[e] but does not do
what he commands is a liar, and the truth
is not in him.[f] 5But if anyone obeys his
word,[g] God's love[d] is truly made complete

1:1 [a] S Jn 1:2 [b] S Lk 24:48; Jn 1:14; 19:35; Ac 4:20; 2Pe 1:16; 1Jn 4:14 [c] Jn 20:27 **1:2** [d] Jn 1:1-4; 11:25; 14:6; 1Ti 3:16; 1Pe 1:20; 1Jn 3:5,8 [e] S Jn 15:27 [f] S Mt 25:46 **1:3** [g] S ver 1 [h] 1Co 1:9 **1:4** [i] 1Jn 2:1 [j] S Jn 3:29 **1:5** [k] 1Jn 3:11 [l] 1Ti 6:16 **1:6** [m] Jn 3:19-21; 8:12; 2Co 6:14; Eph 5:8; 1Jn 2:11 [n] Jn 3:19-21; 1Jn 2:4; 4:20 **1:7** [o] Isa 2:5 [p] Heb 9:14; Rev 1:5; 7:14 **1:8** [q] Pr 20:9; Jer 2:35; Ro 3:9-19; Jas 3:2 [r] Jn 8:44; 1Jn 2:4 **1:9** [s] Ps 32:5; 51:2; Pr 28:13 [t] ver 7; Mic 7:18-20; Heb 10:22 **1:10** [u] ver 8 [v] 1Jn 5:10 [w] Jn 5:38; 1Jn 2:14 **2:1** [x] ver 12,13,28; 1Jn 3:7,18; 4:4; 5:21; S 1Th 2:11 [y] S Ro 8:34; 1Ti 2:5 **2:2** [z] Ro 3:25; 1Jn 4:10 [a] S Mt 1:21; S Jn 3:17 **2:3** [b] ver 5; 1Jn 3:24; 4:13; 5:2 [c] S ver 4 [d] S Jn 14:15 **2:4** [e] ver 3; Tit 1:16; 1Jn 3:6; 4:7,8 [f] 1Jn 1:6,8 **2:5** [g] S Jn 14:15

[a] 4 Some manuscripts *your* [b] 7 Or *every* [c] 2 Or *He is the one who turns aside God's wrath, taking away our sins, and not only ours but also* [d] 5 Or *word, love for God*

1:1–4 The introduction to this letter deals with the same subject and uses several of the same words as the introduction to John's Gospel (1:1–4)—"beginning," "Word," "life," "with."

1:1 *was from the beginning.* Has always existed. *we.* John and the other apostles. *heard ... seen ... looked at ... touched.* The apostle had made a careful examination of the Word of life. He testifies that the one who has existed from eternity "became flesh" (Jn 1:14; see note there)—i.e., a flesh-and-blood man. He was truly divine and truly human. At the outset, John contradicts the heresy of the Gnostics (see Introduction: Gnosticism). *Word of life.* The one who is life and reveals life (see v. 2 and note). "Word" here speaks of revelation (see note on Jn 1:1).

1:2 *The life ... the eternal life.* Christ (cf. Jn 1:4 and note). He is called "the life" because he is the living one who has life in himself (see Jn 11:25; 14:6 and notes). He is also the source of life and sovereign over life (5:11). The letter begins and ends (5:20) with the theme of eternal life.

1:3 *fellowship with us.* Participation with us (vicariously) in our experience of hearing, seeing and touching the incarnate Christ (v. 1). Fellowship (Greek *koinonia*) is the spiritual union of the believer with Christ—as described in the figures of the vine and branches (Jn 15:1–5) and the body and the head (1Co 12:12; Col 1:18)—as well as communion with the Father and with fellow believers (see vv. 6–7).

1:4 *our joy complete.* John's joy in the Lord could not be complete unless his readers shared the true knowledge of the Christ (see 2Jn 12; cf. Php 2:2).

1:5 *from him.* From Christ. *light ... darkness.* Light represents what is good, true and holy, while darkness represents what is evil and false (see Jn 3:19–21).

1:6–7 *walk in the darkness ... in the light.* Two lifestyles—one characterized by wickedness and error, the other by holiness and truth.

1:6 *we.* John and his readers. *to have fellowship with him.* To be in living, spiritual union with God. *walk.* A metaphor for living (see note on Col 1:10). *truth.* See note on Jn 1:14.

1:7 *sin.* A key word in 1 John, occurring 27 times in the Greek.

1:9 *confess our sins.* Cf. Pr 28:13 and note. *faithful and just.* Here the phrase is virtually a single concept (faithful-and-just). It indicates that God's response toward those who confess their sins will be in accordance with his nature and his gracious commitment to his people (see Ps 143:1; Zec 8:8 and note). *faithful.* To his promise to forgive (see Jer 31:34; Mic 7:18–20; Heb 10:22–23 and notes). *will forgive us.* Will provide the forgiveness that restores the communion with God that had been interrupted by sin (as requested in the Lord's Prayer, Mt 6:12).

1:10 *we have not sinned.* Gnostics denied that their immoral actions were sinful.

2:1 *dear children.* John, the aged apostle, often used this expression of endearment (vv. 12–13,28; 3:7,18; 4:4; 5:21; the term in 2:18 translates a different Greek word). *one who speaks ... in our defense.* One Greek word underlies this phrase, which refers to someone who speaks in court in behalf of a defendant (see note on Jn 14:16). *Righteous One.* In God's court the defender must be, and is, sinless (cf. Ac 3:14 and note).

2:2 *atoning sacrifice for our sins.* The NIV text note explains the fuller meaning of the original Greek (see also 4:10). God's holiness demands punishment for human sin. God, therefore, out of love (4:10; Jn 3:16), sent his Son to make substitutionary atonement for the believer's sin. In this way the Father's wrath is satisfied; his wrath against the Christian's sin has been turned away and directed toward Christ. See note on Ro 3:25. *for the sins of the whole world.* Forgiveness through Christ's atoning sacrifice is not limited to one particular group only; it has worldwide application (see Jn 1:29). It must, however, be received by faith (see Jn 3:16). Thus this verse does not teach universalism (that all people ultimately will be saved), but that God is an impartial God.

2:3 *know.* Forty-two times 1 John uses two Greek verbs normally translated "know." One of these verbs is related to the name of the Gnostics, the heretical sect that claimed to have a special knowledge (Greek *gnosis*) of God (see Introduction: Gnosticism). *obey his commands.* Does not mean that only those who never disobey (1:8–9) know God, but simply refers to those whose lives are generally characterized by obedience.

2:5 *God's love is truly made complete in him.* Means either that God's love for the believer is made complete when

in him.[h] This is how we know[i] we are in
him: 6Whoever claims to live in him must
walk as Jesus did.[j]
7Dear friends,[k] I am not writing you a
new command but an old one, which you
have had since the beginning.[l] This old
command is the message you have heard.
8Yet I am writing you a new command;[m]
its truth is seen in him and you, because
the darkness is passing[n] and the true light[o]
is already shining.[p]
9Anyone who claims to be in the light
but hates his brother[q] is still in the darkness.[r] 10Whoever loves his brother lives in
the light,[s] and there is nothing in him[a] to
make him stumble.[t] 11But whoever hates
his brother[u] is in the darkness and walks
around in the darkness;[v] he does not know
where he is going, because the darkness
has blinded him.[w]

12I write to you, dear children,[x]
because your sins have been
forgiven on account of his
name.[y]
13I write to you, fathers,
because you have known him who is
from the beginning.[z]
I write to you, young men,
because you have overcome[a] the evil
one.[b]
I write to you, dear children,[c]
because you have known the Father.
14I write to you, fathers,
because you have known him who is
from the beginning.[d]
I write to you, young men,
because you are strong,[e]
and the word of God[f] lives in you,[g]
and you have overcome the evil
one.[h]

Do Not Love the World

15Do not love the world or anything in
the world.[i] If anyone loves the world, the
love of the Father is not in him.[j] 16For everything in the world—the cravings of
sinful man,[k] the lust of his eyes[l] and the
boasting of what he has and does—comes
not from the Father but from the world.
17The world and its desires pass away,[m]
but the man who does the will of God[n]
lives forever.

Warning Against Antichrists

18Dear children, this is the last hour;[o]
and as you have heard that the antichrist
is coming,[p] even now many antichrists
have come.[q] This is how we know it is
the last hour. 19They went out from us,[r]
but they did not really belong to us. For if
they had belonged to us, they would have

[a] 10 Or *it*

2:5 [h]1Jn 4:12 [i]S ver 3 **2:6** [j]S Mt 11:29 **2:7** [k]S 1Co 10:14 [l]ver 24; 1Jn 3:11,23; 4:21; 2Jn 5,6 **2:8** [m]S Jn 13:34 [n]Ro 13:12; Heb 10:25 [o]Jn 1:9 [p]Eph 5:8; 1Th 5:5 **2:9** [q]ver 11; Lev 19:17; 1Jn 3:10,15,16; 4:20,21 [r]1Jn 1:5 **2:10** [s]1Jn 3:14 [t]ver 11; Ps 119:165 **2:11** [u]S ver 9 [v]S 1Jn 1:6 [w]Jn 11:9; 12:35 **2:12** [x]S ver 1 [y]S 1Jn 3:23 **2:13** [z]S Jn 1:1 [a]S Jn 16:33 [b]ver 14; S Mt 5:37 [c]S ver 1 **2:14** [d]S Jn 1:1 [e]Eph 6:10 [f]S Heb 4:12 [g]Jn 5:38; 1Jn 1:10 [h]S ver 13 **2:15** [i]Ro 12:2 [j]Jas 4:4 **2:16** [k]Ge 3:6; Ro 13:14; Eph 2:3 [l]Pr 27:20 **2:17** [m]S Heb 12:27 [n]Mt 12:50 **2:18** [o]S Ro 13:11 [p]ver 22; 1Jn 4:3; 2Jn 7 [q]1Jn 4:1 **2:19** [r]Ac 20:30

it moves the believer to acts of obedience (see 4:12), or that our love for God (see NIV text note) becomes complete when it expresses itself in acts of obedience (see 3:16–18). *in him.* Spiritual union with God (see Jn 17:21; Eph 1:1 and note).

2:7–8 *new command.* See Jn 13:34–35 and notes. The Biblical command to love was old (see Lev 19:18; also Mt 22:39–40). But its newness is seen in: (1) the new and dramatic illustration of divine love on the cross; (2) Christ's exposition of the OT law (see Mt 5), which seemed new to Christ's hearers; and (3) the daily experience of believers as they grow in love for each other.

2:7 *Dear friends.* Like "dear children" (see note on v. 1), a favorite term of John's (used ten times in two letters: here; 3:2,21; 4:1,7,11; 3Jn 1–2,5,11). *since the beginning.* The beginning of their Christian experience, when they first heard the gospel.

2:8 *true light.* Used in the NT only here and in Jn 1:9 (see note on Jn 1:4), this phrase refers to the gospel of Jesus Christ, who is the light of the world (see Jn 8:12; 2Co 4:6 and notes).

2:9–10 *hates … loves.* In the Bible hatred and love as moral qualities are not primarily emotions, but attitudes expressed in actions (see 3:15–16).

2:9 *light … darkness.* See note on 1:5. *brother.* See note on Ro 1:13.

2:10 *stumble.* Into sin.

2:12–14 *I write to you … because.* By extended repetition in these verses, John assures his readers that, in spite of the rigorous tests contained in the letter, he is confident of their salvation. *dear children … fathers … young men.* As elsewhere in this letter, "dear children" probably refers to all John's readers (see note on v. 1), including fathers and young men. The terms "fathers" and "young men" may, however, describe two different levels of spiritual maturity. Some hold that all three terms refer to levels of spiritual maturity.

2:12 *his name.* Jesus (see 3:23; 5:13; see also note on Ac 4:12).

2:13–14 *him who is from the beginning.* Christ (see note on 1:1).

2:15 *world.* Not the world of people (Jn 3:16) or the created world (Jn 17:24), but here the world, or realm, of sin (v. 16; see Jas 4:4 and note), which is controlled by Satan and organized against God and righteousness (see note on Jn 1:9). *love of the Father.* Love for the Father.

2:18 *last hour.* With other NT writers, John viewed the whole period beginning with Christ's first coming as the last days (see Ac 2:17; 2Ti 3:1 and note). They understood this to be the "last" of the days because neither former prophecy nor new revelation concerning the history of salvation indicated the coming of another era before the return of Christ. The word "last" in "last days," "last times" and "last hour" also expresses a sense of urgency and imminence. The Christian is to be alert, waiting for the return of Christ (Mt 25:1–13). *the antichrist … many antichrists.* John assumed his readers knew that a great enemy of God and his people would arise before Christ's return. That person is called "antichrist" (here), "the man of lawlessness" (2Th 2:3; but see note there) and "the beast" (Rev 13:1–10). But prior to him, there will be many antichrists. These are characterized by the following: (1) They deny the incarnation (see 4:2 and note; 2Jn 7) and that Jesus is the divine Christ (v. 22); (2) they deny the Father (v. 22); (3) they do not have the Father (v. 23); (4) they are liars (v. 22) and deceivers (2Jn 7); (5) they are many (v. 18); (6) in John's day they left the church because they had nothing in common with believers (v. 19). The antichrists referred to in John's letter were the early Gnostics. The "anti" in antichrist means "against" (cf. 2Th 2:4; Rev 13:6–7).

remained with us; but their going showed
that none of them belonged to us.[s]
20But you have an anointing[t] from the
Holy One,[u] and all of you know the truth.[a v]
21I do not write to you because you do not
know the truth, but because you do know
it[w] and because no lie comes from the
truth. 22Who is the liar? It is the man who
denies that Jesus is the Christ. Such a man
is the antichrist — he denies the Father and
the Son.[x] 23No one who denies the Son has
the Father; whoever acknowledges the Son
has the Father also.[y]
24See that what you have heard from
the beginning[z] remains in you. If it does,
you also will remain in the Son and in the
Father.[a] 25And this is what he promised
us — even eternal life.[b]
26I am writing these things to you about
those who are trying to lead you astray.[c]
27As for you, the anointing[d] you received
from him remains in you, and you do
not need anyone to teach you. But as his
anointing teaches you about all things[e]
and as that anointing is real, not counterfeit — just as it has taught you, remain in
him.[f]

Children of God

28And now, dear children,[g] continue in
him, so that when he appears[h] we may be
confident[i] and unashamed before him at
his coming.[j]
29If you know that he is righteous,[k] you
know that everyone who does what is
right has been born of him.[l]
3 How great is the love[m] the Father has
lavished on us, that we should be called
children of God![n] And that is what we are!
The reason the world does not know us is
that it did not know him.[o] 2Dear friends,[p]
now we are children of God,[q] and what
we will be has not yet been made known.
But we know that when he appears,[b r] we
shall be like him,[s] for we shall see him as
he is.[t] 3Everyone who has this hope in him
purifies himself,[u] just as he is pure.[v]
4Everyone who sins breaks the law; in
fact, sin is lawlessness.[w] 5But you know
that he appeared so that he might take
away our sins.[x] And in him is no sin.[y] 6No
one who lives in him keeps on sinning.[z]
No one who continues to sin has either
seen him[a] or known him.[b]
7Dear children,[c] do not let anyone lead
you astray.[d] He who does what is right
is righteous, just as he is righteous.[e] 8He
who does what is sinful is of the devil,[f]
because the devil has been sinning from
the beginning. The reason the Son of God[g]
appeared was to destroy the devil's work.[h]
9No one who is born of God[i] will continue to sin,[j] because God's seed[k] remains in
him; he cannot go on sinning, because he

2:19 [s] 1Co 11:19 **2:20** [t] ver 27; 2Co 1:21 [u] S Mk 1:24 [v] Jer 31:34; Mt 13:11; Jn 14:26 **2:21** [w] 2Pe 1:12; Jude 5 **2:22** [x] 1Jn 4:3; 2Jn 7 **2:23** [y] Jn 8:19; 14:7; 1Jn 4:15; 5:1; 2Jn 9 **2:24** [z] S ver 7 [a] Jn 14:23; 15:4; 1Jn 1:3; 2Jn 9 **2:25** [b] S Mt 25:46 **2:26** [c] 1Jn 3:7 **2:27** [d] ver 20 [e] 1Co 2:12 [f] Jn 15:4 **2:28** [g] S ver 1 [h] Col 3:4; 1Jn 3:2 [i] S Eph 3:12 [j] S 1Th 2:19 **2:29** [k] 1Jn 3:7 [l] S Jn 1:13 **3:1** [m] S Jn 3:16 [n] ver 2,10; S Jn 1:12 [o] Jn 15:21; 16:3 **3:2** [p] S 1Co 10:14 [q] ver 1,10; S Jn 1:12 [r] Col 3:4; 1Jn 2:28 [s] Ro 8:29; 2Pe 1:4 [t] Ps 17:15; Jn 17:24; 2Co 3:18 **3:3** [u] 2Co 7:1; 2Pe 3:13,14 [v] Ps 18:26 **3:4** [w] 1Jn 5:17 **3:5** [x] ver 8; S Jn 3:17 [y] S 2Co 5:21 **3:6** [z] ver 9; 1Jn 5:18 [a] 3Jn 11 [b] S 1Jn 2:4 **3:7** [c] S 1Jn 2:1 [d] 1Jn 2:26 [e] 1Jn 2:29 **3:8** [f] ver 10; Jn 8:44 [g] S Mt 4:3 [h] Heb 2:14 **3:9** [i] S Jn 1:13 [j] ver 6; Ps 119:3; 1Jn 5:18 [k] 1Pe 1:23

[a] 20 Some manuscripts *and you know all things*
[b] 2 Or *when it is made known*

2:20 *anointing.* The Holy Spirit (see v. 27; Jn 14:16–17; 15:26; 16:13; Ac 10:38). *Holy One.* Either Jesus Christ (Mk 1:24; Jn 6:69; Ac 2:27; 3:14; 22:14) or the Father (2Ki 19:22; Job 6:10).
2:22 *Jesus is the Christ.* The man Jesus is the divine Messiah (see the parallel confession in 5:5; see also Introduction: Gnosticism and note on 5:6).
2:23 See 2Jn 9 for the same thought.
2:25 *eternal life.* See Jn 3:15 and note; cf. Mt 19:16 and note.
2:26 One of the statements of purpose for the letter (see Introduction: Occasion and Purpose; see also 5:13 and note).
2:27 *anointing.* See note on v. 20. *do not need anyone to teach you.* Since the Bible constantly advocates teaching (Mt 28:20; 1Co 12:28; Eph 4:11; Col 3:16; 1Ti 4:11; 2Ti 2:2,24), John is not ruling out human teachers. At the time when he wrote, however, Gnostic teachers were insisting that the teaching of the apostles was to be supplemented with the higher knowledge that they (the Gnostics) claimed to possess. John's response was that what the readers were taught under the Spirit's ministry through the apostles not only was adequate but was the only reliable truth. *teaches you.* The teaching ministry of the Holy Spirit (what is commonly called illumination) does not involve revelation of new truth or the explanation of all difficult passages of Scripture to our satisfaction. Rather, it is the development of the capacity to appreciate and appropriate God's truth already revealed — making the Bible meaningful in thought and daily living. *all things.* All things necessary to know for salvation and Christian living.
2:28 *continue in him.* See "remains in" (vv. 24,27). *confident.* See 3:21; 4:17; 5:14.
2:29 *he … him.* God the Father. *does what is right.* Those who are born again are marked by righteous conduct.
3:1 *children of God.* See note on Jn 1:12.
3:2 *he … him.* Christ. *we shall be like him.* Cf. Ro 8:29; 1Co 15:49; Php 3:21.
3:3 *hope.* Not a mere wish, but unshakable confidence concerning the future (see Ro 5:5 and note). *him.* Christ. *purifies himself.* By turning from sin.
3:5 *take away our sins.* See Jn 1:29 and note. *in him is no sin.* Amply confirmed elsewhere in the NT (see 2Co 5:21; Heb 4:15 and notes; 1Pe 3:18).
3:6 *keeps on sinning.* John is not asserting sinless perfection (see 1:8–10; 2:1), but explaining that the believer's life is characterized not by sin but by doing what is right.
3:8 *devil.* In this short letter John says much about the devil: (1) He is called "the devil" (here) and "the evil one" (v. 12; 2:13–14; 5:18–19). (2) He "has been sinning from the beginning" (here), i.e., from the time he first rebelled against God, before the fall of Adam and Eve (see Jn 8:44 and note). (3) He is the instigator of human sin, and those who continue to sin belong to him (vv. 8,12) and are his children (v. 10). (4) He is in the world (4:3) and has "the whole world" of unbelievers under his control (5:19). (5) But he cannot lay hold of believers to harm them (5:18). (6) On the contrary, Christians will overcome him (2:13–14; 4:4), and Christ will destroy his work (see Ro 16:20 and note).
3:9 *God's seed.* The picture is of human reproduction, in which the sperm (the Greek for "seed" is *sperma*) bears the life principle and transfers the paternal characteristics. *cannot go on sinning.* Not a complete cessation of sin, but a life that is not characterized by sin.

has been born of God. 10This is how we know who the children of God[l] are and who the children of the devil[m] are: Anyone who does not do what is right is not a child of God; nor is anyone who does not love[n] his brother.[o]

Love One Another

11This is the message you heard[p] from the beginning:[q] We should love one another.[r] 12Do not be like Cain, who belonged to the evil one[s] and murdered his brother.[t] And why did he murder him? Because his own actions were evil and his brother's were righteous.[u] 13Do not be surprised, my brothers, if the world hates you.[v] 14We know that we have passed from death to life,[w] because we love our brothers. Anyone who does not love remains in death.[x] 15Anyone who hates his brother[y] is a murderer,[z] and you know that no murderer has eternal life in him.[a]

16This is how we know what love is: Jesus Christ laid down his life for us.[b] And we ought to lay down our lives for our brothers.[c] 17If anyone has material possessions and sees his brother in need but has no pity on him,[d] how can the love of God be in him?[e] 18Dear children,[f] let us not love with words or tongue but with actions and in truth.[g] 19This then is how we know that we belong to the truth, and how we set our hearts at rest in his presence 20whenever our hearts condemn us. For God is greater than our hearts, and he knows everything.

21Dear friends,[h] if our hearts do not condemn us, we have confidence before God[i] 22and receive from him anything we ask,[j] because we obey his commands[k] and do what pleases him.[l] 23And this is his command: to believe[m] in the name of his Son, Jesus Christ,[n] and to love one another as he commanded us.[o] 24Those who obey his commands[p] live in him,[q] and he in them. And this is how we know that he lives in us: We know it by the Spirit he gave us.[r]

Test the Spirits

4 Dear friends,[s] do not believe every spirit,[t] but test the spirits to see whether they are from God, because many false prophets have gone out into the world.[u] 2This is how you can recognize the Spirit of God: Every spirit that acknowledges that Jesus Christ has come in the flesh[v] is from God,[w] 3but every spirit that does not acknowledge Jesus is not from God. This is the spirit of the antichrist,[x] which you have heard is coming and even now is already in the world.[y]

4You, dear children,[z] are from God and have overcome them,[a] because the one who is in you[b] is greater than the one who is in the world.[c] 5They are from the world[d] and therefore speak from the viewpoint of the world, and the world listens to them. 6We are from God, and whoever knows God listens to us; but whoever is not from God does not listen to us.[e] This is how we recognize the Spirit[a] of truth[f] and the spirit of falsehood.[g]

God's Love and Ours

7Dear friends, let us love one another,[h]

3:10 [l] ver 1,2; S Jn 1:12 [m] ver 8 [n] 1Jn 4:8 [o] S 1Jn 2:9 **3:11** [p] 1Jn 1:5 [q] S 1Jn 2:7 [r] Jn 13:34,35; 15:12; 1Jn 4:7,11,21; 2Jn 5 **3:12** [s] S Mt 5:37 [t] Ge 4:8 [u] Ps 38:20; Pr 29:10 **3:13** [v] Jn 15:18, 19; 17:14 **3:14** [w] Jn 5:24 [x] S 1Jn 2:9 **3:15** [y] S 1Jn 2:9 [z] Mt 5:21,22; Jn 8:44 [a] Gal 5:20,21; Rev 21:8 **3:16** [b] Jn 10:11 [c] Jn 15:13; Php 2:17; 1Th 2:8 **3:17** [d] Dt 15:7,8; Jas 2:15,16 [e] 1Jn 4:20 **3:18** [f] S 1Jn 2:1 [g] Eze 33:31; Ro 12:9 **3:21** [h] S 1Co 10:14 [i] S Eph 3:12; 1Jn 5:14 **3:22** [j] S Mt 7:7 [k] S Jn 14:15 [l] Jn 8:29; Heb 13:21 **3:23** [m] Jn 6:29 [n] S Lk 24:47; Jn 1:12; 3:18; 20:31; 1Co 6:11; 1Jn 5:13 [o] S Jn 13:34 **3:24** [p] 1Jn 2:3 [q] 1Jn 2:6; 4:15 [r] 1Th 4:8; 1Jn 4:13 **4:1** [s] S 1Co 10:14 [t] Jer 29:8; 1Co 12:10; 2Th 2:2 [u] S Mt 7:15; 1Jn 2:18

[a] 6 Or *spirit*

4:2 [v] S Jn 1:14; 1Jn 2:23 [w] 1Co 12:3 **4:3** [x] 1Jn 2:22; 2Jn 7 [y] 1Jn 2:18 **4:4** [z] S 1Jn 2:1 [a] S Jn 16:33 [b] Ro 8:31 [c] 2Ki 6:16; S Jn 12:31 **4:5** [d] Jn 15:19; 17:14,16 **4:6** [e] Jn 8:47 [f] S Jn 14:17 [g] S Mk 13:5 **4:7** [h] S 1Jn 3:11

3:11 *from the beginning.* See note on 2:7.

3:12 *Cain.* See Heb 11:4 and note.

3:13 *brothers.* See note on Ro 1:13.

3:15 *hates.* See note on 2:9–10; cf. Mt 5:21–22. *murderer.* See Jas 4:2 and note.

3:17–18 See Jas 2:14–17 and note on 2:15–16.

3:17 *love of God.* God's kind of love, which he pours out in the believer's heart (see Ro 5:5 and note) and which in turn enables the Christian to love fellow believers. Or it may speak of the believer's love for God.

3:20 *God is greater than our hearts.* An oversensitive conscience can be quieted by the knowledge that God himself has declared active love to be an evidence of salvation. He knows the hearts of all; he knows whether or not, in spite of shortcomings, they have been born of him (v. 9).

3:23 This command has two parts: (1) Believe in Christ (see Jn 6:29 and note), and (2) love one another (see Jn 13:34–35 and notes). The first part is developed in 4:1–6 and the second part in 4:7–12.

3:24 *We know it by the Spirit.* See Ro 8:16 and note.

4:1 *spirit.* A person moved by a spirit, whether by the Holy Spirit or an evil one. *test the spirits.* Cf. 1Th 5:21 and note. (Mt 7:1 does not refer to such testing or judgment; it speaks of self-righteous moral judgment of others.) *false prophets.* A true prophet speaks from God, being "carried along by the Holy Spirit" (2Pe 1:21; see note there). False prophets, such as the Gnostics of John's day, speak under the influence of spirits alienated from God. Christ warned against false prophets (see Mt 7:15 and note; Mk 13:22), as did Paul (see 1Ti 4:1 and note) and Peter (see 2Pe 2:1 and note).

4:2 *acknowledges.* Not only knows intellectually—for demons know, and shudder (Jas 2:19; cf. Mk 1:24)—but also confesses publicly. *Jesus Christ has come in the flesh.* See note on 1:1. Thus John excludes the Gnostics, especially the Cerinthians, who taught that the divine Christ came upon the human Jesus at his baptism and then left him at the cross, so that it was only the man Jesus who died (see Introduction: Gnosticism).

4:3 *does not acknowledge Jesus.* The incarnate Jesus Christ of 1:2 (see note on 2:18).

4:4 *from God.* An abbreviated form of the expression "born of God" (2:29; 3:9–10; 4:7; 5:1,4,18). *them.* The false prophets (v. 1), who were inspired by the spirit of the antichrist (v. 3). *the one who is in the world.* The devil (see Jn 12:31 and note). In v. 3 "world" means the inhabited earth; in vv. 4–5 it means the community, or system, of those not born of God—including the antichrists (see note on Jn 1:9).

4:6 *Spirit of truth.* Cf. 5:6 and note; see note on Jn 14:17.

4:7—5:3 The word "love" in its various forms is used 43 times in the letter, 32 times in this short section.

for love comes from God. Everyone who
loves has been born of God[i] and knows
God.[j] 8Whoever does not love does not
know God, because God is love.[k] 9This is
how God showed his love among us: He
sent his one and only Son[a][l] into the world
that we might live through him.[m] 10This
is love: not that we loved God, but that
he loved us[n] and sent his Son as an atoning sacrifice for[b] our sins.[o] 11Dear friends,[p]
since God so loved us,[q] we also ought to
love one another.[r] 12No one has ever seen
God;[s] but if we love one another, God
lives in us and his love is made complete
in us.[t]
13We know[u] that we live in him and he
in us, because he has given us of his Spirit.[v] 14And we have seen and testify[w] that
the Father has sent his Son to be the Savior of the world.[x] 15If anyone acknowledges that Jesus is the Son of God,[y] God lives
in him and he in God.[z] 16And so we know
and rely on the love God has for us.
God is love.[a] Whoever lives in love lives
in God, and God in him.[b] 17In this way,
love is made complete[c] among us so that
we will have confidence[d] on the day of
judgment,[e] because in this world we are
like him. 18There is no fear in love. But
perfect love drives out fear,[f] because fear
has to do with punishment. The one who
fears is not made perfect in love.
19We love because he first loved us.[g]
20If anyone says, "I love God," yet hates
his brother,[h] he is a liar.[i] For anyone who
does not love his brother, whom he has
seen,[j] cannot love God, whom he has not
seen.[k] 21And he has given us this command:[l] Whoever loves God must also love
his brother.[m]

Faith in the Son of God

5 Everyone who believes[n] that Jesus is
the Christ[o] is born of God,[p] and everyone who loves the father loves his child
as well.[q] 2This is how we know[r] that we
love the children of God:[s] by loving God
and carrying out his commands. 3This is
love for God: to obey his commands.[t] And
his commands are not burdensome,[u] 4for
everyone born of God[v] overcomes[w] the
world. This is the victory that has overcome the world, even our faith. 5Who is
it that overcomes the world? Only he who
believes that Jesus is the Son of God.[x]
6This is the one who came by water and
blood[y]—Jesus Christ. He did not come by
water only, but by water and blood. And
it is the Spirit who testifies, because the

[a] 9 Or *his only begotten Son* [b] 10 Or *as the one who would turn aside his wrath, taking away*

4:7 [i]S Jn 1:13 [j]S 1Jn 2:4 **4:8** [k]ver 7,16 **4:9** [l]Jn 1:18 [m]Jn 3:16,17; 1Jn 5:11 **4:10** [n]Ro 5:8,10 [o]S Ro 3:25 **4:11** [p]S 1Co 10:14 [q]S Jn 3:16 [r]Jn 15:12; S 1Jn 3:11 **4:12** [s]S Jn 1:18 [t]ver 17; 1Jn 2:5 **4:13** [u]S 1Jn 2:3 [v]1Jn 3:24 **4:14** [w]S Jn 15:27 [x]S Lk 2:11; S Jn 3:17 **4:15** [y]S 1Jn 2:23; 5:5 [z]1Jn 3:24 **4:16** [a]ver 8 [b]ver 12,13; 1Jn 3:24 **4:17** [c]ver 12; 1Jn 2:5 [d]S Eph 3:12 [e]S Mt 10:15 **4:18** [f]Ro 8:15 **4:19** [g]ver 10 **4:20** [h]S 1Jn 2:9 [i]S 1Jn 1:6; 2:4 [j]1Jn 3:17 [k]ver 12; S Jn 1:18 **4:21** [l]1Jn 2:7 [m]S Mt 5:43; S 1Jn 2:9 **5:1** [n]S Jn 3:15 [o]1Jn 2:22; 4:2,15 [p]S Jn 1:13; S 1Jn 2:23 [q]Jn 8:42

5:2 [r]S 1Jn 2:3 [s]1Jn 3:14 **5:3** [t]S Jn 14:15 [u]Mt 11:30; 23:4 **5:4** [v]S Jn 1:13 [w]S Jn 16:33 **5:5** [x]ver 1; S 1Jn 2:23 **5:6** [y]Jn 19:34

4:8 *does not know God.* Only those who are to some degree like him truly know him. *God is love.* In his essential nature and in all his actions, God is loving (see also v. 16). John similarly affirms that God is spirit (see Jn 4:24 and note) and light (see 1:5 and note), as well as righteous (2:29; 3:7), holy (2:20), powerful or great (4:4), faithful (see 1:9 and note), true (5:20) and just (1:9).

4:9 *one and only Son.* See Jn 1:18; 3:16 and notes.

4:10 *atoning sacrifice for our sins.* See note on 2:2.

4:12 *No one has ever seen God.* See note on Jn 1:18. Since our love has its source in God's love, his love reaches full expression (is made complete) when we love fellow Christians. Thus the God whom "no one has ever seen" is seen in those who love, because God lives in them.

4:13–14 *Spirit ... Father ... Son.* See note on Mt 28:19.

4:13 *has given us of his Spirit.* See 3:24 and note.

4:16 *God is love.* See note on v. 8.

4:17 *like him.* Like Christ. The fact that we are like Christ in love is a sign that God, who is love, lives in us; therefore we may have confidence on the day of judgment that we are saved.

4:18 *no fear in love.* There is no fear of God's judgment because genuine love confirms salvation.

4:19 All love comes ultimately from God; genuine love is never self-generated by his creatures.

4:21 *this command.* See Jn 13:34 and note.

5:1 *Everyone who believes that Jesus is the Christ is born of God.* Faith in Jesus as the Messiah is a sign of being born again, just as love is (4:7). *the Christ.* See note on 2:22. *everyone who loves the father loves his child as well.* John wrote at a time when members of a family were closely associated as a unit under the headship of the father. He could therefore use the family as an illustration to show that anyone who loves God the Father will naturally love God's children.

5:3 *This is love for God: to obey his commands.* Cf. Jn 14:15,21 and notes. *his commands are not burdensome.* Not because the commands themselves are light or easy to obey but, as John explains in v. 4, because of the new birth. The one born of God by faith is enabled by the Holy Spirit to obey.

5:4 *overcomes ... has overcome.* To overcome the world is to gain victory over its sinful pattern of life, which is another way of describing obedience to God (v. 3). Such obedience is not impossible for believers because they have been born again and the Holy Spirit dwells within them and gives them strength. John speaks of two aspects of victory: (1) the initial victory of turning in faith from the world to God ("has overcome"); (2) the continuing day-by-day victory of Christian living ("overcomes"). *world.* See note on 2:15.

5:5 *Son of God.* For parallel confessions see 2:22; 4:2; 5:1 and notes.

5:6 *water and blood.* Water symbolizes Jesus' baptism, and blood symbolizes his death. These are mentioned because Jesus' ministry began at his baptism and ended at his death. John is reacting to the Gnostic heretics of his day (see Introduction: Gnosticism) who said that Jesus was born only a man and remained so until his baptism. At that time, they maintained, the Messiah (the Son of God) descended on the human Jesus, but left him before his suffering on the cross—so that it was only the man Jesus who died. Throughout this letter John has been insisting that Jesus Christ is God as well as man (1:1–4; 4:2; 5:5). He now asserts that it was this God-man Jesus Christ who came into our world, was baptized and died. Jesus was the Son of God not only at his baptism but also at his death (v. 6b). This truth is extremely important, because, if Jesus died only as a man, his sacrificial atonement (2:2; 4:10) would not have been sufficient to take away the guilt of human sin. *the Spirit who testifies.* The Holy Spirit testifies that

Spirit is the truth.[z] 7For there are three[a]
that testify: 8the[a] Spirit, the water and the
blood; and the three are in agreement.
9We accept man's testimony,[b] but God's
testimony is greater because it is the testimony of God,[c] which he has given about
his Son. 10Anyone who believes in the Son
of God has this testimony in his heart.[d]
Anyone who does not believe God has
made him out to be a liar,[e] because he has
not believed the testimony God has given
about his Son. 11And this is the testimony:
God has given us eternal life,[f] and this life
is in his Son.[g] 12He who has the Son has
life; he who does not have the Son of God
does not have life.[h]

Concluding Remarks

13I write these things to you who believe in the name of the Son of God[i] so
that you may know that you have eternal
life.[j] 14This is the confidence[k] we have in
approaching God: that if we ask anything
according to his will, he hears us.[l] 15And
if we know that he hears us—whatever
we ask—we know[m] that we have what we
asked of him.[n]
16If anyone sees his brother commit a
sin that does not lead to death, he should
pray and God will give him life.[o] I refer to
those whose sin does not lead to death.
There is a sin that leads to death.[p] I am
not saying that he should pray about that.[q]
17All wrongdoing is sin,[r] and there is sin
that does not lead to death.[s]
18We know that anyone born of God[t]
does not continue to sin; the one who
was born of God keeps him safe, and the
evil one[u] cannot harm him.[v] 19We know
that we are children of God,[w] and that the
whole world is under the control of the
evil one.[x] 20We know also that the Son
of God has come[y] and has given us understanding,[z] so that we may know him
who is true.[a] And we are in him who is
true—even in his Son Jesus Christ. He is
the true God and eternal life.[b]
21Dear children,[c] keep yourselves from
idols.[d]

5:6 [z]S Jn 14:17
5:7 [a]S Mt 18:16
5:9 [b]Jn 5:34 [c]Mt 3:16, 17; Jn 5:32, 37; 8:17, 18
5:10 [d]Ro 8:16; Gal 4:6 [e]Jn 3:33; 1Jn 1:10
5:11 [f]S Mt 25:46 [g]S Jn 1:4
5:12 [h]Jn 3:15, 16, 36
5:13 [i]S 1Jn 3:23 [j]ver 11; S Mt 25:46
5:14 [k]S Eph 3:12; 1Jn 3:21 [l]S Mt 7:7
5:15 [m]ver 18, 19, 20 [n]1Ki 3:12
5:16 [o]Jas 5:15 [p]Ex 23:21; Heb 6:4-6; 10:26 [q]Jer 7:16; 14:11
5:17 [r]1Jn 3:4 [s]ver 16; 1Jn 2:1
5:18 [t]S Jn 1:13 [u]S Mt 5:37 [v]Jn 14:30
5:19 [w]1Jn 4:6 [x]Jn 12:31; 14:30; 17:15
5:20 [y]ver 5 [z]Lk 24:45 [a]Jn 17:3 [b]ver 11; S Mt 25:46
5:21 [c]S 1Jn 2:1 [d]1Co 10:14; 1Th 1:9

[a] 7,8 Late manuscripts of the Vulgate *testify in heaven: the Father, the Word and the Holy Spirit, and these three are one. 8And there are three that testify on earth: the* (not found in any Greek manuscript before the fourteenth century)

Jesus is the Son of God in two ways: (1) The Spirit descended on Jesus at his baptism (Jn 1:32–34), and (2) he continues to confirm in the hearts of believers the apostolic testimony that Jesus' baptism and death verify that he is the Messiah, the Son of God (see 2:27; 1Co 12:3 and notes; cf. Ro 8:16 and note).

5:7 *three.* The OT law required "two or three witnesses" (Dt 17:6; see note there). At the end of this verse, some older English versions add the words found in the NIV text note. But the addition is not found in any Greek manuscript or NT translation prior to the 14th century.

5:9 *God's testimony.* The Holy Spirit's testimony, mentioned in vv. 6–8.

5:11 *has given us eternal life.* As a present possession (see notes on Jn 3:15,36).

5:13 Another statement of the letter's purpose (see 2:26 and note). See Introduction: Occasion and Purpose.

5:14 *if we ask anything according to his will.* Cf. Lk 22:42. For another condition for prayer see 3:21–22.

5:16 Verses 16–17 illustrate the kind of petition we can be sure God will answer (see vv. 14–15). *sin that leads to death.* In the context of this letter directed against Gnostic teaching, which denied the incarnation and threw off all moral restraints, it is probable that the "sin that leads to death" refers to the Gnostics' adamant and persistent denial of the truth and to their shameless immorality. This kind of unrepentant sin leads to spiritual death. Another view is that this is sin that results in physical death. It is held that, because a believer continues to sin, God in judgment takes his or her life (cf. 1Co 11:30). In either case, "sin that does not lead to death" is of a less serious nature.

5:18–20 *We know.* The letter ends with three striking statements, affirming the truths that "we know" and summarizing some of the letter's major themes.

5:18 *the one who was born of God.* Jesus, the Son of God.

5:20 *him who is true.* God the Father. *He is the true God.* Could refer to either God the Father or God the Son. *eternal life.* The letter began with this theme (1:1–2) and now ends with it.

5:21 *idols.* False gods, as opposed to the one true God (v. 20).

2 John

I N T R O D U C T I O N

Author

The author is John the apostle. Obvious similarities to 1 John and the Gospel of John suggest that the same person wrote all three books. Compare the following:

2Jn 5	1Jn 2:7	Jn 13:34–35
2Jn 6	1Jn 5:3	Jn 14:23
2Jn 7	1Jn 4:2–3	
2Jn 12	1Jn 1:4	Jn 15:11; 16:24

See Introductions to 1 John and the Gospel of John: Author.

Date

The letter was probably written about the same time as 1 John (A.D. 85–95), as the above comparisons suggest (see Introduction to 1 John: Date).

Recipient(s)

The person or persons addressed in this letter are unknown (see note on v. 1).

Occasion and Purpose

During the first two centuries the gospel was taken from place to place by traveling evangelists and teachers. Believers customarily took these missionaries into their homes and gave them provisions for their journey when they left. Since false teachers also relied on this practice (see note on 3Jn 5), 2 John was written to urge discernment in supporting traveling teachers; otherwise, someone might unintentionally contribute to the propagation of heresy rather than truth.

Outline

I. Greetings (1–3)
II. Commendation (4)
III. Exhortation and Warning (5–11)
IV. Conclusion and Final Greetings (12–13)

A Quick Look

Author:
The apostle John

Audience:
The "chosen lady," probably a local church in western Asia Minor

Date:
Between A.D. 85 and 95

Theme:
John writes to urge discernment in supporting traveling teachers, since false teachers were also traveling and teaching heresy.

1The elder,[a]

To the chosen[b] lady and her children,
whom I love in the truth[c]—and not I only,
but also all who know the truth[d]— 2be-
cause of the truth,[e] which lives in us[f] and
will be with us forever:

3Grace, mercy and peace from God the
Father and from Jesus Christ,[g] the Father's
Son, will be with us in truth and love.

4It has given me great joy to find some
of your children walking in the truth,[h]
just as the Father commanded us. 5And
now, dear lady, I am not writing you a
new command but one we have had from
the beginning.[i] I ask that we love one another. 6And this is love:[j] that we walk in
obedience to his commands.[k] As you have
heard from the beginning,[l] his command
is that you walk in love.
7Many deceivers, who do not acknowledge Jesus Christ[m] as coming in the flesh,[n]
have gone out into the world.[o] Any such
person is the deceiver and the antichrist.[p]
8Watch out that you do not lose what you
have worked for, but that you may be rewarded fully.[q] 9Anyone who runs ahead
and does not continue in the teaching of
Christ[r] does not have God; whoever continues in the teaching has both the Father
and the Son.[s] 10If anyone comes to you and
does not bring this teaching, do not take
him into your house or welcome him.[t]
11Anyone who welcomes him shares[u] in
his wicked work.

12I have much to write to you, but I do
not want to use paper and ink. Instead, I
hope to visit you and talk with you face to
face,[v] so that our joy may be complete.[w]

13The children of your chosen[x] sister
send their greetings.

1 [a]S Ac 11:30; 3Jn 1 [b]ver 13; Ro 16:13; 1Pe 5:13 [c]ver 3 [d]Jn 8:32; 1Ti 2:4
2 [e]2Pe 1:12 [f]Jn 14:17; 1Jn 1:8
3 [g]S Ro 1:7
4 [h]3Jn 3,4
5 [i]S 1Jn 2:7
6 [j]1Jn 2:5 [k]S Jn 14:15 [l]S 1Jn 2:7
7 [m]1Jn 2:22; 4:2,3 [n]S Jn 1:14 [o]1Jn 4:1 [p]S 1Jn 2:18
8 [q]S Mt 10:42; Mk 10:29,30; 1Co 3:8; Heb 10:35,36; 11:26
9 [r]Jn 8:31 [s]S 1Jn 2:23
10 [t]S Ro 16:17
11 [u]1Ti 5:22
12 [v]3Jn 13,14 [w]S Jn 3:29
13 [x]ver 1

1 *elder.* See note on 1Ti 3:1. In his later years, John functioned as an elder, perhaps of the Ephesian church. The apostle Peter held a similar position (see 1Pe 5:1 and note). *chosen lady.* Either an unknown Christian woman in the province of Asia or a figurative designation of a local church there (see v. 13). *her children.* Children of that Christian lady or members of that local church. *truth.* See note on Jn 1:14.
3 *Grace ... peace.* See note on Ro 1:7. *mercy.* See Ro 9:22–23 and note.
5 *new command.* See note on 1Jn 2:7–8.
6 *from the beginning.* See note on 1Jn 2:7.
7–11 This section deals with the basic Gnostic heresy attacked in 1 John, namely, that the Son of God did not become flesh (see Jn 1:14 and note), but that he temporarily came upon the man Jesus between his baptism and crucifixion (see Introduction to 1 John: Gnosticism).
7 *Jesus Christ as coming in the flesh.* See 1Jn 4:2–3 and notes. *antichrist.* See note on 1Jn 2:18.
8 *worked for ... rewarded.* Work faithfully accomplished on earth brings future reward (see Mk 9:41; 10:29–30; Lk 19:16–19; Heb 11:26).
9 *runs ahead.* A reference to the Gnostics, who believed that they had advanced beyond the teaching of the apostles. *teaching of Christ.* The similarity of this letter to 1 John, the nature of the heresy combated, and the immediate context suggest that John is not referring to teaching given by Christ, but to true teaching about Christ as the incarnate God-man (see 1Jn 2:23).
10 *take him into your house.* A reference to the housing and feeding of traveling teachers (see Introduction: Occasion and Purpose). The instruction does not prohibit greeting or even inviting a person into one's home for conversation. John was warning against providing food and shelter, since this would be an investment in the "wicked work" of false teachers and would give public approval (see v. 11).
12 *paper and ink.* Paper was made from papyrus reeds, which were readily available and cheap. The ink (the Greek for this word comes from a word that means "black") was made by mixing carbon, water and gum or oil. *that our joy may be complete.* See 1Jn 1:4 and note.
13 *chosen sister.* May be taken literally to designate another Christian woman or figuratively to refer to another local church (see note on v. 1).

3 John

INTRODUCTION

Author

The author is John the apostle. In the first verses of both 2 John and 3 John the author identifies himself as "the elder." Note other similarities: "love in the truth" (v. 1 of both letters), "walking in the truth" (v. 4 of both letters) and the similar conclusions. See Introductions to 1 John and the Gospel of John: Author.

Date

The letter was probably written about the same time as 1 and 2 John (A.D. 85 – 95). See Introduction to 1 John: Date.

Recipient

This letter is addressed to a certain Gaius (v. 1), about whom nothing more is known. He must have been a leader in one of the churches in the Roman province of Asia.

Occasion and Purpose

See Introduction to 2 John: Occasion and Purpose. Itinerant teachers sent out by John were rejected in one of the churches in the province of Asia by a dictatorial leader, Diotrephes, who even excommunicated members who showed hospitality to John's messengers. John wrote this letter to commend Gaius for supporting the teachers and, indirectly, to warn Diotrephes.

Outline

I. Greetings (1 – 2)
II. Commendation of Gaius (3 – 8)
III. Condemnation of Diotrephes (9 – 10)
IV. Exhortation to Gaius (11)
V. Example of Demetrius (12)
VI. Conclusion, Benediction and Final Greetings (13 – 14)

A Quick Look

Author:
The apostle John

Audience:
Gaius, perhaps a leader of one of the churches in western Asia Minor

Date:
Between A.D. 85 and 95

Theme:
John writes this letter to commend Gaius for supporting traveling teachers and to rebuke Diotrephes for refusing to welcome them.

1The elder,[a]

To my dear friend Gaius, whom I love
in the truth.

2Dear friend, I pray that you may enjoy
good health and that all may go well with
you, even as your soul is getting along
well. 3It gave me great joy to have some
brothers[b] come and tell about your faithfulness to the truth and how you continue
to walk in the truth.[c] 4I have no greater joy
than to hear that my children[d] are walking
in the truth.[e]

5Dear friend, you are faithful in what
you are doing for the brothers,[f] even
though they are strangers to you.[g] 6They
have told the church about your love. You
will do well to send them on their way[h]
in a manner worthy[i] of God. 7It was for
the sake of the Name[j] that they went out,
receiving no help from the pagans.[k] 8We
ought therefore to show hospitality to
such men so that we may work together
for the truth.

9I wrote to the church, but Diotrephes,
who loves to be first, will have nothing to
do with us. 10So if I come,[l] I will call attention to what he is doing, gossiping maliciously about us. Not satisfied with that,
he refuses to welcome the brothers.[m] He
also stops those who want to do so and
puts them out of the church.[n]

11Dear friend, do not imitate what is evil
but what is good.[o] Anyone who does what
is good is from God.[p] Anyone who does
what is evil has not seen God.[q] 12Deme-
trius is well spoken of by everyone[r]—and
even by the truth itself. We also speak well
of him, and you know that our testimony
is true.[s]

13I have much to write you, but I do not
want to do so with pen and ink. 14I hope
to see you soon, and we will talk face to
face.[t]

Peace to you.[u] The friends here send
their greetings. Greet the friends there by
name.[v]

1 [a]S Ac 11:30; 2Jn 1
3 [b]ver 5, 10; S Ac 1:16 [c]2Jn 4
4 [d]S 1Jn 2:1 [e]ver 3
5 [f]S ver 3 [g]Ro 12:13; Heb 13:2
6 [h]1Co 16:11; 2Co 1:16 [i]S Eph 4:1
7 [j]S Jn 15:21 [k]Ac 20:33, 35
10 [l]ver 14; 2Jn 12 [m]ver 5 [n]Jn 9:22, 34
11 [o]Ps 34:14; 37:27 [p]1Jn 2:29 [q]1Jn 3:6, 9, 10
12 [r]1Ti 3:7 [s]Jn 19:35; 21:24
14 [t]2Jn 12 [u]S Ro 1:7; S Eph 6:23 [v]Jn 10:3

1 *The elder.* See note on 2Jn 1. *dear friend.* A favorite term of John (see note on 1Jn 2:7). *Gaius.* A Christian in one of the churches in the Roman province of Asia. Gaius was a common Roman name. This letter presents two good examples (Gaius [vv. 3–8] and Demetrius [v. 12]) and one bad example (Diotrephes [see vv. 9–10 and notes]). *truth.* See note on Jn 1:14.

3–4 *walk in the truth … walking in the truth.* See 2Jn 4.

4 *my children.* Perhaps John's converts, or believers currently under his spiritual guidance (see 1Jn 2:1 and note).

5 *doing for the brothers.* The early church provided hospitality and support for missionaries. See Introduction to 2 John: Occasion and Purpose; see also note on 2Jn 10.

7 *Name.* Jesus Christ (see note on Ac 4:12; cf. Dt 12:5 and note).

8 *show hospitality.* See v. 5; 1Pe 4:9 and notes.

9 *I wrote.* A previous letter of the apostle that is now lost. *church.* Some identify this church with the chosen lady of 2Jn 1. *Diotrephes.* A church leader who was exercising dictatorial power in the church. He must have had considerable influence since he was able to exclude people from the church fellowship (v. 10). See Introduction: Occasion and Purpose.

10 *gossiping maliciously.* See Pr 18:8; 2Th 3:11 and notes; 1Ti 5:13.

11 *does what is good.* The continual practice of good, not merely doing occasional good deeds (cf. Ro 12:21). *has not seen God.* See 1Jn 3:6.

12 *Demetrius is well spoken of.* In contrast to Diotrephes (see vv. 9–10 and notes; see also note on v. 1). Demetrius was possibly the carrier of this letter. *even by the truth itself.* Possibly in some sense the gospel personified.

13–14 See 2Jn 12–13 for a similar conclusion (see also notes there).

14 *Peace to you.* Not a prayer or wish but a benedictory pronouncement (see note on Ro 1:7).

Jude

INTRODUCTION

Author

The author identifies himself as Jude (v. 1), which is another form of the Hebrew name Judah (Greek "Judas"), a common name among the Jews. Of those so named in the NT, the ones most likely to be author of this letter are: (1) Judas the apostle (see Lk 6:16; Ac 1:13 and note) — not Judas Iscariot — and (2) Judas the brother of the Lord (Mt 13:55; Mk 6:3). The latter is more likely. For example, the author does not claim to be an apostle and even seems to separate himself from the apostles (v. 17). Furthermore, he describes himself as a "brother of James" (v. 1). Ordinarily a person in Jude's day would describe himself as someone's son rather than as someone's brother. The reason for the exception here may have been James's prominence in the church at Jerusalem (see Introduction to James: Author).

Although neither Jude nor James describes himself as a brother of the Lord, others did not hesitate to speak of them in this way (see Mt 13:55; Jn 7:3 – 10; Ac 1:14; 1Co 9:5; Gal 1:19). Apparently they themselves did not ask to be heard because of the special privilege they had as members of the household of Joseph and Mary.

Possible references to the letter of Jude or quotations from it are found at a very early date: e.g., in Clement of Rome (c. A.D. 96). Clement of Alexandria (155 – 215), Tertullian (150 – 222) and Origen (185 – 253) accepted it; it was included in the Muratorian Canon (c. 170) and was accepted by Athanasius (298 – 373) and by the Council of Carthage (397). Eusebius (265 – 340) listed the letter among the questioned books, though he recognized that many considered it as from Jude.

According to Jerome and Didymus, some did not accept the letter as canonical because of the manner in which it uses noncanonical literature (see notes on vv. 9,14). But sound judgment has recognized that an inspired author may legitimately make use of such literature — whether for illustrative purposes or for appropriation of historically reliable or otherwise acceptable material — and such use does not necessarily endorse

A Quick Look

Author:
Most likely Jude, the brother of Jesus

Audience:
Christians who are being threatened by false teachers

Date:
Between A.D. 65 and 80

Theme:
Jude writes to warn believers of false teachers trying to convince believers that being saved by grace gives them license to sin.

that literature as inspired. Under the influence of the Spirit, the church came to the conviction that the authority of God stands behind the letter of Jude. The fact that the letter was questioned and tested but nonetheless was finally accepted by the churches indicates the strength of its claims to authenticity.

Jude thought it imperative that his readers be on guard and be prepared to oppose false teaching with the truth about God's grace.

Date

There is nothing in the letter that requires a date beyond the lifetime of Jude the brother of the Lord. The error the author is combating, like that in 2 Peter, is not the heretical teaching of the second century, but that which could and did develop at an early date (cf. Ac 20:29 – 30; Ro 6:1; 1Co 5:1 – 11; 2Co 12:21; Gal 5:13; Eph 5:3 – 17; 1Th 4:6). (See also Introduction to 2 Peter: Date.) There is, moreover, nothing in the letter that requires a date after the time of the apostles, as some have argued. It may even be that Jude's readers had heard some of the apostles speak (see vv. 17 – 18). Likewise, the use of the word "faith" in the objective sense of the body of truth believed (v. 3) does not require a late dating of the letter. It was used in such a sense as early as Gal 1:23.

The question of the relationship between Jude and 2 Peter has a bearing on the date of Jude. If 2Pe 2 makes use of Jude — a commonly accepted view (see Introduction to 2 Peter: 2 Peter and Jude) — then Jude is to be dated prior to 2 Peter, probably c. A.D. 65. Otherwise, a date as late as c. 80 would be possible.

Recipients

The description of those to whom Jude addressed his letter is very general (see v. 1). It could apply to Jewish Christians, Gentile Christians, or both. Their location is not indicated. It should not be assumed that, since 2Pe 2 and Jude 4 – 18 appear to describe similar situations, they were both written to the same people. The kind of heresy depicted in these two passages was widespread (see Date).

Occasion and Purpose

Although Jude was very eager to write to his readers about salvation, he felt that he must instead warn them about certain immoral men circulating among them who were perverting the grace of God (see v. 4 and note). Apparently these false teachers were trying to convince believers that being saved by grace gave them license to sin since their sins would no longer be held against them. Jude thought it imperative that his readers be on guard against such men and be prepared to oppose their false teaching with the truth about God's grace.

It has generally been assumed that these false teachers were Gnostics. Although this identification is no doubt correct, they must have been forerunners of fully developed, second-century Gnosticism (see Introduction to 2 Peter: Date).

Outline

- I. Greetings (1 – 2)
- II. Occasion for the Letter (3 – 4)
  - A. The Change of Subject (3)
  - B. The Reason for the Change: The Presence of Godless Apostates (4)
- III. Warning against the False Teachers (5 – 16)
  - A. Historical Examples of the Judgment of Apostates (5 – 7)
    1. Unbelieving Israel (5)
    2. Angels who fell (6)
    3. Sodom and Gomorrah (7)
  - B. Description of the Apostates of Jude's Day (8 – 16)
    1. Their slanderous speech deplored (8 – 10)

   2. Their character graphically portrayed (11 – 13)
   3. Their destruction prophesied (14 – 16)

IV. Exhortation to Believers (17 – 23)

V. Concluding Doxology (24 – 25)

1Jude,[a] a servant of Jesus Christ[b] and a
brother of James,

To those who have been called,[c] who
are loved by God the Father and kept by[a]
Jesus Christ:[d]

2Mercy, peace[e] and love be yours in
abundance.[f]

The Sin and Doom of Godless Men

3Dear friends,[g] although I was very eager to write to you about the salvation we
share,[h] I felt I had to write and urge you to
contend[i] for the faith[j] that was once for all
entrusted to the saints.[k] 4For certain men
whose condemnation was written about[b]
long ago have secretly slipped in among
you.[l] They are godless men, who change
the grace of our God into a license for immorality and deny Jesus Christ our only
Sovereign and Lord.[m]
5Though you already know all this,[n] I
want to remind you[o] that the Lord[c] delivered his people out of Egypt, but later
destroyed those who did not believe.[p]
6And the angels who did not keep their
positions of authority but abandoned their
own home—these he has kept in darkness, bound with everlasting chains for
judgment on the great Day.[q] 7In a similar way, Sodom and Gomorrah[r] and the
surrounding towns[s] gave themselves up
to sexual immorality and perversion. They
serve as an example of those who suffer
the punishment of eternal fire.[t]
8In the very same way, these dreamers
pollute their own bodies, reject authority
and slander celestial beings.[u] 9But even
the archangel[v] Michael,[w] when he was
disputing with the devil about the body
of Moses,[x] did not dare to bring a slanderous accusation against him, but said,
"The Lord rebuke you!"[y] 10Yet these men
speak abusively against whatever they do
not understand; and what things they do

1 [a] Mt 13:55; Jn 14:22; Ac 1:13 [b] Ro 1:1 [c] Ro 1:6,7 [d] Jn 17:12
2 [e] Gal 6:16; 1Ti 1:2 [f] S Ro 1:7
3 [g] S 1Co 10:14 [h] Tit 1:4 [i] 1Ti 6:12 [j] ver 20; Ac 6:7 [k] S Ac 9:13
4 [l] Gal 2:4 [m] Tit 1:16; 2Pe 2:1; 1Jn 2:22
5 [n] S 1Jn 2:20 [o] 2Pe 1:12,13; 3:1,2
[p] Nu 14:29; Dt 1:32; 2:15; Ps 106:26; 1Co 10:1-5; Heb 3:16,17
6 [q] S 2Pe 2:4,9
7 [r] S Mt 10:15 [s] Dt 29:23 [t] S Mt 25:41; 2Pe 3:7
8 [u] 2Pe 2:10
9 [v] 1Th 4:16 [w] Da 10:13,21; 12:1; Rev 12:7 [x] Dt 34:6 [y] Zec 3:2

[a] *1* Or *for*; or *in* [b] *4* Or *men who were marked out for condemnation* [c] *5* Some early manuscripts *Jesus*

1 *servant.* See note on Ro 1:1. *brother of James.* See Introduction: Author. *called.* See note on Ro 8:28. *loved by God.* See Jn 3:16; Ro 8:28–39. *kept by Jesus Christ.* He who holds the whole universe together (see Col 1:17; Heb 1:3) will see that God's children are kept in the faith and that they reach their eternal inheritance (see Jn 6:37–40; 17:11–12; 1Pe 1:3–5).

2 *Mercy.* See Ge 19:16; Ro 9:22–23; Tit 3:5 and notes. *peace.* See note on Ro 1:7.

3 *Dear friends.* See vv. 17,20; see also note on 2Pe 3:1. *the salvation we share.* Jude's original intention was to write a general treatment of the doctrine of salvation, probably dealing with such subjects as human sin and guilt, God's love and grace, the forgiveness of sins and the changed lifestyle that follows new birth. *the faith.* Here used of the body of truth held by believers everywhere—the gospel and all its implications (see Introduction: Date; see also 1Ti 4:6). This truth was under attack and had to be defended. *once for all entrusted.* The truth has finality and is not subject to change. *saints.* See notes on Ro 1:7; Eph 1:1.

4 *For.* Introduces the reason Jude felt impelled to change the subject of his letter (see Introduction: Occasion and Purpose). *whose condemnation was written about.* The reference may be to OT denunciations of ungodly people or to Enoch's prophecy (vv. 14–15). Or Jude may mean that judgment has long been about to fall on them because of their sin (see NIV text note and 2Pe 2:3, which may be a clarification of this clause). *godless men.* See vv. 15,18. *change the grace of our God into a license for immorality.* They assume that salvation by grace gives them the right to sin without restraint, either because God in his grace will freely forgive all their sins, or because sin, by contrast, magnifies the grace of God (cf. Ro 5:20; 6:1 and note). *deny ... our only Sovereign and Lord.* The Greek term translated "Sovereign" describes power without limit, or absolute domination. The Greek construction indicates that both "Sovereign" and "Lord" refer to the same person, and this verse, as well as the parallel passage (2 Pe 2:1), clearly states that that person is Christ.

5–7 Three examples of divine judgment.

5 *destroyed those who did not believe.* They did not believe that God would give them the land of Canaan; consequently all that unbelieving generation died in the desert without entering the promised land (see Nu 14:29–30; Dt 1:32–36; 2:15; 1Co 10:1–5 and note on 10:5; Heb 3:16–19 and note).

6 *angels.* See note on 2Pe 2:4. *positions of authority.* See note on 2Pe 2:4. God had assigned differing areas of responsibility and authority to each of the angels (see Da 10:20–21, where the various princes may be angels assigned to various nations). Some of these angels refused to maintain their assignments and thus became the devil and his angels (cf. Mt 25:41). *their own home.* Angels apparently were assigned specific locations as well as responsibilities. Some assume that they left the heavenly realm and came to earth (see note on 2Pe 2:4). *kept ... bound ... for judgment.* See note on 2Pe 2:4. *the great Day.* The final judgment.

7 *In a similar way.* Does not mean that the sin of Sodom and Gomorrah was the same as that of the angels or vice versa. This phrase is used to introduce the third illustration of the fact that God will see to it that the unrighteous will be consigned to eternal punishment on judgment day. *perversion.* Lit. "went after other flesh"; more specifically, homosexual practices (see Ge 19:5 and note). *serve as an example of ... punishment of eternal fire.* God destroyed Sodom and Gomorrah by pouring out "burning sulfur" (Ge 19:24)—a foretaste of the eternal fire that is to come.

8 *dreamers.* The godless men were called "dreamers" either (1) because they claimed to receive revelations or, more likely, (2) because in their passion they were out of touch with truth and reality. *pollute their own bodies.* Probably a reference to the homosexual practices in Sodom and Gomorrah (see vv. 4,7; 1Co 6:9 and note, 18). *reject authority.* See note on 2Pe 2:10. *slander celestial beings.* See note on 2Pe 2:10.

9 According to several church fathers, this verse is based on a noncanonical work called The Testament of Moses (approximately the first century A.D.). Other NT quotations from, or allusions to, non-Biblical works include Paul's quotations of Aratus (see Ac 17:28 and note), Menander (see 1Co 15:33 and note) and Epimenides (see Tit 1:12 and note). Such usage in no way suggests that the quotations, or the books from which they were taken, are divinely inspired. It only means that the Biblical author found the quotations to be a helpful confirmation, clarification or illustration.

10 *whatever they do not understand.* See note on 2Pe 2:12; cf. 1Co 2:14. *like unreasoning animals.* See note on 2Pe 2:12.

understand by instinct, like unreasoning
animals—these are the very things that
destroy them.[z]
11 Woe to them! They have taken the way
of Cain;[a] they have rushed for profit into
Balaam's error;[b] they have been destroyed
in Korah's rebellion.[c]
12 These men are blemishes at your love
feasts,[d] eating with you without the slightest qualm—shepherds who feed only
themselves.[e] They are clouds without
rain,[f] blown along by the wind;[g] autumn
trees, without fruit and uprooted[h]—twice
dead. 13 They are wild waves of the sea,[i]
foaming up their shame;[j] wandering stars,
for whom blackest darkness has been reserved forever.[k]
14 Enoch,[l] the seventh from Adam, prophesied about these men: "See, the Lord is
coming[m] with thousands upon thousands
of his holy ones[n] 15 to judge[o] everyone, and
to convict all the ungodly of all the ungodly acts they have done in the ungodly way,
and of all the harsh words ungodly sinners have spoken against him."[p] 16 These
men are grumblers[q] and faultfinders; they
follow their own evil desires;[r] they boast[s]
about themselves and flatter others for
their own advantage.

A Call to Persevere

17 But, dear friends, remember what the
apostles[t] of our Lord Jesus Christ foretold.[u]
18 They said to you, "In the last times[v] there
will be scoffers who will follow their own
ungodly desires."[w] 19 These are the men
who divide you, who follow mere natural
instincts and do not have the Spirit.[x]
20 But you, dear friends, build yourselves
up[y] in your most holy faith[z] and pray in
the Holy Spirit.[a] 21 Keep yourselves in God's
love as you wait[b] for the mercy of our Lord
Jesus Christ to bring you to eternal life.[c]
22 Be merciful to those who doubt;
23 snatch others from the fire and save
them;[d] to others show mercy, mixed with
fear—hating even the clothing stained by
corrupted flesh.[e]

10 [z] 2Pe 2:12
11 [a] Ge 4:3-8; Heb 11:4; 1Jn 3:12 [b] S 2Pe 2:15 [c] Nu 16:1-3,31-35
12 [d] 2Pe 2:13; 1Co 11:20-22 [e] Eze 34:2,8,10 [f] Pr 25:14; 2Pe 2:17 [g] Eph 4:14 [h] Mt 15:13
13 [i] Isa 57:20 [j] Php 3:19 [k] 2Pe 2:17
14 [l] Ge 5:18,21-24 [m] S Mt 16:27 [n] Dt 33:2; Da 7:10; Zec 14:5; Heb 12:22
15 [o] 2Pe 2:6-9 [p] 1Ti 1:9
16 [q] 1Co 10:10 [r] ver 18; 2Pe 2:10 [s] 2Pe 2:18
17 [t] S Eph 4:11 [u] Heb 2:3; 2Pe 3:2
18 [v] 1Ti 4:1; 2Ti 3:1; 2Pe 3:3 [w] ver 16; 2Pe 2:1; 3:3
19 [x] 1Co 2:14,15
20 [y] Col 2:7; 1Th 5:11 [z] ver 3 [a] Eph 6:18 21 [b] Tit 2:13; Heb 9:28; 2Pe 3:12 [c] S Mt 25:46 23 [d] Am 4:11; Zec 3:2-5; 1Co 3:15 [e] Rev 3:4

11 Three OT examples of the kind of persons Jude warns his readers about. *Woe to them!* A warning that judgment is coming (see Mt 23:13,15–16,23,25,27,29). *way of Cain.* The way of selfishness and greed (see note on Ge 4:3–4) and the way of hatred and murder (see 1Jn 3:12). *Balaam's error.* The error of consuming greed (see note on 2Pe 2:15). *Korah's rebellion.* Korah rose up against God's appointed leadership (see Nu 16). Jude may be suggesting that the false teachers of his day were rebelling against church leadership (cf. 3Jn 9–10).

12–13 These verses contain six graphic metaphors: (1) *blemishes at your love feasts.* See note on 2Pe 2:13. (2) *shepherds who feed only themselves.* Instead of feeding the sheep for whom they are responsible (see Eze 34:8–10). (3) *clouds without rain.* Like clouds promising moisture for the parched land, the false teachers promise soul-satisfying truth, but in reality they have nothing to offer. (4) *autumn trees, without fruit and uprooted—twice dead.* Though the trees ought to be heavy with fruit. (5) *wild waves of the sea.* As wind-tossed waves constantly churn up mire and mud, so these apostates continually stir up moral filth (see Isa 57:20). (6) *wandering stars.* As shooting stars appear in the sky only to fly off into eternal oblivion, so these false teachers are destined for the darkness of eternal hell.

14 *Enoch, the seventh from Adam.* Not the Enoch in the line of Cain (Ge 4:17) but the one in the line of Seth (Ge 5:18–24; 1Ch 1:1–3). He was seventh if Adam is counted as the first. The quotation is from the book of Enoch, which purports to have been written by the Enoch of Ge 5, but actually did not appear until the first century B.C. The book of Enoch was a well-respected writing in NT times. That it was not canonical does not mean that it contained no truth; nor does Jude's quotation of the book mean that he considered it inspired (see Introduction: Author; see also note on v. 9). *the Lord is coming.* Jude uses the quotation to refer to Christ's second coming and to his judgment of the wicked (see 2Th 1:6–10). *holy ones.* Probably angels (see Da 4:13–17; 2Th 1:7). However, some think they are raptured saints who are returning with the Lord (see 1Th 3:13 and note).

15 *ungodly ... ungodly ... ungodly ... ungodly.* This thunderous repetition and the awesome judgment scene that is depicted emphasize the condemnation of the false teachers in v. 4.

16 *These men.* The ungodly men first mentioned in v. 4 and subsequently referred to repeatedly as "these men" (vv. 10,12,14,19; cf. v. 8). They are the libertine false teachers who pervert the grace of God.

17 *remember what the apostles ... foretold.* The coming of these godless men should not take believers by surprise, for it had been predicted by the apostles (Ac 20:29; 1Ti 4:1; 2Ti 3:1–5; 2Pe 2:1–3; 3:2–3).

18 *They said.* The Greek for this phrase indicates that the apostles continually or repeatedly warned that such godless apostates would come. *last times.* See note on Jas 5:3. *scoffers.* In both 2Pe 3:3 and Jude the scoffers are said to be characterized by selfish lusts ("desires").

19 *men who divide you.* At the very least this phrase means that they were divisive, creating factions in the church—the usual practice of heretics. Or Jude may refer to the later Gnostics' division of people into the spiritual (the Gnostics) and the sensual (those for whom there is no hope). *follow mere natural instincts.* An ironic description of the false teachers, who labeled others as sensual (see 1Co 2:14 and note). *not have the Spirit.* Rather than being the spiritual ones—the privileged elite class the Gnostics claimed to be—Jude denies that they even possess the Spirit. A person who does not have the Spirit is clearly not saved (see Ro 8:9).

20 *But you, dear friends.* In contrast to the ungodly false teachers, about whom this letter speaks at length. *most holy faith.* See note on v. 3. *in the Holy Spirit.* According to the Spirit's promptings and with the power of the Spirit (see Ro 8:26–27; Gal 4:6; Eph 6:17–18 and notes).

21 *Keep yourselves in God's love.* God keeps believers in his love (see Ro 8:35–39 and notes), and enables them to keep themselves in his love. *eternal life.* See Jn 3:15 and note.

22–23 *those who doubt ... others.* Perhaps those who have come under the influence of the apostates.

23 *snatch others from the fire.* Rescuing them from the verge of destruction (see Am 4:11; Zec 3:2; 1Co 3:15 and notes).

Doxology

24To him who is able[f] to keep you from
falling and to present you before his glorious presence[g] without fault[h] and with
great joy— 25to the only God[i] our Savior
be glory, majesty, power and authority,
through Jesus Christ our Lord, before all
ages, now and forevermore![j] Amen.[k]

24 [f] S Ro 16:25 [g] S 2Co 4:14 [h] Col 1:22 **25** [i] Jn 5:44; 1Ti 1:17 [j] Heb 13:8 [k] S Ro 11:36

mercy, mixed with fear. Even in showing mercy one may be trapped by the allurement of sin. *clothing stained by corrupted flesh.* The wicked are pictured as so corrupt that even their garments are polluted by their sinful nature.

24–25 After all the attention necessarily given in this letter to the ungodly and their works of darkness, Jude concludes his letter by focusing attention on God, who is fully able to keep from falling those who put their trust in him.

Revelation

INTRODUCTION

Author

Four times the author identifies himself as John (1:1,4,9; 22:8). From as early as Justin Martyr in the second century A.D. it has been held that this John was the apostle, the son of Zebedee (see Mt 10:2). The book itself reveals that the author was a Jew, well versed in Scripture, a church leader who was well known to the seven churches of Asia Minor, and a deeply religious person fully convinced that Christ would soon triumph over the demonic forces at work in the world.

In the third century, however, an African bishop named Dionysius compared the language, style and thought of the Apocalypse (Revelation) with that of the other writings of John and decided that the book could not have been written by the apostle John. He suggested that the author was a certain John the Presbyter, whose name appears elsewhere in ancient writings. Although many today follow Dionysius in his view of authorship, the external evidence seems overwhelmingly supportive of the traditional view.

> **A Quick Look**
>
> **Author:**
> The apostle John
>
> **Audience:**
> Seven churches in western Asia Minor
>
> **Date:**
> About A.D. c. 95
>
> **Theme:**
> John writes to encourage the faithful to stand firm against persecution and compromise in the light of the imminent return of Christ to deliver the righteous and judge the wicked.

Date

Revelation was written when Christians were entering a time of persecution. The two periods most often mentioned are the latter part of Nero's reign (A.D. 54–68) and the latter part of Domitian's reign (81–96). Most interpreters date the book c. 95. (A few suggest a date during the reign of Vespasian: 69–79.)

Occasion

Since Roman authorities at this time were beginning to enforce emperor worship, Christians — who held that Christ, not Caesar, was Lord — were facing increasing hostility. The believers at Smyrna are warned against coming opposition (2:10), and the church at Philadelphia is told of an hour of trial coming on the world (3:10). Antipas has already given his life (2:13) along with others (6:9). John has been exiled to the island of Patmos (probably the site of a Roman penal colony) for his activities as a Christian missionary (1:9). Some within the church are advocating a policy of compromise (2:14–15,20), which has to be corrected before its subtle influence can undermine the determination of believers to stand fast in the perilous days that lie ahead.

Purpose

John writes to encourage the faithful to resist staunchly the demands of emperor worship. He informs his readers that the final showdown between God and Satan is imminent. Satan will increase his persecution of believers, but they must stand fast, even to death. They are sealed against any spiritual harm and will soon be vindicated when Christ returns, when the wicked are forever destroyed, and when God's people enter an eternity of glory and blessedness.

Revelation is apocalyptic, a kind of writing that is highly symbolic.

Literary Form

For an adequate understanding of Revelation, the reader must recognize that it is a distinct kind of literature. Revelation is apocalyptic, a kind of writing that is highly symbolic (see Isa 24–27 and Introduction to Isaiah: Literary Features; Da 7–12 and Introduction to Daniel: Literary Form; Zec 1:7—6:8 and Introduction to Zechariah: Literary Forms and Themes). Although its visions often seem bizarre to the Western reader, fortunately the book provides a number of clues for its own interpretation (e.g., stars are angels, lampstands are churches, 1:20; "the great prostitute," 17:1, is "Babylon" [Rome?], 17:5,18; and the heavenly Jerusalem is the wife of the Lamb, 21:9–10).

Distinctive Feature

A distinctive feature is the frequent use of the number seven (52 times). There are seven beatitudes (see note on 1:3), seven churches (1:4,11), seven spirits (1:4), seven golden lampstands (1:12), seven stars (1:16), seven seals (5:1), seven horns and seven eyes (5:6), seven trumpets (8:2), seven thunders (10:3), seven signs (12:1,3; 13:13–14; 15:1; 16:14; 19:20), seven crowns (12:3), seven plagues (15:6), seven golden bowls (15:7), seven hills (17:9) and seven kings (17:10), as well as other sevens. Symbolically, the number seven stands for completeness.

Interpretation

Interpreters of Revelation normally fall into four groups:

1. *Preterists* understand the book exclusively in terms of its first-century setting, claiming that most of its events have already taken place.
2. *Historicists* take it as describing the long chain of events from Patmos to the end of history.
3. *Futurists* place the book primarily in the end times.
4. *Idealists* view it as symbolic pictures of such timeless truths as the victory of good over evil.

Fortunately, the fundamental truths of Revelation do not depend on adopting a particular point of view. They are available to anyone who will read the book for its overall message and resist the temptation to become overly enamored with the details.

Outline

- I. Introduction (1:1–8)
  - A. Prologue (1:1–3)
  - B. Greetings and Doxology (1:4–8)
- II. Jesus among the Seven Churches (1:9–20)
- III. The Letters to the Seven Churches (chs. 2–3)
  - A. Ephesus (2:1–7)
  - B. Smyrna (2:8–11)
  - C. Pergamum (2:12–17)
  - D. Thyatira (2:18–29)

E. Sardis (3:1–6)
F. Philadelphia (3:7–13)
G. Laodicea (3:14–22)

IV. The Throne, the Scroll and the Lamb (chs. 4–5)
A. The Throne in Heaven (ch. 4)
B. The Seven-Sealed Scroll (5:1–5)
C. The Lamb Slain (5:6–14)

V. The Seven Seals (6:1 — 8:1)
A. First Seal: The White Horse (6:1–2)
B. Second Seal: The Red Horse (6:3–4)
C. Third Seal: The Black Horse (6:5–6)
D. Fourth Seal: The Pale Horse (6:7–8)
E. Fifth Seal: The Souls under the Altar (6:9–11)
F. Sixth Seal: The Great Earthquake (6:12–17)
G. The Sealing of the 144,000 (7:1–8)
H. The Great Multitude (7:9–17)
I. Seventh Seal: Silence in Heaven (8:1)

VI. The Seven Trumpets (8:2 — 11:19)
A. Introduction (8:2–5)
B. First Trumpet: Hail and Fire Mixed with Blood (8:6–7)
C. Second Trumpet: A Mountain Thrown into the Sea (8:8–9)
D. Third Trumpet: The Star Wormwood (8:10–11)
E. Fourth Trumpet: A Third of the Sun, Moon and Stars Struck (8:12–13)
F. Fifth Trumpet: The Plague of Locusts (9:1–12)
G. Sixth Trumpet: Release of the Four Angels (9:13–21)
H. The Angel and the Little Scroll (ch. 10)
I. The Two Witnesses (11:1–14)
J. Seventh Trumpet: Judgments and Rewards (11:15–19)

VII. Interlude: Persecution, Deliverance and Judgment (chs. 12–14)
A. The Woman and the Dragon (ch. 12)
B. The Two Beasts (ch. 13)
C. The Lamb and the 144,000 (14:1–5)
D. The Harvest of the Earth (14:6–20)

VIII. The Seven Bowls (chs. 15–16)
A. Introduction: The Song of Moses and the Seven Angels with the Seven Plagues (ch. 15)
B. First Bowl: Ugly and Painful Sores (16:1–2)
C. Second Bowl: Sea Turns to Blood (16:3)
D. Third Bowl: Rivers and Springs of Water Become Blood (16:4–7)
E. Fourth Bowl: Sun Scorches People with Fire (16:8–9)
F. Fifth Bowl: Darkness (16:10–11)
G. Sixth Bowl: Euphrates River Dries Up (16:12–16)
H. Seventh Bowl: Tremendous Earthquake (16:17–21)

IX. The Destruction of Babylon and the Coming of the New Jerusalem (17:1 — 22:5)
A. The Destruction of Babylon (17:1 — 19:5)
   1. The great prostitute described (ch. 17)
   2. The fall of Babylon (ch. 18)
   3. Praise for Babylon's fall (19:1–5)
B. Praise for the Wedding of the Lamb (19:6–10)
C. The Return of Christ (19:11–21)
D. The Thousand Years (20:1–6)
E. Satan's Doom (20:7–10)
F. Great White Throne Judgment (20:11–15)

- G. The Coming of the New Jerusalem (21:1 — 22:5)
  1. The new heaven and new earth (21:1 – 8)
  2. The new Jerusalem (21:9 – 27)
  3. Eden restored (22:1 – 5)

X. Conclusion and Benediction (22:6 – 21)

Prologue

1 The revelation of Jesus Christ, which God gave[a] him to show his servants what must soon take place.[b] He made it known by sending his angel[c] to his servant John,[d] 2who testifies to everything he saw—that is, the word of God[e] and the testimony of Jesus Christ.[f] 3Blessed is the one who reads the words of this prophecy, and blessed are those who hear it and take to heart what is written in it,[g] because the time is near.[h]

Greetings and Doxology

4John,

To the seven churches[i] in the province of Asia:

Grace and peace to you[j] from him who is, and who was, and who is to come,[k] and from the seven spirits[a][l] before his throne, 5and from Jesus Christ, who is the faithful witness,[m] the firstborn from the dead,[n] and the ruler of the kings of the earth.[o]

To him who loves us[p] and has freed us from our sins by his blood,[q] 6and has made us to be a kingdom and priests[r] to serve his God and Father[s]—to him be glory and power for ever and ever! Amen.[t]

7Look, he is coming with the clouds,[u]
and every eye will see him,
even those who pierced him;[v]
and all the peoples of the earth will
mourn[w] because of him.
So shall it be! Amen.

8"I am the Alpha and the Omega,"[x] says the Lord God, "who is, and who was, and who is to come,[y] the Almighty."[z]

One Like a Son of Man

9I, John,[a] your brother and companion in the suffering[b] and kingdom[c] and patient endurance[d] that are ours in Jesus, was on the island of Patmos because of the word of God[e] and the testimony of Jesus.[f] 10On the Lord's Day[g] I was in the Spirit,[h] and I heard behind me a loud voice like a trumpet,[i] 11which said: "Write on a scroll what you see[j] and send it to the seven churches:[k] to Ephesus,[l] Smyrna,[m] Pergamum,[n] Thyatira,[o] Sardis,[p] Philadelphia[q] and Laodicea."[r]

12I turned around to see the voice that was speaking to me. And when I turned I saw seven golden lampstands,[s] 13and among the lampstands[t] was someone "like a son of man,"[b][u] dressed in a robe

[a] 4 Or *the sevenfold Spirit* [b] 13 Daniel 7:13

1:1 [a] Jn 12:49; 17:8 [b] ver 19; Da 2:28,29; Rev 22:6 [c] Rev 22:16 [d] ver 4,9; Rev 22:8 **1:2** [e] ver 9; S Heb 4:12 [f] ver 9; 1Co 1:6; Rev 6:9; 12:17; 19:10 **1:3** [g] Lk 11:28; Rev 22:7 [h] S Ro 13:11 **1:4** [i] ver 11,20 [j] S Ro 1:7 [k] ver 8; Rev 4:8; 11:17; 16:5 [l] Isa 11:2; Rev 3:1; 4:5; 5:6 **1:5** [m] Isa 55:4; Jn 18:37; Rev 3:14 [n] Ps 89:27; Col 1:18 [o] S 1Ti 6:15 [p] S Ro 8:37 [q] S Ro 3:25 **1:6** [r] S 1Pe 2:5; Rev 5:10; 20:6 [s] Ro 15:6 [t] S Ro 11:36 **1:7** [u] Da 7:13; S Mt 16:27; 24:30; 26:64; S Lk 17:30; S 1Co 1:7; S 1Th 2:19; 4:16,17 [v] Jn 19:34,37 [w] Zec 12:10; Mt 24:30 **1:8** [x] S ver 17; Rev 21:6; 22:13 [y] S ver 4 [z] Rev 4:8; 15:3; 19:6 **1:9** [a] ver 1 [b] S Ac 14:22; 2Co 1:7; Php 4:14 [c] ver 6 [d] 2Ti 2:12 [e] ver 2; S Heb 4:12 [f] S ver 2 **1:10** [g] Ac 20:7 [h] Rev 4:2; 17:3; 21:10 [i] Ex 20:18; Rev 4:1 **1:11** [j] ver 19 [k] ver 4,20 [l] S Ac 18:19 [m] Rev 2:8 [n] Rev 2:12 [o] Ac 16:14; Rev 2:18,24 [p] Rev 3:1 [q] Rev 3:7 [r] S Col 2:1; Rev 3:14 **1:12** [s] ver 20; Ex 25:31-40; Zec 4:2; Rev 2:1 **1:13** [t] Rev 2:1 [u] Eze 1:26; Da 7:13; 10:16; Rev 14:14

1:1 *revelation.* Apocalypse ("unveiling" or "disclosure"). *of Jesus Christ.* Can mean (1) by or from Jesus Christ, (2) about Jesus Christ or (3) both. *servants.* All believers. *soon take place.* See v. 3; 22:6–7,10,20. *his angel.* A mediating angel. "Angel(s)" occurs over 80 times in Revelation. *John.* See Introduction: Author.

1:3 *Blessed.* The first of seven beatitudes in the book (see 14:13; 16:15; 19:9; 20:6; 22:7,14). "Blessed" means much more than "happy." It describes the favorable circumstance granted by God to a person (see notes on Ps 1:1; Mt 5:3). *prophecy.* Includes not only foretelling the future but also proclaiming any word from God—whether command, instruction, warning, history or prediction (see 1Co 14:3 and note). *time is near.* See note on Jas 5:9.

1:4 *seven churches.* Located about 50 miles apart, forming a circle in Asia moving clockwise north from Ephesus and coming around full circle from Laodicea (east of Ephesus; see map, p. 1967). They were perhaps postal centers serving seven geographic regions. Apparently the entire book of Revelation (including the seven letters) was sent to each church (see v. 11). *Asia.* A Roman province lying in modern western Turkey. *Grace and peace.* See note on Ro 1:7. *who is ... was ... is to come.* A paraphrase of the divine name *Yahweh* (see Ex 3:14–15 and notes). Cf. Heb 13:8. *seven spirits.* See NIV text note; see also Isa 11:2; Zec 4:2 and notes.

1:5–6 *has freed us ... has made us.* Emphasizes these blessings as present possessions already enjoyed by the believer (see also 5:9–10).

1:6 *a kingdom and priests.* This OT designation of Israel (see notes on Ex 19:6; Zec 3) is applied in the NT to the church (1Pe 2:5,9).

1:7 *coming with the clouds.* See Mt 24:30 and note. *pierced.* See Ps 22:16; Isa 53:5; Zec 12:10; Jn 19:34,37. *So shall it be! Amen.* A double affirmation, the first translating the second.

1:8 *the Alpha and the Omega.* The first and last letters of the Greek alphabet. God is the beginning and the end (see 21:6). He sovereignly rules over all human history. In 22:13 Jesus applies the same title to himself; see also "the First and the Last" (v. 17; 2:8; 22:13). *Almighty.* Nine of the 12 occurrences of this term in the NT are in Revelation (here; 4:8; 11:17; 15:3; 16:7,14; 19:6,15; 21:22). The other three are in Ro 9:29; 2Co 6:18; Jas 5:4.

1:9 *suffering ... kingdom ... patient endurance.* Three pivotal themes in Revelation: (1) suffering (2:9–10,22; 7:14), (2) kingdom (11:15; 12:10; 16:10; 17:12,17–18), (3) patient endurance (2:2–3,19; 3:10; 13:10; 14:12). *Patmos.* A small (four by eight miles), rocky island in the Aegean Sea some 50 miles southwest of Ephesus, off the coast of modern Turkey (see map, p. 1967). It probably served as a Roman penal settlement. Eusebius, the "father of church history" (A.D. 265–340), reports that John was released from Patmos under the emperor Nerva (96–98).

1:10 *the Lord's Day.* A technical term for the first day of the week—so named because Jesus rose from the dead on that day. It was also the day on which the Christians met for worship, instruction in the faith, and mutual encouragement (Ac 20:7; cf. Eph 5:19; Col 3:16; Heb 10:25 and notes) and for gathering funds for the relief of the poor (see 1Co 16:2 and note). *in the Spirit.* In a state of spiritual exaltation by the power of the Spirit—not a dream, but a vision like Peter's in Ac 10:10.

1:11 *scroll.* Pieces of papyrus or parchment sewn together and rolled on a spindle (see note on Ex 17:14). The book form was not invented until about the second century A.D. *seven churches.* See note on v. 4.

1:12 *seven.* See Introduction: Distinctive Feature. *golden lampstands.* The seven churches (see v. 20).

1:13 *son of man.* See notes on Da 7:13; Mk 8:31. *robe ... to his feet.* The high priest wore a full-length robe (Ex 28:4; 29:5).

reaching down to his feet[v] and with a golden sash around his chest.[w] 14His head and hair were white like wool, as white as snow, and his eyes were like blazing fire.[x] 15His feet were like bronze glowing in a furnace,[y] and his voice was like the sound of rushing waters.[z] 16In his right hand he held seven stars,[a] and out of his mouth came a sharp double-edged sword.[b] His face was like the sun[c] shining in all its brilliance.

17When I saw him, I fell at his feet[d] as though dead. Then he placed his right hand on me[e] and said: "Do not be afraid.[f] I am the First and the Last.[g] 18I am the Living One; I was dead,[h] and behold I am alive for ever and ever![i] And I hold the keys of death and Hades.[j]

19"Write, therefore, what you have seen,[k] what is now and what will take place later. 20The mystery of the seven stars that you saw in my right hand[l] and of the seven golden lampstands[m] is this: The seven stars are the angels[a] of the seven churches,[n] and the seven lampstands are the seven churches.[o]

1:13 [v]Isa 6:1 [w]Da 10:5; Rev 15:6 **1:14** [x]Da 7:9; 10:6; Rev 2:18; 19:12 **1:15** [y]Eze 1:7; Da 10:6; Rev 2:18 [z]Eze 43:2; Rev 14:2; 19:6 **1:16** [a]ver 20; Rev 2:1; 3:1 [b]Isa 1:20; 49:2; Heb 4:12; Rev 2:12,16; 19:15,21 [c]Jdg 5:31; Mt 17:2 **1:17** [d]Eze 1:28; Da 8:17,18 [e]Da 8:18 [f]S Mt 14:27 [g]Isa 41:4; 44:6; 48:12; Rev 2:8; 22:13 **1:18** [h]Ro 6:9; Rev 2:8 [i]Dt 32:40; Da 4:34; 12:7; Rev 4:9,10; 10:6; 15:7 [j]Rev 9:1; 20:1 **1:19** [k]ver 11; Hab 2:2 **1:20** [l]S ver 16 [m]S ver 12 [n]ver 4,11 [o]Mt 5:14,15 **2:1** [p]S Ac 18:19 [q]Rev 1:16 [r]Rev 1:12,13 **2:2** [s]ver 19; Rev 3:1,8,15

To the Church in Ephesus

2 "To the angel[b] of the church in Ephesus[p] write:

These are the words of him who holds the seven stars in his right hand[q] and walks among the seven golden lampstands:[r] 2I know your deeds,[s] your hard work and your perseverance. I know that you cannot tolerate wicked men, that you have tested[t] those who claim to be apostles but are not, and have found them false.[u] 3You have persevered and have endured hardships for my name,[v] and have not grown weary.

4Yet I hold this against you: You have forsaken your first love.[w] 5Remember the height from which you have fallen! Repent[x] and do the things you did at first. If you do not repent, I will come to you and remove your lampstand[y] from its place. 6But you have this in your favor: You hate the practices of the Nicolaitans,[z] which I also hate.

7He who has an ear, let him hear[a] what the Spirit says to the churches. To him who overcomes,[b] I will give the right to eat from the tree of life,[c] which is in the paradise[d] of God.

[a] *20* Or *messengers* [b] *1* Or *messenger*; also in verses 8, 12 and 18

[t]1Jn 4:1 [u]2Co 11:13 **2:3** [v]S Jn 15:21 **2:4** [w]Jer 2:2; Mt 24:12 **2:5** [x]ver 16,22; Rev 3:3,19 [y]Rev 1:20 **2:6** [z]ver 15 **2:7** [a]S Mt 11:15; ver 11,17,29; Rev 3:6,13,22; 13:9 [b]S Jn 16:33 [c]Ge 2:9; 3:22-24; Rev 22:2,14,19 [d]Lk 23:43

1:14 *white like wool.* Cf. Da 7:9; Isa 1:18. The hoary head suggests wisdom and dignity (Lev 19:32; Pr 16:31). *eyes ... like blazing fire.* Penetrating insight (see 4:6).

1:16 *sharp double-edged sword.* Like a long Thracian sword (also in 2:12,16; 6:8; 19:15,21). The sword in 6:4; 13:10,14 was a small sword or dagger. The sword symbolizes divine judgment (see Isa 49:2; Heb 4:12).

1:17 *fell at his feet.* A sign of great respect and awe (4:10; 5:8; 7:11; 19:10; 22:8). *I am.* See note on Jn 6:35. *the First and the Last.* Essentially the same as "the Alpha and the Omega" (v. 8; cf. Isa 44:6; 48:12).

1:18 *Living One.* Based on OT references to the "living God" (e.g., Dt 5:26; Jos 3:10 [see note there]; 1Sa 17:26; Ps 42:2; 84:2). In contrast to the dead gods of paganism, Christ possesses life in his essential nature. *keys of death and Hades.* Absolute control over their domain (see Mt 16:18 and note).

1:19 Many take the threefold division of this verse as a clue to the entire structure of the book. "What you have seen" would be the inaugural vision of ch. 1; "what is now" would be the letters to the seven churches (chs. 2–3); "what will take place later" would be everything from ch. 4 on. An alternative interpretation sees the initial clause as the essential unit (it parallels v. 11), followed by two explanatory clauses. The sense would be: "Write, therefore, what you are about to see, i.e., both what is now and what will take place later." Some who hold the latter view make no attempt to outline the book on this basis, maintaining that there is a mixture of "now" and "later" throughout.

1:20 The first of several places where the symbols are interpreted (see also 17:15,18). *angels.* Lit. "messengers" (see NIV text note), i.e., agents through whom God acts (cf. Heb 1:14)—here, either (1) heavenly messengers or (2) earthly messengers/ministers.

2:1—3:22 Some take the seven letters as a preview of church history in its downward course toward Laodicean lukewarmness. Others interpret them as characteristic of various kinds of Christian congregations that have existed from John's day until the present time. In either case, they were historical churches in Asia Minor (see map, p. 1967, and map No. 13 at the end of this study Bible). A general pattern in the letters is commendation, complaint and correction.

2:1 *angel.* See note on 1:20. *Ephesus.* See Introduction to Ephesians: The City of Ephesus. *holds the seven stars.* See 1:16,20. *seven golden lampstands.* See 1:12,20.

2:2 *tested.* The necessity of testing for correct doctrine and dependable advice was widely recognized in the early church (see 1Co 14:29; 1Th 5:21; 1Jn 4:1).

2:4 *first love.* The love they had at first for one another and/or for Christ.

2:5 *remove your lampstand.* Immediate judgment.

2:6 *Nicolaitans.* A heretical sect within the church that had worked out a compromise with the pagan society. They apparently taught that spiritual liberty gave them sufficient leeway to practice idolatry and immorality. Tradition identifies them with Nicolas, the proselyte of Antioch who was one of the first seven deacons in the Jerusalem church (Ac 6:5), though the evidence is merely circumstantial. A similar group at Pergamum held the teaching of Balaam (vv. 14–15), and some at Thyatira were followers of the woman Jezebel (v. 20). From their heretical tendencies it would appear that all three groups were Nicolaitans.

2:7 *overcomes.* The challenge to be victorious in the battle against evil (see 12:11) occurs in each letter (here; vv. 11,17,26; 3:5,12,21). *paradise.* Originally a Persian word for a pleasure garden (see note on Lk 23:43). In Revelation it symbolizes the eschatological place of blessedness (cf. Lk 23:43) where God and believers are restored to the perfect fellowship that existed before sin entered the world.

To the Church in Smyrna

8"To the angel of the church in Smyrna[e]
write:
These are the words of him who is
the First and the Last,[f] who died and
came to life again.[g] 9I know your afflictions and your poverty—yet you
are rich![h] I know the slander of those
who say they are Jews and are not,[i]
but are a synagogue of Satan.[j] 10Do
not be afraid of what you are about
to suffer. I tell you, the devil will put
some of you in prison to test you,[k]
and you will suffer persecution for
ten days.[l] Be faithful,[m] even to the
point of death, and I will give you the
crown of life.[n]
11He who has an ear, let him hear[o]
what the Spirit says to the churches.
He who overcomes will not be hurt at
all by the second death.[p]

To the Church in Pergamum

12"To the angel of the church in Pergamum[q] write:
These are the words of him who has
the sharp, double-edged sword.[r] 13I
know where you live—where Satan
has his throne. Yet you remain true to
my name. You did not renounce your
faith in me,[s] even in the days of Antipas, my faithful witness,[t] who was
put to death in your city—where Satan lives.[u]
14Nevertheless, I have a few things
against you:[v] You have people there
who hold to the teaching of Balaam,[w] who taught Balak to entice the

2:8 [e]Rev 1:11 [f]S Rev 1:17 [g]Rev 1:18 **2:9** [h]2Co 6:10; Jas 2:5 [i]Rev 3:9 [j]ver 13,24; S Mt 4:10 **2:10** [k]Rev 3:10 [l]Da 1:12,14 [m]ver 13; Rev 17:14 [n]S Mt 10:22; S 1Co 9:25 **2:11** [o]S ver 7 [p]Rev 20:6,14; 21:8 **2:12** [q]Rev 1:11 [r]ver 16; S Rev 1:16 **2:13** [s]Rev 14:12 [t]Rev 1:5; 11:3 [u]ver 9,24; S Mt 4:10 **2:14** [v]ver 20 [w]S 2Pe 2:15

2:8 *Smyrna.* A proud and beautiful Asian city (modern Izmir) closely aligned with Rome and eager to meet its demands for emperor worship. This plus a large and actively hostile Jewish population made it extremely difficult to live there as a Christian. Polycarp, the most famous of the early martyrs, was bishop of Smyrna. *the First and the Last.* See note on 1:17.
2:9 *who say they are Jews.* See Ro 2:28–29. *Satan.* See notes on Mt 16:23; 1Jn 3:8.
2:10 *devil.* Greek *diabolos,* meaning "accuser." Hebrew *śaṭan* also means "accuser" (see Job 1:6 and note). *persecution.* See the warnings by Jesus (Jn 15:20) and Paul (2Ti 3:12). *ten days.* Probably indicates a limited period of suffering. *crown of life.* The crown that is eternal life. "Crown" does not refer to a royal crown (12:3; 13:1; 19:12) but to the garland or wreath awarded to the winner in athletic contests (3:11; 4:4,10; 6:2; 9:7; 12:1; 14:14).
2:11 *overcomes.* See note on v. 7. *second death.* The lake of fire (20:14; see 20:6; 21:8).
2:12 *Pergamum.* Modern Bergama; the ancient capital of the Roman province of Asia, built on a cone-shaped hill rising 1,000 feet above the surrounding valley. Its name in Greek means "citadel." The Greek word is also the origin of our word "parchment," the writing surface of choice for manuscripts in the ancient library at Pergamum. See map below. *double-edged sword.* See note on 1:16.
2:13 *where Satan has his throne.* Satan ruled from Pergamum in that it was the official center of emperor worship in Asia. *Antipas.* First martyr of Asia. According to tradition he was slowly roasted to death in a bronze kettle during the reign of Domitian (81–96). *faithful witness.* The Lord's title in 1:5.
2:14 *teaching of Balaam.* Balaam advised the Midianite women how to lead the Israelites astray (Nu 25:1–2; 31:16; cf. Jude 11 and notes on Nu 22:5,8). He is a fitting prototype of corrupt teachers who deceive believers into compromise with the religions and practices of the non-Christian

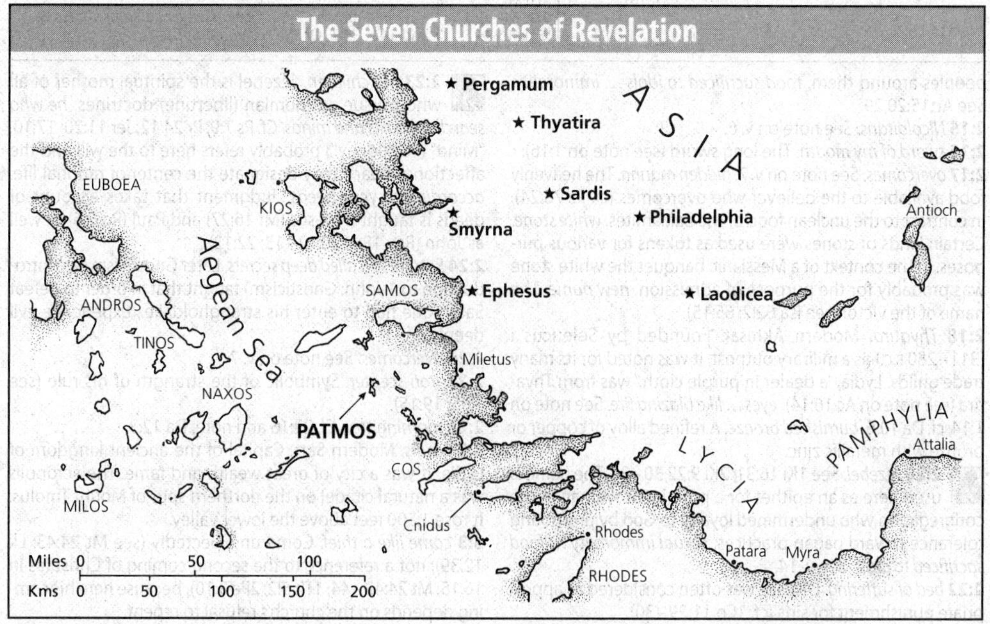

Israelites to sin by eating food sacrificed to idols[x] and by committing sexual immorality.[y] 15Likewise you also
have those who hold to the teaching
of the Nicolaitans.[z] 16Repent[a] therefore! Otherwise, I will soon come to
you and will fight against them with
the sword of my mouth.[b]

17He who has an ear, let him hear[c]
what the Spirit says to the churches.
To him who overcomes,[d] I will give
some of the hidden manna.[e] I will
also give him a white stone with a
new name[f] written on it, known only
to him who receives it.[g]

To the Church in Thyatira

18"To the angel of the church in Thyatira[h]
write:

These are the words of the Son of
God,[i] whose eyes are like blazing fire
and whose feet are like burnished
bronze.[j] 19I know your deeds,[k] your
love and faith, your service and perseverance, and that you are now doing more than you did at first.

20Nevertheless, I have this against
you: You tolerate that woman Jezebel,[l] who calls herself a prophetess.
By her teaching she misleads my servants into sexual immorality and the
eating of food sacrificed to idols.[m] 21I
have given her time[n] to repent of her
immorality, but she is unwilling.[o] 22So
I will cast her on a bed of suffering,
and I will make those who commit
adultery[p] with her suffer intensely,
unless they repent of her ways. 23I
will strike her children dead. Then
all the churches will know that I am
he who searches hearts and minds,[q]
and I will repay each of you according to your deeds.[r] 24Now I say to the
rest of you in Thyatira, to you who do
not hold to her teaching and have not
learned Satan's so-called deep secrets
(I will not impose any other burden
on you):[s] 25Only hold on to what you
have[t] until I come.[u]

26To him who overcomes[v] and does
my will to the end,[w] I will give authority over the nations[x]—

27'He will rule them with an iron
scepter;[y]
he will dash them to pieces
like pottery'[a z]—

just as I have received authority from
my Father. 28I will also give him the
morning star.[a] 29He who has an ear,
let him hear[b] what the Spirit says to
the churches.

To the Church in Sardis

3 "To the angel[b] of the church in Sardis[c]
write:

These are the words of him who
holds the seven spirits[c d] of God
and the seven stars.[e] I know your
deeds;[f] you have a reputation of being alive, but you are dead.[g] 2Wake
up! Strengthen what remains and is
about to die, for I have not found
your deeds complete in the sight of
my God. 3Remember, therefore, what
you have received and heard; obey it,
and repent.[h] But if you do not wake
up, I will come like a thief,[i] and you

2:14 [x] S Ac 15:20 [y] 1Co 6:13 **2:15** [z] ver 6 **2:16** [a] S ver 5 [b] 2Th 2:8; S Rev 1:16 **2:17** [c] S ver 7 [d] S Jn 16:33 [e] Jn 6:49,50 [f] Isa 56:5; 62:2; 65:15 [g] Rev 19:12 **2:18** [h] ver 24; Ac 16:14; Rev 1:11 [i] S Mt 4:3 [j] S Rev 1:14,15 **2:19** [k] S ver 2 **2:20** [l] 1Ki 16:31; 21:25; 2Ki 9:7 [m] ver 14; S Ac 15:20 **2:21** [n] Ro 2:4; 2Pe 3:9 [o] Ro 2:5; Rev 9:20; 16:9,11 **2:22** [p] Rev 17:2; 18:9 **2:23** [q] 1Sa 16:7; 1Ki 8:39; Ps 139:1,2,23; Pr 21:2; Jer 17:10; Lk 16:15; Ro 8:27; 1Th 2:4 [r] S Mt 16:27 **2:24** [s] Ac 15:28 **2:25** [t] Rev 3:11 [u] S Mt 16:27 **2:26** [v] S Jn 16:33 [w] Mt 10:22 [x] Ps 2:8; Rev 3:21 **2:27** [y] Rev 12:5; 19:15 [z] Ps 2:9; Isa 30:14; Jer 19:11 **2:28** [a] Rev 22:16 **2:29** [b] S ver 7 **3:1** [c] Rev 1:11 [d] S Rev 1:4 [e] S Rev 1:16 [f] S Rev 2:2 [g] 1Ti 5:6 **3:3** [h] S Rev 2:5 [i] S Lk 12:39

[a] *27* Psalm 2:9 [b] *1* Or *messenger*; also in verses 7 and 14 [c] *1* Or *the sevenfold Spirit*

peoples around them. *food sacrificed to idols ... immorality.* See Ac 15:20,29.
2:15 *Nicolaitans.* See note on v. 6.
2:16 *sword of my mouth.* The long sword (see note on 1:16).
2:17 *overcomes.* See note on v. 7. *hidden manna.* The heavenly food available to the believer who overcomes (cf. Ps 78:24), in contrast to the unclean food of the Balaamites. *white stone.* Certain kinds of stones were used as tokens for various purposes. In the context of a Messianic banquet the white stone was probably for the purpose of admission. *new name.* The name of the victor (see Isa 62:2; 65:15).
2:18 *Thyatira.* Modern Akhisar. Founded by Seleucus I (311–280 B.C.) as a military outpost, it was noted for its many trade guilds. Lydia, "a dealer in purple cloth," was from Thyatira (see note on Ac 16:14). *eyes ... like blazing fire.* See note on 1:14; cf. Da 10:6. *burnished bronze.* A refined alloy of copper or bronze with metallic zinc.
2:20 *Jezebel.* See 1Ki 16:31; 2Ki 9:22,30–37. The name is used here as an epithet for a prominent woman in the congregation who undermined loyalty to God by promoting tolerance toward pagan practices. *sexual immorality ... food sacrificed to idols.* See v. 14.
2:22 *bed of suffering.* Disease was often considered as appropriate punishment for sins (cf. 1Co 11:29–30).
2:23 *her children.* Jezebel is the spiritual mother of all who pursue antinomian (libertine) doctrines. *he who searches hearts and minds.* Cf. Ps 7:9; Pr 24:12; Jer 11:20; 17:10. "Mind" (lit. "kidney") probably refers here to the will and the affections; "heart" may designate the center of rational life. *according to your deeds.* Judgment that takes account of deeds is taught by Jesus (Mt 16:27) and Paul (Ro 2:6) as well as John (Rev 18:6; 20:12–13; 22:12).
2:24 *Satan's so-called deep secrets.* Later Gnosticism (see Introduction to 1 John: Gnosticism) taught that in order to defeat Satan one had to enter his stronghold, i.e., experience evil deeply.
2:26 *overcomes.* See note on v. 7.
2:27 *iron scepter.* Symbolic of the strength of his rule (see 12:5; 19:15).
2:28 *morning star.* Cf. 22:16 and note; Da 12:3.
3:1 *Sardis.* Modern Sart. Capital of the ancient kingdom of Lydia, it was a city of great wealth and fame. The acropolis was a natural citadel on the northern spur of Mount Tmolus. It rose 1,500 feet above the lower valley.
3:3 *come like a thief.* Come unexpectedly (see Mt 24:43; Lk 12:39); not a reference to the second coming of Christ (as in 16:15; Mt 24:42–44; 1Th 5:2; 2Pe 3:10), because here his coming depends on the church's refusal to repent.

will not know at what time[j] I will
come to you.
4Yet you have a few people in Sardis who have not soiled their clothes.[k]
They will walk with me, dressed
in white,[l] for they are worthy. 5He
who overcomes[m] will, like them, be
dressed in white.[n] I will never blot
out his name from the book of life,[o]
but will acknowledge his name before my Father[p] and his angels. 6He
who has an ear, let him hear[q] what
the Spirit says to the churches.

To the Church in Philadelphia

7"To the angel of the church in Philadelphia[r] write:

These are the words of him who
is holy[s] and true,[t] who holds the key
of David.[u] What he opens no one
can shut, and what he shuts no one
can open. 8I know your deeds.[v] See,
I have placed before you an open
door[w] that no one can shut. I know
that you have little strength, yet you
have kept my word and have not denied my name.[x] 9I will make those
who are of the synagogue of Satan,[y]
who claim to be Jews though they are
not,[z] but are liars—I will make them
come and fall down at your feet[a] and
acknowledge that I have loved you.[b]
10Since you have kept my command
to endure patiently, I will also keep
you[c] from the hour of trial that is going to come upon the whole world[d] to
test[e] those who live on the earth.[f]

3:3 [j] Lk 12:39
3:4 [k] Jude 23 [l] ver 5, 18; Rev 4:4; 6:11; 7:9, 13, 14; 19:14
3:5 [m] S Jn 16:33 [n] S ver 4 [o] S Rev 20:12 [p] Mt 10:32
3:6 [q] S Rev 2:7
3:7 [r] Rev 1:11 [s] S Mk 1:24 [t] 1Jn 5:20; Rev 6:10; 19:11 [u] Isa 22:22; Mt 16:19
3:8 [v] S Rev 2:2 [w] S Ac 14:27 [x] Rev 2:13
3:9 [y] Rev 2:9 [z] Rev 2:9 [a] Isa 49:23 [b] Isa 43:4; S Ro 8:37
3:10 [c] 2Pe 2:9 [d] S Mt 24:14 [e] Rev 2:10 [f] Rev 6:10; 8:13; 11:10; 13:8, 14; 17:8
3:11 [g] S Mt 16:27 [h] Rev 2:25 [i] S 1Co 9:25
3:12 [j] S Jn 16:33 [k] Gal 2:9 [l] Rev 14:1; 22:4 [m] Eze 48:35 [n] Gal 4:26; Rev 21:2, 10
3:13 [o] S Rev 2:7
3:14 [p] S Col 2:1; Rev 1:11 [q] Jn 18:37; Rev 1:5 [r] Pr 8:22; Jn 1:3; Col 1:16, 18
3:15 [s] S Rev 2:2 [t] Ro 12:11
3:17 [u] Hos 12:8; 1Co 4:8 [v] Pr 13:7
3:18 [w] S 1Pe 1:7 [x] S ver 4 [y] Rev 16:15

11I am coming soon.[g] Hold on to
what you have,[h] so that no one will
take your crown.[i] 12Him who overcomes[j] I will make a pillar[k] in the
temple of my God. Never again will
he leave it. I will write on him the
name of my God[l] and the name of the
city of my God,[m] the new Jerusalem,[n]
which is coming down out of heaven
from my God; and I will also write on
him my new name. 13He who has an
ear, let him hear[o] what the Spirit says
to the churches.

To the Church in Laodicea

14"To the angel of the church in Laodicea[p]
write:

These are the words of the Amen,
the faithful and true witness,[q] the ruler of God's creation.[r] 15I know your
deeds,[s] that you are neither cold nor
hot.[t] I wish you were either one or
the other! 16So, because you are lukewarm—neither hot nor cold—I am
about to spit you out of my mouth.
17You say, 'I am rich; I have acquired
wealth and do not need a thing.'[u]
But you do not realize that you are
wretched, pitiful, poor, blind and naked.[v] 18I counsel you to buy from me
gold refined in the fire,[w] so you can
become rich; and white clothes[x] to
wear, so you can cover your shameful
nakedness;[y] and salve to put on your
eyes, so you can see.

3:4 *dressed in white.* Description of the redeemed (3:18; 6:11; 7:9,13–14; cf. 4:4; 19:14).
3:5 *overcomes.* See note on 2:7. *book of life.* A divine ledger is first mentioned in Ex 32:32–33 (see note on Ps 69:28; cf. Da 12:1). It was a register of all citizens in the kingdom community. To have one's name erased from this book would indicate loss of citizenship (see 13:8; 17:8; 20:12,15; 21:27; Php 4:3).
3:7 *Philadelphia.* Modern Alashehir; a city of commercial importance conveniently located as the gateway to the high central plateau of the Roman province of Asia in Asia Minor. The name means "brotherly love" and commemorates the loyalty and devotion of Attalus II (220–130 B.C.), the city's cofounder, to his brother Eumenes II. *holy and true.* See 6:10. For God as the Holy One see Isa 40:25; Hab 3:2–3; Mk 1:24; see also notes on Ex 3:5; Lev 11:44. *key of David.* Christ is the Davidic Messiah with authority to control entrance to the kingdom (see Isa 22:22; Mt 16:19).
3:8 *open door.* Either the door of opportunity or the door to the kingdom. The context favors the latter.
3:9 *synagogue of Satan.* A bold metaphor directed against unbelieving and hostile Jews. Cf. Jesus' scathing rebuke in Jn 8:44; see also 2Co 11:14–15. The Jewish synagogue was a gathering place for worship, study and communal activities. *claim to be Jews.* See Ro 2:28–29. *fall down at your feet.* An appropriate act of worship in the Near East (see Isa 45:14; 60:14; cf. Ac 10:25; Php 2:10; see also note on Rev 1:17).
3:10 *keep you from.* The Greek for this phrase can mean either "keep you from undergoing" or "keep you through." *hour of trial.* The period of testing that precedes the consummation of the kingdom (see 13:5–10; Mt 24:4–28; cf. Da 12:1; Mk 13:19; 2Th 2:1–12). *those who live on the earth.* See 6:10 and note.
3:11 *I am coming soon.* Cf. 1:1; 22:7,12,20 (see note on Jas 5:9). *crown.* See 2:10 and note.
3:12 *overcomes.* See note on 2:7. *temple.* See note on 7:15. *name of my God.* See 14:1; 22:4. *new Jerusalem.* See 21:2,10. *write on him my new name.* Names revealed character. Christ's new name symbolizes all that he is by virtue of his redemptive work for humankind. This awaits the second advent.
3:14 *Laodicea.* Near modern Denizli. The wealthiest city in Phrygia during Roman times, it was widely known for its banking establishments, medical school and textile industry. Its major weakness was lack of an adequate water supply. Each of these characteristics is reflected in the letter. *the Amen.* Isa 65:16 speaks of "the God of the Amen," i.e., "the God of truth." As a personal designation it describes one who is perfectly trustworthy or faithful. *faithful and true witness.* See 1:5; 19:11. *ruler.* The Greek word can mean first in point of time ("beginning") or first in rank ("ruler").
3:16 *lukewarm—neither hot nor cold.* "Hot" may refer to the hot, medicinal waters of nearby Hierapolis. The church in Laodicea supplied neither healing for the spiritually sick nor refreshment for the spiritually weary. *spit.* Lit. "vomit."
3:18 Refers to three items in which Laodicea took great pride: financial wealth, an extensive textile industry and a famous eye salve.

19Those whom I love I rebuke and
discipline.[z] So be earnest, and repent.[a]
20Here I am! I stand at the door[b] and
knock. If anyone hears my voice and
opens the door,[c] I will come in[d] and
eat with him, and he with me.
21To him who overcomes,[e] I will
give the right to sit with me on my
throne,[f] just as I overcame[g] and sat
down with my Father on his throne.
22He who has an ear, let him hear[h]
what the Spirit says to the churches."

The Throne in Heaven

4 After this I looked, and there before me
was a door standing open[i] in heaven.
And the voice I had first heard speaking to
me like a trumpet[j] said, "Come up here,[k]
and I will show you what must take place
after this."[l] 2At once I was in the Spirit,[m]
and there before me was a throne in heav-
en[n] with someone sitting on it. 3And the
one who sat there had the appearance of
jasper[o] and carnelian.[p] A rainbow,[q] resembling an emerald,[r] encircled the throne.
4Surrounding the throne were twenty-four
other thrones, and seated on them were
twenty-four elders.[s] They were dressed
in white[t] and had crowns of gold on their
heads. 5From the throne came flashes of
lightning, rumblings and peals of thunder.[u]
Before the throne, seven lamps[v] were blazing. These are the seven spirits[a][w] of God.
6Also before the throne there was what
looked like a sea of glass,[x] clear as crystal.
In the center, around the throne, were
four living creatures,[y] and they were covered with eyes, in front and in back.[z] 7The
first living creature was like a lion, the second was like an ox, the third had a face
like a man, the fourth was like a flying
eagle.[a] 8Each of the four living creatures[b]
had six wings[c] and was covered with eyes
all around,[d] even under his wings. Day
and night[e] they never stop saying:

"Holy, holy, holy
is the Lord God Almighty,[f]
who was, and is, and is to come."[g]

9Whenever the living creatures give glory,
honor and thanks to him who sits on the
throne[h] and who lives for ever and ever,[i]
10the twenty-four elders[j] fall down before
him[k] who sits on the throne,[l] and worship
him who lives for ever and ever. They lay
their crowns before the throne and say:

11 "You are worthy, our Lord and God,
to receive glory and honor and
power,[m]

[a] 5 Or *the sevenfold Spirit*

3:19 [z] Dt 8:5; Pr 3:12; 1Co 11:32; Heb 12:5,6 [a] S Rev 2:5 **3:20** [b] Mt 24:33; Jas 5:9 [c] Lk 12:36 [d] S Ro 8:10 **3:21** [e] S Jn 16:33 [f] S Mt 19:28 [g] Rev 5:5 **3:22** [h] S Rev 2:7 **4:1** [i] S Mt 3:16 [j] Rev 1:10 [k] Rev 11:12 [l] Rev 1:19; 22:6 **4:2** [m] S Rev 1:10 [n] ver 9,10; 1Ki 22:19; Isa 6:1; Eze 1:26-28; Da 7:9; Rev 20:11 **4:3** [o] Rev 21:11 [p] Rev 21:20 [q] Eze 1:28; Rev 10:1 [r] Rev 21:19 **4:4** [s] ver 10; Rev 5:6,8,14; 11:16; 19:4 [t] S Rev 3:4,5 **4:5** [u] Ex 19:16; Rev 8:5; 11:19; 16:18 [v] Zec 4:2 [w] S Rev 1:4 **4:6** [x] Rev 15:2 [y] ver 8,9; Eze 1:5; Rev 5:6; 6:1; 7:11; 14:3; 15:7; 19:4 [z] Eze 1:18; 10:12 **4:7** [a] Eze 1:10; 10:14 **4:8** [b] S ver 6 [c] Isa 6:2 [d] Eze 1:18 [e] Rev 14:11 [f] Isa 6:3; S Rev 1:8 [g] S Rev 1:4 **4:9** [h] ver 2; Ps 47:8; S Rev 5:1 [i] S Rev 1:18 **4:10** [j] S ver 4 [k] Dt 33:3; Rev 5:8,14; 7:11; 11:16 [l] S ver 2 **4:11** [m] Rev 1:6; 5:12

3:19 *whom I love I ... discipline.* See Job 5:17; Ps 94:12; Pr 3:11–12; 1Co 11:32; Heb 12:5–11.

3:20 *I stand at the door and knock.* Usually taken as a picture of Christ's knocking on the door of an (i.e., any) unbeliever's heart. In context, however, the self-deluded members of the congregation are being addressed.

3:21 *overcomes.* See note on 2:7. *sit with me on my throne.* See 20:4,6; Mt 19:28; 2Ti 2:12.

4:1—5:14 These two chapters constitute an introduction to chs. 6–20. In the throne room of heaven, the Lamb assumes the responsibility of initiating the great final conflict with the forces of evil, the end of which will see the Lamb triumphant and the devil consigned to the lake of fire.

4:1 *Come up here.* Similarly, Moses was called up to the top of Mount Sinai to receive divine direction (Ex 19:20,24). Cf. also the heavenly ascent of the two witnesses (11:12). Some interpreters find the rapture of the church in this verse. *what must take place after this.* See 1:1,19; Da 2:28–29,45.

4:2 *in the Spirit.* In a state of heightened spiritual awareness by the power of the Spirit (see note on 1:10; see also 17:3; 21:10). *throne in heaven.* The depiction of God ruling from his throne in heaven is a regular feature of the OT (e.g., Ps 47:8).

4:3 *jasper ... carnelian ... emerald.* Since God dwells in "unapproachable light" and is one "whom no one has seen or can see" (1Ti 6:16), he is described in terms of the reflected brilliance of precious stones—an emerald rainbow around the throne (cf. Eze 1:26–28).

4:4 *twenty-four elders.* Representative of either the whole company of believers in heaven or an exalted angelic order worshiping and serving God there (see vv. 9–11; 5:5–14; 7:11–17; 11:16–18; 14:3; 19:4). The number 24 is often understood to reflect the 12 Israelite tribes of the OT and the 12 apostles of the NT.

4:5 *flashes of lightning ... thunder ... blazing.* Symbolic of the awesome majesty and power of God (cf. the manifestation of God at Sinai, Ex 19:16–19; cf. also the conventional OT depiction of God's coming in mighty power to deliver his people, Ps 18:12–15; 77:18). In Revelation, thunder and lightning always mark an important event connected with the heavenly temple (8:5; 11:19; 16:18). *seven spirits.* See note on 1:4; "seven" symbolizes fullness, completeness or perfection.

4:6 *sea of glass.* See 15:2. The source of the imagery may be Eze 1:22 (cf. Ex 24:10), but it is also possible that it is the basin in the heavenly temple (cf. 11:19; 14:15,17; 15:5–6,8; 16:1,17), whose counterpart in the earthly temple was referred to as the Sea (1Ki 7:23–25; 2Ki 16:17; 2Ch 4:2,4,10,15; Jer 27:19). Other features of the temple in heaven are: the lamps (v. 5), the altar (6:9), the altar of incense (8:3) and the ark of the covenant (11:19). *four living creatures.* An exalted order of angelic beings whose task is to guard the heavenly throne and lead in worship and adoration of God. *covered with eyes.* Nothing escapes their attention.

4:7 Ezekiel in a vision also saw four living creatures, each of which had four faces—human in front, lion on the right, ox on the left, and eagle behind (Eze 1:6,10). In John's vision the creatures were in the form of a lion, an ox, and a flying eagle, and one had a face like that of a man.

4:8 *six wings.* This feature of the living creatures and the praise they speak seem to be modeled after the seraphs of Isa 6:2–3; thus the living creatures combine features of the cherubim of Eze 1 and 10 (see note on v. 7) and the seraphs of Isa 6. *Holy, holy, holy.* See note on Isa 6:3. *was ... is ... is to come.* An expansion of the divine name in Ex 3:14–15 (see note on Rev 1:4). God's power and holiness extend from eternity past to eternity yet to come (cf. Isa 41:4).

4:10 *lay their crowns.* Acknowledgment that God alone is worthy of ultimate praise and worship.

4:11 *you created all things.* See Ge 1.

for you created all things,
and by your will they were created
and have their being."[n]

The Scroll and the Lamb

5 Then I saw in the right hand of him
who sat on the throne[o] a scroll with
writing on both sides[p] and sealed[q] with
seven seals. 2And I saw a mighty angel[r]
proclaiming in a loud voice, "Who is worthy to break the seals and open the scroll?"
3But no one in heaven or on earth or under the earth could open the scroll or even
look inside it. 4I wept and wept because no
one was found who was worthy to open
the scroll or look inside. 5Then one of the
elders said to me, "Do not weep! See, the
Lion[s] of the tribe of Judah,[t] the Root of
David,[u] has triumphed. He is able to open
the scroll and its seven seals."
6Then I saw a Lamb,[v] looking as if it had
been slain, standing in the center of the
throne, encircled by the four living creatures[w] and the elders.[x] He had seven horns
and seven eyes,[y] which are the seven spirits[a][z] of God sent out into all the earth. 7He
came and took the scroll from the right
hand of him who sat on the throne.[a] 8And
when he had taken it, the four living creatures[b] and the twenty-four elders[c] fell
down before the Lamb. Each one had a
harp[d] and they were holding golden bowls
full of incense, which are the prayers[e] of
the saints. 9And they sang a new song:[f]

"You are worthy[g] to take the scroll
and to open its seals,
because you were slain,
and with your blood[h] you purchased[i]
men for God
from every tribe and language and
people and nation.[j]
10You have made them to be a kingdom
and priests[k] to serve our God,
and they will reign on the earth."[l]

11Then I looked and heard the voice of
many angels, numbering thousands upon
thousands, and ten thousand times ten
thousand.[m] They encircled the throne and
the living creatures[n] and the elders.[o] 12In a
loud voice they sang:

"Worthy is the Lamb,[p] who was slain,[q]
to receive power and wealth and
wisdom and strength
and honor and glory and praise!"[r]

13Then I heard every creature in heaven
and on earth and under the earth[s] and on
the sea, and all that is in them, singing:

"To him who sits on the throne[t] and to
the Lamb[u]
be praise and honor and glory and
power,
for ever and ever!"[v]

14The four living creatures[w] said, "Amen,"[x]
and the elders[y] fell down and worshiped.[z]

The Seals

6 I watched as the Lamb[a] opened the
first of the seven seals.[b] Then I heard
one of the four living creatures[c] say in a

[a] 6 Or *the sevenfold Spirit*

4:11 [n]Ac 14:15; Rev 10:6 **5:1** [o]ver 7,13; Rev 4:2,9; 6:16 [p]Eze 2:9,10 [q]Isa 29:11; Da 12:4 **5:2** [r]Rev 10:1 **5:5** [s]Ge 49:9 [t]S Heb 7:14 [u]Isa 11:1,10; Ro 15:12; Rev 22:16 **5:6** [v]ver 8,9,12,13; S Jn 1:29 [w]S Rev 4:6 [x]S Rev 4:4 [y]Zec 4:10 [z]S Rev 1:4 **5:7** [a]S ver 1 **5:8** [b]S Rev 4:6 [c]S Rev 4:4 [d]Rev 14:2; 15:2 [e]Ps 141:2; Rev 8:3,4 **5:9** [f]Ps 40:3; 98:1; 149:1; Isa 42:10; Rev 14:3,4 [g]Rev 4:11 [h]Heb 9:12 [i]S 1Co 6:20 [j]S Rev 13:7 **5:10** [k]S 1Pe 2:5 [l]Rev 3:21; 20:4 **5:11** [m]Da 7:10; Heb 12:22; Jude 14 [n]S Rev 4:6 [o]S Rev 4:4 **5:12** [p]ver 13 [q]ver 9 [r]Rev 1:6; 4:11 **5:13** [s]ver 3; Php 2:10 [t]S ver 1,7 [u]ver 6; Rev 6:16; 7:10 [v]1Ch 29:11; Mal 1:6; 2:2; S Ro 11:36 **5:14** [w]S Rev 4:6 [x]Rev 4:9 [y]S Rev 4:4 [z]Rev 4:10 **6:1** [a]S Rev 5:6 [b]Rev 5:1 [c]S Rev 4:6,7

5:1 *scroll.* See note on 1:11; cf. the little scroll of 10:2,8–10. *writing on both sides.* Like the stone tablets of the OT covenant law (see Ex 32:15 and note; Eze 2:9–10). The fibers of a papyrus scroll run horizontally on the inside, which makes writing easier than on the reverse side (where the fibers are vertical). *sealed with seven seals.* Indicating absolute inviolability (cf. Isa 29:11; Da 12:4).

5:2 *mighty angel.* Powerful enough to address his challenge to the whole creation (cf. 10:1; 18:21 and the angel with great authority and splendor in 18:2).

5:3 *heaven ... earth ... under the earth.* A conventional phrase used to express the universality of the proclamation—no creature was worthy. It is not intended to teach a threefold division of the universe (cf. Ex 20:4; Php 2:10).

5:5 *Lion of the tribe of Judah.* A Messianic title taken from Ge 49:8–10, where Judah is named a "lion's cub" and promised the right to rule "until he comes to whom it belongs" (see also Eze 21:27). *Root of David.* See Isa 11:1,10, which looks forward to the ideal king in the line of David. The title is interpreted Messianically in Ro 15:12.

5:6 *Lamb.* Pictured as the sacrifice for sin ("slain"; cf. Isa 53:7; Jn 1:29) and as the mighty conqueror (17:14). Revelation uses a special word for "lamb" (29 times in Revelation and only once elsewhere in the NT—Jn 21:15). The idea of the lamb as a victorious military leader seems to come from the apocalyptic tradition (1 Enoch 90:9; Testament of Joseph 19:8). *as if it had been slain.* Bearing the marks of its slaughter—he has come to power through his death. *seven horns.* The horn is an ancient Jewish symbol for power or strength (cf. Dt 33:17). The fourth beast of Da 7:7,20 had ten horns (cf. Da 8:3,5). Seven horns would symbolize full strength. *seven spirits.* See note on 4:5.

5:8 *harp.* An ancient stringed instrument (not the large modern harp) used especially to accompany songs (Ps 33:2). *bowls full of incense.* The bowl was a flat, shallow cup. Incense was a normal feature of Hebrew ritual (see Dt 33:10; cf. Ps 141:2; Rev 8:3–4). *prayers of the saints.* In later Jewish thought, angels often present the prayers of saints to God (Tobit 12:15; 3 Baruch 11). *saints.* See notes on Ro 1:7; Eph 1:1.

5:9 *new song.* Cf. 14:3; Ps 33:3; 96:1; 144:9; Isa 42:10. In the OT a new song celebrated a new act of divine deliverance or blessing. That is also its sense here; notice the theme of the song. *with your blood you purchased men.* The sacrificial death of Christ is central to NT teaching (see Mk 10:45; 1Co 6:20).

5:10 *have made them.* See note on 1:6. *kingdom and priests.* See note on 1:6. *reign on the earth.* See 2:26–27; 20:4,6; 22:5.

5:11 *thousands upon thousands.* A rhetorical phrase for an indefinitely large number (see Da 7:10; cf. Heb 12:22).

5:12 *power ... praise!* See David's farewell prayer in 1Ch 29:10–19. The attributes increase from three in 4:11 to four in 5:13 to seven in 5:12; 7:12.

5:13 *heaven ... earth ... under the earth.* See note on v. 3.

6:1—8:1 The cycle of the seven seals.

6:1 *Lamb.* See v. 16; see also 5:6 and note. *seven seals.* The first of three sevenfold numbered series of judgments (cf. the

voice like thunder,[d] "Come!" 2I looked,
and there before me was a white horse![e]
Its rider held a bow, and he was given a
crown,[f] and he rode out as a conqueror
bent on conquest.[g]
3When the Lamb opened the second
seal, I heard the second living creature[h]
say, "Come!" 4Then another horse came
out, a fiery red one.[i] Its rider was given
power to take peace from the earth[j] and
to make men slay each other. To him was
given a large sword.
5When the Lamb opened the third seal,
I heard the third living creature[k] say,
"Come!" I looked, and there before me
was a black horse![l] Its rider was holding
a pair of scales in his hand. 6Then I heard
what sounded like a voice among the four
living creatures,[m] saying, "A quart[a] of
wheat for a day's wages,[b] and three quarts
of barley for a day's wages,[b][n] and do not
damage[o] the oil and the wine!"
7When the Lamb opened the fourth seal,
I heard the voice of the fourth living creature[p] say, "Come!" 8I looked, and there
before me was a pale horse![q] Its rider was
named Death, and Hades[r] was following
close behind him. They were given power
over a fourth of the earth to kill by sword,
famine and plague, and by the wild beasts
of the earth.[s]
9When he opened the fifth seal, I saw
under[t] the altar[u] the souls of those who
had been slain[v] because of the word of
God[w] and the testimony they had maintained. 10They called out in a loud voice,
"How long,[x] Sovereign Lord,[y] holy and
true,[z] until you judge the inhabitants of
the earth[a] and avenge our blood?"[b] 11Then
each of them was given a white robe,[c] and
they were told to wait a little longer, until
the number of their fellow servants and
brothers who were to be killed as they had
been was completed.[d]
12I watched as he opened the sixth seal.
There was a great earthquake.[e] The sun
turned black[f] like sackcloth[g] made of goat
hair, the whole moon turned blood red,
13and the stars in the sky fell to earth,[h] as
late figs drop from a fig tree[i] when shaken
by a strong wind. 14The sky receded like a
scroll, rolling up,[j] and every mountain and
island was removed from its place.[k]
15Then the kings of the earth, the princes, the generals, the rich, the mighty, and
every slave and every free man[l] hid in
caves and among the rocks of the mountains.[m] 16They called to the mountains and
the rocks, "Fall on us[n] and hide us from
the face of him who sits on the throne[o]
and from the wrath of the Lamb! 17For the
great day[p] of their wrath has come, and
who can stand?"[q]

6:1 [d]Rev 14:2; 19:6 **6:2** [e]Zec 1:8; 6:3; Rev 19:11 [f]Zec 6:11; Rev 14:14; 19:12 [g]Ps 45:4 **6:3** [h]Rev 4:7 **6:4** [i]Zec 1:8; 6:2 [j]Mt 10:34 **6:5** [k]Rev 4:7 [l]Zec 6:2 **6:6** [m]S Rev 4:6,7 [n]Eze 4:16 [o]Rev 7:1,3; 9:4 **6:7** [p]Rev 4:7 **6:8** [q]Zec 6:3 [r]Hos 13:14; Rev 1:18; 20:13,14 [s]Jer 15:2,3; 24:10; Eze 5:12,17 **6:9** [t]Ex 29:12; Lev 4:7 [u]Rev 14:18; 16:7 [v]Rev 20:4 [w]Ro 1:2; S Heb 4:12 **6:10** [x]Ps 119:84; Zec 1:12 [y]Lk 2:29; 2Pe 2:1 [z]S Rev 3:7 [a]S Rev 3:10 [b]Dt 32:43; 2Ki 9:7; Ps 79:10; Rev 16:6; 18:20; 19:2 **6:11** [c]S Rev 3:4 [d]Heb 11:40 **6:12** [e]Ps 97:4; Isa 29:6; Eze 38:19; Rev 8:5; 11:13; 16:18 [f]S Mt 24:29 [g]Isa 50:3

[a] 6 Greek *a choinix* (probably about a liter) [b] 6 Greek *a denarius*

6:13 [h]S Mt 24:29; Rev 8:10; 9:1 [i]Isa 34:4 **6:14** [j]S 2Pe 3:10; Rev 20:11; 21:1 [k]Ps 46:2; Isa 54:10; Jer 4:24; Eze 38:20; Na 1:5; Rev 16:20; 21:1 **6:15** [l]Rev 19:18 [m]Isa 2:10,19,21 **6:16** [n]Hos 10:8; Lk 23:30 [o]S Rev 5:1 **6:17** [p]Joel 1:15; 2:1,2,11,31; Zep 1:14,15; Rev 16:14 [q]Ps 76:7; Na 1:6; Mal 3:2

seven trumpets in chs. 8–9 and the seven bowls in ch. 16). *four living creatures.* See 4:6–7 and notes.

6:2 *white horse.* The imagery of the "four horsemen of the Apocalypse" comes from Zec 1:8–17; 6:1–8 (see note on Zec 6:2–3). The colors in Revelation correspond to the character of the rider; white symbolizes conquest. Major interpretations of the rider on the white horse are: (1) Christ (cf. 19:11), (2) the antichrist and (3) the spirit of conquest. The latter establishes a more natural sequence with the other three riders (which symbolize bloodshed, famine and death). *bow.* A battle weapon.

6:4 *another horse ... a fiery red one.* Symbolizing bloodshed and war (cf. Zec 1:8; 6:2). *men slay each other.* If the white horse is conquest from without, the red horse may be internal revolution. *sword.* See note on 1:16.

6:5 *black horse.* Symbolizing famine (cf. Zec 6:2,6). The sequence is thus conquest, bloodshed, famine. *pair of scales.* A balance beam with scales hung from either end. Weights were originally stones.

6:6 *wheat ... barley.* One quart of wheat would be enough for only one person. Three quarts of the less nutritious barley would be barely enough for a small family. Famine had inflated prices to at least ten times their normal level. *the oil and the wine.* Sets limits on the destruction by the rider of the black horse. The roots of the olive and vine go deeper and would not be immediately affected by a limited drought.

6:8 *pale horse.* Describes the ashen appearance of the dead; it symbolizes death. *Hades.* Equivalent to Hebrew *Sheol* (see 1:18; 20:13–14; see also note on Mt 16:18). *sword ... wild beasts.* See Eze 5:16–17 and note.

6:10 *inhabitants of the earth.* A regular designation in Revelation for humankind in its hostility to God (see 3:10; 8:13; 11:10; 13:8,12; 17:2,8).

6:11 *white robe.* Symbol of blessedness and purity (see 3:5,18; 4:4; 7:9,13; 19:14). *until the number ... was completed.* Jewish thought held that God rules the world according to a predetermined time schedule (in the Apocrypha see 2 Esdras 4:35–37) and that the end awaits the death of a certain number of the righteous (1 Enoch 47:4). *brothers.* See note on Ro 1:13.

6:12 *earthquake.* A common feature of divine visitation (see Ex 19:18; Isa 2:19; Hag 2:6). *sackcloth.* See note on 11:3. *moon turned blood red.* See Joel 2:31, quoted by Peter in his Pentecost sermon (Ac 2:20).

6:13 *stars ... fell.* One of the signs immediately preceding the coming of the Son of Man (Mk 13:25–26). *late figs.* Green figs appearing in the winter and easily blown from the tree, which at that season has no leaves.

6:14 *sky receded like a scroll.* See Isa 34:4. *every mountain and island was removed.* Perhaps suggested by Jer 4:24 or Na 1:5; see 16:20; 20:11.

6:15 *generals.* A general was a Roman officer who commanded a cohort, i.e., about 1,000 men. *hid in caves.* See Jer 4:29.

6:16 *wrath of the Lamb.* Only here is wrath attributed to the Lamb, but it is related to God's wrath (see "their wrath" in v. 17). God's wrath is a subject that permeates NT teaching and is both present (see Ro 1:18 and note) and future (see 19:15). It is prophesied in the OT (Zep 1:14–18; Na 1:6; Mal 3:2).

144,000 Sealed

7 After this I saw four angels standing at
the four corners[r] of the earth, holding
back the four winds[s] of the earth to prevent[t] any wind from blowing on the land
or on the sea or on any tree. 2Then I saw
another angel coming up from the east,
having the seal[u] of the living God.[v] He
called out in a loud voice to the four angels who had been given power to harm
the land and the sea:[w] 3"Do not harm[x] the
land or the sea or the trees until we put a
seal on the foreheads[y] of the servants of
our God." 4Then I heard the number[z] of
those who were sealed: 144,000[a] from all
the tribes of Israel.

5From the tribe of Judah 12,000 were
sealed,
from the tribe of Reuben 12,000,
from the tribe of Gad 12,000,
6from the tribe of Asher 12,000,
from the tribe of Naphtali 12,000,
from the tribe of Manasseh 12,000,
7from the tribe of Simeon 12,000,
from the tribe of Levi 12,000,
from the tribe of Issachar 12,000,
8from the tribe of Zebulun 12,000,
from the tribe of Joseph 12,000,
from the tribe of Benjamin 12,000.

The Great Multitude in White Robes

9After this I looked and there before me
was a great multitude that no one could
count, from every nation, tribe, people
and language,[b] standing before the throne[c]
and in front of the Lamb. They were wearing white robes[d] and were holding palm
branches in their hands. 10And they cried
out in a loud voice:

"Salvation belongs to our God,[e]
who sits on the throne,[f]
and to the Lamb."

11All the angels were standing around the
throne and around the elders[g] and the four
living creatures.[h] They fell down on their
faces[i] before the throne and worshiped
God, 12saying:

"Amen!
Praise and glory
and wisdom and thanks and honor
and power and strength
be to our God for ever and ever.
Amen!"[j]

13Then one of the elders asked me,
"These in white robes[k]—who are they,
and where did they come from?"
14I answered, "Sir, you know."
And he said, "These are they who have
come out of the great tribulation; they
have washed their robes[l] and made them
white in the blood of the Lamb.[m] 15There-
fore,

"they are before the throne of God[n]
and serve him[o] day and night in
his temple;[p]
and he who sits on the throne[q] will
spread his tent over them.[r]
16Never again will they hunger;
never again will they thirst.[s]
The sun will not beat upon them,
nor any scorching heat.[t]

7:1 [r]Isa 11:12 [s]Jer 49:36; Eze 37:9; Da 7:2; Zec 6:5; Mt 24:31 [t]S Rev 6:6 **7:2** [u]Rev 9:4 [v]S Mt 16:16 [w]ver 1 **7:3** [x]S Rev 6:6 [y]Eze 9:4; Rev 9:4; 14:1; 22:4 **7:4** [z]Rev 9:16 [a]Rev 14:1,3 **7:9** [b]S Rev 13:7 [c]ver 15 [d]S Rev 3:4 **7:10** [e]Ps 3:8; Rev 12:10; 19:1 [f]S Rev 5:1 **7:11** [g]S Rev 4:4 [h]S Rev 4:6 [i]S Rev 4:10 **7:12** [j]S Ro 11:36; Rev 5:12-14 **7:13** [k]S Rev 3:4 **7:14** [l]Rev 22:14 [m]Heb 9:14; 1Jn 1:7; Rev 12:11 **7:15** [n]ver 9 [o]Rev 22:3 [p]Rev 11:19 [q]S Rev 5:1 [r]Isa 4:5,6; Rev 21:3 **7:16** [s]Jn 6:35 [t]Isa 49:10

7:1–17 An interlude separating the final seal (8:1) from the preceding six (the same feature is found in the trumpet sequence; see 10:1—11:13). It contains two visions: (1) the sealing of the 144,000 (vv. 1–8) and (2) the innumerable multitude (vv. 9–17).
7:1 *four winds.* Destructive agents of God (see Jer 49:36).
7:2 *seal of the living God.* Ancient documents were folded and tied, and a lump of clay was pressed over the knot. The sender would then stamp the hardening clay with his signet ring or roll it with a cylinder seal, which authenticated and protected the contents. The sealing in ch. 7 results in the name of the Lord being stamped on the forehead of his followers (see 9:4; 14:1; cf. 22:4). Its primary purpose is to protect the people of God in the coming judgments. For the background see Eze 9:4, where the mark was the Hebrew letter *Taw,* made like an *X* or + (see also note on Eze 9:4).
7:4 *144,000.* Some find here a reference to members of actual Jewish tribes, the faithful Jewish remnant of the "great tribulation" (v. 14). Others take the passage as symbolic of all the faithful believers who live during the period of tribulation.
7:5 *Judah.* Perhaps listed before Reuben, his older brother, because the Messiah belonged to the tribe of Judah (but see note on Ge 37:21).
7:6 *Manasseh.* One of the two Joseph tribes (Ephraim and Manasseh), yet mentioned separately, probably to make up 12 tribes since Dan is omitted. This omission is due perhaps to Dan's early connection with idolatry (Jdg 18:30), or to a tradition that the antichrist was to come from that tribe.
7:9 *great multitude.* Identified in v. 14 as those who have come out of the "great tribulation." *every nation, tribe, people and language.* All four are mentioned together also in 5:9; 11:9; 13:7; 14:6. Cf. 10:11; 17:15, in which one of the four is changed. *palm branches.* Used for festive occasions (see Lev 23:40; Jn 12:13).
7:10 *Salvation belongs to our God.* See Ge 49:18 ("deliverance"); Jnh 2:9.
7:11 *elders.* See note on 4:4. *four living creatures.* See note on 4:6.
7:12 *Praise ... strength.* The sevenfold list of attributes expresses complete or perfect praise (see note on 5:12).
7:13 *white robes.* See note on 6:11.
7:14 *the great tribulation.* The period of final hostility prior to Christ's return. Some hold that the beginning of this hostility was already being experienced by the church of John's day.
7:15 *temple.* All 16 references to the temple in Revelation use the word that designates the temple proper rather than the larger precincts. It is the place where God's presence dwells. Thus no longer may only one tribe (Levites) go into God's presence, but all believers serve God there, for they have been made priests in God's service (see 1:6; 5:10; 20:6). *spread his tent.* The imagery would evoke memories of the tabernacle in the desert (Lev 26:11–13).

17 For the Lamb at the center of the
throne will be their shepherd;[u]
he will lead them to springs of living
water.[v]
And God will wipe away every tear
from their eyes."[w]

The Seventh Seal and the Golden Censer

8 When he opened the seventh seal,[x]
there was silence in heaven for about
half an hour.
2 And I saw the seven angels[y] who stand
before God, and to them were given seven
trumpets.[z]
3 Another angel,[a] who had a golden censer, came and stood at the altar. He was
given much incense to offer, with the
prayers of all the saints,[b] on the golden
altar[c] before the throne. 4 The smoke of
the incense, together with the prayers of
the saints, went up before God[d] from the
angel's hand. 5 Then the angel took the
censer, filled it with fire from the altar,[e]
and hurled it on the earth; and there came
peals of thunder,[f] rumblings, flashes of
lightning and an earthquake.[g]

The Trumpets

6 Then the seven angels who had the
seven trumpets[h] prepared to sound them.
7 The first angel[i] sounded his trumpet,
and there came hail and fire[j] mixed with
blood, and it was hurled down upon the
earth. A third[k] of the earth was burned up,
a third of the trees were burned up, and all
the green grass was burned up.[l]
8 The second angel sounded his trumpet,
and something like a huge mountain,[m] all
ablaze, was thrown into the sea. A third[n]
of the sea turned into blood,[o] 9 a third[p] of
the living creatures in the sea died, and a
third of the ships were destroyed.
10 The third angel sounded his trumpet,
and a great star, blazing like a torch, fell
from the sky[q] on a third of the rivers and
on the springs of water[r]— 11 the name of
the star is Wormwood.[a] A third[s] of the waters turned bitter, and many people died
from the waters that had become bitter.[t]
12 The fourth angel sounded his trumpet,
and a third of the sun was struck, a third
of the moon, and a third of the stars, so
that a third[u] of them turned dark.[v] A third
of the day was without light, and also a
third of the night.[w]
13 As I watched, I heard an eagle that
was flying in midair[x] call out in a loud
voice: "Woe! Woe! Woe[y] to the inhabitants of the earth,[z] because of the trumpet
blasts about to be sounded by the other
three angels!"

9 The fifth angel sounded his trumpet,
and I saw a star that had fallen from
the sky to the earth.[a] The star was given
the key[b] to the shaft of the Abyss.[c] 2 When

7:17 [u] S Jn 10:11 [v] S Jn 4:10 [w] Isa 25:8; 35:10; 51:11; 65:19; Rev 21:4 **8:1** [x] Rev 6:1 **8:2** [y] ver 6-13; Rev 9:1, 13; 11:15 [z] S Mt 24:31 **8:3** [a] Rev 7:2 [b] Rev 5:8 [c] ver 5; Ex 30:1-6; Heb 9:4; Rev 9:13 **8:4** [d] Ps 141:2 **8:5** [e] Lev 16:12, 13 [f] S Rev 4:5 [g] S Rev 6:12 **8:6** [h] S ver 2 **8:7** [i] S ver 2 [j] Eze 38:22 [k] ver 7-12; Rev 9:15, 18; 12:4 [l] Rev 9:4 **8:8** [m] Jer 51:25 [n] S ver 7 [o] Rev 16:3 **8:9** [p] S ver 7 **8:10** [q] Isa 14:12; Rev 6:13; 9:1 [r] Rev 14:7; 16:4 **8:11** [s] S ver 7 [t] Jer 9:15; 23:15 **8:12** [u] S ver 7 [v] Ex 10:21-23; Rev 6:12, 13 [w] Eze 32:7 **8:13** [x] Rev 14:6; 19:17 [y] Rev 9:12; 11:14; 12:12 [z] S Rev 3:10 **9:1** [a] Rev 8:10 [b] Rev 1:18 [c] ver 2, 11; S Lk 8:31

[a] *11* That is, Bitterness

7:17 *shepherd.* Ancient kings often referred to themselves as the shepherds of their people (see Ps 23:1 and note).
8:1 *silence in heaven.* A dramatic pause before the next series of plagues—the final act of the drama is left undisclosed here, reserved to be presented later.
8:2—11:19 The cycle of the seven trumpets.
8:2 *seven trumpets.* In OT times the trumpet served to announce important events and give signals in time of war. The seven trumpets of Rev 8–9; 11:15–19 announce a series of plagues more severe than the seals but not as completely devastating as the bowls (ch. 16).
8:3 *censer.* A firepan used to hold live charcoal for the burning of incense (cf. Ex 27:3; 1Ki 7:50). *with the prayers.* Most translations consider the incense to be mingled "with" prayers. The Greek for this phrase also allows a translation that takes the incense "to be" the prayers ("incense ... consisting of the prayers").
8:4 Although the angel is involved in presenting the prayers of the saints to God, he does not make them acceptable. The Jewish apocalyptic concept of angels as mediators finds no place in the NT. Angels did function as mediators in the old covenant era (see Ac 7:38 and note), but there is no record of such a mediatorial function on the part of angels in the new covenant era.
8:5 *thunder ... earthquake.* See note on 4:5.
8:7 *hail and fire mixed with blood.* Cf. the imagery of the seventh plague on Egypt (Ex 9:13–25; cf. Eze 38:22). *A third of the earth was burned up.* This fraction indicates that the punishment announced by the trumpets is not yet complete and final (the same fraction appears in each of the next three plagues: vv. 8–9,10–11,12). A smaller fraction (a fourth) of devastation accompanied the opening of the fourth seal (6:8).
8:8 *sea turned into blood.* Reminiscent of the first plague on Egypt (Ex 7:20–21). This is an eschatological judgment rather than natural pollution resulting from widespread volcanic upheavals.
8:10 *great star ... fell.* See notes on 6:13; 9:1.
8:11 *Wormwood.* A plant with a strong, bitter taste (see NIV text note). It is used here as a metaphor for calamity and sorrow (see Pr 5:3–4; Jer 9:15; La 3:19). It is not poisonous, but its bitterness suggests death. *waters turned bitter.* The reverse of the miracle at Marah, where bitter waters were made sweet (Ex 15:25).
8:12 *a third of the sun was struck.* In the ninth plague on Egypt, thick darkness covered the land for three days (Ex 10:21–23). References to the Egyptian plagues suggest that in Revelation we have the final exodus of God's people from the bondage of a world controlled by hostile powers.
8:13 *Woe! Woe! Woe ... !* These three woes correspond to the three final trumpet plagues (see 9:12; 11:14 [10:1—11:13 is an interlude]; the seven bowl judgments of chs. 15–16 apparently constitute the third woe). The woes fall on the unbelieving world (the phrase "the inhabitants of the earth" refers to the wicked; see note on 6:10), not on the righteous (see 9:4).
9:1 *star that had fallen.* The star in 8:10 was part of a cosmic disturbance; here the star is a divine agent, probably an angel (cf. 20:1). *Abyss.* Conceived of as the subterranean abode of demonic hordes (see 20:1; Lk 8:31). This Greek word (derived ultimately from Sumerian via Akkadian) means "very deep" or "bottomless," and is used in the Septuagint (the pre-Christian Greek translation of the OT) to translate the Hebrew word for the primeval deep (see Ge 1:2; 7:11; Pr 8:28). Eight of the nine NT occurrences of the Greek word *Abyss* are in Revelation.

he opened the Abyss, smoke rose from it
like the smoke from a gigantic furnace.[d]
The sun and sky were darkened[e] by the
smoke from the Abyss.[f] 3And out of the
smoke locusts[g] came down upon the earth
and were given power like that of scorpions[h] of the earth. 4They were told not to
harm[i] the grass of the earth or any plant
or tree,[j] but only those people who did not
have the seal of God on their foreheads.[k]
5They were not given power to kill them,
but only to torture them for five months.[l]
And the agony they suffered was like that
of the sting of a scorpion[m] when it strikes
a man. 6During those days men will seek
death, but will not find it; they will long to
die, but death will elude them.[n]

7The locusts looked like horses prepared
for battle.[o] On their heads they wore something like crowns of gold, and their faces
resembled human faces.[p] 8Their hair was
like women's hair, and their teeth were
like lions' teeth.[q] 9They had breastplates
like breastplates of iron, and the sound
of their wings was like the thundering of
many horses and chariots rushing into battle.[r] 10They had tails and stings like scorpions, and in their tails they had power
to torment people for five months.[s] 11They
had as king over them the angel of the
Abyss,[t] whose name in Hebrew[u] is Abaddon,[v] and in Greek, Apollyon.[a]

12The first woe is past; two other woes
are yet to come.[w]

13The sixth angel sounded his trumpet, and I heard a voice coming from the
horns[b][x] of the golden altar that is before
God.[y] 14It said to the sixth angel who had
the trumpet, "Release the four angels[z]
who are bound at the great river Euphrates."[a] 15And the four angels who had been
kept ready for this very hour and day and
month and year were released[b] to kill a
third[c] of mankind.[d] 16The number of the
mounted troops was two hundred million.
I heard their number.[e]

17The horses and riders I saw in my vision looked like this: Their breastplates
were fiery red, dark blue, and yellow as
sulfur. The heads of the horses resembled
the heads of lions, and out of their mouths[f]
came fire, smoke and sulfur.[g] 18A third[h] of
mankind was killed[i] by the three plagues
of fire, smoke and sulfur[j] that came out of
their mouths. 19The power of the horses
was in their mouths and in their tails; for
their tails were like snakes, having heads
with which they inflict injury.

20The rest of mankind that were not
killed by these plagues still did not repent[k] of the work of their hands;[l] they
did not stop worshiping demons,[m] and
idols of gold, silver, bronze, stone and
wood—idols that cannot see or hear or
walk.[n] 21Nor did they repent[o] of their murders, their magic arts,[p] their sexual immorality[q] or their thefts.

[a] *11* *Abaddon* and *Apollyon* mean *Destroyer.*
[b] *13* That is, projections

9:2 [d]Ge 19:28; Ex 19:18 [e]Joel 2:2,10 [f]ver 1,11; S Lk 8:31 **9:3** [g]Ex 10:12-15 [h]ver 5,10 **9:4** [i]S Rev 6:6 [j]Rev 8:7 [k]S Rev 7:2,3 **9:5** [l]ver 10 [m]ver 3 **9:6** [n]Job 3:21; 7:15; Jer 8:3; Rev 6:16 **9:7** [o]Joel 2:4 [p]Da 7:8 **9:8** [q]Joel 1:6 **9:9** [r]Joel 2:5 **9:10** [s]ver 3,5,19 **9:11** [t]ver 1,2; S Lk 8:31 [u]Rev 16:16 [v]Job 26:6; 28:22; 31:12; Ps 88:11 **9:12** [w]S Rev 8:13 **9:13** [x]Ex 30:1-3 [y]Rev 8:3 **9:14** [z]Rev 7:1 [a]Ge 15:18; Dt 1:7; Jos 1:4; Isa 11:15; Rev 16:12 **9:15** [b]Rev 20:7 [c]S Rev 8:7 [d]ver 18 **9:16** [e]Rev 5:11; 7:4 **9:17** [f]Rev 11:5 [g]ver 18; Ps 11:6; Isa 30:33; Eze 38:22; Rev 14:10; 19:20; 20:10; 21:8 **9:18** [h]S Rev 8:7 [i]ver 15 [j]S ver 17 **9:20** [k]S Rev 2:21 [l]Dt 4:28; 31:29; Jer 1:16; Mic 5:13; Ac 7:41 [m]S 1Co 10:20 [n]Ps 115:4-7; 135:15-17; Da 5:23 **9:21** [o]S Rev 2:21 [p]Isa 47:9,12; Rev 18:23 [q]Rev 17:2,5

9:3 *locusts.* For background see the plague of locusts in Ex 10:1–20. Joel 1:2—2:11 interprets the locust plague as a foreshadowing of the devastations that accompany the day of the Lord. Locusts traveled in enormous swarms and could strip a land of all vegetation. In 1866, 200,000 people died in a famine in Algeria following a locust plague. *scorpions.* Large spider-like organisms that injure or kill by means of a poisonous barb in the tail.

9:4 *people who did not have the seal of God.* The first woe does not affect the "servants of … God" (7:3). Cf. the Israelites, who were protected from the Egyptian plagues (Ex 8:22; 9:4,26; 10:23; 11:7).

9:5 *five months.* A limited period of time suggested by the life cycle of the locust or the dry season (spring through late summer, about five months), in which the danger of a locust invasion is always present.

9:6 *seek death, but will not find it.* Cf. Hos 10:8 (quoted in Lk 23:30). Cornelius Gallus, a Roman poet living in the first century B.C., wrote: "Worse than any wound is the wish to die and yet not be able to do so." Cf. Paul's attitude toward death in Php 1:23–24.

9:7 *human faces.* The locusts appear to have the cunning of intelligent beings. They do not simply use brute force.

9:8 *women's hair.* Perhaps a reference to long antennae. *lions' teeth.* Cruel, inhumane.

9:9 *breastplates.* The breastplate was a coat of mail that protected the front. *like breastplates of iron.* Probably thin iron pieces riveted to a leather base.

9:10 *five months.* See note on v. 5.

9:11 *Abaddon.* A personification of destruction (see NIV text note; cf. Pr 15:11 and NIV text note).

9:12 *first woe.* See note on 8:13.

9:13 *horns of the golden altar.* See 8:3–5. The horns were projections at the four corners of the altar (Ex 27:2). Those fleeing judgment could seek mercy by taking hold of the horns (1Ki 1:50–51; 2:28; see note on Am 3:14).

9:14 *four angels.* Apparently in charge of the demonic horsemen (vv. 15–19). *Euphrates.* See note on Ge 15:18.

9:15 *hour … day … month … year.* Apocalyptic thought views God as acting according to an exact timetable.

9:16 *two hundred million.* The reference is most likely general, intending an incalculable host rather than a specific number (cf. Ps 68:17; Da 7:10; Rev 5:11).

9:17 *breastplates.* See note on v. 9. *out of their mouths came fire.* Cf. the two witnesses in 11:5.

9:19 *tails were like snakes, having heads.* Emphasizes the demonic origin of the horses (cf. 12:9).

9:20 *still did not repent.* Suggests that the purpose of the extreme suffering of some was to call the others to repentance (cf. v. 21; 2:21; 16:9,11; cf. also Am 4:6–11 and note). *demons.* Spiritual beings in league with Satan and exerting an evil influence on human affairs (cf. Dt 4:28; Ps 115:5–7; Lk 4:33 and note; 1Co 10:20).

9:21 *Nor did they repent.* See 16:9,11. Even physical pain will not change the rebellious heart. *magic arts.* Involved the mixing of various ingredients (the Greek for this phrase is *pharmakon,* from which comes the English "pharmacy") for magical purposes. Believers at Ephesus publicly burned their

The Angel and the Little Scroll

10 Then I saw another mighty angel[r]
coming down from heaven.[s] He was
robed in a cloud, with a rainbow[t] above
his head; his face was like the sun,[u] and
his legs were like fiery pillars.[v] 2He was
holding a little scroll,[w] which lay open in
his hand. He planted his right foot on the
sea and his left foot on the land,[x] 3and he
gave a loud shout like the roar of a lion.[y]
When he shouted, the voices of the sev-
en thunders[z] spoke. 4And when the seven
thunders spoke, I was about to write;[a] but
I heard a voice from heaven[b] say, "Seal up
what the seven thunders have said and do
not write it down."[c]
5Then the angel I had seen standing on
the sea and on the land[d] raised his right
hand to heaven.[e] 6And he swore[f] by him
who lives for ever and ever,[g] who created
the heavens and all that is in them, the
earth and all that is in it, and the sea and
all that is in it,[h] and said, "There will be
no more delay![i] 7But in the days when
the seventh angel is about to sound his
trumpet,[j] the mystery[k] of God will be accomplished, just as he announced to his
servants the prophets."[l]
8Then the voice that I had heard from
heaven[m] spoke to me once more: "Go,
take the scroll[n] that lies open in the hand
of the angel who is standing on the sea
and on the land."
9So I went to the angel and asked him
to give me the little scroll. He said to me,
"Take it and eat it. It will turn your stomach sour, but in your mouth it will be as
sweet as honey."[o] 10I took the little scroll
from the angel's hand and ate it. It tasted as sweet as honey in my mouth,[p] but
when I had eaten it, my stomach turned
sour. 11Then I was told, "You must prophesy[q] again about many peoples, nations,
languages and kings."[r]

The Two Witnesses

11 I was given a reed like a measuring
rod[s] and was told, "Go and measure the temple of God and the altar, and
count the worshipers there. 2But exclude
the outer court;[t] do not measure it, because it has been given to the Gentiles.[u]
They will trample on the holy city[v] for 42
months.[w] 3And I will give power to my
two witnesses,[x] and they will prophesy

10:1 [r]Rev 5:2 [s]Rev 18:1; 20:1 [t]Eze 1:28; Rev 4:3 [u]Mt 17:2; Rev 1:16 [v]Rev 1:15 **10:2** [w]ver 8-10; Rev 5:1 [x]ver 5,8 **10:3** [y]Hos 11:10 [z]Rev 4:5 **10:4** [a]Rev 1:11,19 [b]ver 8 [c]Da 8:26; 12:4,9; Rev 22:10 **10:5** [d]ver 1,2 [e]Dt 32:40; Da 12:7 **10:6** [f]Ge 14:22; Ex 6:8; Nu 14:30 [g]S Rev 1:18 [h]Ps 115:15; 146:6; Rev 4:11; 14:7 [i]Rev 16:17 **10:7** [j]S Mt 24:31 [k]S Ro 16:25 [l]Am 3:7 **10:8** [m]ver 4 [n]ver 2 **10:9** [o]Jer 15:16; Eze 2:8-3:3 **10:10** [p]S ver 9 **10:11** [q]Eze 37:4,9 [r]Da 3:4; S Rev 13:7 **11:1** [s]Eze 40:3; Rev 21:15 **11:2** [t]Eze 40:17,20 [u]Lk 21:24 [v]S Rev 21:2 [w]ver 3; Da 7:25; 12:7; Rev 12:6,14; 13:5 **11:3** [x]Rev 1:5; 2:13 [y]S ver 2

books of magic, valued at 50,000 drachmas (Ac 19:19). (A drachma was a silver coin worth about a day's wages.)

10:1—11:13 The second interlude (see note on 7:1–17).

10:1 *mighty angel.* Perhaps the angel of 5:2. *robed in a cloud.* See Mt 17:5; 24:30 and notes. *rainbow.* Cf. Eze 1:26–28. The rainbow became a sign of God's pledge never to destroy the earth again by a flood (see Ge 9:8–17 and note on 9:13). *legs were like fiery pillars.* Since the exodus supplies background for this central part of Revelation (see note on 8:12), this feature may recall the pillars of fire and cloud that guided (Ex 13:21–22) and protected (Ex 14:19,24) the Israelites during their desert journey.

10:2 *little scroll.* Not the same as the scroll of destiny in ch. 5, since that scroll was intended to reveal its contents and this scroll was to be eaten. Furthermore, the term "little scroll" sets this particular scroll off from all others. *right foot on the sea ... left foot on the land.* Indicates his tremendous size and symbolizes that his coming has to do with the destiny of all creation (cf. v. 6).

10:3 *seven thunders.* In 8:5; 11:19; 16:18 thunder is connected with divine punishment. Here, too, it anticipates the judgment to fall on those who refuse God's love and grace.

10:4 *Seal up.* In Da 8:26; 12:4,9 the prophecies are sealed until the last times, when they will be opened. What the seven thunders said will not be revealed until their proper time. Cf. the angel's instructions in 22:10 not to seal the prophecies of Revelation.

10:5 *raised his right hand.* A part of oath taking (see Ge 14:22 and note; Dt 32:40).

10:6 *him who lives for ever and ever.* Of special encouragement in a context of impending martyrdom (cf. 1:18; 4:9–10; 15:7). *no more delay.* The martyrs in 6:9–11 were told to rest for a while, but now the end has come (cf. Da 12:1; Mk 13:19).

10:7 *mystery of God.* In apocalyptic thought mysteries were secrets preserved in heaven and revealed to the apocalyptist. Here the mystery is that God has won the victory over the forces of evil and will reign for ever and ever (cf. 11:15).

10:9 *Take it and eat it.* Grasp and digest fully the contents of the scroll (cf. Ps 119:103). *turn your stomach sour.* The message of the little scroll (11:1–13) will involve suffering—the bad news. *in your mouth ... sweet as honey.* God's eternal purposes will experience no further delay—the good news. Cf. Eze 3:1–3 and notes on 3:1,3.

10:11 *prophesy again.* The prophecies following the sounding of the seventh trumpet in 11:15. *peoples ... kings.* See note on 7:9.

11:1 *reed.* A bamboo-like cane that often reached a height of 20 feet and grew in abundance in the waters along the banks of the Jordan. Straight and light, the reed was a convenient measuring rod (see Eze 40:3; Zec 2:1–2). *temple.* See note on 7:15, though here the sanctuary on earth is what is measured. Some hold that the symbolic reference is to the believing church, others that it refers to believing Israel. Some representatives of the latter view believe that "temple" should be understood more literally as a future rebuilt temple. *altar.* The context of worship suggests that this is the great altar.

11:2 *outer court.* The court of the Gentiles, approximately 26 acres. *trample on the holy city.* Cf. Ps 79:1; Isa 63:18; Lk 21:24. *42 months.* Three and a half years. Some find the background for this period in the time of Jewish suffering under the Syrian tyrant, Antiochus IV Epiphanes (168–165 B.C.). Others point out that, whereas the temple was desolated for three years under Antiochus, the figure used in Revelation is three and a half years, which no doubt looks back to the dividing of the 70th "seven" (Da 9:27) into two equal parts. The same time period is also designated as "1,260 days" (v. 3; 12:6) and as "a time, times and half a time" (12:14; cf. Da 7:25; 12:7). This period of time evidently became a conventional symbol for a limited period of unrestrained wickedness.

11:3 *two witnesses.* Modeled after Moses and Elijah (see notes on vv. 5–6). They may symbolize testifying believers in the final period before Christ returns. Or they may be two actual individuals who will be martyred for the proclamation of the

for 1,260 days,[y] clothed in sackcloth."[z]
4These are the two olive trees[a] and the two
lampstands that stand before the Lord of
the earth.[b] 5If anyone tries to harm them,
fire comes from their mouths and devours
their enemies.[c] This is how anyone who
wants to harm them must die.[d] 6These
men have power to shut up the sky[e] so
that it will not rain during the time they
are prophesying;[f] and they have power to
turn the waters into blood[g] and to strike
the earth with every kind of plague as often as they want.

7Now when they have finished their testimony, the beast[h] that comes up from the
Abyss[i] will attack them,[j] and overpower
and kill them. 8Their bodies will lie in the
street of the great city,[k] which is figuratively called Sodom[l] and Egypt, where also
their Lord was crucified.[m] 9For three and
a half days men from every people, tribe,
language and nation[n] will gaze on their
bodies and refuse them burial.[o] 10The inhabitants of the earth[p] will gloat over them
and will celebrate by sending each other
gifts,[q] because these two prophets had tormented those who live on the earth.

11But after the three and a half days[r] a
breath of life from God entered them,[s] and
they stood on their feet, and terror struck
those who saw them. 12Then they heard
a loud voice from heaven saying to them,
"Come up here."[t] And they went up to
heaven in a cloud,[u] while their enemies
looked on.

13At that very hour there was a severe
earthquake[v] and a tenth of the city collapsed. Seven thousand people were killed
in the earthquake, and the survivors were
terrified and gave glory[w] to the God of
heaven.[x]

14The second woe has passed; the third
woe is coming soon.[y]

The Seventh Trumpet

15The seventh angel sounded his trumpet,[z] and there were loud voices[a] in heav-
en, which said:

"The kingdom of the world has
become the kingdom of our
Lord and of his Christ,[b]
and he will reign for ever and
ever."[c]

16And the twenty-four elders,[d] who were
seated on their thrones before God, fell on
their faces[e] and worshiped God, 17saying:

"We give thanks[f] to you, Lord God
Almighty,[g]
the One who is and who was,[h]
because you have taken your great
power
and have begun to reign.[i]
18The nations were angry;[j]
and your wrath has come.
The time has come for judging the
dead,[k]
and for rewarding your servants the
prophets[l]
and your saints and those who
reverence your name,
both small and great[m]—
and for destroying those who destroy
the earth."

11:3 [z]Ge 37:34; 2Sa 3:31; Ne 9:1; Jnh 3:5 **11:4** [a]Ps 52:8; Jer 11:16; Zec 4:3,11 [b]Zec 4:14 **11:5** [c]2Sa 22:9; 2Ki 1:10; Jer 5:14; Rev 9:17,18 [d]Nu 16:29,35 **11:6** [e]S Lk 4:25 [f]ver 3 [g]Ex 7:17,19; Rev 8:8 **11:7** [h]Rev 13:1-4 [i]S Lk 8:31 [j]Da 7:21; Rev 13:7 **11:8** [k]Rev 16:19 [l]Isa 1:9; Jer 23:14; Eze 16:46 [m]Heb 13:12 **11:9** [n]S Rev 13:7 [o]Ps 79:2,3 **11:10** [p]S Rev 3:10 [q]Ne 8:10,12; Est 9:19,22 **11:11** [r]ver 9 [s]Eze 37:5,9,10,14 **11:12** [t]Rev 4:1 [u]2Ki 2:11; Ac 1:9 **11:13** [v]S Rev 6:12 [w]Rev 14:7; 16:9; 19:7 [x]Rev 16:11 **11:14** [y]S Rev 8:13 **11:15** [z]S Mt 24:31 [a]Rev 16:17; 19:1 [b]Rev 12:10 [c]Ps 145:13; Da 2:44; 7:14,27; Mic 4:7; Zec 14:9; Lk 1:33 **11:16** [d]S Rev 4:4 [e]S Rev 4:10 **11:17** [f]Ps 30:12 [g]S Rev 1:8 [h]S Rev 1:4 [i]Rev 19:6 **11:18** [j]Ps 2:1 [k]Rev 20:12 [l]Rev 10:7 [m]S Rev 19:5

truth. *1,260 days.* See note on v. 2. These are months of 30 days (42 months x 30 days = 1,260 days). *sackcloth.* See 6:12; a coarse, dark cloth woven from the hair of goats or camels. It was worn as a sign of mourning or penitence (Joel 1:13; Jnh 3:5–6; Mt 11:21; see note on Ge 37:34).

11:4 The imagery emphasizes that the power for effective testimony is supplied by the Spirit of God (see notes on Zec 4).

11:5 *fire comes ... and devours.* Cf. Elijah's encounters with the messengers of Ahaziah (2Ki 1:10,12).

11:6 *power to shut up the sky.* Cf. the drought in the days of Elijah (1Ki 17:1; see also Lk 4:25; Jas 5:17). *waters into blood.* God used Moses to bring the same plague on the Egyptians (Ex 7:17–21).

11:7 *the beast.* First mention of the major opponent of God's people in the final days (see chs. 13; 17). That he comes up from the Abyss (see note on 9:1) indicates his demonic character. *kill them.* They will suffer the same fate as their Lord (see v. 8).

11:8 *Their bodies will lie in the street.* In the Near East the denial of burial was a flagrant violation of decency. *great city.* Possibly Jerusalem, though some say Rome, Babylon or some other city. It may be symbolic of the world opposed to God (see 16:19; 17:18; 18:10,16,18–19,21). "Sodom" (see similarly Isa 1:10) refers to its low level of morality (cf. Ge 19:4–11), and "Egypt" emphasizes oppression and slavery. Some say that Jesus could have been crucified in Rome in the sense that her power extended throughout the known world and was immediately responsible for Christ's execution.

11:9 *three and a half days.* A short time when compared with the three and a half years of their ministry. *refuse them burial.* See note on v. 8.

11:11 *a breath of life from God entered them.* A dramatic validation of the true faith (cf. Eze 37:5,10).

11:12 *went up to heaven in a cloud.* Cf. 1Th 4:17. *enemies looked on.* Cf. 1:7.

11:13 *earthquake.* See notes on 6:12; Eze 38:19. *gave glory to the God of heaven.* Not an act of repentance but the terrified realization that Christ, not the antichrist, is the true Lord of all.

11:14 *second woe.* Cf. 9:12.

11:15 *seventh angel sounded.* The series of trumpet blasts is now continued (see 9:13) and completed. *kingdom of our Lord.* Cf. Ex 15:18; Ps 10:16; Zec 14:9. *of our Lord and of his Christ.* Cf. Ps 2:2.

11:16 *twenty-four elders.* See note on 4:4.

11:17 *One who is and who was.* In 1:4,8; 4:8 he is also the one "who is to come." This is now omitted because his reign is here pictured as having begun.

11:18 *nations were angry.* See Ps 48:4. *your wrath.* See note on 6:16. God's wrath triumphs in 14:10–11; 16:15–21; 20:8–9. *judging the dead.* Anticipated in 6:10, carried out in 20:11–15. *your servants the prophets.* See Da 9:6,10; Am 3:7; Zec 1:6.

19Then God's temple[n] in heaven was
opened, and within his temple was seen
the ark of his covenant.[o] And there came
flashes of lightning, rumblings, peals of
thunder,[p] an earthquake and a great hailstorm.[q]

The Woman and the Dragon

12 A great and wondrous sign[r] appeared
in heaven:[s] a woman clothed with
the sun, with the moon under her feet and
a crown of twelve stars[t] on her head. 2She
was pregnant and cried out in pain[u] as
she was about to give birth. 3Then another sign appeared in heaven:[v] an enormous
red dragon[w] with seven heads[x] and ten
horns[y] and seven crowns[z] on his heads.
4His tail swept a third[a] of the stars out of
the sky and flung them to the earth.[b] The
dragon stood in front of the woman who
was about to give birth, so that he might
devour her child[c] the moment it was born.
5She gave birth to a son, a male child, who
will rule all the nations with an iron scepter.[d] And her child was snatched up[e] to
God and to his throne. 6The woman fled
into the desert to a place prepared for her
by God, where she might be taken care of
for 1,260 days.[f]

7And there was war in heaven. Michael[g] and his angels fought against the dragon,[h] and the dragon and his angels[i] fought
back. 8But he was not strong enough, and
they lost their place in heaven. 9The great
dragon was hurled down—that ancient
serpent[j] called the devil,[k] or Satan,[l] who
leads the whole world astray.[m] He was
hurled to the earth,[n] and his angels with
him.

10Then I heard a loud voice in heaven[o]
say:

"Now have come the salvation[p] and
the power and the kingdom of
our God,
and the authority of his Christ.
For the accuser of our brothers,[q]
who accuses them before our God
day and night,
has been hurled down.
11They overcame[r] him
by the blood of the Lamb[s]
and by the word of their testimony;[t]
they did not love their lives so much
as to shrink from death.[u]
12Therefore rejoice, you heavens[v]
and you who dwell in them!
But woe[w] to the earth and the sea,[x]
because the devil has gone down to
you!
He is filled with fury,
because he knows that his time is
short."

13When the dragon[y] saw that he had
been hurled to the earth, he pursued the
woman who had given birth to the male
child.[z] 14The woman was given the two
wings of a great eagle,[a] so that she might
fly to the place prepared for her in the desert, where she would be taken care of for
a time, times and half a time,[b] out of the
serpent's reach. 15Then from his mouth
the serpent[c] spewed water like a river, to
overtake the woman and sweep her away
with the torrent. 16But the earth helped
the woman by opening its mouth and
swallowing the river that the dragon had

11:19 [n] Rev 15:5, 8 [o] Ex 25:10-22; 2Ch 5:7; Heb 9:4 [p] S Rev 4:5 [q] Rev 16:21 **12:1** [r] ver 3 [s] Rev 11:19 [t] Ge 37:9 **12:2** [u] Isa 26:17; Gal 4:19 **12:3** [v] ver 1; Rev 15:1 [w] ver 9,13,16,17; Rev 13:1 [x] Rev 13:1; 17:3,7,9 [y] Da 7:7,20; Rev 13:1; 17:3,7,12,16 [z] Rev 19:12 **12:4** [a] S Rev 8:7 [b] Da 8:10 [c] Mt 2:16 **12:5** [d] Ps 2:9; Rev 2:27; 19:15 [e] S Ac 8:39 **12:6** [f] S Rev 11:2 **12:7** [g] S Jude 9 [h] ver 3 [i] Mt 25:41 **12:9** [j] ver 15; Ge 3:1-7 [k] Mt 25:41; Rev 20:2 [l] S Mt 4:10 [m] Rev 20:3,8,10 [n] Lk 10:18; Jn 12:31

12:10 [o] Rev 11:15 [p] Rev 7:10 [q] Job 1:9-11; Zec 3:1; 1Pe 5:8 **12:11** [r] S Jn 16:33; Rev 15:2 [s] S Rev 7:14 [t] Rev 6:9 [u] Lk 14:26; Rev 2:10 **12:12** [v] Ps 96:11; Isa 44:23; 49:13; Rev 18:20 [w] S Rev 8:13 [x] Rev 10:6

12:13 [y] ver 3 [z] ver 5 **12:14** [a] Ex 19:4 [b] S Rev 11:2 **12:15** [c] ver 9

11:19 *God's temple in heaven.* The sanctuary in heaven (3:12; 7:15; 15:5–8) as distinguished from the sanctuary on earth (11:1). *ark of his covenant.* The OT ark was a chest of acacia wood (Dt 10:1–2). It symbolized the throne or presence of God among his people. It was probably destroyed when Nebuzaradan destroyed the temple in Jerusalem (2Ki 25:8–10). In the NT it symbolizes God's faithfulness in keeping covenant with his people. *lightning ... hailstorm.* See note on 4:5.
12:1—14:20 Interlude: persecution of God's people by the dragon and the great beasts rising out of the sea and the earth (chs. 12–13), which does not prevent the Lamb's deliverance of the redeemed (14:1–5) but does lead to God's judgment on the persecuting powers (14:6–20).
12:1 *sign.* An extraordinary spectacle or event that points beyond itself (cf. Lk 21:11,25; Ac 2:19). *a woman clothed with the sun.* Probably a symbolic reference to the believing Messianic community (see v. 5). *twelve stars.* Cf. the 12 tribes of Israel.
12:2 *cried out in pain.* Cf. the similar language describing the rebirth of Jerusalem in Isa 66:7 (see Mic 4:10).
12:3 *red dragon.* Identified in v. 9 (cf. 20:2). Dragons abound in the mythology of ancient peoples (Leviathan in Canaanite lore and Set-Typhon, the red crocodile, in Egypt). In the OT they are normally used metaphorically to depict the enemies of God and of Israel (see Ps 74:14; Isa 27:1; Eze 29:3). *seven heads.* See 13:1; 17:9–11 and notes. *ten horns.* Symbolizing great power (see 13:1; 17:12 and note).
12:5 *a son, a male child.* The Messiah. *iron scepter.* See note on 2:27. *snatched up to God.* The ascension of Christ.
12:6 *desert.* Not a wasteland but a place of spiritual refuge (cf. Hos 2:14). *1,260 days.* The time of spiritual protection corresponds to the time of persecution (see note on 11:2; cf. 13:5).
12:7 *Michael.* An archangel who defeats Satan in heavenly warfare. In Da 12:1 he is the protector of Israel who will deliver her from tribulation in the last days.
12:9 *dragon was hurled ... to the earth.* Not the original casting of Satan out of heaven, but his final exclusion—an explanation of his intense hostility against God's people in the last days (vv. 12–17). *ancient serpent.* See Ge 3:1 and note. *devil, or Satan.* See notes on 2:9–10. *leads ... astray.* Cf. 2Co 11:3; see also Lk 22:31; Jn 13:2.
12:10 *accuser.* See Job 1:9–11 and notes on 1:6; Mt 16:23; 1Jn 3:8; see also Zec 3:1. Satan (v. 9) in Hebrew means "accuser" or "adversary."
12:11 *blood of the Lamb.* See note on 5:9; see also 1:5; 7:14.
12:12 *his time is short.* The period of final, intense hostility of Satan toward the people of God.
12:13–16 Cf. the similarity to the exodus.
12:14 *desert.* See note on v. 6. *a time, times and half a time.* One year plus two years plus half a year (see note on 11:2).
12:16 *earth helped ... by opening its mouth.* Cf. Nu 16:30–33, where the earth opened and swallowed Korah's men.

spewed out of his mouth. 17 Then the dragon was enraged at the woman and went
off to make war[d] against the rest of her
offspring[e]—those who obey God's commandments[f] and hold to the testimony of
13 Jesus.[g] 1 And the dragon[a] stood on
the shore of the sea.

The Beast out of the Sea

And I saw a beast coming out of the
sea.[h] He had ten horns and seven heads,[i]
with ten crowns on his horns, and on each
head a blasphemous name.[j] 2 The beast I
saw resembled a leopard,[k] but had feet like
those of a bear[l] and a mouth like that of a
lion.[m] The dragon gave the beast his power
and his throne and great authority.[n] 3 One
of the heads of the beast seemed to have
had a fatal wound, but the fatal wound
had been healed.[o] The whole world was
astonished[p] and followed the beast. 4 Men
worshiped the dragon because he had giv-
en authority to the beast, and they also
worshiped the beast and asked, "Who is
like[q] the beast? Who can make war against
him?"
5 The beast was given a mouth to utter
proud words and blasphemies[r] and to exercise his authority for forty-two months.[s]
6 He opened his mouth to blaspheme God,
and to slander his name and his dwelling
place and those who live in heaven.[t] 7 He
was given power to make war[u] against the
saints and to conquer them. And he was
given authority over every tribe, people,
language and nation.[v] 8 All inhabitants of
the earth[w] will worship the beast—all
whose names have not been written in
the book of life[x] belonging to the Lamb[y]
that was slain from the creation of the
world.[b][z]
9 He who has an ear, let him hear.[a]

10 If anyone is to go into captivity,
into captivity he will go.
If anyone is to be killed[c] with the
sword,
with the sword he will be killed.[b]

This calls for patient endurance and faithfulness[c] on the part of the saints.[d]

The Beast out of the Earth

11 Then I saw another beast, coming out of the earth.[e] He had two horns
like a lamb, but he spoke like a dragon.[f] 12 He exercised all the authority[g] of
the first beast on his behalf,[h] and made
the earth and its inhabitants worship the
first beast,[i] whose fatal wound had been
healed.[j] 13 And he performed great and
miraculous signs,[k] even causing fire to
come down from heaven[l] to earth in full
view of men. 14 Because of the signs[m] he
was given power to do on behalf of the
first beast, he deceived[n] the inhabitants
of the earth.[o] He ordered them to set up
an image in honor of the beast who was
wounded by the sword and yet lived.[p]

[a] 1 Some late manuscripts *And I* [b] 8 Or *written from the creation of the world in the book of life belonging to the Lamb that was slain* [c] 10 Some manuscripts *anyone kills*

12:17 [d] Rev 11:7; 13:7 [e] Ge 3:15 [f] S Jn 14:15 [g] S Rev 1:2
13:1 [h] Da 7:1-6; Rev 15:2; 16:13 [i] S Rev 12:3 [j] Da 11:36; Rev 17:3
13:2 [k] Da 7:6 [l] Da 7:5 [m] Da 7:4 [n] Rev 2:13; 16:10
13:3 [o] ver 12,14 [p] Rev 17:8
13:4 [q] Ex 15:11
13:5 [r] Da 7:8,11, 20,25; 11:36; 2Th 2:4 [s] S Rev 11:2
13:6 [t] Rev 12:12
13:7 [u] Da 7:21; Rev 11:7 [v] Rev 5:9; 7:9; 10:11; 17:15
13:8 [w] ver 12,14; S Rev 3:10 [x] S Rev 20:12 [y] S Jn 1:29 [z] S Mt 25:34
13:9 [a] S Rev 2:7
13:10 [b] Jer 15:2; 43:11 [c] S Heb 6:12 [d] Rev 14:12
13:11 [e] ver 1,2 [f] Rev 16:13
13:12 [g] ver 4 [h] ver 14; Rev 19:20 [i] ver 15; Rev 14:9,11; 16:2; 19:20; 20:4 [j] ver 3
13:13 [k] S Mt 24:24 [l] 1Ki 18:38; 2Ki 1:10; Lk 9:54; Rev 20:9
13:14 [m] 2Th 2:9,10 [n] Rev 12:9 [o] S Rev 3:10 [p] ver 3,12

12:17 *rest of her offspring.* Believers in general as contrasted with Christ, the male child of vv. 5,13. *testimony of Jesus.* The testimony that Jesus bore (cf. 1:2,9; 19:10).

13:1 *beast coming out of the sea.* First mentioned in 11:7. According to some, the beast symbolizes the Roman empire, the deification of secular authority. According to others, he is the final, personal antichrist. According to still others, the beast symbolizes anti-Christian political power that came to expression in the Roman empire of John's day, that continues in various ways down through the present era, and that will become manifest in the political power of the final antichrist (see note on 14:8). The background seems to be Daniel's vision of the four great beasts (Da 7:2–7). See 17:8–11 for the interpreting angel's explanation of the beast. *sea.* See 17:15. *ten horns.* See 17:12 and note. *blasphemous name.* Roman emperors tended to assume titles of deity. Domitian, e.g., was addressed as *Dominus et Deus noster* ("Our Lord and God").

13:2 *leopard ... bear ... lion.* John's beast combined characteristics of Daniel's four beasts (Da 7:4–6). *dragon.* See note on 12:3.

13:3 *fatal wound ... healed.* Emphasizes the tremendous recuperative power of the beast. *whole world was astonished.* See 17:8 for the same reaction.

13:5–6 Cf. Da 11:36–39 and note on 11:36.

13:5 *was given.* Four times in the Greek text of vv. 5–7 the passive "was given" occurs, either emphasizing the subordinate role of the beast (see vv. 2,4) or indicating that even the beast operates under the authority granted to it by God (the verbs in vv. 2,4 are active while the verbs here are passive). *forty-two months.* See note on 11:2.

13:7 *make war.* See 12:17; see also Da 7:7.

13:8 *book of life.* See note on 3:5; cf. 20:12,15. *Lamb that was slain.* See note on 5:6; cf. Isa 53:7; Jn 1:29,36. *slain from the creation of the world.* The death of Christ was a redemptive event decreed from eternity. See, however, NIV text note, which affirms that believers' names were written in the book of life from eternity (cf. 17:8).

13:11 *another beast, coming out of the earth.* According to some, he symbolizes religious power in the service of secular authorities. According to others, he is the personal false prophet (see 16:13; 19:20; 20:10). *two horns like a lamb.* He attempts to appear gentle and harmless. *spoke like a dragon.* See Jesus' warning in Mt 7:15 about ravenous wolves who come in sheep's clothing.

13:12 *exercised all the authority of the first beast.* The trinity of evil is now complete. The beast from the earth is under the authority of the beast from the sea. The latter is subject to the dragon. Satan, secular power and religious compromise (or Satan, the antichrist and the false prophet) join against the cause of God: Father, Son and Holy Spirit.

13:13 *miraculous signs.* See the warning in Dt 13:1–3; see also Mt 24:24; 2Th 2:9; cf. Rev 19:20. *fire ... from heaven.* See 1Ki 18:24–39.

13:14 *set up an image.* Cf. Da 3:1–11; 2Th 2:4.

15He was given power to give breath to
the image of the first beast, so that it
could speak and cause all who refused
to worship[q] the image to be killed.[r] 16He
also forced everyone, small and great,[s]
rich and poor, free and slave, to receive
a mark on his right hand or on his forehead,[t] 17so that no one could buy or sell
unless he had the mark,[u] which is the
name of the beast or the number of his
name.[v]
18This calls for wisdom.[w] If anyone has
insight, let him calculate the number of
the beast, for it is man's number.[x] His
number is 666.

The Lamb and the 144,000

14 Then I looked, and there before me
was the Lamb,[y] standing on Mount
Zion,[z] and with him 144,000[a] who had
his name and his Father's name[b] written on their foreheads.[c] 2And I heard a
sound from heaven like the roar of rushing waters[d] and like a loud peal of thunder.[e] The sound I heard was like that of
harpists playing their harps.[f] 3And they
sang a new song[g] before the throne and
before the four living creatures[h] and the
elders.[i] No one could learn the song except the 144,000[j] who had been redeemed
from the earth. 4These are those who did
not defile themselves with women, for
they kept themselves pure.[k] They follow
the Lamb wherever he goes.[l] They were
purchased from among men[m] and offered
as firstfruits[n] to God and the Lamb. 5No
lie was found in their mouths;[o] they are
blameless.[p]

The Three Angels

6Then I saw another angel flying in midair,[q] and he had the eternal gospel to proclaim to those who live on the earth[r]—to
every nation, tribe, language and people.[s]
7He said in a loud voice, "Fear God[t] and
give him glory,[u] because the hour of his
judgment has come. Worship him who
made[v] the heavens, the earth, the sea and
the springs of water."[w]
8A second angel followed and said, "Fall-
en! Fallen is Babylon the Great,[x] which
made all the nations drink the maddening
wine of her adulteries."[y]
9A third angel followed them and said
in a loud voice: "If anyone worships the
beast[z] and his image[a] and receives his
mark on the forehead[b] or on the hand,
10he, too, will drink of the wine of God's
fury,[c] which has been poured full strength
into the cup of his wrath.[d] He will be tormented with burning sulfur[e] in the presence of the holy angels and of the Lamb.

13:15 [q]S ver 12 [r]Da 3:3-6 **13:16** [s]S Rev 19:5 [t]Rev 7:3; 14:9; 20:4 **13:17** [u]Rev 14:9 [v]ver 18; Rev 14:11; 15:2 **13:18** [w]Rev 17:9 [x]Rev 15:2; 21:17 **14:1** [y]S Rev 5:6 [z]Ps 2:6; Heb 12:22 [a]ver 3; Rev 7:4 [b]Rev 3:12; 22:4 [c]S Rev 7:3 **14:2** [d]S Rev 1:15 [e]Rev 6:1 [f]Rev 5:8; 15:2 **14:3** [g]S Rev 5:9 [h]S Rev 4:6 [i]S Rev 4:4 [j]ver 1 **14:4** [k]2Co 11:2; Rev 3:4 [l]Rev 7:17 [m]Rev 5:9 [n]Jer 2:3; Jas 1:18 **14:5** [o]Ps 32:2; Zep 3:13; Jn 1:47; 1Pe 2:22 [p]Eph 5:27 **14:6** [q]Rev 8:13; 19:17 [r]S Rev 3:10 [s]S Rev 13:7 **14:7** [t]Ps 34:9; Rev 15:4 [u]S Rev 11:13 [v]S Rev 10:6 [w]Rev 8:10; 16:4 **14:8** [x]Isa 21:9; Jer 51:8; Rev 16:19; 17:5; 18:2,10 [y]Rev 17:2,4; 18:3,9 **14:9** [z]S Rev 13:12 [a]Rev 13:14 [b]S Rev 13:16 **14:10** [c]Isa 51:17; Jer 25:15 [d]Jer 51:7; Rev 18:6 [e]S Rev 9:17

13:15 *it could speak.* Belief in statues that could speak is widely attested in ancient literature. Ventriloquism and other forms of deception were common.

13:16 *mark.* Whatever its origin—possibly the branding of slaves or enemy soldiers, the sealing and stamping of official documents, or the sign of the cross on the forehead of a new Christian—the mark of the beast apparently symbolized allegiance to the demands of emperor worship. In the final days of the antichrist it will be the ultimate test of loyalty (cf. v. 17; 14:9,11; 15:2; 16:2; 19:20; 20:4). It imitates the sealing of the servants of God in ch. 7.

13:17 *buy or sell.* Economic boycott against all faithful believers. *number of his name.* In ancient times the letters of the alphabet served for numbers. Riddles using numerical equivalents for names were popular.

13:18 *666.* Various schemes for decoding these numbers result in such names as Euanthas, Lateinos, and Nero Caesar. Others take 666 as a symbol for the trinity of evil and imperfection—each digit falls short of the perfect number 7.

14:1 *Lamb.* See note on 5:6. *Mount Zion.* In the OT it was first the fortress of the pre-Israelite city of Jerusalem (2Sa 5:7), captured by David and established as his capital. Later it became a virtual synonym for Jerusalem. In Revelation, as in Heb 12:22–24, it is the heavenly Jerusalem, the eternal dwelling place of God and his people (cf. Gal 4:26). It comes down to the new earth in 21:2–3. *144,000.* See note on 7:4. *name.* Contrast 13:16–18.

14:2 *harps.* See note on 5:8.

14:3 *new song.* See note on 5:9. The theme is deliverance.

14:4 *not defile themselves with women.* Probably a symbolic description of believers who kept themselves from defiling relationships with the pagan world system (cf. note on Ex 34:15). *follow the Lamb.* As his disciples (see Mt 19:21; Mk 8:34). *firstfruits.* See Lev 23:9–14. The word is used figuratively in the NT for the first converts in an area (Ro 16:5) and the first to rise from the dead (1Co 15:20). In Revelation believers are considered as a choice offering to God and the Lamb.

14:5 *No lie.* Contrast Ro 1:25; 2Th 2:9–12 and note on 2:11; cf. Isa 53:9.

14:6 *eternal gospel.* The content of this "good news" is perhaps found in v. 7.

14:7 *him who made the heavens.* See Ex 20:11; Ps 146:6.

14:8 *Babylon the Great.* Ancient Babylon in Mesopotamia was the political, commercial and religious center of a world empire. It was noted for its luxury and moral decadence. The title "Babylon the Great" is taken from Da 4:30. According to some, it is used in Revelation (e.g., here and in 16:19; 17:5; 18:2,10,21) for Rome as the center of opposition to God and his people. According to others, it represents the whole political and religious system of the world in general under the rule of the antichrist (see note on 13:1). According to still others, it is to be understood as literal Babylon—rebuilt and restored. Babylon's fall is proclaimed in Isa 21:9 (see note there); Jer 51:8. *maddening wine of her adulteries.* Here Babylon (Rome?) is pictured as a prostitute whose illicit relations are achieved by intoxication (see note on Ex 34:15).

14:10 *cup of his wrath.* In the OT God's wrath is commonly pictured as a cup of wine to be drunk (Ps 75:8; Isa 51:17; Jer 25:15[see note there]). It is not the outworking of impersonal laws of retribution, but the response of a righteous God to those who refuse his love and grace. *burning sulfur.* Sodom and Gomorrah were destroyed by a rain of burning sulfur (Ge 19:24). Ps 11:6 speaks of a similar fate for the wicked. The figure occurs elsewhere in the OT and the Apocrypha. It is used several times in the final chapters of Revelation (19:20; 20:10; 21:8).

11 And the smoke of their torment rises for ever and ever.[f] There is no rest day or night[g] for those who worship the beast and his image,[h] or for anyone who receives the mark of his name."[i] 12 This calls for patient endurance[j] on the part of the saints[k] who obey God's commandments[l] and remain faithful to Jesus.

13 Then I heard a voice from heaven say, "Write: Blessed are the dead who die in the Lord[m] from now on."

"Yes," says the Spirit,[n] "they will rest from their labor, for their deeds will follow them."

The Harvest of the Earth

14 I looked, and there before me was a white cloud,[o] and seated on the cloud was one "like a son of man"[a][p] with a crown[q] of gold on his head and a sharp sickle in his hand. 15 Then another angel came out of the temple[r] and called in a loud voice to him who was sitting on the cloud, "Take your sickle[s] and reap, because the time to reap has come, for the harvest[t] of the earth is ripe." 16 So he who was seated on the cloud swung his sickle over the earth, and the earth was harvested.

17 Another angel came out of the temple in heaven, and he too had a sharp sickle.[u] 18 Still another angel, who had charge of the fire, came from the altar[v] and called in a loud voice to him who had the sharp sickle, "Take your sharp sickle[w] and gather the clusters of grapes from the earth's vine, because its grapes are ripe." 19 The angel swung his sickle on the earth, gathered its grapes and threw them into the great winepress of God's wrath.[x] 20 They were trampled in the winepress[y] outside the city,[z] and blood[a] flowed out of the press, rising as high as the horses' bridles for a distance of 1,600 stadia.[b]

Seven Angels With Seven Plagues

15 I saw in heaven another great and marvelous sign:[b] seven angels[c] with the seven last plagues[d]—last, because with them God's wrath is completed. 2 And I saw what looked like a sea of glass[e] mixed with fire and, standing beside the sea, those who had been victorious[f] over the beast[g] and his image[h] and over the number of his name.[i] They held harps[j] given them by God 3 and sang the song of Moses[k] the servant of God[l] and the song of the Lamb:[m]

"Great and marvelous are your deeds,[n]
Lord God Almighty.[o]
Just and true are your ways,[p]
King of the ages.
4 Who will not fear you, O Lord,[q]
and bring glory to your name?[r]
For you alone are holy.
All nations will come
and worship before you,[s]
for your righteous acts[t] have been revealed."

5 After this I looked and in heaven the temple,[u] that is, the tabernacle of the Testimony,[v]

a 14 Daniel 7:13 *b* 20 That is, about 180 miles (about 300 kilometers)

14:11 [f]Isa 34:10; Rev 19:3 [g]Rev 4:8 [h]ver 9; S Rev 13:12 [i]Rev 13:17 **14:12** [j]S Heb 6:12 [k]Rev 13:10 [l]S Jn 14:15 **14:13** [m]1Co 15:18; 1Th 4:16 [n]Rev 2:7; 22:17 **14:14** [o]Mt 17:5 [p]Da 7:13; S Rev 1:13 [q]S Rev 6:2 **14:15** [r]ver 17; Rev 11:19 [s]ver 18; Joel 3:13; Mk 4:29 [t]Jer 51:33 **14:17** [u]S ver 15 **14:18** [v]Rev 6:9; 8:5; 16:7 [w]S ver 15 **14:19** [x]Rev 19:15 **14:20** [y]ver 19; Isa 63:3; Joel 3:13; Rev 19:15 [z]Heb 13:12; Rev 11:8 [a]Ge 49:11; Dt 32:14 **15:1** [b]Rev 12:1,3 [c]ver 6-8; Rev 16:1; 17:1; 21:9 [d]Lev 26:21; Rev 9:20 **15:2** [e]Rev 4:6 [f]Rev 12:11 [g]Rev 13:1 [h]Rev 13:14 [i]Rev 13:17 [j]Rev 5:8; 14:2 **15:3** [k]Ex 15:1 [l]Jos 1:1 [m]S Rev 5:9 [n]Ps 111:2 [o]S Rev 1:8 [p]Ps 145:17 **15:4** [q]Jer 10:7 [r]Ps 86:9 [s]Isa 66:23 [t]Rev 19:8 **15:5** [u]Rev 11:19 [v]Ex 38:21; Nu 1:50

14:11 *torment ... for ever and ever.* Revelation offers no support for the doctrine of the annihilation of the wicked (also compare 19:20 with 20:10).

14:13 *Blessed.* The second beatitude (see note on 1:3).

14:14 *seated on the cloud.* Cf. Ps 68:4; Mt 17:5; 24:30 and notes. *son of man.* See 1:13 and notes on Da 7:13; Mk 8:31. *crown of gold.* A victory wreath of gold. See note on 2:10 for the comparison between the victory crown and the royal crown. *sickle.* The Israelite sickle used for cutting grain was normally a flint or iron blade attached to a curved shaft of wood or bone.

14:15 *harvest of the earth.* Symbolizes in a general way the coming judgment (see v. 19; Mt 13:30,40–42). Some interpreters think it refers to the ingathering of the righteous at the return of Christ.

14:18 *another angel, who had charge of the fire.* The angel of 8:3–5. Fire is commonly associated with judgment (see La 1:13 and note; Mt 18:8; Lk 9:54; 2Th 1:7). *sharp sickle.* The context suggests (in contrast to the sickle of v. 14) the smaller grape-knife with which the farmer cut the clusters of grapes from the vine.

14:19 *winepress.* A rock-hewn trough about eight feet square with a channel leading to a lower and smaller trough. Grapes were thrown into the upper vat and tramped with bare feet. The juice was collected in the lower vat (see note on Hag 2:16). At times mechanical pressure was added. The treading of grapes was a common OT figure for the execution of divine wrath (see Isa 63:3; La 1:15; Joel 3:13).

14:20 *outside the city.* Bloodshed would defile the city (see Joel 3:12–14; Zec 14:1–4; cf. Heb 13:12). *1,600 stadia.* See NIV text note; the approximate length of the Holy Land from north to south.

15:1–8 Introduces the last of the three sevenfold series of judgments—the bowls of wrath (see note on 8:2).

15:1 *God's wrath.* See note on 6:16.

15:2 *sea of glass.* See note on 4:6. *victorious over the beast.* Cf. the saints' victory over the devil in 12:11. *number of his name.* See notes on 13:16–18. *harps.* See note on 5:8.

15:3–4 *King of the ages* [TNIV *nations*] ... *fear you.* See Jer 10:7 and note.

15:3 *song of Moses.* See Ex 15; Dt 32. Ex 15:1–18 was sung on Sabbath evenings in the synagogue to celebrate Israel's great deliverance from Egypt. *song of the Lamb.* The risen Lord triumphed over his enemies (including death and Hades, 1:18) in securing spiritual deliverance for his followers (cf. Ps 22). *Great and marvelous are your deeds.* See Ex 15:11; Ps 92:5; 111:2. *Almighty.* See note on 1:8. *King of the ages.* See Jer 10:7,10; cf. 1Ti 1:17.

15:4 Universal recognition of God is taught in both the OT (Ps 86:9; Isa 45:22–23; Mal 1:11) and the NT (Php 2:9–11).

15:5 *tabernacle of the Testimony.* The dwelling place of God during the desert wandering of the Israelites (see Ex 40:34–35). It was so named because the ancient tent

was opened.[w] 6Out of the temple[x] came
the seven angels with the seven plagues.[y]
They were dressed in clean, shining lin-
en[z] and wore golden sashes around their
chests.[a] 7Then one of the four living
creatures[b] gave to the seven angels[c] sev-
en golden bowls filled with the wrath of
God, who lives for ever and ever.[d] 8And
the temple was filled with smoke[e] from
the glory of God and from his power, and
no one could enter the temple[f] until the
seven plagues of the seven angels were
completed.

The Seven Bowls of God's Wrath

16 Then I heard a loud voice from the
temple[g] saying to the seven angels,[h]
"Go, pour out the seven bowls of God's
wrath on the earth."[i]
2The first angel went and poured out his
bowl on the land,[j] and ugly and painful
sores[k] broke out on the people who had
the mark of the beast and worshiped his
image.[l]
3The second angel poured out his bowl
on the sea, and it turned into blood like
that of a dead man, and every living thing
in the sea died.[m]
4The third angel poured out his bowl on
the rivers and springs of water,[n] and they
became blood.[o] 5Then I heard the angel in
charge of the waters say:

"You are just in these judgments,[p]
you who are and who were,[q] the
Holy One,[r]
because you have so judged;[s]
6for they have shed the blood of your
saints and prophets,[t]
and you have given them blood to
drink[u] as they deserve."

7And I heard the altar[v] respond:

"Yes, Lord God Almighty,[w]
true and just are your judgments."[x]

8The fourth angel[y] poured out his bowl
on the sun,[z] and the sun was given power to scorch people with fire.[a] 9They were
seared by the intense heat and they cursed
the name of God,[b] who had control over
these plagues, but they refused to repent[c]
and glorify him.[d]
10The fifth angel poured out his bowl on
the throne of the beast,[e] and his kingdom
was plunged into darkness.[f] Men gnawed
their tongues in agony 11and cursed[g] the
God of heaven[h] because of their pains and
their sores,[i] but they refused to repent of
what they had done.[j]
12The sixth angel poured out his bowl
on the great river Euphrates,[k] and its water
was dried up to prepare the way[l] for the
kings from the East.[m] 13Then I saw three
evil[a] spirits[n] that looked like frogs;[o] they
came out of the mouth of the dragon,[p] out
of the mouth of the beast[q] and out of the
mouth of the false prophet.[r] 14They are
spirits of demons[s] performing miraculous
signs,[t] and they go out to the kings of the
whole world,[u] to gather them for the battle[v] on the great day[w] of God Almighty.
15"Behold, I come like a thief![x] Blessed
is he who stays awake[y] and keeps his
clothes with him, so that he may not go
naked and be shamefully exposed."[z]
16Then they gathered the kings together[a] to the place that in Hebrew[b] is called
Armageddon.[c]

[a] 13 Greek *unclean*

15:5 [w] S Mt 3:16 **15:6** [x] Rev 14:15 [y] S ver 1 [z] Eze 9:2; Da 10:5 [a] Rev 1:13 **15:7** [b] S Rev 4:6 [c] S ver 1 [d] S Rev 1:18 **15:8** [e] Isa 6:4 [f] Ex 40:34,35; 1Ki 8:10,11; 2Ch 5:13,14 **16:1** [g] Rev 11:19 [h] S Rev 15:1 [i] ver 2-21; Ps 79:6; Zep 3:8 **16:2** [j] Rev 8:7 [k] ver 11; Ex 9:9-11; Dt 28:35 [l] Rev 13:15-17; 14:9 **16:3** [m] Ex 7:17-21; Rev 8:8,9; Rev 11:6 **16:4** [n] Rev 8:10 [o] Ex 7:17-21 **16:5** [p] Rev 15:3 [q] S Rev 1:4 [r] Rev 15:4 [s] Rev 6:10 **16:6** [t] Lk 11:49-51 [u] Isa 49:26; Rev 17:6; 18:24 **16:7** [v] Rev 6:9; 14:18 [w] S Rev 1:8 [x] Rev 15:3; 19:2 **16:8** [y] Rev 8:12 [z] Rev 6:12 [a] Rev 14:18 **16:9** [b] ver 11,21 [c] S Rev 2:21 [d] S Rev 11:13 **16:10** [e] Rev 13:2 [f] Ex 10:21-23; Isa 8:22; Rev 8:12; 9:2 **16:11** [g] ver 9,21 [h] Rev 11:13 [i] ver 2 [j] S Rev 2:21 **16:12** [k] S Rev 9:14 [l] Isa 11:15,16 [m] Isa 41:2; 46:11 **16:13** [n] Rev 18:2 [o] Ex 8:6 [p] S Rev 12:3 [q] S Rev 13:1 [r] Rev 19:20; 20:10 **16:14** [s] 1Ti 4:1 [t] S Mt 24:24 [u] S Mt 24:14 [v] Rev 17:14; 19:19; 20:8 [w] S Rev 6:17 **16:15** [x] S Lk 12:39 [y] Lk 12:37 [z] Rev 3:18 **16:16** [a] ver 14 [b] Rev 9:11 [c] Jdg 5:19; 2Ki 23:29,30; Zec 12:11

contained the two tablets of the covenant law brought down from Mount Sinai (Ex 32:15; 38:21; Dt 10:5).

15:6 *seven plagues.* The last series of plagues (see v. 1). *golden sashes.* Symbolic of royal and priestly functions.

15:7 *wrath of God.* Cf. 2Th 1:7–9.

15:8 *filled with smoke.* Cf. Ex 40:34; 1Ki 8:10–11; Eze 44:4. Smoke symbolizes the power and glory of God. *no one could enter the temple.* Both tabernacle and temple provide illustrations: with reference to Moses, Ex 40:35; with reference to the priests, 2Ch 5:14.

16:2 *land.* Compare the first four bowls (vv. 2–9) with the first four trumpets (8:7–12). *ugly and painful sores.* Cf. the boils and abscesses of the sixth Egyptian plague (Ex 9:9–11; see also Job 2:7–8,13). *mark of the beast.* See 13:16 and note.

16:4 *rivers and springs of water.* Cf. 8:10–11; see also Ps 78:44.

16:5 *you who are and who were.* See note on 11:17; cf. Ex 3:14.

16:6 *given them blood to drink.* Punishment is tailored to fit the crime (see Isa 49:26; cf. Gal 6:7 and note).

16:7 *altar.* Personified.

16:8 *fire.* Often connected with judgment in Scripture (see note on 14:18; see also Dt 28:22; 1Co 3:13; 2Pe 3:7).

16:9 *refused to repent.* In 11:13 the nations were dazzled into homage by the great earthquake. Here they curse the name of God (see 13:6).

16:10 *throne of the beast.* Cf. Satan's throne in 2:13. "Throne" occurs 42 times in Revelation. The other 40 references are to the throne of God. *darkness.* Cf. Ex 10:21–23. *gnawed their tongues.* Cf. the scene in 6:15–17.

16:11 *God of heaven.* Used in Da 2:44 of the sovereign God, who destroys the kingdoms of the world and establishes his own universal and eternal reign.

16:12 *Euphrates.* See note on Ge 15:18. *kings from the East.* Evidently Parthian rulers (17:15—18:24), to be distinguished from the "kings of the whole world" (v. 14), who wage the final war against Christ and the armies of heaven (19:11–21).

16:13 *frogs.* Lev 11:10 classifies the frog as an unclean animal. The imagery suggests the deceptive propaganda that will, in the last days, lead people to accept and support the cause of evil.

16:14 *miraculous signs.* Cf. 13:13. *kings of the whole world.* See 6:15. *great day of God.* See 19:11–21 for this battle.

16:15 *Blessed.* The third beatitude (see note on 1:3).

16:16 *Armageddon.* Perhaps stands for Har Mageddon, "the mountain of Megiddo" (see note on Jdg 5:19). Many see no specific geographical reference in the designation and take it to be a symbol of the final overthrow of evil by God. Others understand it more literally.

17The seventh angel poured out his bowl
into the air,[d] and out of the temple[e] came a
loud voice[f] from the throne, saying, "It is
done!"[g] 18Then there came flashes of lightning, rumblings, peals of thunder[h] and a
severe earthquake.[i] No earthquake like
it has ever occurred since man has been
on earth,[j] so tremendous was the quake.
19The great city[k] split into three parts, and
the cities of the nations collapsed. God remembered[l] Babylon the Great[m] and gave
her the cup filled with the wine of the fury
of his wrath.[n] 20Every island fled away and
the mountains could not be found.[o] 21From
the sky huge hailstones[p] of about a hundred pounds each fell upon men. And they
cursed God[q] on account of the plague of
hail,[r] because the plague was so terrible.

The Woman on the Beast

17 One of the seven angels[s] who had the
seven bowls[t] came and said to me,
"Come, I will show you the punishment[u]
of the great prostitute,[v] who sits on many
waters.[w] 2With her the kings of the earth
committed adultery and the inhabitants of
the earth were intoxicated with the wine
of her adulteries."[x]
3Then the angel carried me away in the
Spirit[y] into a desert.[z] There I saw a woman
sitting on a scarlet[a] beast that was covered with blasphemous names[b] and had
seven heads and ten horns.[c] 4The woman was dressed in purple and scarlet, and
was glittering with gold, precious stones
and pearls.[d] She held a golden cup[e] in her
hand, filled with abominable things and
the filth of her adulteries.[f] 5This title was
written on her forehead:

MYSTERY[g]
BABYLON THE GREAT[h]
THE MOTHER OF PROSTITUTES[i]
AND OF THE ABOMINATIONS OF THE EARTH.

6I saw that the woman was drunk with
the blood of the saints,[j] the blood of those
who bore testimony to Jesus.
When I saw her, I was greatly astonished. 7Then the angel said to me: "Why
are you astonished? I will explain to you the
mystery[k] of the woman and of the beast she
rides, which has the seven heads and ten
horns.[l] 8The beast, which you saw, once
was, now is not, and will come up out of
the Abyss[m] and go to his destruction.[n] The
inhabitants of the earth[o] whose names have
not been written in the book of life[p] from
the creation of the world will be astonished[q]
when they see the beast, because he once
was, now is not, and yet will come.
9"This calls for a mind with wisdom.[r]
The seven heads[s] are seven hills on which
the woman sits. 10They are also seven
kings. Five have fallen, one is, the other
has not yet come; but when he does come,
he must remain for a little while. 11The
beast who once was, and now is not,[t] is
an eighth king. He belongs to the seven
and is going to his destruction.
12"The ten horns[u] you saw are ten kings
who have not yet received a kingdom, but
who for one hour[v] will receive authority
as kings along with the beast. 13They have
one purpose and will give their power and
authority to the beast.[w] 14They will make
war[x] against the Lamb, but the Lamb will

16:17 [d] Eph 2:2 [e] Rev 14:15 [f] Rev 11:15 [g] Rev 21:6 **16:18** [h] S Rev 4:5 [i] S Rev 6:12 [j] Da 12:1; Mt 24:21 **16:19** [k] S Rev 17:18 [l] Rev 18:5 [m] S Rev 14:8 [n] Rev 14:10 **16:20** [o] S Rev 6:14 **16:21** [p] Eze 13:13; 38:22; Rev 8:7; 11:19 [q] ver 9,11 [r] Ex 9:23-25 **17:1** [s] S Rev 15:1 [t] Rev 15:7 [u] Rev 16:19 [v] ver 5,15,16; Isa 23:17; Rev 19:2 [w] Jer 51:13 **17:2** [x] S Rev 14:8 **17:3** [y] S Rev 1:10 [z] Rev 12:6,14 [a] Rev 18:12,16 [b] Rev 13:1 [c] S Rev 12:3 **17:4** [d] Eze 28:13; Rev 18:16 [e] Jer 51:7; Rev 18:6 [f] ver 2; S Rev 14:8 **17:5** [g] ver 7 [h] S Rev 14:8 [i] ver 1,2 **17:6** [j] Rev 16:6; 18:24 **17:7** [k] ver 5 [l] ver 3; S Rev 12:3 **17:8** [m] S Lk 8:31 [n] Rev 13:10 [o] S Rev 3:10 [p] S Rev 20:12 [q] Rev 13:3 **17:9** [r] Rev 13:18 [s] ver 3 **17:11** [t] ver 8 **17:12** [u] S Rev 12:3 [v] Rev 18:10,17,19 **17:13** [w] ver 17 **17:14** [x] S Rev 16:14

16:17 *temple.* See 15:5–6. *It is done!* The last of the seven bowls of divine wrath has now been poured out.
16:19 *great city.* See 17:18 and note.
16:21 *plague of hail.* Cf. Ex 9:18–26.
17:1—22:5 The destruction of Babylon (17:1—19:5) and the coming of the new creation and the new Jerusalem in which Eden is restored (21:1—22:5)—together with visionary depictions of decisive redemptive events that culminate in the latter state (19:6—20:15).
17:1—18:24 See note on 14:8.
17:1 *seven angels.* Cf. 15:1; 16. *great prostitute.* See v. 18 for the angel's own identification of this symbol. In v. 5 the harlot is named "Babylon the Great." *sits on many waters.* See v. 15; Ps 137:1; Jer 51:13.
17:2 *wine of her adulteries.* See note on 14:8; cf. 18:3; Isa 23:17; Jer 51:7.
17:3 *in the Spirit.* In a state of spiritual ecstasy by the power of the Spirit (see notes on 1:10; 4:2; see also 21:10). *scarlet beast.* The beast that rose out of the sea in ch. 13. The color scarlet is similar to that of the red dragon in 12:3 (cf. v. 4). *blasphemous names.* See note on 13:1.
17:5 *MYSTERY.* Possibly not a part of the title. The opening part of the verse would then be translated "This mysterious title was written on her forehead: BABYLON . . ." See note on 14:8.
17:6 *saints . . . those who bore testimony.* See 6:9.
17:7 *mystery.* See note on 10:7.
17:8 *once was, now is not, and will come.* An obvious imitation of the description of the Lamb (1:18; 2:8). Cf. the description of God in 1:4,8; 4:8. Here the phrase seems to mean that the beast appeared once, is not presently evident, but will in the future again make his presence known. Evil is persistent. *Abyss.* See note on 9:1. *go to his destruction.* Although evil is real and persistent, there is no uncertainty about its ultimate fate. *book of life.* See note on 3:5.
17:9 *seven hills.* It is perhaps significant that Rome began as a network of seven hill settlements on the east bank of the Tiber River (see map, p. 1735). Her designation as the city on seven hills is commonplace among Roman writers (e.g., Virgil, Martial, Cicero).
17:10 *seven kings.* That seven heads symbolize both seven hills and seven kings illustrates the fluidity of apocalyptic symbolism, unless the hills are figurative for royal (or political) power. *Five . . . one . . . the other.* Taken (1) as seven actual Roman emperors, (2) as seven secular empires or (3) symbolically as the power of the Roman empire as a whole.
17:11 *now is not.* Cf. 13:3. *eighth king.* The antichrist, who plays the role of a king ("belongs to the seven") but is in reality part of the cosmic struggle between God and Satan.
17:12 *ten kings.* Since they are said to have not yet received royal power, they seem to belong to the future. They are likely symbolic and represent the totality of political powers that will align themselves with the beast. *one hour.* A short time.
17:14 *Lamb will overcome.* See 5:6 and note. *Lord of lords and King of kings.* Emphasizes the supreme sovereignty

overcome[y] them because he is Lord of
lords and King of kings[z]—and with him
will be his called, chosen[a] and faithful followers."
15Then the angel said to me, "The waters[b] you saw, where the prostitute sits,
are peoples, multitudes, nations and languages.[c] 16The beast and the ten horns[d]
you saw will hate the prostitute.[e] They will
bring her to ruin[f] and leave her naked;[g]
they will eat her flesh[h] and burn her with
fire.[i] 17For God has put it into their hearts[j]
to accomplish his purpose by agreeing to
give the beast their power to rule,[k] until
God's words are fulfilled.[l] 18The woman
you saw is the great city[m] that rules over
the kings of the earth."

The Fall of Babylon

18 After this I saw another angel[n] coming down from heaven.[o] He had great
authority, and the earth was illuminated
by his splendor.[p] 2With a mighty voice he
shouted:

"Fallen! Fallen is Babylon the Great![q]
She has become a home for
demons
and a haunt for every evil[a] spirit,[r]
a haunt for every unclean and
detestable bird.[s]
3For all the nations have drunk
the maddening wine of her
adulteries.[t]
The kings of the earth committed
adultery with her,[u]
and the merchants of the earth
grew rich[v] from her excessive
luxuries."[w]

4Then I heard another voice from heav-
en say:

"Come out of her, my people,[x]
so that you will not share in her
sins,
so that you will not receive any of
her plagues;[y]
5for her sins are piled up to heaven,[z]
and God has remembered[a] her
crimes.
6Give back to her as she has given;
pay her back[b] double[c] for what she
has done.
Mix her a double portion from her
own cup.[d]
7Give her as much torture and grief
as the glory and luxury she gave
herself.[e]
In her heart she boasts,
'I sit as queen; I am not a widow,
and I will never mourn.'[f]
8Therefore in one day[g] her plagues will
overtake her:
death, mourning and famine.
She will be consumed by fire,[h]
for mighty is the Lord God who
judges her.

9"When the kings of the earth who committed adultery with her[i] and shared her
luxury[j] see the smoke of her burning,[k]
they will weep and mourn over her.[l] 10Ter-
rified at her torment, they will stand far
off[m] and cry:

"'Woe! Woe, O great city,[n]
O Babylon, city of power!
In one hour[o] your doom has come!'

11"The merchants[p] of the earth will
weep and mourn[q] over her because no
one buys their cargoes any more[r]— 12car-
goes of gold, silver, precious stones and
pearls; fine linen, purple, silk and scarlet
cloth; every sort of citron wood, and articles of every kind made of ivory, costly
wood, bronze, iron and marble;[s] 13cargoes
of cinnamon and spice, of incense, myrrh
and frankincense, of wine and olive oil,
of fine flour and wheat; cattle and sheep;
horses and carriages; and bodies and souls
of men.[t]
14"They will say, 'The fruit you longed
for is gone from you. All your riches and
splendor have vanished, never to be recovered.' 15The merchants who sold these
things and gained their wealth from her[u]

[a] 2 Greek *unclean*

17:14 [y]S Jn 16:33 [z]S 1Ti 6:15 [a]Mt 22:14 **17:15** [b]ver 1; Isa 8:7; Jer 47:2 [c]S Rev 13:7 **17:16** [d]S Rev 12:3 [e]ver 1 [f]Rev 18:17,19 [g]Eze 16:37,39 [h]Rev 19:18 [i]Rev 18:8 **17:17** [j]2Co 8:16 [k]ver 13 [l]Jer 39:16; Rev 10:7 **17:18** [m]Rev 16:19; 18:10,18,19,21 **18:1** [n]Rev 17:1 [o]Rev 10:1; 20:1 [p]Eze 43:2 **18:2** [q]S Rev 14:8 [r]Rev 16:13 [s]Isa 13:21,22; 34:11,13-15; Jer 50:39; 51:37; Zep 2:14,15 **18:3** [t]S Rev 14:8 [u]Rev 17:2 [v]ver 11,15,23; Eze 27:9-25 [w]ver 7,9 **18:4** [x]Isa 48:20; Jer 50:8; 51:6,9,45; 2Co 6:17 [y]Ge 19:15 **18:5** [z]2Ch 28:9; Ezr 9:6; Jer 51:9 [a]Rev 16:19 **18:6** [b]Ps 137:8; Jer 50:15,29 [c]Isa 40:2 [d]Rev 14:10; 16:19; 17:4 **18:7** [e]Eze 28:2-8 [f]Ps 10:6; Isa 47:7,8; Zep 2:15 **18:8** [g]ver 10; Isa 9:14; 47:9; Jer 50:31,32 [h]Rev 17:16 **18:9** [i]ver 3; Rev 14:8; 17:2,4 [j]ver 3,7 [k]ver 18; Rev 14:11; 19:3 [l]Jer 51:8; Eze 26:17,18 **18:10** [m]ver 15,17 [n]ver 16,19 [o]ver 17; Rev 17:12 **18:11** [p]Eze 27:27 [q]ver 15,19; Eze 27:31 [r]S ver 3 **18:12** [s]Eze 27:12-22; Rev 17:4 **18:13** [t]Eze 27:13; 1Ti 1:10 **18:15** [u]S ver 3

of the Lamb (cf. 5:6 and note;19:16; Dt 10:17; Ps 136:2–3; Da 2:47; 1Ti 6:15).
17:18 *great city.* Cf. 16:19; 17:1; see notes on 11:8; 14:8.
18:1 *great authority.* See note on 5:2. *earth was illuminated by his splendor.* Cf. Ex 34:29–35; Ps 104:2; Eze 43:1–5; 1Ti 6:16.
18:2 *Fallen is Babylon.* Cf. Isa 21:9; Jer 51:8; see notes on 11:8; 14:8.
18:3 *wine of her adulteries.* See note on 14:8.
18:4 *Come out of her.* A common prophetic warning (cf. Isa 52:11; Jer 51:45; 2Co 6:14—7:1).
18:6 *double.* In full, sufficiently (see note on Isa 40:2). *her own cup.* See 17:4.
18:7 *I am not a widow.* A claim that the men of Babylon have not died on battlefields.
18:9–20 Three groups lament: (1) kings (v. 9), (2) merchants (v. 11) and (3) seamen (v. 17). The passage is modeled after Ezekiel's lament over Tyre (Eze 27). Fifteen of the 29 commodities in vv. 12–13 are also listed in Eze 27:12–22.
18:9 *kings ... weep and mourn over her.* Probably because of their own great financial loss (see v. 11).
18:10 *one hour.* Repeated in vv. 17,19; cf. note on 17:12.
18:12 *purple.* Cloth dyed with an expensive Phoenician dye that had to be extracted a drop at a time from the murex shellfish. *citron wood.* An expensive dark wood from north Africa—used for inlay work in costly furniture. *marble.* Used to decorate public buildings and the homes of the very rich.
18:13 *spice ... incense, myrrh and frankincense.* See Ge 37:25; Ex 25:6; 30:34; SS 1:13; 3:6 and notes. The Magi brought myrrh and frankincense for the child Jesus (Mt 2:11). *bodies and souls of men.* Slave trade.

will stand far off,[v] terrified at her torment.
They will weep and mourn[w] 16and cry
out:

"'Woe! Woe, O great city,[x]
dressed in fine linen, purple and
scarlet,
and glittering with gold, precious
stones and pearls![y]
17In one hour[z] such great wealth has
been brought to ruin!'[a]

"Every sea captain, and all who travel by ship, the sailors, and all who earn
their living from the sea,[b] will stand far
off.[c] 18When they see the smoke of her
burning,[d] they will exclaim, 'Was there
ever a city like this great city[e]?'[f] 19They
will throw dust on their heads,[g] and with
weeping and mourning[h] cry out:

"'Woe! Woe, O great city,[i]
where all who had ships on the sea
became rich through her wealth!
In one hour she has been brought to
ruin![j]
20Rejoice over her, O heaven![k]
Rejoice, saints and apostles and
prophets!
God has judged her for the way she
treated you.'"[l]

21Then a mighty angel[m] picked up a
boulder the size of a large millstone and
threw it into the sea,[n] and said:

"With such violence
the great city[o] of Babylon will be
thrown down,
never to be found again.
22The music of harpists and musicians,
flute players and trumpeters,
will never be heard in you again.[p]
No workman of any trade
will ever be found in you again.
The sound of a millstone
will never be heard in you again.[q]
23The light of a lamp
will never shine in you again.
The voice of bridegroom and bride
will never be heard in you again.[r]
Your merchants were the world's great
men.[s]
By your magic spell[t] all the nations
were led astray.

18:15 [v]ver 10,17 [w]ver 11,19; Eze 27:31 **18:16** [x]ver 10,19 [y]Rev 17:4 **18:17** [z]ver 10; Rev 17:12 [a]Rev 17:16 [b]Eze 27:28-30 [c]ver 10,15 **18:18** [d]ver 9; Rev 19:3 [e]S Rev 17:18 [f]Eze 27:32; Rev 13:4 **18:19** [g]Jos 7:6; La 2:10; Eze 27:30 [h]ver 11,15; Eze 27:31 [i]ver 10,16; Rev 17:18 [j]Rev 17:16 **18:20** [k]Jer 51:48; S Rev 12:12 [l]Rev 19:2 **18:21** [m]Rev 5:2; 10:1 [n]Jer 51:63 [o]S Rev 17:18 **18:22** [p]Isa 24:8; Eze 26:13 [q]Jer 25:10 **18:23** [r]Jer 7:34; 16:9; 25:10 [s]ver 3; Isa 23:8 [t]Na 3:4

18:24 [u]Rev 16:6; 17:6 [v]Jer 51:49; Mt 23:35 **19:1** [w]ver 6; Rev 11:15 [x]ver 3,4,6 [y]Rev 7:10; 12:10 [z]Rev 4:11; 7:12 **19:2** [a]Rev 16:7 [b]S Rev 17:1 [c]S Rev 6:10 **19:3** [d]ver 1,4,6 [e]Isa 34:10; Rev 14:11 **19:4** [f]S Rev 4:4 [g]S Rev 4:6 [h]S Rev 4:10 [i]ver 1,3,6 **19:5** [j]Ps 134:1 [k]ver 18; Ps 115:13; Rev 11:18; 13:16; 20:12 **19:6** [l]ver 1; Rev 11:15 [m]S Rev 1:15 [n]ver 1,3,4 [o]S Rev 1:8 [p]Rev 11:15 **19:7** [q]S Rev 11:13 [r]ver 9; Mt 22:2; 25:10; Eph 5:32

24In her was found the blood of prophets
and of the saints,[u]
and of all who have been killed on
the earth."[v]

Hallelujah!

19 After this I heard what sounded like
the roar of a great multitude[w] in
heaven shouting:

"Hallelujah![x]
Salvation[y] and glory and power[z] belong
to our God,
2 for true and just are his judgments.[a]
He has condemned the great
prostitute[b]
who corrupted the earth by her
adulteries.
He has avenged on her the blood of his
servants."[c]

3And again they shouted:

"Hallelujah![d]
The smoke from her goes up for ever
and ever."[e]

4The twenty-four elders[f] and the four
living creatures[g] fell down[h] and worshiped
God, who was seated on the throne. And
they cried:

"Amen, Hallelujah!"[i]

5Then a voice came from the throne,
saying:

"Praise our God,
all you his servants,[j]
you who fear him,
both small and great!"[k]

6Then I heard what sounded like a great
multitude,[l] like the roar of rushing waters[m]
and like loud peals of thunder, shouting:

"Hallelujah![n]
For our Lord God Almighty[o]
reigns.[p]
7Let us rejoice and be glad
and give him glory![q]
For the wedding of the Lamb[r] has
come,
and his bride[s] has made herself
ready.

[s]Rev 21:2,9; 22:17

18:17 *sea captain.* The pilot of the ship rather than the owner. Both are mentioned in Ac 27:11.
18:19 *throw dust on their heads.* An act of sorrow and dismay (see Eze 27:30). *In one hour.* See vv. 10,17.
18:20 *God has judged her for the way she treated you.* The scales of justice will be balanced.
18:21 *large millstone.* Similar to the large millstone of Mk 9:42, which was actually a "donkey millstone" (one large enough to require a donkey to turn it).
18:24 *blood of prophets.* See 6:10; 17:6; 19:2; cf. Eze 24:7. *prophets ... saints.* Probably not two distinct groups: The first may be a special class within the second (cf. the order in 16:6).
19:1 *great multitude.* See note on 7:9. *Hallelujah!* Occurs four times in vv. 1–6 but nowhere else in the NT. It is derived from two Hebrew words meaning "Praise the LORD" (see note on Ps 150:6).
19:2 *great prostitute.* See 17:1,5,18; see also 14:8 and note. *avenged on her the blood of his servants.* See the prayer in 6:10; cf. 16:6; 18:20.
19:4 *The twenty-four elders and the four living creatures.* See notes on 4:4,6.
19:7 *wedding of the Lamb.* The imagery of a wedding to express the intimate relationship between God and his people ("his bride") has its roots in the prophetic literature of the OT

8Fine linen,[t] bright and clean,
was given her to wear."
(Fine linen stands for the righteous acts[u]
of the saints.)

9Then the angel said to me,[v] "Write:[w] 'Blessed are those who are invited to the wedding supper of the Lamb!' "[x] And he added, "These are the true words of God."[y]

10At this I fell at his feet to worship him.[z] But he said to me, "Do not do it! I am a fellow servant with you and with your brothers who hold to the testimony of Jesus. Worship God![a] For the testimony of Jesus[b] is the spirit of prophecy."

The Rider on the White Horse

11I saw heaven standing open[c] and there before me was a white horse, whose rider[d] is called Faithful and True.[e] With justice he judges and makes war.[f] 12His eyes are like blazing fire,[g] and on his head are many crowns.[h] He has a name written on him[i] that no one knows but he himself.[j] 13He is dressed in a robe dipped in blood,[k] and his name is the Word of God.[l] 14The armies of heaven were following him, riding on white horses and dressed in fine linen,[m] white[n] and clean. 15Out of his mouth comes a sharp sword[o] with which to strike down[p] the nations. "He will rule them with an iron scepter."[a][q] He treads the winepress[r] of the fury of the wrath of God Almighty. 16On his robe and on his thigh he has this name written:[s]

KING OF KINGS AND LORD OF LORDS.[t]

17And I saw an angel standing in the sun, who cried in a loud voice to all the birds[u] flying in midair,[v] "Come,[w] gather together for the great supper of God,[x] 18so that you may eat the flesh of kings, generals, and mighty men, of horses and their riders, and the flesh of all people,[y] free and slave,[z] small and great."[a]

19Then I saw the beast[b] and the kings of the earth[c] and their armies gathered together to make war against the rider on the horse[d] and his army. 20But the beast was captured, and with him the false prophet[e] who had performed the miraculous signs[f] on his behalf.[g] With these signs he had deluded[h] those who had received the mark of the beast[i] and worshiped his image.[j] The two of them were thrown alive into the fiery lake[k] of burning sulfur.[l] 21The rest of them were killed with the sword[m] that came out of the mouth of the rider on the horse,[n] and all the birds[o] gorged themselves on their flesh.

The Thousand Years

20 And I saw an angel coming down out of heaven,[p] having the key[q] to the Abyss[r] and holding in his hand a great chain. 2He seized the dragon, that ancient serpent, who is the devil, or Satan,[s] and bound him for a thousand years.[t]

[a] *15* Psalm 2:9

19:8 [t] ver 14; Rev 15:6 [u] Isa 61:10; Eze 44:17; Zec 3:4; Rev 15:4 **19:9** [v] ver 10 [w] Rev 1:19 [x] Lk 14:15 [y] Rev 21:5; 22:6 **19:10** [z] Rev 22:8 [a] Ac 10:25, 26; Rev 22:9 [b] S Rev 1:2 **19:11** [c] S Mt 3:16 [d] ver 19, 21; Rev 6:2 [e] Rev 3:14 [f] Ex 15:3; Ps 96:13; Isa 11:4 **19:12** [g] S Rev 1:14 [h] Rev 6:2; 12:3 [i] ver 16 [j] S Rev 2:17 **19:13** [k] Isa 63:2, 3 [l] Jn 1:1 **19:14** [m] ver 8 [n] S Rev 3:4 **19:15** [o] ver 21; S Rev 1:16 [p] Isa 11:4; 2Th 2:8 [q] Ps 2:9; Rev 2:27; 12:5 [r] S Rev 14:20 **19:16** [s] ver 12 [t] S 1Ti 6:15 **19:17** [u] ver 21 [v] Rev 8:13; 14:6 [w] Jer 12:9; Eze 39:17 [x] Isa 34:6; Jer 46:10 **19:18** [y] Eze 39:18-20 [z] Rev 6:15 [a] S ver 5 **19:19** [b] S Rev 13:1 [c] Rev 16:14, 16 [d] ver 11, 21 **19:20** [e] Rev 16:13 [f] S Mt 24:24 [g] Rev 13:12 [h] Rev 13:14 [i] Rev 13:16 [j] Rev 13:15 [k] Da 7:11; Rev 20:10, 14, 15; 21:8 [l] S Rev 9:17 **19:21** [m] ver 15; S Rev 1:16 [n] ver 11, 19 [o] ver 17 **20:1** [p] Rev 10:1; 18:1 [q] Rev 1:18 [r] S Lk 8:31 **20:2** [s] S Mt 4:10 [t] Isa 24:22; S 2Pe 2:4

(e.g., Isa 54:5–7; Hos 2:19). Cf. the NT usage (Mt 22:2–14; Eph 5:32).

19:9 *Blessed.* The fourth beatitude (see note on 1:3). *wedding supper.* See Mt 8:11; Lk 14:15; 22:16 and notes.

19:10 *fell at his feet.* See note on 1:17; cf. Ac 10:25. *spirit of prophecy.* Possibly it means that the message attested by Jesus is either the essence of prophetic proclamation or that which the Spirit takes and puts in the mouth of Christian prophets.

19:11 *white horse.* Probably not the white horse of 6:2. The context here indicates that the rider is Christ returning as Warrior-Messiah-King.

19:12 *name written.* A secret name whose meaning is veiled from all created beings.

19:13 *robe dipped in blood.* Either the blood of the enemy shed in conflict (cf. 14:14–20; Isa 63:1–3), or the blood of Christ shed to atone for sin.

19:14 *armies of heaven.* Angelic beings (cf. Dt 33:2; Ps 68:17); possibly also believers (cf. 17:14).

19:15 *sharp sword.* See note on 1:16. *iron scepter.* See note on 2:27. *treads the winepress of the ... wrath of God.* Cf. Isa 63:3 and note. *winepress.* See note on 14:19.

19:16 *KING OF KINGS.* See note on 17:14.

19:17 *great supper of God.* A grim contrast to the "wedding supper of the Lamb" (v. 9; cf. Eze 39:17–20).

19:19 See 16:16 and note.

19:20 *beast ... false prophet.* See notes on 13:1,11. *fiery lake of burning sulfur.* See 20:10,14–15; 21:8. Punishment by fire is prominent in both Biblical (see, e.g., note on La 1:13) and non-Biblical Jewish writings (e.g., 1 Enoch 54:1). Although the designation *gehenna* is not used here, this is what John refers to (see note on Mt 5:22). Originally the site of a shrine where human sacrifices were offered (2Ki 16:3; 23:10; Jer 7:31), it came to be equated with the "hell" of final judgment in apocalyptic literature.

19:21 *birds gorged themselves.* On the "great supper of God" of vv. 17–18.

20:1—22:21 These last three chapters reflect many of the subjects and themes of the first three chapters of Genesis (see Introduction to Genesis: Literary Features).

20:1 *Abyss.* See note on 9:1.

20:2 *dragon.* See note on 12:3. *ancient serpent.* See 12:15; Ge 3:1–5. *thousand years.* The millennium (from the Latin *mille,* "thousand," and *annus,* "year"). It is taken literally by some as 1,000 actual years, while others interpret it metaphorically as a long but undetermined period of time. There are three basic approaches to the subject of the millennium: (1) Amillennialism: The millennium describes the present reign of Christ in heaven over his realm (Mt 28:18–20), along with the souls of deceased believers and in the hearts and lives of living believers on earth (see also note on 1Co 15:25). The present form of God's kingdom will be followed by Christ's return, the general resurrection, the final judgment and Christ's continuing reign over the perfect kingdom on the new earth in the eternal state. (2) Premillennialism: The present form of God's kingdom is moving toward a grand climax when Christ will return, the first resurrection will occur and his kingdom will find expression in a

3He threw him into the Abyss,[u] and locked
and sealed[v] it over him, to keep him from
deceiving the nations[w] anymore until the
thousand years were ended. After that, he
must be set free for a short time.
4I saw thrones[x] on which were seated those who had been given authority
to judge.[y] And I saw the souls of those
who had been beheaded[z] because of their
testimony for Jesus[a] and because of the
word of God.[b] They had not worshiped
the beast[c] or his image and had not received his mark on their foreheads or their
hands.[d] They came to life and reigned[e]
with Christ a thousand years. 5(The rest
of the dead did not come to life until the
thousand years were ended.) This is the
first resurrection.[f] 6Blessed[g] and holy are
those who have part in the first resurrection. The second death[h] has no power over
them, but they will be priests[i] of God and
of Christ and will reign with him[j] for a
thousand years.

Satan's Doom

7When the thousand years are over,[k] Satan will be released from his prison 8and
will go out to deceive the nations[l] in the
four corners of the earth[m]—Gog and Magog[n]—to gather them for battle.[o] In number they are like the sand on the seashore.[p]
9They marched across the breadth of the
earth and surrounded[q] the camp of God's
people, the city he loves.[r] But fire came
down from heaven[s] and devoured them.
10And the devil, who deceived them,[t] was
thrown into the lake of burning sulfur,[u]
where the beast[v] and the false prophet[w]
had been thrown. They will be tormented
day and night for ever and ever.[x]

The Dead Are Judged

11Then I saw a great white throne[y] and
him who was seated on it. Earth and sky
fled from his presence,[z] and there was no
place for them. 12And I saw the dead, great
and small,[a] standing before the throne,
and books were opened.[b] Another book
was opened, which is the book of life.[c]
The dead were judged[d] according to what
they had done[e] as recorded in the books.
13The sea gave up the dead that were in it,
and death and Hades[f] gave up the dead[g]
that were in them, and each person was
judged according to what he had done.[h]
14Then death[i] and Hades[j] were thrown
into the lake of fire.[k] The lake of fire is the
second death.[l] 15If anyone's name was not
found written in the book of life,[m] he was
thrown into the lake of fire.

The New Jerusalem

21 Then I saw a new heaven and a new
earth,[n] for the first heaven and the
first earth had passed away,[o] and there
was no longer any sea. 2I saw the Holy
City,[p] the new Jerusalem, coming down
out of heaven from God,[q] prepared as a
bride[r] beautifully dressed for her husband.
3And I heard a loud voice from the throne
saying, "Now the dwelling of God is with
men, and he will live with them.[s] They
will be his people, and God himself will
be with them and be their God.[t] 4He will
wipe every tear from their eyes.[u] There
will be no more death[v] or mourning or
crying or pain,[w] for the old order of things
has passed away."[x]
5He who was seated on the throne[y] said,
"I am making everything new!"[z] Then he
said, "Write this down, for these words are
trustworthy and true."[a]

20:3 [u]ver 1 [v]Da 6:17; Mt 27:66 [w]ver 8, 10; Rev 12:9 **20:4** [x]Da 7:9 [y]Mt 19:28; Rev 3:21 [z]Rev 6:9 [a]S Rev 1:2 [b]S Heb 4:12 [c]S Rev 13:12 [d]S Rev 13:16 [e]ver 6; Rev 22:5 **20:5** [f]ver 6; Lk 14:14; Php 3:11; 1Th 4:16 **20:6** [g]Rev 14:13 [h]S Rev 2:11 [i]S 1Pe 2:5 [j]ver 4; Rev 22:5 **20:7** [k]ver 2 **20:8** [l]ver 3, 10; Rev 12:9 [m]Isa 11:12; Eze 7:2; Rev 7:1 [n]Eze 38:2; 39:1 [o]S Rev 16:14 [p]Eze 38:9, 15; Heb 11:12 **20:9** [q]Eze 38:9, 16 [r]Ps 87:2 [s]Eze 38:22; 39:6; S Rev 13:13 **20:10** [t]ver 3, 8; Rev 12:9; 19:20 [u]S Rev 9:17 [v]Rev 16:13 [w]Rev 16:13 [x]Rev 14:10, 11 **20:11** [y]S Rev 4:2 [z]S Rev 6:14 **20:12** [a]S Rev 19:5 [b]Da 7:10 [c]ver 15; Ex 32:32; Dt 29:20; Da 12:1; Mal 3:16; Lk 10:20; Rev 3:5; 21:27 [d]Rev 11:18 [e]Jer 17:10; S Mt 16:27 **20:13** [f]Rev 1:18; 6:8 [g]Isa 26:19 [h]S Mt 16:27 **20:14** [i]1Co 15:26 [j]ver 13 [k]S Rev 19:20 [l]S Rev 2:11

20:15 [m]S ver 12 **21:1** [n]S 2Pe 3:13 [o]S Rev 6:14 **21:2** [p]ver 10; Ne 11:18; Isa 52:1; Rev 11:2; 22:19 [q]ver 10; Heb 11:10; 12:22; Rev 3:12 [r]S Rev 19:7 **21:3** [s]Ex 25:8; 2Ch 6:18; Eze 48:35; Zec 2:10 [t]S 2Co 6:16 **21:4** [u]S Rev 7:17 [v]Isa 25:8; 1Co 15:26; Rev 20:14 [w]Isa 35:10; 65:19 [x]S 2Co 5:17 **21:5** [y]Rev 4:9; 20:11 [z]ver 4 [a]Rev 19:9; 22:6

literal, visible reign of peace and righteousness on the earth in space-time history. After the final resurrection, the last judgment and the renewal of the heavens and the earth, this future, temporal kingdom will merge into the eternal kingdom, and the Lord will reign forever on the new earth. (3) Postmillennialism: The world will eventually be Christianized through the preaching of the gospel, resulting in a long period of peace and prosperity called the millennium. This future period will close with Christ's second coming, the resurrection of the dead, the final judgment and the eternal state.

20:3 *free for a short time.* See vv. 7–10.

20:4 *souls of those who had been beheaded.* See 6:9–11. *his mark.* See note on 13:16. *came to life.* The "first resurrection" (v. 5).

20:5 *rest of the dead.* Either the wicked or everyone except the martyrs (see v. 4).

20:6 *Blessed.* The fifth beatitude (see note on 1:3). *second death.* Defined in v. 14 as the "lake of fire" (cf. 2:11; 21:8).

20:7 *thousand years.* See note on v. 2.

20:8 *Gog and Magog.* Symbolize the nations of the world as they band together for a final assault on God. The OT background is Eze 38–39.

20:10 *tormented day and night.* See note on 14:11; cf. 14:10.

20:12 *book of life.* See note on 3:5. *judged according to what they had done.* Divine judgment that takes account of works is spoken of also in Ps 62:12; Jer 17:10; Ro 2:6; 1Pe 1:17 and elsewhere.

20:13 *death and Hades.* See 6:8 and note.

20:14–15 *lake of fire.* See note on 19:20.

21:2—22:5 The "Holy City" combines elements of Jerusalem, the temple and the Garden of Eden (see Introduction to Genesis: Literary Features).

21:2 *new Jerusalem.* See "the Jerusalem that is above" (Gal 4:26; see note there). *bride.* See note on 19:7.

21:3 *dwelling of God.* See Lev 26:11–12; Eze 37:27; 2Co 6:16; Eph 2:21–22. *with ... with ... with.* The most eloquent culmination of the Immanuel theme (see 2Co 13:14 and note). *his people ... their God.* The deepest expression of the intimate fellowship that God had promised to those in covenant relationship with him (see Zec 8:8 and note).

21:4 *wipe every tear.* See 7:17; Isa 25:8.

6He said to me: "It is done.[b] I am the
Alpha and the Omega,[c] the Beginning and
the End. To him who is thirsty I will give
to drink without cost[d] from the spring of
the water of life.[e] 7He who overcomes[f] will
inherit all this, and I will be his God and
he will be my son.[g] 8But the cowardly, the
unbelieving, the vile, the murderers, the
sexually immoral, those who practice magic arts, the idolaters and all liars[h]—their
place will be in the fiery lake of burning
sulfur.[i] This is the second death."[j]

9One of the seven angels who had the
seven bowls full of the seven last plagues[k]
came and said to me, "Come, I will show
you the bride,[l] the wife of the Lamb."
10And he carried me away[m] in the Spirit[n] to a mountain great and high, and
showed me the Holy City, Jerusalem,
coming down out of heaven from God.[o]
11It shone with the glory of God,[p] and its
brilliance was like that of a very precious
jewel, like a jasper,[q] clear as crystal.[r] 12It
had a great, high wall with twelve gates,[s]
and with twelve angels at the gates. On
the gates were written the names of the
twelve tribes of Israel.[t] 13There were three
gates on the east, three on the north, three
on the south and three on the west. 14The
wall of the city had twelve foundations,[u]
and on them were the names of the twelve
apostles[v] of the Lamb.

15The angel who talked with me had
a measuring rod[w] of gold to measure the
city, its gates[x] and its walls. 16The city was
laid out like a square, as long as it was
wide. He measured the city with the rod
and found it to be 12,000 stadia[a] in length,
and as wide and high as it is long. 17He
measured its wall and it was 144 cubits[b]
thick,[c] by man's[y] measurement, which the
angel was using. 18The wall was made of
jasper,[z] and the city of pure gold, as pure
as glass.[a] 19The foundations of the city
walls were decorated with every kind of
precious stone.[b] The first foundation was
jasper,[c] the second sapphire, the third
chalcedony, the fourth emerald, 20the fifth
sardonyx, the sixth carnelian,[d] the seventh
chrysolite, the eighth beryl, the ninth topaz, the tenth chrysoprase, the eleventh
jacinth, and the twelfth amethyst.[d] 21The
twelve gates[e] were twelve pearls,[f] each
gate made of a single pearl. The great
street of the city was of pure gold, like
transparent glass.[g]

22I did not see a temple[h] in the city,
because the Lord God Almighty[i] and the
Lamb[j] are its temple. 23The city does not
need the sun or the moon to shine on it,
for the glory of God[k] gives it light,[l] and
the Lamb[m] is its lamp. 24The nations will
walk by its light, and the kings of the earth
will bring their splendor into it.[n] 25On no
day will its gates[o] ever be shut,[p] for there
will be no night there.[q] 26The glory and
honor of the nations will be brought into
it.[r] 27Nothing impure will ever enter it, nor
will anyone who does what is shameful
or deceitful,[s] but only those whose names
are written in the Lamb's book of life.[t]

The River of Life

22 Then the angel showed me the river[u]
of the water of life,[v] as clear as crystal,[w] flowing[x] from the throne of God and
of the Lamb 2down the middle of the great
street of the city. On each side of the river
stood the tree of life,[y] bearing twelve crops
of fruit, yielding its fruit every month. And
the leaves of the tree are for the healing
of the nations.[z] 3No longer will there be
any curse.[a] The throne of God and of the
Lamb will be in the city, and his servants
will serve him.[b] 4They will see his face,[c]
and his name will be on their foreheads.[d]

21:6 [b]Rev 16:17 [c]Rev 1:8; 22:13 [d]Isa 55:1 [e]S Jn 4:10 **21:7** [f]S Jn 16:33 [g]ver 3; 2Sa 7:14; 2Co 6:16; S Ro 8:14 **21:8** [h]ver 27; Ps 5:6; 1Co 6:9; Heb 12:14; Rev 22:15 [i]S Rev 9:17 [j]S Rev 2:11 **21:9** [k]S Rev 15:1,6,7 [l]S Rev 19:7 **21:10** [m]Eze 40:2; Rev 17:3 [n]S Rev 1:10 [o]S ver 2 **21:11** [p]ver 23; Isa 60:1,2; Eze 43:2; Rev 15:8; 22:5 [q]ver 18,19; Rev 4:3 [r]Rev 4:6 **21:12** [s]ver 15,21,25; Rev 22:14 [t]Eze 48:30-34 **21:14** [u]S Eph 2:20; Heb 11:10 [v]Ac 1:26; Eph 2:20 **21:15** [w]Eze 40:3; Rev 11:1 [x]S ver 12 **21:17** [y]Rev 13:18 **21:18** [z]S ver 11 [a]ver 21 **21:19** [b]Ex 28:17-20; Isa 54:11,12; Eze 28:13 [c]S ver 11 **21:20** [d]Rev 4:3 **21:21** [e]S ver 12 [f]Isa 54:12 [g]ver 18 **21:22** [h]Jn 4:21,23 [i]S Rev 1:8 [j]S Rev 5:6 **21:23** [k]S ver 11 [l]Isa 24:23; 60:19,20; Rev 22:5 [m]S Rev 5:6 **21:24** [n]ver 26; Isa 60:3,5

[a] *16* That is, about 1,400 miles (about 2,200 kilometers)
[b] *17* That is, about 200 feet (about 65 meters)
[c] *17* Or *high*
[d] *20* The precise identification of some of these precious stones is uncertain.

21:25 [o]S ver 12 [p]Isa 60:11 [q]Zec 14:7; Rev 22:5 **21:26** [r]ver 24 **21:27** [s]Isa 52:1; Joel 3:17; Rev 22:14,15 [t]S Rev 20:12 **22:1** [u]Ps 36:8; 46:4 [v]ver 17; S Jn 4:10 [w]Rev 4:6 [x]Eze 47:1; Zec 14:8 **22:2** [y]S Rev 2:7 [z]Eze 47:12 **22:3** [a]Zec 14:11 [b]Rev 7:15 **22:4** [c]S Mt 5:8 [d]S Rev 7:3

21:6 *the Alpha and the Omega.* See note on 1:8. *water of life.* Cf. Ps 36:9; Jn 4:10,14 and notes.
21:7 *He who overcomes.* Cf. the emphasis on overcoming in the seven letters (2:7,11,17,26; 3:5,12,21).
21:8 *cowardly ... liars.* See note on Ro 1:29–31. "Cowardly" heads the list because it stands opposed to the faithfulness of the one who "overcomes" (v. 7). *magic arts.* Cf. Ac 19:19. The magical tradition in ancient times called for the mixing of various herbs to ward off evil. *fiery lake of burning sulfur.* See note on 19:20.
21:9 *seven last plagues.* See 15:1.
21:10 *in the Spirit.* See notes on 1:10; 4:2; 17:3.
21:12 *twelve gates.* See Eze 48:30–35. The number 12 probably emphasizes the continuity of the NT church and the OT people of God. See v. 14, where the 12 foundations bear the names of the 12 apostles.
21:15 *measure the city.* Cf. Eze 40–41. In Rev 11 the measuring was to ensure protection; here it serves to show the size and symmetry of the eternal dwelling place of the faithful.
21:16 *length ... wide ... high.* Thus a perfect cube, as was the Most Holy Place of the tabernacle and the temple.
21:17 *144 cubits.* See NIV text note.
21:20 See NIV text note.
21:27 *Lamb's book of life.* See note on 3:5.
22:1 *river of the water of life.* The description of the river here seems to combine elements taken from the description of Eden (Ge 2:8–14) and the river flowing from the new temple seen by Ezekiel (Eze 47:1–12), as well as certain new elements (see Ps 36:8; 46:4 and notes).
22:2 *tree of life.* See v. 14; Ge 2:9; 3:22; Eze 47:12.
22:4 *They will see his face.* In ancient times criminals were banished from the presence of the king (Est 7:8; cf. 2Sa 14:24). One blessing of eternity will be to see the Lord face to face (cf. Ps 17:15 and note; 1Co 13:12; 1Jn 3:2). *his name.* See note on 3:12.

5There will be no more night.[e] They will
not need the light of a lamp or the light of
the sun, for the Lord God will give them
light.[f] And they will reign for ever and
ever.[g]
6The angel said to me,[h] "These words
are trustworthy and true.[i] The Lord, the
God of the spirits of the prophets,[j] sent his
angel[k] to show his servants the things that
must soon take place."

Jesus Is Coming

7"Behold, I am coming soon![l] Blessed[m]
is he who keeps the words of the prophecy
in this book."[n]

8I, John, am the one who heard and saw
these things.[o] And when I had heard and
seen them, I fell down to worship at the
feet[p] of the angel who had been showing
them to me. 9But he said to me, "Do not
do it! I am a fellow servant with you and
with your brothers the prophets and of all
who keep the words of this book.[q] Worship God!"[r]
10Then he told me, "Do not seal up[s] the
words of the prophecy of this book,[t] because the time is near.[u] 11Let him who does
wrong continue to do wrong; let him who
is vile continue to be vile; let him who
does right continue to do right; and let
him who is holy continue to be holy."[v]

12"Behold, I am coming soon![w] My reward is with me,[x] and I will give to everyone according to what he has done.[y] 13I am
the Alpha and the Omega,[z] the First and
the Last,[a] the Beginning and the End.[b]

14"Blessed are those who wash their
robes,[c] that they may have the right to the
tree of life[d] and may go through the gates[e]
into the city.[f] 15Outside[g] are the dogs,[h]
those who practice magic arts, the sexually immoral, the murderers, the idolaters
and everyone who loves and practices
falsehood.
16"I, Jesus,[i] have sent my angel[j] to give
you[a] this testimony for the churches.[k] I
am the Root[l] and the Offspring of David,[m]
and the bright Morning Star."[n]

17The Spirit[o] and the bride[p] say, "Come!"
And let him who hears say, "Come!" Whoever is thirsty, let him come; and whoever
wishes, let him take the free gift of the
water of life.[q]

18I warn everyone who hears the words
of the prophecy of this book:[r] If anyone
adds anything to them,[s] God will add to
him the plagues described in this book.[t]
19And if anyone takes words away[u] from
this book of prophecy,[v] God will take away
from him his share in the tree of life[w] and
in the holy city, which are described in
this book.
20He who testifies to these things[x] says,
"Yes, I am coming soon."[y]
Amen. Come, Lord Jesus.[z]
21The grace of the Lord Jesus be with
God's people.[a] Amen.

[a] 16 The Greek is plural.

22:5 [e] Rev 21:25; Zec 14:7 [f] Isa 60:19,20; Rev 21:23 [g] Da 7:27; Rev 20:4 **22:6** [h] Rev 1:1 [i] Rev 21:5 [j] 1Co 14:32; Heb 12:9 [k] ver 16; Rev 1:1 **22:7** [l] ver 12,20; S Mt 16:27 [m] Rev 1:3; 16:15 [n] ver 10,18,19 **22:8** [o] S Rev 1:1 [p] Rev 19:10 **22:9** [q] ver 10,18,19 [r] Rev 19:10 **22:10** [s] Da 8:26; Rev 10:4 [t] ver 7,18,19 [u] S Ro 13:11 **22:11** [v] Eze 3:27; Da 12:10 **22:12** [w] ver 7,20; S Mt 16:27 [x] Isa 40:10; 62:11 [y] S Mt 16:27 **22:13** [z] Rev 1:8 [a] S Rev 1:17 [b] Rev 21:6 **22:14** [c] Rev 7:14 [d] S Rev 2:7 [e] S Rev 21:12 [f] S Rev 21:27 **22:15** [g] Dt 23:18; 1Co 6:9,10; Gal 5:19-21; Col 3:5,6; Rev 21:8 [h] Php 3:2 **22:16** [i] Rev 1:1 [j] ver 6 [k] Rev 1:4 [l] S Rev 5:5 [m] S Mt 1:1 [n] 2Pe 1:19; Rev 2:28 **22:17** [o] Rev 2:7; 14:13 [p] S Rev 19:7 [q] S Jn 4:10 **22:18** [r] ver 7,10,19 [s] Dt 4:2; 12:32; Pr 30:6 [t] Rev 15:6-16:21 **22:19** [u] Dt 4:2; 12:32; Pr 30:6 [v] ver 7,10,18 [w] S Rev 2:7 **22:20** [x] Rev 1:2 [y] ver 7,12; S Mt 16:27 [z] 1Co 16:22 **22:21** [a] S Ro 16:20

22:5 *they will reign.* See 5:10; 20:6; Da 7:18,27.
22:6–21 Conclusion and closing benediction.
22:6 *his servants.* See v. 3. *things that must soon take place.* See 1:1,19.
22:7 *I am coming soon!* See vv. 12,20; 2:16; 3:11. *Blessed.* The sixth beatitude (see note on 1:3).
22:8 *fell down to worship.* See note on 1:17.
22:9 *Do not do it!* The episode (here and in 19:10) is no doubt included to remind the reader/listener that the worship of any created being—no matter how noble—is a form of idolatry, a vice sternly warned against (v. 15; 21:8; see notes on Ge 20:9; Ex 34:15).
22:10 *Do not seal up the words.* Contrast Da 12:4.
22:11 "The time is near" (v. 10), so it is too late to change. The unrepentant must now face the consequences of their actions (see v. 12).
22:12 *I am coming soon!* See vv. 7,20; 2:16; 3:11. *according to what he has done.* See notes on 2:23; 20:12.
22:13 *the Alpha and the Omega.* See note on 1:8.
22:14 *Blessed.* The last of the seven beatitudes (see note on 1:3). *wash their robes.* "In the blood of the Lamb" (7:14).
22:15 *dogs ... falsehood.* See note on Ro 1:29–31. *dogs.* A term applied to all types of ceremonially impure persons. In Dt 23:18 it designates a male prostitute.
22:16 *my angel.* Cf. 1:1. *the Root and the Offspring of David.* See note on 5:5; cf. Isa 11:1,10; Ro 1:3. *bright Morning Star.* See Nu 24:17 and note.
22:18–19 Cf. the commands in Dt 4:2; 12:32. The warning here relates specifically to the book of Revelation.
22:20 *I am coming soon.* See vv. 7,12; 2:16; 3:11. *Come, Lord Jesus.* See note on 1Co 16:22.
22:21 *grace.* See note on Ro 1:7. *with.* See note on 2Co 13:14. *Amen.* See notes on Dt 27:15; Ro 1:25.

Study Helps

Table of Weights and Measures 1993

Index to Topics 1994

Index to Notes 2148

Index to Maps 2188

Concordance 2192

Index to Color Maps 2337

Table of Weights and Measures

	Biblical Unit	Approximate American Equivalent	Approximate Metric Equivalent
Weights	talent (60 minas)	75 pounds	34 kilograms
	mina (50 shekels)	1 1/4 pounds	0.6 kilogram
	shekel (2 bekas)	2/5 ounce	11.5 grams
	pim (2/3 shekel)	1/3 ounce	7.6 grams
	beka (10 gerahs)	1/5 ounce	5.5 grams
	gerah	1/50 ounce	0.6 gram
Length	cubit	18 inches	0.5 meter
	span	9 inches	23 centimeters
	handbreadth	3 inches	8 centimeters
Capacity			
Dry Measure	cor [homer] (10 ephahs)	6 bushels	220 liters
	lethek (5 ephahs)	3 bushels	110 liters
	ephah (10 omers)	3/5 bushel	22 liters
	seah (1/3 ephah)	7 quarts	7.3 liters
	omer (1/10 ephah)	2 quarts	2 liters
	cab (1/18 ephah)	1 quart	1 liter
Liquid Measure	bath (1 ephah)	6 gallons	22 liters
	hin (1/6 bath)	4 quarts	4 liters
	log (1/72 bath)	1/3 quart	0.3 liter

The figures of the table are calculated on the basis of a shekel equaling 11.5 grams, a cubit equaling 18 inches and an ephah equaling 22 liters. The quart referred to is either a dry quart (slightly larger than a liter) or a liquid quart (slightly smaller than a liter), whichever is applicable. The ton referred to in the footnotes is the American ton of 2,000 pounds.

This table is based upon the best available information, but it is not intended to be mathematically precise; like the measurement equivalents in the footnotes, it merely gives approximate amounts and distances. Weights and measures differed somewhat at various times and places in the ancient world. There is uncertainty particularly about the ephah and the bath; further discoveries may shed more light on these units of capacity.

Index to Topics

The Index to Topics will lead you to key texts on a variety of subjects covered in the *NIV Study Bible*. Many of these key texts have helpful study notes on these subjects.

AARON

A. Family data
- —Genealogy ... Ex 6:16 – 20; 1Ch 6:3 – 15
- —Son of Amram and Jochebed ... Ex 6:20
- —Older brother of Moses ... Ex 7:1,7
- —Brother of Miriam ... Nu 26:59
- —Married Elisheba ... Ex 6:23
- —Four children ... Ex 6:23; Lev 10:1,6

B. His priesthood
1. His garments ... Ex 28:1 – 43; Ex 39:1 – 31
2. His consecration ... Ex 29:1 – 46
3. His ordination ... Lev 8:1 – 36
4. His duties
   - —To teach God's decrees ... Lev 10:8 – 11
   - —To offer prescribed sacrifices ... Lev 6:9 – 13
   - —To officiate on the Day of Atonement ... Heb 9:7
   - —To make atonement in special situations ... Nu 16:46 – 47
5. Hereditary high priesthood ... Nu 20:25 – 26
6. Established the house of Aaron ... 2Ch 29:21; Ps 115:10,12; Lk 1:5

C. Significant events
- —Spokesman for Moses ... Ex 4:14 – 16,27 – 31; Ex 7:1 – 2
- —Supported Moses' hands ... Ex 17:8 – 13
- —Built golden calf ... Ex 32:1 – 24
- —Saved through Moses' prayer ... Dt 9:20
- —With Miriam, criticized Moses ... Nu 12:1 – 15
- —His staff budded ... Nu 17:1 – 11
- —Forbidden to enter Canaan ... Nu 20:1 – 12
- —His death ... Nu 20:22 – 29; Nu 33:38 – 39

ABEDNEGO
- —Hebrew deported to Babylon ... Da 1:1 – 6
- —Name changed from Azariah ... Da 1:7
- —Refused to be defiled by food ... Da 1:8 – 20
- —Was appointed administrator over Babylon ... Da 2:49
- —Refused to worship idols ... Da 3:1 – 12
- —Saved from fiery furnace ... Da 3:13 – 30

ABEL
- —Second son of Adam ... Ge 4:2
- —The first shepherd ... Ge 4:2
- —Offered proper sacrifice ... Ge 4:4; Heb 11:4
- —Considered righteous ... Mt 23:35
- —Murdered by Cain ... Ge 4:8; 1Jn 3:12
- —Christ's blood superior to his ... Heb 12:24
- —His place taken by Seth ... Ge 4:25

ABIATHAR
- —High priest in days of Saul and David ... Mk 2:26
- —Escaped Saul's slaughter ... 1Sa 22:18 – 23
- —Became high priest under David ... 1Sa 23:6,9
- —Joint high priest with Zadok ... 2Sa 19:11
- —Supported David against Absalom ... 2Sa 15:24 – 29
- —Supported Adonijah ... 1Ki 1:7 – 42
- —Deposed by Solomon ... 1Ki 2:22 – 35

ABIGAIL

A. Stepsister of David ... 2Sa 17:25; 1Ch 2:16 – 17
- —Married Jether ... 2Sa 17:25
- —Mother of Amasa, Absalom's commander ... 2Sa 17:25
- —Aunt of Joab, David's commander ... 2Sa 17:25

B. Wife of Nabal ... 1Sa 25:3
- —Begged David to spare Nabal's life ... 1Sa 25:23 – 35
- —Became David's wife after Nabal's death ... 1Sa 25:36 – 42
- —Captured and rescued ... 1Sa 30:5,18
- —Gave birth to Kileab ... 2Sa 3:3

ABIHU
- —Son of Aaron ... Ex 6:23
- —Went up Mount Sinai ... Ex 24:1,9
- —Consecrated as priest ... Ex 28:1
- —Killed for offering unauthorized fire ... Lev 10:1 – 2; Nu 3:2 – 4
- —Had no sons ... 1Ch 24:2

ABIJAH

A. Second son of Samuel ... 1Ch 6:28
- —A corrupt judge ... 1Sa 8:1 – 5

B. An Aaronic priest ... 1Ch 24:10
- —Ancestor of Zechariah ... Lk 1:5

C. Son of Jeroboam I of Israel ... 1Ki 14:1
- —Died as Ahijah prophesied ... 1Ki 14:1 – 18

D. King of Judah: son of Rehoboam ... 1Ki 14:31; Mt 1:7
- —Reigned three years ... 1Ki 15:1 – 2
- —Fought against Jeroboam ... 2Ch 13:1 – 22
- —A wicked king ... 1Ki 15:3

ABIMELECH

A. King of Gerar
- —Took Abraham's wife Sarah ... Ge 20:1 – 2
- —Warned by God in a dream ... Ge 20:3 – 7
- —Angry with Abraham ... Ge 20:8 – 16
- —Healed by God ... Ge 20:17 – 18
- —Made a covenant with Abraham ... Ge 21:22 – 33

B. Another king of Gerar
- —Discovered truth about Rebekah ... Ge 26:1 – 11
- —Controversy with Isaac over wells ... Ge 26:12 – 22
- —Made a covenant with Isaac ... Ge 26:26 – 31

C. Son of Gideon ... Jdg 8:31
- —Attempted to make himself king ... Jdg 9:1 – 49
- —His death ... Jdg 9:50 – 57

ABISHAG
- —Shunammite virgin who attended David ... 1Ki 1:1 – 4
- —Adonijah killed for wanting to marry her ... 1Ki 2:13 – 25

ABISHAI
- —Son of Zeruiah, David's sister ... 1Ch 2:16
- —Brother of Joab ... 1Sa 26:6
- —One of David's chief warriors ... 1Ch 11:15 – 21

—Wanted to kill Saul 1Sa 26:6–9
—Fought against Edomites 1Ch 18:12–13
—Killed Abner 2Sa 2:18–27
—Fought against Ammonites 2Sa 10:9–10
—Wanted to kill Shimei 2Sa 16:5–12
—Fought against Absalom 2Sa 18:2,5,12
—Fought against Sheba 2Sa 20:1–6,10
—Fought against Philistines 2Sa 21:15–17

ABNER
—Cousin of Saul 1Sa 14:50
—Commander of Saul's army 1Sa 17:55–57
—Chided by David for carelessness 1Sa 26:5–16
—Made Ish-Bosheth king after Saul 2Sa 2:8–10
—Defeated by David's men 2Sa 2:12–17
—Defected to David 2Sa 3:8–21
—Killed by Joab and Abishai 2Sa 3:22–39

ABORTION
A. Law regarding accidental loss of a child .... Ex 21:22
B. What is said about a fetus
—It is called a child .... Mt 1:20
—It has conscious awareness .... Lk 1:36,41,44
—Sinful nature is present at conception .... Ps 51:5
C. How God relates to a fetus
—God cares for a conceived child .... Isa 46:3
—God forms a child .... Ps 139:13–15
Isa 44:2,24
—God plans a child's life .... Ps 139:16
Isa 49:1
Jer 1:5
Gal 1:15

ABRAHAM
A. Family data
—Line of Shem 1Ch 1:24–27
—Son of Terah .... Ge 11:26–27
—Original name: Abram .... Ge 11:27
—Husband of Sarai .... Ge 11:29
—Father of Ishmael with Hagar .... Ge 16:1–4,15–16
—Father of Isaac with Sarah .... Ge 21:1–3
—Father of many children with Keturah .... Ge 25:1–4
—Died at 175 years old .... Ge 25:7–8
B. Covenant with the Lord
1. Called while in Ur .... Ge 12:1–3
Ac 7:2–4
2. Received promises
—Land and descendants .... Ge 13:14–17
Ge 15:18–21
Ge 22:15–18
—A son by Sarah .... Ge 17:16
Ge 18:9–15
3. Given circumcision as a sign .... Ge 17:1–14,23–27
Ro 4:9–12
4. Declared righteous through faith .... Ge 15:6
Ro 4:3,20–24
Gal 3:6–9
5. Covenant sealed by sacrifice .... Ge 15:8–21
6. Name changed to Abraham .... Ge 17:5
Ne 9:7
7. Covenant remembered .... Lk 1:68–75
Heb 6:13–15
C. Travels and significant events
—Left Ur .... Ge 11:31
—Went to Canaan .... Ge 12:1–6
Ac 7:2–4
—Deceived Pharaoh about Sarai .... Ge 12:10–20
—Divided land with Lot, settled in Hebron .... Ge 13:1–18
—Rescued Lot from four kings .... Ge 14:1–16
—Blessed by Melchizedek .... Ge 14:17–20
Heb 7:1–7
—Declared righteous through faith .... Ge 15:6
—Fathered Ishmael with Hagar .... Ge 16:1–16
—Entertained three visitors .... Ge 18:1–15
—Interceded for the city of Sodom .... Ge 18:16–33
—Deceived Abimelech about Sarah .... Ge 20:1–10
—Fathered Isaac with Sarah .... Ge 21:1–3
—Sent Hagar and Ishmael away .... Ge 21:8–21
Gal 4:22–30
—Made a covenant with Abimelech .... Ge 21:22–32
—Tested by command to sacrifice Isaac .... Ge 22:1–18
Heb 11:17–19
—Bought field for Sarah's burial .... Ge 23:1–20
—Secured wife for Isaac .... Ge 24:1–67
—Fathered children with Keturah .... Ge 25:1–6
—Died .... Ge 25:7–11
D. Titles ascribed to him
—Mighty prince .... Ge 23:5–6
—Servant of God .... Ge 26:24
—Friend of God .... Isa 41:8
Jas 2:23
—Prophet .... Ge 20:7
—Father of Israel .... Ex 3:15
Mt 3:9
—Father of all believers .... Ro 4:11–12,16
Gal 3:7
E. Significance in New Testament
—Jesus is a son of Abraham .... Mt 1:1
—His true seed is Christ .... Gal 3:15–16,29
—Jesus preceded him .... Jn 8:57–58
—Rejoiced to see Jesus' day .... Jn 8:56
—Showed greatness of Christ by giving a tithe to Melchizedek .... Heb 7:4–10
—Lived by faith .... Heb 11:8–12,17–19
—Believed in the power of the resurrection .... Ro 4:17–21
—Became the father of believers .... Ro 4:11–12
Gal 3:7
—His faith preceded the law .... Ro 4:9–11,13–16
Gal 3:17–19
—Cast out the sons of the law .... Gal 4:21–31
—Demonstrated faith by works .... Jas 2:20–24

ABSALOM
—Son of David by Maacah 2Sa 3:3
1Ch 3:2
—Killed Amnon for rape of Tamar 2Sa 13:23–33
—Fled to Geshur 2Sa 13:36–38
—Allowed by David to return 2Sa 14:1–24
—Reconciled with David 2Sa 14:28–33
—Rebelled against David 2Sa 15:1–12
—David fled from him 2Sa 15:13–37
—Accepted the advice of Hushai .... 2Sa 16:15—17:23
—Fought against David's men 2Sa 18:1–8
—Killed by Joab 2Sa 18:9–18
—Mourned by David .... 2Sa 18:19—19:8

ACCESS TO GOD
A. The command to approach God
—In the Old Testament .... Isa 55:6
Am 5:4,6
—In the New Testament .... Mt 7:7
Lk 11:9
Jas 4:8
B. How can we approach God?
1. From God's standpoint
—The Father draws us to himself .... Jn 6:44
—Jesus is the way to the Father .... Jn 14:6
Ro 5:2
Eph 3:12
1Pe 3:18

—The Spirit enables us to come near .... Eph 2:18
2. From our standpoint
—We must believe .... Ro 5:2
Heb 11:6
—We must live clean, obedient lives .... Ps 24:3 – 5
Mt 5:8
—We must pray to the Father .... Mt 6:6
—We must call upon God's name .... Ps 145:18
C. Promises to those who approach God
—We will find God .... Dt 4:29
2Ch 15:2
—God will listen to us 2Ki 13:4
—God will forgive us 2Ch 7:14
—God will make a covenant with us .... Isa 55:3
—God will bless us .... Ps 65:4
—We can have confidence before God .... Eph 3:12
Heb 4:16
1Jn 5:14

See also PRAYER

ACHAN

—Son of Carmi, of tribe of Judah .... Jos 7:1
—Stole things from Jericho .... Jos 7:1
—His sin caused defeat at Ai .... Jos 7:3 – 12
—His sin revealed .... Jos 7:13 – 23
—Stoned to death .... Jos 7:24 – 26
—A lesson for Israel .... Jos 22:18 – 20

ACHISH

—King of Gath before whom David feigned insanity .. 1Sa 21:10 – 15
—Gave David town of Ziklag .... 1Sa 27:1 – 7
—Trusted David .... 1Sa 27:10 – 12
—Philistines asked him to expel David .... 1Sa 29:1 – 11
—Still king in time of Solomon .... 1Ki 2:39 – 40

ADAM

A. The first Adam
1. The creation of Adam
—Made in God's image .... Ge 1:26 – 27
—Made from dust of the earth .... Ge 2:7
—Became a living being .... Ge 2:7
1Co 15:45
—Woman was created from him .... Ge 2:21 – 23
2. The work of Adam
—Was placed in Eden .... Ge 2:8
—Took care of Eden .... Ge 2:15
—Named the animals .... Ge 2:19 – 20
—Work cursed after the fall .... Ge 3:17 – 19
—Was banished from Eden .... Ge 3:23 – 24
3. Marriage of Adam and Eve
—Was established by God .... Ge 2:23 – 24
—Eve tempted her husband .... Ge 3:6
1Ti 2:14
—Adam blamed Eve .... Ge 3:12
—Adam and Eve had children .... Ge 4:1 – 2
Ge 4:25—5:4
4. Temptation and fall of Adam
—God warned Adam not to sin .... Ge 2:16 – 17
—Adam disobeyed God .... Ge 3:1 – 6
—God pronounced punishment .... Ge 3:16 – 19
—Adam died .... Ge 5:5
—Sin and death passed on to all humans .... Ro 5:12,15 – 17,19
—God condemns us for Adam's sin .... Ro 5:16,18
B. The second Adam (Christ) 1Co 15:45
1. Prophecy concerning him in Eden .... Ge 3:15
2. Christ as the second Adam
—Descended from the first Adam .... Lk 3:23 – 38
—Obedient to God's will .... Ro 5:19
—Victorious over the devil .... Mt 4:1 – 11
1Jn 3:8
3. Results for believers
—They receive righteousness and life .... Ro 5:15 – 18
1Co 15:22
—They will receive new bodies like his .... 1Co 15:46 – 49
Php 3:20 – 21

ADONIJAH

—Son of David by Haggith 2Sa 3:4
1Ch 3:2
—Attempted to be king after David .... 1Ki 1:5 – 27
—David made Solomon king instead .... 1Ki 1:28 – 53
—Wanted Abishag as wife .... 1Ki 2:13 – 22
—Killed at Solomon's command .... 1Ki 2:23 – 25

ADOPTION

—Becoming someone's child by a legal act
A. In human relationships
—Abram wants to adopt .... Ge 15:2 – 4
—Pharaoh's daughter adopts Moses .... Ex 2:10
—Mordecai adopts Esther .... Est 2:7
—A wife adopts a maid's son .... Ge 16:1 – 3
Ge 30:1 – 5
Ge 30:9 – 12
B. In the God-man relationship
1. It is rooted in God's eternal love .... Eph 1:4 – 5
Ro 8:29
1Jn 3:1
2. Israel is God's adopted son .... Ex 4:22 – 23
Dt 14:2
Jer 31:9
Hos 11:1
Ro 9:4
3. Christians are God's adopted children
—We become children by God's grace .... Eph 1:5 – 6
—We become children through faith in Christ .... Jn 1:12 – 13
Gal 3:26
—We can call God Father .... Mt 6:9
Ro 8:15
Gal 4:6 – 7
—We become siblings of Christ .... Mk 3:34 – 35
Heb 2:11 – 12
—We are united as one body in Christ .... Eph 2:11 – 13,19
Eph 3:6
—Our adoption is completed only at the resurrection .... Ro 8:19,23
1Jn 3:2
4. Results of being God's children
—We receive the rights of inheritance .... Ro 8:17
Gal 4:7
—We must walk in light .... Jn 12:35 – 36
Eph 5:8 – 10
1Th 5:4 – 5
—We must live as obedient children .... 1Pe 1:14 – 16
—We must live in peace .... Mt 5:9
Eph 2:17 – 19
—We must live in love .... Mt 5:44 – 45
Lk 6:35
—We must separate ourselves from evil .... 2Co 6:17 – 18
Php 2:15
—We are subject to God's discipline .... Heb 12:5 – 11
—We can expect suffering .... Ro 8:18,22

ADULLAM

—A city in southwest Judah .... Jos 15:21,33,35
—Judah married a woman from there .... Ge 38:1 – 2
—David hid his followers in a cave near it .... 1Sa 22:1 – 2
—David's men risked getting water from Bethlehem .... 2Sa 23:13 – 17
1Ch 11:15 – 19

—Fortified by Rehoboam .... 2Ch 11:5 – 10
—Judgment prophesied against it .... Mic 1:15
—Established again after the exile .... Ne 11:30

ADULTERY

—Sexual unfaithfulness to one's spouse
A. Related theme
ADULTERY is a theme of Hosea .... Hos 4:13
B. Old Testament perspective
1. Laws against adultery
—In the Ten Commandments .... Ex 20:14; Dt 5:18
—Various laws on adultery .... Lev 20:10; Nu 5:12 – 31; Dt 22:22 – 24
2. Examples of adultery
—Judah and Tamar .... Ge 38:15 – 18
—David and Bathsheba .... 2Sa 11:2 – 5
—Others in Judah .... Jer 5:7 – 9; Jer 29:23
3. Characteristics of adultery
—Is a sin against one's spouse and God .... Ge 39:7 – 9; 2Sa 12:13; Ps 51:4
—Is personally dangerous .... Pr 2:16 – 19; Pr 6:25 – 29,32
—Defiles a whole nation .... Jer 3:1; Jer 23:10 – 15; Eze 33:26
C. New Testament perspective
1. The sin of adultery
—Starts in a sinful heart .... Mt 15:19
—Considered a sinful action .... Ro 7:2 – 3; Jas 2:11; 2Pe 2:14
—Sinful even in thought .... Mt 5:27 – 28
—Remarriage as adultery .... Mt 5:31 – 32; Mt 19:8 – 9
2. Results of adultery
—Leads to God's judgment .... Heb 13:4
—Leads to exclusion from the kingdom .... Gal 5:19 – 21; 1Co 6:9; Rev 22:15
3. Pardon promised for adulterers .... Jn 8:3 – 11; 1Co 6:11
D. Spiritual adultery
—References in the Old Testament .... Jer 3:6 – 10,20; Eze 16:32 – 35; Hos 1:2
—References in the New Testament .... Mt 12:39; Jas 4:4
—God judges spiritual adultery .... Jer 5:11 – 17; Eze 16:37 – 42; Mk 8:38
—God desires faithfulness to Christ 2Co 11:2

See also MARRIAGE

AFFLICTION

See PAIN

AGABUS

—A prophet in the early church .... Ac 11:27 – 28
—Predicted a severe famine for the world .... Ac 11:28
—Predicted Paul's arrest in Jerusalem .... Ac 21:10 – 11

AGAG

—King of Amalekites; spared by Saul .... 1Sa 15:7 – 9,20
—Killed by Samuel .... 1Sa 15:32 – 33

AGRIPPA

—King who visited Festus .... Ac 25:13 – 22
—Paul spoke before him .... Ac 25:23—26:23
—Paul invited him to believe .... Ac 26:25 – 27
—Rejected the gospel .... Ac 26:28
—Declared Paul innocent .... Ac 26:31 – 32

AHAB

A. Personal data
—Son of Omri; king of Israel .... 1Ki 16:28 – 29
—Husband of Jezebel 1Ki 16:31
B. Significant events
—Promoted Baal worship .... 1Ki 16:31 – 33
—Opposed by Elijah 1Ki 17:1
—Contest on Mount Carmel .... 1Ki 18:16 – 39
—Defeated Ben-Hadad .... 1Ki 20:1 – 34
—Coveted Naboth's vineyard .... 1Ki 21:1 – 16
—Fought against king of Aram .... 1Ki 22:29 – 30
—Accidentally killed in battle .... 1Ki 22:34 – 38
C. Prophesied against
—By an unnamed prophet .... 1Ki 20:35 – 43
—By Elijah .... 1Ki 21:17 – 29
—By Micaiah .... 1Ki 22:9 – 28
D. Subsequent history
—Elisha told Jehu to destroy Ahab's family .... 2Ki 9:6 – 10
—House of Ahab destroyed .... 2Ki 10:1 – 17
—Name became a symbol of wickedness .... 2Ch 21:6,13; 2Ch 22:3 – 4; Mic 6:16

AHAZ

—Son of Jotham; king of Judah 2Ki 16:1; 2Ch 28:1
—Worshiped idols .... 2Ki 16:1 – 4,10 – 18; 2Ch 28:1 – 4,22 – 25
—Fought against Aram and Israel .... 2Ki 16:5 – 6; Isa 7:1
—Defeated by Aram and Israel .... 2Ch 28:5 – 15
—Fought against Edom and Philistia .... 2Ch 28:16 – 19
—Sought help from Assyria .... 2Ki 16:7 – 9
—Refused a sign from the Lord .... Isa 7:2 – 17
—His death .... 2Ki 16:19 – 20

AHAZIAH

A. Son of Ahab; king of Israel 1Ki 22:51
—Worshiped idols .... 1Ki 22:52 – 53
—Made an alliance with Jehoshaphat .... 2Ch 20:36 – 37
—Died while seeking advice from Baal .... 2Ki 1:1 – 17
B. Son of Jehoram; king of Judah .... 2Ki 8:25 – 26; 2Ch 22:1 – 2
—Worshiped idols .... 2Ki 8:27; 2Ch 22:3 – 4
—Allied with Joram, king of Israel .... 2Ki 8:28 – 29
—Killed by Jehu while visiting Joram .... 2Ki 9:14 – 29; 2Ch 22:1 – 9
—Only surviving son was Joash .... 2Ki 11:1 – 3

AHIMELECH

A. Priest at Nob during Saul's time 1Sa 21:1
—Gave David consecrated bread .... 1Sa 21:2 – 6
—Gave David Goliath's sword .... 1Sa 21:8 – 9
—Betrayed to Saul by Doeg .... 1Sa 22:9 – 16
—Killed by Doeg with other priests .... 1Sa 22:17 – 19
—Son Abiathar escaped to join David .... 1Sa 22:20 – 23
B. Grandson of Ahimelech 2Sa 8:17
—Co-priest with Zadok during David's reign 1Ch 18:16; 1Ch 24:6,31
C. One of David's warriors 1Sa 26:6

AHITHOPHEL

—A counselor of David 2Sa 15:12
—Joined Absalom against David .... 2Sa 15:31 – 37
—Advised Absalom .... 2Sa 16:15 – 23
—Absalom rejected his counsel .... 2Sa 17:1 – 14
—Committed suicide 2Sa 17:23

AI

—A city in Palestine, east of Bethel .... Jos 7:2
—Abram built an altar near there .... Ge 12:8
—Joshua's troops were initially defeated there .... Jos 7:3 – 5
—After Achan's death, Ai was destroyed .... Jos 8:1 – 29
—Later rebuilt, with Israelites settling there .... Ezr 2:2,28

ALCOHOL

A. Terms used in the Bible
—Beer and wine .... 1Sa 1:15; Pr 31:4,6
—Fermented drink .... Nu 6:3; Jdg 13:4,7
—Mixed wine .... Pr 9:2; Pr 23:30
—Old wine and new wine .... Am 9:13; Lk 5:37 – 39

B. Various uses for alcohol
—In family meals .... Ge 27:25
—In public feasting .... Est 1:7 – 8,10; Da 5:1 – 4
—At weddings .... Jn 2:3
—As an offering to God .... Ex 29:38,40; Lev 23:12 – 13
—As a tithe .... Dt 12:17; Ne 13:5
—In barter exchange 2Ch 2:10
—As a commodity for commerce .... Eze 27:18
—As medicine .... Lk 10:34; 1Ti 5:23
—As a drug for pain .... Pr 31:6; Mk 15:23
—As a means to become drunk .... Ge 9:20 – 21

C. Positive aspects of alcohol
—A blessing from God .... Joel 2:19
—Can help one celebrate .... Jn 2:1 – 11
—Can give enjoyment .... Ps 104:15; Zec 9:17
—Can aid in happiness .... Ecc 10:19
—Can help to refresh someone 2Sa 16:2
—Can help one's health 1Ti 5:23

D. Dangers of using alcohol
—Loosens morals .... Ge 9:21 – 22
—Inflames an individual .... Isa 5:11 – 12
—Destroys health .... 1Sa 25:36 – 37
—Impairs judgment .... Pr 31:4 – 5; Isa 28:7
—Raises tempers .... Pr 20:1
—Leads to poverty .... Pr 23:21
—Leads to sorrow .... Pr 23:29 – 30
—Creates disunity in the church .... 1Co 11:18 – 21

E. Drunkenness forbidden .... Isa 5:11 – 12,22; Ro 13:13; 1Co 5:11; 1Co 6:9 – 10; Eph 5:18

F. Symbolic uses of alcohol
—Symbolizes the blood of Christ .... Mt 26:27 – 29
—Symbolizes the gospel of salvation .... Isa 55:1
—Symbolizes the judgment of God .... Ps 75:8; Jer 25:15 – 16; Rev 14:10
—Symbolizes the sins of the antichrist .... Rev 17:2; Rev 18:3

ALIEN

—A citizen of one country residing in another

A. Aliens within the nation of Israel
1. Who were they?
—Those leaving Egypt with Israelites .... Ex 12:38
—Unconquered nations in Canaan .... Jos 9:26 – 27; 1Ki 9:20 – 21
—Captives taken in war .... Dt 21:10 – 11
—Slaves purchased .... Lev 25:44 – 46
—Foreigners hired in Israel 1Ki 9:27
—Foreigners attracted to Israel .... 2Ch 6:32 – 33
2. How were they to be treated?
—God had a special love for them .... Dt 10:18; Ps 146:9
—They were not to be oppressed .... Ex 22:21; Ex 23:9; Lev 19:33 – 34
—They enjoyed equal protection .... Lev 24:22; Lev 25:35; Dt 1:16 – 17; Dt 24:17 – 21
—They shared equal responsibility .... Ex 20:8 – 10; Nu 15:14 – 16
—Israel condemned for oppressing them .... Ps 94:6; Eze 22:7,29

B. God's people as aliens
1. In the Old Testament
—Abraham in Canaan .... Ge 17:8; Ge 23:4
—Jacob in Canaan .... Ge 28:4
—Moses in Midian .... Ex 18:3
—Israelites in Egypt .... Ge 15:13; Ex 23:9
—Israelites in Canaan .... Lev 25:23; 1Ch 29:15; Ps 39:12; Ps 119:19
—Israelites in Babylon .... La 5:2
—Their true homeland was elsewhere .... Heb 11:13 – 15
2. In the New Testament
—We are called foreigners 1Pe 1:17; 1Pe 2:11
—We are not part of this world .... Jn 17:14,16
—Our true home is heaven .... Php 3:20 – 21; Col 3:1,3; Heb 11:16
—We must not love the world .... Ro 12:2; 1Jn 2:15 – 17
—We may not alienate people in the church .... Eph 2:19 – 22; Heb 13:1 – 2

ALTAR

A. Altars used in heathen religions
1. Such altars built .... Ex 32:5; 1Ki 16:32 – 33; 1Ki 18:26; Ac 17:23
2. Such altars destroyed
—At God's command .... Ex 34:13; Dt 7:5
—By Moses .... Ex 32:20
—By Gideon .... Jdg 6:25 – 28
—By all the Israelites 2Ki 11:18; 2Ch 31:1
—By various kings 2Ki 18:4; 2Ki 23:12; 2Ch 14:3,5
—By the Lord himself .... Hos 10:2

B. Altars used in the worship of the Lord
1. Such altars built or rebuilt by:
—Noah.......Ge 8:20
—Abram.......Ge 12:7–8
Ge 13:18
—Isaac.......Ge 26:25
—Jacob.......Ge 35:6–7
—Moses.......Ex 17:15
—Joshua.......Jos 8:30
—Gideon.......Jdg 6:24
—Samuel.......1Sa 7:17
—Saul.......1Sa 14:35
—David.......2Sa 24:25
—Solomon.......2Ch 8:12
—Asa.......2Ch 15:8
—Elijah.......1Ki 18:30–32
—Hezekiah's men.......2Ch 29:18
—Manasseh.......2Ch 33:16
—Jeshua and Zerubbabel.......Ezr 3:2–3
2. Altars located in
—The tabernacle.......Ex 37:25—38:7
—Solomon's temple.......2Ch 4:1,19
—The second temple.......Ezr 7:17
—Ezekiel's temple.......Eze 43:13–27
—Herod's temple.......Lk 1:11
3. Purpose of altars to the Lord
—To sacrifice to the Lord.......Ge 8:20
Ge 12:7–8
—To make atonement for God's people.......Lev 16:18–20
—To burn incense to the Lord.......Ex 30:1–10
—To function as memorials.......Ex 17:15
Jos 22:26–27
4. Altars in the Christian religion
—Christ's cross is our altar.......Heb 13:10–12
—No need for sacrifice after Christ came.......Heb 9:6–15,23–28
Heb 10:1–18
—The heavenly altar of incense.......Rev 6:9
Rev 8:3–5

AMALEKITES

A. Their identity
—The descendants of Amalek, grandson of Esau..Ge 36:15–16
—Lived in the Negev (south Canaan).......Nu 13:29
B. Their wars
—Defeated by Kedorlaomer and his allies.......Ge 14:5–7
—Defeated by Israelites in the desert.......Ex 17:8–13
—Defeated the disobedient Israelites.......Nu 14:41–45
—Allied with Eglon against Israelites.......Jdg 3:12–13
—Allied with Midianites against Israelites.......Jdg 6:3,33
—Defeated by Gideon.......Jdg 7:12,22–24
—Defeated by King Saul.......1Sa 14:47–48
1Sa 15:1–9
—King Agag killed by Samuel.......1Sa 15:32–33
—Defeated by David.......1Sa 27:8–9
1Sa 30:1–19
—An Amalekite soldier killed King Saul.......2Sa 1:4–15
C. Important data concerning them
—They had no fear of God.......Dt 25:17–18
—Moses prophesied their complete destruction..Ex 17:14
Dt 25:17–19
—Balaam predicted their destruction.......Nu 24:20
—Destruction completed by the Simeonites.......1Ch 4:42–43

AMASA

—Nephew of David.......1Ch 2:17
—Commander of Absalom's forces.......2Sa 17:25
—Came back to David.......2Sa 19:13
—Killed by Joab.......2Sa 20:4–13

AMAZIAH

A. Son of Joash; king of Judah.......2Ki 14:1–2
—Killed his father's assassins.......2Ki 14:5–6
—Raised a large army.......2Ch 25:5–6
—Defeated Edom.......2Ki 14:7
2Ch 25:7–13
—Worshiped Edom's gods.......2Ch 25:14
—Rebuked by a prophet.......2Ch 25:15–16
—Defeated by Israel.......2Ki 14:8–14
2Ch 25:17–24
—Killed by conspirators.......2Ch 25:27
B. Idolatrous priest who opposed Amos.......Am 7:10–17

AMBITION

—A goal one sets in life
A. Related theme
PRIORITIES is a theme of Haggai.......Hag 1:4
B. Examples of proper ambitions
—Witnessing to unbelievers.......Ro 15:20
—Being fully devoted to the Lord.......1Co 7:32,34
—Desiring the greater gifts, especially love.......1Co 12:31—13:7
—Pleasing God in everything.......2Co 5:9
—Striving for perfection, unity and peace.......2Co 13:11
—Forging ahead in service to Christ.......Php 3:12–14
—Leading a quiet, diligent life.......1Th 4:11
—Pursuing righteousness and godliness.......1Ti 6:11
2Ti 2:22
C. Examples of improper ambitions
—Competing with others in the kingdom.......Mk 10:35–45
Php 1:15,17
—Serving one's own selfish wants.......Php 2:3
Jas 2:14–16
—Seeking riches.......1Ki 3:7–12
Lk 12:13–21
1Ti 6:9–10
—Attempting to glorify oneself.......Ge 11:3–4
Da 4:28–30
—Attempting to displace God.......Eze 28:2
2Th 2:3–4

See also PRIDE

AMMONITES

A. Their identity
—Descendants of Ben-Ammi, son of Lot.......Ge 19:38
—Related to the Moabites.......Ge 19:36–38
—Given land east of the Jordan.......Dt 2:19
Dt 3:16
—Served the god Molech.......1Ki 11:7,33
B. Significant Ammonites
—Nahash: besieged Jabesh.......1Sa 11:1–2
—Hanun: opposed David.......2Sa 10:1–4
—Zelek: one of David's mighty men.......1Ch 11:39
—Naamah: the mother of Rehoboam.......1Ki 14:21,31
—Zabad: conspired against Joash.......2Ch 24:26
—Tobiah: opposed Nehemiah.......Ne 2:10,19
Ne 4:3,7–8
C. Their wars
—Allied with Eglon against Israelites.......Jdg 3:12–13
—Allied with Philistines against Israelites.......Jdg 10:7–9,17–18
—Defeated by Jephthah.......Jdg 11:4–33
—Defeated by Saul.......1Sa 11:1–11
1Sa 14:47
—Defeated by David's army.......2Sa 10:1–14
2Sa 12:26–31
1Ch 19:1–15
1Ch 20:1
—Allied with Moabites against Jehoshaphat.......2Ch 20:1
—They and Moabites destroyed each other.......2Ch 20:22–24
—Defeated by Uzziah.......2Ch 26:8

—Defeated by Jotham 2Ch 27:5
—Allied against Jehoiakim 2Ki 24:1 – 2
—Plotted against rebuilding of Jerusalem Ne 2:19
Ne 4:1 – 3,7 – 8

D. Important data concerning them
1. During the time of Moses and Joshua
—Not attacked by the Israelites Dt 2:19,37
—Refused to give food to Israelites Dt 23:4
—Not allowed to join the Israelites Dt 23:4
Ne 13:1 – 8
—Half of their land given to Gad Jos 13:25
2. During the time of the kings
—Israelites worshiped their gods Jdg 10:6
1Ki 11:5,7
—David used them to kill Uriah 2Sa 12:9
—Solomon intermarried with them 1Ki 11:1
1Ki 14:21
3. Numerous Jews intermarried with them Ezr 9:1
Ne 13:23 – 27
4. Prophecies concerning their destruction Isa 11:12 – 14
Jer 49:1 – 5
Eze 21:28 – 32
Eze 25:1 – 7
Am 1:13 – 15
Zep 2:8 – 11

AMNON

—Firstborn of David 2Sa 3:2
—Raped Tamar 2Sa 13:1 – 19
—Killed by Absalom 2Sa 13:20 – 29
—David mourned for him 2Sa 13:37

AMON

A. Son of Manasseh; king of Judah 2Ki 21:18 – 19
—Promoted idolatry 2Ki 21:20 – 22
—Assassinated 2Ki 21:23 – 24
B. Ruler of city of Samaria under Ahab 1Ki 22:26
2Ch 18:25

AMORITES

A. Their identity
—Descendants of Canaan, grandson of Noah Ge 10:6,15 – 16
—One of the Canaanite nations Ex 33:2
—Lived in hill country, east of the Jordan Nu 13:29
Jos 2:10
—Boundaries given Jos 12:2 – 5

B. Significant Amorites
—Mamre, Eshcol, Aner: friends of Abram Ge 14:13
—Sihon and Og: fought against Israelites Nu 21:21,33
Dt 4:46 – 47

C. Their wars
—Defeated by Kedorlaomer and his allies Ge 14:5 – 7
—Sihon and Og defeated by the Israelites Nu 21:21 – 31
—They defeated disobedient Israelites Dt 1:42 – 45
—Five Amorite kings defeated by Joshua Jos 10:5 – 26

D. Important data concerning them
1. Exceptionally sinful Ge 15:16
2Ki 21:11
2. God promised their land to the Israelites Ex 3:8,17
Ex 34:11
3. Political relationship with Israelites
—Land given to tribe of Reuben Jos 13:15,21
—Israelites told to destroy them Dt 7:1 – 6
Dt 20:16 – 18
—Israelites did not destroy them Jos 13:2,4
Jdg 1:34 – 36
—Amorites and Israelites at peace 1Sa 7:14
—Became slaves of Israelites 1Ki 9:20 – 21
2Ch 8:7 – 8
4. Religious relationship with Israelites
—Israelites must not worship their gods Jos 24:14 – 15
—Israelites worshiped their gods Jdg 6:10
5. Intermarried with the Israelites Jdg 3:5 – 6
Ezr 9:1 – 2

AMOS

A. Prophet from Tekoa Am 1:1
—Originally a farmer and shepherd Am 7:14
—Confronted the prophet Amaziah Am 7:10 – 17
B. Ancestor of Jesus Lk 3:25

ANANIAS

A. Husband of Sapphira Ac 5:1
—Kept back part of their money Ac 5:2
—Died for lying to God Ac 5:3 – 10
B. Disciple in Damascus who baptized Saul/Paul Ac 9:10 – 17
—Commissioned Paul Ac 22:12 – 16
C. High priest at Paul's arrest Ac 23:2
Ac 24:1

ANCESTRY

—Those from whom one has descended
A. Related theme
GENEALOGY is a theme of 1 Chronicles 1Ch 9:1
B. Physical ancestry of the Israelites
—Genealogies were important Ge 5:1 – 32
Ge 46:8 – 26
1Ch 1:1—9:44
Ezr 2:3 – 61
Mt 1:1 – 17
Lk 3:23 – 38
—Priests had to prove ancestry Ezr 2:62
Ne 7:64
—Israelites proud of Abraham as father Isa 41:8
Isa 51:2
Lk 3:8
Jn 8:31 – 33
C. Ancestry of Jesus
—A descendant of Adam Lk 3:38
—A descendant of Abraham Mt 1:1
Ro 9:5
—A descendant of David Mt 1:1
Ro 1:3
D. Spiritual ancestry of God's people
1. Physical ancestry insufficient to be saved Ro 9:6 – 7
2. Requirements for becoming true children of Abraham
—We must be chosen by God Ro 9:10 – 13
—We must believe in Jesus Ro 4:11,16
Gal 3:7,26 – 29
—We must do God's will Jn 8:39 – 40
3. True children of Abraham
—Are heirs of God Ro 8:17
Gal 3:29
—Include both Jews and Gentiles Ro 4:16 – 17
Eph 3:6

ANDREW

—Brother of Simon Peter Mt 4:18
—Fisherman Mk 1:16 – 18
—Disciple of John the Baptist Jn 1:35 – 40
—Introduced Peter to Jesus Jn 1:41 – 42
—Became a disciple of Jesus Mt 4:18
—Introduced little boy to Jesus Jn 6:8
—Introduced Greeks to Jesus Jn 12:21 – 22
—Asked Jesus about destruction of temple Mk 13:3
—One of the apostles Ac 1:13

ANGEL

—Spiritual beings created by God

A. Their origin and nature
- —They are spirits...Heb 1:14
- —They were created by God...Ps 148:2,5; Col 1:16
- —They were created early in creation...Job 38:6–7
- —They were created good...Ge 1:31
- —They are not to be worshiped...Col 2:18; Rev 19:10
- —They do not marry or die...Lk 20:35–36
- —Some angels rebelled against God...2Pe 2:4

B. Names and ranks of good angels
- —Michael...Da 12:1; Jude 9; Rev 12:7
- —Gabriel...Da 9:21; Lk 1:19,26
- —Archangels...1Th 4:16
- —Seraphs...Isa 6:2
- —Cherubim...Eze 10:1–3
- —Rulers and authorities...Eph 3:10; Col 1:16
- —Thrones and powers...Col 1:16
- —There are numerous angels...Rev 5:11

C. Duties of good angels
1. General duties
   - —They revealed the law...Ac 7:38; Gal 3:19; Heb 2:2
   - —They bring messages from God...Zec 1:14–17; Ac 10:3–6
   - —They praise and worship God...Heb 1:6; Rev 5:11–12
   - —They provide for God's people...1Ki 19:5–8; Mt 4:11; Heb 1:14
   - —They protect God's people...Ps 91:11; Da 6:22; Ac 12:7–10
   - —Some serve as guardian angels...Mt 18:10; Ac 12:15
   - —They give guidance to God's people...Ac 8:26; Ac 27:23–24
   - —They interpret God's will...Da 7:16; Zec 1:9,13–14
   - —They carry out God's will...Nu 22:22; Ps 103:20–21; Mt 28:2
   - —They punish God's enemies...2Ki 19:35; Ac 12:23; Rev 14:17—16:21
2. Duties connected with Christ
   - —Gabriel announced conception to Mary...Lk 1:26–38
   - —An angel announced conception to Joseph...Mt 1:20–21
   - —An angel announced his birth...Lk 2:9–12
   - —Angels sang at his birth...Lk 2:13–14
   - —An angel warned Joseph to flee to Egypt...Mt 2:13
   - —An angel told Joseph to return...Mt 2:19–20
   - —Angels strengthened Christ...Mt 4:11; Lk 22:43
   - —Angels were available to help him...Mt 26:53
   - —An angel rolled away the stone...Mt 28:2
   - —Angels announced his resurrection...Mt 28:5–7; Lk 24:23; Jn 20:11–13
   - —Angels were present at his ascension...Ac 1:11
   - —Angels will return with Christ...Mt 25:31; 2Th 1:7

D. Evil angels
1. Satan is their leader...Job 1:6; Zec 3:1; Mt 4:10
2. Duties
   - —They oppose good angels...Rev 12:7–9
   - —They work through false teachers...2Th 2:9–10; 1Ti 4:1–2
   - —They try to separate believers from God...Ro 8:38–39
   - —They oppose Christ and his church...Rev 12:3–6,13–17
   - —They do evil to humans...Job 2:6–8; Mt 13:38–39; Lk 13:11,16
   - —They tempt humans to sin...Mt 4:3; 1Pe 5:8
   - —They accuse us before God...Zec 3:1

ANGEL OF THE LORD

A. To whom did he appear?
- —To Hagar...Ge 16:7; Ge 21:17
- —To Abraham...Ge 22:11,15
- —To Jacob...Ge 31:11–13
- —To Moses...Ex 3:2
- —To the Israelites in the exodus...Ex 14:19
- —To Balaam...Nu 22:22–36
- —To Joshua...Jdg 2:1,4
- —To Gideon...Jdg 6:11
- —To Samson's parents...Jdg 13:21–22
- —To David...1Ch 21:16
- —To Elijah...2Ki 1:3–6
- —To Daniel...Da 6:22

B. What tasks did he perform?
- —Delivered messages from the Lord...Ge 22:15–18
- —Protected God's people...2Ki 19:34–35
- —Redeemed God's people...Isa 63:9
- —Punished God's people...2Sa 24:16–17
- —Destroyed God's enemies...Ex 23:23

C. How can we identify him as God (Jesus)?
- —He uses "I" when he brings a message...Ge 16:10; Ge 22:16–17; Ge 31:13; Ex 3:6; Jdg 6:14
- —He describes himself as holy...Ex 3:2,5
- —He carries out God's judgment...2Sa 24:16; 2Ki 19:35
- —God's name is in him...Ex 23:20–23
- —He takes on a human appearance...Jos 5:13–15; Jdg 13:6,10,21

ANGER

A. Human anger
1. Expressed by such people as:
   - —Cain...Ge 4:5–6
   - —Jacob...Ge 30:2
   - —Moses...Ex 11:8
   - —Saul...1Sa 20:30
   - —David...2Sa 6:8
   - —Naaman...2Ki 5:11
   - —Nehemiah...Ne 5:6
   - —Jonah...Jnh 4:1,9
2. Control of our anger
   - —We must refrain from anger...Ps 37:8; Eph 4:31
   - —We must be slow to anger...Jas 1:19–20
   - —We must keep our temper in check...Pr 16:32
   - —In our anger we must not sin...Ps 4:4; Eph 4:26–27

3. Anger puts us in danger of hell .... Mt 5:21–22
4. We must let God avenge sin .... Ps 94:1; Ro 12:19; 2Th 1:6–8

B. The anger of Jesus
—At injustice .... Mk 3:5; Mk 10:14
—At the misuse of God's house .... Jn 2:12–17
—In the final judgment .... Rev 6:16–17

C. The anger of God
1. God's anger is righteous .... Ro 3:5–6; Rev 16:5–6
2. Reasons for his anger
—The worship of idols 1Ki 14:9,15,22; 2Ch 34:25
—Sin .... Dt 9:7; 2Ki 22:13; Ro 1:18
—Unbelief .... Ps 78:21–22; Jn 3:36
—Unjust treatment of others .... Isa 10:1–4; Am 2:6–7
—Refusal to repent .... Isa 9:13,17; Ro 2:5
3. Expressions of his anger
—In temporal judgments .... Nu 11:1,33; Isa 10:5; La 1:12
—In the day of the Lord .... Ps 110:5; Zep 1:15,18; Ro 2:5,8; Rev 11:18
4. God's control of his anger
—God is slow to anger .... Ex 34:6; Ps 103:8
—God's mercy overshadows his anger .... Ps 30:5; Isa 54:8; Hos 11:8–11
—God will turn away his anger .... Ps 78:38; Isa 48:9; Da 9:16
—Believers are spared from God's anger .... Ro 5:9; 1Th 1:10; 1Th 5:9

ANIMALS

A. Animals mentioned in the Bible
—Antelope .... Dt 14:5
—Ape 1Ki 10:22
—Baboon 1Ki 10:22
—Bear 1Sa 17:34–37
—Behemoth .... Job 40:15–24
—Camel .... Lev 11:4
—Cattle (bull, cow, calf) .... 1Sa 6:7; Ps 68:30
—Deer .... Ps 42:1
—Dog .... Mt 15:26–27
—Donkey .... Mt 21:2,5
—Fish .... Jn 21:3–11
—Fox .... Mt 8:20
—Gazelle .... Dt 14:5
—Goat .... Ge 30:35
—Horse .... Ge 47:17
—Hyena .... Isa 13:22
—Hyrax .... Lev 11:5
—Ibex .... Dt 14:5
—Jackal .... Isa 13:21
—Leopard .... Isa 11:6
—Leviathan .... Job 41:1
—Lion .... Ge 49:9
—Mole .... Isa 2:20
—Mule 2Sa 18:9
—Ox .... Ex 22:1,4
—Pig .... Mk 5:11–16
—Rabbit .... Lev 11:6
—Rat .... Isa 66:17
—Sheep (ram, ewe, lamb) .... Ge 32:14; 2Sa 12:1–4
—Weasel .... Lev 11:29
—Wolf .... Isa 11:6

B. Animals used as symbols
1. Behemoth: symbolizes power .... Job 40:15–24
2. Deer
—Symbolizes the thirsty soul .... Ps 42:1
—Symbolizes the joy of the redeemed .... Isa 35:6; Hab 3:19
3. Dog
—Symbolizes God's judgment .... 1Ki 21:19,23–24; Rev 22:15
—Symbolizes a fool .... Pr 26:11
—Symbolizes an enemy .... Ps 22:16,20
4. Donkey: symbolizes gentleness .... Zec 9:9
5. Fish
See FISH
6. Fox
—Symbolizes that which threatens us .... SS 2:15
—Symbolizes slyness .... Lk 13:32
7. Horse
See HORSE
8. Lamb
See LAMB
9. Lion
See LION
10. Ox: symbolizes faithfulness .... Isa 1:3
11. Wolf: symbolizes a false prophet .... Mt 7:15; Ac 20:29

See also BIRDS; INSECTS; REPTILES

ANNA

—A prophetess from the tribe of Asher .... Lk 2:36
—Elderly widow .... Lk 2:36–37
—Witnessed to others about baby Jesus .... Lk 2:28

ANNAS

—High priest when John the Baptist ministered .... Lk 3:2
—Father-in-law of Caiaphas, the high priest .... Jn 18:13
—Jesus on trial before him .... Jn 18:13,19–23
—Sent Jesus to Caiaphas .... Jn 18:24
—Peter and John on trial before him .... Ac 4:5–7

ANOINTING

—Pouring oil on God's servants

A. Purposes of anointing with oil
1. For beautifying oneself .... Ru 3:3; Ps 104:15
2. For healing .... Lk 10:34; Jas 5:14
3. For dedicating officials to God .... Ex 29:7; 1Sa 10:1; 1Ki 19:16
4. For dedicating things to God
—Jacob's stone pillow .... Ge 28:18
—The tabernacle and its utensils .... Ex 40:9–11

B. Which officials received an anointing?
1. In the Old Testament
a. Prophets .... 1Ki 19:16; Ps 105:15
b. Priests .... Ex 29:1,7; Lev 8:12

c. Kings
—Specific examples ... 1Sa 10:1
1Sa 16:1,13
1Ki 19:16
—Kings called "the LORD's anointed" ... 1Sa 12:3
1Sa 26:9
2Ch 6:42
2. In the New Testament
a. Jesus, anointed by the Holy Spirit
—Prophesied ... Ps 2:2
Isa 61:1
Da 9:25 – 26
—Performed at his baptism ... Mt 3:16
Jn 1:32 – 33
b. Christians, anointed by the Holy Spirit ... 2Co 1:21
1Jn 2:20,27

ANTICHRIST

A. Anyone who opposes Christ
—Called an antichrist ... 1Jn 2:18,22
1Jn 4:3
2Jn 7
—Called a false Christ ... Mt 24:24
Mk 13:22
B. *The* antichrist
1. Given the title "the antichrist" ... 1Jn 2:18
2. Symbols of the antichrist
—Daniel's little horn ... Da 7:8,24 – 26
—The king who exalts himself ... Da 11:36 – 45
—The abomination that causes desolation ... Mk 13:14
—The man of lawlessness ... 2Th 2:3 – 4,8 – 10
—The beast ... Rev 11:7
Rev 13:1,11
3. Characteristics of the antichrist
—He is controlled by Satan ... 2Th 2:9
Rev 13:2
—He opposes God ... Da 7:25
Da 11:36
2Th 2:4
Rev 13:6
—He teaches false views of Christ ... 1Jn 2:22
1Jn 4:3
2Jn 7
—He lies and deceives humanity ... 1Jn 2:22
2Jn 7
—He performs counterfeit miracles ... 2Th 2:9
Rev 13:3
Rev 19:20
—He persecutes Christians ... Rev 13:7
—He gains political control of the world ... Da 7:25
Da 11:40 – 45
Rev 13:7
—He gains economic control of the world ... Rev 13:16 – 17
—He gains religious control of the world ... 2Th 2:4
Rev 13:11 – 14
4. The end of the antichrist
—He is now being restrained ... 2Th 2:6 – 7
—He will be destroyed at Christ's return ... 2Th 2:8
—He will be thrown into the lake of fire ... Rev 19:20
Rev 20:10

ANTIOCH

A. The capital of Syria
1. Important Christian events at Antioch
—First Gentile church located there ... Ac 11:19 – 21
—Barnabas sent there ... Ac 11:22 – 24
—Paul brought there by Barnabas ... Ac 11:25 – 26
—Disciples first called Christians there ... Ac 11:26
—Agabus prophesied there ... Ac 11:27
—Peter and Paul had conflict there ... Gal 2:11 – 14
—Sent delegates to council in Jerusalem ... Ac 15:1 – 3
—Church heard report of the council ... Ac 15:22 – 31
2. Antioch as a missionary church
—Church sent out Paul and Barnabas ... Ac 13:1 – 3
—Paul and Barnabas reported to them ... Ac 14:26 – 27
—Paul's second journey began from there ... Ac 15:35 – 40
—Paul returned there after second journey ... Ac 18:22
—Paul's third journey began from there ... Ac 18:23
B. An important town in Pisidia
—Paul preached the gospel there ... Ac 13:14 – 48
—Word spread from there throughout region ... Ac 13:49
—Antioch Jews ran Paul out of town ... Ac 13:50 – 51
—Paul made brief return visit ... Ac 14:21 – 23
—Paul recalled persecution that occurred there ... 2Ti 3:11

ANXIETY

—The experience of worry and concern
A. The experience of anxiety
1. Appropriate concern
—For other family members ... 1Sa 10:2
Lk 2:48
—At the thought of having sinned ... Ps 139:23 – 24
—For not being able to understand a vision ... Da 7:15
—For the welfare of other Christians ... 2Co 11:28 – 29
Php 2:20,26,28
2. Inappropriate anxiety
—For life's basic necessities ... Ecc 2:22 – 23
Eze 4:16 – 17
Mt 6:25 – 34
Lk 12:22 – 31
—For trivial, unnecessary things ... Lk 10:41
—For the cares of this life ... Mk 4:18 – 19
3. Anxiety weighs us down ... Pr 12:25
B. The cure for anxiety
—We must not be anxious ... Ecc 11:10
Mt 6:31
1Co 7:32
—God promises to remove anxiety ... Ps 94:19
—God promises to take care of us ... Mt 6:34
1Pe 5:7
—We must rely on Jesus ... Lk 21:14 – 15
—We must pray ... Php 4:6
See also PROVIDENCE

APOLLOS

—Jewish Christian from Alexandria ... Ac 18:24 – 25
—Instructed by Aquila and Priscilla ... Ac 18:26
—Ministered at Corinth ... Ac 18:27 – 28
Ac 19:1
1Co 3:4 – 9
—Urged to revisit Corinth ... 1Co 16:12
—Messenger for Paul to Titus ... Tit 3:13

APOSTASY

—Falling away from the truth
See FALLING AWAY

APOSTLE

—Someone sent out on an official commission
A. Related themes
PETER AND PAUL is a theme of Acts ... Ac 19:11
DEFENSE is a theme of Galatians ... Gal 1:10
SELF-DEFENSE is a theme of 2 Corinthians ... 2Co 12:19
B. Jesus was an apostle, sent out by God ... Heb 3:1
C. Apostles sent out by Jesus
1. The twelve disciples as apostles
—Commissioned before his resurrection ... Mt 10:5 – 10
—Commissioned after his resurrection ... Mt 28:19
Ac 1:8

2. Paul as an apostle
   —His call from the risen Christ ... Ac 9:5–6
   Ac 22:8–10,18
   Ac 26:15–18
   —His defense of his apostleship ... 1Co 9:1–2
   2Co 10:1—11:33
   2Co 12:11–13
   Gal 1:1—2:10
   —His calling as apostle to the Gentiles ... Ro 11:13
   Ro 15:16
   Gal 2:8–9
3. Others called apostles
   —Barnabas, with Paul ... Ac 14:4
   —James, the Lord's brother ... Gal 1:19
   —Andronicus and Junias ... Ro 16:7
   —Silas and Timothy, with Paul ... 1Th 2:6

D. The duties of Christ's apostles
   —Apostleship is one of God's gifts ... 1Co 12:28
   Eph 4:11
   —Forming the foundation of the church ... Eph 2:20
   Rev 21:14
   —Witnessing about Christ ... Ac 1:8
   —Teaching true doctrine ... Ac 2:42
   —Ministering the word of God ... Ac 6:2,4
   —Making important decisions for the church ... Ac 15:1–2
   Gal 2:1–3,7–10

E. The signs of apostleship
   —Having seen the risen Christ ... Ac 1:21–22
   1Co 9:1
   —Performing signs, wonders and miracles ... 2Co 12:12
   —Being persecuted for the Lord ... Ac 5:40–41
   2Co 11:22–33

AQUILA

—Husband of Priscilla; tentmakers ... Ac 18:1–3
—Invited Paul to live with them ... Ac 18:3
—Traveled with Paul to Ephesus ... Ac 18:18–19
—Instructed Apollos ... Ac 18:26
—Paul considered him a co-worker ... Ro 16:3
—Church met in their house ... Ro 16:4

ARAM, ARAMEANS

See DAMASCUS

ARK OF THE COVENANT LAW

A. Its construction
   —Made of acacia wood, overlaid with gold ... Ex 25:10–11
   Ex 37:1–2
   —Had gold rings for poles ... Ex 25:12–15
   Ex 37:3–5
   —Its lid was the atonement cover ... Ex 25:17–21
   Ex 37:6–9

B. Its contents
   —A jar of manna ... Ex 16:32–34
   —Aaron's staff that had budded ... Nu 17:10–11
   —The Ten Commandments ... Dt 10:1–2
   1Ki 8:9
   —All three mentioned together ... Heb 9:4

C. Its symbolism
   —Symbolized God's presence among his people ... Ex 30:6
   —Symbolized the power of God ... Nu 10:35–36
   Ps 132:8
   —Sprinkled blood symbolized forgiveness of sin ... Lev 16:15–16

D. Its history
1. During the time of Moses and Joshua
   —Placed in the Most Holy Place of tabernacle ... Ex 26:34
   —Went before the Israelites on journey ... Nu 10:33
   —Instrumental in crossing the Jordan ... Jos 3:1–3,14–17
   —Instrumental in the capture of Jericho ... Jos 6:4–11
   —Joshua prayed before the ark after Ai ... Jos 7:6
   —Present at covenant renewal at Mount Ebal ... Jos 8:30–33
2. During the time of the judges
   —Placed at Shiloh during Eli's time ... 1Sa 3:3,21
   —Taken by Israelites into battle ... 1Sa 4:3–5
   —Captured by Philistines ... 1Sa 4:11,17
   —Returned by Philistines ... 1Sa 5:1—6:16
   —Desecrated at Beth Shemesh ... 1Sa 6:19–20
   —Sent to Kiriath Jearim ... 1Sa 6:21—7:2
3. During the time of David and Solomon
   —Uzzah touched the ark and was killed ... 2Sa 6:1–8
   1Ch 13:1–10
   —Ark stationed at the house of Obed-Edom ... 2Sa 6:10–11
   1Ch 13:13–14
   —David brought it to Jerusalem ... 2Sa 6:12–17
   1Ch 15:1—16:1
   —Temporarily removed under Absalom ... 2Sa 15:24–29
   —Placed in the Most Holy Place of the temple ... 1Ki 8:3–9
   2Ch 5:2–10

See also TABERNACLE

ARMAGEDDON

See MEGIDDO

ARTAXERXES

—Permitted Ezra and his group to go to Canaan ... Ezr 7:1,11–26
—Employed Nehemiah as cupbearer ... Ne 2:1
—Issued order to stop rebuilding Jerusalem ... Ezr 4:7–23
—Sent Nehemiah to rebuild walls of Jerusalem ... Ne 2:1–9
—Appointed Nehemiah as governor ... Ne 5:14

ASA

—Son of Abijah; king of Judah ... 1Ki 14:31
1Ki 15:8–10
—A godly reformer ... 1Ki 15:11–12
2Ch 15:1–19
—Removed grandmother as queen ... 1Ki 15:13
—Increased strength of Judah ... 2Ch 14:7–8
—Defeated Cushites ... 2Ch 14:9–15
—Waged war with Israel ... 1Ki 15:16–17
—Made alliance with Ben-Hadad ... 1Ki 15:18–21
2Ch 16:2–6
—Hanani prophesied against him ... 2Ch 16:7–9
—Punished by God in his death ... 2Ch 16:11–14

ASAHEL

—Nephew of David ... 1Ch 2:16
—One of David's warriors ... 1Ch 11:26
—One of David's twelve commanders ... 1Ch 27:7
—Pursued Abner ... 2Sa 2:18–22
—Killed by Abner ... 2Sa 2:23
—Death avenged by Joab ... 2Sa 3:22–27

ASAPH

A. Father of Hezekiah's recorder ... 2Ki 18:18,37
   Isa 36:3,22
B. A Levite musician ... 1Ch 15:19
   1Ch 16:4–7,37
   —Called a seer ... 2Ch 29:30
   —His descendants were singers ... 1Ch 25:1–2,6
   Ezr 2:41
   Ne 11:22–23
   —Wrote various psalms ... 2Ch 29:30
   Ps 50
   Ps 73–83

ASCENSION

—The return of Jesus to heaven

A. The event

—Prophesied in the Old Testament ... Ps 24:7–11; Ps 68:18; Ps 110:1

—Prophesied by Jesus ... Jn 7:33; Jn 13:1,3; Jn 20:17

—Recorded in the New Testament ... Mk 16:19; Lk 24:51; Ac 1:9

—Occurred forty days after the resurrection ... Ac 1:3

B. Activities of the ascended Christ

—He sat at God's right hand ... Ac 2:33; Ac 5:31; Heb 1:3

—He stood at God's right hand ... Ac 7:55–56

—He brought his atoning blood to God ... Heb 9:12

—He sent forth his Spirit ... Jn 16:7; Ac 1:4–5; Ac 2:33

—He gave gifts to humans ... Eph 4:8–10

—He is now enthroned in power ... Eph 1:20–21; Php 2:9–11; 1Pe 3:22; Rev 1:5

—He is crowned with glory and honor ... 1Ti 3:16; Heb 2:9

—He is praised by multitudes in heaven ... Rev 5:6–14; Rev 7:9–12

—He is destroying God's enemies ... 1Co 15:24–26; Heb 10:12–13

—He is interceding for us ... Ro 8:34; Heb 7:25–26; 1Jn 2:1

—He is preparing a place for us ... Jn 14:2–3

—He is preparing for us to reign with him ... 2Ti 2:12; Rev 20:5–6

—He is planning his return ... Jn 14:18,28; Ac 1:11

C. Activities of the ascended Christ on earth

—He identifies himself with believers ... Mt 25:40; Jn 17:21–23; Ac 9:4–5

—He draws believers to himself ... Eph 2:6; Col 3:1–4

—He is with Christians gathered in his name ... Mt 18:20

—He is with us always ... Mt 28:20

—He protects Christians ... Ac 18:9–10

—He directs Christians ... Ac 22:17–21

ASHER

A. Son of Jacob by Zilpah ... Ge 35:26

—Name means "happy" ... Ge 30:12–13

—Went to Egypt with family ... Ge 46:8,17

—Father of five sons ... Ge 46:17

—Blessed by Jacob ... Ge 49:20

B. Tribe descended from Asher

—Blessed by Moses ... Dt 33:24–25

—Numbered ... Nu 1:40–41; Nu 26:44–47

—Allotted land in Canaan ... Jos 19:24–31; Eze 48:2

—Failed to possess land ... Jdg 1:31–32

—Failed to support Deborah ... Jdg 5:17

—Supported Gideon ... Jdg 6:35; Jdg 7:23

—Supported David ... 1Ch 12:36

—Supported Hezekiah ... 2Ch 30:10–11

—Anna from the tribe of Asher ... Lk 2:36

—One of the tribes of the 144,000 ... Rev 7:6

ASIA

—Area east of the Aegean Sea (present-day Turkey)

A. The Jews of Asia

—Were in Jerusalem at Pentecost ... Ac 2:7–9

—Opposed Stephen ... Ac 6:9

—Incited riot against Paul in Jerusalem ... Ac 21:27–31

B. The church in Asia

1. Churches established there

—Ephesus ... Eph 1:1; Rev 2:1

—Colosse ... Col 1:1

—Laodicea ... Col 4:16; Rev 3:14

—Troas ... Ac 20:6–12

—Smyrna ... Rev 2:8

—Pergamum ... Rev 2:12

—Thyatira ... Rev 2:18

—Sardis ... Rev 3:1

—Philadelphia ... Rev 3:7

2. Events

—Paul's first convert was Epenetus ... Ro 16:5

—Paul ministered in Ephesus ... Ac 19:8–10,22; Ac 20:17–18

—Gospel went through Asia from Ephesus ... Ac 19:10,26

—Paul suffered greatly there ... 2Co 1:8–9

—Paul addressed letters to them ... Eph 1:1; Col 1:2; Col 4:16

—Peter addressed his letter to them ... 1Pe 1:1

—Timothy ministered in Ephesus ... 1Ti 1:3

—John wrote to seven churches there ... Rev 1:4

ASSURANCE

—Being certain of our salvation

A. Of what can we be sure?

—Our calling and election ... 2Pe 1:10

—God's abiding love ... Ro 8:38–39

—Being God's children ... Ro 8:16

—Our salvation at the last day ... Php 1:6; 2Ti 1:12

—Our inheritance from God ... Heb 6:11–12

—Our resurrection at the last day ... Job 19:25–26

—Seeing our ascended Lord ... 1Jn 3:2

—Receiving a crown of righteousness ... 2Ti 4:8

—Having eternal life ... 1Jn 5:13

B. How do we obtain assurance?

—By believing God's word ... 1Jn 5:13

—By accepting God's promises ... Jn 3:16,36; Jn 6:39–40; 1Jn 5:12–13

C. On what is our assurance founded?

—On God's choosing of us ... Eph 1:4–8; 1Th 1:4

—On God's keeping us safe ... Jn 6:39; Jn 10:28–30

—On God's powerful love ... Ro 8:35–39

D. What assures us of our salvation?

—The Spirit living within us ... Ro 8:14–16; Gal 4:6

—Our faith ... Ac 13:48; Ro 3:22,30; Ro 10:9–10; Eph 2:8

—Our hope ... Heb 6:11,18–19

—Our life of love and good works ... Mt 7:20
Gal 5:19–24
2Pe 1:5–8,10
1Jn 3:10–14

E. Examples of those who experienced assurance
—David ... Ps 23:6
—Old Testament saints ... Isa 32:17
—Paul ... 2Ti 1:12
2Ti 4:7–8,18
—Christians in general ... 1Jn 2:12–14

F. Assurance is compatible with
—Doubt ... Mk 9:23–24
—Sin in our lives ... Gal 6:1
1Jn 1:8–10
—Partial understanding of God's truth ... 1Co 13:8–12

ASSYRIANS

A. Their identity
—Descendants of Cush, grandson of Noah ... Ge 10:6,8–11
—Capital city is Nineveh ... Ge 10:11
See NINEVEH
—Located by the Euphrates River ... Isa 27:12–13
Jer 2:18

B. Kings of Assyria (in chronological order)
—Pul ... 2Ki 15:19
—Tiglath-Pileser ... 2Ki 15:29
—Shalmaneser ... 2Ki 17:3–4
—Sargon ... Isa 20:1
—Sennacherib ... 2Ki 18:13
—Esarhaddon ... 2Ki 19:37
—Ashurbanipal ... Ezr 4:10

C. Campaigns against God's people
1. Against the northern kingdom
—First invasion ... 2Ki 15:19
—Received tribute money and withdrew ... 2Ki 15:19–20
—Second invasion ... 2Ki 15:29
—Territories annexed and people deported ... 2Ki 15:29
—Hoshea refused to submit ... 2Ki 17:3–4
—Three-year siege of Samaria ... 2Ki 17:5
2Ki 18:9
—Samaria captured and people deported ... 2Ki 17:6
2Ki 18:10–11
—Other people settled in Samaria ... 2Ki 17:24
2. Against the southern kingdom
—King Ahaz allied with Assyria ... 2Ki 16:7–9
2Ch 28:16–18
—Assyria did not help Ahaz ... 2Ch 28:19–21
—Hezekiah refused to pay tribute ... 2Ki 18:7
—Sennacherib attacked cities of Judah ... 2Ki 18:13
—Hezekiah paid tribute from temple riches ... 2Ki 18:14–16
—Sennacherib attacked Jerusalem ... 2Ki 18:17—19:13
2Ch 32:9–19
Isa 36:1—37:13
—Hezekiah prayed for deliverance ... 2Ki 19:14–19
Isa 37:14–20
—Isaiah prophesied the fall of Assyria ... 2Ki 19:20–34
Isa 37:21–35
—The defeat of Assyria and Sennacherib ... 2Ki 19:35–36
2Ch 32:20–21
Isa 37:36–38

D. Important data concerning them
1. Garden of Eden in vicinity of Asshur ... Ge 2:14
2. Country of Assyria was beautiful ... Eze 31:3–9
3. Character of the Assyrians
—A godless nation ... Isa 10:6
—A powerful nation ... 2Ki 19:11,17
Isa 28:2
—A proud nation ... 2Ki 19:23–24
Isa 10:12
Eze 31:3,10
—A cruel nation ... Na 3:1–4
4. God used Assyrians to punish Israelites ... 2Ki 17:7–17
Isa 7:17–25
Isa 10:5–6
5. Prophecies concerning them
—Assyrians to be destroyed ... Isa 10:5,12–19
Isa 30:31–33
Na 2:1–13
Zep 2:13–15
—Israelites to be called back from Assyria ... Isa 11:11–16
Isa 27:12–13
Hos 11:11
Mic 7:11–12
Zec 10:8–12
—Assyrians to worship the Lord someday ... Isa 19:23–25

ATHALIAH

—Daughter of Ahab ... 2Ki 8:26
—Wife of Jehoram and mother of Ahaziah ... 2Ki 8:18,26
2Ch 22:2
—Made herself queen by killing Ahaziah's sons ... 2Ki 11:1–2
2Ch 22:10–12
—Ruled for six years ... 2Ki 11:3
—Killed when Joash was made king ... 2Ki 11:4–16
2Ch 23:1–15

ATHLETICS

A. References to athletic activities in the Bible
—Wrestling ... Ge 32:24–25
—Slinging ... Jdg 20:16
—Archery ... 1Sa 20:18–22, 35–40
—Running ... 2Sa 18:19–26
—Boxing ... 1Co 9:26
—Competing in the games ... 1Co 9:25

B. Athletics used in symbolic ways
1. Archery: Job felt like God's target ... Job 16:12–13
2. Ball-throwing: symbol of God's judgment ... Isa 22:17–18
3. Running races
—Running in the path of God's commands ... Ps 119:32
—Running the Christian race ... Heb 12:1–2
—Not running in vain ... Gal 2:2
Php 2:16
4. Wrestling: symbol of struggling with Satan ... Eph 6:12
5. The games
—The necessity of strict training ... 1Co 9:24–27
—Competing according to the rules ... 2Ti 2:5
6. The crown or prize awaiting believers ... 1Co 9:25
Php 3:13–14
2Ti 2:5
2Ti 4:8
1Pe 5:4

ATONEMENT

—Procedure of reconciling sinners to God

A. Elements involved in atonement
—Sin of humanity ... Isa 6:7
Isa 27:9
Da 9:24
Jn 1:29
—Blood must be shed ... Lev 16:14,18
Heb 9:19–22
—Substitutionary sacrifice is offered ... Lev 4:13–20
Lev 5:5–10
Isa 53:4–7
1Jn 2:2
—Guilt is transferred to the substitute ... Lev 1:3–4
Lev 16:21–22
2Co 5:21
—Forgiveness is granted ... Lev 4:26,31,35
Ro 3:23–25

B. Old Testament Day of Atonement
—Description of the Day of Atonement ... Lev 16:2 – 34
Lev 23:26 – 32
Nu 29:7 – 11
—Involved only the high priest ... Heb 9:7
—Performed in the Most Holy Place ... Lev 16:2,16 – 20
Heb 9:8,25
—Done once a year ... Ex 30:10
Lev 16:34
Heb 9:7
—Year of Jubilee began on Day of Atonement ... Lev 25:9
C. Atonement accomplished by Christ
1. Symbolized in Old Testament sacrifices
—The Passover lamb ... Ex 12:1 – 7,12 – 13
1Co 5:7
—A lamb that takes away sin ... Isa 53:7
Jn 1:29,36
1Pe 1:18 – 19
Rev 5:6
—The Day of Atonement ... Heb 9:7 – 14,23 – 28
2. Fulfilled in the New Testament
—Sacrifice of Christ atones for sin ... Ro 3:25
1Co 5:7
Heb 9:28
1Jn 2:2
1Jn 4:10
—Christ presented his blood to God ... Heb 9:12,14
3. The results of Christ's atoning blood
—Our sins are forgiven ... Eph 1:7
—We are purified from sin ... 1Jn 1:7
—We are freed from sin ... Rev 1:5
—We are redeemed ... Ro 3:24 – 25
1Pe 1:18
—We are saved ... Ro 5:9
—We are reconciled with God ... Ro 5:10
Col 1:20
—We have peace with God ... Col 1:20
—We are made holy ... Heb 13:12
—We are reconciled to other Christians ... Eph 2:14 – 17
—The power of the devil is destroyed ... Col 2:15
Heb 2:14

AUTHORITY

—The ability to exercise power over others
A. Related themes
1. AUTHORITY is a theme of:
—Matthew ... Mt 7:29
—John ... Jn 10:18
2. LEADERSHIP is a theme of:
—Ezra ... Ezr 7:10
—Nehemiah ... Ne 13:25
—1 Timothy ... 1Ti 4:16
B. Human authority
1. Given as a gift from God and Christ
—To humans for ruling creation ... Ge 1:28
Ps 8:6 – 8
—To kings for ruling people ... Ps 72:1
Ro 13:1 – 5
—To prophets for speaking ... Dt 18:18
—To disciples for casting out demons ... Mk 6:7,13
—To apostles for forgiving sins ... Jn 20:22 – 23
—To apostles for founding the church ... Mt 16:19
Mt 18:18
—To church leaders for building the church ... 2Co 10:8
2Co 13:10
Eph 4:11 – 13
Tit 2:15
—To saints for judging the world ... 1Co 6:2 – 3
2. Exercised by humans
—Often done by exerting power ... Mt 20:25
Mk 10:42
Lk 22:25
—Christian authority defined by service ... Mt 20:26 – 28
Mk 10:43 – 45
Lk 22:26 – 27
See SERVANT
3. Misused by humans
—In ascribing power to ourselves, not God ... Dt 8:10 – 18
—In depending on ourselves, not God ... Ps 147:10 – 11
—In oppressing the poor ... Ps 10:2 – 11
—In exalting power rather than wisdom ... Ecc 9:12 – 18
C. Divine authority
1. Authority of God
—Power and authority ascribed to him ... 2Ch 20:6
Ps 66:3,5 – 7
Jude 25
—His authority may not be questioned ... Ro 9:20 – 21
—Even Satan under his control ... Job 1:6 – 12
Job 2:1 – 7
2. Authority of Jesus
a. While on earth
—To cast out evil spirits ... Mk 1:34
—To preach the word ... Mt 7:28 – 29
—To forgive sins ... Mk 2:5 – 12
—To give eternal life ... Jn 17:2
—To control nature ... Mk 4:39 – 41
—To raise the dead ... Jn 10:17 – 18
Jn 11:23 – 27,38 – 44
—To judge ... Jn 5:27 – 30
b. Now in heaven
—All authority given to him ... Mt 28:18
Php 2:9 – 11
—Has authority at God's right hand ... Eph 1:20 – 23
Col 2:9 – 10
—Controls history ... Rev 5:1 – 5
—Is ruler of the kings of the earth ... Rev 1:5
—Is King of kings and Lord of lords ... Rev 17:14
Rev 19:16

AWE

—Reverence for the Lord
See FEAR

BAASHA

—Killed Nadab to become king of Israel ... 1Ki 15:27 – 28
—Killed rest of Jeroboam's family ... 1Ki 15:29 – 30
—Fought against Asa of Judah ... 1Ki 15:16 – 22,32
—Evil reign for twenty-four years ... 1Ki 15:33 – 34
—Jehu prophesied against him ... 1Ki 16:1 – 4
—Family killed by Zimri ... 1Ki 16:9 – 13

BABYLON

A. Identity and early history of the city
—Descendants of Ham ... Ge 10:6,8 – 10
—City is built by Nimrod ... Ge 10:8 – 10
—Rebellion against God at the tower of Babel ... Ge 11:1 – 9
B. The nation of Babylon
1. Significant Babylonians
—Merodach-Baladan: paid visit to Hezekiah ... 2Ki 20:12 – 13
—Nebuchadnezzar ... 2Ki 24:1
See NEBUCHADNEZZAR
—Nebuzaradan: commander of army ... 2Ki 24:8
—Evil-Merodach: released Jehoiachin ... 2Ki 25:27
—Belshazzar: saw handwriting on the wall ... Da 5:1
2. Chronological history
—Under the control of Assyria ... 2Ki 17:24
—Envoys visited Hezekiah ... 2Ki 20:12 – 18
—Invaded Judah during Jehoiakim's reign ... 2Ki 24:1 – 2

—Exiles deported with Jehoiachin .... 2Ki 24:10 – 16
—Nebuchadnezzar's dream .... Da 2:1 – 49
—Nebuchadnezzar's image and fiery furnace .. Da 3:1 – 30
—King Zedekiah's revolt 2Ch 36:13
—Nebuchadnezzar marched on Jerusalem .... Jer 52:4 – 5
—Jerusalem totally destroyed .... 2Ki 25:4,8 – 10
Jer 52:12 – 14
—A second group deported 2Ki 25:11
2Ch 36:20
—Nebuchadnezzar's madness and restoration .... Da 4:1 – 37
—A third group deported .... Jer 52:24 – 27
—King Belshazzar's banquet .... Da 5:1 – 4
—Medes took over Babylon .... Da 5:30 – 31

3. Jews in Babylon
—Three waves of exiles .... Jer 52:28 – 30
—Daniel and friends in royal service .... Da 1:1 – 21
—Ezekiel saw visions .... Eze 1:1 – 28
—Jews encouraged to settle there .... Jer 29:1 – 7
—Seventy years of exile .... Jer 25:11
2Ch 36:21
—Jews experienced grief .... Ps 137:1 – 6
—Jews allowed to return under Persians .... 2Ch 36:22 – 23
Ezr 1:1 – 4

4. Characteristics of the Babylonians
a. A powerful nation
—A naval power .... Isa 43:14
—A military power .... Jer 5:15 – 17
Jer 51:34
—A worldwide kingdom .... Da 2:37 – 38
Da 4:22
—A glorious nation .... Da 4:28 – 30,36
—A wealthy people .... Jer 51:13
b. A wicked nation
—They trusted in wickedness .... Isa 47:10
—They were idolatrous .... Jer 50:38
—They engaged in sacrilegious feasting .... Da 5:1 – 3
—They were cruel .... Isa 14:4,16 – 17
Hab 1:6 – 7
—They showed arrogance against God .... Isa 14:13 – 14

5. Prophecies concerning Babylon
—They will conquer the world .... Jer 21:3 – 10
Jer 27:1 – 11
Eze 21:18 – 23
Eze 29:19
—They will be destroyed .... Isa 13:1—14:23
Isa 14:3 – 22
Isa 21:1 – 10
Isa 47:1 – 15
Jer 50:1—51:58

C. New Testament references to Babylon
1. As a symbol of the Roman Empire 1Pe 5:13
2. As a symbol of the power of the antichrist
—Inspires people to sin .... Rev 14:8
Rev 18:2 – 5
—Persecutes the church .... Rev 17:5 – 6
Rev 18:24
—Makes war with the Lamb .... Rev 17:9 – 18
—Will be destroyed completely .... Rev 18:2 – 10,16 – 24

BALAAM

A. Personal data
—Son of Beor .... Nu 22:5
—Lived in Mesopotamia .... Dt 23:4
—Considered a prophet 2Pe 2:16
—Killed by Israelites .... Nu 31:8
Jos 13:22

B. His history
—Asked by Balak to curse Israelites .... Nu 22:4 – 8
—Commanded by God not to go .... Nu 22:9 – 13
—Asked by Balak a second time .... Nu 22:15 – 17
—Permitted to go .... Nu 22:18 – 20
—Met by an angel on the way .... Nu 22:21 – 35
—Uttered blessings instead of curses .... Nu 23:1—24:10
—Prophesied about Christ .... Nu 24:15 – 19
—Advised Balak to intermarry with Israelites .... Nu 31:15 – 16
—Returned home .... Nu 24:25

C. New Testament references
—Considered an example of greed .... 2Pe 2:14 – 15
Jude 11
—Considered a teacher of immorality .... Rev 2:14

BALAK

—Moabite king, frightened by Israelites .... Nu 22:1 – 4
—Hired Balaam to curse Israelites .... Nu 22:4 – 20
Jos 24:9
—Encouraged Moabites to marry Israelites .... Rev 2:14

BANNER

—A flag or insignia

A. How banners were used
—To designate different families .... Nu 2:2
—To rally troops .... SS 6:4
—To send messages .... Isa 13:2
Isa 18:3

B. The banner used as a symbol
—The Lord as our Banner .... Ex 17:15
—Jesus Christ as a banner for all nations .... Isa 11:10
—The banner of love .... SS 2:4
—God rallies us to his banner .... Ps 60:4
—God rallies all nations to his banner .... Isa 11:12
Isa 49:22 – 23
—We lift up victory banners .... Ps 20:5
—We raise a banner for the nations .... Isa 62:10 – 11
—God rallies armies to use in judgment .... Isa 5:26 – 29
Isa 13:2

BAPTISM

—The sacrament of initiation

A. Baptism of John the Baptist
—Where John baptized .... Jn 1:28
Jn 3:23
—He baptized many people .... Mt 3:5 – 6
—He baptized Jesus .... Mt 3:13 – 15
—His baptism symbolized repentance .... Mt 3:11
—His baptism meant to reveal Jesus .... Jn 1:31
—His baptism looked ahead to Spirit baptism .... Lk 3:16

B. Baptism by Jesus' disciples .... Jn 3:22
Jn 4:1 – 2

C. Christian baptism
1. It was commanded by Jesus .... Mt 28:19 – 20
Mk 16:16
2. It was done in the name
—Of the Father, the Son, the Holy Spirit .... Mt 28:19
—Of Jesus Christ .... Ac 2:38
Ac 10:48
—Of the Lord Jesus .... Ac 19:5
3. It was typified in the Old Testament
—In the story of the flood .... 1Pe 3:19 – 21
—In the rite of circumcision .... Col 2:11 – 12
—In the crossing of the Red Sea 1Co 10:2
4. Occurrences of Christian baptism
—Three thousand on Pentecost .... Ac 2:41
—New believers in Samaria .... Ac 8:12
—Ethiopian eunuch .... Ac 8:36 – 38
—Saul at his conversion .... Ac 9:18
—Cornelius and his friends .... Ac 10:48
—Lydia and her household .... Ac 16:15
—Philippian jailer and his household .... Ac 16:33
—New believers in Corinth .... Ac 18:8

—Gaius, Crispus, household of Stephanas....... 1Co 1:14 – 16
—New believers at Ephesus .... Ac 19:1 – 7

5. Symbolism of Christian baptism
—Forgiveness of sins........ Ac 2:38
—Washing away of sin........ Ac 22:16
—Spiritual rebirth........ Tit 3:5
—Salvation........ 1Pe 3:21
—Dying with Christ........ Ro 6:3 – 4
Col 2:12
—Spiritual circumcision........ Col 2:11 – 12
—Inclusion in the body of Christ........ 1Co 12:13
—Unity in the body of Christ........ Eph 4:3 – 6
—Being clothed with Christ........ Gal 3:27

6. Characteristics of Christian baptism
—Only one baptism........ Eph 4:5
—Done with water........ Ac 8:36 – 38
Ac 10:47
—Faith is essential........ Mk 16:16
Ac 8:12
Ac 16:31 – 34
—Repentance is essential........ Ac 2:38
—Linked with receiving the Holy Spirit........ Ac 2:38
Ac 10:44 – 48
Ac 19:2 – 6
—Separated from receiving the Spirit........ Ac 8:14 – 17
—Administered to households........ Ac 16:15,33
1Co 1:16

BAPTISM OF THE HOLY SPIRIT

A. Jesus was baptized with the Holy Spirit........ Mt 3:16
Jn 1:32 – 33

B. Jesus baptized with the Holy Spirit
—Prophesied by John........ Mt 3:11
Lk 3:16
—Prophesied by Jesus........ Ac 1:5
—Fulfilled at Pentecost........ Ac 2:1 – 4

C. Relationship to water baptism
—Water baptism linked with Spirit baptism........ Ac 2:38 – 39
Ac 9:17 – 18
Ac 10:44 – 48
Ac 19:1 – 6
—Water baptism separated from Spirit baptism........ Ac 8:12,14 – 17
—Born of water and the Spirit........ Jn 3:5
—Baptized by one Spirit into one body........ 1Co 12:13
—Washing of rebirth and renewal by Spirit........ Tit 3:5

BARABBAS

—Prisoner at the time of Jesus........ Mt 27:16
—Committed murder and insurrection........ Mk 15:7
Jn 18:40
—Received freedom in place of Jesus........ Mt 27:17 – 26
Ac 3:13 – 14

BARAK

—Warrior who fought with Deborah against Sisera........ Jdg 4:6 – 16
—Sang song with Deborah........ Jdg 5:1 – 31
—Considered an example of faith........ Heb 11:32

BARNABAS

A. Personal data
—Originally named Joseph........ Ac 4:36
—Full of the Holy Spirit and faith........ Ac 11:24
—Sold property, brought proceeds to the church........ Ac 4:37
—Considered a prophet and teacher........ Ac 13:1
—Considered an apostle........ Ac 14:14

B. Relationship with Paul
—Brought Paul to the apostles........ Ac 9:27
—Brought Paul to Antioch........ Ac 11:25 – 26
—Brought gift with Paul to Jerusalem........ Ac 11:28 – 29
—Accompanied Paul on missionary journey........ Ac 13 – 14
—Went to Jerusalem for conference........ Ac 15:1 – 2,12
Gal 2:1 – 9
—Conflict with Paul over John Mark........ Ac 15:36 – 40
—Conflict with Paul over eating with Gentiles........ Gal 2:11 – 13
—Co-worker with Paul........ 1Co 9:6
Col 4:10

BARTHOLOMEW

—Disciple of Jesus........ Mk 3:18
—One of the apostles........ Mt 10:3
Ac 1:13
—Probably also known as Nathanael........ Jn 1:45 – 49

BARUCH

—Son of Neriah........ Jer 32:12
—Jeremiah's secretary and friend........ Jer 32:12 – 16
Jer 36:4 – 32
—Forced to go to Egypt........ Jer 43:1 – 7
—Received comforting message from Jeremiah........ Jer 45:1 – 5

BARZILLAI

—Gileadite who aided David........ 2Sa 17:27 – 29
—Unable to go with David because of age........ 2Sa 19:31 – 39

BATHSHEBA

—Wife of Uriah........ 2Sa 11:3
—Committed adultery with David........ 2Sa 11:4
—Sent message she was pregnant........ 2Sa 11:5
—Became wife of David after Uriah was killed........ 2Sa 11:27
—First child died........ 2Sa 12:13 – 23
—Mother of Solomon........ 2Sa 12:24
—Influenced David to make Solomon king........ 1Ki 1:11 – 31
—Pleaded with Solomon for Adonijah........ 1Ki 2:13 – 25

BEERSHEBA

A. History of Beersheba
—Southernmost city in the land of Israel........ Jdg 20:1
—Hagar fled there from Sarah........ Ge 21:14 – 19
—Abraham made a treaty with Abimelech there........ Ge 21:22 – 31
—Abraham lived there a while........ Ge 22:19
—Isaac made a treaty with Abimelech there........ Ge 26:23 – 33
—Jacob stopped there on the way to Egypt........ Ge 46:1 – 5
—Allotted to tribe of Judah........ Jos 15:21,28
—Later allotted to tribe of Simeon........ Jos 19:1 – 2
—Samuel's sons served as judges there........ 1Sa 8:1 – 3
—Elijah escaped there from Jezebel........ 1Ki 19:3
—Became a center of idolatry........ 2Ki 23:8
Am 8:14
—Resettled after the exile........ Ne 11:27,30

B. Appearances of God there
—To Hagar, to give her water........ Ge 21:17 – 19
—To Isaac, to bless him........ Ge 26:23 – 25
—To Jacob, to reassure him........ Ge 46:1 – 4
—To Elijah, to strengthen him........ 1Ki 19:3 – 7

BELSHAZZAR

—King of Babylon........ Da 7:1
—Gave a huge feast........ Da 5:1 – 4
—Saw handwriting on the wall........ Da 5:5 – 29
—Killed by the Medes........ Da 5:30 – 31

BENEVOLENCE

See THE RICH AND THE POOR; STEWARDSHIP

BEN-HADAD

A. King of Damascus........ 1Ki 15:18
—Made treaty with Asa........ 1Ki 15:18 – 19
—Fought against Israelite cities........ 1Ki 15:20 – 21

B. Another king of Damascus........ 1Ki 20:1
—Fought against Ahab........ 1Ki 20:2 – 12

—Defeated by Ahab 1Ki 20:13–21
—Fought Israel again the next year........ 1Ki 20:26–28
—Again defeated by Ahab........ 1Ki 20:29–30
—Made peace with Israelites 1Ki 20:31–34
—Later besieged Samaria 2Ki 6:24
—Siege miraculously lifted........ 2Ki 7:5–7
—Killed by Hazael 2Ki 8:7–15
C. Another king of Damascus 2Ki 13:24
—Son of Hazael........ 2Ki 13:24
—Defeated by Jehoash three times........ 2Ki 13:25
—Amos prophesied against him .... Am 1:3–5

BENJAMIN

A. Twelfth son of Jacob, second of Rachel........ Ge 35:16–24
—Name means "son of my right hand"........ Ge 35:16–18
—Favored by Jacob........ Ge 42:4
—Accompanied brothers to Egypt........ Ge 43:1–15
—Royal cup found in his sack .... Ge 44:1–13
—Judah interceded for him........ Ge 44:18–34
—Moved to Egypt with his family........ Ge 46:8,19
—Father of ten sons .... Ge 46:21
—Blessed by Jacob........ Ge 49:27
B. Tribe descended from Benjamin
—Blessed by Moses........ Dt 33:12
—Numbered........ Nu 1:36–37
Nu 26:38–41
—Allotted land........ Jos 18:11–28
—Failed to possess land fully........ Jdg 1:21
—Nearly obliterated........ Jdg 20–21
—King Saul from this tribe 1Sa 10:20–24
—Sided with Ish-Bosheth after Saul's death........ 2Sa 2:8–11
—Turned to David........ 1Ch 12:23,29
—The apostle Paul was from this tribe .... Ro 11:1
Php 3:5
—One of the tribes of the 144,000 .... Rev 7:8

BETHANY

—A town on the Mount of Olives........ Lk 19:29
—Less than two miles from Jerusalem .... Jn 11:18
—The hometown of Mary, Martha and Lazarus........ Jn 11:1
—Jesus stayed there after Triumphal Entry........ Mk 11:11
—Jesus anointed by Mary there........ Mt 26:6–13
Mk 14:3–9
Jn 12:1–8
—Jesus ascended into heaven from there........ Lk 24:50–51

BETHEL

A. Identity of Bethel
—Originally called Luz........ Ge 28:19
—Close to Ai........ Jos 12:9
—On the border between Ephraim and Benjamin........ Jos 16:1–2
Jos 18:11–13
—Originally given to Benjamin .... Jos 18:21–22
—Later belonged to Ephraim .... Jdg 4:5
1Ch 7:20,28
—Southernmost city of northern kingdom 1Ki 12:26–29
B. History of Bethel
—Abram built an altar near there........ Ge 12:8
Ge 13:3
—Jacob had a dream there........ Ge 28:10–17
—Jacob returned there with his family........ Ge 35:1–7
—Ephraim attacked the city and took it .... Jdg 1:22–26
—Samuel served as judge there........ 1Sa 7:15–16
—Prophet spoke against Jeroboam there........ 1Ki 13:1–6
—Abijah captured it from Jeroboam........ 2Ch 13:19–20
—Youths mocked Elisha and were killed........ 2Ki 2:23–24
—Amos prophesied against Israel there........ Am 7:10–13
—Josiah destroyed Jeroboam's altars 2Ki 23:15
—Resettled after exile........ Ne 11:31
C. Religious importance of Bethel
—God appeared to Jacob there .... Ge 28:10–19
Ge 35:9–15
—God was "the God of Bethel"........ Ge 31:13
—People inquired of the Lord there........ Jdg 20:18
Jdg 21:2–3
—The ark was kept there for a while .... Jdg 20:26–27
—Jeroboam set up golden calf there........ 1Ki 12:28–32
—A company of prophets lived there 2Ki 2:2–3,23
—Became known for its idolatry........ Am 4:4
—Prophesied against because of idolatry........ Hos 10:15
Am 3:14
Am 5:5–6

BETHLEHEM

A. Identity of Bethlehem
—Originally called Ephrath........ Ge 35:19
—A city given to Judah........ Ru 1:1
—Known as "the town of David"........ Lk 2:4,11
B. Important events at Bethlehem
—Rachel buried there........ Ge 35:19–20
—Ibzan judged there........ Jdg 12:8–10
—Home of Elimelech and Naomi........ Ru 1:1,19–22
—Ruth married Boaz there........ Ru 4:11–13
—David anointed king there........ 1Sa 16:4–13
—Philistines controlled it for a while........ 2Sa 23:14–17
—Rehoboam fortified it 2Ch 11:5–6
C. Jesus and Bethlehem
—Micah prophesied Messiah to be born there........ Mic 5:2
Mt 2:3–6
Jn 7:42
—Jesus was born in Bethlehem........ Mt 2:1
Lk 2:1–7
—Herod killed babies there .... Mt 2:16–18

BETHSAIDA

—A town in Galilee........ Jn 12:21
—Three of the disciples came from there........ Jn 1:44
—Feeding of five thousand occurred there .... Lk 9:10–17
—Jesus healed a blind man there........ Mk 8:22–26
—Jesus denounced it for unbelief........ Mt 11:20–22
Lk 10:13–14

BEZALEL

—Craftsman filled with God's Spirit........ Ex 31:1–3
Ex 35:30–31
—Supervised building of the tabernacle .... Ex 31:4–11
Ex 36:1–5

BILDAD

—One of Job's friends who tried to comfort him........ Job 2:11–13
—His first speech........ Job 8:1–22
—His second speech........ Job 18:1–21
—His third speech........ Job 25:1–6
—Offered sacrifices to God after Job's restoration........ Job 42:7–9

BILHAH

—Servant of Rachel........ Ge 29:29
—Mother of Dan and Naphtali........ Ge 30:1–7
Ge 35:25
—Reuben slept with her........ Ge 35:22

BIRDS

A. Birds mentioned in the Bible
—Bat........ Lev 11:19
—Birds of prey........ Ge 15:11
—Carrion birds .... Eze 39:4
—Chicken........ Mt 23:37
—Cormorant .... Lev 11:17

—Dove … SS 2:12,14
—Eagle … Jer 49:16
—Falcon … Dt 14:13
—Gull … Lev 11:16
—Hawk … Lev 11:16
—Heron … Lev 11:19
—Hoopoe … Lev 11:19
—Kite (various types) … Lev 11:14
—Mourning dove … Isa 38:14
—Osprey … Lev 11:18
—Ostrich … Job 39:13 – 18
—Owl (various types) … Isa 34:11
—Partridge … 1Sa 26:20
—Pigeon … Lev 5:7,11
—Quail … Nu 11:31 – 32
—Raven … Ge 8:7
—Rooster … Mt 26:74
—Sparrow … Ps 84:3
—Stork … Lev 11:19
—Swallow … Pr 26:2
—Swift … Jer 8:7
—Thrush … Jer 8:7
—Vulture (various types) … Lev 11:13

B. Birds used as symbols
1. The dove
—Symbolizes mourning … Isa 38:14; Isa 59:11
—Symbolizes renewal … Ge 8:10 – 12
—Symbolizes the Holy Spirit … Mt 3:16
—Symbolizes innocence … Mt 10:16
2. The eagle
—Symbolizes deliverance … Ex 19:4; Rev 12:14
—Symbolizes power … Jer 4:13; Eze 17:3,7
—Symbolizes youthfulness … Ps 103:5; Isa 40:31
3. The sparrow
—Symbolizes God's protecting care … Ps 84:3; Mt 10:29 – 31

BLASPHEMY

—Bringing reproach against God

A. How can one blaspheme God?
—By speaking against God … Lev 24:11,16; Mt 26:64 – 65; Ac 6:11
—By speaking against God's word … Ac 6:11
—By engaging in idolatry … Ne 9:18,26; Eze 20:27 – 28
—By persecuting the church … 1Ti 1:13
—By oppressing the poor … Jas 2:2 – 7
—By bearing a sacrilegious name … Rev 13:1

B. Regulations concerning blasphemy
—Prohibited by the law of God … Ex 20:7; Ex 22:28
—Punishable by death … Lev 24:13 – 16,23; Mt 26:65 – 66

C. Jesus is charged with blasphemy
—For claiming to forgive sins … Mt 9:2 – 3; Mk 2:7
—For claiming to be Son of Man … Mt 26:64 – 65
—For claiming to be God … Jn 10:33

D. Blasphemy against Holy Spirit
—Linked with calling Jesus an agent of Satan … Mt 12:24 – 27; Mk 3:22 – 26
—Considered an unforgivable sin … Mt 12:31 – 32; Mk 3:29; Lk 12:10

BLESSING

A. Human blessings
1. Blessing sacred things
—Sacrifices … 1Sa 9:13
—The cup in the Lord's Supper … 1Co 10:16
2. Blessing other human beings
—A father blesses his sons … Ge 27:1 – 40; Ge 48:15 – 16
—A family blesses a daughter leaving … Ge 24:60
—Moses blesses the Israelites … Dt 33
—Leaders bless the people … Ex 39:43; Jos 22:6 – 7; 2Sa 6:18; 1Ki 8:14; 2Ch 31:8
—Priests bless the people … Nu 6:24 – 26; 1Sa 2:20; 2Ch 30:27
—A prophet blesses the people … Nu 23:11,25 – 26
—The people bless the king … 1Ki 8:66
—A blessing used as a greeting … Ru 2:4; 1Sa 15:13
—Children bless their mother … Pr 31:28
—The command to bless one's enemies … Lk 6:28; Ro 12:14

B. Divine blessings
1. What/whom does God bless?
—Nature … Ge 1:22
—The Sabbath … Ex 20:11
—The work of his people … Dt 28:8,12
—Humanity in general … Ge 1:28
—His covenant people … Ge 9:1; Ge 24:1; Dt 2:7
—God-fearing individuals … Ps 1:1 – 3; Pr 3:13; Pr 16:20
—Those who live by godly principles … Ps 41:1; Pr 14:21; Mt 5:3 – 11
—The home of the righteous … Pr 3:33
—Nations other than Israel … Ge 39:5; Isa 19:25; Jer 4:2
2. What are God's blessings?
a. Material blessings given to us
—General statements … Dt 7:13 – 14; Dt 28:2 – 14
—Peace and prosperity … Eze 34:26
—Health, happiness and long life … Ps 21:3 – 5
—Children and a happy home … Ps 128:1 – 6
—Abundant crops and food … Ps 67:6 – 7; Mal 3:10 – 12; Ac 14:17
—Showers of blessing … Eze 34:26 – 30
b. Spiritual blessings given to us
—General statements … Jn 1:16 – 17; 1Co 9:23; Eph 1:3
—God's favor and grace … Ps 5:12
—Forgiveness of sins … Ps 32:1 – 2; Ro 4:7 – 8
—Salvation … Ro 10:12 – 13
—Being part of God's people … Ro 15:27
—Eternal joy … Ps 21:6
—Spiritual strength and peace … Ps 29:11
—Having God as a shepherd … Ps 28:9
c. The blessing of Abraham
—First mentioned to Abram … Ge 12:2 – 3
—Repeated to Abraham … Ge 22:17 – 18

—Repeated to Isaac .... Ge 26:3 – 5
—Repeated to Jacob .... Ge 28:13 – 15
—Repeated regarding David's line .... Ps 72:17
—Fulfilled in Christ for the Jews .... Ac 3:24 – 26
—Fulfilled in Christ for the Gentiles .... Gal 3:8 – 9,14

3. Who are blessed by the Lord?
—Those who avoid sin .... Ps 1:1
—Those who take refuge in the Lord .... Ps 2:12
—Those whose sins are forgiven .... Ps 32:1
—Those who trust in the Lord .... Ps 40:4
—Those who show concern for the weak .... Ps 41:1
—Those chosen by the Lord .... Ps 65:4
—Those who dwell in God's house .... Ps 84:4
—Those disciplined by the Lord .... Ps 94:12
—Those who fear the Lord .... Ps 112:1
—Those who walk according to God's law .... Ps 119:1 – 2
—Those who find wisdom in the Lord .... Pr 3:13
—Those who wait for the Lord .... Isa 30:18
—Those who follow the way of Jesus .... Mt 5:3 – 12; Lk 6:20 – 22
—Those who confess Jesus as God's Son .... Mt 16:16 – 17
—Those who hear and obey God's word .... Lk 11:28
—Those who persevere in their faith .... Jas 1:12
—Those who die in the Lord .... Rev 14:13
—Those invited to Christ's marriage feast .... Rev 19:9

BLOOD

A. Blood referred to literally
—In a human being 2Sa 20:12
—In an animal .... Ge 9:4

B. Blood used as a symbol

1. Blood symbolizes life
—Abel's blood meant his life .... Ge 4:10
—Eating blood means eating life .... Dt 12:23
—"Shedding blood" means taking a life .... Ge 9:5 – 6; Hab 2:8,17; Mt 27:24
—"Being innocent of blood" means not being responsible for physical death .... Mt 27:24
—"Being innocent of blood" means not being responsible for spiritual death .... Eze 3:17 – 19; Ac 18:6

2. Blood used in Old Testament sacrifices
—Examples .... Lev 1:5,11; Lev 3:2,8,13; Lev 16:14 – 16
—Shed blood symbolized forgiveness .... Lev 17:11; Heb 9:22

3. The blood shed by Christ

a. What happened to it
—It flowed from the cross .... Jn 19:34
—It was presented to God in heaven .... Heb 9:12,24 – 28

b. What it accomplishes
—Our forgiveness .... Eph 1:7; Heb 9:22; Rev 1:5
—Our redemption .... Ac 20:28; Heb 9:12; 1Pe 1:18 – 19
—Our atonement .... Ro 3:25
—Our justification .... Ro 5:9
—Our reconciliation .... Eph 2:13 – 16
—Our cleansing .... Heb 9:14; 1Jn 1:7; Rev 7:14
—Our holiness .... Heb 10:29; Heb 13:12
—Our new life .... Jn 6:53 – 56
—Establishment of the new covenant .... Lk 22:20; 1Co 11:25
—Power over Satan .... Rev 12:11

BOASTING

See PRIDE

BOAZ

—Bethlehemite .... Ru 2:1
—Acted kindly to Ruth .... Ru 2:8 – 16
—Married Ruth .... Ru 4:1 – 13
—Became ancestor of David .... Ru 4:18 – 22; 1Ch 2:12 – 15
—Became ancestor of Jesus .... Mt 1:5 – 16; Lk 3:23 – 32

BODY

A. The human body

1. Refers to the physical body
—Originally fashioned by God .... Ge 2:7,22
—Now formed in the womb .... Ps 139:13,15 – 16; Isa 44:2
—Refers to one's outward appearance .... Ge 25:25; SS 5:10 – 16
—We clothe the body .... Mt 6:25
—Refers to the sexual side of humans 1Co 7:4
—The body must be controlled .... 1Th 4:4; Jas 3:2
—The body can be healthy .... Pr 3:8
—The body can become ill .... Ps 38:3,7
—The body can suffer 1Pe 4:1
—The body remains behind at death .... 1Sa 31:10; 1Ki 13:24 – 25

2. Refers to the whole human person
—It experiences life and peace .... Pr 14:30
—It experiences freedom .... Mk 5:29
—We can discipline it 1Co 9:27
—We can love or hate it .... Eph 5:29
—It can be washed by God .... Heb 10:22
—It can yearn for God .... Ps 63:1
—It can please God .... Ro 12:1
—It can reveal the living Jesus .... 2Co 4:10; Php 1:20

3. Effects of sin on the human body/person
—It becomes an instrument of sin .... Ro 6:12 – 13,19; Ro 7:5
—It becomes subject to death .... Ge 3:19; Ps 90:3 – 5; Ro 8:10

4. Effects of salvation on the human body/person
—It receives new life .... Ro 8:11
—It becomes a member of Christ 1Co 6:15
—It becomes a temple of the Spirit 1Co 6:19
—It seeks to do God's will .... Ro 6:13,19
—It must honor God .... Ro 12:1; 1Co 5:20; Php 1:20

5. The future of the Christian's body
—Our bodies will be resurrected .... Jn 5:28 – 29; Jn 11:23 – 24; 1Co 15:42 – 44
—Our bodies will be redeemed .... Ro 8:23
—We will receive new bodies, like Jesus .... 1Co 15:52 – 54; Php 3:21

B. The body of Christ

1. His physical body
—Jesus came in a human body .... 1Ti 3:16; 1Jn 4:2 – 3
—Jesus was conceived by the Holy Spirit .... Lk 1:35
—Jesus suffered in his body 1Pe 4:1
—Jesus sacrificed himself in his body .... Heb 10:10
—Jesus died in his body .... Ro 7:4; 1Pe 3:18
—Jesus' body was buried .... Mt 27:58 – 60; Jn 19:38 – 40

—Jesus' body was raised to life .... Ac 2:31 – 32
—Jesus received a glorified body .... Php 3:21
2. Spiritual significance of his body
a. His body symbolized by bread in the Lord's Supper .... Mt 26:26
1Co 10:16
1Co 11:24
b. The church as the body of Christ
—Identified as such .... Col 1:24
—Christ as the head of his body .... Eph 1:22 – 23
Col 1:18
—Christ as Savior of his body .... Eph 5:23
—Emphasis on one body .... Ro 12:4 – 5
1Co 10:16 – 17
—Emphasis on unity in the body .... 1Co 12:25 – 26
Eph 2:14 – 16
Eph 4:3 – 4,12 – 13
—Each member in the body important .... 1Co 12:14 – 24

BOLDNESS

See COURAGE

BOOK

A. In the Old Testament
1. Books of the law and prophecy
—The book(s) of God .... Ex 32:32 – 33
Ps 139:16
Da 7:10
—The Book of the Covenant .... Ex 24:7
—The Book of the Law .... Dt 28:61
Ne 8:1,3,8,18
—The Book of Moses .... Ezr 6:18
—The book of Jeremiah's prophecies .... Jer 25:13
Jer 30:2 – 3
—The book of the vision of Nahum .... Na 1:1
—The Book of Truth .... Da 10:21
2. Books of history and poetry
—The Book of the Wars of the LORD .... Nu 21:14
—The Book of Jashar .... Jos 10:12 – 13
—The book of the annals of King David 1Ch 27:24
—The book of the annals of Solomon 1Ki 11:41
—The book of the annals of the kings 1Ki 14:19,29
—The book of the Laments 2Ch 35:25
—The book of the annals of Persian kings .... Est 2:23
3. No end to the making of books .... Ecc 12:12
B. In the New Testament
1. References to parts of the Old Testament
—The book of Moses .... Mk 12:26
—The Book of the Law .... Gal 3:10
—The book of the prophets .... Ac 7:42
—The Book of Isaiah .... Lk 3:4
Ac 8:28
—The Book of Psalms .... Lk 20:42
Ac 1:20
2. References to parts of the New Testament
—The Gospel of Luke .... Ac 1:1
—The Gospel of John .... Jn 20:30
—The Revelation of John .... Rev 22:7,18 – 19
3. God's special books
—The scroll of history .... Rev 5:1 – 5
—The book of life .... Php 4:3
Rev 3:5
Rev 21:27
—The books opened on the judgment day .... Rev 20:12

BORN AGAIN

—Spiritual rebirth by the power of Jesus
A. Why is spiritual birth necessary?
—Because we are dead in sin .... Eph 2:1,4 – 5
Col 2:13
—Because we need the Spirit .... Jn 3:3 – 6
B. How does spiritual birth take place?
—By a decision of God .... Jn 1:13
—By a decision of Jesus, the Son of God .... Jn 5:21
—By an act of God through Christ .... Col 2:13
—By the Holy Spirit .... Jn 3:6
Tit 3:5
—Through the word of God .... Jas 1:18
1Pe 1:23
—Through believing in Jesus 1Jn 5:1
C. What does spiritual birth result in?
—Salvation and new life .... Tit 3:5
—Entrance into God's kingdom .... Jn 3:3
—Being a new creation 2Co 5:17
Eph 4:24
—Victory over a sinful life .... Ro 6:4 – 7
1Jn 3:9
1Jn 5:4,18
—Ability to do what is right 1Jn 2:29
—Ability to love one another 1Jn 4:7
—Safety from the evil one 1Jn 5:18

BREAD

A. Physical bread
1. Bread as a food
—Bread is eaten .... Ge 14:18
1Ki 17:6
Mt 14:16 – 17
—Bread stands for life's necessities .... Dt 8:3
Ps 37:25
Pr 30:8
Mt 6:11
2. God's use of bread
—God tested Israel by giving only manna .... Dt 8:3
—God tested Israel by a lack of bread .... Nu 21:5
—God punished Israel by cutting off bread .... Lev 26:26
La 1:11
B. Bread in Old Testament worship
1. Used in fellowship offerings .... Lev 7:11 – 13
2. Used in Aaron's ordination .... Lev 8:2,26,31 – 32
3. The bread of the Presence
—Placed in tabernacle .... Ex 25:30
—Placed in the temple 2Ch 4:19
—Twelve loaves for twelve tribes .... Lev 24:5 – 8
—David was given this bread .... 1Sa 21:3 – 6
Mt 12:3 – 4
4. First bread each harvest offered to God .... Nu 15:19 – 21
5. The Feast of Unleavened Bread
—A reminder of bread used in the exodus .... Ex 12:8 – 20
—Regulations given .... Lev 23:6
Dt 16:3 – 4
—Celebrated in Israel's history .... Jos 5:11
2Ch 30:21 – 27
2Ch 35:17 – 19
Ezr 6:22
—Celebrated at the time of Jesus .... Mt 26:17
—Celebrated in the early church .... Ac 20:6
C. Bread related to Jesus
1. Physical bread
—Feeding of the five thousand .... Mt 14:13 – 21
Mk 6:35 – 44
Lk 9:12 – 17
Jn 6:5 – 13
—Feeding of the four thousand .... Mt 15:29 – 38
Mk 8:1 – 9
—A parable on bread .... Lk 11:5 – 8
—Jesus served bread in the upper room .... Mt 26:26
2. Bread used symbolically
—Jesus as bread of life .... Jn 6:35,41,48,51

—"This [bread] is my body" Mk 14:22; Lk 22:19; 1Co 11:23–24
—Participating in the body of Christ 1Co 10:16
—Being one body in Christ 1Co 10:17

BROTHERS AND SISTERS

A. Natural use of brother and sister
1. People with the same parents Ge 4:2,8; Ge 34:13–15
2. People with the same father Ge 20:12; Ge 37:2,4,8
3. Any relative
—Members of the Israelite nation Hos 2:1
—People with same ancestors (Esau/Jacob) Nu 20:14

B. Brothers and sisters of Jesus
1. Names
—James Mt 13:55; Gal 1:19
—Joseph Mt 13:55
—Simon Mt 13:55
—Judas Mt 13:55; Jude 1
2. Relationship to Jesus
—Wanted to see Jesus Mt 12:46–47
—Gave advice to Jesus Jn 7:3
—Did not believe in Jesus Jn 7:5
—Later became disciples of Jesus Ac 1:14
—Went on missionary excursions 1Co 9:5
—James became a leader of the church Ac 15:13–21; Gal 2:9

C. Spiritual use of brother and sister
—Christ is our brother Ro 8:29; Heb 2:11
—We are brothers and sisters of Christ Mt 12:50
—Christians are brothers and sisters of one another Mt 23:8; 1Co 6:6; Phm 16
—Specific references to sisters Ro 16:1; Phm 2; Jas 2:15; 2Jn 13

D. Living as Christian brothers and sisters
—Be concerned about a brother or sister in need Jas 2:15; 1Jn 3:17
—Forgive each other Mt 5:23–24; Mt 18:15,21–22
—Love each other 1Th 4:9–10; Heb 13:1
—Overlook social differences Phm 15–16; Gal 3:28
—Discipline an errant brother or sister 2Th 3:6
—Do not judge each other Ro 14:10,13; 1Co 6:5–8; Jas 4:11
—Do not destroy each other 1Co 8:9–13

BUILDING

A. Building in a physical sense
1. Things built to honor the Lord
—Altars Ge 12:8; Ge 35:1
—The tabernacle Ex 35:8—38:20
—The temple 1Ki 6:1–38
2. Things built against God's will
—The tower of Babel Ge 11:4
—Altars to pagan gods Ex 32:5; 1Ki 12:26–31

B. Building in a spiritual sense
1. Christians as builders
—Of their own lives on Christ and his words Mt 7:24–27; 1Co 3:12–15; Col 2:7
—Of themselves in the faith Jude 20
—Of the church into a unified body Eph 2:21; Eph 4:16
—Of other Christians in love Ro 15:2; 1Co 8:1; 1Th 5:11
2. The Lord as a builder
—Of Jerusalem Ps 147:2
—Of the house of David 2Sa 7:27; 1Ki 11:38
—Of the nation of Judah Jer 31:4
—Of our homes Ps 127:1
—Of the church Mt 16:18
—Of a place in heaven for his people Jn 14:1–2; 2Co 5:1
—Of the new Jerusalem Heb 11:10
—Christ is the cornerstone Ps 118:22–23; 1Pe 2:6

CAESAREA

—A seacoast city Ac 9:30; Ac 18:22
—Roman capital of Palestine Ac 12:19–20; Ac 23:23–24
—Philip's home and headquarters for preaching Ac 8:40; Ac 21:8
—Cornelius stationed there Ac 10:1
—Peter preached to Cornelius there Ac 10:23–48
—Paul imprisoned for two years there Ac 24:1,27
—Paul on trial before Felix there Ac 24:1–21
—Paul appealed to Caesar there Ac 25:6–12
—Paul spoke to Agrippa there Ac 25:13—26:32

CAIAPHAS

—A high priest at the time of John the Baptist Lk 3:2
—Son-in-law of Annas, the high priest Jn 18:13
—Spoke prophetically about Jesus Jn 11:49–53
—Jesus on trial before him Mt 26:57–67; Jn 18:24
—Peter and John on trial before him Ac 4:5–7

CAIN

A. History in the Old Testament
—Firstborn son of Adam Ge 4:1
—The first farmer Ge 4:2
—Offered an unsatisfactory offering Ge 4:3,5
—Murdered his brother Abel Ge 4:8; 1Jn 3:12
—Became a wanderer Ge 4:10–16
—His marriage and family Ge 4:17–18

B. Significance in the New Testament
—Considered a symbol of evil Jude 11
—Did not offer a sacrifice in faith Heb 11:4
—Serves as warning not to hate others 1Jn 3:11–13

CALEB

—Son of Jephunneh; of tribe of Judah Nu 13:6
—One of the chosen spies of Canaan Nu 13:1–2,6
—Gave a positive report Nu 13:30
—Pled with Israelites to have faith Nu 14:6–9
—Allowed to enter Canaan Nu 14:30–32
—Given city of Hebron Jos 14:6–15; Jdg 1:20
—Gave daughter to be wife of Othniel Jdg 1:12–15

CALENDAR

See MONTH

CALL, CALLING

—God's summoning us to himself

A. Basic meanings of "call"
- —To summon to a conference ... Ge 3:9; Ac 4:18
- —To pray to the Lord ... Ge 4:26; Ro 10:13
- —To name something/someone ... Ge 2:19; Lk 1:60
- —To make someone one's own ... Isa 43:1; 1Pe 2:9
- —To appoint someone to service ... Ex 3:4–5; Mk 1:19–20

B. The call to become God's children

1. What is its nature?
- —It is heavenward ... Php 3:14; Heb 3:1
- —It is irrevocable ... Ro 11:29
- —It is linked to our election ... Ro 8:30; 2Th 2:13–14
- —More are called than chosen ... Mt 22:14

2. What must we do?
- —We must repent ... Lk 5:32; Ac 2:38–39; Ac 17:30
- —We must call on God's name ... Ac 9:21; Ro 10:12
- —We must confirm God's call by our lives ... 2Pe 1:5–10

3. What are its results?
- —We are justified and glorified ... Ro 8:28–30
- —We have fellowship with Jesus ... 1Co 1:9
- —We enter God's kingdom ... 1Th 2:12; 2Pe 1:9–10
- —We enter God's light ... 1Pe 2:9
- —We enter Christ's glory ... 2Th 2:14
- —We have Christian hope ... Eph 4:4
- —We receive our inheritance ... Heb 9:15
- —We will conquer along with the Lamb ... Rev 17:14

C. The call to live a holy life

1. Basic call ... Eph 4:1; 1Th 1:4; 2Ti 1:9

2. What that call involves
- —Patient suffering ... 1Pe 2:20–21
- —Working for peace ... 1Co 7:15; Col 3:15
- —Serving one another ... Gal 5:13
- —Working as an apostle ... Ro 1:1
- —Working as missionaries ... Ac 13:2

D. The means used by God to call us
- —The Holy Spirit ... 1Th 1:5
- —Grace ... Gal 1:15
- —The message of the gospel ... 2Th 2:14; Ro 10:14

CANAAN, CANAANITES

A. Related themes
- SETTLEMENT is a theme of Joshua ... Jos 19:51
- HOMECOMING is a theme of Ezra ... Ezr 2:1

B. Identity
- —Canaanites were descendants of Ham ... Ge 10:6,15–17
- —Various Canaanite nations ... Ge 15:19–21; Ex 3:8; Nu 13:29; Dt 7:1
- —Borders of Canaan given ... Ge 10:18–19

C. Relationship to God's people

1. Land promised to Abraham and descendants ... Ge 15:18–21; Ge 17:8; Ex 6:4; Ps 105:11

2. Brief history of God's people in Canaan
- —Abraham wandered there ... Ge 17:8
- —Isaac lived there ... Ge 26:1–6
- —Jacob left Canaan for Egypt ... Ge 46:5–6
- —Under Joshua, Israelites conquered Canaan ... Jos 12:1–24
- —Land divided out to the twelve tribes ... Jos 14:1–5
- —Northern tribes removed from Canaan ... 2Ki 17:18,22–23
- —People of Judah exiled into Babylon ... 2Ki 24:14
- —Jews returned to Canaan ... Ezr 1:1–5

3. The destruction of the Canaanites
- —God promised to destroy them ... Ex 23:23,27–31; Ex 34:11
- —God ordered Israelites to destroy them ... Nu 33:51–53; Dt 20:16–17
- —Israelites to make no alliance with them ... Ex 23:32; Dt 7:2–4
- —Canaan was never fully taken ... Jos 13:1–5; Jdg 1:27–36
- —Some still existed at time of Jesus ... Mt 15:22

D. Significance of Canaan
- —Promised inheritance for Israelites ... Nu 26:52–56
- *See* INHERITANCE
- —A symbol of God's final land of rest ... Heb 4:1–11

CAPERNAUM

A. Jesus' ministry at Capernaum
- —Headquarters of Jesus' Galilean ministry ... Mt 4:13–17; Jn 2:12
- —Jesus taught there ... Mk 1:21–22; Lk 4:31–32
- —Jesus spoke about the bread of life there ... Jn 6:24–59

B. Miracles of Jesus at Capernaum
- —Demon cast out ... Mk 1:21–27; Lk 4:31–37
- —Healing of Peter's mother-in-law ... Mk 1:29–31; Lk 4:38–39
- —Healing of official's son ... Jn 4:46–54
- —Healing of paralytic man ... Mk 2:1–12
- —Healing of centurion's servant ... Mt 8:5–13; Lk 7:1–10
- —Healing of many people ... Mk 1:32–34; Lk 4:40–41
- —Paying temple tax from a fish ... Mt 17:24–27

C. Jesus denounced Capernaum for unbelief ... Mt 11:23–24; Lk 10:15

CASTING LOTS

A. Occasions for casting lots

1. Decisions of God's people through casting lots
- —Choosing a goat on Day of Atonement ... Lev 16:8
- —Dividing Canaan for the tribes of Israel ... Jos 18:6–10
- —Determining a guilty party ... 1Sa 14:40–44
- —Assigning duties to priests and Levites ... 1Ch 24:5,31; 1Ch 26:13–16; Lk 1:5–9
- —Deciding who would live in Jerusalem ... Ne 11:1
- —Choosing a replacement for Judas ... Ac 1:26

2. Decisions by heathens through casting lots
- —Haman's choice of a day for killing Jews ... Est 3:7
- —Detection of Jonah by sailors ... Jnh 1:7
- —Owners of conquered Israelites ... Joel 3:3; Ob 11; Na 3:10
- —Recipient of Jesus' garment ... Mt 27:35

B. God controls the casting of lots .... Pr 16:33
C. Urim and Thummim likely a form of casting lots .... Ex 28:30
Lev 8:8
Nu 27:21
Dt 33:8
1Sa 28:6

CEPHAS

See PETER

CHARIOT

A. Uses for the chariot
1. For royalty to ride in .... Ge 41:43
1Ki 18:44
2. For important officials to ride in 2Ki 5:21
Ac 8:28 – 30
3. For use in war
—The Egyptians .... Ex 14:7
—The Canaanites .... Jos 11:4,6,9
—The Philistines 1Sa 13:5
—The Arameans .... 1Ki 22:31 – 33
—The Assyrians 2Ki 19:23
—The Israelites 1Ch 18:4
—The Cushites 2Ch 14:9
—The Babylonians .... Eze 23:15,23 – 24
4. For use in pagan worship 2Ki 23:11
B. The chariot referred to symbolically
—Elijah's ascension in a fiery chariot .... 2Ki 2:11 – 12
—The clouds are God's chariot .... Ps 104:3
—God's heavenly host are charioteers .... 2Ki 6:15 – 17
Ps 68:17
—God executes judgment by his chariots .... Isa 66:15 – 16

CHASTISEMENT

See DISCIPLINE

CHILDREN

A. Proper opinion of children
—A gift from God .... Ge 4:1
Ge 33:5
—A heritage from the Lord .... Ps 127:3 – 5
—A blessing from God .... Lk 1:42
—A crown to the aged .... Pr 17:6
B. Familiar stories involving children
—Abraham's willingness to sacrifice Isaac .... Ge 22:1 – 19
—The baby Moses .... Ex 2:1 – 10
—Jephthah's daughter .... Jdg 11:29 – 40
—The call of Samuel .... 1Sa 3:1 – 18
—David anointed king .... 1Sa 16:1 – 13
—David killed a lion and a bear .... 1Sa 17:34 – 37
—Elijah raised a dead boy .... 1Ki 17:17 – 24
—Elisha raised a dead boy .... 2Ki 4:8 – 37
—Joash became king at seven years .... 2Ki 11:4 – 12,21
2Ch 23:1 – 11
2Ch 24:1
—Josiah became king at eight years .... 2Ki 22:1 – 2
2Ch 34:1 – 2
—Jesus raised a girl from the dead .... Mt 9:22 – 25
Mk 5:35 – 43
Lk 8:49 – 56
—Jesus raised a boy from the dead .... Lk 7:11 – 15
—Jesus used a boy's lunch to feed a crowd .... Jn 6:1 – 13
—Jesus called children to come to him .... Mt 19:13 – 15
Mk 10:13 – 16
Lk 18:15 – 17
C. God's relationship to children
1. Blesses barren women with children .... Ps 113:9
—Sarah .... Ge 21:1 – 3
—Rebekah .... Ge 25:21 – 22
—Rachel .... Ge 30:1 – 2
—Hannah .... 1Sa 1:6 – 8
—Elizabeth .... Lk 1:7,24 – 25
2. Forms children in the womb .... Ps 139:13 – 16
3. Knows children even before birth .... Jer 1:5
Gal 1:15
4. Includes children in his covenant .... Ge 17:7
Ac 2:39
5. Considers children of believers holy 1Co 7:14
6. Shows concern for orphans .... Dt 10:18
Ps 10:14
Hos 14:3
Jas 1:27
D. Jesus and children
1. His own childhood
—His conception .... Mt 1:18
Lk 1:26 – 38
—His birth .... Mt 1:25
Lk 2:1 – 7
—His circumcision and dedication .... Lk 2:21 – 38
—His flight into Egypt .... Mt 2:14 – 15
—His visit to the temple at twelve years .... Lk 2:41 – 50
—Summary of his boyhood .... Lk 2:51 – 52
2. His feelings about children
—He wanted children to come to him .... Mt 19:13 – 15
Mk 10:13 – 16
Lk 18:15 – 17
—He used them to teach disciples humility .... Mt 18:1 – 4
Mk 9:36 – 37
Lk 9:46 – 48
—He used them in parables .... Mt 11:16 – 17
—He raised them from the dead .... Mt 9:22 – 25
Mk 5:35 – 43
Lk 7:11 – 15
Lk 8:49 – 56
E. Relationship between parents and children
1. Parents' duties to children
—Give them names .... Ge 21:3
Ge 29:31—30:24
Mt 1:25
Lk 1:59 – 63
—Care for their physical needs .... 1Sa 1:22 – 24
—Educate them .... Dt 6:6 – 7
See EDUCATION
—Discipline them .... Pr 23:13 – 14
See DISCIPLINE
—Lay up inheritance for them 2Co 12:14
2. Children's duties to parents
—Obey them .... Pr 6:20
Eph 6:1
Col 3:20
—Listen to and follow their instruction .... Pr 1:8 – 9
Pr 3:1 – 2
—Honor them .... Ex 20:12
Lev 19:3
—Respect them in their old age .... Pr 23:22
—Care for them 1Ti 5:4
F. Symbolic use of "children"
—Jesus' term for his disciples .... Mk 10:24
—A term for all believers .... Ro 8:16 – 17
See ADOPTION
—An elderly pastor's term for his church 1Jn 2:1,18
—Paul's term for those he led to Christ .... 1Co 4:14 – 17
1Ti 1:2
Tit 1:4

See also FATHER; MOTHER; YOUTH

CHOOSING

A. Related theme
CHOOSING is a theme of Deuteronomy .... Dt 7:6
B. *See* ELECTION

CHRIST

See JESUS CHRIST

CHRISTIAN

A. References in the New Testament
—Disciples first called Christians at Antioch ... Ac 11:26
—Paul wanted Agrippa to become a Christian ... Ac 26:28
—Christians need not be ashamed ... 1Pe 4:16
B. Other titles for Christians
—Foreigners in the world ... 1Pe 2:11
See ALIEN
—Believers ... Ac 2:44
See FAITH
—Brothers and sisters ... Jas 2:15
See BROTHERS AND SISTERS
—Children of God ... Ro 8:16
See CHILDREN
—Children of light ... Eph 5:8
See LIGHT
—Disciples of the Lord ... Ac 9:1
See DISCIPLES
—The elect of God ... 1Pe 1:1
See ELECTION
—Friends of Christ ... Jn 15:14
See FRIENDSHIP
—Heirs of God ... Ro 8:17
See INHERITANCE
—Members of the body of Christ ... Ro 12:4–5
See BODY
—Priests ... Rev 1:6
See PRIEST
—Those sanctified in Christ ... 1Co 1:2
See SANCTIFICATION
—Holy people ... 2Co 1:1
See SANCTIFICATION
—Servants of God ... 1Pe 2:16
See SERVANT

CHURCH

—God's called-out people
A. Related themes
1. CHURCH is a theme of:
—Matthew ... Mt 18:17
—Ephesians ... Eph 3:10
2. CHURCH ORDER is a theme of 1 Timothy ... 1Ti 3:15
B. Definition of church
1. Church as a local group of believers
—In Jerusalem ... Ac 8:1
—In Antioch ... Ac 13:1
—In Caesarea ... Ac 18:22
—In Ephesus ... Ac 20:17
—In Cenchrea ... Ro 16:1
—In Corinth ... 1Co 1:2
—In Laodicea ... Col 4:16
—In Thessalonica ... 1Th 1:1
—Several in Galatia ... Gal 1:2
—Seven in Asia Minor ... Rev 2–3
2. Church as one worldwide church ... Mt 16:18
1Co 10:32
Eph 5:25
Col 1:18
C. Titles ascribed to the church
—God's building ... 1Co 3:9
—God's field ... 1Co 3:9
—The temple of the Holy Spirit ... 1Co 6:19
—The church of God ... 2Co 1:1
—A pure virgin ... 2Co 11:2
—The Jerusalem that is above ... Gal 4:26
—The Israel of God ... Gal 6:16
—The body of Christ ... Eph 1:22–23
—A holy temple ... Eph 2:21
—The bride of Christ ... Eph 5:25–28
Rev 21:9
—A chosen people ... 1Pe 2:9
—A royal priesthood ... 1Pe 2:9
—A holy nation ... 1Pe 2:9
—God's special possession ... 1Pe 2:9
—The flock of God ... 1Pe 5:2
—The wife of the Lamb ... Rev 21:9–10
D. Characteristics of the New Testament church
1. Saved by Christ's blood ... Ac 20:28
Eph 5:25–27
2. Usually met in homes ... Ro 16:5
Col 4:15
Phm 2
3. Held worship services ... Ac 20:7–11
1Co 14:26–28
Heb 10:25
4. Shared in the sacraments
—Baptism ... Ac 18:8
1Co 12:13
—Lord's Supper (breaking bread) ... Ac 2:42
Ac 20:7
1Co 11:23–33
5. Experienced unity
—Into one body ... Ro 12:5
Eph 4:13
—As one flock with one shepherd ... Jn 10:16
6. Enjoyed fellowship ... Ac 2:42
1Jn 1:3–7
7. Helped each other ... Ac 4:32–37
2Co 8:1–5
8. Evangelized others ... Ro 1:8
1Th 1:8–10
9. Grew ... Ac 4:4
Ac 5:14
Ac 16:5
10. Was organized ... Ac 14:23
Php 1:1
1Ti 3:1–13
Tit 1:5–9
11. Had problems ... 1Co 1:11–12
1Co 11:17–22
Gal 3:1–5
12. Had to exercise discipline ... Mt 18:15–17
1Co 5:1–5
2Th 3:11–15
Tit 3:10–11
13. Experienced persecution ... Ac 8:1–3
Ac 17:5–9
1Th 2:14–15

See also BROTHERS AND SISTERS; DEACON; ELDER; FELLOWSHIP; GROWTH; MISSION; SACRAMENT; UNITY; WORSHIP

CIRCUMCISION

—The cutting off of the foreskin
A. Occurrences of circumcision
—Abraham and his household ... Ge 17:23–27
—Isaac ... Ge 21:4
Ac 7:8
—All males in the city of Shechem ... Ge 34:24
—Moses' son ... Ex 4:24–25
—The Israelites at Gilgal ... Jos 5:2–3
—John the Baptist ... Lk 1:59
—Jesus ... Lk 2:21
—The apostle Paul ... Php 3:5
—Timothy ... Ac 16:3
B. Circumcision in the Old Testament
—Done at eight days ... Ge 17:12
—A sign of the covenant ... Ge 17:9–14

—A sign of Abraham's faith ..... Ro 4:11
—Must be accompanied by heart circumcision ..... Dt 10:16
Dt 30:6
Jer 4:4

C. Circumcision in the New Testament
1. Controversy in early church
—A circumcision group in the church ..... Ac 11:2 – 3
Gal 2:12
Gal 6:12 – 13
Tit 1:10
—Discussed by leaders in Jerusalem ..... Ac 15:1 – 22
Gal 2:4
—Decision: circumcision unnecessary ..... Ac 15:6 – 29
Gal 2:1 – 3,15 – 16
2. Discussion in Paul's letters
—Physical circumcision means nothing 1Co 7:19
Gal 5:6
Col 3:11
—Circumcision not needed for salvation ..... Ro 4:9 – 12
Gal 2:2 – 3
1Co 7:18
—True circumcision involves obedience ..... Ro 2:25
—True circumcision is of the heart ..... Ro 2:28 – 29
—True worshipers are true circumcision ..... Php 3:3
—Christians are circumcised in baptism ..... Col 2:11 – 12

CITY

A. Major cities mentioned in the Bible
—Antioch ..... Ac 11:19 – 20
—Athens ..... Ac 17:15
—Babel/Babylon ..... Ge 11:9
Da 4:30
—Caesarea ..... Ac 23:23
—Corinth ..... Ac 18:1
—Damascus 2Sa 8:6
—Ephesus ..... Ac 19:1
—Jericho ..... Jos 6:1
—Jerusalem ..... 2Sa 5:6 – 7
—Nineveh ..... Jnh 1:2
—Philippi ..... Ac 16:12
—Rome ..... Ac 28:14
—Samaria 1Ki 16:24
—Sodom and Gomorrah ..... Ge 18:20
B. Types of Israelite cities
—The capital city ..... 2Sa 5:6 – 9
1Ki 16:24
—Cities for defense ..... 2Ch 11:5 – 12
—Chariot cities 2Ch 1:14
—Cities for storage 2Ch 8:4,6
—Cities for the Levites ..... Nu 35:1 – 5,7
—Cities of refuge ..... Nu 35:6 – 15
Dt 19:1 – 3
Jos 20:1 – 9

C. Critical importance of cities
1. Defense of cities
—Usually fortified with walls ..... Nu 13:28
Dt 3:5
Jos 6:5
2Ch 11:5 – 13
—Besieged by armies 1Ki 20:1
2Ki 16:5
—Kingdom fell when the city was entered ..... 2Ki 17:5 – 6
2Ki 25:1 – 7
2. Cities as centers for missions
a. Jonah sent to Nineveh ..... Jnh 1:2
b. Disciples evangelized cities ..... Mt 10:23
c. Paul preached in cities
—Antioch ..... Ac 11:25 – 26
—Paphos on Cyprus ..... Ac 13:6 – 12
—Antioch of Pisidia ..... Ac 13:14 – 49
—Philippi ..... Ac 16:12 – 40
—Thessalonica ..... 1Th 1:7 – 10
—Corinth ..... Ac 18:1 – 17
—Ephesus ..... Ac 19:1 – 41
D. The city used as a symbol
—Of total rebellion against God ..... Rev 18:1 – 24
See BABYLON
—Of the church and of heaven ..... Heb 12:22 – 23
Rev 21:1 – 4
See JERUSALEM

CLEANNESS

A. The Old Testament regarding clean/unclean
1. How did one become unclean?
—By eating unclean foods ..... Lev 11:1 – 23
—Through childbirth ..... Lev 12:1 – 8
—Through skin diseases ..... Lev 13:1—14:57
—Through discharges from the body ..... Lev 15:1 – 33
—By touching a dead body ..... Nu 5:2
—By worshiping false gods ..... Jer 13:25 – 27
Hos 8:5
—Through a life of sin ..... Isa 64:5 – 7
2. How could one become clean?
—By washing self and clothes ..... Ex 19:10 – 14
Ex 30:18 – 21
Lev 22:6
—By certain sacrifices and ceremonies ..... Lev 12:6 – 8
Lev 14:1 – 11
—By turning to the Lord ..... Ps 51:2,7
Isa 4:4
Isa 6:5 – 7
B. Inward cleansing from sin
1. The need for such cleansing ..... Mt 23:25 – 28
2. God's promise for such cleansing ..... Jer 33:8
Eze 36:25,33
3. The process of such cleansing
—The believer must ask for it ..... Ps 51:2,7
1Jn 1:9
—It takes place in the heart ..... Ps 24:3 – 4
Mk 7:18 – 23
—It occurs through Christ's blood ..... Heb 9:14
Heb 10:19 – 22
1Jn 1:7
—It occurs through the word of God ..... Eph 5:25 – 27
4. The results of such cleansing
—It leads to a life of holiness 2Co 7:1
—It leads to a life of purity 1Jn 3:3
—It leads to a life of love 1Pe 1:22

CLOTHING

A. Purposes and uses of clothing
1. Clothing for natural uses
—To cover nakedness ..... Ge 3:7,21
—To keep warm ..... Pr 31:21
—To trade in business ..... Pr 31:24
Ac 16:14
2. Clothing for religious purposes
—To use in special service to God ..... Ex 28:1 – 5
—To symbolize a message from God ..... 1Ki 11:29 – 32
—To appoint a prophet as successor 1Ki 19:19
2Ki 2:13 – 14
3. Clothing used for display
—Special favor to a child ..... Ge 37:3 – 4
—Honor to a citizen ..... Est 6:11
—One's wealth ..... Mt 11:8
—One's power ..... Ac 12:21
—One's position as ruler ..... Ge 41:42
—One's self-righteousness ..... Mt 23:5
—Mourning ..... Ge 37:34
2Sa 3:31
Job 1:20

—Sorrow for sin .... Ezr 9:3
—Shock .... Mk 14:63
Ac 14:14
B. Significant garments in the Bible
—Garments sewn by God for Adam and Eve .... Ge 3:21
—The robe of Joseph from his father .... Ge 37:3 – 4
—The garments stolen by Achan .... Jos 7:20 – 21
—The purple robe put on Jesus .... Mk 15:17
—The seamless garment of Jesus at the cross .... Mt 27:35
Mk 15:24
Jn 19:23 – 24
C. Clothing used as a symbol
—Taking off a garment means putting off sin .... Eph 4:22
Col 3:9
—Putting on a garment means putting on Jesus .... Ro 13:14
Gal 3:27
—Receiving a new garment symbolizes forgiveness .... Zec 3:3 – 5
Mt 22:11 – 13
Rev 3:5
—Being clothed with white robes in heaven .... Rev 7:9,13 – 14

COMFORT

—Consolation and strength in a time of need

A. Related theme
COMFORT is a theme of Nahum .... Na 2:2
B. People who need comfort
—Those grieving .... Ge 37:33 – 35
Job 2:11
Isa 61:2
Mt 5:4
—Those in a new country .... Ru 2:13
—Those facing troubles .... Ps 71:21
Isa 51:19
—Those downcast 2Co 7:6
—Those being punished for sin .... Isa 40:1
La 1:9,17
2Co 2:6 – 7
C. Sources of comfort
1. Human comfort given by
—Spouses .... Ge 24:67
2Sa 12:24
—Children .... Ge 37:33 – 35
—Friends .... Job 2:11 – 13
Jn 11:19
—Prophets .... Isa 40:1 – 2
1Co 14:3
—Preachers .... Isa 61:1 – 2
2Co 1:4 – 6
1Th 2:11 – 12
—Any Christian .... 2Co 2:6 – 7
Col 4:11
2. Divine comfort given through
—God .... Isa 51:3,12
Isa 57:18
Isa 66:13
Zec 1:17
—The God of all comfort .... Jer 8:18
2Co 1:3
—God's rod and staff .... Ps 23:4
—God's promises .... Ps 119:50,76
—Jesus Christ .... Jn 14:27
Jn 16:33
—Christ's love .... Php 2:1
—The Holy Spirit as Counselor .... Jn 14:16,26
Jn 15:5 – 7

COMPASSION

—Deep feeling of concern for suffering and needy people

A. Related themes
1. CONCERN is a theme of:
—Nehemiah .... Ne 2:2
—1 Thessalonians 1Th 2:17
2. SOCIAL CONCERN is a theme of:
—Deuteronomy .... Dt 26:12
—Luke .... Lk 7:22
B. Human compassion commanded
—In the Old Testament .... Mic 6:8
Zec 7:9
—In the New Testament .... Gal 6:2
Eph 4:32
Col 3:12
1Pe 3:8
C. The compassion of Christ
—To people without leaders .... Mt 9:36
Mk 6:34
—To sick people .... Mt 14:14
Mt 20:34
Mk 1:41
—To hungry people .... Mt 15:32
Mk 8:2
—To a grieving widow .... Lk 7:13
—To all of us in our weaknesses .... Heb 4:15
D. The compassion of God
1. A chief characteristic of God
—God is the God of compassion 2Co 1:3
—He is compassionate .... Ex 34:6
Ps 103:8
Jnh 4:2
—He is full of compassion .... Ps 116:5
Jas 5:11
—His compassions never fail .... La 3:22
2. His expressions of compassion
—To Adam and Eve when they sinned .... Ge 3:15
—To the Israelites in Egypt .... Ex 3:7
—To the Israelites in the desert .... Ne 9:17 – 21
—To the Israelites groaning under enemies .... Jdg 2:18
—To the Israelites in exile .... Isa 54:7 – 8
Jer 42:11 – 12
—To all of us as sinners .... Ps 51:1
Ps 103:8 – 12
Mic 7:19
—To foreigners and the oppressed .... Ex 22:27
Dt 10:18 – 19

See also MERCY

CONFESSION

A. Related theme
CONFESSION is a theme of Psalms .... Ps 51:2
B. Confession of sin before God
1. Examples of people confessing sin
—Aaron .... Nu 12:11
—David 2Sa 12:13
Ps 32:5
Ps 38:18
Ps 51:1 – 5
—Nehemiah .... Ne 1:6 – 7
—Isaiah .... Isa 6:5
—Peter .... Lk 5:8
—A tax collector .... Lk 18:13
2. Those who may confess sin
—Individual sinners .... Lev 5:5
Mt 6:12
—Priests on behalf of the people .... Lev 16:21
Ezr 9:5—10:1
—Prophets on behalf of the people .... Isa 6:5
Isa 59:12 – 15
Jer 14:7,20 – 21
Da 9:7 – 11

3. The results of confessing sin
—We receive God's mercy.......... Pr 28:13
—We receive God's forgiveness.......... Ps 32:5
1Jn 1:9
—We are justified.......... Lk 18:13 – 14
—We receive healing.......... Jas 5:16
—We become purified.......... 1Jn 1:9

C. Confession of faith in Jesus Christ
1. Such confession is necessary to be saved.......... Mt 10:32 – 33
Ro 10:9 – 10
2. Earliest confessions of faith
—"Jesus is Lord".......... Jn 20:28
Ro 10:9
1Co 12:3
Php 2:11
—"Jesus is the Messiah".......... Mt 16:16
Jn 20:31
Ac 17:2 – 3
1Jn 2:22
—"Jesus is the Son of God".......... Mt 16:16
Mt 27:54
Jn 20:31
1Jn 4:15
3. Other elements added to confessions
—Certain teachings about Christ.......... 1Jn 4:2 – 3
2Jn 7
—Trustworthy sayings.......... 1Ti 1:15
1Ti 4:9 – 10
2Ti 2:11
Tit 3:8
4. Brief creeds in the New Testament.......... 1Co 15:3 – 5
1Ti 3:16
2Ti 2:11 – 13
Tit 3:4 – 7

CONFIDENCE
See ASSURANCE

CONSCIENCE
—An inner voice defining right and wrong

A. Everyone has a conscience.......... Ro 2:14 – 15

B. Our conscience and sin
—It helps us do what is right.......... Ro 2:15
2Co 1:12
—It accuses us of sin.......... 2Sa 24:10
Ac 2:37
1Co 8:7
—It can be distorted.......... Pr 30:20
Eph 4:19
1Ti 4:2
—A good conscience can be rejected.......... 1Ti 1:19

C. Our conscience and Christ
—It becomes cleansed through Christ.......... Heb 9:14
Heb 10:19,22
—It inspires us to love others.......... 1Ti 1:5
—It inspires us to obey God's law.......... 1Jn 3:21 – 22
—We must hold a clear conscience.......... Ac 24:16
1Ti 3:9
Heb 13:18

D. Our conscience and other Christians
—A weak Christian has a weak conscience.......... 1Co 8:7,10
1Co 10:27 – 29
—A weak Christian's faith can be destroyed.......... Ro 14:14 – 15
1Co 8:11
—We must protect a weak Christian.......... Ro 14:13,15,19 – 21
1Co 8:9 – 13
1Co 10:27 – 32
—We must not judge another's conscience.......... Ro 14:1 – 13
1Co 10:29

CONTENTMENT
See COVETING

CONVERSION
See REPENTANCE

CORINTH
A. Events of the church in Corinth
—Paul preached there for one and a half years.......... Ac 18:1 – 11
—Paul's trial before Gallio.......... Ac 18:12 – 17
—Apollos sent there.......... Ac 18:27—19:1
—First (lost) letter of Paul to them.......... 1Co 5:9 – 10
—Paul's second letter to them.......... 1Co 1:1 – 2
—Timothy sent there.......... 1Co 4:17
1Co 16:10 – 11
—Paul's third (lost) letter to them.......... 2Co 2:3 – 4
2Co 7:8 – 12
—Titus sent there.......... 2Co 7:5 – 7
—Paul's fourth letter to them.......... 2Co 1:1
—Titus sent there again.......... 2Co 8:16 – 24
—Paul's visit there for three months.......... Ac 20:2 – 3
—Paul's collection among them.......... Ro 15:25 – 27
1Co 16:1 – 4
2Co 8:6 – 15
2Co 9:1 – 15

B. Character of the church in Corinth
—Most held to the teachings of Paul.......... 1Co 11:2
1Co 15:1 – 2
—Disunified.......... 1Co 1:11 – 12
—Spiritually immature.......... 1Co 3:1 – 2
1Co 14:20
—Proud; tolerated sinners.......... 1Co 5:1 – 2
—Lack of concern for weak Christians.......... 1Co 8:9 – 13
—Lack of love for each other.......... 1Co 11:17 – 22
—Trouble over speaking in tongues.......... 1Co 14:1 – 20
—Some denied the resurrection.......... 1Co 15:12
—Some challenged Paul's leadership.......... 2Co 10:1 – 11
2Co 11:13 – 21

CORNELIUS
—Roman centurion who feared God.......... Ac 10:1 – 2
—Received vision from God.......... Ac 10:3 – 8
—Peter preached to him.......... Ac 10:23 – 43
—Received Holy Spirit.......... Ac 10:44 – 46
—Became a baptized Christian.......... Ac 10:47 – 48

COUNSELOR
—One who gives advice and direction for life

A. Human counselors
1. A class of people called counselors.......... Isa 3:3
2. Wise counsel
—Good counsel is necessary.......... Pr 15:22
Pr 22:20 – 21
—Wisdom counsels us.......... Pr 8:12 – 16
—God's law counsels us.......... Ps 119:24
—David had wise counselors.......... 1Ch 27:32 – 33
—Jeremiah was a good counselor.......... Jer 38:14 – 27
3. Foolish counsel
—Wicked counselors must be rejected.......... Job 21:16
Ps 1:1
—Rehoboam followed foolish counselors.......... 1Ki 12:1 – 15
—The Babylonians had poor counselors.......... Isa 47:13

B. God as counselor
—The Lord as counselor.......... Ps 16:7
Ps 73:24
Isa 28:29
—Christ, the Wonderful Counselor.......... Isa 9:6
—The Holy Spirit as Counselor.......... Isa 11:2
Jn 14:16,26
Jn 15:26
Jn 16:7

COURAGE

—The ability to face danger without fear

A. Remarkable stories of courage
- —Moses and Aaron confronting Pharaoh .... Ex 5:1 – 4; Ex 10:24 – 29
- —Ehud killing Eglon .... Jdg 3:15 – 30
- —Gideon against the Midianites .... Jdg 7:1 – 24
- —Jonathan against the Philistines .... 1Sa 14:1 – 14
- —David against Goliath .... 1Sa 17:26 – 50
- —Elijah on Mount Carmel .... 1Sa 18:1 – 40
- —Esther approaching King Xerxes .... Est 5:1 – 8
- —Daniel's three friends and the fiery furnace .... Da 3:1 – 30
- —Daniel and the lions' den .... Da 6:1 – 23
- —The apostles facing the Sanhedrin .... Ac 4:1 – 22; Ac 5:17 – 41
- —Saul (Paul) preaching in Damascus .... Ac 9:20 – 25
- —Paul heading to Jerusalem .... Ac 21:10 – 14

B. The command to be courageous
- —To the Israelites from Moses .... Dt 31:6
- —To the Israelites from Joshua .... Jos 10:25
- —To Joshua from Moses .... Dt 31:7,23
- —To Joshua from the Lord .... Jos 1:6 – 9,18
- —To Solomon from David 1Ch 22:13; 1Ch 28:20
- —To judges from King Jehoshaphat 2Ch 19:11
- —To the Israelites from Hezekiah 2Ch 32:7
- —To Peter from Jesus .... Mt 14:27
- —To the disciples from Jesus .... Mk 6:50
- —To Paul from the Lord .... Ac 23:11
- —To all of us .... 1Co 16:13; Heb 3:6

C. Aspects of courage
1. When do we need courage?
   - —As we face dangers and difficulties .... Jos 1:6 – 9; 1Co 16:13
   - —As we face the future .... Ro 8:37 – 39; 2Co 5:1 – 7
2. Who is our source of courage?
   - —God .... Ge 26:24; Jos 1:9; Ps 18:29 – 50; Ps 46:1 – 2
   - —Christ .... Php 4:13; Col 1:11; Rev 1:17 – 18
   - —The Holy Spirit .... Ac 4:8 – 13

COVENANT

—An agreement established between two parties

A. Related themes
1. COVENANT is a theme of:
   - —Genesis .... Ge 17:4
   - —Exodus .... Ex 24:3
   - —2 Samuel 2Sa 23:5
2. RENEWAL is a theme of:
   - —Deuteronomy .... Dt 29:12
   - —Joshua .... Jos 24:25
   - —Malachi .... Mal 3:7

B. Covenants between humans
1. Examples of human covenants
   - —Between Isaac and Abimelech .... Ge 26:26 – 31
   - —Between Jacob and Laban .... Ge 31:43 – 54
   - —Between Joshua and the Gibeonites .... Jos 9:3 – 15
   - —Between David and Jonathan 1Sa 18:3
   - —Between David and Abner .... 2Sa 3:12 – 16
   - —Between Jehoiada and the guards .... 2Ki 11:4 – 12
   - —Between Joash and the people 2Ki 11:17
   - —Between Zedekiah and the people .... Jer 34:8 – 10
2. Elements in a covenant
   - —Promises .... 1Sa 20:14 – 17
   - —Stipulations 2Sa 3:13
   - —Oaths .... Ge 31:53
   - —Responsibilities 2Ki 12:8
   - —Witnesses .... Ge 31:45 – 48; 1Sa 20:42
   - —Implied threats .... Ge 31:53

C. Covenants between God and humans
1. Examples of such covenants
   - —With Adam before the fall .... Ge 2:15 – 17
   - —With Adam after the fall .... Ge 3:14 – 19
   - —With Noah .... Ge 9:1 – 19
   - —With Abram .... Ge 12:1 – 3
   - —With Israel at Sinai .... Ex 19:5 – 8
   - —With Israel before entering the promised land .... Dt 29 – 30
   - —With Israel in the promised land .... Jos 24:1 – 27
   - —With David .... 2Sa 7:14 – 17
   - —With the returned exiles .... Ne 9:38—10:39
   - —Future covenant of peace .... Eze 34:25 – 31
   - —The new covenant .... Jer 31:33 – 34
2. The covenants with Adam
   - a. First covenant (before the fall)
     - —Requirement was obedience .... Ge 2:16 – 17
     - —Promise was life .... Ge 3:22
     - —Penalty was death .... Ge 2:17
     - —Adam and Eve disobeyed .... Ge 3:1 – 6
     - —God pronounced punishment .... Ge 3:14 – 19
     - —Christ perfectly obeyed God's will .... Jn 6:38; Ro 5:18 – 19; 2Co 5:21; Heb 4:15
     - —Christ's death reversed Adam's .... Ro 5:15 – 19
   - b. Second covenant (after the fall)
     - —Conflict between Satan and humans .... Ge 3:15
     - —God promised Satan's defeat .... Ge 3:15
     - —Fulfilled in Satan's defeat by Christ .... Ro 16:20; Heb 2:14; 1Jn 3:8
3. The covenant with Abraham
   - a. Where is it mentioned?
     - —First mentioned to Abram .... Ge 12:2 – 3
     - —Repeated to Abraham .... Ge 22:17 – 18
     - —Repeated to Isaac .... Ge 26:3 – 5
     - —Repeated to Jacob .... Ge 28:13 – 15
     - —Repeated to Moses .... Ex 6:2 – 4
     - —Celebrated by the psalmists .... Ps 105:7 – 11
     - —Acknowledged by the returned exiles .... Ne 9:7 – 8
   - b. What are its elements?
     - —Several promises .... Ge 12:2 – 3
     - —No conditions attached .... Ge 12:2 – 3
     - —Faith came later .... Ge 15:6
     - —Law of circumcision followed faith .... Ge 17:3 – 14
   - c. How was it fulfilled in Christ?
     - —John the Baptist began fulfillment .... Lk 1:72 – 75
     - —Peter preached its fulfillment .... Ac 3:25
     - —Its center is faith in Christ .... Gal 3:6 – 9
     - —The law follows faith .... Ro 4:9 – 13
4. The covenant of the law made at Mount Sinai
   - a. Where is it mentioned?
     - —First made at Mount Sinai .... Ex 19:3 – 6
     - —Confirmed by the Israelites .... Ex 24:1 – 8
     - —Renewed at the border of Canaan .... Dt 29
     - —Renewed at Mount Ebal .... Jos 8:30 – 35
     - —Renewed at Shechem .... Jos 24:1 – 27
     - —Rejected by the ten tribes .... 2Ki 17:7 – 20
     - —Renewed under Josiah .... 2Ch 34:29 – 33
     - —Broken by the nation of Judah .... Jer 31:32
     - —Renewed by the returned exiles .... Ne 9:38—10:39

b. What are its elements?
—Centered on the law of God .... Ex 34:27–28; Dt 4:13–14
—Required obedience .... Ex 24:7; Ex 34:10–11; Dt 29:9
—Linked with blessings and curses .... Dt 28; Jos 8:34–35
—Did not annul covenant with Abraham ... Gal 3:15–17
—Pointed out human sin .... Ro 3:20,23; Gal 3:19
—Increased sin .... Ro 5:20
—Prepared for the coming of Christ .... Gal 3:23–25

c. How was it fulfilled in Christ?
—He fulfilled the law .... Mt 5:17
—He perfectly obeyed the law .... Ro 5:18–19; 2Co 5:21; Heb 4:15
—He died the death of a curse .... Gal 3:10–13
—His death removed the curse from us .... Gal 3:13–14

5. The covenant with David
a. Where is it mentioned?
—First promised to David 2Sa 7:4–17
—Celebrated by David 2Sa 23:5
—Mentioned to Solomon 1Ki 2:2–4
—Celebrated by Solomon 1Ki 8:22–26
—Mentioned to Jeroboam 1Ki 11:34–36
—Reaffirmed during Jehoram's reign 2Ki 8:19
—Celebrated by psalmists .... Ps 89:3; Ps 132:10–12
—Reaffirmed by Isaiah .... Isa 9:6–7
—Reaffirmed by Ezekiel .... Eze 37:24–25

b. What are its elements?
—Several promises 2Sa 7:9–16
—No conditions attached 2Sa 7:15–16

c. How was it fulfilled in Christ?
—Mentioned by Gabriel to Mary .... Lk 1:32–33
—Preached by Paul .... Ac 13:22–23,34
—Hinted at in book of Hebrews .... Heb 1:8
—Jesus is the Son of David .... Mt 1:1; Ro 1:3
—Jesus is a king who rules .... Jn 18:33–37; 1Co 15:24–25; Rev 19:16

6. The new covenant
a. Where is it promised?
—Through Jeremiah .... Jer 31:33–34; Jer 32:38–40
—Through Ezekiel .... Eze 16:60–62; Eze 34:25–31
—Through Hosea .... Hos 2:18–20

b. What are its elements?
—Several promises .... Jer 31:33–34
—No conditions attached .... Jer 31:33–34

c. How was it fulfilled in Christ?
—Asserted by Christ in the upper room .... Lk 22:20; 1Co 11:25
—Mentioned by Paul 2Co 3:6
—Explained in book of Hebrews .... Heb 8:6–13; Heb 9:15–28; Heb 10:11–18; Heb 12:22–24

7. God's relationship to his covenants
—He establishes his covenant .... Ge 6:18; Ge 17:7; Ex 6:4; Eze 16:60–62
—He is faithful to his covenant .... Dt 7:9; 1Ki 8:23; Ne 9:32; Da 9:4
—He remembers his covenant .... Ex 2:24; Ps 105:8; Ps 111:5; Eze 16:60; Lk 1:72

COVETING

—The sinful desire for what belongs to someone else; greed

A. The command against coveting
—In the Old Testament .... Ex 20:17; Dt 5:21; Dt 7:25
—In the New Testament .... Ro 7:7–11; Eph 5:3; Col 3:5

B. Coveting often leads to other sins 1Ti 6:10; 1Jn 2:15–16
—To deceit (Jacob) .... Ge 27:18–26
—To adultery (David) 2Sa 11:1–5
—To disobedience to God (Achan) .... Jos 7:20–21
—To hypocritical worship (Saul) 1Sa 15:9–23
—To murder (Ahab) 1Ki 21:1–14
—To theft (Gehazi) 2Ki 5:20–24
—To family disharmony .... Pr 15:27
—To lying (Ananias and Sapphira) .... Ac 5:1–10

C. Contentment as the answer to coveting
—The command to be content .... Lk 3:14; 1Ti 6:8; Heb 13:5
—The experience of Paul .... Php 4:11–12

CREATION

A. Related theme
BEGINNINGS is a theme of Genesis .... Ge 1:1

B. The work of creation
—Accounts of creation .... Ge 1:1—2:3; Ge 2:4–24; Job 38:4–38; Ps 104:1–26
—Done out of nothing .... Heb 11:3
—Done in six days .... Ge 1:3–31; Ex 20:11; Ex 31:17

C. Creation as the work of God
—God as the creator .... Ge 1:1; Isa 44:24; Ac 4:24
—Accomplished through Christ .... Jn 1:3,10; Col 1:16; Heb 1:2
—The Holy Spirit involved in creation .... Job 33:4; Ps 104:30

D. Creation reveals God
—His glory .... Ps 19:1
—His power .... Isa 40:26,28
—His divine nature .... Ro 1:20
—His wisdom .... Ps 104:24
—His love .... Ps 33:5–6

E. Creation after Adam and Eve sinned
—Was cursed by God .... Ge 3:14,17–19
—Was subjected to frustration .... Ro 8:20
—Praises God .... Ps 145:10; Ps 148:1–5; Isa 55:12
—Eagerly awaits redemption .... Ro 8:19
—Will someday be liberated .... Ro 8:21
—Will someday be recreated .... Isa 65:17; 2Pe 3:10–13; Rev 21:1

F. Humans commanded to rule creation ... Ge 1:26,28; Ps 8:6–8; Ps 115:16

CREED

See CONFESSION

CROSS

A. Jesus and the cross
1. What it involved
—The means to bring about Jesus' death ... Jn 19:17–18; Ac 5:30
—Was the death of a curse ... Gal 3:13
—Planned by God ... Lk 24:26–27; Ac 2:23
—Carried out by humans ... Ac 2:23; Ac 5:30
—Showed Jesus' obedience ... Php 2:8
2. What it accomplished
—Redeemed us from the curse of God ... Gal 3:10,13
—Took away our sins ... Col 2:13–14; 1Pe 2:24
—Reconciled us with God ... Eph 2:16; Col 1:20
—Gave us eternal life ... Jn 3:14–15
—Brought about victory over Christ's enemies ... Col 2:15
B. The message of the cross
—Was preached by the apostles ... Ac 2:23; Ac 8:32–35; Ac 13:28–29; 1Co 1:23; 1Co 2:1–2
—Was a stumbling block to Jews ... 1Co 1:23
—Was foolishness to Gentiles ... 1Co 1:18,23
C. Believers and the cross
—They are crucified with Christ ... Gal 2:20
—Their sinful nature is put to death ... Ro 6:6; Gal 5:24; 1Pe 2:24
—They are crucified to the world ... Gal 6:14
—They must carry their cross ... Mt 10:38

CROWN

A. Examples of those who wore a crown
—Priests ... Lev 8:9; Zec 6:9–11
—Kings ... 2Sa 12:30; SS 3:11
—Queens ... Est 1:11; Est 2:17
—Christ with a crown of thorns ... Mt 27:29; Jn 19:2,5
—Christ with a royal crown ... Rev 14:14; Rev 19:12
B. Crowns used as a symbol
1. In the present life
—God crowns humans with glory and honor ... Ps 8:5
—God crowns us with salvation ... Ps 149:4
—God crowns us with love ... Ps 103:4
—God crowns us with blessings ... Pr 10:6
—A good wife is her husband's crown ... Pr 12:4
—Gray hair is a crown of splendor ... Pr 16:31
—Grandchildren are a crown to the aged ... Pr 17:6
—Christians are a crown to Paul ... 1Th 2:19; Php 4:1
2. In the life hereafter
—God will be a glorious crown for us ... Isa 28:5
—Christians will be a crown for God ... Isa 62:3
—Everlasting joy will crown us ... Isa 35:10
—We receive an everlasting crown ... 1Co 9:25
—We receive a crown of righteousness ... 2Ti 4:8
—We receive a crown of life ... Jas 1:12; Rev 2:10
—We receive a crown of glory ... 1Pe 5:4

CURSE, CURSING

A. The curse as a result of sin
1. Warnings of the curse
—Principle stated ... Dt 11:26–28; Pr 3:33; Jer 11:3
—Extended list of curses ... Dt 27:15–26; Dt 28:15–68
2. Expressions of the curse
a. In the Old Testament
—On the serpent ... Ge 3:14
—On Cain ... Ge 4:9–12
—On Canaan ... Ge 9:25
—On Simeon and Levi ... Ge 49:7–9
—On any who disobey the law ... Dt 27:26
—On those who dishonor God ... Mal 2:2
—On the land ... Ge 3:17; Isa 24:6; Jer 23:10; Jer 44:22; Mal 4:6
b. In the New Testament
—On those not kind to the needy ... Mt 25:41–46
—On those who refuse the gospel ... Gal 1:8–9
—On those who do not love the Lord ... 1Co 16:22
—On those who fall away from Christ ... Heb 6:4–8
—On all sinners ... Gal 3:10
3. Removal of the curse by Christ's cross ... Gal 3:13
B. Human cursing
1. Cursing God
—Humans may not curse God ... Ex 20:7; Dt 5:11; 1Co 12:3
—Penalty for cursing God was death ... Lev 24:10–16; 1Ki 21:13; Job 2:9

See also BLASPHEMY
2. Cursing other humans
a. Examples
—Balak's desire to curse Israel ... Nu 23:11,25
—Joshua cursed rebuilders of Jericho ... Jos 6:26
—Citizens of Shechem cursed Abimelech ... Jdg 9:26–27
—Goliath cursed David ... 1Sa 17:43
—Shimei cursed David ... 2Sa 16:5–7
—Curses on greedy people ... Pr 11:26
—Non-Christians curse Christians ... 1Co 4:12
b. The command not to curse other humans ... Ex 21:17; Pr 20:20; Pr 30:10–11; Jas 3:10–12
c. We must bless instead of curse ... Lk 6:28; Ro 12:14

CYRUS

—Persian king ... 2Ch 36:22; Da 6:28
—Allowed Israel to return from exile ... 2Ch 36:23
—Commanded rebuilding of the temple ... Ezr 1:1–4
—His decree recalled ... Ezr 6:1–5
—Called shepherd of the Lord ... Isa 44:28
—Called anointed of the Lord ... Isa 45:1–13

DAMASCUS

A. Identity and location
—Capital city of the Arameans/Syrians .... 1Ki 15:18; Isa 7:8
—Arameans were descendants of Shem .... Ge 10:22–23

B. Significant Arameans
—Eliezer: servant of Abram .... Ge 15:2
—Three kings called Ben-Hadad
See BEN-HADAD
—Naaman: the leprous commander 2Ki 5:1
See NAAMAN
—Hazael: king after Ben-Hadad 2Ki 8:15
See HAZAEL
—Rezin: allied with Israel against Ahaz .... Isa 7:1–9

C. Significant events of Damascus/Syria
1. Old Testament
—Abram passed through it .... Ge 14:15
—David conquered it 2Sa 8:5–6; 1Ch 18:5–6
—Twenty thousand Aramean soldiers defeated by Joab 2Sa 10:6–19
—Asa made a treaty with its king 1Ki 15:18–20; 2Ch 16:2
—Elisha prophesied there 2Ki 8:7–13
—Jeroboam II conquered it 2Ki 14:28
—Joash defeated by the Arameans 2Ch 24:23–25
—Israel allied with it against Judah .... 2Ki 16:5; Isa 7:1–2
—Ahaz defeated by the Arameans 2Ch 28:5
—Assyria captured it .... 2Ki 16:9; Isa 8:3–7
2. New Testament
—News of Jesus went to Syria .... Mt 4:24
—Saul went there to persecute Christians .... Ac 9:1–2
—Saul converted near there .... Ac 9:3–9
—Saul/Paul preached there .... Ac 9:19–22; Gal 1:17–18
—Paul escaped from there in a basket .... Ac 9:23–25; 2Co 11:32–33
—Paul traveled through Syria .... Ac 15:41; Gal 1:21

D. Prophecies against Damascus .... Isa 17:1–14; Jer 49:23–27; Am 1:3–5; Zec 9:1

DAN

A. Son of Jacob by Bilhah .... Ge 35:25
—Name means "he has vindicated" .... Ge 30:4–6
—Went to Egypt with family .... Ge 46:8,23
—Father of one son .... Ge 46:23
—Blessed by Jacob .... Ge 49:16–17

B. Tribe descended from Dan .... Nu 26:42
—Blessed by Moses .... Dt 33:22
—Numbered .... Nu 1:38–39; Nu 26:43
—Allotted land .... Jos 19:40–48; Eze 48:1
—Failed to possess the land fully .... Jdg 1:34–35
—Failed to support Deborah .... Jdg 5:17
—Samson was a Danite .... Jdg 13:2,24–25
—Stole Micah's priest .... Jdg 18:1–26

C. A city in Israel .... Ge 14:14
—At one time called Leshem .... Jos 19:47
—Also called Laish .... Jdg 18:27–31
—Northernmost city in land of Israel .... Jdg 20:1
—Jeroboam set up golden calf there 1Ki 12:25–30
—Conquered by Ben-Hadad 1Ki 15:20

DANCING

A. There is a time to dance .... Ecc 3:4

B. Occasions for dancing
1. Appropriate
—To praise and worship God .... Ex 15:20–21; Ps 68:24–25; Ps 149:3; Ps 150:4
—To express human elation .... 1Sa 18:6–7; 2Sa 6:16; Jer 31:4
2. Inappropriate
—In pagan worship .... Ex 32:5–6,19; 1Ki 18:26–29; 1Co 10:7
—Herodias before Herod .... Mt 14:6
3. Dancing ceases at a time of sorrow .... La 5:15; Mt 11:17

C. God's blessing turns sorrow into dancing .... Ps 30:11

DANIEL

A. Hebrew exiled to Babylon .... Da 1:6
—Educated in Babylonia .... Da 1:3–5
—Name changed to Belteshazzar .... Da 1:7
—Refused non-Jewish food .... Da 1:8–21
—Interpreted dreams of Nebuchadnezzar .... Da 2:24–47; Da 4:4–27
—Interpreted handwriting on the wall .... Da 5:1–28
—Survived the lions' den .... Da 6:1–23
—Recorded visions .... Da 7:1—12:13
—Jesus referred to his prophecy .... Mt 24:15

B. Son of David and Abigail 1Ch 3:1

DARIUS

A. King of the Medes; conquered Babylon .... Da 5:31
—Son of Xerxes .... Da 9:1

B. A later king of Persia .... Ezr 4:5; Hag 1:1,15
—Asked to stop rebuilding of temple .... Ezr 5:3–17
—Allowed rebuilding of temple .... Ezr 6:1–12

DARKNESS

A. Physical darkness
—Created by God .... Isa 45:7
—Originally covered the earth .... Ge 1:2
—Separated from light .... Ge 1:4
—Called night .... Ge 1:5
—Comes when the sun sets .... Ge 15:17
—God can see things in the dark .... Ps 139:11–12; Da 2:22

B. Darkness as a symbol
1. For the mysteriousness of God .... Ex 20:21; Ps 18:9; Ps 97:2
2. For afflictions .... Job 18:6,18; Isa 59:9; La 3:1–2
3. For ignorance about God .... Job 37:19; Isa 60:2; 1Jn 2:8
4. For sin and evil
—Sinful deeds are deeds of darkness .... Ro 13:12; Eph 5:11
—The way of the wicked is darkness .... Pr 2:13; Pr 4:19; 1Th 5:4–5
—Living in sin is walking in darkness .... Jn 3:19; 1Jn 1:6; 1Jn 2:9,11

5. For judgment from God ... Joel 2:2
Am 5:18,20
Rev 16:10
6. For the realm of Satan ... Lk 22:53
Eph 6:12
Col 1:13
7. For hell as a place of punishment ... Mt 8:12
2Pe 2:17
Jude 13

C. Antidotes to darkness as evil
1. God
—His first act was to dispel darkness ... Ge 1:2–3
—He surrounds himself with light ... Ps 104:1–2
1Ti 6:16
—He is the God of light ... 1Jn 1:5
2. Jesus
—Jesus came to dispel darkness ... Jn 1:4–9
Jn 3:19–21
Jn 12:46
—Jesus is the light of the world ... Jn 8:12
Jn 9:5
3. Heaven
—God's light permeates heaven ... Isa 60:19–20
Rev 21:23
—Heaven has no night ... Zec 14:7
Rev 22:5

See also LIGHT

DAVID

A. Related theme
DAVID is a theme of 1 Chronicles ... 1Ch 28:4
B. Personal data
1. Ancestry
—Son of Jesse ... Ru 4:17–22
1Ch 2:13–15
—Youngest in the family ... 1Sa 16:10–13
2. Wives
—Michal, daughter of Saul ... 1Sa 18:2–27
—Abigail, widow of Nabal ... 1Sa 25:39–44
—Bathsheba, widow of Uriah ... 2Sa 11
—Many wives and concubines ... 2Sa 5:13–15
3. Descendants
—Solomon ... 2Sa 12:24
—Amnon ... 2Sa 13:1
—Absalom ... 2Sa 13:1
—Adonijah ... 1Ki 1:5–6
—Many sons ... 2Sa 3:2–5
1Ch 3:1–9
—Jesus was the Son of David ... Mt 1:1–17
Lk 3:31
4. Occupations
—A shepherd ... 1Sa 16:11
1Sa 17:20,34–37
—A musician ... 1Sa 16:14–23
2Sa 23:1
—A psalmist ... 1Ch 16:7
Ps 3–34, etc.
Lk 20:42
—A prophet ... 2Sa 23:1–2
Ac 2:25–31
—A king ... 2Sa 5:3–4

C. David's life during Saul's reign
1. His anointing as future king ... 1Sa 16:1–13
2. His work in Saul's service
—Played music for Saul ... 1Sa 16:14–23
1Sa 18:10
—Killed Goliath ... 1Sa 17:4–51
—Became a mighty warrior ... 1Sa 18:2–7
3. Saul's reaction to David
—Was jealous of him ... 1Sa 18:6–9,12,29
—Tried to kill him ... 1Sa 18:10–11
1Sa 19:1–18
4. David's flights
—To Nob ... 1Sa 21:1
—To Gath ... 1Sa 21:10
—To the cave of Adullam ... 1Sa 22:1
—To Keilah ... 1Sa 23:7
—To desert strongholds ... 1Sa 23:14–24
—To the land of the Philistines ... 1Sa 27:1–3
—David spared Saul's life ... 1Sa 24:1–21
1Sa 26:1–25
5. His military victories
—Killed two hundred Philistines ... 1Sa 18:24–27
—Saved town of Keilah ... 1Sa 23:1–6
—Defeated Amalekites ... 1Sa 30:1–31
—Not allowed to fight on side of Philistines ... 1Sa 29:1–11
6. His covenant with Jonathan ... 1Sa 18:1–4
1Sa 20:16–17
1Sa 23:15–18
7. His lament over Saul and Jonathan ... 2Sa 1:17–27

D. David's life as king
1. His fight to become king
—Became king of Judah ... 2Sa 2:1–11
—Fought with Saul's supporters ... 2Sa 2:8—4:12
—Became king of all Israel ... 2Sa 5:1–4
1Ch 11:1–3
2. His military accomplishments
—Conquered Jerusalem ... 2Sa 5:6–10
1Ch 11:4–9
—Conquered Philistines ... 2Sa 5:17–25
2Sa 21:15–22
1Ch 14:8–17
—Conquered Ammonites ... 2Sa 10:1–19
1Ch 19:1–19
—Conquered many others ... 2Sa 8:1–14
1Ch 18:1–13
—Avenged the Gibeonites ... 2Sa 21:1–14
—Organized army and government ... 1Ch 27:1–34
—Had many mighty men ... 2Sa 23:8–39
1Ch 11–12
—Numbered his army, which angered the Lord ... 2Sa 24:1–17
1Ch 21:1–19
3. His involvement in Israel's worship
—Brought ark to Jerusalem ... 2Sa 6:1–19
—Planned the temple ... 1Ch 22:1–19
1Ch 28:8—29:9
—Organized Israel's worship ... 1Ch 15:16—16:43
—Organized priests and Levites ... 1Ch 23:26
4. God's covenant with him ... 2Sa 7:1–17
See COVENANT
5. David's sin and its consequences
—His sin with Bathsheba ... 2Sa 11:1–5
—Attempt at cover-up ... 2Sa 11:6–27
—Sin exposed by Nathan ... 2Sa 12:1–14
—Death of his son ... 2Sa 12:15–23
—Absalom's revolt ... 2Sa 14:1—18:8
—Death of Absalom ... 2Sa 18:9–18
—David mourned Absalom's death ... 2Sa 18:33—19:4
—Return to Jerusalem ... 2Sa 19:9–43
—Sheba's revolt ... 2Sa 20:1–22
6. His last days
—Abishag took care of him ... 1Ki 1:1–4
—Appointed Solomon king ... 1Ki 1:28—2:9
—Gave charge to Solomon ... 1Ki 2:1–9
—His last words ... 2Sa 23:1–7
—His death ... 1Ki 2:10–12

E. His spiritual life
  1. Positive qualities
    —Depended on the Lord .... 1Sa 17:45 – 47; Ps 27:1 – 6
    —Trusted in the Lord .... Ps 25:1 – 5
    —Praised God .... 1Ch 16:7 – 10; Ps 9:1 – 2
    —Was concerned about God's house .... 1Ch 17:1 – 2; 1Ch 22:5
    —Respected those in authority .... 1Sa 24:5; 1Sa 26:9 – 11
    —Was faithful to his promises .... 2Sa 9:1 – 13
    —Repented of his sin .... 2Sa 12:13; Ps 32:3 – 5
  2. Negative qualities
    —Took pride in his military power .... 2Sa 24:1 – 10
    —Committed adultery with Bathsheba .... 2Sa 11:1 – 5
    —Committed a murder indirectly .... 2Sa 11:14 – 17

F. New Testament significance
  —Jesus is David's Son .... Mt 1:1; 2Ti 2:8
  —Jesus is the Root of David .... Rev 5:5; Rev 22:16
  —Jesus sat on David's throne .... Lk 1:30 – 33
  —David confessed Jesus to be Lord .... Mt 22:42 – 43
  —David was not a legalist .... Lk 6:1 – 5
  —David prophesied the resurrection .... Ac 2:25 – 31
  —David believed righteousness came through faith .... Ro 4:6 – 8
  —David was a hero of faith .... Heb 11:32 – 33
  —God spoke through David .... Heb 4:7

DAY

A. Meanings of the word "day"
  1. The period of light after the night
    —Light called "day" by God .... Ge 1:5
    —"Day and night" .... Ge 8:22; Est 4:16; Jn 9:4 – 5
    —Divided into twelve hours .... Mt 20:1 – 12; Jn 11:9
  2. The time period of twenty-four hours .... Ge 1:5,13,19; Ge 8:4 – 5,13 – 14; Ex 2:11,13
  3. A synonym for "time"
    —The day of creation .... Dt 4:32
    —The day of the exodus 1Ki 8:16
    —The day of the giving of the law .... Nu 15:23
    —A day of disaster .... Dt 32:35
    —To the present day .... Jos 4:9
    —The day of one's death .... Jdg 13:7
    —The day Jerusalem was built .... Jer 32:31
    —The day the temple was built .... Hag 2:18
    —The day of salvation 2Co 6:2

B. The day of the Lord
  1. In the Old Testament, it can refer to:
    —The time of God's judgment .... Joel 1:15; Am 5:18; Am 8:11 – 14; Zep 1:14 – 17
    —The time of Israel's restoration .... Isa 10:20; Isa 11:10 – 11; Zec 9:16
    —The first coming of Christ .... Mal 3:1 – 3
    —The outpouring of the Spirit .... Joel 2:28 – 31
    —The kingdom of Christ .... Isa 4:2 – 6; Mic 4:1 – 7
    —The end of the world .... Isa 24:21 – 23; Isa 27:12 – 13; Zec 14:1 – 3
  2. In the New Testament, it can refer to:
    —The day of the final battle .... Rev 16:14
    —The day of Christ's return .... Mk 13:24 – 27; 1Co 1:7 – 8; 2Co 1:14
    —The day of judgment .... 1Co 3:12 – 15; 1Th 5:2 – 3; 2Pe 3:12
    —The day of God's wrath .... Ro 2:5 – 6
    —The day of blessing for Christians 1Co 1:8; 2Ti 4:8

DEACON

A. Often translated "servant" or "minister"
  —Used of Jesus .... Ro 15:8
  —Used of Paul and Apollos 1Co 3:5
  —Used of Timothy 1Ti 4:6
  —Used of any follower of Christ .... Jn 12:26

B. An office in the New Testament church .... Php 1:1
  —Assistants to apostles .... Ac 6:1 – 4
  —Qualifications given .... Ac 6:3; 1Ti 3:8 – 13
  —Possibly women were deaconesses .... Ro 16:1; 1Ti 3:11

DEATH

A. Physical death
  1. Phrases used
    —Dying .... Ge 5:5,8,11
    —Returning to the dust .... Ge 3:19; Ecc 12:7
    —Lying down in the dust .... Job 7:21
    —Going to one's ancestors .... Ge 15:15
    —Resting with one's ancestors .... Dt 31:16; 2Sa 7:12
    —Being gathered to one's people .... Ge 25:8; Ge 49:29
    —Breathing one's last .... Ge 35:29; Lk 23:46
    —Going down to the grave .... Ge 37:35; 1Ki 2:6,9
    —Falling asleep .... Jn 11:11; Ac 7:60
    —Sleeping the last sleep .... Ps 76:5
    —Being away from the body 2Co 5:8
    —Departing .... Php 1:23; 2Ti 4:6; 2Pe 1:15
  2. All human beings die .... Ecc 8:8; Heb 9:27
    —First examples .... Ge 4:8; Ge 5:5 – 20,25 – 31
    —Two exceptions: Enoch and Elijah .... Ge 5:21 – 24; 2Ki 2:11 – 12
  3. Death came as a result of sin
    —A result of Adam's sin .... Ge 2:17; Ro 5:12; 1Co 15:21 – 22
    —The wages of sin for everyone .... Ro 6:23
  4. Death was conquered by Christ
    —He was raised from the dead .... Ro 6:9
    —He holds the keys of death .... Rev 1:18
    —He releases us from fear of death .... Heb 2:15
    —He will destroy death completely .... 1Co 15:26,53 – 57
  5. What is death for believers?
    —Falling asleep in Christ 1Co 15:18; 1Th 4:14
    —Gain .... Php 1:21
    —Precious to God .... Ps 116:15; Rev 14:13

—The entrance into peace....Isa 57:1–2
—The entrance into glory....Ps 73:24
—Clothes us with our heavenly dwelling....2Co 5:4
—Prepares us to receive a crown....2Ti 4:8
6. What is death for the wicked?
—Without salvation....Eze 3:19
Jn 8:21
—Without hope....Job 8:13
Pr 11:7
—A judgment from God....Nu 16:29–30
Lk 12:20
—The pathway to hell....Lk 16:22–23
Ac 1:25
—Not pleasurable to God....Eze 18:23,32
—Something for them to fear....Job 27:19–21
Pr 10:24

B. Spiritual death
1. Its origin
—Came as a result of sin....Ge 2:17
Ro 5:12
Ro 6:23
—Is part of the sinful human nature....Ro 8:6
2. Who are spiritually dead?
—Everyone who does not have Christ....Eph 2:1,5
Col 2:13
1Jn 5:12
—Those seeking personal pleasure....Eph 4:17–19
1Ti 5:6
—Those not serving God by good works....Heb 6:1
Heb 9:14
Rev 3:1–2
3. How can one overcome spiritual death?
—Through faith in Christ....Eph 2:4–5
Eph 5:14
1Jn 5:12
—By repenting and turning to God....Lk 15:17–24
Rev 3:1–3

C. Eternal death
1. Phrases used to describe eternal death
—Eternal punishment....Mt 25:46
—Hell....Mt 5:29–30
—The eternal fire....Mt 25:41
—The fiery lake of burning sulfur....Rev 19:20
—The lake of fire....Rev 20:15
—Shut out from God's presence....2Th 1:9
—The darkness outside....Mt 25:30
—The blackest darkness....Jude 13
—The second death....Rev 20:6
—The coming wrath....1Th 1:10
2. What is its origin?
—Came as a result of sin....Ge 2:17
Ro 5:12
Ro 6:23
Jas 1:15
—Symbolized by removal from Eden....Ge 3:22–24
3. Who are subject to eternal death?
—The devil and his angels....2Pe 2:4
Rev 20:10
—The antichrist....2Th 2:8
Rev 19:20
—Those who worship the beast....Rev 14:9–11
—Those who choose the broad road....Mt 7:13
—Those who live a wicked life....Ro 1:28–31
—Those who do not love the needy....Mt 25:41–46
—Those who do not believe in Jesus....Jn 3:36
—False teachers in the church....2Pe 2:1–17
—Godless, greedy people in the church....Jude 4,8–13
4. Jesus conquered eternal death....1Co 15:20,54–57
2Ti 1:10
5. Who will escape eternal death?
—Those who believe in Jesus....Jn 3:16,18,36
Jn 11:25–26
—Those who are raised with Christ....Ro 6:5–11
—Those who keep the word of God....Jn 8:51
—Those who choose the narrow road....Mt 7:14
—Those who are kind to the needy....Mt 25:34–40
—Those who do not worship the beast....Rev 20:4–6

DEBORAH

A. Rebekah's nurse....Ge 35:8
B. A prophetess....Jdg 4:4
—Judged Israel....Jdg 4:5
—Fought Sisera's army with Barak....Jdg 4:6–10,14–16
—Deborah's song of triumph....Jdg 5:1–31

DEBT

—What is owed to another person
A. Financial debts
1. Regulated by Old Testament laws
—No interest to be charged....Ex 22:25
Lev 25:36–37
Dt 15:8
Dt 23:19–20
—Security to be returned....Ex 22:26–27
Dt 24:10–13
—The seventh year for canceling debts....Dt 15:1–6
—The Year of Jubilee for canceling debts....Lev 25:8–54
2. Examples of oppressed debtors
—Numerous people in David's time....1Sa 22:2
—A widow in Elisha's day....2Ki 4:1–7
—The poor in Amos's day....Am 2:6–8
—Many Israelites in Nehemiah's day....Ne 5:1–13
3. Warnings against cosigning for a debt....Pr 6:1–5
Pr 11:15
Pr 17:18
Pr 22:26–27
4. Debts in the New Testament world
—Borrowing was common....Lk 6:34
—Jesus used imagery of debt in parables....Mt 18:23–35
Lk 7:41–42
Lk 11:5–8
Lk 16:1–9
—Jesus used imagery of interest in parables....Mt 25:14–30
Lk 19:12–27
—We must lend without expecting return....Lk 6:35
—We must pay what is owed....Ro 13:7
B. Debts used as a symbol
1. Debt symbolizes sin....Mt 6:12–15
Mt 18:23–35
Lk 7:41–48
2. Debt symbolizes our Christian obligations
—Paul's debt to preach the gospel....Ro 1:14
1Co 9:16
—Our debt to love others....Ro 13:8
—The Gentile debt to Jews....Ro 15:25–27

DEMETRIUS

—Silversmith in Ephesus....Ac 19:24
—Incited a riot over evangelism there....Ac 19:25–29
—Told to work through legal channels....Ac 19:38–40

DEMONS

—Evil spirits that can afflict humans
A. The characteristics of demons
1. Their identity
—They are related to false gods....Dt 32:17
Ps 106:37
1Co 10:20
Rev 9:20

—They are also called evil spirits — Mk 5:12 – 13
1Ti 4:1

2. Their behavior
—Insane raving — Mk 1:23 – 24
Mk 5:2 – 5
—Self-destructive behavior — Mk 5:5
Mk 9:22
—Convulsions — Mk 9:18,20
—Could cause physical ailments — Mt 12:22
—Could speak — Mk 1:34
Mk 5:12
—Could perform miracles — Rev 16:13 – 14

B. The relationship of demons to Jesus
1. They recognized Jesus — Mt 8:28 – 29
Mk 1:23 – 24
Ac 19:13 – 16
2. They were driven out in the name of Jesus
—By Jesus himself — Mk 1:23 – 24,32 – 34
Mk 5:1 – 13
Mk 9:14 – 27
—By the followers of Jesus — Mk 16:17
Lk 10:17
Ac 5:16
Ac 16:16 – 18
3. Jesus' power over demons demonstrates
—That he was not influenced by Beelzebub — Mt 12:25 – 29
Mk 3:23 – 27
Lk 11:17 – 22
—That the kingdom of God worked in Jesus — Mt 12:28
Lk 11:20

DEPRAVITY

See SIN

DEPRESSION

—The feeling of despair over life's problems

A. Examples of depressed people
—Moses — Nu 11:10 – 15
—Elijah — 1Ki 19:1 – 4
—Job — Job 3:1 – 26
—The psalmist — Ps 42:1 – 11
—The Teacher — Ecc 2:20
—Jonah — Jnh 4:3

B. Perspectives for depressed people
—Being reminded of God's presence — 1Ki 19:11 – 13
—Experiencing the Holy Spirit — Isa 61:1 – 3
Jn 16:6 – 7
—Placing hope and trust in God — Ps 31:24
Ps 42:5,11
Heb 6:18 – 19
—Casting anxiety on God — 1Pe 5:7
—Receiving the support of believers — 1Sa 20:41 – 42
Job 2:11 – 13
Job 42:10 – 11
1Th 5:11

DESPAIR

See DEPRESSION

DEVIL

See SATAN

DEVOTION

See MEDITATION

DINAH

—Daughter of Jacob — Ge 30:21
Ge 46:15
—Raped by Shechem — Ge 34:1 – 4
—Avenged by Simeon and Levi — Ge 34:25 – 29

DISCIPLESHIP

—Following the lifestyle outlined by Jesus

A. Related theme
DISCIPLESHIP is a theme of Matthew — Mt 10:25

B. Who are called disciples?
—Twelve chosen followers of Jesus — Mk 3:16 – 19
—Believers in Jesus — Ac 6:7
Ac 9:1
Ac 11:26

C. What is expected of disciples?
—Commitment to Jesus — Mt 8:19 – 22
Mk 1:17 – 18
Lk 14:26 – 27
—Humble service — Mk 10:43 – 44
—Following teachings of the Sermon on the Mount — Mt 5:1—7:27
—Doing the will of God — Mt 12:49 – 50
—Loving one another — Jn 13:34 – 35
Jn 15:9 – 17
—Sharing with one another — Ac 4:32 – 37
Ac 11:28 – 29
—Making disciples of all nations — Mt 28:19

D. What happens to Jesus' disciples?
—They receive eternal life — Mk 10:29 – 30
—Jesus teaches them — Lk 11:2 – 4
—Jesus acknowledges them before his Father — Mt 10:32
—They are called Christians — Ac 11:26
—They may have to suffer — Jn 15:20
2Ti 3:12
—They may experience rejection — Mt 10:22,34 – 35
Jn 15:18,21
Jn 17:14
—They need strengthening — Ac 14:21 – 22
Ac 18:23

DISCIPLINE

—Measures taken to ensure conformity to the accepted standard

A. Related theme
DISCIPLINE is a theme of 1 Corinthians — 1Co 5:5

B. Methods of discipline
1. Human discipline
—By instruction and warning — Pr 1:2 – 4,8 – 10
2Ti 4:2
Tit 2:15
—By the rod — Pr 13:24
Pr 22:15
2. God's discipline of us
—By instruction and warning — Jer 7:27 – 28
Jer 17:23
—By adversity and affliction — Lev 26:23 – 26
Job 33:19
Ps 39:10 – 11
Jer 2:30

C. Motives of discipline
—Love — 2Sa 7:14 – 15
Pr 3:12
Heb 12:6
Rev 3:19
—Desire for another's growth and improvement — Job 5:17
Pr 25:12
Pr 29:15
Heb 12:10

D. Types of discipline
1. Self-discipline — Ro 6:12 – 14
Ro 8:13
1Co 9:26 – 27
2. Discipline in the home — Pr 13:24
Pr 15:5
Pr 19:18

3. Mutual discipline
—Between friends ... Pr 17:10; Pr 27:5–6; Pr 28:23
—Among believers ... Lk 17:3; 1Th 5:11,14–15; 2Th 3:15

4. Church discipline
a. Done through preaching the word ... 2Ti 3:16–17; 2Ti 4:2; Tit 2:15
b. Done through direct measures
—Rebuke sinners publicly ... 1Ti 5:20; Tit 1:13
—Have nothing to do with sinners ... Ro 16:17; 1Co 5:9–11; 2Th 3:6,14; Tit 3:10
—Remove sinners from the church ... 1Co 5:1–5,13; 1Ti 1:20

DIVORCE

—The breaking of the marital bond

A. Physical divorce
1. Divorce in the Old Testament
—Not part of God's original plan ... Ge 2:24; Mt 19:8
—Allowed and regulated ... Dt 22:13–19,28–29; Dt 24:1–4
—Evidence of human stubbornness ... Mt 19:8
—Priests not to marry divorcees ... Lev 21:7,14
—Hated by God ... Mal 2:16
—Defiled the land ... Jer 3:1–2
—Required for those with idolatrous wives ... Ezr 10:2–17
2. Divorce in the New Testament
—Marriage considered binding ... Mt 19:3–6; Ro 7:2–3
—Permitted by Jesus for unfaithfulness ... Mt 5:31–33; Mt 19:9
—Permitted by Paul in mixed marriages ... 1Co 7:12–15
—Divorce was a pardonable sin ... Jn 4:17–18,39–42

B. Spiritual divorce
1. A result of sin and idolatry ... Isa 50:1; Jer 3:2
2. Northern kingdom (Israel): divorced by God ... Jer 3:8
3. Southern kingdom (Judah)
—Equally as adulterous as Israel ... Jer 3:8–11
—Temporary separation through the exile ... Isa 50:1; Isa 54:7
—Taken back by God as spouse ... Isa 54:6–8; Isa 62:4–5

See also ADULTERY; MARRIAGE

DOCTRINE

—True teachings concerning faith and life

A. Related themes
1. DIRECTION is a theme of Proverbs ... Pr 3:5
2. DEFENSE is a theme of Colossians ... Col 2:8
3. DISCERNMENT is a theme of 2 John ... 2Jn 10
4. FALSE DOCTRINE is a theme of 1 Timothy ... 1Ti 1:3
5. FALSE TEACHERS is a theme of:
—2 Peter ... 2Pe 2:1
—Jude ... Jude 4

B. The importance of knowing doctrine
—Stressed in the Old Testament ... Ps 78:1–8; Pr 7:1–5; Pr 13:14
—Stressed in the New Testament ... 1Co 11:2; 2Th 2:15; 2Ti 1:13; Tit 1:9; Tit 2:1

See also CONFESSION; EDUCATION

C. Concern over false doctrine
1. The identity of false teachers
—The teachers of the law ... Mt 23:2–4,16–22; Mk 12:38–40; Lk 20:46–47; 1Ti 1:6–7
—Teachers of unsound doctrine ... 1Ti 4:1–3; 2Ti 4:3–4; Tit 1:9–11
—Teachers who distort the truth ... Ac 20:29–30; 2Ti 2:17–18
—Teachers who introduce heresies ... 2Pe 2:1; 2Jn 7
—Teachers who cause divisions ... Ro 16:17; 1Ti 6:3–5
—Teachers who promote immorality ... 2Ti 3:6–8; Rev 2:14,20
2. Commands concerning false teachers
—Watch out for them ... Mk 12:38; Lk 20:46; Ac 20:31; 2Jn 8
—Command them to stop teaching ... 1Ti 1:3–4; Tit 1:10–11,13–14
—Withdraw from them ... Ro 16:17; 2Ti 2:16–18; 2Jn 10–11

DOEG

—An Edomite; Saul's head shepherd ... 1Sa 21:7
—Reported to Saul about priests of Nob ... 1Sa 22:9–10
—Killed the priests of Nob for Saul ... 1Sa 22:18–19
—David wrote a psalm about the incident ... Ps 52:1–9

DOG

See ANIMALS

DORCAS

—Disciple in Joppa who died ... Ac 9:36–37
—Raised to life by Peter ... Ac 9:38–41

DOUBT

—A questioning of one's faith

A. Examples of believers who doubted
—Abram ... Ge 12:10–20; Ge 15:2–3; Ge 16:1–4; Ge 20:1–13
—Moses ... Ex 33:15–19
—Gideon ... Jdg 6:36–37,39
—John the Baptist ... Mt 11:2–3
—Peter ... Mt 14:28–31
—Martha ... Jn 11:39
—Some disciples ... Mt 28:17
—Thomas ... Jn 20:24–25

B. Ending doubt
1. How doubts were ended
—Abram, by believing God's word ... Ge 15:6
—Moses, by seeing God's glory ... Ex 33:21–23
—Gideon, by throwing out the fleece ... Jdg 6:36–40
—John, by seeing Christ's miracles ... Mt 11:4–6
—Peter, by reaching out to Christ ... Mt 14:30–31
—Thomas, by seeing the risen Christ ... Jn 20:26–29

2. God wants us to overcome doubt...Mk 11:22–24
Jas 1:6
Jude 22

DOVE

See BIRDS

DREAMS AND VISIONS

A. Dreams and visions in general
—Closely related...Da 7:1–2
—Used by God for revelation...Nu 12:6
—Authenticity must be tested...Dt 13:1–5
—God alone can interpret dreams...Ge 40:8
Ge 41:16
Da 2:27–28
B. Examples of dreams and visions used for revelation
1. Dreams
—Jacob...Ge 28:12–16
—Joseph...Ge 37:5–9
—Pharaoh, interpreted by Joseph...Ge 41:1–36
—Solomon...1Ki 3:5
—Nebuchadnezzar, interpreted by Daniel...Da 2:24–47
Da 4:4–27
—Joseph, husband of Mary...Mt 1:20–21
2. Visions
—Abram...Ge 15:1
—Jacob...Ge 46:2
—Samuel...1Sa 3:10–15
—Various prophets...Isa 1:1
Da 7:1
Ob 1
Mic 1:1
Na 1:1
—Cornelius...Ac 10:3–6
—Peter...Ac 10:9–17
—Paul...Ac 18:9
C. Warnings against those who feign dreams...Jer 23:25–28
Eze 13:3–9
Zec 10:2
Jude 8

DROUGHT

See HUNGER AND THIRST

DRUGS

See ALCOHOL

DRUNKENNESS

See ALCOHOL

DUST

A. Humans are creatures of dust
—Created from the dust of the ground...Ge 2:7
Ecc 3:20
1Co 15:47
—Pictures human frailty...Ps 103:14
—Will return to the dust...Ge 3:19
Ps 104:29
Ecc 12:7
B. Dust used as a symbol
—Dust symbolizes a large number...Ge 13:16
Nu 23:10
—Rain turned into dust as God's judgment...Dt 28:24
—Dust on the head expresses grief...Job 2:12
Isa 47:1
—Sitting in dust expresses repentance...Jnh 3:6
—Lying in dust expresses humiliation...Ps 44:25
Ps 113:7
—Lying down in dust means death...Job 7:21
Ps 7:5
—Enemies licking the dust means defeat...Ps 72:9
Mic 7:17
—Shaking dust off the feet means rejection...Mt 10:14
Ac 13:51
—Throwing dust in the air expresses shock...Ac 22:23

EAGLE

See BIRDS

EAR

A. The human ear
1. Uses for the human ear
—To hear...2Sa 7:22
—To acquire wisdom and knowledge...Pr 2:2
Pr 18:15
—To wear earrings...Ge 35:4
—To designate, by piercing, a permanent servant...Ex 21:6
2. Types of human ears
—The ear eager to listen to Jesus...Mt 11:15
—The ear eager to listen to the Spirit...Rev 2:7,11,17,29
—The understanding ear...Job 13:1
—The deaf ear...Isa 43:8
—The closed ear...Jer 6:10
—The uncircumcised ear...Ac 7:51
—The ear itching to hear falsehood...2Ti 4:3
B. The ears of God
—His ears are attentive to our prayers...Ps 34:15
1Pe 3:12
—His ears hear the cries of the oppressed...Jas 5:4
—His ear is not dull...Isa 59:1
—His ears hear insolence...2Ki 19:28
—He closes his ears to sinners...Eze 8:18
—We can ask God to give ear to us...Ps 5:1
Ps 17:1,6
Ps 130:2

EARTH

A. God and the earth
1. His actions regarding it
—He created it...Ge 1:1
—He laid its foundations...Heb 1:10
—He suspended it in space...Job 26:7
—He called forth plants from it...Ge 1:11
—He called forth animals from it...Ge 1:24
—He made people from it...Ge 2:7
—He filled it with his creatures...Ps 104:24
—He holds it firmly...Ps 75:3
—He governs it...Job 34:12–15
—He will judge it...Ps 96:13
See also CREATION; PROVIDENCE
2. His relationship to it
—He owns it...Ps 24:1
1Co 10:26
—He is King over all of it...Ps 47:2,7,9
—He loves it...Ps 33:5
—His glory fills it...Isa 6:3
—His knowledge will fill it...Isa 11:9
Hab 2:14
—It is his footstool...Isa 66:1
Mt 5:35
B. Humans and the earth
—Made from the earth...Ge 2:7
1Co 15:47
—It is given to humans...Ps 115:16
—Humans must fill and rule it...Ge 1:28
Ge 9:7
Ps 8:6–8
—Believers shall inherit it...Mt 5:5
Ro 4:13

C. The earth and sin
—Ground cursed after Adam's sin........................Ge 3:17 – 19
—Earth groans as a result of sin........................Ro 8:22
—Earth became the domain for Satan................Rev 12:9
—Earth waits for redemption..............................Ro 8:20 – 21
—God will someday make a new earth...............Isa 65:17
2Pe 3:13
Rev 21:1

EARTHQUAKE

—At the Lord's appearance to Elijah........................1Ki 19:11 – 12
—At the Lord's judgment of Jerusalem......................Isa 29:5 – 6
—During the reign of Uzziah..................................Am 1:1
Zec 14:5
—After the death of Christ......................................Mt 27:54
—At the resurrection of Christ.................................Mt 28:2
—During Paul's imprisonment in Philippi.................Ac 16:26
—As a sign of Christ's coming.................................Mt 24:4 – 8
Mk 13:3 – 8
Lk 21:7 – 11
—In the great tribulation...Rev 6:12
Rev 11:13
—In God's final judgment..Rev 16:17 – 18

EDOMITES

A. Their identity
—The descendants of Esau (Edom)......................Ge 25:30
Ge 36:8 – 9
—Lived in hill country, southeast of Israel...........Ge 36:9
—Country also called Mount Seir........................Ge 32:3
—Territory bordered on Judah.............................Jos 15:21
B. Significant Edomites
—Numerous kings listed.......................................Ge 36:31 – 39
1Ch 1:43 – 50
—Doeg: head shepherd of King Saul....................1Sa 21:7
1Sa 22:9,18 – 19
—Hadad: fought against Solomon.......................1Ki 11:14 – 22
C. Their wars
—Defeated by King Saul.......................................1Sa 14:47
—Defeated by David...2Sa 8:11 – 14
1Ch 18:11 – 13
—Defeated Moab with Israel and Judah...............2Ki 3:1 – 27
—Allied with Moab against Jehoshaphat..............2Ch 20:1,10
—Their warriors killed by Moabites and Ammonites...2Ch 20:22 – 24
—Defeated Jehoram of Judah..............................2Ki 8:20 – 22
2Ch 21:8 – 10
—Defeated by King Amaziah................................2Ki 14:7
2Ch 25:10 – 12
—Defeated King Ahaz of Judah...........................2Ch 28:17
D. Important data concerning them
—Refused passage to Israelites in desert.............Nu 20:14 – 21
—Israelites passed around their country.............Nu 21:4
Jdg 11:17 – 18
—Solomon intermarried with them.....................1Ki 11:1
—Prophecies concerning their destruction..........Isa 34:4 – 15
Jer 49:7 – 22
Eze 25:12 – 14
Eze 35:1 – 15
Am 1:11 – 12
Ob 1 – 21

EDUCATION

A. People as educators
1. Primary educators: parents
—A never-ending task..Dt 4:9
Dt 6:4 – 7
Pr 1:8
Pr 6:20
—Usually done by fathers...................................Ge 18:19
Ps 44:1
Eph 6:4
—Could be done by mothers.................................Pr 6:20
2Ti 1:5
2Ti 3:15
2. Officials authorized by a government...............Ezr 7:6,10
2Ch 17:7 – 9
Ne 8:7 – 8
Ac 7:22
3. Authorized religious officials...........................Mk 12:28
Jn 3:10
Ac 22:3
4. The apostles...Mt 28:20
Ac 2:42
Ac 4:2
5. People gifted by the Spirit.................................1Co 12:28 – 29
Eph 4:11
6. Any mature Christian..Heb 5:11 – 14
B. The content of education
—The law of God...Dt 6:6 – 7
Dt 33:10
—The praiseworthy deeds of God........................Ps 78:4 – 6
—The holy Scriptures..2Ti 3:14 – 17
—General knowledge and wisdom......................Da 1:17
Col 2:3
C. The foundation of education
—The fear of God..Ps 111:10
Pr 1:7
Pr 9:10
—Knowing the Lord Jesus Christ........................1Co 1:30
Col 2:3
D. Purpose of education
—To impart information.....................................Ps 78:4 – 6
—To inspire trust and obedience........................Ps 78:7 – 8
Pr 22:19
—To inspire wisdom...Pr 4:5 – 8
—To attain skill in holy living.............................Ge 18:19
Pr 1:2 – 4
2Ti 3:17
—To prepare for adulthood.................................Pr 22:6

EGLON

A. City in Canaan..Jos 10:3
—Its king joined others against city of Gibeon.....Jos 10:3 – 8
—Defeated by Joshua..Jos 10:9 – 14
B. King of Moab...Jdg 3:12 – 14
—Killed by Ehud...Jdg 3:16 – 23

EGYPT

A. Names and geography
1. Other terms for Egypt
—The land of Ham...Ps 105:23
—The land of slavery.....................................Ex 20:2
—The South...Da 11:5
—Rahab...Isa 51:9 – 10
2. Areas of Egypt
—Upper and Lower Egypt..............................Isa 11:11
—The Nile River...Eze 29:3
—The land of Goshen.....................................Ge 47:6
—Rameses, a district in Goshen.....................Ge 47:11
—Pithom and Rameses: built by Israelites.......Ex 1:11
—Memphis, the capital city...........................Hos 9:6
—Thebes..Eze 30:14
—Tahpanhes, the city to which Jews fled.........Jer 43:8
Jer 44:1
B. Important Egyptians
—Their kings were called pharaohs
See PHARAOH
—Hagar: servant of Sarai.....................................Ge 16:1

—Potiphar: owner of Joseph ... Ge 39:1
—Shishak: ransacked the temple ... 1Ki 14:25–26

C. Interaction with God's people
1. During the time of the patriarchs
—Abram went to Egypt during famine ... Ge 12:10–20
—Joseph sold there by merchants ... Ge 37:28
—Joseph became governor of Egypt ... Ge 41:33–45
—Joseph's brothers bought grain there ... Ge 42:1–26; Ge 43:1—44:3
—Jacob and his sons moved there ... Ge 46:1—47:12
2. At the time of the exodus
See EXODUS
3. During the time of the kings
—Solomon intermarried with them ... 1Ki 3:1
—Solomon ruled territory to its border ... 1Ki 4:21
—Solomon traded with them ... 1Ki 10:28–29; 2Ch 1:16–17
—Enemies of Solomon fled there ... 1Ki 11:14–18; 1Ki 11:40
—Gained victory over Rehoboam ... 1Ki 14:25–26; 2Ch 12:1–12
—Hoshea allied with them against Syria ... 2Ki 17:4
—Josiah killed in a battle against them ... 2Ki 23:29–30; 2Ch 35:20–24
—Jehoahaz deposed by king of Egypt ... 2Ki 23:33–35; 2Ch 36:2–4
—Jews fled there after death of Gedaliah ... 2Ki 25:25–26
—Jeremiah forced to go there ... Jer 43:4–7
4. In the New Testament
—Jesus and his parents fled there ... Mt 2:13–15
—Egyptian Jews in Jerusalem on Pentecost ... Ac 2:10

D. Prophecies concerning Egypt
—God's people to be enslaved there ... Ge 15:13
—God's people to be freed ... Ge 15:14; Ex 3:7–10
—Judgment against Egypt ... Isa 19:1–17; Jer 46:2–26; Eze 29:3—30:26
—Judgment on those who seek help from Egypt ... Isa 30:1–3; Isa 31:1–4; Jer 2:18–19,36–37; Jer 42:7–22; Hos 7:11–16
—God will call his people back from Egypt ... Isa 11:10–11; Isa 27:12–13
—God will call his Son from Egypt ... Hos 11:1; Mt 2:15
—Egyptians will someday worship the Lord ... Isa 19:18–25; Isa 45:14; Mic 7:11–13

EHUD

—Left-handed judge of Israel ... Jdg 3:15
—Killed Eglon ... Jdg 3:16–23
—Led Israelites against Moabites ... Jdg 3:26–30

ELAH

—Son of Baasha ... 1Ki 16:6
—Became king of Israel ... 1Ki 16:6,8
—Murdered by Zimri ... 1Ki 16:9–10

ELDER

A. Elders in the Old Testament
—Assisted in government ... Nu 11:16–17
—Advised kings ... 1Ki 12:6–7
—Judged the people ... Dt 22:13–19
—Witnessed legal matters ... Ru 4:2–11
—Performed religious rituals ... Ex 12:21
—Represented the tribes ... 1Ki 8:1–3
—Helped educate the people ... Ex 19:7

B. Elders in the New Testament
1. In Jewish society
—Leaders of the people ... Mt 27:12; Ac 24:1
—Established religious tradition ... Mt 15:2
2. In the church
—Synonymous with "overseer" ... Tit 1:6–7
—Appointed by the apostles ... Ac 14:23; Tit 1:5
—Qualifications given ... 1Ti 3:1–7; Tit 1:5–9
—Directed the affairs of the church ... 1Ti 5:17
—Preached and taught the truth ... 1Ti 3:2; 1Ti 5:17
—Guarded against false teaching ... Ac 20:29–31; Tit 1:9
—Served as pastors ... Ac 20:28; Jas 5:14; 1Pe 5:1–3
—Church members should submit to them ... 1Th 5:12; Heb 13:7,17
3. Twenty-four elders in heaven
—They are seated on thrones ... Rev 4:4; Rev 11:16
—They worship God ... Rev 4:10; Rev 5:8–14; Rev 7:11–12; Rev 19:4

ELEAZAR

—Son of Aaron ... Ex 6:23–25
—Became high priest after Aaron ... Nu 20:26–28; Dt 10:6
—Took census with Moses ... Nu 26:1–4
—Aided Joshua in dividing up Canaan ... Jos 14:1
—His death ... Jos 24:33

ELECTION

—Being chosen by God

A. Related theme
CHOOSING is a theme of Deuteronomy ... Dt 7:6

B. Examples of people chosen by God
1. In the Old Testament
—Abraham ... Ge 18:19
—Jacob ... Ge 25:23
—Moses ... Ps 106:23
—Aaron ... Nu 17:1–8
—Saul ... 1Sa 10:24
—David ... 1Sa 16:1,12; 2Sa 6:21
—People of Israel ... Isa 41:8–9
—Servant of the Lord ... Isa 42:1
2. In the New Testament
—Jesus, God's Son ... Lk 9:35
—The disciples ... Jn 15:16
—Paul ... Ac 9:15; Gal 1:15
—The church ... 1Pe 2:9
—Individual Christians ... Eph 1:4; 1Pe 1:2

C. The basis of election
—God's love ... Dt 10:14–15; Eph 1:4; 2Ti 1:9
—God's grace ... Ro 11:5–6
—God's faithfulness to his promises ... Dt 7:7–8
—God's decision to fulfill his purposes ... Ro 9:11
—God's foreknowledge ... Ro 8:29; 1Pe 1:2
—Not based on human works ... Ro 9:11–12

D. The purposes of election
1. For God
—To show his grace ... Ro 11:5–6; Eph 1:7
—To redeem his children ... Eph 1:5,7; 2Th 2:13
2. For the elect
—To come to faith ... Ac 13:48; 2Th 2:13
—To assure us of salvation ... Isa 41:9–10; Ro 8:33–34; 2Pe 1:10
—To praise God ... Eph 1:11–12
—To become like Christ ... Ro 8:29
—To do good works ... Eph 2:10; Col 3:12
—To bear fruit ... Jn 15:16
—To witness to others ... Isa 42:1,6–7; Ac 9:15

ELI
—High priest ... 1Sa 1:9
—Blessed Hannah ... 1Sa 1:12–18
—Raised Samuel ... 1Sa 2:11–21
—Grieved over his sons' wickedness ... 1Sa 2:22–25
—Did not restrain his sons ... 1Sa 3:13
—Prophet spoke against him ... 1Sa 2:27–36
—His death ... 1Sa 4:12–22

ELIHU
—Younger friend of Job ... Job 32:4
—Angry with Job and his friends ... Job 32:2–3
—Gave a lengthy speech ... Job 32:6—37:24

ELIJAH
A. His life as a prophet of God
—Predicted drought in Israel ... 1Ki 17:1; Jas 5:17
—Fed by ravens ... 1Ki 17:2–6
—Stayed with a widow in Zarephath ... 1Ki 17:7–16
—Raised the widow's dead son ... 1Ki 17:17–24
—Challenged Baal's prophets to a contest ... 1Ki 18:19–26
—Prayed for fire from heaven ... 1Ki 18:30–39
—Killed the prophets of Baal ... 1Ki 18:40
—Prayed for rain ... 1Ki 18:41–45
—Fled from Jezebel ... 1Ki 19:1–3
—Prayed that he might die ... 1Ki 19:4–5
—Strengthened by the Lord ... 1Ki 19:6–18
—Anointed Elisha as successor ... 1Ki 19:19–21
—Confronted Ahab after death of Naboth ... 1Ki 21:17–29
—Prophesied death of Azariah ... 2Ki 1:3–17
—Taken to heaven without dying ... 2Ki 2:11–12
B. Later references
—Malachi prophesied his return ... Mal 4:5–6
—John the Baptist likened to him ... Mt 17:9–13; Mk 9:9–13
—Jesus compared to him ... Mt 16:14
—Jesus compared his rejection to Elijah's ... Lk 4:24–26
—Appeared to Jesus in the transfiguration ... Mt 17:1–8; Mk 9:1–8
—Paul recalled a remnant in Elijah's day ... Ro 11:2–5
—His prayers are an example for us ... Jas 5:17–18

ELIMELECH
—Husband of Naomi ... Ru 1:2
—Fled to Moab during famine ... Ru 1:1
—Died in Moab ... Ru 1:3

ELIPHAZ
A. Firstborn son of Esau ... Ge 36:4,10
B. One of Job's friends who tried to comfort him ... Job 2:11
—His first speech ... Job 4:1—5:27
—His second speech ... Job 15:1–35
—His third speech ... Job 22:1–30
—Offered sacrifices to God after Job's restoration ... Job 42:7–9

ELISHA
A. His association with Elijah
—Anointed by Elijah as successor ... 1Ki 19:16–21
—Accompanied Elijah on his last day ... 2Ki 2:1–8
—Inherited Elijah's cloak ... 2Ki 2:9–13
—Divided the Jordan with Elijah's cloak ... 2Ki 2:14
B. His ministry
—Purified bad water ... 2Ki 2:19–22
—Pronounced a curse on mocking young men ... 2Ki 2:23–25
—Aided Israelites in the defeat of Moab ... 2Ki 3:11–20
—Increased widow's oil ... 2Ki 4:1–7
—Raised Shunammite's son ... 2Ki 4:8–37
—Purified food by a miracle ... 2Ki 4:38–41
—Fed a hundred men by a miracle ... 2Ki 4:42–44
—Healed Naaman's leprosy ... 2Ki 5:1–19
—Caused axhead to float ... 2Ki 6:1–7
—Captured Arameans ... 2Ki 6:8–23
—Advised king of Israel ... 2Ki 6:24—8:6
—Prophesied end to siege of Arameans ... 2Ki 7:1–2
—Prophesied Ben-Hadad's death ... 2Ki 8:7–15
—Anointed Jehu as king of Israel ... 2Ki 9:1–3
—Prophesied victory for Jehoash ... 2Ki 13:14–17
—His death ... 2Ki 13:20
C. Later references
—His dead body raised another one to life ... 2Ki 13:20–21
—Jesus compared his rejection to Elisha's ... Lk 4:24,27

ELIZABETH
—Wife of Zechariah; barren ... Lk 1:5–7
—Relative of the virgin Mary ... Lk 1:36
—Gave birth to John the Baptist ... Lk 1:11–23,57–58
—Visited by Mary ... Lk 1:39–45

ELKANAH
—Husband of Hannah and Peninnah ... 1Sa 1:1–2
—Worshiped every year at Shiloh ... 1Sa 1:3–8
—Father of Samuel ... 1Sa 1:19–20

ENCOURAGEMENT
—Giving support and inspiration
A. Related theme
ENCOURAGEMENT is a theme of Zechariah ... Zec 10:12
B. Human encouragement
1. Those who need encouragement
—Leaders ... Dt 1:38; Dt 3:28
—The oppressed ... Isa 1:17
—The persecuted ... Ac 14:21–22; 1Th 3:1–3
—All Christians ... Ac 20:1; Heb 3:13
2. Those who do the encouraging
—Kings ... 2Sa 19:7; 2Ch 32:6–8
—Prophets ... Ac 15:32
—Apostles ... Ac 16:40; Ac 20:2; 1Th 2:11–12
—Church pastors ... Col 4:7–8; 2Ti 4:2; Tit 2:15; 1Pe 5:12
—Specially gifted Christians ... Ro 12:6,8

—All Christians to each other Ro 1:12
1Th 4:18
Heb 10:25

C. Divine encouragement
—God encourages us Ps 10:17
2Th 2:16 – 17
Heb 6:17 – 18
—Christ encourages us Php 2:1
2Th 2:16 – 17
—The Holy Spirit encourages us Ac 9:31
—The Scriptures encourage us Ro 15:4
Heb 12:5

ENEMY

A. Types of enemies
—Heathen nations Jos 5:13
1Sa 4:3
Jer 12:7
—Personal adversaries 2Sa 4:8
1Ki 21:20
Est 7:6
Pr 16:7
—Spiritual forces Eph 6:12
1Pe 5:8
—Death 1Co 15:26

B. Reactions to one's enemies
1. In Israelite history
—Destroyed in war
See WARFARE
—Occasionally treated kindly 1Sa 26:7 – 12
2. In the psalms
—Prayers for deliverance from them Ps 59:1
Ps 64:1 – 2
Ps 143:9
—Prayers for God to judge them Ps 35:4 – 8,26
Ps 58:6 – 9
Ps 69:22 – 28
Ps 109:6 – 15
3. In the New Testament
—Jesus prayed for them Lk 23:34
—Stephen prayed for them Ac 7:60

C. Commands from God regarding enemies
—Treat them with kindness Pr 25:21 – 22
Ro 12:19 – 21
—Pray for them Mt 5:44
—Love them Mt 5:44
Lk 6:27,35

ENOCH

A. Son of Cain Ge 4:17 – 18
B. Descendant of Seth Ge 5:19 – 20
—Walked with God Ge 5:22 – 24
—Taken by God to heaven without dying Ge 5:24
—An example of faith Heb 11:5

ENVY

—Intense feeling of ill will or malice

A. In the Old Testament
—Examples of envy Ge 37:11
Nu 16:1 – 3
Ps 106:16 – 18
—The command not to envy Pr 3:31
Pr 23:17
Pr 24:1

B. In the New Testament
—Examples of envy Mt 27:18
Mk 15:10
Php 1:15,17
—Negative effects of envy Mk 7:20 – 23
Jas 3:14,16
—A positive result from envy Ro 11:13 – 14
—Envy in a list of vices Ro 1:29
Gal 5:21
1Pe 2:1
—Love does not envy 1Co 13:4

EPHESUS

—Paul left Priscilla and Aquila there Ac 18:19
—Apollos learned about Christ there Ac 18:24 – 26
—Paul converted some disciples of John there Ac 19:1 – 7
—Paul spent two years there Ac 19:8 – 22
—Riot over Paul's evangelism there Ac 19:23 – 41
—Paul wrote letter to the church there Eph 1:1
—Timothy ministered there 1Ti 1:3
—Tychicus ministered there 2Ti 4:12
—Church there lost its first love Rev 2:1 – 7

EPHRAIM

A. Second son of Joseph Ge 41:52
Ge 46:20
—Name means "twice fruitful" Ge 41:52
—Blessed by Jacob ahead of Manasseh Ge 48:12 – 20

B. Tribe descended from Ephraim
—Numbered Nu 1:33
Nu 26:37
—Blessed by Moses Dt 33:17
—Allotted land in Canaan Jos 16:4 – 9
Eze 48:5
—Failed to possess the land Jos 16:10
Jdg 1:29
—Quarreled with Gideon Jdg 8:1 – 3
—Quarreled with Jephthah Jdg 12:1 – 6
—Many joined kingdom of Judah during Asa's reform 2Ch 15:8 – 9

C. A synonym for the northern kingdom Isa 7:17
Hos 5:5

ESAU

A. His birth
—Firstborn of Isaac Ge 25:25
—Twin with Jacob Ge 25:26
—Also called Edom Ge 25:30

B. Significant events
—Became a hunter Ge 25:27
—Sold his birthright Ge 25:29 – 34
—His blessing stolen by Jacob Ge 27:1 – 40
—Wanted to kill Jacob Ge 27:41
—Married pagan women Ge 26:34
Ge 28:6 – 9
—Reconciled to Jacob Ge 33:1 – 17
—With Jacob, buried Isaac Ge 35:29

C. His descendants Ge 36:1 – 43
See EDOMITES

D. Later significance of Esau
—Descendants to be obliterated Ob 1 – 21
Jer 49:7 – 22
—Jacob chosen over him Mal 1:2 – 3
—Demonstrates God's purpose of election Ro 9:11 – 13
—His rejection for not repenting Heb 12:16 – 17

ESTHER

—Daughter of Abihail Est 2:15
—Cousin of Mordecai Est 2:7
—Chosen queen by Xerxes Est 2:8 – 18
—Objected to appearing before Xerxes Est 4:10 – 11
—Asked for a fast Est 4:15 – 16
—Risked her life by approaching Xerxes Est 5:1 – 2
—Foiled Haman's plan to kill Jews Est 7:1 – 8
—Caused Haman's execution Est 7:9 – 10
—Her plan preserved the Jews Est 8:1—9:17
—Decreed celebration of Purim Est 9:18 – 32

ETERNAL

—Without end in time

A. Eternity related to humans

1. The human body does not live forever ... Ecc 12:7
   See DEATH
2. Eternal life for believers
   —Jesus came to give eternal life ... Jn 11:25 – 26; 2Ti 1:10; 1Jn 5:11 – 12
   —We receive eternal life through faith ... Jn 3:16,36; 1Jn 5:13
   —We receive eternal salvation through Christ ... Heb 5:9; Heb 9:12
   —We have an eternal house in heaven ... 2Co 5:1
   —We are called into God's eternal glory ... 1Pe 5:10
   —We enter an eternal kingdom ... 2Pe 1:11
   —We receive an eternal inheritance ... Heb 9:15
3. Eternal punishment for the wicked ... Mt 25:46; 2Th 1:9; Rev 21:8

B. Eternity related to God

1. His being and person
   —God is the eternal God ... Dt 33:27
   —God is the eternal Rock ... Isa 26:4
   —God is from everlasting to everlasting ... Ps 90:2
   —God lives forever ... Isa 57:15
   —God's name endures forever ... Ps 135:13
   —God is not bound by time ... Ps 90:4; 2Pe 3:8; Rev 1:8
2. His attributes
   —He does not change ... Ps 102:27; Mal 3:6; Heb 13:8
   —His love endures forever ... 2Ch 7:3,6; Ps 136:1 – 26
   —His righteousness endures forever ... Ps 111:3; 2Co 9:9
   —His faithfulness endures forever ... Ps 100:5; Ps 117:2
   —His purpose for humanity is eternal ... Eph 3:11
   —His power is eternal ... Ro 1:20
3. His kingdom
   —God is the eternal King ... 1Ti 1:17
   —His kingdom is eternal ... Ps 145:13; Da 4:3,34
   —Christ reigns forever and ever ... Rev 11:15
4. His everlasting covenant
   —With Abraham, Isaac, Jacob ... Ge 17:7 – 8; 1Ch 16:17
   —With David ... 2Sa 7:13 – 16; 2Sa 23:5
   —With us in the new covenant ... Isa 55:3; Jer 32:40; Eze 37:26
5. God's word is eternal ... Ps 119:89; Isa 40:8; 1Pe 1:24 – 25

EUPHRATES

—One of the rivers of Eden ... Ge 2:14
—Abraham came from beyond it ... Jos 24:2 – 3
—Israel's borders to expand there ... Ge 15:18; Dt 11:22 – 25
—Hittites controlled it ... Jos 1:4
—David expanded kingdom to it ... 2Sa 8:3; 1Ch 18:3
—Solomon's kingdom bordered on it ... 1Ki 4:21; Ps 72:8
—Assyrians controlled it ... 2Ki 23:29; Isa 8:7 – 8
—Babylon controlled it ... 2Ki 24:1; Jer 46:2
—Christ's kingdom to reach to it ... Zec 9:9 – 10
—Army of the final battle to come from there ... Rev 9:14; Rev 16:12

EVANGELISM

See MISSION

EVE

A. Eve in the Old Testament

1. Her history
   —Made in God's image ... Ge 1:27; Ge 5:1 – 2
   —Made from Adam's rib ... Ge 2:22
   —Became Adam's wife ... Ge 2:23 – 24
   —Entered conversation with serpent ... Ge 3:1 – 5
   —Ate forbidden fruit with Adam ... Ge 3:6
   —Tried to hide from God ... Ge 3:8
   —Blamed serpent for her sin ... Ge 3:13
   —Received curse from God ... Ge 3:16
   —Banished with Adam from Eden ... Ge 3:23
   —Mother of Cain, Abel and Seth ... Ge 4:1 – 2,25
2. Her significance as mother of all humans ... Ge 3:20

B. Eve in the New Testament

—Significance of Eve being created after Adam ... 1Co 11:8; 1Ti 2:13
—Significance of Eve deceived by serpent ... 2Co 11:3

EXAMPLE

A. Old Testament people as examples

1. As warnings ... 1Co 10:6 – 11; 2Ti 3:8
2. As models for Christian behavior
   —Job in his perseverance ... Jas 5:10 – 11
   —Elijah in his prayers ... Jas 5:16 – 18
   —Numerous saints in their faith ... Heb 11:4 – 40

B. Christ as an example

—His humility ... Php 2:5 – 8
—His love ... Jn 15:12 – 13; Eph 5:2
—His service ... Jn 13:14 – 15
—His gentleness ... Mt 11:29
—His consideration of others ... Ro 15:2 – 3
—His grace of giving ... 2Co 8:7 – 9
—His forgiveness ... Col 3:13
—His purity ... 1Jn 3:3
—His unjust suffering ... 1Pe 2:20 – 23
—His obedience to the Father ... Jn 15:10
—His general walk of life ... 1Jn 2:6

C. Paul as an example

—Thessalonians followed his example ... 1Th 1:6
—Churches encouraged to imitate him ... 1Co 4:16; 1Co 11:1; Php 3:17; 2Th 3:7,9

D. Christians as examples

—The Thessalonians were examples ... 1Th 1:7
—Church leaders must be examples ... 1Ti 4:12; Tit 2:7; 1Pe 5:3
—We must all be examples ... Mt 5:16; Php 2:14 – 15; 1Pe 2:12

EXHORTATION

See ENCOURAGEMENT

EXILE

—The captivity of the people of Judah by the Babylonians

A. Judah carried away into Babylon
- 1. The story of the exile told ... 2Ki 24:11 – 16; 2Ki 25:11
- 2. Three waves of exiles ... Jer 52:28 – 30
  - —Daniel in the first ... Da 1:1 – 6
  - —Ezekiel in the second ... Eze 1:1 – 3
  - —Remainder of the people in the third ... 2Ch 36:20
- 3. Reasons for the exile
  - —Because of the sins of Manasseh ... 2Ki 21:10 – 15; Jer 15:1 – 4
  - —Because of Judah's idolatry ... Dt 28:45 – 52; Isa 40:2; Jer 5:7 – 17; Eze 6:1 – 8
  - —Because Judah failed to heed prophets ... 2Ch 36:15 – 20
- 4. Lessons the Jews learned in the exile
  - —That God was everywhere ... Eze 11:16
  - —That God was Redeemer ... Isa 59:12 – 20
  - —That God still loved them ... Jer 30:10 – 11,18 – 22; Eze 34:20 – 31
  - —That the Law was important ... Ezr 7:10; Ne 8:1 – 9

B. The return from exile
- —Occurred after seventy years ... Jer 25:11
- —God remembered his promises ... Jer 29:10
- —God remembered his covenant ... Eze 16:60
- —Cyrus decreed the Jews could return ... 2Ch 36:23; Ezr 1:2 – 4
- —The Jews returned in two groups ... Ezr 1:5 – 6; Ezr 7:1 – 9

EXODUS

—The escape of the Israelites from Egypt

A. Related themes
- FREEDOM is a theme of Exodus ... Ex 6:6
- JOURNEY is a theme of Numbers ... Nu 9:18

B. Jacob and his sons in Egypt
- —Moved to Egypt ... Ge 46:1 – 27
- —Became slaves of the Egyptians ... Ex 1:8 – 14

C. God's deliverance of his people from Egypt
- 1. God's choosing of a deliverer
  - —Moses preserved at birth ... Ex 2:1 – 10
  - —Moses called as deliverer ... Ex 3:7 – 22
  - —Aaron appointed to assist Moses ... Ex 4:13 – 17,27 – 31
- 2. The process of deliverance
  - —Signs given to Moses ... Ex 4:1 – 9
  - —The first appearance before Pharaoh ... Ex 5:1 – 5
  - —The second appearance before Pharaoh ... Ex 7:10 – 13
  - —The first nine plagues ... Ex 7:14—10:29
  - —The preparation for the tenth plague ... Ex 11:1—12:28
  - —The slaying of the firstborn in Egypt ... Ex 12:29 – 30
  - —The escape from Egypt ... Ex 12:31 – 39
  - —The pursuit of the Israelites ... Ex 14:5 – 9
  - —The crossing of the Red Sea ... Ex 14:10 – 22,29
  - —The drowning of the Egyptians ... Ex 14:23 – 28
- 3. God's motive in the exodus
  - —Faithfulness to his promises ... Ge 15:13 – 16; Dt 7:8 – 9
  - —His love for his people ... Dt 7:8 – 9; Hos 11:1

D. Israelite remembrance of the exodus
- —Sung after crossing the Red Sea ... Ex 15:1 – 21
- —Celebrated annually in the Passover ... Ex 13:3 – 16
- —Recalled in the Ten Commandments ... Ex 20:2; Dt 5:6
- —Celebrated by psalmists ... Ps 66:5 – 6; Ps 78:12 – 14; Ps 105:26 – 39; Ps 106:8 – 12
- —Taught by prophets ... Isa 43:16 – 21; Isa 63:11 – 14; Hos 12:9,13; Na 1:4

E. The exodus in the New Testament
- —As an affirmation of God's power ... Ac 13:17; Ro 9:17
- —As a picture of salvation in Christ ... 1Co 10:1 – 4
- —As an example of God's care ... Jn 6:31 – 33
- —As an example of human faith ... Heb 11:29
- —As a warning against disobedience ... Heb 3:7—4:2; Jude 5

EYE

A. The human eye
- 1. The physical eyes
  - —Leah's weak eyes ... Ge 29:17
  - —Lovers' eyes ... SS 1:15; SS 7:4
  - —Cruelty in eyes being gouged out ... Jdg 16:21; 2Ki 25:7
- 2. Figurative use of eyes
  - —Enlightened eyes symbolize knowledge ... Ps 19:8; Eph 1:18
  - —Opened eyes symbolize knowledge ... Ge 3:5,7
  - —Bright eyes symbolize well-being ... 1Sa 14:27
  - —Dim eyes symbolize grief ... Job 17:7
  - —Winking eyes express mockery ... Ps 35:19
  - —Winking eyes plot perversity ... Pr 16:30
  - —Dissatisfied eyes express greed ... Pr 27:20
  - —Closed eyes express spiritual blindness ... Isa 6:10; Mt 13:15
  - —Lustful eyes ... 1Jn 2:16
  - —Eyes full of adultery ... 2Pe 2:14
  - —Haughty eyes ... Ps 18:27
  - —A jealous eye ... 1Sa 18:9

B. The eye of God
- —Symbolizes God's all-knowing nature ... Ps 139:16; Pr 15:3
- —Symbolizes God's holiness ... Hab 1:13
- —Symbolizes God watching over us ... Ezr 5:5; Ps 33:18
- —Symbolizes Christ's control of history ... Rev 5:6

EZEKIEL

A. Family background and history
- —A priest ... Eze 1:3
- —Carried into exile ... Eze 1:1
- —Called to be a prophet ... Eze 2:1—3:11
- —Married; wife died ... Eze 24:18

B. His symbolic actions as a prophet
- —City of Jerusalem on a clay tablet ... Eze 4:1 – 3
- —Lying immobile for more than a year ... Eze 4:4 – 8
- —Strange diet during the "siege" of Jerusalem ... Eze 4:9 – 17
- —A strange haircut ... Eze 5:1 – 4
- —Packing his belongings for exile ... Eze 12:1 – 16
- —Shuddering while eating his food ... Eze 12:17 – 20
- —Groaning in public ... Eze 20:6 – 7
- —Not mourning when his wife died ... Eze 24:15 – 24
- —A prophecy using sticks ... Eze 37:15 – 28

C. His parables as a prophet
- —The parable of the useless vine ... Eze 15:1 – 8
- —The parable of the wife turned prostitute ... Eze 16:1 – 63
- —The parable of two eagles and a vine ... Eze 17:1 – 24
- —The parable of the lion ... Eze 19:1 – 9
- —The parable of the two adulterous sisters ... Eze 23:1 – 49

EZRA

- —A priest ... Ezr 7:1 – 5
- —A teacher of the Law ... Ezr 7:6 – 10

—Led exiles back to Jerusalem .... Ezr 8:15 – 36
—Concerned about intermarriage .... Ezr 9:1 – 4
—Prayed about intermarriage problem .... Ezr 9:5 – 15
—Corrected intermarriage problem .... Ezr 10:1 – 17
—Read Law at the Feast of Tabernacles .... Ne 8:1 – 8
—Participated in dedication of wall of Jerusalem .... Ne 12:31 – 36

FACE

A. The human face
  1. Significance of the human face
    —Seeing a face means meeting a person .... Ge 43:3,5; 2Sa 14:28,32
    —Talking face to face 2Jn 12; 3Jn 14
    —A radiant face means closeness to God .... Ex 34:29 – 30
    —One can slap a face in anger 1Ki 22:24
    —One can spit in a face in disgust .... Mt 26:67
  2. Emotions expressed by the face
    —The cheerful face .... Pr 15:13
    —The face bowed down in respect .... Ge 48:12; 1Sa 25:23
    —The downcast face .... Ge 4:5 – 6; Lk 24:17
    —The sad face .... Ne 2:3 – 4
    —The face hidden in fear .... Ex 3:6
    —The terrified face .... Da 5:6,9
    —The face bowed down in grief .... Jos 7:10
    —The face turned away in grief 2Ki 20:2
    —The face turned away in shame .... Ezr 9:6
    —The face covered with shame .... Ps 69:7

B. The face of God
  —God's face synonymous with himself .... Hos 5:15
  —God's glory seen in the face of Christ 2Co 4:6
  —Seeing God face to face .... Ge 32:30; 1Co 13:12
  —Seeking God's face in prayer .... Ps 24:6; Ps 27:8
  —God's face shining on us in blessing .... Nu 6:24 – 26; Ps 4:6
  —God's face hidden from our sins .... Ps 51:9
  —God's face hidden in judgment .... Dt 31:17 – 18; Ps 13:1 – 2
  —God's face set against evildoers .... Lev 20:3,5; Ps 34:16; Eze 15:7; 1Pe 3:12

FAITH

—Belief in a person or a teaching

A. Related themes
  1. BELIEVE is a theme of John .... Jn 20:31
  2. FAITH is a theme of:
    —Galatians .... Gal 3:22
    —James .... Jas 5:15
  3. INDIVIDUALISM is a theme of Ezekiel .... Eze 18:4

B. What are the basic elements of faith?
  1. Trust in God and commitment to Christ .... Ge 15:6; Pr 3:5; Ro 3:22; Heb 11:1
  2. True knowledge of God and Christ
    —Truths of the faith are important 1Ti 3:9; 1Ti 4:1
    —They must be based on God's word 2Ti 3:16
    —They are worth fighting for .... Jude 3

C. What must we believe?
  1. We must believe *in*:
    —God .... Ex 14:31; Jn 14:1
    —Christ .... Jn 2:11; Ac 16:31
    —The name of the Son of God 1Jn 3:23
    —The prophets .... Ex 14:31; 2Ch 20:20
  2. We must believe
    a. What God has said
      —The commandments of God .... Ps 119:66
      —The writings of the Old Testament .... Lk 24:25; Jn 5:46 – 47; Ac 26:27
      —The gospel .... Mk 1:15; 1Co 15:1 – 2
      —The holy Scriptures .... 2Ti 3:14 – 15
      —The promises of God .... Ro 4:20 – 21
      —Things God has said to us .... Ge 15:6
    b. What God teaches about Jesus
      —That Jesus is the Christ .... Jn 20:31; 1Jn 5:1
      —That Jesus is God's Son 1Jn 5:5
      —That Jesus was raised from the dead .... Ro 10:9
      —Summary creed .... 1Co 15:3 – 11

See also CONFESSION; DOCTRINE

D. Where does faith come from?
  —From God, as a gift .... Eph 2:8; Php 1:29
  —From the Father and the Son .... Eph 6:23
  —From the power of God in us 1Co 2:5
  —From the Holy Spirit 1Co 12:9
  —From hearing the gospel .... Jn 17:20; Ac 15:7; Ro 10:14,17
  —From reading the Scriptures .... Jn 20:31; 1Jn 5:13

E. What happens when we believe?
  —We receive forgiveness of sin .... Ac 10:43
  —We are justified .... Ro 3:28; Gal 2:16
  —We are saved .... Ac 16:30 – 31; Ro 10:9
  —We receive eternal life .... Jn 3:14 – 16
  —We become free from condemnation .... Jn 3:17
  —We become free from spiritual death .... Jn 11:25 – 26
  —We become God's children .... Jn 1:12; Gal 3:26
  —We become children of light .... Jn 12:36
  —We gain access to God .... Eph 3:12
  —We enter God's rest .... Heb 4:3
  —Our hearts are purified .... Ac 15:9
  —We are sanctified .... Ac 26:18
  —The word of God goes to work in us 1Th 2:13
  —We receive peace with God .... Ro 5:1
  —We experience joy .... Ac 16:34
  —We gain security in God's power 1Pe 1:5

F. What must we do as believers?
  —Live by faith .... 2Co 5:7; Gal 2:20
  —Walk by faith .... Ro 4:12
  —Face everything by faith .... Heb 11:33 – 39
  —Remain true to the faith .... Ac 14:22
  —Continue in the faith .... Col 1:23
  —Stand firm in the faith 1Co 16:13; 1Pe 5:9
  —Fight for the faith .... 1Ti 6:12; Jude 3
  —Increase our faith .... Lk 17:5
  —Grow in faith .... 2Th 1:3; Jude 20
  —Please God by our faith .... Heb 11:6
  —Combine faith with hope and love .... 1Co 13:2,13; Gal 5:6; 1Th 1:3

—Do everything by faith ... Ro 14:22–23
—Pray in faith ... Jas 1:5–6
—Tell others about our faith ... 2Co 4:13–14
—Demonstrate faith by good works ... Jas 2:14–26
—Overcome sin by our faith ... 1Jn 5:4–5
—Fight the devil by our faith ... Eph 6:16

G. Striking examples of faith
—Abraham ... Ro 4:1–3,9–21
—Numerous Old Testament people ... Heb 11:4–40
—Daniel's three friends ... Da 3:16–18
—Daniel ... Da 6:1–11
—A centurion ... Mt 8:5–10
—A sick woman ... Mt 9:20–22
—A Canaanite woman ... Mt 15:22–28
—Blind Bartimaeus ... Mk 10:46–52
—A sinful woman ... Lk 7:36–50
—Martha ... Jn 11:21–27
—Thomas ... Jn 20:24–29
—Philippian jailer ... Ac 16:29–34
—Lois, Eunice and Timothy ... 2Ti 1:5
—Paul ... 2Ti 1:12

FAITHFULNESS

—Remaining steadfast to one's commitments

A. Related themes
FAITHFULNESS is a theme of:
—Judges ... Jdg 2:18
—2 Kings ... 2Ki 8:19
—Lamentations ... La 3:23

B. Human faithfulness
1. Faithfulness is an aspect of the fruit of the Spirit ... Gal 5:22
2. Examples of those who were faithful
—Abraham ... Ne 9:8
—Moses ... Nu 12:7
—Hezekiah ... 2Ch 31:20
—The Zadokite priests ... Eze 48:11
—Timothy ... 1Co 4:17
—Epaphras ... Col 1:7
—Onesimus ... Col 4:9
—Silas ... 1Pe 5:12
3. We must be faithful
—In obeying God's commands ... Dt 11:13
—In our walk before God ... 1Ki 2:4
—In serving God ... 2Ch 19:9
—In our prayer life ... Ro 12:12
—In the use of our gifts ... 1Pe 4:10
—In persevering until death ... Rev 2:10
4. God's promises to those who are faithful
—He is faithful to them ... Ps 18:25
—His eyes are on them ... Ps 101:6
—He preserves them ... Ps 31:23
—He guards their lives ... Ps 97:10
—He protects them ... Pr 2:8
—He blesses them ... Dt 11:13–15
—He rewards them ... Mt 25:21–23
—He does not forsake them ... Ps 37:28
—He guarantees them life ... Eze 18:9

C. God's faithfulness
1. God is faithful in himself
—He is the faithful God ... Dt 7:9; Heb 10:23
—He abounds in faithfulness ... Ps 86:15
—His faithfulness is great ... La 3:23
—He will remain faithful ... 2Ti 2:13
2. God is faithful in his actions
—He is faithful in all he does ... Ps 33:4; Ps 111:7–8
—He is faithful to his covenant ... Ps 78:24–28
—He keeps all his promises ... Ge 21:1–2; 1Ki 8:20; Ac 13:23,32–33
—Christ fulfills all God's promises ... 2Co 1:18,20
3. God is faithful in his relationship to us
—In his love for us ... Ps 89:24; Ps 143:1
—In helping us ... 1Co 10:13
—In protecting us ... Ps 91:4; 2Th 3:3
—In forgiving us ... 1Jn 1:9
4. God's word is faithful ... 2Sa 7:28; Ps 19:7; Rev 21:5

FALLING AWAY

—Falling away from the faith, backsliding, apostasy

A. Falling away in the Old Testament
1. Examples
—At Mount Sinai ... Ex 32:1–35
—During the time of the judges ... Jdg 2:10–12
—In Israel ... 1Ki 16:30–33
—In Judah ... 2Ch 24:17–19
—A regular pattern ... Ps 106:6–47
2. Causes
—Mixed marriages ... Nu 25:1–3; Ne 13:26–27
—Poor examples of kings ... 1Ki 16:29–33; 2Ki 21:1–11
3. Judgment for those who fall away ... Dt 13:13–18; 2Ki 21:12–15

B. Falling away in the New Testament
1. Examples
—At the time of Jesus ... Jn 6:66
—In the early church ... 1Ti 1:19–20; 2Ti 2:17–18; 2Pe 2:20–21
—Future severe apostasy ... Mt 24:12; 2Th 2:3; 2Ti 3:1,5
2. Causes
—Influence of deceiving spirits ... 1Ti 4:1
—False teachers ... Ac 20:29–30; Rev 2:14–15
—Human desires ... 2Ti 4:3–4
—Love of world ... 2Ti 4:10
—Hardened hearts ... Ac 7:51–52; Ac 28:26–27
—Persecution ... Mt 24:9–10
—A time of testing ... Lk 8:13
3. Judgment for those who fell away
—Judgment from God ... Heb 10:26–31; Jude 11–15
—Removal from God's kingdom ... Rev 2:5
—Impossible to renew to repentance ... Heb 6:4–8
4. The antidote to falling away
—Heed the warning not to fall away ... Heb 3:12; 2Pe 3:17
—Depend on God ... Ro 8:35–39; 1Co 10:13; Jude 24
—Remain steadfast in faith ... Heb 6:11–12; Jude 20–21
—Continue reading God's word ... 2Ti 3:14–17
—Keep growing in Christian character ... 2Pe 1:5–10
—Associate with other believers ... Heb 3:13; Heb 10:24

FAMILY

A. Related theme
FAMILY is a theme of Ruth ..... Ru 2:20

B. The establishment of the family
—Marriage begun in the Garden of Eden ..... Ge 2:18–24
—The first children, given by God ..... Ge 4:1–2
—The family built by God ..... Ps 127:1–6
—The family blessed by God ..... Ps 128:1–6
—The central unit in God's covenant ..... Ge 17:7; Jos 24:15

C. Responsibilities in the family
1. The father as head
—Head of the family ..... Ex 6:14
—Head of the wife ..... Eph 5:23–24
—Must love his wife ..... Eph 5:25–33; 1Pe 3:7
—Must supervise religious observances ..... Ge 35:1–7; Ex 12:3; 1Sa 1:21
—Must supervise education of children ..... Ps 44:1; Ps 78:3; Eph 6:4
—Must care for the children's needs ..... 2Co 12:14; Col 3:21
2. The role of the mother
—Submissive to her husband ..... Eph 5:24; 1Pe 3:1–6
—Assist in training of children ..... Pr 1:8; Pr 6:20
—Could take an important role in home ..... 1Sa 1:9–28; Pr 31:10–31; 2Ti 1:5
3. The place of children
—A blessing from the Lord ..... Ps 127:3–5
—Must honor parents ..... Ex 20:12; Lev 19:3
—Must obey parents ..... Dt 21:18–21; Eph 6:1–3; Col 3:20

D. Things that disturb or destroy the family
—Jealousy and hatred ..... Ge 4:3–8
—Lack of respect toward parents ..... Ge 9:21–22
—Parents picking favorites ..... Ge 25:27–28
—Rivalry and selfishness ..... Ge 27:1–41
—Polygamy ..... Ge 30:1–2; 1Sa 1:1–6
—Lack of discipline 1Sa 2:22–25
—Lust and incest 2Sa 13:1–21
—Personal ambition ..... Jdg 9:1–5; 2Sa 15:1–17
—Mixed marriages ..... Ne 13:23–27
—Materialism 1Ti 6:6–10
—False teaching ..... Tit 1:10–11

E. New Testament teachings on the family
—Salvation took place in households ..... Ac 16:15,31–34; Ac 18:8; 1Co 1:16; 1Co 16:15
—Children of believers are holy 1Co 7:14
—A well-ordered family was important ..... 1Ti 3:4–5,12; Tit 1:6
—Care for members in the family circle 1Ti 5:4,8,16

F. The family used figuratively
—As a picture of the nation of Israel ..... Ps 115:9–12
—As a picture of the church ..... Gal 6:10; Eph 2:19; Heb 2:11; 1Pe 4:17

See also CHILDREN; FATHER; MARRIAGE; MOTHER

FAMINE

See HUNGER AND THIRST

FASTING

—Voluntarily depriving oneself of food

A. In the Old Testament
1. Occasions for fasting
—To prepare to receive God's law ..... Ex 34:28; Dt 9:9,18
—To prepare for the Day of Atonement ..... Lev 16:29,31
—To show sorrow at time of death 1Sa 31:13; 2Sa 1:12
—To show sorrow for sin ..... 1Ki 21:27; Ne 9:1; Jnh 3:6–9
—To show humility ..... Ps 35:13
—To pray in time of national need ..... 2Ch 20:3; Ezr 8:21; Est 4:16; Joel 2:15–17
—To accompany deep personal prayer ..... 2Sa 12:16,21; Ne 1:4; Da 9:3–4
2. Prophets criticized fasting as outward show ..... Isa 58:3–7; Jer 14:12; Zec 7:4–10

B. In the New Testament
1. Occasions for fasting
—A regular pattern for many Jews ..... Mt 9:14; Lk 2:37; Ac 23:12–14
—Paul after his conversion ..... Ac 9:9
—To prepare for mission work ..... Ac 13:2–3; Ac 14:23
—Not done by Jesus' disciples ..... Mt 9:14
2. Jesus criticized fasting as outward show ..... Mt 6:16–18; Lk 18:9–14

FATHER

A. Various meanings of father
—Creator ..... Jas 1:17
—Source or originator ..... Ge 4:20–21
—Caretaker ..... Job 29:16
—Counselor ..... Ge 45:8
—A respected prophet 2Ki 6:21
—A respected priest ..... Jdg 17:10
—One's male parent ..... Ge 4:18
—One's grandfather ..... Ge 28:13
—One's great-grandfather 1Ki 15:11
—One's ancestors in general ..... Jos 24:6; 2Ki 21:22

B. The father in the family
1. Duties of a father
—Supervise religious observances ..... Ge 35:1–7; Ex 12:3; 1Sa 1:21
—Responsible for education of children ..... Ge 18:19; Dt 4:9–10; Eph 6:5
—Responsible for discipline of children ..... Dt 8:4; Pr 3:11–12
—Care for his children's needs ..... 2Co 12:14; Col 3:21
—Give blessing to his children ..... Ge 27:27–29,39–40; Ge 49:1–28
2. Responsibility of children
—Respect their fathers ..... Ex 20:12; Lev 19:3

—Obey their fathers .... Ex 20:12; Eph 6:1; Col 3:20

C. Spiritual use of father
- —Abraham as the father of believers .... Ro 4:11,16 – 17; Gal 3:7
- —Paul as the father of his churches .... 1Co 4:15; 1Th 2:11 – 12
- —God as Father of Jesus Christ .... Jn 17:1,5; Eph 1:3
- —God as Father of everyone .... Mal 2:10; Ac 17:28 – 29
- —God as Father of his chosen people .... Isa 63:16; Jer 31:9
- —God as Father of believers in Jesus .... Mt 6:9; Jn 1:12 – 13; Gal 1:1,4
- —Christians can call God "Abba" (Father) .... Ro 8:15; Gal 4:6
- —The devil as father of the ungodly .... Jn 8:44; 1Jn 3:10 – 12

FEAR

—One's apprehension in a frightening situation; reverence

A. Fear as being afraid

1. Why did people experience fear?
   - —Fear of seeing God .... Ex 3:6
   - —Fear of a vision of angels .... Mt 28:4; Lk 2:8 – 9
   - —Fear of the unknown .... Lk 9:34,45
   - —Fear of punishment for sin .... Ge 3:8 – 10; Ge 18:15; Ac 24:25
   - —Fear of danger .... Ac 27:17,29
   - —Fear of being killed .... Ge 26:7; 1Ki 19:3
   - —Fear of losing one's life .... Jnh 1:5; Mt 14:30
   - —Fear of losing one's loved ones .... Ge 31:31; Ge 42:4
   - —Fear of bringing unpleasant news 1Sa 3:15; 2Sa 12:18
   - —Fear of an enemy .... 1Sa 28:5; Jn 20:19
   - —Fear of a person in authority .... Ne 2:2
   - —Fear of what another person might do 1Sa 18:12,15
   - —Fear of what others might say .... Gal 2:12
   - —Fear of the future .... Ge 21:17
2. The command not to be afraid
   - —Given by God .... Ge 21:17; Ge 26:24; Ac 18:9
   - —Given by Moses .... Ex 14:13; Ex 20:20
   - —Given by Joshua .... Jos 10:25
   - —Given by Samuel 1Sa 12:20
   - —Given by Elijah 1Ki 17:13
   - —Given by David 1Ch 22:13
   - —Given by the prophet Jahaziel 2Ch 20:15,17
   - —Given by Hezekiah 2Ch 32:7
   - —Given by Isaiah .... Isa 44:2,8
   - —Given by Jeremiah .... Jer 42:11
   - —Given by Jesus .... Mt 14:27; Mk 5:36; Lk 12:4,7,32; Jn 6:20
   - —Given by an angel .... Lk 1:13,30; Lk 2:10; Ac 27:23 – 24
3. How to conquer fear
   - —By trusting in God .... Ps 56:4,11
   - —By believing in Jesus .... Mk 5:36
   - —By knowing God is with us .... Ge 26:24; Dt 31:6,8; Ps 23:4; Isa 43:5
   - —By knowing Jesus is with us .... Jn 6:20; Ac 18:9 – 10
   - —By knowing God is our Savior .... Ps 27:1,3
   - —By knowing God is our refuge .... Ps 46:1 – 2; Ps 91:1 – 6; Heb 13:6
   - —By knowing God will fight for us .... Dt 3:22; Dt 20:3 – 4; 2Ch 20:15 – 17
   - —By obeying the Lord .... 1Sa 12:20 – 21; 1Ch 22:12 – 13
4. Courage as the answer to fear
   See COURAGE

B. Fear as reverence for the Lord

1. The command to fear the Lord .... Dt 6:13; Jos 24:14; 2Ch 19:7; Ps 33:8; Pr 3:7; Ecc 12:13
2. Examples of those who feared the Lord
   - —Noah .... Heb 11:7
   - —Abraham .... Ge 22:12
   - —Joseph .... Ge 42:18
   - —Job .... Job 1:1
   - —David .... Ps 5:7
   - —Hezekiah .... Jer 26:19
   - —Nehemiah .... Ne 5:15
   - —The early church .... Ac 9:31
3. Reasons for fearing the Lord
   - —His awesome power .... Ex 20:18 – 20
   - —His glory .... Lk 2:9
   - —His holiness .... Rev 15:4
   - —His majesty .... Ps 96:4 – 6
   - —His greatness 1Sa 12:24
   - —His forgiveness .... Ps 130:4
   - —His faithfulness .... Ps 119:38
4. Benefits of fearing God
   - —A way to praise God .... Ps 22:23
   - —A way to serve God .... Ps 2:11
   - —A way to obey God .... Ecc 12:13
   - —A way to fight evil .... Pr 8:13; Pr 16:6
   - —A way to become wise .... Ps 111:10; Pr 1:7
   - —A way to lengthen life .... Pr 10:27
   - —God loves those who fear him .... Ps 103:11,13,17
   - —God saves those who fear him .... Ps 85:9
   - —God protects those who fear him .... Ps 60:4; Pr 14:26 – 27
   - —God blesses those who fear him .... Ps 115:12 – 13
   - —God provides for those who fear him .... Ps 34:9; Ps 111:5

FEASTS

A. Religious feasts

1. Commanded in the Old Testament
   - —Passover .... Ex 12:1 – 14; Lev 23:5; Nu 9:1 – 14; Dt 16:1 – 7

—Unleavened Bread Ex 12:15 – 20
Ex 13:3 – 10
Lev 23:6 – 8
Nu 28:17 – 25
Dt 16:3 – 4,8
—Firstfruits Lev 23:9 – 14
—Weeks (Harvest, Pentecost) Ex 23:16
Lev 23:15 – 21
Nu 28:26 – 31
Dt 16:9 – 12
—Trumpets Lev 23:23 – 25
Nu 29:1 – 6
—Day of Atonement Lev 16:1 – 34
Nu 29:7 – 11
—Tabernacles (Ingathering, Booths) Ex 23:16
Lev 23:33 – 43
Nu 29:12 – 34
Dt 16:13 – 15
—Sacred assembly Lev 23:36
Nu 29:35 – 38
—Purim Est 9:27 – 28

2. Celebrations in the Old Testament
—Passover Jos 5:10
2Ki 23:21 – 23
2Ch 30:1 – 20
2Ch 35:1 – 17
Ezr 6:19 – 21
—Unleavened Bread Jos 5:11
2Ch 30:21 – 27
2Ch 35:17 – 19
Ezr 6:22
—Day of Atonement Ne 9:1 – 38
—Tabernacles (Booths) Ezr 3:4
Ne 8:13 – 18
—Purim Est 9:18 – 32

3. Celebrations in the New Testament
—Passover Mt 26:1 – 2,17 – 29
Mk 14:12 – 25
Lk 22:7 – 38
Jn 2:13 – 25
Jn 11:55 – 56
Jn 13:1 – 30
—Unleavened Bread Mt 26:17
Mk 14:1,12
Lk 22:1,7
—Weeks (Pentecost) Ac 2:1 – 41
—Tabernacles (Booths) Jn 7:2 – 36
—Sacred assembly Jn 7:37 – 44
—Dedication (Hanukkah) Jn 10:22 – 39
—The Lord's Supper Mt 26:26 – 29
Mk 14:22 – 25
Lk 22:17 – 20
1Co 11:17 – 26

4. Criticism when feasts became empty rituals
—In the Old Testament Isa 1:14
Isa 5:12
Hos 2:11
Am 5:21 – 23
—In the New Testament 2Pe 2:13
Jude 12

B. Non-religious occasions for feasting
—At weanings Ge 21:8
—At the signing of a treaty Ge 26:30
—At marriages Ge 29:21 – 22
Jdg 14:10
—At a coronation 1Ki 1:41
—At a family celebration Lk 15:23

FELIX

—Governor of Judea Ac 23:24
—Letter addressed to him Ac 23:26 – 30
—Paul on trial before him Ac 24:1 – 21
—Sought personal interview with Paul Ac 24:24 – 26
—Kept Paul in prison to please the Jews Ac 24:27
—Replaced by Festus Ac 24:27

FELLOWSHIP

—A sharing together between persons

A. Human fellowship among God's people Ge 2:18
1. Basis of such fellowship
—Fellowship with God 1Jn 1:3,7
—The presence of Christ Mt 18:20
—The word of God Ac 2:42
2. The expression of such fellowship
—Prayed for by Christ Jn 17:20 – 23
—Sung by the psalmists Ps 133:1 – 2
—Demonstrated by mutual sharing Ac 2:44 – 45
Ac 4:32 – 35
—Demonstrated by prayers for each other Ac 1:14
Ac 4:24 – 31
Ro 15:30 – 32
—Symbolized in the Lord's Supper Ac 2:46 – 47
1Co 10:16 – 17
—Exercised among church leaders Gal 2:9
3. "One another" commands
—Be devoted to one another Ro 12:10
—Live in harmony with one another Ro 12:16
1Pe 3:8
—Accept one another Ro 15:7
—Instruct one another Ro 15:14
—Use your gifts for one another 1Co 12:7
1Pe 4:10
—Share with one another 2Co 8:7,13 – 15
—Greet one another 2Co 13:12
—Serve one another in love Gal 5:13
—Carry one another's burdens Gal 6:2
—Be kind to one another Eph 4:32
1Th 5:15
—Forgive one another Eph 4:32
—Look to the interest of others Php 2:3 – 4
—Bear with one another Col 3:13
—Love one another Col 3:14
1Jn 4:11 – 12
—Admonish one another Col 3:16
—Encourage one another 1Th 5:11
Heb 10:25
—Build up one another 1Th 5:11
—Live in peace with one another 1Th 5:13
—Spur one another to good works Heb 10:24
—Confess your sins to each other Jas 5:16
—Pray for one another Jas 5:16
—Be hospitable to one another 1Pe 4:9
4. We may have no fellowship with the ungodly 1Co 5:1 – 2
2Co 6:14 – 16
Eph 5:5 – 7,11

B. Fellowship with God
1. Fellowship with the triune God
—With God the Father 1Jn 1:3
—With God the Son Jn 15:3 – 4
1Co 1:9
—With God the Holy Spirit 2Co 13:14
Php 2:1
2. Developing such fellowship
—By desiring it Ps 42:1
Ps 63:1
—By believing in Jesus, God's Son 1Jn 1:2 – 3
—By meditating on God's word Ps 1:2
Ps 119:10 – 15
2Pe 1:4
—By praying to God Mk 1:35
Lk 5:16

—By thinking wholesome thoughts .... Php 4:8–9
—By living a holy life .... Ps 15:1–5
2Co 6:14–18
—By participating in the Lord's Supper 1Co 10:16
1Co 11:23–26

3. Examples of such fellowship
—Enoch .... Ge 5:22–24
—Noah .... Ge 6:9
—Abraham .... Ge 18:17–19
—Jacob .... Ge 48:15
—Moses .... Ex 33:1
—David .... Ps 23
—Jesus .... Mt 26:39–42
—Paul .... Ac 22:17–21
2Co 12:1–4

FESTUS

—Succeeded Felix as governor .... Ac 24:27
—Visited Jerusalem authorities .... Ac 25:1–5
—Convened court to deal with Paul .... Ac 25:6–12
—Paul appealed to Caesar before him .... Ac 25:12
—Consulted Agrippa about Paul .... Ac 25:13–22
—Arranged an audience for Agrippa with Paul .... Ac 25:23—26:29

FIRE

A. Human uses of fire
1. Domestic uses
—For cooking .... Isa 44:15–16
Jn 21:9
—For warmth .... Isa 44:15–16
Mk 14:54
—For metalworking .... Ex 32:24
2. Military uses
—For destroying a city .... Jos 6:24
1Sa 30:1
2Ch 36:19
—For destroying crops 2Sa 14:30
3. Religious uses
—For sacrifices .... Ge 8:20
Lev 1:9
Nu 18:17
—For burning incense .... Ex 30:7–8
1Ki 9:25
Lk 1:9
—For burning unclean substances .... Lev 13:52,55
—Unholy fire could not be used .... Lev 10:1–2

B. God's use of fire
1. God is a consuming fire .... Dt 4:24
Heb 12:29
2. Positive uses of fire
a. To represent his presence
—To Moses in the burning bush .... Ex 3:1–4
—To Israel in the pillar of fire .... Ex 13:21–22
Ex 14:24
—To Israel on Mount Sinai .... Ex 19:18
—To Elijah going into heaven 2Ki 2:11
—To the disciples on Pentecost .... Ac 2:3
b. To burn sacrifices prepared for him .... Ge 15:17
1Ki 18:38–39
2Ch 7:1
c. To purify his people .... Isa 48:10
Mal 3:3
3. Negative uses of fire
—To express his wrath .... Dt 32:22
Ps 89:46
—To judge sinners on earth .... Ge 19:24–25
Lev 10:2
Nu 11:1–2
2Ki 1:10,12
—To punish eternally in hell .... Mt 5:22
2Th 1:7–8
Jas 3:6
Rev 18:17–18

FIRSTFRUITS

A. Firstfruits in the Old Testament
1. Firstfruits to be dedicated to God
—Firstborn son .... Ex 13:1–2
—Firstborn of livestock .... Ex 13:1–2
—Firstfruits of the crops .... Ex 23:16
Lev 23:9
—Firstfruits of grain, wine, oil, wool .... Dt 18:4
2Ch 31:5
—Firstfruits of fruit trees .... Lev 19:23–24
—Firstfruits of everything grown .... Dt 26:2
Pr 3:9
2. Rules and regulations
a. General
—In the Law of Moses .... Lev 2:11–16
Lev 23:9–14
Dt 26:1–15
—After the exile .... Ne 10:35
Ne 12:44
—In the new temple .... Eze 44:30
b. Must be brought to the Lord's house .... Ex 23:19
Ex 34:26
c. Must precede eating of harvested crops .... Lev 23:14

B. Firstfruits as symbol in the New Testament
—Christ as the firstfruits of those raised 1Co 15:20,23
—The Holy Spirit as our first blessing .... Ro 8:23
—The Holy Spirit as a guaranteed deposit 2Co 1:22
2Co 5:5
Eph 1:14
—Early Christians as firstfruits of others .... Jas 1:18

FISH

A. Fish in the Old Testament
—A food for humans .... Nu 11:5
Ne 13:16
—Humans given dominion over fish .... Ge 1:26,28
Ps 8:6–8
—The great fish that swallowed Jonah .... Jnh 1:17
Mt 12:40

B. Fish in the New Testament
1. Several disciples were fishermen .... Mt 4:18–21
Jn 21:1–3
2. Miracles with fish
—Miraculous catch of fish .... Lk 5:4–7
Jn 21:4–11
—Feeding the multitude with two fish .... Mk 6:37–44
Jn 6:1–11
—Tax money in the mouth of a fish .... Mt 17:24–27
3. Parable concerning fish and net .... Mt 13:47–48

FOLLY

A. Characteristics of the fool
—Begins with a denial of God .... Ps 14:1
—Does not trust in God 2Ch 16:7–9
—Trusts in self .... Pr 28:26
—Has no desire to get wisdom .... Pr 1:7,22
Pr 17:16
—Spurns discipline .... Pr 15:5
—Finds pleasure in evil .... Pr 10:23
Tit 3:3
—Is rebellious .... Ps 107:17
—Engages in senseless merriment .... Ecc 7:4–6
—Loves to quarrel .... Pr 20:3
—Does not control anger .... Pr 29:9,11
—Comes to ruin .... Pr 10:8,10,14

See also WISDOM

B. Special aspects of foolishness in the New Testament
—The foolishness of preaching ... 1Co 1:21 – 24
—The foolishness of God is wiser than human wisdom ... 1Co 1:25
—Being fools for Christ's sake ... 1Co 3:18; 1Co 4:10
—Paul's speech of the fool ... 2Co 11:16—12:13

FOOL
See FOLLY

FOOT
A. The human foot
1. Symbolic uses of the human foot
—Washing feet in ceremonial cleansing ... Ex 30:17 – 21
—Washing feet as a sign of courtesy ... Ge 18:4
—Washing feet as a sign of repentance ... Lk 7:37 – 48
—Washing feet as a sign of servanthood ... Jn 13:3 – 15
—Cutting off feet as a punishment ... 2Sa 4:12
2. Metaphors concerning the foot
a. Dominion: everything under our feet ... Ps 8:6
b. Security: feet on solid rock ... Ps 40:2
c. Gratitude: falling down at one's feet ... Lk 17:16
d. Victory
—Trampling underfoot ... Mic 7:10
—Placing feet on the neck ... Jos 10:24
—Enemies as one's footstool ... Ps 110:1; Ac 2:35
e. Submission: falling down at one's feet ... 1Sa 25:24; 2Sa 22:40; Rev 19:10
f. Rejection: shaking dust off one's feet ... Mt 10:14; Ac 13:51
g. Sin
—Straying feet ... Ps 44:18
—Stumbling feet ... Ps 116:8
h. Miscellaneous
—Beautiful feet of gospel preachers ... Isa 52:7; Ro 10:15
—God's word as a lamp to our feet ... Ps 119:105
B. The feet of God
—Bowing down at his feet in submission ... Dt 33:3
—The earth as God's footstool ... Isa 66:1; Mt 5:35
—The ark as God's footstool ... 1Ch 28:2

FOREIGNERS
See ALIEN

FORGET
A. Human forgetting
1. What we ought to forget
—Our troubles ... Ge 41:51; Isa 65:16
—The trials of the past ... Isa 43:18; Php 3:13
—Our sin and the shame it brings ... Isa 54:4; Eze 39:26
2. What we ought not to forget
—The Lord ... Dt 6:12; Isa 17:10; Jer 2:32
—God's mighty acts ... Dt 4:9; Ps 78:7,11
—God's covenant with us ... Dt 4:23,31; 2Ki 17:38
—God's law ... Ps 119:61,83,109
—God's patience with us ... 2Pe 3:9 – 10
—God's benefits to us ... Ps 103:2
—The teachings of our parents ... Pr 3:6; Pr 4:5
B. Divine forgetting
1. What God forgets
—The sins of those who repent ... Isa 43:25; Jer 31:34; Heb 8:12
—Those who persistently refuse to believe ... Jer 23:39 – 40
2. What God does not forget
—His people ... Isa 44:21; Isa 49:21
—Our good deeds and love ... Heb 6:10
—Even the smallest of his creatures ... Lk 12:6
—The sins of those who refuse to repent ... Am 8:7
3. Praying that God will not forget
—Us ... Ps 13:1
—The helpless ... Ps 10:12
—Those who are afflicted ... Ps 74:19
See also REMEMBER

FORGIVENESS
—Pardon for human sins and shortcomings
A. Related theme
FORGIVENESS is a theme of Philemon ... Phm 17
B. Human forgiveness of others
1. Examples
—Esau of his brother Jacob ... Ge 33:4
—Joseph of his brothers ... Ge 50:15 – 21
—The father of his wayward son ... Lk 15:17 – 24
—Jesus of his enemies ... Lk 23:34
—Stephen of his enemies ... Ac 7:60
—Paul of those deserting him ... 2Ti 4:16
2. Required of Christians ... Mt 18:35; Lk 11:4; Eph 4:32; Col 3:13
C. God's forgiveness of us
1. Why does God forgive?
—Because of his compassion ... Ex 34:6 – 7; Mic 7:19
—Because of his love ... Ps 51:1
—Because of his grace ... Ps 103:8
—Because of his mercy ... Isa 55:7
2. How does God forgive?
—Always by shedding of blood ... Heb 9:22
—Foreshadowed by Old Testament sacrifice ... Lev 4:1—5:13
—Fulfilled by the blood of Christ ... Col 1:14; Col 2:13 – 14; Heb 9:14,28
—Jesus can forgive sins ... Mk 2:1 – 11
3. What happens to our sins?
—They go out of sight ... Isa 38:17
—They go out of reach ... Ps 103:12; Mic 7:19
—They go out of mind ... Isa 43:25; Jer 31:34
—They go out of existence ... Ps 51:1 – 2,7,9; Isa 44:22; Ac 3:19
4. How do we receive forgiveness?
—We must confess our sins ... Ps 32:5; 1Jn 1:9
—We must repent of our sins ... Ac 2:38; Ac 3:19
—We must believe in Christ ... Lk 24:47; Ac 10:43; Ac 13:38

FORNICATION
See SEXUAL STANDARDS

FREEDOM

—Being liberated from bondage

A. Related themes

FREEDOM is a theme of:

—Exodus ... Ex 6:6

—Galatians ... Gal 5:13

B. Freedom from human slavery

1. In the Old Testament

—God delivered his enslaved people ... Ex 1:11; Ex 6:6 – 7; Ex 20:2

—God forbade slavery among Hebrews ... Ex 21:2; Dt 15:12 – 15; Jer 34:8 – 17

—Prophets spoke against slavery ... 2Ki 4:1 – 7; Ne 5:4 – 8

2. In the New Testament

—Apostles accepted slavery ... Eph 6:5 – 8; Col 3:22 – 25; 1Pe 2:18 – 19

—Slaves were to be treated as brothers and sisters ... Phm 15 – 16

See also SLAVERY

C. Spiritual freedom

1. Who sets us free?

—God ... Ro 6:17 – 18

—Christ ... Jn 8:34 – 36; Gal 2:4; Gal 5:1

—The Holy Spirit ... Ro 8:15; 2Co 3:17

2. From what are we set free?

—From sin ... Jn 8:36; Ro 6:7

—From sin and death ... Ro 8:2

—From fear of death ... Heb 2:15

—From fear ... Ro 8:15

—From the law ... Ro 7:6; Gal 3:23 – 25; Jas 1:25

—From the curse of the law ... Gal 3:13 – 14

—From bondage to decay ... Ro 8:21

—From the basic principles of the world ... Gal 4:3 – 4; Col 2:20 – 22

3. How are we set free?

—By hearing and believing the truth ... Jn 8:32

—By participating in Christ's death ... Ro 6:6 – 14; Ro 7:4

—By the power of the Holy Spirit ... Ro 7:6; Ro 8:15

4. Our response to being free

—We must thank God ... Ps 116:16 – 17

—We must glorify God ... 1Co 10:31

—We must walk in freedom ... Ps 119:45

—We must serve others ... 1Co 9:19 – 23; 1Co 10:32 – 33

—We must not hurt other Christians ... Ro 14:13 – 21; 1Co 8:9 – 12

—We must not use freedom as excuse to sin ... Gal 5:1,13; 1Pe 2:16

FRIENDSHIP

A. Human friendship

1. Examples of human friendship

—Ruth and Naomi ... Ru 1:15 – 18

—David and Jonathan ... 1Sa 18:1 – 4; 1Sa 20:41 – 42

—Job and three friends ... Job 2:11

2. Characteristics of true friendship

—Loyalty ... Ps 41:9; Pr 17:17; Pr 27:6

—Love and support ... Pr 17:17; Pr 18:24; Ecc 4:10; Ac 24:23

—Comfort in sorrow ... Job 2:11; Jn 11:33 – 36

—Encouragement ... 3Jn 5; Jude 17,20

3. Dangers of bad friendships

—Can give bad advice ... 1Ki 12:8 – 14

—Can double-cross us ... Ps 41:9; Pr 16:28; Pr 17:9; Ps 109:4 – 5

—Can desert us ... Ps 38:11

—Can lead us away from the Lord ... Dt 13:6 – 9; Pr 22:24 – 25; Jas 4:4

B. Friendship with God

1. Examples of God's friends

—Moses ... Ex 33:11

—Abraham ... 2Ch 20:7; Jas 2:23

—Job ... Job 29:4

2. Friendship with Jesus

—Calls his disciples friends ... Jn 15:14 – 15

—Calls tax collectors and sinners friends ... Mt 11:19

—Emphasizes sacrificial love ... Jn 15:13

—Emphasizes obedience ... Jn 15:14

FRUIT OF THE SPIRIT

—Specific listing of aspects of the Spirit's fruit ... Gal 5:22 – 23

—Other listings of these aspects ... Ro 14:17; Eph 3:15 – 16; Eph 4:2 – 3; Col 3:12 – 15; 2Pe 1:5 – 7

See also entries for each aspect

GABRIEL

—An angel ... Lk 1:19

—Interpreted Daniel's visions ... Da 8:16 – 26; Da 9:20 – 27

—Announced birth of John the Baptist ... Lk 1:11 – 20

—Announced birth of Jesus to Mary ... Lk 1:26 – 38

GAD

A. Son of Jacob by Zilpah ... Ge 35:26

—Name means "good fortune" ... Ge 30:11

—Went to Egypt with family ... Ge 46:8,16

—Father of seven sons ... Ge 46:16

—Blessed by Jacob ... Ge 49:19

B. Tribe descended from Gad

—Blessed by Moses ... Dt 33:20 – 21

—Numbered ... Nu 1:25; Nu 26:18

—Asked to settle east of the Jordan ... Nu 32:1 – 27

—Allotted land on east side of the Jordan ... Nu 32:31 – 38; Jos 18:7

—Allotted land on west side of the Jordan ... Eze 48:27 – 28

—One of the tribes of the 144,000 ... Rev 7:5

C. A prophet ... 1Sa 22:5

—A seer of David ... 2Sa 24:11 – 19

—Recorded events of David's reign ... 1Ch 29:29

GALATIA
—Paul preached the gospel there........................Ac 16:6
Ac 18:23
—Paul collected money there........................1Co 16:1–2
—Paul wrote a letter to churches there........................Gal 1:2
—Peter wrote a letter to Christians there........................1Pe 1:1

GALILEE
A. In the the Old Testament
—Land belonging to the tribe of Naphtali........................Jos 20:7
—Key city: Kadesh........................Jos 21:32
—Twenty towns given to Hiram of Tyre........................1Ki 9:11
—Tiglath-Pileser took that land........................2Ki 15:29
—Future blessing for Galilee promised........................Isa 9:1–7
B. In the New Testament
1. A district governed by Herod........................Lk 3:1
Lk 23:5–7
2. Important towns in Galilee
—Nazareth........................Mt 2:22–23
—Capernaum........................Lk 4:31
—Cana........................Jn 2:1
—Bethsaida........................Jn 12:21
3. The Sea of Galilee
—Disciples used to fish there........................Mt 4:18–22
Mk 1:16–20
—Jesus taught from a boat........................Lk 5:3
—Jesus taught on its shore........................Jn 6:1–3
—Jesus stilled a storm on it........................Mt 8:23–27
Mk 4:36–41
Lk 8:22–26
—Jesus walked on it........................Mt 14:25–33
Jn 6:16–21
—Disciples met the risen Christ there........................Jn 21:1–14
4. Jesus and Galilee
—Joseph and Mary were from there........................Lk 1:26
Lk 2:4
—Jesus grew up in Nazareth........................Mt 2:22
Mk 1:9
Lk 2:39
—Jesus called "Jesus of Galilee"........................Mt 26:69
—Jesus fulfilled Isaiah's prophecy........................Mt 4:12–17
—Jesus had extensive ministry there........................Mt 4:23–25
Mt 11:1
Mk 1:14,39
Lk 4:14–15
Jn 7:1
—Great Commission given in Galilee........................Mt 28:16–20
—Church spread through Galilee........................Ac 9:31

GAMBLING
See STEALING; STEWARDSHIP

GATH
—One of the five great Philistine cities........................Jos 13:3
—Giants (including Goliath) came from there........................1Sa 17:4
2Sa 21:19–22
—David fled there from Saul........................1Sa 21:10–11
1Sa 27:2–4
—David feigned insanity there........................1Sa 21:12–15
—King David conquered it........................1Ch 18:1
—Rehoboam fortified it........................2Ch 11:5,8
—Hazael king of Aram took it from Joash........................2Ki 12:17
—Uzziah captured it back........................2Ch 26:6

GAZA
—Originally a Canaanite city........................Ge 10:19
—One of the five great Philistine cities........................1Sa 6:17–18
—Given to tribe of Judah........................Jos 15:47
—Taken by the men of Judah........................Jdg 1:18
—Samson carried away its gates........................Jdg 16:1–3
—Samson died there........................Jdg 16:21–30
—Solomon ruled over it........................1Ki 4:24
—Hezekiah conquered it........................2Ki 18:7–8
—Prophecies against it........................Am 1:6–7
Jer 47:1–7
Zep 2:4
Zec 9:5
—Gospel preached on the road to Gaza........................Ac 8:26–39

GEDALIAH
—Governor of Judah, appointed by Nebuchadnezzar........................2Ki 25:22–23
—Encouraged settling down in Babylon........................2Ki 25:24
—Became guardian of Jeremiah........................Jer 39:14
—Warned of an assassination plot........................Jer 40:13–16
—Assassinated by Ishmael........................2Ki 25:25
Jer 41:1–3

GEHAZI
—Servant of Elisha........................2Ki 4:12
—Unable to raise Shunammite's son from the dead..2Ki 4:29–31
—Sought reward from Naaman........................2Ki 5:20–25
—Inflicted with leprosy........................2Ki 5:26–27
—Told the king about the Shunammite........................2Ki 8:4–6

GENEALOGY
See ANCESTRY

GENTILES
See NATIONS

GENTLENESS
See MEEKNESS

GIBEON
—A city of the Hivites........................Jos 11:19
—Tricked Joshua into making a treaty........................Jos 9:1–27
—Joshua protected it from five kings........................Jos 10:1–14
—Given to the tribe of Benjamin........................Jos 18:21,25
1Ch 6:60
—Saul and David battled there........................2Sa 2:12–28
—David defeated Philistines there........................2Sa 5:25
—Tabernacle kept there for a while........................1Ch 16:39–42
—Solomon offered sacrifices there........................1Ki 3:4
2Ch 1:3–6
—Solomon asked for wisdom there........................1Ki 3:5–15
2Ch 1:7–13
—Gedaliah's assassin fled there........................Jer 41:11–15
—City rebuilt after the exile........................Ne 3:7

GIDEON
A. His background and call as judge
—Youngest son of Joash........................Jdg 6:11,15
—Also called Jerub-Baal........................Jdg 7:1
—Angel called him........................Jdg 6:11–24
—Prepared sacrifice........................Jdg 6:19–22
—Supported by his father........................Jdg 6:25–32
—Needed assurance through throwing out a fleece........................Jdg 6:36–40
—Had many wives........................Jdg 8:30–31
B. His war against Midianites
—Gathered an army........................Jdg 6:34–35
—Reduced size of army to three hundred........................Jdg 7:2–8
—Developed battle plan........................Jdg 7:15–21
—Achieved victory........................Jdg 7:22–25
C. Subsequent events
—Took revenge on men of Succoth........................Jdg 8:4–21
—Refused to be king........................Jdg 8:22–23
—Made an idol for worship........................Jdg 8:24–27
—Served as judge for forty years........................Jdg 8:28
—His death........................Jdg 8:32
—Called a hero of faith........................Heb 11:32

GIFTS OF THE SPIRIT

A. Types of gifts
—Speaking in tongues ... Ac 10:46; Ac 19:6; 1Co 12:10,28,30; 1Co 14:2,6 – 11
—Interpreting tongues ... 1Co 12:10,30; 1Co 14:13,27 – 28
—Prophecy ... Ro 12:6; 1Co 12:10,28 – 29; 1Co 14:3 – 5,22 – 25
—Serving ... Ro 12:7; 1Pe 4:11
—Teaching ... Ro 12:7; 1Co 12:28 – 29
—Being an apostle ... 1Co 12:28 – 29; Eph 4:11
—Contributing to others ... Ro 12:8
—Exercising leadership ... Ro 12:8
—Showing mercy ... Ro 12:8
—Encouraging others ... Ro 12:8
—Being single ... 1Co 7:7 – 8
—Wisdom ... 1Co 12:8
—Knowledge ... 1Co 12:8
—Faith ... 1Co 12:9
—Healing ... 1Co 12:9,28,30
—Miraculous powers ... 1Co 12:10,28 – 29
—Distinguishing between spirits ... 1Co 12:10
—Helping others ... 1Co 12:28
—Administration ... 1Co 12:28
—Doing evangelism ... Eph 4:11
—Being a pastor ... Eph 4:11
—Speaking in public ... 1Pe 4:11
—Skill and knowledge in crafts ... Ex 31:1 – 5

B. The purposes of gifts
—To be enjoyed privately ... 1Co 14:4
—To witness to Christ ... 1Co 12:1 – 3
—To build up the church ... 1Co 12:7; 1Co 14:3,5,12,26; 1Pe 4:10
—To demonstrate God's grace in us ... Ro 12:6
—To praise God ... 1Co 14:24 – 25; 1Pe 4:11

C. Gifts are subordinate to love
—The greatest way is the way of love ... 1Co 12:31—13:3
—Gifts will disappear ... 1Co 13:8 – 10
—Love will always remain ... 1Co 13:13

D. Warning against gifts that deceive
—False prophets can do wonders and signs ... Mt 24:24
—The antichrist will do counterfeit signs ... 2Th 2:9; Rev 13:13 – 14
—We must test the spirits ... 1Jn 4:1

GLORY

—The grandeur and majesty of God

A. Related theme
GLORY OF CHRIST is a theme of Colossians ... Col 1:27

B. God and his glory
1. Glory belongs to God ... 1Ch 29:11; Ps 29:1,3; Ps 96:7; Ro 11:36
2. God dwells in awesome majesty ... Job 37:22; Ps 93:1; Ps 145:5
3. God's name is glorious ... Dt 28:58; 1Ch 29:13; Ps 8:1; Ps 79:9
4. God reveals his glory
—In Jesus Christ ... Isa 40:5; Jn 1:14
—In the tent of meeting ... Ex 40:34 – 35
—In the temple ... 2Ch 5:14; Eze 10:4; Eze 43:5
—In his works ... Ps 19:1; Ps 111:3
—Through Moses ... Ex 34:29 – 35
—On Mount Sinai ... Ex 24:15 – 17
—To Isaiah ... Isa 6:3
—To his people through his redemption ... Isa 44:23; Isa 46:13
—To Ezekiel ... Eze 1:28
—To the shepherds of Bethlehem ... Lk 2:9
—To Stephen ... Ac 7:55
—To the whole world ... Ps 97:6; Isa 66:18; Hab 2:14

C. Jesus and his glory
1. He is the Lord of glory ... 1Co 2:8; Jas 2:1
2. He has God's glory
—Had glory from the beginning ... Jn 17:5
—Surpassed glory of the Old Testament ... 2Co 3:7 – 11
—Now exalted in glory ... 1Ti 3:16; Rev 5:12 – 13
—Will return in glory ... Mt 24:30; Mt 25:31
3. He revealed God's glory
—In human flesh ... Jn 1:14; Heb 1:3
—In his actions ... Jn 2:11; Jn 11:40 – 44
—In his transfiguration ... Lk 9:29 – 30; 2Pe 1:16 – 19
—In his death ... Jn 12:23 – 24
—In the resurrection ... Lk 24:26; Php 3:21

D. The Spirit and his glory
—Called the Spirit of glory ... 1Pe 4:14
—His ministry is glorious ... 2Co 3:8

E. Believers and the glory of God
1. The present
—We fall short of his glory ... Ro 3:23
—Christ came to bring us to glory ... Lk 2:29 – 32; Col 1:27
—We receive God's glory through Christ ... Jn 17:22; 2Co 4:6
—We receive the Spirit of glory ... 1Pe 4:14
—We must reflect his glory ... 1Co 10:31; 2Co 3:18
—We must pray that his glory will endure ... Ps 104:31
2. The future
—We will be brought into his glory ... Heb 2:10; Jude 24
—We will share in Christ's glory ... Ro 8:17 – 18; 1Pe 5:10
—Our new bodies will bear his glory ... 1Co 15:42 – 43; Php 3:21
—We will receive a crown of glory ... 1Pe 5:4

GOD

A. Related themes
1. GOD is a theme of:
—Genesis ... Ge 28:13
—Proverbs ... Pr 16:4
—Isaiah ... Isa 54:5

2. UNIVERSAL GOD is a theme of:
—Ruth ... Ru 1:16
—Ezekiel ... Eze 1:1
—Jonah ... Jnh 1:2

B. The being of God
See HOLY SPIRIT; JESUS CHRIST; TRINITY

C. Names of God
—God ... Ge 1:1
—LORD ... Ge 4:1,4
—LORD God ... Ge 2:4
—God Most High ... Ge 14:18 – 20
—The Sovereign LORD ... Ge 15:2
—God Almighty ... Ge 17:1
—The Eternal God ... Ge 21:33
—The God of Bethel ... Ge 31:13
—God of Abraham, Isaac, Jacob ... Ex 3:6
—I AM WHO I AM ... Ex 3:14
—The God of the Hebrews ... Ex 3:18
—Jealous ... Ex 34:14
—The God of Israel ... 1Sa 1:17
—God, the Rock ... 2Sa 22:47
—The LORD, the God of heaven ... Ezr 1:2
—The Mighty One, God, the LORD ... Ps 50:1
—God the King ... Ps 145:1
—The Holy One of Israel ... Isa 1:4
—The Mighty One of Israel ... Isa 1:24

D. Characteristics of God
1. Divine characteristics
—Holy ... Lev 11:44
—Eternal ... Ps 90:2
—Infinite ... 1Ki 8:27
—Immortal ... 1Ti 1:17
—Invisible ... Jn 1:18
—All-knowing ... Ps 147:5
—Everywhere present ... Ps 139:7 – 21
—All-powerful ... Isa 40:6 – 7
—Unchanging ... Mal 3:6
—Incomparable ... Isa 40:18,25
—Righteous ... Ps 145:17
—Perfect ... Mt 5:48
—Awesome and majestic ... Ex 15:11
—Gracious ... Ex 34:6
—Spirit ... Jn 4:24
2. Human characteristics ascribed to him
a. Physical characteristics
—Face of God ... Nu 6:25 – 26
See FACE
—Ears of God ... Ne 1:6
See EAR
—Eyes of God ... 2Ch 16:9
See EYE
—Nostrils of God ... Ex 15:8
—Mouth of God ... Dt 8:3
See MOUTH
—Voice of God ... Ex 15:26
See VOICE
—Hands of God ... Ezr 7:9
See HAND
—Fingers of God ... Ps 8:3
—Arms of God ... Dt 33:27
—Shoulders of God ... Dt 33:12
—Back of God ... Ex 33:21 – 22
—Feet of God ... Ps 18:9
See FOOT
b. Physical actions
—God sits ... Ps 102:12
—God stands ... Ge 28:13
—God walks ... Ge 3:8
—God comes down ... Ge 11:5
—God goes up ... Ge 17:22
—God marches ... Zec 9:14
—God rides ... Ps 68:33
—God soars ... 2Sa 22:11
—God shoots arrows ... 2Sa 22:15
—God reaches down ... 2Sa 22:17
—God rests ... Ge 2:2
—God sleeps ... Ps 44:23
c. Emotional characteristics
—God loves ... Ex 34:6
1Jn 4:8 – 10
—God is compassionate ... Ex 3:7
—God is patient ... 2Pe 3:9
—God laughs ... Ps 2:4
—God becomes angry ... Dt 9:7
—God grieves ... Ge 6:6
—God is jealous ... Ex 34:14
—God fears ... Dt 32:26 – 27
—God hates ... Ps 5:5

E. Our response to God
—We should trust in him ... Jn 14:1
See TRUST
—We should hope in him ... Ps 131:3
See HOPE
—We should believe him ... Ge 15:6
See FAITH
—We should fear him ... Dt 6:13
See FEAR
—We should praise him ... Ps 150:1 – 6
See PRAISE
—We should worship him ... Ps 96:9
See WORSHIP
—We should stand in awe of him ... Hab 3:2
—We should honor him ... Pr 3:9
—We should glorify him ... Ps 34:3
—We should thirst for him ... Ps 42:2

GOLD

A. Uses for gold
1. In Israelite worship
—The tabernacle structure ... Ex 26:29,32
—The tabernacle furniture ... Ex 25:10 – 40
Ex 30:3 – 5
—Priestly garments ... Ex 28:11 – 36
—The temple structure ... 2Ch 3:4 – 6
—The temple furniture ... 2Ch 4:7 – 8,20 – 22
2. In pagan worship
—The golden calf in the desert ... Ex 32:1 – 4
—The golden calves of Jeroboam ... 1Ki 12:26 – 30
—Other idols ... Isa 2:20
Hos 8:4
3. For personal wealth ... 2Ch 9:13
Ecc 2:8
Mt 10:9
4. For gifts ... 2Ch 9:9
Ezr 2:69
Mt 2:11
5. For jewelry ... Ge 24:22
Ex 32:2
Jdg 8:24,26
6. For royal display ... 2Ch 9:15 – 16
Est 1:6 – 7

B. Value of gold for God's people
1. Positive: a blessing from God ... Ge 13:2
Isa 60:6,17
2. Negative
—Spiritual values worth more than gold ... Ps 19:10
Pr 3:13 – 14
1Pe 1:7
—Gold valueless in redemption ... 1Pe 1:18

C. Gold as a symbol
—For God's people surviving God's testing .... Job 23:10
—For trustworthy spiritual values .... 1Co 3:12 – 13
Rev 3:18
—For the new heaven .... Rev 21:18,21

GOLIATH

—A Philistine giant .... 1Sa 17:4 – 7
—Taunted the Israelite army .... 1Sa 17:8 – 11
—David offered to fight him .... 1Sa 17:32 – 37
—David killed him .... 1Sa 17:48 – 51
—David obtained his sword 1Sa 21:9

GOMORRAH

See SODOM AND GOMORRAH

GOSPEL

—The good news of salvation for humanity
A. Terms used to describe the gospel
—The gospel of God .... Ro 1:1
—The good news of God's grace .... Ac 20:24
—The gospel of God's Son .... Ro 1:9
—The gospel of our Lord Jesus 2Th 1:8
—The gospel of Christ .... Ro 15:19
—The gospel that displays the glory of Christ 2Co 4:4
—The good news about Jesus Christ .... Mk 1:1
—The gospel of the kingdom .... Mt 24:14
—The gospel of salvation .... Eph 1:13
—The gospel of peace .... Eph 6:15
—The eternal gospel .... Rev 14:6
B. The gospel in the Old Testament
—First revealed to Adam and Eve .... Ge 3:15
—Revealed to Abraham .... Ge 12:2 – 3
Ge 18:18
Ge 22:18
Gal 3:8
—Revealed to Israel through prophets .... Isa 40:9
Isa 52:7 – 10
Isa 61:6
Ro 1:1 – 2
C. The gospel in the New Testament
1. The proclaimers of the gospel
—The angel at Christ's birth .... Lk 2:10
—John the Baptist .... Lk 3:18
—Jesus Christ .... Mk 1:14 – 15
Lk 4:43
—The twelve disciples .... Lk 9:6
—The twelve apostles .... Ac 5:42
—Peter and John .... Ac 8:25
Ac 15:7
—Philip .... Ac 8:12,40
—Paul .... Ac 14:7
Ro 15:19
—Unnamed missionaries 1Pe 1:12
—Our responsibility .... Mt 24:14
Mt 28:19
2. The content of the gospel
—The basic story about Jesus .... Mk 1:1
1Co 15:1 – 8,11
—Jesus is the Christ .... Ac 5:42
—Humans should repent .... Mk 1:15
—Salvation is by faith in Jesus .... Ro 1:16 – 17
—God gives us his grace .... Ac 20:24
—Both Jew and Gentile can be saved .... Eph 3:6 – 7
—Jesus will return as judge .... Ro 2:16
—How believers should live .... Php 1:27
3. The characteristics of the gospel
—It reveals the glory of Christ 2Co 4:4
—It is eternal 1Pe 1:25
Rev 14:6
—It demonstrates God's power .... Ro 1:16
—It calls us 2Th 2:14
—It saves us 1Co 15:2
—It gives us peace .... Eph 6:15
—It gives us hope .... Col 1:23
—It gives us life 2Ti 1:10
—It grows and bears fruit .... Col 1:6
—It tolerates no rival .... Gal 1:6 – 9
4. The response to the gospel
—We should believe it .... Heb 4:2
—We should obey it 2Co 9:13
2Th 1:8
Heb 4:6
—We should not be ashamed of it .... Ro 1:16
—We should live in line with its truth .... Gal 2:14
Php 1:27
—We should serve it 2Co 8:18
—We should continue in it .... Col 1:23
—We should promote it 1Co 9:16
—We should defend it .... Php 1:7,16
Jude 3
—We should preach it .... Mk 16:15
Ac 8:4
Ro 15:19 – 20
1Co 9:16
—We may have to suffer for it 2Ti 1:8
2Ti 2:8 – 9

GOVERNMENT

—The rule of humans by other humans
A. Phases of civil government among the Israelites/Jews
1. Rule by the fathers (patriarchs)
—Abram .... Ge 14:13 – 16
—Isaac .... Ge 26:26 – 32
—Jacob .... Ge 34:5,30 – 31
Ge 46:5 – 27
2. Rule by God's chosen leaders
—Moses .... Ex 3:7 – 12
Ex 18:13 – 26
—Moses and Aaron .... Nu 17:1 – 13
—Joshua .... Dt 31:1 – 8
Jos 1:1 – 11
3. Rule by God's chosen judges
See JUDGE, JUDGMENT
4. Rule through God's chosen kings
—Israel asked for a king .... 1Sa 8:4 – 22
—Israel's first king, Saul .... 1Sa 10:20 – 26
—David anointed as king .... 1Sa 16:1 – 13
—David's line to be the royal line .... 2Sa 7:8 – 16
See KING
5. Rule by foreign kings
—The Babylonians .... 2Ch 36:15 – 21
Da 1:1 – 6
—The Persians .... Ezr 1:1 – 4
Isa 44:28—45:6
—The Herods of Idumea .... Mt 2:1 – 8,16 – 22
—The Romans .... Mt 27:11 – 14
Jn 18:28 – 40
B. Principles of government
1. God and human government
—God is the real ruler .... Dt 33:5
Jdg 8:23
1Ch 29:23
Ps 29:10 – 11
Isa 33:22
—God rules through anointed servants .... Ps 45:6 – 7
Isa 45:1
2. Humans in the government
—They derive authority from God .... Da 4:17
Jn 19:11
Ro 13:1,4

—God's people may serve pagan governments .... Ne 2:1–9
Ne 5:14–18
Est 8:1–2
Da 1:17–21

C. Our responsibility to government
—We must respect it 1Sa 14:6–7
1Sa 26:7–11
1Pe 2:17
—We must submit to it .... Ro 13:1,5
Tit 3:1
1Pe 2:13–14
—We must support it with taxes .... Mt 22:15–21
Ro 13:6–7
—We must pray for it 1Ti 2:1–2
—Occasionally we may have to disobey it .... Ac 5:29

GRACE

—God's free and undeserved favor

A. Related themes
GRACE is a theme of:
—Genesis .... Ge 25:33
—Judges .... Jdg 6:13
—Job .... Job 42:10
—Jonah .... Jnh 3:10
—Romans .... Ro 11:6

B. Grace comes as a gift
—From God .... Eph 2:8
1Pe 5:10
—From the Father .... Ps 84:11
Jas 1:17
—From Christ, the Son .... Jn 1:17
1Co 1:4
—From the Holy Spirit .... Zec 12:10
Heb 10:29

C. How can we receive grace?
—We must accept Christ .... Jn 1:14,16
2Co 8:9
Eph 1:6–7
—We must be humble .... Pr 3:34
Jas 4:6
—We cannot earn it by good works .... Ro 11:6
2Ti 1:9
—We cannot earn it by keeping the law .... Ro 6:14
Gal 2:16

D. Examples of those who received grace
—Abraham .... Gal 3:18
—Paul .... Eph 3:2
1Ti 1:12–16
—All believers .... Eph 1:7–8

E. What happens to believers through grace?
—They are chosen .... Ro 11:5
—They are called .... Gal 1:15
—They believe .... Ac 18:27
—They are justified .... Ro 3:24
Tit 3:7
—They receive righteousness .... Ro 5:17
—They are saved .... Ac 15:11
Tit 2:11
—They are redeemed .... Ro 3:24
—They are forgiven .... Eph 1:7
—They receive many good things .... Ro 8:32
Jas 1:17
—They receive spiritual gifts .... Ro 12:6
Eph 4:7–12
—They receive encouragement 2Th 2:16
—They receive help in time of need .... Heb 4:16
—They are able to bear up under suffering 2Co 12:9
—They have hope 2Th 2:16
—They are glorified in Christ 2Th 1:12

F. Relationship of believers to grace
—They are under grace .... Ro 6:14
—They stand in grace .... Ro 5:2
—They are what they are by grace 1Co 15:10
—They abound in grace 2Co 9:8
1Ti 1:14
—They share in God's grace .... Php 1:7
—They may approach God's throne of grace .... Heb 4:16
—They are strengthened by grace .... Heb 13:9
—They must grow in grace 2Pe 3:18
—They must not receive grace in vain 2Co 6:1
—They can fall away from grace .... Gal 5:4
Heb 6:4–6

G. The wicked experience grace .... Isa 26:10
Mt 5:45
Ac 14:17

GRAVE (SHEOL)

—Sheol is a Hebrew word of uncertain meaning

A. Where everyone goes at death .... Isa 14:9–11
—The righteous .... Ge 37:35
Ps 88:3–5
—The wicked .... Nu 16:30
Eze 32:21,27

B. Characteristics
—A place of darkness and corruption .... Job 17:13–16
—A place of inactivity .... Ps 6:5
Ps 31:17
Ecc 9:10
Isa 38:18
—The opposite of the heavens .... Ps 139:8
Am 9:2
—The opposite of life .... Pr 15:24
—It is never satisfied .... Pr 27:20
Isa 5:14
Hab 2:5

C. Resurrection takes place from there .... Ps 16:10–11
Ps 49:14–15

GREAT TRIBULATION

—A time of intense distress at the end of the world

A. General tribulation
See PAIN

B. The great tribulation
—Only use of the specific term .... Rev 7:14
—A time of great distress .... Isa 24:1–20
Da 12:1
Mt 24:15–28
—The time is limited .... Da 9:24–27
—Dominated by the antichrist .... Rev 13:11–17
—Ends with the destruction of Babylon .... Rev 14:8
Rev 18:1–24
—Shortened for the sake of the elect .... Mt 24:22

GREECE, GREEK

—A Roman province, south of Macedonia

A. Paul's ministry in Greece
1. Greece is also called Achaia .... Ac 18:12,27
Ro 15:26
1Co 16:15
2. Ministry in Athens
—Paul preached to Jews and Greeks there .... Ac 17:16–17
—Altar to unknown god located there .... Ac 17:22–23
—Paul's sermon to the Areopagus .... Ac 17:22–31
3. Ministry in Corinth
See CORINTH

B. The Greeks
—Greeks wanted to speak with Jesus .... Jn 12:20–21
—God-fearing Greeks joined with Jews .... Ac 17:4,17

—Grecian Jews in the early church .... Ac 6:1; Ac 9:29
—Paul preached to Jews and Greeks .... Ac 18:4; Ac 20:21
—"Greek" sometimes meant any non-Jew .... 1Co 1:22 – 24; Gal 2:3

GREED

See THE RICH AND THE POOR

GRIEF

A. Related theme
LAMENT is a theme of Lamentations .... La 1:16

B. Human grief
1. Occasions for human grief
—Death of a loved one .... Ge 37:34 – 35; 2Sa 18:33
—A loved one likely to die soon .... 2Sa 12:15 – 17; Mt 17:23
—A loved one departing .... Jn 16:19 – 20
—Experiencing pain and suffering .... Ps 10:12 – 13; Ps 31:9 – 13; 1Pe 1:6
—Seeing the pain of others .... Job 30:25; Jer 48:36
—Feeling sorrow for sin .... Ne 8:8 – 11; Jas 4:8 – 9
—Being punished for sin .... La 1:4 – 5; 2Co 2:5 – 7
—Seeing the sin of others 1Sa 16:1
—Not being able to bear children .... 1Sa 1:10 – 11,15 – 16
—Children marrying outside the faith .... Ge 26:34 – 35
—Children choosing the way of folly .... Pr 10:1; Pr 17:21
—One's relatives not receiving Christ .... Ro 9:2 – 3; 2Co 12:21

2. The answer to human grief
—Receiving comfort from friends .... Job 2:11 – 13; Jn 11:19; Ro 12:15
—Receiving comfort from the Lord .... Ps 23:4; Isa 61:2; Mt 5:4
—Seeing the risen Christ .... Jn 20:20; 1Th 4:13 – 14
—Experiencing salvation .... 2Co 7:9 – 10; 1Pe 1:5 – 6
—Knowing that God does not reject us .... La 3:31 – 33
—Knowing that God turns grief into joy .... Isa 61:3; Jer 31:13; Jn 16:20
—Knowing that God will wipe away all tears .... Isa 25:8; Rev 21:4

C. Divine grief
1. The grief of the triune God
—Grief of the Father .... Ge 6:6 – 7; 1Sa 15:10 – 11
—Grief of the Son .... Lk 19:41 – 44; Jn 11:33 – 35
—Grief of the Holy Spirit .... Isa 63:10; Eph 4:30

2. Occasions for divine grief
—Grief because of human sin .... Ge 3:6 – 7; 1Sa 15:10 – 11; Eze 6:9 – 10
—Grief because of punishment for sin .... 2Sa 24:16; Jer 42:10; Lk 19:41 – 44

GROWTH

A. Related themes
GROWTH is a theme of Esther .... Est 4:8
MATURITY is a theme of Hebrews .... Heb 6:1
SEARCHING is a theme of Ecclesiastes .... Ecc 2:3

B. Natural growth
—Of plants .... Ps 90:5 – 6
—Of human beings .... Lk 1:80; Lk 2:40
—Of political power 2Sa 3:1

C. Numerical growth of the church
1. Parables of growth
—Parable of the sower .... Mt 13:3 – 9,18 – 23
—Parable of the weeds .... Mt 13:24 – 30,36 – 43
—Parable of the mustard seed .... Mt 13:31 – 32
—Parable of the yeast .... Mt 13:33

2. Growth of the New Testament church .... Ac 4:4; Ac 5:14; Ac 6:7; Ac 9:31; Ac 16:5

D. Spiritual growth of Christians
1. What shows lack of growth?
—Inadequate knowledge of God's truth .... Ac 18:24 – 28; Ac 19:1 – 6
—Lack of doctrinal soundness .... Eph 4:14
—Jealousy and quarreling .... 1Co 3:1 – 3
—Living a life of evil 1Co 14:20
—Inability to understand deeper truths .... Heb 5:12 – 14

2. How does growth take place?
—By study of God's word .... 1Pe 2:1 – 3
—By increasing our knowledge of God .... Col 1:10
—By deepening our faith .... Eph 4:13
—By showing love .... Eph 4:15 – 16
—By developing Christian character .... 2Pe 1:5 – 8

3. God wants us to grow and bear fruit .... Ps 1:1 – 3; Ps 92:12 – 15; Jn 15:2,4 – 5,16

GUILT

—The condition of one who breaks the law

A. Guilt in the Old Testament
1. Standing guilty before God
—Because of deliberate sin .... Lev 6:1 – 4
—Because of unintentional sin .... Lev 5:2 – 4,14 – 17
—Guilty even before birth .... Ps 51:5
—Dressed in dirty clothes .... Isa 64:6; Zec 3:3 – 4
—God knows our guilt .... Ps 69:5
—God does not leave guilt unpunished .... Ex 34:7; Na 1:3

2. Feeling guilty because of sin .... 2Sa 24:10; Ezr 9:5 – 7,15; Ps 38:4

3. Resolving guilt before God
—The call to acknowledge guilt .... Jer 3:13; Hos 5:15
—The guilt offering .... Lev 5:14—6:7; Lev 7:1 – 6
—Confession and forgiveness .... Ps 32:5; Isa 6:5 – 7

B. Guilt in the New Testament
1. The reality of guilt
—Christ's coming convicts us of guilt .... Jn 15:22,24
—The Spirit convicts us of guilt .... Jn 16:7 – 8
—One sin makes us guilty of breaking the whole law .... Jas 2:10
—All stand guilty before God .... Ro 3:19,23
—All are guilty because of Adam's sin .... Ro 5:12 – 14

2. The resolution of guilt
—We must confess our sins ... 1Jn 1:9
—We must draw near to God in faith ... Heb 10:22
—We become free of guilt through Christ ... Ro 5:15 – 18

See also CONFESSION; FORGIVENESS; SIN

HAGAR

—Egyptian servant of Sarai ... Ge 16:1
—Given to Abram to conceive a child ... Ge 16:3
—Driven away by Sarai while pregnant ... Ge 16:5 – 16
—Gave birth to Ishmael ... Ge 25:12
—Driven away after birth of Isaac ... Ge 21:9 – 21
—Story interpreted by Paul ... Gal 4:21 – 31

HAGGAI

—A postexilic prophet ... Ezr 5:1
—Encouraged rebuilding of temple ... Ezr 6:14
Hag 1:12 – 13
—Warned God's people of dangers of selfishness ... Hag 1:3 – 11

HAM

—Son of Noah ... Ge 5:32
1Ch 1:4
—Laughed at Noah's nakedness ... Ge 9:20 – 27
—Father of Canaan ... Ge 9:18
1Ch 1:8 – 16

HAMAN

—Agagite noble honored by Xerxes ... Est 3:1 – 2
—Angry when Mordecai would not bow down ... Est 3:2 – 5
—Plotted to execute Jews ... Est 3:6 – 15
—Set up pole upon which to impale Mordecai ... Est 5:9 – 14
—Forced to honor Mordecai ... Est 6:1 – 13
—Plot exposed by Esther ... Est 7:1 – 8
—Impaled on his own pole ... Est 7:9 – 10

HAND

A. The human hand
1. What the human hand does
—Works ... Ps 90:17
—Holds ... Rev 7:9
—Writes ... Gal 6:11
—Touches ... 1Jn 1:1
—Claps ... Ps 47:1
—Fights ... Ps 18:34
—Blesses ... Lev 9:22
—Lifts up in prayer ... 1Ti 2:8
—Lifts up in praise ... Ps 134:2
—Takes oath before God ... Ge 14:22
2. Significance of the right hand
—Place of honor ... Ps 45:9
—Position of power ... 1Ki 2:19
—Used to confirm an agreement ... Gal 2:9
3. Laying on of hands
a. In the Old Testament
—Ordained Levites ... Nu 8:10
—Ordained leaders ... Nu 27:18,22 – 23
—Transferred guilt ... Lev 16:20 – 21
b. In the New Testament
—Conferred healing ... Mk 6:5
Lk 4:40
Ac 28:8
—Transferred the Holy Spirit ... Ac 8:17
Ac 9:17
Ac 19:6
—Ordained missionaries ... Ac 13:3
—Ordained church officers ... Ac 6:6
1Ti 4:14
2Ti 1:6

B. The hand of God
1. What it does
—It saves us ... Ex 6:1
Dt 5:15
—It guides us ... Ezr 7:9
—It provides for us ... Ps 104:28
—It protects us ... Ps 139:10
—It receives our spirits ... Ps 31:5
—It pleads with us ... Isa 65:2
—It chastises us ... Ps 32:4
—It punishes unbelievers ... Ex 7:5
2. Significance of the right hand of God
—His hand of power ... Ps 17:7
Ps 73:23
Ps 118:15 – 16
—Sitting at his right hand as ruler ... Ps 110:1
Ac 2:33
Eph 1:20
Heb 1:3

HANNAH

—Wife of Elkanah ... 1Sa 1:1 – 2
—Prayed to have a child ... 1Sa 1:9 – 18
—Gave birth to Samuel ... 1Sa 1:19 – 20
—Dedicated Samuel to the Lord's work ... 1Sa 1:24 – 28
—Prayed at Samuel's dedication ... 1Sa 2:1 – 10
—Blessed by Eli ... 1Sa 2:18 – 20
—Gave birth to other children ... 1Sa 2:21

HARAN

A. The father of Lot (Haran) ... Ge 11:27
—Died in Ur ... Ge 11:28
B. A city in Mesopotamia (Haran)
—Terah, Abram and Lot emigrated there ... Ge 11:31
Ac 7:4
—Abram set out from there for Canaan ... Ge 12:4
—Abraham sent there to find a wife for Isaac ... Ge 24:1 – 4
—Jacob fled there ... Ge 28:10
—Home of Laban, Leah and Rachel ... Ge 29:4 – 6
—Jacob lived there twenty years ... Ge 31:41
—Belonged to Assyrian Empire ... 2Ki 19:12

HARVEST

A. The importance of harvests
1. Events were calculated by harvest times ... Ge 30:14
Jdg 15:1
Ru 1:22
2. Israelite feasts centered around harvest
—Feast of Firstfruits ... Lev 23:9 – 14
—Feast of Weeks ... Lev 23:15 – 21
—Feast of Tabernacles ... Lev 23:33 – 43
3. Provision made for the poor at harvesttime ... Lev 19:9 – 10
Dt 24:19 – 22
Ru 2:1 – 9

B. God's use of harvests
—Abundant harvest demonstrated his love ... Dt 8:7 – 9
Ps 23:1
Ps 144:12 – 15
—God chastised by means of crop failure and famine ... Isa 17:10 – 11
Joel 1:8 – 12
Hag 1:5 – 6

C. Harvesting used as a metaphor
1. To picture mission work
—Pray for workers in God's harvest ... Mt 9:37 – 38
—The fields ripe for harvest ... Jn 4:35 – 36
2. To picture God's judgment ... Isa 17:1 – 5
Jer 51:33
3. To picture the end of the world
—Gathering God's people ... Mt 13:24 – 30,36 – 43

—Judging God's enemies .... Rev 14:14–19
Joel 3:12–13

4. The law of the harvest
—Reaping what we sow 2Co 9:6
Gal 6:7
—Sowing evil and reaping trouble .... Job 4:8
Pr 22:8
Hos 10:13
—Sowing good and reaping blessing .... Hos 10:12
Gal 6:8–9

HAZAEL

—A servant of King Ben-Hadad of Aram 2Ki 8:7–8
—Anointed by Elijah as king over Aram 1Ki 19:15
—Asked Elisha about Ben-Hadad 2Ki 8:8–9
—Murdered Ben-Hadad 2Ki 8:14–15
—Became king of Aram 2Ki 8:15
—Fought against Israel and Judah 2Ki 8:28
2Ch 22:5–6
—Conquered part of Israel 2Ki 10:32–33
2Ki 13:22
—Gained power over Joash 2Ki 12:17–18
—Succeeded by son Ben-Hadad 2Ki 13:24
—Judgment prophesied against him .... Am 1:3–5

HEAD

A. The human head
1. Literal use
—Hand put on the head in blessing .... Ge 48:14–18
—People were anointed on the head .... Ex 29:7
1Sa 10:1
—Anointing head with oil meant blessings .... Ps 23:5
—Crowns were put on the head 1Ch 20:2
Est 2:17
—No razor on the head of a Nazirite .... Nu 6:5–6
Jdg 13:5
—Cutting off the head, a sign of victory 1Sa 17:51
1Sa 31:9
—Woman's covered head showed submission 1Co 11:5,10
—A bowed head showed reverence .... Ge 24:26
Ge 43:28
Ex 4:31
—A bowed head showed grief .... Ps 35:14
—Dust on one's head showed sorrow 1Sa 4:12
—Pulling hair from the head showed sorrow .. Ezr 9:3
—Shaving hair from the head showed grief .... Job 1:20
Isa 15:2
—Ashes on one's head showed shame 2Sa 13:19
—Shaking the head showed disdain .... Job 16:4
Ps 22:7
Mt 27:39

2. Figurative use
—Blessings crown the head .... Pr 10:6
—Joy crowns the head .... Isa 35:10
Isa 51:11
—Blood on one's head meant guilt 2Sa 1:15–16
Eze 33:4
—Lifting up one's head meant pride .... Ps 83:2
—From head to foot meant the whole body ... Dt 28:35
Isa 1:6
—The Lord gives grace by lifting a head .... Ps 3:3
Ps 27:5–6
—Heaping coals of fire on the head .... Pr 25:22
Ro 12:20
—Jesus had nowhere to lay his head .... Mt 8:20

B. Head used in symbolic ways
1. Political leadership
—Heads as leaders of the clans of Israel .... Nu 1:16
Jos 14:1
—Heads as leaders of the tribes .... Nu 30:1
—Heads as leaders of families 2Ch 1:2
Ezr 2:68
—A head as the king of a country .... Isa 7:8–9

2. Husband as the head of his wife 1Co 11:3,8–10
Eph 5:23

3. Christ as the head
—Of all creation .... Eph 1:10
—Of every man 1Co 11:3
—Of the church .... Eph 5:23
Col 1:18
Col 2:19

HEALING

A. Roles in healing
1. God is the ultimate healer .... Dt 32:39
Ps 103:3
Jer 30:17

2. Human elements that play a role
—Faith .... Mt 13:58
Mk 5:34
Lk 18:42
—Prayer .... Jas 5:14–16
—Intercession .... Nu 12:10–15
1Ki 13:6
—A cheerful heart .... Pr 17:22
—Positive words .... Pr 16:24

B. Physical healing of the body
1. Medical care used 2Ki 20:7
Lk 10:34–35
1Ti 5:23

2. Miracles performed
—Directly by God .... Ge 20:17
—By prophets 1Ki 17:17–24
2Ki 5:1–14
—By Jesus .... Mt 4:24
—By followers of Jesus .... Ac 5:15–16
Ac 28:8
—By agents of Satan 2Th 2:9
Rev 13:3

3. Spiritual gifts of miracles and healing 1Co 12:9–10,28

See also MIRACLE

C. Spiritual healing
—Received by the land 2Ch 7:13–14
—Received by people 2Ch 30:18–20
Hos 14:4
1Pe 2:24
—Performed by Jesus with physical healing .... Mk 2:5–11

HEART

—The center of the human being

A. Basic concept of the heart
1. The wellspring of all life .... Pr 4:23
Lk 6:45

2. Combined with other basic human elements
—The heart and soul .... Dt 6:5
1Sa 14:7
Mt 22:37
—The heart and body .... Ps 16:9
—The heart and mind .... Ps 26:2
Mt 22:37
Rev 2:23
—The heart and spirit .... Ps 51:10,17
Eze 18:31
—The heart and flesh .... Ps 73:26
Ps 84:2
—The heart and thoughts .... Ps 139:23
—The heart and understanding .... Pr 3:5

B. What the heart controls
1. Human emotions
—The glad heart .... Ex 4:14; Ac 2:26
—The singing heart .... Eph 5:19
—The heart that loves .... Dt 6:5; SS 3:1–3
—The heart that takes delight .... Ecc 2:10; Jer 15:16
—The excited heart .... Lk 24:32
—The courageous heart .... 1Sa 10:26; Ps 27:14
—The heart that is encouraged .... Col 2:2; 2Th 2:17
—The thankful heart .... Col 3:16
—The repentant heart .... Ps 51:17
—The humble heart .... Mt 11:29
—The compassionate heart .... Lk 7:13
—The anxious heart .... Pr 12:25
—The discouraged heart .... Jos 2:11
—The troubled heart .... Jn 12:27
—The grieving heart .... 1Sa 2:33; La 2:18
—The tormented heart .... La 2:11
—The broken heart .... Eze 21:6
—The heavy heart .... Pr 25:20
—The anguished heart .... Isa 65:14; Jer 4:19; Ro 9:2
—The fearful heart .... Dt 28:67; Jos 5:1
—The angry heart .... Ps 39:3; Pr 19:3

2. The human will
—To do according to one's heart 1Sa 2:35; 1Ch 28:2
—To decide in the heart 2Ch 6:7
—To devote the heart 1Ch 22:19
—To direct the heart 2Th 3:5
—To turn the heart .... 1Ki 8:58; Ps 119:36
—To incline the heart .... Dt 5:29
—To win over the heart 2Sa 19:14
—To yield the heart .... Jos 24:23
—To agree with one heart .... Jer 32:39; Ac 4:32
—To be moved in the heart .... Ex 35:21
—The purposes of the heart .... Jer 23:20
—The motives of the heart 1Co 4:5
—The desires of the heart .... Ps 21:2; Ro 10:1
—The willing heart 2Ch 29:31
—The unrepentant heart .... Ro 2:5
—The hardened heart .... Ex 4:21; Pr 28:14

3. The human intelligence
—To acknowledge in the heart .... Dt 4:39
—To know in the heart .... Dt 8:5
—To take something to heart .... Ex 7:23; Ecc 7:2
—To fix words in the heart .... Dt 11:18
—To lay up words in the heart .... Job 22:22; Pr 4:21
—To search the heart .... Ps 4:4
—To say in the heart .... Ro 10:6
—To muse in the heart .... Ps 77:6
—To ponder in the heart .... Lk 2:19
—To think in the heart .... Mk 2:8
—To understand in the heart .... Pr 2:2
—To meditate in the heart .... Ps 19:14
—To pray in the heart .... Ge 24:45; 1Sa 1:13
—To believe in the heart .... Ro 10:9
—To be wise in the heart .... Pr 2:10; Pr 10:8
—To doubt in the heart .... Mk 11:23
—To harbor deceit in the heart .... Pr 26:24; Jer 17:9
—To devise evil in the heart .... Ps 140:2
—The thoughts of the heart .... Ge 6:5; Lk 2:35

C. Key elements in the human heart
1. Characteristics of the unregenerate heart
—Proud .... Pr 18:12
—Foolish .... Pr 12:23
—Deceitful .... Jer 17:9
—Rebellious .... Jer 5:23
—Perverse .... Pr 11:20
—Evil .... Ge 6:5
—Wicked .... Pr 6:18
—Callous .... Ps 119:70
—Malicious .... Ps 28:3
—Hardened .... Eph 4:18
—Darkened .... Ro 1:21
—Deluded .... Isa 44:20
—Unrepentant .... Ro 2:5
—Unbelieving .... Heb 3:12
—Gone astray .... Ps 95:10
—Devoted to idols .... Eze 11:21
—Filled with schemes to do wrong .... Ecc 8:11
—Filled with madness .... Ecc 9:3
—Far from God .... Isa 29:13; Mk 7:6

2. What the regenerate heart does
—Cries out for the living God .... Ps 84:2
—Seeks God .... Ps 119:2,10
—Responds to God 2Ki 22:19
—Trusts in the Lord .... Pr 3:5
—Loves the Lord .... Dt 6:5; Mt 22:37
—Praises the Lord .... Ps 9:1
—Sings to the Lord .... Ps 30:12
—Rejoices in the Lord 1Sa 2:1
—Rejoices in salvation .... Ps 13:5
—Is grateful to God .... Col 3:16
—Obeys God's law .... Ps 119:34,69,112; Eph 6:6
—Hides God's word within .... Ps 119:11
—Is on fire for God's word .... Jer 20:9
—Meditates on God and his word .... Ps 19:14
—Is upright .... Ps 7:10
—Speaks the truth .... Ps 15:2
—Is steadfast and secure .... Ps 57:7; Ps 112:7–8
—Is pure .... Ps 24:4; Mt 5:8
—Is wise .... Pr 10:8
—Is sincere .... Ac 2:46; Heb 10:22
—Is unafraid and courageous .... Ps 27:3,14
—Is contrite .... Ps 51:17
—Is circumcised .... Dt 10:16; Ro 2:29
—Walks blamelessly .... Ps 101:2
—Loves others 1Pe 1:22

D. God's relationship to the human heart
—He knows it 1Sa 16:7
—He searches it .... Ps 7:9; Jer 17:10
—He tests it 1Ch 29:17; 1Th 2:4

—He influences it ... Ezr 7:27
—He directs it ... Pr 21:1
—He opens it ... Ac 16:14
—He touches it ... 1Sa 10:26
—He makes light shine in it ... 2Co 4:6
—He cleanses it ... Heb 10:22
—He writes his law on it ... Jer 31:33
—He strengthens it ... 1Th 3:13
—He keeps it loyal ... 1Ch 29:18
—He gives a new heart ... Ps 51:10; Eze 11:19

HEAVEN

A. What is heaven?
1. Part of God's creation ... Ge 1:1
—A component of the universe ... Ex 20:4; Php 2:10
—Where God placed sun, moon and stars ... Ge 1:14–18; Dt 4:19
—Where precipitation comes from ... Ge 8:2; Job 38:29; Isa 55:10
2. The place where God dwells
—His dwelling place ... 1Ki 8:30; Mt 6:9
—His sanctuary ... Ps 102:19
—Where his throne is ... Ps 2:4; Isa 63:15
—Where Christ ascended ... Lk 24:51; Heb 9:24

B. What does God do from heaven?
1. Actions in Bible history
—God talked to his people ... Ge 22:11,15
—God made the Israelites hear him ... Dt 4:36
—God heard his people when they prayed ... Ne 9:27–28
—God sent bread ... Ex 16:4,13–15; Ne 9:15
—God sent fire of judgment ... 2Ki 1:12
—God sent fire for sacrifice ... 1Ch 21:26
—God revealed mysteries ... Da 2:18–19; Ac 10:10–16
2. Continuing actions
—God reigns ... Ps 99:1–2
—God observes human actions ... Ps 14:2; Ps 102:19
—God blesses his people ... Dt 26:15
—God hears our prayers ... 2Ch 6:21,23,25,27
—God saves us ... Ps 57:3
—God sends his Holy Spirit ... 1Pe 1:12
—God reveals his wrath ... Ro 1:18
—Christ prepares a place for us ... Jn 14:2–3
—Christ will return from heaven ... 1Th 4:16

C. Our relationship to heaven
1. How can we enter heaven?
—We must be chosen and called ... 2Pe 1:10–11
—We must be born again ... Jn 3:5
—We must trust in God and in Jesus ... Jn 14:1–2
—We must have our names recorded there ... Lk 10:20
—We must be righteous ... Mt 5:19–20
—We must live holy lives ... Rev 22:14–15
—We must do the will of God ... Mt 7:21
—We must be humble ... Mt 18:3–4
—We must be poor in spirit ... Mt 5:3
—We must overcome ... Rev 2:7; Rev 21:7
—We must receive new bodies ... 1Co 15:50–54
2. What should our attitude be toward heaven?
—We should lay up treasures there ... Mt 6:20
—We should sacrifice everything for it ... Mt 13:44–46
—We should long for it ... 2Co 5:2
—We should eagerly look for it ... 2Pe 3:13
—We should hope for it ... Col 1:5
—In spirit we are already there ... Eph 2:6; Php 3:20; Col 3:1

D. Aspects of the present heaven
1. Positive
—God dwells there ... 1Ki 8:30
—Christ dwells there at God's right hand ... Ac 7:55–56; Eph 1:20
—Christ intercedes for us there ... Heb 9:24
—There is joy there ... Lk 15:7,10
—There is comfort there ... Lk 16:22–25
—Satan has been cast out of there ... Rev 12:7–9
2. Negative
—God reveals his wrath from there ... 1Sa 2:10; Ro 1:18
—Powers of evil intrude there ... Job 1:6–7; Eph 6:12
—Wars occur there ... Rev 12:7
—Saints cry out from there ... Rev 6:9–11
—Saints do not yet have new bodies ... 1Co 15:48–54
—It must be destroyed and renewed ... 2Pe 3:7,10,12–13; Rev 21:1

E. What the new heaven will be like
1. It will be free from:
—Death ... Lk 20:35–36; Rev 21:4
—Pain, sorrow and crying ... Isa 65:19–23; Rev 21:4
—Night ... Rev 22:5
—Hunger and thirst ... Rev 7:16
—The curse of God ... Rev 22:3
—Wicked people ... Rev 22:15
2. For believers, it will be:
—Eternal ... 2Co 5:1
—A place of eternal light ... Rev 22:5
—The home of righteousness ... 2Pe 3:13
—The place of harmony and unity ... Isa 65:25
—The place of eternal praise to God ... Rev 7:15
—The place of exquisite beauty ... Rev 21:10–21
—The place of purity ... Rev 21:27
—The place of the tree of life ... Rev 22:1–2

HEBRON

—A city, originally called Kiriath Arba ... Jos 14:15
—Also called Mamre ... Ge 23:19
—Abram built an altar and lived there ... Ge 13:18
—Abraham and Sarah's burial plot located there ... Ge 23:1–19
—Allied with other cities against Gibeonites ... Jos 10:1–5
—Defeated by Joshua ... Jos 10:6–26; Jos 11:21
—Given to Caleb ... Jos 14:13–15; Jdg 1:9–10,20
—Later given to Kohathites ... 1Ch 6:54–56
—David ruled from there for seven years ... 2Sa 2:1–4; 1Ki 2:11
—Soldiers joined David there ... 1Ch 12:23–40
—David anointed king of all Israel there ... 2Sa 5:1–3; 1Ch 11:1–3
—Absalom crowned king there ... 2Sa 15:7–10

HEIR

See INHERITANCE

HELL

A. A place of punishment
—For fallen angels ... 2Pe 2:4
—For the devil and his angels ... Mt 25:41
—For the beast and the false prophet ... Rev 19:20
—For those who worship the beast ... Rev 14:9–11

—For wicked humans.......Rev 21:8
—For those who reject the gospel.......Mt 10:11 – 15

B. Hints of hell in the Old Testament
—The wicked perish in death.......Ps 49:10 – 15
—There will be judgment for the wicked.......Job 24:21 – 24
—There will be eternal punishment.......Isa 66:24; Da 12:2

C. Description of hell in the New Testament
—A place of separation from God.......2Th 1:9
—The second death.......Rev 21:8
—The place of condemnation.......Mt 23:33
—The place of torment.......Lk 16:23
—The place of weeping and the grinding of teeth.......Mt 8:12; Mt 25:30
—The place where body and soul is destroyed.......Mt 10:28
—Eternal punishment.......Mt 25:46
—Everlasting destruction.......2Th 1:9
—Everlasting chains.......Jude 6
—Eternal fire.......Mt 18:8; Jude 7
—The lake of fire.......Rev 20:15
—The blackest darkness.......Jude 13

HERESY
See DOCTRINE

HEROD
A. Herod the Great
—King of Judea at time of Jesus' birth.......Mt 2:1; Lk 1:5
—Magi contacted him.......Mt 2:1 – 8
—Ordered babies in Bethlehem killed.......Mt 2:16

B. Herod Antipas
—Tetrarch of Galilee.......Mt 14:1; Lk 3:1
—Beheaded John the Baptist.......Mt 14:3 – 12
—Worried about Jesus.......Lk 9:7 – 9
—Jesus called him a fox.......Lk 13:31 – 32
—Participated in trial of Jesus.......Lk 23:6 – 15

C. Herod Agrippa
—Persecuted the early church.......Ac 12:1
—Killed James.......Ac 12:2
—Arrested Peter.......Ac 12:3 – 19
—Died a miserable death from God.......Ac 12:19 – 23

HERODIAS
—Wife of Herod Antipas.......Mt 14:3 – 4; Mk 6:17
—Told daughter to ask for John's severed head.......Mt 14:6 – 11; Mk 6:21 – 27

HEZEKIAH
—King of Judah.......2Ch 29:1
—Purified the temple.......2Ch 29:3 – 19
—Restored proper sacrifices.......2Ch 29:20 – 36
—Celebrated the Passover for two weeks.......2Ch 30:1 – 27
—Cleansed land of idols.......2Ch 31:1
—Organized priests and Levites.......2Ch 31:2 – 19
—Collected Solomon's proverbs.......Pr 25:1
—Sought the Lord for help against Assyria.......2Ch 32:1 – 20; Isa 36:1—37:20
—Witnessed the destruction of Sennacherib.......2Ch 32:21 – 23; Isa 37:36 – 37
—Had fatal illness.......2Ki 20:1
—Illness healed by God through prayer.......2Ki 20:2 – 11; Isa 38:2 – 8
—Sang a song after his recovery.......Isa 38:9 – 20
—Judged for sin of pride.......2Ki 20:12 – 21; Isa 39:1 – 8

HILKIAH
—High priest during time of Josiah.......2Ki 22:4
—Reported his finding of the Book of the Law.......2Ki 22:8; 2Ch 34:14 – 15
—Questioned Huldah about the Law.......2Ki 22:14; 2Ch 34:22
—Ordered by Josiah to cleanse the temple.......2Ki 23:4; 2Ch 34:9 – 11
—Became administrator of the temple.......2Ch 35:8

HIRAM
—King of Tyre.......2Sa 5:11
—Helped David build his palace.......2Sa 5:11 – 12; 1Ch 14:1
—Helped Solomon build the temple.......1Ki 5:1 – 12; 2Ch 2:3 – 18
—Scorned towns that Solomon gave him.......1Ki 9:10 – 13
—Helped build Solomon's navy.......1Ki 9:26 – 28; 2Ch 8:17 – 18
—Engaged in extensive trade.......1Ki 10:11 – 12

HITTITES
A. Their identity
—Descendants of Canaan, grandson of Noah.......Ge 10:6,15
—One of the seven Canaanite nations.......Ex 33:2

B. Significant Hittites
—Ephron: sold Abraham a burial plot.......Ge 23:10 – 20
—Judith and Basemath: wives of Esau.......Ge 26:34
—Ahimelech: a soldier with David.......1Sa 26:6
—Uriah: husband of Bathsheba.......2Sa 11:3 – 24; 1Ki 15:5

C. Their wars
—Allied with others against Joshua.......Jos 11:1 – 5
—Defeated by Joshua.......Jos 12:7 – 8

D. Important data concerning them
—Controlled much land in Moses' time.......Nu 13:27 – 29; Jos 1:4
—God promised their land to his people.......Ex 3:8,17; Ex 34:11
—Israelites told to destroy them completely.......Dt 7:1 – 6; Dt 20:17
—Israelites did not destroy them completely.......Jdg 3:5
—Solomon traded with them.......1Ki 10:29
—Many became Solomon's slaves.......1Ki 9:20 – 21; 2Ch 8:7 – 8
—Intermarried with the Israelites.......Jdg 3:5 – 6; 1Ki 11:1; Ezr 9:1 – 2

HOLINESS
—Being set apart from sin; purity

A. Related theme
HOLINESS is a theme of Leviticus.......Lev 19:12

B. The holiness of God
1. In the Old Testament
—He is holy.......Ps 99:3,5,9
—He is called the Holy One of Israel.......2Ki 19:22; Isa 30:11 – 12,15
—His Spirit is holy.......Isa 63:10
—His name is holy.......Ps 111:9
—His throne is holy.......Ps 47:8
—He is majestic in holiness.......Ex 15:11
—His holiness has splendor.......1Ch 16:29
—He is surrounded by holiness.......Isa 6:3
—He is unique in his holiness.......1Sa 2:2
—He swears by his holiness.......Am 4:2
—He will show himself holy.......Isa 5:16
—His words are holy.......Jer 23:9
—His arm is holy.......Isa 52:10

2. In the New Testament
—The Father is holy ... Mt 6:9
Jn 17:11
—The Son is holy ... Lk 1:35
Ac 4:27,30
—The Spirit is holy ... Ac 2:4
Ro 1:4

C. The holiness of God's people
1. Israel in the Old Testament
—They were holy to the Lord ... Jer 2:3
—They were a holy people ... Ex 19:6
Dt 7:6
—They formed a holy race ... Ezr 9:2
—They were expected to be holy ... Lev 11:44 – 45
Lev 19:12
—The priests were holy ... Lev 21:5 – 6
2. Christians in the New Testament
—They are a holy people ... Col 3:12
1Pe 2:9
—They are a holy temple ... Eph 2:21
—They are sanctified (made holy) ... 1Co 6:11
—They are chosen to be holy ... Eph 1:4
—They are called to a holy life ... 1Th 4:7
—They must live holy lives ... Heb 12:14
1Pe 1:15 – 16
—They are to serve God in holiness ... Lk 1:74 – 75
—They must purify themselves in holiness ... 2Co 7:1
—They will be presented to God as holy ... Col 1:22

D. The holiness of special things
1. Referred to in the Old Testament
—The ground where one meets God ... Ex 3:4 – 5
—The Holy Place and the Most Holy Place ... Ex 26:33
—The altar in the tabernacle ... Ex 29:37
—The garments of the priests ... Ex 28:2 – 4
—The turban of the priest ... Ex 39:30 – 31
—The furnishings used by the priests ... Nu 4:15
—The guilt offering ... Lev 7:1
—Anything given to the Lord ... Lev 27:9,14,21,28
—The camp of the Israelites ... Dt 23:14
—The temple ... Hab 2:20
—The Sabbath ... Ex 16:23
—The Year of Jubilee ... Lev 25:12
—Mount Zion in Jerusalem ... Ps 2:6
Isa 27:13
—The city of Jerusalem ... Ne 11:1
2. Referred to in the New Testament
—The angels ... Ac 10:22
1Th 3:13
—The city of Jerusalem ... Mt 4:5
—The Scriptures ... Ro 1:2
2Ti 3:15
—The law of God ... Ro 7:12
—A Christian's faith ... Jude 20
—A Christian's hands in prayer ... 1Ti 2:8
—The kiss of greeting among Christians ... 1Co 16:20
1Th 5:26

See also SANCTIFICATION

HOLY SPIRIT

A. Related theme
HOLY SPIRIT is a theme of Acts ... Ac 13:2

B. The Spirit's divine nature
1. Called God ... Lk 1:32,35
Ac 5:3 – 4
2. United with the Father and Son ... Mt 28:19
2Co 13:14
3. Has characteristics of God
—Eternal ... Heb 9:14
—Everywhere present ... Ps 139:7 – 10
—All-knowing ... 1Co 2:10 – 11
—Has great power ... Ac 1:8
Ro 15:19
—Raised Christ from the dead ... 1Pe 3:18
—Performs miracles ... Mt 12:28
Ro 15:19
—Involved in creation ... Ge 1:2
—Gives spiritual life to us ... Jn 3:3 – 8

C. The Spirit as a person
—He teaches ... Jn 14:26
—He hears and speaks ... Jn 16:13
—He testifies about Christ ... Jn 15:26
—He encourages ... Ac 9:31
—He counsels ... Jn 14:16
—He convicts people of sin ... Jn 16:8
—He prays for us ... Ro 8:27
—He sends people out ... Ac 13:4
—He experiences grief ... Eph 4:30
—He can be resisted ... Ac 7:51
—He can be tested ... Ac 5:9

D. The Spirit's work
1. In the Old Testament
—Involved in creation ... Ge 1:2
—Gave life to God's creatures ... Ps 104:30
—Guided God's people ... Isa 63:11 – 13
—Instructed God's people ... Ne 9:20
—Led God's people in the right way ... Ps 143:10
—Inspired God's people to do right ... Ps 51:10 – 22
—Admonished God's people ... Ne 9:30
—Reacted to human evil ... Ge 6:3
—Gave artistic ability to individuals ... Ex 31:2 – 3
—Gave his power to Israel's leaders ... Jdg 6:34
1Sa 16:13
Zec 4:6
—Lived among God's people ... Hag 2:5
—Inspired the prophets ... Nu 11:29
Mic 3:8
Zec 7:12
2Pe 1:21
—Spoke through the psalmists ... 2Sa 23:2
Ac 1:16,20
Heb 3:7 – 11
—Old Testament prophecies on the Spirit ... Isa 11:1 – 3
Isa 32:15
Isa 42:1
Isa 44:3
Isa 61:1 – 3
Eze 39:29
Joel 2:28 – 32
2. In the life of Jesus Christ
—Jesus was conceived by the Spirit ... Lk 1:34 – 35
—He received the Spirit at his baptism ... Lk 3:21 – 22
—He was filled with the Spirit ... Lk 4:1
—He ministered in the power of the Spirit ... Mt 12:15 – 21
Lk 4:18 – 21
—He cast out demons by the Spirit ... Mt 12:28
—He offered himself to God through the Spirit ... Heb 9:14
—He was raised by the Spirit ... Ro 8:11
1Ti 3:16
1Pe 3:18
—He promised to send the Spirit ... Jn 15:26
—He sent the Spirit on Pentecost ... Ac 2:33
—The Spirit is the Spirit of Jesus ... Ac 16:7
Ro 8:98
Gal 4:6
3. In the church
—The Spirit came at Pentecost ... Ac 2:1 – 4
—He dwells in the church ... 1Co 3:16 – 17
Eph 2:22
—He appoints officers for the church ... Ac 20:28

—He directs decisions of the church .... Ac 15:28
—He chooses missionaries .... Ac 13:2
—He sends out missionaries .... Ac 13:4
—He directs the mission enterprise .... Ac 8:29,39; Ac 16:6–7

4. In individuals
—The Spirit dwells in us .... Jn 14:16–17; Ro 8:11; 1Co 6:19
—He convicts us of sin .... Jn 16:7–11
—He gives us new life .... Jn 3:5–6; Tit 3:5
—He makes us realize God's love .... Ro 5:5
—He gives us power to witness .... Ac 1:8; Ac 6:9–10
—He teaches us what to say .... Lk 12:12
—He reveals God's secrets to us 1Co 2:10–16
—He brings Christ's presence to us .... Jn 14:16–18
—He keeps us in touch with God .... Ro 8:26; Jude 20
—He teaches us about Christ .... Jn 14:26; Jn 15:26
—He enables us to find the truth 1Jn 4:1–6
—He encourages us .... Ac 9:31
—He controls us .... Ro 8:9
—He gives us joy and peace .... Ro 14:17
—He draws us into fellowship .... 2Co 13:14; Php 2:1
—He enables us to live the Christian life .... Ro 8:5–9
—He works his fruit in us .... Gal 5:16–25
—He sanctifies us .... Ro 15:16; 2Th 2:13
—He gives us gifts 1Co 12:4–11
See GIFTS OF THE SPIRIT
—He gives us his sword to fight Satan .... Eph 6:17
—He prays for us in times of crisis .... Ro 8:26
—He will raise us from the dead .... Ro 8:11

E. The Spirit in our life

1. How to receive the Spirit
—We must repent of our sins .... Ac 2:37–38
—We must believe in Jesus .... Ac 11:15–17; Ro 8:9; Gal 3:2–3,14; Eph 1:13
—We must be baptized in Jesus' name .... Ac 2:38; Ac 19:1–6
—We must pray to receive him .... Lk 11:13; Ac 8:15

2. Being filled with the Holy Spirit

a. His filling is a gift for all believers
—Old Testament promise .... Joel 2:28–29
—New Testament fulfillment .... Ac 2:17–18
—New Testament promise to us .... Ac 2:38; Ro 8:9

b. Persons *filled* with the Holy Spirit
—Bezalel .... Ex 31:2–5
—Samson .... Jdg 14:19
—Saul 1Sa 10:10
—John the Baptist .... Lk 1:15
—Elizabeth .... Lk 1:47
—Zechariah .... Lk 1:67
—The disciples on Pentecost .... Ac 2:4
—Peter before the Jewish council .... Ac 4:8
—The early Christians at prayer .... Ac 4:31
—Paul in his preaching .... Ac 13:9
—New Christians .... Ac 13:52

c. Persons *full* of the Holy Spirit
—Jesus .... Lk 4:1
—The first deacons .... Ac 6:3
—Stephen .... Ac 6:5
—Barnabas .... Ac 11:24

d. The command to be filled with the Spirit
—To Paul at his conversion .... Ac 9:17
—To all Christians .... Eph 5:18

3. Being sealed with the Spirit .... 2Co 1:21–22; 2Co 5:5; Eph 1:13–14

4. Baptized with the Spirit
See BAPTISM OF THE SPIRIT

HOME
See FAMILY

HOMOSEXUALITY
See SEXUAL STANDARDS

HONESTY
See INTEGRITY

HOPE
—Certainty in the present and firm expectation for the future

A. Related themes

1. HOPE is a theme of:
—Isaiah .... Isa 9:7
—Jeremiah .... Jer 23:5
—Amos .... Am 9:11
—Micah .... Mic 4:1
—Zephaniah .... Zep 3:15
—Haggai .... Hag 2:7
—1 Thessalonians 1Th 1:10
—2 Thessalonians 2Th 2:3
—1 Peter 1Pe 1:3
—Revelation .... Rev 21:3

2. RESTORATION is a theme of:
—Ezekiel .... Eze 36:24
—Joel .... Joel 2:32

B. The nature of hope

1. Basic concept of hope
—It is linked with faith .... 1Co 13:13; Heb 11:1
—It is linked with trust .... Ps 33:20–21; Ro 15:13
—It is linked with expectation .... Ro 4:18–19; Tit 1:2

2. In whom/what do we hope?
—In God .... Ps 42:5,11; Ps 130:7; 1Ti 6:17
—In Jesus Christ .... Ro 15:12; 1Co 15:19; Eph 1:12; Php 2:19
—In the name of God .... Ps 52:9
—In the word of God .... Ps 119:74; Ps 130:5
—In the promises of God .... Ac 26:6
—In the resurrection of the dead .... Ac 23:6

3. For what do we hope?
—God's righteousness .... Gal 5:5
—Salvation .... Ro 8:24–25; 1Th 5:8
—God's saving arm .... Isa 51:5
—Liberation from bondage to decay .... Ro 8:20–21
—The resurrection .... Ac 2:26; Ac 26:7
—The glory of God .... Ro 5:2; 2Co 3:11–12
—Our glorious inheritance .... Eph 1:18; Col 1:5

—The appearance of Jesus Christ.......Tit 2:13
1Jn 3:2 – 3
—A crown of righteousness.......2Ti 4:8
—A crown of glory.......1Pe 5:4
—A crown of life.......Rev 2:10
—Eternal life.......Tit 1:2
Tit 3:7

C. Jesus Christ and our hope
1. He is called our hope
—He is our hope.......1Ti 1:1
—He is the hope of Israel.......Ac 28:20
—He is the hope of glory.......Col 1:27
2. He fulfilled the hope of the Old Testament
—Jesus confirms the promises of God.......Ac 26:6 – 7
Ro 15:8
—All promises of God fulfilled in him.......2Co 1:20

D. Hope in the Christian life
1. The choice we face
—Hope in humans or in God.......Ps 33:16 – 19
—Hope in riches or in God.......1Ti 6:17
—Without God, there is no hope.......Eph 2:12
1Th 4:13
2. Attaining hope
—We are called to only one hope.......Eph 1:18
Eph 4:4
—We must set our hope fully on Jesus.......1Pe 1:13
—We must believe the resurrection.......1Pe 1:3
—We must abound in hope.......Ro 15:13
1Co 13:13
—We must never lose our hope.......Ps 25:5
3. The benefits of hope
—Causes us to praise God.......Ps 71:14
—Causes us to rejoice.......Ro 5:2
Ro 12:12
—Renews our strength.......Isa 40:31
—Inspires us to a life of purity.......1Jn 3:3
—Inspires us to persevere.......1Th 1:3
—Cures the downcast soul.......Ps 42:5,11
La 3:20 – 21
—Will never disappoint us.......Isa 49:23
Ro 5:5
—Our hope is like a stabilizing anchor.......Heb 6:18 – 19
4. We should defend our hope.......1Pe 3:15

HOPHNI

—Son of Eli; brother of Phinehas.......1Sa 1:3
—A wicked priest.......1Sa 2:12 – 17
—Scorned his father's rebuke.......1Sa 2:22 – 25
—His death prophesied as a sign.......1Sa 2:30 – 34
—Brought the ark into battle.......1Sa 4:4
—Killed in the battle.......1Sa 4:11,17

HOREB

See SINAI

HORSE

A. Literal uses of horses
1. Military
—Description of the war-horse.......Job 39:19 – 25
—Pharaoh's horses.......Ex 14:9,23
—Canaanite horses.......Jos 11:4
—Solomon's horses.......2Ch 1:14 – 16
—Syrian horses.......2Ki 6:14 – 15
2. Non-military uses
—Horses used to reinforce royal power.......2Sa 15:1
1Ki 1:5
—Horse riding to honor a person.......Est 6:6 – 11
—Horses as livestock.......Ge 47:17
—Horses used in farm labor.......Isa 28:28
—Horses used for transportation.......Isa 66:20
—Horses used to bring messages.......Est 8:10
3. Relying on horses
—They cannot bring victory.......Ps 33:16 – 17
—Trust in God instead of horses.......Ps 20:7
Isa 31:1

B. Figurative use of horses
—Horses of fire carried Elijah to heaven.......2Ki 2:11
—God's people becoming like the proud horse.......Zec 10:3
—God's angels using horses and chariots.......2Ki 6:17
—God's power symbolized in his horses.......Hab 3:8,15
—The returning Lord riding a white horse.......Rev 19:11 – 13

HOSEA

—A prophet; son of Beeri.......Hos 1:1
—His wife pictured unfaithful Israel.......Hos 1:2 – 11
—Became reconciled with his wife.......Hos 3:1 – 3

HOSHEA

A. Original name of Joshua.......Nu 13:16
B. Last king of Israel.......2Ki 17:1
—Murdered Pekah to get throne.......2Ki 15:30
—Captured and deported by Assyria.......2Ki 17:2 – 6

HOSPITALITY

See KINDNESS

HULDAH

—A prophetess.......2Ki 22:14
—Visited by Hilkiah during Josiah's reign.......2Ki 22:12 – 20
2Ch 34:19 – 28

HUMILITY

—Lowliness; freedom from pride
A. Related theme
HUMILITY is a theme of 1 Corinthians.......1Co 1:29
B. What humility involves
—A childlike attitude.......Mt 18:1 – 4
—Repentance.......Isa 66:2
Lk 18:13 – 14
—Submission before God.......2Ch 34:27
Da 5:22 – 23
—Seeking God's face in prayer.......2Ch 7:14
—Fasting.......Ezr 8:21
Ps 35:13
—Following God's laws.......Jer 44:10
Zep 2:3
—Working for justice and mercy.......Mic 6:6 – 8
—Opposite of pride.......Pr 3:34
Da 4:37
1Pe 5:5

C. Humility in our lives
1. The command to be humble
—We must humble ourselves.......Eph 4:2
1Pe 5:6
—We must walk humbly with God.......Mic 6:8
—We must clothe ourselves with humility.......Col 3:12
1Pe 5:5
—We must consider others better than ourselves.......Php 2:3
—We must avoid false humility.......Col 2:18,23
2. The benefits of humility
—God saves the humble.......Ps 18:27
—God shows favor to the humble.......Pr 3:34
Isa 66:2
Jas 4:6
—God lifts up/exalts the lowly.......Mt 23:12
Lk 1:52
—God revives the lowly.......Isa 57:15
—God honors the humble.......Pr 15:33
Pr 18:12

—God rewards the humble .... Pr 22:4
—God blesses the humble 2Ch 7:14
—God guides and teaches the humble .... Ps 25:9
—With humility comes wisdom .... Pr 11:2

D. Examples of humility
1. The supreme example: Jesus Christ
—In his coming to earth 2Co 8:9
—In his lowliness .... Mt 11:29
—In his life of service .... Lk 22:27
—In his submission to God's will .... Jn 6:38
—In his sufferings .... Isa 53:1–9
—In his washing of the disciples' feet .... Jn 13:4–5
—In his Triumphal Entry .... Mt 21:5,7
—In his death on the cross .... Php 2:5–8
2. Other examples
—The Israelites in the desert .... Dt 8:3
—Ahab 1Ki 21:29
—Josiah 2Ki 22:19
—Rehoboam and his people 2Ch 12:5–12
—Job .... Job 42:2–6
—Isaiah .... Isa 6:1–6
—John the Baptist .... Jn 3:27–30
—Peter .... Lk 5:8–9
—Paul .... Ac 20:19

HUNGER AND THIRST

A. Examples of famines and droughts
—Worldwide famine in Joseph's day .... Ge 41:53
—Famine in Bethlehem .... Ru 1:1
—Famine in David's time 2Sa 21:1
—Drought and famine in Elijah's day 1Ki 17:1
—Famine in Elisha's day 2Ki 6:25; 2Ki 8:1
—Famine in Jerusalem 2Ki 25:3
—Famine in Nehemiah's day .... Ne 5:3
—Famine predicted by Agabus .... Ac 11:27–28

B. How times of hunger and thirst were used:
1. By God
—To fulfill his plan for his people .... Ge 15:13–14; Ge 41:56—42:3; Ge 46:3–4
—To humble and teach the Israelites .... Ex 16:2–3; Dt 8:2–3
—To get people to look to him for help .... Jdg 6:3–6; Ps 107:4–9
—To punish stubborn disobedience .... Dt 28:47–48; Isa 65:11–13
—To bring judgment on sinners .... Isa 9:18–21; Am 4:6,9
2. By Jesus
—To demonstrate his compassion .... Mk 6:34–44; Mk 8:1–9
—To show he was bread from heaven .... Jn 6:33,48–51
3. By the church
—To show kindness to the needy .... Ac 11:28–30; 2Co 8:13–15
—To show church unity .... Ro 15:25–27

C. Spiritual hunger and thirst
1. The reality of such hunger and thirst
—Physical bread cannot satisfy .... Dt 8:3; Mt 4:4
—Prediction of a famine of God's word .... Am 8:11–12
2. Satisfying such hunger and thirst
—God promises to satisfy .... Isa 55:1–3; Mt 5:6
—Jesus is the bread of life .... Jn 6:35,48–58; 1Co 10:16
—Jesus is the water of life .... Jn 4:13–14; Jn 7:37–38

HUR

—A chief magistrate of the Israelites .... Ex 24:14
—With Aaron, supported Moses' hand .... Ex 17:10–12

HUSHAI

—Friend of David 2Sa 15:37
—Conspired with David to outwit Absalom 2Sa 15:32–37
—Foiled Absalom's revolt by giving poor advice .... 2Sa 16:15—17:16

HYPOCRISY

—Open display of religion without genuine commitment

A. Related theme
HYPOCRISY is a theme of James .... Jas 3:9

B. Description of hypocrisy
—Displaying religion with no love for God .... Isa 29:13; Mt 6:2–6,16–18; Mt 23:5–7
—Claiming love for God, mistreating others .... Mk 12:38–40; 1Jn 3:17; 1Jn 4:20
—Not practicing what one preaches .... Mt 23:3; Ro 2:17–24
—Sticking only to the letter of the law .... Mt 23:16–23; Lk 13:15–16
—Criticizing another for one's own sins .... Mt 7:3–5; Mk 7:6–13
—Being outwardly beautiful but inwardly rotten .... Mt 23:27–28
—Having only an outward form of godliness 2Co 11:13–15; 2Ti 3:5
—Lying to make oneself look good .... Ac 5:1–10

C. God and human hypocrisy
1. God's reaction to hypocrites
—Is angry with them .... Lk 13:14–15
—Has no reward for them .... Mt 6:2,5,16
—Pronounces woe to them .... Mt 23:13–16,23–29
—Has punishment in store for them .... Lk 20:46–47
—Condemns them to hell .... Mt 23:33
2. God's will for his people
—Wants us to avoid hypocrites 2Ti 3:5
—Warns us against hypocrisy 1Pe 2:1
—Wants us to express our faith by works .... Jas 2:14–17; 1Jn 3:17–19
—Wants us to show genuine love .... Ro 12:9; 1Pe 1:22
—Wants us to exercise a sincere faith 1Ti 1:5; 2Ti 1:5

ICHABOD

—Son born to Phinehas's wife after his death 1Sa 4:19–22
—Name means "no glory" 1Sa 4:21

IDOLATRY

—The worship of false gods

A. Idols mentioned in the Bible
—Adrammelech 2Ki 17:31
—Anammelech 2Ki 17:31
—Artemis .... Ac 19:24,27–28
—Asherah 1Ki 14:15
—Ashima 2Ki 17:30
—Ashtoreth 1Sa 31:10
—Baal 1Ki 16:31–32
—Baal-Berith .... Jdg 8:33
—Baal-Zebub 2Ki 1:3
—Bel .... Isa 46:1
—Chemosh 1Ki 11:7,33
—Dagon 1Sa 5:2–4
—Golden calf 1Ki 12:28
—Hermes .... Ac 14:12
—Ishtar (Queen of Heaven) .... Jer 7:18

—Molech 1Ki 11:5,7
—Marduk ..... Jer 50:2
—Nergal 2Ki 17:30
—Nebo ..... Isa 46:1
—Nibhaz 2Ki 17:31
—Nisroch 2Ki 19:37
—Rephan ..... Ac 7:43
—Rimmon 2Ki 5:18
—Succoth Benoth 2Ki 17:30
—Tammuz ..... Eze 8:14
—Tartak 2Ki 17:31
—Zeus ..... Ac 14:12

B. Principles concerning idols
—They have no real existence 1Co 8:4
—They cannot save ..... Ps 115:4–8
Ps 135:14–18
Isa 46:1–7
Da 5:23
—The worship of idols is mocked 1Ki 18:27
Isa 44:9–20
Jer 10:3–5

C. God's perspective concerning idolatry
1. In the Old Testament
—Israel may not worship idols ..... Ex 20:3–4
2Ki 17:35
Ex 34:14,17
—Israel must destroy idols in Canaan ..... Ex 23:24
Ex 34:13
Dt 7:5
2. In the New Testament
—Idolaters do not inherit the kingdom 1Co 6:9–10
Gal 5:20–21
—We must flee from idolatry 1Co 10:14
1Jn 5:21
—Greed condemned as idolatry ..... Col 3:5
—Money considered a false god ..... Mt 6:24

IMAGE OF GOD

A. Humans created in God's image ..... Ge 1:26–27
Ge 5:1
1Co 11:7

B. The image and humanity's fall into sin
1. The image was lost
—Sin pervades everyone ..... Ro 3:23
Ro 5:12–14
—We need to be restored in God's image ..... Ro 8:29
Col 3:10
2. The image was partially retained
—All humans are in touch with God ..... Ac 17:27–28
—God's image in us rules out murder ..... Ge 9:6
—God's image in us rules out cursing ..... Jas 3:9

C. Christ and the image of God
1. He bears God's perfect image
—He is the image of God *par excellence* 2Co 4:4
Col 1:15
Heb 1:3
—We see God in Christ ..... Jn 1:18
Jn 12:45
Jn 14:9
2. He works in fallen, but redeemed humans
—To restore us to God's image ..... Ro 8:29
2Co 3:18
—To renew us in knowledge ..... Col 3:10
—To renew us in righteousness ..... Eph 4:24
—To renew us in holiness ..... Eph 4:24
—Some day he will completely restore us 1Co 15:49
1Jn 3:2

D. Our responsibility as image-bearers of God
—We must rule creation wisely ..... Ge 1:28
Ps 8:6–8
—We may not worship images created by humans ..... Ex 20:4
Ac 17:29
—We may not murder another person ..... Ge 9:6
—We may not curse another person ..... Jas 3:9

INCARNATION

See JESUS CHRIST

INCENSE

A. Incense burned
1. To pagan gods 1Ki 11:7–8
2Ki 17:9–12
Jer 11:12
2. To the Lord God
a. Two incense offerings
—Daily burning on altar of incense ..... Ex 30:1–8
2Ch 2:4
—Incense on the Day of Atonement ..... Lev 16:12–13
1Ch 6:49
b. Regulations concerning incense ..... Ex 30:9,34–38
Lev 10:1–2
Nu 16:35–38
c. Continued in the New Testament ..... Lk 1:8–9
d. Incense detestable if insincere ..... Isa 1:13
Jer 6:20

B. Incense as symbolic of prayer ..... Ps 141:2
Lk 1:10
Rev 5:8
Rev 8:3–4

INHERITANCE

A. Inheritance in the Old Testament
1. Family inheritance
—Firstborn son received birthright ..... Ge 25:29–34
Dt 21:15–17
—Firstborn son received double share ..... Dt 21:17
—If no sons, daughters inherit ..... Nu 27:1–8
—If no children, next of kin inherit ..... Nu 27:9
—Land had to stay within the tribe ..... Nu 36:7
1Ki 21:3
—Each allotted land was an inheritance ..... Nu 26:53,56
2. Israel's inheritance
—Canaan: the land of God's inheritance ..... Dt 4:21
1Ki 8:36
Ps 78:55
—Promised to Abram ..... Ge 12:7
Ge 15:18–21
—Land divided as inheritance to Israelites ..... Jos 11:23
—To remain an heir required obedience ..... Dt 4:25–27
2Ki 21:12–15
—Inheritance lost in the exile ..... Ps 79:1–8
—Inheritance regained in the return ..... Ne 11:20
Isa 65:8–9
Eze 36:12
3. Spiritualizing the inheritance
—The Lord as the people's inheritance ..... Ps 73:26
Ps 142:5
—The people as the Lord's inheritance ..... Dt 4:20
Isa 47:6
—God's inheritance to include Gentiles ..... Ps 2:8
Jer 10:16

B. Inheritance in the New Testament
1. Jesus is the heir ..... Heb 1:2
2. We become heirs
—When we become sons of God ..... Gal 4:7
—When we believe in Jesus ..... Ro 4:13
Heb 6:12
—When we receive God's grace ..... Gal 3:18
—We become co-heirs with Christ ..... Ro 8:17

3. What we are to inherit
—The earth .... Mt 5:5
—The kingdom of light .... Col 1:12
—The kingdom of heaven .... Mt 25:34
—The kingdom of God 1Co 6:9
—Eternal life .... Mt 19:29; Tit 3:7
—Everything .... Rev 21:7

4. The nature of our inheritance
—It is given by God and his word .... Ac 20:32
—It is received as a reward .... Col 3:24
—It is kept in heaven for us 1Pe 1:4
—It is imperishable .... 1Co 15:50 – 53; 1Pe 1:4
—It is eternal .... Heb 9:15
—It is guaranteed by the Spirit .... Eph 1:13 – 14
—It can be lost through disobedience .... Mt 25:41 – 46; Heb 4:6,11

INSECTS

A. Insects and other small creatures mentioned in the Bible
—Ant .... Pr 6:6
—Bee .... Jdg 14:8
—Cricket .... Lev 11:22
—Flea 1Sa 24:14
—Fly .... Ex 8:21 – 24
—Gadfly .... Jer 46:20
—Gnat .... Ex 8:16 – 18
—Grasshopper .... Ps 78:46
—Hornet .... Jos 24:12
—Katydid .... Lev 11:22
—Leech .... Pr 30:15
—Locust .... Joel 1:4
—Maggot .... Ex 16:20,24
—Moth .... Job 27:18
—Scorpion .... Dt 8:15
—Spider .... Job 8:14
—Worm .... Jnh 4:7

B. God's use of insects
—Some suitable for food, some not .... Lev 11:21 – 24
—Sometimes used as a judgment .... Ex 8:16 – 32; Joel 1:2 – 12
—Ants used to teach us lessons .... Pr 6:6 – 8
—Moths used as a symbol of destruction .... Mt 6:19 – 20
—Honey used as a symbol of God's blessing .... Dt 11:9

INSPIRATION OF SCRIPTURE

—The Bible as God's written word

A. Scripture is inspired by God
1. Basic statement 2Ti 3:16; 2Pe 1:21
2. Affirmations in the Old Testament
—God put words in prophets' mouths .... Dt 18:18; Isa 51:16; Jer 1:9
—The Spirit spoke through David 2Sa 23:2
—"This is what the LORD says" .... Isa 43:1; Jer 6:16
—"The word of the LORD came to . . ." .... 1Ki 17:2; Eze 1:3
3. Affirmations in the New Testament
—David spoke by the Holy Spirit .... Mk 12:36; Ac 4:25
—God speaks in the Old Testament .... Heb 4:3,7; Heb 8:8
—The Spirit speaks in the Old Testament .... Ac 28:25; Heb 3:7
—In the Old Testament, "It is written" .... Mt 4:4,6,10; 1Co 1:19,31
—The Scriptures cannot be broken .... Jn 10:35
—The Scriptures must be fulfilled .... Mt 5:18; Mt 24:35; Lk 24:44

B. Characteristics of the inspired word of God
—Trustworthy .... 2Sa 7:28; Ps 111:7 – 8; Jn 17:17
—Eternally fixed .... Ps 119:89; Isa 40:8
—Unbreakable .... Mt 5:18; Jn 10:35
—A sure guide for life .... Ps 119:105; 2Ti 3:16 – 17
—Effective in its purposes .... Jer 23:29; Heb 4:12

C. How Bible writers received their material
—In various ways .... Heb 1:1
—By direct speech from God .... Ex 34:27 – 28; Nu 12:8; Jer 30:1 – 2
—By angels .... Zec 1:12 – 17; Ac 7:53
—By visions .... Ge 15:1; Mic 1:1
—By dreams .... Da 7:1
See DREAMS AND VISIONS
—By an inner impulse from God .... Jer 20:9; 2Pe 1:21
—By eyewitness accounts .... Lk 1:2; 1Jn 1:1 – 4
—By careful research .... Lk 1:3 – 4

INTEGRITY

—Honesty in life and adherence to moral principle

A. Examples of those showing integrity
—Job .... Job 2:3
—David .... 1Ch 28:17; Ps 78:72
—Financial officials of the temple .... 2Ki 12:9 – 15
—Hananiah .... Ne 7:2
—Jesus .... Mt 22:16

B. Expectation of living in integrity and honesty
—Linked with observing all God's commands 1Ki 9:4
—Preferred above wealth .... Pr 28:6
—Expected of the upright .... Pr 11:3
—Expected of Christian leaders .... Tit 2:7
—Required in business dealings .... Lev 19:36; Dt 25:15; Pr 16:11

C. Blessings of living in integrity and honesty
—We please God 1Ch 29:17
—We gain a good reputation .... Pr 16:13
—We receive God's protection .... Pr 2:7
—We gain security for ourselves .... Ps 25:21; Pr 10:9
—We gain security for future generations .... 1Ki 9:4 – 5

See also TRUTH

INTERCESSION

—The prayer of one person for another

A. Related theme
INTERCESSION is a theme of Numbers .... Nu 14:19

B. Human intercession
1. Examples of intercession by officials
—By leaders .... Ex 32:11 – 14; Nu 14:13 – 19; Jos 7:6 – 9
—By priests .... Lev 5:10; Lev 16:21; Ezr 9:5 – 15

—By prophets 1Sa 7:5–6
1Ki 13:6
Da 9:3–19
Jas 5:17–18
—By kings 2Sa 24:17
1Ki 8:33–51
—By apostles Ac 8:15
Eph 3:14–19
Php 1:9–11
Col 1:9–12
—By elders Jas 5:14

2. Examples of intercession by individuals
a. In the Old Testament
—Abraham for Lot Ge 18:23–32
—David for his sick child 2Sa 12:16
—David for Solomon 1Ch 29:19
—Job for his children Job 1:5
—A psalmist for the people Ps 20:1–5
Ps 25:22
—A psalmist for all nations Ps 67:3–5
b. In the New Testament
—Stephen for his persecutors Ac 7:60
—Peter for Dorcas Ac 9:40
—Paul for a sick man Ac 28:8
—Paul for Timothy 2Ti 1:3
—Paul for Philemon Phm 4
—Christians for their persecutors Mt 5:44
—The church for Peter Ac 12:5,12
—The church for missionaries Mt 9:38
Ac 13:3
Heb 13:18
—The church for Paul Ro 15:31–32
Eph 6:19–20
—The church for each other Jas 5:16
—The church for all people 1Ti 2:1–2

3. The purposes of human intercession
—For averting judgment Ge 18:23–32
Nu 14:13–19
—For escape from danger Ac 12:5,12
Ro 15:31
—For God's blessings Nu 6:24–26
1Ki 18:41–45
—For the Holy Spirit's power Ac 8:15–17
Eph 3:14–17
—For healing 1Ki 17:20–21
Ac 28:8
Jas 5:14–16
—For forgiveness Ezr 9:5–15
Ac 7:60
—For the ability to rule well 1Ch 29:19
1Ti 2:2
—For Christian growth Php 1:9–11
Col 1:10–11
—For effective pastors 2Ti 1:3–7
—For effective mission work Mt 9:38
Eph 6:19–20
—For the salvation of others Ro 10:1–4
—For others to praise God Ps 67:3–5

C. Divine intercession
1. The intercession of Christ
—For his followers Lk 22:32
Jn 14:16
Jn 17:6–26
—For his enemies Lk 23:34
—Continual intercession for us Ro 8:34
Heb 7:24
Heb 9:24
1Jn 2:1
2. The Spirit as intercessor Ro 8:26–27

INTEREST

See DEBT

ISAAC

A. History of Isaac
—Promised son of Abraham and Sarah Ge 17:19
1Ch 1:28
—His birth Ge 21:1–3
—His circumcision Ge 21:4
—Party at his weaning Ge 21:8–13
—Offered up by Abraham Ge 22:1–14
Heb 11:17–19
—Took Rebekah as wife Ge 24:1–67
—Inherited Abraham's estate Ge 25:5
—With Ishmael, buried Abraham Ge 25:7–11
—Fathered Esau and Jacob Ge 25:19–26
1Ch 1:34
—Lied to Abimelech about Rebekah Ge 26:1–11
—Became very wealthy Ge 26:12–13
—Made a covenant with Abimelech Ge 26:14–31
—Tricked into blessing Jacob Ge 27:1–40
—Sent Jacob away to find a wife Ge 28:1–5
—His death Ge 35:27–29

B. Significance of Isaac
—Perpetuated Abrahamic covenant Ge 17:21
Ge 26:2–5
—Shows grace and faithfulness of God Ge 21:1
—Shows who are true children of Abraham Ro 9:7–9
Gal 4:21–31
—Shows God's purpose in election Ro 9:10–13
—Is an example of true faith Heb 11:20

ISAIAH

—A prophet in Judah and Jerusalem Isa 1:1
—Called by God Isa 6:1–13
—Announced judgment to Ahaz Isa 7:1–25
—Married a prophetess and fathered children Isa 8:1–4
—Prophesied Hezekiah's death 2Ki 20:1
Isa 38:1
—Prophesied fifteen more years of life for Hezekiah 2Ki 20:4–6
Isa 38:4–8
—Prophesied Sennacherib's fall 2Ki 19:20–34
Isa 37:21–35
—Prophesied coming victory of Babylon 2Ki 20:14–18
Isa 39:3–7
—Wrote down Judah's history 2Ch 26:22
2Ch 32:32

ISCARIOT

See JUDAS

ISH-BOSHETH

—Son of Saul 1Ch 8:33
—Tried to succeed Saul as king 2Sa 2:8–11
—Had conflict with his general, Abner 2Sa 3:6–11
—Murdered by two supporters of David 2Sa 4:1–12

ISHMAEL

—Son of Abram by Hagar Ge 16:15–16
1Ch 1:28
—Blessed, but not the son of the covenant Ge 17:18–21
Gal 4:21–31
—Teased Isaac at Isaac's weaning Ge 21:8–9
—Sent away with his mother by Sarah Ge 21:8–21
—With Isaac, buried Abraham Ge 25:9–11
—Married and fathered children Ge 25:12–16
1Ch 1:29–31
—His death Ge 25:17

ISRAEL
A. Related theme
JUDAH = ISRAEL is a theme of 2 Chronicles............2Ch 29:24
B. Israel in the Old Testament
1. Name God gave Jacob
—Given after wrestling with God....................Ge 32:28
—His sons called the sons of Israel..................Ge 46:8
See JACOB
2. The nation of God's people
—Each son became a tribe..............................Ge 49:28
—Together became known as Israelites..........Ex 1:9
—Called the house of Israel.............................Ex 40:38
—Called Israel..Jdg 2:7
Ps 14:7
Isa 43:1,22,28
—Specifically, the northern kingdom.............1Ki 12:16 – 17
—Israel (northern kingdom) destroyed...........2Ki 17:18
—Thereupon Judah was called Israel..............2Ch 29:24
—Returned exiles called Israel........................Ezr 2:2,70
Ne 12:47
C. Israel in the New Testament
1. The Jewish nation...Mt 10:6
Jn 3:10
Php 3:5
2. Spiritual use of Israel
—Spiritual descendants of Abraham...............Ro 9:6 – 8
—Jewish Christians as true Israel...................Eph 3:6
—The church is true Israel..............................Gal 6:16
—The total sum of God's people.....................Ro 11:26

ISSACHAR
A. Son of Jacob by Leah..Ge 35:23
1Ch 2:1
—Name means "reward".......................................Ge 30:18
—Went to Egypt with family.................................Ge 46:8,13
—Father of four sons..Ge 46:13
—Blessed by Jacob..Ge 49:14 – 15
B. Tribe descended from Issachar
—Blessed by Moses..Dt 33:18 – 19
—Numbered..Nu 1:29
Nu 26:25
—Allotted land..Jos 19:17 – 23
Eze 48:25
—Assisted Deborah...Jdg 5:15
—One of the tribes of the 144,000........................Rev 7:7

ITHAMAR
—Son of Aaron...Ex 6:23
1Ch 6:3
—Had duties at tabernacle..Ex 38:21
—Served as priest during lifetime of Aaron..............Nu 3:4
—Supervised Gershonites and Merarites...................Nu 4:22,33
—Founded one of the Levitical families....................1Ch 24:4 – 6

JACOB
A. Family data
—Second son of Isaac and Rebekah.......................Ge 25:26
—Twin brother of Esau..Ge 25:24 – 25
—Married Leah and Rachel....................................Ge 29:16 – 30
—Father of twelve sons and one daughter..............Ge 29:31—30:24
Ge 35:16 – 18,23 – 26
Ge 46:8 – 27
1Ch 2:1 – 2
B. History of his life
1. Before his arrival in Haran
—A quiet man who stayed at home.....................Ge 25:27
—Bought Esau's birthright.................................Ge 25:29 – 34
—Tricked Isaac into blessing him........................Ge 27:1 – 37
—Fled to Haran because of Esau's anger..............Ge 27:41
Ge 28:1 – 5
—Had dream at Bethel..Ge 28:10 – 22
—God renewed Abraham's covenant with him..Ge 28:13 – 15
2. At Haran
—Arrived in Haran..Ge 29:1 – 8
—Met and stayed at Uncle Laban's.......................Ge 29:9 – 14
—Served Laban for Leah and Rachel....................Ge 29:16 – 30
—Became father of many children.......................Ge 29:31—30:24
—Worked for wages to be paid in goats................Ge 30:25 – 43
—Decided to return to Canaan.............................Ge 31:1 – 21
—Pursued by Laban..Ge 31:22 – 55
3. Upon return to Canaan
—Devised scheme to make peace with Esau...Ge 32:1 – 21
—Wrestled with God...Ge 32:22 – 26
—Name changed to Israel....................................Ge 32:27 – 30
—Reconciled with Esau.......................................Ge 33:1 – 17
—Settled in Shechem..Ge 33:18 – 20
—Returned to Bethel...Ge 35:1 – 15
—Grieved over disappearance of Joseph...........Ge 37:31 – 35
—Sent sons to Egypt during famine....................Ge 42:1 – 5
Ge 43:1 – 15
4. In Egypt
—Moved to Egypt...Ge 46:1 – 7
—Met Pharaoh..Ge 47:7 – 11
—Blessed Ephraim and Manasseh......................Ge 48:1 – 20
—Blessed each of his sons..................................Ge 49:1 – 28
Heb 11:21
—His death...Ge 49:29 – 33
—Buried back in Canaan....................................Ge 50:1 – 14
C. Significance in the New Testament
—Samaritans considered Jacob their father.........Jn 4:7 – 12
—Demonstrates God's purpose in election...........Ro 9:11 – 13
—Is an example of faith.......................................Heb 11:21
D. Name became a synonym for all Israelites...........Nu 23:7
Ps 14:7
Isa 43:1,22,28
Ro 11:26

JAEL
—Woman who killed Sisera.......................................Jdg 4:17 – 22
—Praised by Deborah..Jdg 5:24 – 27

JAIR
—Judge from Gilead..Jdg 10:3 – 5

JAIRUS
—Synagogue ruler whose daughter Jesus raised.......Mk 5:22 – 43
Lk 8:41 – 56

JAMES
A. A disciple of Jesus
—Son of Zebedee and brother of John..................Mt 4:21 – 22
Mk 3:17
—Originally a fisherman.......................................Mt 4:21
—Wanted hostile Samaritans killed......................Lk 9:52 – 55
—Observed the transfiguration.............................Mt 17:1 – 13
Mk 9:1 – 13
—Sought top place in Jesus' kingdom...................Mk 10:35 – 45
—Accompanied Jesus to Gethsemane.....................Mt 26:36 – 46
—One of the apostles..Ac 1:13
—Killed by Herod...Ac 12:2
B. Another disciple of Jesus
—Son of Alphaeus...Mt 10:3
Mk 3:18
—One of the apostles..Ac 1:13
C. Son of Joseph and Mary..Mt 13:55
—A half brother of the Lord Jesus.........................Gal 1:19
—Brother of Jude..Jude 1
—Did not believe in Jesus.....................................Jn 7:3 – 5
—Met the risen Lord...1Co 15:7
—Stayed with believers before Pentecost..............Ac 1:13

—Became leader of the Jerusalem church ... Ac 12:17
Gal 2:9,12
—Proposed solution at the council in Jerusalem ... Ac 15:12 – 21
—Visited by Paul ... Ac 21:18
Gal 1:19
—Wrote the letter of James ... Jas 1:1

JAPHETH

—Son of Noah ... Ge 5:32
1Ch 1:4 – 5
—With Shem, covered his father with a garment ... Ge 9:23
—Blessed by Noah ... Ge 9:27
—Sons listed ... Ge 10:2 – 5

JEALOUSY

—An emotion expressing possessiveness; related to zeal

A. Jealousy as a positive emotion

1. In humans

—Jealous for the things of the Lord ... Nu 25:11 – 13
1Ki 19:10,14
—Jealous for faithfulness in marriage ... Pr 6:34
SS 8:6
—Jealous for the purity of the church ... 2Co 11:2

2. In God

—He is jealous for his people ... Joel 2:18
Zec 1:14
Zec 8:2
—He jealously tolerates no rivals ... Ex 20:5
Jos 24:19
1Co 10:21 – 22
—Sin arouses him to jealousy ... Ps 78:58
Na 1:2
—His name is Jealous ... Ex 34:14

B. Jealousy as a negative emotion

1. Sins that it leads to

—To envy ... Ge 37:11
Ps 106:16 – 18
—To discontent ... Ge 30:1
—To quarreling ... 1Co 3:3 – 4
—To verbal abuse ... Ac 13:45
—To intense anger ... Pr 27:4
—To persecution ... Ac 5:17 – 18

2. The command to get rid of jealousy ... Ro 13:13
2Co 12:20
Gal 5:20

JECONIAH

See JEHOIACHIN

JEHOAHAZ

A. Son of Jehu; king of Israel ... 2Ki 13:1 – 9
B. Son of Josiah; king of Judah ... 2Ki 23:31 – 34
2Ch 36:1 – 4

JEHOASH

A. A king of Judah
See JOASH
B. Son of Jehoahaz; king of Israel ... 2Ki 13:10 – 11
—Defeated Arameans three times ... 2Ki 13:14 – 25
—Defeated Amaziah, king of Judah ... 2Ki 14:1 – 16
2Ch 25:17 – 24

JEHOIACHIN

—Son of Jehoiakim; king of Judah ... 2Ki 24:8 – 9
2Ch 36:8 – 9
—Brought to Babylon by Nebuchadnezzar ... 2Ki 24:10 – 15
2Ch 36:10
Jer 24:1
—Freed from prison in Babylon ... 2Ki 25:27 – 30
Jer 52:31 – 34

JEHOIADA

—A priest during Athaliah's reign ... 2Ki 11:1 – 4
—Son-in-law of King Jehoram ... 2Ch 22:11
—Helped hide Joash for six years in temple ... 2Ch 22:11 – 12
—Arranged for crowning of Joash as king ... 2Ki 11:5 – 16
2Ch 23:1 – 15
—Decided to rid the land of idols ... 2Ki 11:17 – 20
2Ch 23:16 – 17
—Managed the temple ... 2Ch 23:18 – 21
—Advised Joash ... 2Ki 12:2
2Ch 24:2
—With Joash, repaired the temple ... 2Ki 12:4 – 16
2Ch 24:3 – 14
—His death ... 2Ch 24:15 – 16

JEHOIAKIM

—Son of Josiah; king of Judah ... 2Ki 23:34
—Had conflict with Nebuchadnezzar ... 2Ki 24:1 – 6
2Ch 36:5 – 8
—Killed the prophet Uriah ... Jer 26:20 – 23
—Burned scroll of Jeremiah's prophecies ... Jer 36:16 – 26

JEHORAM

A. Son of Jehoshaphat; king of Judah ... 2Ki 8:16 – 19
2Ch 21:4 – 7
—Warred against Edom ... 2Ki 8:20 – 22
—Prophesied against by Elijah ... 2Ch 21:12 – 15
—Warred against the Philistines ... 2Ch 21:16 – 17
—Killed by the Lord ... 2Ch 21:18 – 19
B. A king of Israel
See JORAM

JEHOSHAPHAT

—Son of Asa; king of Judah ... 1Ki 22:41 – 44
2Ch 17:1
—Strengthened his kingdom ... 2Ch 17:2 – 19
—Joined with Ahab of Israel against Aram ... 1Ki 22:1 – 33
2Ch 18:1 – 32
—Appointed judges ... 2Ch 19:4 – 11
—Joined with Joram of Israel against Moab ... 2Ki 3:5 – 27
—Miraculously delivered from Moab and Ammon ... 2Ch 20:1 – 26
—Prayed intensely to the Lord ... 2Ch 20:5 – 12
—Punished for alliance with Israel ... 2Ch 20:35 – 37

JEHU

A. Prophet who spoke against Baasha ... 1Ki 16:1 – 4,12
B. King of Israel ... 2Ki 9:6
—Elijah told to anoint him king ... 1Ki 19:16
—Anointed by servant of Elisha ... 2Ki 9:1 – 13
—Appointed to obliterate house of Ahab ... 2Ki 9:6 – 10
—Killed Joram and Ahaziah ... 2Ki 9:14 – 29
2Ch 22:7 – 9
—Killed Jezebel ... 2Ki 9:30 – 37
—Killed relatives of Ahab ... 2Ki 10:1 – 17
—Killed ministers of Baal ... 2Ki 10:18 – 29
—His death ... 2Ki 10:30 – 36

JEPHTHAH

—Judge from Gilead ... Jdg 11:1 – 3
—Delivered Israel from Ammon ... Jdg 11:4 – 33
—Made a rash vow affecting his daughter ... Jdg 11:30 – 40
—Punished the Ephraimites ... Jdg 12:1 – 6
—His death ... Jdg 12:7

JEREMIAH

—Prophet to kingdom of Judah ... Jer 1:1 – 3
—Called by the Lord ... Jer 1:4 – 19
—Composed laments at Josiah's death ... 2Ch 35:25
—His life threatened for continuing to prophesy ... Jer 11:18 – 23
Jer 26:1 – 16

—Put in stocks....Jer 20:1 – 3
—Opposed by Hananiah....Jer 28:1 – 17
—Wrote scroll that was burned by king....Jer 36:1 – 26
—Rewrote the scroll....Jer 36:27 – 32
—Imprisoned; Zedekiah sought his advice....Jer 37:1 – 21
—Charged with treason and thrown into cistern....Jer 38:1 – 13
—Zedekiah sought his advice again....Jer 38:14 – 27
—Purchased field just before Jerusalem destroyed....Jer 32:1 – 15
—Taken with some of the people to Egypt....Jer 43:1 – 7

JERICHO

A. Identity
—Located in a valley....Dt 34:3
—Near the Jordan River....Nu 33:50
—Called "City of the Palms"....Dt 34:3

B. History of the city
1. In the Old Testament
—Rahab lived there....Jos 2:1
—Israelites spied it out....Jos 2:1 – 21
—Israelites camped opposite it....Jos 3:16
—Israelites marched around it....Jos 6:1 – 15
—Its walls collapsed....Jos 6:20
—All except Rahab destroyed....Jos 6:21 – 25
—Joshua pronounced curse on rebuilding it....Jos 6:26
—Curse fulfilled when Hiel rebuilt it....1Ki 16:34
—A company of prophets stationed there....2Ki 2:5
—It was reinhabited....2Ch 28:15; Ne 3:2

2. In the New Testament
—Good Samaritan headed toward it....Lk 10:30 – 35
—Jesus healed Bartimaeus there....Mk 10:46 – 52; Lk 18:35 – 43
—Jesus healed two blind men there....Mt 20:29 – 34
—Zacchaeus lived there....Lk 19:1 – 10

JEROBOAM

A. First king of the northern kingdom
—An official of king Solomon....1Ki 11:26 – 28
—Ahijah prophesied he would be king....1Ki 11:29 – 39
—Fled to Egypt....1Ki 11:40
—Led rebellion against Rehoboam....1Ki 12:18 – 19
—Became king of the northern kingdom....1Ki 12:20
—Instituted idolatry....1Ki 12:25 – 33
—Judged for idolatry....1Ki 13:1 – 6; 1Ki 14:1 – 18
—His death....1Ki 14:19 – 20

B. Son of Jehoash; king of Israel....2Ki 14:23 – 29
—Denounced by Amos....Am 7:10 – 11

JERUB-BAAL

See GIDEON

JERUSALEM

A. Related theme
JERUSALEM is a theme of 2 Samuel....2Sa 6:12

B. Important names for this city
—Salem....Ge 14:18; Ps 76:2
—The Jebusite city....Jos 18:28
—Jebus....1Ch 11:4
—Jerusalem....2Sa 5:6
—Zion....2Sa 5:7; Ps 48:12
—The City of David....2Sa 6:12,16; 1Ki 2:10
—The city of the Great King....Ps 48:2
—The city of God....Ps 46:4; Ps 87:3
—The city of the LORD....Isa 60:14
—The City of Righteousness....Isa 1:26
—The City of Truth....Zec 8:3
—The holy city....Ne 11:1,18; Isa 48:2
—THE LORD IS THERE....Eze 48:35
—Moriah....Ge 22:1 – 2; 2Ch 3:1
—Ariel....Isa 29:1

C. Significant historical events of Jerusalem
—Abraham's "sacrifice" of Isaac....Ge 22:1 – 18
—King of Jerusalem conquered by Joshua....Jos 10:1 – 14
—City given to the tribe of Benjamin....Jos 18:28
—Conquered by David; became his capital....2Sa 5:6 – 10
—Temple built there....2Ch 3:1
—Became capital of the southern kingdom....1Ki 14:21
—Destroyed by Nebuchadnezzar....2Ch 36:19
—The center of Jewish life after exile....Ezr 1:5; Mt 2:1,3
—Jesus entered it as king....Mt 21:9 – 10
—Jesus was crucified there....Lk 9:31; Lk 24:18
—Holy Spirit poured out there....Ac 2:1 – 5
—Gospel spread out from there....Lk 24:47; Ac 1:8
—First council of the church held there....Ac 15:1 – 2; Gal 2:1 – 5
—Jesus predicted its destruction....Lk 19:42 – 44; Lk 21:20 – 24

D. Spiritual significance of Jerusalem
—The city chosen by God....1Ki 11:13
—The place where God put his Name....Dt 12:11; 1Ki 14:21
—The city that Jews prayed toward....1Ki 8:44; Da 6:10
—The place from which God's word comes....Isa 2:3
—The place from which God rules....Ps 48:1 – 3,12 – 14; Ps 99:1 – 2
—The place from which the Messiah rules....Isa 9:6 – 7
—The site of history's final battle....Zec 14:1 – 5; Rev 20:7 – 10
—A symbol of the church....Gal 4:26; Heb 12:22
—Heaven as the new Jerusalem....Rev 3:12; Rev 21:2,10 – 27

JESSE

—Grandson of Boaz and Ruth; father of David....Ru 4:17 – 22
—Visited by Samuel....1Sa 16:1 – 13
—Had eight sons....1Sa 16:8 – 11; 1Sa 17:12
—Sent David to enter Saul's service....1Sa 16:18 – 20
—Sent David to visit his brothers at battle....1Sa 17:17 – 19

JESUS CHRIST

A. Related themes
1. SON OF GOD is a theme of Mark....Mk 14:61
2. JESUS = GOD/MAN is a theme of:
—John....Jn 1:1
—Hebrews....Heb 4:15
3. ACTION is a theme of Mark....Mk 1:41

B. His divine nature
1. Preexistence with God
—Asserted in the Old Testament....Isa 9:6 – 7; Mic 5:2
—Asserted in the New Testament....Jn 1:1; Php 2:6; Col 1:15 – 17; Rev 1:4,8

2. Divine names ascribed to him
—God....Jn 1:1; Heb 1:8; 1Jn 5:20

—God the One and Only ... Jn 1:18
—God over all ... Ro 9:5
—Immanuel ("God with us") ... Isa 7:14
Mt 1:23
—Our God and Savior ... Tit 2:13
2Pe 1:1
—Lord ... Ac 2:36
Ro 10:9
Php 2:11
Col 2:6
—Lord of all ... Ac 10:36
—Lord and God ... Jn 20:28
—Lord and Savior ... 2Pe 1:11
2Pe 2:20
2Pe 3:18
—Lord of glory ... 1Co 2:8
—Lord of lords ... Rev 17:14
Rev 19:16
—Alpha and Omega ... Rev 1:8
Rev 21:5–6
—The Living One ... Rev 1:18
—The Holy One of God ... Mk 1:24
—The Holy and Righteous One ... Ac 3:14
—The "I am" ... Jn 8:58

3. His relationship with the Father
—Equal with the Father ... Jn 5:18
Jn 10:33
Php 2:6
—One with the Father ... Jn 10:33
Jn 17:22

4. Divine qualities ascribed to him
—Has the fullness of God ... Col 2:9
—Was involved in creation ... Jn 1:3
Col 1:16
Heb 1:2
—Has the glory of God ... Jn 1:14
Heb 1:3
—Preserves creation ... Col 1:17
Heb 1:3
—Is present everywhere ... Mt 28:20
—Is all-powerful ... Mt 28:18
Php 3:21
—Knows everything ... Jn 2:24–25
Jn 6:61,64
—Is unchanging ... Heb 1:12
Heb 13:8
—Has the power to forgive sins ... Mk 2:5–11
Lk 7:48
—Receives worship from people ... Mt 2:11
Rev 5:11–14
—Receives worship from angels ... Heb 1:6
—We must believe in him as we do in God ... Jn 14:1
Ac 16:31–34

C. His human nature

1. Had a human genealogy ... Mt 1:1–17
Lk 3:23–28

2. His birth and childhood
—Conceived in Mary's womb ... Mt 1:20
Lk 1:26–37
—His human birth ... Mt 1:25
Lk 2:1–7
—Circumcised on the eighth day ... Lk 2:21
—Visited the temple as a boy ... Lk 2:41–51
—Grew as anyone else does ... Lk 2:52

3. His suffering, death and burial
—Bloody sweat in the garden ... Lk 22:44
—Death on the cross ... Mt 27:50
Jn 19:33
Php 2:7–8
—Blood and water flowed from his wound ... Jn 19:34–35
—Body taken down from the cross ... Lk 23:53
—Body prepared and laid in a tomb ... Jn 19:39–41
—Burial clothes used ... Jn 20:6–7

4. His resurrection and ascension
—His resurrection on Easter Sunday ... Mt 28:1–15
Lk 24:1–8
—His appearances for forty days ... Lk 24:9–49
Jn 20:1–29
Ac 1:1–5
—His body still a human body ... Lk 24:40–43
Jn 20:24–29
—His ascension into heaven ... Lk 24:50–51
Ac 1:9–11

5. He had human characteristics
—Could be touched ... Mk 5:27–32
Jn 20:27
1Jn 1:1
—Became hungry ... Mt 4:2
Mt 21:18
—Became thirsty ... Jn 19:28
—Became tired ... Jn 4:6
—Needed sleep ... Mt 8:20
Mk 4:38
—Showed compassion ... Mt 9:36
Mk 8:2
—Showed anger and indignation ... Mk 10:14
Jn 2:13–16
—Wept ... Lk 19:41
Jn 11:35

6. His human nature specifically mentioned
—He became flesh ... Jn 1:14
—He shared our humanity ... Heb 2:14
—He is like us in all things—except sin ... Heb 2:17
Heb 4:15
—We must acknowledge that Jesus came in the flesh ... 1Jn 4:2
2Jn 7

D. His most important names
—Jesus ("the LORD saves") ... Mt 1:21
—Immanuel ... Mt 1:23
—The Messiah ... Mt 16:16
Ac 17:3
—The Son of God ... Lk 1:35
Jn 20:31
—The Holy One of God ... Mk 1:24
—The cornerstone ... Mk 12:10
—The Word of God ... Jn 1:1
Rev 19:13
—The Lamb of God ... Jn 1:36
—The bridegroom of the church ... Jn 3:29
—The Prophet ... Jn 6:14
—The bread of life ... Jn 6:48
—The light of the world ... Jn 8:12
—The good shepherd ... Jn 10:11
Heb 13:20
1Pe 5:4
—The resurrection and the life ... Jn 11:25
—The King of Israel ... Jn 12:13
—The way, the truth, the life ... Jn 14:6
—King of the Jews ... Jn 19:19–21
—The author of life ... Ac 3:15
—Prince and Savior ... Ac 5:31
—Son of Man ... Ac 7:56
—Judge of the living and the dead ... Ac 10:42
—Lord ... Ro 10:9
Php 2:11
—The Lord of glory ... 1Co 2:8
—Our Passover lamb ... 1Co 5:8
—The second Adam ... 1Co 15:45–47
—Husband of the church ... 2Co 11:2

—Head of the church .... Col 1:18
—The mediator 1Ti 2:5
—The righteous Judge 2Ti 4:8
—Great high priest .... Heb 4:14
—Alpha and Omega .... Rev 1:8
—The Lion of the tribe of Judah .... Rev 5:5
—Lord of lords .... Rev 17:14
—The Root and Offspring of David .... Rev 22:16
—The bright Morning Star .... Rev 22:16

E. His work on earth and in heaven
1. His work on earth
—Did his Father's will .... Mt 26:39; Jn 4:34; Jn 6:38
—Fulfilled the Old Testament .... Mt 5:17
—Came to seek and save the lost .... Lk 19:10
—Came to give us eternal life .... Jn 10:10,28
—Gave his life as a ransom for many .... Mk 10:45
—Made an atoning sacrifice .... Ro 3:25; 1Jn 2:2
—Died for our sins .... 1Co 15:3; Gal 1:4; 1Pe 3:18
—Reconciled us to God .... 2Co 5:18 – 19; Eph 2:14 – 17
—Rose again for our justification .... Ro 4:25
—Destroyed the works of Satan .... Heb 2:14; 1Jn 3:8

2. His work as God's Anointed One
—Called God's anointed one .... Ac 4:26
—His anointing as Prophet .... Jn 6:14; Ac 3:21 – 23; Heb 1:1
—His anointing as Priest .... Heb 6:20; Heb 9:11 – 14,23 – 28
—His anointing as King .... Jn 12:13; Rev 19:13 – 16

3. His work as the exalted Lord in heaven
—Sent out the Spirit .... Jn 15:26; Ac 2:32 – 33
—Rules the world at God's right hand .... 1Co 15:25; Heb 1:3 – 4
—Rules the church at God's right hand .... Eph 1:20 – 22; Col 1:18
—Makes intercession for us .... Ro 8:34; Heb 7:25
—Will overcome all his enemies .... 1Co 15:26 – 28; Rev 17:14; Rev 19:11 – 21
—Will come again to take us to himself .... 1Th 5:16 – 17
—Will come again to judge humanity .... Ac 10:42; 2Co 5:10; 2Ti 4:1

See also TRINITY

JETHRO

—Father-in-law of Moses; priest of Midian .... Ex 3:1
—Also called Reuel .... Nu 10:29
—Owned flocks of sheep .... Ex 2:16 – 20
—Permitted Moses to return to Egypt from Midian .... Ex 4:18
—Brought wife and sons to Moses in desert .... Ex 18:1 – 7
—Acknowledged power of the Lord .... Ex 18:9 – 12
—Advised Moses to appoint judges for Israel .... Ex 18:13 – 27

JEW

A. Their identity
—Name given to God's people in Babylon .... Est 3:4 – 6; Est 8:9; Jer 32:12; Jer 44:1
—Jews returned to Jerusalem .... Ezr 5:1,5; Ne 4:1 – 2
—Jews lived all over the world .... Zec 8:23; Ac 24:5

B. The Jews in the New Testament
1. Their history
—Many opposed Jesus .... Jn 5:15 – 16; Jn 9:22
—They asked for Jesus' death .... Jn 19:4 – 12; 1Th 2:14 – 16
—First Christians were Jews .... Ac 2:5 – 14
—Jews continued to become believers .... Ac 14:1; Ac 17:4,12
—The Jews persecuted the apostles .... Ac 9:23; Ac 13:50; Ac 17:5 – 9,13

2. Paul and the Jews
—Paul was proud to be a Jew .... Php 3:4 – 5
—His message was to the Jew first .... Ac 13:46; Ro 1:16
—Jews were as sinful as Gentiles .... Ro 2:9 – 10
—Christ is Savior of Jew and Gentile .... Ro 10:12 – 13; 1Co 1:24
—True Jew is marked by inner regeneration .... Ro 2:28 – 29
—Paul's sorrow over Jews rejecting Jesus .... Ro 9:1 – 5
—Salvation of Gentiles would arouse Jews .... Ro 11:13 – 15

JEZEBEL

—Sidonian wife of Ahab 1Ki 16:31
—Promoted Baal worship .... 1Ki 16:32 – 33
—Killed prophets of the Lord 1Ki 18:4,13
—Opposed Elijah .... 1Ki 19:1 – 2
—Had Naboth killed .... 1Ki 21:1 – 15
—Death prophesied 1Ki 21:23
—Killed by Jehu .... 2Ki 9:30 – 37
—Became a symbol of wickedness .... Rev 2:20

JOAB

—Nephew of David 1Ch 2:16
—Commander of David's army 2Sa 8:16
—Defeated Ish-Bosheth and his army .... 2Sa 2:10 – 32
—Killed Abner .... 2Sa 3:22 – 27
—Captured the city of Jerusalem 1Ch 11:6
—Defeated Ammon .... 2Sa 10:7 – 19; 1Ch 19:8 – 19
—Put Uriah in front line of battle .... 2Sa 11:16 – 24
—Defeated Rabbah .... 1Ch 20:1 – 3
—Devised plan to reconcile David and Absalom .... 2Sa 14:1 – 24
—Killed Absalom .... 2Sa 18:9 – 15
—Rebuked David's grief over Absalom's death .... 2Sa 19:1 – 8
—Put down Sheba's revolt .... 2Sa 20:1 – 22
—Tried to convince David not to number his men .... 2Sa 24:1 – 4
—Numbered David's men 2Sa 24:9
—Supported Adonijah over Solomon 1Ki 1:7
—Killed under Solomon's orders .... 1Ki 2:28 – 34

JOASH

—Son of Ahaziah; king of Judah 2Ki 11:2
—Sheltered from Athaliah .... 2Ki 11:2 – 3; 2Ch 22:11 – 12
—Proclaimed king by Jehoiada at seven years of age .... 2Ki 11:4 – 12,21; 2Ch 23:1 – 11
—Repaired the temple .... 2Ki 12:1 – 16; 2Ch 24:1 – 14
—Gave temple objects to king of Aram .... 2Ki 12:17 – 18
—Later led the people into idolatry .... 2Ch 24:17 – 19
—Assassinated .... 2Ki 12:20; 2Ch 24:23 – 25

JOB
—A God-fearing man from Uz .... Job 1:1
—Very wealthy .... Job 1:1–3
—His righteousness tested by disaster .... Job 1:6–22
—His righteousness tested by affliction .... Job 2:7–8
—His three friends tried to comfort him .... Job 2:11–13
—Cursed the day of his birth .... Job 3:1–26
—Gave rebuttals to Eliphaz .... Job 6:1—7:21
Job 16:1—17:16
Job 23:1—24:25
—Gave rebuttals to Bildad .... Job 9:1—10:22
Job 19:1–29
Job 26:1—31:40
—Gave rebuttals to Zophar .... Job 12:1—13:28
Job 21:1–34
—Repented .... Job 42:1–6
—Prayed for his friends .... Job 42:10
—Was made prosperous again .... Job 42:10–17
—Considered an example of righteousness .... Eze 14:14,20
—Considered an example of perseverance .... Jas 5:11

JOCHEBED
—Mother of Moses and Aaron .... Ex 6:20
Nu 26:59
—Hid Moses from the Egyptians .... Ex 2:1–2
—Hid Moses among the reeds .... Ex 2:3–4
—Was asked to take care of Moses .... Ex 2:7–10
—Considered an example of faith .... Heb 11:23

JOHN
A. John the Baptist
—His birth announced to his father Zechariah .... Lk 1:11–20
—Mother Elizabeth conceived .... Lk 1:23–25
—His birth .... Lk 1:57–66
—Ministered in the Desert of Judea .... Mt 3:1–12
Mk 1:2–8
—Preached a baptism of repentance .... Lk 3:7–14
Ac 13:24
Ac 19:3–4
—Witnessed concerning Jesus .... Mt 3:11–12
Mk 1:7–8
Jn 1:29–36
—Said Jesus must become greater .... Jn 3:25–30
—Baptized Jesus .... Mt 3:13–17
Lk 3:21–22
—Expressed doubts about Jesus .... Mt 11:2–6
Lk 7:18–23
—Arrested by Herod .... Mt 4:12
Mk 1:14
—Beheaded by Herod .... Mt 14:1–12
Mk 6:14–29
—Fulfilled prophecy about Elijah .... Mt 11:7–19
Mk 9:11–13

B. A disciple of Jesus
1. Events during Jesus' lifetime
—Son of Zebedee and brother of James .... Mt 4:21–22
Mk 3:17
—Originally a fisherman .... Mt 4:21
—Uneducated .... Ac 4:13
—Wanted hostile Samaritans killed .... Lk 9:52–55
—Observed the transfiguration .... Mt 17:1–13
Mk 9:2–13
—Sought top place in Jesus' kingdom .... Mk 10:35–45
—With Peter, prepared for the Passover .... Lk 22:8
—Accompanied Jesus to Gethsemane .... Mt 26:36–45
—Was called the disciple whom Jesus loved ... Jn 13:23
Jn 19:26
Jn 20:2
Jn 21:7,20
—Jesus committed his mother to him .... Jn 19:26–27
—Ran to the tomb on Easter Sunday .... Jn 20:2–8
—Breakfast with Jesus after resurrection .... Jn 21:1–14
2. Events after Jesus' ascension
—One of the apostles .... Ac 1:13
—Healed a lame man with Peter .... Ac 3:1–8
—Arrested with Peter .... Ac 4:1–3
—Questioned before the Sanhedrin .... Ac 4:7–21
—Sent to new Christians in Samaria .... Ac 8:14–17
—Involved in the council at Jerusalem .... Gal 2:9
—Wrote letters as "the elder" 2Jn 1
3Jn 1
—Exiled to Patmos .... Rev 1:9
—The prophet who wrote Revelation .... Rev 1:1–33
Rev 22:8

C. Cousin of Barnabas
See MARK

JONAH
—Prophet in the days of Jeroboam II 2Ki 14:25
—Called to preach to city of Nineveh .... Jnh 1:1–2
—Fled to Tarshish .... Jnh 1:3
—His flight caused a storm .... Jnh 1:4–12
—Thrown overboard .... Jnh 1:13–16
—Swallowed by fish .... Jnh 1:17
—Prayed while inside the fish .... Jnh 2:1–9
—Called a second time to preach to Nineveh .... Jnh 3:1–4
—Reproved by the Lord .... Jnh 4:1–11
—His life considered a sign of resurrection .... Mt 12:39–41
Lk 11:29–32

JONATHAN
—Oldest son of King Saul 1Sa 14:49
—Attacked Philistines 1Sa 13:3–4
1Sa 14:1–14
—Ate honey in disobedience to Saul 1Sa 14:24–45
—Became David's best friend 1Sa 18:1
—Made covenant with David 1Sa 18:3–4
1Sa 20:16–17
1Sa 23:16–18
—Informed David of Saul's plans 1Sa 19:1–3
—Interceded for David 1Sa 19:4–6
—Warned David to flee 1Sa 20:18–42
—Killed in battle 1Sa 31:2

JORAM
A. Son of Ahab; king of Israel 2Ki 1:17
2Ki 3:1–3
—Fought with Jehoshaphat against Moab 2Ki 3:4–27
—Wounded in battle against Hazael 2Ki 8:25–29
2Ch 22:5–6
—Killed by Jehu 2Ki 9:14–26
2Ch 22:7–8

B. King of Judah
See JEHORAM

JORDAN
—The river flowing from the Sea of Galilee to the Dead Sea
A. In the time of the patriarchs
—Well-watered plain where Lot settled .... Ge 13:10–11
—Jacob crossed it, going to Haran .... Ge 32:10
—Jacob's sons mourned Jacob's death there .... Ge 50:10–11
B. In the time of Moses and Joshua
—Israelites camped along it .... Nu 22:1
—A census taken there .... Nu 26:1–4
—Some Israelites given land east of the Jordan ... Nu 32:1–33
Nu 34:10–15
—Israelites crossed the Jordan .... Jos 3:1–17
Ps 114:3,5

—Twelve stones from the Jordan formed a memorial .... Jos 4:1 – 9
—Canaanites afraid because of the crossing .... Jos 5:1

C. In the time of the judges and kings
—Controlling the Jordan important in war .... Jdg 3:28
Jdg 7:24 – 25
Jdg 12:5 – 6
—David fled from Absalom across the Jordan .... 2Sa 17:21 – 22
—Elijah miraculously crossed the Jordan .... 2Ki 2:7 – 8
—Elisha miraculously crossed the Jordan .... 2Ki 2:13 – 14
—Naaman cured by washing in the Jordan .... 2Ki 5:9 – 14
—Axhead floated in the Jordan .... 2Ki 6:1 – 7

D. In the New Testament
—John the Baptist baptized there .... Mt 3:6
Mk 1:5
Lk 3:3
—Jesus was baptized in the Jordan .... Mt 3:13 – 17
Mk 1:9 – 11
Lk 3:21 – 22
—Jesus ministered across the Jordan .... Mt 19:1
Mk 10:1
Jn 10:40 – 42

JOSEPH

A. Son of Jacob by Rachel
1. His life in Canaan
—His birth .... Ge 30:24
—Name means "may he add" .... Ge 30:24
—Favored by Jacob, hated by brothers .... Ge 37:3 – 4
—His dreams .... Ge 37:5 – 11
—Sold by brothers to Midianites .... Ge 37:12 – 36
2. His life in Egypt
—Served under Potiphar .... Ge 39:1 – 19
—Put into prison .... Ge 39:20 – 23
—Interpreted dreams of Pharaoh's servants .... Ge 40:1 – 19
—Interpreted dreams of Pharaoh .... Ge 41:14 – 40
—Was appointed ruler in Egypt .... Ge 41:41 – 57
—Father of two sons .... Ge 41:50 – 52
—Treated brothers harshly during famine .... Ge 42:6 – 24
—Ordered return of money to his brothers .... Ge 42:25 – 28
—Had meal with all his brothers .... Ge 43:26 – 34
—Ordered silver cup put in Benjamin's sack .... Ge 44:1 – 13
—Revealed himself to his brothers .... Ge 45:1 – 15
—Invited his family to live in Egypt .... Ge 45:16 – 28
—Brought Jacob and sons to Egypt .... Ge 46:1—47:12
—Joseph's administration .... Ge 47:13 – 26
—Had Jacob bless Ephraim and Manasseh .... Ge 48:1 – 22
—Blessed by Jacob .... Ge 49:22 – 26
—His death .... Ge 50:22 – 26
Heb 11:22
—Bones taken back to Canaan .... Jos 24:32
3. Tribe divided into Ephraim and Manasseh .... Dt 33:13 – 17
See EPHRAIM; MANASSEH
—One of the tribes of the 144,000 .... Rev 7:8

B. Husband of Mary, mother of Jesus .... Mt 1:16
Lk 1:27
—Considered not marrying Mary .... Mt 1:18 – 19
—Visited by angel .... Mt 1:20 – 24
—Went to Bethlehem during census .... Lk 2:1 – 5
—Gave name "Jesus" to Mary's son .... Mt 1:25
—Circumcised Jesus; presented him in the temple .... Lk 2:21 – 24
—Took Mary and Jesus to Egypt .... Mt 2:13 – 15
—Returned and settled in Nazareth .... Mt 2:19 – 23
—Went to Jerusalem for Passover .... Lk 2:41 – 51

C. A rich man from Arimathea .... Mt 27:57
—A member of the Jewish Council .... Mk 15:43
—Had not consented to Jesus' crucifixion .... Lk 23:51
—A secret disciple of Jesus .... Jn 19:38
—With Nicodemus, prepared Jesus' body .... Jn 19:39 – 40
—Buried Jesus in Joseph's own tomb .... Mt 27:58 – 60
Mk 15:43 – 46
Jn 19:41 – 42

D. A companion of Paul
See BARNABAS

JOSHUA

A. Son of Nun; name changed from Hoshea .... Nu 13:8,16
1Ch 7:27
1. Ministry under Moses
—Fought Amalekites .... Ex 17:9 – 14
—Accompanied Moses on Mount Sinai .... Ex 24:13
Ex 32:17
—Spied out Canaan .... Nu 13:8,16 – 25
—Encouraged Israelites to enter Canaan .... Nu 14:6 – 9
—Allowed to enter land .... Nu 14:30
—Appointed as Moses' successor .... Nu 27:12 – 23
Dt 31:1 – 8
2. Leader of Israelites into Canaan
—Encouraged by the Lord as leader .... Jos 1:1 – 9
—Charged Israel to conquer Canaan .... Jos 1:10 – 16
—Led Israelites through the Jordan .... Jos 3:1 – 17
—Had stone memorial built at the Jordan .... Jos 4:1 – 9
—Circumcised Israelites .... Jos 5:1 – 9
—Visited by commander of the Lord .... Jos 5:13 – 15
—Conquered Jericho .... Jos 6:1 – 25
—Defeated at Ai .... Jos 7:1 – 5
—Conquered Ai .... Jos 8:1 – 28
—Deceived by Gibeonites .... Jos 9:1 – 27
—Conquered five kings at Gibeon .... Jos 10:1 – 28
—Conquered southern Canaan .... Jos 10:29 – 43
—Conquered northern Canaan .... Jos 11:1—12:24
—Renewed covenant .... Jos 8:30 – 35
Jos 24:1 – 27
—Divided land among tribes .... Jos 14:1 – 5
—His farewell .... Jos 23:1 – 16
—His death .... Jos 24:28 – 31

B. High priest during time of Zerubbabel .... Hag 1:1,12,14
—Rebuilt the altar of the Lord .... Ezr 3:2 – 6
—Helped rebuild the temple .... Ezr 5:2
—Zechariah's vision of Joshua's trial in heaven .... Zec 3:1 – 9
—A crown for him .... Zec 6:9 – 15

JOSIAH

—Son of Amon; king of Judah 2Ki 21:24
2Ch 33:25
—Began reign when eight years old 2Ki 22:1
2Ch 34:1
—Purged the land of idolatry .... 2Ki 23:4 – 20,24 – 25
2Ch 34:3 – 7
—A prophecy concerning his reign 1Ki 13:2
—Repaired the temple .... 2Ki 22:3 – 7
2Ch 34:8 – 13
—Book of Law discovered .... 2Ki 22:8 – 20
2Ch 34:14 – 28
—Renewed the covenant .... 2Ki 23:1 – 3
2Ch 34:29 – 32
—Celebrated the Passover .... 2Ki 23:21 – 23
2Ch 35:1 – 19
—Killed by Pharaoh Neco .... 2Ki 23:29 – 30
2Ch 35:20 – 27

JOTHAM

A. Youngest son of Gideon .... Jdg 9:5
—Spoke to Shechemites against Abimelech .... Jdg 9:7 – 20
—Fled to Beer .... Jdg 9:21

B. Son of Uzziah; king of Judah .... 2Ki 15:32 – 38
—Reigned while Uzziah had leprosy 2Ch 26:21
—Repaired temple and walls of Jerusalem .... 2Ch 27:1 – 4

—Defeated Ammonites....2Ch 27:5–6
—His death....2Ch 27:8–9

JOY

A. Related themes
JOY is a theme of:
—Luke....Lk 24:52
—Philippians....Php 4:4

B. The nature of true joy
1. It centers in God
—In the Father....Ps 32:11
Ro 5:11
—In the Son....Jn 15:11
Php 4:4
—In the Holy Spirit....Ro 14:17
Ro 15:13
Gal 5:22
2. It can be experienced even while suffering....Mt 5:11–12
Ac 5:41
Ro 5:3
Col 1:24
Jas 1:2–3
1Pe 4:13
3. One aspect of the fruit of the Spirit....Gal 5:22
4. Our joy should never end....Php 4:4
1Th 5:16

C. Reasons for joy
1. Expressed in the Old Testament
a. Personal joy
—For salvation....Isa 12:3
Isa 52:8–9
—For forgiveness....Ps 51:7–8
—For personal well-being....Dt 12:17–18
1Ch 12:40
—For God's protection....Ps 5:11–12
Ps 31:7–8
—For life in the presence of God....Ps 16:11
Ps 21:6
—For a happy home....Pr 5:18
Pr 23:24–25
b. National joy
—At religious feasts....2Ch 30:23–25
Ne 8:12,17
Est 8:16–17
—At coronations....1Sa 11:15
1Ki 1:39–40
—At the dedication of the temple....1Ki 8:65–66
Ezr 3:10–13
—For all that the Lord does....Ps 98:1–9
Ps 100:1–2
—For victory over enemies....1Sa 18:6–7
2Ch 20:27–28
—For the return from exile....Ps 126:1–3
Jer 31:10–13
2. In the New Testament
—For the birth of Jesus....Mt 2:10
Lk 2:10,20
—For the resurrection of Jesus....Mt 28:8
Lk 24:41,52
—For salvation....Ac 13:48
1Pe 1:8–9
—For our names in the book of life....Lk 10:20
—For miraculous healing....Ac 8:7–8
—For privilege of preaching about Christ....Php 1:18
—For one sinner who repents....Lk 15:7,10
—For the wedding of the Lamb....Rev 19:7

JUDAH

A. Son of Jacob by Leah....Ge 35:23
1Ch 2:1
—Name means "praise"....Ge 29:35
—Spoke against killing brother Joseph....Ge 37:25–27
—Married a woman from Adullam....Ge 38:1–5
—Engaged in illicit sex with Tamar....Ge 38:12–24
—Fathered Perez and Zerah by Tamar....Ge 38:27–30
—Promised to be security for Benjamin....Ge 43:8–10
—Interceded for Benjamin before Joseph....Ge 44:18–34
—Went to Egypt with family....Ge 46:8,12
—Father of five sons....Ge 46:12
—Blessed by Jacob....Ge 49:8–12

B. Tribe descended from Judah
—Blessed by Moses....Dt 33:7
—Numbered....Nu 1:27
Nu 26:22
—Allotted land....Jos 15
Eze 48:7
—Failed to fully possess the land....Jos 15:63
Jdg 1:1–20
—David was from this tribe....1Ch 28:2–4
Mt 1:2–6
—David ruled this tribe first....2Sa 2:1–4
—Became the name for the southern kingdom....1Ki 12:21–22
1Ki 14:21–22
—Taken captive to Babylon....2Ki 24:1–16
—Returned from exile....Ezr 1:1–5
—One of the tribes of the 144,000....Rev 7:5

JUDAS

A. Disciple of Jesus, called Iscariot....Mt 10:4
Mk 3:19
—Criticized Mary for wastefulness....Jn 12:4–5
—Treasurer of disciples; pilfered money....Jn 12:6
—Satan entered into him....Lk 22:3
Jn 13:27
—Agreed with Jews to betray Jesus....Mt 26:14–16
Mk 14:10–11
—Identified as betrayer in upper room....Mt 26:25
Jn 13:21–30
—Betrayed Jesus with a kiss....Mt 26:47–49
Mk 14:43–45
Lk 22:47–48
—Returned money to the Jews....Mt 27:3–5
—Committed suicide....Mt 27:5
—Died a horrible death....Ac 1:18–19
—Better not to have been born....Mk 14:21
—Called a devil....Jn 6:70–71
—Jesus said he was doomed to destruction....Jn 17:12
—Replaced by Matthias....Ac 1:15–26

B. Another disciple of Jesus; son of James....Lk 6:16
Jn 14:22
—Probably also called Thaddaeus....Mt 10:3
Mk 3:18
—One of the apostles....Ac 1:13

C. Brother of Jesus and James....Mt 13:55
Mk 6:3
—Also called Jude....Jude 1

D. A Christian prophet....Ac 15:22–32
—Also called Barsabbas....Ac 15:22

JUDE

See JUDAS

JUDEA

A. A district governed by the Romans
—Located west of the Jordan River....Mt 19:1
—Ruled by King Herod at birth of Jesus....Mt 2:1–3
Lk 1:5
—Ruled by Herod's son Archelaus....Mt 2:22
—Governed by Pilate....Lk 3:1
—Ruled by Herod Agrippa....Ac 12:1–3,19

B. Important towns in Judea
—Jerusalem .... Mt 2:1; Ac 26:20
—Bethlehem .... Mt 2:1; Lk 2:4
—Arimathea .... Lk 23:51
C. John the Baptist preached in Desert of Judea .... Mt 3:1
D. Jesus and Judea
—Born in Bethlehem of Judea .... Mt 2:1–6
—Preached in synagogues of Judea .... Lk 4:44
—Ministered in Judean countryside .... Jn 3:22
—News about Jesus spread throughout Judea .... Lk 7:17; Lk 23:5
—Many from Judea followed Jesus .... Mt 4:25; Mk 3:8; Lk 6:17
—Jesus crucified in Judea 1Th 2:14–15
E. The apostles and Judea
—Gospel was to spread throughout Judea .... Ac 1:8
—Residents of Judea present on Pentecost .... Ac 2:5–9
—Christians scattered throughout Judea .... Ac 8:1
—Famine aid for Christians in Judea .... Ac 11:29; Ro 15:25–26
—Christians there suffered persecution 1Th 2:14–16

JUDGE, JUDGMENT

A. Related themes
1. JUDGMENT is a theme of:
—Exodus .... Ex 34:7
—2 Kings 2Ki 17:22
—Isaiah .... Isa 65:6
—Jeremiah .... Jer 6:19
—Ezekiel .... Eze 24:21
—Hosea .... Hos 6:5
—Amos .... Am 6:8
—Obadiah .... Ob 18
—Micah .... Mic 1:6
—Nahum .... Na 3:7
—Zephaniah .... Zep 1:4
—Revelation .... Rev 16:5
2. DEVASTATION is a theme of Joel .... Joel 1:2
B. Judgment done by humans
1. Official judgment
a. In the political realm
—God raised up judges for his people .... Jdg 2:16
—Ehud as judge .... Jdg 3:12–30
—Deborah as judge .... Jdg 4:4–16
—Gideon as judge .... Jdg 6:11—8:32
—Jephthah as judge .... Jdg 10:6—12:7
—Samson as judge .... Jdg 13:1—16:31
—Eli as judge 1Sa 4:18
—Samuel as judge 1Sa 7:15–17
b. In the legal realm
—Judges set up by Moses .... Ex 18:13–26; Dt 16:18–20
—Approved transactions regarding Ruth .... Ru 4:1–12
—Judges set up by Jehoshaphat 2Ch 19:5–7
—Judges set up by Ezra .... Ezr 8:25–27
—Pilate was a judge .... Mt 27:19; Jn 19:13
—Paul on trial before Gallio .... Ac 18:12–16
—Paul on trial before Felix .... Ac 24:1–23
—Paul on trial before Festus .... Ac 25:6–12
—Lawsuits among believers 1Co 6:1–8
—Lawsuits often instituted by the rich .... Jas 2:6–7
c. In the religious realm
—Sanhedrin against Jesus .... Mt 26:57–66
—Sanhedrin against followers of Jesus .... Jn 9:22,28–34
—Sanhedrin against Christians .... Ac 4:5–21; Ac 5:21–40; Ac 22:30—23:7
—Judgment done by the church .... 1Co 5:1–5; 1Ti 1:20; Tit 3:10–11
d. Standards for official judgment
—Two or three witnesses needed .... Dt 19:15; Mt 26:60
—Must be impartial .... Dt 1:17; Dt 16:19; Pr 24:23
—Must be fair and just .... Dt 1:16; Dt 16:20; Isa 56:1
—Oath could be required .... Ex 22:11; Heb 6:16
—Decisions made before witnesses .... Ru 4:9–11
—Casting lots sometimes used .... Pr 18:18
2. The judging attitude
—We must not judge others .... Mt 7:1–5; Ro 14:1–4,13; 1Co 4:5; 1Co 10:29; Jas 4:11–12
—We must judge ourselves .... Mt 7:3–5; Gal 6:1,4
3. Human participation in the final judgment .... Mt 19:28; Lk 22:30; 1Co 6:2–3
C. Judgment done by God
1. God described as a judge
—God as judge of all the earth .... Ge 18:26; Ps 94:2
—Christ as judge .... Jn 5:22; Ac 10:42; 2Ti 4:1
—His judgment is always right .... Dt 32:4; Job 34:10; 2Th 1:5
2. Temporal judgments
a. Examples of those whom God judged
—The world in the flood .... Ge 7:17–23
—Sodom and Gomorrah .... Ge 19:24–26
—The firstborn in Egypt .... Ex 12:29–30
—Pharaoh and his army .... Ex 14:23–28
—The Israelites in the desert .... Nu 14:26–35
—Korah and his men .... Nu 16:31–35
—The Israelites during the judges .... Jdg 2:14–15
—Ahab and his family 2Ki 9:6–10
—The city of Samaria 2Ki 17:16–18
—The Jews in exile 2Ki 24:1–4
—Proud Nebuchadnezzar .... Da 4:29–33
—King Belshazzar .... Da 5:25–30
—The city of Jerusalem .... Lk 19:41–44
—King Herod .... Ac 12:21–23
—The magician Elymas .... Ac 13:9–11
b. Types of temporal judgments
—Drought 1Ki 17:1
—Famine .... La 2:11–12
—Fire from heaven 2Ki 1:10,12
—Flood .... Ge 7:17–23
—An invasion of locusts .... Joel 1:2–7
—Earthquake .... Isa 24:18–20
—Plague 2Sa 24:15–16
—Blight and mildew .... Am 4:9
—Severe storms .... Jos 10:10–11
—Destruction of property .... Eze 33:23–29
—Exile 2Ch 36:20
—Famine of hearing God's word .... Am 8:11
—Death 2Ki 9:8–10,30–33
c. Purposes of temporal judgments
—To punish sin .... Ge 6:5–7; Hos 5:1,8–11

—To reveal himself as God .... Ex 9:14–16; Eze 5:13
—To purify his people .... Mal 3:2–4; Jn 15:2
—To drive his people to repentance .... Am 5:6,15; Lk 13:2–5

3. The final judgment
 a. Names for the final judgment
  —The day of judgment 2Pe 2:9
  —The day of the Lord 1Th 5:2
  —The day of God's wrath .... Ro 2:5–6
  —The great Day .... Jude 6
  —The Day 1Co 3:13
 b. The judges of the final judgment
  —God as the judge .... Ps 96:13; Ecc 3:17
  —Administration given to Christ .... Jn 5:22; Ac 10:42; Ro 2:16
 c. Those who are to be judged
  —The living and the dead .... Ac 10:42
  —All nations .... Mt 25:31–32
  —All people .... 2Co 5:10; Heb 9:27; Rev 20:11–14
 d. Time of the final judgment: unknown .... Mt 24:36–42; Lk 12:40; 1Th 5:1–3
 e. The basis of the final judgment
  —Our faith in Jesus .... Jn 3:16–18; Jn 5:24–26
  —Our sincere commitment to Jesus .... Mt 7:22–23
  —Our being heirs of God .... Mt 25:34
  —Our names being in the book of life .... Rev 20:15
  —Our adherence to God's law .... Ro 2:12–16; Jas 2:12
  —What we've done with God's gifts .... Lk 12:48
  —Our actions .... Ecc 12:14; Mt 25:35–46; 1Co 3:12–15; 2Co 5:10
  —Our words .... Mt 12:36–37; Jas 3:1–2
  —Our inner thoughts 1Co 4:5
  —Our perseverance to the end .... Mt 24:13
  —In God mercy triumphs over judgment .... Jas 2:13
 f. The results of the final judgment
  —Unbelievers will be punished .... Ro 2:5; 2Th 1:8–9; Rev 20:15
  —Believers will receive eternal life .... Jn 3:16; 1Jn 5:11–12
  —Believers will receive salvation .... Ro 13:11; Heb 9:27–28
  —Believers will receive redemption .... Lk 21:28; Eph 4:30
  —Believers will receive a crown .... 2Ti 4:8; Jas 1:12
 g. Attitude toward the final judgment
  —Be on your guard .... Mk 13:23,33
  —Be alert 1Th 5:6
  —Watch .... Mt 25:13

JUSTICE

—Fairness in the treatment of others

A. Related themes
 JUSTICE is a theme of Lamentations .... La 4:13
 SOCIAL JUSTICE is a theme of Amos .... Am 5:24

B. Human justice
 1. Israelites commanded to exercise justice .... Ex 23:1–3,6; Lev 19:15; Dt 1:17; Dt 16:18–20
 2. The prophets and justice
  —They called the people to justice .... Jer 22:3; Hos 12:6; Am 5:24; Mic 6:8
  —They spoke against injustice .... Isa 3:15; Am 2:6–8; Mic 3:1–3
 3. Christians called to exercise justice .... Mt 23:23; Col 4:1; Jas 2:1–4

C. The justice of God
 1. God is just 2Th 1:6
  —His ways are just .... Dt 32:4; Da 4:37; Rev 15:3
  —He loves justice .... Ps 11:7; Ps 33:5
  —He does no wrong .... Zep 3:5
  —He judges justly .... 1Pe 2:23; Rev 16:5,7
 2. The nature of God's justice
  —He is impartial .... 2Ch 19:7; Job 34:19; Ro 2:11
  —He champions victims of injustice .... Ps 10:17–18; Ps 103:6
 3. Expressions of God's justice
  —Requires death for sin .... Ge 2:17; Ro 6:23
  —Is expressed in his forgiveness 1Jn 1:9

See also RIGHTEOUSNESS

JUSTIFICATION

—Being declared right with God; acceptance by God

A. The basis of justification
 —Christ as our righteousness 1Co 1:30
 —Christ's perfect obedience .... Ro 5:19; 2Co 5:21; Heb 4:15; 1Pe 2:22
 —Christ's death on the cross .... Ro 3:24–25; Ro 5:9
 —Christ's resurrection .... Ro 4:25

B. The manner of justification
 —We cannot earn it by obedience .... Ro 3:28; Ro 9:31–32; Gal 2:16; Gal 3:11; Php 3:9
 —We receive it as a gift of God's grace .... Ro 3:24; Ro 4:16; Ro 5:15–17; Gal 2:21
 —We receive it by repenting .... Lk 18:13–14
 —We receive it through faith .... Ac 13:39; Ro 3:22,26–28; Ro 4:10–12; Gal 2:16; Gal 5:5; Php 3:9
 —Faith must be a living faith .... Jas 2:14–26

C. The results of justification
 —We become children of Abraham .... Ro 4:11–12,16–17; Gal 3:6–7

—We are redeemed ... Ro 3:24
—We receive forgiveness of sins ... Ac 13:38–39
—We receive the gift of eternal life ... Ro 5:17–18; Ro 8:10; Tit 3:7
—We are saved from God's wrath ... Ro 5:9
—We become free from condemnation ... Ro 8:1,33–34
—We have peace with God ... Ro 5:1
—We are blessed by God ... Ro 4:6–9; Gal 3:9,14
—We are considered to have kept God's law ... Ro 8:3–4; 2Co 5:21
—We become free from the law ... Gal 5:1
—We share in Christ's sufferings ... Php 3:10
—We go on to live a life of holiness ... Ro 6:19,22; Gal 2:17–19
—We will someday be glorified ... Ro 8:30

KADESH, KADESH BARNEA

—City bordering on Edom ... Nu 20:14–16
—God appeared to Hagar near there ... Ge 16:7–14
—Abraham lived near there ... Ge 20:1
—Moses sent out spies from there ... Nu 13:1–2,26; Dt 1:19–25; Jos 14:6–7
—Israelites rebelled against the Lord there ... Nu 14:1–45; Dt 1:26–45; Dt 9:23–24
—Israelites camped there again for many days ... Dt 1:46; Jdg 11:16–17
—Miriam died there ... Nu 20:1
—Moses struck the rock there to get water ... Nu 20:2–12
—Joshua conquered that area ... Jos 10:41
—Became southernmost town of Judah ... Jos 15:3; Eze 47:19

KETURAH

—Wife of Abraham after Sarah ... Ge 25:1
—Also called Abraham's concubine ... 1Ch 1:32
—Mother of six sons ... Ge 25:2

KINDNESS

—A hospitable, friendly attitude toward others

A. Related theme
HOSPITALITY is a theme of 3 John ... 3Jn 8

B. Human kindness

1. Expected of Christians
—Commanded ... 2Co 6:6; Gal 5:22; Col 3:12; 2Pe 1:7
—One aspect of the fruit of the Spirit ... Gal 5:22

2. Expressions of kindness
—Showing forgiveness ... Ge 50:21
—Sparing someone's life ... Jos 2:12–13
—Healing the sick ... Ac 4:9
—Helping the needy ... 2Sa 9:1–7; Pr 14:21,31; Pr 19:17
—Helping victims of injustice ... Ge 40:14
—Helping strangers ... Ac 28:2; Heb 13:1–2; 3Jn 5–8

C. Kindness of God
—In giving us salvation ... Tit 3:4
—In being faithful to his promises ... 1Ki 3:6
—In watching over us ... Job 10:12
—In showing compassion to us ... Isa 54:8
—In providing for needs ... Ge 32:10; Ru 2:20; Hos 11:4; Ac 14:17
—In helping us in various life situations ... Ge 39:21; Ezr 9:9

See also MERCY

KING

A. Related theme
KINGSHIP is a theme of 1 Samuel ... 1Sa 11:15

B. Human kings

1. Examples of non-Israelite kings
—Four kings warring against five ... Ge 14:8–11
—Melchizedek, king of Salem ... Ge 14:18
—List of the kings of Edom ... Ge 36:32–39
—Pharaoh, king of Egypt ... Ex 1:8,15–22
—Sihon and Og defeated ... Nu 21:21–35
—Various kings in Canaan defeated ... Jos 8:1–2; Jos 10:1–3,16–42; Jos 12
—David defeated various kings ... 2Sa 8:1–14
—The king of Assyria took Israel ... 2Ki 17:3–6
—King Nebuchadnezzar took Judah ... 2Ki 25:1–7
—King Cyrus allowed return to Judah ... Ezr 1:1–4
—Nehemiah served King Artaxerxes ... Ne 2:1
—Esther became wife of King Xerxes ... Est 2:1,17–18
—Caesar as king ... Jn 19:12,15
—The kings of the earth ... Ps 2:2; Ps 102:15; Ps 138:4

2. The kings of Israel and Judah

a. The beginning of kingship
—The people asked for a king ... 1Sa 8:4–5
—Samuel warned them ... 1Sa 8:10–18
—Saul anointed as first king ... 1Sa 10:20–24; 1Sa 11:14–15

b. Kings of the united kingdom
—Saul (42 years) ... 1Sa 13:1
See SAUL
—David (40 years) ... 1Ki 2:11
See DAVID
—Solomon (40 years) ... 1Ki 11:42
See SOLOMON

c. The kings of Israel (in chronological order)
—Jeroboam (22 years) ... 1Ki 12:25—14:20
—Nadab (2 years) ... 1Ki 15:25–31
—Baasha (24 years) ... 1Ki 15:32—16:7
—Elah (2 years) ... 1Ki 16:8–14
—Zimri (7 days) ... 1Ki 16:15–20
—Tibni (with Omri) ... 1Ki 16:21–22
—Omri (12 years) ... 1Ki 16:23–28
—Ahab (22 years) ... 1Ki 16:29—22:40; 2Ch 18:1–34
—Ahaziah (2 years) ... 1Ki 22:51–53; 2Ki 1:1–18
—Joram (12 years) ... 2Ki 3:1–8:15
—Jehu (28 years) ... 2Ki 9:6—10:36
—Jehoahaz (17 years) ... 2Ki 13:1–9
—Jehoash (16 years) ... 2Ki 13:10–25
—Jeroboam II (41 years) ... 2Ki 14:23–29
—Zechariah (6 months) ... 2Ki 15:8–12
—Shallum (1 month) ... 2Ki 15:13–15
—Menahem (10 years) ... 2Ki 15:16–22
—Pekahiah (2 years) ... 2Ki 15:23–26
—Pekah (20 years) ... 2Ki 15:27–31
—Hoshea (9 years) ... 2Ki 17:1–6

See also entries for each of these kings

d. The kings of Judah (in chronological order)
—Rehoboam (17 years) 1Ki 12:1–24
1Ki 14:21–31
2Ch 10:1—12:16
—Abijah (3 years) 1Ki 15:1–8
2Ch 13:1—14:1
—Asa (41 years) 1Ki 15:9–24
2Ch 14:2—16:14
—Jehoshaphat (25 years) 1Ki 22:41–50
2Ch 17:1—21:3
—Jehoram (8 years) 2Ki 8:16–24
2Ch 21:4–20
—Ahaziah (1 year) 2Ki 8:25–29
2Ch 22:1–9
—Athaliah (7 years) 2Ki 11:1–21
2Ch 22:10—23:21
—Joash (40 years) 2Ki 12:1–21
2Ch 24:1–27
—Amaziah (29 years) 2Ki 14:1–22
2Ch 25:1–28
—Azariah/Uzziah (52 years) 2Ki 15:1–7
2Ch 26:1–23
—Jotham (16 years) 2Ki 15:32–38
2Ch 27:1–8
—Ahaz (16 years) 2Ki 16:1–20
2Ch 28:1–27
—Hezekiah (29 years) .... 2Ki 18:1—20:21
2Ch 29:1—32:33
Isa 36:1—39:8
—Manasseh (55 years) 2Ki 21:1–18
2Ch 33:1–20
—Amon (2 years) 2Ki 21:19–26
2Ch 33:21–25
—Josiah (31 years) .... 2Ki 22:1—23:30
2Ch 34:1—35:27
—Jehoahaz (3 months) 2Ki 23:31–33
2Ch 36:1–4
—Jehoiakim (11 years) .... 2Ki 23:24—24:7
2Ch 36:5–8
—Jehoiachin (3 months) 2Ki 24:8–17
2Ch 36:9–10
—Zedekiah (11 years) .... 2Ki 24:18—25:26
2Ch 36:11–21

See also entries for each of these kings

C. God as a king
1. God called a king
—The King of heaven .... Da 4:37
—The King of glory .... Ps 24:10
—The eternal, immortal, invisible King 1Ti 1:17
—The great King .... Ps 47:2
—He rules over all the earth 2Ch 20:6
Ps 99:1–2
Isa 52:7
—He rules from his throne 1Ki 22:19
Ps 9:4,7–8
Isa 6:1–3
2. Christ is a king
a. Prophesied in the Old Testament
—The coming one will have a scepter .... Ge 49:10
Nu 24:17
—He will rule on David's throne .... Ps 132:11–12
Isa 9:6–7
Jer 33:17
—He will rule at God's right hand .... Ps 110:1
—He will rule eternally .... Da 2:44–45
—He will rule with authority .... Da 7:13–14
—He will rule as a shepherd .... Isa 40:10–11
Eze 34:23–24
Mic 5:2–4
—He will rule wisely .... Isa 52:13
Jer 23:5
—He will rule with justice .... Isa 32:1
Jer 33:15–16
—He will rule humbly .... Zec 9:9
—He will function as a priest .... Ps 110:4
Zec 6:12–13
b. Fulfilled in the New Testament
—He is the King of the Jews .... Mt 2:2
Jn 19:19–21
—He is the King of Israel .... Jn 1:49
—He claimed kingship .... Mt 27:11
Jn 18:37
—He entered Jerusalem as king .... Mt 21:1–9
—He came to rule on David's throne .... Lk 1:32–33
Ac 2:29–33
—He now rules at God's right hand .... Eph 1:20–23
Heb 1:3–8
—He is ruling over his enemies 1Co 15:25–27
—He will sit as a King who judges .... Mt 25:31–34

KINGDOM

—The rule of humans or God over others

A. Related themes
KINGDOM is a theme of:
—2 Samuel 2Sa 5:12
—1 Kings 1Ki 4:21

B. Human kingdoms
1. General kingdoms of Bible history
—Kingdom of Bashan .... Nu 32:33
—Kingdom of the Amorites .... Nu 32:33
—The Aramean kingdom 1Ch 18:6
—The kingdom of Babylon .... Da 1:20
Da 4:36
—The kingdom of Media and Persia .... Est 1:2–4
Da 5:28,30
—Four kingdoms in Nebuchadnezzar's dream .... Da 2:36–43
—All the kingdoms of the earth .... Dt 28:25
2Ki 19:15,19
Jer 15:4
Mt 4:8
2. The kingdom(s) of Israel and Judah
—The kingdom taken away from Saul 1Sa 13:13–14
—The kingdom united under David 2Sa 5:1–5,12
—The kingdom expanded under David 2Sa 8:11–14
—The kingdom given to Solomon 1Ki 1:28–40
—The kingdom to be divided after Solomon 1Ki 11:9–13
—The kingdom divided under Rehoboam 1Ki 12:16–24
—The kingdom of Israel destroyed 2Ki 17:7–23
—The kingdom of Judah destroyed 2Ki 25:1–21

C. Kingdom of God
1. When and where is that kingdom?
a. The kingdom is present in Jesus
—John preached it was near .... Mt 3:2
—Jesus preached it was near .... Mk 1:15
—Jesus preached good news of the kingdom .... Mt 4:23
—Some parables describe its life .... Mt 13:11–52
—Jesus' miracles proved its presence .... Lk 7:18–22
—Casting out demons proved it .... Lk 11:20
—"The kingdom of God is in our midst" .... Lk 17:20–21
—It comes through Jesus' death .... Lk 23:42–43
—It comes through Jesus' resurrection 1Co 15:20–25
—The apostles preached the kingdom .... Ac 8:12
Ac 19:8
Ac 28:23,28
—Christ brings us into his kingdom .... Col 1:12–13
b. The kingdom is yet to come
—Jesus prayed, "Your kingdom come" .... Mt 6:10

—Some parables describe it as future........Mt 25:1 – 34
—It comes with the return of Jesus............2Ti 4:1
—It is something we will inherit...............Mt 25:34
1Co 15:50
Jas 2:5
—It is a heavenly kingdom........................2Ti 4:18
Heb 12:26 – 28
—It is a kingdom we will receive...............2Pe 1:11
—The millennial kingdom.........................Rev 20:1 – 6

2. How can we enter the kingdom?
—By experiencing new birth..........................Jn 3:3
—By receiving it as a gift from Jesus ....Lk 22:29
—By responding to God's call 1Th 2:12
—By repenting of our sins...............................Mk 1:15
—By being redeemed through Christ.................Col 1:12 – 14
—By accepting Christ's righteousness ....Mt 5:20
—By following Jesus ....Mt 19:21 – 24
Lk 9:61 – 62
—By loving God ....Jas 2:5
—By persevering in the faith.............................Ac 14:22
2Th 1:4 – 5
—By doing the will of God ....Mt 7:21 – 23

3. What is life in the kingdom like?
—Described in the Sermon on the Mount ....Mt 5:1—7:27
—Described in the Sermon on the Plain..........Lk 6:17 – 49
—Described in many parables of Jesus............Mt 13:11 – 52
Mt 18:23 – 35
Mt 20:1 – 16
Mt 21:28—22:14
—A life of childlike humility..........................Mt 18:1 – 4
—A life of joy and peace..................................Ro 14:17
—A life free from sin's control.........................1Co 6:9 – 11
Gal 5:16 – 21
Eph 5:3 – 5
—A life of producing the fruit of the Spirit ......Gal 5:21 – 23

4. How must we relate to the kingdom?
—We must pray for it ....Mt 6:10
—We must seek it first ....Mt 6:33
—We must preach it..Ac 8:22
Ac 28:31
—We must work for it ....Col 4:11
—We may have to suffer for it...........................Ac 14:22
2Ti 4:16 – 18

KISS

A. Legitimate uses
—To say hello ....Ge 29:13
Ge 33:4
—To say good-bye ....Ge 31:55
Ru 1:9
1Sa 20:41
—To accompany a blessing...............................Ge 27:26 – 27
—To express deep affection...............................1Sa 20:41
—To express sexual love ....SS 1:2
—To express grief ....Ge 50:1
Ac 20:37
—To demonstrate forgiveness ....Ge 33:4
Ge 45:15
Lk 15:20
—To show honor and respect 1Sa 10:1
Lk 7:38
—To express submission...................................Ps 2:12
—To show Christian love...................................Ro 16:16
1Pe 5:14

B. Pagan use: kissing idols 1Ki 19:18
Job 31:26 – 27
Hos 13:2

C. Hypocritical uses
—Absalom trying to gain popularity 2Sa 15:5
—Joab when he killed Amasa.............................2Sa 20:9
—Judas when he betrayed Jesus ....Mt 26:48 – 49
Mk 14:44 – 45
Lk 22:47 – 48
—A prostitute seducing a man ....Pr 7:13
—Can be used by any enemy.............................Pr 27:6

KNOWLEDGE

A. Related theme
KNOWLEDGE is a theme of 2 Peter 2Pe 1:3

B. Human knowledge of God and his ways

1. Source of our knowledge
—God himself ....Pr 2:6
Jer 9:23 – 24
—Christ...Col 2:3,8
—The Holy Spirit ....1Co 2:9 – 16
—The world around us ....Ps 19:1
Ro 1:19 – 20
—God's word...Pr 2:1 – 5
Jn 17:17
2Ti 3:15 – 16
—God's mighty acts for his people ....Ex 6:6 – 7
Eze 37:13 – 14

2. Corruption of human knowledge of God
—First sin: seeking knowledge apart from God ....Ge 3:4 – 7
—Humans suppress the truth about God ....Ro 1:18
2Ti 3:7
Tit 1:16
—Idolatry is evidence of this ....Ro 1:21 – 23

3. Proper attitude to the knowledge of God
—We must know God...Jer 9:24
—To know God is to do his will ....Jer 22:15 – 16
—We must know Christ.....................................Php 3:8,10
—We must pray for knowledge..........................Ps 119:66
—We must grow in knowledge ....Eph 4:13
Heb 5:12—6:1
2Pe 1:5 – 8
2Pe 3:18
—We must recognize its limitations..................1Co 13:8 – 12
—We must realize love surpasses it..................1Co 8:1
Eph 3:19
—We must not become proud of it....................1Co 8:1
—We must not wander away from it..................1Ti 6:20 – 21

4. Benefits of the knowledge of God
—Gives stability to life ....Pr 24:3 – 6
—Enables us to know the love of God 1Jn 3:1
—Enables us to fight sin and evil......................2Pe 1:3 – 4
—Keeps us from destruction by God.................Hos 4:6
—Essential to eternal life ....Jn 17:3

C. Knowledge possessed by God
—God is all-knowing...Ps 139:1 – 6
Isa 46:10
1Jn 3:20
—God's knowledge of us precedes our birth......Ps 139:15 – 16
Jer 1:5
—God knows what is inside us 1Sa 16:7
Ps 44:21
—God knows our needs.....................................Ps 103:13 – 14
Mt 6:31 – 32
—Little things do not escape his notice ....Mt 10:29 – 30
—God cannot be taught by humans...................Job 21:22
Isa 40:12 – 14
—Jesus knew God's will for him........................Lk 18:31 – 33
Jn 13:1
—Jesus knows us completely ....Jn 2:25
Jn 4:16 – 18
Jn 6:64
—All knowledge is hidden in Christ...................Col 2:3

KORAH

—A descendant of Levi ... Ex 6:19,21,24
—Led a rebellion against Moses ... Nu 16:1 – 3
—Killed by the Lord for this rebellion ... Nu 16:4 – 35
—His descendants became temple gatekeepers ... 1Ch 9:17,19; 1Ch 26:1
—His descendants became temple musicians ... 1Ch 6:31 – 32,37; 2Ch 20:19
—Sons of Korah wrote various psalms ... Ps 44 – 49,85 – 88
—His rebellion illustrates God's judgment ... Jude 11

LABAN

—Son of Bethuel ... Ge 24:24
—Brother of Rebekah ... Ge 24:29
—Father of Leah and Rachel ... Ge 29:16
—Deceived Jacob into marrying Leah ... Ge 29:22 – 27
—Became Jacob's boss ... Ge 29:18 – 20; Ge 30:25 – 34
—Became jealous of Jacob's prosperity ... Ge 31:1 – 2
—Disinherited his daughters ... Ge 31:14 – 16
—Pursued the fleeing Jacob ... Ge 31:22 – 25
—Made a covenant with Jacob ... Ge 31:43 – 55

LAMB

A. Uses for lambs
—For food ... Dt 32:14; Am 6:4
—For clothing ... Pr 27:26
—For sealing a treaty ... Ge 21:27 – 31
—For the payment of tribute ... 2Ki 3:4
—For a sacrifice in place of Isaac ... Ge 22:8,13
—For a regular burnt offering ... Ex 29:38 – 42
—For offerings at special feasts ... Nu 28:27; Nu 29:2
—For the Passover ... Ex 12:3 – 6; Nu 28:16 – 19

B. The lamb as a symbol
—Of extraordinary joy ... Ps 114:1 – 4
—Of innocence ... 2Sa 12:1 – 4
—Of weak people ... Isa 40:11; Jn 21:15
—Of peace-loving missionaries ... Lk 10:3
—Of the age of peace ... Isa 11:6; Isa 65:25

C. Jesus as the Lamb of God
—Prophesied by Isaiah ... Isa 53:4 – 7
—Fulfilled in Jesus ... Ac 8:32 – 35
—Called the Lamb of God ... Jn 1:29,36
—Called the Passover lamb ... 1Co 5:7
—Shed his blood as a lamb without blemish ... 1Pe 1:19
—Receives praise as the slain Lamb ... Rev 5:6 – 13; Rev 7:9 – 11
—Celebrates with his 144,000 ... Rev 14:1 – 5
—Conquers the antichrist ... Rev 17:14
—Marries the church as a bride ... Rev 19:7,9; Rev 21:9

LANGUAGE

A. Languages mentioned in the Bible
—Hebrew ... Isa 36:11,13
—Babylonian ... Da 1:4
—Aramaic ... Ezr 4:7
—Ashdod ... Ne 13:23 – 24
—Lycaonian ... Ac 14:11
—Latin ... Jn 19:20
—Greek ... Ac 21:37
—Numerous languages ... Ge 10:5,20,31; Ac 2:5 – 11

B. Language barriers begun at Babel ... Ge 11:1 – 9

C. Language barriers removed
—At Pentecost ... Ac 2:4 – 11
—Through gift of tongues ... Ac 10:46; Ac 19:6; 1Co 12:10,28 – 30; 1Co 13:1
—Through the interpretation of tongues ... 1Co 12:10,30; 1Co 14:5,13,27
—In heaven ... Rev 5:9; Rev 7:9

LAW

A. Related themes
LAW is a theme of:
—Leviticus ... Lev 7:37
—1 Chronicles ... 1Ch 22:12
—2 Chronicles ... 2Ch 8:13

B. Meanings of the word "law"
—A general principle ... Ro 7:23
—Rules of conduct in the conscience ... Ro 2:14
—Edicts made by human governments ... Da 6:12
—Rules revealed by God through Moses ... Ex 21:1; Ro 5:13; Ac 15:5
—The first five books of the Bible ... Gal 3:10
—The whole Old Testament ... Jn 15:25; 1Co 14:21

C. The law of God
1. Characteristics
—True ... Ps 119:142,151
—Perfect ... Ps 19:7; Jas 1:25
—Trustworthy ... Ps 19:7; Ps 119:86,138
—Enduring ... Ps 119:91,160; Mt 5:18
—Right and righteous ... Ps 19:8; Ps 119:75,137; Ro 7:12
—Holy ... Ro 7:12
—Good ... Ro 7:12,16; 1Ti 1:8
—Spiritual ... Ro 7:14
—Love is its summary ... Mt 22:37 – 40; Ro 13:8 – 10; Gal 5:14

2. Brief history of God's law revealed to Moses
—Spoken directly by God ... Ex 20:1,18 – 19; Dt 5:4,22
—Spoken by Moses to the Israelites ... Ex 20:22
—Written on tablets of stone ... Ex 24:12; Ex 31:18
—Tablets broken by Moses ... Ex 32:15 – 19
—Written on tablets a second time ... Ex 34:1 – 5,27 – 28
—Repeated in Deuteronomy ... Dt 4:44 – 46
—Placed in the ark of the covenant ... Dt 31:24 – 26
—Repeated by Joshua ... Jos 24:25 – 26
—Honored by David ... 1Ch 16:40
—Disobeyed by God's people ... 2Ki 17:12 – 20
—Taught by Jehoshaphat ... 2Ch 17:9; 2Ch 19:8
—Honored during Joash's reign ... 2Ch 23:18 – 19
—Honored during Hezekiah's reign ... 2Ch 31:3 – 4,21
—Rediscovered during Josiah's reign ... 2Ch 34:14 – 18
—Studied by Ezra ... Ezr 7:10
—Reintroduced by Ezra to the people ... Ne 8:1 – 18
—Read in the synagogues ... Ac 15:21
—Fulfilled by Jesus Christ ... Mt 5:17 – 18

3. Purpose of the law of God
—To show the way to life .... Lev 18:4–5; Dt 30:15–20; Gal 3:12
—To point out our sin .... Ro 3:20; Gal 3:19
—To increase sin .... Ro 5:20
—To show that we are under its curse .... Gal 3:10,13
—To lead us to Christ .... Gal 3:24

4. The Israelites and the law of God
—Must know it .... Ex 33:12–13
—Must fix it in their hearts .... Dt 11:18; Ps 119:11
—Must teach it .... Dt 4:9–10; Dt 11:19–21
—Must observe it .... Dt 4:1,6; Dt 29:9
—Must remember it .... Nu 15:38–40; Mal 4:4
—Must love it .... Ps 119:47,97
—Must delight in it .... Ps 1:2; Ps 112:1

5. Jesus Christ and the law of God
—Came to fulfill it .... Mt 5:17–18
—Born under it .... Gal 4:4
—Circumcised according to it .... Lk 2:21
—Consecrated according to it .... Lk 2:22–24
—Attended feasts prescribed in it .... Mk 14:12–16; Jn 2:23
—Perfectly obeyed it .... 2Co 5:21; Heb 4:15; 1Pe 2:22–23
—Completed what it pointed to .... Heb 8:5–6; Heb 9:11–15,23–28
—Bore its curse on the cross .... Gal 3:13
—Ended its burden .... Ro 7:4–6; Ro 10:1–5; Gal 3:24–25
—Gave us freedom from it .... Jn 8:31–36; Gal 5:1

6. Christians and the law of God
—Cannot keep it perfectly .... Ro 3:19–20,23; Ro 7:4–5
—Cannot be justified through it .... Ro 3:20,28; Gal 3:11
—Have met its requirements .... Ro 8:4
—Are free from its condemnation .... Ro 8:2
—Are free from its curse .... Gal 3:13–14
—Are free from its burden .... Gal 2:1–5; Gal 5:1
—Have it written on their hearts .... Heb 8:10–13
—Are under the law of Christ .... Jn 14:15; 1Co 9:21; Gal 6:2
—Must keep the law of love .... Jn 13:34–35; Ro 13:8–10; Gal 5:13–14; 1Jn 3:11–18
—Must keep the Ten Commandments .... Eph 6:2; Jas 2:8–11

7. The Spirit and the law
—Sets us free from it .... Ro 8:2,13; 2Co 3:17
—Enables us to keep its spirit .... Ro 7:6; 2Co 3:6; Gal 5:16–17,22–25

LAZARUS

A. Poor man in Jesus' parable .... Lk 16:19–31
B. Brother of Mary and Martha .... Jn 11:1
—Became sick and died .... Jn 11:2–15
—Raised from the dead .... Jn 11:38–44
—Present at a meal with Jesus .... Jn 12:2
—His resurrection caused a stir .... Jn 12:17–19

LEADER

A. Related themes
LEADERSHIP is a theme of:
—Ezra .... Ezr 7:10
—Nehemiah .... Ne 13:25
—1 Timothy 1Ti 4:6

B. Types of leaders
—Moses as God's chosen leader .... Nu 33:1; Mic 6:4
—Joshua as Moses' successor .... Dt 1:38; Jos 1:6
—Tribal leaders .... Nu 2:3,5,7,10; Nu 7:2
—Judges .... Jdg 4:4; Jdg 12:7–14
—Kings 1Sa 8:5–6,20; 1Ch 11:2; 2Ch 1:10
—Priests .... Ne 9:38
—The shepherds of Israel .... Jer 25:34–36
—Church officials .... Ac 15:22; Heb 13:7,17,24

C. Principles of leadership
1. Positive principles
—Depend on the Lord's strength .... Jos 1:6
—Obey the law of God .... Jos 1:7–8
—Use wisdom and knowledge from God .... 2Ch 1:10; Jer 3:15
—Exercise justice .... Mic 3:1–3
—Live an exemplary life 1Ti 4:12; 1Pe 5:3
—Serve the people selflessly .... Mt 20:26; Lk 22:26–27; 1Pe 5:2
—Govern diligently .... Ro 12:8

2. Negative principles
—Do not be rebellious against God .... Jer 2:8–9; Hos 9:15–17
—Do not lead the people astray .... Isa 3:12–15; Jer 23:30–32; 1Jn 3:7
—Do not be a poor example .... Ezr 9:1–2
—Do not exert power .... Mt 20:25–26; 1Pe 5:3
—Do not seek your own needs and wants first .... Eze 34:1–6; Am 5:11–13

See also KING; SHEPHERD

D. God as leader of his people
—God the Father as leader .... Ex 15:13; Dt 8:2,15; 2Ch 13:12; Ps 23:1–3; Ps 139:23–24
—Jesus the Son as leader .... Jn 10:2–3,10–14; Jn 13:12–15
—The Holy Spirit as leader .... Ro 8:14; Gal 5:18

LEAH

—Older daughter of Laban .... Ge 29:16
—First wife of Jacob .... Ge 29:22–27
—Not loved by Jacob .... Ge 29:31

—Bore six sons and one daughter ..... Ge 29:31 – 35
Ge 30:17 – 21
Ge 35:23
—Buried with Abraham and Sarah ..... Ge 49:31

LEAVEN
See YEAST

LEBANON
A. Location of Lebanon
—Northeast part of the promised land ..... Dt 11:24
Jos 13:5 – 6
—Land of mountains and valleys ..... Jos 12:7
Jdg 3:3
—Contained Mount Hermon ..... Jos 11:17
B. Importance of Lebanon to Israelites
—Never totally occupied by Israelites ..... Jos 13:5 – 6
—Its wood used in the first temple ..... 1Ki 5:6 – 10
—Its wood used in Solomon's palace ..... 1Ki 7:2 – 3
—Its wood used in the second temple ..... Ezr 3:7
C. Lebanon used as a symbol
—Of the majesty of the Creator ..... Ps 104:16
—Of the power of the Creator ..... Ps 29:4 – 6
—Of the fruitfulness of God's people ..... Ps 72:16
Ps 92:12 – 14
—Of the new world of the redeemed ..... Isa 35:1 – 2
Isa 60:13
—Of one's beauty and majesty ..... SS 3:6 – 9
SS 5:15
—Of the importance of the royal house ..... Jer 22:6 – 7
—Of the arrogance of humanity ..... Isa 2:12 – 18

LEGALISM
See FREEDOM

LEISURE
See REST

LEVI, LEVITE
A. Son of Jacob by Leah ..... Ge 35:23
1Ch 2:1
—Name means "attached" ..... Ge 29:34
—With Simeon, avenged rape of sister Dinah ..... Ge 34:25 – 31
—Went to Egypt with family ..... Ge 46:8,11
—Father of three sons ..... Ge 46:11
—Blessed by Jacob ..... Ge 49:5 – 7
B. Tribe descended from Levi
1. History of the tribe
—Moses and Aaron from that tribe ..... Ex 2:1
—Tribe blessed by Moses ..... Dt 33:8 – 11
—Tribe chosen to serve as priests ..... Nu 3:1—4:49
—Made ceremonially clean ..... Nu 8:5 – 26
—Numbered ..... Nu 3:39
Nu 26:62
—Allotted cities, but not land ..... Nu 18:20,24
Nu 35:1 – 5
—Allotted land ..... Eze 48:8 – 22
—One of the tribes of the 144,000 ..... Rev 7:7
2. Duties
—Belonged to the Lord ..... Nu 3:11 – 13
—Were Israel's religious leaders ..... Dt 10:8
—Were in charge of the tabernacle ..... Nu 1:50 – 53
Nu 4:1 – 33
—Assisted Aaron ..... Nu 3:5 – 9
Nu 18:1 – 7
—Prepared the sacrifices ..... 2Ch 35:10 – 14
Ezr 6:19 – 21
—Gathered tithes and offerings ..... Nu 18:20 – 24
Dt 18:1 – 2
Ne 10:37 – 39
—Served as judges of the people ..... Dt 17:8 – 9
1Ch 23:3 – 4
1Ch 26:29
—Recited the curses of God ..... Dt 27:14 – 26
—Supervised the work of the temple ..... 1Ch 23:3 – 4,28 – 32
1Ch 26:20 – 28
—Instructed the people in the law ..... Ne 8:7 – 9
—Some were gatekeepers ..... 1Ch 23:3 – 5
1Ch 26:1 – 19
—Some were musicians ..... 1Ch 23:3 – 5
1Ch 25:1 – 31
Ne 12:24,27 – 43
C. One of Jesus' disciples
See MATTHEW

LIFE
A. Related themes
1. LIFE is a theme of:
—John ..... Jn 3:16
—1 John 1Jn 5:20
2. LIFE'S PURPOSE is a theme of Ecclesiastes ..... Ecc 12:13
B. God and life
—God is a living God ..... Dt 5:26
Ps 42:2
1Th 1:9
—God has life in himself ..... Jn 5:26
—Jesus is the Living One ..... Rev 1:18
—Jesus is the life ..... Jn 11:25
Jn 14:6
1Jn 1:1 – 2
—Jesus has life in himself ..... Jn 1:4
—The Spirit of life ..... Ro 8:2
C. Physical life
1. Plant and animal life
—Created by God ..... Ge 1:11 – 12,20 – 25
Ps 104:24 – 25,30
—Preserved by God ..... Ps 104:21,24 – 28
Ps 145:15 – 16
Ps 147:8 – 9
2. Human life
—God is its source ..... Ge 2:7
Job 33:4
Isa 42:5
Ac 17:26,28
—God preserves it ..... Job 12:10
Ps 138:7
—God removes it as punishment for sin ..... Ge 3:19
Ro 5:12
—Human life should be reproduced ..... Ge 1:28
Ge 9:1,7
—Human life is fleeting and fragile ..... Job 20:4 – 11
Ps 90:3 – 10
Ps 103:14 – 16
—God's kingdom is more important ..... Mt 6:25 – 34
Mt 10:38 – 39
Jn 12:25
—Taking a human life is forbidden ..... Ge 9:5 – 6
Ex 20:13
Ro 13:9 – 10
D. Spiritual life
1. The source of spiritual life
—God, the Father ..... Eph 2:4 – 5
Col 2:13
—Jesus Christ, God's Son ..... Jn 1:4
Jn 10:10
Ac 3:15
—The Holy Spirit ..... Eze 37:14
Jn 3:5 – 6
Ro 8:2,11
—The word of God ..... Jas 1:18
1Pe 1:23

2. Phrases describing spiritual life
 —Being born again .... Jn 3:3 – 8
 —Being crucified with Christ .... Gal 2:20; Ro 6:8 – 10
 —Being raised with Christ .... Ro 6:4; Col 3:1 – 3
 —Being a new creation 2Co 5:17
 —Walking/living by the Spirit .... Gal 5:16,25
 —Having names in the book of life .... Lk 10:20; Php 4:3
 —Already having eternal life .... Jn 3:36; Jn 6:47; 1Jn 5:11 – 13
 —Not being subject to the second death .... Rev 20:6
3. How to obtain spiritual life
 —We must choose it .... Dt 30:19 – 20
 —We must hear the word of God .... Ac 16:14; Ro 10:13 – 14
 —We must be called by God .... 2Th 2:13 – 14
 —We must repent of our sins .... Ac 2:38
 —We must believe in Jesus .... Jn 3:15 – 16; Jn 20:31
4. Stages of spiritual life
 —The time of birth .... Jn 3:3 – 8; 1Pe 1:23
 —Being infants in Christ 1Co 3:1; 1Pe 2:2
 —Growth must take place .... Eph 4:14 – 16; Col 1:10; 1Pe 2:2
 —Becoming mature Christians .... 1Co 2:6; Eph 4:13; Heb 5:14 — 6:1; Jas 1:4
 —We must not slip back .... Php 3:13 – 16; Heb 5:12 – 14

See also GROWTH

E. Eternal life
1. How can we receive eternal life?
 —By being appointed to it by God .... Ac 13:48
 —By being called to it 1Ti 6:12
 —By reading the Scriptures .... Jn 5:39
 —By receiving it as a gift from God .... Ro 6:23
 —By receiving it as a gift from Jesus .... Jn 5:40; Jn 10:28
 —By taking hold of it 1Ti 6:12,19
 —By realizing Jesus is eternal life 1Jn 1:2; 1Jn 5:20
 —By believing in Jesus .... Jn 3:15 – 16
 —By trusting in Jesus .... Jn 14:1 – 3
 —By drinking of Jesus as water of life .... Jn 4:13 – 14
 —By eating of Jesus as bread of life .... Jn 6:48 – 51
 —By eating of the tree of life .... Ge 3:22; Rev 2:7
 —By dying with Christ 2Ti 2:11
 —By knowing God .... Jn 17:3
 —By being righteous .... Mt 25:46
 —By obeying the commands of God .... Jn 12:50
 —By pleasing the Spirit .... Gal 6:8
2. Eternal life begins now
 —We have eternal life .... Jn 3:36; Jn 5:24
 —We are already with Christ in heaven .... Eph 2:6; Col 3:3
3. Eternal life is still in the future
 —We have been promised it 1Ti 4:8
 —We have hope of it .... Tit 1:2; Tit 3:7
 —We will rise again to receive it .... Jn 5:28 – 29
 —We will receive it as a crown 1Pe 5:4
 —We will inherit it .... Mt 19:29
 —We will reap it .... Gal 6:8
 —We will reign in it .... Ro 5:17
 —Jesus will bring us to it .... Jude 21
 —We will someday be in paradise .... Lk 23:43; Rev 2:7

LIGHT

A. God and light
 —God is light 1Jn 1:5
 —He created light .... Ge 1:3; Isa 45:7
 —He is the Father of lights .... Jas 1:17
 —He lives in light .... Ps 104:2; 1Ti 6:16
 —Jesus reflects the Father's light .... Heb 1:3
 —Jesus is the light of the world .... Jn 1:9; Jn 8:12; Jn 9:5

B. God's word as a light
 —God's word is a light .... Ps 119:105; Pr 6:23; 2Pe 1:19
 —God's word gives light .... Ps 119:130
 —The gospel proclaims light .... Ac 26:18,23; 2Co 4:4
 —In God's light we see light .... Ps 19:8; Ps 36:9
 —God's light guides us .... Ps 43:3; Isa 51:4

C. Believers and the light of God
 —We are enlightened .... Heb 6:4; Heb 10:32
 —We are children of the light .... 1Th 5:5; Mt 5:14
 —We are called into God's light 1Pe 2:9
 —We confess that the Lord is our light .... Ps 27:1; Mic 7:8 – 9
 —We walk in the light .... Isa 2:5; 1Jn 1:5,7
 —Our path gets ever brighter .... Pr 4:18
 —We put on the armor of light .... Ro 13:12
 —We live as children of light .... Eph 5:8 – 11
 —We must be light to the world .... Mt 5:14 – 16; Php 2:15
 —We shall someday enter the kingdom of light .... Col 1:12 – 13
 —We look for a new heaven of only light .... Isa 60:19; Rev 21:23; Rev 22:5
 —We have no fellowship with darkness .... Lk 11:35; 2Co 6:14; Eph 5:11

See DARKNESS

LION

A. Lion stories in the Bible
 —Samson killed a lion .... Jdg 14:5 – 6
 —David killed a lion .... 1Sa 17:34 – 35
 —A lion killed a prophet 1Ki 13:24; 1Ki 20:36
 —Settlers in Samaria killed by lions .... 2Ki 17:25 – 26
 —Daniel in the lions' den .... Da 6:16 – 24

B. The lion as a symbol
1. Characteristics that stand out
 —Majestic .... Pr 30:29 – 30
 —Fierce .... Am 3:8
 —Stealthy .... Job 10:16
 —Mean when hungry .... Ps 17:12
2. As a symbol of evil
 —Of the devil 1Pe 5:8

—Of enemies attacking God's people .... Isa 5:29
—Of cruel rulers of the people .... Zep 3:3
—Of one's persecutors .... Ps 17:10–12
Ps 22:13,21
2Ti 4:17

3. As a symbol of God and good
—Of Christ, the triumphant Ruler .... Rev 5:5
—Of the protecting power of God .... Isa 31:4–5
—Of the anger of God against sin .... Hos 5:14
Hos 13:8
—Of the powerful Israelites .... Nu 24:9
—Of the tribe of Judah .... Ge 49:9
Mic 5:8
—Of the bravery of humans 2Sa 1:23
—Of the boldness of believers .... Pr 28:1
—Of the victory of believers .... Ps 91:13
—The lion lies peacefully with the lamb .... Isa 11:6–9
Isa 65:25

LORD

A. Human lords
—Used to refer to someone in authority .... Ge 44:16,18
2Sa 24:3
—Used as a title of respect .... Ge 23:15
Jdg 4:18
1Sa 1:15

B. God as the Lord
1. The God of Israel
—First revealed as LORD to Moses .... Ex 3:13–14
Ex 6:2–8
—Called the Lord of lords .... Dt 10:17
Ps 136:3
1Ti 6:15
—Reigns in majesty and strength .... Ps 93:1
Ps 96:6
—Expects trust and reverence as Lord .... Dt 28:58
Ps 96:4
Pt 3:5–6

2. Jesus as Lord
—The Lord Jesus Christ 2Co 13:14
2Th 1:2
—Our Lord Jesus Christ 1Th 5:9
Eph 6:24
—Jesus Christ our Lord 1Co 1:9
1Ti 1:2
—Designated Lord through his resurrection .... Ro 10:9
Php 2:8–11
—He is the Old Testament "LORD" .... Ac 2:21
Ro 10:13
2Ti 2:19
—He is Lord of all .... Ac 10:36
Ro 14:9
—He is the Lord of lords .... Rev 17:14
Rev 19:13–16
—He is the only Lord 1Co 8:6
Eph 4:5

3. Believers confess Jesus as Lord
—Confession of Thomas .... Jn 20:28
—Confession of early Christians .... Ac 2:36
1Co 1:2
1Co 12:3
Col 2:6
—Confession commanded of us .... Ro 10:9
Php 2:11

LORD'S SUPPER

—The sacramental meal of God's people

A. Titles for this feast
—The Lord's Supper 1Co 11:20
—The breaking of bread .... Ac 2:42
Ac 20:7
—Participation in body and blood of Christ 1Co 10:16

B. Celebration of this feast
—Commanded by Christ .... Lk 22:17–20
1Co 11:23–24
—Done frequently in the early church .... Ac 2:42,46–47
Ac 20:7,11
—Sometimes done in the wrong spirit 1Co 11:20–22

C. Purpose of this feast
—To remember the death of Christ .... Lk 22:19
1Co 11:24–25
—To symbolize Christ's body and blood .... Mt 26:26,28
Jn 6:51–56
1Co 10:16
—To participate in Christ's body and blood 1Co 10:16
—To proclaim the death of Christ 1Co 11:26
—To recall eating with the risen Lord .... Lk 24:30,35,41–43
Jn 21:13
Ac 1:4
—To introduce the new covenant .... Mt 26:28
1Co 11:25
—To have fellowship with one another .... Ac 2:42,46–47
1Co 10:16–17
—To anticipate Christ's return .... Mt 26:29
1Co 11:26

LOT

A. Nephew of Abram .... Ge 11:27
—Went with Abram to Canaan .... Ge 12:5
—Chose to live in Sodom .... Ge 13:5–12
—Rescued from four kings .... Ge 14:11–16
—Rescued from Sodom .... Ge 19:1–29
2Pe 2:7
—His wife killed while fleeing Sodom .... Ge 19:26
Lk 17:32
—Fathered Moab and Ammon by his daughters .... Ge 19:30–38

B. Casting the lot
See CASTING LOTS

LOVE

A. Related themes
LOVE is a theme of:
—Song of Songs .... SS 1:2
—Hosea .... Hos 2:23
—John .... Jn 15:9
—1 Corinthians 1Co 13:13
—1 John 1Jn 4:19

B. Human love
1. Love for God
a. Expressions of this love
—Expressed by the psalmist .... Ps 18:1
Ps 116:1
—Commanded in the Old Testament .... Dt 6:5
Ps 31:23
—The first and great commandment .... Mt 22:37–38

b. What we receive through this love
—God's love .... Ex 20:6
Ps 119:132
—God's protecting care .... Ps 91:14
Ps 145:20
Ro 8:28
—Blessing from God .... Dt 11:13–15
—A life of joy .... Ps 5:11
—Life in the promised land .... Ps 69:35–36
—The kingdom as inheritance .... Jas 2:5
—A crown of life .... Jas 1:12

c. What we do through this love
—Love others 1Jn 4:20–21
—Obey God's law .... Dt 13:3–4
1Jn 5:2–3
—Hate evil .... Ps 97:10

2. Love for Christ

a. Expressing this love

—Should be foremost in our lives ... Mt 10:37
—Should be a permanent love ... Eph 6:24
—Linked with faith in Christ ... 1Pe 1:8
—Linked with love for God ... Jn 8:42; 1Jn 5:1
—Linked with obedience to God ... Jn 14:21,23
—Expressed by loving others ... Mt 25:40

b. Results of this love

—Results in God's love for us ... Jn 14:21; Jn 16:27
—Results in a call to care for the church ... Jn 21:15 – 17
—Lack of such love strongly rebuked ... 1Co 16:22

3. Love for other Christians

a. The command for such love

—Commanded by God ... 1Jn 4:21; 2Jn 6
—Commanded by Jesus ... Jn 13:34 – 35; Jn 15:12,17; 1Jn 3:11,23
—Commanded by Paul ... Ro 12:9 – 10; Gal 5:13; Eph 5:2; Php 2:2 – 4; Col 3:14; 1Th 4:9 – 10; 1Ti 1:5
—Commanded in Hebrews ... Heb 10:24; Heb 13:1
—Commanded by Peter ... 1Pe 1:22; 1Pe 2:17; 1Pe 4:8; 2Pe 1:7
—Encouraged by John ... 1Jn 3:18; 1Jn 4:7,11 – 12; 2Jn 5
—We should pray for it to increase ... Php 1:9; 1Th 3:12

b. Expressions of this love

—An aspect of the fruit of the Spirit ... Gal 5:22; Col 1:8
—Linked with faith and hope ... 1Co 13:13; Col 1:4 – 5
—Expresses itself in self-sacrifice ... Jn 15:13; 1Co 13:4 – 7
—Involves concern for the weak ... Ro 14:1,13 – 16
—Involves caring for the needy ... 2Co 8:7 – 8; Phm 9 – 10
—No fear in such love ... 1Jn 4:18

c. Results of this love

—Demonstrates we are true disciples ... Jn 13:35
—Assures us of eternal life ... 1Jn 3:14 – 15
—Builds the church ... 1Co 8:1; Eph 4:15 – 16

4. Love for all humans

a. Love your neighbor as yourself

—Commanded in the Old Testament ... Lev 19:18
—Commanded by Jesus ... Mt 22:39
—Commanded by the apostles ... Ro 13:9; Gal 5:14; Jas 2:8

b. Love for strangers ... Lev 19:34; Dt 10:19; Heb 13:2

c. Do good to all humans ... Gal 6:10

d. Love even for enemies

—Commanded in the Old Testament ... Ex 23:4 – 5; Pr 25:21 – 22
—Commanded by Jesus ... Mt 5:43 – 45
—Commanded by Paul ... Ro 12:20 – 21
—Commanded by Peter ... 1Pe 3:9

5. The "song of love" ... 1Co 13

—Highest of all Christian virtues ... 1Co 13:13
—Everything valueless without it ... 1Co 13:1 – 3
—Central nature is selflessness ... 1Co 13:4 – 7
—Endures throughout eternity ... 1Co 13:8 – 13

C. Love of Christ

1. Love of Christ for the Father ... Jn 14:31

2. Love of Christ for his people

—His love for Mary, Martha, Lazarus ... Jn 11:3,5,36
—His love for his disciples ... Jn 13:1,34; Jn 15:9,12
—The disciple whom Jesus loved ... Jn 13:23; Jn 19:26; Jn 20:2; Jn 21:7,20
—His love for the church ... Eph 5:25
—His love expressed by his sacrifice ... Jn 15:13; Gal 2:20; Eph 5:2,25

3. Our relationship to this love

—We must realize how extensive it is ... Eph 3:17 – 19
—We must remain in it ... Jn 15:9 – 10
—Nothing can separate us from it ... Ro 8:35 – 37
—It motivates us to love others ... Jn 13:34; Jn 15:12; Eph 5:2
—It serves as a pattern for husbands ... Eph 5:25 – 28
—It motivates us to mission work ... 2Co 5:14

D. Love of God

1. God is love ... 1Jn 4:8,16

2. God loves the Son

—Prophesied in the Old Testament ... Isa 42:1; Mt 12:18
—Expressed at Jesus' baptism ... Mt 3:17
—Expressed at the transfiguration ... Mt 17:5; 2Pe 1:17
—Acknowledged by Jesus ... Jn 5:20; Jn 10:17; Jn 15:9 – 10; Jn 17:23 – 24,26

3. God loves the sinful world

—His love for the world stated ... Jn 3:16
—His love in spite of sin ... Ro 5:8; Tit 3:3 – 4
—His love expressed in sending his Son ... Jn 3:16; 1Jn 4:9 – 10

4. God expresses a special love for his people

—In his love for Jesus ... Jn 16:27; Jn 17:23
—In our election ... Eph 1:4; 1Th 1:4
—In our being called ... Ro 1:7; Jude 1
—In our receiving his grace ... 2Th 2:16
—In our adoption ... 1Jn 3:1
—In our salvation ... 2Th 2:13; Tit 3:4 – 5
—In our redemption ... Dt 7:8; Isa 63:9
—In our forgiveness ... Isa 38:17
—In our being made alive with Christ ... Eph 2:4 – 5
—In our receiving the Holy Spirit ... Ro 5:5
—In our being disciplined ... Heb 12:5 – 7
—In our obedience ... 1Jn 2:5
—In our love for others ... 1Jn 3:17; 1Jn 4:12
—In our receiving eternal life ... Jude 21

5. Our relationship to this love
—It is everlasting ... Jer 31:3
—We must be directed into it ... 2Th 3:5
—We must keep ourselves in it ... Jude 21
—Nothing can separate us from it ... Ro 8:35 – 39

LUKE
—The beloved doctor ... Col 4:14
—Co-worker with Paul ... 2Ti 4:11
Phm 24
—Likely a travel companion with Paul ... Ac 16:10 – 17
Ac 20:5—21:18
Ac 27:1—28:16

LUST
See SEXUAL STANDARDS

LYDIA
—Seller of cloth from Thyatira ... Ac 16:14
—Responded to Paul's preaching ... Ac 16:14
—Invited Paul to stay at her house in Philippi ... Ac 16:15
—Church met in her house ... Ac 16:40

LYING
—Misrepresenting or falsifying the truth
A. Perspectives on lying
—God does not lie ... Tit 1:2
—Denying that Jesus is the Christ is lying ... 1Jn 2:22
1Jn 5:10
—Hypocrites are liars ... Ps 62:4
1Jn 4:20
—The antichrist deceives humanity ... 2Th 2:9 – 10
—Satan is the father of lies ... Jn 8:44
Ac 13:10
—Lying will be exposed ... Pr 12:19
B. The prohibition against lying
—Ninth commandment prohibits lying ... Ex 20:16
Dt 5:20
—Other laws prohibit lying ... Lev 19:11
Eph 4:25
Col 3:9
—Lying is detestable to God ... Pr 6:16 – 17
—Pray to be kept from lying ... Pr 30:8
C. The punishment for lying
—Severe punishment for false witnesses ... Dt 19:16 – 19
Pr 19:5
—God silences liars ... Ps 63:11
—God punishes liars ... Ps 120:3 – 4
—God destroys liars ... Ps 5:6
Mic 6:12 – 13
—God excludes liars from heaven ... Rev 21:8,27
D. Examples of lying in the Bible
1. Sinful lying
—Satan in the Garden of Eden ... Ge 3:4
—Cain to God ... Ge 4:9
—Abram about Sarai ... Ge 12:10 – 20
—Sarah to God ... Ge 18:15
—Jacob to his father ... Ge 27:14 – 25
—Joseph's brothers to Jacob ... Ge 37:31 – 33
—Gibeonites to Joshua ... Jos 9:1 – 13
—Saul to Samuel ... 1Sa 15:1 – 3,13 – 22
—False witnesses about Naboth ... 1Ki 21:11 – 12
—Lying prophets to Ahab ... 1Ki 22:6,19 – 28
—Gehazi to Naaman ... 2Ki 5:20 – 24
—False prophets to the people ... Eze 13:1 – 9
—False witnesses about Jesus ... Mt 26:59 – 62
—Peter about Jesus ... Mt 26:69 – 74
—Ananias and Sapphira to God ... Ac 5:1 – 10
2. Lying with God's approval
—Midwives lie to spare babies ... Ex 1:15 – 21
—Rahab lies to save the spies ... Jos 2:1 – 14
—Ehud deceives King Eglon ... Jdg 3:15 – 18
—Jael deceives Sisera ... Jdg 4:17 – 21
Jdg 5:24 – 27
See also HYPOCRISY; TRUTH

MACEDONIA
—A Roman province, north of Achaia (Greece)
A. Paul in the main cities of Macedonia
—Paul's vision of man of Macedonia ... Ac 16:9
—Philippi ... Ac 16:12 – 40
—Thessalonica ... Ac 17:1 – 9
—Berea ... Ac 17:10 – 15
See also PAUL
B. Christians in Macedonia
—Suffered persecution ... Ac 17:5 – 8,13
1Th 1:6
—Were dedicated believers ... 1Th 1:7 – 10
2Co 8:1,5
—Were poor ... 2Co 8:1 – 2
—Gave generously to the poor ... Ro 15:25 – 26
2Co 8:2 – 4
—Helped Paul financially ... 2Co 11:7 – 9
Php 4:14 – 18

MACHPELAH
—Cave purchased by Abraham from Ephron ... Ge 23:7 – 18
—Sarah buried there ... Ge 23:19
—Abraham buried there ... Ge 25:9 – 10
—Isaac, Rebekah and Leah buried there ... Ge 49:29 – 31
—Jacob buried there ... Ge 50:12 – 13

MAGIC, WITCHCRAFT AND SORCERY
A. Terms used
—Divination ... Dt 18:10
—Sorcery ... Dt 18:10
—Interpreting omens ... Dt 18:10
—Witchcraft ... Dt 18:10
—Casting spells ... Dt 18:11
—Mediums and spiritists ... Dt 18:11
—Consulting the dead ... Dt 18:11
—Magic ... Eze 13:18,20
B. Purpose of magic and sorcery
—To determine the future ... Ge 44:15
1Sa 28:5 – 7
Da 2:2,27
—To control the future ... Ge 30:14
Nu 23:23
C. Warnings against magic and sorcery
—In the law ... Ex 22:18
Lev 19:26,31
Lev 20:6,27
Dt 18:10 – 12,20 – 21
—In the prophets ... Isa 2:6
Isa 47:10 – 14
Jer 27:9
Mic 5:12
Mal 3:5
—In the early church ... Ac 8:9 – 24
Ac 13:6 – 12
Ac 16:16 – 18
Ac 19:13 – 19
Gal 5:20
Rev 21:8

MANASSEH
A. Firstborn of Joseph ... Ge 41:51
Ge 46:20
—Name means "forget" ... Ge 41:51
—Blessed by Jacob, but not as firstborn ... Ge 48:12 – 20

B. Tribe descended from Manasseh
—Blessed by Moses .... Dt 33:17
—Numbered .... Nu 1:35
Nu 26:34
—Allotted land east of the Jordan .... Nu 32:33,39 – 42
Jos 13:8 – 33
—Allotted land west of the Jordan .... Jos 17:1 – 11
Eze 48:4
—Failed to fully possess the land .... Jos 17:12 – 13
Jdg 1:27
—One of the tribes of the 144,000 .... Rev 7:6
C. Son of Hezekiah; king of Judah 2Ki 20:21
2Ch 32:33
—Judah's most wicked king .... 2Ki 21:1 – 11
2Ch 33:1 – 10
—Captured by Assyrians 2Ch 33:11
—Repented of his sins .... 2Ch 33:12 – 13
—Began to clear land of idols .... 2Ch 33:15 – 16
—Judah exiled for his sins .... 2Ki 21:10 – 15

MARK

—Jewish name is John .... Ac 12:25
—A cousin of Barnabas .... Col 4:10
—A close friend of Peter 1Pe 5:13
—Believers gathered at his home to pray .... Ac 12:12
—Went to Antioch with Barnabas and Saul .... Ac 12:25
—Did mission work with Barnabas and Saul .... Ac 13:4 – 5
—Deserted Paul in Pamphylia .... Ac 15:37 – 38
—Returned with Barnabas to Cyprus .... Ac 15:39
—Later became fellow worker with Paul again .... Phm 24
2Ti 4:11

MARRIAGE

A. God and marriage
1. God honors marriage
—Established it in Garden of Eden .... Ge 2:18,21 – 24
—Command repeated in New Testament .... Mt 19:5
Eph 5:31
—Regulated it by Old Testament laws .... Lev 20:10 – 21
Nu 36:1 – 12
Dt 25:5 – 10
—Jesus attended a wedding .... Jn 2:1 – 2
—Marriage must be honored .... Mal 2:15
Heb 13:4
2. Monogamy versus polygamy
—Ideal is monogamy .... Ge 2:24
1Ti 3:2,12
—Polygamy practiced in Old Testament .... Ge 29:16 – 30
1Sa 1:1 – 2
1Sa 25:42 – 43
1Ki 11:1 – 3
—Polygamy often caused friction .... Ge 30:1
Lev 18:18
1Sa 1:3 – 8
3. Adultery
—In all cases forbidden .... Ex 20:14
Lev 18:20
—Excludes one from the kingdom of God .... Gal 5:19 – 21
1Co 6:9
See ADULTERY
4. Marriage with unbelievers forbidden
—In the Old Testament law .... Ex 34:15 – 16
Dt 7:3 – 4
—By Old Testament examples .... Jdg 16:4 – 21
1Ki 11:1 – 8
Ezr 9:1 – 5,10 – 15
Ne 13:23 – 27
—In the New Testament .... 1Co 7:12 – 16
2Co 6:14 – 18
5. Permanency of marriage
—Marriage is union for life .... Mt 19:3 – 6,9
Ro 7:2 – 3
1Co 7:39
—God hates divorce .... Mal 2:16
—Divorce allowed for hardness of heart .... Dt 24:1 – 4
Mt 19:7 – 8
See DIVORCE
B. Being single and being married
1. Remaining single is an option
—It is a gift from God .... 1Co 7:7 – 8
—It is preferable in times of crisis .... 1Co 7:25 – 28
—It frees one to serve God totally .... 1Co 7:32 – 35
2. Purposes of marriage
—To inspire human happiness .... Ge 2:18
—To express love intimately .... Pr 5:15 – 20
SS 2:3 – 7
SS 8:5 – 7
—To have children .... Ge 1:27 – 28
Mal 2:15
1Ti 5:14
—To prevent immorality .... 1Co 7:2,8 – 9
C. Weddings in the Bible
—The wedding of Isaac .... Ge 24:62 – 67
—The weddings of Jacob .... Ge 29:21 – 28
—The wedding of Samson .... Jdg 14:10 – 19
—The wedding of a king .... Ps 45:1 – 17
—Jesus at a wedding in Cana .... Jn 2:1 – 11
—Wedding parables of Jesus .... Mt 22:1 – 14
Mt 25:1 – 13
Lk 14:8 – 11
D. Duties of marriage partners
—Husband to love and respect his wife .... Eph 5:25
Col 3:19
1Pe 3:7
—Wife to submit to her husband .... Eph 5:22
Col 3:18
1Pe 3:1
—Equal responsibility .... 1Co 7:1 – 5,32 – 35
E. Marriage as a symbol
—God as the husband of Israel .... Isa 54:5
Jer 3:14
Hos 2:16,19 – 20
—Christ as the bridegroom of the church .... Mk 2:19 – 20
Jn 3:29
—Christ as the husband of the church 2Co 11:2
Eph 5:22 – 32
—Church as the bride of Christ .... Eph 5:22 – 24
Rev 21:2,9 – 10
—Heaven begins with a wedding .... Mt 22:1 – 10
Mt 25:1 – 10
Rev 19:7,9

MARTHA

—Sister of Mary and Lazarus .... Lk 10:38 – 39
Jn 11:1
—Kept busy in the kitchen .... Lk 10:40
—Rebuked by Jesus .... Lk 10:41 – 42
—Went to meet Jesus after Lazarus died .... Jn 11:20
—Confessed the resurrection .... Jn 11:20 – 27
—Objected to opening Lazarus's tomb .... Jn 11:38 – 40

MARY

A. Mother of Jesus .... Mt 1:16
—Angel announced her pregnancy .... Lk 1:26 – 38
—Visited cousin Elizabeth .... Lk 1:39 – 40
—Sang a song .... Lk 1:46 – 55
—Her virgin birth announced to Joseph .... Mt 1:18 – 25
—Gave birth to Jesus in Bethlehem .... Lk 2:1 – 7
—Presented Jesus in the temple .... Lk 2:21 – 24

—Fled with Joseph and baby to Egypt.......Mt 2:13 – 15
—Returned and settled in Nazareth.......Mt 2:19 – 23
—With twelve-year-old Jesus in temple.......Lk 2:41 – 52
—Had other children.......Mk 6:3
—Went to a wedding in Cana.......Jn 2:1 – 5
—Questioned Jesus' sanity.......Mk 3:21
—Observed Jesus' crucifixion.......Mt 27:55 – 56
—Entrusted to John at the cross.......Jn 19:25 – 27
—Among the disciples after ascension.......Ac 1:14

B. Mary Magdalene
—Former demoniac.......Lk 8:2
—Helped support Jesus' ministry.......Lk 8:1 – 3
—Present at the cross.......Mt 27:56; Mk 15:40
—Present at Jesus' burial.......Mt 27:61; Mk 15:47
—Went to the tomb early on Easter Sunday.......Mt 28:1
—Saw angel after the resurrection.......Mt 28:2 – 10; Mk 16:1 – 8
—Saw Jesus after the resurrection.......Mk 16:9; Jn 20:1 – 2,10 – 18

C. Sister of Martha and Lazarus
—Jesus visited them.......Lk 10:38 – 39
—Went to meet Jesus after Lazarus died.......Jn 11:28 – 32
—Listened to Jesus' teaching.......Lk 10:39
—Washed Jesus' feet.......Jn 11:2; Jn 12:1 – 8
—Commended by Jesus.......Mt 26:6 – 13; Lk 10:41 – 42

MATTHEW
—A disciple of Jesus.......Mt 10:3; Mk 3:18
—A tax collector, called by Jesus to follow him.......Mt 9:9
—Also called Levi.......Mk 2:14 – 17; Lk 5:27 – 32
—Held dinner for Jesus.......Mt 9:10 – 13
—One of the apostles.......Ac 1:13

MATTHIAS
—Apostle, chosen to replace Judas.......Ac 1:26

MEDES AND PERSIANS
A. Two related nations.......Est 1:14; Da 6:8,12,15; Da 8:20

B. Significance for God's people
—Northern kingdom deported there.......2Ki 17:6; 2Ki 18:11
—Defeated Babylonians.......Isa 13:17; Jer 51:11,28; Da 5:28,30 – 31
—Allowed Jews to rebuild temple.......2Ch 36:20 – 23

C. Kings of the Medes and Persians, in chronological order
—Darius the Mede.......Da 5:31
—Cyrus.......Ezr 1:1 – 2
—Darius the Persian.......Ezr 4:5,24
—Xerxes.......Est 1:1
—Artaxerxes.......Ezr 7:1; Ne 2:1

See entries for each individual king

MEDIATOR
—Someone who helps bring reconciliation between two parties

A. Related theme
MEDIATOR is a theme of Job.......Job 9:33

B. Human mediators at work
—Judah spoke to Joseph for Benjamin.......Ge 44:18 – 34
—Moses spoke to Pharaoh for the Israelites.......Ex 5:1 – 5
—Jonathan spoke to Saul for David.......1Sa 19:1 – 7
—Abigail spoke to David for her husband.......1Sa 25:14 – 35
—Esther spoke to the king for her people.......Est 7:1 – 6

C. Mediators between God and humans
1. The need for a mediator
—Israelites desired one at Mount Sinai.......Ex 20:18 – 19
—Job cried out for one.......Job 9:33
—Job knew one existed.......Job 16:19 – 21
—The task of a mediator.......1Sa 2:25; Job 33:23 – 25; Gal 3:20
2. Human mediators between God and his people
—Moses.......Ex 32:7 – 14; Nu 14:11 – 20; Dt 5:5; Gal 3:19
—Prophets.......1Ki 21:17 – 19; Jer 23:21 – 22; Da 9:3 – 19; Heb 1:1
—Priests.......Lev 16:20 – 21; Nu 6:22 – 27; Ezr 9:3 – 15
—Kings.......1Ki 8:22 – 53; 1Ch 21:16 – 17
3. Jesus as mediator between us and God
a. Described as a mediator
—Our mediator with God.......Heb 8:6; Heb 9:15; Heb 12:24
—The only mediator needed.......1Ti 2:5
b. His qualifications as a mediator
—He is fully God.......Jn 1:1; Heb 1:3; 1Jn 5:20
—He is fully human.......Jn 1:14; Php 2:6 – 8; Heb 2:14,17; 1Jn 4:2
c. His tasks as our mediator
—Isaiah prophesied Jesus' task.......Isa 53:3 – 12
—Reversed consequences of Adam's sin.......Ro 5:15 – 19; 1Co 15:21 – 22
—Reconciled us to God through death.......2Co 5:18 – 21; Col 1:21 – 22
—Intercedes with God on our behalf.......Jn 17:6 – 26; Ro 8:34; Heb 7:25; 1Jn 2:1
—Brings messages from God to us.......Jn 12:49 – 50; Heb 1:1 – 2

MEDITATION
—Reflecting on God and his word

A. On what are we to meditate?
—On God.......Ps 63:6
—On God's law.......Ps 1:2; Ps 119:15,48,97
—On God's promises.......Ps 119:148
—On God's unfailing love.......Ps 48:9
—On God's works.......Ps 77:12; Ps 143:5; Ps 145:5

B. What does meditation accomplish?
—Gives us a sense of peace.......Php 4:6 – 9
—Develops close relationship with God.......Ps 63:6 – 8
—Prepares us for important decisions.......Lk 6:12 – 13
—Gives us strength for Christian living.......Ps 1:2 – 3; 2Co 12:7 – 9
—Helps give us direction for life.......Ac 22:17 – 21

C. When did people meditate?
—In the morning .... Ps 5:1 – 3
Mk 1:35
—All day long .... Ps 119:97
—Day and night .... Jos 1:8
Ps 1:2
—In the evening .... Ge 24:63
—Through the watches of the night .... Ps 119:148

D. Examples of those who meditated
—Isaac .... Ge 24:63
—Psalmists .... Ps 48:9
Ps 119:48,97,148
Ps 143:5
—Jesus .... Mt 14:23
Mk 1:35
Lk 5:16
—Jesus' followers .... Ac 9:11 – 12
Ac 10:2,9 – 16
Ac 22:17 – 18

MEEKNESS

—The quality of a gentle spirit

A. Human meekness
1. Meekness is required of us
—A Christian quality .... Col 3:12
1Ti 6:11
—An aspect of the fruit of the Spirit .... Gal 5:22 – 23
—We must act with gentleness .... Eph 4:2
Php 4:5
1Pe 3:15
2. Meekness is a powerful force
—A gentle tongue is persuasive .... Pr 25:15
—A gentle answer turns away anger .... Pr 15:1
—A gentle spirit wins people to Christ .... 1Pe 3:1 – 4
3. The meek are blessed .... Ps 37:11
Mt 5:5

See also HUMILITY

B. God's meekness
—The gentle whisper of God 1Ki 19:12
—The meekness and gentleness of Christ .... Zec 9:9
Mt 21:5
2Co 10:1

MEGIDDO

—Its king defeated by Joshua .... Jos 12:21
—A city given to Manasseh .... Jos 17:11
—Manasseh did not conquer it .... Jdg 1:27
—Deborah and Barak fought there .... Jdg 5:19
—Solomon built it up 1Ki 9:15
—King Ahaziah died there 2Ki 9:27
—Josiah was killed there .... 2Ki 23:29 – 30
2Ch 35:20 – 27
—Final battle at Armageddon ("hill of Megiddo") .... Rev 16:14 – 16

MELCHIZEDEK

—King of Salem; priest of God Most High .... Ge 14:18
—Blessed Abram .... Ge 14:19 – 20
—Called a high priest forever .... Ps 110:4
—His priesthood prophetic of Jesus .... Heb 5:6
Heb 6:20
—His priesthood explained .... Heb 7:1 – 28

MENAHEM

—King of Israel .... 2Ki 15:17 – 22
—Assassinated Shallum to become king 2Ki 15:14
—Extremely cruel 2Ki 15:16

MEPHIBOSHETH

—Son of Jonathan 2Sa 4:4
—Shown kindness by David .... 2Sa 9:1 – 13
—Accused by Ziba of siding with Absalom .... 2Sa 16:1 – 4
—Explained his story to David .... 2Sa 19:24 – 30
—Spared from death 2Sa 21:7

MERCY

—Underserved kindness and compassion

A. Human mercy
1. The command to be merciful
—Be merciful .... Lk 6:36
Ro 12:8
Jude 22
—Mercy is more important than sacrifice .... Hos 6:6
Mic 6:6 – 8
Mt 9:13
2. Expressions of human mercy
—Being forgiving .... Mt 18:23 – 35
—Being kind to the hurting .... Lk 10:30 – 37
—Being kind to the poor .... Lk 16:19 – 26

B. The mercy of God
1. A part of his nature
—God is merciful .... Dt 4:31
Ne 9:31
Lk 6:36
—God exercises mercy freely .... Ex 33:19
Ro 9:15 – 18
—Mercy triumphs over judgment .... Jas 2:13
2. Expressions of his mercy
—Forgiving our sins .... Ps 51:1 – 2
Da 9:9
1Ti 1:13 – 16
—Saving us in Christ .... Eph 2:4 – 5
Tit 3:4 – 5
1Pe 1:3 – 4
—Being faithful to his covenant .... Dt 4:31
Dt 13:17 – 18
Ne 9:31
—Receiving us back to himself .... Jer 3:12 – 13
—Healing us when ill .... Php 2:27
—Sparing his own from destruction .... Ge 19:16
Ps 116:1 – 6
—Keeping us safe from the enemy .... Ps 6:9 – 10
Ps 28:6 – 7
3. Praying for God's mercy
—"Have mercy" .... Ps 4:1
Ps 9:13
—"Hear my cry for mercy" .... Ps 28:2
Ps 86:6
—"Remember your great mercy" .... Ps 25:6
—"Have mercy on me, a sinner" .... Lk 18:13
—"Have mercy on us, Son of David" .... Mt 9:27
Mt 20:30 – 31

See also GRACE; COMPASSION

MESHACH

—Hebrew deported to Babylon .... Da 1:1 – 6
—Name changed from Mishael .... Da 1:7
—Refused to be defiled by food .... Da 1:8 – 20
—Appointed administrator over Babylon .... Da 2:49
—Refused to worship idols .... Da 3:1 – 12
—Saved from the fiery furnace .... Da 3:13 – 30

MESSIAH

See JESUS CHRIST

METHUSELAH

—Son of Enoch, father of Lamech .... Ge 5:21 – 27
—Lived 969 years .... Ge 5:27

MICAIAH

—Prophet of the Lord .... 1Ki 22:7 – 8

—Warned Ahab of disaster 1Ki 22:9–28
2Ch 18:1–27

MICHAEL

—An archangel .... Jude 9
—Stood against the forces of evil .... Da 10:13,21
—Conducted war in heaven against Satan .... Rev 12:7

MICHAL

—Daughter of Saul 1Sa 14:49
—Became wife of David 1Sa 18:20–28
—Warned David of Saul's plot 1Sa 19:11–17
—Given by Saul to Paltiel 1Sa 25:44
—Retrieved by David 2Sa 3:13–16
—Criticized David for dancing before the ark 2Sa 6:16–23
1Ch 15:29

MIDIANITES

A. Their identity
—Descendants of Abraham through Keturah .... Ge 25:1–4
—Very wealthy .... Jdg 8:24–26
B. Important Midianites
—Jethro: priest of Midian .... Ex 3:1
—Zipporah: Moses' wife .... Ex 2:21
—Cozbi: killed for marrying an Israelite .... Nu 25:14–15
—Oreb and Zeeb: kings killed by Gideon .... Jdg 7:25–26
—Zeba and Zalmunna: kings killed by Gideon .... Jdg 8:12,21
C. Their interactions with God's people
—Brought Joseph to Egypt .... Ge 37:36
—Allied with Moabites against Israelites .... Nu 22:4,7
—Intermarried with the Israelites .... Nu 25:6
—Were considered enemies of Israel .... Nu 25:16–18
—Defeated by Moses .... Nu 31:1–12
—Oppressed the Israelites .... Jdg 6:1–6
—Defeated by Gideon .... Jdg 7:1–25

MILK

A. Sources of milk
—Cattle .... Dt 32:14
—Cows 2Sa 17:29
—Goats .... Pr 27:27
—Mothers .... Isa 28:9
B. Importance of milk
1. As a staple food
—For infants .... Isa 28:9
—For adults .... Ge 18:8
Jdg 4:19
2. As a figure of speech
—A land flowing with milk and honey .... Ex 3:8,17
Nu 16:13–14
Dt 6:3
—A special blessing from God .... Isa 7:21–22
—A symbol of whiteness .... Ge 49:12
—A symbol of a lover's charms .... SS 4:11
—A symbol of spiritual blessings .... Isa 55:1
Joel 3:17–18
—A symbol of instruction for the immature 1Co 3:1–2
Heb 5:12–13
—A symbol of pure doctrine 1Pe 2:2

MIND

A. What does the mind do?
1. Involved with the human will
—Can be made up 2Co 2:1
—Can make decisions 1Ch 12:38
—Can make plans 2Sa 7:1–3
—Can be willing to do things 1Ch 28:9
—Can give guidance .... Ecc 2:3
—Can sing and pray 1Co 14:15
—Can vacillate (double-minded) .... Jas 1:8
—Can change 2Ki 24:1
—Can plot evil .... Ps 83:5
2. Involved with human intelligence
—Can be opened .... Lk 24:45
—Can think .... Ne 5:7
—Can seek knowledge 1Ki 10:1–2
—Can understand .... Da 5:12
—Can remember .... Ge 37:11
—Can be made dull 2Co 3:14
—Can be blinded 2Co 4:4
—Can be closed .... Isa 44:18
3. Involved with human emotions
—The troubled mind .... Ge 41:8
—A disturbed mind .... Da 7:15
—The anxious mind .... Dt 28:65
—The doubting mind .... Lk 24:38
4. A person can be out of his or her mind .... Mk 3:21
Mk 5:3–5,15
Ac 26:24
2Co 5:13
B. The believer's mind
1. God and our minds
—God searches them .... Ps 7:9
Ps 26:2
—God tests them .... Jer 11:20
—God puts his law in them .... Jer 31:33
Heb 8:10
—God guards them .... Php 4:7
—Christ searches them .... Rev 2:23
—The Spirit shapes them .... Ro 8:5
—We have the mind of Christ 1Co 2:16
2. Our responsibility to our minds
—They must be made new .... Ro 12:2
Eph 4:23
—We must set them on things above .... Col 3:2
—We must prepare them to serve God 1Pe 1:13
—We must love God with all the mind .... Mt 22:37
Mk 12:30
Lk 10:27
—We must be of one mind as Christians .... Ac 4:32
1Co 1:10
2Co 13:11

MIRACLE

A. Related theme
MIRACLES is a theme of Exodus .... Ex 15:11
B. Words used to designate miracles
—Miracles .... Ex 7:9
Jn 7:21
—Signs .... Ex 4:8
Mt 12:38–39
—Wonders .... Dt 13:1–2
Jn 4:48
C. Purposes of miracles
1. In the Old Testament
—To demonstrate God is Lord .... Ex 9:14
1Ki 18:36–39
2Ki 5:8–15
—To designate God's messengers .... Ex 4:1–9
1Ki 17:17–24
2Ki 1:10,12
—To confirm one's faith .... Jdg 6:37–40
2Ki 2:13–14
—To deliver God's people .... Ex 14:21–30
Jos 10:12–14
—To care for God's people .... Ex 17:1–6
Nu 11:31–32
—To care for the needy 1Ki 17:10–16
2Ki 4:1–7
—To punish sinners .... Ge 19:24–26
Nu 16:28–35

2. In the life of Jesus
—To show compassion ..... Mt 14:14
Mt 15:32
—To prove he was God ..... Mk 2:8–12
Jn 20:30–31
—To prove he was the Messiah ..... Mt 11:2–5
Jn 5:36
—To demonstrate the kingdom of God ..... Lk 11:20
Jn 10:37–38
—To secure redemption of believers ..... Ro 4:25
1Co 15:17–20
—Not to dazzle crowds ..... Mt 16:1–4
Lk 23:8–9

3. In the early church
—To demonstrate Jesus is Savior and Lord ..... Ac 4:8–12
Ac 14:3
—To lead people to faith ..... Ac 13:12
Ac 9:42
—To advance the gospel ..... Ac 12:1–11
Ac 16:16–18
—To show compassion ..... Ac 9:32–41
Ac 20:9–10
—To judge sinners ..... Ac 5:1–11
Ac 13:8–11

D. People who performed miracles
—Moses and Aaron ..... Ex 7:8–21
Ps 105:26–27
—Joshua ..... Jos 3:9–17
Jos 10:12–14
—A prophet of Judah 1Ki 13:4–6
—Elijah 1Ki 17:15–23
1Ki 18:30–38
—Elisha 2Ki 2:19–22
2Ki 4:1–7
—Isaiah 2Ki 20:7–11
—Daniel's three friends ..... Da 3:19–27
—Daniel ..... Da 6:16–24
—Jesus ..... Mt 4:23–24
Jn 20:30–31
—The seventy-two sent out by Jesus ..... Lk 10:9,17
—The apostles as a group ..... Ac 2:43
Ac 5:12
—Peter ..... Ac 3:1–7
Ac 5:15–16
—Stephen ..... Ac 6:8
—Philip ..... Ac 8:6–7,13
—Paul and Barnabas ..... Ac 14:3
—Paul ..... Ac 14:8–10
Ac 19:11–12
—One of the gifts given to the church 1Co 12:10,29
Gal 3:5

E. Miracles of Jesus
—Turned water into wine ..... Jn 2:1–11
—Healed official's son at Capernaum ..... Jn 4:43–65
—Cast out demon in Capernaum ..... Mk 1:23–26
Lk 4:33–35
—Healed Peter's mother-in-law ..... Mt 8:14–17
Mk 1:29–31
Lk 4:38–39
—Healed leper ..... Mt 8:2–4
Mk 1:40–45
Lk 5:12–13
—Net full of fish ..... Lk 5:4–11
—Healed paralytic ..... Mt 9:1–8
Mk 2:1–12
Lk 5:18–25
—Healed crippled man ..... Jn 5:1–9
—Healed shriveled hand ..... Mt 12:10–13
Mk 3:1–5
Lk 6:6–10
—Healed centurion's servant ..... Mt 8:5–13
Lk 7:1–10
—Raised widow's son ..... Lk 7:11–17
—Cast out demon ..... Mt 12:22–23
Lk 11:14
—Stilled a storm ..... Mt 8:23–27
Mk 4:37–41
Lk 8:22–25
—Cast out demons in Gerasenes ..... Mt 8:28–34
Mk 5:1–20
Lk 8:27–35
—Healed woman's bleeding and raised Jairus's daughter ..... Mt 9:18–26
Mk 5:21–43
Lk 8:26–41
—Healed two blind men ..... Mt 9:27–31
—Healed mute man ..... Mt 9:32–33
—Fed five thousand ..... Mt 14:15–21
Mk 6:35–44
Lk 9:12–17
Jn 6:5–13
—Walked on water ..... Mt 14:25–33
Mk 6:48–52
Jn 6:19–21
—Healed Canaanite woman's daughter ..... Mt 15:21–28
Mk 7:24–30
—Fed four thousand ..... Mt 15:32–39
Mk 8:1–9
—Healed deaf man ..... Mk 7:31–37
—Healed blind man at Bethsaida ..... Mk 8:22–26
—Cast demon out of boy ..... Mt 17:14–18
Mk 9:14–29
Lk 9:38–43
—Provided temple tax from fish's mouth ..... Mt 17:24–27
—Healed ten lepers ..... Lk 17:11–19
—Healed man born blind ..... Jn 9:1–7
—Raised Lazarus ..... Jn 11:1–44
—Healed crippled woman ..... Lk 13:11–17
—Healed man with dropsy ..... Lk 14:1–6
—Healed two blind men ..... Mt 20:29–34
Mk 10:46–52
Lk 18:35–43
—Cursed a fig tree ..... Mt 21:18–22
Mk 11:12–14
—Healed Malchus's ear ..... Lk 22:50–51
—Helped disciples catch 153 fish ..... Jn 21:1–14

F. Counterfeit miracles
—Performed by Egyptian magicians ..... Ex 7:11,22
—Performed by Simon the sorcerer ..... Ac 8:9–11
—Performed by false prophets ..... Dt 13:1–3
Mt 24:24
—Performed by the antichrist 2Th 2:9
Rev 13:13
Rev 19:20

MIRIAM

—Sister of Moses and Aaron ..... Nu 26:59
—Watched over baby Moses ..... Ex 2:3–4
—Arranged for Moses' mother to care for Moses ..... Ex 2:5–10
—Led dancing at Red Sea ..... Ex 15:20–21
—Criticized Moses; struck with leprosy ..... Nu 12:1–15
—Her death ..... Nu 20:1

MISSION

—Being sent out on a task
A. Related themes
WORLDWIDE MISSION is a theme of:
—Matthew ..... Mt 21:43
—Acts ..... Ac 28:14
—Romans ..... Ro 15:19

B. Examples of those sent by God on a mission
1. People
—Abram ... Ge 12:1–3
—Joseph ... Ge 45:5–7; Ps 105:17
—Moses ... Ex 3:10,14
—Moses and Aaron ... Ps 105:26
—Isaiah ... Isa 6:8
—Jeremiah ... Jer 26:16
—Ezekiel ... Eze 3:4–5
—Amos ... Am 7:14–15
—Jonah ... Jnh 1:1–2; Jnh 3:1–2
—Haggai ... Hag 1:12
—Zechariah ... Zec 2:9,11
—Prophets in general ... Jer 7:25; Jer 25:4; Zec 7:12
—John the Baptist ... Mal 3:1; Mk 1:2
—The twelve disciples ... Mt 10:1–10
—The seventy-two messengers ... Lk 10:1–7
—The apostles as missionaries ... Mt 28:19–20; Jn 17:18; Jn 20:21; Ac 13:4; Ac 22:21; Gal 1:1
2. Jesus, God's Son ... Lk 4:18–19; Jn 17:3; Gal 4:4–6
3. The Holy Spirit ... Jn 14:26; Jn 15:26
4. The angels
—To Abraham's servant ... Ge 24:7,40
—To the Israelites ... Ex 23:20–23
—To the inhabitants of Jerusalem ... 1Ch 21:15–18
—To God's people in general ... Ps 91:11
—To Daniel's three friends ... Da 3:28
—To Daniel ... Da 6:22
—To Mary ... Lk 1:26–38
—To Peter ... Ac 12:6–11
—To all of us ... Heb 1:14

C. For what purpose were they sent?
1. Jesus' unique mission
—To atone for sin ... Mk 10:45; Gal 4:4–5; 1Jn 4:9–10
—To preach and to heal ... Mt 9:35–36; Lk 4:18–21
2. Leaders, prophets and missionaries
—To lead God's people ... 1Sa 12:8
—To prepare the way before the Lord ... Mal 3:1; Mt 11:10
—To bring a message of redemption ... Isa 61:1; Jnh 1:1–2; Mk 3:14; Mt 28:19–20; Ro 10:13–15; 1Co 1:17
—To call the people to repent ... Jer 35:15; Jer 42:21
—To heal hurting people ... Isa 61:1–3; Mt 10:8
—To warn God's people ... Jer 26:15; Eze 3:18–21
—To pronounce judgment ... Jer 26:12; Eze 2:3–8; Mt 23:33–36
3. Angels
See ANGEL

MOABITES

A. Their identity
—Descendants of Moab, son of Lot ... Ge 19:37
—Related to Ammonites ... Ge 19:36–38
—Held land east of the Jordan ... Nu 33:48–49; Dt 2:9
—Served the god Chemosh ... 1Ki 11:7

B. Important Moabites
—Balak: hired Balaam to curse Israelites ... Nu 22:2—24:25
—Eglon: killed by Ehud ... Jdg 3:12,15–23
—Ruth: married Boaz ... Ru 1:22
See RUTH

C. Their wars against Israelites
—Allied with Midianites against Israel ... Nu 22:4,7
—Allied with Ammonites against Israel ... Jdg 3:12–13
—Defeated by Israelites under Ehud ... Jdg 3:28–30
—Defeated by King Saul ... 1Sa 14:47
—Defeated by David ... 2Sa 8:11–12; 1Ch 18:11
—Rebelled against Israel ... 2Ki 3:5
—Defeated by Joram and Jehoshaphat ... 2Ki 3:6–25
—Allied with Ammonites against Judah ... 2Ch 20:1
—They and Ammonites destroyed each other ... 2Ch 20:22–24
—Raided the land of Israel ... 2Ki 13:20
—Allied against Jehoiakim ... 2Ki 24:1–2

D. Important data concerning them
1. Before the time of the kings
—Intermarried with Israelites ... Nu 25:1–3
—Israelites did not pass through Moab ... Jdg 11:17–18
—Not allowed to join Israelites ... Dt 23:3; Ne 13:1–3
—Moses died on Mount Pisgah in Moab ... Dt 34:1–5
—Elimelech and Naomi lived there ... Ru 1:1–5
2. During the time of the kings
—David brought his parents there ... 1Sa 22:3–4
—Solomon intermarried with them ... 1Ki 11:1
—Israelites worshiped their gods ... 1Ki 11:7
—Paid tribute to Ahab ... 2Ki 3:4
3. Numerous Jews intermarried with them ... Ezr 9:1; Ne 13:23–27
4. Prophecies concerning their destruction ... Isa 15:1—16:14; Jer 48:1–47; Eze 25:8–11; Am 2:1–3; Zep 2:8–11

MONEY

See THE RICH AND THE POOR; STEWARDSHIP

MONTH

—Twelve time segments per year, based on the moon
—Abib or Nisan, the first month ... Ex 13:4; Ne 2:1
—Ziv or Iyyar, the second month ... 1Ki 6:1
—Sivan, the third month ... Est 8:9
—Tammuz, the fourth month ... Jer 52:6
—Ab, the fifth month ... Nu 33:38
—Elul, the sixth month ... Ne 6:15
—Ethanim or Tishri, the seventh month ... 1Ki 8:2
—Bul or Heshvan, the eighth month ... 1Ki 6:38
—Kislev, the ninth month ... Zec 7:1
—Tebeth, the tenth month ... Est 2:16
—Shebat, the eleventh month ... Zec 1:7
—Adar, the twelfth month ... Ezr 6:15

MOON

A. Data concerning the moon
—Created by God ... Ge 1:16; Ps 8:3

—Controlled by God .... Jos 10:12 – 13; Jer 31:35
—Governs the night .... Ge 1:16; Ps 136:9
—Marks off the seasons .... Ge 1:14; Ps 104:19
—New Moon festivals .... Nu 10:10; 1Sa 20:5,18,24; Am 8:5
—Involved in the blessing of productive land .... Dt 33:13 – 14
—Must praise God .... Ps 148:3
—Believed to cause mental illness .... Ps 121:6
—Worshiped by the heathen .... 2Ki 23:5; Jer 8:2
—No moon needed in heaven .... Isa 60:19 – 20; Rev 21:23

B. The moon used in a symbolic way
—Of stability and endurance .... Ps 72:5,7
—Of judgment at the end of time .... Isa 13:10 – 11; Mt 24:29; Rev 6:12

MORDECAI

—Benjamite exile who brought up Esther .... Est 2:5 – 10
—Exposed plot to kill Xerxes .... Est 2:19 – 23
—Refused to honor Haman .... Est 3:1 – 6; Est 5:9 – 14
—Pole made to impale him .... Est 5:14
—Begged Esther to foil Haman's plot .... Est 4:1 – 17
—Haman forced to honor him .... Est 6:1 – 11
—Exalted by the king .... Est 8:1 – 2,15; Est 9:3 – 4
—With Esther, established Purim .... Est 9:18 – 32

MORIAH

—Region where Abraham went to "sacrifice" Isaac .... Ge 22:1 – 18
—Mountain on which temple was built .... 2Ch 3:1 – 2

MOSES

A. Family data
—Son of Amram and Jochebed .... Ex 6:20; 1Ch 6:3
—Tribe of Levi .... Ex 2:1
—Brother of Aaron .... Ex 4:14
—Name means "draw out" .... Ex 2:10
—Married Zipporah .... Ex 2:21
—Father of Gershom and Eliezer .... Ex 2:22; Ex 18:2 – 4

B. His history
1. His youth
—Hid by his parents for three months .... Ex 2:2; Heb 11:23
—Hid in a basket in the Nile .... Ex 2:3 – 4
—Discovered by Pharaoh's daughter .... Ex 2:5 – 9
—Brought up by Pharaoh's daughter .... Ex 2:10
—Killed an Egyptian .... Ex 2:11 – 12
—Fled to Midian .... Ex 2:13 – 15
—Became a shepherd .... Ex 3:1
2. Delivered Israel from Egypt
—Called by God .... Ex 3:2—4:17
—Explained his call to Israelites .... Ex 4:29 – 31
—Made demands to Pharaoh .... Ex 5:1 – 5
—The ten plagues .... Ex 7:14—11:9
—Arranged the Passover .... Ex 12:1 – 28
—Led Israelites out of Egypt .... Ex 12:29 – 42
—Led them to the border of the Red Sea .... Ex 13:17—14:4
—Led them across the Red Sea .... Ex 14:21 – 31
—Sang song of deliverance .... Ex 15:1 – 21
3. Led Israel to Mount Sinai
—Water at Marah and Elim .... Ex 15:22 – 27
—Asked God for food; received manna .... Ex 16:1 – 16
—Brought water from the rock .... Ex 17:1 – 7
—Raised hands to defeat Amalekites .... Ex 17:8 – 16
—Delegated judges .... Ex 18:13 – 27; Dt 1:9 – 18
—Received law at Mount Sinai .... Ex 19:3 – 25; Ex 24:12 – 18; Jn 1:17
—Announced law to Israel .... Ex 24:3 – 7
—Broke tablets because of golden calf .... Ex 32:19 – 20; Dt 9:7 – 17
—Received law a second time .... Ex 34:1 – 4,27 – 28
—Saw glory of the Lord .... Ex 33:18 – 23
—His face reflected glory of God .... Ex 34:29 – 35
—Supervised building of tabernacle .... Ex 35:4—36:7
—Set apart Aaron and priests .... Lev 8:1—9:24
—Numbered tribes .... Nu 1:1—4:49
4. From Sinai to the border of Canaan
—Left Sinai .... Nu 10:11 – 13
—Handled the people's complaints .... Nu 11:1 – 34
—Opposed by Aaron and Miriam .... Nu 12:1 – 15
—Sent spies into Canaan .... Nu 13:1 – 33
—Prayed for the rebellious people .... Nu 14:1 – 25
—Announced forty years of wandering .... Nu 14:26 – 40
—Opposed by Korah .... Nu 16:1 – 50
—Struck rock; forbidden to enter Canaan .... Nu 20:1 – 13; Dt 1:37
—Put bronze snake on a pole for healing .... Nu 21:4 – 9; Jn 3:14
—Defeated kings in battle .... Nu 21:1 – 3,21 – 31
—Numbered tribes a second time .... Nu 26:1 – 65
—Designated Joshua as successor .... Nu 27:12 – 23; Dt 34:9
—Gave final address (Deuteronomy) .... Dt 1:5
—Sang a song .... Dt 31:30—32:43
—Blessed the twelve tribes .... Dt 33:1 – 29
—Saw the promised land .... Dt 34:1 – 4
—His death .... Dt 34:5 – 8

C. Titles ascribed to him
—The man of God .... Ezr 3:2
—God's chosen one .... Ps 106:23
—The servant of God .... 2Ch 24:6,9; Ps 105:26
—The lawgiver .... Jn 1:17
—Prophet of the Lord .... Dt 18:15,18
—Intimate friend of God .... Ex 33:11
—Leader of God's people .... Mic 6:4
—Shepherd of God's people .... Ps 77:20

D. Moses in the New Testament
—Appeared to Jesus at the transfiguration .... Mt 17:2 – 4
—Respected for giving the Law .... Mt 19:7 – 8; Jn 7:19,23
—Exemplified true faith .... Heb 11:24 – 28
—Foreshadowed Jesus as the Prophet .... Ac 3:21 – 23
—His writings prophetic of Jesus .... Jn 1:45
—His lifting up of snake pictured Jesus' death .... Jn 3:14 – 15
—Crossing the Red Sea pictured baptism .... 1Co 10:1 – 2
—His veil symbolized the old covenant .... 2Co 3:7 – 16
—His faithfulness foreshadowed that of Jesus .... Heb 3:1 – 6
—God, not Moses, gave manna .... Jn 6:30 – 33

MOTHER

A. Motherhood in the Bible
1. The experience of motherhood
—It is a gift from God .... Ps 113:9; Ps 127:3
—It can be painful .... Ge 3:16; Isa 13:8; Jn 16:21

—Infertility can cause frustration ... Ge 25:21
Ge 30:1
1Sa 1:1 – 20
2. Women saved through childbearing ... 1Ti 2:15
3. Significant experiences of motherhood
—Eve, the mother of the living ... Ge 3:20
Ge 4:1 – 2,25
—Sarah ... Ge 21:1 – 5
—Rebekah ... Ge 25:21 – 26
—Leah ... Ge 29:31 – 35
Ge 30:17 – 21
—Rachel ... Ge 30:1 – 8,22 – 23
Ge 35:16 – 18
—Jochabed (Moses' mother) ... Ex 2:1 – 10
—Samson's mother ... Jdg 13:1 – 24
—Ruth ... Ru 4:13 – 15
—Hannah ... 1Sa 1:1 – 20
—Bathsheba ... 2Sa 12:24 – 25
—Isaiah's wife ... Isa 8:3 – 4
—Hosea's wife ... Hos 1:2 – 9
—Elizabeth ... Lk 1:24 – 25,39 – 44
—The virgin Mary ... Lk 1:26 – 38
Lk 2:4 – 7

B. The mother in the family
1. Duties of a mother to her children
—Loves them ... 1Ki 3:26
Isa 49:15
—Comforts and cares for them ... Ru 4:16
Isa 66:13
1Th 2:13
—Protects them ... Ex 2:1 – 3
Heb 11:23
—With their husbands, educates them ... Pr 1:8
Pr 31:1,26
—Educates them alone, if necessary ... 2Ti 1:5
2Ti 3:15
—Watches over their affairs ... Ge 27:5 – 17
1Ki 1:11 – 31
Pr 31:15,27
2. Responsibility of children to mothers
—Obey them ... Dt 21:18
Eph 6:1 – 2
—Respect them ... Ex 20:12
Lev 19:3
Pr 23:22
—Listen to them ... Pr 1:8
Pr 6:20

C. Mother used as a symbol
—God compared to a mother ... Isa 49:15
Isa 66:13
—The church as mother ... Isa 66:10 – 11
Gal 4:26

MOUNTAIN

A. Mountains mentioned in the Bible
—Mount Ararat ... Ge 8:4
—Mount Baalah ... Jos 15:11
—Mount Carmel ... 1Ki 18:19
—Mount Ebal ... Dt 11:29
—Mount Ephron ... Jos 15:9
—Mount Gaash ... Jos 24:30
—Mount Gerizim ... Dt 11:29
—Mount Gilboa ... 1Sa 31:1
—Mount Gilead ... Jdg 7:3
—Mount Halak ... Jos 11:17
—Mount Heres ... Jdg 1:35
—Mount Hermon ... Dt 3:8
—Mount Hor ... Nu 20:22
—Mount Horeb ... Ex 33:6
—Mount Jearim ... Jos 15:10
—Mount Mizar ... Ps 42:6
—Mount Moriah ... 2Ch 3:1
—Mount Nebo ... Dt 32:49
—Mount of Olives ... Zec 14:4
See OLIVES, MOUNT OF
—Mount Paran ... Dt 33:2
—Mount Perazim ... Isa 28:21
—Mount Pisgah ... Jos 12:3
—Mount Samaria ... Am 4:1
—Mount Seir ... Dt 1:2
—Mount Shepher ... Nu 33:23
—Mount Sinai ... Ex 19:11
See SINAI
—Mount Sirion ... Dt 4:48
—Mount Tabor ... Jdg 4:6
—Mount Zalmon ... Jdg 9:48
—Mount Zemaraim ... 2Ch 13:4
—Mount Zion ... Ps 48:2
See ZION

B. Mountains used in illustrations
—Of God's creative power ... Am 4:13
—Of God's continuing power ... Ps 65:5 – 7
—Of God's redemptive power ... Isa 40:4 – 5
—Of the power of God's judgment ... Rev 6:14 – 16
—Of God's righteousness ... Ps 36:6
—Of God's glory in the new age ... Isa 2:2 – 3
—Of prosperity for God's people ... Ps 72:3
Am 9:13
—Of the strength of human faith ... Mt 17:20 – 21
—Of the joy of the redeemed ... Isa 44:23

MOUTH

A. The human mouth
1. Appropriate functions of our mouths
—To praise God ... Ps 63:5
—To sing to the Lord ... Ps 40:3
—To testify concerning God ... Ps 89:1
—To confess Jesus as Lord ... Ro 10:9 – 10
—To reveal God's word ... Dt 18:18
—To reveal what is in the heart ... Mt 12:34 – 35
—To speak words ... Ps 19:14
—To laugh with joy ... Ps 126:2
—To eat ... 1Sa 14:26 – 27
—To drink ... Jdg 7:6
—To kiss ... SS 1:2
2. Responsibilities to our mouths
a. Negative
—Keep them from sin ... Ecc 5:6
—Keep them from perversity ... Pr 4:24
—Keep them from flattery ... Pr 26:28
—Keep them from arrogance ... 1Sa 2:3
—Keep them from lies ... Rev 14:5
—Keep them from unwholesome talk ... Eph 4:29
—Keep them from cursing ... Jas 3:9 – 10
b. Positive
—Speak what is true and just ... Pr 8:7 – 8
—Speak what is wise ... Ps 37:30
—Guide them properly ... Pr 16:23
—Guard them properly ... Pr 21:23

B. The mouth of God
—God created with his mouth ... Ps 33:6
—God gave his law with his mouth ... Ps 119:13,72
—God gives promises with his mouth ... Isa 40:3 – 5
—God teaches with his mouth ... Dt 8:3
—God pronounces judgment with his mouth ... Isa 1:20
—God rejects by spitting us out of his mouth ... Rev 3:16
—God destroys with his mouth ... Ps 18:8
—Jesus destroys with a sword in his mouth ... Rev 2:16
Rev 19:15

MURDER

—The deliberate killing of another human

A. The command against murder
- —The sixth commandment .... Ex 20:13; Dt 5:17; Jas 2:10 – 11
- —Anger as the root of murder .... Mt 5:21 – 22
- —Hatred as the root of murder 1Jn 3:15
- —Murder comes out of a sinful heart .... Mt 15:18 – 19

B. What happens after a murder
- —One can be cursed by God .... Ge 4:11
- —One can be excluded from heaven .... 1Jn 3:15; Rev 22:15
- —One is subject to capital punishment .... Ge 9:5 – 6; Ex 21:12 – 14,23
- —More than one witness required .... Nu 35:30; Dt 19:15
- —Cities of refuge in Israel .... Nu 35:16 – 32; Dt 19:1 – 14
- —Murderers can be forgiven .... Lk 23:34; Ac 7:60

C. Examples of murder in the Bible
- —Cain killed Abel .... Ge 4:8
- —Moses killed an Egyptian .... Ex 2:11 – 12
- —Abimelech killed his brothers .... Jdg 9:5
- —David killed Uriah 2Sa 12:9
- —Absalom killed Amnon .... 2Sa 13:28 – 33
- —Jezebel killed Naboth .... 1Ki 21:8 – 14
- —Hazael killed Ben-Hadad .... 2Ki 8:14 – 15
- —Athaliah killed the royal family 2Ki 11:1
- —Herod killed the babies in Bethlehem .... Mt 2:16
- —Herod killed John the Baptist .... Mt 14:6 – 11
- —The Jews killed Jesus .... Ac 2:23; 1Th 2:15
- —The Jews killed Stephen .... Ac 7:57 – 60
- —Herod killed James .... Ac 12:2

MUSIC AND SONG

A. Related theme
- MUSIC is a theme of 2 Chronicles 2Ch 5:13

B. Musical instruments
1. Begun by Jubal .... Ge 4:21
2. Types of instruments in the Bible
   - —Bells .... Ex 28:33 – 35
   - —Castanets 2Sa 6:5
   - —Cymbals 2Sa 6:5
   - —Harp 1Ch 25:3
   - —Flute .... Da 3:5,7,10,15
   - —Horn .... Da 3:5,7,10,15
   - —Lyre 2Sa 6:5
   - —Pipe .... Da 3:5,10,15
   - —Sistrum 2Sa 6:5
   - —Timbrel 2Sa 6:5
   - —Trumpet .... Nu 10:2
   - —Zither .... Da 3:5,10,15
3. Used in Israelite worship
   - —Organized by David 1Ch 25:1,6; 2Ch 7:6
   - —Mentioned in the psalms .... Ps 47:6; Ps 98:5 – 6; Ps 150:4 – 5
4. Used when Jesus returns 1Co 15:52; 1Th 4:16

C. Songs
1. In the Old Testament
   a. Occasions for singing
      - —In sacred processions 2Sa 6:5; 1Ch 13:8
      - —At dedications .... 2Ch 5:12 – 13; Ezr 3:10 – 11; Ne 12:27 – 28,40
      - —On feast days 2Ch 30:21
      - —At coronations 2Ch 23:13
      - —To celebrate victories .... Ex 15:1 – 18; Nu 21:17; Jdg 5:1 – 31
   b. The psalmist's intention to sing .... Ps 27:6; Ps 57:7,9; Ps 61:8; Ps 101:1; Ps 104:33
   c. Instructions to sing .... Ps 30:4; Ps 68:32; Ps 98:1; Ps 149:1
   d. All creation should sing .... Ps 148:1 – 12; Isa 44:23; Isa 49:13
2. In the New Testament
   - —Songs at the birth of Jesus .... Lk 1:46 – 55,68 – 79; Lk 2:14,29 – 32
   - —Songs in the worshiping church .... 1Co 14:15; Eph 5:19; Col 3:16; Jas 5:13
   - —Songs in heaven .... Rev 5:9 – 10,12 – 13; Rev 7:10,12,15 – 17; Rev 15:3 – 4; Rev 19:1 – 8

MYSTERY

—Secret truths revealed by God

A. Related theme
- MYSTERY is a theme of Mark .... Mk 4:11

B. God and his secret truths
1. God discloses mysteries
   - —To his prophets .... Ge 40:8; Isa 48:6; Am 3:7; Da 2:18,27 – 28; Ro 16:25 – 26
   - —To his apostles .... Mk 4:10 – 12; Eph 3:4 – 5; Rev 1:19 – 20
2. Only believers understand mysteries .... Mk 4:10 – 12; 1Co 2:6 – 11; 2Co 4:3 – 6

C. Mysteries revealed to God's people
1. In the Old Testament
   - —Future events revealed to Joseph .... Ge 40:8 – 22; Ge 41:1 – 32
   - —Future events revealed to Daniel .... Da 2:24 – 47; Da 4:19 – 27
2. In the New Testament
   - —Basic teachings about Christ 1Ti 3:16
   - —Basic message of the gospel .... Col 4:3
   - —All wisdom hidden in Christ .... Col 2:2 – 3
   - —The nature of the kingdom of God .... Lk 8:10 – 15
   - —The union of Christ and his church .... Eph 5:29 – 32
   - —Christ's care for his church .... Rev 1:19 – 20
   - —What happens at Christ's return .... 1Co 15:51 – 52
   - —Inclusion of Gentiles in the kingdom .... Eph 3:6; Col 1:26
   - —Plan to reach the Jews with gospel .... Ro 11:25 – 26

D. Love is preferable to knowing mysteries 1Co 13:2

NAAMAN

- —Aramean general afflicted with leprosy 2Ki 5:1
- —Cured by Elisha .... 2Ki 5:2 – 14
- —Took Israelite soil back to Damascus .... 2Ki 5:15 – 19
- —His cure mentioned by Jesus .... Lk 4:27

NABAL

—Wealthy Carmelite; husband of Abigail .... 1Sa 25:1 – 3
—Name means "fool" 1Sa 25:25
—Refused to help David .... 1Sa 25:4 – 13
—Abigail pleaded for his life .... 1Sa 25:14 – 25
—His death .... 1Sa 25:36 – 38

NABOTH

—Owner of a vineyard in Jezreel 1Ki 21:1
—Refused to sell vineyard to King Ahab .... 1Ki 21:2 – 3
—Killed by Jezebel .... 1Ki 21:4 – 14
—Ahab's family destroyed for this .... 1Ki 21:17 – 24
—Joram killed in Naboth's vineyard .... 2Ki 9:21 – 26

NADAB

A. Firstborn of Aaron .... Ex 6:23
—Went up Mount Sinai .... Ex 24:1,9
—Consecrated as priest .... Ex 28:1
—Killed for offering unauthorized fire .... Lev 10:1 – 3; Nu 3:2 – 4
—Had no sons 1Ch 24:2
B. Son of Jeroboam I; king of Israel 1Ki 15:25
—Killed all his brothers 1Ki 15:29
—Killed by Baasha .... 1Ki 15:27 – 28

NAME

A. Human names
1. Giving a name implied authority .... Ge 2:19; Ge 41:45; 2Ki 23:34; Da 1:7
2. Bible names could express
—The feelings of the mother at birth .... Ge 4:1,25; Ge 29:31 – 35; Ge 30:4 – 24
—The feelings of the father at birth .... Ge 35:16 – 18; Ge 41:51 – 52
—Circumstances of the child's conception .... Ge 17:17,19; 1Sa 1:20
—Circumstances of the child's birth .... Ge 25:24 – 26; Ge 38:27 – 30; Ex 2:10
—Historical situation at time of birth .... 1Sa 4:19 – 22; Isa 8:1 – 4; Hos 1:6 – 9
—How a person's life would develop .... Ge 3:20; Ge 27:36; 1Sa 25:25; 1Ch 22:9; Mt 1:21
—A name directly given by God .... Lk 1:13,60
3. A name change meant a new role
—From Abram to Abraham .... Ge 17:5 – 6
—From Sarai to Sarah .... Ge 17:15 – 16
—From Jacob to Israel .... Ge 32:28
—From Simon to Peter .... Jn 1:42
—Promise of new names for us .... Isa 62:2; Rev 2:17
4. The names of believers
—Are called Christians .... Ac 11:26
—Are known by Christ .... Jn 10:3 – 4
—Are acknowledged before the Father .... Mt 10:32; Rev 3:5
—Are entered into the book of life .... Lk 10:20; Php 4:3; Rev 20:15

B. The name of God and Christ
1. God's name describes him
—It is identical with himself .... 2Sa 7:5,13; Ps 99:6
—It defines his nature .... Isa 9:6
—It defines his power .... Heb 1:4
2. God's name has power
—It delivers us .... Ex 3:13 – 15
—It saves us .... Ps 54:1; Mt 1:21,23; Ac 4:12
—It gives us life .... Jn 20:31
—It justifies us 1Co 6:11
—It sanctifies us 1Co 6:11
—It protects us .... Pr 18:10
—It helps us .... Ps 116:3 – 4; Jn 14:13 – 14
3. Our attitude toward God's name
—Praise it .... Ps 68:4; Ps 99:3
—Glorify it .... Ps 86:12; Ps 105:3
—Exalt it .... Ps 34:3
—Hallow it .... Mt 6:9
—Rejoice in it .... Ps 89:16
—Love it .... Isa 56:6
—Give thanks to it .... Ps 106:47
—Trust in it .... Ps 33:21
—Hope in it .... Ps 52:9
—Fear it .... Ps 86:11; Isa 59:19
—Call on it .... Ps 116:4,13,17; Joel 2:32
—Declare it .... Ps 22:22
—Live to reflect it .... Dt 28:9 – 10; Ro 2:21 – 24
—Don't misuse it .... Ex 20:7; Mal 1:6
4. Our attitude toward Christ's name
—Bow before it .... Php 2:10 – 11
—Believe in it .... Jn 2:23; 1Jn 3:23
—Confess it .... Ro 10:9; Heb 13:15
—Be baptized into it .... Ac 10:48
—Call on it 1Co 1:2
—Pray in it .... Jn 14:13 – 14; Jn 16:23 – 24
—Give thanks in it .... Eph 5:20
—Assemble in it 1Co 5:4
—Preach it .... Ac 8:12; Ac 9:27 – 28
—Live to reflect it 2Th 1:12
—Do miracles in it .... Mk 16:17; Ac 3:16; Ac 4:30
—May have to suffer for it .... Ac 5:40 – 41; Ac 9:16; Rev 2:3

NAOMI

—Wife of Elimelech; mother-in-law of Ruth .... Ru 1:2,4
—Left Bethlehem for Moab during famine .... Ru 1:1
—Returned as a widow with Ruth .... Ru 1:6 – 22
—Advised Ruth to seek marriage with Boaz .... Ru 2:17—3:4
—Cared for Ruth's son Obed .... Ru 4:13 – 17

NAPHTALI

A. Son of Jacob by Bilhah .... Ge 35:25; 1Ch 2:2
—Name means "my struggle" .... Ge 30:7 – 8
—Went to Egypt with family .... Ge 46:8,24
—Father of four sons .... Ge 46:24
—Blessed by Jacob .... Ge 49:21

B. Tribe descended from Naphtali
—Blessed by Moses .... Dt 33:23
—Numbered .... Nu 1:43
Nu 26:50
—Allotted land .... Jos 19:32 – 39
Eze 48:3
—Failed to fully possess the land .... Jdg 1:33
—Supported Deborah .... Jdg 4:10
Jdg 5:18
—Supported David 1Ch 12:34
—One of the tribes of the 144,000 .... Rev 7:6

NATHAN
—A prophet and chronicler 1Ch 29:29
2Ch 9:29
—Announced God's covenant with David .... 2Sa 7:1 – 17
1Ch 17:1 – 15
—Denounced David's sin with Bathsheba .... 2Sa 12:1 – 15
—Revealed Adonijah's plot to David .... 1Ki 1:10 – 27
—Participated in Solomon's coronation .... 1Ki 1:28 – 40

NATHANAEL
—One of Jesus' disciples .... Jn 1:45 – 51
Jn 21:2
—Probably also called Bartholomew .... Mt 10:3
Ac 1:13

NATIONS
A. The origin of nations
—Came from one family .... Ac 17:26
—Began after the flood .... Ge 10:1 – 32
—God divided up the nations .... Dt 32:8
B. God's intentions for the nations
1. God is king over all nations 2Ch 20:6
Ps 47:2
Jer 10:7,10
2. God chose a special nation
—Began with God's choice of Abram .... Ge 12:2
—Israelites were a holy, chosen nation .... Ex 19:5 – 6
Am 3:1 – 2
—Israelites commanded to remain separate .... Ex 34:15 – 16
Dt 7:1 – 6
—God's choice intended to bless all nations .... Ge 12:3
Ge 18:18
Ge 22:18
3. God prophesied salvation for all nations .... Ps 22:27 – 28
Ps 67:2
Isa 45:22 – 23
Isa 52:10
Zec 8:20 – 23
4. The nations are called to salvation
—Called by Jonah in the Old Testament .... Jnh 3:1 – 10
—Gospel to be preached to all nations .... Mt 24:14
Mt 28:19
Mk 16:15
Lk 24:47
Ac 1:8
—Apostles preached to all nations .... Ac 2:5 – 14
Ac 10:34 – 35
Ro 1:16
Ro 15:8 – 12,19
—Church composed of all nations .... Eph 2:11 – 22
Rev 5:9
Rev 7:9

NATURE
See CREATION

NAZARETH
—A Galilean town .... Mt 4:13
—Had a poor reputation .... Jn 1:46
—Gabriel appeared to Mary there .... Lk 1:26 – 38
—Jesus grew up there .... Mt 2:23
Lk 2:39,51 – 52
—Jesus called "Jesus of Nazareth" .... Jn 18:5,7
Jn 19:19
Ac 2:22
—Jesus was rejected by the town .... Mt 13:54 – 58
Mk 6:1 – 6
Lk 4:16 – 30

NEBUCHADNEZZAR
—Babylonian king 2Ki 24:1
—Campaigned against Judah .... 2Ki 24:1 – 4,10 – 16
2Ch 36:6 – 10
—Destroyed Jerusalem and the temple .... 2Ki 25:1 – 17
2Ch 36:15 – 21
Jer 39:1 – 10
—Was kind to Jeremiah .... Jer 39:11 – 14
—Was impressed with Daniel and his friends .... Da 1:18 – 20
—Dreams interpreted by Daniel .... Da 2:14 – 47
Da 4:9 – 27
—Put Daniel's three friends in fiery furnace .... Da 3:1 – 27
—Lived seven years like an animal .... Da 4:28 – 33
—Worshiped God .... Da 3:28 – 29
Da 4:34 – 37

NECO
See PHARAOH

NEEDY
See THE RICH AND THE POOR

NEHEMIAH
—Cupbearer for Artaxerxes .... Ne 1:11
—Became sad over condition of the exiles .... Ne 1:2 – 11
—Became governor of Jews .... Ne 8:9
—Inspected walls of Jerusalem .... Ne 2:11 – 20
—Rebuilt walls of Jerusalem .... Ne 3:1—4:23
Ne 6:15 – 19
—Showed concern for the poor .... Ne 5:1 – 13
—With Ezra, reestablished true worship .... Ne 8:1 – 12
—Signed a renewed covenant with the Lord .... Ne 9:38—10:1
—Dedicated walls of Jerusalem .... Ne 12:27 – 47
—Made a later visit to Jerusalem .... Ne 13:1 – 30

NEIGHBOR
—Anyone near you; any fellow human being
A. How not to treat your neighbors
—Do not give false testimony against them .... Ex 20:16
—Do not covet what is theirs .... Ex 20:17
—Do not deceive them .... Lev 6:2
—Do not rob them .... Lev 19:13
—Do not kill them .... Dt 22:26
—Do not plot harm against them .... Pr 3:29
—Do not despise them .... Pr 14:21
—Do not deceive them .... Pr 26:19
—Do not flatter them .... Pr 29:5
—Do not judge them .... Jas 4:12
—Do not commit adultery with neighbor's wife .... Lev 20:10
B. How to treat your neighbors
—Love them as yourself .... Lev 19:18
Mt 22:39
Ro 13:9
Jas 2:8
—Be kind to them .... Lk 10:29 – 37
—Speak the truth to them .... Eph 4:25

NICODEMUS
—Pharisee who visited Jesus at night .... Jn 3:1 – 21

—Argued for fair treatment of Jesus....Jn 7:50 – 52
—With Joseph, prepared Jesus for burial....Jn 19:38 – 42

NIGHT

See DARKNESS

NINEVEH

—A city founded by Nimrod....Ge 10:11 – 12
—The capital of Assyria....2Ki 19:36; Isa 37:37
—Jonah told to preach against it....Jnh 1:1 – 2; Jnh 3:1 – 3
—The people of Nineveh repented....Jnh 3:5 – 10
—The people of Nineveh condemn unbelievers....Mt 12:41; Lk 11:32
—Prophecies concerning its destruction....Na 1:8—3:19; Zep 2:13 – 15

NOAH

—A righteous man....Eze 14:14,20
—Called to build the ark....Ge 6:11 – 22
—Entered the ark....Ge 7:1 – 9
—Survived the flood....Ge 8:15 – 19
—Worshiped the Lord after the flood....Ge 8:20 – 22
—God made covenant with him....Ge 9:1 – 17
—Became drunk....Ge 9:18 – 23
—Blessed Shem and Japheth and cursed Canaan....Ge 9:24 – 27

NUMBERS

A. Numbers used as a literary device
—In poetry....Ps 62:11; Pr 6:16 – 19; Pr 30:15 – 29
—In prophecy....Am 1:3—2:6; Mic 5:5
—In genealogies....Mt 1:17

B. Numbers used in a symbolic fashion

1. The number "one"
—One God....Dt 6:4; 1Co 8:6; Eph 4:6; Jas 2:19
—One Lord....1Co 8:6; Eph 4:5
—One Spirit....1Co 12:13; Eph 4:4
—Father and Son are one....Jn 10:30
—One body....Ro 12:4 – 5; Eph 4:4
—One in Christ....Jn 17:11,21; Gal 3:28; Eph 2:14 – 15
—One hope....Eph 4:4
—One faith and one baptism....Eph 4:5
—One father of the human race, Adam....Ac 17:26; Ro 5:12; 1Co 15:21 – 22
—One flesh in marriage....Ge 2:24; Eph 5:31

2. The number "two"
—Two ways to choose....Jos 24:15; 1Ki 18:21; Mt 7:13 – 14
—The two-edged sword....Heb 4:12; Rev 1:16
—Male and female....Ge 1:27
—Two by two into the ark....Ge 7:8 – 9,15 – 16
—Two tablets of the law....Ex 32:15
—Disciples sent out two by two....Mk 6:7
—Two witnesses....Nu 35:30; Jn 8:17 – 18; 2Co 13:1

3. The number "three"
—Father, Son, Holy Spirit....Mt 28:19; 2Co 13:14
See TRINITY
—Three annual festivals in Israel....Ex 23:14 – 17
—Threefold benediction by priests....Nu 6:24 – 26
—Job's three friends....Job 2:11
—Jonah's three days in the fish....Jnh 1:17; Mt 12:40
—Three temptations of Jesus....Mt 4:3 – 10
—Three prayers in Gethsemane....Mt 26:39 – 44
—Three denials of Peter....Mt 26:34,69 – 75
—Jesus' resurrection on the third day....Mt 16:21; Lk 24:46; 1Co 15:4
—Three questions for Peter....Jn 21:15 – 17
—Peter's three visions....Ac 10:10 – 16
—Faith, hope, love....1Co 13:13

4. The number "four"
—The four rivers in Eden....Ge 2:10 – 14
—The four winds....Jer 49:36
—The four corners of the earth....Eze 7:2
—Series of fours in Zechariah's visions....Zec 1:8,18 – 21
—Four creatures around God's throne....Eze 1:4 – 14; Rev 4:6 – 8
—Four kingdoms seen in a vision....Da 2:36 – 43; Da 7:2 – 7,17

5. The number "seven"
—Creation in seven days....Ge 1:1—2:3
—The Sabbath on the seventh day....Ex 20:8 – 11
—The sabbath year....Lev 25:1 – 7
—The Year of Jubilee (seven sabbath years)....Lev 25:8 – 12
—Seven lamps on the lampstand....Ex 25:37
—Feast of Unleavened Bread for seven days....Ex 34:18
—Feast of Tabernacles for seven days....Lev 23:34
—Seven sprinklings for a cleansed leper....Lev 14:7,16
—Seven dippings for leper Naaman....2Ki 5:10,14
—Seven days marching around Jericho....Jos 6:1 – 16
—Seven deacons....Ac 6:3 – 5
—Numerous series of sevens in Revelation....Rev 1:12 – 20; Rev 5:1; Rev 8:1 – 2; Rev 15:1,6 – 8

6. The number "ten"
—Ten righteous men to save Sodom....Ge 18:32
—The ten plagues....Ex 7:14—12:36
—The Ten Commandments....Ex 34:28
—Ten testings of the Israelites....Nu 14:22
—The tithe (a tenth)....Ge 14:20
See TITHES AND OFFERINGS
—Ten virgins in Jesus' parable....Mt 25:1 – 13
—Ten horns and crowns on a beast....Rev 13:1

7. The number "twelve"
—Twelve sons of Jacob....Ge 35:22 – 26
—Twelve tribes....Ex 24:4
—Twelve stones from the Jordan....Jos 4:9
—Twelve stones in Elijah's altar....1Ki 18:31
—Twelve disciples of Jesus....Mt 10:1 – 5
—Twelve hours of daylight....Jn 11:9
—A crown of twelve stars....Rev 12:1
—Twelve apostles....Ac 1:26
—Several twelves in the new Jerusalem....Rev 21:12 – 14,21

8. The number "forty"
—Rain for forty days and nights....Ge 7:12
—Moses for forty days on Mount Sinai....Ex 24:18
—Forty years wandering in the desert....Nu 14:33 – 34

—Moses' life divided into three forties .... Ac 7:23,30,36
—David's reign of forty years 1Ki 2:11
—Solomon's reign of forty years 1Ki 11:42
—Elijah for forty days on the mountain 1Ki 19:8
—Jesus for forty days in the desert .... Mt 4:2
—Jesus ascended after forty days .... Ac 1:3

9. The number "seventy"
—Seventy people came to Egypt .... Ge 46:27
—Seventy elders in Israel .... Ex 24:1,9
—Seventy years of exile .... Jer 25:11 – 12
—Seventy "sevens" in Daniel's visions .... Da 9:20 – 27
—Forgiving seventy-seven times .... Mt 18:22
—The sending of the seventy-two .... Lk 10:1,17

10. "Thousands"
—One thousand years (the Millennium) .... Rev 20:1 – 7
—A thousand years as one day .... Ps 90:4; 2Pe 3:8
—Three thousand converts on Pentecost .... Ac 2:41
—Feeding the four thousand .... Mt 15:29 – 38
—Feeding the five thousand .... Mt 14:13 – 21
—Seven thousand not bowing to Baal .... 1Ki 19:18; Ro 11:4
—Thousands who love and obey the Lord .... Ex 20:6
—Thousands of thousands of chariots .... Ps 68:17
—Thousands and thousands before God .... Da 7:10
—Thousands and thousands praising God .... Heb 12:22; Rev 5:11
—One hundred forty-four thousand .... Rev 7:4 – 8; Rev 14:1 – 3

11. Mysterious numbers
—Forty-two months .... Rev 11:2; Rev 13:5
—One thousand, two hundred sixty days .... Rev 11:3; Rev 12:6
—Six hundred sixty-six .... Rev 13:18

OATH

A. The human oath

1. Expressions of the oath
—"May God . . . judge between us" .... Ge 31:53
—"As surely as the LORD lives" .... Ru 3:13
—"May God deal with you . . . severely" 1Sa 3:17
—"As surely as you live" 1Sa 17:55
—"The LORD is witness between you and me" 1Sa 20:23,42
—"I am telling the truth, I am not lying" 1Ti 2:7
—"God . . . is my witness" .... Ro 1:9
—"I speak the truth in Christ" .... Ro 9:1

2. Features of the oath

a. Purposes
—To settle an issue .... Ex 22:10 – 11
—To confirm an agreement with someone .... Ge 31:45 – 54
—To confirm a covenant with a people .... Jos 9:3 – 15
—To confirm a covenant with God .... 2Ch 15:12 – 15
—To ensure obedience to a master .... Ge 24:1 – 4
—To ensure obedience to a king .... Ecc 8:2
—To ensure obedience to the Lord .... Ne 10:29

b. Other aspects of the oath
—Must be fulfilled .... Nu 30:1 – 2
—Could bind future generations .... Ge 50:24 – 25
—Conditions sometimes attached .... Jos 2:12 – 21
—Not necessary for Christians .... Mt 5:33 – 37; Jas 5:12
—Christ responded to an oath .... Mt 26:63 – 64

B. God's oath

1. Content of God's oaths
—To give Canaan to Abraham's descendants .... Ge 22:15 – 18; Ge 50:24
—To keep someone on David's throne .... 2Sa 7:10 – 16
—To set up a priesthood like Melchizedek's .... Ps 110:4

2. Character of God's oaths
—He swears by himself .... Ge 22:16; Heb 6:13 – 15
—God does not lie .... Nu 23:19; Heb 6:16 – 18
—God fulfills his oaths .... Ps 105:42 – 43; Lk 1:69 – 75; Lk 1:32 – 33; Heb 6:19—7:22

See also CURSE; VOW

OBADIAH

A. Servant of King Ahab 1Ki 18:3
—Sheltered one hundred prophets from Jezebel 1Ki 18:4
—Notified Ahab of Elijah's return .... 1Ki 18:7 – 16

B. Prophet against Edom .... Ob 1

OBEDIENCE

A. Related themes

1. OBEDIENCE is a theme of:
—1 Samuel 1Sa 12:14
—2 Samuel 2Sa 12:10
—1 Kings 1Ki 9:4
—2 Kings 2Ki 22:19
—Daniel .... Da 1:8
—1 Corinthians 1Co 7:19

2. TRUST AND OBEY is a theme of Joshua .... Jos 10:25

B. Obedience in the Old Testament

1. Relationships of obedience
—Israelites obey the Lord their God .... Ex 19:5; Dt 4:30
—Israelites obey the law of God .... Ex 34:11; Dt 11:13,27,32
—Citizens obey the king .... 1Ki 2:43; Ecc 8:2
—Children obey parents .... Ex 20:12; Pr 1:8 – 9; Pr 6:20 – 21

2. Rewards for obedience .... Ex 19:5 – 6; Dt 28:1 – 14; Jos 1:7 – 8

3. Punishment for disobedience .... Dt 28:15 – 68; 1Sa 12:15; 2Ki 17:7 – 20; Jer 11:1 – 3

4. Obedience more important than outward ritual .... 1Sa 15:22; Ps 40:6 – 8; Pr 21:3; Jer 7:22 – 23

C. Obedience in the New Testament

1. Relationships of obedience
—Christians obey God .... Heb 12:9; Jas 4:7; 1Jn 5:3
—Christians obey Christ .... Jn 14:13,23; Ro 1:5; 1Co 9:21; Gal 6:2; Heb 5:9
—Citizens obey government authorities .... Ro 13:1 – 5; 1Pe 2:13 – 14
—Christians obey church leaders .... Heb 13:17
—Servants obey masters .... Eph 6:5 – 8; Col 3:22
—Children obey parents .... Eph 6:1; Col 3:20

2. Obeying God precedes obeying humans .... Ac 4:19 – 20; Ac 5:29

OCCULT
See MAGIC, WITCHCRAFT AND SORCERY

OFFERINGS
See TITHES AND OFFERINGS

OG
—King of Bashan .... Nu 21:33; Dt 1:4
—Destroyed by the Israelites .... Nu 21:34 – 35; Dt 3:1 – 11
—Victory sung by the Israelites .... Ps 136:20

OLIVES, MOUNT OF
—A hill east of Jerusalem .... Eze 11:23; Zec 14:4
—David climbed it while fleeing from Absalom 2Sa 15:30
—Jesus often went there .... Lk 22:39; Jn 8:1
—Triumphal Entry began from there .... Mt 21:1 – 9; Mk 11:1 – 10; Lk 19:29 – 40
—Jesus predicted destruction of Jerusalem there .... Mt 24:3 – 34; Mk 13:3 – 31
—Gethsemane located there .... Mt 26:30,36; Mk 14:26,32
—Jesus ascended into heaven from there .... Ac 1:9 – 12

OMRI
—King of Israel .... 1Ki 16:21 – 28
—Father of Ahab 1Ki 16:28

ORDER
A. Related theme
  ORGANIZATION is a theme of Numbers .... Nu 2:34
  CHURCH ORDER is a theme of 1 Timothy 1Ti 3:15
B. Order needed among God's people
  —For the Israelites in the desert .... Nu 2:1 – 34
  —In Christian worship 1Co 14:40
  —In the Christian life .... Col 2:5
  —In presenting the truth about Christ .... Lk 1:3
See also CHURCH; DEACON; ELDER

ORPAH
—Moabitess; daughter-in-law of Naomi .... Ru 1:3 – 5
—Remained in Moab .... Ru 1:14

OTHNIEL
—Nephew of Caleb; married Caleb's daughter .... Jos 15:15 – 19; Jdg 1:12 – 15
—Became a judge .... Jdg 3:10
—Freed Israelites from Arameans .... Jdg 3:7 – 11

PAIN
—Various types of suffering experienced in our lives
A. Related themes
  1. SUFFERING is a theme of:
    —Job .... Job 2:13
    —Jeremiah .... Jer 15:18
    —Mark .... Mk 8:31
    —2 Corinthians 2Co 1:8
    —1 Peter 1Pe 4:12
  2. COMPLAINT is a theme of:
    —Psalms .... Ps 123:4
    —Habakkuk .... Hab 1:2
  3. HARD TIMES is a theme of 2 Timothy 2Ti 1:8
  4. UNJUST PERSECUTION is a theme of Acts .... Ac 12:2
B. Pain and suffering as a universal experience
  1. In humans
    —The righteous .... Ps 22:1 – 2,12 – 18
    —The wicked .... Pr 10:16; Pr 12:21
  2. In creation as a whole .... Ro 8:20 – 22
C. The problem of pain and suffering for God's people
  1. Examples of those who experienced pain
    —Joseph .... Ge 39:11 – 20
    —The Israelites in Egypt .... Ex 1:8 – 14
    —The poor .... Ne 5:1 – 5; Am 2:6 – 7
    —Job .... Job 2:7 – 13
    —David .... Ps 22:1 – 18
    —Asaph .... Ps 73:2 – 14
    —Daniel's three friends .... Da 3:13 – 23
    —Daniel .... Da 6:16 – 17
    —Peter and John .... Ac 5:40 – 41
    —Paul .... Ac 14:19; 2Co 11:23 – 26
    —The Hebrew Christians .... Heb 10:33 – 34
    —Other Christians .... 1Th 2:14 – 15; 1Pe 2:19 – 21
    —Christians in Smyrna .... Rev 2:9 – 10
    —Saints in John's vision .... Rev 6:9 – 10
  2. Christian attitude toward pain
    —We must expect it .... Mt 24:9; Jn 16:1 – 4,33; 2Ti 3:12
    —We may have to endure it 2Ti 2:3; 2Ti 4:5
    —We must realize not all are delivered .... Heb 11:35 – 38
    —We must be patient in it .... Ro 12:12; 1Pe 2:20 – 21
    —We can rejoice in it .... Ro 5:3; Col 1:24; Jas 1:2 – 3; 1Pe 4:12 – 14
    —We must overcome it .... Ro 8:35 – 37; Rev 2:10 – 11
    —We must not become discouraged .... Eph 3:13
    —We must not lose heart .... 2Co 4:7 – 10,16 – 17; 1Th 3:3
    —We do complain against it .... Job 3:3 – 26; Ps 74:1,10 – 11; 2Co 12:7 – 8
  3. Why does God allow such pain?
    —To punish sins .... 2Sa 12:9 – 18; 2Ch 33:10 – 11
    —To test us .... Dt 8:2; Job 2:1 – 6; Isa 48:10
    —To teach us his will .... Ps 119:71,75
    —To teach us patience .... Ro 5:3; Jas 1:3
    —To humble us .... Dt 8:3; 2Ch 7:13 – 14
    —To discipline us in love .... Heb 12:4 – 11
    —To drive us to repentance .... Jdg 6:1 – 6; Ps 107:4 – 6,10 – 13; Hos 5:15
    —To get us to rely on his grace .... 2Co 12:7 – 10
    —To purify us .... Zec 13:7 – 9; Mal 3:2 – 3; Jn 15:2
    —To promote his glory .... Jn 9:1 – 3
    —To further the gospel .... Ac 8:3 – 4; 2Ti 4:16 – 17
  4. How does God relate to pain?
    —He is in control .... Job 1:6 – 12; Ro 8:38 – 39
    —He causes good to triumph .... Ps 49:13 – 15; Ps 73:16 – 20; Ro 8:28

—He is a refuge for believers ..... Ps 16:1,8
Ps 46:1
Isa 25:4
—He shares our pain ..... Isa 53:2–4
Isa 63:9
—He walks with us through pain ..... Ps 23:4
Ps 46:7,11
Isa 43:2
—He comforts us ..... Isa 49:13
Zec 1:17
2Co 1:4–5
Mt 11:28–30
—He will terminate pain at Christ's return 2Th 1:4–7
Rev 21:1–4

5. How should believers relate to those in pain?
—We should pray for them ..... Ac 12:5
Ro 15:30–31
2Co 1:10–11
Jas 5:13–16
—We should comfort them ..... Job 2:11–13
2Co 1:6–8
—We should share their burdens ..... Job 30:25
Ro 12:15
Gal 6:2
Heb 13:3
—We should encourage them 1Th 5:11
—We should give them help ..... Isa 58:7
Lk 10:30–37
Php 4:14
1Jn 3:17–18

PARABLE

—Stories that illustrate spiritual truths

A. The purposes of parables
—To teach things to children ..... Ps 78:2–4
Pr 1:1–6
—To make an important point ..... Jdg 9:7–20
1Sa 12:1–7
—To give a prophetic message ..... Isa 5:1–7
Eze 17:1–18
Hos 12:10
—To teach us about the kingdom ..... Mk 4:2,10
—To obscure teaching from unbelievers ..... Mt 13:11–15

B. Parables and fables in the Old Testament
—The fable of Jotham to Abimelech ..... Jdg 9:7–15
—The parable of Nathan to David 2Sa 12:1–6
—The fable of Jehoash to Amaziah 2Ki 14:9
—The parable of Isaiah to the people ..... Isa 5:1–7
—The parables of Ezekiel to the people ..... Eze 17:1–8,22–24
Eze 20:45–49
Eze 24:1–5

C. Jesus' use of parables
—He used them regularly ..... Mk 4:33–34
—He explained things to the disciples alone ..... Mt 13:10–13
Mk 4:3–8,14–20
Lk 8:9–10
—He taught about the kingdom of God ..... Mk 4:11,26,30–32

D. Parables of Jesus
—Lamp on a stand ..... Mt 5:14–15
Mk 4:21–22
Lk 8:16
—Wise and foolish builders ..... Mt 7:24–27
Lk 6:47–49
—New cloth on an old garment ..... Mt 9:16
Mk 2:21
Lk 5:36
—New wine in old wineskins ..... Mt 9:17
Mk 2:22
Lk 5:37–38
—Sower ..... Mt 13:3–23
Mk 4:3–25
Lk 8:5–15
—Growing seed ..... Mk 4:25–29
—Wheat and weeds ..... Mt 13:24–30,36–43
—Mustard seed ..... Mt 13:31–32
Mk 4:30–32
Lk 13:18–19
—Yeast ..... Mt 13:33
Lk 13:20–21
—Hidden treasure ..... Mt 13:43
—Valuable pearl ..... Mt 13:45–46
—Net ..... Mt 13:47–51
—House owner ..... Mt 13:52
—Good Samaritan ..... Lk 10:25–37
—Wandering sheep ..... Mt 18:10–14
Lk 15:3–7
—Lost coin ..... Lk 15:8–10
—Lost son ..... Lk 15:11–32
—Unmerciful servant ..... Mt 18:15–35
—Shrewd manager ..... Lk 16:1–9
—Rich man and Lazarus ..... Lk 16:19–31
—Persistent widow ..... Lk 18:1–8
—Pharisee and tax collector ..... Lk 18:9–14
—Workers in the vineyard ..... Mt 20:1–16
—Two sons ..... Mt 21:28–32
—Tenants ..... Mt 21:33–46
Mk 12:1–6
Lk 20:9–18
—Wedding banquet ..... Mt 22:1–14
—Faithful servant ..... Mt 24:45–51
Lk 12:42–48
—Ten virgins ..... Mt 25:1–13
—Bags of gold/Ten minas ..... Mt 25:14–30
Lk 19:12–27
—Sheep and goats ..... Mt 25:31–46

PATIENCE

—Long-suffering, perseverance

A. Human patience
1. The command to be patient
—Be patient ..... Ro 12:12
1Th 5:14
Heb 12:1
Jas 5:7–8
—Bear with others' shortcomings ..... Eph 4:2
Col 3:12–13
2. The manner of achieving patience
—By dependence on God ..... Ro 15:5
Col 1:11
—Through hope in Christ 1Th 1:3
Jas 5:7
—As part of the fruit of the Spirit ..... Gal 5:22
3. Examples of patience
—Abraham ..... Heb 6:15
—Job ..... Jas 5:11
—The prophets ..... Jas 5:10
—Paul 2Ti 3:10
—John ..... Rev 1:9

See also PERSEVERANCE

B. Patience of God
1. Statements of God's patience
—God is slow to anger ..... Ex 34:6
Nu 14:18
Ps 30:5
Ps 78:38
—Jesus is patient with us 1Ti 1:16
2. Purpose: to call humans to repentance ..... Ro 2:4
2Pe 3:9,15
3. God's patience at time of Noah 1Pe 3:20

PAUL

A. Related themes
 PETER AND PAUL is a theme of Acts ... Ac 19:11
 MINISTRY is a theme of 2 Corinthians ... 2Co 4:1
 DEFENSE is a theme of Galatians ... Gal 1:10

B. His background
 —Originally called Saul ... Ac 13:9
 —From Tarsus ... Ac 9:11
 Ac 21:39
 —From the tribe of Benjamin ... Php 3:5
 —A Pharisee ... Php 3:5
 —Educated by Gamaliel ... Ac 22:3
 —Unmarried ... 1Co 7:8

C. His life as a persecutor of Christians
 —Assisted in stoning of Stephen ... Ac 7:58
 Ac 8:1
 —Zealously persecuted church ... Ac 9:1
 Gal 1:13 – 14
 Php 3:6
 —Cast vote against Christians ... Ac 26:9 – 10
 —Went to Damascus to persecute ... Ac 9:2
 Ac 22:4 – 5
 —Converted on the way to Damascus ... Ac 9:3 – 19
 Ac 22:6 – 21
 Ac 26:12 – 18

D. His life as an apostle
 1. From conversion to first missionary journey
  —Called as missionary to Gentiles ... Ac 22:17 – 21
  Ac 26:16 – 18
  —Went to Arabia ... Gal 1:17
  —Preached in Damascus; escaped in basket ... Ac 9:19 – 25
  2Co 11:32 – 33
  —Went to Jerusalem ... Ac 9:26 – 29
  —Went to Tarsus ... Ac 9:30
  —Brought to Antioch by Barnabas ... Ac 11:22 – 26
  —Brought offering to Jerusalem ... Ac 11:29 – 30
  —Returned to Antioch ... Ac 12:25
 2. First missionary journey
  —Called by God ... Ac 13:2 – 4
  —Preached throughout Cyprus ... Ac 13:5 – 12
  —Preached in Pisidian Antioch ... Ac 13:14 – 52
  —Was persecuted in Iconium ... Ac 14:1 – 7
  —Preached and stoned at Lystra ... Ac 14:8 – 20
  —Preached at Derbe ... Ac 14:20 – 21
  —Returned to Antioch ... Ac 14:21 – 28
 3. The Jerusalem council
  —Sent to Jerusalem ... Ac 15:1 – 4
  Gal 2:1 – 2
  —Discussed circumcision privately ... Gal 2:3 – 10
  —Open meeting on circumcision issue ... Ac 15:5 – 22
  —Letter drafted and sent with them ... Ac 15:23 – 31
  —Friction developed with Peter ... Gal 2:11 – 14
 4. Second missionary journey
  —Split with Barnabas over John Mark ... Ac 15:36 – 41
  —Took Silas along ... Ac 15:40
  —Visited previous churches ... Ac 15:41
  —Added Timothy to his group ... Ac 16:1 – 4
  —At Troas, called to Macedonia ... Ac 16:6 – 10
  —Preached to women at Philippi ... Ac 16:13 – 15
  —Imprisoned and freed in Philippi ... Ac 16:16 – 40
  —Ministered in Thessalonica ... Ac 17:1 – 9
  —Ministered in Berea ... Ac 17:10 – 15
  —Preached in Athens ... Ac 17:16 – 33
  —Ministered in Corinth for eighteen months ... Ac 18:1 – 11
  —Attacked by Jews ... Ac 18:12 – 17
  —Left Corinth and returned to Antioch ... Ac 18:18 – 22
 5. Third missionary journey
  —Arrived at Ephesus in Asia ... Ac 19:1
  —Ministered for two years there ... Ac 19:2 – 22
  —Suffered many hardships there ... 2Co 1:3 – 10
  —Visited with leaders from Corinth ... 1Co 16:17 – 18
  —Riot in Ephesus ... Ac 19:23 – 41
  —Left for Macedonia ... Ac 20:1
  —Met Titus in Macedonia ... 2Co 7:5 – 7
  —Gathered money for Jerusalem ... 2Co 8:1 – 5
  Ro 15:26
  —Arrived in Greece ... Ac 20:2 – 3
  —Gathered more money for Jerusalem ... Ro 15:26
  —Left Greece for Jerusalem ... Ac 20:3 – 6
  Ro 15:25
  —Spoke all night at Troas ... Ac 20:7 – 12
  —Said farewell to elders of Ephesus ... Ac 20:17 – 38
  —Sailed for Jerusalem ... Ac 21:1 – 6
  —Traveled to Jerusalem ... Ac 21:7 – 17
  —Reported to Jerusalem leaders ... Ac 21:17 – 25
 6. Paul's period of imprisonment
  —Attacked and beaten by Jews from Asia ... Ac 21:27 – 32
  —Arrested by Roman commander ... Ac 21:33 – 35
  —Addressed the Jewish crowd ... Ac 22:1 – 21
  —Addressed Sanhedrin ... Ac 23:1 – 11
  —Transferred to Caesarea ... Ac 23:12 – 35
  —On trial before Felix ... Ac 24:1 – 21
  —Kept in prison in Caesarea ... Ac 24:22 – 27
  —On trial before Festus ... Ac 25:1 – 12
  —Appealed to Caesar ... Ac 25:12
  —Spoke before Agrippa ... Ac 25:13—26:32
  —Sailed for Rome; shipwrecked ... Ac 27:1 – 44
  —Stranded on island of Malta ... Ac 28:1 – 10
  —Arrived in Rome ... Ac 28:11 – 16
  —Preached to Jews of Rome ... Ac 28:17 – 28
  —Remained two years in Rome ... Ac 28:30 – 31
  —Freed after trial before emperor ... 2Ti 4:16 – 17
 7. Travels after release from imprisonment
  —In Macedonia ... 1Ti 1:3
  —In Crete ... Tit 1:5
  —In Nicopolis ... Tit 3:12
  —In Miletus ... 2Ti 4:20
  —In Troas ... 2Ti 4:13
  —Imprisoned again ... 2Ti 2:8 – 9
  —Probably killed this time ... 2Ti 4:6 – 8

E. Significant issues in Paul's letters
 —His apostleship ... 1Co 9:1 – 3
 2Co 11:4—12:13
 Gal 1:1—2:14
 —Salvation possible only in the name of Jesus ... Ro 3:21 – 26
 Ro 5:1 – 2
 Ro 10:3 – 13
 2Co 5:18 – 21
 Gal 3:10 – 14,24 – 29
 Eph 2:1 – 22
 Php 3:7 – 14
 Col 1:13 – 23
 1Ti 1:12 – 16
 —Salvation through faith alone ... Ro 3:21—5:1
 Gal 2:15 – 21
 Eph 2:8 – 9
 Php 3:9
 —Circumcision not necessary for salvation ... Ro 4:9 – 12
 Gal 2:3
 Gal 5:1 – 6
 Col 2:11 – 12
 —Christian freedom ... Ro 14:1—15:13
 1Co 8:1 – 13
 1Co 11:23 – 33
 Gal 4:31—5:13
 —Concern for the salvation of Jews ... Ro 9:1 – 5
 Ro 10:1 – 4
 —Proper use of spiritual gifts ... Ro 12:3 – 8
 1Co 12:1—14:40

—Life led by the Spirit of God ... Ro 8:1–17; Gal 5:16–26
—Proper order needed in the church ... 1Co 11:17–34; 1Co 14:26–40; 1Ti 2:1—3:15; Tit 1:5—2:15

PEACE

—Wholeness and well-being in all areas of life

A. Basic meanings of peace
1. Peace ("Shalom") is a basic greeting
—Hello ... Da 10:19; Jn 20:19; Gal 1:3
—Good-bye ... 1Sa 25:35; 2Sa 15:9; 1Pe 5:14; 3Jn 14
2. Peace in a political sense
—On the international scene ... 1Sa 7:14; 1Ki 4:24; Ac 24:2
—On the national scene ... 2Sa 3:21–23; 1Ki 22:44; 2Ch 14:1
3. Peace in human relationships
—In relationships with others ... Ro 12:18; Heb 12:14; 1Pe 3:11
—Among the Israelite people ... Ps 34:14; Ps 122:6–7
—In relationships in the church ... Ac 9:31; Ro 14:19; 2Co 13:11; Eph 2:14–17
—In relationships in the home ... Ge 44:17; Pr 17:1; Pr 29:17; 1Co 7:15
4. Personal sense of peace
—In relationship with oneself ... Ps 4:8; Pr 14:30; 2Co 2:13
—In relationship with God ... Nu 6:26; Isa 26:3; Ro 5:1; Php 4:7–9; Col 1:20

B. The source of peace
1. It comes as a divine gift
—From God the Father ... Ro 1:7; Ro 15:33; Php 4:7
—From the Lord Jesus Christ ... Isa 9:6–7; Lk 2:14; Jn 14:27; Ro 1:7; Eph 2:14; 2Th 3:16
—From the Holy Spirit ... Ro 14:17; Gal 5:22; Eph 4:3
—God promises a covenant of peace ... Isa 54:10; Eze 34:25; Eze 37:26
—We must pray to God for peace ... Ps 122:6–7; Jer 29:7; 1Ti 2:1
2. It comes through human effort
—We must let peace rule in us ... Col 3:15
—We must live in peace ... 2Co 13:11; 1Th 5:13
—We must seek peace ... Ps 34:14; 1Pe 3:11
—We must try to live in peace ... Ro 12:18; Ro 14:19; Heb 12:14
—We must pursue peace ... Ps 34:14; 2Ti 2:22
—We must obey God to receive peace ... Lev 26:3,6

C. Jesus and our peace
—Prophesied to be the Prince of Peace ... Isa 9:6
—Peace proclaimed at his birth ... Lk 2:14
—Peace promised to his disciples ... Jn 14:27; Jn 16:33
—Peace achieved on the cross ... Isa 53:5; Col 1:20
—Began the good news of peace ... Isa 52:7; Ac 10:36
—He is our peace ... Eph 2:14
—Enables us to have peace with God ... Ro 5:1
—Establishes peace within the church ... Eph 2:15
—Guides us in the way of peace ... Lk 1:79
—Blesses us with peace ... Nu 6:24–26; Ps 29:11; 1Co 1:3
—Enables us to die in peace ... Lk 2:29–31

D. The wicked and peace
—They proclaim a false peace ... Jer 6:14; Eze 13:10
—They do not know the way of peace ... Isa 59:8; Lk 19:42
—They hate peace ... Ps 120:6–7
—They have no peace ... Isa 48:18,22; Isa 57:21

PEKAH

—King of Israel ... 2Ki 15:27–31
—Assassinated Pekahiah to become king ... 2Ki 15:25
—Allied with Syria against Judah ... 2Ki 15:37; Isa 7:1–2
—Inflicted much destruction on Judah ... 2Ch 28:5–8
—Destruction of the alliance foretold ... Isa 7:3–9
—Failed in attempt to take Jerusalem ... 2Ki 16:5–6

PEKAHIAH

—King of Israel ... 2Ki 15:23–26
—Assassinated by Pekah, an officer ... 2Ki 15:25

PERFECTION

—Complete and without sin or error

A. Perfection as a human goal
1. The goal stated ... Mt 5:48; 2Co 13:9,11
2. Perfection possible only in the Lord
—Animal sacrifice cannot make us perfect ... Heb 10:1
—The law cannot make us perfect ... Ro 3:20; Heb 7:11,19
—God makes our way perfect ... 2Sa 22:33
—God's strength makes us perfect ... 2Co 12:7–10
—Jesus is the perfecter of our faith ... Heb 12:2
—Jesus makes us perfect by his sacrifice ... Heb 10:14
—The Spirit helps us attain perfection ... Gal 3:3
3. Perfection requires various human actions
—Learning God's wisdom ... Col 1:28
—Knowing God's word ... 2Ti 3:14–17
—Pressing forward in faith ... Php 3:12–14
—Self-sacrifice ... Mt 19:21
—Love ... Col 3:14
—Purifying ourselves ... 2Co 7:1

—Controlling what we say ... Jas 3:2
—Not being afraid ... 1Jn 4:18
4. Perfection attained only in the hereafter ... 1Co 13:8 – 10; Heb 12:22 – 23

See also HOLINESS; SANCTIFICATION

B. Perfection as the nature of God
1. God the Father
—He is perfect ... Mt 5:48
—His works are perfect ... Dt 32:4
—His way is perfect ... 2Sa 22:31
—His law is perfect ... Ps 19:7; Jas 1:25
—His will is perfect ... Ro 12:2
—He is perfect in knowledge ... Job 37:16
—He is perfect in faithfulness ... Isa 25:1
2. Christ the Son
—He is without sin ... 2Co 5:21; Heb 7:26; 1Jn 3:5
—He was made perfect through suffering ... Heb 2:10; Heb 5:8 – 9; Heb 7:28

PERSECUTION

—Oppression because of one's faith

A. Examples of persecution
1. The prophets
—Prophets in general ... 2Ch 36:15 – 16; Mt 5:12; Mt 23:31,37; Ac 7:52
—Elijah ... 1Ki 19:1 – 3
—Micaiah ... 1Ki 22:9 – 28
—Jeremiah ... Jer 26:1 – 19; Jer 37:11—38:13
—Uriah son of Shemaiah ... Jer 26:20 – 22
2. The apostles
—Persecution prophesied ... Mt 24:9; Jn 15:18 – 21; Jn 16:1 – 4
—The apostles as a group ... Ac 5:27,40
—James ... Ac 12:1 – 2
—Peter ... Ac 12:3 – 5
—Paul ... Ac 14:5 – 6,19 – 20; Ac 16:22 – 24; Ac 22:27 – 36; 2Co 11:23 – 26
—John ... Rev 1:9
3. Christians in general
—Stephen ... Ac 7:57 – 60
—Christians in Judea ... Ac 8:1 – 3; 1Th 2:14 – 15
—Christians outside Judea ... Ac 9:1 – 2; Ac 26:11
—Christians in Thessalonica ... 1Th 2:14 – 15
—Christians in Smyrna ... Rev 2:9 – 10
—To be expected for all ... 2Ti 3:12

B. Attitudes in relationship to persecution
—Commit yourself to God ... 1Pe 4:19
—Persevere under it ... Mk 13:13; Heb 10:32 – 36; Jas 1:12; Rev 2:10
—Rejoice in it ... Mt 5:12; Ac 5:41; Php 2:17; Col 1:24
—Flee from it ... Mt 10:23; Ac 14:6
—Do not be ashamed ... 1Pe 4:16
—Pray for persecutors ... Mt 5:44; Lk 23:34; Ac 7:60

PERSEVERANCE

—Remaining firm in our faith

A. Related themes
PERSEVERANCE is a theme of:
—2 Timothy ... 2Ti 2:3
—Hebrews ... Heb 10:36

B. God preserves us in our faith
—He draws us firmly to himself ... Jn 6:37
—He holds us in his hand ... Ps 37:24; Jn 10:27 – 29
—He keeps us in his love ... Ro 8:35 – 39
—He watches over us ... Ps 121:3 – 8; Ps 145:20
—He protects us from the evil one ... 2Th 3:3; 1Jn 5:18
—He keeps our commitment firm ... 1Co 1:8; 2Ti 1:12
—He will keep us until the final day ... Php 1:6; 1Pe 1:4 – 5

C. We must persevere in our faith
—The command to persevere ... Heb 10:35 – 36; Heb 12:2; Jas 1:12
—The command to use spiritual armor ... Eph 6:10 – 17; 1Th 5:8
—The warning not to turn away from God ... Heb 3:12; Heb 6:1 – 6; Heb 10:26 – 31; Rev 2:4 – 5
—The possibility of rejecting the faith ... 1Ti 1:19 – 20; 1Ti 6:20 – 21; 2Ti 2:17 – 18; Heb 3:16 – 18

PERSIA

See MEDES AND PERSIANS

PETER

A. Related themes
PETER AND PAUL is a theme of Acts ... Ac 19:11

B. Background information
—Father's name was John ... Jn 1:42
—Given name: Simon ... Jn 1:42
—Brother of Andrew ... Mt 10:2
—A native of Bethsaida ... Jn 1:44
—Originally a fisherman ... Lk 5:1 – 5
—Uneducated ... Ac 4:13
—Married ... Mk 1:30; 1Co 9:5

C. Events during Jesus' public ministry
—Let Jesus use his boat to speak from ... Lk 5:3
—Caught numerous fish at Jesus' command ... Lk 5:5 – 7
—Given the name Cephas (Peter) ... Mt 16:17 – 18; Jn 1:42
—Called by Jesus to fish for people ... Mt 4:18 – 20; Mk 1:16 – 18
—Witnessed raising of Jairus's daughter ... Mk 5:37 – 41
—Walked on water at Jesus' bidding ... Mt 14:28 – 31
—Confessed Christ as Son of God ... Mt 16:13 – 16; Mk 8:27 – 30; Lk 9:18 – 20
—Rebuked by Jesus ... Mt 16:21 – 23; Mk 8:31 – 33
—Observed the transfiguration ... Mt 17:1 – 8; Mk 9:2 – 8
—Caught fish that had coin in its mouth ... Mt 17:24 – 27

—Inquired about limits of forgiveness.................Mt 18:21
—Did not want Jesus to wash his feet ....Jn 13:6 – 10
—Jesus prayed for him ....Lk 22:31 – 32
—His denial of Jesus predicted.................Mt 26:31 – 35
Mk 14:27 – 31
Lk 22:33 – 34
—Accompanied Jesus to Gethsemane ....Mt 26:36 – 45
Mk 14:32 – 42
—Cut off ear of the high priest's servant.................Jn 18:10 – 11
—Denied Jesus three times ....Mt 26:69 – 75
Mk 14:66 – 72
Lk 22:54 – 62
Jn 18:15 – 18,25 – 27

D. Events between resurrection and Pentecost
—Ran to tomb on Easter Sunday.................Lk 24:12
Jn 20:2 – 8
—Jesus appeared to him ....Lk 24:33 – 34
1Co 15:5
—Decided to go fishing.................Jn 21:3
—Had breakfast with Jesus ....Jn 21:4 – 14
—Was asked three times, "Do you love me?".................Jn 21:15 – 17
—One of the apostles in upper room.................Ac 1:13
—Suggested that Judas's vacancy be filled.................Ac 1:15 – 22

E. Events after Pentecost
—Preached a sermon on Pentecost Sunday.................Ac 2:14 – 36
—Called the people to repent.................Ac 2:37 – 40
—With John, healed a lame man ....Ac 3:1 – 8
—Preached in the temple.................Ac 3:11 – 26
—Arrested with John.................Ac 4:1 – 3
—Questioned before the Sanhedrin ....Ac 4:7 – 21
Ac 5:27 – 32
—Spoke judgment against Ananias and Sapphira ....Ac 5:1 – 10
—His shadow healed people ....Ac 5:15 – 16
—Was sent to new Christians in Samaria.................Ac 8:14 – 17
—Through a vision, was sent to Cornelius.................Ac 10:9 – 48
—Explained how God was saving Gentiles ....Ac 11:1 – 18
—Imprisoned by Herod ....Ac 12:3 – 5
—Freed from prison by an angel ....Ac 12:6 – 11
—Left Jerusalem ....Ac 12:17
—Did missionary work among the Jews.................1Co 9:5
Gal 2:9
—Had conflict with Paul at Antioch.................Gal 2:11 – 14
—Spoke at council in Jerusalem ....Ac 15:7 – 11

F. His character and significance
1. Often spoke impulsively
—Asked to come to Jesus on the water ....Mt 14:28
—Rebuked Jesus ....Mt 16:22
—Said he was willing to die with Jesus.................Lk 22:33
—Claimed he would never deny Jesus ....Mt 26:33 – 35
—Did not want Jesus to wash his feet.................Jn 13:6 – 9
2. A leader among the disciples
—His name always mentioned first.................Mt 10:2
Mk 3:16
Lk 6:14
Ac 1:13
—Often the spokesman for the rest.................Mt 16:16
Mt 26:33 – 35
Ac 2:14
Ac 4:29
3. One of the major leaders of the church
—Called "rock" by Jesus.................Mt 16:18
—Led the church in Jerusalem ....Ac 5:1 – 9
—Paul met specifically with him.................Gal 1:18
—Spoke at Jerusalem council.................Ac 15:7 – 11
—Called a "pillar" ....Gal 2:9
—A party at Corinth called by his name 1Co 1:12
—Wrote two letters.................1Pe 1:1
2Pe 1:1

PETITION

—Asking God for personal things in prayer

A. Why must we ask?
—God commands it.................Mt 7:7 – 9
—We have needs.................Php 4:19
—We follow the example of God's holy people.................1Ch 16:4
Da 6:11
Da 9:17 – 18

B. How must we ask?
—In faith.................Mk 11:24
Jn 14:12 – 14
—With thanksgiving ....Php 4:6
—In Jesus' name.................Jn 14:6,13
Jn 15:16
Jn 16:23 – 24
Ro 5:2
—Without worry ....Mt 6:25 – 34
Lk 12:22 – 31

C. For what may we ask?
—For daily bread ....Mt 6:11
—For forgiveness.................Da 9:19
Mt 6:12
—For freedom from temptation ....Mt 6:13
—For the Holy Spirit ....Lk 11:13
—For the ability to witness with boldness.................Ac 4:29 – 30
—For safety in travel ....Ezr 8:21 – 23
—For healing.................Isa 38:2
Mk 1:40
—For a child 1Sa 1:11
—For anything ....Jn 14:14

PHARAOH

—The title given to the king of Egypt

A. Pharaohs mentioned in the Bible
1. The pharaoh at the time of Abram
—Sarai taken into his palace ....Ge 12:14 – 15
—Diseases inflicted on his household ....Ge 12:17
—Expelled Abram from Egypt ....Ge 12:18 – 20
2. The pharaoh at the time of Joseph
—Put butler and baker in prison ....Ge 40:1 – 4
—Had dreams, interpreted by Joseph ....Ge 41:1 – 32
—Made Joseph second in command ....Ge 41:37 – 43
—Gave Joseph a wife ....Ge 41:44 – 45
—Invited Jacob to live in Egypt ....Ge 45:16 – 20
—Greeted Jacob and his family ....Ge 47:1 – 10
—Settled Jacob and family in Goshen ....Ge 47:5 – 6
—Allowed Joseph to bury Jacob in Canaan ....Ge 50:4 – 6
3. The pharaoh at the time of the exodus
a. Oppression of the Israelites
—Did not know about Joseph ....Ex 1:8
—Turned the Israelites into slaves.................Ex 1:9 – 11
—Ordered the death of baby boys.................Ex 1:15 – 22
—Tried to kill Moses ....Ex 2:15
—Increased burden of slavery.................Ex 5:1 – 18
b. Interaction with Moses and Aaron
—First appearance before him ....Ex 5:1 – 5
—Second appearance, first miracles ....Ex 7:10 – 21
—Asked for plagues to be stopped.................Ex 8:8,28
Ex 9:27 – 28
Ex 10:16 – 17
—Agreed to let Israelites worship ....Ex 8:25 – 29
Ex 9:27 – 28
Ex 10:8 – 10,24
—Hardened his heart.................Ex 7:13,22
Ex 8:15,32
Ex 9:7,12,34 – 35
Ex 10:1,20,27
c. The exodus
—His firstborn son killed.................Ex 12:29 – 30
—Ordered Israelites to leave ....Ex 12:31 – 32

—Changed mind and pursued Israelites..... Ex 14:5 – 9
—Followed Israelites into the sea............. Ex 14:23 – 25
—Drowned.. Ex 14:26 – 28
Ps 106:10 – 11
4. The pharaoh at the time of Solomon
—Alliance between him and Solomon 1Ki 3:1
—Solomon married his daughter.................... 1Ki 3:1
1Ki 11:1
—Conquered Gezer and gave it to Solomon 1Ki 9:16
5. Shishak, at the end of Solomon's reign
—Befriended Hadad, adversary of Solomon.... 1Ki 11:14 – 22
—Befriended Jeroboam 1Ki 11:40
—Attacked and defeated Rehoboam............... 1Ki 14:25 – 26
2Ch 12:1 – 11
6. The pharaoh in Hoshea's time
—Possibly called So... 2Ki 17:4
—Hoshea made alliance with him.................. 2Ki 17:4
7. The pharaoh in Hezekiah's time
—Made alliance with Hezekiah .... Isa 30:1 – 2
—Advanced against Sennacherib.................... 2Ki 19:9
—A weak pharaoh.. 2Ki 18:21
Isa 36:6
—Unable to save Judah .... Isa 30:3 – 5
Isa 31:1 – 3
8. Pharaoh Neco
—Allied with Assyria against Babylon............ 2Ki 23:29
2Ch 35:20
—Fought and defeated Josiah........................ 2Ki 23:29 – 30
2Ch 35:20 – 24
—Deposed Jehoahaz... 2Ki 23:33
2Ch 36:3
—Made Jehoiakim king..................................... 2Ki 23:34 – 35
2Ch 36:4
—Defeated by the Babylonians .... Jer 46:2
9. Hophra, at the time of the exile
—Zedekiah asked his help against Babylon..... Eze 17:15
—Marched against the Babylonians................ Jer 37:5
—Deserted Zedekiah.. Jer 37:7
—His defeat to Nebuchadnezzar prophesied... Jer 44:30
Eze 29:19 – 20

B. Prophecies against Pharaoh
—By Jeremiah .... Jer 44:30
Jer 46:14 – 19
—By Ezekiel.. Eze 29:1 – 5
Eze 32:1 – 15

PHARISEES

—A Jewish party, prominent at the time of Jesus
A. Major characteristics
—Political leaders of the Jews........................ Mt 27:62 – 64
—Members of the Sanhedrin (Jewish council) ..... Ac 23:6
—Leaders of the synagogue............................ Jn 9:13 – 16,22
—Official interpreters of the law .... Mt 23:2
—Strict observers of the Law of Moses............ Mt 12:2,8 – 14
Mt 23:23
—Strict adherents of Jewish traditions............ Mk 7:2 – 3
Gal 1:14
—Believed circumcision was necessary .... Ac 15:5
—Believed in the resurrection and in angels .... Ac 23:8
—Tried to remain separate from sinners........... Mt 9:11
—Promoted Judaism throughout the world......... Mt 23:15
B. Prominent Pharisees in the Bible
—Nicodemus.. Jn 3:1
—Gamaliel... Ac 5:34
—Paul .... Ac 23:6
Php 3:5
C. The Pharisees and Jesus
1. Regularly questioned and tested Jesus .... Lk 11:53 – 54
—About eating with sinners .... Mt 9:11
Mk 2:16
Lk 5:30
—About fasting... Mt 9:14
Mk 2:18
Lk 5:33
—About failing to keep the Sabbath .... Mt 12:2
Mk 2:24
Lk 6:2
—About not keeping traditions....................... Mt 15:1 – 2
Mk 7:5
—About marriage and divorce .... Mt 19:3
Mk 10:2
—About a woman caught in adultery .... Jn 8:1 – 6
—About paying taxes to Caesar....................... Mt 22:15 – 17
Mk 12:13 – 15
—About the most important commandment.. Mt 22:34 – 36
—About the kingdom of God .... Lk 17:20 – 21
—About the validity of Jesus' testimony.......... Jn 8:12 – 13
—About their own blindness........................... Jn 8:40
—Asked for a miraculous sign .... Mt 12:38
—Asked for a sign from heaven....................... Mt 16:1
Mk 8:11
2. Criticized Jesus
—Said he was controlled by a demon .... Mt 9:34
Mt 12:24
—Said he spoke blasphemy .... Lk 5:21
—Said he failed to keep the Sabbath .... Lk 6:6 – 7
—Criticized his association with sinners.......... Lk 7:36 – 39
Lk 15:1 – 2
—Criticized his acceptance of praise................ Lk 19:38 – 39
3. Desired to get rid of Jesus
—Tried to arrest him... Jn 7:32
Jn 18:1 – 3
—Sought to kill him .... Mt 12:14
Mk 3:6
Jn 11:46 – 50
—Asked for soldiers to guard the tomb .... Mt 27:62 – 64
4. Some secretly believed in Jesus .... Jn 12:42 – 43
D. Jesus criticized the Pharisees
—For their lack of true righteousness............... Mt 5:20
—For their questionable teachings.................... Mt 16:6,11 – 12
—For persecuting God's messengers .... Mt 21:33 – 46
Mt 23:33 – 36
—For failing to understand Scripture .... Mt 22:41 – 45
—For their hypocrisy .... Mt 23:1 – 32
Lk 11:37 – 44
Lk 18:9 – 14
—For their lack of concern for people .... Lk 14:1 – 14
—For their love of money .... Lk 16:14 – 15

PHILIP

A. Disciple of Jesus .... Mt 10:3
Mk 3:18
—Brought Nathanael to Jesus .... Jn 1:44 – 46
—Jesus tested him at feeding of five thousand .... Jn 6:5 – 7
—Introduced Greeks to Jesus............................. Jn 12:20 – 22
—Wanted to see the Father .... Jn 14:8 – 9
—One of the apostles .... Ac 1:13
B. One of the seven deacons................................. Ac 6:1 – 7
—Became an evangelist in Samaria .... Ac 8:5 – 13
—Witnessed to and baptized Ethiopian eunuch ... Ac 8:26 – 39
—Continued preaching the gospel .... Ac 8:40
—Had four daughters who prophesied.............. Ac 21:9

PHILISTINES

A. Their identity
—Descendants of Egypt, son of Ham .... Ge 10:6,13 – 14
—Came from Caphtor (Crete) .... Am 9:7
—Five main cities .... Jos 13:3
1Sa 6:17
—Advanced in culture and war techniques .... 1Sa 13:5 – 7,19 – 21

—Their land not fully taken over by Joshua Jos 13:2
Jdg 3:1–3

B. Prominent Philistines
—Abimelech: wanted Rebekah as wife Ge 26:1,7–11
—Delilah: Samson's lover and deceiver Jdg 16:4–20
—Goliath: giant killed by David 1Sa 17:4,41–49
—Achish: king of Gath, friend of David 1Sa 21:10–15
1Sa 27:1–7

C. Their wars
1. The period of the judges
a. Defeated by Shamgar Jdg 3:31
b. Fought Israel at time of Jephthah Jdg 10:7–9
c. Fought Israel at time of Samson Jdg 13:1,5
See SAMSON
d. Fought Israel at time of Samuel
—Captured the ark in battle 1Sa 4:1–11
—Returned the ark 1Sa 6:1–12
—Defeated by Samuel at Mizpah 1Sa 7:2–14
2. The period of the kings
a. During Saul's reign
—Attacked by Jonathan 1Sa 13:3–7
—Defeated by Jonathan and troops 1Sa 14:1–47
—Defeated after death of Goliath 1Sa 17:1–53
—Two hundred killed by David 1Sa 18:24–27
—Defeated by David 1Sa 19:8
1Sa 23:1–5
—Attacked King Saul 1Sa 28:1,4–5
—Defeated Israelites; Saul died 1Sa 31:1–7
1Ch 10:1–7
b. During David's reign
—God promised to defeat them 2Sa 3:18
—David's victories over them 2Sa 5:17–25
2Sa 8:1
2Sa 21:15–22
1Ch 14:8–17
1Ch 18:1
1Ch 20:4–8
—Exploits of David's mighty men 2Sa 23:9–17
1Ch 11:12–19
c. Solomon ruled them 1Ki 4:21
2Ch 9:26
d. Jehoshaphat ruled them 2Ch 17:10–11
e. They defeated Jehoram 2Ch 21:16–17
f. Uzziah defeated them 2Ch 26:6–7
g. They defeated Ahaz 2Ch 28:18
h. Hezekiah defeated them 2Ki 18:8

D. Important data concerning them
—Isaac made treaty with Abimelech Ge 26:26–31
—David hid from Saul among them 1Sa 27:1–7
1Sa 29:1–11
—Prophecies against them Isa 14:28–32
Jer 47:1–7
Eze 25:15–17
Am 1:6–8
Zep 2:4–7
Zec 9:5–7
—Promise concerning their salvation Ps 87:4

PHINEHAS

A. Son of Eleazar and grandson of Aaron Ex 6:25
—Killed Zimri and Cozbi to end plague Nu 25:6–15
—Investigated an altar across the Jordan Jos 22:13–31
B. Son of Eli; brother of Hophni 1Sa 1:3
—A wicked priest 1Sa 2:12–17
—Scorned his father's rebuke 1Sa 2:22–25
—His death prophesied as a sign to Eli 1Sa 2:30–34
—Brought the ark into battle 1Sa 4:4
—Killed in the battle 1Sa 4:11,17

PHOEBE

—Christian from Cenchrea commended by Paul Ro 16:1–2

PIETY

See MEDITATION; SPIRITUALITY

PILATE

—Governor of Judea Jn 18:28–29
—Presided over Jesus' trial Mt 27:11–26
Mk 15:1–15
Lk 23:1–5,13–25
Jn 18:28—19:16
—Sent Jesus to Herod Lk 23:6–12
—Washed his hands as sign of innocence Mt 27:24–25
—Consented to Jesus' crucifixion Mt 27:15–26
Mk 15:6–15
—Gave body of Jesus to Joseph and Nicodemus Mt 27:57–60
Jn 19:38–42
—Authorized a guard at the tomb Mt 27:62–66
—His name forever associated with Jesus' death Ac 3:13
Ac 4:27
Ac 13:28
1Ti 6:13

PITY

See COMPASSION; MERCY

POTIPHAR

—Egyptian official who bought Joseph Ge 37:36
—Put Joseph in charge of his household Ge 39:1–6
—Sent Joseph to prison, unjustly Ge 39:7–20

POVERTY

See THE RICH AND THE POOR

POWER

See AUTHORITY

PRAISE

A. Related theme
PRAISE is a theme of Psalms Ps 150:6
B. Praising God is a command
1. Commanded throughout the Bible
—In the Mosaic Law Dt 8:10
—In the Prophets 1Ch 29:20
Isa 61:11
Jer 20:13
Joel 2:26
—In the Psalms Ps 103:1
Ps 104:1
Ps 145–150
—In the New Testament Eph 1:3,6,12,14
1Pe 1:3,7
Rev 19:5
2. Praise is commanded of:
—God's people Ps 30:4
Ps 135:1–2,19–21
—Children Ps 8:2
Mt 21:16
—The nations Ps 67:3–5
Ps 117:1
Ro 15:11
—The angels Ps 103:20
Ps 148:2
—Everything that breathes Ps 150:6
—All creation Ps 98:8
Ps 148:3–12
Isa 44:23
C. Reasons for praise
—God's greatness Ps 145:3
—God's splendor and majesty Ps 96:4–6
—God's glory Ps 66:1–2
—God's holiness Ps 99:3
Isa 6:3

—God's love and faithfulness ... Ps 57:9–10; Ps 89:1–2
—God's acts of power ... Ps 150:2
—God's marvelous deeds ... Isa 25:1
—God's glorious grace ... Eph 1:6
—God's salvation ... Ps 106:1–5; Lk 1:68–75; Lk 2:14,20
—God's benefits to his people ... Ps 103:1–18; Ps 111:1–10; Isa 63:7
—God's deliverance of us ... Ps 40:1–3; Ps 124:6–8

D. Methods of praise
—By public worship ... Ps 100:4
—By singing ... Ps 146:1; Ps 147:1
—By musical instruments ... Ps 150:3–5
—By speaking ... Ps 51:15; Heb 13:15
—By dancing ... Ps 149:3
—By witnessing to unbelievers ... 1Pe 2:9

PRAYER

—Communication with God

A. Related themes
PRAYER is a theme of Luke ... Lk 11:1
PRAY AND WORK is a theme of Nehemiah ... Ne 4:9

B. What is prayer?
—Calling on the name of the Lord ... Ge 4:26; Ge 12:8; Zep 3:9
—Calling to God ... Ps 4:1,3; Ps 17:6
—Seeking God's face ... 2Ch 7:14; Ps 27:8
—Seeking the Lord ... Ps 34:4; Isa 55:6
—Crying out to God ... Ps 3:4; Ps 66:1
—Lifting up the soul to God ... Ps 25:1; Ps 86:4
—Lifting up one's hands to God ... Ps 28:2; Ps 141:2
—Approaching God's throne of grace ... Heb 4:16
—Drawing near to God ... Heb 10:22

C. To whom should we pray?
—To God ... 2Ch 20:5–6; Ezr 9:6; Ac 4:24
—To the Father ... Eph 1:17; Eph 3:14; Col 1:3
—To the Lord ... 2Ch 20:5–6; Ac 4:24; 2Co 12:8
—To Jesus Christ ... Lk 23:42; Ac 7:59

D. What are the elements of prayer?
—Praise ... Ps 150; Mt 11:25–26
See PRAISE
—Thanksgiving ... Ps 136; Php 4:6
See THANKSGIVING
—Confession ... Ps 51; Mt 6:12
See CONFESSION
—Intercession ... Ps 122:6–9; Jn 17:6–26
See INTERCESSION
—Petition ... Ps 27:7–12; Mt 26:39,42
See PETITION

E. How should we pray?

1. Divine elements
—Through Jesus Christ ... Ro 1:8
—In the name of Jesus Christ ... Jn 14:13–14; Eph 5:20
—In the Holy Spirit ... Eph 6:18; Jude 20

2. Human elements
—In the fear of the Lord ... Ps 145:19; Pr 1:28–29
—In faith ... Mk 11:24; Jas 1:6; Jas 5:15
—In humility ... 2Ch 7:14; 2Ch 33:12–13
—In repentance ... 2Ch 6:37; Ac 3:19
—With all our heart ... Dt 4:29; Jer 29:13
—With a heart free from sin ... Ps 66:18–19; Isa 1:15–16; Jn 9:31
—With a life free from selfishness ... Lk 18:9–14; Jas 4:3
—With a heart free from doubt ... Mt 21:21; Jas 1:5–7
—With a forgiving spirit ... Mt 6:14–15; Mk 11:25
—With confidence ... Eph 3:12; Heb 10:19,35; 1Jn 3:21–22
—With persistence ... Lk 11:5–10; Lk 18:1–7; 1Th 5:17
—With sincerity and simplicity ... Mt 6:5–8; Mk 12:38–40
—In accordance with God's will ... Mt 26:42; 1Jn 5:14
—By accompanying prayer with obedience ... 1Jn 3:22

F. Does God answer the prayers of his people?

1. Remarkable answers to prayers
—Abraham's servant for a wife for Isaac ... Ge 24:12–27
—Moses for the defeat of Amalek ... Ex 17:8–13
—Gideon and his fleece ... Jdg 6:36–40
—Samson for strength ... Jdg 16:25–30
—Hannah for a child ... 1Sa 1:9–20
—Elijah for return to life of a dead boy ... 1Ki 17:19–23
—Elijah for fire from heaven ... 1Ki 18:30–38
—Elijah for rain ... 1Ki 18:41–45; Jas 5:17–18
—Elisha for return to life of a dead boy ... 2Ki 4:32–35
—Hezekiah for healing ... 2Ki 20:1–7
—Daniel for safety in the lions' den ... Da 6:10,16–22
—Zechariah for a child ... Lk 1:7,11–17
—The thief on the cross for salvation ... Lk 23:42–43
—Early Christians for Peter in prison ... Ac 12:3–11
—Paul and Silas in prison ... Ac 16:25–26

2. God's promises to answer us
—In the Old Testament ... Ps 86:7; Isa 30:19; Isa 58:9
—In the words of Jesus ... Mt 7:7–11; Jn 14:13–14
—In New Testament letters ... Jas 1:5–8; 1Jn 5:14–15

3. The basis of God's answers
   - —God's glory .... Nu 14:13 – 16; Jn 17:1 – 5
   - —God's grace .... Ex 32:31 – 32; Nu 14:17 – 19; Isa 30:19; 2Co 12:8 – 9
   - —God's faithfulness to his word .... Ex 32:12 – 13; 2Ch 20:7 – 9
4. The manner of God's answers
   - —Sometimes immediately .... Nu 14:20; 1Ki 17:20 – 21; Lk 23:43
   - —Sometimes after a delay .... Lk 18:1 – 7
   - —Sometimes more than asked for .... 1Ki 18:24,36 – 38; Eph 3:20
   - —Sometimes different from the request .... 1Ki 19:1 – 9; 2Co 12:7 – 9
   - —Sometimes "No" .... 2Sa 12:15 – 20
   - —God requires action on our part .... Ne 4:9

G. Various aspects of prayer
1. Postures of prayer
   - —Standing .... 1Ki 8:22; Ne 9:4 – 5
   - —Sitting .... 1Ch 17:16; Lk 10:13
   - —Kneeling .... Ezr 9:5; Da 6:10; Ac 20:36
   - —Bowing down .... Ex 34:8; Ps 5:7; Ps 95:6
   - —Lying on the ground .... 2Sa 12:16; Mt 26:39
   - —Lifting up hands .... Ps 28:2; Isa 1:15; 1Ti 2:8
2. Manner of prayer
   - —Alone, silently 1Sa 1:18
   - —Alone, aloud .... Eze 11:13
   - —With two or three .... Mt 18:19
   - —In a larger group .... Ps 35:18
3. Time of prayer
   - —In the morning .... Ps 5:1 – 3; Mk 1:35
   - —In the evening .... Ge 24:63
   - —At fixed times .... Ps 55:17; Da 6:10
   - —Always .... Lk 18:1; Ro 1:10; 1Th 5:17
4. Possible places of prayer
   - —In secret .... Mt 6:6
   - —In bed .... Ps 63:6
   - —In a family setting .... Ac 10:1 – 2
   - —Out in the open .... Ge 24:11 – 12
   - —In the battlefield .... Jos 10:12 – 13
   - —By the riverside .... Ac 16:13
   - —In the temple 2Ki 19:14
   - —In the church gathered together .... Ac 4:23 – 24,31
   - —Anywhere 1Ti 2:8

PREACHING

A. Preachers in the Bible
1. Old Testament saints who preached
   - —Noah 2Pe 2:5
   - —Jonah .... Jnh 1:2; Jnh 3:2
   - —Isaiah .... Isa 61:1
   - —Ezekiel .... Eze 21:2
   - —Amos .... Am 7:16
   - —Haggai and Zechariah .... Ezr 6:14
2. New Testament saints who preached
   - —John the Baptist .... Mt 3:1
   - —Jesus .... Mt 4:17
   - —Peter and John .... Ac 8:25
   - —Philip .... Ac 8:40
   - —Paul .... Ac 9:27; 1Co 9:16
   - —Timothy 1Ti 4:13
   - —Numerous believers .... Ac 8:4; Ac 15:35
   - —All Christians .... Mt 28:19; Mk 16:15

B. The content of preaching
1. In the Old Testament
   - —A message of judgment .... Eze 20:46; Eze 21:2; Am 7:16; Jnh 3:4
   - —A message of hope .... Isa 40:1 – 2,9; Isa 52:7 – 10; Am 9:11 – 15
2. In the New Testament
   - —The good news of the kingdom .... Lk 9:2; Lk 16:16; Ac 20:25
   - —The good news of salvation .... 1Co 1:21; 1Co 15:1 – 2
   - —The cross of Christ .... 1Co 2:1 – 2
   - —The resurrection of Christ .... Ac 17:18,31; 1Co 15:12 – 14
   - —Jesus Christ is Lord 2Co 4:5
   - —Fulfillment of the Scriptures in Christ .... Ac 2:14 – 36; Ac 4:12 – 26; Ac 13:16 – 41; 1Co 15:3 – 5
   - —The coming judgment .... Ac 10:42; Ac 17:31
   - —The call to repent and believe .... Mk 1:15; Ac 2:38; Ac 10:43; Ac 26:20

PREDESTINATION

See ELECTION; PROVIDENCE

PRIDE

A. Legitimate pride
1. Occasions for such pride
   - —Boasting in the Lord .... Ps 34:2; Ps 44:8; Jer 9:24; 1Co 1:31
   - —Boasting in the cross of Christ .... Gal 6:14
   - —Boasting about God-fearing churches .... 2Co 1:14; 2Co 7:4; Php 2:16
2. The glory of such pride
   - —Must be in God's grace 2Co 1:12
   - —Must be in Jesus Christ .... Ro 15:17 – 18
   - —Must be in the Holy Spirit .... Ro 15:18 – 19

B. Sinful pride
1. Characteristics of a proud person
   - —Tries to be like God .... Ge 3:5 – 6
   - —Thinks himself or herself better than others .... Lk 18:10 – 12
   - —Boasts about ancestry .... Lk 3:8; Jn 8:33
   - —Takes pride in the temple .... Jer 7:4

—Takes pride in self-accomplishment............Isa 10:12 – 15
Eze 28:1 – 7
1Co 4:7

2. Notable examples
—Adam and Eve............Ge 3:5 – 6
—David............1Ch 21:1 – 7
—Uzziah............2Ch 26:16
—Hezekiah............2Ch 32:25
—Nebuchadnezzar............Da 4:30
—Herod............Ac 12:21 – 23

3. Results of such pride
—Deceives the heart............Jer 49:16
—Hardens the heart............Da 5:20
—Produces quarrels............Pr 13:10
—Brings disgrace............Pr 11:2
—Leads to destruction............Pr 16:18
—Brings opposition from God............Pr 3:34
Jas 4:6
—Brings judgment from God............Lev 26:18 – 20
Zep 2:10 – 11
Mal 4:1

4. Warnings against such pride............Pr 8:13
Pr 16:5,18
Pr 21:4,24
Lk 18:9
Ro 12:16
1Jn 2:16

See also HUMILITY

PRIEST

A. Basic requirements for being priests
—Must belong to the tribe of Levi............Ex 29:9,44
Ezr 2:61 – 62
—Had to follow special marriage laws............Lev 21:7 – 9,13 – 15
—Had to remain unshaven............Lev 21:5 – 6
—Had to honor proper procedures............Lev 10:1 – 7
—Non-priests punished for doing priestly work...Nu 18:7
1Sa 13:8 – 14
2Ch 26:16 – 21

B. Basic tasks of the priests (including Levites)
—Presented needs of the people to God............Heb 5:1 – 3
—Made atonement for sin............Lev 16:1 – 22
—Sprinkled blood of the sacrifices............Lev 1:5,11
Lev 17:11
—Offered sacrifices on the altar............Lev 6:8 – 9
—Kept fire burning on the altar............Lev 6:13
—Burned incense on the altar............Ex 30:7 – 9
Lk 1:5 – 9
—Took care of the sanctuary............Nu 3:38
—Responsible for the treasury............1Ch 26:20
—Supervised the work of the temple............1Ch 23:4
—Carried the ark............Nu 4:15
—Led the people in music............Ne 12:27 – 43
—Blessed the people............Nu 6:23 – 27
—Prayed for the people............Lev 16:20 – 21
Ezr 9:5 – 15
—Made diagnosis regarding leprosy............Lev 13:1 – 8
—Taught the law............Ne 8:7 – 8
Mal 2:7
—Made judgments according to the law............Dt 21:5
1Ch 23:4

C. Christ fulfilled the Old Testament priesthood
—Compared to a high priest............Heb 8:1 – 6
—Sacrificed himself............Heb 9:26,28
Heb 10:12
1Jn 2:2
—Brought his blood into heaven............Heb 9:12
—Justifies us............Ro 3:24 – 28
—Reconciles us to God............2Co 5:18 – 19
—Continues to pray for us............Ro 8:34
Heb 7:25
1Jn 2:1

D. Priesthood of all believers
—Believers are called a holy priesthood............1Pe 2:5,9
Rev 1:6
—We can approach God directly through Christ...Jn 14:6
Ro 5:2
Eph 2:18
—We can confess sins directly to God............Mt 6:12
Lk 18:13
Ac 2:37 – 38
Ac 17:30
—Our lives must be spiritual sacrifices............Ro 12:1
Heb 13:15 – 16
1Pe 2:5

PRISCILLA

—Wife of Aquila; tentmakers............Ac 18:1 – 3
—Invited Paul to live with them............Ac 18:3
—Traveled with Paul to Ephesus............Ac 18:18 – 19
—Instructed Apollos............Ac 18:26
—Paul considered her a co-worker............Ro 16:3
—Church met in their house............Ro 16:4

PROMISE

—God's pledge for the future

A. Major promises of God
1. Concerning Christ
—Coming offspring of the woman............Ge 3:15
—Abraham as a father of many............Ge 12:1 – 3
—Scepter to come from Judah............Ge 49:10
—Star to come from Jacob............Nu 24:17
—Prophet like Moses............Dt 18:15,18
—David's throne to be established forever......2Sa 7:16
—The virgin birth............Isa 7:14
—The coming Prince of Peace............Isa 9:6 – 7
—The suffering servant of God............Isa 53:1 – 12
—The new covenant............Jer 31:31 – 34
—The coming shepherd............Eze 34:23
—The coming Holy Spirit............Joel 2:28 – 32
—A king born in Bethlehem............Mic 5:2 – 4
—Jesus riding into Jerusalem............Zec 9:9
—The forerunner of the Messiah............Mal 3:1

2. Concerning believers
—God will forgive sin............1Jn 1:9
—God will give us peace............Ps 85:8
—God will bless us............Ps 67:6 – 7
—God will lead us............Ps 23:1 – 6
—God will never leave us............Heb 13:5
—Jesus will never leave us............Mt 28:20
—God will answer prayer............1Jn 5:14 – 15
—Jesus will answer prayer............Jn 14:13 – 14
—God will help us overcome temptation............1Co 10:13
—God will protect us from Satan............2Th 3:3
—God will give us eternal life............1Jn 2:25
—God will give us the kingdom............Jas 2:5
—God will make us his heirs............Gal 3:29

B. God's attitude to his promises
—Gives us many promises............2Pe 1:4
—Confirms his promises by an oath............Heb 6:13 – 20
—Remembers his promises............Ps 105:42
—Keeps his promises............Jos 23:15
Isa 38:7
Ac 13:23,32 – 33
2Pe 3:9
—Is faithful to his promises............1Th 5:24
Heb 10:23
—Fulfills all his promises in Christ............2Co 1:18,20
—God's promises never fail............1Ki 8:56

C. Believers and God's promises
—We have them from God 2Co 7:1
—We must believe them Ps 106:12,24
Ro 4:16–21
—We must share in them Eph 3:6
—We must rejoice in them Ps 119:162
—We must meditate on them Ps 119:148
—We must not fall short of them Heb 4:1

PROPHET

A. Related themes
1. PROPHETS is a theme of:
—1 Kings 1Ki 11:29
—2 Kings 2Ki 6:12
2. FULFILLMENT is a theme of:
—Matthew Mt 5:17
—Hebrews Heb 7:27
B. How did one become a prophet?
—Called directly by God Isa 6:8
Jer 1:4–5
Am 7:14–15
—Inspired by God to prophesy 1Sa 10:6,9–11
1Sa 19:23–24
—Appointed by another prophet 1Ki 19:19–21
—Some joined the company of the prophets 2Ki 2:3,5,7
2Ki 6:1–4
C. What did a prophet do?
1. Spoke messages from God to the people
—God commanded them to speak Dt 18:18
Jnh 3:2
—The Spirit moved them to speak 2Pe 1:21
—They said, "This is what the LORD says" Isa 44:6
Jer 6:16
2. Served as watchmen for the people Jer 6:16–17
Eze 3:16–21
3. Pointed out the sins of kings 2Sa 12:1–12
1Ki 18:18–19
4. Pronounced judgment on the people 1Ki 21:20–24
Isa 2:6–21
Jer 4:5–18
5. Predicted the future 1Sa 9:9
—The near future 1Ki 17:1
Ac 11:28
—The distant future Isa 65:17–25
Joel 2:28–32
Mic 5:2–5
Lk 24:25–27
6. Called the people to repentance 2Ki 17:13
Jer 18:11
Am 5:4–6,14–15
7. Gave hope to the people Jer 23:3–8
Am 9:11–15
Zep 3:9–17
8. Interpreted dreams Da 2:17–45
Da 3:9–28
9. Wrote down messages from God Jer 30:2
Hab 2:2
Rev 1:11,19
D. Tests for determining the true prophet
—Does the prophecy come true? Dt 18:21–22
Jer 28:1–17
—Does it correspond with God's word? Dt 13:1–3
1Ki 22:17–28,37
1Jn 4:1–3
—Does the prophet live a God-fearing life? Jer 23:9–18
2Pe 2:1–3,13–18
E. Responses to the prophets
1. Positive
—They were to be heeded Dt 18:15
—They were to be trusted 2Ch 20:20
2. Negative
—They were often persecuted 2Ch 36:16
Ac 7:52
—They were sometimes put in prison 2Ch 18:25–26
Jer 37:15–16
—They were even killed 1Ki 19:10
Mt 21:35–36
1Th 2:15
F. Jesus Christ as God's final prophet
—He fulfilled God's promise of a prophet Dt 18:15,18
Ac 3:21–23
Ac 7:37
—He fulfilled all Old Testament prophecies Mt 5:17
2Co 1:20
1Pe 1:10–11
—He is called "the Prophet" Jn 6:14–15
Jn 7:40
—He called himself a prophet Mt 13:57
Lk 13:33
—He perfectly spoke God's word Jn 7:16
Jn 12:49–50
Heb 1:1–2
—He is the Word of God in human flesh Jn 1:14
G. Prophets in the New Testament church
1. Names
—Agabus Ac 11:28
Ac 21:10
—Judas and Silas Ac 15:32
—Twelve men in Ephesus Ac 19:6
—Daughters of Philip Ac 21:9
—Paul 1Co 13:2
1Th 4:13–17
—Peter 2Pe 3:10–13
—John Rev 1:1
2. Prophecy as a gift of the Spirit
—Mentioned by Peter on Pentecost Ac 2:17
—Mentioned by Paul 1Co 12:10
1Co 14:1
Eph 4:11
—Distinct from the gift of teaching Ac 13:1
1Co 12:28
Eph 4:11
3. Function of prophets in the church
—Served as foundation of the church Eph 2:20
—Their gift preferred to tongues 1Co 14:1–5
—Message must edify the church 1Co 14:4–5,12
—Message must reach unbelievers 1Co 14:23–25
—Message must be tested by other prophets 1Co 14:29–32
1Th 5:19–20
1Jn 4:1

PROVIDENCE

—God's care over creation and his control of history
A. Related themes
1. PROVIDENCE is a theme of:
—Numbers Nu 21:3
—Ruth Ru 4:14
—Ezra Ezr 8:31
—Esther Est 6:4
2. PLAN OF GOD is a theme of:
—Luke Lk 16:16
—Ephesians Eph 1:10
3. GOD'S CONTROL is a theme of:
—Jeremiah Jer 10:10
—Daniel Da 4:35
—Habakkuk Hab 2:13
—Zechariah Zec 12:1
4. GOD'S FREEDOM is a theme of Job Job 40:8

B. God's care for his whole creation
1. Aspects of God's providence
—Cares for all his creatures .... Ps 145:9; Mt 10:29
—Provides food for his creatures .... Ps 104:14,27–28; Ps 145:16; Mt 6:26
—Preserves his creatures .... Ne 9:6; Ps 36:6
—Determines the events of history .... Ge 50:20; Ps 33:10–11; Ac 2:22–23
—Determines the ways of humans .... Pr 16:1,9; Pr 19:21
—Controls everything that happens .... Isa 40:22–26; Da 4:35; Ac 17:26; Eph 1:11
—Controls the weather .... Ps 68:9; Mt 5:45; Ac 14:15–17
—Controls the smallest details .... Mt 10:29–30
—Controls evil .... Job 2:1–8; Isa 14:24–27; Isa 45:7; Am 3:6
2. Means of God's control
—By his powerful word .... Ps 29:3–9; Heb 1:3
—By Jesus Christ .... Col 1:17

C. God's special care for his own people
1. General statements .... Ps 91:1–16; Isa 31:5; Ro 8:35–39; 1Pe 3:12
2. Specific statements
—Opens hearts to believe the gospel .... Lk 24:45; Ac 16:14
—Controls specific events .... Ge 22:8,13–14; Ps 105:5–44; Ps 136:10–24; Isa 38:17
—Works for good of those who love him .... Ge 50:20; Ro 8:28

D. Our response to God's providence
—Acknowledge it 1Sa 2:6–10; 1Ch 29:11–12
—Rejoice in it .... Ps 4:7–8; Ps 16:7–11
—Trust in it .... Ps 13:6; Ps 28:7
—Humble ourselves in the face of it .... Dt 8:2–3; Job 1:20–22; Job 42:1–6
—Do not worry about tomorrow .... Mt 6:25–34; Mt 10:28–31

PUNISHMENT

—Penalty inflicted because of sin

A. Related theme
CYCLES is a theme of Judges .... Jdg 10:6

B. Human punishment through law
1. Principles of punishment
—Power to punish given to government .... Ro 13:4
—Eye for eye, tooth for tooth .... Ex 21:23–25; Lev 24:19–20; Dt 19:21
—Restitution to be made .... Ex 22:1–9; Nu 5:5–8
—Must be impartial .... Lev 24:22; Dt 1:16–17
—Innocent must be acquitted .... Dt 25:1
2. Methods of punishment
a. Non-capital punishments
—Fines .... Ex 21:22; Am 2:8
—Confiscation of property .... Ezr 7:26
—Beating .... Dt 25:2–3; 2Co 11:23–25
—Gouging out eyes .... Jdg 16:21
—Imprisonment .... 1Ki 22:27; Ac 12:4
—Confinement in a dungeon .... Jer 38:6
—Chains .... 2Ki 23:33; Php 1:7,13
—Banishment .... Ezr 7:26; Rev 1:9
—Excommunication from synagogue .... Jn 9:22; Jn 16:2
b. Capital punishment
—Stoning .... Dt 22:24; Ac 7:59
—Burning .... Lev 20:14
—Killing by the sword .... Ac 12:2
—Impaling on a pole .... Est 7:9–10
—Crucifying .... Mk 15:20,24
—Beheading .... Ge 40:19
—Sawing in pieces .... Heb 11:37
—Throwing to wild beasts .... Da 6:16,24

C. God's punishment
1. Basic reasons for God's punishment
—Human sin .... Am 1:3—2:16; Ro 6:23
—Idolatry .... 2Ki 17:14–20; Jer 2:9–13
—Disobedience to God's law .... Dt 28:15–68; Ne 9:26–27
2. Methods of God's punishments
a. Temporal
—Sickness 2Ch 26:19–20
—Death of a loved one 2Sa 12:14
—Drought 1Ki 17:1
—Famine .... La 2:11–12
—Violent storms .... Jnh 1:4
—Plagues .... Joel 1:2–11
—Defeat by foreign armies .... Jdg 2:10–15
—Exile 2Ch 36:15–20
b. Eternal punishment
See HELL

QUEEN

A. Queen of Sheba
—Came to visit Solomon 1Ki 10:1–2; 2Ch 9:1
—Overwhelmed at Solomon's wisdom 1Ki 10:3–9; 2Ch 9:2–8
—Gave Solomon many gifts 1Ki 10:10; 2Ch 9:9
—Received gifts from Solomon 1Ki 10:13; 2Ch 9:12
—Jesus used her as an example .... Mt 12:42; Lk 11:31

B. Queen Athaliah
See ATHALIAH

C. Queen Vashti
See VASHTI

D. Queen Esther
See ESTHER

E. Queen of Heaven (goddess Ishtar) .... Jer 7:18
Jer 44:17 – 19,25
F. Babylon pictured as a queen .... Isa 47:5 – 8
Rev 18:7

RACHEL
—Younger daughter of Laban .... Ge 29:16
—Second wife of Jacob .... Ge 29:28
—Loved by Jacob more than Leah .... Ge 29:30
—Bore two sons .... Ge 30:22 – 24
Ge 35:16 – 18,24
—Stole Laban's gods .... Ge 31:19,32 – 35
—Her death .... Ge 35:19 – 20
—Prophecy concerning her .... Jer 31:15
—Prophecy fulfilled at the birth of Jesus .... Mt 2:16 – 18

RAHAB
—Prostitute at Jericho who hid spies .... Jos 2:1 – 21
—Spared when Jericho was destroyed .... Jos 6:22 – 25
—Mother of Boaz .... Mt 1:5
—An example of true faith .... Heb 11:31
Jas 2:25 – 26

RAIN
See WEATHER

RANSOM
See REDEMPTION

REBEKAH
—Sister of Laban .... Ge 24:29
—Secured as bride for Isaac .... Ge 24:34 – 61
—Mother of Esau and Jacob .... Ge 25:19 – 26
—Abimelech discovered that she was Isaac's wife .... Ge 26:1 – 11
—Helped Jacob deceitfully get Isaac's blessing .... Ge 27:1 – 17
—Convinced Isaac that Jacob should leave .... Ge 27:42—28:4
—Buried in cave of Machpelah .... Ge 49:29 – 31

RECONCILIATION
—Establishing harmony between conflicting parties
A. The need for reconciliation
1. Between humans
—Adam and Eve argued in Eden .... Ge 3:12 – 13
—Abram and Lot could not agree .... Ge 13:5 – 11
—Sarai and Hagar could not get along .... Ge 16:3 – 6
—Jacob fled from Esau .... Ge 27:41 – 45
—There will always be conflicts .... Mt 24:6
2. Between God and humans
—Adam and Eve hid from God .... Ge 3:8
—Sinners are hostile to God .... Ro 8:7
Col 1:21
—Sinners cannot stand in God's presence .... Ps 5:5 – 6
—Isaiah fearful of God's presence .... Isa 6:5
3. Between God and nature
—Nature cursed by God .... Ge 3:14 – 18
—Nature groans because of sin .... Ro 8:20,22
B. The process of reconciliation
1. Only God can reconcile us to himself
—God took the initiative 2Co 5:18
—God reconciles sinners to himself 2Co 5:19
Col 1:22
—He reconciles all things to himself .... Eph 1:10
Col 1:20
2. Accomplished through the cross .... Ro 5:10
2Co 5:18 – 19
Col 1:22
Heb 2:17
3. Reconciliation among humans rooted in Christ
—Christ is our peace .... Eph 2:14 – 17
—We are one in Christ .... Jn 17:11,22 – 23
Gal 3:28
Col 3:11
—Harmony experienced in the early church .... Ac 2:44 – 45
Ac 4:32 – 35
C. Believers and reconciliation
1. Reconciliation with God
—We must be reconciled to God 2Co 5:20
—We must proclaim reconciliation .... 2Co 5:19 – 20
2. Reconciliation among believers
—Conflicts resolved in the early church .... Ac 15:1 – 29
Gal 2:1 – 10
—We may show no partiality in the church .... Jas 2:1 – 4,9
1Pe 1:17
—There may be no divisions in the church .... 1Co 1:10 – 13
1Co 11:18 – 22
—We must work for harmony in the church .... Gal 6:1 – 2
Eph 4:29 – 32
Php 2:1 – 5
—We must end personal conflicts .... Mt 5:23 – 24
Mt 18:15 – 16
1Co 6:1 – 8
Php 4:2 – 3

REDEMPTION
—Freedom obtained through a price paid
A. Related theme
REDEMPTION is a theme of Isaiah .... Isa 43:1
B. Redemption among humans
1. Redemption of an Israelite slave
—Slave could redeem himself .... Lev 25:49
—Slave could be redeemed by relatives .... Lev 25:48 – 49
—Slave released in Year of Jubilee .... Lev 25:54
2. Redemption of property
—A person could redeem his own land .... Lev 25:26 – 27
—A relative could redeem the land .... Lev 25:25,48 – 53
—Land returned in the Year of Jubilee .... Lev 25:28,39 – 43
—Land could be redeemed through marriage .... Ru 4:1 – 12
C. Redemption by God
1. Natural redemption for Israelites
—Israelites were slaves in Egypt .... Ge 15:13
Ex 1:11 – 14
Dt 5:15
—Israelites redeemed through the exodus .... Ex 6:6
2Sa 7:22 – 24
Ps 106:8 – 10
Mic 6:4
—Price paid was the destruction of Egypt .... Isa 43:3
—Judah redeemed from Babylon .... Isa 54:5 – 8
Jer 31:10 – 11
Mic 4:10
2. Spiritual redemption from sin
a. We need redemption
—We are all slaves to sin .... Jn 8:34
Ro 6:17
—Humans cannot redeem themselves .... Ps 49:7 – 8
b. God redeemed the Israelites .... Ps 130:8
Isa 44:21 – 22
Lk 1:68 – 71
c. Christ redeems us
—Redemption accomplished in Christ .... Ro 3:24
Col 1:13 – 14
—The ransom paid was his blood .... Eph 1:7
1Pe 1:19
Rev 5:9
—The ransom paid was his death .... Mk 10:45
Heb 9:15
1Ti 2:6

d. The purpose of redemption
—To justify us before God........ Ro 3:24
—To free us from wickedness........ Ro 6:7,22
Tit 2:14
—To free us from the law........ Gal 4:5
—To free us from the curse........ Gal 3:13
—To free us from an empty way of life........ 1Pe 1:18
e. The results of redemption
—We are forgiven........ Eph 1:7
Col 1:14
—We can now live free lives........ Gal 5:1,13
—We can now serve God........ 1Pe 2:16
—We await our final redemption........ Lk 21:27 – 28
Ro 8:23
Eph 1:14

REGENERATION
See BORN AGAIN

REHOBOAM
—Son of Solomon; king of Judah........ 1Ki 11:43
1Ch 3:10
—Had various wives........ 2Ch 11:18 – 21
—Was asked to lighten Israelite yoke........ 1Ki 12:1 – 4
2Ch 10:1 – 4
—Refused to ease the Israelites' burden........ 1Ki 12:5 – 15
2Ch 10:5 – 15
—Caused division in the kingdom........ 1Ki 12:16 – 24
2Ch 10:16 – 19
—Told not to fight to regain ten tribes........ 2Ch 11:1 – 4
—Built up defenses of Judah........ 2Ch 11:5 – 12
—Supported by Levites from Israel........ 2Ch 11:13 – 17
—Led Judah into idolatry........ 1Ki 14:21 – 24
2Ch 12:1,14
—Fought with Shishak of Egypt........ 1Ki 14:25 – 28
2Ch 12:2 – 11
—Humbled himself........ 2Ch 12:12
—His death........ 1Ki 14:31
2Ch 12:16

REJOICE
See JOY

REMEMBER
A. Human remembrance
1. Examples of what humans must remember
—The day of the exodus........ Ex 13:3
—The Sabbath day........ Ex 20:8
—God's care during forty years in wilderness........ Dt 8:2
—Rebellion against God........ Dt 9:7
—The power of God........ Ne 4:14
—The miracles of God........ Ps 77:11
—The name of God........ Ps 119:55
—The Creator........ Ecc 12:1,6
—The body and blood of the Lord........ 1Co 11:24 – 25
—The poor........ Gal 2:10
—The stranger........ Heb 13:2
2. What do humans do when they remember?
—They celebrate the Passover........ Ex 13:3 – 10
—They keep the Sabbath holy........ Ex 20:8
—They trust God........ Dt 8:17 – 18
—They obey and serve God........ Dt 10:12 – 13
—They fight for the Lord........ Ne 4:14
—They meditate on God and his mighty acts........ Ps 77:11 – 20
—They keep God's law........ Ps 119:55
—They fear God and obey his commandments........ Ecc 12:13
—They celebrate the Lord's Supper........ 1Co 11:26 – 29
—They give on behalf of the poor........ Gal 2:10
—They show hospitality........ Heb 13:2

B. Divine remembrance
1. Examples of what/whom God remembers
—His covenant with Noah........ Ge 9:14 – 15
—His covenant with Abraham........ Ex 2:23 – 25
Ps 105:8
—His promises........ Ps 105:42
—His love and faithfulness........ Ps 98:3
—Noah........ Ge 8:1
—Abraham........ Ge 19:29
—Rachel........ Ge 30:22
—Hannah........ 1Sa 1:19 – 20
—The wickedness of his people........ Jer 14:10
Hos 8:13
2. What does God do when he remembers?
—He spares the world from a flood........ Ge 9:14 – 15
—He rescues his people from Egypt........ Ex 3:7 – 9
Ps 105:43 – 44
—He saves his people........ Ps 98:3
—He dries up the earth........ Ge 8:1
—He brings Lot out of Sodom........ Ge 19:29
—He gives children to barren women........ Ge 30:22 – 24
1Sa 1:20
—He punishes sin........ Jer 14:10
Hos 8:13

See also FORGET

REMNANT
—A small but faithful number of God's people preserved
A. Basis of God's promise to keep a remnant
—The honor of his name........ 1Sa 12:22
—His promise to Abraham........ Ge 17:7
—His promise to David........ 1Ki 6:13
B. God kept his promise to preserve a remnant
—Remnant kept at the time of Elijah........ 1Ki 19:18
Ro 11:4
—A remnant of Israel joined with Judah........ 2Ch 30:25
2Ch 34:9
Isa 10:20 – 22
Ro 9:27 – 29
—The entire nation of Judah was a remnant........ 2Ki 17:18
Hos 1:7
—Remnant preserved from Assyria........ 2Ki 19:4,29 – 31
Mic 5:6 – 8
—Remnant kept after Jerusalem was destroyed........ 2Ch 36:20
Jer 40:11
Jer 42:2
Eze 11:13
—Remnant returned from the exile........ Ezr 9:8,13 – 15
Ne 1:2
Jer 23:3
Eze 34:12 – 14
Hag 1:12,14
—Believing Jews were a remnant of Israel........ Ro 11:5
C. God's promise to preserve the church
—Promise of Jesus to Peter........ Mt 16:18
—Promise of Jesus for the end times........ Mt 24:21 – 22
—Remnant preserved in Thyatira........ Rev 2:24 – 25
—Remnant preserved in Sardis........ Rev 3:4 – 5

REPENTANCE
—Sorrow for sin and turning to God
A. Related themes
REPENTANCE is a theme of:
—Joel........ Joel 2:13
—Zechariah........ Zec 1:3
B. The command to repent
—God calls all people to repent........ Jer 18:11
Eze 18:30 – 32
Ac 17:30
2Pe 3:9

—Christ calls people to repent ... Mk 1:14–15
Lk 13:1–5
Rev 2:5,16
Rev 3:3
—John the Baptist called people to repent ... Mt 3:2
—The apostles called people to repent ... Mk 6:12
Ac 2:38
Ac 3:19–20
Ac 26:20
—The call must go out today ... Lk 24:46–48

C. Essential aspects of repentance
—Acknowledging we are lost ... Lk 15:3–7
—Expressing sorrow for sin ... Lk 5:32
Ac 2:37–38
Ac 8:22
2Co 7:9–10
—Returning to the Father ... Lk 15:17–20
—Believing in Jesus Christ ... Mk 1:15
Ac 20:21
Rev 3:19–20
—Doing good works ... Jer 18:11–12
Mt 3:8
Ac 26:20
Rev 2:4–5

D. The results of repentance
—Escape from disaster ... Jer 18:7–8
—Forgiveness ... 1Ki 8:46–50
Ac 2:38
—Salvation ... 2Co 7:10
—A new heart and spirit ... Eze 18:30–31
—A knowledge of the truth ... 2Ti 2:25
—Eternal life ... Ac 11:18
—Regret without repentance brings death ... Mt 27:3–5
2Co 7:10

REPTILES

A. Reptiles mentioned in the Bible
—Adder ... Isa 30:6
—Chameleon ... Lev 11:30
—Cobra ... Isa 11:8
—Frog ... Ex 8:2–13
—Gecko ... Lev 11:30
—Lizard ... Lev 11:29–30
—Serpent ... Job 26:13
—Snake ... Ps 58:4
—Viper ... Ac 28:3
—Worm ... Jnh 4:7

B. Serpents and snakes used symbolically
—As a symbol of healing ... Nu 21:8–9
Jn 3:14–15
—As a symbol of shrewdness ... Mt 10:16
—As a symbol of alcohol's effects ... Pr 23:31–32
—As a symbol of hypocrites ... Mt 23:23
Lk 3:7–8
—As a symbol of evil people ... Dt 32:33
Ps 140:1–3
—As a symbol of God's judgment ... Nu 21:6–7
Isa 14:28–29
—As a symbol of Satan ... Ge 3:1–5
Rev 12:9
Rev 20:2

REST

A. Types of rest
—The Sabbath day ... Ex 20:8–11
—Sleep ... Pr 3:23–24
—Life in the land of Canaan ... Jos 1:13
—Absence of war ... 1Ch 22:9
—Getting away from trouble ... Ps 55:6–8
—Getting away from people ... Mk 6:31
—Death ... 1Ki 2:10
1Th 4:13,15
—Heaven as the land of rest ... Heb 4:8–11
Rev 14:13

B. The human need for rest
—Because of six days of work ... Ex 20:8–10
—Because of fatigue ... Mt 8:24
Mt 26:43
—Because of overwork ... Mk 6:30–31
—Because of depression ... 1Ki 19:3–6
—Because of anxiety ... Ecc 2:22–23
2Co 2:13
—Because of the storms of life ... Job 3:20–26
Ps 55:4–8

C. The realization of true rest
—Through trusting in God ... Ps 37:3–7
Ps 91:1–2
—Through resting in God ... Ps 23:1–3
Ps 62:1,5
—Through experiencing God's presence ... Ex 33:14
Ps 31:19–20
—Through coming to Jesus ... Mt 11:28–29
Jn 16:33
—Through the Spirit of God ... Isa 63:14

RESURRECTION

—Resuscitation of a dead body

A. The resurrection of Christ
1. Prophecies of Christ's resurrection
a. The Old Testament in general ... Lk 24:25–26,44–46
Jn 20:9
1Co 15:4
b. Specific prophecies in the Old Testament
—David ... Ps 16:3–11
Ac 2:24–32
—Isaiah ... Isa 55:3
Ac 13:34
—Jonah ... Jnh 1:17
Mt 12:39–40
c. Prophesied by Jesus before his death ... Mk 8:31
Mk 9:9,31
Mk 10:33–34
Jn 2:19–22
2. The event of Christ's resurrection ... Mt 28:1–7
Mk 16:1–8
Lk 24:1–8
Jn 20:1–8
3. The power used to raise Christ
—The power of God ... Ac 2:24
Eph 1:19–20
Col 2:12
—Christ's own power ... Jn 10:18
—Jesus is *the* resurrection ... Jn 11:25–26
—The power of the Spirit ... Ro 8:11
1Pe 3:18
4. The nature of Christ's resurrected body
a. The same body that died was raised ... Lk 24:39–40
Jn 20:27
b. It was a physical body
—He ate ... Lk 24:41–43
Jn 21:12–13
Ac 10:40–41
—He could be touched ... Jn 20:27
1Jn 1:1
c. It was a glorified body ... 1Co 15:42–44
Php 3:21
—He passed through locked doors ... Jn 20:19,26
—He ascended into heaven ... Ac 1:9

5. The appearances of the risen Christ
   —To Mary Magdalene .... Mk 16:9; Jn 20:10–18
   —To several women .... Mt 28:8–10
   —To Peter .... Lk 24:34; 1Co 15:5
   —To two disciples going to Emmaus .... Lk 24:13–31
   —To a group of disciples .... Lk 24:36–44
   —To the disciples, minus Thomas .... Jn 20:19–25
   —To the disciples, with Thomas .... Jn 20:26–29; 1Co 15:5
   —To disciples at the Sea of Galilee .... Jn 21:1–14
   —To the disciples in Galilee .... Mt 28:16–20
   —To a group of five hundred 1Co 15:6
   —To James 1Co 15:7
   —To all the apostles in Jerusalem .... Ac 1:4–9; 1Co 15:7
   —To Paul .... Ac 9:3–6; 1Co 15:8
   —Jesus gave many convincing proofs .... Ac 1:3
6. The significance of Christ's resurrection
   —Declares his deity .... Ro 1:4
   —Declares his Lordship .... Ro 10:9
   —Justifies us .... Ro 4:25
   —Forgives us 1Co 15:17
   —Saves us .... Ro 10:9; 1Pe 3:21
   —Gives us living hope 1Co 15:18–19; 1Pe 1:3
   —Gives us victory over death .... Ro 6:9–11; 1Co 15:57
   —Guarantees our resurrection .... 1Co 15:20,23; Php 3:10–11
   —Guarantees the coming judgment .... Ac 17:31
7. The proclamation of Christ's resurrection
   —Proclaimed by angels .... Mt 28:5–7; Lk 24:3–7
   —Acknowledged by Christ's enemies .... Mt 28:11–15
   —Preached by Peter .... Ac 2:24–32; Ac 10:40–41
   —Preached by Paul .... Ac 13:30–37; Ac 17:31; 1Co 15:3–5

B. The resurrection of humans
1. Resurrection miracles
   a. In the Old Testament
      —By Elijah 1Ki 17:17–23
      —By Elisha 2Ki 4:19–37; 2Ki 13:21
   b. In the New Testament
      —By Jesus .... Mk 5:38–42; Lk 7:11–15; Jn 11:38–44
      —At Jesus' death .... Mt 27:52–53
      —By Peter .... Ac 9:32–35
      —By Paul .... Ac 20:9–10
      —In Hebrews .... Heb 11:35
2. The resurrection at the last day
   a. Affirmed in the Old Testament .... Job 19:26; Ps 16:10; Isa 26:19; Da 12:2
   b. Affirmed in the New Testament
      —Believed by the Jews .... Jn 11:24; Ac 23:6; Ac 24:15
      —Denied by the Sadducees .... Mt 22:23; Ac 23:7–8
      —Prophesied by Jesus .... Mk 12:26–27; Jn 5:28–29; Jn 5:39,44
      —Proclaimed by the apostles .... Ac 24:14–15; Ro 2:7–8; Ro 8:11; 1Co 15:50–57; 1Th 4:13–17; Rev 20:4–5,12–13
3. The nature of the resurrection
   a. For believers
      —Have already risen to a new life .... Ro 6:3–4; Eph 2:6; Col 2:12
      —Will rise first .... 1Th 4:6; Rev 20:4–5
      —Will receive bodies like Christ's .... Php 3:21; 1Jn 3:2
      —Will receive imperishable bodies 1Co 15:42
      —Will receive glorious bodies 1Co 15:43
      —Will receive spiritual bodies 1Co 15:44
   b. For unbelievers
      —Will go to everlasting contempt .... Da 12:2
      —Will be condemned .... Jn 5:28–29
      —Will be judged .... Rev 20:14–15

REUBEN

A. Firstborn of Jacob by Leah .... Ge 35:23; 1Ch 2:1
   —Name means "He has seen my misery" .... Ge 29:32
   —Slept with his father's concubine .... Ge 35:22; Ge 49:4
   —Attempted to rescue Joseph .... Ge 37:21–30
   —Went to Egypt with family .... Ge 46:8–9
   —Father of four sons .... Ge 46:9
   —Blessed by Jacob .... Ge 49:3–4
B. Tribe descended from Reuben
   —Blessed by Moses .... Dt 33:6
   —Numbered .... Nu 1:21; Nu 26:7
   —Allotted land east of the Jordan .... Nu 32:1–33; Nu 34:14
   —Allotted land west of the Jordan .... Eze 48:6
   —Failed to help Deborah .... Jdg 5:15–16
   —Supported David 1Ch 12:37
   —One of the tribes of the 144,000 .... Rev 7:5

REVELATION

—God's disclosure of himself and his truth
A. God's revelation in nature
   —It reveals God's glory .... Ps 19:1–6
   —It reveals God's kindness .... Ac 14:17
   —It proclaims his majesty .... Ps 8:1
   —It proclaims his righteousness .... Ps 50:6; Ps 97:6
   —It proclaims his eternal power .... Ro 1:19–20
B. God's special revelation to his people
1. Direct revelation
   —By speaking .... Ge 17:1–2; Ex 33:11; Rev 1:10–11
   —By dreams .... Ge 20:3; Nu 12:6
   —By visions .... Ge 15:1; Job 33:14–15; 2Co 12:1–4
2. Revelation in events of Bible history .... Dt 3:24; Eze 6:13–14; Eze 37:13–14
3. Revelation in his written word
   —God revealed to prophets 2Ti 3:15–16; 2Pe 1:21

—God revealed to apostles ... 1Co 2:10; 2Co 12:7; 2Pe 3:15

4. His key revelation is Jesus Christ
   —Jesus reveals the Father ... Jn 1:18; Jn 14:9; Heb 1:1–2
   —Jesus is the Word of God ... Jn 1:1,14; Rev 19:11–13

C. God's continuing revelation to the church
   —Revelation is a gift of the Spirit ... 1Co 14:26; Eph 1:17
   —Revelations must witness to Christ ... 1Co 12:3
   —Revelations must be evaluated by the church ... 1Co 14:29–32

See also DREAMS AND VISIONS; WORD OF GOD

REWARD

—What God has in store for humans

A. In the Old Testament
   1. Rewarded according to one's deeds
      —Stated in the Mosaic Law ... Lev 26:3–39; Dt 28:1–68
      —Stated in the Psalms ... Ps 19:11; Ps 28:4; Ps 62:12
      —Stated in Proverbs ... Pr 1:29–31; Pr 12:14; Pr 14:14
      —Stated in the Prophets ... Isa 59:18; Isa 66:6; Jer 17:10; Jer 21:13–14; Eze 9:9–10
   2. Cannot always be applied to this life ... Job 1:1—2:10; Job 9:21–22; Ps 73:1–14; Ecc 9:1–12
   3. God does not treat us as our sin deserves ... Ezr 9:13; Job 33:26–28; Ps 103:8–10
   4. God's final reward is in the world to come ... Ps 73:16–20; Ecc 12:13–14

B. In the New Testament
   1. Whom does God reward with good?
      —Those who receive God's grace ... Ro 6:23; Ro 11:6
      —Those who believe in Jesus ... Jn 14:1–3; Ro 4:5,16
      —Those who have an obedient faith ... Lk 14:12–14; 1Co 3:8,12–14; Eph 6:8; Col 3:23–24; Jas 2:14–24
      —Those persecuted for Jesus' sake ... Mt 5:11–12
   2. Do we earn our reward?
      —We *inherit* our reward ... Mt 25:34; Ac 20:32; Col 1:12; Rev 21:7
      —Good works are not done for rewards ... Mt 6:1–6,16–18; Lk 17:7–10
   3. What is our reward?
      —A crown of righteousness ... 2Ti 4:8
      —A crown of glory ... 1Pe 5:4
      —A crown of life ... Jas 1:12
      —A crown that lasts forever ... 1Co 9:25
      —The kingdom prepared for us ... Mt 25:34
      —A place in heaven ... Jn 14:2–3; 2Co 5:1; 2Ti 4:8
      —Eternal life ... Ro 2:7; Gal 6:8
      —Eternal glory ... 2Co 4:17
   4. Judgment in store for the disobedient ... Ro 1:18; Ro 2:8–9; Rev 21:8; Rev 22:14–15

THE RICH AND THE POOR

A. Related themes
   1. MONEY is a theme of 2 Corinthians ... 2Co 9:7
   2. SOCIAL CONCERN is a theme of:
      —Deuteronomy ... Dt 26:12
      —Luke ... Lk 7:22

B. God is the source of all wealth
   —He owns everything ... Ex 19:5; Ps 24:1; Hag 2:8; 1Co 10:26
   —He gives wealth ... Ge 26:12–13; Dt 8:16–18; 1Co 4:7
   —He decides who is rich or poor ... 1Sa 2:7; Pr 10:22; Pr 22:2

C. Riches
   1. Examples of wealthy people
      —Abraham ... Ge 24:34–35
      —Isaac ... Ge 26:12–14
      —Esau ... Ge 36:7
      —Laban ... Ge 30:29–30
      —Jacob ... Ge 30:43
      —Nabal ... 1Sa 25:2–3
      —David ... 2Sa 5:9–13
      —Solomon ... 1Ki 10:14–29
      —Jehoshaphat ... 2Ch 17:5
      —Job ... Job 1:1–3
      —Joseph of Arimathea ... Mt 27:57
   2. Means of gaining wealth
      —Prosperity as God's reward to righteous ... Ps 25:12–13; Ps 112:1–3; Pr 10:22
      —The wicked can also be wealthy ... Job 21:7–13; Ps 73:3,12; Jer 12:1–2
      —Wealth gained by taking bribes ... Isa 1:23; Eze 22:12; Am 5:12
      —Wealth gained by usury and extortion ... Ne 5:1–7; Pr 28:8; Jer 22:17; Eze 22:12
      —Wealth gained by exploiting the poor ... Isa 3:14–15; Jer 2:34; Am 2:6–8; Jas 2:6
   3. Reactions of the rich to their wealth
      a. Unwholesome reactions
         —Hoard it up for themselves ... Ecc 5:13; Lk 12:16–19; Jas 5:3
         —Become greedy and fall into sin ... Pr 15:27; 1Ti 6:9–10
         —Trust in it ... Job 31:24–28; Ps 49:5–6; Ps 52:7; 1Ti 6:17
         —Become proud because of it ... Eze 28:5; Hos 12:8; Rev 3:17

—Reject God because of it .... Dt 8:12–14
Dt 32:15
Ne 9:25–26
Mt 19:16–22

b. Wholesome reactions
—Use it to help the poor .... Ne 5:14–19
Job 29:11–17
Lk 19:8–9
Ac 4:34–37
2Co 8:1–4
—Use it to help bring about peace .... Ge 32:13–21
Ge 43:11–15
1Sa 25:18–35
Pr 18:16

4. God's commands concerning wealth
—We must acknowledge God as the source .... Dt 8:18
1Ch 29:12
Hos 2:8
—We must use wealth in God's service .... Ex 35:4–9
1Ch 29:3
Mal 3:8–10
—We must help the poor .... Ps 82:3–4
Mt 19:16–21
Eph 4:28
1Ti 6:18
—We must not store up treasures on earth .... Mt 6:19–21
—We should not trust in wealth .... Ps 62:10
1Ti 6:17
—We should not be greedy .... Eph 5:3
Col 3:5
1Pe 5:2
—We cannot serve God and Money .... Mt 6:24–25

5. Riches are considered
—Fleeting .... Pr 23:5
Pr 27:24
—Corruptible .... Mt 6:19
Jas 5:2–3
—Perishable 1Pe 1:18
—Uncertain 1Ti 6:17
—Unsatisfying .... Ecc 4:8
Ecc 5:10
—Deceitful .... Mt 13:22
—Spiritually dangerous .... Lk 18:18–25

6. Judgments often spoken against the rich
—In the Old Testament .... Isa 1:23–25
Jer 17:11
Am 4:1–3
Mic 2:1–5
Hab 2:6–8
Zec 7:8–14
—In the New Testament .... Lk 6:24–25
Lk 16:13–15
Ac 8:20–23
Jas 5:1–6
2Pe 2:3,14–15

7. True riches are spiritual
—Having Jesus is worth everything .... Mt 13:44–47
Php 3:7–8
Heb 10:34
—Believing in Jesus brings true wealth 1Pe 1:7
Rev 3:17–18
—God's grace brings spiritual riches .... Eph 1:7,18
Eph 3:8,16
Col 1:27
—All things are ours in Christ 1Co 3:21–23
—We should store up treasures in heaven .... Mt 6:20
1Ti 6:19

D. Poverty
1. Examples of poor people
—Lot .... Ge 19:23–30
—Naomi and Ruth .... Ru 1:20–2:2
—Widow of Zarephath 1Ki 17:10–12
—Jesus .... Mt 8:20
2Co 8:9
—Lazarus .... Lk 16:20
—Paul (on occasion) .... Php 4:12

2. Reasons for becoming poor
a. God's choice for us 1Sa 2:7
b. Exploitation by the rich .... Isa 3:14–15
Jer 2:34
Am 2:6–8
Mic 3:1–3
Jas 2:6
c. The result of
—Laziness .... Pr 6:9–11
—Haste .... Pr 21:5
—Alcohol .... Pr 23:21
—Greed .... Pr 22:16

3. Laws given to protect the poor
—There must be no poor .... Dt 15:4
—Poor must not be taken advantage of .... Ex 22:22–23
—The poor must be paid daily .... Dt 24:14–15
—Poor allowed to glean in fields .... Lev 19:10
Dt 24:19–21
—Laws regarding security on loans .... Dt 24:10–13
—No interest may be charged to the poor .... Ex 22:25
Lev 25:36
—The year for canceling debts .... Dt 15:1–11
—The Year of Jubilee .... Lev 25:5–55
—Equal justice for rich and poor .... Ex 23:2–3,6
Dt 1:17
Pr 31:9

4. Blessings for those who show kindness to the poor
—Their throne will be secure .... Ps 72:1–5
Pr 29:14
—Their righteousness endures forever .... Ps 112:9
Isa 58:6–8
—God will answer their prayers .... Isa 58:6–7,9
—They will be rewarded by God .... Pr 14:21
Pr 19:17
Pr 22:9
Pr 28:27
—They will have treasure in heaven .... Mt 19:21
Lk 12:33
Lk 19:8–9

5. God as the hope of the poor
—He is their refuge .... Ps 14:6
Isa 25:4
—He is their protector .... Ps 12:5
—He is their deliverer 1Sa 2:8
Ps 34:6
Ps 113:7
—He is their helper .... Ps 40:17
Ps 70:5
Isa 41:17
—He is their provider .... Ps 132:15
Isa 61:1–3
Lk 4:18–19

RIGHTEOUSNESS

—The state of being perfect and without sin

A. Related theme
RIGHTEOUSNESS is a theme of Romans .... Ro 1:17

B. The righteousness of humans
1. In themselves humans are unrighteous
—No one is righteous .... Ps 14:1–3
Ps 53:1–3
Ro 3:10–12,23
—Our righteous acts are like filthy rags .... Isa 64:6

—We deserve God's wrath........Ro 1:18
Eph 2:3
2. God gives us righteousness
a. Experienced in the Old Testament
—By Abram........Ge 15:6
—By David........Ps 32:1 – 2
Ps 103:17
—By Isaiah........Isa 45:8,24
Isa 46:13
Isa 61:10
b. Experienced by believers in Christ
—God declares us righteous........Ro 3:21 – 22
Ro 4:1 – 8
Gal 3:21 – 22
Php 3:8 – 9
—God credits us with Christ's righteousness........Ro 4:11,22 – 24
—His righteousness is a gift........Ro 5:17
—We become God's righteousness........2Co 5:21
3. Believers are called "the righteous"
—In the Old Testament........Ps 1:5 – 6
Pr 10:3,6 – 7,20 – 21
Isa 26:7
Hos 14:9
—In the New Testament........Mt 25:37,46
Heb 12:23
Jas 5:16
4. Responsibilities regarding a righteous way of life
—Be instruments of righteousness........Ro 6:13
—Be slaves to righteousness........Ro 6:18 – 19
—Long for righteousness........Mt 5:6
—Perform righteousness........Am 5:24
Mt 5:20
—Pursue righteousness........Isa 51:1
1Ti 6:11
2Ti 2:22
—Put on righteousness........Eph 4:24
Eph 6:14
—Seek righteousness........Mt 6:33
—Bring forth fruits of righteousness........Hos 10:12
2Co 9:10
Heb 12:11
—Live for righteousness........1Pe 2:24
—Do what is right........1Jn 2:29
1Jn 3:7
—Shun wickedness........2Co 6:14 – 15
5. God's word teaches how to be righteous........2Ti 3:16 – 17
6. Our final righteousness
—Heaven is the home of righteousness........2Pe 3:13
—We receive a crown of righteousness........2Ti 4:8

See also JUSTIFICATION

C. The righteousness of God
1. God the Father
—God is righteous........Ps 7:9
Isa 45:21
Jer 12:1
Jn 17:25
—He always acts righteously........1Sa 12:7
Ps 145:17
Jer 9:24
Mic 6:5
—He judges righteously........Ps 9:4
Ps 98:9
Jer 11:20
—His commandments are righteous........Ps 19:9
Ps 119:138,160
Ro 1:32
Ro 7:12
—His righteousness endures forever........Ps 111:3
Ps 112:3
2. Jesus is righteous
a. Old Testament prophecies
—His name is "The LORD Our Righteousness"........Jer 23:6
Jer 33:16
—He is the righteous servant........Isa 53:11
—He is the sun of righteousness........Mal 4:2
—He is clothed in righteousness........Isa 11:5
Isa 59:16 – 17
—He loves righteousness........Ps 45:7
—He judges in righteousness........Ps 72:2
Isa 11:4
—He reigns in righteousness........Isa 32:1
Zec 9:9
b. New Testament assertions
—He is the Righteous One........Ac 3:14
Ac 7:52
1Jn 2:1
—He fulfilled all righteousness........Mt 3:15
—He lived a righteous life........Ro 5:18
2Co 5:21
1Pe 3:18
—He is our righteousness........1Co 1:30
—He loves righteousness........Heb 1:8 – 9
—He is the righteous Judge........2Ti 4:8
3. Believers and God's righteousness
—They acknowledge it........Ezr 9:15
Da 9:7
—They see it........Mic 7:9
—They speak of it........Ps 35:28
—They proclaim it........Ps 22:31
Ps 71:15 – 16
—They sing of it........Ps 51:14
—They exult in it........Ps 89:16
—They give thanks for it........Ps 7:17
—They are led in it........Ps 5:8
—They are upheld by it........Isa 41:10
—They pray for it........Ps 31:1
Ps 143:11

RIVER

A. Rivers and streams mentioned in the Bible
—Abana........2Ki 5:12
—Ahava........Ezr 8:15,21
—Arnon........Nu 21:13,24
—Besor........1Sa 30:9,21
—Egypt........Ge 15:18
—Euphrates........Dt 1:7
See EUPHRATES
—Gihon........1Ki 1:33,38
—Gozan........1Ch 5:26
—Jabbok........Ge 32:22
—Jordan........Ge 13:10
See JORDAN
—Kanah........Jos 16:8
—Kebar........Eze 10:15
—Kerith........1Ki 17:3 – 5
—Kidron........Jn 18:1
—Kishon........Jdg 4:7,13
—Nile........Ge 41:1,3,17
—Pharpar........2Ki 5:12
—Pishon........Ge 2:11
—Shihor........Jos 13:3
—Tigris........Ge 2:14
—Ulai........Da 8:2
—Zered........Dt 2:13 – 14
B. How were rivers and streams used?
1. Literally
—For drinking........1Ki 17:3 – 4
—For bathing........Ex 2:5

—For irrigation ... Ge 2:10
—For transportation ... Isa 23:3
—For fishing ... Lev 11:9 – 10
—For healing ... 2Ki 5:14
—For baptism ... Mk 1:5
2. As a symbol
—Of an enemy's strength ... Ps 124:1 – 4
—Of God's judgment ... Ps 88:16 – 17
Isa 42:15
—Of God's blessings ... Ps 36:8
Isa 41:17 – 18
—Of God's peace ... Isa 48:18
Isa 66:12
—Of wisdom ... Pr 18:4
—Of life in the Spirit ... Jn 7:38 – 39
—Of healing, life-giving power ... Eze 47:1 – 12
Rev 22:1 – 2

ROCK

A. Uses for rocks
—As a pillow ... Ge 28:11
—As an altar ... Jdg 6:20 – 21
—As a landmark ... Jdg 15:8
—As a memorial ... Jos 4:1 – 9
—As a habitat for animals ... Ps 104:18
—As a hiding place ... 1Sa 13:6
—As a tomb ... Mt 27:60
—As a place from which water flowed ... Ex 17:6
Nu 20:8 – 11
B. The rock as a symbol
1. Of Simon, named Peter ... Mt 16:18
Jn 1:42
2. Of the apostles as the church's foundation ... Eph 2:20
Rev 21:14
3. Of Christ
—The rock in the wilderness ... 1Co 10:4
—The foundation of the church ... 1Co 3:11
—The cornerstone of the church ... Eph 2:20
1Pe 2:6
—A stone over which people stumble ... Ro 9:33
1Pe 2:8
4. Of God who protects and saves ... Dt 32:4,15
Ps 18:2
Isa 26:4
Hab 1:12

ROME

—The capital city of the New Testament world
A. The government of Rome
—Ruled the world at the time of Christ ... Lk 2:1
Jn 18:28
Ac 16:12
—Expelled Jews from the city ... Ac 18:2
—Gave privileges to Roman citizens ... Ac 16:37 – 38
Ac 22:25 – 29
B. Christianity and Rome
1. Jews from Rome in Jerusalem at Pentecost ... Ac 2:10
2. Paul and Rome
—Paul wrote to the church in Rome ... Ro 1:7
—Paul wanted to go to Rome ... Ro 1:15
Ro 15:23 – 24
—Paul arrived in Rome as a prisoner ... Ac 28:14 – 16
—Paul visited with Christians of Rome ... Ac 28:15
—Paul preached in Rome ... Ac 28:23 – 31
Php 1:12 – 13
—Paul was probably killed in Rome ... 2Ti 4:6 – 8
3. Peter may have referred to Rome as Babylon ... 1Pe 5:13

RUTH

—Moabitess; widowed daughter-in-law of Naomi ... Ru 1:3 – 5
—Went with Naomi to Bethlehem ... Ru 1:22
—Gleaned in field of Boaz ... Ru 2:2 – 17
—Proposed marriage to Boaz ... Ru 3:1 – 14
—Married Boaz ... Ru 4:1 – 13
—Gave birth to Obed ... Ru 4:13 – 17
—Ancestor of David ... Ru 4:17 – 22
—Ancestor of Jesus ... Mt 1:5

SABBATH

—Seventh day of the week, the day of rest
A. The Sabbath in the Old Testament
1. The Sabbath day of rest
a. God rested on the Sabbath ... Ge 2:2 – 3
b. Israel observed it before law was given ... Ex 16:23,25
c. Laws concerning the Sabbath
—The fourth commandment ... Ex 20:8 – 11
—No work to be done ... Ex 31:14 – 15
Ex 35:2 – 3
—A day of sacred assembly ... Lev 23:2 – 3
—A day for special offerings ... Nu 28:9 – 10
2. Purposes of the Sabbath
—To be a sign of the covenant ... Ex 31:16 – 17
Isa 56:6
Eze 20:12,20
—To honor God ... Isa 58:13
—To worship God ... Lev 23:3
—To remember God's salvation ... Dt 5:15
—To rest from work ... Dt 5:12 – 14
3. The sabbath year ... Lev 25:1 – 7
Eze 46:3
4. The Israelites and the Sabbath
—Disobeyed the Sabbath ... Jer 17:20 – 23
—Desecrated the Sabbath ... Eze 20:21,24
Eze 22:8
Eze 23:38 – 39
—Couldn't wait for Sabbath to be over ... Am 8:4 – 5
—Wanted to work on Sabbath ... Ne 13:20 – 21
—Nehemiah reinstituted Sabbath laws ... Ne 13:15 – 22
B. In the New Testament
1. The Jews and the Sabbath
—Worshiped regularly on that day ... Lk 4:16,31
Ac 13:14 – 15
Ac 17:2
—Used it as a focal point for legalism ... Mt 12:2,10
Lk 13:14
Jn 9:13 – 16
2. Jesus and the Sabbath
—Is Lord of the Sabbath ... Mt 12:8
Mk 2:28
—Tried to restore its proper spirit ... Lk 13:10 – 16
Lk 14:1 – 6
Jn 5:16 – 18
—Taught Sabbath was for our good ... Mk 2:27
3. Symbolism of the Sabbath
—Symbolizes the rest God wants for us ... Heb 4:3 – 4
—Symbolizes the eternal Sabbath ... Heb 4:8 – 11
4. The day of worship in the early church
a. The Sabbath ... Ac 13:14
Ac 17:2
Ac 18:4
b. The first day of the week
—Christ's resurrection on that day ... Lk 24:1 – 7
Jn 20:1,19
—Pentecost on that day ... Ac 2:1
—Worship on that day ... Ac 20:7
—Offerings set aside on that day ... 1Co 16:2
—John's vision on the Lord's Day ... Rev 1:10

SACRIFICE

A. Related theme
SACRIFICE is a theme of Philippians ... Php 2:17

B. Sacrifices in the Old Testament
1. Persons performing them
—Cain and Abel.......Ge 4:3 – 5
—Noah.......Ge 8:20 – 21
—Abram.......Ge 12:7 – 8
Ge 15:9 – 11
—Jacob.......Ge 31:54
Ge 46:1
—Job.......Job 1:5
—Regular duties of priests.......Lev 1:3 – 17
2. Types of sacrifices
a. According to substances used
—Various animal sacrifices.......Lev 1:2 – 17
Lev 3:1—4:35
—Grain sacrifices.......Lev 2:1 – 16
Lev 6:14 – 23
b. According to time performed
—Daily sacrifices.......Ex 29:38 – 41
Nu 28:1 – 8
—Weekly sacrifices.......Nu 28:9 – 10
—Monthly sacrifices.......Nu 28:11 – 15
—Annual sacrifices.......Nu 28:16—29:38
3. Purpose of sacrifices
a. As cleansing for sin
—Burnt offerings.......Lev 1:3 – 17
—Sin offerings.......Lev 4:1—5:13
—Guilt offerings.......Lev 5:14—6:7
b. As thanksgiving to God
—Grain offerings.......Lev 2:1 – 16
—Fellowship offerings.......Lev 3:1 – 16
4. The insufficiency of sacrifices alone
a. Had to be accompanied by
—A true faith.......Heb 11:4
—A humble heart.......Ps 51:17
Isa 66:2 – 3
—A repentant heart.......Isa 1:11 – 16
—A life of obedience.......1Sa 15:22
Ps 40:6 – 8
—A life of justice.......Mic 6:6 – 8
—A desire to give one's best.......Mal 1:6 – 14
b. Despised if offered by unjust people.......Isa 1:11 – 15
Am 5:21 – 24

C. Sacrifice in the New Testament
1. View of Old Testament sacrifices
—They cannot take away sin.......Heb 9:9 – 10,23
Heb 10:1 – 4,11
—They point to the sacrifice of Christ.......Heb 9:11 – 14,24 – 26
2. The sacrifice of Christ
—He is the Lamb who was sacrificed.......Jn 1:29
1Co 5:7
Rev 5:6
—He is the atoning sacrifice.......Ro 3:25
Heb 7:27
Heb 9:28
1Jn 4:10
3. Sacrifices expected of the Christian
—Total commitment to Christ.......Mt 16:24 – 25
See SELF-DENIAL
—Lives of service to God.......Ro 12:1
1Pe 2:5
—Praising and confessing God.......Heb 13:15
—Deeds of kindness.......Heb 13:16
—Gifts of money for use in God's work.......Php 4:18

SADDUCEES

—A Jewish party, prominent at the time of Jesus
A. Major characteristics
—Members of the Sanhedrin (Jewish council).......Ac 23:6
—Did not believe in the resurrection of the dead.......Mt 22:23
Ac 23:8

B. The Sadducees and Jesus
1. The Sadducees questioned and tested Jesus
—About a sign from heaven.......Mt 16:1
Mk 8:11
—About the resurrection of the dead.......Mt 22:23 – 27
Mk 12:18 – 23
Lk 20:27 – 33
2. Jesus criticized the Sadducees.......Mt 16:6,11 – 12
C. The Sadducees and the early church
—Persecuted the church.......Ac 4:1 – 3
Ac 5:17 – 18
—Put the apostles on trial.......Ac 5:21 – 32
—Put Paul on trial.......Ac 22:30—23:6

SALOME

—The mother of James and John, sons of Zebedee.......Mt 27:56
Mk 15:40
—Wanted a high position for her sons.......Mt 20:20 – 23
—Watched Jesus die on the cross.......Mk 15:40
—Went to the empty tomb.......Mk 16:1

SALT

A. Uses for salt
—For seasoning food.......Job 6:6
—For seasoning sacrifices.......Lev 2:13
Eze 43:24
—For ratifying a covenant.......Nu 18:19
2Ch 13:5
—For rubbing a newborn child.......Eze 16:4
B. Symbolism of salt
—Symbol of judgment.......Ge 19:26
Jer 48:9
—Symbol of permanency of covenant.......Nu 18:19
—Symbol of preservation.......Mt 5:13
—Symbol of peace.......Mk 9:50
Col 4:6

SALVATION

A. Related theme
WORLDWIDE SAVIOR is a theme of Luke.......Lk 19:9
B. Definition of salvation
1. "Save" translated as "heal".......Mk 10:52
Mk 6:56
Ac 14:9
2. "Save" as rescue from physical danger.......Da 6:27
Mt 8:25
Lk 23:39
Ac 27:20,31
Heb 5:7
3. "Save" as rescue from personal enemies.......Ps 18:3
Ps 59:2
4. "Save" as deliverance from political oppression
—Salvation from Egypt.......Ex 14:13,30
Ps 106:8 – 11
—Salvation from enemies invading Canaan.......Jdg 3:9,31
Jdg 8:22
2Ki 14:27
5. "Save" as deliverance from sin
a. In the Old Testament
—Asking for salvation from sin.......Ps 39:8
—Promise of salvation through Messiah.......Jer 23:5 – 6
Eze 37:23
b. In the New Testament, it embraces
—The past: "have been saved"/"saved".......Eph 2:5,8
2Ti 1:9
Tit 3:5
—The present: "are being saved".......1Co 1:18
2Co 2:15
—The future: "will be saved".......Ro 5:9 – 10
1Pe 1:5

C. God as the source of salvation
1. Israel's God in the Old Testament
a. He is called "Savior" ... 1Ch 16:35; Ps 25:5; Isa 43:11; Isa 45:15,21; Mic 7:7
b. He is Israel's salvation ... Ex 15:1–2; Ps 27:1; Isa 12:2; Jnh 2:9
c. He promised worldwide salvation ... Ps 67:2; Isa 49:6; Isa 52:10
2. Christ as Savior
—Salvation is in his name alone ... Ac 4:12; Ac 10:43; Ro 10:13
—He is called Savior ... Lk 2:11; Eph 5:23; Tit 1:4
—He saves his people from sin ... Mt 1:21; Ac 5:31; Tit 2:13–14
—He saves the lost ... Lk 15:3–10; Lk 19:10
—He saves the world ... Jn 3:16–17; Jn 12:47; 1Jn 4:14

D. The process of salvation
1. Salvation required the work of Christ
—His coming to this earth ... 2Co 8:9; Php 2:6–8
—His death on the cross ... Jn 3:14–15; 1Co 1:18; 1Co 15:2–3
—The shedding of his blood ... 1Pe 1:18–19; Rev 5:9
—His resurrection from the dead ... Ro 10:9; 1Pe 1:3–5
—His ascension into heaven ... Ac 5:31
2. Salvation comes as a gift from God
—A gift of his love ... Ro 5:8–9; Tit 3:5; 1Jn 4:9–10
—A gift of his grace ... Eph 2:5,8; Tit 2:11
—A gift of his mercy ... Tit 3:4–5; 1Pe 1:3
3. Requirements for salvation
—Read the Scriptures ... 2Ti 3:15
—Believe in Jesus Christ ... Jn 3:16; Ac 16:30–31; Eph 2:8
—Repent of our sins ... Isa 30:15; Ac 2:37–38; Ac 3:19; 2Co 7:10
—Accept salvation as a free gift ... Isa 55:1; Rev 21:6
—Realize we can do nothing to earn salvation ... Eph 2:8–9; 2Ti 1:9; Tit 3:5
—Give our all in response to salvation ... Mt 13:44–46; Lk 14:33; Php 3:7–8

E. Our relationship to God's salvation
—We long for it ... Ps 119:81,174
—We wait for it ... La 3:26
—We hope for it ... 1Th 5:8–9
—We pray for it ... Ps 54:1; Ps 85:7; Jer 31:7
—We realize that it is *now* ... 2Co 6:2
—We must count its cost ... Lk 14:25–33
—We are clothed with it ... 2Ch 6:41; Isa 61:10
—We rejoice in it ... Ps 9:14; Isa 25:9
—We delight in it ... Ps 35:9
—We love it ... Ps 40:16
—We make it known ... Ps 67:2
—We proclaim it ... 1Ch 16:23; Ps 96:2
—We grow in it ... 1Pe 2:2
—We work it out ... Php 2:12

F. Pictures of salvation
—Horn of salvation ... 2Sa 22:3; Ps 18:2
—Fortress of salvation ... Ps 28:8
—Cup of salvation ... Ps 116:13
—Wells of salvation ... Isa 12:3
—Walls and ramparts of salvation ... Isa 26:1
—A rich store of salvation ... Isa 33:6
—Springs of salvation ... Isa 45:8
—Helmet of salvation ... Isa 59:17; Eph 6:17
—Garments of salvation ... Isa 61:10
—Torch of salvation ... Isa 62:1
—Gospel of salvation ... Eph 1:13

SAMARIA

A. Identity of Samaria
—City built by Omri, king of Israel ... 1Ki 16:23–24
—Became capital of northern kingdom ... 1Ki 16:29,32; 1Ki 21:18
—Became synonymous with the northern kingdom ... 1Ki 21:1; Hos 7:1

B. History in the Old Testament
—Besieged by Ben-Hadad ... 2Ki 6:24–25
—Besieged by Assyria ... 2Ki 17:5
—City taken; people deported ... 2Ki 17:6; 2Ki 18:10–12
—City plundered ... Isa 8:4
—Other people settled in the region ... 2Ki 17:24
—Capital city of Trans-Euphrates province ... Ezr 4:17; Ne 4:1–2

C. History in the New Testament
—Jesus visited it ... Lk 17:11; Jn 4:4–6
—Gospel must be preached there ... Ac 1:8
—Gospel spread there ... Ac 8:1
—Philip preached there ... Ac 8:5–7
—Holy Spirit was poured out there ... Ac 8:14–17
—Simon the sorcerer lived there ... Ac 8:9–13,18–24
—Paul traveled through there ... Ac 15:3

SAMARITANS

A. In the Old Testament
—A mixed race resettled in Samaria ... 2Ki 17:24
—Had a polytheistic religion ... 2Ki 17:25–33
—Wanted to help rebuild the temple ... Ezr 4:1–2
—Offer to rebuild the temple refused ... Ezr 4:3
—Tried to frustrate rebuilding of the temple ... Ezr 4:4–5,24; Ezr 5:3–17
—Tried to frustrate rebuilding of Jerusalem ... Ezr 4:7–23; Ne 4:1–23; Ne 6:1–14

B. In the New Testament
—Jews and Samaritans did not associate............Jn 4:9
—Jesus told parable of Good Samaritan..............Lk 10:30 – 35
—A Samaritan leper returned to thank Jesus.......Lk 17:11 – 19
—A Samaritan town rejected Jesus.....................Lk 9:52 – 53
—James and John wanted to destroy the town....Lk 9:54 – 55
—Jesus talked with a Samaritan woman.............Jn 4:7 – 26
—Many Samaritans believed in Jesus..................Jn 4:39 – 42
Ac 8:5,12

SAMSON

A. History of his life
—Judge from the tribe of Dan.............................Jdg 13:2,24 – 25
—Birth promised...Jdg 13:2 – 14
—Married Philistine woman................................Jdg 14:1 – 18
—Took revenge on Philistines..............................Jdg 15:1 – 20
—Betrayed by Delilah...Jdg 16:1 – 20
—Captured and eyes gouged out.........................Jdg 16:21 – 22
—His death...Jdg 16:23 – 31
B. Feats of strength
—Killed a lion...Jdg 14:6
—Killed thirty Philistines.....................................Jdg 14:19
—Killed a thousand Philistines with jawbone......Jdg 15:13 – 17
—Carried off gates of Gaza...................................Jdg 16:3
—Pushed down temple of Dagon, at cost of his life...Jdg 16:25 – 30
C. An example of faith..Heb 11:32

SAMUEL

A. Early life
—Hannah prayed that God would give her a son..1Sa 1:10 – 18
—Dedicated to God's service...............................1Sa 1:21 – 28
—Raised by Eli..1Sa 2:11,18 – 26
—Called by God to be a prophet..........................1Sa 3:1 – 20
B. His life as prophet and judge
—Judged Israel many years..................................1Sa 7:15 – 17
—Functioned as prophet......................................1Sa 9:9,19
—Led Israel to victory over Philistines.................1Sa 7:2 – 14
—Israelites asked him to anoint a king................1Sa 8:1 – 22
—Anointed Saul as king..1Sa 10:1,17 – 24
Ac 13:20 – 21
—Gave farewell speech as Israel's leader.............1Sa 12:1 – 25
—Rebuked Saul for offering a sacrifice................1Sa 13:8 – 14
—Rebuked Saul for disobedience.........................1Sa 15:12 – 23
—Announced God's rejection of Saul...................1Sa 15:24 – 29
—Anointed David as king......................................1Sa 16:1 – 13
Ac 13:22
—David fled to him for protection.......................1Sa 19:18 – 24
—Wrote about the events of his day....................1Ch 29:29
—His death..1Sa 25:1
C. Importance after his death
—Summoned by a medium to speak to Saul.........1Sa 28:5 – 20
—Seen as a prophet who spoke of Jesus..............Ac 3:24
—Considered an example of faith........................Ps 99:6
Heb 11:32

SANBALLAT

—Chief political opponent of Nehemiah..............Ne 2:10
—Ridiculed rebuilding of Jerusalem.......................Ne 2:19
Ne 4:1 – 2
—Opposed rebuilding of Jerusalem........................Ne 4:7 – 12
—Schemed to harm Nehemiah...............................Ne 6:1 – 14
—His daughter married high priest's son..............Ne 13:28

SANCTIFICATION

—Being holy and becoming holy
A. Christians have been sanctified
—Sanctified in Christ...1Co 1:2
1Co 6:11
—Sanctified through Christ's blood......................Heb 10:29
—Sanctified by the Holy Spirit..............................Ro 15:16
—Sanctified by faith..Ac 26:18
—Christians are called God's holy people.............1Co 1:2
2Co 1:1
Php 1:1
B. Christians are being sanctified..........................Ac 20:32
—Through the word of God....................................Jn 17:17 – 19
—Through the work of God.....................................1Th 5:23
—Through the work of the Holy Spirit...................2Th 2:13
1Pe 1:2
—Through resisting sin...1Th 4:3 – 7

See also HOLINESS

SANHEDRIN

—The Jewish political and religious council
A. Its structure
1. Members
—Elders, chief priests, teachers of law..............Mt 16:21
Mt 27:41
—Chief priests and Pharisees.............................Jn 11:47
—Pharisees and Sadducees.................................Ac 23:6
2. Led by high priest...Mt 26:59,62 – 66
B. Meetings and decisions mentioned in the Bible
1. Concerning Jesus
—Decided that he should be put to death..........Jn 11:47 – 50
—Made agreement with Judas to betray him...Mt 26:14 – 16
Mk 14:10 – 11
Lk 22:3 – 6
—Condemned him to death................................Mt 26:57 – 66
Mk 14:53 – 64
Jn 18:12 – 14,19 – 24
—Asked Pilate for a guard at the tomb...............Mt 27:62 – 65
2. Concerning the apostles
—Interviewed Peter and John.............................Ac 4:5 – 17
—Ordered them not to preach about Jesus.........Ac 4:18 – 21
—Interviewed them a second time.....................Ac 5:27 – 40
—Flogged the apostles...Ac 5:40 – 41
—Brought Stephen before their assembly...........Ac 6:12—7:56
—Decided to kill Stephen....................................Ac 7:57 – 58
—Voted to kill numerous believers.....................Ac 26:10
—Authorized Saul to persecute believers in Damascus...Ac 9:1 – 2
—Interviewed Paul in Jerusalem.........................Ac 22:30—23:9
—Prosecuted Paul before Felix............................Ac 24:1 – 9
—Prosecuted Paul before Festus.........................Ac 25:6 – 7

SAPPHIRA

—Wife of Ananias..Ac 5:1
—Deceitfully kept back part of their money...........Ac 5:2
—Died for lying to God...Ac 5:7 – 10

SARAH

A. Her life
—Original name: Sarai..Ge 11:29
—Wife of Abram; barren.......................................Ge 11:29 – 30
—Went with Abram to Canaan...............................Ge 12:4 – 5
—Thought by Pharaoh to be Abram's sister..........Ge 12:10 – 20
—Gave Hagar to Abram as concubine..................Ge 16:3
—Mistreated Hagar so that Hagar ran away..........Ge 16:4 – 6
—Name changed to Sarah.....................................Ge 17:15
—Birth of Isaac promised.....................................Ge 17:16 – 21
—Laughed about a possible pregnancy................Ge 18:10 – 15
—Thought by Abimelech to be Abraham's sister...Ge 20:1 – 18
—Isaac born...Ge 21:1 – 7
—Wanted Abraham to send Hagar and Ishmael away...Ge 21:8 – 21
—Her death and burial..Ge 23:1 – 19
B. Significance of Sarah
—Mother of the Israelites......................................Isa 51:2

—Birth of Isaac shows God's election ....Ro 9:6–9
—Sending Hagar away illustrates our freedom ....Gal 4:21–31
—An example of true faith with Abraham...........Heb 11:11–13
—An example of a submissive wife 1Pe 3:5–6

SATAN

—An angel who became the archenemy of God

A. Terms for Satan
—The accuser..Zec 3:1; Rev 12:10
—The devil ....Mt 4:1; Rev 12:9
—The tempter ....Mt 4:3; 1Th 3:5
—The evil one..Mt 6:13; 1Jn 2:13–14
—Beelzebub...Mt 12:24
—Belial 2Co 6:15
—A murderer from the beginning ....Jn 8:44
—The father of lies ....Jn 8:44
—The prince of this world...................................Jn 12:31; Jn 14:30
—The god of this age...2Co 4:4
—Ruler of the kingdom of the air ....Eph 2:2
—The angel of the Abyss ....Rev 9:11
—Abaddon or Apollyon ....Rev 9:11
—The ancient serpent ....Rev 12:9

B. Activities of Satan
1. Activities in the past
—Originally created as good ....Ge 1:31
—Led revolt of angels in heaven ....2Pe 2:4; Rev 12:7–8
—Tempted Adam and Eve ....Ge 3:1–7
—Incited David to sin 1Ch 21:1–2
—Afflicted Job..Job 1:6–19; Job 2:1–10
—Tempted Jesus ....Mt 4:1–11
—Involved in effort to put Jesus to death..........Lk 22:3; Jn 14:30–31
2. Activities in the present
—Rules a kingdom opposed to God.....................Mt 12:25–26; Mt 25:41
—Controls the present sinful world ....1Jn 5:19; Rev 12:9
—Afflicts people with illness..............................Job 2:7; Lk 13:16; Ac 10:38; 2Co 12:7
—Tempts believers to sin....................................1Ch 21:1; Mt 16:23; Ac 5:3; 1Th 3:5
—Tries to keep people from true worship ....Mt 13:19; 1Pe 5:8–9
—Thwarts the spread of the gospel...................Mt 13:19; 2Co 4:3–4; 1Th 2:18
—Wants people to worship him ....Mt 4:9
—Masquerades as an angel of light 2Co 11:14
—Uses many schemes..2Co 2:11; Eph 6:11
—Persecutes the church ....Rev 2:10; Rev 12:13–17
—Holds the power of death ....Heb 2:14–15
3. Future activities
—Will be bound in the Millennium ....Rev 20:2–3
—Will be set free during the great tribulation ....Rev 20:7–9
—Will empower the antichrist ....2Th 2:9; Rev 13:2–4

C. Victory over Satan
1. God has power over him ....Job 1:6–12; Job 2:1–6; Lk 22:31–32
2. Christ has disarmed him
—Prophesied in Eden ....Ge 3:15
—Christ came to destroy him 1Jn 3:8
—Demonstrated in Christ's victory over temptation ....Mt 4:1–11
—Demonstrated by casting out demons ....Lk 10:18; Lk 11:20
—The cross of Christ sealed his defeat..............Jn 12:31–33; Col 2:15; Rev 12:11
3. Believers must fight against him
—We must pray for deliverance ....Mt 6:13
—We must keep busy for the Lord.....................1Ti 5:13–15
—We must resist his temptations.......................1Co 7:5; Jas 4:7
—We must extinguish his flaming arrows by our faith...Eph 6:16
—We must overcome him ....1Jn 2:13; Rev 2:10–11; Rev 12:10–11
—Christ prays for the victory of our faith.........Lk 22:31–32
4. Final defeat of Satan
—Prophesied by Paul ....Ro 16:20
—Satan bound in the Millennium ....Rev 20:2–3
—Final victory at Christ's return ....Mt 25:31,41; Rev 20:10,14

SAUL

A. First king of Israel
1. Family data and early life
—A member of the tribe of Benjamin 1Sa 9:1–2
—Son of Kish...1Sa 9:1–2
—His family..1Sa 14:49–50; 1Ch 8:33
—Searched for his father's donkeys...................1Sa 9:3–4
—Consulted Samuel..1Sa 9:5–20
—Anointed king by Samuel.................................1Sa 10:1
—Prophesied..1Sa 10:9–13; 1Sa 19:23–24
—Chosen as king at Mizpah 1Sa 10:20–26
2. Early events as king
—Defeated Ammonites at Jabesh Gilead 1Sa 11:1–11
—Confirmed as king..1Sa 11:12–15
—Fought the Philistines.......................................1Sa 13:1–7,16–22
—Did not wait for Samuel to offer sacrifice 1Sa 13:8–14
—Disobeyed God regarding Amalekites 1Sa 15:1–23
—Repented 1Sa 15:24–31
3. His interaction with David
—Employed David as musician..........................1Sa 16:14–23
—Approved David's offer to fight Goliath 1Sa 17:31–39
—Became jealous of David..................................1Sa 18:1–9
—Tried to kill David, who was playing music...1Sa 18:10–11
—Gave David his daughter Michal as wife.........1Sa 18:20–28
—Again tried to kill David 1Sa 19:1–17
—Angry at Jonathan for befriending David.....1Sa 20:26–34
—Pursued David; killed priests at Nob.............1Sa 22:6–19
—Went to Keilah and Ziph 1Sa 23:7–28
—Spared by David in a cave at En Gedi.............1Sa 24:1–21
—Spared by David while sleeping in camp.......1Sa 26:1–25
4. Saul's death
—Sought Samuel's advice through a medium...1Sa 28:1–14
—Rebuked by Samuel's spirit 1Sa 28:15–20
—Wounded by Philistines; killed himself...........1Sa 31:1–6; 1Ch 10:1–6
—His death lamented by David.........................2Sa 1:17–27

B. One of Christ's apostles
See PAUL

SEA

A. Seas mentioned in the Bible
1. The Mediterranean Sea....Ex 23:31; Nu 34:5; Nu 34:6–7; Dt 11:24
2. The Red Sea....Ac 7:36
—The Sea of Reeds....Ex 10:19
—The Egyptian sea....Isa 11:15
3. The Sea of Galilee....Mt 4:18; Nu 34:11
—The Sea of Tiberias....Jn 6:1
4. The Dead Sea....Nu 34:3; Zec 14:8
—The Sea of the Arabah....Dt 3:17
5. The Adriatic Sea....Ac 27:27

B. The sea used as a symbol
1. Negative
—Of human sin and restlessness....Ge 49:4; Isa 57:20; Eph 4:14
—Of human instability....Jas 1:6
—Of the lifestyle of heretics....Jude 13
—Of God's judgment....Jer 49:23–24; La 2:13
—Of the abode of satanic powers....Da 7:2–3; Rev 13:1
—No sea in heaven....Rev 21:1
2. Positive
—Of the vast mysteries of God....Job 11:7–9
—Of God's presence everywhere....Ps 139:9
—Of the wide expanse of a kingdom....Ps 72:8
—Of God's great forgiveness....Mic 7:19
—Of God's promise of righteousness....Isa 48:18
—Of the extension of the gospel....Isa 11:9; Hab 2:14

See also WATER

SEAL

A. Literal uses of the seal
—A plate on the high priest's turban....Ex 39:30–31
—An item for personal identification....Ge 38:18,25
—A mark for identifying correspondence....1Ki 21:8
—A governmental mark warning people....Mt 27:66
—A mark securing a title deed....Jer 32:9–14

B. Figurative use of the seal
—Circumcision: a seal of the covenant....Ro 4:11
—Zerubbabel: a seal of the coming Messiah....Hag 2:23
—The Holy Spirit: a seal of salvation....2Co 1:22; Eph 1:14; Eph 4:30
—Christians: a seal of apostleship....1Co 9:2
—God's word: a seal for the church....2Ti 2:19
—The seven seals: Jesus' control of history....Rev 5:1—6:17
—The sealed 144,000: God's elect....Rev 7:1–8
—The sealed Abyss: God's control of Satan....Rev 20:3

SECOND COMING

—The return of Jesus at the end of history

A. Terms for the second coming
—The day of the Lord....1Co 1:8; Php 1:6,10; 1Th 5:2
—The day of God....2Pe 3:12
—The last day....Jn 12:48
—The Day....1Co 3:13; Heb 10:25
—The last time....1Pe 1:5
—The appearing of the glory of Jesus Christ....Tit 2:13

B. Prophecies of his second coming
—By Jesus before the crucifixion....Mt 24:30–31; Mt 26:64; Jn 14:3
—By Jesus after the resurrection....Jn 21:22
—By two angels at Jesus' ascension....Ac 1:10–11
—By the apostles in their preaching....Ac 3:20; Ac 17:31
—By the apostles in their writings....Php 3:20; 1Th 4:14–17; 1Ti 6:14; Tit 2:13

C. The event of the second coming
1. Time of the return
—It is unknown....Mk 13:32
—It will be sudden....Mt 24:27; Mk 13:36
—It will be unexpected....Lk 12:40; 2Pe 3:10
—It will be after the great tribulation....Mt 24:29–31; 2Th 2:2–3
2. Characteristics of the return
—It will be on the clouds....Mt 24:30; Mk 14:62; 1Th 4:17
—It will be visible....Rev 1:7
—It will be a bodily return....Ac 1:11
—It will be with his angels....Mt 16:27; 2Th 1:7
—It will be with great glory....Mt 16:27; Mt 25:31; 2Th 2:8
—It will be with power....Mt 24:30
—It will be with a great noise....1Co 15:51–52; 1Th 4:16

D. The purposes of the second coming
—That he might be glorified in his people....2Th 1:10
—That he might deliver the kingdom to God....1Co 15:24
—That he might reign over all....Rev 11:15
—That he might expose the secrets of human hearts....1Co 4:5
—That he might judge the human race....Mt 25:31–46; Ac 10:42; 2Ti 4:1; 1Pe 4:5
—That he might complete salvation for believers....Heb 9:28
—That he might take his people to be with him....Jn 14:3
—That he might gather the elect....Mk 13:27

E. Believers and the second coming
1. The attitude of believers toward it
—Should live holy lives until that day....2Pe 3:11–12
—Should long for it....2Ti 4:8
—Should watch for it....Mk 13:35–37; Lk 12:35–40
—Should wait for it....1Co 1:7; Php 3:20; Tit 2:13
—Should look forward to it....2Pe 3:12–13
—Should be patient until it....Jas 5:7–8
—Should persevere until it....Rev 2:10–11; Rev 3:11–12
—Should pray for its fulfillment....1Co 16:22; Rev 22:20
2. Promises for believers when it occurs
—We will be preserved by Christ....Php 1:6; Jude 24
—We will be found blameless....1Co 1:8; 1Th 3:13

—We will be clothed anew by God.................2Co 5:4–5
—We will receive new bodies.................1Co 15:42–53
—We will be made like Christ.................1Co 15:49
Php 3:20–21
1Jn 3:2
—We will receive a crown.................1Co 9:25
2Ti 4:8
1Pe 5:4
Jas 1:12
—We will reign with Christ.................2Ti 2:12
Rev 22:5
—We will be incredibly happy.................1Pe 4:13

SELF-CONTROL

—Control of one's body and emotions

A. Self-control as a Christian trait
—Expressed negatively.................Pr 25:28
2Ti 3:3
—Expressed positively.................1Ti 3:2
Tit 2:2,5–6,12
2Pe 1:6
—An aspect of the Spirit's fruit.................Gal 5:22–23

B. Reasons for self-control
—To control anger.................Pr 16:32
Pr 29:11
—To avoid sexual sins.................1Co 7:3–5
1Th 4:3–4
—To prepare for Christ's return.................1Th 5:6–8
—To enable us to pray properly.................1Pe 4:7
—To show resistance to Satan.................1Pe 5:8–9

SELF-DENIAL

—Rejection of a self-centered life

A. Jesus exemplified self-denial
—In coming to this earth.................2Co 8:9
Php 2:6–7
—In resisting temptations of Satan.................Mt 4:3–4,8–10
—In doing his Father's will.................Jn 6:38
Mt 26:39,42
—In washing his disciples' feet.................Jn 13:4–5,12–15
—In dying on the cross.................Mk 10:45
1Pe 2:21–24

B. Christians called to self-denial
—The call to self-denial.................Mt 16:24–26
Mk 8:34–37
Lk 9:23–25
—The priority of love for Jesus.................Mt 10:37–39
Lk 14:25–33
—Giving of ourselves to others.................Mt 5:38–42
1Co 10:24
—The necessity of being a servant.................Mk 10:42–44
Lk 22:25–27
Jn 12:24–26

See SERVANT

—Renouncing selfish desires.................Gal 5:24
Tit 2:12
—The life of self-sacrifice.................Ro 12:2
2Co 4:10–11

SELFISHNESS

See SELF-DENIAL

SENNACHERIB

—An Assyrian king.................2Ki 18:13
—Attempted siege of Jerusalem.................2Ki 18:13–37
2Ch 32:1–19
Isa 36:1–22
—His army destroyed by the angel of the Lord.................2Ki 19:35–36
2Ch 32:21
Isa 37:36–37
—His death by murder.................2Ki 19:37
2Ch 32:21
Isa 37:38

SERVANT

A. Essential qualities of a servant
—Must have only one master.................Lk 16:13
—Must be submissive to a master's will.................Ps 123:2
Eph 6:5
1Pe 2:18
—Must be faithful to a master.................1Co 4:2

B. Servants on a human level
1. Servants in the home
—Hagar.................Ge 16:1
—Abraham's servant (Eliezer).................Ge 24:1–2
—Zilpah.................Ge 29:24
—Bilhah.................Ge 29:29
—Joseph.................Ge 39:1–4
2. Servants in the economic realm
—Laws concerning servants and slaves.................Ex 21:2–11
Lev 25:39–46
—Hired servants.................2Ch 24:12
Mt 20:1–15
Lk 15:17–19
3. Servants on a political level
—Servants of a king.................1Sa 16:16,18
2Sa 12:18–19
2Ki 9:28
—The king's children are called servants.................2Sa 13:24
1Ki 1:17
—The king as servant of the people.................1Ki 12:7
—A king as servant to another king.................2Ki 16:7
2Ki 24:1

C. Believers as servants of one another
—We are called to serve as Jesus did.................Jn 13:14–16
1Pe 2:21
—We are commanded to serve others.................Gal 5:13
Eph 5:21
—Paul as a servant of others.................1Co 9:19–23
2Co 4:5

D. Servants of the Lord
1. Examples of servants of the Lord
—Abraham, Isaac and Jacob.................Ex 32:13
—Moses.................Nu 12:7
—Joshua.................Jdg 2:8
—Samson.................Jdg 15:18
—David.................2Sa 7:5
—Elijah.................1Ki 18:36
—The prophets.................2Ki 9:7
Zec 1:6
Rev 10:7
—The apostles.................1Co 4:1
2Co 6:4
Php 1:1
—All Christians.................Ro 6:22
Eph 6:6
1Pe 2:16
—The 144,000.................Rev 7:4
2. Isaiah's servant songs.................Isa 42:1–4
Isa 49:1–6
Isa 50:4–9
Isa 52:13—53:12
3. Jesus as the servant of the Lord
—Fulfilled the servant songs of Isaiah.................Mt 12:17–21
Ac 8:32–35
1Pe 2:22–25
—Took the nature of a servant.................Php 2:7
—Called himself a servant.................Mk 10:45
Lk 22:27
—Compared himself to a servant.................Lk 12:37

—Demonstrated servanthood by washing feet ..... Jn 13:4–11
—Demonstrated servanthood by his cross ..... Isa 53:4–6; Php 2:7–8
—Exalted as servant ..... Isa 52:13

SETH

—Third son of Adam and Eve ..... Ge 4:25
—Took the place of Abel ..... Ge 4:25
—Made in Adam's likeness ..... Ge 5:3
—His family ..... Ge 5:6–8
—An ancestor of Jesus ..... Lk 3:38

SEXUAL STANDARDS

A. Sexual sins condemned in the Bible
—Adultery ..... Ex 20:14; Pr 5:1–23
—Incest ..... Lev 20:19–21
—Sex with animals ..... Lev 20:15–16
—Loss of virginity before marriage ..... Dt 22:20–21
—Prostitution ..... Dt 23:17–18; Pr 7:10–27
—Homosexuality ..... Ro 1:26–27; 1Co 6:9
—Obscenity ..... Eph 5:4
—Lust ..... Mt 5:27–28; 1Th 4:5

B. God's will regarding sexual standards
1. In negative terms
—Laws against illicit sexual behavior ..... Ex 20:14; Lev 20:10–21; Dt 23:17–18
—The command to flee immorality ..... 1Co 6:18; Eph 5:3; Col 3:5; 1Th 4:3
—Sexual sin excludes one from the kingdom ..... 1Co 6:9–10; Gal 5:19–21; Eph 5:3–5; Rev 22:15
2. In positive terms
—Strive for purity 1Th 4:4,7; 1Pe 3:2
—Be faithful in marriage 1Co 7:2–4
—Exercise self-control ..... 1Co 7:8–9; Gal 5:23; 1Th 4:4

See also MARRIAGE; ADULTERY; DIVORCE

SHADRACH

—Hebrew deported to Babylon ..... Da 1:6
—Name changed from Hananiah ..... Da 1:7
—Refused to be defiled by food ..... Da 1:8–20
—Appointed administrator over Babylon ..... Da 2:49
—Refused to worship idols ..... Da 3:1–18
—Saved from fiery furnace ..... Da 3:19–30

SHALLUM

—King of Israel 2Ki 15:10–15
—Assassinated by Menahem 2Ki 15:14

SHAME

A. Reasons for feeling ashamed
—Being naked ..... Ge 3:7; Eze 23:29
—Experiencing defeat ..... Ps 6:10; Isa 29:22–23
—Being humiliated ..... Eze 16:63; Zec 13:3–5; 1Co 1:27–29
—Experiencing sin ..... Ezr 9:6; Jer 22:22; 2Th 3:14
—Being taunted by one's enemies ..... Ps 44:15–16
—Having an undisciplined child ..... Pr 19:26
—Falsely accusing someone ..... Pr 25:8–10; 1Pe 3:16
—Giving less than poorer people 2Co 9:3–4
—Being inconsistent with one's principles ..... Ezr 8:22

B. When the Christian need not be ashamed
—When looking to the Lord ..... Ps 34:5
—When hoping in the Lord ..... Ps 25:3
—When taking refuge in the Lord ..... Ps 25:20
—When trusting in the Lord ..... Ro 9:33; 1Pe 2:6
—When believing in Christ ..... Mk 8:38; 2Ti 1:12
—When believing Christ and his word ..... Mk 8:38; Lk 9:26
—When preaching the gospel ..... Ro 1:16; 2Ti 1:8
—When suffering for Christ's sake 1Pe 4:16
—When obeying God's law ..... Ps 119:5–6
—When doing one's best for the Lord 2Ti 2:15
—When the Lord returns 1Jn 2:28

SHAMGAR

—Judge; killed six hundred Philistines ..... Jdg 3:31

SHAPHAN

—Secretary during Josiah's reign 2Ki 22:3
—Supervised finances for temple repairs 2Ki 22:3–7; 2Ch 34:8–13,16–17
—Brought newly discovered Book of the Law to Josiah 2Ki 22:8–10; 2Ch 34:14–17
—Read the Book of the Law to Josiah 2Ki 22:10; 2Ch 34:18
—With others, visited prophetess Huldah 2Ki 22:14–20; 2Ch 34:20–28

SHECHEM

A. A man who raped Jacob's daughter Dinah ..... Ge 34:1–4
—Agreed to circumcision and marriage ..... Ge 34:11–24
—Killed by Simeon and Levi ..... Ge 34:25–29

B. A city in Canaan
—The Lord appeared to Abram there ..... Ge 12:6–7
—Jacob purchased land there ..... Ge 33:18–19
—Pillaged by the sons of Jacob ..... Ge 34:26–29
—Joseph went there to find his brothers ..... Ge 37:14–17
—One of the cities of refuge ..... Jos 20:7
—Joshua renewed the covenant there ..... Jos 24:1–27
—Gideon's son Abimelech was crowned its king ..... Jdg 9:1–6
—Civil war between Abimelech and Shechem ..... Jdg 9:22–57
—Rehoboam was made king there 1Ki 12:1
—Jeroboam fortified it as his capital 1Ki 12:25
—In New Testament, Shechem is Sychar ..... Jn 4:5

SHEEP

See LAMB

SHEM

—Son of Noah ..... Ge 5:32; 1Ch 1:4
—With Japheth, covered his father with a garment ..... Ge 9:23
—Blessed by Noah ..... Ge 9:26
—Sons listed ..... Ge 10:21–31
—Abram came from his line ..... Ge 11:10–26

SHEOL
See GRAVE

SHEPHERD
A. Related theme
PASTORAL ADVICE is a theme of Titus .... Tit 3:8
B. The shepherd as an human occupation
1. Examples of shepherds .... Ge 4:2; Ge 29:9; 1Sa 16:11; Lk 2:8
2. Responsibilities of shepherds
—Find pasture for flocks .... Eze 34:2,13 – 14
—Provide water for flocks .... Ge 29:2 – 8; Ex 2:16
—Protect the flocks .... 1Sa 17:34 – 36; Lk 2:8
—Seek lost sheep .... Eze 34:16; Mt 18:10 – 13
—Care for injured sheep .... Mt 12:11
—Regularly account for the sheep .... Jn 10:2 – 5
—Know what happens to the sheep .... Ge 31:38 – 39
—Shear the sheep .... Ge 38:12; 1Sa 25:2,7
C. Figurative use of shepherd
1. Leaders of God's people as shepherds
a. Old Testament leaders
—Joshua .... Nu 27:15 – 18
—David .... 2Sa 5:2; Ps 78:70 – 72
—Cyrus .... Isa 44:28
—Selfish shepherds .... Isa 56:10 – 11; Jer 10:21; Eze 34:2 – 6; Zec 10:2 – 3
b. Church leaders .... Jn 21:15 – 17; Ac 20:28 – 31; 1Pe 5:2 – 3
2. God as a shepherd
—God is called a shepherd .... Ps 23:1; Ps 80:1
—We are his sheep .... Ps 95:7; Ps 100:3
—God acted as a shepherd in the exodus .... Ps 77:20; Ps 78:52; Isa 63:11
—God cares for us like a shepherd .... Isa 40:11; Eze 34:11 – 16; Mic 7:14
3. Jesus Christ as a shepherd
a. He is called a shepherd
—The good shepherd .... Jn 10:11,14
—The great Shepherd .... Heb 13:20
—The Chief Shepherd 1Pe 5:4
—The Shepherd and Overseer 1Pe 2:25
b. He acts as a shepherd
—Old Testament prophecies .... Isa 40:11; Eze 34:23; Mic 5:2 – 4; Zec 13:7
—He died for the sheep .... Jn 10:15
—He has compassion for the sheep .... Mt 9:36
—He knows his sheep .... Jn 10:3 – 4,14
—He searches for wandering sheep .... Mt 18:12 – 14; Lk 15:3 – 7
—He will judge like a shepherd .... Mt 25:32

SHILOH
—Located in Ephraim, near Bethel .... Jdg 21:19
—The first religious center in Canaan .... Jos 18:1; Jdg 18:31
—Joshua's political center .... Jos 21:1 – 2
—Joshua divided the land there .... Jos 18:9
—Benjamites seized women there .... Jdg 21:19 – 23
—Hannah asked for a son there .... 1Sa 1:3 – 18
—Eli and sons ministered there .... 1Sa 2:12 – 14
—God appeared to Samuel there 1Sa 3:21
—Ark taken into battle from there .... 1Sa 4:3 – 6; Ps 78:60 – 61
—Eli died there .... 1Sa 4:12 – 18
—Prophet Ahijah ministered there 1Ki 11:29; 1Ki 14:2
—City lay in ruins in Jeremiah's day .... Jer 7:12 – 14; Jer 26:9

SHIMEI
—A Benjamite who cursed David .... 2Sa 16:5 – 14
—Spared from execution .... 2Sa 19:16 – 23
—Killed on Solomon's orders .... 1Ki 2:8 – 9,36 – 46

SIDON
A. Identity and location
—A chief city of Phoenicia .... Isa 23:11 – 12
—A seacoast city .... Ac 27:3
—Often linked with Tyre .... Isa 23:1 – 2; Mt 15:21
—Sidonians were descendants of Ham .... Ge 10:6,15
—A peaceful, prosperous people .... Jdg 18:7
—Skillful in felling timber .... 1Ki 5:6; 1Ch 22:4; Zec 9:2
—Served the goddess Ashtoreth 1Ki 11:5,33
B. Significance of Sidon
1. In the Old Testament
—Territory given to tribe of Asher .... Jos 19:24,28
—Asher did not drive out its inhabitants .... Jdg 1:31
—Cut timber for the temple 1Ki 5:6
—Solomon intermarried with them 1Ki 11:1
—Ahab married Jezebel, a Sidonian 1Ki 16:31
—Elijah stayed with a Sidonian widow .... 1Ki 17:9 – 16
—Prophecies against them .... Isa 23:2,4,11 – 12; Eze 28:20 – 23; Joel 3:4 – 8
2. In the New Testament
—Jesus ministered there .... Mt 15:21 – 28; Mk 7:24 – 30
—Paul spent a night there .... Ac 27:3

SIDONIANS
See SIDON

SIGN
—An outward event with a spiritual significance
A. Miracles as signs
1. In the Old Testament
—Signs for Israel .... Ex 4:29 – 31; Nu 14:11
—Signs for Pharaoh .... Ex 10:1 – 2
—Signs for Gideon .... Jdg 6:17 – 24,36 – 40
—Signs for Saul 1Sa 10:7,9
—A sign for Jeroboam .... 1Ki 13:3 – 5
—A sign for Ahaz .... Isa 7:11 – 14
2. In the New Testament
—Jesus' miracles were signs .... Jn 2:11,23; Jn 12:37; Jn 20:30
—The Jews wanted miraculous signs .... Mt 12:38 – 40; Mt 16:1 – 4; Jn 2:18; 1Co 1:22

—The apostles performed signs ..... Ac 4:16,30
Ac 8:6
Ac 14:3

B. Signs of the covenant
1. In the Old Testament
—The rainbow with Noah ..... Ge 9:12 – 16
—Circumcision with Abraham ..... Ge 17:11
Ro 4:11
—The blood of the Passover at the exodus ..... Ex 12:13
—The Sabbath at Mount Sinai ..... Ex 31:12 – 17
—The altar at the crossing of the Jordan ..... Jos 4:5 – 7
2. In the New Testament
—The water of baptism ..... Mt 28:19
1Pe 3:21
—Bread and wine of the Lord's Supper ..... 1Co 11:23 – 26

C. Signs of the end times
1. Jesus is asked to reveal these signs ..... Mk 13:1 – 4
2. Listing of these signs
—Wars and rumors of wars ..... Mk 13:7 – 8
—Persecution of Christians ..... Mk 13:9
Jn 15:18 – 21
—False teachers and false Christs ..... Mk 13:6,22
1Jn 2:18 – 19
—The worldwide spread of the gospel ..... Mt 24:14
Rev 7:9 – 10
—The antichrist ..... 2Th 2:3 – 4,8
Rev 13:1 – 9
—The great tribulation ..... Mk 13:14 – 20
Rev 7:14
—Signs in the heavens ..... Lk 21:11,25

D. The purpose of signs
—To bring about faith in God ..... Nu 14:11
Jn 20:30
—To strengthen faith in God ..... Jos 24:16 – 17
Ro 4:11
—To confirm a message from God ..... 2Ki 19:28 – 29
Lk 2:12,16 – 20
—To protect God's people from danger ..... Ex 12:13
—To bring to mind God's care and promises ..... Ge 9:12 – 16
Ex 13:7 – 9
1Co 11:23 – 26

SIHON

—King of the Amorites ..... Nu 21:21
Dt 1:4
—Marched out against Israelites ..... Nu 21:23
—Destroyed by Israelites ..... Nu 21:24 – 31
Dt 2:32 – 36
—Victory sung by the Israelites ..... Nu 21:27 – 30
Ps 136:19

SILAS

—A prophet of the early church ..... Ac 15:32
—Delegated to report on council in Jerusalem ..... Ac 15:22
—Traveled with Paul on second missionary journey .. Ac 15:40
—With Paul in prison at Philippi ..... Ac 16:19 – 36
—With Paul in Thessalonica and Berea ..... Ac 17:1 – 10
—Stayed behind in Berea ..... Ac 17:14
—Came to Paul in Corinth ..... Ac 18:5
—Preached with Paul in Corinth 2Co 1:19
—Co-writer with Paul 1Th 1:1
2Th 1:1
—Co-writer with Peter 1Pe 5:12

SILVER

A. Uses for silver
1. In Israelite worship
—The tabernacle furniture ..... Ex 26:19 – 25
Ex 27:9 – 11,17
—Offerings ..... Nu 7:13,19,25
Ezr 1:4,6,9 – 11
—The temple building ..... 1Ch 29:2 – 5
—The temple furniture ..... 1Ch 28:14 – 17
2. In crafting idol gods ..... Isa 2:20
Hos 8:4
Ac 19:24
3. For personal wealth ..... Ge 13:2
Ecc 2:8
4. For gifts ..... 1Ki 15:18 – 19
Ezr 2:69
5. For payment as money ..... Ge 42:25 – 27
Jdg 9:4
Mt 26:15
6. For jewelry ..... Ge 24:53
Eze 16:17
7. For royal display ..... Ge 44:2
Est 1:6 – 7

B. Value of silver for God's people
1. Positive: a blessing from God ..... Ge 13:2
Isa 60:9,17
2. Negative
—Wisdom worth more than silver ..... Job 28:12 – 15
Pr 3:13 – 14
Pr 16:16
—Silver valueless in redemption 1Pe 1:18

C. Silver as a symbol
—For saints surviving God's testing ..... Isa 48:10
Zec 13:9
—For God's dependable word ..... Ps 12:6
—For trustworthy spiritual values ..... 1Co 3:12 – 13

SIMEON

A. Son of Jacob by Leah ..... Ge 35:23
1Ch 2:1
—Name means "one who hears" ..... Ge 29:33
—With Levi, avenged rape of Dinah ..... Ge 34:25 – 31
—Held hostage by Joseph in Egypt ..... Ge 42:24—43:23
—Went to Egypt with family ..... Ge 46:8,10
—Father of six sons ..... Ge 46:10
—Blessed by Jacob ..... Ge 49:5 – 7

B. Tribe descended from Simeon
—Numbered ..... Nu 1:23
Nu 26:14
—Allotted land ..... Jos 19:1 – 9
Eze 48:24
—One of the tribes of the 144,000 ..... Rev 7:7

C. A righteous man who blessed Jesus ..... Lk 2:25 – 35
—Sang a song ..... Lk 2:29 – 32

SIMON

A. One of Jesus' disciples
See PETER

B. Another disciple of Jesus
—Called the Zealot ..... Mt 10:4
Mk 3:18
—One of the apostles ..... Ac 1:13

C. A Samaritan sorcerer ..... Ac 8:9 – 11
—Baptized as a Christian ..... Ac 8:12
—Offered Peter money for power to impart the Holy Spirit ..... Ac 8:18 – 19
—Severely rebuked by Peter ..... Ac 8:20 – 23

SIN

A. Related themes
SIN is a theme of:
—Genesis ..... Ge 6:5
—Judges ..... Jdg 21:25
—Isaiah ..... Isa 1:4
—Malachi ..... Mal 1:8
—Romans ..... Ro 2:12
—1 John 1Jn 3:6

B. Words for sin
—Transgression ... Ps 32:1
—Iniquity ... Ps 51:2,9
—Wickedness ... Ge 6:5
—Evil ... Ge 8:21
—Rebellion ... Ex 34:7
—Uncleanness ... Lev 16:16
—Disobedience ... Jos 22:22
—Wrongdoing ... 1Sa 24:11
—Guilt ... Isa 1:4
—Unrighteousness ... 1Jn 1:9
—Lawlessness ... 1Jn 3:4
—Depravity ... 2Pe 2:19
—Faults ... Ps 19:12

C. The origin and extent of sin
1. Original sin
—Adam and Eve disobeyed God's command ... Ge 3:1 – 7
—Their sin passed down to all humans ... Ro 5:12,15
1Co 15:22
2. Present extent of sin
—There is sin in everyone ... Ps 14:2 – 3
Ro 3:10 – 20,23
—Present already at conception ... Ps 51:5
—Permeates to the heart of people ... Ge 6:5
Jer 17:9
Mt 15:18 – 20
—Christ alone was without sin ... 2Co 5:21
Heb 4:15
1Pe 2:22
1Jn 3:5

D. God and human sin
1. His negative reaction
—He is grieved over sin ... Ge 6:6
—He is angry over sin ... Ps 78:19 – 21,56 – 59
Jn 3:36
Ro 1:18
—He hates sin ... Ps 5:5
Pr 6:16 – 19
—He punishes sin ... Ge 3:15 – 19
Isa 3:11 – 26
Am 3:2
2. His positive reaction
—He sent his Son to die for sinners ... Jn 3:16
Ro 5:8
1Jn 4:10
—He forgives sin ... Ex 34:6 – 7
1Jn 1:9
—He removes sin far away ... Ps 103:8 – 12
—He sweeps away sin ... Isa 44:22
—He hurls sin away ... Mic 7:19
—He puts sin behind his back ... Isa 38:17
—He no longer remembers our sin ... Jer 31:34

E. Christ and human sin
—He was sinless ... 2Co 5:21
Heb 4:15
Heb 7:26
1Pe 2:22
1Jn 3:5
—He paid the penalty for sin ... Ro 4:25
Ro 8:3
Col 2:13 – 14
1Pe 2:24
—He forgives sin ... Mk 2:5 – 12
Lk 7:48
Col 1:13 – 14
—His blood redeems us from sin ... Eph 1:7
—His blood cleanses us from sin ... 1Jn 1:7
—He takes away the sin of the world ... Jn 1:29
1Jn 2:2

F. Humans and their sin
1. How has sin affected us?
—We are responsible for our sin ... Eze 18:10 – 18
—We are accountable to God for sin ... Jer 17:10
2Co 5:10
Rev 20:12
—We are subject to death because of sin ... Ge 2:17
Ro 6:23
Jas 1:15
—We cannot atone for our own sin ... Ps 49:7
Mt 16:26
2. What should we do with our sin?
—We should confess it ... Ps 32:1 – 5
Pr 28:13
1Jn 1:9
—We should repent of it ... Eze 18:30 – 31
Ac 3:19 – 20
—We should turn from it ... Ps 34:14
Isa 1:16
3Jn 11
—We should hate it ... Ps 97:10
Am 5:15
Ro 12:9
—We should throw it off ... Heb 12:1
—We should fight against it ... Eph 6:12 – 13
Heb 12:4
3. What are the blessings after confession?
—We are forgiven our sin ... Ps 32:5
Ac 2:38
Ac 10:43
—God considers us righteous ... Ro 4:5 – 8
Php 3:9
—We are purified from sin ... 1Jn 1:9
—We are freed from sin ... Ro 6:7,18,22
Rev 1:5
—We are no longer slaves to sin ... Ro 6:6,17
—We do not continue a life of sin ... 1Jn 3:6,9
1Jn 5:18
—We are dead to sin ... Ro 6:2,11
—We pass from death to life ... Ro 6:23

SINAI

A. A desert area where the Israelites camped ... Ex 19:1 – 2
—Census taken there ... Nu 1:1 – 4,19
—Passover celebrated there ... Nu 9:1 – 5
—Israelites stayed there nearly a year ... Nu 10:12

B. Mount Sinai, in the above area
1. Identity
—Called Mount Horeb ... Ex 33:6
—Called the mountain of God ... Ex 3:1
Ex 24:13
—God came down from Mount Sinai ... Dt 33:2
—God is the God of Mount Sinai ... Ps 68:8
2. History and significance
—God appeared to Moses there ... Ex 3:1 – 6
—God spoke his law from there ... Ex 19:20—20:17
Dt 5:4 – 21
—Israelites frightened at the mountain ... Ex 20:18 – 19
Dt 5:5,22 – 27
—Moses received the law there ... Ex 24:15 – 18
Dt 9:9 – 11
—Israelites worshiped golden calf there ... Ex 32:1 – 20
Dt 9:8 – 17
Ps 106:19 – 23
—Moses received the law a second time ... Ex 34:1 – 32
Lev 7:38
Dt 10:1 – 5,10
—Elijah talked with God there ... 1Ki 19:8 – 18

SINGLES
See MARRIAGE

SISERA
—Canaanite commander ... Jdg 4:2
—Fought against Deborah and Barak ... Jdg 4:12–16
—Killed by Jael ... Jdg 4:21; Jdg 5:24–30

SISTER
See BROTHERS AND SISTERS

SLAVERY
A. Slavery in the Old Testament
1. Slavery common
—Abraham had slaves ... Ge 20:14; Ge 21:10
—Israelites were slaves in Egypt ... Ex 1:11; Dt 6:20–21
—David had slaves ... 2Sa 6:20,22
—Solomon conscripted slaves ... 1Ki 9:20–22
—The Teacher had slaves ... Ecc 2:7
—Sons were made slaves to pay debts ... 2Ki 4:1
—Israelites were slaves to Babylon ... La 1:1
—Israelites were slaves to Persia ... Ne 9:36
—There were slaves among returning Jews ... Ne 5:5
2. God and human slavery
a. Delivered Israelites from slavery ... Ex 13:3; Ex 20:2
b. Regulated slavery in Israel
—Treatment of slaves ... Ex 21:5–11,20–21; Dt 15:12–18; Dt 23:15–16
—Release in the Year of Jubilee ... Lev 25:39–55
c. Gave rights to slaves
—Were members of the covenant ... Ge 17:12–13
—Rested on the Sabbath ... Ex 20:10; Dt 5:12–15
—Included in religious meals ... Ex 12:44; Dt 16:11,14
—Could expect equal justice ... Job 31:13
—Could become an heir ... Ge 15:2–3
B. Slavery in the New Testament
1. Common in Roman society ... Ac 16:16,19; 1Co 7:21; 1Ti 1:10
2. Messages for Christian slaves
—Slave and master are equal in Christ ... 1Co 12:13; Gal 3:28; Col 3:11; Phm 15–16
—Slaves must respect their masters ... 1Ti 6:1–2
—Slaves must submit to their masters ... Tit 2:9–10; 1Pe 2:18
—Slaves must obey their masters ... Eph 6:5–8; Col 3:22–25
—If possible, try to gain freedom ... 1Co 7:21
3. Messages given to Christian masters
—Masters must treat slaves kindly ... Eph 6:9; Phm 17
—Masters must treat slaves justly ... Col 4:1
C. Slavery as a symbol
—By nature we are slaves to sin ... Jn 8:34; Ro 6:16–17; Ro 7:14; 2Pe 2:19
—The Old Testament era saw slavery to the law ... Gal 4:3–5; Gal 5:1
—We must become slaves to righteousness ... Ro 6:18
—We must become slaves to God and Christ ... Ro 6:22; 1Co 7:22; Eph 6:6

SNOW
See WEATHER

SODOM AND GOMORRAH
A. Their identity and location
—Wealthy cities in the Jordan plain ... Ge 13:10
—Extremely wicked inhabitants ... Ge 13:13; Ge 18:20–21
B. History of Sodom and Gomorrah
—Lot went to live there ... Ge 13:11–12
—Cities defeated by four kings ... Ge 14:8–12
—Abram rescued the cities ... Ge 14:13–16
—Abraham interceded for the cities ... Ge 18:23–33
—Sodom and Gomorrah destroyed ... Ge 19:1–29
—God's promise of restoration ... Eze 16:53–57
C. Sodom and Gomorrah used as symbols
—A symbol of total wickedness ... Isa 3:9; Jer 23:14; Eze 16:46–50; Mt 10:15
—A symbol of evil Jerusalem ... Rev 11:8
—A symbol of God's judgment ... Isa 13:19; Jer 49:18; Am 4:11; Zep 2:9
—A symbol of eternal punishment ... 2Pe 2:6; Jude 7

SOLOMON
A. Family data
—Son of David by Bathsheba ... 2Sa 12:24; 1Ch 3:5
—Married Pharaoh's daughter ... 1Ki 3:1
—Later married numerous pagan women ... 1Ki 11:1–3
B. His early life as king
—Appointed as king by David ... 1Ki 1:11–53
—Given parting charge ... 1Ki 2:1–9
—Had Adonijah and his supporters killed ... 1Ki 2:13–46
—Asked for wisdom ... 1Ki 3:4–15; 2Ch 1:2–13
—Judged between two prostitutes ... 1Ki 3:16–28
—Known widely for his wisdom ... 1Ki 4:29–31,34
—Wrote three thousand proverbs ... 1Ki 4:32; Pr 1:1
—Wrote one thousand and five songs ... 1Ki 4:32; SS 1:1
—Built temple ... 1Ki 5:1—6:38; 2Ch 2:1—3:17
—Built palace ... 1Ki 7:1–12
—Furnished the temple ... 1Ki 7:13–51; 2Ch 4:1—5:1
—Brought ark into the temple ... 1Ki 8:1–11; 2Ch 5:2–14
—Offered prayer of dedication for temple ... 1Ki 8:22–53; 2Ch 6:14–42
—Dedicated the temple with sacrifices ... 1Ki 8:62–66; 2Ch 7:1–10
—God made promises to Solomon ... 1Ki 9:1–9; 2Ch 7:11–22
—Administrated his kingdom ... 1Ki 9:10–28; 2Ch 8:1–18
—Visited by the queen of Sheba ... 1Ki 10:1–13; 2Ch 9:1–12
—Had a glorious kingdom ... 1Ki 10:14–29; 2Ch 9:13–28

C. His later life as king
—Wives turned his heart from God .... 1Ki 11:1 – 13
—Hadad and Rezon rebelled against him............ 1Ki 11:14 – 25
—Jeroboam rebelled against him........................ 1Ki 11:26 – 40
—His death .... 1Ki 11:41 – 43
2Ch 9:29 – 31
D. Solomon remembered after his death
—For his organization of temple service.............. 2Ch 35:3 – 4
Ne 12:45
—For marrying idolatrous wives .... Ne 13:26
—For his splendor .... Mt 6:29
—For his wisdom.. Mt 12:42
—For his building of the temple........................... Ac 7:47

SON OF MAN

A. "Son of man" denotes someone merely human
—"Son of man" means "man"................................ Ps 80:17
—Ezekiel called "son of man"................................ Eze 2:1
Eze 3:1
B. Jesus as the Son of Man
—Prophesied in the Old Testament .... Da 7:13 – 14
—Identified himself as such .... Mk 2:10
Lk 7:34
Lk 9:58
Jn 9:35 – 37
—Died and rose again .... Mk 8:31
Mk 9:31
Mk 10:33 – 34
Jn 3:14 – 15
—Is in heaven... Mt 26:64
Ac 7:56
Rev 1:13
—Will return... Mt 13:41
Mk 13:26
Mk 14:62
—We must feed on him... Jn 6:53

SONG

See MUSIC AND SONG

SORROW

See GRIEF

SOUL

—The non-physical element in humans
A. Defining the soul
1. Basic concepts
—Humans were created as whole people .... Ge 2:7
—Soul referred to in the context of death .... Mt 10:28
Rev 6:9
2. Soul often synonymous with:
—Spirit.. Ecc 12:7
Lk 1:46 – 47
—Heart.. Ps 19:7 – 8
Ps 84:2
—Life .... Ps 26:9
—One's whole being .... Ps 35:9 – 10
3. Sometimes soul appears distinct from:
—Heart.. Dt 4:29
Dt 6:5
—Spirit.. 1Th 5:23
Heb 4:12
B. What does the soul do?
1. Expresses human emotions
—Peace.. Ps 23:2 – 3
—Refreshment... Ps 19:7
—Joy.. Ps 35:9
—Courage .... Jdg 5:21
—Support 1Sa 14:7
—Grief.. 1Sa 1:10,15
Job 30:25
—Sorrow .... Mt 26:38
—Bitterness .... Job 7:11
—Anguish .... Ps 6:3
—Depression.. Ps 42:5,11
La 3:20
2. Has spiritual desires
—Thirsts for God.. Ps 42:1 – 2
—Yearns for God.. Ps 84:2
—Seeks God .... Dt 4:29
2Ch 15:12
—Finds rest in God .... Ps 62:1,5
—Turns to God.. Dt 30:10
1Ki 8:48
—Loves God .... Dt 6:5
Dt 13:3
—Serves God.. Dt 10:12
Jos 22:5
—Obeys God .... Dt 30:2
2Ki 23:3
—Praises God .... Ps 103:1 – 2,22
—Cries out to God .... Rev 6:9 – 10
C. What does God do for the soul?
—He saves the soul 1Pe 1:9
—Gives hope as an anchor for the soul.................. Heb 6:19

SPIRIT

—An immaterial being
A. The human spirit
1. Defining the spirit
See SOUL
2. What does the spirit do?
a. Involved with the emotions
—The compelled spirit .... Job 32:18 – 20
—The stirred-up spirit.................................. 1Ch 5:26
—The revived spirit .... Ge 45:27
—The stubborn spirit .... Dt 2:30
—The bitter spirit... 1Sa 30:6
—The fainting spirit .... Ps 142:3
—The broken spirit....................................... Ps 51:17
—The troubled spirit.................................... Jn 13:21
—The anguished spirit .... Job 7:11
—The crushed spirit .... Ps 34:18
—The provoked spirit .... Ecc 7:9
—The haughty spirit .... Pr 16:18
—The lowly spirit... Isa 57:15
—The contrite spirit...................................... Isa 66:2
—The joyful spirit... Lk 1:47
—The gentle, quiet spirit............................. 1Pe 3:4
b. Involved with the will
—The spirit that follows God....................... Nu 14:24
—The spirit that follows itself .... Eze 13:3
—The steadfast spirit .... Ps 51:10
—The willing spirit....................................... Ps 51:12
—The wayward spirit .... Isa 29:24
c. Involved with the intellect
—The inquiring spirit .... Ps 77:6
—The understanding spirit .... Isa 29:24
3. What does God do for the spirit?
—He can stir it up.. Hag 1:14
—He searches it.. Pr 20:27
—He gives us a new one .... Eze 36:26
—He gives it new birth..................................... Jn 3:6
—He testifies with our spirit............................. Ro 8:16
—It returns to him.. Ecc 12:7
—He receives it .... Ps 31:5
B. The Holy Spirit
See HOLY SPIRIT

C. Spirit beings
  1. God sends out spirits
    —Angels are spirits he sends out ...... Heb 1:14
    See ANGEL
    —A reporting spirit sent to Sennacherib ...... Isa 37:7
    —An evil spirit sent to Abimelech ...... Jdg 9:23
    —An evil spirit sent to Saul 1Sa 16:14–15,23
    —A lying spirit sent to false prophets 1Ki 22:19–23
  2. Evil spirits
    —Have influence over humans ...... 1Ti 4:1; Rev 16:13–14
    —Were cast out by Jesus ...... Mt 8:16; Mk 1:23–27
    —Were cast out by the apostles ...... Ac 5:16; Ac 16:16–18

SPIRITUALITY
See HOLINESS; MEDITATION

STARS
A. Data concerning the stars
  —Created by God ...... Ge 1:16; Ps 8:3
  —Controlled by God ...... Ps 147:4; Jer 31:35
  —Show God's power ...... Isa 40:26
  —Must praise God ...... Ps 148:3
  —Were worshiped by the heathen ...... 2Ki 21:3; Jer 19:13; Ac 7:43
B. Stars and constellations mentioned in the Bible
  —The Bear ...... Job 9:9
  —Orion ...... Job 9:9
  —Pleiades ...... Am 5:8
  —The star of Bethlehem ...... Mt 2:2,9
C. Stars used as symbols
  —Of Jesus the Messiah ...... Nu 24:17; Rev 22:16
  —Of an innumerable number ...... Ge 22:17; Ne 9:23
  —Of Christians as witnesses ...... Php 2:15–16
  —Of the saints in heaven ...... Da 12:3
  —Of angels ...... Rev 1:16,20
  —Of heretics ...... Jude 13
  —Of judgment at the end of time ...... Isa 13:10–11; Mt 24:29; Rev 6:12

STEADFASTNESS
See PERSEVERANCE

STEALING
—Taking what belongs to someone else
A. The command against stealing
  —The eighth commandment ...... Ex 20:15; Dt 5:19; Mt 19:17–18
  —Fraud and dishonest weights outlawed ...... Lev 19:13; Pr 20:10,23
  —Theft prohibited in Paul's writings ...... Ro 13:8–9; Eph 4:28
  —Theft profanes the name of God ...... Lev 19:11–12; Jer 7:9–11
  —Theft often accompanied by greed ...... Ps 62:10
B. The punishment for thieves
  —Expected to make restitution ...... Ex 22:1–9; Nu 5:5–8
  —Are subject to God's judgment ...... Hab 2:6
  —Can be excluded from the kingdom of God 1Co 6:9–10
C. Examples of stealing in the Bible
  —Rachel and the household gods ...... Ge 31:19,30–32
  —Achan and goods from Jericho ...... Jos 7:11
  —Micah and eleven hundred shekels of silver ...... Jdg 17:2
  —Ahab and Naboth's vineyard 1Ki 21:16,19
  See also THE RICH AND THE POOR
D. Theft used as a metaphor
  —For gaining admiration (stealing hearts) 2Sa 15:6
  —For withholding tithes (robbing God) ...... Mal 3:8–9
  —For claiming to speak God's word (stealing words from others) ...... Jer 23:30
  —For the unexpectedness of Christ's return ...... Lk 12:39–40; 1Th 5:2; 2Pe 3:10; Rev 3:3

STEPHEN
—One of the seven deacons ...... Ac 6:5
—Spoke eloquently ...... Ac 6:8–10
—Arrested by the Jews ...... Ac 6:11–15
—Gave powerful speech to the Sanhedrin ...... Ac 7:1–53
—Stoned to death ...... Ac 7:54–60; Ac 22:20

STEWARDSHIP
—How one handles what God has given
A. God's relationship to what we have
  1. God owns everything ...... Ex 19:5; Ps 24:1; Hag 2:8
  2. God is the source of everything
    —All our wealth ...... Ge 26:12–13; 1Co 4:7
    —Our personal talents ...... Ro 12:3,6; 1Co 12:7–11
    —Our ability to work ...... Dt 8:17–18; Ecc 2:24–25
    —Every moment of our lives ...... Ps 39:4–5; Mt 6:27
    —Everything we have ...... Job 1:21; Jn 3:27
B. Our relationship to what we have
  1. Our gifts and talents
    —Must use them faithfully ...... Mt 25:14–27; 1Co 4:2
    —Must be trustworthy with them ...... Lk 16:10–12
    —Must use them for God's glory ...... 1Sa 17:45–46; Ro 14:7–8; 1Co 10:31; 1Pe 4:11
    —Must use them to serve others ...... Ro 14:19; 1Co 12:7; 1Co 14:12; 1Pe 4:10
  2. Our time
    —Recognize the brevity of time ...... Job 7:7; Ps 89:47; Ecc 9:11–12
    —Must be faithful in use of time ...... Ps 90:12,17; Eph 5:15–16
  3. Our wealth and possessions
    a. Basic attitude
      —Must believe that God will provide ...... Mt 6:25–34; Php 4:19
      —Cannot take credit for what we have ...... Da 4:28–35; 1Co 4:7
      —Must be content with what we have ...... Php 4:11–12; 1Ti 6:6–8; Heb 13:5

b. Principles of giving to the Lord
- —Giving should be proportionate ... Pr 3:9; Mal 3:8 – 10; 1Co 16:1 – 2
- —Giving should be willing ... Ex 25:1 – 2; 1Ch 29:6 – 9; 2Co 8:1 – 5,11 – 12
- —Giving should be spontaneous ... 2Co 9:2 – 5
- —Giving should be cheerful ... 2Ch 24:10; 2Co 9:7
- —Giving should be generous ... 2Co 8:2; 2Co 9:5,11,13

c. Blessings await a giver
- —On earth ... Dt 15:4; Ac 20:35; 2Co 9:6,10
- —In heaven ... Mt 19:21; 1Ti 6:19

STRANGERS
See ALIEN

SUFFERING
See PAIN

SUN
A. Data concerning the sun
- —Created by God ... Ge 1:16; Ps 74:16
- —Governs the day ... Ge 1:16; Ps 136:8
- —Controlled by God ... Jos 10:12 – 13; Ps 19:4 – 6; Jer 31:35
- —Needed for crops ... Dt 33:13 – 14
- —Needed for warmth ... Ps 19:6
- —Must praise God ... Ps 148:3
- —Can harm a person ... Ps 121:6
- —Worshiped by the heathen ... 2Ki 23:5,11; Jer 8:2
- —No sun needed in heaven ... Isa 60:19 – 20; Rev 21:23

B. The sun used as a symbol
- —Of God ... Ps 84:11
- —Of God's glory ... Ps 19:1 – 6
- —Of Christ ... Mal 4:2
- —Of Christ's glory ... Mt 17:2; Ac 26:13 – 15; Rev 1:16
- —Of the future glory of believers ... Mt 13:43
- —Of stability and endurance ... Ps 72:5,17
- —Of judgment at the end of time ... Isa 13:10 – 11; Mt 24:29; Rev 6:12

SWEARING
See CURSE

SYMPATHY
See COMPASSION

SYRIA, SYRIANS
See DAMASCUS

TABERNACLE
A. Related theme
- TABERNACLE is a theme of Exodus ... Ex 40:34

B. Also called "the tent of meeting" ... Nu 4:25; Nu 9:17 – 18

C. The building of the tabernacle

1. Planning the tabernacle
- —Extensive plans outlined by God ... Ex 25:8—30:38
- —Based on pattern of heaven ... Heb 8:5; Heb 9:24

2. Building the tabernacle
- —Material collected ... Ex 35:4 – 29; Ex 36:3 – 7
- —Supervisers chosen ... Ex 35:30—36:2
- —Work performed ... Ex 36:8—39:31
- —Inspected by Moses ... Ex 39:32 – 43
- —The completed tabernacle set up ... Ex 40:1 – 33

3. Structure of the tabernacle

a. Contents of the courtyard
- —Its construction ... Ex 38:9 – 20
- —Altar of burnt offering ... Ex 38:1 – 7
- —Basin for washing ... Ex 38:8

b. Contents of the Holy Place
- —Table for bread of the Presence ... Ex 25:23 – 30
- —Golden lampstand ... Ex 37:17 – 24
- —Altar of incense ... Ex 37:25 – 29

c. Contents of the Most Holy Place ... Ex 37:1 – 9; Heb 9:4

See ARK OF THE COVENANT LAW

d. Two parts separated by a curtain ... Ex 26:33; Heb 9:3

D. History of the tent of meeting
- —God talked with Moses there ... Lev 1:1; Nu 7:89
- —Aaron and his sons were consecrated there ... Ex 29:1 – 4,10 – 11
- —Filled with God's glory at dedication ... Ex 40:34 – 35
- —Covered by the cloud ... Nu 9:15 – 23
- —Used in Israelite sacrifices ... Lev 1:3 – 5; Lev 3:2,8
- —Placed in the center of the camp ... Nu 2:1 – 2,17
- —Joshua was commissioned there ... Dt 31:14 – 15,23
- —Set up at Shiloh in Canaan ... Jos 18:1; Jdg 18:31; 1Sa 2:14,22
- —Located at Nob during Saul's time ... 1Sa 21:1 – 6
- —Located at Gibeon during David's time ... 1Ch 16:37 – 40
- —Brought to Jerusalem during David's reign ... 1Ch 23:25 – 26,32; 2Ch 1:4,13
- —Solomon replaced it with the temple ... 2Ch 5:4 – 6

E. Symbolism of the tabernacle

1. Symbol of God's presence among the people ... Ex 25:8; Ex 29:43; Ex 40:34 – 35

2. Its contents symbolized Christ
- —He made his dwelling ("tabernacle") among men ... Jn 1:14
- —His death is the atoning sacrifice ... 1Jn 4:10
- —His body is sacred bread ... Jn 6:27 – 59
- —His body is the curtain ... Heb 10:20
- —His blood washes and purifies us ... 1Jn 1:7

TAMAR
A. Wife of Judah's sons Er and Onan ... Ge 38:1 – 10
- —Tricked Judah into fathering children ... Ge 38:11 – 26
- —Gave birth to twins ... Ge 38:27 – 30
- —An ancestor of Jesus ... Mt 1:3

B. Daughter of David, sister of Absalom ... 2Sa 13:1
- —Raped by half brother Amnon ... 2Sa 13:2 – 21
- —Rape avenged by Absalom ... 2Sa 13:23 – 33

TEACHING
See DOCTRINE; EDUCATION

TEMPLE

A. Related themes
1. TEMPLE is a theme of:
—1 Kings ... 1Ki 6:1
—2 Chronicles ... 2Ch 7:1
2. REBUILDING is a theme of Ezra ... Ezr 5:2

B. The first temple
1. Its construction
—The idea conceived by David ... 2Sa 7:1 – 2
—David not allowed to construct it ... 2Sa 7:4 – 13
—Planned by David ... 1Ch 28:11 – 19
—Gifts collected by David ... 1Ch 29:1 – 9
—Built by Solomon ... 2Ch 3:1—5:1
2. Its structure based on the tabernacle
—Contained the Most Holy Place ... 2Ch 3:8 – 14
—Its parts separated by a curtain ... 2Ch 3:14; Mt 27:51
3. Its history
—Ark brought into it ... 2Ch 5:2 – 10
—Filled with the glory of God ... 2Ch 5:13 – 14; 2Ch 7:1 – 3
—Dedicated by Solomon ... 2Ch 6:1 – 13; 2Ch 7:4 – 7
—Ransacked by Shishak of Egypt ... 2Ch 12:9
—Refurbished by Asa ... 2Ch 15:8,18
—Joash hidden there ... 2Ch 22:12
—Restored by Joash ... 2Ch 24:4 – 14
—Furnishings sent by Ahaz to Assyria ... 2Ch 28:21,24
—Purified by Hezekiah ... 2Ch 29:3 – 19
—Desecrated by Manasseh ... 2Ch 33:3 – 7
—Purified by Josiah ... 2Ch 34:8 – 11
—Ransacked by Nebuchadnezzar ... 2Ch 36:7
—Destroyed by Nebuchadnezzar ... 2Ch 36:18 – 19

C. The second temple
1. Its construction
—Cyrus ordered its rebuilding ... Ezr 1:1 – 4
—Rebuilding begun under Zerubbabel ... Ezr 3:7 – 13
—Opposition to its rebuilding ... Ezr 4:1 – 4
—Work resumed ... Ezr 5:1 – 2
—Completed ... Ezr 6:13 – 15
—Dedicated ... Ezr 6:16 – 18
—Repaired and beautified by Herod ... Jn 2:20
2. New Testament events in the temple
—Zechariah met by an angel there ... Lk 1:8 – 20
—Jesus presented there ... Lk 2:22,27
—Jesus there at twelve years old ... Lk 2:42 – 50
—Jesus taught there ... Mt 26:55; Mk 12:35; Jn 7:14,28
—Jesus drove out money changers ... Mt 21:12 – 13; Jn 2:14 – 17
—Curtain torn at Jesus' death ... Mt 27:51
—Early Christians worshiped there ... Ac 2:46
—Apostles taught there ... Ac 3:1—4:2; Ac 5:21,42
—Paul arrested there ... Ac 21:27 – 33; Ac 26:21

D. Prophecies regarding the temple
1. Temple should not give false sense of security
—Jeremiah ... Jer 7:2 – 8
—Micah ... Mic 3:9 – 12
—Stephen ... Ac 7:47 – 50
2. Predictions of its destruction
—The first temple ... Jer 7:14; Eze 24:20 – 21
—The second temple ... Mk 13:1 – 2
3. Prophets bemoaned its destruction ... Isa 64:10 – 11; La 1:9 – 10
4. Prophets stirred up the people to rebuild ... Ezr 5:1; Ezr 6:14; Hag 1:2 – 15; Zec 4:8 – 9
5. Predictions of its future glory ... Isa 60:7,13; Hag 2:3,7 – 9
6. Ezekiel's new temple ... Eze 40:1—43:27; Eze 47:1 – 12
7. The new Jerusalem has no temple ... Rev 21:22

E. Symbolism of the temple
1. Symbol in the Old Testament
—Of God dwelling with his people ... 2Ch 6:20,33; Ps 18:6
—Of God's favor to his people ... Ps 65:4
2. Symbol in the New Testament
—Jesus Christ as a temple ... Jn 2:19 – 22
—The church as a temple ... 1Co 3:16 – 17; 2Co 6:16; Eph 2:21 – 22; Heb 3:6
—The human body as a temple ... 1Co 6:19

TEMPTATION

—Enticing one to sin against God

A. The source of temptation
1. God does not tempt us to sin ... Jas 1:13
2. Satan entices us to sin
—Adam and Eve ... Ge 3:1 – 4
—David ... 1Ch 21:1
—Job ... Job 1:6 – 12
—Jesus ... Mt 4:1 – 11
—Ananias and Sapphira ... Ac 5:1 – 3
3. Situations tempt us to sin
—Taking the easy way ... Mt 7:13 – 14; Mt 16:21 – 23
—The things of the world ... Mt 18:7 – 9
—Weakness of faith ... Lk 22:31 – 32
—Sexual desire ... 1Co 7:3 – 5
—Pride in one's own strength ... Gal 6:1
—Persecution ... 1Th 3:4 – 5
—Riches ... 1Ti 6:9
—Evil desires ... Jas 1:14 – 15

B. The fight against temptation
—We must beware of the devil's schemes ... 2Co 2:11; Eph 6:11
—We must watch out for temptation ... Mt 26:41; Lk 22:40,46; 1Pe 5:8
—God helps us overcome temptation ... 1Co 10:13
—Christ helps us overcome temptation ... Heb 2:17 – 18; Heb 4:15 – 16
—We must pray for help against temptation ... Mt 6:13

TEN COMMANDMENTS

—Given by God from Mount Sinai ... Ex 20:1 – 17; Ex 34:28; Dt 5:7 – 21
—Written on stone tablets ... Ex 34:1; Dt 4:13; Dt 10:4
—Stored in the ark of the covenant law ... Dt 10:1 – 2; 1Ki 8:9
—Summary of commandments is love ... Mt 22:37 – 40; Ro 13:9 – 10
—Ten individual commandments ... Ex 34:28; Dt 4:13

See ADULTERY; CHILDREN; COVETING; CURSE; IDOLATRY; LYING; MURDER; SABBATH; SEXUAL STANDARDS; STEALING; WORSHIP

TESTAMENT

See COVENANT

TESTING

A. Humans' testing
1. Testing God
a. Positive examples
—Gideon testing God's call .... Jdg 6:36 – 40
—Ahaz invited to test God .... Isa 7:10 – 12
—Israelites invited to test God .... Mal 3:10
b. Negative examples
—Grumbling over water .... Ex 17:1 – 2,7
Dt 33:8
Ps 95:9
—Grumbling over food .... Ps 78:17 – 18
Ps 106:14 – 15
—Many times of testing .... Nu 14:22
Ps 78:41
—Pharisees tested Jesus .... Mt 16:1
Mt 19:3
Mk 8:11
—Ananias and Sapphira test the Spirit .... Ac 5:1 – 10
c. The command not to test God .... Dt 6:16
Mt 4:7
1Co 10:9
2. The testing of ourselves
—The Teacher tests himself .... Ecc 2:1 – 11
—We must test our faith .... 2Co 13:5 – 7
—We must test our actions .... Gal 6:4
—We must test everything 1Th 5:21
—We must test the spirits 1Jn 4:1

B. God's testing of humans
1. God as a testing God
—God tests our hearts 1Ch 29:17
Pr 17:3
Jer 11:20
1Th 2:4
—His testing refines us .... Ps 66:10
Isa 48:10
Jer 9:7
—We may ask God to test us .... Ps 26:2
Ps 139:23
2. Examples of God's testing
—Abraham, with sacrifice of Isaac .... Ge 22:1
Heb 11:17
—The Israelites, with lack of water .... Ex 15:22 – 26
—The Israelites, with rules on manna .... Ex 16:4 – 5
Dt 8:2 – 3,16
—The Israelites, with thunder on Mount Sinai .... Ex 20:18 – 20
—The Israelites, with false prophets .... Dt 13:1 – 3
—The Israelites, with heathen nations .... Jdg 2:20—3:4
—Hezekiah, with envoys from Babylon 2Ch 32:31
—Job, with suffering .... Job 23:10
—Christians, with trials and suffering .... Jas 1:2 – 3,12
Rev 3:10
3. Purpose of God's testing
—To humble us .... Dt 8:2 – 3
—To see if we will love him .... Dt 13:3
—To see if we will fear him .... Ex 20:18 – 20
—To see if we will obey him .... Ge 22:1
Ex 16:4 – 5
—To see if we will persevere in our faith .... Jas 1:2 – 3
Rev 3:10 – 11

THADDAEUS

—Disciple of Jesus .... Mt 10:3
Mk 3:18
—Probably also known as Judas son of James .... Lk 6:16
Jn 14:22
—One of the apostles .... Ac 1:13

THANKSGIVING

A. Related theme
THANKSGIVING is a theme of Psalms .... Ps 100:4
B. Thanksgiving is a command
—A command in the Psalms .... Ps 75:1
Ps 107:1
Ps 118:1
Ps 136:1 – 3
—A command in the Prophets .... Isa 12:4
Jer 33:11
—A command in the New Testament .... Eph 5:20
Php 4:6
Col 3:15,17
1Th 5:18
—The command to give thank offerings .... Lev 7:12 – 15
2Ch 29:31
Ps 107:22
—The duty of certain Levites to give thanks .... 1Ch 16:4 – 7
1Ch 23:28 – 30
C. Reasons for thanksgiving
—For God's goodness and love 1Ch 16:34
2Ch 20:21
Ps 118:29
—For God's wonderful deeds .... Ps 75:1
Ps 107:8,15,21,31
—For God's protection .... Ps 56:12 – 13
—For salvation 1Ch 16:35
Ps 118:21
Ro 7:24 – 25
—For daily provisions .... Mt 14:19
2Co 9:12
1Ti 4:3 – 5
—For faith, hope and love .... Ro 1:8
Col 1:3 – 5
1Th 1:2 – 4
2Th 1:3 – 4
—For God's grace 1Co 1:4
—For healing .... Lk 17:16
—For victory over sin and death 1Co 15:57
—For all people 1Ti 2:1
—For everything .... Eph 5:20
1Th 5:18
D. Methods of thanksgiving
—Singing .... Ps 28:7
Ne 12:27,31,40
Col 3:16 – 17
—Playing musical instruments 1Ch 25:1
—Praying .... Ro 1:8 – 10
1Co 1:4 – 9
—Giving offerings .... Lev 7:12 – 15
Ps 56:12
2Co 9:12 – 15
—Worshiping God .... Ps 100:2 – 4
Heb 12:28
—Speaking about Jesus .... Lk 2:38
—Living holy lives .... Ro 12:1
1Co 6:20

THEFT

See STEALING

THIRST

See HUNGER AND THIRST

THOMAS

—Disciple of Jesus .... Mt 10:3
Mk 3:18
—Ready to die with Christ .... Jn 11:16
—Asked where Jesus was going .... Jn 14:5
—Doubted Jesus' resurrection .... Jn 20:24 – 25

—Convinced of Jesus' resurrection ... Jn 20:26–27
—Confessed Jesus as Lord and God ... Jn 20:28–29

THRONE

A. The human throne
1. Examples
—The throne of Pharaoh ... Ge 41:40
—The throne of David ... 2Sa 3:10
—The throne of Solomon ... 1Ki 2:12
—The throne of Elah ... 1Ki 16:11
—The thrones of Ahab and Jehoshaphat ... 1Ki 22:10
—The throne of Xerxes ... Est 1:2
—The throne of Nebuchadnezzar ... Da 4:36
—The throne of Herod ... Ac 12:21
2. God and human thrones
—All thrones established by God ... 2Sa 7:13; Ps 47:7–8
—Those on thrones must rule righteously ... 2Ch 9:8; Pr 16:12; Isa 16:5
—David's throne is the Lord's throne ... 1Ch 29:23
—God can destroy thrones ... Jer 22:2–5; Hag 2:20–22
B. The throne of Christ
—He came to sit on David's throne ... Lk 1:32–33; Ac 2:30
—He sits on his heavenly throne ... Mt 19:28; Heb 8:1; Heb 12:2
—His throne lasts forever ... Heb 1:8
—His throne is one of righteousness ... Mt 25:31–46; Heb 1:8
—We will someday sit with him on his throne ... Rev 3:21
C. The throne of God
—His throne is in heaven ... Ps 11:4; Ps 103:19
—His throne is a throne of grace ... Heb 4:16
—His throne is glorious ... Isa 6:1; Eze 1:26–28
—His throne is eternal ... Ps 45:6; Ps 93:2
—His throne is one of righteousness ... Ps 9:4; Ps 45:6–7
—His throne is surrounded by praise ... Rev 4:2–11; Rev 7:9–17

TIME

A. Time as chronological time
1. God and time
—Time created by God "in the beginning" ... Ge 1:1
—God is above time ... Ps 90:4; 2Pe 3:8
2. Human division of time
—Hours ... Mt 20:1–12; Jn 11:9; Ac 5:7
—Days and seasons ... Ge 8:22; Ex 34:21
—Weeks ... Dt 16:9; Ac 28:14
—Months ... Ex 12:2; Lk 1:24,56
—Years ... Ge 1:14; Ge 15:13
3. Phrases used in God's timetable of history
—"The time has come" ... Mk 1:15
—"When the set time had fully come" ... Gal 4:4
—"The times of the Gentiles" ... Lk 21:24
—"In the last days" ... Ac 2:17; 2Ti 3:1
—"At the last day" ... Jn 12:48
4. The end of time
—Time is moving toward final victory ... Ac 1:6–7
—Time ends at Christ's return ... Mt 16:27; Ac 1:11; 1Th 4:15–17
—Time ends with final judgment ... Rev 20:11–15
B. Time as opportunity
—A time for everything ... Ecc 3:1–8,17; Ecc 8:6
—Our times are in God's hands ... Ps 31:15
—We must make proper use of time ... Ps 90:12; 1Co 7:29–31; Eph 5:15; Col 4:5

TIMOTHY

A. Early life
—From Lystra ... Ac 16:1–2
—From a mixed marriage; uncircumcised ... Ac 16:1,3
—Brought up as a good Jewish boy ... 2Ti 3:15
—Taught by mother and grandmother ... 2Ti 1:5
—Became a believer through Paul ... 1Co 4:17; 1Ti 1:1
—Circumcised by Paul ... Ac 16:3
—A young man ... 1Ti 4:12
B. His life as co-worker with Paul
—Went with Paul on second missionary journey ... Ac 16:3–4
—Stayed in Berea with Silas ... Ac 17:14
—Sent to Thessalonica ... 1Th 3:2
—Came to Paul in Corinth ... Ac 18:5; 1Th 3:6
—Sent to Macedonia ... Ac 19:22
—Sent to settle problems at Corinth ... 1Co 4:17; 1Co 16:10
—Accompanied Paul as he headed to Jerusalem ... Ac 20:1–4
—Co-writer with Paul ... 2Co 1:1; Col 1:1; 1Th 1:1
—Ministered to Paul in Philippi ... Php 2:19–24
—Led church at Ephesus ... 1Ti 1:3
—A pastor responsible for worship ... 1Ti 2:1–10; 2Ti 4:2–5
—Spent some time in prison ... Heb 13:23
C. His character
—A hard worker for the Lord ... Php 2:19–24; 2Ti 2:15; 2Ti 4:5
—A good follower of Paul ... 1Co 4:17; Php 2:22; 2Ti 1:13–14
—Somewhat timid ... 2Ti 1:6–7
—Needed encouragement ... 1Ti 4:11–16; 1Ti 6:11–14,20
—Tendency to get sick ... 1Ti 5:23

TITHES AND OFFERINGS

A. Tithes
1. In the Old Testament
—Tithing commanded ... Lev 27:30–33; Dt 12:6–7; 2Ch 31:4–8
—A tenth of everything required ... Ge 14:20; Ge 28:22; Dt 14:23
—Tithes used to support Levites ... Nu 18:21–24; Dt 14:22–27
—Israelites stopped tithing ... Ne 13:10–12; Mal 3:8–10

2. In the New Testament
—Tithing became hypocritical....Mt 23:23
Lk 11:42
—Tithers were self-righteous....Lk 18:9 – 12

B. Offerings
1. In the Old Testament
a. The burnt offering....Lev 1:1 – 17
Lev 6:8 – 13
Lev 8:18 – 21
b. The grain offering....Lev 2:1 – 16
Lev 6:14 – 23
c. The fellowship offering....Lev 3:1 – 17
Lev 7:11 – 34
d. The sin offering....Lev 4:1—5:13
Lev 6:24 – 30
Lev 8:14 – 17
e. The guilt offering....Lev 5:14—6:7
Lev 7:1 – 6
f. Freewill offerings
—For the tabernacle....Ex 25:1 – 7
Ex 35:4 – 9,29
—For the first temple....1Ch 29:6 – 9
2Ch 24:8 – 11
—For the second temple....Ezr 2:68
—In the Feast of Weeks....Dt 16:10
—As one of the fellowship offerings....Lev 7:16
g. Offerings sometimes given hypocritically....Isa 1:11 – 13
Hag 2:14
Mal 1:6 – 14
Mal 3:8 – 9
2. Freewill offerings in the New Testament
—Given for the poor....Lk 19:8
Ac 11:28 – 30
Ro 15:25 – 27
—Given to support Paul....2Co 11:8 – 9
Php 4:15 – 18
3. Principles of giving offerings
—Freely....Mt 10:8
—Joyfully....2Co 9:7
—In proportion to income....Dt 16:17
Pr 3:9
1Co 16:2
—Generously....Ps 37:26
2Co 9:5 – 6
1Ti 6:18

See also THE RICH AND THE POOR; SACRIFICE; STEWARDSHIP

TITUS

—A Christian led by Paul to the Lord....Tit 1:4
—Gentile co-worker of Paul....2Co 8:23
Gal 2:1 – 3
—Sent to Corinth....2Co 2:13
2Co 8:6,16 – 18
2Co 12:18
—Sent to Crete....Tit 1:4 – 5
—Sent to Dalmatia....2Ti 4:10

TONGUES

See GIFTS OF THE SPIRIT; LANGUAGE

TRADITION

—Teachings and religious observances handed down

A. Teachings passed down
—By parents to children....Ps 78:3 – 6
Pr 1:7
—By the Jewish elders....Mk 7:3,5
—By the apostles....1Co 11:2,23 – 26
1Co 15:3 – 7
2Th 2:15

B. Dangers of traditions
—Can obscure God's word....Mt 15:1 – 9
Mk 7:1 – 13
—Can misdirect a person's life....Mic 6:16
Gal 1:14

C. Reactions to traditions
—Consider bad ones to be rubbish....Php 3:4 – 8
—Hold fast to good ones....1Co 15:1 – 5
2Th 2:15

TREE

A. Kinds of trees mentioned in the Bible
—Acacia....Ex 25:5
—Algum....2Ch 2:8
—Almond....Ge 30:37
—Apple....SS 2:3
—Broom....1Ki 19:4
—Cedar....1Ki 4:33
—Citron....Rev 18:12
—Cypress....Ge 6:14
—Ebony....Eze 27:15
—Fig....Mt 21:19
—Fir....Isa 41:19
—Juniper....Isa 41:19
—Myrtle....Ne 8:15
—Nut....SS 6:11
—Oak....Ge 35:4
—Olive....Jdg 9:8
—Palm....Ex 15:27
—Pine....Isa 44:14
—Plane....Ge 30:37
—Pomegranate....1Sa 14:2
—Poplar....Ps 137:2
—Sycamore....Lk 19:4
—Tamarisk....Ge 21:33
—Terebinth....Hos 4:13
—Willow....Eze 17:5

B. Trees used in a symbolic way
1. Significant trees
—The tree of the knowledge of good and evil....Ge 2:17
—The tree of life....Ge 3:22,24
Rev 22:2
2. Comparison to trees
—The righteous are like a tree....Ps 1:3
Ps 92:12 – 15
Isa 61:3
—Wisdom is like a tree....Pr 3:18
—The Branch is a symbol of Christ....Isa 11:1
Jer 23:5 – 6
3. Illustrations connected with trees
—Parable of the trees and thornbush....Jdg 9:7 – 20
—Parable of the coming new tree....Eze 17:22 – 24
—Parable of the tree and its fruit....Mt 7:17 – 19
—Parable of the mustard seed....Mt 13:31 – 32
—Parable of the barren fig tree....Lk 13:6 – 9
—Cursing of the fig tree....Mk 11:12 – 14, 20 – 21
—A lesson from the fig tree....Mt 24:32 – 33
—Parable of the two olive trees....Ro 11:17 – 24

TRIBULATION

See GREAT TRIBULATION; PAIN

TRINITY

—One God in three persons—Father, Son and Holy Spirit

A. There is only one God
—Expressed in the Old Testament....Dt 4:35,39
Dt 6:4
Isa 45:21

—Expressed in the New Testament ... 1Co 8:5–6
Eph 4:6
1Ti 2:5
Jas 2:19

B. Hints of a plurality in God in the Old Testament
—God speaks of himself as "us" ... Ge 1:26–27
Ge 3:22
Ge 11:7
Isa 6:8
—Someone coming from God is God ... Isa 7:14
Isa 9:6
—The angel of the Lord speaks as God
See ANGEL OF THE LORD

C. The Son as God
See JESUS CHRIST

D. The Holy Spirit as God
See HOLY SPIRIT

E. Father, Son and Spirit together
—One name for the three ... Mt 28:19
—The three persons mentioned together ... Mt 3:16–17
Jn 15:26
Ro 5:5–6
Ro 8:11,16–17
1Co 12:4–6
2Co 13:14
Gal 4:4–6
Eph 4:4–6
1Th 1:2–5
2Th 2:13
Tit 3:4–6
1Pe 1:2
1Jn 4:2
Jude 20–21

F. Similar divine characteristics for all three
1. Holiness
—Of the Father ... Jn 17:11
—Of the Son ... 1Co 1:30
—Of the Spirit ... Ro 1:4
2. Eternity
—Of the Father ... 1Ti 1:17
—Of the Son ... Heb 1:2–3,8
—Of the Spirit ... Heb 9:14
3. All-knowing
—Of the Father ... Mt 6:8,32
—Of the Son ... Jn 2:24–25
—Of the Spirit ... 1Co 2:10–11
4. All-powerful
—Of the Father ... Ps 135:5–7
—Of the Son ... 1Co 15:24–27
—Of the Spirit ... Ro 15:13,19
5. Everywhere present
—Of the Father ... Jer 23:24
—Of the Son ... Mt 28:20
—Of the Spirit ... Ps 139:7–10

G. Similar divine activities for all three
1. Creating
—By the Father ... Ge 1:1
—By the Son ... Jn 1:3
—By the Spirit ... Ps 104:30
2. Giving of spiritual life
—By the Father ... Eph 2:4–5
—By the Son ... Jn 10:10
—By the Spirit ... Eze 37:14
3. Performing miracles
—By the Father ... 1Ki 18:38
—By the Son ... Mt 4:23–24
—By the Spirit ... Ro 15:19
4. Teaching
—By the Father ... Ps 71:17
Isa 48:17
—By the Son ... Jn 13:13
—By the Spirit ... Jn 14:26
5. Experiencing grief because of sin
—By the Father ... Ge 6:6
—By the Son ... Lk 19:41–44
—By the Spirit ... Eph 4:30

TRUST

—Confidence put in someone or something

A. Related themes
TRUST is a theme of Psalms ... Ps 62:5
TRUST AND OBEY is a theme of Joshua ... Jos 10:25

B. In whom/what must we trust?
—In God ... Ps 56:3–4,11
Ps 91:2
—In the Lord ... Ps 4:5
Pr 3:5
Na 1:7
Ac 14:23
—In Jesus Christ ... Jn 14:1
Ro 10:11
1Pe 2:6
—In the name of the Lord ... Ps 20:7
Isa 50:10
Zep 3:12
—In God's word ... Ps 119:42
—In God's unfailing love ... Ps 52:8

C. What are the results of trusting in God?
—We become righteous and just ... Ps 37:5–6
—We are saved ... Isa 25:9
—We are blessed ... Ps 40:4
—We experience joy ... Ps 33:21
—We are released from fear ... Ps 56:3–4
—We receive direction from the Lord ... Pr 3:5–6
—We stand firm ... Ps 20:7–8
—We prosper ... Pr 28:25
—God keeps us safe ... Jer 39:17–18
—God delivers us ... Ps 22:4
—God cares for us ... Na 1:7
—God surrounds us with his love ... Ps 32:10
—Jesus prepares a place for us ... Jn 14:1–2

D. In what ought we *not* trust?
—In idols ... 2Ki 17:14–15
Isa 42:17
Jer 13:25
—In other people ... Ps 118:8–9
Ps 146:3
Jer 17:5–7
—In ourselves ... Pr 28:26
—In fortified cities ... Jer 5:17
—In horses and chariots ... Ps 20:7
Isa 31:1–3
—In weapons ... Ps 44:6
—In riches ... Job 31:24–28
Ps 52:7
Lk 12:13–21
1Ti 6:17

TRUTH

—What is accurate and agrees with reality

A. Related theme
TRUTH is a theme of 1 John ... 1Jn 2:8

B. Of whom/what is truth characteristic?
1. God
—The Father ... Ps 31:5
Isa 65:16
—Jesus ... Jn 1:14
Jn 14:6
—The Spirit ... Jn 14:17
1Jn 5:6

2. God's revelation
—God's law .... Ps 119:43
—God's word 2Sa 7:28
Isa 45:19
Jn 17:17
—The testimony of Jesus .... Jn 8:45 – 46
Jn 18:37
—The word of the prophets 1Ki 18:24
1Ki 22:16
Jer 26:15
—The gospel proclaimed by the apostles 2Co 4:2
Gal 2:5,14
Eph 1:13
3. The church, the pillar of truth 1Ti 3:15

C. How must believers relate to the truth?
—Must know it .... Ps 51:6
1Ti 2:4
—Must come to a knowledge of it 2Ti 2:25
Tit 1:1
Heb 10:26
—Must seek it .... Jer 5:1
—Must choose it .... Ps 119:30
—Must buy it .... Pr 23:23
—Must believe it 2Th 2:13
—Must love it .... Zec 8:19
—Must walk in it .... Ps 26:3
3Jn 3 – 5
—Must live by it .... Jn 3:21
1Jn 1:6
—Must obey it .... Gal 5:7
—Must worship in it .... Jn 4:23 – 24
—Must speak it .... Ps 15:2
Zec 8:16
Eph 4:25

D. What does the truth do for us?
—Protects us .... Ps 40:11
—Guides us .... Ps 43:3
—Sets us free .... Jn 8:31 – 32
—Sanctifies us .... Jn 17:17,19
—Purifies us 1Pe 1:22

E. What do the wicked do with respect to truth?
—Reject it .... Isa 59:14 – 15
Ro 2:8
—Do not speak it .... Jer 9:5
—Distort it .... Ac 20:30
—Suppress it .... Ro 1:18
—Exchange it for a lie .... Ro 1:25
—Wander away from it 2Ti 2:18
—Oppose it 2Ti 3:8
—Turn away from it 2Ti 4:4

TYRE

A. Identity and location
—A merchant city .... Ne 13:16
—A seacoast city .... Lk 6:17
—Often linked with Sidon .... Isa 23:1 – 2
Mt 15:21

See SIDON

B. Significance of Tyre
1. In the Old Testament
—Territory given to tribe of Asher .... Jos 19:24,29
—King Hiram sent wood for David's palace .... 2Sa 5:11 – 12
1Ch 14:1 – 2
—King Hiram sent wood for the temple .... 1Ki 5:7 – 12
2Ch 2:11 – 16
—Huram of Tyre was a temple craftsman .... 1Ki 7:13 – 14
—Prophecies against them .... Isa 23:1 – 18
Eze 26:1—28:19
Joel 3:4 – 8
Am 1:9 – 10

2. In the New Testament
—Jesus ministered there .... Mt 15:21 – 28
Mk 7:24 – 30
—Paul spent seven days there .... Ac 21:3 – 6

UNION WITH CHRIST

A. Related theme
IN CHRIST is a theme of Ephesians .... Eph 2:6

B. Christians are:
—In Christ 1Th 2:14
—New creatures in Christ 2Co 5:17
—The faithful in Christ .... Eph 1:1

C. Our participation in events of Christ's life
—We suffer with him .... Ro 8:17
Php 3:10
1Pe 4:13
—We share in his broken body .... 1Co 10:16 – 17
—We share in his shed blood .... 1Co 10:16 – 17
—We are crucified with him .... Ro 6:6,8
Col 2:20
—We are buried with him .... Ro 6:4
Col 2:12
—We are raised with him .... Eph 2:6
Col 2:12
Col 3:1
—We sit at God's right hand with him .... Eph 2:6
Col 3:1
—We will return with him 1Th 4:14
—We will share in his glory .... Ro 8:17
—We will reign with him 2Ti 2:12

D. Our involvement in Christ
—We are chosen in him .... Eph 1:4,11
—We are justified in him .... Gal 2:17
—We who are in him are free from condemnation .... Ro 8:1
—We are baptized into him .... Gal 3:27
Col 2:11 – 13
—We are infants in him 1Co 3:1
—We are found in him .... Php 3:9
—We are one with him .... Jn 14:20
Jn 17:21,23
1Co 6:17
—We must remain in him .... Jn 15:4 – 5,7
—We live in him 1Jn 3:24
—Our way of life is in him 1Co 4:17
—We grow in him .... Eph 4:16
—We pray in him .... Eph 2:18
Eph 3:12
—We are blessed in him .... Eph 1:3
—We are sanctified in him 1Co 1:2
—We fall asleep (die) in him 1Th 4:14,16
1Co 15:18
—We will be made alive in him 1Co 15:22

E. Pictures of union with Christ
—Vine and branches .... Jn 15:1 – 7
—Foundation and building .... 1Co 3:10 – 11
Eph 2:20 – 21
—Head and members of the body .... Ro 12:4 – 5
1Co 12:14 – 27
—Husband and wife .... Eph 5:23 – 32
—Shepherd and sheep .... Jn 10:11,14 – 16

UNITY

A. Related themes
UNITY is a theme of:
—Acts .... Ac 4:32
—1 Corinthians 1Co 12:13

B. Expressions of the unity of the church
—One nation and people .... 1Pe 2:9 – 10

—One body ... Ro 12:4–5
1Co 12:13,27
—One family ... Eph 2:19
—One bride/spouse ... 2Co 11:2
Eph 5:23–30
—One temple ... 1Co 3:16–17
—One building with one foundation ... 1Co 3:9–11
Eph 2:20–21
—One spiritual house ... 1Pe 2:5
—One field/vineyard ... Jn 15:5
1Co 3:9
—One flock ... Jn 10:16
—One city ... Heb 12:22–23
C. The basis of unity
—Christ's unity with the Father ... Jn 17:20–23
—Christ's death on the cross ... Eph 2:14–16
—Our unity with Christ ... Gal 3:26–28
—The one Holy Spirit ... Eph 4:3–4
—Our common faith and hope ... Eph 4:4–5,13
D. Demonstrations of unity
—The life of the early church ... Ac 2:42–47
Ac 4:32
—The Lord's Supper ... 1Co 10:16–17
E. Important elements of unity
—Unity is good and pleasant ... Ps 133:1
—Unity makes God's people fruitful ... Ps 133:3
—Unity is a challenge we must strive to achieve ... Eph 4:12–16
Php 1:27
Php 2:1–3
1Th 5:13
1Pe 3:8
—Unity requires that we love one another ... Eph 4:15–16
—Diversity in gifts is consistent with unity ... Ro 12:4–8
1Co 12:7–30
—Diversity in thinking is consistent with unity ... Ro 14:1–6
F. Causes of disunity
—Quarreling ... Ac 15:36–39
1Co 3:3
—Favoritism ... Jas 2:1–4
—Spiritual immaturity ... 1Co 1:10–12
1Co 3:1–2
—Hypocrisy ... Gal 2:11–14
1Pe 2:1

URIAH

—Hittite husband of Bathsheba ... 2Sa 11:2–3
—One of David's brave warriors ... 2Sa 23:39
—Devoted to duty ... 2Sa 11:8–13
—Killed on David's orders ... 2Sa 11:16–25

URIM AND THUMMIM

See CASTING LOTS

USURY

See DEBT

UZZIAH

—Son of Amaziah; king of Judah ... 2Ch 26:1–5
—Also called Azariah ... 2Ki 15:1
—An effective and powerful king ... 2Ch 26:6–15
—Became proud and unlawfully burnt incense ... 2Ch 26:16–19
—Punished with leprosy ... 2Ki 15:5
2Ch 26:20–21

VASHTI

—Wife of Xerxes; queen of Persia ... Est 1:9
—Refused to display her beauty ... Est 1:10–12
—Deposed as queen ... Est 1:15–21
—Replaced by Esther ... Est 2:17

VICTORY

See WARFARE

VINEYARD

A. Significant vineyards in the Bible
—Noah's ... Ge 9:20
—Those in Canaan ... Nu 13:23–24
Dt 8:8
—Naboth's ... 1Ki 21:1–16
—Vineyards in Jesus' parables ... Mt 20:1–15
Mt 21:28–31,33–40
B. Design and care of vineyards
1. The design
—Had protecting walls ... Nu 22:24
Pr 24:30–31
—Had a tower for watchmen ... Isa 5:1–2
Mt 21:33
—Had a winepress in it ... Isa 5:2
Mt 21:33
2. The care
—Clearing the field ... Isa 5:2
—Planting ... Ps 107:37
Ecc 2:4
Isa 5:2
—Cultivating ... Dt 28:39
Isa 7:25
—Pruning ... Lev 25:3
Jn 15:2
—Harvesting ... Lev 19:10
Jdg 9:27
—Treading the winepress ... Isa 16:10
C. Vineyards used as a symbol
1. A symbol of prosperity and security
—To sit in one's vineyard meant security ... 1Ki 4:25
Mic 4:4
—To eat from one's vineyard meant prosperity ... 2Ki 18:31
Ps 107:37–38
Isa 36:16
2. Spiritual symbols
—A symbol of the Israelite nation ... Ps 80:8–11
Isa 5:7
Jer 2:21
Hos 10:1
—A symbol of the followers of Jesus ... Jn 15:1–6
—A symbol of the kingdom of heaven ... Mt 20:1–15
Mt 21:28–33

VISION

See DREAMS AND VISIONS

VOICE

A. The human voice
1. Uses of the human voice
—Ordinary communication ... 1Sa 24:16
—Recognizing a person ... Ge 27:22
1Sa 26:17
Ac 12:14
—Expressing unity (one voice) ... Ex 24:3
—Praying ... Ps 66:19
—Requesting a favor ... Lk 17:13
—Preaching ... Ac 2:14
2. Expressions of the human voice
—The praising voice ... 2Ch 20:19
Lk 17:15
—The shouting voice ... Isa 40:9
—The complaining voice ... Ps 64:1
—The weeping voice ... Jer 31:15–16

B. The voice of God
1. Expressions of God's voice
a. People called by his voice
—Moses .... Ex 3:4 – 6; Ac 7:31 – 32
—Samuel .... 1Sa 3:1 – 14
—Isaiah .... Isa 6:8 – 10
b. The power of his voice
—Accompanied by fire .... Dt 4:33
—Sounds like thunder .... 2Sa 22:14; Job 37:4 – 5; Ps 29:3 – 4
—Accomplishes great things .... Ps 29:5 – 9; Ps 46:6
—Can come as a gentle whisper .... 1Ki 19:12 – 13
c. Messages of his voice
—His law from Mount Sinai .... Dt 5:22 – 26
—Affirmation of Jesus as his Son .... Mt 3:17; Lk 9:35 – 36
—Glorification of Jesus .... Jn 12:28 – 30
2. The voice of Jesus
—Jesus proclaimed with a loud voice .... Jn 7:37 – 38
—Jesus cried out with a loud voice .... Mt 27:46,50
—His voice raised Lazarus .... Jn 11:43
—His voice called Paul to be an apostle .... Ac 9:4 – 6
—His voice revealed things to John .... Rev 1:10 – 13
—His voice calls his sheep .... Jn 10:16,27
—His voice will raise the dead .... Jn 5:25,28
3. Our response to God's voice
—We must recognize his voice .... Jn 10:3 – 5
—We must listen to his voice .... Ex 15:26; Dt 30:20
—We must obey his voice .... 1Sa 15:22; Hag 1:12

VOW

—A solemn promise made to God
A. Significant vows in the Bible
—Jacob's vow at Bethel .... Ge 28:20 – 22
—The Nazirite vow .... Nu 6:1 – 21
—Jephthah's vow .... Jdg 11:30 – 31
—Nazirite vow required for Samson .... Jdg 13:1 – 7
—Hannah's vow regarding Samuel 1Sa 1:11
—David's vow regarding a temple for the Lord .... Ps 132:1 – 5
—Paul's Nazirite vow .... Ac 18:18
B. The nature of the vow
—Often arose in times of distress .... Ge 28:20 – 22; Nu 21:1 – 2; Ps 66:13 – 14; Ps 116:7 – 14
—Made only to God .... Lev 27:2,9; Dt 23:21 – 23; Isa 19:21
—Was completely voluntary .... Dt 23:22; Ecc 5:5
—Had to be fulfilled .... Dt 23:21,23; Ecc 5:4,6
—Should not be made rashly .... Pr 20:25
—Rules for redeeming vows .... Lev 27:1 – 33
—Could be abused at times .... Mk 7:9 – 13

WALK OF LIFE

—The Christian way of life
A. Related themes
1. CHRISTIAN LIVING is a theme of:
—Romans .... Ro 12:1
—Ephesians .... Eph 4:1
—Philippians .... Php 1:27
—Colossians .... Col 3:12
—1 Thessalonians 1Th 4:1
—James .... Jas 1:27
—1 Peter 1Pe 5:6
2. RESPONSE is a theme of Deuteronomy .... Dt 13:4
3. ATTITUDE is a theme of Proverbs .... Pr 10:12
B. What the Christian walk is not
—Not walking according to the sinful nature .... Ro 8:4; Gal 5:16 – 21
—Not walking in the ways of evildoers .... 1Ki 15:26,34; Pr 4:14
—Not walking in dark ways .... Pr 2:13
—Not walking in darkness .... Jn 8:12; 1Jn 1:6; 1Jn 2:11
—Not walking in the counsel of the wicked .... Ps 1:1
—Not walking in pride .... Da 4:37; Mic 2:3
C. What the Christian walk is
—Walking with God .... Ps 56:13; Mic 6:8; Rev 3:4
—Walking in God's ways .... Dt 5:33; Dt 10:12; Jos 22:5
—Walking before God 1Ki 2:4; 2Ch 7:17
—Walking in truth .... Ps 26:3; 3Jn 3 – 4
—Walking in the light .... Ps 89:15; Isa 2:5; 1Jn 1:7
—Walking in the name of God .... Mic 4:5
—Walking in the fear of God .... Ne 5:9
—Walking in the law of God .... Ps 119:1
—Walking in love and obedience 2Jn 6
—Walking in the Spirit .... Ro 8:4
—Walking in the paths of the righteous .... Pr 2:20
—Walking as Jesus walked 1Jn 2:6
D. Examples of those who walked with God
—Enoch .... Ge 5:22 – 24
—Noah .... Ge 6:9
—Abraham .... Ge 24:40
—Isaac .... Ge 48:15
—Levi .... Mal 2:4 – 6
—Jotham 2Ch 27:6
—Hezekiah .... Isa 38:3
E. God's promise to walk with us .... Lev 26:12; 2Co 6:16

WARFARE

A. Related themes
1. CONFLICT is a theme of Revelation .... Rev 12:7
2. GOD'S HELP is a theme of 1 Samuel 1Sa 17:45
3. GOD'S INTERVENTION is a theme of 2 Chronicles 2Ch 20:17
4. DELIVERANCE is a theme of Esther .... Est 8:11
5. VICTORY is a theme of:
—Joshua .... Jos 21:43
—Daniel .... Da 6:27
6. CHRIST'S VICTORY is a theme of Revelation .... Rev 11:15
B. Physical Warfare
1. Wars in the Bible
a. First recorded war .... Ge 14:1 – 17
b. Israelite wars on the way to Canaan .... Ex 17:8 – 13; Nu 21:1 – 3,21 – 35
c. Wars of Joshua
—The battle against Jericho .... Jos 6:1 – 25
—The battle against Ai .... Jos 7:3 – 5; Jos 8:1 – 29
—The battle against five kings .... Jos 10:1 – 28
—The southern cities defeated .... Jos 10:29 – 43

—The northern cities defeated .... Jos 11:1 – 23
d. Wars in the period of the judges
—Deborah and Barak .... Jdg 4:12 – 23
—Gideon .... Jdg 7:1 – 25
—Jephthah .... Jdg 11:4 – 33
—During Eli's judgeship .... 1Sa 4:1 – 10; 1Sa 7:2 – 14
e. Wars during the time of Saul
—Saul rescued the city of Jabesh .... 1Sa 11:1 – 11
—Against the Philistines .... 1Sa 13:2 – 7; 1Sa 14:1 – 46; 1Sa 17:1 – 54; 1Sa 31:1 – 7
—Against the Amalekites .... 1Sa 15:4 – 9; 1Sa 30:1 – 20
f. Wars during the time of David
—Gained control of all Israel .... 2Sa 2:8—4:12
—Against the Philistines .... 2Sa 5:17 – 25; 2Sa 21:15 – 22
—Against the Ammonites .... 2Sa 10:1 – 14
—Against the Arameans .... 2Sa 10:15 – 19
—Civil war against Absalom .... 2Sa 15:1—18:18
—Summary of wars .... 2Sa 8:1 – 14
g. Wars of the northern kingdom
—Against the southern kingdom .... 1Ki 15:16 – 17,32; 2Ki 13:12; 2Ki 14:9 – 14; 2Ki 16:5 – 6
—Against the Philistines .... 1Ki 16:15 – 17
—Against the Arameans .... 1Ki 20:1 – 34; 1Ki 22:1 – 37; 2Ki 6:8—7:11; 2Ki 8:28 – 29; 2Ki 13:3 – 7
—Against Assyria .... 2Ki 15:19 – 20,29 – 30; 2Ki 16:7 – 10; 2Ki 17:1 – 6
h. Wars of the southern kingdom
—Against the Egyptians .... 1Ki 14:25 – 26
—Against the Edomites .... 2Ki 8:20 – 22; 2Ki 14:7
—Against the Ammonites and Moabites .... 2Ch 20:1 – 26
—Against Assyria .... 2Ch 32:1 – 22; 2Ch 33:10 – 11
—Against Babylon .... 2Ki 24:1 – 4,10 – 16; 2Ki 25:1 – 21

2. Victory for God's people
a. God is the source of victory .... Nu 21:3; Dt 20:1 – 4; Jos 11:7 – 8; 2Ch 20:15 – 17; Ps 18:29,34 – 43; Pr 21:31
b. Principles of victory
—Success when faithful to the Lord .... Jdg 7:1 – 25; 1Sa 17:41 – 50; 2Ch 20:20
—Defeat when unfaithful .... 2Ki 17:5 – 20; 2Ki 21:10 – 15
c. God controls foreign armies .... Isa 13:3 – 5; Jer 25:8 – 9; Eze 21:18 – 22

C. Spiritual warfare
1. God is at war with Satan
—At the time of Job .... Job 1:6 – 12; Job 26:6 – 13
—In the days of Israel .... Isa 27:1
—At the time of Christ .... Mt 4:1 – 11; Lk 10:18
—In heaven .... Rev 12:7 – 9

2. Christians are at war
—With the devil .... Ge 3:1 – 15; 2Co 2:11; 1Pe 5:8
—With the powers of darkness .... Eph 6:12
—With the world .... Jn 15:18 – 19; 1Jn 2:15 – 17
—With the old self .... Ro 6:6,12
—With the sinful nature .... Ro 8:5 – 9; Gal 5:16 – 25
—With sinful desires .... Ro 7:15 – 20; 1Pe 2:11
—With death .... 1Co 15:26; Heb 2:14 – 15
3. How Christians ought to fight
—By depending on God .... Ps 18:29,32; Ps 27:1 – 2
—By being dedicated to Jesus Christ 2Ti 2:4; 1Pe 5:10
—By standing firm in the Lord .... Eph 6:10 – 14
—By holding on to the faith .... 1Ti 1:18 – 19; 1Jn 5:4 – 5
—By laying hold of eternal life 1Ti 6:12
—By being good soldiers 2Ti 2:3
—By enduring hardship 2Ti 2:3
—By exercising self-denial .... 1Co 9:26 – 27
—By praying .... Eph 6:18
—By resisting the devil .... 1Pe 5:8 – 9
4. Protection provided by the Lord
—The full armor of God .... Eph 6:11,13
—The armor of light .... Ro 13:12
—God as our shield .... Ge 15:1; Dt 33:29; Ps 115:9 – 11
—The shield of faith .... Eph 6:16
—The belt of righteousness .... Isa 11:5
—The belt of truth .... Eph 6:14
—The breastplate of righteousness .... Isa 59:17; Eph 6:14
—The breastplate of faith and love 1Th 5:8
—Feet ready to run to bring the good news .... Isa 52:7; Eph 6:15
—The helmet of salvation .... Eph 6:17; 1Th 5:8
—The sword of the Spirit, the word of God .... Eph 6:17; Heb 4:12
5. Victory is certain
a. Accomplished by Christ
—On the cross .... Jn 12:31 – 33; Col 2:15; Heb 2:14
—In his ascension .... Eph 1:20 – 21; Php 2:9 – 11
—In his return .... 1Co 15:24 – 28; Rev 19:11 – 16
b. Our victory given through Christ
—God gives us the victory .... Ro 7:25; 1Co 15:55 – 57
—We can do all things in Christ .... Php 4:13
—God will crush Satan under our feet .... Ro 16:20
c. Victory over sin through the Spirit .... Ro 8:9 – 13; Gal 5:16 – 18

WATCHFULNESS

A. God watches over people
—His protective watch .... Ge 31:49; Ps 121:3 – 8; Isa 27:2 – 3; Jer 31:10

—His watch over good and evil .... Job 7:17–21
Job 13:27
Pr 15:3
Jer 31:28

B. God's people must be watchful
1. What we must watch
—Ourselves and our manner of life .... Dt 4:9
Dt 4:15
Ps 39:1
1Ti 4:16
—For false teachers .... Mk 13:5–6
Ac 20:28–31
Php 3:2–3
2Jn 8
—For those who divide the church .... Ro 16:17
—For hypocrites .... Mk 12:38–40
—For the second coming of Jesus .... Mt 25:13
1Th 5:5–6
Rev 16:15
2. How we must watch
—With prayer .... Mk 14:38
Eph 6:18
—With alertness .... Mk 13:33
1Th 5:6
—With care not to fall into temptation .... Mk 14:38
Gal 6:1
—With care not to forget what God has done .... Dt 4:9
—With hope .... Mic 7:7
—With thankfulness .... Col 4:2

WATER

A. Uses of water
1. Water for washing
a. Simple cleansing
—Washing body .... Ru 3:3
—Washing face .... Ge 43:31
—Washing feet .... Ge 18:4
2Sa 11:8
Jn 13:4–5
b. Ritual cleansing
—Washing clothes at Mount Sinai .... Ex 19:10,14
—Washing necessary for priests .... Ex 30:17–21
—Washing necessary for Levites .... Nu 8:5–7
—Washing parts of a sacrifice .... Lev 1:9,13
—Washing after a skin disease .... Lev 14:8–9
—Washing after uncleanness .... Lev 15:5–13,21–22
Nu 19:11–13
—Various Jewish washing rituals .... Mt 23:25–26
Mk 7:3–4
2. Water for drinking
a. Water drunk by humans and animals .... Ge 24:11–19
Jdg 7:4–5
Mt 10:42
b. God provided water for his people
—Hagar .... Ge 21:15–19
—The Israelites in the desert .... Ex 17:1–6
Nu 20:1–11
Ps 78:20
—The Israelites in the time of Elisha 2Ki 3:15–20

B. God and water
1. God is the source of living water .... Ps 23:2
Isa 55:1
Jer 2:13
2. Christ is the source of living water .... Jn 4:10–14
Jn 7:37–38
Rev 21:6
Rev 22:1–2
3. Water used in judgment by God
—The flood .... Ge 7:17–24
1Pe 3:20
—The destruction of the Egyptians .... Ex 14:26–30
Ps 106:9–11
—The destruction of the Philistines .... Jer 47:2–5
—The storm in the story of Jonah .... Jnh 1:3–15
—Sea storms in general .... Ps 107:23–30

C. Water used as a symbol
1. As a symbol of evil people .... Ge 49:4
Isa 57:20
Jude 13
2. As a symbol of personal affliction
—Waters overwhelming someone .... Ps 42:7
Ps 69:1–2,14–15
Jer 49:23
—God protects his people from the waters .... Ps 18:16–17
Ps 124:1–5
Isa 43:2
—Heaven has no sea .... Rev 21:1
3. As a symbol of cleansing from sin .... Isa 1:16
Eze 36:25
Eph 5:26
Heb 10:22
4. As a cleansing symbol in baptism .... Ac 8:36
Ac 22:16
1Pe 3:21
5. As a symbol of the Holy Spirit .... Isa 44:3
Jn 7:38–39
6. As a symbol of heavenly peace .... Isa 35:6–7
Isa 43:19–21
Jer 31:11–12
Zec 14:6–9
Rev 22:1–2

WEALTH

See THE RICH AND THE POOR

WEATHER

A. God and the weather
1. God controls the weather
—He sends sunshine .... Ps 19:4–6
Mt 5:45
—He sends rain and snow .... Job 5:10
Job 38:22–30
Ps 147:16–17
—He sends wind .... Ex 10:13
Ps 78:26
Ps 147:18
—He sends storms .... Ps 107:25–26
Jnh 1:4
Eze 13:13
2. God uses weather elements
a. To exhibit his power .... Ex 19:16
b. To bless his people .... Dt 11:13–15
Ps 65:9–11
Ps 147:7–9
c. To help his people in battle .... Jos 10:11–14
1Sa 7:10
2Sa 22:13–15
d. To judge people
—By withholding rain .... Lev 26:18–20
1Ki 17:1
Am 4:7
—By sending floods .... Ge 7:11–24
Isa 8:6–8
Na 1:8
—By sending violent storms .... Ex 9:22–26
Ps 107:25–27
Na 1:3–4
Hag 2:17

B. Weather elements used as symbols
1. The sun
See SUN
2. Clouds
—God's presence among his people .... Ex 13:21 – 22; Ps 104:3
—The mystery of God .... Ps 97:2
—Sin and forgiveness .... Isa 44:22
—Departed Christians who surround us as witnesses .... Heb 12:1
—God's judgment .... Joel 2:2
—An advancing army .... Jer 4:13
3. Wind
—God's presence around us .... Ps 104:3
—The Holy Spirit .... Jn 3:8; Ac 2:2
—Meaninglessness .... Ecc 1:6,14
—False teaching .... Eph 4:14
4. Gentle rain showers
—The word of God .... Isa 55:10 – 12
—God's blessings .... Eze 34:26; Hos 6:3
5. Snow
—Forgiveness .... Ps 51:7; Isa 1:18
—Leprosy .... Nu 12:10
—God's wonders .... Job 38:22
—Brightness .... Mt 28:3
—Glory of Christ .... Rev 1:14
6. Hail
—God's wonders .... Job 38:22
—God's power and majesty .... Ps 18:12
—God's judgment .... Rev 8:7
7. Thunder
—God's voice .... Ps 18:13; Ps 29:3 – 7; Ps 68:32 – 33
—God's majesty .... Rev 4:5
8. Lightning
—Christ's return .... Mt 24:27; Lk 17:24
—Satan's fall .... Lk 10:18
9. Violent storms, as God's final judgment .... Eze 38:22; Rev 11:19; Rev 16:18 – 21

See also HUNGER AND THIRST; WATER

WICKEDNESS
See SIN

WILL OF GOD
A. God's will: what God wants us to do
1. What does God's will include?
—His law in general .... Ro 2:18; 1Pe 4:2 – 3
—His word in general .... Ac 20:27
—Doing what is good 1Pe 2:15
—Avoiding sexual immorality 1Th 4:3
—Giving thanks in all circumstances 1Th 5:18
2. How did Jesus relate to God's will?
—He came to do God's will .... Jn 4:34; Jn 6:38; Heb 10:5,7
—He was obedient to God's will .... Php 2:7 – 8
—He submitted to God's will for him .... Mt 26:39,42
3. How must we relate to God's will
—We must know his will .... Col 1:9
—We must understand his will .... Eph 5:17
—We must choose to do his will .... Jn 7:17
—We must do his will .... Ps 40:8; Ps 143:10; Mt 12:50
—We must approve his will by obedience .... Ro 12:2
—We must stand firm in his will .... Col 4:12

B. God's will: what God plans in history
1. Aspects of God's will
—God does whatever he pleases .... Ps 115:3; Ps 135:6; Da 4:35; Ro 9:18 – 21
—Everything occurs according to his will .... Eph 1:11
2. What can we know about God's plan?
a. His plan may be kept secret
—Hidden in the Old Testament .... Eph 1:9; Eph 3:4 – 5
—Hidden from learned people .... Mt 11:25 – 26
—Even now we may not understand it .... Ro 9:18 – 24
b. Some parts of his plan are revealed
—That salvation is in Christ .... Gal 1:4
—That God saves both Jew and Gentile .... Eph 3:6
—That everyone should be saved 1Ti 2:4; 2Pe 3:9
—That all God's children come to him .... Mt 18:14; Jn 6:39 – 40
—That Paul was called as an apostle 1Co 1:1
3. God's will and human suffering
—His will may include suffering .... Job 1:6 – 22; 1Pe 3:17; 1Pe 4:19
—God works for his people's good .... Ge 50:20; Jer 29:11; Ro 8:28

See also PAIN

4. Our relationship to God's plan for us
—Pray that God's will be done .... Mt 6:10
—Pray that things happen by God's will .... Ac 18:21; Ro 15:31 – 32; 1Co 16:7; Jas 4:13 – 15
—Submit to God's plan for us .... Ac 21:14

WIND
See WEATHER

WINE
See ALCOHOL

WISDOM
—Comprehensive knowledge that is put into practice
A. Related theme
WISDOM is a theme of Proverbs .... Pr 2:6
B. Human wisdom
1. Source of wisdom
—Received as a gift from God .... 1Ki 3:11 – 12; Pr 2:6; Ecc 2:26; Da 2:21; Jas 1:5
—Received as a gift from the Spirit .... 1Co 12:8; Eph 1:17
—Starts with the fear of the Lord .... Job 28:28; Ps 111:10; Pr 9:10
—Comes from listening to the wise .... Pr 1:2; Pr 4:1 – 11; Pr 13:20
—Comes from research and education .... Ecc 1:13,17; Ecc 7:25
—Comes from discipline .... Pr 29:15
—Comes from admonishing one another .... Col 3:16

2. Expressions of wisdom
—Serving as craftsman .... Ex 28:3
—Following God's law .... Dt 4:6
Hos 14:9
Mt 7:24–26
—Writing proverbs and songs 1Ki 4:29,32
—Studying God's creation 1Ki 4:29,33
—Administering justice 1Ki 3:16–28
1Ki 10:8–9
—Avoiding evil .... Pr 5:1–6
—Taking advice .... Pr 13:10
—Giving advice .... Da 1:20
—Interpreting visions and dreams .... Da 2:23,30
—Preparing for the future .... Mt 25:1–13
—Exercising patience .... Pr 19:11
—Living the Christian lifestyle .... Pr 2:20–21
Jas 3:17
—Defending the gospel .... Ac 6:3,10
3. Benefits of wisdom
—Makes us blessed .... Pr 3:13
—Leads to a long life .... Pr 3:16
—Preserves our lives .... Ecc 7:12
—Protects us .... Pr 4:6
—Exalts us .... Pr 4:8–9
—Brings us joy .... Pr 29:3
Pr 27:11
—Gives us strength .... Ecc 7:19
—Brings us healing .... Pr 12:18
—Saves us from evil ways .... Pr 2:12–19

C. Divine wisdom
1. True wisdom centers in God
—God has wisdom .... Job 12:13
Job 28:20–24
Da 2:20
—Christ is the wisdom of God 1Co 1:24,30
Col 2:3
—The Spirit is the Spirit of wisdom .... Isa 11:2
Eph 1:17
2. The nature of God's wisdom
—Profound .... Job 9:4
—Precious .... Pr 8:18–19
—Deep and rich .... Ro 11:33
—Magnificent .... Isa 28:29
—Manifold .... Eph 3:10
—Unsurpassable .... Jer 10:7
3. Activities of God's wisdom
—Operative in creation .... Ps 104:24
Pr 3:19
Pr 8:22–31
Jer 10:12
—Controls nature .... Job 26:12
Job 39:26
—Controls history .... Isa 10:12–13
—Counsels rulers .... Pr 8:14–16

WITCHCRAFT

See MAGIC, WITCHCRAFT AND SORCERY

WITNESS

—One who bears testimony to something or someone

A. Types of witnesses
—God as a witness .... Ge 31:50
Jdg 11:10
—People as witnesses .... Jos 24:22
Ru 4:9–11
Jer 32:12
—Things as witnesses .... Dt 31:19–21
Jos 24:27
Isa 19:19–20

B. Legal witnesses
—Two or three necessary to convict someone .... Dt 17:6
Mt 26:60–61
2Co 13:1
—No false testimony to be given .... Ex 20:16
Dt 19:16–18
Pr 24:28–29

C. Witnesses to God's truth and salvation
—Israel as witnesses .... Isa 43:10–12
Isa 44:8
—The prophets as witnesses .... Ac 10:43
Ac 26:22–23
—John the Baptist as witness .... Jn 1:7,15,32–34
Jn 5:33–34
—Jesus Christ as the faithful witness .... Jn 8:18
Jn 18:37
Rev 1:5–6
—The Holy Spirit as witness .... Jn 15:26
Ac 5:30–32
Ro 8:16
—Signs and wonders as witnesses .... Jn 2:11
Jn 20:30–31
Heb 2:3–4
—Jesus' followers as witnesses .... Lk 1:2
Ac 1:8
Ac 3:15–16
Ac 5:30–32
Ac 10:41–42

WOMEN

A. Status of women
1. In creation
—Created in the image of God .... Ge 1:27
—Equal responsibility and blessing .... Ge 1:26,28–30
—Created as a companion for man .... Ge 2:18,20
—Created second, from man .... Ge 2:21–22
1Co 11:3,7–8,12
2. In and after the fall
—Eve was tempted and sinned first .... Ge 3:1–6
2Co 11:3
1Ti 2:14
—Were subordinated to husbands .... Ge 3:16
—Were considered weak and insecure .... Isa 19:16
Jer 50:37
1Pe 3:7
3. In the covenant of the Old Testament
—Circumcision only for males .... Ge 17:10–14
—Only males instructed to appear before the Lord .... Ex 23:17
—Value of woman was less than that of a man .... Lev 27:1–8
—Sons had priority over daughters .... Nu 36:1–9
Ps 127:3–4
—Women served in the worship of God .... Ex 15:20
Ex 38:8
Ezr 2:65
—Women also expected to keep the feasts .... Dt 16:9–15
4. Jesus' attitude toward women
—Healed women as well as men .... Mk 1:30–31
Mk 5:25–34
Lk 13:10–17
—Used women as examples in parables .... Lk 13:20–21
Lk 15:8–10
Lk 17:35
Lk 18:1–8
—Was supported by women .... Lk 8:1–3
—Affirmed women eager to learn .... Lk 10:38–42
Jn 4:7–26
—Praised a poor widow and her gift .... Lk 21:1–4
—Praised Martha's confession .... Jn 11:24–27

—Women were first witnesses to resurrection .... Mt 28:1 – 10
Mk 16:1 – 8
Lk 24:1 – 11
Jn 20:1 – 2,10 – 18

5. In the redemption won by Christ
—In Christ no male or female .... Gal 3:28
—Salvation came through woman .... Gal 4:4 – 5
—Woman saved through childbearing 1Ti 2:15
—Spirit poured out on sons and daughters .... Joel 2:28 – 29
Ac 2:17 – 18
—Women filled with the Holy Spirit .... Lk 1:41 – 45
Ac 2:1 – 4
—Women and men both saved .... Ac 9:36 – 39
Ac 17:4,12
—Women prayed and prophesied .... Ac 1:14
1Co 11:5
—Women were to be silent in the churches .... 1Co 14:33 – 35
1Ti 2:11 – 12

B. Roles and occupations of women
—Wife
See MARRIAGE
—Mother
See MOTHER
—Shepherdess .... Ge 29:6
Ex 2:16
—Businesswoman .... Pr 31:13 – 19
Ac 16:14
—Judge .... Jdg 4:4 – 5
—Prophetess .... 2Ki 22:14 – 20
Ac 21:8 – 9
—Teacher .... Ac 18:26
—Workers in the church .... Ro 16:1 – 2
Php 4:2 – 3

C. Prominent women in the Bible
—Abigail 1Sa 25:3
—Anna .... Lk 2:36
—Athaliah 2Ki 11:1
—Bathsheba 2Sa 11:3
—Deborah .... Jdg 4:4
—Dorcas .... Ac 9:36
—Elizabeth .... Lk 1:5
—Esther .... Est 2:7
—Eve .... Ge 3:20
—Hagar .... Ge 16:1
—Hannah 1Sa 1:2
—Huldah 2Ki 22:14
—Jael .... Jdg 4:17
—Jezebel 1Ki 16:31
—Leah .... Ge 29:16
—Lydia .... Ac 16:14
—Mary the mother of Jesus .... Lk 1:27
—Mary Magdalene .... Lk 8:2
—Mary and Martha .... Lk 10:38 – 39
—Miriam .... Ex 15:20
—Phoebe .... Ro 16:1
—Priscilla .... Ac 18:2
—Rachel .... Ge 29:16
—Rahab .... Jos 2:3
—Rebekah .... Ge 24:29
—Ruth .... Ru 1:4
—Salome .... Mk 15:40
—Sapphira .... Ac 5:1
—Sarah .... Ge 12:5
—Tamar .... Ge 38:6
See also entries for each of these women

WORD OF GOD

A. What is the word of God?
—The word God spoke in creation .... Ps 33:6 – 9
—The word God spoke to the prophets 1Ki 17:2,8
Jer 1:2,4,11 – 13
Eze 6:1 – 3
—The Old Testament revelation .... Jn 10:34 – 45
—The word spoken by Jesus .... Lk 5:1
—Jesus himself as the Word become flesh .... Jn 1:1,14
—The word spoken by the apostles .... Ac 13:44
1Th 2:13
1Pe 1:25
—Instructions given by pastors .... Gal 6:6
2Ti 4:2

B. What power does the word of God have?
—The power to create .... Ps 33:6
Heb 11:3
2Pe 3:5
—The power to sustain all of creation .... Ps 147:15 – 18
Heb 1:3
—The power to heal .... Ps 107:20
Mt 8:8
—The power to judge our hearts .... Heb 4:12
—The power to give us new birth .... Jas 1:18
1Pe 1:23
—The power to lead us to faith .... Ro 10:17
—The power to save us 2Ti 3:15
—The power to make us holy .... Eph 5:26
—The power to fight against Satan .... Eph 6:17
Rev 19:13 – 15
—The power to destroy the world 2Pe 3:7

C. Characteristics of God's word
—It is reliable 2Sa 7:28
—It is true 1Ki 17:24
Jn 17:17
—It is flawless .... Pr 30:5
—It is alive and active .... Heb 4:12
—It is eternal .... Ps 119:89
—It will endure .... Isa 40:8
Mt 5:18
Mt 24:35
—It will not return empty .... Isa 55:11

D. Our reaction to the word of God
—We must hear it .... Isa 1:10
Jer 7:1 – 2
—We must understand it .... Mt 13:23
—We must accept it .... Mk 4:20
Ac 2:41
1Th 2:13
—We must hide it in our hearts .... Ps 119:11
—We must retain it .... Lk 8:15
—We must let it dwell in us .... Col 3:16
—We must trust in it .... Ps 119:42
—We must hope in it .... Ps 119:74,81,114
Ps 130:5
—We must praise it .... Ps 56:4,10
—We must live according to it .... Ps 119:9
—We must obey it .... Ps 119:17,67
Jas 1:22 – 24
—We must handle it correctly 2Ti 2:15
—We must preach it .... Ac 8:4

E. Pictures used for the word of God
—Lamp and light .... Ps 119:105
—Rain producing fruit .... Isa 55:10 – 11
—Consuming fire .... Jer 5:14
—Destroying hammer .... Jer 23:29
—Seed .... Mk 4:14
—Sword .... Eph 6:17
Heb 4:12

F. Scripture as the word of God
See INSPIRATION OF SCRIPTURE

G. Jesus as the Word of God
—He is the Word of God .... Jn 1:1

—He is the creative Word.......Jn 1:3
—He is the Word become flesh.......Jn 1:14
—He is the Word of life.......1Jn 1:2
—He is the victorious Word.......Rev 19:13–16

WORK

A. Related themes
PRAY AND WORK is a theme of Nehemiah.......Ne 4:9
DAILY WORK is a theme of 2 Thessalonians.......2Th 3:6
B. The work of humans
1. Humans in general
a. Nature of work
—Required of Adam before the fall.......Ge 1:28
Ge 2:15,19–20
—Required of humans after the fall.......Ex 20:9
Eph 4:28
1Th 4:11
—Became hard work.......Ge 3:17–19
Ecc 3:9–10
—Can seem meaningless.......Ecc 1:14
Ecc 2:11,17
b. God's relationship to human work
—He commands it.......Dt 5:13
—He expects it.......Ps 104:23
—He blesses honest toil.......Pr 14:23
Pr 27:23–27
—He speaks against laziness.......Pr 6:6–11
Pr 10:4–5
2. Daily work for Christians
—We must earn our daily bread.......2Th 3:10
—We must pray for God to establish it.......Ps 90:17
—We must depend on God in it.......Ps 127:1–2
Isa 26:12
—We must bring glory to God's name through it.......1Co 10:31
Col 3:17
—We must accompany it with prayer.......Ne 4:6–9
—Our work is not in vain.......1Co 15:58
C. The work of God
1. Aspects of his work
—Created the world.......Ge 1:1–2:3
Ps 8:3
—Preserves the world.......Ps 36:6
—Governs the world.......Ac 17:26
Eph 1:11
—Redeems the world.......Jn 3:16–17
Jn 12:47
—Always at work in the world.......Jn 5:17
2. His works described as:
—Numerous.......Ps 104:24
—Great.......Ps 92:5
—Awesome.......Ps 66:5
—Marvelous.......Rev 15:3
—Wonderful.......Ps 139:14
—Faithful.......Ps 111:7
3. Our reaction to God's works
—We should see them.......Ps 46:8
Ps 66:5
—We should have regard for them.......Ps 28:5
—We should consider them.......Ps 8:3
—We should meditate on them.......Ps 77:12
Ps 143:5
—We should sing for joy at them.......Ps 92:4
—We should praise them.......Job 36:24
—We should tell others about them.......Ps 107:21–22
Ps 145:4–6

WORLD

A. Related themes
1. WORLDWIDE MISSION is a theme of:
—Matthew.......Mt 21:43
—Acts.......Ac 28:14
—Romans.......Ro 15:19
2. WORLDWIDE SAVIOR is a theme of Luke.......Lk 19:9
B. Meaning of the word "world"
—The entire created universe.......Jer 10:12
—All men and women on earth.......Ge 11:1,9
1Sa 17:46
Isa 12:5
Jn 3:16
—People opposed to God.......Jn 14:30–31
1Jn 5:19
—Natural life as opposed to spiritual life.......1Co 7:33
C. God's relationship to the sinful world
1. God the Father
—He loves it.......Jn 3:16
—He sent Jesus to save it.......Jn 3:16–17
Jn 17:18,23
—He reconciled it through Christ.......2Co 5:19
—He holds it accountable to him.......Ro 3:19
—He will judge it.......Ps 96:13
Ps 98:9
2. Jesus the Son
—He is its light.......Jn 3:19
Jn 8:12
Jn 9:5
—He takes away its sin.......Jn 1:29
—He is its Savior.......Lk 2:10–11
Jn 4:42
1Ti 1:15
1Jn 4:14
—He gives it life.......Jn 6:33,51
—He has overcome it.......Jn 16:33
—He will judge it.......Ac 17:31
D. Our relationship to the sinful world
1. How we relate to the world
—We are in it.......Jn 17:15
2Co 10:3
—We are strangers in it.......1Pe 2:11
—We are not of it.......Jn 15:19
Jn 17:14,16
Jas 4:4
—We may not adopt its standards.......Ro 12:2
Tit 2:12
Jas 1:27
—We must not love it.......2Ti 4:10
1Jn 2:15–16
—We must be crucified to it.......Ro 6:6
Gal 6:14
—We must overcome it.......Jn 16:33
1Jn 5:4–5
—We must proclaim the gospel to it.......Mt 24:14
Mt 28:19
Mk 16:15
—We will judge it.......1Co 6:2
2. How the world relates to us
—The world hates us.......Jn 15:18
Jn 17:14
1Jn 3:13
—The world persecutes us.......Jn 15:20–21
2Ti 3:12
—The world has false prophets.......1Jn 4:1,3
2Jn 7

WORSHIP

A. Related themes
WORSHIP is a theme of:
—Leviticus.......Lev 23:2
—1 Chronicles.......1Ch 25:1

B. The call to worship
  1. Commanded by God ..... 2Ki 17:35 – 39; Ps 29:2; Ps 96:9
  2. Affirmed by believers ..... Ps 95:6; Ps 100:1 – 2; Ps 132:6 – 7; Heb 10:25

C. Examples of people at worship
  1. The formal worship of God
    —Cain and Abel ..... Ge 4:3 – 4
    —Noah ..... Ge 8:20
    —Abraham ..... Ge 22:5
    —Isaac ..... Ge 26:23 – 25
    —Jacob ..... Ge 35:1 – 7
    —The Israelites under Moses ..... Ex 24:1 – 8
    —The Israelites under David ..... 1Ch 23:28 – 31
    —Daniel ..... Da 6:10
    —The returned exiles ..... Ezr 3:10 – 11; Ne 8:2 – 18
    —Jesus ..... Lk 4:15 – 27
    —The apostles ..... Ac 3:1
    —The early church ..... Ac 2:42,46 – 47; Ac 20:7 – 11
    —The hosts of heaven ..... Rev 5:8 – 14; Rev 7:9 – 17
  2. The worship of Christ
    —The Magi ..... Mt 2:11
    —Christ's disciples ..... Mt 14:33; Mt 28:17; Lk 24:52
    —A blind man who received his sight ..... Jn 9:38
    —The heavenly hosts ..... Rev 5:8 – 14

D. The day for worship
  See SABBATH

E. Characteristics of true worship
  1. Principles to follow
    —Worship God alone ..... Ex 20:4 – 5; Ex 23:24 – 25; Mt 4:10
    —Love God with all your heart ..... Dt 6:4 – 6; Dt 10:12 – 13
    —Be humble in heart ..... Ps 51:17; Isa 66:2; Mic 6:6 – 8
    —Depend on the Holy Spirit ..... Jn 4:20 – 24; Php 3:3
    —Formal ritual alone is insufficient ..... Isa 1:11 – 15; Am 5:21 – 24
  2. Specific elements in Christian worship
    —Reading Scripture 1Ti 4:13
    —Preaching ..... Ac 20:7; 2Ti 4:2
    See PREACHING
    —Praying 1Ti 2:1,8
    See PRAYER
    —Singing ..... Col 3:16
    See MUSIC AND SONG
    —Giving an offering ..... 1Co 16:1 – 2
    See TITHES AND OFFERINGS
    —Exercising spiritual gifts ..... 1Co 14:26 – 33
    See GIFTS OF THE SPIRIT
    —Celebrating the sacraments ..... Ac 2:41 – 42; 1Co 11:18 – 29
    See BAPTISM; LORD'S SUPPER

WRATH

See ANGER

XERXES

—King of Persia ..... Est 1:1 – 2
—Deposed Queen Vashti ..... Est 1:15 – 21
—Made Esther queen ..... Est 2:17
—Signed edict to annihilate the Jews ..... Est 3:12 – 15
—Received Esther without having summoned her ..... Est 5:1 – 8
—Honored Mordecai ..... Est 6:1 – 11
—Furious at Haman ..... Est 7:1 – 8
—Impaled Haman on a pole ..... Est 7:9 – 10
—Signed edict allowing Jews to defend themselves ..... Est 8:3 – 14
—Exalted Mordecai ..... Est 8:1 – 2,15; Est 9:4

YEAR OF JUBILEE

See THE RICH AND THE POOR; SLAVERY

YEAST

—A leavening substance for bread

A. Leaven and bread
  —Allowed in some offerings ..... Lev 7:13; Lev 23:17
  —Not allowed in other offerings ..... Ex 23:15 – 16; Lev 2:11; Dt 16:1 – 8
  —The Feast of Unleavened Bread
  See FEASTS

B. Leaven as a symbol
  —A symbol of corruption and evil ..... Mt 16:6,12; Gal 5:7 – 9; 1Co 5:6 – 8
  —A symbol of the penetrating influence of the kingdom ..... Mt 13:33; Lk 13:21

YOKE

A. Uses for the yoke
  —To use on animals at work ..... 1Ki 19:19 – 21
  —To control slaves 1Ti 6:1
  —To wear as a prophetic symbol ..... Jer 27:2

B. The yoke as a symbol
  1. Positive
    —A symbol of service to God's law ..... Jer 2:20
    —A symbol of discipleship ..... Mt 11:28 – 30
  2. Negative
    —A symbol of oppression ..... 1Ki 12:4,9 – 11; Jer 28:10 – 14
    —A symbol of bondage to sin ..... La 1:14
    —A symbol of legalism ..... Ac 15:10; Gal 5:1
    —A symbol of union with unbelievers 2Co 6:14

YOUTH

A. Characteristics of youth
  —Strong ..... Pr 20:29; Isa 40:30; 1Jn 2:14
  —Devoted and zealous ..... 1Ki 18:12; Jer 2:2; Gal 1:13 – 14
  —Inexperienced ..... 1Sa 17:33; 1Ch 22:5; Jer 1:6
  —Sinful and foolish ..... Job 13:26; 1Sa 2:17; 1Ki 12:8 – 15; Ps 25:7; 2Ti 2:22
  —Lacking in knowledge and judgment ..... Ge 37:2 – 11; Pr 1:4; Pr 7:7

B. Encouragement to youth
—To commit their lives to God ... Ps 119:9
Ecc 12:1
La 3:27
—To seek knowledge from God ... 1Ki 3:7–9
—To enjoy life ... Pr 5:18
Ecc 11:9
—To see visions and to prophesy ... Joel 2:28
Ac 2:17
—To exercise self-control ... Tit 2:6
C. Familiar stories involving youths
—Joseph sold into Egypt ... Ge 37:12–28
—Joseph serving faithfully in Egypt ... Ge 39:1–12
—Gideon called to be military leader ... Jdg 6:15–16
—David killing Goliath ... 1Sa 17:26–50
—Joash repairing the temple ... 2Ch 24:4–14
—Josiah purifying the land and the temple ... 2Ch 34:3–13
—Jeremiah called to serve as prophet ... Jer 1:4–19
—James and John following Jesus ... Mk 1:19–20
—Timothy accompanying Paul ... Ac 16:1–3
—Timothy serving as pastor ... 1Ti 4:12

ZACCHAEUS
—Tax collector ... Lk 19:1–2
—Climbed a tree to see Jesus ... Lk 19:3–4
—Welcomed Jesus into his house ... Lk 19:5–7
—Saved by Jesus ... Lk 19:8–9

ZADOK
—A priest in the time of David ... 2Sa 8:17
—Ministered in Hebron after Saul's death ... 1Ch 12:23–28
—Helped bring the ark to Jerusalem ... 1Ch 15:11–13
—Became David's priest ... 1Ch 16:39–40
1Ch 24:6
—Loyal to David during Absalom's rebellion ... 2Sa 15:24–36
2Sa 17:15,17–21
—Loyal to David during Adonijah's rebellion ... 1Ki 1:8
—Anointed Solomon king ... 1Ki 1:32–40
—Became Solomon's priest ... 1Ki 2:35
1Ki 4:4
1Ch 29:22

ZEAL
See JEALOUSY

ZEBULUN
A. Son of Jacob by Leah ... Ge 35:23
1Ch 2:1
—Name means "honor" ... Ge 30:20
—Went to Egypt with family ... Ge 46:8,14
—Father of three sons ... Ge 46:14
—Blessed by Jacob ... Ge 49:13
B. Tribe descended from Zebulun
—Blessed by Moses ... Dt 33:18–19
—Numbered ... Nu 1:31
Nu 26:27
—Allotted land ... Jos 19:10–16
Eze 48:26
—Failed to fully possess the land ... Jdg 1:30
—Supported Deborah ... Jdg 4:6–10
Jdg 5:14,18
—Supported David ... 1Ch 12:33
—One of the tribes of the 144,000 ... Rev 7:8

ZECHARIAH
A. Son of Jeroboam II; king of Israel ... 2Ki 15:8–9
—Assassinated by Shallum ... 2Ki 15:10
B. A postexilic prophet
—Encouraged rebuilding of temple ... Ezr 5:1
Ezr 6:14
—Received various visions and prophecies ... Zec 1:1,7
Zec 7:1,8
C. Father of John the Baptist
—Took his turn as priest in temple ... Lk 1:5,8–10
—Received announcement of the birth of a son ... Lk 1:11–20
—Could not speak for nine months ... Lk 1:20–22
—Gave name "John" to his son ... Lk 1:59–63
—Praised God with a song ... Lk 1:64–79

ZEDEKIAH
A. A false prophet ... 1Ki 22:11
2Ch 18:10
—Slapped true prophet Micaiah in the face ... 1Ki 22:24
2Ch 18:23
B. Son of Josiah ... 1Ch 3:15
—Also called Mattaniah ... 2Ki 24:17
—Made king of Judah by Nebuchadnezzar ... 2Ki 24:17–20
2Ch 36:10
—Asked Jeremiah to pray for Jerusalem ... Jer 37:3
—Consulted with Jeremiah ... Jer 38:14–27
—Rebelled against Nebuchadnezzar ... 2Ki 24:20
2Ch 36:13
—Jerusalem destroyed during his time ... 2Ki 25:1–17
2Ch 36:15–19
—Saw his sons killed ... Jer 39:5–6
—Blinded and taken to Babylon ... Jer 39:7

ZERUBBABEL
—Descendant of David ... 1Ch 3:19
Mt 1:3
—Led return of Jews from exile ... Ezr 2:2
Ne 7:7
—Restored worship in Judah ... Ezr 3:1–8
—Helped rebuild temple ... Ezr 3:8–13
Hag 1:1–12
Zec 4:1–9
—Handled opposition to rebuilding ... Ezr 4:1–5

ZILPAH
—Servant of Leah ... Ge 29:24
—Mother of Gad and Asher ... Ge 30:9–12
Ge 35:26

ZIMRI
—King of Israel ... 1Ki 16:9–20
—Gained throne by assassination ... 1Ki 16:9–10
—Committed suicide ... 1Ki 16:18

ZION
A. Zion as an earthly place
—The Jebusite city captured by David ... 2Sa 5:6–7
—The place where David built his palace ... 2Ch 5:2
—The temple of the Lord ... Ps 20:2
Isa 18:7
—The holy mountain of God in Jerusalem ... Ps 74:2
Joel 3:17,21
—The whole city of Jerusalem ... 2Ki 19:31
Ps 48:1–2
Isa 33:20
Am 1:2
—The whole nation of Judah ... Ps 78:68
Isa 51:16
B. Zion as a symbolic place
—The heavenly throne of God ... Ps 9:7,11
Mic 4:7
—The prophetic kingdom of Jesus ... Ps 2:6
Ps 110:2
Isa 28:16
Isa 59:20
—The heavenly Jerusalem ... Heb 12:22
—The place from which Christ rules ... Rev 14:1

ZIPPORAH
—Daughter of Reuel; wife of Moses....Ex 2:18,21 – 22
—Moved with Moses back to Egypt....Ex 4:20
—Had two sons....Ex 18:2 – 4
—Circumcised her son....Ex 4:24 – 26
—Visited Moses in the desert....Ex 18:5 – 6

ZOPHAR
—One of Job's friends who tried to comfort him....Job 2:11 – 13
—His first speech....Job 11:1 – 20
—His second speech....Job 20:1 – 29
—Offered sacrifices to God after Job's restoration....Job 42:7 – 9

Index to Notes

All entries are words or concepts in the study notes, charts, essays and book introductions, *not* in the NIV text. For references to key words in the text, consult either the Index to Topics or the Concordance. For location of geographical names, check both the Index to Maps and the Index to Color Maps.

A

AARON
anointing of
Ps 133:2
death of
Nu 20:24 – 29
family of
Ex 6:13; Ex 6:20
and golden calf
Ex 32:4; Ex 32:22 – 24; Ex 32:24
as Moses' representative
Ex 7:1 – 2; Ex 7:19
priesthood of
Ex 24:1; 1Sa 2:30; 1Ch 6:1 – 3; Eze 44:15; Heb 7:11
ABADDON
Job 26:6; Rev 9:11
ABANA RIVER
2Ki 5:12
ABEDNEGO
Da 1:7; Heb 11:34
ABEL
Ge 4:2; Ge 4:3 – 4; Ge 4:10; Job 16:18; Heb 11:4; Heb 12:23; Heb 12:24
ABIATHAR
1Sa 2:31; 1Sa 22:20; 1Sa 28:6; 2Sa 8:17; 1Ki 2:28; 1Ki 4:4; 1Ch 6:8; 1Ch 16:39; 1Ch 24:3; Mk 2:26
ABIEZER
Jdg 8:2
ABIEZRITE
Jdg 6:11
ABIGAIL
1Sa 25:1 – 44; 2Sa 17:25; Pr 11:22
ABIHAIL
Nu 3:35
ABIHU
Ex 24:1; Lev 10:1 – 3; Nu 3:4; 1Ch 6:1 – 3; 1Ch 24:2; Ac 5:1
ABIJAH (head of priestly division)
1Ch 24:10; Lk 1:5
ABIJAH (son of Jeroboam)
1Ki 14:1; 1Ki 14:12; 1Ki 14:13; 1Ki 14:14
ABIJAH (son of Rehoboam)
1Ki 12:21; 1Ki 12:24; 1Ki 15:2; 1Ki 15:15; 1Ki 15:19; 1Ki 15:26; 2Ch 11:23; 2Ch 13:1 — 14:1; 2Ch 28:6; 2Ch 28:24 – 25
ABIMELECH
Ge 20:2; Ge 26:1; Jdg 8:31; Jdg 9:1 – 57
ABINADAB (keeper of ark)
1Sa 7:1; 2Sa 6:3; 1Ch 13:7
ABINADAB (one of Jesse's sons)
1Sa 16:8
ABIRAM
Nu 16:12
ABISHAG
1Ki 1:3; 1Ki 2:17
ABISHAI
1Sa 26:6; 1Ch 2:10 – 17
ABISHALOM
1Ki 15:2
ABNER
1Sa 20:25; 1Sa 26:5
ABORTION
Ps 139:13 – 16; Ps 139:15; Jer 1:5
ABRAHAM
his call
Ac 7:2
and the church
Gal 6:16
and circumcision
Ge 17:10; Jn 7:22; Ro 4:11
and descendants
Ge 12:2 – 3; Ge 13:16; Ge 15:5; Ge 17:6; Lk 19:9; Ro 4:12,13; Gal 3:7; Gal 3:29; Heb 2:16
and eternity
Lk 16:22
and faith
Ge 12:4; Ge 15:6; Ge 17:1; Ro 4:1; Heb 11:8; Heb 11:19; Heb 12:23; Jas 2:21
friend of God
Ge 18:17; Jas 2:23
and God's covenant promises
Ge 12:2 – 3; Ge 15:18; Ge 17:2 – 8; Ge 22:17 – 18; 1Ki 2:4; 1Ki 3:8; Mic 7:20; Zec 2:11; Ro 9:4; Ro 15:8; 1Co 7:14; Gal 3:19; Heb 6:13; Heb 6:18; "Major Covenants in the Old Testament," 19
and Jesus
Jn 8:53; Jn 8:56; Ac 3:22,26
meaning of name
Ge 17:5
and Melchizedek
Ge 14:18 – 23; Heb 7:3; Heb 7:4
his obedience
Ge 12:4; Ge 17:1 – 27; Ge 17:9; Ge 26:5
his wealth
Ge 13:2,9; Ge 14:14; Ge 15:1
ABRAHAMIC COVENANT
Ge 12:2 – 3; Ge 15:18; Ge 17:2; Ge 17:6 – 11; "Major Covenants in the Old Testament," 19
ABRAM. *See* ABRAHAM
ABSALOM
2Sa 3:3; 2Sa 13:1 – 39; 2Sa 14:1; 2Sa 15:1; 2Sa 16:18; 2Sa 17:1 – 4; 2Sa 18:5 – 6; 2Sa 19:5; 1Ki 15:2; 2Ch 11:20
ABSTINENCE
from alcoholic beverages
Nu 6:4; Jer 35:6; Lk 1:15
from food sacrificed to idols
Ac 15:20; 1Co 8:1; 1Co 8:7; 1Co 8:9; 1Co 8:11; 1Co 8:13
from sexual relations
Ex 19:15
ABYSS
Lk 8:31; Rev 9:1; Rev 11:7
ACACIA WOOD
Ex 25:5; Isa 41:19
ACBOR
2Ki 22:12
ACCOUNTABILITY
Ge 2:9; Isa 7:15; Eze 33:10
ACCUSER. *See also* SATAN
Job 1:6; Job 1:8; Job 1:9; Job 1:12; Job 19:6; Rev 12:10
ACHAIA
Ac 18:11; Ac 18:12; Ac 18:27; 1Co 16:15; 2Co 1:1; Php 4:15; 1Th 1:7
ACHAN
Jos 7:1 – 26; 1Ch 2:7; Ac 5:1
ACHAR
1Ch 2:7
ACHISH
1Sa 27:2; 1Sa 27:12; 1Sa 29:6; 1Ki 2:39; Ne 11:28
ACHOR. *See* VALLEY: of Achor
ACROCORINTH
1Co 7:2

ACZIB
Mic 1:14
ADAD
Jdg 2:13
ADADNIRARI III
2Ki 13:5
ADAM
Ge 2:4; Ge 2:9; Mt 4:1; Ro 5:12; Ro 5:13; Ro 5:14; 1Co 15:22; 1Co 15:44–49; Col 1:20; 1Ti 2:13–14
ADAR
Est 9:31; "Hebrew Calendar and Selected Events," 104
ADMAH
Hos 11:8
ADONAI. *See* NAMES OF GOD: Lord (*Adonai*)
ADONI-BEZEK
Jdg 1:5
ADONI-ZEDEK
Jos 10:1; Ecc 1:16
ADONIJAH
2Sa 3:4; 2Sa 12:10; 2Sa 15:1; 1Ki 1:5; 1Ki 1:7; 1Ki 1:9; 1Ki 1:24; 1Ki 1:50; 1Ki 2:15; 1Ki 2:28; 1Ch 3:1–9; 1Ch 29:24
ADONIRAM
2Sa 20:24; 1Ki 4:6; 1Ki 12:6; 1Ki 12:18; 2Ch 10:18
ADOPTION
physical
Ge 15:3–4
spiritual
Ro 8:15; Ro 8:23; Gal 3:25–26; Gal 4:5
symbolic
Ge 30:3; Ge 48:10
ADRAMMELECH
2Ki 19:37; Isa 36:19
ADRAMYTTIUM
Ac 27:2
ADRIATIC SEA
Ac 27:27
ADULTERY
consequences of
Pr 6:26; Jn 8:5
and divorce, remarriage
Mk 10:12; Lk 16:18
eyes full of
Mt 5:28–30; 2Pe 2:14
as sin against God, others
Ex 20:14; 1Co 6:9; 1Co 6:13; 1Th 4:6
spiritual
Ex 34:15; Mt 12:39; Jas 4:4
woman caught in
Jn 8:3; Jn 8:4; Jn 8:5
AEGEAN SEA
Ac 16:11; Rev 1:9
AENEAS
Ac 9:33
AENON
Jn 3:23
AGABUS
Ac 11:28; Ac 15:2; Ac 21:10
AGAPE (love feast)
1Co 11:21; 1Co 11:33; 2Pe 2:13
AGORA
Ac 17:19
AGUR
Job 38:4–5; Pr 30:1
AHAB
1Ki 16:25; 1Ki 16:27; 1Ki 16:32; 1Ki 17:1; 1Ki 18:5; 1Ki 20:1; 2Ch 18:1; 2Ch 18:2; 2Ch 18:29; Isa 16:1
AHAVA
Ezr 8:15
AHAZ
1Ki 15:19; 2Ki 16:1; 2Ki 16:3; 2Ch 28:17–18; 2Ch 28:24–25; Isa 7:1; Isa 7:3; Isa 7:9; Isa 7:11; Isa 7:14; Isa 7:17; Isa 8:3
AHAZIAH (king of Israel)
1Ki 16:30; 1Ki 16:31; 1Ki 22:40; 1Ki 22:44; 1Ki 22:48; 2Ki 1:2; 2Ki 1:3; 2Ki 1:4; 2Ki 1:5; 2Ki 1:8; 2Ki 1:9; 2Ki 1:10; 2Ki 1:11; 2Ki 1:13; 2Ki 1:17; Rev 11:5
AHAZIAH (king of Judah)
2Ki 8:28; 2Ch 22:7; 2Ch 22:9
AHIJAH (priest)
1Sa 14:3
AHIJAH (prophet)
1Ki 11:40; 1Ki 12:26; 1Ki 14:2; 1Ki 14:6
AHIKAM
2Ki 22:12; Jer 26:24
AHIMAAZ (son of Zadok)
2Sa 18:19; 2Sa 18:27; 2Sa 18:29
AHIMELECH (Hittite officer)
1Sa 26:6
AHIMELECH (relative of Abiathar)
2Sa 8:17; 1Ch 24:3; Mk 2:26
AHIMELECH (son of Ahitub)
1Sa 14:3; 1Sa 21:1; 1Sa 21:2; 1Sa 21:4
AHINOAM
1Sa 14:50; 2Sa 12:8
AHIO
1Ch 13:7; 1Ch 13:10
AHITHOPHEL
2Sa 11:3; 2Sa 15:12; 2Sa 17:1–3; 2Sa 17:14; 2Sa 17:23; 1Ch 27:33
AHITUB (father of Zadok)
2Sa 8:17; 1Ch 6:8; Ezr 7:2
AHITUB (son of Phinehas)
1Sa 14:3
AHMOSE
Ex 1:8
AI
Jos 7:2; Jos 8:17; Jos 8:28
AIJALON
1Sa 14:31; "Conquest of Canaan," 309
ALBINUS
Ac 24:27
ALEXANDER (the Great)
Ne 5:4; Ne 13:28; Eze 26:14; Da 7:4–7; Joel 3:4; Hag 2:6; Ac 13:14; Ac 16:12; "Ptolemies and Seleucids," 1330; "The Time Between the Testaments," 1451
ALEXANDER (Jewish spokesman)
Ac 19:33
ALEXANDRIA
Ac 2:10; Ac 18:24; Ac 27:5
ALMIGHTY
Ge 17:1; 1Sa 1:3
ALMUGWOOD
1Ki 10:11
ALOES
SS 4:14
ALPHA
Rev 1:8; Rev 1:17
AMALEK
1Sa 15:5
AMALEKITES
Ge 14:7; Jdg 6:3; 1Sa 15:2; 2Sa 1:8; Est 3:1; Est 9:5–10
AMANA
SS 4:8
AMARNA TABLETS
Ge 14:13; Ge 33:3; Ecc 1:16; "Ancient Texts Relating to the Old Testament," xxii
AMASA
2Sa 17:25; 2Sa 19:13; 2Sa 20:4; 2Sa 20:8; 2Sa 20:11; 1Ki 2:5; 1Ki 2:29; 1Ch 2:10–17
AMASIAH
Am 1:1
AMAZIAH (king of Judah)
2Ki 8:22; 2Ki 12:21; 2Ki 14:2; 2Ki 14:3; 2Ki 14:7; 2Ki 14:13; 2Ki 14:21; 2Ch 17:2; Isa 44:17
AMAZIAH (priest at Bethel)
Am 7:11; Am 7:12; Am 7:13; Am 7:17
AMEN
Dt 27:15; Ro 1:25; 1Co 14:15–17; Gal 6:18
AMENEMOPE'S WISDOM
1Ki 4:30; Pr 22:20; "Ancient Texts Relating to the Old Testament," xxii
AMESTRIS
Ne 2:6; Est 1:11
AMILLENNIALISM
Rev 20:2
AMMAN
Eze 21:20; Am 1:13
AMMIHUD
2Sa 13:37
AMMINADAB
1Ch 6:22; Mt 1:4
AMMON
Ge 19:36–38; 2Sa 12:30; Am 1:13
AMMONITES
Ge 19:36–38; 1Sa 11:1; 2Sa 10:2; Zep 1:5
AMNON
2Sa 3:2–5; 2Sa 3:3; 2Sa 12:10; 2Sa 13:13; 2Sa 13:15; 2Sa 13:21
AMON
2Ki 21:20; 2Ki 21:24; 2Ki 23:5; 2Ki 23:12; 2Ch 33:21–25; Ezr 4:10
AMORITES
Ge 10:16; Ge 15:16; Jos 5:1; Jos 10:5; Jdg 1:34; Jdg 6:10; 2Sa 21:2; 1Ki 21:26; Am 2:9

AMOS
1Ki 13:1; Eze 7:7; Hos 1:1; Am 1:1; Introduction to Hosea: Author and Date; Introduction to Amos: Author
AMOZ
Isa 1:1
AMPHIPOLIS
Ac 16:12; Ac 17:1
AMPLIATUS
Ro 16:8 – 10
AMRAM
Ex 6:20; Nu 3:27
AMUNHOTEP II
1Ki 6:1; Introduction to Exodus: Chronology
ANAKITES
Nu 13:22; Dt 1:28; Jos 11:21; 2Sa 21:16; 2Sa 21:18; 2Sa 21:20; 2Sa 21:22
ANAMMELECH
Isa 36:19
ANANIAH
Ne 11:32
ANANIAS (high priest)
Ac 22:5; Ac 22:12; Ac 23:2; Ac 24:1
ANANIAS (husband of Sapphira)
Ac 5:1; Ac 5:13
ANANIAS (of Damascus)
Ac 9:10
ANATA
Jer 1:1
ANATH
Jdg 3:31; Jer 1:1
ANATHEMA
Ro 9:3; Gal 1:8
ANATHOTH
Isa 10:30; Jer 1:1
ANCIENT OF DAYS
Da 7:9
ANDREW
Mk 1:29; Mk 1:36; Lk 21:7; Jn 1:35
ANDRONICUS
Mk 6:30
ANGEL OF THE LORD
Ge 16:7; 2Ki 1:3; Zec 1:8
ANGELS
as agents of God
Ge 32:1,24; Ex 12:23; Job 1:6; Ps 78:25; 1Co 11:10; 2Th 1:7; Heb 1:4; Heb 2:2; Heb 2:5
elect
1Ti 5:21
fallen, theories about
1Pe 3:19 – 20; 2Pe 2:4; Jude 6
guardian
Mt 18:10; Ac 12:15; Heb 1:14
hierarchy
Col 1:16
as mediators
Rev 1:1; Rev 8:4
place of
Heb 1:4; Heb 1:5 – 14; Heb 1:6; Heb 1:7; Heb 2:5; Heb 12:23
of the seven churches
Rev 1:20
worship of
Col 1:16; Col 2:18; Introduction to Colossians: The Colossian Heresy
ANGER
Jnh 4:1; Jnh 4:2; Eph 4:26
ANGER, GOD'S
Rev 6:16
as eternal judgment
Ro 5:9; Ro 9:3; 1Th 2:16
just
Nu 16:24; Ps 2:5; Jn 3:36; Ro 1:18; Col 3:6; Rev 14:10
and kindness
Ro 11:22
nature of
Ex 4:14
against the nations
Ps 16:5; Jer 25:15; Ob 16; Hab 2:16; Mt 20:22; Rev 14:10
against his people
Ex 4:14; Nu 11:10; 2Sa 24:1; Eze 23:31; Zec 1:2; Heb 3:16 – 19; Introduction to Numbers: Theological Teaching
satisfaction of
Ro 3:25; Eph 2:8; Heb 2:17; 1Jn 2:2
ANNA
Lk 2:36; Lk 2:37
ANNAS
Mt 26:3; Mk 8:31; Mk 14:53 — 15:15; Lk 3:2; Jn 18:13; Jn 18:19; Ac 4:6; Ac 5:17
ANOINTING
Ex 29:7; Nu 3:3; 1Sa 2:10; 1Sa 9:16; Mt 16:16; Mk 14:3; Jn 1:25; Jas 5:14
ANTI-LEBANON MOUNTAINS
Eze 27:5
ANTICHRIST
as beast
Rev 13:1; Rev 13:12; Rev 13:16
characteristics of
1Jn 2:18; 1Jn 4:4
images of
Da 7:8; Da 9:27; Da 11:36 – 45; Zec 11:17; Mt 24:15; Rev 6:2; Rev 13:14; Rev 17:11
as "man of lawlessness"
2Th 2:3
origin of
Rev 11:7; Rev 13:12
predicted in Daniel
Mt 24:15
ANTINOMIANISM
Ro 3:31; Ro 6:1; Php 3:19; Rev 2:23
ANTIOCH
Da 11:7; Ac 6:5; Ac 11:19; Gal 2:11; Rev 2:6
of Pisidia
Ac 13:14; 2Ti 3:11
ANTIOCHUS II (Theos)
Da 11:6
ANTIOCHUS III (the Great)
Ezr 7:22; Ezr 7:24; Da 11:10; Da 11:11; Da 11:12; Da 11:13; Da 11:16; Da 11:18; Da 11:19; Da 11:20; Joel 3:4
ANTIOCHUS IV (Epiphanes)
1Sa 2:35; Ps 30 title; Da 8:9 – 12; Da 8:23 – 25; Da 11:21; Da 11:28; Da 12:11 – 12; Mt 24:15; Jn 10:22; Rev 11:2; "The Time Between the Testaments," 1451
ANTIPAS
Rev 2:13
ANTIPATRIS
Ac 23:31
ANTONIA, TOWER OF
Ac 12:9
ANXIETY
Php 2:28; Php 4:6
APELLES
Ro 16:8 – 10
APHEK
1Sa 4:1; 1Sa 29:1; 1Ki 20:26; 1Ki 20:30; 2Ki 13:17
APHRODITE
1Co 6:18; 1Co 7:2; 1Co 10:14
APIRU
Ge 14:13; "The Exodus," 108
APIS
Ex 9:3; Ex 32:4; Jos 24:14; Jer 46:15
APOCALYPTIC LITERATURE
Introduction to Daniel: Literary Form; Introduction to Zechariah: Literary Form and Themes; Introduction to Revelation: Literary Form
APOCRYPHAL BOOKS
Ezr 1:8; Ezr 6:2; "The Time Between the Testaments," 1451
APOLLO
1Co 10:14
APOLLOS
Ac 18:25; Ac 19:1; 1Co 1:1; 1Co 3:6; 1Co 16:12; Tit 3:13; Introduction to Hebrews: Author
APOSTASY
Heb 10:26
APOSTLE
authority of
1Co 1:1
distinguished from disciple
Lk 6:13
foundation of church
Eph 2:20; Eph 4:11
Paul as
1Co 1:1; 1Co 9:1; Gal 2:7
word, meaning of
Mk 6:30; Lk 6:13; Ac 14:4; Ro 1:1; Ro 16:7; 1Co 1:1; 1Co 12:28; Gal 1:1; Php 2:25; Heb 3:1
APPHIA
Phm 1:2
APRIES. *See* HOPHRA
AQABA, GULF OF
1Ki 9:26; 2Ch 20:35 – 37; Ac 7:29
AQUILA
Ac 18:18; 1Co 16:19; Col 4:15
ARABAH
Dt 1:1; 2Ki 14:25; Isa 33:9; Eze 47:8; Am 6:14

ARABIA
Ac 9:23; Gal 1:17; Gal 1:18
ARABS
Ge 17:12; Ge 25:13,16; Ne 2:19
ARAH
Ezr 2:5
ARAM
Ge 10:22; Dt 26:5; Isa 7:1; Isa 7:2; Isa 7:4
ARAM MAACAH
1Ch 19:6
ARAM NAHARAIM
Ge 24:10; Ge 25:20; 1Ch 19:6
ARAMAIC
2Ki 18:26; Ezr 4:8; Ezr 4:18; Da 2:4; Mk 5:41; Introduction to Ezra: Languages
ARAMEANS
Ge 22:23 – 24; Dt 26:5; 1Ch 18:5; "The Divided Kingdom," 497
ARARAT
Ge 8:4; Isa 37:38
ARAUNAH
2Sa 24:16; 1Ch 21:20 – 21; 2Ch 7:1 – 3
ARCHAEOLOGY
"Ancient Texts Relating to the OT," xxii; "Solomon's Temple," 484; "Major Archaeological Finds Relating to the New Testament," 1667
ARCHELAUS
Mt 2:22; Lk 3:1; Lk 19:14
ARCHIPPUS
Col 4:9 – 17
AREOPAGUS
Ac 17:19; Ac 17:33; Ac 17:34
ARETAS IV
Lk 3:19; Ac 9:23; 2Co 11:32
ARIEL (leader of the Jews)
Ezr 8:16
ARIEL (Jerusalem)
Isa 29:1,2,7; Eze 43:15
ARIMATHEA
1Sa 1:1; Mt 27:57
ARIOCH
Da 2:14
ARISTARCHUS
Ac 19:29; Col 4:9 – 17
ARISTIDES
1Co 1:19
ARISTOBULUS
Ac 12:1; Ro 16:10
ARK. *See also* ARK NARRATIVES; ARK OF THE COVENANT
Ge 6:14; Ex 2:3
ARK NARRATIVES
Introduction to 1 Samuel: Contents and Theme
ARK OF THE COVENANT (ARK OF THE TESTIMONY)
Ex 25:10; Ex 25:22; Ex 26:31 – 35; Jos 3:3; 1Sa 4:3; 1Sa 4:11; 1Sa 4:21; 1Sa 5:3; 1Sa 5:8; 1Sa 5:11; 1Sa 6:19; 1Sa 6:20; 1Sa 14:18; 2Sa 15:25; 1Ki 6:19; 1Ch 13:1 – 4; 1Ch 13:10; 2Ch 5:2; 2Ch 5:10; 2Ch 35:3; Jer 3:16; Heb 9:4; Heb 9:5; "Tabernacle Furnishings," 127; "Temple Furnishings," 487
ARKITES
2Sa 15:32
ARMAGEDDON
Da 11:40 – 45; Rev 16:16
ARMENIA
Eze 27:14
ARNON GORGE
Jos 12:1
ARNON RIVER
Jos 13:9; Jos 13:15; 2Ki 3:25
AROER
Jos 13:9; Isa 17:2
ARPAD
2Ki 18:34; Isa 10:9
ARSAMES
Ne 2:7
ARTAXERXES I
Ezr 4:7; Ezr 4:21 – 23; Ezr 6:14; Ezr 7:1; Ezr 7:11; Ezr 9:9; Ne 1:3; Ne 2:6; Ne 11:23; Isa 60:10
ARTAXERXES II
Ezr 4:7
ARTAXERXES III
Ezr 4:7
ARTEMIS
Ac 19:24; Ac 19:25; 1Co 16:9
ARVAD
Eze 27:8
ASA
1Ki 15:13; 1Ki 15:14; 1Ki 15:15; 1Ki 15:19; 1Ki 15:22; 2Ch 14:1; 2Ch 14:5; 2Ch 16:1; 2Ch 16:2 – 9
ASAHEL
1Sa 26:6; 2Sa 3:27; 1Ch 2:10 – 17
ASAPH. *See* EBIASAPH
ASAPH (descendant of Gershon)
1Ch 6:31 – 48; Ps 39 title
ASCENSION OF CHRIST. *See* CHRIST: ascension of
ASCENSION OF ISAIAH, THE
Introduction to Isaiah: Author
ASCLEPIUS
1Co 10:14
ASHDOD
1Sa 5:1; Ne 4:7; Isa 20:1; Introduction to Micah: Historical Background; "Five Cities of the Philistines," 331
ASHER
Ex 1:2 – 4; Jos 19:24; Jos 19:32; Eze 48:2
ASHERAH
Ex 34:13; Jdg 2:13; Job 9:8; Eze 8:3
ASHERAH POLES
Ex 34:13; Dt 7:5; 1Ki 14:15
ASHKELON
Jdg 1:18; 2Sa 1:20; Am 1:8; "Five Cities of the Philistines," 331
ASHTORETH
Jdg 2:13; 1Sa 7:3
ASHUR-UBALLIT
2Ki 23:29
ASHURBANIPAL
2Ch 33:11; Ezr 4:9; Ezr 4:10; Na 1:11; Na 3:10
ASHURNASIRPAL II
2Ki 10:8; Ne 5:17
ASIA MINOR
Eze 27:14; Ob 20; Ac 6:9; 2Co 1:8; Gal 1:2; Gal 1:21; 1Pe 1:1; Rev 3:7
ASIARCHON
Ac 19:31
ASSEMBLY
Dt 16:8; Joel 2:16; Mt 16:18; Ac 5:11; 1Co 1:2; Gal 1:13
ASSHUR
Eze 27:23
ASSIR
1Ch 6:22 – 23
ASSOS
Ac 20:13; Ac 27:2
ASSYRIA
Ge 10:22; 2Ki 15:29; 2Ki 16:7; 2Ki 18:7; 2Ch 33:11; Isa 13:1 — 14:27; "Assyrian Campaigns against Israel and Judah," 552; "Exile of the Northern Kingdom," 558
ASSYRIAN KING LIST
1Ch 1:4
ASWAN
Eze 29:10; Ac 8:27
ATER
Ezr 2:16
ATHALIAH
1Ki 12:24; 2Ki 8:18; 2Ch 18:1; 2Ch 22:10 – 12; 2Ch 24:4; Ezr 8:7; Ne 3:28
ATHEISM
Ps 14:1; Introduction to Genesis: Theological Theme and Message
ATHENS
Ac 17:14; Ac 17:15; Php 4:15; 1Th 3:1 – 2
ATONEMENT. *See also* DEATH, CHRIST'S: as atonement
Ex 25:17; Lev 4:4; Lev 16:20 – 22; Lev 17:11; Jos 2:18; Ro 3:25; Heb 2:17; Heb 9:5; Heb 9:7; 1Pe 2:24; 1Jn 2:2
ATRAHASIS
Introduction to Genesis: Background
ATRAHASIS EPIC
"Ancient Texts Relating to the Old Testament," xxii
ATTALIA
Ac 14:25
ATTRIBUTES OF GOD. *See* GOD: attributes/character of
AUGUSTINE
Jn 7:17; "The Book of the Twelve, or the Minor Prophets," 1333
AVENGER
Dt 32:35; Jos 20:3; Ru 2:20; Ps 8:2; Isa 41:14
AVVA
2Ki 17:24
AVVIM
Jos 18:23

AVVITES
Dt 2:23
AZARIAH (Abednego)
Da 1:6
AZARIAH (Uzziah; son of Amaziah)
2Ki 14:21; 2Ki 14:22; 2Ki 15:1; 2Ch 26:1; 2Ch 26:11; Isa 6:1
AZARIAH (son of Hilkiah)
Ezr 7:1
AZARIAH (son of Zadok)
1Sa 2:35; 1Ki 4:2; 1Ki 4:4
AZEKAH
1Sa 17:1; Jer 34:7
AZEL
Zec 14:5
AZGAD
Ezr 2:12
AZIZUS
Ac 24:24
AZOTUS
Ac 8:40

BAAL
Jos 24:14; Jdg 2:13; 1Sa 5:2; 2Sa 2:8; 1Ki 16:31; 1Ki 16:32; 1Ki 17:1; 1Ki 18:24; Eze 43:7; Hos 2:5; Hos 2:8
BAAL GAD
Jos 11:17
BAAL HAMON
SS 8:11
BAAL MEON
Eze 25:9
BAAL PEOR
Nu 31:1–24; Hos 9:10; 1Co 10:8
BAAL PERAZIM
2Sa 5:20
BAAL TAMAR
Jdg 20:33
BAAL ZEPHON
Ex 14:2
BAAL-BERITH
Jdg 8:33
BAAL-ZEBUB
Jdg 10:6; Mt 10:25
BAAL-ZEBUL
Jdg 10:6; Mt 10:25
BAALAH OF JUDAH
1Ch 13:6
BAALATH
1Ki 9:18
BAANA (son of Ahilud)
1Ki 4:12
BAANA (son of Hushai)
1Ki 4:16
BAANAH
2Sa 4:8
BAASHA
1Ki 12:24; 1Ki 15:19; 1Ki 15:28; 2Ch 16:1; 2Ch 16:2–9
BABEL
Ge 11:4; Ge 11:9
BABEL, TOWER OF
Ge 11:4; Introduction to Genesis: Background
BABYLON
Ge 11:4; Ge 11:9; Isa 13:1 — 14:27; Isa 13:19; Isa 14:22–23; Isa 21:9; Jer 50:1 — 51:64; Jer 51:44; Da 4:30; Hab 1:6,11; Hab 2:3; Hab 2:6–20; Rev 14:8; Rev 17:1; Rev 18:2; "The Neo-Babylonian Empire," 1318
BABYLONIAN CHRONICLES
Na 2:6; Na 2:10
BABYLONIAN THEODICY
"Ancient Texts Relating to the Old Testament," xxii
BACKSLIDING
Jer 2:19; Jer 3:22
BAGOHI
Ne 2:10; Ne 13:7
BAHURIM
2Sa 3:16; 2Sa 16:5
BALAAM
Nu 22:5; Nu 22:8; Nu 22:9; Nu 22:23; Nu 23:19; Jos 13:22; Jos 24:10; Job 3:8; 2Pe 2:15; Jude 11; Rev 2:14; Rev 2:17; Introduction to Numbers: Theological Teaching
BALAK
Nu 22:1–5; Nu 22:37; Nu 23:2; Nu 23:13; Nu 24:11
BALIKH RIVER
Isa 37:12
BALM
Ge 37:25; Jer 8:22; Eze 27:17
BANIAS
Mt 16:13
BAPTISM
and circumcision
Col 2:11–12
for the dead
1Co 15:29
figurative
Mk 10:38; Lk 12:50; 1Co 10:2
of households
1Co 1:16
meaning of
Ac 2:38; Ac 22:16; Ro 6:3–4; Eph 4:5; Tit 3:5; 1Pe 3:21
Paul and
1Co 1:17
of repentance
Mk 1:4; Ac 2:14–40; Ac 19:4
significance of Christ's
Mt 3:15
spiritual
1Co 12:13
BAR MITZVAH
Ro 7:9
BAR-JESUS
Ac 13:6
BARABBAS
Mt 27:16; Mk 15:7; Lk 23:18; Jn 18:40
BARADA RIVER
2Ki 5:12
BARAK
Jdg 4:6
BARBARIANS
Ro 1:14
BARLEY
Ex 9:18; Jdg 7:13; Ru 1:22
BARNABAS
Isa 49:6; Mk 6:30; Ac 4:36; Ac 12:1; Ac 13:1; Ac 13:5; Ac 13:9; Ac 14:1; Ac 14:4; Ac 14:12; Ac 14:23; Ac 15:12; Ac 15:39; 1Co 9:4; 2Co 8:18; Gal 2:1; Col 4:10; 2Ti 4:11; Introduction to Hebrews: Author
BARRENNESS
Ge 30:23; Nu 5:21; 2Sa 6:23; Ps 113:9; Lk 1:25
BARSABBAS
Ac 1:23
BARTHOLOMEW
Lk 6:14; Ac 1:13
BARTIMAEUS
Lk 18:35; Lk 19:37
BARUCH
Ezr 7:6; Jer 32:12; Jer 36:32; Jer 45:1–5; Introduction to Jeremiah: Author and Date
BARZILLAI
2Sa 17:27; 2Sa 21:8
BASHAN
Nu 21:33; Isa 2:13; Eze 39:18; Am 4:1; Na 1:4; Zec 11:2
BATH RABBIM
SS 7:4
BATHSHEBA
2Sa 5:14; 2Sa 11:4; 2Sa 11:5; 2Sa 11:27; 2Sa 23:34; 1Ki 1:11; SS 3:11
BAY OF NAPLES
Ac 28:13
BEALOTH
1Ki 9:18
BEAR
Job 9:9
BEAST, THE
Rev 11:7; Rev 13:1; Rev 13:3; Rev 13:5; Rev 13:11; Rev 13:12; Rev 13:16
BEATITUDES, THE
Mt 5:1 — 7:29; Lk 6:20–49; Lk 6:20–23; Rev 1:3
BEELIADA
1Ch 14:7
BEELZEBUB. *See also* BAAL-ZEBUB; BAAL-ZEBUL; SATAN
Mt 10:25; Lk 11:15; Lk 11:22
BEER
Jdg 9:21
BEER ELIM
Isa 15:8
BEEROTH
2Sa 4:2
BEERSHEBA
Ge 21:31; 1Sa 3:20; 1Ki 19:3; Am 5:5
BEHISTUN INSCRIPTION
Ezr 4:24; Ezr 6:12; Ne 6:6; Est 2:23; Hag 1:1
BEIT JIBRIN
Ne 11:29

BEL
Isa 46:1; Da 1:7; Da 4:8
BELA
1Ch 7:6 – 12
BELIAL. *See also* SATAN
Dt 13:13; 2Co 6:15
BELSHAZZAR
Da 5:1; Da 5:22 – 23; Da 7:1
BELTESHAZZAR
Da 1:7
BEN-ABINADAB
1Ki 4:11
BENAIAH
2Sa 23:20; 1Ki 2:46; 1Ki 4:4
BENEDICTION
Nu 6:24 – 26; 2Co 13:14; Heb 13:20 – 21
BENEDICTUS
1Sa 2:1; Lk 1:68 – 79
BEN-HADAD I
1Ki 15:20; 1Ki 20:1; 1Ki 20:4; 1Ki 20:9; 1Ki 20:22; 1Ki 20:32; 1Ki 20:42; 1Ki 22:1; 2Ki 15:29
BEN-HADAD II
1Ki 20:1; 2Ki 5:6; 2Ki 5:7; 2Ki 8:9
BEN-HADAD III
2Ki 13:3; Am 1:4
BEN-HUR
1Ki 4:8
BENJAMIN (son of Jacob)
Ge 35:18; Ge 42:4
BENJAMIN (tribe of Israel)
Jdg 3:15; 1Ki 12:21; 1Ch 8:1 – 40
BEQAA VALLEY
2Sa 8:3
BEREA
Ac 17:10; Php 4:15; 1Th 3:1 – 2
BEREKIAH
Ne 2:10
BERENICE
Da 11:6; Da 11:7
BERGAMA
Rev 2:12
BERNICE
Ac 25:13
BEROSSUS
Ezr 4:15
BEROTHAH
Eze 47:16
BETH ANATH
Jdg 1:33
BETH ARBEL
Hos 10:14
BETH AVEN
Jos 7:2; Hos 4:15; Hos 10:5
BETH BARAH
Jdg 7:24
BETH DIBLATHAIM
Eze 6:14
BETH EDEN
Am 1:5
BETH GILGAL
Ne 12:29
BETH HAKKEREM
Ne 3:14
BETH HORON
Jos 10:11; 1Ki 9:17; 1Ki 9:18; 2Ch 8:5
BETH JESHIMOTH
Eze 25:9
BETH MILLO
Jdg 9:6; 2Ki 12:20
BETH PELET
Ne 11:26
BETH PEOR
Dt 3:29; Hos 9:10
BETH REHOB
1Ch 18:5; 1Ch 19:6
BETH SHAN
Jos 17:11; Jn 3:23
BETH SHEMESH
Jdg 1:33; 1Sa 6:9; 1Sa 6:14 – 15; 1Sa 6:19; 2Ki 14:11
BETH TOGARMAH
Eze 27:14
BETH ZUR
Ne 3:16
BETHANY
Ne 11:32; Mt 21:17; Mk 11:11; Lk 19:29; Jn 1:28
BETHEL
Ge 12:8; Jos 8:17; Jdg 20:18; 1Ki 12:29; 2Ki 2:23; 2Ki 17:28; Ezr 2:28; Hos 4:15; Hos 8:5; Hos 10:5; Hos 12:3; Hos 12:4; Am 3:14; Am 4:4; Am 5:6; Am 7:15; Zec 7:3; Introduction to Amos: Author
BETHESDA, POOL OF
Jn 5:2
BETHLEHEM
Jdg 12:8; Jdg 17:7; Ru 1:1; 1Sa 16:1; Mic 5:2; Mt 2:1; Mt 2:16; Lk 2:4; Lk 2:8; Lk 2:22
BETHPHAGE
Mt 21:1; Lk 19:29
BETHSAIDA
Mt 11:21; Mk 6:32; Mk 6:44; Jn 6:5
BETROTHAL
Mt 1:18
BEZALEL
Ex 31:2; Ex 37:1; 1Ch 2:18 – 24; 2Ch 1:5; Introduction to 2 Chronicles: The Building of the Temple in Chronicles
BEZEK
Jdg 1:4; 1Sa 11:8
BEZER
Dt 4:43
BIBLE. *See* SCRIPTURE
BIER
Lk 7:14
BIGTHANA
Est 2:23
BIGVAI
Ne 2:10; Ne 13:7
BILDAD
Job 2:11; Job 8:5 – 6; Job 8:20; Job 18:1 – 4; Job 18:17; Job 19:6; Job 26:5 – 14; Job 32:15 – 16
BILHAH
Ex 1:2 – 4; 1Ch 7:13
BIRTHRIGHT
Ge 25:31; Ge 27:36
BISHOP
Tit 1:7
BISITUN INSCRIPTION. *See* BEHISTUN INSCRIPTION
BIT ADINI
Isa 37:12
BITHYNIA
Ac 16:7; 1Pe 1:1
BLACK OBELISK
2Ki 10:34; "Ancient Texts Relating to the Old Testament," xxii
BLASPHEMY
Mk 2:7; Mk 14:64; Lk 5:21; Jn 8:59; Jn 10:31; Jn 10:33; Jn 19:7; Ac 6:11; Ac 14:5; Ac 26:11; 1Ti 1:20
BLASTUS
Ac 12:20
BLESSED
Ps 1:1; Pr 31:28; Mt 5:3; Rev 1:3
BLESSING
Ge 12:2 – 3; Ge 27:33; Ge 27:36; Ge 33:11; Ge 35:11 – 12; Ge 49:2 – 27; Lev 26:3; Eze 34:26; Eph 1:3
BLESSINGS AND CURSES
Ge 27:33; Lev 26:4; Dt 4:25; Dt 27:12,15,26; Dt 28:1 – 14
BLOOD
Ge 9:4; Ex 12:7; Lev 4:5; Lev 17:11; Mk 14:24; Heb 9:18; Heb 12:24; 1Pe 1:18 – 19; Introduction to Leviticus: Theological Themes
BLOOD REVENGE
Ge 27:45; Nu 35:6 – 15; Jos 20:1 – 9; 2Sa 14:7; "Cities of Refuge," 239
BOASTING. *See also* PRIDE
Ro 15:17; 2Co 11:30; Gal 6:14
BOAZ
Ru 2:1; Ru 3:1; Ru 4:1; Introduction to Ruth: Theme and Theology; Literary Features
BOOK
of the Covenant
Ex 20:22 — 23:19; Ex 24:7; 2Ki 23:2
of the Dead
Eze 29:5
of Jashar
Jos 10:13; Introduction to 1 Samuel: Literary Features, Authorship and Date
of the Law
Jos 1:8; Jos 23:6; 2Ki 22:8; 2Ch 34:3 – 7; Ne 8:1
of Life
Ps 69:28; Rev 3:5
of Moses
Ezr 6:18; Ne 8:1
of Truth
Da 10:21
of the Twelve
"The Book of the Twelve, or the Minor Prophets," 1333

of the Wars of the Lord
Nu 21:14; Ps 60:5–8
BOOTHS, FEAST OF. *See also* FEAST: of Ingathering; of Tabernacles
Ex 23:16; Lev 23:42
BOUNDARY STONE
Dt 19:14; Pr 15:25
BOZKATH
2Ki 22:1
BOZRAH
Isa 34:6; Jer 49:13; Am 1:12
BRANCH
Isa 4:2; Jer 23:5; Zec 3:8
BREAD OF LIFE
Jesus as
Jn 6:35
BREAD OF THE PRESENCE
Ex 25:30; Lev 24:8; 1Sa 21:4
BREASTPLATE
Rev 9:9
BRIBES
Pr 17:8
BRIDEGROOM. *See* CHRIST: as bridegroom
BROAD WALL
Ne 3:8; Ne 11:9
BRONZE PILLARS
1Ki 7:15
BRONZE SEA
1Ki 7:23
BROOM TREE
1Ki 19:4; Job 30:4; Ps 120:4
BUBASTIS
Eze 30:17
BUCKTHORN
Jdg 9:14
BURIAL CUSTOMS, JEWISH
Mk 14:8; Mk 16:1; Lk 23:56
BURNT OFFERING
Lev 1:3; Lev 3:5; Ne 8:10; Eze 40:39; "Tabernacle Furnishings," 127; "Old Testament Sacrifices," 153
BUSYBODIES
2Th 3:11
BUZITE
Job 32:2
BYBLOS
Jos 13:5; Eze 27:9

C

CAESAR (Augustus)
Mt 11:21; Lk 2:1; Ac 10:1
CAESAR (Claudius)
Ac 12:21; Ac 17:7
CAESAR (Tiberius)
Lk 20:22; Jn 19:12
CAESAREA
Lk 23:1; Ac 8:40; Ac 10:1; Ac 12:19; Ac 19:6; Ac 21:8; Ac 23:33
CAESAREA PHILIPPI
Mt 16:13
CAIAPHAS
Mt 26:3; Mk 14:53—15:15; Lk 3:2; Jn 11:50; Jn 11:51; Ac 4:6; Ac 5:17; Jas 5:12
CAIN
Ge 4:3–4; Ge 4:5; Ge 4:11; Ge 4:13; Ge 4:17; 1Sa 20:11; Heb 11:4; Jude 11
CALAH
Jnh 1:2; Jnh 3:3
CALAMUS
SS 4:14; Isa 43:24; Jer 6:20; Eze 27:19
CALCOL
1Ch 2:6
CALEB
Nu 14:24; Jdg 1:12; 1Sa 25:3
CALENDAR, HEBREW
Ex 12:2; Lev 23:5,24; "Hebrew Calendar and Selected Events," 104
CALF WORSHIP
Ex 32:4; Ex 32:5; Ex 32:6; 1Ki 12:28
CALIGULA
2Co 11:32
CALNEH
Am 6:2
CALNO
Isa 10:9
CALVARY
Mk 15:22; Lk 23:33; Jn 19:17
CAMBYSES
Ezr 6:8; Ezr 6:9; Ezr 9:9; Da 11:2; Da 11:8
CAMELS
Ge 12:16; Jdg 6:5
CANA
Jn 2:1
CANAAN
Ge 10:6; Jos 1:4
people of
Ge 9:25; Ge 34:9; Ex 3:8; Jos 2:2; Jos 5:1
promised land
Ge 23:19; Ge 37:1; Ex 3:8; Jos 3:10
religious practices
Ge 15:16; Dt 18:9; Jdg 2:13; 1Ki 14:24; 2Ki 16:4; Zec 14:21
CANAANITE
Mt 15:22
CANDACE
Ac 8:27
CANNEH
Eze 27:23
CANNIBALISM
Dt 28:53; Isa 49:26; Jer 19:9; Eze 5:10
CANON
"The Time Between the Testaments," 1451
CAPERNAUM
Mt 4:13; Mk 3:8; Mk 3:21; Lk 10:15; "Capernaum Synagogue," 1572
CAPHTOR
Ge 10:14
CAPITAL PUNISHMENT
Ge 9:6
CAPPADOCIA
Ac 2:9
CARCHEMISH
2Ch 35:21; Isa 10:9; Isa 10:19; Joel 1:15; Introduction to Habakkuk: Date
CARIA/CARITES
2Ki 11:4; 2Ch 23:1
CARMEL
1Sa 15:12; Isa 33:9; Isa 35:2; Na 1:4
CARMEL, MOUNT. *See* MOUNT: Carmel
CARTHAGE
Isa 23:7
CASIPHIA
Ezr 8:17
CASSANDER
Da 7:4–7
CASSIA
Ex 25:6; Eze 27:19
CASTOR
Ac 28:11
CAUDA
Ac 27:16
CEDARS OF LEBANON
Jdg 9:15; 2Sa 5:11; 1Ki 5:6; 1Ki 7:2; SS 5:15; Isa 9:10; Isa 14:8; Isa 37:24
CENCHREA
Ac 18:1; Ac 20:3; Ro 16:1
CENSER
Lev 10:1; Nu 16:37; Rev 8:3
CENSUS
Ex 30:12; Nu 1:2; Nu 26:1–51; 2Sa 24:1; 1Ch 21:1—22:1; Lk 2:1
CENTURION
Mt 8:5; Lk 7:2; Ac 10:1
CHALDEANS
Ezr 5:12; Job 1:17; Eze 23:23; Hab 1:6; Ac 7:4; "Nebuchadnezzar's Campaigns against Judah," 572
CHEMOSH
Jdg 11:24; Ru 1:15; Ne 13:26; Isa 44:19; Am 2:2
CHERUBIM
Ge 3:24; Ex 25:18; 1Sa 4:4; 2Sa 22:11; 1Ki 6:23; Ps 18:10; Eze 1:5; Eze 10:1; Eze 10:7; Eze 10:14; Eze 41:18; Heb 9:5
CHIEF PRIEST
Mt 2:4
CHILDREN. *See also* FAMILY; PARENTS
the blessing of. *See also* BARRENNESS
Ps 112:2; Ps 127:3,5
disciplining. *See* DISCIPLINE: of children
their responsibility to parents
Isa 51:18; Mk 7:11; Jn 19:27; Eph 6:1
teaching/influencing
Pr 27:11; 1Co 7:14; Eph 6:4; 2Ti 3:15; Introduction to Proverbs: Purpose and Teaching; "The Wise Man According to Proverbs: An Outline," 957
CHILD SACRIFICE
Jdg 11:30; 2Ki 3:27; 2Ki 16:3; 2Ki 23:10; Jer 7:31; Eze 16:20

CHRIST. *See also* SON: of the Blessed One, of David, of Man, of the Most High
"The Life of Christ," 1508
"Jesus in Judea and Samaria," 1629; "Jesus in Galilee," 1635; "Harmony of the Gospels," 1668
ascension of
Lk 24:53; Jn 16:10; Ac 1:2; Ac 1:12; Ac 2:38; Eph 4:9; Php 3:21; 1Ti 3:16; Heb 4:14; 1Pe 3:19–20a; 1Pe 3:22; Rev 12:5
baptism of
Mt 3:15; Lk 3:21; Jn 5:37; 1Jn 5:6; "Jesus' Baptism and Temptation," 1468
believer in
Eph 1:1
as bread of life
Ex 16:4; Jn 6:35
as bridegroom
2Co 11:2
as cornerstone
1Pe 2:6
death of. See DEATH, CHRIST'S
deity of
Jn 1:1; Jn 1:18; Ro 9:5; Ro 10:9; Php 2:6; Tit 2:13; Heb 1:2–3; Heb 1:6; Heb 1:8; 2Pe 1:1
exaltation of
Isa 52:13; Eph 1:3; Php 2:9–10; Heb 1:2–3; Heb 12:2
as example
Php 2:5; 1Pe 2:21; 1Pe 3:18
fullness of
Eph 4:13; Eph 4:15; Col 1:19; Col 2:9
glory of
Jn 12:41; 1Pe 1:11
humanity of
Mk 4:38; Jn 1:14; Php 2:8
humility of
Jn 13:5; Jn 13:14–15; Php 2:8
incarnation of
Jn 1:9; Jn 8:56; Ro 8:3; Ro 11:25; 2Co 8:9; Eph 4:9; Php 2:6; 1Ti 3:16; Heb 1:2–3; Heb 2:11; Heb 2:13; 1Jn 2:18
and Israel
Isa 49:3; Mt 2:15; Mt 15:26; Jn 1:51
judgment and
Jn 12:47; 2Co 5:10
law of
1Co 9:21; Gal 6:2
as Lord
Mt 2:2; Lk 2:11; Ro 10:9; Ro 14:9; 1Co 12:3; Php 2:9–11; 1Th 1:1; Rev 17:14
his natural family
Lk 8:19,21
obedience of
Jn 4:34; Jn 17:4; Jn 19:30; Php 2:8; Heb 5:8
priesthood of
Ex 20:19; Lev 4:3; Lev 16:3; Heb 2:17; Heb 4:14; Heb 4:16; Heb 5:5; Heb 7:25; Heb 7:27; Heb 8:2
resurrection of. See RESURRECTION, CHRIST'S
as Savior
Lk 2:11; Jn 4:42; Tit 1:4
second coming of. See SECOND COMING
suffering of
Isa 52:14; Isa 53:1–12; Lk 2:35; Lk 17:25; Heb 5:7; 1Pe 1:11; 1Pe 2:21; 1Pe 3:18; 1Pe 4:13
temptation of
Mt 4:1–11; Mt 4:1; Lk 4:2; Lk 4:3; Lk 4:7; Lk 4:9; Lk 4:13; Lk 22:43; "Jesus' Baptism and Temptation," 1468
transfiguration of
Mt 16:28; Mt 17:1–10; Mt 17:1; Mt 17:2; Lk 9:28; 1Pe 5:1; 2Pe 1:16,19–21
trial of
Mk 14:53—15:15
triumphal entry of
Zec 9:9; Mk 11:1–11; Lk 19:28–44; "The Life of Christ," 1508; "Passion Week," 1552
virgin birth and conception of
Isa 7:14; Mt 1:25; Lk 1:26–35; Lk 2:33; Lk 3:23–38; Lk 3:23
CHRISTIANS
characteristics of
Lk 18:17; Jn 15:11; Ac 2:46; Ac 4:13; Gal 5:22–23
demands of. See DISCIPLESHIP
the name
Ac 11:26
treatment of each other
Ne 5:9; Mk 9:50; Lk 6:37; Jn 13:14,34,35; Jn 16:2; Ac 11:1; Php 2:1–5; Jas 2:1
unity of. See UNITY, CHRISTIAN
and the world
Jn 15:21
CHRISTOPHANY
Jos 5:13
CHURCH
description of
Mt 16:18; Mt 18:17; Ac 5:11; Ac 9:31; 1Co 1:2; 2Co 1:1; Gal 1:13; Eph 2:22; Eph 3:10; 2Ti 2:19
discipline. See CHURCH DISCIPLINE
foundation of
Mt 16:18; Eph 2:20
growth of
Ac 4:4; Ac 5:14; Ac 6:1; Ac 6:7
opposition to
Ac 8:1; Ac 12:2; 1Co 15:9; Php 1:28
unity of
1Co 10:17; 1Co 12:12–13; Eph 4:1–16; Php 2:1–4
CHURCH DISCIPLINE
Mt 18:17; 1Co 5:2; 1Co 5:5; 1Co 5:9; 1Co 5:11; 1Co 5:12; 2Co 2:5–11; Gal 6:1; Th 3:14–15; 1Ti 1:20
CHURCH OF THE HOLY SEPULCHRE
Mk 15:46
CICERO
1Co 5:1
CILICIA
Eze 27:11; Ac 6:9; Ac 15:23; Ac 27:5; Gal 1:21
CILICIAN GATES
Ac 22:3
CINNAMON
Ex 25:6; SS 4:14
CIRCUMCISION
Ex 4:25; Eze 28:10
and the covenant
Ge 17:10; Ge 17:11; Isa 56:4; Isa 56:6; Col 2:11–12
and legalism
Ac 15:1; Ro 2:25; Ro 2:29; Gal 2:12; Gal 6:12
meaning of
Ge 17:10; Ge 17:11; Ge 17:12; Jn 7:22; Ro 2:25; Ro 4:11
and the passover
Jos 5:2
spiritual
Ro 2:29; Php 3:3
CITADEL
Ne 2:8
CITIES
five, of the Philistines
Jdg 3:3; Am 1:6; Am 1:8; "Five Cities of the Philistines," 331
of refuge
Nu 35:6–15; Nu 35:22; Nu 35:24; Nu 35:32; Jos 20:1–9; "Cities of Refuge," 239
CITRON WOOD
Rev 18:12
CITY
of David
2Sa 5:7; 1Ki 2:10; 1Ki 3:1; Ne 3:26
of destruction
Isa 19:18
CIVIL AUTHORITY
Ro 13:1; Ro 13:3; Ro 13:4; 1Ti 2:1–2; Tit 3:1–2; 1Pe 2:13—3:6; 1Pe 2:13,15–17
CLAUDIUS (Roman emperor)
Ac 11:28; Ac 23:34; Ac 28:17
CLAUDIUS (Lysias)
Ac 21:31
CLEAN/UNCLEAN
Lev 4:12; Lev 11:1—15:33; Lev 11:2,44; Nu 5:2–10; Nu 9:1–14; Mk 7:19–20; Ac 10:14,15; Introduction to Leviticus: Title
CLEMENT
Php 4:3; Introduction to 1 Corinthians: Author and Date
CLEOPAS
Lk 24:13
CLEOPATRA I
Da 11:17; "Ptolemies and Seleucids," 1330
CNIDUS
Ac 27:7
COLOSSE
1Co 16:19; Introduction to Colossians: Colosse

COMFORT
2Co 1:3; Php 2:1
COMMANDMENTS. *See* TEN COMMANDMENTS
CONCUBINE
Ge 25:1; Ge 25:6; Ge 30:4; Ge 30:5–12; Jdg 8:31; Ecc 2:8
CONFUSION OF LANGUAGES
Ge 11:9
CONIAH
Jer 22:24–30
CONVERSION
Ac 15:5; Ac 16:14; Ac 26:20; 1Th 1:9–10
COPPER
Dt 8:9
CORBAN
Lev 1:2; Mk 7:11; Mk 7:13
CORINTH
Ro 16:23; Introduction to 1 Corinthians: The City of Corinth; "Corinth in the Time of Paul," 1766
CORNELIUS
Ac 10:1; Ac 10:2; Ac 10:3; Ac 10:26; Ac 10:30; Ac 10:34; 1Co 1:16
CORNER GATE
2Ki 14:13; 2Ch 25:23; 2Ch 26:9; Zec 14:10
CORNERSTONE. *See* CHRIST: as cornerstone
CORPORATE SOLIDARITY
Jos 7:24; Ps 44:4
COUNCIL OF TRENT
"The Time Between the Testaments," 1451
COUNSELOR
Jn 14:16
COURT OF THE GENTILES
Mt 21:12; Mk 11:15; Mk 11:17; Lk 19:45; Ac 3:2
COVENANT
Ge 9:8–17; Ge 9:9; Ge 17:7; "Major Covenants in the Old Testament," 19; "Major Social Concerns in the Covenant," 268
Abrahamic
Ge 15:17; Ge 15:18; Ge 17:1–23
blessings and/or curses
Ex 1:7; Lev 26:14; Nu 1:46; Dt 5:2; 1Ki 2:4; 1Ki 8:33; 1Ki 9:4–5; 1Ki 14:15; 2Ki 2:24; 2Ki 17:7–23; Introduction to Numbers: Theological Teaching
Davidic
2Sa 7:1–29; 2Sa 7:11; 1Ki 8:53; 2Ki 11:1; 2Ki 16:5; Ps 89:30–37; Isa 42:6; Isa 54:10; Isa 55:3
demands of
Ge 22:2; Ge 26:5; Ex 24:6; Dt 30:12,14; 1Sa 12:14; 1Ki 17:13; Introduction to 1 Samuel: Contents and Theme
document
Ex 31:18; Dt 1:5; 1Sa 10:25; Introduction to Deuteronomy: Structure and Outline
everlasting
2Sa 23:5; Isa 24:5; Isa 55:3; Jer 31:36–37
God's faithfulness to
1Sa 12:7; 1Ki 2:4; Jer 33:17–26; Introduction to Judges: Theme and Theology; Introduction to Jeremiah: Themes and Message
Levitical
Nu 25:11
of love
Dt 7:9; Dt 7:12
messenger of
Mal 3:1
Mosaic/Sinaitic
Ex 19:5; Ex 20:2; Dt 5:2; 2Ki 11:17; 2Ki 17:17; 2Ki 17:35; Jer 31:32; Gal 3:20
new
Isa 42:6; Jer 31:31–34; Eze 34:25; Heb 8:8–12
Noahic
Ge 9:9
and oaths
Dt 4:31
of peace (new covenant)
Eze 34:25
of salt
Nu 18:19
sign of
Ge 9:12,13; Ge 17:10,11; Ex 20:10; Ex 31:16–17
types of (in ancient Near East)
"Major Types of Royal Covenants/Treaties in the Ancient Near East," 19
COVENANT-MAKING
practices and their significance
Ge 15:17–18; Ge 26:30; Ge 31:54; Ex 18:12; Ex 24:6,11; Dt 4:31; Dt 30:19; Jos 24:2; 1Sa 11:15
terminology
Ge 21:23; Ex 20:5–6; Lev 25:55; Lev 26:12; Dt 26:17; Dt 27:9; "Major Types of Royal Covenants/Treaties in the Ancient Near East," 19
COVET
Ex 20:17; Mt 19:21
CREATION
Ge 1:1—2:3; Ge 1:1–4; Ge 1:11; Ge 2:2; Ge 2:4; Ge 2:7; Ge 2:18–25; Ge 8:1–22; Ge 9:1–29; Ps 33:6; Ps 104:2,7,19–30; Ro 8:19; Ro 8:22; 2Co 4:6; Heb 4:3; introduction to Ps 104
CREMATION
1Sa 31:12; Am 6:10
CRETE
Ge 10:14; Ac 27:7; Tit 1:5; Introduction to Titus: Crete
CRISPUS
Ac 18:8
CROSS
Mt 10:38; Mk 8:34; Lk 4:7; Lk 9:23; Jn 12:32; Jn 12:41; Jn 19:17; Ac 5:30; 1Co 1:23; Gal 6:14; Introduction to Mark: Emphases
CROWNS
2Ti 4:8; Jas 1:12; Rev 2:10; Rev 4:10
CRUCIFIXION
Mt 20:19; Mk 15:24
CTESIAS
Ne 2:6
CUMMIN
Isa 28:25; Mt 23:23
CUNEIFORM
Da 1:4
CUP. *See also* ANGER, GOD'S
Ps 16:5; Isa 51:17; Jer 25:15; Eze 23:31; Mt 20:22; Mt 26:39; Mk 10:38; Mk 14:24; Mk 14:36; Jn 18:11; 1Co 11:25
CUPBEARER
Ne 1:11
CURSE
Ge 3:14; Ge 4:11; Ge 8:21; Ge 9:25; Ge 12:3; Lev 26:14; Dt 27:26; Dt 28:1–14; 1Sa 3:17; Jer 15:3; 1Co 16:22
CUSH (son of Ham)
Nu 12:1
CUSH (nation)
Ge 10:6–8; 2Ch 14:9; Isa 18:1
CUSHAN
Hab 3:7
CUSHAN-RISHATHAIM
Jdg 3:8
CUTHAH
2Ki 17:24
CYAXARES
Na 2:1
CYBELE
Ac 19:24
CYMBALS
Ne 12:27
CYPRUS
Isa 23:1; Eze 27:6; Ac 4:36; Ac 11:19; Ac 13:4
CYRENE
Mk 15:21; Ac 2:10; Ac 6:9
CYRUS
2Ch 36:22–23; Ezr 1:1; Ezr 1:3; Ezr 6:8; Isa 41:2; Isa 44:28; Isa 45:1,3–4,8; Da 1:21; Da 2:32–43; Da 5:31
CYRUS CYLINDER
Ezr 6:10; "Ancient Texts Relating to the Old Testament," xxii

DAGON
Jdg 10:6; 1Sa 5:2; 1Sa 5:3
DALMANUTHA
Mk 8:10
DALMATIA
2Ti 4:10
DAMARIS
Ac 17:34
DAMASCUS
2Ch 28:20; Isa 7:4; Isa 17:1; Eze

27:18; Eze 47:16; Am 1:3; Am 3:12; Ac 9:2; Gal 1:17; "Roman Damascus," 1695

DAN
Jdg 18:7; Jdg 20:1; 1Sa 3:20; 1Ki 12:29; Eze 48:1

DAN (tribe)
Rev 7:6

DANIEL
2Ki 24:1; Ezr 7:11; Est 1:2; Est 2:9; Est 2:19; Eze 14:14,20; Da 1:2; Da 1:6; Da 1:8; Da 1:9; Da 1:17; Rev 13:1; Rev 13:2; Introduction to Daniel: Author, Date and Authenticity

DARIC
1Ch 29:7; Ezr 2:69

DARIUS I
1Ch 29:7; Ezr 4:6; Ezr 4:24; Ezr 5:6–7; Ezr 6:8; Ezr 6:9; Ezr 6:11; Ezr 6:12; Ezr 6:22; Ezr 9:9; Ne 11:23; Est 1:1; Est 1:5–6; Da 11:2; Hag 1:1; Zec 1:1

DARIUS II
Ezr 6:9; Ezr 7:16; Ne 12:22; Est 2:5

DARIUS III
Ne 12:22

DARIUS (the Mede)
Da 5:31

DARKNESS
Ge 1:3; Ps 107:10; Ps 112:4; Isa 45:7; Isa 59:9; Isa 60:2; Joel 2:2; Am 5:18; Lk 1:79; Lk 22:53; Jn 1:5; Jn 8:12; 2Co 4:6; Eph 5:8; Col 1:12–13; 1Jn 1:5–7

DAUGHTER OF ZION/JERUSALEM
2Ki 19:21; Isa 1:8

DAUGHTERS OF JERUSALEM/ZION
SS 1:5; SS 3:11

DAVID
"David's Family Tree," 402; "David the Fugitive," 409; "Exploits of David," 418; "The City of the Jebusites/David's Jerusalem," 432; "David's Conquests," 444

anointing of
1Sa 16:13; 1Sa 16:14; 2Sa 2:4

and Bathsheba
2Sa 11:4; 2Sa 11:6; 2Sa 11:8; 2Sa 11:15; 2Sa 11:27

brings ark to Jerusalem
2Sa 6:12

and Christ
Mt 1:1; Mt 1:16; Mt 2:1; Lk 1:32; Lk 2:4; Lk 2:5; Lk 2:11

confession of
2Sa 12:13; Ps 51:3–6; introduction to Ps 51

death of
2Sa 23:1; 1Ki 1:1; 1Ki 2:10

and death of Absalom
2Sa 19:5

defeats the Philistines
2Sa 5:17

faith of
1Sa 17:32; 1Sa 17:45

as a father See FATHER: David as

and Goliath
1Sa 17:32; 1Sa 17:45; 1Sa 17:46; 1Sa 17:54

and Jonathan
1Sa 18:3; 1Sa 18:4; 1Sa 19:4; 2Sa 1:23; 2Sa 1:26; 2Sa 9:1

judgment on
2Sa 12:10; 2Sa 12:11; 2Sa 13:28

as king over Israel
2Sa 5:1

and Nathan
2Sa 7:3; 1Ki 2:4

palace of
2Sa 5:11; 2Sa 5:12; 2Sa 7:2

prayers of
2Sa 7:18–29; Ps 6:1–10; Ps 72:20

royal line of
2Sa 7:12

and Saul
1Sa 16:14—17:58; 1Sa 16:16; 1Sa 16:19; 1Sa 17:15; 1Sa 17:37; 1Sa 17:55; 1Sa 18:1; 1Sa 18:7; 1Sa 18:13; 1Sa 19:1

as shepherd
1Sa 9:3; 2Sa 7:7

and Solomon
1Ki 3:7; 1Ch 17:1; 1Ch 17:10; Introduction to 1 Chronicles: Portrait of David and Solomon

DAY OF ATONEMENT
Lev 4:5; Lev 16:1–34; Lev 23:27; Nu 29:7–11; 2Ch 7:9; Ezr 6:15; Ne 9:1; Isa 6:6; Joel 1:14; Lk 18:12; Ac 27:9; Gal 4:10; Heb 4:14; Heb 9:4; Heb 9:5; Heb 9:7; Heb 13:10; "Old Testament Feasts and Other Sacred Days," 178

DAY OF JUDGMENT
Jas 2:13; Jas 5:5; 1Pe 4:5; 1Pe 4:6

DAY OF THE LORD
Isa 2:11,17,20; Isa 10:20,27; Eze 7:7; Joel 1:15; Joel 2:2; Joel 2:11; Joel 2:30–31; Am 5:18; Am 8:9; Mal 3:2; Mal 4:1; 1Th 5:2; 2Pe 3:12; Rev 9:3; Introduction to Joel: Theological Message; Introduction to Zephaniah: Purpose and Theological Theme

DEACON
Ne 13:13; Ac 6:6; 1Co 12:5; Php 1:1; 1Ti 3:8; 1Ti 3:11; "Qualifications for Elders/Overseers and Deacons," 1874

DEAD, RAISING OF
1Ki 17:22; Lk 7:14; Ac 9:40

DEAD SEA
Ge 14:3; Ge 14:10; Eze 47:8; Mk 1:4; Lk 3:20

DEAD SEA SCROLLS
Ge 12:11; Ex 7:11; Dt 32:43; Jos 6:5; 1Sa 1:23; Ezr 8:15; Jer 6:23; Da 2:18; Joel 2:23; Lk 9:35; Jn 3:25; Jn 5:2; Heb 1:4; "The Time Between the Testaments," 1451; "Ancient Texts Relating to the Old Testament," xxii

DEATH
Ge 2:17; Ge 3:19,22; Ge 5:5; Ps 6:5; Hos 13:14; Jn 11:11; Ro 5:12–21; 1Co 15:56–57; Php 1:23–24; Php 1:23; 1Th 4:13; Heb 2:14

DEATH, CHRIST'S
Jn 2:4; 1Co 15:44–49; 2Co 4:10; 2Ti 2:11; 1Pe 3:19–21

as atonement
Lev 6:2,5; Jos 2:18; Ro 3:25; 2Co 5:14; 2Co 8:9; Col 1:24; Heb 13:10; 1Pe 2:24; 1Pe 3:18; 1Jn 2:2; Introduction to Hebrews: Theme

baptism as symbol of
Ro 6:3–4; 1Pe 3:21

meaning of
2Co 5:14; 2Co 5:21; Col 1:20; 1Pe 1:18–19; 1Pe 3:21; 1Jn 5:6

as mystery
Ro 11:25

predictions of
Isa 52:13—53:12; Zec 13:7

substitutionary character of
Mk 10:45; Ro 3:24; Ro 5:6–7,9; Eph 2:13; Col 1:2; Col 1:14; 1Pe 1:18; 1Pe 1:19; 1Pe 2:24; Rev 5:9

DEATH PENALTY
Ge 9:6; Lev 20:1–27; Jos 1:18; 2Sa 4:11; 2Sa 11:5; 2Sa 12:13; Ro 13:4

DEBIR
Jos 10:38

DEBORAH
Jdg 4:1—5:31; Lk 2:36

DECAPOLIS
Mt 4:25; Mk 8:1; "The Decapolis and the Lands Beyond the Jordan," 1530; "The Territories of Tyre and Sidon," 1537

DEDICATION, FEAST OF
Jn 10:22; "Old Testament Feasts and Other Sacred Days," 178

DEITY OF CHRIST. *See* CHRIST: deity of

DEMAS
Col 4:9–17; Col 4:14

DEMETRIUS
Ac 19:24

DEMETRIUS I
Da 11:21

DEMON POSSESSION
Mk 1:23; Lk 4:33; Jn 7:20

DEMONS
Lk 4:33; Rev 9:20

DENARIUS
Mt 20:2; Mt 22:19; Mt 26:15

DEPOSIT/DOWN PAYMENT
Ro 8:23; 2Co 1:22

DEPRAVITY, TOTAL
Ge 6:5; Ge 8:21

DERBE
Ac 14:6; Ac 14:20

DESERT
of Edom
2Ki 3:8

of Paran
Ge 21:21; Nu 12:16; 1Ki 11:18
of Shur
Ex 15:22
of Sin
Ex 16:1
of Sinai
Ex 19:2; Nu 1:1
of Zin
Nu 13:21
DEVIL. *See* SATAN
DIADOCHI
"Ptolemies and Seleucids," 1330
DIANA
Ac 19:24
DIASPORA
Ne 1:8; "The Time Between the Testaments," 1451
DIBON
Isa 15:2; Isa 15:9
DIDYMUS
Jn 11:16
DIMON
Isa 15:9
DIONYSIUS
Ac 17:34
DIOTREPHES
3Jn 9; Introduction to 3 John: Occasion and Purpose
DISCIPLESHIP
Mt 8:22; Mt 10:38; Mt 11:12; Mk 1:17; Mk 8:34 – 35; Mk 9:39; Mk 9:50; Mk 10:30; Mk 10:43; Lk 9:23; Lk 14:28; Lk 14:33
DISCIPLINE
of believers
Job 5:17 – 26; Pr 3:11 – 12; Hos 5:2; 1Co 11:32; Heb 12:5; Heb 12:7; Heb 12:11
of children
2Sa 13:21; 1Ki 1:6; Pr 13:24
church
Mt 18:17 – 20; 1Co 5:1 – 12; 2Co 2:5 – 11; Gal 6:1; 2Th 3:14 – 15; 1Ti 1:20
self
1Co 9:27; Tit 1:8
DIVINATION
Ge 30:27; Nu 22:40; Dt 18:9; 1Sa 15:23
DIVINE ELECTION. *See* ELECTION, DIVINE
DIVORCE
Dt 22:19; Dt 24:1 – 4; Ezr 10:3; Isa 50:1; Jer 3:1; Hos 2:2; Mal 2:10 – 16; Mt 1:18; Mt 1:19; Mt 19:3; Mk 10:2; Mk 10:5; Mk 10:9; Mk 10:11; Lk 16:18; Jn 4:18; 1Co 7:11 – 12; 1Co 7:15
DOME OF THE ROCK
Ge 22:2
DOMITIAN
Rev 13:1; Introduction to Revelation: Date
DOTHAN
Ge 37:17; 2Ki 6:13
DOUBT
Ge 3:1; Lk 7:19; Lk 7:23; Jn 20:25; Ro 14:1; 1Co 10:28
DOVE
Ge 8:11; Ps 68:13; Ps 74:19; Mk 1:10; Introduction to Jonah: Title
DOXOLOGY
Ro 11:33 – 36; Eph 1:3 – 14; Php 4:20; Jude 24 – 25; Introduction to Psalms: Collection, Arrangement and Date
DRACHMA
Ezr 2:69; Lk 15:8
DRAGON, THE
Rev 12:3; Rev 12:9; Rev 20:2
DREAM
Ge 20:3; Ge 40:5; Jdg 7:13 – 14; 1Ki 3:5; Job 4:12 – 21; Da 1:17; Mt 1:20
DRINK OFFERING
Isa 57:6; Joel 1:9; Php 2:17; 2Ti 4:6
DROPSY
Lk 14:2
DRUNKENNESS
Ge 9:21; Ge 19:33; 1Sa 1:13; Pr 20:1; Pr 23:20; Pr 23:29 – 35; Isa 5:11 – 13; Eze 23:42; Joel 1:5; Hab 2:15; Eph 5:18
DRUSILLA
Ac 23:34; Ac 24:24
DUNG GATE
Ne 2:13
DURA
Da 3:1
DUST
Ge 3:14,19; Ge 13:16; Ne 9:1; Job 2:8; Job 30:19; Job 42:6; Jnh 3:5 – 6

E

EARTHQUAKE
Eze 38:19; Am 1:1; Zec 14:15; Rev 6:12
EAST GATE
1Ch 26:14; Ne 3:29
EBED
Ezr 8:6
EBENEZER
1Sa 4:1
EBER
Ge 10:21
EBIASAPH
1Ch 6:22 – 23; 1Ch 26:1
EBLA TABLETS
Introduction to Genesis: Background; "Ancient Texts Relating to the Old Testament," xxii
ECBATANA
Ezr 6:2; Est 1:2
ECCLESIASTICUS
"The Book of the Twelve, or the Minor Prophets," 1333
EDEN
Ge 2:8; 2Ki 19:12; Joel 2:3; Isa 37:12; Eze 27:23; Eze 28:13; Rev 21:2 — 22:5
EDOMITES
Ge 25:26; 2Ki 3:8; 1Ch 1:43 – 54; 2Ch 21:8 – 10; Job 1:1; Job 2:11; Job 4:1; Isa 21:11; Isa 34:5; Isa 34:8; Isa 63:1; La 4:21; Am 1:11; Am 9:12; Ob 1:1; Ob 1:8 – 19; Mal 1:4; Mal 1:5
EFFECTUAL CALLING
Ro 8:28
EGLON
Jdg 3:12 – 30
EGNATIAN WAY
Ac 17:1; Ac 17:6; Ac 27:6
EGYPT
Isa 19:4; Isa 19:7; Isa 19:22; Isa 19:25; Isa 36:6; Isa 37:36; Eze 29:1; Mt 2:15; Ac 2:10; Ac 27:5; Ac 27:6; Introduction to Genesis: Background
EGYPTIAN HALLEL
Ps 113 – 118; Mt 26:30
EHUD
Jdg 3:12 – 30
EKRON
1Sa 5:10; 2Ki 1:2; Am 1:8; Zec 9:5; "Five Cities of the Philistines," 331
EL OLAM. *See* NAMES OF GOD: Eternal God (*El Olam*)
EL SHADDAI. *See* NAMES OF GOD: God Almighty (*El Shaddai*)
ELAH
1Ki 16:9; 2Ch 16:1; Hos 7:5
ELAM
Ezr 4:9; Isa 11:11; Eze 32:24
ELAMITES
Ezr 4:10; Isa 21:2
EL-BERITH
Jdg 8:33
ELDERS
church officers
Ac 11:30; Ac 20:17; Ac 20:28; 1Ti 3:1; 1Ti 3:8; 1Ti 5:17; 1Ti 5:20; 1Ti 5:22; Tit 1:5; Tit 1:6 – 9; Tit 1:6; Tit 1:7; 1Pe 2:25; 1Pe 5:1; 1Pe 5:2; 1Pe 5:5; 2Jn 1:1 – 13; "Qualifications for Elders/Overseers and Deacons," 1874
in Israel
Ex 3:16; 2Sa 3:17; Job 29:7; Jer 19:1; Eze 14:1; Joel 1:2; Mt 15:2; Ac 24:1
qualifications for
"Qualifications for Elders/Overseers and Deacons," 1874
tradition of
Mt 15:2
ELEAZAR (high priest)
Lk 3:2; Ac 4:6
ELEAZAR (son of Aaron)
Nu 20:25; Jos 14:1; 1Ch 6:1 – 3; 1Ch 6:4 – 15; Ezr 7:5
ELECT, THE
Ro 11:7; 2Ti 2:10; 1Pe 1:2; 1Pe 2:9
ELECTION, DIVINE
Ge 25:23; Ro 8:29; Ro 8:34; Ro 9:6; Ro 9:11; Ro 9:13; Eph 1:4; Eph 1:6; Col 3:12; 2Th 2:13; 1Ti 2:4; 1Ti 4:10; Introduction to 1 Chronicles: Purpose and Themes, 2

ELEPHANTINE PAPYRI
Ezr 6:3 – 5; Ezr 6:8; Ezr 6:9; Ezr 6:10; Ezr 7:16; Ezr 9:1; Ezr 9:9; Ne 1:2; Ne 2:10; Ne 12:11; "Ancient Texts Relating to the Old Testament," xxii
ELI
1Sa 1:13; 1Sa 2:23; 1Sa 2:25; 1Sa 3:5; 1Sa 3:18; 1Sa 4:18
ELIAB (brother of David)
1Sa 16:6; 1Sa 17:28; 1Ch 27:18
ELIAKIM (Jehoiakim)
2Ki 23:34; 2Ch 36:4
ELIAKIM (son of Hilkiah)
Isa 22:20 – 21
ELIAM
2Sa 11:3; 2Sa 23:34
ELIASAPH
Nu 3:24
ELIASHIB
Ne 3:1; Ne 12:10; Ne 13:5
ELIEHOENAI
Ezr 8:4
ELIEZER
Ex 4:20
ELIHU (brother of David)
1Ch 27:18
ELIHU (friend of Job)
Job 13:27; Job 32:1 — 37:24; Job 32:2 – 3; Job 32:14; Job 33:8; Job 33:11; Job 33:12; Job 33:19; Job 33:30; Job 38:1
ELIJAH
"Lives of Elijah and Elisha," 518
and the drought
1Ki 18:1; 1Ki 18:17
and Elisha
2Ki 2:2; 2Ki 2:3; 2Ki 2:9; 2Ki 2:10; 2Ki 2:11; 2Ki 2:12; 2Ki 2:13; 2Ki 2:14; 2Ki 2:15
and God's Spirit
1Ki 18:12
and Jezebel
1Ki 17:6,9; 1Ki 19:1,3
and John the Baptist
Mal 4:5; Mk 9:12; Jn 1:21
meaning of name
1Ki 17:1
and Moses
1Ki 17:1; 2Ki 1:10; 2Ki 2:8; 2Ki 2:11; Mt 17:3; Lk 9:30; Rev 11:6
and the prophets of Baal
1Ki 18:21; 1Ki 18:24; 1Ki 18:27; 1Ki 18:31; 1Ki 18:33; 1Ki 18:40; 1Ki 18:41; 1Ki 18:42
sustained by God
1Ki 17:4; 1Ki 17:12; 1Ki 17:13; 1Ki 17:14; 1Ki 17:15; 1Ki 19:4; 1Ki 19:7; 1Ki 19:10
and the transfiguration
Mt 17:3; Mt 17:10; Lk 9:30
and the widow of Zarephath
1Ki 17:9; 1Ki 17:10; 1Ki 17:12; 1Ki 17:13; 1Ki 17:14; 1Ki 17:15; 1Ki 17:18; 1Ki 17:21 – 22,24
ELIMELECH
Ru 1:2; Ru 4:3; Ru 4:6
ELIPHAZ (friend of Job)
Job 4:2; Job 4:6 – 7; Job 5:2; Job 5:17 – 26; Job 5:27; Job 6:4; Job 8:8; Job 15:7 – 10; Job 15:11 – 13; Job 15:20 – 35; Job 22:2 – 4; Job 22:5 – 11; Job 22:12 – 20; Job 22:21 – 30; Job 25:4 – 6; Job 34:7; Job 42:7 – 9
ELIPHAZ (son of Esau)
1Ch 1:36
ELIPHELET
1Ch 3:1 – 9
ELISHA
"Lives of Elijah and Elisha," 518
birth of
2Ki 13:14
and cursing young men
2Ki 2:23; 2Ki 2:24
and Elijah
1Ki 19:19; 1Ki 19:21; 2Ki 2:2; 2Ki 2:10; 2Ki 2:12; 2Ki 2:14
and judgment on Israel
2Ki 8:12
meaning of name
1Ki 19:16
and Naaman
2Ki 5:16; 2Ki 5:19; 2Ki 5:22
and servant
2Ki 4:12,30; 2Ki 5:22,26 – 27; 2Ki 6:16; 2Ki 6:17; 2Ki 6:18
and Shunammite woman
2Ki 4:9; 2Ki 4:10; 2Ki 4:16; 2Ki 4:17; 2Ki 4:23; 2Ki 4:29; 2Ki 4:33; 2Ki 4:37
ELISHAH
Ge 10:4; Eze 27:7
ELISHAMA (father of Nethaniah)
2Ki 25:23
ELISHAMA (son of Jekamiah)
1Ch 2:34 – 41
ELISHAPHAT
2Ch 23:1
ELIZABETH
Mt 3:1; Lk 1:36; Lk 1:67
ELIZAPHAN
Nu 3:30; 1Ch 15:4 – 10; 2Ch 29:13
ELKANAH
1Sa 1:1; 1Sa 1:21; 1Ch 6:22 – 23
ELKOSH
Introduction to Nahum: Author
ELNATHAN
2Ki 22:12; Jer 26:22
ELOHIM. *See* NAMES OF GOD (*Elohim*)
ELON
Jdg 12:11
ELYMAS
Ac 13:8
EMBALMING
Ge 50:2
EN EGLAIM
Eze 47:10
EN GEDI
SS 1:14; Eze 47:10; Eze 47:18
EN RIMMON
Ne 11:29; Zec 14:10
EN ROGEL
2Sa 17:17; 1Ki 1:9; Ne 2:13
ENDOR
1Sa 28:7
ENOCH
Ge 5:24; Heb 11:6; Jude 1:14
ENUMA ELISH
Introduction to Genesis: Background; "Ancient Texts Relating to the Old Testament," xxii
EPAPHRAS
Col 1:7; Col 4:9 – 17
EPAPHRODITUS
Php 2:25 – 30; Php 4:16
EPHAH (measure)
Ru 2:17; Mic 6:10; "Table of Weights and Measures," 1995
EPHAH (son of Midian)
Isa 60:6
EPHESUS
Ac 18:19; Ac 19:19; Ac 19:38; 1Co 4:11 – 13; 1Co 15:32; 1Co 16:5; 1Co 16:19; Eph 1:1; 1Ti 1:3; 1Ti 5:9; Tit 3:9; Rev 1:4; Rev 1:9; Rev 2:1 – 7; Rev 9:21; Introduction to Ephesians: The City of Ephesus; "Ephesus in the Time of Paul," 1823
EPHOD
Ex 28:6; Jdg 8:27; 1Sa 2:18; 1Sa 2:28
EPHRAIM (son of Joseph)
Ge 48:5; Ge 48:6; Ge 48:7; Jos 14:4
EPHRAIM (territory)
Ge 48:19; Jos 14:4; Isa 7:2; Isa 7:8; Isa 7:17; Isa 17:3; Hos 9:11; Hos 12:8; Hos 13:1
EPHRAIM GATE
2Ki 14:13; 2Ch 25:23; Ne 8:16
EPHRATH
1Sa 16:1
EPHRATHAH
Ru 1:2; Mic 5:2
EPHRON
Ge 23:9; Ge 23:15; Ge 23:17
EPICUREAN PHILOSOPHY
Ac 17:18; Ac 17:26
ER
1Ch 2:3 – 9
ERASTUS
Ac 19:22; Ro 16:23; 1Co 16:10; 1Co 16:11
ERECH
Ge 10:10; Ezr 6:8
ESARHADDON
2Ki 19:28; 2Ch 33:11; Ne 9:32; Isa 7:8; Isa 19:4; Isa 23:12
ESAU
Ge 25:34; Ge 26:34; Ge 36:1; Am 1:11; Ob 1:18; Ob 1:21; Mal 1:3; Ro 9:13; Ro 9:14; Heb 12:16
ESDRAS
Ezr 7:1; Introduction to Ezra: Ezra and Nehemiah
ESH-BAAL. *See* ISH-BOSHETH
ESSENES
"The Time Between the Testaments," 1451; "Jewish Sects," 1502

ESTHER
Est 1:9; Est 2:1; Est 2:7; Est 2:9; Est 2:10; Est 2:16
ETERNAL LIFE
Ge 2:9; Ge 3:22; Ge 3:24; Mt 19:16; Mt 19:17; Jn 3:15; Jn 3:36; Jn 6:27; Jn 6:28; Ac 13:48; Ro 2:6–7; Ro 6:22; Gal 6:8; 1Ti 6:12; 1Jn 1:2; 1Jn 5:20
ETHAN (musician)
1Ch 2:6; 1Ch 6:31–48; Ps 39 title
ETHANIM
2Ch 5:3; "Hebrew Calendar and Selected Events," 104
ETHBAAL
1Ki 16:25; 1Ki 16:31; 1Ki 17:9
ETHIOPIA
Am 8:8; Ac 8:27
EUCHARIST
Mk 14:23
EUNICE
2Ti 1:5
EUNUCH
Isa 56:3; Mt 19:12
EUODIA
Php 4:2–3
EUPHRATES RIVER
Ge 2:14; Ge 15:18; 2Sa 8:3; Ezr 4:10
EUROQUILO
Ac 27:14
EUTYCHUS
Ac 20:9; Ac 20:10
EVANGELISTS
Eph 4:11
EVE
Ge 2:4; Ge 2:9; Ge 3:20; Col 1:20; 1Ti 2:13–14
EVERLASTING LIFE. *See* ETERNAL LIFE
EVIL ONE
Mt 6:13; 1Jn 3:8
EVIL SPIRITS
1Sa 16:14; Lk 4:33; Lk 9:39
EVIL-MERODACH
2Ki 25:27; Da 5:26–28
EXCOMMUNICATION
Mt 18:17; Jn 9:22; 1Co 5:2; 1Co 5:5
EXECUTION, FORMS OF
Est 2:23
EXILE
Isa 27:8; Da 1:2; "Exile of the Northern Kingdom," 558; "Exile of the Southern Kingdom," 576; "Return from Exile," 672
EXODUS, THE
Isa 55:13; Ro 9:17; Gal 3:19; Heb 3:7–11; Introduction to Genesis: Author and Date of Writing; Introduction to Exodus: Title; Introduction to Exodus: Author and Date of Writing; "The Exodus," 108; Introduction to Judges: Background
EXPANSE
Ge 1:6
EZEKIEL
Introduction to Ezekiel: Author
denounces Edom
Ob 1:15
and the exile
Da 1:2
prophecy of
2Ki 25:7
temple of
2Ch 4:2; Ne 8:16; Eze 40:48—42:20; "Ezekiel's Temple," 1297
visions of
Ne 8:16; Rev 4:7
EZION GEBER
1Ki 9:26
EZRA
1Ch 6:8; Ezr 7:6; Ezr 7:7–9; Ne 2:9; Ne 8:1; Ne 12:31; Mal 2:11; Jn 9:22; Introduction to Ezra: Ezra and Nehemiah; "Chronology: Ezra-Nehemiah," 675

FACTIONS
1Co 3:17; 1Co 11:19; Jude 19
FAITH
Da 3:18; Da 3:28; Hab 2:4; Hab 3:18–19; Mk 9:24; Mk 13:32; Lk 17:5; Lk 17:19; Lk 18:8; Jn 7:17; Heb 6:1–2; Heb 11:6; Heb 11:32–38; Heb 11:40; Introduction to Ecclesiastes: Purpose and Teaching; introduction to Ps 27
Abraham's
Ge 12:4; Ge 15:6; Ge 17:1; Ge 17:11; Ge 22:2; Ge 22:5; Ge 22:12; Ro 4:19; Heb 11:8; Heb 11:19
Daniel's
Da 6:23
dead
Jas 2:14–26
defense of
1Pe 3:15; Jude 3
God's response to
Ge 15:6
and healing
Jn 5:9; Jas 5:14
Noah's
Heb 11:7
saving
Jn 1:7; Jn 14:11; Ro 3:24; Ro 3:28; Ro 4:22; Ro 6:3–4; Ro 8:24; Gal 5:6; Eph 2:8–9; Jas 2:14–26; Jas 2:21
strong
Lk 7:9; Lk 17:5; 1Co 12:9; 1Co 13:2
FAITHFULNESS
Ps 4:3; Ro 3:3; 1Co 1:9; 2Ti 2:2; 1Jn 1:9
FALSE WITNESS
Pr 6:19
FAMILY. *See also* CHILDREN; FATHER; MOTHER; PARENTS
Ge 6:18; Ex 20:5; Ezr 1:5; Ps 109:12; Lk 8:21; Eph 3:15; 1Jn 5:1
FAMILY GUARDIAN
Ru 2:20
FAMINE
Ge 12:10; Ge 41:27; Ge 47:13; Ru 1:1; 1Ki 17:1; 1Ki 18:18; Ne 5:3; Hag 1:6
FASTING
Lev 16:29,31; Ne 1:4; Est 4:16; Est 9:31; Joel 1:14; Zec 8:19; Mt 6:1; Mk 2:18; Lk 5:33; Lk 18:12; Ac 13:3; Ac 27:9; Jas 1:26
FAT OF RAMS
1Sa 15:22
FAT OF SACRIFICES
Ex 29:13; Lev 3:16; Isa 34:6
FATHER. *See also* CHILDREN; FAMILY; PARENTS
Jdg 14:2; Jdg 17:10; Pr 27:11; Eph 6:4; 1Jn 5:1
David as a
2Sa 13:21; 2Sa 18:33; 1Ki 1:6
Eli as a
1Sa 4:18
FAVORITISM
Ge 27:6; 1Ti 5:21; Jas 2:1; Jas 2:5–13
FEAR
1Sa 17:11; 2Sa 6:9
FEAR OF GOD. *See* GOD: fear (reverence) of
FEAST
of Booths. See of Tabernacles (Booths or Ingathering)
Day of Atonement. See DAY OF ATONEMENT
"OT Feasts and Other Sacred Days," 178
of Dedication (Hanukkah)
Jn 10:22
of Firstfruits
Ex 23:19; 1Co 16:8; Jas 1:18
of Harvest. See of Weeks (Pentecost or Harvest)
Ac 2:1
of Ingathering. See of Tabernacles (Booths or Ingathering)
of Passover
Ex 1:14; Ex 12:11; Ex 12:26; Ex 12:48; Nu 9:1–14; Jos 5:10; 2Ki 23:21; 2Ki 23:22; 2Ch 30:2; 2Ch 30:5; 2Ch 30:8; 2Ch 35:1; Est 3:7; Mt 26:17; Mk 14:1; Mk 14:2; Mk 14:5; Mk 14:12; Mk 14:14; Lk 2:41; Lk 21:37; Lk 22:1; Lk 22:7; Lk 22:13; Lk 22:16; Lk 23:7; Jn 1:29; Jn 2:13; Jn 5:1; Jn 7:1; Jn 12:12; Jn 13:2; Jn 19:14; Jn 19:31; Ac 20:6; 1Co 5:6; 1Co 5:7; 1Co 5:8; 1Co 10:16; 1Co 11:25; 1Co 16:8
of Pentecost. See of Weeks (Pentecost or Harvest)
Purim. See PURIM
of Tabernacles (Booths or Ingathering)
Ex 23:16; Lev 23:34; Lev 23:42;

Jdg 21:19; 1Sa 1:3; 1Ki 8:2; 1Ki 8:65; 1Ki 9:25; 1Ki 12:32; 2Ch 5:3; 2Ch 7:9; 2Ch 31:7; Ne 8:15; Ne 8:16; Ne 8:17; Ps 47:1 – 9; Ps 81:3; Eze 45:25; Zec 14:16; Jn 7:2; Ac 27:9; introduction to Ps 47
of Trumpets
Nu 29:1 – 6; Ne 8:2
of Unleavened Bread
Ex 12:17; Ex 23:15; Lev 23:6; 1Ki 9:25; Ezr 6:9; Mt 26:17; Mk 14:1; Mk 14:2; Mk 14:12; Ac 20:6; 1Co 5:8
of Weeks (Pentecost or Harvest)
Ex 23:16; Lev 23:16; Nu 28:26 – 31; 1Ki 9:25; 2Ch 15:10; 2Ch 31:7; Lk 2:41; Ac 2:1; "Old Testament Feasts and Other Sacred Days," 178
FELIX, ANTONIUS
Ac 23:34; Ac 24:2 – 3; Ac 24:22; Ac 24:24; Ac 24:25; Ac 24:26; Ac 24:27
FELLOWSHIP
Mk 10:30; Ac 2:42; Php 2:1; 1Jn 1:3; 1Jn 1:6
FELLOWSHIP OFFERING
Lev 3:1; Lev 3:5; Pr 7:14; Eze 43:27; "Old Testament Sacrifices," 153
FESTUS
Ac 24:27; Ac 25:1; Ac 25:9; Ac 25:26; Ac 26:1; Ac 26:3; Ac 26:8
FIELD OF BLOOD
Mt 27:8
FINGER OF GOD
Ex 8:19; Ex 31:18
FIRE AS JUDGMENT
La 1:13
FIRST GATE
Zec 14:10
FIRSTBORN
Ge 4:3 – 4; Ex 4:22; Ex 11:5; Ex 13:2; Dt 21:17; Col 1:15; Col 1:18; Heb 12:23
FIRSTFRUITS. *See also* FEAST: of Firstfruits
Nu 15:20; Dt 26:2; Ne 10:35; Pr 3:9; Jer 2:3; Ac 2:1; Ro 8:23; Ro 11:16; 1Co 15:20; 1Co 15:23; Jas 1:18; Rev 14:4
FISH GATE
Ne 3:3
FIVE PHILISTINE CITIES
Jdg 3:3; Am 1:6; Am 1:8
FLESH
Eze 36:26; Gal 3:3; Php 3:3
FLOGGING
Mk 15:15
FLOOD, THE
Ge 6:17; 2Pe 3:6
FOOL
Ps 14:1; Pr 1:7; Ecc 5:4; Ecc 10:15
FOREKNOWLEDGE
Ro 8:29; 1Pe 2:8
FORGIVENESS
Pr 16:6; Mt 18:35; Mk 2:5; Mk 2:7; Lk 3:3; Lk 11:4; Lk 17:4; Lk 24:47; Jn 20:23; Ac 2:38; Ac 3:19; Ac 13:39; Ac 19:4; Ro 11:27; Eph 4:32; Eph 5:1; Php 2:1; Heb 8:5; Heb 8:8 – 12; Heb 12:24; 1Pe 1:18; 1Jn 1:9; introduction to Ps 32
FORMER PROPHETS
Introduction to Joshua: Title and Theological Theme
FORNICATION. *See* ADULTERY
FORTRESS OF ANTONIA
Ac 21:31; Ac 21:37
FORTY
Ge 7:4
FORUM OF APPIUS
Ac 28:15
FOUNTAIN GATE
Ne 2:14
FRANKINCENSE
Ex 30:34
FREE WILL
Jn 12:39; 1Ti 2:4
FREEDOM
1Co 7:21; Gal 2:4; Gal 5:1; Gal 5:13; Jas 1:25; 1Pe 2:16
FUTURIST
Introduction to Revelation: Interpretation

G

GABRIEL
Lk 1:19; 1Th 4:16
GAD (David's seer)
1Sa 22:5
GAD (Jacob's seventh son and tribe of)
Ex 1:2 – 4; Jos 13:24; 1Ch 5:11 – 22; Eze 48:27
GADARA
Mt 8:28
GADATES INSCRIPTION
Ezr 7:24
GAIUS (of Derbe)
Ac 20:4
GAIUS (friend of John)
3Jn 1
GAIUS (of Macedonia)
Ac 14:6
GAIUS (Titius Justus)
Ro 16:23
GALATIA
Ac 16:6; Ac 18:23; 2Ti 4:10
GALBANUM
Ex 25:6
GALEED
Ge 31:51
GALILEE
Isa 9:1; Mt 2:22; Mk 2:14; Mk 5:43; Mk 7:24; Lk 4:23; Lk 19:37; Lk 22:59; Jn 4:45; Jn 7:52
GALILEE, SEA OF
Mk 1:16; Mk 4:37; Lk 5:1; Jn 6:1
GALL
Ps 69:21; Pr 5:4; Mt 27:34
GALLIO
Ac 18:12
GAMALIEL
Ac 5:34; Ac 9:1; Ac 22:3
GAMMAD
Eze 27:11
GATE
Benjamin
Ne 3:1; Zec 14:10
city
Ge 19:1 – 2; Ge 22:17; Ge 23:10; Ru 4:1; Pr 1:21
of Ephraim
Ne 3:6
of the guard
Ne 12:31
GATH
1Sa 21:10; 2Sa 1:20; 1Ki 2:39; 1Ch 7:20 – 29; Am 1:8; Mic 1:10; "Five Cities of the Philistines," 331
GATH HEPHER
2Ki 14:25; Jnh 1:2
GATH RIMMON
2Sa 6:10
GAUMATA
Da 11:2
GAZA
Jos 10:41; Jdg 1:18; Jdg 16:1; Jdg 16:21; 1Ki 4:24; Isa 20:1; Am 1:6; Ac 8:26; Ac 8:36; Ac 8:40; "Five Cities of the Philistines," 331
GAZELLE
SS 2:9; SS 2:16; SS 6:2
GEBA
1Sa 13:3; 1Ki 15:22; 2Ki 23:8; Zec 14:10
GEBALITES
Jos 13:5; Eze 27:9
GEDALIAH
2Ki 22:12; 2Ki 25:22; 2Ki 25:24; 2Ki 25:25; Jer 26:24; Zec 8:19
GEHAZI
2Ki 4:12; 2Ki 4:30; 2Ki 5:22; 2Ki 5:26
GEHENNA
Isa 66:24; Mt 5:22; Lk 12:5
GELILOTH
Jos 22:10
GEMARIAH
Jer 36:10
GENEALOGIES
Ge 4:17 – 18; Ge 5:5; Ge 11:10 – 26; Ru 4:18 – 22; 1Ch 1:5 – 23; Introduction to 1 Chronicles: Genealogies
GENERAL LETTERS
1914
GENERATION
Ge 15:16
GENEROSITY. *See also* GIVING
Pr 11:24; Pr 14:21
GENESIS
Introduction to Genesis: Title
GENESIS APOCRYPHON
Ge 12:11
GENNESARET
plain of
Mt 14:34

sea of (lake of)
Mk 1:16; Lk 5:1
GENTILES
Nu 15:14; Ru 1:17; 2Ki 5:14; Ps 117:1; Mt 2:2; Mt 21:41; Lk 2:31; Lk 4:26–27; Jn 12:32; Ac 9:43; Ac 10:23,28; Ac 10:45; Ac 10:47; Ro 11:17; Ro 15:19; Introduction to Jonah: Literary Characteristics
GERA
2Sa 16:5; 1Ki 2:8
GERAR
Ge 20:1
GERASA
Mk 5:1; Lk 8:26
GERSHOM (family of Phinehas)
Ezr 8:2
GERSHOM (father of Jonathan the Levite)
Jdg 18:30
GERSHOM (son of Moses)
Ex 4:20; Ac 7:29
GERSHONITES
Jos 21:27; Zec 12:13
GESHEM
Ne 2:19
GESHURITES
Dt 3:14; 1Sa 27:8; 2Sa 3:3
GETHSEMANE
Mt 26:36; Mk 14:32; Lk 22:39; Heb 5:7
GEZER
Jos 10:33; Jos 16:1; Jos 16:10; 1Ki 3:1
GEZER CALENDAR
"Ancient Texts Relating to the Old Testament," xxii
GIBBETHON
1Ki 15:27; 1Ki 16:9
GIBEAH
in Benjamin
Jdg 9:32; Jdg 19:14; 1Sa 10:5; 1Sa 26:1; Ezr 2:28; Hos 10:9
near Shiloh
Jos 24:33
GIBEON
Jos 9:3; Jos 10:2; 1Sa 7:1; 2Sa 2:12; 1Ch 16:39; 2Ch 7:12; Hab 3:11
GIBEONITES
Jos 9:1–27; Jos 10:2; 2Sa 21:1; 2Sa 21:4; 2Sa 21:6; 1Ki 3:4
GIDEON
Jdg 2:16; Jdg 6:1–40; Jdg 7:1–25; Jdg 8:1–35; Jdg 9:1–57; Isa 9:4; "Gideon's Battles," 342
GIFTS
of administration
1Co 12:28
spiritual
Ex 31:3; Nu 11:29; Nu 12:1; Nu 12:2; Ro 12:6; 1Co 1:7; 1Co 12:1; 1Co 12:4–6; 1Co 12:6; 1Co 12:7; 1Co 12:8; 1Co 12:9; 1Co 12:11; 1Co 12:12; 1Co 12:14; 1Co 12:21–26; 1Co 12:28; 1Co 12:31; 1Co 14:1–5; 1Co 14:20; 1Co 14:26–27; 1Co 14:32; Eph 4:11; Eph 4:12; 2Ti 1:6; Heb 2:4
GIHON (city)
1Ki 1:41
GIHON (spring)
2Ki 20:20; Ne 3:26
GILBOA
1Sa 28:4; 2Sa 1:21
GILEADITES
Ge 31:21; Jdg 10:18; Jdg 11:8; Hos 12:11
GILGAL
Jos 4:19; Jos 10:9; Jdg 1:1; Jdg 2:1; 1Sa 11:14; 1Sa 15:12; Ne 12:29; Hos 4:15; Am 4:4
GILGAMESH
Introduction to Genesis: Background
GILGAMESH EPIC
"Ancient Texts Relating to the Old Testament," xxii
GILONITE
2Sa 15:12
GITTITE
2Sa 6:10; 2Sa 15:18
GIVING. *See also* GENEROSITY
2Co 8:5; 2Co 8:6; 2Co 8:8; 2Co 8:12; 2Co 9:12; 2Co 9:15
GLEANING
Jdg 8:2; Ru 1:22; Ru 2:2
GLORY OF ISRAEL
1Sa 15:29
GLORY OF THE LORD. *See* GOD: glory of
GLUTTONY
1Co 11:20
GNOSTICISM
Col 1:19; Col 1:28; Col 2:3; Col 2:10–15; Col 2:18; 1Ti 1:3–11; 1Ti 4:3; 1Ti 6:20; 2Ti 2:14–18; 2Pe 2:12; 1Jn 1:10; 1Jn 2:3; 1Jn 2:18; 1Jn 2:27; 1Jn 4:1; 1Jn 4:2; 1Jn 5:6; 1Jn 5:16; 2Jn 1:7–11; 2Jn 1:9; Jude 1:19; Rev 2:24; Introduction to 1 John: Gnosticism
GOAT
SS 4:1
GOBLET
SS 7:2
GOD
anger/wrath of. See ANGER, GOD'S
attributes/character of
Ex 34:6–7; Nu 14:17–19; Nu 23:19; 1Sa 15:29; Jnh 4:2; Jnh 4:11; Ro 9:17; 1Jn 4:8; Introduction to Amos: Theme and Message
call of
Ro 11:29
as Creator
Ge 1:1; Ge 1:2; Ge 1:3; Ge 1:4; Ge 1:11; Ge 1:16; Ge 1:22; Ge 1:26; Ge 2:4; Ps 29:1–11; Isa 40:21; Isa 43:1
faithfulness of
Ps 3:1–8; Ro 3:3; 1Co 1:9; 1Jn 1:9; Introduction to Judges: Theme and Theology
as Father
2Sa 7:14; Jn 5:18; Jn 8:44; Ro 8:14; Eph 1:3; Heb 1:5
fear (reverence) of
Ge 20:11; Jos 4:24; 2Ch 19:7; Ps 15:4; Ps 34:8–14; Ps 111:10; Pr 1:7; Ecc 7:18; Ecc 12:13; Mal 4:2; Lk 12:5; Ro 3:18; 2Co 5:11; 1Pe 1:17; 1Pe 3:14; 1Jn 4:18; Introduction to Proverbs: Purpose and Teaching
fellowship with
Mk 7:20; 1Jn 1:3
glory of
Ex 29:43; Ex 40:34; 1Ki 8:10; 2Ch 5:14; Ps 26:8; Eze 1:1–28; Eze 1:28; Eze 10:3; Eze 43:2; Hag 2:7; Jn 12:41; Ro 1:23; Ro 3:23; Ro 6:4; 2Co 3:7; 2Co 3:18
guidance of
Dt 31:6; 1Sa 2:4–5; 1Co 10:1
jealousy of
Ex 20:5
as judge
Ge 18:25; Ex 2:14; Jdg 11:27
judgment of. See JUDGMENT, GOD'S
love of
Dt 4:37; Dt 7:8; 2Sa 7:15; Jn 3:16; Jn 5:42; Ro 8:37; Ro 8:39; Ro 11:32; 2Th 3:5; Tit 3:4; 1Jn 2:5; 1Jn 3:17; 1Jn 4:8; 1Jn 4:17; Introduction to Ruth: Theme and Theology
mercy of
Ex 25:17; Nu 18:1–7; Lk 15:28; Ro 11:25; Ro 11:27; Ro 12:1; Jas 2:13
name of. See NAMES OF GOD
patience of
Ro 2:4; Ro 9:22; 2Pe 3:8,9; Introduction to Judges: Theme and Theology
power of
Ge 18:14; Ex 14:14; Nu 11:23; Nu 14:9; Dt 3:22; Ps 97:1–6; 2Co 12:9
presence of
Nu 14:9; Dt 1:43; Dt 4:7; 1Sa 4:3,4; 1Ki 6:13; Jer 23:23; Lk 11:25
righteousness of
Ps 4:1; Ro 3:5
as shepherd
Jn 10:1–42; Zec 10:2
sovereignty of
Ge 25:23; Nu 3:38; Jos 11:20; 1Sa 2:6–8; 2Sa 24:1; 1Ki 12:15; 1Ki 18:1; 2Ki 20:5; Est 4:12–16; Ps 9:1; Ecc 3:1–22; Jer 18:7–10; Jnh 1:4; Ro 9:21; 1Ti 2:4; Introduction to Ezekiel: Themes; Introduction to Daniel: Theme; Introduction to Zechariah: Theological Teaching
voice of
2Sa 22:14

will of
Jn 7:6; Jn 7:17; Jn 17:24; Ro 12:2; 1Co 12:10; Php 2:7; Php 2:14; Php 2:15; Heb 5:7; Heb 6:3; Heb 8:8–12; Heb 10:5; Heb 10:7; 1Pe 2:19; 1Pe 4:1
GOD OF HEAVEN
Ezr 1:2
GODLINESS
Zec 8:23; 1Ti 2:2; 1Ti 4:7; 2Pe 1:6
GOG
Eze 38:2; Rev 20:8
GOLD
1Ki 6:20
GOLDEN CALF
Ex 32:4; Ex 32:5; Ex 32:6; 2Ki 23:15
GOLDEN GATE
Ne 3:29; Eze 44:2
GOLDEN LAMPSTAND
Ex 25:37; 1Sa 3:3; Heb 9:2
GOLDEN RULE
Mt 7:12; Lk 6:27
GOLGOTHA
Jn 19:17
GOLIATH
1Sa 17:54; 2Sa 9:8
GOMER (son of Japheth)
Ge 10:2; Eze 38:6
GOMER (wife of Hosea)
Hos 3:1; Hos 3:2; Introduction to Hosea: Special Problems
GOMORRAH
Ge 13:10; Am 4:11; Zep 2:9
GOOD SHEPHERD
Zec 11:8; Zec 11:9; Zec 11:11; Zec 11:17; Jn 10:1–42
GOSHEN
Ge 45:10; Jos 10:41
GOSPEL
Mk 1:1; 2Co 2:16; 2Co 11:9; Php 1:27; 1Jn 2:8
GOSSIP
Pr 18:8
GOVERNMENT. *See* CIVIL AUTHORITY
GOZAN
2Ki 17:6; Isa 37:12
GRACE
Ge 3:16; Ge 3:17–19; Ge 17:21; Isa 26:10; Eze 36:22; Da 9:18; Mt 25:34–40; Mk 10:27; Jn 1:12; Ro 3:24; Ro 6:14; Ro 11:5; 2Co 2:14; 2Co 8:5; 2Co 9:14; 2Co 12:9; Gal 1:3; Eph 2:8; Eph 3:8; Tit 2:11–14; Tit 2:11
GRAIN OFFERING
Lev 2:1; Joel 1:9; Ac 10:4; "Old Testament Sacrifices," 153
GRANDCHILDREN
Pr 17:6
GRAVE
Ge 37:35; Jnh 2:2
GREAT HALLEL
Ps 120:1
GREAT TRIBULATION
Mt 24:16; Mt 24:21; Mt 24:22; Mt 25:31–46; Rev 7:4; Rev 7:9; Rev 7:14
GREAT WHITE THRONE JUDGMENT
1Co 15:26
GREECE
Da 2:32–43; Da 7:4–7; Da 8:5; 1Co 16:6; "The Neo-Babylonian Empire," 1318; "From Malachi to Christ," 1450
GREED
Job 31:24–28; Lk 12:13; Ac 5:1; Eph 5:3; Eph 5:5; 2Pe 2:3
GRIEF. *See also* MOURNING
2Sa 1:12,17; 2Sa 13:31; Ezr 9:3; Jn 11:31,33
GUBARU
Da 5:31
GUILT OFFERING
Lev 5:15; 1Sa 6:3; Isa 53:10; "Old Testament Sacrifices," 153
GYGES
Eze 38:2

HABAKKUK
Introduction to Habakkuk: Author
HABIRU
Ge 14:13; "The Exodus," 108
HACALIAH
Ne 1:1
HACMONITE
2Sa 23:8
HADAD
1Ki 11:14; 1Ki 11:21; 1Ki 11:22
HADAD RIMMON
Zec 12:11
HADADEZER
2Sa 8:3; 2Sa 10:19; 1Ki 11:24; 1Ki 22:1
HADES
Mt 16:18; Lk 12:5; Lk 16:23; 1Co 15:26; Rev 1:18; Rev 6:8
HADID
Ne 11:34
HAGAR
Ge 16:1; 1Ch 5:10; Ezr 10:3
HAGGAI
Ezr 4:24; Ezr 5:1; Ezr 6:13–14; Ne 10:39; Introduction to Haggai: Author
HAGRITES
1Ch 5:10; Ps 83:6
HAKKATAN
Ezr 8:12
HALLEL PSALMS
Ps 120:1; Mt 26:30; Mk 11:9
HALLELUJAH
Ps 111:1–10; Ps 146:1–10; Rev 19:1
HAM
Ge 10:6
HAMAN
Est 3:1; Est 3:2–6; Est 3:9; Est 3:13; Est 5:9; Est 5:11; Est 7:8; Est 8:2
HAMATH
2Sa 8:9; Isa 10:9; Eze 47:15; Eze 47:16; Am 6:2; Zec 9:1; Zec 9:2
HAMATH ZOBAH
1Ki 11:24
HAMMEDATHA
Est 3:1
HAMMURAPI
Ge 14:1; Ge 16:2; Ge 39:7; Lev 24:20; Ezr 8:34; Ezr 10:3; Job 13:27; "Ancient Texts Relating to the Old Testament," xxii
HAMOR
Jdg 9:28
HANAN
Ezr 2:46
HANANI (brother of Nehemiah)
Ne 1:2; Ne 13:7
HANANI (father of Jehu)
1Ki 15:19; 2Ch 19:2
HANANIAH (false prophet)
Jer 28:1; Jer 28:2; Jer 28:3; Jer 28:16
HANANIAH (priest)
Ne 1:2
HANANIAH (Shadrach)
Da 1:6
HANANIAH (son of Zerubbabel)
1Ch 3:20
HANES
Isa 30:4
HANNAH
1Sa 1:3; 1Sa 2:1; 1Sa 2:4–5; 1Sa 2:6–8
HANUKKAH
Ezr 6:16; Ps 30 title; Da 8:9–12; Jn 10:22; "Old Testament Feasts and Other Sacred Days," 178
HANUN
2Sa 17:27
HARAM ESH-SHARIF
Eze 44:2
HARAN
Ge 11:31; 2Ki 19:12; Isa 37:12; Eze 27:23; Ac 7:2,4
HAREM
Ecc 2:8
HAROD
Jdg 7:1
HARP
Ge 31:27; Ne 12:27
HARVEST
Jos 3:15; Ru 1:22; Ru 3:3
HARVEST, FEAST OF. *See* FEAST: of Weeks (Pentecost or Harvest)
HASIDIM
Mk 2:16
HATHACH
Est 4:4–12
HATSHEPSUT, QUEEN
Ex 2:5
HAURAN
Ne 2:10
HAVILAH
Ge 2:11; 1Sa 15:7
HAWK
Job 39:26
HAZAEL
1Ki 19:15; 2Ki 8:12; 2Ki 8:13; Am 1:4; Am 6:13
HAZAR SHUAL
Ne 11:27

HAZAZON TAMAR
Eze 47:18
HAZER HATTICON
Eze 47:16
HAZOR
Jos 11:1,10; Jdg 4:2; 1Ki 9:15
HEAD
1Co 11:3; 1Co 11:4
HEALING
1Co 12:9; Jas 5:14
HEART
1Sa 16:7; Ps 7:9
definition of
Ps 4:7; Mt 5:8; Ro 10:9
hardness of
Job 36:13–15; Mk 6:52
HEAVEN
Mk 11:30; Gal 4:26; Heb 3:2; Heb 11:13
HEBER THE KENITE
Jdg 4:11
HEBREW
Ge 10:21; Ge 14:13; 2Ki 18:26; Isa 36:11
HEBRON
Ge 23:2; Nu 13:22; Jos 14:12; Jos 21:11; Ac 7:16
HELAM
2Sa 10:16
HELBON
Eze 27:18
HELECH
Eze 27:11
HELIODORUS
Da 11:20
HELIOPOLIS
Ge 41:45; Isa 19:18; Eze 30:17
HELL. *See also* ABADDON; GEHENNA; HADES
Jer 7:31; Mt 5:22
HEMAN
1Ch 2:6; 1Ch 6:31–48; 2Ch 29:13–14
HENA
2Ki 18:34
HENNA
SS 1:14
HEQT
Ex 8:2
HERESIES
Eph 4:14; Col 1:16; Col 2:3; Col 2:8; Col 2:17; Col 2:19; Col 2:21; Col 2:23; 1Ti 1:3–11; 1Ti 6:20; 2Pe 2:1; 2Pe 2:12
HERMES
Ac 14:12
HERMON, MOUNT. *See* MOUNT: Hermon
HEROD (Agrippa I)
Ac 9:15; Ac 12:1; Ac 12:19; Ac 12:21; Ac 12:23; Ac 15:2; Ac 24:24; Ac 25:22; Ac 25:26; Ac 26:1; Ac 26:3; Ac 26:8; Ac 26:27; Ro 16:10
HEROD (Antipas)
Ne 11:1; Mt 14:1; Mk 8:15; Mk 10:2; Lk 3:19; Ac 12:1; Ac 23:31; Ac 25:22; Ro 16:10
HEROD (of Chalcis)
Ac 25:13
HEROD (the Great)
Mt 2:1; Mt 2:15; Lk 1:5; Ac 12:1; Ac 23:31; Ac 23:35; Ro 16:10; "House of Herod," 1465; "Herod's Temple," 1470; "The Holy Land Under Herod the Great," 1570
HEROD (Philip)
Mt 14:3
HERODIANS
Mt 22:15–17; Mk 3:6
HERODIAS
Mt 14:3; Mt 14:6; Lk 3:19
HERODOTUS
Ezr 4:8; Ezr 6:11; Ezr 7:14; Est 1:1; Est 1:13–14; Est 3:9; Est 4:11; Est 5:11; Est 8:1; Isa 37:36
HESHBON
SS 7:4
HEZEKIAH
2Ki 16:20; 2Ki 20:3; 2Ki 20:5; 2Ki 20:6; 2Ki 23:6; 2Ch 15:12; 2Ch 29:5–11; 2Ch 30:2; 2Ch 32:27–29; Ezr 6:17; Ne 2:14; Isa 10:20–22; Isa 20:5; Isa 29:15; Isa 33:8; Hos 1:1; Zep 1:1; "Jerusalem During the Time of the Prophets," 1333
HEZIR
1Ch 24:15
HEZRON
1Ch 2:3–9
HIEL
1Ki 16:34
HIEROPOLIS
1Co 16:19; Col 1:7; Col 4:13; Rev 3:16
HIGH PLACES
1Sa 9:12; 1Ki 3:2; 1Ki 15:14; 2Ki 12:3
HILKIAH
2Ki 22:4; 2Ki 25:18; 1Ch 6:13; Ezr 7:1; Jer 1:1; Jer 29:3
HILLEL, SCHOOL OF
Lev 24:20; Mt 19:3; Ac 5:34
HINNOM VALLEY
2Ki 23:10; 2Ch 28:3; Isa 66:24; Jer 7:31; Zep 1:5; Mt 5:22
HIRAM
2Sa 5:11; 1Ki 5:1; 1Ki 5:9; 1Ki 5:11; 1Ki 9:11; 1Ki 10:11; 1Ch 14:1; 2Ch 2:3–10; 2Ch 8:1–2
HISTORICIST
Introduction to Revelation: Interpretation
HITTITES
Ge 10:15; Ge 23:9; Jdg 1:26; 1Sa 26:6; Eze 16:3
HIVITES
Jos 9:7; Jdg 3:3; 2Sa 21:2
HOBAB
Nu 10:29
HOLINESS
Ex 3:5; Lev 11:44; Dt 7:6; Ro 1:7; Ro 6:22; 1Co 1:2; 1Co 5:6; Eph 1:4; Eph 5:26; Php 1:10; Col 1:2; 1Pe 1:16; Introduction to Leviticus: Theological Themes
HOLOCAUST OFFERING
Lev 1:3
HOLY CITY
Isa 64:10
HOLY KISS
Ro 16:16; 1Co 16:20; 2Co 13:12; 1Th 5:26
HOLY LAND
Zec 2:12; Zec 5:11
HOLY ONE OF GOD
Mk 1:24
HOLY ONE OF ISRAEL
2Ki 19:22; Isa 1:4
HOLY PLACE
Ex 26:31–35; 1Sa 3:3; Ezr 6:15
HOLY SPIRIT
Ge 1:2; Jdg 11:29; Ps 51:11
and God
Ac 5:3; Ro 8:27; Php 1:19
and Pentecost
Mt 3:11; Ac 2:2; Ac 2:4; 1Pe 1:12
baptism of
Ac 2:14; Ac 19:2; Ac 19:6; 1Co 12:13
coming of
Jn 14:16; Jn 14:18; Jn 14:26; Jn 16:7; Jn 20:22; Ac 5:32
description of
Mk 1:10; Jn 14:17
fruit of
Ro 8:23; Ro 14:17; Gal 5:22–23
gifts of
Ex 31:3; Ro 15:13; 1Co 1:7; 1Co 12:4; 1Co 12:10; 2Co 3:6; 2Co 3:8–9; 1Th 5:19; 2Ti 1:6
grieving of
Eph 4:30; Eph 4:31
indwelling of
Ac 2:38; Ac 8:16; 1Co 3:16; 1Co 6:18; Eph 2:22; Eph 5:18; Php 1:11; Php 2:1
and Jesus
Mt 3:16; 2Co 3:17; Php 1:19
need of
1Co 2:14; 1Co 2:15
power of
Ex 31:3; Zec 4:7; Ro 8:2; Ro 8:4; Gal 5:16; 1Th 1:5
as a seal
Hag 2:23; Eph 1:13
sovereignty of
Jn 3:8; 1Co 12:11
work of
Jn 7:39; Jn 14:26; Jn 16:13; Jn 16:14; Ac 1:2; Ac 2:34; Ac 9:31; Ac 15:28; Ro 2:29; Ro 12:11; 1Co 7:40; 1Co 12:3; Eph 6:17–18; 1Pe 1:2; 1Jn 2:27
HOLY TO THE LORD
Zec 14:20
HOLY WEEK
"Passion Week," 1552
HOMOSEXUALITY
Ge 19:5; Dt 22:5; Jdg 19:22; Jdg 19:23; Ro 1:27; 1Co 6:9; 2Pe 2:10; Jude 1:8
HONEY
Ge 43:11; Dt 32:13

HONOR
Ex 20:12
HOPE
Ro 4:18; Ro 5:2; Ro 5:5; Ro 8:24; Ro 12:12; Ro 15:13; Eph 1:18; Eph 4:4; Col 1:5; 1Th 1:3; 1Ti 1:1; Heb 6:19; Heb 7:19; 1Pe 1:3
HOPHNI
1Sa 4:4; 1Sa 4:11
HOPHRA
2Ki 24:20; Jer 37:5; Jer 44:30; Eze 17:7; Eze 29:6; Eze 30:21
HOREB, MOUNT. *See* MOUNT: Horeb
HORITES
Ge 14:6; Jos 9:7
HORMAH
Nu 21:3
HORNS
Ex 27:2; Lev 4:7; 1Ki 1:50
HORONITE
Ne 2:10
HORSE GATE
Ne 3:28
HORSEMEN, FOUR
Rev 6:2; Rev 6:4; Rev 6:5; Rev 6:6; Rev 6:8; Rev 9:14
HOSANNA
Jer 31:7; Mt 21:9
HOSEA
2Ki 15:19; Mic 1:1; Introduction to Hosea: Author and Date
HOSHEA
2Ki 17:3; Hos 7:11; Hos 8:9
HOSPITALITY
Ge 18:2; Ge 19:8; Jdg 4:21; Jdg 13:15; Jdg 19:21; 3Jn 1:5
HOUSE OF DAVID
1Ki 12:19
HOUSE OF JOSEPH
2Sa 19:20
HOUSE OF THE HEROES
Ne 3:16
HOUSEHOLD GODS
Ge 31:19; Jdg 17:5; Eze 21:21
HOUSES, PALESTINIAN
Jdg 3:10; Mk 2:4; Lk 15:8
HULDAH
2Ki 22:14; Isa 57:1
HUMILITY
Jdg 6:15; 1Sa 9:21; 1Sa 23:17; Ps 147:6; Zep 2:3; Mk 9:34; Lk 5:8; Lk 14:11; Jn 13:5; Jn 13:8; Php 2:3; Php 2:5; Col 2:18; 1Pe 5:5
HUR
Ex 17:10
HURAM-ABI
1Ki 7:13; 1Ki 7:14; 1Ch 2:18–24; 2Ch 2:7; 2Ch 2:13
HURRIANS
Ge 14:6; Jos 9:7
HUSBAND
1Co 14:34–35; Eph 5:22; Eph 5:23; Eph 5:25; Eph 5:28–29; Tit 1:6; Tit 2:4; 1Pe 3:1
HUSHAI
2Sa 15:32; 2Sa 15:37; 2Sa 17:12; 2Sa 17:16; 1Ki 4:16
HYMENAEUS
2Ti 2:14–18
HYMN TO THE ATEN
"Ancient Texts Relating to the Old Testament," xxii
HYPERBOLE
Ps 68:13; Mt 18:8–9; Mk 7:3; Lk 6:41; Lk 14:26; Jn 12:19; Jn 21:25; Gal 4:15; Col 1:6
HYPOCRISY
Mt 6:2; 23:23; Lk 13:15; Ac 5:9
HYSSOP
Ex 12:22; Lev 14:4; Jn 19:29

I

I AM WHO I AM. *See* NAMES OF GOD: "I Am"
ICONIUM
Ac 13:51; Ac 14:6; Ac 16:6; 2Ti 3:11
IDDO
Introduction to Zechariah: Author and Unity
IDEALIST
Introduction to Revelation: Interpretation
IDOL
Eze 6:4; Eze 21:21
IDOLATRY
Ex 20:4; Ex 34:15; Lev 26:1; 2Ki 9:22; 2Ki 17:16; Job 31:24–28; Isa 44:9–20; Eze 21:21; Hab 2:18; Hab 2:20; 1Co 8:5; 1Co 8:7; 1Co 8:9; 1Co 8:10; 1Co 8:12; 1Co 8:13; 1Co 10:7; 1Co 10:14; 1Co 10:18; 1Co 10:22; Eph 5:5
IDUMEANS
Ne 11:25; Ne 11:26; Mk 3:8
ILLYRICUM
Ro 15:19; 2Ti 4:10
IMAGE OF GOD
Ge 1:26; Col 1:15
IMITATORS OF CHRIST
1Th 1:6
IMMANUEL
Isa 7:14; Isa 8:8; 2Co 13:14
IMMEDIATE RETRIBUTION, THEORY OF
Introduction to 1 Chronicles: Purpose and Themes
IMMORALITY
Ex 32:6; Lev 18:1 — 20:27; Pr 2:18; Ac 15:20; 1Co 6:9; 1Co 6:13; 1Co 6:16; 1Co 6:19; 1Co 7:2; 1Co 7:5; 1Co 10:8; 1Th 4:3; 1Th 4:6; 1Th 4:8
IMMORTALITY
Pr 12:28; Ro 2:6–7
INCARNATION. *See* CHRIST: incarnation of
INCENSE
Ex 30:1; Lev 2:1; Rev 5:8
INCEST
Ge 19:33; Lev 18:6; 1Co 5:1
INDIVIDUAL RESPONSIBILITY
Jer 31:30; Eze 3:16; Eze 14:20; Eze 18:4; Mt 22:13; Introduction to Jeremiah: Themes and Message
INGATHERING, FEAST OF. *See* FEAST: of Tabernacles (Booths or Ingathering)
INHERITANCE
Ge 25:5; Ps 127:3; Jer 2:7; Jer 3:19; Ro 8:17; Ro 8:23; Eph 1:18; 1Pe 1:4
INJUSTICE
Zec 8:16
INSPIRATION (OF SCRIPTURE)
2Ti 3:16; 2Pe 1:21
INTEREST
Ex 22:25–27; Lev 25:36; Dt 23:20; Ne 5:10
INTERMARRIAGE
Ge 26:35; Dt 7:4; Jos 23:12; Jdg 14:1; Ru 1:4; 1Ki 11:1; Ezr 9:1; 2Co 6:14
IRON
Dt 8:9
ISAAC
burial of
Ac 7:16
chosen by God
Ge 17:21; Ro 9:15
and law of primogeniture
Ge 25:5
meaning of name
Ge 17:17
offered as sacrifice
Ge 22:2; Heb 11:19; Jas 2:21
as patriarch
Ro 9:5
promise of birth
Ge 18:10; Ro 4:17
ISAIAH
2Ki 18:17; 2Ki 19:2; 2Ki 19:20; Ezr 9:9; Job 18:14; Eze 5:1; Eze 12:2; Eze 15:4; Hos 1:1; Hos 7:5; Joel 2:11; Mic 1:1; Zep 1:1; Zec 1:4; Mt 27:9; Mk 1:2–3; Mk 7:6; Mk 10:45; Lk 1:17; Lk 5:8; Introduction to Isaiah: Author
ISH-BOSHETH
1Sa 31:2; 2Sa 2:8; 2Sa 2:11; 2Sa 3:14; 2Sa 4:4; 1Ch 10:6
ISHMAEL
Ge 37:25; Jdg 13:3; 2Ki 25:23; 1Ch 5:10; Isa 60:7
ISHTAR
Est 2:7; Jer 7:18; Jer 44:18; Jer 44:19
ISHTAR'S DESCENT
"Ancient Texts Relating to the Old Testament," xxii
ISRAEL
Ge 32:28; Ge 34:9; Ex 40:38; 1Ki 1:35; 1Ki 18:31; Ro 9:4; "The Divided Kingdom," 497; "Rulers of the Divided Kingdom of Israel and Judah," 504; "Assyrian Campaigns against Israel and Judah," 552; "Exile of the Northern Kingdom," 558
and aliens
Ex 22:21–27; Nu 15:14; Jos 8:33; Jos 20:9; Ru 1:22

as a chosen people
Ex 19:5; 2Sa 7:23; Ro 1:16; 1Pe 2:9
corporate unity of
Jos 7:1–26,11,24
disobedience/unfaithfulness of
Nu 14:1–11,34; Nu 16:41; Nu 20:2; Nu 21:4–5; Nu 25:1; Dt 1:43; Dt 4:25
faithfulness of
Jos 24:31
as a theocracy
Jdg 8:23; 1Sa 8:7; 1Sa 11:14; 1Sa 12:12; 1Sa 13:13; 1Sa 15:23; 1Sa 17:11; 2Ki 1:10; Ps 93:1–5; Introduction to Judges: Theme and Theology; Introduction to 1 Samuel: Contents and Theme; Introduction to 2 Samuel: Contents and Theme
ITHAMAR
1Ch 6:1–3; Ezr 8:2

JAAZANIAH (Jewish captain)
2Ki 25:23; Ne 5:18
JAAZANIAH (Recabite)
Jer 35:3
JAAZANIAH (son of Shaphan)
Eze 8:11
JABBOK RIVER
Ge 32:22
JABESH GILEAD
Jdg 21:11; 1Sa 11:1
JABIN
Jos 11:1; Jdg 4:2
JACKAL WELL
Ne 2:13
JACOB
Ge 25:26; Ge 29:25; Ge 30:2; Ge 31:26; Ge 32:24; Ge 32:26; Ge 32:28; Ge 33:20; Ge 35:11–12; Ge 47:9; Heb 11:22; "Jacob's Journeys," 56; "The Tribes of Israel," 82
JACOB'S WELL
Jn 4:11
JAEL
Jdg 4:18; Jdg 4:21; Jdg 5:28
JAFFA
Ac 9:36
JAHAZ
Isa 15:4
JAIR (judge of Israel)
Jdg 10:3
JAIRUS
Mt 9:18; Ac 9:40
JAKIN
2Ki 11:14; Eze 40:49
JAMBRES
Ex 7:11; 2Ti 3:8
JAMES (brother of Christ)
Mk 6:30; Lk 8:19; Ac 1:14; Ac 9:26; Ac 12:17; Ac 15:13; Ac 15:14; Ac 21:18; Gal 1:19; Gal 2:2; Tit 1:1; Introduction to James: Author
JAMES (son of Alphaeus)
Lk 6:15; Ac 1:13
JAMES (son of Zebedee)
Mk 5:37; Lk 9:28; Lk 9:54; Ac 3:1; Ac 12:2; Ac 12:17; 1Co 15:7
JANNES
Ex 7:11; 2Ti 3:8
JAPHETHITES
Ge 10:2
JARMUTH
Ne 11:29
JASHAR, BOOK OF
Jos 10:13
JASON
Ac 17:5; Ac 17:9; Ro 16:21
JEBEL DRUZE
Ps 68:14
JEBUSITES
Ge 10:16; Jos 15:63; 2Sa 5:6; 2Sa 5:8; Zec 9:7; "The City of the Jebusites/David's Jerusalem," 432
JECONIAH
Mt 1:11
JEDIDIAH
2Sa 12:25
JEDUTHUN
1Ch 9:15–16; 2Ch 29:13–14; Ps 39:1
JEHEZKEL
Eze 1:3
JEHOAHAZ
2Ki 23:30; 2Ki 23:33; 1Ch 3:15–16; 2Ch 36:4; Jer 22:11; Eze 19:3
JEHOASH. *See also* JOASH
2Ki 13:5; 2Ki 13:19; 2Ki 14:8; 2Ki 14:13; 2Ch 26:9; Am 6:13
JEHOHANAN
Ne 2:10; Ne 6:17–18
JEHOIACHIN
2Ki 24:8; 2Ki 24:17; 1Ch 3:15–16; 2Ch 36:9–10; Ezr 1:8; Ezr 5:2; Eze 1:2; Eze 7:27; Eze 17:4; Eze 17:5; Eze 19:5; Mt 1:11
JEHOIACHIN'S RATION DOCKETS
"Ancient Texts Relating to the Old Testament," xxii
JEHOIADA (high priest)
2Ki 11:2; 2Ki 11:14; 2Ki 12:20; 2Ch 15:12; 2Ch 24:5; 2Ch 24:14; 2Ch 24:15–22
JEHOIAKIM
2Ki 23:30; 2Ki 23:37; 2Ki 24:1; 2Ki 24:5; 1Ch 3:15–16; 2Ch 36:4; 2Ch 36:5–8; Ezr 1:1; Eze 17:5; Mt 1:11
JEHOIARIB
1Ch 24:7
JEHONADAB
2Ki 10:15; 2Ki 10:16; Jer 35:6
JEHORAM. *See also* JORAM
1Ki 12:24; 1Ki 22:50; 2Ki 1:17; 2Ki 8:16; 2Ki 8:17; 2Ki 8:18; 2Ki 11:2; 2Ch 21:5; 2Ch 21:8–10; 2Ch 21:12–15; 2Ch 22:1; Mt 1:8
JEHOSHAPHAT
1Ki 4:3; 1Ki 4:12; 1Ki 22:2; 1Ki 22:4; 1Ki 22:5; 1Ki 22:7; 1Ki 22:15; 1Ki 22:41; 1Ki 22:44; 1Ki 22:48; 2Ki 1:17; 2Ki 3:7; 2Ki 3:9; 2Ki 3:11; 2Ki 3:14; 2Ki 8:28; 2Ch 17:6; 2Ch 18:1; 2Ch 19:4; 2Ch 19:5; 2Ch 20:5–12; 2Ch 20:35–37
JEHOSHEBA
2Ki 11:2
JEHOVAH. *See* NAMES OF GOD: LORD (Yahweh/Jehovah)
JEHOZADAK
2Ki 25:18; 1Ch 6:14; Ezr 2:2; Hag 1:1
JEHU (king of Judah)
1Ki 1:39; 1Ki 19:16; 2Ki 9:27; 2Ki 9:31; 2Ki 10:1; 2Ki 10:7; 2Ki 10:30
JEHU (prophet)
1Ki 16:1; 2Ch 22:6
JEHUCAL
Jer 37:3
JEPHTHAH
Jdg 11:1; Jdg 11:30
JERAHMEELITES
1Sa 27:10; 1Ch 2:25–33
JEREMIAH
2Ki 22:11; 2Ki 22:12; 2Ch 35:25; 2Ch 36:5–8; 2Ch 36:22–23; Isa 10:30; Mt 27:9; Lk 22:20; Gal 3:19; Heb 13:20; Introduction to Jeremiah: Author and Date
JERICHO
Jos 6:1; 1Ki 16:34; Mk 10:46; Lk 10:30; Heb 11:30
JEROBOAM I
1Ki 11:40; 1Ki 12:28; 1Ki 12:30; 1Ki 12:32; 1Ki 13:7; 1Ki 13:24; 1Ki 14:1; 1Ki 14:2; 1Ki 14:7–8; 1Ki 14:9; 1Ki 14:12; 1Ki 14:13; 1Ki 15:26; 1Ki 16:7; 2Ki 14:23; 2Ki 16:3; 2Ki 17:6; 2Ch 30:2; Hos 8:5; Hos 8:6; Hos 13:10
JEROBOAM II
1Ki 13:1; 2Ki 13:5; 2Ki 13:19; 2Ki 13:25; 2Ki 14:25; 2Ch 26:6–8; Hos 1:1; Hos 1:4; Hos 4:2; Hos 8:4; Hos 10:1; Am 6:2; Am 6:13
JEROME
Introduction to Ezra: Ezra and Nehemiah
JERUB-BAAL/JERUB-BESHETH
Jdg 6:32; 2Sa 11:21
JERUSALEM
conquest/destruction of
"Nebuchadnezzar's Campaign against Judah," 572
geographical/physical aspects of
Jdg 1:8; 2Sa 5:6; Ne 3:1–32; Ps 48:2; "The City of the Jebusites/David's Jerusalem," 432; "Solomon's Jerusalem," 477; "Jerusalem of the Returning Exiles," 695; "Jerusalem During the Time of the Prophets," 1333; "Jerusalem During the Ministry of Jesus," 1527

names of
Ge 14:18; 2Sa 5:7; Isa 1:26; Jer 33:16; Eze 48:35
religious significance of
1Ki 11:13; Ps 9:11; Ps 24:7–10; Ps 48:1–14; Ps 76:1–12; Ps 87:1–7; Eze 38:12; Gal 4:25,26; Introduction to Psalms: Theology
JESHANAH GATE
Ne 3:6
JESHUA
1Ch 6:14; Ezr 1:8; Ezr 2:2; Ezr 3:2; Ezr 6:13–14
JESHURUN
Isa 44:2
JESSE
1Sa 16:1; 2Sa 17:25; 1Ch 2:10–17
JESUS. *See* CHRIST
JETHRO
Ex 2:16
JEZEBEL
1Ki 16:25; 1Ki 16:31; 1Ki 18:13; 1Ki 21:9; 1Ki 21:19; 2Ki 9:31; Mk 9:13; Rev 2:20; Rev 2:23
JEZREEL (son of Hosea)
Hos 1:4; Hos 1:11; Hos 2:22
JEZREEL (city)
1Sa 25:43; 1Ki 18:46; 1Ki 21:11; 2Ki 8:28
JOAB
1Sa 26:6; 2Sa 2:13; 2Sa 3:25; 2Sa 3:29; 2Sa 5:8; 2Sa 14:2; 2Sa 19:5; 2Sa 20:10; 2Sa 20:23; 1Ki 1:7; 1Ch 21:6; 1Ch 27:24
JOANNA
Lk 24:10
JOASH
2Ki 12:2; 2Ki 12:6; 2Ki 12:17; 2Ch 24:5; 2Ch 24:15–22; Ezr 3:10; Ne 10:32
JOB
Jas 5:11; Introduction to Job: Author
JOCHEBED
Ex 6:20
JOEL
Ac 2:4; Ac 2:17; Introduction to Joel: Author
JOHANAN
1Ch 3:15–16; Ezr 2:46; Ne 12:11
JOHANAN BEN ZACCAI
Ac 4:6
JOHN (the apostle)
Mt 20:20; Mk 5:37; Mk 15:40; Lk 9:54; Ac 3:1; Ac 4:13; Ac 8:14; Ac 10:37; Ac 12:2; Ac 12:17; Gal 2:2; Rev 1:9; Introduction to John: Author
JOHN (the Baptist)
baptism of
Mt 3:11; Mk 1:4; Ac 2:38; Ac 18:25; Ac 19:4
beheading of
Ac 12:1; Ac 12:2
birth date and childhood of
Mt 3:1; Lk 1:80
and Christ's baptism
Mt 3:15
compared to Jesus
Mt 4:17; Mt 17:12; Lk 5:33; Jn 1:15
compared to others
Mal 4:5; Mt 11:11
disciples of
Mk 2:18; Ac 19:1
imprisonment of
Mt 4:12; Mk 6:17
lifestyle of
Mt 3:4; Lk 1:15; Lk 5:33
ministry of
Mal 3:1; Mal 4:1; Mal 4:6; Mt 3:3; Mt 4:17; Lk 16:16; Jn 1:7; Jn 1:23; Jn 3:30
name, meaning of
Ezr 2:46; Mk 1:4
JOHN (Hyrcanus)
Mk 2:16; "The Time Between the Testaments," 1451
JOHN MARK. *See* MARK, JOHN
JONADAB
Jer 35:6
JONAH
Lk 11:30; Lk 11:31–32; Introduction to Jonah: Author; "The Book of Jonah," 1384
JONATHAN (son of Annas)
Ac 4:6
JONATHAN (son of Gershom)
Jdg 18:30
JONATHAN (son of Saul)
1Sa 13:2; 1Sa 14:24–26; 1Sa 15:23; 1Sa 18:3; 1Sa 18:4; 1Sa 19:4; 1Sa 20:11; 1Sa 20:15; 1Sa 20:16; Ezr 8:6
JOPPA
Jos 19:40; Ac 9:32; Ac 9:36
JORAM
1Ki 16:30; 1Ki 16:31; 2Ki 6:30; 2Ki 6:33; 2Ch 22:6; 2Ch 22:7
JORDAN RIVER
Jos 1:2; 2Sa 19:41; 1Ki 20:26; 2Ki 5:10; 1Ch 12:8–15; Isa 33:9; Zec 11:3; Mk 1:5; Mk 1:16
JORDAN VALLEY
Ge 13:10; 1Ki 20:26
JOSEPH (of Arimathea)
Isa 53:9; Lk 23:50; Jn 19:38
JOSEPH (Barsabbas)
Ac 1:23; Ac 15:22
JOSEPH (brother of Christ)
Lk 8:19
JOSEPH (husband of Mary)
Mt 1:16; Mt 1:18; Mt 1:20; Mt 13:55; Lk 1:32; Lk 3:23–38
JOSEPH (son of Jacob)
and covenant of God
Ge 37:2
and Daniel
Da 1:9
death of
Ge 50:25; Ge 50:26
faith of
Heb 11:22
and his brothers
Ge 43:30; Ge 50:17; Isa 42:14; Ac 7:9
interpreter of dreams
Jdg 7:13–14
name of
Ge 41:45
as representative of Israel
Ge 39:1; Ge 39:6; Ge 40:8
as ruler over Egypt
Ge 41:40; Ne 5:5
tribe of
1Ch 2:1–2; 1Ch 5:1–10; Isa 9:21; Eze 47:13; Eze 48:31; Am 5:6
JOSEPHUS
Ge 31:19; Mt 24:21; Introduction to Ezra: Ezra and Nehemiah; "The Book of the Twelve, or the Minor Prophets," 1333; "The Time Between the Testaments," 1451
JOSHUA (Moses' aide)
Ex 17:9; Jos 1:1–18; Jos 1:10; Jos 3:7; Jos 24:1–33; Ne 8:17; 1Co 10:5; Heb 4:1; Heb 4:6–8; Heb 11:30; Introduction to Joshua: The Life of Joshua; "Conquest of Canaan," 309
JOSHUA (priest)
Zec 3:1; Zec 3:7; Zec 4:1–14; Zec 4:3
JOSIAH
1Ki 13:2; 2Ki 22:3; 2Ki 22:20; 2Ki 23:22; 2Ki 23:34; 2Ch 28:3; 2Ch 36:2; Isa 57:1; Zep 1:4–6; Mt 1:11
JOTBAH
2Ki 21:19
JOTHAM (king of Judah)
2Ki 15:5; 2Ki 15:33; 2Ki 16:2; Introduction to Micah: Date
JOY
in the Lord
Dt 12:12; 1Sa 11:15; Ps 45:7; Jn 3:29; Php 1:21; Php 1:26; Php 2:17–18; 1Th 5:16; 1Jn 1:4
in suffering
Ro 5:3; Php 4:4; Jas 1:2
JUBILEE, YEAR OF. *See* YEAR OF JUBILEE
JUDAH
Ge 43:3; Ge 43:9; Ge 49:8–11; Nu 2:3–7; Jdg 1:2; "The Divided Kingdom," 497; "Rulers of the Divided Kingdom of Israel and Judah," 504; "Assyrian Campaigns against Israel and Judah," 552; "Nebuchadnezzar's Campaigns against Judah," 572; "Exile of the Southern Kingdom," 576
JUDAISM
Gal 1:13; Gal 4:15; Gal 4:25; Gal 5:9; "The Time Between the Testaments," 1451
JUDAIZERS
Ro 14:1; Gal 2:4; Gal 2:11; Gal 2:12; Gal 4:30; Gal 5:7; Gal 6:12;

Introduction to Galatians: Occasion and Purpose

JUDAS (Barsabbas)
Ac 1:23; Ac 15:22

JUDAS (brother of Christ)
Lk 8:19

JUDAS (the Galilean)
Ac 5:37

JUDAS (Iscariot)
Mt 26:23; Mt 28:16; Lk 24:9; Jn 6:71; Jn 13:26–27; Jn 17:12; Ac 1:11; Ac 1:18; Ac 1:20; 1Co 15:5; 2Th 2:3

JUDAS (son of James)
Lk 6:16; Ac 1:13

JUDAS MACCABEUS
Da 8:9–12; Da 8:14; Da 11:34; Jn 10:22; "The Time Between the Testaments," 1451

JUDEANS
Mk 10:1; Lk 23:5; Ac 1:8; Ac 8:1; Ac 15:1; Ro 15:31

JUDGING OTHERS
Mt 7:1; Ro 2:1; Ro 14:1; Ro 14:10; 1Co 5:4; 1Co 5:12

JUDGMENT, GOD'S. *See also* GOD: as judge
as act of purification
Zep 3:9–20; Jn 15:2; 1Pe 4:17
agents of
Jer 1:16
of all people
Ge 3:14; Gal 6:5; 2Ti 4:1
of believers
Jer 1:16; Ro 14:10; 2Co 5:10; Gal 6:5; Jas 2:12
disciplinary
Eze 5:13; 1Co 11:29
eternal
Mic 7:4; 1Co 3:13; 1Th 1:10; 1Th 5:2; Heb 6:1–2; Jas 2:13; Jude 1:12
imagery of
Eze 13:11; Rev 14:15
on Israel and Judah
Am 1:2–15; Am 2:1–16; Introduction to Jeremiah: Themes and Message; Introduction to Amos: Theological Theme and Message
just
Ge 18:25; Ps 58:1–11; Ecc 3:17; Eze 18:30; Ob 15; Jn 16:11; 2Th 1:5
and mercy
Jas 2:13; Introduction to Jeremiah: Themes and Message
and salvation
Ge 18:17; Jn 12:47; Heb 9:27
time of
Mt 13:47–51; 1Co 4:5; 1Th 5:2
on wicked cities
Ge 18:21; Eze 25:1–17; Eze 26:1–21; Eze 27:1–36; Eze 28:1–26; Eze 29:1–21; Eze 30:1–26; Eze 31:1–18; Eze 32:1–32; Introduction to Nahum: Theological Themes
of works
Ecc 11:9; Ecc 12:14; Ro 2:1–16; Ro 14:10; 1Co 3:13; 2Co 5:10; Rev 20:12

JULIUS
Ac 27:1; Ac 27:2; Ac 27:6

JUNIAS
Mk 6:30; Ro 16:7

JUSTICE
Ge 18:25; Ps 5:10; Ps 89:14; Isa 42:1; Zec 7:9; Zec 8:16; Introduction to Amos: Theological Theme and Message

JUSTIFICATION
before God
Lk 18:14
declared righteous
Ro 3:24
and faith
Ro 4:12; Ro 4:24; Gal 2:16; Jas 2:14–26
and forgiveness of sins
Ac 13:39
and the Holy Spirit
Ro 8:10; Gal 4:22–23

JUSTIN MARTYR
Ro 16:16; 1Co 16:2

JUSTUS
Ac 1:23

K

KADESH BARNEA
Ge 14:7; Nu 20:1; Eze 47:19

KADESH IN NAPHTALI
Jdg 4:6

KARNAK
2Ch 12:2; Eze 30:14; Na 3:8

KAVALLA
Ac 16:11; Ac 17:1

KEBAR RIVER
Ezr 2:59; Eze 1:1

KEDAR
Isa 21:16; Jer 2:10

KEILAH
Ne 3:17–18

KENITES
Nu 24:21; 1Sa 15:6; 1Ch 2:55

KEREN-HAPPUCH
Job 42:14

KERETHITES
1Sa 30:14; 2Sa 8:18; 1Ch 18:17; Eze 25:16

KERIOTH
Am 2:2; Mk 3:19; Jn 6:71

KERIOTH-HEZRON
Mk 3:19

KERITH RAVINE
1Ki 17:3

KETURAH
Job 2:11

KEZIAH
Job 42:14

KHAMSIN
Ex 10:21

KHARGAH OASIS
Ezr 6:8

KHERSA
Mk 5:1

KHOSER RIVER
Na 2:6

KIDRON VALLEY
2Ch 29:16; Ne 3:28; Jn 18:1

KILEAB
2Sa 3:3; 2Sa 13:28

KINDNESS
Jos 2:12; 1Ki 3:6

KING LISTS
"Ancient Texts Relating to the Old Testament," xxii

KING OF KINGS
Ezr 7:12; Zec 6:11; Zec 14:9; Rev 17:14

KINGDOM
of God
Mt 3:2; Mt 13:44–45; Mt 19:16; Lk 4:43; Lk 17:21; 1Co 4:20; 1Co 15:24; 1Co 15:25
of heaven
Da 4:26; Mt 3:2; Mt 19:16

KING'S FOREST
Ne 2:8

KING'S GATE
Est 2:19

KING'S HIGHWAY
"The Book of Ruth," 367

KING'S POOL
Ne 2:14

KING'S VALLEY
2Sa 18:18

KINGSHIP IN ANCIENT TIMES
Ps 2:7; Ps 3:3; Ps 11:7; Ps 17:8; Ps 23:1

KINNERETH
Dt 3:17
Sea of
Mk 1:16

KINSMAN-REDEEMER
Ge 38:8; Ru 2:20; Ru 3:12; Ru 4:3; Ru 4:6

KIRIATH ARBA
Ge 23:2; Jos 14:15; Ne 11:25

KIRIATH BAAL
1Ch 13:6

KIRIATH JEARIM
2Ki 23:37; 1Ch 13:6

KISLEV
Ne 1:1; Ne 2:1; "Hebrew Calendar and Selected Events," 104

KISS
Ge 41:40; Ps 2:12

KITTIM
Nu 24:24; Jer 2:10

KNOWING GOD
Ex 6:3; 1Sa 2:12; 1Sa 3:7; Pr 2:5; Jer 22:16; 1Co 13:12

KNOWLEDGE, CHRISTIAN
1Co 8:2; Tit 1:16

KNOWLEDGE OF GOOD AND EVIL
Ge 2:9; Heb 5:14

KODRANTES
Lk 12:6

KOHATHITES
Jos 21:4; 1Ch 6:22–23; 1Ch 15:4–10

KONYA
Ac 13:51
KORAH
Nu 16:1 – 7; Nu 16:24; Ps 42:1; Jude 11
KORAZIN
Mt 11:21

L

LABAN
Ge 30:37
LABOR, FORCED
2Sa 20:24; 1Ki 5:13; 1Ki 9:15
LACHISH
2Ki 14:19; 2Ki 25:1; Isa 36:2; Mic 1:13
LACHISH OSTRACA (LETTERS)
2Ki 25:1; Jer 34:7; "Ancient Texts Relating to the Old Testament," xxii
LAEL
Nu 3:24
LAISH
Ge 14:14; Jdg 18:7
LAKE OF FIRE
Rev 2:11
LAMB
Ge 22:8; Rev 5:6; Rev 14:4; Rev 15:3; Rev 17:8; Rev 17:14; Rev 19:7; Rev 19:17
LAMB OF GOD
Ge 22:8; Jn 1:29; 1Co 5:7
LAMENTS
2Sa 1:17; Eze 19:1; Am 5:1; Am 5:16 – 17; Introduction to Lamentations
LAMP
Ex 25:37; 2Sa 22:29; 1Ki 11:36; Ps 18:28
LAMPSTAND
Ex 25:37; Zec 4:2; Heb 9:2; "Tabernacle Furnishings," 127; "Temple Furnishings," 487
LAODICEA
1Co 16:19; Col 2:1; Rev 3:14; Rev 3:16; Rev 3:18
LASEA
Ac 27:8
LAST DAYS (LATER TIMES, ETC.)
Nu 24:14; Isa 2:2; Joel 2:28; Ac 2:17; 1Ti 4:1; 2Ti 3:1; Heb 1:1 – 2; Jas 5:9; 2Pe 3:3; 1Jn 2:18
LAST SUPPER. *See* LORD'S SUPPER: and the Passover
LATTER PROPHETS
Introduction to Isaiah: Position in the Hebrew Bible
LAW
Ex 18:16; Lev 18:5; Isa 8:16; Mt 5:17; Ac 28:23; Ro 3:21; Ro 7:4; Ro 7:5; Ro 7:6; Ro 7:7; Ro 7:12; Ro 8:2; 1Co 9:20; 1Co 9:21; Gal 4:25; Gal 5:14; Heb 7:18; Heb 7:19
case, in Israel
Nu 27:5; Jos 20:1 – 9; 1Ki 3:16
of love
Jas 2:8
of retaliation
Ex 21:23 – 25
LAW OF MOSES. *See also* MOSES: law of
applications/interpretations of
Mt 15:2; Lk 11:46; Jn 5:10; Jn 7:49
LAYING ON OF HANDS
Ex 29:10; Ac 6:6; Ac 13:3; 2Ti 1:6; Heb 6:1 – 2
LAZARUS
Ezr 7:5; Jn 11:1; Jn 11:4; Jn 11:17; Jn 11:22
LEAH
Ge 29:31 – 35; Mal 1:3
LEAVEN
1Co 5:6
LEBANON
SS 4:8; SS 4:15; SS 5:15; Eze 31:3; Mk 7:24; Ac 11:19
LEBO HAMATH
2Ki 14:25; Eze 47:15; Am 6:14
LEGALISM
1Sa 21:4; Ecc 7:18; Mt 5:18 – 20; Mk 2:16; Mk 2:25; Mk 7:11; Mk 7:13; Mk 10:20; Lk 5:33; Lk 11:46; Ac 15:1; Ac 21:24; Ro 9:31; Ro 14:1; Gal 2:16; Gal 4:9; Gal 4:15; Php 3:6
LEGION
Mk 5:9
LEHI
Jdg 15:9
LENTIL
Ge 25:34
LEPROSY
Lev 13:2; 2Ki 5:11; 2Ch 26:23; Mt 8:2; Mk 1:44; Lk 5:12; Lk 5:14; Lk 17:16
LEPTON
Lk 12:59
LEVI. *See also* MATTHEW
tribe of
1Ch 2:6; 1Ch 6:1 – 3; 1Ch 15:4 – 10; "The Tribes of Israel," 82; Introduction to Leviticus: Title
LEVIATHAN
Job 3:8; Job 26:13; Job 41:1; Ps 104:26; Isa 27:1; Jnh 1:17; Rev 12:3
LEVIRATE LAW. *See* MARRIAGE: levirate
LEVIRATE MARRIAGE. *See* MARRIAGE: levirate
LEVITES
Introduction to Leviticus: Title
and the ark
1Ch 13:10
census of
1Ch 23:3
cities of
Nu 3:1 – 5; Nu 3:6 – 15
cleansing of
Nu 8:5 – 26; Mal 3:3
duties of
Nu 8:24; Nu 8:26; 1Ch 9:28 – 34; 2Ch 30:17; Ne 12:30; Ne 13:30; Jn 1:19
set apart
Ex 32:29
LEVITICAL PRIESTHOOD. *See* PRIESTHOOD, LEVITICAL
LIBERTINISM
Ecc 7:18; Gal 5:22 – 23; Php 3:19; Rev 2:23
LIBNAH
2Ki 8:22; 2Ch 21:10
LIBYA
Eze 27:10; Ac 6:9
LIFE
the blessing/sacredness of
Ge 9:4,6; Lev 17:11; 1Ki 17:22; Ps 69:32; Jn 5:21,25,26
descriptive of the Lord
Dt 30:20; Jn 1:4; Jn 11:25
God's purpose for humanity
Ge 2:9; Ge 50:20; Dt 30:20; Eze 16:6
identified with light
Ps 27:1; Ps 36:9; 2Co 4:6
resurrection
Ro 6:8; 1Co 4:11,16
LIGHT
Ge 1:3; Ps 27:1; Jn 1:4; Jn 8:12; 2Co 4:6; Col 1:12; 1Jn 1:5; 1Jn 1:6 – 7
LILY
SS 2:1
LION
Ge 49:9; Rev 5:5
LO DEBAR
2Sa 9:4; Am 6:13
LO-AMMI
Hos 1:9
LOCUSTS
and day of the Lord
Rev 9:3
destruction by
Joel 1:5; Joel 1:9
as food
Mt 3:4
plague of
Ex 10:4; Joel 1:6; Introduction to Joel: Message
LOIS
2Ti 1:5
LONGEVITY
Ge 5:5; Ge 5:27; Isa 65:20
LO-RUHAMAH
Hos 1:6; Hos 2:19
LORD. *See* NAMES OF GOD: LORD (Yahweh/Jehovah)
LORD ALMIGHTY. *See* NAMES OF GOD: LORD Almighty (*Yahweh Sabaoth*)
LORD'S ANOINTED
1Sa 2:10; 1Sa 9:16; 1Sa 24:6; Ps 2:1 – 12
LORD'S DAY
Rev 1:10
LORD'S PRAYER
Lk 11:1; Lk 11:4
LORD'S SUPPER
desecration of
Nu 9:13; 1Co 11:20; 1Co 11:21; 1Co 11:27

explanation of
Mk 14:22
and faith
Jn 6:53 – 58; 1Co 11:28
foreshadowed
Ex 24:11
frequency of
1Co 11:26
and Messianic banquet
1Ch 12:38 – 40
and the Passover
Ex 12:48; Lk 22:16
symbol of
1Co 10:16; 1Co 11:24; 1Co 11:25
and the worship service
Ac 20:7; Ac 28:14
LOT
Ge 13:12; Ge 13:14; Ge 14:12; Ge 19:1; Ge 19:14; 2Sa 8:2; Isa 15:5
LOTS, CASTING OF
Ex 28:30; Jos 7:14; Ne 11:1; Pr 16:33; Eze 21:21; Jnh 1:7; Ac 1:26
LOT'S WIFE
Ge 19:26
LOVE
brotherly
1Th 4:9
as a debt
Ro 13:8
for enemies
Ex 23:4 – 5; Lev 19:18; Lk 6:27; Lk 10:31 – 33; Ro 12:20
and forgiveness
Pr 10:12
God's
Dt 4:37; Jos 2:12; Lk 15:31; 1Co 13:13; 2Co 5:14; 1Th 1:4; 2Th 2:13; 2Th 3:5; Tit 3:4; 1Jn 2:7 – 8; 1Jn 4:12
and the great commandment
Lk 10:27; Ro 13:9; 1Pe 1:22
marital
Ex 20:5; SS 8:6 – 7; Tit 2:4; Introduction to Song of Songs: Theme and Theology
meaning of
Ex 20:5; Ex 20:6; Jos 22:5; Mt 22:37; Mt 22:39; Jn 21:15 – 17; 1Co 13:1
sincere
Ro 12:9; 2Co 8:8; 2Pe 1:7
and spiritual gifts
1Co 14:1
LOVE FEAST. *See* AGAPE
LOWER POOL
Ne 3:15; Isa 22:9
LUCIFER
Isa 14:12
LUCIUS (of Cyrene)
Ac 13:1
LUKE
Ac 1:1; 2Co 8:18; Col 4:14; Introduction to Luke: Author; Introduction to Acts: Author
LUST
Pr 6:25; Eph 5:3
LUTHER, MARTIN
Ps 46:1 – 11; Ro 3:28; Phm 17,19; Jas 2:14 – 26
LYCAONIA
Ac 14:6
LYDDA
Ezr 2:33; Ac 9:32
LYDIA (woman)
Ac 16:14; 1Co 1:16; Rev 2:18
LYDIA (territory)
Da 7:4 – 7; Rev 3:1
LYRE
Ne 12:27
LYSANIAS
Lk 3:1
LYSTRA
Ac 14:6; Ac 14:12; 2Ti 3:11

M

MAACAH (daughter of Absalom)
2Sa 14:27; 1Ki 15:2; 1Ki 15:13; 2Ch 11:20
MAACAH (wife of David)
2Sa 3:3; 2Sa 13:1
MAACATHITES
Dt 3:14
MACCABEES
Da 11:5; Da 11:34; Mk 2:16; Heb 11:35; "Ptolemies and Seleucids," 1330; "From Malachi to Christ," 1450; "The Time Between the Testaments," 1451
MACEDON
Da 7:4 – 7
MACEDONIA
Ac 16:9; 1Co 16:5; 1Co 16:10; Php 4:15; 1Th 1:7
MACHAERUS
Mk 6:17
MACHPELAH
Ge 23:9
MAGADAN
Mt 15:39; Mk 8:10
MAGDALA
Mk 8:10
MAGI
Mt 2:1; Mt 2:2; Mt 2:11
MAGICIANS
Ge 41:8; Dt 18:9; Ac 19:19; Rev 9:21
MAGNIFICAT
Hannah's
1Sa 2:1
Mary's
Lk 1:46 – 55
MAGOG
Ge 10:2; Eze 38:2; Rev 20:8
MAHANAIM
Ge 32:2; 2Sa 2:8; 2Sa 2:11; 2Sa 17:24
MAHER-SHALAL-HASH-BAZ
Isa 5:19; Isa 7:14; Isa 8:1 – 2; Isa 8:3
MAHLON
Ru 1:5; Ru 4:5
MAKIR
Ge 50:23; Jos 13:29; Jdg 5:13 – 18; 2Sa 9:4
MAKKEDAH
Jos 10:16
MALCHUS
Mk 14:47; Lk 22:51; Lk 22:59
MALKIJAH
Jer 35:6
MALTA
Ac 28:1
MALTHACE
Mt 14:3; "House of Herod," 1465
MAN
creation of
Ge 1:26; Ge 2:7; Ge 9:5,6; Ps 139:14
his dominion over the earth
Ge 1:26,28; Ge 2:15; Ge 9:2; Ps 8:6 – 8; Heb 2:6 – 8; Heb 8:1; Heb 9:1 – 28
fall of
Ge 3:1,7,14; Ro 5:12 – 21,14; Ro 16:17 – 20; 1Co 15:22,56
MANAEN
Ac 13:1
MANASSEH (grandfather of Jonathan)
Jdg 18:30
MANASSEH (son of Hezekiah)
2Ki 20:18; 2Ki 21:1; 2Ki 21:3; 2Ki 21:15; 2Ki 21:16; 2Ki 21:20; 2Ki 23:6; 2Ch 33:11 – 17; 2Ch 33:20; Ezr 4:10; Isa 9:21; Isa 39:6; Na 1:11; Zep 1:5; Mt 5:22
MANASSEH (son of Joseph)
Ge 48:5 – 7; Ge 48:13; Jos 13:29; Jos 14:4; Jdg 10:3; 2Ki 17:16; Ac 7:14; Rev 7:6
MANDRAKE
Ge 30:14
MANNA
Nu 11:7; Nu 21:5; Jos 5:12; 2Ch 5:10; Mt 4:4; Jn 6:31; Jn 6:58; 1Co 10:3 – 4; Rev 2:17
MARAH
Ex 15:23; Rev 8:11
MARDIKH
Introduction to Genesis: Background
MARDUK
Est 2:5; Isa 45:4; Isa 46:1; Da 1:7; Da 4:8; Introduction to Genesis: Background
MARI
Ge 24:10; Introduction to Genesis: Background
MARI TABLETS
"Ancient Texts Relating to the Old Testament," xxiii
MARIAMNE
Mt 14:3; "House of Herod," 1465
MARK, JOHN
Mk 14:51; Ac 1:13; Ac 10:37; Ac 12:25; Ac 13:5; Ac 13:13; Ac 15:38; Ac 15:39; Col 4:10; 2Ti 4:11; 1Pe 5:13; Introduction to Mark: John Mark in the NT
MARKET DISTRICT
Ne 11:9

MARRIAGE. *See also* DIVORCE
Mal 2:14; 1Co 6:16; 1Co 6:17; 1Co 6:18; 1Co 7:1; 1Co 7:3; 1Co 7:5; 1Co 7:6; 1Co 7:10; 1Co 7:11; 1Co 7:14; 1Co 7:15; 1Co 7:36; 1Co 7:37; 1Co 7:39; 1Co 11:5–6; Eph 5:22; Eph 5:23; Eph 5:25; 1Ti 3:2; Tit 1:6
customs of ancient Near East
Ge 21:21; Ge 29:22; Ex 22:16; Jdg 14:2,10; Ru 3:4,9; 1Sa 18:25; SS 8:8; Mt 1:18; Mt 22:11; Mk 2:19; Jn 2:1
levirate
Ge 38:8; Ru 1:11; Ru 4:5; 1Ch 3:19; Mt 22:24
MARTHA
Lk 19:29; Jn 11:22; Jn 11:27; Jn 11:37
MARTYRDOM
1Co 13:3; Heb 12:1; Rev 10:6
MARY (of Bethany)
Lk 19:29; Jn 11:20; Jn 11:21; Jn 11:31; Jn 12:3
MARY (Magdalene)
Mk 15:40; Lk 8:2; Jn 20:16; Jn 20:17
MARY (mother of Jesus)
Mt 1:16; Mt 1:18; Mt 1:20; Mt 2:11; Lk 1:32; Lk 2:5; Lk 2:35; Lk 8:19; Lk 24:10; Ac 1:14
MARY (mother of Mark)
Ac 1:13; Ac 12:12; Col 4:15
MARY (wife of Clopas)
Mt 28:1
MASORETIC TEXT
1Ch 14:12; 2Ch 2:18
MASSAH
Ex 17:7; Nu 20:13
MATERIALISM
Jdg 17:10; 2Ki 1:8; 2Ki 5:26; Mk 10:22; Lk 12:13
MATTANIAH
2Ki 24:17; 2Ch 36:4
MATTATHIAS
1Ch 24:7; Da 11:34; "The Time Between the Testaments," 1451
MATTHEW
Hos 11:1; Mk 2:14; Lk 5:27; Lk 5:28; Lk 5:29; Lk 6:15; Introduction to Matthew: Author
MATTHIAS
Ac 2:1
MATURITY
1Co 2:14–23; 1Co 3:1–4; Heb 5:14; Heb 13:22
MEANINGLESSNESS
Ecc 1:2
MEDEBA
2Ki 1:1; 1Ch 19:7; Isa 15:2
MEDES
Ezr 6:2; Isa 13:17; Na 1:14; Ac 2:9
MEDIATOR
Ge 28:12; Ex 20:19; Ex 32:30; Job 5:1; Gal 3:20; Heb 8:6
MEDIUM (at Endor)
1Sa 28:7; 1Sa 28:12; 1Sa 28:21
MEDIUMS
Lev 20:6; Dt 18:9
MEDO-PERSIA
Da 2:32–43; Da 7:4–7; Da 8:3
MEEKNESS
Ps 37:11; Mt 5:5
MEGIDDO
Jos 17:11; Jdg 5:19; 1Ki 9:15; 1Ki 22:39; Rev 16:16
MELCHIZEDEK
Ge 14:18–20; Ps 110:4; Ecc 1:16; Heb 5:5; Heb 7:1; Heb 7:3; Heb 7:4; Heb 7:11; Heb 7:16; Heb 8:7; Heb 13:10
MELITA
Ac 28:1
MELQART
1Ki 16:31
MEMPHIS
Isa 19:13; Eze 30:13; Hos 9:6
MENAHEM
2Ki 15:12; 2Ki 15:14; Hos 5:13; Hos 7:11; Hos 8:9
MENANDER
1Co 15:33
MENELAUS
1Sa 2:35
MENSTRUATION
Ge 31:35; Lev 15:24; Dt 22:14
MEPHIBOSHETH
Jdg 6:32; 2Sa 9:2; 2Sa 9:7; 2Sa 19:27
MERARI
Ex 6:16; 1Ch 15:4–10
MERATHAIM
Jer 50:21
MERCY
Ge 19:16; Hos 6:6; Ro 9:18,22–23; Ro 12:8; Tit 3:5; Introduction to Jeremiah: Themes and Message
MERIB-BAAL
Jdg 6:32; 2Sa 4:4
MERIBAH
Ex 17:7; Nu 20:13
MERIBAH KADESH
Eze 47:19
MERODACH-BALADAN
2Ki 20:1; 2Ki 20:12
MEROM
Jos 11:5
MEROZ
Jdg 5:23
MESHA
2Ki 3:27; Isa 16:1
MESHA (MOABITE) STONE (INSCRIPTION)
Ge 49:19; 2Ki 1:1
MESHACH
Da 1:7
MESHECH (son of Japheth)
Ge 10:2
MESHECH (son of Shem)
Eze 32:26; Eze 38:2
MESHULLAM (leader in return from exile)
Ezr 8:16; Ezr 10:15
MESHULLAM (son of Berekiah)
Ne 2:10; Ne 3:4; Ne 6:17–18
MESOPOTAMIA
Ge 24:10; 1Ki 4:30; Ezr 2:59; Ezr 2:69; Ac 2:9
MESSIAH. *See also* CHRIST
Nu 3:3; Ps 2:2; Isa 9:6; Isa 45:1; Da 9:25–27; Am 9:12; Mic 5:3; Mic 5:4; Mt 16:16; Mk 14:61; Jn 1:25
MESSIANIC REFERENCES
Ge 49:10; Dt 18:15; 2Sa 7:16; Ps 110:1–7; Isa 42:1–4; Jer 23:5; Da 7:18; Introduction to Zechariah: Theological Teaching
MESSIANIC AGE
Isa 2:2; Isa 11:6–9; Lk 4:19; Heb 1:1
MESSIANIC BANQUET
1Ch 12:38–40; Mt 8:11; Lk 14:15
MESSIANIC SECRET
Mt 8:4; Mt 16:20; Mk 3:12; Mk 5:19; Mk 5:43; Lk 9:21; Introduction to Mark: Emphases
MEUNITES
Jdg 10:12; 2Ch 20:1
MEZUZOT
Dt 6:8–9
MICAH (Ephraimite)
Jdg 16:5; Jdg 17:2; Jdg 18:24
MICAH (prophet)
Job 30:29; Mt 2:6; Introduction to Micah: Author
MICAIAH
1Ki 22:15; 1Ki 22:16; 1Ki 22:17
MICHAEL
Ezr 8:8; Da 10:13; Lk 1:19; 1Th 4:16; Heb 1:4; Rev 12:7
MICHAL
1Sa 15:23; 1Sa 18:28; 1Sa 19:24; 2Sa 3:13; 2Sa 6:23
MICMASH
1Sa 13:2; Isa 10:28
MIDIAN
Ex 2:15; Ac 7:29; Heb 11:27
MIDIANITES
Ge 37:25; Jdg 6:1; Jdg 7:24; 1Ki 11:18; "Gideon's Battles," 342
MIDRASH
Zec 6:12
MIGDOL
Ex 14:2; Eze 29:10
MILCOM
Jdg 10:6; 1Ki 11:5; Jer 49:1
MILDEW
Lev 13:47
MILETUS
Ac 20:15; 2Ti 4:20
MILK AND HONEY
Ex 3:8; SS 4:11
MILLENNIUM, THE
1Co 15:25; Rev 20:2
MILLO
Jdg 9:6
MILLSTONES
Dt 24:6; Jdg 9:53; Mk 9:42
MINA
Ezr 2:69; Da 5:26–28; Lk 19:13

MINISTERS
"manual" for
1Th 2:1–12
payment of
Nu 18:12; Ne 5:14; 1Co 9:4,11,18,19; 2Co 2:17; 2Co 11:7,12; 1Th 2:6
a warning to
Nu 3:4
MINNITH
Eze 27:17
MINOR PROPHETS
1333
MIRACLES OF JESUS. *See also* MIRACLES OF OTHERS
feeding of the 5,000
Mt 15:37; Mk 6:42; Mk 6:43; Mk 6:44
feeding of the 4,000
Mt 15:37; Mk 8:4
healing of lame man
Jn 7:21
list of "Miracles of Jesus," 1625
purpose of
Mk 2:10; Jn 2:11
MIRACLES OF OTHERS. *See also* MIRACLES OF JESUS
Ex 4:8; Ex 8:19; 1Co 12:12
of Elijah
1Ki 17:4; 1Ki 17:16; 1Ki 18:38; 2Ki 1:10; 2Ki 2:8
of Elisha
2Ki 2:14; 2Ki 2:21; 2Ki 2:24; 2Ki 4:4; 2Ki 4:33; 2Ki 5:10; 2Ki 5:14; 2Ki 6:6; 2Ki 6:18; 2Ki 13:21
of Joshua
Jos 3:1–17; Jos 4:1–24; Jos 3:7; Jos 3:10; Jos 3:13; Jos 6:1; Jos 10:13
of Moses
Ex 7:12; Ex 7:17; Ex 14:21; Ex 15:25; Ex 17:6; Nu 20:11; Nu 21:8–9
of Samuel
1Sa 12:19
MIRIAM
Ex 15:20; Lk 2:36
MISHAEL
Da 1:6
MISHNAH
Ne 10:34; Jer 35:19; Mt 15:2; Mk 2:24; Mk 11:15
MISHNEH
Ne 3:6
MITHREDATH
Ezr 1:8
MITYLENE
Ac 20:14
MIZPAH
Ge 31:49; Jdg 10:17; 1Sa 7:5; 1Ki 15:22; 2Ki 25:23; Hos 5:1; "Jacob's Journeys," 52
MNASON
Ac 21:16
MOAB
Ge 19:36–38; Ru 1:15; 2Ki 3:23; Isa 15:1; Isa 15:9; Isa 16:3; "The Book of Ruth," 367
MOABITE STONE
Introduction to 1 Kings: Theme; "Ancient Texts Relating to the Old Testament," xxiii
MOABITES
Ru 1:4; 2Sa 8:2; 2Ki 3:23; Isa 15:9; Isa 16:3; "The Book of Ruth," 367
MOLECH
Lev 18:21; Jdg 10:6; 1Ki 11:5; Isa 44:19; Isa 57:9; Jer 49:1; Zep 1:5; Zep 3:10
MONEY
blessings of
Pr 3:2,10; Pr 10:15,22; Ecc 10:19; Lk 16:9
dangers of
1Ki 9:4–5; Mk 4:19; Mk 10:21; Lk 12:33
love of
Pr 23:4; Ecc 5:10; Ac 5:1
true wealth
Lk 16:11; 2Co 6:10
using religion for
2Ki 5:26; Eze 13:19; 2Co 2:17; 2Co 11:7
and the wicked
Ps 49:1–20; Ps 73:18–20; Isa 53:9
MONOGAMY
Ge 2:24; Ge 4:19; 1Ti 3:2; Tit 1:6
MONOTHEISM
Dt 4:35; Introduction to Genesis: Theme and Message
MOON
Ge 1:16
MORDECAI
Ezr 2:2; Est 2:5; Est 2:19; Est 3:2–6; Est 5:9; Est 6:1; Est 7:8; Est 7:9; Est 8:2; Est 8:3–6; Est 8:15; Est 9:1; Est 9:20
MORESHETH
Introduction to Micah: Author
MORIAH, MOUNT. *See* MOUNT: Moriah
MOSES. *See also* MIRACLES: of Moses
birth of
Ex 2:2; Ex 2:10
call of
Ac 7:22; Ac 7:23; Ac 7:29; Ac 7:37; Heb 3:2
and Christ
Dt 18:15; Dt 34:12; Mt 17:3; Mt 22:24; Jn 6:31; Jn 6:32; Ac 7:35; Heb 3:2; Heb 3:5–6
death of
Jos 1:1; Heb 11:29
and fasting
Ezr 10:6
and the Holy Spirit
Hag 2:5
and John the Baptist
Mt 4:2
law of
1Ki 14:23; 1Ki 14:24; 1Ki 18:27; 1Ki 21:10; 2Ki 4:1; 1Ch 23:3; Job 31:29–32; Isa 47:6; Jn 5:10; Jn 5:45; Jn 7:22; Gal 2:16; Heb 7:11; Heb 10:5–6; Introduction to Genesis: Author and Date of Writing
leadership of
Nu 11:29; Nu 16:1–7; Nu 27:20; Introduction to Deuteronomy: Historical Setting
as mediator
Ex 20:19; Ex 24:2; Ex 32:30; Ex 33:11; Nu 7:89; Nu 11:12; Dt 9:19; Ac 7:38
obedience of
Nu 3:16; Nu 8:20
as prophet
Nu 1:1; Nu 9:23; Nu 11:29; Nu 12:6–8,8; Dt 18:15; Ac 3:22–26
punishment of
Nu 20:11; Nu 27:12–23
song of
Dt 32:4; Isa 44:8; Introduction to Numbers: Author and Date
MOST HIGH. *See* NAMES OF GOD
MOST HOLY PLACE
Ex 26:31–35; Ex 27:12–13; 1Ki 6:2; 1Ki 6:16; 1Ki 6:23; 2Ch 3:8; Ezr 6:15; Ps 28:2; Eze 41:22; Mt 27:51; Lk 1:9; Heb 4:14; Heb 8:2; Heb 9:4; Heb 9:28; Heb 10:19; Heb 10:20
MOT
Jdg 10:6; Job 18:14; Jer 9:21
MOTHER. *See also* BARRENNESS; CHILDREN; PARENTS
Ps 113:9; Pr 31:1,26
MOUNT
Carmel
1Ki 18:19; SS 7:5; Am 1:2
Ebal
Jos 8:30; Jn 4:20
Gerizim
Jn 4:20
Gilboa
Jdg 7:3; 2Sa 1:21
Gilead
Jdg 7:3; SS 4:1
Hermon
Dt 3:8; Jos 12:1; Lk 9:28
Horeb
Ex 3:1; Dt 1:2; 1Ki 19:7; 2Ki 8:7
Mizar
Ps 42:6
Moriah
Ge 22:2; 2Ch 3:1
of Olives
Eze 11:23; Zep 1:5; Zec 14:4; Mt 24:3; Mk 11:1; Lk 19:29; Ac 1:12; Ac 21:38
Olympus
Ps 48:2; Isa 14:13
Paran
Jdg 5:4; Hab 3:3
Perazim
Isa 28:21
Seir
Ge 36:8; Eze 35:2
Sinai
Ex 3:1; Ex 19:5; Ex 19:12–13; 1Ki 19:8; Ps 68:1–35; 2Co

3:7 – 18; Gal 4:24; Heb 8:6; Heb 12:18 – 21; Heb 12:25; Rev 4:1; Rev 15:5
Tabor
Jdg 4:6; Hos 5:1; Lk 9:28
of Transfiguration
Lk 3:22; Lk 9:28
Zaphon
Ps 48:2; Isa 14:13
Zion
2Sa 5:7; 2Ch 3:1; Ne 3:16; Ps 2:4 – 6; Ps 48:2; Isa 2:2 – 4; Eze 40:2; Ob 1:17; Ob 1:21; Zec 6:1; Heb 12:22; Rev 14:1
MOUNTAIN OF THE LORD
Isa 2:2 – 4; "The City of the Jebusites/David's Jerusalem," 432
MOURNING. *See also* GRIEF
Ge 37:34; 2Sa 13:19; 2Sa 15:30; Joel 1:5; Am 8:10; Mk 5:38; Jn 11:19
MURDER
Ge 1:26; Ge 4:8; Ge 4:23; Ge 9:6; Ex 20:13; Ex 21:13; Nu 35:33; Dt 21:23; Mt 5:21
MUSIC
instruments of
Nu 10:10; Ezr 3:10; Ne 12:27,35; Ps 150:3 – 5; Isa 38:20
songs/hymns
Ex 15:1 – 18; Jdg 5:1 – 31; Eph 5:19; Col 3:16
MUSICIANS
1Sa 16:14 – 23; 1Sa 17:1 – 58; 1Sa 16:16; 1Ch 25:1; Ezr 2:65; Ne 12:9; Ps 4:1
MUSTARD SEED
Mt 13:32; Lk 13:19
MYRA
Ac 27:5
MYRRH
Ge 37:25; Ex 25:6; SS 1:13; Mt 2:11; Mk 15:23; Rev 18:13
MYSIA
Ac 16:7
MYSTERY
Da 2:18; Ro 11:25; 1Co 2:7; 1Co 13:2; 1Co 14:2; 1Co 15:51; Eph 3:3; Eph 5:32; Col 1:26; 2Th 2:7; 1Ti 3:16; Rev 10:7; Rev 17:5

N

NAAMAN
1Sa 9:7; 2Ki 5:10; 2Ki 5:11; 2Ki 5:14; 2Ki 5:15; 2Ki 5:19
NABAL
1Sa 25:2 – 44
NABONIDUS
Da 5:1; Da 5:7; Da 5:10; Da 5:26 – 28
NABOPOLASSAR
2Ki 23:29; 2Ki 24:1; 2Ch 35:21; Ezr 5:12; Eze 31:11; Na 2:1
NABOTH
1Ki 21:3; 1Ki 21:13; 1Ki 21:19
NABU
Ezr 10:43; Isa 46:1; Da 3:2
NADAB
Ex 24:1; 1Ki 14:14; Ac 5:1
NAHUM
Jnh 1:2; Introduction to Nahum: Author
NAIOTH
1Sa 19:18
NAME
Ge 11:4; Ge 17:5; Ex 33:19; Dt 6:13; 1Sa 25:25; Ps 5:11; Jer 16:21; Eze 20:9; 2Th 1:12; Heb 1:4
NAMES OF GOD
Ex 34:6 – 7; 1Ki 5:5; Eze 20:9; Introduction, xvii
Eternal God (*El Olam*)
Ge 21:33
God (*Elohim*)
Ge 1:1; Ge 2:4; Ge 7:16; Ecc 1:13
God Almighty (*El Shaddai*)
Ge 17:1; Job 5:17
God Most High (*El Elyon*)
Ge 14:19; Dt 32:8
"I Am"
Ex 3:14; Jn 6:35; Jn 8:58
Lord (*Adonai*)
Ge 18:27; Zec 4:14
LORD (*Yahweh/Jehovah*)
Ge 2:4; Ge 7:16; Ex 3:14 – 15; Ex 6:3,6; Lev 18:2; Dt 28:58
LORD Almighty (*Yahweh Sabaoth*)
1Sa 1:3
NAMING
Ge 1:5; Ge 2:19; Ge 17:5; Ge 17:15; Ge 32:28
NAOMI
Ru 1:1 – 4; Ru 3:4
NAPHTALI
Ex 1:2 – 4; Jos 19:32; 1Ki 15:20; 2Ki 15:29; 1Ch 7:13; 2Ch 2:13; Isa 9:1
NARD
SS 1:12; Mk 14:3; Jn 12:3
NATHAN
2Sa 7:3; 2Sa 12:13; 1Ki 1:24; 1Ki 2:4; Ac 3:24; Introduction to 1 Samuel: Literary Features, Authorship and Date
NATHANAEL
Lk 6:14; Jn 1:49; Ac 1:13
NAZARENE
Mt 2:23
NAZARETH
Mt 2:23; Lk 4:23
NAZIRITE VOW
Nu 6:2; Nu 6:4; Nu 6:5; Nu 6:6; Nu 6:9 – 12; Jdg 13:5; 1Sa 1:11; Jer 7:29; Am 2:11; Lk 1:15; Ac 18:18; Ac 21:23
NEAPOLIS
Ac 8:5; Ac 16:11
NEBAIOTH
Isa 60:7
NEBO
Ezr 10:43; Isa 15:2; Da 1:7
NEBUCHADNEZZAR
as commander
2Ki 24:1; 2Ch 35:21
as conqueror
2Ch 36:4; 2Ch 36:5 – 8; Ne 1:3; "Nebuchadnezzar's Campaigns against Judah," 572
death of
Da 5:11
and fall of Jerusalem
2Ki 24:8; 2Ki 24:11; 2Ki 25:1; Eze 26:8; Introduction to Jeremiah: Background
NEBUZARADAN
Jer 40:2 – 3; Rev 11:19
NECO II. *See* PHARAOH: Neco II
NEGEV
Ge 12:9; 1Sa 27:10; Isa 30:6
NEHEMIAH
Ezr 2:70; Ezr 4:5; Ezr 7:11; Ezr 7:26; Ezr 9:3; Ne 1:1; Eze 44:9; Introduction to Ezra: The Order of Ezra and Nehemiah; "Chronology: Ezra-Nehemiah," 671
NEIGHBOR. *See* LOVE: of neighbor
NEPHILIM
Ge 6:4; Nu 13:33
NERGAL-SHAREZER
Jer 39:3
NERI
1Ch 3:19
NERO
Ac 25:11; 1Ti 2:2; 1Pe 2:13
NEW BIRTH
Jn 3:3; Jn 3:5; Ro 6:8; 1Co 2:14; 1Co 4:20; 2Co 4:6; Eph 4:24; Tit 3:5; Jas 2:5; 1Pe 1:23; 1Jn 5:3
NEW COVENANT
Jer 31:31 – 34; Heb 7:19; Heb 8:8 – 12; Heb 9:10; Heb 10:15 – 18; Heb 13:20
NEW GATE
Jer 26:10
NEW HEAVENS AND NEW EARTH
Isa 65:17; 2Pe 3:13
NEW JERUSALEM
2Ch 3:8; Rev 21:2 – 27; Rev 22:1 – 5
NEW MOON FESTIVAL
1Sa 20:5; 1Sa 20:6; Isa 1:14; Hag 1:1
NEW QUARTER
2Ki 22:14; Ne 3:6; Ne 11:9
NEW YEAR
Ex 12:2; Lev 23:34; Eze 40:1; "Old Testament Feasts and Other Sacred Days," 178
NICANOR GATE
Ac 3:2
NICODEMUS
Jn 3:2; Jn 7:50 – 51; Jn 19:39
NICOLAITANS
Rev 2:6
NICOLAS
Ac 6:5; Rev 2:6
NICOPOLIS
Tit 3:12
NILE RIVER
Ex 7:17; Ex 7:20; Ex 7:24; Am 8:8
NIMROD
Ge 10:8; Jnh 1:2

NINEVEH
2Ki 19:36; 2Ki 23:29; Jnh 1:2; Jnh 3:3; Na 1:8; Na 3:17; Na 3:19; Introduction to Ezekiel: Background
NIPPUR
Ezr 2:59; Est 2:5
NISROCH
2Ki 19:37
NO AMON
Na 3:8
NOAH
Ge 6:8–9; Ge 6:18; Ge 6:22; Ge 7:1; Ge 9:9; Heb 11:7; 1Pe 3:19–20; "Table of Nations," 22
NOAHIC COVENANT
Ge 9:9; Ge 9:11–13; "Major Covenants in the Old Testament," 19
NORTH GALATIAN THEORY
Introduction to Galatians: Date and Destination
NUNC DIMITTIS
Lk 2:29–32
NUZI TABLETS
Ge 15:3–4; Ge 21:11; Ge 25:5; Ru 4:7; Introduction to Genesis: Background; "Ancient Texts Relating to the Old Testament," xxiii

O

OATH
Ge 42:15; Ex 20:7; Dt 6:13; 2Sa 14:11; 1Ki 1:17; 1Ki 8:31; Heb 6:13; Heb 7:20; Jas 5:12
OBADIAH (governor of Ahab's palace)
1Ki 18:3; 1Ki 18:8; 1Ki 18:12
OBADIAH (prophet)
Introduction to Obadiah: Author
OBED
Ru 4:14; Ru 4:17
OBED-EDOM (David's bodyguard)
2Sa 6:10; 2Sa 6:12; 1Ki 8:1; 1Ch 13:13; 1Ch 26:4
OBED-EDOM (son of Jeduthun)
2Ch 25:24
OBEDIENCE
Ge 12:4; Ge 17:1; Ge 17:9–10; Ge 17:23; Ge 21:14; Ge 22:2–3; Lev 26:3; Dt 4:1; 1Sa 15:22; Jer 13:1–2; Jer 13:4–7; Da 3:12; Am 5:25; Mk 9:7; Jn 14:21; Jn 15:10; Ac 6:7; Ro 6:17; 1Co 15:28; Eph 5:22; Php 2:8; Php 2:12; Heb 5:8; Heb 10:5; Heb 11:8; 1Pe 1:2; 1Jn 2:3; 1Jn 2:5; 1Jn 5:4; Introduction to Haggai: Themes and Teaching
OCCULT
Lev 20:6; Isa 3:2–3; Eze 13:18
ODED
1Ki 15:13; 2Ch 28:9–15
OFFERINGS TO THE LORD
Ge 4:3–4; Lev 1:2; Lev 1:3; Lev 2:1; Lev 3:1; Lev 4:5; Lev 5:15; 2Ch 31:5–6; 1Co 16:2; 1Co 16:3; "Old Testament Sacrifices," 153
OG
Nu 21:35; Zec 11:2
OHOLIAB
Ex 31:6; 1Ch 2:18–24; 2Ch 2:7; 2Ch 2:13
OHOLIBAH
Eze 23:4
OIL
Hag 1:11; Mk 6:13; Jas 5:14
OLD GATE
Ne 3:6
OLIVE TREE
Jdg 9:9–13; Ne 8:15; Mk 14:32; Ro 11:17
OLIVES, MOUNT OF. *See* MOUNT: of Olives
OLIVET DISCOURSE
Mt 24:1–51; Mt 25:1–46; Mk 13:1–37
OLYMPIC GAMES
1Co 9:24
OMEGA
Rev 1:8; Rev 1:17
OMRI
1Ki 14:17; 1Ki 16:16; 1Ki 16:23; 1Ki 16:24; 1Ki 16:25; 1Ki 16:27; 1Ki 16:30; 2Ki 9:31
ON
Ge 41:45; Eze 30:17
ONAN
Ge 38:9
144,000
Rev 7:4
ONESIMUS
Col 3:22–25; Col 4:1; Col 4:9–17; Tit 1:4; Phm 1:1,11,20; Introduction to Philemon: Recipient, Background and Purpose
ONIAS III
Da 11:22
ONIAS IV
Isa 19:19
ONO
Ne 6:2
ONYCHA
Ex 25:6
OPHEL
Ne 3:26
OPHIR
Ge 10:29; 1Ki 9:11; 1Ki 9:28; Job 22:24; Isa 13:12
OPPRESSION
Jdg 2:6–23; Jdg 3:1–6; Jdg 3:7–11; Ecc 4:1; Am 2:7; Introduction to Exodus: Chronology; Introduction to Judges: Theme and Theology; Introduction to Amos: Date and Historical Situation
ORACLE
Nu 23:7; Ps 36:1; Pr 30:1; Isa 13:1; Hab 1:1; Zec 9:1
ORCHARD
SS 4:13
ORDINATION OF ELDERS
Nu 3:3; 1Ti 5:22
OREB
Jdg 7:25; Isa 10:26
ORIGEN
Introduction to Ezra: Ezra and Nehemiah
ORIGINAL SIN
Ge 6:5; Ge 8:21; Isa 53:4
ORION
Job 9:9; Am 5:8
ORPAH
Ru 1:14; Ru 4:6
ORPHAN
Ex 22:21–27; Isa 1:17
OSORKON I
2Ch 14:9
OSTRACA
Jer 34:7
OTHNIEL
Jdg 1:13; 1Ch 4:13
OVERSEER
Ac 20:28; Php 1:1; 1Ti 3:1; Tit 1:7; 1Pe 2:25; 1Pe 5:2; "Qualifications for Elders/Overseers and Deacons," 1874
OXGOAD
Jdg 3:31

P

PADDAN ARAM
Ge 25:20
PADI
2Ki 18:8
PAHATH-MOAB
Ezr 2:6
PALACE OF THE FOREST OF LEBANON
1Ki 7:2; 1Ki 7:7
PALESTINE
Ge 10:6; Zec 9:6; Mt 14:1; "The Holy Land Under Herod the Great," 1570
PAMPHYLIA
Ac 2:10; Ac 13:13; Ac 14:24; Col 4:10
PANEAS
Mt 16:13
PANTHEISM
Introduction to Genesis: Theological Theme and Message
PAPHOS
Ac 13:6
PAPYRUS
Ex 2:3; Isa 35:7
PARABLE
Mt 13:3; Mk 4:2; Mk 4:34; Lk 8:4; "Parables of Jesus," 1598
of the good Samaritan
2Ch 28:9–15; Lk 10:29; Lk 10:30; Lk 10:31–33; Lk 10:35; Lk 10:36
of the hidden treasure
Mt 13:44–46
of the lost sheep
Lk 15:4
of the net
Mt 13:47–51

of the prodigal son
Lk 15:12; Lk 15:13; Lk 15:15; Lk 15:22 – 23; Lk 15:28; Lk 15:29; Lk 15:30; Lk 15:31; Lk 15:32
of the sower
Isa 6:9 – 10; Mk 4:26 – 29
of the tenants
Isa 5:1; Lk 20:10
of the weeds
Mt 13:25; Mt 13:47 – 51
PARADISE
Ge 2:8; Ne 2:8; Lk 23:43; 2Co 12:2 – 4; Rev 2:7
PARAN, DESERT OF
Ge 21:21; Nu 12:16; 1Ki 11:18
PARCHMENTS
2Ti 4:13
PARENTS. *See also* CHILDREN; FAMILY; FATHER; MOTHER
as examples to children
2Sa 13:28
hatred of
Mal 1:3; Lk 14:26
honoring
Ex 20:12
obedience to
Lk 2:49
responsibility of
Ge 6:18; Pr 14:26
showing favoritism to children
Ge 27:6
PAROSH
Ezr 2:3
PARTHIANS
Ac 2:9
PARVAIM
2Ch 3:6
PASHHUR
Jer 20:1; Jer 20:6
PASSION WEEK
Lk 13:34; Lk 19:45; Lk 20:1; Lk 22:7; "Passion Week," 1552
PASSOVER, FEAST OF. *See* FEAST: of Passover
PASTORAL LETTERS
Ac 28:30; "The Pastoral Letters," 1867; Introduction to 1 Timothy: Background and Purpose
PASTORS. *See also* MINISTERS
Ac 20:28; Eph 4:11; 1Pe 5:2
PATARA
Ac 21:1
PATIENCE
Pr 16:32; Ro 12:12
PATMOS
Rev 1:9
PAUL
Ac 9:1; Ro 1:1; Php 3:4 – 14; 2Ti 4:7; "Timeline of Paul's Life," 1695; "Corinth in the Time of Paul," 1696; "Ephesus in the Time of Paul," 1823; "Philippi in the Time of Paul," 1836
appeal to Caesar
Ac 25:11
arrested
Ac 22:30; Ac 24:23
at Stephen's execution
Ac 7:58; Ac 9:1
before Agrippa
Ac 26:8
before Felix
Ac 23:34; Ac 24:26
before Festus
Ac 24:27; Ac 25:9
born in Tarsus
Ac 6:9; Ac 22:3
conversion of
Ac 9:5; Ac 9:17
and council of Jerusalem
Ac 12:1; Ac 15:1; Ac 15:2; Gal 2:1
directed by the Holy Spirit
Ac 20:22
first missionary journey of
Ac 13:2; Ac 13:4; Ac 13:13; Ac 16:1; "Paul's First Missionary Journey," 1704
fourth missionary journey of
Ac 28:30; "The Pastoral Letters," 1867; "Paul's Fourth Missionary Journey," 1872; Introduction to 1 Timothy
and his vow
Ac 18:18
imprisonment of
Ac 16:32; Ac 28:16; Ac 28:30; Introduction to Colossians: Author, Date and Place of Writing
message of
Ac 9:20; Ac 9:29; Ac 13:14
name changed from Saul
Ac 13:9
return to Jerusalem
Ac 21:1
second missionary journey of
Ac 13:4; Ac 16:1; Ac 16:6; Ac 16:8; "Paul's Second Missionary Journey," 1711
stoning of
Ac 14:19
student of Gamaliel
Ac 5:34
suffering of
2Co 11:23 – 26; Gal 6:17; Col 1:24
third missionary journey of
Ac 18:23; Ac 19:1; Ac 27:1; Introduction to Romans: Date and Place of Writing; "Paul's Third Missionary Journey," 1718
trip to Rome
Ac 27:1; Ac 28:22; "Paul's Journey to Rome," 1731; "Rome in the Time of Paul," 1735
PAX ROMANA
Lk 2:1; Lk 2:14
PEACE
Ge 8:11; Nu 6:26; Isa 39:8; Isa 48:18; Jer 6:14; Eze 34:25; Mic 5:5; Mt 10:34; Lk 2:14; Jn 14:27; Jn 20:19; Ro 1:7; Ro 5:1; Ro 12:18; Php 4:7; Col 3:15; 3Jn 14
PEACE OFFERING. *See* FELLOWSHIP OFFERING
PEDAIAH
1Ch 3:19
PEKAH
2Ki 15:25; 2Ki 15:27; 2Ki 16:5; 2Ch 28:5; 2Ch 28:6; Isa 7:1; Isa 7:9; Isa 8:6
PEKAHIAH
2Ki 15:25
PEKOD
Jer 50:21; Eze 23:23
PELATIAH
1Ch 3:21; Eze 11:1
PELETHITES
2Sa 8:18; 1Ch 18:17
PELUSIUM
Eze 30:15
PENIEL
Jdg 8:8; 1Ki 12:25
PENINNAH
1Sa 2:3
PENTATEUCH
1Sa 8:7; 1Ki 1:50; 2Ki 22:8; Ne 10:34; Mt 22:24; Jn 4:25; Jn 10:34; Ro 8:2; Introduction to Genesis: Author and Date of Writing
PENTECOST. *See also* FEAST: of Weeks (Pentecost or Harvest)
Ex 23:16; Lev 23:16; Joel 2:28 – 32; Mt 3:11; Mt 16:19; Mt 16:28; Jn 1:33; Ac 1:5; Ac 2:1; Ac 2:2; Ac 2:3; Ac 2:15; Ac 4:4; Ac 8:16; 1Co 12:10; 1Co 16:8; Col 1:6; 1Pe 1:12; "Countries of People Mentioned at Pentecost," 1680
PEOR
Nu 31:1 – 24; Jos 22:17
PERATH
Jer 13:4
PERAZIM
1Ch 14:11
PEREA
Lk 13:31
PEREZ
Ge 38:29; Ru 4:12; 1Ch 9:4 – 6
PERFUME
SS 1:3; SS 1:12; Mk 14:3; Mk 14:8; Lk 7:38; Jn 12:3
PERGA
Ac 13:13
PERGAMUM
Rev 2:12; Rev 2:13
PERIZZITES
Ge 13:7; Jos 17:15
PERJURY
Ex 20:7; Zec 5:3
PERSECUTION
Jn 15:21; Ac 9:4; 1Co 16:1; 2Co 5:13; Php 1:28; Col 1:24; 2Ti 3:12; Heb 10:32; Heb 12:4; Heb 12:5; Rev 2:10
PERSEPOLIS
Ezr 5:6 – 7; Ezr 6:1; Ezr 6:2
PERSEVERANCE
1Co 15:2; Php 2:12; Heb 3:6; Heb 3:14; Heb 6:11; Heb 11:35; Heb 12:1; Jas 5:11; 1Pe 1:5
PERSIA
Ezr 5:28; Ezr 7:4 – 7; Ezr 8:3;

Ezr 9:9; Ezr 10:13; Isa 41:2; Da 7:4–7; Hag 1:1; Hag 2:6; Zec 1:20; Mt 2:1; Introduction to Esther: Author and Date
Gulf of
Isa 21:1; Isa 43:14; Ac 2:9
PERSIANS
Ezr 1:1; Ezr 4:14; Ezr 6:2; Ne 5:4; Est 2:23; Est 5:11; Isa 43:3; Isa 47:11; Da 7:4–7; "From Malachi to Christ," 1450
PETER
Introduction to 1 Peter: Author and Date
call of
Mk 1:17
and Christ's forgiveness
Jn 21:7; Jn 21:15–17; Jn 21:15
and Christ's resurrection
Lk 24:12; 1Co 15:5
in garden of Gethsemane
Mk 14:47; Mk 14:66; Mk 14:70; Jn 18:10; Jn 18:15
and his concept of Christ
Mt 16:18; Mk 8:32; Mk 8:33; Lk 9:20; Jn 6:68; Jn 13:37
and his denial of Christ
Mt 26:31; Mt 26:73; Mk 14:37; Mk 16:7; Lk 22:61; Jn 13:38; Jn 18:17; Jn 18:18
and his ministry
Ac 8:14; Ac 11:17; Ac 15:7; 1Co 1:12; "Philip's and Peter's Missionary Journeys," 1698
and his vision from God
Ac 10:10; Ac 10:14; Ac 10:23; Ac 10:26; Ac 10:28
house of
Mt 4:13; Mk 1:29; Mk 9:33
marriage of
Mk 1:30; 1Co 9:5
and Pentecost
Ac 2:4; Ac 2:14; Ac 2:17; Ac 2:34
and the transfiguration
Mk 9:5; Lk 9:28
and the washing of feet
Jn 13:8; Jn 13:9
PETHUEL
Introduction to Joel: Author
PETRA
2Ki 14:7; Ac 2:11
PHARAOH
Amunhotep II
1Ki 6:1; Introduction to Exodus: Chronology
Apries (Hophra)
2Ki 24:20; Eze 17:7; Eze 30:21
Neco II
Jdg 5:19; 2Ki 22:20; 2Ki 23:29; 2Ki 23:33; 2Ki 23:34; 2Ki 23:35; 2Ch 36:2; 2Ch 36:4; Isa 36:10; Eze 31:3
Osorkon I
2Ch 14:9
Psammeticus II
Eze 17:7
Psusennes II
1Ki 3:1
Rameses II
1Ki 6:1; La 4:20; Heb 11:27; Introduction to Exodus: Chronology
Seti I
Introduction to Exodus: Chronology
Shabako
Isa 18:1; Isa 30:1
Shebitku
Isa 37:9
Shishak
1Ki 3:1; 1Ki 11:40; 1Ki 14:25; 2Ch 12:2; "Ancient Texts Relating to the Old Testament," xxiii
Siamun
1Ki 3:1
Thutmose III
Ex 1:11; Ex 2:15; Jdg 4:3; Jdg 5:19; Introduction to Exodus: Chronology
PHARISEES
Mt 3:7; Mt 3:11; Mt 10:14; Mt 22:15–17; Mt 23:24; Mk 2:16; Mk 2:18; Mk 3:4; Mk 3:6; Mk 7:1; Mk 8:15; Mk 10:2; Mk 12:18; Lk 5:17; Lk 5:21; Lk 5:30; Lk 6:11; Lk 11:39; Lk 13:31; Lk 15:28; Lk 18:12; Jn 1:24; Jn 4:1; Jn 7:47; Jn 7:49; Jn 7:50–51; Jn 7:52; Jn 8:15; Jn 9:40; Jn 9:41; Jn 11:47; Jn 17:8; Ac 5:34; Ac 15:1; Ac 15:5; Ac 22:30; Ac 24:21; Gal 4:10; "The Time Between the Testaments," 1451; "Jewish Sects," 1502
PHICOL
Ge 21:22
PHILADELPHIA
Rev 3:7
PHILEMON
Col 3:22–25; Col 4:1; Col 4:10; Introduction to Philemon: Recipient, Background and Purpose
PHILETUS
2Ti 2:14–18
PHILIP (the apostle)
Jn 12:21
PHILIP (the evangelist)
Ac 8:5; Ac 8:14; Ac 8:34; Ac 8:40; Ac 21:8; "Philip's and Peter's Missionary Journeys," 1692
PHILIP (Herod I)
Mt 14:3
PHILIP (the tetrarch)
Mt 11:21; Mt 14:6; Ac 12:1
PHILIPPI
Ac 16:11; Ac 16:12; Ac 16:13; Introduction to Philippians: Recipients; "Philippi in the Time of Paul," 1836
PHILISTINES
Ge 10:14; Jdg 4:1–2; Jdg 10:6; Jdg 14:3; Jdg 16:5; 1Sa 4:7; 1Sa 4:8; 1Sa 5:2; 1Sa 5:3; 1Sa 5:6; 1Sa 5:8; 1Sa 14:24; 1Sa 17:32; 1Sa 17:51; 1Sa 21:11; 1Sa 28:4; 1Sa 29:1; 1Sa 31:4; 2Sa 1:20; 2Sa 2:9; 2Sa 5:17; 2Sa 5:21; 2Ki 12:17; 2Ki 16:6; Isa 14:29; Eze 25:15; Eze 25:16; Joel 3:4
PHILISTINES, FIVE CITIES OF
Jdg 3:3; Am 1:6; Am 1:8; "Five Cities of the Philistines," 331
PHINEHAS (son of Eleazar)
Ex 32:28; Nu 25:11; Nu 31:6; Jdg 20:18; Jdg 20:28; 1Ch 9:17–21; Mal 2:5; "Major Covenants in the Old Testament," 19
PHINEHAS (son of Eli)
1Sa 4:4; 1Sa 4:11; 1Ch 9:17–21; Mal 2:5
PHOEBE
Ro 16:1
PHOENICIANS
Ge 10:6; Eze 28:10; Mk 7:24; Ac 11:19
PHOENIX
Ac 27:12
PHRYGIA
Ac 16:6; Ac 18:23
PHYLACTERIES
Ex 13:9; Dt 6:8–9; Mt 23:5
PILATE
Mt 8:5; Mt 27:2; Mt 27:65; Mk 15:1; Lk 23:1; Lk 23:7; Lk 23:16; Lk 23:18; Lk 23:25; Lk 23:38; Lk 23:44; Jn 18:29; Jn 18:33; Jn 18:34; Jn 19:6; Jn 19:10; Jn 19:22; 1Co 2:8
PILLAR
Ge 28:18
PISIDIA
Ac 14:24
PISTACHIO
Ge 43:11
PLAGUES
Ex 7:14–25; Ex 8:1–32; Ex 9:1–35; Ex 10:1–29; Ps 105:28–36; Rev 8:2; Rev 8:7; Rev 8:8; Rev 8:12; Rev 9:3; Rev 9:4
PLAINS
of Aram
Ge 28:1
of Megiddo
Jdg 5:19
of Moab
Nu 22:1
PLEIADES
Job 9:9; Am 5:8
PLUMB LINE
Am 7:8; Zec 4:10
POLEMON
Ac 25:13
POLLUX
Ac 28:11
POLYBIUS
Da 11:12
POLYCARP
Rev 2:8
POLYGAMY
Ge 4:19; Ge 25:6; 2Sa 3:2–5; 1Ki 11:1; 1Ti 3:2
POLYTHEISM
1Ki 5:7; Introduction to Genesis:

Theological Theme and Message
PONTUS
Ac 18:2; 1Pe 1:1
POOR
Ex 22:21 – 27; Lev 25:4; Lev 25:13; Dt 15:4; Dt 15:11; Ps 14:6; Ps 34:6; Am 2:7; Zec 7:10; Mk 14:7; Jas 2:5 – 13
PORTION OF JACOB
Jer 10:16
POSTMILLENNIALISM
Rev 20:2
POTSHERD GATE
Jer 19:2
POZZUOLI
Ac 28:13
PRAETORIUM
Mt 27:27; Mk 15:16
PRAISE
Ps 8:1 – 9; Ps 9:1; Ps 26:6; Ps 29:1 – 11; Ps 33:1 – 22; Ps 34:1; Ps 150:3 – 5
PRAYER
Dt 4:7; Introduction to Psalms: Psalm Types
and faith
Jn 15:7
faithfulness in
Ne 2:4; Lk 11:1; Ro 12:12; 1Th 3:10
and fasting
Ezr 8:23; Ne 1:4; Ac 13:3
for forgiveness
Ps 51:1 – 19; Lk 11:4
and God's will
Jn 14:13; 1Jn 5:14
hindrances to
1Pe 3:7
importance of
Mk 9:29; Jn 15:16; Ac 2:42; Eph 6:17 – 18
instruction in
Lk 11:1; Lk 11:4
intercessory
2Ki 19:4; Job 42:10
in Jesus' name
Jn 14:13
posture
1Ch 17:16
and praise
Ps 7:17; Ps 66:1 – 20
stated time for
Lk 18:10; Ac 3:1
and thanksgiving
Php 1:3 – 4; Php 4:6; Col 3:16; Introduction to Psalms: Psalm Types
PREDESTINATION
Ro 8:29; Ro 8:30; Eph 1:4
PREMILLENNIALISM
Rev 20:2
PRETERIST
Introduction to Revelation: Interpretation
PRIDE
Ps 31:23; Ps 101:5; Ps 123:4; Ps 131:1; Pr 11:2; 1Co 4:8; 1Co 8:1; Introduction to Psalms: Theology: Major Themes, No. 3
PRIEST
garments of
Ex 28:2; Ex 28:6; Ex 28:8; Ex 28:35; Lev 16:1 – 34
role of
Ex 20:19; Ex 28:1; Ex 28:12; Lev 4:5; Lev 6:6; Lev 16:1 – 34; Lev 21:17; Nu 3:4; Nu 18:7; Dt 20:2; Dt 31:11; 1Sa 2:28; 1Ki 1:39; 2Ch 15:3
PRIESTHOOD
Ex 19:22
Aaronic
Nu 17:10; Nu 18:1 – 7
Levitical
Eze 1:1; Heb 7:27; Heb 8:7; Heb 10:1; Heb 10:11 – 14
PRIMOGENITURE, LAW OF
Ge 25:5; Ge 25:23; Dt 21:17
PRINCE OF THIS WORLD. *See* SATAN
PRISCA. *See* PRISCILLA
PRISCILLA
Ac 18:2; Ac 18:18; Ac 18:19; 1Co 16:19
PRISON LETTERS
Introduction to Colossians: Author, Date and Place of Writing
PRISONERS. *See* WAR: prisoners of
PROMISED LAND
Jos 1:1 – 18; Ps 95:11; Introduction to Joshua: Title and Theme
PROPHECY
definition of
Lk 1:67; Jn 11:51; Ac 11:27; 1Co 12:10; Rev 1:3
end of
1Co 13:8
false
Dt 13:1 – 5; Dt 18:21 – 22; 1Ki 13:20; Eze 13:6; 1Jn 4:1; 1Jn 4:4; Rev 13:11; Rev 13:12
gift of
1Co 13:1 – 3; 1Co 14:1 – 5
purpose of
Nu 11:25; 1Co 14:3; 1Co 14:5; 1Co 14:24; 1Co 14:30; 1Ti 1:18
PROPHESY
1Sa 10:5; 1Sa 18:10; Mt 7:22; 1Co 14:24
PROPHET
Ex 3:4; Ex 7:1 – 2; Nu 12:8; Dt 18:15; 1Sa 9:9; 1Sa 10:5; 1Ki 1:39; 1Ki 22:19; 2Ki 19:4; Eze 3:17; Eze 22:30; Am 2:11; Jnh 3:2; Zec 1:1; Ac 13:1; Eph 2:20; Eph 4:11; 1Th 2:15
PROPHETESS
Ex 15:20; Jdg 4:4; Lk 2:36
PROPHETS, THE
Mt 5:17; Ro 1:2; Heb 1:1; 1Pe 1:10
PROPITIATION
Ro 3:25; 1Jn 2:2
PROSTITUTE, SHRINE
Ge 38:21; Jer 2:20; Hos 4:13; Hos 4:14
PROSTITUTION. *See also* PROSTITUTE, SHRINE
Ge 20:9; Ex 34:15; Dt 23:18; Jdg 2:17; 1Ki 14:24; Ps 73:27; Pr 6:26; Eze 16:15; Eze 16:24; Eze 23:5; Eze 43:7; Lk 7:37; 1Co 6:9; 1Co 6:18; 1Co 7:2; Rev 14:8; Rev 22:15
PROVERB
Introduction to Proverbs: The Nature of a Proverb
PRUDENCE
Pr 1:4
PSAMMETICUS II
Eze 17:7
PSEUDEPIGRAPHA
"The Time Between the Testaments," 1451
PTAHHOTEP
1Ki 4:30
PTOLEMAIS
Ac 21:7
PTOLEMIES
Da 11:5,6,7,11,14,22; "Ptolemies and Seleucids," 1330; "The Time Between the Testaments," 1451
PUAH
Ex 1:15; Jdg 10:1
PUBLICANS
Mt 5:46
PUBLIUS
Ac 28:7
PUL
2Ki 15:19; 1Ch 5:26; Ne 9:32
PURIM
Est 2:9; Est 3:7; Est 9:18 – 19; "Old Testament Feasts and Other Sacred Days," 178; Introduction to Esther: Author and Date; Introduction to Esther: Purpose, Themes and Literary Features
PURPLE
Ex 25:4; Ac 16:14
PUT
Ge 10:6; Eze 27:10; Na 3:9
PUTEOLI
Ac 28:13

Q

Q (Quelle)
"Dating the Synoptic Gospels," 1457
QARQAR, BATTLE OF
1Ki 4:26; 2Ki 5:1; 2Ki 13:7; "The Divided Kingdom," 497
QOS
Ezr 2:53
QUALIFICATIONS FOR ELDERS AND DEACONS
1Ti 3:2; Tit 1:6 – 9; "Qualifications for Elders/Overseers and Deacons," 1874
QUARRELS
1Co 1:11; 1Co 3:17
QUEEN
of Heaven
Jer 7:18

of Sheba
1Ki 10:1; 1Ki 10:9; 2Ch 9:1–12; Mt 12:42; Lk 11:31–32
QUIRINIUS
Lk 2:2; Ac 5:37
QUMRAN
Ezr 7:2; Ezr 8:15; Ne 8:16; Ne 10:34; Ne 12:9; Jer 32:14; Eze 44:15; Joel 2:23; Zec 6:13; Jn 1:23; Jn 3:25; "The Time Between the Testaments," 1451
QUOTATIONS OF OLD TESTAMENT
Ro 3:10–18

R

RABBAH
Dt 3:11; 2Sa 12:26
RABBI
Mt 26:49
RACA
Mt 5:22
RACHEL
Ge 29:30; Ge 31:19; Ru 4:11; Jer 31:15
RAHAB
Jos 2:1–24; Jos 2:1; Jos 2:8–11; Jos 2:12; Jos 7:1–26; Ru 1:4; Isa 30:7; Mt 1:5; Heb 11:31; Jas 2:25
RAINBOW
Ge 9:13
RAM
Lev 5:15; Ezr 10:19; horn. *See* TRUMPET
RAMAH
1Sa 1:1; 1Sa 15:34; 1Ki 15:17; Isa 10:29; Jer 31:15
RAMATHAIM
1Sa 1:1
RAMESES
Ge 47:11; Eze 30:14; Introduction to Exodus: Chronology
RAMESES II
1Ki 6:1; La 4:20; Heb 11:27; Introduction to Exodus: Chronology
RAMOTH GILEAD
1Ki 22:3; 2Ki 5:2; 2Ki 8:28; 2Ch 22:5; 2Ch 22:6
RAMPARTS
Isa 26:1
RANSOM
Ex 13:13; Mt 20:28; Mk 10:45; Eph 1:7; Heb 9:15; 1Pe 1:18
RAPHA
2Sa 21:16
RAPTURE, THE
1Co 15:52; 2Co 12:2–4; 1Th 4:17; Rev 4:1
RAS SHAMRA TABLETS
Ge 15:16; "Ancient Texts Relating to the Old Testament," xxiii; Introduction to Joshua: Historical Setting
REBEKAH
Ge 27:6; Ge 27:8
RECABITES
2Sa 4:8; 2Ki 10:15; Jer 35:1–19
RECONCILIATION
Ro 5:10; Ro 5:11; 2Co 5:18; 2Co 5:21; Eph 2:11–22; Col 1:20; Heb 12:24
RED SEA
Ex 13:18; Ex 14:2; Dt 2:1; 1Ki 9:26
REDEMPTION
Ex 6:6–8; Ex 13:13; Ps 65:6–7; Mt 20:28; Ro 3:24; 2Co 5:17; 2Co 5:18; Eph 1:7; Col 1:14; 1Pe 1:2; 1Pe 1:18; Introduction to Exodus: Themes and Theology
REHOBOAM
1Ki 2:24; 1Ki 12:8; 1Ki 12:14; 1Ki 12:15; 2Ch 11:5–10; 2Ch 11:18–22; 2Ch 11:23; 2Ch 13:7
REHOBOTH IR
Jnh 1:2; Jnh 3:3
REHUM
Ezr 4:8; Ne 1:3
REMEMBER
Ge 8:1; 1Sa 1:11; Ne 1:8; Ne 13:31
REMINDER OFFERING
Nu 5:15,18
REMNANT
2Ki 19:4; 2Ki 19:30–31; 2Ki 21:14; Isa 1:9; Isa 6:13; Isa 10:20–22; Isa 24:14; Am 5:15; Mic 4:7; Ro 9:27–29; Ro 11:5; Ro 11:7; Rev 7:4
REPENTANCE
Mt 3:2; Mt 4:17; Mk 1:4; Lk 24:47; Ac 2:38; Ac 3:19; Ac 11:18; Ac 19:4; Ro 2:4; 1Co 5:5; 2Co 2:5–11; 2Co 7:8–9; 2Co 7:10; 2Th 3:14; Heb 6:1–2; Jas 5:1; Introduction to Jeremiah: Themes and Message; Introduction to Hosea: Theme and Message
REPHAITES
Dt 2:11; Jos 17:15; 2Sa 21:16; 1Ch 20:4
RESEN
Jnh 1:2; Jnh 3:3
RESHEPH
Job 5:7
REST
Dt 3:20; Jos 1:13,15; 1Ki 5:4; 1Ki 8:56; Ps 95:11; Heb 4:1; Heb 4:3; Heb 4:10; Heb 4:11
RESURRECTION
Ps 6:5; Isa 53:11; Da 12:2; Mk 9:10; 1Co 15:42–44; 1Co 15:44–49; 1Co 15:51; 1Co 15:52; 1Co 15:57; 1Th 4:13; Heb 6:1–2; 1Pe 3:18
RESURRECTION, CHRIST'S
appearances after
Ac 1:2; Ac 1:3; 1Co 15:3–5; 1Co 15:5; 1Co 15:6; "Resurrection Appearances," 1615
evidence for
1Co 15:3–5; 1Co 15:12; 1Co 15:20; 1Co 15:34
meaning of
Ro 10:9; 1Co 15:21; 1Co 15:57; 1Co 15:58; Gal 1:1; 2Ti 2:8; 1Pe 3:21
Paul and
Ac 26:8; Ro 4:17; Eph 4:9
prediction of
Isa 53:11
and that of believers
Ro 8:11; 1Co 15:22; 1Co 15:23; 1Co 15:44–49; Php 3:10; Php 3:21; 1Pe 1:3
theories about
1Pe 3:19–20
timing of
1Co 15:4
RETALIATION
Ex 21:23–25; Lev 24:20; Job 31:1–40; Lk 6:29; "Cities of Refuge," 239
REUBEN
Ge 35:22; Ge 37:21; Ge 42:37; Ge 48:5; 1Ch 5:1–10; 1Ch 5:23–26
REUEL
Ex 2:16
REVELATION
1Co 14:30
REWARDS (CROWNS)
2Ti 4:8
REZIN
2Ki 16:5; 2Ch 28:5; Isa 8:6
REZON
1Ki 11:24
RHEGIUM
Ac 28:13
RHODA
Ac 12:13
RHODES
Ge 10:4; Eze 27:15; Ac 21:2
RICH YOUNG RULER
Mk 10:17; Mk 10:18; Mk 10:19; Mk 10:20; Mk 10:21; Mk 10:22; Lk 10:25; Lk 10:27; Lk 10:29
RICHES. *See* MONEY
RIGHTEOUS, THE
Ps 1:5; Ps 4:1; introduction to Ps 37
RIGHTEOUSNESS
Ge 7:1; Ge 15:6; Dt 6:25; 2Sa 22:21; Ps 1:1–6; Ps 89:14; Pr 12:28; Pr 14:34; Isa 45:8; Isa 46:13; Mt 1:19; Mt 6:1; Jn 16:10; Ro 1:17; Ro 3:24; Ro 4:1; Ro 9:31; Ro 10:3; Ro 10:4; Ro 10:5; Ro 10:6–7; Ro 10:8; Ro 14:17; 1Co 1:30; 2Co 3:8–9; Gal 5:5; Php 1:11; 2Ti 4:8; Heb 11:7; Heb 12:11; 2Pe 1:1
RIMMON
Jdg 10:6; 2Ki 5:18; Zec 14:10
RIVER
Abana
2Ki 5:12
Arnon
Jos 13:9; Jos 13:15; 2Ki 3:25
Balikh
Isa 37:12
Barada
2Ki 5:12

of Egypt
Ge 15:18
Euphrates
Ge 2:14; 2Sa 8:3; Ezr 4:10; Rev 9:14
Jabbok
Ge 32:22
Jordan
Jos 1:2; 2Sa 19:41; 1Ki 20:26; 2Ki 5:10; 1Ch 12:8 – 15; Isa 33:9; Zec 11:3; Mk 1:5; Mk 1:16
Kebar
Ezr 2:59; Eze 1:1
Khoser
Na 2:6
Nile
Ex 7:17; Ex 7:20; Ex 7:24; Am 8:8
Pharpar
2Ki 5:12
Shihor
Jos 13:3; 1Ch 13:15; Isa 23:3

RIZPAH
1Sa 14:50; 2Sa 12:8

ROCK
Ge 49:24; 1Sa 2:2; 2Sa 22:2; Ps 18:2

ROME
"The Neo-Babylonian Empire," 1318; "From Malachi to Christ," 1450; "Paul's Journey to Rome," 1731; "Rome in the Time of Paul," 1735; Introduction to Romans: Recipients

ROOT OF JESSE
Isa 11:10

ROSH HASHANAH
Nu 29:1 – 6; Eze 40:1; "Old Testament Feasts and Other Sacred Days," 178

RUFUS
Mk 15:21; Lk 23:26

RUTH
Ru 1:4; Ru 1:16; "The Book of Ruth," 367

S

SABBATH
Ge 2:3; Ex 16:23; Ex 20:9 – 10; Ex 31:13; Ex 31:16 – 17; Nu 15:32; Ne 9:14; Ne 10:31; Ne 13:15; Isa 56:2; Isa 56:4,6; Eze 20:12; Am 8:5; Mt 4:23; Mt 12:10; Mt 24:20; Mt 27:62; Mk 1:21; Mk 2:25; Mk 2:27; Lk 4:40; Lk 6:9; Lk 14:1; Jn 5:17; Jn 7:22; Ac 1:12; Ro 14:5; "Old Testament Feasts and Other Sacred Days," 178

SABEANS
Job 1:15; Eze 23:42; Joel 3:8

SACKCLOTH
Ge 37:34; 2Ki 6:30; Ps 30:11; Isa 20:2; Jnh 3:5 – 6; Rev 11:3

SACRED
1Co 3:17

SACRIFICES
Ex 12:7; Nu 28:1 – 31; Nu 29:1 – 40; 1Sa 15:22; Ps 50:8 – 13; Ps 51:17; Isa 53:11; Introduction to Leviticus: Themes; "Old Testament Sacrifices," 153

SADDUCEES
Ezr 7:2; Mt 2:4; Mt 3:7; Mt 3:11; Mt 22:24; Mk 12:18; Lk 20:27; Ac 4:1; Ac 23:6; "The Time Between the Testaments," 1451; "Jewish Sects," 1502

SAFFRON
SS 4:14

SAHRA
Eze 27:18

SAINTS
1Sa 2:9; Ps 4:3; Ro 1:7; Ro 15:25; 1Co 1:2; 1Co 6:1; 2Co 1:1; Eph 1:1; Eph 1:18; Php 1:1

SALEM
Ge 14:18

SALOME
Ezr 8:10; Mt 14:6; Mk 15:40

SALT
Ge 19:26; Mk 9:50

SALT OF THE COVENANT
Lev 2:13; Nu 18:19

SALVATION
at the last day
Ro 10:9
available to all
Ro 5:18
based on faith
Ro 11:26; 2Ti 1:9; Tit 2:11; Heb 3:14
day of
Isa 49:8; Ro 13:11; Php 1:6
freely offered
Ac 16:30; Ac 16:31; 1Ti 4:10
meaning of
Mk 5:34; Eph 2:8; Php 2:1; Php 2:12; 2Th 1:9; 1Ti 4:16; Tit 2:14; Jas 2:14 – 26; Jas 2:21; 1Pe 1:5
work of God
Mk 10:27; 1Co 1:26 – 31; 2Th 2:13; 1Ti 2:4; Tit 3:5; Introduction to Exodus: Themes and Theology

SAMARIA (city)
1Ki 16:24; 1Ki 21:1; 1Ki 21:19; 2Ki 5:3; 2Ki 6:8; 2Ki 6:25; 2Ki 17:5; 2Ki 17:6; Isa 28:1; Am 3:12; Am 3:13; Am 3:15; Ac 8:5

SAMARIA (territory)
1Ki 13:32; 1Ki 21:1; 2Ki 17:29; 2Ki 23:18; Ezr 4:10; Ne 2:10; Ne 2:19; Isa 10:10; Hos 7:1; Na 1:9; Jn 4:4; Ac 1:8; Ac 12:1

SAMARIA OSTRACA
1Ch 7:14 – 19

SAMARITAN
2Ki 17:29; Mt 10:5; Lk 9:52; Lk 10:31 – 33; Jn 4:9; Jn 4:20; Jn 4:25; Jn 8:48

SAMOS
Ac 20:15

SAMOTHRACE
Ac 16:11

SAMSON
Jdg 13:1 – 25; Jdg 14:1 – 20; Jdg 15:1 – 20; Jdg 16:1 – 31; Jdg 13:24; Jdg 14:10; Jdg 15:2; Jdg 16:1; Jdg 16:7; Jdg 16:13; Jdg 16:20; Jdg 16:21; Jdg 16:30

SAMUEL
Introduction to 1 Samuel: Title
and David
1Sa 16:7; 1Sa 16:13; 2Sa 2:4
death of
1Sa 25:1
and Eli
1Sa 3:1; 1Sa 3:11 – 14
as intercessor
1Sa 7:5
and Israel
1Sa 10:25; 1Sa 12:15; 1Sa 12:24
as prophet
1Sa 3:19; 1Sa 10:5
and Saul
1Sa 9:6; 1Sa 11:15; 1Sa 12:6; 1Sa 15:21; 1Sa 15:31; 1Sa 15:35; Introduction to Judges: Title; Introduction to 1 Samuel: Contents and Theme; Literary Features, Authorship and Date

SANBALLAT
Ne 2:10; Ne 6:5; Ne 13:28

SANCTIFICATION
Jn 17:17; Jn 17:20; Ro 8:29; 1Co 1:2; 2Co 3:8 – 9; 2Co 3:18; Eph 2:9; 1Th 3:13; 1Th 4:8; Heb 10:10; 1Pe 1:5; 1Pe 2:24; 1Pe 4:1

SANHEDRIN
Mt 27:1; Mt 27:2; Mk 14:53 — 15:15; Mk 14:55; Lk 23:1; Ac 4:5; Ac 5:21; Ac 22:20; Ac 22:30; Ac 24:1

SAPPHIRA
Ac 5:1

SARAH. *See also* SARAI
Ro 4:19; Gal 4:30

SARAI. *See also* SARAH
Ge 12:11; Ge 17:15
SARDIS
Ob 20; Rev 3:1

SARGON II
2Ki 17:6; 2Ki 17:24; 2Ki 20:12; Ezr 4:7; Ne 2:19; Isa 20:1

SARGON LEGEND
"Ancient Texts Relating to the Old Testament," xxiii

SARGON'S DISPLAY INSCRIPTION
"Ancient Texts Relating to the Old Testament," xxiii

SATAN
and Ananias
Ac 5:3
and believers, unbelievers
Job 1:12; 1Th 3:5; 1Jn 3:8
and David
2Sa 24:1
and Eve
Ge 3:1
fall of
Lk 8:31; Lk 10:18; Jn 12:31; Ro 16:20; 1Th 3:5; Rev 12:7
and Jesus
Mt 4:1 – 11; Mk 8:33; Lk 4:2; Lk 4:13; Jn 14:30

and Job
Job 1:6; Job 1:8
and Judas
Lk 22:3
names for
Dt 13:13; Mt 10:25; Mt 16:23; 1Th 3:5; 1Jn 3:8; Rev 2:9
and the unpardonable sin
Mt 12:31
SAUL (king)
and the ark
1Sa 14:18
called by God
1Sa 11:5; 1Sa 11:13
and David
1Sa 16:19; 1Sa 17:37; 1Sa 17:55; 1Sa 19:24; 2Sa 3:13; 2Sa 3:14
death of
2Sa 1:10
disobedience of
1Sa 13:9; 1Sa 13:13; 1Sa 14:24–26; 1Sa 15:12; 1Sa 15:23; 1Sa 17:33
origins of
1Sa 9:21; 1Sa 10:5
and Samuel
1Sa 9:6; 1Sa 10:8; 1Sa 11:15; 1Sa 15:13; 1Sa 15:31; 1Sa 15:35
and Spirit of God
1Sa 16:14; 1Sa 19:24
SAUL (of Tarsus). *See* PAUL
SCAPEGOAT
Lev 16:5; Isa 53:6
SCEVA
Ac 19:14
SCRIBES, THE
Ezr 7:6; Jer 8:8; Lk 20:19
SCRIPTURE. *See also* WORD OF GOD
1Ti 5:18; 2Ti 3:16
divine origin of
Mt 1:22; 2Pe 1:21
purpose of
Ro 15:4
SCROLL
Ex 17:14; 2Ti 4:13
SCYTHIANS
Na 1:14; Na 2:1; Col 3:11
SEA
Adriatic
Ac 27:27
Aegean
Ac 16:11; Rev 1:9
of the Arabah
2Ki 14:25
Bronze
1Ki 7:23; 1Ki 7:24
Dead
Ge 14:3; Ge 14:10; Eze 47:8; Mk 1:4; Lk 3:20
of Galilee
Mk 1:16; Mk 4:37; Lk 5:1; Jn 6:1
of Gennesaret
Mk 1:16; Lk 5:1
of Kinnereth
Mk 1:16
Mediterranean
Ge 28:12; Heb 8:6
Red
Ex 13:18; Ex 14:2; Dt 2:1; 1Ki 9:26
of Tiberias
Mk 1:16; Lk 5:1; Jn 6:1
SEA PEOPLES
"The Exodus," 108; "Conquest of Canaan," 310
SEAL
Ge 38:18; Hag 2:23
SECOND COMING
Jn 14:3; Jn 14:18; Jn 21:22; 2Co 1:14; Php 1:6; Col 3:4; 2Th 2:1; 2Ti 4:8; Tit 2:13; Heb 10:25
judgment at
1Th 5:2; Jas 5:9
and "last days"
1Ti 4:1; 2Ti 3:1; 1Jn 2:18
literary treatment of
Mt 3:12
manner of
Mk 13:26
outcome of
Isa 52:7; Ro 13:11; 1Co 13:10; 1Co 15:23; 1Co 15:24; 1Co 15:26; 1Co 15:44–49; 1Co 15:58; 2Co 4:4; Php 1:6; Php 1:10; Rev 14:15
participants in
Lk 21:35; 1Th 4:15; 2Th 1:7
predictions of
Lk 21:27
signs of
Isa 66:19; Mk 13:29; Lk 18:8; Heb 12:27
timing of
Lk 12:40; Lk 17:23; Lk 21:32; Jn 16:16; 1Th 5:2; 1Ti 4:1; 1Ti 6:15; 2Ti 3:1; Jas 5:9; 1Pe 4:7; Rev 22:12
waiting for
1Th 1:9–10; 1Jn 2:18
SECOND DISTRICT
Ne 11:9
SECULARISM
Ecc 4:13–16
SEIR
Ge 36:8; Jdg 5:4; Isa 21:11; Eze 25:8
SELA
2Ki 14:7; Isa 16:1; Ob 1:3
SELAH
Introduction to Psalms: Authorship and Titles (last paragraph)
SELEUCIA
Ac 13:4
SELEUCIDS
Da 11:5,7,10,20,21; Rev 2:18; "Ptolemies and Seleucids," 1330; "The Time Between the Testaments," 1451
SELF-CONTROL
Pr 16:32; 2Pe 1:6
SELF-DENIAL
Lk 9:23; Lk 9:48; Ro 14:7; Ro 15:1; 1Co 9:12; 1Co 9:19
SEMITES
Ge 10:21; Ne 12:31
SENAAH
Ezr 2:35
SENIR
SS 4:8; Eze 27:5
SENNACHERIB
2Ki 18:13; 2Ki 18:14; 2Ki 19:4; 2Ki 19:29; 2Ki 19:37; 2Ch 32:21; Ne 11:27; Isa 8:8; Isa 36:1; 1Co 1:19
SENNACHERIB'S PRISM
"Ancient Texts Relating to the Old Testament," xxiii
SEPHARVAIM
Isa 36:19; Eze 47:16
SEPTUAGINT
Ecc 1:1; Am 5:26; Introduction to Leviticus: Title; Introduction to Numbers: Title; Introduction to 1 Samuel: Title; Introduction to Ezra: Ezra and Nehemiah; Introduction to Psalms: Name; "The Book of the Twelve, or the Minor Prophets," 1333; "The Time Between the Testaments," 1451
SERAIAH
2Ki 25:18; 1Ch 6:14; Ezr 7:1
SERAPH
Isa 6:2
SERIAH
2Sa 8:17
SERMON ON THE MOUNT/PLAIN
Mt 5:1–48; Mt 6:1–34; Mt 7:1–29; Lk 6:20–49; Lk 11:1
SERPENT
Ge 3:1; Ge 3:14; Ge 3:15; Am 9:3
SERVANT OF THE LORD
Ex 14:31; Dt 34:5; Jdg 2:8; Ps 18:1; Isa 41:8–9; Isa 42:1–4; Ro 1:1; Ro 6:18; Ro 16:1; 2Co 11:23; Gal 1:10; Gal 6:17; Php 1:1; Php 2:7
SERVANTHOOD
Mk 10:35–36; Mk 10:45; Lk 22:26; Jn 13:5
SETI I
Introduction to Exodus: Chronology
SEVEN
Ge 4:17–18; Lev 4:6; Jos 6:4; Ru 4:15; Ps 12:6; Pr 9:1; Introduction to Genesis: Literary Features; Introduction to Revelation: Distinctive Feature
SEVEN, THE
Ac 6:6; Ac 8:5; Ac 14:23
SEVEN LEAN YEARS TRADITION
"Ancient Texts Relating to the Old Testament," xxiii
SEVENTY
Ge 10:2; Ge 46:27
SEXUAL SIN. *See* ADULTERY; HOMOSEXUALITY
SHABAKO
Isa 18:1; Isa 30:1
SHABBETHAI
Ezr 10:15; Ne 13:15
SHADDAI. *See* NAMES OF GOD: God Almighty (*El Shaddai*)

SHADRACH
Da 1:7
SHALLUM
2Ki 15:27; 2Ki 22:14; 2Ki 23:30; 1Ch 3:15 – 16; Jer 22:11; Hos 7:7
SHALMANESER III
1Ki 18:5; 1Ki 22:1; 2Ki 8:7; 2Ki 10:8; 2Ki 10:34; 2Ki 13:7; 2Ki 19:12; Na 3:3
SHALMANESER IV
2Ki 14:25
SHALMANESER V
2Ki 17:3; 2Ki 17:6; Isa 10:10
SHALMANESER'S BLACK OBELISK
"Ancient Texts Relating to the Old Testament," xxiii
SHAMASH
Ezr 1:8
SHAMASH-SHUM-UKIN
2Ch 33:11; Ezr 4:9
SHAMGAR
Jdg 3:31
SHAMMAH
1Sa 16:9; 2Sa 13:3; 2Sa 21:21
SHAMMAI, SCHOOL OF
Lev 19:18; Lev 24:20; Mt 19:3
SHAPHAN
2Ki 22:3; Ezr 7:6; Jer 29:3; Jer 36:10
SHAPHAT
1Ki 19:16; 2Ki 3:11
SHAREZER
2Ki 19:37
SHARON
SS 2:1; Isa 33:9; Ac 9:35
SHEALTIEL
1Ch 3:19; Ezr 5:2; Ne 12:1; Hag 1:1; Mt 1:12
SHEAR-JASHUB
Isa 7:3
SHEBA (son of Bicri)
2Sa 20:1; 2Sa 20:14; 2Sa 20:21; 1Ch 18:17
SHEBA (son of Joktan)
Ge 10:28
SHEBA (Arabian home of queen)
1Ki 10:1; Isa 60:6; Jer 6:20; Eze 38:13; Mt 12:42
SHEBITKU
Isa 37:9
SHEBNA
Isa 22:15; Isa 22:16; Isa 22:21
SHECANIAH (head of Davidic family)
1Ch 3:21; 1Ch 3:22
SHECANIAH (son of Jehiel)
Ezr 10:2
SHECHEM
Ge 33:18; Jos 8:30 – 35; Jdg 9:1; 1Ki 12:1; Ac 7:16
SHEEP GATE
Ne 3:1; Ne 3:32
SHEKEL
Ge 20:16; Ezr 2:69
SHELAH
1Ch 2:3 – 9; 1Ch 9:4 – 6
SHELANITES
1Ch 9:4 – 6
SHELOMITH
Ezr 8:10
SHEM
Ge 10:2; Ge 10:21; 1Ch 1:5 – 23
SHEMA
Dt 4:1; Dt 6:4 – 9; Mk 12:29; Mk 12:31; Jas 2:19
SHEMAIAH (prophet)
1Ki 12:22; Jer 29:24
SHEMAIAH (son of Delaiah)
Ne 6:10; Ne 6:12
SHEMAIAH (son of Shechaniah)
1Ch 3:22
SHENAZZAR
1Ch 3:18; Ezr 1:8
SHEOL
Ge 37:35; Mt 16:18; Rev 6:8
SHEPHELAH
Jos 15:33; Mic 1:10 – 15; "Five Cities of the Philistines," 331
SHEPHERD
Ge 48:15; Ps 23:1; Ps 119:176; Eze 34:2; Zec 10:2; Mk 6:42; Jn 10:1 – 30; 1Pe 2:25; 1Pe 5:2
SHESHACH
Jer 25:26
SHESHBAZZAR
1Ch 3:18; Ezr 1:8; Ezr 1:11; Ezr 2:63; Ne 5:15
SHIBBOLETH
Jdg 12:6
SHIELD
Ge 15:1; Ps 3:3
SHIHOR RIVER
Jos 13:3; 1Ch 13:5; Isa 23:3
SHILOAH
Isa 8:6
SHILOH
Jos 18:1; Jdg 21:19; 1Sa 1:3; 1Sa 2:32; 1Sa 9:12
SHILONITES
1Ch 9:4 – 6
SHIMEI (Benjamite)
2Sa 16:8; 2Sa 16:10; 2Sa 19:17; 2Sa 19:23; 1Ki 2:8; 1Ki 2:36; 1Ki 2:46
SHIMEI (son of Kish)
Est 2:5
SHIMEON
Ezr 10:31
SHIMSHAI
Ezr 4:8; Ne 1:3
SHIPHRAH
Ex 1:15
SHIPS OF TARSHISH
1Ki 10:22
SHISHAK
1Ki 11:40; 1Ki 14:25; 2Ch 12:2; "Ancient Texts Relating to the Old Testament," xxiii
SHISHAK'S GEOGRAPHICAL LIST
"Ancient Texts Relating to the Old Testament," xxiii
SHITTIM
Nu 25:1
SHOBI
2Sa 17:27
SHRINE PROSTITUTE. *See* PROSTITUTE, SHRINE
SHUAH
Job 2:11
SHUHAM
Jdg 18:19
SHULAMMITE
SS 6:13
SHUNAMMITE
2Ki 4:13; SS 6:13
SHUNEM
1Sa 28:4; 1Ki 1:3
SHUR, DESERT OF
Ex 15:22; 1Sa 15:7
SIAMUN
1Ki 3:1
SIBMAH
Isa 16:8
SIDON
Jdg 3:3; Jdg 10:6; Jdg 18:7; Eze 27:8; Da 11:15; Joel 3:4; Lk 4:26; Lk 10:14; Ac 12:20; Ac 27:3; "The Territories of Tyre and Sidon," 1537
SIGN
Ex 3:12; Ex 4:8; 1Ki 13:3; Isa 7:14; Mt 12:38; Lk 1:18; Lk 11:29; Lk 11:33; Jn 2:11
SIGNET RING
Hag 2:23
SIHON
Nu 21:21 – 26; SS 7:4; Isa 15:4
SILAS
Ac 15:22; Ac 15:40; Ac 16:6; Ac 16:32; Ac 16:37; Ac 17:10; Ac 18:5; 1Th 1:1; 1Th 1:5; 1Th 3:1 – 2; 1Pe 5:12
SILLA
2Ki 12:20
SILOAM, POOL OF
Ne 2:13; Ne 2:14; Ne 3:15; Job 28:10; Jn 9:7
SILOAM, TOWER OF
Lk 13:4
SILOAM, TUNNEL OF
Ne 2:14; "Jerusalem During the Ministry of Jesus," 1527
SILOAM INSCRIPTION
2Ki 20:20; "Ancient Texts Relating to the Old Testament," xxiii
SILVER
Dt 14:25
SILVERSMITH
Jdg 17:4; Ac 19:24
SIMEON (high priest)
Lk 1:6; Lk 2:25; Lk 2:29 – 32
SIMEON (Niger)
Ac 13:1
SIMEON (son of Jacob)
1Ch 4:24 – 43; 2Ch 34:6; Ezr 10:31
SIMEON (tribe)
Ge 49:7; Jdg 1:3
SIMEON BAR KOSIBA (Kokhba)
Zec 11:17
SIMON (of Cyrene)
Mk 15:21; Lk 23:26; Jn 19:17

SIMON (the Zealot)
Mt 10:4
SIMON MAGUS (sorcerer)
Ac 8:9; Ac 8:10; Ac 8:13; Ac 8:18
SIMON PETER. *See* PETER
SIMON THE LEPER
Mt 26:6
SIN
freed from
Ro 6:6; Ro 6:7; Ro 6:22
inherited by all
Ge 6:5; Ge 8:21
nature
Ro 7:5; Ro 7:25
offering
Ex 29:10; Lev 4:3; Lev 4:20; 2Ki 12:16; Ne 8:10; Eze 43:19; "Old Testament Sacrifices," 153
power of
Ge 4:7; Ge 4:13; Ge 4:23; Jn 8:34; Ro 3:10–18; Ro 6:14; 1Co 15:56
universality of
Ro 3:9; Ro 3:22–23
unpardonable
Mt 12:31
victory over
Mt 4:1–11; 1Co 15:57; 1Jn 1:7; 1Jn 1:9; 1Jn 3:6
wages of
Ge 2:17; Ge 3:22; Ge 5:5; Lev 15:31; Nu 15:2; Ro 5:12; Ro 6:23; Ro 7:9; 1Co 7:10
SIN, DESERT OF
Ex 16:1
SIN-SHAR-ISHKUN
Na 3:18
SINAI, DESERT OF
Ex 19:2; Nu 1:1
SINAI, MOUNT. *See* MOUNT: Sinai
SINUHE
Ne 9:25; Introduction to Genesis: Background; "Ancient Texts Relating to the Old Testament," xxiii
SINUHE'S STORY
"Ancient Texts Relating to the Old Testament," xxiii
SIROCCO
Ge 41:6; Job 15:2
SISERA
Jdg 4:7; Jdg 4:18; Jdg 4:22; 1Sa 13:5
SLANDER
Pr 15:4; 2Co 8:21; 2Pe 2:10
SLAVERY
Ex 1:11; Ex 5:6; Ex 6:7–8; Ex 21:2; Ex 21:32; Lev 25:55; 1Ki 9:15; 2Ki 4:1; Ne 5:5; 1Co 7:21; 1Co 7:22; 1Co 7:23; Gal 5:1; Eph 6:5; Col 3:22—4:1; Tit 2:9–10; 1Pe 2:18
to God
Ro 6:18,22; Gal 1:10
SLEDGE
Am 1:3
SLINGSTONE
Jdg 20:16; 1Sa 17:40
SLUGGARD
Pr 6:6
SMYRNA
Rev 2:8
SNARE
Ex 4:3; Nu 21:8–9; 2Ki 18:4
SOCIAL JUSTICE
Introduction to Amos: Theme and Message
SOCIAL RESPONSIBILITY
Zec 7:10; Ro 12:13
SOCOH
1Sa 17:1
SODOM
Ge 13:10; Ge 13:12; Ge 18:20; Ge 19:13; Eze 16:47; Zep 2:9; Lk 10:12; Rev 11:8; Rev 14:10
SODOMY
Ge 19:5
SOLOMON
"Solomon's Jerusalem," 477
anointed by Zadok
1Ki 1:39
birth of
1Ki 3:7
failures of
1Ki 3:3; 1Ki 3:14; 1Ki 11:11
idealized by Chronicler
Introduction to 1 Chronicles: Portrait of David and Solomon
marriages of
1Ki 3:1; 1Ki 11:1; 1Ki 11:4; 2Ch 9:28; 2Ch 21:6
palace of
1Ki 7:1–12
and queen of Sheba
1Ki 10:1; 1Ki 10:9; 1Ki 10:13; 2Ch 9:1–12
receives wisdom from God
2Ch 1:5
son of Bathsheba
2Sa 5:14; 1Ki 1:11
successor to David
1Ki 1:13; 1Ki 2:4; 1Ch 22:5
temple of
1Ki 6:2; 1Ki 8:27; "Solomon's Temple," 484; Introduction to 2 Chronicles: The Building of the Temple in Chronicles
wealth of
1Ki 4:26
SOLOMON'S COLONNADE
Jn 10:23; Ac 3:11
SON
of Abraham
Mk 1:1
of the Blessed One
Mk 14:61
of David
Mt 1:1; Mt 1:16; Mt 1:20; Mt 2:1; Mt 9:27; Mk 10:47; Mk 12:35; Jn 7:42
of God
Jn 3:16
of man
Eze 2:1; Da 7:13; Mk 8:31; Lk 19:10; Jn 12:34; Ac 7:56; Eph 1:22; Rev 6:13
of the Most High
Lk 1:32; Lk 8:28
SONG
of David
2Sa 22:1
of Deborah
Jdg 5:1–31
of Hannah
1Sa 2:1
of Mary
Lk 1:46–55
of Moses
Ex 15:1–18; Dt 31:30; Dt 32:1–43; Dt 32:4; Rev 15:3
of the Vineyard
Isa 5:7
of Zechariah
Lk 1:68–79
SONS
of God
Ge 6:2; Job 5:1; Ro 8:14; Ro 8:15; Ro 8:19; Ro 8:23; Gal 4:5; Heb 2:10; Heb 12:7
of thunder
Mk 3:17; Lk 9:54
SOOTHSAYER'S TREE
Jdg 9:37
SOPATER
Ac 20:4; Ro 16:21
SOREK VALLEY
Jdg 14:5
SOSIPATER
Ac 20:4; Ro 16:21
SOSTHENES
Ac 18:17; 1Co 1:1
SOUL
Ps 6:3; Mt 10:28
SOUND DOCTRINE
Tit 1:9; Tit 2:2–10; "The Pastoral Letters," 1867
SOUTH GALATIAN THEORY, THE
Introduction to Galatians: Date and Destination
SOUTH GATE
1Ch 26:15
SOVEREIGNTY OF GOD. *See* GOD: sovereignty of
SPAIN
Ro 15:24; 2Co 10:16
SPELT
Ex 9:32
SPICE
SS 4:10
SPIES
Nu 13:2; Jos 2:1–24
SPIRIT OF BONDAGE
2Co 11:4
SPIRIT OF THE LORD
Jdg 3:10; Jdg 6:34; Jdg 11:29; 1Sa 11:6; 1Sa 16:14; 1Sa 19:24; 2Sa 23:2; 1Ki 18:12; Introduction to Judges: Theme and Theology
SPIRITS, EVIL. *See* EVIL SPIRITS
SPIRITUAL GIFTS. *See* GIFTS: spiritual
STEPHANUS
1Co 16:15

STEPHEN
Ac 6:5; Ac 6:8; Ac 6:9; Ac 6:11; Ac 6:13; Ac 7:9; Ac 7:14; Ac 7:16; Ac 7:23; Ac 7:35; Ac 7:43; Ac 7:44–50; Ac 7:49
STOICISM
Ac 17:18
STRAIGHT STREET
Ac 9:11; "Roman Damascus," 1695
SUBMISSION
Ex 20:2; Ps 2:12; Ro 13:1; Eph 5:21; Eph 5:22; Heb 13:17; 1Pe 3:1; 1Pe 5:5
SUBSTITUTION
Ge 22:13; Ex 12:7; Ex 29:10; Lev 1:5; Lev 16:20–22; Nu 8:10; Mt 20:28; Mk 10:45
SUCCOTH
Ex 12:37; Jdg 7:24; 1Ki 7:46
SUFFERING
Rev 1:9; Introduction to Job: Theme and Message; Introduction to Psalms: Theology; Introduction to 1 Peter: Themes
for Christ
1Co 7:28; 1Co 13:3; 2Co 1:8; Php 1:13; Php 1:20; Php 1:29; 1Th 3:3; 2Ti 2:11–13,12; 2Ti 3:11; 1Pe 3:14; 1Pe 4:1; 1Pe 4:4; 1Pe 4:13
of Christ
Isa 52:14; Heb 2:10; Heb 5:8; Heb 12:2; 1Pe 2:21
rejoicing in
Ro 5:3,4
of the righteous
Job 10:3; Ps 22:1–31; Ps 73:1–28; Lk 13:2,4; Ro 8:36; 2Co 4:17; Jas 1:9–10
and spiritual gain
Job 2:10; Heb 12:5; 1Pe 4:17
SUKKITES
2Ch 12:3
SUN
Ge 1:16; Ex 10:21; Ps 19:4–6; Ps 104:19–23
SUN OF RIGHTEOUSNESS
Mal 4:2
SUSA
Ezr 4:9; Ezr 6:2; Ne 5:4; Est 1:2; Est 1:5–6; Est 2:5
SWEARING
Dt 6:13; Jas 5:12
SYCAMORE (FIG) TREE
Am 7:14; Lk 19:4
SYCHAR
Jn 4:5
SYNAGOGUE
description of
Eze 8:1; Mk 1:21; Lk 21:12; Ac 13:14; "The Time Between the Testaments," 1451; "Capernaum Synagogue," 1572
ruler of
Mk 5:22
SYNOPTIC GOSPELS
Mt 3:3; Mt 13:3; Mt 19:16; Mt 20:30; Mt 21:12–17; Lk 5:12–16; Lk 9:12; Lk 19:45; Jn 6:68; Jn 18:11; "Dating the Synoptic Gospels," 1457; "Parables of Jesus," 1598
SYNTYCHE
Php 4:2–3
SYRACUSE
Ac 28:12
SYRIA
Isa 30:1; Da 7:4–7; Da 11:6; Gal 1:17; Gal 1:21; "The Time Between the Testaments," 1451
SYRO-EPHRAIMITE WAR
Isa 7:1

TAANACH
Jdg 5:19
TABEEL
Isa 7:6
TABERNACLE
Ex 25:9; Ex 26:1; Ex 26:31–35; 1Sa 1:9; Rev 15:5; "The Tabernacle," 126; "Tabernacle Furnishings," 127
TABERNACLES, FEAST OF. *See* FEAST: of Tabernacles
TABITHA
Ac 9:40
TABLE OF NATIONS
Ge 10:2; 1Ch 1:5–23; "Table of Nations," 22
TABLETS
Ex 31:18; 2Co 3:3; 2Co 3:6
TABRIMMON
1Ki 15:19
TAHPANHES
Jer 2:16; Eze 30:18
TALE OF TWO BROTHERS
"Ancient Texts Relating to the Old Testament," xxiii
TALENT, THE
1Ki 20:39; Mt 25:15; Lk 19:13
TALMAI
2Sa 3:3; 2Sa 13:37
TALMANUTHA
Mk 8:10
TALMUD
Zec 6:12; Mk 5:26; Mk 15:23; Lk 16:22; Introduction to Ezra: Ezra and Nehemiah
TAMAR
Ge 38:11; Ru 1:4; Ru 3:4; 2Sa 3:2; 2Sa 3:3; 2Sa 13:1; 2Sa 13:13; 2Sa 13:15; 2Sa 13:21; 2Sa 14:27; 1Ki 15:2; 2Ch 11:20; Eze 47:18
TAMARISK
Ge 21:33
TAMMUZ
Eze 8:14
TANIS
Isa 19:11; Eze 30:14
TAPPUAH
2Ki 15:16
TARGUM
Ne 8:8; Zec 6:12; Zec 10:4; Introduction to Job: Date
TARSHISH
Ps 72:10; Isa 23:6; Eze 27:12; Jnh 1:3
TARSUS
Ac 6:9; Ac 9:30; Ac 22:3; Gal 1:21
TARTARUS
2Pe 2:4
TARTESSUS
Isa 23:6; Jnh 1:3
TAWILAN
Ob 1:9
TAX COLLECTOR
Mt 5:46; Mk 2:15; Lk 3:12; Lk 18:13; Lk 19:2
TAXES
1Ch 27:25–31; Ne 5:4; Mt 17:24; Mt 22:15–17; Mk 12:14; Ro 13:6
TEACHER OF RIGHTEOUSNESS
Joel 2:23
TEACHERS OF THE LAW
Mt 2:4; Mk 2:16; Mk 12:40; Lk 5:17
TEACHING
1Co 12:28; Eph 4:11; Eph 4:14
false
2Co 2:17; 2Co 3:1; 2Co 4:2; 2Co 4:5; 2Co 5:11; 2Co 6:14; 2Co 7:2; 2Co 7:3; 2Co 10:4; 2Co 10:7; 2Co 10:12; 2Co 10:13; 2Co 11:1; 2Co 11:2; 2Co 11:6; 2Co 11:11; 2Co 11:13; 2Co 11:19; 2Co 11:22; 2Co 12:12; 2Co 12:16; 2Co 13:5; Php 3:2; 1Ti 1:3–11; 1Ti 4:1; Tit 1:9; 2Pe 2:15; Rev 2:14
TEBAH
1Ch 18:8
TEKOA
2Sa 14:1; Ne 3:5; Ne 3:27; Introduction to Amos: Author
TEL ABIB
Eze 3:15; Ac 9:36
TEL MELAH
Ezr 2:59
TELL (mound)
Jos 11:13; Ezr 2:59; Jer 30:18
TELL BEIT MIRSIM
Jos 10:38; 2Ch 26:10
TELL ED-DUWEIR
2Ki 14:19
TELL EL-MASKHUTAH
Ex 12:37; Ne 2:19
TEMA
Job 1:15; Isa 21:14
TEMAN
Job 2:11; Job 4:1; Jer 49:7; Eze 25:13; Am 1:12; Ob 1:9; Hab 3:3
TEMPLE
curtain of
Ex 26:31; Nu 3:25–26; Mt 27:51; Mk 15:38; Lk 23:45
early
1Sa 1:9; Ps 24:2
Ezekiel's
Ne 8:16; "Ezekiel's Temple," 1297
Herod's
Mt 2:1; Mt 4:5; Lk 4:9; Lk 21:5; Jn 2:20; Ac 3:2; "Herod's Temple," 1470

Solomon's
1Ki 6:1 – 38; 1Ki 8:2; Ezr 5:11; Ezr 6:15; Hag 2:3; Jnh 2:4; "Solomon's Temple," 484; "Temple Furnishings," 487; Introduction to 2 Chronicles: The Building of the Temple in Chronicles
Zerubbabel's
Ezr 4:24; Ezr 6:3; Ezr 6:15; Hag 1:2; Hag 2:3; Zec 4:1 – 14; Zec 4:6; Zec 4:10; "Zerubbabel's Temple," 677
Scroll
Ezr 8:15; Ne 8:16; Ne 10:34
Treasury
Lk 21:1
TEMPTATION
Ge 3:6; Ge 22:1; Mt 4:1 – 11; Mt 4:1; 1Co 10:13; 1Th 3:5; Heb 4:15; Heb 4:16; Jas 1:13
TEN COMMANDMENTS
Ex 20:1 – 17; Ex 20:1; Ex 31:18; Dt 5:6 – 21
TENDON
Ge 32:32
TENT OF MEETING
Ex 27:21; Lev 1:1; Lev 16:16; Nu 2:17; Jos 18:1; 1Sa 7:1; 1Ki 8:4; Jn 1:14
TENTMAKING
Ac 18:3; 1Co 4:12
TERAH
Ge 11:31; Jos 24:14; Ac 7:4
TERAPHIM. *See* HOUSEHOLD GODS
TERTIUS
Ac 24:1; Ro 16:22
TERTULLUS
Ac 24:1; Ac 24:10
TESTING
Ge 22:1 – 2; Ex 15:25; Nu 11:10; Dt 4:20; Ps 66:10; Mt 4:1; Rev 3:10
TETRARCH
Mt 14:1
THADDAEUS
Mk 3:18; Lk 6:16; Ac 1:13
THANK OFFERING
Ps 7:17; "Old Testament Sacrifices," 153
THANKSGIVING
Ro 1:8; Ro 1:21; Eph 5:4; Php 1:3 – 4; Php 4:6; Php 4:18; Col 1:3; Col 3:16; 1Th 3:9; 1Th 5:18; Introduction to Psalms: Psalm Types
THEBES. *See* KARNAK
THEOCRACY. *See also* ISRAEL: as a theocracy
Ge 9:5; Ge 9:6
THEOPHANY
Nu 12:5; Nu 14:10; Jos 5:13
THEOPHILUS
Ac 1:1; Introduction to Luke: Recipient and Purpose
THESSALONICA
Ac 16:12; Php 4:15; Php 4:16; Introduction to 1 Thessalonians: Thessalonica
THIRTY, THE
2Sa 23:24; 1Ch 27:9 – 15
THOMAS
Jn 11:16; Jn 14:5
THORNBUSH
Jdg 9:14
THREE, THE
2Sa 23:8
THREE TAVERNS
Ac 28:15
THRESHING
Ge 50:10; Ru 1:22; Ru 2:17; Am 1:3
THUCYDIDES
Ne 1:3
THUTMOSE III
Ex 1:11; Ex 2:15; Jdg 4:3; Jdg 5:19; Ne 5:18; Introduction to Exodus: Chronology
THYATIRA
Ac 16:14; Rev 2:18
TIBERIAS (city)
Ne 11:1; Lk 23:7; Lk 23:8; Jn 6:1
TIBERIAS, SEA OF
Mk 1:16; Lk 5:1; Jn 6:1
TIBERIUS, EMPEROR
Mt 22:19; Lk 3:1; Ro 16:11
TIBNI
1Ki 16:22; 1Ki 16:23
TIGLATH-PILESER III
1Ki 15:20; 1Ki 16:27; 2Ki 15:19; 2Ki 15:30; 2Ki 16:9; 1Ch 5:6; 1Ch 5:26; 2Ch 26:11; 2Ch 28:20; Isa 17:3; Hos 5:13; Hos 7:9; "Assyrian Campaigns against Israel and Judah," 552
TIKVAH
Ezr 10:15
TIMNA
1Ch 1:36
TIMNAH
Jdg 14:1; Jdg 14:5
TIMNATH SERAH
Jos 19:50
TIMOTHY
Ac 14:6; Ac 14:20; Ac 16:1; Ac 16:6; Ac 17:10; Ac 18:5; Ac 19:22; Ac 20:4; Ac 21:24; 1Co 16:10; 2Co 1:1; Php 1:1; Php 2:19 – 23; Col 1:1; 1Th 1:1; 2Ti 1:5; 2Ti 1:7; 2Ti 3:15; Tit 1:6 – 9; Heb 13:23; Introduction to 1 Timothy: Recipient
TIPHSAH
1Ki 4:24; 2Ki 15:16
TIRATHITES
1Ch 2:55
TIRHAKAH
Isa 37:9
TIRZAH
1Ki 14:17; 2Ki 15:14; SS 6:4
TISHRI
2Ch 5:3; Ezr 3:1; Ne 8:1; "Hebrew Calendar and Selected Events," 104
TITHE
Ge 14:20; Ge 28:22; Lev 27:30; Nu 18:26 – 32; Dt 14:22 – 29; Am 4:4; Lk 18:12
TITIUS JUSTUS
Ac 18:7
TITUS
Ac 16:3; 2Co 2:12; 2Co 7:5 – 6; 2Co 8:6; 2Co 8:16; 2Co 12:13; Gal 2:1; Introduction to Titus: Recipient
TOB
Jdg 11:3; 1Ch 19:6
TOBIAH
Ne 2:10; Ne 3:4; Ne 6:17 – 18; Ne 13:5; Eze 44:9
TOLA
Jdg 10:1
TONGUE
Ps 5:9; Ps 10:7; Ps 120:4; Pr 13:3
TONGUES
of fire
Ac 2:3
languages and/or spiritual gift
Ac 2:4; Ac 2:6; Ac 10:47; 1Co 12:10; 1Co 12:28; 1Co 13:1 – 3; 1Co 13:8; 1Co 14:1 – 5; 1Co 14:2; 1Co 14:5; 1Co 14:6; 1Co 14:9; 1Co 14:10; 1Co 14:14; 1Co 14:15 – 17; 1Co 14:19; 1Co 14:20; 1Co 14:23; 1Co 14:27 – 28; 1Co 14:29; 1Co 14:32; 1Co 14:34; Heb 2:4
TOPHETH
2Ki 23:10; Isa 30:33; Jer 7:31
TORAH
Ne 9:13; Ps 119:1; "The Time Between the Testaments," 1451
TOTAL DEPRAVITY. *See* DEPRAVITY, TOTAL
TOWER
of Babel
Ge 11:4
of Hananel
Ne 3:1; Zec 14:10
of the hundred
Ne 3:1
of the ovens
Ne 3:11
TRADITION OF ELDERS
Mt 15:2
TRANSFIGURATION
Mt 16:28; Mt 17:1 – 9; Mt 17:1; Mt 17:2; Mk 9:2; Lk 9:28; 1Pe 5:1
TRANSFIGURATION, MOUNT OF. *See* MOUNT: of Transfiguration
TRANSGRESSION
Ro 4:15
TRANSJORDAN
1Ch 12:8 – 15; Ne 2:19; Mt 19:1
TRANSVESTISM
Dt 22:5
TREE OF LIFE
Ge 2:9
TRINITY, THE
Mt 3:16 – 17; Mt 28:19; Mk 1:10 – 11; Jn 14:17; 1Co 12:4 – 6; 1Co 15:28; 2Co 13:14; 1Th 1:1; 2Th 2:13; Heb 1:2 – 3; 1Pe 1:2
TRIUMPHAL ENTRY
"Passion Week," 1552

TROAS
Ac 16:8; Ac 20:1; Ac 20:5; 2Co 2:12; 2Co 7:5–6
TROPHIMUS
Ac 20:4; Ac 21:29
TRUMPET
Nu 10:10; Nu 29:1–6; Jdg 7:16; Jdg 7:22; Ezr 3:10; Joel 2:1; Joel 2:15
TRUMPETS, FEAST OF
Nu 29:1–6; Ne 8:2
TRUST
Ps 16:1–11; Ps 31:1–24; Pr 3:5; Da 6:23; Jn 14:1; Jn 14:11; Heb 2:13; Heb 10:22; Heb 11:7; Introduction to Psalms: Psalm Types
TRUTH
1Ki 17:24; Ps 51:6; Mk 3:28; Jn 1:14; Ac 5:9
TUBAL
Ge 10:2; Isa 66:19; Eze 32:26; Eze 38:2
TURKEY
1Co 16:19; Col 4:13; Col 4:16; 2Ti 1:15; 2Ti 4:10
TUTANKHAMUN
Heb 11:26; "The Tabernacle," 126; "Tabernacle Furnishings," 127
TWELVE, THE
Lk 10:1; Jn 6:71; Ac 1:11; Ac 6:2; Ac 14:4; Ac 21:18; Ro 16:7; 1Co 15:5
TYCHICUS
Ac 20:4; Eph 6:21; Col 3:22–25; Col 4:1; Col 4:10; Col 4:16
TYRANNUS
Ac 19:9
TYRE
2Sa 5:11; 2Ch 2:3–10; Ps 45:12; Isa 23:1; Isa 23:7; Eze 26:1—28:19; Hos 9:13; Am 1:9; Am 1:10; Zec 9:3; Mt 11:21; Mk 7:24; Lk 10:14; Ac 12:20; Ac 21:3; "The Territories of Tyre and Sidon," 1537
TYROPOEON VALLEY
Ne 11:9; map No. 10 at the end of this study Bible

U

UGARITIC
Ge 15:16; Ezr 9:11; Eze 14:14; Eze 14:20; "Ancient Texts Relating to the Old Testament," xxiii; Introduction to Joshua: Historical Setting
UNBELIEF
2Co 4:4; Heb 3:16–19
UNBELIEVERS
2Co 6:14; 1Pe 2:8; 1Pe 2:12; 1Pe 2:15; 1Pe 3:14; 1Pe 3:15; 1Jn 3:8
UNDER THE SUN
Ecc 1:3
UNITY, CHRISTIAN
Ps 133:2; Ps 133:3; Jn 17:11; Jn 17:21; Ac 4:32; Ro 12:5; Ro 14:1; Ro 15:5; 1Co 1:10; 1Co 3:17; 1Co 8:12; 1Co 10:17; Eph 3:6; Eph 3:10; Eph 3:11; Eph 4:3; Eph 4:4; Eph 4:5; Eph 4:13; Eph 4:16; Php 1:27; Php 2:2; Php 2:3; 1Th 5:13
UNLEAVENED BREAD
Ex 12:15; Jos 5:11
UNLEAVENED BREAD, FEAST OF.
See FEAST: of Unleavened Bread
UNPARDONABLE SIN
Mt 12:31; Mk 3:29
UPPER GATE OF BENJAMIN
Jer 20:2
UPPER MILLSTONE
Jdg 9:53
UPPER ROOM DISCOURSE
Jn 13:1–38; Jn 14:1–31; Jn 15:1–27; Jn 16:1–33; Jn 17:1–26
UR
Ge 11:28; Ne 12:27
URARTU
Ge 8:4; Ezr 4:7; Isa 37:38
URIAH (the Hittite)
2Sa 11:3; 2Sa 11:6; 2Sa 11:11; 2Sa 11:15; 2Sa 11:21
URIEL (Levite)
1Ki 15:2; 1Ch 6:24
URIEL (man of Gibeah)
2Ch 11:20
URIM AND THUMMIM
Ex 28:30; 1Sa 2:28; 2Sa 15:27
USURY
Ne 5:10; Eze 18:8
UZ
Job 1:1
UZZAH
2Sa 6:3; 2Sa 6:7; 1Ch 13:7; 1Ch 13:10; 1Ch 14:11; Ac 5:1
UZZIAH
2Ki 15:13; 2Ch 26:1; 2Ch 26:6–8; 2Ch 26:23; 2Ch 28:27; Ne 2:13; Ne 3:11; Ne 6:11; Isa 6:1; Introduction to Amos: Date and Historical Situation
UZZIEL
Nu 3:30; 1Ch 15:4–10

VALLEY
of Achor
Jos 7:26; Isa 65:10; Hos 2:15
of the Arabah. See ARABAH
of Aven
Am 1:5
of Ben Hinnom. See HINNOM VALLEY
Beqaa
2Sa 8:3; Am 1:5
of the Craftsmen
Ne 11:35
of Decision
Joel 3:2; Joel 3:14
of Elah
1Sa 17:2; Ac 8:36
of Eshcol
Nu 13:23
of Gibeon
Isa 28:21
Huleh
Job 40:21–23
Indus River
Ne 5:18
of Jehoshaphat
Joel 3:2; Joel 3:14
of Jezreel
Jos 19:17; Jdg 5:19; Jdg 7:1; 1Ki 1:3; Hos 1:5
Jordan
Ge 13:10; 1Ki 20:26
Kidron
2Ch 29:16; Ne 3:28; Jn 18:1
King's
2Sa 18:18
of Rephaim
Isa 17:5
of Salt
2Ki 14:7; 2Ki 14:25
of Slaughter
Jer 7:32
of Vision
Isa 22:1
of Wickedness
Am 1:5
of Zeboiim
1Sa 13:18
of Zephathah
2Ch 14:10
VALLEY GATE
2Ch 26:9; Ne 2:13; Ne 11:30; Ne 12:31
VASHTI
Est 1:11; Est 1:19; Est 2:19; Est 7:9
VATICANUS
"The Book of the Twelve, or the Minor Prophets," 1333
VEIL
Ge 24:65; SS 1:7; SS 4:1
VESPASIAN
Ac 25:13
VICES
Ro 1:29–31
VINEYARD
SS 1:6; SS 2:15
VIRGIN
Isa 7:14; Joel 1:8; Mt 1:18; 1Co 7:25
VIRGIN DAUGHTER OF ZION
2Ki 19:21
VIRTUES
Gal 5:22–23
VISIONS
Nu 12:6–8; Pr 29:18; Eze 1:1; Eze 1:26; Eze 1:28
VIZIER
Ge 41:43
VOW. *See also* NAZIRITE VOW
Lev 7:16; Nu 30:1–16; Jdg 11:30; 1Sa 1:21; Ps 7:17; Ecc 5:6; Jnh 2:9; Ac 18:18
VULGATE
Isa 14:12; Lk 1:46–55; Lk

1:68–79; Lk 2:29–32; 1Th 4:17; Introduction to 1 Samuel: Title; Introduction to Ezra: Ezra and Nehemiah

W

WADI EL-ARISH
Ge 15:18; Isa 27:12; Eze 47:19
WAR
and accession to the throne
1Sa 20:14; 2Sa 16:21; 1Ki 1:12; 1Ki 2:22
as a contest between deities
Jdg 11:21; 2Sa 5:21
ethics and
"The Conquest and the Ethical Question of War," 286
implements of (in ancient times)
Jos 11:6; Jos 17:16; Jdg 3:16; Jdg 20:16; 1Sa 13:19; 2Ch 26:15
Lord as leader in
Nu 31:1–24,26–35; 2Sa 5:23; 2Sa 24:14
practices of (in ancient times)
Jos 10:24; Jdg 7:25; 1Ki 22:34; 2Ki 8:12; 2Ki 10:8; Hos 10:14; Na 3:3; "Assyrian Campaigns against Israel and Judah," 552
prisoners of (treatment in ancient times)
Jdg 1:6; Jdg 16:21; 2Sa 10:4; 2Sa 12:31; 2Sa 20:24; Am 4:2; "Exile of the Northern Kingdom," 558
representative combat in
1Sa 17:4; 2Sa 2:17
WARNING
Heb 2:1–4; Heb 3:7–11; Heb 10:26–31
WASHERMAN'S FIELD
Isa 7:3
WATCHES OF THE NIGHT
Jdg 7:19; Mt 14:25; Lk 12:38
WATCHMEN
SS 3:3; Eze 3:17
WATER
Ge 26:20; Ex 7:20; Nu 5:18; Nu 20:2; Jn 4:7
and baptism
Jn 3:5; 1Jn 5:6
ceremonial use of
1Sa 7:6; Eze 36:25; Jn 2:6
figurative use of
Job 22:11; Job 33:18; Isa 55:1
imagery of
Ps 32:6; Ps 36:8; Ps 42:7; Ps 74:13–14; Ps 89:9–10
in miracles
Ex 7:17; Ex 14:22; Jos 3:10; Jos 3:13; Jdg 15:19; 2Ki 2:8; 2Ki 2:21; 2Ki 5:10
symbolism of
Ps 36:8; Jn 3:5; Jn 4:10; Eph 5:26; Heb 10:22; 1Jn 5:6
WATERS
chaotic
Ps 32:6; Ps 74:13–14; Ps 89:9–10; Ps 93:3; Ps 107:24; SS 8:7
restful
Ps 23:2
WATER GATE
Ne 3:26; Ne 8:1; Ne 12:31
WAY, THE
Jer 10:2; Jn 14:6; Ac 9:2; Ac 24:14; Ac 24:22
WAY OF HOLINESS
Isa 35:8
WEALTH. *See* MONEY
WEDDING, JEWISH
Joel 1:8; Mt 1:18; Mk 2:19
WEEKS, FEAST OF. *See* FEAST: of Weeks (Pentecost or Harvest)
Nu 28:26–31; 1Ki 9:25; 2Ch 15:10; Ac 2:1
WICKED, THE
Ps 36:2–4; introduction to Ps 37
WIDOWS
Ex 22:21–27; 1Ki 17:22; 2Ki 4:14; Isa 1:17; Ac 6:1; 2Co 8:12; 1Ti 5:9; 1Ti 5:12
WIFE. *See* WOMEN: as wives
WINE
Jn 2:3
WINEPRESS
Isa 5:2; Rev 14:19
WINE VAT
Hag 2:16
WINGS
Ru 2:12; Ru 3:9
WINNOWING
Ru 1:22; Ru 3:2
WISDOM
Job 28:28; Pr 1:2; Pr 2:12–19; Pr 3:19–20; Pr 8:22–31; Ecc 12:13; Eph 5:15; Jas 1:5; "Wisdom Literature," 727; Introduction to Ecclesiastes: Purpose and Method
of the world
1Co 1:20; 1Co 1:21; 1Co 2:1
WITCH. *See* MEDIUM
WITCHCRAFT
2Ki 9:22
WITNESSING
Jn 1:7; Ac 1:8; Heb 12:1
WOMEN
as wives
Pr 31:10; Eph 5:22; 1Pe 1:1–6; 1Pe 3:6; 1Pe 3:7
in the church
1Co 11:3; 1Co 11:5; 1Co 14:34–35; 1Ti 2:8–14; 1Ti 3:11
status of (in ancient times)
Ex 10:11; Nu 5:21; Jn 4:27; Jn 11:28; Ac 17:4
WORD OF GOD. *See also* SCRIPTURE
Ps 119:1–176; Lk 3:2; Jn 1:1; Heb 4:12; 1Pe 1:23; 1Pe 1:25; 1Pe 2:2
WORD OF LIFE
1Jn 1:1
WORK/LAZINESS
Pr 10:4; Pr 10:5
WORKS RIGHTEOUSNESS
1Sa 1:11–15; Mt 19:16; Mt 19:17; Ro 4:1; Ro 4:3; Ro 14:1; Eph 2:9; Php 3:6; Jas 2:14–26
WORMWOOD
Rev 8:11
WORSHIP
of God
Ex 10:11; Ex 27:21; Lev 1:3; 1Sa 15:22; Ne 8:6; Ps 4:1; Ps 22:22–31; Ps 24:1–2; Ps 24:4; Ps 67:1–7; Ps 74:8; Ps 100:1; Isa 1:11–15; Jer 7:1—10:25; Jer 7:1—8:3; Mic 6:6–8; Lk 4:16; Jn 4:24; Ro 12:1; 1Co 11:3–16; 1Co 14:26; Introduction to Exodus: Themes and Theology; Introduction to Leviticus: Title
of idols
Ex 20:4; Ex 32:6; Lev 17:4; Lev 26:1; Ex 19:4–6; Ex 29:1–46; Ps 97:7
place of
Jn 4:20; Jn 4:24
of stars
2Ki 17:16; 2Ki 23:12; Isa 40:26; Jer 19:13

XERXES I
Ezr 4:6; Ezr 7:1; Ezr 9:9; Ne 1:11; Ne 2:6; Est 1:1; Est 1:2; Est 2:1; Est 3:9; Est 8:1; Introduction to Esther: Purpose, Themes and Literary Features

YAHWEH. *See* NAMES OF GOD: LORD (*Yahweh*/Jehovah)
YEAR OF JUBILEE
Lev 25:10; Eze 46:17; Lk 4:19; "Old Testament Feasts and Other Sacred Days," 178
YEAST
Ex 12:15; Mt 13:33; Mk 8:15; Lk 13:21
YEMEN
Eze 23:42; Eze 27:19; Eze 38:13; Joel 3:8; Mt 12:42
YOKE
Eze 34:27
YOM KIPPUR. *See also* DAY OF ATONEMENT
Lev 23:27; "Old Testament Feasts and Other Sacred Days," 178
YUGOSLAVIA
Ro 15:19; 2Ti 4:10

ZABUD
Introduction to 1 Samuel: Literary Features, Authorship and Date
ZACCHAEUS
Lk 19:2
ZADOK
1Sa 2:35; 2Sa 8:17; 1Ki 4:2; 1Ki

4:4; 1Ch 6:8; 1Ch 16:39; Ezr 7:2; Eze 44:15
ZAHAR
Eze 27:18
ZALMON
Ps 68:14
ZAMZUMMITES
Dt 2:20
ZANOAH
Ne 11:30
ZAREPHATH
1Ki 17:9; 2Ki 4:37
ZEALOTS
Mt 10:4; Ac 5:37; "Jewish Sects," 1502
ZEBEDEE
Mt 20:20
ZEBOIIM
Hos 11:8
ZEBULUN
Jos 19:10; Jdg 5:13 – 18; Jdg 12:8; Jdg 12:11; Mt 4:15 – 16
ZECHARIAH (father of John the Baptist)
Mt 3:1; Lk 1:5; Lk 1:21; Lk 1:67; Lk 1:78
ZECHARIAH (prophet)
Hos 1:3; Hos 7:7; Introduction to Zechariah: Author and Unity
ZECHARIAH (son of Hosah)
Ezr 5:1; Ezr 6:13 – 14; Ezr 8:3
ZECHARIAH (son of Jehoiada)
2Ki 12:17; 2Ki 12:20; 2Ki 14:29; 1Ch 25:1; 2Ch 24:25; 2Ch 26:5; Heb 11:37
ZEDEKIAH (king of Judah)
Ge 49:10; 2Ki 24:17; 2Ki 24:19; 2Ki 24:20; 2Ki 25:7; 1Ch 3:15 – 16; 2Ch 36:4; 2Ch 36:9 – 10; 2Ch 36:11 – 14; Ezr 7:1; Eze 7:27; Eze 17:5; Eze 17:7; Eze 19:5; Eze 32:3; Mic 5:1
ZEDEKIAH (son of Kenaanah)
1Ki 22:11; 1Ki 22:24
ZELOPHEHAD
Nu 36:1 – 13; 1Ch 7:14 – 19
ZENAS
Tit 3:13
ZEPHANIAH
2Ki 22:2; 2Ki 22:14; Introduction to Zephaniah: Author
ZERAH (Cushite king)
2Ch 14:1; 2Ch 14:9; 2Ch 15:10
ZERAH (twin born to Judah)
1Ch 9:4 – 6; Ps 88:1
ZERUBBABEL
1Ch 3:18; 1Ch 3:19; 1Ch 3:20; 1Ch 3:21; 2Ch 19:11; Ezr 1:8; Ezr 3:2; Ezr 5:2; Ezr 6:13 – 14; Hag 2:3; Hag 2:8; Zec 4:1 – 14; Zec 4:6; Zec 4:10; Mt 1:12; "Zerubbabel's Temple," 677
ZERUIAH
1Sa 26:6; 2Sa 2:13
ZEUS
Da 11:31; Ac 14:12
ZEUS OLYMPIUS
Da 11:31
ZIBA
2Sa 9:2; 2Sa 9:3; 2Sa 16:2; 2Sa 19:27
ZIGGURAT
Ge 11:4; Ge 28:12; Ge 28:13; Ge 28:17; Introduction to Psalms: Literary Features
ZIKLAG
1Sa 27:6; 1Sa 27:7; Ne 11:28
ZILPAH
Ex 1:2 – 4; Eze 48:2
ZIMRI
1Ki 16:12; 2Ki 9:31; Jer 25:25
ZIN, DESERT OF. *See* DESERT: of Zin
ZION. *See also* JERUSALEM
2Sa 5:7; Ps 9:11; Ps 87:1 – 7; Joel 2:1; Am 1:2
ZION, MOUNT. *See* MOUNT: Zion
ZIPPORAH
Ex 4:25; Ex 18:2; Nu 12:1
ZOAN
Isa 19:11; Isa 30:4; Eze 30:14
ZOAR
Isa 15:5
ZOBAH
2Sa 8:3; 1Ch 18:5; 1Ch 19:6; 2Ch 8:3 – 4
ZOPHAR
Job 11:2 – 3; Job 11:4; Job 11:5; Job 11:6; Job 11:8 – 9; Job 11:11 – 12; Job 17:10 – 16; Job 20:2 – 3; Job 20:4 – 11; Job 20:29
ZORAH
Jdg 13:2
ZURIEL
Nu 3:35

Index to Maps

All entries are place-names found on the maps within this study Bible. References are to the page on which the map is located. For additional information on place-names, see Index to Topics.

Abana River 1572, 1702
Abel Beth Maacah 562
Abel Meholah 342, 518
Abel Shittim 309, 310, 311
Abila 1530, 1547
Abilene 1572
Acco 239, 309, 310, 311, 562, 1570
Achaia 1711, 1731, 1735, 1872
Acshaph 309, 3110, 311
Acrocorinth 1776
Acropolis 1836
Aczib 562
Adam 342
Addon 672
Adriatic Sea 1736, 1872
Adullam 309, 310, 311, 331, 409
Aegean Sea 1967
Aenon 1635
Agora 1702, 1766, 1823
Agrippa, Baths of 1735
Ai 309, 310, 311
Aiath 562
Aijalon 331
Alalakh 56
Aleppo 56, 568, 572
Alexandria 1872
Alexandrium 1570
Ammon 108, 497, 576
Amphipolis 1711, 1728
Amphitheater 1735, 1766
Anathoth 562
Andros 1967
Anio Vetus 1735
Antioch (of Pisidia) 1704, 1711, 1718, 1731, 1967
Antioch (Syria) 1704, 1710, 1711, 1718, 1731, 1872
Antipatris 1570, 1697
Antonia Fortress 1530
Aphek 331, 418, 497, 518
Aphrodite, Temple of 1766
Apollo, Temple of 1766
Apollonia 1711, 1718
Aqua Alsietina 1735
Aqua Appia 1735
Aqua Claudia 1735
Aqua Julia 1735
Aqua Marcia 1735
Aqua Virgo 1735
Arabia 572, 1570, 1680
Arabian Desert 1318
Arad 497, 518
Aram 22, 1318
Ararat, Mt 22, 562
Arbela 562
Arcadian Way 1823
Arimathea 1570
Arnon River 367, 444, 497, 1570, 1635
Aroer 367
Arphaxad 22
Arrapkha 562
Artemis, Temple of 1823
Arvad 562, 1384
Arubu (Arabs) 562
Asclepion 1766
Ashdod 108, 331, 409, 562, 672, 1570
Ashkelon 331, 562, 1467, 1570
Ashpot Gate 1527
Ashtaroth 497
Asia 1680, 1710, 1711, 1718, 1967
Asshur (nation) 22
Asshur 562, 563, 576, 1384
Assos 1718
Assyria 545, 562, 1318, 1384
Athens 1702, 1711, 1718, 1872
Athribis 1467
Attalia 1710, 1967
Auranitis 1530, 1570
Aventine 1735
Azekah 309, 311, 312, 331, 572
Azotus 1570, 1695

Babylon 563, 572, 576, 672, 1318
Babylonia 563, 1318
Balbus, Theater of 1735
Barada (Abana) River 1695
Basilica Aemilia 1735
Basilica Julia 1735
Batanea 1530, 1570
Beersheba 56, 108, 239, 309, 310, 311, 497, 518, 1467, 1570
Behistun 563
Berea 1702, 1711, 1718
Beth Horon, Lower 309, 310, 311, 331
Beth Horon, Upper 309, 310, 311
Beth Nimrah 309, 310, 311
Beth Shan 239, 309, 310, 311, 342, 444, 1468
Beth Shemesh 309, 310, 311, 331
Bethany 1635
Bethany beyond Jordan 1468, 1530
Bethel 56, 309, 310, 311, 497, 518
Bethesda, Pool of 1527
Bethlehem 367, 409, 417, 1467, 1570, 1635
Bethsaida 1530, 1537, 1570
Bethsura 1695
Betogabris 1695
Bezer 239
Bezetha 1527
Bithynia 1711, 1872
Black Sea 1680, 1711, 1718, 1872
Bozrah 497
Brundisium 1872
Byblos 568, 576, 672, 1384
Byzantium 1872

Caelian 1735
Caesarea 1537, 1570, 1629, 1635, 1695, 1702, 1711, 1718, 1731
Caesarea Philippi 1530, 1537, 1570
Calah 562, 563
Campus Martius 1735
Campus Vaticanus 1735
Cana 1629, 1635
Canaan (nation) 22, 56, 108
Canatha 1530
Capernaum 1468, 1537, 1570, 1629, 1635, 1702

Capitoline 1735
Cappadocia 1680, 1710, 1711, 1872
Carchemish 56, 563, 568, 576, 1318, 1384
Carmel 331, 417
Carmel, Mount 518, 1570, 1635
Carthage 1731, 1872
Carthage Nova 1872
Caspian Sea 1318, 1680
Cauda 1731
Cayster River 1823
Cecilia Metella, Tomb of 1735
Cenchrea 1711
Cestius, Pyramid of 1735
Chios (Kios) 1718, 1967
Cilicia 1710, 1872
Cilician Gates 1710, 1718
Circus Flaminius 1735
Circus Maximus 1735
Cnidus 1710, 1731, 1967
Colosse 1702, 1710, 1718, 1872
Coressus, Mt. 1823
Corinth 1702, 1711, 1718, 1766
Corsica 1872
Cos 1710, 1718, 1967
Crete 1680, 1702, 1711, 1718, 1731, 1872
Curetes Street 1823
Cush (nation) 22
Cuthah 572
Cyprus 1702, 1710, 1711, 1718, 1731, 1872
Cyrenaica 1711, 1718
Cyrene 1680, 1711, 1718, 1731, 1872

Damascus 56, 309, 310, 311, 444, 497, 518, 562, 568, 576, 672, 1318, 1384, 1530, 1537, 1570, 1695
Damascus, Desert of 518
Damascus Gate 1527
Dan 497
David, City of 1527
Dead Sea 367, 572, 1467, 1468, 1530, 1570, 1635, 1695
Debir 309, 310, 311, 331
Decapolis 1530, 1537, 1570
Derbe 1702, 1710, 1711, 1718
Dibon 309, 310, 311, 367, 497
Dophkah 108
Dor 239, 309, 310, 311, 444, 562 1570
Dothan 309, 310, 311, 342, 518, 562
Dion 1530, 1537, 1570
Dumah 572, 672
Dur Sharrukin 568, 1384

Ebal, Mt. 309, 310, 311, 342, 1570
Ecbatana 568, 572, 672, 1680
Edom 108, 409, 497, 572
Edom, Way of 518
Edrei 56, 309, 310, 311
Eglon 309, 310, 311, 331, 409
Egypt 108, 497, 562, 572, 1467, 1680, 1872
Egypt, River of 1467
Egypt, Wadi of 108, 562, 572
Ekron 309, 310, 311, 331, 563
Elah, Valley of 409
Elam (nation) 22, 1318, 1680
Elath 497
Elim 108
Eltekeh 562
Emmaus 1635
En Gedi 417
Endor 342
Ephesus 1702, 1710, 1711, 1718, 1823, 1872, 1967
Ephraim 1570
Ephrath 56
Erech 576
Esquiline 1735
Essene Gate 1527
Euboea 1967
Euphrates River 22, 56, 444, 563, 568, 572, 576, 1318, 1384
Ezion Geber 108, 1467

Fair Havens 1731
Forum 1735
Forum of Appius 1731

Gadara 1468, 1530, 1537
Gades 1872
Galatia 1710, 1711, 1718, 1872
Galilee 1467, 1530, 1537, 1570, 1635
Galilee, Sea of 572, 1468, 1530, 1570, 1635, 1635
Gallia 1872
"Garden Tomb" 1527
Gaulanitis 1530, 1570
Gath 309, 310, 311, 331, 409, 417, 563
Gaza 108, 331, 497, 562, 576, 1467, 1570, 1695
Geba 563
Gerar 331
Gerasa 1530
Gerizim, Mt. 309, 310, 311, 342, 1570, 1635, 1695
Geshur 444, 497
Gezer 239, 309, 310, 311, 331, 497, 562
Gibbethon 331, 497
Gibeah 409, 563
Gibeon 309, 310, 311, 572
Gihon Spring 1527
Gilboa, Mt. 342
Gilead 56
Gilgal 309, 310, 311, 518
Gimarrai (Gomer) 563
Gischala 1537
Golan 239
Gomer (nation) 22
Goshen 108
Gozan 568
Great Rift Valley 1467
Great Sea (Mediterranean) 444, 497, 518, 572, 576, 1318, 1384, 1570

Habor River 562
Halys River 1711, 1718
Hamath 444, 563, 568, 572, 576, 1318
Haran 56, 562, 563, 672, 1318
Harod, Spring of 342
Hasmonean Palace 1527
Hazeroth 108
Hazor 309, 310, 311, 497, 562, 1570
Hebron 108, 239, 309, 310, 311, 331, 417, 444, 497, 562, 572, 1467, 1570
Heliopolis 1467
Hereth, Forest of 409
Hermon, Mt. 309, 311, 1530, 1537, 1570
Herodium 1570
Herod's Royal Palace 1527
Herod's Towers 1527
Heshbon 108, 239, 309, 310, 311, 367
Hinnom Valley 432, 477, 695, 1333, 1527
Hippodrome 1527
Hippos 1537
Hispania 1872
Huldah Gates and Stairways 1527

Ibleam 309, 310, 311, 342
Iconium 1702, 1710, 1711, 1718
Idumaea 1570
Ijon 562
Illyricum 1872
Immer 672
Isis and Serapis, Temple of 1735

Israel (Kingdom of) 367, 497
Italia (Italy) 1731, 1872
Iturea 1570

Jabbok River 56, 342, 444, 497, 1570, 1635
Jabesh Gilead 342
Jahaz 309, 310, 311
Jamnia 1570, 1695
Janiculum 1735
Janoah 562
Javan (nation) 22
Jebus 409, 417
Jericho 108, 309, 310, 311, 1468, 1570, 1635417, 444, 497, 562, 572, 576, 672, 1318, 1467, 1468, 1530, 1570, 1635, 1680, 1695, 1702, 1711, 1718, 1731, 1872
Jezreel 342, 497, 518
Joppa 331, 497, 562, 1384, 1570, 1695, 1702
Jordan River 56, 108, 309, 310, 311, 342, 367, 417, 444, 497, 518, 1467, 1468, 1530, 1570, 1635, 1635, 1695
Jotapata 1537
Judah 497, 562, 572, 576, 1384
Judea 331, 1467, 1570, 1635, 1680
Julius Caesar, Temple of 1735
Juno, Temple of 1735
Jupiter, Temple of 1735

Kadesh Barnea 108, 497
Kedar 572
Kedesh 239, 562
Keilah 331, 409
Kerith Ravine 518
Kerub 672
Khorsabad 1318
Kidron Valley 432, 477, 695, 1333, 1527
King's highway 367
Kinnereth 309, 311, 311
Kinnereth, Sea of 108, 309, 310, 311, 342, 497
Kios (Chios) 1718, 1967
Kir Hareseth 367, 497
Kir of Moab 518
Kiriath Arba 56
Kiriath Jearim 309, 310, 311
Kishon River 342, 444, 1635
Kishon Valley 518
Kittim 1384
Korazin 1570, 1635

Lachish 108, 309, 310, 311, 331, 497, 563, 572
Laodicea 1702, 1967
Lasea 1731
Lebonah 1467
Lechaeum Road 1766
Leontes River 1570
Lerna 1766
Libnah 309, 310, 311, 331
Litani River 444
Lod 331
Lower Sea 1318
Lud (nation) 22
Lycia 1710, 1731, 1967
Lydda 1570, 1695, 1702
Lydia 572
Lystra 1702, 1710, 1711, 1718

Macedonia 1711, 1718, 1731, 1872
Machaerus 1468, 1570, 1635
Madai (nation) 22
Madon 309, 310, 311
Magdala 1635
Magnesian Gate 1823
Mahanaim 56
Malta 1731
Mamre 56
Maon 331, 417
Maon, Desert of 417
Marah 108
Marcellus, Theater of 1735
Mari 1384
Masada 1570
Massilia 1872
Media 563, 568, 572, 1680
Mediterranean Sea 1467, 1530, 1570, 1635, 1635, 1680, 1695, 1711, 1718, 1731, 1872
Megiddo 331, 342, 444, 497, 562, 572
Meiron, Mt. 1570
Memphis 108, 572, 1467, 1872
Menzaleh, Lake 108
Merom, Waters of 309, 310, 311
Meshech (nation) 22
Mesopotamia 1680
Micmash 563
Midian 108
Migdol 108, 572
Migron 563
Miletus 1702, 1718, 1872, 1967
Milos 1967
Mitylene 1710, 1718
Mizpah 56, 409, 572
Mizraim (nation) 22
Moab 367, 409, 497

Moreh, Hill of 342
Myra 1710, 1731, 1967
Mysia 1711

Nabatean Kingdom 1570
Nain 1570, 1635, 1635
Naxos 1967
Nazareth 1467, 1468, 1570, 1635, 1635
Neapolis 1695, 1711, 1718, 1872
Nebo, Mt. 108, 309, 310, 311, 367, 1570
Nero, Baths of 1735
Nicomedia 1872
Nicopolis 1872
Nile River 22, 108, 562, 1467, 1872
Nineveh 562, 563, 576, 1318, 1384
Nippur 572, 576, 672, 1318
Nob 409, 563
North Market (Macellum) 1766

Olives, Mt. of 477, 695, 1333, 1527
On 108, 572
Ophrah 342
Orontes, River 56, 444, 562, 563, 1710

Paddan Aram 56
Palatine 1735
Pamphylia 1680, 1710, 1731, 1967
Paphos 1702, 1710
Paran, Desert of 108
Parthian empire 1680
Pasargadae 572
Patara 1710, 1718, 1967
Patmos 1710, 1967
Pella 1530, 1570, 1635
Pelusium 1467
Peniel 56, 239, 342, 497
Perea 1530, 1570
Perga 1710
Pergamum 1872, 1967
Persepolis 572
Persia 572
Persian Empire 672
Persian Gulf 572, 576
Pharpar River 1570
Phasaelis 1570
Philadelphia 1530, 1570, 1967
Philip, Tetrarchy of 1537
Philippi 1702, 1711, 1718, 1836, 1872
Philistia 108, 331, 563, 1467
Phoenicia 1570, 1718
Phoenix 1731
Phrygia 1680, 1711, 1718

Pion, Mt. 1823
Pisidia 1710
Pithom 108, 1467
Pompey, Theater of 1735
Pontus 1680, 1711, 1872
Porta Capena 1735
Psephinus Tower 1527
Ptolemais 1537, 1570, 1635, 1718
Punon 108
Put (nation) 22
Puteoli 1702, 1731

Quirinal 1735
Qumran 1468, 1570

Rabbah 108, 444, 497
Rabbah of the Ammonites 672
Ramah 563, 572, 1570
Rameses 108
Ramoth 239
Ramoth Gilead 56, 497, 518
Raphana 1530, 1537, 1570
Rapha 497, 563
Red Sea 108, 444, 497, 1318, 1467, 1680
Rephidim 108
Rhegium 1702, 1731
Rhodes (city) 1710, 1718, 1967
Rhodes (island) 1710, 1711, 1718, 1967
Riblah 572, 576
Rome 1680, 1702, 1731, 1735, 1872

Salamis 1702, 1710
Salim (Tell Shalem) 1468, 1635
Salmone 1731
Salt Sea (Dead Sea) 56, 108, 309, 310, 311, 409, 417, 497, 518
Samaria (city) 497, 518, 562, 572, 672, 1570, 1635, 1695, 1702
Samaria (nation) 562, 563, 1570, 1635
Samos 1710, 1718, 1967
Samothrace 1711
Sardinia 1872
Sardis 1967
Scythopolis (Beth Shan) 1468, 1530, 1537, 1570, 1635, 1635
Sebaste (Samaria) 1695
Seir 56
Seleucia 1710
Semechonitis, Lake 1570, 1635
Sepphoris 1468, 1537
Serapis, Temple of 1823
Servian wall 1735
Shechem 56, 239, 342, 497, 572
Shephelah 331
Shiloh 342, 572
Shimron 309, 310, 311
Shunem 518
Shur, Desert of 108
Sicily 1702, 1731, 1872
Sidon (city) 518, 562, 572, 1318, 1537, 1570, 1702, 1731
Sidon (territory) 1537
Siloam, Pool of 1527
Sin, Desert of 108
Sinai 108, 1467
Sinai, Desert of 108
Sinai, Mt. 108
Smyrna 1710, 1967
Succoth 56, 108, 342, 1467
Susa 572, 672, 1318, 1680
Sychar 1570, 1635
Syracuse 1702, 1731, 1872
Syria 1710

Taanach 309, 310, 311, 444
Tabbath 342
Tabor, Mt. 342, 1468, 1570, 1635, 1635
Tadmor 568, 576, 672, 1384
Tahpanhes 572
Tamar 497
Tarraco 1872
Tarshish 1384
Tarsus 568, 1702, 1710, 1711, 1718, 1731, 1872
Tekoa 563
Tel Harsha 672
Tel Melah 672
Tel Qasile 331
Tell Shalem 1468
Tema 1318
Teman 497
Thebes 1872
Thessalonica 1702, 1711, 1718
Thrace 1718, 1872
Three Taverns 1731
Thyatira 1967
Tiber Island 1735
Tiber River 1735
Tiberias 1468, 1570, 1635, 1635
Tigris River 22, 563, 568, 576, 672, 1318, 1384
Til Barsip 56
Timnah 331, 563
Tingis 1872
Tinos 1967
Tiphsah 563, 572, 576, 672
Tiras (nation) 22
Tirzah 342, 497
Tishbe 518
Toletum 1872
Traconitis 1530, 1570
Trans-Euphrates 672
Troas 1702, 1711, 1718, 1872
Tubal (nation) 22
Tyre (city) 444, 497, 518, 563, 568, 572, 672, 1318, 1384, 1537, 1570, 1702, 1718
Tyre (territory) 1537
Tyropoeon Street 1527

Ugarit 56
Upper Pirene 1766
Ur 572, 576, 1318
Urartu (Ararat) 568
Urmia, Lake 562, 568

Van, Lake 568
Via Appia 1735
Via Aurelia 1735
Via Egnatia 1836
Via Flaminia 1735
Via Labicana 1735
Via Lata 1735
Via Latina 1735
Via Pinciana 1735
Via Triumphalis 1735
Vicus Longus 1735
Vicus Patricius 1735
Viminal 1735

"Wadi El Arabah" 1467
"Wilson's Arch" 1527

Xystus 1527

Yarkon River 331
Yarmuk River 342, 444, 497, 1530, 1570, 1635, 1635

Zarephath 518
Zarethan 342
Zered River 444, 497
Ziklag 331, 417
Zin, Desert of 108
Zion, Mt. 1527
Ziph 409
Ziph, Desert of 409

Concordance

This NIV Concordance is a condensation of *The NIV Complete Concordance*, taking over 35,000 references from the latter's 250,000. These 35,000 references have been selected as the most helpful for the average Bible student or layperson.

When determining whether or not to include a verse reference, we gave careful consideration to the passage in which the verse is located. We also encourage you to always consider the larger context of the passage, giving special attention to the flow of the thought from beginning to end. Whenever you look up a verse, your goal should be to discover the intended meaning of the verse in context. Do not use this concordance, or any concordance, merely as a *verse-finder;* it should also be used as a *passage-finder*. The contexts surrounding each entry are longer than those usually found in concordances; but even so, the context excerpts are too brief for study purposes. They serve only to help you locate familiar verses.

In some cases the usual short contextual phrases are ineffective in helping you locate a passage. This is especially true in studying key events in a Bible character's life. Therefore, we have incorporated 260 "block entries" in which we use descriptive phrases that mark the breadth of a passage containing episodes of that person's life. The descriptive phrases replace the brief context surrounding each occurrence of the name.

Often more than one Bible character has the same name. For example, there are more than thirty Zechariahs in the Bible. In these cases we have given the name a block entry, assigning each person a number (1), (2), etc., and have included a descriptive phrase to distinguish each. Insignificant names are not included.

In this concordance there are 1,239 key-word entries that have an exhaustive list of every appearance of that word. When this occurs, the word or block entry is marked with an asterisk (*).

Two entries are marked with a dagger (†) and two with a double-dagger (‡). LORD† and LORD'S† list occurrences of the title "Lord," spelled "Lord" and "lord," "Lord's" and "lord's" in the NIV. LORD‡ and LORD'S‡ list occurrences of the proper name of God, *Yahweh,* spelled "LORD" and "LORD'S" in the NIV. See the Preface to the New International Version on page xi.

This miniconcordance includes some words not found in *The NIV Complete Concordance.* These words include: boy, boy's, boys, daughter, daughters, girl, man, man's, men, men's, people, peoples, woman, and women.

Since this concordance can only serve one translation—the New International Version—it is difficult for readers familiar with the Authorized Version to make the transition from its older, more archaic language to that of the NIV. We have tried, therefore, to make this transition a bit easier by including some forty-four prominent Authorized Version words and linking them to NIV words that have taken their place. We wish to thank Dr. Daniel E. Sauerwein of Multnomah Bible College for supplying the data for these additional words.

We pray that this concordance will be used by NIV readers to introduce them to the full scope of God's truth in every book of the Bible.

John R. Kohlenberger III
Edward W. Goodrick

AARON

Genealogy of (Ex 6:16 – 20; Jos 21:4, 10; 1Ch 6:3 – 15).

Priesthood of (Ex 28:1; Nu 17; Heb 5:1 – 4; 7), garments (Ex 28; 39), consecration (Ex 29), ordination (Lev 8).

Spokesman for Moses (Ex 4:14 – 16, 27 – 31; 7:1 – 2). Supported Moses' hands in battle (Ex 17:8 – 13). Built golden calf (Ex 32; Dt 9:20). Talked against Moses (Nu 12). Priesthood opposed (Nu 16); staff budded (Nu 17). Forbidden to enter land (Nu 20:1 – 12). Death (Nu 20:22 – 29; 33:38 – 39).

ABADDON*

Rev 9: 11 whose name in Hebrew is *A,*

ABANDON (ABANDONED)

Dt 4: 31 he will not *a* or destroy you
1Ki 6: 13 and will not *a* my people Israel."
Ne 9: 19 compassion you did not *a* them
9: 31 an end to them or *a* them,
Ps 16: 10 you will not *a* me to the grave,
Ac 2: 27 you will not *a* me to the grave,
1Ti 4: 1 in later times some will *a* the faith

ABANDONED (ABANDON)

Ge 24: 27 who has not *a* his kindness
2Co 4: 9 persecuted, but not *a;* struck down,

ABBA*

Mk 14: 36 "*A,* Father," he said, "everything is
Ro 8: 15 And by him we cry, "*A,* Father."
Gal 4: 6 the Spirit who calls out, "*A,* Father

ABEDNEGO

Deported to Babylon with Daniel (Da 1:1 – 6). Name changed from Azariah (Da 1:7). Refused defilement by food (Da 1:8 – 20). Refused idol worship (Da 3:1 – 12); saved from furnace (Da 3:13 – 30).

ABEL

Second son of Adam (Ge 4:2). Offered proper sacrifice (Ge 4:4; Heb 11:4). Murdered by Cain (Ge 4:8; Mt 23:35; Lk 11:51; 1Jn 3:12).

ABHOR (ABHORS)

Lev 26: 30 of your idols, and I will *a* you.
Dt 7: 26 Utterly *a* and detest it,
Ps 26: 5 I *a* the assembly of evildoers
119: 163 I hate and *a* falsehood
139: 21 and *a* those who rise up against you
Am 6: 8 "I *a* the pride of Jacob
Ro 2: 22 You who *a* idols, do you rob

ABHORS (ABHOR)

Pr 11: 1 The Lord *a* dishonest scales,

ABIATHAR

High priest in days of Saul and David (1Sa 22; 2Sa 15; 1Ki 1 – 2; Mk 2:26). Escaped Saul's slaughter of priests (1Sa 22:18 – 23). Supported David in Absalom's revolt (2Sa 15:24 – 29). Supported Adonijah (1Ki 1:7 – 42); deposed by Solomon (1Ki 2:22 – 35; cf. 1Sa 2:31 – 35).

ABIGAIL

1. Sister of David (1Ch 2:16 – 17).

2. Wife of Nabal (1Sa 25:30); pled for his life with David (1Sa 25:14 – 35). Became David's wife after Nabal's death (1Sa 25:36 – 42); bore him Kileab (2Sa 3:3) also known as Daniel (1Ch 3:1).

ABIHU

Son of Aaron (Ex 6:23; 24:1, 9); killed for offering unauthorized fire (Lev 10; Nu 3:2 – 4; 1Ch 24:1 – 2).

ABIJAH

1. Second son of Samuel (1Ch 6:28); a corrupt judge (1Sa 8:1 – 5).

2. An Aaronic priest (1Ch 24:10; Lk 1:5).

3. Son of Jeroboam I of Israel; died as prophesied by Ahijah (1Ki 14:1 – 18).

4. Son of Rehoboam; king of Judah who fought Jeroboam I attempting to reunite the kingdom (1Ki 14:31 – 15:8; 2Ch 12:16 – 14:1; Mt 1:7).

ABILITY (ABLE)

Ex 35: 34 tribe of Dan, the *a* to teach others.
Dt 8: 18 for it is he who gives you the *a*
Ezr 2: 69 According to their *a* they gave
Mt 25: 15 one talent, each according to his *a.*
Ac 11: 29 disciples, each according to his *a,*
2Co 1: 8 far beyond our *a* to endure,
8: 3 were able, and even beyond their *a.*

ABIMELECH

1. King of Gerar who took Abraham's wife Sarah, believing her to be his sister (Ge 20). Later made a covenant with Abraham (Ge 21:22 – 33).

2. King of Gerar who took Isaac's wife Rebekah, believing her to be his sister (Ge 26:1 – 11). Later made a covenant with Isaac (Ge 26:12 – 31).

3. Son of Gideon (Jdg 8:31). Attempted to make himself king (Jdg 9).

ABISHAG*

Shunammite virgin; attendant of David in his old age (1Ki 1:1 – 15; 2:17 – 22).

ABISHAI

Son of Zeruiah, David's sister (1Sa 26:6; 1Ch 2:16). One of David's chief warriors (1Ch 11:15 – 21): against Edom (1Ch 18:12 – 13), Ammon (2Sa 10), Absalom (2Sa 18), Sheba (2Sa 20). Wanted to kill Saul (1Sa 26), killed Abner (2Sa 2:18 – 27; 3:22 – 39), wanted to kill Shimei (2Sa 16:5 – 13; 19:16 – 23).

ABLE (ABILITY ENABLE ENABLED ENABLES ENABLING)

Nu 14: 16 'The Lord was not *a*
1Ch 29: 14 that we should be *a* to give
2Ch 2: 6 who is *a* to build a temple for him,
Eze 7: 19 and gold will not be *a* to save them
Da 3: 17 the God we serve is *a* to save us
4: 37 walk in pride he is *a* to humble.
Mt 9: 28 "Do you believe that I am *a*
Lk 13: 24 will try to enter and will not be *a* to
14: 30 to build and was not *a* to finish.'
21: 15 none of your adversaries will be *a*
21: 36 and that you may be *a* to stand
Ac 5: 39 you will not be *a* to stop these men;
Ro 8: 39 will be *a* to separate us
14: 4 for the Lord is *a* to make him stand
16: 25 to him who is *a* to establish you
2Co 9: 8 God is *a* to make all grace abound
Eph 3: 20 him who is *a* to do immeasurably
6: 13 you may be *a* to stand your ground,
1Ti 3: 2 respectable, hospitable, *a* to teach,
2Ti 1: 12 and am convinced that he is *a*
2: 24 kind to everyone, *a* to teach,
3: 15 which are *a* to make you wise
Heb 2: 18 he is *a* to help those who are being
7: 25 he is *a* to save completely
Jas 3: 2 *a* to keep his whole body in check.
Jude : 24 To him who is *a* to keep you
Rev 5: 5 He is *a* to open the scroll

ABNER

Cousin of Saul and commander of his army (1Sa 14:50; 17:55 – 57; 26). Made Ish-Bosheth king after Saul (2Sa 2:8 – 10), but later defected to David (2Sa 3:6 – 21). Killed Asahel (2Sa 2:18 – 32), for which he was killed by Joab and Abishai (2Sa 3:22 – 39).

ABOLISH (ABOLISHED ABOLISHING)

Hos 2: 18 I will *a* from the land,
Mt 5: 17 that I have come to *a* the Law

ABOLISHED (ABOLISH)

Gal 5: 11 the offense of the cross has been *a.*

ABOLISHING* (ABOLISH)

Eph 2: 15 by *a* in his flesh the law

ABOMINATION*

Da 11: 31 set up the *a* that causes desolation.
12: 11 *a* that causes desolation is set up,
Mt 24: 15 the holy place 'the *a* that causes
Mk 13: 14 you see 'the *a* that causes

ABOUND (ABOUNDING)

2Co 9: 8 able to make all grace *a* to you,
9: 8 you will *a* in every good work.
Php 1: 9 that your love may *a* more

ABOUNDING (ABOUND)

Ex 34: 6 slow to anger, *a* in love
Nu 14: 18 *a* in love and forgiving sin
Ne 9: 17 slow to anger and *a* in love.
Ps 86: 5 *a* in love to all who call to you.
86: 15 slow to anger, *a* in love
103: 8 slow to anger, *a* in love.
Joel 2: 13 slow to anger and *a* in love,
Jnh 4: 2 slow to anger and *a* in love,

ABRAHAM

Abram, son of Terah (Ge 11:26 – 27), husband of Sarah (Ge 11:29).

Covenant relation with the Lord (Ge 12:1 – 3; 13:14 – 17; 15; 17; 22:15 – 18; Ex 2:24; Ne 9:8; Ps 105; Mic 7:20; Lk 1:68 – 75; Ro 4; Heb 6:13 – 15).

Called from Ur, via Haran, to Canaan (Ge 12:1; Ac 7:2 – 4; Heb 11:8 – 10). Moved to Egypt, nearly lost Sarah to Pharoah (Ge 12:10 – 20). Divided the land with Lot; settled in Hebron (Ge 13). Saved Lot from four kings (Ge 14:1 – 16); blessed by Melchizedek (Ge 14:17 – 20; Heb 7:1 – 20). Declared righteous by faith (Ge 15:6; Ro 4:3; Gal 3:6 – 9). Fathered Ishmael by Hagar (Ge 16).

Name changed from Abram (Ge 17:5; Ne 9:7). Circumcised (Ge 17; Ro 4:9 – 12). Entertained three visitors (Ge 18); promised a son by Sarah (Ge 18:9 – 15; 17:16). Questioned destruction of Sodom and Gomorrah (Ge 18:16 – 33). Moved to Gerar; nearly lost Sarah to Abimelech (Ge 20). Fathered Isaac by Sarah (Ge 21:1 – 7; Ac 7:8; Heb 11:11 – 12); sent away Hagar and Ishmael (Ge 21:8 – 21; Gal 4:22 – 30). Covenant with Abimelech (Ge 21:22 – 32). Tested by offering Isaac (Ge 22; Heb 11:17 – 19; Jas 2:21 – 24). Sarah died; bought field of Ephron for burial (Ge 23). Secured wife for Isaac (Ge 24). Fathered children by Keturah (Ge 25:1 – 6; 1Ch 1:32 – 33). Death (Ge 25:7 – 11).

Called servant of God (Ge 26:24), friend of God (2Ch 20:7; Isa 41:8; Jas 2:23), prophet (Ge 20:7), father of Israel (Ex 3:15; Isa 51:2; Mt 3:9; Jn 8:39 – 58).

ABSALOM

Son of David by Maacah (2Sa 3:3; 1Ch 3:2). Killed Amnon for rape of his sister Tamar; banished by David (2Sa 13). Returned to Jerusalem; received by David (2Sa 14). Rebelled against David; seized kingdom (2Sa 15 – 17). Killed (2Sa 18).

ABSENT

Col 2: 5 though I am *a* from you in body,

ABSOLUTE*

1Ti 5: 2 women as sisters, with *a* purity.

ABSTAIN (ABSTAINS)

Ex 19: 15 *A* from sexual relations."
Nu 6: 3 he must *a* from wine and other
Ac 15: 20 them to *a* from food polluted
1Pe 2: 11 to *a* from sinful desires,

ABSTAINS* (ABSTAIN)

Ro 14: 6 thanks to God; and he who *a,*

ABUNDANCE (ABUNDANT)

Ge 41: 29 Seven years of great *a* are coming
Job 36: 31 and provides food in *a.*
Ps 66: 12 but you brought us to a place of *a.*
Ecc 5: 12 but the *a* of a rich man
Isa 66: 11 and delight in her overflowing *a."*
Jer 2: 22 and use an *a* of soap,
Mt 13: 12 given more, and he will have an *a.*
25: 29 given more, and he will have an *a.*
Lk 12: 15 consist in the *a* of his possessions."
1Pe 1: 2 Grace and peace be yours in *a.*
2Pe 1: 2 yours in *a* through the knowledge
Jude : 2 peace and love be yours in *a.*

ABUNDANT (ABUNDANCE)

Dt 28: 11 will grant you *a* prosperity —
32: 2 like *a* rain on tender plants.
Job 36: 28 and *a* showers fall on mankind.
Ps 68: 9 You gave *a* showers, O God;
78: 15 gave them water as *a* as the seas;
132: 15 I will bless her with *a* provisions;
145: 7 will celebrate your *a* goodness
Pr 12: 11 works his land will have *a* food,
28: 19 works his land will have *a* food,
Jer 33: 9 and will tremble at the *a* prosperity
Ro 5: 17 who receive God's *a* provision

ABUSIVE

2Ti 3: 2 *a,* disobedient to their parents,

ABYSS*

Lk 8: 31 not to order them to go into the *A.*
Rev 9: 1 the key to the shaft of the *A.*
9: 2 When he opened the *A,* smoke rose
9: 2 darkened by the smoke from the *A.*
9: 11 king over them the angel of the *A,*
11: 7 up from the *A* will attack them,
17: 8 and will come up out of the *A*
20: 1 having the key to the *A*
20: 3 He threw him into the *A,*

ACCEPT (ACCEPTABLE ACCEPTANCE ACCEPTED ACCEPTS)

Ex 23: 8 "Do not *a* a bribe,
Dt 16: 19 Do not *a* a bribe, for a bribe blinds
Job 42: 8 and I will *a* his prayer and not deal
Pr 10: 8 The wise in heart *a* commands,
19: 20 Listen to advice and *a* instruction,
Ro 15: 7 *A* one another, then, just
Jas 1: 21 humbly *a* the word planted in you,

ACCEPTABLE (ACCEPT)

Pr 21: 3 is more *a* to the Lord

ACCEPTANCE* (ACCEPT)

Ro 11: 15 what will their *a* be but life
1Ti 1: 15 saying that deserves full *a:*
4: 9 saying that deserves full *a*

ACCEPTED (ACCEPT)

Ge 4: 7 will you not be *a?* But if you do not
Job 42: 9 and the Lord *a* Job's prayer.
Lk 4: 24 "no prophet is *a* in his hometown.
Gal 1: 9 you a gospel other than what you *a,*

ACCEPTS (ACCEPT)

Ps 6: 9 the Lord *a* my prayer.
Jn 13: 20 whoever *a* anyone I send *a* me;
13: 20 whoever *a* me *a* the one who sent

ACCESS
Ro 5: 2 through whom we have gained *a*
Eph 2: 18 For through him we both have *a*

ACCOMPANIED (ACCOMPANY)
1Co 10: 4 from the spiritual rock that *a* them,
Jas 2: 17 if it is not *a* by action, is dead.

ACCOMPANIES (ACCOMPANY)
2Co 9: 13 obedience that *a* your confession

ACCOMPANY (ACCOMPANIED ACCOMPANIES)
Dt 28: 2 *a* you if you obey the LORD your
Mk 16: 17 these signs will *a* those who believe
Heb 6: 9 your case — things that *a* salvation.

ACCOMPLISH
Ecc 2: 2 And what does pleasure *a?*"
Isa 44: 28 and will *a* all that I please;
55: 11 but will *a* what I desire

ACCORD
Nu 24: 13 not do anything of my own *a,*
Jn 10: 18 but I lay it down of my own *a.*
12: 49 For I did not speak of my own *a,*

ACCOUNT (ACCOUNTABLE)
Ge 2: 4 This is the *a* of the heavens
5: 1 This is the written *a* of Adam's line
6: 9 This is the *a* of Noah.
10: 1 This is the *a* of Shem, Ham
11: 10 This is the *a* of Shem.
11: 27 This is the *a* of Terah.
25: 12 This is the *a* of Abraham's son
25: 19 This is the *a* of Abraham's son
36: 1 This is the *a* of Esau (that is, Edom
36: 9 This is the *a* of Esau the father
37: 2 This is the *a* of Jacob.
Mt 12: 36 to give *a* on the day of judgment
Lk 16: 2 Give an *a* of your management,
Ro 14: 12 each of us will give an *a* of himself
Heb 4: 13 of him to whom we must give *a.*

ACCOUNTABLE* (ACCOUNT)
Eze 3: 18 and I will hold you *a* for his blood.
3: 20 and I will hold you *a* for his blood.
33: 6 but I will hold the watchman *a*
33: 8 and I will hold you *a* for his blood.
34: 10 and will hold them *a* for my flock.
Da 6: 2 The satraps were made *a* to them
Jnh 1: 14 Do not hold us *a* for killing
Ro 3: 19 and the whole world held *a* to God.

ACCURATE
Dt 25: 15 You must have *a* and honest
Pr 11: 1 but *a* weights are his delight.

ACCURSED (CURSE)
2Pe 2: 14 experts in greed — an *a* brood!

ACCUSATION (ACCUSE)
1Ti 5: 19 Do not entertain an *a*

ACCUSATIONS (ACCUSE)
2Pe 2: 11 do not bring slanderous *a*

ACCUSE (ACCUSATION ACCUSATIONS ACCUSER ACCUSES ACCUSING)
Pr 3: 30 Do not *a* a man for no reason —
Lk 3: 14 and don't *a* people falsely —

ACCUSER (ACCUSE)
Jn 5: 45 Your *a* is Moses, on whom your
Rev 12: 10 For the *a* of our brothers,

ACCUSES (ACCUSE)
Job 40: 2 Let him who *a* God answer him!"
Rev 12: 10 who *a* them before our God day

ACCUSING (ACCUSE)
Ro 2: 15 and their thoughts now *a,*

ACHAN*
Sin at Jericho caused defeat at Ai; stoned (Jos 7; 22:20; 1Ch 2:7).

ACHE*
Pr 14: 13 Even in laughter the heart may *a,*

ACHIEVE
Isa 55: 11 *a* the purpose for which I sent it.

ACHISH
King of Gath before whom David feigned insanity (1Sa 21:10 – 15). Later "ally" of David (2Sa 27 – 29).

ACKNOWLEDGE (ACKNOWLEDGED ACKNOWLEDGES)
Pr 3: 6 in all your ways *a* him,
Jer 3: 13 Only *a* your guilt —
Hos 6: 3 let us press on to *a* him.
Mt 10: 32 *a* him before my Father in heaven.
Lk 12: 8 *a* him before the angels of God.
1Jn 4: 3 spirit that does not *a* Jesus is not

ACKNOWLEDGED (ACKNOWLEDGE)
Lk 7: 29 *a* that God's way was right,

ACKNOWLEDGES* (ACKNOWLEDGE)
Ps 91: 14 for he *a* my name.
Mt 10: 32 "Whoever *a* me before men,
Lk 12: 8 whoever *a* me before men,
1Jn 2: 23 whoever *a* the Son has the Father
4: 2 Every spirit that *a* that Jesus Christ
4: 15 If anyone *a* that Jesus is the Son

ACQUIRES (ACQUIRING)
Pr 18: 15 of the discerning *a* knowledge;

ACQUIRING* (ACQUIRES)
Pr 1: 3 for *a* a disciplined and prudent life,

ACQUIT (ACQUITTING)
Ex 23: 7 to death, for I will not *a* the guilty.

ACQUITTING* (ACQUIT)
Dt 25: 1 *a* the innocent and condemning
Pr 17: 15 *A* the guilty and condemning

ACT (ACTION ACTIONS ACTIVE ACTIVITY ACTS)
Ps 119: 126 It is time for you to *a,* O LORD;

ACTION (ACT)
2Co 9: 2 has stirred most of them to *a.*
Jas 2: 17 if it is not accompanied by *a,*
1Pe 1: 13 minds for *a;* be self-controlled;

ACTIONS (ACT)
Mt 11: 19 wisdom is proved right by her *a.*"
Gal 6: 4 Each one should test his own *a.*
Tit 1: 16 but by their *a* they deny him.

ACTIVE* (ACT)
Phm : 6 I pray that you may be *a*
Heb 4: 12 For the word of God is living and *a*

ACTIVITY (ACT)
Ecc 3: 1 a season for every *a* under heaven:
3: 17 for there will be a time for every *a,*

ACTS (ACT)
1Ch 16: 9 tell of all his wonderful *a.*
Ps 71: 16 proclaim your mighty *a,*
71: 24 tell of your righteous *a*
105: 2 tell of all his wonderful *a.*
106: 2 Who can proclaim the mighty *a*
145: 4 they will tell of your mighty *a.*
145: 12 all men may know of your mighty *a*
150: 2 Praise him for his *a* of power;
Isa 64: 6 all our righteous *a* are like filthy
Mt 6: 1 not to do your '*a* of righteousness'

ADAM
1. First man (Ge 1:26 – 2:25; Ro 5:14; 1Ti 2:13). Sin of (Ge 3; Hos 6:7; Ro 5:12 – 21). Children of (Ge 4:1 – 5:5). Death of (Ge 5:5; Ro 5:12 – 21; 1Co 15:22).
2. City (Jos 3:16).

ADD (ADDED)
Dt 4: 2 Do not *a* to what I command you
12: 32 do not *a* to it or take away from it.
Pr 1: 5 let the wise listen and *a*
9: 9 he will *a* to his learning.
30: 6 Do not *a* to his words,
Mt 6: 27 by worrying can *a* a single hour
Lk 12: 25 by worrying can *a* a single hour
Rev 22: 18 God will *a* to him the plagues

ADDED (ADD)
Ecc 3: 14 nothing can be *a* to it and nothing
Ac 2: 47 Lord *a* to their number daily those
Ro 5: 20 The law was *a* so that the trespass
Gal 3: 19 It was *a* because of transgressions

ADDICTED*
Tit 2: 3 to be slanderers or *a* to much wine,

ADMINISTRATION*
1Co 12: 28 with gifts of *a,* and those speaking
Eph 3: 2 Surely you have heard about the *a*
3: 9 to everyone the *a* of this mystery,

ADMIRABLE*
Php 4: 8 whatever is lovely, whatever is *a* —

ADMIT
Hos 5: 15 until they *a* their guilt.

ADMONISH* (ADMONISHING)
Col 3: 16 and *a* one another with all wisdom,
1Th 5: 12 you in the Lord and who *a* you.

ADMONISHING* (ADMONISH)
Col 1: 28 *a* and teaching everyone

ADONIJAH
1. Son of David by Haggith (2Sa 3:4; 1Ch 3:2). Attempted to be king after David; killed by Solomon's order (1Ki 1 – 2).
2. Levite; teacher of the Law (2Ch 17:8).

ADOPTED (ADOPTION)
Eph 1: 5 In love he predestined us to be *a*

ADOPTION* (ADOPTED)
Ro 8: 23 as we wait eagerly for our *a* as sons,
9: 4 Theirs is the *a* as sons; theirs

ADORE*
SS 1: 4 How right they are to *a* you!

ADORNMENT* (ADORNS)
1Pe 3: 3 should not come from outward *a,*

ADORNS* (ADORNMENT)
Ps 93: 5 holiness *a* your house
Isa 61: 10 as a bride *a* herself with her jewels.
61: 10 bridegroom *a* his head like a priest,

ADULTERER (ADULTERY)
Lev 20: 10 both the *a* and the adulteress must
Heb 13: 4 for God will judge the *a*

ADULTERERS (ADULTERY)
1Co 6: 9 idolaters nor *a* nor male prostitutes
1Ti 1: 10 for murderers, for *a* and perverts,

ADULTERESS (ADULTERY)
Hos 3: 1 she is loved by another and is an *a.*

ADULTERIES (ADULTERY)
Jer 3: 8 sent her away because of all her *a.*

ADULTEROUS (ADULTERY)
Mk 8: 38 in this *a* and sinful generation,
Jas 4: 4 You *a* people, don't you know that

ADULTERY (ADULTERER ADULTERERS ADULTERESS ADULTERIES ADULTEROUS)
Ex 20: 14 "You shall not commit *a.*
Dt 5: 18 "You shall not commit *a.*
Mt 5: 27 that it was said, 'Do not commit *a.*'
5: 28 lustfully has already committed *a*
5: 32 the divorced woman commits *a.*
15: 19 murder, *a,* sexual immorality, theft
19: 9 marries another woman commits *a*
19: 18 do not commit *a,* do not steal,
Mk 7: 21 theft, murder, *a,* greed, malice,
10: 11 marries another woman commits *a*
10: 12 another man, she commits *a.*"
10: 19 do not commit *a,* do not steal,
Lk 16: 18 a divorced woman commits *a.*
16: 18 marries another woman commits *a*
18: 20 'Do not commit *a,* do not murder,
Jn 8: 4 woman was caught in the act of *a.*
Rev 18: 3 of the earth committed *a* with her,

ADULTS*
1Co 14: 20 but in your thinking be *a.*

ADVANCE (ADVANCED)
Ps 18: 29 With your help I can *a*
Php 1: 12 has really served to *a* the gospel.

ADVANCED (ADVANCE)
Job 32: 7 *a* years should teach wisdom.'

ADVANTAGE
Ex 22: 22 "Do not take *a* of a widow
Dt 24: 14 Do not take *a* of a hired man who is
Ro 3: 1 What *a,* then, is there
2Co 11: 20 or exploits you or takes *a* of you
1Th 4: 6 should wrong his brother or take *a*

ADVERSITY*
Pr 17: 17 and a brother is born for *a.*
Isa 30: 20 the Lord gives you the bread of *a*

ADVICE (ADVISERS)
1Ki 12: 8 rejected the *a* the elders
12: 14 he followed the *a* of the young men
2Ch 10: 8 rejected the *a* the elders
Pr 12: 5 but the *a* of the wicked is deceitful.
12: 15 but a wise man listens to *a.*
19: 20 Listen to *a* and accept instruction,
20: 18 Make plans by seeking *a;*

ADVISERS (ADVICE)
Pr 11: 14 but many *a* make victory sure.

ADVOCATE*
Job 16: 19 my *a* is on high.

AFFLICTED (AFFLICTION)
Job 2: 7 and *a* Job with painful sores
36: 6 but gives the *a* their rights.
Ps 9: 12 he does not ignore the cry of the *a.*
9: 18 nor the hope of the *a* ever perish.
119: 67 Before I was *a* I went astray,
119: 71 It was good for me to be *a*
119: 75 and in faithfulness you have *a* me.
Isa 49: 13 will have compassion on his *a* ones.
53: 4 smitten by him, and *a.*
53: 7 He was oppressed and *a,*

Na 1: 12 Although I have *a* you, ⌞O Judah,⌟

AFFLICTION (AFFLICTED AFFLICTIONS)
Dt 16: 3 bread of *a*, because you left Egypt
Ps 107: 41 he lifted the needy out of their *a*
Isa 30: 20 of adversity and the water of *a*,
48: 10 in the furnace of *a*.
La 3: 33 For he does not willingly bring *a*
Ro 12: 12 patient in *a*, faithful in prayer.

AFFLICTIONS (AFFLICTION)
Col 1: 24 lacking in regard to Christ's *a*,

AFRAID (FEAR)
Ge 3: 10 and I was *a* because I was naked;
26: 24 Do not be *a*, for I am with you;
Ex 2: 14 Then Moses was *a* and thought,
3: 6 because he was *a* to look at God.
Dt 1: 21 Do not be *a*; do not be discouraged
1: 29 "Do not be terrified; do not be *a*
20: 1 do not be *a* of them,
20: 3 Do not be fainthearted or *a*;
2Ki 25: 24 "Do not be *a* of the Babylonian
1Ch 13: 12 David was *a* of God that day
Ps 27: 1 of whom shall I be *a*?
56: 3 When I am *a*, / I will trust in you.
56: 4 in God I trust; I will not be *a*.
Pr 3: 24 lie down, you will not be *a*;
Isa 10: 24 do not be *a* of the Assyrians,
12: 2 I will trust and not be *a*.
44: 8 Do not tremble, do not be *a*.
Jer 1: 8 Do not be *a* of them, for I am
Mt 8: 26 You of little faith, why are you so *a*
10: 28 be *a* of the One who can destroy
10: 31 So don't be *a*; you are worth more
Mk 5: 36 "Don't be *a*; just believe."
Lk 9: 34 and they were *a* as they entered
Jn 14: 27 hearts be troubled and do not be *a*.
Ac 27: 24 beside me and said, 'Do not be *a*,
Ro 11: 20 Do not be arrogant, but be *a*.
Heb 13: 6 Lord is my helper; I will not be *a*.

AGAG (AGAGITE)
King of Amalekites not killed by Saul (1Sa 15).

AGAGITE (AGAG)
Est 8: 3 to the evil plan of Haman the *A*,

AGED (AGES)
Job 12: 12 Is not wisdom found among the *a*?
Pr 17: 6 children are a crown to the *a*,

AGES (AGED)
Ro 16: 25 the mystery hidden for long *a* past,
Eph 2: 7 that in the coming *a* he might show
3: 9 which for *a* past was kept hidden
Col 1: 26 that has been kept hidden for *a*
Rev 15: 3 King of the *a*.

AGONY
Lk 16: 24 because I am in *a* in this fire.'
Rev 16: 10 Men gnawed their tongues in *a*

AGREE (AGREEMENT AGREES)
Mt 18: 19 on earth *a* about anything you ask
Ro 7: 16 want to do, I *a* that the law is good.
Php 4: 2 with Syntyche to *a* with each other

AGREEMENT (AGREE)
2Co 6: 16 What *a* is there between the temple

AGREES* (AGREE)
Ac 7: 42 This *a* with what is written
24: 14 I believe everything that *a*
1Co 4: 17 which *a* with what I teach

AGRIPPA*
Descendant of Herod; king before whom Paul pled his case in Caesarea (Ac 25:13 – 26:32).

AHAB
1. Son of Omri; king of Israel (1Ki 16:28 – 22:40), husband of Jezebel (1Ki 16:31). Promoted Baal worship (1Ki 16:31 – 33); opposed by Elijah (1Ki 17:1; 18; 21), a prophet (1Ki 20:35 – 43), Micaiah (1Ki 22:1 – 28). Defeated Ben-Hadad (1Ki 20). Killed for failing to kill Ben-Hadad and for murder of Naboth (1Ki 20:35 – 21:40).
2. A false prophet (Jer 29:21 – 22).

AHAZ
1. Son of Jotham; king of Judah, (2Ki 16; 2Ch 28). Idolatry of (2Ki 16:3 – 4, 10 – 18; 2Ch 28:1 – 4, 22 – 25). Defeated by Aram and Israel (2Ki 16:5 – 6; 2Ch 28:5 – 15). Sought help from Assyria rather than the LORD (2Ki 16:7 – 9; 2Ch 28:16 – 21; Isa 7).
2. Benjamite, descendant of Saul (1Ch 8:35 – 36).

AHAZIAH
1. Son of Ahab; king of Israel (1Ki 22:51 – 2Ki 1:18; 2Ch 20:35 – 37). Made an unsuccessful alliance with Jehoshaphat of Judah (2Ch 20:35 – 37). Died for seeking Baal rather than the LORD (2Ki 1).
2. Son of Jehoram; king of Judah (2Ki 8:25 – 29; 9:14 – 29), also called Jehoahaz (2Ch 21:17 – 22:9; 25:23). Killed by Jehu while visiting Joram (2Ki 9:14 – 29; 2Ch 22:1 – 9).

AHIJAH
1Sa 14: 18 Saul said to *A*, "Bring the ark
1Ki 14: 2 *A* the prophet is there — the one

AHIMELECH
1. Priest who helped David in his flight from Saul (1Sa 21 – 22).
2. One of David's warriors (1Sa 26:6).

AHITHOPHEL
One of David's counselors who sided with Absalom (2Sa 15:12, 31 – 37; 1Ch 27:33 – 34); committed suicide when his advice was ignored (2Sa 16:15 – 17:23).

AI
Jos 7: 4 they were routed by the men of *A*,
8: 28 So Joshua burned *A* and made it

AID
Isa 38: 14 troubled; O Lord, come to my *a*!"
Php 4: 16 you sent me *a* again and again

AIM
1Co 7: 34 Her *a* is to be devoted to the Lord
2Co 13: 11 *A* for perfection, listen

AIR
Mt 8: 20 and birds of the *a* have nests,
Lk 9: 58 and birds of the *a* have nests,
1Co 9: 26 not fight like a man beating the *a*.
14: 9 You will just be speaking into the *a*
Eph 2: 2 of the ruler of the kingdom of the *a*,
1Th 4: 17 clouds to meet the Lord in the *a*.

ALABASTER*
Mt 26: 7 came to him with an *a* jar
Mk 14: 3 a woman came with an *a* jar
Lk 7: 37 she brought an *a* jar of perfume,

ALARM (ALARMED)
2Co 7: 11 indignation, what *a*, what longing,

ALARMED (ALARM)
Mk 13: 7 and rumors of wars, do not be *a*.
2Th 2: 2 not to become easily unsettled or *a*

ALERT*
Jos 8: 4 All of you be on the *a*.
Ps 17: 11 with eyes *a*, to throw me
Isa 21: 7 let him be *a*, / fully *a*."
Mk 13: 33 Be *a*! You do not know
Eph 6: 18 be *a* and always keep on praying
1Th 5: 6 but let us be *a* and self-controlled.
1Pe 5: 8 Be self-controlled and *a*.

ALIEN (ALIENATED ALIENS)
Ex 22: 21 "Do not mistreat an *a*
Lev 24: 22 are to have the same law for the *a*
Ps 146: 9 The LORD watches over the *a*

ALIENATED (ALIEN)
Gal 5: 4 by law have been *a* from Christ;
Col 1: 21 Once you were *a* from God

ALIENS (ALIEN)
Ex 23: 9 know how it feels to be *a*,
1Pe 2: 11 as *a* and strangers in the world,

ALIVE (LIVE)
1Sa 2: 6 LORD brings death and makes *a*;
Lk 24: 23 vision of angels, who said he was *a*.
Ac 1: 3 convincing proofs that he was *a*.
Ro 6: 11 but *a* to God in Christ Jesus.
1Co 15: 22 so in Christ all will be made *a*.
Eph 2: 5 made us *a* with Christ

ALMIGHTY (MIGHT)
Ge 17: 1 "I am God *A*; walk before me
Ex 6: 3 to Isaac and to Jacob as God *A*,
Ru 1: 20 the *A* has made my life very bitter.
Job 11: 7 Can you probe the limits of the *A*?
33: 4 the breath of the *A* gives me life.
Ps 89: 8 O LORD God *A*, who is like you?
91: 1 will rest in the shadow of the *A*.
Isa 6: 3 "Holy, holy, holy is the LORD *A*;
45: 13 says the LORD *A*."
47: 4 the LORD *A* is his name —
48: 2 the LORD *A* is his name:
51: 15 the LORD *A* is his name.
54: 5 the LORD *A* is his name —
Am 5: 14 the LORD God *A* will be with you,
5: 15 the LORD God *A* will have mercy
Rev 4: 8 holy is the Lord God *A*, who was,
19: 6 For our Lord God *A* reigns.

ALPHA*
Rev 1: 8 "I am the *A* and the Omega,"
21: 6 I am the *A* and the Omega,
22: 13 I am the *A* and the Omega,

ALTAR
Ge 8: 20 Then Noah built an *a* to the LORD
12: 7 So he built an *a* there to the LORD
13: 18 where he built an *a* to the LORD.
22: 9 Abraham built an *a* there
22: 9 his son Isaac and laid him on the *a*,
26: 25 Isaac built an *a* there and called
35: 1 and build an *a* there to God,
Ex 17: 15 Moses built an *a* and called it
27: 1 "Build an *a* of acacia wood,
30: 1 "Make an *a* of acacia wood
37: 25 They made the *a* of incense out
Dt 27: 5 an *a* to the LORD your God, an *a*
Jos 8: 30 on Mount Ebal an *a* to the LORD,
22: 10 built an imposing *a* there
Jdg 6: 24 So Gideon built an *a* to the LORD
21: 4 the next day the people built an *a*
1Sa 7: 17 he built an *a* there to the LORD.
14: 35 Then Saul built an *a* to the LORD;
2Sa 24: 25 David built an *a* to the LORD
1Ki 12: 33 sacrifices on the *a* he had built
13: 2 "O *a*, *a*! This is what the LORD
16: 32 He set up an *a* for Baal
18: 30 and he repaired the *a* of the LORD
2Ki 16: 11 So Uriah the priest built an *a*
1Ch 21: 26 David built an *a* to the LORD
2Ch 4: 1 made a bronze *a* twenty cubits
4: 19 the golden *a*; the tables
15: 8 He repaired the *a* of the LORD
32: 12 'You must worship before one *a*
33: 16 he restored the *a* of the LORD
Ezr 3: 2 to build the *a* of the God of Israel
Isa 6: 6 taken with tongs from the *a*.
Eze 40: 47 the *a* was in front of the temple.
Mt 5: 23 if you are offering your gift at the *a*
Ac 17: 23 found an *a* with this inscription:
Heb 13: 10 We have an *a* from which those
Rev 6: 9 I saw under the *a* the souls

ALTER*
Ps 89: 34 or *a* what my lips have uttered.

ALWAYS
Dt 15: 11 There will *a* be poor people
Ps 16: 8 I have set the LORD *a* before me.
51: 3 and my sin is *a* before me.
Pr 23: 7 who is *a* thinking about the cost.
Mt 26: 11 The poor you will *a* have with you,
28: 20 And surely I am with you *a*,
Mk 14: 7 The poor you will *a* have with you,
Jn 12: 8 You will *a* have the poor
1Co 13: 7 *a* protects, *a* trusts, *a* hopes, *a*
Php 4: 4 Rejoice in the Lord *a*.
1Pe 3: 15 *A* be prepared to give an answer

AMALEKITES
Ex 17: 8 *A* came and attacked the Israelites
1Sa 15: 2 'I will punish the *A*

AMASA
Nephew of David (1Ch 2:17). Commander of Absalom's forces (2Sa 17:24 – 27). Returned to David (2Sa 19:13). Killed by Joab (2Sa 20:4 – 13).

AMASSES*
Pr 28: 8 *a* it for another, who will be kind

AMAZED
Mt 7: 28 the crowds were *a* at his teaching,
Mk 6: 6 And he was *a* at their lack of faith.
10: 24 The disciples were *a* at his words.
Ac 2: 7 Utterly *a*, they asked: "Are not all
13: 12 for he was *a* at the teaching about

AMAZIAH
1. Son of Joash; king of Judah (2Ki 14; 2Ch 25). Defeated Edom (2Ki 14:7; 2Ch 25:5 – 13); defeated by Israel for worshiping Edom's gods (2Ki 14:8 – 14; 2Ch 25:14 – 24).
2. Idolatrous priest who opposed Amos (Am 7:10 – 17).

AMBASSADOR* (AMBASSADORS)
Eph 6: 20 for which I am an *a* in chains.

AMBASSADORS (AMBASSADOR)
2Co 5: 20 We are therefore Christ's *a*,

AMBITION*
Ro 15: 20 It has always been my *a*
Gal 5: 20 fits of rage, selfish *a*, dissensions,
Php 1: 17 preach Christ out of selfish *a*,
2: 3 Do nothing out of selfish *a*
1Th 4: 11 Make it your *a* to lead a quiet life,
Jas 3: 14 and selfish *a* in your hearts,
3: 16 where you have envy and selfish *a*,

AMENDS
Pr 14: 9 Fools mock at making *a* for sin,

AMNON
Firstborn of David (2Sa 3:2; 1Ch 3:1). Killed by Absalom for raping his sister Tamar (2Sa 13).

AMON
1. Son of Manasseh; king of Judah (2Ki 21:18 – 26; 1Ch 3:14; 2Ch 33:21 – 25).
2. Ruler of Samaria under Ahab (1Ki 22:26; 2Ch 18:25).

AMOS
1. Prophet from Tekoa (Am 1:1; 7:10 – 17).
2. Ancestor of Jesus (Lk 3:25).

ANAK (ANAKITES)
Nu 13: 28 even saw descendants of *A* there.

ANAKITES (ANAK)
Dt 1: 28 We even saw the *A* there.'"
2: 10 and numerous, and as tall as the *A*.
9: 2 "Who can stand up against the *A*?"

ANANIAS
1. Husband of Sapphira; died for lying to God (Ac 5:1 – 11).
2. Disciple who baptized Saul (Ac 9:10 – 19).
3. High priest at Paul's arrest (Ac 22:30 – 24:1).

ANCESTORS (ANCESTRY)
1Ki 19: 4 I am no better than my *a*."

ANCESTRY (ANCESTORS)
Ro 9: 5 from them is traced the human *a*

ANCHOR
Heb 6: 19 We have this hope as an *a*

ANCIENT
Da 7: 9 and the *A* of Days took his seat.
7: 13 He approached the *A* of Days
7: 22 until the *A* of Days came

ANDREW*
Apostle; brother of Simon Peter (Mt 4:18; 10:2; Mk 1:16 – 18, 29; 3:18; 13:3; Lk 6:14; Jn 1:35 – 44; 6:8 – 9; 12:22; Ac 1:13).

ANGEL (ANGELS ARCHANGEL)
Ge 16: 7 The *a* of the LORD found Hagar
22: 11 But the *a* of the LORD called out
Ex 23: 20 I am sending an *a* ahead of you
Nu 22: 23 When the donkey saw the *a*
Jdg 2: 1 The *a* of the LORD went up
6: 22 Gideon realized that it was the *a*
13: 15 Manoah said to the *a* of the LORD
2Sa 24: 16 The *a* of the LORD was then
1Ki 19: 7 The *a* of the LORD came back
2Ki 19: 35 That night the *a* of the LORD went
Ps 34: 7 The *a* of the LORD encamps
Hos 12: 4 He struggled with the *a*
Mt 2: 13 an *a* of the Lord appeared
28: 2 for an *a* of the Lord came
Lk 1: 26 God sent the *a* Gabriel
2: 9 An *a* of the Lord appeared to them,
22: 43 An *a* from heaven appeared to him
Ac 6: 15 his face was like the face of an *a*.
12: 7 Suddenly an *a* of the Lord
2Co 11: 14 Satan himself masquerades as an *a*
Gal 1: 8 or an *a* from heaven should preach

ANGELS (ANGEL)
Ps 91: 11 command his *a* concerning you
Mt 4: 6 command his *a* concerning you,
13: 39 of the age, and the harvesters are *a*.
13: 49 The *a* will come and separate
18: 10 For I tell you that their *a*
25: 41 prepared for the devil and his *a*.
Lk 4: 10 command his *a* concerning you
20: 36 for they are like the *a*.
1Co 6: 3 you not know that we will judge *a*?
13: 1 in the tongues of men and of *a*,
Col 2: 18 and the worship of *a* disqualify you
Heb 1: 4 as much superior to the *a*
1: 6 "Let all God's *a* worship him."
1: 7 "He makes his *a* winds,
1: 14 Are not all *a* ministering spirits
2: 7 made him a little lower than the *a*;
2: 9 was made a little lower than the *a*,
13: 2 some people have entertained *a*
1Pe 1: 12 Even *a* long to look
2Pe 2: 4 For if God did not spare *a*
Jude : 6 *a* who did not keep their positions

ANGER (ANGERED ANGRY)
Ex 15: 7 You unleashed your burning *a*;
22: 24 My *a* will be aroused, and I will kill
32: 10 alone so that my *a* may burn
32: 11 "why should your *a* burn
32: 12 Turn from your fierce *a*; relent
32: 19 his *a* burned and he threw
34: 6 slow to *a*, abounding in love
Lev 26: 28 then in my *a* I will be hostile
Nu 14: 18 slow to *a*, abounding in love
25: 11 has turned my *a* away
32: 10 LORD's *a* was aroused that day
32: 13 The LORD's *a* burned
Dt 9: 19 I feared the *a* and wrath
29: 28 In furious *a* and in great wrath
Jdg 14: 19 Burning with *a*, he went up
2Sa 12: 5 David burned with *a*
2Ki 22: 13 Great is the LORD's *a* that burns
Ne 9: 17 slow to *a* and abounding in love.
Ps 30: 5 For his *a* lasts only a moment,
78: 38 Time after time he restrained his *a*
86: 15 slow to *a*, abounding in love
90: 7 We are consumed by your *a*
103: 8 slow to *a*, abounding in love.
Pr 15: 1 but a harsh word stirs up *a*.
29: 11 A fool gives full vent to his *a*,
30: 33 so stirring up *a* produces strife."
Jnh 4: 2 slow to *a* and abounding in love,
Eph 4: 26 "In your *a* do not sin": Do not let
Jas 1: 20 for man's *a* does not bring about

ANGERED (ANGER)
Pr 22: 24 do not associate with one easily *a*,
1Co 13: 5 it is not easily *a*, it keeps no record

ANGRY (ANGER)
Ps 2: 12 Kiss the Son, lest he be *a*
95: 10 For forty years I was *a*
Pr 29: 22 An *a* man stirs up dissension,
Mt 5: 22 But I tell you that anyone who is *a*
Jas 1: 19 slow to speak and slow to become *a*

ANGUISH
Ps 118: 5 In my *a* I cried to the LORD,
Jer 4: 19 Oh, my *a*, my *a*!
Zep 1: 15 a day of distress and *a*,
Lk 21: 25 nations will be in *a* and perplexity
22: 44 in *a*, he prayed more earnestly,
Ro 9: 2 and unceasing *a* in my heart.

ANIMALS
Ge 1: 24 wild *a*, each according to its kind."
7: 16 The *a* going in were male
Dt 14: 4 These are the *a* you may eat: the ox
Job 12: 7 ask the *a*, and they will teach you,
Isa 43: 20 The wild *a* honor me,

ANNOUNCE (ANNOUNCED)
Mt 6: 2 give to the needy, do not *a* it

ANNOUNCED (ANNOUNCE)
Isa 48: 5 before they happened I *a* them
Gal 3: 8 and *a* the gospel in advance

ANNOYANCE*
Pr 12: 16 A fool shows his *a* at once,

ANNUAL*
Ex 30: 10 This *a* atonement must be made
Jdg 21: 19 there is the *a* festival of the LORD
1Sa 1: 21 family to offer the *a* sacrifice
2: 19 husband to offer the *a* sacrifice.
20: 6 an *a* sacrifice is being made there
2Ch 8: 13 New Moons and the three *a* feasts
Heb 10: 3 those sacrifices are an *a* reminder

ANOINT (ANOINTED ANOINTING)
Ex 30: 26 use it to *a* the Tent of Meeting,
30: 30 "*A* Aaron and his sons
1Sa 9: 16 *A* him leader over my people Israel
15: 1 to *a* you king over his people Israel;
2Ki 9: 3 what the LORD says: I *a* you king
Ps 23: 5 You *a* my head with oil;
Da 9: 24 prophecy and to *a* the most holy.
Jas 5: 14 and *a* him with oil in the name

ANOINTED (ANOINT)
1Ch 16: 22 "Do not touch my *a* ones;
Ps 105: 15 "Do not touch my *a* ones;
Isa 61: 1 because the LORD has *a* me
Da 9: 26 the *A* One will be cut off
Lk 4: 18 because he has *a* me
Ac 10: 38 how God *a* Jesus of Nazareth

ANOINTING (ANOINT)
Lev 8: 12 some of the *a* oil on Aaron's head
1Ch 29: 22 *a* him before the LORD to be ruler
Ps 45: 7 by *a* you with the oil of joy.
Heb 1: 9 by *a* you with the oil of joy."
1Jn 2: 20 you have an *a* from the Holy One,
2: 27 about all things and as that *a* is real,

ANT* (ANTS)
Pr 6: 6 Go to the *a*, you sluggard;

ANTICHRIST* (ANTICHRISTS)
1Jn 2: 18 have heard that the *a* is coming,
2: 22 a man is the *a* — he denies
4: 3 of the *a*, which you have heard is
2Jn : 7 person is the deceiver and the *a*.

ANTICHRISTS* (ANTICHRIST)
1Jn 2: 18 even now many *a* have come.

ANTIOCH
Ac 11: 26 were called Christians first at *A*.

ANTS* (ANT)
Pr 30: 25 *A* are creatures of little strength,

ANXIETIES* (ANXIOUS)
Lk 21: 34 drunkenness and the *a* of life,

ANXIETY (ANXIOUS)
1Pe 5: 7 Cast all your *a* on him

ANXIOUS (ANXIETIES ANXIETY)
Pr 12: 25 An *a* heart weighs a man down,
Php 4: 6 Do not be *a* about anything,

APOLLOS*
Christian from Alexandria, learned in the Scriptures; instructed by Aquila and Priscilla (Ac 18:24 – 28). Ministered at Corinth (Ac 19:1; 1Co 1:12; 3; Tit 3:13).

APOLLYON*
Rev 9: 11 is Abaddon, and in Greek, *A*.

APOSTLE (APOSTLES APOSTLES')
Ro 11: 13 as I am the *a* to the Gentiles,
1Co 9: 1 Am I not an *a*? Have I not seen
2Co 12: 12 The things that mark an *a* — signs,
Gal 2: 8 of Peter as an *a* to the Jews,
1Ti 2: 7 was appointed a herald and an *a* —
2Ti 1: 11 I was appointed a herald and an *a*
Heb 3: 1 *a* and high priest whom we confess.

APOSTLES (APOSTLE)
See also Andrew, Bartholomew, James, John, Judas, Matthew, Matthias, Nathanael, Paul, Peter, Philip, Simon, Thaddaeus, Thomas.
Mk 3: 14 twelve — designating them *a* —
Lk 11: 49 'I will send them prophets and *a*,
Ac 1: 26 so he was added to the eleven *a*.
2: 43 signs were done by the *a*.
1Co 12: 28 God has appointed first of all *a*,
15: 9 For I am the least of the *a*
2Co 11: 13 masquerading as *a* of Christ.
Eph 2: 20 built on the foundation of the *a*
4: 11 It was he who gave some to be *a*,
Rev 21: 14 names of the twelve *a* of the Lamb.

APOSTLES' (APOSTLE)
Ac 5: 2 the rest and put it at the *a'* feet.
8: 18 at the laying on of the *a'* hands,

APPEAL
Ac 25: 11 I *a* to Caesar!" After Festus had
Phm : 9 yet I *a* to you on the basis of love.

APPEAR (APPEARANCE APPEARANCES APPEARED APPEARING APPEARS)
Ge 1: 9 to one place, and let dry ground *a*."
Lev 16: 2 I *a* in the cloud over the atonement
Mt 24: 30 of the Son of Man will *a* in the sky,
Mk 13: 22 false prophets will *a* and perform
Lk 19: 11 of God was going to *a* at once.
2Co 5: 10 we must all *a* before the judgment
Col 3: 4 also will *a* with him in glory.
Heb 9: 24 now to *a* for us in God's presence.
9: 28 and he will *a* a second time,

APPEARANCE (APPEAR)
1Sa 16: 7 Man looks at the outward *a*,
Isa 52: 14 his *a* was so disfigured beyond that
53: 2 in his *a* that we should desire him.
Gal 2: 6 God does not judge by external *a* —

APPEARANCES* (APPEAR)
Jn 7: 24 Stop judging by mere *a*,

APPEARED (APPEAR)
Nu 14: 10 glory of the LORD *a* at the Tent
Mt 1: 20 an angel of the Lord *a* to him
Lk 2: 9 An angel of the Lord *a* to them,
1Co 15: 5 and that he *a* to Peter,
Heb 9: 26 now he has *a* once for all at the end

APPEARING (APPEAR)
1Ti 6: 14 until the *a* of our Lord Jesus Christ,
2Ti 1: 10 through the *a* of our Savior,
4: 8 to all who have longed for his *a*.
Tit 2: 13 the glorious *a* of our great God

APPEARS (APPEAR)
Mal 3: 2 Who can stand when he *a*?
Col 3: 4 When Christ, who is your life, *a*,
1Pe 5: 4 And when the Chief Shepherd *a*,
1Jn 3: 2 But we know that when he *a*,

APPETITE
Pr 16: 26 The laborer's *a* works for him;

Ecc 6: 7 yet his *a* is never satisfied.
Jer 50: 19 his *a* will be satisfied

APPLES
Pr 25: 11 is like *a* of gold in settings of silver.

APPLY (APPLYING)
Pr 22: 17 *a* your heart to what I teach,
23: 12 *A* your heart to instruction

APPLYING (APPLY)
Pr 2: 2 and *a* your heart to understanding,

APPOINT (APPOINTED)
Ps 61: 7 *a* your love and faithfulness
1Th 5: 9 For God did not *a* us
Tit 1: 5 and *a* elders in every town,

APPOINTED (APPOINT)
Dt 1: 15 *a* them to have authority over you
Pr 8: 23 I was *a* from eternity,
Da 11: 27 an end will still come at the *a* time.
Hab 2: 3 For the revelation awaits an *a* time;
Jn 15: 16 Chose you and *a* you to go
Ro 9: 9 "At the *a* time I will return,

APPROACH (APPROACHING)
Ex 24: 2 but Moses alone is to *a* the LORD;
Eph 3: 12 in him we may *a* God with freedom
Heb 4: 16 Let us then *a* the throne of grace

APPROACHING (APPROACH)
Heb 10: 25 all the more as you see the Day *a*.
1Jn 5: 14 is the confidence we have in *a* God:

APPROPRIATE
1Ti 2: 10 *a* for women who profess

APPROVAL (APPROVE)
Jdg 18: 6 Your journey has the LORD's *a*."
Jn 6: 27 the Father has placed his seal of *a*."
1Co 11: 19 to show which of you have God's *a*
Gal 1: 10 trying to win the *a* of men,

APPROVE (APPROVAL APPROVED APPROVES)
Ro 2: 18 if you know his will and *a*
12: 2 and *a* what God's will is —

APPROVED* (APPROVE)
Ro 14: 18 pleasing to God and *a* by men.
16: 10 Greet Apelles, tested and *a*
2Co 10: 18 who commends himself who is *a*,
1Th 2: 4 as men *a* by God to be entrusted
2Ti 2: 15 to present yourself to God as one *a*,

APPROVES* (APPROVE)
Ro 14: 22 not condemn himself by what he *a*.

APT*
Pr 15: 23 A man finds joy in giving an *a* reply

AQUILA*
Husband of Priscilla; co-worker with Paul, instructor of Apollos (Ac 18; Ro 16:3; 1Co 16:19; 2Ti 4:19).

ARABIA
Gal 1: 17 but I went immediately into *A*
4: 25 Hagar stands for Mount Sinai in *A*

ARARAT
Ge 8: 4 came to rest on the mountains of *A*.

ARAUNAH
2Sa 24: 16 threshing floor of *A* the Jebusite.

ARBITER* (ARBITRATE)
Lk 12: 14 who appointed me a judge or an *a*

ARBITRATE* (ARBITER)
Job 9: 33 If only there were someone to *a*

ARCHANGEL* (ANGEL)
1Th 4: 16 with the voice of the *a*
Jude : 9 *a* Michael, when he was disputing

ARCHER
Pr 26: 10 Like an *a* who wounds at random

ARCHIPPUS*
Col 4: 17 Tell *A*: "See to it that you complete
Phm : 2 to *A* our fellow soldier

ARCHITECT*
Heb 11: 10 whose *a* and builder is God.

AREOPAGUS*
Ac 17: 19 brought him to a meeting of the *A*,
17: 22 up in the meeting of the *A*
17: 34 of the *A*, also a woman named

ARGUE (ARGUMENT ARGUMENTS)
Job 13: 3 and to *a* my case with God.
13: 8 Will you *a* the case for God?
Pr 25: 9 If you *a* your case with a neighbor,

ARGUMENT (ARGUE)
Heb 6: 16 is said and puts an end to all *a*.

ARGUMENTS (ARGUE)
Isa 41: 21 "Set forth your *a*," says Jacob's
Col 2: 4 you by fine-sounding *a*.
2Ti 2: 23 to do with foolish and stupid *a*,
Tit 3: 9 and *a* and quarrels about the law,

ARK
Ge 6: 14 So make yourself an *a*
Ex 25: 21 and put in the *a* the Testimony,
Dt 10: 5 put the tablets in the *a* I had made,
1Sa 4: 11 The *a* of God was captured,
7: 2 that the *a* remained at Kiriath
2Sa 6: 17 They brought the *a* of the LORD
1Ki 8: 9 There was nothing in the *a*
1Ch 13: 9 out his hand to steady the *a*,
2Ch 35: 3 "Put the sacred *a* in the temple that
Heb 9: 4 This *a* contained the gold jar
11: 7 in holy fear built an *a*
Rev 11: 19 within his temple was seen the *a*

ARM (ARMY)
Nu 11: 23 "Is the LORD's *a* too short?
Dt 4: 34 hand and an outstretched *a*,
7: 19 mighty hand and outstretched *a*,
Ps 44: 3 it was your right hand, your *a*,
98: 1 his right hand and his holy *a*
Jer 27: 5 outstretched *a* I made the earth
1Pe 4: 1 *a* yourselves also with the same

ARMAGEDDON*
Rev 16: 16 that in Hebrew is called *A*.

ARMIES (ARMY)
1Sa 17: 26 Philistine that he should defy the *a*
Rev 19: 14 *a* of heaven were following him,

ARMOR (ARMY)
1Ki 20: 11 on his *a* should not boast like one
Jer 46: 4 put on your *a*!
Ro 13: 12 deeds of darkness and put on the *a*
Eph 6: 11 Put on the full *a* of God
6: 13 Therefore put on the full *a* of God,

ARMS (ARMY)
Dt 33: 27 underneath are the everlasting *a*.
Ps 18: 32 It is God who *a* me with strength
Pr 31: 17 her *a* are strong for her tasks.
31: 20 She opens her *a* to the poor
Isa 40: 11 He gathers the lambs in his *a*
Mk 10: 16 And he took the children in his *a*,
Heb 12: 12 strengthen your feeble *a*

ARMY (ARM ARMIES ARMOR ARMS)
Ps 33: 16 No king is saved by the size of his *a*
Joel 2: 2 a large and mighty *a* comes,
2: 5 like a mighty *a* drawn up for battle.
2: 11 thunders at the head of his *a*;
Rev 19: 19 the rider on the horse and his *a*.

AROMA
Ge 8: 21 The LORD smelled the pleasing *a*
Ex 29: 18 a pleasing *a*, an offering made
Lev 3: 16 made by fire, a pleasing *a*.
2Co 2: 15 For we are to God the *a* of Christ

AROUSE (AROUSED)
Ro 11: 14 I may somehow *a* my own people

AROUSED (AROUSE)
Ps 78: 58 they *a* his jealousy with their idols.

ARRANGED
1Co 12: 18 But in fact God has *a* the parts

ARRAYED*
Ps 110: 3 *A* in holy majesty,
Isa 61: 10 and *a* me in a robe of righteousness

ARREST
Mt 10: 19 But when they *a* you, do not worry

ARROGANCE (ARROGANT)
1Sa 2: 3 or let your mouth speak such *a*,
Pr 8: 13 I hate pride and *a*,
Mk 7: 22 lewdness, envy, slander, *a* and folly
2Co 12: 20 slander, gossip, *a* and disorder.

ARROGANT (ARROGANCE)
Ps 5: 5 The *a* cannot stand
119: 78 May the *a* be put to shame
Pr 17: 7 *A* lips are unsuited to a fool —
21: 24 *a* man — "Mocker" is his name;
Ro 1: 30 God-haters, insolent, *a*
11: 20 Do not be *a*, but be afraid.
1Ti 6: 17 in this present world not to be *a*

ARROW (ARROWS)
Ps 91: 5 nor the *a* that flies by day,
Pr 25: 18 Like a club or a sword or a sharp *a*

ARROWS (ARROW)
Ps 64: 3 and aim their words like deadly *a*.
64: 7 But God will shoot them with *a*;
127: 4 Like *a* in the hands of a warrior
Pr 26: 18 firebrands or deadly *a*
Eph 6: 16 you can extinguish all the flaming *a*

ARTAXERXES
King of Persia; allowed rebuilding of temple under Ezra (Ezr 4; 7), and of walls of Jerusalem under his cupbearer Nehemiah (Ne 2; 5:14; 13:6).

ARTEMIS
Ac 19: 28 "Great is *A* of the Ephesians!"

ASA
King of Judah (1Ki 15:8 – 24; 1Ch 3:10; 2Ch 14 – 16). Godly reformer (2Ch 15); in later years defeated Israel with help of Aram, not the LORD (1Ki 15:16 – 22; 2Ch 16).

ASAHEL
1. Nephew of David, one of his warriors (2Sa 23:24; 1Ch 2:16; 11:26; 27:7). Killed by Abner (2Sa 2); avenged by Joab (2Sa 3:22 – 39).
2. Levite; teacher (2Ch 17:8).

ASAPH
1. Recorder to Hezekiah (2Ki 18:18, 37; Isa 36:3, 22).
2. Levitical musician (1Ch 6:39; 15:17 – 19; 16:4 – 7, 37). Sons of (1Ch 25; 2Ch 5:12; 20:14; 29:13; 35:15; Ezr 2:41; 3:10; Ne 7:44; 11:17; 12:27 – 47). Psalms of (2Ch 29:30; Ps 50; 73 – 83).

ASCEND* (ASCENDED ASCENDING)
Dt 30: 12 "Who will *a* into heaven to get it
Ps 24: 3 Who may *a* the hill of the LORD?
Isa 14: 13 "I will *a* to heaven;
14: 14 I will *a* above the tops of the clouds
Jn 6: 62 of Man *a* to where he was before!
Ac 2: 34 For David did not *a* to heaven,
Ro 10: 6 'Who will *a* into heaven?'" (that is,

ASCENDED (ASCEND)
Ps 68: 18 When you *a* on high,
Eph 4: 8 "When he *a* on high,

ASCENDING (ASCEND)
Ge 28: 12 and the angels of God were *a*
Jn 1: 51 and the angels of God *a*

ASCRIBE*
1Ch 16: 28 *A* to the LORD, O families
16: 28 *a* to the LORD glory and strength,
16: 29 *a* to the LORD the glory due his
Job 36: 3 I will *a* justice to my Maker.
Ps 29: 1 *A* to the LORD, O mighty ones,
29: 1 *a* to the LORD glory and strength.
29: 2 *A* to the LORD the glory due his
96: 7 *A* to the LORD, O families
96: 7 *a* to the LORD glory and strength.
96: 8 *A* to the LORD the glory due his

ASHAMED (SHAME)
Mk 8: 38 If anyone is *a* of me and my words
Lk 9: 26 If anyone is *a* of me and my words,
Ro 1: 16 I am not *a* of the gospel,
2Ti 1: 8 So do not be *a* to testify about our
2: 15 who does not need to be *a*

ASHER
Son of Jacob by Zilpah (Ge 30:13; 35:26; 46:17; Ex 1:4; 1Ch 2:2). Tribe of blessed (Ge 49:20; Dt 33:24 – 25), numbered (Nu 1:40 – 41; 26:44 – 47), allotted land (Jos 10:24 – 31; Eze 48:2), failed to fully possess (Jdg 1:31 – 32), failed to support Deborah (Jdg 5:17), supported Gideon (Jdg 6:35; 7:23) and David (1Ch 12:36), 12,000 from (Rev 7:6).

ASHERAH (ASHERAHS)
Ex 34: 13 and cut down their *A* poles.
1Ki 18: 19 the four hundred prophets of *A*,

ASHERAHS* (ASHERAH)
Jdg 3: 7 and served the Baals and the *A*.

ASHES
Job 42: 6 and repent in dust and *a*."
Mt 11: 21 ago in sackcloth and *a*.

ASHTORETHS
Jdg 2: 13 and served Baal and the *A*.
1Sa 7: 4 put away their Baals and *A*,

ASLEEP (SLEEP)
1Co 15: 18 who have fallen *a* in Christ are lost.
1Th 4: 13 be ignorant about those who fall *a*,

ASSEMBLY
Ps 1: 5 nor sinners in the *a* of the righteous
35: 18 I will give you thanks in the great *a*
82: 1 God presides in the great *a*;
149: 1 his praise in the *a* of the saints.

ASSIGNED
1Ki 7: 14 and did all the work *a* to him.
Mk 13: 34 with his *a* task, and tells the one
1Co 3: 5 as the Lord has *a* to each his task.
7: 17 place in life that the Lord *a* to him
2Co 10: 13 to the field God has *a* to us,

ASSOCIATE
Pr 22: 24 do not *a* with one easily angered,
Jn 4: 9 (For Jews do not *a* with Samaritans
Ac 10: 28 law for a Jew to *a* with a Gentile
Ro 12: 16 but be willing to *a* with people
1Co 5: 9 to *a* with sexually immoral people
5: 11 am writing you that you must not *a*
2Th 3: 14 Do not *a* with him,

ASSURANCE (ASSURED)
Heb 10: 22 with a sincere heart in full *a* of faith

ASSURED (ASSURANCE)
Col 4: 12 the will of God, mature and fully *a*.

ASTRAY
Ps 119: 67 Before I was afflicted I went *a*,
Pr 10: 17 ignores correction leads others *a*.
20: 1 whoever is led *a* by them is not
Isa 53: 6 We all, like sheep, have gone *a*,
Jer 50: 6 their shepherds have led them *a*
Jn 16: 1 you so that you will not go *a*.
1Pe 2: 25 For you were like sheep going *a*,
1Jn 3: 7 do not let anyone lead you *a*.

ASTROLOGERS
Isa 47: 13 Let your *a* come forward,
Da 2: 2 *a* to tell him what he had dreamed.

ATE (EAT)
Ge 3: 6 wisdom, she took some and *a* it.
27: 25 Jacob brought it to him and he *a*;
2Sa 9: 11 Mephibosheth *a* at David's table
Ps 78: 25 Men *a* the bread of angels;
Jer 15: 16 When your words came, I *a* them;
Eze 3: 3 So I *a* it, and it tasted as sweet
Mt 14: 20 They all *a* and were satisfied,
15: 37 They all *a* and were satisfied.
Mk 6: 42 They all *a* and were satisfied,
Lk 9: 17 They all *a* and were satisfied,

ATHALIAH
Granddaughter of Omri; wife of Jehoram and mother of Ahaziah; encouraged their evil ways (2Ki 8:18, 27; 2Ch 22:2). At death of Ahaziah she made herself queen, killing all his sons but Joash (2Ki 11:1 – 3; 2Ch 22:10 – 12); killed six years later when Joash was revealed (2Ki 11:4 – 16; 2Ch 23:1 – 15).

ATHLETE*
2Ti 2: 5 if anyone competes as an *a*,

ATONE* (ATONEMENT)
Ex 30: 15 to the LORD to *a* for your lives.
2Ch 29: 24 for a sin offering to *a* for all Israel,
Da 9: 24 an end to sin, to *a* for wickedness,

ATONED* (ATONEMENT)
Dt 21: 8 And the bloodshed will be *a* for.
1Sa 3: 14 guilt of Eli's house will never be *a*
Pr 16: 6 faithfulness sin is *a* for;
Isa 6: 7 guilt is taken away and your sin *a*
22: 14 your dying day this sin will not be *a*
27: 9 then, will Jacob's guilt be *a* for,

ATONEMENT (ATONE ATONED)
Ex 25: 17 "Make an *a* cover of pure gold —
30: 10 Once a year Aaron shall make *a*
Lev 17: 11 it is the blood that makes *a*
23: 27 this seventh month is the Day of *A*.
Nu 25: 13 and made *a* for the Israelites."
Ro 3: 25 presented him as a sacrifice of *a*,
Heb 2: 17 that he might make *a* for the sins

ATTACK
Ps 109: 3 they *a* me without cause.

ATTAINED
Php 3: 16 up to what we have already *a*.
Heb 7: 11 If perfection could have been *a*

ATTENTION (ATTENTIVE)
Pr 4: 1 pay *a* and gain understanding.
4: 20 My son, pay *a* to what I say;
5: 1 My son, pay *a* to my wisdom,
7: 24 pay *a* to what I say.
22: 17 Pay *a* and listen to the sayings
Ecc 7: 21 Do not pay *a* to every word people
Isa 42: 20 many things, but have paid no *a*;
Tit 1: 14 and will pay no *a* to Jewish myths
Heb 2: 1 We must pay more careful *a*,

ATTENTIVE (ATTENTION)
Ne 1: 11 let your ear be *a* to the prayer
1Pe 3: 12 and his ears are *a* to their prayer,

ATTITUDE (ATTITUDES)
Eph 4: 23 new in the *a* of your minds;
Php 2: 5 Your *a* should be the same
1Pe 4: 1 yourselves also with the same *a*,

ATTITUDES (ATTITUDE)
Heb 4: 12 it judges the thoughts and *a*

ATTRACTIVE
Tit 2: 10 teaching about God our Savior *a*.

AUDIENCE
Pr 29: 26 Many seek an *a* with a ruler,

AUTHORITIES (AUTHORITY)
Ro 13: 1 *a* that exist have been established
13: 5 it is necessary to submit to the *a*,
13: 6 for the *a* are God's servants,
Eph 3: 10 and *a* in the heavenly realms,
6: 12 but against the rulers, against the *a*,
Col 1: 16 thrones or powers or rulers or *a*;
2: 15 having disarmed the powers and *a*,
Tit 3: 1 people to be subject to rulers and *a*,
1Pe 3: 22 *a* and powers in submission to him.

AUTHORITY (AUTHORITIES)
Mt 7: 29 because he taught as one who had *a*
9: 6 the Son of Man has *a* on earth
28: 18 "All *a* in heaven and on earth has
Mk 1: 22 he taught them as one who had *a*,
2: 10 the Son of Man has *a* on earth
Lk 4: 32 because his message had *a*.
5: 24 the Son of Man has *a* on earth
Jn 10: 18 *a* to lay it down and *a*
Ac 1: 7 the Father has set by his own *a*.
Ro 7: 1 that the law has *a* over a man only
13: 1 for there is no *a* except that which
13: 2 rebels against the *a* is rebelling
1Co 11: 10 to have a sign of *a* on her head.
15: 24 he has destroyed all dominion, *a*
1Ti 2: 2 for kings and all those in *a*,
2: 12 to teach or to have *a* over a man;
Tit 2: 15 Encourage and rebuke with all *a*.
Heb 13: 17 your leaders and submit to their *a*.

AUTUMN*
Dt 11: 14 both *a* and spring rains,
Ps 84: 6 the *a* rains also cover it with pools.
Jer 5: 24 who gives *a* and spring rains
Joel 2: 23 both *a* and spring rains, as before.
Jas 5: 7 and how patient he is for the *a*
Jude : 12 blown along by the wind; *a* trees,

AVENGE (VENGEANCE)
Lev 26: 25 sword upon you to *a* the breaking
Dt 32: 35 It is mine to *a*; I will repay.
32: 43 for he will *a* the blood
Ro 12: 19 "It is mine to *a*; I will repay,"
Heb 10: 30 "It is mine to *a*; I will repay,"
Rev 6: 10 of the earth and *a* our blood?"

AVENGER (VENGEANCE)
Nu 35: 27 the *a* of blood may kill the accused
Jos 20: 3 find protection from the *a* of blood.
Ps 8: 2 to silence the foe and the *a*.

AVENGES (VENGEANCE)
Ps 94: 1 O LORD, the God who *a*,

AVENGING (VENGEANCE)
1Sa 25: 26 and from *a* yourself with your own
Na 1: 2 The LORD is a jealous and *a* God;

AVOID (AVOIDS)
Pr 4: 15 *A* it, do not travel on it;
20: 3 It is to a man's honor to *a* strife,
20: 19 so *a* a man who talks too much.
Ecc 7: 18 who fears God will *a* all ⌊extremes⌋.
1Th 4: 3 you should *a* sexual immorality;
5: 22 *A* every kind of evil.
2Ti 2: 16 *A* godless chatter, because those
Tit 3: 9 But *a* foolish controversies

AVOIDS* (AVOID)
Pr 16: 6 of the LORD a man *a* evil.
16: 17 The highway of the upright *a* evil;

AWAITS (WAIT)
Pr 15: 10 Stern discipline *a* him who leaves
28: 22 and is unaware that poverty *a* him.

AWAKE (WAKE)
Ps 17: 15 when I *a*, I will be satisfied
Pr 6: 22 when you *a*, they will speak to you.

AWARD*
2Ti 4: 8 will *a* to me on that day —

AWARE
Ex 34: 29 he was not *a* that his face was
Mt 24: 50 and at an hour he is not *a* of.
Lk 12: 46 and at an hour he is not *a* of.

AWE* (AWESOME OVERAWED)
1Sa 12: 18 So all the people stood in *a*
1Ki 3: 28 they held the king in *a*,
Job 25: 2 "Dominion and *a* belong to God;
Ps 119: 120 I stand in *a* of your laws.
Ecc 5: 7 Therefore stand in *a* of God.
Isa 29: 23 will stand in *a* of the God of Israel.
Jer 2: 19 and have no *a* of me,"
33: 9 they will be in *a* and will tremble
Hab 3: 2 I stand in *a* of your deeds,
Mal 2: 5 and stood in *a* of my name.
Mt 9: 8 they were filled with *a*;
Lk 1: 65 The neighbors were all filled with *a*
5: 26 They were filled with *a* and said,
7: 16 They were all filled with *a*
Ac 2: 43 Everyone was filled with *a*,
Heb 12: 28 acceptably with reverence and *a*,

AWESOME* (AWE)
Ge 28: 17 and said, "How *a* is this place!
Ex 15: 11 *a* in glory,
34: 10 among will see how *a* is the work
Dt 4: 34 or by great and *a* deeds,
7: 21 is among you, is a great and *a* God.
10: 17 the great God, mighty and *a*,
10: 21 and *a* wonders you saw
28: 58 revere this glorious and *a* name —
34: 12 performed the *a* deeds that Moses
Jdg 13: 6 like an angel of God, very *a*.
2Sa 7: 23 *a* wonders by driving out nations
1Ch 17: 21 *a* wonders by driving out nations
Ne 1: 5 of heaven, the great and *a* God,
4: 14 and *a*, and fight for your brothers,
9: 32 the great, mighty and *a* God,
Job 10: 16 again display your *a* power
37: 22 God comes in *a* majesty.
Ps 45: 4 let your right hand display *a* deeds.
47: 2 How *a* is the LORD Most High,
65: 5 us with *a* deeds of righteousness,
66: 3 to God, "How *a* are your deeds!
66: 5 how *a* his works in man's behalf!
68: 35 You are *a*, O God,
89: 7 he is more *a* than all who surround
99: 3 praise your great and *a* name —
106: 22 and *a* deeds by the Red Sea.
111: 9 holy and *a* is his name.
145: 6 of the power of your *a* works,
Isa 64: 3 when you did *a* things that we did
Eze 1: 18 Their rims were high and *a*,
1: 22 expanse, sparkling like ice, and *a*.
Da 2: 31 dazzling statue, *a* in appearance.
9: 4 "O Lord, the great and *a* God,
Zep 2: 11 The LORD will be *a* to them

AX
Mt 3: 10 The *a* is already at the root
Lk 3: 9 The *a* is already at the root

BAAL
Jdg 6: 25 Tear down your father's altar to *B*
1Ki 16: 32 *B* in the temple of *B* that he built
18: 25 Elijah said to the prophets of *B*,
19: 18 knees have not bowed down to *B*
2Ki 10: 28 Jehu destroyed *B* worship in Israel.
Jer 19: 5 places of *B* to burn their sons
Ro 11: 4 have not bowed the knee to *B*."

BAASHA
King of Israel (1Ki 15:16 – 16:7; 2Ch 16:1 – 6).

BABBLER* (BABBLING)
Ac 17: 18 "What is this *b* trying to say?"

BABBLING* (BABBLER)
Mt 6: 7 do not keep on *b* like pagans,

BABIES* (BABY)
Ge 25: 22 The *b* jostled each other within her
Ex 2: 6 "This is one of the Hebrew *b*,"
Lk 18: 15 also bringing *b* to Jesus
Ac 7: 19 them to throw out their newborn *b*
1Pe 2: 2 Like newborn *b*, crave pure

BABY* (BABIES BABY'S)
Ex 2: 6 She opened it and saw the *b*.
2: 7 women to nurse the *b* for you?"
2: 9 So the woman took the *b*
2: 9 "Take this *b* and nurse him for me,
1Ki 3: 17 I had a *b* while she was there
3: 18 was born, this woman also had a *b*.
3: 26 give her the living *b*! Don't kill him
3: 27 Give the living *b* to the first woman
Isa 49: 15 "Can a mother forget the *b*
Lk 1: 41 the *b* leaped in her womb,
1: 44 the *b* in my womb leaped for joy.
1: 57 time for Elizabeth to have her *b*,
2: 6 the time came for the *b* to be born,
2: 12 You will find a *b* wrapped in strips

Lk 2: 16 the *b,* who was lying in the manger.
Jn 16: 21 but when her *b* is born she forgets

BABY'S* (BABY)
Ex 2: 8 the girl went and got the *b* mother.

BABYLON
Ps 137: 1 By the rivers of *B* we sat and wept
Jer 29: 10 seventy years are completed for *B,*
51: 37 *B* will be a heap of ruins,
Rev 14: 8 "Fallen! Fallen is *B* the Great,
17: 5 MYSTERY *B* THE GREAT

BACKS
2Pe 2: 21 and then to turn their *b*

BACKSLIDING* (BACKSLIDINGS)
Jer 2: 19 your *b* will rebuke you.
3: 22 I will cure you of *b.*"
14: 7 For our *b* is great;
15: 6 "You keep on *b.*
Eze 37: 23 them from all their sinful *b,*

BACKSLIDINGS* (BACKSLIDING)
Jer 5: 6 and their *b* many.

BALAAM
Prophet who attempted to curse Israel (Nu 22 – 24; Dt 23:4 – 5; 2Pe 2:15; Jude 11). Killed in Israel's vengeance on Midianites (Nu 31:8; Jos 13:22).

BALAK
Moabite king who hired Balaam to curse Israel (Nu 22 – 24; Jos 24:9).

BALDHEAD
2Ki 2: 23 "Go on up, you *b!*" they said.

BALM
Jer 8: 22 Is there no *b* in Gilead?

BANISH (BANISHED)
Jer 25: 10 I will *b* from them the sounds of joy

BANISHED (BANISH)
Dt 30: 4 Even if you have been *b*

BANNER
Ex 17: 15 and called it The LORD is my *B.*
SS 2: 4 and his *b* over me is love.
Isa 11: 10 the Root of Jesse will stand as a *b*

BANQUET
SS 2: 4 He has taken me to the *b* hall,
Lk 14: 13 when you give a *b,* invite the poor,

BAPTISM* (BAPTIZE)
Mt 21: 25 John's *b* — where did it come from?
Mk 1: 4 and preaching a *b* of repentance
10: 38 baptized with the *b* I am baptized
10: 39 baptized with the *b* I am baptized
11: 30 John's *b* — was it from heaven,
Lk 3: 3 preaching a *b* of repentance
12: 50 But I have a *b* to undergo,
20: 4 John's *b* — was it from heaven,
Ac 1: 22 beginning from John's *b*
10: 37 after the *b* that John preached —
13: 24 and *b* to all the people of Israel.
18: 25 though he knew only the *b* of John.
19: 3 did you receive?" "John's *b,*"
19: 3 "Then what *b* did you receive?"
19: 4 "John's *b* was a *b* of repentance.
Ro 6: 4 with him through *b* into death
Eph 4: 5 one Lord, one faith, one *b;*
Col 2: 12 having been buried with him in *b*
1Pe 3: 21 this water symbolizes *b* that now

BAPTISMS* (BAPTIZE)
Heb 6: 2 instruction about *b,* the laying

BAPTIZE* (BAPTISM BAPTISMS BAPTIZED BAPTIZING)
Mt 3: 11 He will *b* you with the Holy Spirit
3: 11 "I *b* you with water for repentance.
Mk 1: 8 I *b* you with water, but he will
1: 8 he will *b* you with the Holy Spirit."
Lk 3: 16 He will *b* you with the Holy Spirit
3: 16 John answered them all, "I *b* you
Jn 1: 25 "Why then do you *b*
1: 26 nor the Prophet?" "I *b* with water,"
1: 33 and remain is he who will *b*
1: 33 me to *b* with water told me,
1Co 1: 14 I am thankful that I did not *b* any
1: 17 For Christ did not send me to *b,*

BAPTIZED* (BAPTIZE)
Mt 3: 6 they were *b* by him in the Jordan
3: 13 to the Jordan to be *b* by John.
3: 14 saying, "I need to be *b* by you,
3: 16 as Jesus was *b,* he went up out
Mk 1: 5 they were *b* by him in the Jordan
1: 9 and was *b* by John in the Jordan.
Mk 10: 38 or be *b* with the baptism I am
10: 38 with the baptism I am *b* with?"
10: 39 and be *b* with the baptism I am
10: 39 with the baptism I am *b* with,
16: 16 believes and is *b* will be saved,
Lk 3: 7 to the crowds coming out to be *b*
3: 12 Tax collectors also came to be *b.*
3: 21 were being *b,* Jesus was *b* too.
7: 29 because they had been *b* by John.
7: 30 they had not been *b* by John.)
Jn 3: 22 spent some time with them, and *b.*
3: 23 were constantly coming to be *b.*
4: 2 in fact it was not Jesus who *b,*
Ac 1: 5 For John *b* with water,
1: 5 but in a few days you will be *b*
2: 38 Repent and be *b,* every one of you,
2: 41 who accepted his message were *b,*
8: 12 they were *b,* both men and women.
8: 13 Simon himself believed and was *b.*
8: 16 they had simply been *b*
8: 36 Why shouldn't I be *b?*"
8: 38 into the water and Philip *b* him.
9: 18 was *b,* and after taking some food,
10: 47 people from being *b* with water?
10: 48 So he ordered that they be *b*
11: 16 what the Lord had said, 'John *b*
11: 16 you will be *b* with the Holy Spirit.'
16: 15 members of her household were *b,*
16: 33 he and all his family were *b.*
18: 8 heard him believed and were *b.*
19: 5 they were *b* into the name
22: 16 be *b* and wash your sins away,
Ro 6: 3 *b* into Christ Jesus were *b*
1Co 1: 13 Were you *b* into the name of Paul?
1: 15 so no one can say that you were *b*
1: 16 I also *b* the household of Stephanas
1: 16 I don't remember if I *b* anyone else
10: 2 They were all *b* into Moses
12: 13 For we were all *b* by one Spirit
15: 29 what will those do who are *b*
15: 29 why are people *b* for them?
Gal 3: 27 all of you who were *b*

BAPTIZING* (BAPTIZE)
Mt 3: 7 coming to where he was *b,*
28: 19 *b* them in the name of the Father
Mk 1: 4 *b* in the desert region
Jn 1: 28 of the Jordan, where John was *b.*
1: 31 but the reason I came *b*
3: 23 also was *b* at Aenon near Salim,
3: 26 he is *b,* and everyone is going
4: 1 and *b* more disciples than John,
10: 40 to the place where John had been *b*

BAR-JESUS*
Ac 13: 6 and false prophet named *B,*

BARABBAS
Mt 27: 26 Then he released *B* to them.

BARAK*
Judge who fought with Deborah against Canaanites (Jdg 4 – 5; 1Sa 12:11; Heb 11:32).

BARBARIAN*
Col 3: 11 circumcised or uncircumcised, *b,*

BARBS*
Nu 33: 55 allow to remain will become *b*

BARE
Hos 2: 3 as *b* as on the day she was born;
Heb 4: 13 and laid *b* before the eyes of him

BARNABAS*
Disciple, originally Joseph (Ac 4:36), prophet (Ac 13:1), apostle (Ac 14:14). Brought Paul to apostles (Ac 9:27), Antioch (Ac 11:22 – 29; Gal 2:1 – 13), on the first missionary journey (Ac 13 – 14). Together at Jerusalem Council, they separated over John Mark (Ac 15). Later co-workers (1Co 9:6; Col 4:10).

BARREN
Ge 11: 30 Sarai was *b;* she had no children.
29: 31 her womb, but Rachel was *b.*
Ps 113: 9 He settles the *b* woman
Isa 54: 1 "Sing, O *b* woman,
Lk 1: 7 children, because Elizabeth was *b;*
Gal 4: 27 "Be glad, O *b* woman,
Heb 11: 11 and Sarah herself was *b* —

BARTHOLOMEW*
Apostle (Mt 10:3; Mk 3:18; Lk 6:14; Ac 1:13). Possibly also known as Nathanael (Jn 1:45 – 49; 21:2).

BARUCH
Jeremiah's secretary (Jer 32:12 – 16; 36; 43:1 – 6; 45:1 – 2).

BARZILLAI
1. Gileadite who aided David during Absalom's revolt (2Sa 17:27; 19:31 – 39).
2. Son-in-law of 1. (Ezr 2:61; Ne 7:63).

BASHAN
Jos 22: 7 Moses had given land in *B,*
Ps 22: 12 strong bulls of *B* encircle me.

BASIN
Ex 30: 18 "Make a bronze *b,*

BASKET
Ex 2: 3 she got a papyrus *b* for him
Ac 9: 25 him in a *b* through an opening
2Co 11: 33 I was lowered in a *b* from a window

BATCH*
Ro 11: 16 then the whole *b* is holy;
1Co 5: 6 through the whole *b* of dough?
5: 7 old yeast that you may be a new *b*
Gal 5: 9 through the whole *b* of dough."

BATH (BATHING)
Jn 13: 10 person who has had a *b* needs only

BATHING (BATH)
2Sa 11: 2 From the roof he saw a woman *b.*

BATHSHEBA*
Wife of Uriah who committed adultery with and became wife of David (2Sa 11), mother of Solomon (2Sa 12:24; 1Ki 1 – 2; 1Ch 3:5).

BATTLE (BATTLES)
1Sa 17: 47 for the *b* is the LORD's,
2Ch 20: 15 For the *b* is not yours, but God's.
Ps 24: 8 the LORD mighty in *b.*
Ecc 9: 11 or the *b* to the strong,
Isa 31: 4 down to do *b* on Mount Zion
Eze 13: 5 in the *b* on the day of the LORD.
Rev 16: 14 them for the *b* on the great day
20: 8 and Magog — to gather them for *b.*

BATTLES* (BATTLE)
1Sa 8: 20 to go out before us and fight our *b.*"
18: 17 and fight the *b* of the LORD."
25: 28 because he fights the LORD's *b.*
2Ch 32: 8 God to help us and to fight our *b.*"

BEAR (BEARING BEARS BIRTH BIRTHRIGHT BORE BORN CHILDBEARING CHILDBIRTH FIRSTBORN NEWBORN REBIRTH)
Ge 4: 13 punishment is more than I can *b.*
Ps 38: 4 like a burden too heavy to *b.*
Isa 11: 7 The cow will feed with the *b,*
53: 11 and he will *b* their iniquities.
Da 7: 5 beast, which looked like a *b.*
Mt 7: 18 A good tree cannot *b* bad fruit,
Jn 15: 2 branch that does *b* fruit he prunes
15: 8 glory, that you *b* much fruit,
15: 16 appointed you to go and *b* fruit —
Ro 7: 4 in order that we might *b* fruit
15: 1 ought to *b* with the failings
1Co 10: 13 tempted beyond what you can *b.*
Col 3: 13 *B* with each other and forgive

BEARD
Lev 19: 27 or clip off the edges of your *b.*
Isa 50: 6 to those who pulled out my *b;*

BEARING (BEAR)
Eph 4: 2 *b* with one another in love.
Col 1: 10 *b* fruit in every good work,
Heb 13: 13 outside the camp, *b* the disgrace he

BEARS (BEAR)
1Ki 8: 43 house I have built *b* your Name.
Ps 68: 19 who daily *b* our burdens.

BEAST (BEASTS)
Rev 13: 18 him calculate the number of the *b,*
16: 2 people who had the mark of the *b*
19: 20 who had received the mark of the *b*

BEASTS (BEAST)
Da 7: 3 Four great *b,* each different
1Co 15: 32 If I fought wild *b* in Ephesus

BEAT (BEATEN BEATING BEATINGS)
Isa 2: 4 They will *b* their swords
Joel 3: 10 *B* your plowshares into swords
Mic 4: 3 They will *b* their swords
1Co 9: 27 I *b* my body and make it my slave

BEATEN (BEAT)
Lk 12: 47 do what his master wants will be *b*
12: 48 deserving punishment will be *b*
2Co 11: 25 Three times I was *b* with rods,

BEATING (BEAT)
1Co 9: 26 I do not fight like a man *b* the air.
1Pe 2: 20 if you receive a *b* for doing wrong

BEATINGS (BEAT)
Pr 19: 29 and *b* for the backs of fools.

BEAUTIFUL* (BEAUTY)
Ge 6: 2 that the daughters of men were *b,*
12: 11 "I know what a *b* woman you are.
12: 14 saw that she was a very *b* woman.
24: 16 The girl was very *b,* a virgin;
26: 7 of Rebekah, because she is *b.*"
29: 17 Rachel was lovely in form, and *b.*
49: 21 that bears *b* fawns.
Nu 24: 5 "How *b* are your tents, O Jacob,
Dt 21: 11 among the captives a *b* woman
Jos 7: 21 saw in the plunder a *b* robe
1Sa 25: 3 was an intelligent and *b* woman,
2Sa 11: 2 The woman was very *b,*
13: 1 the *b* sister of Absalom son
14: 27 and she became a *b* woman.
1Ki 1: 3 throughout Israel for a *b* girl
1: 4 The girl was very *b;* she took care
Est 2: 2 for *b* young virgins for the king,
2: 3 realm to bring all these *b* girls
Job 38: 31 "Can you bind the *b* Pleiades?
42: 15 land were there found women as *b*
Ps 48: 2 It is *b* in its loftiness,
Pr 11: 22 is a *b* woman who shows no
24: 4 filled with rare and *b* treasures.
Ecc 3: 11 He has made everything *b*
SS 1: 8 *Lover* If you do not know, most *b*
1: 10 Your cheeks are *b* with earrings,
1: 15 Oh, how *b!*
1: 15 *Lover* How *b* you are, my darling!
2: 10 my *b* one, and come with me.
2: 13 my *b* one, come with me."
4: 1 How *b* you are, my darling!
4: 1 Oh, how *b!*
4: 7 All *b* you are, my darling;
5: 9 most *b* of women?
6: 1 most *b* of women?
6: 4 *Lover* You are *b,* my darling,
7: 1 How *b* your sandaled feet,
7: 6 How *b* you are and how pleasing,
Isa 4: 2 of the LORD will be *b*
28: 5 a *b* wreath
52: 7 How *b* on the mountains
Jer 3: 19 the most *b* inheritance
6: 2 so *b* and delicate,
11: 16 with fruit *b* in form.
46: 20 "Egypt is a *b* heifer,
Eze 7: 20 They were proud of their *b* jewelry
16: 7 and became the most *b* of jewels.
16: 12 and a *b* crown on your head.
16: 13 You became very *b* and rose
20: 6 and honey, the most *b* of all lands.
20: 15 and honey, most *b* of all lands —
23: 42 and *b* crowns on their heads.
27: 24 traded with you *b* garments,
31: 3 with *b* branches overshadowing
31: 9 I made it *b*
33: 32 who sings love songs with a *b* voice
Da 4: 12 Its leaves were *b,* its fruit abundant
4: 21 with *b* leaves and abundant fruit,
8: 9 to the east and toward the *B* Land.
11: 16 will establish himself in the *B* Land
11: 41 He will also invade the *B* Land.
11: 45 the seas at the *b* holy mountain.
Zec 9: 17 How attractive and *b* they will be!
Mt 23: 27 which look *b* on the outside
26: 10 She has done a *b* thing to me.
Mk 14: 6 She has done a *b* thing to me.
Lk 21: 5 temple was adorned with *b* stones
Ac 3: 2 carried to the temple gate called *B,*
3: 10 at the temple gate called *B,*
Ro 10: 15 "How *b* are the feet
1Pe 3: 5 in God used to make themselves *b.*

BEAUTY* (BEAUTIFUL)
Est 1: 11 order to display her *b* to the people
2: 3 let *b* treatments be given to them.
2: 9 her with her *b* treatments
2: 12 months of *b* treatments prescribed
Ps 27: 4 to gaze upon the *b* of the LORD
37: 20 LORD's enemies will be like the *b*
45: 11 The king is enthralled by your *b;*
50: 2 From Zion, perfect in *b,*
Pr 6: 25 lust in your heart after her *b*
31: 30 is deceptive, and *b* is fleeting;
Isa 3: 24 instead of *b,* branding.
28: 1 to the fading flower, his glorious *b,*
28: 4 That fading flower, his glorious *b,*
33: 17 Your eyes will see the king in his *b*
53: 2 He had no *b* or majesty
61: 3 to bestow on them a crown of *b*
La 2: 15 the perfection of *b,*
Eze 16: 14 had given you made your *b* perfect,
16: 14 the nations on account of your *b,*
16: 15 passed by and your *b* became his.
16: 15 "'But you trusted in your *b*
Eze 16: 25 lofty shrines and degraded your *b,*
27: 3 "I am perfect in *b.*"
27: 4 your builders brought your *b*
27: 11 they brought your *b* to perfection.
28: 7 draw their swords against your *b*
28: 12 full of wisdom and perfect in *b.*
28: 17 proud on account of your *b,*
31: 7 It was majestic in *b,*
31: 8 could match its *b.*
Jas 1: 11 blossom falls and its *b* is destroyed.
1Pe 3: 3 Your *b* should not come
3: 4 the unfading *b* of a gentle

BED (SICKBED)
Isa 28: 20 The *b* is too short to stretch out on,
Lk 11: 7 and my children are with me in *b.*
17: 34 night two people will be in one *b;*
Heb 13: 4 and the marriage *b* kept pure,

BEELZEBUB*
Mt 10: 25 of the house has been called *B,*
12: 24 "It is only by *B,* the prince
12: 27 And if I drive out demons by *B,*
Mk 3: 22 possessed by *B!* By the prince
Lk 11: 15 "By *B,* the prince of demons,
11: 18 claim that I drive out demons by *B.*
11: 19 Now if I drive out demons by *B,*

BEER
Pr 20: 1 Wine is a mocker and *b* a brawler;

BEERSHEBA
Ge 21: 14 and wandered in the desert of *B.*
Jdg 20: 1 all the Israelites from Dan to *B*
1Sa 3: 20 to *B* recognized that Samuel was
2Sa 3: 10 and Judah from Dan to *B.*"
17: 11 Let all Israel, from Dan to *B* —
24: 2 the tribes of Israel from Dan to *B*
24: 15 of the people from Dan to *B* died.
1Ki 4: 25 from Dan to *B,* lived in safety,
1Ch 21: 2 count the Israelites from *B* to Dan.
2Ch 30: 5 throughout Israel, from *B* to Dan,

BEFALLS*
Pr 12: 21 No harm *b* the righteous,

BEGGING
Ps 37: 25 or their children *b* bread.
Ac 16: 9 of Macedonia standing and *b* him,

BEGINNING
Ge 1: 1 In the *b* God created the heavens
Ps 102: 25 In the *b* you laid the foundations
111: 10 of the LORD is the *b* of wisdom;
Pr 1: 7 of the LORD is the *b* of knowledge
9: 10 of the LORD is the *b* of wisdom,
Ecc 3: 11 fathom what God has done from *b*
Isa 40: 21 Has it not been told you from the *b*
46: 10 I make known the end from the *b,*
Mt 24: 8 All these are the *b* of birth pains.
Lk 1: 3 investigated everything from the *b,*
Jn 1: 1 In the *b* was the Word,
1Jn 1: 1 That which was from the *b,*
Rev 21: 6 and the Omega, the *B* and the End.
22: 13 and the Last, the *B* and the End.

BEHAVE (BEHAVIOR)
Ro 13: 13 Let us *b* decently, as in the daytime

BEHAVIOR (BEHAVE)
1Pe 3: 1 without words by the *b* of their wives,
3: 16 maliciously against your good *b*

BEHEMOTH*
Job 40: 15 "Look at the *b,*

BELIEVE (BELIEVED BELIEVER BELIEVERS BELIEVES BELIEVING)
Ex 4: 1 "What if they do not *b* me
1Ki 10: 7 I did not *b* these things until I came
2Ch 9: 6 But I did not *b* what they said
Ps 78: 32 of his wonders, they did not *b.*
Hab 1: 5 that you would not *b,*
Mt 18: 6 one of these little ones who *b* in me
21: 22 If you *b,* you will receive whatever
27: 42 from the cross, and we will *b* in him
Mk 1: 15 Repent and *b* the good news!"
5: 36 ruler, "Don't be afraid; just *b.*"
9: 24 "I do *b;* help me overcome my
9: 42 one of these little ones who *b* in me
11: 24 *b* that you have received it,
15: 32 the cross, that we may see and *b.*"
16: 16 but whoever does not *b* will be
16: 17 signs will accompany those who *b:*
Lk 8: 12 so that they may not *b* and be saved.
8: 13 They *b* for a while, but in the time
8: 50 just *b,* and she will be healed."
22: 67 you will not *b* me,
24: 25 to *b* all that the prophets have
Jn 1: 7 that through him all men might *b.*
3: 18 does not *b* stands condemned
4: 42 "We no longer *b* just
5: 38 for you do not *b* the one he sent.
5: 46 believed Moses, you would *b* me,
6: 29 to *b* in the one he has sent."
6: 69 We *b* and know that you are
7: 5 his own brothers did not *b* in him.
8: 24 if you do not *b* that I am _the one I
9: 35 "Do you *b* in the Son of Man?"
9: 36 "Tell me so that I may *b* in him."
9: 38 "Lord, I *b,*" and he worshiped him.
10: 26 you do not *b* because you are not
10: 37 Do not *b* me unless I do what my
10: 38 you do not *b* me, *b* the miracles,
11: 27 "I *b* that you are the Christ,
12: 37 they still would not *b* in him.
12: 39 For this reason they could not *b,*
12: 44 in me, he does not *b* in me only,
13: 19 does happen you will *b* that I am
14: 10 Don't you *b* that I am in the Father
14: 11 *B* me when I say that I am
14: 11 or at least *b* on the evidence
16: 30 This makes us *b* that you came
16: 31 "You *b* at last!" Jesus answered.
17: 21 that the world may *b* that you have
19: 35 he testifies so that you also may *b.*
20: 27 Stop doubting and *b.*"
20: 31 written that you may *b* that Jesus is
Ac 16: 31 They replied, "*B* in the Lord Jesus,
19: 4 the people to *b* in the one coming
24: 14 I *b* everything that agrees
26: 27 Agrippa, do you *b* the prophets?
Ro 3: 22 faith in Jesus Christ to all who *b.*
4: 11 he is the father of all who *b*
10: 9 *b* in your heart that God raised him
10: 10 For it is with your heart that you *b*
10: 14 And how can they *b* in the one
16: 26 so that all nations might *b*
1Co 1: 21 preached to save those who *b.*
Gal 3: 22 might be given to those who *b.*
Php 1: 29 of Christ not only to *b* on him,
1Th 4: 14 We *b* that Jesus died and rose again
2Th 2: 11 delusion so that they will *b* the lie
1Ti 4: 10 and especially of those who *b.*
Tit 1: 6 a man whose children *b*
Heb 11: 6 comes to him must *b* that he exists
Jas 1: 6 But when he asks, he must *b*
2: 19 Even the demons *b* that —
2: 19 You *b* that there is one God.
1Pe 2: 7 to you who *b,* this stone is precious
1Jn 3: 23 to *b* in the name of his Son,
4: 1 Dear friends, do not *b* every spirit,
5: 13 things to you who *b* in the name

BELIEVED (BELIEVE)
Ge 15: 6 Abram *b* the LORD, and he
Ex 4: 31 signs before the people, and they *b.*
Isa 53: 1 Who has *b* our message
Jnh 3: 5 The Ninevites *b* God.
Lk 1: 45 is she who has *b* that what the Lord
Jn 1: 12 to those who *b* in his name,
2: 22 Then they *b* the Scripture
3: 18 because he has not *b* in the name
5: 46 If you *b* Moses, you would believe
7: 39 whom those who *b*
11: 40 "Did I not tell you that if you *b,*
12: 38 "Lord, who has *b* our message
20: 8 He saw and *b.*
20: 29 who have not seen and yet have *b.*"
Ac 13: 48 were appointed for eternal life *b.*
19: 2 the Holy Spirit when you *b?*"
Ro 4: 3 Scripture say? "Abraham *b* God,
10: 14 call on the one they have not *b* in?
10: 16 "Lord, who has *b* our message?"
1Co 15: 2 Otherwise, you have *b* in vain.
Gal 3: 6 Consider Abraham: "He *b* God,
2Th 2: 12 who have not *b* the truth
1Ti 3: 16 was *b* on in the world,
2Ti 1: 12 because I know whom I have *b,*
Jas 2: 23 that says, "Abraham *b* God,

BELIEVER* (BELIEVE)
1Ki 18: 3 (Obadiah was a devout *b*
Ac 16: 1 whose mother was a Jewess and a *b*
16: 15 "If you consider me a *b* in the Lord
1Co 7: 12 brother has a wife who is not a *b*
7: 13 has a husband who is not a *b*
2Co 6: 15 What does a *b* have in common
1Ti 5: 16 any woman who is a *b* has widows

BELIEVERS* (BELIEVE)
Jn 4: 41 of his words many more became *b.*
Ac 1: 15 among the *b* (a group numbering
2: 44 All the *b* were together
4: 32 All the *b* were one in heart

Ac 5: 12 And all the *b* used to meet together
9: 41 he called the *b* and the widows
10: 45 The circumcised *b* who had come
11: 2 the circumcised *b* criticized him
15: 2 along with some other *b,*
15: 5 Then some of the *b* who belonged
15: 23 To the Gentile *b* in Antioch,
21: 25 for the Gentile *b,* we have written
1Co 6: 5 to judge a dispute between *b?*
14: 22 is for *b,* not for unbelievers.
14: 22 not for *b* but for unbelievers;
Gal 6: 10 who belong to the family of *b.*
1Th 1: 7 a model to all the *b* in Macedonia
1Ti 4: 12 set an example for the *b* in speech,
6: 2 benefit from their service are *b,*
Jas 2: 1 *b* in our glorious Lord Jesus Christ,
1Pe 2: 17 Love the brotherhood of *b,*

BELIEVES* (BELIEVE)
Pr 14: 15 A simple man *b* anything,
Mk 9: 23 is possible for him who *b."*
11: 23 *b* that what he says will happen,
16: 16 Whoever *b* and is baptized will be
Jn 3: 15 that everyone who *b*
3: 16 that whoever *b* in him shall not
3: 18 Whoever *b* in him is not
3: 36 Whoever *b* in the Son has eternal
5: 24 *b* him who sent me has eternal life
6: 35 and he who *b* in me will never be
6: 40 and *b* in him shall have eternal life,
6: 47 he who *b* has everlasting life.
7: 38 Whoever *b* in me, as the Scripture
11: 25 He who *b* in me will live, even
11: 26 and *b* in me will never die.
12: 44 Jesus cried out, "When a man *b*
12: 46 so that no one who *b*
Ac 10: 43 about him that everyone who *b*
13: 39 him everyone who *b* is justified
Ro 1: 16 for the salvation of everyone who *b*
10: 4 righteousness for everyone who *b.*
1Jn 5: 1 Everyone who *b* that Jesus is
5: 5 Only he who *b* that Jesus is the Son
5: 10 Anyone who *b* in the Son

BELIEVING* (BELIEVE)
Jn 20: 31 and that by *b* you may have life
Ac 9: 26 not *b* that he really was a disciple.
1Co 7: 14 sanctified through her *b* husband.
7: 15 A *b* man or woman is not bound
9: 5 right to take a *b* wife along with us,
Gal 3: 2 or by *b* what you heard? Are you
1Ti 6: 2 Those who have *b* masters are not

BELLY
Ge 3: 14 You will crawl on your *b*
Da 2: 32 its *b* and thighs of bronze,
Mt 12: 40 three nights in the *b* of a huge fish,

BELONG (BELONGING BELONGS)
Ge 40: 8 "Do not interpretations *b* to God?
Lev 25: 55 for the Israelites *b* to me
Dt 10: 14 LORD your God *b* the heavens,
29: 29 The secret things *b*
Job 12: 13 "To God *b* wisdom and power;
12: 16 To him *b* strength and victory;
25: 2 "Dominion and awe *b* to God;
Ps 47: 9 for the kings of the earth *b* to God;
95: 4 and the mountain peaks *b* to him.
115: 16 The highest heavens *b*
Jer 5: 10 for these people do not *b*
Jn 8: 44 You *b* to your father, the devil,
15: 19 As it is, you do not *b* to the world,
Ro 1: 6 called to *b* to Jesus Christ.
7: 4 that you might *b* to another,
8: 9 of Christ, he does not *b* to Christ.
14: 8 we live or die, we *b* to the Lord.
1Co 7: 39 but he must *b* to the Lord.
15: 23 when he comes, those who *b*
Gal 3: 29 If you *b* to Christ, then you are
5: 24 Those who *b* to Christ Jesus have
1Th 5: 5 We do not *b* to the night
5: 8 But since we *b* to the day, let us be
1Jn 3: 19 then is how we know that we *b*

BELONGING (BELONG)
1Pe 2: 9 a holy nation, a people *b* to God,

BELONGS (BELONG)
Lev 27: 30 *b* to the LORD; it is holy
Dt 1: 17 of any man, for judgment *b* to God.
Job 41: 11 Everything under heaven *b* to me.
Ps 22: 28 for dominion *b* to the LORD
89: 18 Indeed, our shield *b* to the LORD,
111: 10 To him *b* eternal praise.
Eze 18: 4 For every living soul *b* to me,
Jn 8: 47 He who *b* to God hears what God
Ro 12: 5 each member *b* to all the others.
Rev 7: 10 "Salvation *b* to our God,

BELOVED* (LOVE)
Dt 33: 12 "Let the *b* of the LORD rest secure
SS 5: 9 How is your *b* better than others,
5: 9 *Friends* How is your *b* better
Jer 11: 15 "What is my *b* doing in my temple

BELSHAZZAR
King of Babylon in days of Daniel (Da 5).

BELT
Ex 12: 11 with your cloak tucked into your *b,*
1Ki 18: 46 and, tucking his cloak into his *b,*
2Ki 4: 29 "Tuck your cloak into your *b,*
9: 1 "Tuck your cloak into your *b,*
Isa 11: 5 Righteousness will be his *b*
Eph 6: 14 with the *b* of truth buckled

BENEFICIAL* (BENEFIT)
1Co 6: 12 for me"—but not everything is *b.*
10: 23 but not everything is *b.*

BENEFIT (BENEFICIAL BENEFITS)
Job 22: 2 "Can a man be of *b* to God?
Isa 38: 17 Surely it was for my *b*
Ro 6: 22 the *b* you reap leads to holiness,
2Co 4: 15 All this is for your *b,*

BENEFITS (BENEFIT)
Ps 103: 2 and forget not all his *b.*
Jn 4: 38 you have reaped the *b* of their labor

BENJAMIN
Twelfth son of Jacob by Rachel (Ge 35:16–24; 46:19–21; 1Ch 2:2). Jacob refused to send him to Egypt, but relented (Ge 42–45). Tribe of blessed (Ge 49:27; Dt 33:12), numbered (Nu 1:37; 26:41), allotted land (Jos 18:11–28; Eze 48:23), failed to fully possess (Jdg 1:21), nearly obliterated (Jdg 20–21), sided with Ish-Bosheth (2Sa 2), but turned to David (1Ch 12:2, 29). 12,000 from (Rev 7:8).

BEREANS*
Ac 17: 11 the *B* were of more noble character

BESTOWING* (BESTOWS)
Pr 8: 21 *b* wealth on those who love me

BESTOWS (BESTOWING)
Ps 84: 11 the LORD *b* favor and honor;

BETHANY
Mk 11: 1 and *B* at the Mount of Olives,

BETHEL
Ge 28: 19 He called that place *B,*

BETHLEHEM
Ru 1: 19 went on until they came to *B.*
1Sa 16: 1 I am sending you to Jesse of *B.*
2Sa 23: 15 from the well near the gate of *B!"*
Mic 5: 2 "But you, *B* Ephrathah,
Mt 2: 1 After Jesus was born in *B* in Judea,
2: 6 "'But you, *B,* in the land of Judah,

BETHPHAGE
Mt 21: 1 came to *B* on the Mount of Olives,

BETHSAIDA
Jn 12: 21 who was from *B* in Galilee,

BETRAY (BETRAYED BETRAYS)
Ps 89: 33 nor will I ever *b* my faithfulness.
Pr 25: 9 do not *b* another man's confidence,
Mt 10: 21 "Brother will *b* brother to death,
26: 21 the truth, one of you will *b* me."

BETRAYED (BETRAY)
Mt 27: 4 "for I have *b* innocent blood."

BETRAYS (BETRAY)
Pr 11: 13 A gossip *b* a confidence,
20: 19 A gossip *b* a confidence;

BEULAH*
Isa 62: 4 and your land *B;*

BEWITCHED*
Gal 3: 1 foolish Galatians! Who has *b* you?

BEZALEL
Judahite craftsman in charge of building the tabernacle (Ex 31:1–11; 35:30–39:31).

BIDDING*
Ps 103: 20 you mighty ones who do his *b,*
148: 8 stormy winds that do his *b,*

BILDAD
One of Job's friends (Job 8; 18; 25).

BILHAH
Servant of Rachel, mother of Jacob's sons Dan and Naphtali (Ge 30:1–7; 35:25; 46:23–25).

BIND (BINDS BOUND)
Dt 6: 8 and *b* them on your foreheads.
Pr 3: 3 *b* them around your neck,
6: 21 *B* them upon your heart forever;
7: 3 *B* them on your fingers;
Isa 61: 1 me to *b* up the brokenhearted,
Mt 16: 19 whatever you *b* on earth will be

BINDS (BIND)
Ps 147: 3 and *b* up their wounds.
Isa 30: 26 when the LORD *b* up the bruises

BIRD (BIRDS)
Pr 27: 8 Like a *b* that strays from its nest
Ecc 10: 20 a *b* of the air may carry your words,

BIRDS (BIRD)
Mt 8: 20 and *b* of the air have nests,
Lk 9: 58 and *b* of the air have nests,

BIRTH (BEAR)
Ps 51: 5 Surely I was sinful at *b,*
58: 3 Even from *b* the wicked go astray;
Isa 26: 18 but we gave *b* to wind.
Mt 1: 18 This is how the *b* of Jesus Christ
24: 8 these are the beginning of *b* pains.
Jn 3: 6 Flesh gives *b* to flesh, but the Spirit
1Pe 1: 3 great mercy he has given us new *b*

BIRTHRIGHT (BEAR)
Ge 25: 34 So Esau despised his *b.*

BITTEN
Nu 21: 8 anyone who is *b* can look at it

BITTER (BITTERNESS EMBITTER)
Ex 12: 8 along with *b* herbs, and bread made
Pr 27: 7 what is *b* tastes sweet.

BITTERNESS (BITTER)
Pr 14: 10 Each heart knows its own *b,*
17: 25 and *b* to the one who bore him.
Ro 3: 14 full of cursing and *b."*
Eph 4: 31 Get rid of all *b,* rage and anger,

BLACK
Zec 6: 6 The one with the *b* horses is going
Rev 6: 5 and there before me was a *b* horse!

BLAMELESS* (BLAMELESSLY)
Ge 6: 9 *b* among the people of his time,
17: 1 walk before me and be *b.*
Dt 18: 13 You must be *b* before the LORD
2Sa 22: 24 I have been *b* before him
22: 26 to the *b* you show yourself *b,*
Job 1: 1 This man was *b* and upright;
1: 8 one on earth like him; he is *b*
2: 3 one on earth like him; he is *b*
4: 6 and your *b* ways your hope?
8: 20 God does not reject a *b* man
9: 20 if I were *b,* it would pronounce me
9: 21 "Although I am *b,*
9: 22 'He destroys both the *b*
12: 4 though righteous and *b!*
22: 3 gain if your ways were *b?*
31: 6 and he will know that I am *b*—
Ps 15: 2 He whose walk is *b*
18: 23 I have been *b* before him
18: 25 to the *b* you show yourself *b,*
19: 13 Then will I be *b,*
26: 1 for I have led a *b* life;
26: 11 But I lead a *b* life;
37: 18 The days of the *b* are known
37: 37 Consider the *b,* observe the upright
84: 11 from those whose walk is *b.*
101: 2 I will be careful to lead a *b* life—
101: 2 house with *b* heart.
101: 6 he whose walk is *b*
119: 1 Blessed are they whose ways are *b,*
119: 80 May my heart be *b*
Pr 2: 7 a shield to those whose walk is *b,*
2: 21 and the *b* will remain in it;
11: 5 of the *b* makes a straight way
11: 20 in those whose ways are *b.*
19: 1 Better a poor man whose walk is *b*
20: 7 The righteous man leads a *b* life;
28: 6 Better a poor man whose walk is *b*
28: 10 *b* will receive a good inheritance.
28: 18 He whose walk is *b* is kept safe,
Eze 28: 15 You were *b* in your ways
1Co 1: 8 so that you will be *b* on the day
Eph 1: 4 world to be holy and *b* in his sight.
5: 27 any other blemish, but holy and *b.*
Php 1: 10 and *b* until the day of Christ,
2: 15 so that you may become *b* and pure
1Th 2: 10 and *b* we were among you who
3: 13 hearts so that you will be *b*
5: 23 and body be kept *b* at the coming
Tit 1: 6 An elder must be *b,* the husband of
1: 7 he must be *b*—not overbearing,
Heb 7: 26 *b,* pure, set apart from sinners,

2Pe 3: 14 effort to be found spotless, *b*
Rev 14: 5 found in their mouths; they are *b*.

BLAMELESSLY* (BLAMELESS)
Lk 1: 6 commandments and regulations *b*.

BLASPHEME* (BLASPHEMED BLASPHEMER BLASPHEMES BLASPHEMIES BLASPHEMING BLASPHEMOUS BLASPHEMY)
Ex 22: 28 "Do not *b* God or curse the ruler
Ac 26: 11 and I tried to force them to *b*.
1Ti 1: 20 over to Satan to be taught not to *b*.
2Pe 2: 12 these men *b* in matters they do not
Rev 13: 6 He opened his mouth to *b* God,

BLASPHEMED* (BLASPHEME)
Lev 24: 11 of the Israelite woman *b* the Name
2Ki 19: 6 of the king of Assyria have *b* me.
19: 22 Who is it you have insulted and *b*?
Isa 37: 6 of the king of Assyria have *b* me.
37: 23 Who is it you have insulted and *b*?
52: 5 my name is constantly *b*.
Eze 20: 27 your fathers *b* me by forsaking me:
Ac 19: 37 robbed temples nor *b* our goddess.
Ro 2: 24 name is *b* among the Gentiles

BLASPHEMER* (BLASPHEME)
Lev 24: 14 "Take the *b* outside the camp.
24: 23 they took the *b* outside the camp
1Ti 1: 13 I was once a *b* and a persecutor

BLASPHEMES* (BLASPHEME)
Lev 24: 16 anyone who *b* the name
24: 16 native-born, when he *b* the Name,
Nu 15: 30 native-born or alien, *b* the LORD,
Mk 3: 29 whoever *b* against the Holy Spirit
Lk 12: 10 but anyone who *b* against the Holy

BLASPHEMIES* (BLASPHEME)
Ne 9: 18 or when they committed awful *b*.
9: 26 to you; they committed awful *b*.
Mk 3: 28 and *b* of men will be forgiven them.
Rev 13: 5 and *b* and to exercise his authority

BLASPHEMING* (BLASPHEME)
Mt 9: 3 "This fellow is *b*!" Knowing their
Mk 2: 7 He's *b*! Who can forgive sins

BLASPHEMOUS* (BLASPHEME)
Rev 13: 1 and on each head a *b* name.
17: 3 that was covered with *b* names

BLASPHEMY* (BLASPHEME)
Mt 12: 31 and *b* will be forgiven men,
12: 31 the *b* against the Spirit will not be
26: 65 Look, now you have heard the *b*.
26: 65 "He has spoken *b*! Why do we
Mk 14: 64 "You have heard the *b*.
Lk 5: 21 "Who is this fellow who speaks *b*?
Jn 10: 33 replied the Jews, "but for *b*,
10: 36 Why then do you accuse me of *b*
Ac 6: 11 words of *b* against Moses

BLAST*
Ex 15: 8 By the *b* of your nostrils
19: 13 horn sounds a long *b* may they go
19: 16 and a very loud trumpet *b*.
Nu 10: 5 When a trumpet *b* is sounded,
10: 6 At the sounding of a second *b*,
10: 6 The *b* will be the signal
10: 9 sound a *b* on the trumpets.
Jos 6: 5 you hear them sound a long *b*
6: 16 the priests sounded the trumpet *b*,
2Sa 22: 16 at the *b* of breath from his nostrils.
Job 4: 9 at the *b* of his anger they perish.
39: 25 At the *b* of the trumpet he snorts,
Ps 18: 15 the *b* of breath from your nostrils.
98: 6 and the *b* of the ram's horn—
147: 17 Who can withstand his icy *b*?
Isa 27: 8 with his fierce *b* he drives her out,
Eze 22: 20 a furnace to melt it with a fiery *b*,
Am 2: 2 tumult amid war cries and the *b*
Heb 12: 19 to a trumpet *b* or to such a voice

BLEATING*
1Sa 15: 14 "What then is this *b* of sheep

BLEMISH (BLEMISHES)
Lev 22: 21 be without defect or *b*
Eph 5: 27 or wrinkle or any other *b*,
Col 1: 22 without *b* and free from accusation
1Pe 1: 19 a lamb without *b* or defect.

BLEMISHES* (BLEMISH)
2Pe 2: 13 and *b*, reveling in their pleasures
Jude : 12 These men are *b* at your love feasts

BLESS (BLESSED BLESSES BLESSING BLESSINGS)
Ge 12: 3 I will *b* those who *b* you,
32: 26 not let you go unless you *b* me."
Dt 7: 13 He will love you and *b* you
33: 11 *B* all his skills, O LORD,
Ps 72: 15 and *b* him all day long.
Ro 12: 14 Bless those who persecute you; *b*

BLESSED (BLESS)
Ge 1: 22 God *b* them and said, "Be fruitful
2: 3 And God *b* the seventh day
22: 18 nations on earth will be *b*,
Nu 24: 9 "May those who bless you be *b*
1Ch 17: 27 have *b* it, and it will be *b* forever."
Ps 1: 1 *B* is the man
2: 12 *B* are all who take refuge in him.
32: 2 *B* is the man
33: 12 *B* is the nation whose God is
40: 4 *B* is the man
41: 1 *B* is he who has regard for the weak
84: 5 *B* are those whose strength is
89: 15 *B* are those who have learned
94: 12 *B* is the man you discipline,
106: 3 *B* are they who maintain justice,
112: 1 *B* is the man who fears the LORD,
118: 26 *B* is he who comes in the name
119: 1 *B* are they whose ways are
119: 2 *B* are they who keep his statutes
127: 5 *B* is the man
Pr 3: 13 *B* is the man who finds wisdom,
8: 34 *B* is the man who listens to me,
28: 20 A faithful man will be richly *b*,
29: 18 but *b* is he who keeps the law.
31: 28 Her children arise and call her *b*;
Isa 30: 18 *B* are all who wait for him!
Mal 3: 12 Then all the nations will call you *b*,
3: 15 But now we call the arrogant *b*.
Mt 5: 3 saying: "*B* are the poor in spirit,
5: 4 *B* are those who mourn,
5: 5 *B* are the meek,
5: 6 *B* are those who hunger
5: 7 *B* are the merciful,
5: 8 *B* are the pure in heart,
5: 9 *B* are the peacemakers,
5: 10 *B* are those who are persecuted
5: 11 "*B* are you when people insult you,
Lk 1: 48 on all generations will call me *b*,
Jn 12: 13 "*B* is he who comes in the name
Ac 20: 35 'It is more *b* to give than to receive
Tit 2: 13 while we wait for the *b* hope—
Jas 1: 12 *B* is the man who perseveres
Rev 1: 3 *B* is the one who reads the words
22: 7 *B* is he who keeps the words
22: 14 "*B* are those who wash their robes,

BLESSES (BLESS)
Ps 29: 11 the LORD *b* his people with peace.
Ro 10: 12 and richly *b* all who call on him,

BLESSING (BLESS)
Ge 27: 4 so that I may give you my *b*
Dt 23: 5 turned the curse into a *b* for you,
33: 1 This is the *b* that Moses the man
Pr 10: 22 The *b* of the LORD brings wealth,
Eze 34: 26 there will be showers of *b*.

BLESSINGS (BLESS)
Dt 11: 29 proclaim on Mount Gerizim the *b*,
Jos 8: 34 all the words of the law—the *b*
Pr 10: 6 *B* crown the head of the righteous,
Ro 15: 27 shared in the Jews' spiritual *b*,

BLIND (BLINDED)
Mt 15: 14 a *b* man leads a *b* man, both will fall
23: 16 "Woe to you, *b* guides! You say,
Mk 10: 46 a *b* man, Bartimaeus (that is,
Lk 6: 39 "Can a *b* man lead a *b* man?
Jn 9: 25 I was *b* but now I see!"

BLINDED (BLIND)
Jn 12: 40 elsewhere: "He has *b* their eyes
2Co 4: 4 The god of this age has *b* the minds

BLOOD (BLOODSHED BLOODTHIRSTY)
Ge 4: 10 Your brother's *b* cries out to me
9: 6 "Whoever sheds the *b* of man,
Ex 12: 13 and when I see the *b*, I will pass
24: 8 "This is the *b* of the covenant that
Lev 16: 15 and take its *b* behind the curtain
17: 11 For the life of a creature is in the *b*,
Dt 12: 23 eat the *b*, because the *b* is the life,
Ps 72: 14 for precious is their *b* in his sight.
Pr 6: 17 hands that shed innocent *b*,
Isa 1: 11 pleasure in the *b* of bulls and lambs
Mt 26: 28 This is my *b* of the covenant,
27: 24 "I am innocent of this man's *b*,"
Mk 14: 24 "This is my *b* of the covenant,
Lk 22: 44 drops of *b* falling to the ground.
Jn 6: 53 of the Son of Man and drink his *b*,
Ac 15: 20 of strangled animals and from *b*.
20: 26 innocent of the *b* of all men.
Ro 3: 25 of atonement, through faith in his *b*
5: 9 have now been justified by his *b*,
1Co 11: 25 cup is the new covenant in my *b*;
Eph 1: 7 we have redemption through his *b*,
2: 13 near through the *b* of Christ.
Col 1: 20 by making peace through his *b*,
Heb 9: 7 once a year, and never without *b*,
9: 12 once for all by his own *b*,
9: 20 "This is the *b* of the covenant,
9: 22 of *b* there is no forgiveness.
12: 24 word than the *b* of Abel.
1Pe 1: 19 but with the precious *b* of Christ,
1Jn 1: 7 and the *b* of Jesus, his Son,
Rev 1: 5 has freed us from our sins by his *b*,
5: 9 with your *b* you purchased men
7: 14 white in the *b* of the Lamb.
12: 11 him by the *b* of the Lamb
19: 13 He is dressed in a robe dipped in *b*,

BLOODSHED (BLOOD)
Jer 48: 10 on him who keeps his sword from *b*
Eze 35: 6 did not hate *b*, *b* will pursue you.
Hab 2: 12 to him who builds a city with *b*

BLOODTHIRSTY* (BLOOD)
Ps 5: 6 *b* and deceitful men
26: 9 my life with *b* men,
55: 23 *b* and deceitful men
59: 2 and save me from *b* men.
139: 19 Away from me, you *b* men!
Pr 29: 10 *B* men hate a man of integrity

BLOSSOM
Isa 35: 1 the wilderness will rejoice and *b*.

BLOT (BLOTS)
Ex 32: 32 then *b* me out of the book you have
Ps 51: 1 *b* out my transgressions.
Rev 3: 5 I will never *b* out his name

BLOTS (BLOT)
Isa 43: 25 "I, even I, am he who *b* out

BLOWN
Eph 4: 14 and *b* here and there by every wind
Jas 1: 6 doubts is like a wave of the sea, *b*
Jude : 12 without rain, *b* along by the wind;

BLUSH
Jer 6: 15 they do not even know how to *b*.

BOAST (BOASTS)
1Ki 20: 11 armor should not *b* like one who
Ps 34: 2 My soul will *b* in the LORD;
44: 8 In God we make our *b* all day long,
Pr 27: 1 Do not *b* about tomorrow,
Jer 9: 23 or the rich man *b* of his riches,
1Co 1: 31 Let him who boasts *b* in the Lord."
2Co 10: 17 Let him who boasts *b* in the Lord."
11: 30 I do not inwardly burn? If I must *b*,
Gal 6: 14 May I never *b* except in the cross
Eph 2: 9 not by works, so that no one can *b*.

BOASTS (BOAST)
Jer 9: 24 but let him who *b* boast about this:

BOAZ
Wealthy Bethlehemite who showed favor to Ruth (Ru 2), married her (Ru 4). Ancestor of David (Ru 4:18–22; 1Ch 2:12–15), Jesus (Mt 1:5–16; Lk 3:23–32).

BODIES (BODY)
Isa 26: 19 their *b* will rise.
Ro 12: 1 to offer your *b* as living sacrifices,
1Co 6: 15 not know that your *b* are members
Eph 5: 28 to love their wives as their own *b*.

BODILY (BODY)
Col 2: 9 of the Deity lives in *b* form,

BODY (BODIES BODILY EMBODIMENT)
Zec 13: 6 What are these wounds on your *b*?'
Mt 10: 28 afraid of those who kill the *b*
26: 26 saying, "Take and eat; this is my *b*
26: 41 spirit is willing, but the *b* is weak."
Mk 14: 22 saying, "Take it; this is my *b*."
Lk 22: 19 saying, "This is my *b* given for you;
Jn 13: 10 wash his feet; his whole *b* is clean.
Ro 6: 13 Do not offer the parts of your *b*
12: 4 us has one *b* with many members,
1Co 6: 19 not know that your *b* is a temple
6: 20 Therefore honor God with your *b*.
11: 24 "This is my *b*, which is for you;
12: 12 The *b* is a unit, though it is made up
12: 13 baptized by one Spirit into one *b*—
15: 44 a natural *b*, it is raised a spiritual *b*.
Eph 1: 23 which is his *b*, the fullness
4: 25 for we are all members of one *b*.
5: 30 for we are members of his *b*.
Php 1: 20 Christ will be exalted in my *b*,
Col 1: 24 sake of his *b*, which is the church.

BOLD (BOLDNESS)
Ps 138: 3 you made me *b* and stouthearted.
Pr 21: 29 A wicked man puts up a *b* front,
28: 1 but the righteous are as *b* as a lion.

BOLDNESS* (BOLD)
Lk 11: 8 of the man's *b* he will get up
Ac 4: 29 to speak your word with great *b.*

BONDAGE
Ezr 9: 9 God has not deserted us in our *b.*

BONES
Ge 2: 23 "This is now bone of my *b*
Ps 22: 14 and all my *b* are out of joint.
22: 17 I can count all my *b;*
Eze 37: 1 middle of a valley; it was full of *b.*
Jn 19: 36 "Not one of his *b* will be broken,"

BOOK (BOOKS)
Ex 32: 33 against me I will blot out of my *b.*
Jos 1: 8 Do not let this *B* of the Law depart
2Ki 22: 8 "I have found the *B* of the Law
2Ch 34: 15 "I have found the *B* of the Law
Ne 8: 8 They read from the *B* of the Law
Ps 69: 28 May they be blotted out of the *b*
Da 12: 1 name is found written in the *b*—
Jn 20: 30 which are not recorded in this *b.*
Php 4: 3 whose names are in the *b* of life.
Rev 3: 5 never blot out his name from the *b*
20: 12 *b* was opened, which is the *b*
20: 15 was not found written in the *b*
21: 27 written in the Lamb's *b* of life.
22: 18 him the plagues described in this *b.*

BOOKS* (BOOK)
Ecc 12: 12 Of making many *b* there is no end,
Da 7: 10 and the *b* were opened.
Jn 21: 25 for the *b* that would be written.
Rev 20: 12 the throne, and *b* were opened.
20: 12 they had done as recorded in the *b.*

BORE (BEAR)
Isa 53: 12 For he *b* the sin of many,
1Pe 2: 24 He himself *b* our sins in his body

BORN (BEAR)
Ecc 3: 2 a time to be *b* and a time to die,
Isa 9: 6 For to us a child is *b,*
66: 8 Can a country be *b* in a day
Lk 2: 11 of David a Savior has been *b* to you
Jn 3: 3 see the kingdom of God unless he is *b* again.
3: 4 How can a man be *b* when he is old
3: 5 unless he is *b* of water
3: 7 at my saying, 'You must be *b* again
3: 8 it is with everyone *b* of the Spirit."
1Pe 1: 23 For you have been *b* again,
1Jn 3: 9 because he has been *b* of God.
4: 7 Everyone who loves has been *b*
5: 1 believes that Jesus is the Christ is *b*
5: 4 for everyone *b* of God overcomes
5: 18 We know that anyone *b*

BORROWER
Pr 22: 7 and the *b* is servant to the lender.

BOTHER (BOTHERING)
Lk 11: 7 one inside answers, 'Don't *b* me.

BOTHERING (BOTHER)
Lk 18: 5 yet because this widow keeps *b* me,

BOUGHT (BUY)
Ac 20: 28 which he *b* with his own blood.
1Co 6: 20 You are not your own; you were *b*
7: 23 You were *b* at a price; do not
2Pe 2: 1 the sovereign Lord who *b* them—

BOUND (BIND)
Is 56: 3 Let no foreigner who has *b* himself
Mt 16: 19 bind on earth will be *b* in heaven,
18: 18 bind on earth will be *b* in heaven,
Ro 7: 2 by law a married woman is *b*
1Co 7: 39 A woman is *b* to her husband
Jude : 6 *b* with everlasting chains
Rev 20: 2 and *b* him for a thousand years.

BOUNDARY (BOUNDS)
Nu 34: 3 your southern *b* will start
Pr 23: 10 Do not move an ancient *b* stone
Hos 5: 10 who move *b* stones.

BOUNDS (BOUNDARY)
2Co 7: 4 all our troubles my joy knows no *b.*

BOUNTY*
Ge 49: 26 than the *b* of the age-old hills.
Dt 28: 12 heavens, the storehouse of his *b,*
1Ki 10: 13 he had given her out of his royal *b.*
Ps 65: 11 You crown the year with your *b,*
68: 10 from your *b,* O God, you provided

Jer 31: 12 rejoice in the *b* of the LORD—
31: 14 my people will be filled with my *b*

BOW (BOWED BOWS)
Dt 5: 9 You shall not *b* down to them
1Ki 22: 34 But someone drew his *b* at random
Ps 5: 7 in reverence will I *b* down
44: 6 I do not trust in my *b,*
95: 6 Come, let us *b* down in worship,
138: 2 I will *b* down toward your holy
Isa 44: 19 Shall I *b* down to a block of wood?"
45: 23 Before me every knee will *b;*
Ro 14: 11 'every knee will *b* before me;
Php 2: 10 name of Jesus every knee should *b,*

BOWED (BOW)
Ps 145: 14 and lifts up all who are *b* down.
146: 8 the LORD lifts up those who are *b*

BOWS (BOW)
Isa 44: 15 he makes an idol and *b* down to it.
44: 17 he *b* down to it and worships.

BOY (BOY'S BOYS)
Ge 21: 17 God heard the *b* crying,
22: 12 not lay a hand on the *b*
Jdg 13: 5 *b* is to be a Nazirite,
1Sa 2: 11 *b* ministered before the LORD.
3: 8 the LORD was calling the *b.*
Isa 7: 16 before the *b* knows enough
Mt 17: 18 demon, and it came out of the *b*
Lk 2: 43 the *b* Jesus stayed behind

BOY'S (BOY)
1Ki 17: 22 the *b* life returned to him
2Ki 4: 34 the *b* body grew warm

BOYS (BOY)
Ge 25: 24 twin *b* in her womb
Ex 1: 18 they let the *b* live.

BRACE*
Job 38: 3 *B* yourself like a man;
40: 7 out of the storm: "*B* yourself like
Na 2: 1 *b* yourselves,

BRAG*
Am 4: 5 and *b* about your freewill offerings
Ro 2: 17 *b* about your relationship to God;
2: 23 temples? You who *b* about the law,
Jas 4: 16 As it is, you boast and *b.*

BRAIDED
1Ti 2: 9 not with *b* hair or gold or pearls
1Pe 3: 3 as *b* hair and the wearing

BRANCH (BRANCHES)
Isa 4: 2 In that day the *B* of the LORD will
Jer 23: 5 up to David a righteous *B,*
33: 15 I will make a righteous *B* sprout
Zec 3: 8 going to bring my servant, the *B.*
6: 12 is the man whose name is the *B,*
Jn 15: 2 while every *b* that does bear fruit
15: 4 No *b* can bear fruit by itself;

BRANCHES (BRANCH)
Jn 15: 5 "I am the vine; you are the *b.*
Ro 11: 21 if God did not spare the natural *b,*

BRAVE
2Sa 2: 7 Now then, be strong and *b,*
13: 28 you this order? Be strong and *b.*"

BREACH (BREAK)
Ps 106: 23 stood in the *b* before him

BREACHING (BREAK)
Pr 17: 14 Starting a quarrel is like *b* a dam;

BREAD
Ex 12: 8 and *b* made without yeast.
23: 15 the Feast of Unleavened *B;*
25: 30 Put the *b* of the Presence
Dt 8: 3 that man does not live on *b* alone
Ps 78: 25 Men ate the *b* of angels;
Pr 30: 8 but give me only my daily *b.*
Ecc 11: 1 Cast your *b* upon the waters,
Isa 55: 2 Why spend money on what is not *b*
Mt 4: 3 tell these stones to become *b.*"
4: 4 'Man does not live on *b* alone,
6: 11 Give us today our daily *b.*
26: 26 Jesus took *b,* gave thanks
Mk 14: 22 Jesus took *b,* gave thanks
Lk 4: 3 tell this stone to become *b.*"
4: 4 'Man does not live on *b* alone.'"
9: 13 "We have only five loaves of *b*
11: 3 Give us each day our daily *b.*
22: 19 And he took *b,* gave thanks
Jn 6: 33 For the *b* of God is he who comes
6: 35 Jesus declared, "I am the *b* of life.
6: 41 "I am the *b* that came

Jn 6: 48 I am the *b* of life.
6: 51 I am the living *b* that came
6: 51 This *b* is my flesh, which I will give
21: 13 took the *b* and gave it to them,
1Co 10: 16 And is not the *b* that we break
11: 23 took *b,* and when he had given
11: 26 For whenever you eat this *b*

BREAK (BREACH BREACHING BREAKERS BREAKING BREAKS BROKE BROKEN BROKENNESS)
Nu 30: 2 he must not *b* his word
Jdg 2: 1 'I will never *b* my covenant
Pr 25: 15 and a gentle tongue can *b* a bone.
Isa 42: 3 A bruised reed he will not *b,*
Mal 2: 15 and do not *b* faith with the wife
Mt 12: 20 A bruised reed he will not *b,*
Ac 20: 7 week we came together to *b* bread.
1Co 10: 16 the bread that we *b* a participation
Rev 5: 2 "Who is worthy to *b* the seals

BREAKERS* (BREAK)
Ps 42: 7 all your waves and *b*
93: 4 mightier than the *b* of the sea—
Jnh 2: 3 all your waves and *b*

BREAKING (BREAK)
Jos 9: 20 fall on us for *b* the oath we swore
Eze 16: 59 oath by *b* the covenant.
17: 18 the oath by *b* the covenant.
Ac 2: 42 to the *b* of bread and to prayer.
Jas 2: 10 at just one point is guilty of *b* all

BREAKS (BREAK)
Jer 23: 29 "and like a hammer that *b* a rock
1Jn 3: 4 Everyone who sins *b* the law;

BREASTPIECE (BREASTPLATE)
Ex 28: 15 Fashion a *b* for making decisions—

BREASTPLATE* (BREASTPIECE)
Isa 59: 17 He put on righteousness as his *b,*
Eph 6: 14 with the *b* of righteousness in place
1Th 5: 8 putting on faith and love as a *b,*

BREASTS
La 4: 3 Even jackals offer their *b*

BREATH (BREATHED GOD-BREATHED)
Ge 2: 7 into his nostrils the *b* of life,

BREATHED (BREATH)
Ge 2: 7 *b* into his nostrils the breath of life,
Mk 15: 37 With a loud cry, Jesus *b* his last.
Jn 20: 22 And with that he *b* on them

BREEDS*
Pr 13: 10 Pride only *b* quarrels,

BRIBE
Ex 23: 8 "Do not accept a *b,*
Dt 16: 19 for a *b* blinds the eyes of the wise
27: 25 "Cursed is the man who accepts a *b*
Pr 6: 35 will refuse the *b,* however great it

BRIDE
Isa 62: 5 as a bridegroom rejoices over his *b,*
Rev 19: 7 and his *b* has made herself ready.
21: 2 as a *b* beautifully dressed
21: 9 I will show you the *b,* the wife
22: 17 The Spirit and the *b* say, "Come!"

BRIDEGROOM
Ps 19: 5 which is like a *b* coming forth
Mt 25: 1 and went out to meet the *b.*
25: 5 The *b* was a long time in coming,

BRIGHTENS* (BRIGHTNESS)
Pr 16: 15 When a king's face *b,* it means life;
Ecc 8: 1 Wisdom *b* a man's face

BRIGHTER (BRIGHTNESS)
Pr 4: 18 shining ever *b* till the full light

BRIGHTNESS* (BRIGHTENS BRIGHTER)
2Sa 22: 13 Out of the *b* of his presence
23: 4 like the *b* after rain
Ps 18: 12 of the *b* of his presence clouds
Isa 59: 9 for *b,* but we walk in deep shadows.
60: 3 and kings to the *b* of your dawn.
60: 19 will the *b* of the moon shine on you
Da 12: 3 who are wise will shine like the *b*
Am 5: 20 pitch-dark, without a ray of *b?*

BRILLIANCE* (BRILLIANT)
Ac 22: 11 the *b* of the light had blinded me.
Rev 1: 16 was like the sun shining in all its *b.*
21: 11 its *b* was like that of a very precious

BRILLIANT* (BRILLIANCE)
Ecc 9: 11 or wealth to the *b*
Eze 1: 4 and surrounded by *b* light.
1: 27 and *b* light surrounded him.

BRINK*
Pr 5: 14 I have come to the *b* of utter ruin

BRITTLE
Da 2: 42 will be partly strong and partly *b.*

BROAD
Mt 7: 13 and *b* is the road that leads

BROKE (BREAK)
Mt 26: 26 took bread, gave thanks and *b* it,
Mk 14: 22 took bread, gave thanks and *b* it,
Ac 2: 46 They *b* bread in their homes
20: 11 he went upstairs again and *b* bread
1Co 11: 24 when he had given thanks, he *b* it

BROKEN (BREAK)
Ps 34: 20 not one of them will be *b.*
51: 17 The sacrifices of God are a *b* spirit;
Ecc 4: 12 of three strands is not quickly *b.*
Lk 20: 18 on that stone will be *b* to pieces,
Jn 7: 23 the law of Moses may not be *b,*
10: 35 and the Scripture cannot be *b*—
19: 36 "Not one of his bones will be *b,*"
Ro 11: 20 they were *b* off because of unbelief,

BROKENHEARTED* (HEART)
Ps 34: 18 The Lord is close to the *b*
109: 16 and the needy and the *b.*
147: 3 He heals the *b*
Isa 61: 1 He has sent me to bind up the *b,*

BROKENNESS* (BREAK)
Isa 65: 14 and wail in *b* of spirit.

BRONZE
Ex 27: 2 and overlay the altar with *b.*
30: 18 "Make a *b* basin, with its *b* stand,
Nu 21: 9 So Moses made a *b* snake
Da 2: 32 and thighs of *b,* its legs of iron,
10: 6 legs like the gleam of burnished *b,*
Rev 1: 15 His feet were like *b* glowing
2: 18 whose feet are like burnished *b.*

BROTHER (BROTHER'S BROTHERHOOD BROTHERLY BROTHERS)
Pr 17: 17 and a *b* is born for adversity.
18: 24 a friend who sticks closer than a *b.*
27: 10 neighbor nearby than a *b* far away.
Mt 5: 24 and be reconciled to your *b;*
18: 15 "If your *b* sins against you,
Mk 3: 35 Whoever does God's will is my *b*
Lk 17: 3 "If your *b* sins, rebuke him,
Ro 14: 15 not by your eating destroy your *b*
14: 21 anything else that will cause your *b*
1Co 8: 13 if what I eat causes my *b* to fall
2Th 3: 6 away from every *b* who is idle
3: 15 as an enemy, but warn him as a *b.*
Phm : 16 but better than a slave, as a dear *b.*
Jas 2: 15 Suppose a *b* or sister is
4: 11 Anyone who speaks against his *b*
1Jn 2: 9 hates his *b* is still in the darkness.
2: 10 Whoever loves his *b* lives
2: 11 But whoever hates his *b* is
3: 10 is anyone who does not love his *b.*
3: 15 who hates his *b* is a murderer,
3: 17 material possessions and sees his *b*
4: 20 For anyone who does not love his *b*
4: 20 yet hates his *b,* he is a liar.
4: 21 loves God must also love his *b.*
5: 16 If anyone sees his *b* commit a sin

BROTHER'S (BROTHER)
Ge 4: 9 "Am I my *b* keeper?" The Lord
Mt 7: 5 remove the speck from your *b* eye.
Ro 14: 13 or obstacle in your *b* way.

BROTHERHOOD (BROTHER)
1Pe 2: 17 Love the *b* of believers, fear God,

ROTHERLY* (BROTHER)
12: 10 devoted to one another in *b* love.
4: 9 Now about *b* love we do not need
1: 7 and to godliness, *b* kindness;
1: 7 kindness; and to *b* kindness,

RS (BROTHER)
14 You are to help your *b*
is when *b* live together in unity!
who stirs up dissension among *b.*
"Here are my mother and my *b.*
veryone who has left houses or *b*
of the least of these *b* of mine,
o are my mother and my *b?*"
sisters or mother or father
betrayed even by parents, *b,*
ack, strengthen your *b.*"
did not believe in him.
e and strengthen the *b.*
st for the sake of my *b*

1Co 8: 12 sin against your *b* in this way
2Co 11: 26 and in danger from false *b.*
Gal 2: 4 some false *b* had infiltrated our
1Th 4: 10 you do love all the *b*
5: 26 Greet all the *b* with a holy kiss.
1Ti 6: 2 for them because they are *b.*
Heb 2: 11 Jesus is not ashamed to call them *b.*
2: 17 to be made like his *b* in every way,
13: 1 Keep on loving each other as *b.*
1Pe 1: 22 you have sincere love for your *b,*
3: 8 be sympathetic, love as *b,*
1Jn 3: 14 death to life, because we love our *b.*
3: 16 to lay down our lives for our *b.*
3Jn : 10 he refuses to welcome the *b.*
Rev 12: 10 For the accuser of our *b,*

BROW
Ge 3: 19 By the sweat of your *b*

BRUISED (BRUISES)
Isa 42: 3 A *b* reed he will not break,
Mt 12: 20 A *b* reed he will not break,

BRUISES (BRUISED)
Isa 30: 26 when the Lord binds up the *b*

BRUTAL (BRUTE)
2Ti 3: 3 slanderous, without self-control, *b,*

BRUTE* (BRUTAL)
Ps 73: 22 I was a *b* beast before you.
2Pe 2: 12 They are like *b* beasts, creatures

BUBBLING*
Pr 18: 4 the fountain of wisdom is a *b* brook
Isa 35: 7 the thirsty ground *b* springs.

BUCKET*
Isa 40: 15 the nations are like a drop in a *b;*

BUCKLED* (BUCKLER)
Eph 6: 14 belt of truth *b* around your waist,

BUCKLER* (BUCKLED)
Ps 35: 2 Take up shield and *b;*

BUD (BUDDED)
Isa 27: 6 Israel will *b* and blossom

BUDDED (BUD)
Heb 9: 4 Aaron's staff that had *b,*

BUILD (BUILDER BUILDERS BUILDING BUILDS BUILT REBUILD REBUILT)
2Sa 7: 5 Are you the one to *b* me a house
1Ki 6: 1 he began to *b* the temple
Ecc 3: 3 a time to tear down and a time to *b,*
Mt 16: 18 and on this rock I will *b* my church,
Ac 20: 32 which can *b* you up and give you
Ro 15: 2 neighbor for his good, to *b* him up.
1Co 14: 12 excel in gifts that *b* up the church.
1Th 5: 11 one another and *b* each other up,
Jude : 20 *b* yourselves up in your most holy

BUILDER* (BUILD)
1Co 3: 10 I laid a foundation as an expert *b,*
Heb 3: 3 the *b* of a house has greater honor
3: 4 but God is the *b* of everything.
11: 10 whose architect and *b* is God.

BUILDERS (BUILD)
Ps 118: 22 The stone the *b* rejected
Mt 21: 42 "'The stone the *b* rejected
Mk 12: 10 "'The stone the *b* rejected
Lk 20: 17 "'The stone the *b* rejected
Ac 4: 11 "'the stone you *b* rejected,
1Pe 2: 7 "The stone the *b* rejected

BUILDING (BUILD)
Ezr 3: 8 to supervise the *b* of the house
Ne 4: 17 of Judah who were *b* the wall.
Ro 15: 20 so that I would not be *b*
1Co 3: 9 you are God's field, God's *b.*
2Co 5: 1 we have a *b* from God, an eternal
10: 8 us for *b* you up rather
13: 10 the Lord gave me for *b* you up,
Eph 2: 21 him the whole *b* is joined together
4: 29 helpful for *b* others up according

BUILDS (BUILD)
Ps 127: 1 Unless the Lord *b* the house,
Pr 14: 1 The wise woman *b* her house,
1Co 3: 10 one should be careful how he *b.*
3: 12 If any man *b* on this foundation
8: 1 Knowledge puffs up, but love *b* up.
Eph 4: 16 grows and *b* itself up in love,

BUILT (BUILD)
1Ki 6: 14 So Solomon *b* the temple
Mt 7: 24 is like a wise man who *b* his house
Lk 6: 49 is like a man who *b* a house
Ac 17: 24 does not live in temples *b* by hands.

1Co 3: 14 If what he has *b* survives, he will
2Co 5: 1 in heaven, not *b* by human hands.
Eph 2: 20 *b* on the foundation of the apostles
4: 12 the body of Christ may be *b* up
Col 2: 7 live in him, rooted and *b* up in him,
1Pe 2: 5 are being *b* into a spiritual house

BULL (BULLS)
Lev 4: 3 bring to the Lord a young *b*

BULLS (BULL)
1Ki 7: 25 The Sea stood on twelve *b,*
Heb 10: 4 it is impossible for the blood of *b*

BURDEN (BURDENED BURDENS BURDENSOME)
Ps 38: 4 like a *b* too heavy to bear.
Ecc 1: 13 What a heavy *b* God has laid
Mt 11: 30 my yoke is easy and my *b* is light."
Ac 15: 28 to us not to *b* you with anything
2Co 11: 9 from being a *b* to you in any way,
12: 14 and I will not be a *b* to you,
1Th 2: 9 day in order not to be a *b* to anyone
2Th 3: 8 so that we would not be a *b* to any
Heb 13: 17 not a *b,* for that would be

BURDENED* (BURDEN)
Isa 43: 23 have not *b* you with grain offerings
43: 24 But you have *b* me with your sins
Mic 6: 3 How have I *b* you? Answer me.
Mt 11: 28 all you who are weary and *b,*
2Co 5: 4 are in this tent, we groan and are *b,*
Gal 5: 1 do not let yourselves be *b* again
1Ti 5: 16 not let the church be *b* with them,

BURDENS (BURDEN)
Ps 68: 19 who daily bears our *b.*
Lk 11: 46 down with *b* they can hardly carry,
Gal 6: 2 Carry each other's *b,*

BURDENSOME (BURDEN)
1Jn 5: 3 And his commands are not *b,*

BURIED (BURY)
Ru 1: 17 die I will die, and there I will be *b.*
Ro 6: 4 *b* with him through baptism
1Co 15: 4 that he was *b,* that he was raised
Col 2: 12 having been *b* with him in baptism

BURN (BURNING BURNT)
Dt 7: 5 and *b* their idols in the fire.
Ps 79: 5 long will your jealousy *b* like fire?
1Co 7: 9 to marry than to *b* with passion.

BURNING (BURN)
Ex 27: 20 so that the lamps may be kept *b.*
Lev 6: 9 the fire must be kept *b* on the altar.
Ps 18: 28 You, O Lord, keep my lamp *b;*
Pr 25: 22 you will heap *b* coals on his head,
Ro 12: 20 you will heap *b* coals on his head."
Rev 19: 20 alive into the fiery lake of *b* sulfur.

BURNISHED*
1Ki 7: 45 of the Lord were of *b* bronze.
Eze 1: 7 and gleamed like *b* bronze.
Da 10: 6 and legs like the gleam of *b* bronze,
Rev 2: 18 and whose feet are like *b* bronze.

BURNT (BURN)
Ge 8: 20 he sacrificed *b* offerings on it.
22: 2 as a *b* offering on one
Ex 10: 25 and *b* offerings to present
18: 12 brought a *b* offering and other
40: 6 Place the altar of *b* offering in front
Lev 1: 3 "'If the offering is a *b* offering
Jos 8: 31 offered to the Lord *b* offerings
Jdg 6: 26 offer the second bull as a *b* offering
13: 16 But if you prepare a *b* offering,
1Ki 3: 4 offered a thousand *b* offerings
9: 25 year Solomon sacrificed *b* offerings
10: 5 and the *b* offerings he made
Ezr 3: 2 Israel to sacrifice *b* offerings on it,
Eze 43: 18 for sacrificing *b* offerings

BURST
Ps 98: 4 *b* into jubilant song with music;
Isa 44: 23 *B* into song, you mountains,
49: 13 *b* into song, O mountains!
52: 9 *B* into songs of joy together,
54: 1 *b* into song, shout for joy,
55: 12 will *b* into song before you,

BURY (BURIED)
Mt 8: 22 and let the dead *b* their own dead."
Lk 9: 60 "Let the dead *b* their own dead,

BUSH
Ex 3: 2 the *b* was on fire it did not burn up.
Mk 12: 26 the account of the *b,* how God said
Lk 20: 37 But in the account of the *b,*
Ac 7: 35 who appeared to him in the *b.*

BUSINESS
Ecc 4: 8 a miserable *b!*
Da 8: 27 and went about the king's *b.*
1Co 5: 12 What *b* is it of mine to judge those
1Th 4: 11 to mind your own *b* and to work
Jas 1: 11 even while he goes about his *b.*

BUSY*
1Ki 18: 27 Perhaps he is deep in thought, or *b,*
20: 40 While your servant was *b* here
Isa 32: 6 his mind is *b* with evil:
Hag 1: 9 of you is *b* with his own house.
2Th 3: 11 They are not *b;* they are
Tit 2: 5 to be *b* at home, to be kind,

BUSYBODIES*
2Th 3: 11 They are not busy; they are *b.*
1Ti 5: 13 *b,* saying things they ought not to.

BUY (BOUGHT BUYS)
Pr 23: 23 *B* the truth and do not sell it;
Isa 55: 1 Come, *b* wine and milk
Rev 13: 17 so that no one could *b* or sell

BUYS (BUY)
Pr 31: 16 She considers a field and *b* it;

BYWORD (WORD)
1Ki 9: 7 Israel will then become a *b*
Ps 44: 14 You have made us a *b*
Joel 2: 17 a *b* among the nations.

CAESAR
Mt 22: 21 "Give to *C* what is Caesar's,

CAIN
Firstborn of Adam (Ge 4:1), murdered brother Abel (Ge 4:1–16; 1Jn 3:12).

CAKE
Hos 7: 8 Ephraim is a flat *c* not turned over.

CALEB
Judahite who spied out Canaan (Nu 13:6); allowed to enter land because of faith (Nu 13:30–14:38; Dt 1:36). Possessed Hebron (Jos 14:6–15:19).

CALF
Ex 32: 4 into an idol cast in the shape of a *c,*
Pr 15: 17 than a fattened *c* with hatred.
Lk 15: 23 Bring the fattened *c* and kill it.
Ac 7: 41 made an idol in the form of a *c.*

CALL (CALLED CALLING CALLS)
1Ki 18: 24 I will *c* on the name of the LORD.
2Ki 5: 11 *c* on the name of the LORD his
1Ch 16: 8 to the LORD, *c* on his name;
Ps 105: 1 to the LORD, *c* on his name;
116: 13 and *c* on the name of the LORD.
116: 17 and *c* on the name of the LORD.
145: 18 near to all who *c* on him,
Pr 31: 28 children arise and *c* her blessed;
Isa 5: 20 Woe to those who *c* evil good
12: 4 to the LORD, *c* on his name;
55: 6 *c* on him while he is near.
65: 24 Before they *c* I will answer;
Jer 33: 3 '*C* to me and I will answer you
Zep 3: 9 that all of them may *c* on the name
Zec 13: 9 They will *c* on my name
Mt 9: 13 come to *c* the righteous,
Mk 2: 17 I have not come to *c* the righteous,
Lk 5: 32 I have not come to *c* the righteous,
Ac 2: 39 all whom the Lord our God will *c.*"
9: 14 to arrest all who *c* on your name."
9: 21 among those who *c* on this name?
Ro 10: 12 and richly blesses all who *c* on him,
11: 29 gifts and his *c* are irrevocable.
1Co 1: 2 with all those everywhere who *c*
1Th 4: 7 For God did not *c* us to be impure,
2Ti 2: 22 along with those who *c*

CALLED (CALL)
Ge 2: 23 she shall be *c* 'woman,'
5: 2 he blessed them and *c* them "man
12: 8 and *c* on the name of the LORD.
21: 33 and there he *c* upon the name
26: 25 and *c* on the name of the LORD.
1Sa 3: 5 and said, "Here I am; you *c* me."
2Ch 7: 14 if my people, who are *c*
Ps 34: 6 This poor man *c,* and the LORD
116: 4 Then I *c* on the name of the LORD
Isa 56: 7 for my house will be *c*
La 3: 55 I *c* on your name, O LORD,
Hos 11: 1 and out of Egypt I *c* my son.
Mt 1: 16 was born Jesus, who is *c* Christ.
2: 15 "Out of Egypt I *c* my son."
21: 13 "'My house will be *c* a house
Mk 11: 17 "'My house will be *c*
Lk 1: 32 will be *c* the Son of the Most High.
1: 35 to be born will be *c* the Son of God.
Ro 1: 1 *c* to be an apostle and set apart
1: 6 among those who are *c* to belong
1: 7 loved by God and *c* to be saints:
8: 28 who have been *c* according
8: 30 And those he predestined, he also *c*
1Co 1: 1 *c* to be an apostle of Christ Jesus
1: 2 in Christ Jesus and *c* to be holy,
1: 24 but to those whom God has *c,*
1: 26 of what you were when you were *c.*
7: 15 God has *c* us to live in peace.
7: 17 and to which God has *c* him.
Gal 1: 6 deserting the one who *c* you
1: 15 from birth and *c* me by his grace,
5: 13 You, my brothers, were *c* to be free
Eph 1: 18 the hope to which he has *c* you,
4: 4 as you were *c* to one hope
Col 3: 15 of one body you were *c* to peace.
2Th 2: 14 He *c* you to this through our gospel
1Ti 6: 12 life to which you were *c*
2Ti 1: 9 who has saved us and *c* us
Heb 9: 15 that those who are *c* may receive
1Pe 1: 15 But just as he who *c* you is holy,
2: 9 of him who *c* you out of darkness
3: 9 to this you were *c* so that you may
5: 10 who *c* you to his eternal glory
2Pe 1: 3 of him who *c* us by his own glory
Jude : 1 To those who have been *c,*

CALLING (CALL)
Isa 40: 3 A voice of one *c:*
Mt 3: 3 "A voice of one *c* in the desert,
Mk 1: 3 "a voice of one *c* in the desert,
10: 49 Cheer up! On your feet! He's *c* you
Lk 3: 4 "A voice of one *c* in the desert,
Jn 1: 23 I am the voice of one *c* in the desert
Ac 22: 16 wash your sins away, *c* on his name
Eph 4: 1 worthy of the *c* you have received.
2Th 1: 11 may count you worthy of his *c,*
2Pe 1: 10 all the more eager to make your *c*

CALLOUS* (CALLOUSED)
Ps 17: 10 They close up their *c* hearts,
73: 7 From their *c* hearts comes iniquity;
119: 70 Their hearts are *c* and unfeeling,

CALLOUSED* (CALLOUS)
Isa 6: 10 Make the heart of this people *c;*
Mt 13: 15 this people's heart has become *c;*
Ac 28: 27 this people's heart has become *c;*

CALLS (CALL)
Ps 147: 4 and *c* them each by name.
Isa 40: 26 and *c* them each by name.
Joel 2: 32 And everyone who *c*
Mt 22: 43 speaking by the Spirit, *c* him 'Lord
Jn 10: 3 He *c* his own sheep by name
Ac 2: 21 And everyone who *c*
Ro 10: 13 "Everyone who *c* on the name
1Th 2: 12 who *c* you into his kingdom
5: 24 The one who *c* you is faithful

CALM (CALMS)
Ps 107: 30 They were glad when it grew *c,*
Isa 7: 4 keep *c* and don't be afraid.
Eze 16: 42 I will be *c* and no longer angry.

CALMS* (CALM)
Pr 15: 18 but a patient man *c* a quarrel.

CAMEL
Mt 19: 24 it is easier for a *c* to go
23: 24 strain out a gnat but swallow a *c.*
Mk 10: 25 It is easier for a *c* to go
Lk 18: 25 it is easier for a *c* to go

CAMP (ENCAMPS)
Heb 13: 13 outside the *c,* bearing the disgrace

CANAAN (CANAANITE CANAANITES)
Ge 10: 15 *C* was the father of Sidon his
Lev 14: 34 "When you enter the land of *C,*
25: 38 of Egypt to give you the land of *C*
Nu 13: 2 men to explore the land of *C,*
33: 51 'When you cross the Jordan into *C,*
Jdg 4: 2 a king of *C,* who reigned in Hazor.
1Ch 16: 18 "To you I will give the land of *C*
Ps 105: 11 "To you I will give the land of *C*
Ac 13: 19 he overthrew seven nations in *C*

CANAANITE (CANAAN)
Ge 10: 18 Later the *C* clans scattered
28: 1 "Do not marry a *C* woman.
Jos 5: 1 all the *C* kings along the seacoast
Jdg 1: 32 lived among the *C* inhabitants

CANAANITES (CANAAN)
Ex 33: 2 before you and drive out the *C,*

CANCEL (CANCELED)
Dt 15: 1 seven years you must *c* debts.

CANCELED (CANCEL)
Mt 18: 27 pity on him, *c* the debt
Lk 7: 42 so he *c* the debts of both.
Col 2: 14 having *c* the written code,

CANDLESTICKS see LAMPSTANDS

CANOPY*
2Sa 22: 12 He made darkness his *c*
2Ki 16: 18 away the Sabbath *c* that had been
Ps 18: 11 made darkness his covering, his *c*
Isa 4: 5 over all the glory will be a *c.*
40: 22 stretches out the heavens like a *c,*
Jer 43: 10 he will spread his royal *c*

CAPERNAUM
Mt 4: 13 Nazareth, he went and lived in *C,*
Jn 6: 59 teaching in the synagogue in *C.*

CAPITAL
Dt 21: 22 guilty of a *c* offense is put to death

CAPSTONE* (STONE)
Ps 118: 22 has become the *c;*
Zec 4: 7 he will bring out the *c* to shouts
Mt 21: 42 has become the *c;*
Mk 12: 10 has become the *c;*
Lk 20: 17 has become the *c*'?
Ac 4: 11 which has become the *c.*'
1Pe 2: 7 has become the *c,*"

CAPTIVATE* (CAPTIVE)
Pr 6: 25 or let her *c* you with her eyes,

CAPTIVATED* (CAPTIVE)
Pr 5: 19 may you ever be *c* by her love.
5: 20 Why be *c,* my son, by an adulteress

CAPTIVE (CAPTIVATE CAPTIVATED CAPTIVES CAPTIVITY CAPTURED)
Ac 8: 23 full of bitterness and *c* to sin."
2Co 10: 5 and we take *c* every thought
Col 2: 8 See to it that no one takes you *c*
2Ti 2: 26 who has taken them *c* to do his will.

CAPTIVES (CAPTIVE)
Ps 68: 18 you led *c* in your train;
Isa 61: 1 to proclaim freedom for the *c*
Eph 4: 8 he led *c* in his train

CAPTIVITY (CAPTIVE)
Dt 28: 41 because they will go into *c.*
2Ki 25: 21 So Judah went into *c,* away
Jer 30: 3 Israel and Judah back from *c*
52: 27 So Judah went into *c,* away
Eze 29: 14 I will bring them back from *c*

CAPTURED (CAPTIVE)
1Sa 4: 11 The ark of God was *c,*
2Sa 5: 7 David *c* the fortress of Zion,
2Ki 17: 6 the king of Assyria *c* Samaria

CARCASS
Jdg 14: 9 taken the honey from the lion's *c.*
Mt 24: 28 there is a *c,* there the vultures

CARE (CAREFUL CARES CARING)
Ps 8: 4 the son of man that you *c* for him?
65: 9 You *c* for the land and water it;
144: 3 what is man that you *c* for him,
Pr 29: 7 The righteous *c* about justice
Mk 5: 26 deal under the *c* of many doctors
Lk 10: 34 him to an inn and took *c* of him.
18: 4 I don't fear God or *c* about men,
Jn 21: 16 Jesus said, "Take *c* of my sheep."
1Ti 3: 5 how can he take *c* of God's church
6: 20 what has been entrusted to your *c.*
Heb 2: 6 the son of man that you *c* for him?
1Pe 5: 2 of God's flock that is under your *c,*

CAREFUL* (CARE)
Ge 31: 24 "Be *c* not to say anything to Jacob,
31: 29 'Be *c* not to say anything to Jacob,
Ex 19: 12 'Be *c* that you do not go up
23: 13 "Be *c* to do everything I have said
34: 12 Be *c* not to make a treaty
34: 15 "Be *c* not to make a treaty
Lev 18: 4 and be *c* to follow my decrees.
25: 18 "'Follow my decrees and be *c*
26: 3 and are *c* to obey my commands,
Dt 2: 4 afraid of you, but be very *c.*
4: 9 before you today? Only be *c,*
4: 23 Be *c* not to forget the covenant
5: 32 So be *c* to do what the LORD your
6: 3 be *c* to obey so that it may go well
6: 12 be *c* that you do not forget
6: 25 And if we are *c* to obey all this law
7: 12 attention to these laws and are *c*
8: 1 Be *c* to follow every command I am
8: 11 Be *c* that you do not forget
11: 16 Be *c,* or you will be enticed

Dt 12: 1 and laws you must be *c* to follow
12: 13 Be *c* not to sacrifice your burnt
12: 19 Be *c* not to neglect the Levites
12: 28 Be *c* to obey all these regulations I
12: 30 be *c* not to be ensnared
15: 5 are *c* to follow all these commands
15: 9 Be *c* not to harbor this wicked
17: 10 Be *c* to do everything they direct
24: 8 cases of leprous diseases be very *c*
Jos 1: 7 Be *c* to obey all the law my servant
1: 8 so that you may be *c*
22: 5 But be very *c* to keep
23: 6 be *c* to obey all that is written
23: 11 be very *c* to love the LORD your
1Ki 8: 25 if only your sons are *c* in all they do
2Ki 10: 31 Yet Jehu was not *c* to keep the law
17: 37 You must always be *c*
21: 8 if only they will be *c*
1Ch 22: 13 if you are *c* to observe the decrees
28: 8 Be *c* to follow all the commands
2Ch 6: 16 if only your sons are *c* in all they do
33: 8 if only they will be *c*
Ezr 4: 22 Be *c* not to neglect this matter.
Job 36: 18 Be *c* that no one entices you
Ps 101: 2 I will be *c* to lead a blameless life —
Pr 13: 24 he who loves him is *c*
27: 23 give *c* attention to your herds;
Isa 7: 4 Be *c*, keep calm and don't be afraid.
Jer 17: 21 Be *c* not to carry a load
17: 24 But if you are *c* to obey me,
22: 4 For if you are *c* to carry out these
Eze 11: 20 will follow my decrees and be *c*
18: 19 has been *c* to keep all my decrees,
20: 19 follow my decrees and be *c*
20: 21 they were not *c* to keep my laws —
36: 27 you to follow my decrees and be *c*
37: 24 and be *c* to keep my decrees.
Mic 7: 5 be *c* of your words.
Hag 1: 5 "Give *c* thought to your ways.
1: 7 "Give *c* thought to your ways.
2: 15 give *c* thought to this from this day
2: 18 Give *c* thought: Is there yet any
2: 18 give *c* thought to the day
Mt 2: 8 and make a *c* search for the child.
6: 1 "Be *c* not to do your 'acts
16: 6 "Be *c*," Jesus said to them.
Mk 8: 15 "Be *c*," Jesus warned them.
Lk 21: 34 Be *c*, or your hearts will be weighed
Ro 12: 17 Be *c* to do what is right in the eyes
1Co 3: 10 each one should be *c* how he builds
8: 9 Be *c*, however, that the exercise
10: 12 standing firm, be *c* that you don't
Eph 5: 15 Be very *c*, then, how you live —
2Ti 4: 2 great patience and *c* instruction.
Tit 3: 8 may be *c* to devote themselves
Heb 2: 1 We must pay more *c* attention,
4: 1 let us be *c* that none

CARELESS*
Mt 12: 36 for every *c* word they have spoken.

CARES* (CARE)
Dt 11: 12 It is a land the LORD your God *c*
Job 39: 16 she *c* not that her labor was in vain,
Ps 55: 22 Cast your *c* on the LORD
142: 4 no one *c* for my life.
Pr 12: 10 A righteous man *c* for the needs
Ecc 5: 3 when there are many *c*,
Jer 12: 11 because there is no one who *c*.
30: 17 Zion for whom no one *c*.'
Na 1: 7 He *c* for those who trust in him,
Jn 10: 13 and *c* nothing for the sheep.
Eph 5: 29 but he feeds and *c* for it, just
1Pe 5: 7 on him because he *c* for you.

CARING* (CARE)
1Th 2: 7 like a mother *c* for her little
1Ti 5: 4 practice by *c* for their own family

CARPENTER (CARPENTER'S)
Mk 6: 3 does miracles! Isn't this the *c*?

CARPENTER'S* (CARPENTER)
Mt 13: 55 "Isn't this the *c* son? Isn't his

CARRIED (CARRY)
Ex 19: 4 and how I *c* you on eagles' wings
Dt 1: 31 how the LORD your God *c* you,
Isa 53: 4 and *c* our sorrows,
63: 9 he lifted them up and *c* them
Mt 8: 17 and *c* our diseases."
Heb 13: 9 Do not be *c* away by all kinds
2Pe 1: 21 as they were *c* along by the Holy
3: 17 so that you may not be *c* away

CARRIES (CARRY)
Dt 32: 11 and *c* them on its pinions.
Isa 40: 11 and *c* them close to his heart;

CARRY (CARRIED CARRIES CARRYING)
Lev 16: 22 goat will *c* on itself all their sins
26: 15 and fail to *c* out all my commands
Isa 46: 4 I have made you and I will *c* you;
Lk 14: 27 anyone who does not *c* his cross
Gal 6: 2 *C* each other's burdens,
6: 5 for each one should *c* his own load.

CARRYING (CARRY)
Jn 19: 17 *C* his own cross, he went out
1Jn 5: 2 loving God and *c* out his

CARVED (CARVES)
Nu 33: 52 Destroy all their *c* images
Mic 5: 13 I will destroy your *c* images

CARVES* (CARVED)
Dt 27: 15 "Cursed is the man who *c* an image

CASE
Pr 18: 17 to present his *c* seems right,
22: 23 for the LORD will take up their *c*
23: 11 he will take up their *c* against you.

CAST (CASTING)
Ex 34: 17 "Do not make *c* idols.
Lev 16: 8 He is to *c* lots for the two goats —
Ps 22: 18 and *c* lots for my clothing.
55: 22 *C* your cares on the LORD
Pr 16: 33 The lot is *c* into the lap,
Ecc 11: 1 *C* your bread upon the waters,
Jn 19: 24 and *c* lots for my clothing."
1Pe 5: 7 *C* all your anxiety on him

CASTING (CAST)
Pr 18: 18 *C* the lot settles disputes
Mt 27: 35 divided up his clothes by *c* lots.

CATCH (CATCHES CAUGHT)
Lk 5: 4 and let down the nets for a *c*."
5: 10 from now on you will *c* men."

CATCHES (CATCH)
Job 5: 13 He *c* the wise in their craftiness,
1Co 3: 19 "He *c* the wise in their craftiness";

CATTLE
Ps 50: 10 and the *c* on a thousand hills.

CAUGHT (CATCH)
Ge 22: 13 there in a thicket he saw a ram *c*
2Co 12: 2 who fourteen years ago was *c* up
1Th 4: 17 and are left will be *c* up together with them

CAUSE (CAUSES)
Pr 24: 28 against your neighbor without *c*,
Ecc 8: 3 Do not stand up for a bad *c*,
Mt 18: 7 of the things that *c* people to sin!
Ro 14: 21 else that will *c* your brother
1Co 10: 32 Do not *c* anyone to stumble,

CAUSES (CAUSE)
Ps 7: 16 The trouble he *c* recoils on himself;
Isa 8: 14 a stone that *c* men to stumble
Mt 5: 29 If your right eye *c* you to sin,
5: 30 And if your right hand *c* you to sin,
18: 6 if anyone *c* one of these little ones
18: 8 or your foot *c* you to sin,
Ro 14: 20 to eat anything that *c* someone else
1Co 8: 13 if what I eat *c* my brother to fall
1Pe 2: 8 "A stone that *c* men to stumble

CAUTIOUS*
Pr 12: 26 A righteous man is *c* in friendship,

CEASE
Ps 46: 9 He makes wars *c* to the ends

CELEBRATE*
Ex 10: 9 we are to *c* a festival to the LORD
12: 14 generations to come you shall *c* it
12: 17 *C* this day as a lasting ordinance
12: 17 "*C* the Feast of Unleavened Bread,
12: 47 community of Israel must *c* it.
12: 48 to *c* the LORD's Passover must
23: 14 are to *c* a festival to me.
23: 15 "*C* the Feast of Unleavened Bread;
23: 16 "*C* the Feast of Harvest
23: 16 "*C* the Feast of Ingathering
34: 18 "*C* the Feast of Unleavened Bread.
34: 22 "*C* the Feast of Weeks
Lev 23: 39 *c* the festival to the LORD
23: 41 *C* this as a festival to the LORD
23: 41 for the generations to come; *c* it
Nu 9: 2 "Have the Israelites *c* the Passover
9: 3 *C* it at the appointed time,
9: 4 told the Israelites to *c* the Passover,
9: 6 of them could not *c* the Passover
9: 10 they may still *c* the LORD's
9: 11 are to *c* it on the fourteenth day
9: 12 When they *c* the Passover,
9: 13 on a journey fails to *c* the Passover,
9: 14 to *c* the LORD's Passover must do
29: 12 *C* a festival to the LORD
Dt 16: 1 *c* the Passover of the LORD your
16: 10 Then *c* the Feast of Weeks
16: 13 *C* the Feast of Tabernacles
16: 15 For seven days *c* the Feast
Jdg 16: 23 to Dagon their god and to *c*,
2Sa 6: 21 the LORD's people Israel — I will *c*
2Ki 23: 21 "*C* the Passover to the LORD your
2Ch 30: 1 and *c* the Passover to the LORD,
30: 2 decided to *c* the Passover
30: 3 able to *c* it at the regular time
30: 5 and *c* the Passover to the LORD,
30: 13 in Jerusalem to *c* the Feast
30: 23 to *c* the festival seven more days;
Ne 8: 12 of food and to *c* with great joy,
12: 27 to *c* joyfully the dedication
Est 9: 21 to have them *c* annually
Ps 145: 7 They will *c* your abundant
Isa 30: 29 as on the night you *c* a holy festival
Na 1: 15 *C* your festivals, O Judah,
Zec 14: 16 and to *c* the Feast of Tabernacles.
14: 18 up to *c* the Feast of Tabernacles.
14: 19 up to *c* the Feast of Tabernacles.
Mt 26: 18 I am going to *c* the Passover
Lk 15: 23 Let's have a feast and *c*.
15: 24 So they began to *c*.
15: 29 goat so I could *c* with my friends.
15: 32 But we had to *c* and be glad,
Rev 11: 10 will *c* by sending each other gifts,

CELESTIAL*
2Pe 2: 10 afraid to slander *c* beings;
Jude : 8 authority and slander *c* beings.

CENSER (CENSERS)
Lev 16: 12 is to take a *c* full of burning coals
Rev 8: 3 Another angel, who had a golden *c*,

CENSERS (CENSER)
Nu 16: 6 Take *c* and tomorrow put fire

CENTURION
Mt 8: 5 had entered Capernaum, a *c* came
27: 54 When the *c* and those
Mk 15: 39 And when the *c*, who stood there
Lk 7: 3 The *c* heard of Jesus and sent some
23: 47 The *c*, seeing what had happened,
Ac 10: 1 a *c* in what was known
27: 1 handed over to a *c* named Julius,

CEPHAS* (PETER)
Jn 1: 42 You will be called *C*" (which,
1Co 1: 12 another, "I follow *C*"; still another,
3: 22 Paul or Apollos or *C* or the world
9: 5 and the Lord's brothers and *C*?

CEREMONIAL* (CEREMONY)
Lev 14: 2 at the time of his *c* cleansing,
15: 13 off seven days for his *c* cleansing;
Mk 7: 3 they give their hands a *c* washing,
Jn 2: 6 used by the Jews for *c* washing,
3: 25 Jew over the matter of *c* washing.
11: 55 to Jerusalem for their *c* cleansing
18: 28 to avoid *c* uncleanness the Jews did
Heb 9: 10 drink and various *c* washings —
13: 9 not by *c* foods, which are

CEREMONIALLY* (CEREMONY)
Lev 4: 12 outside the camp to a place *c* clean,
5: 2 touches anything *c* unclean —
6: 11 the camp to a place that is *c* clean.
7: 19 anyone *c* clean may eat it.
7: 19 touches anything *c* unclean must
10: 14 Eat them in a *c* clean place;
11: 4 not have a split hoof; it is *c* unclean
12: 2 birth to a son will be *c* unclean
12: 7 and then she will be *c* clean
13: 3 he shall pronounce him *c* unclean.
14: 8 with water; then he will be *c* clean.
15: 28 and after that she will be *c* clean.
15: 33 lies with a woman who is *c* unclean.
17: 15 he will be *c* unclean till evening.
21: 1 must not make himself *c* unclean
22: 3 of your descendants is *c* unclean
27: 11 he vowed is a *c* unclean animal —
Nu 5: 2 who is *c* unclean because of a dead
6: 7 must not make himself *c* unclean
8: 6 Israelites and make them *c* clean.
9: 6 they were *c* unclean on account
9: 13 But if a man who is *c* clean
18: 11 household who is *c* clean may eat
18: 13 household who is *c* clean may eat
19: 7 but he will be *c* unclean till evening
19: 9 and put them in a *c* clean place
19: 18 Then a man who is *c* clean is

Dt 12: 15 Both the *c* unclean and the clean
12: 22 Both the *c* unclean and the clean
14: 7 they are *c* unclean for you.
15: 22 Both the *c* unclean and the clean
1Sa 20: 26 to David to make him *c* unclean—
2Ch 13: 11 the bread on the *c* clean table
30: 17 for all those who were not *c* clean
Ezr 6: 20 themselves and were all *c* clean.
Ne 12: 30 Levites had purified themselves *c*,
Isa 66: 20 of the LORD in *c* clean vessels.
Eze 22: 10 period, when they are *c* unclean.
Ac 24: 18 I was *c* clean when they found me
Heb 9: 13 those who are *c* unclean sanctify

CEREMONY* (CEREMONIAL CEREMONIALLY)
Ge 50: 11 Egyptians are holding a solemn *c*
Ex 12: 25 as he promised, observe this *c*.
12: 26 'What does this *c* mean to you?'
13: 5 are to observe this *c* in this month:

CERTAIN (CERTAINTY)
2Pe 1: 19 word of the prophets made more *c*,

CERTAINTY* (CERTAIN)
Lk 1: 4 so that you may know the *c*
Jn 17: 8 They knew with *c* that I came

CERTIFICATE* (CERTIFIED)
Dt 24: 1 and he writes her a *c* of divorce,
24: 3 and writes her a *c* of divorce,
Isa 50: 1 "Where is your mother's *c*
Jer 3: 8 I gave faithless Israel her *c*
Mt 5: 31 divorces his wife must give her a *c*
19: 7 that a man give his wife a *c*
Mk 10: 4 a man to write a *c* of divorce

CERTIFIED* (CERTIFICATE)
Jn 3: 33 has accepted it has *c* that God is

CHAFF
Ps 1: 4 They are like *c*
35: 5 May they be like *c* before the wind,
Da 2: 35 became like *c* on a threshing floor
Mt 3: 12 up the *c* with unquenchable fire."

CHAINED (CHAINS)
2Ti 2: 9 But God's word is not *c*.

CHAINS (CHAINED)
Eph 6: 20 for which I am an ambassador in *c*.
Col 4: 18 Remember my *c*.
2Ti 1: 16 and was not ashamed of my *c*.
Jude : 6 with everlasting *c* for judgment

CHAMPION
Ps 19: 5 like a *c* rejoicing to run his course.

CHANCE
Ecc 9: 11 but time and *c* happen to them all.

CHANGE (CHANGED)
1Sa 15: 29 of Israel does not lie or *c* his mind;
Ps 110: 4 and will not *c* his mind:
Jer 7: 5 If you really *c* your ways
Mal 3: 6 "I the LORD do not *c*.
Mt 18: 3 unless you *c* and become like little
Heb 7: 21 and will not *c* his mind:
Jas 1: 17 who does not *c* like shifting

CHANGED (CHANGE)
1Sa 10: 6 you will be *c* into a different person
Hos 11: 8 My heart is *c* within me;
1Co 15: 51 but we will all be *c*— in a flash,

CHARACTER*
Ru 3: 11 that you are a woman of noble *c*.
Pr 12: 4 of noble *c* is her husband's crown,
31: 10 A wife of noble *c* who can find?
Ac 17: 11 noble *c* than the Thessalonians,
Ro 5: 4 perseverance, *c*; and *c*, hope.
1Co 15: 33 "Bad company corrupts good *c*."

CHARGE (CHARGES)
Job 34: 13 him in *c* of the whole world?
Ro 8: 33 Who will bring any *c*
1Co 9: 18 the gospel I may offer it free of *c*,
2Co 11: 7 the gospel of God to you free of *c*?
2Ti 4: 1 I give you this *c*: Preach the Word;
Phm : 18 or owes you anything, *c* it to me.

CHARGES (CHARGE)
Isa 50: 8 Who then will bring *c* against me?

CHARIOT (CHARIOTS)
2Ki 2: 11 suddenly a *c* of fire and horses
Ps 104: 3 He makes the clouds his *c*
Ac 8: 28 sitting in his *c* reading the book

CHARIOTS (CHARIOT)
2Ki 6: 17 and *c* of fire all around Elisha.
Ps 20: 7 Some trust in *c* and some in horses,
68: 17 The *c* of God are tens of thousands

CHARM* (CHARMING)
Pr 17: 8 bribe is a *c* to the one who gives it;
31: 30 *C* is deceptive, and beauty is

CHARMING* (CHARM)
Pr 26: 25 his speech is *c*, do not believe
SS 1: 16 Oh, how *c*!

CHASE (CHASES)
Lev 26: 8 Five of you will *c* a hundred,

CHASES* (CHASE)
Pr 12: 11 he who *c* fantasies lacks judgment.
28: 19 one who *c* fantasies will have his

CHASM*
Lk 16: 26 and you a great *c* has been fixed,

CHATTER* (CHATTERING)
1Ti 6: 20 Turn away from godless *c*
2Ti 2: 16 Avoid godless *c*, because those

CHATTERING* (CHATTER)
Pr 10: 8 but a *c* fool comes to ruin.
10: 10 and a *c* fool comes to ruin.

CHEAT* (CHEATED CHEATING CHEATS)
Mal 1: 14 "Cursed is the *c* who has
1Co 6: 8 you yourselves *c* and do wrong,

CHEATED* (CHEAT)
Ge 31: 7 yet your father has *c* me
1Sa 12: 3 Whom have I *c*? Whom have I
12: 4 "You have not *c* or oppressed us,"
Lk 19: 8 if I have *c* anybody out of anything,
1Co 6: 7 Why not rather be *c*? Instead,

CHEATING* (CHEAT)
Am 8: 5 and *c* with dishonest scales,

CHEATS* (CHEAT)
Lev 6: 2 or if he *c* him, or if he finds lost

CHEEK (CHEEKS)
Mt 5: 39 someone strikes you on the right *c*,
Lk 6: 29 If someone strikes you on one *c*,

CHEEKS (CHEEK)
Isa 50: 6 my *c* to those who pulled out my

CHEERFUL* (CHEERS)
Pr 15: 13 A happy heart makes the face *c*,
15: 15 but the *c* heart has a continual feast
15: 30 A *c* look brings joy to the heart,
17: 22 A *c* heart is good medicine,
2Co 9: 7 for God loves a *c* giver.

CHEERS (CHEERFUL)
Pr 12: 25 but a kind word *c* him up.

CHEMOSH
2Ki 23: 13 for *C* the vile god of Moab,

CHERISH (CHERISHED CHERISHES)
Ps 17: 14 You still the hunger of those you *c*;

CHERISHED (CHERISH)
Ps 66: 18 If I had *c* sin in my heart,

CHERISHES* (CHERISH)
Pr 19: 8 he who *c* understanding prospers.

CHERUB (CHERUBIM)
Ex 25: 19 Make one *c* on one end
Eze 28: 14 You were anointed as a guardian *c*,

CHERUBIM (CHERUB)
Ge 3: 24 side of the Garden of Eden *c*
1Sa 4: 4 who is enthroned between the *c*.
2Sa 6: 2 enthroned between the *c* that are
22: 11 He mounted the *c* and flew;
1Ki 6: 23 a pair of *c* of olive wood,
2Ki 19: 15 of Israel, enthroned between the *c*,
1Ch 13: 6 who is enthroned between the *c*—
Ps 18: 10 He mounted the *c* and flew;
80: 1 who sit enthroned between the *c*,
99: 1 he sits enthroned between the *c*,
Isa 37: 16 of Israel, enthroned between the *c*,
Eze 10: 1 was over the heads of the *c*.

CHEST
Ex 25: 10 "Have them make a *c*
2Ki 12: 9 Jehoiada the priest took a *c*
Da 2: 32 its *c* and arms of silver, its belly
Rev 1: 13 with a golden sash around his *c*.

CHEWS
Lev 11: 3 divided and that *c* the cud.

CHIEF
1Pe 5: 4 And when the *C* Shepherd appears,

CHILD (CHILDISH CHILDREN CHILDREN'S GRANDCHILDREN)
Pr 20: 11 Even a *c* is known by his actions,
22: 6 Train a *c* in the way he should go,
22: 15 Folly is bound up in the heart of a *c*
23: 13 not withhold discipline from a *c*;
29: 15 *c* left to himself disgraces his mother.
Isa 7: 14 The virgin will be with *c*
9: 6 For to us a *c* is born,
11: 6 and a little *c* will lead them.
66: 13 As a mother comforts her *c*,
Mt 1: 23 "The virgin will be with *c*
18: 2 He called a little *c* and had him
Lk 1: 42 and blessed is the *c* you will bear!
1: 80 And the *c* grew and became strong
1Co 13: 11 When I was a *c*, I talked like a *c*,
1Jn 5: 1 who loves the father loves his *c*

CHILDBEARING (BEAR)
Ge 3: 16 greatly increase your pains in *c*;

CHILDBIRTH (BEAR)
Gal 4: 19 the pains of *c* until Christ is formed

CHILDISH* (CHILD)
1Co 13: 11 When I became a man, I put *c* ways

CHILDREN (CHILD)
Ex 20: 5 punishing the *c* for the sin
Dt 4: 9 Teach them to your *c*
6: 7 Impress them on your *c*.
11: 19 them to your *c*, talking about them
14: 1 You are the *c* of the LORD your
24: 16 nor *c* put to death for their fathers;
30: 19 so that you and your *c* may live
32: 46 so that you may command your *c*
Job 1: 5 "Perhaps my *c* have sinned
Ps 8: 2 From the lips of *c* and infants
78: 5 forefathers to teach their *c*,
Pr 17: 6 Children's *c* are a crown
20: 7 blessed are his *c* after him.
31: 28 Her *c* arise and call her blessed;
Joel 1: 3 Tell it to your *c*,
Mal 4: 6 the hearts of the fathers to their *c*,
Mt 7: 11 how to give good gifts to your *c*,
11: 25 and revealed them to little *c*.
18: 3 you change and become like little *c*
19: 14 "Let the little *c* come to me,
21: 16 "'From the lips of *c* and infants
Mk 9: 37 one of these little *c* in my name
10: 14 "Let the little *c* come to me,
10: 16 And he took the *c* in his arms,
13: 12 *C* will rebel against their parents
Lk 10: 21 and revealed them to little *c*.
18: 16 "Let the little *c* come to me,
Jn 1: 12 the right to become *c* of God—
Ac 2: 39 The promise is for you and your *c*
Ro 8: 16 with our spirit that we are God's *c*.
1Co 14: 20 Brothers, stop thinking like *c*.
2Co 12: 14 parents, but parents for their *c*.
Eph 6: 1 *C*, obey your parents in the Lord,
6: 4 do not exasperate your *c*; instead,
Col 3: 20 *C*, obey your parents in everything,
3: 21 Fathers, do not embitter your *c*,
1Ti 3: 4 and see that his *c* obey him
3: 12 and must manage his *c* and his
5: 10 bringing up *c*, showing hospitality,
Heb 2: 13 and the *c* God has given me."
1Jn 3: 1 that we should be called *c* of God!

CHILDREN'S (CHILD)
Isa 54: 13 and great will be your *c* peace.

CHOKE
Mk 4: 19 come in and *c* the word,

CHOOSE (CHOOSES CHOSE CHOSEN)
Dt 30: 19 Now *c* life, so that you
Jos 24: 15 then *c* for yourselves this day
Pr 8: 10 *C* my instruction instead of silver,
16: 16 to *c* understanding rather
Jn 15: 16 You did not *c* me, but I chose you

CHOOSES (CHOOSE)
Mt 11: 27 to whom the Son *c* to reveal him.
Lk 10: 22 to whom the Son *c* to reveal him."
Jn 7: 17 If anyone *c* to do God's will,

CHOSE (CHOOSE)
Ge 13: 11 So Lot *c* for himself the whole plain
Ps 33: 12 the people he *c* for his inheritance.
Jn 15: 16 but I *c* you and appointed you to go
1Co 1: 27 But God *c* the foolish things
Eph 1: 4 he *c* us in him before the creation
2Th 2: 13 from the beginning God *c* you

CHOSEN (CHOOSE)
Isa 41: 8 Jacob, whom I have *c*,
Mt 22: 14 For many are invited, but few are *c*

Lk 10: 42 Mary has *c* what is better,
23: 35 the Christ of God, the *C* One."
Jn 15: 19 but I have *c* you out of the world.
1Pe 1: 20 He was *c* before the creation
2: 9 But you are a *c* people, a royal

CHRIST (CHRIST'S CHRISTIAN CHRISTIANS CHRISTS)
Mt 1: 16 was born Jesus, who is called *C*.
16: 16 Peter answered, "You are the *C*,
22: 42 "What do you think about the *C*?
Mk 1: 1 of the gospel about Jesus *C*,
8: 29 Peter answered, "You are the *C*."
14: 61 "Are you the *C*, the Son
Lk 9: 20 Peter answered, "The *C* of God."
Jn 1: 41 found the Messiah" (that is, the *C*).
20: 31 you may believe that Jesus is the *C*,
Ac 2: 36 you crucified, both Lord and *C*."
5: 42 the good news that Jesus is the *C*.
9: 22 by proving that Jesus is the *C*.
9: 34 said to him, "Jesus *C* heals you.
17: 3 proving that the *C* had to suffer
18: 28 the Scriptures that Jesus was the *C*.
26: 23 that the *C* would suffer and,
Ro 1: 4 from the dead: Jesus *C* our Lord.
3: 22 comes through faith in Jesus *C*
5: 1 God through our Lord Jesus *C*,
5: 6 we were still powerless, *C* died
5: 8 While we were still sinners, *C* died
5: 11 in God through our Lord Jesus *C*,
5: 17 life through the one man, Jesus *C*.
6: 4 as *C* was raised from the dead
6: 9 that since *C* was raised
6: 23 life in *C* Jesus our Lord.
7: 4 to the law through the body of *C*,
8: 1 for those who are in *C* Jesus,
8: 9 Spirit of *C*, he does not belong to *C*.
8: 17 heirs of God and co-heirs with *C*,
8: 34 Who is he that condemns? *C* Jesus,
8: 35 us from the love of *C*?
9: 5 is traced the human ancestry of *C*,
10: 4 *C* is the end of the law
12: 5 so in *C* we who are many form one
13: 14 yourselves with the Lord Jesus *C*,
14: 9 *C* died and returned to life
15: 3 For even *C* did not please himself
15: 5 yourselves as you follow *C* Jesus,
15: 7 then, just as *C* accepted you,
16: 18 people are not serving our Lord *C*,
1Co 1: 2 to those sanctified in *C* Jesus
1: 7 for our Lord Jesus *C* to be revealed.
1: 13 Is *C* divided? Was Paul crucified
1: 17 For *C* did not send me to baptize,
1: 23 but we preach *C* crucified:
1: 30 of him that you are in *C* Jesus,
2: 2 except Jesus *C* and him crucified.
3: 11 one already laid, which is Jesus *C*.
5: 7 For *C*, our Passover lamb,
6: 15 bodies are members of *C* himself?
8: 6 and there is but one Lord, Jesus *C*,
8: 12 conscience, you sin against *C*.
10: 4 them, and that rock was *C*.
11: 1 as I follow the example of *C*.
11: 3 the head of every man is *C*,
12: 27 Now you are the body of *C*,
15: 3 that *C* died for our sins according
15: 14 And if *C* has not been raised,
15: 22 so in *C* all will be made alive.
15: 57 victory through our Lord Jesus *C*.
2Co 1: 5 as the sufferings of *C* flow
2: 14 us in triumphal procession in *C*
3: 3 show that you are a letter from *C*,
3: 14 because only in *C* is it taken away.
4: 4 light of the gospel of the glory of *C*,
4: 5 not preach ourselves, but Jesus *C*
4: 6 of the glory of God in the face of *C*.
5: 10 before the judgment seat of *C*,
5: 17 Therefore, if anyone is in *C*,
6: 15 What harmony is there between *C*
10: 1 the meekness and gentleness of *C*,
11: 2 you to one husband, to *C*,
Gal 1: 7 are trying to pervert the gospel of *C*
2: 4 on the freedom we have in *C* Jesus
2: 16 but by faith in Jesus *C*.
2: 17 does that mean that *C* promotes sin
2: 20 I have been crucified with *C*
2: 21 *C* died for nothing!" You foolish
3: 13 *C* redeemed us from the curse
3: 16 meaning one person, who is *C*.
3: 26 of God through faith in *C* Jesus,
4: 19 of childbirth until *C* is formed
5: 1 for freedom that *C* has set us free.
5: 4 by law have been alienated from *C*;
5: 24 to *C* Jesus have crucified the sinful
6: 14 in the cross of our Lord Jesus *C*,
Eph 1: 3 with every spiritual blessing in *C*.
1: 10 together under one head, even *C*.
1: 20 which he exerted in *C*
2: 5 made us alive with *C*
2: 10 created in *C* Jesus
2: 12 time you were separate from *C*,
2: 20 with *C* Jesus himself as the chief
3: 8 the unsearchable riches of *C*,
3: 17 so that *C* may dwell in your hearts
4: 7 has been given as *C* apportioned it.
4: 13 measure of the fullness of *C*.
4: 15 into him who is the Head, that is, *C*
4: 32 just as in *C* God forgave you.
5: 2 as *C* loved us and gave himself up
5: 21 out of reverence for *C*.
5: 23 as *C* is the head of the church,
5: 25 just as *C* loved the church
Php 1: 18 motives or true, *C* is preached.
1: 21 to live is *C* and to die is gain.
1: 23 I desire to depart and be with *C*,
1: 27 worthy of the gospel of *C*.
1: 29 on behalf of *C* not only to believe
2: 5 be the same as that of *C* Jesus:
3: 7 now consider loss for the sake of *C*.
3: 10 I want to know *C* and the power
3: 18 as enemies of the cross of *C*.
4: 19 to his glorious riches in *C* Jesus.
Col 1: 4 heard of your faith in *C* Jesus
1: 27 which is *C* in you, the hope of glory
1: 28 may present everyone perfect in *C*.
2: 2 the mystery of God, namely, *C*,
2: 6 as you received *C* Jesus as Lord,
2: 9 For in *C* all the fullness
2: 13 God made you alive with *C*.
2: 17 the reality, however, is found in *C*.
3: 1 then, you have been raised with *C*,
3: 3 and your life is now hidden with *C*
3: 15 Let the peace of *C* rule
1Th 5: 9 through our Lord Jesus *C*.
2Th 2: 1 the coming of our Lord Jesus *C*
2: 14 in the glory of our Lord Jesus *C*.
1Ti 1: 12 I thank *C* Jesus our Lord, who has
1: 15 *C* Jesus came into the world
1: 16 *C* Jesus might display his unlimited
2: 5 the man *C* Jesus, who gave himself
2Ti 1: 9 us in *C* Jesus before the beginning
1: 10 appearing of our Savior, *C* Jesus,
2: 1 in the grace that is in *C* Jesus.
2: 3 us like a good soldier of *C* Jesus.
2: 8 Remember Jesus *C*, raised
2: 10 the salvation that is in *C* Jesus,
3: 12 life in *C* Jesus will be persecuted,
3: 15 salvation through faith in *C* Jesus.
4: 1 presence of God and of *C* Jesus,
Tit 2: 13 our great God and Savior, Jesus *C*,
Heb 3: 6 But *C* is faithful as a son
3: 14 to share in *C* if we hold firmly
5: 5 So *C* also did not take
6: 1 the elementary teachings about *C*
9: 11 When *C* came as high priest
9: 14 more, then, will the blood of *C*,
9: 15 For this reason *C* is the mediator
9: 24 For *C* did not enter a man-made
9: 26 Then *C* would have had
9: 28 so *C* was sacrificed once
10: 10 of the body of Jesus *C* once for all.
13: 8 Jesus *C* is the same yesterday
1Pe 1: 2 for obedience to Jesus *C*
1: 3 of Jesus *C* from the dead,
1: 11 he predicted the sufferings of *C*
1: 19 but with the precious blood of *C*,
2: 21 because *C* suffered for you,
3: 15 in your hearts set apart *C* as Lord.
3: 18 For *C* died for sins once for all,
3: 21 you by the resurrection of Jesus *C*,
4: 13 participate in the sufferings of *C*,
4: 14 insulted because of the name of *C*,
2Pe 1: 1 and Savior Jesus *C* have received
1: 16 and coming of our Lord Jesus *C*,
1Jn 2: 1 Jesus *C*, the Righteous One.
2: 22 man who denies that Jesus is the *C*.
3: 16 Jesus *C* laid down his life for us.
3: 23 in the name of his Son, Jesus *C*,
4: 2 that Jesus *C* has come
5: 1 believes that Jesus is the *C* is born
5: 20 even in his Son Jesus *C*.
2Jn : 9 teaching of *C* does not have God;
Jude : 4 deny Jesus *C* our only Sovereign
Rev 1: 1 The revelation of Jesus *C*,
1: 5 from Jesus *C*, who is the faithful
11: 15 kingdom of our Lord and of his *C*,
20: 4 reigned with *C* a thousand years.
20: 6 they will be priests of God and of *C*

CHRIST'S (CHRIST)
1Co 9: 21 from God's law but am under *C* law
2Co 5: 14 For *C* love compels us,
5: 20 We are therefore *C* ambassadors,
12: 9 so that *C* power may rest on me.
Col 1: 22 by *C* physical body through death

CHRISTIAN* (CHRIST)
Ac 26: 28 you can persuade me to be a *C*?"
1Pe 4: 16 as a *C*, do not be ashamed,

CHRISTIANS* (CHRIST)
Ac 11: 26 The disciples were called *C* first

CHRISTS* (CHRIST)
Mt 24: 24 For false *C* and false prophets will
Mk 13: 22 For false *C* and false prophets will

CHURCH
Mt 16: 18 and on this rock I will build my *c*,
18: 17 if he refuses to listen even to the *c*,
Ac 20: 28 Be shepherds of the *c* of God,
1Co 5: 12 of mine to judge those outside the *c*
14: 4 but he who prophesies edifies the *c*.
14: 12 to excel in gifts that build up the *c*.
14: 26 done for the strengthening of the *c*.
15: 9 because I persecuted the *c* of God.
Gal 1: 13 how intensely I persecuted the *c*
Eph 5: 23 as Christ is the head of the *c*,
Col 1: 18 he is the head of the body, the *c*;
1: 24 the sake of his body, which is the *c*.

CHURNING
Pr 30: 33 For as *c* the milk produces butter,

CIRCLE
Isa 40: 22 enthroned above the *c* of the earth,

CIRCUMCISE (CIRCUMCISED CIRCUMCISION)
Dt 10: 16 *C* your hearts, therefore,

CIRCUMCISED (CIRCUMCISE)
Ge 17: 10 Every male among you shall be *c*.
17: 12 who is eight days old must be *c*,
Jos 5: 3 and *c* the Israelites at Gibeath
Gal 5: 2 that if you let yourselves be *c*,

CIRCUMCISION (CIRCUMCISE)
Ro 2: 25 *C* has value if you observe the law,
2: 29 and *c* is *c* of the heart, by the Spirit,
1Co 7: 19 *C* is nothing and uncircumcision is

CIRCUMSTANCES
Php 4: 11 to be content whatever the *c*.
1Th 5: 18 continually; give thanks in all *c*,

CITIES (CITY)
Lk 19: 17 small matter, take charge of ten *c*.'
19: 19 'You take charge of five *c*.'

CITIZENS (CITIZENSHIP)
Eph 2: 19 but fellow *c* with God's people

CITIZENSHIP* (CITIZENS)
Ac 22: 28 "I had to pay a big price for my *c*."
Eph 2: 12 excluded from *c* in Israel
Php 3: 20 But our *c* is in heaven.

CITY (CITIES)
Mt 5: 14 A *c* on a hill cannot be hidden.
Ac 18: 10 I have many people in this *c*."
Heb 13: 14 here we do not have an enduring *c*,
Rev 21: 2 saw the Holy *C*, the new

CIVILIAN*
2Ti 2: 4 a soldier gets involved in *c* affairs—

CLAIM (CLAIMS RECLAIM)
Pr 25: 6 do not *c* a place among great men;
1Jn 1: 6 If we *c* to have fellowship
1: 8 If we *c* to be without sin, we
1: 10 If we *c* we have not sinned,

CLAIMS (CLAIM)
Jas 2: 14 if a man *c* to have faith
1Jn 2: 6 Whoever *c* to live in him must walk
2: 9 Anyone who *c* to be in the light

CLANGING*
1Co 13: 1 a resounding gong or a *c* cymbal.

CLAP* (CLAPPED CLAPS)
Job 21: 5 *c* your hand over your mouth.
Ps 47: 1 *C* your hands, all you nations;
98: 8 Let the rivers *c* their hands,
Pr 30: 32 *c* your hand over your mouth!
Isa 55: 12 will *c* their hands.
La 2: 15 *c* their hands at you;

CLAPPED* (CLAP)
2Ki 11: 12 and the people *c* their hands
Eze 25: 6 Because you have *c* your hands

CLAPS* (CLAP)
Job 27: 23 It *c* its hands in derision

Job 34: 37 scornfully he *c* his hands among us
Na 3: 19 *c* his hands at your fall,

CLASSIFY*
2Co 10: 12 dare to *c* or compare ourselves

CLAUDIUS
Ac 11: 28 happened during the reign of *C.*)
18: 2 because *C* had ordered all the Jews

CLAY
Isa 45: 9 Does the *c* say to the potter,
64: 8 We are the *c*, you are the potter;
Jer 18: 6 "Like *c* in the hand of the potter,
La 4: 2 are now considered as pots of *c*,
Da 2: 33 partly of iron and partly of baked *c*.
Ro 9: 21 of the same lump of *c* some pottery
2Co 4: 7 we have this treasure in jars of *c*
2Ti 2: 20 and *c*; some are for noble purposes

CLEAN (CLEANNESS CLEANSE CLEANSED CLEANSES CLEANSING)
Ge 7: 2 seven of every kind of *c* animal,
Lev 4: 12 the camp to a place ceremonially *c*,
16: 30 you will be *c* from all your sins.
Ps 24: 4 He who has *c* hands and a pure
51: 7 with hyssop, and I will be *c*;
Pr 20: 9 I am *c* and without sin"?
Eze 36: 25 I will sprinkle *c* water on you,
Mt 8: 2 are willing, you can make me *c*."
12: 44 the house unoccupied, swept *c*
23: 25 You *c* the outside of the cup
Mk 7: 19 Jesus declared all foods "*c*.")
Jn 13: 10 to wash his feet; his whole body is *c*
15: 3 are already *c* because of the word
Ac 10: 15 impure that God has made *c*."
Ro 14: 20 All food is *c*, but it is wrong

CLEANNESS (CLEAN)
2Sa 22: 25 according to my *c* in his sight.

CLEANSE (CLEAN)
Ps 51: 2 and *c* me from my sin.
51: 7 *C* me with hyssop, and I will be
Pr 20: 30 Blows and wounds *c* away evil,
Heb 9: 14 *c* our consciences from acts that
10: 22 having our hearts sprinkled to *c* us

CLEANSED (CLEAN)
Heb 9: 22 requires that nearly everything be *c*
2Pe 1: 9 has forgotten that he has been *c*

CLEANSES* (CLEAN)
2Ti 2: 21 If a man *c* himself from the latter,

CLEANSING (CLEAN)
Eph 5: 26 *c* her by the washing with water

CLEFT*
Ex 33: 22 I will put you in a *c* in the rock

CLEVER
Isa 5: 21 and *c* in their own sight.

CLING
Ro 12: 9 Hate what is evil; *c* to what is good.

CLINGS
Ps 63: 8 My soul *c* to you;

CLOAK
Ex 12: 11 with your *c* tucked into your belt,
2Ki 4: 29 "Tuck your *c* into your belt,
9: 1 "Tuck your *c* into your belt,
Mt 5: 40 let him have your *c* as well.

CLOSE (CLOSER CLOSES)
2Ki 11: 8 Stay *c* to the king wherever he goes
2Ch 23: 7 Stay *c* to the king wherever he goes
Ps 34: 18 LORD is *c* to the brokenhearted
148: 14 of Israel, the people *c* to his heart.
Isa 40: 11 and carries them *c* to his heart;
Jer 30: 21 himself to be *c* to me?'

CLOSER (CLOSE)
Ex 3: 5 "Do not come any *c*," God said.
Pr 18: 24 there is a friend who sticks *c*

CLOSES (CLOSE)
Pr 28: 27 he who *c* his eyes to them receives

CLOTHE (CLOTHED CLOTHES CLOTHING)
Ps 45: 3 *c* yourself with splendor
Isa 52: 1 *c* yourself with strength.
Ro 13: 14 *c* yourselves with the Lord Jesus
Col 3: 12 *c* yourselves with compassion,
1Pe 5: 5 *c* yourselves with humility

CLOTHED (CLOTHE)
Ps 30: 11 removed my sackcloth and *c* me
104: 1 you are *c* with splendor
Pr 31: 22 she is *c* in fine linen and purple.
31: 25 She is *c* with strength and dignity;
Isa 61: 10 For he has *c* me with garments
Lk 24: 49 until you have been *c* with power
Gal 3: 27 into Christ have *c* yourselves

CLOTHES (CLOTHE)
Dt 8: 4 Your *c* did not wear out
Mt 6: 25 the body more important than *c*?
6: 28 "And why do you worry about *c*?
27: 35 they divided up his *c* by casting lots
Jn 11: 44 Take off the grave *c* and let him go

CLOTHING (CLOTHE)
Dt 22: 5 A woman must not wear men's *c*,
Job 29: 14 I put on righteousness as my *c*;
Ps 22: 18 and cast lots for my *c*.
Mt 7: 15 They come to you in sheep's *c*,
1Ti 6: 8 But if we have food and *c*,

CLOUD (CLOUDS)
Ex 13: 21 them in a pillar of *c* to guide them
1Ki 18: 44 *c* as small as a man's hand is rising
Pr 16: 15 his favor is like a rain *c* in spring.
Isa 19: 1 See, the LORD rides on a swift *c*
Lk 21: 27 of Man coming in a *c* with power
Heb 12: 1 by such a great *c* of witnesses,
Rev 14: 14 seated on the *c* was one "like a son

CLOUDS (CLOUD)
Dt 33: 26 and on the *c* in his majesty.
Ps 68: 4 extol him who rides on the *c*—
104: 3 He makes the *c* his chariot
Pr 25: 14 Like *c* and wind without rain
Da 7: 13 coming with the *c* of heaven.
Mt 24: 30 of Man coming on the *c* of the sky,
26: 64 and coming on the *c* of heaven."
Mk 13: 26 coming in *c* with great power
1Th 4: 17 with them in the *c* to meet the Lord
Rev 1: 7 Look, he is coming with the *c*,

CLUB
Pr 25: 18 Like a *c* or a sword or a sharp arrow

CO-HEIRS* (INHERIT)
Ro 8: 17 heirs of God and *c* with Christ,

COALS
Pr 25: 22 you will heap burning *c* on his head
Ro 12: 20 you will heap burning *c* on his head

COARSE*
Eph 5: 4 or *c* joking, which are out of place,

CODE*
Ro 2: 27 even though you have the written *c*
2: 29 by the Spirit, not by the written *c*.
7: 6 not in the old way of the written *c*.
Col 2: 14 having canceled the written *c*,

COINS
Mt 26: 15 out for him thirty silver *c*.
Lk 15: 8 suppose a woman has ten silver *c*

COLD
Pr 25: 25 Like *c* water to a weary soul
Mt 10: 42 if anyone gives even a cup of *c* water
24: 12 the love of most will grow *c*,

COLLECTION
1Co 16: 1 Now about the *c* for God's people:

COLT
Zec 9: 9 on a *c*, the foal of a donkey.
Mt 21: 5 on a *c*, the foal of a donkey.'"

COMB
Ps 19: 10 than honey from the *c*.

COMFORT* (COMFORTED COMFORTER COMFORTERS COMFORTING COMFORTS)
Ge 5: 29 "He will *c* us in the labor
37: 35 and daughters came to *c* him,
Ru 2: 13 "You have given me *c*
1Ch 7: 22 and his relatives came to *c* him.
Job 2: 11 sympathize with him and *c* him.
7: 13 When I think my bed will *c* me
16: 5 *c* from my lips would bring you
36: 16 to the *c* of your table laden
Ps 23: 4 rod and your staff, they *c* me.
71: 21 and *c* me once again.
119: 50 My *c* in my suffering is this:
119: 52 and I find *c* in them.
119: 76 May your unfailing love be my *c*,
119: 82 I say, "When will you *c* me?"
Isa 40: 1 *C*, *c* my people,
51: 3 The LORD will surely *c* Zion
51: 19 who can *c* you?—
57: 18 I will guide him and restore *c*
61: 2 to *c* all who mourn,
66: 13 so will I *c* you;
Jer 16: 7 food to *c* those who mourn
31: 13 I will give them *c* and joy instead
La 1: 2 there is none to *c* her.
1: 9 there was none to *c* her.
1: 16 No one is near to *c* me,
1: 17 but there is no one to *c* her.
1: 21 but there is no one to *c* me.
2: 13 that I may *c* you,
Eze 16: 54 all you have done in giving them *c*.
Na 3: 7 Where can I find anyone to *c* you?"
Zec 1: 17 and the LORD will again *c* Zion
10: 2 they give *c* in vain.
Lk 6: 24 you have already received your *c*.
Jn 11: 19 and Mary to *c* them in the loss
1Co 14: 3 encouragement and *c*.
2Co 1: 3 of compassion and the God of all *c*,
1: 4 so that we can *c* those
1: 4 with the *c* we ourselves have
1: 5 through Christ our *c* overflows.
1: 6 if we are comforted, it is for your *c*,
1: 6 it is for your *c* and salvation;
1: 7 so also you share in our *c*.
2: 7 you ought to forgive and *c* him,
7: 7 also by the *c* you had given him.
Php 2: 1 if any *c* from his love,
Col 4: 11 and they have proved a *c* to me.

COMFORTED* (COMFORT)
Ge 24: 67 Isaac was *c* after his mother's death
37: 35 comfort him, but he refused to be *c*.
2Sa 12: 24 Then David *c* his wife Bathsheba,
Job 42: 11 They *c* and consoled him
Ps 77: 2 and my soul refused to be *c*.
86: 17 have helped me and *c* me.
Isa 12: 1 and you have *c* me.
52: 9 for the LORD has *c* his people,
54: 11 lashed by storms and not *c*,
66: 13 and you will be *c* over Jerusalem."
Jer 31: 15 and refusing to be *c*,
Mt 2: 18 and refusing to be *c*,
5: 4 for they will be *c*.
Lk 16: 25 but now he is *c* here and you are
Ac 20: 12 man home alive and were greatly *c*.
2Co 1: 6 if we are *c*, it is for your comfort,
7: 6 *c* us by the coming of Titus,

COMFORTER* (COMFORT)
Ecc 4: 1 and they have no *c*;
4: 1 and they have no *c*.
Jer 8: 18 O my *C* in sorrow,

COMFORTERS* (COMFORT)
Job 16: 2 miserable *c* are you all!
Ps 69: 20 for *c*, but I found none.

COMFORTING* (COMFORT)
Isa 66: 11 satisfied at her *c* breasts;
Zec 1: 13 *c* words to the angel who talked
Jn 11: 31 *c* her, noticed how quickly she got
1Th 2: 12 *c* and urging you to live lives

COMFORTS* (COMFORT)
Job 29: 25 I was like one who *c* mourners.
Isa 49: 13 For the LORD *c* his people
51: 12 "I, even I, am he who *c* you.
66: 13 As a mother *c* her child,
2Co 1: 4 who *c* us in all our troubles,
7: 6 But God, who *c* the downcast,

COMMAND (COMMANDED COMMANDING COMMANDMENT COMMANDMENTS COMMANDS)
Ex 7: 2 You are to say everything I *c* you,
Nu 14: 41 are you disobeying the LORD's *c*?
24: 13 to go beyond the *c* of the LORD—
Dt 4: 2 Do not add to what I *c* you
8: 1 to follow every *c* I am giving you
12: 32 See that you do all I *c* you;
15: 11 I *c* you to be openhanded
30: 16 For I *c* you today to love
32: 46 so that you may *c* your children
Ps 91: 11 For he will *c* his angels concerning
Pr 13: 13 but he who respects a *c* is rewarded
Ecc 8: 2 Obey the king's *c*, I say,
Jer 1: 7 you to and say whatever I *c* you.
1: 17 and say to them whatever I *c* you.
7: 23 Walk in all the ways I *c* you,
11: 4 Obey me and do everything I *c* you
26: 2 Tell them everything I *c* you;
Joel 2: 11 mighty are those who obey his *c*.
Mt 4: 6 He will *c* his angels concerning you
15: 3 why do you break the *c* of God
Lk 4: 10 "'He will *c* his angels concerning
Jn 14: 15 love me, you will obey what I *c*.
15: 12 My *c* is this: Love each other
15: 14 friends if you do what I *c*.
15: 17 This is my *c*: Love each other.
1Co 14: 37 writing to you is the Lord's *c*.
Gal 5: 14 law is summed up in a single *c*:
1Ti 1: 5 goal of this *c* is love, which comes

1Ti 6: 14 to you keep this *c* without spot
6: 17 *C* those who are rich
Heb 11: 3 universe was formed at God's *c*,
2Pe 2: 21 on the sacred *c* that was passed
3: 2 and the *c* given by our Lord
1Jn 2: 7 I am not writing you a new *c*
3: 23 this is his *c*: to believe in the name
4: 21 And he has given us this *c*:
2Jn : 6 his *c* is that you walk in love.

COMMANDED (COMMAND)
Ge 2: 16 And the LORD God *c* the man,
7: 5 Noah did all that the LORD *c* him.
50: 12 Jacob's sons did as he had *c* them:
Ex 7: 6 did just as the LORD *c* them.
19: 7 all the words the LORD had *c* him
Dt 4: 5 laws as the LORD my God *c* me,
6: 24 The LORD *c* us to obey all these
Jos 1: 9 Have I not *c* you? Be strong
1: 16 Whatever you have *c* us we will do,
2Sa 5: 25 So David did as the LORD *c* him,
2Ki 17: 13 the entire Law that I *c* your fathers
21: 8 careful to do everything I *c* them
2Ch 33: 8 do everything I *c* them concerning
Ps 33: 9 he *c*, and it stood firm.
78: 5 which he *c* our forefathers
148: 5 for he *c* and they were created.
Mt 28: 20 to obey everything I have *c* you.
1Co 9: 14 Lord has *c* that those who preach
1Jn 3: 23 and to love one another as he *c* us.
2Jn : 4 in the truth, just as the Father *c* us.

COMMANDING (COMMAND)
2Ti 2: 4 he wants to please his *c* officer.

COMMANDMENT* (COMMAND)
Jos 22: 5 But be very careful to keep the *c*
Mt 22: 36 which is the greatest *c* in the Law?"
22: 38 This is the first and greatest *c*.
Mk 12: 31 There is no *c* greater than these."
Lk 23: 56 the Sabbath in obedience to the *c*.
Jn 13: 34 "A new *c* I give you: Love one
Ro 7: 8 the opportunity afforded by the *c*,
7: 9 when the *c* came, sin sprang to life
7: 10 that the very *c* that was intended
7: 11 and through the *c* put me to death.
7: 11 the opportunity afforded by the *c*,
7: 12 and the *c* is holy, righteous
7: 13 through the *c* sin might become
13: 9 and whatever other *c* there may be,
Eph 6: 2 which is the first *c* with a promise
Heb 9: 19 Moses had proclaimed every *c*

COMMANDMENTS* (COMMAND)
Ex 20: 6 who love me and keep my *c*.
34: 28 of the covenant — the Ten *C*.
Dt 4: 13 to you his covenant, the Ten *C*,
5: 10 who love me and keep my *c*.
5: 22 These are the *c* the LORD
6: 6 These *c* that I give you today are
9: 10 were all the *c* the LORD
10: 4 The Ten *C* he had proclaimed
Ecc 12: 13 Fear God and keep his *c*,
Mt 5: 19 one of the least of these *c*
19: 17 If you want to enter life, obey the *c*
22: 40 the Prophets hang on these two *c*."
Mk 10: 19 You know the *c*: 'Do not murder,
12: 28 "Of all the *c*, which is the most
Lk 1: 6 observing all the Lord's *c*
18: 20 You know the *c*: 'Do not commit
Ro 13: 9 The *c*, "Do not commit adultery,"
Eph 2: 15 in his flesh the law with its *c*
Rev 12: 17 those who obey God's *c*
14: 12 part of the saints who obey God's *c*

COMMANDS (COMMAND)
Ex 24: 12 and *c* I have written for their
25: 22 give you all my *c* for the Israelites.
34: 32 gave them all the *c* the LORD had
Lev 22: 31 "Keep my *c* and follow them.
Nu 15: 39 and so you will remember all the *c*
Dt 7: 9 those who love him and keep his *c*.
7: 11 Therefore, take care to follow the *c*
11: 1 decrees, his laws and his *c* always.
11: 27 the blessing if you obey the *c*
28: 1 carefully follow all his *c* I give you
30: 10 LORD your God and keep his *c*
Jos 22: 5 to walk in all his ways, to obey his *c*
1Ki 2: 3 and keep his decrees and *c*,
8: 58 in all his ways and to keep the *c*,
8: 61 to live by his decrees and obey his *c*
1Ch 28: 7 unswerving in carrying out my *c*
29: 19 devotion to keep your *c*,
2Ch 31: 21 in obedience to the law and the *c*,
Ne 1: 5 those who love him and obey his *c*,
Ps 78: 7 but would keep his *c*.
112: 1 who finds great delight in his *c*.
Ps 119: 10 do not let me stray from your *c*.
119: 32 I run in the path of your *c*,
119: 35 Direct me in the path of your *c*,
119: 47 for I delight in your *c*
119: 48 I lift up my hands to your *c*,
119: 73 me understanding to learn your *c*.
119: 86 All your *c* are trustworthy;
119: 96 but your *c* are boundless.
119: 98 Your *c* make me wiser
119: 115 that I may keep the *c* of my God!
119: 127 Because I love your *c*
119: 131 longing for your *c*.
119: 143 but your *c* are my delight.
119: 151 and all your *c* are true.
119: 172 for all your *c* are righteous.
119: 176 for I have not forgotten your *c*.
Pr 2: 1 and store up my *c* within you,
3: 1 but keep my *c* in your heart,
6: 23 For these *c* are a lamp,
10: 8 The wise in heart accept *c*,
Isa 48: 18 you had paid attention to my *c*,
Da 9: 4 all who love him and obey his *c*,
Mt 5: 19 teaches these *c* will be called great
Mk 7: 8 You have let go of the *c* of God
7: 9 way of setting aside the *c* of God
Jn 14: 21 Whoever has my *c* and obeys them,
15: 10 If you obey my *c*, you will remain
Ac 17: 30 but now he *c* all people everywhere
1Co 7: 19 Keeping God's *c* is what counts.
1Jn 2: 3 come to know him if we obey his *c*.
2: 4 but does not do what he *c* is a liar,
3: 22 we obey his *c* and do what pleases
3: 24 Those who obey his *c* live in him,
5: 2 loving God and carrying out his *c*.
5: 3 And his *c* are not burdensome,
5: 3 This is love for God: to obey his *c*.
2Jn : 6 that we walk in obedience to his *c*.

COMMEMORATE
Ex 12: 14 "This is a day you are to *c*;

COMMEND* (COMMENDABLE COMMENDED COMMENDS)
Ps 145: 4 One generation will *c* your works
Ecc 8: 15 So I *c* the enjoyment of life,
Ro 13: 3 do what is right and he will *c* you.
16: 1 I *c* to you our sister Phoebe,
2Co 3: 1 beginning to *c* ourselves again?
4: 2 the truth plainly we *c* ourselves
5: 12 trying to *c* ourselves to you again,
6: 4 as servants of God we *c* ourselves
10: 12 with some who *c* themselves.
1Pe 2: 14 and to *c* those who do right.

COMMENDABLE* (COMMEND)
1Pe 2: 19 For it is *c* if a man bears up
2: 20 you endure it, this is *c* before God.

COMMENDED* (COMMEND)
Ne 11: 2 The people *c* all the men who
Job 29: 11 and those who saw me *c* me,
Lk 16: 8 master *c* the dishonest manager
Ac 15: 40 *c* by the brothers to the grace
2Co 12: 11 I ought to have been *c* by you,
Heb 11: 2 This is what the ancients were *c* for
11: 4 By faith he was *c* as a righteous
11: 5 he was *c* as one who pleased God.
11: 39 These were all *c* for their faith,

COMMENDS* (COMMEND)
Pr 15: 2 of the wise *c* knowledge,
2Co 10: 18 but the one whom the Lord *c*.
10: 18 not the one who *c* himself who is

COMMIT (COMMITS COMMITTED)
Ex 20: 14 "You shall not *c* adultery.
Dt 5: 18 "You shall not *c* adultery.
1Sa 7: 3 and *c* yourselves to the LORD
Ps 31: 5 Into your hands I *c* my spirit;
37: 5 *C* your way to the LORD;
Pr 16: 3 *C* to the LORD whatever you do,
Mt 5: 27 that it was said, 'Do not *c* adultery.'
5: 32 causes her to *c* adultery,
19: 18 do not *c* adultery, do not steal,
Mk 10: 19 do not *c* adultery, do not steal,
Lk 18: 20 'Do not *c* adultery, do not murder,
23: 46 into your hands I *c* my spirit."
Ac 20: 32 I *c* you to God and to the word
Ro 2: 22 do you *c* adultery? You who abhor
2: 22 that people should not *c* adultery,
13: 9 "Do not *c* adultery,"
1Co 10: 8 We should not *c* sexual immorality,
Jas 2: 11 do not *c* adultery but do *c* murder,
1Pe 4: 19 to God's will should *c* themselves
Rev 2: 22 I will make those who *c* adultery

COMMITS (COMMIT)
Pr 6: 32 man who *c* adultery lacks
Pr 29: 22 a hot-tempered one *c* many sins.
Ecc 8: 12 a wicked man *c* a hundred crimes
Eze 18: 12 He *c* robbery.
18: 14 who sees all the sins his father *c*,
18: 24 from his righteousness and *c* sin
18: 26 from his righteousness and *c* sin,
22: 11 you one man *c* a detestable offense
Mt 5: 32 the divorced woman *c* adultery.
19: 9 marries another woman *c* adultery
Mk 10: 11 marries another woman *c* adultery
10: 12 another man, she *c* adultery."
Lk 16: 18 a divorced woman *c* adultery.
16: 18 marries another woman *c* adultery,

COMMITTED (COMMIT)
Nu 5: 7 and must confess the sin he has *c*.
1Ki 8: 61 But your hearts must be fully *c*
15: 14 Asa's heart was fully *c*
2Ch 16: 9 those whose hearts are fully *c*
Mt 5: 28 lustfully has already *c* adultery
11: 27 "All things have been *c* to me
Lk 10: 22 "All things have been *c* to me
Ac 14: 23 *c* them to the Lord,
14: 26 where they had been *c* to the grace
1Co 9: 17 I am simply discharging the trust *c*
2Co 5: 19 And he has *c* to us the message
1Pe 2: 22 "He *c* no sin,
Rev 17: 2 the kings of the earth *c* adultery
18: 3 of the earth *c* adultery with her,
18: 9 kings of the earth who *c* adultery

COMMON
Ge 11: 1 had one language and a *c* speech.
Lev 10: 10 between the holy and the *c*,
Pr 22: 2 Rich and poor have this in *c*:
29: 13 the oppressor have this in *c*:
Ac 2: 44 together and had everything in *c*.
1Co 10: 13 has seized you except what is *c*
2Co 6: 14 and wickedness have in *c*?

COMPANION (COMPANIONS)
Ps 55: 13 my *c*, my close friend,
55: 20 My *c* attacks his friends;
Pr 13: 20 but a *c* of fools suffers harm.
28: 7 a *c* of gluttons disgraces his father.
29: 3 *c* of prostitutes squanders his
Rev 1: 9 your brother and *c* in the suffering

COMPANIONS (COMPANION)
Ps 45: 7 your God, has set you above your *c*
Pr 18: 24 A man of many *c* may come to ruin
Heb 1: 9 your God, has set you above your *c*

COMPANY
Ps 14: 5 present in the *c* of the righteous.
Pr 21: 16 comes to rest in the *c* of the dead.
24: 1 do not desire their *c*;
Jer 15: 17 I never sat in the *c* of revelers,
1Co 15: 33 "Bad *c* corrupts good character."

COMPARE* (COMPARED COMPARING COMPARISON)
Job 28: 17 Neither gold nor crystal can *c*
28: 19 The topaz of Cush cannot *c* with it;
39: 13 but they cannot *c* with the pinions
Ps 86: 8 no deeds can *c* with yours.
89: 6 skies above can *c* with the LORD?
Pr 3: 15 nothing you desire can *c* with her.
8: 11 nothing you desire can *c* with her.
Isa 40: 18 To whom, then, will you *c* God?
40: 18 What image will you *c* him to?
40: 25 "To whom will you *c* me?
46: 5 "To whom will you *c* me
La 2: 13 With what can I *c* you,
Eze 31: 8 *c* with its branches —
Da 1: 13 Then *c* our appearance with that
Mt 11: 16 "To what can I *c* this generation?
Lk 7: 31 I *c* the people of this generation?
13: 18 What shall I *c* it to? It is like
13: 20 What shall I *c* the kingdom of God
2Co 10: 12 and *c* themselves with themselves,
10: 12 or *c* ourselves with some who

COMPARED* (COMPARE)
Jdg 8: 2 What have I accomplished *c* to you
8: 3 What was I able to do *c* to you?"
Isa 46: 5 you liken me that we may be *c*?
Eze 31: 2 Who can be *c* with you in majesty?
31: 18 the trees of Eden can be *c* with you
Php 3: 8 I consider everything a loss *c*

COMPARING* (COMPARE)
Ro 8: 18 present sufferings are not worth *c*
2Co 8: 8 the sincerity of your love by *c* it
Gal 6: 4 without *c* himself to somebody else

COMPARISON* (COMPARE)
2Co 3: 10 now in *c* with the surpassing glory.

COMPASSION* (COMPASSIONATE COMPASSIONS)

Ex 33: 19 I will have *c* on whom I will have *c*.
Dt 13: 17 he will show you mercy, have *c*
28: 54 man among you will have no *c*
30: 3 restore your fortunes and have *c*
32: 36 and have *c* on his servants
Jdg 2: 18 for the LORD had *c* on them
1Ki 3: 26 son was alive was filled with *c*
2Ki 13: 23 and had *c* and showed concern
2Ch 30: 9 and your children will be shown *c*
Ne 9: 19 of your great *c* you did not
9: 27 and in your great *c* you gave them
9: 28 in your *c* you delivered them time
Ps 51: 1 according to your great *c*
77: 9 Has he in anger withheld his *c*?"
90: 13 Have *c* on your servants.
102: 13 You will arise and have *c* on Zion,
103: 4 and crowns you with love and *c*.
103: 13 As a father has *c* on his children,
103: 13 so the LORD has *c*
116: 5 our God is full of *c*.
119: 77 Let your *c* come to me that I may
119: 156 Your *c* is great, O LORD;
135: 14 and have *c* on his servants.
145: 9 he has *c* on all he has made.
Isa 13: 18 will they look with *c* on children.
14: 1 The LORD will have *c* on Jacob;
27: 11 so their Maker has no *c* on them,
30: 18 he rises to show you *c*.
49: 10 He who has *c* on them will guide
49: 13 and will have *c* on his afflicted ones
49: 15 and have no *c* on the child she has
51: 3 and will look with *c* on all her ruins
54: 7 with deep *c* I will bring you back.
54: 8 I will have *c* on you,"
54: 10 says the LORD, who has *c* on you.
60: 10 in favor I will show you *c*.
63: 7 to his *c* and many kindnesses.
63: 15 and *c* are withheld from us.
Jer 12: 15 I will again have *c* and will bring
13: 14 *c* to keep me from destroying them
15: 6 I can no longer show *c*.
21: 7 show them no mercy or pity or *c*.'
30: 18 and have *c* on his dwellings;
31: 20 I have great *c* for him,"
33: 26 restore their fortunes and have *c*
42: 12 I will show you *c* so that he will
42: 12 so that he will have *c* on you
La 3: 32 he brings grief, he will show *c*,
Eze 9: 5 without showing pity or *c*.
16: 5 or had *c* enough to do any
39: 25 and will have *c* on all the people
Hos 2: 19 in love and *c*.
11: 8 all my *c* is aroused.
13: 14 "I will have no *c*,
14: 3 for in you the fatherless find *c*."
Am 1: 11 stifling all *c*,
Jnh 3: 9 with *c* turn from his fierce anger
3: 10 he had *c* and did not bring
Mic 7: 19 You will again have *c* on us;
Zec 7: 9 show mercy and *c* to one another.
10: 6 because I have *c* on them.
Mal 3: 17 as in *c* a man spares his son who
Mt 9: 36 When he saw the crowds, he had *c*
14: 14 he had *c* on them and healed their
15: 32 "I have *c* for these people;
20: 34 Jesus had *c* on them and touched
Mk 1: 41 with *c*, Jesus reached out his hand
6: 34 and saw a large crowd, he had *c*
8: 2 "I have *c* for these people;
Lk 15: 20 and was filled with *c* for him;
Ro 9: 15 and I will have *c* on whom I have *c*
2Co 1: 3 the Father of *c* and the God
Php 2: 1 and *c*, then make my joy complete
Col 3: 12 clothe yourselves with *c*, kindness,
Jas 5: 11 The Lord is full of *c* and mercy.

COMPASSIONATE* (COMPASSION)

Ex 22: 27 out to me, I will hear, for I am *c*.
34: 6 the LORD, the *c* and gracious God
2Ch 30: 9 LORD your God is gracious and *c*.
Ne 9: 17 gracious and *c*, slow to anger
Ps 86: 15 O Lord, are a *c* and gracious God,
103: 8 The LORD is *c* and gracious,
111: 4 the LORD is gracious and *c*.
112: 4 the gracious and *c* and righteous
145: 8 The LORD is gracious and *c*,
La 4: 10 With their own hands *c* women
Joel 2: 13 for he is gracious and *c*,
Jnh 4: 2 that you are a gracious and *c* God,
Eph 4: 32 Be kind and *c* to one another,
1Pe 3: 8 love as brothers, be *c* and humble.

COMPASSIONS* (COMPASSION)

La 3: 22 for his *c* never fail.

COMPELLED (COMPULSION)

Ac 20: 22 "And now, *c* by the Spirit,
1Co 9: 16 I cannot boast, for I am *c* to preach.

COMPELS (COMPULSION)

Job 32: 18 and the spirit within me *c* me;
2Co 5: 14 For Christ's love *c* us, because we

COMPETENCE* (COMPETENT)

2Co 3: 5 but our *c* comes from God.

COMPETENT* (COMPETENCE)

Ro 15: 14 and *c* to instruct one another.
1Co 6: 2 are you not *c* to judge trivial cases?
2Co 3: 5 Not that we are *c* in ourselves to claim
3: 6 He has made us *c* as ministers

COMPETES*

1Co 9: 25 Everyone who *c* in the games goes
2Ti 2: 5 Similarly, if anyone *c* as an athlete,
2: 5 unless he *c* according to the rules.

COMPLACENCY* (COMPLACENT)

Pr 1: 32 and the *c* of fools will destroy them
Eze 30: 9 ships to frighten Cush out of her *c*.

COMPLACENT* (COMPLACENCY)

Isa 32: 9 You women who are so *c*,
32: 11 Tremble, you *c* women;
Am 6: 1 Woe to you who are *c* in Zion,
Zep 1: 12 and punish those who are *c*,

COMPLAINING*

Php 2: 14 Do everything without *c* or arguing

COMPLETE

Dt 16: 15 your hands, and your joy will be *c*.
Jn 3: 29 That joy is mine, and it is now *c*.
15: 11 and that your joy may be *c*.
16: 24 will receive, and your joy will be *c*.
17: 23 May they be brought to *c* unity
Ac 20: 24 *c* the task the Lord Jesus has given
Php 2: 2 then make my joy *c*
Col 4: 17 to it that you *c* the work you have
Jas 1: 4 so that you may be mature and *c*,
2: 22 his faith was made *c* by what he did
1Jn 1: 4 We write this to make our joy *c*.
2: 5 God's love is truly made *c* in him.
4: 12 and his love is made *c* in us.
4: 17 love is made *c* among us
2Jn : 12 to face, so that our joy may be *c*.

COMPLIMENTS*

Pr 23: 8 and will have wasted your *c*.

COMPREHEND* (COMPREHENDED)

Job 28: 13 Man does not *c* its worth;
Ecc 8: 17 No one can *c* what goes
8: 17 he knows, he cannot really *c* it.

COMPREHENDED* (COMPREHEND)

Job 38: 18 Have you *c* the vast expanses

COMPULSION (COMPELLED COMPELS)

2Co 9: 7 not reluctantly or under *c*,

CONCEAL (CONCEALED CONCEALS)

Ps 40: 10 I do not *c* your love and your truth
Pr 25: 2 It is the glory of God to *c* a matter;

CONCEALED (CONCEAL)

Jer 16: 17 nor is their sin *c* from my eyes.
Mt 10: 26 There is nothing *c* that will not be
Mk 4: 22 and whatever is *c* is meant
Lk 8: 17 nothing *c* that will not be known
12: 2 There is nothing *c* that will not be

CONCEALS* (CONCEAL)

Pr 10: 18 He who *c* his hatred has lying lips,
28: 13 He who *c* his sins does not prosper,

CONCEIT* (CONCEITED CONCEITS)

Isa 16: 6 her overweening pride and *c*,
Jer 48: 29 her overweening pride and *c*,
Php 2: 3 out of selfish ambition or vain *c*,

CONCEITED* (CONCEIT)

1Sa 17: 28 I know how *c* you are and how
Ro 11: 25 brothers, so that you may not be *c*:
12: 16 Do not be *c*.
2Co 12: 7 To keep me from becoming *c*
Gal 5: 26 Let us not become *c*, provoking
1Ti 3: 6 or he may become *c* and fall
6: 4 he is *c* and understands nothing.
2Ti 3: 4 of the good, treacherous, rash, *c*,

CONCEITS* (CONCEIT)

Ps 73: 7 evil *c* of their minds know no

CONCEIVED (CONCEIVES)

Ps 51: 5 from the time my mother *c* me.
Mt 1: 20 what is *c* in her is from the Holy
1Co 2: 9 no mind has *c*

Jas 1: 15 after desire has *c*, it gives birth

CONCEIVES* (CONCEIVED)

Ps 7: 14 *c* trouble gives birth

CONCERN* (CONCERNED)

Ge 39: 6 he did not *c* himself with anything
39: 8 "my master does not *c* himself
1Sa 23: 21 "The LORD bless you for your *c*
2Ki 13: 23 and had compassion and showed *c*
Job 9: 21 I have no *c* for myself;
19: 4 my error remains my *c* alone.
Ps 131: 1 I do not *c* myself with great matters
Pr 29: 7 but the wicked have no such *c*.
Eze 36: 21 I had *c* for my holy name, which
Ac 15: 14 God at first showed his *c* by taking
18: 17 But Gallio showed no *c* whatever.
1Co 7: 32 I would like you to be free from *c*.
12: 25 that its parts should have equal *c*
2Co 7: 7 your deep sorrow, your ardent *c*
7: 11 what alarm, what longing, what *c*,
8: 16 of Titus the same *c* I have for you.
11: 28 of my *c* for all the churches.
Php 4: 10 at last you have renewed your *c*

CONCERNED (CONCERN)

Ex 2: 25 Israelites and was *c* about them.
Ps 142: 4 no one is *c* for me.
Jnh 4: 10 "You have been *c* about this vine,
4: 11 Should I not be *c* about that great
1Co 7: 32 An unmarried man is *c* about
9: 9 Is it about oxen that God is *c*?
Php 4: 10 you have been *c*, but you had no

CONCESSION*

1Co 7: 6 I say this as a *c*, not as a command.

CONDEMN* (CONDEMNATION CONDEMNED CONDEMNING CONDEMNS)

Job 9: 20 innocent, my mouth would *c* me;
10: 2 I will say to God: Do not *c* me,
34: 17 Will you *c* the just and mighty One
34: 29 if he remains silent, who can *c* him?
40: 8 Would you *c* me to justify yourself?
Ps 94: 21 and *c* the innocent to death.
109: 7 and may his prayers *c* him.
109: 31 from those who *c* him.
Isa 50: 9 Who is he that will *c* me?
Mt 12: 41 with this generation and *c* it;
12: 42 with this generation and *c* it;
20: 18 They will *c* him to death
Mk 10: 33 They will *c* him to death
Lk 6: 37 Do not *c*, and you will not be
11: 31 men of this generation and *c* them;
11: 32 with this generation and *c* it;
Jn 3: 17 Son into the world to *c* the world,
7: 51 "Does our law *c* anyone
8: 11 "Then neither do I *c* you,"
12: 48 very word which I spoke will *c* him
Ro 2: 27 yet obeys the law will *c* you who,
14: 3 everything must not *c* the man who
14: 22 is the man who does not *c* himself
2Co 7: 3 this to *c* you; I have said
1Jn 3: 20 presence whenever our hearts *c* us.
3: 21 if our hearts do not *c* us,

CONDEMNATION* (CONDEMN)

Jer 42: 18 of *c* and reproach; you will never
44: 12 and horror, of *c* and reproach.
Ro 3: 8 may result"? Their *c* is deserved.
5: 16 followed one sin and brought *c*,
5: 18 of one trespass was *c* for all men,
8: 1 there is now no *c* for those who are
2Pe 2: 3 Their *c* has long been hanging
Jude : 4 certain men whose *c* was written

CONDEMNED* (CONDEMN)

Dt 13: 17 of those *c* things shall be found
Job 32: 3 to refute Job, and yet had *c* him.
Ps 34: 21 the foes of the righteous will be *c*.
34: 22 will be *c* who takes refuge in him.
37: 33 let them be *c* when brought to trial.
79: 11 preserve those *c* to die.
102: 20 and release those *c* to death."
Mt 12: 7 you would not have *c* the innocent.
12: 37 and by your words you will be *c*."
23: 33 How will you escape being *c* to hell
27: 3 betrayed him, saw that Jesus was *c*,
Mk 14: 64 They all *c* him as worthy of death.
16: 16 whoever does not believe will be *c*.
Lk 6: 37 condemn, and you will not be *c*.
Jn 3: 18 Whoever believes in him is not *c*,
3: 18 does not believe stands *c* already
5: 24 has eternal life and will not be *c*;
5: 29 who have done evil will rise to be *c*.
8: 10 Has no one *c* you?" "No one, sir,"
16: 11 prince of this world now stands *c*.
Ac 25: 15 against him and asked that he be *c*.

Ro 3: 7 why am I still *c* as a sinner?"
8: 3 And so he *c* sin in sinful man,
14: 23 But the man who has doubts is *c*
1Co 4: 9 like men *c* to die in the arena.
11: 32 disciplined so that we will not be *c*
Gal 1: 8 let him be eternally *c*! As we have
1: 9 let him be eternally *c*! Am I now
2Th 2: 12 that all will be *c* who have not
Tit 2: 8 of speech that cannot be *c*,
Heb 11: 7 By his faith he *c* the world
Jas 5: 6 You have *c* and murdered innocent
5: 12 and your "No," no, or you will be *c*
2Pe 2: 6 if he *c* the cities of Sodom
Rev 19: 2 He has *c* the great prostitute

CONDEMNING* (CONDEMN)
Dt 25: 1 the innocent and *c* the guilty.
1Ki 8: 32 *c* the guilty and bringing
Pr 17: 15 the guilty and *c* the innocent—
Ac 13: 27 yet in *c* him they fulfilled the words
Ro 2: 1 judge the other, you are *c* yourself,

CONDEMNS* (CONDEMN)
Job 15: 6 Your own mouth *c* you, not mine;
Pr 12: 2 but the LORD *c* a crafty man.
Ro 8: 34 Who is he that *c*? Christ Jesus,
2Co 3: 9 the ministry that *c* men is glorious,

CONDITION
Pr 27: 23 Be sure you know the *c*

CONDUCT (CONDUCTED CONDUCTS)
Pr 10: 23 A fool finds pleasure in evil *c*,
20: 11 by whether his *c* is pure and right.
21: 8 but the *c* of the innocent is upright.
Ecc 6: 8 how to *c* himself before others?
Jer 4: 18 "Your own *c* and actions
17: 10 to reward a man according to his *c*,
Eze 7: 3 I will judge you according to your *c*
Php 1: 27 *c* yourselves in a manner worthy
1Ti 3: 15 to *c* themselves in God's household

CONDUCTED* (CONDUCT)
2Co 1: 12 testifies that we have *c* ourselves

CONDUCTS* (CONDUCT)
Ps 112: 5 who *c* his affairs with justice.

CONFESS* (CONFESSED CONFESSES CONFESSING CONFESSION)
Lev 5: 5 he must *c* in what way he has
16: 21 and *c* over it all the wickedness
26: 40 "'But if they will *c* their sins
Nu 5: 7 must *c* the sin he has committed.
1Ki 8: 33 back to you and *c* your name,
8: 35 toward this place and *c* your name
2Ch 6: 24 they turn back and *c* your name,
6: 26 toward this place and *c* your name
Ne 1: 6 I *c* the sins we Israelites, including
Ps 32: 5 I said, "I will *c*
38: 18 I *c* my iniquity;
Jn 1: 20 fail to *c*, but confessed freely,
12: 42 they would not *c* their faith
Ro 10: 9 That if you *c* with your mouth,
10: 10 it is with your mouth that you *c*
14: 11 every tongue will *c* to God.'"
Php 2: 11 every tongue *c* that Jesus Christ is
Heb 3: 1 and high priest whom we *c*.
13: 15 the fruit of lips that *c* his name.
Jas 5: 16 Therefore *c* your sins to each other
1Jn 1: 9 If we *c* our sins, he is faithful

CONFESSED* (CONFESS)
1Sa 7: 6 day they fasted and there they *c*,
Ne 9: 2 in their places and *c* their sins
Da 9: 4 to the LORD my God and *c*:
Jn 1: 20 but *c* freely, "I am not the Christ."
Ac 19: 18 and openly *c* their evil deeds.

CONFESSES* (CONFESS)
Pr 28: 13 whoever *c* and renounces them
2Ti 2: 19 and, "Everyone who *c* the name

CONFESSING* (CONFESS)
Ezr 10: 1 While Ezra was praying and *c*,
Da 9: 20 *c* my sin and the sin
Mt 3: 6 *C* their sins, they were baptized
Mk 1: 5 *C* their sins, they were baptized

CONFESSION* (CONFESS)
Ezr 10: 11 Now make *c* to the LORD,
Ne 9: 3 and spent another quarter in *c*
2Co 9: 13 obedience that accompanies your *c*
1Ti 6: 12 called when you made your good *c*
6: 13 Pontius Pilate made the good *c*,

CONFIDENCE* (CONFIDENT)
Jdg 9: 26 and its citizens put their *c* in him.
2Ki 18: 19 On what are you basing this *c*
2Ch 32: 8 And the people gained *c*
2Ch 32: 10 On what are you basing your *c*,
Job 4: 6 Should not your piety be your *c*
Ps 71: 5 my *c* since my youth.
Pr 3: 26 for the LORD will be your *c*
3: 32 but takes the upright into his *c*.
11: 13 A gossip betrays a *c*,
20: 19 A gossip betrays a *c*;
25: 9 do not betray another man's *c*,
31: 11 Her husband has full *c* in her
Isa 32: 17 will be quietness and *c* forever.
36: 4 On what are you basing this *c*
Jer 17: 7 whose *c* is in him.
49: 31 which lives in *c*,"
Eze 29: 16 a source of *c* for the people of Israel
Mic 7: 5 put no *c* in a friend.
2Co 2: 3 I had *c* in all of you, that you would
3: 4 Such *c* as this is ours
7: 4 I have great *c* in you; I take great
7: 16 I am glad I can have complete *c*
8: 22 so because of his great *c* in you.
Eph 3: 12 God with freedom and *c*.
Php 3: 3 and who put no *c* in the flesh—
3: 4 I myself have reasons for such *c*.
3: 4 reasons to put *c* in the flesh,
2Th 3: 4 We have *c* in the Lord that you are
Heb 3: 14 till the end the *c* we had at first.
4: 16 the throne of grace with *c*,
10: 19 since we have *c* to enter the Most
10: 35 So do not throw away your *c*;
13: 6 So we say with *c*,
1Jn 3: 21 we have *c* before God and receive
4: 17 us so that we will have *c* on the day
5: 14 This is the *c* we have

CONFIDENT* (CONFIDENCE)
Job 6: 20 because they had been *c*;
Ps 27: 3 even then will I be *c*.
27: 13 I am still *c* of this:
Lk 18: 9 To some who were *c*
2Co 1: 15 Because I was *c* of this, I planned
5: 6 Therefore we are always *c*
5: 8 We are *c*, I say, and would prefer
9: 4 ashamed of having been so *c*.
10: 7 If anyone is *c* that he belongs
Gal 5: 10 I am *c* in the Lord that you will
Php 1: 6 day until now, being *c* of this,
2: 24 I am *c* in the Lord that I myself will
Phm : 21 *C* of your obedience, I write to you,
Heb 6: 9 we are *c* of better things
1Jn 2: 28 that when he appears we may be *c*

CONFIDES*
Ps 25: 14 The LORD *c* in those who fear him

CONFORM* (CONFORMED CONFORMITY CONFORMS)
Ro 12: 2 Do not *c* any longer to the pattern
1Pe 1: 14 do not *c* to the evil desires you had

CONFORMED* (CONFORM)
Eze 5: 7 *c* to the standards of the nations
11: 12 but have *c* to the standards
Ro 8: 29 predestined to be *c* to the likeness

CONFORMITY* (CONFORM)
Eph 1: 11 in *c* with the purpose of his will,

CONFORMS* (CONFORM)
1Ti 1: 11 to the sound doctrine that *c*

CONQUEROR* (CONQUERORS)
Mic 1: 15 I will bring a *c* against you
Rev 6: 2 he rode out as a *c* bent on conquest.

CONQUERORS (CONQUEROR)
Ro 8: 37 than *c* through him who loved us.

CONSCIENCE* (CONSCIENCE-STRICKEN CONSCIENCES CONSCIENTIOUS)
Ge 20: 5 I have done this with a clear *c*
20: 6 I know you did this with a clear *c*,
1Sa 25: 31 have on his *c* the staggering burden
Job 27: 6 my *c* will not reproach me as long
Ac 23: 1 to God in all good *c* to this day."
24: 16 to keep my *c* clear before God
Ro 9: 1 my *c* confirms it in the Holy Spirit
13: 5 punishment but also because of *c*.
1Co 4: 4 My *c* is clear, but that does not
8: 7 since their *c* is weak, it is defiled.
8: 10 with a weak *c* sees you who have
8: 12 in this way and wound their weak *c*
10: 25 without raising questions of *c*,
10: 27 you without raising questions of *c*.
10: 28 man who told you and for *c'* sake—
10: 29 freedom be judged by another's *c*?
10: 29 the other man's *c*, I mean,
2Co 1: 12 Our *c* testifies that we have
4: 2 to every man's *c* in the sight of God
5: 11 and I hope it is also plain to your *c*.
1Ti 1: 5 and a good *c* and a sincere faith.
1: 19 holding on to faith and a good *c*.
3: 9 truths of the faith with a clear *c*.
2Ti 1: 3 as my forefathers did, with a clear *c*
Heb 9: 9 able to clear the *c* of the worshiper.
10: 22 to cleanse us from a guilty *c*
13: 18 We are sure that we have a clear *c*
1Pe 3: 16 and respect, keeping a clear *c*,
3: 21 the pledge of a good *c* toward God.

CONSCIENCE-STRICKEN* (CONSCIENCE)
1Sa 24: 5 David was *c* for having cut
2Sa 24: 10 David was *c* after he had counted

CONSCIENCES* (CONSCIENCE)
Ro 2: 15 their *c* also bearing witness,
1Ti 4: 2 whose *c* have been seared
Tit 1: 15 their minds and *c* are corrupted.
Heb 9: 14 cleanse our *c* from acts that lead

CONSCIENTIOUS* (CONSCIENCE)
2Ch 29: 34 for the Levites had been more *c*

CONSCIOUS*
Ro 3: 20 through the law we become *c* of sin
1Pe 2: 19 of unjust suffering because he is *c*

CONSECRATE (CONSECRATED)
Ex 13: 2 "*C* to me every firstborn male.
40: 9 *c* it and all its furnishings,
Lev 20: 7 "'*C* yourselves and be holy,
25: 10 *C* the fiftieth year and proclaim
1Ch 15: 12 fellow Levites are to *c* yourselves

CONSECRATED (CONSECRATE)
Ex 29: 43 and the place will be *c* by my glory.
Lev 8: 30 So he *c* Aaron and his garments
2Ch 7: 16 *c* this temple so that my Name may
Lk 2: 23 is to be *c* to the Lord"),
1Ti 4: 5 because it is *c* by the word of God

CONSENT
1Co 7: 5 except by mutual *c* and for a time,

CONSIDER (CONSIDERATE CONSIDERED CONSIDERS)
1Sa 12: 24 *c* what great things he has done
16: 7 "Do not *c* his appearance
2Ch 19: 6 "*C* carefully what you do,
Job 37: 14 stop and *c* God's wonders.
Ps 8: 3 When I *c* your heavens,
77: 12 and *c* all your mighty deeds.
107: 43 and *c* the great love of the LORD.
143: 5 and *c* what your hands have done.
Pr 6: 6 *c* its ways and be wise!
20: 25 and only later to *c* his vows.
Ecc 7: 13 *C* what God has done:
Lk 12: 24 *C* the ravens: They do not sow
12: 27 about the rest? "*C* how the lilies
Php 2: 3 but in humility *c* others better
3: 8 I *c* everything a loss compared
Heb 10: 24 And let us *c* how we may spur one
Jas 1: 2 *C* it pure joy, my brothers,

CONSIDERATE* (CONSIDER)
Tit 3: 2 to be peaceable and *c*,
Jas 3: 17 then peace-loving, *c*, submissive,
1Pe 2: 18 only to those who are good and *c*,
3: 7 in the same way be *c* as you live

CONSIDERED (CONSIDER)
Job 1: 8 "Have you *c* my servant Job?
2: 3 "Have you *c* my servant Job?
Ps 44: 22 we are *c* as sheep to be slaughtered.
Isa 53: 4 yet we *c* him stricken by God,
Ro 8: 36 we are *c* as sheep to be slaughtered

CONSIDERS (CONSIDER)
Pr 31: 16 She *c* a field and buys it;
Ro 14: 5 One man *c* one day more sacred
Jas 1: 26 If anyone *c* himself religious

CONSIST (CONSISTS)
Lk 12: 15 a man's life does not *c*

CONSISTS (CONSIST)
Eph 5: 9 fruit of the light *c* in all goodness,

CONSOLATION
Ps 94: 19 your *c* brought joy to my soul.

CONSPIRE
Ps 2: 1 Why do the nations *c*

CONSTANT
Dt 28: 66 You will live in *c* suspense,
Pr 19: 13 wife is like a *c* dripping.
27: 15 a *c* dripping on a rainy day;
Ac 27: 33 "you have been in *c* suspense
Heb 5: 14 by *c* use have trained themselves

CONSTRUCTIVE*
1Co 10: 23 but not everything is *c*.

CONSULT
Pr 15: 12 he will not *c* the wise.
Gal 1: 16 I did not *c* any man, nor did I go up

CONSUME (CONSUMES CONSUMING)
Jn 2: 17 "Zeal for your house will *c* me."

CONSUMES (CONSUME)
Ps 69: 9 for zeal for your house *c* me,

CONSUMING (CONSUME)
Dt 4: 24 For the LORD your God is a *c* fire,
Heb 12: 29 and awe, for our "God is a *c* fire."

CONTAIN* (CONTAINED CONTAINS)
1Ki 8: 27 the highest heaven, cannot *c* you.
2Ch 2: 6 the highest heavens, cannot *c* him?
6: 18 the highest heavens, cannot *c* you.
Ecc 8: 8 power over the wind to *c* it;
2Pe 3: 16 His letters *c* some things that are

CONTAINED (CONTAIN)
Heb 9: 4 This ark *c* the gold jar of manna,

CONTAINS (CONTAIN)
Pr 15: 6 of the righteous *c* great treasure,

CONTAMINATES*
2Co 7: 1 from everything that *c* body

CONTEMPT
Pr 14: 31 He who oppresses the poor shows *c*
17: 5 He who mocks the poor shows *c*
18: 3 When wickedness comes, so does *c*
Da 12: 2 others to shame and everlasting *c*.
Mal 1: 6 O priests, who show *c* for my name.
Ro 2: 4 Or do you show *c* for the riches
Gal 4: 14 you did not treat me with *c*
1Th 5: 20 do not treat prophecies with *c*.

CONTEND (CONTENDED CONTENDING CONTENTIOUS)
Ge 6: 3 "My Spirit will not *c*
Ps 35: 1 *C*, O LORD, with those who
Isa 49: 25 I will *c* with those who *c* with you,
Jude : 3 you to *c* for the faith that was once

CONTENDED (CONTEND)
Php 4: 3 help these women who have *c*

CONTENDING* (CONTEND)
Php 1: 27 *c* as one man for the faith

CONTENT* (CONTENTMENT)
Jos 7: 7 If only we had been *c* to stay
Pr 13: 25 The righteous eat to their hearts' *c*,
19: 23 one rests *c*, untouched by trouble.
Ecc 4: 8 yet his eyes were not *c*
Lk 3: 14 don't accuse people falsely — be *c*
Php 4: 11 to be *c* whatever the circumstances
4: 12 I have learned the secret of being *c*
1Ti 6: 8 and clothing, we will be *c* with that.
Heb 13: 5 and be *c* with what you have,

CONTENTIOUS* (CONTEND)
1Co 11: 16 If anyone wants to be *c* about this,

CONTENTMENT* (CONTENT)
Job 36: 11 and their years in *c*.
SS 8: 10 like one bringing *c*.
1Ti 6: 6 But godliness with *c* is great gain.

CONTEST*
Heb 10: 32 in a great *c* in the face of suffering.

CONTINUAL (CONTINUE)
Pr 15: 15 but the cheerful heart has a *c* feast.
Eph 4: 19 of impurity, with a *c* lust for more.

CONTINUE (CONTINUAL CONTINUES CONTINUING)
1Ki 8: 23 servants who *c* wholeheartedly
2Ch 6: 14 servants who *c* wholeheartedly
Ps 36: 10 *C* your love to those who know you
Ac 13: 43 urged them to *c* in the grace of God
Ro 11: 22 provided that you *c* in his kindness.
Gal 3: 10 Cursed is everyone who does not *c*
Php 2: 12 *c* to work out your salvation
Col 1: 23 if you *c* in your faith, established
2: 6 received Christ Jesus as Lord, *c*
1Ti 2: 15 if they *c* in faith, love and holiness
2Ti 3: 14 *c* in what you have learned
1Jn 2: 28 And now, dear children, *c* in him,
3: 9 born of God will *c* to sin,
5: 18 born of God does not *c* to sin;
2Jn : 9 and does not *c* in the teaching
Rev 22: 11 and let him who is holy *c* to be holy
22: 11 let him who does right *c* to do right;

CONTINUES (CONTINUE)
Ps 100: 5 *c* through all generations.
119: 90 Your faithfulness *c*

2Co 10: 15 Our hope is that, as your faith *c*
1Jn 3: 6 No one who *c* to sin has

CONTINUING (CONTINUE)
Ro 13: 8 the *c* debt to love one another,

CONTRIBUTION (CONTRIBUTIONS)
Ro 15: 26 pleased to make a *c* for the poor

CONTRIBUTIONS (CONTRIBUTION)
2Ch 24: 10 all the people brought their *c* gladly
31: 12 they faithfully brought in the *c*,

CONTRITE*
Ps 51: 17 a broken and *c* heart,
Isa 57: 15 also with him who is *c* and lowly
57: 15 and to revive the heart of the *c*.
66: 2 he who is humble and *c* in spirit,

CONTROL (CONTROLLED CONTROLS SELF-CONTROL SELF-CONTROLLED)
Pr 29: 11 a wise man keeps himself under *c*.
1Co 7: 9 But if they cannot *c* themselves,
7: 37 but has *c* over his own will,
1Th 4: 4 you should learn to *c* his own body

CONTROLLED (CONTROL)
Ps 32: 9 but must be *c* by bit and bridle
Ro 8: 6 but the mind *c* by the Spirit is life
8: 8 Those *c* by the sinful nature cannot

CONTROLS* (CONTROL)
Job 37: 15 you know how God *c* the clouds
Pr 16: 32 a man who *c* his temper

CONTROVERSIES*
Ac 26: 3 with all the Jewish customs and *c*.
1Ti 1: 4 These promote *c* rather
6: 4 He has an unhealthy interest in *c*
Tit 3: 9 But avoid foolish *c* and genealogies

CONVERSATION
Col 4: 6 Let your *c* be always full of grace,

CONVERT
1Ti 3: 6 He must not be a recent *c*,

CONVICT (CONVICTION)
Pr 24: 25 with those who *c* the guilty,
Jn 16: 8 he will *c* the world of guilt in regard
Jude : 15 and to *c* all the ungodly

CONVICTION* (CONVICT)
1Th 1: 5 the Holy Spirit and with deep *c*.

CONVINCE* (CONVINCED CONVINCING)
Ac 28: 23 and tried to *c* them about Jesus

CONVINCED* (CONVINCE)
Ge 45: 28 "I'm *c*! My son Joseph is still alive.
Lk 16: 31 will not be *c* even if someone rises
Ac 19: 26 and hear how this fellow Paul has *c*
26: 9 "I too was *c* that I ought
26: 26 I am *c* that none of this has escaped
28: 24 Some were *c* by what he said,
Ro 2: 19 if you are *c* that you are a guide
8: 38 For I am *c* that neither death
14: 5 Each one should be fully *c*
14: 14 I am fully *c* that no food is unclean
15: 14 I myself am *c*, my brothers,
1Co 14: 24 he will be *c* by all that he is a sinner
2Co 5: 14 we are *c* that one died for all,
Php 1: 25 *C* of this, I know that I will remain,
2Ti 1: 12 and am *c* that he is able
3: 14 have learned and have become *c*

CONVINCING* (CONVINCE)
Ac 1: 3 and gave many *c* proofs that he was

COOLNESS*
Pr 25: 13 Like the *c* of snow at harvest time

COPIES (COPY)
Heb 9: 23 for the *c* of the heavenly things

COPY (COPIES)
Dt 17: 18 for himself on a scroll a *c* of this law
Heb 8: 5 They serve at a sanctuary that is a *c*
9: 24 sanctuary that was only a *c*

CORBAN*
Mk 7: 11 received from me is *C*' (that is,

CORD (CORDS)
Jos 2: 18 you have tied this scarlet *c*
Ecc 4: 12 *c* of three strands is not quickly

CORDS (CORD)
Pr 5: 22 the *c* of his sin hold him fast.
Isa 54: 2 lengthen your *c*,
Hos 11: 4 them with *c* of human kindness,

CORINTH
Ac 18: 1 Paul left Athens and went to *C*.

1Co 1: 2 To the church of God in *C*,
2Co 1: 1 To the church of God in *C*,

CORNELIUS*
Roman to whom Peter preached; first Gentile Christian (Ac 10).

CORNER (CORNERS)
Ru 3: 9 "Spread the *c* of your garment
Pr 21: 9 Better to live on a *c* of the roof
25: 24 Better to live on a *c* of the roof
Ac 26: 26 because it was not done in a *c*.

CORNERS (CORNER)
Mt 6: 5 on the street *c* to be seen by men.
22: 9 Go to the street *c* and invite

CORNERSTONE* (STONE)
Job 38: 6 or who laid its *c* —
Isa 28: 16 a precious *c* for a sure foundation;
Jer 51: 26 rock will be taken from you for a *c*,
Zec 10: 4 From Judah will come the *c*,
Eph 2: 20 Christ Jesus himself as the chief *c*.
1Pe 2: 6 a chosen and precious *c*,

CORRECT* (CORRECTED CORRECTING CORRECTION CORRECTIONS CORRECTS)
Job 6: 26 Do you mean to *c* what I say,
40: 2 contends with the Almighty *c* him?
Jer 10: 24 *C* me, LORD, but only with justice
2Ti 4: 2 *c*, rebuke and encourage —

CORRECTED* (CORRECT)
Pr 29: 19 A servant cannot be *c*

CORRECTING* (CORRECT)
2Ti 3: 16 *c* and training in righteousness,

CORRECTION* (CORRECT)
Lev 26: 23 things you do not accept my *c*
Job 36: 10 He makes them listen to *c*
Pr 5: 12 How my heart spurned *c*!
10: 17 whoever ignores *c* leads others
12: 1 but he who hates *c* is stupid.
13: 18 but whoever heeds *c* is honored.
15: 5 whoever heeds *c* shows prudence.
15: 10 he who hates *c* will die.
15: 12 A mocker resents *c*;
15: 32 whoever heeds *c* gains
29: 15 The rod of *c* imparts wisdom,
Jer 2: 30 they did not respond to *c*.
5: 3 crushed them, but they refused *c*.
7: 28 LORD its God or responded to *c*.
Zep 3: 2 she accepts no *c*.
3: 7 you will fear me / and accept *c*!'

CORRECTIONS* (CORRECT)
Pr 6: 23 and the *c* of discipline

CORRECTS* (CORRECT)
Job 5: 17 "Blessed is the man whom God *c*;
Pr 9: 7 Whoever *c* a mocker invites insult;

CORRUPT (CORRUPTED CORRUPTION CORRUPTS)
Ge 6: 11 Now the earth was *c* in God's sight
Ps 14: 1 They are *c*, their deeds are vile;
14: 3 they have together become *c*;
Pr 4: 24 keep *c* talk far from your lips.
6: 12 who goes about with a *c* mouth,
19: 28 A *c* witness mocks at justice,

CORRUPTED (CORRUPT)
2Co 7: 2 wronged no one, we have *c* no one,
Tit 1: 15 but to those who are *c* and do not

CORRUPTION (CORRUPT)
2Pe 1: 4 escape the *c* in the world caused
2: 20 If they have escaped the *c*

CORRUPTS* (CORRUPT)
Ecc 7: 7 and a bribe *c* the heart.
1Co 15: 33 "Bad company *c* good character."
Jas 3: 6 It *c* the whole person, sets

COST (COSTS)
Nu 16: 38 sinned at the *c* of their lives.
Pr 4: 7 Though it *c* all you have, get
7: 23 little knowing it will *c* him his life.
Isa 55: 1 milk without money and without *c*.
Lk 14: 28 and estimate the *c* to see
Rev 21: 6 to drink without *c* from the spring

COSTS (COST)
Pr 6: 31 it *c* him all the wealth of his house.

COUNCIL
Ps 89: 7 In the *c* of the holy ones God is
107: 32 and praise him in the *c* of the elders

COUNSEL (COUNSELOR COUNSELS)
1Ki 22: 5 "First seek the *c* of the LORD."

2Ch 18: 4 "First seek the c of the LORD."
Job 38: 2 "Who is this that darkens my c
42: 3 'Who is this that obscures my c
Ps 1: 1 walk in the c of the wicked
73: 24 You guide me with your c,
107: 11 despised the c of the Most High.
Pr 8: 14 C and sound judgment are mine;
15: 22 Plans fail for lack of c,
27: 9 from his earnest c.
Isa 28: 29 wonderful in c and magnificent
1Ti 5: 14 So I c younger widows to marry,
Rev 3: 18 I c you to buy from me gold refined

COUNSELOR (COUNSEL)
Isa 9: 6 Wonderful C, Mighty God,
Jn 14: 16 he will give you another C to be
14: 26 But the C, the Holy Spirit,
15: 26 "When the C comes, whom I will
16: 7 the C will not come to you;
Ro 11: 34 Or who has been his c?"

COUNSELS (COUNSEL)
Ps 16: 7 I will praise the LORD, who c me;

COUNT (COUNTED COUNTING COUNTS)
Ps 22: 17 I can c all my bones;
Ro 4: 8 whose sin the Lord will never c
6: 11 c yourselves dead to sin
2Th 1: 11 that our God may c you worthy

COUNTED (COUNT)
Ac 5: 41 because they had been c worthy
2Th 1: 5 and as a result you will be c worthy

COUNTERFEIT*
2Th 2: 9 displayed in all kinds of c miracles,
1Jn 2: 27 not c — just as it has taught you,

COUNTING (COUNT)
2Co 5: 19 not c men's sins against them.

COUNTRY
Pr 28: 2 When a c is rebellious, it has many
29: 4 By justice a king gives a c stability,
Isa 66: 8 Can a c be born in a day
Lk 15: 13 off for a distant c and there
Jn 4: 44 prophet has no honor in his own c.)
2Co 11: 26 in danger in the c, in danger at sea;
Heb 11: 14 looking for a c of their own.

COUNTRYMEN
2Co 11: 26 danger from my own c, in danger

COUNTS (COUNT)
Jn 6: 63 The Spirit gives life; the flesh c
1Co 7: 19 God's commands is what c.
Gal 5: 6 only thing that c is faith expressing

COURAGE* (COURAGEOUS)
Jos 2: 11 everyone's c failed because of you,
5: 1 and they no longer had the c
2Sa 4: 1 he lost c, and all Israel became
7: 27 So your servant has found c
1Ch 17: 25 So your servant has found c to pray
2Ch 15: 8 son of Oded the prophet, he took c.
19: 11 Act with c, and may the LORD be
Ezr 7: 28 I took c and gathered leading men
10: 4 We will support you, so take c
Ps 107: 26 in their peril their c melted away.
Eze 22: 14 Will your c endure or your hands
Da 11: 25 and c against the king of the South.
Mt 14: 27 said to them: "Take c!
Mk 6: 50 spoke to them and said, "Take c!
Ac 4: 13 When they saw the c of Peter
23: 11 "Take c! As you have testified
27: 22 now I urge you to keep up your c,
27: 25 So keep up your c, men,
1Co 16: 13 stand firm in the faith; be men of c;
Php 1: 20 will have sufficient c so that now
Heb 3: 6 if we hold on to our c and the hope

COURAGEOUS* (COURAGE)
Dt 31: 6 Be strong and c.
31: 7 of all Israel, "Be strong and c,
31: 23 son of Nun: "Be strong and c,
Jos 1: 6 and c, because you will lead these
1: 7 Be strong and very c.
1: 9 commanded you? Be strong and c.
1: 18 Only be strong and c!"
10: 25 Be strong and c.
1Ch 22: 13 Be strong and c.
28: 20 "Be strong and c, and do the work.
2Ch 26: 17 priest with eighty other c priests
32: 7 with these words: "Be strong and c.

COURSE
Ps 19: 5 a champion rejoicing to run his c.
Pr 2: 8 for he guards the c of the just
15: 21 of understanding keeps a straight c.
16: 9 In his heart a man plans his c,
Pr 17: 23 to pervert the c of justice.
Jas 3: 6 sets the whole c of his life on fire,

COURT (COURTS)
Pr 22: 22 and do not crush the needy in c,
25: 8 do not bring hastily to c,
Mt 5: 25 adversary who is taking you to c.
1Co 4: 3 judged by you or by any human c;

COURTS (COURT)
Ps 84: 10 Better is one day in your c
100: 4 and his c with praise;
Am 5: 15 maintain justice in the c.
Zec 8: 16 and sound judgment in your c;

COURTYARD
Ex 27: 9 "Make a c for the tabernacle.

COUSIN
Col 4: 10 as does Mark, the c of Barnabas.

COVENANT (COVENANTS)
Ge 9: 9 "I now establish my c with you
17: 2 I will confirm my c between me
Ex 19: 5 if you obey me fully and keep my c,
24: 7 Then he took the Book of the C
Dt 4: 13 declared to you his c, the Ten
29: 1 in addition to the c he had made
Jdg 2: 1 'I will never break my c with you,
1Sa 23: 18 of them made a c before the LORD
1Ki 8: 21 in which is the c of the LORD that
8: 23 you who keep your c of love
2Ki 23: 2 the words of the Book of the C,
1Ch 16: 15 He remembers his c forever,
2Ch 6: 14 you who keep your c of love
34: 30 the words of the Book of the C,
Ne 1: 5 who keeps his c of love
Job 31: 1 "I made a c with my eyes
Ps 105: 8 He remembers his c forever,
Pr 2: 17 ignored the c she made before God
Isa 42: 6 you to be a c for the people
61: 8 make an everlasting c with them.
Jer 11: 2 "Listen to the terms of this c
31: 31 "when I will make a new c
31: 32 It will not be like the c
31: 33 "This is the c I will make
Eze 37: 26 I will make a c of peace with them;
Da 9: 27 He will confirm a c with many
Hos 6: 7 Like Adam, they have broken the c
Mal 2: 14 the wife of your marriage c.
3: 1 of the c, whom you desire,
Mt 26: 28 blood of the c, which is poured out
Mk 14: 24 "This is my blood of the c,
Lk 22: 20 "This cup is the new c in my blood,
1Co 11: 25 "This cup is the new c in my blood;
2Co 3: 6 as ministers of a new c —
Gal 4: 24 One c is from Mount Sinai
Heb 8: 6 as the c of which he is mediator is
8: 8 when I will make a new c
9: 15 Christ is the mediator of a new c,
12: 24 to Jesus the mediator of a new c,

COVENANTS (COVENANT)
Ro 9: 4 theirs the divine glory, the c,
Gal 4: 24 for the women represent two c.

COVER (COVER-UP COVERED COVERING COVERINGS COVERS)
Ex 25: 17 "Make an atonement c of pure gold
25: 21 Place the c on top of the ark
33: 22 and c you with my hand
Lev 16: 2 in the cloud over the atonement c.
Ps 32: 5 and did not c up my iniquity.
91: 4 He will c you with his feathers,
Hos 10: 8 say to the mountains, "C us!"
Lk 23: 30 and to the hills, "C us!" '
1Co 11: 6 If a woman does not c her head,
11: 6 shaved off, she should c her head.
11: 7 A man ought not to c his head,
Jas 5: 20 and c over a multitude of sins.

COVER-UP* (COVER)
1Pe 2: 16 but do not use your freedom as a c

COVERED (COVER)
Ps 32: 1 whose sins are c.
85: 2 and c all their sins.
Isa 6: 2 With two wings they c their faces,
51: 16 c you with the shadow of my hand
Ro 4: 7 whose sins are c.
1Co 11: 4 with his head c dishonors his head.

COVERING (COVER)
1Co 11: 15 For long hair is given to her as a c.

COVERINGS (COVER)
Ge 3: 7 and made c for themselves.
Pr 31: 22 She makes c for her bed;

COVERS (COVER)
Pr 10: 12 but love c over all wrongs.
17: 9 He who c over an offense promotes
2Co 3: 15 Moses is read, a veil c their hearts.
1Pe 4: 8 love c over a multitude of sins.

COVET* (COVETED COVETING COVETOUS)
Ex 20: 17 You shall not c your neighbor's
20: 17 "You shall not c your neighbor's
34: 24 and no one will c your land
Dt 5: 21 "You shall not c your neighbor's
7: 25 Do not c the silver and gold
Mic 2: 2 They c fields and seize them,
Ro 7: 7 if the law had not said, "Do not c."
13: 9 "Do not steal," "Do not c,"
Jas 4: 2 c, but you cannot have what you

COVETED* (COVET)
Jos 7: 21 weighing fifty shekels, I c them
Ac 20: 33 I have not c anyone's silver or gold

COVETING
Ro 7: 7 what c really was if the law

COVETOUS* (COVET)
Ro 7: 8 in me every kind of c desire.

COWARDLY*
Rev 21: 8 But the c, the unbelieving, the vile,

COWS
Ge 41: 2 of the river there came up seven c,
Ex 25: 5 skins dyed red and hides of sea c;
Nu 4: 6 are to cover this with hides of sea c,
1Sa 6: 7 Hitch the c to the cart,

CRAFTINESS* (CRAFTY)
Job 5: 13 He catches the wise in their c,
1Co 3: 19 "He catches the wise in their c";
Eph 4: 14 and c of men in their deceitful

CRAFTSMAN
Pr 8: 30 Then I was the c at his side.

CRAFTY* (CRAFTINESS)
Ge 3: 1 the serpent was more c than any
1Sa 23: 22 They tell me he is very c.
Job 5: 12 He thwarts the plans of the c,
15: 5 you adopt the tongue of the c.
Pr 7: 10 like a prostitute and with c intent.
12: 2 but the LORD condemns a c man.
14: 17 and a c man is hated.
2Co 12: 16 c fellow that I am, I caught you

CRAVE* (CRAVED CRAVES CRAVING CRAVINGS)
Nu 11: 4 with them began to c other food,
Dt 12: 20 you c meat and say, "I would like
Pr 23: 3 Do not c his delicacies,
23: 6 do not c his delicacies;
31: 4 not for rulers to c beer,
Mic 7: 1 none of the early figs that I c.
1Pe 2: 2 newborn babies, c pure spiritual

CRAVED* (CRAVE)
Nu 11: 34 the people who had c other food.
Ps 78: 18 by demanding the food they c.
78: 29 for he had given them what they c.
78: 30 turned from the food they c,

CRAVES* (CRAVE)
Pr 13: 4 The sluggard c and gets nothing,
21: 10 The wicked man c evil;
21: 26 All day long he c for more,

CRAVING* (CRAVE)
Job 20: 20 he will have no respite from his c;
Ps 106: 14 In the desert they gave in to their c;
Pr 10: 3 but he thwarts the c of the wicked.
13: 2 the unfaithful have a c for violence.
21: 25 The sluggard's c will be the death
Jer 2: 24 sniffing the wind in her c —

CRAVINGS* (CRAVE)
Ps 10: 3 He boasts of the c of his heart;
Eph 2: 3 gratifying the c of our sinful nature
1Jn 2: 16 in the world — the c of sinful man,

CRAWL
Ge 3: 14 You will c on your belly

CREATE* (CREATED CREATES CREATING CREATION CREATOR)
Ps 51: 10 C in me a pure heart, O God,
Isa 4: 5 Then the LORD will c over all
45: 7 I bring prosperity and c disaster;
45: 7 I form the light and c darkness,
45: 18 he did not c it to be empty,
65: 17 "Behold, I will c / new heavens
65: 18 for I will c Jerusalem to be a delight
65: 18 forever in what I will c,
Jer 31: 22 The LORD will c a new thing

Mal 2: 10 one Father? Did not one God c us?
Eph 2: 15 His purpose was to c

CREATED* (CREATE)
Ge 1: 1 In the beginning God c the heavens
1: 21 God c the great creatures of the sea
1: 27 So God c man in his own image,
1: 27 in the image of God he c him;
1: 27 male and female he c them.
2: 4 and the earth when they were c.
5: 1 When God c man, he made him
5: 2 He c them male and female
5: 2 when they were c, he called them
6: 7 whom I have c, from the face
Dt 4: 32 from the day God c man
Ps 89: 12 You c the north and the south;
89: 47 what futility you have c all men!
102: 18 a people not yet c may praise
104: 30 you send your Spirit, / they are c,
139: 13 For you c my inmost being;
148: 5 for he commanded and they were c
Isa 40: 26 Who c all these?
41: 20 that the Holy One of Israel has c it.
42: 5 he who c the heavens and stretched
43: 1 he who c you, O Jacob,
43: 7 whom I c for my glory,
45: 8 I, the LORD, have c it.
45: 12 and c mankind upon it.
45: 18 he who c the heavens,
48: 7 They are c now, and not long ago;
54: 16 And it is I who have c the destroyer
54: 16 "See, it is I who c the blacksmith
57: 16 the breath of man that I have c.
Eze 21: 30 In the place where you were c,
28: 13 the day you were c they were
28: 15 ways from the day you were c
Mk 13: 19 when God c the world, until now—
Ro 1: 25 and served c things rather
1Co 11: 9 neither was man c for woman,
Eph 2: 10 c in Christ Jesus to do good works,
3: 9 hidden in God, who c all things.
4: 24 c to be like God in true
Col 1: 16 For by him all things were c:
1: 16 all things were c by him
1Ti 4: 3 which God c to be received
4: 4 For everything God c is good,
Heb 12: 27 c things—so that what cannot be
Jas 1: 18 a kind of firstfruits of all he c.
Rev 4: 11 and by your will they were c
4: 11 for you c all things,
10: 6 who c the heavens and all that is

CREATES* (CREATE)
Am 4: 13 c the wind,

CREATING* (CREATE)
Ge 2: 3 the work of c that he had done.
Isa 57: 19 c praise on the lips of the mourners

CREATION* (CREATE)
Hab 2: 18 he who makes it trusts in his own c;
Mt 13: 35 hidden since the c of the world."
25: 34 for you since the c of the world.
Mk 10: 6 of c God 'made them male
16: 15 and preach the good news to all c.
Jn 17: 24 me before the c of the world.
Ro 1: 20 For since the c of the world God's
8: 19 The c waits in eager expectation
8: 20 For the c was subjected
8: 21 in hope that the c itself will be
8: 22 that the whole c has been groaning
8: 39 depth, nor anything else in all c,
2Co 5: 17 he is a new c; the old has gone,
Gal 6: 15 anything; what counts is a new c.
Eph 1: 4 us in him before the c of the world
Col 1: 15 God, the firstborn over all c.
Heb 4: 3 finished since the c of the world.
4: 13 Nothing in all c is hidden
9: 11 that is to say, not a part of this c.
9: 26 times since the c of the world.
1Pe 1: 20 chosen before the c of the world,
2Pe 3: 4 as it has since the beginning of c."
Rev 3: 14 true witness, the ruler of God's c.
13: 8 slain from the c of the world.
17: 8 life from the c of the world will be

CREATOR* (CREATE)
Ge 14: 19 C of heaven and earth.
14: 22 God Most High, C of heaven
Dt 32: 6 Is he not your Father, your C,
Ecc 12: 1 Remember your C
Isa 27: 11 and their C shows them no favor.
40: 28 the C of the ends of the earth.
43: 15 Israel's C, your King."
Mt 19: 4 the beginning the C 'made them
Ro 1: 25 created things rather than the C—
Col 3: 10 in knowledge in the image of its C.
1Pe 4: 19 themselves to their faithful C

CREATURE (CREATURES)
Lev 17: 11 For the life of a c is in the blood,
17: 14 the life of every c is its blood.
Ps 136: 25 and who gives food to every c.
Eze 1: 15 beside each c with its four faces.
Rev 4: 7 The first living c was like a lion,

CREATURES (CREATURE)
Ge 6: 19 bring into the ark two of all living c,
8: 21 again will I destroy all living c,
Ps 104: 24 the earth is full of your c.
Eze 1: 5 was what looked like four living c.

CREDIT (CREDITED CREDITOR CREDITS)
Lk 6: 33 what c is that to you? Even
Ro 4: 24 to whom God will c righteousness
1Pe 2: 20 it to your c if you receive a beating

CREDITED (CREDIT)
Ge 15: 6 and he c it to him as righteousness.
Ps 106: 31 This was c to him as righteousness
Eze 18: 20 of the righteous man will be c
Ro 4: 3 and it was c to him as righteousness
4: 4 his wages are not c to him as a gift,
4: 5 his faith is c as righteousness.
4: 9 saying that Abraham's faith was c
4: 23 The words "it was c
Gal 3: 6 and it was c to him as righteousness
Php 4: 17 for what may be c to your account.
Jas 2: 23 and it was c to him as righteousness

CREDITOR (CREDIT)
Dt 15: 2 Every c shall cancel the loan he has

CREDITS (CREDIT)
Ro 4: 6 whom God c righteousness apart

CRETANS (CRETE)
Tit 1: 12 "C are always liars, evil brutes,

CRETE (CRETANS)
Ac 27: 12 harbor in C, facing both southwest

CRIED (CRY)
Ex 2: 23 groaned in their slavery and c out,
14: 10 They were terrified and c out
Nu 20: 16 but when we c out to the LORD,
Jos 24: 7 But they c to the LORD for help,
Jdg 3: 9 But when they c out to the LORD,
3: 15 Again the Israelites c out
4: 3 they c to the LORD for help.
6: 6 the Israelites that they c out
10: 12 Maonites oppressed you and you c
1Sa 7: 9 He c out to the LORD
12: 8 they c to the LORD for help,
12: 10 They c out to the LORD and said,
Ps 18: 6 I c to my God for help.

CRIMINALS
Lk 23: 32 both c, were also led out with him

CRIMSON
Isa 1: 18 though they are red as c,
63: 1 with his garments stained c?

CRIPPLED
2Sa 9: 3 of Jonathan; he is c in both feet."
Mk 9: 45 better for you to enter life c

CRISIS*
1Co 7: 26 of the present c, I think that it is

CRITICISM*
2Co 8: 20 We want to avoid any c

CROOKED*
Dt 32: 5 but a warped and c generation.
2Sa 22: 27 to the c you show yourself shrewd.
Ps 18: 26 to the c you show yourself shrewd.
125: 5 But those who turn to c ways
Pr 2: 15 whose paths are c
5: 6 her paths are c, but she knows it
8: 8 none of them is c or perverse.
10: 9 he who takes c paths will be found
Ecc 7: 13 what he has made c?
Isa 59: 8 have turned them into c roads;
La 3: 9 he has made my paths c.
Lk 3: 5 The c roads shall become straight,
Php 2: 15 children of God without fault in a c

CROP (CROPS)
Mt 13: 8 where it produced a c—a hundred,
21: 41 share of the c at harvest time."

CROPS (CROP)
Pr 3: 9 with the firstfruits of all your c;
10: 5 He who gathers c in summer is
28: 3 like a driving rain that leaves no c.
2Ti 2: 6 the first to receive a share of the c.

CROSS (CROSSED CROSSING)
Dt 4: 21 swore that I would not c the Jordan
12: 10 But you will c the Jordan
Mt 10: 38 and anyone who does not take his c
16: 24 and take up his c and follow me.
Mk 8: 34 and take up his c and follow me.
Lk 9: 23 take up his c daily and follow me.
14: 27 anyone who does not carry his c
Jn 19: 17 Carrying his own c, he went out
Ac 2: 23 to death by nailing him to the c.
1Co 1: 17 lest the c of Christ be emptied
1: 18 the message of the c is foolishness
Gal 5: 11 offense of the c has been abolished.
6: 12 persecuted for the c of Christ.
6: 14 in the c of our Lord Jesus Christ,
Eph 2: 16 both of them to God through the c,
Php 2: 8 even death on a c!
3: 18 as enemies of the c of Christ.
Col 1: 20 through his blood, shed on the c.
2: 14 he took it away, nailing it to the c.
2: 15 triumphing over them by the c.
Heb 12: 2 set before him endured the c,

CROSSED (CROSS)
Jos 4: 7 When it c the Jordan, the waters
Jn 5: 24 he has c over from death to life.

CROSSING (CROSS)
Ge 48: 14 he was the younger, and c his arms,

CROSSROADS (ROAD)
Jer 6: 16 "Stand at the c and look;

CROUCHING
Ge 4: 7 sin is c at your door; it desires

CROWD (CROWDS)
Ex 23: 2 Do not follow the c in doing wrong.

CROWDS (CROWD)
Mt 9: 36 he saw the c, he had compassion

CROWED (CROWS)
Mt 26: 74 the man!" Immediately a rooster c.

CROWN (CROWNED CROWNS)
Pr 4: 9 present you with a c of splendor."
10: 6 Blessings c the head
12: 4 noble character is her husband's c,
16: 31 Gray hair is a c of splendor;
17: 6 Children's children are a c
Isa 35: 10 everlasting joy will c their heads.
51: 11 everlasting joy will c their heads.
61: 3 to bestow on them a c of beauty
62: 3 You will be a c of splendor
Eze 16: 12 and a beautiful c on your head.
Zec 9: 16 like jewels in a c.
Mt 27: 29 and then twisted together a c of thorns
Mk 15: 17 then twisted together a c of thorns
Jn 19: 2 The soldiers twisted together a c
19: 5 When Jesus came out wearing the c
1Co 9: 25 it to get a c that will last forever.
9: 25 it to get a c that will not last;
Php 4: 1 and long for, my joy and c,
1Th 2: 19 or the c in which we will glory
2Ti 2: 5 he does not receive the victor's c
4: 8 store for me the c of righteousness,
Jas 1: 12 he will receive the c
1Pe 5: 4 you will receive the c
Rev 2: 10 and I will give you the c of life.
3: 11 so that no one will take your c.
14: 14 a son of man" with a c of gold

CROWNED* (CROWN)
Ps 8: 5 and c him with glory and honor.
Pr 14: 18 the prudent are c with knowledge.
SS 3: 11 crown with which his mother c him
Heb 2: 7 you c him with glory and honor
2: 9 now c with glory and honor

CROWNS (CROWN)
Ps 103: 4 and c me with love and compassion
149: 4 he c the humble with salvation.
Pr 11: 26 blessing c him who is willing to sell.
Rev 4: 4 and had c of gold on their heads.
4: 10 They lay their c before the throne
12: 3 ten horns and seven c on his heads.
19: 12 and on his head are many c.

CROWS (CROWED)
Mt 26: 34 this very night, before the rooster c

CRUCIFIED* (CRUCIFY)
Mt 20: 19 to be mocked and flogged and c.
26: 2 of Man will be handed over to be c
27: 26 and handed him over to be c.
27: 35 When they had c him, they divided
27: 38 Two robbers were c with him,
27: 44 same way the robbers who were c
28: 5 looking for Jesus, who was c.

Mk 15: 15 and handed him over to be *c*.
15: 24 And they *c* him.
15: 25 the third hour when they *c* him.
15: 27 They *c* two robbers with him,
15: 32 Those *c* with him also heaped
16: 6 for Jesus the Nazarene, who was *c*.
Lk 23: 23 insistently demanded that he be *c*,
23: 33 *c* him, along with the criminals —
24: 7 be *c* and on the third day be raised
24: 20 sentenced to death, and they *c* him;
Jn 19: 16 him over to them to be *c*.
19: 18 Here they *c* him, and with him two
19: 20 for the place where Jesus was *c* was
19: 23 When the soldiers *c* Jesus,
19: 32 of the first man who had been *c*
19: 41 At the place where Jesus was *c*,
Ac 2: 36 whom you *c*, both Lord and Christ
4: 10 whom you *c* but whom God raised
Ro 6: 6 For we know that our old self was *c*
1Co 1: 13 Is Christ divided? Was Paul *c*
1: 23 but we preach Christ *c*: a stumbling
2: 2 except Jesus Christ and him *c*.
2: 8 they would not have *c* the Lord
2Co 13: 4 to be sure, he was *c* in weakness,
Gal 2: 20 I have been *c* with Christ
3: 1 Christ was clearly portrayed as *c*.
5: 24 Christ Jesus have *c* the sinful
6: 14 which the world has been *c*
Rev 11: 8 where also their Lord was *c*.

CRUCIFY* (CRUCIFIED CRUCIFYING)
Mt 23: 34 Some of them you will kill and *c*;
27: 22 They all answered, "*C* him!" "Why
27: 23 they shouted all the louder, "*C* him
27: 31 Then they led him away to *c* him.
Mk 15: 13 "*C* him!" they shouted.
15: 14 they shouted all the louder, "*C* him
15: 20 Then they led him out to *c* him.
Lk 23: 21 they kept shouting, "*C* him! *C* him
Jn 19: 6 they shouted, "*C*! *C*!"
19: 6 "You take him and *c* him.
19: 10 either to free you or to *c* you?"
19: 15 Crucify him!" "Shall I *c* your king
19: 15 away! Take him away! *C* him!"

CRUCIFYING* (CRUCIFY)
Heb 6: 6 to their loss they are *c* the Son

CRUSH (CRUSHED)
Ge 3: 15 he will *c* your head,
Isa 53: 10 it was the LORD's will to *c* him
Ro 16: 20 The God of peace will soon *c* Satan

CRUSHED (CRUSH)
Ps 34: 18 and saves those who are *c* in spirit.
Pr 17: 22 but a *c* spirit dries up the bones.
18: 14 but a *c* spirit who can bear?
Isa 53: 5 he was *c* for our iniquities;
2Co 4: 8 not *c*; perplexed, but not in despair;

CRY (CRIED)
Ex 2: 23 *c* for help because of their slavery
Ps 5: 2 Listen to my *c* for help,
34: 15 and his ears are attentive to their *c*;
40: 1 he turned to me and heard my *c*.
130: 1 Out of the depths I *c* to you,
Pr 21: 13 to the *c* of the poor,
La 2: 18 *c* out to the Lord.
Hab 2: 11 The stones of the wall will *c* out,
Lk 19: 40 keep quiet, the stones will *c* out."

CUNNING
2Co 11: 3 deceived by the serpent's *c*,
Eph 4: 14 and by the *c* and craftiness of men

CUP
Ps 23: 5 my *c* overflows.
Isa 51: 22 from that *c*, the goblet of my wrath,
51: 22 the *c* that made you stagger;
Mt 10: 42 if anyone gives even a *c* of cold water
20: 22 "Can you drink the *c* I am going
23: 25 You clean the outside of the *c*
23: 26 First clean the inside of the *c*
26: 27 Then he took the *c*, gave thanks
26: 39 may this *c* be taken from me.
26: 42 possible for this *c* to be taken away
Mk 9: 41 anyone who gives you a *c* of water
10: 38 "Can you drink the *c* I drink
10: 39 "You will drink the *c* I drink
14: 23 Then he took the *c*, gave thanks
14: 36 Take this *c* from me.
Lk 11: 39 Pharisees clean the outside of the *c*
22: 17 After taking the *c*, he gave thanks
22: 20 after the supper he took the *c*,
22: 20 "This *c* is the new covenant
22: 42 if you are willing, take this *c*
Jn 18: 11 I not drink the *c* the Father has
1Co 10: 16 Is not the *c* of thanksgiving
10: 21 the *c* of the Lord and the *c*
11: 25 after supper he took the *c*, saying,
11: 25 "This *c* is the new covenant

CUPBEARER
Ge 40: 1 the *c* and the baker of the king
Ne 1: 11 I was *c* to the king.

CURE (CURED)
Jer 17: 9 and beyond *c*.
30: 15 your pain that has no *c*?
Hos 5: 13 But he is not able to *c* you,
Lk 9: 1 out all demons and to *c* diseases,

CURED (CURE)
Mt 11: 5 those who have leprosy are *c*,
Lk 6: 18 troubled by evil spirits were *c*,

CURSE (ACCURSED CURSED CURSES CURSING)
Ge 4: 11 Now you are under a *c*
8: 21 "Never again will I *c* the ground
12: 3 and whoever curses you I will *c*;
Dt 11: 26 before you today a blessing and a *c*
11: 28 the *c* if you disobey the commands
21: 23 hung on a tree is under God's *c*.
23: 5 turned the *c* into a blessing for you,
Job 1: 11 he will surely *c* you to your face."
2: 5 he will surely *c* you to your face."
2: 9 *C* God and die!" He replied,
Ps 109: 28 They may *c*, but you will bless;
Pr 3: 33 The LORD's *c* is on the house
24: 24 peoples will *c* him and nations
Mal 2: 2 and I will *c* your blessings.
Lk 6: 28 bless those who *c* you, pray
Ro 12: 14 persecute you; bless and do not *c*.
Gal 3: 10 on observing the law are under a *c*,
3: 13 of the law by becoming a *c* for us,
Jas 3: 9 with it we *c* men, who have been
Rev 22: 3 No longer will there be any *c*.

CURSED (CURSE)
Ge 3: 17 "*C* is the ground because of you;
Dt 27: 15 "*C* is the man who carves an image
27: 16 "*C* is the man who dishonors his
27: 17 "*C* is the man who moves his
27: 18 "*C* is the man who leads the blind
27: 19 *C* is the man who withholds justice
27: 20 "*C* is the man who sleeps
27: 21 "*C* is the man who has sexual
27: 22 "*C* is the man who sleeps
27: 23 "*C* is the man who sleeps
27: 24 "*C* is the man who kills his
27: 25 "*C* is the man who accepts a bribe
27: 26 "*C* is the man who does not uphold
Jer 17: 5 "*C* is the one who trusts in man,
Mal 1: 14 "*C* is the cheat who has
Ro 9: 3 I could wish that I myself were *c*
1Co 4: 12 When we are *c*, we bless;
12: 3 "Jesus be *c*," and no one can say,
Gal 3: 10 "*C* is everyone who does not
3: 13 *C* is everyone who is hung on a tree

CURSES (CURSE)
Ex 21: 17 "Anyone who *c* his father
Lev 20: 9 "'If anyone *c* his father or mother,
Nu 5: 23 is to write these *c* on a scroll
Jos 8: 34 the blessings and the *c* — just
Pr 20: 20 If a man *c* his father or mother,
28: 27 to them receives many *c*.
Mt 15: 4 and 'Anyone who *c* his father
Mk 7: 10 and, 'Anyone who *c* his father

CURSING (CURSE)
Ps 109: 18 He wore *c* as his garment;
Ro 3: 14 "Their mouths are full of *c*
Jas 3: 10 the same mouth come praise and *c*.

CURTAIN
Ex 26: 31 "Make a *c* of blue, purple
26: 33 The *c* will separate the Holy Place
Mt 27: 51 At that moment the *c*
Mk 15: 38 The *c* of the temple was torn in two
Lk 23: 45 the *c* of the temple was torn in two.
Heb 6: 19 the inner sanctuary behind the *c*,
9: 3 Behind the second *c* was a room
10: 20 opened for us through the *c*,

CUSTOM
Job 1: 5 This was Job's regular *c*.
Mk 10: 1 and as was his *c*, he taught them.
Lk 4: 16 into the synagogue, as was his *c*.
Ac 17: 2 As his *c* was, Paul went

CUT
Lev 19: 27 "'Do not *c* the hair at the sides
21: 5 of their beards or *c* their bodies.
1Ki 3: 25 "*C* the living child in two
Isa 51: 1 to the rock from which you were *c*
53: 8 For he was *c* off from the land
Da 2: 45 of the rock *c* out of a mountain,
9: 26 the Anointed One will be *c* off
Mt 3: 10 not produce good fruit will be *c*
24: 22 If those days had not been *c* short,
1Co 11: 6 for a woman to have her hair *c*

CYMBAL* (CYMBALS)
1Co 13: 1 a resounding gong or a clanging *c*.

CYMBALS (CYMBAL)
1Ch 15: 16 instruments: lyres, harps and *c*.
2Ch 5: 12 dressed in fine linen and playing *c*,
Ps 150: 5 praise him with resounding *c*.

CYRUS
Persian king who allowed exiles to return (2Ch 36:22 – Ezr 1:8), to rebuild temple (Ezr 5:13 – 6:14), as appointed by the LORD (Isa 44:28 – 45:13).

DAGON
Jdg 16: 23 offer a great sacrifice to *D* their god
1Sa 5: 2 Dagon's temple and set it beside *D*.

DAMASCUS
Ac 9: 3 As he neared *D* on his journey,

DAN
1. Son of Jacob by Bilhah (Ge 30:4 – 6; 35:25; 46:23). Tribe of blessed (Ge 49:16 – 17; Dt 33:22), numbered (Nu 1:39; 26:43), allotted land (Jos 19:40 – 48; Eze 48:1), failed to fully possess (Jdg 1:34 – 35), failed to support Deborah (Jdg 5:17), possessed Laish/Dan (Jdg 18).
2. Northernmost city in Israel (Ge 14:14; Jdg 18; 20:1).

DANCE (DANCED DANCING)
Ecc 3: 4 a time to mourn and a time to *d*,
Mt 11: 17 and you did not *d*;

DANCED (DANCE)
2Sa 6: 14 *d* before the LORD
Mk 6: 22 of Herodias came in and *d*,

DANCING (DANCE)
Ps 30: 11 You turned my wailing into *d*;
149: 3 Let them praise his name with *d*

DANGER
Pr 22: 3 A prudent man sees *d*
27: 12 The prudent see *d* and take refuge,
Mt 5: 22 will be in *d* of the fire of hell.
Ro 8: 35 famine or nakedness or *d* or sword?
2Co 11: 26 I have been in *d* from rivers,

DANIEL
1. Hebrew exile to Babylon, name changed to Belteshazzar (Da 1:6 – 7). Refused to eat unclean food (Da 1:8 – 21). Interpreted Nebuchadnezzar's dreams (Da 2; 4), writing on the wall (Da 5). Thrown into lion's den (Da 6). Visions of (Da 7 – 12).
2. Son of David (1Ch 3:1).

DARIUS
1. King of Persia (Ezr 4:5), allowed rebuilding of temple (Ezr 5 – 6).
2. Mede who conquered Babylon (Da 5:31).

DARK (DARKENED DARKENS DARKNESS)
Job 34: 22 There is no *d* place, no deep
Ps 18: 9 *d* clouds were under his feet.
Pr 31: 15 She gets up while it is still *d*;
SS 1: 6 Do not stare at me because I am *d*,
Jn 12: 35 in the *d* does not know where he is
Ro 2: 19 a light for those who are in the *d*,
2Pe 1: 19 as to a light shining in a *d* place,

DARKENED (DARK)
Joel 2: 10 the sun and moon are *d*,
Mt 24: 29 "'the sun will be *d*,
Ro 1: 21 and their foolish hearts were *d*.
Eph 4: 18 They are *d* in their understanding

DARKENS (DARK)
Job 38: 2 "Who is this that *d* my counsel

DARKNESS (DARK)
Ge 1: 2 *d* was over the surface of the deep,
1: 4 he separated the light from the *d*.
Ex 10: 22 and total *d* covered all Egypt
20: 21 approached the thick *d* where God
2Sa 22: 29 the LORD turns my *d* into light.
Ps 18: 28 my God turns my *d* into light.
91: 6 the pestilence that stalks in the *d*,
112: 4 Even in *d* light dawns
139: 12 even the *d* will not be dark to you;
Pr 4: 19 the way of the wicked is like deep *d*
Isa 5: 20 and light for *d*,
42: 16 I will turn the *d* into light
45: 7 I form the light and create *d*,
58: 10 then your light will rise in the *d*,
61: 1 and release from *d*,
Joel 2: 31 The sun will be turned to *d*
Mt 4: 16 the people living in *d*
6: 23 how great is that *d*! "No one can

Lk 11: 34 are bad, your body also is full of *d*.
23: 44 and *d* came over the whole land
Jn 1: 5 The light shines in the *d*,
3: 19 but men loved *d* instead of light
Ac 2: 20 The sun will be turned to *d*
2Co 4: 6 who said, "Let light shine out of *d*
6: 14 fellowship can light have with *d*?
Eph 5: 8 For you were once *d*, but now you
5: 11 to do with the fruitless deeds of *d*,
1Pe 2: 9 out of *d* into his wonderful light.
2Pe 2: 17 Blackest *d* is reserved for them.
1Jn 1: 5 in him there is no *d* at all.
2: 9 but hates his brother is still in the *d*.
Jude : 6 in *d*, bound with everlasting chains
: 13 for whom blackest *d* has been

DASH
Ps 2: 9 you will *d* them to pieces like

DAUGHTER (DAUGHTERS)
Ex 1: 10 she took him to Pharaoh's *d*
Jdg 11: 40 to commemorate the *d* of Jephthah
Est 2: 7 Mordecai had taken her as his own *d*
Ps 9: 14 praises in the gates of the *D* of Zion
137: 8 O *D* of Babylon, doomed
Isa 62: 11 "Say to the *D* of Zion,
Zec 9: 9 Shout, *D* of Jerusalem!
Mk 5: 34 "*D*, your faith has healed you.
7: 29 the demon has left your *d*.

DAUGHTERS (DAUGHTER)
Ge 6: 2 the *d* of men were beautiful,
19: 36 Lot's *d* became pregnant
Nu 36: 10 Zelophehad's *d* did as the LORD
Joel 2: 28 sons and *d* will prophesy,

DAVID

Son of Jesse (Ru 4:17 – 22; 1Ch 2:13 – 15), ancestor of Jesus (Mt 1:1 – 17; Lk 3:31). Wives and children (1Sa 18; 25:39 – 44; 2Sa 3:2 – 5; 5:13 – 16; 11:27; 1Ch 3:1 – 9).

Anointed king by Samuel (1Sa 16:1 – 13). Musician to Saul (1Sa 16:14 – 23; 18:10). Killed Goliath (1Sa 17). Relation with Jonathan (1Sa 18:1 – 4; 19 – 20; 23:16 – 18; 2Sa 1). Disfavor of Saul (1Sa 18:6 – 23:29). Spared Saul's life (1Sa 24; 26). Among Philistines (1Sa 21:10 – 14; 27 – 30). Lament for Saul and Jonathan (2Sa 1).

Anointed king of Judah (2Sa 2:1 – 11). Conflict with house of Saul (2Sa 2 – 4). Anointed king of Israel (2Sa 5:1 – 4; 1Ch 11:1 – 3). Conquered Jerusalem (2Sa 5:6 – 10; 1Ch 11:4 – 9). Brought ark to Jerusalem (2Sa 6; 1Ch 13; 15 – 16). The LORD promised eternal dynasty (2Sa 7; 1Ch 17; Ps 132). Showed kindness to Mephibosheth (2Sa 9). Adultery with Bathsheba, murder of Uriah (2Sa 11 – 12). Son Amnon raped daughter Tamar; killed by Absalom (2Sa 13). Absalom's revolt (2Sa 14 – 17); death (2Sa 18). Sheba's revolt (2Sa 20). Victories: Philistines (2Sa 5:17 – 25; 1Ch 14:8 – 17; 2Sa 21:15 – 22; 1Ch 20:4 – 8), Ammonites (2Sa 10; 1Ch 19), various (2Sa 8; 1Ch 18). Mighty men (2Sa 23:8 – 39; 1Ch 11 – 12). Punished for numbering army (2Sa 24; 1Ch 21). Appointed Solomon king (1Ki 1:28 – 2:9). Prepared for building of temple (1Ch 22 – 29). Last words (2Sa 23:1 – 7). Death (1Ki 2:10 – 12; 1Ch 29:28).

Psalmist (Mt 22:43 – 45), musician (Am 6:5), prophet (2Sa 23:2 – 7; Ac 1:16; 2:30).

Psalms of: 2 (Ac 4:25), 3 – 32, 34 – 41, 51 – 65, 68 – 70, 86, 95 (Heb 4:7), 101, 103, 108 – 110, 122, 124, 131, 133, 138 – 145.

DAWN (DAWNED DAWNS)
Ps 37: 6 your righteousness shine like the *d*,
Pr 4: 18 is like the first gleam of *d*,
Isa 14: 12 O morning star, son of the *d*!
Am 4: 13 he who turns *d* to darkness,
5: 8 who turns blackness into *d*

DAWNED (DAWN)
Isa 9: 2 a light has *d*.
Mt 4: 16 a light has *d*."

DAWNS* (DAWN)
Ps 65: 8 where morning *d* and evening
112: 4 in darkness light *d* for the upright,
Hos 10: 15 When that day *d*,
2Pe 1: 19 until the day *d* and the morning

DAY (DAYS)
Ge 1: 5 God called the light "*d*,"
1: 5 and there was morning — the first *d*
1: 8 there was morning — the second *d*.
1: 13 there was morning — the third *d*.
1: 19 there was morning — the fourth *d*.
1: 23 there was morning — the fifth *d*.
1: 31 there was morning — the sixth *d*.
2: 2 so on the seventh *d* he rested
8: 22 *d* and night
Ex 16: 30 the people rested on the seventh *d*.
20: 8 "Remember the Sabbath *d*
Lev 16: 30 on this *d* atonement will be made
23: 28 because it is the *D* of Atonement,
Nu 14: 14 before them in a pillar of cloud by *d*
Jos 1: 8 meditate on it *d* and night,
2Ki 7: 9 This is a *d* of good news
25: 30 *D* by *d* the king gave Jehoiachin
1Ch 16: 23 proclaim his salvation *d* after *d*.
Ne 8: 18 *D* after *d*, from the first *d*
Ps 84: 10 Better is one *d* in your courts
96: 2 proclaim his salvation *d* after *d*.
118: 24 This is the *d* the LORD has made;
Pr 27: 1 not know what a *d* may bring forth.
Isa 13: 9 a cruel *d*, with wrath and fierce
Jer 46: 10 But that *d* belongs to the Lord,
50: 31 "for your *d* has come,
Eze 30: 2 "Alas for that *d*!"
Joel 1: 15 "Alas for that *d*!
2: 31 and dreadful *d* of the LORD.
Am 3: 14 On the *d* I punish Israel for her sins
5: 20 Will not the *d* of the LORD be
Ob : 15 "The *d* of the LORD is near
Zep 1: 14 The great *d* of the LORD is near —
Zec 2: 11 joined with the LORD in that *d*
14: 1 A *d* of the LORD is coming
14: 7 It will be a unique *d*,
Mal 4: 5 dreadful *d* of the LORD comes.
Mt 24: 38 up to the *d* Noah entered the ark;
Lk 11: 3 Give us each *d* our daily bread.
17: 24 in his *d* will be like the lightning,
Ac 5: 42 *D* after *d*, in the temple courts
17: 11 examined the Scriptures every *d*
17: 17 as in the marketplace *d* by *d*
Ro 14: 5 man considers every *d* alike.
1Co 5: 5 his spirit saved on the *d* of the Lord
2Co 4: 16 we are being renewed *d* by *d*.
11: 25 I spent a night and a *d*
1Th 5: 2 for you know very well that the *d*
5: 4 so that this *d* should surprise you
2Th 2: 2 saying that the *d* of the Lord has
Heb 7: 27 need to offer sacrifices *d* after *d*,
2Pe 3: 8 With the Lord a *d* is like
3: 10 *d* of the Lord will come like a thief.
Rev 6: 17 For the great *d* of their wrath has
16: 14 on the great *d* of God Almighty.

DAYS (DAY)
Dt 17: 19 he is to read it all the *d* of his life
32: 7 Remember the *d* of old;
Ps 23: 6 all the *d* of my life,
34: 12 and desires to see many good *d*,
39: 5 have made my *d* a mere
90: 10 The length of our *d* is seventy years
90: 12 Teach us to number our *d* aright,
103: 15 As for man, his *d* are like grass,
128: 5 all the *d* of your life;
Pr 31: 12 all the *d* of her life.
Ecc 9: 9 all the *d* of this meaningless life
12: 1 Creator in the *d* of your youth,
Isa 38: 20 all the *d* of our lives
Da 7: 9 and the Ancient of *D* took his seat.
7: 13 He approached the Ancient of *D*
7: 22 until the Ancient of *D* came
Hos 3: 5 and to his blessings in the last *d*.
Joel 2: 29 I will pour out my Spirit in those *d*.
Mic 4: 1 In the last *d*
Lk 19: 43 The *d* will come upon you
Ac 2: 17 by the prophet Joel: "'In the last *d*,
2Ti 3: 1 will be terrible times in the last *d*.
Heb 1: 2 in these last *d* he has spoken to us
2Pe 3: 3 that in the last *d* scoffers will come,

DAZZLING*
Da 2: 31 *d* statue, awesome in appearance.
Mk 9: 3 His clothes became *d* white,

DEACON* (DEACONS)
1Ti 3: 12 A *d* must be the husband of

DEACONS* (DEACON)
Php 1: 1 together with the overseers and *d*:
1Ti 3: 8 *D*, likewise, are to be men worthy
3: 10 against them, let them serve as *d*.

DEAD (DIE)
Lev 17: 15 who eats anything found *d*
Dt 18: 11 or spiritist or who consults the *d*.
Isa 8: 19 Why consult the *d* on behalf
Mt 8: 22 and let the *d* bury their own *d*."
28: 7 'He has risen from the *d*
Lk 15: 24 For this son of mine was *d*
24: 46 rise from the *d* on the third day,
Ro 6: 11 count yourselves *d* to sin
1Co 15: 29 do who are baptized for the *d*?
Eph 2: 1 you were *d* in your transgressions
1Th 4: 16 and the *d* in Christ will rise first.
Jas 2: 17 is not accompanied by action, is *d*.
2: 26 so faith without deeds is *d*.
Rev 14: 13 Blessed are the *d* who die
20: 12 And I saw the *d*, great and small,

DEADENED* (DIE)
Jn 12: 40 and *d* their hearts,

DEAR* (DEARER)
2Sa 1: 26 you were very *d* to me.
Ps 102: 14 For her stones are *d*
Jer 31: 20 Is not Ephraim my *d* son,
Jn 2: 4 "*D* woman, why do you involve me
19: 26 he said to his mother, "*D* woman,
Ac 15: 25 to you with our *d* friends Barnabas
Ro 16: 5 Greet my *d* friend Epenetus,
16: 9 in Christ, and my *d* friend Stachys.
16: 12 Greet my *d* friend Persis, another
1Co 4: 14 but to warn you, as my *d* children.
10: 14 my *d* friends, flee from idolatry.
15: 58 Therefore, my *d* brothers,
2Co 7: 1 we have these promises, *d* friends,
12: 19 and everything we do, *d* friends,
Gal 4: 19 My *d* children, for whom I am
Eph 6: 21 the *d* brother and faithful servant
Php 2: 12 my *d* friends, as you have always
4: 1 firm in the Lord, *d* friends!
Col 1: 7 Epaphras, our *d* fellow servant,
4: 7 He is a *d* brother, a faithful
4: 9 our faithful and *d* brother,
4: 14 Our *d* friend Luke, the doctor,
1Th 2: 8 because you had become so *d* to us.
1Ti 6: 2 their service are believers, and *d*
2Ti 1: 2 To Timothy, my *d* son: Grace,
Phm : 1 To Philemon our *d* friend
: 16 He is very *d* to me but
: 16 better than a slave, as a *d* brother.
Heb 6: 9 we speak like this, *d* friends,
Jas 1: 16 Don't be deceived, my *d* brothers.
1: 19 My *d* brothers, take note of this:
2: 5 thoughts? Listen, my *d* brothers:
1Pe 2: 11 *D* friends, I urge you, as aliens
4: 12 *D* friends, do not be surprised
2Pe 3: 1 *D* friends, this is now my second
3: 8 not forget this one thing, *d* friends:
3: 14 *d* friends, since you are looking
3: 15 just as our *d* brother Paul
3: 17 *d* friends, since you already know
1Jn 2: 1 My *d* children, I write this to you
2: 7 *D* friends, I am not writing you
2: 12 I write to you, *d* children,
2: 13 I write to you, *d* children,
2: 18 *D* children, this is the last hour;
2: 28 *d* children, continue in him,
3: 2 *D* friends, now we are children
3: 7 *D* children, do not let anyone lead
3: 18 love of God be in him? *D* children,
3: 21 *D* friends, if our hearts do not
4: 1 *D* friends, do not believe every
4: 4 *d* children, are from God
4: 7 *D* friends, let us love one another,
4: 11 *D* friends, since God so loved us,
5: 21 *D* children, keep yourselves
2Jn : 5 *d* lady, I am not writing you a new
3Jn : 1 The elder, To my *d* friend Gaius,
: 2 *D* friend, I pray that you may enjoy
: 5 *D* friend, you are faithful
: 11 *D* friend, do not imitate what is evil
Jude : 3 *D* friends, although I was very
: 17 But, *d* friends, remember what
: 20 *d* friends, build yourselves up

DEARER* (DEAR)
Phm : 16 dear to me but even *d* to you,

DEATH (DIE)
Ex 21: 12 kills him shall surely be put to *d*.
Nu 35: 16 the murderer shall be put to *d*.
Dt 30: 19 set before you life and *d*,
Ru 1: 17 if anything but *d* separates you
2Ki 4: 40 O man of God, there is *d* in the pot
Job 26: 6 *D* is naked before God;
Ps 23: 4 the valley of the shadow of *d*,
44: 22 for your sake we face *d* all day long
89: 48 What man can live and not see *d*,
116: 15 is the *d* of his saints.
Pr 8: 36 all who hate me love *d*."
11: 19 he who pursues evil goes to his *d*.
14: 12 but in the end it leads to *d*.
15: 11 *D* and Destruction lie open
16: 25 but in the end it leads to *d*.
18: 21 tongue has the power of life and *d*,
19: 18 do not be a willing party to his *d*.
23: 14 and save his soul from *d*.
Ecc 7: 2 for *d* is the destiny of every man;
Isa 25: 8 he will swallow up *d* forever.
53: 12 he poured out his life unto *d*,
Eze 18: 23 pleasure in the *d* of the wicked?
18: 32 pleasure in the *d* of anyone,
33: 11 pleasure in the *d* of the wicked,
Hos 13: 14 Where, O *d*, are your plagues?
Jn 5: 24 he has crossed over from *d* to life.

Ro 4: 25 delivered over to *d* for our sins
5: 12 and in this way *d* came to all men,
5: 14 *d* reigned from the time of Adam
6: 3 Jesus were baptized into his *d*?
6: 23 For the wages of sin is *d*,
7: 24 me from this body of *d*?
8: 13 put to *d* the misdeeds of the body,
8: 36 your sake we face *d* all day long;
1Co 15: 21 For since *d* came through a man,
15: 26 The last enemy to be destroyed is *d*
15: 55 Where, O *d*, is your sting?"
2Ti 1: 10 who has destroyed *d* and has
Heb 2: 14 him who holds the power of *d* —
1Jn 5: 16 There is a sin that leads to *d*.
Rev 1: 18 And I hold the keys of *d* and Hades
2: 11 hurt at all by the second *d*.
20: 6 The second *d* has no power
20: 14 The lake of fire is the second *d*.
20: 14 Then *d* and Hades were thrown
21: 4 There will be no more *d*
21: 8 This is the second *d*."

DEBAUCHERY*
Ro 13: 13 not in sexual immorality and *d*,
2Co 12: 21 and *d* in which they have indulged.
Gal 5: 19 impurity and *d*; idolatry
Eph 5: 18 drunk on wine, which leads to *d*.
1Pe 4: 3 living in *d*, lust, drunkenness,

DEBORAH*
1. Prophetess who led Israel to victory over Canaanites (Jdg 4–5).
2. Rebekah's nurse (Ge 35:8).

DEBT* (DEBTOR DEBTORS DEBTS)
Dt 15: 3 must cancel any *d* your brother
24: 6 the upper one — as security for a *d*,
1Sa 22: 2 or in *d* or discontented gathered
Job 24: 9 of the poor is seized for a *d*.
Mt 18: 25 that he had be sold to repay the *d*.
18: 27 canceled the *d* and let him go.
18: 30 into prison until he could pay the *d*.
18: 32 'I canceled all that *d* of yours
Lk 7: 43 who had the bigger *d* canceled."
Ro 13: 8 Let no *d* remain outstanding,
13: 8 continuing *d* to love one another,

DEBTOR* (DEBT)
Isa 24: 2 for *d* as for creditor.

DEBTORS* (DEBT)
Hab 2: 7 Will not your *d* suddenly arise?
Mt 6: 12 as we also have forgiven our *d*.
Lk 16: 5 called in each one of his master's *d*.

DEBTS* (DEBT)
Dt 15: 1 seven years you must cancel *d*.
15: 2 time for canceling *d* has been
15: 9 the year for canceling *d*, is near,"
31: 10 in the year for canceling *d*,
2Ki 4: 7 "Go, sell the oil and pay your *d*.
Ne 10: 31 the land and will cancel all *d*.
Pr 22: 26 or puts up security for *d*;
Mt 6: 12 Forgive us our *d*,
Lk 7: 42 so he canceled the *d* of both.

DECAY*
Ps 16: 10 will you let your Holy One see *d*.
49: 9 and not see *d*.
49: 14 their forms will *d* in the grave,
Pr 12: 4 a disgraceful wife is like *d*
Isa 5: 24 so their roots will *d*
Hab 3: 16 *d* crept into my bones,
Ac 2: 27 will you let your Holy One see *d*.
2: 31 to the grave, nor did his body see *d*.
13: 34 never to *d*, is stated in these words:
13: 35 will not let your Holy One see *d*.'
13: 37 raised from the dead did not see *d*.
Ro 8: 21 liberated from its bondage to *d*

DECEIT (DECEIVE)
Ps 5: 9 with their tongue they speak *d*.
Isa 53: 9 nor was any *d* in his mouth.
Da 8: 25 He will cause *d* to prosper,
Zep 3: 13 nor will *d* be found in their mouths.
Mk 7: 22 greed, malice, *d*, lewdness, envy,
Ac 13: 10 You are full of all kinds of *d*
Ro 1: 29 murder, strife, *d* and malice.
3: 13 their tongues practice *d*."
1Pe 2: 1 yourselves of all malice and all *d*,
2: 22 and no *d* was found in his mouth."

DECEITFUL (DECEIVE)
Jer 17: 9 The heart is *d* above all things
Hos 10: 2 Their heart is *d*,
2Co 11: 13 men are false apostles, *d* workmen,
Eph 4: 14 of men in their *d* scheming.
4: 22 is being corrupted by its *d* desires;
1Pe 3: 10 and his lips from *d* speech.

Rev 21: 27 who does what is shameful or *d*,

DECEITFULNESS* (DECEIVE)
Ps 119: 118 for their *d* is in vain.
Mt 13: 22 and the *d* of wealth choke it,
Mk 4: 19 the *d* of wealth and the desires
Heb 3: 13 of you may be hardened by sin's *d*.

DECEIVE (DECEIT DECEITFUL DECEITFULNESS DECEIVED DECEIVER DECEIVERS DECEIVES DECEIVING DECEPTION DECEPTIVE)
Lev 19: 11 "'Do not *d* one another.
Pr 14: 5 A truthful witness does not *d*,
24: 28 or use your lips to *d*.
Jer 37: 9 Do not *d* yourselves, thinking,
Zec 13: 4 garment of hair in order to *d*.
Mt 24: 5 'I am the Christ,' and will *d* many.
24: 11 will appear and *d* many people.
24: 24 and miracles to *d* even the elect —
Mk 13: 6 'I am he,' and will *d* many.
13: 22 and miracles to *d* the elect —
Ro 16: 18 and flattery they *d* the minds
1Co 3: 18 Do not *d* yourselves.
Eph 5: 6 Let no one *d* you with empty words
Col 2: 4 this so that no one may *d* you
2Th 2: 3 Don't let anyone *d* you in any way,
Jas 1: 22 to the word, and so *d* yourselves.
1Jn 1: 8 we *d* ourselves and the truth is not
Rev 20: 8 and will go out to *d* the nations

DECEIVED (DECEIVE)
Ge 3: 13 "The serpent *d* me, and I ate."
Lk 21: 8 "Watch out that you are not *d*.
1Co 6: 9 the kingdom of God? Do not be *d*:
2Co 11: 3 Eve was *d* by the serpent's cunning
Gal 6: 7 Do not be *d*: God cannot be
1Ti 2: 14 And Adam was not the one *d*;
2Ti 3: 13 to worse, deceiving and being *d*.
Tit 3: 3 *d* and enslaved by all kinds
Jas 1: 16 Don't be *d*, my dear brothers.
Rev 13: 14 he *d* the inhabitants of the earth.
20: 10 And the devil, who *d* them,

DECEIVER (DECEIVE)
Mt 27: 63 while he was still alive that *d* said,
2Jn : 7 Any such person is the *d*

DECEIVERS* (DECEIVE)
Ps 49: 5 when wicked *d* surround me —
Tit 1: 10 and *d*, especially those
2Jn : 7 Many *d*, who do not acknowledge

DECEIVES (DECEIVE)
Pr 26: 19 is a man who *d* his neighbor
Mt 24: 4 "Watch out that no one *d* you.
Mk 13: 5 "Watch out that no one *d* you.
Gal 6: 3 when he is nothing, he *d* himself.
2Th 2: 10 sort of evil that *d* those who are
Jas 1: 26 he *d* himself and his religion is

DECEIVING* (DECEIVE)
Lev 6: 2 by *d* his neighbor about something
1Ti 4: 1 follow *d* spirits and things taught
2Ti 3: 13 go from bad to worse, *d*
Rev 20: 3 him from *d* the nations anymore

DECENCY* (DECENTLY)
1Ti 2: 9 women to dress modestly, with *d*

DECENTLY* (DECENCY)
Ro 13: 13 Let us behave *d*, as in the daytime,

DECEPTION (DECEIVE)
Pr 14: 8 but the folly of fools is *d*.
26: 26 His malice may be concealed by *d*,
Mt 27: 64 This last *d* will be worse
2Co 4: 2 we do not use *d*, nor do we distort

DECEPTIVE (DECEIVE)
Pr 11: 18 The wicked man earns *d* wages,
31: 30 Charm is *d*, and beauty is fleeting;
Jer 7: 4 Do not trust in *d* words and say,
Col 2: 8 through hollow and *d* philosophy,

DECIDED (DECISION)
2Co 9: 7 man should give what he has *d*

DECISION (DECIDED)
Ex 28: 29 heart on the breastpiece of *d*
Joel 3: 14 multitudes in the valley of *d*!

DECLARE (DECLARED DECLARING)
1Ch 16: 24 *D* his glory among the nations,
Ps 19: 1 The heavens *d* the glory of God;
96: 3 *D* his glory among the nations,
Isa 42: 9 and new things I *d*;

DECLARED (DECLARE)
Mk 7: 19 Jesus *d* all foods "clean.")
Ro 2: 13 the law who will be *d* righteous.
3: 20 no one will be *d* righteous

DECLARING (DECLARE)
Ps 71: 8 *d* your splendor all day long.
Ac 2: 11 we hear them *d* the wonders

DECREE (DECREED DECREES)
Ex 15: 25 There the LORD made a *d*
1Ch 16: 17 He confirmed it to Jacob as a *d*,
Ps 2: 7 I will proclaim the *d* of the LORD:
7: 6 Awake, my God; *d* justice.
81: 4 this is a *d* for Israel,
148: 6 he gave a *d* that will never pass
Da 4: 24 and this is the *d* the Most High has
Lk 2: 1 Augustus issued a *d* that a census
Ro 1: 32 know God's righteous *d* that those

DECREED (DECREE)
Ps 78: 5 He *d* statutes for Jacob
Jer 40: 2 LORD your God *d* this disaster
La 3: 37 happen if the Lord has not *d* it?
Da 9: 24 "Seventy 'sevens' are *d*
9: 26 and desolations have been *d*.
Lk 22: 22 Son of Man will go as it has been *d*,

DECREES (DECREE)
Ge 26: 5 my commands, my *d* and my laws
Ex 15: 26 to his commands and keep all his *d*,
18: 16 inform them of God's *d* and laws."
18: 20 Teach them the *d* and laws,
Lev 10: 11 Israelites all the *d* the LORD has
18: 4 and be careful to follow my *d*.
18: 5 Keep my *d* and laws,
18: 26 you must keep my *d* and my laws.
Ps 119: 12 teach me your *d*.
119: 16 I delight in your *d*;
119: 48 and I meditate on your *d*.
119: 112 My heart is set on keeping your *d*

DEDICATE (DEDICATED DEDICATION)
Nu 6: 12 He must *d* himself to the LORD
Pr 20: 25 for a man to *d* something rashly

DEDICATED (DEDICATE)
Lev 21: 12 he has been *d* by the anointing oil
Nu 6: 9 thus defiling the hair he has *d*,
6: 18 shave off the hair that he *d*.
18: 6 *d* to the LORD to do the work
1Ki 8: 63 and all the Israelites *d* the temple
2Ch 29: 31 "You have now *d* yourselves
Ne 3: 1 They *d* it and set its doors in place,

DEDICATION (DEDICATE)
Nu 6: 19 shaved off the hair of his *d*,
Jn 10: 22 came the Feast of *D* at Jerusalem.
1Ti 5: 11 sensual desires overcome their *d*

DEED (DEEDS)
Jer 32: 10 and sealed the *d*, had it witnessed,
32: 16 After I had given the *d* of purchase
Col 3: 17 you do, whether in word or *d*,
2Th 2: 17 and strengthen you in every good *d*

DEEDS (DEED)
Dt 3: 24 or on earth who can do the *d*
4: 34 or by great and awesome *d*,
34: 12 the awesome *d* that Moses
1Sa 2: 3 and by him *d* are weighed.
1Ch 16: 24 his marvelous *d* among all peoples.
Job 34: 25 Because he takes note of their *d*,
Ps 26: 7 and telling of all your wonderful *d*.
45: 4 right hand display awesome *d*.
65: 5 with awesome *d* of righteousness,
66: 3 "How awesome are your *d*!
71: 17 day I declare your marvelous *d*.
72: 18 who alone does marvelous *d*.
73: 28 I will tell of all your *d*.
75: 1 men tell of your wonderful *d*.
77: 11 I will remember the *d* of the LORD
77: 12 and consider all your mighty *d*.
78: 4 the praiseworthy *d* of the LORD,
78: 7 and would not forget his *d*
86: 8 no *d* can compare with yours.
86: 10 you are great and do marvelous *d*;
88: 12 or your righteous *d* in the land
90: 16 May your *d* be shown
92: 4 For you make me glad by your *d*,
96: 3 his marvelous *d* among all peoples.
107: 8 and his wonderful *d* for men,
107: 15 and his wonderful *d* for men,
107: 21 and his wonderful *d* for men.
107: 24 his wonderful *d* in the deep.
107: 31 and his wonderful *d* for men.
111: 3 Glorious and majestic are his *d*,
145: 6 and I will proclaim your great *d*.
Jer 32: 19 purposes and mighty are your *d*.
Hab 3: 2 I stand in awe of your *d*, O LORD.
Mt 5: 16 that they may see your good *d*
Lk 1: 51 He has performed mighty *d*
23: 41 we are getting what our *d* deserve.

Ac 26: 20 prove their repentance by their *d.*
1Ti 6: 18 rich in good *d,* and to be generous
Heb 10: 24 on toward love and good *d.*
Jas 2: 14 claims to have faith but has no *d?*
2: 18 Show me your faith without *d,*
2: 20 faith without *d* is useless?
2: 26 so faith without *d* is dead.
1Pe 2: 12 they may see your good *d*
Rev 2: 19 I know your *d,* your love and faith,
2: 23 each of you according to your *d.*
3: 1 I know your *d;* you have
3: 2 I have not found your *d* complete
3: 8 I know your *d.*
3: 15 I know your *d,* that you are neither
14: 13 for their *d* will follow them."
15: 3 "Great and marvelous are your *d,*

DEEP (DEPTH DEPTHS)
Ge 1: 2 was over the surface of the *d,*
8: 2 Now the springs of the *d*
Ps 42: 7 *D* calls to *d*
Lk 5: 4 to Simon, "Put out into *d* water,
1Co 2: 10 all things, even the *d* things
1Ti 3: 9 hold of the *d* truths of the faith

DEER
Ps 42: 1 As the *d* pants for streams of water,

DEFAMED*
Isa 48: 11 How can I let myself be *d?*

DEFEATED
1Co 6: 7 have been completely *d* already.

DEFEND (DEFENDED DEFENDER DEFENDING DEFENDS DEFENSE)
Ps 72: 4 He will *d* the afflicted
74: 22 Rise up, O God, and *d* your cause;
82: 2 "How long will you *d* the unjust
82: 3 *D* the cause of the weak
119: 154 *D* my cause and redeem me;
Pr 31: 9 *d* the rights of the poor and needy
Isa 1: 17 *D* the cause of the fatherless,
1: 23 They do not *d* the cause
Jer 5: 28 they do not *d* the rights of the poor.
50: 34 He will vigorously *d* their cause

DEFENDED (DEFEND)
Jer 22: 16 He *d* the cause of the poor

DEFENDER (DEFEND)
Ex 22: 2 the *d* is not guilty of bloodshed;
Ps 68: 5 to the fatherless, a *d* of widows,
Pr 23: 11 for their *D* is strong;

DEFENDING (DEFEND)
Ps 10: 18 *d* the fatherless and the oppressed,
Ro 2: 15 now accusing, now even *d* them.)
Php 1: 7 or *d* and confirming the gospel,

DEFENDS* (DEFEND)
Dt 10: 18 He *d* the cause of the fatherless
33: 7 With his own hands he *d* his cause.
Isa 51: 22 your God, who *d* his people:

DEFENSE (DEFEND)
Ps 35: 23 Awake, and rise to my *d!*
Php 1: 16 here for the *d* of the gospel.
1Jn 2: 1 speaks to the Father in our *d*—

DEFERRED*
Pr 13: 12 Hope *d* makes the heart sick,

DEFIED
1Sa 17: 45 armies of Israel, whom you have *d.*
1Ki 13: 26 the man of God who *d* the word

DEFILE (DEFILED)
Da 1: 8 Daniel resolved not to *d* himself
Rev 14: 4 are those who did not *d* themselves

DEFILED (DEFILE)
Isa 24: 5 The earth is *d* by its people;

DEFRAUD
Lev 19: 13 Do not *d* your neighbor or rob him.
Mk 10: 19 do not *d,* honor your father

DEITY*
Col 2: 9 of the *D* lives in bodily form,

DELAY
Ecc 5: 4 vow to God, do not *d* in fulfilling it.
Isa 48: 9 my own name's sake I *d* my wrath;
Heb 10: 37 is coming will come and will not *d.*
Rev 10: 6 and said, "There will be no more *d!*

DELICACIES
Ps 141: 4 let me not eat of their *d.*
Pr 23: 3 Do not crave his *d,*
23: 6 do not crave his *d;*

DELICIOUS*
Pr 9: 17 food eaten in secret is *d!"*

DELIGHT* (DELIGHTED DELIGHTFUL DELIGHTING DELIGHTS)
Lev 26: 31 and I will take no *d* in the pleasing
Dt 30: 9 The LORD will again *d* in you
1Sa 2: 1 for I *d* in your deliverance.
15: 22 "Does the LORD *d*
Ne 1: 11 the prayer of your servants who *d*
Job 22: 26 Surely then you will find *d*
27: 10 Will he find *d* in the Almighty?
Ps 1: 2 But his *d* is in the law of the LORD
16: 3 in whom is all my *d.*
35: 9 and *d* in his salvation.
35: 27 those who *d* in my vindication
37: 4 *D* yourself in the LORD
43: 4 to God, my joy and my *d.*
51: 16 You do not *d* in sacrifice,
51: 19 whole burnt offerings to *d* you;
62: 4 they take *d* in lies.
68: 30 Scatter the nations who *d* in war.
111: 2 by all who *d* in them.
112: 1 who finds great *d* in his commands.
119: 16 I *d* in your decrees;
119: 24 Your statutes are my *d;*
119: 35 for there I find *d.*
119: 47 for I *d* in your commands
119: 70 but I *d* in your law.
119: 77 for your law is my *d.*
119: 92 If your law had not been my *d,*
119: 143 but your commands are my *d.*
119: 174 and your law is my *d.*
147: 10 nor his *d* in the legs of a man;
149: 4 For the LORD takes *d*
Pr 1: 22 How long will mockers *d*
2: 14 who *d* in doing wrong
8: 30 I was filled with *d* day after day,
11: 1 but accurate weights are his *d.*
29: 17 he will bring *d* to your soul.
Ecc 2: 10 My heart took *d* in all my work,
SS 1: 4 We rejoice and *d* in you;
2: 3 I *d* to sit in his shade,
Isa 5: 7 are the garden of his *d.*
11: 3 he will *d* in the fear of the LORD.
13: 17 and have no *d* in gold.
32: 14 the *d* of donkeys, a pasture
42: 1 my chosen one in whom I *d;*
55: 2 and your soul will *d* in the richest
58: 13 if you call the Sabbath a *d*
61: 10 I *d* greatly in the LORD;
62: 4 for the LORD will take *d* in you,
65: 18 for I will create Jerusalem to be a *d*
65: 19 and take *d* in my people;
66: 3 their souls *d* in their abominations;
66: 11 *d* in her overflowing abundance."
Jer 9: 24 for in these I *d,"*
15: 16 they were my joy and my heart's *d,*
31: 20 the child in whom I *d?*
49: 25 the town in which I *d?*
Eze 24: 16 away from you the *d* of your eyes.
24: 21 in which you take pride, the *d*
24: 25 and glory, the *d* of their eyes,
Hos 7: 3 *d* the king with their wickedness,
Mic 1: 16 for the children in whom you *d;*
7: 18 but *d* to show mercy.
Zep 3: 17 He will take great *d* in you,
Mt 12: 18 the one I love, in whom I *d;*
Mk 12: 37 large crowd listened to him with *d.*
Lk 1: 14 He will be a joy and *d* to you,
Ro 7: 22 in my inner being I *d* in God's law;
1Co 13: 6 Love does not *d* in evil
2Co 12: 10 for Christ's sake, I *d* in weaknesses,
Col 2: 5 and *d* to see how orderly you are

DELIGHTED (DELIGHT)
2Sa 22: 20 he rescued me because he *d* in me.
1Ki 10: 9 who has *d* in you and placed you
2Ch 9: 8 who has *d* in you and placed you
Ps 18: 19 he rescued me because he *d* in me.
Lk 13: 17 but the people were *d* with all

DELIGHTFUL* (DELIGHT)
Ps 16: 6 surely I have a *d* inheritance.
SS 1: 2 for your love is more *d* than wine.
4: 10 How *d* is your love, my sister,
Mal 3: 12 for yours will be a *d* land,"

DELIGHTING* (DELIGHT)
Pr 8: 31 and *d* in mankind.

DELIGHTS (DELIGHT)
Est 6: 6 for the man the king *d* to honor?"
Ps 22: 8 since he *d* in him."
35: 27 who *d* in the well-being
36: 8 from your river of *d.*
37: 23 if the LORD *d* in a man's way
147: 11 the LORD *d* in those who fear him,
Pr 3: 12 as a father the son he *d* in.
10: 23 of understanding *d* in wisdom.
11: 20 he *d* in those whose ways are
12: 22 but he *d* in men who are truthful.
14: 35 A king *d* in a wise servant,
18: 2 but *d* in airing his own opinions.
23: 24 he who has a wise son *d* in him.
Col 2: 18 Do not let anyone who *d*

DELILAH*
Woman who betrayed Samson (Jdg 16:4 – 22).

DELIVER (DELIVERANCE DELIVERED DELIVERER DELIVERS)
Dt 32: 39 and no one can *d* out of my hand.
Ps 22: 8 Let him *d* him,
72: 12 For he will *d* the needy who cry out
79: 9 *d* us and forgive our sins
109: 21 of the goodness of your love, *d* me.
119: 170 *d* me according to your promise.
Mt 6: 13 but *d* us from the evil one.'
2Co 1: 10 hope that he will continue to *d* us,

DELIVERANCE (DELIVER)
1Sa 2: 1 for I delight in your *d.*
Ps 3: 8 From the LORD comes *d.*
32: 7 and surround me with songs of *d.*
33: 17 A horse is a vain hope for *d;*
Ob : 17 But on Mount Zion will be *d;*

DELIVERED (DELIVER)
Ps 34: 4 he *d* me from all my fears.
107: 6 and he *d* them from their distress.
116: 8 have *d* my soul from death,
Da 12: 1 written in the book — will be *d.*
Ro 4: 25 He was *d* over to death for our sins

DELIVERER* (DELIVER)
Jdg 3: 9 for them a *d,* Othniel son of Kenaz,
3: 15 and he gave them a *d* — Ehud,
2Sa 22: 2 is my rock, my fortress and my *d;*
2Ki 13: 5 The LORD provided a *d* for Israel,
Ps 18: 2 is my rock, my fortress and my *d;*
40: 17 You are my help and my *d;*
70: 5 You are my help and my *d;*
140: 7 O Sovereign LORD, my strong *d,*
144: 2 my stronghold and my *d,*
Ac 7: 35 sent to be their ruler and *d*
Ro 11: 26 "The *d* will come from Zion;

DELIVERS (DELIVER)
Ps 34: 17 he *d* them from all their troubles.
34: 19 but the LORD *d* him from them all
37: 40 The LORD helps them and *d* them
37: 40 he *d* them from the wicked

DELUSION*
2Th 2: 11 God sends them a powerful *d*

DEMAND (DEMANDED)
Lk 6: 30 belongs to you, do not *d* it back.

DEMANDED (DEMAND)
Lk 12: 20 This very night your life will be *d*
12: 48 been given much, much will be *d;*

DEMETRIUS
Ac 19: 24 A silversmith named *D,* who made

DEMON* (DEMONS)
Mt 9: 33 And when the *d* was driven out,
11: 18 and they say, 'He has a *d.*'
17: 18 Jesus rebuked the *d,* and it came
Mk 7: 26 to drive the *d* out of her daughter.
7: 29 the *d* has left your daughter."
7: 30 lying on the bed, and the *d* gone.
Lk 4: 33 there was a man possessed by a *d,*
4: 35 Then the *d* threw the man
7: 33 wine, and you say, 'He has a *d.*'
8: 29 driven by the *d* into solitary places.
9: 42 the *d* threw him to the ground
11: 14 When the *d* left, the man who had
11: 14 was driving out a *d* that was mute.
Jn 8: 49 "I am not possessed by a *d,"*
10: 21 Can a *d* open the eyes of the blind
10: 21 sayings of a man possessed by a *d.*

DEMON-POSSESSED* (DEMON-POSSESSION)
Mt 4: 24 those suffering severe pain, the *d,*
8: 16 many who were *d* were brought
8: 28 two *d* men coming
8: 33 what had happened to the *d* men.
9: 32 man who was *d* and could not talk
12: 22 they brought him a *d* man who was
Mk 1: 32 brought to Jesus all the sick and *d.*
5: 16 what had happened to the *d* man —
5: 18 the man who had been *d* begged
Lk 8: 27 met by a *d* man from the town.
8: 36 the people how the *d* man had been

Jn 7: 20 "You are *d*," the crowd answered.
8: 48 that you are a Samaritan and *d*?"
8: 52 "Now we know that you are *d*!
10: 20 Many of them said, "He is *d*
Ac 19: 13 Jesus over those who were *d*.

DEMON-POSSESSION* (DEMON-POSSESSED)
Mt 15: 22 is suffering terribly from *d*."

DEMONS* (DEMON)
Dt 32: 17 to *d*, which are not God —
Ps 106: 37 and their daughters to *d*.
Mt 7: 22 and in your name drive out *d*
8: 31 *d* begged Jesus, "If you drive us
9: 34 prince of *d* that he drives out *d*."
10: 8 who have leprosy, drive out *d*.
12: 24 of *d*, that this fellow drives out
12: 24 that this fellow drives out *d*."
12: 27 And if I drive out *d* by Beelzebub,
12: 28 if I drive out *d* by the Spirit of God,
Mk 1: 34 He also drove out many *d*,
1: 34 but he would not let the *d* speak
1: 39 their synagogues and driving out *d*.
3: 15 to have authority to drive out *d*.
3: 22 the prince of *d* he is driving out *d*."
5: 12 The *d* begged Jesus, "Send us
5: 15 possessed by the legion of *d*,
6: 13 They drove out many *d*
9: 38 "we saw a man driving out *d*
16: 9 out of whom he had driven seven *d*
16: 17 In my name they will drive out *d*;
Lk 4: 41 *d* came out of many people,
8: 2 from whom seven *d* had come out;
8: 30 because many *d* had gone into him.
8: 32 The *d* begged Jesus to let them go
8: 33 When the *d* came out of the man,
8: 35 from whom the *d* had gone out,
8: 38 from whom the *d* had gone out
9: 1 and authority to drive out all *d*
9: 49 "we saw a man driving out *d*
10: 17 the *d* submit to us in your name."
11: 15 the prince of *d*, he is driving out *d*."
11: 18 you claim that I drive out *d*
11: 19 Now if I drive out *d* by Beelzebub,
11: 20 if I drive out *d* by the finger of God,
13: 32 'I will drive out *d* and heal people
Ro 8: 38 neither angels nor *d*, neither
1Co 10: 20 of pagans are offered to *d*,
10: 20 you to be participants with *d*.
10: 21 of the Lord and the cup of *d* too;
10: 21 the Lord's table and the table of *d*.
1Ti 4: 1 spirits and things taught by *d*.
Jas 2: 19 Good! Even the *d* believe that —
Rev 9: 20 they did not stop worshiping *d*,
16: 14 of *d* performing miraculous signs,
18: 2 She has become a home for *d*

DEMONSTRATE* (DEMONSTRATES DEMONSTRATION)
Ro 3: 25 He did this to *d* his justice,
3: 26 he did it to *d* his justice

DEMONSTRATES* (DEMONSTRATE)
Ro 5: 8 God *d* his own love for us in this:

DEMONSTRATION* (DEMONSTRATE)
1Co 2: 4 but with a *d* of the Spirit's power,

DEN
Da 6: 16 and threw him into the lions' *d*.
Mt 21: 13 you are making it a '*d* of robbers.'"
Mk 11: 17 you have made it 'a *d* of robbers.'"
Lk 19: 46 but you have made it 'a *d* of robbers

DENARII* (DENARIUS)
Mt 18: 28 who owed him a hundred *d*.
Lk 7: 41 One owed him five hundred *d*,

DENARIUS (DENARII)
Mt 20: 2 agreed to pay them a *d* for the day
Mk 12: 15 Bring me a *d* and let me look at it."

DENIED (DENY)
Mt 26: 70 But he *d* it before them all.
Mk 14: 68 But he *d* it.
Lk 22: 57 But he *d* it.
Jn 18: 25 He *d* it, saying, "I am not."
1Ti 5: 8 he has *d* the faith and is worse
Rev 3: 8 my word and have not *d* my name.

DENIES (DENY)
1Jn 2: 22 It is the man who *d* that Jesus is
2: 23 No one who *d* the Son has

DENY (DENIED DENIES DENYING)
Ex 23: 6 "Do not *d* justice to your poor
Job 27: 5 till I die, I will not *d* my integrity.
Isa 5: 23 but *d* justice to the innocent.
La 3: 35 to *d* a man his rights
Am 2: 7 and *d* justice to the oppressed.
Mt 16: 24 he must *d* himself and take up his
Mk 8: 34 he must *d* himself and take up his
Lk 9: 23 he must *d* himself and take up his
22: 34 you will *d* three times that you
Ac 4: 16 miracle, and we cannot *d* it.
Tit 1: 16 but by their actions they *d* him.
Jas 3: 14 do not boast about it or *d* the truth.
Jude : 4 *d* Jesus Christ our only Sovereign

DENYING* (DENY)
Eze 22: 29 mistreat the alien, *d* them justice.
2Ti 3: 5 a form of godliness but *d* its power.
2Pe 2: 1 *d* the sovereign Lord who bought

DEPART (DEPARTED DEPARTS DEPARTURE)
Ge 49: 10 The scepter will not *d* from Judah,
Job 1: 21 and naked I will *d*.
Mt 25: 41 '*D* from me, you who are cursed,
Php 1: 23 I desire to *d* and be with Christ,

DEPARTED (DEPART)
1Sa 4: 21 "The glory has *d* from Israel" —
Ps 119: 102 I have not *d* from your laws,

DEPARTS (DEPART)
Ecc 5: 15 and as he comes, so he *d*.

DEPARTURE (DEPART)
Lk 9: 31 spoke about his *d*, which he was
2Ti 4: 6 and the time has come for my *d*.
2Pe 1: 15 after my *d* you will always be able

DEPEND
Ps 62: 7 My salvation and my honor *d*

DEPOSES*
Da 2: 21 he sets up kings and *d* them.

DEPOSIT
Mt 25: 27 money on *d* with the bankers,
Lk 19: 23 didn't you put my money on *d*,
2Co 1: 22 put his Spirit in our hearts as a *d*,
5: 5 and has given us the Spirit as a *d*,
Eph 1: 14 who is a *d* guaranteeing our
2Ti 1: 14 Guard the good *d* that was

DEPRAVED* (DEPRAVITY)
Eze 16: 47 ways you soon became more *d*
23: 11 and prostitution she was more *d*
Ro 1: 28 he gave them over to a *d* mind,
Php 2: 15 fault in a crooked and *d* generation,
2Ti 3: 8 oppose the truth — men of *d* minds,

DEPRAVITY* (DEPRAVED)
Ro 1: 29 of wickedness, evil, greed and *d*.
2Pe 2: 19 they themselves are slaves of *d* —

DEPRIVE
Dt 24: 17 Do not *d* the alien or the fatherless
Pr 18: 5 or to *d* the innocent of justice.
31: 5 *d* all the oppressed of their rights.
Isa 10: 2 to *d* the poor of their rights
29: 21 with false testimony *d* the innocent
La 3: 36 to *d* a man of justice —
1Co 7: 5 Do not *d* each other
9: 15 die than have anyone *d* me

DEPTH (DEEP)
Ro 8: 39 any powers, neither height nor *d*,
11: 33 the *d* of the riches of the wisdom

DEPTHS (DEEP)
Ps 130: 1 Out of the *d* I cry to you, O LORD;

DERIDES*
Pr 11: 12 who lacks judgment *d* his neighbor,

DERIVES*
Eph 3: 15 in heaven and on earth *d* its name.

DESCEND (DESCENDED DESCENDING)
Ro 10: 7 "or 'Who will *d* into the deep?'"

DESCENDED (DESCEND)
Eph 4: 9 except that he also *d* to the lower,
Heb 7: 14 For it is clear that our Lord *d*

DESCENDING (DESCEND)
Ge 28: 12 of God were ascending and *d* on it.
Mt 3: 16 the Spirit of God *d* like a dove
Mk 1: 10 and the Spirit *d* on him like a dove.
Jn 1: 51 and *d* on the Son of Man."

DESECRATING*
Ne 13: 17 you are doing — *d* the Sabbath day?
13: 18 against Israel by *d* the Sabbath."
Isa 56: 2 who keeps the Sabbath without *d* it
56: 6 who keep the Sabbath without *d* it
Eze 44: 7 *d* my temple while you offered me

DESERT
Nu 32: 13 wander in the *d* forty years,
Dt 8: 16 He gave you manna to eat in the *d*,
29: 5 years that I led you through the *d*,
Ne 9: 19 you did not abandon them in the *d*.
Ps 78: 19 "Can God spread a table in the *d*?
78: 52 led them like sheep through the *d*.
Pr 21: 19 Better to live in a *d*
Isa 32: 2 like streams of water in the *d*
32: 15 and the *d* becomes a fertile field,
35: 6 and streams in the *d*.
43: 20 because I provide water in the *d*
Mk 1: 3 "a voice of one calling in the *d*,
1: 13 and he was in the *d* forty days,
Rev 12: 6 fled into the *d* to a place prepared

DESERTED (DESERTS)
Ezr 9: 9 our God has not *d* us
Mt 26: 56 all the disciples *d* him and fled.
2Ti 1: 15 in the province of Asia has *d* me,

DESERTING (DESERTS)
Gal 1: 6 are so quickly *d* the one who called

DESERTS (DESERTED DESERTING)
Zec 11: 17 who *d* the flock!

DESERVE* (DESERVED DESERVES)
Ge 40: 15 to *d* being put in a dungeon."
Lev 26: 21 times over, as your sins *d*.
Jdg 20: 10 it can give them what they *d*
1Sa 26: 16 you and your men *d* to die,
1Ki 2: 26 You *d* to die, but I will not put you
Ps 28: 4 bring back upon them what they *d*.
94: 2 pay back to the proud what they *d*.
103: 10 he does not treat us as our sins *d*
Pr 3: 27 from those who *d* it,
Ecc 8: 14 men who get what the righteous *d*,
8: 14 men who get what the wicked *d*,
Isa 66: 6 repaying his enemies all they *d*.
Jer 14: 16 out on them the calamity they *d*.
17: 10 according to what his deeds *d*."
21: 14 I will punish you as your deeds *d*,
32: 19 to his conduct and as his deeds *d*.
49: 12 "If those who do not *d*
La 3: 64 Pay them back what they *d*,
Eze 16: 59 I will deal with you as you *d*,
Zec 1: 6 to us what our ways and practices *d*
Mt 8: 8 I do not *d* to have you come
22: 8 those I invited did not *d* to come.
Lk 7: 6 for I do not *d* to have you come
23: 15 he has done nothing to *d* death.
23: 41 for we are getting what our deeds *d*
Ro 1: 32 those who do such things *d* death,
1Co 15: 9 even *d* to be called an apostle,
16: 18 Such men *d* recognition.
2Co 11: 15 end will be what their actions *d*.
Rev 16: 6 blood to drink as they *d*."

DESERVED* (DESERVE)
2Sa 19: 28 descendants *d* nothing
Ezr 9: 13 less than our sins have *d*
Job 33: 27 but I did not get what I *d*.
Ac 23: 29 charge against him that *d* death
Ro 3: 8 Their condemnation is *d*.

DESERVES* (DESERVE)
Nu 35: 31 the life of a murderer, who *d* to die.
Dt 25: 2 If the guilty man *d* to be beaten,
25: 2 the number of lashes his crime *d*,
Jdg 9: 16 and if you have treated him as he *d*
2Sa 12: 5 the man who did this *d* to die!
Job 34: 11 upon him what his conduct *d*.
Jer 51: 6 he will pay her what she *d*.
Lk 7: 4 "This man *d* to have you do this,
10: 7 for the worker *d* his wages.
Ac 26: 31 is not doing anything that *d* death
1Ti 1: 15 saying that *d* full acceptance:
4: 9 saying that *d* full acceptance
5: 18 and "The worker *d* his wages."
Heb 10: 29 severely do you think a man *d*

DESIGNATED
Lk 6: 13 also *d* apostles: Simon (whom he
Heb 5: 10 and was *d* by God to be high priest

DESIRABLE* (DESIRE)
Ge 3: 6 and also *d* for gaining wisdom,
Pr 22: 1 A good name is more *d*
Jer 3: 19 and give you a *d* land,

DESIRE* (DESIRABLE DESIRED DESIRES)
Ge 3: 16 Your *d* will be for your husband,
Dt 5: 21 You shall not set your *d*
1Sa 9: 20 to whom is all the *d* of Israel turned
2Sa 19: 38 anything you *d* from me I will do
23: 5 and grant me my every *d*?
1Ch 29: 18 keep this *d* in the hearts
2Ch 1: 11 "Since this is your heart's *d*
9: 8 and his *d* to uphold them forever,
Job 13: 3 But I *d* to speak to the Almighty

Job 21: 14 We have no *d* to know your ways.
Ps 10: 17 O LORD, the *d* of the afflicted;
20: 4 May he give you the *d*
21: 2 You have granted him the *d*
27: 12 me over to the *d* of my foes,
40: 6 Sacrifice and offering you did not *d*
40: 8 I *d* to do your will, O my God;
40: 14 may all who *d* my ruin
41: 2 him to the *d* of his foes.
51: 6 Surely you *d* truth
70: 2 may all who *d* my ruin
73: 25 earth has nothing I *d* besides you
Pr 3: 15 nothing you *d* can compare
8: 11 and nothing you *d* can compare
10: 24 what the righteous *d* will be
11: 23 The *d* of the righteous ends only
12: 12 The wicked *d* the plunder
17: 16 since he has no *d* to get wisdom?
24: 1 do not *d* their company;
Ecc 12: 5 and *d* no longer is stirred.
SS 6: 12 my *d* set me among the royal
7: 10 and his *d* is for me.
Isa 26: 8 are the *d* of our hearts.
53: 2 appearance that we should *d* him.
55: 11 but will accomplish what I *d*
Eze 24: 25 delight of their eyes, their heart's *d*,
Hos 6: 6 For I *d* mercy, not sacrifice,
Mic 7: 3 the powerful dictate what they *d* —
Mal 3: 1 whom you *d*, will come," says
Mt 9: 13 learn what this means: 'I *d* mercy,
12: 7 what these words mean, 'I *d* mercy,
Jn 8: 44 want to carry out your father's *d*.
Ro 7: 8 in me every kind of covetous *d*.
7: 18 For I have the *d* to do what is good,
9: 16 depend on man's *d* or effort,
10: 1 my heart's *d* and prayer to God
1Co 12: 31 But eagerly *d* the greater gifts.
14: 1 and eagerly *d* spiritual gifts,
2Co 8: 10 but also to have the *d* to do so.
8: 13 Our *d* is not that others might be
Php 1: 23 I *d* to depart and be with Christ,
Heb 10: 5 Sacrifice and offering you did not *d*
10: 8 and sin offerings you did not *d*,
13: 18 *d* to live honorably in every way.
Jas 1: 14 by his own evil *d*, he is dragged
1: 15 Then, after *d* has conceived,
2Pe 2: 10 of those who follow the corrupt *d*

DESIRED (DESIRE)
Hag 2: 7 and the *d* of all nations will come,
Lk 22: 15 "I have eagerly *d* to eat this

DESIRES* (DESIRE)
Ge 4: 7 at your door; it *d* to have you,
41: 16 will give Pharaoh the answer he *d*."
2Sa 3: 21 rule over all that your heart *d*."
1Ki 11: 37 rule over all that your heart *d*;
Job 17: 11 and so are the *d* of my heart.
31: 16 "If I have denied the *d* of the poor
Ps 34: 12 and *d* to see many good days,
37: 4 he will give you the *d* of your heart.
103: 5 who satisfies your *d* with good things,
140: 8 do not grant the wicked their *d*,
145: 16 satisfy the *d* of every living thing.
145: 19 He fulfills the *d* of those who fear
Pr 11: 6 the unfaithful are trapped by evil *d*.
13: 4 *d* of the diligent are fully satisfied.
19: 22 What a man *d* is unfailing love;
Ecc 6: 2 so that he lacks nothing his heart *d*,
SS 2: 7 or awaken love / until it so *d*.
3: 5 or awaken love / until it so *d*.
8: 4 or awaken love / until it so *d*.
Hab 2: 4 his *d* are not upright —
Mk 4: 19 and the *d* for other things come in
Ro 1: 24 over in the sinful *d* of their hearts
6: 12 body so that you obey its evil *d*.
8: 5 set on what that nature *d*;
8: 5 set on what the Spirit *d*.
13: 14 to gratify the *d* of the sinful nature.
Gal 5: 16 and you will not gratify the *d*
5: 17 the sinful nature *d* what is contrary
5: 24 nature with its passions and *d*.
Eph 2: 3 and following its *d* and thoughts.
4: 22 being corrupted by its deceitful *d*;
Col 3: 5 impurity, lust, evil *d* and greed,
1Ti 3: 1 an overseer, he *d* a noble task.
5: 11 their sensual *d* overcome their
6: 9 and harmful *d* that plunge men
2Ti 2: 22 Flee the evil *d* of youth,
3: 6 are swayed by all kinds of evil *d*,
4: 3 Instead, to suit their own *d*,
Jas 1: 20 about the righteous life that God *d*.
4: 1 from your *d* that battle within you?
1Pe 1: 14 conform to the evil *d* you had
2: 11 to abstain from sinful *d*, which war
4: 2 of his earthly life for evil human *d*,
2Pe 1: 4 in the world caused by evil *d*.
2: 18 to the lustful *d* of sinful human
3: 3 and following their own evil *d*.
1Jn 2: 17 The world and its *d* pass away,
Jude : 16 they follow their own evil *d*;
: 18 will follow their own ungodly *d*."

DESOLATE (DESOLATION)
Isa 54: 1 are the children of the *d* woman
Gal 4: 27 are the children of the *d* woman

DESOLATION (DESOLATE)
Da 11: 31 up the abomination that causes *d*.
12: 11 abomination that causes *d* is set up,
Mt 24: 15 'the abomination that causes *d*,'

DESPAIR (DESPAIRED)
Isa 61: 3 instead of a spirit of *d*.
2Co 4: 8 perplexed, but not in *d*; persecuted,

DESPAIRED* (DESPAIR)
2Co 1: 8 ability to endure, so that we *d*

DESPERATE*
2Sa 12: 18 He may do something *d*."
Ps 60: 3 have shown your people *d* times;
79: 8 for we are in *d* need.
142: 6 for I am in *d* need;

DESPISE (DESPISED DESPISES)
2Sa 12: 9 Why did you *d* the word
Job 5: 17 so do not *d* the discipline
36: 5 God is mighty, but does not *d* men;
42: 6 Therefore I *d* myself
Ps 51: 17 O God, you will not *d*.
102: 17 he will not *d* their plea.
Pr 1: 7 but fools *d* wisdom and discipline.
3: 11 do not *d* the LORD's discipline
6: 30 Men do not *d* a thief if he steals
23: 22 do not *d* your mother
Jer 14: 21 of your name do not *d* us;
Am 5: 10 and *d* him who tells the truth.
5: 21 "I hate, I *d* your religious feasts;
Mt 6: 24 devoted to the one and *d* the other.
Lk 16: 13 devoted to the one and *d* the other.
1Co 11: 22 Or do you *d* the church of God
Tit 2: 15 Do not let anyone *d* you.
2Pe 2: 10 of the sinful nature and *d* authority.

DESPISED (DESPISE)
Ge 25: 34 So Esau *d* his birthright.
Ps 22: 6 by men and *d* by the people.
Pr 12: 8 but men with warped minds are *d*.
Isa 53: 3 He was *d* and rejected by men,
53: 3 he was *d*, and we esteemed him not
1Co 1: 28 of this world and the *d* things —

DESPISES (DESPISE)
Pr 14: 21 He who *d* his neighbor sins,
15: 20 but a foolish man *d* his mother.
15: 32 who ignores discipline *d* himself,
Zec 4: 10 "Who *d* the day of small things?

DESTINED (DESTINY)
Lk 2: 34 "This child is *d* to cause the falling
1Co 2: 7 and that God *d* for our glory
Col 2: 22 These are all *d* to perish with use,
1Th 3: 3 know quite well that we were *d*
Heb 9: 27 Just as man is *d* to die once,
1Pe 2: 8 which is also what they were *d* for.

DESTINY* (DESTINED PREDESTINED)
Job 8: 13 Such is the *d* of all who forget God;
Ps 73: 17 then I understood their final *d*.
Ecc 7: 2 for death is the *d* of every man;
9: 2 share a common *d* — the righteous
9: 3 the sun: The same *d* overtakes all.
Isa 65: 11 and fill bowls of mixed wine for *D*,
Php 3: 19 Their *d* is destruction, their god is

DESTITUTE
Ps 102: 17 to the prayer of the *d*;
Pr 31: 8 for the rights of all who are *d*.
Heb 11: 37 *d*, persecuted and mistreated —

DESTROY (DESTROYED DESTROYING DESTROYS DESTRUCTION DESTRUCTIVE)
Ge 6: 17 floodwaters on the earth to *d* all life
9: 11 will there be a flood to *d* the earth."
Pr 1: 32 complacency of fools will *d* them;
Mt 10: 28 of the One who can *d* both soul
Mk 14: 58 'I will *d* this man-made temple
Lk 4: 34 to *d* us? I know who you are —
Jn 10: 10 only to steal and kill and *d*;
Ac 8: 3 But Saul began to *d* the church.
Rev 11: 18 destroying those who *d* the earth."

DESTROYED (DESTROY)
Dt 8: 19 you today that you will surely be *d*.
Job 19: 26 And after my skin has been *d*,
Pr 6: 15 he will suddenly be *d* —
11: 3 the unfaithful are *d*
21: 28 listens to him will be *d* forever.
29: 1 will suddenly be *d* —
Isa 55: 13 which will not be *d*."
Da 2: 44 up a kingdom that will never be *d*,
6: 26 his kingdom will not be *d*,
1Co 5: 5 so that the sinful nature may be *d*
8: 11 for whom Christ died, is *d*
15: 24 Father after he has *d* all dominion,
15: 26 The last enemy to be *d* is death.
2Co 4: 9 abandoned; struck down, but not *d*.
5: 1 if the earthly tent we live in is *d*,
Gal 5: 15 or you will be *d* by each other.
Eph 2: 14 the two one and has *d* the barrier,
2Ti 1: 10 who has *d* death and has brought
Heb 10: 39 of those who shrink back and are *d*,
2Pe 2: 12 born only to be caught and *d*,
3: 10 the elements will be *d* by fire,
3: 11 Since everything will be *d*
Jude : 5 later *d* those who did not believe.
: 11 have been *d* in Korah's rebellion.

DESTROYING (DESTROY)
Jer 23: 1 "Woe to the shepherds who are *d*

DESTROYS (DESTROY)
Pr 6: 32 whoever does so *d* himself.
11: 9 mouth the godless *d* his neighbor,
18: 9 is brother to one who *d*.
28: 24 he is partner to him who *d*.
Ecc 9: 18 but one sinner *d* much good.
1Co 3: 17 If anyone *d* God's temple,

DESTRUCTION (DESTROY)
Nu 32: 15 and you will be the cause of their *d*
Pr 16: 18 Pride goes before *d*,
17: 19 he who builds a high gate invites *d*.
24: 22 for those two will send sudden *d*
Hos 13: 14 Where, O grave, is your *d*?
Mt 7: 13 broad is the road that leads to *d*,
Lk 6: 49 it collapsed and its *d* was complete
Jn 17: 12 except the one doomed to *d*
Ro 9: 22 of his wrath — prepared for *d*?
Gal 6: 8 from that nature will reap *d*;
Php 3: 19 Their destiny is *d*, their god is their
1Th 5: 3 *d* will come on them suddenly,
2Th 1: 9 punished with everlasting *d*
2: 3 is revealed, the man doomed to *d*.
1Ti 6: 9 that plunge men into ruin and *d*.
2Pe 2: 1 bringing swift *d* on themselves.
2: 3 and their *d* has not been sleeping.
3: 7 of judgment and *d* of ungodly men.
3: 12 That day will bring about the *d*
3: 16 other Scriptures, to their own *d*.
Rev 17: 8 out of the Abyss and go to his *d*.
17: 11 to the seven and is going to his *d*.

DESTRUCTIVE (DESTROY)
2Pe 2: 1 will secretly introduce *d* heresies,

DETERMINED (DETERMINES)
Job 14: 5 Man's days are *d*;
Isa 14: 26 This is the plan *d* for the whole
Da 11: 36 for what has been *d* must take place
Ac 17: 26 and he *d* the times set for them

DETERMINES* (DETERMINED)
Ps 147: 4 He *d* the number of the stars
Pr 16: 9 but the LORD *d* his steps.
1Co 12: 11 them to each one, just as he *d*.

DETEST (DETESTABLE DETESTED DETESTS)
Lev 11: 10 in the water — you are to *d*.
Pr 8: 7 for my lips *d* wickedness.
13: 19 but fools *d* turning from evil.
16: 12 Kings *d* wrongdoing,
24: 9 and men *d* a mocker.
29: 27 The righteous *d* the dishonest;
29: 27 the wicked *d* the upright.

DETESTABLE (DETEST)
Pr 6: 16 seven that are *d* to him:
21: 27 The sacrifice of the wicked is *d* —
28: 9 even his prayers are *d*.
Isa 1: 13 Your incense is *d* to me.
41: 24 he who chooses you is *d*.
44: 19 Shall I make a *d* thing
Jer 44: 4 'Do not do this *d* thing that I hate!'
Eze 8: 13 doing things that are even more *d*."
Lk 16: 15 among men is *d* in God's sight.
Tit 1: 16 They are *d*, disobedient
1Pe 4: 3 orgies, carousing and *d* idolatry.

DETESTED* (DETEST)
Zec 11: 8 The flock *d* me, and I grew weary

DETESTS* (DETEST)
Dt 22: 5 LORD your God *d* anyone who

Dt 23: 18 the LORD your God *d* them both.
25: 16 LORD your God *d* anyone who
Pr 3: 32 for the LORD *d* a perverse man
11: 20 The LORD *d* men
12: 22 The LORD *d* lying lips,
15: 8 The LORD *d* the sacrifice
15: 9 The LORD *d* the way
15: 26 The LORD *d* the thoughts
16: 5 The LORD *d* all the proud of heart
17: 15 the LORD *d* them both.
20: 10 the LORD *d* them both.
20: 23 The LORD *d* differing weights,

DEVIATE*
2Ch 8: 15 They did not *d* from the king's

DEVICES*
Ps 81: 12 to follow their own *d.*

DEVIL* (DEVIL'S)
Mt 4: 1 the desert to be tempted by the *d.*
4: 5 the *d* took him to the holy city
4: 8 *d* took him to a very high mountain
4: 11 the *d* left him, and angels came
13: 39 the enemy who sows them is the *d.*
25: 41 the eternal fire prepared for the *d*
Lk 4: 2 forty days he was tempted by the *d.*
4: 3 *d* said to him, "If you are the Son
4: 5 The *d* led him up to a high place
4: 9 The *d* led him to Jerusalem
4: 13 When the *d* had finished all this
8: 12 then the *d* comes and takes away
Jn 6: 70 of you is a *d!*" (He meant Judas,
8: 44 You belong to your father, the *d,*
13: 2 the *d* had already prompted Judas
Ac 10: 38 were under the power of the *d,*
13: 10 "You are a child of the *d*
Eph 4: 27 and do not give the *d* a foothold.
1Ti 3: 6 under the same judgment as the *d.*
2Ti 2: 26 and escape from the trap of the *d,*
Heb 2: 14 the *d* — and free those who all their
Jas 3: 15 but is earthly, unspiritual, of the *d.*
4: 7 Resist the *d,* and he will flee
1Pe 5: 8 Your enemy the *d* prowls
1Jn 3: 8 because the *d* has been sinning
3: 8 who does what is sinful is of the *d,*
3: 10 and who the children of the *d* are:
Jude : 9 with the *d* about the body of Moses
Rev 2: 10 the *d* will put some of you in prison
12: 9 that ancient serpent called the *d*
12: 12 the *d* has gone down to you!
20: 2 that ancient serpent, who is the *d,*
20: 10 And the *d,* who deceived them,

DEVIL'S* (DEVIL)
Eph 6: 11 stand against the *d* schemes.
1Ti 3: 7 into disgrace and into the *d* trap.
1Jn 3: 8 was to destroy the *d* work.

DEVIOUS*
Pr 2: 15 and who are *d* in their ways.
14: 2 he whose ways are *d* despises him.
21: 8 The way of the guilty is *d,*

DEVOTE* (DEVOTED DEVOTING DEVOTION DEVOUT)
1Ch 22: 19 Now *d* your heart and soul
2Ch 31: 4 Levites so they could *d* themselves
Job 11: 13 "Yet if you *d* your heart to him
Jer 30: 21 for who is he who will *d* himself
Mic 4: 13 You will *d* their ill-gotten gains
1Co 7: 5 so that you may *d* yourselves
Col 4: 2 *D* yourselves to prayer, being
1Ti 1: 4 nor to *d* themselves to myths
4: 13 *d* yourself to the public reading
Tit 3: 8 may be careful to *d* themselves
3: 14 people must learn to *d* themselves

DEVOTED (DEVOTE)
1Ki 11: 4 and his heart was not fully *d*
Ezr 7: 10 For Ezra had *d* himself to the study
Ps 86: 2 Guard my life, for I am *d* to you.
Mt 6: 24 or he will be *d* to the one
Mk 7: 11 from me is Corban' (that is, a gift *d*
Ac 2: 42 They *d* themselves
18: 5 Paul *d* himself exclusively
Ro 12: 10 Be *d* to one another
1Co 7: 34 Her aim is to be *d* to the Lord
16: 15 and they have *d* themselves
2Co 7: 12 for yourselves how *d* to us you are.

DEVOTING* (DEVOTE)
1Ti 5: 10 *d* herself to all kinds of good deeds.

DEVOTION* (DEVOTE)
2Ki 20: 3 and with wholehearted *d* and have
1Ch 28: 9 and serve him with wholehearted *d*
29: 3 in my *d* to the temple
29: 19 son Solomon the wholehearted *d*
2Ch 32: 32 and his acts of *d* are written
35: 26 of Josiah's reign and his acts of *d,*
Job 6: 14 despairing man should have the *d*
15: 4 and hinder *d* to God.
Isa 38: 3 and with wholehearted *d* and have
Jer 2: 2 "'I remember the *d* of your youth,
Eze 33: 31 With their mouths they express *d,*
1Co 7: 35 way in undivided *d* to the Lord.
2Co 11: 3 from your sincere and pure *d*

DEVOUR (DEVOURED DEVOURING DEVOURS)
2Sa 2: 26 "Must the sword *d* forever?
Mk 12: 40 They *d* widows' houses
1Pe 5: 8 lion looking for someone to *d.*

DEVOURED (DEVOUR)
Jer 30: 16 But all who devour you will be *d;*

DEVOURING (DEVOUR)
Gal 5: 15 keep on biting and *d* each other,

DEVOURS (DEVOUR)
2Sa 11: 25 the sword *d* one as well as another.
Pr 21: 20 but a foolish man *d* all he has.

DEVOUT* (DEVOTE)
1Ki 18: 3 (Obadiah was a *d* believer
Isa 57: 1 *d* men are taken away,
Lk 2: 25 Simeon, who was righteous and *d.*
Ac 10: 2 his family were *d* and God-fearing;
10: 7 a *d* soldier who was one of his attendants
13: 43 and *d* converts to Judaism followed
22: 12 He was a *d* observer of the law

DEW
Jdg 6: 37 If there is *d* only on the fleece

DICTATED
Jer 36: 4 and while Jeremiah *d* all the words

DIE (DEAD DEADENED DEATH DIED DIES DYING)
Ge 2: 17 when you eat of it you will surely *d*
3: 3 you must not touch it, or you will *d*
3: 4 will not surely *d,*" the serpent said
Ex 11: 5 Every firstborn son in Egypt will *d,*
Ru 1: 17 Where you *d* I will *d,* and there I
2Ki 14: 6 each is to *d* for his own sins."
Job 2: 9 Curse God and *d!*" He replied,
Pr 5: 23 He will *d* for lack of discipline,
10: 21 but fools *d* for lack of judgment.
15: 10 he who hates correction will *d.*
23: 13 with the rod, he will not *d.*
Ecc 3: 2 a time to be born and a time to *d,*
Isa 22: 13 "for tomorrow we *d!*"
66: 24 their worm will not *d,* nor will their
Jer 31: 30 everyone will *d* for his own sin;
Eze 3: 18 that wicked man will *d* for his sin,
3: 19 he will *d* for his sin; but you will
3: 20 block before him, he will *d.*
18: 4 soul who sins is the one who will *d.*
18: 20 soul who sins is the one who will *d.*
18: 31 Why will you *d,* O house of Israel?
33: 8 'O wicked man, you will surely *d,*'
Mt 26: 52 "for all who draw the sword will *d*
Mk 9: 48 "'their worm does not *d,*
Jn 8: 21 and you will *d* in your sin.
11: 26 and believes in me will never *d.*
Ro 5: 7 Very rarely will anyone *d*
14: 8 and if we *d,* we *d* to the Lord.
1Co 15: 22 in Adam all *d,* so in Christ all will
15: 31 I *d* every day — I mean that,
15: 32 for tomorrow we *d.*"
Php 1: 21 to live is Christ and to *d* is gain.
Heb 9: 27 Just as man is destined to *d* once,
1Pe 2: 24 so that we might *d* to sins
Rev 14: 13 Blessed are the dead who *d*

DIED (DIE)
1Ki 16: 18 So he *d,* because of the sins he had
1Ch 1: 51 Hadad also *d.*
10: 13 Saul *d* because he was unfaithful
Lk 16: 22 "The time came when the beggar *d*
Ro 5: 6 we were still powerless, Christ *d*
5: 8 we were still sinners, Christ *d*
6: 2 By no means! We *d* to sin;
6: 7 anyone who has *d* has been freed
6: 8 if we *d* with Christ, we believe that
6: 10 The death he *d,* he *d* to sin once
14: 9 Christ *d* and returned to life
14: 15 brother for whom Christ *d.*
1Co 8: 11 for whom Christ *d,* is destroyed
15: 3 that Christ *d* for our sins according
2Co 5: 14 *d* for all, and therefore all *d.*
5: 15 he *d* for all, that those who live
Col 2: 20 Since you *d* with Christ
3: 3 For you *d,* and your life is now
1Th 4: 14 We believe that Jesus *d*
5: 10 He *d* for us so that, whether we are
2Ti 2: 11 If we *d* with him,
Heb 9: 15 now that he has *d* as a ransom
9: 17 in force only when somebody has *d*
1Pe 3: 18 For Christ *d* for sins once for all,
Rev 2: 8 who *d* and came to life again.

DIES (DIE)
Job 14: 14 If a man *d,* will he live again?
Pr 11: 7 a wicked man *d,* his hope perishes;
26: 20 without gossip a quarrel *d* down.
Jn 11: 25 in me will live, even though he *d;*
12: 24 But if it *d,* it produces many seeds.
Ro 7: 2 but if her husband *d,* she is released
14: 7 and none of us *d* to himself alone.
1Co 7: 39 But if her husband *d,* she is free
15: 36 does not come to life unless it *d.*

DIFFERENCE* (DIFFERENT)
2Sa 19: 35 Can I tell the *d* between what is
2Ch 12: 8 so that they may learn the *d*
Eze 22: 26 they teach that there is no *d*
44: 23 are to teach my people the *d*
Ro 3: 22 There is no *d,* for all have sinned
10: 12 For there is no *d* between Jew
Gal 2: 6 whatever they were makes no *d*

DIFFERENCES* (DIFFERENT)
1Co 11: 19 to be *d* among you to show which

DIFFERENT* (DIFFERENCE DIFFERENCES DIFFERING DIFFERS)
Lev 19: 19 "'Do not mate *d* kinds of animals.
Nu 14: 24 my servant Caleb has a *d* spirit
1Sa 10: 6 you will be changed into a *d* person
Est 1: 7 each one *d* from the other,
3: 8 whose customs are *d* from those
Da 7: 3 Four great beasts, each *d*
7: 7 It was *d* from all the former beasts,
7: 19 which was *d* from all the others
7: 23 It will be *d* from all the other
7: 24 them another king will arise, *d*
11: 29 but this time the outcome will be *d*
Mk 16: 12 Jesus appeared in a *d* form
Ro 12: 6 We have *d* gifts, according
1Co 4: 7 For who makes you *d*
12: 4 There are *d* kinds of gifts,
12: 5 There are *d* kinds of service,
12: 6 There are *d* kinds of working,
12: 10 speaking in *d* kinds of tongues,
12: 28 and those speaking in *d* kinds
2Co 11: 4 or a *d* gospel from the one you
11: 4 or if you receive a *d* spirit
Gal 1: 6 and are turning to a *d* gospel —
4: 1 he is no *d* from a slave,
Heb 7: 13 are said belonged to a *d* tribe,
Jas 2: 25 and sent them off in a *d* direction?

DIFFERING* (DIFFERENT)
Dt 25: 13 Do not have two *d* weights
25: 14 Do not have two *d* measures
Pr 20: 10 Differing weights and *d* measures
20: 10 *D* weights and differing measures
20: 23 The LORD detests *d* weights,

DIFFERS* (DIFFERENT)
1Co 15: 41 and star *d* from star in splendor.

DIFFICULT (DIFFICULTIES)
Ex 18: 22 but have them bring every *d* case
Dt 30: 11 commanding you today is not too *d*
2Ki 2: 10 "You have asked a *d* thing,"
Eze 3: 5 of obscure speech and *d* language,
Ac 15: 19 that we should not make it *d*

DIFFICULTIES* (DIFFICULT)
Dt 31: 17 and *d* will come upon them,
31: 21 when many disasters and *d* come
2Co 12: 10 in hardships, in persecutions, in *d.*

DIGNITY
Pr 31: 25 She is clothed with strength and *d;*

DIGS
Pr 26: 27 If a man *d* a pit, he will fall into it;

DILIGENCE (DILIGENT)
Ezr 5: 8 The work is being carried on with *d*
Heb 6: 11 to show this same *d* to the very end

DILIGENT (DILIGENCE)
Pr 10: 4 but *d* hands bring wealth.
12: 24 *D* hands will rule,
12: 27 the *d* man prizes his possessions.
13: 4 of the *d* are fully satisfied.
21: 5 The plans of the *d* lead to profit
1Ti 4: 15 Be *d* in these matters; give yourself

DINAH*
Only daughter of Jacob, by Leah (Ge 30:21; 46:15). Raped by Shechem; avenged by Simeon and Levi (Ge 34).

DINE
Pr 23: 1 When you sit to *d* with a ruler,

DIOTREPHES*
3Jn : 9 but *D,* who loves to be first,

DIRECT (DIRECTED DIRECTIVES DIRECTS)
Ge 18: 19 so that he will *d* his children
Dt 17: 10 to do everything they *d* you to do.
Ps 119: 35 *D* me in the path of your
119: 133 *D* my footsteps according
Jer 10: 23 it is not for man to *d* his steps.
2Th 3: 5 May the Lord *d* your hearts
1Ti 5: 17 The elders who *d* the affairs

DIRECTED (DIRECT)
Ge 24: 51 master's son, as the LORD has *d.*"
Nu 16: 40 as the LORD *d* him through Moses
Dt 2: 1 Sea, as the LORD had *d* me.
6: 1 laws the LORD your God *d* me
Jos 11: 9 did to them as the LORD had *d:*
11: 23 just as the LORD had *d* Moses,
Pr 20: 24 A man's steps are *d* by the LORD.
Jer 13: 2 as the LORD *d,* and put it
Ac 7: 44 It had been made as God *d* Moses,
Tit 1: 5 elders in every town, as I *d* you.

DIRECTIVES* (DIRECT)
1Co 11: 17 In the following *d* I have no praise

DIRECTS (DIRECT)
Ps 42: 8 By day the LORD *d* his love,
Isa 48: 17 who *d* you in the way you should

DIRGE*
Mt 11: 17 we sang a *d,*
Lk 7: 32 we sang a *d,*

DISABLED*
Jn 5: 3 number of *d* people used to lie —
Heb 12: 13 so that the lame may not be *d,*

DISAGREEMENT*
Ac 15: 39 had such a sharp *d* that they parted

DISAPPEAR (DISAPPEARED DISAPPEARS)
Mt 5: 18 will by any means *d* from the Law
Lk 16: 17 earth to *d* than for the least stroke
Heb 8: 13 is obsolete and aging will soon *d.*
2Pe 3: 10 The heavens will *d* with a roar;

DISAPPEARED (DISAPPEAR)
1Ki 20: 40 busy here and there, the man *d.*"

DISAPPEARS (DISAPPEAR)
1Co 13: 10 perfection comes, the imperfect *d.*

DISAPPOINT* (DISAPPOINTED)
Ro 5: 5 And hope does not *d* us,

DISAPPOINTED (DISAPPOINT)
Ps 22: 5 in you they trusted and were not *d.*

DISAPPROVE*
Pr 24: 18 or the LORD will see and *d*

DISARMED*
Col 2: 15 And having *d* the powers

DISASTER
Ex 32: 12 and do not bring *d* on your people.
Ps 57: 1 wings until the *d* has passed.
Pr 1: 26 I in turn will laugh at your *d;*
3: 25 Have no fear of sudden *d*
6: 15 Therefore *d* will overtake him
16: 4 even the wicked for a day of *d.*
17: 5 over *d* will not go unpunished.
27: 10 house when *d* strikes you —
Isa 45: 7 I bring prosperity and create *d;*
Jer 17: 17 you are my refuge in the day of *d.*
Eze 7: 5 An unheard-of *d* is coming.

DISCERN (DISCERNED DISCERNING DISCERNMENT)
Ps 19: 12 Who can *d* his errors?
139: 3 You *d* my going out and my lying
Php 1: 10 you may be able to *d* what is best

DISCERNED (DISCERN)
1Co 2: 14 because they are spiritually *d.*

DISCERNING (DISCERN)
1Ki 3: 9 So give your servant a *d* heart
3: 12 I will give you a wise and *d* heart,
Pr 1: 5 and let the *d* get guidance —
8: 9 To the *d* all of them are right;
10: 13 on the lips of the *d,*
14: 6 knowledge comes easily to the *d.*
14: 33 in the heart of the *d*
15: 14 The *d* heart seeks knowledge,
16: 21 The wise in heart are called *d,*
17: 24 A *d* man keeps wisdom in view,
Pr 17: 28 and *d* if he holds his tongue.
18: 15 heart of the *d* acquires knowledge;
19: 25 rebuke a *d* man, and he will gain
28: 7 He who keeps the law is a *d* son,

DISCERNMENT (DISCERN)
Ps 119: 125 I am your servant; give me *d*
Pr 3: 21 preserve sound judgment and *d,*
17: 10 A rebuke impresses a man of *d*
28: 11 a poor man who has *d* sees

DISCHARGED* (DISCHARGING)
Ecc 8: 8 As no one is *d* in time of war,

DISCHARGING* (DISCHARGED)
1Co 9: 17 I am simply *d* the trust committed

DISCIPLE (DISCIPLES DISCIPLES')
Mt 10: 42 these little ones because he is my *d,*
Lk 14: 26 his own life — he cannot be my *d.*
14: 27 and follow me cannot be my *d.*
14: 33 everything he has cannot be my *d.*
Jn 13: 23 of them, the *d* whom Jesus loved,
19: 26 and the *d* whom he loved standing
21: 7 Then the *d* whom Jesus loved said
21: 20 saw that the *d* whom Jesus loved

DISCIPLES (DISCIPLE)
Mt 10: 1 He called his twelve *d* to him
26: 56 Then all the *d* deserted him
28: 19 Therefore go and make *d*
Mk 3: 7 withdrew with his *d* to the lake,
16: 20 Then the *d* went out and preached
Lk 6: 13 he called his *d* to him and chose
Jn 2: 11 and his *d* put their faith in him.
6: 66 many of his *d* turned back
8: 31 to my teaching, you are really my *d.*
12: 16 At first his *d* did not understand all
13: 35 men will know that you are my *d*
15: 8 showing yourselves to be my *d.*
20: 20 The *d* were overjoyed
Ac 6: 1 the number of *d* was increasing,
11: 26 The *d* were called Christians first
14: 22 strengthening the *d*
18: 23 Phrygia, strengthening all the *d.*

DISCIPLES' (DISCIPLE)
Jn 13: 5 and began to wash his *d* feet,

DISCIPLINE* (DISCIPLINED DISCIPLINES SELF-DISCIPLINE)
Dt 4: 36 made you hear his voice to *d* you.
11: 2 and experienced the *d*
21: 18 listen to them when they *d* him,
Job 5: 17 so do not despise the *d*
Ps 6: 1 or *d* me in your wrath.
38: 1 or *d* me in your wrath.
39: 11 You rebuke and *d* men for their sin;
94: 12 Blessed is the man you *d,* O LORD
Pr 1: 2 for attaining wisdom and *d;*
1: 7 but fools despise wisdom and *d.*
3: 11 do not despise the LORD's *d*
5: 12 You will say, "How I hated *d!*
5: 23 He will die for lack of *d,*
6: 23 and the corrections of *d*
10: 17 He who heeds *d* shows the way
12: 1 Whoever loves *d* loves knowledge,
13: 18 He who ignores *d* comes to poverty
13: 24 who loves him is careful to *d* him.
15: 5 A fool spurns his father's *d,*
15: 10 Stern *d* awaits him who leaves
15: 32 He who ignores *d* despises himself,
19: 18 *D* your son, for in that there is hope
22: 15 the rod of *d* will drive it far
23: 13 Do not withhold *d* from a child;
23: 23 get wisdom, *d* and understanding.
29: 17 *D* your son, and he will give you
Jer 17: 23 would not listen or respond to *d.*
30: 11 I will *d* you but only with justice;
32: 33 would not listen or respond to *d.*
46: 28 I will *d* you but only with justice;
Hos 5: 2 I will *d* all of them.
Heb 12: 5 do not make light of the Lord's *d,*
12: 7 as *d;* God is treating you
12: 8 (and everyone undergoes *d*),
12: 11 No *d* seems pleasant at the time,
Rev 3: 19 Those whom I love I rebuke and *d.*

DISCIPLINED* (DISCIPLINE)
Pr 1: 3 for acquiring a *d* and prudent life,
Isa 26: 16 when you *d* them,
Jer 31: 18 and I have been *d.*
31: 18 'You *d* me like an unruly calf,
1Co 11: 32 we are being *d* so that we will not
Tit 1: 8 upright, holy and *d.*
Heb 12: 7 For what son is not *d* by his father?
12: 8 you are not *d* (and everyone
12: 9 all had human fathers who *d* us
Heb 12: 10 Our fathers *d* us for a little while

DISCIPLINES* (DISCIPLINE)
Dt 8: 5 your heart that as a man *d* his son,
8: 5 so the LORD your God *d* you.
Ps 94: 10 Does he who *d* nations not punish?
Pr 3: 12 the LORD *d* those he loves,
Heb 12: 6 because the Lord *d* those he loves,
12: 10 but God *d* us for our good,

DISCLOSED
Lk 8: 17 is nothing hidden that will not be *d,*
Col 1: 26 and generations, but is now *d*
Heb 9: 8 Holy Place had not yet been *d*

DISCORD
Gal 5: 20 idolatry and witchcraft; hatred, *d,*

DISCOURAGED* (DISCOURAGEMENT)
Nu 32: 9 they *d* the Israelites
Dt 1: 21 Do not be afraid; do not be *d.*"
31: 8 Do not be afraid; do not be *d.*"
Jos 1: 9 Do not be terrified; do not be *d,*
8: 1 "Do not be afraid; do not be *d.*
10: 25 "Do not be afraid; do not be *d.*
1Ch 22: 13 Do not be afraid or *d.*
28: 20 or *d,* for the LORD God,
2Ch 20: 15 or *d* because of this vast army.
20: 17 Do not be afraid; do not be *d.*
32: 7 or *d* because of the king of Assyria
Job 4: 5 to you, and you are *d;*
Isa 42: 4 he will not falter or be *d*
Eph 3: 13 to be *d* because of my sufferings
Col 3: 21 children, or they will become *d.*

DISCOURAGEMENT* (DISCOURAGED)
Ex 6: 9 of their *d* and cruel bondage.

DISCOVERED
2Ki 23: 24 book that Hilkiah the priest had *d*

DISCREDIT* (DISCREDITED)
Ne 6: 13 would give me a bad name to *d* me.
Job 40: 8 "Would you *d* my justice?

DISCREDITED (DISCREDIT)
2Co 6: 3 so that our ministry will not be *d.*

DISCRETION*
1Ch 22: 12 May the LORD give you *d*
Pr 1: 4 knowledge and *d* to the young —
2: 11 *D* will protect you,
5: 2 that you may maintain *d*
8: 12 I possess knowledge and *d.*
11: 22 a beautiful woman who shows no *d.*

DISCRIMINATED*
Jas 2: 4 have you not *d* among yourselves

DISEASE (DISEASES)
Mt 4: 23 and healing every *d* and sickness
9: 35 and healing every *d* and sickness.
10: 1 and to heal every *d* and sickness.

DISEASES (DISEASE)
Ps 103: 3 and heals all my *d;*
Mt 8: 17 and carried our *d.*"
Mk 3: 10 those with *d* were pushing forward
Lk 9: 1 drive out all demons and to cure *d,*

DISFIGURE* (DISFIGURED)
Mt 6: 16 for they *d* their faces

DISFIGURED (DISFIGURE)
Isa 52: 14 his appearance was so *d*

DISGRACE (DISGRACEFUL DISGRACES)
Ps 44: 15 My *d* is before me all day long,
52: 1 you who are a *d* in the eyes of God?
74: 21 not let the oppressed retreat in *d;*
Pr 6: 33 Blows and *d* are his lot,
11: 2 When pride comes, then comes *d,*
14: 34 but sin is a *d* to any people.
19: 26 is a son who brings shame and *d.*
Mt 1: 19 want to expose her to public *d,*
Ac 5: 41 of suffering *d* for the Name.
1Co 11: 6 and if it is a *d* for a woman
11: 14 it is a *d* to him, but that
1Ti 3: 7 so that he will not fall into *d*
Heb 6: 6 and subjecting him to public *d.*
11: 26 He regarded *d* for the sake
13: 13 the camp, bearing the *d* he bore.

DISGRACEFUL (DISGRACE)
Pr 10: 5 during harvest is a *d* son.
12: 4 a *d* wife is like decay in his bones.
17: 2 wise servant will rule over a *d* son,
1Co 14: 35 for it is *d* for a woman to speak

DISGRACES (DISGRACE)
Pr 28: 7 of gluttons *d* his father.
29: 15 but a child left to himself *d* his mother

DISGUISES*
Pr 26:24 A malicious man *d* himself

DISH
Pr 19:24 sluggard buries his hand in the *d*;
Mt 23:25 the outside of the cup and *d*,

DISHONEST*
Ex 18:21 trustworthy men who hate *d* gain
Lev 19:35 "'Do not use *d* standards
1Sa 8:3 They turned aside after *d* gain
Pr 11:1 The LORD abhors *d* scales,
13:11 *D* money dwindles away,
20:23 and *d* scales do not please him.
29:27 The righteous detest the *d*;
Jer 22:17 are set only on *d* gain,
Eze 28:18 By your many sins and *d* trade
Hos 12:7 The merchant uses *d* scales;
Am 8:5 and cheating with *d* scales,
Mic 6:11 Shall I acquit a man with *d* scales,
Lk 16:8 master commended the *d* manager
16:10 whoever is *d* with very little will
16:10 with very little will also be *d*
1Ti 3:8 wine, and not pursuing *d* gain.
Tit 1:7 not violent, not pursuing *d* gain.
1:11 and that for the sake of *d* gain.

DISHONOR* (DISHONORED DISHONORS)
Lev 18:7 "'Do not *d* your father
18:8 wife; that would *d* your father.
18:10 daughter; that would *d* you.
18:14 "'Do not *d* your father's brother
18:16 that would *d* your brother.
20:19 for that would *d* a close relative;
Dt 22:30 he must not *d* his father's bed.
Pr 30:9 and so *d* the name of my God.
Jer 14:21 do not *d* your glorious throne.
20:11 their *d* will never be forgotten.
La 2:2 princes down to the ground in *d*.
Eze 22:10 are those who *d* their fathers' bed;
Jn 8:49 I honor my Father and you *d* me.
Ro 2:23 do you *d* God by breaking the law?
1Co 15:43 it is sown in *d*, it is raised in glory;
2Co 6:8 through glory and *d*, bad report

DISHONORED* (DISHONOR)
Lev 20:11 father's wife, he has *d* his father.
20:17 He has *d* his sister and will be held
20:20 with his aunt, he has *d* his uncle.
20:21 of impurity; he has *d* his brother.
Dt 21:14 as a slave, since you have *d* her.
Ezr 4:14 proper for us to see the king *d*,
1Co 4:10 You are honored, we are *d*!

DISHONORS* (DISHONOR)
Dt 27:16 Cursed is the man who *d* his father
27:20 for he *d* his father's bed."
Job 20:3 I hear a rebuke that *d* me,
Mic 7:6 For a son *d* his father,
1Co 11:4 with his head covered *d* his head.
11:5 her head uncovered *d* her head—

DISILLUSIONMENT*
Ps 7:14 conceives trouble gives birth to *d*.

DISMAYED
Isa 28:16 the one who trusts will never be *d*.
41:10 do not be *d*, for I am your God.

DISOBEDIENCE* (DISOBEY)
Jos 22:22 in rebellion or *d* to the LORD,
Jer 43:7 So they entered Egypt in *d*
Ro 5:19 as through the *d* of the one man
11:30 mercy as a result of their *d*,
11:32 to *d* so that he may have mercy
2Co 10:6 ready to punish every act of *d*,
Heb 2:2 and *d* received its just punishment,
4:6 go in, because of their *d*.
4:11 fall by following their example of *d*.

DISOBEDIENT* (DISOBEY)
Ne 9:26 "But they were *d* and rebelled
Lk 1:17 and the *d* to the wisdom
Ac 26:19 I was not *d* to the vision
Ro 10:21 hands to a *d* and obstinate people."
11:30 as you who were at one time *d*
11:31 so they too have now become *d*
Eph 2:2 now at work in those who are *d*.
5:6 comes on those who are *d*.
5:12 to mention what the *d* do in secret.
2Ti 3:2 proud, abusive, *d* to their parents,
Tit 1:6 to the charge of being wild and *d*.
1:16 *d* and unfit for doing anything
3:3 At one time we too were foolish, *d*,
Heb 11:31 killed with those who were *d*.

DISOBEY* (DISOBEDIENCE DISOBEDIENT DISOBEYED DISOBEYING DISOBEYS)
Dt 11:28 the curse if you *d* the commands
2Ch 24:20 'Why do you *d* the LORD's
Est 3:3 Why do you *d* the king's command
Jer 42:13 and so *d* the LORD your God,
Ro 1:30 they *d* their parents; they are
1Pe 2:8 because they *d* the message—

DISOBEYED* (DISOBEY)
Nu 14:22 and in the desert but who *d* me
27:14 both of you *d* my command
Jdg 2:2 Yet you have *d* me.
Ne 9:29 arrogant and *d* your commands.
Isa 24:5 they have *d* the laws,
Jer 43:4 and all the people *d* the LORD's
Lk 15:29 for you and never *d* your orders.
Heb 3:18 rest if not to those who *d*?
1Pe 3:20 the spirits in prison who *d* long ago

DISOBEYING* (DISOBEY)
Nu 14:41 "Why are you *d* the LORD's

DISOBEYS* (DISOBEY)
Eze 33:12 man will not save him when he *d*,

DISORDER
1Co 14:33 For God is not a God of *d*
2Co 12:20 slander, gossip, arrogance and *d*.
Jas 3:16 there you find *d* and every evil

DISOWN (DISOWNS)
Pr 30:9 I may have too much and *d* you
Mt 10:33 I will *d* him before my Father
26:35 to die with you, I will never *d* you."
2Ti 2:12 If we *d* him,

DISOWNS (DISOWN)
Lk 12:9 he who *d* me before men will be

DISPENSATION see ADMINISTRATION, TRUST

DISPLACES
Pr 30:23 a maidservant who *d* her mistress.

DISPLAY (DISPLAYED DISPLAYS)
Ps 45:4 your right hand *d* awesome deeds.
Eze 39:21 I will *d* my glory among the nations
Ro 9:17 that I might *d* my power in you
1Co 4:9 on *d* at the end of the procession,
1Ti 1:16 Christ Jesus might *d* his unlimited

DISPLAYED (DISPLAY)
Jn 9:3 work of God might be *d* in his life.
2Th 2:9 the work of Satan *d* in all kinds

DISPLAYS (DISPLAY)
Isa 44:23 he *d* his glory in Israel.

DISPLEASE (DISPLEASED)
1Th 2:15 They *d* God and are hostile

DISPLEASED (DISPLEASE)
2Sa 11:27 David had done *d* the LORD.

DISPUTABLE* (DISPUTE)
Ro 14:1 passing judgment on *d* matters.

DISPUTE (DISPUTABLE DISPUTES DISPUTING)
Pr 17:14 before a *d* breaks out.
1Co 6:1 If any of you has a *d* with another,

DISPUTES (DISPUTE)
Pr 18:18 Casting the lot settles *d*

DISPUTING (DISPUTE)
1Ti 2:8 in prayer, without anger or *d*.

DISQUALIFIED*
1Co 9:27 I myself will not be *d* for the prize.

DISREPUTE*
2Pe 2:2 will bring the way of truth into *d*.

DISSENSION* (DISSENSIONS)
Pr 6:14 he always stirs up *d*.
6:19 and a man who stirs up *d*
10:12 Hatred stirs up *d*,
15:18 A hot-tempered man stirs up *d*,
16:28 A perverse man stirs up *d*,
28:25 A greedy man stirs up *d*,
29:22 An angry man stirs up *d*,
Ro 13:13 debauchery, not in *d* and jealousy.

DISSENSIONS* (DISSENSION)
Gal 5:20 selfish ambition, *d*, factions

DISSIPATION*
Lk 21:34 will be weighed down with *d*,
1Pe 4:4 with them into the same flood of *d*,

DISTINCTION
Ac 15:9 He made no *d* between us

DISTINGUISH (DISTINGUISHING)
1Ki 3:9 and to *d* between right and wrong.
Heb 5:14 themselves to *d* good from evil.

DISTINGUISHING
1Co 12:10 the *d* between spirits,

DISTORT
Ac 20:30 and *d* the truth in order
2Co 4:2 nor do we *d* the word of God.
2Pe 3:16 ignorant and unstable people *d*,

DISTRACTED*
Lk 10:40 But Martha was *d* by all

DISTRESS (DISTRESSED)
2Ch 15:4 in their *d* they turned to the LORD
Ps 18:6 In my *d* I called to the LORD;
81:7 In your *d* you called and I rescued
120:1 I call on the LORD in my *d*,
Jnh 2:2 "In my *d* I called to the LORD,
Mt 24:21 For then there will be great *d*,
Jas 1:27 after orphans and widows in their *d*

DISTRESSED (DISTRESS)
Lk 12:50 how *d* I am until it is completed!
Ro 14:15 If your brother is *d*

DIVIDE (DIVIDED DIVIDING DIVISION DIVISIONS DIVISIVE)
Ps 22:18 They *d* my garments among them

DIVIDED (DIVIDE)
Mt 12:25 household *d* against itself will not
Lk 23:34 they *d* up his clothes by casting lots
1Co 1:13 Is Christ *d*? Was Paul crucified

DIVIDING (DIVIDE)
Eph 2:14 destroyed the barrier, the *d* wall
Heb 4:12 it penetrates even to *d* soul

DIVINATION
Lev 19:26 "'Do not practice *d* or sorcery.

DIVINE
Ro 1:20 his eternal power and *d* nature—
2Co 10:4 they have *d* power
2Pe 1:4 you may participate in the *d* nature

DIVISION (DIVIDE)
Lk 12:51 on earth? No, I tell you, but *d*.
1Co 12:25 so that there should be no *d*

DIVISIONS (DIVIDE)
Ro 16:17 to watch out for those who cause *d*
1Co 1:10 another so that there may be no *d*
11:18 there are *d* among you,

DIVISIVE* (DIVIDE)
Tit 3:10 Warn a *d* person once,

DIVORCE* (DIVORCED DIVORCES)
Dt 22:19 he must not *d* her as long as he lives
22:29 He can never *d* her as long
24:1 and he writes her a certificate of *d*,
24:3 and writes her a certificate of *d*,
Isa 50:1 is your mother's certificate of *d*
Jer 3:8 faithless Israel her certificate of *d*
Mal 2:16 "I hate *d*," says the LORD God
Mt 1:19 he had in mind to *d* her quietly.
5:31 must give her a certificate of *d*.'
19:3 for a man to *d* his wife for any
19:7 man give his wife a certificate of *d*
19:8 permitted you to *d* your wives
Mk 10:2 Is it lawful for a man to *d* his wife?"
10:4 a man to write a certificate of *d*
1Co 7:11 And a husband must not *d* his wife.
7:12 to live with him, he must not *d* her.
7:13 to live with her, she must not *d* him
7:27 Are you married? Do not seek a *d*.

DIVORCED* (DIVORCE)
Lev 21:7 or *d* from their husbands,
21:14 not marry a widow, a *d* woman,
22:13 daughter becomes a widow or is *d*,
Nu 30:9 or *d* woman will be binding on her.
Dt 24:4 then her first husband, who *d* her,
1Ch 8:8 after he had *d* his wives Hushim
Eze 44:22 not marry widows or *d* women;
Mt 5:32 marries the *d* woman commits adultery.
Lk 16:18 who marries a *d* woman commits

DIVORCES* (DIVORCE)
Jer 3:1 "If a man *d* his wife
Mt 5:31 'Anyone who *d* his wife must give
5:32 tell you that anyone who *d* his wife,
19:9 tell you that anyone who *d* his wife,
Mk 10:11 "Anyone who *d* his wife
10:12 And if she *d* her husband
Lk 16:18 "Anyone who *d* his wife

DOCTOR
Mt 9:12 "It is not the healthy who need a *d*,

DOCTRINE* (DOCTRINES)
1Ti 1:10 to the sound *d* that conforms

1Ti 4: 16 Watch your life and *d* closely.
2Ti 4: 3 men will not put up with sound *d.*
Tit 1: 9 can encourage others by sound *d*
2: 1 is in accord with sound *d.*

DOCTRINES* (DOCTRINE)
1Ti 1: 3 not to teach false *d* any longer
6: 3 If anyone teaches false *d*

DOEG*
Edomite; Saul's head shepherd; responsible for murder of priests at Nob (1Sa 21:7; 22:6 – 23; Ps 52).

DOG (DOGS)
Pr 26: 11 As a *d* returns to its vomit,
Ecc 9: 4 a live *d* is better off than a dead lion
2Pe 2: 22 "A *d* returns to its vomit," and,

DOGS (DOG)
Mt 7: 6 "Do not give *d* what is sacred;
15: 26 bread and toss it to their *d.*"

DOMINION
Job 25: 2 "*D* and awe belong to God;
Ps 22: 28 for *d* belongs to the LORD

DONKEY
Nu 22: 30 *d* said to Balaam, "Am I not your
Zec 9: 9 gentle and riding on a *d,*
Mt 21: 5 gentle and riding on a *d,*
2Pe 2: 16 for his wrongdoing by a *d*—

DOOR (DOORS)
Job 31: 32 for my *d* was always open
Ps 141: 3 keep watch over the *d* of my lips.
Mt 6: 6 close the *d* and pray to your Father
7: 7 and the *d* will be opened to you.
Ac 14: 27 how he had opened the *d* of faith
1Co 16: 9 a great *d* for effective work has
2Co 2: 12 found that the Lord had opened a *d*
Rev 3: 20 I stand at the *d* and knock.

DOORFRAMES
Dt 6: 9 Write them on the *d* of your houses

DOORKEEPER
Ps 84: 10 I would rather be a *d* in the house

DOORS (DOOR)
Ps 24: 7 be lifted up, you ancient *d,*

DORCAS
Ac 9: 36 is *D),* who was always doing good

DOUBLE
2Ki 2: 9 "Let me inherit a *d* portion
1Ti 5: 17 church well are worthy of *d* honor,

DOUBLE-EDGED (EDGE)
Heb 4: 12 Sharper than any *d* sword,
Rev 1: 16 of his mouth came a sharp *d* sword.
2: 12 of him who has the sharp, *d* sword.

DOUBLE-MINDED* (MIND)
Ps 119: 113 I hate *d* men,
Jas 1: 8 he is a *d* man, unstable
4: 8 and purify your hearts, you *d.*

DOUBT (DOUBTING DOUBTS)
Mt 14: 31 he said, "why did you *d?*"
21: 21 if you have faith and do not *d,*
Mk 11: 23 and does not *d* in his heart
Jas 1: 6 he must believe and not *d,*
Jude : 22 Be merciful to those who *d;*

DOUBTING* (DOUBT)
Jn 20: 27 Stop *d* and believe."

DOUBTS* (DOUBT)
Lk 24: 38 and why do *d* rise in your minds?
Ro 14: 23 the man who has *d* is condemned
Jas 1: 6 he who *d* is like a wave of the sea,

DOVE (DOVES)
Ge 8: 8 Then he sent out a *d* to see
Mt 3: 16 Spirit of God descending like a *d*

DOVES (DOVE)
Lev 12: 8 is to bring two *d* or two young
Mt 10: 16 as snakes and as innocent as *d.*
Lk 2: 24 "a pair of *d* or two young pigeons."

DOWNCAST
Ps 42: 5 Why are you *d,* O my soul?
2Co 7: 6 But God, who comforts the *d,*

DOWNFALL
Hos 14: 1 Your sins have been your *d!*

DRAGON
Rev 12: 7 and his angels fought against the *d,*
13: 2 The *d* gave the beast his power
20: 2 He seized the *d,* that ancient

DRAW (DRAWING DRAWS)
Mt 26: 52 "for all who *d* the sword will die
Jn 12: 32 up from the earth, will *d* all men
Heb 10: 22 let us *d* near to God

DRAWING (DRAW)
Lk 21: 28 because your redemption is *d* near

DRAWS (DRAW)
Jn 6: 44 the Father who sent me *d* him,

DREAD (DREADFUL)
Ps 53: 5 they were, overwhelmed with *d,*

DREADFUL (DREAD)
Mt 24: 19 How *d* it will be in those days
Heb 10: 31 It is a *d* thing to fall into the hands

DREAM
Joel 2: 28 your old men will *d* dreams,
Ac 2: 17 your old men will *d* dreams.

DRESS
1Ti 2: 9 I also want women to *d* modestly,

DRIFT*
Heb 2: 1 so that we do not *d* away.

DRINK (DRINKING DRINKS DRUNK DRUNKARD DRUNKARD'S DRUNKARDS DRUNKENNESS)
Ex 29: 40 of a hin of wine as a *d* offering.
Nu 6: 3 He must not *d* grape juice
Jdg 7: 5 from those who kneel down to *d.*"
2Sa 23: 15 that someone would get me a *d*
Pr 5: 15 *D* water from your own cistern,
Mt 20: 22 "Can you *d* the cup I am going to *d*
26: 27 saying, "*D* from it, all of you.
Mk 16: 18 and when they *d* deadly poison,
Lk 12: 19 Take life easy; eat, *d* and be merry
Jn 7: 37 let him come to me and *d.*
18: 11 Shall I not *d* the cup the Father has
1Co 10: 4 and drank the same spiritual *d;*
12: 13 were all given the one Spirit to *d.*
Php 2: 17 being poured out like a *d* offering
2Ti 4: 6 being poured out like a *d* offering,
Rev 14: 10 too, will *d* of the wine of God's fury
21: 6 to *d* without cost from the spring

DRINKING (DRINK)
Ro 14: 17 God is not a matter of eating and *d,*

DRINKS (DRINK)
Isa 5: 22 and champions at mixing *d,*
Jn 4: 13 "Everyone who *d* this water will be
6: 54 and *d* my blood has eternal life,
1Co 11: 27 or *d* the cup of the Lord

DRIPPING
Pr 19: 13 wife is like a constant *d.*
27: 15 a constant *d* on a rainy day;

DRIVE (DRIVES)
Ex 23: 30 Little by little I will *d* them out
Nu 33: 52 *d* out all the inhabitants of the land
Jos 13: 13 Israelites did not *d* out the people
23: 13 will no longer *d* out these nations
Pr 22: 10 *D* out the mocker, and out goes
Mt 10: 1 authority to *d* out evil spirits
Jn 6: 37 comes to me I will never *d* away.

DRIVES (DRIVE)
Mt 12: 26 If Satan *d* out Satan, he is divided
1Jn 4: 18 But perfect love *d* out fear,

DROP (DROPS)
Pr 17: 14 so *d* the matter before a dispute
Isa 40: 15 Surely the nations are like a *d*

DROPS (DROP)
Lk 22: 44 his sweat was like *d* of blood falling

DROSS
Ps 119: 119 of the earth you discard like *d;*
Pr 25: 4 Remove the *d* from the silver,

DROUGHT
Jer 17: 8 It has no worries in a year of *d*

DROWNED
Ex 15: 4 are *d* in the Red Sea.
Mt 18: 6 and to be *d* in the depths of the sea.
Heb 11: 29 tried to do so, they were *d.*

DROWSINESS*
Pr 23: 21 and *d* clothes them in rags.

DRUNK (DRINK)
1Sa 1: 13 Eli thought she was *d* and said
Ac 2: 15 men are not *d,* as you suppose.
Eph 5: 18 Do not get *d* on wine, which leads

DRUNKARD (DRINK)
Mt 11: 19 and a *d,* a friend of tax collectors
1Co 5: 11 or a slanderer, a *d* or a swindler.

DRUNKARD'S* (DRINK)
Pr 26: 9 Like a thornbush in a *d* hand

DRUNKARDS (DRINK)
Pr 23: 21 for *d* and gluttons become poor,
1Co 6: 10 nor the greedy nor *d* nor slanderers

DRUNKENNESS (DRINK)
Lk 21: 34 weighed down with dissipation, *d*
Ro 13: 13 and *d,* not in sexual immorality
Gal 5: 21 factions and envy; *d,* orgies,
1Ti 3: 3 not given to *d,* not violent
1Pe 4: 3 living in debauchery, lust, *d,* orgies,

DRY
Ge 1: 9 place, and let *d* ground appear."
Ex 14: 16 go through the sea on *d* ground.
Jos 3: 17 the crossing on *d* ground.
Isa 53: 2 and like a root out of *d* ground.
Eze 37: 4 '*D* bones, hear the word

DULL
Isa 6: 10 make their ears *d*
2Co 3: 14 But their minds were made *d,*

DUST
Ge 2: 7 man from the *d* of the ground
3: 19 for *d* you are
Job 42: 6 and repent in *d* and ashes."
Ps 22: 15 you lay me in the *d* of death.
103: 14 he remembers that we are *d.*
Ecc 3: 20 all come from *d,* and to *d* all return.
Mt 10: 14 shake the *d* off your feet
1Co 15: 47 was of the *d* of the earth,

DUTIES (DUTY)
2Ti 4: 5 discharge all the *d* of your ministry

DUTY (DUTIES)
Ecc 12: 13 for this is the whole *d* of man.
Ac 23: 1 I have fulfilled my *d* to God
1Co 7: 3 husband should fulfill his marital *d*

DWELL (DWELLING DWELLINGS DWELLS DWELT)
Ex 25: 8 for me, and I will *d* among them.
2Sa 7: 5 the one to build me a house to *d* in?
1Ki 8: 27 "But will God really *d* on earth?
Ps 23: 6 I will *d* in the house of the LORD
37: 3 *d* in the land and enjoy safe pasture
61: 4 I long to *d* in your tent forever
Pr 8: 12 wisdom, *d* together with prudence;
Isa 33: 14 of us can *d* with the consuming fire
43: 18 do not *d* on the past.
Jn 5: 38 nor does his word *d* in you,
Eph 3: 17 so that Christ may *d* in your hearts
Col 1: 19 to have all his fullness *d* in him,
3: 16 the word of Christ *d* in you richly

DWELLING (DWELL)
Lev 26: 11 I will put my *d* place among you,
Dt 26: 15 from heaven, your holy *d* place,
Ps 90: 1 Lord, you have been our *d* place
2Co 5: 2 to be clothed with our heavenly *d,*
Eph 2: 22 to become a *d* in which God lives

DWELLINGS (DWELL)
Lk 16: 9 will be welcomed into eternal *d.*

DWELLS (DWELL)
Ps 46: 4 holy place where the Most High *d.*
91: 1 He who *d* in the shelter

DWELT (DWELL)
Dt 33: 16 of him who *d* in the burning bush.

DYING (DIE)
Ro 7: 6 by *d* to what once bound us,
2Co 6: 9 yet regarded as unknown; *d,*

EAGER
Pr 31: 13 and works with *e* hands.
Ro 8: 19 The creation waits in *e* expectation
1Co 14: 12 Since you are *e* to have spiritual
14: 39 my brothers, be *e* to prophesy,
Tit 2: 14 a people that are his very own, *e*
1Pe 5: 2 greedy for money, but *e* to serve;

EAGLE (EAGLE'S EAGLES)
Dt 32: 11 like an *e* that stirs up its nest
Eze 1: 10 each also had the face of an *e.*
Rev 4: 7 the fourth was like a flying *e.*
12: 14 given the two wings of a great *e,*

EAGLE'S (EAGLE)
Ps 103: 5 your youth is renewed like the *e.*

EAGLES (EAGLE)
Isa 40: 31 They will soar on wings like *e;*

EAR (EARS)
Ex 21: 6 and pierce his *e* with an awl.
Ps 5: 1 Give *e* to my words, O LORD,
Pr 2: 2 turning your *e* to wisdom
1Co 2: 9 no *e* has heard,
12: 16 if the *e* should say, "Because I am
Rev 2: 7 He who has an *e*, let him hear what

EARN (EARNED EARNINGS)
2Th 3: 12 down and *e* the bread they eat.

EARNED (EARN)
Pr 31: 31 Give her the reward she has *e*,

EARNESTNESS
2Co 7: 11 what *e*, what eagerness
8: 7 in complete *e* and in your love

EARNINGS (EARN)
Pr 31: 16 out of her *e* she plants a vineyard.

EARRING (EARRINGS)
Pr 25: 12 Like an *e* of gold or an ornament

EARRINGS (EARRING)
Ex 32: 2 Take off the gold *e* that your wives,

EARS (EAR)
Job 42: 5 My *e* had heard of you
Ps 34: 15 and his *e* are attentive to their cry;
Pr 21: 13 If a man shuts his *e* to the cry
26: 17 Like one who seizes a dog by the *e*
Isa 6: 10 hear with their *e*,
Mt 11: 15 He who has *e*, let him hear.
2Ti 4: 3 to say what their itching *e* want
1Pe 3: 12 his *e* are attentive to their prayer,

EARTH (EARTH'S EARTHLY)
Ge 1: 1 God created the heavens and the *e*.
1: 2 Now the *e* was formless and empty,
7: 24 The waters flooded the *e*
14: 19 Creator of heaven and *e*.
1Ki 8: 27 "But will God really dwell on *e*?
Job 26: 7 he suspends the *e* over nothing.
Ps 24: 1 *e* is the LORD's, and everything
46: 6 he lifts his voice, the *e* melts.
90: 2 or you brought forth the *e*
97: 5 before the Lord of all the *e*.
102: 25 you laid the foundations of the *e*,
108: 5 and let your glory be over all the *e*.
Pr 8: 26 before he made the *e* or its fields
Isa 6: 3 the whole *e* is full of his glory."
24: 20 The *e* reels like a drunkard,
37: 16 You have made heaven and *e*.
40: 22 enthroned above the circle of the *e*,
51: 6 the *e* will wear out like a garment
54: 5 he is called the God of all the *e*.
55: 9 the heavens are higher than the *e*,
65: 17 new heavens and a new *e*.
66: 1 and the *e* is my footstool.
Jer 10: 10 When he is angry, the *e* trembles;
23: 24 "Do not I fill heaven and *e*?"
33: 25 and the fixed laws of heaven and *e*,
Hab 2: 20 let all the *e* be silent before him."
Mt 5: 5 for they will inherit the *e*.
5: 35 or by the *e*, for it is his footstool;
6: 10 done on *e* as it is in heaven.
16: 19 bind on *e* will be bound
24: 35 Heaven and *e* will pass away,
28: 18 and on *e* has been given to me.
Lk 2: 14 on *e* peace to men
Jn 12: 32 when I am lifted up from the *e*,
Ac 4: 24 "you made the heaven and the *e*
7: 49 and the *e* is my footstool.
1Co 10: 26 The *e* is the Lord's, and everything
Eph 3: 15 in heaven and on *e* derives its name
Php 2: 10 in heaven and on *e* and under the *e*,
Heb 1: 10 you laid the foundations of the *e*,
2Pe 3: 13 to a new heaven and a new *e*,
Rev 8: 7 A third of the *e* was burned up,
12: 12 But woe to the *e* and the sea,
20: 11 *E* and sky fled from his presence,
21: 1 I saw a new heaven and a new *e*,
21: 1 and the first *e* had passed away,

EARTH'S (EARTH)
Job 38: 4 when I laid the *e* foundation?

EARTHENWARE
Pr 26: 23 Like a coating of glaze over *e*

EARTHLY (EARTH)
Eph 4: 9 descended to the lower, *e* regions?
Php 3: 19 Their mind is on *e* things.
Col 3: 2 on things above, not on *e* things.
3: 5 whatever belongs to your *e* nature:

EARTHQUAKE (EARTHQUAKES)
Eze 38: 19 at that time there shall be a great *e*
Mt 28: 2 There was a violent *e*, for an angel
Rev 6: 12 There was a great *e*.

EARTHQUAKES (EARTHQUAKE)
Mt 24: 7 There will be famines and *e*

EASE
Pr 1: 33 and be at *e*, without fear of harm."

EASIER (EASY)
Lk 16: 17 It is *e* for heaven and earth
18: 25 it is *e* for a camel to go

EAST
Ge 2: 8 God had planted a garden in the *e*,
Ps 103: 12 as far as the *e* is from the west,
Eze 43: 2 God of Israel coming from the *e*.
Mt 2: 1 Magi from the *e* came to Jerusalem
2: 2 We saw his star in the *e*

EASY (EASIER)
Mt 11: 30 For my yoke is *e* and my burden is

EAT (ATE EATEN EATER EATING EATS)
Ge 2: 16 "You are free to *e* from any tree
2: 17 but you must not *e* from the tree
3: 19 you will *e* your food
Ex 12: 11 *E* it in haste; it is the LORD's
Lev 11: 2 these are the ones you may *e*:
17: 12 "None of you may *e* blood,
Dt 8: 16 He gave you manna to *e*
14: 4 These are the animals you may *e*:
Jdg 14: 14 "Out of the eater, something to *e*;
2Sa 9: 7 and you will always *e* at my table."
Pr 31: 27 and does not *e* the bread of idleness
Isa 55: 1 come, buy and *e*!
65: 25 and the lion will *e* straw like the ox,
Eze 3: 1 *e* what is before you, *e* this scroll;
Mt 14: 16 You give them something to *e*."
15: 2 wash their hands before they *e*!"
26: 26 "Take and *e*; this is my body."
Mk 14: 14 where I may *e* the Passover
Lk 10: 8 and are welcomed, *e* what is set
12: 19 Take life easy; *e*, drink
12: 22 what you will *e*; or about your body
Jn 4: 32 to *e* that you know nothing about."
6: 31 bread from heaven to *e*.'"
6: 52 can this man give us his flesh to *e*?"
Ac 10: 13 Kill and *e*."
Ro 14: 2 faith allows him to *e* everything,
14: 15 is distressed because of what you *e*,
14: 20 to *e* anything that causes someone
14: 21 It is better not to *e* meat
1Co 5: 11 With such a man do not even *e*.
8: 13 if what I *e* causes my brother to fall
10: 25 *E* anything sold in the meat market
10: 27 *e* whatever is put before you
10: 31 So whether you *e* or drink
11: 26 For whenever you *e* this bread
2Th 3: 10 man will not work, he shall not *e*."
Rev 2: 7 the right to *e* from the tree of life,
3: 20 I will come in and *e* with him,

EATEN (EAT)
Ge 3: 11 Have you *e* from the tree that I
Ac 10: 14 "I have never *e* anything impure
Rev 10: 10 when I had *e* it, my stomach turned

EATER (EAT)
Isa 55: 10 for the sower and bread for the *e*,

EATING (EAT)
Ex 34: 28 and forty nights without *e* bread
Ro 14: 15 not by your *e* destroy your brother
14: 17 kingdom of God is not a matter of *e*
14: 23 because his *e* is not from faith;
1Co 8: 4 about *e* food sacrificed to idols:
8: 10 you who have this knowledge *e*
Jude : 12 *e* with you without the slightest

EATS (EAT)
1Sa 14: 24 "Cursed be any man who *e* food
Lk 15: 2 "This man welcomes sinners and *e*
Jn 6: 51 If anyone *e* of this bread, he will live
6: 54 Whoever *e* my flesh and drinks my
Ro 14: 2 faith is weak, *e* only vegetables.
14: 3 man who *e* everything must not
14: 6 He who *e* meat, *e* to the Lord,
14: 23 has doubts is condemned if he *e*,
1Co 11: 27 whoever *e* the bread or drinks

EBAL
Dt 11: 29 and on Mount *E* the curses.
Jos 8: 30 Joshua built on Mount *E* an altar

EBENEZER
1Sa 7: 12 He named it *E*, saying, "Thus far

EDEN
Ge 2: 8 in *E*; and there he put the man
Eze 28: 13 You were in *E*,

EDGE (DOUBLE-EDGED)
Mt 9: 20 and touched the *e* of his cloak.

EDICT
Heb 11: 23 they were not afraid of the king's *e*.

EDIFICATION (EDIFIED EDIFIES)
Ro 14: 19 leads to peace and to mutual *e*.

EDIFIED* (EDIFICATION)
1Co 14: 5 so that the church may be *e*.
14: 17 but the other man is not *e*.

EDIFIES* (EDIFICATION)
1Co 14: 4 but he who prophesies *e* the church
14: 4 speaks in a tongue *e* himself,

EDOM
Ge 36: 1 the account of Esau (that is, *E*).
36: 8 *E*) settled in the hill country of Seir
Isa 63: 1 Who is this coming from *E*,
Ob : 1 Sovereign LORD says about *E*—

EDUCATED*
Ac 7: 22 Moses was *e* in all the wisdom

EFFECT* (EFFECTIVE)
Job 41: 26 sword that reaches him has no *e*,
Isa 32: 17 *e* of righteousness will be quietness
Ac 7: 53 put into *e* through angels
1Co 15: 10 his grace to me was not without *e*.
Gal 3: 19 put into *e* through angels
Eph 1: 10 put into *e* when the times will have
Heb 9: 17 it never takes *e* while the one who
9: 18 put into *e* without blood.

EFFECTIVE* (EFFECT)
1Co 16: 9 a great door for *e* work has opened
Jas 5: 16 a righteous man is powerful and *e*.

EFFORT*
Ecc 2: 19 into which I have poured my *e*
Da 6: 14 and made every *e* until sundown
Lk 13: 24 "Make every *e* to enter
Jn 5: 44 yet make no *e* to obtain the praise
Ro 9: 16 depend on man's desire or *e*,
14: 19 make every *e* to do what leads
Gal 3: 3 to attain your goal by human *e*?
Eph 4: 3 Make every *e* to keep the unity
1Th 2: 16 to all men in their *e* to keep us
2: 17 intense longing we made every *e*
Heb 4: 11 make every *e* to enter that rest,
12: 14 Make every *e* to live in peace
2Pe 1: 5 make every *e* to add
1: 15 And I will make every *e* to see that
3: 14 make every *e* to be found spotless,

EGG
Lk 11: 12 for an *e*, will give him a scorpion?

EGLON
1. Fat king of Moab killed by Ehud (Jdg 3:12–30).
2. City in Canaan (Jos 10).

EGYPT (EGYPTIANS)
Ge 12: 10 went down to *E* to live there
37: 28 Ishmaelites, who took him to *E*.
42: 3 went down to buy grain from *E*.
45: 20 the best of all *E* will be yours.'"
46: 6 and all his offspring went to *E*.
47: 27 Now the Israelites settled in *E*
Ex 3: 11 and bring the Israelites out of *E*?"
12: 40 lived in *E* was 430 years.
12: 41 all the LORD's divisions left *E*.
32: 1 Moses who brought us up out of *E*,
Nu 11: 18 We were better off in *E*!"
14: 4 choose a leader and go back to *E*."
24: 8 "God brought them out of *E*;
Dt 6: 21 "We were slaves of Pharaoh in *E*,
1Ki 4: 30 greater than all the wisdom of *E*.
10: 28 horses were imported from *E*
11: 40 but Jeroboam fled to *E*,
14: 25 king of *E* attacked Jerusalem.
2Ch 35: 20 Neco king of *E* went up to fight
36: 3 The king of *E* dethroned him
Isa 19: 23 a highway from *E* to Assyria.
Hos 11: 1 and out of *E* I called my son.
Mt 2: 15 "Out of *E* I called my son."
Heb 11: 27 By faith he left *E*, not fearing
Rev 11: 8 is figuratively called Sodom and *E*,

EGYPTIANS (EGYPT)
Nu 14: 13 "Then the *E* will hear about it!

EHUD
Left-handed judge who delivered Israel from Moabite king, Eglon (Jdg 3:12–30).

EKRON
1Sa 5: 10 So they sent the ark of God to *E*.

ELAH
Son of Baasha; king of Israel (1Ki 16:6–14).

ELATION
Pr 28: 12 righteous triumph, there is great *e;*

ELDER* (ELDERLY ELDERS)
Isa 3: 2 the soothsayer and *e,*
1Ti 5: 19 an accusation against an *e*
Tit 1: 6 *e* must be blameless, the husband
1Pe 5: 1 among you, I appeal as a fellow *e,*
2Jn : 1 The *e,* To the chosen lady
3Jn : 1 The *e,* To my dear friend Gaius,

ELDERLY* (ELDER)
Lev 19: 32 show respect for the *e*

ELDERS (ELDER)
1Ki 12: 8 rejected the advice the *e* gave him
Mt 15: 2 break the tradition of the *e?*
Mk 7: 3 holding to the tradition of the *e.*
7: 5 to the tradition of the *e* instead
Ac 11: 30 gift to the *e* by Barnabas
14: 23 and Barnabas appointed *e* for them
15: 2 the apostles and *e* about this
15: 4 the church and the apostles and *e,*
15: 6 and *e* met to consider this question.
15: 22 and *e,* with the whole church,
15: 23 The apostles and *e,* your brothers,
16: 4 and *e* in Jerusalem for the people
20: 17 to Ephesus for the *e* of the church.
21: 18 and all the *e* were present.
23: 14 They went to the chief priests and *e*
24: 1 to Caesarea with some of the *e*
1Ti 4: 14 when the body of *e* laid their hands
5: 17 The *e* who direct the affairs
Tit 1: 5 and appoint *e* in every town,
Jas 5: 14 He should call the *e* of the church
1Pe 5: 1 To the *e* among you, I appeal
Rev 4: 4 seated on them were twenty-four *e.*
4: 10 the twenty-four *e* fall

ELEAZAR
Third son of Aaron (Ex 6:23–25). Succeeded Aaron as high priest (Nu 20:26; Dt 10:6). Allotted land to tribes (Jos 14:1). Death (Jos 24:33).

ELECT* (ELECTION)
Mt 24: 22 the sake of the *e* those days will be
24: 24 miracles to deceive even the *e*—
24: 31 and they will gather his *e*
Mk 13: 20 sake of the *e,* whom he has chosen,
13: 22 and miracles to deceive the *e*—
13: 27 gather his *e* from the four winds,
Ro 11: 7 it did not obtain, but the *e* did.
1Ti 5: 21 and Christ Jesus and the *e* angels,
2Ti 2: 10 everything for the sake of the *e,*
Tit 1: 1 Christ for the faith of God's *e*
1Pe 1: 1 To God's *e,* strangers in the world,

ELECTION* (ELECT)
Ro 9: 11 God's purpose in *e* might stand:
11: 28 but as far as *e* is concerned,
2Pe 1: 10 to make your calling and *e* sure.

ELEMENTARY* (ELEMENTS)
Heb 5: 12 someone to teach you the *e* truths
6: 1 us leave the *e* teachings about

ELEMENTS* (ELEMENTARY)
2Pe 3: 10 the *e* will be destroyed by fire,
3: 12 and the *e* will melt in the heat.

ELEVATE*
2Co 11: 7 to *e* you by preaching the gospel

ELI
High priest in youth of Samuel (1Sa 1–4). Blessed Hannah (1Sa 1:12–18); raised Samuel (1Sa 2:11–26). Prophesied against because of wicked sons (1Sa 2:27–36). Death of Eli and sons (1Sa 4:11–22).

ELIHU
One of Job's friends (Job 32–37).

ELIJAH
Prophet; predicted famine in Israel (1Ki 17:1; Jas 5:17). Fed by ravens (1Ki 17:2–6). Raised Sidonian widow's son (1Ki 17:7–24). Defeated prophets of Baal at Carmel (1Ki 18:16–46). Ran from Jezebel (1Ki 19:1–9). Prophesied death of Azariah (2Ki 1). Succeeded by Elishah (1Ki 19:19–21; 2Ki 2:1–18). Taken to heaven in whirlwind (2Ki 2:11–12).
Return prophesied (Mal 4:5–6); equated with John the Baptist (Mt 17:9–13; Mk 9:9–13; Lk 1:17). Appeared with Moses in transfiguration of Jesus (Mt 17:1–8; Mk 9:1–8).

ELIMELECH
Ru 1: 3 Now *E,* Naomi's husband, died,

ELIPHAZ
1. Firstborn of Esau (Ge 36).
2. One of Job's friends (Job 4–5; 15; 22).

ELISHA
Prophet; successor of Elijah (1Ki 19:16–21); inherited his cloak (2Ki 2:1–18). Purified bad water (2Ki 2:19–22). Cursed young men (2Ki 2:23–25). Aided Israel's defeat of Moab (2Ki 3). Provided widow with oil (2Ki 4:1–7). Raised Shunammite woman's son (2Ki 4:8–37). Purified food (2Ki 4:38–41). Fed 100 men (2Ki 4:42–44). Healed Naaman's leprosy (2Ki 5). Made axhead float (2Ki 6:1–7). Captured Arameans (2Ki 6:8–23). Political adviser to Israel (2Ki 6:24–8:6; 9:1–3; 13:14–19), Damascus (2Ki 8:7–15). Death (2Ki 13:20).

ELIZABETH*
Mother of John the Baptist, relative of Mary (Lk 1:5–58).

ELKANAH
Husband of Hannah, father of Samuel (1Sa 1–2).

ELOI*
Mt 27: 46 *"E, E, lama sabachthani?"*—
Mk 15: 34 *"E, E, lama sabachthani?"*—

ELOQUENCE* (ELOQUENT)
1Co 2: 1 come with *e* or superior wisdom

ELOQUENT* (ELOQUENCE)
Ex 4: 10 "O Lord, I have never been *e,*

ELYMAS
Ac 13: 8 *E* the sorcerer (for that is what his

EMBEDDED*
Ecc 12: 11 sayings like firmly *e* nails—

EMBERS
Pr 26: 21 As charcoal to *e* and as wood to fire

EMBITTER* (BITTER)
Col 3: 21 Fathers, do not *e* your children,

EMBODIMENT* (BODY)
Ro 2: 20 have in the law the *e* of knowledge

EMPTIED (EMPTY)
1Co 1: 17 the cross of Christ be *e* of its power.

EMPTY (EMPTIED)
Ge 1: 2 Now the earth was formless and *e,*
Job 26: 7 the northern ⌞skies⌟ over *e* space;
Isa 45: 18 he did not create it to be *e,*
55: 11 It will not return to me *e,*
Jer 4: 23 and it was formless and *e;*
Lk 1: 53 but has sent the rich away *e.*
Eph 5: 6 no one deceive you with *e* words,
1Pe 1: 18 from the *e* way of life handed
2Pe 2: 18 For they mouth *e,* boastful words

ENABLE (ABLE)
Lk 1: 74 to *e* us to serve him without fear
Ac 4: 29 *e* your servants to speak your word

ENABLED* (ABLE)
Lev 26: 13 *e* you to walk with heads held high.
Ru 4: 13 And the LORD *e* her to conceive,
Jn 6: 65 unless the Father has *e* him."
Ac 2: 4 other tongues as the Spirit *e* them.
7: 10 and *e* him to gain the goodwill
Heb 11: 11 was *e* to become a father

ENABLES (ABLE)
Php 3: 21 by the power that *e* him

ENABLING* (ABLE)
Ac 14: 3 the message of his grace by *e* them

ENCAMPS* (CAMP)
Ps 34: 7 The angel of the LORD *e*

ENCOURAGE* (ENCOURAGED ENCOURAGEMENT ENCOURAGES ENCOURAGING)
Dt 1: 38 *E* him, because he will lead Israel
3: 28 and *e* and strengthen him,
2Sa 11: 25 Say this to *e* Joab."
19: 7 Now go out and *e* your men.
Job 16: 5 But my mouth would *e* you;
Ps 10: 17 you *e* them, and you listen
64: 5 They *e* each other in evil plans,
Isa 1: 17 *e* the oppressed.
Jer 29: 8 to the dreams you *e* them to have.
Ac 15: 32 to *e* and strengthen the brothers.
Ro 12: 8 if it is encouraging, let him *e;*
Eph 6: 22 how we are, and that he may *e* you.
Col 4: 8 and that he may *e* your hearts.
1Th 3: 2 to strengthen and *e* you
4: 18 Therefore *e* each other
5: 11 Therefore *e* one another
5: 14 those who are idle, *e* the timid,
2Th 2: 17 *e* your hearts and strengthen you
2Ti 4: 2 rebuke and *e*— with great patience
Tit 1: 9 so that he can *e* others
2: 6 *e* the young men to be
2: 15 *E* and rebuke with all authority.
Heb 3: 13 But *e* one another daily, as long
10: 25 but let us *e* one another—

ENCOURAGED* (ENCOURAGE)
Jdg 7: 11 you will be *e* to attack the camp."
20: 22 But the men of Israel *e* one another
2Ch 22: 3 for his mother *e* him
32: 6 and *e* them with these words:
35: 2 and *e* them in the service
Eze 13: 22 you *e* the wicked not to turn
Ac 9: 31 It was strengthened; and *e*
11: 23 and *e* them all to remain true
16: 40 met with the brothers and *e* them.
18: 27 the brothers *e* him and wrote
27: 36 They were all *e* and ate some food
28: 15 men Paul thanked God and was *e.*
Ro 1: 12 and I may be mutually *e*
1Co 14: 31 everyone may be instructed and *e.*
2Co 7: 4 I am greatly *e;* in all our troubles
7: 13 By all this we are *e.*
Php 1: 14 brothers in the Lord have been *e*
Col 2: 2 My purpose is that they may be *e*
1Th 3: 7 persecution we were *e* about you
Heb 6: 18 offered to us may be greatly *e.*

ENCOURAGEMENT* (ENCOURAGE)
Ac 4: 36 Barnabas (which means Son of *E),*
13: 15 a message of *e* for the people,
20: 2 speaking many words of *e*
Ro 15: 4 *e* of the Scriptures we might have
15: 5 and *e* give you a spirit of unity
1Co 14: 3 to men for their strengthening, *e*
2Co 7: 13 to our own *e,* we were especially
Php 2: 1 If you have any *e* from being united
2Th 2: 16 and by his grace gave us eternal *e*
Phm : 7 love has given me great joy and *e,*
Heb 12: 5 word of *e* that addresses you

ENCOURAGES* (ENCOURAGE)
Isa 41: 7 The craftsman *e* the goldsmith,

ENCOURAGING* (ENCOURAGE)
Ac 14: 22 *e* them to remain true to the faith.
15: 31 and were glad for its *e* message.
20: 1 for the disciples and, after *e* them,
Ro 12: 8 if it is *e,* let him encourage;
1Th 2: 12 *e,* comforting and urging you
1Pe 5: 12 *e* you and testifying that this is

ENCROACH
Pr 23: 10 or *e* on the fields of the fatherless,

END (ENDS)
Ps 119: 33 then I will keep them to the *e.*
119: 112 to the very *e.*
Pr 1: 19 Such is the *e* of all who go
5: 4 but in the *e* she is bitter as gall,
5: 11 At the *e* of your life you will groan,
14: 12 but in the *e* it leads to death.
14: 13 and joy may *e* in grief.
16: 25 but in the *e* it leads to death.
19: 20 and in the *e* you will be wise.
20: 21 will not be blessed at the *e.*
23: 32 In the *e* [illegible] a snake
25: 8 for [illegible] the *e*
28: 23 [illegible] favor
29: 21 he will bring grief in the *e.*
Ecc 3: 11 done from beginning to *e.*
7: 8 The *e* of a matter is better
12: 12 making many books there is no *e,*
Eze 7: 2 The *e!* The *e* has come
Mt 10: 22 firm to the *e* will be saved.
24: 13 firm to the *e* will be saved.
24: 14 nations, and then the *e* will come.
Lk 21: 9 but the *e* will not come right away
Ro 10: 4 Christ is the *e* of the law
1Co 15: 24 the *e* will come, when he hands
Rev 21: 6 Omega, the Beginning and the *E.*
22: 13 the Last, the Beginning and the *E.*

ENDS (END)
Ps 19: 4 their words to the *e* of the world.
Pr 20: 17 he *e* up with a mouth full of gravel.
Isa 49: 6 salvation to the *e* of the earth."
62: 11 proclamation to the *e* of the earth:
Ac 13: 47 salvation to the *e* of the earth.'"
Ro 10: 18 their words to the *e* of the world."

ENDURANCE* (ENDURE)
Ro 15: 4 through *e* and the encouragement
15: 5 May the God who gives *e*
2Co 1: 6 which produces in you patient *e*
6: 4 in great *e;* in troubles, hardships
Col 1: 11 might so that you may have great *e*
1Th 1: 3 and your *e* inspired by hope
1Ti 6: 11 faith, love, *e* and gentleness.
2Ti 3: 10 patience, love, *e,* persecutions,
Tit 2: 2 and sound in faith, in love and in *e.*
Rev 1: 9 and patient *e* that are ours in Jesus,

Rev 13: 10 This calls for patient *e*
14: 12 This calls for patient *e* on the part

ENDURE (ENDURANCE ENDURED ENDURES ENDURING)
Ps 72: 17 May his name *e* forever;
Pr 12: 19 Truthful lips *e* forever,
27: 24 for riches do not *e* forever,
Ecc 3: 14 everything God does will *e* forever;
Da 2: 44 to an end, but it will itself *e* forever.
Mal 3: 2 who can *e* the day of his coming?
1Co 4: 12 when we are persecuted, we *e* it;
2Co 1: 8 far beyond our ability to *e*,
2Ti 2: 3 *E* hardship with us like a good
2: 10 Therefore I *e* everything
2: 12 if we *e*, / we will also reign
4: 5 head in all situations, *e* hardship,
Heb 12: 7 *E* hardship as discipline; God is
1Pe 2: 20 a beating for doing wrong and *e* it?
2: 20 suffer for doing good and you *e* it,
Rev 3: 10 kept my command to *e* patiently,

ENDURED* (ENDURE)
Ps 123: 3 for we have *e* much contempt.
123: 4 We have *e* much ridicule
132: 1 and all the hardships he *e*.
Ac 13: 18 and *e* their conduct forty years
2Ti 3: 11 and Lystra, the persecutions I *e*.
Heb 12: 2 set before him *e* the cross,
12: 3 him who *e* such opposition
Rev 2: 3 and have *e* hardships for my name,

ENDURES (ENDURE)
Ps 102: 12 renown *e* through all generations.
112: 9 his righteousness *e* forever;
136: 1 *His love e forever.*
Da 9: 15 made for yourself a name that *e*
2Co 9: 9 his righteousness *e* forever."

ENDURING (ENDURE)
2Th 1: 4 persecutions and trials you are *e*.
1Pe 1: 23 through the living and *e* word

ENEMIES (ENEMY)
Ps 23: 5 in the presence of my *e*.
110: 1 hand until I make your *e*
Pr 16: 7 his *e* live at peace with him.
Isa 59: 18 wrath to his *e*
Mic 7: 6 a man's *e* are the members
Mt 5: 44 Love your *e* and pray
10: 36 a man's *e* will be the members
Lk 6: 27 Love your *e*, do good
6: 35 But love your *e*, do good to them,
20: 43 hand until I make your *e*
Ro 5: 10 For if, when we were God's *e*,
1Co 15: 25 reign until he has put all his *e*
Php 3: 18 many live as *e* of the cross of Christ
Heb 1: 13 hand until I make your *e*
10: 13 for his *e* to be made his footstool,

ENEMY (ENEMIES ENMITY)
Pr 24: 17 Do not gloat when your *e* falls;
25: 21 If your *e* is hungry, give him food
27: 6 but an *e* multiplies kisses.
29: 24 of a thief is his own *e*;
Lk 10: 19 to overcome all the power of the *e*;
Ro 12: 20 "If your *e* is hungry, feed him;
1Co 15: 26 The last *e* to be destroyed is death.
1Ti 5: 14 and to give the *e* no opportunity
1Pe 5: 8 Your *e* the devil prowls

ENERGY*
Col 1: 29 struggling with all his *e*, which

ENGRAVED
Isa 49: 16 I have *e* you on the palms
2Co 3: 7 which was *e* in letters on stone,

ENHANCES*
Ro 3: 7 my falsehood *e* God's truthfulness

ENJOY (JOY)
Dt 6: 2 and so that you may *e* long life.
Ps 37: 3 dwell in the land and *e* safe pasture.
Pr 28: 16 ill-gotten gain will *e* a long life.
Ecc 3: 22 better for a man than to *e* his work,
Eph 6: 3 and that you may *e* long life
Heb 11: 25 rather than to *e* the pleasures of sin
3Jn : 2 I pray that you may *e* good health

ENJOYMENT (JOY)
Ecc 4: 8 and why am I depriving myself of *e*
1Ti 6: 17 us with everything for our *e*.

ENLARGE (ENLARGES)
2Co 9: 10 *e* the harvest of your righteousness.

ENLARGES (ENLARGE)
Dt 33: 20 Blessed is he who *e* Gad's domain!

ENLIGHTENED* (LIGHT)
Eph 1: 18 that the eyes of your heart may be *e*
Heb 6: 4 for those who have once been *e*,

ENMITY* (ENEMY)
Ge 3: 15 And I will put *e*

ENOCH
1. Son of Cain (Ge 4:17–18).
2. Descendant of Seth; walked with God and taken by him (Ge 5:18–24; Heb 11:5). Prophet (Jude 14).

ENSLAVED (SLAVE)
Gal 4: 9 Do you wish to be *e* by them all
Tit 3: 3 and *e* by all kinds of passions

ENSNARE (SNARE)
Pr 5: 22 of a wicked man *e* him;
Ecc 7: 26 but the sinner she will *e*.

ENSNARED* (SNARE)
Dt 7: 25 for yourselves, or you will be *e* by it
12: 30 be careful not to be *e*
Ps 9: 16 the wicked are *e* by the work
Pr 6: 2 *e* by the words of your mouth,
22: 25 and get yourself *e*.

ENTANGLED (ENTANGLES)
2Pe 2: 20 and are again *e* in it and overcome,

ENTANGLES* (ENTANGLED)
Heb 12: 1 and the sin that so easily *e*,

ENTER (ENTERED ENTERING ENTERS ENTRANCE)
Ps 95: 11 "They shall never *e* my rest."
100: 4 *E* his gates with thanksgiving
Pr 2: 10 For wisdom will *e* your heart,
Mt 5: 20 will certainly not *e* the kingdom
7: 13 "*E* through the narrow gate.
7: 21 Lord,' will *e* the kingdom of heaven
18: 3 you will never *e* the kingdom
18: 8 It is better for you to *e* life maimed
19: 17 to *e* life, obey the commandments
19: 23 man to *e* the kingdom of heaven.
Mk 9: 43 It is better for you to *e* life maimed
9: 45 It is better for you to *e* life crippled
9: 47 for you to *e* the kingdom of God
10: 15 like a little child will never *e* it."
10: 23 is for the rich to *e* the kingdom
Lk 13: 24 will try to *e* and will not be able to.
13: 24 "Make every effort to *e*
18: 17 like a little child will never *e* it."
18: 24 is for the rich to *e* the kingdom
Jn 3: 5 no one can *e* the kingdom of God.
Heb 3: 11 'They shall never *e* my rest.'"
4: 11 make every effort to *e* that rest,

ENTERED (ENTER)
Ps 73: 17 me till I *e* the sanctuary of God;
Eze 4: 14 meat has ever *e* my mouth."
Ac 11: 8 or unclean has ever *e* my mouth.'
Ro 5: 12 as sin *e* the world through one man,
Heb 9: 12 but he *e* the Most Holy Place once

ENTERING (ENTER)
Mt 21: 31 the prostitutes are *e* the kingdom
Lk 11: 52 have hindered those who were *e*."
Heb 4: 1 the promise of *e* his rest still stands,

ENTERS (ENTER)
Mk 7: 18 you see that nothing that *e* a man
Jn 10: 2 The man who *e* by the gate is

ENTERTAIN* (ENTERTAINED ENTERTAINMENT)
Jdg 16: 25 "Bring out Samson to *e* us."
Mt 9: 4 "Why do you *e* evil thoughts
1Ti 5: 19 Do not *e* an accusation
Heb 13: 2 Do not forget to *e* strangers,

ENTERTAINED* (ENTERTAIN)
Ac 28: 7 and for three days *e* us hospitably.
Heb 13: 2 so doing some people have *e* angels

ENTERTAINMENT* (ENTERTAIN)
Da 6: 18 without any *e* being brought to him

ENTHRALLED*
Ps 45: 11 The king is *e* by your beauty;

ENTHRONED* (THRONE)
1Sa 4: 4 who is *e* between the cherubim.
2Sa 6: 2 who is *e* between the cherubim that
2Ki 19: 15 of Israel, *e* between the cherubim,
1Ch 13: 6 who is *e* between the cherubim —
Ps 2: 4 The One *e* in heaven laughs;
9: 11 to the LORD, *e* in Zion;
22: 3 Yet you are *e* as the Holy One;
29: 10 The LORD sits *e* over the flood;
29: 10 the LORD is *e* as King forever.
55: 19 God, who is *e* forever,
61: 7 May he be *e* in God's presence
80: 1 who sit *e* between the cherubim,
99: 1 he sits *e* between the cherubim,
102: 12 But you, O LORD, sit *e* forever;
113: 5 the One who sits *e* on high,
132: 14 here I will sit *e*, for I have desired it
Isa 14: 13 I will sit *e* on the mount
37: 16 of Israel, *e* between the cherubim,
40: 22 He sits *e* above the circle
52: 2 rise up, sit *e*, O Jerusalem.

ENTHRONES* (THRONE)
Job 36: 7 he *e* them with kings

ENTHUSIASM*
2Co 8: 17 he is coming to you with much *e*
9: 2 and your *e* has stirred most of them

ENTICE* (ENTICED ENTICES)
Pr 1: 10 My son, if sinners *e* you,
2Pe 2: 18 they *e* people who are just escaping
Rev 2: 14 who taught Balak to *e* the Israelites

ENTICED* (ENTICE)
Dt 4: 19 do not be *e* into bowing
11: 16 or you will be *e* to turn away
2Ki 17: 21 Jeroboam *e* Israel away
Job 31: 9 If my heart has been *e* by a woman,
31: 27 so that my heart was secretly *e*
Jas 1: 14 desire, he is dragged away and *e*.

ENTICES* (ENTICE)
Dt 13: 6 your closest friend secretly *e* you,
Job 36: 18 Be careful that no one *e* you
Pr 16: 29 A violent man *e* his neighbor

ENTIRE
Gal 5: 14 The *e* law is summed up

ENTRANCE (ENTER)
Mt 27: 60 stone in front of the *e* to the tomb
Mk 15: 46 a stone against the *e* of the tomb.
16: 3 away from the *e* of the tomb?"
Jn 11: 38 cave with a stone laid across the *e*.
20: 1 had been removed from the *e*.

ENTRUST (TRUST)
Jn 2: 24 Jesus would not *e* himself to them,
2Ti 2: 2 the presence of many witnesses *e*

ENTRUSTED (TRUST)
Jer 13: 20 Where is the flock that was *e* to you
Jn 5: 22 but has *e* all judgment to the Son,
Ro 3: 2 they have been *e* with the very
6: 17 of teaching to which you were *e*.
1Co 4: 1 as those *e* with the secret things
1Th 2: 4 by God to be *e* with the gospel.
1Ti 1: 11 of the blessed God, which he *e*
6: 20 guard what has been *e* to your care.
2Ti 1: 12 able to guard what I have *e* to him
1: 14 Guard the good deposit that was *e*
Tit 1: 3 light through the preaching *e* to me
1: 7 Since an overseer is *e*
1Pe 2: 23 he *e* himself to him who judges
5: 3 not lording it over those *e* to you,
Jude : 3 once for all *e* to the saints.

ENVIES
Jas 4: 5 spirit he caused to live in us *e*

ENVIOUS (ENVY)
Dt 32: 21 I will make them *e*
Pr 24: 19 or be *e* of the wicked,
Ro 10: 19 "I will make you *e*

ENVOY
Pr 13: 17 but a trustworthy *e* brings healing.

ENVY (ENVIOUS ENVYING)
Pr 3: 31 Do not *e* a violent man
14: 30 but *e* rots the bones.
23: 17 Do not let your heart *e* sinners,
24: 1 Do not *e* wicked men,
Mk 7: 22 malice, deceit, lewdness, *e*, slander
Ro 1: 29 They are full of *e*, murder, strife,
11: 14 arouse my own people to *e*
1Co 13: 4 It does not *e*, it does not boast,
Gal 5: 21 factions and *e*; drunkenness, orgies
Php 1: 15 that some preach Christ out of *e*
1Ti 6: 4 and quarrels about words that result in *e*,
Tit 3: 3 lived in malice and *e*, being hated
Jas 3: 14 But if you harbor bitter *e*
3: 16 where you have *e* and selfish
1Pe 2: 1 *e*, and slander of every kind.

ENVYING* (ENVY)
Gal 5: 26 provoking and *e* each other.

EPHAH
Eze 45: 11 The *e* and the bath are

EPHESUS
Ac 18: 19 at *E*, where Paul left Priscilla
19: 1 the interior and arrived at *E*.
Eph 1: 1 To the saints in *E*, the faithful
Rev 2: 1 the angel of the church in *E* write:

EPHRAIM
1. Second son of Joseph (Ge 41:52; 46:20). Blessed as firstborn by Jacob (Ge 48). Tribe of numbered (Nu 1:33; 26:37), blessed (Dt 33:17), allotted land (Jos 16:4 – 9; Eze 48:5), failed to fully possess (Jos 16:10; Jdg 1:29).
2. Synonymous with Northern Kingdom (Isa 7:17; Hos 5).

EQUAL (EQUALITY EQUITY)
Dt 33: 25 and your strength will *e* your days.
1Sa 9: 2 without *e* among the Israelites —
Isa 40: 25 who is my *e*?" says the Holy One.
46: 5 you compare me or count me *e*?
Da 1: 19 and he found none *e* to Daniel,
Jn 5: 18 making himself *e* with God.
1Co 12: 25 that its parts should have *e* concern
2Co 2: 16 And who is *e* to such a task?

EQUALITY* (EQUAL)
2Co 8: 13 pressed, but that there might be *e*.
8: 14 Then there will be *e*, as it is written:
Php 2: 6 did not consider *e*

EQUIP* (EQUIPPED)
Heb 13: 21 *e* you with everything good

EQUIPPED (EQUIP)
2Ti 3: 17 man of God may be thoroughly *e*

EQUITY* (EQUAL)
Ps 96: 10 he will judge the peoples with *e*.
98: 9 and the peoples with *e*.
99: 4 you have established *e*;

ERODES*
Job 14: 18 "But as a mountain *e* and crumbles

ERROR (ERRORS)
Jas 5: 20 Whoever turns a sinner from the *e*
2Pe 2: 18 escaping from those who live in *e*.

ERRORS* (ERROR)
Ps 19: 12 Who can discern his *e*?
Ecc 10: 4 calmness can lay great *e* to rest.

ESAU
Firstborn of Isaac, twin of Jacob (Ge 25:21 – 26). Also called Edom (Ge 25:30). Sold Jacob his birthright (Ge 25:29 – 34); lost blessing (Gen 27). Married Hittites (Ge 26:34), Ishmaelites (Ge 28:6 – 9). Reconciled to Jacob (Gen 33). Genealogy (Ge 36). The LORD chose Jacob over Esau (Mal 1:2 – 3), but gave Esau land (Dt 2:2 – 12). Descendants eventually obliterated (Ob 1 – 21; Jer 49:7 – 22).

ESCAPE (ESCAPED ESCAPES ESCAPING)
Ps 68: 20 from the Sovereign LORD comes *e*
Pr 11: 9 through knowledge the righteous *e*.
Ro 2: 3 think you will *e* God's judgment?
1Th 5: 3 woman, and they will not *e*.
2Ti 2: 26 and *e* from the trap of the devil,
Heb 2: 3 how shall we *e* if we ignore such
12: 25 If they did not *e* when they refused
2Pe 1: 4 and *e* the corruption in the world

ESCAPED (ESCAPE)
2Pe 2: 20 If they have *e* the corruption

ESCAPES (ESCAPE)
Pr 12: 13 but a righteous man *e* trouble.

ESCAPING (ESCAPE)
1Co 3: 15 only as one *e* through the flames.
2Pe 2: 18 they entice people who are just *e*

ESTABLISH (ESTABLISHED ESTABLISHES)
Ge 6: 18 But I will *e* my covenant with you,
17: 21 But my covenant I will *e* with Isaac
2Sa 7: 11 the LORD himself will *e* a house
1Ki 9: 5 I will *e* your royal throne
1Ch 28: 7 I will *e* his kingdom forever
Ps 90: 17 *e* the work of our hands for us —
Isa 26: 12 LORD, you *e* peace for us;
Ro 10: 3 God and sought to *e* their own,
16: 25 able to *e* you by my gospel
Heb 10: 9 sets aside the first to *e* the second.

ESTABLISHED (ESTABLISH)
Ge 9: 17 the sign of the covenant I have *e*
Ex 6: 4 also *e* my covenant with them
Pr 16: 12 a throne is *e* through righteousness.

ESTABLISHES (ESTABLISH)
Job 25: 2 he *e* order in the heights of heaven.
Isa 42: 4 till he *e* justice on earth.

ESTATE
Ps 136: 23 who remembered us in our low *e*

ESTEEMED
Pr 22: 1 to be *e* is better than silver or gold.
Isa 53: 3 he was despised, and we *e* him not.

ESTHER
Jewess, originally named Hadassah, who lived in Persia; cousin of Mordecai (Est 2:7). Chosen queen of Xerxes (Est 2:8 – 18). Persuaded by Mordecai to foil Haman's plan to exterminate the Jews (Est 3 – 4). Revealed Haman's plans to Xerxes, resulting in Haman's death (Est 7), the Jews' preservation (Est 8 – 9), Mordecai's exaltation (Est 8:15; 9:4; 10). Decreed celebration of Purim (Est 9:18 – 32).

ETERNAL* (ETERNALLY ETERNITY)
Ge 21: 33 the name of the LORD, the *E* God.
Dt 33: 27 The *e* God is your refuge,
1Ki 10: 9 of the LORD's *e* love for Israel,
Ps 16: 11 with *e* pleasures at your right hand.
21: 6 you have granted him *e* blessings
111: 10 To him belongs *e* praise.
119: 89 Your word, O LORD, is *e*;
119: 160 all your righteous laws are *e*.
Ecc 12: 5 Then man goes to his *e* home
Isa 26: 4 LORD, the LORD, is the Rock *e*.
47: 7 the *e* queen!'
Jer 10: 10 he is the living God, the *e* King.
Da 4: 3 His kingdom is an *e* kingdom;
4: 34 His dominion is an *e* dominion;
Hab 3: 6 His ways are *e*.
Mt 18: 8 two feet and be thrown into *e* fire.
19: 16 good thing must I do to get *e* life?"
19: 29 as much and will inherit *e* life.
25: 41 into the *e* fire prepared for the devil
25: 46 but the righteous to *e* life."
25: 46 they will go away to *e* punishment,
Mk 3: 29 be forgiven; he is guilty of an *e* sin."
10: 17 "what must I do to inherit *e* life?"
10: 30 and in the age to come, *e* life.
Lk 10: 25 "what must I do to inherit *e* life?"
16: 9 will be welcomed into *e* dwellings.
18: 18 what must I do to inherit *e* life?"
18: 30 and, in the age to come, *e* life."
Jn 3: 15 believes in him may have *e* life.
3: 16 him shall not perish but have *e* life.
3: 36 believes in the Son has *e* life,
4: 14 spring of water welling up to *e* life."
4: 36 now he harvests the crop for *e* life,
5: 24 believes him who sent me has *e* life
5: 39 that by them you possess *e* life.
6: 27 but for food that endures to *e* life,
6: 40 believes in him shall have *e* life,
6: 54 and drinks my blood has *e* life,
6: 68 You have the words of *e* life.
10: 28 I give them *e* life, and they shall
12: 25 in this world will keep it for *e* life.
12: 50 that his command leads to *e* life.
17: 2 all people that he might give *e* life
17: 3 this is *e* life: that they may know
Ac 13: 46 yourselves worthy of *e* life,
13: 48 were appointed for *e* life believed.
Ro 1: 20 his *e* power and divine nature —
2: 7 and immortality, he will give *e* life.
5: 21 righteousness to bring *e* life
6: 22 to holiness, and the result is *e* life.
6: 23 but the gift of God is *e* life
16: 26 by the command of the *e* God,
2Co 4: 17 for us an *e* glory that far outweighs
4: 18 temporary, but what is unseen is *e*.
5: 1 from God, an *e* house in heaven,
Gal 6: 8 from the Spirit will reap *e* life.
Eph 3: 11 to his *e* purpose which he
2Th 2: 16 his grace gave us *e* encouragement
1Ti 1: 16 believe on him and receive *e* life.
1: 17 Now to the King *e*, immortal,
6: 12 Take hold of the *e* life
2Ti 2: 10 is in Christ Jesus, with *e* glory.
Tit 1: 2 resting on the hope of *e* life,
3: 7 heirs having the hope of *e* life.
Heb 5: 9 he became the source of *e* salvation
6: 2 of the dead, and *e* judgment.
9: 12 having obtained *e* redemption.
9: 14 through the *e* Spirit offered himself
9: 15 the promised *e* inheritance —
13: 20 of the *e* covenant brought back
1Pe 5: 10 you to his *e* glory in Christ,
2Pe 1: 11 into the *e* kingdom of our Lord
1Jn 1: 2 and we proclaim to you the *e* life,
2: 25 what he promised us — even *e* life.
3: 15 know that no murderer has *e* life
5: 11 God has given us *e* life,
5: 13 you may know that you have *e* life.
5: 20 He is the true God and *e* life.
Jude : 7 who suffer the punishment of *e* fire.
: 21 Christ to bring you to *e* life.
Rev 14: 6 and he had the *e* gospel to proclaim

ETERNALLY* (ETERNAL)
Gal 1: 8 let him be *e* condemned! As we
1: 9 let him be *e* condemned! Am I now

ETERNITY* (ETERNAL)
Ps 93: 2 you are from all *e*.
Pr 8: 23 I was appointed from *e*,
Ecc 3: 11 also set *e* in the hearts of men;

ETHIOPIAN*
Jer 13: 23 Can the *E* change his skin
Ac 8: 27 and on his way he met an *E* eunuch

EUNUCH (EUNUCHS)
Ac 8: 27 on his way he met an Ethiopian *e*,

EUNUCHS (EUNUCH)
Isa 56: 4 "To the *e* who keep my Sabbaths,
Mt 19: 12 For some are *e* because they were

EUTYCHUS*
Ac 20: 9 was a young man named *E*,

EVANGELIST* (EVANGELISTS)
Ac 21: 8 stayed at the house of Philip the *e*,
2Ti 4: 5 hardship, do the work of an *e*,

EVANGELISTS* (EVANGELIST)
Eph 4: 11 some to be prophets, some to be *e*,

EVE*
Ge 3: 20 Adam named his wife *E*,
4: 1 Adam lay with his wife *E*,
2Co 11: 3 as *E* was deceived by the serpent's
1Ti 2: 13 For Adam was formed first, then *E*

EVEN-TEMPERED* (TEMPER)
Pr 17: 27 and a man of understanding is *e*.

EVENING
Ge 1: 5 there was *e*, and there was morning

EVER (EVERLASTING FOREVER FOREVERMORE)
Ex 15: 18 LORD will reign for *e* and *e*."
Dt 8: 19 If you *e* forget the LORD your
1Ki 3: 12 anyone like you, nor will there *e* be.
Job 4: 7 were the upright *e* destroyed?
Ps 5: 11 let them *e* sing for joy.
10: 16 The LORD is King for *e* and *e*;
21: 4 length of days, for *e* and *e*.
25: 3 will *e* be put to shame,
25: 15 My eyes are *e* on the LORD,
26: 3 for your love is *e* before me,
45: 6 O God, will last for *e* and *e*;
45: 17 nations will praise you for *e* and *e*.
48: 14 For this God is our God for *e* and *e*;
52: 8 God's unfailing love for *e* and *e*.
61: 8 will I *e* sing praise to your name
71: 6 I will *e* praise you.
84: 4 they are *e* praising you.
89: 33 nor will I *e* betray my faithfulness.
111: 8 They are steadfast for *e* and *e*,
119: 44 your law, for *e* and *e*.
119: 98 for they are *e* with me.
132: 12 sit on your throne for *e* and *e*."
145: 1 I will praise your name for *e* and *e*.
145: 2 and extol your name for *e* and *e*.
145: 21 his holy name for *e* and *e*.
Pr 4: 18 shining *e* brighter till the full light
5: 19 may you *e* be captivated
Isa 66: 8 Who has *e* heard of such a thing?
66: 8 Who has *e* seen such things?
Jer 7: 7 I gave your forefathers for *e* and *e*.
25: 5 and your fathers for *e* and *e*.
31: 36 the descendants of Israel *e* cease
Da 2: 20 be to the name of God for *e* and *e*;
7: 18 it forever — yes, for *e* and *e*.'
12: 3 like the stars for *e* and *e*.
Mic 4: 5 our God for *e* and *e*.
Mt 13: 14 you will be *e* seeing but never
13: 14 "'You will be *e* hearing
Mk 4: 12 *e* hearing but never understanding;
Jn 1: 18 No one has *e* seen God,
Gal 1: 5 to whom be glory for *e* and *e*.
Eph 3: 21 all generations, for *e* and *e*!
Php 4: 20 and Father be glory for *e* and *e*.
1Ti 1: 17 be honor and glory for *e* and *e*.
2Ti 4: 18 To him be glory for *e* and *e*.
Heb 1: 8 O God, will last for *e* and *e*,
13: 21 to whom be glory for *e* and *e*.
1Pe 4: 11 the glory and the power for *e* and *e*.
5: 11 To him be the power for *e* and *e*.
1Jn 4: 12 No one has *e* seen God;
Rev 1: 6 him be glory and power for *e* and *e*!
1: 18 and behold I am alive for *e* and *e*!
21: 27 Nothing impure will *e* enter it,
22: 5 And they will reign for *e* and *e*.

EVER-INCREASING* (INCREASE)
Ro 6: 19 to impurity and to *e* wickedness,

2Co 3: 18 into his likeness with *e* glory,

EVERLASTING* (EVER)
Ge 9: 16 and remember the *e* covenant
17: 7 an *e* covenant between me and you
17: 8 I will give as an *e* possession to you
17: 13 in your flesh is to be an *e* covenant.
17: 19 an *e* covenant for his descendants
48: 4 *e* possession to your descendants
Nu 18: 19 It is an *e* covenant of salt
Dt 33: 15 and the fruitfulness of the *e* hills;
33: 27 and underneath are the *e* arms.
2Sa 23: 5 made with me an *e* covenant,
1Ch 16: 17 to Israel as an *e* covenant:
16: 36 from *e* to *e.*
29: 10 from *e* to *e.*
Ezr 9: 12 to your children as an *e* inheritance
Ne 9: 5 your God, who is from *e* to *e.*"
Ps 41: 13 from *e* to *e.*
52: 5 God will bring you down to *e* ruin:
74: 3 toward these *e* ruins,
78: 66 he put them to *e* shame.
90: 2 from *e* to *e* you are God.
103: 17 But from *e* to *e*
105: 10 to Israel as an *e* covenant:
106: 48 from *e* to *e.*
119: 142 Your righteousness is *e*
139: 24 and lead me in the way *e.*
145: 13 Your kingdom is an *e* kingdom,
Isa 9: 6 *E* Father, Prince of Peace.
24: 5 and broken the *e* covenant.
30: 8 it may be an *e* witness.
33: 14 Who of us can dwell with *e* burning
35: 10 *e* joy will crown their heads.
40: 28 The LORD is the *e* God,
45: 17 the LORD with an *e* salvation;
45: 17 to ages *e.*
51: 11 *e* joy will crown their heads.
54: 8 but with *e* kindness
55: 3 I will make an *e* covenant with you,
55: 13 for an *e* sign,
56: 5 I will give them an *e* name
60: 15 I will make you the *e* pride
60: 19 for the LORD will be your *e* light,
60: 20 the LORD will be your *e* light,
61: 7 and *e* joy will be theirs.
61: 8 and make an *e* covenant with them.
63: 12 to gain for himself *e* renown,
Jer 5: 22 an *e* barrier it cannot cross.
23: 40 I will bring upon you *e* disgrace—
23: 40 *e* shame that will not be forgotten."
25: 9 of horror and scorn, and an *e* ruin.
31: 3 "I have loved you with an *e* love;
32: 40 I will make an *e* covenant
50: 5 the LORD in an *e* covenant
Eze 16: 60 and I will establish an *e* covenant
37: 26 with them; it will be an *e* covenant.
Da 7: 14 dominion is an *e* dominion that will
7: 27 His kingdom will be an *e* kingdom,
9: 24 to bring in *e* righteousness,
12: 2 others to shame and *e* contempt.
12: 2 some to *e* life, others to shame
Mic 6: 2 you *e* foundations of the earth.
Hab 1: 12 O LORD, are you not from *e?*
Jn 6: 47 the truth, he who believes has *e* life.
2Th 1: 9 punished with *e* destruction
Jude : 6 bound with *e* chains for judgment

EVER-PRESENT*
Ps 46: 1 an *e* help in trouble

EVIDENCE (EVIDENT)
Jn 14: 11 on the *e* of the miracles themselves.
Ac 11: 23 and saw the *e* of the grace of God,
2Th 1: 5 All this is *e* that God's judgment is
Jas 2: 20 do you want *e* that faith

EVIDENT (EVIDENCE)
Php 4: 5 Let your gentleness be *e* to all.

EVIL (EVILDOER EVILDOERS EVILS)
Ge 2: 9 of the knowledge of good and *e.*
3: 5 be like God, knowing good and *e.*"
6: 5 of his heart was only *e* all the time.
Ex 32: 22 how prone these people are to *e.*
Jdg 2: 11 Then the Israelites did *e* in the eyes
3: 7 The Israelites did *e* in the eyes
3: 12 Once again the Israelites did *e*
4: 1 the Israelites once again did *e*
6: 1 Again the Israelites did *e*
10: 6 Again the Israelites did *e*
13: 1 Again the Israelites did *e*
1Ki 11: 6 So Solomon did *e* in the eyes
16: 25 But Omri did *e* in the eyes
2Ki 15: 24 Pekahiah did *e* in the eyes
Job 1: 1 he feared God and shunned *e.*
1: 8 a man who fears God and shuns *e.*"
Job 34: 10 Far be it from God to do *e,*
36: 21 Beware of turning to *e,*
Ps 5: 4 not a God who takes pleasure in *e;*
23: 4 I will fear no *e,*
34: 13 keep your tongue from *e*
34: 14 Turn from *e* and do good;
34: 16 is against those who do *e,*
37: 1 Do not fret because of *e* men
37: 8 do not fret—it leads only to *e.*
37: 27 Turn from *e* and do good;
49: 5 fear when *e* days come,
51: 4 and done what is *e* in your sight,
97: 10 those who love the LORD hate *e,*
101: 4 I will have nothing to do with *e.*
141: 4 not my heart be drawn to what is *e,*
Pr 4: 27 keep your foot from *e.*
8: 13 To fear the LORD is to hate *e;*
10: 23 A fool finds pleasure in *e* conduct,
11: 19 he who pursues *e* goes to his death.
11: 27 *e* comes to him who searches for it.
14: 16 man fears the LORD and shuns *e,*
17: 13 If a man pays back *e* for good,
20: 30 Blows and wounds cleanse away *e,*
24: 19 Do not fret because of *e* men
24: 20 for the *e* man has no future hope,
26: 23 are fervent lips with an *e* heart.
28: 5 *E* men do not understand justice,
29: 6 An *e* man is snared by his own sin,
Ecc 12: 14 whether it is good or *e.*
Isa 5: 20 Woe to those who call *e* good
13: 11 I will punish the world for its *e,*
55: 7 and the *e* man his thoughts.
Jer 4: 14 wash the *e* from your heart
18: 8 nation I warned repents of its *e,*
18: 11 So turn from your *e* ways,
Eze 33: 11 Turn! Turn from your *e* ways!
33: 13 he will die for the *e* he has done.
33: 15 and does no *e,* he will surely live;
Am 5: 13 for the times are *e.*
Hab 1: 13 Your eyes are too pure to look on *e;*
Zec 8: 17 do not plot *e* against your neighbor,
Mt 5: 45 He causes his sun to rise on the *e*
6: 13 but deliver us from the *e* one.'
7: 11 If you, then, though you are *e,*
12: 34 you who are *e* say anything good?
12: 35 and the *e* man brings *e* things out
12: 35 out of the *e* stored up in him.
12: 43 "When an *e* spirit comes out
15: 19 out of the heart come *e* thoughts,
Mk 7: 21 come *e* thoughts, sexual
Lk 6: 45 and the *e* man brings *e* things out
11: 13 If you then, though you are *e,*
Jn 3: 19 of light because their deeds were *e.*
3: 20 Everyone who does *e* hates
17: 15 you protect them from the *e* one.
Ro 1: 30 they invent ways of doing *e;*
2: 8 who reject the truth and follow *e,*
2: 9 for every human being who does *e:*
3: 8 "Let us do *e* that good may result"?
6: 12 body so that you obey its *e* desires.
7: 19 no, the *e* I do not want to do—
7: 21 to do good, *e* is right there with me.
12: 9 Hate what is *e;* cling
12: 17 Do not repay anyone *e* for *e.*
12: 21 Do not be overcome by *e,*
14: 16 good to be spoken of as *e.*
16: 19 and innocent about what is *e.*
1Co 13: 6 Love does not delight in *e*
14: 20 In regard to *e* be infants,
Eph 5: 16 because the days are *e.*
6: 12 forces of *e* in the heavenly realms.
6: 16 all the flaming arrows of the *e* one.
Col 3: 5 impurity, lust, *e* desires and greed,
1Th 5: 22 Avoid every kind of *e.*
2Th 3: 3 and protect you from the *e* one.
1Ti 6: 10 of money is a root of all kinds of *e.*
2Ti 2: 22 Flee the *e* desires of youth,
3: 6 are swayed by all kinds of *e* desires,
3: 13 while *e* men and impostors will go
Heb 5: 14 to distinguish good from *e.*
Jas 1: 13 For God cannot be tempted by *e,*
1: 21 and the *e* that is so prevalent,
3: 6 a world of *e* among the parts
3: 8 It is a restless *e,* full
1Pe 2: 16 your freedom as a cover-up for *e;*
3: 9 Do not repay *e* with *e* or insult
3: 10 must keep his tongue from *e*
3: 17 for doing good than for doing *e.*
1Jn 2: 13 you have overcome the *e* one.
2: 14 and you have overcome the *e* one.
3: 12 who belonged to the *e* one
5: 18 and the *e* one cannot harm him.
5: 19 is under the control of the *e* one.
3Jn : 11 do not imitate what is *e*

EVILDOER* (EVIL)
2Sa 3: 39 the LORD repay the *e* according
Ps 101: 8 I will cut off every *e*
Mal 4: 1 and every *e* will be stubble,

EVILDOERS* (EVIL)
1Sa 24: 13 saying goes, 'From *e* come evil
Job 8: 20 or strengthen the hands of *e.*
34: 8 He keeps company with *e;*
34: 22 where *e* can hide.
Ps 14: 4 Will *e* never learn—
14: 6 You *e* frustrate the plans
26: 5 I abhor the assembly of *e*
36: 12 See how the *e* lie fallen—
53: 4 Will the *e* never learn—
59: 2 Deliver me from *e*
64: 2 from that noisy crowd of *e.*
92: 7 and all *e* flourish,
92: 9 all *e* will be scattered.
94: 4 all the *e* are full of boasting.
94: 16 will take a stand for me against *e?*
119: 115 Away from me, you *e,*
125: 5 the LORD will banish with the *e.*
141: 4 deeds with men who are *e;*
141: 5 ever against the deeds of *e;*
141: 9 from the traps set by *e.*
Pr 21: 15 but terror to *e.*
Isa 1: 4 a brood of *e,*
31: 2 against those who help *e.*
Jer 23: 14 They strengthen the hands of *e,*
Hos 10: 9 the *e* in Gibeah?
Mal 3: 15 Certainly the *e* prosper, and
Mt 7: 23 you *e!*' "Therefore everyone who
Lk 13: 27 Away from me, all you *e!*'
18: 11 *e,* adulterers—or even like this tax

EVILS* (EVIL)
Mk 7: 23 All these *e* come from inside

EWE
2Sa 12: 3 one little *e* lamb he had bought.

EXACT*
Ge 43: 21 the *e* weight—in the mouth
Est 4: 7 including the *e* amount
Mt 2: 7 from them the *e* time the star had
Jn 4: 53 realized that this was the *e* time
Ac 17: 26 the *e* places where they should live.
Heb 1: 3 the *e* representation of his being,

EXALT* (EXALTED EXALTS)
Ex 15: 2 my father's God, and I will *e* him.
Jos 3: 7 begin to *e* you in the eyes
1Sa 2: 10 and *e* the horn of his anointed."
1Ch 25: 5 the promises of God to *e* him.
29: 12 power to *e* and give strength to all.
Job 19: 5 If indeed you would *e* yourselves
Ps 30: 1 I will *e* you, O LORD,
34: 3 let us *e* his name together.
35: 26 may all who *e* themselves over me
37: 34 He will *e* you to inherit the land;
38: 16 *e* themselves over me
75: 6 or from the desert can *e* a man.
89: 17 and by your favor you *e* our horn.
99: 5 *E* the LORD our God
99: 9 *E* the LORD our God
107: 32 Let them *e* him in the assembly
118: 28 you are my God, and I will *e* you.
145: 1 I will *e* you, my God the King;
Pr 4: 8 Esteem her, and she will *e* you;
25: 6 Do not *e* yourself in the king's
Isa 24: 15 *e* the name of the LORD, the God
25: 1 I will *e* you and praise your name,
Eze 29: 15 and will never again *e* itself
Da 4: 37 *e* and glorify the King of heaven,
11: 36 He will *e* and magnify himself
11: 37 but will *e* himself above them all.
Hos 11: 7 he will by no means *e* them.
2Th 2: 4 will *e* himself over everything that is

EXALTED* (EXALT)
Ex 15: 1 for he is highly *e.*
15: 21 for he is highly *e.*
Nu 24: 7 their kingdom will be *e.*
Jos 4: 14 That day the LORD *e* Joshua
2Sa 5: 12 and had *e* his kingdom for the sake
22: 47 *E* be God, the Rock, my Savior!
22: 49 You *e* me above my foes;
23: 1 of the man *e* by the Most High,
1Ch 14: 2 that his kingdom had been highly *e*
17: 17 as though I were the most *e* of men,
29: 11 you are *e* as head over all.
29: 25 The LORD highly *e* Solomon
Ne 9: 5 and may it be *e* above all blessing
Job 24: 24 For a little while they are *e,*
36: 22 "God is *e* in his power.
37: 23 beyond our reach and *e* in power;

Ps 18: 46 *E* be God my Savior!
18: 48 You *e* me above my foes;
21: 13 Be *e,* O LORD, in your strength;
27: 6 Then my head will be *e*
35: 27 they always say, "The LORD be *e,*
40: 16 "The LORD be *e!*"
46: 10 I will be *e* among the nations,
46: 10 I will be *e* in the earth."
47: 9 he is greatly *e.*
57: 5 Be *e,* O God, above the heavens;
57: 11 Be *e,* O God, above the heavens;
70: 4 "Let God be *e!*"
89: 13 hand is strong, your right hand *e.*
89: 19 I have *e* a young man
89: 24 through my name his horn will be *e*
89: 27 the most *e* of the kings of the earth.
89: 42 You have *e* the right hand
92: 8 But you, O LORD, are *e* forever.
92: 10 You have *e* my horn like that
97: 9 you are *e* far above all gods.
99: 2 he is *e* over all the nations.
108: 5 Be *e,* O God, above the heavens,
113: 4 The LORD is *e* over all the nations
138: 2 for you have *e* above all things
148: 13 for his name alone is *e;*
Pr 11: 11 of the upright a city is *e,*
30: 32 have played the fool and *e* yourself,
Isa 2: 11 the LORD alone will be *e*
2: 12 for all that is *e*
2: 17 the LORD alone will be *e*
5: 16 the LORD Almighty will be *e*
6: 1 *e,* and the train of his robe filled
12: 4 and proclaim that his name is *e.*
24: 4 the *e* of the earth languish.
33: 5 The LORD is *e,* for he dwells
33: 10 "Now will I be *e;*
52: 13 be raised and lifted up and highly *e.*
Jer 17: 12 A glorious throne, *e*
La 2: 17 he has *e* the horn of your foes.
Eze 21: 26 The lowly will be *e* and the *e* will be
Hos 13: 1 he was *e* in Israel.
Mic 6: 6 and bow down before the *e* God?
Mt 23: 12 whoever humbles himself will be *e.*
Lk 14: 11 he who humbles himself will be *e.*"
18: 14 he who humbles himself will be *e.*"
Ac 2: 33 *E* to the right hand of God,
5: 31 God *e* him to his own right hand
Php 1: 20 always Christ will be *e* in my body,
2: 9 Therefore God *e* him
Heb 7: 26 from sinners, *e* above the heavens.

EXALTS* (EXALT)
1Sa 2: 7 he humbles and he *e.*
Job 36: 7 and *e* them forever.
Ps 75: 7 He brings one down, he *e* another.
Pr 14: 34 Righteousness *e* a nation,
Mt 23: 12 For whoever *e* himself will be
Lk 14: 11 For everyone who *e* himself will be
18: 14 For everyone who *e* himself will be

EXAMINE (EXAMINED EXAMINES)
Ps 11: 4 his eyes *e* them.
17: 3 you probe my heart and *e* me
26: 2 *e* my heart and my mind;
Jer 17: 10 and *e* the mind,
20: 12 Almighty, you who *e* the righteous
La 3: 40 Let us *e* our ways and test them,
1Co 11: 28 A man ought to *e* himself
2Co 13: 5 *E* yourselves to see whether you

EXAMINED (EXAMINE)
Job 13: 9 Would it turn out well if he *e* you?
Ac 17: 11 *e* the Scriptures every day to see

EXAMINES (EXAMINE)
Ps 11: 5 The LORD *e* the righteous,
Pr 5: 21 and he *e* all his paths.

EXAMPLE* (EXAMPLES)
2Ki 14: 3 In everything he followed the *e*
Ecc 9: 13 also saw under the sun this *e*
Eze 14: 8 and make him an *e* and a byword.
Jn 13: 15 have set you an *e* that you should
Ro 7: 2 as long as he lives? For *e,*
1Co 11: 1 Follow my *e,* as I follow
11: 1 as I follow the *e* of Christ.
Gal 3: 15 let me take an *e* from everyday life.
Php 3: 17 Join with others in following my *e,*
2Th 3: 7 how you ought to follow our *e.*
1Ti 1: 16 as an *e* for those who would believe
4: 12 set an *e* for the believers in speech,
Tit 2: 7 In everything set them an *e*
Heb 4: 11 fall by following their *e*
Jas 3: 4 Or take ships as an *e.*
5: 10 as an *e* of patience in the face
1Pe 2: 21 leaving you an *e,* that you should
2Pe 2: 6 made them an *e* of what is going
Jude : 7 as an *e* of those who suffer

EXAMPLES* (EXAMPLE)
1Co 10: 6 Now these things occurred as *e*
10: 11 as *e* and were written down
1Pe 5: 3 to you, but being *e* to the flock.

EXASPERATE*
Eph 6: 4 Fathers, do not *e* your children;

EXCEL* (EXCELLENT)
Ge 49: 4 as the waters, you will no longer *e,*
1Co 14: 12 to *e* in gifts that build up the church
2Co 8: 7 But just as you *e* in everything—
8: 7 also *e* in this grace of giving.

EXCELLENT (EXCEL)
1Co 12: 31 now I will show you the most *e* way
Php 4: 8 if anything is *e* or praiseworthy—
1Ti 3: 13 have served well gain an *e* standing
Tit 3: 8 These things are *e* and profitable

EXCESSIVE
Eze 18: 8 or take *e* interest.
2Co 2: 7 not be overwhelmed by *e* sorrow.

EXCHANGE (EXCHANGED)
Mt 16: 26 Or what can a man give in *e*
Mk 8: 37 Or what can a man give in *e*
2Co 6: 13 As a fair *e*— I speak

EXCHANGED (EXCHANGE)
Ps 106: 20 They *e* their Glory
Jer 2: 11 But my people have *e* their Glory
Hos 4: 7 they *e* their Glory
Ro 1: 23 *e* the glory of the immortal God
1: 25 They *e* the truth of God for a lie,
1: 26 their women *e* natural relations

EXCLAIM
Ps 35: 10 My whole being will *e,*

EXCUSE* (EXCUSES)
Ps 25: 3 who are treacherous without *e.*
Lk 14: 18 Please *e* me.'
14: 19 Please *e* me.'
Jn 15: 22 they have no *e* for their sin.
Ro 1: 20 so that men are without *e.*
2: 1 You, therefore, have no *e,*

EXCUSES* (EXCUSE)
Lk 14: 18 "But they all alike began to make *e.*

EXERTED*
Eph 1: 20 which he *e* in Christ

EXHORT*
1Ti 5: 1 but *e* him as if he were your father.

EXILE
2Ki 17: 23 taken from their homeland into *e*
25: 11 into *e* the people who remained

EXISTED* (EXISTS)
2Pe 3: 5 ago by God's word the heavens *e*

EXISTS (EXISTED)
Heb 2: 10 and through whom everything *e,*
11: 6 to him must believe that he *e*

EXPANSE
Ge 1: 7 So God made the *e* and separated
1: 8 God called the *e* "sky."

EXPECT (EXPECTATION EXPECTED EXPECTING)
Mt 24: 44 at an hour when you do not *e* him.
Lk 12: 40 at an hour when you do not *e* him."
Php 1: 20 I eagerly *e* and hope that I will

EXPECTATION (EXPECT)
Ro 8: 19 waits in eager *e* for the sons
Heb 10: 27 but only a fearful *e* of judgment

EXPECTED (EXPECT)
Pr 11: 7 all he *e* from his power comes
Hag 1: 9 "You *e* much, but see, it turned out

EXPECTING (EXPECT)
Lk 6: 35 and lend to them without *e*

EXPEL* (EXPELLED)
1Co 5: 13 *E* the wicked man from among you

EXPELLED (EXPEL)
Eze 28: 16 and I *e* you, O guardian cherub,

EXPENSE (EXPENSIVE)
1Co 9: 7 Who serves as a soldier at his own *e*

EXPENSIVE* (EXPENSE)
Mt 26: 7 jar of very *e* perfume,
Mk 14: 3 jar of very *e* perfume,
Lk 7: 25 those who wear *e* clothes
Jn 12: 3 a pint of pure nard, an *e* perfume;
1Ti 2: 9 or gold or pearls or *e* clothes,

EXPERT
1Co 3: 10 I laid a foundation as an *e* builder,

EXPLAINING (EXPLAINS)
Ac 17: 3 *e* and proving that the Christ had

EXPLAINS* (EXPLAINING)
Ac 8: 31 he said, "unless someone *e* it to me

EXPLOIT* (EXPLOITED EXPLOITING EXPLOITS)
Pr 22: 22 Do not *e* the poor because they are
Isa 58: 3 and *e* all your workers.
2Co 12: 17 Did I *e* you through any
12: 18 Titus did not *e* you, did he?
2Pe 2: 3 greed these teachers will *e* you

EXPLOITED* (EXPLOIT)
2Co 7: 2 no one, we have *e* no one.

EXPLOITING* (EXPLOIT)
Jas 2: 6 Is it not the rich who are *e* you?

EXPLOITS (EXPLOIT)
2Co 11: 20 or *e* you or takes advantage of you

EXPLORE
Nu 13: 2 "Send some men to *e* the land

EXPOSE (EXPOSED)
1Co 4: 5 will *e* the motives of men's hearts.
Eph 5: 11 of darkness, but rather *e* them.

EXPOSED (EXPOSE)
Jn 3: 20 for fear that his deeds will be *e.*
Eph 5: 13 everything *e* by the light becomes

EXPRESS (EXPRESSING)
Ro 8: 26 us with groans that words cannot *e.*

EXPRESSING* (EXPRESS)
1Co 2: 13 *e* spiritual truths in spiritual words.
Gal 5: 6 thing that counts is faith *e* itself

EXTENDS (EXTENT)
Pr 31: 20 and *e* her hands to the needy.
Lk 1: 50 His mercy *e* to those who fear him,

EXTENT (EXTENDS)
Jn 13: 1 he now showed them the full *e*

EXTERNAL
Gal 2: 6 judge by *e* appearance—

EXTINGUISH (EXTINGUISHED)
Eph 6: 16 which you can *e* all the flaming

EXTINGUISHED (EXTINGUISH)
2Sa 21: 17 the lamp of Israel will not be *e.*"

EXTOL*
Job 36: 24 Remember to *e* his work,
Ps 34: 1 I will *e* the LORD at all times;
68: 4 *e* him who rides on the clouds—
95: 2 and *e* him with music and song.
109: 30 mouth I will greatly *e* the LORD;
111: 1 I will *e* the LORD with all my heart
115: 18 it is we who *e* the LORD,
117: 1 *e* him, all you peoples.
145: 2 and *e* your name for ever and ever.
145: 10 your saints will *e* you.
147: 12 *E* the LORD, O Jerusalem;

EXTORT*
Lk 3: 14 "Don't *e* money and don't accuse

EXTRAORDINARY*
Ac 19: 11 God did *e* miracles through Paul,

EXTREME (EXTREMES)
2Co 8: 2 and their *e* poverty welled up

EXTREMES* (EXTREME)
Ecc 7: 18 who fears God will avoid all ⌞*e*⌟.

EXULT
Ps 89: 16 they *e* in your righteousness.
Isa 45: 25 will be found righteous and will *e.*

EYE (EYES)
Ge 3: 6 good for food and pleasing to the *e,*
Ex 21: 24 you are to take life for life, *e* for *e,*
Dt 19: 21 life for life, *e* for *e,* tooth for tooth,
Ps 94: 9 Does he who formed the *e* not see?
Mt 5: 29 If your right *e* causes you to sin,
5: 38 '*E* for *e,* and tooth for tooth.'
6: 22 "The *e* is the lamp of the body.
7: 3 of sawdust in your brother's *e*
1Co 2: 9 "No *e* has seen,
12: 16 I am not an *e,* I do not belong
15: 52 of an *e,* at the last trumpet.
Eph 6: 6 favor when their *e* is on you,
Col 3: 22 not only when their *e* is on you
Rev 1: 7 and every *e* will see him,

EYES (EYE)
Nu 15: 39 the lusts of your own hearts and *e*.
33: 55 remain will become barbs in your *e*
Dt 11: 12 the *e* of the LORD your God are
12: 25 right in the *e* of the LORD.
16: 19 for a bribe blinds the *e* of the wise
Jos 23: 13 on your backs and thorns in your *e*,
1Sa 15: 17 you were once small in your own *e*,
1Ki 10: 7 I came and saw with my own *e*.
2Ki 9: 30 heard about it, she painted her *e*,
2Ch 16: 9 For the *e* of the LORD range
Job 31: 1 "I made a covenant with my *e*
36: 7 He does not take his *e*
Ps 25: 15 My *e* are ever on the LORD,
36: 1 God before his *e*.
101: 6 My *e* will be on the faithful
118: 23 and it is marvelous in our *e*.
119: 18 Open my *e* that I may see
119: 37 my *e* away from worthless things;
121: 1 I lift up my *e* to the hills —
123: 1 I lift up my *e* to you,
139: 16 your *e* saw my unformed body.
141: 8 But my *e* are fixed on you,
Pr 3: 7 Do not be wise in your own *e*;
4: 25 Let your *e* look straight ahead,
15: 3 The *e* of the LORD are everywhere
17: 24 a fool's *e* wander to the ends
Isa 6: 5 and my *e* have seen the King,
33: 17 Your *e* will see the king
42: 7 to open *e* that are blind,
Jer 24: 6 My *e* will watch over them
Hab 1: 13 Your *e* are too pure to look on evil;
Mt 6: 22 If your *e* are good, your whole
21: 42 and it is marvelous in our *e*?
Lk 16: 15 ones who justify yourselves in the *e*
24: 31 Then their *e* were opened
Jn 4: 35 open your *e* and look at the fields!
Ac 1: 9 he was taken up before their very *e*,
2Co 4: 18 So we fix our *e* not on what is seen,
8: 21 not only in the *e* of the Lord but
Eph 1: 18 also that the *e* of your heart may be
Heb 12: 2 Let us fix our *e* on Jesus, the author
Jas 2: 5 poor in the *e* of the world to be rich
1Pe 3: 12 For the *e* of the Lord are
Rev 7: 17 wipe away every tear from their *e*."
21: 4 He will wipe every tear from their *e*.

EYEWITNESSES* (WITNESS)
Lk 1: 2 by those who from the first were *e*
2Pe 1: 16 but we were *e* of his majesty.

EZEKIEL*
Priest called to be prophet to the exiles (Eze 1 – 3). Symbolically acted out destruction of Jerusalem (Eze 4 – 5; 12; 24).

EZRA*
Priest and teacher of the Law who led a return of exiles to Israel to reestablish temple and worship (Ezr 7 – 8). Corrected intermarriage of priests (Ezr 9 – 10). Read Law at celebration of Feast of Tabernacles (Ne 8). Participated in dedication of Jerusalem's walls (Ne 12).

FACE (FACES)
Ge 32: 30 "It is because I saw God *f* to *f*,
Ex 3: 6 Moses hid his *f*, because he was
33: 11 would speak to Moses *f* to *f*,
33: 20 But," he said, "you cannot see my *f*,
34: 29 was not aware that his *f* was radiant
Nu 6: 25 the LORD make his *f* shine
12: 8 With him I speak *f* to *f*,
14: 14 O LORD, have been seen *f* to *f*,
Dt 5: 4 The LORD spoke to you *f* to *f* out
31: 17 I will hide my *f* from them,
34: 10 whom the LORD knew *f* to *f*,
Jdg 6: 22 the angel of the LORD *f* to *f*!"
2Ki 14: 8 challenge: "Come, meet me *f* to *f*."
1Ch 16: 11 seek his *f* always.
2Ch 7: 14 and seek my *f* and turn
25: 17 of Israel: "Come, meet me *f* to *f*."
Ezr 9: 6 and disgraced to lift up my *f* to you,
Ps 4: 6 Let the light of your *f* shine upon us
27: 8 Your *f*, LORD, I will seek.
31: 16 Let your *f* shine on your servant;
44: 3 and the light of your *f*,
44: 22 Yet for your sake we *f* death all day
51: 9 Hide your *f* from my sins
67: 1 and make his *f* shine upon us; *Selah*
80: 3 make your *f* shine upon us,
105: 4 seek his *f* always.
119: 135 Make your *f* shine
SS 2: 14 and your *f* is lovely.
Isa 50: 7 Therefore have I set my *f* like flint,
50: 8 Let us *f* each other!
54: 8 I hid my *f* from you for a moment,
Jer 32: 4 and will speak with him *f* to *f*
34: 3 and he will speak with you *f* to *f*.
Eze 1: 10 Each of the four had the *f* of a man,
Eze 20: 35 *f* to *f*, I will execute judgment
Mt 17: 2 His *f* shone like the sun,
18: 10 angels in heaven always see the *f*
Lk 9: 29 the appearance of his *f* changed,
Ro 8: 36 "For your sake we *f* death all day
1Co 13: 12 mirror; then we shall see *f* to *f*.
2Co 3: 7 could not look steadily at the *f*
4: 6 the glory of God in the *f* of Christ.
10: 1 who am "timid" when *f* to *f*
1Pe 3: 12 but the *f* of the Lord is
2Jn : 12 to visit you and talk with you *f* to *f*,
3Jn : 14 see you soon, and we will talk *f* to *f*.
Rev 1: 16 His *f* was like the sun shining
22: 4 They will see his *f*, and his name

FACES (FACE)
2Co 3: 18 who with unveiled *f* all reflect

FACTIONS
2Co 12: 20 outbursts of anger, *f*, slander,
Gal 5: 20 selfish ambition, dissensions, *f*

FADE (FADING)
Jas 1: 11 the rich man will *f* away
1Pe 5: 4 of glory that will never *f* away.

FADING (FADE)
2Co 3: 7 *f* though it was, will not
3: 11 if what was *f* away came with glory,
3: 13 at it while the radiance was *f* away.

FAIL (FAILED FAILING FAILINGS FAILS FAILURE)
Lev 26: 15 and *f* to carry out all my commands
1Ki 2: 4 you will never *f* to have a man
1Ch 28: 20 He will not *f* you or forsake you
2Ch 34: 33 they did not *f* to follow the LORD,
Ps 89: 28 my covenant with him will never *f*.
Pr 15: 22 Plans *f* for lack of counsel,
Isa 51: 6 my righteousness will never *f*.
La 3: 22 for his compassions never *f*.
Lk 22: 32 Simon, that your faith may not *f*.
2Co 13: 5 unless, of course, you *f* the test?

FAILED (FAIL)
Jos 23: 14 has been fulfilled; not one has *f*.
1Ki 8: 56 Not one word has *f*
Ps 77: 8 Has his promise *f* for all time?
Ro 9: 6 as though God's word had *f*.
2Co 13: 6 discover that we have not *f* the test.

FAILING (FAIL)
1Sa 12: 23 sin against the LORD by *f* to pray

FAILINGS (FAIL)
Ro 15: 1 ought to bear with the *f* of the weak

FAILS (FAIL)
Jer 14: 6 their eyesight *f*
Joel 1: 10 the oil *f*.
1Co 13: 8 Love never *f*.

FAILURE* (FAIL)
1Th 2: 1 that our visit to you was not a *f*.

FAINT
Isa 40: 31 they will walk and not be *f*.

FAINTHEARTED* (HEART)
Dt 20: 3 Do not be *f* or afraid; do not be
20: 8 shall add, "Is any man afraid or *f*?

FAIR (FAIRNESS)
Pr 1: 3 doing what is right and just and *f*;
Col 4: 1 slaves with what is right and *f*,

FAIRNESS* (FAIR)
Pr 29: 14 If a king judges the poor with *f*,

FAITH* (FAITHFUL FAITHFULLY FAITHFULNESS FAITHLESS)
Ex 21: 8 because he has broken *f* with her.
Dt 32: 51 both of you broke *f* with me
Jos 22: 16 'How could you break *f*
Jdg 9: 16 and in good *f* when you made
9: 19 and in good *f* toward Jerub-Baal
1Sa 14: 33 "You have broken *f*," he said.
2Ch 20: 20 Have *f* in the LORD your God
20: 20 have *f* in his prophets and you will
Isa 7: 9 If you do not stand firm in your *f*,
26: 2 the nation that keeps *f*.
Hab 2: 4 but the righteous will live by his *f* —
Mal 2: 10 by breaking *f* with one another?
2: 11 one another? Judah has broken *f*.
2: 14 because you have broken *f* with her
2: 15 and do not break *f* with the wife
2: 16 in your spirit, and do not break *f*.
Mt 6: 30 O you of little *f*? So do not worry,
8: 10 anyone in Israel with such great *f*.
8: 26 He replied, "You of little *f*,
9: 2 When Jesus saw their *f*, he said
9: 22 he said, "your *f* has healed you."
Mt 9: 29 According to your *f* will it be done
13: 58 there because of their lack of *f*.
14: 31 of little *f*," he said, "why did you
15: 28 "Woman, you have great *f*!
16: 8 Jesus asked, "You of little *f*,
17: 20 if you have *f* as small as a mustard
17: 20 "Because you have so little *f*.
21: 21 if you have *f* and do not doubt,
24: 10 many will turn away from the *f*
Mk 2: 5 When Jesus saw their *f*, he said
4: 40 still have no *f*?" They were
5: 34 "Daughter, your *f* has healed you.
6: 6 he was amazed at their lack of *f*.
10: 52 said Jesus, "your *f* has healed you."
11: 22 "Have *f* in God," Jesus answered.
16: 14 he rebuked them for their lack of *f*
Lk 5: 20 When Jesus saw their *f*, he said,
7: 9 I have not found such great *f*
7: 50 the woman, "Your *f* has saved you;
8: 25 "Where is your *f*?" he asked his
8: 48 "Daughter, your *f* has healed you.
12: 28 will he clothe you, O you of little *f*!
17: 5 "Increase our *f*!" He replied,
17: 6 "If you have *f* as small
17: 19 your *f* has made you well."
18: 8 will he find *f* on the earth?"
18: 42 your sight; your *f* has healed you."
22: 32 Simon, that your *f* may not fail.
Jn 2: 11 and his disciples put their *f* in him.
7: 31 in the crowd put their *f* in him.
8: 30 he spoke, many put their *f* in him.
11: 45 had seen what Jesus did, put their *f*
12: 11 to Jesus and putting their *f* in him.
12: 42 they would not confess their *f*
14: 12 anyone who has *f* in me will do
Ac 3: 16 By *f* in the name of Jesus, this man
3: 16 *f* that comes through him that has
6: 5 full of *f* and of the Holy Spirit;
6: 7 of priests became obedient to the *f*.
11: 24 full of the Holy Spirit and *f*,
13: 8 to turn the proconsul from the *f*.
14: 9 saw that he had *f* to be healed
14: 22 them to remain true to the *f*.
14: 27 the door of *f* to the Gentiles.
15: 9 for he purified their hearts by *f*.
16: 5 were strengthened in the *f*
20: 21 and have *f* in our Lord Jesus.
24: 24 as he spoke about *f* in Christ Jesus.
26: 18 those who are sanctified by *f*
27: 25 for I have *f* in God that it will
Ro 1: 5 to the obedience that comes from *f*.
1: 8 because your *f* is being reported all
1: 12 encouraged by each other's *f*.
1: 17 is by *f* from first to last,
1: 17 "The righteous will live by *f*."
3: 3 What if some did not have *f*?
3: 3 lack of *f* nullify God's faithfulness?
3: 22 comes through *f* in Jesus Christ
3: 25 a sacrifice of atonement, through *f*
3: 26 one who justifies those who have *f*
3: 27 the law? No, but on that of *f*.
3: 28 by *f* apart from observing the law.
3: 30 through that same *f*.
3: 30 will justify the circumcised by *f*
3: 31 nullify the law by this *f*? Not at all!
4: 5 his *f* is credited as righteousness.
4: 9 that Abraham's *f* was credited
4: 11 had by *f* while he was still
4: 12 of the *f* that our father Abraham
4: 13 the righteousness that comes by *f*.
4: 14 *f* has no value and the promise is
4: 16 Therefore, the promise comes by *f*,
4: 16 are of the *f* of Abraham.
4: 19 Without weakening in his *f*,
4: 20 but was strengthened in his *f*
5: 1 we have been justified through *f*,
5: 2 access by *f* into this grace
9: 30 a righteousness that is by *f*;
9: 32 Because they pursued it not by *f*
10: 6 the righteousness that is by *f* says:
10: 8 the word of *f* we are proclaiming:
10: 17 *f* comes from hearing the message,
11: 20 of unbelief, and you stand by *f*.
12: 3 measure of *f* God has given you.
12: 6 let him use it in proportion to his *f*.
14: 1 Accept him whose *f* is weak,
14: 2 One man's *f* allows him
14: 2 but another man, whose *f* is weak,
14: 23 because his eating is not from *f*;
14: 23 that does not come from *f* is sin.
1Co 2: 5 so that your *f* might not rest
12: 9 to another *f* by the same Spirit,
13: 2 and if I have a *f* that can move
13: 13 And now these three remain: *f*,
15: 14 is useless and so is your *f*.

1Co 15: 17 has not been raised, your f is futile;
16: 13 stand firm in the f; be men
2Co 1: 24 Not that we lord it over your f,
1: 24 because it is by f you stand firm.
4: 13 With that same spirit of f we
5: 7 We live by f, not by sight.
8: 7 in f, in speech, in knowledge,
10: 15 as your f continues to grow,
13: 5 to see whether you are in the f;
Gal 1: 23 now preaching the f he once tried
2: 16 Jesus that we may be justified by f
2: 16 but by f in Jesus Christ.
2: 16 have put our f in Christ Jesus that
2: 20 I live by f in the Son of God,
3: 8 would justify the Gentiles by f,
3: 9 So those who have f are blessed
3: 9 along with Abraham, the man of f.
3: 11 "The righteous will live by f."
3: 12 based on f; on the contrary,
3: 14 by f we might receive the promise
3: 22 being given through f
3: 23 Before this f came, we were held
3: 23 up until f should be revealed.
3: 24 that we might be justified by f.
3: 25 that f has come, we are no longer
3: 26 of God through f in Christ Jesus,
5: 5 But by f we eagerly await
5: 6 that counts is f expressing itself
Eph 1: 15 ever since I heard about your f
2: 8 through f— and this not
3: 12 through f in him we may approach
3: 17 dwell in your hearts through f.
4: 5 one Lord, one f, one baptism;
4: 13 up until we all reach unity in the f
6: 16 to all this, take up the shield of f,
6: 23 love with f from God the Father
Php 1: 25 for your progress and joy in the f,
1: 27 as one man for the f of the gospel
2: 17 and service coming from your f,
3: 9 comes from God and is by f.
3: 9 that which is through f in Christ—
Col 1: 4 heard of your f in Christ Jesus
1: 5 the f and love that spring
1: 23 continue in your f, established
2: 5 and how firm your f in Christ is.
2: 7 in the f as you were taught,
2: 12 him through your f in the power
1Th 1: 3 Father your work produced by f,
1: 8 your f in God has become known
3: 2 and encourage you in your f,
3: 5 I sent to find out about your f.
3: 6 brought good news about your f
3: 7 about you because of your f.
3: 10 supply what is lacking in your f.
5: 8 on f and love as a breastplate,
2Th 1: 3 because your f is growing more
1: 4 and f in all the persecutions
1: 11 and every act prompted by your f.
3: 2 evil men, for not everyone has f.
1Ti 1: 2 To Timothy my true son in the f:
1: 4 than God's work—which is by f.
1: 5 a good conscience and a sincere f.
1: 14 along with the f and love that are
1: 19 and so have shipwrecked their f.
1: 19 on to f and a good conscience.
2: 7 of the true f to the Gentiles.
2: 15 if they continue in f, love
3: 9 of the f with a clear conscience.
3: 13 assurance in their f in Christ Jesus.
4: 1 later times some will abandon the f
4: 6 brought up in the truths of the f
4: 12 in life, in love, in f and in purity.
5: 8 he has denied the f and is worse
6: 10 have wandered from the f
6: 11 pursue righteousness, godliness, f,
6: 12 Fight the good fight of the f.
6: 21 so doing have wandered from the f.
2Ti 1: 5 been reminded of your sincere f,
1: 13 with f and love in Christ Jesus.
2: 18 and they destroy the f of some.
2: 22 and pursue righteousness, f,
3: 8 as far as the f is concerned,
3: 10 my purpose, f, patience, love,
3: 15 wise for salvation through f
4: 7 finished the race, I have kept the f.
Tit 1: 1 Christ for the f of God's elect
1: 2 a f and knowledge resting
1: 4 my true son in our common f:
1: 13 so that they will be sound in the f
2: 2 self-controlled, and sound in f,
3: 15 Greet those who love us in the f.
Phm : 5 because I hear about your f
: 6 may be active in sharing your f,
Heb 4: 2 heard did not combine it with f.
4: 14 firmly to the f we profess.

Heb 6: 1 and of f in God, instruction about
6: 12 but to imitate those who through f
10: 22 heart in full assurance of f,
10: 38 But my righteous one will live by f.
11: 1 f is being sure of what we hope for
11: 3 By f we understand that
11: 4 And by f he still speaks, even
11: 4 By f Abel offered God a better
11: 4 By f he was commended
11: 5 By f Enoch was taken from this life
11: 6 And without f it is impossible
11: 7 By his f he condemned the world
11: 7 By f Noah, when warned about
11: 7 the righteousness that comes by f.
11: 8 By f Abraham, when called to go
11: 9 By f he made his home
11: 11 By f Abraham, even though he was
11: 13 living by f when they died.
11: 17 By f Abraham, when God tested
11: 20 By f Isaac blessed Jacob
11: 21 By f Jacob, when he was dying,
11: 22 By f Joseph, when his end was near
11: 23 By f Moses' parents hid him
11: 24 By f Moses, when he had grown up
11: 27 By f he left Egypt, not fearing
11: 28 By f he kept the Passover
11: 29 By f the people passed
11: 30 By f the walls of Jericho fell,
11: 31 By f the prostitute Rahab,
11: 33 through f conquered kingdoms,
11: 39 were all commended for their f,
12: 2 the author and perfecter of our f,
13: 7 way of life and imitate their f.
Jas 1: 3 of your f develops perseverance.
2: 5 the eyes of the world to be rich in f
2: 14 has no deeds? Can such f save him?
2: 14 if a man claims to have f
2: 17 In the same way, f by itself,
2: 18 I will show you my f by what I do.
2: 18 Show me your f without deeds,
2: 18 "You have f; I have deeds."
2: 20 do you want evidence that f
2: 22 You see that his f and his actions
2: 22 and his f was made complete
2: 24 by what he does and not by f alone.
2: 26 so f without deeds is dead.
5: 15 in f will make the sick person well;
1Pe 1: 5 who through f are shielded
1: 7 These have come so that your f—
1: 9 you are receiving the goal of your f,
1: 21 and so your f and hope are in God.
5: 9 Resist him, standing firm in the f,
2Pe 1: 1 Jesus Christ have received a f
1: 5 effort to add to your f goodness;
1Jn 5: 4 overcome the world, even our f.
Jude : 3 to contend for the f that was once
: 20 up in your most holy f
Rev 2: 13 You did not renounce your f in me,
2: 19 your love and f, your service

FAITHFUL* (FAITH)

Nu 12: 7 he is f in all my house.
Dt 7: 9 your God is God; he is the f God,
32: 4 A f God who does no wrong,
1Sa 2: 35 I will raise up for myself a f priest,
2Sa 20: 19 We are the peaceful and f in Israel.
22: 26 "To the f you show yourself f,
1Ki 3: 6 because he was f to you
2Ch 31: 18 were f in consecrating themselves.
31: 20 and f before the LORD his God.
Ne 9: 8 You found his heart f to you,
Ps 12: 1 the f have vanished
18: 25 To the f you show yourself f,
25: 10 of the LORD are loving and f
31: 23 The LORD preserves the f,
33: 4 he is f in all he does.
37: 28 and will not forsake his f ones.
78: 8 whose spirits were not f to him.
78: 37 they were not f to his covenant.
89: 19 to your f people you said:
89: 24 My f love will be with him,
89: 37 the f witness in the sky."
97: 10 for he guards the lives of his f ones
101: 6 My eyes will be on the f in the land,
111: 7 The works of his hands are f
145: 13 The LORD is f to all his promises
146: 6 the LORD, who remains f forever.
Pr 2: 8 and protects the way of his f ones.
20: 6 but a f man who can find?
28: 20 A f man will be richly blessed,
31: 26 and f instruction is on her tongue.
Isa 1: 21 See how the f city has become
1: 26 the F City."
49: 7 because of the LORD, who is f,
55: 3 my f love promised to David.
Jer 42: 5 f witness against us if we do not act

Eze 43: 11 so that they may be f to its design
48: 11 who were f in serving me
Hos 11: 12 even against the f Holy One.
Zec 8: 8 I will be f and righteous to them
Mt 24: 45 Who then is the f and wise servant,
25: 21 'Well done, good and f servant!
25: 21 You have been f with a few things;
25: 23 You have been f with a few things;
25: 23 'Well done, good and f servant!
Lk 12: 42 then is the f and wise manager,
Ro 12: 12 patient in affliction, f in prayer.
1Co 1: 9 his Son Jesus Christ our Lord, is f.
4: 2 been given a trust must prove f.
4: 17 my son whom I love, who is f
10: 13 And God is f; he will not let you be
2Co 1: 18 no"? But as surely as God is f,
Eph 1: 1 in Ephesus, the f in Christ Jesus:
6: 21 the dear brother and f servant
Col 1: 2 and f brothers in Christ at Colosse:
1: 7 who is a f minister of Christ
4: 7 a f minister and fellow servant
4: 9 He is coming with Onesimus, our f
1Th 5: 24 The one who calls you is f
2Th 3: 3 the Lord is f, and he will strengthen
1Ti 1: 12 he considered me f, appointing me
5: 9 has been f to her husband,
2Ti 2: 13 he will remain f,
Heb 2: 17 and f high priest in service to God,
3: 2 He was f to the one who appointed
3: 2 as Moses was f in all God's house.
3: 5 Moses was f as a servant
3: 6 But Christ is f as a son
8: 9 because they did not remain f
10: 23 for he who promised is f.
11: 11 he considered him f who had made
1Pe 4: 19 themselves to their f Creator
5: 12 whom I regard as a f brother,
1Jn 1: 9 he is f and just and will forgive us
3Jn : 5 you are f in what you are doing
Rev 1: 5 who is the f witness, the firstborn
2: 10 Be f, even to the point of death,
2: 13 the days of Antipas, my f witness,
3: 14 the words of the Amen, the f
14: 12 commandments and remain f
17: 14 his called, chosen and f followers."
19: 11 whose rider is called F and True.

FAITHFULLY* (FAITH)

Dt 11: 13 if you f obey the commands I am
Jos 2: 14 f when the LORD gives us the land
1Sa 12: 24 and serve him f with all your heart;
1Ki 2: 4 and if they walk f before me
2Ki 20: 3 how I have walked before you f
22: 7 because they are acting f."
2Ch 19: 9 must serve f and wholeheartedly
31: 12 they f brought in the contributions,
31: 15 and Shecaniah assisted him f
32: 1 all that Hezekiah had so f done,
34: 12 The men did the work f.
Ne 9: 33 you have acted f, while we did
13: 14 so f done for the house of my God
Isa 38: 3 how I have walked before you f
Jer 23: 28 one who has my word speak it f.
Eze 18: 9 and f keeps my laws.
44: 15 and who f carried out the duties
1Pe 4: 10 f administering God's grace

FAITHFULNESS* (FAITH)

Ge 24: 27 not abandoned his kindness and f
24: 49 if you will show kindness and f
32: 10 and f you have shown your servant.
47: 29 you will show me kindness and f.
Ex 34: 6 f, maintaining love to thousands,
Jos 24: 14 the LORD and serve him with all f.
1Sa 26: 23 man for his righteousness and f.
2Sa 2: 6 now show you kindness and f,
15: 20 May kindness and f be with you."
Ps 30: 9 Will it proclaim your f?
36: 5 your f to the skies.
40: 10 I speak of your f and salvation.
54: 5 in your f destroy them.
57: 3 God sends his love and his f.
57: 10 your f reaches to the skies.
61: 7 appoint your love and f
71: 22 the harp for your f, O my God;
85: 10 Love and f meet together;
85: 11 F springs forth from the earth,
86: 15 to anger, abounding in love and f.
88: 11 your f in Destruction?
89: 1 mouth I will make your f known
89: 2 that you established your f
89: 5 your f too, in the assembly
89: 8 and your f surrounds you.
89: 14 love and f go before you.
89: 33 nor will I ever betray my f.
89: 49 which in your f you swore to David

Ps 91: 4 his f will be your shield
92: 2 and your f at night,
98: 3 and his f to the house of Israel;
100: 5 f continues through all
108: 4 your f reaches to the skies.
111: 8 done in f and uprightness.
115: 1 because of your love and f.
117: 2 the f of the LORD endures forever.
119: 75 and in f you have afflicted me.
119: 90 f continues through all
138: 2 name for your love and your f,
143: 1 in your f and righteousness
Pr 3: 3 Let love and f never leave you;
14: 22 plan what is good find love and f.
16: 6 Through love and f sin is atoned for
20: 28 Love and f keep a king safe;
Isa 11: 5 and f the sash around his waist.
16: 5 in f a man will sit on it —
25: 1 for in perfect f
38: 18 cannot hope for your f.
38: 19 about your f.
42: 3 In f he will bring forth justice;
61: 8 In my f I will reward them
La 3: 23 great is your f.
Hos 2: 20 I will betroth you in f,
4: 1 "There is no f, no love,
Mt 23: 23 of the law — justice, mercy and f.
Ro 3: 3 lack of faith nullify God's f?
Gal 5: 22 patience, kindness, goodness, f,
3Jn : 3 and tell about your f to the truth
Rev 13: 10 and f on the part of the saints.

FAITHLESS* (FAITH)
Ps 78: 57 fathers they were disloyal and f,
101: 3 The deeds of f men I hate;
119: 158 I look on the f with loathing,
Pr 14: 14 The f will be fully repaid
Jer 3: 6 you seen what f Israel has done?
3: 8 I gave f Israel her certificate
3: 11 "F Israel is more righteous
3: 12 f Israel,' declares the LORD,
3: 14 f people," declares the LORD,
3: 22 "Return, f people;
12: 1 Why do all the f live at ease?
Ro 1: 31 they are senseless, f, heartless,
2Ti 2: 13 if we are f,

FALL (FALLEN FALLING FALLS)
Ps 37: 24 though he stumble, he will not f,
55: 22 he will never let the righteous f.
69: 9 of those who insult you f on me.
145: 14 The LORD upholds all those who f
Pr 11: 28 Whoever trusts in his riches will f,
Isa 40: 7 The grass withers and the flowers f,
Mt 7: 25 yet it did not f, because it had its
Lk 10: 18 "I saw Satan f like lightning
11: 17 a house divided against itself will f.
23: 30 say to the mountains, "F on us!"
Ro 3: 23 and f short of the glory of God,
Heb 6: 6 if they f away, to be brought back

FALLEN (FALL)
2Sa 1: 19 How the mighty have f!
Isa 14: 12 How you have f from heaven,
1Co 11: 30 and a number of you have f asleep.
15: 6 though some have f asleep.
15: 18 who have f asleep in Christ are lost.
15: 20 of those who have f asleep.
Gal 5: 4 you have f away from grace.
1Th 4: 15 precede those who have f asleep.

FALLING (FALL)
Jude : 24 able to keep you from f

FALLS (FALL)
Pr 11: 14 For lack of guidance a nation f,
24: 17 Do not gloat when your enemy f;
28: 14 he who hardens his heart f
Mt 13: 21 of the word, he quickly f away.
21: 44 He who f on this stone will be
Jn 12: 24 a kernel of wheat f to the ground
Ro 14: 4 To his own master he stands or f.

FALSE (FALSEHOOD FALSELY)
Ex 20: 16 "You shall not give f testimony
23: 1 "Do not spread f reports.
23: 7 Have nothing to do with a f charge
Dt 5: 20 "You shall not give f testimony
Pr 12: 17 but a f witness tells lies.
13: 5 The righteous hate what is f,
14: 5 but a f witness pours out lies.
14: 25 but a f witness is deceitful.
19: 5 A f witness will not go unpunished,
19: 9 A f witness will not go unpunished,
21: 28 A f witness will perish,
25: 18 is the man who gives f testimony
Isa 44: 25 who foils the signs of f prophets
Jer 23: 16 they fill you with f hopes.
Mt 7: 15 "Watch out for f prophets.
15: 19 theft, f testimony, slander.
19: 18 not steal, do not give f testimony,
24: 11 and many f prophets will appear
24: 24 For f Christs and f prophets will
Mk 10: 19 do not give f testimony, do not
13: 22 For f Christs and f prophets will
Lk 6: 26 their fathers treated the f prophets.
18: 20 not steal, do not give f testimony,
Jn 1: 47 in whom there is nothing f."
1Co 15: 15 found to be f witnesses about God,
2Co 11: 13 For such men are f apostles,
11: 26 and in danger from f brothers.
Gal 2: 4 some f brothers had infiltrated our
Php 1: 18 whether from f motives or true,
Col 2: 18 anyone who delights in f humility
2: 23 their f humility and their harsh
1Ti 1: 3 not to teach f doctrines any longer
6: 3 If anyone teaches f doctrines
2Pe 2: 1 also f prophets among the people,
2: 1 there will be f teachers among you.
1Jn 4: 1 many f prophets have gone out
Rev 16: 13 out of the mouth of the f prophet.
19: 20 with him the f prophet who had
20: 10 and the f prophet had been thrown.

FALSEHOOD* (FALSE)
Job 21: 34 left of your answers but f!"
31: 5 "If I have walked in f
Ps 52: 3 f rather than speaking the truth.
119: 163 I hate and abhor f
Pr 30: 8 Keep f and lies far from me;
Isa 28: 15 and f our hiding place."
Ro 3: 7 "If my f enhances God's
Eph 4: 25 each of you must put off f
1Jn 4: 6 Spirit of truth and the spirit of f.
Rev 22: 15 everyone who loves and practices f

FALSELY (FALSE)
Lev 19: 12 "'Do not swear f by my name
Mt 5: 11 f say all kinds of evil against you
Lk 3: 14 and don't accuse people f —
1Ti 6: 20 ideas of what is f called knowledge,

FALTER*
Pr 24: 10 If you f in times of trouble,
Isa 42: 4 he will not f or be discouraged

FAME
Jos 9: 9 of the f of the LORD your God.
Isa 66: 19 islands that have not heard of my f
Hab 3: 2 LORD, I have heard of your f;

FAMILIES (FAMILY)
Ps 68: 6 God sets the lonely in f,

FAMILY (FAMILIES)
Pr 15: 27 greedy man brings trouble to his f,
31: 15 she provides food for her f
Mk 5: 19 to your f and tell them how much
Lk 9: 61 go back and say good-by to my f."
12: 52 in one f divided against each other,
Ac 10: 2 He and all his f were devout
16: 33 and all his f were baptized.
16: 34 he and his whole f.
1Ti 3: 4 He must manage his own f well
3: 5 how to manage his own f,
5: 4 practice by caring for their own f
5: 8 and especially for his immediate f,

FAMINE
Ge 12: 10 Now there was a f in the land,
26: 1 Now there was a f in the land —
41: 30 seven years of f will follow them.
Ru 1: 1 the judges ruled, there was a f
1Ki 18: 2 Now the f was severe in Samaria,
Am 8: 11 but a f of hearing the words
Ro 8: 35 or persecution or f or nakedness

FAN*
2Ti 1: 6 you to f into flame the gift of God,

FANTASIES*
Ps 73: 20 you will despise them as f.
Pr 12: 11 but he who chases f lacks judgment
28: 19 one who chases f will have his fill

FAST (FASTING)
Dt 10: 20 Hold f to him and take your oaths
11: 22 in all his ways and to hold f to him
13: 4 serve him and hold f to him.
30: 20 to his voice, and hold f to him.
Jos 22: 5 to hold f to him and to serve him
23: 8 to hold f to the LORD your God,
2Ki 18: 6 He held f to the LORD
Ps 119: 31 I hold f to your statutes, O LORD;
139: 10 your right hand will hold me f.
Mt 6: 16 "When you f, do not look somber
1Pe 5: 12 Stand f in it.

FASTING (FAST)
Ps 35: 13 and humbled myself with f.
Ac 13: 2 were worshiping the Lord and f,
14: 23 and f, committed them to the Lord

FATHER (FATHER'S FATHERED FATHERLESS FATHERS FOREFATHERS)
Ge 2: 24 this reason a man will leave his f
17: 4 You will be the f of many nations.
Ex 20: 12 "Honor your f and your mother,
21: 15 "Anyone who attacks his f
21: 17 "Anyone who curses his f
Lev 18: 7 "'Do not dishonor your f
19: 3 you must respect his mother and f,
20: 9 "'If anyone curses his f or mother,
Dt 1: 31 carried you, as a f carries his son,
5: 16 "Honor your f and your mother,
21: 18 son who does not obey his f
32: 6 Is he not your F, your Creator,
2Sa 7: 14 I will be his f, and he will be my son
1Ch 17: 13 I will be his f, and he will be my son
22: 10 will be my son, and I will be his f.
28: 6 to be my son, and I will be his f.
Job 38: 28 Does the rain have a f?
Ps 2: 7 today I have become your F.
27: 10 Though my f and mother forsake
68: 5 A f to the fatherless, a defender
89: 26 to me, 'You are my F,
103: 13 As a f has compassion
Pr 3: 12 as a f the son he delights in.
10: 1 A wise son brings joy to his f,
17: 21 there is no joy for the f of a fool.
17: 25 A foolish son brings grief to his f
23: 22 Listen to your f, who gave you life,
23: 24 f of a righteous man has great joy;
28: 7 of gluttons disgraces his f.
28: 24 He who robs his f or mother
29: 3 loves wisdom brings joy to his f,
Isa 9: 6 Everlasting F, Prince of Peace.
45: 10 Woe to him who says to his f,
63: 16 But you are our F,
Jer 2: 27 They say to wood, 'You are my f,'
3: 19 I thought you would call me 'F'
31: 9 because I am Israel's f,
Eze 18: 19 the son not share the guilt of his f?'
Mic 7: 6 For a son dishonors his f,
Mal 1: 6 If I am a f, where is the honor due
2: 10 we not all one F? Did not one God
Mt 3: 9 'We have Abraham as our f.'
5: 16 and praise your F in heaven.
6: 9 "'Our F in heaven,
6: 26 yet your heavenly F feeds them.
10: 37 "Anyone who loves his f
11: 27 no one knows the F except the Son
15: 4 'Honor your f and mother'
18: 10 the face of my F in heaven.
19: 5 this reason a man will leave his f
19: 19 honor your f and mother,'
19: 29 or brothers or sisters or f or mother
23: 9 And do not call anyone on earth 'f,'
Mk 7: 10 'Honor your f and your mother,' and,
Lk 9: 59 "Lord, first let me go and bury my f
12: 53 f against son and son against f,
14: 26 and does not hate his f and mother,
18: 20 honor your f and mother.'"
23: 34 Jesus said, "F, forgive them,
Jn 3: 35 The F loves the Son and has placed
4: 21 you will worship the F neither
5: 17 "My F is always at his work
5: 18 he was even calling God his own F,
5: 20 For the F loves the Son
6: 44 the F who sent me draws him,
6: 46 No one has seen the F
8: 19 "You do not know me or my F,"
8: 28 speak just what the F has taught me
8: 41 The only F we have is God himself
8: 42 God were your F, you would love
8: 44 You belong to your f, the devil,
10: 17 reason my F loves me is that I lay
10: 30 I and the F are one."
10: 38 and understand that the F is in me,
14: 6 No one comes to the F
14: 9 who has seen me has seen the F.
14: 28 for the F is greater than I.
15: 9 "As the F has loved me,
15: 23 He who hates me hates my F
20: 17 'I am returning to my F and your F,
Ac 13: 33 today I have become your F.'
Ro 4: 11 he is the f of all who believe
4: 16 He is the f of us all.
8: 15 And by him we cry, "Abba, F."
1Co 4: 15 for in Christ Jesus I became your f
2Co 6: 18 "I will be a F to you,
Eph 5: 31 this reason a man will leave his f
6: 2 "Honor your f and mother" —

Php 2: 11 to the glory of God the *F*.
Heb 1: 5 today I have become your *F*"?
12: 7 what son is not disciplined by his *f*?
1Jn 1: 3 And our fellowship is with the *F*
2: 15 the love of the *F* is not in him.
2: 22 he denies the *F* and the Son.

FATHER'S (FATHER)
Pr 13: 1 A wise son heeds his *f* instruction,
15: 5 A fool spurns his *f* discipline,
19: 13 A foolish son is his *f* ruin,
Mt 16: 27 going to come in his *F* glory
Lk 2: 49 had to be in my *F* house?"
Jn 2: 16 How dare you turn my *F* house
10: 29 can snatch them out of my *F* hand.
14: 2 In my *F* house are many rooms;
15: 8 to my *F* glory, that you bear much

FATHERED (FATHER)
Dt 32: 18 You deserted the Rock, who *f* you;

FATHERLESS (FATHER)
Dt 10: 18 He defends the cause of the *f*
14: 29 the *f* and the widows who live
24: 17 Do not deprive the alien or the *f*
24: 19 Leave it for the alien, the *f*
26: 12 the alien, the *f* and the widow,
Ps 68: 5 A father to the *f*, a defender
82: 3 Defend the cause of the weak and *f*
Pr 23: 10 or encroach on the fields of the *f*,

FATHERS (FATHER)
Ex 20: 5 for the sin of the *f* to the third
Jer 31: 29 'The *f* have eaten sour grapes,
Mal 4: 6 the hearts of the children to their *f*;
Lk 1: 17 the hearts of the *f* to their children
11: 11 "Which of you *f*, if your son asks
Jn 4: 20 Our *f* worshiped on this mountain,
1Co 4: 15 you do not have many *f*,
Eph 6: 4 *F*, do not exasperate your children;
Col 3: 21 *F*, do not embitter your children,
Heb 12: 9 all had human *f* who disciplined us

FATHOM* (FATHOMED)
Job 11: 7 "Can you *f* the mysteries of God?
Ps 145: 3 his greatness no one can *f*.
Ecc 3: 11 yet they cannot *f* what God has
Isa 40: 28 and his understanding no one can *f*
1Co 13: 2 and can *f* all mysteries and all

FATHOMED* (FATHOM)
Job 5: 9 performs wonders that cannot be *f*,
9: 10 performs wonders that cannot be *f*,

FATTENED
Pr 15: 17 than a *f* calf with hatred.
Lk 15: 23 Bring the *f* calf and kill it.

FAULT (FAULTS)
1Sa 29: 3 I have found no *f* in him."
Mt 18: 15 and show him his *f*, just
Php 2: 15 of God without *f* in a crooked
Jas 1: 5 generously to all without finding *f*,
Jude : 24 his glorious presence without *f*

FAULTFINDERS*
Jude : 16 These men are grumblers and *f*;

FAULTLESS*
Pr 8: 9 they are *f* to those who have
Php 3: 6 as for legalistic righteousness, *f*.
Jas 1: 27 Father accepts as pure and *f* is this:

FAULTS* (FAULT)
Job 10: 6 that you must search out my *f*
Ps 19: 12 Forgive my hidden *f*.

FAVOR (FAVORITISM)
Ge 4: 4 The LORD looked with *f* on Abel
6: 8 But Noah found *f* in the eyes
Ex 33: 12 and you have found *f* with me.'
34: 9 if I have found *f* in your eyes,"
Lev 26: 9 "'I will look on you with *f*
Nu 11: 15 if I have found *f* in your eyes—
Jdg 6: 17 "If now I have found *f* in your eyes,
1Sa 2: 26 in *f* with the LORD and with men.
2Sa 2: 6 and I too will show you the same *f*
2Ki 13: 4 Jehoahaz sought the LORD's *f*,
2Ch 33: 12 In his distress he sought the *f*
Est 7: 3 "If I have found *f* with you, O king,
Ps 90: 17 May the *f* of the Lord our God rest
Pr 8: 35 and receives *f* from the LORD.
18: 22 and receives *f* from the LORD.
19: 6 Many curry *f* with a ruler,
Isa 61: 2 proclaim the year of the LORD's *f*
Zec 11: 7 called one *F* and the other Union,
Lk 1: 30 Mary, you have found *f* with God.
2: 14 to men on whom his *f* rests."
2: 52 and in *f* with God and men.
4: 19 to proclaim the year of the Lord's *f*
2Co 6: 2 now is the time of God's *f*,

FAVORITISM* (FAVOR)
Ex 23: 3 and do not show *f* to a poor man
Lev 19: 15 to the poor or *f* to the great,
Ac 10: 34 true it is that God does not show *f*
Ro 2: 11 For God does not show *f*.
Eph 6: 9 and there is no *f* with him.
Col 3: 25 for his wrong, and there is no *f*.
1Ti 5: 21 and to do nothing out of *f*.
Jas 2: 1 Lord Jesus Christ, don't show *f*.
2: 9 But if you show *f*, you sin

FEAR (AFRAID FEARED FEARS FRIGHTENED GOD-FEARING)
Dt 6: 13 *F* the LORD your God, serve him
10: 12 but to *f* the LORD your God,
31: 12 and learn to *f* the LORD your God
31: 13 and learn to *f* the LORD your God
Jos 4: 24 you might always *f* the LORD
24: 14 "Now *f* the LORD and serve him
1Sa 12: 14 If you *f* the LORD and serve
12: 24 But be sure to *f* the LORD
2Sa 23: 3 when he rules in the *f* of God,
2Ch 19: 7 let the *f* of the LORD be upon you.
26: 5 who instructed him in the *f* of God.
Job 1: 9 "Does Job *f* God for nothing?"
Ps 2: 11 Serve the LORD with *f*
19: 9 The *f* of the LORD is pure,
23: 4 I will *f* no evil,
27: 1 whom shall I *f*?
33: 8 Let all the earth *f* the LORD;
34: 7 around those who *f* him,
34: 9 *F* the LORD, you his saints,
46: 2 Therefore we will not *f*,
86: 11 that I may *f* your name.
90: 11 great as the *f* that is due you.
91: 5 You will not *f* the terror of night,
111: 10 *f* of the LORD is the beginning
118: 4 Let those who *f* the LORD say:
128: 1 Blessed are all who *f* the LORD,
145: 19 of those who *f* him;
147: 11 delights in those who *f* him,
Pr 1: 7 *f* of the LORD is the beginning
1: 33 and be at ease, without *f* of harm."
8: 13 To *f* the LORD is to hate evil;
9: 10 *f* of the LORD is the beginning
10: 27 The *f* of the LORD adds length
14: 27 The *f* of the LORD is a fountain
15: 33 *f* of the LORD teaches a man
16: 6 through the *f* of the LORD a man
19: 23 The *f* of the LORD leads to life:
22: 4 Humility and the *f* of the LORD
29: 25 *F* of man will prove to be a snare,
31: 21 she has no *f* for her household;
Ecc 12: 13 *F* God and keep his
Isa 11: 3 delight in the *f* of the LORD.
33: 6 the *f* of the LORD is the key
35: 4 "Be strong, do not *f*;
41: 10 So do not *f*, for I am with you;
41: 13 and says to you, Do not *f*;
43: 1 "*F* not, for I have redeemed you;
51: 7 Do not *f* the reproach of men
54: 14 you will have nothing to *f*.
Jer 17: 8 It does not *f* when heat comes;
Lk 12: 5 I will show you whom you should *f*:
2Co 5: 11 we know what it is to *f* the Lord,
Php 2: 12 to work out your salvation with *f*
1Jn 4: 18 But perfect love drives out *f*,
Jude : 23 to others show mercy, mixed with *f*
Rev 14: 7 "*F* God and give him glory,

FEARED (FEAR)
Job 1: 1 he *f* God and shunned evil.
Ps 76: 7 You alone are to be *f*.
Mal 3: 16 those who *f* the LORD talked

FEARS (FEAR)
Job 1: 8 a man who *f* God and shuns evil."
2: 3 a man who *f* God and shuns evil.
Ps 34: 4 he delivered me from all my *f*.
112: 1 is the man who *f* the LORD,
Pr 14: 16 A wise man *f* the LORD
14: 26 He who *f* the LORD has a secure
31: 30 a woman who *f* the LORD is
2Co 7: 5 conflicts on the outside, *f* within.
1Jn 4: 18 The one who *f* is not made perfect

FEAST (FEASTING FEASTS)
Pr 15: 15 the cheerful heart has a continual *f*.
2Pe 2: 13 pleasures while they *f* with you.

FEASTING (FEAST)
Pr 17: 1 than a house full of *f*, with strife.

FEASTS (FEAST)
Am 5: 21 "I hate, I despise your religious *f*;
Jude : 12 men are blemishes at your love *f*,

FEATHERS
Ps 91: 4 He will cover you with his *f*,

FEEBLE
Job 4: 3 you have strengthened *f* hands.
Isa 35: 3 Strengthen the *f* hands,
Heb 12: 12 strengthen your *f* arms

FEED (FEEDS)
Jn 21: 15 Jesus said, "*F* my lambs."
21: 17 Jesus said, "*F* my sheep.
Ro 12: 20 "If your enemy is hungry, *f* him;
Jude : 12 shepherds who *f* only themselves.

FEEDS (FEED)
Pr 15: 14 but the mouth of a fool *f* on folly.
Mt 6: 26 yet your heavenly Father *f* them.
Jn 6: 57 so the one who *f* on me will live

FEEL
Jdg 16: 26 me where I can *f* the pillars that
Ps 115: 7 they have hands, but cannot *f*,

FEET (FOOT)
Ru 3: 8 discovered a woman lying at his *f*.
Ps 8: 6 you put everything under his *f*:
22: 16 have pierced my hands and my *f*.
40: 2 he set my *f* on a rock
56: 13 and my *f* from stumbling,
66: 9 and kept our *f* from slipping.
73: 2 as for me, my *f* had almost slipped;
110: 1 a footstool for your *f*."
119: 105 Your word is a lamp to my *f*
Pr 4: 26 Make level paths for your *f*
Isa 52: 7 are the *f* of those who bring good
Da 2: 33 its *f* partly of iron and partly
Na 1: 15 the *f* of one who brings good news,
Mt 10: 14 shake the dust off your *f*
22: 44 enemies under your *f*."'
Lk 1: 79 to guide our *f* into the path of peace
20: 43 a footstool for your *f*."'
24: 39 Look at my hands and my *f*.
Jn 13: 5 and began to wash his disciples' *f*,
13: 14 also should wash one another's *f*.
Ro 3: 15 "Their *f* are swift to shed blood;
10: 15 "How beautiful are the *f*
16: 20 will soon crush Satan under your *f*.
1Co 12: 21 And the head cannot say to the *f*,
15: 25 has put all his enemies under his *f*.
Eph 1: 22 God placed all things under his *f*
1Ti 5: 10 washing the *f* of the saints,
Heb 1: 13 a footstool for your *f*"?
2: 8 and put everything under his *f*."
12: 13 "Make level paths for your *f*,"
Rev 1: 15 His *f* were like bronze glowing

FELIX
Governor before whom Paul was tried (Ac 23:23 – 24:27).

FELLOWSHIP
Ex 20: 24 burnt offerings and *f* offerings,
Lev 3: 1 If someone's offering is a *f* offering,
1Co 1: 9 who has called you into *f*
5: 2 out of your *f* the man who did this?
2Co 6: 14 what *f* can light have with darkness
13: 14 and the *f* of the Holy Spirit be
Gal 2: 9 and Barnabas the right hand of *f*
Php 2: 1 if any *f* with the Spirit,
3: 10 the *f* of sharing in his sufferings,
1Jn 1: 3 And our *f* is with the Father
1: 3 so that you also may have *f* with us.
1: 6 claim to have *f* with him yet walk
1: 7 we have *f* with one another,

FEMALE
Ge 1: 27 male and *f* he created them.
5: 2 He created them male and *f*
Mt 19: 4 Creator 'made them male and *f*,'
Mk 10: 6 God 'made them male and *f*.'
Gal 3: 28 *f*, for you are all one in Christ Jesus

FEROCIOUS
Mt 7: 15 but inwardly they are *f* wolves.

FERTILE (FERTILIZE)
Isa 32: 15 and the desert becomes a *f* field,
Jer 2: 7 I brought you into a *f* land

FERTILIZE* (FERTILE)
Lk 13: 8 and I'll dig around it and *f* it.

FERVOR*
Ac 18: 25 and he spoke with great *f*
Ro 12: 11 but keep your spiritual *f*, serving

FESTIVAL
1Co 5: 8 Therefore let us keep the *F*,
Col 2: 16 or with regard to a religious *f*,

FESTUS
Successor of Felix; sent Paul to Caesar (Ac 25 – 26).

FEVER
Job 30: 30 my body burns with *f.*
Mt 8: 14 mother-in-law lying in bed with a *f.*
Lk 4: 38 was suffering from a high *f,*
Jn 4: 52 "The *f* left him yesterday
Ac 28: 8 suffering from *f* and dysentery.

FIELD (FIELDS)
Ge 4: 8 Abel, "Let's go out to the *f.*"
Lev 19: 9 reap to the very edges of your *f*
19: 19 Do not plant your *f* with two kinds
Pr 31: 16 She considers a *f* and buys it;
Isa 40: 6 glory is like the flowers of the *f.*
Mt 6: 28 See how the lilies of the *f* grow.
6: 30 how God clothes the grass of the *f,*
13: 38 *f* is the world, and the good seed
13: 44 is like treasure hidden in a *f.*
Lk 14: 18 I have just bought a *f,* and I must go
1Co 3: 9 you are God's *f,* God's building.
1Pe 1: 24 glory is like the flowers of the *f;*

FIELDS (FIELD)
Ru 2: 2 go to the *f* and pick up the leftover
Lk 2: 8 were shepherds living out in the *f*
Jn 4: 35 open your eyes and look at the *f!*

FIG (FIGS SYCAMORE-FIG)
Ge 3: 7 so they sewed *f* leaves together
Jdg 9: 10 "Next, the trees said to the *f* tree,
1Ki 4: 25 man under his own vine and *f* tree.
Pr 27: 18 He who tends a *f* tree will eat its
Mic 4: 4 and under his own *f* tree,
Zec 3: 10 to sit under his vine and *f* tree,'
Mt 21: 19 Seeing a *f* tree by the road,
Lk 13: 6 "A man had a *f* tree, planted
Jas 3: 12 brothers, can a *f* tree bear olives,
Rev 6: 13 drop from a *f* tree when shaken

FIGHT (FIGHTING FIGHTS FOUGHT)
Ex 14: 14 The LORD will *f* for you; you need
Dt 1: 30 going before you, will *f* for you,
3: 22 the LORD your God himself will *f*
Ne 4: 20 Our God will *f* for us!"
Ps 35: 1 *f* against those who *f* against me.
Jn 18: 36 my servants would *f*
1Co 9: 26 I do not *f* like a man beating the air.
2Co 10: 4 The weapons we *f*
1Ti 1: 18 them you may *f* the good *f,*
6: 12 Fight the good *f* of the faith.
2Ti 4: 7 fought the good *f,* I have finished

FIGHTING (FIGHT)
Jos 10: 14 Surely the LORD was *f* for Israel!

FIGHTS (FIGHT)
Jos 23: 10 the LORD your God *f* for you,
1Sa 25: 28 because he *f* the LORD's battles.
Jas 4: 1 What causes *f* and quarrels

FIGS (FIG)
Lk 6: 44 People do not pick *f*
Jas 3: 12 grapevine bear *f?* Neither can a salt

FILL (FILLED FILLING FILLS FULL FULLNESS FULLY)
Ge 1: 28 and increase in number; *f* the earth
Ps 16: 11 you will *f* me with joy
81: 10 wide your mouth and I will *f* it.
Pr 28: 19 who chases fantasies will have his *f*
Hag 2: 7 and I will *f* this house with glory,'
Jn 6: 26 you ate the loaves and had your *f.*
Ac 2: 28 you will *f* me with joy
Ro 15: 13 the God of hope *f* you with all joy

FILLED (FILL)
Ex 31: 3 I have *f* him with the Spirit of God,
35: 31 he has *f* him with the Spirit of God,
Dt 34: 9 son of Nun was *f* with the spirit
1Ki 8: 10 the cloud *f* the temple
8: 11 glory of the LORD *f* his temple.
2Ch 5: 14 of the LORD *f* the temple of God.
7: 1 the glory of the LORD *f* the temple
Ps 72: 19 may the whole earth be *f*
119: 64 The earth is *f* with your love,
Isa 6: 4 and the temple was *f* with smoke.
Eze 10: 3 and a cloud *f* the inner court.
10: 4 The cloud *f* the temple,
43: 5 the glory of the LORD *f* the temple
Hab 2: 14 For the earth will be *f*
3: 3 and his praise *f* the earth.
Mt 5: 6 for they will be *f.*
Lk 1: 15 and he will be *f* with the Holy Spirit
1: 41 and Elizabeth was *f* with the Holy
1: 67 His father Zechariah was *f*
2: 40 and became strong; he was *f*
Jn 12: 3 the house was *f* with the fragrance
Ac 2: 2 *f* the whole house where they were
2: 4 All of them were *f*
4: 8 Then Peter, *f* with the Holy Spirit,
Ac 4: 31 they were all *f* with the Holy Spirit
9: 17 and be *f* with the Holy Spirit."
13: 9 called Paul, *f* with the Holy Spirit,
Eph 5: 18 Instead, be *f* with the Spirit.
Php 1: 11 *f* with the fruit of righteousness
Rev 15: 8 And the temple was *f* with smoke

FILLING (FILL)
Eze 44: 4 the glory of the LORD *f* the temple

FILLS (FILL)
Nu 14: 21 of the LORD *f* the whole earth,
Ps 107: 9 and *f* the hungry with good things.
Eph 1: 23 fullness of him who *f* everything

FILTH (FILTHY)
Isa 4: 4 The Lord will wash away the *f*
Jas 1: 21 rid of all moral *f* and the evil that is

FILTHY (FILTH)
Isa 64: 6 all our righteous acts are like *f* rags;
Col 3: 8 and *f* language from your lips.
2Pe 2: 7 by the *f* lives of lawless men

FINAL (FINALITY)
Ps 73: 17 then I understood their *f* destiny.

FINALITY* (FINAL)
Ro 9: 28 on earth with speed and *f.*"

FINANCIAL*
1Ti 6: 5 that godliness is a means to *f* gain.

FIND (FINDS FOUND)
Nu 32: 23 be sure that your sin will *f* you out.
Dt 4: 29 you will *f* him if you look for him
1Sa 23: 16 and helped him *f* strength in God.
Job 23: 3 If only I knew where to *f* him;
Ps 36: 7 *f* refuge in the shadow
62: 5 *F* rest, O my soul, in God alone;
91: 4 under his wings you will *f* refuge;
Pr 8: 17 and those who seek me *f* me.
14: 22 those who plan what is good *f* love
20: 6 but a faithful man who can *f?*
24: 14 if you *f* it, there is a future hope
31: 10 A wife of noble character who can *f*
Jer 6: 16 and you will *f* rest for your souls.
29: 13 and *f* me when you seek me
Mt 7: 7 seek and you will *f;* knock
11: 29 and you will *f* rest for your souls.
16: 25 loses his life for me will *f* it.
22: 9 invite to the banquet anyone you *f.*'
Lk 11: 9 seek and you will *f;* knock
18: 8 will he *f* faith on the earth?"
Jn 10: 9 come in and go out, and *f* pasture.

FINDS (FIND)
Ps 62: 1 My soul *f* rest in God alone;
112: 1 who *f* great delight
119: 162 like one who *f* great spoil.
Pr 3: 13 Blessed is the man who *f* wisdom,
8: 35 For whoever *f* me *f* life
11: 27 He who seeks good *f* good will,
18: 22 He who *f* a wife *f* what is good
Mt 7: 8 he who seeks *f;* and to him who
10: 39 Whoever *f* his life will lose it,
Lk 11: 10 he who seeks *f;* and to him who
12: 37 whose master *f* them watching
12: 43 servant whom the master *f* doing
15: 4 go after the lost sheep until he *f* it?
15: 8 and search carefully until she *f* it?

FINE-SOUNDING* (SOUND)
Col 2: 4 may deceive you by *f* arguments.

FINGER
Ex 8: 19 to Pharaoh, "This is the *f* of God."
31: 18 of stone inscribed by the *f* of God.
Dt 9: 10 two stone tablets inscribed by the *f*
Lk 11: 20 But if I drive out demons by the *f*
16: 24 to dip the tip of his *f* in water
Jn 8: 6 to write on the ground with his *f.*
20: 25 and put my *f* where the nails were,

FINISH (FINISHED)
Jn 4: 34 him who sent me and to *f* his work.
5: 36 that the Father has given me to *f,*
Ac 20: 24 if only I may *f* the race
2Co 8: 11 Now *f* the work, so that your eager
Jas 1: 4 Perseverance must *f* its work

FINISHED (FINISH)
Ge 2: 2 seventh day God had *f* the work he
Jn 19: 30 the drink, Jesus said, "It is *f.*"
2Ti 4: 7 I have *f* the race, I have kept

FIRE
Ex 3: 2 in flames of *f* from within a bush.
13: 21 in a pillar of *f* to give them light,
Lev 6: 12 *f* on the altar must be kept burning;
9: 24 *F* came out from the presence
1Ki 18: 38 Then the *f* of the LORD fell
2Ki 2: 11 suddenly a chariot of *f*
Isa 5: 24 as tongues of *f* lick up straw
30: 27 and his tongue is a consuming *f.*
Jer 23: 29 my word like *f,*" declares
Da 3: 25 four men walking around in the *f,*
Zec 3: 2 stick snatched from the *f?*"
Mal 3: 2 For he will be like a refiner's *f*
Mt 3: 11 you with the Holy Spirit and with *f.*
3: 12 the chaff with unquenchable *f.*"
5: 22 will be in danger of the *f* of hell.
18: 8 and be thrown into eternal *f.*
25: 41 into the eternal *f* prepared
Mk 9: 43 where the *f* never goes out.
9: 48 and the *f* is not quenched.'
9: 49 Everyone will be salted with *f.*
Lk 3: 16 you with the Holy Spirit and with *f.*
12: 49 I have come to bring *f* on the earth,
Ac 2: 3 to be tongues of *f* that separated
1Co 3: 13 It will be revealed with *f,*
1Th 5: 19 Do not put out the Spirit's *f;*
Heb 12: 29 for our "God is a consuming *f.*"
Jas 3: 5 set on *f* by a small spark.
3: 6 also is a *f,* a world of evil
2Pe 3: 10 the elements will be destroyed by *f,*
Jude : 7 suffer the punishment of eternal *f.*
: 23 snatch others from the *f*
Rev 1: 14 and his eyes were like blazing *f.*
20: 14 The lake of *f* is the second death.

FIRM*
Ex 14: 13 Stand *f* and you will see
15: 8 surging waters stood *f* like a wall;
Jos 3: 17 the covenant of the LORD stood *f*
2Ch 20: 17 stand *f* and see the deliverance
Ezr 9: 8 giving us a *f* place in his sanctuary,
Job 11: 15 you will stand *f* and without fear.
36: 5 he is mighty, and *f* in his purpose.
41: 23 they are *f* and immovable.
Ps 20: 8 but we rise up and stand *f.*
30: 7 you made my mountain stand *f;*
33: 9 he commanded, and it stood *f.*
33: 11 of the LORD stand *f* forever,
37: 23 he makes his steps *f;*
40: 2 and gave me a *f* place to stand.
75: 3 it is I who hold its pillars *f.*
78: 13 made the water stand *f* like a wall.
89: 2 that your love stands *f* forever,
89: 4 and make your throne *f*
93: 5 Your statutes stand *f;*
119: 89 it stands *f* in the heavens.
Pr 4: 26 and take only ways that are *f.*
10: 25 but the righteous stand *f* forever.
12: 7 the house of the righteous stands *f.*
Isa 7: 9 If you do not stand *f* in your faith,
22: 17 about to take *f* hold of you
22: 23 drive him like a peg into a *f* place;
22: 25 into the *f* place will give way;
Eze 13: 5 so that it will stand *f* in the battle
Zec 8: 23 nations will take *f* hold of one Jew
Mt 10: 22 he who stands *f* to the end will be
24: 13 he who stands *f* to the end will be
Mk 13: 13 he who stands *f* to the end will be
Lk 21: 19 By standing *f* you will gain life.
1Co 10: 12 So, if you think you are standing *f,*
15: 58 my dear brothers, stand *f.*
16: 13 on your guard; stand *f* in the faith;
2Co 1: 7 for you is *f,* because we know that
1: 21 who makes both us and you stand *f*
1: 24 because it is by faith you stand *f.*
Gal 5: 1 Stand *f,* then, and do not let
Eph 6: 14 Stand *f* then, with the belt
Php 1: 27 I will know that you stand *f*
4: 1 that is how you should stand *f*
Col 1: 23 in your faith, established and *f,*
2: 5 and how *f* your faith in Christ is.
4: 12 that you may stand *f* in all the will
1Th 3: 8 since you are standing *f* in the Lord
2Th 2: 15 stand *f* and hold to the teachings
1Ti 6: 19 a *f* foundation for the coming age,
2Ti 2: 19 God's solid foundation stands *f,*
Heb 6: 19 an anchor for the soul, *f* and secure
Jas 5: 8 You too, be patient and stand *f,*
1Pe 5: 9 Resist him, standing *f* in the faith,
5: 10 make you strong, *f* and steadfast.

FIRST
Ge 1: 5 and there was morning — the *f* day.
13: 4 and where he had *f* built an altar.
Ex 34: 19 *f* offspring of every womb belongs
1Ki 22: 5 "*F* seek the counsel of the LORD."
Pr 18: 17 *f* to present his case seems right,
Isa 44: 6 I am the *f* and I am the last;
48: 12 I am the *f* and I am the last.
Mt 5: 24 *F* go and be reconciled
6: 33 But seek *f* his kingdom

Mt 7: 5 *f* take the plank out
19: 30 But many who are *f* will be last,
20: 16 last will be *f,* and the *f* will be last."
20: 27 wants to be *f* must be your slave —
22: 38 This is the *f* and greatest
23: 26 *F* clean the inside of the cup
Mk 9: 35 to be *f,* he must be the very last,
10: 31 are *f* will be last, and the last *f.*"
10: 44 wants to be *f* must be slave
13: 10 And the gospel must *f* be preached
Lk 13: 30 will be *f,* and *f* who will be last."
Jn 8: 7 let him be the *f* to throw a stone
Ac 11: 26 disciples were called Christians *f*
Ro 1: 16 *f* for the Jew, then for the Gentile.
1: 17 is by faith from *f* to last,
2: 9 *f* for the Jew, then for the Gentile;
2: 10 *f* for the Jew, then for the Gentile.
1Co 12: 28 in the church God has appointed *f*
15: 45 "The *f* man Adam became a living
2Co 8: 5 they gave themselves *f* to the Lord
Eph 6: 2 which is the *f* commandment
1Th 4: 16 and the dead in Christ will rise *f.*
1Ti 2: 13 For Adam was formed *f,* then Eve.
Heb 10: 9 He sets aside the *f*
Jas 3: 17 comes from heaven is *f* of all pure;
1Jn 4: 19 We love because he *f* loved us.
3Jn : 9 but Diotrephes, who loves to be *f,*
Rev 1: 17 I am the *F* and the Last.
2: 4 You have forsaken your *f* love.
22: 13 and the Omega, the *F* and the Last,

FIRSTBORN (BEAR)
Ex 11: 5 Every *f* son in Egypt will die,
34: 20 Redeem all your *f* sons.
Ps 89: 27 I will also appoint him my *f,*
Lk 2: 7 and she gave birth to her *f,* a son.
Ro 8: 29 that he might be the *f*
Col 1: 15 image of the invisible God, the *f*
1: 18 and the *f* from among the dead,
Heb 1: 6 when God brings his *f*
12: 23 of the *f,* whose names are written
Rev 1: 5 who is the faithful witness, the *f*

FIRSTFRUITS
Ex 23: 16 the Feast of Harvest with the *f*
23: 19 "Bring the best of the *f* of your soil
Ro 8: 23 who have the *f* of the Spirit,
1Co 15: 23 Christ, the *f;* then, when he comes,
Rev 14: 4 offered as *f* to God and the Lamb.

FISH (FISHERS)
Ge 1: 26 let them rule over the *f* of the sea
Jnh 1: 17 But the LORD provided a great *f*
Mt 7: 10 asks for a *f,* will give him a snake?
12: 40 three nights in the belly of a huge *f,*
14: 17 loaves of bread and two *f,*"
Mk 6: 38 they said, "Five — and two *f.*"
Lk 5: 6 of *f* that their nets began to break.
9: 13 loaves of bread and two *f* —
Jn 6: 9 small barley loaves and two small *f,*
21: 5 haven't you any *f?*" "No,"
21: 11 It was full of large *f,* 153, but

FISHERMEN
Mk 1: 16 a net into the lake, for they were *f.*

FISHERS (FISH)
Mt 4: 19 "and I will make you *f* of men."
Mk 1: 17 "and I will make you *f* of men."

FISHHOOK*
Job 41: 1 pull in the leviathan with a *f*

FISTS
Mt 26: 67 and struck him with their *f.*

FIT (FITTING)
Jdg 17: 6 no king; everyone did as he saw *f.*
21: 25 no king; everyone did as he saw *f.*

FITTING* (FIT)
Ps 33: 1 it is *f* for the upright to praise him.
147: 1 how pleasant and *f* to praise him!
Pr 10: 32 of the righteous know what is *f,*
19: 10 It is not *f* for a fool to live in luxury
26: 1 honor is not *f* for a fool.
1Co 14: 40 everything should be done in a *f*
Col 3: 18 to your husbands, as is *f* in the Lord
Heb 2: 10 sons to glory, it was *f* that God,

FIX* (FIXED)
Dt 11: 18 *F* these words of mine
Job 14: 3 Do you *f* your eye on such a one?
Pr 4: 25 *f* your gaze directly before you.
Isa 46: 8 "Remember this, *f* it in mind,
Am 9: 4 I will *f* my eyes upon them
2Co 4: 18 we *f* our eyes not on what is seen,
Heb 3: 1 heavenly calling, *f* your thoughts
12: 2 Let us *f* our eyes on Jesus,

FIXED* (FIX)
2Ki 8: 11 stared at him with a *f* gaze
Job 38: 10 when I *f* limits for it
Ps 141: 8 my eyes are *f* on you, O Sovereign
Pr 8: 28 *f* securely the fountains of the deep
Jer 33: 25 and night and the *f* laws of heaven
Lk 16: 26 and you a great chasm has been *f,*

FLAME (FLAMES FLAMING)
2Ti 1: 6 you to fan into *f* the gift of God,

FLAMES (FLAME)
1Co 3: 15 only as one escaping through the *f.*
13: 3 and surrender my body to the *f,*

FLAMING (FLAME)
Eph 6: 16 you can extinguish all the *f* arrows

FLANK
Eze 34: 21 Because you shove with *f*

FLASH
1Co 15: 52 in a *f,* in the twinkling of an eye,

FLATTER* (FLATTERING FLATTERS FLATTERY)
Job 32: 21 nor will I *f* any man;
Ps 78: 36 But then they would *f* him
Jude : 16 *f* others for their own advantage.

FLATTERING* (FLATTER)
Ps 12: 2 their *f* lips speak with deception.
12: 3 May the LORD cut off all *f* lips
Pr 26: 28 and a *f* mouth works ruin.
28: 23 than he who has a *f* tongue.
Eze 12: 24 or *f* divinations among the people

FLATTERS* (FLATTER)
Ps 36: 2 For in his own eyes he *f* himself
Pr 29: 5 Whoever *f* his neighbor

FLATTERY* (FLATTER)
Job 32: 22 for if I were skilled in *f,*
Da 11: 32 With *f* he will corrupt those who
Ro 16: 18 and *f* they deceive the minds
1Th 2: 5 You know we never used *f,*

FLAWLESS*
2Sa 22: 31 the word of the LORD is *f.*
Job 11: 4 You say to God, 'My beliefs are *f*
Ps 12: 6 And the words of the LORD are *f,*
18: 30 the word of the LORD is *f.*
Pr 30: 5 "Every word of God is *f;*
SS 5: 2 my dove, my *f* one.

FLEE (FLEES)
Ps 139: 7 Where can I *f* from your presence?
1Co 6: 18 *F* from sexual immorality.
10: 14 my dear friends, *f* from idolatry.
1Ti 6: 11 But you, man of God, *f* from all this
2Ti 2: 22 *F* the evil desires of youth,
Jas 4: 7 Resist the devil, and he will *f*

FLEECE
Jdg 6: 37 I will place a wool *f*

FLEES (FLEE)
Pr 28: 1 The wicked man *f* though no one

FLEETING*
Job 14: 2 like a *f* shadow, he does not endure
Ps 39: 4 let me know how *f* is my life.
89: 47 Remember how *f* is my life.
144: 4 his days are like a *f* shadow.
Pr 21: 6 is a *f* vapor and a deadly snare.
31: 30 Charm is deceptive, and beauty is *f*

FLESH
Ge 2: 23 and *f* of my *f;*
2: 24 and they will become one *f.*
2Ch 32: 8 With him is only the arm of *f,*
Job 19: 26 yet in my *f* I will see God;
Eze 11: 19 of stone and give them a heart of *f.*
36: 26 of stone and give you a heart of *f.*
Mt 19: 5 and the two will become one *f*'?
Mk 10: 8 and the two will become one *f.*'
Jn 1: 14 The Word became *f* and made his
6: 51 This bread is my *f,* which I will give
1Co 6: 16 "The two will become one *f.*"
15: 39 All *f* is not the same: Men have one
Eph 5: 31 and the two will become one *f.*"
6: 12 For our struggle is not against *f*
Php 3: 2 do evil, those mutilators of the *f.*
1Jn 4: 2 come in the *f* is from God,
Jude : 23 the clothing stained by corrupted *f.*

FLIGHT
Dt 32: 30 or two put ten thousand to *f,*

FLINT
Isa 50: 7 Therefore have I set my face like *f,*
Zec 7: 12 They made their hearts as hard as *f*

FLIRTING*
Isa 3: 16 *f* with their eyes,

FLOCK (FLOCKS)
Ps 77: 20 You led your people like a *f*
78: 52 he brought his people out like a *f;*
95: 7 the *f* under his care.
Isa 40: 11 He tends his *f* like a shepherd:
Jer 10: 21 and all their *f* is scattered.
23: 2 "Because you have scattered my *f*
31: 10 watch over his *f* like a shepherd.'
Eze 34: 2 not shepherds take care of the *f?*
Zec 11: 17 who deserts the *f!*
Mt 26: 31 the sheep of the *f* will be scattered.'
Lk 12: 32 little *f,* for your Father has been
Jn 10: 16 shall be one *f* and one shepherd.
Ac 20: 28 all the *f* of which the Holy Spirit
1Co 9: 7 Who tends a *f* and does not drink
1Pe 5: 2 Be shepherds of God's *f* that is
5: 3 but being examples to the *f.*

FLOCKS (FLOCK)
Lk 2: 8 keeping watch over their *f* at night.

FLOG (FLOGGED FLOGGING)
Pr 19: 25 *F* a mocker, and the simple will
Ac 22: 25 to *f* a Roman citizen who hasn't

FLOGGED (FLOG)
Jn 19: 1 Pilate took Jesus and had him *f.*
Ac 5: 40 the apostles in and had them *f.*
16: 23 After they had been severely *f,*
2Co 11: 23 frequently, been *f* more severely,

FLOGGING (FLOG)
Heb 11: 36 *f,* while still others were chained

FLOOD (FLOODGATES)
Ge 7: 7 ark to escape the waters of the *f.*
Mal 2: 13 You *f* the LORD's altar with tears.
Mt 24: 38 For in the days before the *f,*
2Pe 2: 5 world when he brought the *f*

FLOODGATES (FLOOD)
Ge 7: 11 the *f* of the heavens were opened.
Mal 3: 10 see if I will not throw open the *f*

FLOOR
Jas 2: 3 or "Sit on the *f* by my feet,"

FLOUR
Lev 2: 1 his offering is to be of fine *f.*
Nu 7: 13 filled with fine *f* mixed with oil
28: 9 of an ephah of fine *f* mixed with oil.

FLOURISH (FLOURISHES FLOURISHING)
Ps 72: 7 In his days the righteous will *f;*
92: 7 and all evildoers *f,*
92: 12 The righteous will *f* like a palm tree
Pr 14: 11 but the tent of the upright will *f.*

FLOURISHES (FLOURISH)
Pr 12: 12 but the root of the righteous *f.*

FLOURISHING (FLOURISH)
Ps 52: 8 *f* in the house of God;

FLOW (FLOWING)
Nu 13: 27 and it does *f* with milk and honey!
Jn 7: 38 streams of living water will *f*

FLOWER (FLOWERS)
Job 14: 2 up like a *f* and withers away;
Ps 103: 15 he flourishes like a *f* of the field;
Jas 1: 10 he will pass away like a wild *f.*

FLOWERS (FLOWER)
Isa 40: 6 and all their glory is like the *f*
40: 7 The grass withers and the *f* fall,
1Pe 1: 24 and all their glory is like the *f*

FLOWING (FLOW)
Ex 3: 8 a land *f* with milk and honey —
33: 3 Go up to the land *f* with milk
Nu 16: 14 us into a land *f* with milk
Jos 5: 6 a land *f* with milk and honey.
Ps 107: 33 *f* springs into thirsty ground,
107: 35 the parched ground into *f* springs;
Jer 32: 22 a land *f* with milk and honey.
Eze 20: 6 a land *f* with milk and honey,
Rev 22: 1 *f* from the throne of God

FLUTE
Ps 150: 4 praise him with the strings and *f,*
Mt 11: 17 "'We played the *f* for you,
1Co 14: 7 that make sounds, such as the *f*

FOAL*
Zec 9: 9 on a colt, the *f* of a donkey.
Mt 21: 5 on a colt, the *f* of a donkey.'"

FOILS*
Ps 33: 10 The LORD *f* the plans
Isa 44: 25 who *f* the signs of false prophets

FOLDING* (FOLDS)
Pr 6: 10 a little *f* of the hands to rest —
24: 33 a little *f* of the hands to rest —

FOLDS (FOLDING)
Ecc 4: 5 The fool *f* his hands

FOLLOW (FOLLOWED FOLLOWING FOLLOWS)
Ex 23: 2 Do not *f* the crowd in doing wrong.
Lev 18: 4 and be careful to *f* my decrees.
Dt 5: 1 Learn them and be sure to *f* them.
17: 19 *f* carefully all the words of this law
1Ki 11: 6 he did not *f* the LORD completely,
2Ch 34: 33 they did not fail to *f* the LORD,
Ps 23: 6 Surely goodness and love will *f* me
119: 166 and I *f* your commands.
Mt 4: 19 *f* me," Jesus said, "and I will make
8: 19 I will *f* you wherever you go."
8: 22 But Jesus told him, "*F* me,
16: 24 and take up his cross and *f* me.
19: 27 "We have left everything to *f* you!
Lk 9: 23 take up his cross daily and *f* me.
9: 61 Still another said, "I will *f* you,
Jn 10: 4 his sheep *f* him because they know
10: 5 But they will never *f* a stranger;
10: 27 I know them, and they *f* me.
12: 26 Whoever serves me must *f* me;
21: 19 Then he said to him, "*F* me!"
1Co 1: 12 One of you says, "I *f* Paul";
11: 1 *F* my example, as I follow
14: 1 *F* the way of love and eagerly
2Th 3: 9 ourselves a model for you to *f*.
1Pe 2: 21 that you should *f* in his steps.
Rev 14: 4 They *f* the Lamb wherever he goes.

FOLLOWED (FOLLOW)
Nu 32: 11 they have not *f* me wholeheartedly,
Dt 1: 36 he *f* the LORD wholeheartedly."
Jos 14: 14 he *f* the LORD, the God of Israel,
2Ch 10: 14 he *f* the advice of the young men
Mt 4: 20 once they left their nets and *f* him.
9: 9 and Matthew got up and *f* him.
26: 58 But Peter *f* him at a distance,
Lk 18: 43 he received his sight and *f* Jesus,

FOLLOWING (FOLLOW)
Ps 119: 14 I rejoice in *f* your statutes
Php 3: 17 Join with others in *f* my example,
1Ti 1: 18 by *f* them you may fight the good

FOLLOWS (FOLLOW)
Jn 8: 12 Whoever *f* me will never walk

FOLLY (FOOL)
Pr 14: 29 a quick-tempered man displays *f*.
19: 3 A man's own *f* ruins his life,
Ecc 10: 1 so a little *f* outweighs wisdom
Mk 7: 22 envy, slander, arrogance and *f*.
2Ti 3: 9 their *f* will be clear to everyone.

FOOD (FOODS)
Ge 1: 30 I give every green plant for *f*."
Pr 12: 9 to be somebody and have no *f*.
12: 11 his land will have abundant *f*,
20: 13 you will have *f* to spare.
20: 17 *F* gained by fraud tastes sweet
21: 20 of the wise are stores of choice *f*
22: 9 for he shares his *f* with the poor.
23: 3 for that *f* is deceptive.
23: 6 Do not eat the *f* of a stingy man,
25: 21 If your enemy is hungry, give him *f*
31: 14 bringing her *f* from afar.
31: 15 she provides *f* for her family
Isa 58: 7 not to share your *f* with the hungry
Eze 18: 7 but gives his *f* to the hungry
Da 1: 8 to defile himself with the royal *f*
Mt 3: 4 His *f* was locusts and wild honey.
6: 25 Is not life more important than *f*,
Jn 4: 32 "I have *f* to eat that you know
4: 34 have brought him *f*?" "My *f*,"
6: 27 Do not work for *f* that spoils,
6: 55 my flesh is real *f* and my blood is
Ac 15: 20 to abstain from *f* polluted by idols,
Ro 14: 14 fully convinced that no *f* is unclean
1Co 8: 1 Now about *f* sacrificed to idols:
8: 8 But *f* does not bring us near to God
2Co 11: 27 and have often gone without *f*;
1Ti 6: 8 But if we have *f* and clothing,
Heb 5: 14 But solid *f* is for the mature,
Jas 2: 15 sister is without clothes and daily *f*.

FOODS (FOOD)
Mk 7: 19 Jesus declared all *f* "clean.")

FOOL (FOLLY FOOL'S FOOLISH FOOLISHNESS FOOLS)
1Sa 25: 25 his name is *F*, and folly goes
Ps 14: 1 The *f* says in his heart,
Pr 10: 10 and a chattering *f* comes to ruin.
10: 18 and whoever spreads slander is a *f*.
12: 15 The way of a *f* seems right to him,
12: 16 A *f* shows his annoyance at once,
14: 16 but a *f* is hotheaded and reckless.
15: 5 A *f* spurns his father's discipline,
17: 12 than a *f* in his folly.
17: 16 use is money in the hand of a *f*,
17: 21 To have a *f* for a son brings grief;
17: 28 Even a *f* is thought wise
18: 2 A *f* finds no pleasure
20: 3 but every *f* is quick to quarrel.
23: 9 Do not speak to a *f*,
24: 7 Wisdom is too high for a *f*;
26: 4 Do not answer a *f* according
26: 5 Answer a *f* according to his folly,
26: 7 is a proverb in the mouth of a *f*.
26: 11 so a *f* repeats his folly.
26: 12 for a *f* than for him.
27: 22 Though you grind a *f* in a mortar,
28: 26 He who trusts in himself is a *f*,
29: 11 A *f* gives full vent to his anger,
29: 20 for a *f* than for him.
Mt 5: 22 But anyone who says, 'You *f*!'
Lk 12: 20 "But God said to him, 'You *f*!
1Co 3: 18 he should become a "*f*"
2Co 11: 21 I am speaking as a *f* — I

FOOL'S (FOOL)
Pr 14: 3 A *f* talk brings a rod to his back,
18: 7 A *f* mouth is his undoing,

FOOLISH (FOOL)
Pr 10: 1 but a *f* son grief to his mother.
14: 1 her own hands the *f* one tears hers
15: 20 but a *f* man despises his mother.
17: 25 A *f* son brings grief to his father
19: 13 A *f* son is his father's ruin,
Mt 7: 26 practice is like a *f* man who built
25: 2 of them were *f* and five were wise.
Lk 11: 40 You *f* people! Did not the one who
24: 25 He said to them, "How *f* you are,
1Co 1: 20 Has not God made *f* the wisdom
1: 27 God chose the *f* things of the world
Gal 3: 1 died for nothing!" You *f* Galatians!
Eph 5: 4 should there be obscenity, *f* talk
5: 17 Therefore do not be *f*,
Tit 3: 9 But avoid *f* controversies

FOOLISHNESS (FOOL)
1Co 1: 18 of the cross is *f* to those who are
1: 21 through the *f* of what was preached
1: 23 block to Jews and *f* to Gentiles,
1: 25 For the *f* of God is wiser
2: 14 for they are *f* to him, and he cannot
3: 19 of this world is *f* in God's sight.

FOOLS (FOOL)
Pr 1: 7 but *f* despise wisdom and discipline
3: 35 but *f* he holds up to shame.
12: 23 but the heart of *f* blurts out folly.
13: 19 but *f* detest turning from evil.
13: 20 but a companion of *f* suffers harm.
14: 9 *F* mock at making amends for sin,
14: 24 but the folly of *f* yields folly.
Ecc 7: 5 than to listen to the song of *f*.
7: 6 so is the laughter of *f*.
10: 6 *F* are put in many high positions,
Mt 23: 17 You blind *f*! Which is greater:
Ro 1: 22 they became *f* and exchanged
1Co 4: 10 We are *f* for Christ, but you are

FOOT (FEET FOOTHOLD)
Jos 1: 3 every place where you set your *f*,
Ps 121: 3 He will not let your *f* slip —
Pr 3: 23 and your *f* will not stumble;
4: 27 keep your *f* from evil.
25: 17 Seldom set *f* in your neighbor's
Isa 1: 6 From the sole of your *f* to the top
Mt 18: 8 or your *f* causes you to sin,
Lk 4: 11 so that you will not strike your *f*
1Co 12: 15 If the *f* should say, "Because I am
Rev 10: 2 He planted his right *f* on the sea

FOOTHOLD* (FOOT)
Ps 69: 2 where there is no *f*.
73: 2 I had nearly lost my *f*.
Eph 4: 27 and do not give the devil a *f*.

FOOTSTEPS (STEP)
Ps 119: 133 Direct my *f* according

FOOTSTOOL
Ps 99: 5 and worship at his *f*;
110: 1 a *f* for your feet."
Isa 66: 1 and the earth is my *f*.
Mt 5: 35 for it is his *f*; or by Jerusalem,
Ac 7: 49 and the earth is my *f*.
Heb 1: 13 a *f* for your feet"?
10: 13 for his enemies to be made his *f*,

FORBEARANCE*
Ro 3: 25 because in his *f* he had left the sins

FORBID
1Co 14: 39 and do not *f* speaking in tongues.
1Ti 4: 3 They *f* people to marry

FORCE (FORCED FORCEFUL FORCES FORCING)
Jn 6: 15 to come and make him king by *f*,
Ac 26: 11 and I tried to *f* them to blaspheme.
Gal 2: 14 that you *f* Gentiles

FORCED (FORCE)
Mt 27: 32 and they *f* him to carry the cross.
Phm : 14 do will be spontaneous and not *f*.

FORCEFUL* (FORCE)
Mt 11: 12 forcefully advancing, and *f* men lay
2Co 10: 10 "His letters are weighty and *f*,

FORCES (FORCE)
Mt 5: 41 If someone *f* you to go one mile,
Eph 6: 12 and against the spiritual *f* of evil

FORCING (FORCE)
Lk 16: 16 and everyone is *f* his way into it.

FOREFATHERS (FATHER)
Heb 1: 1 spoke to our *f* through the prophets
1Pe 1: 18 handed down to you from your *f*,

FOREHEAD (FOREHEADS)
Ex 13: 9 a reminder on your *f* that the law
13: 16 on your *f* that the LORD brought
1Sa 17: 49 and struck the Philistine on the *f*.
Rev 13: 16 a mark on his right hand or on his *f*,

FOREHEADS (FOREHEAD)
Dt 6: 8 hands and bind them on your *f*.
Rev 9: 4 not have the seal of God on their *f*.
14: 1 his Father's name written on their *f*

FOREIGN (FOREIGNER FOREIGNERS)
Ge 35: 2 "Get rid of the *f* gods you have
2Ch 14: 3 He removed the *f* altars
33: 15 He got rid of the *f* gods
Isa 28: 11 with *f* lips and strange tongues

FOREIGNER (FOREIGN)
Lk 17: 18 give praise to God except this *f*?"
1Co 14: 11 I am a *f* to the speaker,

FOREIGNERS (FOREIGN)
Eph 2: 12 *f* to the covenants of the promise,
2: 19 you are no longer *f* and aliens,

FOREKNEW* (KNOW)
Ro 8: 29 For those God *f* he
11: 2 not reject his people, whom he *f*.

FOREKNOWLEDGE* (KNOW)
Ac 2: 23 to you by God's set purpose and *f*;
1Pe 1: 2 to the *f* of God the Father,

FORESAW*
Gal 3: 8 Scripture *f* that God would justify

FOREST
Jas 3: 5 Consider what a great *f* is set

FOREVER (EVER)
Ge 3: 22 the tree of life and eat, and live *f*."
6: 3 Spirit will not contend with man *f*,
Ex 3: 15 This is my name *f*, the name
2Sa 7: 26 so that your name will be great *f*.
1Ki 2: 33 may there be the LORD's peace *f*."
9: 3 by putting my Name there *f*.
1Ch 16: 15 He remembers his covenant *f*,
16: 34 his love endures *f*.
16: 41 "for his love endures *f*."
17: 24 and that your name will be great *f*.
2Ch 5: 13 his love endures *f*."
20: 21 for his love endures *f*."
Ps 9: 7 The LORD reigns *f*;
23: 6 dwell in the house of the LORD *f*.
28: 9 be their shepherd and carry them *f*.
29: 10 the LORD is enthroned as King *f*.
33: 11 the plans of the LORD stand firm *f*
37: 28 They will be protected *f*,
44: 8 and we will praise your name *f*.
61: 4 I long to dwell in your tent *f*
72: 19 Praise be to his glorious name *f*;
73: 26 and my portion *f*.
77: 8 Has his unfailing love vanished *f*?
79: 13 will praise you *f*;
81: 15 and their punishment would last *f*.
86: 12 I will glorify your name *f*.
89: 1 of the LORD's great love *f*;
92: 8 But you, O LORD, are exalted *f*.

Ps 100: 5 is good and his love endures *f*;
102: 12 But you, O LORD, sit enthroned *f*;
104: 31 of the LORD endure *f*;
107: 1 his love endures *f*.
110: 4 "You are a priest *f*,
111: 3 and his righteousness endures *f*.
112: 6 man will be remembered *f*.
117: 2 of the LORD endures *f*.
118: 1 his love endures *f*.
119: 111 Your statutes are my heritage *f*;
119: 152 that you established them to last *f*.
136: 1 *His love endures f*.
146: 6 the LORD, who remains faithful *f*.
Pr 10: 25 but the righteous stand firm *f*.
27: 24 for riches do not endure *f*,
Isa 25: 8 he will swallow up death *f*.
26: 4 Trust in the LORD *f*,
32: 17 will be quietness and confidence *f*.
40: 8 but the word of our God stands *f*."
51: 6 But my salvation will last *f*,
51: 8 But my righteousness will last *f*,
57: 15 he who lives *f*, whose name is holy:
59: 21 from this time on and *f*,"
Jer 33: 11 his love endures *f*."
Eze 37: 26 put my sanctuary among them *f*.
Da 2: 44 to an end, but it will itself endure *f*.
3: 9 live *f*! You have issued a decree,
Jn 6: 51 eats of this bread, he will live *f*.
14: 16 Counselor to be with you *f*—
Ro 9: 5 who is God over all, *f* praised!
16: 27 to the only wise God be glory *f*
1Co 9: 25 it to get a crown that will last *f*.
1Th 4: 17 And so we will be with the Lord *f*.
Heb 5: 6 "You are a priest *f*,
7: 17 "You are a priest *f*,
7: 24 Jesus lives *f*, he has a permanent
13: 8 same yesterday and today and *f*.
1Pe 1: 25 but the word of the Lord stands *f*."
1Jn 2: 17 who does the will of God lives *f*.
2Jn : 2 lives in us and will be with us *f*:

FOREVERMORE (EVER)
Ps 113: 2 both now and *f*.

FORFEIT
Mk 8: 36 the whole world, yet *f* his soul?
Lk 9: 25 and yet lose or *f* his very self?

FORGAVE (FORGIVE)
Ps 32: 5 and you *f*
65: 3 you *f* our transgressions
78: 38 you *f* their iniquities
Eph 4: 32 just as in Christ God *f* you.
Col 2: 13 He *f* us all our sins, having
3: 13 Forgive as the Lord *f* you.

FORGET (FORGETS FORGETTING FORGOT FORGOTTEN)
Dt 4: 23 Be careful not to *f* the covenant
6: 12 that you do not *f* the LORD,
2Ki 17: 38 Do not *f* the covenant I have made
Ps 9: 17 all the nations that *f* God.
10: 12 Do not *f* the helpless.
50: 22 "Consider this, you who *f* God,
78: 7 and would not *f* his deeds
103: 2 and *f* not all his benefits.
119: 93 I will never *f* your precepts,
137: 5 may my right hand *f* its skill.
Pr 3: 1 My son, do not *f* my teaching,
4: 5 do not *f* my words or swerve
Isa 49: 15 "Can a mother *f* the baby
51: 13 that you *f* the LORD your Maker,
Jer 2: 32 Does a maiden *f* her jewelry,
23: 39 I will surely *f* you and cast you out
Heb 6: 10 he will not *f* your work
13: 2 Do not *f* to entertain strangers,
13: 16 And do not *f* to do good
2Pe 3: 8 But do not *f* this one thing,

FORGETS (FORGET)
Jn 16: 21 her baby is born she *f* the anguish
Jas 1: 24 immediately *f* what he looks like.

FORGETTING* (FORGET)
Php 3: 13 *F* what is behind and straining
Jas 1: 25 to do this, not *f* what he has heard,

FORGIVE* (FORGAVE FORGIVENESS FORGIVES FORGIVING)
Ge 50: 17 I ask you to *f* your brothers the sins
50: 17 please *f* the sins of the servants
Ex 10: 17 Now *f* my sin once more
23: 21 he will not *f* your rebellion,
32: 32 But now, please *f* their sin—
34: 9 *f* our wickedness and our sin,
Nu 14: 19 with your great love, *f* the sin
Dt 29: 20 will never be willing to *f* him;
Jos 24: 19 He will not *f* your rebellion
1Sa 15: 25 *f* my sin and come back with me,
25: 28 Please *f* your servant's offense,
1Ki 8: 30 place, and when you hear, *f*.
8: 34 and *f* the sin of your people Israel
8: 36 and *f* the sin of your servants,
8: 39 *F* and act; deal with each man
8: 50 *f* all the offenses they have
8: 50 *f* your people, who have sinned
2Ki 5: 18 But may the LORD *f* your servant
5: 18 may the LORD *f* your servant
24: 4 and the LORD was not willing to *f*.
2Ch 6: 21 place; and when you hear, *f*.
6: 25 and *f* the sin of your people Israel
6: 27 and *f* the sin of your servants,
6: 30 *F*, and deal with each man
6: 39 *f* your people, who have sinned
7: 14 will *f* their sin and will heal their
Job 7: 21 and *f* my sins?
Ps 19: 12 *F* my hidden faults.
25: 11 *f* my iniquity, though it is great.
79: 9 deliver us and *f* our sins
Isa 2: 9 do not *f* them.
Jer 5: 1 I will *f* this city.
5: 7 "Why should I *f* you?
18: 23 Do not *f* their crimes
31: 34 "For I will *f* their wickedness
33: 8 and will *f* all their sins of rebellion
36: 3 then I will *f* their wickedness
50: 20 for I will *f* the remnant I spare.
Da 9: 19 O Lord, listen! O Lord, *f*! O Lord,
Hos 1: 6 that I should at all *f* them.
14: 2 "*F* all our sins
Am 7: 2 *f*! How can Jacob survive?
Mt 6: 12 *F* us our debts,
6: 14 For if you *f* men when they sin
6: 14 heavenly Father will also *f* you.
6: 15 But if you do not *f* men their sins,
6: 15 your Father will not *f* your sins.
9: 6 authority on earth to *f* sins. . . .
18: 21 many times shall I *f* my brother
18: 35 you *f* your brother from your heart
Mk 2: 7 Who can *f* sins but God alone?"
2: 10 authority on earth to *f* sins
11: 25 anything against anyone, *f* him,
11: 25 in heaven may *f* you your sins."
Lk 5: 21 Who can *f* sins but God alone?"
5: 24 authority on earth to *f* sins. . . .
6: 37 *F*, and you will be forgiven.
11: 4 *F* us our sins,
11: 4 *f* everyone who sins against us.
17: 3 rebuke him, and if he repents, *f* him
17: 4 and says, 'I repent,' *f* him."
23: 34 Jesus said, "Father, *f* them,
Jn 20: 23 If you *f* anyone his sins, they are
20: 23 if you do not *f* them, they are not
Ac 8: 22 Perhaps he will *f* you
2Co 2: 7 you ought to *f* and comfort him,
2: 10 If you *f* anyone, I also *f* him.
2: 10 if there was anything to *f*—
12: 13 a burden to you? *F* me this wrong!
Col 3: 13 and *f* whatever grievances you may
3: 13 *F* as the Lord forgave you.
Heb 8: 12 For I will *f* their wickedness
1Jn 1: 9 and just and will *f* us our sins

FORGIVENESS* (FORGIVE)
Ps 130: 4 But with you there is *f*;
Mt 26: 28 out for many for the *f* of sins.
Mk 1: 4 of repentance for the *f* of sins.
Lk 1: 77 salvation through the *f* of their sins,
3: 3 of repentance for the *f* of sins.
24: 47 and *f* of sins will be preached
Ac 5: 31 that he might give repentance and *f*
10: 43 believes in him receives *f* of sins
13: 38 that through Jesus the *f*
26: 18 so that they may receive *f* of sins
Eph 1: 7 through his blood, the *f* of sins,
Col 1: 14 in whom we have redemption, the *f*
Heb 9: 22 the shedding of blood there is no *f*.

FORGIVES* (FORGIVE)
Ps 103: 3 He *f* all my sins
Mic 7: 18 pardons sin and *f* the transgression
Lk 7: 49 "Who is this who even *f* sins?"

FORGIVING* (FORGIVE)
Ex 34: 7 and *f* wickedness, rebellion and sin.
Nu 14: 18 abounding in love and *f* sin
Ne 9: 17 But you are a *f* God, gracious
Ps 86: 5 You are *f* and good, O Lord,
99: 8 you were to Israel a *f* God,
Da 9: 9 The Lord our God is merciful and *f*
Eph 4: 32 to one another, *f* each other,

FORGOT (FORGET)
Dt 32: 18 you *f* the God who gave you birth.
Ps 78: 11 They *f* what he had done,
106: 13 But they soon *f* what he had done

FORGOTTEN (FORGET)
Job 11: 6 God has even *f* some of your sin.
Ps 44: 20 If we had *f* the name of our God
Isa 17: 10 You have *f* God your Savior;
Hos 8: 14 Israel has *f* his Maker
Lk 12: 6 Yet not one of them is *f* by God.
2Pe 1: 9 and has *f* that he has been cleansed

FORM (FORMED)
Isa 52: 14 *f* marred beyond human likeness—
2Ti 3: 5 having a *f* of godliness

FORMED (FORM)
Ge 2: 7 —the LORD God *f* the man
2: 19 Now the LORD God had *f* out
Ps 103: 14 for he knows how we are *f*,
Ecc 11: 5 or how the body is *f* in a mother's
Isa 29: 16 Shall what is *f* say to him who *f* it,
45: 18 but *f* it to be inhabited—
49: 5 he who *f* me in the womb
Jer 1: 5 "Before I *f* you in the womb I knew
Ro 9: 20 "Shall what is *f* say to him who *f* it,
Gal 4: 19 of childbirth until Christ is *f* in you,
1Ti 2: 13 For Adam was *f* first, then Eve.
Heb 11: 3 understand that the universe was *f*
2Pe 3: 5 and the earth was *f* out of water

FORMLESS*
Ge 1: 2 Now the earth was *f* and empty,
Jer 4: 23 and it was *f* and empty;

FORSAKE (FORSAKEN)
Dt 31: 6 he will never leave you nor *f* you."
Jos 1: 5 I will never leave you nor *f* you.
24: 16 "Far be it from us to *f* the LORD
2Ch 15: 2 but if you *f* him, he will *f* you.
Ps 27: 10 Though my father and mother *f* me
94: 14 he will never *f* his inheritance.
Isa 55: 7 Let the wicked *f* his way
Heb 13: 5 never will I *f* you."

FORSAKEN (FORSAKE)
Ps 22: 1 my God, why have you *f* me?
37: 25 I have never seen the righteous *f*
Mt 27: 46 my God, why have you *f* me?"
Rev 2: 4 You have *f* your first love.

FORTRESS
2Sa 22: 2 "The LORD is my rock, my *f*
Ps 18: 2 The LORD is my rock, my *f*
31: 2 a strong *f* to save me.
59: 16 for you are my *f*,
71: 3 for you are my rock and my *f*.
Pr 14: 26 who fears the LORD has a secure *f*,

FORTUNE-TELLING*
Ac 16: 16 deal of money for her owners by *f*.

FORTY
Ge 7: 4 on the earth for *f* days and *f* nights,
18: 29 "What if only *f* are found there?"
Ex 16: 35 The Israelites ate manna *f* years,
24: 18 on the mountain *f* days and *f* nights
Nu 14: 34 For *f* years—one year for each
Jos 14: 7 I was *f* years old when Moses
1Sa 4: 18 He had led Israel *f* years.
2Sa 5: 4 king, and he reigned *f* years.
1Ki 19: 8 he traveled *f* days and *f* nights
2Ki 12: 1 and he reigned in Jerusalem *f* years
2Ch 9: 30 in Jerusalem over all Israel *f* years.
Eze 29: 12 her cities will lie desolate *f* years
Jnh 3: 4 "*F* more days and Nineveh will be
Mt 4: 2 After fasting *f* days and *f* nights,

FOUGHT (FIGHT)
1Co 15: 32 If I *f* wild beasts in Ephesus
2Ti 4: 7 I have *f* the good fight, I have

FOUND (FIND)
2Ki 22: 8 "I have *f* the Book of the Law
1Ch 28: 9 If you seek him, he will be *f* by you;
2Ch 15: 15 sought God eagerly, and he was *f*
Isa 55: 6 Seek the LORD while he may be *f*;
65: 1 I was *f* by those who did not seek
Da 5: 27 on the scales and *f* wanting.
Mt 1: 18 she was *f* to be with child
Lk 15: 6 with me; I have *f* my lost sheep.'
15: 9 with me; I have *f* my lost coin.'
15: 24 is alive again; he was lost and is *f*.'
Ac 4: 12 Salvation is *f* in no one else,
Ro 10: 20 "I was *f* by those who did not seek
Jas 2: 8 If you really keep the royal law *f*
Rev 5: 4 no one was *f* who was worthy

FOUNDATION (FOUNDATIONS FOUNDED)
Isa 28: 16 a precious cornerstone for a sure *f*;
Mt 7: 25 because it had its *f* on the rock.
Lk 14: 29 For if he lays the *f* and is not able

Ro 15: 20 building on someone else's f.
1Co 3: 10 I laid a f as an expert builder,
3: 11 For no one can lay any f other
Eph 2: 20 built on the f of the apostles
1Ti 3: 15 the pillar and f of the truth.
2Ti 2: 19 God's solid f stands firm,
Heb 6: 1 not laying again the f of repentance

FOUNDATIONS (FOUNDATION)
Ps 102: 25 In the beginning you laid the f
Heb 1: 10 O Lord, you laid the f of the earth,

FOUNDED (FOUNDATION)
Jer 10: 12 he f the world by his wisdom
Heb 8: 6 and it is f on better promises.

FOUNTAIN
Ps 36: 9 For with you is the f of life;
Pr 14: 27 The fear of the LORD is a f of life,
18: 4 the f of wisdom is a bubbling brook.
Zec 13: 1 "On that day a f will be opened

FOX (FOXES)
Lk 13: 32 He replied, "Go tell that f,

FOXES (FOX)
SS 2: 15 the little f
Mt 8: 20 "F have holes and birds

FRAGRANCE (FRAGRANT)
Ex 30: 38 it to enjoy its f must be cut
Jn 12: 3 filled with the f of the perfume.
2Co 2: 14 us spreads everywhere the f
2: 16 of death; to the other, the f of life.

FRAGRANT (FRAGRANCE)
Eph 5: 2 as a f offering and sacrifice to God.
Php 4: 18 They are a f offering, an acceptable

FREE (FREED FREEDOM FREELY)
Ge 2: 16 "You are f to eat from any tree
Ps 118: 5 and he answered by setting me f.
119: 32 for you have set my heart f.
146: 7 The LORD sets prisoners f,
Pr 6: 3 then do this, my son, to f yourself,
Jn 8: 32 and the truth will set you f."
8: 36 if the Son sets you f, you will be f
Ro 6: 18 You have been set f from sin
8: 2 of life set me f from the law of sin
1Co 12: 13 whether Jews or Greeks, slave or f
Gal 3: 28 slave nor f, male nor female,
5: 1 for freedom that Christ has set us f.
1Pe 2: 16 f men, but do not use your freedom

FREED (FREE)
Ps 116: 16 you have f me from my chains.
Ro 6: 7 anyone who has died has been f
Rev 1: 5 has f us from our sins by his blood,

FREEDOM (FREE)
Ps 119: 45 I will walk about in f,
Isa 61: 1 to proclaim f for the captives
Lk 4: 18 me to proclaim f for the prisoners
Ro 8: 21 into the glorious f of the children
1Co 7: 21 although if you can gain your f,
2Co 3: 17 the Spirit of the Lord is, there is f.
Gal 2: 4 ranks to spy on the f we have
5: 13 But do not use your f to indulge
Jas 1: 25 into the perfect law that gives f,
1Pe 2: 16 but do not use your f as a cover-up

FREELY (FREE)
Isa 55: 7 and to our God, for he will f pardon
Mt 10: 8 Freely you have received, f give.
Ro 3: 24 and are justified f by his grace
Eph 1: 6 which he has f given us

FRESH
Jas 3: 11 Can both f water and salt water

FRET*
Ps 37: 1 Do not f because of evil men
37: 7 do not f when men succeed
37: 8 do not f— it leads only to evil.
Pr 24: 19 Do not f because of evil men

FRICTION
1Ti 6: 5 and constant f between men

FRIEND (FRIENDS FRIENDSHIP)
Ex 33: 11 as a man speaks with his f.
2Ch 20: 7 descendants of Abraham your f?
Pr 17: 17 A f loves at all times,
18: 24 there is a f who sticks closer
27: 6 Wounds from a f can be trusted
27: 10 Do not forsake your f and the f
Isa 41: 8 you descendants of Abraham my f,
Mt 11: 19 a f of tax collectors and "sinners." '
Lk 11: 8 him the bread because he is his f,
Jn 19: 12 "If you let this man go, you are no f
Jas 2: 23 and he was called God's f.
4: 4 Anyone who chooses to be a f

FRIENDS (FRIEND)
Pr 16: 28 and a gossip separates close f.
17: 9 the matter separates close f.
Zec 13: 6 given at the house of my f.'
Jn 15: 13 that he lay down his life for his f.
15: 14 You are my f if you do what I

FRIENDSHIP (FRIEND)
Jas 4: 4 don't you know that f

FRIGHTENED (FEAR)
Php 1: 28 gospel without being f in any way
1Pe 3: 14 fear what they fear; do not be f."

FROGS
Ex 8: 2 plague your whole country with f.
Rev 16: 13 three evil spirits that looked like f;

FRUIT (FRUITFUL)
Jdg 9: 11 'Should I give up my f, so good
Ps 1: 3 which yields its f in season
Pr 11: 30 The f of the righteous is a tree
12: 14 From the f of his lips a man is filled
27: 18 He who tends a fig tree will eat its f
Isa 11: 1 from his roots a Branch will bear f.
27: 6 and fill all the world with f.
32: 17 The f of righteousness will be peace
Jer 17: 8 and never fails to bear f."
Hos 10: 12 reap the f of unfailing love,
14: 2 that we may offer the f of our lips.
Am 8: 1 showed me: a basket of ripe f.
Mt 3: 8 Produce f in keeping
3: 10 does not produce good f will be cut
7: 16 By their f you will recognize them.
7: 17 good f, but a bad tree bears bad f.
7: 20 by their f you will recognize them.
12: 33 a tree good and its f will be good,
Lk 3: 9 does not produce good f will be cut
6: 43 nor does a bad tree bear good f.
13: 6 and he went to look for f on it,
Jn 15: 2 branch in me that bears no f,
15: 16 and bear f— f that will last.
Ro 7: 4 in order that we might bear f
Gal 5: 22 But the f of the Spirit is love, joy,
Php 1: 11 with the f of righteousness that
Col 1: 10 bearing f in every good work,
Heb 13: 15 the f of lips that confess his name.
Jas 3: 17 and good f, impartial and sincere.
Jude : 12 autumn trees, without f
Rev 22: 2 of f, yielding its f every month.

FRUITFUL (FRUIT)
Ge 1: 22 "Be f and increase in number
9: 1 "Be f and increase in number
35: 11 be f and increase in number
Ex 1: 7 the Israelites were f and multiplied
Ps 128: 3 Your wife will be like a f vine
Jn 15: 2 prunes so that it will be even more f.
Php 1: 22 this will mean f labor for me.

FRUITLESS*
Eph 5: 11 to do with the f deeds of darkness,

FRUSTRATION
Ro 8: 20 For the creation was subjected to f,

FUEL
Isa 44: 19 "Half of it I used for f;

FULFILL (FULFILLED FULFILLMENT FULFILLS)
Nu 23: 19 Does he promise and not f?
Ps 61: 8 and f my vows day after day.
116: 14 I will f my vows to the LORD
138: 8 The LORD will f ⌊his purpose⌋
Ecc 5: 5 than to make a vow and not f it.
Isa 46: 11 far-off land, a man to f my purpose.
Jer 33: 14 'when I will f the gracious promise
Mt 1: 22 place to f what the Lord had said
3: 15 us to do this to f all righteousness."
4: 14 f what was said
5: 17 come to abolish them but to f them.
8: 17 This was to f what was spoken
12: 17 This was to f what was spoken
21: 4 place to f what was spoken
Jn 12: 38 This was to f the word
13: 18 But this is to f the scripture:
15: 25 But this is to f what is written
1Co 7: 3 husband should f his marital duty

FULFILLED (FULFILL)
Jos 21: 45 of Israel failed; every one was f.
23: 14 Every promise has been f;
Pr 13: 12 but a longing f is a tree of life.
13: 19 A longing f is sweet to the soul,
Mt 2: 15 so was f what the Lord had said
2: 17 the prophet Jeremiah was f:
2: 23 So was f what was said
13: 14 In them is f the prophecy of Isaiah:
13: 35 So was f what was spoken
26: 54 would the Scriptures be f that say it
26: 56 of the prophets might be f."
27: 9 by Jeremiah the prophet was f:
Mk 13: 4 that they are all about to be f?"
14: 49 But the Scriptures must be f."
Lk 4: 21 "Today this scripture is f
18: 31 about the Son of Man will be f.
24: 44 Everything must be f that is
Jn 18: 9 words he had spoken would be f:
19: 24 the Scripture might be f which said,
19: 28 and so that the Scripture would be f
19: 36 so that the Scripture would be f:
Ac 1: 16 to be f which the Holy Spirit spoke
Ro 13: 8 loves his fellowman has f the law.
Jas 2: 23 And the scripture was f that says,

FULFILLMENT (FULFILL)
Ro 13: 10 Therefore love is the f of the law.

FULFILLS (FULFILL)
Ps 57: 2 to God, who f ⌊his purpose⌋ for me.
145: 19 He f the desires of those who fear

FULL (FILL)
2Ch 24: 10 them into the chest until it was f.
Ps 127: 5 whose quiver is f of them.
Pr 27: 7 He who is f loathes honey,
31: 11 Her husband has f confidence
Isa 6: 3 the whole earth is f of his glory."
11: 9 for the earth will be f
Lk 4: 1 Jesus, f of the Holy Spirit,
Jn 10: 10 may have life, and have it to the f.
Ac 6: 3 known to be f of the Spirit
6: 5 a man f of faith and of the Holy
7: 55 But Stephen, f of the Holy Spirit,
11: 24 f of the Holy Spirit and faith,

FULL-GROWN* (GROW)
Jas 1: 15 when it is f, gives birth to death.

FULLNESS* (FILL)
Dt 33: 16 gifts of the earth and its f
Jn 1: 16 From the f of his grace we have all
Ro 11: 12 greater riches will their f bring!
Eph 1: 23 the f of him who fills everything
3: 19 to the measure of all the f of God.
4: 13 to the whole measure of the f
Col 1: 19 to have all his f dwell in him,
1: 25 to you the word of God in its f—
2: 9 in Christ all the f of the Deity lives
2: 10 and you have been given f in Christ

FULLY (FILL)
1Ki 8: 61 your hearts must be f committed
2Ch 16: 9 whose hearts are f committed
Ps 119: 4 that are to be f obeyed.
119: 138 they are f trustworthy.
Pr 13: 4 of the diligent are f satisfied.
Lk 6: 40 everyone who is f trained will be
Ro 4: 21 being f persuaded that God had
14: 5 Each one should be f convinced
1Co 13: 12 shall know f, even as I am f known.
15: 58 Always give yourselves f
2Ti 4: 17 the message might be f proclaimed

FURIOUS (FURY)
Dt 29: 28 In f anger and in great wrath
Jer 32: 37 where I banish them in my f anger

FURNACE
Isa 48: 10 in the f of affliction.
Da 3: 6 be thrown into a blazing f."
Mt 13: 42 will throw them into the fiery f,

FURY (FURIOUS)
Isa 14: 6 and in f subdued nations
Jer 21: 5 and a mighty arm in anger and f
Rev 14: 10 will drink of the wine of God's f,
16: 19 with the wine of the f of his wrath.
19: 15 the winepress of the f of the wrath

FUTILE (FUTILITY)
Mal 3: 14 You have said, 'It is f to serve God.
1Co 3: 20 that the thoughts of the wise are f."

FUTILITY (FUTILE)
Eph 4: 17 in the f of their thinking.

FUTURE
Ps 37: 37 there is a f for the man of peace.
Pr 23: 18 There is surely a f hope for you,
Ecc 7: 14 anything about his f.
8: 7 Since no man knows the f,
Jer 29: 11 plans to give you hope and a f.
31: 17 So there is hope for your f,"
Ro 8: 38 neither the present nor the f,
1Co 3: 22 life or death or the present or the f

GABRIEL*
Angel who interpreted Daniel's visions (Da 8:16–26; 9:20–27); announced births of John (Lk 1:11–20), Jesus (Lk 1:26–38).

GAD

1. Son of Jacob by Zilpah (Ge 30:9 – 11; 35:26; 1Ch 2:2). Tribe of blessed (Ge 49:19; Dt 33:20 – 21), numbered (Nu 1:25; 26:18), allotted land east of the Jordan (Nu 32; 34:14; Jos 18:7; 22), west (Eze 48:27 – 28), 12,000 from (Rev 7:5).

2. Prophet; seer of David (1Sa 22:5; 2Sa 24:11 – 19; 1Ch 29:29).

GAIN (GAINED GAINS)

Ex 14: 17 And I will *g* glory through Pharaoh
Ps 60: 12 With God we will *g* the victory,
Pr 4: 1 pay attention and *g* understanding.
8: 5 You who are simple, *g* prudence;
28: 16 he who hates ill-gotten *g* will enjoy
28: 23 in the end *g* more favor
Isa 63: 12 to *g* for himself everlasting renown
Da 2: 8 that you are trying to *g* time,
Mk 8: 36 it for a man to *g* the whole world,
Lk 9: 25 it for a man to *g* the whole world,
21: 19 standing firm you will *g* life.
1Co 13: 3 but have not love, I *g* nothing.
Php 1: 21 to live is Christ and to die is *g*.
3: 8 that I may *g* Christ and be found
1Ti 3: 13 have served well *g* an excellent
6: 5 godliness is a means to financial *g*.
6: 6 with contentment is great *g*.

GAINED (GAIN)

Jer 32: 20 have *g* the renown that is still yours
Ro 5: 2 through whom we have *g* access

GAINS (GAIN)

Pr 3: 13 the man who *g* understanding,
11: 16 A kindhearted woman *g* respect,
15: 32 heeds correction *g* understanding.
29: 23 but a man of lowly spirit *g* honor.
Mt 16: 26 for a man if he *g* the whole world,

GALILEE

Isa 9: 1 but in the future he will honor *G*
Mt 4: 15 *G* of the Gentiles —
26: 32 I will go ahead of you into *G*."
28: 10 Go and tell my brothers to go to *G*;

GALL

Mt 27: 34 mixed with *g*; but after tasting it,

GALLIO

Ac 18: 12 While *G* was proconsul of Achaia,

GALLOWS

Est 7: 10 Haman on the *g* he had prepared

GAMALIEL

Ac 5: 34 But a Pharisee named *G*, a teacher

GAMES

1Co 9: 25 in the *g* goes into strict training.

GAP

Eze 22: 30 stand before me in the *g* on behalf

GAPE*

Ps 35: 21 They *g* at me and say, "Aha! Aha!

GARDEN (GARDENER)

Ge 2: 8 the LORD God had planted a *g*
2: 15 put him in the *G* of Eden to work it
SS 4: 12 You are a *g* locked up, my sister,
Isa 58: 11 You will be like a well-watered *g*,
Jer 31: 12 They will be like a well-watered *g*,
Eze 28: 13 the *g* of God;
31: 9 Eden in the *g* of God.

GARDENER (GARDEN)

Jn 15: 1 true vine, and my Father is the *g*.

GARLAND*

Pr 1: 9 They will be a *g* to grace your head
4: 9 She will set a *g* of grace

GARMENT (GARMENTS)

Ps 102: 26 they will all wear out like a *g*.
Isa 50: 9 They will all wear out like a *g*;
51: 6 the earth will wear out like a *g*
61: 3 and a *g* of praise
Mt 9: 16 of unshrunk cloth on an old *g*,
Jn 19: 23 This *g* was seamless, woven
Heb 1: 11 they will all wear out like a *g*.

GARMENTS (GARMENT)

Ge 3: 21 The LORD God made *g* of skin
Ex 28: 2 Make sacred *g* for your brother
Lev 16: 23 and take off the linen *g* he put
16: 24 holy place and put on his regular *g*.
Isa 61: 10 me with *g* of salvation
63: 1 with his *g* stained crimson?
Joel 2: 13 and not your *g*.
Zec 3: 4 and I will put rich *g* on you."
Jn 19: 24 "They divided my *g* among them

GATE (GATES)

Ps 118: 20 This is the *g* of the LORD
Pr 31: 23 husband is respected at the city *g*,
31: 31 works bring her praise at the city *g*.
Mt 7: 13 For wide is the *g* and broad is
7: 13 "Enter through the narrow *g*.
Jn 10: 1 not enter the sheep pen by the *g*,
10: 2 enters by the *g* is the shepherd
10: 7 "I tell you the truth, I am the *g*
10: 9 I am the *g*; whoever enters
Heb 13: 12 also suffered outside the city *g*
Rev 21: 21 each *g* made of a single pearl.

GATES (GATE)

Ps 24: 7 Lift up your heads, O you *g*;
24: 9 Lift up your heads, O you *g*;
100: 4 Enter his *g* with thanksgiving
118: 19 Open for me the *g* of righteousness
Isa 60: 11 Your *g* will always stand open,
60: 18 and your *g* Praise.
62: 10 Pass through, pass through the *g*!
Mt 16: 18 the *g* of Hades will not overcome it
Rev 21: 12 On the *g* were written the names
21: 21 The twelve *g* were twelve pearls,
21: 25 On no day will its *g* ever be shut,
22: 14 may go through the *g* into the city.

GATH

1Sa 17: 23 the Philistine champion from *G*,
2Sa 1: 20 "Tell it not in *G*,
Mic 1: 10 Tell it not in *G*;

GATHER (GATHERED GATHERS)

Ps 106: 47 and *g* us from the nations,
Isa 11: 12 and *g* the exiles of Israel;
Jer 3: 17 and all nations will *g* in Jerusalem
23: 3 "I myself will *g* the remnant
31: 10 who scattered Israel will *g* them
Zep 2: 1 *G* together, *g* together,
3: 20 At that time I will *g* you;
Zec 14: 2 I will *g* all the nations to Jerusalem
Mt 12: 30 he who does not *g* with me scatters
13: 30 then *g* the wheat and bring it
23: 37 longed to *g* your children together,
24: 31 and they will *g* his elect
25: 26 *g* where I have not scattered seed?
Mk 13: 27 and *g* his elect from the four winds,
Lk 3: 17 and to *g* the wheat into his barn,
11: 23 and he who does not *g* with me,
13: 34 longed to *g* your children together,

GATHERED (GATHER)

Ex 16: 18 and he who *g* little did not have too
Pr 30: 4 Who has *g* up the wind
Mt 25: 32 All the nations will be *g* before him
2Co 8: 15 and he who *g* little did not have too
2Th 2: 1 Lord Jesus Christ and our being *g*
Rev 16: 16 Then they *g* the kings together

GATHERS (GATHER)

Ps 147: 2 he *g* the exiles of Israel.
Pr 10: 5 He who *g* crops in summer is a wise
Isa 40: 11 He *g* the lambs in his arms
Mt 23: 37 a hen *g* her chicks under her wings,

GAVE (GIVE)

Ge 2: 20 man *g* names to all the livestock,
3: 6 She also *g* some to her husband,
14: 20 Abram *g* him a tenth of everything.
28: 4 the land God *g* to Abraham."
35: 12 The land I *g* to Abraham
39: 23 *g* him success in whatever he did.
47: 11 *g* them property in the best part
Ex 4: 11 to him, "Who *g* man his mouth?
31: 18 he *g* him the two tablets
Dt 2: 12 did in the land the LORD *g* them
2: 36 The LORD our God *g* us all
3: 12 I *g* the Reubenites and the Gadites
3: 13 I *g* to the half tribe of Manasseh.
3: 15 And I *g* Gilead to Makir.
3: 16 Gadites I *g* the territory extending
8: 16 He *g* you manna to eat in the desert
26: 9 us to this place and *g* us this land,
32: 8 the Most High *g* the nations their
Jos 11: 23 and he *g* it as an inheritance
13: 14 tribe of Levi he *g* no inheritance,
14: 13 *g* him Hebron as his inheritance.
21: 44 The LORD *g* them rest
24: 13 I *g* you a land on which you did not
1Sa 27: 6 So on that day Achish *g* him Ziklag
2Sa 12: 8 I *g* you the house of Israel
1Ki 4: 29 God *g* Solomon wisdom
5: 12 The LORD *g* Solomon wisdom,
Ezr 2: 69 According to their ability they *g*
Ne 9: 15 In their hunger you *g* them bread
9: 20 You *g* your good Spirit
9: 22 You *g* them kingdoms and nations,
9: 27 compassion you *g* them deliverers,
Job 1: 21 LORD *g* and the LORD has taken
42: 10 prosperous again and *g* him twice
Ps 69: 21 and *g* me vinegar for my thirst.
135: 12 he *g* their land as an inheritance,
Ecc 12: 7 the spirit returns to God who *g* it.
Eze 3: 2 and he *g* me the scroll to eat.
Mt 1: 25 And he *g* him the name Jesus.
25: 35 and you *g* me something to drink,
25: 42 and you *g* me nothing to drink,
26: 26 Jesus took bread, *g* thanks
27: 50 in a loud voice, he *g* up his spirit.
Mk 6: 7 *g* them authority over evil spirits.
Jn 1: 12 he *g* the right to become children
3: 16 so loved the world that he *g* his one
17: 4 by completing the work you *g* me
17: 6 you *g* them to me and they have
19: 30 bowed his head and *g* up his spirit.
Ac 1: 3 *g* many convincing proofs that he
2: 45 they *g* to anyone as he had need.
11: 17 *g* them the same gift as he *g* us,
Ro 1: 24 Therefore God *g* them
1: 26 God *g* them over to shameful lusts.
1: 28 he *g* them over to a depraved mind,
8: 32 not spare his own Son, but *g* him up
2Co 5: 18 *g* us the ministry of reconciliation:
8: 3 For I testify that they *g* as much
8: 5 they *g* themselves first to the Lord
Gal 1: 4 who *g* himself for our sins
2: 20 who loved me and *g* himself for me
Eph 4: 8 and *g* gifts to men."
5: 2 as Christ loved us and *g* himself up
5: 25 and *g* himself up for her
2Th 2: 16 and by his grace *g* us eternal
1Ti 2: 6 who *g* himself as a ransom
Tit 2: 14 who *g* himself for us to redeem us
1Jn 3: 24 We know it by the Spirit he *g* us.

GAZE

Ps 27: 4 to *g* upon the beauty of the LORD
Pr 4: 25 fix your *g* directly before you.

GEDALIAH

Governor of Judah appointed by Nebuchadnezzar (2Ki 25:22 – 26; Jer 39 – 41).

GEHAZI*

Servant of Elisha (2Ki 4:12 – 5:27; 8:4 – 5).

GENEALOGIES

1Ti 1: 4 themselves to myths and endless *g*.
Tit 3: 9 avoid foolish controversies and *g*

GENERATION (GENERATIONS)

Ex 3: 15 am to be remembered from *g* to *g*.
Nu 32: 13 until the whole *g* of those who had
Dt 1: 35 of this evil *g* shall see the good land
Jdg 2: 10 After that whole *g* had been
Ps 24: 6 Such is the *g* of those who seek him
48: 13 tell of them to the next *g*.
71: 18 I declare your power to the next *g*,
78: 4 we will tell the next *g*
102: 18 Let this be written for a future *g*,
112: 2 the *g* of the upright will be blessed
145: 4 One *g* will commend your works
La 5: 19 your throne endures from *g* to *g*.
Da 4: 3 his dominion endures from *g* to *g*.
4: 34 his kingdom endures from *g* to *g*.
Joel 1: 3 and their children to the next *g*.
Mt 12: 39 adulterous *g* asks for a miraculous
17: 17 "O unbelieving and perverse *g*,"
23: 36 all this will come upon this *g*.
24: 34 this *g* will certainly not pass away
Mk 9: 19 "O unbelieving *g*," Jesus replied,
13: 30 this *g* will certainly not pass away
Lk 1: 50 who fear him, from *g* to *g*.
11: 29 Jesus said, "This is a wicked *g*.
11: 30 will the Son of Man be to this *g*.
11: 50 Therefore this *g* will be held
21: 32 this *g* will certainly not pass away
Ac 2: 40 Save yourselves from this corrupt *g*
Php 2: 15 fault in a crooked and depraved *g*,

GENERATIONS (GENERATION)

Ge 9: 12 a covenant for all *g* to come:
17: 7 after you for the *g* to come,
17: 9 after you for the *g* to come.
Ex 20: 6 a thousand *g* of those
31: 13 and you for the *g* to come,
Dt 7: 9 covenant of love to a thousand *g*
32: 7 consider the *g* long past.
1Ch 16: 15 he commanded, for a thousand *g*,
Job 8: 8 "Ask the former *g*
Ps 22: 30 future *g* will be told about the Lord
33: 11 of his heart through all *g*.
45: 17 your memory through all *g*;
89: 1 faithfulness known through all *g*.
90: 1 throughout all *g*.

Ps 100: 5 continues through all *g*.
102: 12 your renown endures through all *g*.
105: 8 he commanded, for a thousand *g*,
119: 90 continues through all *g*;
135: 13 renown, O LORD, through all *g*.
145: 13 dominion endures through all *g*.
146: 10 your God, O Zion, for all *g*.
Pr 27: 24 and a crown is not secure for all *g*.
Isa 41: 4 forth the *g* from the beginning?
51: 8 my salvation through all *g*."
Lk 1: 48 now on all *g* will call me blessed,
Eph 3: 5 not made known to men in other *g*
3: 21 in Christ Jesus throughout all *g*,
Col 1: 26 been kept hidden for ages and *g*,

GENEROSITY* (GENEROUS)
2Co 8: 2 poverty welled up in rich *g*.
9: 11 and through us your *g* will result
9: 13 and for your *g* in sharing with them

GENEROUS* (GENEROSITY)
Ps 37: 26 They are always *g* and lend freely;
112: 5 Good will come to him who is *g*
Pr 11: 25 A *g* man will prosper;
22: 9 A *g* man will himself be blessed,
Mt 20: 15 Or are you envious because I am *g*
2Co 9: 5 Then it will be ready as a *g* gift,
9: 5 for the *g* gift you had promised.
9: 11 way so that you can be *g*
1Ti 6: 18 and to be *g* and willing to share.

GENTILE (GENTILES)
Ac 21: 25 As for the *G* believers, we have
Ro 1: 16 first for the Jew, then for the *G*.
2: 9 first for the Jew, then for the *G*;
2: 10 first for the Jew, then for the *G*.
10: 12 difference between Jew and *G* —

GENTILES (GENTILE)
Isa 42: 6 and a light for the *G*,
49: 6 also make you a light for the *G*,
49: 22 "See, I will beckon to the *G*,
Lk 2: 32 a light for revelation to the *G*
21: 24 on by the *G* until the times
Ac 9: 15 to carry my name before the *G*
10: 45 been poured out even on the *G*.
11: 18 granted even the *G* repentance unto
13: 16 and you *G* who worship God,
13: 46 of eternal life, we now turn to the *G*
13: 47 I have made you a light for the *G*,
14: 27 opened the door of faith to the *G*.
15: 14 by taking from the *G* a people
18: 6 From now on I will go to the *G*."
22: 21 I will send you far away to the *G*.'"
26: 20 and in all Judea, and to the *G* also,
28: 28 salvation has been sent to the *G*,
Ro 2: 14 when *G*, who do not have the law,
3: 9 and *G* alike are all under sin.
3: 29 Is he not the God of *G* too? Yes,
9: 24 from the Jews but also from the *G*?
11: 11 to the *G* to make Israel envious.
11: 12 their loss means riches for the *G*,
11: 13 as I am the apostle to the *G*,
15: 9 I will praise you among the *G*;
15: 9 so that the *G* may glorify God
1Co 1: 23 block to Jews and foolishness to *G*,
Gal 1: 16 I might preach him among the *G*,
2: 2 gospel that I preach among the *G*.
2: 8 my ministry as an apostle to the *G*.
2: 9 agreed that we should go to the *G*,
3: 8 that God would justify the *G*
3: 14 to the *G* through Christ Jesus,
Eph 3: 6 the gospel the *G* are heirs together
3: 8 to the *G* the unsearchable riches
Col 1: 27 among the *G* the glorious riches
1Ti 2: 7 a teacher of the true faith to the *G*.
2Ti 4: 17 and all the *G* might hear it.

GENTLE* (GENTLENESS)
Dt 28: 54 Even the most *g* and sensitive man
28: 56 The most *g* and sensitive woman
28: 56 and *g* that she would not venture
2Sa 18: 5 Be *g* with the young man Absalom
1Ki 19: 12 And after the fire came a *g* whisper
Job 41: 3 Will he speak to you with *g* words?
Pr 15: 1 A *g* answer turns away wrath,
25: 15 and a *g* tongue can break a bone.
Jer 11: 19 I had been like a *g* lamb led
Zec 9: 9 *g* and riding on a donkey,
Mt 11: 29 for I am *g* and humble in heart,
21: 5 *g* and riding on a donkey,
Ac 27: 13 When a *g* south wind began
1Co 4: 21 or in love and with a *g* spirit?
Eph 4: 2 Be completely humble and *g*;
1Th 2: 7 but we were *g* among you,
1Ti 3: 3 not violent but *g*, not quarrelsome,
1Pe 3: 4 the unfading beauty of a *g*

GENTLENESS* (GENTLE)
2Co 10: 1 By the meekness and *g* of Christ,
Gal 5: 23 faithfulness, *g* and self-control.
Php 4: 5 Let your *g* be evident to all.
Col 3: 12 kindness, humility, *g* and patience.
1Ti 6: 11 faith, love, endurance and *g*.
1Pe 3: 15 But do this with *g* and respect,

GENUINE*
2Co 6: 8 *g*, yet regarded as impostors;
Php 2: 20 who takes a *g* interest
1Pe 1: 7 may be proved *g* and may result

GERIZIM
Dt 27: 12 on Mount *G* to bless the people:

GERSHOM
Ex 2: 22 and Moses named him *G*, saying,

GETHSEMANE*
Mt 26: 36 disciples to a place called *G*,
Mk 14: 32 They went to a place called *G*,

GHOST see also SPIRIT
Lk 24: 39 a *g* does not have flesh and bones,

GIBEON
Jos 10: 12 "O sun, stand still over *G*,

GIDEON*
Judge, also called Jerub-Baal; freed Israel from Midianites (Jdg 6–8; Heb 11:32). Given sign of fleece (Jdg 6:36–40).

GIFT (GIFTED GIFTS)
Pr 18: 16 A *g* opens the way for the giver
21: 14 A *g* given in secret soothes anger,
Ecc 3: 13 in all his toil — this is the *g* of God.
Mt 5: 23 if you are offering your *g*
Jn 4: 10 "If you knew the *g* of God
Ac 1: 4 wait for the *g* my Father promised,
2: 38 And you will receive the *g*
11: 17 So if God gave them the same *g*
Ro 6: 23 but the *g* of God is eternal life
12: 6 If a man's *g* is prophesying,
1Co 7: 7 each man has his own *g* from God;
2Co 8: 12 the *g* is acceptable according
9: 15 be to God for his indescribable *g*!
Eph 2: 8 it is the *g* of God — not by works,
1Ti 4: 14 not neglect your *g*, which was
2Ti 1: 6 you to fan into flame the *g* of God,
Heb 6: 4 who have tasted the heavenly *g*,
Jas 1: 17 and perfect *g* is from above,
1Pe 3: 7 with you of the gracious *g* of life,
4: 10 should use whatever *g* he has
Rev 22: 17 let him take the free *g* of the water

GIFTED* (GIFT)
1Co 14: 37 he is a prophet or spiritually *g*,

GIFTS (GIFT)
Ps 76: 11 bring *g* to the One to be feared.
112: 9 He has scattered abroad his *g*
Pr 25: 14 of *g* he does not give.
Mt 2: 11 and presented him with *g* of gold
7: 11 Father in heaven give good *g*
7: 11 to give good *g* to your children,
Lk 11: 13 to give good *g* to your children,
Ac 10: 4 and *g* to the poor have come up
Ro 11: 29 for God's *g* and his call are
12: 6 We have different *g*, according
1Co 12: 1 Now about spiritual *g*, brothers,
12: 4 There are different kinds of *g*,
12: 28 those with *g* of administration,
12: 30 all work miracles? Do all have *g*
12: 31 But eagerly desire the greater *g*.
14: 1 and eagerly desire spiritual *g*,
14: 12 eager to have spiritual *g*,
14: 12 excel in *g* that build up the church.
2Co 9: 9 "He has scattered abroad his *g*
Eph 4: 8 and gave *g* to men."
Heb 2: 4 and *g* of the Holy Spirit distributed
9: 9 indicating that the *g* and sacrifices

GILEAD
1Ch 27: 21 the half-tribe of Manasseh in *G*:
Jer 8: 22 Is there no balm in *G*?
46: 11 "Go up to *G* and get balm,

GILGAL
Jos 5: 9 So the place has been called *G*

GIRD*
Ps 45: 3 *G* your sword upon your side,

GIRL
Ge 24: 16 *g* was very beautiful, a virgin;
2Ki 5: 2 a young *g* from Israel.
Mk 5: 41 Little *g*, I say to you, get up!

GIVE (GAVE GIVEN GIVER GIVES GIVING LIFE-GIVING)
Ge 28: 4 you and your descendants the blessing *g* to Abraham
28: 22 that you *g* me I will *g* you a tenth."
Ex 20: 16 "You shall not *g* false testimony
30: 15 The rich are not to *g* more
Nu 6: 26 and *g* you peace."'
Dt 5: 20 "You shall not *g* false testimony
15: 10 *G* generously to him and do
15: 14 *G* to him as the LORD your God
1Sa 1: 11 then I will *g* him to the LORD
1: 28 So now I *g* him to the LORD.
2Ch 15: 7 be strong and do not *g* up,
Pr 21: 26 but the righteous *g* without sparing
23: 26 My son, *g* me your heart
25: 21 if he is thirsty, *g* him water to drink
30: 8 but *g* me only my daily bread.
31: 31 *G* her the reward she has earned,
Ecc 3: 6 a time to search and a time to *g* up,
Isa 42: 8 I will not *g* my glory to another
Eze 36: 26 I will *g* you a new heart
Mt 6: 11 *G* us today our daily bread.
7: 11 know how to *g* good gifts
10: 8 Freely you have received, freely *g*.
16: 19 I will *g* you the keys
22: 21 "*G* to Caesar what is Caesar's,
Mk 8: 37 Or what can a man *g* in exchange
10: 19 not steal, do not *g* false testimony,
Lk 6: 38 *G*, and it will be given to you.
11: 3 *G* us each day our daily bread.
11: 13 Father in heaven *g* the Holy Spirit
14: 33 who does not *g* up everything he
Jn 10: 28 I *g* them eternal life, and they shall
13: 34 "A new commandment I *g* you:
14: 16 he will *g* you another Counselor
14: 27 I do not *g* to you as the world gives.
14: 27 leave with you; my peace I *g* you.
17: 2 people that he might *g* eternal life
Ac 20: 35 blessed to *g* than to receive.'"
Ro 2: 7 immortality, he will *g* eternal life.
8: 32 with him, graciously *g* us all things
12: 8 let him *g* generously;
13: 7 *G* everyone what you owe him:
14: 12 each of us will *g* an account
2Co 9: 7 Each man should *g* what he has
Gal 2: 5 We did not *g* in to them
6: 9 reap a harvest if we do not *g* up.
Heb 10: 25 Let us not *g* up meeting together,
Rev 14: 7 "Fear God and *g* him glory,

GIVEN (GIVE)
Nu 8: 16 are to be *g* wholly to me.
Dt 26: 11 things the LORD your God has *g*
Job 3: 23 Why is life *g* to a man
Ps 115: 16 but the earth he has *g* to man.
Isa 9: 6 to us a son is *g*,
Mt 6: 33 and all these things will be *g* to you
7: 7 "Ask and it will be *g* to you;
13: 12 Whoever has will be *g* more,
22: 30 people will neither marry nor be *g*
25: 29 everyone who has will be *g* more,
Lk 6: 38 Give, and it will be *g* to you.
8: 10 kingdom of God has been *g* to you,
11: 9 Ask and it will be *g* to you;
22: 19 saying, "This is my body *g* for you;
Jn 3: 27 man can receive only what is *g* him
15: 7 you wish, and it will be *g* you.
17: 24 I want those you have *g* me to be
17: 24 the glory you have *g* me
18: 11 the cup the Father has *g* me?"
Ac 5: 32 whom God has *g* to those who
20: 24 the task the Lord Jesus has *g* me —
Ro 5: 5 the Holy Spirit, whom he has *g* us.
1Co 4: 2 those who have been *g* a trust must
11: 24 and when he had *g* thanks,
12: 13 we were all *g* the one Spirit to drink
2Co 5: 5 and has *g* us the Spirit as a deposit,
Eph 1: 6 which he has freely *g* us
4: 7 to each one of us grace has been *g*
1Ti 4: 14 was *g* you through a prophetic
1Jn 4: 13 because he has *g* us of his Spirit.

GIVER* (GIVE)
Pr 18: 16 A gift opens the way for the *g*
2Co 9: 7 for God loves a cheerful *g*.

GIVES (GIVE)
Job 35: 10 who *g* songs in the night,
Ps 119: 130 The unfolding of your words *g* light;
Pr 3: 34 but *g* grace to the humble.
11: 24 One man *g* freely, yet gains
14: 30 A heart at peace *g* life to the body,
15: 30 good news *g* health to the bones.
19: 6 of a man who *g* gifts.
25: 26 is a righteous man who *g* way

Pr 28: 27 He who *g* to the poor will lack
29: 4 justice a king *g* a country stability,
Isa 40: 29 He *g* strength to the weary
Hab 2: 15 "Woe to him who *g* drink
Mt 10: 42 if anyone *g* even a cup of cold water
Jn 5: 21 even so the Son *g* life to whom he is
6: 63 The Spirit *g* life; the flesh counts
1Co 15: 57 He *g* us the victory
2Co 3: 6 the letter kills, but the Spirit *g* life.
1Th 4: 8 who *g* you his Holy Spirit.
Jas 1: 25 into the perfect law that *g* freedom,
4: 6 but *g* grace to the humble."
1Pe 5: 5 but *g* grace to the humble."

GIVING (GIVE)

Ne 8: 8 *g* the meaning so that the people
Est 9: 19 a day for *g* presents to each other.
Ps 19: 8 *g* joy to the heart.
Pr 15: 23 A man finds joy in *g* an apt reply—
Mt 6: 4 so that your *g* may be in secret.
24: 38 marrying and *g* in marriage,
Ac 15: 8 them by *g* the Holy Spirit to them,
2Co 8: 7 also excel in this grace of *g*.
Php 4: 15 shared with me in the matter of *g*

GLAD* (GLADDENS GLADNESS)

Ex 4: 14 his heart will be *g* when he sees you
Jos 22: 33 They were *g* to hear the report
Jdg 8: 25 "We'll be *g* to give them."
18: 20 household?" Then the priest was *g*.
1Sa 19: 5 and you saw it and were *g*.
2Sa 1: 20 daughters of the Philistines be *g*,
1Ki 8: 66 *g* in heart for all the good things
1Ch 16: 31 heavens rejoice, let the earth be *g*;
2Ch 7: 10 and *g* in heart for the good things
Ps 5: 11 let all who take refuge in you be *g*;
9: 2 I will be *g* and rejoice in you;
14: 7 let Jacob rejoice and Israel be *g*!
16: 9 Therefore my heart is *g*
21: 6 made him *g* with the joy
31: 7 I will be *g* and rejoice in your love,
32: 11 Rejoice in the LORD and be *g*,
40: 16 rejoice and be *g* in you;
45: 8 music of the strings makes you *g*.
46: 4 whose streams make *g* the city
48: 11 the villages of Judah are *g*
53: 6 let Jacob rejoice and Israel be *g*!
58: 10 The righteous will be *g*
67: 4 May the nations be *g* and sing
68: 3 But may the righteous be *g*
69: 32 The poor will see and be *g*—
70: 4 rejoice and be *g* in you;
90: 14 for joy and be *g* all our days.
90: 15 Make us *g* for as many days
92: 4 For you make me *g* by your deeds,
96: 11 heavens rejoice, let the earth be *g*;
97: 1 LORD reigns, let the earth be *g*;
97: 8 and the villages of Judah are *g*
105: 38 Egypt was *g* when they left,
107: 30 They were *g* when it grew calm,
118: 24 let us rejoice and be *g* in it.
149: 2 of Zion be *g* in their King.
Pr 23: 15 then my heart will be *g*;
23: 25 May your father and mother be *g*;
29: 6 a righteous one can sing and be *g*.
Ecc 8: 15 sun than to eat and drink and be *g*.
Isa 25: 9 let us rejoice and be *g*
35: 1 and the parched land will be *g*;
65: 18 But be *g* and rejoice forever
66: 10 with Jerusalem and be *g* for her,
Jer 20: 15 who made him very *g*, saying,
31: 13 Then maidens will dance and be *g*,
41: 13 were with him, they were *g*.
50: 11 "Because you rejoice and are *g*,
La 4: 21 be *g*, O Daughter of Edom,
Joel 2: 21 be *g* and rejoice.
2: 23 Be *g*, O people of Zion,
Hab 1: 15 and so he rejoices and is *g*.
Zep 3: 14 Be *g* and rejoice with all your heart
Zec 2: 10 and be *g*, O Daughter of Zion.
8: 19 will become joyful and *g* occasions
10: 7 their hearts will be *g* as with wine.
Mt 5: 12 be *g*, because great is your reward
Lk 15: 32 But we had to celebrate and be *g*,
Jn 4: 36 and the reaper may be *g* together.
8: 56 my day; he saw it and was *g*."
11: 15 for your sake I am *g* I was not there
14: 28 you would be *g* that I am going
Ac 2: 26 Therefore my heart is *g*
2: 46 together with *g* and sincere hearts,
11: 23 he was *g* and encouraged them all
13: 48 they were *g* and honored the word
15: 3 news made all the brothers very *g*.
15: 31 were *g* for its encouraging message.
1Co 16: 17 was *g* when Stephanas, Fortunatus
2Co 2: 2 who is left to make me *g*
7: 16 I am *g* I can have complete
13: 9 We are *g* whenever we are weak
Gal 4: 27 "Be *g*, O barren woman,
Php 2: 17 I am *g* and rejoice with all of you.
2: 18 So you too should be *g* and rejoice
2: 28 you see him again you may be *g*
Rev 19: 7 Let us rejoice and be *g*

GLADDENS* (GLAD)

Ps 104: 15 wine that *g* the heart of man,

GLADNESS* (GLAD)

2Ch 29: 30 So they sang praises with *g*
Est 8: 16 a time of happiness and joy, *g*
8: 17 there was joy and *g*
Job 3: 22 who are filled with *g*
Ps 35: 27 shout for joy and *g*;
45: 15 They are led in with joy and *g*;
51: 8 Let me hear joy and *g*;
65: 12 the hills are clothed with *g*.
100: 2 Worship the LORD with *g*;
Ecc 5: 20 God keeps him occupied with *g*
9: 7 Go, eat your food with *g*,
Isa 16: 10 *g* are taken away from the orchards
35: 10 *G* and joy will overtake them,
51: 3 Joy and *g* will be found in her,
51: 11 *G* and joy will overtake them,
61: 3 the oil of *g* / instead of mourning,
Jer 7: 34 and *g* and to the voices of bride
16: 9 and *g* and to the voices of bride
25: 10 from them the sounds of joy and *g*,
31: 13 I will turn their mourning into *g*;
33: 11 once more the sounds of joy and *g*,
48: 33 Joy and *g* are gone
Joel 1: 16 joy and *g*

GLAZE*

Pr 26: 23 of *g* over earthenware

GLEAM*

Pr 4: 18 of the righteous is like the first *g*
Da 10: 6 legs like the *g* of burnished bronze,

GLOAT (GLOATS)

Pr 24: 17 Do not *g* when your enemy falls;

GLOATS* (GLOAT)

Pr 17: 5 whoever *g* over disaster will not go

GLORIES* (GLORY)

1Pe 1: 11 and the *g* that would follow.

GLORIFIED* (GLORY)

Isa 66: 5 'Let the LORD be *g*,
Eze 39: 13 day I am *g* will be a memorable day
Da 4: 34 and *g* him who lives forever.
Jn 7: 39 since Jesus had not yet been *g*.
11: 4 glory so that God's Son may be *g*
12: 16 after Jesus was *g* did they realize
12: 23 come for the Son of Man to be *g*.
12: 28 "I have *g* it, and will glorify it again
13: 31 Son of Man *g* and God is *g* in him.
13: 32 If God is *g* in him, God will glorify
Ac 3: 13 our fathers, has *g* his servant Jesus.
Ro 1: 21 they neither *g* him as God
8: 30 those he justified, he also *g*.
2Th 1: 10 comes to be *g* in his holy people
1: 12 of our Lord Jesus may be *g* in you,
1Pe 1: 21 him from the dead and *g* him,

GLORIFIES* (GLORY)

Lk 1: 46 My soul *g* the Lord
Jn 8: 54 as your God, is the one who *g* me.

GLORIFY* (GLORY)

Ps 34: 3 *G* the LORD with me;
63: 3 my lips will *g* you.
69: 30 and *g* him with thanksgiving.
86: 12 I will *g* your name forever.
Isa 60: 13 and I will *g* the place of my feet.
Da 4: 37 and exalt and *g* the King of heaven,
Jn 8: 54 Jesus replied, "If I *g* myself,
12: 28 glorified it, and will *g* it again."
12: 28 *g* your name!" Then a voice came
13: 32 God will *g* the Son in himself,
13: 32 in himself, and will *g* him at once.
17: 1 *G* your Son, that your Son may
17: 1 your Son, that your Son may *g* you.
17: 5 *g* me in your presence
21: 19 death by which Peter would *g* God.
Ro 15: 6 and mouth you may *g* the God
15: 9 so that the Gentiles may *g* God
1Pe 2: 12 and *g* God on the day he visits us.
Rev 16: 9 they refused to repent and *g* him.

GLORIFYING* (GLORY)

Lk 2: 20 *g* and praising God

GLORIOUS* (GLORY)

Dt 28: 58 not revere this *g* and awesome
33: 29 and your *g* sword.
1Ch 29: 13 and praise your *g* name.
Ne 9: 5 "Blessed be your *g* name,
Ps 16: 3 they are the *g* ones
45: 13 All *g* is the princess
66: 2 make his praise *g*.
72: 19 Praise be to his *g* name forever;
87: 3 *G* things are said of you,
111: 3 *G* and majestic are his deeds,
145: 5 of the *g* splendor of your majesty,
145: 12 the *g* splendor of your kingdom.
Isa 3: 8 defying his *g* presence.
4: 2 the LORD will be beautiful and *g*,
11: 10 and his place of rest will be *g*.
12: 5 for he has done *g* things;
28: 1 to the fading flower, his *g* beauty,
28: 4 That fading flower, his *g* beauty,
28: 5 will be a *g* crown,
42: 21 to make his law great and *g*.
60: 7 and I will adorn my *g* temple.
63: 12 who sent his *g* arm of power
63: 14 to make for yourself a *g* name.
63: 15 from your lofty throne, holy and *g*.
64: 11 *g* temple, where our fathers praised
Jer 13: 18 for your *g* crowns
14: 21 do not dishonor your *g* throne.
17: 12 A *g* throne, exalted
48: 17 how broken the *g* staff!'
Mt 19: 28 the Son of Man sits on his *g* throne,
Lk 9: 31 appeared in *g* splendor, talking
Ac 2: 20 of the great and *g* day of the Lord.
Ro 8: 21 and brought into the *g* freedom
2Co 3: 8 of the Spirit be even more *g*?
3: 9 how much more *g* is the ministry
3: 9 ministry that condemns men is *g*,
3: 10 For what was *g* has no glory now
Eph 1: 6 to the praise of his *g* grace,
1: 17 *g* Father, may give you the Spirit
1: 18 the riches of his *g* inheritance
3: 16 of his *g* riches he may strengthen
Php 3: 21 so that they will be like his *g* body.
4: 19 to his *g* riches in Christ Jesus.
Col 1: 11 all power according to his *g* might
1: 27 among the Gentiles the *g* riches
1Ti 1: 11 to the *g* gospel of the blessed God,
Tit 2: 13 the *g* appearing of our great God
Jas 2: 1 believers in our *g* Lord Jesus Christ
1Pe 1: 8 with an inexpressible and *g* joy,
Jude : 24 before his *g* presence without fault

GLORIOUSLY* (GLORY)

Isa 24: 23 and before its elders, *g*.

GLORY (GLORIES GLORIFIED GLORIFIES GLORIFY GLORIFYING GLORIOUS GLORIOUSLY)

Ex 14: 4 But I will gain *g* for myself
14: 17 And I will gain *g* through Pharaoh
15: 11 awesome in *g*,
16: 10 and there was the *g* of the LORD
24: 16 and the *g* of the LORD settled
33: 18 Moses said, "Now show me your *g*
40: 34 and the *g* of the LORD filled
Nu 14: 21 the *g* of the LORD fills the whole
Dt 5: 24 LORD our God has shown us his *g*
Jos 7: 19 "My son, give *g* to the LORD,
1Sa 4: 21 "The *g* has departed from Israel"—
1Ch 16: 10 *G* in his holy name;
16: 24 Declare his *g* among the nations,
16: 28 ascribe to the LORD *g*
29: 11 and the *g* and the majesty
Ps 8: 1 You have set your *g*
8: 5 and crowned him with *g* and honor
19: 1 The heavens declare the *g* of God;
24: 7 that the King of *g* may come in.
26: 8 the place where your *g* dwells.
29: 1 ascribe to the LORD *g*
29: 9 And in his temple all cry, "*G*!"
57: 5 let your *g* be over all the earth.
66: 2 Sing the *g* of his name;
72: 19 the whole earth be filled with his *g*.
96: 3 Declare his *g* among the nations,
102: 15 of the earth will revere your *g*.
108: 5 and let your *g* be over all the earth.
149: 9 This is the *g* of all his saints.
Pr 19: 11 it is to his *g* to overlook an offense.
25: 2 It is the *g* of God to conceal
Isa 4: 5 over all the *g* will be a canopy.
6: 3 the whole earth is full of his *g*."
24: 16 "*G* to the Righteous One."
26: 15 You have gained *g* for yourself;
35: 2 they will see the *g* of the LORD,
40: 5 the *g* of the LORD will be revealed
42: 8 I will not give my *g* to another
42: 12 Let them give *g* to the LORD
43: 7 whom I created for my *g*,
44: 23 he displays his *g* in Israel.

Isa 48: 11 I will not yield my *g* to another.
66: 18 and they will come and see my *g*.
66: 19 They will proclaim my *g*
Eze 1: 28 the likeness of the *g* of the LORD.
10: 4 the radiance of the *g* of the LORD.
43: 2 and the land was radiant with his *g*.
44: 4 and saw the *g* of the LORD filling
Hab 2: 14 knowledge of the *g* of the LORD,
3: 3 His *g* covered the heavens
Zec 2: 5 'and I will be its *g* within.'
Mt 16: 27 in his Father's *g* with his angels,
24: 30 of the sky, with power and great *g*.
25: 31 sit on his throne in heavenly *g*.
25: 31 the Son of Man comes in his *g*,
Mk 8: 38 in his Father's *g* with the holy
13: 26 in clouds with great power and *g*.
Lk 2: 9 and the *g* of the Lord shone
2: 14 saying, "*G* to God in the highest,
9: 26 and in the *g* of the Father
9: 26 of him when he comes in his *g*
9: 32 they saw his *g* and the two men
19: 38 in heaven and *g* in the highest!"
21: 27 in a cloud with power and great *g*.
24: 26 these things and then enter his *g*?"
Jn 1: 14 We have seen his *g*, the *g* of the One
2: 11 He thus revealed his *g*,
8: 50 I am not seeking *g* for myself;
8: 54 myself, my *g* means nothing.
11: 4 for God's *g* so that God's Son may
11: 40 you would see the *g* of God?"
12: 41 he saw Jesus' *g* and spoke about
14: 13 so that the Son may bring *g*
15: 8 is to my Father's *g*, that you bear
16: 14 He will bring *g* to me by taking
17: 4 I have brought you *g* on earth
17: 5 presence with the *g* I had with you
17: 10 *g* has come to me through them.
17: 22 given them the *g* that you gave
17: 24 to see my *g*, the *g* you have given
Ac 7: 2 The God of *g* appeared
7: 55 up to heaven and saw the *g* of God,
Ro 1: 23 exchanged the *g* of the immortal
2: 7 by persistence in doing good seek *g*
2: 10 then for the Gentile; but *g*,
3: 7 truthfulness and so increases his *g*,
3: 23 and fall short of the *g* of God,
4: 20 in his faith and gave *g* to God,
8: 17 that we may also share in his *g*.
8: 18 with the *g* that will be revealed
9: 4 theirs the divine *g*, the covenants,
9: 23 riches of his *g* known to the objects
9: 23 whom he prepared in advance for *g*
11: 36 To him be the *g* forever! Amen.
15: 17 Therefore I *g* in Christ Jesus
16: 27 to the only wise God be *g* forever
1Co 2: 7 for our *g* before time began.
10: 31 whatever you do, do it all for the *g*
11: 7 but the woman is the *g* of man.
11: 7 since he is the image and *g* of God;
11: 15 it is her *g*? For long hair is given
15: 43 it is raised in *g*; it is sown
2Co 1: 20 spoken by us to the *g* of God.
3: 7 in letters on stone, came with *g*,
3: 7 the face of Moses because of its *g*,
3: 10 comparison with the surpassing *g*.
3: 10 what was glorious has no *g* now
3: 11 how much greater is the *g*
3: 11 what was fading away came with *g*,
3: 18 faces all reflect the Lord's *g*,
3: 18 likeness with ever-increasing *g*,
4: 4 of the gospel of the *g* of Christ,
4: 6 of the knowledge of the *g* of God
4: 15 to overflow to the *g* of God.
4: 17 us an eternal *g* that far outweighs
Gal 1: 5 to whom be *g* for ever and ever.
Eph 1: 12 might be for the praise of his *g*.
1: 14 to the praise of his *g*.
3: 13 for you, which are your *g*.
3: 21 to him be *g* in the church
Php 1: 11 to the *g* and praise of God.
2: 11 to the *g* of God the Father.
3: 3 of God, who *g* in Christ Jesus,
4: 20 and Father be *g* for ever and ever.
Col 1: 27 Christ in you, the hope of *g*.
3: 4 also will appear with him in *g*.
1Th 2: 12 you into his kingdom and *g*.
2: 19 in which we will *g* in the presence
2: 20 Indeed, you are our *g* and joy.
2Th 2: 14 in the *g* of our Lord Jesus Christ.
1Ti 1: 17 be honor and *g* for ever and ever.
3: 16 was taken up in *g*.
2Ti 2: 10 is in Christ Jesus, with eternal *g*.
4: 18 To him be *g* for ever and ever.
Heb 1: 3 The Son is the radiance of God's *g*
2: 7 you crowned him with *g* and honor
Heb 2: 9 now crowned with *g* and honor
2: 10 In bringing many sons to *g*,
5: 5 take upon himself the *g*
9: 5 the ark were the cherubim of the *G*,
13: 21 to whom be *g* for ever and ever.
1Pe 1: 7 *g* and honor when Jesus Christ is
1: 24 and all their *g* is like the flowers
4: 11 To him be the *g* and the power
4: 13 overjoyed when his *g* is revealed.
4: 14 for the Spirit of *g* and of God rests
5: 1 will share in the *g* to be revealed:
5: 4 of *g* that will never fade away.
5: 10 you to his eternal *g* in Christ,
2Pe 1: 3 of him who called us by his own *g*
1: 17 and *g* from God the Father
1: 17 came to him from the Majestic *G*,
3: 18 To him be *g* both now and forever!
Jude : 25 to the only God our Savior be *g*,
Rev 1: 6 to him be *g* and power for ever
4: 9 the living creatures give *g*,
4: 11 to receive *g* and honor and power,
5: 12 and honor and *g* and praise!"
5: 13 and honor and *g* and power,
7: 12 Praise and *g*
11: 13 and gave *g* to the God of heaven.
14: 7 "Fear God and give him *g*,
15: 4 and bring *g* to your name?
15: 8 with smoke from the *g* of God
19: 1 *g* and power belong to our God,
19: 7 and give him *g*!
21: 11 It shone with the *g* of God,
21: 23 for the *g* of God gives it light,
21: 26 *g* and honor of the nations will be

GLOWING
Eze 8: 2 was as bright as *g* metal.
Rev 1: 15 His feet were like bronze *g*

GLUTTONS* (GLUTTONY)
Pr 23: 21 for drunkards and *g* become poor,
28: 7 of *g* disgraces his father.
Tit 1: 12 always liars, evil brutes, lazy *g*."

GLUTTONY* (GLUTTONS)
Pr 23: 2 throat if you are given to *g*.

GNASHING
Mt 8: 12 where there will be weeping and *g*

GNAT* (GNATS)
Mt 23: 24 You strain out a *g* but swallow

GNATS (GNAT)
Ex 8: 16 of Egypt the dust will become *g*."

GOADS
Ecc 12: 11 The words of the wise are like *g*,
Ac 26: 14 hard for you to kick against the *g*.'

GOAL*
Lk 13: 32 on the third day I will reach my *g*.'
2Co 5: 9 So we make it our *g* to please him,
Gal 3: 3 to attain your *g* by human effort?
Php 3: 14 on toward the *g* to win the prize
1Ti 1: 5 The *g* of this command is love,
1Pe 1: 9 for you are receiving the *g*

GOAT (GOATS SCAPEGOAT)
Ge 15: 9 "Bring me a heifer, a *g* and a ram,
30: 32 and every spotted or speckled *g*.
37: 31 slaughtered a *g* and dipped
Ex 26: 7 Make curtains of *g* hair for the tent
Lev 16: 9 shall bring the *g* whose lot falls
Nu 7: 16 one male *g* for a sin offering;
Isa 11: 6 the leopard will lie down with the *g*
Da 8: 5 suddenly a *g* with a prominent

GOATS (GOAT)
Nu 7: 17 five male *g* and five male lambs
Mt 25: 32 separates the sheep from the *g*.
Heb 10: 4 of bulls and *g* to take away sins.

GOD (GOD'S GODLINESS GODLY GODS)
Ge 1: 1 In the beginning *G* created
1: 2 and the Spirit of *G* was hovering
1: 3 And *G* said, "Let there be light,"
1: 7 So *G* made the expanse
1: 9 And *G* said, "Let the water
1: 11 Then *G* said, "Let the land produce
1: 20 And *G* said, "Let the water teem
1: 21 So *G* created the great creatures
1: 25 *G* made the wild animals according
1: 26 Then *G* said, "Let us make man
1: 27 So *G* created man in his own image
1: 31 *G* saw all that he had made,
2: 3 And *G* blessed the seventh day
2: 7 And the LORD *G* formed the man
2: 8 the LORD *G* had planted a garden
2: 18 The LORD *G* said, "It is not good
Ge 2: 22 Then the LORD *G* made a woman
3: 1 to the woman, "Did *G* really say,
3: 5 you will be like *G*, knowing good
3: 8 from the LORD *G* among the trees
3: 9 But the LORD *G* called to the man
3: 21 The LORD *G* made garments
3: 22 LORD *G* said, "The man has now
3: 23 So the LORD *G* banished him
5: 1 When *G* created man, he made him
5: 22 Enoch walked with *G* 300 years
5: 24 because *G* took him away.
6: 2 sons of *G* saw that the daughters
6: 9 of his time, and he walked with *G*.
6: 12 *G* saw how corrupt the earth had
8: 1 But *G* remembered Noah
9: 1 Then *G* blessed Noah and his sons,
9: 6 for in the image of *G*
9: 16 everlasting covenant between *G*
14: 18 He was priest of *G* Most High,
14: 19 Blessed be Abram by *G* Most High,
16: 13 "You are the *G* who sees me,"
17: 1 "I am *G* Almighty; walk before me
17: 7 to be your *G* and the *G*
21: 4 him, as *G* commanded him.
21: 6 "*G* has brought me laughter,
21: 20 *G* was with the boy as he grew up.
21: 22 *G* is with you in everything you do.
21: 33 name of the LORD, the Eternal *G*.
22: 1 Some time later *G* tested Abraham.
22: 8 "*G* himself will provide the lamb
22: 12 Now I know that you fear *G*,
25: 11 Abraham's death, *G* blessed his
28: 12 and the angels of *G* were ascending
28: 17 other than the house of *G*;
31: 42 But *G* has seen my hardship
31: 50 remember that *G* is a witness
32: 1 and the angels of *G* met him.
32: 28 because you have struggled with *G*
32: 30 "It is because I saw *G* face to face,
33: 11 for *G* has been gracious to me
35: 1 and build an altar there to *G*,
35: 5 and the terror of *G* fell
35: 10 *G* said to him, "Your name is Jacob
35: 11 *G* said to him, "I am *G* Almighty;
41: 51 *G* has made me forget all my
41: 52 *G* has made me fruitful in the land
50: 20 but *G* intended it for good
50: 24 But *G* will surely come to your aid
Ex 2: 24 *G* heard their groaning
3: 5 "Do not come any closer," *G* said.
3: 6 because he was afraid to look at *G*.
3: 12 And *G* said, "I will be with you.
3: 14 what shall I tell them?" *G* said
4: 27 he met Moses at the mountain of *G*
6: 7 own people, and I will be your *G*.
8: 10 is no one like the LORD our *G*.
10: 16 sinned against the LORD your *G*
13: 18 So *G* led the people
15: 2 He is my *G*, and I will praise him,
16: 12 that I am the LORD your *G*.'"
17: 9 with the staff of *G* in my hands."
18: 5 camped near the mountain of *G*.
19: 3 Then Moses went up to *G*,
20: 1 And *G* spoke all these words:
20: 2 the LORD your *G*, who brought
20: 5 the LORD your *G*, am a jealous *G*,
20: 7 the name of the LORD your *G*,
20: 10 a Sabbath to the LORD your *G*.
20: 12 the LORD your *G* is giving you.
20: 19 But do not have *G* speak to us
20: 20 the fear of *G* will be with you
22: 20 "Whoever sacrifices to any *g* other
22: 28 "Do not blaspheme *G*
23: 19 to the house of the LORD your *G*.
31: 18 inscribed by the finger of *G*.
34: 6 the compassionate and gracious *G*,
34: 14 name is Jealous, is a jealous *G*.
Lev 2: 13 salt of the covenant of your *G* out
11: 44 the LORD your *G*; consecrate
18: 21 not profane the name of your *G*.
19: 2 the LORD your *G*, am holy.
20: 7 because I am the LORD your *G*.
21: 6 They must be holy to their *G*
22: 33 out of Egypt to be your *G*.
26: 12 walk among you and be your *G*,
Nu 15: 40 and will be consecrated to your *G*.
22: 18 the command of the LORD my *G*.
22: 38 I must speak only what *G* puts
23: 19 *G* is not a man, that he should lie,
25: 13 zealous for the honor of his *G*
Dt 1: 17 for judgment belongs to *G*.
1: 21 the LORD your *G* has given you
1: 30 The LORD your *G*, who is going
3: 22 LORD your *G* himself will fight
3: 24 For what *g* is there in heaven

Dt 4:24 is a consuming fire, a jealous *G*.
4:29 there you seek the LORD your *G*,
4:31 the LORD your *G* is a merciful *G*;
4:39 heart this day that the LORD is *G*
5:9 the LORD your *G*, am a jealous *G*,
5:11 the name of the LORD your *G*,
5:12 the LORD your *G* has commanded
5:14 a Sabbath to the LORD your *G*.
5:15 the LORD your *G* brought you out
5:16 the LORD your *G* has commanded
5:16 the LORD your *G* is giving you.
5:24 LORD our *G* has shown us his
5:26 of the living *G* speaking out of fire,
6:2 them may fear the LORD your *G*
6:4 LORD our *G*, the LORD is one.
6:5 Love the LORD your *G*
6:13 the LORD your *G*, serve him only
6:16 Do not test the LORD your *G*
7:6 holy to the LORD your *G*.
7:9 your *G* is *G*; he is the faithful *G*,
7:12 the LORD your *G* will keep his
7:19 LORD your *G* will do the same
7:21 is a great and awesome *G*.
8:5 the LORD your *G* disciplines you.
8:11 do not forget the LORD your *G*,
8:18 But remember the LORD your *G*,
9:10 inscribed by the finger of *G*.
10:12 but to fear the LORD your *G*,
10:14 the LORD your *G* belong
10:17 For the LORD your *G* is *G* of gods
10:21 He is your praise; he is your *G*,
11:1 Love the LORD your *G*
11:13 to love the LORD your *G*
12:12 rejoice before the LORD your *G*,
12:28 in the eyes of the LORD your *G*.
13:3 The LORD your *G* is testing you
13:4 the LORD your *G* you must
15:6 the LORD your *G* will bless you
15:19 the LORD your *G* every firstborn
16:11 rejoice before the LORD your *G*
16:17 the LORD your *G* has blessed you.
18:13 before the LORD your *G*.
18:15 The LORD your *G* will raise up
19:9 to love the LORD your *G*
22:5 the LORD your *G* detests anyone
23:5 the LORD your *G* loves you.
23:14 the LORD your *G* moves about
23:21 a vow to the LORD your *G*,
25:16 the LORD your *G* detests anyone
26:5 declare before the LORD your *G*:
29:13 that he may be your *G*
29:29 belong to the LORD our *G*,
30:2 return to the LORD your *G*
30:4 the LORD your *G* will gather you
30:6 The LORD your *G* will circumcise
30:16 today to love the LORD your *G*,
30:20 you may love the LORD your *G*,
31:6 for the LORD your *G* goes
32:3 Oh, praise the greatness of our *G*!
32:4 A faithful *G* who does no wrong,
33:27 The eternal *G* is your refuge,
Jos 1:9 for the LORD your *G* will be
14:8 the LORD my *G* wholeheartedly.
14:9 the LORD my *G* wholeheartedly.'
14:14 the *G* of Israel, wholeheartedly.
22:5 to love the LORD your *G*,
22:22 The Mighty One, *G*, the LORD!
22:34 Between Us that the LORD is *G*.
23:8 to hold fast to the LORD your *G*,
23:11 careful to love the LORD your *G*.
23:14 the LORD your *G* gave you has
23:15 of the LORD your *G* has come true
24:19 He is a holy *G*; he is a jealous *G*.
24:23 to the LORD, the *G* of Israel."
Jdg 5:3 to the LORD, the *G* of Israel.
16:28 O *G*, please strengthen me just
Ru 1:16 be my people and your *G* my *G*.
2:12 by the LORD, the *G* of Israel,
1Sa 2:2 there is no Rock like our *G*.
2:3 for the LORD is a *G* who knows,
2:25 another man, *G* may mediate
10:26 men whose hearts *G* had touched.
12:12 the LORD your *G* was your king.
16:15 spirit from *G* is tormenting you.
17:26 defy the armies of the living *G*?"
17:36 defied the armies of the living *G*.
17:45 the *G* of the armies of Israel,
17:46 world will know that there is a *G*
23:16 and helped him find strength in *G*.
28:15 and *G* has turned away from me.
30:6 strength in the LORD his *G*.
2Sa 7:22 and there is no *G* but you,
7:23 on earth that *G* went out to redeem
14:14 But *G* does not take away life;
21:14 *G* answered prayer in behalf
2Sa 22:3 my *G* is my rock, in whom I take
22:31 "As for *G*, his way is perfect;
22:32 And who is the Rock except our *G*
22:33 It is *G* who arms me with strength
22:47 Exalted be *G*, the Rock, my Savior!
1Ki 2:3 what the LORD your *G* requires:
4:29 *G* gave Solomon wisdom
5:5 for the Name of the LORD my *G*,
8:23 there is no *G* like you in heaven
8:27 "But will *G* really dwell on earth?
8:60 may know that the LORD is *G*
8:61 committed to the LORD our *G*,
10:24 to hear the wisdom *G* had put
15:30 he provoked the LORD, the *G*
18:21 If the LORD is *G*, follow him;
18:36 it be known today that you are *G*
18:37 are *G*, and that you are turning
20:28 a *g* of the hills and not a *g*
2Ki 5:15 "Now I know that there is no *G*
18:5 in the LORD, the *G* of Israel.
19:15 *G* of Israel, enthroned
19:19 Now, O LORD our *G*, deliver us
1Ch 12:18 for your *G* will help you."
13:2 if it is the will of the LORD our *G*,
16:35 Cry out, "Save us, O *G* our Savior;
17:20 and there is no *G* but you,
17:24 the *G* over Israel, is Israel's *G*!'
21:8 said to *G*, "I have sinned greatly
22:1 house of the LORD *G* is to be here,
22:19 soul to seeking the LORD your *G*.
28:2 for the footstool of our *G*,
28:9 acknowledge the *G* of your father,
28:20 for the LORD *G*, my *G*, is with you
29:1 not for man but for the LORD *G*.
29:2 provided for the temple of my *G* —
29:3 of my *G* I now give my personal
29:10 *G* of our father Israel,
29:13 Now, our *G*, we give you thanks,
29:16 O LORD our *G*, as for all this
29:17 my *G*, that you test the heart
29:18 *G* of our fathers Abraham,
2Ch 2:4 for the Name of the LORD my *G*
5:14 of the LORD filled the temple of *G*
6:4 be to the LORD, the *G* of Israel,
6:14 there is no *G* like you in heaven
6:18 "But will *G* really dwell on earth
10:15 for this turn of events was from *G*,
13:12 *G* is with us; he is our leader.
15:3 was without the true *G*,
15:12 the *G* of their fathers,
15:15 They sought *G* eagerly,
18:13 I can tell him only what my *G* says
19:3 have set your heart on seeking *G*."
19:7 with the LORD our *G* there is no
20:6 are you not the *G* who is in heaven?
20:20 Have faith in the LORD your *G*
25:8 for *G* has the power to help
26:5 sought the LORD, *G* gave him
30:9 for the LORD your *G* is gracious
30:19 who sets his heart on seeking *G* —
31:21 he sought his *G* and worked
32:31 *G* left him to test him
33:12 the favor of the LORD his *G*
34:33 fail to follow the LORD, the *G*
Ezr 6:21 to seek the LORD, the *G* of Israel.
7:18 accordance with the will of your *G*.
7:23 Whatever the *G* of heaven has
8:22 "The gracious hand of our *G* is
8:31 The hand of our *G* was on us,
9:6 "O my *G*, I am too ashamed
9:9 our *G* has not deserted us
9:13 our *G*, you have punished us less
9:15 *G* of Israel, you are righteous!
Ne 1:5 the great and awesome *G*,
5:9 fear of our *G* to avoid the reproach
5:15 for *G* I did not act like that.
7:2 feared *G* more than most men do.
8:8 from the Book of the Law of *G*,
8:18 from the Book of the Law of *G*.
9:5 and praise the LORD your *G*,
9:17 But you are a forgiving *G*,
9:31 you are a gracious and merciful *G*.
9:32 the great, mighty and awesome *G*,
10:29 oath to follow the Law of *G* given
10:39 not neglect the house of our *G*."
12:43 *G* had given them great joy.
13:11 Why is the house of *G* neglected?"
13:26 He was loved by his *G*,
13:31 Remember me with favor, O my *G*.
Job 1:1 he feared *G* and shunned evil.
1:22 by charging *G* with wrongdoing.
2:10 Shall we accept good from *G*,
4:17 a mortal be more righteous than *G*?
5:17 is the man whom *G* corrects;
8:3 Does *G* pervert justice?
Job 8:20 "Surely *G* does not reject
9:2 a mortal be righteous before *G*?
11:7 Can you fathom the mysteries of *G*
12:13 "To *G* belong wisdom and power;
16:7 Surely, O *G*, you have worn me out
19:26 yet in my flesh I will see *G*;
21:19 '*G* stores up a man's punishment
21:22 Can anyone teach knowledge to *G*,
22:12 "Is not *G* in the heights of heaven?
22:13 Yet you say, 'What does *G* know?
22:21 "Submit to *G* and be at peace
25:2 "Dominion and awe belong to *G*;
25:4 can a man be righteous before *G*?
26:6 Death is naked before *G*;
30:20 O *G*, but you do not answer;
31:6 let *G* weigh me in honest scales
31:14 do when *G* confronts me?
32:13 let *G* refute him, not man.'
33:6 I am just like you before *G*;
33:14 For *G* does speak — now one way,
33:26 He prays to *G* and finds favor
34:10 Far be it from *G* to do evil,
34:12 is unthinkable that *G* would do
34:23 *G* has no need to examine men
34:33 Should *G* then reward you
36:5 "*G* is mighty, but does not despise
36:26 is *G* — beyond our understanding!
37:22 *G* comes in awesome majesty.
Ps 5:4 You are not a *G* who takes pleasure
7:11 *G* is a righteous judge,
10:14 O *G*, do see trouble and grief;
14:5 for *G* is present in the company
18:2 my *G* is my rock, in whom I take
18:28 my *G* turns my darkness into light.
18:30 As for *G*, his way is perfect;
18:31 And who is the Rock except our *G*
18:32 It is *G* who arms me with strength
18:46 Exalted be *G* my Savior!
19:1 The heavens declare the glory of *G*;
22:1 *G*, my *G*, why have you forsaken
22:10 womb you have been my *G*.
27:9 O *G* my Savior.
29:3 the *G* of glory thunders,
31:5 redeem me, O LORD, the *G*
31:14 I say, "You are my *G*."
33:12 the nation whose *G* is the LORD,
35:24 righteousness, O LORD my *G*;
37:31 The law of his *G* is in his heart;
40:3 a hymn of praise to our *G*.
40:8 I desire to do your will, O my *G*;
42:1 so my soul pants for you, O *G*.
42:2 thirsts for *G*, for the living *G*.
42:5 Put your hope in *G*,
42:8 a prayer to the *G* of my life.
42:11 Put your hope in *G*,
43:4 to *G*, my joy and my delight.
44:8 In *G* we make our boast all day
45:6 O *G*, will last for ever and ever;
45:7 therefore *G*, your *G*, has set you
46:1 *G* is our refuge and strength,
46:5 *G* will help her at break of day.
46:10 "Be still, and know that I am *G*;
47:1 shout to *G* with cries of joy.
47:6 Sing praises to *G*, sing praises;
47:7 For *G* is the King of all the earth;
48:9 Within your temple, O *G*,
49:7 or give to *G* a ransom for him —
50:2 *G* shines forth.
50:3 Our *G* comes and will not be silent;
51:1 Have mercy on me, O *G*,
51:10 Create in me a pure heart, O *G*,
51:17 O *G*, you will not despise.
53:2 any who seek *G*.
54:4 Surely *G* is my help;
55:19 *G*, who is enthroned forever,
56:4 In *G*, whose word I praise,
56:10 In *G*, whose word I praise,
56:13 that I may walk before *G*
57:3 *G* sends his love and his
57:7 My heart is steadfast, O *G*,
59:17 are my fortress, my loving *G*.
62:1 My soul finds rest in *G* alone;
62:7 my honor depend on *G*;
62:8 for *G* is our refuge.
62:11 One thing *G* has spoken,
63:1 O *G*, you are my *G*,
65:5 O *G* our Savior,
66:1 Shout with joy to *G*, all the earth!
66:3 Say to *G*, "How awesome are your
66:5 Come and see what *G* has done,
66:16 listen, all you who fear *G*;
66:20 Praise be to *G*,
68:4 Sing to *G*, sing praise to his name,
68:6 *G* sets the lonely in families,
68:20 Our *G* is a *G* who saves;

Ps 68: 24 has come into view, O *G*,
68: 35 You are awesome, O *G*,
69: 5 You know my folly, O *G*;
70: 1 Hasten, O *G*, to save me;
70: 4 "Let *G* be exalted!"
70: 5 come quickly to me, O *G*.
71: 17 my youth, O *G*, you have taught
71: 18 do not forsake me, O *G*,
71: 19 reaches to the skies, O *G*,
71: 22 harp for your faithfulness, O my *G*;
73: 17 me till I entered the sanctuary of *G*;
73: 26 but *G* is the strength of my heart
76: 11 Make vows to the LORD your *G*
77: 13 What *g* is so great as our God?
77: 14 You are the *G* who performs
78: 19 Can *G* spread a table in the desert?
79: 9 Help us, O *G* our Savior,
81: 1 Sing for joy to *G* our strength;
82: 1 *G* presides in the great assembly;
84: 2 out for the living *G*.
84: 10 a doorkeeper in the house of my *G*
84: 11 For the LORD *G* is a sun
86: 12 O Lord my *G*, with all my heart;
86: 15 a compassionate and gracious *G*,
87: 3 O city of *G*: *Selah*
89: 7 of the holy ones *G* is greatly feared;
90: 2 to everlasting you are *G*.
91: 2 my *G*, in whom I trust."
94: 22 my *G* the rock in whom I take
95: 7 for he is our *G*
99: 8 you were to Israel a forgiving *G*,
99: 9 Exalt the LORD our *G*
100: 3 Know that the LORD is *G*.
108: 1 My heart is steadfast, O *G*;
113: 5 Who is like the LORD our *G*,
115: 3 Our *G* is in heaven;
116: 5 our *G* is full of compassion.
123: 2 look to the LORD our *G*,
136: 2 Give thanks to the *G* of gods.
136: 26 Give thanks to the *G* of heaven.
139: 17 to me are your thoughts, O *G*!
139: 23 Search me, O *G*, and know my
143: 10 for you are my *G*;
144: 2 He is my loving *G* and my fortress,
147: 1 is to sing praises to our *G*,
Pr 3: 4 in the sight of *G* and man.
14: 31 to the needy honors *G*.
25: 2 of *G* to conceal a matter;
30: 5 "Every word of *G* is flawless;
Ecc 2: 26 *G* gives wisdom, knowledge
3: 11 cannot fathom what *G* has done
3: 13 in all his toil — this is the gift of *G*.
3: 14 *G* does it so that men will revere him.
5: 4 When you make a vow to *G*,
5: 19 in his work — this is a gift of *G*.
8: 12 who are reverent before *G*.
11: 5 cannot understand the work of *G*,
12: 7 the spirit returns to *G* who gave it.
12: 13 Fear *G* and keep his
Isa 5: 16 the holy *G* will show himself holy
9: 6 Wonderful Counselor, Mighty *G*,
12: 2 Surely *G* is my salvation;
25: 9 "Surely this is our *G*;
28: 11 *G* will speak to this people,
29: 23 will stand in awe of the *G* of Israel.
30: 18 For the LORD is a *G* of justice.
35: 4 your *G* will come,
37: 16 you alone are *G* over all
40: 1 says your *G*.
40: 3 a highway for our *G*.
40: 8 the word of our *G* stands forever."
40: 18 then, will you compare *G*?
40: 28 The LORD is the everlasting *G*,
41: 10 not be dismayed, for I am your *G*.
41: 13 For I am the LORD, your *G*,
43: 10 Before me no *g* was formed,
44: 6 apart from me there is no *G*.
44: 15 he also fashions a *g* and worships it;
45: 18 he is *G*;
48: 17 "I am the LORD your *G*,
52: 7 "Your *G* reigns!"
52: 12 *G* of Israel will be your rear guard.
55: 7 to our *G*, for he will freely pardon.
57: 21 says my *G*, "for the wicked."
59: 2 you from your *G*;
60: 19 and your *G* will be your glory.
61: 2 and the day of vengeance of our *G*,
61: 10 my soul rejoices in my *G*.
62: 5 so will your *G* rejoice over you.
Jer 7: 23 I will be your *G* and you will be my
10: 10 But the LORD is the true *G*;
10: 12 But *G* made the earth by his power;
23: 23 "Am I only a *G* nearby,"
23: 36 distort the words of the living *G*,
31: 33 I will be their *G*,
Jer 32: 27 "I am the LORD, the *G*
42: 6 for we will obey the LORD our *G*."
51: 10 what the LORD our *G* has done.'
51: 56 For the LORD is a *G* of retribution
Eze 28: 13 the garden of *G*;
34: 31 and I am your *G*, declares
Da 2: 28 there is a *G* in heaven who reveals
3: 17 the *G* we serve is able to save us
3: 29 for no other *g* can save in this way
6: 16 "May your *G*, whom you serve
9: 4 O Lord, the great and awesome *G*,
10: 12 to humble yourself before your *G*,
11: 36 things against the *G* of gods.
Hos 1: 9 my people, and I am not your *G*.
1: 10 will be called 'sons of the living *G*.'
4: 6 you have ignored the law of your *G*
6: 6 acknowledgment of *G* rather
9: 8 The prophet, along with my *G*,
12: 6 and wait for your *G* always.
Joel 2: 13 Return to the LORD your *G*,
2: 23 rejoice in the LORD your *G*,
Am 4: 12 prepare to meet your *G*, O Israel."
4: 13 the LORD *G* Almighty is his name
Jnh 1: 6 Get up and call on your *g*!
4: 2 a gracious and compassionate *G*,
Mic 6: 8 and to walk humbly with your *G*.
7: 7 I wait for *G* my Savior;
7: 18 Who is a *G* like you,
Na 1: 2 LORD is a jealous and avenging *G*;
Hab 3: 18 I will be joyful in *G* my Savior.
Zep 3: 17 The LORD your *G* is with you,
Zec 14: 5 Then the LORD my *G* will come,
Mal 2: 10 Father? Did not one *G* create us?
2: 16 says the LORD *G* of Israel,
3: 8 Will a man rob *G*? Yet you rob me.
Mt 1: 23 which means, "*G* with us."
4: 4 comes from the mouth of *G*.'"
4: 7 'Do not put the Lord your *G*
4: 10 'Worship the Lord your *G*,
5: 8 for they will see *G*.
6: 24 You cannot serve both *G*
19: 6 Therefore what *G* has joined
19: 26 but with *G* all things are possible."
22: 21 and to *G* what is God's."
22: 32 He is not the *G* of the dead
22: 37 "'Love the Lord your *G*
27: 46 which means, "My *G*, my *G*,
Mk 2: 7 Who can forgive sins but *G* alone?"
7: 13 Thus you nullify the word of *G*
10: 6 of creation *G* 'made them male
10: 9 Therefore what *G* has joined
10: 18 "No one is good — except *G* alone.
10: 27 all things are possible with *G*."
11: 22 "Have faith in *G*," Jesus answered.
12: 17 and to *G* what is God's."
12: 29 the Lord our *G*, the Lord is one.
12: 30 Love the Lord your *G*
15: 34 which means, "My *G*, my *G*,
16: 19 and he sat at the right hand of *G*.
Lk 1: 30 Mary, you have found favor with *G*
1: 37 For nothing is impossible with *G*."
1: 47 my spirit rejoices in *G* my Savior,
2: 14 "Glory to *G* in the highest,
2: 52 and in favor with *G* and men.
4: 8 'Worship the Lord your *G*
5: 21 Who can forgive sins but *G* alone?"
8: 39 tell how much *G* has done for you."
10: 9 'The kingdom of *G* is near you.'
10: 27 "'Love the Lord your *G*
13: 18 "What is the kingdom of *G* like?
18: 19 "No one is good — except *G* alone.
18: 27 with men is possible with *G*."
20: 25 and to *G* what is God's."
20: 38 He is not the *G* of the dead,
22: 69 at the right hand of the mighty *G*."
Jn 1: 1 was with *G*, and the Word was *G*.
1: 18 ever seen *G*, but *G* the One and Only,
1: 29 Lamb of *G*, who takes away the sin
3: 16 "For *G* so loved the world that he
3: 34 the one whom *G* has sent speaks
4: 24 *G* is spirit, and his worshipers must
5: 44 praise that comes from the only *G*?
6: 29 answered, "The work of *G* is this:
7: 17 my teaching comes from *G* or
8: 42 to them, "If *G* were your Father,
8: 47 belongs to *G* hears what *G* says.
11: 40 you would see the glory of *G*?"
13: 3 from *G* and was returning to *G*;
13: 31 of Man glorified and *G* is glorified
14: 1 Trust in *G*; trust also in me.
17: 3 the only true *G*, and Jesus Christ,
20: 17 your Father, to my *G* and your *G*
20: 28 "My Lord and my *G*!"
20: 31 the Son of *G*, and that
Ac 2: 11 wonders of *G* in our own tongues!"
Ac 2: 24 But *G* raised him from the dead,
2: 33 Exalted to the right hand of *G*,
2: 36 *G* has made this Jesus, whom you
3: 15 but *G* raised him from the dead.
3: 19 Repent, then, and turn to *G*,
4: 31 and spoke the word of *G* boldly.
5: 4 You have not lied to men but to *G*
5: 29 "We must obey *G* rather than men!
5: 31 *G* exalted him to his own right
5: 32 whom *G* has given
7: 55 to heaven and saw the glory of *G*,
8: 21 your heart is not right before *G*.
11: 9 anything impure that *G* has made
12: 24 But the word of *G* continued
13: 32 What *G* promised our fathers he
15: 10 to test *G* by putting on the necks
17: 23 TO AN UNKNOWN *G*.
17: 30 In the past *G* overlooked such
20: 27 to you the whole will of *G*.
20: 32 "Now I commit you to *G*
24: 16 keep my conscience clear before *G*
Ro 1: 16 the power of *G* for the salvation
1: 17 a righteousness from *G* is revealed,
1: 18 The wrath of *G* is being revealed
1: 24 Therefore *G* gave them
1: 26 *G* gave them over to shameful lusts
2: 11 For *G* does not show favoritism.
2: 16 when *G* will judge men's secrets
3: 4 Let *G* be true, and every man a liar.
3: 19 world held accountable to *G*.
3: 23 and fall short of the glory of *G*,
3: 29 Is *G* the *G* of Jews only? Is he not
4: 3 say? "Abraham believed *G*,
4: 6 to whom *G* credits righteousness
4: 17 the *G* who gives life to the dead
4: 24 to whom *G* will credit
5: 1 we have peace with *G*
5: 5 because *G* has poured out his love
5: 8 *G* demonstrates his own love for us
6: 22 and have become slaves to *G*,
6: 23 but the gift of *G* is eternal life
8: 7 the sinful mind is hostile to *G*.
8: 17 heirs of *G* and co-heirs with Christ,
8: 28 in all things *G* works for the good
9: 14 What then shall we say? Is *G* unjust
9: 18 Therefore *G* has mercy
10: 9 in your heart that *G* raised him
11: 2 *G* did not reject his people,
11: 22 the kindness and sternness of *G*:
11: 32 For *G* has bound all men
13: 1 exist have been established by *G*.
14: 12 give an account of himself to *G*.
16: 20 *G* of peace will soon crush Satan
1Co 1: 18 are being saved it is the power of *G*.
1: 20 Has not *G* made foolish
1: 25 For the foolishness of *G* is wiser
1: 27 But *G* chose the foolish things
2: 9 what *G* has prepared
2: 11 of *G* except the Spirit of *G*.
3: 6 watered it, but *G* made it grow.
3: 17 God's temple, *G* will destroy
6: 20 Therefore honor *G* with your body.
7: 7 each man has his own gift from *G*;
7: 15 *G* has called us to live in peace.
7: 20 was in when *G* called him.
7: 24 each man, as responsible to *G*,
8: 3 man who loves *G* is known by *G*.
8: 8 food does not bring us near to *G*;
10: 13 *G* is faithful; he will not let you be
10: 31 do it all for the glory of *G*.
12: 24 But *G* has combined the members
14: 33 For *G* is not a *G* of disorder
15: 24 over the kingdom to *G* the Father
15: 28 so that *G* may be all in all.
15: 34 are some who are ignorant of *G* —
15: 57 be to *G*! He gives us the victory
2Co 1: 9 rely on ourselves but on *G*,
2: 14 be to *G*, who always leads us
2: 15 For we are to *G* the aroma of Christ
2: 17 we do not peddle the word of *G*
3: 5 but our competence comes from *G*.
4: 2 nor do we distort the word of *G*.
4: 7 this all-surpassing power is from *G*
5: 5 Now it is *G* who has made us
5: 19 that *G* was reconciling the world
5: 20 though *G* were making his appeal
5: 21 *G* made him who had no sin
6: 16 we are the temple of the living *G*.
9: 7 for *G* loves a cheerful giver.
9: 8 *G* is able to make all grace abound
10: 13 to the field *G* has assigned to us,
Gal 2: 6 *G* does not judge by external
3: 5 Does *G* give you his Spirit
3: 6 Abraham: "He believed *G*,
3: 11 justified before *G* by the law,

Gal 3: 26 You are all sons of *G* through faith
6: 7 not be deceived: *G* cannot be
Eph 1: 22 *G* placed all things under his feet
2: 8 it is the gift of *G* — not by works,
2: 10 which *G* prepared in advance for us
2: 22 in which *G* lives by his Spirit.
4: 6 one baptism; one *G* and Father
4: 24 to be like *G* in true righteousness
5: 1 Be imitators of *G*, therefore,
6: 6 doing the will of *G* from your heart.
Php 2: 6 Who, being in very nature *G*,
2: 9 Therefore *G* exalted him
2: 13 for it is *G* who works in you to will
4: 7 peace of *G*, which transcends all
4: 19 And my *G* will meet all your needs
Col 1: 19 For *G* was pleased
2: 13 *G* made you alive with Christ.
1Th 2: 4 trying to please men but *G*,
2: 13 but as it actually is, the word of *G*,
3: 9 How can we thank *G* enough
4: 7 For *G* did not call us to be impure,
4: 9 taught by *G* to love each other.
5: 9 For *G* did not appoint us
1Ti 2: 5 one mediator between *G* and men,
4: 4 For everything *G* created is good,
5: 4 for this is pleasing to *G*.
2Ti 1: 6 you to fan into flame the gift of *G*,
Tit 1: 2 which *G*, who does not lie,
2: 13 glorious appearing of our great *G*
Heb 1: 1 In the past *G* spoke
3: 4 but *G* is the builder of everything.
4: 4 "And on the seventh day *G* rested
4: 12 For the word of *G* is living
6: 10 *G* is not unjust; he will not forget
6: 18 in which it is impossible for *G* to lie
7: 19 by which we draw near to *G*.
7: 25 come to *G* through him,
10: 22 draw near to *G* with a sincere heart
10: 31 to fall into the hands of the living *G*
11: 5 commended as one who pleased *G*.
11: 6 faith it is impossible to please *G*,
12: 7 as discipline; *G* is treating you
12: 10 but *G* disciplines us for our good,
12: 29 for our "*G* is a consuming fire."
13: 15 offer to *G* a sacrifice of praise —
Jas 1: 12 crown of life that *G* has promised
1: 13 For *G* cannot be tempted by evil,
1: 27 Religion that *G* our Father accepts
2: 19 You believe that there is one *G*.
2: 23 "Abraham believed *G*,
4: 4 the world becomes an enemy of *G*.
4: 6 "*G* opposes the proud
4: 8 Come near to *G* and he will come
1Pe 1: 23 the living and enduring word of *G*.
2: 20 this is commendable before *G*.
3: 18 the unrighteous, to bring you to *G*.
4: 11 it with the strength *G* provides,
5: 5 because, "*G* opposes the proud
2Pe 1: 21 but men spoke from *G*
2: 4 For if *G* did not spare angels
1Jn 1: 5 *G* is light; in him there is no
2: 17 the will of *G* lives forever.
3: 1 we should be called children of *G*!
3: 9 born of *G* will continue to sin,
3: 10 we know who the children of *G* are
3: 20 For *G* is greater than our hearts,
4: 7 for love comes from *G*.
4: 8 not know *G*, because *G* is love.
4: 9 This is how *G* showed his love
4: 11 Dear friends, since *G* so loved us,
4: 12 No one has ever seen *G*;
4: 15 *G* lives in him and he in *G*.
4: 16 *G* is love.
4: 20 "I love *G*," yet hates his brother,
4: 21 Whoever loves *G* must
5: 2 that we love the children of *G*:
5: 3 love for *G*: to obey his commands.
5: 4 born of *G* overcomes the world.
5: 10 does not believe *G* has made him
5: 14 have in approaching *G*:
5: 18 born of *G* does not continue to sin;
Rev 4: 8 holy is the Lord *G* Almighty,
7: 12 be to our *G* for ever and ever.
7: 17 *G* will wipe away every tear
11: 16 fell on their faces and worshiped *G*,
15: 3 Lord *G* Almighty.
17: 17 For *G* has put it into their hearts
19: 6 For our Lord *G* Almighty reigns.
21: 3 Now the dwelling of *G* is with men,
21: 23 for the glory of *G* gives it light,

GOD-BREATHED* (BREATH)
2Ti 3: 16 All Scripture is *G* and is useful

GOD-FEARING* (FEAR)
Ecc 8: 12 that it will go better with *G* men,

Ac 2: 5 staying in Jerusalem *G* Jews
10: 2 all his family were devout and *G*;
10: 22 He is a righteous and *G* man,
13: 26 of Abraham, and you *G* Gentiles,
13: 50 But the Jews incited the *G* women
17: 4 as did a large number of *G* Greeks
17: 17 with the Jews and the *G* Greeks,

GOD-HATERS* (HATE)
Ro 1: 30 They are gossips, slanderers, *G*,

GOD'S (GOD)
2Ch 20: 15 For the battle is not yours, but *G*.
Job 37: 14 stop and consider *G* wonders.
Ps 52: 8 I trust in *G* unfailing love
69: 30 I will praise *G* name in song
Mk 3: 35 Whoever does *G* will is my brother
Jn 7: 17 If anyone chooses to do *G* will,
10: 36 'I am *G* Son'? Do not believe me
Ro 2: 3 think you will escape *G* judgment?
2: 4 not realizing that *G* kindness leads
3: 3 lack of faith nullify *G* faithfulness?
7: 22 in my inner being I delight in *G* law
9: 16 or effort, but on *G* mercy.
11: 29 for *G* gifts and his call are
12: 2 and approve what *G* will is —
12: 13 Share with *G* people who are
13: 6 for the authorities are *G* servants,
1Co 7: 19 Keeping *G* commands is what
2Co 6: 2 now is the time of *G* favor,
Eph 1: 7 riches of *G* grace that he lavished
1Th 4: 3 It is *G* will that you should be sanctified;
5: 18 for this is *G* will for you
1Ti 6: 1 so that *G* name and our teaching
2Ti 2: 19 *G* solid foundation stands firm,
Tit 1: 7 overseer is entrusted with *G* work,
Heb 1: 3 The Son is the radiance of *G* glory
9: 24 now to appear for us in *G* presence.
11: 3 was formed at *G* command,
1Pe 2: 15 For it is *G* will that
3: 4 which is of great worth in *G* sight.
1Jn 2: 5 *G* love is truly made complete

GODLESS
Job 20: 5 the joy of the *g* lasts but a moment.
1Ti 6: 20 Turn away from *g* chatter

GODLINESS (GOD)
1Ti 2: 2 and quiet lives in all *g* and holiness.
4: 8 but *g* has value for all things,
6: 5 and who think that *g* is a means
6: 6 *g* with contentment is great gain.
6: 11 and pursue righteousness, *g*, faith,
2Pe 1: 6 and to perseverance, *g*;

GODLY (GOD)
Ps 4: 3 that the LORD has set apart the *g*
2Co 7: 10 *G* sorrow brings repentance that
11: 2 jealous for you with a *g* jealousy.
2Ti 3: 12 everyone who wants to live a *g* life
2Pe 3: 11 You ought to live holy and *g* lives

GODS (GOD)
Ex 20: 3 "You shall have no other *g*
Dt 5: 7 "You shall have no other *g*
1Ch 16: 26 For all the *g* of the nations are idols
Ps 82: 6 "I said, 'You are "*g*";
Jn 10: 34 have said you are *g*'? If he called
Ac 19: 26 He says that man-made *g* are no *g*.

GOG
Eze 38: 18 When *G* attacks the land of Israel,
Rev 20: 8 *G* and Magog — to gather them

GOLD
1Ki 20: 3 'Your silver and *g* are mine,
Job 22: 25 then the Almighty will be your *g*,
23: 10 tested me, I will come forth as *g*.
28: 15 cannot be bought with the finest *g*,
31: 24 "If I have put my trust in *g*
Ps 19: 10 They are more precious than *g*,
119: 127 more than *g*, more than pure *g*,
Pr 3: 14 and yields better returns than *g*.
22: 1 esteemed is better than silver or *g*.
Hag 2: 8 The silver is mine and the *g* is mine
Mt 2: 11 and presented him with gifts of *g*
Rev 3: 18 to buy from me *g* refined in the fire,

GOLGOTHA*
Mt 27: 33 to a place called *G* (which means
Mk 15: 22 to the place called *G* (which means
Jn 19: 17 (which in Aramaic is called *G*).

GOLIATH
Philistine giant killed by David (1Sa 17; 21:9).

GOMORRAH
Ge 19: 24 sulfur on Sodom and *G* —
Mt 10: 15 and *G* on the day of judgment

2Pe 2: 6 and *G* by burning them to ashes,
Jude : 7 *G* and the surrounding towns gave

GOOD
Ge 1: 4 God saw that the light was *g*,
1: 10 And God saw that it was *g*.
1: 12 And God saw that it was *g*.
1: 18 And God saw that it was *g*.
1: 21 And God saw that it was *g*.
1: 25 And God saw that it was *g*.
1: 31 he had made, and it was very *g*.
2: 9 and the tree of the knowledge of *g*
2: 9 pleasing to the eye and *g* for food.
2: 18 "It is not *g* for the man to be alone.
3: 22 become like one of us, knowing *g*
50: 20 but God intended it for *g*
2Ch 7: 3 "He is *g*; / his love endures
31: 20 doing what was *g* and right
Job 2: 10 Shall we accept *g* from God,
Ps 14: 1 there is no one who does *g*.
34: 8 Taste and see that the LORD is *g*;
34: 14 Turn from evil and do *g*;
37: 3 Trust in the LORD and do *g*;
37: 27 Turn from evil and do *g*;
52: 9 for your name is *g*.
53: 3 there is no one who does *g*,
84: 11 no *g* thing does he withhold
86: 5 You are forgiving and *g*, O Lord
100: 5 For the LORD is *g* and his love
103: 5 satisfies your desires with *g* things,
112: 5 *G* will come to him who is
119: 68 You are *g*, and what you do is *g*;
133: 1 How *g* and pleasant it is
145: 9 The LORD is *g* to all;
147: 1 How *g* it is to sing praises
Pr 3: 4 you will win favor and a *g* name
3: 27 Do not withhold *g*
11: 27 He who seeks *g* finds *g* will,
13: 22 A *g* man leaves an inheritance
14: 22 those who plan what is *g* find love
15: 3 on the wicked and the *g*.
15: 23 and how *g* is a timely word!
15: 30 *g* news gives health to the bones.
17: 22 A cheerful heart is *g* medicine,
18: 22 He who finds a wife finds what is *g*
19: 2 It is not *g* to have zeal
22: 1 A *g* name is more desirable
31: 12 She brings him *g*, not harm,
Ecc 12: 14 whether it is *g* or evil.
Isa 5: 20 Woe to those who call evil *g*
40: 9 You who bring *g* tidings
52: 7 the feet of those who bring *g* news,
61: 1 me to preach *g* news to the poor.
Jer 6: 16 ask where the *g* way is,
13: 23 Neither can you do *g*
32: 39 the *g* of their children after them.
Eze 34: 14 I will tend them in a *g* pasture,
Mic 6: 8 has showed you, O man, what is *g*.
Na 1: 15 the feet of one who brings *g* news,
Mt 5: 45 sun to rise on the evil and the *g*,
7: 11 Father in heaven give *g* gifts
7: 17 Likewise every *g* tree bears *g* fruit,
7: 18 A *g* tree cannot bear bad fruit,
12: 35 The *g* man brings *g* things out
13: 8 Still other seed fell on *g* soil,
13: 24 is like a man who sowed *g* seed
13: 48 and collected the *g* fish in baskets,
19: 17 "There is only One who is *g*.
22: 10 both *g* and bad, and the wedding
25: 21 'Well done, *g* and faithful servant!
Mk 1: 15 Repent and believe the *g* news!"
3: 4 lawful on the Sabbath: to do *g*
4: 8 Still other seed fell on *g* soil.
8: 36 What *g* is it for a man
10: 18 "No one is *g* — except God alone.
16: 15 preach the *g* news to all creation.
Lk 2: 10 I bring you *g* news
3: 9 does not produce *g* fruit will be
6: 27 do *g* to those who hate you,
6: 43 nor does a bad tree bear *g* fruit.
6: 45 The *g* man brings *g* things out
8: 8 Still other seed fell on *g* soil.
9: 25 What *g* is it for a man
14: 34 "Salt is *g*, but if it loses its saltiness,
18: 19 "No one is *g* — except God alone.
19: 17 "'Well done, my *g* servant!'
Jn 10: 11 "I am the *g* shepherd.
Ro 3: 12 there is no one who does *g*,
7: 12 is holy, righteous and *g*.
7: 16 want to do, I agree that the law is *g*.
7: 18 I have the desire to do what is *g*,
8: 28 for the *g* of those who love him,
10: 15 feet of those who bring *g* news!"
12: 2 his *g*, pleasing and perfect will.
12: 9 Hate what is evil; cling to what is *g*.
13: 4 For he is God's servant to do you *g*

Ro 16: 19 you to be wise about what is *g*,
1Co 7: 1 It is *g* for a man not to marry.
10: 24 should seek his own *g*, but the *g*
15: 33 Bad company corrupts *g* character
2Co 9: 8 you will abound in every *g* work.
Gal 4: 18 provided the purpose is *g*,
6: 9 us not become weary in doing *g*,
6: 10 as we have opportunity, let us do *g*
Eph 2: 10 in Christ Jesus to do *g* works,
6: 8 everyone for whatever *g* he does,
Php 1: 6 that he who began a *g* work
Col 1: 10 bearing fruit in every *g* work,
1Th 5: 21 Hold on to the *g*.
1Ti 3: 7 have a *g* reputation with outsiders,
4: 4 For everything God created is *g*,
6: 12 Fight the *g* fight of the faith.
6: 18 them to do *g*, to be rich in *g* deeds,
2Ti 3: 17 equipped for every *g* work.
4: 7 I have fought the *g* fight, I have
Tit 1: 8 loves what is *g*, who is
2: 7 an example by doing what is *g*.
2: 14 his very own, eager to do what is *g*.
Heb 5: 14 to distinguish *g* from evil.
10: 24 on toward love and *g* deeds.
12: 10 but God disciplines us for our *g*,
13: 16 do not forget to do *g* and to share
Jas 4: 17 who knows the *g* he ought to do
1Pe 2: 3 you have tasted that the Lord is *g*.
2: 12 Live such *g* lives among the pagans
2: 18 not only to those who are *g*
3: 17 to suffer for doing *g*

GOODS
Ecc 5: 11 As *g* increase,

GORGE
Pr 23: 20 or *g* themselves on meat,

GOSHEN
Ge 45: 10 You shall live in the region of *G*
Ex 8: 22 differently with the land of *G*,

GOSPEL
Ro 1: 16 I am not ashamed of the *g*,
15: 16 duty of proclaiming the *g* of God,
15: 20 to preach the *g* where Christ was
1Co 1: 17 to preach the *g* — not with words
9: 12 rather than hinder the *g* of Christ.
9: 14 who preach the *g* should receive
9: 16 Woe to me if I do not preach the *g*!
15: 1 you of the *g* I preached to you,
15: 2 By this *g* you are saved,
2Co 4: 4 light of the *g* of the glory of Christ,
9: 13 your confession of the *g*
Gal 1: 7 a different *g* — which is really no *g*
Eph 6: 15 comes from the *g* of peace.
Php 1: 27 in a manner worthy of the *g*
Col 1: 23 This is the *g* that you heard
1Th 2: 4 by God to be entrusted with the *g*.
2Th 1: 8 do not obey the *g* of our Lord Jesus
2Ti 1: 10 immortality to light through the *g*.
Rev 14: 6 he had the eternal *g* to proclaim

GOSSIP*
Pr 11: 13 A *g* betrays a confidence,
16: 28 and a *g* separates close friends.
18: 8 of a *g* are like choice morsels;
20: 19 A *g* betrays a confidence;
26: 20 without *g* a quarrel dies down.
26: 22 of a *g* are like choice morsels;
2Co 12: 20 slander, *g*, arrogance and disorder.

GOVERN (GOVERNMENT)
Ge 1: 16 the greater light to *g* the day
Job 34: 17 Can he who hates justice *g*?
Ro 12: 8 it is leadership, let him *g* diligently;

GOVERNMENT (GOVERN)
Isa 9: 6 and the *g* will be on his shoulders.

GRACE* (GRACIOUS)
Ps 45: 2 lips have been anointed with *g*,
Pr 1: 9 will be a garland to *g* your head
3: 22 an ornament to *g* your neck.
3: 34 but gives *g* to the humble.
4: 9 She will set a garland of *g*
Isa 26: 10 Though *g* is shown to the wicked,
Jnh 2: 8 forfeit the *g* that could be theirs.
Zec 12: 10 of Jerusalem a spirit of *g*
Lk 2: 40 and the *g* of God was upon him.
Jn 1: 14 who came from the Father, full of *g*
1: 16 of his *g* we have all received one
1: 17 *g* and truth came through Jesus
Ac 4: 33 and much *g* was upon them all.
6: 8 a man full of God's *g* and power,
11: 23 saw the evidence of the *g* of God,
13: 43 them to continue in the *g* of God.
14: 3 message of his *g* by enabling them
Ac 14: 26 they had been committed to the *g*
15: 11 We believe it is through the *g*
15: 40 by the brothers to the *g* of the Lord
18: 27 to those who by *g* had believed.
20: 24 testifying to the gospel of God's *g*.
20: 32 to God and to the word of his *g*,
Ro 1: 5 we received *g* and apostleship
1: 7 *G* and peace to you
3: 24 and are justified freely by his *g*
4: 16 be by *g* and may be guaranteed
5: 2 access by faith into this *g*
5: 15 came by the *g* of the one man,
5: 15 how much more did God's *g*
5: 17 God's abundant provision of *g*
5: 20 where sin increased, *g* increased all
5: 21 also *g* might reign
6: 1 on sinning so that *g* may increase?
6: 14 you are not under law, but under *g*.
6: 15 we are not under law but under *g*?
11: 5 there is a remnant chosen by *g*.
11: 6 if by *g*, then it is no longer by works
11: 6 if it were, *g* would no longer be *g*.
12: 3 For by the *g* given me I say
12: 6 according to the *g* given us.
15: 15 because of the *g* God gave me
16: 20 The *g* of our Lord Jesus be
1Co 1: 3 *G* and peace to you
1: 4 of his *g* given you in Christ Jesus.
3: 10 By the *g* God has given me,
15: 10 But by the *g* of God I am what I am
15: 10 but the *g* of God that was with me.
15: 10 his *g* to me was not without effect.
16: 23 The *g* of the Lord Jesus be with you
2Co 1: 2 *G* and peace to you
1: 12 wisdom but according to God's *g*.
4: 15 so that the *g* that is reaching more
6: 1 not to receive God's *g* in vain.
8: 1 to know about the *g* that God has
8: 6 also to completion this act of *g*
8: 7 also excel in this *g* of giving.
8: 9 For you know the *g*
9: 8 able to make all *g* abound to you,
9: 14 of the surpassing *g* God has given
12: 9 "My *g* is sufficient for you,
13: 14 May the *g* of the Lord Jesus Christ,
Gal 1: 3 *G* and peace to you
1: 6 the one who called you by the *g*
1: 15 from birth and called me by his *g*,
2: 9 when they recognized the *g* given
2: 21 I do not set aside the *g* of God,
3: 18 God in his *g* gave it to Abraham
5: 4 you have fallen away from *g*.
6: 18 The *g* of our Lord Jesus Christ be
Eph 1: 2 *G* and peace to you
1: 6 to the praise of his glorious *g*,
1: 7 riches of God's *g* that he lavished
2: 5 it is by *g* you have been saved.
2: 7 the incomparable riches of his *g*,
2: 8 For it is by *g* you have been saved,
3: 2 of God's *g* that was given to me
3: 7 by the gift of God's *g* given me
3: 8 God's people, this *g* was given me:
4: 7 to each one of us *g* has been given
6: 24 *G* to all who love our Lord Jesus
Php 1: 2 *G* and peace to you
1: 7 all of you share in God's *g* with me.
4: 23 The *g* of the Lord Jesus Christ be
Col 1: 2 *G* and peace to you
1: 6 understood God's *g* in all its truth.
4: 6 conversation be always full of *g*,
4: 18 *G* be with you.
1Th 1: 1 and the Lord Jesus Christ: *G*
5: 28 The *g* of our Lord Jesus Christ be
2Th 1: 2 *G* and peace to you
1: 12 according to the *g* of our God
2: 16 and by his *g* gave us eternal
3: 18 The *g* of our Lord Jesus Christ be
1Ti 1: 2 my true son in the faith: *G*,
1: 14 The *g* of our Lord was poured out
6: 21 *G* be with you.
2Ti 1: 2 To Timothy, my dear son: *G*,
1: 9 This *g* was given us in Christ Jesus
1: 9 because of his own purpose and *g*.
2: 1 be strong in the *g* that is
4: 22 *G* be with you.
Tit 1: 4 *G* and peace from God the Father
2: 11 For the *g* of God that brings
3: 7 having been justified by his *g*,
3: 15 *G* be with you all.
Phm : 3 *G* to you and peace
: 25 The *g* of the Lord Jesus Christ be
Heb 2: 9 that by the *g* of God he might taste
4: 16 find *g* to help us in our time of need
4: 16 the throne of *g* with confidence,
10: 29 and who has insulted the Spirit of *g*
Heb 12: 15 See to it that no one misses the *g*
13: 9 hearts to be strengthened by *g*,
13: 25 *G* be with you all.
Jas 4: 6 but gives *g* to the humble."
4: 6 But he gives us more *g*. That is why
1Pe 1: 2 *G* and peace be yours in abundance
1: 10 who spoke of the *g* that was
1: 13 fully on the *g* to be given you
4: 10 faithfully administering God's *g*
5: 5 but gives *g* to the humble."
5: 10 the God of all *g*, who called you
5: 12 and testifying that this is the true *g*
2Pe 1: 2 *G* and peace be yours in abundance
3: 18 But grow in the *g* and knowledge
2Jn : 3 and will be with us forever: *G*,
Jude : 4 who change the *g* of our God
Rev 1: 4 *G* and peace to you
22: 21 The *g* of the Lord Jesus be

GRACIOUS (GRACE)
Ex 34: 6 the compassionate and *g* God,
Nu 6: 25 and be *g* to you;
Ne 9: 17 But you are a forgiving God, *g*
Ps 67: 1 May God be *g* to us and bless us
Pr 22: 11 a pure heart and whose speech is *g*
Isa 30: 18 Yet the LORD longs to be *g* to you

GRAIN
Lev 2: 1 When someone brings a *g* offering
Lk 17: 35 women will be grinding *g* together;
1Co 9: 9 ox while it is treading out the *g*."

GRANDCHILDREN (CHILD)
1Ti 5: 4 But if a widow has children or *g*,

GRANDMOTHER (MOTHER)
2Ti 1: 5 which first lived in your *g* Lois

GRANT (GRANTED)
Ps 20: 5 May the LORD *g* all your requests
51: 12 *g* me a willing spirit, to sustain me.

GRANTED (GRANT)
Pr 10: 24 what the righteous desire will be *g*.
Mt 15: 28 great faith! Your request is *g*."
Php 1: 29 For it has been *g* to you on behalf

GRAPES
Nu 13: 23 branch bearing a single cluster of *g*.
Jer 31: 29 'The fathers have eaten sour *g*,
Eze 18: 2 "'The fathers eat sour *g*,
Mt 7: 16 Do people pick *g* from thornbushes
Rev 14: 18 and gather the clusters of *g*

GRASPED
Php 2: 6 with God something to be *g*,

GRASS
Ps 103: 15 As for man, his days are like *g*,
Isa 40: 6 "All men are like *g*,
Mt 6: 30 If that is how God clothes the *g*
1Pe 1: 24 "All men are like *g*,

GRASSHOPPERS
Nu 13: 33 We seemed like *g* in our own eyes,

GRATIFY* (GRATITUDE)
Ro 13: 14 think about how to *g* the desires
Gal 5: 16 and you will not *g* the desires

GRATITUDE (GRATIFY)
Col 3: 16 and spiritual songs with *g*

GRAVE (GRAVES)
Nu 19: 16 who touches a human bone or a *g*,
Dt 34: 6 day no one knows where his *g* is.
Ps 5: 9 Their throat is an open *g*;
49: 15 will redeem my life from the *g*;
Pr 7: 27 Her house is a highway to the *g*,
Hos 13: 14 Where, O *g*, is your destruction?
Jn 11: 44 "Take off the *g* clothes
Ac 2: 27 you will not abandon me to the *g*,

GRAVES (GRAVE)
Eze 37: 12 I am going to open your *g*
Jn 5: 28 are in their *g* will hear his voice
Ro 3: 13 "Their throats are open *g*;

GRAY
Pr 16: 31 *G* hair is a crown of splendor;
20: 29 *g* hair the splendor of the old.

GREAT (GREATER GREATEST GREATNESS)
Ge 12: 2 I will make your name *g*,
12: 2 "I will make you into a *g* nation
Ex 32: 11 out of Egypt with *g* power
Nu 14: 19 In accordance with your *g* love,
Dt 4: 32 so *g* as this ever happened,
10: 17 the *g* God, mighty and awesome,
29: 28 in *g* wrath the LORD uprooted
Jos 7: 9 do for your own *g* name?"

Jdg 16: 5 you the secret of his *g* strength
2Sa 7: 22 "How *g* you are, O Sovereign
22: 36 you stoop down to make me *g*.
24: 14 for his mercy is *g*; but do not let me
1Ch 17: 19 made known all these *g* promises.
Ps 18: 35 you stoop down to make me *g*.
19: 11 in keeping them there is *g* reward.
47: 2 the *g* King over all the earth!
57: 10 For *g* is your love, reaching
68: 11 and *g* was the company
89: 1 of the LORD's *g* love forever;
103: 11 so *g* is his love for those who fear
107: 43 consider the *g* love of the LORD.
108: 4 For *g* is your love, higher
117: 2 For *g* is his love toward us,
119: 165 *G* peace have they who love your
145: 3 *G* is the LORD and most worthy
Pr 22: 1 is more desirable than *g* riches;
23: 24 of a righteous man has *g* joy;
Isa 42: 21 to make his law *g* and glorious.
Jer 27: 5 With my *g* power and outstretched
32: 19 *g* are your purposes and mighty are
La 3: 23 *g* is your faithfulness.
Da 9: 4 "O Lord, the *g* and awesome God,
Joel 2: 11 The day of the LORD is *g*;
2: 20 Surely he has done *g* things.
Zep 1: 14 "The *g* day of the LORD is near—
Mal 1: 11 My name will be *g*
4: 5 the prophet Elijah before that *g*
Mt 20: 26 whoever wants to become *g*
Mk 10: 43 whoever wants to become *g*
Lk 6: 23 because *g* is your reward in heaven.
6: 35 Then your reward will be *g*,
21: 27 in a cloud with power and *g* glory.
Eph 1: 19 and his incomparably *g* power
2: 4 But because of his *g* love for us,
1Ti 6: 6 with contentment is *g* gain.
Tit 2: 13 glorious appearing of our *g* God
Heb 2: 3 if we ignore such a *g* salvation?
1Jn 3: 1 How *g* is the love the Father has
Rev 6: 17 For the *g* day of their wrath has
20: 11 Then I saw a *g* white throne

GREATER (GREAT)
Mt 11: 11 there has not risen anyone *g*
12: 6 I tell you that one *g*
12: 41 and now one *g* than Jonah is here.
12: 42 now one *g* than Solomon is here.
Mk 12: 31 There is no commandment *g*
Jn 1: 50 You shall see *g* things than that."
3: 30 He must become *g*; I must become
14: 12 He will do even *g* things than these
15: 13 *G* love has no one than this,
1Co 12: 31 But eagerly desire the *g* gifts.
2Co 3: 11 how much *g* is the glory
Heb 3: 3 the builder of a house has *g* honor
3: 3 worthy of *g* honor than Moses,
7: 7 lesser person is blessed by the *g*.
11: 26 as of *g* value than the treasures
1Jn 3: 20 For God is *g* than our hearts,
4: 4 is in you is *g* than the one who is

GREATEST (GREAT)
Mt 22: 38 is the first and *g* commandment.
23: 11 *g* among you will be your servant.
Lk 9: 48 least among you all—he is the *g*."
1Co 13: 13 But the *g* of these is love.

GREATNESS* (GREAT)
Ex 15: 7 In the *g* of your majesty
Dt 3: 24 to show to your servant your *g*
32: 3 Oh, praise the *g* of our God!
1Ch 29: 11 O LORD, is the *g* and the power
2Ch 9: 6 half the *g* of your wisdom was told
Est 10: 2 account of the *g* of Mordecai
Ps 145: 3 his *g* no one can fathom.
150: 2 praise him for his surpassing *g*.
Isa 63: 1 forward in the *g* of his strength?
Eze 38: 23 I will show my *g* and my holiness,
Da 4: 22 your *g* has grown until it reaches
5: 18 and *g* and glory and splendor.
7: 27 and *g* of the kingdoms
Mic 5: 4 will live securely, for then his *g*
Lk 9: 43 And they were all amazed at the *g*
Php 3: 8 compared to the surpassing *g*

GREED (GREEDY)
Lk 12: 15 on your guard against all kinds of *g*
Ro 1: 29 kind of wickedness, evil, *g*
Eph 5: 3 or of any kind of impurity, or of *g*,
Col 3: 5 evil desires and *g*, which is idolatry
2Pe 2: 14 experts in *g*—an accursed brood!

GREEDY (GREED)
Pr 15: 27 A *g* man brings trouble
1Co 6: 10 nor thieves nor the *g* nor drunkards
Eph 5: 5 No immoral, impure or *g* person—

1Pe 5: 2 not *g* for money, but eager to serve;

GREEK (GREEKS)
Gal 3: 28 There is neither Jew nor *G*,
Col 3: 11 Here there is no *G* or Jew,

GREEKS (GREEK)
1Co 1: 22 miraculous signs and *G* look

GREEN
Ps 23: 2 makes me lie down in *g* pastures,

GREW (GROW)
Lk 1: 80 And the child *g* and became strong
2: 52 And Jesus *g* in wisdom and stature,
Ac 9: 31 by the Holy Spirit, it *g* in numbers,
16: 5 in the faith and *g* daily in numbers.

GRIEF (GRIEFS GRIEVANCES GRIEVE GRIEVED)
Ps 10: 14 O God, do see trouble and *g*;
Pr 10: 1 but a foolish son *g* to his mother.
14: 13 and joy may end in *g*.
17: 21 To have a fool for a son brings *g*;
Ecc 1: 18 the more knowledge, the more *g*.
La 3: 32 Though he brings *g*, he will show
Jn 16: 20 but your *g* will turn to joy.
1Pe 1: 6 had to suffer *g* in all kinds of trials.

GRIEFS* (GRIEF)
1Ti 6: 10 pierced themselves with many *g*.

GRIEVANCES* (GRIEF)
Col 3: 13 forgive whatever *g* you may have

GRIEVE (GRIEF)
Eph 4: 30 do not *g* the Holy Spirit of God,
1Th 4: 13 or to *g* like the rest of men,

GRIEVED (GRIEF)
Isa 63: 10 and *g* his Holy Spirit.

GRINDING
Lk 17: 35 women will be *g* grain together;

GROAN (GROANING GROANS)
Ro 8: 23 *g* inwardly as we wait eagerly
2Co 5: 4 For while we are in this tent, we *g*

GROANING (GROAN)
Ex 2: 24 God heard their *g* and he
Eze 21: 7 'Why are you *g*?' you shall say,
Ro 8: 22 that the whole creation has been *g*

GROANS (GROAN)
Ro 8: 26 with *g* that words cannot express.

GROUND
Ge 1: 10 God called the dry *g* "land,"
3: 17 "Cursed is the *g* because of you;
4: 10 blood cries out to me from the *g*.
Ex 3: 5 where you are standing is holy *g*."
15: 19 walked through the sea on dry *g*.
Isa 53: 2 and like a root out of dry *g*.
Mt 10: 29 fall to the *g* apart from the will
25: 25 and hid your talent in the *g*.
Jn 8: 6 to write on the *g* with his finger.
Eph 6: 13 you may be able to stand your *g*,

GROW (FULL-GROWN GREW GROWING GROWS)
Pr 13: 11 by little makes it *g*.
20: 13 not love sleep or you will *g* poor;
Isa 40: 31 they will run and not *g* weary,
Mt 6: 28 See how the lilies of the field *g*.
1Co 3: 6 watered it, but God made it *g*.
2Pe 3: 18 But *g* in the grace and knowledge

GROWING (GROW)
Col 1: 6 this gospel is bearing fruit and *g*,
1: 10 *g* in the knowledge of God,
2Th 1: 3 your faith is *g* more and more,

GROWS (GROW)
Eph 4: 16 *g* and builds itself up in love,
Col 2: 19 *g* as God causes it to grow.

GRUMBLE (GRUMBLED GRUMBLERS GRUMBLING)
1Co 10: 10 And do not *g*, as some of them did
Jas 5: 9 Don't *g* against each other,

GRUMBLED (GRUMBLE)
Ex 15: 24 So the people *g* against Moses,
Nu 14: 29 and who has *g* against me.

GRUMBLERS* (GRUMBLE)
Jude : 16 These men are *g* and faultfinders;

GRUMBLING (GRUMBLE)
Jn 6: 43 "Stop *g* among yourselves,"
1Pe 4: 9 to one another without *g*.

GUARANTEE (GUARANTEEING)
Heb 7: 22 Jesus has become the *g*

GUARANTEEING* (GUARANTEE)
2Co 1: 22 as a deposit, *g* what is to come.
5: 5 as a deposit, *g* what is to come.
Eph 1: 14 who is a deposit *g* our inheritance

GUARD (GUARDS)
1Sa 2: 9 He will *g* the feet of his saints,
Ps 141: 3 Set a *g* over my mouth, O LORD;
Pr 2: 11 and understanding will *g* you.
4: 13 *g* it well, for it is your life.
4: 23 Above all else, *g* your heart,
7: 2 *g* my teachings as the apple
Isa 52: 12 the God of Israel will be your rear *g*
Mk 13: 33 Be on *g*! Be alert! You do not know
Lk 12: 1 "Be on your *g* against the yeast
12: 15 Be on your *g* against all kinds
Ac 20: 31 So be on your *g*! Remember that
1Co 16: 13 Be on your *g*; stand firm in the faith
Php 4: 7 will *g* your hearts and your minds
1Ti 6: 20 *g* what has been entrusted
2Ti 1: 14 *G* the good deposit that was

GUARDS (GUARD)
Pr 13: 3 He who *g* his lips *g* his life,
19: 16 who obeys instructions *g* his life,
21: 23 He who *g* his mouth and his tongue
22: 5 he who *g* his soul stays far

GUIDANCE (GUIDE)
Pr 1: 5 and let the discerning get *g*—
11: 14 For lack of *g* a nation falls,
24: 6 for waging war you need *g*,

GUIDE (GUIDANCE GUIDED GUIDES)
Ex 13: 21 of cloud to *g* them on their way
15: 13 In your strength you will *g* them
Ne 9: 19 cease to *g* them on their path,
Ps 25: 5 *g* me in your truth and teach me,
43: 3 let them *g* me;
48: 14 he will be our *g* even to the end.
67: 4 and *g* the nations of the earth.
73: 24 You *g* me with your counsel,
139: 10 even there your hand will *g* me,
Pr 4: 11 I *g* you in the way of wisdom
6: 22 When you walk, they will *g* you;
Isa 58: 11 The LORD will *g* you always;
Jn 16: 13 comes, he will *g* you into all truth.

GUIDED (GUIDE)
Ps 107: 30 he *g* them to their desired haven.

GUIDES (GUIDE)
Ps 23: 3 He *g* me in paths of righteousness
25: 9 He *g* the humble in what is right
Pr 11: 3 The integrity of the upright *g* them,
16: 23 A wise man's heart *g* his mouth,
Mt 23: 16 "Woe to you, blind *g*! You say,
23: 24 You blind *g*! You strain out a gnat

GUILT (GUILTY)
Lev 5: 15 It is a *g* offering.
Ps 32: 5 the *g* of my sin.
38: 4 My *g* has overwhelmed me
Isa 6: 7 your *g* is taken away and your sin
Jer 2: 22 the stain of your *g* is still before me
Eze 18: 19 'Why does the son not share the *g*

GUILTY (GUILT)
Ex 34: 7 does not leave the *g* unpunished;
Mk 3: 29 Spirit will never be forgiven; he is *g*
Jn 8: 46 Can any of you prove me *g* of sin?
1Co 11: 27 in an unworthy manner will be *g*
Heb 10: 2 and would no longer have felt *g*
10: 22 to cleanse us from a *g* conscience
Jas 2: 10 at just one point is *g* of breaking all

HABAKKUK*
Prophet to Judah (Hab 1:1; 3:1).

HABIT
1Ti 5: 13 they get into the *h* of being idle
Heb 10: 25 as some are in the *h* of doing,

HADAD
Edomite adversary of Solomon (1Ki 11:14–25).

HADES*
Mt 16: 18 the gates of *H* will not overcome it.
Rev 1: 18 And I hold the keys of death and *H*
6: 8 *H* was following close behind him.
20: 13 and *H* gave up the dead that were
20: 14 *H* were thrown into the lake of fire.

HAGAR
Servant of Sarah, wife of Abraham, mother of Ishmael (Ge 16:1–6; 25:12). Driven away by Sarah while pregnant (Ge 16:5–16); after birth of Isaac (Ge 21:9–21; Gal 4:21–31).

HAGGAI*
Post-exilic prophet who encouraged rebuilding of the temple (Ezr 5:1; 6:14; Hag 1–2).

HAIL
Ex 9: 19 the *h* will fall on every man
Rev 8: 7 and there came *h* and fire mixed

HAIR (HAIRS HAIRY)
Lev 19: 27 "'Do not cut the *h* at the sides
Nu 6: 5 he must let the *h* of his head grow
Pr 16: 31 Gray *h* is a crown of splendor;
20: 29 gray *h* the splendor of the old.
Lk 7: 44 and wiped them with her *h*.
21: 18 But not a *h* of your head will perish
Jn 11: 2 and wiped his feet with her *h*.
12: 3 and wiped his feet with her *h*.
1Co 11: 6 for a woman to have her *h* cut
11: 6 she should have her *h* cut off;
11: 14 that if a man has long *h*,
11: 15 For long *h* is given to her
11: 15 but that if a woman has long *h*,
1Ti 2: 9 not with braided *h* or gold or pearls
1Pe 3: 3 as braided *h* and the wearing
Rev 1: 14 and *h* were white like wool,

HAIRS (HAIR)
Mt 10: 30 even the very *h* of your head are all
Lk 12: 7 the very *h* of your head are all

HAIRY (HAIR)
Ge 27: 11 "But my brother Esau is a *h* man,

HALF
Ex 30: 13 This *h* shekel is an offering
Jos 8: 33 *H* of the people stood in front
1Ki 3: 25 give *h* to one and *h* to the other."
10: 7 Indeed, not even *h* was told me;
Est 5: 3 Even up to *h* the kingdom,
Da 7: 25 him for a time, times and *h* a time.
Mk 6: 23 up to *h* my kingdom."

HALF-TRIBE (TRIBE)
Nu 32: 33 and the *h* of Manasseh son

HALLELUJAH*
Rev 19: 1, 3, 4, 6.

HALLOWED* (HOLY)
Mt 6: 9 *h* be your name,
Lk 11: 2 *h* be your name,

HALT
Job 38: 11 here is where your proud waves *h*'?

HALTER*
Pr 26: 3 for the horse, a *h* for the donkey,

HAM
Son of Noah (Ge 5:32; 1Ch 1:4), father of Canaan (Ge 9:18; 10:6–20; 1Ch 1:8–16). Saw Noah's nakedness (Ge 9:20–27).

HAMAN
Agagite nobleman honored by Xerxes (Est 3:1–2). Plotted to exterminate the Jews because of Mordecai (Est 3:3–15). Forced to honor Mordecai (Est 5–6). Plot exposed by Esther (Est 5:1–8; 7:1–8). Hanged (Est 7:9–10).

HAMPERED*
Pr 4: 12 you walk, your steps will not be *h*;

HAND (HANDED HANDFUL HANDS OPENHANDED)
Ge 24: 2 "Put your *h* under my thigh.
47: 29 put your *h* under my thigh
Ex 13: 3 out of it with a mighty *h*.
15: 6 Your right *h*, O LORD,
33: 22 and cover you with my *h*
Dt 12: 7 in everything you have put your *h*
1Ki 8: 42 and your mighty *h* and your
13: 4 But the *h* he stretched out
1Ch 29: 14 you only what comes from your *h*.
29: 16 it comes from your *h*, and all
2Ch 6: 15 with your *h* you have fulfilled it—
Ne 4: 17 materials did their work with one *h*
Job 40: 4 I put my *h* over my mouth.
Ps 16: 8 Because he is at my right *h*,
32: 4 your *h* was heavy upon me;
37: 24 the LORD upholds him with his *h*.
44: 3 it was your right *h*, your arm,
45: 9 at your right *h* is the royal bride
63: 8 your right *h* upholds me.
75: 8 In the *h* of the LORD is a cup
91: 7 ten thousand at your right *h*,
98: 1 his right *h* and his holy arm
109: 31 at the right *h* of the needy one,
110: 1 "Sit at my right *h*
137: 5 may my right *h* forget *its skill*.
139: 10 even there your *h* will guide me,
145: 16 You open your *h*
Pr 27: 16 or grasping oil with the *h*.
Ecc 5: 15 that he can carry in his *h*.
9: 10 Whatever your *h* finds to do,
Isa 11: 8 the young child put his *h*
40: 12 the waters in the hollow of his *h*,
41: 13 who takes hold of your right *h*
44: 5 still another will write on his *h*,
48: 13 My own *h* laid the foundations
64: 8 we are all the work of your *h*.
La 3: 3 he has turned his *h* against me
Da 10: 10 *h* touched me and set me trembling
Jnh 4: 11 people who cannot tell their right *h*
Hab 3: 4 rays flashed from his *h*,
Mt 5: 30 if your right *h* causes you to sin,
6: 3 know what your right *h* is doing,
12: 10 a man with a shriveled *h* was there.
18: 8 If your *h* or your foot causes you
22: 44 "Sit at my right *h*
26: 64 at the right *h* of the Mighty One
Mk 3: 1 a man with a shriveled *h* was there.
9: 43 If your *h* causes you to sin, cut it off
12: 36 "Sit at my right *h*
16: 19 and he sat at the right *h* of God.
Lk 6: 6 there whose right *h* was shriveled.
20: 42 "Sit at my right *h*
22: 69 at the right *h* of the mighty God."
Jn 10: 28 one can snatch them out of my *h*.
20: 27 Reach out your *h* and put it
Ac 7: 55 Jesus standing at the right *h* of God
1Co 12: 15 I am not a *h*, I do not belong
Heb 1: 13 "Sit at my right *h*
Rev 13: 16 to receive a mark on his right *h*

HANDED (HAND)
Da 7: 25 The saints will be *h* over to him
1Ti 1: 20 whom I have *h* over to Satan

HANDFUL (HAND)
Ecc 4: 6 Better one *h* with tranquillity

HANDLE (HANDLES)
Col 2: 21 "Do not *h*! Do not taste! Do not

HANDLES (HANDLE)
2Ti 2: 15 who correctly *h* the word of truth.

HANDS (HAND)
Ge 27: 22 but the *h* are the *h* of Esau."
Ex 17: 11 As long as Moses held up his *h*,
29: 10 his sons shall lay their *h* on its head
Dt 6: 8 Tie them as symbols on your *h*
Jdg 7: 6 lapped with their *h* to their mouths.
2Ki 11: 12 and the people clapped their *h*
2Ch 6: 4 who with his *h* has fulfilled what he
Ps 22: 16 they have pierced my *h*
24: 4 He who has clean *h* and a pure
31: 5 Into your *h* I commit my spirit;
31: 15 My times are in your *h*;
47: 1 Clap your *h*, all you nations;
63: 4 and in your name I will lift up my *h*
Pr 10: 4 Lazy *h* make a man poor,
21: 25 because his *h* refuse to work.
31: 13 and works with eager *h*.
31: 20 and extends her *h* to the needy.
Ecc 10: 18 if his *h* are idle, the house leaks.
Isa 35: 3 Strengthen the feeble *h*,
49: 16 you on the palms of my *h*;
55: 12 will clap their *h*.
65: 2 All day long I have held out my *h*
La 3: 41 Let us lift up our hearts and our *h*
Lk 23: 46 into your *h* I commit my spirit."
Ac 6: 6 who prayed and laid their *h*
8: 18 at the laying on of the apostles' *h*,
13: 3 they placed their *h* on them
19: 6 When Paul placed his *h* on them,
28: 8 placed his *h* on him and healed him
1Th 4: 11 and to work with your *h*,
1Ti 2: 8 to lift up holy *h* in prayer,
4: 14 body of elders laid their *h* on you.
5: 22 hasty in the laying on of *h*,
2Ti 1: 6 you through the laying on of my *h*.
Heb 6: 2 the laying on of *h*, the resurrection

HANDSOME*
Ge 39: 6 Now Joseph was well-built and *h*,
1Sa 16: 12 a fine appearance and *h* features.
17: 42 ruddy and *h*, and he despised him.
2Sa 14: 25 praised for his *h* appearance
1Ki 1: 6 also very *h* and was born next
SS 1: 16 *Beloved* How *h* you are, my lover!
Eze 23: 6 all of them *h* young men,
23: 12 horsemen, all *h* young men.
23: 23 with them, *h* young men,
Da 1: 4 without any physical defect, *h*,
Zec 11: 13 the *h* price at which they priced me

HANG (HANGED HANGING HUNG)
Mt 22: 40 and the Prophets *h* on these two

HANGED (HANG)
Mt 27: 5 Then he went away and *h* himself.

HANGING (HANG)
Ac 10: 39 They killed him by *h* him on a tree,

HANNAH*
Wife of Elkanah, mother of Samuel (1Sa 1). Prayer at dedication of Samuel (1Sa 2:1–10). Blessed (1Sa 2:18–21).

HAPPIER (HAPPY)
Mt 18: 13 he is *h* about that one sheep
1Co 7: 40 she is *h* if she stays as she is—

HAPPINESS* (HAPPY)
Dt 24: 5 bring *h* to the wife he has married.
Est 8: 16 For the Jews it was a time of *h*
Job 7: 7 my eyes will never see *h* again.
Ecc 2: 26 gives wisdom, knowledge and *h*,
Mt 25: 21 Come and share your master's *h*!'
25: 23 Come and share your master's *h*!'

HAPPY* (HAPPIER HAPPINESS)
Ge 30: 13 The women will call me *h*."
30: 13 Then Leah said, "How *h* I am!
1Ki 4: 20 they drank and they were *h*.
10: 8 How *h* your men must be!
10: 8 men must be! How *h* your officials,
2Ch 9: 7 How *h* your men must be!
9: 7 men must be! How *h* your officials,
Est 5: 9 Haman went out that day *h*
5: 14 the king to the dinner and be *h*."
Ps 10: 6 I'll always be *h* and never have
68: 3 may they be *h* and joyful.
113: 9 as a *h* mother of children.
137: 8 *h* is he who repays you
Pr 15: 13 A *h* heart makes the face cheerful,
Ecc 3: 12 better for men than to be *h*
5: 19 to accept his lot and be *h*
7: 14 When times are good, be *h*;
11: 9 Be *h*, young man, while you are
Jnh 4: 6 Jonah was very *h* about the vine.
Zec 8: 19 and glad occasions and *h* festivals
1Co 7: 30 those who are *h*, as if they were not
2Co 7: 9 yet now I am *h*, not because you
7: 13 delighted to see how *h* Titus was,
Jas 5: 13 Is anyone *h*? Let him sing songs

HARD (HARDEN HARDENED HARDENING HARDENS HARDER HARDSHIP HARDSHIPS)
Ge 18: 14 Is anything too *h* for the LORD?
1Ki 10: 1 came to test him with *h* questions.
Pr 14: 23 All *h* work brings a profit,
Jer 32: 17 Nothing is too *h* for you.
Zec 7: 12 They made their hearts as *h* as flint
Mt 19: 23 it is *h* for a rich man
Mk 10: 5 your hearts were *h* that Moses
Jn 6: 60 disciples said, "This is a *h* teaching.
Ac 20: 35 of *h* work we must help the weak,
26: 14 It is *h* for you to kick
Ro 16: 12 woman who has worked very *h*
1Co 4: 12 We work *h* with our own hands.
2Co 6: 5 imprisonments and riots; in *h* work
1Th 5: 12 to respect those who work *h*
Rev 2: 2 your *h* work and your

HARDEN (HARD)
Ex 4: 21 I will *h* his heart so that he will not
Ps 95: 8 do not *h* your hearts as you did
Ro 9: 18 he hardens whom he wants to *h*.
Heb 3: 8 do not *h* your hearts

HARDENED (HARD)
Ex 10: 20 But the LORD *h* Pharaoh's heart,

HARDENING* (HARD)
Ro 11: 25 Israel has experienced a *h* in part
Eph 4: 18 in them due to the *h* of their hearts.

HARDENS* (HARD)
Pr 28: 14 he who *h* his heart falls into trouble
Ro 9: 18 and he *h* whom he wants to harden.

HARDER (HARD)
1Co 15: 10 No, I worked *h* than all of them—
2Co 11: 23 I have worked much *h*, been

HARDHEARTED* (HEART)
Dt 15: 7 do not be *h* or tightfisted

HARDSHIP (HARD)
Ro 8: 35 Shall trouble or *h* or persecution
2Ti 2: 3 Endure *h* with us like a good
4: 5 endure *h*, do the work
Heb 12: 7 Endure *h* as discipline; God is

HARDSHIPS (HARD)
Ac 14: 22 go through many *h* to enter
2Co 6: 4 in troubles, *h* and distresses;
12: 10 in insults, in *h*, in persecutions,
Rev 2: 3 and have endured *h* for my name,

HARM (HARMS)
1Ch 16: 22 do my prophets no *h*."
Ps 105: 15 do my prophets no *h*."
121: 6 the sun will not *h* you by day,
Pr 3: 29 not plot *h* against your neighbor,
12: 21 No *h* befalls the righteous,
31: 12 She brings him good, not *h*,
Jer 10: 5 they can do no *h*
29: 11 to prosper you and not to *h* you,
Ro 13: 10 Love does no *h* to its neighbor.
1Co 11: 17 for your meetings do more *h*
1Jn 5: 18 the evil one cannot *h* him.

HARMONY*
Zec 6: 13 there will be *h* between the two.'
Ro 12: 16 Live in *h* with one another.
2Co 6: 15 What *h* is there between Christ
1Pe 3: 8 live in *h* with one another;

HARMS* (HARM)
Pr 8: 36 whoever fails to find me *h* himself;

HARP (HARPS)
Ge 4: 21 the father of all who play the *h*
1Sa 16: 23 David would take his *h* and play.
Ps 33: 2 Praise the LORD with the *h*;
98: 5 with the *h* and the sound of singing
150: 3 praise him with the *h* and lyre,
Rev 5: 8 Each one had a *h* and they were

HARPS (HARP)
Ps 137: 2 we hung our *h*,

HARSH
Pr 15: 1 but a *h* word stirs up anger.
Col 2: 23 and their *h* treatment of the body,
3: 19 and do not be *h* with them.
1Pe 2: 18 but also to those who are *h*.
Jude : 15 of all the *h* words ungodly sinners

HARVEST (HARVESTERS)
Ge 8: 22 seedtime and *h*,
Ex 23: 16 the Feast of *H* with the firstfruits
Dt 16: 15 God will bless you in all your *h*
Pr 10: 5 during *h* is a disgraceful son.
Jer 8: 20 "The *h* is past,
Joel 3: 13 for the *h* is ripe.
Mt 9: 37 *h* is plentiful but the workers are
Lk 10: 2 He told them, "The *h* is plentiful,
Jn 4: 35 at the fields! They are ripe for *h*.
1Co 9: 11 if we reap a material *h* from you?
2Co 9: 10 the *h* of your righteousness.
Gal 6: 9 at the proper time we will reap a *h*
Heb 12: 11 it produces a *h* of righteousness
Jas 3: 18 in peace raise a *h* of righteousness.
Rev 14: 15 for the *h* of the earth is ripe."

HARVESTERS (HARVEST)
Ru 2: 3 to glean in the fields behind the *h*.

HASTE (HASTEN HASTY)
Ex 12: 11 it in *h*; it is the LORD's Passover.
Pr 21: 5 as surely as *h* leads to poverty.
29: 20 Do you see a man who speaks in *h*?

HASTEN (HASTE)
Ps 70: 1 *H*, O God, to save me;
119: 60 I will *h* and not delay

HASTY* (HASTE)
Pr 19: 2 nor to be *h* and miss the way.
Ecc 5: 2 do not be *h* in your heart
1Ti 5: 22 Do not be *h* in the laying

HATE (GOD-HATERS HATED HATES HATING HATRED)
Lev 19: 17 "'Do not *h* your brother
Ps 5: 5 you *h* all who do wrong.
36: 2 too much to detect or *h* his sin.
45: 7 righteousness and *h* wickedness;
97: 10 those who love the LORD *h* evil,
119: 104 therefore I *h* every wrong path.
119: 163 I *h* and abhor falsehood
139: 21 Do I not *h* those who *h* you,
Pr 8: 13 To fear the LORD is to *h* evil;
9: 8 rebuke a mocker or he will *h* you;
13: 5 The righteous *h* what is false,
25: 17 too much of you, and he will *h* you.
29: 10 Bloodthirsty men *h* a man
Ecc 3: 8 a time to love and a time to *h*,
Isa 61: 8 I *h* robbery and iniquity.
Eze 35: 6 Since you did not *h* bloodshed,
Am 5: 15 *H* evil, love good;
Mal 2: 16 "I *h* divorce," says the LORD God
Mt 5: 43 your neighbor and *h* your enemy.'
10: 22 All men will *h* you because of me,
Lk 6: 22 Blessed are you when men *h* you,
6: 27 do good to those who *h* you,
14: 26 does not *h* his father and mother,
Ro 12: 9 *H* what is evil; cling to what is good

HATED (HATE)
Mal 1: 3 loved Jacob, but Esau I have *h*,
Jn 15: 18 keep in mind that it *h* me first.
Ro 9: 13 "Jacob I loved, but Esau I *h*."
Eph 5: 29 no one ever *h* his own body,
Heb 1: 9 righteousness and *h* wickedness;

HATES (HATE)
Pr 6: 16 There are six things the LORD *h*,
13: 24 He who spares the rod *h* his son,
15: 27 but he who *h* bribes will live.
26: 28 A lying tongue *h* those it hurts,
Jn 3: 20 Everyone who does evil *h* the light,
12: 25 while the man who *h* his life
1Jn 2: 9 *h* his brother is still in the darkness.
4: 20 "I love God," yet *h* his brother,

HATING (HATE)
Jude : 23 *h* even the clothing stained

HATRED (HATE)
Pr 10: 12 *H* stirs up dissension,
15: 17 than a fattened calf with *h*.
Jas 4: 4 with the world is *h* toward God?

HAUGHTY
Pr 6: 17 detestable to him: / *h* eyes,
16: 18 a *h* spirit before a fall.

HAVEN
Ps 107: 30 he guided them to their desired *h*.

HAY
1Co 3: 12 costly stones, wood, *h* or straw,

HEAD (HEADS HOTHEADED)
Ge 3: 15 he will crush your *h*,
Nu 6: 5 no razor may be used on his *h*.
Jdg 16: 17 If my *h* were shaved, my strength
1Sa 9: 2 a *h* taller than any of the others.
2Sa 18: 9 Absalom's *h* got caught in the tree.
Ps 23: 5 You anoint my *h* with oil;
133: 2 is like precious oil poured on the *h*,
Pr 10: 6 Blessings crown the *h*
25: 22 will heap burning coals on his *h*,
Isa 59: 17 and the helmet of salvation on his *h*
Eze 33: 4 his blood will be on his own *h*.
Mt 8: 20 of Man has no place to lay his *h*."
Jn 19: 2 crown of thorns and put it on his *h*.
Ro 12: 20 will heap burning coals on his *h*."
1Co 11: 3 and the *h* of Christ is God.
11: 5 her *h* uncovered dishonors her *h* —
12: 21 And the *h* cannot say to the feet,
Eph 1: 22 him to be *h* over everything
5: 23 For the husband is the *h* of the wife
Col 1: 18 And he is the *h* of the body,
2Ti 4: 5 keep your *h* in all situations,
Rev 14: 14 with a crown of gold on his *h*
19: 12 and on his *h* are many crowns.

HEADS (HEAD)
Lev 26: 13 you to walk with *h* held high.
Ps 22: 7 they hurl insults, shaking their *h*:
24: 7 Lift up your *h*, O you gates;
Isa 35: 10 everlasting joy will crown their *h*.
51: 11 everlasting joy will crown their *h*.
Mt 27: 39 shaking their *h* and saying,
Lk 21: 28 stand up and lift up your *h*,
Ac 18: 6 "Your blood be on your own *h*!
Rev 4: 4 and had crowns of gold on their *h*.

HEAL* (HEALED HEALING HEALS)
Nu 12: 13 please *h* her!" The LORD replied
Dt 32: 39 I have wounded and I will *h*,
2Ki 20: 5 and seen your tears; I will *h* you.
20: 8 the sign that the LORD will *h* me
2Ch 7: 14 their sin and will *h* their land.
Job 5: 18 he injures, but his hands also *h*.
Ps 6: 2 *h* me, for my bones are in agony.
41: 4 *h* me, for I have sinned against you
Ecc 3: 3 a time to kill and a time to *h*,
Isa 19: 22 he will strike them and *h* them.
19: 22 respond to their pleas and *h* them.
57: 18 seen his ways, but I will *h* him;
57: 19 "And I will *h* them."
Jer 17: 14 *H* me, O LORD, and I will be
30: 17 and *h* your wounds,'
33: 6 I will *h* my people and will let them
La 2: 13 Who can *h* you?
Hos 5: 13 not able to *h* your sores.
6: 1 but he will *h* us;
7: 1 whenever I would *h* Israel,
14: 4 "I will *h* their waywardness
Na 3: 19 Nothing can *h* your wound;
Zec 11: 16 or seek the young, or *h* the injured,
Mt 8: 7 said to him, "I will go and *h* him."
10: 1 to *h* every disease and sickness.
10: 8 *H* the sick, raise the dead,
12: 10 "Is it lawful to *h* on the Sabbath?"
Mt 13: 15 and turn, and I would *h* them.'
17: 16 but they could not *h* him."
Mk 3: 2 if he would *h* him on the Sabbath.
6: 5 on a few sick people and *h* them.
Lk 4: 23 to me: 'Physician, *h* yourself!
5: 17 present for him to *h* the sick.
6: 7 to see if he would *h* on the Sabbath.
7: 3 him to come and *h* his servant.
8: 43 years, but no one could *h* her.
9: 2 kingdom of God and to *h* the sick.
10: 9 *H* the sick who are there
13: 32 and *h* people today and tomorrow,
14: 3 "Is it lawful to *h* on the Sabbath
Jn 4: 47 begged him to come and *h* his son,
12: 40 nor turn — and I would *h* them."
Ac 4: 30 Stretch out your hand to *h*
28: 27 and turn, and I would *h* them.'

HEALED* (HEAL)
Ge 20: 17 to God, and God *h* Abimelech,
Ex 21: 19 and see that he is completely *h*.
Lev 13: 37 hair has grown in it, the itch is *h*.
14: 3 If the person has been *h*
Jos 5: 8 were in camp until they were *h*.
1Sa 6: 3 you will be *h*, and you will know
2Ki 2: 21 LORD says: 'I have *h* this water.
2Ch 30: 20 heard Hezekiah and *h* the people.
Ps 30: 2 and you *h* me.
107: 20 He sent forth his word and *h* them;
Isa 6: 10 and turn and be *h*."
53: 5 and by his wounds we are *h*.
Jer 14: 19 us so that we cannot be *h*?
17: 14 Heal me, O LORD, and I will be *h*;
51: 8 perhaps she can be *h*.
51: 9 but she cannot be *h*;
51: 9 "'We would have *h* Babylon,
Eze 34: 4 the weak or *h* the sick
Hos 11: 3 it was I who *h* them.
Mt 4: 24 and the paralyzed, and he *h* them.
8: 8 the word, and my servant will be *h*.
8: 13 his servant was *h* at that very hour.
8: 16 with a word and *h* all the sick.
9: 21 If I only touch his cloak, I will be *h*
9: 22 he said, "your faith has *h* you."
9: 22 woman was *h* from that moment.
12: 15 him, and he *h* all their sick,
12: 22 Jesus *h* him, so that he could both
14: 14 on them and *h* their sick.
14: 36 and all who touched him were *h*.
15: 28 And her daughter was *h*
15: 30 laid them at his feet; and he *h* them
17: 18 and he was *h* from that moment.
19: 2 followed him, and he *h* them there.
21: 14 to him at the temple, and he *h* them
Mk 1: 34 and Jesus *h* many who had various
3: 10 For he had *h* many, so that those
5: 23 hands on her so that she will be *h*
5: 28 If I just touch his clothes, I will be *h*
5: 34 "Daughter, your faith has *h* you.
6: 13 people with oil and *h* them.
6: 56 and all who touched him were *h*.
10: 52 said Jesus, "your faith has *h* you."
Lk 4: 40 hands on each one, he *h* them.
5: 15 and to be *h* of their sicknesses.
6: 18 and to be *h* of their diseases.
7: 7 the word, and my servant will be *h*.
8: 47 and how she had been instantly *h*.
8: 48 "Daughter, your faith has *h* you.
8: 50 just believe, and she will be *h*."
9: 11 and *h* those who needed healing.
9: 42 *h* the boy and gave him back
13: 14 Jesus had *h* on the Sabbath,
13: 14 So come and be *h* on those days,
14: 4 he *h* him and sent him away.
17: 15 when he saw he was *h*, came back,
18: 42 your sight; your faith has *h* you."
22: 51 touched the man's ear and *h* him.
Jn 5: 10 said to the man who had been *h*,
5: 13 man who was *h* had no idea who it
Ac 4: 9 and are asked how he was *h*,
4: 10 stands before you *h*.
4: 14 who had been *h* standing there
4: 22 man who was miraculously *h* was
5: 16 evil spirits, and all of them were *h*.
8: 7 paralytics and cripples were *h*.
14: 9 saw that he had faith to be *h*
28: 8 placed his hands on him and *h* him.
Heb 12: 13 may not be disabled, but rather *h*.
Jas 5: 16 for each other so that you may be *h*
1Pe 2: 24 by his wounds you have been *h*.
Rev 13: 3 but the fatal wound had been *h*.
13: 12 whose fatal wound had been *h*.

HEALING* (HEAL)
2Ch 28: 15 food and drink, and *h* balm.
Pr 12: 18 but the tongue of the wise brings *h*.

Pr 13: 17 but a trustworthy envoy brings *h.*
15: 4 The tongue that brings *h* is a tree
16: 24 sweet to the soul and *h* to the bones
Isa 58: 8 and your *h* will quickly appear;
Jer 8: 15 for a time of *h*
8: 22 Why then is there no *h*
14: 19 for a time of *h*
30: 12 your injury beyond *h.*
30: 13 no *h* for you.
33: 6 I will bring health and *h* to it;
46: 11 there is no *h* for you.
Eze 30: 21 It has not been bound up for *h*
47: 12 for food and their leaves for *h."*
Mal 4: 2 rise with *h* in its wings.
Mt 4: 23 and *h* every disease and sickness
9: 35 and *h* every disease and sickness.
Lk 6: 19 coming from him and *h* them all.
9: 6 gospel and *h* people everywhere.
9: 11 and healed those who needed *h.*
Jn 7: 23 angry with me for *h* the whole man
Ac 3: 16 him that has given this complete *h*
10: 38 *h* all who were under the power
1Co 12: 9 to another gifts of *h*
12: 28 also those having gifts of *h,*
12: 30 Do all have gifts of *h?* Do all speak
Rev 22: 2 are for the *h* of the nations.

HEALS* (HEAL)
Ex 15: 26 for I am the LORD, who *h* you."
Lev 13: 18 a boil on his skin and it *h,*
Ps 103: 3 and *h* all your diseases;
147: 3 He *h* the brokenhearted
Isa 30: 26 and *h* the wounds he inflicted.
Ac 9: 34 said to him, "Jesus Christ *h* you.

HEALTH* (HEALTHIER HEALTHY)
1Sa 25: 6 And good *h* to all that is yours!
25: 6 Good *h* to you and your household
Ps 38: 3 of your wrath there is no *h*
38: 7 there is no *h* in my body.
Pr 3: 8 This will bring *h* to your body
4: 22 and *h* to a man's whole body.
15: 30 and good news gives *h* to the bones
Isa 38: 16 You restored me to *h*
Jer 30: 17 But I will restore you to *h*
33: 6 I will bring *h* and healing to it;
3Jn : 2 I pray that you may enjoy good *h*

HEALTHIER* (HEALTH)
Da 1: 15 end of the ten days they looked *h*

HEALTHY* (HEALTH)
Ge 41: 5 Seven heads of grain, *h* and good,
41: 7 of grain swallowed up the seven *h,*
Ps 73: 4 their bodies are *h* and strong.
Zec 11: 16 or heal the injured, or feed the *h,*
Mt 9: 12 "It is not the *h* who need a doctor,
Mk 2: 17 "It is not the *h* who need a doctor,
Lk 5: 31 "It is not the *h* who need a doctor,

HEAP
Pr 25: 22 you will *h* burning coals
Ro 12: 20 you will *h* burning coals

HEAR (HEARD HEARING HEARS)
Ex 15: 14 The nations will *h* and tremble;
22: 27 I will *h,* for I am compassionate.
Nu 14: 13 Then the Egyptians will *h* about it!
Dt 1: 16 *H* the disputes between your
4: 36 heaven he made you *h* his voice
6: 4 *H,* O Israel: The LORD our God,
19: 20 The rest of the people will *h* of this
31: 13 must *h* it and learn
Jos 7: 9 of the country will *h* about this
1Ki 8: 30 *H* the supplication of your servant
2Ki 19: 16 O LORD, and *h;* open your eyes,
2Ch 7: 14 then will I *h* from heaven
Job 31: 35 ("Oh, that I had someone to *h* me!
Ps 94: 9 he who implanted the ear not *h?*
95: 7 Today, if you *h* his voice,
Ecc 7: 21 or you may *h* your servant cursing
Isa 21: 3 I am staggered by what I *h,*
29: 18 that day the deaf will *h* the words
30: 21 your ears will *h* a voice behind you,
51: 7 *H* me, you who know what is right,
59: 1 nor his ear too dull to *h.*
65: 24 while they are still speaking I will *h*
Jer 5: 21 who have ears but do not *h:*
Eze 33: 7 so *h* the word I speak and give
37: 4 'Dry bones, *h* the word
Mt 11: 5 the deaf *h,* the dead are raised,
11: 15 He who has ears, let him *h.*
13: 17 and to *h* what you *h* but did not *h* it
Mk 12: 29 answered Jesus, "is this: '*H,*
Lk 7: 22 the deaf *h,* the dead are raised,
Jn 8: 47 reason you do not *h* is that you do
Ac 13: 7 he wanted to *h* the word of God.
13: 44 gathered to *h* the word of the Lord.
17: 32 "We want to *h* you again
Ro 2: 13 is not those who *h* the law who are
10: 14 they *h* without someone preaching
2Ti 4: 3 what their itching ears want to *h.*
Heb 3: 7 "Today, if you *h* his voice,
Rev 1: 3 and blessed are those who *h* it

HEARD (HEAR)
Ex 2: 24 God *h* their groaning and he
Dt 4: 32 has anything like it ever been *h* of?
2Sa 7: 22 as we have *h* with our own ears.
Job 42: 5 My ears had *h* of you
Isa 40: 21 Have you not *h?*
40: 28 Have you not *h?*
66: 8 Who has ever *h* of such a thing?
Jer 18: 13 Who has ever *h* anything like this?
Da 10: 12 your words were *h,* and I have
12: 8 I *h,* but I did not understand.
Hab 3: 16 I *h* and my heart pounded,
Mt 5: 21 "You have *h* that it was said
5: 27 "You have *h* that it was said,
5: 33 you have *h* that it was said
5: 38 "You have *h* that it was said,
5: 43 "You have *h* that it was said,
Lk 12: 3 in the dark will be *h* in the daylight,
Jn 8: 26 and what I have *h* from him I tell
Ac 2: 6 because each one *h* them speaking
1Co 2: 9 no ear has *h,*
2Co 12: 4 He *h* inexpressible things,
1Th 2: 13 word of God, which you *h* from us,
2Ti 1: 13 What you *h* from me, keep
Jas 1: 25 not forgetting what he has *h,*
Rev 22: 8 am the one who *h* and saw these

HEARING (HEAR)
Isa 6: 9 Be ever *h,* but never understanding
Mt 13: 14 will be ever *h* but never
Mk 4: 12 ever *h* but never understanding;
Ac 28: 26 will be ever *h* but never
Ro 10: 17 faith comes from *h* the message,
1Co 12: 17 where would the sense of *h* be?

HEARS (HEAR)
Jn 5: 24 whoever *h* my word and believes
1Jn 5: 14 according to his will, he *h* us.
Rev 3: 20 If anyone *h* my voice and opens

HEART (BROKENHEARTED FAINT-HEARTED HARDHEARTED HEART'S HEARTACHE HEARTS KINDHEARTED SIMPLEHEARTED STOUTHEARTED WHOLEHEARTED WHOLEHEARTEDLY)
Ge 6: 5 of his *h* was only evil all the time.
Ex 4: 21 But I will harden his *h*
25: 2 each man whose *h* prompts him
35: 21 and whose *h* moved him came
Lev 19: 17 Do not hate your brother in your *h.*
Dt 4: 9 or let them slip from your *h* as long
4: 29 if you look for him with all your *h*
6: 5 LORD your God with all your *h*
10: 12 LORD your God with all your *h*
11: 13 and to serve him with all your *h*
13: 3 you love him with all your *h*
15: 10 and do so without a grudging *h;*
26: 16 observe them with all your *h*
29: 18 you today whose *h* turns away
30: 2 and obey him with all your *h*
30: 6 you may love him with all your *h*
30: 10 LORD your God with all your *h*
Jos 22: 5 and to serve him with all your *h*
23: 14 You know with all your *h*
1Sa 10: 9 God changed Saul's *h,*
12: 20 serve the LORD with all your *h.*
12: 24 serve him faithfully with all your *h;*
13: 14 sought out a man after his own *h*
14: 7 I am with you *h* and soul."
16: 7 but the LORD looks at the *h."*
17: 32 "Let no one lose *h* on account
1Ki 2: 4 faithfully before me with all their *h*
3: 9 So give your servant a discerning *h*
3: 12 give you a wise and discerning *h,*
8: 48 back to you with all their *h*
9: 3 and my *h* will always be there.
9: 4 walk before me in integrity of *h*
10: 24 the wisdom God had put in his *h.*
11: 4 and his *h* was not fully devoted
14: 8 and followed me with all his *h,*
15: 14 Asa's *h* was fully committed
2Ki 22: 19 Because your *h* was responsive
23: 3 with all his *h* and all his soul,
1Ch 28: 9 for the LORD searches every *h*
2Ch 6: 38 back to you with all their *h*
7: 16 and my *h* will always be there.
15: 12 of their fathers, with all their *h*
15: 17 Asa's *h* was fully committed
17: 6 His *h* was devoted to the ways
22: 9 sought the LORD with all his *h."*
2Ch 34: 31 with all his *h* and all his soul,
36: 13 stiff-necked and hardened his *h*
Ezr 1: 5 everyone whose *h* God had moved
Ne 4: 6 the people worked with all their *h.*
Job 19: 27 How my *h* yearns within me!
22: 22 and lay up his words in your *h.*
37: 1 "At this my *h* pounds
Ps 9: 1 you, O LORD, with all my *h;*
14: 1 The fool says in his *h,*
16: 9 Therefore my *h* is glad
19: 14 and the meditation of my *h*
20: 4 he give you the desire of your *h*
24: 4 who has clean hands and a pure *h,*
26: 2 examine my *h* and my mind;
37: 4 will give you the desires of your *h.*
37: 31 The law of his God is in his *h;*
44: 21 since he knows the secrets of the *h*
45: 1 My *h* is stirred by a noble theme
51: 10 Create in me a pure *h,* O God,
51: 17 a broken and contrite *h,*
53: 1 The fool says in his *h,*
66: 18 If I had cherished sin in my *h,*
73: 1 to those who are pure in *h.*
73: 26 My flesh and my *h* may fail,
86: 11 give me an undivided *h,*
90: 12 that we may gain a *h* of wisdom.
97: 11 and joy on the upright in *h.*
108: 1 My *h* is steadfast, O God;
109: 22 and my *h* is wounded within me.
111: 1 will extol the LORD with all my *h*
112: 7 his *h* is steadfast, trusting
112: 8 His *h* is secure, he will have no fear
119: 2 and seek him with all their *h.*
119: 10 I seek you with all my *h;*
119: 11 I have hidden your word in my *h*
119: 30 I have set my *h* on your laws.
119: 32 for you have set my *h* free.
119: 34 and obey it with all my *h.*
119: 36 Turn my *h* toward your statutes
119: 58 sought your face with all my *h;*
119: 69 I keep your precepts with all my *h.*
119: 111 they are the joy of my *h.*
119: 112 My *h* is set on keeping your
119: 145 I call with all my *h;* answer me,
125: 4 to those who are upright in *h.*
138: 1 you, O LORD, with all my *h;*
139: 23 Search me, O God, and know my *h*
Pr 2: 2 applying your *h* to understanding,
3: 1 but keep my commands in your *h,*
3: 3 write them on the tablet of your *h.*
3: 5 Trust in the LORD with all your *h*
4: 4 hold of my words with all your *h;*
4: 21 keep them within your *h;*
4: 23 Above all else, guard your *h,*
6: 21 Bind them upon your *h* forever;
7: 3 write them on the tablet of your *h.*
10: 8 The wise in *h* accept commands,
13: 12 Hope deferred makes the *h* sick,
14: 13 Even in laughter the *h* may ache,
14: 30 A *h* at peace gives life to the body,
15: 13 A happy *h* makes the face cheerful,
15: 15 the cheerful *h* has a continual feast.
15: 28 *h* of the righteous weighs its
15: 30 A cheerful look brings joy to the *h,*
16: 23 A wise man's *h* guides his mouth,
17: 22 A cheerful *h* is good medicine,
20: 9 can say, "I have kept my *h* pure;
22: 11 He who loves a pure *h*
22: 17 apply your *h* to what I teach,
22: 18 when you keep them in your *h*
23: 15 My son, if your *h* is wise,
23: 19 and keep your *h* on the right path.
23: 26 My son, give me your *h*
24: 17 stumbles, do not let your *h* rejoice,
27: 19 so a man's *h* reflects the man.
Ecc 5: 2 do not be hasty in your *h*
8: 5 wise *h* will know the proper time
11: 10 banish anxiety from your *h*
SS 3: 1 I looked for the one my *h* loves;
4: 9 You have stolen my *h,* my sister,
5: 2 *Beloved* I slept but my *h* was awake
5: 4 my *h* began to pound for him.
8: 6 Place me like a seal over your *h,*
Isa 6: 10 Make the *h* of this people calloused
40: 11 and carries them close to his *h;*
57: 15 and to revive the *h* of the contrite.
66: 14 you see this, your *h* will rejoice
Jer 3: 15 give you shepherds after my own *h,*
4: 14 wash the evil from your *h*
9: 26 of Israel is uncircumcised in *h."*
17: 9 The *h* is deceitful above all things
20: 9 is in my *h* like a fire,
24: 7 I will give them a *h* to know me,
29: 13 when you seek me with all your *h.*
32: 39 I will give them singleness of *h*

Jer 32: 41 them in this land with all my *h*
51: 46 Do not lose *h* or be afraid
Eze 11: 19 I will give them an undivided *h*
18: 31 and get a new *h* and a new spirit.
36: 26 I will give you a new *h*
44: 7 foreigners uncircumcised in *h*
Da 7: 4 and the *h* of a man was given to it.
Joel 2: 12 "return to me with all your *h*,
2: 13 Rend your *h*
Zep 3: 14 Be glad and rejoice with all your *h*,
Mt 5: 8 Blessed are the pure in *h*,
5: 28 adultery with her in his *h*.
6: 21 treasure is, there your *h* will be
11: 29 for I am gentle and humble in *h*,
12: 34 of the *h* the mouth speaks.
13: 15 For this people's *h* has become
15: 18 out of the mouth come from the *h*,
15: 19 For out of the *h* come evil thoughts
18: 35 forgive your brother from your *h*."
22: 37 the Lord your God with all your *h*
Mk 11: 23 and does not doubt in his *h*
12: 30 the Lord your God with all your *h*
12: 33 To love him with all your *h*,
Lk 2: 19 and pondered them in her *h*.
2: 51 treasured all these things in her *h*.
6: 45 out of the good stored up in his *h*,
6: 45 overflow of his *h* his mouth speaks.
8: 15 for those with a noble and good *h*,
10: 27 the Lord your God with all your *h*
12: 34 treasure is, there your *h* will be
Jn 12: 27 "Now my *h* is troubled,
Ac 1: 24 "Lord, you know everyone's *h*.
2: 37 they were cut to the *h*
4: 32 All the believers were one in *h*
8: 21 your *h* is not right before God.
15: 8 who knows the *h*, showed that he
16: 14 The Lord opened her *h* to respond
28: 27 For this people's *h* has become
Ro 1: 9 with my whole *h* in preaching
2: 29 is circumcision of the *h*,
10: 9 in your *h* that God raised him
10: 10 is with your *h* that you believe
15: 6 with one *h* and mouth you may
1Co 14: 25 the secrets of his *h* will be laid bare.
2Co 2: 4 anguish of *h* and with many tears,
4: 1 this ministry, we do not lose *h*.
4: 16 Therefore we do not lose *h*.
9: 7 give what he has decided in his *h*
Eph 1: 18 eyes of your *h* may be enlightened
5: 19 make music in your *h* to the Lord,
6: 5 and with sincerity of *h*, just
6: 6 doing the will of God from your *h*.
Php 1: 7 since I have you in my *h*; for
Col 2: 2 is that they may be encouraged in *h*
3: 22 but with sincerity of *h*
3: 23 work at it with all your *h*,
1Ti 1: 5 which comes from a pure *h*
3: 1 If anyone sets his *h*
2Ti 2: 22 call on the Lord out of a pure *h*.
Phm : 12 who is my very *h* — back to you.
: 20 in the Lord; refresh my *h* in Christ.
Heb 4: 12 the thoughts and attitudes of the *h*.
1Pe 1: 22 one another deeply, from the *h*.

HEART'S* (HEART)
2Ch 1: 11 "Since this is your *h* desire
Jer 15: 16 they were my joy and my *h* delight,
Eze 24: 25 delight of their eyes, their *h* desire,
Ro 10: 1 my *h* desire and prayer to God

HEARTACHE* (HEART)
Pr 15: 13 but *h* crushes the spirit.

HEARTLESS*
La 4: 3 but my people have become *h*
Ro 1: 31 they are senseless, faithless, *h*,

HEARTS (HEART)
Lev 26: 41 their uncircumcised *h* are humbled
Dt 6: 6 are to be upon your *h*.
10: 16 Circumcise your *h*, therefore,
11: 18 Fix these words of mine in your *h*
30: 6 your God will circumcise your *h*
Jos 11: 20 himself who hardened their *h*
24: 23 and yield your *h* to the LORD,
1Sa 7: 3 to the LORD with all your *h*,
10: 26 valiant men whose *h* God had
2Sa 15: 6 and so he stole the *h* of the men
1Ki 8: 39 for you alone know the *h* of all men
8: 61 your *h* must be fully committed
18: 37 are turning their *h* back again."
1Ch 29: 18 and keep their *h* loyal to you.
2Ch 6: 30 (for you alone know the *h* of men),
11: 16 tribe of Israel who set their *h*
29: 31 all whose *h* were willing brought
Ps 7: 9 who searches minds and *h*,
33: 21 In him our *h* rejoice,
Ps 62: 8 pour out your *h* to him,
95: 8 do not harden your *h* as you did
Ecc 3: 11 also set eternity in the *h* of men;
Isa 26: 8 are the desire of our *h*.
29: 13 but their *h* are far from me.
35: 4 say to those with fearful *h*,
51: 7 people who have my law in your *h*:
63: 17 harden our *h* so we do not revere
65: 14 out of the joy of their *h*,
Jer 4: 4 circumcise your *h*,
12: 2 but far from their *h*.
17: 1 on the tablets of their *h*
31: 33 and write it on their *h*.
Mal 4: 6 He will turn the *h* of the fathers
Mt 15: 8 but their *h* are far from me.
Mk 6: 52 the loaves; their *h* were hardened.
7: 6 but their *h* are far from me.
7: 21 out of men's *h*, come evil thoughts,
Lk 1: 17 to turn the *h* of the fathers
16: 15 of men, but God knows your *h*.
24: 32 "Were not our *h* burning within us
Jn 5: 42 not have the love of God in your *h*.
14: 1 "Do not let your *h* be troubled.
14: 27 Do not let your *h* be troubled
Ac 7: 51 with uncircumcised *h* and ears!
11: 23 true to the Lord with all their *h*.
15: 9 for he purified their *h* by faith.
28: 27 understand with their *h*
Ro 1: 21 and their foolish *h* were darkened.
2: 15 of the law are written on their *h*,
5: 5 love into our *h* by the Holy Spirit,
8: 27 who searches our *h* knows
1Co 4: 5 will expose the motives of men's *h*.
2Co 1: 22 put his Spirit in our *h* as a deposit,
3: 2 written on our *h*, known
3: 3 but on tablets of human *h*.
4: 6 shine in our *h* to give us the light
6: 11 and opened wide our *h* to you.
6: 13 to my children — open wide your *h*
7: 2 Make room for us in your *h*.
Gal 4: 6 the Spirit of his Son into our *h*,
Eph 3: 17 dwell in your *h* through faith.
Php 4: 7 will guard your *h* and your minds
Col 3: 1 set your *h* on things above,
3: 15 the peace of Christ rule in your *h*,
3: 16 with gratitude in your *h* to God.
1Th 2: 4 men but God, who tests our *h*.
3: 13 May he strengthen your *h*
2Th 2: 17 encourage your *h* and strengthen
Phm : 7 have refreshed the *h* of the saints.
Heb 3: 8 do not harden your *h*
8: 10 and write them on their *h*.
10: 16 I will put my laws in their *h*,
10: 22 having our *h* sprinkled
Jas 4: 8 purify your *h*, you double-minded.
2Pe 1: 19 the morning star rises in your *h*.
1Jn 3: 20 For God is greater than our *h*,

HEAT
Ps 19: 6 nothing is hidden from its *h*.
2Pe 3: 12 and the elements will melt in the *h*.

HEAVEN (HEAVENLY HEAVENS HEAVENWARD)
Ge 14: 19 Creator of *h* and earth.
28: 12 with its top reaching to *h*,
Ex 16: 4 rain down bread from *h* for you.
20: 22 that I have spoken to you from *h*:
Dt 26: 15 from *h*, your holy dwelling place,
30: 12 "Who will ascend into *h* to get it
1Ki 8: 27 the highest *h*, cannot contain you.
8: 30 Hear from *h*, your dwelling place,
22: 19 the host of *h* standing around him
2Ki 2: 1 up to *h* in a whirlwind,
19: 15 You have made *h* and earth.
2Ch 7: 14 then will I hear from *h*
Isa 14: 12 How you have fallen from *h*,
66: 1 "*H* is my throne,
Da 7: 13 coming with the clouds of *h*.
Mt 3: 2 for the kingdom of *h* is near."
3: 16 At that moment *h* was opened,
4: 17 for the kingdom of *h* is near."
5: 12 because great is your reward in *h*,
5: 19 great in the kingdom of *h*.
6: 9 "'Our Father in *h*,
6: 10 done on earth as it is in *h*.
6: 20 up for yourselves treasures in *h*,
7: 21 Lord,' will enter the kingdom of *h*,
16: 19 bind on earth will be bound in *h*,
18: 3 will never enter the kingdom of *h*.
18: 18 bind on earth will be bound in *h*,
19: 14 the kingdom of *h* belongs to such
19: 21 and you will have treasure in *h*.
19: 23 man to enter the kingdom of *h*.
23: 13 the kingdom of *h* in men's faces.
24: 35 *H* and earth will pass away,
26: 64 and coming on the clouds of *h*."
Mt 28: 18 "All authority in *h*
Mk 1: 10 he saw *h* being torn open
10: 21 and you will have treasure in *h*.
13: 31 *H* and earth will pass away,
14: 62 and coming on the clouds of *h*."
16: 19 he was taken up into *h*
Lk 3: 21 *h* was opened and the Holy Spirit
10: 18 saw Satan fall like lightning from *h*.
10: 20 that your names are written in *h*."
12: 33 in *h* that will not be exhausted,
15: 7 in *h* over one sinner who repents
18: 22 and you will have treasure in *h*.
21: 33 *H* and earth will pass away,
24: 51 left them and was taken up into *h*.
Jn 3: 13 No one has ever gone into *h*
6: 38 down from *h* not to do my will
12: 28 Then a voice came from *h*,
Ac 1: 11 has been taken from you into *h*,
7: 49 the prophet says: "'*H* is my
7: 55 looked up to *h* and saw the glory
9: 3 a light from *h* flashed around him.
26: 19 disobedient to the vision from *h*.
Ro 10: 6 'Who will ascend into *h*?'" (that is,
1Co 15: 47 the earth, the second man from *h*.
2Co 5: 1 an eternal house in *h*, not built
12: 2 ago was caught up to the third *h*.
Eph 1: 10 to bring all things in *h*
Php 2: 10 *h* and on earth and under the earth,
3: 20 But our citizenship is in *h*.
Col 1: 16 things in *h* and on earth, visible
4: 1 that you also have a Master in *h*.
1Th 1: 10 and to wait for his Son from *h*,
4: 16 himself will come down from *h*,
Heb 1: 3 hand of the Majesty in *h*.
8: 5 and shadow of what is in *h*.
9: 24 he entered *h* itself, now to appear
12: 23 whose names are written in *h*.
1Pe 1: 4 spoil or fade — kept in *h* for you,
3: 22 who has gone into *h* and is
2Pe 3: 13 we are looking forward to a new *h*
Rev 5: 13 Then I heard every creature in *h*
11: 19 God's temple in *h* was opened,
12: 7 And there was war in *h*.
15: 5 this I looked and in *h* the temple,
19: 1 of a great multitude in *h* shouting:
19: 11 I saw *h* standing open and there
21: 1 Then I saw a new *h* and a new earth
21: 10 coming down out of *h* from God.

HEAVENLY (HEAVEN)
Ps 8: 5 him a little lower than the *h* beings
2Co 5: 2 to be clothed with our *h* dwelling,
Eph 1: 3 in the *h* realms with every spiritual
1: 20 at his right hand in the *h* realms,
2Ti 4: 18 bring me safely to his *h* kingdom.
Heb 12: 22 to the *h* Jerusalem, the city

HEAVENS (HEAVEN)
Ge 1: 1 In the beginning God created the *h*
11: 4 with a tower that reaches to the *h*,
Dt 33: 26 who rides on the *h* to help you
1Ki 8: 27 The *h*, even the highest heaven,
2Ch 2: 6 since the *h*, even the highest
Ezr 9: 6 and our guilt has reached to the *h*.
Ne 9: 6 You made the *h*, even the highest
Job 11: 8 They are higher than the *h* —
38: 33 Do you know the laws of the *h*?
Ps 8: 3 When I consider your *h*,
19: 1 The *h* declare the glory of God;
33: 6 of the LORD were the *h* made,
57: 5 Be exalted, O God, above the *h*;
102: 25 the *h* are the work of your hands.
103: 11 as high as the *h* are above the earth,
108: 4 is your love, higher than the *h*;
115: 16 The highest *h* belong to the LORD
119: 89 it stands firm in the *h*.
135: 6 in the *h* and on the earth,
139: 8 If I go up to the *h*, you are there;
148: 1 Praise the LORD from the *h*,
Isa 40: 26 Lift your eyes and look to the *h*:
45: 8 "You *h* above, rain
51: 6 Lift up your eyes to the *h*,
55: 9 "As the *h* are higher than the earth,
65: 17 new *h* and a new earth.
Jer 31: 37 if the *h* above can be measured
32: 17 you have made the *h* and the earth
Eze 1: 1 *h* were opened and I saw visions
Da 12: 3 shine like the brightness of the *h*,
Joel 2: 30 I will show wonders in the *h*
Mt 24: 31 from one end of the *h* to the other.
Mk 13: 27 of the earth to the ends of the *h*.
Eph 4: 10 who ascended higher than all the *h*,
Heb 4: 14 priest who has gone through the *h*,
7: 26 from sinners, exalted above the *h*.
2Pe 3: 5 ago by God's word the *h* existed
3: 10 The *h* will disappear with a roar;

HEAVENWARD (HEAVEN)
Php 3: 14 for which God has called me *h*

HEAVIER (HEAVY)
Pr 27: 3 provocation by a fool is *h* than both

HEAVY (HEAVIER)
1Ki 12: 4 and the *h* yoke he put on us,
Ecc 1: 13 What a *h* burden God has laid
Isa 47: 6 you laid a very *h* yoke.
Mt 23: 4 They tie up *h* loads and put them

HEBREW (HEBREWS)
Ge 14: 13 and reported this to Abram the *H.*
2Ki 18: 26 speak to us in *H* in the hearing
Php 3: 5 tribe of Benjamin, a *H* of Hebrews;

HEBREWS (HEBREW)
Ex 9: 1 of the *H,* says: "Let my people go,
2Co 11: 22 Are they *H?* So am I.

HEBRON
Ge 13: 18 near the great trees of Mamre at *H,*
23: 2 died at Kiriath Arba (that is, *H)*
Jos 14: 13 and gave him *H* as his inheritance.
20: 7 *H)* in the hill country of Judah.
21: 13 the priest they gave *H* (a city
2Sa 2: 11 king in *H* over the house

HEDGE
Job 1: 10 "Have you not put a *h* around him

HEED (HEEDS)
Ecc 7: 5 It is better to *h* a wise man's rebuke

HEEDS (HEED)
Pr 13: 1 wise son *h* his father's instruction,
13: 18 whoever *h* correction is honored.
15: 5 whoever *h* correction shows
15: 32 whoever *h* correction gains

HEEL
Ge 3: 15 and you will strike his *h."*

HEIR (INHERIT)
Gal 4: 7 God has made you also an *h.*
Heb 1: 2 whom he appointed *h* of all things,

HEIRS (INHERIT)
Ro 8: 17 then we are *h* — *h* of God
Gal 3: 29 and *h* according to the promise.
Eph 3: 6 gospel the Gentiles are *h* together
1Pe 3: 7 as *h* with you of the gracious gift

HELD (HOLD)
Ex 17: 11 As long as Moses *h* up his hands,
Dt 4: 4 but all of you who *h* fast
2Ki 18: 6 He *h* fast to the LORD
SS 3: 4 I *h* him and would not let him go
Isa 65: 2 All day long I have *h* out my hands
Ro 10: 21 day long I have *h* out my hands
Col 2: 19 and *h* together by its ligaments

HELL*
Mt 5: 22 will be in danger of the fire of *h.*
5: 29 body to be thrown into *h.*
5: 30 for your whole body to go into *h.*
10: 28 destroy both soul and body in *h.*
18: 9 and be thrown into the fire of *h.*
23: 15 as much a son of *h* as you are.
23: 33 you escape being condemned to *h?*
Mk 9: 43 than with two hands to go into *h,*
9: 45 have two feet and be thrown into *h.*
9: 47 two eyes and be thrown into *h,*
Lk 12: 5 has power to throw you into *h.*
16: 23 In *h,* where he was in torment,
Jas 3: 6 and is itself set on fire by *h.*
2Pe 2: 4 but sent them to *h,* putting them

HELMET
Isa 59: 17 and the *h* of salvation on his head;
Eph 6: 17 Take the *h* of salvation
1Th 5: 8 and the hope of salvation as a *h.*

HELP (HELPED HELPER HELPFUL HELPING HELPLESS HELPS)
Ex 23: 5 leave it there; be sure you *h* him
Lev 25: 35 *h* him as you would an alien
Dt 33: 26 who rides on the heavens to *h* you
2Ch 16: 12 even in his illness he did not seek *h*
Ps 18: 6 I cried to my God for *h.*
30: 2 my God, I called to you for *h*
33: 20 he is our *h* and our shield.
46: 1 an ever-present *h* in trouble.
72: 12 the afflicted who have no one to *h.*
79: 9 *H* us, O God our Savior,
108: 12 for the *h* of man is worthless.
115: 9 he is their *h* and shield.
121: 1 where does my *h* come from?
Ecc 4: 10 his friend can *h* him up.
Isa 41: 10 I will strengthen you and *h* you;
Jnh 2: 2 depths of the grave I called for *h,*
Mk 9: 24 *h* me overcome my unbelief!"
Lk 11: 46 will not lift one finger to *h* them.
Ac 16: 9 Come over to Macedonia and *h* us
18: 27 he was a great *h* to those who
20: 35 of hard work we must *h* the weak,
26: 22 I have had God's *h* to this very day,
1Co 12: 28 those able to *h* others, those
2Co 9: 2 For I know your eagerness to *h,*
1Ti 5: 16 she should *h* them and not let

HELPED (HELP)
1Sa 7: 12 "Thus far has the LORD *h* us."

HELPER (HELP)
Ge 2: 18 I will make a *h* suitable for him."
Ps 10: 14 you are the *h* of the fatherless.
Heb 13: 6 Lord is my *h;* I will not be afraid.

HELPFUL (HELP)
Eph 4: 29 only what is *h* for building others

HELPING (HELP)
Ac 9: 36 always doing good and *h* the poor.
1Ti 5: 10 *h* those in trouble and devoting

HELPLESS (HELP)
Ps 10: 12 Do not forget the *h.*
Mt 9: 36 because they were harassed and *h,*

HELPS (HELP)
Ro 8: 26 the Spirit *h* us in our weakness.

HEN
Mt 23: 37 as a *h* gathers her chicks
Lk 13: 34 as a *h* gathers her chicks

HERALD
1Ti 2: 7 for this purpose I was appointed a *h*
2Ti 1: 11 of this gospel I was appointed a *h*

HERBS
Ex 12: 8 with bitter *h,* and bread made

HERITAGE (INHERIT)
Ps 61: 5 you have given me the *h*
119: 111 Your statutes are my *h* forever;
127: 3 Sons are a *h* from the LORD,

HEROD
1. King of Judea who tried to kill Jesus (Mt 2; Lk 1:5).
2. Son of 1. Tetrarch of Galilee who arrested and beheaded John the Baptist (Mt 14:1 – 12; Mk 6:14 – 29; Lk 3:1, 19 – 20; 9:7 – 9); tried Jesus (Lk 23:6 – 15).
3. Grandson of 1. King of Judea who killed James (Ac 12:2); arrested Peter (Ac 12:3 – 19). Death (Ac 12:19 – 23).

HERODIAS
Wife of Herod the Tetrarch who persuaded her daughter to ask for John the Baptist's head (Mt 14:1 – 12; Mk 6:14 – 29).

HEWN
Isa 51: 1 the quarry from which you were *h;*

HEZEKIAH
King of Judah. Restored the temple and worship (2Ch 29 – 31). Sought the LORD for help against Assyria (2Ki 18 – 19; 2Ch 32:1 – 23; Isa 36 – 37). Illness healed (2Ki 20:1 – 11; 2Ch 32:24 – 26; Isa 38). Judged for showing Babylonians his treasures (2Ki 20:12 – 21; 2Ch 32:31; Isa 39).

HID (HIDE)
Ge 3: 8 and they *h* from the LORD God
Ex 2: 2 she *h* him for three months.
Jos 6: 17 because she *h* the spies we sent.
1Ki 18: 13 I *h* a hundred of the LORD's
2Ch 22: 11 she *h* the child from Athaliah
Isa 54: 8 I *h* my face from you for a moment,
Mt 13: 44 When a man found it, he *h* it again,
25: 25 and *h* your talent in the ground.
Heb 11: 23 By faith Moses' parents *h* him

HIDDEN (HIDE)
1Sa 10: 22 has *h* himself among the baggage."
Job 28: 11 and brings *h* things to light.
Ps 19: 12 Forgive my *h* faults.
78: 2 I will utter *h* things, things from of old —
119: 11 I have *h* your word in my heart
Pr 2: 4 and search for it as for *h* treasure,
27: 5 rebuke than *h* love.
Isa 59: 2 your sins have *h* his face from you,
Da 2: 22 He reveals deep and *h* things;
Mt 5: 14 A city on a hill cannot be *h.*
10: 26 or *h* that will not be made known.
11: 25 because you have *h* these things
13: 35 I will utter things *h*
13: 44 of heaven is like treasure *h*
Mk 4: 22 For whatever is *h* is meant
Ro 16: 25 of the mystery *h* for long ages past,
1Co 2: 7 a wisdom that has been *h*
Eph 3: 9 for ages past was kept *h* in God,
Col 1: 26 the mystery that has been kept *h*
2: 3 in whom are *h* all the treasures
3: 3 and your life is now *h* with Christ

HIDE (HID HIDDEN HIDING)
Dt 31: 17 I will *h* my face from them,
Ps 17: 8 *h* me in the shadow of your wings
27: 5 he will *h* me in the shelter
143: 9 for I *h* myself in you.
Isa 53: 3 one from whom men *h* their faces

HIDING (HIDE)
Ps 32: 7 You are my *h* place;
Pr 28: 12 to power, men go into *h.*

HIGH
Ge 14: 18 He was priest of God Most *H,*
14: 22 God Most *H,* Creator of heaven
Ps 21: 7 the unfailing love of the Most *H*
82: 6 you are all sons of the Most *H.'*
Isa 14: 14 I will make myself like the Most *H*
Da 4: 17 know that the Most *H* is sovereign
Mk 5: 7 Jesus, Son of the Most *H* God?
Heb 7: 1 and priest of God Most *H.*

HIGHWAY
Isa 40: 3 a *h* for our God.

HILL (HILLS)
Ps 24: 3 ascend the *h* of the LORD?
Isa 40: 4 every mountain and *h* made low;
Mt 5: 14 A city on a *h* cannot be hidden.
Lk 3: 5 every mountain and *h* made low.

HILLS (HILL)
1Ki 20: 23 "Their gods are gods of the *h.*
Ps 50: 10 and the cattle on a thousand *h.*
121: 1 I lift up my eyes to the *h* —
Hos 10: 8 and to the *h,* "Fall on us!"
Lk 23: 30 and to the *h,* "Cover us!"'
Rev 17: 9 The seven heads are seven *h*

HINDER (HINDERED HINDERS)
1Sa 14: 6 Nothing can *h* the LORD
Mt 19: 14 come to me, and do not *h* them,
1Co 9: 12 anything rather than *h* the gospel
1Pe 3: 7 so that nothing will *h* your prayers.

HINDERED (HINDER)
Lk 11: 52 and you have *h* those who were

HINDERS (HINDER)
Heb 12: 1 let us throw off everything that *h*

HINT*
Eph 5: 3 even a *h* of sexual immorality,

HIP
Ge 32: 32 socket of Jacob's *h* was touched

HIRAM
King of Tyre; helped David build his palace (2Sa 5:11 – 12; 1Ch 14:1); helped Solomon build the temple (1Ki 5; 2Ch 2) and his navy (1Ki 9:10 – 27; 2Ch 8).

HIRED
Lk 15: 15 and *h* himself out to a citizen
Jn 10: 12 *h* hand is not the shepherd who

HOARDED (HOARDS)
Ecc 5: 13 wealth *h* to the harm of its owner,
Jas 5: 3 You have *h* wealth in the last days.

HOARDS (HOARDED)
Pr 11: 26 People curse the man who *h* grain,

HOLD (HELD HOLDS)
Ex 20: 7 LORD will not *h* anyone guiltless
Lev 19: 13 "'Do not *h* back the wages
Dt 5: 11 LORD will not *h* anyone guiltless
11: 22 in all his ways and to *h* fast to him
13: 4 serve him and *h* fast to him.
30: 20 listen to his voice, and *h* fast to him
Jos 22: 5 to *h* fast to him and to serve him
2Ki 4: 16 "you will *h* a son in your arms."
Ps 18: 16 from on high and took *h* of me;
73: 23 you *h* me by my right hand.
Pr 4: 4 "Lay *h* of my words
Isa 41: 13 who takes *h* of your right hand
54: 2 do not *h* back;
Eze 3: 18 and I will *h* you accountable
3: 20 and I will *h* you accountable
33: 6 I will *h* the watchman accountable
Zec 8: 23 nations will take firm *h* of one Jew
Mk 11: 25 if you *h* anything against anyone,
Jn 20: 17 Jesus said, "Do not *h* on to me,
Php 2: 16 as you *h* out the word of life —
3: 12 but I press on to take *h* of that
Col 1: 17 and in him all things *h* together.
1Th 5: 21 *H* on to the good.
1Ti 6: 12 Take *h* of the eternal life
Heb 10: 23 Let us *h* unswervingly

HOLDS (HOLD)
Pr 10: 19 but he who *h* his tongue is wise.
17: 28 and discerning if he *h* his tongue.

HOLES
Hag 1: 6 to put them in a purse with *h* in it."
Mt 8: 20 "Foxes have *h* and birds

HOLINESS* (HOLY)
Ex 15: 11 majestic in *h*,
Dt 32: 51 because you did not uphold my *h*
1Ch 16: 29 the LORD in the splendor of his *h*.
2Ch 20: 21 him for the splendor of his *h*
Ps 29: 2 in the splendor of his *h*.
89: 35 Once for all, I have sworn by my *h*
93: 5 *h* adorns your house
96: 9 in the splendor of his *h*;
Isa 29: 23 they will acknowledge the *h*
35: 8 it will be called the Way of *H*.
Eze 36: 23 I will show the *h* of my great name,
38: 23 I will show my greatness and my *h*,
Am 4: 2 LORD has sworn by his *h*:
Lk 1: 75 fear in *h* and righteousness
Ro 1: 4 the Spirit of *h* was declared
6: 19 to righteousness leading to *h*.
6: 22 the benefit you reap leads to *h*,
1Co 1: 30 our righteousness, *h*
2Co 1: 12 in the *h* and sincerity that are
7: 1 perfecting *h* out of reverence
Eph 4: 24 God in true righteousness and *h*.
1Ti 2: 2 quiet lives in all godliness and *h*.
2: 15 love and *h* with propriety.
Heb 12: 10 that we may share in his *h*.
12: 14 without *h* no one will see the Lord.

HOLY (HALLOWED HOLINESS)
Ge 2: 3 the seventh day and made it *h*,
Ex 3: 5 you are standing is *h* ground."
16: 23 a *h* Sabbath to the LORD.
19: 6 kingdom of priests and a *h* nation.'
20: 8 the Sabbath day by keeping it *h*.
26: 33 Place from the Most *H* Place.
26: 33 curtain will separate the *H* Place
28: 36 seal: *H* TO THE LORD.
29: 37 Then the altar will be most *h*,
30: 10 It is most *h* to the LORD."
30: 29 them so they will be most *h*,
31: 13 I am the LORD, who makes you *h*.
40: 9 all its furnishings, and it will be *h*.
Lev 10: 3 I will show myself *h*;
10: 10 must distinguish between the *h*
10: 13 in a *h* place, because it is your share
11: 44 and be *h*, because I am *h*.
11: 45 therefore be *h*, because I am *h*.
19: 2 'Be *h* because I, the LORD your
19: 8 he has desecrated what is *h*
19: 24 the fourth year all its fruit will be *h*,
20: 3 and profaned my *h* name.
20: 7 "'Consecrate yourselves and be *h*,
20: 8 I am the LORD, who makes you *h*.
20: 26 You are to be *h* to me because I,
21: 6 They must be *h* to their God
21: 8 Consider them *h*, because I
22: 9 am the LORD, who makes them *h*.
22: 32 Do not profane my *h* name.
25: 12 For it is a jubilee and is to be *h*
27: 9 given to the LORD becomes *h*.
Nu 4: 15 they must not touch the *h* things
6: 5 He must be *h* until the period
20: 12 as *h* in the sight of the Israelites,
20: 13 and where he showed himself *h*
Dt 5: 12 the Sabbath day by keeping it *h*,
23: 14 Your camp must be *h*,
26: 15 from heaven, your *h* dwelling place
33: 2 He came with myriads of *h* ones
Jos 5: 15 place where you are standing is *h*."
24: 19 He is a *h* God; he is a jealous God.
1Sa 2: 2 "There is no one *h* like the LORD;
6: 20 of the LORD, this *h* God?
21: 5 even on missions that are not *h*.
2Ki 4: 9 often comes our way is a *h* man
1Ch 16: 10 Glory in his *h* name;
16: 35 may give thanks to your *h* name,
29: 3 I have provided for this *h* temple:
2Ch 30: 27 heaven, his *h* dwelling place.
Ezr 9: 2 and have mingled the *h* race
Ne 11: 1 the *h* city, while the remaining nine
Job 6: 10 not denied the words of the *H* One.
Ps 2: 6 King on Zion, my *h* hill."
11: 4 The LORD is in his *h* temple;
16: 10 will you let your *H* One see decay.
22: 3 you are enthroned as the *H* One;
24: 3 Who may stand in his *h* place?
30: 4 praise his *h* name.
77: 13 Your ways, O God, are *h*.
78: 54 to the border of his *h* land,
Ps 99: 3 he is *h*.
99: 5 he is *h*.
99: 9 for the LORD our God is *h*.
105: 3 Glory in his *h* name;
111: 9 *h* and awesome is his name.
Pr 9: 10 of the *H* One is understanding.
Isa 5: 16 the *h* God will show himself *h*
6: 3 *H*, *h*, *h* is the LORD Almighty;
8: 13 is the one you are to regard as *h*,
29: 23 they will keep my name *h*;
40: 25 who is my equal?" says the *H* One.
43: 3 the *H* One of Israel, your Savior;
54: 5 *H* One of Israel is your Redeemer;
57: 15 who lives forever, whose name is *h*:
58: 13 and the LORD's *h* day honorable,
Jer 17: 22 but keep the Sabbath day *h*,
Eze 20: 41 I will show myself *h* among you
22: 26 to my law and profane my *h* things;
28: 22 and show myself *h* within her.
28: 25 I will show myself *h* among them
36: 20 nations they profaned my *h* name,
38: 16 when I show myself *h* through you
44: 23 the difference between the *h*
Da 9: 24 prophecy and to anoint the most *h*.
Hab 2: 20 But the LORD is in his *h* temple;
Zec 14: 5 and all the *h* ones with him.
14: 20 On that day *H* TO THE LORD
Mt 24: 15 in the *h* place 'the abomination
Mk 1: 24 the *H* One of God!" "Be quiet!"
Lk 1: 35 the *h* one to be born will be called
1: 49 *h* is his name.
4: 34 the *H* One of God!" "Be quiet!"
Jn 6: 69 and know that you are the *H* One
Ac 2: 27 will you let your *H* One see decay.
13: 35 will not let your *H* One see decay.'
Ro 1: 2 prophets in the *H* Scriptures
7: 12 and the commandment is *h*,
11: 16 if the root is *h*, so are the branches.
12: 1 as living sacrifices, *h* and pleasing
1Co 1: 2 in Christ Jesus and called to be *h*,
7: 14 be unclean, but as it is, they are *h*.
Eph 1: 4 the creation of the world to be *h*
2: 21 and rises to become a *h* temple
3: 5 by the Spirit to God's *h* apostles
5: 3 improper for God's *h* people.
5: 26 up for her to make her *h*,
Col 1: 22 death to present you *h* in his sight,
1Th 2: 10 and so is God, of how *h*,
3: 13 and *h* in the presence of our God
3: 13 comes with all his *h* ones.
4: 7 us to be impure, but to live a *h* life.
2Th 1: 10 to be glorified in his *h* people
1Ti 2: 8 to lift up *h* hands in prayer,
2Ti 1: 9 saved us and called us to a *h* life —
2: 21 for noble purposes, made *h*,
3: 15 you have known the *h* Scriptures,
Tit 1: 8 upright, *h* and disciplined.
Heb 2: 11 Both the one who makes men *h*
7: 26 one who is *h*, blameless, pure,
10: 10 we have been made *h*
10: 14 those who are being made *h*.
10: 19 to enter the Most *H* Place
12: 14 in peace with all men and to be *h*;
13: 12 gate to make the people *h*
1Pe 1: 15 But just as he who called you is *h*,
1: 16 is written: "Be *h*, because I am *h*."
2: 5 house to be a *h* priesthood,
2: 9 a royal priesthood, a *h* nation,
3: 5 For this is the way the *h* women
2Pe 3: 11 You ought to live *h* and godly lives
Jude : 14 upon thousands of his *h* ones
Rev 3: 7 are the words of him who is *h*
4: 8 "*H*, *h*, *h* is the Lord God
15: 4 For you alone are *h*.
20: 6 and *h* are those who have part
22: 11 let him who is *h* continue to be *h*."

HOME (HOMES)
Dt 6: 7 Talk about them when you sit at *h*
11: 19 about them when you sit at *h*
20: 5 Let him go *h*, or he may die
24: 5 is to be free to stay at *h*
Ru 1: 11 "Return *h*, my daughters.
2Sa 7: 10 them so that they can have a *h*
1Ch 16: 43 and David returned *h* to bless his
Ps 84: 3 Even the sparrow has found a *h*,
113: 9 settles the barren woman in her *h*
Pr 3: 33 but he blesses the *h* of the righteous
27: 8 is a man who strays from his *h*.
Ecc 12: 5 Then man goes to his eternal *h*
Eze 36: 8 for they will soon come *h*.
Mic 2: 2 They defraud a man of his *h*,
Mt 1: 24 and took Mary *h* as his wife.
Mk 10: 29 "no one who has left *h* or brothers
Lk 10: 38 named Martha opened her *h*
Jn 14: 23 to him and make our *h* with him.
Jn 19: 27 this disciple took her into his *h*.
Ac 16: 15 baptized, she invited us to her *h*.
Tit 2: 5 to be busy at *h*, to be kind,

HOMELESS*
1Co 4: 11 we are brutally treated, we are *h*.

HOMES (HOME)
Ne 4: 14 daughters, your wives and your *h*."
Isa 32: 18 in secure *h*,
Mk 10: 30 as much in this present age (*h*,
1Ti 5: 14 to manage their *h* and to give

HOMETOWN
Mt 13: 57 "Only in his *h*
Lk 4: 24 "no prophet is accepted in his *h*.

HOMOSEXUAL*
1Co 6: 9 male prostitutes nor *h* offenders

HONEST (HONESTY)
Lev 19: 36 Use *h* scales and *h* weights,
Dt 25: 15 and *h* weights and measures,
Job 31: 6 let God weigh me in *h* scales
Pr 12: 17 truthful witness gives *h* testimony,

HONESTY (HONEST)
2Ki 12: 15 they acted with complete *h*.

HONEY (HONEYCOMB)
Ex 3: 8 a land flowing with milk and *h* —
Jdg 14: 8 a swarm of bees and some *h*,
1Sa 14: 26 they saw the *h* oozing out,
Ps 19: 10 than *h* from the comb.
119: 103 sweeter than *h* to my mouth!
Pr 25: 16 If you find *h*, eat just enough —
SS 4: 11 milk and *h* are under your tongue.
Isa 7: 15 and *h* when he knows enough
Eze 3: 3 it tasted as sweet as *h* in my mouth.
Mt 3: 4 His food was locusts and wild *h*.
Rev 10: 9 mouth it will be as sweet as *h*."

HONEYCOMB (HONEY)
SS 4: 11 Your lips drop sweetness as the *h*,
5: 1 I have eaten my *h* and my honey;

HONOR (HONORABLE HONORABLY HONORED HONORS)
Ex 20: 12 "*H* your father and your mother,
Nu 20: 12 trust in me enough to *h* me
25: 13 he was zealous for the *h* of his God
Dt 5: 16 "*H* your father and your mother,
Jdg 4: 9 going about this, the *h* will not be
1Sa 2: 8 and has them inherit a throne of *h*.
2: 30 Those who *h* me I will *h*,
1Ch 29: 12 Wealth and *h* come from you;
2Ch 1: 11 or *h*, nor for the death
18: 1 had great wealth and *h*,
Est 6: 6 for the man the king delights to *h*
Ps 8: 5 and crowned him with glory and *h*.
45: 11 *h* him, for he is your lord.
84: 11 the LORD bestows favor and *h*;
Pr 3: 9 *H* the LORD with your wealth,
3: 35 The wise inherit *h*,
15: 33 and humility comes before *h*.
18: 12 but humility comes before *h*.
20: 3 It is to a man's *h* to avoid strife,
25: 27 is it honorable to seek one's own *h*.
Isa 29: 13 and *h* me with their lips,
Jer 33: 9 and *h* before all nations
Mt 13: 57 own house is a prophet without *h*."
15: 4 '*H* your father and mother'
15: 8 These people *h* me with their lips,
19: 19 *h* your father and mother,'
23: 6 they love the place of *h* at banquets
Mk 6: 4 own house is a prophet without *h*."
Lk 14: 8 do not take the place of *h*,
Jn 5: 23 that all may *h* the Son just
7: 18 does so to gain *h* for himself,
12: 26 My Father will *h* the one who
Ro 12: 10 *H* one another above yourselves.
1Co 6: 20 Therefore *h* God with your body.
Eph 6: 2 "*H* your father and mother" —
1Ti 5: 17 well are worthy of double *h*,
Heb 2: 7 you crowned him with glory and *h*
Rev 4: 9 *h* and thanks to him who sits

HONORABLE (HONOR)
1Th 4: 4 body in a way that is holy and *h*,

HONORABLY (HONOR)
Heb 13: 18 and desire to live *h* in every way.

HONORED (HONOR)
Ps 12: 8 when what is vile is *h* among men.
Pr 13: 18 but whoever heeds correction is *h*.
Da 4: 34 I *h* and glorified him who lives
1Co 12: 26 if one part is *h*, every part rejoices
Heb 13: 4 Marriage should be *h* by all,

HONORS (HONOR)
Ps 15: 4 but *h* those who fear the LORD,
Pr 14: 31 to the needy *h* God.

HOOF
Ex 10: 26 not a *h* is to be left behind.

HOOKS
Isa 2: 4 and their spears into pruning *h*.
Joel 3: 10 and your pruning *h* into spears.
Mic 4: 3 and their spears into pruning *h*.

HOPE (HOPES)
Job 13: 15 Though he slay me, yet will I *h*
Ps 25: 3 No one whose *h* is in you
33: 17 A horse is a vain *h* for deliverance;
33: 18 on those whose *h* is
42: 5 Put your *h* in God,
62: 5 my *h* comes from him.
119: 74 for I have put my *h* in your word.
130: 5 and in his word I put my *h*.
130: 7 O Israel, put your *h* in the LORD,
146: 5 whose *h* is in the LORD his God,
147: 11 who put their *h* in his unfailing love
Pr 13: 12 *H* deferred makes the heart sick,
23: 18 There is surely a future *h* for you,
Isa 40: 31 but those who *h* in the LORD
Jer 29: 11 plans to give you *h* and a future.
La 3: 21 and therefore I have *h*:
Zec 9: 12 to your fortress, O prisoners of *h*;
Ro 5: 4 character; and character, *h*.
8: 20 in *h* that the creation itself will be
8: 24 But *h* that is seen is no *h* at all.
8: 25 if we *h* for what we do not yet have,
12: 12 Be joyful in *h*, patient in affliction,
15: 4 of the Scriptures we might have *h*.
15: 13 May the God of *h* fill you
1Co 13: 13 now these three remain: faith, *h*
15: 19 for this life we have *h* in Christ,
Eph 2: 12 without *h* and without God
Col 1: 27 Christ in you, the *h* of glory.
1Th 1: 3 and your endurance inspired by *h*
5: 8 and the *h* of salvation as a helmet.
1Ti 4: 10 that we have put our *h*
6: 17 but to put their *h* in God,
Tit 1: 2 resting on the *h* of eternal life,
2: 13 while we wait for the blessed *h* —
Heb 6: 19 We have this *h* as an anchor
10: 23 unswervingly to the *h* we profess,
11: 1 faith is being sure of what we *h* for
1Jn 3: 3 Everyone who has this *h*

HOPES (HOPE)
1Co 13: 7 always *h*, always perseveres.

HORN (HORNS)
Ex 19: 13 when the ram's *h* sounds a long
27: 2 Make a *h* at each of the four
Da 7: 8 This *h* had eyes like the eyes

HORNS (HORN)
Da 7: 24 ten *h* are ten kings who will come
Rev 5: 6 He had seven *h* and seven eyes,
12: 3 and ten *h* and seven crowns
13: 1 He had ten *h* and seven heads,
17: 3 and had seven heads and ten *h*.

HORRIBLE (HORROR)
Jer 5: 30 "A *h* and shocking thing

HORROR (HORRIBLE)
Jer 2: 12 and shudder with great *h*,"

HORSE
Ps 147: 10 not in the strength of the *h*,
Pr 26: 3 A whip for the *h*, a halter
Zec 1: 8 before me was a man riding a red *h*
Rev 6: 2 and there before me was a white *h*!
6: 4 Come!" Then another *h* came out,
6: 5 and there before me was a black *h*!
6: 8 and there before me was a pale *h*!
19: 11 and there before me was a white *h*,

HOSANNA
Mt 21: 9 "*H* in the highest!"
Mk 11: 9 "*H*!"
Jn 12: 13 "*H*!"

HOSEA
Prophet whose wife and family pictured the unfaithfulness of Israel (Hos 1 – 3).

HOSHEA (JOSHUA)
1. Original name of Joshua (Nu 13:16).
2. Last king of Israel (2Ki 15:30; 17:1 – 6).

HOSPITABLE* (HOSPITALITY)
1Ti 3: 2 self-controlled, respectable, *h*,
Tit 1: 8 Rather he must be *h*, one who loves

HOSPITABLY* (HOSPITALITY)
Ac 28: 7 and for three days entertained us *h*.

HOSPITALITY* (HOSPITABLE HOSPITABLY)
Ro 12: 13 Practice *h*.
16: 23 whose *h* I and the whole church
1Ti 5: 10 as bringing up children, showing *h*,
1Pe 4: 9 Offer *h* to one another
3Jn : 8 therefore to show *h* to such men

HOSTILE (HOSTILITY)
Ro 8: 7 the sinful mind is *h* to God.

HOSTILITY (HOSTILE)
Eph 2: 14 wall of *h*, by abolishing
2: 16 by which he put to death their *h*.

HOT
1Ti 4: 2 have been seared as with a *h* iron.
Rev 3: 15 that you are neither cold nor *h*.

HOT-TEMPERED (TEMPER)
Pr 15: 18 A *h* man stirs up dissension,
19: 19 A *h* man must pay the penalty;
22: 24 Do not make friends with a *h* man,
29: 22 and a *h* one commits many sins.

HOTHEADED (HEAD)
Pr 14: 16 but a fool is *h* and reckless.

HOUR
Ecc 9: 12 knows when his *h* will come:
Mt 6: 27 you by worrying can add a single *h*
Lk 12: 40 the Son of Man will come at an *h*
Jn 12: 23 The *h* has come for the Son of Man
12: 27 for this very reason I came to this *h*

HOUSE (HOUSEHOLD HOUSEHOLDS HOUSES STOREHOUSE)
Ex 12: 22 the door of his *h* until morning.
20: 17 shall not covet your neighbor's *h*.
Nu 12: 7 he is faithful in all my *h*.
Dt 5: 21 desire on your neighbor's *h*
2Sa 7: 11 LORD himself will establish a *h*
1Ch 17: 23 and his *h* be established forever.
Ne 10: 39 "We will not neglect the *h*
Ps 23: 6 I will dwell in the *h* of the LORD
27: 4 dwell in the *h* of the LORD
69: 9 for zeal for your *h* consumes me,
84: 10 a doorkeeper in the *h* of my God
122: 1 "Let us go to the *h* of the LORD."
127: 1 Unless the LORD builds the *h*,
Pr 7: 27 Her *h* is a highway to the grave,
21: 9 than share a *h* with a quarrelsome
Isa 56: 7 a *h* of prayer for all nations."
Jer 7: 11 Has this *h*, which bears my Name,
18: 2 "Go down to the potter's *h*,
Eze 33: 7 made you a watchman for the *h*
Joel 3: 18 will flow out of the LORD's *h*
Zec 13: 6 given at the *h* of my friends.'
Mt 7: 24 is like a wise man who built his *h*
10: 11 and stay at his *h* until you leave.
12: 29 can anyone enter a strong man's *h*
21: 13 My *h* will be called a *h* of prayer,'
Mk 3: 25 If a *h* is divided against itself,
11: 17 "'My *h* will be called
Lk 6: 48 He is like a man building a *h*,
10: 7 Do not move around from *h* to *h*.
11: 17 a *h* divided against itself will fall.
11: 24 'I will return to the *h* I left.'
15: 8 sweep the *h* and search carefully
19: 9 Today salvation has come to this *h*,
Jn 2: 16 How dare you turn my Father's *h*
2: 17 "Zeal for your *h* will consume me."
12: 3 the *h* was filled with the fragrance
14: 2 In my Father's *h* are many rooms;
Ac 20: 20 you publicly and from *h* to *h*.
Ro 16: 5 the church that meets at their *h*.
Heb 3: 3 the builder of a *h* has greater honor
1Pe 2: 5 built into a spiritual *h* to be a holy

HOUSEHOLD (HOUSE)
Ex 12: 3 lamb for his family, one for each *h*.
Jos 24: 15 my *h*, we will serve the LORD."
Pr 31: 21 it snows, she has no fear for her *h*;
31: 27 over the affairs of her *h*
Mic 7: 6 are the members of his own *h*.
Mt 10: 36 will be the members of his own *h*.'
12: 25 or *h* divided against itself will not
Ac 16: 31 you will be saved — you and your *h*
Eph 2: 19 people and members of God's *h*,
1Ti 3: 12 manage his children and his *h* well.
3: 15 to conduct themselves in God's *h*,

HOUSEHOLDS (HOUSE)
Tit 1: 11 because they are ruining whole *h*

HOUSES (HOUSE)
Ex 12: 27 passed over the *h* of the Israelites
Mt 19: 29 everyone who has left *h* or brothers

HOVERING* (HOVERS)
Ge 1: 2 of God was *h* over the waters.
Isa 31: 5 Like birds *h* overhead,

HOVERS* (HOVERING)
Dt 32: 11 and *h* over its young,

HULDAH*
Prophetess inquired by Hilkiah for Josiah (2Ki 22; 2Ch 34:14 – 28).

HUMAN (HUMANITY)
Lev 24: 17 If anyone takes the life of a *h* being,
Isa 52: 14 his form marred beyond *h* likeness
Jn 8: 15 You judge by *h* standards;
Ro 1: 3 as to his *h* nature was a descendant
9: 5 from them is traced the *h* ancestry
1Co 1: 17 not with words of *h* wisdom,
1: 26 of you were wise by *h* standards;
2: 13 not in words taught us by *h* wisdom
2Co 3: 3 of stone but on tablets of *h* hearts.
Gal 3: 3 to attain your goal by *h* effort?
2Pe 2: 18 lustful desires of sinful *h* nature,

HUMANITY* (HUMAN)
Heb 2: 14 he too shared in their *h* so that

HUMBLE (HUMBLED HUMBLES HUMILIATE HUMILIATED HUMILITY)
Nu 12: 3 (Now Moses was a very *h* man,
2Ch 7: 14 will *h* themselves and pray
Ps 18: 27 You save the *h*
25: 9 He guides the *h* in what is right
149: 4 he crowns the *h* with salvation.
Pr 3: 34 but gives grace to the *h*.
Isa 66: 2 he who is *h* and contrite in spirit,
Mt 11: 29 for I am gentle and *h* in heart,
Eph 4: 2 Be completely *h* and gentle;
Jas 4: 6 but gives grace to the *h*."
4: 10 *H* yourselves before the Lord,
1Pe 5: 5 but gives grace to the *h*."
5: 6 *H* yourselves,

HUMBLED (HUMBLE)
Mt 23: 12 whoever exalts himself will be *h*,
Lk 14: 11 who exalts himself will be *h*,
Php 2: 8 he *h* himself

HUMBLES* (HUMBLE)
1Sa 2: 7 he *h* and he exalts.
Isa 26: 5 He *h* those who dwell on high,
Mt 18: 4 whoever *h* himself like this child is
23: 12 whoever *h* himself will be exalted.
Lk 14: 11 he who *h* himself will be exalted."
18: 14 he who *h* himself will be exalted."

HUMILIATE* (HUMBLE)
Pr 25: 7 than for him to *h* you
1Co 11: 22 and *h* those who have nothing?

HUMILIATED (HUMBLE)
Jer 31: 19 I was ashamed and *h*
Lk 14: 9 *h*, you will have to take the least

HUMILITY* (HUMBLE)
Ps 45: 4 of truth, *h* and righteousness;
Pr 11: 2 but with *h* comes wisdom.
15: 33 and *h* comes before honor.
18: 12 but *h* comes before honor.
22: 4 *H* and the fear of the LORD
Zep 2: 3 Seek righteousness, seek *h*;
Ac 20: 19 I served the Lord with great *h*
Php 2: 3 but in *h* consider others better
Col 2: 18 let anyone who delights in false *h*
2: 23 their false *h* and their harsh
3: 12 *h*, gentleness and patience.
Tit 3: 2 and to show true *h* toward all men.
Jas 3: 13 in the *h* that comes from wisdom.
1Pe 5: 5 clothe yourselves with *h*

HUNG (HANG)
Dt 21: 23 anyone who is *h* on a tree is
Mt 18: 6 him to have a large millstone *h*
Lk 19: 48 all the people *h* on his words.
Gal 3: 13 "Cursed is everyone who is *h*

HUNGER (HUNGRY)
Ne 9: 15 In their *h* you gave them bread
Pr 6: 30 to satisfy his *h* when he is starving.
Mt 5: 6 Blessed are those who *h*
Lk 6: 21 Blessed are you who *h* now,
2Co 6: 5 sleepless nights and *h*; in purity,
11: 27 I have known *h* and thirst
Rev 7: 16 Never again will they *h*;

HUNGRY (HUNGER)
Job 24: 10 carry the sheaves, but still go *h*.
Ps 107: 9 and fills the *h* with good things.
146: 7 and gives food to the *h*.

Pr 19: 15 and the shiftless man goes *h*.
25: 21 If your enemy is *h*, give him food
27: 7 to the *h* even what is bitter tastes
Isa 58: 7 not to share your food with the *h*
58: 10 spend yourselves in behalf of the *h*
Eze 18: 7 but gives his food to the *h*
18: 16 but gives his food to the *h*
Mt 15: 32 I do not want to send them away *h*,
25: 35 For I was *h* and you gave me
25: 42 For I was *h* and you gave me
Lk 1: 53 He has filled the *h* with good things
Jn 6: 35 comes to me will never go *h*,
Ro 12: 20 "If your enemy is *h*, feed him;
1Co 4: 11 To this very hour we go *h*
Php 4: 12 whether well fed or *h*,

HUR
Ex 17: 12 Aaron and *H* held his hands up —

HURL
Mic 7: 19 *h* all our iniquities into the depths

HURT (HURTS)
Ecc 8: 9 it over others to his own *h*.
Mk 16: 18 deadly poison, it will not *h* them
Rev 2: 11 He who overcomes will not be *h*

HURTS* (HURT)
Ps 15: 4 even when it *h*,
Pr 26: 28 A lying tongue hates those it *h*,

HUSBAND (HUSBAND'S HUSBANDS)
Pr 31: 11 Her *h* has full confidence in her
31: 23 Her *h* is respected at the city gate,
31: 28 her *h* also, and he praises her:
Isa 54: 5 For your Maker is your *h* —
Jer 3: 14 the LORD, "for I am your *h*.
3: 20 like a woman unfaithful to her *h*,
Jn 4: 17 "I have no *h*," she replied.
Ro 7: 2 a married woman is bound to her *h*
1Co 7: 2 and each woman her own *h*.
7: 3 The *h* should fulfill his marital duty
7: 10 wife must not separate from her *h*.
7: 11 And a *h* must not divorce his wife.
7: 13 And if a woman has a *h* who is not
7: 14 For the unbelieving *h* has been
7: 39 A woman is bound to her *h* as long
7: 39 But if her *h* dies, she is free
2Co 11: 2 I promised you to one *h*, to Christ,
Gal 4: 27 woman than of her who has a *h*."
Eph 5: 23 For the *h* is the head of the wife
5: 33 and the wife must respect her *h*.
1Ti 3: 2 the *h* of but one wife, temperate,
3: 12 A deacon must be the *h* of
5: 9 has been faithful to her *h*,
Tit 1: 6 An elder must be blameless, the *h*

HUSBANDMAN see GARDENER

HUSBAND'S (HUSBAND)
Dt 25: 5 Her *h* brother shall take her
Pr 12: 4 of noble character is her *h* crown,
1Co 7: 4 the *h* body does not belong

HUSBANDS (HUSBAND)
Eph 5: 22 submit to your *h* as to the Lord.
5: 25 *H*, love your wives, just
5: 28 *h* ought to love their wives
Col 3: 18 submit to your *h*, as is fitting
3: 19 *H*, love your wives and do not be
Tit 2: 4 the younger women to love their *h*
2: 5 and to be subject to their *h*,
1Pe 3: 1 same way be submissive to your *h*
3: 7 *H*, in the same way be considerate

HUSHAI
Wise man of David who frustrated Ahithophel's advice and foiled Absalom's revolt (2Sa 15:32 – 37; 16:15 – 17:16; 1Ch 27:33).

HYMN* (HYMNS)
Ps 40: 3 a *h* of praise to our God.
Mt 26: 30 they had sung a *h*, they went out
Mk 14: 26 they had sung a *h*, they went out
1Co 14: 26 everyone has a *h*, or a word

HYMNS* (HYMN)
Ac 16: 25 Silas were praying and singing *h*
Ro 15: 9 I will sing *h* to your name."
Eph 5: 19 to one another with psalms, *h*
Col 3: 16 *h* and spiritual songs with gratitude

HYPOCRISY* (HYPOCRITE HYPOCRITES HYPOCRITICAL)
Mt 23: 28 but on the inside you are full of *h*
Mk 12: 15 we?" But Jesus knew their *h*.
Lk 12: 1 yeast of the Pharisees, which is *h*.
Gal 2: 13 The other Jews joined him in his *h*,
2: 13 by their *h* even Barnabas was led
1Pe 2: 1 *h*, envy, and slander of every kind.

HYPOCRITE* (HYPOCRISY)
Mt 7: 5 You *h*, first take the plank out
Lk 6: 42 You *h*, first take the plank out

HYPOCRITES* (HYPOCRISY)
Ps 26: 4 nor do I consort with *h*;
Mt 6: 2 as the *h* do in the synagogues
6: 5 when you pray, do not be like the *h*
6: 16 do not look somber as the *h* do,
15: 7 You *h*! Isaiah was right
22: 18 their evil intent, said, "You *h*,
23: 13 of the law and Pharisees, you *h*!
23: 15 of the law and Pharisees, you *h*!
23: 23 of the law and Pharisees, you *h*!
23: 25 of the law and Pharisees, you *h*!
23: 27 you *h*! You are like whitewashed
23: 29 of the law and Pharisees, you *h*!
24: 51 and assign him a place with the *h*,
Mk 7: 6 when he prophesied about you *h*;
Lk 12: 56 *H*! You know how
13: 15 The Lord answered him, "You *h*!

HYPOCRITICAL* (HYPOCRISY)
1Ti 4: 2 teachings come through *h* liars,

HYSSOP
Ex 12: 22 Take a bunch of *h*, dip it
Ps 51: 7 with *h*, and I will be clean;
Jn 19: 29 the sponge on a stalk of the *h* plant,

ICHABOD
1Sa 4: 21 She named the boy *I*, saying,

IDLE* (IDLENESS IDLERS)
Dt 32: 47 They are not just *i* words for you —
Job 11: 3 Will your *i* talk reduce men
Ecc 10: 18 if his hands are *i*, the house leaks.
11: 6 at evening let not your hands be *i*,
Isa 58: 13 as you please or speaking *i* words,
Col 2: 18 mind puffs him up with *i* notions.
1Th 5: 14 those who are *i*, encourage
2Th 3: 6 away from every brother who is *i*
3: 7 We were not *i* when we were
3: 11 We hear that some among you are *i*
1Ti 5: 13 they get into the habit of being *i*

IDLENESS* (IDLE)
Pr 31: 27 and does not eat the bread of *i*.

IDLERS* (IDLE)
1Ti 5: 13 And not only do they become *i*,

IDOL (IDOLATER IDOLATERS IDOLATRY IDOLS)
Ex 20: 4 make for yourself an *i* in the form
32: 4 made it into an *i* cast in the shape
Isa 40: 19 As for an *i*, a craftsman casts it,
41: 7 He nails down the *i*
44: 15 he makes an *i* and bows down to it.
44: 17 From the rest he makes a god, his *i*;
Hab 2: 18 "Of what value is an *i*,
1Co 8: 4 We know that an *i* is nothing at all

IDOLATER* (IDOL)
1Co 5: 11 an *i* or a slanderer, a drunkard
Eph 5: 5 greedy person — such a man is an *i*

IDOLATERS (IDOL)
1Co 5: 10 or the greedy and swindlers, or *i*.
6: 9 Neither the sexually immoral nor *i*

IDOLATRY (IDOL)
1Sa 15: 23 and arrogance like the evil of *i*.
1Co 10: 14 my dear friends, flee from *i*.
Gal 5: 20 and debauchery; *i* and witchcraft;
Col 3: 5 evil desires and greed, which is *i*.
1Pe 4: 3 orgies, carousing and detestable *i*.

IDOLS (IDOL)
Dt 32: 16 angered him with their detestable *i*.
Ps 78: 58 aroused his jealousy with their *i*.
Isa 44: 9 All who make *i* are nothing,
Eze 23: 39 sacrificed their children to their *i*,
Ac 15: 20 to abstain from food polluted by *i*,
21: 25 abstain from food sacrificed to *i*,
1Co 8: 1 Now about food sacrificed to *i*:
1Jn 5: 21 children, keep yourselves from *i*.
Rev 2: 14 to sin by eating food sacrificed to *i*

IGNORANT (IGNORE)
1Co 15: 34 for there are some who are *i* of God
Heb 5: 2 to deal gently with those who are *i*
1Pe 2: 15 good you should silence the *i* talk
2Pe 3: 16 which *i* and unstable people distort

IGNORE (IGNORANT IGNORED IGNORES)
Dt 22: 1 do not *i* it but be sure
Ps 9: 12 he does not *i* the cry of the afflicted
Heb 2: 3 if we *i* such a great salvation?

IGNORED (IGNORE)
Hos 4: 6 you have *i* the law of your God,
1Co 14: 38 he ignores this, he himself will be *i*.

IGNORES* (IGNORE)
Pr 10: 17 whoever *i* correction leads others
13: 18 He who *i* discipline comes
15: 32 He who *i* discipline despises
1Co 14: 38 If he *i* this, he himself will be

ILL (ILLNESS)
Mt 4: 24 brought to him all who were *i*

ILL-GOTTEN
Pr 1: 19 the end of all who go after *i* gain;
10: 2 *I* treasures are of no value,

ILL-TEMPERED* (TEMPER)
Pr 21: 19 than with a quarrelsome and *i* wife.

ILLEGITIMATE
Heb 12: 8 then you are *i* children

ILLNESS (ILL)
2Ki 8: 9 'Will I recover from this *i*?' "
2Ch 16: 12 even in his *i* he did not seek help
Ps 41: 3 and restore him from his bed of *i*.
Isa 38: 9 king of Judah after his *i*

ILLUMINATED*
Rev 18: 1 and the earth was *i* by his splendor.

IMAGE (IMAGES)
Ge 1: 26 "Let us make man in our *i*,
1: 27 So God created man in his own *i*,
9: 6 for in the *i* of God
Dt 27: 15 "Cursed is the man who carves an *i*
Isa 40: 18 What *i* will you compare him to?
Da 3: 1 King Nebuchadnezzar made an *i*
1Co 11: 7 since he is the *i* and glory of God;
2Co 4: 4 glory of Christ, who is the *i* of God.
Col 1: 15 He is the *i* of the invisible God,
3: 10 in knowledge in the *i* of its Creator.
Rev 13: 14 them to set up an *i* in honor

IMAGES (IMAGE)
Ps 97: 7 All who worship *i* are put to shame,
Jer 10: 14 His *i* are a fraud;
Ro 1: 23 of the immortal God for *i* made

IMAGINATION (IMAGINE)
Eze 13: 2 who prophesy out of their own *i*:

IMAGINE (IMAGINATION)
Eph 3: 20 more than all we ask or *i*,

IMITATE (IMITATORS)
1Co 4: 16 Therefore I urge you to *i* me.
Heb 6: 12 but to *i* those who through faith
13: 7 of their way of life and *i* their faith.
3Jn : 11 do not *i* what is evil but what is

IMITATORS* (IMITATE)
Eph 5: 1 Be *i* of God, therefore,
1Th 1: 6 You became *i* of us and of the Lord
2: 14 became *i* of God's churches

IMMANUEL*
Isa 7: 14 birth to a son, and will call him *I*.
8: 8 O *I*!"
Mt 1: 23 and they will call him *I*" —

IMMORAL* (IMMORALITY)
Pr 6: 24 keeping you from the *i* woman,
1Co 5: 9 to associate with sexually *i* people
5: 10 the people of this world who are *i*,
5: 11 but is sexually *i* or greedy,
6: 9 Neither the sexually *i* nor idolaters
Eph 5: 5 No *i*, impure or greedy person —
Heb 12: 16 See that no one is sexually *i*,
13: 4 the adulterer and all the sexually *i*.
Rev 21: 8 the murderers, the sexually *i*,
22: 15 the sexually *i*, the murderers,

IMMORALITY* (IMMORAL)
Nu 25: 1 in sexual *i* with Moabite women,
Jer 3: 9 Because Israel's *i* mattered so little
Mt 15: 19 murder, adultery, sexual *i*, theft,
Mk 7: 21 sexual *i*, theft, murder, adultery,
Ac 15: 20 from sexual *i*, from the meat
15: 29 animals and from sexual *i*.
21: 25 animals and from sexual *i*."
Ro 13: 13 not in sexual *i* and debauchery,
1Co 5: 1 reported that there is sexual *i*
6: 13 The body is not meant for sexual *i*,
6: 18 Flee from sexual *i*.
7: 2 But since there is so much *i*,
10: 8 We should not commit sexual *i*,
Gal 5: 19 sexual *i*, impurity and debauchery;
Eph 5: 3 must not be even a hint of sexual *i*,
Col 3: 5 sexual *i*, impurity, lust, evil desires
1Th 4: 3 that you should avoid sexual *i*;
Jude : 4 grace of our God into a license for *i*
: 7 gave themselves up to sexual *i*
Rev 2: 14 and by committing sexual *i*.

Rev 2: 20 misleads my servants into sexual *i*
2: 21 given her time to repent of her *i*,
9: 21 their sexual *i* or their thefts.

IMMORTAL* (IMMORTALITY)
Ro 1: 23 glory of the *i* God for images made
1Ti 1: 17 Now to the King eternal, *i*,
6: 16 who alone is *i* and who lives

IMMORTALITY* (IMMORTAL)
Pr 12: 28 along that path is *i*.
Ro 2: 7 honor and *i*, he will give eternal life
1Co 15: 53 and the mortal with *i*.
15: 54 with *i*, then the saying that is
2Ti 1: 10 and *i* to light through the gospel.

IMPARTIAL*
Jas 3: 17 and good fruit, *i* and sincere.

IMPARTS*
Pr 29: 15 The rod of correction *i* wisdom,

IMPERFECT*
1Co 13: 10 perfection comes, the *i* disappears.

IMPERISHABLE
1Co 15: 42 it is raised *i*; it is sown in dishonor,
15: 50 nor does the perishable inherit the *i*
1Pe 1: 23 not of perishable seed, but of *i*,

IMPLANTED*
Ps 94: 9 Does he who *i* the ear not hear?

IMPLORE*
Mal 1: 9 "Now *i* God to be gracious to us.
2Co 5: 20 We *i* you on Christ's behalf:

IMPORTANCE* (IMPORTANT)
1Co 15: 3 passed on to you as of first *i*:

IMPORTANT (IMPORTANCE)
Mt 6: 25 Is not life more *i* than food,
23: 23 have neglected the more *i* matters
Mk 12: 29 "The most *i* one," answered Jesus,
12: 33 as yourself is more *i* than all burnt
Php 1: 18 The *i* thing is that in every way,

IMPOSSIBLE
Mt 17: 20 Nothing will be *i* for you."
19: 26 "With man this is *i*,
Mk 10: 27 "With man this is *i*, but not
Lk 1: 37 For nothing is *i* with God."
18: 27 "What is *i* with men is possible
Ac 2: 24 it was *i* for death to keep its hold
Heb 6: 4 It is *i* for those who have once been
6: 18 things in which it is *i* for God to lie,
10: 4 because it is *i* for the blood of bulls
11: 6 without faith it is *i* to please God,

IMPOSTORS
2Ti 3: 13 and *i* will go from bad to worse,

IMPRESS* (IMPRESSES)
Dt 6: 7 *I* them on your children.

IMPRESSES* (IMPRESS)
Pr 17: 10 A rebuke *i* a man of discernment

IMPROPER*
Eph 5: 3 these are *i* for God's holy people.

IMPURE (IMPURITY)
Ac 10: 15 not call anything *i* that God has
Eph 5: 5 No immoral, *i* or greedy person—
1Th 2: 3 spring from error or *i* motives,
4: 7 For God did not call us to be *i*,
Rev 21: 27 Nothing *i* will ever enter it,

IMPURITY (IMPURE)
Ro 1: 24 hearts to sexual *i* for the degrading
Gal 5: 19 sexual immorality, *i*
Eph 4: 19 as to indulge in every kind of *i*,
5: 3 or of any kind of *i*, or of greed,
Col 3: 5 *i*, lust, evil desires and greed,

INCENSE
Ex 30: 1 altar of acacia wood for burning *i*.
40: 5 Place the gold altar of *i* in front
Ps 141: 2 my prayer be set before you like *i*;
Mt 2: 11 him with gifts of gold and of *i*
Heb 9: 4 which had the golden altar of *i*
Rev 5: 8 were holding golden bowls full of *i*,
8: 4 The smoke of the *i*, together

INCLINATION (INCLINES)
Ge 6: 5 and that every *i* of the thoughts

INCLINES* (INCLINATION)
Ecc 10: 2 The heart of the wise *i* to the right,

INCOME
Ecc 5: 10 wealth is never satisfied with his *i*.
1Co 16: 2 sum of money in keeping with his *i*,

INCOMPARABLE*
Eph 2: 7 ages he might show the *i* riches

INCREASE (EVER-INCREASING INCREASED INCREASES INCREASING)
Ge 1: 22 "Be fruitful and *i* in number
3: 16 "I will greatly *i* your pains
8: 17 be fruitful and *i* in number upon it
Ps 62: 10 though your riches *i*,
Pr 22: 16 oppresses the poor to *i* his wealth
Isa 9: 7 Of the *i* of his government
Mt 24: 12 Because of the *i* of wickedness,
Lk 17: 5 said to the Lord, "*I* our faith!"
Ac 12: 24 But the word of God continued to *i*
Ro 5: 20 added so that the trespass might *i*.
1Th 3: 12 May the Lord make your love *i*

INCREASED (INCREASE)
Ac 6: 7 of disciples in Jerusalem *i* rapidly,
Ro 5: 20 But where sin *i*, grace *i* all the more

INCREASES (INCREASE)
Pr 24: 5 and a man of knowledge *i* strength;

INCREASING (INCREASE)
Ac 6: 1 when the number of disciples was *i*,
2Th 1: 3 one of you has for each other is *i*.
2Pe 1: 8 these qualities in *i* measure,

INCREDIBLE*
Ac 26: 8 of you consider it *i* that God raises

INDECENT
Ro 1: 27 Men committed *i* acts

INDEPENDENT*
1Co 11: 11 however, woman is not *i* of man,
11: 11 of man, nor is man *i* of woman.

INDESCRIBABLE*
2Co 9: 15 Thanks be to God for his *i* gift!

INDESTRUCTIBLE*
Heb 7: 16 on the basis of the power of an *i* life

INDIGNANT
Mk 10: 14 When Jesus saw this, he was *i*.

INDISPENSABLE*
1Co 12: 22 seem to be weaker are *i*,

INEFFECTIVE*
2Pe 1: 8 they will keep you from being *i*

INEXPRESSIBLE*
2Co 12: 4 He heard *i* things, things that man
1Pe 1: 8 are filled with an *i* and glorious joy,

INFANCY* (INFANTS)
2Ti 3: 15 from *i* you have known the holy

INFANTS (INFANCY)
Ps 8: 2 From the lips of children and *i*
Mt 21: 16 "'From the lips of children and *i*
1Co 3: 1 but as worldly—mere *i* in Christ.
14: 20 In regard to evil be *i*,
Eph 4: 14 Then we will no longer be *i*,

INFIRMITIES*
Isa 53: 4 Surely he took up our *i*
Mt 8: 17 "He took up our *i*

INFLAMED
Ro 1: 27 were *i* with lust for one another.

INFLUENTIAL*
1Co 1: 26 not many were *i*; not many were

INHABITANTS (INHABITED)
Nu 33: 55 "'But if you do not drive out the *i*
Rev 8: 13 Woe! Woe to the *i* of the earth,

INHABITED (INHABITANTS)
Isa 45: 18 but formed it to be *i*—

INHERIT (CO-HEIRS HEIR HEIRS HERITAGE INHERITANCE)
Dt 1: 38 because he will lead Israel to *i* it.
Jos 1: 6 people to *i* the land I swore
Ps 37: 11 But the meek will *i* the land
37: 29 the righteous will *i* the land
Zec 2: 12 The LORD will *i* Judah
Mt 5: 5 for they will *i* the earth.
19: 29 as much and will *i* eternal life.
Mk 10: 17 "what must I do to *i* eternal life?"
Lk 10: 25 "what must I do to *i* eternal life?"
18: 18 what must I do to *i* eternal life?"
1Co 6: 9 the wicked will not *i* the kingdom
15: 50 blood cannot *i* the kingdom of God
Rev 21: 7 He who overcomes will *i* all this,

INHERITANCE (INHERIT)
Lev 20: 24 I will give it to you as an *i*,
Dt 4: 20 to be the people of his *i*,
10: 9 the LORD is their *i*, as the LORD
Jos 14: 3 two-and-a-half tribes their *i* east
Ps 16: 6 surely I have a delightful *i*.
33: 12 the people he chose for his *i*.
136: 21 and gave their land as an *i*,
Pr 13: 22 A good man leaves an *i*
Mt 25: 34 blessed by my Father; take your *i*,
Eph 1: 14 who is a deposit guaranteeing our *i*
5: 5 has any *i* in the kingdom of Christ
Col 1: 12 you to share in the *i* of the saints
3: 24 you know that you will receive an *i*
Heb 9: 15 receive the promised eternal *i*—
1Pe 1: 4 and into an *i* that can never perish,

INIQUITIES (INIQUITY)
Ps 78: 38 he forgave their *i*
103: 10 or repay us according to our *i*.
Isa 53: 5 he was crushed for our *i*;
53: 11 and he will bear their *i*.
59: 2 But your *i* have separated
Mic 7: 19 and hurl all our *i* into the depths

INIQUITY (INIQUITIES)
Ps 25: 11 forgive my *i*, though it is great.
32: 5 and did not cover up my *i*.
51: 2 Wash away all my *i*
51: 9 and blot out all my *i*.
Isa 53: 6 the *i* of us all.

INJURED
Eze 34: 16 will bind up the *i* and strengthen
Zec 11: 16 or heal the *i*, or feed the healthy,

INJUSTICE
2Ch 19: 7 the LORD our God there is no *i*

INK
2Co 3: 3 not with *i* but with the Spirit

INN*
Lk 2: 7 there was no room for them in the *i*
10: 34 took him to an *i* and took care

INNOCENT
Ex 23: 7 do not put an *i* or honest person
Dt 25: 1 acquitting the *i* and condemning
Pr 6: 17 hands that shed *i* blood,
17: 26 It is not good to punish an *i* man,
Mt 10: 16 shrewd as snakes and as *i* as doves.
27: 4 "for I have betrayed *i* blood."
27: 24 I am *i* of this man's blood," he said.
Ac 20: 26 declare to you today that I am *i*
Ro 16: 19 what is good, and *i* about what is
1Co 4: 4 but that does not make me *i*.

INQUIRE
Isa 8: 19 should not a people *i* of their God?

INSCRIPTION
Mt 22: 20 And whose *i*?" "Caesar's,"
2Ti 2: 19 with this *i*: "The Lord knows those

INSIGHT
1Ki 4: 29 Solomon wisdom and very great *i*,
Ps 119: 99 I have more *i* than all my teachers,
Pr 5: 1 listen well to my words of *i*,
21: 30 There is no wisdom, no *i*, no plan
Php 1: 9 more in knowledge and depth of *i*,
2Ti 2: 7 for the Lord will give you *i*

INSOLENT
Ro 1: 30 God-haters, *i*, arrogant

INSPIRED*
Hos 9: 7 the *i* man a maniac.
1Th 1: 3 and your endurance *i* by hope

INSTALLED
Ps 2: 6 "I have *i* my King

INSTINCT* (INSTINCTS)
2Pe 2: 12 are like brute beasts, creatures of *i*,
Jude : 10 things they do understand by *i*,

INSTINCTS* (INSTINCT)
Jude : 19 who follow mere natural *i*

INSTITUTED
Ro 13: 2 rebelling against what God has *i*,
1Pe 2: 13 to every authority *i* among men:

INSTRUCT (INSTRUCTED INSTRUCTION INSTRUCTIONS INSTRUCTOR)
Ps 32: 8 I will *i* you and teach you
105: 22 to *i* his princes as he pleased
Pr 9: 9 *I* a wise man and he will be wiser
Ro 15: 14 and competent to *i* one another.
1Co 2: 16 that he may *i* him?"
14: 19 to *i* others than ten thousand words
2Ti 2: 25 who oppose him he must gently *i*,

INSTRUCTED (INSTRUCT)
2Ch 26: 5 who *i* him in the fear of God.
Pr 21: 11 a wise man is *i*, he gets knowledge.
Isa 50: 4 LORD has given me an *i* tongue,
Mt 13: 52 who has been *i* about the kingdom
1Co 14: 31 in turn so that everyone may be *i*

INSTRUCTION (INSTRUCT)
Pr 1: 8 Listen, my son, to your father's *i*
4: 1 Listen, my sons, to a father's *i*;
4: 13 Hold on to *i*, do not let it go;
8: 10 Choose my *i* instead of silver,
8: 33 Listen to my *i* and be wise;
13: 1 A wise son heeds his father's *i*,
13: 13 He who scorns *i* will pay for it,
16: 20 Whoever gives heed to *i* prospers,
16: 21 and pleasant words promote *i*.
19: 20 Listen to advice and accept *i*,
23: 12 Apply your heart to *i*
1Co 14: 6 or prophecy or word of *i*?
14: 26 or a word of *i*, a revelation,
Eph 6: 4 up in the training and *i* of the Lord.
1Th 4: 8 he who rejects this *i* does not reject
2Th 3: 14 If anyone does not obey our *i*
1Ti 1: 18 I give you this *i* in keeping
6: 3 to the sound *i* of our Lord Jesus
2Ti 4: 2 with great patience and careful *i*.

INSTRUCTIONS (INSTRUCT)
1Ti 3: 14 I am writing you these *i* so that,

INSTRUCTOR (INSTRUCT)
Gal 6: 6 share all good things with his *i*.

INSTRUMENT* (INSTRUMENTS)
Eze 33: 32 beautiful voice and plays an *i* well,
Ac 9: 15 This man is my chosen *i*
2Ti 2: 21 he will be an *i* for noble purposes,

INSTRUMENTS (INSTRUMENT)
Ro 6: 13 as *i* of wickedness, but rather offer

INSULT (INSULTED INSULTS)
Pr 9: 7 corrects a mocker invites *i*;
12: 16 but a prudent man overlooks an *i*.
Mt 5: 11 Blessed are you when people *i* you,
Lk 6: 22 when they exclude you and *i* you
1Pe 3: 9 evil with evil or *i* with *i*,

INSULTED (INSULT)
Heb 10: 29 and who has *i* the Spirit of grace?
Jas 2: 6 love him? But you have *i* the poor.
1Pe 4: 14 If you are *i* because of the name

INSULTS (INSULT)
Ps 22: 7 they hurl *i*, shaking their heads:
69: 9 the *i* of those who insult you fall
Pr 22: 10 quarrels and *i* are ended.
Mk 15: 29 passed by hurled *i* at him,
Jn 9: 28 Then they hurled *i* at him and said,
Ro 15: 3 "The *i* of those who insult you have
2Co 12: 10 in *i*, in hardships, in persecutions,
1Pe 2: 23 When they hurled their *i* at him,

INTEGRITY*
Dt 9: 5 or your *i* that you are going
1Ki 9: 4 if you walk before me in *i* of heart
1Ch 29: 17 the heart and are pleased with *i*.
Ne 7: 2 because he was a man of *i*
Job 2: 3 And he still maintains his *i*,
2: 9 "Are you still holding on to your *i*?
6: 29 reconsider, for my *i* is at stake.
27: 5 till I die, I will not deny my *i*.
Ps 7: 8 according to my *i*, O Most High.
25: 21 May *i* and uprightness protect me,
41: 12 In my *i* you uphold me
78: 72 David shepherded them with *i*
Pr 10: 9 The man of *i* walks securely,
11: 3 The *i* of the upright guides them,
13: 6 Righteousness guards the man of *i*,
17: 26 or to flog officials for their *i*.
29: 10 Bloodthirsty men hate a man of *i*
Isa 45: 23 my mouth has uttered in all *i*
59: 4 no one pleads his case with *i*.
Mt 22: 16 "we know you are a man of *i*
Mk 12: 14 we know you are a man of *i*.
Tit 2: 7 your teaching show *i*, seriousness

INTELLIGENCE (INTELLIGENT)
Isa 29: 14 the *i* of the intelligent will vanish."
1Co 1: 19 *i* of the intelligent I will frustrate."

INTELLIGENT (INTELLIGENCE)
Isa 29: 14 the intelligence of the *i* will vanish

INTELLIGIBLE
1Co 14: 19 I would rather speak five *i* words

INTENDED
Ge 50: 20 place of God? You *i* to harm me,

INTENSE
1Th 2: 17 out of our *i* longing we made every
Rev 16: 9 They were seared by the *i* heat

INTERCEDE (INTERCEDES INTERCEDING INTERCESSION INTERCESSOR)
Heb 7: 25 he always lives to *i* for them.

INTERCEDES* (INTERCEDE)
Ro 8: 26 but the Spirit himself *i* for us
8: 27 because the Spirit *i* for the saints

INTERCEDING* (INTERCEDE)
Ro 8: 34 hand of God and is also *i* for us.

INTERCESSION* (INTERCEDE)
Isa 53: 12 and made *i* for the transgressors.
1Ti 2: 1 *i* and thanksgiving be made

INTERCESSOR* (INTERCEDE)
Job 16: 20 My *i* is my friend

INTEREST (INTERESTS)
Lev 25: 36 Do not take *i* of any kind from him,
Dt 23: 20 You may charge a foreigner *i*,
Mt 25: 27 would have received it back with *i*.
Php 2: 20 who takes a genuine *i*

INTERESTS (INTEREST)
1Co 7: 34 his wife—and his *i* are divided.
Php 2: 4 only to your own *i*, but also to the *i*
2: 21 everyone looks out for his own *i*,

INTERFERE*
Ezr 6: 7 Do not *i* with the work

INTERMARRY (MARRY)
Dt 7: 3 Do not *i* with them.
Ezr 9: 14 and *i* with the peoples who commit

INTERPRET (INTERPRETATION INTERPRETER INTERPRETS)
Ge 41: 15 "I had a dream, and no one can *i* it.
Mt 16: 3 you cannot *i* the signs of the times.
1Co 12: 30 Do all *i*? But eagerly desire
14: 13 pray that he may *i* what he says.
14: 27 one at a time, and someone must *i*.

INTERPRETATION (INTERPRET)
1Co 12: 10 and to still another the *i* of tongues.
14: 26 a revelation, a tongue or an *i*.
2Pe 1: 20 about by the prophet's own *i*.

INTERPRETER (INTERPRET)
1Co 14: 28 If there is no *i*, the speaker should

INTERPRETS (INTERPRET)
1Co 14: 5 he *i*, so that the church may be

INVADED
2Ki 17: 5 king of Assyria *i* the entire land,
24: 1 king of Babylon *i* the land,

INVENT* (INVENTED)
Ro 1: 30 boastful; they *i* ways of doing evil;

INVENTED* (INVENT)
2Pe 1: 16 We did not follow cleverly *i* stories

INVESTIGATED
Lk 1: 3 I myself have carefully *i* everything

INVISIBLE*
Ro 1: 20 of the world God's *i* qualities—
Col 1: 15 He is the image of the *i* God,
1: 16 and on earth, visible and *i*,
1Ti 1: 17 immortal, *i*, the only God,
Heb 11: 27 because he saw him who is *i*.

INVITE (INVITED INVITES)
Mt 22: 9 *i* to the banquet anyone you find.'
25: 38 did we see you a stranger and *i* you
Lk 14: 12 do not *i* your friends, your brothers
14: 13 you give a banquet, *i* the poor,

INVITED (INVITE)
Zep 1: 7 he has consecrated those he has *i*.
Mt 22: 14 For many are *i*, but few are chosen
25: 35 I was a stranger and you *i* me in,
Lk 14: 10 But when you are *i*, take the lowest
Rev 19: 9 'Blessed are those who are *i*

INVITES (INVITE)
Pr 18: 6 and his mouth *i* a beating.
1Co 10: 27 If some unbeliever *i* you to a meal

INVOLVED
2Ti 2: 4 a soldier gets *i* in civilian affairs—

IRON
2Ki 6: 6 threw it there, and made the *i* float.
Ps 2: 9 will rule them with an *i* scepter;
Pr 27: 17 As *i* sharpens *i*,
Da 2: 33 and thighs of bronze, its legs of *i*,
1Ti 4: 2 have been seared as with a hot *i*.
Rev 2: 27 He will rule them with an *i* scepter;
12: 5 all the nations with an *i* scepter.
19: 15 He will rule them with an *i* scepter

IRRELIGIOUS*
1Ti 1: 9 and sinful, the unholy and *i*;

IRREVOCABLE*
Ro 11: 29 for God's gifts and his call are *i*.

ISAAC
Son of Abraham by Sarah (Ge 17:19; 21:1–7; 1Ch 1:28). Abrahamic covenant perpetuated through (Ge 17:21; 26:2–5). Offered up by Abraham (Ge 22; Heb 11:17–19). Rebekah taken as wife (Ge 24). Inherited Abraham's estate (Ge 25:5). Fathered Esau and Jacob (Ge 25:19–26; 1Ch 1:34). Nearly lost Rebekah to Abimelech (Ge 26:1–11). Covenant with Abimelech (Ge 26:12–31). Tricked into blessing Jacob (Ge 27). Death (Ge 35:27–29). Father of Israel (Ex 3:6; Dt 29:13; Ro 9:10).

ISAIAH
Prophet to Judah (Isa 1:1). Called by the LORD (Isa 6). Announced judgment to Ahaz (Isa 7), deliverance from Assyria to Hezekiah (2Ki 19; Isa 36–37), deliverance from death to Hezekiah (2Ki 20:1–11; Isa 38). Chronicler of Judah's history (2Ch 26:22; 32:32).

ISH-BOSHETH*
Son of Saul who attempted to succeed him as king (2Sa 2:8–4:12; 1Ch 8:33).

ISHMAEL
Son of Abraham by Hagar (Ge 16; 1Ch 1:28). Blessed, but not son of covenant (Ge 17:18–21; Gal 4:21–31). Sent away by Sarah (Ge 21:8–21). Children (Ge 25:12–18; 1Ch 1:29–31). Death (Ge 25:17).

ISLAND
Rev 1: 9 was on the *i* of Patmos
16: 20 Every *i* fled away

ISRAEL (ISRAEL'S ISRAELITE ISRAELITES)
1. Name given to Jacob (see JACOB).
2. Corporate name of Jacob's descendants; often specifically Northern Kingdom.
Ex 28: 11 Engrave the names of the sons of *I*
28: 29 of the sons of *I* over his heart
Nu 24: 17 a scepter will rise out of *I*.
Dt 6: 4 Hear, O *I*: The LORD our God,
10: 12 O *I*, what does the LORD your
Jos 4: 22 *I* crossed the Jordan on dry ground
Jdg 17: 6 In those days *I* had no king;
Ru 2: 12 of *I*, under whose wings you have
1Sa 3: 20 *I* from Dan to Beersheba
4: 21 "The glory has departed from *I*"—
14: 23 So the LORD rescued *I* that day,
15: 26 has rejected you as king over *I*!"
17: 46 will know that there is a God in *I*.
18: 16 But all *I* and Judah loved David,
2Sa 5: 2 'You will shepherd my people *I*,
5: 3 they anointed David king over *I*.
14: 25 In all *I* there was not a man
1Ki 1: 35 I have appointed him ruler over *I*
10: 9 of the LORD's eternal love for *I*,
18: 17 "Is that you, you troubler of *I*?"
19: 18 Yet I reserve seven thousand in *I*—
2Ki 5: 8 know that there is a prophet in *I*."
1Ch 17: 22 made your people *I* your very own
21: 1 incited David to take a census of *I*.
29: 25 Solomon in the sight of all *I*
2Ch 9: 8 of the love of your God for *I*
Ps 73: 1 Surely God is good to *I*,
81: 8 if you would but listen to me, O *I*!
98: 3 his faithfulness to the house of *I*;
99: 8 you were to *I* a forgiving God,
Isa 11: 12 and gather the exiles of *I*;
27: 6 *I* will bud and blossom
44: 21 O *I*, I will not forget you.
46: 13 my splendor to *I*.
Jer 2: 3 *I* was holy to the LORD,
23: 6 and *I* will live in safety.
31: 2 I will come to give rest to *I*."
31: 10 'He who scattered *I* will gather
31: 31 covenant with the house of *I*
33: 17 sit on the throne of the house of *I*,
Eze 3: 17 you a watchman for the house of *I*;
33: 7 you a watchman for the house of *I*;
34: 2 prophesy against the shepherds of *I*
37: 28 that I the LORD make *I* holy,
39: 23 of *I* went into exile for their sin,
Da 9: 20 my sin and the sin of my people *I*
Hos 11: 1 "When *I* was a child, I loved him,
Am 4: 12 prepare to meet your God, O *I*."
7: 11 and *I* will surely go into exile,
8: 2 "The time is ripe for my people *I*;
9: 14 I will bring back my exiled people *I*
Mic 5: 2 one who will be ruler over *I*,

Zep 3: 13 The remnant of I will do no wrong;
Zec 11: 14 brotherhood between Judah and I.
Mal 1: 5 even beyond the borders of I!'
Mt 2: 6 be the shepherd of my people I.' "
10: 6 Go rather to the lost sheep of I.
15: 24 only to the lost sheep of I."
Mk 12: 29 'Hear, O I, the Lord our God,
Lk 22: 30 judging the twelve tribes of I.
Ac 1: 6 going to restore the kingdom to I?"
9: 15 and before the people of I.
Ro 9: 4 of my own race, the people of I.
9: 6 all who are descended from I are I.
9: 31 but I, who pursued a law
11: 7 What I sought so earnestly it did
11: 26 And so all I will be saved,
Gal 6: 16 who follow this rule, even to the I
Eph 2: 12 excluded from citizenship in I
3: 6 Gentiles are heirs together with I,
Heb 8: 8 covenant with the house of I
Rev 7: 4 144,000 from all the tribes of I.
21: 12 the names of the twelve tribes of I.

ISRAEL'S (ISRAEL)

Jdg 10: 16 he could bear I misery no longer.
2Sa 23: 1 I singer of songs:
Isa 44: 6 I King and Redeemer, the LORD
Jer 3: 9 Because I immorality mattered
31: 9 because I am I father,
Jn 3: 10 "You are I teacher," said Jesus,

ISRAELITE (ISRAEL)

Ex 16: 1 The whole I community set out
35: 29 All the I men and women who
Nu 8: 16 offspring from every I woman.
20: 1 the whole I community arrived
20: 22 The whole I community set out
Jn 1: 47 "Here is a true I, in whom there is
Ro 11: 1 I am an I myself, a descendant

ISRAELITES (ISRAEL)

Ex 1: 7 the I were fruitful and multiplied
2: 23 The I groaned in their slavery
3: 9 the cry of the I has reached me,
12: 35 The I did as Moses instructed
12: 37 The I journeyed from Rameses
14: 22 and the I went through the sea
16: 12 I have heard the grumbling of the I.
16: 35 The I ate manna forty years,
24: 17 To the I the glory of the LORD
28: 30 decisions for the I over his heart
29: 45 Then I will dwell among the I
31: 16 The I are to observe the Sabbath,
33: 5 "Tell the I, 'You are a stiff-necked
39: 42 The I had done all the work just
Lev 22: 32 be acknowledged as holy by the I.
25: 46 rule over your fellow I ruthlessly.
25: 55 for the I belong to me as servants.
Nu 2: 32 These are the I, counted according
6: 23 'This is how you are to bless the I.
9: 2 "Have the I celebrate the Passover
9: 17 the I set out; wherever the cloud
10: 12 Then the I set out from the Desert
14: 2 All the I grumbled against Moses
20: 12 as holy in the sight of the I,
21: 6 they bit the people and many I died
26: 65 had told those I they would surely
27: 12 and see the land I have given the I.
33: 3 The I set out from Rameses
35: 10 "Speak to the I and say to them:
Dt 33: 1 on the I before his death.
Jos 1: 2 about to give to them — to the I.
5: 6 The I had moved about
7: 1 the I acted unfaithfully in regard
8: 32 There in the presence of the I,
18: 1 of the I gathered at Shiloh
21: 3 the I gave the Levites the following
22: 9 of Manasseh left the I at Shiloh
Jdg 2: 11 Then the I did evil in the eyes
3: 12 Once again the I did evil
4: 1 the I once again did evil in the eyes
6: 1 Again the I did evil in the eyes
10: 6 Again the I did evil in the eyes
13: 1 Again the I did evil in the eyes
1Sa 17: 2 Saul and the I assembled
1Ki 8: 63 and all the I dedicated the temple
9: 22 did not make slaves of any of the I;
12: 1 for all the I had gone there
12: 17 But as for the I who were living
2Ki 17: 24 towns of Samaria to replace the I.
1Ch 9: 2 in their own towns were some I,
10: 1 fought against Israel; the I fled
11: 4 and all the I marched to Jerusalem,
2Ch 7: 6 and all the I were standing.
Ne 1: 6 the sins we I, including myself
Jer 16: 14 who brought the I up out of Egypt,'
Hos 1: 10 "Yet the I will be like the sand
3: 1 Love her as the LORD loves the I,

Am 4: 5 boast about them, you I,
Mic 5: 3 return to join the I.
Ro 9: 27 the number of the I be like the sand
10: 1 for the I is that they may be saved.
10: 16 But not all the I accepted the good
2Co 11: 22 Are they I? So am I.

ISSACHAR

Son of Jacob by Leah (Ge 30:18; 35:23; 1Ch 2:1). Tribe of blessed (Ge 49:14–15; Dt 33:18–19), numbered (Nu 1:29; 26:25), allotted land (Jos 19:17–23; Eze 48:25), assisted Deborah (Jdg 5:15), 12,000 from (Rev 7:7).

ISSUING*

Da 9: 25 From the i of the decree to restore

ITALY

Ac 27: 1 decided that we would sail for I,
Heb 13: 24 from I send you their greetings.

ITCHING*

2Ti 4: 3 to say what their i ears want to hear

ITHAMAR

Son of Aaron (Ex 6:23; 1Ch 6:3). Duties at tabernacle (Ex 38:21; Nu 4:21–33; 7:8).

ITTAI

2Sa 15: 19 The king said to I the Gittite,

IVORY

1Ki 10: 22 silver and i, and apes and baboons.
22: 39 the palace he built and inlaid with i

JABBOK

Ge 32: 22 and crossed the ford of the J.
Dt 3: 16 and out to the J River,

JABESH

1Sa 11: 1 And all the men of J said to him,
31: 12 wall of Beth Shan and went to J,
1Ch 10: 12 and his sons and brought them to J.

JABESH GILEAD

Jdg 21: 8 that no one from J had come to
2Sa 2: 4 the men of J who had buried Saul,
1Ch 10: 11 the inhabitants of J heard

JACOB

Second son of Isaac, twin of Esau (Ge 25:21–26; 1Ch 1:34). Bought Esau's birthright (Ge 25:29–34); tricked Isaac into blessing him (Ge 27:1–37). Fled to Haran (Ge 28:1–5). Abrahamic covenant perpetuated through (Ge 28:13–15; Mal 1:2). Vision at Bethel (Ge 28:10–22). Served Laban for Rachel and Leah (Ge 29:1–30). Children (Ge 29:31–30:24; 35:16–26; 1Ch 2–9). Flocks increased (Ge 30:25–43). Returned to Canaan (Ge 31). Wrestled with God; name changed to Israel (Ge 32:22–32). Reconciled to Esau (Ge 33). Returned to Bethel (Ge 35:1–15). Favored Joseph (Ge 37:3). Sent sons to Egypt during famine (Ge 42–43). Settled in Egypt (Ge 46). Blessed Ephraim and Manasseh (Ge 48). Blessed sons (Ge 49:1–28; Heb 11:21). Death (Ge 49:29–33). Burial (Ge 50:1–14).

JAEL*

Woman who killed Canaanite general, Sisera (Jdg 4:17–22; 5:24–27).

JAIR

Judge from Gilead (Jdg 10:3–5).

JAIRUS*

Synagogue ruler whose daughter Jesus raised (Mk 5:22–43; Lk 8:41–56).

JAMES

1. Apostle; brother of John (Mt 4:21–22; 10:2; Mk 3:17; Lk 5:1–10). At transfiguration (Mt 17:1–13; Mk 9:1–13; Lk 9:28–36). Killed by Herod (Ac 12:2).

2. Apostle; son of Alphaeus (Mt 10:3; Mk 3:18; Lk 6:15).

3. Brother of Jesus (Mt 13:55; Mk 6:3; Lk 24:10; Gal 1:19) and Judas (Jude 1). With believers before Pentecost (Ac 1:13). Leader of church at Jerusalem (Ac 12:17; 15; 21:18; Gal 2:9, 12). Author of epistle (Jas 1:1).

JAPHETH

Son of Noah (Ge 5:32; 1Ch 1:4–5). Blessed (Ge 9:18–28). Sons of (Ge 10:2–5).

JAR (JARS)

Ge 24: 14 let down your j that I may have
1Ki 17: 14 'The j of flour will not be used up
Jer 19: 1 "Go and buy a clay j from a potter.
Lk 8: 16 hides it in a j or puts it under a bed.

JARS (JAR)

Jn 2: 6 Nearby stood six stone water j,
2Co 4: 7 we have this treasure in j of clay

JASPER

Ex 28: 20 row a chrysolite, an onyx and a j.
Eze 28: 13 chrysolite, onyx and j,
Rev 4: 3 sat there had the appearance of j
21: 19 The first foundation was j,

JAVELIN

1Sa 17: 45 me with sword and spear and j,

JAWBONE

Jdg 15: 15 Finding a fresh j of a donkey,

JEALOUS (JEALOUSY)

Ex 20: 5 the LORD your God, am a j God,
34: 14 whose name is Jealous, is a j God.
Dt 4: 24 God is a consuming fire, a j God.
6: 15 is a j God and his anger will burn
32: 21 They made me j by what is no god
Jos 24: 19 He is a holy God; he is a j God.
Eze 16: 38 of my wrath and j anger.
16: 42 my j anger will turn away from you
23: 25 I will direct my j anger against you,
36: 6 in my j wrath because you have
Joel 2: 18 the LORD will be j for his land
Na 1: 2 LORD is a j and avenging God;
Zep 3: 8 consumed by the fire of my j anger.
Zec 1: 14 I am very j for Jerusalem and Zion,
8: 2 "I am very j for Zion; I am burning
2Co 11: 2 I am j for you with a godly jealousy

JEALOUSY (JEALOUS)

Ps 79: 5 How long will your j burn like fire?
Pr 6: 34 for j arouses a husband's fury,
27: 4 but who can stand before j?
SS 8: 6 its j unyielding as the grave.
Zep 1: 18 In the fire of his j
Zec 8: 2 I am burning with j for her."
Ro 13: 13 debauchery, not in dissension and j
1Co 3: 3 For since there is j and quarreling
10: 22 trying to arouse the Lord's j?
2Co 11: 2 I am jealous for you with a godly j.
12: 20 j, outbursts of anger, factions,
Gal 5: 20 hatred, discord, j, fits of rage,

JEERS*

Heb 11: 36 Some faced j and flogging,

JEHOAHAZ

1. Son of Jehu; king of Israel (2Ki 13:1–9).

2. Son of Josiah; king of Judah (2Ki 23:31–34; 2Ch 36:1–4).

JEHOASH

1. See JOASH.

2. Son of Jehoahaz; king of Israel. Defeat of Aram prophesied by Elisha (2Ki 13:10–25). Defeated Amaziah in Jerusalem (2Ki 14:1–16; 2Ch 25:17–24).

JEHOIACHIN

Son of Jehoiakim; king of Judah exiled by Nebuchadnezzar (2Ki 24:8–17; 2Ch 36:8–10; Jer 22:24–30; 24:1). Raised from prisoner status (2Ki 25:27–30; Jer 52:31–34).

JEHOIADA

Priest who sheltered Joash from Athaliah (2Ki 11–12; 2Ch 22:11–24:16).

JEHOIAKIM

Son of Josiah; made king of Judah by Pharaoh Neco (2Ki 23:34–24:6; 2Ch 36:4–8; Jer 22:18–23). Burned scroll of Jeremiah's prophecies (Jer 36).

JEHORAM

1. Son of Jehoshaphat; king of Judah (2Ki 8:16–24). Prophesied against by Elijah; killed by the LORD (2Ch 21).

2. See JORAM.

JEHOSHAPHAT

Son of Asa; king of Judah. Strengthened his kingdom (2Ch 17). Joined with Ahab against Aram (2Ki 22; 2Ch 18). Established judges (2Ch 19). Joined with Joram against Moab (2Ki 3; 2Ch 20).

JEHU

1. Prophet against Baasha (2Ki 16:1–7).

2. King of Israel. Anointed by Elijah to obliterate house of Ahab (1Ki 19:16–17); anointed by servant of Elisha (2Ki 9:1–13). Killed Joram and Ahaziah (2Ki 9:14–29; 2Ch 22:7–9), Jezebel (2Ki 9:30–37), relatives of Ahab (2Ki 10:1–17), ministers of Baal (2Ki 10:18–29). Death (2Ki 10:30–36).

JEPHTHAH

Judge from Gilead who delivered Israel from Ammon (Jdg 10:6–12:7). Made rash vow concerning his daughter (Jdg 11:30–40).

JEREMIAH

Prophet to Judah (Jer 1:1–3). Called by the LORD (Jer 1). Put in stocks (Jer 20:1–3). Threatened for prophesying (Jer 11:18–23; 26). Opposed by Hananiah (Jer 28). Scroll burned (Jer 36). Imprisoned (Jer 37). Thrown into cistern (Jer 38). Forced to Egypt with those fleeing Babylonians (Jer 43).

JERICHO

Nu 22: 1 along the Jordan across from J.
Jos 3: 16 the people crossed over opposite J.
5: 10 camped at Gilgal on the plains of J,

Lk 10: 30 going down from Jerusalem to J,
Heb 11: 30 By faith the walls of J fell,

JEROBOAM

1. Official of Solomon; rebelled to become first king of Israel (1Ki 11:26–40; 12:1–20; 2Ch 10). Idolatry (1Ki 12:25–33); judgment for (1Ki 13–14; 2Ch 13).
2. Son of Jehoash; king of Israel (1Ki 14:23–29).

JERUSALEM

Jos 10: 1 of J heard that Joshua had taken Ai
15: 8 of the Jebusite city (that is, J).
Jdg 1: 8 The men of Judah attacked J also
1Sa 17: 54 head and brought it to J,
2Sa 5: 5 and in J he reigned over all Israel
5: 6 and his men marched to J
9: 13 And Mephibosheth lived in J,
11: 1 But David remained in J.
15: 29 took the ark of God back to J
24: 16 stretched out his hand to destroy J,
1Ki 3: 1 the LORD, and the wall around J.
9: 15 the wall of J, and Hazor, Megiddo
9: 19 whatever he desired to build in J,
10: 26 cities and also with him in J.
10: 27 as common in J as stones,
11: 7 of J, Solomon built a high place
11: 13 my servant and for the sake of J,
11: 36 always have a lamp before me in J,
11: 42 Solomon reigned in J
12: 27 at the temple of the LORD in J,
14: 21 and he reigned seventeen years in J
14: 25 Shishak king of Egypt attacked J.
15: 2 and he reigned in J three years.
15: 10 and he reigned in J forty-one years.
22: 42 he reigned in J twenty-five years.
2Ki 8: 17 and he reigned in J eight years.
8: 26 and he reigned in J one year.
12: 1 and he reigned in J forty years.
12: 17 Then he turned to attack J.
14: 2 he reigned in J twenty-nine years.
14: 13 Then Jehoash went to J
15: 2 and he reigned in J fifty-two years.
15: 33 and he reigned in J sixteen years.
16: 2 and he reigned in J sixteen years.
16: 5 Israel marched up to fight against J
18: 2 he reigned in J twenty-nine years.
18: 17 Lachish to King Hezekiah at J.
19: 31 For out of J will come a remnant,
21: 1 and he reigned in J fifty-five years.
21: 12 going to bring such disaster on J
21: 19 and he reigned in J two years.
22: 1 he reigned in J thirty-one years.
23: 27 and I will reject J, the city I chose,
23: 31 and he reigned in J three months.
23: 36 and he reigned in J eleven years.
24: 8 and he reigned in J three months.
24: 10 king of Babylon advanced on J
24: 14 He carried into exile all J:
24: 18 and he reigned in J eleven years.
24: 20 anger that all this happened to J
25: 1 king of Babylon marched against J
25: 9 royal palace and all the houses of J.
1Ch 11: 4 and all the Israelites marched to J,
21: 16 sword in his hand extended over J.
2Ch 1: 4 he had pitched a tent for it in J.
3: 1 the LORD in J on Mount Moriah,
6: 6 now I have chosen J for my Name
9: 1 she came to J to test him
20: 15 and all who live in Judah and J!
20: 27 and J returned joyfully to J,
29: 8 LORD has fallen on Judah and J;
36: 19 and broke down the wall of J;
Ezr 1: 2 a temple for him at J in Judah.
2: 1 to Babylon (they returned to J
3: 1 people assembled as one man in J.
4: 12 up to us from you have gone to J
4: 24 of God in J came to a standstill
6: 12 or to destroy this temple in J.
7: 8 Ezra arrived in J in the fifth month
9: 9 a wall of protection in Judah and J.
10: 7 for all the exiles to assemble in J.
Ne 1: 2 the exile, and also about J.
1: 3 The wall of J is broken down,
2: 11 to J, and after staying there three
2: 17 Come, let us rebuild the wall of J,
2: 20 you have no share in J or any claim
3: 8 They restored J as far as the Broad
4: 8 fight against J and stir up trouble
11: 1 leaders of the people settled in J,
12: 27 At the dedication of the wall of J,
12: 43 in J could be heard far away.
Ps 51: 18 build up the walls of J.
79: 1 they have reduced J to rubble.
122: 2 in your gates, O J.
122: 3 J is built like a city
122: 6 Pray for the peace of J:
Ps 125: 2 As the mountains surround J,
128: 5 may you see the prosperity of J,
137: 5 If I forget you, O J,
147: 2 The LORD builds up J;
147: 12 Extol the LORD, O J;
SS 6: 4 lovely as J,
Isa 1: 1 and J that Isaiah son of Amoz saw
2: 1 saw concerning Judah and J:
3: 1 is about to take from J and Judah
3: 8 J staggers,
4: 3 recorded among the living in J.
8: 14 And for the people of J he will be
27: 13 LORD on the holy mountain in J.
31: 5 the LORD Almighty will shield J;
33: 20 your eyes will see J,
40: 2 Speak tenderly to J,
40: 9 You who bring good tidings to J,
52: 1 O J, the holy city.
52: 2 rise up, sit enthroned, O J.
62: 6 on your walls, O J;
62: 7 give him no rest till he establishes J
65: 18 for I will create J to be a delight
Jer 2: 2 and proclaim in the hearing of J:
3: 17 time they will call J The Throne
4: 5 and proclaim in J and say:
4: 14 O J, wash the evil from your heart
5: 1 "Go up and down the streets of J,
6: 6 and build siege ramps against J.
8: 5 Why does J always turn away?
9: 11 "I will make J a heap of ruins,
13: 27 Woe to you, O J!
23: 14 And among the prophets of J
24: 1 into exile from J to Babylon
26: 18 J will become a heap of rubble,
32: 2 of Babylon was then besieging J,
33: 10 the streets of J that are deserted,
39: 1 This is how J was taken: In
51: 50 and think on J."
52: 14 broke down all the walls around J.
La 1: 7 J remembers all the treasures
Eze 14: 21 send against J my four dreadful
16: 2 confront J with her detestable
Da 6: 10 the windows opened toward J.
9: 2 of J would last seventy years.
9: 12 done like what has been done to J.
9: 25 and rebuild J until the Anointed
Joel 3: 1 restore the fortunes of Judah and J,
3: 16 and thunder from J;
3: 17 J will be holy;
Am 2: 5 will consume the fortresses of J."
Ob : 11 and cast lots for J,
Mic 1: 5 Is it not J?
4: 2 the word of the LORD from J.
Zep 3: 16 On that day they will say to J,
Zec 1: 14 'I am very jealous for J and Zion,
1: 17 comfort Zion and choose J.'"
2: 2 He answered me, "To measure J,
2: 4 'J will be a city without walls
8: 3 I will return to Zion and dwell in J.
8: 8 I will bring them back to live in J;
8: 15 determined to do good again to J
8: 22 powerful nations will come to J
9: 9 Shout, Daughter of J!
9: 10 and the war-horses from J,
12: 3 I will make J an immovable rock
12: 10 the inhabitants of J a spirit of grace
14: 2 the nations to J to fight against it;
14: 8 living water will flow out from J,
14: 16 that have attacked J will go up
Mt 16: 21 to his disciples that he must go to J
20: 18 said to them, "We are going up to J
21: 10 When Jesus entered J, the whole
23: 37 "O J, J, you who kill the prophets
Mk 10: 33 "We are going up to J," he said,
Lk 2: 22 Mary took him to J to present him
2: 41 Every year his parents went to J
2: 43 the boy Jesus stayed behind in J,
4: 9 The devil led him to J
9: 31 about to bring to fulfillment at J.
9: 51 Jesus resolutely set out for J,
13: 34 die outside J! "O J, J,
18: 31 told them, "We are going up to J,
19: 41 As he approached J and saw
21: 20 "When you see J being surrounded
21: 24 J will be trampled
24: 47 name to all nations, beginning at J.
Jn 4: 20 where we must worship is in J."
Ac 1: 4 this command: "Do not leave J,
1: 8 and you will be my witnesses in J,
6: 7 of disciples in J increased rapidly,
20: 22 by the Spirit, I am going to J,
23: 11 As you have testified about me in J
Ro 15: 19 So from J all the way
Gal 4: 25 corresponds to the present city of J
4: 26 But the J that is above is free,
Heb 12: 22 to the heavenly J, the city
Rev 3: 12 the new J, which is coming
21: 2 I saw the Holy City, the new J,
21: 10 and showed me the Holy City, J,

JESSE

Father of David (Ru 4:17–22; 1Sa 16; 1Ch 2:12–17).

JESUS

LIFE: Genealogy (Mt 1:1–17; Lk 3:21–37). Birth announced (Mt 1:18–25; Lk 1:26–45). Birth (Mt 2:1–12; Lk 2:1–40). Escape to Egypt (Mt 2:13–23). As a boy in the temple (Lk 2:41–52). Baptism (Mt 3:13–17; Mk 1:9–11; Lk 3:21–22; Jn 1:32–34). Temptation (Mt 4:1–11; Mk 1:12–13; Lk 4:1–13). Ministry in Galilee (Mt 4:12–18:35; Mk 1:14–9:50; Lk 4:14–13:9; Jn 1:35–2:11; 4; 6), Transfiguration (Mt 17:1–8; Mk 9:2–8; Lk 9:28–36), on the way to Jerusalem (Mt 19–20; Mk 10; Lk 13:10–19:27), in Jerusalem (Mt 21–25; Mk 11–13; Lk 19:28–21:38; Jn 2:12–3:36; 5; 7–12). Last supper (Mt 26:17–35; Mk 14:12–31; Lk 22:1–38; Jn 13–17). Arrest and trial (Mt 26:36–27:31; Mk 14:43–15:20; Lk 22:39–23:25; Jn 18:1–19:16). Crucifixion (Mt 27:32–66; Mk 15:21–47; Lk 23:26–55; Jn 19:28–42). Resurrection and appearances (Mt 28; Mk 16; Lk 24; Jn 20–21; Ac 1:1–11; 7:56; 9:3–6; 1Co 15:1–8; Rev 1:1–20).

MIRACLES. Healings: official's son (Jn 4:43–54), demoniac in Capernaum (Mk 1:23–26; Lk 4:33–35), Peter's mother-in-law (Mt 8:14–17; Mk 1:29–31; Lk 4:38–39), leper (Mt 8:2–4; Mk 1:40–45; Lk 5:12–16), paralytic (Mt 9:1–8; Mk 2:1–12; Lk 5:17–26), cripple (Jn 5:1–9), shriveled hand (Mt 12:10–13; Mk 3:1–5; Lk 6:6–11), centurion's servant (Mt 8:5–13; Lk 7:1–10), widow's son raised (Lk 7:11–17), demoniac (Mt 12:22–23; Lk 11:14), Gadarene demoniacs (Mt 8:28–34; Mk 5:1–20; Lk 8:26–39), woman's bleeding and Jairus' daughter (Mt 9:18–26; Mk 5:21–43; Lk 8:40–56), blind man (Mt 9:27–31), mute man (Mt 9:32–33), Canaanite woman's daughter (Mt 15:21–28; Mk 7:24–30), deaf man (Mk 7:31–37), blind man (Mk 8:22–26), demoniac boy (Mt 17:14–18; Mk 9:14–29; Lk 9:37–43), ten lepers (Lk 17:11–19), man born blind (Jn 9:1–7), Lazarus raised (Jn 11), crippled woman (Lk 13:11–17), man with dropsy (Lk 14:1–6), two blind men (Mt 20:29–34; Mk 10:46–52; Lk 18:35–43), Malchus' ear (Lk 22:50–51). Other Miracles: water to wine (Jn 2:1–11), catch of fish (Lk 5:1–11), storm stilled (Mt 8:23–27; Mk 4:37–41; Lk 8:22–25), 5,000 fed (Mt 14:15–21; Mk 6:35–44; Lk 9:10–17; Jn 6:1–14), walking on water (Mt 14:25–33; Mk 6:48–52; Jn 6:15–21), 4,000 fed (Mt 15:32–39; Mk 8:1–9), money from fish (Mt 17:24–27), fig tree cursed (Mt 21:18–22; Mk 11:12–14), catch of fish (Jn 21:1–14).

MAJOR TEACHING; Sermon on the Mount (Mt 5–7; Lk 6:17–49), to Nicodemus (Jn 3), to Samaritan woman (Jn 4), Bread of Life (Jn 6:22–59), at Feast of Tabernacles (Jn 7–8), woes to Pharisees (Mt 23; Lk 11:37–54), Good Shepherd (Jn 10:1–18), Olivet Discourse (Mt 24–25; Mk 13; Lk 21:5–36), Upper Room Discourse (Jn 13–16).

PARABLES: Sower (Mt 13:3–23; Mk 4:3–25; Lk 8:5–18), seed's growth (Mk 4:26–29), wheat and weeds (Mt 13:24–30, 36–43), mustard seed (Mt 13:31–32; Mk 4:30–32), yeast (Mt 13:33; Lk 13:20–21), hidden treasure (Mt 13:44), valuable pearl (Mt 13:45–46), net (Mt 13:47–51), house owner (Mt 13:52), good Samaritan (Lk 10:25–37), unmerciful servant (Mt 18:15–35), lost sheep (Mt 18:10–14; Lk 15:4–7), lost coin (Lk 15:8–10), lost son (Lk 15:11–32), dishonest manager (Lk 16:1–13), rich man and Lazarus (Lk 16:19–31), persistent widow (Lk 18:1–8), Pharisee and tax collector (Lk 18:9–14), payment of workers (Mt 20:1–16), tenants and the vineyard (Mt 21:28–46; Mk 12:1–12; Lk 20:9–19), wedding banquet (Mt 22:1–14), faithful servant (Mt 24:45–51), ten virgins (Mt 25:1–13), talents (Mt 25:14–30; Lk 19:12–27).

DISCIPLES see APOSTLES. Call of (Jn 1:35–51; Mt 4:18–22; 9:9; Mk 1:16–20; 2:13–14; Lk 5:1–11, 27–28). Named Apostles (Mk 3:13–19; Lk 6:12–16). Twelve sent out (Mt 10; Mk 6:7–11; Lk 9:1–5). Seventy sent out (Lk 10:1–24). Defection of (Jn 6:60–71; Mt 26:56; Mk 14:50–52). Final commission (Mt 28:16–20; Jn 21:15–23; Ac 1:3–8).

Ac 2: 32 God has raised this J to life,
9: 5 "I am J, whom you are persecuting
9: 34 said to him, "J Christ heals you.
15: 11 of our Lord J that we are saved,
16: 31 "Believe in the Lord J,
20: 24 the task the Lord J has given me—
Ro 3: 24 redemption that came by Christ J.
5: 17 life through the one man, J Christ.
8: 1 for those who are in Christ J,
1Co 1: 7 for our Lord J Christ to be revealed
2: 2 except J Christ and him crucified.
6: 11 in the name of the Lord J Christ
8: 6 and there is but one Lord, J Christ,
12: 3 and no one can say, "J is Lord,"
2Co 4: 5 not preach ourselves, but J Christ
13: 5 Do you not realize that Christ J is
Gal 2: 16 but by faith in J Christ.
3: 28 for you are all one in Christ J.
5: 6 in Christ J neither circumcision
6: 17 bear on my body the marks of J.

Eph 1: 5 as his sons through *J* Christ,
2: 10 created in Christ *J*
2: 20 with Christ *J* himself as the chief
Php 1: 6 until the day of Christ *J*.
2: 5 be the same as that of Christ *J*:
2: 10 name of *J* every knee should bow,
Col 3: 17 do it all in the name of the Lord *J*,
1Th 1: 10 whom he raised from the dead — *J*,
4: 14 We believe that *J* died
5: 23 at the coming of our Lord *J* Christ.
2Th 1: 7 when the Lord *J* is revealed
2: 1 the coming of our Lord *J* Christ
1Ti 1: 15 Christ *J* came into the world
2Ti 1: 10 appearing of our Savior, Christ *J*,
2: 3 us like a good soldier of Christ *J*.
3: 12 life in Christ *J* will be persecuted,
Tit 2: 13 our great God and Savior, *J* Christ,
Heb 2: 9 But we see *J*, who was made a little
2: 11 So *J* is not ashamed to call them
3: 1 fix your thoughts on *J*, the apostle
3: 3 *J* has been found worthy
4: 14 through the heavens, *J* the Son
6: 20 where *J*, who went before us,
7: 22 *J* has become the guarantee
7: 24 but because *J* lives forever,
8: 6 But the ministry *J* has received is
12: 2 Let us fix our eyes on *J*, the author
12: 24 to *J* the mediator of a new
1Pe 1: 3 the resurrection of *J* Christ
2Pe 1: 16 and coming of our Lord *J* Christ,
1Jn 1: 7 and the blood of *J*, his Son,
2: 1 *J* Christ, the Righteous One.
2: 6 to live in him must walk as *J* did.
4: 15 anyone acknowledges that *J* is
Rev 1: 1 The revelation of *J* Christ,
22: 16 *J*, have sent my angel
22: 20 Come, Lord *J*.

JETHRO

Father-in-law and adviser of Moses (Ex 3:1; 18). Also known as Reuel (Ex 2:18).

JEW (JEWS JEWS' JUDAISM)

Est 2: 5 of Susa a *J* of the tribe of Benjamin,
Zec 8: 23 of one *J* by the hem of his robe
Ac 21: 39 "I am a *J*, from Tarsus in Cilicia,
Ro 1: 16 first for the *J*, then for the Gentile.
2: 28 A man is not a *J* if he is only one
10: 12 there is no difference between *J*
1Co 9: 20 To the Jews I became like a *J*,
Gal 2: 14 "You are a *J*, yet you live like
3: 28 There is neither *J* nor Greek,
Col 3: 11 Here there is no Greek or *J*,

JEWEL (JEWELRY JEWELS)

Pr 20: 15 that speak knowledge are a rare *j*.
SS 4: 9 with one *j* of your necklace.
Rev 21: 11 that of a very precious *j*,

JEWELRY (JEWEL)

Ex 35: 22 and brought gold *j* of all kinds:
Jer 2: 32 Does a maiden forget her *j*,
Eze 16: 11 you with *j*: I put bracelets
1Pe 3: 3 wearing of gold *j* and fine clothes.

JEWELS (JEWEL)

Isa 54: 12 your gates of sparkling *j*,
61: 10 as a bride adorns herself with her *j*.
Zec 9: 16 like *j* in a crown.

JEWS (JEW)

Ne 4: 1 He ridiculed the *J*,
Est 3: 13 kill and annihilate all the *J* —
4: 14 and deliverance for the *J* will arise
Mt 2: 2 who has been born king of the *J*?
27: 11 "Are you the king of the *J*?" "Yes,
Jn 4: 9 (For *J* do not associate
4: 22 for salvation is from the *J*.
19: 3 saying, "Hail, king of the *J*!"
Ac 20: 21 I have declared to both *J*
Ro 3: 29 Is God the God of *J* only?
9: 24 not only from the *J* but
15: 27 they owe it to the *J* to share
1Co 1: 22 *J* demand miraculous signs
9: 20 To the *J* I became like a Jew,
12: 13 whether *J* or Greeks, slave or free
Gal 2: 8 of Peter as an apostle to the *J*,
Rev 2: 9 slander of those who say they are *J*
3: 9 claim to be *J* though they are not,

JEWS' (JEW)

Ro 15: 27 shared in the *J* spiritual blessings,

JEZEBEL

Sidonian wife of Ahab (1Ki 16:31). Promoted Baal worship (1Ki 16:32 – 33). Killed prophets of the LORD (1Ki 18:4, 13). Opposed Elijah (1Ki 19:1 – 2). Had Naboth killed (1Ki 21). Death prophesied (1Ki 21:17 – 24). Killed by Jehu (2Ki 9:30 – 37).

JEZREEL

2Ki 9: 36 at *J* dogs will devour Jezebel's flesh
10: 7 and sent them to Jehu in *J*.
Hos 1: 4 house of Jehu for the massacre at *J*,

JOAB

Nephew of David (1Ch 2:16). Commander of his army (2Sa 8:16). Victorious over Ammon (2Sa 10; 1Ch 19), Rabbah (2Sa 11; 1Ch 20), Jerusalem (1Ch 11:6), Absalom (2Sa 18), Sheba (2Sa 20). Killed Abner (2Sa 3:22 – 39), Amasa (2Sa 20:1 – 13). Numbered David's army (2Sa 24; 1Ch 21). Sided with Adonijah (1Ki 1:17, 19). Killed by Benaiah (1Ki 2:5 – 6, 28 – 35).

JOASH

Son of Ahaziah; king of Judah. Sheltered from Athaliah by Jehoiada (2Ki 11; 2Ch 22:10 – 23:21). Repaired temple (2Ki 12; 2Ch 24).

JOB

Wealthy man from Uz; feared God (Job 1:1 – 5). Righteousness tested by disaster (Job 1:6 – 22), personal affliction (Job 2). Maintained innocence in debate with three friends (Job 3 – 31), Elihu (Job 32 – 37). Rebuked by the LORD (Job 38 – 41). Vindicated and restored to greater stature by the LORD (Job 42). Example of righteousness (Eze 14:14, 20).

JOCHEBED*

Mother of Moses and Aaron (Ex 6:20; Nu 26:59).

JOEL

Prophet (Joel 1:1; Ac 2:16).

JOHN

1. Son of Zechariah and Elizabeth (Lk 1). Called the Baptist (Mt 3:1 – 12; Mk 1:2 – 8). Witness to Jesus (Mt 3:11 – 12; Mk 1:7 – 8; Lk 3:15 – 18; Jn 1:6 – 35; 3:27 – 30; 5:33 – 36). Doubts about Jesus (Mt 11:2 – 6; Lk 7:18 – 23). Arrest (Mt 4:12; Mk 1:14). Execution (Mt 14:1 – 12; Mk 6:14 – 29; Lk 9:7 – 9). Ministry compared to Elijah (Mt 11:7 – 19; Mk 9:11 – 13; Lk 7:24 – 35).

2. Apostle; brother of James (Mt 4:21 – 22; 10:2; Mk 3:17; Lk 5:1 – 10). At transfiguration (Mt 17:1 – 13; Mk 9:1 – 13; Lk 9:28 – 36). Desire to be greatest (Mk 10:35 – 45). Leader of church at Jerusalem (Ac 4:1 – 3; Gal 2:9). Elder who wrote epistles (2Jn 1; 3Jn 1). Prophet who wrote Revelation (Rev 1:1; 22:8).

3. Cousin of Barnabas, co-worker with Paul, (Ac 12:12 – 13:13; 15:37), see MARK.

JOIN (JOINED JOINS)

Ne 10: 29 all these now *j* their brothers
Pr 23: 20 Do not *j* those who drink too much
24: 21 and do not *j* with the rebellious,
Jer 3: 18 of Judah will *j* the house of Israel,
Eze 37: 17 *J* them together into one stick
Da 11: 34 who are not sincere will *j* them.
Ro 15: 30 to *j* me in my struggle by praying
2Ti 1: 8 *j* with me in suffering for the gospel

JOINED (JOIN)

Zec 2: 11 "Many nations will be *j*
Mt 19: 6 Therefore what God has *j* together,
Mk 10: 9 Therefore what God has *j* together,
Ac 1: 14 They all *j* together constantly
Eph 2: 21 him the whole building is *j* together
4: 16 *j* and held together

JOINS (JOIN)

1Co 16: 16 and to everyone who *j* in the work,

JOINT (JOINTS)

Ps 22: 14 and all my bones are out of *j*.

JOINTS (JOINT)

Heb 4: 12 even to dividing soul and spirit, *j*

JOKING*

Ge 19: 14 his sons-in-law thought he was *j*.
Pr 26: 19 and says, "I was only *j*!"
Eph 5: 4 or coarse *j*, which are out of place,

JONAH

Prophet in days of Jeroboam II (2Ki 14:25). Called to Nineveh; fled to Tarshish (Jnh 1:1 – 3). Cause of storm; thrown into sea (Jnh 1:4 – 16). Swallowed by fish (Jnh 1:17). Prayer (Jnh 2). Preached to Nineveh (Jnh 3). Attitude reproved by the LORD (Jnh 4). Sign of (Mt 12:39 – 41; Lk 11:29 – 32).

JONATHAN

Son of Saul (1Sa 13:16; 1Ch 8:33). Valiant warrior (1Sa 13 – 14). Relation to David (1Sa 18:1 – 4; 19 – 20; 23:16 – 18). Killed at Gilboa (1Sa 31). Mourned by David (2Sa 1).

JOPPA

Ezr 3: 7 logs by sea from Lebanon to *J*,
Jnh 1: 3 to *J*, where he found a ship bound
Ac 9: 43 Peter stayed in *J* for some time

JORAM

1. Son of Ahab; king of Israel. Fought with Jehoshaphat against Moab (2Ki 3). Killed with Ahaziah by Jehu (2Ki 8:25 – 29; 9:14 – 26; 2Ch 22:5 – 9).

2. See JEHORAM.

JORDAN

Ge 13: 10 plain of the *J* was well watered,
Nu 22: 1 and camped along the *J*
34: 12 boundary will go down along the *J*
Dt 3: 27 you are not going to cross this *J*.
Jos 1: 2 get ready to cross the *J* River
3: 11 go into the *J* ahead of you.
3: 17 ground in the middle of the *J*,
4: 22 Israel crossed the *J* on dry ground.'
2Ki 2: 7 and Elisha had stopped at the *J*.
2: 13 and stood on the bank of the *J*.
5: 10 wash yourself seven times in the *J*,
6: 4 They went to the *J* and began
Ps 114: 3 the *J* turned back;
Isa 9: 1 along the *J* — The people walking
Jer 12: 5 manage in the thickets by the *J*?
Mt 3: 6 baptized by him in the *J* River.
4: 15 the way to the sea, along the *J*,
Mk 1: 9 and was baptized by John in the *J*.

JOSEPH

1. Son of Jacob by Rachel (Ge 30:24; 1Ch 2:2). Favored by Jacob, hated by brothers (Ge 37:3 – 4). Dreams (Ge 37:5 – 11). Sold by brothers (Ge 37:12 – 36). Served Potiphar; imprisoned by false accusation (Ge 39). Interpreted dreams of Pharaoh's servants (Ge 40), of Pharaoh (Ge 41:4 – 40). Made greatest in Egypt (Ge 41:41 – 57). Sold grain to brothers (Ge 42 – 45). Brought Jacob and sons to Egypt (Ge 46 – 47). Sons Ephraim and Manasseh blessed (Ge 48). Blessed (Ge 49:22 – 26; Dt 33:13 – 17). Death (Ge 50:22 – 26; Ex 13:19; Heb 11:22). 12,000 from (Rev 7:8).

2. Husband of Mary, mother of Jesus (Mt 1:16 – 24; 2:13 – 19; Lk 1:27; 2; Jn 1:45).

3. Disciple from Arimathea, who gave his tomb for Jesus' burial (Mt 27:57 – 61; Mk 15:43 – 47; Lk 23:50 – 52).

4. Original name of Barnabas (Ac 4:36).

JOSHUA (HOSHEA)

1. Son of Nun; name changed from Hoshea (Nu 13:8, 16; 1Ch 7:27). Fought Amalekites under Moses (Ex 17:9 – 14). Servant of Moses on Sinai (Ex 24:13; 32:17). Spied Canaan (Nu 13). With Caleb, allowed to enter land (Nu 14:6, 30). Succeeded Moses (Dt 1:38; 31:1 – 8; 34:9).

Charged Israel to conquer Canaan (Jos 1). Crossed Jordan (Jos 3 – 4). Circumcised sons of wilderness wanderings (Jos 5). Conquered Jericho (Jos 6), Ai (Jos 7 – 8), five kings at Gibeon (Jos 10:1 – 28), southern Canaan (Jos 10:29 – 43), northern Canaan (Jos 11 – 12). Defeated at Ai (Jos 7). Deceived by Gibeonites (Jos 9). Renewed covenant (Jos 8:30 – 35; 24:1 – 27). Divided land among tribes (Jos 13 – 22). Last words (Jos 23). Death (Jos 24:28 – 31).

2. High priest during rebuilding of temple (Hag 1 – 2; Zec 3:1 – 9; 6:11).

JOSIAH

Son of Amon; king of Judah (2Ki 21:26; 1Ch 3:14). Prophesied (1Ki 13:2). Book of Law discovered during his reign (2Ki 22; 2Ch 34:14 – 31). Reforms (2Ki 23:1 – 25; 2Ch 34:1 – 13; 35:1 – 19). Killed by Pharaoh Neco (2Ki 23:29 – 30; 2Ch 35:20 – 27).

JOTHAM

1. Son of Gideon (Jdg 9).

2. Son of Azariah (Uzziah); king of Judah (2Ki 15:32 – 38; 2Ch 26:21 – 27:9).

JOURNEY

Dt 1: 33 who went ahead of you on your *j*,
2: 7 over your *j* through this vast desert
Jdg 18: 6 Your *j* has the LORD's approval."
Ezr 8: 21 and ask him for a safe *j* for us
Job 16: 22 before I go on the *j* of no return.
Isa 35: 8 The unclean will not *j* on it;
Mt 25: 14 it will be like a man going on a *j*,
Ro 15: 24 to have you assist me on my *j* there

JOY* (ENJOY ENJOYMENT JOYFUL JOYOUS OVERJOYED REJOICE REJOICES REJOICING)

Ge 31: 27 so I could send you away with *j*
Lev 9: 24 shouted for *j* and fell facedown.
Dt 16: 15 and your *j* will be complete.
Jdg 9: 19 may Abimelech be your *j*,
1Ch 12: 40 and sheep, for there was *j* in Israel.
16: 27 strength and *j* in his dwelling place.
16: 33 sing for *j* before the LORD,
29: 17 with *j* how willingly your people
29: 22 drank with great *j* in the presence
2Ch 30: 26 There was great *j* in Jerusalem,
Ezr 3: 12 while many others shouted for *j*.
3: 13 of the shouts of *j* from the sound
6: 16 of the house of God with *j*.
6: 22 with *j* by changing the attitude
6: 22 *j* the Feast of Unleavened Bread,
Ne 8: 10 for the *j* of the LORD is your
8: 12 and to celebrate with great *j*,
8: 17 And their *j* was very great.
12: 43 God had given them great *j*.

Est 8: 16 a time of happiness and *j*,
8: 17 there was *j* and gladness
9: 17 and made it a day of feasting and *j*.
9: 18 and made it a day of feasting and *j*.
9: 19 as a day of *j* and feasting,
9: 22 and *j* and giving presents of food
9: 22 their sorrow was turned into *j*
Job 3: 7 may no shout of *j* be heard in it.
6: 10 my *j* in unrelenting pain—
8: 21 and your lips with shouts of *j*.
9: 25 they fly away without a glimpse of *j*
10: 20 from me so I can have a moment's *j*
20: 5 the *j* of the godless lasts
33: 26 he sees God's face and shouts for *j*;
38: 7 and all the angels shouted for *j*?
Ps 4: 7 have filled my heart with greater *j*
5: 11 let them ever sing for *j*.
16: 11 me with *j* in your presence,
19: 8 giving *j* to the heart.
20: 5 We will shout for *j*
21: 1 How great is his *j* in the victories
21: 6 with the *j* of your presence.
27: 6 will I sacrifice with shouts of *j*;
28: 7 My heart leaps for *j*
30: 11 sackcloth and clothed me with *j*,
33: 3 play skillfully, and shout for *j*.
35: 27 shout for *j* and gladness;
42: 4 with shouts of *j* and thanksgiving
43: 4 to God, my *j* and my delight.
45: 7 by anointing you with the oil of *j*.
45: 15 They are led in with *j* and gladness;
47: 1 shout to God with cries of *j*.
47: 5 God has ascended amid shouts of *j*,
48: 2 the *j* of the whole earth.
51: 8 Let me hear *j* and gladness;
51: 12 to me the *j* of your salvation
65: 8 you call forth songs of *j*.
65: 13 they shout for *j* and sing.
66: 1 Shout with *j* to God, all the earth!
67: 4 the nations be glad and sing for *j*,
71: 23 My lips will shout for *j*
81: 1 Sing for *j* to God our strength;
86: 4 Bring *j* to your servant,
89: 12 Hermon sing for *j* at your name.
90: 14 for *j* and be glad all our days.
92: 4 I sing for *j* at the works
94: 19 your consolation brought *j*
95: 1 let us sing for *j* to the LORD;
96: 12 the trees of the forest will sing for *j*;
97: 11 and *j* on the upright in heart.
98: 4 for *j* to the LORD, all the earth,
98: 6 shout for *j* before the LORD,
98: 8 the mountains sing together for *j*;
100: 1 for *j* to the LORD, all the earth.
105: 43 his chosen ones with shouts of *j*;
106: 5 share in the *j* of your nation
107: 22 and tell of his works with songs of *j*
118: 15 Shouts of *j* and victory
119: 111 they are the *j* of my heart.
126: 2 our tongues with songs of *j*.
126: 3 and we are filled with *j*.
126: 5 will reap with songs of *j*.
126: 6 will return with songs of *j*,
132: 9 may your saints sing for *j*."
132: 16 and her saints will ever sing for *j*.
137: 3 tormentors demanded songs of *j*;
137: 6 my highest *j*.
149: 5 and sing for *j* on their beds.
Pr 10: 1 A wise son brings *j* to his father,
10: 28 The prospect of the righteous is *j*,
11: 10 wicked perish, there are shouts of *j*.
12: 20 but *j* for those who promote peace.
14: 10 and no one else can share its *j*.
14: 13 and *j* may end in grief.
15: 20 A wise son brings *j* to his father,
15: 23 A man finds *j* in giving an apt reply
15: 30 A cheerful look brings *j*
17: 21 there is no *j* for the father of a fool.
21: 15 it brings *j* to the righteous
23: 24 of a righteous man has great *j*;
27: 9 incense bring *j* to the heart,
27: 11 my son, and bring *j* to my heart;
29: 3 A man who loves wisdom brings *j*
Ecc 8: 15 Then *j* will accompany him
11: 9 let your heart give you *j* in the days
Isa 9: 3 and increased their *j*;
12: 3 With *j* you will draw water
12: 6 Shout aloud and sing for *j*,
16: 9 shouts of *j* over your ripened fruit
16: 10 *J* and gladness are taken away
22: 13 But see, there is *j* and revelry,
24: 11 all *j* turns to gloom,
24: 14 raise their voices, they shout for *j*;
26: 19 wake up and shout for *j*.
35: 2 will rejoice greatly and shout for *j*.

Isa 35: 6 the mute tongue shout for *j*.
35: 10 Gladness and *j* will overtake them,
35: 10 everlasting *j* will crown their heads
42: 11 Let the people of Sela sing for *j*;
44: 23 Sing for *j*, O heavens,
48: 20 Announce this with shouts of *j*
49: 13 Shout for *j*, O heavens;
51: 3 *J* and gladness will be found in her,
51: 11 Gladness and *j* will overtake them,
51: 11 everlasting *j* will crown their heads
52: 8 together they shout for *j*.
52: 9 Burst into songs of *j* together,
54: 1 burst into song, shout for *j*,
55: 12 You will go out in *j*
56: 7 give them *j* in my house of prayer.
58: 14 then you will find your *j*
60: 5 heart will throb and swell with *j*;
60: 15 and the *j* of all generations.
61: 7 and everlasting *j* will be theirs.
65: 14 out of the *j* of their hearts,
65: 18 and its people a *j*.
66: 5 that we may see your *j*!'
Jer 7: 34 will bring an end to the sounds of *j*
15: 16 they were my *j* and my heart's
16: 9 will bring an end to the sounds of *j*
25: 10 banish from them the sounds of *j*
31: 7 "Sing with *j* for Jacob;
31: 12 shout for *j* on the heights of Zion;
31: 13 give them comfort and *j* instead
33: 9 this city will bring me renown, *j*,
33: 11 be heard once more the sounds of *j*
48: 33 *J* and gladness are gone
48: 33 no one treads them with shouts of *j*
48: 33 they are not shouts of *j*.
51: 48 will shout for *j* over Babylon,
La 2: 15 the *j* of the whole earth?"
5: 15 *J* is gone from our hearts;
Eze 7: 7 not *j*, upon the mountains.
24: 25 their *j* and glory, the delight
Joel 1: 12 Surely the *j* of mankind
1: 16 *j* and gladness
Mt 13: 20 and at once receives it with *j*.
13: 44 in his *j* went and sold all he had
28: 8 afraid yet filled with *j*,
Mk 4: 16 and at once receive it with *j*.
Lk 1: 14 He will be a *j* and delight to you,
1: 44 the baby in my womb leaped for *j*.
1: 58 great mercy, and they shared her *j*.
2: 10 news of great *j* that will be
6: 23 "Rejoice in that day and leap for *j*,
8: 13 the word with *j* when they hear it,
10: 17 The seventy-two returned with *j*
10: 21 full of *j* through the Holy Spirit,
24: 41 still did not believe it because of *j*
24: 52 returned to Jerusalem with great *j*.
Jn 3: 29 That *j* is mine, and it is now
3: 29 full of *j* when he hears
15: 11 and that your *j* may be complete.
15: 11 this so that my *j* may be in you
16: 20 but your grief will turn to *j*.
16: 21 because of her *j* that a child is born
16: 22 and no one will take away your *j*.
16: 24 and your *j* will be complete.
17: 13 measure of my *j* within them.
Ac 2: 28 with *j* in your presence.'
8: 8 So there was great *j* in that city.
13: 52 And the disciples were filled with *j*
14: 17 and fills your hearts with *j*."
16: 34 he was filled with *j* because he had come
Ro 14: 17 peace and *j* in the Holy Spirit,
15: 13 the God of hope fill you with all *j*
15: 32 will I may come to you with *j*
16: 19 so I am full of *j* over you;
2Co 1: 24 but we work with you for your *j*,
2: 3 that you would all share my *j*.
7: 4 our troubles my *j* knows no
7: 7 so that my *j* was greater than ever.
8: 2 their overflowing *j* and their
Gal 4: 15 What has happened to all your *j*?
5: 22 *j*, peace, patience, kindness,
Php 1: 4 I always pray with *j*
1: 25 for your progress and *j* in the faith,
1: 26 being with you again your *j*
2: 2 then make my *j* complete
2: 29 him in the Lord with great *j*,
4: 1 and long for, my *j* and crown,
1Th 1: 6 with the *j* given by the Holy Spirit.
2: 19 For what is our hope, our *j*,
2: 20 Indeed, you are our glory and *j*.
3: 9 you in return for all the *j* we have
2Ti 1: 4 so that I may be filled with *j*.
Phm : 7 Your love has given me great *j*
Heb 1: 9 by anointing you with the oil of *j*."
12: 2 for the *j* set before him endured
13: 17 them so that their work will be a *j*,

Jas 1: 2 Consider it pure *j*, my brothers,
4: 9 to mourning and your *j* to gloom.
1Pe 1: 8 with an inexpressible and glorious *j*
1Jn 1: 4 this to make our *j* complete.
2Jn : 4 It has given me great *j* to find some
: 12 so that our *j* may be complete.
3Jn : 3 It gave me great *j* to have some
: 4 I have no greater *j*
Jude : 24 without fault and with great *j*—

JOYFUL* (JOY)
Dt 16: 14 Be *j* at your Feast—you, your sons
1Sa 18: 6 with *j* songs and with tambourines
1Ki 8: 66 *j* and glad in heart
1Ch 15: 16 as singers to sing *j* songs,
2Ch 7: 10 *j* and glad in heart
Ps 68: 3 may they be happy and *j*.
100: 2 come before him with *j* songs.
Ecc 9: 7 and drink your wine with a *j* heart,
Isa 24: 8 the *j* harp is silent.
Jer 31: 4 and go out to dance with the *j*.
Hab 3: 18 I will be *j* in God my Savior.
Zec 8: 19 and tenth months will become *j*
10: 7 Their children will see it and be *j*;
Ro 12: 12 Be *j* in hope, patient in affliction,
1Th 5: 16 Be *j* always; pray continually;
Heb 12: 22 thousands of angels in *j* assembly,

JOYOUS* (JOY)
Est 8: 15 the city of Susa held a *j* celebration.

JUBILANT
Ps 96: 12 let the fields be *j*, and everything
98: 4 burst into *j* song with music;

JUBILEE
Lev 25: 11 The fiftieth year shall be a *j* for you;

JUDAH (JUDEA)
1. Son of Jacob by Leah (Ge 29:35; 35:23; 1Ch 2:1). Did not want to kill Joseph (Ge 37:26–27). Among Canaanites, fathered Perez by Tamar (Ge 38). Tribe of blessed as ruling tribe (Ge 49:8–12; Dt 33:7), numbered (Nu 1:27; 26:22), allotted land (Jos 15; Eze 48:7), failed to fully possess (Jos 15:63; Jdg 1:1–20).
2. Name used for people and land of Southern Kingdom.
Ru 1: 7 take them back to the land of *J*.
2Sa 2: 4 king over the house of *J*.
Isa 1: 1 The vision concerning *J*
3: 8 *J* is falling;
Jer 13: 19 All *J* will be carried into exile,
30: 3 bring my people Israel and *J* back
Hos 1: 7 I will show love to the house of *J*;
Zec 10: 4 From *J* will come the cornerstone,
Mt 2: 6 least among the rulers of *J*;
Heb 7: 14 that our Lord descended from *J*,
8: 8 and with the house of *J*.
Rev 5: 5 of the tribe of *J*, the Root of David,

JUDAISM (JEW)
Ac 13: 43 devout converts to *J* followed Paul
Gal 1: 13 of my previous way of life in *J*,
1: 14 advancing in *J* beyond many Jews

JUDAS
1. Apostle; son of James (Lk 6:16; Jn 14:22; Ac 1:13). Probably also called Thaddaeus (Mt 10:3; Mk 3:18).
2. Brother of James and Jesus (Mt 13:55; Mk 6:3), also called Jude (Jude 1).
3. Christian prophet (Ac 15:22–32).
4. Apostle, also called Iscariot, who betrayed Jesus (Mt 10:4; 26:14–56; Mk 3:19; 14:10–50; Lk 6:16; 22:3–53; Jn 6:71; 12:4; 13:2–30; 18:2–11). Suicide of (Mt 27:3–5; Ac 1:16–25).

JUDEA (JUDAH)
Mt 2: 1 born in Bethlehem in *J*,
24: 16 are in *J* flee to the mountains.
Lk 3: 1 Pontius Pilate was governor of *J*,
Ac 1: 8 and in all *J* and Samaria,
9: 31 Then the church throughout *J*,
1Th 2: 14 imitators of God's churches in *J*,

JUDGE (JUDGED JUDGES JUDGING JUDGMENT JUDGMENTS)
Ge 16: 5 May the LORD *j* between you
18: 25 Will not the *J* of all the earth do
Lev 19: 15 but *j* your neighbor fairly.
Dt 1: 16 between your brothers and *j* fairly,
17: 12 man who shows contempt for the *j*
32: 36 The LORD will *j* his people
Jdg 2: 18 Whenever the LORD raised up a *j*
1Sa 2: 10 the LORD will *j* the ends
3: 13 that I would *j* his family forever
7: 15 *j* over Israel all the days of his life.
24: 12 May the LORD *j* between you
1Ki 8: 32 *J* between your servants,
1Ch 16: 33 for he comes to *j* the earth.
2Ch 6: 23 *J* between your servants, repaying

2Ch 19: 7 J carefully, for with the LORD our
Job 9: 15 plead with my J for mercy.
Ps 7: 8 J me, O LORD, according
7: 8 let the LORD j the peoples.
7: 11 God is a righteous j,
9: 8 He will j the world in righteousness
50: 6 for God himself is j.
51: 4 and justified when you j.
75: 2 it is I who j uprightly.
76: 9 when you, O God, rose up to j,
82: 8 Rise up, O God, j the earth,
94: 2 Rise up, O J of the earth;
96: 10 he will j the peoples with equity.
96: 13 He will j the world in righteousness
98: 9 He will j the world in righteousness
110: 6 He will j the nations, heaping up
Pr 31: 9 Speak up and j fairly;
Isa 2: 4 He will j between the nations
3: 13 he rises to j the people.
11: 3 He will not j by what he sees
33: 22 For the LORD is our j,
Jer 11: 20 Almighty, you who j righteously
Eze 7: 3 I will j you according
7: 27 by their own standards I will j them
18: 30 O house of Israel, I will j you,
20: 36 so I will j you, declares
22: 2 "Son of man, will you j her?
34: 17 I will j between one sheep
Joel 3: 12 sit to j all the nations on every side.
Mic 3: 11 Her leaders j for a bribe,
4: 3 He will j between many peoples
Mt 7: 1 Do not j, or you too will be judged.
Lk 6: 37 "Do not j, and you will not be
18: 2 there was a j who neither feared
Jn 5: 27 And he has given him authority to j
5: 30 By myself I can do nothing; I j only
8: 16 But if I do j, my decisions are right,
12: 47 For I did not come to j the world,
12: 48 There is a j for the one who rejects
Ac 10: 42 as j of the living and the dead.
17: 31 a day when he will j the world
Ro 2: 16 day when God will j men's secrets
3: 6 how could God j the world?
14: 10 then, why do you j your brother?
1Co 4: 3 indeed, I do not even j myself.
4: 5 Therefore j nothing
6: 2 And if you are to j the world,
6: 2 that the saints will j the world?
Gal 2: 6 not j by external appearance—
Col 2: 16 Therefore do not let anyone j you
2Ti 4: 1 who will j the living and the dead,
4: 8 which the Lord, the righteous J,
Heb 10: 30 "The Lord will j his people."
12: 23 come to God, the j of all men,
13: 4 for God will j the adulterer
Jas 4: 12 There is only one Lawgiver and J,
4: 12 who are you to j your neighbor?
1Pe 4: 5 to him who is ready to j the living
Rev 20: 4 who had been given authority to j.

JUDGED (JUDGE)

Mt 7: 1 "Do not judge, or you too will be j.
1Co 4: 3 I care very little if I am j by you
10: 29 For why should my freedom be j
11: 31 But if we j ourselves, we would not
14: 24 all that he is a sinner and will be j
Jas 3: 1 who teach will be j more strictly.
Rev 20: 12 The dead were j according

JUDGES (JUDGE)

Jdg 2: 16 Then the LORD raised up j,
Job 9: 24 he blindfolds its j.
Ps 58: 11 there is a God who j the earth."
75: 7 But it is God who j:
Pr 29: 14 If a king j the poor with fairness,
Jn 5: 22 Moreover, the Father j no one,
1Co 4: 4 It is the Lord who j me.
Heb 4: 12 it j the thoughts and attitudes
1Pe 1: 17 on a Father who j each man's work
2: 23 himself to him who j justly.
Rev 19: 11 With justice he j and makes war.

JUDGING (JUDGE)

Ps 9: 4 on your throne, j righteously.
Pr 24: 23 To show partiality in j is not good:
Isa 16: 5 one who in j seeks justice
Mt 19: 28 j the twelve tribes of Israel.
Jn 7: 24 Stop j by mere appearances,

JUDGMENT (JUDGE)

Nu 33: 4 for the LORD had brought j
Dt 1: 17 of any man, for j belongs to God.
32: 41 and my hand grasps it in j,
1Sa 25: 33 May you be blessed for your good j
Ps 1: 5 the wicked will not stand in the j,
9: 7 he has established his throne for j.
76: 8 From heaven you pronounced j,
82: 1 he gives j among the "gods":
119: 66 Teach me knowledge and good j,
143: 2 Do not bring your servant into j,
Pr 3: 21 preserve sound j and discernment,
6: 32 man who commits adultery lacks j;
8: 14 Counsel and sound j are mine;
10: 21 but fools die for lack of j.
11: 12 man who lacks j derides his
12: 11 but he who chases fantasies lacks j.
17: 18 A man lacking in j strikes hands
18: 1 he defies all sound j.
28: 16 A tyrannical ruler lacks j,
Ecc 12: 14 God will bring every deed into j,
Isa 3: 14 The LORD enters into j
28: 6 justice to him who sits in j,
53: 8 By oppression and j he was taken
66: 16 the LORD will execute j
Jer 2: 35 But I will pass j on you
25: 31 he will bring j on all mankind
51: 18 when their j comes, they will
Eze 11: 10 and I will execute j on you
Da 7: 22 pronounced j in favor of the saints
Am 7: 4 Sovereign LORD was calling for j
Zec 8: 16 and sound j in your courts;
Mal 3: 5 "So I will come near to you for j.
Mt 5: 21 who murders will be subject to j.'
5: 22 with his brother will be subject to j.
10: 15 on the day of j than for that town.
11: 24 on the day of j than for you."
12: 36 have to give account on the day of j
12: 41 up at the j with this generation
Jn 5: 22 but has entrusted all j to the Son,
5: 30 as I hear, and my j is just,
7: 24 appearances, and make a right j."
8: 26 "I have much to say in j of you.
9: 39 "For j I have come into this world,
12: 31 Now is the time for j on this world;
16: 8 to sin and righteousness and j:
16: 11 in regard to j, because the prince
Ac 24: 25 self-control and the j to come,
Ro 2: 1 you who pass j on someone else,
2: 2 Now we know that God's j
5: 16 The j followed one sin
12: 3 rather think of yourself with sober j
14: 10 stand before God's j seat.
14: 13 Therefore let us stop passing j
1Co 7: 40 In my j, she is happier if she stays
11: 29 body of the Lord eats and drinks j
2Co 5: 10 appear before the j seat of Christ,
2Th 1: 5 is evidence that God's j is right,
1Ti 3: 6 fall under the same j as the devil.
5: 12 Thus they bring j on themselves,
Heb 6: 2 of the dead, and eternal j.
9: 27 to die once, and after that to face j,
10: 27 but only a fearful expectation of j
Jas 2: 13 j without mercy will be shown
4: 11 are not keeping it, but sitting in j
1Pe 4: 17 For it is time for j to begin
2Pe 2: 9 the unrighteous for the day of j,
3: 7 being kept for the day of j
1Jn 4: 17 have confidence on the day of j,
Jude : 6 bound with everlasting chains for j
Rev 14: 7 because the hour of his j has come.

JUDGMENTS (JUDGE)

Jer 1: 16 I will pronounce my j on my people
Da 9: 11 and sworn j written in the Law
Hos 6: 5 my j flashed like lightning
Ro 11: 33 How unsearchable his j,
1Co 2: 15 spiritual man makes j about all
Rev 16: 7 true and just are your j."

JUG

1Sa 26: 12 and water j near Saul's head,
1Ki 17: 12 of flour in a jar and a little oil in a j.

JUST* (JUSTICE JUSTIFICATION JUSTIFIED JUSTIFIES JUSTIFY JUSTIFYING JUSTLY)

Ge 18: 19 LORD by doing what is right and j,
Dt 2: 12 j as Israel did in the land
6: 3 j as the LORD, the God
27: 3 and honey, j as the LORD,
30: 9 j as he delighted in your fathers,
32: 4 and all his ways are j.
32: 4 upright and j is he.
32: 47 They are not j idle words for you—
32: 50 j as your brother Aaron died
2Sa 8: 15 doing what was j and right
1Ch 18: 14 doing what was j and right
2Ch 12: 6 and said, "The LORD is j."
Ne 9: 13 and laws that are j and right,
9: 33 you have been j; you have acted
Job 34: 17 Will you condemn the j
35: 2 Elihu said: "Do you think this is j?
Ps 37: 28 For the LORD loves the j
37: 30 and his tongue speaks what is j.
99: 4 what is j and right.
111: 7 of his hands are faithful and j;
119: 121 I have done what is righteous and j;
Pr 1: 3 doing what is right and j and fair;
2: 8 for he guards the course of the j
2: 9 will understand what is right and j
8: 8 All the words of my mouth are j;
8: 15 and rulers make laws that are j;
12: 5 The plans of the righteous are j,
21: 3 To do what is right and j
Isa 32: 7 even when the plea of the needy is j
58: 2 They ask me for j decisions
Jer 4: 2 if in a truthful, j and righteous way
22: 3 what the LORD says: Do what is j
22: 15 He did what was right and j,
23: 5 do what is j and right in the land.
33: 15 he will do what is j and right
Eze 18: 5 who does what is j and right.
18: 19 Since the son has done what is j
18: 21 and does what is j and right,
18: 25 'The way of the Lord is not j.'
18: 27 and does what is j and right,
18: 29 'The way of the Lord is not j.'
33: 14 and does what is j and right—
33: 16 He has done what is j and right;
33: 17 But it is their way that is not j.
33: 17 'The way of the Lord is not j.'
33: 19 and does what is j and right,
33: 20 'The way of the Lord is not j.'
45: 9 and oppression and do what is j
Da 4: 37 does is right and all his ways are j.
Jn 5: 30 as I hear, and my judgment is j,
Ro 3: 26 as to be j and the one who justifies
2Th 1: 6 God is j: He will pay back trouble
Heb 2: 2 received its j punishment,
1Jn 1: 9 and j and will forgive us our sins
Rev 15: 3 J and true are your ways,
16: 5 "You are j in these judgments,
16: 7 true and j are your judgments."
19: 2 for true and j are his judgments.

JUSTICE* (JUST)

Ge 49: 16 "Dan will provide j for his people
Ex 23: 2 do not pervert j by siding
23: 6 "Do not deny j to your poor people
Lev 19: 15 "'Do not pervert j; do not show
Dt 16: 19 Do not pervert j or show partiality.
16: 20 Follow j and j alone,
24: 17 the alien or the fatherless of j,
27: 19 Cursed is the man who withholds j
1Sa 8: 3 accepted bribes and perverted j.
2Sa 15: 4 and I would see that he gets j."
15: 6 came to the king asking for j,
1Ki 3: 11 for discernment in administering j,
3: 28 wisdom from God to administer j.
7: 7 the Hall of J, where he was to judge
10: 9 to maintain j and righteousness."
2Ch 9: 8 to maintain j and righteousness."
Ezr 7: 25 and judges to administer j
Est 1: 13 experts in matters of law and j,
Job 8: 3 Does God pervert j?
9: 19 matter of j, who will summon him?
19: 7 though I call for help, there is no j.
27: 2 as God lives, who has denied me j,
29: 14 j was my robe and my turban.
31: 13 "If I have denied j
34: 5 but God denies me j.
34: 12 that the Almighty would pervert j.
34: 17 Can he who hates j govern?
36: 3 I will ascribe j to my Maker.
36: 17 j have taken hold of you.
37: 23 in his j and great righteousness,
40: 8 "Would you discredit my j?
Ps 7: 6 Awake, my God; decree j.
9: 8 he will govern the peoples with j.
9: 16 The LORD is known by his j;
11: 7 he loves j;
33: 5 LORD loves righteousness and j;
36: 6 your j like the great deep.
37: 6 j of your cause like the noonday
45: 6 a scepter of j will be the scepter
72: 1 Endow the king with your j, O God
72: 2 your afflicted ones with j.
89: 14 j are the foundation of your throne;
97: 2 j are the foundation of his throne.
99: 4 The King is mighty, he loves j—
101: 1 I will sing of your love and j;
103: 6 and j for all the oppressed.
106: 3 Blessed are they who maintain j,
112: 5 who conducts his affairs with j.
140: 12 I know that the LORD secures j
Pr 8: 20 along the paths of j,
16: 10 and his mouth should not betray j.
17: 23 to pervert the course of j.
18: 5 or to deprive the innocent of j.
19: 28 A corrupt witness mocks at j,

Pr 21: 15 When *j* is done, it brings joy
28: 5 Evil men do not understand *j*,
29: 4 By *j* a king gives a country stability
29: 7 The righteous care about *j*
29: 26 from the LORD that man gets *j*.
Ecc 3: 16 place of *j* — wickedness was there.
5: 8 poor oppressed in a district, and *j*
Isa 1: 17 Seek *j*,
1: 21 She once was full of *j*;
1: 27 Zion will be redeemed with *j*,
5: 7 he looked for *j*, but saw bloodshed;
5: 16 Almighty will be exalted by his *j*,
5: 23 but deny *j* to the innocent.
9: 7 it with *j* and righteousness
10: 2 and withhold *j* from the oppressed of
11: 4 with *j* he will give decisions
16: 5 one who in judging seeks *j*
28: 6 He will be a spirit of *j*
28: 17 I will make *j* the measuring line
29: 21 deprive the innocent of *j*.
30: 18 For the LORD is a God of *j*.
32: 1 and rulers will rule with *j*.
32: 16 *J* will dwell in the desert
33: 5 with *j* and righteousness.
42: 1 and he will bring *j* to the nations.
42: 3 In faithfulness he will bring forth *j*;
42: 4 till he establishes *j* on earth.
51: 4 my *j* will become a light
51: 5 my arm will bring *j* to the nations.
56: 1 "Maintain *j*
59: 4 No one calls for *j*;
59: 8 there is no *j* in their paths.
59: 9 So *j* is far from us,
59: 11 We look for *j*, but find none;
59: 14 So *j* is driven back,
59: 15 that there was no *j*.
61: 8 "For I, the LORD, love *j*;
Jer 9: 24 *j* and righteousness on earth,
10: 24 Correct me, LORD, but only with *j*
12: 1 speak with you about your *j*:
21: 12 "'Administer *j* every morning;
30: 11 I will discipline you but only with *j*;
46: 28 I will discipline you but only with *j*;
La 3: 36 to deprive a man of *j* —
Eze 22: 29 mistreat the alien, denying them *j*.
34: 16 I will shepherd the flock with *j*.
Hos 2: 19 you in righteousness and *j*,
12: 6 maintain love and *j*,
Am 2: 7 and deny *j* to the oppressed.
5: 7 You who turn *j* into bitterness
5: 12 and you deprive the poor of *j*
5: 15 maintain *j* in the courts.
5: 24 But let *j* roll on like a river,
6: 12 But you have turned *j* into poison
Mic 3: 1 Should you not know *j*,
3: 8 and with *j* and might,
3: 9 who despise *j*
Hab 1: 4 and *j* never prevails.
1: 4 so that *j* is perverted.
Zep 3: 5 by morning he dispenses his *j*,
Zec 7: 9 'Administer true *j*; show mercy
Mal 2: 17 or "Where is the God of *j*?"
3: 5 and deprive aliens of *j*,
Mt 12: 18 he will proclaim *j* to the nations.
12: 20 till he leads *j* to victory.
23: 23 important matters of the law — *j*,
Lk 11: 42 you neglect *j* and the love of God.
18: 3 'Grant me *j* against my adversary.'
18: 5 I will see that she gets *j*,
18: 7 And will not God bring about *j*
18: 8 he will see that they get *j*,
Ac 8: 33 humiliation he was deprived of *j*.
17: 31 with *j* by the man he has appointed.
28: 4 *J* has not allowed him to live."
Ro 3: 25 He did this to demonstrate his *j*,
3: 26 it to demonstrate his *j*
2Co 7: 11 what readiness to see *j* done.
Heb 11: 33 administered *j*, and gained what
Rev 19: 11 With *j* he judges and makes war.

JUSTIFICATION* (JUST)
Eze 16: 52 for you have furnished some *j*
Ro 4: 25 and was raised to life for our *j*.
5: 16 many trespasses and brought *j*.
5: 18 of righteousness was *j* that brings

JUSTIFIED* (JUST)
Ps 51: 4 and *j* when you judge.
Lk 18: 14 rather than the other, went home *j*
Ac 13: 39 from everything you could not be *j*
13: 39 him everyone who believes is *j*
Ro 3: 24 and are *j* freely by his grace
3: 28 For we maintain that a man is *j*
4: 2 If, in fact, Abraham was *j* by works,
5: 1 since we have been *j* through faith,
5: 9 Since we have now been *j*
8: 30 those he called, he also *j*; those he *j*,
10: 10 heart that you believe and are *j*,
1Co 6: 11 you were *j* in the name
Gal 2: 16 in Christ Jesus that we may be *j*
2: 16 observing the law no one will be *j*.
2: 16 sinners' know that a man is not *j*
2: 17 "If, while we seek to be *j* in Christ,
3: 11 Clearly no one is *j* before God
3: 24 to Christ that we might be *j* by faith
5: 4 to be *j* by law have been alienated
Tit 3: 7 so that, having been *j* by his grace,
Jas 2: 24 You see that a person is *j*

JUSTIFIES* (JUST)
Ro 3: 26 one who *j* those who have faith
4: 5 but trusts God who *j* the wicked,
8: 33 God has chosen? It is God who *j*.

JUSTIFY* (JUST)
Est 7: 4 such distress would *j* disturbing
Job 40: 8 you condemn me to *j* yourself?
Isa 53: 11 my righteous servant will *j* many,
Lk 10: 29 But he wanted to *j* himself,
16: 15 "You are the ones who *j* yourselves
Ro 3: 30 who will *j* the circumcised by faith
Gal 3: 8 that God would *j* the Gentiles

JUSTIFYING* (JUST)
Job 32: 2 angry with Job for *j* himself rather

JUSTLY* (JUST)
Ps 58: 1 Do you rulers indeed speak *j*?
67: 4 for you rule the peoples *j*
Jer 7: 5 and deal with each other *j*,
Mic 6: 8 To act *j* and to love mercy
Lk 23: 41 We are punished *j*,
1Pe 2: 23 himself to him who judges *j*.

KADESH
Nu 20: 1 of Zin, and they stayed at *K*.
Dt 1: 46 And so you stayed in *K* many days

KADESH BARNEA
Nu 32: 8 I sent them from *K* to look over

KEBAR
Eze 1: 1 among the exiles by the *K* River,

KEDORLAOMER
Ge 14: 17 Abram returned from defeating *K*

KEEP (KEEPER KEEPING KEEPS KEPT)
Ge 31: 49 "May the LORD *k* watch
Ex 15: 26 his commands and *k* all his
20: 6 and *k* my commandments.
Lev 15: 31 You must *k* the Israelites separate
Nu 6: 24 and *k* you;
Dt 4: 2 but *k* the commands of the LORD
6: 17 Be sure to *k* the commands
7: 9 who love him and *k* his commands.
7: 12 your God will *k* his covenant
11: 1 your God and *k* his requirements,
13: 4 *K* his commands and obey him;
30: 10 your God and *k* his commands
30: 16 and to *k* his commands, decrees
Jos 22: 5 careful to *k* the commandment
1Ki 8: 58 and to *k* the commands,
2Ki 17: 19 Judah did not *k* the commands
23: 3 the LORD and *k* his commands,
1Ch 29: 18 and *k* their hearts loyal to you.
2Ch 6: 14 you who *k* your covenant of love
34: 31 the LORD and *k* his commands,
Job 14: 16 but not *k* track of my sin.
Ps 18: 28 You, O LORD, *k* my lamp burning
19: 13 *K* your servant also from willful
78: 10 they did not *k* God's covenant
119: 2 Blessed are they who *k* his statutes
119: 9 can a young man *k* his way pure?
121: 7 The LORD will *k* you
141: 3 *k* watch over the door of my lips.
Pr 4: 21 *k* them within your heart;
4: 24 *k* corrupt talk far from your lips.
30: 8 *K* falsehood and lies far from me;
Ecc 3: 6 a time to *k* and a time
12: 13 and *k* his commandments,
Isa 26: 3 You will *k* in perfect peace
42: 6 I will *k* you and will make you
58: 13 "If you *k* your feet
Jer 16: 11 forsook me and did not *k* my law.
Eze 20: 19 and be careful to *k* my laws.
Mt 10: 10 for the worker is worth his *k*.
Lk 12: 35 and *k* your lamps burning,
17: 33 tries to *k* his life will lose it,
Jn 10: 24 How long will you *k* us in suspense
12: 25 in this world will *k* it for eternal life
Ac 2: 24 for death to *k* its hold on him.
18: 9 "Do not be afraid; *k* on speaking,
Ro 7: 19 want to do — this I *k* on doing.
12: 11 but *k* your spiritual fervor,
14: 22 you believe about these things *k*
16: 17 *K* away from them.
1Co 1: 8 He will *k* you strong to the end,
2Co 12: 7 To *k* me from becoming conceited
Gal 5: 25 let us *k* in step with the Spirit.
Eph 4: 3 Make every effort to *k* the unity
2Th 3: 6 to *k* away from every brother who
1Ti 5: 22 *K* yourself pure.
2Ti 4: 5 *k* your head in all situations,
Heb 9: 20 God has commanded you to *k*."
13: 5 *K* your lives free from the love
Jas 1: 26 and yet does not *k* a tight rein
2: 8 If you really *k* the royal law found
3: 2 able to *k* his whole body in check.
2Pe 1: 8 will *k* you from being ineffective
Jude : 21 *K* yourselves in God's love
: 24 able to *k* you from falling
Rev 3: 10 also *k* you from the hour
22: 9 of all who *k* the words of this book.

KEEPER (KEEP)
Ge 4: 9 I my brother's *k*?" The LORD

KEEPING (KEEP)
Ex 20: 8 the Sabbath day by *k* it holy.
Dt 5: 12 the Sabbath day by *k* it holy,
13: 18 *k* all his commands that I am
Ps 19: 11 in *k* them there is great reward.
119: 112 My heart is set on *k* your decrees
Pr 15: 3 *k* watch on the wicked
Mt 3: 8 Produce fruit in *k* with repentance.
Lk 2: 8 *k* watch over their flocks at night.
1Co 7: 19 *K* God's commands is what counts.
2Co 8: 5 and then to us in *k* with God's will.
Jas 4: 11 you are not *k* it, but sitting
1Pe 3: 16 and respect, *k* a clear conscience,
2Pe 3: 9 Lord is not slow in *k* his promise,

KEEPS (KEEP)
Ne 1: 5 who *k* his covenant of love
Ps 15: 4 who *k* his oath
Pr 12: 23 A prudent man *k* his knowledge
15: 21 of understanding *k* a straight
17: 28 a fool is thought wise if he *k* silent,
29: 11 a wise man *k* himself under control
Isa 56: 2 who *k* the Sabbath
Da 9: 4 who *k* his covenant of love
Am 5: 13 Therefore the prudent man *k* quiet
Jn 7: 19 Yet not one of you *k* the law.
8: 51 if anyone *k* my word, he will never
1Co 13: 5 is not easily angered, it *k* no record
Jas 2: 10 For whoever *k* the whole law
Rev 22: 7 Blessed is he who *k* the words

KEILAH
1Sa 23: 13 that David had escaped from *K*,

KEPT (KEEP)
Ex 12: 42 Because the LORD *k* vigil that
Dt 7: 8 and *k* the oath he swore
2Ki 18: 6 he *k* the commands the LORD had
Ne 9: 8 You have *k* your promise
Ps 130: 3 If you, O LORD, *k* a record of sins,
Isa 38: 17 In your love you *k* me
Mt 19: 20 these I have *k*," the young man
2Co 11: 9 I have *k* myself from being
2Ti 4: 7 finished the race, I have *k* the faith.
1Pe 1: 4 spoil or fade — *k* in heaven for you,

KERNEL
Mk 4: 28 then the full *k* in the head.
Jn 12: 24 a *k* of wheat falls to the ground

KEY (KEYS)
Isa 33: 6 the fear of the LORD is the *k*
Rev 20: 1 having the *k* to the Abyss

KEYS* (KEY)
Mt 16: 19 I will give you the *k* of the kingdom
Rev 1: 18 And I hold the *k* of death

KICK*
Ac 26: 14 for you to *k* against the goads.'

KILL (KILLED KILLS)
Ecc 3: 3 a time to *k* and a time to heal,
Mt 10: 28 *k* the body but cannot *k* the soul.
17: 23 They will *k* him, and on the third
Mk 9: 31 will *k* him, and after three days
10: 34 spit on him, flog him and *k* him.

KILLED (KILL)
Ge 4: 8 his brother Abel and *k* him.
Ex 2: 12 he *k* the Egyptian and hid him
13: 15 the LORD *k* every firstborn
Nu 35: 11 who has *k* someone accidentally
1Sa 17: 50 down the Philistine and *k* him.
Ne 9: 26 They *k* your prophets, who had
Hos 6: 5 I *k* you with the words

Lk 11: 48 they *k* the prophets, and you build
Ac 3: 15 You *k* the author of life,

KILLS (KILL)
Ex 21: 12 *k* him shall surely be put to death.
Lev 24: 21 but whoever *k* a man must be put
2Co 3: 6 for the letter *k*, but the Spirit gives

KIND (KINDNESS KINDNESSES KINDS)
Ge 1: 24 animals, each according to its *k*."
2Ch 10: 7 "If you will be *k* to these people
Pr 11: 17 A *k* man benefits himself,
12: 25 but a *k* word cheers him up.
14: 21 blessed is he who is *k* to the needy.
14: 31 whoever is *k* to the needy honors
19: 17 He who is *k* to the poor lends
Da 4: 27 by being *k* to the oppressed.
Lk 6: 35 because he is *k* to the ungrateful
1Co 13: 4 Love is patient, love is *k*.
15: 35 With what *k* of body will they
Eph 4: 32 Be *k* and compassionate
1Th 5: 15 but always try to be *k* to each other
2Ti 2: 24 instead, he must be *k* to everyone,
Tit 2: 5 to be busy at home, to be *k*,

KINDHEARTED* (HEART)
Pr 11: 16 A *k* woman gains respect,

KINDNESS (KIND)
Ge 24: 12 and show *k* to my master Abraham
32: 10 I am unworthy of all the *k*
39: 21 he showed him *k* and granted him
Jdg 8: 35 failed to show *k* to the family
Ru 2: 20 has not stopped showing his *k*
2Sa 9: 3 to whom I can show God's *k*?"
22: 51 he shows unfailing *k*
Ps 18: 50 he shows unfailing *k*
141: 5 righteous man strike me — it is a *k*;
Isa 54: 8 but with everlasting *k*
Jer 9: 24 I am the LORD, who exercises *k*,
Hos 11: 4 I led them with cords of human *k*,
Ac 14: 17 He has shown *k* by giving you rain
Ro 11: 22 Consider therefore the *k*
2Co 6: 6 understanding, patience and *k*;
Gal 5: 22 peace, patience, *k*, goodness,
Eph 2: 7 expressed in his *k* to us
Col 3: 12 yourselves with compassion, *k*,
Tit 3: 4 But when the *k* and love
2Pe 1: 7 brotherly *k*; and to brotherly *k*,

KINDNESSES* (KIND)
Ps 106: 7 did not remember your many *k*,
Isa 63: 7 I will tell of the *k* of the LORD,
63: 7 to his compassion and many *k*.

KINDS (KIND)
Ge 1: 12 bearing seed according to their *k*
1Co 12: 4 There are different *k* of gifts,
1Ti 6: 10 of money is a root of all *k* of evil.
1Pe 1: 6 had to suffer grief in all *k* of trials.

KING (KING'S KINGDOM KINGDOMS KINGS)
1. Kings of Judah and Israel: see Saul, David, Solomon.

2. Kings of Judah: see Rehoboam, Abijah, Asa, Jehoshaphat, Jehoram, Ahaziah, Athaliah (Queen), Joash, Amaziah, Azariah (Uzziah), Jotham, Ahaz, Hezekiah, Manasseh, Amon, Josiah, Jehoahaz, Jehoiakim, Jehoiachin, Zedekiah.

3. Kings of Israel: see Jeroboam I, Nadab, Baasha, Elah, Zimri, Tibni, Omri, Ahab, Ahaziah, Joram, Jehu, Jehoahaz, Jehoash, Jeroboam II, Zechariah, Shallum, Menahem, Pekah, Pekahiah, Hoshea.

Ex 1: 8 a new *k*, who did not know about
Dt 17: 14 "Let us set a *k* over us like all
Jdg 17: 6 In those days Israel had no *k*;
1Sa 8: 5 now appoint a *k* to lead us,
11: 15 as *k* in the presence of the LORD.
12: 12 the LORD your God was your *k*.
2Sa 2: 4 and there they anointed David *k*
1Ki 1: 30 Solomon your son shall be *k*
Ps 2: 6 "I have installed my *K*
24: 7 that the *K* of glory may come in.
44: 4 You are my *K* and my God,
47: 7 For God is the *K* of all the earth;
Isa 32: 1 See, a *k* will reign in righteousness
Jer 30: 9 and David their *k*,
Hos 3: 5 their God and David their *k*.
Mic 2: 13 *k* will pass through before them,
Zec 9: 9 See, your *k* comes to you,
Mt 2: 2 is the one who has been born *k*
27: 11 "Are you the *k* of the Jews?" "Yes,
Lk 19: 38 "Blessed is the *k* who comes
23: 3 "Are you the *k* of the Jews?" "Yes,
23: 38 THE *K* OF THE JEWS.
Jn 1: 49 of God; you are the *K* of Israel."
12: 13 "Blessed is the *K* of Israel!"
Ac 17: 7 saying that there is another *k*,
1Ti 1: 17 Now to the *K* eternal, immortal,
6: 15 the *K* of kings and Lord of lords,
Heb 7: 1 This Melchizedek was *k* of Salem
1Pe 2: 13 to the *k*, as the supreme authority,
2: 17 of believers, fear God, honor the *k*.
Rev 15: 3 *K* of the ages.
17: 14 he is Lord of lords and *K* of kings —
19: 16 *K* OF KINGS AND LORD

KING'S (KING)
Pr 21: 1 The *k* heart is in the hand
Ecc 8: 3 in a hurry to leave the *k* presence.

KINGDOM (KING)
Ex 19: 6 you will be for me a *k* of priests
Dt 17: 18 When he takes the throne of his *k*,
2Sa 7: 12 body, and I will establish his *k*.
1Ki 11: 31 to tear the *k* out of Solomon's hand
1Ch 17: 11 own sons, and I will establish his *k*.
29: 11 Yours, O LORD, is the *k*;
Ps 45: 6 justice will be the scepter of your *k*.
103: 19 and his *k* rules over all.
145: 11 They will tell of the glory of your *k*
Eze 29: 14 There they will be a lowly *k*.
Da 2: 39 "After you, another *k* will rise,
4: 3 His *k* is an eternal *k*;
7: 27 His *k* will be an everlasting *k*,
Ob : 21 And the *k* will be the LORD's.
Mt 3: 2 Repent, for the *k* of heaven is near
4: 17 Repent, for the *k* of heaven is near
4: 23 preaching the good news of the *k*,
5: 3 for theirs is the *k* of heaven.
5: 10 for theirs is the *k* of heaven.
5: 19 great in the *k* of heaven.
5: 19 least in the *k* of heaven,
5: 20 you will certainly not enter the *k*
6: 10 your *k* come,
6: 33 But seek first his *k* and his
7: 21 Lord,' will enter the *k* of heaven,
8: 11 Isaac and Jacob in the *k* of heaven.
8: 12 the subjects of the *k* will be thrown
9: 35 preaching the good news of the *k*
10: 7 preach this message: 'The *k*
11: 11 least in the *k* of heaven is greater
11: 12 the *k* of heaven has been forcefully
12: 25 "Every *k* divided against itself will
12: 26 How then can his *k* stand?
12: 28 then the *k* of God has come
13: 11 knowledge of the secrets of the *k*
13: 19 hears the message about the *k*
13: 24 "The *k* of heaven is like a man who
13: 31 *k* of heaven is like a mustard seed,
13: 33 "The *k* of heaven is like yeast that
13: 38 stands for the sons of the *k*.
13: 41 of his *k* everything that causes sin
13: 43 the sun in the *k* of their Father.
13: 44 *k* of heaven is like treasure hidden
13: 45 the *k* of heaven is like a merchant
13: 47 *k* of heaven is like a net that was let
13: 52 has been instructed about the *k*
16: 19 the keys of the *k* of heaven;
16: 28 the Son of Man coming in his *k*."
18: 1 the greatest in the *k* of heaven?"
18: 3 you will never enter the *k*
18: 4 the greatest in the *k* of heaven.
18: 23 the *k* of heaven is like a king who
19: 12 because of the *k* of heaven.
19: 14 for the *k* of heaven belongs to such
19: 23 man to enter the *k* of heaven.
19: 24 for a rich man to enter the *k* of God
20: 1 "For the *k* of heaven is like
20: 21 the other at your left in your *k*."
21: 31 the prostitutes are entering the *k*
21: 43 "Therefore I tell you that the *k*
22: 2 "The *k* of heaven is like a king who
23: 13 You shut the *k* of heaven
24: 7 rise against nation, and *k* against *k*.
24: 14 gospel of the *k* will be preached
25: 1 "At that time the *k*
25: 34 the *k* prepared for you
26: 29 anew with you in my Father's *k*."
Mk 1: 15 "The *k* of God is near.
3: 24 If a *k* is divided against itself,
3: 24 against itself, that *k* cannot stand.
4: 11 "The secret of the *k*
4: 26 "This is what the *k* of God is like.
4: 30 "What shall we say the *k*
6: 23 I will give you, up to half my *k*."
9: 1 before they see the *k* of God come
9: 47 better for you to enter the *k* of God
10: 14 for the *k* of God belongs to such
10: 15 anyone who will not receive the *k*
10: 23 for the rich to enter the *k* of God!"
10: 24 how hard it is to enter the *k* of God
10: 25 for a rich man to enter the *k* of God
11: 10 "Blessed is the coming *k*
12: 34 "You are not far from the *k* of God
13: 8 rise against nation, and *k* against *k*.
Mk 14: 25 day when I drink it anew in the *k*
15: 43 who was himself waiting for the *k*
Lk 1: 33 Jacob forever; his *k* will never
4: 43 of the *k* of God to the other towns
6: 20 for yours is the *k* of God.
7: 28 in the *k* of God is greater than he."
8: 1 proclaiming the good news of the *k*
8: 10 knowledge of the secrets of the *k*
9: 2 out to preach the *k* of God
9: 11 spoke to them about the *k* of God,
9: 27 before they see the *k* of God."
9: 60 you go and proclaim the *k* of God
9: 62 fit for service in the *k* of God."
10: 9 'The *k* of God is near you.'
10: 11 sure of this: The *k* of God is near.'
11: 2 your *k* come.
11: 17 "Any *k* divided against itself will
11: 18 himself, how can his *k* stand?
11: 20 then the *k* of God has come to you.
12: 31 seek his *k*, and these things will be
12: 32 has been pleased to give you the *k*.
13: 18 "What is the *k* of God like?
13: 20 What shall I compare the *k* of God
13: 28 all the prophets in the *k* of God,
13: 29 places at the feast in the *k* of God.
14: 15 eat at the feast in the *k* of God."
16: 16 the good news of the *k*
17: 20 when the *k* of God would come,
17: 20 *k* of God does not come with careful
17: 21 because the *k* of God is within you
18: 16 for the *k* of God belongs to such
18: 17 anyone who will not receive the *k*
18: 24 for the rich to enter the *k* of God!
18: 25 for a rich man to enter the *k* of God
18: 29 for the sake of the *k* of God will fail
19: 11 and the people thought that the *k*
21: 10 rise against nation, and *k* against *k*.
21: 31 you know that the *k* of God is near.
22: 16 until it finds fulfillment in the *k*
22: 18 the vine until the *k* of God comes."
22: 29 And I confer on you a *k*, just
22: 30 and drink at my table in my *k*
23: 42 me when you come into your *k*."
23: 51 he was waiting for the *k* of God.
Jn 3: 3 no one can see the *k* of God.
3: 5 no one can enter the *k* of God.
18: 36 now my *k* is from another place."
18: 36 "My *k* is not of this world.
Ac 1: 3 and spoke about the *k* of God.
1: 6 going to restore the *k* to Israel?"
8: 12 he preached the good news of the *k*
14: 22 hardships to enter the *k* of God,"
19: 8 arguing persuasively about the *k*
20: 25 about preaching the *k* will ever see
28: 23 and declared to them the *k* of God
28: 31 hindrance he preached the *k*
Ro 14: 17 For the *k* of God is not a matter
1Co 4: 20 For the *k* of God is not a matter
6: 9 the wicked will not inherit the *k*
6: 10 swindlers will inherit the *k* of God.
15: 24 hands over the *k* to God the Father
15: 50 blood cannot inherit the *k* of God,
Gal 5: 21 live like this will not inherit the *k*
Eph 2: 2 and of the ruler of the *k* of the air,
5: 5 has any inheritance in the *k*
Col 1: 12 of the saints in the *k* of light.
1: 13 and brought us into the *k*
4: 11 among my fellow workers for the *k*
1Th 2: 12 who calls you into his *k* and glory.
2Th 1: 5 will be counted worthy of the *k*
2Ti 4: 1 in view of his appearing and his *k*,
4: 18 bring me safely to his heavenly *k*.
Heb 1: 8 will be the scepter of your *k*.
12: 28 we are receiving a *k* that cannot be
Jas 2: 5 to inherit the *k* he promised those
2Pe 1: 11 into the eternal *k* of our Lord
Rev 1: 6 has made us to be a *k* and priests
1: 9 companion in the suffering and *k*
5: 10 You have made them to be a *k*
11: 15 of the world has become the *k*
11: 15 "The *k* of the world has become
12: 10 the power and the *k* of our God,
16: 10 his *k* was plunged into darkness.
17: 12 who have not yet received a *k*,

KINGDOMS (KING)
2Ki 19: 15 God over all the *k* of the earth.
19: 19 so that all *k* on earth may know
2Ch 20: 6 rule over all the *k* of the nations.
Ps 68: 32 Sing to God, O *k* of the earth,
Isa 37: 16 God over all the *k* of the earth.
37: 20 so that all *k* on earth may know
Eze 29: 15 It will be the lowliest of *k*
37: 22 or be divided into two *k*.
Da 4: 17 Most High is sovereign over the *k*
7: 17 great beasts are four *k* that will rise
Zep 3: 8 to gather the *k*

KINGS (KING)
Ps 2: 2 The *k* of the earth take their stand
47: 9 for the *k* of the earth belong to God
68: 29 *k* will bring you gifts.
72: 11 All *k* will bow down to him
110: 5 he will crush *k* on the day
149: 8 to bind their *k* with fetters,
Pr 16: 12 *K* detest wrongdoing,
Isa 24: 21 and the *k* on the earth below.
52: 15 and *k* will shut their mouths
60: 11 their *k* led in triumphal procession.
Da 2: 21 he sets up *k* and deposes them.
7: 24 ten horns are ten *k* who will come
Lk 21: 12 and you will be brought before *k*
1Co 4: 8 You have become *k* —
1Ti 2: 2 for *k* and all those in authority,
6: 15 the King of *k* and Lord of lords,
Rev 1: 5 and the ruler of the *k* of the earth.
17: 14 he is Lord of lords and King of *k* —
19: 16 KING OF *K* AND LORD

KINSMAN-REDEEMER (REDEEM)
Ru 3: 9 over me, since you are a *k*."
4: 14 day has not left you without a *k*.

KISS (KISSED KISSES)
Ps 2: 12 *K* the Son, lest he be angry
Pr 24: 26 is like a *k* on the lips.
SS 1: 2 *Beloved* Let him *k* me
8: 1 I would *k* you,
Lk 22: 48 the Son of Man with a *k*?"
Ro 16: 16 Greet one another with a holy *k*.
1Co 16: 20 Greet one another with a holy *k*.
2Co 13: 12 Greet one another with a holy *k*.
1Th 5: 26 Greet all the brothers with a holy *k*
1Pe 5: 14 Greet one another with a *k* of love.

KISSED (KISS)
Mk 14: 45 Judas said, "Rabbi!" and *k* him.
Lk 7: 38 *k* them and poured perfume

KISSES* (KISS)
Pr 27: 6 but an enemy multiplies *k*.
SS 1: 2 with the *k* of his mouth —

KNEE (KNEES)
Isa 45: 23 Before me every *k* will bow;
Ro 14: 11 'every *k* will bow before me;
Php 2: 10 name of Jesus every *k* should bow,

KNEEL (KNELT)
Est 3: 2 But Mordecai would not *k* down
Ps 95: 6 let us *k* before the LORD our
Eph 3: 14 For this reason I *k*

KNEES (KNEE)
1Ki 19: 18 all whose *k* have not bowed
Isa 35: 3 steady the *k* that give way;
Da 6: 10 times a day he got down on his *k*
Lk 5: 8 he fell at Jesus' *k* and said,
Heb 12: 12 your feeble arms and weak *k*.

KNELT* (KNEEL)
1Ki 1: 16 Bathsheba bowed low and *k*
2Ch 6: 13 and then *k* down before the whole
7: 3 they *k* on the pavement
29: 29 everyone present with him *k* down
Est 3: 2 officials at the king's gate *k* down
Mt 8: 2 and *k* before him and said,
9: 18 a ruler came and *k* before him
15: 25 The woman came and *k* before him
17: 14 a man approached Jesus and *k*
27: 29 *k* in front of him and mocked him.
Lk 22: 41 *k* down and prayed, "Father,
Ac 20: 36 he *k* down with all of them
21: 5 there on the beach we *k* to pray.

KNEW (KNOW)
2Ch 33: 13 Manasseh *k* that the LORD is God
Job 23: 3 If only I *k* where to find him;
Pr 24: 12 "But we *k* nothing about this,"
Jer 1: 5 you in the womb I *k* you,
Jnh 4: 2 I *k* that you are a gracious
Mt 7: 23 tell them plainly, 'I never *k* you.
12: 25 Jesus *k* their thoughts
Jn 2: 24 himself to them, for he *k* all men.
14: 7 If you really *k* me, you would know

KNIFE
Ge 22: 10 and took the *k* to slay his son.
Pr 23: 2 and put a *k* to your throat

KNOCK* (KNOCKS)
Mt 7: 7 *k* and the door will be opened
Lk 11: 9 *k* and the door will be opened
Rev 3: 20 I am! I stand at the door and *k*.

KNOCKS (KNOCK)
Mt 7: 8 and to him who *k*, the door will be

KNOW (FOREKNEW FOREKNOWLEDGE KNEW KNOWING KNOWLEDGE KNOWN KNOWS)
Ge 22: 12 Now I *k* that you fear God,
Ex 6: 7 you will *k* that I am the LORD
14: 4 and the Egyptians will *k* that I am
33: 13 teach me your ways so I may *k* you
Dt 7: 9 *K* therefore that the LORD your
18: 21 "How can we *k* when a message
Jos 4: 24 of the earth might *k* that the hand
23: 14 You *k* with all your heart
1Sa 17: 46 the whole world will *k* that there is
1Ki 8: 39 heart (for you alone *k* the hearts
Job 11: 6 *K* this: God has even forgotten
19: 25 I *k* that my Redeemer lives,
42: 3 things too wonderful for me to *k*.
Ps 9: 10 Those who *k* your name will trust
46: 10 "Be still, and *k* that I am God;
100: 3 *K* that the LORD is God.
139: 1 and you *k* me.
139: 23 Search me, O God, and *k* my heart;
145: 12 so that all men may *k*
Pr 27: 1 for you do not *k* what a day may
30: 4 Tell me if you *k*!
Ecc 8: 5 wise heart will *k* the proper time
Isa 29: 15 "Who sees us? Who will *k*?"
40: 21 Do you not *k*?
Jer 6: 15 they do not even *k* how to blush.
22: 16 Is that not what it means to *k* me?"
24: 7 I will give them a heart to *k* me,
31: 34 his brother, saying, '*K* the LORD,'
33: 3 unsearchable things you do not *k*.'
Eze 2: 5 they will *k* that a prophet has been
6: 10 they will *k* that I am the LORD;
Da 11: 32 people who *k* their God will firmly
Mt 6: 3 let your left hand *k* what your right
7: 11 *k* how to give good gifts
9: 6 But so that you may *k* that the Son
22: 29 you do not *k* the Scriptures
24: 42 you do not *k* on what day your
26: 74 "I don't *k* the man!" Immediately
Mk 12: 24 you do not *k* the Scriptures
Lk 1: 4 so that you may *k* the certainty
11: 13 *k* how to give good gifts
12: 48 But the one who does not *k*
13: 25 'I don't *k* you or where you come
21: 31 you *k* that the kingdom of God is
23: 34 for they do not *k* what they are
Jn 1: 26 among you stands one you do not *k*
3: 11 we speak of what we *k*,
4: 22 we worship what we do *k*,
4: 42 and we *k* that this man really is
6: 69 and *k* that you are the Holy One
7: 28 You do not *k* him, but I *k* him
8: 14 for I *k* where I came from
8: 19 "You do not *k* me or my Father,"
8: 32 Then you will *k* the truth,
8: 55 Though you do not *k* him, I *k* him.
9: 25 One thing I do *k*.
10: 4 him because they *k* his voice.
10: 14 I *k* my sheep and my sheep *k* me —
10: 27 I *k* them, and they follow me.
12: 35 the dark does not *k* where he is
13: 17 Now that you *k* these things,
13: 35 all men will *k* that you are my
14: 17 you *k* him, for he lives with you
15: 21 for they do not *k* the One who sent
16: 30 we can see that you *k* all things
17: 3 that they may *k* you, the only true
17: 23 to let the world *k* that you sent me
21: 15 he said, "you *k* that I love you."
21: 24 We *k* that his testimony is true.
Ac 1: 7 "It is not for you to *k* the times
1: 24 "Lord, you *k* everyone's heart.
Ro 3: 17 and the way of peace they do not *k*
6: 3 Or don't you *k* that all
6: 6 For we *k* that our old self was
6: 16 Don't you *k* that when you offer
7: 14 We *k* that the law is spiritual;
7: 18 I *k* that nothing good lives in me,
8: 22 We *k* that the whole creation has
8: 26 We do not *k* what we ought to pray
8: 28 we *k* that in all things God works
1Co 1: 21 through its wisdom did not *k* him,
2: 2 For I resolved to *k* nothing
3: 16 Don't you *k* that you yourselves
5: 6 Don't you *k* that a little yeast
6: 2 Do you not *k* that the saints will
6: 15 Do you not *k* that your bodies are
6: 16 Do you not *k* that he who unites
6: 19 Do you not *k* that your body is
7: 16 How do you *k*, wife, whether you
8: 2 does not yet *k* as he ought to *k*.
9: 13 Don't you *k* that those who work
9: 24 Do you not *k* that
13: 9 For we *k* in part and we prophesy
1Co 13: 12 Now I *k* in part; then I shall *k* fully,
15: 58 because you *k* that your labor
2Co 5: 1 we *k* that if the earthly tent we live
5: 11 we *k* what it is to fear the Lord,
8: 9 For you *k* the grace
Gal 1: 11 you to *k*, brothers, that the gospel I
2: 16 not 'Gentile sinners' *k* that a man
Eph 1: 17 so that you may *k* him better.
1: 18 in order that you may *k* the hope
6: 8 you *k* that the Lord will reward
6: 9 since you *k* that he who is both
Php 3: 10 I want to *k* Christ and the power
4: 12 I *k* what it is to be in need,
Col 2: 2 order that they may *k* the mystery
4: 1 because you *k* that you
4: 6 so that you may *k* how
1Th 3: 3 You *k* quite well that we were
5: 2 for you *k* very well that the day
2Th 1: 8 punish those who do not *k* God
1Ti 1: 7 they do not *k* what they are talking
3: 5 (If anyone does not *k* how
3: 15 you will *k* how people ought
2Ti 1: 12 because I *k* whom I have believed,
2: 23 you *k* they produce quarrels.
3: 14 you *k* those from whom you
Heb 8: 11 because they will all *k* me,
11: 8 he did not *k* where he was going.
Jas 1: 3 because you *k* that the testing
3: 1 you *k* that we who teach will be
4: 4 don't you *k* that friendship
4: 14 *k* what will happen tomorrow.
1Pe 1: 18 For you *k* that it was not
2Pe 1: 12 even though you *k* them
1Jn 2: 3 We *k* that we have come
2: 4 The man who says, "I *k* him,"
2: 5 This is how we *k* we are in him:
2: 11 he does not *k* where he is going,
2: 20 and all of you *k* the truth.
2: 29 you *k* that everyone who does
3: 1 not *k* us is that it did not *k* him.
3: 2 But we *k* that when he appears,
3: 10 This is how we *k* who the children
3: 14 We *k* that we have passed
3: 16 This is how we *k* what love is:
3: 19 then is how we *k* that we belong
3: 24 We *k* it by the Spirit he gave us.
4: 8 does not love does not *k* God,
4: 13 We *k* that we live in him
4: 16 so we *k* and rely on the love God
5: 2 This is how we *k* that we love
5: 13 so that you may *k* that you have
5: 15 And if we *k* that he hears us —
5: 18 We *k* that anyone born
5: 20 We *k* also that the Son
Rev 2: 2 I *k* your deeds, your hard work
2: 9 I *k* your afflictions and your
2: 19 I *k* your deeds, your love and faith,
3: 3 you will not *k* at what time I will
3: 15 I *k* your deeds, that you are neither

KNOWING (KNOW)
Ge 3: 5 and you will be like God, *k* good
3: 22 now become like one of us, *k* good
Jn 19: 28 *k* that all was now completed,
Php 3: 8 of *k* Christ Jesus my Lord,
Phm : 21 *k* that you will do even more
Heb 13: 2 entertained angels without *k* it.

KNOWLEDGE (KNOW)
Ge 2: 9 the tree of the *k* of good and evil.
2: 17 eat from the tree of the *k* of good
2Ch 1: 10 and *k*, that I may lead this people,
Job 21: 22 "Can anyone teach *k* to God,
38: 2 counsel with words without *k*?
42: 3 obscures my counsel without *k*?'
Ps 19: 2 night after night they display *k*.
73: 11 Does the Most High have *k*?"
94: 10 Does he who teaches man lack *k*?
119: 66 Teach me *k* and good judgment,
139: 6 Such *k* is too wonderful for me,
Pr 1: 4 *k* and discretion to the young —
1: 7 of the LORD is the beginning of *k*,
2: 5 and find the *k* of God.
2: 6 from his mouth come *k*
2: 10 and *k* will be pleasant to your soul.
3: 20 by his *k* the deeps were divided,
8: 10 *k* rather than choice gold,
8: 12 I possess *k* and discretion.
9: 10 *k* of the Holy One is understanding
10: 14 Wise men store up *k*,
12: 1 Whoever loves discipline loves *k*,
12: 23 A prudent man keeps his *k*
13: 16 Every prudent man acts out of *k*,
14: 6 *k* comes easily to the discerning.
15: 7 The lips of the wise spread *k*;
15: 14 The discerning heart seeks *k*,

Pr 17:27 A man of *k* uses words
18:15 heart of the discerning acquires *k*;
19:2 to have zeal without *k*,
19:25 discerning man, and he will gain *k*.
20:15 lips that speak *k* are a rare jewel.
23:12 and your ears to words of *k*.
24:4 through *k* its rooms are filled
Ecc 7:12 but the advantage of *k* is this:
Isa 11:2 the Spirit of *k* and of the fear
11:9 full of the *k* of the LORD
40:14 Who was it that taught him *k*
Jer 3:15 who will lead you with *k*
Hos 4:6 are destroyed from lack of *k*.
Hab 2:14 filled with the *k* of the glory
Mal 2:7 lips of a priest ought to preserve *k*,
Mt 13:11 The *k* of the secrets of the kingdom
Lk 8:10 The *k* of the secrets of the kingdom
11:52 you have taken away the key to *k*.
Ac 18:24 with a thorough *k* of the Scriptures
Ro 1:28 worthwhile to retain the *k* of God,
10:2 but their zeal is not based on *k*.
11:33 riches of the wisdom and *k* of God!
1Co 8:1 *K* puffs up, but love builds up.
8:11 Christ died, is destroyed by your *k*.
12:8 to another the message of *k*
13:2 can fathom all mysteries and all *k*,
13:8 where there is *k*, it will pass away.
2Co 2:14 everywhere the fragrance of the *k*
4:6 light of the *k* of the glory of God
8:7 in *k*, in complete earnestness
11:6 a trained speaker, but I do have *k*.
Eph 3:19 to know this love that surpasses *k*
4:13 and in the *k* of the Son of God
Php 1:9 and more in *k* and depth of insight,
Col 1:9 God to fill you with the *k* of his will
1:10 every good work, growing in the *k*
2:3 all the treasures of wisdom and *k*.
3:10 which is being renewed in *k*
1Ti 2:4 and to come to a *k* of the truth.
6:20 ideas of what is falsely called *k*,
Tit 1:1 and the *k* of the truth that leads
Heb 10:26 after we have received the *k*
2Pe 1:5 and to goodness, *k*; and to *k*,
3:18 grow in the grace and *k* of our Lord

KNOWN (KNOW)
Ex 6:3 the LORD I did not make myself *k*
Ps 16:11 You have made *k* to me the path
89:1 I will make your faithfulness *k*
98:2 LORD has made his salvation *k*
105:1 make *k* among the nations what he
119:168 for all my ways are *k* to you.
Pr 20:11 Even a child is *k* by his actions,
Isa 12:4 make *k* among the nations what he
46:10 *k* the end from the beginning,
61:9 Their descendants will be *k*
Eze 38:23 I will make myself *k* in the sight
39:7 "'I will make *k* my holy name
Mt 10:26 or hidden that will not be made *k*.
24:43 of the house had *k* at what time
Lk 19:42 had only *k* on this day what would
Jn 15:15 from my Father I have made *k*
16:14 from what is mine and making it *k*
17:26 I have made you *k* to them,
Ac 2:28 You have made *k* to me the paths
Ro 1:19 since what may be *k* about God is
3:21 apart from law, has been made *k*,
9:22 his wrath and make his power *k*,
11:34 "Who has *k* the mind of the Lord?
15:20 the gospel where Christ was not *k*,
16:26 and made *k* through the prophetic
1Co 2:16 "For who has *k* the mind
8:3 But the man who loves God is *k*
13:12 know fully, even as I am fully *k*.
2Co 3:2 written on our hearts, *k*
Gal 4:9 or rather are *k* by God —
Eph 3:5 which was not made *k* to men
6:19 will fearlessly make *k* the mystery
2Ti 3:15 infancy you have *k* the holy
2Pe 2:21 than to have *k* it and then

KNOWS (KNOW)
1Sa 2:3 for the LORD is a God who *k*,
Est 4:14 And who *k* but that you have come
Job 23:10 But he *k* the way that I take;
Ps 44:21 since he *k* the secrets of the heart?
94:11 The LORD *k* the thoughts of man;
103:14 for he *k* how we are formed,
Ecc 8:7 Since no man *k* the future,
8:17 Even if a wise man claims he *k*,
9:12 no man *k* when his hour will come:
Isa 29:16 "He *k* nothing"?
Jer 9:24 that he understands and *k* me,
Mt 6:8 for your Father *k* what you need
11:27 No one *k* the Son
24:36 "No one *k* about that day or hour,
Lk 12:47 "That servant who *k* his master's
16:15 of men, but God *k* your hearts.
Ac 15:8 who *k* the heart, showed that he
Ro 8:27 who searches our hearts *k* the mind
1Co 2:11 who among men *k* the thoughts
8:2 who thinks he *k* something does
2Ti 2:19 The Lord *k* those who are his," and
Jas 4:17 who *k* the good he ought to do
1Jn 4:6 and whoever *k* God listens to us;
4:7 born of God and *k* God.

KOHATHITE (KOHATHITES)
Nu 3:29 The *K* clans were to camp

KOHATHITES (KOHATHITE)
Nu 3:28 The *K* were responsible
4:15 *K* are to carry those things that are

KORAH
Levite who led rebellion against Moses and Aaron (Nu 16; Jude 11).

KORAZIN
Mt 11:21 "Woe to you, *K!* Woe to you,

LABAN
Brother of Rebekah (Ge 24:29), father of Rachel and Leah (Ge 29:16). Received Abraham's servant (Ge 24:29–51). Provided daughters as wives for Jacob in exchange for Jacob's service (Ge 29:1–30). Provided flocks for Jacob's service (Ge 30:25–43). After Jacob's departure, pursued and covenanted with him (Ge 31).

LABOR (LABORING)
Ex 1:11 to oppress them with forced *l*,
20:9 Six days you shall *l* and do all your
Dt 5:13 Six days you shall *l* and do all your
Ps 127:1 its builders *l* in vain.
128:2 You will eat the fruit of your *l*;
Pr 12:24 but laziness ends in slave *l*.
Isa 54:1 you who were never in *l*;
55:2 and your *l* on what does not satisfy
Mt 6:28 They do not *l* or spin.
Jn 4:38 have reaped the benefits of their *l*."
1Co 3:8 rewarded according to his own *l*.
15:58 because you know that your *l*
Gal 4:27 you who have no *l* pains;
Php 2:16 day of Christ that I did not run or *l*
Rev 14:13 "they will rest from their *l*,

LABORING* (LABOR)
2Th 3:8 *l* and toiling so that we would not

LACK (LACKED LACKING LACKS)
Ps 34:9 for those who fear him *l* nothing.
Pr 5:23 He will die for *l* of discipline,
10:21 but fools die for *l* of judgment.
11:14 For *l* of guidance a nation falls,
15:22 Plans fail for *l* of counsel,
28:27 to the poor will *l* nothing,
Mk 6:6 he was amazed at their *l* of faith.
16:14 he rebuked them for their *l* of faith
Ro 3:3 Will their *l* of faith nullify God's
1Co 1:7 you do not *l* any spiritual gift
7:5 because of your *l* of self-control.
Col 2:23 *l* any value in restraining sensual

LACKED (LACK)
Dt 2:7 and you have not *l* anything.
Ne 9:21 them in the desert; they *l* nothing,
1Co 12:24 honor to the parts that *l* it,

LACKING (LACK)
Pr 17:18 A man *l* in judgment strikes hands
Ro 12:11 Never be *l* in zeal, but keep your
Jas 1:4 and complete, not *l* anything.

LACKS (LACK)
Pr 6:32 who commits adultery *l* judgment;
11:12 man who *l* judgment derides his
12:11 he who chases fantasies *l* judgment
15:21 delights a man who *l* judgment,
24:30 of the man who *l* judgment;
25:28 is a man who *l* self-control.
28:16 A tyrannical ruler *l* judgment,
31:11 and *l* nothing of value.
Eze 34:8 because my flock *l* a shepherd
Jas 1:5 any of you *l* wisdom, he should ask

LAID (LAY)
Isa 53:6 and the LORD has *l* on him
Mk 6:29 took his body and *l* it in a tomb.
Lk 6:48 and *l* the foundation on rock.
Ac 6:6 and *l* their hands on them.
1Co 3:11 other than the one already *l*,
1Ti 4:14 body of elders *l* their hands on you.
1Jn 3:16 Jesus Christ *l* down his life for us.

LAKE
Mt 8:24 a furious storm came up on the *l*,
14:25 out to them, walking on the *l*.
Mk 4:1 into a boat and sat in it out on the *l*,
Lk 8:33 down the steep bank into the *l*
Jn 6:25 him on the other side of the *l*,
Rev 19:20 into the fiery *l* of burning sulfur.
20:14 The *l* of fire is the second death.

LAMB (LAMB'S LAMBS)
Ge 22:8 "God himself will provide the *l*
Ex 12:21 and slaughter the Passover *l*.
Nu 9:11 are to eat the *l*, together
2Sa 12:4 he took the ewe *l* that belonged
Isa 11:6 The wolf will live with the *l*,
53:7 he was led like a *l* to the slaughter,
Mk 14:12 to sacrifice the Passover *l*,
Jn 1:29 *L* of God, who takes away the sin
Ac 8:32 as a *l* before the shearer is silent,
1Co 5:7 our Passover *l*, has been sacrificed.
1Pe 1:19 a *l* without blemish or defect.
Rev 5:6 Then I saw a *L*, looking
5:12 "Worthy is the *L*, who was slain,
7:14 white in the blood of the *L*.
14:4 They follow the *L* wherever he
15:3 of God and the song of the *L*:
17:14 but the *L* will overcome them
19:9 to the wedding supper of the *L*!'"
21:23 gives it light, and the *L* is its lamp.

LAMB'S (LAMB)
Rev 21:27 written in the *L* book of life.

LAMBS (LAMB)
Lk 10:3 I am sending you out like *l*
Jn 21:15 Jesus said, "Feed my *l*."

LAME
Isa 33:23 even the *l* will carry off plunder.
35:6 Then will the *l* leap like a deer,
Mt 11:5 The blind receive sight, the *l* walk,
15:31 the *l* walking and the blind seeing.
Lk 14:21 the crippled, the blind and the *l*.'

LAMENT
2Sa 1:17 took up this *l* concerning Saul
Eze 19:1 Take up a *l* concerning the princes

LAMP (LAMPS LAMPSTAND LAMPSTANDS)
2Sa 22:29 You are my *l*, O LORD;
Ps 18:28 You, O LORD, keep my *l* burning;
119:105 Your word is a *l* to my feet
132:17 and set up a *l* for my anointed one.
Pr 6:23 For these commands are a *l*,
20:27 *l* of the LORD searches the spirit
31:18 and her *l* does not go out at night.
Mt 6:22 "The eye is the *l* of the body.
Lk 8:16 "No one lights a *l* and hides it
Rev 21:23 gives it light, and the Lamb is its *l*.
22:5 They will not need the light of a *l*

LAMPS (LAMP)
Mt 25:1 be like ten virgins who took their *l*
Lk 12:35 for service and keep your *l* burning,
Rev 4:5 the throne, seven *l* were blazing.

LAMPSTAND (LAMP)
Ex 25:31 "Make a *l* of pure gold
Zec 4:2 "I see a solid gold *l* with a bowl
4:11 on the right and the left of the *l*?"
Heb 9:2 In its first room were the *l*,
Rev 2:5 and remove your *l* from its place.

LAMPSTANDS (LAMP)
2Ch 4:7 He made ten gold *l* according
Rev 1:12 when I turned I saw seven golden *l*,
1:20 and of the seven golden *l* is this:

LAND (LANDS)
Ge 1:10 God called the dry ground "*l*,"
1:11 "Let the *l* produce vegetation:
1:24 "Let the *l* produce living creatures
12:1 and go to the *l* I will show you.
12:7 To your offspring I will give this *l*."
13:15 All the *l* that you see I will give
15:18 "To your descendants I give this *l*,
50:24 out of this *l* to the *l* he promised
Ex 3:8 a *l* flowing with milk and honey —
6:8 to the *l* I swore with uplifted hand
33:3 Go up to the *l* flowing with milk
Lev 25:23 *l* must not be sold permanently,
Nu 14:8 us into that *l*, a *l* flowing with milk
35:33 Do not pollute the *l* where you are.
Dt 1:8 See, I have given you this *l*.
8:7 God is bringing you into a good *l* —
11:10 The *l* you are entering to take
28:21 you from the *l* you are entering
29:19 will bring disaster on the watered *l*
34:1 LORD showed him the whole *l* —
Jos 13:2 "This is the *l* that remains:
14:4 Levites received no share of the *l*

Jos 14: 9 l on which your feet have walked
2Sa 21: 14 answered prayer in behalf of the l.
2Ki 17: 5 of Assyria invaded the entire l,
24: 1 king of Babylon invaded the l,
25: 21 into captivity, away from her l.
2Ch 7: 14 their sin and will heal their l.
7: 20 then I will uproot Israel from my l,
36: 21 The l enjoyed its sabbath rests;
Ezr 9: 11 entering to possess is a l polluted
Ne 9: 36 in the l you gave our forefathers
Ps 37: 11 But the meek will inherit the l
37: 29 the righteous will inherit the l
136: 21 and gave their l as an inheritance,
142: 5 my portion in the l of the living."
Pr 2: 21 For the upright will live in the l,
12: 11 who works his l will have abundant
Isa 6: 13 though a tenth remains in the l,
53: 8 cut off from the l of the living;
Jer 2: 7 But you came and defiled my l
Eze 36: 24 and bring you back into your own l.

LANDS (LAND)
Ps 111: 6 giving them the l of other nations.
Eze 20: 6 honey, the most beautiful of all l.
Zec 10: 9 in distant l they will remember me.

LANGUAGE (LANGUAGES)
Ge 11: 1 Now the whole world had one l
11: 9 there the LORD confused the l
Ps 19: 3 There is no speech or l
Jn 8: 44 When he lies, he speaks his native l
Ac 2: 6 heard them speaking in his own l.
Col 3: 8 slander, and filthy l from your lips.
Rev 5: 9 from every tribe and l and people
7: 9 every nation, tribe, people and l,
14: 6 to every nation, tribe, l and people.

LANGUAGES (LANGUAGE)
Zec 8: 23 "In those days ten men from all l

LAODICEA
Rev 3: 14 the angel of the church in L write:

LAP
Jdg 7: 5 "Separate those who l the water

LASHES
Pr 17: 10 more than a hundred l a fool.
2Co 11: 24 from the Jews the forty l minus one

LAST (LASTING LASTS LATTER)
Ex 14: 24 During the l watch of the night
2Sa 23: 1 These are the l words of David:
Isa 2: 2 and Jerusalem: In the l days
41: 4 and with the l — I am he."
44: 6 I am the first and I am the l;
48: 12 I am the first and I am the l.
Hos 3: 5 and to his blessings in the l days.
Mic 4: 1 In the l days
Mt 19: 30 But many who are first will be l,
20: 8 beginning with the l ones hired
21: 37 L of all, he sent his son to them.
Mk 9: 35 must be the very l, and the servant
10: 31 are first will be l, and the l first."
15: 37 a loud cry, Jesus breathed his l.
Jn 6: 40 and I will raise him up at the l day."
15: 16 and bear fruit — fruit that will l.
Ac 2: 17 "'In the l days, God says,
Ro 1: 17 is by faith from first to l,
1Co 15: 26 l enemy to be destroyed is death.
15: 52 of an eye, at the l trumpet.
2Ti 3: 1 will be terrible times in the l days.
2Pe 3: 3 in the l days scoffers will come,
Jude : 18 "In the l times there will be
Rev 1: 17 I am the First and the L.
22: 13 the First and the L, the Beginning

LASTING (LAST)
Ex 12: 14 to the LORD — a l ordinance.
Lev 24: 8 of the Israelites, as a l covenant.
Nu 25: 13 have a covenant of a l priesthood,
Heb 10: 34 had better and l possessions.

LASTS (LAST)
Ps 30: 5 For his anger l only a moment,
2Co 3: 11 greater is the glory of that which l!

LATTER (LAST)
Job 42: 12 The LORD blessed the l part
Mt 23: 23 You should have practiced the l,
Php 1: 16 l do so in love, knowing that I am

LAUGH (LAUGHED LAUGHS LAUGHTER)
Ps 59: 8 But you, O LORD, l at them;
Pr 31: 25 she can l at the days to come.
Ecc 3: 4 a time to weep and a time to l,
Lk 6: 21 for you will l.
6: 25 Woe to you who l now,

LAUGHED (LAUGH)
Ge 17: 17 Abraham fell facedown; he l
18: 12 So Sarah l to herself as she thought,

LAUGHS (LAUGH)
Ps 2: 4 The One enthroned in heaven l;
37: 13 but the Lord l at the wicked,

LAUGHTER (LAUGH)
Ge 21: 6 Sarah said, "God has brought me l,
Ps 126: 2 Our mouths were filled with l,
Pr 14: 13 Even in l the heart may ache,
Jas 4: 9 Change your l to mourning

LAVISHED
Eph 1: 8 of God's grace that he l on us
1Jn 3: 1 great is the love the Father has l

LAW (LAWFUL LAWGIVER LAWS)
Lev 24: 22 are to have the same l for the alien
Nu 6: 13 "'Now this is the l for the Nazirite
Dt 1: 5 Moses began to expound this l,
6: 25 to obey all this l before the LORD
27: 26 of this l by carrying them out."
31: 11 you shall read this l before them
31: 26 "Take this Book of the L
Jos 1: 7 to obey all the l my servant Moses
1: 8 of the L depart from your mouth;
22: 5 and the l that Moses the servant
2Ki 22: 8 of the L in the temple of the LORD
2Ch 6: 16 walk before me according to my l,
17: 9 the Book of the L of the LORD;
34: 14 of the L of the LORD that had
Ezr 7: 6 versed in the L of Moses,
Ne 8: 2 Ezra the priest brought the L
8: 8 from the Book of the L of God,
Ps 1: 2 and on his l he meditates day
19: 7 The l of the LORD is perfect,
37: 31 The l of his God is in his heart;
40: 8 your l is within my heart."
119: 18 wonderful things in your l.
119: 70 but I delight in your l.
119: 72 l from your mouth is more precious
119: 77 for your l is my delight.
119: 97 Oh, how I love your l!
119: 163 but I love your l.
119: 165 peace have they who love your l,
Pr 28: 9 If anyone turns a deaf ear to the l,
29: 18 but blessed is he who keeps the l.
Isa 2: 3 The l will go out from Zion,
8: 20 To the l and to the testimony!
42: 21 to make his l great and glorious.
Jer 2: 8 deal with the l did not know me;
8: 8 for we have the l of the LORD,"
31: 33 "I will put my l in their minds
Mic 4: 2 The l will go out from Zion,
Hab 1: 7 they are a l to themselves
Zec 7: 12 as flint and would not listen to the l
Mt 5: 17 that I have come to abolish the L
7: 12 sums up the L and the Prophets.
22: 36 greatest commandment in the L?"
22: 40 All the L and the Prophets hang
23: 23 more important matters of the l —
Lk 11: 52 "Woe to you experts in the l,
16: 17 stroke of a pen to drop out of the L.
24: 44 me in the L of Moses,
Jn 1: 17 For the l was given through Moses;
Ac 13: 39 justified from by the l of Moses.
Ro 2: 12 All who sin apart from the l will
2: 15 of the l are written on their hearts,
2: 20 you have in the l the embodiment
2: 25 value if you observe the l,
3: 19 we know that whatever the l says,
3: 20 in his sight by observing the l;
3: 21 apart from l, has been made known
3: 28 by faith apart from observing the l.
3: 31 Not at all! Rather, we uphold the l.
4: 13 It was not through l that Abraham
4: 15 worthless, because l brings wrath.
4: 16 not only to those who are of the l
5: 13 for before the l was given,
5: 20 l was added so that the trespass
6: 14 because you are not under l,
6: 15 we are not under l but under grace?
7: 1 that the l has authority
7: 4 also died to the l through the body
7: 5 aroused by the l were at work
7: 6 released from the l so that we serve
7: 7 then? Is the l sin? Certainly not!
7: 8 For apart from l, sin is dead.
7: 12 l is holy, and the commandment is
7: 14 We know that the l is spiritual;
7: 22 my inner being I delight in God's l;
7: 25 in my mind am a slave to God's l,
8: 2 because through Christ Jesus the l
8: 3 For what the l was powerless to do
8: 4 of the l might be fully met in us,
8: 7 It does not submit to God's l,
Ro 9: 4 covenants, the receiving of the l,
9: 31 who pursued a l of righteousness,
10: 4 Christ is the end of the l
13: 8 his fellowman has fulfilled the l.
13: 10 love is the fulfillment of the l.
1Co 6: 6 goes to l against another —
9: 9 For it is written in the L of Moses:
9: 20 the l I became like one under the l
9: 21 I became like one not having the l
15: 56 and the power of sin is the l.
Gal 2: 16 justified by observing the l,
2: 19 For through the l I died to the l
3: 2 the Spirit by observing the l,
3: 5 you because you observe the l,
3: 10 on observing the l are under a curse
3: 11 justified before God by the l,
3: 13 curse of the l by becoming a curse
3: 17 The l, introduced 430 years later,
3: 19 then, was the purpose of the l?
3: 21 Is the l, therefore, opposed
3: 23 we were held prisoners by the l,
3: 24 So the l was put in charge to lead us
4: 21 you who want to be under the l,
5: 3 obligated to obey the whole l.
5: 4 justified by l have been alienated
5: 14 The entire l is summed up
5: 18 by the Spirit, you are not under l.
6: 2 and in this way you will fulfill the l
Eph 2: 15 flesh the l with its commandments
Php 3: 9 of my own that comes from the l,
1Ti 1: 8 We know that the l is good
Heb 7: 12 there must also be a change of the l.
7: 19 (for the l made nothing perfect),
10: 1 The l is only a shadow
Jas 1: 25 intently into the perfect l that gives
2: 8 If you really keep the royal l found
2: 10 For whoever keeps the whole l
4: 11 or judges him speaks against the l
1Jn 3: 4 Everyone who sins breaks the l;

LAWFUL (LAW)
Mt 12: 12 Therefore it is l to do good

LAWGIVER* (LAW)
Isa 33: 22 the LORD is our l,
Jas 4: 12 There is only one L and Judge,

LAWLESS (LAWLESSNESS)
2Th 2: 8 And then the l one will be revealed
Heb 10: 17 "Their sins and l acts

LAWLESSNESS* (LAWLESS)
2Th 2: 3 and the man of l is revealed,
2: 7 power of l is already at work;
1Jn 3: 4 sins breaks the law; in fact, sin is l.

LAWS (LAW)
Ex 21: 1 "These are the l you are to set
Lev 25: 18 and be careful to obey my l,
Dt 4: 1 and l I am about to teach you.
30: 16 decrees and l; then you will live
Ps 119: 30 I have set my heart on your l.
119: 43 for I have put my hope in your l.
119: 120 I stand in awe of your l.
119: 164 for your righteous l.
119: 175 and may your l sustain me.
Eze 36: 27 and be careful to keep my l.
Heb 8: 10 I will put my l in their minds
10: 16 I will put my l in their hearts,

LAWSUITS
Hos 10: 4 therefore l spring up
1Co 6: 7 The very fact that you have l

LAY (LAID LAYING LAYS)
Ex 29: 10 and his sons shall l their hands
Lev 1: 4 He is to l his hand on the head
4: 15 the community are to l their hands
Nu 8: 10 the Israelites are to l their hands
27: 18 whom is the spirit, and l your hand
1Sa 26: 9 Who can l a hand on the LORD's
Job 1: 12 on the man himself do not l a finger
22: 22 and l up his words in your heart.
Ecc 10: 4 calmness can l great errors to rest.
Isa 28: 16 "See, I l a stone in Zion,
Mt 8: 20 of Man has no place to l his head."
28: 6 Come and see the place where he l.
Mk 6: 5 l his hands on a few sick people
Lk 9: 58 of Man has no place to l his head."
Jn 10: 15 and I l down my life for the sheep.
10: 18 but I l it down of my own accord.
15: 13 that he l down his life
Ac 8: 19 on whom I l my hands may receive
Ro 9: 33 I l in Zion a stone that causes men
1Co 3: 11 no one can l any foundation other
1Pe 2: 6 "See, I l a stone in Zion,
1Jn 3: 16 And we ought to l down our lives
Rev 4: 10 They l their crowns

LAYING (LAY)
Lk 4: 40 and *l* his hands on each one,
Ac 8: 18 at the *l* on of the apostles' hands,
1Ti 5: 22 Do not be hasty in the *l* on of hands
2Ti 1: 6 is in you through the *l*
Heb 6: 1 not *l* again the foundation
6: 2 instruction about baptisms, the *l*

LAYS (LAY)
Jn 10: 11 The good shepherd *l* down his life

LAZARUS
1. Poor man in Jesus' parable (Lk 16:19 – 31).
2. Brother of Mary and Martha whom Jesus raised from the dead (Jn 11:1 – 12:19).

LAZINESS* (LAZY)
Pr 12: 24 but *l* ends in slave labor.
19: 15 *L* brings on deep sleep,

LAZY* (LAZINESS)
Ex 5: 8 They are *l*; that is why they are
5: 17 Pharaoh said, "*L*, that's what you
5: 17 "Lazy, that's what you are — *l*!
Pr 10: 4 *L* hands make a man poor,
12: 27 The *l* man does not roast his game,
26: 15 he is too *l* to bring it back
Ecc 10: 18 If a man is *l*, the rafters sag;
Mt 25: 26 replied, 'You wicked, *l* servant!
Tit 1: 12 liars, evil brutes, *l* gluttons."
Heb 6: 12 We do not want you to become *l*,

LEAD (LEADER LEADERS LEADERSHIP LEADS LED)
Ex 15: 13 "In your unfailing love you will *l*
Nu 14: 8 with us, he will *l* us into that land,
Dt 31: 2 and I am no longer able to *l* you.
Jos 1: 6 because you will *l* these people
1Sa 8: 5 now appoint a king to *l* us,
2Ch 1: 10 knowledge, that I may *l* this people
Ps 27: 11 *l* me in a straight path
61: 2 *l* me to the rock that is higher
139: 24 and *l* me in the way everlasting.
143: 10 *l* me on level ground.
Pr 4: 11 and *l* you along straight paths.
Ecc 5: 6 Do not let your mouth *l* you
Isa 11: 6 and a little child will *l* them.
49: 10 and *l* them beside springs of water.
Da 12: 3 those who *l* many to righteousness,
Mt 6: 13 And *l* us not into temptation,
Lk 11: 4 And *l* us not into temptation.'"
Gal 3: 24 So the law was put in charge to *l* us
1Th 4: 11 it your ambition to *l* a quiet life,
1Jn 3: 7 do not let anyone *l* you astray.
Rev 7: 17 he will *l* them to springs

LEADER (LEAD)
1Sa 7: 6 Samuel was *l* of Israel at Mizpah.
10: 1 Has not the Lord anointed you *l*
12: 2 I have been your *l* from my youth
13: 14 and appointed him *l* of his people,

LEADERS (LEAD)
Heb 13: 7 Remember your *l*, who spoke
13: 17 Obey your *l* and submit

LEADERSHIP* (LEAD)
Nu 33: 1 by divisions under the *l* of Moses
Ps 109: 8 may another take his place of *l*.
Ac 1: 20 "'May another take his place of *l*.'
Ro 12: 8 if it is *l*, let him govern diligently;

LEADS (LEAD)
Dt 27: 18 is the man who *l* the blind astray
Ps 23: 2 he *l* me beside quiet waters,
37: 8 do not fret — it *l* only to evil.
68: 6 he *l* forth the prisoners
Pr 2: 18 For her house *l* down to death
10: 17 ignores correction *l* others astray.
14: 23 but mere talk *l* only to poverty.
16: 25 but in the end it *l* to death.
19: 23 The fear of the Lord *l* to life:
20: 7 righteous man *l* a blameless life;
21: 5 as surely as haste *l* to poverty.
Isa 40: 11 he gently *l* those that have young.
Mt 7: 13 and broad is the road that *l*
12: 20 till he *l* justice to victory.
15: 14 If a blind man *l* a blind man,
Jn 10: 3 sheep by name and *l* them out.
Ro 6: 16 which *l* to death, or to obedience,
6: 22 the benefit you reap *l* to holiness,
14: 19 effort to do what *l* to peace
2Co 2: 14 always *l* us in triumphal procession
7: 10 sorrow brings repentance that *l*
Tit 1: 1 of the truth that *l* to godliness —

LEAH
Wife of Jacob (Ge 29:16 – 30); bore six sons and one daughter (Ge 29:31 – 30:21; 34:1; 35:23).

LEAN (LEANED)
Pr 3: 5 *l* not on your own understanding;

LEANED (LEAN)
Ge 47: 31 as he *l* on the top of his staff.
Jn 21: 20 (This was the one who had *l* back
Heb 11: 21 as he *l* on the top of his staff.

LEAP (LEAPED LEAPS)
Isa 35: 6 Then will the lame *l* like a deer,
Mal 4: 2 *l* like calves released from the stall.
Lk 6: 23 "Rejoice in that day and *l* for joy,

LEAPED (LEAP)
Lk 1: 41 heard Mary's greeting, the baby *l*

LEAPS (LEAP)
Ps 28: 7 My heart *l* for joy

LEARN (LEARNED LEARNING LEARNS)
Dt 4: 10 so that they may *l* to revere me
5: 1 *L* them and be sure to follow them.
31: 12 and *l* to fear the Lord your God
Ps 119: 7 as I *l* your righteous laws.
Isa 1: 17 *l* to do right!
26: 9 of the world *l* righteousness.
Mt 11: 29 yoke upon you and *l* from me,
Jn 14: 31 world must *l* that I love the Father
1Th 4: 4 that each of you should *l*
1Ti 2: 11 A woman should *l* in quietness
5: 4 these should *l* first of all

LEARNED (LEARN)
Ps 119: 152 Long ago I *l* from your statutes
Mt 11: 25 things from the wise and *l*,
Php 4: 9 Whatever you have *l* or received
4: 11 for I have *l* to be content whatever
2Ti 3: 14 continue in what you have *l*
Heb 5: 8 he *l* obedience from what he

LEARNING (LEARN)
Pr 1: 5 let the wise listen and add to their *l*,
9: 9 man and he will add to his *l*.
Isa 44: 25 who overthrows the *l* of the wise
Jn 7: 15 "How did this man get such *l*
2Ti 3: 7 always *l* but never able

LEARNS (LEARN)
Jn 6: 45 and *l* from him comes to me.

LEATHER
2Ki 1: 8 and with a *l* belt around his waist."
Mt 3: 4 and he had a *l* belt around his waist

LEAVES
Ge 3: 7 so they sewed fig *l* together
Eze 47: 12 for food and their *l* for healing."
Rev 22: 2 the *l* of the tree are for the healing

LEBANON
Dt 11: 24 from the desert to *L*,
1Ki 4: 33 from the cedar of *L*

LED (LEAD)
Ex 3: 1 and he *l* the flock to the far side
Dt 8: 2 the Lord your God *l* you all
1Ki 11: 3 and his wives *l* him astray.
2Ch 26: 16 his pride *l* to his downfall.
Ne 13: 26 he was *l* into sin by foreign women.
Ps 68: 18 you *l* captives in your train;
78: 52 he *l* them like sheep
Pr 7: 21 persuasive words she *l* him astray;
20: 1 whoever is *l* astray
Isa 53: 7 he was *l* like a lamb to the slaughter
Jer 11: 19 I had been like a gentle lamb *l*
Am 2: 10 and I *l* you forty years in the desert
Mt 4: 1 Then Jesus was *l* by the Spirit
27: 31 they *l* him away to crucify him.
Lk 4: 1 was *l* by the Spirit in the desert,
Ac 8: 32 "He was *l* like a sheep
Ro 8: 14 those who are *l* by the Spirit
2Co 7: 9 your sorrow *l* you to repentance.
Gal 5: 18 But if you are *l* by the Spirit,
Eph 4: 8 he *l* captives in his train

LEEKS*
Nu 11: 5 melons, *l*, onions and garlic.

LEFT
Dt 28: 14 or to the *l*, following other gods
Jos 1: 7 turn from it to the right or to the *l*,
23: 6 aside to the right or to the *l*.
2Ki 22: 2 aside to the right or to the *l*.
Pr 4: 27 Do not swerve to the right or the *l*;
Isa 30: 21 turn to the right or to the *l*,
Mt 6: 3 do not let your *l* hand know what
25: 33 on his right and the goats on his *l*.

LEGALISTIC*
Php 3: 6 as for *l* righteousness, faultless.

LEGION
Mk 5: 9 "My name is *L*," he replied,

LEND (LENDER LENDS MONEYLENDER)
Lev 25: 37 You must not *l* him money
Dt 15: 8 freely *l* him whatever he needs.
Ps 37: 26 are always generous and *l* freely;
Eze 18: 8 He does not *l* at usury
Lk 6: 34 if you *l* to those from whom you

LENDER (LEND)
Pr 22: 7 and the borrower is servant to the *l*.
Isa 24: 2 for borrower as for *l*,

LENDS (LEND)
Ps 15: 5 who *l* his money without usury
112: 5 to him who is generous and *l* freely,
Pr 19: 17 to the poor *l* to the Lord,

LENGTH (LONG)
Ps 90: 10 The *l* of our days is seventy years —
Pr 10: 27 The fear of the Lord adds *l* to life

LENGTHY* (LONG)
Mk 12: 40 and for a show make *l* prayers.
Lk 20: 47 and for a show make *l* prayers.

LEOPARD
Isa 11: 6 the *l* will lie down with the goat,
Da 7: 6 beast, one that looked like a *l*.
Rev 13: 2 The beast I saw resembled a *l*,

LEPROSY (LEPROUS)
Nu 12: 10 toward her and saw that she had *l*;
2Ki 5: 1 was a valiant soldier, but he had *l*.
7: 3 men with *l* at the entrance
2Ch 26: 21 King Uzziah had *l*
Mt 11: 5 those who have *l* are cured,
Lk 17: 12 ten men who had *l* met him.

LEPROUS (LEPROSY)
Ex 4: 6 and when he took it out, it was *l*,

LETTER (LETTERS)
Mt 5: 18 not the smallest *l*, not the least
2Co 3: 2 You yourselves are our *l*, written
3: 6 for the *l* kills, but the Spirit gives
2Th 3: 14 not obey our instruction in this *l*,

LETTERS (LETTER)
2Co 3: 7 which was engraved in *l* on stone,
10: 10 "His *l* are weighty and forceful,
2Pe 3: 16 His *l* contain some things that are

LEVEL
Ps 143: 10 lead me on *l* ground.
Pr 4: 26 Make *l* paths for your feet
Isa 26: 7 The path of the righteous is *l*;
40: 4 the rough ground shall become *l*,
Jer 31: 9 on a *l* path where they will not
Heb 12: 13 "Make *l* paths for your feet,"

LEVI (LEVITE LEVITES LEVITICAL)
1. Son of Jacob by Leah (Ge 29:34; 46:11; 1Ch 2:1). With Simeon avenged rape of Dinah (Ge 34). Tribe of blessed (Ge 49:5 – 7; Dt 33:8 – 11), chosen as priests (Nu 3 – 4), numbered (Nu 3:39; 26:62), allotted cities, but not land (Nu 18; 35; Dt 10:9; Jos 13:14; 21), land (Eze 48:8 – 22), 12,000 from (Rev 7:7).
2. See MATTHEW.

LEVIATHAN
Job 41: 1 pull in the *l* with a fishhook
Ps 74: 14 you who crushed the heads of *L*
Isa 27: 1 *L* the gliding serpent,

LEVITE (LEVI)
Dt 26: 12 you shall give it to the *L*, the alien,
Jdg 19: 1 a *L* who lived in a remote area

LEVITES (LEVI)
Nu 1: 53 The *L* are to be responsible
3: 12 "I have taken the *L*
8: 6 "Take the *L* from among the other
18: 21 I give to the *L* all the tithes in Israel
35: 7 must give the *L* forty-eight towns,
2Ch 31: 2 assigned the priests and *L*
Mal 3: 3 he will purify the *L* and refine them

LEVITICAL (LEVI)
Heb 7: 11 attained through the *L* priesthood

LEWDNESS
Mk 7: 22 malice, deceit, *l*, envy, slander,

LIAR* (LIE)
Dt 19: 18 and if the witness proves to be a *l*,
Job 34: 6 I am considered a *l*;
Pr 17: 4 *l* pays attention to a malicious
19: 22 better to be poor than a *l*.
30: 6 will rebuke you and prove you a *l*.

Mic 2: 11 If a *l* and deceiver comes and says,
Jn 8: 44 for he is a *l* and the father of lies.
8: 55 I did not, I would be a *l* like you,
Ro 3: 4 Let God be true, and every man a *l*.
1Jn 1: 10 we make him out to be a *l*
2: 4 not do what he commands is a *l*,
2: 22 Who is the *l*? It is the man who
4: 20 yet hates his brother, he is a *l*.
5: 10 God has made him out to be a *l*,

LIARS* (LIE)
Ps 63: 11 the mouths of *l* will be silenced.
116: 11 "All men are *l*."
Isa 57: 4 the offspring of *l*?
Mic 6: 12 her people are *l*
1Ti 1: 10 for slave traders and *l* and perjurers
4: 2 come through hypocritical *l*,
Tit 1: 12 "Cretans are always *l*, evil brutes,
Rev 3: 9 though they are not, but are *l*—
21: 8 magic arts, the idolaters and all *l*—

LIBERATED*
Ro 8: 21 that the creation itself will be *l*

LICENSE
Jude : 4 of our God into a *l* for immorality

LICK
Ps 72: 9 and his enemies will *l* the dust.
Isa 49: 23 they will *l* the dust at your feet.
Mic 7: 17 They will *l* dust like a snake,

LIE (LIAR LIARS LIED LIES LYING)
Lev 18: 22 "'Do not *l* with a man
19: 11 "'Do not *l*.
Nu 23: 19 God is not a man, that he should *l*,
Dt 6: 7 when you *l* down and when you get
25: 2 the judge shall make him *l* down
1Sa 15: 29 the Glory of Israel does not *l*
Ps 4: 8 I will *l* down and sleep in peace,
23: 2 me *l* down in green pastures,
89: 35 and I will not *l* to David—
Pr 3: 24 when you *l* down, you will not be
Isa 11: 6 leopard will *l* down with the goat,
28: 15 for we have made a *l* our refuge
Jer 9: 5 They have taught their tongues to *l*
23: 14 They commit adultery and live a *l*.
Eze 13: 6 are false and their divinations a *l*.
34: 14 they will *l* down in good grazing
Ro 1: 25 exchanged the truth of God for a *l*,
Col 3: 9 Do not *l* to each other,
2Th 2: 11 so that they will believe the *l*
Tit 1: 2 which God, who does not *l*,
Heb 6: 18 which it is impossible for God to *l*,
1Jn 2: 21 because no *l* comes from the truth.
Rev 14: 5 No *l* was found in their mouths;

LIED (LIE)
Ac 5: 4 You have not *l* to men but to God."

LIES (LIE)
Lev 6: 3 finds lost property and *l* about it,
Ps 5: 6 You destroy those who tell *l*;
10: 7 His mouth is full of curses and *l*
12: 2 Everyone *l* to his neighbor;
34: 13 and your lips from speaking *l*.
58: 3 they are wayward and speak *l*.
144: 8 whose mouths are full of *l*,
Pr 6: 19 a false witness who pours out *l*
12: 17 but a false witness tells *l*.
19: 5 he who pours out *l* will not go free.
19: 9 and he who pours out *l* will perish.
29: 12 If a ruler listens to *l*,
30: 8 Keep falsehood and *l* far from me;
Isa 59: 3 Your lips have spoken *l*,
Jer 5: 31 The prophets prophesy *l*,
9: 3 like a bow, to shoot *l*;
14: 14 "The prophets are prophesying *l*
Hos 11: 12 Ephraim has surrounded me with *l*,
Jn 8: 44 for he is a liar and the father of *l*.

LIFE (LIVE)
Ge 1: 30 everything that has the breath of *l*
2: 7 into his nostrils the breath of *l*,
2: 9 of the garden were the tree of *l*
6: 17 to destroy all *l* under the heavens,
9: 5 for the *l* of his fellow man.
9: 11 Never again will all *l* be cut
Ex 21: 6 Then he will be his servant for *l*.
21: 23 you are to take *l* for *l*, eye for eye,
23: 26 I will give you a full *l* span.
Lev 17: 14 the *l* of every creature is its blood.
24: 17 "'If anyone takes the *l*
24: 18 must make restitution—*l* for *l*.
Nu 35: 31 a ransom for the *l* of a murderer,
Dt 4: 42 one of these cities and save his *l*.
12: 23 because the blood is the *l*,
19: 21 Show no pity: *l* for *l*, eye for eye,
Dt 30: 15 I set before you today *l*
30: 19 Now choose *l*, so that you
30: 20 For the LORD is your *l*,
32: 39 I put to death and I bring to *l*,
32: 47 words for you—they are your *l*.
1Sa 19: 5 He took his *l* in his hands
Job 2: 6 hands; but you must spare his *l*."
33: 4 of the Almighty gives me *l*.
33: 30 that the light of *l* may shine on him.
Ps 16: 11 known to me the path of *l*;
17: 14 this world whose reward is in this *l*.
23: 6 all the days of my *l*,
27: 1 LORD is the stronghold of my *l*—
34: 12 Whoever of you loves *l*
36: 9 For with you is the fountain of *l*;
39: 4 let me know how fleeting is my *l*.
41: 2 will protect him and preserve his *l*;
49: 7 No man can redeem the *l*
49: 8 the ransom for a *l* is costly,
63: 3 Because your love is better than *l*,
69: 28 they be blotted out of the book of *l*
91: 16 With long *l* will I satisfy him
104: 33 I will sing to the LORD all my *l*;
119: 25 preserve my *l* according to your word
Pr 1: 3 a disciplined and prudent *l*,
3: 2 will prolong your *l* many years
3: 18 of *l* to those who embrace her;
4: 23 for it is the wellspring of *l*.
6: 23 are the way to *l*,
6: 26 adulteress preys upon your very *l*.
7: 23 little knowing it will cost him his *l*.
8: 35 For whoever finds me finds *l*
10: 11 of the righteous is a fountain of *l*,
10: 27 of the LORD adds length to *l*,
11: 30 of the righteous is a tree of *l*,
13: 3 He who guards his lips guards his *l*,
13: 12 but a longing fulfilled is a tree of *l*.
13: 14 of the wise is a fountain of *l*,
14: 27 of the LORD is a fountain of *l*,
15: 4 that brings healing is a tree of *l*,
16: 22 Understanding is a fountain of *l*
19: 3 A man's own folly ruins his *l*,
19: 23 The fear of the LORD leads to *l*:
21: 21 finds *l*, prosperity and honor.
Isa 53: 10 LORD makes his *l* a guilt offering,
53: 11 he will see the light ⌞of *l*⌟
53: 12 he poured out his *l* unto death,
Jer 10: 23 that a man's *l* is not his own;
La 3: 58 you redeemed my *l*.
Eze 18: 27 and right, he will save his *l*.
37: 5 enter you, and you will come to *l*.
Da 12: 2 some to everlasting *l*, others
Jnh 2: 6 you brought my *l* up from the pit,
Mal 2: 5 a covenant of *l* and peace,
Mt 6: 25 Is not *l* more important than food,
7: 14 and narrow the road that leads to *l*,
10: 39 Whoever finds his *l* will lose it,
16: 21 and on the third day be raised to *l*.
16: 25 wants to save his *l* will lose it,
18: 8 better for you to enter *l* maimed
19: 16 thing must I do to get eternal *l*?"
19: 29 as much and will inherit eternal *l*.
20: 28 to give his *l* as a ransom for many."
25: 46 but the righteous to eternal *l*."
Mk 8: 35 but whoever loses his *l* for me
9: 43 better for you to enter *l* maimed
10: 17 "what must I do to inherit eternal *l*
10: 30 and in the age to come, eternal *l*.
10: 45 to give his *l* as a ransom for many."
Lk 6: 9 to save *l* or to destroy it?"
9: 22 and on the third day be raised to *l*."
9: 24 wants to save his *l* will lose it,
12: 15 a man's *l* does not consist
12: 22 do not worry about your *l*,
12: 25 can add a single hour to his *l*?
14: 26 even his own *l*—he cannot be my
17: 33 tries to keep his *l* will lose it,
21: 19 standing firm you will gain *l*.
Jn 1: 4 In him was *l*, and that *l* was
3: 15 believes in him may have eternal *l*.
3: 36 believes in the Son has eternal *l*,
4: 14 of water welling up to eternal *l*."
5: 21 raises the dead and gives them *l*,
5: 24 him who sent me has eternal *l*
5: 26 For as the Father has *l* in himself,
5: 39 that by them you possess eternal *l*.
5: 40 refuse to come to me to have *l*.
6: 27 for food that endures to eternal *l*,
6: 33 down from heaven and gives *l*
6: 35 Jesus declared, "I am the bread of *l*
6: 40 believes in him shall have eternal *l*,
6: 47 he who believes has everlasting *l*.
6: 48 I am the bread of *l*.
6: 51 give for the *l* of the world."
6: 53 and drink his blood, you have no *l*
Jn 6: 63 The Spirit gives *l*; the flesh counts
6: 68 You have the words of eternal *l*.
8: 12 but will have the light of *l*."
10: 10 I have come that they may have *l*,
10: 15 and I lay down my *l* for the sheep.
10: 17 loves me is that I lay down my *l*—
10: 28 I give them eternal *l*, and they shall
11: 25 "I am the resurrection and the *l*.
12: 25 The man who loves his *l* will lose it,
12: 50 his command leads to eternal *l*.
13: 37 I will lay down my *l* for you."
14: 6 am the way and the truth and the *l*.
15: 13 lay down his *l* for his friends.
17: 2 people that he might give eternal *l*
17: 3 Now this is eternal *l*: that they may
20: 31 that by believing you may have *l*
Ac 2: 32 God has raised this Jesus to *l*,
3: 15 You killed the author of *l*,
11: 18 the Gentiles repentance unto *l*."
13: 48 appointed for eternal *l* believed.
Ro 2: 7 immortality, he will give eternal *l*.
4: 25 was raised to *l* for our justification.
5: 10 shall we be saved through his *l*!
5: 18 was justification that brings *l*
5: 21 righteousness to bring eternal *l*
6: 4 the Father, we too may live a new *l*.
6: 13 have been brought from death to *l*;
6: 22 holiness, and the result is eternal *l*.
6: 23 but the gift of God is eternal *l*
8: 6 mind controlled by the Spirit is *l*
8: 11 also give *l* to your mortal bodies
8: 38 convinced that neither death nor *l*,
1Co 15: 19 If only for this *l* we have hope
15: 36 What you sow does not come to *l*
2Co 2: 16 to the other, the fragrance of *l*.
3: 6 letter kills, but the Spirit gives *l*.
4: 10 so that the *l* of Jesus may
5: 4 is mortal may be swallowed up by *l*.
Gal 2: 20 The *l* I live in the body, I live
3: 21 had been given that could impart *l*,
6: 8 from the Spirit will reap eternal *l*.
Eph 4: 1 I urge you to live a *l* worthy
Php 2: 16 as you hold out the word of *l*—
4: 3 whose names are in the book of *l*.
Col 1: 10 order that you may live a *l* worthy
3: 3 your *l* is now hidden with Christ
1Th 4: 12 so that your daily *l* may win
1Ti 1: 16 on him and receive eternal *l*.
4: 8 for both the present *l* and the *l*
4: 12 in *l*, in love, in faith and in purity.
4: 16 Watch your *l* and doctrine closely.
6: 12 Take hold of the eternal *l*
6: 19 hold of the *l* that is truly *l*.
2Ti 1: 9 saved us and called us to a holy *l*—
1: 10 destroyed death and has brought *l*
3: 12 to live a godly *l* in Christ Jesus will
Tit 1: 2 resting on the hope of eternal *l*,
3: 7 heirs having the hope of eternal *l*.
Heb 7: 16 of the power of an indestructible *l*.
Jas 1: 12 crown of *l* that God has promised
3: 13 Let him show it by his good *l*,
1Pe 3: 7 with you of the gracious gift of *l*,
3: 10 "Whoever would love *l*
4: 2 rest of his earthly *l* for evil human
2Pe 1: 3 given us everything we need for *l*
1Jn 1: 1 proclaim concerning the Word of *l*.
2: 25 he promised us—even eternal *l*.
3: 14 we have passed from death to *l*,
3: 16 Jesus Christ laid down his *l* for us.
5: 11 has given us eternal *l*, and this *l* is
5: 20 He is the true God and eternal *l*.
Jude : 21 Christ to bring you to eternal *l*.
Rev 2: 7 the right to eat from the tree of *l*,
2: 8 who died and came to *l* again.
2: 10 and I will give you the crown of *l*.
3: 5 name from the book of *l*,
13: 8 written in the book of *l* belonging
17: 8 in the book of *l* from the creation
20: 12 was opened, which is the book of *l*.
20: 15 not found written in the book of *l*,
21: 6 from the spring of the water of *l*.
21: 27 written in the Lamb's book of *l*.
22: 1 me the river of the water of *l*,
22: 2 side of the river stood the tree of *l*,
22: 14 may have the right to the tree of *l*
22: 17 take the free gift of the water of *l*.
22: 19 from him his share in the tree of *l*

LIFE-GIVING (GIVE)
Pr 15: 31 He who listens to a *l* rebuke
1Co 15: 45 being"; the last Adam, a *l* spirit.

LIFETIME (LIVE)
Ps 30: 5 but his favor lasts a *l*;
Lk 16: 25 in your *l* you received your good

LIFT (LIFTED LIFTING LIFTS)
Ps 3: 3 you bestow glory on me and *l*
28: 2 as I *l* up my hands
63: 4 in your name I will *l* up my hands.
91: 12 they will *l* you up in their hands,
121: 1 I *l* up my eyes to the hills —
123: 1 I *l* up my eyes to you,
134: 2 *L* up your hands in the sanctuary
143: 8 for to you I *l* up my soul.
Isa 40: 9 *l* up your voice with a shout,
La 2: 19 *L* up your hands to him
3: 41 Let us *l* up our hearts and our
Mt 4: 6 they will *l* you up in their hands,
Lk 21: 28 stand up and *l* up your heads,
1Ti 2: 8 everywhere to *l* up holy hands
Jas 4: 10 the Lord, and he will *l* you up.
1Pe 5: 6 that he may *l* you up in due time.

LIFTED (LIFT)
Ne 8: 6 and all the people *l* their hands
Ps 24: 7 be *l* up, you ancient doors,
40: 2 He *l* me out of the slimy pit,
41: 9 has *l* up his heel against me.
Isa 52: 13 *l* up and highly exalted.
63: 9 he *l* them up and carried them
Jn 3: 14 Moses *l* up the snake in the desert,
8: 28 "When you have *l* up the Son
12: 32 when I am *l* up from the earth,
12: 34 'The Son of Man must be *l* up'?
13: 18 shares my bread has *l* up his heel

LIFTING (LIFT)
Ps 141: 2 may the *l* up of my hands be like

LIFTS (LIFT)
Ps 113: 7 and *l* the needy from the ash heap;

LIGAMENT* (LIGAMENTS)
Eph 4: 16 held together by every supporting *l*

LIGAMENTS* (LIGAMENT)
Col 2: 19 held together by its *l* and sinews,

LIGHT (ENLIGHTENED LIGHTS)
Ge 1: 3 "Let there be *l*," and there was *l*.
Ex 13: 21 in a pillar of fire to give them *l*,
25: 37 it so that they *l* the space in front
2Sa 22: 29 LORD turns my darkness into *l*.
Job 38: 19 "What is the way to the abode of *l*?
Ps 4: 6 Let the *l* of your face shine upon us
18: 28 my God turns my darkness into *l*.
19: 8 giving *l* to the eyes.
27: 1 LORD is my *l* and my salvation —
36: 9 in your *l* we see *l*.
56: 13 God in the *l* of life.
76: 4 You are resplendent with *l*,
89: 15 who walk in the *l* of your presence,
104: 2 He wraps himself in *l*
119: 105 and a *l* for my path.
119: 130 The unfolding of your words gives *l*;
139: 12 for darkness is as *l* to you.
Pr 4: 18 till the full *l* of day.
Isa 2: 5 let us walk in the *l* of the LORD.
9: 2 have seen a great *l*;
42: 6 and a *l* for the Gentiles,
45: 7 I form the *l* and create darkness,
49: 6 also make you a *l* for the Gentiles,
53: 11 he will see the *l* of life
60: 1 "Arise, shine, for your *l* has come,
60: 19 LORD will be your everlasting *l*,
Eze 1: 27 and brilliant *l* surrounded him.
Mic 7: 8 the LORD will be my *l*.
Mt 4: 16 have seen a great *l*;
5: 14 "You are the *l* of the world.
5: 15 it gives *l* to everyone in the house.
5: 16 let your *l* shine before men,
6: 22 your whole body will be full of *l*.
11: 30 yoke is easy and my burden is *l*."
17: 2 his clothes became as white as the *l*
24: 29 and the moon will not give its *l*;
Mk 13: 24 and the moon will not give its *l*;
Lk 2: 32 a *l* for revelation to the Gentiles
8: 16 those who come in can see the *l*.
11: 33 those who come in may see the *l*.
Jn 1: 4 and that life was the *l* of men.
1: 5 The *l* shines in the darkness,
1: 7 witness to testify concerning that *l*,
1: 9 The true *l* that gives *l*
3: 19 but men loved darkness instead of *l*
3: 20 Everyone who does evil hates the *l*,
8: 12 he said, "I am the *l* of the world.
9: 5 in the world, I am the *l* of the world
12: 35 Walk while you have the *l*,
12: 46 I have come into the world as a *l*,
Ac 13: 47 "'I have made you a *l*
Ro 13: 12 darkness and put on the armor of *l*.
2Co 4: 6 made his *l* shine in our hearts
6: 14 Or what fellowship can *l* have
11: 14 masquerades as an angel of *l*.
Eph 5: 8 but now you are *l* in the Lord.
1Th 5: 5 You are all sons of the *l*
1Ti 6: 16 and who lives in unapproachable *l*,
1Pe 2: 9 of darkness into his wonderful *l*.
2Pe 1: 19 as to a *l* shining in a dark place,
1Jn 1: 5 God is *l*; in him there is no
1: 7 But if we walk in the *l*,
2: 9 Anyone who claims to be in the *l*
Rev 21: 23 for the glory of God gives it *l*,
22: 5 for the Lord God will give them *l*.

LIGHTNING
Ex 9: 23 and *l* flashed down to the ground.
20: 18 and *l* and heard the trumpet
Ps 18: 12 with hailstones and bolts of *l*.
Eze 1: 13 it was bright, and *l* flashed out of it.
Da 10: 6 his face like *l*, his eyes like flaming
Mt 24: 27 For as the *l* that comes from the east
28: 3 His appearance was like *l*,
Lk 10: 18 "I saw Satan fall like *l* from heaven.
Rev 4: 5 From the throne came flashes of *l*,

LIGHTS (LIGHT)
Ge 1: 14 "Let there be *l* in the expanse
Lk 8: 16 No one *l* a lamp and hides it in a jar

LIKE-MINDED* (MIND)
Php 2: 2 make my joy complete by being *l*,

LIKENESS
Ge 1: 26 man in our image, in our *l*,
Ps 17: 15 I will be satisfied with seeing your *l*
Isa 52: 14 his form marred beyond human *l* —
Ro 8: 3 Son in the *l* of sinful man
8: 29 to be conformed to the *l* of his Son,
2Co 3: 18 his *l* with ever-increasing glory,
Php 2: 7 being made in human *l*.
Jas 3: 9 who have been made in God's *l*.

LILIES (LILY)
Lk 12: 27 "Consider how the *l* grow.

LILY (LILIES)
SS 2: 1 a *l* of the valleys.
2: 2 *Lover* Like a *l* among thorns

LIMIT
Ps 147: 5 his understanding has no *l*.
Jn 3: 34 for God gives the Spirit without *l*.

LINEN
Lev 16: 4 He is to put on the sacred *l* tunic,
Pr 31: 22 she is clothed in fine *l* and purple.
31: 24 She makes *l* garments
Mk 15: 46 So Joseph bought some *l* cloth,
Jn 20: 6 He saw the strips of *l* lying there,
Rev 15: 6 shining *l* and wore golden sashes
19: 8 Fine *l*, bright and clean,

LINGER
Hab 2: 3 Though it *l*, wait for it;

LION (LION'S LIONS')
Jdg 14: 6 power so that he tore the *l* apart
1Sa 17: 34 When a *l* or a bear came
Isa 11: 7 and the *l* will eat straw like the ox.
65: 25 and the *l* will eat straw like the ox,
Eze 1: 10 right side each had the face of a *l*,
10: 14 the third the face of a *l*,
Da 7: 4 "The first was like a *l*,
1Pe 5: 8 around like a roaring *l* looking
Rev 4: 7 The first living creature was like a *l*
5: 5 See, the *L* of the tribe of Judah,

LION'S (LION)
Ge 49: 9 You are a *l* cub, O Judah;

LIONS' (LION)
Da 6: 7 shall be thrown into the *l* den.

LIPS
Ps 8: 2 From the *l* of children and infants
34: 1 his praise will always be on my *l*.
40: 9 I do not seal my *l*,
63: 3 my *l* will glorify you.
119: 171 May my *l* overflow with praise,
140: 3 the poison of vipers is on their *l*.
141: 3 keep watch over the door of my *l*.
Pr 10: 13 on the *l* of the discerning,
10: 18 who conceals his hatred has lying *l*,
10: 32 *l* of the righteous know what is
12: 22 The LORD detests lying *l*,
13: 3 He who guards his *l* guards his life,
14: 7 will not find knowledge on his *l*.
24: 26 is like a kiss on the *l*.
26: 23 are fervent *l* with an evil heart.
27: 2 someone else, and not your own *l*.
Isa 6: 5 For I am a man of unclean *l*,
28: 11 with foreign *l* and strange tongues
29: 13 and honor me with their *l*,
Mal 2: 7 "For the *l* of a priest ought
Mt 15: 8 These people honor me with their *l*
21: 16 "'From the *l* of children
Lk 4: 22 words that came from his *l*.
Ro 3: 13 "The poison of vipers is on their *l*."
Col 3: 8 and filthy language from your *l*.
Heb 13: 15 the fruit of *l* that confess his name.
1Pe 3: 10 and his *l* from deceitful speech.

LISTEN (LISTENED LISTENING LISTENS)
Dt 18: 15 You must *l* to him.
30: 20 *l* to his voice, and hold fast to him.
1Ki 4: 34 came to *l* to Solomon's wisdom,
2Ki 21: 9 But the people did not *l*.
Pr 1: 5 let the wise *l* and add
Ecc 5: 1 Go near to *l* rather
Eze 2: 5 And whether they *l* or fail to *l* —
Mt 12: 42 earth to *l* to Solomon's wisdom,
Mk 9: 7 *L* to him!" Suddenly,
Jn 10: 27 My sheep *l* to my voice; I know
Ac 3: 22 you must *l* to everything he tells
Jas 1: 19 Everyone should be quick to *l*,
1: 22 Do not merely *l* to the word,
1Jn 4: 6 not from God does not *l* to us.

LISTENED (LISTEN)
Ne 8: 3 And all the people *l* attentively
Isa 66: 4 when I spoke, no one *l*.
Da 9: 6 We have not *l* to your servants

LISTENING (LISTEN)
1Sa 3: 9 Speak, LORD, for your servant is *l*
Pr 18: 13 He who answers before *l* —
Lk 10: 39 at the Lord's feet *l* to what he said.

LISTENS (LISTEN)
Pr 12: 15 but a wise man *l* to advice.
Lk 10: 16 "He who *l* to you *l*
1Jn 4: 6 and whoever knows God *l* to us;

LIVE (ALIVE LIFE LIFETIME LIVES LIVING)
Ge 3: 22 tree of life and eat, and *l* forever."
Ex 20: 12 so that you may *l* long
33: 20 for no one may see me and *l*."
Nu 21: 8 who is bitten can look at it and *l*."
Dt 5: 24 we have seen that a man can *l*
6: 2 as you *l* by keeping all his decrees
8: 3 to teach you that man does not *l*
Job 14: 14 If a man dies, will he *l* again?
Ps 15: 1 Who may *l* on your holy hill?
24: 1 the world, and all who *l* in it;
26: 8 I love the house where you *l*,
119: 175 Let me *l* that I may praise you,
Pr 21: 9 Better to *l* on a corner of the roof
21: 19 Better to *l* in a desert
Ecc 9: 4 a *l* dog is better off than a dead lion
Isa 26: 19 But your dead will *l*;
55: 3 hear me, that your soul may *l*.
Eze 17: 19 LORD says: As surely as I *l*,
20: 11 for the man who obeys them will *l*
37: 3 can these bones *l*?" I said,
Am 5: 6 Seek the LORD and *l*,
Hab 2: 4 but the righteous will *l* by his faith
Zec 2: 11 I will *l* among you and you will
Mt 4: 4 'Man does not *l* on bread alone,
Lk 4: 4 'Man does not *l* on bread alone.'"
Jn 14: 19 Because I *l*, you also will *l*.
Ac 17: 24 does not *l* in temples built by hands
17: 28 'For in him we *l* and move
Ro 1: 17 "The righteous will *l* by faith."
2Co 5: 7 We *l* by faith, not by sight.
6: 16 "I will *l* with them and walk
Gal 2: 20 The life I *l* in the body, I *l* by faith
3: 11 "The righteous will *l* by faith."
5: 25 Since we *l* by the Spirit, let us keep
Eph 4: 17 that you must no longer *l*
Php 1: 21 to *l* is Christ and to die is gain.
Col 1: 10 order that you may *l* a life worthy
1Th 4: 1 we instructed you how to *l* in order
5: 13 *L* in peace with each other.
1Ti 2: 2 that we may *l* peaceful
2Ti 3: 12 who wants to *l* a godly life
Tit 2: 12 and to *l* self-controlled, upright
Heb 10: 38 But my righteous one will *l* by faith
12: 14 Make every effort to *l* in peace
1Pe 1: 17 *l* your lives as strangers here
3: 8 *l* in harmony with one another;

LIVES (LIVE)
Ge 45: 7 and to save your *l* by a great
Job 19: 25 I know that my Redeemer *l*,
Pr 1: 19 it takes away the *l*
Isa 57: 15 he who *l* forever, whose name is
Da 3: 28 to give up their *l* rather than serve
Jn 14: 17 for he *l* with you and will be in you.

Ro 6: 10 but the life he *l*, he *l* to God.
7: 18 I know that nothing good *l* in me,
8: 9 if the Spirit of God *l* in you.
14: 7 For none of us *l* to himself alone
1Co 3: 16 and that God's Spirit *l* in you?
Gal 2: 20 I no longer live, but Christ *l* in me.
1Th 2: 8 only the gospel of God but our *l*
1Ti 2: 2 quiet *l* in all godliness and holiness.
Tit 2: 12 and godly *l* in this present age,
Heb 7: 24 but because Jesus *l* forever,
13: 5 Keep your *l* free from the love
1Pe 3: 2 the purity and reverence of your *l*.
2Pe 3: 11 You ought to live holy and godly *l*
1Jn 3: 16 to lay down our *l* for our brothers.
4: 16 Whoever *l* in love *l* in God,

LIVING (LIVE)
Ge 2: 7 and the man became a *l* being.
1Sa 17: 26 defy the armies of the *l* God?"
Isa 53: 8 cut off from the land of the *l*;
Jer 2: 13 the spring of *l* water,
Eze 1: 5 what looked like four *l* creatures.
Zec 14: 8 On that day *l* water will flow out
Mt 22: 32 the God of the dead but of the *l*."
Jn 4: 10 he would have given you *l* water."
6: 51 I am the *l* bread that came
7: 38 streams of *l* water will flow
Ro 8: 11 Jesus from the dead is *l* in you,
12: 1 to offer your bodies as *l* sacrifices,
1Co 9: 14 the gospel should receive their *l*
Heb 4: 12 For the word of God is *l* and active.
10: 20 and *l* way opened for us
10: 31 to fall into the hands of the *l* God.
1Pe 1: 23 through the *l* and enduring word
Rev 1: 18 I am the *L* One; I was dead,
4: 6 the throne, were four *l* creatures,
7: 17 to springs of *l* water.

LOAD (LOADS)
Gal 6: 5 for each one should carry his own *l*.

LOADS (LOAD)
Mt 23: 4 They tie up heavy *l* and put them

LOAF (LOAVES)
1Co 10: 17 for we all partake of the one *l*.

LOAVES (LOAF)
Mk 6: 41 Taking the five *l* and the two fish
8: 6 When he had taken the seven *l*
Lk 11: 5 'Friend, lend me three *l* of bread,

LOCKED
Jn 20: 26 the doors were *l*, Jesus came
Gal 3: 23 *l* up until faith should be revealed.

LOCUSTS
Ex 10: 4 I will bring *l* into your country
Joel 2: 25 you for the years the *l* have eaten —
Mt 3: 4 His food was *l* and wild honey.
Rev 9: 3 And out of the smoke *l* came

LOFTY
Ps 139: 6 too *l* for me to attain.
Isa 57: 15 is what the high and *l* One says —

LONELY
Ps 68: 6 God sets the *l* in families,
Lk 5: 16 Jesus often withdrew to *l* places

LONG (LENGTH LENGTHY LONGED LONGING LONGINGS LONGS)
Ex 17: 11 As *l* as Moses held up his hands,
Nu 6: 5 the hair of his head grow *l*.
1Ki 18: 21 "How *l* will you waver
Ps 119: 97 I meditate on it all day *l*.
119: 174 I *l* for your salvation, O LORD,
Hos 7: 13 I *l* to redeem them
Am 5: 18 Why do you *l* for the day
Mt 25: 5 The bridegroom was a *l* time
Jn 9: 4 As *l* as it is day, we must do
1Co 11: 14 that if a man has *l* hair,
Eph 3: 18 to grasp how wide and *l* and high
Php 1: 8 God can testify how I *l* for all
1Pe 1: 12 Even angels *l* to look

LONGED (LONG)
Mt 13: 17 righteous men *l* to see what you see
23: 37 how often I have *l*
Lk 13: 34 how often I have *l*
2Ti 4: 8 to all who have *l* for his appearing.

LONGING* (LONG)
Dt 28: 65 with *l*, and a despairing heart.
Job 7: 2 Like a slave *l* for the evening
Ps 119: 20 My soul is consumed with *l*
119: 81 with *l* for your salvation,
119: 131 *l* for your commands.
143: 7 my spirit faints with *l*.
Pr 13: 12 but a *l* fulfilled is a tree of life.
Pr 13: 19 A *l* fulfilled is sweet to the soul,
Eze 23: 27 look on these things with *l*
Lk 16: 21 and *l* to eat what fell from the rich
Ro 15: 23 since I have been *l* for many years
2Co 5: 2 *l* to be clothed with our heavenly
7: 7 He told us about your *l* for me,
7: 11 what alarm, what *l*, what concern,
1Th 2: 17 out of our intense *l* we made every
Heb 11: 16 they were *l* for a better country —

LONGINGS* (LONG)
Ps 38: 9 All my *l* lie open before you,
112: 10 the *l* of the wicked will come

LONGS* (LONG)
Ps 63: 1 my body *l* for you,
Isa 26: 9 in the morning my spirit *l* for you.
30: 18 Yet the LORD *l* to be gracious
Php 2: 26 For he *l* for all of you and is

LOOK (LOOKED LOOKING LOOKS)
Ge 19: 17 "Flee for your lives! Don't *l* back,
Ex 3: 6 because he was afraid to *l* at God.
Nu 21: 8 anyone who is bitten can *l* at it
32: 8 Kadesh Barnea to *l* over the land.
Dt 4: 29 you will find him if you *l* for him
1Sa 16: 7 The LORD does not *l*
Job 31: 1 not to *l* lustfully at a girl.
Ps 34: 5 Those who *l* to him are radiant;
105: 4 *L* to the LORD and his strength;
113: 6 who stoops down to *l*
123: 2 As the eyes of slaves *l* to the hand
Pr 1: 28 they will *l* for me but will not find
4: 25 Let your eyes *l* straight ahead,
15: 30 A cheerful *l* brings joy to the heart,
Isa 17: 7 In that day men will *l*
31: 1 do not *l* to the Holy One of Israel,
40: 26 Lift your eyes and *l* to the heavens:
60: 5 Then you will *l* and be radiant,
Jer 3: 3 Yet you have the brazen *l*
6: 16 "Stand at the crossroads and *l*;
Eze 34: 11 for my sheep and *l* after them.
Hab 1: 13 Your eyes are too pure to *l* on evil;
Zec 12: 10 They will *l* on me, the one they
Mt 18: 10 "See that you do not *l* down on one
18: 12 go to *l* for the one that wandered
23: 27 which *l* beautiful on the outside
Mk 13: 21 '*L*, here is the Christ!' or, '*L*,
Lk 6: 41 "Why do you *l* at the speck
24: 39 *L* at my hands and my feet.
Jn 1: 36 he said, "*L*, the Lamb of God!"
4: 35 open your eyes and *l* at the fields!
19: 37 "They will *l* on the one they have
Ro 14: 10 why do you *l* down on your brother
Php 2: 4 Each of you should *l* not only
1Ti 4: 12 Don't let anyone *l* down on you
Jas 1: 27 to *l* after orphans and widows
1Pe 1: 12 long to *l* into these things.
2Pe 3: 12 as you *l* forward to the day of God

LOOKED (LOOK)
Ge 19: 26 Lot's wife *l* back, and she became
Ex 2: 25 So God *l* on the Israelites
1Sa 6: 19 because they had *l* into the ark
SS 3: 1 I *l* for the one my heart loves;
Eze 22: 30 "I *l* for a man among them who
34: 6 and no one searched or *l* for them.
44: 4 I *l* and saw the glory
Da 7: 9 "As I *l*,
10: 5 I *l* up and there before me was
Hab 3: 6 he *l*, and made the nations tremble.
Mt 25: 36 I was sick and you *l* after me,
Lk 18: 9 and *l* down on everybody else,
22: 61 The Lord turned and *l* straight
1Jn 1: 1 which we have *l* at and our hands

LOOKING (LOOK)
Ps 69: 3 *l* for my God.
119: 82 My eyes fail, *l* for your promise;
119: 123 My eyes fail, *l* for your salvation,
Mk 16: 6 "You are *l* for Jesus the Nazarene,
2Co 10: 7 You are *l* only on the surface
Php 4: 17 Not that I am *l* for a gift,
1Th 2: 6 We were not *l* for praise from men,
2Pe 3: 13 with his promise we are *l* forward
Rev 5: 6 I saw a Lamb, *l* as if it had been

LOOKS (LOOK)
1Sa 16: 7 Man *l* at the outward appearance,
Ezr 8: 22 is on everyone who *l* to him,
Ps 104: 32 who *l* at the earth, and it trembles;
138: 6 on high, he *l* upon the lowly,
Pr 27: 18 he who *l* after his master will be
Eze 34: 12 As a shepherd *l* after his scattered
Mt 5: 28 But I tell you that anyone who *l*
16: 4 and adulterous generation *l*
Lk 9: 62 and *l* back is fit for service
Jn 6: 40 Father's will is that everyone who *l*
12: 45 When he *l* at me, he sees the one
Php 2: 21 For everyone *l* out
Jas 1: 25 But the man who *l* intently

LOOSE
Isa 33: 23 Your rigging hangs *l*:
Mt 16: 19 and whatever you *l* on earth will be
18: 18 and whatever you *l* on earth will be

LORD† (LORD'S† LORDED LORDING)
Ge 18: 27 been so bold as to speak to the *L*,
Ex 15: 17 O *L*, your hands established.
Nu 16: 13 now you also want to *l* it over us?
Dt 10: 17 God of gods and *L* of lords,
Jos 3: 13 the *L* of all the earth — set foot
1Ki 3: 10 *L* was pleased that Solomon had
Ne 4: 14 Remember the *L*, who is great
Job 28: 28 'The fear of the *L* — that is wisdom,
Ps 37: 13 but the *L* laughs at the wicked,
38: 22 O *L* my Savior.
54: 4 the *L* is the one who sustains me.
62: 12 and that you, O *L*, are loving.
69: 6 O *L*, the LORD Almighty;
86: 5 You are forgiving and good, O *L*,
86: 8 gods there is none like you, O *L*;
89: 49 O *L*, where is your former great
110: 1 The LORD says to my *L*:
110: 5 The *L* is at your right hand;
130: 3 O *L*, who could stand?
135: 5 that our *L* is greater than all gods.
136: 3 Give thanks to the *L* of lords:
147: 5 Great is our *L* and mighty in power
Isa 6: 1 I saw the *L* seated on a throne,
Da 2: 47 and the *L* of kings and a revealer
9: 4 "O *L*, the great and awesome God,
9: 7 "*L*, you are righteous,
9: 9 The *L* our God is merciful
9: 19 O *L*, listen! O *L*, forgive! O *L*,
Mt 3: 3 'Prepare the way for the *L*,
4: 7 'Do not put the *L* your God
4: 10 'Worship the *L* your God,
7: 21 "Not everyone who says to me, '*L*,
9: 38 Ask the *L* of the harvest, therefore,
12: 8 Son of Man is *L* of the Sabbath."
20: 25 of the Gentiles *l* it over them,
21: 9 comes in the name of the *L*!"
22: 37 "'Love the *L* your God
22: 44 For he says, "'The *L* said to my *L*:
23: 39 comes in the name of the *L*.'"
Mk 1: 3 'Prepare the way for the *L*,
12: 11 the *L* has done this,
12: 29 the *L* our God, the *L* is one.
12: 30 Love the *L* your God
Lk 2: 9 glory of the *L* shone around them,
6: 5 The Son of Man is *L* of the Sabbath
6: 46 "Why do you call me, '*L*, *L*,'
10: 27 "'Love the *L* your God
11: 1 one of his disciples said to him, "*L*,
24: 34 The *L* has risen and has appeared
Jn 1: 23 'Make straight the way for the *L*.'"
Ac 2: 21 on the name of the *L* will be saved.'
2: 25 "'I saw the *L* always before me.
2: 34 "'The *L* said to my *L*:
8: 16 into the name of the *L* Jesus.
9: 5 "Who are you, *L*?" Saul asked.
10: 36 through Jesus Christ, who is *L*
11: 23 true to the *L* with all their hearts.
16: 31 replied, "Believe in the *L* Jesus,
Ro 4: 24 in him who raised Jesus our *L*
5: 11 in God through our *L* Jesus Christ,
6: 23 life in Christ Jesus our *L*.
8: 39 of God that is in Christ Jesus our *L*.
10: 9 with your mouth, "Jesus is *L*,"
10: 13 on the name of the *L* will be saved
10: 16 *L*, who has believed our message?"
11: 34 Who has known the mind of the *L*?
12: 11 your spiritual fervor, serving the *L*.
13: 14 yourselves with the *L* Jesus Christ,
14: 4 for the *L* is able to make him stand.
14: 8 we live to the *L*; and if we die,
1Co 1: 31 Let him who boasts boast in the *L*."
3: 5 the *L* has assigned to each his task.
4: 5 time; wait till the *L* comes.
6: 13 for the *L*, and the *L* for the body.
6: 14 By his power God raised the *L*
7: 32 affairs — how he can please the *L*.
7: 34 to be devoted to the *L* in both body
7: 35 in undivided devotion to the *L*.
7: 39 but he must belong to the *L*.
8: 6 and there is but one *L*, Jesus Christ,
10: 9 We should not test the *L*,
11: 23 For I received from the *L* what I
12: 3 "Jesus is *L*," except by the Holy
15: 57 victory through our *L* Jesus Christ.
15: 58 fully to the work of the *L*,

1Co 16: 22 If anyone does not love the *L* —
2Co 1: 24 Not that we *l* it over your faith,
2: 12 found that the *L* had opened a door
3: 17 Now the *L* is the Spirit,
4: 5 but Jesus Christ as *L*, and ourselves
5: 6 in the body we are away from the *L*
8: 5 they gave themselves first to the *L*
8: 21 not only in the eyes of the *L* but
10: 17 Let him who boasts boast in the *L*."
10: 18 but the one whom the *L* commends
13: 10 the authority the *L* gave me
Gal 6: 14 in the cross of our *L* Jesus Christ,
Eph 4: 5 one *L*, one faith, one baptism;
5: 8 but now you are light in the *L*.
5: 10 and find out what pleases the *L*.
5: 19 make music in your heart to the *L*,
5: 22 submit to your husbands as to the *L*
6: 1 obey your parents in the *L*,
6: 7 as if you were serving the *L*,
6: 8 know that the *L* will reward
6: 10 in the *L* and in his mighty power.
Php 2: 11 confess that Jesus Christ is *L*,
3: 1 my brothers, rejoice in the *L*!
3: 8 of knowing Christ Jesus my *L*,
4: 1 you should stand firm in the *L*,
4: 4 Rejoice in the *L* always.
4: 5 The *L* is near.
Col 1: 10 you may live a life worthy of the *L*
2: 6 as you received Christ Jesus as *L*,
3: 13 Forgive as the *L* forgave you.
3: 17 do it all in the name of the *L* Jesus,
3: 18 your husbands, as is fitting in the *L*.
3: 20 in everything, for this pleases the *L*
3: 23 as working for the *L*, not for men,
3: 24 It is the *L* Christ you are serving.
3: 24 receive an inheritance from the *L*
4: 17 work you have received in the *L*."
1Th 3: 8 since you are standing firm in the *L*
3: 12 May the *L* make your love increase
4: 1 and urge you in the *L* Jesus
4: 6 The *L* will punish men
4: 15 who are left till the coming of the *L*
5: 2 day of the *L* will come like a thief
5: 23 at the coming of our *L* Jesus Christ.
2Th 1: 7 when the *L* Jesus is revealed
1: 12 of our *L* Jesus may be glorified
2: 1 the coming of our *L* Jesus Christ
2: 8 whom the *L* Jesus will overthrow
3: 3 *L* is faithful, and he will strengthen
3: 5 May the *L* direct your hearts
1Ti 6: 15 the King of kings and *L* of lords,
2Ti 1: 8 ashamed to testify about our *L*,
2: 19 "The *L* knows those who are his,"
4: 8 which the *L*, the righteous Judge,
4: 17 But the *L* stood at my side
Heb 1: 10 O *L*, you laid the foundations
10: 30 "The *L* will judge his people."
12: 14 holiness no one will see the *L*.
13: 6 *L* is my helper; I will not be afraid.
Jas 3: 9 With the tongue we praise our *L*
4: 10 Humble yourselves before the *L*,
5: 11 The *L* is full of compassion
1Pe 1: 25 the word of the *L* stands forever."
2: 3 you have tasted that the *L* is good.
3: 12 eyes of the *L* are on the righteous
3: 15 in your hearts set apart Christ as *L*.
2Pe 1: 11 into the eternal kingdom of our *L*
1: 16 and coming of our *L* Jesus Christ,
2: 1 the sovereign *L* who bought
2: 9 then the *L* knows how
3: 9 The *L* is not slow in keeping his
3: 18 and knowledge of our *L* and Savior
Jude : 14 the *L* is coming with thousands
Rev 4: 8 holy, holy is the *L* God Almighty,
4: 11 "You are worthy, our *L* and God,
11: 15 has become the kingdom of our *L*
17: 14 he is *L* of lords and King of kings —
19: 16 KINGS AND *L* OF LORDS.
22: 5 for the *L* God will give them light.
22: 20 Come, *L* Jesus.

LORD'S† (LORD†)
Lk 1: 38 "I am the *L* servant," Mary
Ac 11: 21 The *L* hand was with them,
21: 14 and said, "The *L* will be done."
1Co 7: 32 is concerned about the *L* affairs —
10: 26 "The earth is the *L*, and everything
11: 26 you proclaim the *L* death
2Co 3: 18 faces all reflect the *L* glory,
Eph 5: 17 but understand what the *L* will is.
2Ti 2: 24 And the *L* servant must not quarrel
Heb 12: 5 light of the *L* discipline,
Jas 4: 15 you ought to say, "If it is the *L* will,
5: 8 because the *L* coming is near.
1Pe 2: 13 Submit yourselves for the *L* sake

LORDED* (LORD†)
Ne 5: 15 Their assistants also *l* it

LORDING* (LORD†)
1Pe 5: 3 not *l* it over those entrusted to you,

LORD‡ (LORD'S‡)
2: 4 When the *L* God made the earth
2: 7 the *L* God formed the man
2: 22 Then the *L* God made a woman
3: 21 The *L* God made garments of skin
3: 23 So the *L* God banished him
4: 4 The *L* looked with favor on Abel
4: 26 began to call on the name of the *L*.
6: 7 So the *L* said, "I will wipe mankind
7: 16 Then the *L* shut him in.
9: 26 Blessed be the *L*, the God of Shem!
11: 9 there the *L* confused the language
12: 1 *L* had said to Abram, "Leave your
15: 6 Abram believed the *L*,
15: 18 On that day the *L* made a covenant
17: 1 the *L* appeared to him and said,
18: 1 The *L* appeared to Abraham
18: 14 Is anything too hard for the *L*?
18: 19 way of the *L* by doing what is right
21: 1 Now the *L* was gracious to Sarah
22: 14 that place The *L* Will Provide.
24: 1 the *L* had blessed him in every way
26: 2 The *L* appeared to Isaac and said,
28: 13 There above it stood the *L*,
31: 49 "May the *L* keep watch
39: 2 The *L* was with Joseph
39: 21 in the prison, the *L* was with him;
Ex 3: 2 the angel of the *L* appeared to him
4: 11 Is it not I, the *L*? Now go;
4: 31 heard that the *L* was concerned
6: 2 also said to Moses, "I am the *L*.
9: 12 the *L* hardened Pharaoh's heart
12: 27 'It is the Passover sacrifice to the *L*,
12: 43 The *L* said to Moses and Aaron,
13: 9 For the *L* brought you out of Egypt
13: 21 By day the *L* went ahead of them
14: 13 the deliverance the *L* will bring
14: 30 That day the *L* saved Israel
15: 3 The *L* is a warrior;
15: 11 among the gods is like you, O *L*?
15: 26 for I am the *L*, who heals you."
16: 12 know that I am the *L* your God.'"
16: 23 day of rest, a holy Sabbath to the *L*.
17: 15 and called it The *L* is my Banner.
19: 8 will do everything the *L* has said."
19: 20 The *L* descended to the top
20: 2 "I am the *L* your God, who
20: 5 the *L* your God, am a jealous God,
20: 7 for the *L* will not hold anyone
20: 10 a Sabbath to the *L* your God.
20: 11 in six days the *L* made the heavens
20: 12 in the land the *L* your God is giving
23: 25 Worship the *L* your God,
24: 3 "Everything the *L* has said we will
24: 12 The *L* said to Moses, "Come up
24: 16 and the glory of the *L* settled
25: 1 The *L* said to Moses, "Tell
28: 36 HOLY TO THE *L*
30: 11 Then the *L* said to Moses,
31: 13 so you may know that I am the *L*,
31: 18 When the *L* finished speaking
33: 11 The *L* would speak to Moses face
33: 19 And the *L* said, "I will cause all my
34: 1 *L* said to Moses, "Chisel out two
34: 6 proclaiming, "The *L*, the *L*,
34: 10 awesome is the work that I, the *L*,
34: 29 because he had spoken with the *L*.
40: 34 glory of the *L* filled the tabernacle.
40: 38 So the cloud of the *L* was
Lev 8: 36 did everything the *L* commanded
9: 23 and the glory of the *L* appeared
10: 2 and they died before the *L*.
19: 2 'Be holy because I, the *L* your God,
20: 8 I am the *L*, who makes you holy.
20: 26 to be holy to me because I, the *L*,
23: 40 and rejoice before the *L* your God
Nu 6: 24 Say to them: "'"The *L* bless you
8: 5 *L* said to Moses: "Take the Levites
11: 1 hardships in the hearing of the *L*,
14: 14 O *L*, have been seen face to face,
14: 18 you have declared: 'The *L* is slow
14: 21 glory of the *L* fills the whole earth,
21: 6 Then the *L* sent venomous snakes
22: 31 Then the *L* opened Balaam's eyes,
23: 12 "Must I not speak what the *L* puts
30: 2 When a man makes a vow to the *L*
32: 12 followed the *L* wholeheartedly.'
Dt 1: 21 and take possession of it as the *L*,
2: 7 forty years the *L* your God has
4: 29 there you seek the *L* your God,
Dt 5: 6 And he said: "I am the *L* your God,
5: 9 the *L* your God, am a jealous God,
6: 4 The *L* our God, the *L* is one.
6: 5 Love the *L* your God
6: 16 Do not test the *L* your God
6: 25 law before the *L* our God,
7: 1 When the *L* your God brings you
7: 6 holy to the *L* your God.
7: 8 But it was because the *L* loved you
7: 9 that the *L* your God is God;
7: 12 then the *L* your God will keep his
8: 5 so the *L* your God disciplines you.
9: 10 The *L* gave me two stone tablets
10: 12 but to fear the *L* your God,
10: 14 To the *L* your God belong
10: 17 For the *L* your God is God of gods
10: 20 Fear the *L* your God and serve him
10: 22 now the *L* your God has made you
11: 1 Love the *L* your God and keep his
11: 13 to love the *L* your God
16: 1 the Passover of the *L* your God,
17: 15 the king the *L* your God chooses.
28: 1 If you fully obey the *L* your God
28: 15 if you do not obey the *L* your God
29: 1 covenant the *L* commanded Moses
29: 29 things belong to the *L* our God,
30: 4 from there the *L* your God will
30: 6 *L* your God will circumcise your
30: 10 if you obey the *L* your God
30: 16 today to love the *L* your God,
30: 20 For the *L* is your life, and he will
31: 6 for the *L* your God goes with you;
34: 5 of the *L* died there in Moab,
Jos 10: 14 a day when the *L* listened to a man.
22: 5 to love the *L* your God, to walk
23: 11 careful to love the *L* your God.
24: 15 my household, we will serve the *L*
24: 18 We too will serve the *L*,
Jdg 2: 12 They forsook the *L*, the God
Ru 1: 8 May the *L* show kindness to you,
4: 13 And the *L* enabled her to conceive,
1Sa 1: 11 him to the *L* for all the days
1: 15 I was pouring out my soul to the *L*.
1: 28 So now I give him to the *L*.
2: 2 "There is no one holy like the *L*;
2: 25 but if a man sins against the *L*,
2: 26 in favor with the *L* and with men.
3: 9 *L*, for your servant is listening.'"
3: 19 The *L* was with Samuel
7: 12 "Thus far has the *L* helped us."
9: 17 sight of Saul, the *L* said to him,
11: 15 as king in the presence of the *L*.
12: 18 all the people stood in awe of the *L*
12: 22 his great name the *L* will not reject
12: 24 But be sure to fear the *L*
13: 14 the *L* has sought out a man
14: 6 Nothing can hinder the *L*
15: 22 "Does the *L* delight
16: 13 Spirit of the *L* came upon David
17: 45 you in the name of the *L* Almighty,
2Sa 6: 14 danced before the *L*
7: 22 How great you are, O Sovereign *L*!
8: 6 *L* gave David victory everywhere
12: 7 This is what the *L*, the God
22: 2 "The *L* is my rock, my fortress
22: 29 You are my lamp, O *L*;
22: 31 the word of the *L* is flawless.
1Ki 1: 30 today what I swore to you by the *L*,
2: 3 and observe what the *L* your God
3: 7 O *L* my God, you have made your
5: 5 for the Name of the *L* my God,
5: 12 The *L* gave Solomon wisdom,
8: 11 the glory of the *L* filled his temple.
8: 23 toward heaven and said: "O *L*,
8: 61 fully committed to the *L* our God,
9: 3 The *L* said to him: "I have heard
10: 9 Praise be to the *L* your God,
15: 14 committed to the *L* all his life.
18: 21 If the *L* is God, follow him;
18: 36 "O *L*, God of Abraham, Isaac
18: 39 "The *L* — he is God! The *L* —
21: 23 also concerning Jezebel the *L* says:
2Ki 13: 23 But the *L* was gracious to them
17: 18 So the *L* was very angry with Israel
18: 5 Hezekiah trusted in the *L*,
19: 1 and went into the temple of the *L*.
20: 11 *L* made the shadow go back the ten
21: 12 Therefore this is what the *L*,
22: 2 right in the eyes of the *L*
22: 8 of the Law in the temple of the *L*."
23: 3 to follow the *L* and keep his
23: 21 the Passover to the *L* your God,
23: 25 a king like him who turned to the *L*
24: 2 The *L* sent Babylonian, Aramean,
24: 4 and the *L* was not willing to forgive

1Ch 10: 13 because he was unfaithful to the *L*;
11: 3 with them at Hebron before the *L*,
11: 9 the *L* Almighty was with him.
13: 6 from there the ark of God the *L*, who
16: 8 Give thanks to the *L*, call
16: 11 Look to the *L* and his strength;
16: 14 He is the *L* our God;
16: 23 Sing to the *L*, all the earth;
17: 1 covenant of the *L* is under a tent."
21: 24 take for the *L* what is yours,
22: 5 to be built for the *L* should be
22: 11 build the house of the *L* your God,
22: 13 and laws that the *L* gave Moses
22: 16 Now begin the work, and the *L* be
22: 19 soul to seeking the *L* your God.
25: 7 and skilled in music for the *L* —
28: 9 for the *L* searches every heart
28: 20 for the *L* God, my God, is with you
29: 1 not for man but for the *L* God.
29: 11 O *L*, is the greatness and the power
29: 18 O *L*, God of our fathers Abraham,
29: 25 The *L* highly exalted Solomon
2Ch 1: 1 for the *L* his God was with him
5: 13 to give praise and thanks to the *L*.
5: 14 the glory of the *L* filled the temple
6: 16 "Now *L*, God of Israel, keep
6: 41 O *L* God, and come
6: 42 O *L* God, do not reject your
7: 1 the glory of the *L* filled the temple.
7: 12 the *L* appeared to him at night
7: 21 'Why has the *L* done such a thing
9: 8 as king to rule for the *L* your God.
13: 12 do not fight against the *L*,
14: 2 right in the eyes of the *L* his God.
15: 14 to the *L* with loud acclamation,
16: 9 of the *L* range throughout the earth
17: 9 the Book of the Law of the *L*;
18: 13 said, "As surely as the *L* lives,
19: 6 judging for man but for the *L*,
19: 9 wholeheartedly in the fear of the *L*.
20: 15 This is what the *L* says to you:
20: 20 Have faith in the *L* your God
20: 21 appointed men to sing to the *L*
26: 5 As long as he sought the *L*,
26: 16 He was unfaithful to the *L* his God,
29: 30 to praise the *L* with the words
30: 9 for the *L* your God is gracious
31: 20 and faithful before the *L* his God.
32: 8 with us is the *L* our God to help us
34: 14 Law of the *L* that had been given
34: 31 to follow the *L* and keep his
Ezr 3: 10 foundation of the temple of the *L*,
7: 6 for the hand of the *L* his God was
7: 10 observance of the Law of the *L*,
9: 5 hands spread out to the *L* my God
9: 8 the *L* our God has been gracious
9: 15 O *L*, God of Israel, you are
Ne 1: 5 Then I said: "O *L*, God of heaven,
8: 1 which the *L* had commanded
9: 6 You alone are the *L*.
Job 1: 6 to present themselves before the *L*,
1: 21 *L* gave and the *L* has taken away;
38: 1 the *L* answered Job out
42: 9 and the *L* accepted Job's prayer.
42: 12 The *L* blessed the latter part
Ps 1: 2 But his delight is in the law of the *L*
1: 6 For the *L* watches over the way
4: 6 of your face shine upon us, O *L*.
4: 8 for you alone, O *L*,
5: 3 In the morning, O *L*,
6: 1 O *L*, do not rebuke me
8: 1 O *L*, our Lord,
9: 9 The *L* is a refuge for the oppressed,
9: 19 Arise, O *L*, let not man triumph;
10: 16 The *L* is King for ever and ever;
12: 6 And the words of the *L* are flawless
16: 5 *L*, you have assigned me my
16: 8 I have set the *L* always before me.
18: 1 I love you, O *L*, my strength.
18: 6 In my distress I called to the *L*;
18: 30 the word of the *L* is flawless.
19: 7 The law of the *L* is perfect,
19: 14 O *L*, my Rock and my Redeemer.
20: 5 May the *L* grant all your requests.
20: 7 in the name of the *L* our God.
22: 8 let the *L* rescue him.
23: 1 The *L* is my shepherd, I shall
23: 6 I will dwell in the house of the *L*
24: 3 Who may ascend the hill of the *L*?
24: 8 The *L* strong and mighty,
25: 10 All the ways of the *L* are loving
27: 1 The *L* is my light and my salvation
27: 4 to gaze upon the beauty of the *L*
27: 6 I will sing and make music to the *L*.
29: 1 Ascribe to the *L*, O mighty ones,
Ps 29: 4 The voice of the *L* is powerful;
30: 4 Sing to the *L*, you saints of his;
31: 5 redeem me, O *L*, the God of truth.
32: 2 whose sin the *L* does not count
33: 1 joyfully to the *L*, you righteous;
33: 6 of the *L* were the heavens made,
33: 12 is the nation whose God is the *L*,
33: 18 But the eyes of the *L* are
34: 1 I will extol the *L* at all times;
34: 3 Glorify the *L* with me;
34: 4 I sought the *L*, and he answered me
34: 7 The angel of the *L* encamps
34: 8 Taste and see that the *L* is good;
34: 9 Fear the *L*, you his saints,
34: 15 The eyes of the *L* are
34: 18 The *L* is close to the brokenhearted
37: 4 Delight yourself in the *L*
37: 5 Commit your way to the *L*;
39: 4 "Show me, O *L*, my life's end
40: 1 I waited patiently for the *L*;
40: 5 Many, O *L* my God,
46: 8 Come and see the works of the *L*,
47: 2 How awesome is the *L* Most High,
48: 1 Great is the *L*, and most worthy
50: 1 The Mighty One, God, the *L*,
55: 22 Cast your cares on the *L*
59: 8 But you, O *L*, laugh at them;
68: 4 his name is the *L* —
68: 18 O *L* God, might dwell there.
68: 20 from the Sovereign *L* comes escape
69: 31 This will please the *L* more
72: 18 Praise be to the *L* God, the God
75: 8 In the hand of the *L* is a cup
78: 4 the praiseworthy deeds of the *L*,
84: 8 my prayer, O *L* God Almighty;
84: 11 For the *L* God is a sun and shield;
85: 7 Show us your unfailing love, O *L*,
86: 11 Teach me your way, O *L*,
87: 2 the *L* loves the gates of Zion
89: 5 heavens praise your wonders, O *L*,
89: 8 O *L* God Almighty, who is like you
91: 2 I will say of the *L*, "He is my refuge
92: 1 It is good to praise the *L*
92: 4 by your deeds, O *L*;
92: 13 planted in the house of the *L*,
93: 1 The *L* reigns, he is robed in majesty
93: 5 house for endless days, O *L*.
94: 1 O *L*, the God who avenges,
94: 12 is the man you discipline, O *L*,
94: 18 your love, O *L*, supported me.
95: 1 Come, let us sing for joy to the *L*;
95: 3 For the *L* is the great God,
95: 6 let us kneel before the *L* our Maker
96: 1 Sing to the *L* a new song;
96: 5 but the *L* made the heavens.
96: 8 to the *L* the glory due his name;
96: 9 Worship the *L* in the splendor
96: 13 they will sing before the *L*,
97: 1 The *L* reigns, let the earth be glad;
97: 9 O *L*, are the Most High
98: 1 Sing to the *L* a new song,
98: 2 *L* has made his salvation known
98: 4 Shout for joy to the *L*, all the earth,
99: 1 The *L* reigns,
99: 2 Great is the *L* in Zion;
99: 5 Exalt the *L* our God
99: 9 Exalt the *L* our God
100: 1 Shout for joy to the *L*, all the earth.
100: 2 Worship the *L* with gladness;
100: 3 Know that the *L* is God.
100: 5 For the *L* is good and his love
101: 1 to you, O *L*, I will sing praise.
102: 12 But you, O *L*, sit enthroned forever
103: 1 Praise the *L*, O my soul;
103: 8 The *L* is compassionate
103: 19 The *L* has established his throne
104: 1 O *L* my God, you are very great;
104: 24 How many are your works, O *L*!
104: 33 I will sing to the *L* all my life;
105: 4 Look to the *L* and his strength;
105: 7 He is the *L* our God;
106: 2 proclaim the mighty acts of the *L*
107: 1 Give thanks to the *L*, for he is good
107: 8 to the *L* for his unfailing love
107: 21 to the *L* for his unfailing love
107: 43 and consider the great love of the *L*
108: 3 I will praise you, O *L*,
109: 26 Help me, O *L* my God;
110: 1 The *L* says to my Lord:
110: 4 The *L* has sworn
111: 2 Great are the works of the *L*;
111: 4 *L* is gracious and compassionate.
111: 10 The fear of the *L* is the beginning
112: 1 Blessed is the man who fears the *L*,
113: 1 Praise, O servants of the *L*,
Ps 113: 2 Let the name of the *L* be praised,
113: 4 *L* is exalted over all the nations,
113: 5 Who is like the *L* our God,
115: 1 Not to us, O *L*, not to us
115: 18 it is we who extol the *L*,
116: 12 How can I repay the *L*
116: 15 Precious in the sight of the *L*
117: 1 Praise the *L*, all you nations;
118: 1 Give thanks to the *L*, for he is good
118: 5 In my anguish I cried to the *L*,
118: 8 It is better to take refuge in the *L*
118: 18 The *L* has chastened me severely,
118: 23 the *L* has done this,
118: 24 This is the day the *L* has made;
118: 26 comes in the name of the *L*.
119: 1 to the law of the *L*.
119: 64 with your love, O *L*;
119: 89 Your word, O *L*, is eternal;
119: 126 It is time for you to act, O *L*;
119: 159 O *L*, according to your love.
120: 1 I call on the *L* in my distress,
121: 2 My help comes from the *L*,
121: 5 The *L* watches over you —
121: 8 the *L* will watch over your coming
122: 1 "Let us go to the house of the *L*."
123: 2 so our eyes look to the *L* our God,
124: 1 If the *L* had not been on our side —
124: 8 Our help is in the name of the *L*,
125: 2 so the *L* surrounds his people
126: 3 The *L* has done great things for us,
126: 4 Restore our fortunes, O *L*,
127: 1 Unless the *L* builds the house,
127: 3 Sons are a heritage from the *L*,
128: 1 Blessed are all who fear the *L*,
130: 1 O *L*; O Lord, hear my voice.
130: 3 If you, O *L*, kept a record of sins,
130: 5 I wait for the *L*, my soul waits,
131: 3 O Israel, put your hope in the *L*
132: 1 O *L*, remember David
132: 13 For the *L* has chosen Zion,
133: 3 For there the *L* bestows his
134: 3 May the *L*, the Maker of heaven
135: 4 For the *L* has chosen Jacob
135: 6 The *L* does whatever pleases him,
136: 1 Give thanks to the *L*, for he is good
137: 4 How can we sing the songs of the *L*
138: 1 I will praise you, O *L*,
138: 8 The *L* will fulfill ⌞his purpose⌟
139: 1 O *L*, you have searched me
140: 1 Rescue me, O *L*, from evil men;
141: 1 O *L*, I call to you; come quickly
141: 3 Set a guard over my mouth, O *L*;
142: 5 I cry to you, O *L*;
143: 9 Rescue me from my enemies, O *L*,
144: 3 O *L*, what is man that you care
145: 3 Great is the *L* and most worthy
145: 8 *L* is gracious and compassionate,
145: 9 The *L* is good to all;
145: 17 The *L* is righteous in all his ways
145: 18 The *L* is near to all who call on him
146: 5 whose hope is in the *L* his God,
146: 7 The *L* sets prisoners free,
147: 2 The *L* builds up Jerusalem;
147: 7 Sing to the *L* with thanksgiving;
147: 11 *L* delights in those who fear him,
147: 12 Extol the *L*, O Jerusalem;
148: 1 Praise the *L* from the heavens,
148: 7 Praise the *L* from the earth,
149: 4 For the *L* takes delight
150: 1 Praise the *L*.
150: 6 that has breath praise the *L*.
Pr 1: 7 The fear of the *L* is the beginning
1: 29 and did not choose to fear the *L*,
2: 5 will understand the fear of the *L*
2: 6 For the *L* gives wisdom,
3: 5 Trust in the *L* with all your heart
3: 7 fear the *L* and shun evil.
3: 9 Honor the *L* with your wealth,
3: 12 the *L* disciplines those he loves,
3: 19 By wisdom the *L* laid the earth's
5: 21 are in full view of the *L*,
6: 16 There are six things the *L* hates,
8: 13 To fear the *L* is to hate evil;
9: 10 "The fear of the *L* is the beginning
10: 27 The fear of the *L* adds length to life
11: 1 The *L* abhors dishonest scales,
12: 22 The *L* detests lying lips,
14: 2 whose walk is upright fears the *L*,
14: 26 He who fears the *L* has a secure
14: 27 The fear of the *L* is a fountain
15: 3 The eyes of the *L* are everywhere,
15: 16 Better a little with the fear of the *L*
15: 33 of the *L* teaches a man wisdom,
16: 2 but motives are weighed by the *L*.
16: 3 Commit to the *L* whatever you do,

Pr 16: 4 The *L* works out everything
16: 5 The *L* detests all the proud of heart
16: 9 but the *L* determines his steps.
16: 33 but its every decision is from the *L*.
18: 10 The name of the *L* is a strong tower
18: 22 and receives favor from the *L*.
19: 14 but a prudent wife is from the *L*.
19: 17 to the poor lends to the *L*,
19: 23 The fear of the *L* leads to life:
20: 10 the *L* detests them both.
21: 2 but the *L* weighs the heart.
21: 3 to the *L* than sacrifice.
21: 30 that can succeed against the *L*.
21: 31 but victory rests with the *L*.
22: 2 The *L* is the Maker of them all.
22: 23 for the *L* will take up their case
23: 17 for the fear of the *L*.
24: 18 or the *L* will see and disapprove
24: 21 Fear the *L* and the king, my son,
25: 22 and the *L* will reward you.
28: 14 is the man who always fears the *L*,
29: 26 from the *L* that man gets justice.
30: 7 "Two things I ask of you, O *L*;
31: 30 a woman who fears the *L* is
Isa 2: 3 up to the mountain of the *L*,
2: 10 the ground from dread of the *L*
3: 17 the *L* will make their scalps bald."
4: 2 of the *L* will be beautiful
5: 16 the *L* Almighty will be exalted
6: 3 holy, holy is the *L* Almighty;
9: 7 The zeal of the *L* Almighty
11: 2 The Spirit of the *L* will rest on him
11: 9 full of the knowledge of the *L*
12: 2 The *L*, the *L*, is my strength
18: 7 of the Name of the *L* Almighty.
24: 1 the *L* is going to lay waste the earth
25: 1 O *L*, you are my God;
25: 6 this mountain the *L* Almighty will
25: 8 The Sovereign *L* will wipe away
26: 4 Trust in the *L* forever,
26: 8 *L*, walking in the way of your laws,
26: 13 O *L*, our God, other lords
26: 21 the *L* is coming out of his dwelling
27: 1 the *L* will punish with his sword,
27: 12 In that day the *L* will thresh
28: 5 In that day the *L* Almighty
29: 6 the *L* Almighty will come
29: 15 to hide their plans from the *L*,
30: 18 For the *L* is a God of justice.
30: 26 when the *L* binds up the bruises
30: 27 the Name of the *L* comes from afar
30: 30 The *L* will cause men
33: 2 O *L*, be gracious to us;
33: 6 the fear of the *L* is the key
33: 22 For the *L* is our judge,
34: 2 The *L* is angry with all nations;
35: 2 they will see the glory of the *L*,
35: 10 the ransomed of the *L* will return.
38: 7 to you that the *L* will do what he
40: 3 the way for the *L*;
40: 5 the glory of the *L* will be revealed,
40: 7 the breath of the *L* blows on them.
40: 10 the Sovereign *L* comes with power,
40: 14 Whom did the *L* consult
40: 28 The *L* is the everlasting God,
40: 31 but those who hope in the *L*
41: 14 will help you," declares the *L*,
41: 20 that the hand of the *L* has done this
42: 6 the *L*, have called you
42: 8 "I am the *L*; that is my name!
42: 13 The *L* will march out like a mighty
42: 21 It pleased the *L*
43: 3 For I am the *L*, your God,
43: 11 I, even I, am the *L*,
44: 6 "This is what the *L* says —
44: 24 I am the *L*,
45: 5 I am the *L*, and there is no other;
45: 7 I, the *L*, do all these things.
45: 21 Was it not I, the *L*?
48: 17 "I am the *L* your God,
50: 4 Sovereign *L* has given me
50: 10 Who among you fears the *L*
51: 1 and who seek the *L*:
51: 11 The ransomed of the *L* will return.
51: 15 the *L* Almighty is his name.
53: 1 the arm of the *L* been revealed?
53: 6 and the *L* has laid on him
53: 10 and the will of the *L* will prosper
54: 5 the *L* Almighty is his name —
55: 6 Seek the *L* while he may be found;
55: 7 to the *L*, and he will have mercy
56: 6 who bind themselves to the *L*
58: 8 of the *L* will be your rear guard.
58: 11 The *L* will guide you always;
59: 1 the arm of the *L* is not too short
Isa 60: 1 the glory of the *L* rises upon you.
60: 16 Then you will know that I, the *L*,
60: 20 the *L* will be your everlasting light,
61: 1 Spirit of the Sovereign *L* is on me,
61: 3 a planting of the *L*
61: 10 I delight greatly in the *L*;
61: 11 so the Sovereign *L* will make
62: 4 for the *L* will take delight in you,
63: 7 I will tell of the kindnesses of the *L*,
64: 8 Yet, O *L*, you are our Father.
66: 15 See, the *L* is coming with fire,
Jer 1: 9 Then the *L* reached out his hand
2: 19 when you forsake the *L* your God
3: 25 sinned against the *L* our God,
4: 4 Circumcise yourselves to the *L*,
8: 7 the requirements of the *L*.
9: 24 I am the *L*, who exercises kindness,
10: 6 No one is like you, O *L*;
10: 10 But the *L* is the true God;
12: 1 You are always righteous, O *L*,
14: 7 O *L*, do something for the sake
14: 20 O *L*, we acknowledge our
16: 15 will say, 'As surely as the *L* lives,
16: 19 O *L*, my strength and my fortress,
17: 7 is the man who trusts in the *L*,
17: 10 "I the *L* search the heart
20: 11 *L* is with me like a mighty warrior;
23: 6 The *L* Our Righteousness.
24: 7 heart to know me, that I am the *L*.
28: 9 as one truly sent by the *L* only
31: 11 For the *L* will ransom Jacob
31: 22 The *L* will create a new thing
31: 34 his brother, saying, 'Know the *L*,'
32: 27 I am the *L*, the God of all mankind.
33: 16 The *L* Our Righteousness.'
36: 6 the words of the *L* that you wrote
40: 3 now the *L* has brought it about;
42: 3 Pray that the *L* your God will tell
42: 4 I will tell you everything the *L* says
42: 6 we will obey the *L* our God,
50: 4 go in tears to seek the *L* their God.
51: 10 "'The *L* has vindicated us;
51: 56 For the *L* is a God of retribution;
La 3: 24 to myself, "The *L* is my portion;
3: 25 *L* is good to those whose hope is
3: 40 and let us return to the *L*.
Eze 1: 3 the word of the *L* came
1: 28 of the likeness of the glory of the *L*.
4: 14 Sovereign *L*! I have never defiled
10: 4 Then the glory of the *L* rose
15: 7 you will know that I am the *L*.
30: 3 the day of the *L* is near —
36: 23 nations will know that I am the *L*,
37: 4 'Dry bones, hear the word of the *L*!
43: 4 glory of the *L* entered the temple
44: 4 LORD filling the temple of the *L*,
Da 9: 2 to the word of the *L* given
Hos 1: 7 horsemen, but by the *L* their God."
2: 20 and you will acknowledge the *L*.
3: 1 as the *L* loves the Israelites,
3: 5 They will come trembling to the *L*
6: 1 "Come, let us return to the *L*.
6: 3 Let us acknowledge the *L*;
10: 12 for it is time to seek the *L*,
12: 5 the *L* is his name of renown!
14: 1 O Israel, to the *L* your God.
Joel 1: 1 The word of the *L* that came
1: 15 For the day of the *L* is near;
2: 1 for the day of the *L* is coming.
2: 11 The day of the *L* is great;
2: 13 Return to the *L* your God,
2: 23 rejoice in the *L* your God,
2: 31 the great and dreadful day of the *L*.
2: 32 on the name of the *L* will be saved;
3: 14 For the day of the *L* is near
3: 16 the *L* will be a refuge for his people,
Am 4: 13 the *L* God Almighty is his name.
5: 6 Seek the *L* and live,
5: 15 Perhaps the *L* God Almighty will
5: 18 long for the day of the *L*?
7: 15 *L* took me from tending the flock
8: 12 searching for the word of the *L*,
9: 5 The Lord, the *L* Almighty,
Ob : 15 "The day of the *L* is near
Jnh 1: 3 But Jonah ran away from the *L*
1: 4 the *L* sent a great wind on the sea,
1: 17 But the *L* provided a great fish
2: 9 Salvation comes from the *L*."
4: 2 He prayed to the *L*, "O *L*,
4: 6 Then the *L* God provided a vine
Mic 1: 1 The word of the *L* that came to Micah
4: 2 up to the mountain of the *L*,
5: 4 flock in the strength of the *L*,
6: 2 For the *L* has a case
6: 8 And what does the *L* require of you
Mic 7: 7 as for me, I watch in hope for the *L*,
Na 1: 2 The *L* takes vengeance on his foes
1: 3 The *L* is slow to anger
Hab 2: 14 knowledge of the glory of the *L*,
2: 20 But the *L* is in his holy temple;
3: 2 I stand in awe of your deeds, O *L*.
Zep 1: 1 The word of the *L* that came
1: 7 for the day of the *L* is near.
3: 17 The *L* your God is with you,
Hag 1: 1 the word of the *L* came
1: 8 and be honored," says the *L*.
2: 23 that day,' declares the *L* Almighty,
Zec 1: 1 the word of the *L* came
1: 17 and the *L* will again comfort Zion
3: 1 standing before the angel of the *L*,
4: 6 by my Spirit,' says the *L* Almighty.
6: 12 and build the temple of the *L*.
8: 21 the *L* and seek the *L* Almighty.
9: 16 The *L* their God will save them
14: 5 Then the *L* my God will come,
14: 9 The *L* will be king
14: 16 the *L* Almighty, and to celebrate
Mal 1: 1 The word of the *L* to Israel
3: 6 "I the *L* do not change.
4: 5 and dreadful day of the *L* comes.

LORD'S‡ (LORD‡)

Ex 4: 14 the *L* anger burned against Moses
12: 11 Eat it in haste; it is the *L* Passover.
34: 34 he entered the *L* presence
Lev 23: 4 "'These are the *L* appointed feasts,
Nu 9: 23 At the *L* command they encamped
14: 41 you disobeying the *L* command?
32: 13 The *L* anger burned against Israel
Dt 6: 18 is right and good in the *L* sight,
10: 13 and to observe the *L* commands
32: 9 For the *L* portion is his people,
Jos 21: 45 Not one of all the *L* good promises
1Sa 24: 10 because he is the *L* anointed.'
1Ki 10: 9 Because of the *L* eternal love
Ps 24: 1 The earth is the *L*, and everything
32: 10 but the *L* unfailing love
89: 1 of the *L* great love forever;
103: 17 *L* love is with those who fear him,
118: 15 "The *L* right hand has done mighty
Pr 3: 11 do not despise the *L* discipline
19: 21 but it is the *L* purpose that prevails.
Isa 24: 14 west they acclaim the *L* majesty.
30: 9 to listen to the *L* instruction.
49: 4 Yet what is due me is in the *L* hand
53: 10 Yet it was the *L* will to crush him
55: 13 This will be for the *L* renown,
61: 2 to proclaim the year of the *L* favor
62: 3 of splendor in the *L* hand,
Jer 25: 17 So I took the cup from the *L* hand
48: 10 lax in doing the *L* work!
51: 7 was a gold cup in the *L* hand;
La 3: 22 of the *L* great love we are not
Eze 7: 19 them in the day of the *L* wrath.
Joel 3: 18 will flow out of the *L* house
Ob : 21 And the kingdom will be the *L*.
Mic 4: 1 of the *L* temple will be established
6: 2 O mountains, the *L* accusation;
Hab 2: 16 from the *L* right hand is coming
Zep 2: 3 sheltered on the day of the *L* anger.

LOSE (LOSES LOSS LOST)

Dt 1: 28 Our brothers have made us *l* heart.
1Sa 17: 32 "Let no one *l* heart on account
Isa 7: 4 Do not *l* heart because of these two
Mt 10: 39 Whoever finds his life will *l* it,
Lk 9: 25 and yet *l* or forfeit his very self?
Jn 6: 39 that I shall *l* none of all that he has
2Co 4: 1 this ministry, we do not *l* heart.
4: 16 Therefore we do not *l* heart.
Heb 12: 3 will not grow weary and *l* heart.
12: 5 do not *l* heart when he rebukes you
2Jn : 8 that you do not *l* what you have

LOSES (LOSE)

Mt 5: 13 But if the salt *l* its saltiness,
Lk 15: 4 you has a hundred sheep and *l* one
15: 8 has ten silver coins and *l* one.

LOSS (LOSE)

Ro 11: 12 and their *l* means riches
1Co 3: 15 he will suffer *l*; he himself will be
Php 3: 8 I consider everything a *l* compared

LOST (LOSE)

Ps 73: 2 I had nearly *l* my foothold.
Jer 50: 6 "My people have been *l* sheep;
Eze 34: 4 the strays or searched for the *l*.
34: 16 for the *l* and bring back the strays.
Mt 18: 14 any of these little ones should be *l*.
Lk 15: 4 go after the *l* sheep until he finds it?
15: 6 with me; I have found my *l* sheep.'

Lk 15: 9 with me; I have found my l coin.'
15: 24 is alive again; he was l and is found
19: 10 to seek and to save what was l."
Php 3: 8 for whose sake I have l all things.

LOT (LOTS)

Nephew of Abraham (Ge 11:27; 12:5). Chose to live in Sodom (Ge 13). Rescued from four kings (Ge 14). Rescued from Sodom (Ge 19:1 – 29; 2Pe 2:7). Fathered Moab and Ammon by his daughters (Ge 19:30 – 38).

Est 3: 7 the l) in the presence of Haman
9: 24 the l) for their ruin and destruction.
Pr 16: 33 The l is cast into the lap,
18: 18 Casting the l settles disputes
Ecc 3: 22 his work, because that is his l.
Ac 1: 26 Then they cast lots, and the l fell

LOTS (LOT)

Jos 18: 10 Joshua then cast l for them
Ps 22: 18 and cast l for my clothing.
Joel 3: 3 They cast l for my people
Ob : 11 and cast l for Jerusalem,
Mt 27: 35 divided up his clothes by casting l.
Ac 1: 26 Then they cast l, and the lot fell

LOVE* (BELOVED LOVED LOVELY LOVER LOVER'S LOVERS LOVES LOVING LOVING-KINDNESS)

Ge 20: 13 'This is how you can show your l
22: 2 your only son, Isaac, whom you l,
29: 18 Jacob was in l with Rachel and said
29: 20 days to him because of his l for her.
29: 32 Surely my husband will l me now."
Ex 15: 13 "In your unfailing l you will lead
20: 6 showing l to a thousand generations
20: 6 of those who l me
21: 5 'I l my master and my wife
34: 6 abounding in l and faithfulness,
34: 7 maintaining l to thousands,
Lev 19: 18 but l your neighbor as yourself.
19: 34 L him as yourself,
Nu 14: 18 abounding in l and forgiving sin
14: 19 In accordance with your great l,
Dt 5: 10 showing l to a thousand generations
5: 10 of those who l me
6: 5 L the LORD your God
7: 9 generations of those who l him
7: 9 keeping his covenant of l
7: 12 God will keep his covenant of l
7: 13 He will l you and bless you
10: 12 to walk in all his ways, to l him,
10: 19 you are to l those who are aliens,
11: 1 L the LORD your God
11: 13 to l the LORD your God
11: 22 to l the LORD your God,
13: 3 you l him with all your heart
13: 6 wife you l, or your closest friend
19: 9 to l the LORD your God
21: 15 the son of the wife he does not l,
21: 16 the son of the wife he does not l.
30: 6 so that you may l him
30: 16 today to l the LORD your God,
30: 20 and that you may l the LORD your
33: 3 Surely it is you who l the people;
Jos 22: 5 to l the LORD your God, to walk
23: 11 careful to l the LORD your God.
Jdg 5: 31 may they who l you be like the sun
14: 16 You hate me! You don't really l me
16: 4 he fell in l with a woman
16: 15 "How can you say, 'I l you,'
1Sa 18: 20 Saul's daughter Michal was in l
20: 17 had David reaffirm his oath out of l
2Sa 1: 26 Your l for me was wonderful,
7: 15 But my l will never be taken away
13: 1 son of David fell in l with Tamar,
13: 4 said to him, "I'm in l with Tamar,
16: 17 "Is this the l you show your friend?
19: 6 You l those who hate you
19: 6 hate you and hate those who l you.
1Ki 3: 3 Solomon showed his l
8: 23 you who keep your covenant of l
10: 9 of the LORD's eternal l for Israel,
11: 2 Solomon held fast to them in l.
1Ch 16: 34 his l endures forever.
16: 41 "for his l endures forever."
17: 13 I will never take my l away
2Ch 5: 13 his l endures forever."
6: 14 you who keep your covenant of l
6: 42 Remember the great l promised
7: 3 his l endures forever."
7: 6 saying, "His l endures forever."
9: 8 Because of the l of your God
19: 2 and l those who hate the LORD?
20: 21 for his l endures forever."
Ezr 3: 11 his l to Israel endures forever."
Ne 1: 5 covenant of l with those who l him
9: 17 slow to anger and abounding in l.
Ne 9: 32 who keeps his covenant of l,
13: 22 to me according to your great l.
Job 15: 34 of those who l bribes.
19: 19 those I l have turned against me.
37: 13 or to water his earth and show his l.
Ps 4: 2 How long will you l delusions
5: 11 that those who l your name may
6: 4 save me because of your unfailing l.
11: 5 wicked and those who l violence
13: 5 But I trust in your unfailing l;
17: 7 Show the wonder of your great l,
18: 1 I l you, O LORD, my strength.
21: 7 through the unfailing l
23: 6 Surely goodness and l will follow
25: 6 O LORD, your great mercy and l,
25: 7 according to your l remember me,
26: 3 for your l is ever before me,
26: 8 I l the house where you live,
31: 7 I will be glad and rejoice in your l,
31: 16 save me in your unfailing l.
31: 21 for he showed his wonderful l
31: 23 L the LORD, all his saints!
32: 10 but the LORD's unfailing l
33: 5 the earth is full of his unfailing l.
33: 18 whose hope is in his unfailing l,
33: 22 May your unfailing l rest upon us,
36: 5 Your l, O LORD, reaches
36: 7 How priceless is your unfailing l!
36: 10 Continue your l to those who know
40: 10 I do not conceal your l
40: 11 may your l and your truth always
40: 16 may those who l your salvation
42: 8 By day the LORD directs his l,
44: 26 of your unfailing l.
45: 7 You l righteousness and hate
48: 9 we meditate on your unfailing l.
51: 1 according to your unfailing l;
52: 3 You l evil rather than good,
52: 4 You l every harmful word,
52: 8 I trust in God's unfailing l
57: 3 God sends his l and his faithfulness
57: 10 For great is your l, reaching
59: 16 in the morning I will sing of your l;
60: 5 that those you l may be delivered.
61: 7 appoint your l and faithfulness
63: 3 Because your l is better than life,
66: 20 or withheld his l from me!
69: 13 in your great l, O God,
69: 16 out of the goodness of your l;
69: 36 and those who l his name will dwell
70: 4 may those who l your salvation
77: 8 Has his unfailing l vanished forever
85: 7 Show us your unfailing l, O LORD
85: 10 L and faithfulness meet together;
86: 5 abounding in l to all who call
86: 13 For great is your l toward me;
86: 15 abounding in l and faithfulness.
88: 11 Is your l declared in the grave,
89: 1 of the LORD's great l forever;
89: 2 declare that your l stands firm
89: 14 l and faithfulness go before you.
89: 24 My faithful l will be with him,
89: 28 I will maintain my l to him forever,
89: 33 but I will not take my l from him,
89: 49 where is your former great l,
90: 14 with your unfailing l,
92: 2 to proclaim your l in the morning
94: 18 your l, O LORD, supported me.
97: 10 Let those who l the LORD hate
98: 3 He has remembered his l
100: 5 is good and his l endures forever;
101: 1 I will sing of your l and justice;
103: 4 crowns you with l and compassion.
103: 8 slow to anger, abounding in l.
103: 11 so great is his l for those who fear
103: 17 LORD's l is with those who fear
106: 1 his l endures forever.
106: 45 and out of his great l he relented.
107: 1 his l endures forever.
107: 8 to the LORD for his unfailing l
107: 15 to the LORD for his unfailing l
107: 21 to the LORD for his unfailing l
107: 31 to the LORD for his unfailing l
107: 43 consider the great l of the LORD.
108: 4 For great is your l, higher
108: 6 that those you l may be delivered.
109: 21 out of the goodness of your l,
109: 26 save me in accordance with your l.
115: 1 because of your l and faithfulness.
116: 1 I l the LORD, for he heard my
117: 2 For great is his l toward us,
118: 1 his l endures forever.
118: 2 "His l endures forever."
118: 3 "His l endures forever."
118: 4 "His l endures forever."
Ps 118: 29 his l endures forever.
119: 41 May your unfailing l come to me,
119: 47 because I l them.
119: 48 to your commands, which I l,
119: 64 The earth is filled with your l,
119: 76 May your unfailing l be my
119: 88 my life according to your l,
119: 97 Oh, how I l your law!
119: 113 but I l your law.
119: 119 therefore I l your statutes.
119: 124 your servant according to your l
119: 127 Because I l your commands
119: 132 to those who l your name.
119: 149 in accordance with your l;
119: 159 O LORD, according to your l.
119: 159 See how I l your precepts;
119: 163 but I l your law.
119: 165 peace have they who l your law,
119: 167 for I l them greatly.
122: 6 "May those who l you be secure.
130: 7 for with the LORD is unfailing l
136: 1 -26 His l endures forever.
138: 2 for your l and your faithfulness,
138: 8 your l, O LORD, endures forever
143: 8 of your unfailing l,
143: 12 In your unfailing l, silence my
145: 8 slow to anger and rich in l.
145: 20 over all who l him,
147: 11 who put their hope in his unfailing l
Pr 1: 22 you simple ones l your simple
3: 3 Let l and faithfulness never leave
4: 6 l her, and she will watch over you.
5: 19 you ever be captivated by her l.
7: 18 let's drink deep of l till morning;
7: 18 let's enjoy ourselves with l!
8: 17 I l those who l me,
8: 21 wealth on those who l me
8: 36 all who hate me l death."
9: 8 rebuke a wise man and he will l you
10: 12 but l covers over all wrongs.
14: 22 those who plan what is good find l
15: 17 of vegetables where there is l
16: 6 Through l and faithfulness sin is
17: 9 over an offense promotes l,
18: 21 and those who l it will eat its fruit.
19: 22 What a man desires is unfailing l;
20: 6 claims to have unfailing l,
20: 13 Do not l sleep or you will grow
20: 28 L and faithfulness keep a king safe;
20: 28 through l his throne is made secure
21: 21 who pursues righteousness and l
27: 5 rebuke than hidden l.
Ecc 3: 8 a time to l and a time to hate,
9: 1 but no man knows whether l
9: 6 Their l, their hate
9: 9 life with your wife, whom you l,
SS 1: 2 for your l is more delightful
1: 3 No wonder the maidens l you!
1: 4 we will praise your l more
1: 7 you whom I l, where you graze
2: 4 and his banner over me is l.
2: 5 for I am faint with l.
2: 7 Do not arouse or awaken l
3: 5 Do not arouse or awaken l
4: 10 How delightful is your l, my sister,
4: 10 How much more pleasing is your l
5: 8 Tell him I am faint with l.
7: 6 O l, with your delights!
7: 12 there I will give you my l.
8: 4 Do not arouse or awaken l
8: 6 for l is as strong as death,
8: 7 Many waters cannot quench l;
8: 7 all the wealth of his house for l,
Isa 1: 23 they all l bribes
5: 1 I will sing for the one I l
16: 5 In l a throne will be established;
38: 17 In your l you kept me
43: 4 and because I l you,
54: 10 yet my unfailing l for you will not
55: 3 my faithful l promised to David.
56: 6 to l the name of the LORD,
56: 10 they l to sleep.
57: 8 a pact with those whose beds you l,
61: 8 "For I, the LORD, l justice;
63: 9 In his l and mercy he redeemed
66: 10 all you who l her;
Jer 2: 25 I l foreign gods,
2: 33 How skilled you are at pursuing l!
5: 31 and my people l it this way.
12: 7 I will give the one I l
14: 10 "They greatly l to wander;
16: 5 my l and my pity from this people
31: 3 you with an everlasting l;
32: 18 You show l to thousands
33: 11 his l endures forever."

La 3: 22 of the LORD's great l we are not
3: 32 so great is his unfailing l.
Eze 16: 8 saw that you were old enough for l,
23: 17 of l, and in their lust they defiled
33: 32 more than one who sings l songs
Da 9: 4 covenant of l with all who l him
Hos 1: 6 for I will no longer show l
1: 7 Yet I will show l to the house
2: 4 I will not show my l to her children
2: 19 in l and compassion.
2: 23 I will show my l to the one I called
3: 1 Go, show your l to your wife again,
3: 1 and l the sacred raisin cakes."
3: 1 L her as the LORD loves
4: 1 "There is no faithfulness, no l,
4: 18 their rulers dearly l shameful ways.
6: 4 Your l is like the morning mist,
9: 1 you l the wages of a prostitute
9: 15 I will no longer l them;
10: 12 reap the fruit of unfailing l,
11: 4 with ties of l;
12: 6 maintain l and justice,
14: 4 and l them freely,
Joel 2: 13 slow to anger and abounding in l,
Am 4: 5 for this is what you l to do,"
5: 15 Hate evil, l good;
Jnh 4: 2 slow to anger and abounding in l,
Mic 3: 2 you who hate good and l evil;
6: 8 To act justly and to l mercy
Zep 3: 17 he will quiet you with his l,
Zec 8: 17 and do not l to swear falsely.
8: 19 Therefore l truth and peace."
Mt 3: 17 "This is my Son, whom I l;
5: 43 'L your neighbor and hate your
5: 44 L your enemies and pray
5: 46 you l those who l you, what reward
6: 5 for they l to pray standing
6: 24 he will hate the one and l the other,
12: 18 the one I l, in whom I delight;
17: 5 "This is my Son, whom I l;
19: 19 and 'l your neighbor as yourself.'"
22: 37 "'L the Lord your God
22: 39 'L your neighbor as yourself.'
23: 6 they l the place of honor
23: 7 they l to be greeted
24: 12 the l of most will grow cold,
Mk 1: 11 "You are my Son, whom I l;
9: 7 "This is my Son, whom I l.
12: 30 L the Lord your God
12: 31 'L your neighbor as yourself.'
12: 33 To l him with all your heart,
12: 33 and to l your neighbor
Lk 3: 22 "You are my Son, whom I l;
6: 27 you who hear me: L your enemies,
6: 32 Even 'sinners' l those who l them.
6: 32 you l those who l you, what credit
6: 35 l your enemies, do good to them,
7: 42 which of them will l him more?"
10: 27 and, 'L your neighbor as yourself
10: 27 "'L the Lord your God
11: 42 you neglect justice and the l of God
11: 43 you l the most important seats
16: 13 he will hate the one and l the other,
20: 13 whom I l; perhaps they will respect
20: 46 l to be greeted in the marketplaces
Jn 5: 42 I know that you do not have the l
8: 42 were your Father, you would l me,
11: 3 "Lord, the one you l is sick."
13: 1 them the full extent of his l.
13: 34 I give you: L one another.
13: 34 so you must l one another.
13: 35 disciples, if you l one another."
14: 15 "If you l me, you will obey what I
14: 21 I too will l him and show myself
14: 23 My Father will l him, and we will
14: 24 He who does not l me will not obey
14: 31 world must learn that I l the Father
15: 9 Now remain in my l.
15: 10 commands and remain in his l.
15: 10 you will remain in my l,
15: 12 L each other as I have loved you.
15: 13 Greater l has no one than this,
15: 17 This is my command: L each other.
15: 19 to the world, it would l you
17: 26 known in order that the l you have
21: 15 do you truly l me more than these
21: 15 he said, "you know that I l you."
21: 16 Yes, Lord, you know that I l you."
21: 16 do you truly l me?" He answered,
21: 17 all things; you know that I l you."
21: 17 "Do you l me?" He said, "Lord,
21: 17 "Simon son of John, do you l me?"
Ro 5: 5 because God has poured out his l
5: 8 God demonstrates his own l for us
8: 28 for the good of those who l him,
Ro 8: 35 us from the l of Christ?
8: 39 us from the l of God that is
12: 9 L must be sincere.
12: 10 to one another in brotherly l.
13: 8 continuing debt to l one another,
13: 9 "L your neighbor as yourself."
13: 10 Therefore l is the fulfillment
13: 10 L does no harm to its neighbor.
14: 15 you are no longer acting in l.
15: 30 and by the l of the Spirit,
16: 8 Greet Ampliatus, whom I l
1Co 2: 9 prepared for those who l him"—
4: 17 my son whom I l, who is faithful
4: 21 or in l and with a gentle spirit?
8: 1 Knowledge puffs up, but l builds up
13: 1 have not l, I am only a resounding
13: 2 but have not l, I am nothing.
13: 3 but have not l, I gain nothing.
13: 4 Love is patient, l is kind.
13: 4 L is patient, love is kind.
13: 6 L does not delight in evil
13: 8 L never fails.
13: 13 But the greatest of these is l.
13: 13 three remain: faith, hope and l.
14: 1 way of l and eagerly desire spiritual
16: 14 Do everything in l.
16: 22 If anyone does not l the Lord—
16: 24 My l to all of you in Christ Jesus.
2Co 2: 4 to let you know the depth of my l
2: 8 therefore, to reaffirm your l for him
5: 14 For Christ's l compels us,
6: 6 in the Holy Spirit and in sincere l;
8: 7 complete earnestness and in your l
8: 8 sincerity of your l by comparing it
8: 24 show these men the proof of your l
11: 11 Why? Because I do not l you?
12: 15 If I l you more, will you l me less?
13: 11 And the God of l and peace will be
13: 14 of the Lord Jesus Christ, and the l
Gal 5: 6 is faith expressing itself through l.
5: 13 rather, serve one another in l.
5: 14 "L your neighbor as yourself."
5: 22 But the fruit of the Spirit is l, joy,
Eph 1: 4 In l he predestined us
1: 15 and your l for all the saints,
2: 4 But because of his great l for us,
3: 17 being rooted and established in l,
3: 18 and high and deep is the l of Christ,
3: 19 and to know this l that surpasses
4: 2 bearing with one another in l.
4: 15 Instead, speaking the truth in l,
4: 16 grows and builds itself up in l,
5: 2 loved children and live a life of l,
5: 25 l your wives, just as Christ loved
5: 28 husbands ought to l their wives
5: 33 each one of you also must l his wife
6: 23 l with faith from God the Father
6: 24 Christ with an undying l.
6: 24 to all who l our Lord Jesus Christ
Php 1: 9 that your l may abound more
1: 16 so in l, knowing that I am put here
2: 1 from his l, if any fellowship
2: 2 having the same l, being one
4: 1 you whom I l and long for,
Col 1: 4 of the l you have for all the saints—
1: 5 l that spring from the hope that is
1: 8 also told us of your l in the Spirit.
2: 2 in heart and united in l,
3: 14 And over all these virtues put on l,
3: 19 l your wives and do not be harsh
1Th 1: 3 your labor prompted by l,
3: 6 good news about your faith and l.
3: 12 May the Lord make your l increase
4: 9 about brotherly l we do not need
4: 9 taught by God to l each other.
4: 10 you do l all the brothers
5: 8 on faith and l as a breastplate,
5: 13 them in the highest regard in l
2Th 1: 3 and the l every one of you has
2: 10 because they refused to l the truth
3: 5 direct your hearts into God's l
1Ti 1: 5 The goal of this command is l,
1: 14 and l that are in Christ Jesus.
2: 15 l and holiness with propriety.
4: 12 in life, in l, in faith and in purity.
6: 10 For the l of money is a root
6: 11 faith, l, endurance and gentleness.
2Ti 1: 7 of power, of l and of self-discipline.
1: 13 with faith and l in Christ Jesus.
2: 22 and pursue righteousness, faith, l
3: 3 unholy, without l, unforgiving,
3: 10 faith, patience, l, endurance,
Tit 2: 2 in faith, in l and in endurance.
2: 4 women to l their husbands
3: 4 and l of God our Savior appeared,
Tit 3: 15 Greet those who l us in the faith.
Phm : 5 and your l for all the saints.
: 7 Your l has given me great joy
: 9 yet I appeal to you on the basis of l.
Heb 6: 10 and the l you have shown him
10: 24 may spur one another on toward l
13: 5 free from the l of money
Jas 1: 12 promised to those who l him.
2: 5 he promised those who l him?
2: 8 "L your neighbor as yourself,"
1Pe 1: 8 you have not seen him, you l him;
1: 22 the truth so that you have sincere l
1: 22 l one another deeply,
2: 17 L the brotherhood of believers,
3: 8 be sympathetic, l as brothers,
3: 10 "Whoever would l life
4: 8 Above all, l each other deeply,
4: 8 l covers over a multitude of sins.
5: 14 Greet one another with a kiss of l.
2Pe 1: 7 and to brotherly kindness, l.
1: 17 "This is my Son, whom I l;
1Jn 2: 5 God's l is truly made complete
2: 15 Do not l the world or anything
2: 15 the l of the Father is not in him.
3: 1 How great is the l the Father has
3: 10 anyone who does not l his brother.
3: 11 We should l one another.
3: 14 Anyone who does not l remains
3: 14 because we l our brothers.
3: 16 This is how we know what l is:
3: 17 how can the l of God be in him?
3: 18 let us not l with words or tongue
3: 23 to l one another as he commanded
4: 7 Dear friends, let us l one another,
4: 7 for l comes from God.
4: 8 Whoever does not l does not know
4: 8 not know God, because God is l.
4: 9 This is how God showed his l
4: 10 This is l: not that we loved God,
4: 11 we also ought to l one another.
4: 12 seen God; but if we l one another,
4: 12 and his l is made complete in us.
4: 16 God is l.
4: 16 Whoever lives in l lives in God,
4: 16 and rely on the l God has for us.
4: 17 l is made complete among us
4: 18 But perfect l drives out fear,
4: 18 There is no fear in l.
4: 18 who fears is not made perfect in l.
4: 19 We l because he first loved us.
4: 20 If anyone says, "I l God,"
4: 20 anyone who does not l his brother,
4: 20 whom he has seen, cannot l God,
4: 21 loves God must also l his brother.
5: 2 we know that we l the children
5: 3 This is l for God: to obey his
2Jn : 1 whom I l in the truth—
: 3 will be with us in truth and l.
: 5 I ask that we l one another.
: 6 his command is that you walk in l.
: 6 this is l: that we walk in obedience
3Jn : 1 To my dear friend Gaius, whom I l
: 6 have told the church about your l.
Jude : 2 peace and l be yours in abundance.
: 12 men are blemishes at your l feasts,
: 21 Keep yourselves in God's l
Rev 2: 4 You have forsaken your first l.
2: 19 I know your deeds, your l and faith
3: 19 Those whom I l I rebuke
12: 11 they did not l their lives so much

LOVED* (LOVE)

Ge 24: 67 she became his wife, and he l her;
25: 28 l Esau, but Rebekah l Jacob.
29: 30 and he l Rachel more than Leah.
29: 31 the LORD saw that Leah was not l,
29: 33 the LORD heard that I am not l,
34: 3 and he l the girl and spoke tenderly
37: 3 Now Israel l Joseph more than any
37: 4 saw that their father l him more
Dt 4: 37 Because he l your forefathers
7: 8 But it was because the LORD l you
10: 15 on your forefathers and l them,
1Sa 1: 5 a double portion because he l her,
18: 1 in spirit with David, and he l him
18: 3 with David because he l him
18: 16 But all Israel and Judah l David,
18: 28 that his daughter Michal l David,
20: 17 because he l him as he l himself.
2Sa 1: 23 in life they were l and gracious,
12: 24 The LORD l him; and
12: 25 and because the LORD l him,
13: 15 hated her more than he had l her.
1Ki 11: 1 l many foreign women
2Ch 11: 21 Rehoboam l Maacah daughter
26: 10 in the fertile lands, for he l the soil.

Ne 13: 26 He was l by his God, and God
Ps 44: 3 light of your face, for you l them.
47: 4 the pride of Jacob, whom he l.
78: 68 Mount Zion, which he l.
88: 18 taken my companions and l ones
109: 17 He l to pronounce a curse —
Isa 5: 1 My l one had a vineyard
Jer 2: 2 how as a bride you l me
8: 2 which they have l and served
31: 3 "I have l you with an everlasting
Eze 16: 37 those you l as well as those you
Hos 2: 1 and of your sisters, 'My l one.'
2: 23 to the one I called 'Not my l one.'
3: 1 though she is l by another
9: 10 became as vile as the thing they l.
11: 1 "When Israel was a child, I l him,
Mal 1: 2 "But you ask, 'How have you l us?'
1: 2 "I have l you," says the LORD.
1: 2 "Yet I have l Jacob, but Esau I
Mk 10: 21 Jesus looked at him and l him.
12: 6 left to send, a son, whom he l.
Lk 7: 47 been forgiven — for she l much.
16: 14 The Pharisees, who l money,
Jn 3: 16 so l the world that he gave his one
3: 19 but men l darkness instead of light
11: 5 Jesus l Martha and her sister
11: 36 "See how he l him!" But some
12: 43 for they l praise from men more
13: 1 Having l his own who were
13: 23 the disciple whom Jesus l,
13: 34 As I have l you, so you must love
14: 21 He who loves me will be l
14: 28 If you l me, you would be glad that
15: 9 the Father has l me, so have I l you.
15: 12 Love each other as I have l you.
16: 27 loves you because you have l me
17: 23 have l them even as you have l me.
17: 24 you l me before the creation
19: 26 the disciple whom he l standing
20: 2 one Jesus l, and said, "They have
21: 7 the disciple whom Jesus l said
21: 20 whom Jesus l was following
Ro 1: 7 To all in Rome who are l by God
8: 37 conquerors through him who l us.
9: 13 "Jacob I l, but Esau I hated."
9: 25 her 'my l one' who is not my l one,"
11: 28 they are l on account
Gal 2: 20 who l me and gave himself for me.
Eph 5: 1 as dearly l children and live a life
5: 2 as Christ l us and gave himself up
5: 25 just as Christ l the church
Col 3: 12 and dearly l, clothe yourselves
1Th 1: 4 For we know, brothers l by God,
2: 8 We l you so much that we were
2Th 2: 13 for you, brothers l by the Lord,
2: 16 who l us and by his grace gave us
2Ti 4: 10 for Demas, because he l this world,
Heb 1: 9 You have l righteousness
2Pe 2: 15 who l the wages of wickedness.
1Jn 4: 10 This is love: not that we l God,
4: 10 but that he l us and sent his Son
4: 11 Dear friends, since God so l us,
4: 19 We love because he first l us.
Jude : 1 who are l by God the Father
Rev 3: 9 and acknowledge that I have l you.

LOVELY* (LOVE)
Ge 29: 17 but Rachel was l in form,
Est 1: 11 and nobles, for she was l to look at.
2: 7 was l in form and features,
Ps 84: 1 How l is your dwelling place,
SS 1: 5 Dark am I, yet l,
2: 14 and your face is l.
4: 3 your mouth is l.
5: 16 he is altogether l.
6: 4 l as Jerusalem,
Am 8: 13 l young women and strong young
Php 4: 8 whatever is l, whatever is

LOVER* (LOVE)
SS 1: 13 My l is to me a sachet of myrrh
1: 14 My l is to me a cluster
1: 16 How handsome you are, my l!
2: 3 is my l among the young men.
2: 8 Listen! My l!
2: 9 My l is like a gazelle or a young
2: 10 My l spoke and said to me,
2: 16 Beloved My l is mine and I am his;
2: 17 turn, my l,
4: 16 Let my l come into his garden
5: 2 Listen! My l is knocking:
5: 4 My l thrust his hand
5: 5 I arose to open for my l,
5: 6 I opened for my l,
5: 6 but my l had left; he was gone.
5: 8 if you find my l,
SS 5: 10 Beloved My l is radiant and ruddy,
5: 16 This is my l, this my friend,
6: 1 Where has your l gone,
6: 1 Which way did your l turn,
6: 2 Beloved My l has gone
6: 3 I am my lover's and my l is mine;
7: 9 May the wine go straight to my l,
7: 10 I belong to my l,
7: 11 my l, let us go to the countryside,
7: 13 that I have stored up for you, my l.
8: 5 leaning on her l?
8: 14 Beloved Come away, my l,
1Ti 3: 3 not quarrelsome, not a l of money.

LOVER'S* (LOVE)
SS 6: 3 I am my l and my lover is mine;

LOVERS* (LOVE)
SS 5: 1 drink your fill, O l.
Jer 3: 1 as a prostitute with many l —
3: 2 the roadside you sat waiting for l,
4: 30 Your l despise you;
La 1: 2 Among all her l
Eze 16: 33 but you give gifts to all your l,
16: 36 in your promiscuity with your l,
16: 37 I am going to gather all your l,
16: 39 Then I will hand you over to your l,
16: 41 and you will no longer pay your l.
23: 5 she lusted after her l, the Assyrians
23: 9 I handed her over to her l,
23: 20 There she lusted after her l,
23: 22 I will stir up your l against you,
Hos 2: 5 She said, 'I will go after my l,
2: 7 She will chase after her l
2: 10 lewdness before the eyes of her l;
2: 12 she said were her pay from her l;
2: 13 and went after her l,
8: 9 Ephraim has sold herself to l.
2Ti 3: 2 People will be l of themselves,
3: 2 l of money, boastful, proud,
3: 3 without self-control, brutal, not l
3: 4 l of pleasure rather than l of God —

LOVES* (LOVE)
Ge 44: 20 sons left, and his father l him.'
Dt 10: 18 and l the alien, giving him food
15: 16 because he l you and your family
21: 15 and he l one but not the other,
21: 16 son of the wife he l in preference
23: 5 because the LORD your God l you
28: 54 wife he l or his surviving children,
28: 56 will begrudge the husband she l
33: 12 and the one the LORD l rests
Ru 4: 15 who l you and who is better to you
2Ch 2: 11 "Because the LORD l his people,
Ps 11: 7 he l justice;
33: 5 The LORD l righteousness
34: 12 Whoever of you l life
37: 28 For the LORD l the just
87: 2 the LORD l the gates of Zion
91: 14 Because he l me," says the LORD,
99: 4 The King is mighty, he l justice —
119: 140 and your servant l them.
127: 2 for he grants sleep to those he l.
146: 8 the LORD l the righteous.
Pr 3: 12 the LORD disciplines those he l,
12: 1 Whoever l discipline l knowledge,
13: 24 he who l him is careful
15: 9 he l those who pursue
17: 17 A friend l at all times,
17: 19 He who l a quarrel l sin;
19: 8 He who gets wisdom l his own soul
21: 17 He who l pleasure will become
21: 17 whoever l wine and oil will never
22: 11 He who l a pure heart and whose
29: 3 A man who l wisdom brings joy
Ecc 5: 10 Whoever l money never has
5: 10 whoever l wealth is never satisfied
SS 3: 1 I looked for the one my heart l;
3: 2 I will search for the one my heart l.
3: 3 "Have you seen the one my heart l
3: 4 when I found the one my heart l.
Hos 3: 1 as the LORD l the Israelites,
10: 11 that l to thresh;
12: 7 he l to defraud.
Mal 2: 11 the sanctuary the LORD l,
Mt 10: 37 anyone who l his son or daughter
10: 37 "Anyone who l his father
Lk 7: 5 because he l our nation
7: 47 has been forgiven little l little."
Jn 3: 35 Father l the Son and has placed
5: 20 For the Father l the Son
10: 17 reason my Father l me is that I lay
12: 25 The man who l his life will lose it,
14: 21 He who l me will be loved
14: 21 obeys them, he is the one who l me.
Jn 14: 23 Jesus replied, "If anyone l me,
16: 27 the Father himself l you
Ro 13: 8 for he who l his fellowman has
1Co 8: 3 But the man who l God is known
2Co 9: 7 for God l a cheerful giver.
Eph 1: 6 has freely given us in the One he l.
5: 28 He who l his wife l himself.
5: 33 must love his wife as he l himself,
Col 1: 13 us into the kingdom of the Son he l,
Tit 1: 8 one who l what is good, who is
Heb 12: 6 the Lord disciplines those he l,
1Jn 2: 10 Whoever l his brother lives
2: 15 If anyone l the world, the love
4: 7 Everyone who l has been born
4: 21 Whoever l God must also love his
5: 1 who l the father l his child
3Jn : 9 but Diotrephes, who l to be first,
Rev 1: 5 To him who l us and has freed us
20: 9 camp of God's people, the city he l.
22: 15 and everyone who l and practices

LOVING* (LOVE)
Ps 25: 10 All the ways of the LORD are l
59: 10 my l God.
59: 17 O God, are my fortress, my l God.
62: 12 and that you, O Lord, are l.
144: 2 He is my l God and my fortress,
145: 13 and l toward all he has made.
145: 17 and l toward all he has made.
Pr 5: 19 A l doe, a graceful deer —
Heb 13: 1 Keep on l each other as brothers.
1Jn 5: 2 by l God and carrying out his

LOVING-KINDNESS* (LOVE)
Jer 31: 3 I have drawn you with l.

LOWER
Ps 8: 5 You made him a little l
2Co 11: 7 a sin for me to l myself in order
Heb 2: 7 You made him a little l

LOWING
1Sa 15: 14 What is this l of cattle that I hear?"

LOWLY
Job 5: 11 The l he sets on high,
Ps 138: 6 on high, he looks upon the l,
Pr 29: 23 but a man of l spirit gains honor.
Isa 57: 15 also with him who is contrite and l
Eze 21: 26 l will be exalted and the exalted
1Co 1: 28 He chose the l things of this world

LOYAL
1Ch 29: 18 and keep their hearts l to you.
Ps 78: 8 whose hearts were not l to God,

LUKE*
Co-worker with Paul (Col 4:14; 2Ti 4:11; Phm 24).

LUKEWARM*
Rev 3: 16 So, because you are l — neither hot

LUST (LUSTED LUSTS)
Pr 6: 25 Do not l in your heart
Eze 20: 30 and l after their vile images?
Col 3: 5 sexual immorality, impurity, l,
1Th 4: 5 not in passionate l like the heathen,
1Pe 4: 3 in debauchery, l, drunkenness,
1Jn 2: 16 the l of his eyes and the boasting

LUSTED (LUST)
Eze 23: 5 she l after her lovers, the Assyrians

LUSTS* (LUST)
Nu 15: 39 yourselves by going after the l
Ro 1: 26 God gave them over to shameful l.

LUXURY
Jas 5: 5 You have lived on earth in l

LYDIA'S*
Ac 16: 40 went to L house, where they met

LYING (LIE)
Pr 6: 17 a l tongue,
12: 22 The LORD detests l lips,
21: 6 A fortune made by a l tongue
26: 28 A l tongue hates those it hurts,

MACEDONIA
Ac 16: 9 "Come over to M and help us."

MAD
Dt 28: 34 The sights you see will drive you m

MADE (MAKE)
Ge 1: 7 So God m the expanse
1: 16 God m two great lights —
1: 16 He also m the stars.
1: 25 God m the wild animals according
1: 31 God saw all that he had m,
2: 22 Then the LORD God m a woman

Ge 6: 6 was grieved that he had *m* man
9: 6 has God *m* man.
15: 18 that day the LORD *m* a covenant
Ex 20: 11 six days the LORD *m* the heavens
20: 11 the Sabbath day and *m* it holy.
24: 8 the covenant that the LORD has *m*
32: 4 *m* it into an idol cast in the shape
Lev 16: 34 Atonement is to be *m* once a year
Dt 32: 6 who *m* you and formed you?
Jos 24: 25 On that day Joshua *m* a covenant
2Ki 19: 15 You have *m* heaven and earth.
2Ch 2: 12 the God of Israel, who *m* heaven
Ne 9: 6 You *m* the heavens,
9: 10 You *m* a name for yourself,
Ps 33: 6 of the LORD were the heavens *m*,
95: 5 The sea is his, for he *m* it,
96: 5 but the LORD *m* the heavens.
100: 3 It is he who *m* us, and we are his;
118: 24 This is the day the LORD has *m*;
136: 7 who *m* the great lights—
139: 14 I am fearfully and wonderfully *m*;
Ecc 3: 11 He has *m* everything beautiful
Isa 43: 7 whom I formed and *m*."
45: 12 It is I who *m* the earth
45: 18 he who fashioned and *m* the earth,
66: 2 Has not my hand *m* all these things
Jer 10: 12 But God *m* the earth by his power;
27: 5 and outstretched arm I *m* the earth
32: 17 you have *m* the heavens
33: 2 LORD says, he who *m* the earth,
51: 15 "He *m* the earth by his power;
Eze 3: 17 I have *m* you a watchman
33: 7 I have *m* you a watchman
Am 5: 8 (he who *m* the Pleiades and Orion,
Jnh 1: 9 who *m* the sea and the land."
Mk 2: 27 "The Sabbath was *m* for man,
Jn 1: 3 Through him all things were *m*;
Ac 17: 24 "The God who *m* the world
1Co 3: 6 watered it, but God *m* it grow.
Heb 1: 2 through whom he *m* the universe.
Jas 3: 9 who have been *m* in God's likeness
Rev 14: 7 Worship him who *m* the heavens,

MAGDALENE
Lk 8: 2 Mary (called *M*) from whom seven

MAGI
Mt 2: 1 *M* from the east came to Jerusalem

MAGIC (MAGICIANS)
Eze 13: 20 I am against your *m* charms
Rev 21: 8 those who practice *m* arts,
22: 15 those who practice *m* arts,

MAGICIANS (MAGIC)
Ex 7: 11 the Egyptian *m* also did the same
Da 2: 2 So the king summoned the *m*,

MAGNIFICENCE* (MAGNIFICENT)
1Ch 22: 5 for the LORD should be of great *m*

MAGNIFICENT (MAGNIFICENCE)
1Ki 8: 13 I have indeed built a *m* temple
Isa 28: 29 in counsel and *m* in wisdom.
Mk 13: 1 stones! What *m* buildings!"

MAGOG
Eze 38: 2 of the land of *M*, the chief prince
39: 6 I will send fire on *M*
Rev 20: 8 and *M*— to gather them for battle.

MAIDEN (MAIDENS)
Pr 30: 19 and the way of a man with a *m*.
Isa 62: 5 As a young man marries a *m*,
Jer 2: 32 Does a *m* forget her jewelry,

MAIDENS (MAIDEN)
SS 1: 3 No wonder the *m* love you!

MAIMED
Mt 18: 8 It is better for you to enter life *m*

MAINTAIN (MAINTAINING)
Ps 82: 3 *m* the rights of the poor
106: 3 Blessed are they who *m* justice,
Hos 12: 6 *m* love and justice,
Am 5: 15 *m* justice in the courts.
Ro 3: 28 For we *m* that a man is justified

MAINTAINING* (MAINTAIN)
Ex 34: 7 faithfulness, *m* love to thousands,

MAJESTIC* (MAJESTY)
Ex 15: 6 was *m* in power.
15: 11 *m* in holiness,
Job 37: 4 he thunders with his *m* voice.
Ps 8: 1 how *m* is your name in all the earth
8: 9 how *m* is your name in all the earth
29: 4 the voice of the LORD is *m*.
68: 15 of Bashan are *m* mountains;
76: 4 more *m* than mountains rich
111: 3 Glorious and *m* are his deeds,
SS 6: 4 *m* as troops with banners.
6: 10 *m* as the stars in procession?
Isa 30: 30 men to hear his *m* voice
Eze 31: 7 It was *m* in beauty,
2Pe 1: 17 came to him from the *M* Glory,

MAJESTY* (MAJESTIC)
Ex 15: 7 In the greatness of your *m*
Dt 5: 24 has shown us his glory and his *m*,
11: 2 his *m*, his mighty hand, his
33: 17 In *m* he is like a firstborn bull;
33: 26 and on the clouds in his *m*.
1Ch 16: 27 Splendor and *m* are before him;
29: 11 and the *m* and the splendor,
Est 1: 4 the splendor and glory of his *m*.
7: 3 if it pleases your *m*, grant me my
Job 37: 22 God comes in awesome *m*.
40: 10 and clothe yourself in honor and *m*
Ps 21: 5 on him splendor and *m*.
45: 3 with splendor and *m*.
45: 4 In your *m* ride forth victoriously
68: 34 whose *m* is over Israel,
93: 1 The LORD reigns, he is robed in *m*
93: 1 the LORD is robed in *m*
96: 6 Splendor and *m* are before him;
104: 1 clothed with splendor and *m*.
110: 3 Arrayed in holy *m*,
145: 5 of the glorious splendor of your *m*,
Isa 2: 10 and the splendor of his *m*!
2: 19 and the splendor of his *m*,
2: 21 and the splendor of his *m*,
24: 14 west they acclaim the LORD's *m*.
26: 10 and regard not the *m* of the LORD.
53: 2 or *m* to attract us to him,
Eze 31: 2 can be compared with you in *m*?
31: 18 with you in splendor and *m*?
Da 4: 30 and for the glory of my *m*?"
Mic 5: 4 in the *m* of the name
Zec 6: 13 and he will be clothed with *m*
Ac 19: 27 will be robbed of her divine *m*."
25: 26 to write to His *M* about him.
2Th 1: 9 and from the *m* of his power
Heb 1: 3 hand of the *M* in heaven.
8: 1 of the throne of the *M* in heaven,
2Pe 1: 16 but we were eyewitnesses of his *m*.
Jude : 25 only God our Savior be glory, *m*,

MAKE (MADE MAKER MAKERS MAKES MAKING MAN-MADE)
Ge 1: 26 "Let us *m* man in our image,
2: 18 I will *m* a helper suitable for him."
6: 14 *m* yourself an ark of cypress wood;
12: 2 "I will *m* you into a great nation
Ex 22: 3 thief must certainly *m* restitution,
25: 9 *M* this tabernacle and all its
25: 40 See that you *m* them according
Nu 6: 25 the LORD *m* his face shine
2Sa 7: 9 Now I will *m* your name great,
Job 7: 17 "What is man that you *m* so much
Ps 4: 8 *m* me dwell in safety.
20: 4 and *m* all your plans succeed.
108: 1 *m* music with all my soul.
110: 1 hand until I *m* your enemies
119: 165 and nothing can *m* them stumble.
Pr 3: 6 and he will *m* your paths straight.
4: 26 *M* level paths for your feet
20: 18 *M* plans by seeking advice;
Isa 14: 14 I will *m* myself like the Most High
29: 16 "He did not *m* me"?
55: 3 I will *m* an everlasting covenant
61: 8 and *m* an everlasting covenant
Jer 31: 31 "when I will *m* a new covenant
Eze 37: 26 I will *m* a covenant of peace
Mt 3: 3 *m* straight paths for him.'"
28: 19 and *m* disciples of all nations,
Mk 1: 17 "and I will *m* you fishers of men."
Lk 13: 24 "*M* every effort to enter
14: 23 country lanes and *m* them come in,
Ro 14: 19 *m* every effort to do what leads
2Co 5: 9 So we *m* it our goal to please him,
Eph 4: 3 *M* every effort to keep the unity
Col 4: 5 *m* the most of every opportunity.
1Th 4: 11 *M* it your ambition
Heb 4: 11 *m* every effort to enter that rest,
8: 5 it that you *m* everything according
12: 14 *M* every effort to live in peace
2Pe 1: 5 *m* every effort to add
3: 14 *m* every effort to be found spotless,

MAKER* (MAKE)
Job 4: 17 Can a man be more pure than his *M*
9: 9 He is the *M* of the Bear and Orion,
32: 22 my *M* would soon take me away.
35: 10 no one says, 'Where is God my *M*,
36: 3 I will ascribe justice to my *M*.
40: 19 yet his *M* can approach him
Ps 95: 6 kneel before the LORD our *M*;
115: 15 the *M* of heaven and earth.
121: 2 the *M* of heaven and earth.
124: 8 the *M* of heaven and earth.
134: 3 the *M* of heaven and earth,
146: 6 the *M* of heaven and earth,
149: 2 Let Israel rejoice in their *M*;
Pr 14: 31 poor shows contempt for their *M*,
17: 5 poor shows contempt for their *M*;
22: 2 The LORD is the *M* of them all.
Ecc 11: 5 the *M* of all things.
Isa 17: 7 that day men will look to their *M*
27: 11 so their *M* has no compassion
45: 9 to him who quarrels with his *M*,
45: 11 the Holy One of Israel, and its *M*:
51: 13 that you forget the LORD your *M*,
54: 5 For your *M* is your husband—
Jer 10: 16 for he is the *M* of all things,
51: 19 for he is the *M* of all things,
Hos 8: 14 Israel has forgotten his *M*

MAKERS* (MAKE)
Isa 45: 16 All the *m* of idols will be put

MAKES (MAKE)
Ps 23: 2 *m* me lie down in green pastures,
Pr 13: 12 Hope deferred *m* the heart sick,
1Co 3: 7 but only God, who *m* things grow.

MAKING (MAKE)
Ps 19: 7 *m* wise the simple.
Ecc 12: 12 Of *m* many books there is no end,
Jn 5: 18 *m* himself equal with God.
Eph 5: 16 *m* the most of every opportunity,

MALACHI*
Mal 1: 1 of the LORD to Israel through *M*.

MALE
Ge 1: 27 *m* and female he created them.
Ex 13: 2 to me every firstborn *m*.
Nu 8: 16 the first *m* offspring
Mt 19: 4 the Creator 'made them *m*
Gal 3: 28 slave nor free, *m* nor female,

MALICE (MALICIOUS)
Mk 7: 22 adultery, greed, *m*, deceit,
Ro 1: 29 murder, strife, deceit and *m*.
1Co 5: 8 the yeast of *m* and wickedness,
Eph 4: 31 along with every form of *m*.
Col 3: 8 *m*, slander, and filthy language
1Pe 2: 1 rid yourselves of all *m*

MALICIOUS (MALICE)
Pr 26: 24 A *m* man disguises himself
1Ti 3: 11 not *m* talkers but temperate
6: 4 *m* talk, evil suspicions

MALIGN
Tit 2: 5 so that no one will *m* the word

MAN (MAN'S MANKIND MEN MEN'S WOMAN WOMEN)
Ge 1: 26 "Let us make *m* in our image,
2: 7 God formed the *m* from the dust
2: 8 *m* became a living being
2: 15 God took the *m* and put
2: 18 for the *m* to be alone
2: 20 *m* gave names to all the
2: 23 she was taken out of *m*,
2: 25 *m* and his wife were both
3: 9 God called to the *m*,
3: 22 *m* has now become like
4: 1 I have brought forth a *m*.
6: 3 not contend with *m* forever,
6: 6 grieved that he had made *m*
9: 6 Whoever sheds the blood of *m*,
Dt 8: 3 *m* does not live on bread
1Sa 13: 14 a *m* after his own heart
15: 29 he is not a *m* that he
16: 7 at the things *m* looks at.
Job 14: 1 *M* born of woman is of few
14: 14 If a *m* dies, will he live
Ps 1: 1 Blessed is the *m* who does
8: 4 what is *m* that you are
32: 2 Blessed is the *m* whose sin
40: 4 Blessed is the *m* who makes
84: 12 blessed is the *m* who trusts
103: 15 As for *m*, his days are
112: 1 Blessed is the *m* who fears
119: 9 can a young *m* keep his
127: 5 Blessed is the *m* whose quiver
144: 3 what is *m* that you care
Pr 3: 13 Blessed is the *m* who finds
9: 9 Instruct a wise *m*
14: 12 that seems right to a *m*,
30: 19 way of a *m* with a maiden.

Isa 53: 3 a *m* of sorrows,
Jer 17: 5 the one who trusts in *m*,
17: 7 blessed is the *m* who trusts
Eze 22: 30 I looked for a *m*
Mt 4: 4 *M* does not live on bread
19: 5 a *m* will leave his father
Mk 8: 36 What good is it for a *m*
Lk 4: 4 '*M* does not live on bread
Ro 5: 12 entered the world through one *m*
1Co 2: 15 spiritual *m* makes judgments
3: 12 If any *m* builds on this
7: 1 good for a *m* not to marry.
7: 2 each *m* should have his own
11: 3 head of every *m* is Christ,
11: 3 head of woman is *m*
13: 11 When I became a *m*,
15: 21 death came through a *m*,
15: 45 first *m* Adam became a
15: 47 the second *m* from heaven
2Co 12: 2 I know a *m* in Christ
Eph 2: 15 create in himself one new *m*
5: 31 a *m* will leave his father
Php 2: 8 found in appearance as a *m*,
1Ti 2: 5 the *m* Christ Jesus,
2: 12 have authority over a *m*;
2Ti 3: 17 that the *m* of God may be
Heb 2: 6 what is *m* that you are
9: 27 as *m* is destined to die

MAN'S (MAN)
Pr 20: 24 A *m* steps are directed by
Jer 10: 23 a *m* life is not his own;
1Co 1: 25 is wiser than *m* wisdom,

MAN-MADE (MAKE)
Heb 9: 11 perfect tabernacle that is not *m*,
9: 24 not enter a *m* sanctuary that was

MANAGE (MANAGER)
Jer 12: 5 how will you *m* in the thickets
1Ti 3: 4 He must *m* his own family well
3: 12 one wife and must *m* his children
5: 14 to *m* their homes and to give

MANAGER (MANAGE)
Lk 12: 42 Who then is the faithful and wise *m*
16: 1 a rich man whose *m* was accused

MANASSEH
1. Firstborn of Joseph (Ge 41:51; 46:20). Blessed by Jacob but not firstborn (Ge 48). Tribe of blessed (Dt 33:17), numbered (Nu 1:35; 26:34), half allotted land east of Jordan (Nu 32; Jos 13:8–33), half west (Jos 17; Eze 48:4), failed to fully possess (Jos 17:12–13; Jdg 1:27), 12,000 from (Rev 7:6).
2. Son of Hezekiah; king of Judah (2Ki 21:1–18; 2Ch 33:1–20). Judah exiled for his detestable sins (2Ki 21:10–15). Repentance (2Ch 33:12–19).

MANDRAKES
Ge 30: 14 give me some of your son's *m*."

MANGER
Lk 2: 12 in strips of cloth and lying in a *m*."

MANIFESTATION*
1Co 12: 7 to each one the *m* of the Spirit is

MANKIND (MAN)
Ge 6: 7 I will wipe *m*, whom I have created
Ps 33: 13 and sees all *m*;
Pr 8: 31 and delighting in *m*.
Ecc 7: 29 God made *m* upright,
Isa 40: 5 and all *m* together will see it.
45: 12 and created *m* upon it.
Jer 32: 27 "I am the LORD, the God of all *m*.
Zec 2: 13 Be still before the LORD, all *m*,
Lk 3: 6 And all *m* will see God's salvation

MANNA
Ex 16: 31 people of Israel called the bread *m*.
Dt 8: 16 He gave you *m* to eat in the desert,
Jn 6: 49 Your forefathers ate the *m*
Rev 2: 17 I will give some of the hidden *m*.

MANNER
1Co 11: 27 in an unworthy *m* will be guilty
Php 1: 27 conduct yourselves in a *m* worthy

MANSIONS*
Ps 49: 14 far from their princely *m*.
Isa 5: 9 the fine *m* left without occupants.
Am 3: 15 and the *m* will be demolished,"
5: 11 though you have built stone *m*,

MARCH
Jos 6: 4 *m* around the city seven times,
Isa 42: 13 LORD will *m* out like a mighty

MARITAL* (MARRY)
Ex 21: 10 of her food, clothing and *m* rights.
Mt 5: 32 except for *m* unfaithfulness,
19: 9 except for *m* unfaithfulness,
1Co 7: 3 husband should fulfill his *m* duty

MARK (MARKS)
Cousin of Barnabas (Col 4:10; 2Ti 4:11; Phm 24; 1Pe 5:13), see JOHN.
Ge 4: 15 Then the LORD put a *m* on Cain
Rev 13: 16 to receive a *m* on his right hand

MARKET (MARKETPLACE MARKETPLACES)
Jn 2: 16 turn my Father's house into a *m*!"

MARKETPLACE (MARKET)
Lk 7: 32 are like children sitting in the *m*

MARKETPLACES (MARKET)
Mt 23: 7 they love to be greeted in the *m*

MARKS (MARK)
Jn 20: 25 Unless I see the nail *m* in his hands
Gal 6: 17 bear on my body the *m* of Jesus.

MARRED
Isa 52: 14 his form *m* beyond human likeness

MARRIAGE (MARRY)
Mt 22: 30 neither marry nor be given in *m*;
24: 38 marrying and giving in *m*,
Ro 7: 2 she is released from the law of *m*.
Heb 13: 4 by all, and the *m* bed kept pure,

MARRIED (MARRY)
Dt 24: 5 happiness to the wife he has *m*.
Ezr 10: 10 you have *m* foreign women,
Pr 30: 23 an unloved woman who is *m*,
Mt 1: 18 pledged to be *m* to Joseph,
Mk 12: 23 since the seven were *m* to her?"
Ro 7: 2 by law a *m* woman is bound
1Co 7: 27 Are you *m*? Do not seek a divorce.
7: 33 But a *m* man is concerned about
7: 36 They should get *m*.

MARRIES (MARRY)
Mt 5: 32 anyone who *m* the divorced woman
19: 9 and *m* another woman commits
Lk 16: 18 the man who *m* a divorced woman

MARROW
Heb 4: 12 joints and *m*; it judges the thoughts

MARRY (INTERMARRY MARITAL MARRIAGE MARRIED MARRIES)
Dt 25: 5 brother shall take her and *m* her
Mt 22: 30 resurrection people will neither *m*
1Co 7: 1 It is good for a man not to *m*.
7: 9 control themselves, they should *m*,
7: 28 if you do *m*, you have not sinned;
1Ti 4: 3 They forbid people to *m*
5: 14 So I counsel younger widows to *m*,

MARTHA*
Sister of Mary and Lazarus (Lk 10:38–42; Jn 11; 12:2).

MARVELED* (MARVELOUS)
Lk 2: 33 mother *m* at what was said about
2Th 1: 10 and to be *m* at among all those who

MARVELING* (MARVELOUS)
Lk 9: 43 While everyone was *m*

MARVELOUS* (MARVELED MARVELING)
1Ch 16: 24 his *m* deeds among all peoples.
Job 37: 5 God's voice thunders in *m* ways;
Ps 71: 17 to this day I declare your *m* deeds.
72: 18 who alone does *m* deeds.
86: 10 For you are great and do *m* deeds;
96: 3 his *m* deeds among all peoples.
98: 1 for he has done *m* things;
118: 23 and it is *m* in our eyes.
Isa 25: 1 you have done *m* things,
Zec 8: 6 but will it seem *m* to me?"
8: 6 "It may seem *m* to the remnant
Mt 21: 42 and it is *m* in our eyes'?
Mk 12: 11 and it is *m* in our eyes'?"
Rev 15: 1 in heaven another great and *m* sign
15: 3 "Great and *m* are your deeds,

MARY
1. Mother of Jesus (Mt 1:16–25; Lk 1:27–56; 2:1–40). With Jesus at temple (Lk 2:41–52), at the wedding in Cana (Jn 2:1–5), questioning his sanity (Mk 3:21), at the cross (Jn 19:25–27). Among disciples after Ascension (Ac 1:14).
2. Magdalene; former demoniac (Lk 8:2). Helped support Jesus' ministry (Lk 8:1–3). At the cross (Mt 27:56; Mk 15:40; Jn 19:25), burial (Mt 27:61; Mk 15:47). Saw angel after resurrection (Mt 28:1–10; Mk 16:1–9; Lk 24:1–12); also Jesus (Jn 20:1–18).
3. Sister of Martha and Lazarus (Jn 11). Washed Jesus' feet (Jn 12:1–8).

MASQUERADES*
2Co 11: 14 for Satan himself *m* as an angel

MASTER (MASTER'S MASTERED MASTERS MASTERY)
Ge 4: 7 to have you, but you must *m* it."
Hos 2: 16 you will no longer call me 'my *m*.'
Mal 1: 6 If I am a *m*, where is the respect
Mt 10: 24 nor a servant above his *m*.
23: 8 for you have only one *M*
24: 46 that servant whose *m* finds him
25: 21 "His *m* replied, 'Well done,
25: 23 "His *m* replied, 'Well done,
Ro 6: 14 For sin shall not be your *m*,
14: 4 To his own *m* he stands or falls.
Col 4: 1 you know that you also have a *M*
2Ti 2: 21 useful to the *M* and prepared

MASTER'S (MASTER)
Mt 25: 21 Come and share your *m* happiness

MASTERED* (MASTER)
1Co 6: 12 but I will not be *m* by anything.
2Pe 2: 19 a slave to whatever has *m* him.

MASTERS (MASTER)
Pr 25: 13 he refreshes the spirit of his *m*.
Mt 6: 24 "No one can serve two *m*.
Lk 16: 13 "No servant can serve two *m*.
Eph 6: 5 obey your earthly *m* with respect
6: 9 And *m*, treat your slaves
Col 3: 22 obey your earthly *m* in everything;
4: 1 *M*, provide your slaves
1Ti 6: 1 should consider their *m* worthy
6: 2 who have believing *m* are not
Tit 2: 9 subject to their *m* in everything,
1Pe 2: 18 to your *m* with all respect,

MASTERY* (MASTER)
Ro 6: 9 death no longer has *m* over him.

MAT
Mk 2: 9 'Get up, take your *m* and walk'?
Ac 9: 34 Get up and take care of your *m*."

MATCHED*
2Co 8: 11 do it may be *m* by your completion

MATTHEW*
Apostle; former tax collector (Mt 9:9–13; 10:3; Mk 3:18; Lk 6:15; Ac 1:13). Also called Levi (Mk 2:14–17; Lk 5:27–32).

MATTHIAS
Ac 1: 26 the lot fell to *M*; so he was added

MATURE* (MATURITY)
Lk 8: 14 and pleasures, and they do not *m*.
1Co 2: 6 a message of wisdom among the *m*,
Eph 4: 13 of the Son of God and become *m*,
Php 3: 15 of us who are *m* should take such
Col 4: 12 firm in all the will of God, *m*
Heb 5: 14 But solid food is for the *m*,
Jas 1: 4 work so that you may be *m*

MATURITY* (MATURE)
Heb 6: 1 about Christ and go on to *m*,

MEAL
Pr 15: 17 Better a *m* of vegetables where
1Co 10: 27 some unbeliever invites you to a *m*
Heb 12: 16 for a single *m* sold his inheritance

MEANING
Ne 8: 8 and giving the *m* so that the people

MEANINGLESS
Ecc 1: 2 "*M*! *M*!" says the Teacher.
1Ti 1: 6 from these and turned to *m* talk.

MEANS
1Co 9: 22 by all possible *m* I might save some

MEASURE (MEASURED MEASURES)
Ps 71: 15 though I know not its *m*.
Eze 45: 3 In the sacred district, *m*
Zec 2: 2 He answered me, "To *m* Jerusalem
Lk 6: 38 A good *m*, pressed
Eph 3: 19 to the *m* of all the fullness of God.
4: 13 to the whole *m* of the fullness
Rev 11: 1 "Go and *m* the temple of God

MEASURED (MEASURE)
Isa 40: 12 Who has *m* the waters
Jer 31: 37 if the heavens above can be *m*

MEASURES (MEASURE)
Dt 25: 14 Do not have two differing *m*
Pr 20: 10 Differing weights and differing *m*

MEAT
Pr 23: 20 or gorge themselves on *m*,
Ro 14: 6 He who eats *m*, eats to the Lord,
14: 21 It is better not to eat *m*
1Co 8: 13 I will never eat *m* again,
10: 25 *m* market without raising questions

MEDDLER* (MEDDLES)
1Pe 4: 15 kind of criminal, or even as a *m*.

MEDDLES* (MEDDLER)
Pr 26: 17 is a passer-by who *m*

MEDIATOR
1Ti 2: 5 and one *m* between God and men,
Heb 8: 6 of which he is *m* is superior
9: 15 For this reason Christ is the *m*
12: 24 to Jesus the *m* of a new covenant,

MEDICINE*
Pr 17: 22 A cheerful heart is good *m*,

MEDITATE* (MEDITATED MEDITATES MEDITATION)
Ge 24: 63 out to the field one evening to *m*,
Jos 1: 8 from your mouth; *m* on it day
Ps 48: 9 we *m* on your unfailing love.
77: 12 I will *m* on all your works
119: 15 I *m* on your precepts
119: 23 your servant will *m*
119: 27 then I will *m* on your wonders.
119: 48 and I *m* on your decrees.
119: 78 but I will *m* on your precepts.
119: 97 I *m* on it all day long.
119: 99 for I *m* on your statutes.
119: 148 that I may *m* on your promises.
143: 5 I *m* on all your works
145: 5 I will *m* on your wonderful works.

MEDITATED* (MEDITATE)
Ps 39: 3 and as I *m*, the fire burned;

MEDITATES* (MEDITATE)
Ps 1: 2 and on his law he *m* day and night.

MEDITATION* (MEDITATE)
Ps 19: 14 of my mouth and the *m* of my heart
104: 34 May my *m* be pleasing to him,

MEDIUM
Lev 20: 27 "'A man or woman who is a *m*

MEEK* (MEEKNESS)
Ps 37: 11 But the *m* will inherit the land
Zep 3: 12 the *m* and humble,
Mt 5: 5 Blessed are the *m*,

MEEKNESS* (MEEK)
2Co 10: 1 By the *m* and gentleness of Christ,

MEET (MEETING MEETINGS MEETS)
Ps 42: 2 When can I go and *m* with God?
85: 10 Love and faithfulness *m* together;
Am 4: 12 prepare to *m* your God, O Israel."
1Co 11: 34 when you *m* together it may not
1Th 4: 17 them in the clouds to *m* the Lord

MEETING (MEET)
Ex 40: 34 the cloud covered the Tent of *M*,
Heb 10: 25 Let us not give up *m* together,

MEETINGS* (MEET)
1Co 11: 17 for your *m* do more harm

MEETS (MEET)
Heb 7: 26 Such a high priest *m* our need—

MELCHIZEDEK
Ge 14: 18 *M* king of Salem brought out bread
Ps 110: 4 in the order of *M*."
Heb 7: 11 in the order of *M*, not in the order

MELT (MELTS)
2Pe 3: 12 and the elements will *m* in the heat.

MELTS (MELT)
Am 9: 5 he who touches the earth and it *m*,

MEMBER (MEMBERS)
Ro 12: 5 each *m* belongs to all the others.

MEMBERS (MEMBER)
Mic 7: 6 a man's enemies are the *m*
Mt 10: 36 a man's enemies will be the *m*
Ro 7: 23 law at work in the *m* of my body,
12: 4 of us has one body with many *m*,
1Co 6: 15 not know that your bodies are *m*
12: 24 But God has combined the *m*
Eph 3: 6 *m* together of one body,
4: 25 for we are all *m* of one body.
5: 30 for we are *m* of his body.
Col 3: 15 as *m* of one body you were called

MEMORABLE* (MEMORY)
Eze 39: 13 day I am glorified will be a *m* day

MEMORIES* (MEMORY)
1Th 3: 6 us that you always have pleasant *m*

MEMORY (MEMORABLE MEMORIES)
Pr 10: 7 *m* of the righteous will be
Mt 26: 13 she has done will also be told, in *m*

MEN (MAN)
Ge 6: 2 daughter of *m* were beautiful,
6: 4 heroes of old, *m* of renown
Ps 9: 20 nations know they are but *m*.
11: 4 He observes the sons of *m*;
Mt 4: 19 will make you fishers of *m*
5: 16 your light shine before *m*
6: 14 if you forgive *m* when
10: 32 acknowledges me before *m*
12: 31 blasphemy will be forgiven *m*,
12: 36 *m* will have to give account
23: 5 is done for *m* to see:
Mk 7: 7 are but rules taught by *m*.
Lk 6: 22 Blessed are you when *m*
6: 26 Woe to you when all *m*
Jn 1: 4 life was the light of *m*.
2: 24 for he knew all *m*.
3: 19 *m* loved darkness instead
12: 32 will draw all *m* to myself
13: 35 all *m* will know that you
Ac 5: 29 obey God rather than *m*!
Ro 1: 18 wickedness of *m*
1: 27 indecent acts with other *m*,
5: 12 death came to all *m*,
1Co 2: 11 among *m* knows the thoughts
3: 3 acting like mere *m*?
3: 21 no more boasting about *m*!
9: 22 all things to all *m*
13: 1 tongues of *m* and of angels
16: 13 be *m* of courage;
16: 18 Such *m* deserve recognition.
2Co 5: 11 we try to persuade *m*.
8: 21 but also in the eyes of *m*.
Gal 1: 1 sent not from *m* nor
1: 10 to win approval of *m*, or
Eph 4: 8 and gave gifts to *m*.
1Th 2: 4 as *m* approved by God
2: 13 not as the word of *m*,
1Ti 2: 4 wants all *m* to be saved
2: 6 as a ransom for all *m*—
4: 10 the Savior of all *m*
5: 2 younger *m* as brothers
2Ti 2: 2 entrust to reliable *m*
Tit 2: 11 has appeared to all *m*.
Heb 5: 1 is selected from among *m*
7: 28 high priests *m* who are weak;
2Pe 1: 21 but *m* spoke from God
Rev 21: 3 dwelling of God is with *m*,

MEN'S (MAN)
2Ki 19: 18 fashioned by *m* hands.
2Ch 32: 19 the work of *m* hands.
1Co 2: 5 not rest on *m* wisdom,

MENAHEM*
King of Israel (2Ki 15:17–22).

MENE
Da 5: 25 that was written: *M, M*,

MEPHIBOSHETH
Son of Jonathan shown kindness by David (2Sa 4:4; 9; 21:7). Accused of siding with Absalom (2Sa 16:1–4; 19:24–30).

MERCHANT
Pr 31: 14 She is like the *m* ships,
Mt 13: 45 of heaven is like a *m* looking

MERCIFUL (MERCY)
Dt 4: 31 the LORD your God is a *m* God;
Ne 9: 31 for you are a gracious and *m* God.
Ps 77: 9 Has God forgotten to be *m*?
78: 38 Yet he was *m*;
Jer 3: 12 for I am *m*,' declares the LORD,
Da 9: 9 The Lord our God is *m*
Mt 5: 7 Blessed are the *m*,
Lk 1: 54 remembering to be *m*
6: 36 Be *m*, just as your Father is *m*.
Heb 2: 17 in order that he might become a *m*
Jas 2: 13 to anyone who has not been *m*.
Jude : 22 Be *m* to those who doubt; snatch

MERCY (MERCIFUL)
Ex 33: 19 *m* on whom I will have *m*,
2Sa 24: 14 of the LORD, for his *m* is great;
1Ch 21: 13 for his *m* is very great;
Ne 9: 31 But in your great *m* you did not put
Ps 25: 6 O LORD, your great *m* and love,
28: 6 for he has heard my cry for *m*.
57: 1 Have *m* on me, O God, have *m*
Pr 28: 13 renounces them finds *m*.
Isa 63: 9 and *m* he redeemed them;
Da 9: 18 but because of your great *m*.
Hos 6: 6 For I desire *m*, not sacrifice,
Am 5: 15 LORD God Almighty will have *m*
Mic 6: 8 To act justly and to love *m*
7: 18 but delight to show *m*.
Hab 3: 2 in wrath remember *m*.
Zec 7: 9 show *m* and compassion
Mt 5: 7 for they will be shown *m*.
9: 13 learn what this means: 'I desire *m*,
12: 7 'I desire *m*, not sacrifice,' you
18: 33 Shouldn't you have had *m*
23: 23 justice, *m* and faithfulness.
Lk 1: 50 His *m* extends to those who fear
Ro 9: 15 "I will have *m* on whom I have *m*,
9: 18 Therefore God has *m*
11: 32 so that he may have *m* on them all.
12: 1 brothers, in view of God's *m*,
12: 8 if it is showing *m*, let him do it
Eph 2: 4 who is rich in *m*, made us alive
1Ti 1: 13 I was shown *m* because I acted
1: 16 for that very reason I was shown *m*
Tit 3: 5 we had done, but because of his *m*.
Heb 4: 16 so that we may receive *m*
Jas 2: 13 judgment without *m* will be shown
2: 13 *M* triumphs over judgment!
3: 17 submissive, full of *m* and good fruit
5: 11 full of compassion and *m*.
1Pe 1: 3 In his great *m* he has given us new
2: 10 once you had not received *m*,
Jude : 23 to others show *m*, mixed with fear

MERRY
Lk 12: 19 Take life easy; eat, drink and be *m*

MESHACH
Hebrew exiled to Babylon; name changed from Mishael (Da 1:6–7). Refused defilement by food (Da 1:8–20). Refused to worship idol (Da 3:1–18); saved from furnace (Da 3:19–30).

MESSAGE (MESSENGER)
Isa 53: 1 Who has believed our *m*
Jn 12: 38 "Lord, who has believed our *m*
Ac 5: 20 "and tell the people the full *m*
10: 36 You know the *m* God sent
17: 11 for they received the *m*
Ro 10: 16 who has believed our *m*?"
10: 17 faith comes from hearing the *m*,
1Co 1: 18 For the *m* of the cross is
2: 4 My *m* and my preaching were not
2Co 5: 19 to us the *m* of reconciliation.
2Th 3: 1 pray for us that the *m*
Tit 1: 9 firmly to the trustworthy *m*
Heb 4: 2 the *m* they heard was of no value
1Pe 2: 8 because they disobey the *m*—

MESSENGER (MESSAGE)
Pr 25: 13 is a trustworthy *m*
Mal 3: 1 I will send my *m*, who will prepare
Mt 11: 10 "'I will send my *m* ahead of you,
2Co 12: 7 a *m* of Satan, to torment me.

MESSIAH*
Jn 1: 41 "We have found the *M*" (that is,
4: 25 "I know that *M*" (called Christ) "is

METHUSELAH
Ge 5: 27 Altogether, *M* lived 969 years,

MICAH
1. Idolater from Ephraim (Jdg 17–18).
2. Prophet from Moresheth (Jer 26:18–19; Mic 1:1).

MICAIAH
Prophet of the LORD who spoke against Ahab (1Ki 22:1–28; 2Ch 18:1–27).

MICHAEL
Archangel (Jude 9); warrior in angelic realm, protector of Israel (Da 10:13, 21; 12:1; Rev 12:7).

MICHAL
Daughter of Saul, wife of David (1Sa 14:49; 18:20–28). Warned David of Saul's plot (1Sa 19). Saul gave her to Paltiel (1Sa 25:44); David retrieved her (2Sa 3:13–16). Criticized David for dancing before the ark (2Sa 6:16–23); 1Ch 15:29).

MIDIAN
Ex 2: 15 Pharaoh and went to live in *M*,
Jdg 7: 2 me to deliver *M* into their hands.

MIDWIVES
Ex 1: 17 The *m*, however, feared God

MIGHT (ALMIGHTY MIGHTIER MIGHTY)
Jdg 16: 30 Then he pushed with all his *m*,
2Sa 6: 5 with all their *m* before the LORD,
6: 14 before the LORD with all his *m*,
2Ch 20: 6 Power and *m* are in your hand,
Ps 21: 13 we will sing and praise your *m*.
54: 1 vindicate me by your *m*.
Isa 63: 15 Where are your zeal and your *m*?
Mic 3: 8 and with justice and *m*,
Zec 4: 6 'Not by *m* nor by power,'
Col 1: 11 power according to his glorious *m*
1Ti 6: 16 To him be honor and *m* forever.

MIGHTIER (MIGHT)
Ps 93: 4 *M* than the thunder

MIGHTY (MIGHT)
Ge 49: 24 of the hand of the *M* One of Jacob,
Ex 6: 1 of my *m* hand he will drive them
13: 3 out of it with a *m* hand.
Dt 5: 15 out of there with a *m* hand
7: 8 he brought you out with a *m* hand
10: 17 the great God, *m* and awesome,
34: 12 one has ever shown the *m* power
2Sa 1: 19 How the *m* have fallen!
23: 8 the names of David's *m* men:
Ne 9: 32 the great, *m* and awesome God,
Job 36: 5 God is *m*, but does not despise men
Ps 24: 8 The LORD strong and *m*,
45: 3 upon your side, O *m* one;
50: 1 The *M* One, God, the LORD,
62: 7 he is my *m* rock, my refuge.
68: 33 who thunders with *m* voice.
71: 16 proclaim your *m* acts,
77: 12 and consider all your *m* deeds.
77: 15 With your *m* arm you redeemed
89: 8 You are *m*, O LORD,
93: 4 the LORD on high is *m*.
99: 4 The King is *m*, he loves justice—
110: 2 LORD will extend your *m* scepter
118: 15 right hand has done *m* things!
136: 12 with a *m* hand and outstretched
145: 4 they will tell of your *m* acts.
145: 12 all men may know of your *m* acts
147: 5 Great is our Lord and *m* in power;
SS 8: 6 like a *m* flame.
Isa 9: 6 Wonderful Counselor, *M* God,
60: 16 your Redeemer, the *M* One
63: 1 *m* to save."
Jer 10: 6 and your name is *m* in power.
20: 11 with me like a *m* warrior;
32: 19 your purposes and *m* are your
Eze 20: 33 I will rule over you with a *m* hand
Zep 3: 17 he is *m* to save.
Mt 26: 64 at the right hand of the *M* One
Eph 1: 19 like the working of his *m* strength,
6: 10 in the Lord and in his *m* power.
1Pe 5: 6 therefore, under God's *m* hand,

MILE*
Mt 5: 41 If someone forces you to go one *m*,

MILK
Ex 3: 8 a land flowing with *m* and honey—
23: 19 a young goat in its mother's *m*.
Pr 30: 33 as churning the *m* produces butter,
Isa 55: 1 Come, buy wine and *m*
1Co 3: 2 I gave you *m*, not solid food,
Heb 5: 12 You need *m*, not solid food!
1Pe 2: 2 babies, crave pure spiritual *m*,

MILLSTONE (STONE)
Lk 17: 2 sea with a *m* tied around his neck

MIND (DOUBLE-MINDED LIKE-MINDED MINDED MINDFUL MINDS)
Nu 23: 19 that he should change his *m*.
Dt 28: 65 LORD will give you an anxious *m*,
1Sa 15: 29 Israel does not lie or change his *m*;
1Ch 28: 9 devotion and with a willing *m*,
2Ch 30: 12 the people to give them unity of *m*
Ps 26: 2 examine my heart and my *m*;
110: 4 and will not change his *m*:
Isa 26: 3 him whose *m* is steadfast,
Jer 17: 10 and examine the *m*,
Mt 22: 37 all your soul and with all your *m*.'
Mk 12: 30 with all your *m* and with all your
Lk 10: 27 your strength and with all your *m*';
Ac 4: 32 believers were one in heart and *m*.
Ro 1: 28 he gave them over to a depraved *m*
7: 25 I myself in my *m* am a slave
8: 6 The *m* of sinful man is death,
8: 7 the sinful *m* is hostile to God.
12: 2 by the renewing of your *m*.
14: 13 make up your *m* not
1Co 1: 10 you may be perfectly united in *m*
2: 9 no *m* has conceived
14: 14 spirit prays, but my *m* is unfruitful.
2Co 13: 11 be of one *m*, live in peace.
Php 3: 19 Their *m* is on earthly things.
Col 2: 18 and his unspiritual *m* puffs him up
1Th 4: 11 to *m* your own business
Heb 7: 21 and will not change his *m*:

MINDED* (MIND)
1Pe 4: 7 be clear *m* and self-controlled

MINDFUL* (MIND)
Ps 8: 4 what is man that you are *m* of him,
Lk 1: 48 God my Savior, for he has been *m*
Heb 2: 6 What is man that you are *m* of him,

MINDS (MIND)
Dt 11: 18 of mine in your hearts and *m*;
Ps 7: 9 who searches *m* and hearts,
Jer 31: 33 "I will put my law in their *m*
Lk 24: 38 and why do doubts rise in your *m*?
24: 45 Then he opened their *m*
Ro 8: 5 to the sinful nature have their *m* set
2Co 4: 4 god of this age has blinded the *m*
Eph 4: 23 new in the attitude of your *m*;
Col 3: 2 Set your *m* on things above,
Heb 8: 10 I will put my laws in their *m*
10: 16 and I will write them on their *m*."
1Pe 1: 13 prepare your *m* for action;
Rev 2: 23 I am he who searches hearts and *m*,

MINISTER (MINISTERING MINISTERS MINISTRY)
Ps 101: 6 will *m* to me.
1Ti 4: 6 you will be a good *m*

MINISTERING (MINISTER)
Heb 1: 14 Are not all angels *m* spirits sent

MINISTERS (MINISTER)
2Co 3: 6 as *m* of a new covenant—

MINISTRY (MINISTER)
Ac 6: 4 to prayer and the *m* of the word."
Ro 11: 13 I make much of my *m*
2Co 4: 1 God's mercy we have this *m*,
5: 18 gave us the *m* of reconciliation:
6: 3 so that our *m* will not be
Gal 2: 8 who was at work in the *m* of Peter
2Ti 4: 5 discharge all the duties of your *m*.
Heb 8: 6 But the *m* Jesus has received is

MIRACLE* (MIRACLES MIRACULOUS)
Ex 7: 9 'Perform a *m*,' then say to Aaron,
Mk 9: 39 "No one who does a *m*
Lk 23: 8 hoped to see him perform some *m*.
Jn 7: 21 "I did one *m*, and you are all
Ac 4: 16 they have done an outstanding *m*,

MIRACLES* (MIRACLE)
1Ch 16: 12 his *m*, and the judgments he
Ne 9: 17 to remember the *m* you performed
Job 5: 9 *m* that cannot be counted.
9: 10 *m* that cannot be counted.
Ps 77: 11 I will remember your *m* of long ago
77: 14 You are the God who performs *m*;
78: 12 He did *m* in the sight
105: 5 his *m*, and the judgments he
106: 7 they gave no thought to your *m*;
106: 22 *m* in the land of Ham
Mt 7: 22 out demons and perform many *m*?'
11: 20 most of his *m* had been performed,
11: 21 If the *m* that were performed
11: 23 If the *m* that were performed
13: 58 And he did not do many *m* there
24: 24 and perform great signs and *m*
Mk 6: 2 does *m*! Isn't this the carpenter?
6: 5 He could not do any *m* there,
13: 22 and *m* to deceive the elect—
Lk 10: 13 For if the *m* that were performed
19: 37 for all the *m* they had seen:
Jn 7: 3 disciples may see the *m* you do.
10: 25 *m* I do in my Father's name speak
10: 32 "I have shown you many great *m*
10: 38 do not believe me, believe the *m*,
14: 11 the evidence of the *m* themselves.
15: 24 But now they have seen these *m*,
Ac 2: 22 accredited by God to you by *m*,
8: 13 by the great signs and *m* he saw.
19: 11 God did extraordinary *m*
Ro 15: 19 by the power of signs and *m*,
1Co 12: 28 third teachers, then workers of *m*,
12: 29 Are all teachers? Do all work *m*?
2Co 12: 12 and *m*— were done among you
Gal 3: 5 work *m* among you because you
2Th 2: 9 in all kinds of counterfeit *m*,
Heb 2: 4 it by signs, wonders and various *m*,

MIRACULOUS (MIRACLE)
Dt 13: 1 and announces to you a *m* sign
Mt 12: 39 generation asks for a *m* sign!
13: 54 this wisdom and these *m* powers?"
Jn 2: 11 This, the first of his *m* signs,
2: 23 people saw the *m* signs he was
3: 2 could perform the *m* signs you are
4: 48 "Unless you people see *m* signs
7: 31 will he do more *m* signs
9: 16 "How can a sinner do such *m* signs
12: 37 Jesus had done all these *m* signs
20: 30 Jesus did many other *m* signs
Ac 2: 43 *m* signs were done by the apostles.
5: 12 apostles performed many *m* signs
1Co 1: 22 Jews demand *m* signs and Greeks
12: 10 to another *m* powers,

MIRE
Ps 40: 2 out of the mud and *m*;
Isa 57: 20 whose waves cast up *m* and mud.

MIRIAM
Sister of Moses and Aaron (Nu 26:59). Led dancing at Red Sea (Ex 15:20–21). Struck with leprosy for criticizing Moses (Nu 12). Death (Nu 20:1).

MIRROR
1Co 13: 12 but a poor reflection as in a *m*;
Jas 1: 23 a man who looks at his face in a *m*

MISDEEDS*
Ps 99: 8 though you punished their *m*.
Ro 8: 13 put to death the *m* of the body,

MISERY
Ex 3: 7 "I have indeed seen the *m*
Jdg 10: 16 he could bear Israel's *m* no longer.
Hos 5: 15 in their *m* they will earnestly seek
Ro 3: 16 ruin and *m* mark their ways,
Jas 5: 1 of the *m* that is coming upon you.

MISFORTUNE
Ob : 12 brother in the day of his *m*,

MISLEAD (MISLED)
Isa 47: 10 wisdom and knowledge *m* you

MISLED (MISLEAD)
1Co 15: 33 Do not be *m*: "Bad company

MISS (MISSES)
Pr 19: 2 nor to be hasty and *m* the way.

MISSES (MISS)
Heb 12: 15 See to it that no one *m* the grace

MIST
Hos 6: 4 Your love is like the morning *m*,
Jas 4: 14 You are a *m* that appears for a little

MISTREAT (MISTREATED)
Ex 22: 21 "Do not *m* an alien or oppress him,
Eze 22: 29 and needy and *m* the alien,
Lk 6: 28 pray for those who *m* you.

MISTREATED (MISTREAT)
Eze 22: 7 *m* the fatherless and the widow.
Heb 11: 25 to be *m* along with the people
11: 37 destitute, persecuted and *m*—
13: 3 who are *m* as if you yourselves

MISUSE* (MISUSES)
Ex 20: 7 "You shall not *m* the name
Dt 5: 11 "You shall not *m* the name
Ps 139: 20 your adversaries *m* your name.

MISUSES* (MISUSE)
Ex 20: 7 anyone guiltless who *m* his name.
Dt 5: 11 anyone guiltless who *m* his name.

MIXED (MIXING)
Da 2: 41 even as you saw iron *m* with clay.

MIXING (MIXED)
Isa 5: 22 and champions at *m* drinks,

MOAB (MOABITESS)
Ge 19: 37 she named him *M*; he is the father
Dt 34: 6 He buried him in *M*, in the valley
Ru 1: 1 live for a while in the country of *M*.
Isa 15: 1 An oracle concerning *M*:
Jer 48: 16 "The fall of *M* is at hand;
Am 2: 1 "For three sins of *M*,

MOABITESS (MOAB)
Ru 1: 22 accompanied by Ruth the *M*,

MOAN
Ps 90: 9 we finish our years with a *m*.

MOCK (MOCKED MOCKER MOCKERS MOCKING MOCKS)
Ps 22: 7 All who see me *m* me;
119: 51 The arrogant *m* me
Pr 1: 26 I will *m* when calamity overtakes
14: 9 Fools *m* at making amends for sin,
Mk 10: 34 who will *m* him and spit on him,

MOCKED (MOCK)
Ps 89: 51 with which they have *m* every step
Mt 27: 29 knelt in front of him and *m* him.
27: 41 of the law and the elders *m* him.
Gal 6: 7 not be deceived: God cannot be *m*.

MOCKER (MOCK)
Pr 9: 7 corrects a *m* invites insult;
9: 12 if you are a *m*, you alone will suffer
20: 1 Wine is a *m* and beer a brawler;
22: 10 Drive out the *m*, and out goes strife

MOCKERS (MOCK)
Ps 1: 1 or sit in the seat of *m.*
Pr 29: 8 *M* stir up a city,

MOCKING (MOCK)
Isa 50: 6 face from *m* and spitting.

MOCKS (MOCK)
Pr 17: 5 He who *m* the poor shows
30: 17 "The eye that *m* a father,

MODEL*
Eze 28: 12 "'You were the *m* of perfection,
1Th 1: 7 And so you became a *m*
2Th 3: 9 to make ourselves a *m* for you

MODESTY*
1Co 12: 23 are treated with special *m,*

MOLDED*
Job 10: 9 Remember that you *m* me like clay

MOLDY
Jos 9: 5 of their food supply was dry and *m.*

MOLECH
Lev 20: 2 of his children to *M* must be put
1Ki 11: 33 and *M* the god of the Ammonites,

MOMENT (MOMENTARY)
Job 20: 5 the joy of the godless lasts but a *m.*
Ps 2: 12 for his wrath can flare up in a *m.*
30: 5 For his anger lasts only a *m,*
Pr 12: 19 but a lying tongue lasts only a *m.*
Isa 54: 7 "For a brief *m* I abandoned you,
66: 8 or a nation be brought forth in a *m?*
Gal 2: 5 We did not give in to them for a *m,*

MOMENTARY* (MOMENT)
2Co 4: 17 and *m* troubles are achieving

MONEY
Pr 13: 11 Dishonest *m* dwindles away,
Ecc 5: 10 Whoever loves *m* never has *m*
Isa 55: 1 and you who have no *m,*
Mt 6: 24 You cannot serve both God and *M.*
27: 5 Judas threw the *m* into the temple
Lk 3: 14 "Don't extort *m* and don't accuse
9: 3 no bread, no *m,* no extra tunic.
16: 13 You cannot serve both God and *M*
Ac 5: 2 part of the *m* for himself,
1Co 16: 2 set aside a sum of *m* in keeping
1Ti 3: 3 not quarrelsome, not a lover of *m.*
6: 10 For the love of *m* is a root
2Ti 3: 2 lovers of *m,* boastful, proud,
Heb 13: 5 free from the love of *m*
1Pe 5: 2 not greedy for *m,* but eager to serve

MONEYLENDER* (LEND)
Ex 22: 25 not be like a *m;* charge him no
Lk 7: 41 men owed money to a certain *m.*

MONTH (MONTHS)
Ex 12: 2 "This *m* is to be for you the first
Eze 47: 12 Every *m* they will bear,
Rev 22: 2 of fruit, yielding its fruit every *m.*

MONTHS (MONTH)
Gal 4: 10 and *m* and seasons and years!
Rev 11: 2 trample on the holy city for 42 *m.*
13: 5 his authority for forty-two *m.*

MOON
Jos 10: 13 and the *m* stopped,
Ps 8: 3 the *m* and the stars,
74: 16 you established the sun and *m.*
89: 37 be established forever like the *m,*
104: 19 The *m* marks off the seasons,
121: 6 nor the *m* by night.
136: 9 the *m* and stars to govern the night;
148: 3 Praise him, sun and *m,*
SS 6: 10 fair as the *m,* bright as the sun,
Joel 2: 31 and the *m* to blood
Hab 3: 11 and *m* stood still in the heavens
Mt 24: 29 and the *m* will not give its light;
Ac 2: 20 and the *m* to blood
1Co 15: 41 *m* another and the stars another;
Col 2: 16 a New *M* celebration or a Sabbath
Rev 6: 12 the whole *m* turned blood red,
21: 23 city does not need the sun or the *m*

MORAL*
Jas 1: 21 rid of all *m* filth and the evil that is

MORDECAI
Benjamite exile who raised Esther (Est 2:5 – 15). Exposed plot to kill Xerxes (Est 2:19 – 23). Refused to honor Haman (Est 3:1 – 6; 5:9 – 14). Charged Esther to foil Haman's plot against the Jews (Est 4). Xerxes forced Haman to honor Mordecai (Est 6). Mordecai exalted (Est 8 – 10). Established Purim (Est 9:18 – 32).

MORIAH*
Ge 22: 2 and go to the region of *M.*
2Ch 3: 1 LORD in Jerusalem on Mount *M,*

MORNING
Ge 1: 5 and there was *m* — the first day.
Dt 28: 67 In the *m* you will say, "If only it
2Sa 23: 4 he is like the light of *m* at sunrise
Ps 5: 3 In the *m,* O LORD,
Pr 27: 14 blesses his neighbor early in the *m,*
Isa 14: 12 O *m* star, son of the dawn!
La 3: 23 They are new every *m;*
2Pe 1: 19 and the *m* star rises in your hearts.
Rev 2: 28 I will also give him the *m* star.
22: 16 of David, and the bright *M* Star."

MORTAL
Ge 6: 3 for he is *m;* his days will be
Job 10: 4 Do you see as a *m* sees?
Ro 8: 11 also give life to your *m* bodies
1Co 15: 53 and the *m* with immortality.
2Co 5: 4 that what is *m* may be swallowed

MOSES
Levite; brother of Aaron (Ex 6:20; 1Ch 6:3). Put in basket into Nile; discovered and raised by Pharaoh's daughter (Ex 2:1 – 10). Fled to Midian after killing Egyptian (Ex 2:11 – 15). Married to Zipporah, fathered Gershom (Ex 2:16 – 22).

Called by the LORD to deliver Israel (Ex 3 – 4). Pharaoh's resistance (Ex 5). Ten plagues (Ex 7 – 11). Passover and Exodus (Ex 12 – 13). Led Israel through Red Sea (Ex 14). Song of deliverance (Ex 15:1 – 21). Brought water from rock (Ex 17:1 – 7). Raised hands to defeat Amalekites (Ex 17:8 – 16). Delegated judges (Ex 18; Dt 1:9 – 18).

Received Law at Sinai (Ex 19 – 23; 25 – 31; Jn 1:17). Announced Law to Israel (Ex 19:7 – 8; 24; 35). Broke tablets because of golden calf (Ex 32; Dt 9). Saw glory of the LORD (Ex 33 – 34). Supervised building of tabernacle (Ex 36 – 40). Set apart Aaron and priests (Lev 8 – 9). Numbered tribes (Nu 1 – 4; 26). Opposed by Aaron and Miriam (Nu 12). Sent spies into Canaan (Nu 13). Announced forty years of wandering for failure to enter land (Nu 14). Opposed by Korah (Nu 16). Forbidden to enter land for striking rock (Nu 20:1 – 13; Dt 1:37). Lifted bronze snake for healing (Nu 21:4 – 9; Jn 3:14). Final address to Israel (Dt 1 – 33). Succeeded by Joshua (Nu 27:12 – 23; Dt 34). Death (Dt 34:5 – 12).

"Law of Moses" (1Ki 2:3; Ezr 3:2; Mk 12:26; Lk 24:44). "Book of Moses" (2Ch 25:12; Ne 13:1). "Song of Moses" (Ex 15:1 – 21; Rev 15:3). "Prayer of Moses" (Ps 90).

MOTH
Mt 6: 19 where *m* and rust destroy,

MOTHER (GRANDMOTHER MOTHER-IN-LAW MOTHER'S)
Ge 2: 24 and *m* and be united to his wife,
3: 20 because she would become the *m*
Ex 20: 12 "Honor your father and your *m,*
Lev 20: 9 "'If anyone curses his father or *m,*
Dt 5: 16 "Honor your father and your *m,*
21: 18 who does not obey his father and *m*
27: 16 who dishonors his father or his *m."*
Jdg 5: 7 arose a *m* in Israel.
1Sa 2: 19 Each year his *m* made him a little
Ps 113: 9 as a happy *m* of children.
Pr 10: 1 but a foolish son grief to his *m.*
23: 22 do not despise your *m*
23: 25 May your father and *m* be glad;
29: 15 a child left to himself disgraces his *m.*
30: 17 that scorns obedience to a *m,*
31: 1 an oracle his *m* taught him:
Isa 49: 15 "Can a *m* forget the baby
66: 13 As a *m* comforts her child,
Jer 20: 17 with my *m* as my grave,
Mic 7: 6 a daughter rises up against her *m,*
Mt 10: 35 a daughter against her *m,*
10: 37 or *m* more than me is not worthy
12: 48 He replied to him, "Who is my *m,*
15: 4 'Honor your father and *m'*
19: 5 and *m* and be united to his wife,
19: 19 honor your father and *m,'*
Mk 7: 10 'Honor your father and your *m,'* and,
10: 19 honor your father and *m.'"*
Lk 11: 27 "Blessed is the *m* who gave you
12: 53 daughter and daughter against *m,*
18: 20 honor your father and *m.'"*
Jn 19: 27 to the disciple, "Here is your *m."*
Gal 4: 26 is above is free, and she is our *m.*
Eph 5: 31 and *m* and be united to his wife,
6: 2 "Honor your father and *m"* —
1Th 2: 7 like a *m* caring for her little
2Ti 1: 5 and in your *m* Eunice and,

MOTHER-IN-LAW (MOTHER)
Ru 2: 19 Ruth told her *m* about the one
Mt 10: 35 a daughter-in-law against her *m* —

MOTHER'S (MOTHER)
Job 1: 21 "Naked I came from my *m* womb,
Pr 1: 8 and do not forsake your *m* teaching
Ecc 5: 15 from his *m* womb,
11: 5 the body is formed in a *m* womb,
Jn 3: 4 time into his *m* womb to be born!"

MOTIVE* (MOTIVES)
1Ch 28: 9 and understands every *m*

MOTIVES* (MOTIVE)
Pr 16: 2 but *m* are weighed by the LORD.
1Co 4: 5 will expose the *m* of men's hearts.
Php 1: 18 whether from false *m* or true,
1Th 2: 3 spring from error or impure *m,*
Jas 4: 3 because you ask with wrong *m,*

MOUNT (MOUNTAIN MOUNTAINS MOUNTAINTOPS)
Ps 89: 9 when its waves *m* up, you still them
Isa 14: 13 enthroned on the *m* of assembly,
Eze 28: 14 You were on the holy *m* of God;
Zec 14: 4 stand on the *M* of Olives,

MOUNTAIN (MOUNT)
Ge 22: 14 "On the *m* of the LORD it will be
Ex 24: 18 And he stayed on the *m* forty days
Dt 5: 4 face to face out of the fire on the *m.*
Job 14: 18 "But as a *m* erodes and crumbles
Ps 48: 1 in the city of our God, his holy *m.*
Isa 40: 4 every *m* and hill made low;
Mic 4: 2 let us go up to the *m* of the LORD,
Mt 4: 8 the devil took him to a very high *m*
17: 20 say to this *m,* 'Move from here
Mk 9: 2 with him and led them up a high *m,*
Lk 3: 5 every *m* and hill made low.
Jn 4: 21 the Father neither on this *m*
2Pe 1: 18 were with him on the sacred *m.*

MOUNTAINS (MOUNT)
Ps 36: 6 righteousness is like the mighty *m,*
46: 2 the *m* fall into the heart of the sea,
90: 2 Before the *m* were born
Isa 52: 7 How beautiful on the *m*
54: 10 Though the *m* be shaken
55: 12 the *m* and hills
Eze 34: 6 My sheep wandered over all the *m*
Mt 24: 16 are in Judea flee to the *m.*
Lk 23: 30 they will say to the *m,* "Fall on us!"
1Co 13: 2 if I have a faith that can move *m,*
Rev 6: 16 They called to the *m* and the rocks,

MOUNTAINTOPS (MOUNT)
Isa 42: 11 let them shout from the *m.*

MOURN (MOURNING MOURNS)
Ecc 3: 4 a time to *m* and a time to dance,
Isa 61: 2 to comfort all who *m,*
Mt 5: 4 Blessed are those who *m,*
Ro 12: 15 *m* with those who *m.*

MOURNING (MOURN)
Isa 61: 3 instead of *m,*
Jer 31: 13 I will turn their *m* into gladness;
Rev 21: 4 There will be no more death or *m*

MOURNS (MOURN)
Zec 12: 10 as one *m* for an only child,

MOUTH (MOUTHS)
Nu 22: 38 only what God puts in my *m."*
Dt 8: 3 comes from the *m* of the LORD.
18: 18 I will put my words in his *m,*
30: 14 it is in your *m* and in your heart
Jos 1: 8 of the Law depart from your *m;*
2Ki 4: 34 *m* to *m,* eyes to eyes, hands
Ps 10: 7 His *m* is full of curses and lies
17: 3 resolved that my *m* will not sin.
19: 14 May the words of my *m*
37: 30 *m* of the righteous man utters
40: 3 He put a new song in my *m,*
71: 8 My *m* is filled with your praise,
119: 103 sweeter than honey to my *m!*
141: 3 Set a guard over my *m,* O LORD;
Pr 2: 6 and from his *m* come knowledge
4: 24 Put away perversity from your *m;*
10: 11 The *m* of the righteous is a fountain
10: 31 *m* of the righteous brings forth
16: 23 A wise man's heart guides his *m,*
26: 28 and a flattering *m* works ruin.
27: 2 praise you, and not your own *m;*
Ecc 5: 2 Do not be quick with your *m,*
SS 1: 2 with the kisses of his *m* —
5: 16 His *m* is sweetness itself;
Isa 29: 13 come near to me with their *m*
40: 5 For the *m* of the LORD has spoken
45: 23 my *m* has uttered in all integrity
51: 16 I have put my words in your *m*
53: 7 so he did not open his *m.*

Isa 55: 11 my word that goes out from my *m:*
59: 21 *m* will not depart from your *m,*
Eze 3: 2 So I opened my *m,* and he gave me
Mal 2: 7 and from his *m* men should seek
Mt 4: 4 comes from the *m* of God.'"
12: 34 overflow of the heart the *m* speaks.
15: 11 into a man's *m* does not make him
15: 18 out of the *m* come from the heart,
Lk 6: 45 overflow of his heart his *m* speaks.
Ro 10: 9 That if you confess with your *m,*
15: 6 and *m* you may glorify the God
1Pe 2: 22 and no deceit was found in his *m."*
Rev 1: 16 and out of his *m* came a sharp
2: 16 them with the sword of my *m.*
3: 16 I am about to spit you out of my *m.*
19: 15 Out of his *m* comes a sharp sword

MOUTHS (MOUTH)
Ps 78: 36 would flatter him with their *m,*
Eze 33: 31 With their *m* they express devotion
Ro 3: 14 "Their *m* are full of cursing
Eph 4: 29 talk come out of your *m,*
Jas 3: 3 bits into the *m* of horses

MOVE (MOVED MOVES)
Dt 19: 14 Do not *m* your neighbor's
Pr 23: 10 Do not *m* an ancient boundary
Ac 17: 28 and *m* and have our being.'
1Co 13: 2 have a faith that can *m* mountains,
15: 58 Let nothing *m* you.

MOVED (MOVE)
Ex 35: 21 and whose heart *m* him came
2Ch 36: 22 the LORD *m* the heart
Ezr 1: 5 everyone whose heart God had *m*
Ps 93: 1 it cannot be *m.*
Jn 11: 33 he was deeply *m* in spirit
Col 1: 23 not *m* from the hope held out

MOVES (MOVE)
Dt 23: 14 For the LORD your God *m* about

MUD (MUDDIED)
Ps 40: 2 out of the *m* and mire;
Isa 57: 20 whose waves cast up mire and *m.*
Jn 9: 6 made some *m* with the saliva,
2Pe 2: 22 back to her wallowing in the *m."*

MUDDIED (MUD)
Pr 25: 26 Like a *m* spring or a polluted well
Eze 32: 13 or *m* by the hoofs of cattle.

MULBERRY*
Lk 17: 6 you can say to this *m* tree,

MULTITUDE (MULTITUDES)
Isa 31: 1 who trust in the *m* of their chariots
Jas 5: 20 and cover over a *m* of sins.
1Pe 4: 8 love covers over a *m* of sins.
Rev 7: 9 me was a great *m* that no one could
19: 1 of a great *m* in heaven shouting:

MULTITUDES (MULTITUDE)
Ne 9: 6 and the *m* of heaven worship you.
Da 12: 2 *M* who sleep in the dust
Joel 3: 14 *M, m* in the valley of decision!

MURDER (MURDERED MURDERER MURDERERS)
Ex 20: 13 "You shall not *m.*
Dt 5: 17 "You shall not *m.*
Pr 28: 17 A man tormented by the guilt of *m*
Mt 5: 21 'Do not *m,* and anyone who
15: 19 *m,* adultery, sexual immorality,
Ro 1: 29 *m,* strife, deceit and malice.
13: 9 "Do not *m,"* "Do not steal,"
Jas 2: 11 adultery," also said, "Do not *m."*

MURDERED (MURDER)
Mt 23: 31 of those who *m* the prophets.
Ac 7: 52 now you have betrayed and *m* him
1Jn 3: 12 to the evil one and *m* his brother.

MURDERER (MURDER)
Nu 35: 16 he is a *m;* the *m* shall be put
Jn 8: 44 He was a *m* from the beginning,
1Jn 3: 15 who hates his brother is a *m,*

MURDERERS (MURDER)
1Ti 1: 9 for *m,* for adulterers and perverts,
Rev 21: 8 the *m,* the sexually immoral,
22: 15 the sexually immoral, the *m,*

MUSIC* (MUSICAL MUSICIAN MUSICIANS)
Ge 31: 27 singing to the *m* of tambourines
Jdg 5: 3 I will make *m* to the LORD,
1Ch 6: 31 put in charge of the *m* in the house
6: 32 They ministered with *m*
25: 6 fathers for the *m* of the temple
25: 7 and skilled in *m* for the LORD—
Ne 12: 27 and with the *m* of cymbals,
Job 21: 12 They sing to the *m* of tambourine
Ps 27: 6 and make *m* to the LORD.
33: 2 make *m* to him on the ten-stringed
45: 8 the *m* of the strings makes you glad
57: 7 I will sing and make *m.*
81: 2 Begin the *m,* strike the tambourine,
87: 7 As they make *m* they will sing,
92: 1 and make *m* to your name,
92: 3 to the *m* of the ten-stringed lyre
95: 2 and extol him with *m* and song.
98: 4 burst into jubilant song with *m;*
98: 5 make *m* to the LORD
108: 1 make *m* with all my soul.
144: 9 the ten-stringed lyre I will make *m*
147: 7 make *m* to our God on the harp.
149: 3 make *m* to him with tambourine
Isa 30: 32 will be to the *m* of tambourines
La 5: 14 young men have stopped their *m.*
Eze 26: 13 *m* of your harps will be heard no
Da 3: 5 lyre, harp, pipes and all kinds of *m,*
3: 7 and all kinds of *m,* all the peoples,
3: 10 and all kinds of *m* must fall down
3: 15 lyre, harp, pipes and all kinds of *m,*
Am 5: 23 to the *m* of your harps.
Hab 3: 19 For the director of *m.*
Lk 15: 25 came near the house, he heard *m*
Eph 5: 19 make *m* in your heart to the Lord,
Rev 18: 22 The *m* of harpists and musicians,

MUSICAL* (MUSIC)
1Ch 15: 16 accompanied by *m* instruments:
23: 5 with the *m* instruments I have
2Ch 7: 6 with the LORD's *m* instruments,
23: 13 with *m* instruments were leading
34: 12 skilled in playing *m* instruments—
Ne 12: 36 with *m* instruments prescribed
Am 6: 5 and improvise on *m* instruments.

MUSICIAN* (MUSIC)
1Ch 6: 33 Heman, the *m,* the son of Joel,

MUSICIANS* (MUSIC)
1Ki 10: 12 to make harps and lyres for the *m.*
1Ch 9: 33 Those who were *m,* heads
15: 19 The *m* Heman, Asaph
2Ch 5: 12 All the Levites who were *m*—
9: 11 to make harps and lyres for the *m.*
35: 15 The *m,* the descendants of Asaph,
Ps 68: 25 are the singers, after them the *m;*
Rev 18: 22 The music of harpists and *m,*

MUSTARD
Mt 13: 31 kingdom of heaven is like a *m* seed,
17: 20 you have faith as small as a *m* seed,
Mk 4: 31 It is like a *m* seed, which is

MUTILATORS*
Php 3: 2 those men who do evil, those *m*

MUTUAL* (MUTUALLY)
Ro 14: 19 leads to peace and to *m* edification.
1Co 7: 5 by *m* consent and for a time,

MUTUALLY* (MUTUAL)
Ro 1: 12 and I may be *m* encouraged

MUZZLE*
Dt 25: 4 Do not *m* an ox while it is treading
Ps 39: 1 I will put a *m* on my mouth
1Co 9: 9 "Do not *m* an ox while it is
1Ti 5: 18 "Do not *m* the ox while it is

MYRRH
Ps 45: 8 All your robes are fragrant with *m*
SS 1: 13 My lover is to me a sachet of *m*
Mt 2: 11 of gold and of incense and of *m.*
Mk 15: 23 offered him wine mixed with *m,*
Jn 19: 39 Nicodemus brought a mixture of *m*
Rev 18: 13 of incense, *m* and frankincense,

MYSTERIES* (MYSTERY)
Job 11: 7 "Can you fathom the *m* of God?
Da 2: 28 a God in heaven who reveals *m.*
2: 29 of *m* showed you what is going
2: 47 Lord of kings and a revealer of *m,*
1Co 13: 2 can fathom all *m* and all knowledge
14: 2 he utters *m* with his spirit.

MYSTERY* (MYSTERIES)
Da 2: 18 God of heaven concerning this *m,*
2: 19 the night the *m* was revealed
2: 27 to the king the *m* he has asked
2: 30 this *m* has been revealed to me,
2: 47 for you were able to reveal this *m."*
4: 9 and no *m* is too difficult for you.
Ro 11: 25 you to be ignorant of this *m,*
16: 25 to the revelation of the *m* hidden
1Co 15: 51 I tell you a *m:* We will not all sleep,
Eph 1: 9 to us the *m* of his will according
3: 3 the *m* made known to me
Eph 3: 4 insight into the *m* of Christ,
3: 6 This *m* is that through the gospel
3: 9 the administration of this *m,*
5: 32 This is a profound *m*—
6: 19 I will fearlessly make known the *m*
Col 1: 26 the *m* that has been kept hidden
1: 27 the glorious riches of this *m,*
2: 2 in order that they may know the *m*
4: 3 so that we may proclaim the *m*
1Ti 3: 16 the *m* of godliness is great:
Rev 1: 20 *m* of the seven stars that you saw
10: 7 the *m* of God will be accomplished,
17: 5 written on her forehead: *M*
17: 7 explain to you the *m* of the woman

MYTHS*
1Ti 1: 4 nor to devote themselves to *m*
4: 7 Have nothing to do with godless *m*
2Ti 4: 4 from the truth and turn aside to *m.*
Tit 1: 14 will pay no attention to Jewish *m*

NAAMAN
Aramean general whose leprosy was cleansed by Elisha (2Ki 5).

NABAL
Wealthy Carmelite the LORD killed for refusing to help David (1Sa 25). David married Abigail, his widow (1Sa 25:39–42).

NABOTH*
Jezreelite killed by Jezebel for his vineyard (1Ki 21). Ahab's family destroyed for this (1Ki 21:17–24; 2Ki 9:21–37).

NADAB
1. Firstborn of Aaron (Ex 6:23); killed with Abihu for offering unauthorized fire (Lev 10; Nu 3:4).
2. Son of Jeroboam I; king of Israel (1Ki 15:25–32).

NAHUM
Prophet against Nineveh (Na 1:1).

NAIL* (NAILING)
Jn 20: 25 "Unless I see the *n* marks

NAILING* (NAIL)
Ac 2: 23 him to death by *n* him to the cross.
Col 2: 14 he took it away, *n* it to the cross.

NAIVE
Ro 16: 18 they deceive the minds of *n* people.

NAKED
Ge 2: 25 The man and his wife were both *n,*
Job 1: 21 *N* I came from my mother's womb,
Isa 58: 7 when you see the *n,* to clothe him,
2Co 5: 3 are clothed, we will not be found *n.*

NAME (NAMES)
Ge 2: 19 man to see what he would *n* them;
4: 26 to call on the *n* of the LORD.
11: 4 so that we may make a *n*
12: 2 I will make your *n* great,
32: 29 Jacob said, "Please tell me your *n."*
Ex 3: 15 This is my *n* forever, the *n*
20: 7 "You shall not misuse the *n*
34: 14 for the LORD, whose *n* is Jealous,
Lev 24: 11 Israelite woman blasphemed the *N*
Dt 5: 11 "You shall not misuse the *n*
12: 11 choose as a dwelling for his *N*—
18: 5 minister in the LORD's *n* always.
25: 6 carry on the *n* of the dead brother
28: 58 this glorious and awesome *n*—
Jos 7: 9 do for your own great *n?"*
Jdg 13: 17 "What is your *n,* so that we may
1Sa 12: 22 of his great *n* the LORD will not
2Sa 6: 2 which is called by the *N,* the name
7: 9 Now I will make your *n* great,
1Ki 5: 5 will build the temple for my *N.'*
8: 29 you said, 'My *N* shall be there,'
1Ch 17: 8 I will make your *n* like the names
2Ch 7: 14 my people, who are called by my *n,*
Ne 9: 10 You made a *n* for yourself,
Ps 8: 1 how majestic is your *n*
9: 10 Those who know your *n* will trust
20: 7 in the *n* of the LORD our God.
29: 2 to the LORD the glory due his *n;*
34: 3 let us exalt his *n* together.
44: 20 If we had forgotten the *n*
66: 2 Sing the glory of his *n;*
68: 4 Sing to God, sing praise to his *n,*
79: 9 for the glory of your *n;*
96: 8 to the LORD the glory due his *n;*
103: 1 my inmost being, praise his holy *n.*
115: 1 but to your *n* be the glory,
138: 2 your *n* and your word.
145: 1 I will praise your *n* for ever
147: 4 and calls them each by *n.*
Pr 3: 4 you will win favor and a good *n*
18: 10 *n* of the LORD is a strong tower;

Pr 22: 1 A good *n* is more desirable
30: 4 What is his *n*, and the *n* of his son?
Ecc 7: 1 A good *n* is better
SS 1: 3 your *n* is like perfume poured out.
Isa 12: 4 thanks to the Lord, call on his *n;*
26: 8 your *n* and renown
40: 26 and calls them each by *n*.
42: 8 "I am the Lord; that is my *n!*
56: 5 I will give them an everlasting *n*
57: 15 who lives forever, whose *n* is holy:
63: 14 to make for yourself a glorious *n*.
Jer 14: 7 do something for the sake of your *n*
15: 16 for I bear your *n*,
Eze 20: 9 of my *n* I did what would keep it
20: 14 of my *n* I did what would keep it
20: 22 of my *n* I did what would keep it
Da 12: 1 everyone whose *n* is found written
Hos 12: 5 the Lord is his *n* of renown!
Joel 2: 32 on the *n* of the Lord will be saved
Mic 5: 4 in the majesty of the *n*
Zep 3: 9 call on the *n* of the Lord
Zec 6: 12 is the man whose *n* is the Branch,
14: 9 one Lord, and his *n* the only *n*.
Mal 1: 6 O priests, who show contempt for my *n*.
Mt 1: 21 and you are to give him the *n* Jesus,
6: 9 hallowed be your *n*,
18: 20 or three come together in my *n*,
24: 5 For many will come in my *n*,
28: 19 them in the *n* of the Father
Mk 9: 41 gives you a cup of water in my *n*
Lk 11: 2 hallowed be your *n*,
Jn 10: 3 He calls his own sheep by *n*
14: 13 I will do whatever you ask in my *n*,
16: 24 asked for anything in my *n*.
Ac 2: 21 on the *n* of the Lord will be saved.'
4: 12 for there is no other *n*
Ro 10: 13 "Everyone who calls on the *n*
Php 2: 9 him the *n* that is above every *n*,
2: 10 at the *n* of Jesus every knee should
Col 3: 17 do it all in the *n* of the Lord Jesus,
Heb 1: 4 as the *n* he has inherited is superior
Jas 5: 14 him with oil in the *n* of the Lord.
1Jn 5: 13 believe in the *n* of the Son of God
Rev 2: 17 stone with a new *n* written on it,
3: 5 I will never blot out his *n*
3: 12 I will also write on him my new *n*.
19: 13 and his *n* is the Word of God.
20: 15 If anyone's *n* was not found written

NAMES (NAME)
Ex 28: 9 engrave on them the *n* of the sons
Lk 10: 20 but rejoice that your *n* are written
Php 4: 3 whose *n* are in the book of life.
Heb 12: 23 whose *n* are written in heaven.
Rev 21: 27 but only those whose *n* are written

NAOMI
Wife of Elimelech, mother-in-law of Ruth (Ru 1:2, 4). Left Bethlehem for Moab during famine (Ru 1:1). Returned a widow, with Ruth (Ru 1:6 – 22). Advised Ruth to seek marriage with Boaz (Ru 2:17 – 3:4). Cared for Ruth's son Obed (Ru 4:13 – 17).

NAPHTALI
Son of Jacob by Bilhah (Ge 30:8; 35:25; 1Ch 2:2). Tribe of blessed (Ge 49:21; Dt 33:23), numbered (Nu 1:43; 26:50), allotted land (Jos 19:32 – 39; Eze 48:3), failed to fully possess (Jdg 1:33), supported Deborah (Jdg 4:10; 5:18), David (1Ch 12:34), 12,000 from (Rev 7:6).

NARROW
Mt 7: 13 "Enter through the *n* gate.
7: 14 and *n* the road that leads to life,

NATHAN
Prophet and chronicler of Israel's history (1Ch 29:29; 2Ch 9:29). Announced the Davidic covenant (2Sa 7; 1Ch 17). Denounced David's sin with Bathsheba (2Sa 12). Supported Solomon (1Ki 1).

NATHANAEL*
Apostle (Jn 1:45 – 49; 21:2). Probably also called Bartholomew (Mt 10:3).

NATION (NATIONS)
Ge 12: 2 "I will make you into a great *n*
Ex 19: 6 a kingdom of priests and a holy *n*.'
Dt 4: 7 What other *n* is so great
Jos 5: 8 And after the whole *n* had been
2Sa 7: 23 one *n* on earth that God went out
Ps 33: 12 Blessed is the *n* whose God is
Pr 11: 14 For lack of guidance a *n* falls,
14: 34 Righteousness exalts a *n*,
Isa 2: 4 *N* will not take up sword
26: 2 that the righteous *n* may enter,
60: 12 For the *n* or kingdom that will not
65: 1 To a *n* that did not call on my name
66: 8 a *n* be brought forth in a moment?
Mic 4: 3 *N* will not take up sword
Mt 24: 7 *N* will rise against *n*,
Mk 13: 8 *N* will rise against *n*,
1Pe 2: 9 a royal priesthood, a holy *n*,
Rev 5: 9 and language and people and *n*.
7: 9 from every *n*, tribe, people
14: 6 to every *n*, tribe, language

NATIONS (NATION)
Ge 17: 4 You will be the father of many *n*.
18: 18 and all *n* on earth will be blessed
Ex 19: 5 of all *n* you will be my treasured
Lev 20: 26 apart from the *n* to be my own.
Dt 7: 1 drives out before you many *n* —
15: 6 You will rule over many *n*
Jdg 3: 1 These are the *n* the Lord left
2Ch 20: 6 rule over all the kingdoms of the *n*.
Ne 1: 8 I will scatter you among the *n*,
Ps 2: 1 Why do the *n* conspire
2: 8 I will make the *n* your inheritance,
9: 5 You have rebuked the *n*
22: 28 and he rules over the *n*.
46: 10 I will be exalted among the *n*,
47: 8 God reigns over the *n;*
66: 7 his eyes watch the *n* —
67: 2 your salvation among all *n*.
68: 30 Scatter the *n* who delight in war.
72: 17 All *n* will be blessed through him,
96: 3 Declare his glory among the *n*,
99: 2 he is exalted over all the *n*.
106: 35 but they mingled with the *n*
110: 6 He will judge the *n*, heaping up
113: 4 The Lord is exalted over all the *n*
Isa 2: 2 and all *n* will stream to it.
11: 10 the *n* will rally to him,
12: 4 among the *n* what he has done,
40: 15 Surely the *n* are like a drop
42: 1 and he will bring justice to the *n*.
51: 4 justice will become a light to the *n*.
52: 15 so will he sprinkle many *n*,
56: 7 a house of prayer for all *n*."
60: 3 *N* will come to your light,
66: 18 and gather all *n* and tongues,
Jer 1: 5 you as a prophet to the *n*."
3: 17 and all *n* will gather in Jerusalem
31: 10 "Hear the word of the Lord, O *n;*
33: 9 and honor before all *n*
46: 28 I completely destroy all the *n*
Eze 22: 4 you an object of scorn to the *n*
34: 13 I will bring them out from the *n*
36: 23 *n* will know that I am the Lord,
37: 22 and they will never again be two *n*
39: 21 I will display my glory among the *n*
Hos 7: 8 "Ephraim mixes with the *n;*
Joel 2: 17 a byword among the *n*.
3: 2 I will gather all *n*
Am 9: 12 and all the *n* that bear my name,"
Zep 3: 8 I have decided to assemble the *n*,
Hag 2: 7 and the desired of all *n* will come,
Zec 8: 13 an object of cursing among the *n*,
8: 23 *n* will take firm hold of one Jew
9: 10 He will proclaim peace to the *n*.
14: 2 I will gather all the *n* to Jerusalem
Mt 12: 18 he will proclaim justice to the *n*.
24: 9 and you will be hated by all *n*
24: 14 whole world as a testimony to all *n*,
25: 32 All the *n* will be gathered
28: 19 and make disciples of all *n*,
Mk 11: 17 a house of prayer for all *n*'?
Ac 4: 25 "'Why do the *n* rage
Ro 15: 12 who will arise to rule over the *n;*
Gal 3: 8 All *n* will be blessed through you."
1Ti 3: 16 was preached among the *n*,
Rev 15: 4 All *n* will come
21: 24 The *n* will walk by its light,
22: 2 are for the healing of the *n*.

NATURAL (NATURE)
Ro 6: 19 you are weak in your *n* selves.
1Co 15: 44 If there is a *n* body, there is

NATURE (NATURAL)
Ro 1: 20 his eternal power and divine *n* —
7: 18 lives in me, that is, in my sinful *n*.
8: 4 do not live according to the sinful *n*
8: 5 to the sinful *n* have their minds set
8: 8 by the sinful *n* cannot please God.
13: 14 to gratify the desires of the sinful *n*.
Gal 5: 13 freedom to indulge the sinful *n;*
5: 19 The acts of the sinful *n* are obvious:
5: 24 Jesus have crucified the sinful *n*
Php 2: 6 Who, being in very *n* God,
Col 3: 5 whatever belongs to your earthly *n*
2Pe 1: 4 you may participate in the divine *n*

NAZARENE* (NAZARETH)
Mt 2: 23 prophets: "He will be called a *N*."
Mk 14: 67 "You also were with that *N*, Jesus,"
16: 6 "You are looking for Jesus the *N*,
Ac 24: 5 He is a ringleader of the *N* sect and

NAZARETH (NAZARENE)
Mt 4: 13 Leaving *N*, he went and lived
Lk 4: 16 to *N*, where he had been brought
Jn 1: 46 "*N!* Can anything good come

NAZIRITE
Nu 6: 2 of separation to the Lord as a *N*,
Jdg 13: 7 because the boy will be a *N* of God

NEBO
Dt 34: 1 Then Moses climbed Mount *N*

NEBUCHADNEZZAR
Babylonian king. Subdued and exiled Judah (2Ki 24 – 25; 2Ch 36; Jer 39). Dreams interpreted by Daniel (Da 2; 4). Worshiped God (Da 3:28 – 29; 4:34 – 37).

NECESSARY*
Ac 1: 21 Therefore it is *n* to choose one
Ro 13: 5 it is *n* to submit to the authorities,
2Co 9: 5 I thought it *n* to urge the brothers
Php 1: 24 it is more *n* for you that I remain
2: 25 But I think it is *n* to send back
Heb 8: 3 and so it was *n* for this one
9: 16 it is *n* to prove the death
9: 23 It was *n*, then, for the copies

NECK (STIFF-NECKED)
Pr 3: 22 an ornament to grace your *n*.
6: 21 fasten them around your *n*.
Mt 18: 6 a large millstone hung around his *n*

NECO
Pharaoh who killed Josiah (2Ki 23:29 – 30; 2Ch 35:20 – 22), deposed Jehoahaz (2Ki 23:33 – 35; 2Ch 36:3 – 4).

NEED (NEEDS NEEDY)
1Ki 8: 59 Israel according to each day's *n*,
Ps 79: 8 for we are in desperate *n*.
116: 6 when I was in great *n*, he saved me.
142: 6 for I am in desperate *n;*
Mt 6: 8 for your Father knows what you *n*
Lk 15: 14 country, and he began to be in *n*.
Ac 2: 45 they gave to anyone as he had *n*.
Ro 12: 13 with God's people who are in *n*.
1Co 12: 21 say to the hand, "I don't *n* you!"
Eph 4: 28 something to share with those in *n*.
1Ti 5: 3 to those widows who are really in *n*
Heb 4: 16 grace to help us in our time of *n*.
1Jn 3: 17 sees his brother in *n* but has no pity

NEEDLE
Mt 19: 24 go through the eye of a *n*

NEEDS (NEED)
Isa 58: 11 he will satisfy your *n*
Php 2: 25 sent to take care of my *n*.
4: 19 God will meet all your *n* according
Jas 2: 16 does nothing about his physical *n*,

NEEDY (NEED)
Dt 15: 11 toward the poor and *n* in your land.
1Sa 2: 8 and lifts the *n* from the ash heap;
Ps 35: 10 and *n* from those who rob them."
69: 33 The Lord hears the *n*
72: 12 he will deliver the *n* who cry out,
140: 12 and upholds the cause of the *n*.
Pr 14: 21 blessed is he who is kind to the *n*.
14: 31 to the *n* honors God.
22: 22 and do not crush the *n* in court,
31: 9 defend the rights of the poor and *n*
31: 20 and extends her hands to the *n*.
Mt 6: 2 "So when you give to the *n*,

NEGLECT* (NEGLECTED)
Dt 12: 19 Be careful not to *n* the Levites
14: 27 And do not *n* the Levites living
Ezr 4: 22 Be careful not to *n* this matter.
Ne 10: 39 We will not *n* the house of our God
Est 6: 10 Do not *n* anything you have
Ps 119: 16 I will not *n* your word.
Lk 11: 42 you *n* justice and the love of God.
Ac 6: 2 for us to *n* the ministry of the word
1Ti 4: 14 Do not *n* your gift, which was

NEGLECTED (NEGLECT)
Mt 23: 23 But you have *n* the more important

NEHEMIAH
Cupbearer of Artaxerxes (Ne 2:1); governor of Israel (Ne 8:9). Returned to Jerusalem to rebuild walls (Ne 2 – 6). With Ezra, reestablished worship (Ne 8). Prayer confessing nation's sin (Ne 9). Dedicated wall (Ne 12).

NEIGHBOR (NEIGHBOR'S)
Ex 20: 16 give false testimony against your *n*.
20: 17 or anything that belongs to your *n*

Lev 19: 13 Do not defraud your *n* or rob him.
19: 17 Rebuke your *n* frankly
19: 18 but love your *n* as yourself.
Ps 15: 3 who does his *n* no wrong
Pr 3: 29 Do not plot harm against your *n*,
11: 12 who lacks judgment derides his *n*,
14: 21 He who despises his *n* sins,
16: 29 A violent man entices his *n*
24: 28 against your *n* without cause,
25: 18 gives false testimony against his *n*.
27: 10 better a *n* nearby than a brother far
27: 14 If a man loudly blesses his *n*
29: 5 Whoever flatters his *n*
Jer 31: 34 No longer will a man teach his *n*,
Zec 8: 17 do not plot evil against your *n*,
Mt 5: 43 Love your *n* and hate your enemy.'
19: 19 and 'love your *n* as yourself.'"
Mk 12: 31 The second is this: 'Love your *n*
Lk 10: 27 and, 'Love your *n* as yourself.'"
10: 29 who is my *n*?" In reply Jesus said:
Ro 13: 9 "Love your *n* as yourself."
13: 10 Love does no harm to its *n*.
15: 2 Each of us should please his *n*
Gal 5: 14 "Love your *n* as yourself."
Eph 4: 25 and speak truthfully to his *n*,
Heb 8: 11 No longer will a man teach his *n*,
Jas 2: 8 "Love your *n* as yourself,"

NEIGHBOR'S (NEIGHBOR)
Ex 20: 17 You shall not covet your *n* wife,
Dt 5: 21 not set your desire on your *n* house
19: 14 not move your *n* boundary stone
27: 17 who moves his *n* boundary stone."
Pr 25: 17 Seldom set foot in your *n* house—

NESTS
Mt 8: 20 and birds of the air have *n*,

NET (NETS)
Pr 1: 17 How useless to spread a *n*
Hab 1: 15 he catches them in his *n*,
Mt 13: 47 of heaven is like a *n* that was let
Jn 21: 6 "Throw your *n* on the right side

NETS (NET)
Ps 141: 10 Let the wicked fall into their own *n*
Mt 4: 20 At once they left their *n*
Lk 5: 4 and let down the *n* for a catch."

NEVER-FAILING*
Am 5: 24 righteousness like a *n* stream!

NEW
Ps 40: 3 He put a *n* song in my mouth,
98: 1 Sing to the LORD a *n* song,
Ecc 1: 9 there is nothing *n* under the sun.
Isa 42: 9 and *n* things I declare;
62: 2 you will be called by a *n* name
65: 17 *n* heavens and a *n* earth.
66: 22 "As the *n* heavens and the *n* earth
Jer 31: 31 "when I will make a *n* covenant
La 3: 23 They are *n* every morning;
Eze 11: 19 undivided heart and put a *n* spirit
18: 31 and get a *n* heart and a *n* spirit.
36: 26 give you a *n* heart and put a *n* spirit
Zep 3: 5 and every *n* day he does not fail,
Mt 9: 17 Neither do men pour *n* wine
Mk 16: 17 they will speak in *n* tongues;
Lk 5: 39 after drinking old wine wants the *n*
22: 20 "This cup is the *n* covenant
Jn 13: 34 "A *n* commandment I give you:
Ac 5: 20 the full message of this *n* life."
Ro 6: 4 the Father, we too may live a *n* life.
1Co 5: 7 old yeast that you may be a *n* batch
11: 25 "This cup is the *n* covenant
2Co 3: 6 as ministers of a *n* covenant—
5: 17 he is a *n* creation; the old has gone,
Gal 6: 15 what counts is a *n* creation.
Eph 4: 23 to be made *n* in the attitude
4: 24 and to put on the *n* self, created
Col 3: 10 and have put on the *n* self,
Heb 8: 8 when I will make a *n* covenant
9: 15 is the mediator of a *n* covenant,
10: 20 by a *n* and living way opened for us
12: 24 Jesus the mediator of a *n* covenant,
1Pe 1: 3 great mercy he has given us *n* birth
2Pe 3: 13 to a *n* heaven and a *n* earth,
1Jn 2: 8 Yet I am writing you a *n* command;
Rev 2: 17 stone with a *n* name written on it,
3: 12 the *n* Jerusalem, which is coming
21: 1 I saw a *n* heaven and a *n* earth,

NEWBORN (BEAR)
1Pe 2: 2 Like *n* babies, crave pure spiritual

NEWS
2Ki 7: 9 This is a day of good *n*
Ps 112: 7 He will have no fear of bad *n*;
Pr 15: 30 good *n* gives health to the bones.
25: 25 is good *n* from a distant land.
Isa 52: 7 the feet of those who bring good *n*,
61: 1 me to preach good *n* to the poor.
Na 1: 15 the feet of one who brings good *n*,
Mt 4: 23 preaching the good *n*
9: 35 preaching the good *n*
11: 5 the good *n* is preached to the poor.
Mk 1: 15 Repent and believe the good *n*!"
16: 15 preach the good *n* to all creation.
Lk 1: 19 and to tell you this good *n*.
2: 10 I bring you good *n*
3: 18 and preached the good *n* to them.
4: 43 "I must preach the good *n*
8: 1 proclaiming the good *n*
16: 16 the good *n* of the kingdom
Ac 5: 42 proclaiming the good *n* that Jesus
10: 36 telling the good *n* of peace
14: 7 continued to preach the good *n*.
14: 21 They preached the good *n*
17: 18 preaching the good *n* about Jesus
Ro 10: 15 feet of those who bring good *n*!"

NICODEMUS*
Pharisee who visited Jesus at night (Jn 3). Argued fair treatment of Jesus (Jn 7:50–52). With Joseph, prepared Jesus for burial (Jn 19:38–42).

NIGHT (NIGHTS NIGHTTIME)
Ge 1: 5 and the darkness he called "*n*."
1: 16 and the lesser light to govern the *n*.
Ex 13: 21 and by *n* in a pillar of fire
14: 24 During the last watch of the *n*.
Dt 28: 66 filled with dread both *n* and day,
Jos 1: 8 and *n*, so that you may be careful
Job 35: 10 who gives songs in the *n*,
Ps 1: 2 on his law he meditates day and *n*.
19: 2 *n* after *n* they display knowledge.
42: 8 at *n* his song is with me—
63: 6 of you through the watches of the *n*
77: 6 I remembered my songs in the *n*.
90: 4 or like a watch in the *n*.
91: 5 You will not fear the terror of *n*,
119: 148 through the watches of the *n*,
121: 6 nor the moon by *n*.
136: 9 the moon and stars to govern the *n*;
Pr 31: 18 and her lamp does not go out at *n*.
Isa 21: 11 Watchman, what is left of the *n*?"
58: 10 and your *n* will become like
Jer 33: 20 and my covenant with the *n*,
Lk 2: 8 watch over their flocks at *n*.
6: 12 and spent the *n* praying to God.
Jn 3: 2 He came to Jesus at *n* and said,
9: 4 *N* is coming, when no one can work
1Th 5: 2 Lord will come like a thief in the *n*.
5: 5 We do not belong to the *n*
Rev 21: 25 for there will be no *n* there.

NIGHTS (NIGHT)
Jnh 1: 17 the fish three days and three *n*.
Mt 4: 2 After fasting forty days and forty *n*
12: 40 three *n* in the belly of a huge fish,
2Co 6: 5 in hard work, sleepless *n*

NIGHTTIME* (NIGHT)
Zec 14: 7 or *n*— a day known to the LORD.

NIMROD
Ge 10: 9 "Like *N*, a mighty hunter

NINEVEH
Jnh 1: 2 "Go to the great city of *N*
Na 1: 1 An oracle concerning *N*.
Mt 12: 41 The men of *N* will stand up

NOAH
Righteous man (Eze 14:14, 20) called to build ark (Ge 6–8; Heb 11:7; 1Pe 3:20; 2Pe 2:5). God's covenant with (Ge 9:1–17). Drunkenness of (Ge 9:18–23). Blessed sons, cursed Canaan (Ge 9:24–27).

NOBLE
Ru 3: 11 you are a woman of *n* character.
Ps 45: 1 My heart is stirred by a *n* theme
Pr 12: 4 of *n* character is her husband's
31: 10 A wife of *n* character who can find?
31: 29 "Many women do *n* things,
Isa 32: 8 But the *n* man makes *n* plans,
Lk 8: 15 good soil stands for those with a *n*
Ro 9: 21 of clay some pottery for *n* purposes
Php 4: 8 whatever is *n*, whatever is right,
2Ti 2: 20 some are for *n* purposes

NOSTRILS
Ge 2: 7 and breathed into his *n* the breath
Ex 15: 8 By the blast of your *n*
Ps 18: 15 at the blast of breath from your *n*.

NOTE
Ac 4: 13 and they took *n* that these men had
Php 3: 17 take *n* of those who live according

NOTHING
2Sa 24: 24 offerings that cost me *n*."
Ne 9: 21 in the desert; they lacked *n*,
Ps 73: 25 earth has *n* I desire besides you
Jer 32: 17 *N* is too hard for you
Jn 15: 5 apart from me you can do *n*.

NOURISH
Pr 10: 21 The lips of the righteous *n* many,

NULLIFY
Mt 15: 6 Thus you *n* the word of God
Ro 3: 31 Do we, then, *n* the law by this faith

OATH
Ex 33: 1 up to the land I promised on *o*
Nu 30: 2 or takes an *o* to obligate himself
Dt 6: 18 promised on *o* to your forefathers,
7: 8 and kept the *o* he swore
29: 12 you this day and sealing with an *o*,
Ps 95: 11 So I declared on *o* in my anger,
119: 106 I have taken an *o* and confirmed it,
132: 11 The LORD swore an *o* to David,
Ecc 8: 2 because you took an *o* before God.
Mt 5: 33 'Do not break your *o*, but keep
Heb 7: 20 And it was not without an *o*!

OBADIAH
1. Believer who sheltered 100 prophets from Jezebel (1Ki 18:1–16).
2. Prophet against Edom (Ob 1).

OBEDIENCE* (OBEY)
Ge 49: 10 and the *o* of the nations is his.
Jdg 2: 17 of *o* to the LORD's commands.
1Ch 21: 19 So David went up in *o*
2Ch 31: 21 in *o* to the law and the commands,
Pr 30: 17 that scorns *o* to a mother,
Lk 23: 56 Sabbath in *o* to the commandment.
Ac 21: 24 but that you yourself are living in *o*
Ro 1: 5 to the *o* that comes from faith.
5: 19 also through the *o* of the one man
6: 16 to *o*, which leads to righteousness?
16: 19 Everyone has heard about your *o*,
2Co 9: 13 for the *o* that accompanies your
10: 6 once your *o* is complete.
Phm : 21 Confident of your *o*, I write to you,
Heb 5: 8 he learned *o* from what he suffered
1Pe 1: 2 for *o* to Jesus Christ and sprinkling
2Jn : 6 that we walk in *o* to his commands.

OBEDIENT* (OBEY)
Dt 30: 17 heart turns away and you are not *o*,
Isa 1: 19 If you are willing and *o*,
Lk 2: 51 with them and was *o* to them.
Ac 6: 7 of priests became *o* to the faith.
2Co 2: 9 if you would stand the test and be *o*
7: 15 he remembers that you were all *o*,
10: 5 thought to make it *o* to Christ.
Php 2: 8 and became *o* to death—
Tit 3: 1 to be *o*, to be ready
1Pe 1: 14 As *o* children, do not conform

OBEY (OBEDIENCE OBEDIENT OBEYED OBEYING OBEYS)
Ex 12: 24 "*O* these instructions as a lasting
19: 5 Now if you *o* me fully and keep my
24: 7 the LORD has said; we will *o*."
Lev 18: 4 You must *o* my laws and be careful
25: 18 and be careful to *o* my laws,
Nu 15: 40 remember to *o* all my commands
Dt 5: 27 We will listen and *o*."
6: 3 careful to *o* so that it may go well
6: 24 us to *o* all these decrees
11: 13 if you faithfully *o* the commands I
12: 28 to *o* all these regulations I am
13: 4 Keep his commands and *o* him;
21: 18 son who does not *o* his father
28: 1 If you fully *o* the LORD your God
28: 15 if you do not *o* the LORD your
30: 2 and *o* him with all your heart
30: 10 if you *o* the LORD your God
30: 14 and in your heart so you may *o* it.
32: 46 children to *o* carefully all the words
Jos 1: 7 to *o* all the law my servant Moses
22: 5 in all his ways, to *o* his commands,
24: 24 the LORD our God and *o* him."
1Sa 15: 22 To *o* is better than sacrifice,
1Ki 8: 61 by his decrees and *o* his commands
2Ki 17: 13 that I commanded your fathers to *o*
2Ch 34: 31 and to *o* the words of the covenant
Ne 1: 5 who love him and *o* his commands,
Ps 103: 18 and remember to *o* his precepts.
103: 20 who *o* his word.

Ps 119: 17 I will *o* your word.
119: 34 and *o* it with all my heart.
119: 57 I have promised to *o* your words.
119: 67 but now I *o* your word.
119: 100 for I *o* your precepts.
119: 129 therefore I *o* them.
119: 167 I *o* your statutes,
Pr 5: 13 I would not *o* my teachers
Jer 7: 23 I gave them this command: *O* me,
11: 4 '*O* me and do everything I
11: 7 and again, saying, "*O* me."
42: 6 we will *o* the LORD our God,
Da 9: 4 who love him and *o* his commands,
Mt 8: 27 the winds and the waves *o* him!"
19: 17 to enter life, *o* the commandments
28: 20 to *o* everything I have commanded
Lk 11: 28 hear the word of God and *o* it."
Jn 14: 15 you will *o* what I command.
14: 23 loves me, he will *o* my teaching.
14: 24 not love me will not *o* my teaching.
15: 10 If you *o* my commands, you will
Ac 5: 29 "We must *o* God rather than men!
5: 32 given to those who *o* him."
Ro 2: 13 it is those who *o* the law who will
6: 12 body so that you *o* its evil desires.
6: 16 slaves to the one whom you *o* —
6: 16 yourselves to someone to *o* him
15: 18 in leading the Gentiles to *o* God
16: 26 nations might believe and *o* him —
Gal 5: 3 obligated to *o* the whole law.
Eph 6: 1 *o* your parents in the Lord,
6: 5 *o* your earthly masters with respect
Col 3: 20 *o* your parents in everything,
3: 22 *o* your earthly masters
2Th 3: 14 anyone does not *o* our instruction
1Ti 3: 4 and see that his children *o* him
Heb 5: 9 eternal salvation for all who *o* him
13: 17 *O* your leaders and submit
1Pe 4: 17 for those who do not *o* the gospel
1Jn 3: 24 Those who *o* his commands live
5: 3 love for God: to *o* his commands.
Rev 12: 17 those who *o* God's commandments
14: 12 the saints who *o* God's

OBEYED (OBEY)
Ge 22: 18 blessed, because you have *o* me."
Jos 1: 17 we fully *o* Moses, so we will obey
Ps 119: 4 that are to be fully *o*.
Da 9: 10 we have not *o* the LORD our God
Jnh 3: 3 Jonah *o* the word of the LORD
Mic 5: 15 the nations that have not *o* me."
Jn 15: 10 as I have *o* my Father's commands
15: 20 If they *o* my teaching, they will
17: 6 and they have *o* your word.
Ac 7: 53 through angels but have not *o* it."
Ro 6: 17 you wholeheartedly *o* the form
Php 2: 12 as you have always *o* — not only
Heb 11: 8 *o* and went, even though he did not
1Pe 3: 6 who *o* Abraham and called him her

OBEYING (OBEY)
1Sa 15: 22 as in *o* the voice of the LORD?
Ps 119: 5 steadfast in *o* your decrees!
Gal 5: 7 and kept you from *o* the truth?
1Pe 1: 22 purified yourselves by *o* the truth

OBEYS (OBEY)
Lev 18: 5 for the man who *o* them will live
Pr 19: 16 He who *o* instructions guards his
Eze 20: 11 for the man who *o* them will live
Jn 14: 21 has my commands and *o* them,
Ro 2: 27 and yet *o* the law will condemn you
1Jn 2: 5 if anyone *o* his word, God's love is

OBLIGATED (OBLIGATION)
Ro 1: 14 I am *o* both to Greeks
Gal 5: 3 himself be circumcised that he is *o*

OBLIGATION (OBLIGATED)
Ro 8: 12 Therefore, brothers, we have an *o*

OBSCENITY*
Eph 5: 4 Nor should there be *o*, foolish talk

OBSCURES*
Job 42: 3 'Who is this that *o* my counsel

OBSERVE (OBSERVING)
Ex 31: 13 'You must *o* my Sabbaths.
Lev 25: 2 the land itself must *o* a sabbath
Dt 4: 6 *O* them carefully, for this will show
5: 12 "*O* the Sabbath day
8: 6 *O* the commands of the LORD
11: 22 If you carefully *o* all these
26: 16 carefully *o* them with all your heart
Ps 37: 37 the blameless, *o* the upright;

OBSERVING (OBSERVE)
Ro 3: 27 principle? On that of *o* the law?
Gal 2: 16 a man is not justified by *o* the law,
3: 2 you receive the Spirit by *o* the law,
3: 10 All who rely on *o* the law are

OBSOLETE
Heb 8: 13 he has made the first one *o*;

OBSTACLE* (OBSTACLES)
Ro 14: 13 or *o* in your brother's way.

OBSTACLES (OBSTACLE)
Ro 16: 17 put *o* in your way that are contrary

OBSTINATE
Isa 65: 2 hands to an *o* people,
Ro 10: 21 to a disobedient and *o* people."

OBTAIN (OBTAINED OBTAINS)
Ro 11: 7 sought so earnestly it did not *o*,
2Ti 2: 10 they too may *o* the salvation that

OBTAINED (OBTAIN)
Ro 9: 30 not pursue righteousness, have *o* it,
Php 3: 12 Not that I have already *o* all this,
Heb 9: 12 having *o* eternal redemption.

OBTAINS* (OBTAIN)
Pr 12: 2 A good man *o* favor

OBVIOUS*
Mt 6: 18 so that it will not be *o*
Gal 5: 19 The acts of the sinful nature are *o*:
1Ti 5: 24 The sins of some men are *o*,
5: 25 In the same way, good deeds are *o*,

OCCASIONS
Eph 6: 18 in the Spirit on all *o* with all kinds

OFFENDED (OFFENSE)
Pr 18: 19 An *o* brother is more unyielding

OFFENDERS* (OFFENSE)
1Co 6: 9 nor homosexual *o* nor thieves

OFFENSE (OFFENDED OFFENDERS OFFENSES OFFENSIVE)
Pr 17: 9 over an *o* promotes love,
19: 11 it is to his glory to overlook an *o*.
Gal 5: 11 In that case the *o* of the cross has

OFFENSES (OFFENSE)
Isa 44: 22 swept away your *o* like a cloud,
59: 12 For our *o* are many in your sight,
Eze 18: 30 Repent! Turn away from all your *o*;
33: 10 "Our *o* and sins weigh us down,

OFFENSIVE (OFFENSE)
Ps 139: 24 See if there is any *o* way in me,

OFFER (OFFERED OFFERING OFFERINGS OFFERS)
Ps 4: 5 *O* right sacrifices
Ro 6: 13 Do not *o* the parts of your body
12: 1 to *o* your bodies as living sacrifices,
Heb 9: 25 he enter heaven to *o* himself again
13: 15 therefore, let us continually *o*

OFFERED (OFFER)
Isa 50: 6 I *o* my back to those who beat me,
1Co 9: 13 share in what is *o* on the altar?
10: 20 of pagans are *o* to demons,
Heb 7: 27 once for all when he *o* himself.
9: 14 the eternal Spirit *o* himself
11: 4 By faith Abel *o* God a better
11: 17 when God tested him, *o* Isaac
Jas 5: 15 prayer *o* in faith will make the sick

OFFERING (OFFER)
Ge 4: 3 of the soil as an *o* to the LORD.
22: 2 a burnt *o* on one of the mountains I
22: 8 provide the lamb for the burnt *o*,
Ex 29: 24 before the LORD as a wave *o*.
29: 40 quarter of a hin of wine as a drink *o*.
Lev 1: 3 If the *o* is a burnt *o* from the herd,
2: 4 "'If you bring a grain *o* baked
3: 1 "'If someone's *o* is a fellowship *o*,
4: 3 a sin *o* for the sin he has committed
5: 15 It is a guilt *o*.
7: 37 ordination *o* and the fellowship *o*,
9: 24 and consumed the burnt *o*
22: 18 to fulfill a vow or as a freewill *o*,
22: 21 a special vow or as a freewill *o*,
1Sa 13: 9 And Saul offered up the burnt *o*.
1Ch 21: 26 from heaven on the altar of burnt *o*.
2Ch 7: 1 and consumed the burnt *o*
Ps 40: 6 Sacrifice and *o* you did not desire,
116: 17 I will sacrifice a thank *o* to you
Isa 53: 10 the LORD makes his life a guilt *o*,
Mt 5: 23 if you are *o* your gift at the altar
Ro 8: 3 likeness of sinful man to be a sin *o*.
Eph 5: 2 as a fragrant *o* and sacrifice to God.
Php 2: 17 I am being poured out like a drink *o*
4: 18 are a fragrant *o*, an acceptable
2Ti 4: 6 being poured out like a drink *o*,
Heb 10: 5 "Sacrifice and *o* you did not desire,
1Pe 2: 5 *o* spiritual sacrifices acceptable

OFFERINGS (OFFER)
1Sa 15: 22 Does the LORD delight in burnt *o*
2Ch 35: 7 and goats for the Passover *o*,
Isa 1: 13 Stop bringing meaningless *o*!
Hos 6: 6 of God rather than burnt *o*.
Mal 3: 8 do we rob you?' "In tithes and *o*.
Mk 12: 33 is more important than all burnt *o*
Heb 10: 8 First he said, "Sacrifices and *o*,

OFFERS (OFFER)
Heb 10: 11 and again he *o* the same sacrifices,

OFFICER (OFFICIALS)
2Ti 2: 4 wants to please his commanding *o*.

OFFICIALS (OFFICER)
Ex 5: 21 a stench to Pharaoh and his *o*.
Pr 17: 26 or to flog *o* for their integrity.
29: 12 all his *o* become wicked.

OFFSPRING
Ge 3: 15 and between your *o* and hers;
12: 7 "To your *o* I will give this land."
13: 16 I will make your *o* like the dust
26: 4 and through your *o* all nations
28: 14 blessed through you and your *o*.
Ex 13: 2 The first *o* of every womb
Ru 4: 12 Through the *o* the LORD gives
Isa 44: 3 I will pour out my Spirit on your *o*,
53: 10 he will see his *o* and prolong his
Ac 3: 25 'Through your *o* all peoples
17: 28 own poets have said, 'We are his *o*.'
17: 29 "Therefore since we are God's *o*,
Ro 4: 18 said to him, "So shall your *o* be."
9: 8 who are regarded as Abraham's *o*.

OG
Nu 21: 33 *O* king of Bashan and his whole
Ps 136: 20 and *O* king of Bashan —

OIL
Ex 29: 7 Take the anointing *o* and anoint
30: 25 It will be the sacred anointing *o*.
Dt 14: 23 tithe of your grain, new wine and *o*,
1Sa 10: 1 Then Samuel took a flask of *o*
16: 13 So Samuel took the horn of *o*
1Ki 17: 16 and the jug of *o* did not run dry,
2Ki 4: 6 Then the *o* stopped flowing.
Ps 23: 5 You anoint my head with *o*;
45: 7 by anointing you with the *o* of joy.
104: 15 *o* to make his face shine,
133: 2 It is like precious *o* poured
Pr 21: 17 loves wine and *o* will never be
Isa 1: 6 or soothed with *o*.
61: 3 the *o* of gladness
Mt 25: 3 but did not take any *o* with them.
Heb 1: 9 by anointing you with the *o* of joy."

OLIVE (OLIVES)
Ge 8: 11 beak was a freshly plucked *o* leaf!
Jdg 9: 8 said to the *o* tree, 'Be our king.'
Jer 11: 16 LORD called you a thriving *o* tree
Zec 4: 3 Also there are two *o* trees by it,
Ro 11: 17 and you, though a wild *o* shoot,
11: 24 of an *o* tree that is wild by nature,
Rev 11: 4 These are the two *o* trees

OLIVES (OLIVE)
Zec 14: 4 stand on the Mount of *O*,
Mt 24: 3 sitting on the Mount of *O*,
Jas 3: 12 a fig tree bear *o*, or a grapevine bear

OMEGA*
Rev 1: 8 "I am the Alpha and the *O*,"
21: 6 I am the Alpha and the *O*,
22: 13 I am the Alpha and the *O*,

OMIT*
Jer 26: 2 I command you; do not *o* a word.

OMRI
King of Israel (1Ki 16:21 – 26).

ONESIMUS*
Col 4: 9 He is coming with *O*, our faithful
Phm : 10 I appeal to you for my son *O*,

ONESIPHORUS*
2Ti 1: 16 mercy to the household of *O*,
4: 19 Aquila and the household of *O*.

ONIONS*
Nu 11: 5 melons, leeks, *o* and garlic.

ONYX
Ex 28: 9 "Take two *o* stones and engrave
28: 20 in the fourth row a chrysolite, an *o*

OPENHANDED* (HAND)
Dt 15: 8 Rather be *o* and freely lend him
15: 11 you to be *o* toward your brothers

OPINIONS*
1Ki 18: 21 will you waver between two *o*?
Pr 18: 2 but delights in airing his own *o*.

OPPONENTS (OPPOSE)
Pr 18: 18 and keeps strong *o* apart.

OPPORTUNE (OPPORTUNITY)
Lk 4: 13 he left him until an *o* time.

OPPORTUNITY* (OPPORTUNE)
1Sa 18: 21 "Now you have a second *o*
Jer 46: 17 he has missed his *o*.'
Mt 26: 16 watched for an *o* to hand him over.
Mk 14: 11 So he watched for an *o* to hand him
Lk 22: 6 and watched for an *o* to hand Jesus
Ac 25: 16 and has had an *o* to defend himself
Ro 7: 8 seizing the *o* afforded
7: 11 seizing the *o* afforded
1Co 16: 12 but he will go when he has the *o*.
2Co 5: 12 are giving you an *o* to take pride
11: 12 from under those who want an *o*
Gal 6: 10 as we have *o*, let us do good
Eph 5: 16 making the most of every *o*,
Php 4: 10 but you had no *o* to show it.
Col 4: 5 make the most of every *o*.
1Ti 5: 14 to give the enemy no *o* for slander.
Heb 11: 15 they would have had *o* to return.

OPPOSE (OPPONENTS OPPOSED OPPOSES OPPOSING OPPOSITION)
Ex 23: 22 and will *o* those who *o* you.
1Sa 2: 10 those who *o* the LORD will be
Job 23: 13 he stands alone, and who can *o* him
Ac 11: 17 I to think that I could *o* God?"
2Ti 2: 25 Those who *o* him he must gently
Tit 1: 9 doctrine and refute those who *o* it.
2: 8 so that those who *o* you may be

OPPOSED (OPPOSE)
Gal 2: 11 to Antioch, I *o* him to his face,
3: 21 therefore, *o* to the promises of God

OPPOSES (OPPOSE)
Jas 4: 6 "God *o* the proud
1Pe 5: 5 because, "God *o* the proud

OPPOSING (OPPOSE)
1Ti 6: 20 the *o* ideas of what is falsely called

OPPOSITION (OPPOSE)
Heb 12: 3 Consider him who endured such *o*

OPPRESS (OPPRESSED OPPRESSES OPPRESSION OPPRESSOR)
Ex 1: 11 masters over them to *o* them
22: 21 "Do not mistreat an alien or *o* him,
Isa 3: 5 People will *o* each other—
Eze 22: 29 they *o* the poor and needy
Da 7: 25 the Most High and *o* his saints
Am 5: 12 You *o* the righteous and take bribes
Zec 7: 10 Do not *o* the widow
Mal 3: 5 who *o* the widows

OPPRESSED (OPPRESS)
Jdg 2: 18 as they groaned under those who *o*
Ps 9: 9 The LORD is a refuge for the *o*,
82: 3 the rights of the poor and *o*.
146: 7 He upholds the cause of the *o*
Pr 16: 19 in spirit and among the *o*
31: 5 and deprive all the *o* of their rights.
Isa 1: 17 encourage the *o*.
53: 7 He was *o* and afflicted,
58: 10 and satisfy the needs of the *o*,
Zec 10: 2 *o* for lack of a shepherd.
Lk 4: 18 to release the *o*,

OPPRESSES (OPPRESS)
Pr 14: 31 He who *o* the poor shows contempt
22: 16 He who *o* the poor
Eze 18: 12 He *o* the poor and needy.

OPPRESSION (OPPRESS)
Ps 12: 5 "Because of the *o* of the weak
72: 14 He will rescue them from *o*
119: 134 Redeem me from the *o* of men,
Isa 53: 8 By *o* and judgment he was taken
58: 9 "If you do away with the yoke of *o*,

OPPRESSOR (OPPRESS)
Ps 72: 4 he will crush the *o*.
Isa 51: 13 For where is the wrath of the *o*?
Jer 22: 3 hand of his *o* the one who has been

ORDAINED
Ps 8: 2 you have *o* praise
111: 9 he *o* his covenant forever—
139: 16 All the days *o* for me
Eze 28: 14 for so I *o* you.
Hab 1: 12 you have *o* them to punish.
Mt 21: 16 you have *o* praise'?"

ORDER (ORDERLY ORDERS)
Nu 9: 23 They obeyed the LORD's *o*,
Ps 110: 4 in the *o* of Melchizedek."
Heb 5: 10 priest in the *o* of Melchizedek.
9: 10 until the time of the new *o*.
Rev 21: 4 for the old *o* of things has passed

ORDERLY (ORDER)
1Co 14: 40 done in a fitting and *o* way.
Col 2: 5 and delight to see how *o* you are

ORDERS (ORDER)
Mk 1: 27 He even gives *o* to evil spirits
3: 12 But he gave them strict *o* not
9: 9 Jesus gave them *o* not

ORDINARY
Ac 4: 13 that they were unschooled, *o* men,

ORGIES*
Ro 13: 13 not in *o* and drunkenness,
Gal 5: 21 drunkenness, *o*, and the like.
1Pe 4: 3 *o*, carousing and detestable

ORIGIN (ORIGINATE ORIGINS)
2Pe 1: 21 For prophecy never had its *o*

ORIGINATE* (ORIGIN)
1Co 14: 36 Did the word of God *o* with you?

ORIGINS* (ORIGIN)
Mic 5: 2 whose *o* are from of old,

ORNAMENT* (ORNAMENTED)
Pr 3: 22 an *o* to grace your neck.
25: 12 of gold or an *o* of fine gold

ORNAMENTED (ORNAMENT)
Ge 37: 3 and he made a richly *o* robe for him

ORPHAN* (ORPHANS)
Ex 22: 22 advantage of a widow or an *o*.

ORPHANS (ORPHAN)
Jn 14: 18 will not leave you as *o*; I will come
Jas 1: 27 to look after *o* and widows

OTHNIEL
Nephew of Caleb (Jos 15:15–19; Jdg 1:12–15). Judge who freed Israel from Aram (Jdg 3:7–11).

OUTBURSTS*
2Co 12: 20 jealousy, *o* of anger, factions,

OUTCOME
Heb 13: 7 Consider the *o* of their way of life
1Pe 4: 17 what will the *o* be for those who do

OUTNUMBER
Ps 139: 18 they would *o* the grains of sand.

OUTSIDERS*
Col 4: 5 wise in the way you act toward *o*;
1Th 4: 12 daily life may win the respect of *o*
1Ti 3: 7 also have a good reputation with *o*,

OUTSTANDING
SS 5: 10 *o* among ten thousand.
Ro 13: 8 no debt remain *o*,

OUTSTRETCHED
Ex 6: 6 and will redeem you with an *o* arm
Dt 4: 34 by a mighty hand and an *o* arm,
5: 15 with a mighty hand and an *o* arm.
1Ki 8: 42 your mighty hand and your *o* arm
Ps 136: 12 with a mighty hand and *o* arm;
Jer 27: 5 and *o* arm I made the earth
32: 17 by your great power and *o* arm.
Eze 20: 33 an *o* arm and with outpoured wrath

OUTWEIGHS (WEIGH)
2Co 4: 17 an eternal glory that far *o* them all.

OUTWIT*
2Co 2: 11 in order that Satan might not *o* us.

OVERAWED* (AWE)
Ps 49: 16 Do not be *o* when a man grows rich

OVERBEARING*
Tit 1: 7 not *o*, not quick-tempered,

OVERCAME (OVERCOME)
Rev 3: 21 as I *o* and sat down with my Father
12: 11 They *o* him

OVERCOME (OVERCAME OVERCOMES)
Mt 16: 18 and the gates of Hades will not *o* it.
Mk 9: 24 I do believe; help me *o* my unbelief
Lk 10: 19 to *o* all the power of the enemy;
Jn 16: 33 But take heart! I have *o* the world."
Ro 12: 21 Do not be *o* by evil, but *o* evil
2Pe 2: 20 and are again entangled in it and *o*,
1Jn 2: 13 because you have *o* the evil one.
4: 4 are from God and have *o* them,
5: 4 is the victory that has *o* the world,
Rev 17: 14 but the Lamb will *o* them

OVERCOMES* (OVERCOME)
1Jn 5: 4 born of God *o* the world.
5: 5 Who is it that *o* the world?
Rev 2: 7 To him who *o*, I will give the right
2: 11 He who *o* will not be hurt at all
2: 17 To him who *o*, I will give some
2: 26 To him who *o* and does my will
3: 5 He who *o* will, like them, be
3: 12 Him who *o* I will make a pillar
3: 21 To him who *o*, I will give the right
21: 7 He who *o* will inherit all this,

OVERFLOW (OVERFLOWING OVERFLOWS)
Ps 65: 11 and your carts *o* with abundance.
119: 171 May my lips *o* with praise,
La 1: 16 and my eyes *o* with tears.
Mt 12: 34 out of the *o* of the heart the mouth
Lk 6: 45 out of the *o* of his heart his mouth
Ro 5: 15 Jesus Christ, *o* to the many! Again,
15: 13 so that you may *o* with hope
2Co 4: 15 to *o* to the glory of God.
1Th 3: 12 *o* for each other and for everyone

OVERFLOWING (OVERFLOW)
Pr 3: 10 then your barns will be filled to *o*,
2Co 8: 2 their *o* joy and their extreme
9: 12 *o* in many expressions of thanks
Col 2: 7 as you were taught, and *o*

OVERFLOWS* (OVERFLOW)
Ps 23: 5 my cup *o*.
2Co 1: 5 also through Christ our comfort *o*.

OVERJOYED* (JOY)
Da 6: 23 The king was *o* and gave orders
Mt 2: 10 they saw the star, they were *o*.
Jn 20: 20 The disciples were *o*
Ac 12: 14 she was so *o* she ran back
1Pe 4: 13 so that you may be *o*

OVERLOOK
Pr 19: 11 it is to his glory to *o* an offense.

OVERSEER* (OVERSEERS)
Pr 6: 7 no *o* or ruler,
1Ti 3: 1 anyone sets his heart on being an *o*,
3: 2 Now the *o* must be above reproach,
Tit 1: 7 Since an *o* is entrusted
1Pe 2: 25 returned to the Shepherd and *O*

OVERSEERS* (OVERSEER)
Ac 20: 28 the Holy Spirit has made you *o*.
Php 1: 1 together with the *o* and deacons:
1Pe 5: 2 as *o*—not because you must,

OVERSHADOW* (OVERSHADOWING)
Lk 1: 35 power of the Most High will *o* you.

OVERSHADOWING (OVERSHADOW)
Ex 25: 20 wings spread upward, *o* the cover
Heb 9: 5 the glory, *o* the atonement cover.

OVERTHROW (OVERTHROWS)
2Th 2: 8 whom the Lord Jesus will *o*

OVERTHROWS (OVERTHROW)
Pr 13: 6 but wickedness *o* the sinner.
Isa 44: 25 who *o* the learning of the wise

OVERWHELMED (OVERWHELMING)
2Sa 22: 5 the torrents of destruction *o* me.
1Ki 10: 5 temple of the LORD, she was *o*.
Ps 38: 4 My guilt has *o* me
65: 3 When we were *o* by sins,
Mt 26: 38 "My soul is *o* with sorrow
Mk 7: 37 People were *o* with amazement.
9: 15 they were *o* with wonder
2Co 2: 7 so that he will not be *o*

OVERWHELMING (OVERWHELMED)
Pr 27: 4 Anger is cruel and fury *o*,
Isa 10: 22 *o* and righteous.
28: 15 When an *o* scourge sweeps by,

OWE
Ro 13: 7 If you *o* taxes, pay taxes; if revenue
Phm : 19 to mention that you *o* me your very

OWNER'S (OWNERSHIP)
Isa 1: 3 the donkey his *o* manger,

OWNERSHIP* (OWNER'S)
2Co 1: 22 He anointed us, set his seal of *o*

OX (OXEN)
Dt 25: 4 Do not muzzle an *o*
Isa 11: 7 and the lion will eat straw like the *o*
Eze 1: 10 and on the left the face of an *o;*
Lk 13: 15 of you on the Sabbath untie his *o*
1Co 9: 9 "Do not muzzle an *o*
1Ti 5: 18 "Do not muzzle the *o*
Rev 4: 7 second was like an *o,* the third had

OXEN (OX)
1Ki 19: 20 Elisha then left his *o* and ran
Lk 14: 19 'I have just bought five yoke of *o,*

PAGAN (PAGANS)
Mt 18: 17 as you would a *p* or a tax collector.
Lk 12: 30 For the *p* world runs

PAGANS* (PAGAN)
Isa 2: 6 and clasp hands with *p.*
Mt 5: 47 Do not even *p* do that? Be perfect,
6: 7 do not keep on babbling like *p,*
6: 32 For the *p* run after all these things,
1Co 5: 1 that does not occur even among *p:*
10: 20 but the sacrifices of *p* are offered
12: 2 You know that when you were *p,*
1Pe 2: 12 such good lives among the *p* that,
4: 3 in the past doing what *p* choose
3Jn : 7 receiving no help from the *p.*

PAID (PAY)
Isa 40: 2 that her sin has been *p* for,
Zec 11: 12 So they *p* me thirty pieces of silver.

PAIN (PAINFUL PAINS)
Ge 3: 16 with *p* you will give birth
6: 6 and his heart was filled with *p.*
Job 6: 10 my joy in unrelenting *p* —
33: 19 may be chastened on a bed of *p*
Jer 4: 19 I writhe in *p.*
15: 18 Why is my *p* unending
Mt 4: 24 suffering severe *p,*
Jn 16: 21 woman giving birth to a child has *p*
1Pe 2: 19 up under the *p* of unjust suffering
Rev 21: 4 or mourning or crying or *p,*

PAINFUL (PAIN)
Ge 3: 17 through *p* toil you will eat of it
5: 29 and *p* toil of our hands caused
Job 6: 25 How *p* are honest words!
Eze 28: 24 neighbors who are *p* briers
2Co 2: 1 I would not make another *p* visit
Heb 12: 11 seems pleasant at the time, but *p.*
1Pe 4: 12 at the *p* trial you are suffering,

PAINS (PAIN)
Ge 3: 16 "I will greatly increase your *p*
Mt 24: 8 these are the beginning of birth *p.*
Ro 8: 22 as in the *p* of childbirth right up
Gal 4: 19 again in the *p* of childbirth
1Th 5: 3 as labor *p* on a pregnant woman,

PAIRS
Ge 7: 8 *P* of clean and unclean animals,

PALACE (PALACES)
2Sa 7: 2 "Here I am, living in a *p* of cedar,
Jer 22: 6 is what the LORD says about the *p*
22: 13 "Woe to him who builds his *p*

PALACES (PALACE)
Mt 11: 8 wear fine clothes are in kings' *p.*
Lk 7: 25 and indulge in luxury are in *p.*

PALE
Isa 29: 22 no longer will their faces grow *p.*
Jer 30: 6 every face turned deathly *p?*
Da 10: 8 my face turned deathly *p*
Rev 6: 8 and there before me was a *p* horse!

PALM (PALMS)
Jn 12: 13 They took *p* branches and went out
Rev 7: 9 and were holding *p* branches

PALMS (PALM)
Isa 49: 16 you on the *p* of my hands;

PAMPERS*
Pr 29: 21 If a man *p* his servant from youth,

PANIC
Dt 20: 3 or give way to *p* before them.
1Sa 14: 15 It was a *p* sent by God.
Eze 7: 7 there is *p,* not joy,
Zec 14: 13 by the LORD with great *p.*

PANTS
Ps 42: 1 As the deer *p* for streams of water,

PARABLES
See also JESUS: PARABLES
Ps 78: 2 I will open my mouth in *p,*
Mt 13: 35 "I will open my mouth in *p,*
Lk 8: 10 but to others I speak in *p,* so that,

PARADISE*
Lk 23: 43 today you will be with me in *p.*"
2Co 12: 4 God knows — was caught up to *p.*
Rev 2: 7 of life, which is in the *p* of God.

PARALYTIC
Mt 9: 2 Some men brought to him a *p,*
Mk 2: 3 bringing to him a *p,* carried by four
Ac 9: 33 a *p* who had been bedridden

PARCHED
Ps 143: 6 my soul thirsts for you like a *p* land.

PARCHMENTS*
2Ti 4: 13 and my scrolls, especially the *p.*

PARDON* (PARDONED PARDONS)
2Ch 30: 18 *p* everyone who sets his heart
Job 7: 21 Why do you not *p* my offenses
Isa 55: 7 and to our God, for he will freely *p.*
Joel 3: 21 I will *p.*"

PARDONED* (PARDON)
Nu 14: 19 as you have *p* them from the time
Joel 3: 21 bloodguilt, which I have not *p,*

PARDONS* (PARDON)
Mic 7: 18 who *p* sin and forgives

PARENTS
Pr 17: 6 and *p* are the pride of their children
19: 14 wealth are inherited from *p,*
Mt 10: 21 children will rebel against their *p*
Lk 18: 29 left home or wife or brothers or *p*
21: 16 You will be betrayed even by *p,* brothers,
Jn 9: 3 Neither this man nor his *p* sinned,"
Ro 1: 30 they disobey their *p;* they are
2Co 12: 14 for their *p,* but *p* for their children.
Eph 6: 1 Children, obey your *p* in the Lord,
Col 3: 20 obey your *p* in everything,
1Ti 5: 4 repaying their *p* and grandparents,
2Ti 3: 2 disobedient to their *p,* ungrateful,

PARTAKE*
1Co 10: 17 for we all *p* of the one loaf.

PARTIAL* (PARTIALITY)
Pr 18: 5 It is not good to be *p* to the wicked

PARTIALITY (PARTIAL)
Lev 19: 15 do not show *p* to the poor
Dt 1: 17 Do not show *p* in judging;
10: 17 who shows no *p* and accepts no
16: 19 Do not pervert justice or show *p.*
2Ch 19: 7 our God there is no injustice or *p*
Job 32: 21 I will show *p* to no one,
34: 19 who shows no *p* to princes
Pr 24: 23 To show *p* in judging is not good:
Mal 2: 9 have shown *p* in matters of the law
Lk 20: 21 and that you do not show *p*
1Ti 5: 21 keep these instructions without *p,*

PARTICIPANTS (PARTICIPATE)
1Co 10: 20 you to be *p* with demons.

PARTICIPATE (PARTICIPANTS PARTICIPATION)
1Pe 4: 13 rejoice that you *p* in the sufferings
2Pe 1: 4 that through them you may *p*

PARTICIPATION (PARTICIPATE)
1Co 10: 16 is not the bread that we break a *p*

PARTNER (PARTNERS PARTNERSHIP)
Pr 2: 17 who has left the *p* of her youth
Mal 2: 14 though she is your *p,* the wife
1Pe 3: 7 them with respect as the weaker *p*

PARTNERS (PARTNER)
Eph 5: 7 Therefore do not be *p* with them.

PARTNERSHIP* (PARTNER)
Php 1: 5 because of your *p* in the gospel

PASS (PASSED PASSER-BY PASSING)
Ex 12: 13 and when I see the blood, I will *p*
33: 19 goodness to *p* in front of you,
1Ki 9: 8 all who *p* by will be appalled
19: 11 for the LORD is about to *p* by."
Ps 90: 10 for they quickly *p,* and we fly away.
105: 19 till what he foretold came to *p,*
Isa 31: 5 he will '*p* over' it and will rescue it
43: 2 When you *p* through the waters,
62: 10 *P* through, *p* through the gates!
Jer 22: 8 "People from many nations will *p*
La 1: 12 to you, all you who *p* by?
Da 7: 14 dominion that will not *p* away,
Am 5: 17 for I will *p* through your midst,"
Mt 24: 34 will certainly not *p* away
24: 35 Heaven and earth will *p* away,
Mk 13: 31 Heaven and earth will *p* away,
Lk 21: 33 Heaven and earth will *p* away,
1Co 13: 8 there is knowledge, it will *p* away.
Jas 1: 10 he will *p* away like a wild flower.
1Jn 2: 17 The world and its desires *p* away,

PASSED (PASS)
Ge 15: 17 a blazing torch appeared and *p*
Ex 33: 22 you with my hand until I have *p* by.
2Ch 21: 20 He *p* away, to no one's regret,
Ps 57: 1 wings until the disaster has *p.*
Lk 10: 32 saw him, *p* by on the other side.
1Co 15: 3 For what I received I *p* on to you
Heb 11: 29 By faith the people *p*

PASSER-BY* (PASS)
Pr 26: 10 is he who hires a fool or any *p.*
26: 17 is a *p* who meddles

PASSING (PASS)
1Co 7: 31 world in its present form is *p* away.
1Jn 2: 8 because the darkness is *p*

PASSION* (PASSIONATE PASSIONS)
Hos 7: 6 Their *p* smolders all night;
1Co 7: 9 better to marry than to burn with *p.*

PASSIONATE* (PASSION)
1Th 4: 5 not in *p* lust like the heathen,

PASSIONS* (PASSION)
Ro 7: 5 the sinful *p* aroused
Gal 5: 24 crucified the sinful nature with its *p*
Tit 2: 12 to ungodliness and worldly *p,*
3: 3 and enslaved by all kinds of *p*

PASSOVER
Ex 12: 11 Eat it in haste; it is the LORD'S *P.*
Nu 9: 2 Have the Israelites celebrate the *P*
Dt 16: 1 celebrate the *P* of the LORD your
Jos 5: 10 the Israelites celebrated the *P.*
2Ki 23: 21 "Celebrate the *P* to the LORD
Ezr 6: 19 the exiles celebrated the *P.*
Mk 14: 12 customary to sacrifice the *P* lamb,
Lk 22: 1 called the *P,* was approaching,
1Co 5: 7 our *P* lamb, has been sacrificed.
Heb 11: 28 he kept the *P* and the sprinkling

PAST
Isa 43: 18 do not dwell on the *p.*
65: 16 For the *p* troubles will be forgotten
Ro 15: 4 in the *p* was written to teach us,
16: 25 the mystery hidden for long ages *p,*
Eph 3: 9 which for ages *p* was kept hidden
Heb 1: 1 In the *p* God spoke

PASTORS*
Eph 4: 11 and some to be *p* and teachers,

PASTURE (PASTURES)
Ps 37: 3 dwell in the land and enjoy safe *p.*
95: 7 and we are the people of his *p,*
100: 3 we are his people, the sheep of his *p*
Jer 50: 7 against the LORD, their true *p,*
Eze 34: 13 I will *p* them on the mountains
Zec 11: 4 "*P* the flock marked for slaughter.
Jn 10: 9 come in and go out, and find *p.*

PASTURES (PASTURE)
Ps 23: 2 He makes me lie down in green *p,*

PATCH
Jer 10: 5 Like a scarecrow in a melon *p,*
Mt 9: 16 No one sews a *p* of unshrunk cloth

PATH (PATHS)
Ps 16: 11 known to me the *p* of life;
27: 11 lead me in a straight *p*
119: 32 I run in the *p* of your commands,
119: 105 and a light for my *p.*
Pr 2: 9 and fair — every good *p.*
12: 28 along that *p* is immortality.
15: 10 awaits him who leaves the *p;*
15: 19 the *p* of the upright is a highway.
15: 24 The *p* of life leads upward
21: 16 from the *p* of understanding
Isa 26: 7 The *p* of the righteous is level;
Jer 31: 9 on a level *p* where they will not
Mt 13: 4 fell along the *p,* and the birds came
Lk 1: 79 to guide our feet into the *p* of peace
2Co 6: 3 no stumbling block in anyone's *p,*

PATHS (PATH)
Ps 23: 3 He guides me in *p* of righteousness
25: 4 teach me your *p;*
Pr 2: 13 who leave the straight *p*
3: 6 and he will make your *p* straight.
4: 11 and lead you along straight *p.*
4: 26 Make level *p* for your feet
5: 21 and he examines all his *p.*
8: 20 along the *p* of justice,
22: 5 In the *p* of the wicked lie thorns
Isa 2: 3 so that we may walk in his *p.*"
Jer 6: 16 ask for the ancient *p,*

Mic 4: 2 so that we may walk in his *p*."
Mt 3: 3 make straight *p* for him.'"
Ac 2: 28 to me the *p* of life;
Ro 11: 33 and his *p* beyond tracing out!
Heb 12: 13 "Make level *p* for your feet,"

PATIENCE* (PATIENT)
Pr 19: 11 A man's wisdom gives him *p;*
25: 15 Through *p* a ruler can be persuaded
Ecc 7: 8 and *p* is better than pride.
Isa 7: 13 Is it not enough to try the *p* of men?
7: 13 Will you try the *p* of my God also?
Ro 2: 4 and *p,* not realizing that God's
9: 22 bore with great *p* the objects
2Co 6: 6 understanding, *p* and kindness;
Gal 5: 22 joy, peace, *p,* kindness, goodness,
Col 1: 11 may have great endurance and *p,*
3: 12 humility, gentleness and *p.*
1Ti 1: 16 Jesus might display his unlimited *p*
2Ti 3: 10 my purpose, faith, *p,* love,
4: 2 with great *p* and careful instruction
Heb 6: 12 *p* inherit what has been promised.
Jas 5: 10 as an example of *p* in the face
2Pe 3: 15 that our Lord's *p* means salvation,

PATIENT* (PATIENCE PATIENTLY)
Ne 9: 30 For many years you were *p*
Job 6: 11 What prospects, that I should be *p?*
Pr 14: 29 A *p* man has great understanding,
15: 18 but a *p* man calms a quarrel.
16: 32 Better a *p* man than a warrior,
Mt 18: 26 'Be *p* with me,' he begged,
18: 29 'Be *p* with me, and I will pay you
Ro 12: 12 Be joyful in hope, *p* in affliction,
1Co 13: 4 Love is *p,* love is kind.
2Co 1: 6 produces in you *p* endurance
Eph 4: 2 humble and gentle; be *p,*
1Th 5: 14 help the weak, be *p* with everyone.
Jas 5: 7 Be *p,* then, brothers,
5: 7 and how *p* he is for the autumn
5: 8 You too, be *p* and stand firm,
2Pe 3: 9 He is *p* with you, not wanting
Rev 1: 9 *p* endurance that are ours in Jesus,
13: 10 This calls for *p* endurance
14: 12 This calls for *p* endurance

PATIENTLY* (PATIENT)
Ps 37: 7 still before the LORD and wait *p*
40: 1 I waited *p* for the LORD;
Isa 38: 13 I waited *p* till dawn,
Hab 3: 16 Yet I will wait *p* for the day
Ac 26: 3 I beg you to listen to me *p.*
Ro 8: 25 we do not yet have, we wait for it *p.*
Heb 6: 15 after waiting *p,* Abraham received
1Pe 3: 20 ago when God waited *p* in the days
Rev 3: 10 kept my command to endure *p,*

PATTERN
Ex 25: 40 according to the *p* shown you
Ro 5: 14 who was a *p* of the one to come.
12: 2 longer to the *p* of this world,
2Ti 1: 13 keep as the *p* of sound teaching,
Heb 8: 5 according to the *p* shown you

PAUL

Also called Saul (Ac 13:9). Pharisee from Tarsus (Ac 9:11; Php 3:5). Apostle (Gal 1). At stoning of Stephen (Ac 8:1). Persecuted Church (Ac 9:1–2; Gal 1:13). Vision of Jesus on road to Damascus (Ac 9:4–9; 26:12–18). In Arabia (Gal 1:17). Preached in Damascus; escaped death through the wall in a basket (Ac 9:19–25). In Jerusalem; sent back to Tarsus (Ac 9:26–30).

Brought to Antioch by Barnabas (Ac 11:22–26). First missionary journey to Cyprus and Galatia (Ac 13–14). Stoned at Lystra (Ac 14:19–20). At Jerusalem council (Ac 15). Split with Barnabas over Mark (Ac 15:36–41).

Second missionary journey with Silas (Ac 16–20). Called to Macedonia (Ac 16:6–10). Freed from prison in Philippi (Ac 16:16–40). In Thessalonica (Ac 17:1–9). Speech in Athens (Ac 17:16–33). In Corinth (Ac 18). In Ephesus (Ac 19). Return to Jerusalem (Ac 20). Farewell to Ephesian elders (Ac 20:13–38). Arrival in Jerusalem (Ac 21:1–26). Arrested (Ac 21:27–36). Addressed crowds (Ac 22), Sanhedrin (Ac 23:1–11). Transferred to Caesarea (Ac 23:12–35). Trial before Felix (Ac 24), Festus (Ac 25:1–12). Before Agrippa (Ac 25:13–26:32). Voyage to Rome; shipwreck (Ac 27). Arrival in Rome (Ac 28).

Epistles: Romans, 1 and 2 Corinthians, Galatians, Ephesians, Philippians, Colossians, 1 and 2 Thessalonians, 1 and 2 Timothy, Titus, Philemon.

PAVEMENT
Jn 19: 13 as the Stone *P* (which

PAY (PAID PAYMENT PAYS REPAID REPAY REPAYING)
Lev 26: 43 They will *p* for their sins
Dt 7: 12 If you *p* attention to these laws
Pr 4: 1 *p* attention and gain understanding
4: 20 My son, *p* attention to what I say;
Pr 5: 1 My son, *p* attention to my wisdom,
6: 31 if he is caught, he must *p* sevenfold,
19: 19 man must *p* the penalty;
22: 17 *P* attention and listen
24: 29 I'll *p* that man back for what he did
Eze 40: 4 and *p* attention to everything I am
Zec 11: 12 give me my *p;* but if not, keep it."
Mt 20: 2 He agreed to *p* them a denarius
22: 16 you *p* no attention to who they are.
22: 17 Is it right to *p* taxes to Caesar
Lk 3: 14 falsely — be content with your *p.*"
19: 8 I will *p* back four times the amount
Ro 13: 6 This is also why you *p* taxes,
2Pe 1: 19 you will do well to *p* attention to it,

PAYMENT (PAY)
Ps 49: 8 no *p* is ever enough —
Php 4: 18 I have received full *p* and

PAYS (PAY)
Pr 17: 13 If a man *p* back evil for good,
1Th 5: 15 sure that nobody *p* back wrong

PEACE (PEACEABLE PEACEFUL PEACEMAKERS)
Lev 26: 6 "'I will grant *p* in the land,
Nu 6: 26 and give you *p.*"'
25: 12 him I am making my covenant of *p*
Dt 20: 10 make its people an offer of *p.*
Jdg 3: 11 So the land had *p* for forty years,
3: 30 and the land had *p* for eighty years.
5: 31 Then the land had *p* forty years.
6: 24 and called it The LORD is *P.*
8: 28 the land enjoyed *p* forty years.
1Sa 7: 14 And there was *p* between Israel
2Sa 10: 19 they made *p* with the Israelites
1Ki 2: 33 may there be the LORD's *p* forever
22: 44 also at *p* with the king of Israel.
2Ki 9: 17 come in *p?*'" The horseman rode
1Ch 19: 19 they made *p* with David
22: 9 and I will grant Israel *p*
2Ch 14: 1 and in his days the country was at *p*
20: 30 kingdom of Jehoshaphat was at *p,*
Job 3: 26 I have no *p,* no quietness;
22: 21 to God and be at *p* with him;
Ps 29: 11 LORD blesses his people with *p.*
34: 14 seek *p* and pursue it.
37: 11 and enjoy great *p.*
37: 37 there is a future for the man of *p.*
85: 10 righteousness and *p* kiss each other
119: 165 Great *p* have they who love your
120: 7 I am a man of *p;*
122: 6 Pray for the *p* of Jerusalem:
147: 14 He grants *p* to your borders
Pr 12: 20 but joy for those who promote *p.*
14: 30 A heart at *p* gives life to the body,
16: 7 his enemies live at *p* with him.
17: 1 Better a dry crust with *p* and quiet
Ecc 3: 8 a time for war and a time for *p.*
Isa 9: 6 Everlasting Father, Prince of *P.*
14: 7 All the lands are at rest and at *p;*
26: 3 You will keep in perfect *p*
32: 17 The fruit of righteousness will be *p;*
48: 18 your *p* would have been like a river,
48: 22 "There is no *p,*" says the LORD,
52: 7 who proclaim *p,*
53: 5 punishment that brought us *p* was
54: 10 nor my covenant of *p* be removed,"
55: 12 and be led forth in *p;*
57: 2 enter into *p;*
57: 19 *P, p,* to those far and near,"
57: 21 "There is no *p,*" says my God,
59: 8 The way of *p* they do not know;
Jer 6: 14 '*P, p,*' they say,
8: 11 "*P, p,*" . . . there is no *p.*
30: 10 Jacob will again have *p*
46: 27 Jacob will again have *p*
Eze 13: 10 "*P,*" when there is no *p,*
34: 25 "'I will make a covenant of *p*
37: 26 I will make a covenant of *p*
Mic 5: 5 And he will be their *p.*
Zec 8: 19 Therefore love truth and *p.*"
9: 10 He will proclaim *p* to the nations.
Mal 2: 5 a covenant of life and *p,*
2: 6 He walked with me in *p*
Mt 10: 34 I did not come to bring *p,*
Mk 9: 50 and be at *p* with each other."
Lk 1: 79 to guide our feet into the path of *p*
2: 14 on earth *p* to men on whom his
19: 38 "*P* in heaven and glory
Jn 14: 27 *P* I leave with you; my *p*
16: 33 so that in me you may have *p.*
Ro 1: 7 and *p* to you from God our Father
2: 10 and *p* for everyone who does good:
5: 1 we have *p* with God
8: 6 by the Spirit is life and *p;*
12: 18 on you, live at *p* with everyone.
14: 19 effort to do what leads to *p*
1Co 7: 15 God has called us to live in *p.*
14: 33 a God of disorder but of *p.*
2Co 13: 11 be of one mind, live in *p.*
Gal 5: 22 joy, *p,* patience, kindness,
Eph 2: 14 he himself is our *p,* who has made
2: 15 thus making *p,* and in this one body
2: 17 and *p* to those who were near.
6: 15 comes from the gospel of *p.*
Php 4: 7 the *p* of God, which transcends all
Col 1: 20 by making *p* through his blood,
3: 15 Let the *p* of Christ rule
3: 15 of one body you were called to *p.*
1Th 5: 3 While people are saying, "*P*
5: 13 Live in *p* with each other.
5: 23 the God of *p,* sanctify you through
2Th 3: 16 the Lord of *p* himself give you *p*
2Ti 2: 22 righteousness, faith, love and *p,*
Heb 7: 2 "king of Salem" means "king of *p.*"
12: 11 *p* for those who have been trained
12: 14 effort to live in *p* with all men
13: 20 May the God of *p,* who
1Pe 3: 11 he must seek *p* and pursue it.
2Pe 3: 14 blameless and at *p* with him.
Rev 6: 4 power to take *p* from the earth

PEACEABLE* (PEACE)
Tit 3: 2 to slander no one, to be *p*

PEACEFUL (PEACE)
1Ti 2: 2 that we may live *p* and quiet lives

PEACE-LOVING
Jas 3: 17 then *p,* considerate

PEACEMAKERS* (PEACE)
Mt 5: 9 Blessed are the *p,*
Jas 3: 18 *P* who sow in peace raise a harvest

PEARL* (PEARLS)
Rev 21: 21 each gate made of a single *p.*

PEARLS (PEARL)
Mt 7: 6 do not throw your *p* to pigs.
13: 45 like a merchant looking for fine *p.*
1Ti 2: 9 or gold or *p* or expensive clothes,
Rev 21: 21 The twelve gates were twelve *p,*

PEDDLE*
2Co 2: 17 we do not *p* the word of God

PEG
Jdg 4: 21 She drove the *p* through his temple

PEKAH

King of Israel (2Ki 15:25–31; Isa 7:1).

PEKAHIAH*

Son of Menahem; king of Israel (2Ki 15:22–26).

PEN
Ps 45: 1 my tongue is the *p*
Mt 5: 18 letter, not the least stroke of a *p,*
Jn 10: 1 who does not enter the sheep *p*

PENETRATES*
Heb 4: 12 it *p* even to dividing soul and spirit,

PENNIES* (PENNY)
Lk 12: 6 not five sparrows sold for two *p?*

PENNY* (PENNIES)
Mt 5: 26 out until you have paid the last *p.*
10: 29 Are not two sparrows sold for a *p?*
Mk 12: 42 worth only a fraction of a *p.*
Lk 12: 59 out until you have paid the last *p.*"

PENTECOST*
Ac 2: 1 of *P* came, they were all together
20: 16 if possible, by the day of *P.*
1Co 16: 8 I will stay on at Ephesus until *P,*

PEOPLE (PEOPLES)
Ge 11: 6 as one *p* speaking the same
Ex 5: 1 Let my *p* go,
6: 7 take you as my own *p,*
8: 23 between my *p* and your *p.*
15: 13 the *p* you have redeemed.
19: 8 The *p* all responded together,
24: 3 Moses went and told the *p*
32: 1 When the *p* saw that Moses
32: 9 they are a stiff-necked *p.*
33: 13 this nation is your *p.*
Lev 9: 7 for yourself and the *p;*
16: 24 the burnt offering for the *p,*
26: 12 and you will be my *p.*
Nu 11: 11 burden of all these *p* on
14: 11 *p* treat me with contempt?
14: 19 forgive the sin of these *p,*
22: 5 A *p* has come out of Egypt
Dt 4: 6 a wise and understanding *p.*
4: 20 the *p* of his inheritance,
5: 28 what this *p* said to you.

Dt 7: 6 a *p* holy to the LORD
26: 18 that you are his *p*,
31: 7 you must go with this *p*
31: 16 these *p* will soon prostitute
32: 9 the LORD's portion is his *p*,
32: 43 atonement for his land and *p*.
33: 29 a *p* saved by the LORD?
Jos 1: 6 you will lead this *p*
24: 24 the *p* said to Joshua,
Jdg 2: 7 *p* served the LORD throughout
Ru 1: 16 Your *p* will be my *p*
1Sa 8: 7 the *p* are saying to you;
12: 22 LORD will not reject his *p*,
2Sa 5: 2 will shepherd my *p* Israel
7: 10 provide a place for my *p*
1Ki 3: 8 among the *p* you have chosen,
8: 30 your *p* Israel when they pray
8: 56 has given rest to his *p*
18: 39 when all the *p* saw this,
2Ki 23: 3 all the *p* pledged themselves
1Ch 17: 21 to redeem *p* for himself
29: 17 how willingly your *p* who are
2Ch 2: 11 Because the LORD loves his *p*,
7: 5 *p* dedicated the temple
7: 14 if my *p*, who are called
30: 6 "*P* of Israel, return to
36: 16 was aroused against his *p*
Ezr 2: 1 These are the *p* of the
3: 1 *p* assembled as one man
Ne 1: 10 your *p*, whom you redeemed
4: 6 *p* worked with all their heart
8: 1 *p* assembled as one man
Est 3: 6 to destroy all Mordecai's *p*,
Job 12: 2 Doubtless you are the *p*,
Ps 29: 11 gives strength to his *p*;
33: 12 *p* he chose for his inheritance
50: 4 that he may judge his *p*
53: 6 restores the fortunes of his *p*,
81: 13 If my *p* would but listen
94: 14 LORD will not reject his *p*;
95: 7 we are the *p* of his pasture,
95: 10 a *p* whose hearts go astray,
125: 2 the LORD surrounds his *p*
135: 14 LORD will vindicate his *p*
144: 15 *p* whose God is the LORD.
Pr 14: 34 sin is a disgrace to any *p*.
29: 2 righteous thrive, the *p* rejoice
29: 18 the *p* cast off restraint
Isa 1: 3 my *p* do not understand.
1: 4 a *p* loaded with guilt,
5: 13 my *p* will go into exile
6: 10 the heart of this *p* calloused;
9: 2 the *p* walking in darkness
12: 12 will assemble the scattered *p*
19: 25 Blessed be Egypt my *p*,
25: 8 remove the disgrace of his *p*
29: 13 These *p* come near to me
40: 1 Comfort, comfort my *p*
40: 7 Surely the *p* are grass.
42: 6 a covenant for the *p*
49: 13 the LORD comforts his *p*
51: 4 "Listen to me, my *p*;
52: 6 my *p* will know my name;
53: 8 for the transgression of my *p*
60: 21 will all your *p* be righteous
62: 12 will be called the Holy *P*,
65: 23 they will be a *p* blessed
Jer 2: 11 my *p* have exchanged their
2: 13 *p* have committed two sins:
2: 32 my *p* have forgotten me,
4: 22 My *p* are fools;
5: 14 Because the *p* have spoken
5: 31 my *p* love it this way
7: 16 do not pray for this *p*
7: 23 you will be my *p*,
18: 15 my *p* have forgotten me;
30: 3 I will bring my *p* Israel
Eze 13: 23 I will save my *p* from
36: 8 fruit for my *p* Israel,
36: 28 you will be my *p*,
36: 38 be filled with flocks of *p*.
37: 13 Then you, my *p*, will know
38: 14 *p* Israel are living in safety
39: 7 name among my *p* Israel.
Da 7: 27 saints, the *p* of the Most High.
8: 24 mighty men and the holy *p*
9: 19 your *p* bear your name
9: 24 are decreed for your *p*
9: 26 *p* of the ruler who will come
10: 14 will happen to your *p*
11: 32 *p* who know their God will
12: 1 prince who protects your *p*,
Hos 1: 10 'You are not my *p*,'
2: 23 'You are my *p*';
4: 14 a *p* without understanding
Joel 2: 18 and take pity on his *p*.
3: 16 be a refuge for his *p*,
Am 9: 14 back my exiled *p* Israel;
Mic 6: 2 a case against his *p*;
7: 14 Shepherd your *p* with
Hag 1: 12 remnant of the *p* obeyed
Zec 2: 11 and will become my *p*.
8: 7 I will save my *p*
13: 9 will say, 'They are my *p*,'
Mk 7: 6 *p* honor me with their lips
8: 27 "Who do *p* say I am?"
Lk 1: 17 make ready a *p* prepared
1: 68 and has redeemed his *p*.
2: 10 joy that will be for all the *p*.
21: 23 and wrath against this *p*.
Jn 11: 50 one man die for the *p*
18: 14 if one man died for the *p*.
Ac 15: 14 from the Gentiles a *p*.
18: 10 have many *p* in this city.
Ro 9: 25 will call them 'my *p*;'
11: 1 Did God reject his *p*?
15: 10 O Gentiles, with his *p*."
2Co 6: 16 and they will be my *p*."
Tit 2: 14 a *p* that are his very own,
Heb 2: 17 for the sins of the *p*.
4: 9 a Sabbath-rest for the *p*
5: 3 for the sins of the *p*.
10: 30 Lord will judge his *p*.
11: 25 mistreated along with the *p*
13: 12 to make the *p* holy
1Pe 2: 9 you are a chosen *p*,
2: 10 Once you were not a *p*,
2: 10 you are the *p* of God;
2Pe 2: 1 false prophets among the *p*,
3: 11 kind of *p* ought you to be?
Rev 18: 4 "Come out of her, my *p*,
21: 3 They will be his *p*,

PEOPLES (PEOPLE)
Ge 17: 16 kings of *p* will come from her
25: 23 two *p* from within you will
27: 29 and *p* bow down to you
28: 3 become a community of *p*.
48: 4 you a community of *p*,
Dt 14: 2 of all the *p* on the face of
28: 10 Then all the *p* on earth
32: 8 set up boundaries for the *p*
Jos 4: 24 all the *p* of the earth might
1Ki 8: 43 all the *p* of the earth may
2Ch 7: 20 of ridicule among all *p*.
Ps 9: 8 he will govern the *p*
67: 5 may all the *p* praise you.
87: 6 in the register of the *p*:
96: 10 he will judge the *p*
Isa 2: 4 settle disputes for many *p*.
17: 12 Oh, the uproar of the *p*—
25: 6 of rich food for all *p*,
34: 1 pay attention, you *p*!
55: 4 him a witness to the *p*,
Jer 10: 3 customs of the *p* are worthless
Da 7: 14 all *p*, nations and men
Mic 4: 1 and *p* will stream to it.
4: 3 will judge between many *p*
5: 7 in the midst of many *p*
Zep 3: 9 purify the lips of the *p*,
3: 20 among all the *p* of the
Zec 8: 20 Many *p* and the inhabitants
12: 2 all the surrounding *p* reeling.
Rev 10: 11 prophesy again about many *p*,
17: 15 the prostitute sits, are *p*,

PEOR
Nu 25: 3 joined in worshiping the Baal of *P*.
Dt 4: 3 who followed the Baal of *P*,

PERCEIVE (PERCEIVING)
Ps 139: 2 you *p* my thoughts from afar.
Pr 24: 12 not he who weighs the heart *p* it?

PERCEIVING* (PERCEIVE)
Isa 6: 9 be ever seeing, but never *p*.'
Mt 13: 14 you will be ever seeing but never *p*.
Mk 4: 12 may be ever seeing but never *p*,
Ac 28: 26 you will be ever seeing but never *p*

PERFECT* (PERFECTER PERFECTING PERFECTION)
Dt 32: 4 He is the Rock, his works are *p*,
2Sa 22: 31 "As for God, his way is *p*;
22: 33 and makes my way *p*.
Job 36: 4 one *p* in knowledge is with you.
37: 16 of him who is *p* in knowledge?
Ps 18: 30 As for God, his way is *p*;
18: 32 and makes my way *p*.
19: 7 The law of the LORD is *p*,
50: 2 From Zion, *p* in beauty,
64: 6 "We have devised a *p* plan!"
SS 6: 9 but my dove, my *p* one, is unique,
Isa 25: 1 for in *p* faithfulness
26: 3 You will keep in *p* peace
Eze 16: 14 had given you made your beauty *p*,
27: 3 "I am *p* in beauty."
28: 12 full of wisdom and *p* in beauty.
Mt 5: 48 Do not even pagans do that? Be *p*,
5: 48 as your heavenly Father is *p*.
19: 21 answered, "If you want to be *p*,
Ro 12: 2 his good, pleasing and *p* will.
2Co 12: 9 for my power is made *p*
Php 3: 12 or have already been made *p*,
Col 1: 28 so that we may present everyone *p*
3: 14 binds them all together in *p* unity.
Heb 2: 10 the author of their salvation *p*
5: 9 what he suffered and, once made *p*,
7: 19 useless (for the law made nothing *p*
7: 28 who has been made *p* forever.
9: 11 and more *p* tabernacle that is not
10: 1 make *p* those who draw
10: 14 he has made *p* forever those who
11: 40 with us would they be made *p*.
12: 23 spirits of righteous men made *p*,
Jas 1: 17 Every good and *p* gift is from above
1: 25 into the *p* law that gives freedom,
3: 2 he is a *p* man, able
1Jn 4: 18 But *p* love drives out fear,
4: 18 The one who fears is not made *p*

PERFECTER* (PERFECT)
Heb 12: 2 the author and *p* of our faith,

PERFECTING* (PERFECT)
2Co 7: 1 *p* holiness out of reverence for God

PERFECTION* (PERFECT)
Ps 119: 96 To all *p* I see a limit;
La 2: 15 the *p* of beauty,
Eze 27: 4 builders brought your beauty to *p*.
27: 11 they brought your beauty to *p*.
28: 12 "'You were the model of *p*,
1Co 13: 10 but when *p* comes, the imperfect
2Co 13: 9 and our prayer is for your *p*.
13: 11 Aim for *p*, listen to my appeal,
Heb 7: 11 If *p* could have been attained

PERFORM (PERFORMED PERFORMS)
Ex 3: 20 with all the wonders that I will *p*
2Sa 7: 23 to *p* great and awesome wonders
Jn 3: 2 no one could *p* the miraculous

PERFORMED (PERFORM)
Mt 11: 21 If the miracles that were *p*
Jn 10: 41 John never *p* a miraculous

PERFORMS (PERFORM)
Ps 77: 14 You are the God who *p* miracles;

PERFUME
Ecc 7: 1 A good name is better than fine *p*,
SS 1: 3 your name is like *p* poured out.
Mk 14: 3 jar of very expensive *p*,

PERIL
2Co 1: 10 us from such a deadly *p*,

PERISH (PERISHABLE PERISHED PERISHES PERISHING)
Ge 6: 17 Everything on earth will *p*.
Est 4: 16 And if I *p*, I *p*."
Ps 1: 6 but the way of the wicked will *p*.
37: 20 But the wicked will *p*:
73: 27 Those who are far from you will *p*;
102: 26 They will *p*, but you remain;
Pr 11: 10 when the wicked *p*, there are
19: 9 and he who pours out lies will *p*.
21: 28 A false witness will *p*,
28: 28 when the wicked *p*, the righteous
Isa 1: 28 who forsake the LORD will *p*.
29: 14 the wisdom of the wise will *p*,
60: 12 that will not serve you will *p*;
Zec 11: 9 the dying die, and the perishing *p*.
Lk 13: 3 unless you repent, you too will all *p*
13: 5 unless you repent, you too will all *p*
21: 18 But not a hair of your head will *p*.
Jn 3: 16 whoever believes in him shall not *p*
10: 28 eternal life, and they shall never *p*;
Ro 2: 12 apart from the law will also *p* apart
Col 2: 22 These are all destined to *p* with use,
2Th 2: 10 They *p* because they refused
Heb 1: 11 They will *p*, but you remain;
1Pe 1: 4 into an inheritance that can never *p*
2Pe 3: 9 not wanting anyone to *p*,

PERISHABLE (PERISH)
1Co 15: 42 The body that is sown is *p*,
1Pe 1: 18 not with *p* things such
1: 23 not of *p* seed, but of imperishable,

PERISHED (PERISH)
Ps 119: 92 I would have *p* in my affliction.

PERISHES (PERISH)
Job 8: 13 so *p* the hope of the godless.
1Pe 1: 7 which *p* even though refined by fire

PERISHING (PERISH)
1Co 1: 18 foolishness to those who are *p,*
2Co 2: 15 being saved and those who are *p.*
4: 3 it is veiled to those who are *p.*

PERJURERS* (PERJURY)
Mal 3: 5 and *p,* against those who defraud
1Ti 1: 10 for slave traders and liars and *p* —

PERJURY* (PERJURERS)
Jer 7: 9 murder, commit adultery and *p,*

PERMANENT
Heb 7: 24 lives forever, he has a *p* priesthood.

PERMISSIBLE (PERMIT)
1Co 6: 12 "Everything is *p* for me" —
10: 23 "Everything is *p*" — but not

PERMIT (PERMISSIBLE PERMITTED)
Hos 5: 4 "Their deeds do not *p* them
1Ti 2: 12 I do not *p* a woman to teach

PERMITTED (PERMIT)
Mt 19: 8 Moses *p* you to divorce your wives
2Co 12: 4 things that man is not *p* to tell.

PERSECUTE (PERSECUTED PERSECUTION PERSECUTIONS)
Ps 119: 86 for men *p* me without cause.
Mt 5: 11 *p* you and falsely say all kinds
5: 44 and pray for those who *p* you,
Jn 15: 20 they persecuted me, they will *p* you
Ac 9: 4 why do you *p* me?" "Who are you,
Ro 12: 14 Bless those who *p* you; bless

PERSECUTED (PERSECUTE)
Mt 5: 10 Blessed are those who are *p*
5: 12 same way they *p* the prophets who
Jn 15: 20 If they *p* me, they will persecute
1Co 4: 12 when we are *p,* we endure it;
15: 9 because I *p* the church of God.
2Co 4: 9 in despair; *p,* but not abandoned;
1Th 3: 4 kept telling you that we would be *p.*
2Ti 3: 12 life in Christ Jesus will be *p,*
Heb 11: 37 destitute, *p* and mistreated —

PERSECUTION (PERSECUTE)
Mt 13: 21 When trouble or *p* comes
Ro 8: 35 or hardship or *p* or famine

PERSECUTIONS (PERSECUTE)
Mk 10: 30 and with them, *p)* and in the age
2Co 12: 10 in hardships, in *p,* in difficulties.
2Th 1: 4 faith in all the *p* and trials you are
2Ti 3: 11 love, endurance, *p,* sufferings —

PERSEVERANCE* (PERSEVERE)
Ro 5: 3 we know that suffering produces *p;*
5: 4 *p,* character; and character, hope.
2Co 12: 12 were done among you with great *p.*
2Th 1: 4 churches we boast about your *p*
3: 5 into God's love and Christ's *p.*
Heb 12: 1 run with *p* the race marked out
Jas 1: 3 the testing of your faith develops *p.*
1: 4 *P* must finish its work
5: 11 You have heard of Job's *p*
2Pe 1: 6 *p;* and to *p,* godliness;
Rev 2: 2 your hard work and your *p.*
2: 19 and faith, your service and *p,*

PERSEVERE* (PERSEVERANCE PERSEVERED PERSEVERES PERSEVERING)
1Ti 4: 16 *P* in them, because if you do,
Heb 10: 36 You need to *p* so that

PERSEVERED* (PERSEVERE)
Heb 11: 27 he *p* because he saw him who is
Jas 5: 11 consider blessed those who have *p.*
Rev 2: 3 You have *p* and have endured

PERSEVERES* (PERSEVERE)
1Co 13: 7 trusts, always hopes, always *p.*
Jas 1: 12 Blessed is the man who *p*

PERSEVERING* (PERSEVERE)
Lk 8: 15 retain it, and by *p* produce a crop.

PERSIANS
Da 6: 15 law of the Medes and *P* no decree

PERSISTENCE*
Ro 2: 7 To those who by *p*

PERSUADE (PERSUADED PERSUASIVE)
Ac 18: 4 trying to *p* Jews and Greeks.
2Co 5: 11 is to fear the Lord, we try to *p* men.

PERSUADED (PERSUADE)
Ro 4: 21 being fully *p* that God had power

PERSUASIVE (PERSUADE)
1Co 2: 4 not with wise and *p* words,

PERVERSION* (PERVERT)
Lev 18: 23 sexual relations with it; that is a *p.*
20: 12 What they have done is a *p;*
Ro 1: 27 the due penalty for their *p.*
Jude : 7 up to sexual immorality and *p.*

PERVERT (PERVERSION PERVERTED PERVERTS)
Ex 23: 2 do not *p* justice by siding
Dt 16: 19 Do not *p* justice or show partiality.
Job 34: 12 that the Almighty would *p* justice.
Pr 17: 23 to *p* the course of justice.
Gal 1: 7 are trying to *p* the gospel of Christ.

PERVERTED (PERVERT)
1Sa 8: 3 and accepted bribes and *p* justice.

PERVERTS* (PERVERT)
1Ti 1: 10 for murderers, for adulterers and *p,*

PESTILENCE (PESTILENCES)
Ps 91: 6 nor the *p* that stalks in the darkness

PESTILENCES (PESTILENCE)
Lk 21: 11 famines and *p* in various places,

PETER
Apostle, brother of Andrew, also called Simon (Mt 10:2; Mk 3:16; Lk 6:14; Ac 1:13), and Cephas (Jn 1:42). Confession of Christ (Mt 16:13 – 20; Mk 8:27 – 30; Lk 9:18 – 27). At transfiguration (Mt 17:1 – 8; Mk 9:2 – 8; Lk 9:28 – 36; 2Pe 1:16 – 18). Caught fish with coin (Mt 17:24 – 27). Denial of Jesus predicted (Mt 26:31 – 35; Mk 14:27 – 31; Lk 22:31 – 34; Jn 13:31 – 38). Denied Jesus (Mt 26:69 – 75; Mk 14:66 – 72; Lk 22:54 – 62; Jn 18:15 – 27). Commissioned by Jesus to shepherd his flock (Jn 21:15 – 23).

Speech at Pentecost (Ac 2). Healed beggar (Ac 3:1 – 10). Speech at temple (Ac 3:11 – 26), before Sanhedrin (Ac 4:1 – 22). In Samaria (Ac 8:14 – 25). Sent by vision to Cornelius (Ac 10). Announced salvation of Gentiles in Jerusalem (Ac 11; 15). Freed from prison (Ac 12). Inconsistency at Antioch (Gal 2:11 – 21). At Jerusalem Council (Ac 15).

Epistles: 1 – 2 Peter.

PETITION (PETITIONS)
1Ch 16: 4 to make *p,* to give thanks,
Php 4: 6 by prayer and *p,* with thanksgiving,

PETITIONS (PETITION)
Heb 5: 7 he offered up prayers and *p*

PHANTOM*
Ps 39: 6 Man is a mere *p* as he goes to

PHARAOH (PHARAOH'S)
Ge 12: 15 her to *P,* and she was taken
41: 14 So *P* sent for Joseph, and he was
Ex 14: 4 glory for myself through *P*
14: 17 And I will gain glory through *P*

PHARAOH'S (PHARAOH)
Ex 7: 3 But I will harden *P* heart, and

PHARISEE (PHARISEES)
Ac 23: 6 brothers, I am a *P,* the son of a *P.*
Php 3: 5 in regard to the law, a *P;* as for zeal,

PHARISEES (PHARISEE)
Mt 5: 20 surpasses that of the *P*
16: 6 guard against the yeast of the *P*
23: 13 of the law and *P,* you hypocrites!
Jn 3: 1 a man of the *P* named Nicodemus,

PHILADELPHIA
Rev 3: 7 the angel of the church in *P* write:

PHILEMON*
Phm : 1 To *P* our dear friend and fellow

PHILIP
1. Apostle (Mt 10:3; Mk 3:18; Lk 6:14; Jn 1:43 – 48; 14:8; Ac 1:13).

2. Deacon (Ac 6:1 – 7); evangelist in Samaria (Ac 8:4 – 25), to Ethiopian (Ac 8:26 – 40).

PHILIPPI
Ac 16: 12 From there we traveled to *P,*
Php 1: 1 To all the saints in Christ Jesus at *P*

PHILISTINE (PHILISTINES)
Jos 13: 3 of the five *P* rulers in Gaza,
1Sa 14: 1 let's go over to the *P* outpost
17: 26 is this uncircumcised *P* that he
17: 37 me from the hand of this *P.*"

PHILISTINES (PHILISTINE)
Jdg 10: 7 them into the hands of the *P*
Jdg 13: 1 the hands of the *P* for forty years.
16: 5 The rulers of the *P* went to her
1Sa 4: 1 at Ebenezer, and the *P* at Aphek.
5: 8 together all the rulers of the *P*
13: 23 a detachment of *P* had gone out
17: 1 the *P* gathered their forces for war
23: 1 the *P* are fighting against Keilah
27: 1 is to escape to the land of the *P.*
31: 1 Now the *P* fought against Israel;
2Sa 5: 17 When the *P* heard that David had
8: 1 David defeated the *P* and subdued
21: 15 there was a battle between the *P*
2Ki 18: 8 he defeated the *P,* as far as Gaza
Am 1: 8 Ekron till the last of the *P* is dead,"

PHILOSOPHER* (PHILOSOPHY)
1Co 1: 20 Where is the *p* of this age?

PHILOSOPHY* (PHILOSOPHER)
Col 2: 8 through hollow and deceptive *p,*

PHINEHAS
Nu 25: 7 When *P* son of Eleazar, the son
Ps 106: 30 But *P* stood up and intervened,

PHOEBE*
Ro 16: 1 I commend to you our sister *P,*

PHYLACTERIES*
Mt 23: 5 They make their *p* wide

PHYSICAL
Ro 2: 28 merely outward and *p.*
Col 1: 22 by Christ's *p* body through death
1Ti 4: 8 For *p* training is of some value,
Jas 2: 16 but does nothing about his *p* needs,

PICK (PICKED)
Mk 16: 18 they will *p* up snakes

PICKED (PICK)
Lk 14: 7 noticed how the guests *p* the places
Jn 5: 9 he *p* up his mat and walked.

PIECE (PIECES)
Jn 19: 23 woven in one *p* from top to bottom.

PIECES (PIECE)
Ge 15: 17 and passed between the *p.*
Jer 34: 18 and then walked between its *p.*
Zec 11: 12 So they paid me thirty *p* of silver.
Mt 14: 20 of broken *p* that were left over.

PIERCE (PIERCED)
Ex 21: 6 and *p* his ear with an awl.
Pr 12: 18 Reckless words *p* like a sword,
Lk 2: 35 a sword will *p* your own soul too."

PIERCED (PIERCE)
Ps 22: 16 they have *p* my hands and my feet.
40: 6 but my ears you have *p;*
Isa 53: 5 But he was *p* for our transgressions,
Zec 12: 10 look on me, the one they have *p,*
Jn 19: 37 look on the one they have *p.*"
Rev 1: 7 even those who *p* him;

PIG'S (PIGS)
Pr 11: 22 Like a gold ring in a *p* snout

PIGEONS
Lev 5: 11 afford two doves or two young *p,*
Lk 2: 24 "a pair of doves or two young *p.*"

PIGS (PIG'S)
Mt 7: 6 do not throw your pearls to *p.*
Mk 5: 11 A large herd of *p* was feeding on

PILATE
Governor of Judea. Questioned Jesus (Mt 27:1 – 26; Mk 15:15; Lk 22:66 – 23:25; Jn 18:28 – 19:16); sent him to Herod (Lk 23:6 – 12); consented to his crucifixion when crowds chose Barabbas (Mt 27:15 – 26; Mk 15:6 – 15; Lk 23:13 – 25; Jn 19:1 – 10).

PILLAR (PILLARS)
Ge 19: 26 and she became a *p* of salt.
Ex 13: 21 ahead of them in a *p* of cloud
1Ti 3: 15 the *p* and foundation of the truth.
Rev 3: 12 who overcomes I will make a *p*

PILLARS (PILLAR)
Gal 2: 9 and John, those reputed to be *p,*

PINIONS
Dt 32: 11 and carries them on its *p.*

PISGAH
Dt 3: 27 Go up to the top of *P* and look west

PIT
Ps 7: 15 falls into the *p* he has made.
40: 2 He lifted me out of the slimy *p,*
103: 4 who redeems your life from the *p*

Pr 23: 27 for a prostitute is a deep *p*
26: 27 If a man digs a *p*, he will fall into it;
Isa 24: 17 Terror and *p* and snare await you,
38: 17 me from the *p* of destruction;
Mt 15: 14 a blind man, both will fall into a *p*."

PITCH
Ge 6: 14 and coat it with *p* inside and out.
Ex 2: 3 and coated it with tar and *p*.

PITIED (PITY)
1Co 15: 19 we are to be *p* more than all men.

PITY (PITIED)
Ps 72: 13 He will take *p* on the weak
Ecc 4: 10 But *p* the man who falls
Lk 10: 33 when he saw him, he took *p* on him

PLAGUE (PLAGUED PLAGUES)
2Ch 6: 28 "When famine or *p* comes
Ps 91: 6 nor the *p* that destroys at midday.

PLAGUED* (PLAGUE)
Ps 73: 5 they are not *p* by human ills.
73: 14 All day long I have been *p*;

PLAGUES (PLAGUE)
Hos 13: 14 Where, O death, are your *p*?
Rev 21: 9 full of the seven last *p* came
22: 18 to him the *p* described in this book.

PLAIN
Isa 40: 4 the rugged places a *p*.
Ro 1: 19 what may be known about God is *p*

PLAN (PLANNED PLANS)
Ex 26: 30 according to the *p* shown you
Job 42: 2 no *p* of yours can be thwarted.
Pr 14: 22 those who *p* what is good find love
21: 30 is no wisdom, no insight, no *p*
Am 3: 7 nothing without revealing his *p*
Eph 1: 11 predestined according to the *p*

PLANK
Mt 7: 3 attention to the *p* in your own eye?
Lk 6: 41 attention to the *p* in your own eye?

PLANNED (PLAN)
Ps 40: 5 The things you *p* for us
Isa 14: 24 "Surely, as I have *p*, so it will be,
23: 9 The Lord Almighty *p* it,
46: 11 what I have *p*, that will I do.
Heb 11: 40 God had *p* something better for us

PLANS (PLAN)
Ps 20: 4 and make all your *p* succeed.
33: 11 *p* of the Lord stand firm forever,
Pr 15: 22 *P* fail for lack of counsel,
16: 3 and your *p* will succeed.
19: 21 Many are the *p* in a man's heart,
20: 18 Make *p* by seeking advice;
Isa 29: 15 to hide their *p* from the Lord,
30: 1 those who carry out *p* that are not
32: 8 But the noble man makes noble *p*,
2Co 1: 17 Or do I make my *p* in a worldly

PLANT (PLANTED PLANTING PLANTS)
Am 9: 15 I will *p* Israel in their own land,
Mt 15: 13 "Every *p* that my heavenly Father

PLANTED (PLANT)
Ge 2: 8 the Lord God had *p* a garden
Ps 1: 3 He is like a tree *p* by streams
Jer 17: 8 He will be like a tree *p* by the water
Mt 15: 13 Father has not *p* will be pulled
21: 33 was a landowner who *p* a vineyard.
Lk 13: 6 "A man had a fig tree, *p*
1Co 3: 6 I *p* the seed, Apollos watered it,
Jas 1: 21 humbly accept the word *p* in you,

PLANTING (PLANT)
Isa 61: 3 a *p* of the Lord

PLANTS (PLANT)
Pr 31: 16 out of her earnings she *p* a vineyard
1Co 3: 7 So neither he who *p* nor he who
9: 7 Who *p* a vineyard and does not eat

PLATTER
Mk 6: 25 head of John the Baptist on a *p*."

PLAY (PLAYED)
1Sa 16: 23 David would take his harp and *p*.
Isa 11: 8 The infant will *p* near the hole

PLAYED (PLAY)
Lk 7: 32 "'We *p* the flute for you,
1Co 14: 7 anyone know what tune is being *p*

PLEA (PLEAD PLEADED PLEADS)
1Ki 8: 28 to your servant's prayer and his *p*
Ps 102: 17 he will not despise their *p*.
La 3: 56 You heard my *p*: "Do not close

PLEAD (PLEA)
Isa 1: 17 *p* the case of the widow.

PLEADED (PLEA)
2Co 12: 8 Three times I *p* with the Lord

PLEADS (PLEA)
Job 16: 21 on behalf of a man he *p* with God

PLEASANT (PLEASE)
Ge 49: 15 and how *p* is his land,
Ps 16: 6 for me in *p* places;
133: 1 How good and *p* it is
135: 3 sing praise to his name, for that is *p*
147: 1 how *p* and fitting to praise him!
Pr 2: 10 knowledge will be *p* to your soul.
3: 17 Her ways are *p* ways,
16: 21 and *p* words promote instruction.
16: 24 *P* words are a honeycomb,
Isa 30: 10 Tell us *p* things,
1Th 3: 6 that you always have *p* memories
Heb 12: 11 No discipline seems *p* at the time,

PLEASANTNESS* (PLEASE)
Pr 27: 9 the *p* of one's friend springs

PLEASE (PLEASANT PLEASANTNESS PLEASED PLEASES PLEASING PLEASURE PLEASURES)
Ps 69: 31 This will *p* the Lord more
Pr 20: 23 and dishonest scales do not *p* him.
Isa 46: 10 and I will do all that I *p*.
Jer 6: 20 your sacrifices do not *p* me."
27: 5 and I give it to anyone I *p*.
Jn 5: 30 for I seek not to *p* myself
Ro 8: 8 by the sinful nature cannot *p* God.
15: 1 of the weak and not to *p* ourselves.
15: 2 Each of us should *p* his neighbor
1Co 7: 32 affairs — how he can *p* the Lord.
10: 33 I try to *p* everybody in every way.
2Co 5: 9 So we make it our goal to *p* him,
Gal 1: 10 or of God? Or am I trying to *p* men
6: 8 the one who sows to *p* the Spirit,
Col 1: 10 and may *p* him in every way:
1Th 2: 4 We are not trying to *p* men
4: 1 how to live in order to *p* God,
2Ti 2: 4 wants to *p* his commanding officer.
Tit 2: 9 to try to *p* them, not to talk back
Heb 11: 6 faith it is impossible to *p* God,

PLEASED (PLEASE)
Dt 28: 63 as it *p* the Lord to make you
1Sa 12: 22 Lord was *p* to make you his own.
1Ki 3: 10 The Lord was *p* that Solomon had
1Ch 29: 17 that you test the heart and are *p*
Mic 6: 7 Will the Lord be *p*
Mal 1: 10 I am not *p* with you," says
Mt 3: 17 whom I love; with him I am well *p*
17: 5 whom I love; with him I am well *p*.
Mk 1: 11 whom I love; with you I am well *p*
Lk 3: 22 whom I love; with you I am well *p*
1Co 1: 21 God was *p* through the foolishness
Col 1: 19 For God was *p* to have all his
Heb 10: 6 you were not *p*.
10: 8 nor were you *p* with them"
10: 38 I will not be *p* with him."
11: 5 commended as one who *p* God.
13: 16 for with such sacrifices God is *p*.
2Pe 1: 17 whom I love; with him I am well *p*

PLEASES (PLEASE)
Job 23: 13 He does whatever he *p*.
Ps 115: 3 he does whatever *p* him.
135: 6 The Lord does whatever *p* him,
Pr 15: 8 but the prayer of the upright *p* him.
21: 1 it like a watercourse wherever he *p*.
Ecc 2: 26 To the man who *p* him, God gives
7: 26 man who *p* God will escape her,
Da 4: 35 He does as he *p*
Jn 3: 8 The wind blows wherever it *p*.
8: 29 for I always do what *p* him."
Eph 5: 10 truth) and find out what *p* the Lord
Col 3: 20 in everything, for this *p* the Lord.
1Ti 2: 3 This is good, and *p* God our Savior,
1Jn 3: 22 his commands and do what *p* him.

PLEASING (PLEASE)
Ge 2: 9 trees that were *p* to the eye
Lev 1: 9 an aroma *p* to the Lord.
Ps 19: 14 be *p* in your sight,
104: 34 May my meditation be *p* to him,
Pr 15: 26 but those of the pure are *p* to him.
16: 7 When a man's ways are *p*
SS 1: 3 *P* is the fragrance of your perfumes
4: 10 How much more *p* is your love
7: 6 How beautiful you are and how *p*,
Ro 12: 1 *p* to God — this is your spiritual
14: 18 Christ in this way is *p* to God
Php 4: 18 an acceptable sacrifice, *p* to God.
1Ti 5: 4 grandparents, for this is *p* to God.
Heb 13: 21 may he work in us what is *p* to him,

PLEASURE (PLEASE)
Ps 5: 4 You are not a God who takes *p*
51: 16 you do not take *p* in burnt offerings
147: 10 His *p* is not in the strength
Pr 10: 23 A fool finds *p* in evil conduct,
18: 2 A fool finds no *p* in understanding
21: 17 He who loves *p* will become poor;
Isa 1: 11 I have no *p*
Jer 6: 10 they find no *p* in it.
Eze 18: 23 Do I take any *p* in the death
18: 32 For I take no *p* in the death
33: 11 I take no *p* in the death
Lk 10: 21 Father, for this was your good *p*.
Eph 1: 5 in accordance with his *p* and will —
1: 9 of his will according to his good *p*,
1Ti 5: 6 the widow who lives for *p* is dead
2Ti 3: 4 lovers of *p* rather than lovers
2Pe 2: 13 Their idea of *p* is to carouse

PLEASURES* (PLEASE)
Ps 16: 11 with eternal *p* at your right hand.
Lk 8: 14 and *p*, and they do not mature.
Tit 3: 3 by all kinds of passions and *p*.
Heb 11: 25 rather than to enjoy the *p* of sin
Jas 4: 3 may spend what you get on your *p*.
2Pe 2: 13 reveling in their *p* while they feast

PLEDGE
Dt 24: 17 take the cloak of the widow as a *p*.
1Pe 3: 21 but the *p* of a good conscience

PLEIADES
Job 38: 31 "Can you bind the beautiful *P*?
Am 5: 8 (he who made the *P* and Orion,

PLENTIFUL (PLENTY)
Mt 9: 37 harvest is *p* but the workers are
Lk 10: 2 harvest is *p*, but the workers are

PLENTY (PLENTIFUL)
2Co 8: 14 the present time your *p* will supply
Php 4: 12 whether living in *p* or in want.

PLOT (PLOTS)
Est 2: 22 Mordecai found out about the *p*
Ps 2: 1 and the peoples *p* in vain?
Pr 3: 29 not *p* harm against your neighbor,
Zec 8: 17 do not *p* evil against your neighbor,
Ac 4: 25 and the peoples *p* in vain?

PLOTS (PLOT)
Pr 6: 14 who *p* evil with deceit in his heart

PLOW (PLOWMAN PLOWSHARES)
Lk 9: 62 "No one who puts his hand to the *p*

PLOWMAN (PLOW)
1Co 9: 10 because when the *p* plows

PLOWSHARES (PLOW)
1Sa 13: 20 to the Philistines to have their *p*,
Isa 2: 4 They will beat their swords into *p*
Joel 3: 10 Beat your *p* into swords
Mic 4: 3 They will beat their swords into *p*

PLUCK
Mk 9: 47 your eye causes you to sin, *p* it out.

PLUNDER (PLUNDERED)
Ex 3: 22 And so you will *p* the Egyptians."
Est 3: 13 of Adar, and to *p* their goods.
8: 11 to *p* the property of their enemies.
9: 10 did not lay their hands on the *p*.
Pr 22: 23 and will *p* those who *p* them.
Isa 3: 14 the *p* from the poor is

PLUNDERED (PLUNDER)
Eze 34: 8 lacks a shepherd and so has been *p*

PLUNGE
1Ti 6: 9 and harmful desires that *p* men
1Pe 4: 4 think it strange that you do not *p*

PODS
Lk 15: 16 with the *p* that the pigs were eating,

POINT
Mt 4: 5 on the highest *p* of the temple.
26: 38 with sorrow to the *p* of death.
Jas 2: 10 yet stumbles at just one *p* is guilty
Rev 2: 10 Be faithful, even to the *p* of death,

POISON
Ps 140: 3 the *p* of vipers is on their lips.
Mk 16: 18 and when they drink deadly *p*,
Ro 3: 13 "The *p* of vipers is on their lips."
Jas 3: 8 It is a restless evil, full of deadly *p*.

POLE (POLES)
Nu 21: 8 "Make a snake and put it up on a *p*;

Dt 16: 21 not set up any wooden Asherah *p*

POLES (POLE)
Ex 25: 13 Then make *p* of acacia wood

POLISHED
Isa 49: 2 he made me into a *p* arrow

POLLUTE* (POLLUTED POLLUTES)
Nu 35: 33 "'Do not *p* the land where you are.
Jude : 8 these dreamers *p* their own bodies,

POLLUTED* (POLLUTE)
Ezr 9: 11 entering to possess is a land *p*
Pr 25: 26 Like a muddied spring or a *p* well
Ac 15: 20 to abstain from food *p* by idols,
Jas 1: 27 oneself from being *p* by the world.

POLLUTES* (POLLUTE)
Nu 35: 33 Bloodshed *p* the land,

PONDER (PONDERED)
Ps 64: 9 and *p* what he has done.
119: 95 but I will *p* your statutes.

PONDERED (PONDER)
Ps 111: 2 they are *p* by all who delight
Lk 2: 19 up all these things and *p* them

POOR (POVERTY)
Lev 19: 10 Leave them for the *p* and the alien.
23: 22 Leave them for the *p* and the alien.
27: 8 If anyone making the vow is too *p*
Dt 15: 4 there should be no *p* among you,
15: 7 is a *p* man among your brothers
15: 11 There will always be *p* people
24: 12 If the man is *p*, do not go to sleep
24: 14 advantage of a hired man who is *p*
Job 5: 16 So the *p* have hope,
24: 4 force all the *p* of the land
Ps 14: 6 frustrate the plans of the *p*,
34: 6 This *p* man called, and the LORD
35: 10 You rescue the *p* from those too
40: 17 Yet I am *p* and needy;
68: 10 O God, you provided for the *p*.
82: 3 maintain the rights of the *p*
112: 9 scattered abroad his gifts to the *p*,
113: 7 He raises the *p* from the dust
140: 12 the LORD secures justice for the *p*
Pr 10: 4 Lazy hands make a man *p*,
13: 7 to be *p*, yet has great wealth.
14: 20 The *p* are shunned
14: 31 oppresses the *p* shows contempt
17: 5 who mocks the *p* shows contempt
19: 1 Better a *p* man whose walk is
19: 17 to the *p* lends to the LORD,
19: 22 better to be *p* than a liar.
20: 13 not love sleep or you will grow *p*;
21: 13 to the cry of the *p*,
21: 17 who loves pleasure will become *p*;
22: 2 Rich and *p* have this in common:
22: 9 for he shares his food with the *p*.
22: 22 not exploit the *p* because they are *p*
28: 6 Better a *p* man whose walk is
28: 27 to the *p* will lack nothing,
29: 7 care about justice for the *p*,
31: 9 defend the rights of the *p*
31: 20 She opens her arms to the *p*
Ecc 4: 13 Better a *p* but wise youth
Isa 3: 14 the plunder from the *p* is
10: 2 to deprive the *p* of their rights
14: 30 of the *p* will find pasture,
25: 4 You have been a refuge for the *p*,
32: 7 schemes to destroy the *p* with lies,
61: 1 me to preach good news to the *p*.
Jer 22: 16 He defended the cause of the *p*
Eze 18: 12 He oppresses the *p* and needy.
Am 2: 7 They trample on the heads of the *p*
4: 1 you women who oppress the *p*
5: 11 You trample on the *p*
Zec 7: 10 or the fatherless, the alien or the *p*.
Mt 5: 3 saying: "Blessed are the *p* in spirit,
11: 5 the good news is preached to the *p*.
19: 21 your possessions and give to the *p*,
26: 11 The *p* you will always have
Mk 12: 42 But a *p* widow came and put
14: 7 The *p* you will always have
Lk 4: 18 me to preach good news to the *p*.
6: 20 "Blessed are you who are *p*,
11: 41 is inside the dish to the *p*,
14: 13 invite the *p*, the crippled, the lame,
21: 2 also saw a *p* widow put
Jn 12: 8 You will always have the *p*
Ac 9: 36 doing good and helping the *p*.
10: 4 and gifts to the *p* have come up
24: 17 to bring my people gifts for the *p*
Ro 15: 26 for the *p* among the saints
1Co 13: 3 If I give all I possess to the *p*
2Co 6: 10 sorrowful, yet always rejoicing; *p*,
8: 9 yet for your sakes he became *p*,
Gal 2: 10 continue to remember the *p*,
Jas 2: 2 and a *p* man in shabby clothes
2: 5 not God chosen those who are *p*
2: 6 But you have insulted the *p*.

POPULATION*
Pr 14: 28 A large *p* is a king's glory,

PORTION
Nu 18: 29 as the LORD's *p* the best
Dt 32: 9 For the LORD's *p* is his people,
1Sa 1: 5 But to Hannah he gave a double *p*
2Ki 2: 9 "Let me inherit a double *p*
Ps 73: 26 and my *p* forever.
119: 57 You are my *p*, O LORD;
Isa 53: 12 Therefore I will give him a *p*
Jer 10: 16 He who is the *P* of Jacob is not like
La 3: 24 to myself, "The LORD is my *p*;
Zec 2: 12 LORD will inherit Judah as his *p*

PORTRAIT
Lk 20: 24 Whose *p* and inscription are on it?"

PORTRAYED
Gal 3: 1 very eyes Jesus Christ was clearly *p*

POSITION (POSITIONS)
Ro 12: 16 to associate with people of low *p*.
Jas 1: 9 ought to take pride in his high *p*.
2Pe 3: 17 and fall from your secure *p*.

POSITIONS (POSITION)
2Ch 20: 17 Take up your *p*; stand firm
Jude : 6 the angels who did not keep their *p*

POSSESS (POSSESSED POSSESSING POSSESSION POSSESSIONS)
Nu 33: 53 for I have given you the land to *p*.
Dt 4: 14 you are crossing the Jordan to *p*.
Pr 8: 12 I *p* knowledge and discretion.
Jn 5: 39 that by them you *p* eternal life.

POSSESSED (POSSESS)
Jn 10: 21 the sayings of a man *p* by a demon.

POSSESSING* (POSSESS)
2Co 6: 10 nothing, and yet *p* everything.

POSSESSION (POSSESS)
Ge 15: 7 to give you this land to take *p* of it
Ex 6: 8 I will give it to you as a *p*.
19: 5 nations you will be my treasured *p*.
Nu 13: 30 "We should go up and take *p*
Dt 7: 6 to be his people, his treasured *p*.
Jos 1: 11 take *p* of the land the LORD your
Ps 2: 8 the ends of the earth your *p*.
135: 4 Israel to be his treasured *p*.
Eph 1: 14 of those who are God's *p* —

POSSESSIONS (POSSESS)
Mt 19: 21 go, sell your *p* and give to the poor,
Lk 11: 21 guards his own house, his *p* are safe
12: 15 consist in the abundance of his *p*."
19: 8 now I give half of my *p* to the poor,
Ac 4: 32 any of his *p* was his own,
2Co 12: 14 what I want is not your *p* but you.
Heb 10: 34 yourselves had better and lasting *p*.
1Jn 3: 17 If anyone has material *p*

POSSIBLE
Mt 19: 26 but with God all things are *p*."
26: 39 if it is *p*, may this cup be taken
Mk 9: 23 "Everything is *p* for him who
10: 27 all things are *p* with God."
14: 35 prayed that if *p* the hour might pass
Ro 12: 18 If it is *p*, as far as it depends on you,
1Co 6: 5 Is it *p* that there is nobody
9: 19 to everyone, to win as many as *p*.
9: 22 by all *p* means I might save some.

POT (POTSHERD POTTER POTTER'S POTTERY)
2Ki 4: 40 there is death in the *p*!"
Jer 18: 4 But the *p* he was shaping

POTIPHAR*
Egyptian who bought Joseph (Ge 37:36), set him over his house (Ge 39:1 – 6), sent him to prison (Ge 39:7 – 30).

POTSHERD (POT)
Isa 45: 9 a *p* among the potsherds

POTTER (POT)
Isa 29: 16 Can the pot say of the *p*,
45: 9 Does the clay say to the *p*,
64: 8 We are the clay, you are the *p*;
Jer 18: 6 "Like clay in the hand of the *p*,
Zec 11: 13 it to the *p*" — the handsome price
Ro 9: 21 Does not the *p* have the right

POTTER'S (POT)
Mt 27: 7 to use the money to buy the *p* field

POTTERY (POT)
Ro 9: 21 of clay some *p* for noble purposes

POUR (POURED POURS)
Ps 62: 8 *p* out your hearts to him,
Isa 44: 3 I will *p* out my Spirit
Eze 20: 8 So I said I would *p* out my wrath
39: 29 for I will *p* out my Spirit
Joel 2: 28 I will *p* out my Spirit on all people.
Zec 12: 10 I will *p* out on the house of David
Mal 3: 10 *p* out so much blessing that you
Ac 2: 17 I will *p* out my Spirit on all people.

POURED (POUR)
Ps 22: 14 I am *p* out like water,
Isa 32: 15 till the Spirit is *p* upon us
Mt 26: 28 which is *p* out for many
Lk 22: 20 in my blood, which is *p* out for you.
Ac 2: 33 and has *p* out what you now see
10: 45 of the Holy Spirit had been *p* out
Ro 5: 5 because God has *p* out his love
Php 2: 17 even if I am being *p* out like a drink
2Ti 4: 6 I am already being *p* out like
Tit 3: 6 whom he *p* out on us generously
Rev 16: 2 and *p* out his bowl on the land,

POURS (POUR)
Lk 5: 37 And no one *p* new wine

POVERTY* (POOR)
Dt 28: 48 and thirst, in nakedness and dire *p*,
1Sa 2: 7 The LORD sends *p* and wealth;
Pr 6: 11 *p* will come on you like a bandit
10: 15 but *p* is the ruin of the poor.
11: 24 withholds unduly, but comes to *p*.
13: 18 who ignores discipline comes to *p*
14: 23 but mere talk leads only to *p*.
21: 5 as surely as haste leads to *p*.
22: 16 to the rich — both come to *p*.
24: 34 *p* will come on you like a bandit
28: 19 fantasies will have his fill of *p*.
28: 22 and is unaware that *p* awaits him.
30: 8 give me neither *p* nor riches,
31: 7 let them drink and forget their *p*
Ecc 4: 14 born in *p* within his kingdom.
Mk 12: 44 out of her *p*, put in everything —
Lk 21: 4 she out of her *p* put in all she had
2Co 8: 2 and their extreme *p* welled up
8: 9 through his *p* might become rich.
Rev 2: 9 I know your afflictions and your *p*

POWER (POWERFUL POWERS)
Ex 15: 6 was majestic in *p*.
32: 11 out of Egypt with great *p*
Dt 8: 17 "My *p* and the strength
34: 12 one has ever shown the mighty *p*
1Sa 10: 6 LORD will come upon you in *p*,
10: 10 Spirit of God came upon him in *p*,
11: 6 Spirit of God came upon him in *p*,
16: 13 the LORD came upon David in *p*.
1Ch 29: 11 LORD, is the greatness and the *p*
2Ch 20: 6 *P* and might are in your hand,
32: 7 for there is a greater *p* with us
Job 9: 4 wisdom is profound, his *p* is vast.
36: 22 "God is exalted in his *p*.
37: 23 beyond our reach and exalted in *p*;
Ps 20: 6 with the saving *p* of his right hand.
63: 2 and beheld your *p* and your glory.
66: 3 So great is your *p*
68: 34 Proclaim the *p* of God,
77: 14 you display your *p*
89: 13 Your arm is endued with *p*;
145: 6 of the *p* of your awesome works,
147: 5 Great is our Lord and mighty in *p*;
150: 2 Praise him for his acts of *p*;
Pr 3: 27 when it is in your *p* to act.
18: 21 The tongue has the *p* of life
24: 5 A wise man has great *p*,
Isa 11: 2 the Spirit of counsel and of *p*,
40: 10 the Sovereign LORD comes with *p*
40: 26 of his great *p* and mighty strength,
63: 12 who sent his glorious arm of *p*
Jer 10: 6 and your name is mighty in *p*.
10: 12 But God made the earth by his *p*;
27: 5 With my great *p* and outstretched
32: 17 and the earth by your great *p*
Hos 13: 14 from the *p* of the grave;
Na 1: 3 to anger and great in *p*;
Zec 4: 6 nor by *p*, but by my Spirit,'
Mt 22: 29 do not know the Scriptures or the *p*
24: 30 on the clouds of the sky, with *p*
Lk 1: 35 and the *p* of the Most High will
4: 14 to Galilee in the *p* of the Spirit,
9: 1 he gave them *p* and authority

Lk 10: 19 to overcome all the *p* of the enemy;
24: 49 clothed with *p* from on high."
Ac 1: 8 you will receive *p* when the Holy
4: 28 They did what your *p* and will had
4: 33 With great *p* the apostles
10: 38 with the Holy Spirit and *p*,
26: 18 and from the *p* of Satan to God,
Ro 1: 16 it is the *p* of God for the salvation
1: 20 his eternal *p* and divine nature—
4: 21 fully persuaded that God had *p*
9: 17 that I might display my *p* in you
15: 13 overflow with hope by the *p*
15: 19 through the *p* of the Spirit.
1Co 1: 17 cross of Christ be emptied of its *p*.
1: 18 to us who are being saved it is the *p*
2: 4 a demonstration of the Spirit's *p*,
6: 14 By his *p* God raised the Lord
15: 24 all dominion, authority and *p*.
15: 56 of death is sin, and the *p*
2Co 4: 7 to show that this all-surpassing *p* is
6: 7 in truthful speech and in the *p*
10: 4 they have divine *p*
12: 9 for my *p* is made perfect
13: 4 weakness, yet he lives by God's *p*.
Eph 1: 19 and his incomparably great *p*
3: 16 you with *p* through his Spirit
3: 20 according to his *p* that is at work
6: 10 in the Lord and in his mighty *p*.
Php 3: 10 and the *p* of his resurrection
3: 21 by the *p* that enables him
Col 1: 11 strengthened with all *p* according
2: 10 who is the head over every *p*
1Th 1: 5 also with *p*, with the Holy Spirit
2Ti 1: 7 but a spirit of *p*, of love
3: 5 form of godliness but denying its *p*.
Heb 2: 14 might destroy him who holds the *p*
7: 16 of the *p* of an indestructible life.
1Pe 1: 5 by God's *p* until the coming
2Pe 1: 3 His divine *p* has given us
Jude : 25 *p* and authority, through Jesus
Rev 4: 11 to receive glory and honor and *p*,
5: 12 to receive *p* and wealth
11: 17 you have taken your great *p*
19: 1 and glory and *p* belong to our God,
20: 6 The second death has no *p*

POWERFUL (POWER)
2Ch 27: 6 Jotham grew *p* because he walked
Est 9: 4 and he became more and more *p*.
Ps 29: 4 The voice of the LORD is *p*;
Jer 32: 18 *p* God, whose name is the LORD
Zec 8: 22 *p* nations will come to Jerusalem
Mk 1: 7 "After me will come one more *p*
Lk 24: 19 *p* in word and deed before God
2Th 1: 7 in blazing fire with his *p* angels.
Heb 1: 3 sustaining all things by his *p* word.
Jas 5: 16 The prayer of a righteous man is *p*

POWERLESS
Ro 5: 6 when we were still *p*, Christ died
8: 3 For what the law was *p* to do

POWERS (POWER)
Da 4: 35 pleases with the *p* of heaven
Ro 8: 38 nor any *p*, neither height nor depth
1Co 12: 10 to another miraculous *p*,
Eph 6: 12 against the *p* of this dark world
Col 1: 16 whether thrones or *p* or rulers
2: 15 And having disarmed the *p*
Heb 6: 5 and the *p* of the coming age,
1Pe 3: 22 and *p* in submission to him.

PRACTICE (PRACTICED PRACTICES)
Lev 19: 26 "'Do not *p* divination or sorcery.
Ps 119: 56 This has been my *p*:
Eze 33: 31 but they do not put them into *p*.
Mt 7: 24 into *p* is like a wise man who built
23: 3 for they do not *p* what they preach.
Lk 8: 21 hear God's word and put it into *p*."
Ro 12: 13 *P* hospitality.
Php 4: 9 or seen in me—put it into *p*.
1Ti 5: 4 to put their religion into *p* by caring

PRACTICED (PRACTICE)
Mt 23: 23 You should have *p* the latter,

PRACTICES (PRACTICE)
Ps 101: 7 No one who *p* deceit
Mt 5: 19 but whoever *p* and teaches these
Col 3: 9 taken off your old self with its *p*

PRAISE (PRAISED PRAISES PRAISEWORTHY PRAISING)
Ex 15: 2 He is my God, and I will *p* him,
Dt 10: 21 He is your *p*; he is your God,
26: 19 declared that he will set you in *p*,
32: 3 Oh, *p* the greatness of our God!
Ru 4: 14 said to Naomi: "*P* be to the LORD,
2Sa 22: 4 to the LORD, who is worthy of *p*,
22: 47 The LORD lives! *P* be to my Rock
1Ch 16: 25 is the LORD and most worthy of *p*;
16: 35 that we may glory in your *p*."
23: 5 four thousand are to *p* the LORD
29: 10 "*P* be to you, O LORD,
2Ch 5: 13 they raised their voices in *p*
20: 21 and to *p* him for the splendor
29: 30 to *p* the LORD with the words
Ezr 3: 10 took their places to *p* the LORD,
Ne 9: 5 and *p* the LORD your God,
Ps 8: 2 you have ordained *p*
9: 1 I will *p* you, O LORD,
16: 7 I will *p* the LORD, who counsels
26: 7 proclaiming aloud your *p*
30: 4 *p* his holy name.
33: 1 it is fitting for the upright to *p* him.
34: 1 his *p* will always be on my lips.
40: 3 a hymn of *p* to our God.
42: 5 for I will yet *p* him,
43: 5 for I will yet *p* him,
45: 17 the nations will *p* you for ever
47: 7 sing to him a psalm of *p*.
48: 1 the LORD, and most worthy of *p*,
51: 15 and my mouth will declare your *p*.
56: 4 In God, whose word I *p*,
57: 9 I will *p* you, O Lord,
63: 4 I will *p* you as long as I live,
65: 1 *P* awaits you, O God, in Zion;
66: 2 make his *p* glorious.
66: 8 *P* our God, O peoples,
68: 19 *P* be to the Lord, to God our Savior,
68: 26 *p* the LORD in the assembly
69: 30 I will *p* God's name in song
69: 34 Let heaven and earth *p* him,
71: 8 My mouth is filled with your *p*,
71: 14 I will *p* you more and more.
71: 22 I will *p* you with the harp
74: 21 the poor and needy *p* your name.
86: 12 I will *p* you, O Lord my God,
89: 5 The heavens *p* your wonders,
92: 1 It is good to *p* the LORD
96: 2 Sing to the LORD, *p* his name;
100: 4 and his courts with *p*;
101: 1 to you, O LORD, I will sing *p*.
102: 18 not yet created may *p* the LORD:
103: 1 *P* the LORD, O my soul;
103: 20 *P* the LORD, you his angels,
104: 1 *P* the LORD, O my soul.
105: 2 Sing to him, sing *p* to him;
106: 1 *P* the LORD.
108: 3 I will *p* you, O LORD,
111: 1 *P* the LORD.
113: 1 *P* the LORD.
117: 1 *P* the LORD, all you nations;
119: 175 Let me live that I may *p* you,
135: 1 *P* the LORD.
135: 20 you who fear him, *p* the LORD.
138: 1 I will *p* you, O LORD,
139: 14 I *p* you because I am fearfully
144: 1 *P* be to the LORD my Rock,
145: 3 is the LORD and most worthy of *p*;
145: 10 All you have made will *p* you,
145: 21 Let every creature *p* his holy name
146: 1 *P* the LORD, O my soul.
147: 1 how pleasant and fitting to *p* him!
148: 1 *P* the LORD from the heavens,
148: 13 Let them *p* the name of the LORD,
149: 1 his *p* in the assembly of the saints.
149: 6 May the *p* of God be
149: 9 *P* the LORD.
150: 2 *p* him for his surpassing greatness.
150: 6 that has breath *p* the LORD.
Pr 27: 2 Let another *p* you, and not your
27: 21 man is tested by the *p* he receives.
31: 31 let her works bring her *p*
SS 1: 4 we will *p* your love more than wine
Isa 12: 1 "I will *p* you, O LORD.
42: 10 his *p* from the ends of the earth,
61: 3 and a garment of *p*
Jer 33: 9 *p* and honor before all nations
Da 2: 20 "*P* be to the name of God for ever
4: 37 *p* and exalt and glorify the King
Mt 5: 16 and *p* your Father in heaven.
21: 16 you have ordained *p*'?"
Lk 19: 37 to *p* God in loud voices
Jn 5: 44 effort to obtain the *p* that comes
12: 43 for they loved *p* from men more
Ro 2: 29 Such a man's *p* is not from men,
15: 7 in order to bring *p* to God.
2Co 1: 3 *P* be to the God and Father
Eph 1: 3 *P* be to the God and Father
1: 6 to the *p* of his glorious grace,
1: 12 might be for the *p* of his glory.
1: 14 to the *p* of his glory.
1Th 2: 6 We were not looking for *p*
Heb 13: 15 offer to God a sacrifice of *p*—
Jas 3: 9 With the tongue we *p* our Lord
5: 13 happy? Let him sing songs of *p*.
Rev 5: 13 be *p* and honor and glory
7: 12 *P* and glory

PRAISED (PRAISE)
1Ch 29: 10 David *p* the LORD in the presence
Ne 8: 6 Ezra *p* the LORD, the great God;
Job 1: 21 may the name of the LORD be *p*."
Ps 113: 2 Let the name of the LORD be *p*,
Pr 31: 30 who fears the LORD is to be *p*.
Isa 63: 7 the deeds for which he is to be *p*,
Da 2: 19 Then Daniel *p* the God of heaven
4: 34 Then I *p* the Most High; I honored
Lk 18: 43 the people saw it, they also *p* God.
23: 47 seeing what had happened, *p* God
Ro 9: 5 who is God over all, forever *p*!
Gal 1: 24 And they *p* God because of me.
1Pe 4: 11 that in all things God may be *p*

PRAISES (PRAISE)
2Sa 22: 50 I will sing *p* to your name.
Ps 18: 49 I will sing *p* to your name.
47: 6 Sing *p* to God, sing *p*;
147: 1 How good it is to sing *p* to our God,
Pr 31: 28 her husband also, and he *p* her:
1Pe 2: 9 that you may declare the *p*

PRAISEWORTHY* (PRAISE)
Ps 78: 4 the *p* deeds of the LORD,
Php 4: 8 if anything is excellent or *p*—

PRAISING (PRAISE)
Lk 2: 13 *p* God and saying, "Glory to God
2: 20 *p* God for all the things they had
Ac 2: 47 *p* God and enjoying the favor
10: 46 speaking in tongues and *p* God.
1Co 14: 16 If you are *p* God with your spirit,

PRAY (PRAYED PRAYER PRAYERS PRAYING PRAYS)
Dt 4: 7 is near us whenever we *p* to him?
1Sa 12: 23 the LORD by failing to *p* for you.
1Ki 8: 30 when they *p* toward this place.
2Ch 7: 14 will humble themselves and *p*
Ezr 6: 10 and *p* for the well-being of the king
Job 42: 8 My servant Job will *p* for you,
Ps 5: 2 for to you I *p*.
32: 6 let everyone who is godly *p*
122: 6 *P* for the peace of Jerusalem:
Jer 29: 7 *P* to the LORD for it,
29: 12 upon me and come and *p* to me,
42: 3 *P* that the LORD your God will
Mt 5: 44 and *p* for those who persecute you,
6: 5 "And when you *p*, do not be like
6: 9 "This, then, is how you should *p*:
14: 23 up on a mountainside by himself to *p*.
19: 13 hands on them and *p* for them.
26: 36 Sit here while I go over there and *p*
Lk 6: 28 *p* for those who mistreat you.
11: 1 us to *p*, just as John taught his
18: 1 them that they should always *p*
22: 40 "*P* that you will not fall
Jn 17: 20 I *p* also for those who will believe
Ro 8: 26 do not know what we ought to *p* for,
1Co 14: 13 in a tongue should *p* that he may
Eph 1: 18 I *p* also that the eyes
3: 16 I *p* that out of his glorious riches he
6: 18 And *p* in the Spirit on all occasions
Col 1: 10 we *p* this in order that you may live
4: 3 *p* for us, too, that God may open
1Th 5: 17 Be joyful always; *p* continually;
2Th 1: 11 in mind, we constantly *p* for you,
Jas 5: 13 one of you in trouble? He should *p*.
5: 16 *p* for each other so that you may be
1Pe 4: 7 self-controlled so that you can *p*.
Jude : 20 up in your most holy faith and *p*

PRAYED (PRAY)
1Sa 1: 27 I *p* for this child, and the LORD
1Ki 18: 36 Elijah stepped forward and *p*:
19: 4 under it and *p* that he might die.
2Ki 6: 17 And Elisha *p*, "O LORD,
2Ch 30: 18 But Hezekiah *p* for them, saying,
Ne 4: 9 we *p* to our God and posted a guard
Job 42: 10 After Job had *p* for his friends,
Da 6: 10 got down on his knees and *p*,
9: 4 I *p* to the LORD my God
Jnh 2: 1 From inside the fish Jonah *p*
Mt 26: 39 with his face to the ground and *p*,
Mk 1: 35 off to a solitary place, where he *p*.
14: 35 *p* that if possible the hour might
Lk 22: 41 knelt down and *p*, "Father,
Jn 17: 1 he looked toward heaven and *p*:
Ac 4: 31 After they *p*, the place where they

Ac 6: 6 who *p* and laid their hands on them
8: 15 they *p* for them that they might
13: 3 So after they had fasted and *p*,

PRAYER (PRAY)
2Ch 30: 27 for their *p* reached heaven,
Ezr 8: 23 about this, and he answered our *p*.
Ps 4: 1 be merciful to me and hear my *p*.
6: 9 the LORD accepts my *p*.
17: 1 Give ear to my *p* —
17: 6 give ear to me and hear my *p*.
65: 2 O you who hear *p*,
66: 20 who has not rejected my *p*
86: 6 Hear my *p*, O LORD;
Pr 15: 8 but the *p* of the upright pleases him
15: 29 but he hears the *p* of the righteous.
Isa 56: 7 a house of *p* for all nations."
Mt 21: 13 house will be called a house of *p*,'
21: 22 receive whatever you ask for in *p*."
Mk 9: 29 This kind can come out only by *p*."
11: 24 whatever you ask for in *p*,
Jn 17: 15 My *p* is not that you take them out
Ac 1: 14 all joined together constantly in *p*,
2: 42 to the breaking of bread and to *p*.
6: 4 and will give our attention to *p*
10: 31 has heard your *p* and remembered
16: 13 expected to find a place of *p*.
Ro 12: 12 patient in affliction, faithful in *p*.
1Co 7: 5 you may devote yourselves to *p*.
2Co 13: 9 and our *p* is for your perfection.
Php 1: 9 this is my *p*: that your love may
4: 6 but in everything, by *p* and petition
Col 4: 2 yourselves to *p*, being watchful
1Ti 2: 8 to lift up holy hands in *p*,
4: 5 by the word of God and *p*.
Jas 5: 15 *p* offered in faith will make the sick
1Pe 3: 12 and his ears are attentive to their *p*,

PRAYERS (PRAY)
1Ch 5: 20 He answered their *p*, because they
Isa 1: 15 even if you offer many *p*,
Mk 12: 40 and for a show make lengthy *p*.
2Co 1: 11 as you help us by your *p*.
Eph 6: 18 on all occasions with all kinds of *p*
1Ti 2: 1 then, first of all, that requests, *p*,
1Pe 3: 7 so that nothing will hinder your *p*.
Rev 5: 8 which are the *p* of the saints.
8: 3 with the *p* of all the saints,

PRAYING (PRAY)
Ge 24: 45 "Before I finished *p* in my heart,
1Sa 1: 12 As she kept on *p* to the LORD,
Mk 11: 25 And when you stand *p*,
Lk 3: 21 as he was *p*, heaven was opened
6: 12 and spent the night *p* to God.
9: 29 As he was *p*, the appearance
Jn 17: 9 I am not *p* for the world,
Ac 9: 11 from Tarsus named Saul, for he is *p*
16: 25 and Silas were *p* and singing hymns
Ro 15: 30 in my struggle by *p* to God for me.
Eph 6: 18 always keep on *p* for all the saints.

PRAYS (PRAY)
1Co 14: 14 my spirit *p*, but my mind is

PREACH (PREACHED PREACHING)
Isa 61: 1 me to *p* good news to the poor.
Mt 10: 7 As you go, *p* this message:
23: 3 they do not practice what they *p*.
Mk 16: 15 and *p* the good news to all creation.
Lk 4: 18 me to *p* good news to the poor.
Ac 9: 20 At once he began to *p*
16: 10 us to *p* the gospel to them.
Ro 1: 15 am so eager to *p* the gospel
10: 15 how can they *p* unless they are sent
15: 20 to *p* the gospel where Christ was
1Co 1: 17 to *p* the gospel — not with words
1: 23 wisdom, but we *p* Christ crucified:
9: 14 that those who *p* the gospel should
9: 16 Woe to me if I do not *p* the gospel!
2Co 4: 5 For we do not *p* ourselves,
10: 16 so that we can *p* the gospel
Gal 1: 8 from heaven should *p* a gospel
2Ti 4: 2 I give you this charge: *P* the Word;

PREACHED (PREACH)
Mt 24: 14 gospel of the kingdom will be *p*
Mk 6: 12 and *p* that people should repent.
13: 10 And the gospel must first be *p*
14: 9 wherever the gospel is *p*
Ac 8: 4 had been scattered *p* the word
28: 31 hindrance he *p* the kingdom
1Co 9: 27 so that after I have *p* to others,
15: 1 you of the gospel I *p* to you,
2Co 11: 4 other than the Jesus we *p*,
Gal 1: 8 other than the one we *p* to you,
Eph 2: 17 *p* peace to you who were far away
Php 1: 18 false motives or true, Christ is *p*.
1Ti 3: 16 was *p* among the nations,
1Pe 1: 25 this is the word that was *p* to you.
3: 19 and *p* to the spirits in prison who

PREACHING (PREACH)
Lk 9: 6 *p* the gospel and healing people
Ac 18: 5 devoted himself exclusively to *p*,
Ro 10: 14 hear without someone *p* to them?
1Co 2: 4 and my *p* were not with wise
9: 18 in *p* the gospel I may offer it free
Gal 1: 9 If anybody is *p* to you a gospel
1Ti 4: 13 the public reading of Scripture, to *p*
5: 17 especially those whose work is *p*

PRECEDE*
1Th 4: 15 will certainly not *p* those who have

PRECEPTS*
Dt 33: 10 He teaches your *p* to Jacob
Ps 19: 8 The *p* of the LORD are right,
103: 18 and remember to obey his *p*.
105: 45 that they might keep his *p*
111: 7 all his *p* are trustworthy.
111: 10 who follow his *p* have good
119: 4 You have laid down *p*
119: 15 I meditate on your *p*
119: 27 understand the teaching of your *p*;
119: 40 How I long for your *p*!
119: 45 for I have sought out your *p*.
119: 56 I obey your *p*.
119: 63 to all who follow your *p*.
119: 69 I keep your *p* with all my heart.
119: 78 but I will meditate on your *p*.
119: 87 but I have not forsaken your *p*.
119: 93 I will never forget your *p*,
119: 94 I have sought out your *p*.
119: 100 for I obey your *p*.
119: 104 I gain understanding from your *p*;
119: 110 but I have not strayed from your *p*.
119: 128 because I consider all your *p* right,
119: 134 that I may obey your *p*.
119: 141 I do not forget your *p*.
119: 159 See how I love your *p*;
119: 168 I obey your *p* and your statutes,
119: 173 for I have chosen your *p*.

PRECIOUS
Ps 19: 10 They are more *p* than gold,
72: 14 for *p* is their blood in his sight.
116: 15 *P* in the sight of the LORD
119: 72 from your mouth is more *p* to me
139: 17 How *p* to me are your thoughts,
Pr 8: 11 for wisdom is more *p* than rubies,
Isa 28: 16 a *p* cornerstone for a sure
1Pe 1: 19 but with the *p* blood of Christ,
2: 4 but chosen by God and *p* to him —
2: 6 a chosen and *p* cornerstone,
2Pe 1: 1 Christ have received a faith as *p*
1: 4 us his very great and *p* promises,

PREDESTINED* (DESTINY)
Ro 8: 29 *p* to be conformed to the likeness
8: 30 And those he *p*, he also called;
Eph 1: 5 In love he *p* us to be adopted
1: 11 having been *p* according

PREDICTED (PREDICTION)
1Sa 28: 17 The LORD has done what he *p*
Ac 7: 52 killed those who *p* the coming
1Pe 1: 11 when he *p* the sufferings of Christ

PREDICTION* (PREDICTED PREDICTIONS)
Jer 28: 9 only if his *p* comes true."

PREDICTIONS (PREDICTION)
Isa 44: 26 and fulfills the *p* of his messengers,

PREGNANT
Ex 21: 22 who are fighting hit a *p* woman
Mt 24: 19 be in those days for *p* women
1Th 5: 3 as labor pains on a *p* woman,

PREPARE (PREPARED)
Ps 23: 5 You *p* a table before me
Isa 25: 6 the LORD Almighty will *p*
40: 3 "In the desert *p*
Am 4: 12 *p* to meet your God, O Israel."
Mal 3: 1 who will *p* the way before me.
Mt 3: 3 '*P* the way for the Lord,
Jn 14: 2 there to *p* a place for you.
Eph 4: 12 to *p* God's people for works
1Pe 1: 13 Therefore, *p* your minds for action;

PREPARED (PREPARE)
Ex 23: 20 to bring you to the place I have *p*.
Mt 25: 34 the kingdom *p* for you
Ro 9: 22 of his wrath — *p* for destruction?
1Co 2: 9 what God has *p* for those who love
Eph 2: 10 which God *p* in advance for us
2Ti 2: 21 and *p* to do any good work.
4: 2 be *p* in season and out of season;
1Pe 3: 15 Always be *p* to give an answer

PRESCRIBED
Ezr 7: 23 Whatever the God of heaven has *p*,

PRESENCE (PRESENT)
Ex 25: 30 Put the bread of the *P* on this table
33: 14 The LORD replied, "My *P* will go
Nu 4: 7 "Over the table of the *P* they are
1Sa 6: 20 in the *p* of the LORD, this
21: 6 of the *P* that had been removed
2Sa 22: 13 Out of the brightness of his *p*
2Ki 17: 23 LORD removed them from his *p*,
23: 27 also from my *p* as I removed Israel,
Ezr 9: 15 one of us can stand in your *p*."
Ps 16: 11 you will fill me with joy in your *p*,
21: 6 with the joy of your *p*.
23: 5 in the *p* of my enemies.
31: 20 the shelter of your *p* you hide them
41: 12 and set me in your *p* forever.
51: 11 Do not cast me from your *p*
52: 9 in the *p* of your saints.
89: 15 who walk in the light of your *p*,
90: 8 our secret sins in the light of your *p*
114: 7 O earth, at the *p* of the Lord,
139: 7 Where can I flee from your *p*?
Isa 26: 17 so were we in your *p*, O LORD.
Jer 5: 22 "Should you not tremble in my *p*?
Eze 38: 20 of the earth will tremble at my *p*.
Hos 6: 2 that we may live in his *p*.
Na 1: 5 The earth trembles at his *p*,
Mal 3: 16 in his *p* concerning those who
Ac 2: 28 you will fill me with joy in your *p*.'
1Th 3: 9 have in the *p* of our God
3: 13 and holy in the *p* of our God
2Th 1: 9 and shut out from the *p* of the Lord
Heb 9: 24 now to appear for us in God's *p*.
1Jn 3: 19 rest in his *p* whenever our hearts
Jude : 24 before his glorious *p* without fault

PRESENT (PRESENCE)
1Co 3: 22 life or death or the *p* or the future —
7: 26 of the *p* crisis, I think that it is good
2Co 11: 2 so that I might *p* you as a pure
Eph 5: 27 and to *p* her to himself
1Ti 4: 8 holding promise for both the *p* life
2Ti 2: 15 Do your best to *p* yourself to God
Jude : 24 and to *p* you before his glorious

PRESERVE
Lk 17: 33 and whoever loses his life will *p* it.

PRESERVES
Ps 119: 50 Your promise *p* my life.

PRESS (PRESSED PRESSURE)
Php 3: 12 but I *p* on to take hold of that
3: 14 I *p* on toward the goal

PRESSED (PRESS)
Lk 6: 38 *p* down, shaken together

PRESSURE (PRESS)
2Co 1: 8 We were under great *p*, far
11: 28 I face daily the *p* of my concern

PRETENDED
1Sa 21: 13 So he *p* to be insane

PREVAILS
1Sa 2: 9 "It is not by strength that one *p*;
Pr 19: 21 but it is the LORD's purpose that *p*

PRICE (PRICELESS)
Job 28: 18 the *p* of wisdom is beyond rubies.
1Co 6: 20 your own; you were bought at a *p*.
7: 23 bought at a *p*; do not become slaves

PRICELESS* (PRICE)
Ps 36: 7 How *p* is your unfailing love!

PRIDE (PROUD)
Pr 8: 13 I hate *p* and arrogance,
11: 2 When *p* comes, then comes
13: 10 *P* only breeds quarrels,
16: 18 *P* goes before destruction,
29: 23 A man's *p* brings him low,
Isa 25: 11 God will bring down their *p*
Da 4: 37 And those who walk in *p* he is able
Am 8: 7 The LORD has sworn by the *P*
2Co 5: 12 giving you an opportunity to take *p*
7: 4 in you; I take great *p* in you.
8: 24 and the reason for our *p* in you,
Gal 6: 4 Then he can take *p* in himself,
Jas 1: 9 ought to take *p* in his high position.

PRIEST (PRIESTHOOD PRIESTLY PRIESTS)
Ge 14: 18 He was *p* of God Most High,

Nu 5: 10 to the *p* will belong to the *p.*'"
2Ch 13: 9 and seven rams may become a *p*
Ps 110: 4 "You are a *p* forever,
Heb 2: 17 faithful high *p* in service to God,
3: 1 and high *p* whom we confess.
4: 14 have a great high *p* who has gone
4: 15 do not have a high *p* who is unable
5: 6 "You are a *p* forever,
6: 20 He has become a high *p* forever,
7: 3 Son of God he remains a *p* forever.
7: 15 clear if another *p* like Melchizedek
7: 26 Such a high *p* meets our need —
8: 1 We do have such a high *p,*
10: 11 Day after day every *p* stands
13: 11 The high *p* carries the blood

PRIESTHOOD (PRIEST)
Heb 7: 24 lives forever, he has a permanent *p.*
1Pe 2: 5 into a spiritual house to be a holy *p,*
2: 9 you are a chosen people, a royal *p,*

PRIESTLY (PRIEST)
Ro 15: 16 to the Gentiles with the *p* duty

PRIESTS (PRIEST)
Ex 19: 6 you will be for me a kingdom of *p*
Lev 21: 1 "Speak to the *p,* the sons of Aaron,
Eze 42: 13 where the *p* who approach
46: 2 *p* are to sacrifice his burnt offering
Mal 1: 6 O *p,* who show contempt for my name.
Rev 5: 10 to be a kingdom and *p*
20: 6 but they will be *p* of God

PRIME
Isa 38: 10 recovery: I said, "In the *p* of my life

PRINCE (PRINCES PRINCESS)
Isa 9: 6 Everlasting Father, *P* of Peace.
Eze 34: 24 and my servant David will be *p*
37: 25 my servant will be their *p* forever.
Da 8: 25 stand against the *P* of princes.
Jn 12: 31 now the *p* of this world will be
Ac 5: 31 as *P* and Savior that he might give

PRINCES (PRINCE)
Ps 118: 9 than to trust in *p.*
148: 11 you *p* and all rulers on earth,
Isa 40: 23 He brings *p* to naught

PRINCESS* (PRINCE)
Ps 45: 13 All glorious is the *p*

PRISCILLA*
Wife of Aquila; co-worker with Paul (Ac 18; Ro 16:3; 1Co 16:19; 2Ti 4:19); instructor of Apollos (Ac 18:24 – 28).

PRISON (PRISONER PRISONERS)
Ps 66: 11 You brought us into *p*
142: 7 Set me free from my *p,*
Isa 42: 7 to free captives from *p*
Mt 25: 36 I was in *p* and you came to visit me
2Co 11: 23 been in *p* more frequently,
Heb 11: 36 others were chained and put in *p.*
13: 3 Remember those in *p*
1Pe 3: 19 spirits in *p* who disobeyed long ago
Rev 20: 7 Satan will be released from his *p*

PRISONER (PRISON)
Ro 7: 23 and making me a *p* of the law of sin
Gal 3: 22 declares that the whole world is a *p*
Eph 3: 1 the *p* of Christ Jesus for the sake

PRISONERS (PRISON)
Ps 68: 6 he leads forth the *p* with singing;
79: 11 groans of the *p* come before you;
107: 10 *p* suffering in iron chains,
146: 7 The LORD sets *p* free,
Zec 9: 12 to your fortress, O *p* of hope;
Lk 4: 18 me to proclaim freedom for the *p*
Gal 3: 23 we were held *p* by the law,

PRIVILEGE*
2Co 8: 4 pleaded with us for the *p* of sharing

PRIZE*
1Co 9: 24 Run in such a way as to get the *p.*
9: 24 but only one gets the *p*? Run
9: 27 will not be disqualified for the *p.*
Php 3: 14 on toward the goal to win the *p*
Col 2: 18 of angels disqualify you for the *p.*

PROBE
Job 11: 7 Can you *p* the limits
Ps 17: 3 Though you *p* my heart

PROCEDURE
Ecc 8: 6 For there is a proper time and *p*

PROCESSION
Ps 68: 24 Your *p* has come into view, O God,
118: 27 boughs in hand, join in the festal *p*

1Co 4: 9 on display at the end of the *p,*
2Co 2: 14 us in triumphal *p* in Christ

PROCLAIM (PROCLAIMED PROCLAIMING PROCLAIMS PROCLAMATION)
Ex 33: 19 and I will *p* my name, the LORD,
Lev 25: 10 and *p* liberty throughout the land
Dt 30: 12 and *p* it to us so we may obey it?"
2Sa 1: 20 *p* it not in the streets of Ashkelon,
1Ch 16: 23 *p* his salvation day after day.
Ne 8: 15 and that they should *p* this word
Ps 2: 7 I will *p* the decree of the LORD:
9: 11 *p* among the nations what he has
19: 1 the skies *p* the work of his hands.
22: 31 They will *p* his righteousness
40: 9 I *p* righteousness in the great
50: 6 the heavens *p* his righteousness,
64: 9 they will *p* the works of God
68: 34 *P* the power of God,
71: 16 I will come and *p* your mighty acts,
92: 2 to *p* your love in the morning
96: 2 *p* his salvation day after day.
97: 6 The heavens *p* his righteousness,
106: 2 Who can *p* the mighty acts
118: 17 will *p* what the LORD has done.
145: 6 and I will *p* your great deeds.
Isa 12: 4 and *p* that his name is exalted.
42: 12 and *p* his praise in the islands.
52: 7 who *p* salvation,
61: 1 to *p* freedom for the captives
66: 19 They will *p* my glory
Jer 7: 2 house and there *p* this message:
50: 2 lift up a banner and *p* it;
Hos 5: 9 I *p* what is certain.
Zec 9: 10 He will *p* peace to the nations.
Mt 10: 27 in your ear, *p* from the roofs.
12: 18 and he will *p* justice to the nations.
Lk 4: 18 me to *p* freedom for the prisoners
9: 60 you go and *p* the kingdom of God."
Ac 17: 23 unknown I am going to *p*
20: 27 hesitated to *p* to you the whole will
1Co 11: 26 you *p* the Lord's death
Col 1: 28 We *p* him, admonishing
4: 4 Pray that I may *p* it clearly,
1Jn 1: 1 this we *p* concerning the Word

PROCLAIMED (PROCLAIM)
Ex 9: 16 and that my name might be *p*
34: 5 there with him and *p* his name,
Ps 68: 11 was the company of those who *p* it:
Ro 15: 19 I have fully *p* the gospel of Christ.
Col 1: 23 that has been *p* to every creature
2Ti 4: 17 me the message might be fully *p*

PROCLAIMING (PROCLAIM)
Ps 26: 7 *p* aloud your praise
92: 15 *p,* "The LORD is upright;
Ac 5: 42 and *p* the good news that Jesus is
Ro 10: 8 the word of faith we are *p*:

PROCLAIMS (PROCLAIM)
Dt 18: 22 If what a prophet *p* in the name

PROCLAMATION (PROCLAIM)
Isa 62: 11 The LORD has made *p*

PRODUCE (PRODUCES)
Mt 3: 8 *P* fruit in keeping with repentance.
3: 10 tree that does not *p* good fruit will

PRODUCES (PRODUCE)
Pr 30: 33 so stirring up anger *p* strife."
Ro 5: 3 that suffering *p* perseverance;
Heb 12: 11 it *p* a harvest of righteousness

PROFANE (PROFANED)
Lev 19: 12 and so *p* the name of your God.
22: 32 Do not *p* my holy name.
Mal 2: 10 Why do we *p* the covenant

PROFANED (PROFANE)
Eze 36: 20 the nations they *p* my holy name,

PROFESS*
1Ti 2: 10 for women who *p* to worship God.
Heb 4: 14 let us hold firmly to the faith we *p.*
10: 23 unswervingly to the hope we *p,*

PROFIT (PROFITABLE)
Pr 14: 23 All hard work brings a *p,*
21: 5 The plans of the diligent lead to *p*
Isa 44: 10 which can *p* him nothing?
2Co 2: 17 not peddle the word of God for *p.*
Php 3: 7 was to my *p* I now consider loss

PROFITABLE* (PROFIT)
Pr 3: 14 for she is more *p* than silver
31: 18 She sees that her trading is *p,*
Tit 3: 8 These things are excellent and *p*

PROFOUND
Job 9: 4 His wisdom is *p,* his power is vast.
Ps 92: 5 how *p* your thoughts!
Eph 5: 32 This is a *p* mystery — but I am

PROGRESS
Php 1: 25 continue with all of you for your *p*
1Ti 4: 15 so that everyone may see your *p.*

PROLONG*
Dt 5: 33 *p* your days in the land that you
Ps 85: 5 Will you *p* your anger
Pr 3: 2 for they will *p* your life many years
Isa 53: 10 will see his offspring and *p* his days,
La 4: 22 he will not *p* your exile.

PROMISE (PROMISED PROMISES)
Nu 23: 19 Does he *p* and not fulfill?
Jos 23: 14 Every *p* has been fulfilled;
2Sa 7: 25 keep forever the *p* you have made
1Ki 8: 20 The LORD has kept the *p* he made
8: 24 You have kept your *p*
Ne 5: 13 man who does not keep this *p.*
9: 8 have kept your *p* because you are
Ps 77: 8 Has his *p* failed for all time?
119: 41 your salvation according to your *p;*
119: 50 Your *p* preserves my life.
119: 58 to me according to your *p.*
119: 162 I rejoice in your *p*
Ac 2: 39 The *p* is for you and your children
Ro 4: 13 offspring received the *p* that he
4: 20 unbelief regarding the *p* of God,
Gal 3: 14 that by faith we might receive the *p*
Eph 2: 12 foreigners to the covenants of the *p*
1Ti 4: 8 holding *p* for both the present life
Heb 6: 13 When God made his *p* to Abraham
11: 11 him faithful who had made the *p.*
2Pe 3: 9 Lord is not slow in keeping his *p,*
3: 13 with his *p* we are looking forward

PROMISED (PROMISE)
Ge 21: 1 did for Sarah what he had *p.*
24: 7 who spoke to me and *p* me on oath,
Ex 3: 17 And I have *p* to bring you up out
Nu 10: 29 for the LORD has *p* good things
Dt 15: 6 your God will bless you as he has *p,*
26: 18 his treasured possession as he *p,*
2Sa 7: 28 and you have *p* these good things
1Ki 9: 5 I *p* David your father when I said,
2Ch 6: 15 with your mouth you have *p*
Ps 119: 57 I have *p* to obey your words.
Lk 24: 49 to send you what my Father has *p;*
Ac 1: 4 but wait for the gift my Father *p,*
13: 32 What God *p* our fathers he has
Ro 4: 21 power to do what he had *p.*
Tit 1: 2 *p* before the beginning of time,
Heb 10: 23 for he who *p* is faithful.
10: 36 you will receive what he has *p.*
Jas 1: 12 the crown of life that God has *p*
2: 5 the kingdom he *p* those who love
2Pe 3: 4 "Where is this 'coming' he *p*?
1Jn 2: 25 And this is what he *p* us —

PROMISES (PROMISE)
Jos 21: 45 one of all the LORD's good *p*
23: 14 of all the good *p* the LORD your
1Ki 8: 56 failed of all the good *p* he gave
1Ch 17: 19 and made known all these great *p.*
Ps 85: 8 he *p* peace to his people, his saints
106: 12 Then they believed his *p*
119: 140 Your *p* have been thoroughly
119: 148 that I may meditate on your *p.*
145: 13 The LORD is faithful to all his *p*
Ro 9: 4 the temple worship and the *p.*
2Co 1: 20 matter how many *p* God has made,
7: 1 Since we have these *p,* dear friends,
Heb 8: 6 and it is founded on better *p.*
2Pe 1: 4 us his very great and precious *p,*

PROMOTE (PROMOTES)
Pr 12: 20 but joy for those who *p* peace.
16: 21 and pleasant words *p* instruction.
1Ti 1: 4 These *p* controversies rather

PROMOTES (PROMOTE)
Pr 17: 9 over an offense *p* love,

PROMPTED
1Th 1: 3 your labor *p* by love, and your
2Th 1: 11 and every act *p* by your faith.

PRONOUNCE (PRONOUNCED)
1Ch 23: 13 to *p* blessings in his name forever.

PRONOUNCED (PRONOUNCE)
1Ch 16: 12 miracles, and the judgments he *p,*

PROOF (PROVE)
Ac 17: 31 He has given *p* of this to all men
2Co 8: 24 Therefore show these men the *p*

PROPER
Ps 104: 27 give them their food at the *p* time.
145: 15 give them their food at the *p* time.
Ecc 5: 18 Then I realized that it is good and *p*
8: 5 the wise heart will know the *p* time
Mt 24: 45 give them their food at the *p* time?
Lk 1: 20 which will come true at their *p* time
1Co 11: 13 Is it *p* for a woman to pray to God
Gal 6: 9 at the *p* time we will reap a harvest
1Ti 2: 6 the testimony given in its *p* time.
1Pe 2: 17 Show *p* respect to everyone:

PROPERTY
Heb 10: 34 the confiscation of your *p*,

PROPHECIES (PROPHESY)
1Co 13: 8 where there are *p*, they will cease;
1Th 5: 20 do not treat *p* with contempt.

PROPHECY (PROPHESY)
Da 9: 24 to seal up vision and *p*
1Co 12: 10 miraculous powers, to another *p*,
13: 2 of *p* and can fathom all mysteries
14: 1 gifts, especially the gift of *p*.
14: 6 or *p* or word of instruction?
14: 22 *p*, however, is for believers,
2Pe 1: 20 you must understand that no *p*
Rev 22: 18 the words of the *p* of this book:

PROPHESIED (PROPHESY)
Nu 11: 25 the Spirit rested on them, they *p*,
1Sa 19: 24 and also *p* in Samuel's presence.
Jn 11: 51 that year he *p* that Jesus would
Ac 19: 6 and they spoke in tongues and *p*.
21: 9 four unmarried daughters who *p*.

PROPHESIES (PROPHESY)
Jer 28: 9 the prophet who *p* peace will be
Eze 12: 27 and he *p* about the distant future.'
1Co 11: 4 *p* with his head covered dishonors
14: 3 But everyone who *p* speaks to men

PROPHESY (PROPHECIES PROPHECY PROPHESIED PROPHESIES PROPHESYING PROPHET PROPHET'S PROPHETESS PROPHETS)
1Sa 10: 6 and you will *p* with them;
Eze 13: 2 Say to those who *p* out
13: 17 daughters of your people who *p* out
34: 2 *p* against the shepherds of Israel;
37: 4 "*P* to these bones and say to them,
Joel 2: 28 Your sons and daughters will *p*,
Mt 7: 22 Lord, did we not *p* in your name,
Ac 2: 17 Your sons and daughters will *p*,
1Co 13: 9 know in part and we *p* in part,
14: 39 my brothers, be eager to *p*,
Rev 11: 3 and they will *p* for 1,260 days,

PROPHESYING (PROPHESY)
1Ch 25: 1 and Jeduthun for the ministry of *p*,
Ro 12: 6 If a man's gift is *p*, let him use it

PROPHET (PROPHESY)
Ex 7: 1 your brother Aaron will be your *p*.
Nu 12: 6 "When a *p* of the LORD is
Dt 13: 1 If a *p*, or one who foretells
18: 18 up for them a *p* like you
18: 22 If what a *p* proclaims in the name
1Sa 3: 20 that Samuel was attested as a *p*
9: 9 because the *p* of today used
1Ki 1: 8 son of Jehoiada, Nathan the *p*,
18: 36 the *p* Elijah stepped forward
2Ki 5: 8 and he will know that there is a *p*
6: 12 "but Elisha, the *p* who is in Israel,
20: 1 The *p* Isaiah son of Amoz went
2Ch 35: 18 since the days of the *p* Samuel;
36: 12 himself before Jeremiah the *p*,
Ezr 5: 1 Haggai the *p* and Zechariah the *p*,
Eze 2: 5 they will know that a *p* has been
33: 33 they will know that a *p* has been
Hos 9: 7 the *p* is considered a fool,
Am 7: 14 "I was neither a *p* nor a prophet's
Hab 1: 1 that Habakkuk the *p* received.
Hag 1: 1 came through the *p* Haggai
Zec 1: 1 to the *p* Zechariah son of Berekiah,
13: 4 that day every *p* will be ashamed
Mal 4: 5 I will send you the *p* Elijah
Mt 10: 41 Anyone who receives a *p*
11: 9 what did you go out to see? A *p*?
12: 39 except the sign of the *p* Jonah.
Lk 1: 76 will be called a *p* of the Most High;
4: 24 "no *p* is accepted in his hometown.
7: 16 A great *p* has appeared among us,"
24: 19 "He was a *p*, powerful in word
Jn 1: 21 "Are you the *P*?" He answered,
Ac 7: 37 'God will send you a *p* like me
21: 10 a *p* named Agabus came
1Co 14: 37 If anybody thinks he is a *p*
Rev 16: 13 and out of the mouth of the false *p*.

PROPHET'S (PROPHESY)
2Pe 1: 20 about by the *p* own interpretation.

PROPHETESS (PROPHESY)
Ex 15: 20 Then Miriam the *p*, Aaron's sister,
Jdg 4: 4 a *p*, the wife of Lappidoth,
Isa 8: 3 I went to the *p*, and she conceived
Lk 2: 36 a *p*, Anna, the daughter of Phanuel,

PROPHETS (PROPHESY)
Nu 11: 29 that all the LORD's people were *p*
1Sa 10: 11 Is Saul also among the *p*?"
28: 6 him by dreams or Urim or *p*.
1Ki 19: 10 put your *p* to death with the sword.
1Ch 16: 22 do my *p* no harm."
Ps 105: 15 do my *p* no harm."
Jer 23: 9 Concerning the *p*:
23: 30 "I am against the *p* who steal
Eze 13: 2 prophesy against the *p*
Mt 5: 17 come to abolish the Law or the *P*;
7: 12 for this sums up the Law and the *P*.
7: 15 "Watch out for false *p*.
22: 40 and the *P* hang on these two
23: 37 you who kill the *p* and stone those
24: 24 false Christs and false *p* will appear
26: 56 of the *p* might be fulfilled."
Lk 10: 24 For I tell you that many *p*
11: 49 'I will send them *p* and apostles,
24: 25 believe all that the *p* have spoken!
24: 44 me in the Law of Moses, the *P*
Ac 3: 24 "Indeed, all the *p* from Samuel on,
10: 43 All the *p* testify about him that
13: 1 the church at Antioch there were *p*
26: 22 nothing beyond what the *p*
28: 23 the Law of Moses and from the *P*.
Ro 1: 2 through his *p* in the Holy
3: 21 to which the Law and the *P* testify.
11: 3 they have killed your *p*
1Co 12: 28 second *p*, third teachers, then
12: 29 Are all *p*? Are all teachers?
14: 32 The spirits of *p* are subject
Eph 2: 20 foundation of the apostles and *p*,
3: 5 Spirit to God's holy apostles and *p*.
4: 11 some to be *p*, some
Heb 1: 1 through the *p* at many times
1Pe 1: 10 Concerning this salvation, the *p*,
2Pe 1: 19 word of the *p* made more certain,
3: 2 spoken in the past by the holy *p*
1Jn 4: 1 because many false *p* have gone out
Rev 11: 10 these two *p* had tormented those
18: 20 Rejoice, saints and apostles and *p*!

PROPORTION
Dt 16: 10 by giving a freewill offering in *p*
16: 17 Each of you must bring a gift in *p*

PROPRIETY*
1Ti 2: 9 with decency and *p*,
2: 15 in faith, love and holiness with *p*.

PROSPECT*
Pr 10: 28 The *p* of the righteous is joy,

PROSPER (PROSPERED PROSPERITY PROSPEROUS PROSPERS)
Dt 5: 33 so that you may live and *p*
28: 63 pleased the LORD to make you *p*
29: 9 that you may *p* in everything you
1Ki 2: 3 so that you may *p* in all you do
Ezr 6: 14 and *p* under the preaching
Pr 11: 10 When the righteous *p*, the city
11: 25 A generous man will *p*;
17: 20 A man of perverse heart does not *p*
28: 13 who conceals his sins does not *p*,
28: 25 he who trusts in the LORD will *p*.
Isa 53: 10 of the LORD will *p* in his hand.
Jer 12: 1 Why does the way of the wicked *p*?

PROSPERED (PROSPER)
Ge 39: 2 was with Joseph and he *p*,
2Ch 14: 7 So they built and *p*.
31: 21 And so he *p*.

PROSPERITY (PROSPER)
Dt 28: 11 will grant you abundant *p*—
30: 15 I set before you today life and *p*,
Job 36: 11 will spend the rest of their days in *p*
Ps 73: 3 when I saw the *p* of the wicked.
122: 9 I will seek your *p*.
128: 2 blessings and *p* will be yours.
Pr 3: 2 and bring you *p*.
13: 21 but *p* is the reward of the righteous.
21: 21 finds life, *p* and honor.
Isa 45: 7 I bring *p* and create disaster;

PROSPEROUS (PROSPER)
Dt 30: 9 your God will make you most *p*
Jos 1: 8 Then you will be *p* and successful.
Job 42: 10 the LORD made him *p* again

PROSPERS (PROSPER)
Ps 1: 3 Whatever he does *p*.
Pr 16: 20 gives heed to instruction *p*,
19: 8 he who cherishes understanding *p*.

PROSTITUTE (PROSTITUTES PROSTITUTION)
Lev 20: 6 and spiritists to *p* himself
Nu 15: 39 and not *p* yourselves by going
Jos 2: 1 the house of a *p* named Rahab
Pr 6: 26 for the *p* reduces you to a loaf
7: 10 like a *p* and with crafty intent.
23: 27 for a *p* is a deep pit
Eze 16: 15 and used your fame to become a *p*.
23: 7 a *p* to all the elite of the Assyrians
Hos 3: 3 you must not be a *p* or be intimate
1Co 6: 15 of Christ and unite them with a *p*?
6: 16 with a *p* is one with her in body?
Rev 17: 1 you the punishment of the great *p*,

PROSTITUTES (PROSTITUTE)
Pr 29: 3 of *p* squanders his wealth.
Mt 21: 31 and the *p* are entering the kingdom
Lk 15: 30 property with *p* comes home,
1Co 6: 9 male *p* nor homosexual offenders

PROSTITUTION (PROSTITUTE)
Eze 16: 16 where you carried on your *p*.
23: 3 engaging in *p* from their youth.
Hos 4: 10 engage in *p* but not increase,

PROSTRATE
Dt 9: 18 again I fell *p* before the LORD
1Ki 18: 39 they fell *p* and cried, "The LORD

PROTECT (PROTECTED PROTECTION PROTECTS)
Dt 23: 14 about in your camp to *p* you
Ps 25: 21 integrity and uprightness *p* me,
32: 7 you will *p* me from trouble
40: 11 your truth always *p* me.
41: 2 The LORD will *p* him
91: 14 I will *p* him, for he acknowledges
140: 1 *p* me from men of violence,
Pr 2: 11 Discretion will *p* you,
4: 6 forsake wisdom, and she will *p* you;
Jn 17: 11 *p* them by the power of your name
17: 15 that you *p* them from the evil one.
2Th 3: 3 and *p* you from the evil one.

PROTECTED (PROTECT)
Jos 24: 17 He *p* us on our entire journey
1Sa 30: 23 He has *p* us and handed
Ps 37: 28 They will be *p* forever,
Jn 17: 12 I *p* them and kept them safe

PROTECTION (PROTECT)
Ezr 9: 9 he has given us a wall of *p* in Judah
Ps 5: 11 Spread your *p* over them,

PROTECTS (PROTECT)
Ps 116: 6 The LORD *p* the simplehearted;
Pr 2: 8 and *p* the way of his faithful ones.
1Co 13: 7 It always *p*, always trusts,

PROUD (PRIDE)
Ps 31: 23 but the *p* he pays back in full.
101: 5 has haughty eyes and a *p* heart,
138: 6 but the *p* he knows from afar.
Pr 3: 34 He mocks *p* mockers
16: 5 The LORD detests all the *p*
16: 19 than to share plunder with the *p*.
18: 12 his downfall a man's heart is *p*,
21: 4 Haughty eyes and a *p* heart,
Isa 2: 12 store for all the *p* and lofty,
Ro 12: 16 Do not be *p*, but be willing
1Co 13: 4 it does not boast, it is not *p*.
2Ti 3: 2 lovers of money, boastful, *p*,
Jas 4: 6 "God opposes the *p*
1Pe 5: 5 because, "God opposes the *p*

PROVE (PROOF PROVED PROVING)
Pr 29: 25 Fear of man will *p* to be a snare,
Jn 8: 46 Can any of you *p* me guilty of sin?
Ac 26: 20 *p* their repentance by their deeds.
1Co 4: 2 been given a trust must *p* faithful.

PROVED (PROVE)
Ps 51: 4 so that you are *p* right
Mt 11: 19 wisdom is *p* right by her actions."
Ro 3: 4 "So that you may be *p* right
1Pe 1: 7 may be *p* genuine and may result

PROVIDE (PROVIDED PROVIDES PROVISION)
Ge 22: 8 "God himself will *p* the lamb
22: 14 that place "The LORD will *P*."
Isa 43: 20 because I *p* water in the desert
61: 3 and *p* for those who grieve in Zion
1Co 10: 13 *p* a way out so that you can stand
1Ti 5: 8 If anyone does not *p*
Tit 3: 14 in order that they may *p*

PROVIDED (PROVIDE)
Ps 68: 10 O God, you *p* for the poor.
111: 9 He *p* redemption for his people;
Jnh 1: 17 But the LORD *p* a great fish
4: 6 Then the LORD God *p* a vine
4: 7 dawn the next day God *p* a worm,
4: 8 God *p* a scorching east wind,
Gal 4: 18 to be zealous, *p* the purpose is good
Heb 1: 3 After he had *p* purification for sins,

PROVIDES (PROVIDE)
Ps 111: 5 He *p* food for those who fear him;
Pr 31: 15 she *p* food for her family
Eze 18: 7 and *p* clothing for the naked.
1Ti 6: 17 who richly *p* us with everything
1Pe 4: 11 it with the strength God *p*,

PROVING* (PROVE)
Ac 9: 22 by *p* that Jesus is the Christ.
17: 3 and *p* that the Christ had to suffer
18: 28 *p* from the Scriptures that Jesus

PROVISION (PROVIDE)
Ro 5: 17 who receive God's abundant *p*

PROVOKED
Ecc 7: 9 Do not be quickly *p* in your spirit,
Jer 32: 32 Judah have *p* me by all the evil they

PROWLS
1Pe 5: 8 Your enemy the devil *p*

PRUDENCE* (PRUDENT)
Pr 1: 4 for giving *p* to the simple,
8: 5 You who are simple, gain *p*;
8: 12 "I, wisdom, dwell together with *p*;
15: 5 whoever heeds correction shows *p*.
19: 25 and the simple will learn *p*;

PRUDENT* (PRUDENCE)
Pr 1: 3 acquiring a disciplined and *p* life,
12: 16 but a *p* man overlooks an insult.
12: 23 A *p* man keeps his knowledge
13: 16 Every *p* man acts out of knowledge
14: 8 The wisdom of the *p* is
14: 15 a *p* man gives thought to his steps.
14: 18 the *p* are crowned with knowledge.
19: 14 but a *p* wife is from the LORD.
22: 3 *p* man sees danger and takes
27: 12 The *p* see danger and take refuge,
Jer 49: 7 Has counsel perished from the *p*?
Am 5: 13 Therefore the *p* man keeps quiet

PRUNES (PRUNING)
Jn 15: 2 that does bear fruit he *p*

PRUNING (PRUNES)
Isa 2: 4 and their spears into *p* hooks.
Joel 3: 10 and your *p* hooks into spears.

PSALMS
Eph 5: 19 Speak to one another with *p*,
Col 3: 16 and as you sing *p*, hymns

PUBLICLY
Ac 20: 20 have taught you *p* and from house
1Ti 5: 20 Those who sin are to be rebuked *p*,

PUFFS
1Co 8: 1 Knowledge *p* up, but love builds up

PULLING
2Co 10: 8 building you up rather than *p* you

PUNISH (PUNISHED PUNISHES PUNISHMENT)
Ge 15: 14 But I will *p* the nation they serve
Ex 32: 34 I will *p* them for their sin."
Pr 17: 26 It is not good to *p* an innocent man,
23: 13 if you *p* him with the rod, he will
Isa 13: 11 I will *p* the world for its evil,
Jer 2: 19 Your wickedness will *p* you;
21: 14 I will *p* you as your deeds deserve,
Zep 1: 12 and *p* those who are complacent,
Ac 7: 7 But I will *p* the nation they serve
2Th 1: 8 He will *p* those who do not know
1Pe 2: 14 by him to *p* those who do wrong

PUNISHED (PUNISH)
Ezr 9: 13 you have *p* us less than our sins
Ps 99: 8 though you *p* their misdeeds.
La 3: 39 complain when *p* for his sins?
Mk 12: 40 Such men will be *p* most severely."
Lk 23: 41 the same sentence? We are *p* justly,
2Th 1: 9 be *p* with everlasting destruction
Heb 10: 29 to be *p* who has trampled the Son

PUNISHES (PUNISH)
Heb 12: 6 and he *p* everyone he accepts

PUNISHMENT (PUNISH)
Isa 53: 5 the *p* that brought us peace was
Jer 4: 18 This is your *p*.
Mt 25: 46 Then they will go away to eternal *p*
Lk 12: 48 and does things deserving *p* will be
21: 22 For this is the time of *p*
Ro 13: 4 wrath to bring *p* on the wrongdoer.
Heb 2: 2 disobedience received its just *p*,
2Pe 2: 9 while continuing their *p*.

PURCHASED
Ps 74: 2 Remember the people you *p* of old,
Rev 5: 9 with your blood you *p* men for God

PURE (PURIFICATION PURIFIED PURIFIES PURIFY PURITY)
2Sa 22: 27 to the *p* you show yourself *p*,
Job 14: 4 Who can bring what is *p*
Ps 19: 9 The fear of the LORD is *p*,
24: 4 who has clean hands and a *p* heart,
51: 10 Create in me a *p* heart, O God,
119: 9 can a young man keep his way *p*?
Pr 15: 26 those of the *p* are pleasing to him.
20: 9 can say, "I have kept my heart *p*;
Isa 52: 11 Come out from it and be *p*,
Hab 1: 13 Your eyes are too *p* to look on evil;
Mt 5: 8 Blessed are the *p* in heart,
2Co 11: 2 I might present you as a *p* virgin
Php 4: 8 whatever is *p*, whatever is lovely,
1Ti 1: 5 which comes from a *p* heart
5: 22 Keep yourself *p*.
2Ti 2: 22 call on the Lord out of a *p* heart.
Tit 1: 15 To the *p*, all things are *p*,
2: 5 to be self-controlled and *p*,
Heb 7: 26 blameless, *p*, set apart from sinners
13: 4 and the marriage bed kept *p*,
Jas 1: 27 that God our Father accepts as *p*
3: 17 comes from heaven is first of all *p*;
1Jn 3: 3 him purifies himself, just as he is *p*.

PURGE
Pr 20: 30 and beatings *p* the inmost being.

PURIFICATION (PURE)
Heb 1: 3 After he had provided *p* for sins,

PURIFIED (PURE)
Ac 15: 9 for he *p* their hearts by faith.
1Pe 1: 22 Now that you have *p* yourselves

PURIFIES* (PURE)
1Jn 1: 7 of Jesus, his Son, *p* us from all sin.
3: 3 who has this hope in him *p* himself,

PURIFY (PURE)
Nu 19: 12 He must *p* himself with the water
2Co 7: 1 us *p* ourselves from everything that
Tit 2: 14 to *p* for himself a people that are
Jas 4: 8 you sinners, and *p* your hearts,
1Jn 1: 9 and *p* us from all unrighteousness.

PURIM
Est 9: 26 Therefore these days were called *P*

PURITY* (PURE)
Hos 8: 5 long will they be incapable of *p*?
2Co 6: 6 in *p*, understanding, patience
1Ti 4: 12 in life, in love, in faith and in *p*.
5: 2 as sisters, with absolute *p*.
1Pe 3: 2 when they see the *p* and reverence

PURPLE
Pr 31: 22 she is clothed in fine linen and *p*.
Mk 15: 17 They put a *p* robe on him, then

PURPOSE (PURPOSED PURPOSES)
Ex 9: 16 I have raised you up for this very *p*,
Job 36: 5 he is mighty, and firm in his *p*.
Pr 19: 21 but it is the LORD's *p* that prevails
Isa 46: 10 I say: My *p* will stand,
55: 11 and achieve the *p* for which I sent it
Ac 2: 23 handed over to you by God's set *p*
Ro 8: 28 have been called according to his *p*.
9: 11 in order that God's *p*
9: 17 "I raised you up for this very *p*,
1Co 3: 8 the man who waters have one *p*,
2Co 5: 5 who has made us for this very *p*
Gal 4: 18 be zealous, provided the *p* is good,
Eph 1: 11 in conformity with the *p* of his will,
3: 11 according to his eternal *p* which he
Php 2: 2 love, being one in spirit and *p*.
2: 13 and to act according to his good *p*.
2Ti 1: 9 but because of his own *p* and grace.

PURPOSED (PURPOSE)
Isa 14: 24 and as I have *p*, so it will stand.
14: 27 For the LORD Almighty has *p*,
Eph 1: 9 which he *p* in Christ, to be put

PURPOSES (PURPOSE)
Ps 33: 10 he thwarts the *p* of the peoples.
Jer 23: 20 the *p* of his heart.
32: 19 great are your *p* and mighty are

PURSE (PURSES)
Hag 1: 6 to put them in a *p* with holes in it."
Lk 10: 4 Do not take a *p* or bag or sandals;
22: 36 "But now if you have a *p*, take it,

PURSES (PURSE)
Lk 12: 33 Provide *p* for yourselves that will

PURSUE (PURSUES)
Ps 34: 14 seek peace and *p* it.
Pr 15: 9 he loves those who *p* righteousness
Ro 9: 30 who did not *p* righteousness,
1Ti 6: 11 and *p* righteousness, godliness,
2Ti 2: 22 and *p* righteousness, faith,
1Pe 3: 11 he must seek peace and *p* it.

PURSUES (PURSUE)
Pr 21: 21 He who *p* righteousness and love
28: 1 wicked man flees though no one *p*,

QUAIL
Ex 16: 13 That evening *q* came and covered
Nu 11: 31 and drove *q* in from the sea.

QUALITIES* (QUALITY)
Da 6: 3 by his exceptional *q* that the king
Ro 1: 20 of the world God's invisible *q*—
2Pe 1: 8 For if you possess these *q*

QUALITY (QUALITIES)
1Co 3: 13 and the fire will test the *q*

QUARREL (QUARRELING QUARRELS QUARRELSOME)
Pr 15: 18 but a patient man calms a *q*.
17: 14 Starting a *q* is like breaching a dam;
17: 19 He who loves a *q* loves sin;
20: 3 but every fool is quick to *q*.
26: 17 in a *q* not his own.
26: 20 without gossip a *q* dies down.
2Ti 2: 24 And the Lord's servant must not *q*;
Jas 4: 2 You *q* and fight.

QUARRELING (QUARREL)
1Co 3: 3 For since there is jealousy and *q*
2Ti 2: 14 before God against *q* about words;

QUARRELS (QUARREL)
Pr 13: 10 Pride only breeds *q*,
Isa 45: 9 Woe to him who *q* with his Maker,
2Ti 2: 23 because you know they produce *q*.
Jas 4: 1 What causes fights and *q*

QUARRELSOME (QUARREL)
Pr 19: 13 a *q* wife is like a constant dripping.
21: 9 than share a house with a *q* wife.
26: 21 so is a *q* man for kindling strife.
1Ti 3: 3 not violent but gentle, not *q*,

QUEEN
1Ki 10: 1 When the *q* of Sheba heard about
2Ch 9: 1 When the *q* of Sheba heard
Mt 12: 42 The *Q* of the South will rise

QUENCH (QUENCHED)
SS 8: 7 Many waters cannot *q* love;

QUENCHED (QUENCH)
Isa 66: 24 nor will their fire be *q*,
Mk 9: 48 and the fire is not *q*.'

QUICK-TEMPERED* (TEMPER)
Pr 14: 17 A *q* man does foolish things,
14: 29 but a *q* man displays folly.
Tit 1: 7 not *q*, not given to drunkenness,

QUIET (QUIETNESS)
Ps 23: 2 he leads me beside *q* waters,
Pr 17: 1 Better a dry crust with peace and *q*
Ecc 9: 17 The *q* words of the wise are more
Am 5: 13 Therefore the prudent man keeps *q*
Zep 3: 17 he will *q* you with his love,
Lk 19: 40 he replied, "if they keep *q*,
1Th 4: 11 it your ambition to lead a *q* life,
1Ti 2: 2 we may live peaceful and *q* lives
1Pe 3: 4 beauty of a gentle and *q* spirit,

QUIETNESS (QUIET)
Isa 30: 15 in *q* and trust is your strength,
32: 17 the effect of righteousness will be *q*
1Ti 2: 11 A woman should learn in *q*

QUIVER
Ps 127: 5 whose *q* is full of them.

RACE
Ecc 9: 11 The *r* is not to the swift
Ac 20: 24 if only I may finish the *r*
1Co 9: 24 that in a *r* all the runners run,
Gal 2: 2 that I was running or had run my *r*
5: 7 You were running a good *r*.
2Ti 4: 7 I have finished the *r*, I have kept
Heb 12: 1 perseverance the *r* marked out

RACHEL
Daughter of Laban (Ge 29:16); wife of Jacob (Ge 29:28); bore two sons (Ge 30:22–24; 35:16–24; 46:19). Stole Laban's gods (Ge 31:19, 32–35). Death (Ge 35:19–20).

RADIANCE (RADIANT)
Eze 1: 28 so was the *r* around him.
Heb 1: 3 The Son is the *r* of God's glory

RADIANT (RADIANCE)
Ex 34: 29 he was not aware that his face was *r*
Ps 34: 5 Those who look to him are *r;*
SS 5: 10 *Beloved* My lover is *r* and ruddy,
Isa 60: 5 Then you will look and be *r,*
Eph 5: 27 her to himself as a *r* church,

RAGE
Ac 4: 25 "'Why do the nations *r*
Col 3: 8 *r,* malice, slander, and filthy

RAGS
Isa 64: 6 our righteous acts are like filthy *r;*

RAHAB
Prostitute of Jericho who hid Israelite spies (Jos 2; 6:22–25; Heb 11:31; Jas 2:25). Mother of Boaz (Mt 1:5).

RAIN (RAINBOW)
Ge 7: 4 from now I will send *r* on the earth
1Ki 17: 1 nor *r* in the next few years
18: 1 and I will send *r* on the land."
Mt 5: 45 and sends *r* on the righteous
Jas 5: 17 it did not *r* on the land for three
Jude : 12 They are clouds without *r,*

RAINBOW (RAIN)
Ge 9: 13 I have set my *r* in the clouds,

RAISE (RISE)
Jn 6: 39 but *r* them up at the last day.
1Co 15: 15 he did not *r* him if in fact the dead

RAISED (RISE)
Isa 52: 13 he will be *r* and lifted up
Mt 17: 23 on the third day he will be *r* to life
Lk 7: 22 the deaf hear, the dead are *r,*
Ac 2: 24 But God *r* him from the dead,
Ro 4: 25 was *r* to life for our justification.
6: 4 as Christ was *r* from the dead
8: 11 And if the Spirit of him who *r* Jesus
10: 9 in your heart that God *r* him
1Co 15: 4 that he was *r* on the third day
15: 20 But Christ has indeed been *r*

RALLY*
Isa 11: 10 the nations will *r* to him,

RAM (RAMS)
Ge 22: 13 there in a thicket he saw a *r* caught
Da 8: 3 before me was a *r* with two horns,

RAMPART*
Ps 91: 4 will be your shield and *r.*

RAMS (RAM)
1Sa 15: 22 to heed is better than the fat of *r.*
Mic 6: 7 pleased with thousands of *r,*

RAN (RUN)
Jnh 1: 3 But Jonah *r* away from the LORD

RANSOM (RANSOMED)
Isa 50: 2 Was my arm too short to *r* you?
Hos 13: 14 "I will *r* them from the power
Mt 20: 28 and to give his life as a *r* for many."
Mk 10: 45 and to give his life as a *r* for many."
1Ti 2: 6 who gave himself as a *r* for all men
Heb 9: 15 as a *r* to set them free

RANSOMED (RANSOM)
Isa 35: 10 and the *r* of the LORD will return.

RARE
Pr 20: 15 that speak knowledge are a *r* jewel.

RAVEN (RAVENS)
Ge 8: 7 made in the ark and sent out a *r,*
Job 38: 41 Who provides food for the *r*

RAVENS (RAVEN)
1Ki 17: 6 The *r* brought him bread
Ps 147: 9 and for the young *r* when they call.
Lk 12: 24 Consider the *r:* They do not sow

READ (READING READS)
Dt 17: 19 he is to *r* it all the days of his life
Jos 8: 34 Joshua *r* all the words of the law—
2Ki 23: 2 He *r* in their hearing all the words
Ne 8: 8 They *r* from the Book of the Law
Jer 36: 6 and *r* to the people from the scroll
2Co 3: 2 known and *r* by everybody.

READING (READ)
1Ti 4: 13 to the public *r* of Scripture,

READS (READ)
Rev 1: 3 Blessed is the one who *r* the words

REAFFIRM
2Co 2: 8 therefore, to *r* your love for him.

REAL* (REALITIES REALITY)
Jn 6: 55 is *r* food and my blood is *r* drink.
1Jn 2: 27 all things and as that anointing is *r,*

REALITIES* (REAL)
Heb 10: 1 are coming—not the *r* themselves.

REALITY* (REAL)
Col 2: 17 the *r,* however, is found in Christ.

REALM (REALMS)
Hab 2: 9 "Woe to him who builds his *r*

REALMS (REALM)
Eph 1: 3 the heavenly *r* with every spiritual
2: 6 in the heavenly *r* in Christ Jesus,

REAP (REAPER REAPS)
Job 4: 8 and those who sow trouble *r* it.
Ps 126: 5 will *r* with songs of joy.
Hos 8: 7 and *r* the whirlwind.
10: 12 *r* the fruit of unfailing love,
Jn 4: 38 you to *r* what you have not worked
Ro 6: 22 the benefit you *r* leads to holiness,
2Co 9: 6 generously will also *r* generously.
Gal 6: 8 from that nature will *r* destruction;

REAPER (REAP)
Jn 4: 36 and the *r* may be glad together.

REAPS (REAP)
Pr 11: 18 who sows righteousness *r* a sure
22: 8 He who sows wickedness *r* trouble,
Gal 6: 7 A man *r* what he sows.

REASON (REASONED)
Ge 2: 24 For this *r* a man will leave his
Isa 1: 18 "Come now, let us *r* together,"
Mt 19: 5 'For this *r* a man will leave his
Jn 12: 27 it was for this very *r* I came
15: 25 'They hated me without *r.*'
1Pe 3: 15 to give the *r* for the hope that you
2Pe 1: 5 For this very *r,* make every effort

REASONED (REASON)
1Co 13: 11 thought like a child, I *r* like a child.

REBEKAH
Sister of Laban, secured as bride for Isaac (Ge 24). Mother of Esau and Jacob (Ge 25:19–26). Taken by Abimelech as sister of Isaac; returned (Ge 26:1–11). Encouraged Jacob to trick Isaac out of blessing (Ge 27:1–17).

REBEL (REBELLED REBELLION REBELS)
Nu 14: 9 Only do not *r* against the LORD.
1Sa 12: 14 and do not *r* against his commands,
Mt 10: 21 children will *r* against their parents

REBELLED (REBEL)
Ps 78: 56 and *r* against the Most High;
Isa 63: 10 Yet they *r*

REBELLION (REBEL)
Ex 34: 7 and forgiving wickedness, *r* and sin
Nu 14: 18 in love and forgiving sin and *r.*
1Sa 15: 23 For *r* is like the sin of divination,
2Th 2: 3 will not come until the *r* occurs

REBELS (REBEL)
Ro 13: 2 he who *r* against the authority is
1Ti 1: 9 but for lawbreakers and *r,*

REBIRTH* (BEAR)
Tit 3: 5 us through the washing of *r*

REBUILD (BUILD)
Ezr 5: 2 set to work to *r* the house of God
Ne 2: 17 let us *r* the wall of Jerusalem,
Ps 102: 16 For the LORD will *r* Zion
Da 9: 25 and *r* Jerusalem until the Anointed
Am 9: 14 they will *r* the ruined cities
Ac 15: 16 Its ruins I will *r,*

REBUILT (BUILD)
Zec 1: 16 and there my house will be *r.*

REBUKE (REBUKED REBUKES REBUKING)
Lev 19: 17 *R* your neighbor frankly
Ps 141: 5 let him *r* me—it is oil on my head.
Pr 3: 11 and do not resent his *r,*
9: 8 *r* a wise man and he will love you.
15: 31 He who listens to a life-giving *r*
17: 10 A *r* impresses a man
19: 25 *r* a discerning man, and he will gain
25: 12 is a wise man's *r* to a listening ear.
27: 5 Better is open *r*
30: 6 or he will *r* you and prove you a liar
Ecc 7: 5 It is better to heed a wise man's *r*
Isa 54: 9 never to *r* you again.
Jer 2: 19 your backsliding will *r* you.
Lk 17: 3 "If your brother sins, *r* him,
1Ti 5: 1 Do not *r* an older man harshly,
2Ti 4: 2 correct, *r* and encourage—
Tit 1: 13 Therefore, *r* them sharply,
2: 15 Encourage and *r* with all authority.
Rev 3: 19 Those whom I love I *r*

REBUKED (REBUKE)
Mk 16: 14 he *r* them for their lack of faith
1Ti 5: 20 Those who sin are to be *r* publicly,

REBUKES (REBUKE)
Job 22: 4 "Is it for your piety that he *r* you
Pr 28: 23 He who *r* a man will
29: 1 remains stiff-necked after many *r*
Heb 12: 5 do not lose heart when he *r* you,

REBUKING (REBUKE)
2Ti 3: 16 *r,* correcting and training

RECEIVE (RECEIVED RECEIVES)
Mt 10: 41 a righteous man will *r* a righteous
Mk 10: 15 anyone who will not *r* the kingdom
Jn 20: 22 and said, "*R* the Holy Spirit.
Ac 1: 8 you will *r* power when the Holy
2: 38 you will *r* the gift of the Holy Spirit
19: 2 "Did you *r* the Holy Spirit
20: 35 'It is more blessed to give than to *r*
1Co 9: 14 the gospel should *r* their living
2Co 6: 17 and I will *r* you."
1Ti 1: 16 believe on him and *r* eternal life.
Jas 1: 7 should not think he will *r* anything
2Pe 1: 11 and you will *r* a rich welcome
1Jn 3: 22 and *r* from him anything we ask,
Rev 4: 11 to *r* glory and honor and power,
5: 12 to *r* power and wealth and wisdom

RECEIVED (RECEIVE)
Mt 6: 2 they have *r* their reward in full.
10: 8 Freely you have *r,* freely give.
Mk 11: 24 believe that you have *r* it,
Jn 1: 12 Yet to all who *r* him,
1: 16 his grace we have all *r* one blessing
Ac 8: 17 and they *r* the Holy Spirit.
10: 47 They have *r* the Holy Spirit just
Ro 8: 15 but you *r* the Spirit of sonship.
1Co 11: 23 For I *r* from the Lord what I
2Co 1: 4 the comfort we ourselves have *r*
Col 2: 6 just as you *r* Christ Jesus as Lord,
1Pe 4: 10 should use whatever gift he has *r*

RECEIVES (RECEIVE)
Pr 18: 22 and *r* favor from the LORD.
27: 21 but man is tested by the praise he *r.*
Mt 7: 8 everyone who asks *r;* he who seeks
10: 40 he who *r* me *r* the one who sent me.
10: 40 "He who *r* you *r* me, and he who
Ac 10: 43 believes in him *r* forgiveness of sins

RECITE
Ps 45: 1 as I *r* my verses for the king;

RECKLESS
Pr 12: 18 *R* words pierce like a sword,
14: 16 but a fool is hotheaded and *r.*

RECKONING
Isa 10: 3 What will you do on the day of *r,*
Hos 9: 7 the days of *r* are at hand.

RECLAIM* (CLAIM)
Isa 11: 11 time to *r* the remnant that is left

RECOGNITION (RECOGNIZE)
1Co 16: 18 Such men deserve *r.*
1Ti 5: 3 Give proper *r* to those widows who

RECOGNIZE (RECOGNITION RECOGNIZED)
Mt 7: 16 By their fruit you will *r* them.
1Jn 4: 2 This is how you can *r* the Spirit
4: 6 This is how we *r* the Spirit of truth

RECOGNIZED (RECOGNIZE)
Mt 12: 33 for a tree is *r* by its fruit.
Ro 7: 13 in order that sin might be *r* as sin,

RECOMPENSE*
Isa 40: 10 and his *r* accompanies him.
62: 11 and his *r* accompanies him.'"

RECONCILE* (RECONCILED RECONCILIATION RECONCILING)
Ac 7: 26 He tried to *r* them by saying, 'Men,
Eph 2: 16 in this one body to *r* both of them
Col 1: 20 him to *r* to himself all things,

RECONCILED* (RECONCILE)
Mt 5: 24 First go and be *r* to your brother;

Lk 12: 58 try hard to be *r* to him on the way,
Ro 5: 10 how much more, having been *r*,
5: 10 we were *r* to him through the death
1Co 7: 11 or else be *r* to her husband.
2Co 5: 18 who *r* us to himself through Christ
5: 20 you on Christ's behalf: Be *r* to God.
Col 1: 22 he has *r* you by Christ's physical

RECONCILIATION* (RECONCILE)
Ro 5: 11 whom we have now received *r*.
11: 15 For if their rejection is the *r*
2Co 5: 18 and gave us the ministry of *r*:
5: 19 committed to us the message of *r*.

RECONCILING* (RECONCILE)
2Co 5: 19 that God was *r* the world to himself

RECORD (RECORDED)
Ps 130: 3 If you, O LORD, kept a *r* of sins,
Hos 13: 12 his sins are kept on *r*.
1Co 13: 5 is not easily angered, it keeps no *r*

RECORDED (RECORD)
Job 19: 23 "Oh, that my words were *r*,
Jn 20: 30 which are not *r* in this book.

RECOUNT*
Ps 40: 5 no one can *r* to you;
79: 13 we will *r* your praise.
119: 13 With my lips I *r*

RED
Ex 15: 4 are drowned in the *R* Sea.
Ps 106: 9 He rebuked the *R* Sea,
Pr 23: 31 Do not gaze at wine when it is *r*,
Isa 1: 18 though they are *r* as crimson,

REDEEM (KINSMAN-REDEEMER REDEEMED REDEEMER REDEEMS REDEMPTION)
Ex 6: 6 will *r* you with an outstretched arm
2Sa 7: 23 on earth that God went out to *r*
Ps 44: 26 *r* us because of your unfailing love.
49: 7 No man can *r* the life of another
49: 15 God will *r* my life from the grave;
130: 8 He himself will *r* Israel
Hos 13: 14 I will *r* them from death.
Gal 4: 5 under law, to *r* those under law,
Tit 2: 14 for us to *r* us from all wickedness

REDEEMED (REDEEM)
Job 33: 28 He *r* my soul from going
Ps 71: 23 I, whom you have *r*.
107: 2 Let the *r* of the LORD say this—
Isa 35: 9 But only the *r* will walk there,
63: 9 In his love and mercy he *r* them;
Gal 3: 13 Christ *r* us from the curse
1Pe 1: 18 or gold that you were *r*

REDEEMER (REDEEM)
Job 19: 25 I know that my *R* lives,
Ps 19: 14 O LORD, my Rock and my *R*.
Isa 44: 6 and *R*, the LORD Almighty:
48: 17 your *R*, the Holy One of Israel:
59: 20 "The *R* will come to Zion,

REDEEMS (REDEEM)
Ps 34: 22 The LORD *r* his servants;
103: 4 he *r* my life from the pit

REDEMPTION (REDEEM)
Ps 130: 7 and with him is full *r*.
Lk 21: 28 because your *r* is drawing near."
Ro 3: 24 grace through the *r* that came
8: 23 as sons, the *r* of our bodies.
1Co 1: 30 our righteousness, holiness and *r*.
Eph 1: 7 In him we have *r* through his blood
1: 14 until the *r* of those who are God's
4: 30 you were sealed for the day of *r*.
Col 1: 14 in whom we have *r*, the forgiveness
Heb 9: 12 having obtained eternal *r*.

REED
Isa 42: 3 A bruised *r* he will not break,
Mt 12: 20 A bruised *r* he will not break,

REFINE*
Jer 9: 7 "See, I will *r* and test them,
Zec 13: 9 I will *r* them like silver
Mal 3: 3 and *r* them like gold and silver.

REFLECT (REFLECTS)
2Co 3: 18 unveiled faces all *r* the Lord's

REFLECTS (REFLECT)
Pr 27: 19 As water *r* a face,

REFRESH (REFRESHED REFRESHING)
Phm : 20 in the Lord; *r* my heart in Christ.

REFRESHED (REFRESH)
Pr 11: 25 refreshes others will himself be *r*.

REFRESHING* (REFRESH)
Ac 3: 19 that times of *r* may come

REFUGE
Nu 35: 11 towns to be your cities of *r*,
Dt 33: 27 The eternal God is your *r*,
Jos 20: 2 to designate the cities of *r*,
Ru 2: 12 wings you have come to take *r*."
2Sa 22: 3 God is my rock, in whom I take *r*,
22: 31 a shield for all who take *r* in him.
Ps 2: 12 Blessed are all who take *r* in him.
5: 11 But let all who take *r* in you be glad
9: 9 The LORD is a *r* for the oppressed,
16: 1 for in you I take *r*.
17: 7 those who take *r* in you
18: 2 God is my rock, in whom I take *r*.
31: 2 be my rock of *r*,
34: 8 blessed is the man who takes *r*
36: 7 find *r* in the shadow of your wings.
46: 1 God is our *r* and strength,
62: 8 for God is our *r*.
71: 1 In you, O LORD, I have taken *r*;
91: 2 "He is my *r* and my fortress,
144: 2 my shield, in whom I take *r*,
Pr 14: 26 and for his children it will be a *r*.
30: 5 a shield to those who take *r* in him.
Na 1: 7 a *r* in times of trouble.

REFUSE (REFUSED)
Jn 5: 40 yet you *r* to come to me to have life

REFUSED (REFUSE)
2Th 2: 10 because they *r* to love the truth
Rev 16: 9 but they *r* to repent and glorify him

REGARD (REGARDS)
1Th 5: 13 Hold them in the highest *r* in love

REGARDS (REGARD)
Ro 14: 14 But if anyone *r* something

REGRET
2Co 7: 10 leads to salvation and leaves no *r*,

REHOBOAM
Son of Solomon (1Ki 11:43; 1Ch 3:10). Harsh treatment of subjects caused divided kingdom (1Ki 12:1–24; 14:21–31; 2Ch 10–12).

REIGN (REIGNED REIGNS)
Ex 15: 18 The LORD will *r*
Ps 68: 16 mountain where God chooses to *r*,
Isa 9: 7 He will *r* on David's throne
24: 23 for the LORD Almighty will *r*
32: 1 See, a king will *r* in righteousness
Jer 23: 5 a King who will *r* wisely
Lk 1: 33 and he will *r* over the house
Ro 6: 12 Therefore do not let sin *r*
1Co 15: 25 For he must *r* until he has put all
2Ti 2: 12 we will also *r* with him.
Rev 11: 15 and he will *r* for ever and ever."
20: 6 will *r* with him for a thousand years
22: 5 And they will *r* for ever and ever.

REIGNED (REIGN)
Ro 5: 21 so that, just as sin *r* in death,
Rev 20: 4 and *r* with Christ a thousand years.

REIGNS (REIGN)
Ps 9: 7 The LORD *r* forever;
47: 8 God *r* over the nations;
93: 1 The LORD *r*, he is robed
96: 10 among the nations, "The LORD *r*
97: 1 The LORD *r*, let the earth be glad;
99: 1 The LORD *r*, / let the nations tremble;
146: 10 The LORD *r* forever,
Isa 52: 7 "Your God *r*!"
Rev 19: 6 For our Lord God Almighty *r*.

REIN
Jas 1: 26 and yet does not keep a tight *r*

REJECT (REJECTED REJECTION REJECTS)
Ps 94: 14 For the LORD will not *r* his people
Ro 11: 1 I ask then: Did God *r* his people?

REJECTED (REJECT)
1Sa 8: 7 it is not you they have *r*,
1Ki 19: 10 The Israelites have *r* your covenant
2Ki 17: 15 They *r* his decrees
Ps 66: 20 who has not *r* my prayer
118: 22 The stone the builders *r*
Isa 5: 24 for they have *r* the law
41: 9 chosen you and have not *r* you.
53: 3 He was despised and *r* by men,
Jer 8: 9 Since they have *r* the word
Mt 21: 42 "The stone the builders *r*
1Ti 4: 4 nothing is to be *r* if it is received
1Pe 2: 4 *r* by men but chosen by God
2: 7 "The stone the builders *r*

REJECTION* (REJECT)
Ro 11: 15 For if their *r* is the reconciliation

REJECTS (REJECT)
Lk 10: 16 but he who *r* me *r* him who sent me
Jn 3: 36 whoever *r* the Son will not see life,
1Th 4: 8 he who *r* this instruction does not

REJOICE (JOY)
Dt 12: 7 shall *r* in everything you have put
1Ch 16: 10 of those who seek the LORD *r*.
16: 31 Let the heavens *r*, let the earth be
Ps 2: 11 and *r* with trembling.
5: 11 those who love your name may *r*
9: 14 and there *r* in your salvation.
34: 2 let the afflicted hear and *r*.
63: 11 But the king will *r* in God;
66: 6 come, let us *r* in him.
68: 3 and *r* before God;
105: 3 of those who seek the LORD *r*.
118: 24 let us *r* and be glad in it.
119: 14 I *r* in following your statutes
119: 162 I *r* in your promise
149: 2 Let Israel *r* in their Maker;
Pr 5: 18 may you *r* in the wife of your youth
23: 25 may she who gave you birth *r*!
24: 17 stumbles, do not let your heart *r*,
Isa 9: 3 as men *r*
35: 1 the wilderness will *r* and blossom.
61: 7 they will *r* in their inheritance;
62: 5 so will your God *r* over you.
Jer 31: 12 they will *r* in the bounty
Zep 3: 17 he will *r* over you with singing."
Zec 9: 9 *R* greatly, O Daughter of Zion!
Lk 6: 23 "*R* in that day and leap for joy,
10: 20 but *r* that your names are written
15: 6 '*R* with me; I have found my lost
15: 9 '*R* with me; I have found my lost
Ro 5: 2 And we *r* in the hope of the glory
12: 15 Rejoice with those who *r*; mourn
Php 2: 17 I am glad and *r* with all of you.
3: 1 Finally, my brothers, *r* in the Lord!
4: 4 *R* in the Lord always.
1Pe 4: 13 But *r* that you participate
Rev 19: 7 Let us *r* and be glad

REJOICES (JOY)
Ps 13: 5 my heart *r* in your salvation.
16: 9 my heart is glad and my tongue *r*;
Isa 61: 10 my soul *r* in my God.
62: 5 as a bridegroom *r* over his bride,
Lk 1: 47 and my spirit *r* in God my Savior,
Ac 2: 26 my heart is glad and my tongue *r*;
1Co 12: 26 if one part is honored, every part *r*
13: 6 delight in evil but *r* with the truth.

REJOICING (JOY)
2Sa 6: 12 to the City of David with *r*.
Ne 12: 43 *r* because God had given them
Ps 30: 5 but *r* comes in the morning.
Lk 15: 7 in the same way there will be more *r*
Ac 5: 41 *r* because they had been counted
2Co 6: 10 sorrowful, yet always *r*; poor,

RELATIVES
Pr 19: 7 A poor man is shunned by all his *r*
Mk 6: 4 among his *r* and in his own house is
Lk 21: 16 betrayed even by parents, brothers, *r*
1Ti 5: 8 If anyone does not provide for his *r*

RELEASE (RELEASED)
Isa 61: 1 and *r* from darkness,
Lk 4: 18 to *r* the oppressed,

RELEASED (RELEASE)
Ro 7: 6 we have been *r* from the law
Rev 20: 7 Satan will be *r* from his prison

RELENTED (RELENTS)
Ex 32: 14 the LORD *r* and did not bring
Ps 106: 45 and out of his great love he *r*.

RELENTS* (RELENTED)
Joel 2: 13 and he *r* from sending calamity.
Jnh 4: 2 a God who *r* from sending calamity

RELIABLE (RELY)
Pr 22: 21 teaching you true and *r* words,
Jn 8: 26 But he who sent me is *r*,
2Ti 2: 2 witnesses entrust to *r* men who will

RELIANCE* (RELY)
Pr 25: 19 is *r* on the unfaithful in times

RELIED (RELY)
2Ch 13: 18 were victorious because they *r*
16: 8 Yet when you *r* on the LORD,
Ps 71: 6 From birth I have *r* on you;

RELIEF
Job 35: 9 they plead for *r* from the arm
Ps 94: 13 you grant him *r* from days
143: 1 come to my *r*.
La 3: 49 without *r*,
3: 56 to my cry for *r*."
2Th 1: 7 and give *r* to you who are troubled,

RELIGION* (RELIGIOUS)
Ac 25: 19 dispute with him about their own *r*
26: 5 to the strictest sect of our *r*,
1Ti 5: 4 all to put their *r* into practice
Jas 1: 26 himself and his *r* is worthless.
1: 27 *R* that God our Father accepts

RELIGIOUS (RELIGION)
Jas 1: 26 If anyone considers himself *r*

RELY (RELIABLE RELIANCE RELIED)
Isa 50: 10 and *r* on his God.
Eze 33: 26 you then possess the land? You *r*
2Co 1: 9 this happened that we might not *r*
Gal 3: 10 All who *r* on observing the law are
1Jn 4: 16 and *r* on the love God has for us.

REMAIN (REMAINS)
Nu 33: 55 allow to *r* will become barbs
Ps 102: 27 But you *r* the same,
Jn 1: 32 from heaven as a dove and *r* on him
15: 4 *R* in me, and I will *r* in you.
15: 7 If you *r* in me and my words
15: 9 Now *r* in my love.
Ro 13: 8 Let no debt *r* outstanding,
1Co 13: 13 And now these three *r*: faith,
2Ti 2: 13 he will *r* faithful,
Heb 1: 11 They will perish, but you *r*;
1Jn 2: 27 just as it has taught you, *r* in him.

REMAINS (REMAIN)
Ps 146: 6 the LORD, who *r* faithful forever.
Heb 7: 3 Son of God he *r* a priest forever.

REMEDY
Isa 3: 7 "I have no *r*.

REMEMBER (REMEMBERED REMEMBERS REMEMBRANCE)
Ge 9: 15 I will *r* my covenant between me
Ex 20: 8 "*R* the Sabbath day
33: 13 *R* that this nation is your people."
Dt 5: 15 *R* that you were slaves in Egypt
1Ch 16: 12 *R* the wonders he has done,
Job 36: 24 *R* to extol his work,
Ps 25: 6 *R*, O LORD, your great mercy
63: 6 On my bed I *r* you;
74: 2 *R* the people you purchased of old,
77: 11 I will *r* the deeds of the LORD;
Ecc 12: 1 *R* your Creator
Isa 46: 8 "*R* this, fix it in mind,
Jer 31: 34 and will *r* their sins no more."
Hab 3: 2 in wrath *r* mercy.
Lk 1: 72 and to *r* his holy covenant,
Gal 2: 10 we should continue to *r* the poor,
Php 1: 3 I thank my God every time I *r* you.
2Ti 2: 8 *R* Jesus Christ, raised
Heb 8: 12 and will *r* their sins no more."

REMEMBERED (REMEMBER)
Ex 2: 24 he *r* his covenant with Abraham,
3: 15 am to be *r* from generation
Ps 98: 3 He has *r* his love
106: 45 for their sake he *r* his covenant
111: 4 He has caused his wonders to be *r*;
136: 23 to the One who *r* us
Isa 65: 17 The former things will not be *r*,
Eze 18: 22 offenses he has committed will be *r*
33: 13 things he has done will be *r*;

REMEMBERS (REMEMBER)
Ps 103: 14 he *r* that we are dust.
111: 5 he *r* his covenant forever.
Isa 43: 25 and *r* your sins no more.

REMEMBRANCE (REMEMBER)
Lk 22: 19 given for you; do this in *r* of me."
1Co 11: 24 which is for you; do this in *r* of me
11: 25 whenever you drink it, in *r* of me."

REMIND
Jn 14: 26 will *r* you of everything I have said
2Pe 1: 12 I will always *r* you of these things,

REMNANT
Ezr 9: 8 has been gracious in leaving us a *r*
Isa 11: 11 time to reclaim the *r* that is left
Jer 23: 3 "I myself will gather the *r*
Zec 8: 12 inheritance to the *r* of this people.
Ro 11: 5 the present time there is a *r* chosen

REMOVED
Ps 30: 11 you *r* my sackcloth and clothed me
103: 12 so far has he *r* our transgressions
Jn 20: 1 and saw that the stone had been *r*

REND
Joel 2: 13 *R* your heart

RENEW (RENEWAL RENEWED RENEWING)
Ps 51: 10 and *r* a steadfast spirit within me.
Isa 40: 31 will *r* their strength.

RENEWAL (RENEW)
Isa 57: 10 You found *r* of your strength,
Tit 3: 5 of rebirth and *r* by the Holy Spirit,

RENEWED (RENEW)
Ps 103: 5 that your youth is *r* like the eagle's.
2Co 4: 16 yet inwardly we are being *r* day

RENEWING* (RENEW)
Ro 12: 2 transformed by the *r* of your mind.

RENOUNCE (RENOUNCED RENOUNCES)
Da 4: 27 *R* your sins by doing what is right,

RENOUNCED (RENOUNCE)
2Co 4: 2 we have *r* secret and shameful

RENOUNCES (RENOUNCE)
Pr 28: 13 confesses and *r* them finds

RENOWN*
Ge 6: 4 were the heroes of old, men of *r*.
Ps 102: 12 *r* endures through all generations.
135: 13 *r*, O LORD, through all
Isa 26: 8 your name and *r*
55: 13 This will be for the LORD's *r*,
63: 12 to gain for himself everlasting *r*,
Jer 13: 11 to be my people for my *r* and praise
32: 20 have gained the *r* that is still yours.
33: 9 Then this city will bring me *r*, joy,
49: 25 the city of *r* not been abandoned,
Eze 26: 17 How you are destroyed, O city of *r*,
Hos 12: 5 the LORD is his name of *r*!

REPAID (PAY)
Lk 6: 34 to 'sinners,' expecting to be *r* in full
14: 14 you will be *r* at the resurrection
Col 3: 25 Anyone who does wrong will be *r*

REPAY (PAY)
Dt 7: 10 But those who hate him he will *r*
32: 35 It is mine to avenge; I will *r*.
Ru 2: 12 May the LORD *r* you
Ps 103: 10 or *r* us according to our iniquities.
116: 12 How can I *r* the LORD
Jer 25: 14 I will *r* them according
Ro 12: 17 Do not *r* anyone evil for evil.
12: 19 "It is mine to avenge; I will *r*,"
1Pe 3: 9 Do not *r* evil with evil

REPAYING (PAY)
2Ch 6: 23 *r* the guilty by bringing
1Ti 5: 4 so *r* their parents and grandparents

REPEATED
Heb 10: 1 the same sacrifices *r* endlessly year

REPENT (REPENTANCE REPENTED REPENTS)
1Ki 8: 47 *r* and plead with you in the land
Job 36: 10 commands them to *r* of their evil.
42: 6 and *r* in dust and ashes."
Jer 15: 19 "If you *r*, I will restore you
Eze 18: 30 *R*! Turn away from all your
18: 32 *R* and live! "Take up a lament
Mt 3: 2 "*R*, for the kingdom of heaven is
4: 17 "*R*, for the kingdom of heaven is
Mk 6: 12 and preached that people should *r*.
Lk 13: 3 unless you *r*, you too will all perish.
Ac 2: 38 Peter replied, "*R* and be baptized,
3: 19 *R*, then, and turn to God,
17: 30 all people everywhere to *r*.
26: 20 also, I preached that they should *r*
Rev 2: 5 *R* and do the things you did at first.

REPENTANCE (REPENT)
Isa 30: 15 "In *r* and rest is your salvation,
Mt 3: 8 Produce fruit in keeping with *r*.
Mk 1: 4 a baptism of *r* for the forgiveness
Lk 3: 8 Produce fruit in keeping with *r*.
5: 32 call the righteous, but sinners to *r*."
24: 47 and *r* and forgiveness of sins will be
Ac 20: 21 that they must turn to God in *r*
26: 20 and prove their *r* by their deeds.
Ro 2: 4 kindness leads you toward *r*?
2Co 7: 10 Godly sorrow brings *r* that leads
2Pe 3: 9 but everyone to come to *r*.

REPENTED (REPENT)
Mt 11: 21 they would have *r* long ago

REPENTS (REPENT)
Lk 15: 7 in heaven over one sinner who *r*
15: 10 of God over one sinner who *r*."
17: 3 rebuke him, and if he *r*, forgive him

REPORTS
Ex 23: 1 "Do not spread false *r*.

REPOSES*
Pr 14: 33 Wisdom *r* in the heart

REPRESENTATION*
Heb 1: 3 and the exact *r* of his being,

REPROACH
Job 27: 6 my conscience will not *r* me
Isa 51: 7 Do not fear the *r* of men
1Ti 3: 2 Now the overseer must be above *r*,

REPUTATION
1Ti 3: 7 also have a good *r* with outsiders,

REQUESTS
Ps 20: 5 May the LORD grant all your *r*.
Php 4: 6 with thanksgiving, present your *r*

REQUIRE (REQUIRED REQUIRES)
Mic 6: 8 And what does the LORD *r* of you

REQUIRED (REQUIRE)
1Co 4: 2 it is *r* that those who have been

REQUIRES (REQUIRE)
1Ki 2: 3 what the LORD your God *r*:
Heb 9: 22 the law *r* that nearly everything be

RESCUE (RESCUED RESCUES)
Ps 22: 8 let the LORD *r* him.
31: 2 come quickly to my *r*;
69: 14 *R* me from the mire,
91: 14 says the LORD, "I will *r* him;
143: 9 *R* me from my enemies, O LORD,
Da 6: 20 been able to *r* you from the lions?"
Ro 7: 24 Who will *r* me from this body
Gal 1: 4 himself for our sins to *r* us
2Pe 2: 9 how to *r* godly men from trials

RESCUED (RESCUE)
Ps 18: 17 He *r* me from my powerful enemy,
Pr 11: 8 The righteous man is *r*
Col 1: 13 For he has *r* us from the dominion

RESCUES (RESCUE)
Da 6: 27 He *r* and he saves;
1Th 1: 10 who *r* us from the coming wrath.

RESENT* (RESENTFUL RESENTS)
Pr 3: 11 and do not *r* his rebuke,

RESENTFUL* (RESENT)
2Ti 2: 24 to everyone, able to teach, not *r*.

RESENTS* (RESENT)
Pr 15: 12 A mocker *r* correction;

RESERVE (RESERVED)
1Ki 19: 18 Yet I *r* seven thousand in Israel—

RESERVED (RESERVE)
Ro 11: 4 "I have *r* for myself seven

RESIST (RESISTED RESISTS)
Da 11: 32 know their God will firmly *r* him.
Mt 5: 39 I tell you, Do not *r* an evil person.
Lk 21: 15 of your adversaries will be able to *r*
Jas 4: 7 *R* the devil, and he will flee
1Pe 5: 9 *R* him, standing firm in the faith,

RESISTED (RESIST)
Job 9: 4 Who has *r* him and come out

RESISTS* (RESIST)
Ro 9: 19 For who *r* his will?" But who are

RESOLVED
Ps 17: 3 I have *r* that my mouth will not sin.
Da 1: 8 But Daniel *r* not to defile himself
1Co 2: 2 For I *r* to know nothing while I was

RESOUNDING*
Ps 150: 5 praise him with *r* cymbals.
1Co 13: 1 I am only a *r* gong or a clanging

RESPECT (RESPECTABLE RESPECTED RESPECTS)
Lev 19: 3 "'Each of you must *r* his mother
19: 32 show *r* for the elderly and revere
Pr 11: 16 A kindhearted woman gains *r*,
Mal 1: 6 where is the *r* due me?" says
Eph 5: 33 and the wife must *r* her husband.
6: 5 obey your earthly masters with *r*
1Th 4: 12 so that your daily life may win the *r*
5: 12 to *r* those who work hard
1Ti 3: 4 children obey him with proper *r*.
3: 8 are to be men worthy of *r*, sincere,

1Ti 3: 11 are to be women worthy of r,
6: 1 their masters worthy of full r,
Tit 2: 2 worthy of r, self-controlled,
1Pe 2: 17 Show proper r to everyone:
3: 7 them with r as the weaker partner
3: 15 But do this with gentleness and r,

RESPECTABLE* (RESPECT)
1Ti 3: 2 self-controlled, r, hospitable,

RESPECTED (RESPECT)
Pr 31: 23 Her husband is r at the city gate,

RESPECTS (RESPECT)
Pr 13: 13 he who r a command is rewarded.

RESPLENDENT*
Ps 76: 4 You are r with light,
132: 18 but the crown on his head will be r

RESPOND
Ps 102: 17 He will r to the prayer
Hos 2: 21 "I will r to the skies,

RESPONSIBILITY (RESPONSIBLE)
Ac 18: 6 your own heads! I am clear of my r.

RESPONSIBLE (RESPONSIBILITY)
Nu 1: 53 The Levites are to be r for the care
1Co 7: 24 Brothers, each man, as r to God,

REST (RESTED RESTS SABBATH-REST)
Ex 31: 15 the seventh day is a Sabbath of r,
33: 14 go with you, and I will give you r."
Lev 25: 5 The land is to have a year of r.
Dt 31: 16 going to r with your fathers,
Jos 14: 15 Then the land had r from war.
21: 44 The LORD gave them r
1Ki 5: 4 The LORD my god has given me r
1Ch 22: 9 who will be a man of peace and r,
Job 3: 17 and there the weary are at r.
Ps 16: 9 my body also will r secure,
33: 22 May your unfailing love r upon us,
62: 1 My soul finds r in God alone;
62: 5 Find r, O my soul, in God alone;
90: 17 of the Lord our God r upon us;
91: 1 will r in the shadow
95: 11 "They shall never enter my r."
Pr 6: 10 a little folding of the hands to r—
Isa 11: 2 Spirit of the LORD will r on him—
11: 10 and his place of r will be glorious.
30: 15 "In repentance and r is your
32: 18 in undisturbed places of r.
57: 20 which cannot r,
Jer 6: 16 and you will find r for your souls.
47: 6 'how long till you r?
Mt 11: 28 and burdened, and I will give you r.
2Co 12: 9 so that Christ's power may r on me
Heb 3: 11 'They shall never enter my r.' "
4: 3 'They shall never enter my r.' "
4: 10 for anyone who enters God's r
Rev 14: 13 "they will r from their labor,

RESTED (REST)
Ge 2: 2 so on the seventh day he r
Heb 4: 4 "And on the seventh day God r

RESTITUTION
Ex 22: 3 "A thief must certainly make r,
Lev 6: 5 He must make r in full, add a fifth
Nu 5: 8 the r belongs to the LORD

RESTORE (RESTORES)
Ps 51: 12 R to me the joy of your salvation
80: 3 R us, O God;
126: 4 R our fortunes, O LORD,
Jer 31: 18 R me, and I will return,
La 5: 21 R us to yourself, O LORD,
Da 9: 25 From the issuing of the decree to r
Na 2: 2 The LORD will r the splendor
Gal 6: 1 are spiritual should r him gently.
1Pe 5: 10 will himself r you and make you

RESTORES (RESTORE)
Ps 23: 3 he r my soul.

RESTRAINED (RESTRAINT)
Ps 78: 38 Time after time he r his anger

RESTRAINING (RESTRAINT)
Pr 27: 16 r her is like r the wind
Col 2: 23 value in r sensual indulgence.

RESTRAINT (RESTRAINED RESTRAINING)
Pr 17: 27 of knowledge uses words with r,
23: 4 have the wisdom to show r.
29: 18 no revelation, the people cast off r;

RESTS (REST)
Dt 33: 12 and the one the LORD loves r
Pr 19: 23 one r content, untouched
Lk 2: 14 to men on whom his favor r."

RESULT
Lk 21: 13 This will r in your being witnesses
Ro 6: 22 to holiness, and the r is eternal life.
11: 31 as a r of God's mercy to you.
2Co 3: 3 from Christ, the r of our ministry,
2Th 1: 5 as a r you will be counted worthy
1Pe 1: 7 may be proved genuine and may r

RESURRECTION*
Mt 22: 23 who say there is no r, came to him
22: 28 at the r, whose wife will she be
22: 30 At the r people will neither marry
22: 31 But about the r of the dead—
27: 53 and after Jesus' r they went
Mk 12: 18 who say there is no r, came to him
12: 23 At the r whose wife will she be,
Lk 14: 14 repaid at the r of the righteous."
20: 27 who say there is no r, came to Jesus
20: 33 at the r whose wife will she be,
20: 35 in the r from the dead will neither
20: 36 since they are children of the r.
Jn 11: 24 again in the r at the last day."
11: 25 Jesus said to her, "I am the r
Ac 1: 22 become a witness with us of his r."
2: 31 he spoke of the r of the Christ,
4: 2 in Jesus the r of the dead.
4: 33 to testify to the r of the Lord Jesus,
17: 18 good news about Jesus and the r.
17: 32 When they heard about the r
23: 6 of my hope in the r of the dead."
23: 8 Sadducees say that there is no r,
24: 15 that there will be a r
24: 21 'It is concerning the r
Ro 1: 4 Son of God by his r from the dead:
6: 5 also be united with him in his r.
1Co 15: 12 some of you say that there is no r
15: 13 If there is no r of the dead,
15: 21 the r of the dead comes
15: 29 if there is no r, what will those do
15: 42 So will it be with the r of the dead.
Php 3: 10 power of his r and the fellowship
3: 11 to attain to the r from the dead.
2Ti 2: 18 say that the r has already taken
Heb 6: 2 on of hands, the r of the dead,
11: 35 so that they might gain a better r.
1Pe 1: 3 hope through the r of Jesus Christ
3: 21 It saves you by the r of Jesus Christ
Rev 20: 5 This is the first r.
20: 6 those who have part in the first r.

RETALIATE*
1Pe 2: 23 he did not r; when he suffered,

RETRIBUTION
Ps 69: 22 may it become r and a trap.
Jer 51: 56 For the LORD is a God of r;
Ro 11: 9 a stumbling block and a r for them.

RETURN (RETURNED RETURNS)
Ge 3: 19 and to dust you will r."
2Sa 12: 23 go to him, but he will not r to me."
2Ch 30: 9 If you r to the LORD, then your
Ne 1: 9 but if you r to me and obey my
Job 10: 21 joy before I go to the place of no r,
16: 22 before I go on the journey of no r.
22: 23 If you r to the Almighty, you will
Ps 80: 14 R to us, O God Almighty!
126: 6 will r with songs of joy,
Isa 10: 21 A remnant will r, a remnant
35: 10 the ransomed of the LORD will r.
55: 11 It will not r to me empty,
Jer 24: 7 for they will r to me
31: 8 a great throng will r.
La 3: 40 and let us r to the LORD.
Hos 6: 1 "Come, let us r to the LORD.
12: 6 But you must r to your God;
14: 1 R, O Israel, to the LORD your
Joel 2: 12 "r to me with all your heart,
Zec 1: 3 'R to me,' declares the LORD
10: 9 and they will r.

RETURNED (RETURN)
Ps 35: 13 When my prayers r
Am 4: 6 yet you have not r to me,"
1Pe 2: 25 now you have r to the Shepherd

RETURNS (RETURN)
Pr 3: 14 and yields better r than gold.
Isa 52: 8 When the LORD r to Zion,
Mt 24: 46 finds him doing so when he r.

REUBEN
Firstborn of Jacob by Leah (Ge 29:32; 46:8; 1Ch 2:1). Attempted to rescue Joseph (Ge 37:21–30). Lost birthright for sleeping with Bilhah (Ge 35:22; 49:4). Tribe of blessed (Ge 49:3–4; Dt 33:6), numbered (Nu 1:21; 26:7), allotted land east of Jordan (Nu 32; 34:14; Jos 13:15), west (Eze 48:6), failed to help Deborah (Jdg 5:15–16), supported David (1Ch 12:37), 12,000 from (Rev 7:5).

REVEAL (REVEALED REVEALS REVELATION REVELATIONS)
Mt 11: 27 to whom the Son chooses to r him.
Gal 1: 16 was pleased to r his Son in me

REVEALED (REVEAL)
Dt 29: 29 but the things r belong to us
Isa 40: 5 the glory of the LORD will be r,
43: 12 I have r and saved and proclaimed
53: 1 the arm of the LORD been r?
65: 1 I r myself to those who did not ask
Mt 11: 25 and r them to little children.
Jn 12: 38 the arm of the Lord been r?"
17: 6 "I have r you to those whom you
Ro 1: 17 a righteousness from God is r,
8: 18 with the glory that will be r in us.
10: 20 I r myself to those who did not ask
16: 26 but now r and made known
1Co 2: 10 but God has r it to us by his Spirit.
2Th 1: 7 happen when the Lord Jesus is r
2: 3 and the man of lawlessness is r,
1Pe 1: 7 and honor when Jesus Christ is r.
1: 20 but was r in these last times
4: 13 overjoyed when his glory is r.

REVEALS* (REVEAL)
Nu 23: 3 Whatever he r to me I will tell you
Job 12: 22 He r the deep things of darkness
Da 2: 22 He r deep and hidden things;
2: 28 a God in heaven who r mysteries.
Am 4: 13 and r his thoughts to man,

REVELATION* (REVEAL)
2Sa 7: 17 David all the words of this entire r.
1Ch 17: 15 David all the words of this entire r.
Pr 29: 18 Where there is no r, the people cast
Da 10: 1 a r was given to Daniel (who was
Hab 2: 2 "Write down the r
2: 3 For the r awaits an appointed time;
Lk 2: 32 a light for r to the Gentiles
Ro 16: 25 according to the r
1Co 14: 6 I bring you some r or knowledge
14: 26 a r, a tongue or an interpretation.
14: 30 And if a r comes to someone who is
Gal 1: 12 I received it by r from Jesus Christ.
2: 2 I went in response to a r
Eph 1: 17 you the Spirit of wisdom and r,
3: 3 mystery made known to me by r,
Rev 1: 1 r of Jesus Christ, which God gave

REVELATIONS* (REVEAL)
2Co 12: 1 on to visions and r from the Lord.
12: 7 of these surpassingly great r,

REVELED* (REVELRY)
Ne 9: 25 they r in your great goodness.

REVELRY (REVELED)
Ex 32: 6 drink and got up to indulge in r.
1Co 10: 7 and got up to indulge in pagan r."

REVENGE (VENGEANCE)
Lev 19: 18 " 'Do not seek r or bear a grudge
Ro 12: 19 Do not take r, my friends,

REVERE* (REVERENCE REVERENT REVERING)
Lev 19: 32 for the elderly and r your God.
Dt 4: 10 so that they may learn to r me
13: 4 must follow, and him you must r.
14: 23 to r the LORD your God always.
17: 19 learn to r the LORD his God
28: 58 and do not r this glorious
Job 37: 24 Therefore, men r him,
Ps 22: 23 R him, all you descendants
33: 8 let all the people of the world r him
102: 15 of the earth will r your glory.
Ecc 3: 14 God does it so that men will r him.
Isa 25: 3 cities of ruthless nations will r you.
59: 19 of the sun, they will r his glory.
63: 17 hearts so we do not r you?
Jer 10: 7 Who should not r you,
Hos 10: 3 because we did not r the LORD.
Mal 4: 2 But for you who r my name,

REVERENCE (REVERE)
Lev 19: 30 and have r for my sanctuary.
Ne 5: 15 of r for God I did not act like that.
Ps 5: 7 in r will I bow down
Da 6: 26 people must fear and r the God
2Co 7: 1 perfecting holiness out of r for God
Eph 5: 21 to one another out of r for Christ.
Col 3: 22 of heart and r for the Lord.
1Pe 3: 2 when they see the purity and r
Rev 11: 18 and those who r your name,

REVERENT* (REVERE)
Ecc 8: 12 with God-fearing men, who are r
Tit 2: 3 women to be r in the way they live,
Heb 5: 7 because of his r submission.
1Pe 1: 17 as strangers here in r fear.

REVERING* (REVERE)
Dt 8: 6 walking in his ways and *r* him.
Ne 1: 11 who delight in *r* your name.

REVERSE*
Isa 43: 13 When I act, who can *r* it?"

REVIVE* (REVIVING)
Ps 80: 18 *r* us, and we will call on your name.
85: 6 Will you not *r* us again,
Isa 57: 15 and to *r* the heart of the contrite.
57: 15 to *r* the spirit of the lowly
Hos 6: 2 After two days he will *r* us;

REVIVING* (REVIVE)
Ps 19: 7 *r* the soul.

REVOKED
Isa 45: 23 a word that will not be *r*:

REWARD (REWARDED REWARDING REWARDS)
Ge 15: 1 your very great *r*."
1Sa 24: 19 May the LORD *r* you well
Ps 19: 11 in keeping them there is great *r*.
62: 12 Surely you will *r* each person
127: 3 children a *r* from him.
Pr 9: 12 are wise, your wisdom will *r* you;
11: 18 sows righteousness reaps a sure *r*.
13: 21 prosperity is the *r* of the righteous.
19: 17 he will *r* him for what he has done.
25: 22 and the LORD will *r* you.
31: 31 Give her the *r* she has earned,
Isa 40: 10 See, his *r* is with him,
49: 4 and my *r* is with my God."
61: 8 In my faithfulness I will *r* them
62: 11 See, his *r* is with him,
Jer 17: 10 to *r* a man according to his conduct
32: 19 you *r* everyone according
Mt 5: 12 because great is your *r* in heaven,
6: 1 you will have no *r*
6: 5 they have received their *r* in full.
10: 41 a prophet will receive a prophet's *r*,
16: 27 and then he will *r* each person
Lk 6: 23 because great is your *r* in heaven.
6: 35 Then your *r* will be great,
1Co 3: 14 built survives, he will receive his *r*.
Eph 6: 8 know that the Lord will *r* everyone
Col 3: 24 an inheritance from the Lord as a *r*.
Heb 11: 26 he was looking ahead to his *r*.
Rev 22: 12 I am coming soon! My *r* is with me

REWARDED (REWARD)
Ru 2: 12 May you be richly *r* by the LORD,
2Sa 22: 21 of my hands he has *r* me.
2Ch 15: 7 for your work will be *r*."
Ps 18: 24 The LORD has *r* me according
Pr 13: 13 he who respects a command is *r*.
14: 14 and the good man *r* for his.
Jer 31: 16 for your work will be *r*,"
1Co 3: 8 and each will be *r* according
Heb 10: 35 your confidence; it will be richly *r*.
2Jn : 8 but that you may be *r* fully.

REWARDING* (REWARD)
Rev 11: 18 for *r* your servants the prophets

REWARDS (REWARD)
1Sa 26: 23 The LORD *r* every man
Pr 12: 14 the work of his hands *r* him.
Heb 11: 6 that he *r* those who earnestly seek

RIBS
Ge 2: 21 he took one of the man's *r*

RICH (RICHES RICHEST)
Job 34: 19 does not favor the *r* over the poor,
Ps 49: 16 overawed when a man grows *r*,
145: 8 slow to anger and *r* in love.
Pr 21: 17 loves wine and oil will never be *r*.
22: 2 *R* and poor have this in common:
23: 4 Do not wear yourself out to get *r*;
28: 6 than a *r* man whose ways are
28: 20 to get *r* will not go unpunished.
28: 22 A stingy man is eager to get *r*
Ecc 5: 12 but the abundance of a *r* man
Isa 33: 6 a *r* store of salvation and wisdom
53: 9 and with the *r* in his death,
Jer 9: 23 or the *r* man boast of his riches,
Zec 3: 4 and I will put *r* garments on you."
Mt 19: 23 it is hard for a *r* man
Lk 1: 53 but has sent the *r* away empty.
6: 24 "But woe to you who are *r*,
12: 21 for himself but is not *r* toward God
16: 1 "There was a *r* man whose
21: 1 Jesus saw the *r* putting their gifts
2Co 6: 10 yet making many *r*; having nothing
8: 2 poverty welled up in *r* generosity.
8: 9 he was *r*, yet for your sakes he
9: 11 You will be made *r* in every way
Eph 2: 4 love for us, God, who is *r* in mercy,
1Ti 6: 9 want to get *r* fall into temptation
6: 17 Command those who are *r*
6: 18 to do good, to be *r* in good deeds,
Jas 1: 10 the one who is *r* should take pride
2: 5 the eyes of the world to be *r* in faith
5: 1 you *r* people, weep and wail
Rev 2: 9 and your poverty — yet you are *r*!
3: 18 you can become *r*; and white

RICHES (RICH)
Job 36: 18 that no one entices you by *r*;
Ps 49: 6 and boast of their great *r*?
49: 12 despite his *r*, does not endure;
62: 10 though your *r* increase,
119: 14 as one rejoices in great *r*.
Pr 3: 16 in her left hand are *r* and honor.
11: 28 Whoever trusts in his *r* will fall,
22: 1 is more desirable than great *r*;
27: 24 for *r* do not endure forever,
30: 8 give me neither poverty nor *r*,
Isa 10: 3 Where will you leave your *r*?
60: 5 to you the *r* of the nations will
Jer 9: 23 or the rich man boast of his *r*,
Lk 8: 14 *r* and pleasures, and they do not
Ro 9: 23 to make the *r* of his glory known
11: 33 the depth of the *r* of the wisdom
Eph 2: 7 he might show the incomparable *r*
3: 8 to the Gentiles the unsearchable *r*
Col 1: 27 among the Gentiles the glorious *r*
2: 2 so that they may have the full *r*

RICHEST (RICH)
Isa 55: 2 and your soul will delight in the *r*

RID
Ge 21: 10 "Get *r* of that slave woman
1Co 5: 7 Get *r* of the old yeast that you may
Gal 4: 30 "Get *r* of the slave woman

RIDE (RIDER RIDING)
Ps 45: 4 In your majesty *r* forth victoriously

RIDER (RIDE)
Rev 6: 2 was a white horse! Its *r* held a bow,
19: 11 whose *r* is called Faithful and True.

RIDING (RIDE)
Zec 9: 9 gentle and *r* on a donkey,
Mt 21: 5 gentle and *r* on a donkey,

RIGGING
Isa 33: 23 Your *r* hangs loose:

RIGHT (RIGHTS)
Ge 4: 7 But if you do not do what is *r*,
18: 19 of the LORD by doing what is *r*
18: 25 the Judge of all the earth do *r*?"
48: 13 on his left toward Israel's *r* hand,
Ex 15: 6 Your *r* hand, O LORD,
15: 26 and do what is *r* in his eyes,
Dt 5: 32 do not turn aside to the *r*
6: 18 Do what is *r* and good
13: 18 and doing what is *r* in his eyes.
Jos 1: 7 do not turn from it to the *r*
1Sa 12: 23 you the way that is good and *r*.
1Ki 3: 9 to distinguish between *r* and wrong
15: 5 For David had done what was *r*
2Ki 7: 9 to each other, "We're not doing *r*.
Ne 9: 13 and laws that are just and *r*,
Ps 16: 8 Because he is at my *r* hand,
16: 11 eternal pleasures at your *r* hand.
17: 7 you who save by your *r* hand
18: 35 and your *r* hand sustains me;
19: 8 The precepts of the LORD are *r*,
25: 9 He guides the humble in what is *r*
33: 4 For the word of the LORD is *r*
44: 3 it was your *r* hand, your arm,
45: 4 let your *r* hand display awesome
51: 4 so that you are proved *r*
63: 8 your *r* hand upholds me.
73: 23 you hold me by my *r* hand.
91: 7 ten thousand at your *r* hand,
98: 1 his *r* hand and his holy arm
106: 3 who constantly do what is *r*.
110: 1 "Sit at my *r* hand
118: 15 LORD's *r* hand has done mighty
119: 144 Your statutes are forever *r*;
137: 5 may my *r* hand forget ⌊its skill⌋.
139: 10 your *r* hand will hold me fast.
Pr 1: 3 doing what is *r* and just and fair;
4: 27 Do not swerve to the *r* or the left;
14: 12 There is a way that seems *r*
18: 17 The first to present his case seems *r*
Ecc 7: 20 who does what is *r* and never sins.
SS 1: 4 How *r* they are to adore you!
Isa 1: 17 learn to do *r*!
7: 15 reject the wrong and choose the *r*.
30: 10 us no more visions of what is *r*!
30: 21 Whether you turn to the *r*
41: 10 you with my righteous *r* hand.
41: 13 who takes hold of your *r* hand
48: 13 my *r* hand spread out the heavens;
64: 5 to the help of those who gladly do *r*
Jer 23: 5 and do what is just and *r* in the land
Eze 18: 5 who does what is just and *r*.
18: 21 and does what is just and *r*,
33: 14 and does what is just and *r*—
Hos 14: 9 The ways of the LORD are *r*;
Mt 5: 29 If your *r* eye causes you to sin,
6: 3 know what your *r* hand is doing,
22: 44 "Sit at my *r* hand
25: 33 He will put the sheep on his *r*
Jn 1: 12 he gave the *r* to become children
Ac 2: 34 "Sit at my *r* hand
7: 55 Jesus standing at the *r* hand of God
Ro 3: 4 "So that you may be proved *r*
8: 34 is at the *r* hand of God and is
9: 21 Does not the potter have the *r*
12: 17 careful to do what is *r* in the eyes
1Co 9: 4 Don't we have the *r* to food
2Co 8: 21 we are taking pains to do what is *r*,
Eph 1: 20 and seated him at his *r* hand
6: 1 parents in the Lord, for this is *r*.
Php 4: 8 whatever is *r*, whatever is pure,
2Th 3: 13 never tire of doing what is *r*.
Heb 1: 3 down at the *r* hand of the Majesty
Jas 2: 8 as yourself," you are doing *r*.
1Pe 3: 14 if you should suffer for what is *r*,
1Jn 2: 29 who does what is *r* has been born
Rev 2: 7 I will give the *r* to eat from the tree
3: 21 I will give the *r* to sit with me
22: 11 let him who does *r* continue to do *r*

RIGHTEOUS (RIGHTEOUSLY RIGHTEOUSNESS)
Ge 6: 9 Noah was a *r* man, blameless
18: 23 "Will you sweep away the *r*
Nu 23: 10 Let me die the death of the *r*,
Ne 9: 8 your promise because you are *r*.
Job 36: 7 He does not take his eyes off the *r*;
Ps 1: 5 nor sinners in the assembly of the *r*.
5: 12 O LORD, you bless the *r*;
11: 7 For the LORD is *r*,
15: 2 and who does what is *r*,
34: 15 The eyes of the LORD are on the *r*
37: 16 Better the little that the *r* have
37: 21 but the *r* give generously;
37: 25 yet I have never seen the *r* forsaken
37: 30 of the *r* man utters wisdom,
55: 22 he will never let the *r* fall.
64: 10 Let the *r* rejoice in the LORD
68: 3 But may the *r* be glad
112: 4 compassionate and *r* man.
118: 20 through which the *r* may enter.
119: 7 as I learn your *r* laws.
119: 137 *R* are you, O LORD,
140: 13 Surely the *r* will praise your name
143: 2 for no one living is *r* before you.
145: 17 The LORD is *r* in all his ways
Pr 3: 33 but he blesses the home of the *r*.
4: 18 of the *r* is like the first gleam
10: 7 of the *r* will be a blessing,
10: 11 The mouth of the *r* is a fountain
10: 16 The wages of the *r* bring them life,
10: 20 The tongue of the *r* is choice silver,
10: 24 what the *r* desire will be granted.
10: 28 The prospect of the *r* is joy,
10: 32 of the *r* know what is fitting,
11: 23 The desire of the *r* ends only
11: 30 The fruit of the *r* is a tree of life,
12: 10 A *r* man cares for the needs
12: 21 No harm befalls the *r*,
13: 9 The light of the *r* shines brightly,
15: 28 of the *r* weighs its answers,
15: 29 but he hears the prayer of the *r*.
16: 31 it is attained by a *r* life.
18: 10 the *r* run to it and are safe.
20: 7 The *r* man leads a blameless life;
21: 15 justice is done, it brings joy to the *r*
23: 24 The father of a *r* man has great joy;
28: 1 but the *r* are as bold as a lion.
29: 6 but a *r* one can sing and be glad.
29: 7 The *r* care about justice
29: 27 The *r* detest the dishonest;
Ecc 7: 20 There is not a *r* man on earth
Isa 26: 7 The path of the *r* is level;
41: 10 you with my *r* right hand.
45: 21 a *r* God and a Savior;
53: 11 his knowledge my *r* servant will
64: 6 and all our *r* acts are like filthy rags
Jer 23: 5 up to David a *r* Branch,
Eze 3: 20 when a *r* man turns
18: 5 "Suppose there is a *r* man
18: 20 of the *r* man will be credited
33: 12 The *r* man, if he sins, will not be

Da 9: 18 requests of you because we are *r*,
Hab 2: 4 but the *r* will live by his faith —
Zec 9: 9 *r* and having salvation,
Mal 3: 18 see the distinction between the *r*
Mt 5: 45 rain on the *r* and the unrighteous.
9: 13 For I have not come to call the *r*,
10: 41 and anyone who receives a *r* man
13: 43 Then the *r* will shine like the sun
13: 49 and separate the wicked from the *r*
25: 37 "Then the *r* will answer him, 'Lord,
25: 46 to eternal punishment, but the *r*
Ac 24: 15 will be a resurrection of both the *r*
Ro 1: 17 as it is written: "The *r* will live
2: 5 when his *r* judgment will be
2: 13 the law who will be declared *r*.
3: 10 "There is no one *r*, not even one;
3: 20 Therefore no one will be declared *r*
5: 19 one man the many will be made *r*.
Gal 3: 11 because, "The *r* will live by faith."
1Ti 1: 9 that law is made not for the *r*
2Ti 4: 8 which the Lord, the *r* Judge,
Tit 3: 5 because of *r* things we had done,
Heb 10: 38 But my *r* one will live by faith.
Jas 5: 16 The prayer of a *r* man is powerful
1Pe 3: 12 the eyes of the Lord are on the *r*
3: 18 the *r* for the unrighteous,
4: 18 "If it is hard for the *r* to be saved,
1Jn 2: 1 defense — Jesus Christ, the *R* One.
3: 7 does what is right is *r*, just as he is *r*.
Rev 19: 8 stands for the *r* acts of the saints.)

RIGHTEOUSLY* (RIGHTEOUS)
Ps 9: 4 on your throne, judging *r*.
Isa 33: 15 He who walks *r*
Jer 11: 20 LORD Almighty, you who judge *r*

RIGHTEOUSNESS (RIGHTEOUS)
Ge 15: 6 and he credited it to him as *r*.
Dt 9: 4 of this land because of my *r*."
1Sa 26: 23 LORD rewards every man for his *r*
1Ki 10: 9 to maintain justice and *r*."
Job 37: 23 great *r*, he does not oppress.
Ps 7: 17 to the LORD because of his *r*
9: 8 He will judge the world in *r*;
17: 15 And I — in *r* I will see your face;
23: 3 He guides me in paths of *r*
33: 5 The LORD loves *r* and justice;
35: 28 My tongue will speak of your *r*
36: 6 Your *r* is like the mighty
37: 6 He will make your *r* shine like
40: 9 I proclaim *r* in the great assembly;
45: 4 in behalf of truth, humility and *r*;
45: 7 You love *r* and hate wickedness;
48: 10 your right hand is filled with *r*.
65: 5 us with awesome deeds of *r*,
71: 2 Rescue me and deliver me in your *r*
71: 15 My mouth will tell of your *r*,
71: 19 Your *r* reaches to the skies, O God,
85: 10 *r* and peace kiss each other.
89: 14 *R* and justice are the foundation
96: 13 He will judge the world in *r*
98: 9 He will judge the world in *r*
103: 6 The LORD works *r*
103: 17 his *r* with their children's children
106: 31 This was credited to him as *r*
111: 3 and his *r* endures forever.
118: 19 Open for me the gates of *r*;
132: 9 May your priests be clothed with *r*;
145: 7 and joyfully sing of your *r*.
Pr 11: 5 *r* of the blameless makes a straight
11: 18 he who sows *r* reaps a sure reward.
13: 6 *R* guards the man of integrity,
14: 34 *R* exalts a nation,
16: 8 Better a little with *r*
16: 12 a throne is established through *r*.
21: 21 He who pursues *r* and love
Isa 5: 16 will show himself holy by his *r*.
9: 7 it with justice and *r*
11: 4 but with *r* he will judge the needy,
16: 5 and speeds the cause of *r*.
26: 9 the people of the world learn *r*.
32: 17 The fruit of *r* will be peace;
42: 6 "I, the LORD, have called you in *r*;
42: 21 the LORD for the sake of his *r*
45: 8 "You heavens above, rain down *r*;
51: 1 "Listen to me, you who pursue *r*
51: 6 my *r* will never fail.
51: 8 But my *r* will last forever,
58: 8 then your *r* will go before you,
59: 17 He put on *r* as his breastplate,
61: 10 and arrayed me in a robe of *r*,
63: 1 "It is I, speaking in *r*,
Jer 9: 24 justice and *r* on earth,
23: 6 The LORD Our *R*.
Eze 3: 20 a righteous man turns from his *r*
14: 20 save only themselves by their *r*.
Eze 18: 20 The *r* of the righteous man will be
33: 12 *r* of the righteous man will not save
Da 9: 24 to bring in everlasting *r*,
12: 3 and those who lead many to *r*,
Hos 10: 12 Sow for yourselves *r*,
Am 5: 24 *r* like a never-failing stream!
Mic 7: 9 I will see his *r*.
Zep 2: 3 Seek *r*, seek humility;
Mal 4: 2 the sun of *r* will rise with healing
Mt 5: 6 those who hunger and thirst for *r*,
5: 10 who are persecuted because of *r*,
5: 20 unless your *r* surpasses that
6: 1 to do your 'acts of *r*' before men,
6: 33 But seek first his kingdom and his *r*
Jn 16: 8 world of guilt in regard to sin and *r*
Ac 24: 25 Paul discoursed on *r*, self-control
Ro 1: 17 For in the gospel a *r* from God is
3: 5 brings out God's *r* more clearly,
3: 22 This *r* from God comes
4: 3 and it was credited to him as *r*."
4: 5 wicked, his faith is credited as *r*.
4: 6 man to whom God credits *r* apart
4: 9 faith was credited to him as *r*.
4: 13 through the *r* that comes by faith.
4: 22 why "it was credited to him as *r*."
5: 18 of *r* was justification that brings life
6: 13 body to him as instruments of *r*.
6: 16 or to obedience, which leads to *r*?
6: 18 and have become slaves to *r*.
6: 19 in slavery to *r* leading to holiness.
8: 10 yet your spirit is alive because of *r*.
9: 30 did not pursue *r*, have obtained it,
10: 3 they did not know the *r* that comes
14: 17 but of *r*, peace and joy
1Co 1: 30 our *r*, holiness and redemption.
2Co 3: 9 is the ministry that brings *r*!
5: 21 that in him we might become the *r*
6: 7 with weapons of *r* in the right hand
6: 14 For what do *r* and wickedness have
9: 9 his *r* endures forever."
Gal 2: 21 for if *r* could be gained
3: 6 and it was credited to him as *r*."
3: 21 then *r* would certainly have come
Eph 4: 24 created to be like God in true *r*
5: 9 *r* and truth) and find out what
6: 14 with the breastplate of *r* in place,
Php 1: 11 filled with the fruit of *r* that comes
3: 6 as for legalistic *r*, faultless.
3: 9 not having a *r* of my own that
1Ti 6: 11 and pursue *r*, godliness, faith, love,
2Ti 2: 22 and pursue *r*, faith, love and peace,
3: 16 correcting and training in *r*,
4: 8 is in store for me the crown of *r*,
Heb 1: 8 and *r* will be the scepter
5: 13 with the teaching about *r*.
7: 2 his name means "king of *r*";
11: 7 became heir of the *r* that comes
12: 11 it produces a harvest of *r*
Jas 2: 23 and it was credited to him as *r*,"
3: 18 sow in peace raise a harvest of *r*.
1Pe 2: 24 die to sins and live for *r*;
2Pe 2: 21 not to have known the way of *r*,
3: 13 and a new earth, the home of *r*.

RIGHTS (RIGHT)
Ps 82: 3 maintain the *r* of the poor
Pr 31: 8 for the *r* of all who are destitute.
Isa 10: 2 to deprive the poor of their *r*
La 3: 35 to deny a man his *r*
Gal 4: 5 that we might receive the full *r*

RING
Pr 11: 22 Like a gold *r* in a pig's snout
Lk 15: 22 Put a *r* on his finger and sandals

RIOTS
2Co 6: 5 imprisonments and *r*; in hard work,

RIPE
Joel 3: 13 for the harvest is *r*.
Am 8: 1 showed me: a basket of *r* fruit.
Jn 4: 35 at the fields! They are *r* for harvest.
Rev 14: 15 for the harvest of the earth is *r*."

RISE (RAISE RAISED RISEN ROSE)
Lev 19: 32 "'*R* in the presence of the aged,
Nu 24: 17 a scepter will *r* out of Israel.
Isa 26: 19 their bodies will *r*.
Mal 4: 2 of righteousness will *r* with healing
Mt 27: 63 'After three days I will *r* again.'
Mk 8: 31 and after three days *r* again.
Lk 18: 33 On the third day he will *r* again."
Jn 5: 29 those who have done good will *r*
20: 9 had to *r* from the dead.)
Ac 17: 3 had to suffer and *r* from the dead.
1Th 4: 16 and the dead in Christ will *r* first.

RISEN (RISE)
Mt 28: 6 He is not here; he has *r*, just
Mk 16: 6 He has *r*! He is not here.
Lk 24: 34 The Lord has *r* and has appeared

RIVER (RIVERS)
Ps 46: 4 There is a *r* whose streams make
Isa 66: 12 "I will extend peace to her like a *r*,
Eze 47: 12 grow on both banks of the *r*.
Rev 22: 1 Then the angel showed me the *r*

RIVERS (RIVER)
Ps 137: 1 By the *r* of Babylon we sat

ROAD (CROSSROADS ROADS)
Mt 7: 13 and broad is the *r* that leads

ROADS (ROAD)
Lk 3: 5 crooked *r* shall become straight,

ROARING
1Pe 5: 8 prowls around like a *r* lion looking

ROB (ROBBERS ROBBERY ROBS)
Mal 3: 8 "Will a man *r* God? Yet you *r* me.

ROBBERS (ROB)
Jer 7: 11 become a den of *r* to you?
Mk 15: 27 They crucified two *r* with him,
Lk 19: 46 but you have made it 'a den of *r*.'"
Jn 10: 8 came before me were thieves and *r*,

ROBBERY (ROB)
Isa 61: 8 I hate *r* and iniquity.

ROBE (ROBED ROBES)
Ge 37: 3 and he made a richly ornamented *r*
Isa 6: 1 the train of his *r* filled the temple.
61: 10 arrayed me in a *r* of righteousness,
Rev 6: 11 each of them was given a white *r*,

ROBED (ROBE)
Ps 93: 1 the LORD is *r* in majesty
Isa 63: 1 Who is this, *r* in splendor,

ROBES (ROBE)
Ps 45: 8 All your *r* are fragrant with myrrh
Rev 7: 13 "These in white *r* — who are they,

ROBS* (ROB)
Pr 19: 26 He who *r* his father and drives out
28: 24 He who *r* his father or mother

ROCK
Ge 49: 24 of the Shepherd, the *R* of Israel,
Ex 17: 6 Strike the *r*, and water will come
Nu 20: 8 Speak to that *r* before their eyes
Dt 32: 4 He is the *R*, his works are perfect,
32: 13 him with honey from the *r*,
2Sa 22: 2 "The LORD is my *r*, my fortress
Ps 18: 2 The LORD is my *r*, my fortress
19: 14 O LORD, my *R* and my Redeemer
40: 2 he set my feet on a *r*
61: 2 lead me to the *r* that is higher
92: 15 he is my *R*, and there is no
Isa 26: 4 the LORD, is the *R* eternal.
51: 1 to the *r* from which you were cut
Da 2: 34 you were watching, a *r* was cut out,
Mt 7: 24 man who built his house on the *r*.
16: 18 and on this *r* I will build my church
Ro 9: 33 and a *r* that makes them fall,
1Co 10: 4 the spiritual *r* that accompanied
1Pe 2: 8 and a *r* that makes them fall."

ROD (RODS)
2Sa 7: 14 I will punish him with the *r* of men,
Ps 23: 4 your *r* and your staff,
Pr 13: 24 He who spares the *r* hates his son,
22: 15 the *r* of discipline will drive it far
23: 13 if you punish him with the *r*,
29: 15 *r* of correction imparts wisdom,
Isa 11: 4 the earth with the *r* of his mouth;

RODS (ROD)
2Co 11: 25 Three times I was beaten with *r*,

ROLL (ROLLED)
Mk 16: 3 "Who will *r* the stone away

ROLLED (ROLL)
Lk 24: 2 They found the stone *r* away

ROMAN
Ac 16: 37 even though we are *R* citizens,
22: 25 you to flog a *R* citizen who hasn't

ROOF (ROOFS)
Pr 21: 9 Better to live on a corner of the *r*

ROOFS
Mt 10: 27 in your ear, proclaim from the *r*.

ROOM (ROOMS)
Mt 6: 6 But when you pray, go into your *r*,
Mk 14: 15 He will show you a large upper *r*,
Lk 2: 7 there was no *r* for them in the inn.
Jn 8: 37 because you have no *r* for my word
21: 25 the whole world would not have *r*
2Co 7: 2 Make *r* for us in your hearts.

ROOMS (ROOM)
Jn 14: 2 In my Father's house are many *r*;

ROOSTER
Mt 26: 34 this very night, before the *r* crows,

ROOT (ROOTED ROOTS)
Isa 11: 10 In that day the *R* of Jesse will stand
53: 2 and like a *r* out of dry ground.
Mt 3: 10 already at the *r* of the trees,
13: 21 But since he has no *r*, he lasts only
Ro 11: 16 if the *r* is holy, so are the branches.
15: 12 "The *R* of Jesse will spring up,
1Ti 6: 10 of money is a *r* of all kinds of evil.
Rev 5: 5 the *R* of David, has triumphed.
22: 16 I am the *R* and the Offspring

ROOTED (ROOT)
Eph 3: 17 being *r* and established in love,

ROOTS (ROOT)
Isa 11: 1 from his *r* a Branch will bear fruit.

ROSE (RISE)
SS 2: 1 I am a *r* of Sharon,
1Th 4: 14 believe that Jesus died and *r* again

ROTS
Pr 14: 30 but envy *r* the bones.

ROUGH
Isa 42: 16 and make the *r* places smooth.
Lk 3: 5 the *r* ways smooth.

ROUND
Ecc 1: 6 *r* and *r* it goes,

ROYAL
Ps 45: 9 at your right hand is the *r* bride
Da 1: 8 not to defile himself with the *r* food
Jas 2: 8 If you really keep the *r* law found
1Pe 2: 9 a *r* priesthood, a holy nation,

RUBBISH*
Php 3: 8 I consider them *r*, that I may gain

RUBIES
Job 28: 18 the price of wisdom is beyond *r*.
Pr 3: 15 She is more precious than *r*;
8: 11 for wisdom is more precious than *r*,
31: 10 She is worth far more than *r*.

RUDDER*
Jas 3: 4 by a very small *r* wherever the pilot

RUDDY
1Sa 16: 12 He was *r*, with a fine appearance
SS 5: 10 *Beloved* My lover is radiant and *r*,

RUDE*
1Co 13: 5 It is not *r*, it is not self-seeking,

RUIN (RUINED RUINING RUINS)
Pr 10: 8 but a chattering fool comes to *r*.
10: 10 and a chattering fool comes to *r*.
10: 14 but the mouth of a fool invites *r*.
10: 29 but it is the *r* of those who do evil.
18: 24 many companions may come to *r*,
19: 13 A foolish son is his father's *r*,
26: 28 and a flattering mouth works *r*.
SS 2: 15 that *r* the vineyards,
Eze 21: 27 A *r*! A *r*! I will make it a *r*!
1Ti 6: 9 desires that plunge men into *r*

RUINED (RUIN)
Isa 6: 5 "I am *r*! For I am a man
Mt 9: 17 and the wineskins will be *r*.
12: 25 divided against itself will be *r*,

RUINING* (RUIN)
Tit 1: 11 they are *r* whole households

RUINS (RUIN)
Pr 19: 3 A man's own folly *r* his life,
Ecc 4: 5 and *r* himself.
2Ti 2: 14 and only *r* those who listen.

RULE (RULER RULERS RULES)
Ge 1: 26 let them *r* over the fish of the sea
3: 16 and he will *r* over you."
Jdg 8: 22 said to Gideon, "*R* over us —
1Sa 12: 12 'No, we want a king to *r* over us' —
Ps 2: 9 You will *r* them with an iron
67: 4 for you *r* the peoples justly
119: 133 let no sin *r* over me.
Pr 17: 2 A wise servant will *r*
Isa 28: 10 *r* on *r*, *r* on *r*;
Eze 20: 33 I will *r* over you with a mighty
Zec 6: 13 and will sit and *r* on his throne.
9: 10 His *r* will extend from sea to sea
Ro 13: 9 are summed up in this one *r*:
15: 12 arise to *r* over the nations;
1Co 7: 17 This is the *r* I lay down in all
Gal 6: 16 and mercy to all who follow this *r*,
Eph 1: 21 far above all *r* and authority,
Col 3: 15 the peace of Christ *r* in your hearts,
2Th 3: 10 we gave you this *r*: "If a man will
Rev 2: 27 He will *r* them with an iron scepter;
12: 5 who will *r* all the nations
19: 15 He will *r* them with an iron scepter

RULER (RULE)
Ps 8: 6 You made him *r* over the works
Pr 19: 6 Many curry favor with a *r*,
23: 1 When you sit to dine with a *r*,
25: 15 Through patience a *r* can be
29: 26 Many seek an audience with a *r*,
Isa 60: 17 and righteousness your *r*.
Da 9: 25 the *r*, comes, there will be seven
Mic 5: 2 one who will be *r* over Israel,
Mt 2: 6 for out of you will come a *r*
Eph 2: 2 of the *r* of the kingdom of the air,
1Ti 6: 15 God, the blessed and only *R*,
Rev 1: 5 and the *r* of the kings of the earth.

RULERS (RULE)
Ps 2: 2 and the *r* gather together
119: 161 *R* persecute me without cause,
Isa 40: 23 reduces the *r* of this world
Da 7: 27 and all *r* will worship and obey him
Mt 20: 25 "You know that the *r*
Ac 13: 27 and their *r* did not recognize Jesus,
Ro 13: 3 For *r* hold no terror
1Co 2: 6 of this age or of the *r* of this age,
Eph 3: 10 should be made known to the *r*
6: 12 the *r*, against the authorities,
Col 1: 16 or powers or *r* or authorities;

RULES (RULE)
Nu 15: 15 is to have the same *r* for you
2Sa 23: 3 when he *r* in the fear of God,
Ps 22: 28 and he *r* over the nations.
66: 7 He *r* forever by his power,
103: 19 and his kingdom *r* over all.
Isa 29: 13 is made up only of *r* taught by men.
40: 10 and his arm *r* for him.
Mt 15: 9 their teachings are but *r* taught
Lk 22: 26 one who *r* like the one who serves.
2Ti 2: 5 he competes according to the *r*.

RUMORS
Jer 51: 46 afraid when *r* are heard in the land;
Mt 24: 6 You will hear of wars and *r* of wars,

RUN (RAN RUNNERS RUNNING RUNS)
Ps 19: 5 champion rejoicing to *r* his course.
Pr 4: 12 when you *r*, you will not stumble.
18: 10 the righteous *r* to it and are safe.
Isa 10: 3 To whom will you *r* for help?
40: 31 they will *r* and not grow weary,
Joel 3: 18 ravines of Judah will *r* with water.
Hab 2: 2 so that a herald may *r* with it.
1Co 9: 24 *R* in such a way as to get the prize.
Gal 2: 2 that I was running or had *r* my race
Php 2: 16 on the day of Christ that I did not *r*
Heb 12: 1 let us *r* with perseverance the race

RUNNERS* (RUN)
1Co 9: 24 that in a race all the *r* run,

RUNNING (RUN)
Ps 133: 2 *r* down on Aaron's beard,
Lk 17: 23 Do not go *r* off after them.
1Co 9: 26 I do not run like a man *r* aimlessly;
Gal 5: 7 You were *r* a good race.

RUNS (RUN)
Jn 10: 12 he abandons the sheep and *r* away.

RUSH
Pr 1: 16 for their feet *r* into sin,
6: 18 feet that are quick to *r* into evil,
Isa 59: 7 Their feet *r* into sin;

RUST
Mt 6: 19 where moth and *r* destroy,

RUTH*
Moabitess; widow who went to Bethlehem with mother-in-law Naomi (Ru 1). Gleaned in field of Boaz; shown favor (Ru 2). Proposed marriage to Boaz (Ru 3). Married (Ru 4:1 – 12); bore Obed, ancestor of David (Ru 4:13 – 22), Jesus (Mt 1:5).

RUTHLESS
Pr 11: 16 but *r* men gain only wealth.
Ro 1: 31 are senseless, faithless, heartless, *r*.

SABBATH (SABBATHS)
Ex 20: 8 "Remember the *S* day
31: 14 " 'Observe the *S*, because it is holy
Lev 25: 2 the land itself must observe a *s*
Dt 5: 12 "Observe the *S* day
Isa 56: 2 keeps the *S* without desecrating it,
56: 6 all who keep the *S*
58: 13 if you call the *S* a delight
Jer 17: 21 not to carry a load on the *S* day
Mt 12: 1 through the grainfields on the *S*.
Lk 13: 10 On a *S* Jesus was teaching in one
Col 2: 16 a New Moon celebration or a *S* day

SABBATH-REST* (REST)
Heb 4: 9 then, a *S* for the people of God;

SABBATHS (SABBATH)
2Ch 2: 4 evening and on *S* and New Moons
Eze 20: 12 Also I gave them my *S*

SACKCLOTH
Ps 30: 11 you removed my *s* and clothed me
Da 9: 3 in fasting, and in *s* and ashes.
Mt 11: 21 would have repented long ago in *s*

SACRED
Lev 23: 2 are to proclaim as *s* assemblies.
Mt 7: 6 "Do not give dogs what is *s*;
Ro 14: 5 One man considers one day more *s*
1Co 3: 17 for God's temple is *s*, and you are
2Pe 1: 18 were with him on the *s* mountain.
2: 21 on the *s* command that was

SACRIFICE (SACRIFICED SACRIFICES)
Ge 22: 2 *S* him there as a burnt offering
Ex 12: 27 'It is the Passover *s* to the LORD,
1Sa 15: 22 To obey is better than *s*,
1Ki 18: 38 the LORD fell and burned up the *s*,
1Ch 21: 24 or *s* a burnt offering that costs me
Ps 40: 6 *S* and offering you did not desire,
50: 14 *S* thank offerings to God,
51: 16 You do not delight in *s*,
54: 6 I will *s* a freewill offering to you;
107: 22 Let them *s* thank offerings
141: 2 of my hands be like the evening *s*.
Pr 15: 8 The LORD detests the *s*
21: 3 to the LORD than *s*.
Da 9: 27 the 'seven' he will put an end to *s*
12: 11 time that the daily *s* is abolished
Hos 6: 6 For I desire mercy, not *s*,
Mt 9: 13 this means: 'I desire mercy, not *s*.'
Ro 3: 25 God presented him as a *s*
Eph 5: 2 as a fragrant offering and *s* to God.
Php 4: 18 an acceptable *s*, pleasing to God.
Heb 9: 26 away with sin by the *s* of himself.
10: 5 "*S* and offering you did not desire,
10: 10 holy through the *s* of the body
10: 14 by one *s* he has made perfect
10: 18 there is no longer any *s* for sin.
11: 4 faith Abel offered God a better *s*
13: 15 offer to God a *s* of praise —
1Jn 2: 2 He is the atoning *s* for our sins,
4: 10 as an atoning *s* for our sins.

SACRIFICED (SACRIFICE)
Ac 15: 29 are to abstain from food *s* to idols,
1Co 5: 7 our Passover lamb, has been *s*.
8: 1 Now about food *s* to idols:
Heb 7: 27 He *s* for their sins once for all
9: 28 so Christ was *s* once

SACRIFICES (SACRIFICE)
Ps 51: 17 The *s* of God are a broken spirit;
Mk 12: 33 than all burnt offerings and *s*."
Ro 12: 1 to offer your bodies as living *s*,
Heb 9: 23 with better *s* than these.
13: 16 for with such *s* God is pleased.
1Pe 2: 5 offering spiritual *s* acceptable

SAD
Lk 18: 23 he heard this, he became very *s*,

SADDUCEES
Mt 16: 6 the yeast of the Pharisees and *S*."
Mk 12: 18 *S*, who say there is no resurrection,
Ac 23: 8 *S* say that there is no resurrection,

SAFE (SAVE)
Ps 27: 5 he will keep me *s* in his dwelling;
37: 3 in the land and enjoy *s* pasture.
Pr 18: 10 the righteous run to it and are *s*.
28: 26 he who walks in wisdom is kept *s*.
29: 25 in the LORD is kept *s*.
Jer 12: 5 If you stumble in *s* country,
Jn 17: 12 kept them *s* by that name you gave
1Jn 5: 18 born of God keeps him *s*,

SAFETY (SAVE)
Ps 4: 8 make me dwell in *s*.
Hos 2: 18 so that all may lie down in *s*.
1Th 5: 3 people are saying, "Peace and *s*,"

SAINTS
1Sa 2: 9 He will guard the feet of his *s*,
Ps 16: 3 As for the *s* who are in the land,
30: 4 Sing to the LORD, you *s* of his;
31: 23 Love the LORD, all his *s*!
34: 9 Fear the LORD, you his *s*,
116: 15 is the death of his *s*.
149: 1 his praise in the assembly of the *s*.
149: 5 Let the *s* rejoice in this honor
Da 7: 18 the *s* of the Most High will receive
Ro 8: 27 intercedes for the *s* in accordance
1Co 6: 2 not know that the *s* will judge
Eph 1: 15 Jesus and your love for all the *s*,
1: 18 of his glorious inheritance in the *s*,
6: 18 always keep on praying for all the *s*
Phm : 7 have refreshed the hearts of the *s*.
Rev 5: 8 which are the prayers of the *s*.
19: 8 for the righteous acts of the *s*.)

SAKE (SAKES)
1Sa 12: 22 For the *s* of his great name
Ps 23: 3 righteousness for his name's *s*.
44: 22 Yet for your *s* we face death all day
106: 8 Yet he saved them for his name's *s*,
Isa 42: 21 for the *s* of his righteousness
43: 25 your transgressions, for my own *s*,
48: 9 For my own name's *s* I delay my
48: 11 For my own *s*, for my own *s*,
Jer 14: 7 for the *s* of your name.
14: 21 For the *s* of your name do not
Eze 20: 9 But for the *s* of my name I did what
20: 14 But for the *s* of my name I did what
20: 22 and for the *s* of my name I did what
36: 22 but for the *s* of my holy name,
Da 9: 17 For your *s*, O Lord, look with favor
Mt 10: 39 life for my *s* will find it.
19: 29 for my *s* will receive a hundred
1Co 9: 23 I do all this for the *s* of the gospel,
2Co 12: 10 for Christ's *s*, I delight
Php 3: 7 loss for the *s* of Christ.
Heb 11: 26 He regarded disgrace for the *s*
1Pe 2: 13 for the Lord's *s* to every authority
3Jn : 7 was for the *s* of the Name that they

SAKES* (SAKE)
2Co 8: 9 yet for your *s* he became poor,

SALEM
Ge 14: 18 king of *S* brought out bread
Heb 7: 2 "king of *S*" means "king of peace."

SALT
Ge 19: 26 and she became a pillar of *s*.
Nu 18: 19 covenant of *s* before the LORD
Mt 5: 13 "You are the *s* of the earth.
Col 4: 6 with *s*, so that you may know how
Jas 3: 11 *s* water flow from the same spring?

SALVATION* (SAVE)
Ex 15: 2 he has become my *s*.
2Sa 22: 3 my shield and the horn of my *s*.
23: 5 Will he not bring to fruition my *s*
1Ch 16: 23 proclaim his *s* day after day.
2Ch 6: 41 O LORD God, be clothed with *s*,
Ps 9: 14 and there rejoice in your *s*.
13: 5 my heart rejoices in your *s*.
14: 7 that *s* for Israel would come out
18: 2 is my shield and the horn of my *s*,
27: 1 The LORD is my light and my *s*—
28: 8 a fortress of *s* for his anointed one.
35: 3 "I am your *s*."
35: 9 and delight in his *s*.
37: 39 The *s* of the righteous comes
40: 10 I speak of your faithfulness and *s*.
40: 16 those who love your *s* always say,
50: 23 way so that I may show him the *s*
51: 12 Restore to me the joy of your *s*
53: 6 that *s* for Israel would come out
62: 1 my *s* comes from him.
62: 2 He alone is my rock and my *s*;
62: 6 He alone is my rock and my *s*;
62: 7 My *s* and my honor depend
67: 2 your *s* among all nations.
69: 13 answer me with your sure *s*.
69: 27 do not let them share in your *s*.
69: 29 may your *s*, O God, protect me.
70: 4 those who love your *s* always say,
71: 15 of your *s* all day long,
74: 12 you bring *s* upon the earth.
85: 7 and grant us your *s*.
85: 9 Surely his *s* is near those who fear
91: 16 and show him my *s*."
Ps 95: 1 to the Rock of our *s*.
96: 2 proclaim his *s* day after day.
98: 1 have worked *s* for him.
98: 2 The LORD has made his *s* known
98: 3 the *s* of our God.
116: 13 I will lift up the cup of *s*
118: 14 he has become my *s*.
118: 21 you have become my *s*.
119: 41 your *s* according to your promise;
119: 81 with longing for your *s*,
119: 123 My eyes fail, looking for your *s*,
119: 155 *S* is far from the wicked,
119: 166 I wait for your *s*, O LORD,
119: 174 I long for your *s*, O LORD,
132: 16 I will clothe her priests with *s*,
149: 4 he crowns the humble with *s*.
Isa 12: 2 Surely God is my *s*;
12: 2 he has become my *s*."
12: 3 from the wells of *s*.
25: 9 let us rejoice and be glad in his *s*."
26: 1 God makes *s*
26: 18 We have not brought *s* to the earth;
30: 15 "In repentance and rest is your *s*,
33: 2 our *s* in time of distress.
33: 6 a rich store of *s* and wisdom
45: 8 let *s* spring up,
45: 17 the LORD with an everlasting *s*;
46: 13 I will grant *s* to Zion,
46: 13 and my *s* will not be delayed.
49: 6 that you may bring my *s*
49: 8 and in the day of *s* I will help you;
51: 5 my *s* is on the way,
51: 6 But my *s* will last forever,
51: 8 my *s* through all generations."
52: 7 who proclaim *s*,
52: 10 the *s* of our God.
56: 1 for my *s* is close at hand
59: 16 so his own arm worked *s* for him,
59: 17 and the helmet of *s* on his head;
60: 18 but you will call your walls *S*
61: 10 me with garments of *s*
62: 1 her *s* like a blazing torch.
63: 5 so my own arm worked *s* for me,
Jer 3: 23 is the *s* of Israel.
La 3: 26 quietly for the *s* of the LORD.
Jnh 2: 9 *S* comes from the LORD."
Zec 9: 9 righteous and having *s*,
Lk 1: 69 He has raised up a horn of *s* for us
1: 71 of long ago), *s* from our enemies
1: 77 give his people the knowledge of *s*
2: 30 For my eyes have seen your *s*,
3: 6 And all mankind will see God's *s*
19: 9 "Today *s* has come to this house,
Jn 4: 22 for *s* is from the Jews.
Ac 4: 12 *S* is found in no one else,
13: 26 message of *s* has been sent.
13: 47 that you may bring *s* to the ends
28: 28 to know that God's *s* has been sent
Ro 1: 16 for the *s* of everyone who believes:
11: 11 *s* has come to the Gentiles
13: 11 because our *s* is nearer now
2Co 1: 6 it is for your comfort and *s*;
6: 2 and in the day of *s* I helped you."
6: 2 of God's favor, now is the day of *s*.
7: 10 brings repentance that leads to *s*
Eph 1: 13 word of truth, the gospel of your *s*.
6: 17 Take the helmet of *s* and the sword
Php 2: 12 to work out your *s* with fear
1Th 5: 8 and the hope of *s* as a helmet.
5: 9 to receive *s* through our Lord Jesus
2Ti 2: 10 they too may obtain the *s* that is
3: 15 wise for *s* through faith
Tit 2: 11 of God that brings *s* has appeared
Heb 1: 14 to serve those who will inherit *s*?
2: 3 This *s*, which was first announced
2: 3 escape if we ignore such a great *s*?
2: 10 of their *s* perfect through suffering.
5: 9 of eternal *s* for all who obey him
6: 9 case — things that accompany *s*.
9: 28 to bring *s* to those who are waiting
1Pe 1: 5 the coming of the *s* that is ready
1: 9 of your faith, the *s* of your souls.
1: 10 Concerning this *s*, the prophets,
2: 2 by it you may grow up in your *s*,
2Pe 3: 15 that our Lord's patience means *s*,
Jude : 3 to write to you about the *s* we share
Rev 7: 10 "*S* belongs to our God,
12: 10 have come the *s* and the power
19: 1 *S* and glory and power belong

SAMARIA (SAMARITAN)
1Ki 16: 24 He bought the hill of *S*
2Ki 17: 6 the king of Assyria captured *S*
Jn 4: 4 Now he had to go through *S*.
4: 5 came to a town in *S* called Sychar,

SAMARITAN (SAMARIA)
Lk 10: 33 But a *S*, as he traveled, came where
17: 16 and thanked him — and he was a *S*.
Jn 4: 7 When a *S* woman came

SAMSON
Danite judge. Birth promised (Jdg 13). Married to Philistine, but wife given away (Jdg 14). Vengeance on Philistines (Jdg 15). Betrayed by Delilah (Jdg 16:1 – 22). Death (Jdg 16:23 – 31). Feats of strength: killed lion (Jdg 14:6), 30 Philistines (Jdg 14:19), 1,000 Philistines with jawbone (Jdg 15:13 – 17), carried off gates of Gaza (Jdg 16:3), pushed down temple of Dagon (Jdg 16:25 – 30).

SAMUEL
Ephraimite judge and prophet (Heb 11:32). Birth prayed for (1Sa 1:10 – 18). Dedicated to temple by Hannah (1Sa 1:21 – 28). Raised by Eli (1Sa 2:11, 18 – 26). Called as prophet (1Sa 3). Led Israel to victory over Philistines (1Sa 7). Asked by Israel for a king (1Sa 8). Anointed Saul as king (1Sa 9 – 10). Farewell speech (1Sa 12). Rebuked Saul for sacrifice (1Sa 13). Announced rejection of Saul (1Sa 15). Anointed David as king (1Sa 16). Protected David from Saul (1Sa 19:18 – 24). Death (1Sa 25:1). Returned from dead to condemn Saul (1Sa 28).

SANBALLAT
Led opposition to Nehemiah's rebuilding of Jerusalem (Ne 2:10, 19; 4; 6).

SANCTIFIED* (SANCTIFY)
Jn 17: 19 that they too may be truly *s*.
Ac 20: 32 among all those who are *s*.
26: 18 among those who are *s* by faith
Ro 15: 16 to God, *s* by the Holy Spirit.
1Co 1: 2 to those *s* in Christ Jesus
6: 11 But you were washed, you were *s*,
7: 14 and the unbelieving wife has been *s*
7: 14 the unbelieving husband has been *s*
1Th 4: 3 It is God's will that you should be *s*
Heb 10: 29 blood of the covenant that *s* him,

SANCTIFY* (SANCTIFIED SANCTIFYING)
Jn 17: 17 *S* them by the truth; your word is
17: 19 For them I *s* myself, that they too
1Th 5: 23 *s* you through and through.
Heb 9: 13 are ceremonially unclean *s* them

SANCTIFYING* (SANCTIFY)
2Th 2: 13 through the *s* work of the Spirit
1Pe 1: 2 through the *s* work of the Spirit,

SANCTUARY
Ex 25: 8 "Then have them make a *s* for me,
Lev 19: 30 and have reverence for my *s*,
Ps 15: 1 LORD, who may dwell in your *s*?
63: 2 I have seen you in the *s*
68: 24 of my God and King into the *s*.
68: 35 are awesome, O God, in your *s*;
73: 17 me till I entered the *s* of God;
102: 19 looked down from his *s* on high,
134: 2 Lift up your hands in the *s*
150: 1 Praise God in his *s*;
Eze 37: 26 I will put my *s* among them forever
41: 1 the man brought me to the outer *s*
Da 9: 26 will destroy the city and the *s*.
Heb 6: 19 It enters the inner *s*
8: 2 in the *s*, the true tabernacle set up
8: 5 They serve at a *s* that is a copy
9: 24 enter a man-made *s* that was only

SAND
Ge 22: 17 and as the *s* on the seashore.
Mt 7: 26 man who built his house on *s*.

SANDAL (SANDALS)
Ru 4: 7 one party took off his *s*

SANDALS (SANDAL)
Ex 3: 5 off your *s*, for the place where you
Dt 25: 9 take off one of his *s*, spit in his face
Jos 5: 15 off your *s*, for the place where you
Mt 3: 11 whose *s* I am not fit to carry.

SANG (SING)
Ex 15: 1 and the Israelites *s* this song
15: 21 Miriam *s* to them:
Nu 21: 17 Then Israel *s* this song:
Jdg 5: 1 Barak son of Abinoam *s* this song:
1Sa 18: 7 As they danced, they *s*:
2Sa 22: 1 David *s* to the LORD the words
2Ch 5: 13 in praise to the LORD and *s*:
29: 30 So they *s* praises with gladness
Ezr 3: 11 thanksgiving they *s* to the LORD:
Job 38: 7 while the morning stars *s* together
Ps 106: 12 and *s* his praise.
Rev 5: 9 And they *s* a new song:
5: 12 In a loud voice they *s*:
14: 3 they *s* a new song before the throne
15: 3 and *s* the song of Moses the servant

SAP
Ro 11: 17 share in the nourishing *s*

SAPPHIRA*
Ac 5: 1 together with his wife *S*,

SARAH
Wife of Abraham, originally named Sarai; barren (Ge 11:29–31; 1Pe 3:6). Taken by Pharaoh as Abraham's sister; returned (Ge 12:10–20). Gave Hagar to Abraham; sent her away in pregnancy (Ge 16). Name changed; Isaac promised (Ge 17:15–21; 18:10–15; Heb 11:11). Taken by Abimelech as Abraham's sister; returned (Ge 20). Isaac born; Hagar and Ishmael sent away (Ge 21:1–21; Gal 4:21–31). Death (Ge 23).

SARDIS
Rev 3: 1 the angel of the church in *S* write:

SASH (SASHES)
Rev 1: 13 with a golden *s* around his chest.

SASHES (SASH)
Rev 15: 6 wore golden *s* around their chests.

SAT (SIT)
Ps 137: 1 By the rivers of Babylon we *s*
Mk 16: 19 and he *s* at the right hand of God.
Lk 10: 39 who *s* at the Lord's feet listening
Heb 1: 3 he *s* down at the right hand
8: 1 who *s* down at the right hand
10: 12 he *s* down at the right hand of God.
12: 2 and *s* down at the right hand

SATAN
Job 1: 6 and *S* also came with them.
Zec 3: 2 said to *S*, "The LORD rebuke you,
Mt 12: 26 If *S* drives out *S*, he is divided
16: 23 *S!* You are a stumbling block to me;
Mk 4: 15 *S* comes and takes away the word
Lk 10: 18 "I saw *S* fall like lightning
22: 3 *S* entered Judas, called Iscariot,
Ro 16: 20 The God of peace will soon crush *S*
1Co 5: 5 is present, hand this man over to *S*,
2Co 11: 14 for *S* himself masquerades
12: 7 a messenger of *S*, to torment me.
1Ti 1: 20 handed over to *S* to be taught not
Rev 12: 9 serpent called the devil, or *S*,
20: 2 or *S*, and bound him for a thousand
20: 7 *S* will be released from his prison

SATISFIED (SATISFY)
Ps 17: 15 I will be *s* with seeing your likeness
22: 26 The poor will eat and be *s*;
63: 5 My soul will be *s* as with the richest
104: 28 they are *s* with good things.
105: 40 *s* them with the bread of heaven.
Pr 13: 4 the desires of the diligent are fully *s*
30: 15 are three things that are never *s*,
Ecc 5: 10 whoever loves wealth is never *s*
Isa 53: 11 he will see the light ⌊of life⌋ and be *s*
Mt 14: 20 They all ate and were *s*,
Lk 6: 21 for you will be *s*.

SATISFIES* (SATISFY)
Ps 103: 5 who *s* your desires with good things,
107: 9 for he *s* the thirsty
147: 14 and *s* you with the finest of wheat.

SATISFY (SATISFIED SATISFIES)
Ps 90: 14 *S* us in the morning
145: 16 *s* the desires of every living thing.
Pr 5: 19 may her breasts *s* you always,
Isa 55: 2 and your labor on what does not *s*?
58: 10 and *s* the needs of the oppressed,

SAUL
1. Benjamite; anointed by Samuel as first king of Israel (1Sa 9–10). Defeated Ammonites (1Sa 11). Rebuked for offering sacrifice (1Sa 13:1–15). Defeated Philistines (1Sa 14). Rejected as king for failing to annihilate Amalekites (1Sa 15). Soothed from evil spirit by David (1Sa 16:14–23). Sent David against Goliath (1Sa 17). Jealousy and attempted murder of David (1Sa 18:1–11). Gave David Michal as wife (1Sa 18:12–30). Second attempt to kill David (1Sa 19). Anger at Jonathan (1Sa 20:26–34). Pursued David: killed priests at Nob (1Sa 22), went to Keilah and Ziph (1Sa 23), life spared by David at En Gedi (1Sa 24) and in his tent (1Sa 26). Rebuked by Samuel's spirit for consulting witch at Endor (1Sa 28). Wounded by Philistines; took his own life (1Sa 31; 1Ch 10). Lamented by David (2Sa 1:17–27). Children (1Sa 14:49–51; 1Ch 8).
2. See PAUL

SAVAGE
Ac 20: 29 *s* wolves will come in among you

SAVE (SAFE SAFETY SALVATION SAVED SAVES SAVIOR)
Ge 45: 5 to *s* lives that God sent me ahead
1Ch 16: 35 Cry out, "*S* us, O God our Savior;
Job 40: 14 that your own right hand can *s* you.
Ps 17: 7 you who *s* by your right hand
18: 27 You *s* the humble
28: 9 *S* your people and bless your
31: 16 *s* me in your unfailing love.
69: 35 for God will *s* Zion
71: 2 turn your ear to me and *s* me.
72: 13 and *s* the needy from death.
89: 48 or *s* himself from the power
91: 3 Surely he will *s* you
109: 31 to *s* his life from those who
146: 3 in mortal men, who cannot *s*.
Pr 2: 16 will *s* you also from the adulteress,
Isa 35: 4 he will come to *s* you."
38: 20 The LORD will *s* me,
46: 7 it cannot *s* him from his troubles.
59: 1 of the LORD is not too short to *s*,
63: 1 mighty to *s*."
Jer 17: 14 *s* me and I will be saved,
Eze 3: 18 ways in order to *s* his life,
7: 19 able to *s* them in the day
14: 14 they could *s* only themselves
33: 12 of the righteous man will not *s* him
34: 22 I will *s* my flock, and they will no
Da 3: 17 the God we serve is able to *s* us
Hos 1: 7 and I will *s* them—not by bow,
Zep 1: 18 will be able to *s* them
3: 17 he is mighty to *s*.
Zec 8: 7 "I will *s* my people
Mt 1: 21 he will *s* his people from their sins
16: 25 wants to *s* his life will lose it,
Lk 19: 10 to seek and to *s* what was lost."
Jn 3: 17 but to *s* the world through him.
12: 47 come to judge the world, but to *s* it.
Ro 11: 14 people to envy and *s* some of them.
1Co 7: 16 whether you will *s* your husband?
1Ti 1: 15 came into the world to *s* sinners—
Heb 7: 25 to *s* completely those who come
Jas 5: 20 of his way will *s* him from death
Jude : 23 others from the fire and *s* them;

SAVED (SAVE)
Ps 22: 5 They cried to you and were *s*;
33: 16 No king is *s* by the size of his army;
34: 6 he *s* him out of all his troubles.
106: 21 They forgot the God who *s* them,
116: 6 when I was in great need, he *s* me.
Isa 25: 9 we trusted in him, and he *s* us.
45: 22 "Turn to me and be *s*,
64: 5 How then can we be *s*?
Jer 4: 14 from your heart and be *s*.
8: 20 and we are not *s*."
Eze 3: 19 but you will have *s* yourself.
33: 5 warning, he would have *s* himself.
Joel 2: 32 on the name of the LORD will be *s*;
Mt 10: 22 firm to the end will be *s*.
24: 13 firm to the end will be *s*.
Mk 13: 13 firm to the end will be *s*.
16: 16 believes and is baptized will be *s*,
Jn 10: 9 enters through me will be *s*.
Ac 2: 21 on the name of the Lord will be *s*.'
2: 47 daily those who were being *s*.
4: 12 to men by which we must be *s*."
15: 11 of our Lord Jesus that we are *s*,
16: 30 do to be *s*?" They replied,
Ro 5: 9 how much more shall we be *s*
9: 27 only the remnant will be *s*.
10: 1 the Israelites is that they may be *s*.
10: 9 him from the dead, you will be *s*.
10: 13 on the name of the Lord will be *s*."
11: 26 so all Israel will be *s*, as it is written:
1Co 1: 18 to us who are being *s* it is the power
3: 15 will suffer loss; he himself will be *s*,
5: 5 his spirit *s* on the day of the Lord.
10: 33 of many, so that they may be *s*.
15: 2 By this gospel you are *s*,
Eph 2: 5 it is by grace you have been *s*.
2: 8 For it is by grace you have been *s*,
2Th 2: 13 you to be *s* through the sanctifying
1Ti 2: 4 who wants all men to be *s*
2: 15 But women will be *s*
2Ti 1: 9 who has *s* us and called us
Tit 3: 5 He *s* us through the washing
Heb 10: 39 but of those who believe and are *s*.

SAVES (SAVE)
Ps 7: 10 who *s* the upright in heart.
68: 20 Our God is a God who *s*;
145: 19 he hears their cry and *s* them.
1Pe 3: 21 It *s* you by the resurrection

SAVIOR* (SAVE)
Dt 32: 15 and rejected the Rock his *S*.
2Sa 22: 3 stronghold, my refuge and my *s*—
22: 47 Exalted be God, the Rock, my *S!*
1Ch 16: 35 Cry out, "Save us, O God our *S*;
Ps 18: 46 Exalted be God my *S!*
24: 5 and vindication from God his *S*.
25: 5 for you are God my *S*,
27: 9 O God my *S*.
38: 22 O Lord my *S*.
42: 5 my *S* and
42: 11 my *S* and my God.
43: 5 my *S* and my God.
65: 5 O God our *S*,
68: 19 Praise be to the Lord, to God our *S*,
79: 9 Help us, O God our *S*,
85: 4 Restore us again, O God our *S*,
89: 26 my God, the Rock my *S*.'
Isa 17: 10 You have forgotten God your *S*;
19: 20 he will send them a *s* and defender,
43: 3 the Holy One of Israel, your *S*;
43: 11 and apart from me there is no *s*.
45: 15 O God and *S* of Israel.
45: 21 a righteous God and a *S*;
49: 26 that I, the LORD, am your *S*,
60: 16 know that I, the LORD, am your *S*,
62: 11 'See, your *S* comes!
63: 8 and so he became their *S*.
Jer 14: 8 its *S* in times of distress,
Hos 13: 4 no *S* except me.
Mic 7: 7 I wait for God my *S*;
Hab 3: 18 I will be joyful in God my *S*.
Lk 1: 47 and my spirit rejoices in God my *S*,
2: 11 of David a *S* has been born to you;
Jn 4: 42 know that this man really is the *S*
Ac 5: 31 *S* that he might give repentance
13: 23 God has brought to Israel the *S*
Eph 5: 23 his body, of which he is the *S*.
Php 3: 20 we eagerly await a *S* from there,
1Ti 1: 1 by the command of God our *S*
2: 3 This is good, and pleases God our *S*
4: 10 who is the *S* of all men,
2Ti 1: 10 through the appearing of our *S*,
Tit 1: 3 me by the command of God our *S*,
1: 4 the Father and Christ Jesus our *S*.
2: 10 about God our *S* attractive.
2: 13 appearing of our great God and *S*,
3: 4 and love of God our *S* appeared,
3: 6 through Jesus Christ our *S*,
2Pe 1: 1 *S* Jesus Christ have received a faith
1: 11 eternal kingdom of our Lord and *S*
2: 20 and *S* Jesus Christ and are again
3: 2 and *S* through your apostles.
3: 18 and knowledge of our Lord and *S*
1Jn 4: 14 Son to be the *S* of the world.
Jude : 25 to the only God our *S* be glory,

SCALE (SCALES)
Ps 18: 29 with my God I can *s* a wall.

SCALES (SCALE)
Lev 11: 9 may eat any that have fins and *s*.
19: 36 Use honest *s* and honest weights,
Pr 11: 1 The LORD abhors dishonest *s*,
Da 5: 27 You have been weighed on the *s*
Rev 6: 5 Its rider was holding a pair of *s*

SCAPEGOAT (GOAT)
Lev 16: 10 by sending it into the desert as a *s*.

SCARECROW*
Jer 10: 5 Like a *s* in a melon patch,

SCARLET
Jos 2: 21 she tied the *s* cord in the window.
Isa 1: 18 "Though your sins are like *s*,
Mt 27: 28 They stripped him and put a *s* robe

SCATTER (SCATTERED SCATTERS)
Dt 4: 27 The LORD will *s* you
Ne 1: 8 I will *s* you among the nations,
Jer 9: 16 I will *s* them among nations that
30: 11 the nations among which I *s* you,
Zec 10: 9 I *s* them among the peoples,

SCATTERED (SCATTER)
Isa 11: 12 he will assemble the *s* people
Jer 31: 10 'He who *s* Israel will gather them
Zec 2: 6 "for I have *s* you to the four winds
13: 7 and the sheep will be *s*,
Mt 26: 31 and the sheep of the flock will be *s*.'
Jn 11: 52 but also for the *s* children of God,
Ac 8: 4 who had been *s* preached the word
Jas 1: 1 To the twelve tribes *s*
1Pe 1: 1 *s* throughout Pontus, Galatia,

SCATTERS (SCATTER)
Mt 12: 30 he who does not gather with me *s*.

SCEPTER
Ge 49: 10 The *s* will not depart from Judah,
Nu 24: 17 a *s* will rise out of Israel.
Ps 2: 9 You will rule them with an iron *s*;
45: 6 a *s* of justice will be the *s*
Heb 1: 8 and righteousness will be the *s*

Rev 2: 27 'He will rule them with an iron *s*;
12: 5 rule all the nations with an iron *s*.
19: 15 "He will rule them with an iron *s*."

SCHEMES
Pr 6: 18 a heart that devises wicked *s*,
24: 9 The *s* of folly are sin,
2Co 2: 11 For we are not unaware of his *s*.
Eph 6: 11 stand against the devil's *s*.

SCHOLAR*
1Co 1: 20 Where is the *s*? Where is

SCOFFERS
2Pe 3: 3 that in the last days *s* will come,

SCORN (SCORNED SCORNING SCORNS)
Ps 69: 7 For I endure *s* for your sake,
69: 20 *S* has broken my heart
89: 41 he has become the *s*
109: 25 I am an object of *s* to my accusers;
119: 22 Remove from me *s* and contempt,
Mic 6: 16 you will bear the *s* of the nations."

SCORNED (SCORN)
Ps 22: 6 *s* by men and despised

SCORNING (SCORN)
Heb 12: 2 him endured the cross, *s* its shame,

SCORNS (SCORN)
Pr 13: 13 He who *s* instruction will pay for it,
30: 17 that *s* obedience to a mother,

SCORPION
Lk 11: 12 will give him a *s*? If you then,
Rev 9: 5 sting of a *s* when it strikes a man.

SCOUNDREL
Pr 6: 12 A *s* and villain,

SCRIPTURE (SCRIPTURES)
Jn 2: 22 Then they believed the *S*
7: 42 Does not the *S* say that the Christ
10: 35 and the *S* cannot be broken —
Ac 8: 32 was reading this passage of *S*:
1Ti 4: 13 yourself to the public reading of *S*,
2Ti 3: 16 All *S* is God-breathed
2Pe 1: 20 that no prophecy of *S* came about

SCRIPTURES (SCRIPTURE)
Mt 22: 29 because you do not know the *S*
Lk 24: 27 said in all the *S* concerning himself.
24: 45 so they could understand the *S*.
Jn 5: 39 These are the *S* that testify about
Ac 17: 11 examined the *S* every day to see
2Ti 3: 15 you have known the holy *S*,
2Pe 3: 16 as they do the other *S*,

SCROLL
Ps 40: 7 it is written about me in the *s*.
Isa 34: 4 and the sky rolled up like a *s*;
Eze 3: 1 eat what is before you, eat this *s*;
Heb 10: 7 it is written about me in the *s* —
Rev 6: 14 The sky receded like a *s*, rolling up,
10: 8 take the *s* that lies open in the hand

SCUM
1Co 4: 13 this moment we have become the *s*

SEA (SEASHORE)
Ex 14: 16 go through the *s* on dry ground.
Dt 30: 13 "Who will cross the *s* to get it
1Ki 7: 23 He made the *S* of cast metal,
Job 11: 9 and wider than the *s*.
Ps 93: 4 mightier than the breakers of the *s*
95: 5 The *s* is his, for he made it,
Ecc 1: 7 All streams flow into the *s*,
Isa 57: 20 the wicked are like the tossing *s*,
Jnh 1: 4 LORD sent a great wind on the *s*,
Mic 7: 19 iniquities into the depths of the *s*.
Hab 2: 14 as the waters cover the *s*.
Zec 9: 10 His rule will extend from *s* to *s*
Mt 18: 6 drowned in the depths of the *s*.
1Co 10: 1 that they all passed through the *s*.
Jas 1: 6 who doubts is like a wave of the *s*,
Jude : 13 They are wild waves of the *s*,
Rev 10: 2 He planted his right foot on the *s*
13: 1 I saw a beast coming out of the *s*.
20: 13 The *s* gave up the dead that were
21: 1 and there was no longer any *s*.

SEAL (SEALED SEALS)
Ps 40: 9 I do not *s* my lips,
SS 8: 6 Place me like a *s* over your heart,
Da 12: 4 and *s* the words of the scroll
Jn 6: 27 God the Father has placed his *s*
1Co 9: 2 For you are the *s* of my apostleship
2Co 1: 22 set his *s* of ownership on us,
Eph 1: 13 you were marked in him with a *s*,
Rev 6: 3 the Lamb opened the second *s*,
6: 5 When the Lamb opened the third *s*,
6: 7 the Lamb opened the fourth *s*,
6: 9 When he opened the fifth *s*,
6: 12 I watched as he opened the sixth *s*.
8: 1 When he opened the seventh *s*,
9: 4 people who did not have the *s*
22: 10 "Do not *s* up the words

SEALED (SEAL)
Eph 4: 30 with whom you were *s* for the day
2Ti 2: 19 solid foundation stands firm, *s*
Rev 5: 1 on both sides and *s* with seven seals

SEALS (SEAL)
Rev 5: 2 "Who is worthy to break the *s*
6: 1 opened the first of the seven *s*.

SEAMLESS*
Jn 19: 23 This garment was *s*, woven

SEARCH (SEARCHED SEARCHES SEARCHING)
Ps 4: 4 *s* your hearts and be silent.
139: 23 *S* me, O God, and know my heart;
Pr 2: 4 and *s* for it as for hidden treasure,
25: 2 to *s* out a matter is the glory
SS 3: 2 I will *s* for the one my heart loves.
Jer 17: 10 "I the LORD *s* the heart
Eze 34: 11 I myself will *s* for my sheep
34: 16 I will *s* for the lost and bring back
Lk 15: 8 and *s* carefully until she finds it?

SEARCHED (SEARCH)
Ps 139: 1 O LORD, you have *s* me
Ecc 12: 10 The Teacher *s* to find just the right
1Pe 1: 10 *s* intently and with the greatest

SEARCHES (SEARCH)
1Ch 28: 9 for the LORD *s* every heart
Ps 7: 9 who *s* minds and hearts,
Pr 11: 27 but evil comes to him who *s* for it.
20: 27 The lamp of the LORD *s* the spirit
Ro 8: 27 And he who *s* our hearts knows
1Co 2: 10 The Spirit *s* all things,
Rev 2: 23 will know that I am he who *s* hearts

SEARCHING (SEARCH)
Jdg 5: 15 there was much *s* of heart.
Am 8: 12 *s* for the word of the LORD,

SEARED
1Ti 4: 2 whose consciences have been *s*

SEASHORE (SEA)
Jos 11: 4 as numerous as the sand on the *s*.
1Ki 4: 29 as measureless as the sand on the *s*.

SEASON (SEASONED SEASONS)
Lev 26: 4 I will send you rain in its *s*,
Ps 1: 3 which yields its fruit in *s*
2Ti 4: 2 be prepared in *s* and out of *s*;

SEASONED* (SEASON)
Col 4: 6 full of grace, *s* with salt,

SEASONS (SEASON)
Ge 1: 14 signs to mark *s* and days and years,
Gal 4: 10 and months and *s* and years!

SEAT (SEATED SEATS)
Ps 1: 1 or sit in the *s* of mockers.
Pr 31: 23 where he takes his *s*
Da 7: 9 and the Ancient of Days took his *s*.
Lk 14: 9 say to you, 'Give this man your *s*.'
2Co 5: 10 before the judgment *s* of Christ,

SEATED (SEAT)
Ps 47: 8 God is *s* on his holy throne.
Isa 6: 1 I saw the Lord *s* on a throne,
Lk 22: 69 of Man will be *s* at the right hand
Eph 1: 20 and *s* him at his right hand
2: 6 and *s* us with him in the heavenly
Col 3: 1 where Christ is *s* at the right hand
Rev 14: 14 *s* on the cloud was one "like a son
20: 11 white throne and him who was *s*

SEATS (SEAT)
Lk 11: 43 you love the most important *s*

SECLUSION*
Lk 1: 24 and for five months remained in *s*.

SECRET (SECRETLY SECRETS)
Dt 29: 29 The *s* things belong
Jdg 16: 6 Tell me the *s* of your great strength
Ps 90: 8 our *s* sins in the light
139: 15 when I was made in the *s* place.
Pr 11: 13 but a trustworthy man keeps a *s*.
21: 14 A gift given in *s* soothes anger,
Jer 23: 24 Can anyone hide in *s* places
Mt 6: 4 so that your giving may be in *s*.
6: 18 who sees what is done in *s*,
Mk 4: 11 "The *s* of the kingdom
1Co 2: 7 No, we speak of God's *s* wisdom,
4: 1 entrusted with the *s* things of God.
2Co 4: 2 we have renounced *s* and shameful
Eph 5: 12 what the disobedient do in *s*.
Php 4: 12 I have learned the *s*

SECRETLY (SECRET)
2Pe 2: 1 They will *s* introduce destructive
Jude : 4 about long ago have *s* slipped

SECRETS (SECRET)
Ps 44: 21 since he knows the *s* of the heart?
Ro 2: 16 day when God will judge men's *s*
1Co 14: 25 the *s* of his heart will be laid bare.
Rev 2: 24 Satan's so-called deep *s* (I will not

SECURE (SECURITY)
Dt 33: 12 beloved of the LORD rest *s* in him,
Ps 16: 5 you have made my lot *s*.
16: 9 my body also will rest *s*,
112: 8 His heart is *s*, he will have no fear;
Pr 14: 26 fears the LORD has a *s* fortress,
Heb 6: 19 an anchor for the soul, firm and *s*.
2Pe 3: 17 and fall from your *s* position.

SECURITY (SECURE)
Job 31: 24 or said to pure gold, 'You are my *s*,'

SEED (SEEDS SEEDTIME)
Ge 1: 11 on the land that bear fruit with *s*
Isa 55: 10 so that it yields *s* for the sower
Mt 13: 3 "A farmer went out to sow his *s*.
13: 31 of heaven is like a mustard *s*,
17: 20 have faith as small as a mustard *s*,
Lk 8: 11 of the parable: The *s* is the word
1Co 3: 6 I planted the *s*, Apollos watered it,
2Co 9: 10 he who supplies *s* to the sower
Gal 3: 29 then you are Abraham's *s*,
1Pe 1: 23 not of perishable *s*,
1Jn 3: 9 because God's *s* remains in him;

SEEDS (SEED)
Jn 12: 24 But if it dies, it produces many *s*.
Gal 3: 16 Scripture does not say "and to *s*,"

SEEDTIME* (SEED)
Ge 8: 22 *s* and harvest,

SEEK (SEEKING SEEKS SELF-SEEKING SOUGHT)
Lev 19: 18 Do not *s* revenge or bear a grudge
Dt 4: 29 if from there you *s* the LORD your
1Ki 22: 5 "First *s* the counsel of the LORD."
1Ch 28: 9 If you *s* him, he will be found
2Ch 7: 14 themselves and pray and *s* my face
15: 2 If you *s* him, he will be found
Ps 34: 10 those who *s* the LORD lack no
105: 3 of those who *s* the LORD rejoice.
105: 4 *s* his face always.
119: 2 and *s* him with all their heart.
119: 10 I *s* you with all my heart;
119: 176 *S* your servant,
Pr 8: 17 and those who *s* me find me.
18: 15 the ears of the wise *s* it out.
25: 27 is it honorable to *s* one's own honor
28: 5 those who *s* the LORD understand
Isa 55: 6 *S* the LORD while he may be
65: 1 found by those who did not *s* me.
Jer 29: 13 You will *s* me and find me
Hos 10: 12 for it is time to *s* the LORD,
Am 5: 4 "*S* me and live;
Zep 2: 3 *S* the LORD, all you humble
Mt 6: 33 But *s* first his kingdom
7: 7 and it will be given to you; *s*
Lk 12: 31 *s* his kingdom, and these things will
19: 10 For the Son of Man came to *s*
Jn 5: 30 for I *s* not to please myself
Ro 10: 20 found by those who did not *s* me;
1Co 7: 27 you married? Do not *s* a divorce.
10: 24 Nobody should *s* his own good,
Heb 11: 6 rewards those who earnestly *s* him.
1Pe 3: 11 he must *s* peace and pursue it.

SEEKING (SEEK)
2Ch 30: 19 who sets his heart on *s* God —
Pr 20: 18 Make plans by *s* advice;
Mal 3: 1 the Lord you are *s* will come
Jn 8: 50 I am not *s* glory for myself;
1Co 10: 33 For I am not *s* my own good

SEEKS (SEEK)
Pr 11: 27 He who *s* good finds good will,
Mt 7: 8 he who *s* finds; and to him who
Jn 4: 23 the kind of worshipers the Father *s*.
Ro 3: 11 no one who *s* God.

SEER
1Sa 9: 9 of today used to be called a *s*.)

SELF-CONTROL* (CONTROL)
Pr 25: 28 is a man who lacks *s*.

Ac 24: 25 s and the judgment to come,
1Co 7: 5 you because of your lack of s.
Gal 5: 23 faithfulness, gentleness and s.
2Ti 3: 3 slanderous, without s, brutal,
2Pe 1: 6 and to knowledge, s; and to s,

SELF-CONTROLLED* (CONTROL)
1Th 5: 6 are asleep, but let us be alert and s.
5: 8 let us be s, putting on faith and love
1Ti 3: 2 s, respectable, hospitable,
Tit 1: 8 who is s, upright, holy
2: 2 worthy of respect, s, and sound
2: 5 to be s and pure, to be busy at home
2: 6 encourage the young men to be s.
2: 12 to live s, upright and godly lives
1Pe 1: 13 prepare your minds for action; be s;
4: 7 and s so that you can pray.
5: 8 Be s and alert.

SELF-DISCIPLINE* (DISCIPLINE)
2Ti 1: 7 a spirit of power, of love and of s.

SELF-INDULGENCE*
Mt 23: 25 inside they are full of greed and s.
Jas 5: 5 lived on earth in luxury and s.

SELF-SEEKING* (SEEK)
Ro 2: 8 But for those who are s
1Co 13: 5 it is not s, it is not easily angered,

SELFISH*
Ps 119: 36 and not toward s gain.
Pr 18: 1 An unfriendly man pursues s ends;
Gal 5: 20 fits of rage, s ambition, dissensions,
Php 1: 17 preach Christ out of s ambition,
2: 3 Do nothing out of s ambition
Jas 3: 14 and s ambition in your hearts,
3: 16 you have envy and s ambition,

SELL (SELLING SELLS SOLD)
Ge 25: 31 "First s me your birthright."
Mk 10: 21 s everything you have
Rev 13: 17 or s unless he had the mark,

SELLING (SELL)
Lk 17: 28 buying and s, planting and building

SELLS (SELL)
Pr 31: 24 makes linen garments and s them,

SEND (SENDING SENDS SENT)
Ps 43: 3 S forth your light and your truth,
Isa 6: 8 S me!" He said, "Go and tell this
Mal 3: 1 "See, I will s my messenger,
Mt 9: 38 to s out workers into his harvest
24: 31 And he will s his angels
Mk 1: 2 I will s my messenger ahead of you,
Lk 20: 13 I will s my son, whom I love;
Jn 3: 17 For God did not s his Son
16: 7 but if I go, I will s him to you.
1Co 1: 17 For Christ did not s me to baptize,

SENDING (SEND)
Mt 10: 16 I am s you out like sheep
Jn 20: 21 Father has sent me, I am s you."
Ro 8: 3 God did by s his own Son

SENDS (SEND)
Ps 57: 3 God s his love and his faithfulness.

SENNACHERIB
Assyrian king whose siege of Jerusalem was overthrown by the LORD following prayer of Hezekiah and Isaiah (2Ki 18:13 – 19:37; 2Ch 32:1 – 21; Isa 36 – 37).

SENSES*
Lk 15: 17 "When he came to his s, he said,
1Co 15: 34 Come back to your s as you ought,
2Ti 2: 26 and that they will come to their s

SENSITIVITY*
Eph 4: 19 Having lost all s, they have given

SENSUAL* (SENSUALITY)
Col 2: 23 value in restraining s indulgence.
1Ti 5: 11 For when their s desires overcome

SENSUALITY* (SENSUAL)
Eph 4: 19 have given themselves over to s

SENT (SEND)
Ex 3: 14 to the Israelites: 'I AM has s me
Isa 55: 11 achieve the purpose for which I s it.
61: 1 He has s me to bind up
Jer 28: 9 as one truly s by the LORD only
Mt 10: 40 me receives the one who s me.
Mk 6: 7 he s them out two by two
Lk 4: 18 He has s me to proclaim freedom
9: 2 and he s them out to preach
10: 16 rejects me rejects him who s me."
Jn 1: 6 There came a man who was s
4: 34 "is to do the will of him who s me
5: 24 believes him who s me has eternal
8: 16 I stand with the Father, who s me.
9: 4 must do the work of him who s me.
16: 5 "Now I am going to him who s me,
17: 3 and Jesus Christ, whom you have s.
17: 18 As you s me into the world,
20: 21 As the Father has s me, I am
Ro 10: 15 can they preach unless they are s?
Gal 4: 4 God s his Son, born of a woman,
1Jn 4: 10 but that he loved us and s his Son

SENTENCE
2Co 1: 9 in our hearts we felt the s of death.

SEPARATE (SEPARATED SEPARATES SEPARATION)
Mt 19: 6 has joined together, let man not s."
Ro 8: 35 Who shall s us from the love
1Co 7: 10 wife must not s from her husband.
2Co 6: 17 and be s, says the Lord.
Eph 2: 12 at that time you were s from Christ,

SEPARATED (SEPARATE)
Isa 59: 2 But your iniquities have s
Eph 4: 18 in their understanding and s

SEPARATES (SEPARATE)
Pr 16: 28 and a gossip s close friends.
17: 9 repeats the matter s close friends.
Mt 25: 32 as a shepherd s the sheep

SEPARATION (SEPARATE)
Nu 6: 2 a vow of s to the LORD

SERAPHS*
Isa 6: 2 Above him were s, each
6: 6 Then one of the s flew to me

SERIOUSNESS*
Tit 2: 7 s and soundness of speech that

SERPENT (SERPENT'S)
Ge 3: 1 the s was more crafty than any
Isa 27: 1 Leviathan the coiling s;
Rev 12: 9 that ancient s called the devil
20: 2 that ancient s, who is the devil,

SERPENT'S (SERPENT)
2Co 11: 3 Eve was deceived by the s cunning,

SERVANT (SERVANTS)
Ex 14: 31 trust in him and in Moses his s.
21: 2 "If you buy a Hebrew s, he is
1Sa 3: 10 "Speak, for your s is listening."
2Sa 7: 19 the future of the house of your s.
1Ki 20: 40 While your s was busy here
Job 1: 8 "Have you considered my s Job?
Ps 19: 11 By them is your s warned;
19: 13 Keep your s also from willful sins;
31: 16 Let your face shine on your s;
89: 3 I have sworn to David my s,
Pr 14: 35 A king delights in a wise s,
17: 2 wise s will rule over a disgraceful
22: 7 and the borrower is s to the lender.
31: 15 and portions for her s girls.
Isa 41: 8 "But you, O Israel, my s,
49: 3 He said to me, "You are my s,
53: 11 my righteous s will justify
Zec 3: 8 going to bring my s, the Branch.
Mal 1: 6 his father, and a s his master.
Mt 8: 13 his s was healed at that very hour.
20: 26 great among you must be your s,
24: 45 Who then is the faithful and wise s,
25: 21 'Well done, good and faithful s!
Lk 1: 38 I am the Lord's s," Mary answered.
16: 13 "No s can serve two masters.
Jn 12: 26 and where I am, my s also will be.
Ro 1: 1 a s of Christ Jesus, called
13: 4 For he is God's s to do you good.
Php 2: 7 taking the very nature of a s,
Col 1: 23 of which I, Paul, have become a s.
2Ti 2: 24 And the Lord's s must not quarrel;

SERVANTS (SERVANT)
Lev 25: 55 for the Israelites belong to me as s.
2Ki 17: 13 to you through my s the prophets."
Ezr 5: 11 "We are the s of the God of heaven
Ps 34: 22 The LORD redeems his s;
103: 21 you his s who do his will.
104: 4 flames of fire his s.
Isa 44: 26 who carries out the words of his s
65: 8 so will I do in behalf of my s;
65: 13 my s will drink,
Lk 17: 10 should say, 'We are unworthy s;
Jn 15: 15 longer call you s, because a servant
Ro 13: 6 for the authorities are God's s,
1Co 3: 5 And what is Paul? Only s,
Heb 1: 7 his s flames of fire."

SERVE (SERVED SERVES SERVICE SERVING)
Dt 10: 12 to s the LORD your God
11: 13 and to s him with all your heart
13: 4 s him and hold fast to him.
28: 47 you did not s the LORD your
Jos 22: 5 and to s him with all your heart
24: 15 this day whom you will s,
24: 18 We too will s the LORD,
1Sa 7: 3 to the LORD and s him only,
12: 20 but s the LORD with all your heart
12: 24 s him faithfully with all your heart;
2Ch 19: 9 "You must s faithfully
Job 36: 11 If they obey and s him,
Ps 2: 11 S the LORD with fear
Da 3: 17 the God we s is able to save us
Mt 4: 10 Lord your God, and s him only.'"
6: 24 "No one can s two masters.
20: 28 but to s, and to give his life
Ro 12: 7 If it is serving, let him s;
Gal 5: 13 rather, s one another in love.
Eph 6: 7 S wholeheartedly,
1Ti 6: 2 they are to s them even better,
Heb 9: 14 so that we may s the living God!
1Pe 4: 10 gift he has received to s others,
5: 2 greedy for money, but eager to s;
Rev 5: 10 kingdom and priests to s our God,

SERVED (SERVE)
Mt 20: 28 Son of Man did not come to be s,
Jn 12: 2 Martha s, while Lazarus was
Ac 17: 25 And he is not s by human hands,
Ro 1: 25 and s created things rather
1Ti 3: 13 Those who have s well gain

SERVES (SERVE)
Lk 22: 26 one who rules like the one who s.
22: 27 But I am among you as one who s.
Jn 12: 26 Whoever s me must follow me;
Ro 14: 18 because anyone who s Christ
1Pe 4: 11 If anyone s, he should do it

SERVICE (SERVE)
Lk 9: 62 fit for s in the kingdom
12: 35 "Be dressed ready for s
Ro 15: 17 in Christ Jesus in my s to God.
1Co 12: 5 There are different kinds of s,
16: 15 themselves to the s of the saints.
2Co 9: 12 This s that you perform is not only
Eph 4: 12 God's people for works of s,
Rev 2: 19 and faith, your s and perseverance,

SERVING (SERVE)
Jos 24: 15 if s the LORD seems undesirable
2Ch 12: 8 learn the difference between s me
Ro 12: 7 If it is s, let him serve;
12: 11 your spiritual fervor, s the Lord.
16: 18 people are not s our Lord Christ,
Eph 6: 7 as if you were s the Lord, not men,
Col 3: 24 It is the Lord Christ you are s.
2Ti 2: 4 No one s as a soldier gets involved

SETH
Ge 4: 25 birth to a son and named him S,

SETTLE
Mt 5: 25 "S matters quickly
2Th 3: 12 in the Lord Jesus Christ to s down

SEVEN (SEVENS SEVENTH)
Ge 7: 2 Take with you s of every kind
Jos 6: 4 march around the city s times,
1Ki 19: 18 Yet I reserve s thousand in Israel —
Pr 6: 16 s that are detestable to him:
24: 16 a righteous man falls s times,
Isa 4: 1 In that day s women
Da 9: 25 comes, there will be s 'sevens,'
Mt 18: 21 Up to s times?" Jesus answered,
Lk 11: 26 takes s other spirits more wicked
Ro 11: 4 for myself s thousand who have not
Rev 1: 4 To the s churches in the province
6: 1 opened the first of the s seals.
8: 2 and to them were given s trumpets.
10: 4 And when the s thunders spoke,
15: 7 to the s angels s golden bowls filled

SEVENS* (SEVEN)
Da 9: 24 "Seventy 's' are decreed
9: 25 will be seven 's,' and sixty-two 's.'
9: 26 the sixty-two 's,' the Anointed

SEVENTH (SEVEN)
Ge 2: 2 By the s day God had finished
Ex 20: 10 but the s day is a Sabbath
23: 11 but during the s year let the land lie
23: 12 but on the s day do not work,
Heb 4: 4 "And on the s day God rested

SEVERE
2Co 8: 2 Out of the most s trial, their
1Th 1: 6 of the Lord; in spite of s suffering,

SEWED (SEWS)
Ge 3: 7 so they *s* fig leaves together

SEWS (SEWED)
Mt 9: 16 No one *s* a patch of unshrunk cloth

SEXUAL (SEXUALLY)
Ex 22: 19 "Anyone who has *s* relations
Lev 18: 6 relative to have *s* relations.
18: 7 father by having *s* relations
18: 20 Do not have *s* relations with
Mt 15: 19 murder, adultery, *s* immorality,
Ac 15: 20 by idols, from *s* immorality,
1Co 5: 1 reported that there is *s* immorality
6: 13 body is not meant for *s* immorality,
6: 18 Flee from *s* immorality.
10: 8 should not commit *s* immorality,
2Co 12: 21 *s* sin and debauchery
Gal 5: 19 *s* immorality, impurity
Eph 5: 3 even a hint of *s* immorality,
Col 3: 5 *s* immorality, impurity, lust,
1Th 4: 3 that you should avoid *s* immorality

SEXUALLY (SEXUAL)
1Co 5: 9 to associate with *s* immoral people
6: 9 Neither the *s* immoral nor idolaters
6: 18 he who sins *s* sins against his own
Heb 12: 16 See that no one is *s* immoral,
13: 4 the adulterer and all the *s* immoral.
Rev 21: 8 the murderers, the *s* immoral,

SHADE
Ps 121: 5 the LORD is your *s*
Isa 25: 4 and a *s* from the heat.

SHADOW
Ps 17: 8 hide me in the *s* of your wings
23: 4 through the valley of the *s* of death,
36: 7 find refuge in the *s* of your wings.
91: 1 will rest in the *s* of the Almighty.
Isa 51: 16 covered you with the *s* of my hand
Col 2: 17 These are a *s* of the things that
Heb 8: 5 and *s* of what is in heaven.
10: 1 The law is only a *s*

SHADRACH
Hebrew exiled to Babylon; name changed from Hananiah (Da 1:6–7). Refused defilement by food (Da 1:8–20). Refused to worship idol (Da 3:1–18); saved from furnace (Da 3:19–30).

SHAKE (SHAKEN SHAKING)
Ps 64: 8 all who see them will *s* their heads
99: 1 let the earth *s*.
Hag 2: 6 I will once more *s* the heavens
Heb 12: 26 "Once more I will *s* not only

SHAKEN (SHAKE)
Ps 16: 8 I will not be *s*.
30: 6 "I will never be *s*."
62: 2 he is my fortress, I will never be *s*.
112: 6 Surely he will never be *s*;
Isa 54: 10 Though the mountains be *s*
Mt 24: 29 and the heavenly bodies will be *s*.'
Lk 6: 38 *s* together and running over,
Ac 2: 25 I will not be *s*.
Heb 12: 27 that what cannot be *s* may remain.

SHAKING* (SHAKE)
Ps 22: 7 they hurl insults, *s* their heads:
Mt 27: 39 insults at him, *s* their heads
Mk 15: 29 *s* their heads and saying, "So!

SHALLUM
King of Israel (2Ki 15:10–16).

SHAME (ASHAMED SHAMED SHAMEFUL)
Ps 25: 3 will ever be put to *s*,
34: 5 their faces are never covered with *s*
69: 6 not be put to *s* because of me,
Pr 13: 18 discipline comes to poverty and *s*,
18: 13 that is his folly and his *s*.
Jer 8: 9 The wise will be put to *s*;
8: 12 No, they have no *s* at all;
Ro 9: 33 trusts in him will never be put to *s*."
10: 11 trusts in him will never be put to *s*."
1Co 1: 27 things of the world to *s* the wise;
Heb 12: 2 endured the cross, scorning its *s*,

SHAMED (SHAME)
Jer 10: 14 every goldsmith is *s* by his idols.
Joel 2: 26 never again will my people be *s*.

SHAMEFUL (SHAME)
2Co 4: 2 have renounced secret and *s* ways;
2Pe 2: 2 Many will follow their *s* ways
Rev 21: 27 nor will anyone who does what is *s*

SHAMGAR
Judge; killed 600 Philistines (Jdg 3:31).

SHAPE (SHAPES SHAPING)
Job 38: 14 The earth takes *s* like clay

SHAPES (SHAPE)
Isa 44: 10 Who *s* a god and casts an idol,

SHAPING (SHAPE)
Jer 18: 4 the pot he was *s* from the clay was

SHARE (SHARED SHARERS SHARES SHARING)
Ge 21: 10 that slave woman's son will never *s*
Lev 19: 17 frankly so you will not *s* in his guilt.
Dt 10: 9 That is why the Levites have no *s*
1Sa 30: 24 All will *s* alike."
Eze 18: 20 The son will not *s* the guilt
Mt 25: 21 and *s* your master's happiness!'
Lk 3: 11 "The man with two tunics should *s*
Ro 8: 17 if indeed we *s* in his sufferings
12: 13 *S* with God's people who are
2Co 1: 7 as you *s* in our sufferings,
Gal 4: 30 the slave woman's son will never *s*
6: 6 in the word must *s* all good things
Eph 4: 28 something to *s* with those in need.
Col 1: 12 you to *s* in the inheritance
2Th 2: 14 that you might *s* in the glory
1Ti 5: 22 and do not *s* in the sins of others.
6: 18 and to be generous and willing to *s*.
2Ti 2: 6 the first to receive a *s* of the crops.
Heb 12: 10 that we may *s* in his holiness.
13: 16 to do good and to *s* with others,
Rev 22: 19 from him his *s* in the tree of life

SHARED (SHARE)
Ps 41: 9 he who *s* my bread,
Ac 4: 32 but they *s* everything they had.
Heb 2: 14 he too *s* in their humanity so that

SHARERS* (SHARE)
Eph 3: 6 and *s* together in the promise

SHARES (SHARE)
Pr 22: 9 for he *s* his food with the poor.
Jn 13: 18 'He who *s* my bread has lifted up

SHARING (SHARE)
1Co 9: 10 so in the hope of *s* in the harvest.
2Co 9: 13 for your generosity in *s* with them
Php 3: 10 the fellowship of *s* in his sufferings,
Phm : 6 you may be active in *s* your faith,

SHARON
SS 2: 1 I am a rose of *S*,

SHARP (SHARPENED SHARPENS SHARPER)
Pr 5: 4 *s* as a double-edged sword.
Isa 5: 28 Their arrows are *s*,
Rev 1: 16 came a *s* double-edged sword.
19: 15 Out of his mouth comes a *s* sword

SHARPENED (SHARP)
Eze 21: 9 *s* and polished—

SHARPENS* (SHARP)
Pr 27: 17 As iron *s* iron,
27: 17 so one man *s* another.

SHARPER* (SHARP)
Heb 4: 12 *S* than any double-edged sword,

SHATTER (SHATTERED SHATTERS)
Jer 51: 20 with you I *s* nations,

SHATTERED (SHATTER)
1Sa 2: 10 who oppose the LORD will be *s*.
Job 16: 12 All was well with me, but he *s* me;
17: 11 days have passed, my plans are *s*,
Ecc 12: 6 before the pitcher is *s* at the spring,

SHATTERS (SHATTER)
Ps 46: 9 he breaks the bow and *s* the spear,

SHAVED
Jdg 16: 17 my head were *s*, my strength would
1Co 11: 5 it is just as though her head were *s*.

SHEAF (SHEAVES)
Lev 23: 11 is to wave the *s* before the LORD

SHEARER* (SHEARERS)
Ac 8: 32 and as a lamb before the *s* is silent,

SHEARERS (SHEARER)
Isa 53: 7 and as a sheep before her *s* is silent,

SHEAVES (SHEAF)
Ge 37: 7 while your *s* gathered around mine
Ps 126: 6 carrying *s* with him.

SHEBA
1. Benjamite who rebelled against David (2Sa 20).
2. See QUEEN.

SHECHEM
1. Raped Jacob's daughter Dinah; killed by Simeon and Levi (Ge 34).
2. City where Joshua renewed the covenant (Jos 24).

SHED (SHEDDING SHEDS)
Ge 9: 6 by man shall his blood be *s*;
Pr 6: 17 hands that *s* innocent blood,
Ro 3: 15 "Their feet are swift to *s* blood;
Col 1: 20 through his blood, *s* on the cross.

SHEDDING (SHED)
Heb 9: 22 without the *s* of blood there is no

SHEDS (SHED)
Ge 9: 6 "Whoever *s* the blood of man,

SHEEP (SHEEP'S SHEEPSKINS)
Nu 27: 17 LORD's people will not be like *s*
Dt 17: 1 a *s* that has any defect or flaw in it,
1Sa 15: 14 "What then is this bleating of *s*
Ps 44: 22 we are considered as *s*
78: 52 led them like *s* through the desert.
100: 3 we are his people, the *s*
119: 176 I have strayed like a lost *s*.
SS 4: 2 teeth are like a flock of *s* just shorn,
Isa 53: 6 We all, like *s*, have gone astray,
53: 7 as a *s* before her shearers is silent,
Jer 50: 6 "My people have been lost *s*;
Eze 34: 11 I myself will search for my *s*
Zec 13: 7 and the *s* will be scattered,
Mt 9: 36 helpless, like *s* without a shepherd.
10: 16 I am sending you out like *s*
12: 11 "If any of you has a *s* and it falls
18: 13 he is happier about that one *s*
25: 32 as a shepherd separates the *s*
Jn 10: 1 man who does not enter the *s* pen
10: 3 He calls his own *s* by name
10: 7 the truth, I am the gate for the *s*.
10: 15 and I lay down my life for the *s*.
10: 27 My *s* listen to my voice; I know
21: 17 Jesus said, "Feed my *s*.
1Pe 2: 25 For you were like *s* going astray,

SHEEP'S* (SHEEP)
Mt 7: 15 They come to you in *s* clothing,

SHEEPSKINS* (SHEEP)
Heb 11: 37 They went about in *s* and goatskins

SHEKEL
Ex 30: 13 This half *s* is an offering

SHELTER
Ps 27: 5 me in the *s* of his tabernacle
31: 20 In the *s* of your presence you hide
55: 8 I would hurry to my place of *s*,
61: 4 take refuge in the *s* of your wings.
91: 1 in the *s* of the Most High
Ecc 7: 12 Wisdom is a *s*
Isa 4: 6 It will be a *s* and shade
25: 4 a *s* from the storm
32: 2 Each man will be like a *s*
58: 7 the poor wanderer with *s*—

SHEM
Son of Noah (Ge 5:32; 6:10). Blessed (Ge 9:26). Descendants (Ge 10:21–31; 11:10–32).

SHEPHERD (SHEPHERDS)
Ge 48: 15 the God who has been my *s*
49: 24 because of the *S*, the Rock of Israel
Nu 27: 17 will not be like sheep without a *s*."
2Sa 7: 7 commanded to *s* my people Israel,
1Ki 22: 17 on the hills like sheep without a *s*,
Ps 23: 1 LORD is my *s*, I shall not be in want.
28: 9 be their *s* and carry them forever.
80: 1 Hear us, O *S* of Israel,
Isa 40: 11 He tends his flock like a *s*:
Jer 31: 10 will watch over his flock like a *s*.'
Eze 34: 5 scattered because there was no *s*,
34: 12 As a *s* looks after his scattered
Zec 11: 9 and said, "I will not be your *s*.
11: 17 "Woe to the worthless *s*,
13: 7 "Strike the *s*,
Mt 2: 6 who will be the *s* of my people
9: 36 and helpless, like sheep without a *s*.
26: 31 "'I will strike the *s*,
Jn 10: 11 The good *s* lays down his life
10: 14 "I am the good *s*; I know my sheep
10: 16 there shall be one flock and one *s*.
Heb 13: 20 that great *S* of the sheep, equip you
1Pe 5: 4 And when the Chief *S* appears,
Rev 7: 17 of the throne will be their *s*;

SHEPHERDS (SHEPHERD)
Jer 23: 1 "Woe to the *s* who are destroying
50: 6 their *s* have led them astray
Eze 34: 2 prophesy against the *s* of Israel;

Lk 2: 8 there were *s* living out in the fields
Ac 20: 28 Be *s* of the church of God,
1Pe 5: 2 Be *s* of God's flock that is
Jude : 12 *s* who feed only themselves.

SHIBBOLETH*
Jdg 12: 6 No," they said, "All right, say '*S*.'"

SHIELD (SHIELDED SHIELDS)
Ge 15: 1 I am your *s*,
2Sa 22: 3 my *s* and the horn of my salvation.
22: 36 You give me your *s* of victory;
Ps 3: 3 But you are a *s* around me,
5: 12 with your favor as with a *s*.
7: 10 My *s* is God Most High,
18: 2 He is my *s* and the horn
28: 7 LORD is my strength and my *s*;
33: 20 he is our help and our *s*.
84: 11 For the LORD God is a sun and *s*;
91: 4 his faithfulness will be your *s*
115: 9 he is their help and *s*.
119: 114 You are my refuge and my *s*;
144: 2 my *s*, in whom I take refuge,
Pr 2: 7 he is a *s* to those whose walk is
30: 5 he is a *s* to those who take refuge
Eph 6: 16 to all this, take up the *s* of faith,

SHIELDED (SHIELD)
1Pe 1: 5 through faith are *s* by God's power

SHIELDS (SHIELD)
Dt 33: 12 for he *s* him all day long,

SHIFTLESS*
Pr 19: 15 and the *s* man goes hungry.

SHIMEI
Cursed David (2Sa 16:5–14); spared (2Sa 19:16–23). Killed by Solomon (1Ki 2:8–9, 36–46).

SHINE (SHINES SHINING SHONE)
Nu 6: 25 the LORD make his face *s*
Job 33: 30 that the light of life may *s* on him.
Ps 4: 6 Let the light of your face *s* upon us,
37: 6 make your righteousness *s* like
67: 1 and make his face *s* upon us; *Selah*
80: 1 between the cherubim, *s* forth
118: 27 and he has made his light *s* upon us.
Isa 60: 1 "Arise, *s*, for your light has come,
Da 12: 3 are wise will *s* like the brightness
Mt 5: 16 let your light *s* before men,
13: 43 the righteous will *s* like the sun
2Co 4: 6 made his light *s* in our hearts
Eph 5: 14 and Christ will *s* on you."
Php 2: 15 in which you *s* like stars

SHINES (SHINE)
Ps 50: 2 God *s* forth.
Pr 13: 9 The light of the righteous *s* brightly
Jn 1: 5 The light *s* in the darkness,

SHINING (SHINE)
Pr 4: 18 *s* ever brighter till the full light
2Pe 1: 19 as to a light *s* in a dark place,
Rev 1: 16 His face was like the sun *s*

SHIPS
Pr 31: 14 She is like the merchant *s*,

SHIPWRECKED*
2Co 11: 25 I was stoned, three times I was *s*,
1Ti 1: 19 and so have *s* their faith.

SHISHAK
1Ki 14: 25 *S* king of Egypt attacked Jerusalem
2Ch 12: 2 *S* king of Egypt attacked Jerusalem

SHOCKING*
Jer 5: 30 "A horrible and *s* thing

SHONE (SHINE)
Mt 17: 2 His face *s* like the sun,
Lk 2: 9 glory of the Lord *s* around them,
Rev 21: 11 It *s* with the glory of God,

SHOOT
Isa 53: 2 up before him like a tender *s*,
Ro 11: 17 and you, though a wild olive *s*,

SHORE
Lk 5: 3 asked him to put out a little from *s*.

SHORT (SHORTENED)
Nu 11: 23 "Is the LORD's arm too *s*?
Isa 50: 2 Was my arm too *s* to ransom you?
59: 1 of the LORD is not too *s* to save,
Mt 24: 22 If those days had not been cut *s*,
Ro 3: 23 and fall *s* of the glory of God,
1Co 7: 29 brothers, is that the time is *s*.
Heb 4: 1 of you be found to have fallen *s* of it
Rev 20: 3 he must be set free for a *s* time.

SHORTENED (SHORT)
Mt 24: 22 of the elect those days will be *s*.

SHOULDER (SHOULDERS)
Zep 3: 9 and serve him *s* to *s*.

SHOULDERS (SHOULDER)
Dt 33: 12 LORD loves rests between his *s*."
Isa 9: 6 and the government will be on his *s*
Lk 15: 5 he joyfully puts it on his *s*

SHOUT (SHOUTED)
Ps 47: 1 *s* to God with cries of joy.
66: 1 *S* with joy to God, all the earth!
95: 1 let us *s* aloud to the Rock
98: 4 *S* for joy to the LORD, all the earth
100: 1 *S* for joy to the LORD, all the earth
Isa 12: 6 *S* aloud and sing for joy, people
26: 19 wake up and *s* for joy.
35: 6 the mute tongue *s* for joy.
40: 9 lift up your voice with a *s*,
42: 2 He will not *s* or cry out,
44: 23 *s* aloud, O earth beneath.
54: 1 burst into song, *s* for joy,
Zec 9: 9 *S*, Daughter of Jerusalem!

SHOUTED (SHOUT)
Job 38: 7 and all the angels *s* for joy?

SHOW (SHOWED)
Ex 18: 20 and *s* them the way to live
33: 18 Moses said, "Now *s* me your glory
2Sa 22: 26 the faithful you *s* yourself faithful,
1Ki 2: 2 "So be strong, *s* yourself a man,
Ps 17: 7 *S* the wonder of your great love,
25: 4 *S* me your ways, O LORD,
39: 4 "*S* me, O LORD, my life's end
85: 7 *S* us your unfailing love, O LORD,
143: 8 *S* me the way I should go,
Pr 23: 4 have the wisdom to *s* restraint.
SS 2: 14 *s* me your face,
Isa 5: 16 the holy God will *s* himself holy
30: 18 he rises to *s* you compassion.
Eze 28: 25 I will *s* myself holy among them
Joel 2: 30 I will *s* wonders in the heavens
Zec 7: 9 *s* mercy and compassion
Ac 2: 19 I will *s* wonders in the heaven
10: 34 it is that God does not *s* favoritism
1Co 12: 31 now I will *s* you the most excellent
Eph 2: 7 ages he might *s* the incomparable
Tit 2: 7 In your teaching *s* integrity,
Jas 2: 18 I will *s* you my faith by what I do.
Jude : 23 to others *s* mercy, mixed with fear

SHOWED (SHOW)
1Ki 3: 3 Solomon *s* his love for the LORD
Lk 24: 40 he *s* them his hands and feet.
1Jn 4: 9 This is how God *s* his love

SHOWERS
Eze 34: 26 in season; there will be *s* of blessing
Hos 10: 12 and *s* righteousness on you.

SHREWD
2Sa 22: 27 to the crooked you show yourself *s*.
Mt 10: 16 Therefore be as *s* as snakes and

SHRINK (SHRINKS)
Heb 10: 39 But we are not of those who *s* back

SHRINKS* (SHRINK)
Heb 10: 38 And if he *s* back,

SHRIVEL
Isa 64: 6 we all *s* up like a leaf,

SHUDDER
Eze 32: 10 and their kings will *s* with horror

SHUHITE
Job 2: 11 Bildad the *S* and Zophar

SHUN* (SHUNS)
Job 28: 28 and to *s* evil is understanding.'"
Pr 3: 7 fear the LORD and *s* evil.

SHUNS (SHUN)
Job 1: 8 a man who fears God and *s* evil."
Pr 14: 16 man fears the LORD and *s* evil,

SHUT
Ge 7: 16 Then the LORD *s* him in.
Isa 22: 22 what he opens no one can *s*,
60: 11 they will never be *s*, day or night,
Da 6: 22 and he *s* the mouths of the lions.
Heb 11: 33 who *s* the mouths of lions,
Rev 3: 7 no one can *s*, and what he shuts
21: 25 On no day will its gates ever be *s*,

SICK (SICKNESS)
Pr 13: 12 Hope deferred makes the heart *s*,
Eze 34: 4 or healed the *s* or bound up
Mt 9: 12 who need a doctor, but the *s*.
10: 8 Heal the *s*, raise the dead, cleanse
25: 36 I was *s* and you looked after me,
1Co 11: 30 many among you are weak and *s*,
Jas 5: 14 of you *s*? He should call the elders

SICKBED* (BED)
Ps 41: 3 LORD will sustain him on his *s*

SICKLE
Joel 3: 13 Swing the *s*,
Rev 14: 14 gold on his head and a sharp *s*

SICKNESS (SICK)
Mt 4: 23 and healing every disease and *s*

SIDE (SIDES)
Ps 91: 7 A thousand may fall at your *s*,
124: 1 If the LORD had not been on our *s*
Jn 18: 37 Everyone on the *s* of truth listens
20: 20 he showed them his hands and *s*.
2Ti 4: 17 But the Lord stood at my *s*
Heb 10: 33 at other times you stood *s* by *s*

SIDES (SIDE)
Nu 33: 55 in your eyes and thorns in your *s*.

SIFT
Lk 22: 31 Satan has asked to *s* you as wheat.

SIGHING
Isa 35: 10 and sorrow and *s* will flee away.

SIGHT
Ps 51: 4 and done what is evil in your *s*,
90: 4 For a thousand years in your *s*
116: 15 Precious in the *s* of the LORD
Pr 3: 4 in the *s* of God and man.
Mt 11: 5 The blind receive *s*, the lame walk,
Ac 4: 19 right in God's *s* to obey you rather
1Co 3: 19 this world is foolishness in God's *s*.
2Co 5: 7 We live by faith, not by *s*.
1Pe 3: 4 which is of great worth in God's *s*.

SIGN (SIGNS)
Ge 9: 12 "This is the *s* of the covenant I am
17: 11 and it will be the *s* of the covenant
Isa 7: 14 the Lord himself will give you a *s*:
55: 13 for an everlasting *s*,
Eze 20: 12 I gave them my Sabbaths as a *s*
Mt 12: 38 to see a miraculous *s* from you."
24: 3 what will be the *s* of your coming
24: 30 "At that time the *s* of the Son
Lk 2: 12 This will be a *s* to you: You will
11: 29 It asks for a miraculous *s*,
Ro 4: 11 he received the *s* of circumcision,
1Co 11: 10 to have a *s* of authority on her head
14: 22 are a *s*, not for believers

SIGNS (SIGN)
Ge 1: 14 let them serve as *s* to mark seasons
Ps 78: 43 day he displayed his miraculous *s*
105: 27 They performed his miraculous *s*
Da 6: 27 he performs *s* and wonders
Mt 24: 24 and perform great *s* and miracles
Mk 16: 17 these *s* will accompany those who
Jn 3: 2 perform the miraculous *s* you are
20: 30 Jesus did many other miraculous *s*
Ac 2: 19 and *s* on the earth below,
1Co 1: 22 Jews demand miraculous *s*
2Co 12: 12 *s*, wonders and miracles—
2Th 2: 9 *s* and wonders, and in every sort

SIHON
Nu 21: 21 to say to *S* king of the Amorites:
Ps 136: 19 *S* king of the Amorites

SILAS*
Prophet (Ac 15:22–32); co-worker with Paul on second missionary journey (Ac 16–18; 2Co 1:19). Co-writer with Paul (1Th 1:1; 2Th 1:1); Peter (1Pe 5:12).

SILENCE (SILENCED SILENT)
1Pe 2: 15 good you should *s* the ignorant talk
Rev 8: 1 there was *s* in heaven

SILENCED (SILENCE)
Ro 3: 19 so that every mouth may be *s*
Tit 1: 11 They must be *s*, because they are

SILENT (SILENCE)
Est 4: 14 For if you remain *s* at this time,
Ps 30: 12 to you and not be *s*.
32: 3 When I kept *s*,
39: 2 But when I was *s* and still,
Pr 17: 28 a fool is thought wise if he keeps *s*,
Ecc 3: 7 a time to be *s* and a time to speak,
Isa 53: 7 as a sheep before her shearers is *s*,
62: 1 For Zion's sake I will not keep *s*,
Hab 2: 20 let all the earth be *s* before him."
Ac 8: 32 and as a lamb before the shearer is *s*

1Co 14: 34 women should remain s
1Ti 2: 12 over a man; she must be s.

SILVER
Ps 12: 6 like s refined in a furnace of clay,
66: 10 you refined us like s.
Pr 2: 4 and if you look for it as for s
3: 14 for she is more profitable than s
8: 10 Choose my instruction instead of s,
22: 1 to be esteemed is better than s
25: 4 Remove the dross from the s,
25: 11 is like apples of gold in settings of s.
Isa 48: 10 I have refined you, though not as s;
Eze 22: 18 They are but the dross of s.
Da 2: 32 its chest and arms of s, its belly
Hag 2: 8 'The s is mine and the gold is mine,'
Zec 13: 9 I will refine them like s
Ac 3: 6 Peter said, "S or gold I do not have,
1Co 3: 12 s, costly stones, wood, hay or straw
1Pe 1: 18 not with perishable things such as s

SILVERSMITH
Ac 19: 24 A s named Demetrius, who made

SIMEON
Son of Jacob by Leah (Ge 29:33; 35:23; 1Ch 2:1). With Levi killed Shechem for rape of Dinah (Ge 34:25–29). Held hostage by Joseph in Egypt (Ge 42:24–43:23). Tribe of blessed (Ge 49:5–7), numbered (Nu 1:23; 26:14), allotted land (Jos 19:1–9; Eze 48:24), 12,000 from (Rev 7:7).

SIMON
1. See PETER.
2. Apostle, called the Zealot (Mt 10:4; Mk 3:18; Lk 6:15; Ac 1:13).
3. Samaritan sorcerer (Ac 8:9–24).

SIMPLE
Ps 19: 7 making wise the s.
119: 130 it gives understanding to the s.
Pr 8: 5 You who are s, gain prudence;
14: 15 A s man believes anything,

SIMPLEHEARTED* (HEART)
Ps 116: 6 The LORD protects the s;

SIN (SINFUL SINNED SINNER SINNERS SINNING SINS)
Ge 4: 7 s is crouching at your door;
Ex 32: 32 please forgive their s— but if not,
Nu 5: 7 and must confess the s he has
32: 23 be sure that your s will find you
Dt 24: 16 each is to die for his own s.
1Sa 12: 23 it from me that I should s
15: 23 For rebellion is like the s
1Ki 8: 46 for there is no one who does not s
2Ch 7: 14 and will forgive their s and will heal
Job 1: 22 Job did not s by charging God
Ps 4: 4 In your anger do not s;
17: 3 resolved that my mouth will not s.
32: 2 whose s the LORD does not count
32: 5 Then I acknowledged my s to you
36: 2 too much to detect or hate his s.
38: 18 I am troubled by my s.
39: 1 and keep my tongue from s;
51: 2 and cleanse me from my s.
66: 18 If I had cherished s in my heart,
119: 11 that I might not s against you.
119: 133 let no s rule over me.
Pr 5: 22 the cords of his s hold him fast.
10: 19 words are many, s is not absent,
14: 9 Fools mock at making amends for s
16: 6 faithfulness s is atoned for;
17: 19 He who loves a quarrel loves s;
20: 9 I am clean and without s"?
Isa 3: 9 they parade their s like Sodom;
6: 7 is taken away and your s atoned
64: 5 But when we continued to s
Jer 31: 30 everyone will die for his own s;
Eze 3: 18 that wicked man will die for his s,
18: 26 his righteousness and commits s,
33: 8 that wicked man will die for his s,
Am 4: 4 "Go to Bethel and s;
Mic 6: 7 of my body for the s of my soul?
7: 18 who pardons s and forgives
Zec 3: 4 "See, I have taken away your s,
Mt 18: 6 little ones who believe in me to s,
Mk 3: 29 he is guilty of an eternal s."
9: 43 If your hand causes you to s,
Lk 17: 1 people to s are bound to come,
Jn 1: 29 who takes away the s of the world!
8: 7 "If any one of you is without s,
8: 34 everyone who sins is a slave to s.
8: 46 Can any of you prove me guilty of s
Ro 2: 12 All who s apart from the law will
5: 12 as s entered the world
5: 20 where s increased, grace increased
6: 2 By no means! We died to s;
6: 11 count yourselves dead to s
6: 14 For s shall not be your master,
6: 23 For the wages of s is death,
7: 7 I would not have known what s was
7: 25 sinful nature a slave to the law of s.
14: 23 that does not come from faith is s.
1Co 8: 12 When you s against your brothers
15: 56 The sting of death is s,
2Co 5: 21 God made him who had no s to be s
Gal 6: 1 if someone is caught in a s,
1Ti 5: 20 Those who s are to be rebuked
Heb 4: 15 just as we are—yet was without s.
9: 26 to do away with s by the sacrifice
11: 25 the pleasures of s for a short time.
12: 1 and the s that so easily entangles,
Jas 1: 15 it gives birth to s; and s,
1Pe 2: 22 "He committed no s,
1Jn 1: 7 his Son, purifies us from all s.
1: 8 If we claim to be without s,
2: 1 But if anybody does s, we have one
3: 4 in fact, s is lawlessness.
3: 5 And in him is no s.
3: 6 No one who continues to s has
3: 9 born of God will continue to s,
5: 16 There is a s that leads to death.
5: 17 All wrongdoing is s, and there is s
5: 18 born of God does not continue to s;

SINAI
Ex 19: 20 descended to the top of Mount S
31: 18 speaking to Moses on Mount S,
Ps 68: 17 from S into his sanctuary.

SINCERE* (SINCERITY)
Da 11: 34 many who are not s will join them.
Ac 2: 46 ate together with glad and s hearts,
Ro 12: 9 Love must be s.
2Co 6: 6 in the Holy Spirit and in s love;
11: 3 somehow be led astray from your s
1Ti 1: 5 a good conscience and a s faith.
3: 8 s, not indulging in much wine,
2Ti 1: 5 have been reminded of your s faith,
Heb 10: 22 near to God with a s heart
Jas 3: 17 and good fruit, impartial and s.
1Pe 1: 22 the truth so that you have s love

SINCERITY* (SINCERE)
1Co 5: 8 bread without yeast, the bread of s
2Co 1: 12 in the holiness and s that are
2: 17 speak before God with s,
8: 8 but I want to test the s of your love
Eph 6: 5 and with s of heart, just
Col 3: 22 but with s of heart and reverence

SINFUL (SIN)
Ps 51: 5 Surely I was s at birth,
51: 5 s from the time my mother
Lk 5: 8 from me, Lord; I am a s man!"
Ro 7: 5 we were controlled by the s nature,
7: 18 lives in me, that is, in my s nature.
7: 25 but in the s nature a slave to the law
8: 3 Son in the likeness of s man
8: 4 not live according to the s nature
8: 7 the s mind is hostile to God.
8: 8 by the s nature cannot please God.
8: 9 are controlled not by the s nature
8: 13 if you live according to the s nature
13: 14 to gratify the desires of the s nature
1Co 5: 5 so that the s nature may be
Gal 5: 13 freedom to indulge the s nature;
5: 16 gratify the desires of the s nature.
5: 19 The acts of the s nature are obvious
5: 24 Jesus have crucified the s nature
6: 8 sows to please his s nature,
Col 2: 11 in the putting off of the s nature,
Heb 3: 12 brothers, that none of you has a s,
1Pe 2: 11 abstain from s desires, which war
1Jn 3: 8 He who does what is s is

SING (SANG SINGER SINGING SINGS SONG SONGS SUNG)
Ex 15: 1 "I will s to the LORD,
Ps 5: 11 let them ever s for joy.
13: 6 I will s to the LORD,
30: 4 S to the LORD, you saints of his;
33: 1 S joyfully to the LORD, you
47: 6 S praises to God, s praises;
57: 7 I will s and make music.
59: 16 But I will s of your strength,
63: 7 I s in the shadow of your wings.
66: 2 S to the glory of his name;
89: 1 I will s of the LORD's great love
95: 1 Come, let us s for joy to the LORD
96: 1 S to the LORD a new song;
98: 1 S to the LORD a new song,
101: 1 I will s of your love and justice;
108: 1 I will s and make music
137: 3 "S us one of the songs of Zion!"
147: 1 is to s praises to our God,
149: 1 S to the LORD a new song,
Isa 54: 1 "S, O barren woman,
1Co 14: 15 also pray with my mind; I will s
Eph 5: 19 S and make music in your heart
Col 3: 16 and as you s psalms, hymns
Jas 5: 13 Is anyone happy? Let him s songs

SINGER* (SING)
2Sa 23: 1 Israel's s of songs:

SINGING (SING)
Ps 63: 5 with s lips my mouth will praise
68: 6 he leads forth the prisoners with s;
98: 5 with the harp and the sound of s,
Isa 35: 10 They will enter Zion with s;
Zep 3: 17 he will rejoice over you with s."
Ac 16: 25 Silas were praying and s hymns
Rev 5: 13 on the sea, and all that is in them, s:

SINGLE
Ex 23: 29 I will not drive them out in a s year,
Mt 6: 27 you by worrying can add a s hour
Gal 5: 14 law is summed up in a s command:

SINGS (SING)
Eze 33: 32 more than one who s love songs

SINNED (SIN)
Lev 5: 5 confess in what way he has s
1Sa 15: 24 Then Saul said to Samuel, "I have s
2Sa 12: 13 "I have s against the LORD."
24: 10 I have s greatly in what I have done
2Ch 6: 37 'We have s, we have done wrong
Job 1: 5 "Perhaps my children have s
33: 27 'I s, and perverted what was right,
Ps 51: 4 Against you, you only, have I s
Jer 2: 35 because you say, 'I have not s.'
14: 20 we have indeed s against you.
Da 9: 5 we have s and done wrong.
Mic 7: 9 Because I have s against him,
Mt 27: 4 "I have s," he said,
Lk 15: 18 I have s against heaven
Ro 3: 23 for all have s and fall short
5: 12 all s— for before the law was given,
2Pe 2: 4 did not spare angels when they s,
1Jn 1: 10 claim we have not s, we make him

SINNER (SIN)
Ecc 9: 18 but one s destroys much good.
Lk 15: 7 in heaven over one s who repents
18: 13 'God, have mercy on me, a s.'
1Co 14: 24 convinced by all that he is a s
Jas 5: 20 Whoever turns a s from the error
1Pe 4: 18 become of the ungodly and the s?"

SINNERS (SIN)
Ps 1: 1 or stand in the way of s
37: 38 But all s will be destroyed;
Pr 1: 10 My son, if s entice you,
23: 17 Do not let your heart envy s,
Mt 9: 13 come to call the righteous, but s."
Ro 5: 8 While we were still s, Christ died
Gal 2: 17 evident that we ourselves are s,
1Ti 1: 15 came into the world to save s—
Heb 7: 26 set apart from s, exalted

SINNING (SIN)
Ex 20: 20 be with you to keep you from s."
1Co 15: 34 stop s; for there are some who are
Heb 10: 26 If we deliberately keep on s
1Jn 3: 6 No one who lives in him keeps on s
3: 9 go on s, because he has been born

SINS (SIN)
Lev 5: 1 "'If a person s because he does not
16: 30 you will be clean from all your s.
26: 40 "'But if they will confess their s
Nu 15: 30 "'But anyone who s defiantly,
1Sa 2: 25 If a man s against another man,
2Ki 14: 6 each is to die for his own s."
Ezr 9: 6 our s are higher than our heads
9: 13 less than our s have deserved
Ps 19: 13 your servant also from willful s;
32: 1 whose s are covered.
51: 9 Hide your face from my s
79: 9 deliver us and forgive our s
85: 2 and covered all their s.
103: 3 who forgives all your s
103: 10 does not treat us as our s deserve
130: 3 O LORD, kept a record of s,
Pr 14: 21 He who despises his neighbor s,
28: 13 who conceals his s does not
29: 22 one commits many s.
Ecc 7: 20 who does what is right and never s.
Isa 1: 18 "Though your s are like scarlet,

Isa 38: 17 you have put all my *s*
43: 25 and remembers your *s* no more.
59: 2 your *s* have hidden his face
64: 6 like the wind our *s* sweep us away.
Jer 31: 34 and will remember their *s* no more
La 3: 39 complain when punished for his *s*?
Eze 18: 4 soul who *s* is the one who will die.
33: 10 Our offenses and *s* weigh us down,
36: 33 day I cleanse you from all your *s*,
Hos 14: 1 Your *s* have been your downfall!
Mt 1: 21 he will save his people from their *s*
6: 15 if you do not forgive men their *s*,
9: 6 authority on earth to forgive *s* ..."
18: 15 "If your brother *s* against you,
26: 28 for many for the forgiveness of *s*.
Lk 5: 24 authority on earth to forgive *s* ..."
11: 4 Forgive us our *s*,
17: 3 "If your brother *s*, rebuke him,
Jn 8: 24 you will indeed die in your *s*."
20: 23 If you forgive anyone his *s*,
Ac 2: 38 for the forgiveness of your *s*.
3: 19 so that your *s* may be wiped out,
10: 43 forgiveness of *s* through his name."
22: 16 be baptized and wash your *s* away,
26: 18 they may receive forgiveness of *s*
Ro 4: 7 whose *s* are covered.
4: 25 delivered over to death for our *s*
1Co 15: 3 died for our *s* according
2Co 5: 19 not counting men's *s* against them.
Gal 1: 4 himself for our *s* to rescue us
Eph 2: 1 dead in your transgressions and *s*,
Col 2: 13 us all our *s*, having canceled
1Ti 5: 22 and do not share in the *s* of others.
Heb 1: 3 he had provided purification for *s*,
2: 17 atonement for the *s* of the people.
7: 27 He sacrificed for their *s* once for all
8: 12 and will remember their *s* no more
9: 28 to take away the *s* of many people;
10: 4 of bulls and goats to take away *s*.
10: 12 for all time one sacrifice for *s*,
10: 26 of the truth, no sacrifice for *s* is left,
Jas 4: 17 ought to do and doesn't do it, *s*.
5: 16 Therefore confess your *s*
5: 20 and cover over a multitude of *s*.
1Pe 2: 24 He himself bore our *s* in his body
3: 18 For Christ died for *s* once for all,
4: 8 love covers over a multitude of *s*.
1Jn 1: 9 If we confess our *s*, he is faithful
2: 2 He is the atoning sacrifice for our *s*,
3: 5 so that he might take away our *s*.
4: 10 as an atoning sacrifice for our *s*.
Rev 1: 5 has freed us from our *s* by his blood

SISERA
Jdg 4: 2 The commander of his army was *S*,
5: 26 She struck *S*, she crushed his head,

SISTER (SISTERS)
Lev 18: 9 have sexual relations with your *s*,
Mk 3: 35 does God's will is my brother and *s*

SISTERS (SISTER)
Mt 19: 29 or brothers or *s* or father or mother
1Ti 5: 2 as *s*, with absolute purity.

SIT (SAT SITS SITTING)
Dt 6: 7 them when you *s* at home
1Ki 8: 25 fail to have a man to *s* before me
Ps 1: 1 or *s* in the seat of mockers.
26: 5 and refuse to *s* with the wicked.
80: 1 you who *s* enthroned
110: 1 "*S* at my right hand
139: 2 You know when I *s* and when I rise
SS 2: 3 I delight to *s* in his shade,
Isa 16: 5 in faithfulness a man will *s* on it—
Mic 4: 4 Every man will *s* under his own
Mt 20: 23 to *s* at my right or left is not for me
22: 44 "*S* at my right hand
Lk 22: 30 in my kingdom and *s* on thrones,
Heb 1: 13 "*S* at my right hand
Rev 3: 21 right to *s* with me on my throne,

SITS (SIT)
Ps 99: 1 *s* enthroned between the cherubim,
Isa 40: 22 He *s* enthroned above the circle
Mt 19: 28 of Man *s* on his glorious throne,
Rev 4: 9 thanks to him who *s* on the throne

SITTING (SIT)
Est 2: 19 Mordecai was *s* at the king's gate.
Mt 26: 64 the Son of Man *s* at the right hand
Rev 4: 2 in heaven with someone *s* on it.

SITUATION (SITUATIONS)
1Co 7: 24 remain in the *s* God called him
Php 4: 12 of being content in any and every *s*,

SITUATIONS* (SITUATION)
2Ti 4: 5 head in all *s*, endure hardship,

SKIES (SKY)
Ps 19: 1 the *s* proclaim the work
71: 19 Your righteousness reaches to the *s*
108: 4 your faithfulness reaches to the *s*.

SKILL (SKILLED SKILLFUL)
Ps 137: 5 may my right hand forget its *s*.
Ecc 10: 10 but *s* will bring success.

SKILLED (SKILL)
Pr 22: 29 Do you see a man *s* in his work?

SKILLFUL (SKILL)
Ps 45: 1 my tongue is the pen of a *s* writer.
78: 72 with *s* hands he led them.

SKIN (SKINS)
Job 19: 20 with only the *s* of my teeth.
19: 26 And after my *s* has been destroyed,
Jer 13: 23 Can the Ethiopian change his *s*

SKINS (SKIN)
Ex 25: 5 ram *s* dyed red and hides
Lk 5: 37 the new wine will burst the *s*,

SKULL
Mt 27: 33 (which means The Place of the *S*).

SKY (SKIES)
Ge 1: 8 God called the expanse "*s*."
Pr 30: 19 the way of an eagle in the *s*,
Isa 34: 4 and the *s* rolled up like a scroll;
Jer 33: 22 stars of the *s* and as measureless
Mt 24: 29 the stars will fall from the *s*,
24: 30 coming on the clouds of the *s*,
Rev 20: 11 Earth and *s* fled from his presence,

SLACK*
Pr 18: 9 One who is *s* in his work

SLAIN (SLAY)
1Sa 18: 7 "Saul has *s* his thousands,
Eze 37: 9 into these *s*, that they may live.'"
Rev 5: 6 as if it had been *s*, standing
5: 12 "Worthy is the Lamb, who was *s*,
6: 9 the souls of those who had been *s*

SLANDER (SLANDERED SLANDERER SLANDERERS SLANDEROUS)
Lev 19: 16 "'Do not go about spreading *s*
Ps 15: 3 and has no *s* on his tongue,
Pr 10: 18 and whoever spreads *s* is a fool.
2Co 12: 20 outbursts of anger, factions, *s*,
Eph 4: 31 rage and anger, brawling and *s*,
1Ti 5: 14 the enemy no opportunity for *s*.
Tit 3: 2 to *s* no one, to be peaceable
1Pe 3: 16 in Christ may be ashamed of their *s*
2Pe 2: 10 afraid to *s* celestial beings;

SLANDERED (SLANDER)
1Co 4: 13 when we are *s*, we answer kindly.

SLANDERER (SLANDER)
1Co 5: 11 an idolater or a *s*, a drunkard

SLANDERERS (SLANDER)
Ro 1: 30 They are gossips, *s*, God-haters,
1Co 6: 10 nor the greedy nor drunkards nor *s*
Tit 2: 3 not to be *s* or addicted

SLANDEROUS (SLANDER)
2Ti 3: 3 unforgiving, *s*, without self-control
2Pe 2: 11 do not bring *s* accusations

SLAUGHTER (SLAUGHTERED)
Isa 53: 7 he was led like a lamb to the *s*,
Jer 11: 19 been like a gentle lamb led to the *s*;
Ac 8: 32 "He was led like a sheep to the *s*,

SLAUGHTERED (SLAUGHTER)
Ps 44: 22 we are considered as sheep to be *s*.
Ro 8: 36 we are considered as sheep to be *s*

SLAVE (ENSLAVED SLAVERY SLAVES)
Ge 21: 10 "Get rid of that *s* woman
Mt 20: 27 wants to be first must be your *s*—
Jn 8: 34 everyone who sins is a *s* to sin.
Ro 7: 14 I am unspiritual, sold as a *s* to sin.
1Co 7: 21 Were you a *s* when you were called
12: 13 whether Jews or Greeks, *s* or free
Gal 3: 28 *s* nor free, male nor female,
4: 7 So you are no longer a *s*, but a son;
4: 30 Get rid of the *s* woman and her son
Col 3: 11 barbarian, Scythian, *s* or free,
1Ti 1: 10 for *s* traders and liars and perjurers
Phm : 16 no longer as a *s*, but better than a *s*,
2Pe 2: 19 a man is a *s* to whatever has

SLAVERY (SLAVE)
Ex 2: 23 The Israelites groaned in their *s*
Ro 6: 19 parts of your body in *s* to impurity
Gal 4: 3 were in *s* under the basic principles

1Ti 6: 1 of *s* should consider their masters

SLAVES (SLAVE)
Ps 123: 2 As the eyes of *s* look to the hand
Ecc 10: 7 I have seen *s* on horseback,
Ro 6: 6 that we should no longer be *s* to sin
6: 16 you are *s* to sin, which leads
6: 22 and have become *s* to God,
Gal 2: 4 in Christ Jesus and to make us *s*.
4: 8 you were *s* to those who
Eph 6: 5 *S*, obey your earthly masters
Col 3: 22 *S*, obey your earthly masters
4: 1 provide your *s* with what is right
Tit 2: 9 Teach *s* to be subject

SLAY (SLAIN)
Job 13: 15 Though he *s* me, yet will I hope

SLEEP (ASLEEP SLEEPER SLEEPING SLEEPS)
Ge 2: 21 the man to fall into a deep *s*;
15: 12 Abram fell into a deep *s*,
28: 11 it under his head and lay down to *s*.
Ps 4: 8 I will lie down and *s* in peace,
121: 4 will neither slumber nor *s*.
127: 2 for he grants *s* to those he loves.
Pr 6: 9 When will you get up from your *s*?
Ecc 5: 12 The *s* of a laborer is sweet,
1Co 15: 51 We will not all *s*, but we will all be
1Th 5: 7 For those who *s*, *s* at night,

SLEEPER (SLEEP)
Eph 5: 14 "Wake up, O *s*,

SLEEPING (SLEEP)
Mk 13: 36 suddenly, do not let him find you *s*.

SLEEPLESS*
2Co 6: 5 in hard work, *s* nights and hunger;

SLEEPS (SLEEP)
Pr 10: 5 he who *s* during harvest is

SLIMY
Ps 40: 2 He lifted me out of the *s* pit,

SLING
1Sa 17: 50 over the Philistine with a *s*

SLIP (SLIPPING)
Dt 4: 9 let them *s* from your heart as long
Ps 121: 3 He will not let your foot *s*—

SLIPPING (SLIP)
Ps 66: 9 and kept our feet from *s*.

SLOW
Ex 34: 6 and gracious God, *s* to anger,
Jas 1: 19 *s* to speak and *s* to become angry,
2Pe 3: 9 The Lord is not *s* in keeping his

SLUGGARD
Pr 6: 6 Go to the ant, you *s*;
13: 4 The *s* craves and gets nothing,
20: 4 A *s* does not plow in season;
26: 15 The *s* buries his hand in the dish;

SLUMBER
Ps 121: 3 he who watches over you will not *s*;
Pr 6: 10 A little sleep, a little *s*,
Ro 13: 11 for you to wake up from your *s*,

SLUR
Ps 15: 3 and casts no *s* on his fellow man,

SMELL
Ecc 10: 1 As dead flies give perfume a bad *s*,
2Co 2: 16 To the one we are the *s* of death;

SMITTEN
Isa 53: 4 *s* by him, and afflicted.

SMOKE
Ex 19: 18 Mount Sinai was covered with *s*,
Ps 104: 32 touches the mountains, and they *s*.
Isa 6: 4 and the temple was filled with *s*.
Joel 2: 30 blood and fire and billows of *s*.
Ac 2: 19 blood and fire and billows of *s*.
Rev 15: 8 filled with *s* from the glory

SMYRNA
Rev 2: 8 the angel of the church in *S* write:

SNAKE (SNAKES)
Nu 21: 8 "Make a *s* and put it up on a pole;
Pr 23: 32 In the end it bites like a *s*
Jn 3: 14 Moses lifted up the *s* in the desert,

SNAKES (SNAKE)
Mt 10: 16 as shrewd as *s* and as innocent
Mk 16: 18 they will pick up *s* with their hands;

SNARE (ENSNARE ENSNARED SNARED)
Dt 7: 16 for that will be a *s* to you.
Ps 69: 22 before them become a *s*;

Ps 91: 3 from the fowler's *s*
Pr 29: 25 Fear of man will prove to be a *s*,
Ro 11: 9 "May their table become a *s*

SNARED (SNARE)
Pr 3: 26 will keep your foot from being *s*.

SNATCH
Jn 10: 28 no one can *s* them out of my hand.
Jude : 23 *s* others from the fire and save

SNOUT
Pr 11: 22 Like a gold ring in a pig's *s*

SNOW
Ps 51: 7 and I will be whiter than *s*.
Isa 1: 18 they shall be as white as *s*;

SNUFF (SNUFFED)
Isa 42: 3 a smoldering wick he will not *s* out.
Mt 12: 20 a smoldering wick he will not *s* out,

SNUFFED (SNUFF)
Pr 13: 9 but the lamp of the wicked is *s* out.

SOAP
Mal 3: 2 a refiner's fire or a launderer's *s*.

SOAR (SOARED)
Isa 40: 31 They will *s* on wings like eagles;

SOARED (SOAR)
2Sa 22: 11 he *s* on the wings of the wind.

SOBER
Ro 12: 3 think of yourself with *s* judgment,

SODOM
Ge 13: 12 and pitched his tents near *S*.
19: 24 rained down burning sulfur on *S*
Isa 1: 9 we would have become like *S*,
Lk 10: 12 on that day for *S* than for that town
Ro 9: 29 we would have become like *S*,
Rev 11: 8 which is figuratively called *S*

SOIL
Ge 4: 2 kept flocks, and Cain worked the *s*.
Mt 13: 23 on good *s* is the man who hears

SOLD (SELL)
1Ki 21: 25 who *s* himself to do evil in the eyes
Mt 10: 29 Are not two sparrows *s* for a penny
13: 44 then in his joy went and *s* all he had
Ro 7: 14 I am unspiritual, *s* as a slave to sin.

SOLDIER
1Co 9: 7 as a *s* at his own expense?
2Ti 2: 3 with us like a good *s* of Christ Jesus

SOLE
Dt 28: 65 place for the *s* of your foot.
Isa 1: 6 From the *s* of your foot to the top

SOLID
2Ti 2: 19 God's *s* foundation stands firm,
Heb 5: 12 You need milk, not *s* food!

SOLOMON
Son of David by Bathsheba; king of Judah (2Sa 12:24; 1Ch 3:5, 10). Appointed king by David (1Ki 1); adversaries Adonijah, Joab, Shimei killed by Benaiah (1Ki 2). Asked for wisdom (1Ki 3; 2Ch 1). Judged between two prostitutes (1Ki 3:16–28). Built temple (1Ki 5–7; 2Ch 2–5); prayer of dedication (1Ki 8; 2Ch 6). Visited by Queen of Sheba (1Ki 10; 2Ch 9). Wives turned his heart from God (1Ki 11:1–13). Jeroboam rebelled against (1Ki 11:26–40). Death (1Ki 11:41–43; 2Ch 9:29–31).
Proverbs of (1Ki 4:32; Pr 1:1; 10:1; 25:1); psalms of (Ps 72; 127); song of (SS 1:1).

SON (SONS SONSHIP)
Ge 17: 19 your wife Sarah will bear you a *s*,
21: 10 rid of that slave woman and her *s*,
22: 2 "Take your *s*, your only *s*, Isaac,
Ex 11: 5 Every firstborn *s* in Egypt will die,
Dt 1: 31 father carries his *s*, all the way you
6: 20 In the future, when your *s* asks you,
8: 5 as a man disciplines his *s*,
21: 18 rebellious *s* who does not obey his
2Sa 7: 14 be his father, and he will be my *s*.
1Ki 3: 20 and put her dead *s* by my breast.
Ps 2: 7 He said to me, "You are my *S*;
2: 12 Kiss the *S*, lest he be angry
8: 4 the *s* of man that you care for him?
Pr 3: 12 as a father the *s* he delights in.
6: 20 My *s*, keep your father's
10: 1 A wise *s* brings joy to his father,
13: 24 He who spares the rod hates his *s*,
29: 17 Discipline your *s*, and he will give
Isa 7: 14 with child and will give birth to a *s*,
Eze 18: 20 The *s* will not share the guilt
Da 3: 25 the fourth looks like a *s* of the gods
7: 13 before me was one like a *s* of man,
Hos 11: 1 and out of Egypt I called my *s*.
Am 7: 14 neither a prophet nor a prophet's *s*,
Mt 1: 1 of Jesus Christ the *s* of David,
1: 21 She will give birth to a *s*,
2: 15 "Out of Egypt I called my *s*."
3: 17 "This is my *S*, whom I love;
4: 3 "If you are the *S* of God, tell these
8: 20 but the *S* of Man has no place
11: 27 one knows the *S* except the Father,
12: 8 For the *S* of Man is Lord
12: 32 a word against the *S* of Man will be
12: 40 so the *S* of Man will be three days
13: 41 *S* of Man will send out his angels,
13: 55 "Isn't this the carpenter's *s*?
14: 33 "Truly you are the *S* of God."
16: 16 "You are the Christ, the *S*
16: 27 For the *S* of Man is going to come
17: 5 "This is my *S*, whom I love;
19: 28 when the *S* of Man sits
20: 18 and the *S* of Man will be betrayed
20: 28 as the *S* of Man did not come
21: 9 "Hosanna to the *S* of David!"
22: 42 Whose *s* is he?" "The *s* of David,"
24: 27 so will be the coming of the *S*
24: 30 They will see the *S* of Man coming
24: 44 the *S* of Man will come at an hour
25: 31 "When the *S* of Man comes
26: 63 if you are the Christ, the *S* of God."
27: 54 "Surely he was the *S* of God!"
28: 19 and of the *S* and of the Holy Spirit,
Mk 1: 11 "You are my *S*, whom I love;
2: 28 So the *S* of Man is Lord
8: 38 the *S* of Man will be ashamed
9: 7 "This is my *S*, whom I love.
10: 45 even the *S* of Man did not come
13: 32 nor the *S*, but only the Father.
14: 62 you will see the *S* of Man sitting
Lk 1: 32 and will be called the *S*
2: 7 she gave birth to her firstborn, a *s*.
3: 22 "You are my *S*, whom I love;
9: 35 This is my *S*, whom I have chosen;
9: 58 but the *S* of Man has no place
12: 8 the *S* of Man will also acknowledge
15: 20 he ran to his *s*, threw his arms
18: 8 when the *S* of Man comes,
18: 31 written by the prophets about the *S*
19: 10 For the *S* of Man came to seek
Jn 1: 34 I testify that this is the *S* of God."
3: 14 so the *S* of Man must be lifted up,
3: 16 that he gave his one and only *S*,
3: 36 believes in the *S* has eternal life,
5: 19 the *S* can do nothing by himself;
6: 40 is that everyone who looks to the *S*
11: 4 so that God's *S* may be glorified
17: 1 Glorify your *S*, that your *S* may
Ac 7: 56 and the *S* of Man standing
13: 33 "'You are my *S*;
Ro 1: 4 with power to be the *S* of God
5: 10 to him through the death of his *S*,
8: 3 did by sending his own *S*
8: 29 conformed to the likeness of his *S*,
8: 32 He who did not spare his own *S*,
1Co 15: 28 then the *S* himself will be made
Gal 2: 20 I live by faith in the *S* of God,
4: 4 God sent his *S*, born of a woman,
4: 30 rid of the slave woman and her *s*,
1Th 1: 10 and to wait for his *S* from heaven,
Heb 1: 2 days he has spoken to us by his *S*,
1: 5 "You are my *S*;
2: 6 the *s* of man that you care for him?
4: 14 Jesus the *S* of God, let us hold
5: 5 "You are my *S*;
7: 28 appointed the *S*, who has been
10: 29 punished who has trampled the *S*
12: 6 everyone he accepts as a *s*."
2Pe 1: 17 saying, "This is my *S*, whom I love;
1Jn 1: 3 is with the Father and with his *S*,
1: 7 his *S*, purifies us from all sin.
2: 23 whoever acknowledges the *S* has
3: 8 reason the *S* of God appeared was
4: 9 only *S* into the world that we might
4: 14 that the Father has sent his *S*
5: 5 he who believes that Jesus is the *S*
5: 11 eternal life, and this life is in his *S*.
Rev 1: 13 lampstands was someone "like a *s*
14: 14 on the cloud was one "like a *s*

SONG (SING)
Ex 15: 2 LORD is my strength and my *s*;
Ps 40: 3 He put a new *s* in my mouth,
69: 30 I will praise God's name in *s*
96: 1 Sing to the LORD a new *s*;
98: 4 burst into jubilant *s* with music;
119: 54 Your decrees are the theme of my *s*
149: 1 Sing to the LORD a new *s*,
Isa 49: 13 burst into *s*, O mountains!
Isa 55: 12 will burst into *s* before you,
Rev 5: 9 And they sang a new *s*:
15: 3 and sang the *s* of Moses the servant

SONGS (SING)
2Sa 23: 1 Israel's singer of *s*:
Job 35: 10 who gives *s* in the night,
Ps 100: 2 come before him with joyful *s*.
126: 6 will return with *s* of joy,
137: 3 "Sing us one of the *s* of Zion!"
Eph 5: 19 with psalms, hymns and spiritual *s*.
Jas 5: 13 Is anyone happy? Let him sing *s*

SONS (SON)
Ge 6: 2 the *s* of God saw that the daughters
10: 20 These are the *s* of Ham
Ru 4: 15 who is better to you than seven *s*,
Ps 127: 3 *S* are a heritage from the LORD,
132: 12 if your *s* keep my covenant
Hos 1: 10 they will be called '*s*
Joel 2: 28 Your *s* and daughters will prophesy
Mt 5: 9 for they will be called *s* of God.
Lk 6: 35 and you will be *s* of the Most High,
Jn 12: 36 so that you may become *s* of light."
Ro 8: 14 by the Spirit of God are *s* of God.
9: 26 they will be called '*s*
2Co 6: 18 and you will be my *s* and daughters
Gal 3: 26 You are all *s* of God through faith
4: 5 we might receive the full rights of *s*.
4: 6 Because you are *s*, God sent
Heb 12: 7 discipline; God is treating you as *s*.

SONSHIP* (SON)
Ro 8: 15 but you received the Spirit of *s*.

SORCERY
Lev 19: 26 "'Do not practice divination or *s*.

SORROW (SORROWS)
Ps 6: 7 My eyes grow weak with *s*;
116: 3 I was overcome by trouble and *s*.
Isa 60: 20 and your days of *s* will end.
Jer 31: 12 and they will *s* no more.
Ro 9: 2 I have great *s* and unceasing
2Co 7: 10 Godly *s* brings repentance that

SORROWS (SORROW)
Isa 53: 3 a man of *s*, and familiar

SOUGHT (SEEK)
2Ch 26: 5 As long as he *s* the LORD,
31: 21 he *s* his God and worked
Ps 34: 4 I *s* the LORD, and he answered me
119: 58 I have *s* your face with all my heart;

SOUL (SOULS)
Dt 6: 5 with all your *s* and with all your
10: 12 all your heart and with all your *s*,
30: 6 all your heart and with all your *s*,
Jos 22: 5 with all your heart and all your *s*."
2Ki 23: 25 and with all his *s* and with all his
Ps 23: 3 he restores my *s*.
34: 2 My *s* will boast in the LORD;
42: 1 so my *s* pants for you, O God.
42: 11 Why are you downcast, O my *s*?
62: 5 Find rest, O my *s*, in God alone;
63: 8 My *s* clings to you;
94: 19 consolation brought joy to my *s*.
103: 1 Praise the LORD, O my *s*;
Pr 13: 19 A longing fulfilled is sweet to the *s*,
16: 24 sweet to the *s* and healing
22: 5 he who guards his *s* stays far
Isa 55: 2 your *s* will delight in the richest
La 3: 20 and my *s* is downcast within me.
Eze 18: 4 For every living *s* belongs to me,
Mt 10: 28 kill the body but cannot kill the *s*.
16: 26 yet forfeits his *s*? Or what can
22: 37 with all your *s* and with all your
Heb 4: 12 even to dividing *s* and spirit,
3Jn : 2 even as your *s* is getting along well.

SOULS (SOUL)
Pr 11: 30 and he who wins *s* is wise.
Jer 6: 16 and you will find rest for your *s*.
Mt 11: 29 and you will find rest for your *s*.

SOUND (FINE-SOUNDING)
Ge 3: 8 and his wife heard the *s*
Pr 3: 21 preserve *s* judgment
Eze 3: 12 I heard behind me a loud rumbling *s*
Jn 3: 8 You hear its *s*, but you cannot tell
Ac 2: 2 Suddenly a *s* like the blowing
1Co 14: 8 if the trumpet does not *s* a clear call
15: 52 the trumpet will *s*, the dead will
1Ti 1: 10 to the *s* doctrine that conforms
2Ti 4: 3 men will not put up with *s* doctrine.
Tit 1: 9 can encourage others by *s* doctrine
2: 1 is in accord with *s* doctrine.

SOUR
Eze 18: 2 "'The fathers eat *s* grapes,

SOURCE
Heb 5: 9 became the *s* of eternal salvation

SOVEREIGN (SOVEREIGNTY)
Ge 15: 2 But Abram said, "O *S* LORD,
2Sa 7: 18 O *S* LORD, and what is my family,
Ps 71: 16 your mighty acts, O *S* LORD;
Isa 25: 8 *S* LORD will wipe away the tears
40: 10 the *S* LORD comes with power,
50: 4 *S* LORD has given me
61: 1 The Spirit of the *S* LORD is on me,
61: 11 so the *S* LORD will make
Jer 32: 17 to the LORD: "Ah, *S* LORD,
Eze 12: 28 fulfilled, declares the *S* LORD.'"
Da 4: 25 that the Most High is *s*
2Pe 2: 1 denying the *s* Lord who bought
Jude : 4 and deny Jesus Christ our only *S*

SOVEREIGNTY (SOVEREIGN)
Da 7: 27 Then the *s*, power and greatness

SOW (SOWER SOWN SOWS)
Job 4: 8 and those who *s* trouble reap it.
Ps 126: 5 Those who *s* in tears
Hos 8: 7 "They *s* the wind
10: 12 *S* for yourselves righteousness,
Mt 6: 26 they do not *s* or reap or store away
13: 3 "A farmer went out to *s* his seed.
1Co 15: 36 What you *s* does not come to life
Jas 3: 18 Peacemakers who *s*
2Pe 2: 22 and, "A *s* that is washed goes back

SOWER (SOW)
Isa 55: 10 so that it yields seed for the *s*
Mt 13: 18 to what the parable of the *s* means:
Jn 4: 36 so that the *s* and the reaper may be
2Co 9: 10 Now he who supplies seed to the *s*

SOWN (SOW)
Mt 13: 8 sixty or thirty times what was *s*.
Mk 4: 15 along the path, where the word is *s*.
1Co 15: 42 The body that is *s* is perishable,

SOWS (SOW)
Pr 11: 18 he who *s* righteousness reaps a sure
22: 8 He who *s* wickedness reaps trouble
2Co 9: 6 Whoever *s* sparingly will
Gal 6: 7 A man reaps what he *s*.

SPARE (SPARES SPARING)
Est 7: 3 *s* my people — this is my request.
Ro 8: 32 He who did not *s* his own Son,
11: 21 natural branches, he will not *s* you
2Pe 2: 4 For if God did not *s* angels
2: 5 if he did not *s* the ancient world

SPARES (SPARE)
Pr 13: 24 He who *s* the rod hates his son,

SPARING (SPARE)
Pr 21: 26 but the righteous give without *s*.

SPARKLE
Zec 9: 16 They will *s* in his land

SPARROW (SPARROWS)
Ps 84: 3 Even the *s* has found a home,

SPARROWS (SPARROW)
Mt 10: 29 Are not two *s* sold for a penny?

SPEAR (SPEARS)
1Sa 19: 10 as Saul drove the *s* into the wall.
Ps 46: 9 breaks the bow and shatters the *s*,

SPEARS (SPEAR)
Isa 2: 4 and their *s* into pruning hooks.
Joel 3: 10 and your pruning hooks into *s*.
Mic 4: 3 and their *s* into pruning hooks.

SPECIAL
Jas 2: 3 If you show *s* attention

SPECK
Mt 7: 3 look at the *s* of sawdust

SPECTACLE
1Co 4: 9 We have been made a *s*
Col 2: 15 he made a public *s* of them,

SPEECH
Ps 19: 3 There is no *s* or language
Pr 22: 11 pure heart and whose *s* is gracious
2Co 8: 7 in faith, in *s*, in knowledge,
1Ti 4: 12 set an example for the believers in *s*

SPEND (SPENT)
Pr 31: 3 do not *s* your strength on women,
Isa 55: 2 Why *s* money on what is not bread,
2Co 12: 15 So I will very gladly *s*

SPENT (SPEND)
Mk 5: 26 many doctors and had *s* all she had,
Lk 6: 12 and *s* the night praying to God.
15: 14 After he had *s* everything,

SPIN
Mt 6: 28 They do not labor or *s*.

SPIRIT (SPIRIT'S SPIRITS SPIRITUAL SPIRITUALLY)
Ge 1: 2 and the *S* of God was hovering
6: 3 "My *S* will not contend
Ex 31: 3 I have filled him with the *S* of God,
Nu 11: 25 and put the *S* on the seventy elders.
Dt 34: 9 filled with the *s* of wisdom
Jdg 6: 34 Then the *S* of the LORD came
11: 29 Then the *S* of the LORD came
13: 25 and the *S* of the LORD began
1Sa 10: 10 the *S* of God came upon him
16: 13 day on the *S* of the LORD came
16: 14 the *S* of the LORD had departed
2Sa 23: 2 "The *S* of the LORD spoke
2Ki 2: 9 inherit a double portion of your *s*,"
Ne 9: 20 You gave your good *S*
9: 30 By your *S* you admonished them
Job 33: 4 The *S* of God has made me;
Ps 31: 5 Into your hands I commit my *s*;
34: 18 saves those who are crushed in *s*.
51: 10 and renew a steadfast *s* within me.
51: 11 or take your Holy *S* from me.
51: 17 sacrifices of God are a broken *s*;
106: 33 rebelled against the *S* of God,
139: 7 Where can I go from your *S*?
143: 10 may your good *S*
Isa 11: 2 The *S* of the LORD will rest
30: 1 an alliance, but not by my *S*,
32: 15 till the *S* is poured upon us
44: 3 I will pour out my *S*
57: 15 him who is contrite and lowly in *s*,
61: 1 The *S* of the Sovereign LORD is
63: 10 and grieved his Holy *S*.
Eze 11: 19 an undivided heart and put a new *s*
13: 3 prophets who follow their own *s*
36: 26 you a new heart and put a new *s*
Da 4: 8 and the *s* of the holy gods is in him
Joel 2: 28 I will pour out my *S* on all people.
Zec 4: 6 but by my *S*,' says the LORD
Mt 1: 18 to be with child through the Holy *S*
3: 11 will baptize you with the Holy *S*
3: 16 he saw the *S* of God descending
4: 1 led by the *S* into the desert
5: 3 saying: "Blessed are the poor in *s*,
10: 20 but the *S* of your Father speaking
12: 31 against the *S* will not be forgiven.
26: 41 *s* is willing, but the body is weak."
28: 19 and of the Son and of the Holy *S*,
Mk 1: 8 he will baptize you with the Holy *S*
Lk 1: 35 "The Holy *S* will come upon you,
1: 80 child grew and became strong in *s*;
3: 16 will baptize you with the Holy *S*
4: 18 "The *S* of the Lord is on me,
11: 13 Father in heaven give the Holy *S*
23: 46 into your hands I commit my *s*."
Jn 1: 33 who will baptize with the Holy *S*.'
3: 5 a man is born of water and the *S*,
4: 24 God is *s*, and his worshipers must
6: 63 The *S* gives life; the flesh counts
7: 39 Up to that time the *S* had not been
14: 26 But the Counselor, the Holy *S*,
16: 13 But when he, the *S* of truth, comes,
20: 22 and said, "Receive the Holy *S*.
Ac 1: 5 will be baptized with the Holy *S*."
1: 8 when the Holy *S* comes on you;
2: 4 of them were filled with the Holy *S*
2: 17 I will pour out my *S* on all people.
2: 38 will receive the gift of the Holy *S*.
4: 31 they were all filled with the Holy *S*
5: 3 that you have lied to the Holy *S*
6: 3 who are known to be full of the *S*
8: 15 that they might receive the Holy *S*,
9: 17 and be filled with the Holy *S*."
11: 16 will be baptized with the Holy *S*.'
13: 2 and fasting, the Holy *S* said,
19: 2 "Did you receive the Holy *S*
Ro 8: 4 nature but according to the *S*.
8: 5 set on what the *S* desires.
8: 9 And if anyone does not have the *S*
8: 13 but if by the *S* you put
8: 16 The *S* himself testifies
8: 23 who have the firstfruits of the *S*,
8: 26 the *S* helps us in our weakness.
1Co 2: 10 God has revealed it to us by his *S*.
2: 14 man without the *S* does not accept
5: 3 present, I am with you in *s*.
6: 19 body is a temple of the Holy *S*,
12: 13 baptized by one *S* into one body —
2Co 1: 22 and put his *S* in our hearts
3: 3 but with the *S* of the living God,
3: 6 the letter kills, but the *S* gives life.
3: 17 Now the Lord is the *S*,
5: 5 and has given us the *S* as a deposit,
7: 1 that contaminates body and *s*,
Gal 3: 2 Did you receive the *S*
5: 16 by the *S*, and you will not gratify
5: 22 But the fruit of the *S* is love, joy,
5: 25 let us keep in step with the *S*.
6: 8 from the *S* will reap eternal life.
Eph 1: 13 with a seal, the promised Holy *S*,
2: 22 in which God lives by his *S*.
4: 4 There is one body and one *S* —
4: 30 do not grieve the Holy *S* of God,
5: 18 Instead, be filled with the *S*.
6: 17 of salvation and the sword of the *S*,
Php 2: 2 being one in *s* and purpose.
1Th 5: 23 May your whole *s*, soul
2Th 2: 13 the sanctifying work of the *S*
1Ti 3: 16 was vindicated by the *S*,
2Ti 1: 7 For God did not give us a *s*
Heb 2: 4 of the Holy *S* distributed according
4: 12 even to dividing soul and *s*,
10: 29 and who has insulted the *S* of grace
1Pe 3: 4 beauty of a gentle and quiet *s*,
2Pe 1: 21 carried along by the Holy *S*.
1Jn 3: 24 We know it by the *S* he gave us.
4: 1 Dear friends, do not believe every *s*
4: 13 because he has given us of his *S*.
Jude : 20 holy faith and pray in the Holy *S*.
Rev 2: 7 let him hear what the *S* says

SPIRIT'S* (SPIRIT)
1Co 2: 4 a demonstration of the *S* power,
1Th 5: 19 not put out the *S* fire; do not treat

SPIRITS (SPIRIT)
1Co 12: 10 to another distinguishing between *s*,
14: 32 The *s* of prophets are subject
1Jn 4: 1 test the *s* to see whether they are

SPIRITUAL (SPIRIT)
Ro 12: 1 to God — this is your *s* act of worship.
12: 11 but keep your *s* fervor, serving
1Co 2: 13 expressing *s* truths in *s* words.
3: 1 I could not address you as *s* but
12: 1 Now about *s* gifts, brothers,
14: 1 of love and eagerly desire *s* gifts,
15: 44 a natural body, it is raised a *s* body.
Gal 6: 1 you who are *s* should restore him
Eph 1: 3 with every *s* blessing in Christ.
5: 19 with psalms, hymns and *s* songs.
6: 12 and against the *s* forces of evil
1Pe 2: 2 newborn babies, crave pure *s* milk,
2: 5 are being built into a *s* house

SPIRITUALLY (SPIRIT)
1Co 2: 14 because they are *s* discerned.

SPIT
Mt 27: 30 They *s* on him, and took the staff
Rev 3: 16 I am about to *s* you out

SPLENDOR
1Ch 16: 29 the LORD in the *s* of his holiness.
29: 11 the glory and the majesty and the *s*,
Job 37: 22 of the north he comes in golden *s*;
Ps 29: 2 in the *s* of his holiness.
45: 3 clothe yourself with *s* and majesty.
96: 6 *S* and majesty are before him;
96: 9 in the *s* of his holiness;
104: 1 you are clothed with *s* and majesty.
145: 5 of the glorious *s* of your majesty,
145: 12 and the glorious *s* of your kingdom.
148: 13 his *s* is above the earth
Pr 4: 9 and present you with a crown of *s*."
16: 31 Gray hair is a crown of *s*;
20: 29 gray hair the *s* of the old.
Isa 55: 5 for he has endowed you with *s*."
60: 21 for the display of my *s*.
61: 3 the LORD for the display of his *s*.
63: 1 Who is this, robed in *s*,
Hab 3: 4 His *s* was like the sunrise;
Mt 6: 29 in all his *s* was dressed like one
Lk 9: 31 appeared in glorious *s*, talking
2Th 2: 8 and destroy by the *s* of his coming.

SPOIL (SPOILS)
Ps 119: 162 like one who finds great *s*.

SPOILS (SPOIL)
Isa 53: 12 he will divide the *s* with the strong,
Jn 6: 27 Do not work for food that *s*,

SPONTANEOUS*
Phm : 14 so that any favor you do will be *s*

SPOTLESS
2Pe 3: 14 make every effort to be found *s*,

SPOTS (SPOTTED)
Jer 13: 23 or the leopard its *s*?

SPOTTED (SPOTS)
Ge 30: 32 and every *s* or speckled goat.

SPREAD (SPREADING SPREADS)
Ps 78: 19 "Can God *s* a table in the desert?
Ac 6: 7 So the word of God *s*.
12: 24 of God continued to increase and *s*.
13: 49 of the Lord *s* through the whole
19: 20 the word of the Lord *s* widely
2Th 3: 1 message of the Lord may *s* rapidly

SPREADING (SPREAD)
Pr 29: 5 is *s* a net for his feet.
1Th 3: 2 God's fellow worker in *s* the gospel

SPREADS (SPREAD)
Pr 10: 18 and whoever *s* slander is a fool.

SPRING (SPRINGS WELLSPRING)
Jer 2: 13 the *s* of living water,
Jn 4: 14 in him a *s* of water welling up
Jas 3: 12 can a salt *s* produce fresh water.

SPRINGS (SPRING)
2Pe 2: 17 These men are *s* without water

SPRINKLE (SPRINKLED SPRINKLING)
Lev 16: 14 and with his finger *s* it on the front

SPRINKLED (SPRINKLE)
Heb 10: 22 having our hearts *s* to cleanse us

SPRINKLING (SPRINKLE)
1Pe 1: 2 to Jesus Christ and *s* by his blood:

SPROUT
Pr 23: 5 for they will surely *s* wings
Jer 33: 15 I will make a righteous Branch *s*

SPUR*
Heb 10: 24 how we may *s* one another

SPURNS*
Pr 15: 5 A fool *s* his father's discipline,

SPY
Gal 2: 4 ranks to *s* on the freedom we have

SQUANDERED (SQUANDERS)
Lk 15: 13 there *s* his wealth in wild living.

SQUANDERS* (SQUANDERED)
Pr 29: 3 of prostitutes *s* his wealth.

SQUARE
Rev 21: 16 The city was laid out like a *s*,

STABILITY*
Pr 29: 4 By justice a king gives a country *s*,

STAFF
Ge 49: 10 the ruler's *s* from between his feet,
Ex 7: 12 Aaron's *s* swallowed up their staffs.
Nu 17: 6 and Aaron's *s* was among them.
Ps 23: 4 your rod and your *s*,

STAIN (STAINED)
Eph 5: 27 without *s* or wrinkle or any other

STAINED (STAIN)
Isa 63: 1 with his garments *s* crimson?

STAKES
Isa 54: 2 strengthen your *s*.

STAND (STANDING STANDS STOOD)
Ex 14: 13 *S* firm and you will see
Jos 10: 12 "O sun, *s* still over Gibeon,
2Ch 20: 17 *s* firm and see the deliverance
Job 19: 25 in the end he will *s* upon the earth.
Ps 1: 1 or *s* in the way of sinners
1: 5 Therefore the wicked will not *s*
24: 3 Who may *s* in his holy place?
33: 11 of the LORD *s* firm forever,
40: 2 and gave me a firm place to *s*.
76: 7 Who can *s* before you
93: 5 Your statutes *s* firm;
119: 120 I *s* in awe of your laws.
130: 3 O Lord, who could *s*?
Ecc 5: 7 Therefore *s* in awe of God.
Isa 7: 9 If you do not *s* firm in your faith,
29: 23 will *s* in awe of the God of Israel.
Eze 22: 30 *s* before me in the gap on behalf
Hab 3: 2 I *s* in awe of your deeds, O LORD.
Zec 14: 4 On that day his feet will *s*
Mal 3: 2 Who can *s* when he appears?
Mt 12: 25 divided against itself will not *s*.
Ro 14: 4 for the Lord is able to make him *s*.
14: 10 we will all *s* before God's judgment
1Co 10: 13 out so that you can *s* up under it.
15: 58 Therefore, my dear brothers, *s* firm
16: 13 Be on your guard; *s* firm in the faith
Gal 5: 1 *S* firm, then, and do not let
Eph 6: 14 *S* firm then, with the belt
2Th 2: 15 *s* firm and hold to the teachings we
Jas 5: 8 You too, be patient and *s* firm,
Rev 3: 20 Here I am! I *s* at the door

STANDING (STAND)
Ex 3: 5 where you are *s* is holy ground."
Jos 5: 15 the place where you are *s* is holy."
Ru 2: 1 a man of *s*, whose name was Boaz.
4: 11 May you have *s* in Ephrathah
Lk 21: 19 By *s* firm you will gain life.
1Ti 3: 13 have served well gain an excellent *s*
1Pe 5: 9 Resist him, *s* firm in the faith,

STANDS (STAND)
Ps 89: 2 that your love *s* firm forever,
119: 89 it *s* firm in the heavens.
Pr 12: 7 the house of the righteous *s* firm.
Isa 40: 8 but the word of our God *s* forever."
Mt 10: 22 but he who *s* firm to the end will be
2Ti 2: 19 God's solid foundation *s* firm,
1Pe 1: 25 but the word of the Lord *s* forever

STAR (STARS)
Nu 24: 17 A *s* will come out of Jacob;
Isa 14: 12 O morning *s*, son of the dawn!
Mt 2: 2 We saw his *s* in the east
2Pe 1: 19 the morning *s* rises in your hearts.
Rev 2: 28 I will also give him the morning *s*.
22: 16 and the bright Morning *S*."

STARS (STAR)
Ge 1: 16 He also made the *s*.
Job 38: 7 while the morning *s* sang together
Da 12: 3 like the *s* for ever and ever.
Php 2: 15 in which you shine like *s*

STATURE
1Sa 2: 26 boy Samuel continued to grow in *s*
Lk 2: 52 And Jesus grew in wisdom and *s*,

STATUTES
Ps 19: 7 *s* of the LORD are trustworthy,
93: 5 Your *s* stand firm;
119: 2 Blessed are they who keep his *s*
119: 14 I rejoice in following your *s*
119: 24 Your *s* are my delight;
119: 36 Turn my heart toward your *s*
119: 99 for I meditate on your *s*.
119: 111 Your *s* are my heritage forever;
119: 125 that I may understand your *s*.
119: 129 Your *s* are wonderful;
119: 138 The *s* you have laid
119: 152 Long ago I learned from your *s*
119: 167 I obey your *s*,

STEADFAST*
Ps 51: 10 and renew a *s* spirit within me.
57: 7 My heart is *s*, O God,
57: 7 my heart is *s*;
108: 1 My heart is *s*, O God;
111: 8 They are *s* for ever and ever,
112: 7 his heart is *s*, trusting in the LORD
119: 5 Oh, that my ways were *s*
Isa 26: 3 him whose mind is *s*,
1Pe 5: 10 and make you strong, firm and *s*.

STEADY
Isa 35: 3 *s* the knees that give way;

STEAL (STOLEN)
Ex 20: 15 "You shall not *s*.
Lev 19: 11 "'Do not *s*.
Dt 5: 19 "You shall not *s*.
Mt 19: 18 do not *s*, do not give false
Ro 13: 9 "Do not *s*," "Do not covet,"
Eph 4: 28 has been stealing must *s* no longer,

STEP (FOOTSTEPS STEPS)
Job 34: 21 he sees their every *s*.
Gal 5: 25 let us keep in *s* with the Spirit.

STEPHEN
Deacon (Ac 6:5). Arrested (Ac 6:8–15). Speech to Sanhedrin (Ac 7). Stoned (Ac 7:54–60; 22:20).

STEPS (STEP)
Ps 37: 23 he makes his *s* firm;
Pr 14: 15 prudent man gives thought to his *s*.
16: 9 but the LORD determines his *s*.
20: 24 A man's *s* are directed
Jer 10: 23 it is not for man to direct his *s*.
1Pe 2: 21 that you should follow in his *s*.

STERN (STERNNESS)
Pr 15: 10 *S* discipline awaits him who leaves

STERNNESS* (STERN)
Ro 11: 22 and *s* of God: *s* to those who fell,

STICKS
Pr 18: 24 there is a friend who *s* closer

STIFF-NECKED (NECK)
Ex 34: 9 Although this is a *s* people,
Pr 29: 1 A man who remains *s*

STILL
Jos 10: 13 So the sun stood *s*,
Ps 37: 7 Be *s* before the LORD
46: 10 "Be *s*, and know that I am God;
89: 9 its waves mount up, you *s* them.
Zec 2: 13 Be *s* before the LORD, all mankind
Mk 4: 39 said to the waves, "Quiet! Be *s*!"

STIMULATE*
2Pe 3: 1 as reminders to *s* you

STING
1Co 15: 55 Where, O death, is your *s*?"

STINGY
Pr 28: 22 A *s* man is eager to get rich

STIRRED (STIRS)
Ps 45: 1 My heart is *s* by a noble theme

STIRS (STIRRED)
Pr 6: 19 and a man who *s* up dissension
10: 12 Hatred *s* up dissension,
15: 1 but a harsh word *s* up anger.
15: 18 hot-tempered man *s* up dissension,
16: 28 A perverse man *s* up dissension,
28: 25 A greedy man *s* up dissension,
29: 22 An angry man *s* up dissension,

STOLEN (STEAL)
Lev 6: 4 he must return what he has *s*
SS 4: 9 You have *s* my heart, my sister,

STOMACH
1Co 6: 13 Food for the *s* and the *s* for food"—
Php 3: 19 their god is their *s*, and their glory

STONE (CAPSTONE CORNERSTONE MILLSTONE STONED STONES)
Ex 24: 4 set up twelve *s* pillars representing
28: 10 on one *s* and the remaining six
34: 1 "Chisel out two *s* tablets like
Dt 4: 13 then wrote them on two *s* tablets.
19: 14 your neighbor's boundary *s* set up
1Sa 17: 50 the Philistine with a sling and a *s*;
Ps 91: 12 will not strike your foot against a *s*.
118: 22 The *s* the builders rejected
Pr 22: 28 not move an ancient boundary *s*
Isa 8: 14 a *s* that causes men to stumble
28: 16 "See, I lay a *s* in Zion,
Eze 11: 19 remove from them their heart of *s*
36: 26 remove from you your heart of *s*
Mt 7: 9 will give him a *s*? Or if he asks
21: 42 "'The *s* the builders rejected
24: 2 not one *s* here will be left
Mk 16: 3 "Who will roll the *s* away
Lk 4: 3 tell this *s* to become bread."
Jn 8: 7 the first to throw a *s* at her."
Ac 4: 11 "'the *s* you builders rejected,
Ro 9: 32 stumbled over the "stumbling *s*."
2Co 3: 3 not on tablets of *s* but on tablets
1Pe 2: 6 "See, I lay a *s* in Zion,
Rev 2: 17 also give him a white *s*

STONED (STONE)
2Co 11: 25 once I was *s*, three times I was
Heb 11: 37 They were *s*; they were sawed

STONES (STONE)
Ex 28: 21 are to be twelve *s*, one for each
Jos 4: 3 to take up twelve *s* from the middle
1Sa 17: 40 chose five smooth *s*
Mt 3: 9 out of these *s* God can raise up
1Co 3: 12 silver, costly *s*, wood, hay or straw,
1Pe 2: 5 also, like living *s*, are being built

STOOD (STAND)
Jos 10: 13 So the sun *s* still,
Lk 22: 28 You are those who have *s* by me
2Ti 4: 17 But the Lord *s* at my side
Jas 1: 12 because when he has *s* the test,

STOOP (STOOPS)
2Sa 22: 36 you *s* down to make me great.

STOOPS (STOOP)
Ps 113: 6 who *s* down to look

STOP
Job 37: 14 *s* and consider God's wonders.
Isa 1: 13 *S* bringing meaningless offerings!
1: 16 *S* doing wrong,
2: 22 *S* trusting in man,
Jer 32: 40 I will never *s* doing good to them,

Mk 9: 39 "Do not *s* him," Jesus said.
Jn 6: 43 "*S* grumbling among yourselves,"
7: 24 *S* judging by mere appearances,
20: 27 *S* doubting and believe."
Ro 14: 13 Therefore let us *s* passing judgment
1Co 14: 20 Brothers, *s* thinking like children.

STORE (STORED)
Pr 2: 1 and *s* up my commands within you,
7: 1 and *s* up my commands within you.
10: 14 Wise men *s* up knowledge,
Isa 33: 6 a rich *s* of salvation and wisdom
Mt 6: 19 not *s* up for yourselves treasures
6: 26 or reap or *s* away in barns,
2Ti 4: 8 Now there is in *s* for me the crown

STORED (STORE)
Lk 6: 45 out of the good *s* up in his heart,
Col 1: 5 from the hope that is *s* up for you

STOREHOUSE (HOUSE)
Mal 3: 10 Bring the whole tithe into the *s*,

STORIES*
2Pe 1: 16 did not follow cleverly invented *s*
2: 3 you with *s* they have made up.

STORM
Job 38: 1 LORD answered Job out of the *s*.
Ps 107: 29 He stilled the *s* to a whisper;
Lk 8: 24 the *s* subsided, and all was calm.

STOUTHEARTED* (HEART)
Ps 138: 3 you made me bold and *s*.

STRAIGHT
Ps 27: 11 lead me in a *s* path
107: 7 He led them by a *s* way
Pr 2: 13 who leave the *s* paths
3: 6 and he will make your paths *s*.
4: 11 and lead you along *s* paths.
4: 25 Let your eyes look *s* ahead,
11: 5 of the blameless makes a *s* way
15: 21 of understanding keeps a *s* course.
Isa 40: 3 make *s* in the wilderness
Mt 3: 3 make *s* paths for him.'"
Jn 1: 23 'Make *s* the way for the Lord.'"
2Pe 2: 15 They have left the *s* way

STRAIN (STRAINING)
Mt 23: 24 You *s* out a gnat but swallow

STRAINING (STRAIN)
Php 3: 13 and *s* toward what is ahead,

STRANGE (STRANGER STRANGERS)
Isa 28: 11 with foreign lips and *s* tongues
1Co 14: 21 "Through men of *s* tongues
1Pe 4: 4 They think it *s* that you do not

STRANGER (STRANGE)
Ps 119: 19 I am a *s* on earth;
Mt 25: 35 I was a *s* and you invited me in,
Jn 10: 5 But they will never follow a *s*;

STRANGERS (STRANGE)
Heb 13: 2 Do not forget to entertain *s*,
1Pe 2: 11 as aliens and *s* in the world,

STRAW
Isa 11: 7 and the lion will eat *s* like the ox.
1Co 3: 12 silver, costly stones, wood, hay or *s*

STRAYED (STRAYS)
Ps 119: 176 I have *s* like a lost sheep.
Jer 31: 19 After I *s*,

STRAYS (STRAYED)
Pr 21: 16 A man who *s* from the path
Eze 34: 16 for the lost and bring back the *s*.

STREAM (STREAMS)
Am 5: 24 righteousness like a never-failing *s*!

STREAMS (STREAM)
Ps 1: 3 He is like a tree planted by *s*
46: 4 is a river whose *s* make glad
Ecc 1: 7 All *s* flow into the sea,
Jn 7: 38 *s* of living water will flow

STREET
Mt 6: 5 on the *s* corners to be seen by men.
22: 9 Go to the *s* corners and invite
Rev 21: 21 The great *s* of the city was of pure gold,

STRENGTH (STRONG)
Ex 15: 2 The LORD is my *s* and my song;
Dt 4: 37 by his Presence and his great *s*,
6: 5 all your soul and with all your *s*.
Jdg 16: 15 told me the secret of your great *s*."
2Sa 22: 33 It is God who arms me with *s*
2Ki 23: 25 with all his soul and with all his *s*,
1Ch 16: 11 Look to the LORD and his *s*;
1Ch 16: 28 ascribe to the LORD glory and *s*,
29: 12 In your hands are *s* and power
Ne 8: 10 for the joy of the LORD is your *s*."
Ps 18: 1 I love you, O LORD, my *s*.
21: 13 Be exalted, O LORD, in your *s*;
28: 7 The LORD is my *s* and my shield;
29: 11 The LORD gives *s* to his people;
33: 16 no warrior escapes by his great *s*.
46: 1 God is our refuge and *s*,
59: 17 O my *S*, I sing praise to you;
65: 6 having armed yourself with *s*,
73: 26 but God is the *s* of my heart
84: 5 Blessed are those whose *s* is in you,
96: 7 ascribe to the LORD glory and *s*.
105: 4 Look to the LORD and his *s*;
118: 14 The LORD is my *s* and my song;
147: 10 not in the *s* of the horse,
Pr 24: 5 a man of knowledge increases *s*;
30: 25 Ants are creatures of little *s*,
Isa 12: 2 the LORD, is my *s* and my song;
31: 1 and in the great *s* of their horsemen
40: 26 of his great power and mighty *s*,
40: 31 will renew their *s*.
63: 1 forward in the greatness of his *s*?
Jer 9: 23 or the strong man boast of his *s*
Mic 5: 4 flock in the *s* of the LORD,
Hab 3: 19 The Sovereign LORD is my *s*;
Mk 12: 30 all your mind and with all your *s*.'
1Co 1: 25 of God is stronger than man's *s*.
Eph 1: 19 is like the working of his mighty *s*,
Php 4: 13 through him who gives me *s*.
Heb 11: 34 whose weakness was turned to *s*;
1Pe 4: 11 it with the *s* God provides,

STRENGTHEN (STRONG)
2Ch 16: 9 to *s* those whose hearts are fully
Ps 119: 28 *s* me according to your word.
Isa 35: 3 *S* the feeble hands,
41: 10 I will *s* you and help you;
Lk 22: 32 have turned back, *s* your brothers."
Eph 3: 16 of his glorious riches he may *s* you
1Th 3: 13 May he *s* your hearts
2Th 2: 17 and *s* you in every good deed
Heb 12: 12 *s* your feeble arms and weak knees.

STRENGTHENED (STRONG)
Col 1: 11 being *s* with all power according
Heb 13: 9 good for our hearts to be *s* by grace,

STRENGTHENING (STRONG)
1Co 14: 26 done for the *s* of the church.

STRETCHES
Ps 104: 2 he *s* out the heavens like a tent

STRICKEN (STRIKE)
Isa 53: 8 of my people he was *s*.

STRICT
1Co 9: 25 in the games goes into *s* training.

STRIFE (STRIVE)
Pr 17: 1 than a house full of feasting, with *s*.
20: 3 It is to a man's honor to avoid *s*,
22: 10 out the mocker, and out goes *s*;
30: 33 so stirring up anger produces *s*."
1Ti 6: 4 *s*, malicious talk, evil suspicions

STRIKE (STRIKES STROKE)
Ge 3: 15 and you will *s* his heel."
Zec 13: 7 "*S* the shepherd,
Mt 4: 6 so that you will not *s* your foot
26: 31 "'I will *s* the shepherd,

STRIKES (STRIKE)
Mt 5: 39 If someone *s* you on the right

STRIPS
Lk 2: 12 You will find a baby wrapped in *s*
Jn 20: 5 in at the *s* of linen lying there

STRIVE* (STRIFE)
Ac 24: 16 I *s* always to keep my conscience
1Ti 4: 10 (and for this we labor and *s*),

STROKE (STRIKE)
Mt 5: 18 the smallest letter, not the least *s*

STRONG (STRENGTH STRENGTHEN STRENGTHENED STRENGTHENING STRONGER)
Dt 3: 24 your greatness and your *s* hand.
31: 6 Be *s* and courageous.
Jos 1: 6 "Be *s* and courageous,
Jdg 5: 21 March on, my soul; be *s*!
2Sa 10: 12 Be *s* and let us fight bravely
1Ki 2: 2 "So be *s*, show yourself a man,
1Ch 28: 20 "Be *s* and courageous,
2Ch 32: 7 them with these words: "Be *s*
Ps 24: 8 The LORD *s* and mighty,
31: 2 a *s* fortress to save me.
Ps 62: 11 that you, O God, are *s*,
Pr 18: 10 The name of the LORD is a *s* tower
31: 17 her arms are *s* for her tasks.
Ecc 9: 11 or the battle to the *s*,
SS 8: 6 for love is as *s* as death,
Isa 35: 4 "Be *s*, do not fear;
53: 12 he will divide the spoils with the *s*,
Jer 9: 23 or the *s* man boast of his strength
50: 34 Yet their Redeemer is *s*;
Hag 2: 4 Be *s*, all you people of the land,'
Mt 12: 29 can anyone enter a *s* man's house
Lk 2: 40 And the child grew and became *s*;
Ro 15: 1 We who are *s* ought to bear
1Co 1: 8 He will keep you *s* to the end,
1: 27 things of the world to shame the *s*.
16: 13 in the faith; be men of courage; be *s*
2Co 12: 10 For when I am weak, then I am *s*.
Eph 6: 10 be *s* in the Lord and in his mighty
2Ti 2: 1 be *s* in the grace that is
1Pe 5: 10 restore you and make you *s*,

STRONGER (STRONG)
Dt 4: 38 before you nations greater and *s*
1Co 1: 25 of God is *s* than man's strength.

STRONGHOLD (STRONGHOLDS)
2Sa 22: 3 He is my *s*, my refuge and my
Ps 9: 9 a *s* in times of trouble.
18: 2 the horn of my salvation, my *s*.
27: 1 The LORD is the *s* of my life—
144: 2 my *s* and my deliverer,

STRONGHOLDS (STRONGHOLD)
Zep 3: 6 their *s* are demolished.
2Co 10: 4 have divine power to demolish *s*.

STRUGGLE (STRUGGLED STRUGGLING)
Ro 15: 30 me in my *s* by praying to God
Eph 6: 12 For our *s* is not against flesh
Heb 12: 4 In your *s* against sin, you have not

STRUGGLED (STRUGGLE)
Ge 32: 28 because you have *s* with God

STRUGGLING* (STRUGGLE)
Col 1: 29 To this end I labor, *s*
2: 1 to know how much I am *s* for you

STUDENT (STUDY)
Mt 10: 24 "A *s* is not above his teacher,

STUDY (STUDENT)
Ezr 7: 10 Ezra had devoted himself to the *s*
Ecc 12: 12 and much *s* wearies the body.
Jn 5: 39 You diligently *s* the Scriptures

STUMBLE (STUMBLES STUMBLING)
Ps 37: 24 though he *s*, he will not fall,
119: 165 and nothing can make them *s*.
Pr 3: 23 and your foot will not *s*;
Isa 8: 14 a stone that causes men to *s*
Jer 13: 16 before your feet *s*
31: 9 a level path where they will not *s*,
Eze 7: 19 for it has made them *s* into sin.
Hos 14: 9 but the rebellious *s* in them.
Mal 2: 8 teaching have caused many to *s*;
Jn 11: 9 A man who walks by day will not *s*,
Ro 9: 33 in Zion a stone that causes men to *s*
14: 20 that causes someone else to *s*.
1Co 10: 32 Do not cause anyone to *s*,
Jas 3: 2 We all *s* in many ways.
1Pe 2: 8 and, "A stone that causes men to *s*
1Jn 2: 10 nothing in him to make him *s*.

STUMBLES (STUMBLE)
Pr 24: 17 when he *s*, do not let your heart
Jn 11: 10 is when he walks by night that he *s*,
Jas 2: 10 and yet *s* at just one point is guilty

STUMBLING (STUMBLE)
Lev 19: 14 put a *s* block in front of the blind,
Ps 56: 13 and my feet from *s*,
Mt 16: 23 Satan! You are a *s* block to me;
Ro 9: 32 They stumbled over the "*s* stone."
11: 9 a *s* block and a retribution for them
14: 13 up your mind not to put any *s* block
1Co 1: 23 a *s* block to Jews and foolishness
8: 9 freedom does not become a *s* block
2Co 6: 3 We put no *s* block in anyone's path,

STUMP
Isa 6: 13 so the holy seed will be the *s*
11: 1 up from the *s* of Jesse;

STUPID
Pr 12: 1 but he who hates correction is *s*.
2Ti 2: 23 to do with foolish and *s* arguments,

STUPOR
Ro 11: 8 "God gave them a spirit of *s*,

SUBDUE (SUBDUED)
Ge 1: 28 in number; fill the earth and *s* it.

SUBDUED (SUBDUE)
Jos 10: 40 So Joshua *s* the whole region,
Ps 47: 3 He *s* nations under us,

SUBJECT (SUBJECTED)
Mt 5: 22 angry with his brother will be *s*
1Co 14: 32 of prophets are *s* to the control
15: 28 then the Son himself will be made *s*
Tit 2: 5 and to be *s* to their husbands,
2: 9 slaves to be *s* to their masters
3: 1 Remind the people to be *s* to rulers

SUBJECTED (SUBJECT)
Ro 8: 20 For the creation was *s*

SUBMISSION (SUBMIT)
1Co 14: 34 but must be in *s*, as the Law says.
1Ti 2: 11 learn in quietness and full *s*.

SUBMISSIVE (SUBMIT)
Jas 3: 17 then peace-loving, considerate, *s*,
1Pe 3: 1 in the same way be *s*
5: 5 in the same way be *s*

SUBMIT (SUBMISSION SUBMISSIVE SUBMITS)
Ro 13: 1 Everyone must *s* himself
13: 5 necessary to *s* to the authorities,
1Co 16: 16 to *s* to such as these
Eph 5: 21 *S* to one another out of reverence
Col 3: 18 Wives, *s* to your husbands,
Heb 12: 9 How much more should we *s*
13: 17 Obey your leaders and *s*
Jas 4: 7 *S* yourselves, then, to God.
1Pe 2: 18 *s* yourselves to your masters

SUBMITS* (SUBMIT)
Eph 5: 24 Now as the church *s* to Christ,

SUBTRACT*
Dt 4: 2 what I command you and do not *s*

SUCCEED (SUCCESS SUCCESSFUL)
Ps 20: 4 and make all your plans *s*.
Pr 15: 22 but with many advisers they *s*.
16: 3 and your plans will *s*.
21: 30 that can *s* against the LORD.

SUCCESS (SUCCEED)
Ge 39: 23 and gave him *s* in whatever he did.
1Sa 18: 14 In everything he did he had great *s*,
1Ch 12: 18 *S*, *s* to you, and *s*
22: 13 you will have *s* if you are careful
2Ch 26: 5 the LORD, God gave him *s*.
Ecc 10: 10 but skill will bring *s*.

SUCCESSFUL (SUCCEED)
Jos 1: 7 that you may be *s* wherever you go.
2Ki 18: 7 he was *s* in whatever he undertook.
2Ch 20: 20 in his prophets and you will be *s*."

SUFFER (SUFFERED SUFFERING SUFFERINGS SUFFERS)
Job 36: 15 those who *s* he delivers
Isa 53: 10 to crush him and cause him to *s*,
Mk 8: 31 the Son of Man must *s* many things
Lk 24: 26 the Christ have to *s* these things
24: 46 The Christ will *s* and rise
2Co 1: 6 of the same sufferings we *s*.
Php 1: 29 to *s* for him, since you are going
Heb 9: 26 would have had to *s* many times
1Pe 3: 17 to *s* for doing good
4: 16 However, if you *s* as a Christian,

SUFFERED (SUFFER)
Heb 2: 9 and honor because he *s* death,
2: 18 Because he himself *s*
1Pe 2: 21 Christ *s* for you, leaving you
4: 1 he who has *s* in his body is done

SUFFERING (SUFFER)
Job 36: 15 who suffer he delivers in their *s*;
Ps 22: 24 the *s* of the afflicted one;
Isa 53: 3 of sorrows, and familiar with *s*.
53: 11 After the *s* of his soul,
La 1: 12 Is any *s* like my *s*
Ac 5: 41 worthy of *s* disgrace for the Name.
Ro 5: 3 know that *s* produces
2Ti 1: 8 But join with me in *s* for the gospel,
Heb 2: 10 of their salvation perfect through *s*.
13: 3 as if you yourselves were *s*.
1Pe 4: 12 at the painful trial you are *s*,

SUFFERINGS (SUFFER)
Ro 5: 3 but we also rejoice in our *s*,
8: 17 share in his *s* in order that we may
8: 18 that our present *s* are not worth
2Co 1: 5 as the *s* of Christ flow
Php 3: 10 the fellowship of sharing in his *s*,
1Pe 4: 13 rejoice that you participate in the *s*
5: 9 are undergoing the same kind of *s*.

SUFFERS (SUFFER)
Pr 13: 20 but a companion of fools *s* harm.
1Co 12: 26 If one part *s*, every part *s* with it;

SUFFICIENT
2Co 12: 9 said to me, "My grace is *s* for you,

SUITABLE
Ge 2: 18 I will make a helper *s* for him."

SUMMED* (SUMS)
Ro 13: 9 there may be, are *s* up
Gal 5: 14 The entire law is *s* up

SUMMONS
Ps 50: 1 speaks and *s* the earth
Isa 45: 3 God of Israel, who *s* you by name.

SUMS* (SUMMED)
Mt 7: 12 for this *s* up the Law

SUN (SUNRISE)
Jos 10: 13 So the *s* stood still,
Jdg 5: 31 may they who love you be like the *s*
Ps 84: 11 For the LORD God is a *s*
121: 6 the *s* will not harm you by day,
136: 8 the *s* to govern the day,
Ecc 1: 9 there is nothing new under the *s*.
Isa 60: 19 The *s* will no more be your light
Mal 4: 2 the *s* of righteousness will rise
Mt 5: 45 He causes his *s* to rise on the evil
13: 43 the righteous will shine like the *s*
17: 2 His face shone like the *s*,
Lk 23: 45 for the *s* stopped shining.
Eph 4: 26 Do not let the *s* go
Rev 1: 16 His face was like the *s* shining
21: 23 The city does not need the *s*

SUNG (SING)
Mt 26: 30 When they had *s* a hymn, they

SUNRISE (SUN)
2Sa 23: 4 he is like the light of morning at *s*
Hab 3: 4 His splendor was like the *s*;

SUPERIOR
Heb 1: 4 he became as much *s* to the angels
8: 6 ministry Jesus has received is as *s*

SUPERVISION
Gal 3: 25 longer under the *s* of the law.

SUPPER
Lk 22: 20 after the *s* he took the cup, saying,
1Co 11: 25 after *s* he took the cup,
Rev 19: 9 to the wedding *s* of the Lamb!'"

SUPPLIED (SUPPLY)
Ac 20: 34 of mine have *s* my own needs
Php 4: 18 and even more; I am amply *s*,

SUPPLY (SUPPLIED SUPPLYING)
2Co 8: 14 your plenty will *s* what they need,
1Th 3: 10 and *s* what is lacking in your faith.

SUPPLYING* (SUPPLY)
2Co 9: 12 you perform is not only *s* the needs

SUPPORT (SUPPORTED SUPPORTING)
Ps 18: 18 but the LORD was my *s*.
Ro 11: 18 consider this: You do not *s* the root
1Co 9: 12 If others have this right of *s*

SUPPORTED (SUPPORT)
Ps 94: 18 your love, O LORD, *s* me.
Col 2: 19 *s* and held together by its ligaments

SUPPORTING (SUPPORT)
Eph 4: 16 held together by every *s* ligament,

SUPPRESS*
Ro 1: 18 wickedness of men who *s* the truth

SUPREMACY* (SUPREME)
Col 1: 18 in everything he might have the *s*.

SUPREME (SUPREMACY)
Pr 4: 7 Wisdom is *s*; therefore get wisdom.

SURE
Nu 28: 31 Be *s* the animals are without defect
32: 23 you may be *s* that your sin will find
Dt 6: 17 Be *s* to keep the commands
14: 22 Be *s* to set aside a tenth
29: 18 make *s* there is no root
Jos 23: 13 then you may be *s* that the LORD
1Sa 12: 24 But be *s* to fear the LORD
Ps 19: 9 The ordinances of the LORD are *s*
132: 11 a *s* oath that he will not revoke:
Pr 27: 23 Be *s* you know the condition
Isa 28: 16 cornerstone for a *s* foundation;
Eph 5: 5 of this you can be *s*: No immoral,
Heb 11: 1 faith is being *s* of what we hope for
2Pe 1: 10 to make your calling and election *s*.

SURFACE
2Co 10: 7 You are looking only on the *s*

SURPASS* (SURPASSED SURPASSES SURPASSING)
Pr 31: 29 but you *s* them all."

SURPASSED* (SURPASS)
Jn 1: 15 'He who comes after me has *s* me
1: 30 man who comes after me has *s* me

SURPASSES* (SURPASS)
Pr 8: 19 what I yield *s* choice silver.
Mt 5: 20 unless your righteousness *s* that
Eph 3: 19 to know this love that *s* knowledge

SURPASSING* (SURPASS)
Ps 150: 2 praise him for his *s* greatness.
2Co 3: 10 in comparison with the *s* glory.
9: 14 of the *s* grace God has given you.
Php 3: 8 the *s* greatness of knowing Christ

SURPRISE (SURPRISED)
1Th 5: 4 that this day should *s* you like

SURPRISED (SURPRISE)
1Pe 4: 12 do not be *s* at the painful trial you
1Jn 3: 13 Do not be *s*, my brothers,

SURRENDER
1Co 13: 3 and *s* my body to the flames,

SURROUND (SURROUNDED SURROUNDS)
Ps 5: 12 you *s* them with your favor
32: 7 and *s* me with songs of deliverance.
89: 7 awesome than all who *s* him.
125: 2 As the mountains *s* Jerusalem,
Jer 31: 22 a woman will *s* a man."

SURROUNDED (SURROUND)
Heb 12: 1 since we are *s* by such a great cloud

SURROUNDS* (SURROUND)
Ps 32: 10 *s* the man who trusts in him.
89: 8 and your faithfulness *s* you.
125: 2 so the LORD *s* his people

SUSA
Ezr 4: 9 and Babylon, the Elamites of *S*,
Ne 1: 1 while I was in the citadel of *S*,

SUSPENDS*
Job 26: 7 he *s* the earth over nothing.

SUSPICIONS*
1Ti 6: 4 evil *s* and constant friction

SUSTAIN (SUSTAINING SUSTAINS)
Ps 55: 22 and he will *s* you;
Isa 46: 4 I am he, I am he who will *s* you.

SUSTAINING* (SUSTAIN)
Heb 1: 3 *s* all things by his powerful word.

SUSTAINS (SUSTAIN)
Ps 18: 35 and your right hand *s* me;
146: 9 and *s* the fatherless and the widow,
147: 6 The LORD *s* the humble
Isa 50: 4 to know the word that *s* the weary.

SWALLOW (SWALLOWED)
Isa 25: 8 he will *s* up death forever.
Jnh 1: 17 provided a great fish to *s* Jonah,
Mt 23: 24 You strain out a gnat but *s* a camel.

SWALLOWED (SWALLOW)
1Co 15: 54 "Death has been *s* up in victory."
2Co 5: 4 so that what is mortal may be *s* up

SWAYED
Mt 11: 7 A reed *s* by the wind? If not,
22: 16 You aren't *s* by men, because you
2Ti 3: 6 are *s* by all kinds of evil desires,

SWEAR (SWORE SWORN)
Lev 19: 12 "'Do not *s* falsely by my name
Ps 24: 4 or *s* by what is false.
Isa 45: 23 by me every tongue will *s*.
Mt 5: 34 Do not *s* at all: either by heaven,
Jas 5: 12 Above all, my brothers, do not *s*—

SWEAT*
Ge 3: 19 By the *s* of your brow
Lk 22: 44 his *s* was like drops of blood falling

SWEET (SWEETER SWEETNESS)
Job 20: 12 "Though evil is *s* in his mouth
Ps 119: 103 How *s* are your words
Pr 9: 17 "Stolen water is *s*;
13: 19 A longing fulfilled is *s* to the soul,

Pr 16: 24 *s* to the soul and healing
20: 17 by fraud tastes *s* to a man,
24: 14 also that wisdom is *s* to your soul;
Ecc 5: 12 The sleep of a laborer is *s*,
Isa 5: 20 and *s* for bitter.
Eze 3: 3 it tasted as *s* as honey in my mouth.
Rev 10: 10 It tasted as *s* as honey in my mouth

SWEETER (SWEET)
Ps 19: 10 they are *s* than honey,
119: 103 *s* than honey to my mouth!

SWEETNESS* (SWEET)
SS 4: 11 Your lips drop *s* as the honeycomb,
5: 16 His mouth is *s* itself;

SWEPT
Mt 12: 44 finds the house unoccupied, *s* clean

SWERVE*
Pr 4: 5 do not forget my words or *s*
4: 27 Do not *s* to the right or the left;

SWIFT
Pr 1: 16 they are *s* to shed blood.
Ecc 9: 11 The race is not to the *s*
Isa 59: 7 they are *s* to shed innocent blood.
Ro 3: 15 "Their feet are *s* to shed blood;
2Pe 2: 1 bringing *s* destruction

SWINDLER* (SWINDLERS)
1Co 5: 11 or a slanderer, a drunkard or a *s*.

SWINDLERS* (SWINDLER)
1Co 5: 10 or the greedy and *s*, or idolaters.
6: 10 *s* will inherit the kingdom of God.

SWORD (SWORDS)
Ge 3: 24 and a flaming *s* flashing back
Dt 32: 41 when I sharpen my flashing *s*
Jos 5: 13 of him with a drawn *s* in his hand.
1Sa 17: 45 "You come against me with *s*
17: 47 here will know that it is not by *s*
31: 4 so Saul took his own *s* and fell on it.
2Sa 12: 10 therefore, the *s* will never depart
Ps 44: 6 my *s* does not bring me victory;
45: 3 Gird your *s* upon your side,
Pr 12: 18 Reckless words pierce like a *s*,
Isa 2: 4 Nation will not take up *s*
Mic 4: 3 Nation will not take up *s*
Mt 10: 34 come to bring peace, but a *s*.
26: 52 all who draw the *s* will die by the *s*.
Lk 2: 35 a *s* will pierce your own soul too."
Ro 13: 4 for he does not bear the *s*
Eph 6: 17 of salvation and the *s* of the Spirit,
Heb 4: 12 Sharper than any double-edged *s*,
Rev 1: 16 came a sharp double-edged *s*.
19: 15 Out of his mouth comes a sharp *s*

SWORDS (SWORD)
Ps 64: 3 who sharpen their tongues like *s*
Isa 2: 4 They will beat their *s*
Joel 3: 10 Beat your plowshares into *s*

SWORE (SWEAR)
Heb 6: 13 for him to swear by, he *s* by himself

SWORN (SWEAR)
Ps 110: 4 The LORD has *s*
Eze 20: 42 the land I had *s* with uplifted hand
Heb 7: 21 "The Lord has *s*

SYCAMORE-FIG (FIG)
Am 7: 14 and I also took care of *s* trees.
Lk 19: 4 and climbed a *s* tree to see him,

SYMBOLIZES*
1Pe 3: 21 this water *s* baptism that now saves

SYMPATHETIC* (SYMPATHY)
1Pe 3: 8 in harmony with one another; be *s*,

SYMPATHIZED* (SYMPATHY)
Heb 10: 34 You *s* with those in prison

SYMPATHY (SYMPATHETIC SYMPATHIZED)
Ps 69: 20 I looked for *s*, but there was none,

SYNAGOGUE
Lk 4: 16 the Sabbath day he went into the *s*,
Ac 17: 2 custom was, Paul went into the *s*,

TABERNACLE (TABERNACLES)
Ex 40: 34 the glory of the LORD filled the *t*.
Heb 8: 2 the true *t* set up by the Lord,
9: 11 and more perfect *t* that is not
9: 21 sprinkled with the blood both the *t*
Rev 15: 5 that is, the *t* of the Testimony,

TABERNACLES (TABERNACLE)
Lev 23: 34 the LORD's Feast of *T* begins,
Dt 16: 16 Feast of Weeks and the Feast of *T*.
Zec 14: 16 and to celebrate the Feast of *T*.

TABLE (TABLES)
Ex 25: 23 "Make a *t* of acacia wood —
Ps 23: 5 You prepare a *t* before me

TABLES (TABLE)
Jn 2: 15 changers and overturned their *t*.
Ac 6: 2 word of God in order to wait on *t*.

TABLET (TABLETS)
Pr 3: 3 write them on the *t* of your heart.
7: 3 write them on the *t* of your heart.

TABLETS (TABLET)
Ex 31: 18 he gave him the two *t*
Dt 10: 5 and put the *t* in the ark I had made,
2Co 3: 3 not on *t* of stone but on *t*

TAKE (TAKEN TAKES TAKING TOOK)
Ge 15: 7 land to *t* possession of it."
22: 17 Your descendants will *t* possession
Ex 3: 5 "*T* off your sandals,
21: 23 you are to *t* life for life, eye for eye,
22: 22 "Do not *t* advantage of a widow
Lev 10: 17 given to you to *t* away the guilt
25: 14 do not *t* advantage of each other.
Nu 13: 30 and *t* possession of the land,
Dt 1: 8 and *t* possession of the land that
12: 32 do not add to it or *t* away from it.
31: 26 "*T* this Book of the Law
1Sa 8: 11 He will *t* your sons and make them
1Ch 17: 13 I will never *t* my love away
Job 23: 10 But he knows the way that I *t*;
Ps 2: 12 Blessed are all who *t* refuge in him.
25: 18 and *t* away all my sins.
27: 14 be strong and *t* heart
31: 24 Be strong and *t* heart,
49: 17 for he will *t* nothing with him
51: 11 or *t* your Holy Spirit from me.
73: 24 afterward you will *t* me into glory.
118: 8 It is better to *t* refuge in the LORD
Pr 22: 23 for the LORD will *t* up their case
Isa 62: 4 for the LORD will *t* delight in you,
Eze 3: 10 and *t* to heart all the words I speak
33: 11 I *t* no pleasure in the death
Mt 10: 38 anyone who does not *t* his cross
11: 29 *T* my yoke upon you and learn
16: 24 deny himself and *t* up his cross
26: 26 saying, "*T* and eat; this is my body
Mk 14: 36 *T* this cup from me.
1Ti 6: 12 *T* hold of the eternal life

TAKEN (TAKE)
Ge 2: 23 for she was *t* out of man."
Lev 6: 4 must return what he has stolen or *t*
Nu 8: 16 I have *t* them as my own in place
19: 3 it is to be *t* outside the camp
Ecc 3: 14 added to it and nothing *t* from it.
Isa 6: 7 your guilt is *t* away and your sin
Zec 3: 4 "See, I have *t* away your sin,
Mt 13: 12 even what he has will be *t* from him
24: 40 one will be *t* and the other left.
26: 39 may this cup be *t* from me.
Mk 16: 19 he was *t* up into heaven
Ac 1: 9 he was *t* up before their very eyes,
Ro 5: 13 But sin is not *t* into account
1Ti 3: 16 was *t* up in glory.

TAKES (TAKE)
1Ki 20: 11 should not boast like one who *t* it
Ps 5: 4 You are not a God who *t* pleasure
34: 8 blessed is the man who *t* refuge
Lk 6: 30 and if anyone *t* what belongs to you
Jn 1: 29 who *t* away the sin of the world!
10: 18 No one *t* it from me, but I lay it
Rev 22: 19 And if anyone *t* words away

TAKING (TAKE)
Ac 15: 14 by *t* from the Gentiles a people
Php 2: 7 *t* the very nature of a servant,

TALENT
Mt 25: 15 to another one *t*, each according

TALES*
1Ti 4: 7 with godless myths and old wives' *t*

TALL
1Sa 17: 4 He was over nine feet *t*.
1Ch 11: 23 who was seven and a half feet *t*.

TAMAR
1. Wife of Judah's sons Er and Onan (Ge 38:1 – 10). Tricked Judah into fathering children when he refused her his third son (Ge 38:11 – 30).
2. Daughter of David, raped by Amnon (2Sa 13).

TAMBOURINE
Ps 150: 4 praise him with *t* and dancing,

TAME* (TAMED)
Jas 3: 8 but no man can *t* the tongue.

TAMED* (TAME)
Jas 3: 7 the sea are being *t* and have been *t*

TARSHISH
Jnh 1: 3 from the LORD and headed for *T*.

TARSUS
Ac 9: 11 ask for a man from *T* named Saul,

TASK (TASKS)
1Ch 29: 1 The *t* is great, because this palatial
Mk 13: 34 each with his assigned *t*,
Ac 20: 24 complete the *t* the Lord Jesus has
1Co 3: 5 the Lord has assigned to each his *t*.
2Co 2: 16 And who is equal to such a *t*?
1Ti 3: 1 an overseer, he desires a noble *t*.

TASKS (TASK)
Pr 31: 17 her arms are strong for her *t*.

TASTE (TASTED TASTY)
Ps 34: 8 *T* and see that the LORD is good;
119: 103 sweet are your words to my *t*,
Pr 24: 13 from the comb is sweet to your *t*.
SS 2: 3 and his fruit is sweet to my *t*.
Col 2: 21 Do not *t*! Do not touch!"?
Heb 2: 9 the grace of God he might *t* death

TASTED (TASTE)
Eze 3: 3 it *t* as sweet as honey in my mouth.
1Pe 2: 3 now that you have *t* that the Lord
Rev 10: 10 It *t* as sweet as honey in my mouth,

TASTY (TASTE)
Ge 27: 4 Prepare me the kind of *t* food I like

TATTOO*
Lev 19: 28 or put *t* marks on yourselves.

TAUGHT (TEACH)
1Ki 4: 33 He also *t* about animals and birds,
2Ki 17: 28 *t* them how to worship the LORD.
2Ch 17: 9 They *t* throughout Judah,
Ps 119: 102 for you yourself have *t* me.
Pr 4: 4 he *t* me and said,
31: 1 an oracle his mother *t* him:
Isa 29: 13 is made up only of rules *t* by men.
50: 4 ear to listen like one being *t*.
Mt 7: 29 he *t* as one who had authority,
15: 9 their teachings are but rules *t*
Lk 4: 15 He *t* in their synagogues,
Ac 20: 20 have *t* you publicly and from house
1Co 2: 13 but in words *t* by the Spirit,
Gal 1: 12 nor was I *t* it; rather, I received it
1Ti 1: 20 to Satan to be *t* not to blaspheme.
1Jn 2: 27 just as it has *t* you, remain in him.

TAX (TAXES)
Mt 11: 19 a friend of *t* collectors and "sinners
17: 24 of the two-drachma *t* came to Peter

TAXES (TAX)
Mt 22: 17 Is it right to pay *t* to Caesar or not
Ro 13: 7 If you owe *t*, pay *t*; if revenue,

TEACH (TAUGHT TEACHER TEACHERS TEACHES TEACHING TEACHINGS)
Ex 4: 12 and will *t* you what to say."
18: 20 *T* them the decrees and laws,
33: 13 *t* me your ways so I may know you
Lev 10: 11 and you must *t* the Israelites all
Dt 4: 9 *T* them to your children
6: 1 me to *t* you to observe
8: 3 to *t* you that man does not live
11: 19 *T* them to your children, talking
1Sa 12: 23 I will *t* you the way that is good
1Ki 8: 36 *T* them the right way to live,
Job 12: 7 ask the animals, and they will *t* you
Ps 32: 8 *t* you in the way you should go;
34: 11 I will *t* you the fear of the LORD.
51: 13 I will *t* transgressors your ways,
78: 5 forefathers to *t* their children,
90: 12 *T* us to number our days aright,
119: 33 *T* me, O LORD, to follow your
143: 10 *T* me to do your will,
Pr 9: 9 *t* a righteous man and he will add
Jer 31: 34 No longer will a man *t* his neighbor
Mic 4: 2 He will *t* us his ways,
Lk 11: 1 said to him, "Lord, *t* us to pray,
12: 12 for the Holy Spirit will *t* you
Jn 14: 26 will *t* you all things and will remind
Ro 2: 21 who *t* others, do you not *t* yourself?
15: 4 in the past was written to *t* us,
1Ti 2: 12 I do not permit a woman to *t*
3: 2 respectable, hospitable, able to *t*,
2Ti 2: 2 also be qualified to *t* others.
2: 24 kind to everyone, able to *t*,

Tit 2: 1 You must *t* what is in accord
2: 15 then, are the things you should *t*.
Heb 8: 11 No longer will a man *t* his neighbor
Jas 3: 1 know that we who *t* will be judged
1Jn 2: 27 you do not need anyone to *t* you.

TEACHER (TEACH)
Ecc 1: 1 The words of the *T*, son of David,
Mt 10: 24 "A student is not above his *t*,
13: 52 "Therefore every *t*
23: 10 Nor are you to be called '*t*,'
Lk 6: 40 A student is not above his *t*,
Jn 3: 2 we know you are a *t* who has come
13: 14 and *T*, have washed your feet,

TEACHERS (TEACH)
Ps 119: 99 I have more insight than all my *t*,
Pr 5: 13 I would not obey my *t*
Lk 20: 46 "Beware of the *t* of the law.
1Co 12: 28 third *t*, then workers of miracles,
Eph 4: 11 and some to be pastors and *t*,
2Ti 4: 3 around them a great number of *t*
Heb 5: 12 by this time you ought to be *t*,
Jas 3: 1 of you should presume to be *t*,
2Pe 2: 1 as there will be false *t* among you.

TEACHES (TEACH)
Ps 25: 9 and *t* them his way.
94: 10 Does he who *t* man lack
Pr 15: 33 of the LORD *t* a man wisdom,
Isa 48: 17 who *t* you what is best for you,
Mt 5: 19 *t* these commands will be called
1Ti 6: 3 If anyone *t* false doctrines
Tit 2: 12 It *t* us to say "No" to ungodliness
1Jn 2: 27 his anointing *t* you about all things

TEACHING (TEACH)
Ezr 7: 10 to *t* its decrees and laws in Israel.
Pr 1: 8 and do not forsake your mother's *t*.
3: 1 My son, do not forget my *t*,
6: 23 this *t* is a light,
Mt 28: 20 *t* them to obey everything I have
Jn 7: 17 whether my *t* comes from God or
8: 31 to my *t*, you are really my disciples.
14: 23 loves me, he will obey my *t*.
Ac 2: 42 themselves to the apostles' *t*
Ro 12: 7 let him serve; if it is *t*, let him teach;
Eph 4: 14 and there by every wind of *t*
2Th 3: 6 to the *t* you received from us.
1Ti 4: 13 of Scripture, to preaching and to *t*.
5: 17 whose work is preaching and *t*.
6: 3 Lord Jesus Christ and to godly *t*,
2Ti 3: 16 is God-breathed and is useful for *t*,
Tit 1: 11 by *t* things they ought not
2: 7 In your *t* show integrity,
Heb 5: 13 with the *t* about righteousness.
2Jn : 9 and does not continue in the *t*

TEACHINGS (TEACH)
Pr 7: 2 guard my *t* as the apple of your eye.
2Th 2: 15 hold to the *t* we passed on to you,
Heb 6: 1 leave the elementary *t* about Christ

TEAR (TEARS)
Rev 7: 17 God will wipe away every *t*
21: 4 He will wipe every *t*

TEARS (TEAR)
Ps 126: 5 Those who sow in *t*
Isa 25: 8 LORD will wipe away the *t*
Jer 31: 16 and your eyes from *t*,
50: 4 in *t* to seek the LORD their God.
Lk 7: 38 she began to wet his feet with her *t*.
2Co 2: 4 anguish of heart and with many *t*,
Php 3: 18 and now say again even with *t*,

TEETH (TOOTH)
Job 19: 20 with only the skin of my *t*.
Ps 35: 16 they gnashed their *t* at me.
Jer 31: 29 and the children's *t* are set on edge
Mt 8: 12 will be weeping and gnashing of *t*."

TEMPER (EVEN-TEMPERED HOT-TEMPERED ILL-TEMPERED QUICK-TEMPERED)
Pr 16: 32 a man who controls his *t*

TEMPERANCE see SELF-CONTROL

TEMPERATE*
1Ti 3: 2 *t*, self-controlled, respectable,
3: 11 not malicious talkers but *t*
Tit 2: 2 Teach the older men to be *t*,

TEMPEST
Ps 50: 3 and around him a *t* rages.
55: 8 far from the *t* and storm."

TEMPLE (TEMPLES)
1Ki 6: 1 began to build the *t* of the LORD.
6: 38 the *t* was finished in all its details
8: 10 the cloud filled the *t* of the LORD.
8: 27 How much less this *t* I have built!
2Ch 36: 19 They set fire to God's *t*
36: 23 me to build a *t* for him at Jerusalem
Ezr 6: 14 finished building the *t* according
Ps 27: 4 and to seek him in his *t*.
Isa 6: 1 and the train of his robe filled the *t*.
Eze 10: 4 cloud filled the *t*, and the court was
43: 4 glory of the LORD entered the *t*
Hab 2: 20 But the LORD is in his holy *t*;
Mt 12: 6 that one greater than the *t* is here.
26: 61 'I am able to destroy the *t* of God
27: 51 of the *t* was torn in two from top
Lk 21: 5 about how the *t* was adorned
Jn 2: 14 In the *t* courts he found men selling
1Co 3: 16 that you yourselves are God's *t*
6: 19 you not know that your body is a *t*
2Co 6: 16 For we are the *t* of the living God.
Rev 21: 22 I did not see a *t* in the city,

TEMPLES (TEMPLE)
Ac 17: 24 does not live in *t* built by hands.

TEMPORARY
2Co 4: 18 what is seen is *t*, but what is unseen

TEMPT* (TEMPTATION TEMPTED TEMPTER TEMPTING)
1Co 7: 5 again so that Satan will not *t* you
Jas 1: 13 does he *t* anyone; but each one is

TEMPTATION* (TEMPT)
Mt 6: 13 And lead us not into *t*,
26: 41 pray so that you will not fall into *t*.
Mk 14: 38 pray so that you will not fall into *t*.
Lk 11: 4 And lead us not into *t*.'"
22: 40 "Pray that you will not fall into *t*."
22: 46 pray so that you will not fall into *t*
1Co 10: 13 No *t* has seized you except what is
1Ti 6: 9 want to get rich fall into *t*

TEMPTED* (TEMPT)
Mt 4: 1 into the desert to be *t* by the devil.
Mk 1: 13 was in the desert forty days, being *t*
Lk 4: 2 for forty days he was *t* by the devil.
1Co 10: 13 But when you are *t*, he will
10: 13 he will not let you be *t*
Gal 6: 1 yourself, or you also may be *t*.
1Th 3: 5 way the tempter might have *t* you
Heb 2: 18 able to help those who are being *t*.
2: 18 he himself suffered when he was *t*,
4: 15 but we have one who has been *t*
Jas 1: 13 For God cannot be *t* by evil,
1: 13 When *t*, no one should say,
1: 14 each one is *t* when, by his own evil

TEMPTER* (TEMPT)
Mt 4: 3 The *t* came to him and said,
1Th 3: 5 some way the *t* might have

TEMPTING* (TEMPT)
Lk 4: 13 the devil had finished all this *t*,
Jas 1: 13 no one should say, "God is *t* me."

TEN (TENTH TITHE TITHES)
Ex 34: 28 covenant — the *T* Commandments.
Lev 26: 8 of you will chase *t* thousand,
Dt 4: 13 covenant, the *T* Commandments,
10: 4 The *T* Commandments he had
Ps 91: 7 *t* thousand at your right hand,
Da 7: 24 *t* horns are *t* kings who will come
Mt 25: 1 will be like *t* virgins who took
25: 28 it to the one who has the *t* talents.
Lk 15: 8 suppose a woman has *t* silver coins
Rev 12: 3 and *t* horns and seven crowns

TENANTS
Mt 21: 34 servants to the *t* to collect his fruit.

TEND
Jer 23: 2 to the shepherds who *t* my people:
Eze 34: 14 I will *t* them in a good pasture,

TENDERNESS*
Isa 63: 15 Your *t* and compassion are
Php 2: 1 fellowship with the Spirit, if any *t*

TENT (TENTMAKER TENTS)
Ex 27: 21 In the *T* of Meeting,
40: 2 "Set up the tabernacle, the *T*
Isa 54: 2 "Enlarge the place of your *t*,
2Co 5: 1 that if the earthly *t* we live
2Pe 1: 13 as long as I live in the *t* of this body,

TENTH (TEN)
Ge 14: 20 Abram gave him a *t* of everything.
Nu 18: 26 you must present a *t* of that tithe
Dt 14: 22 Be sure to set aside a *t*
1Sa 8: 15 He will take a *t* of your grain
Lk 11: 42 you give God a *t* of your mint,
18: 12 I fast twice a week and give a *t*
Heb 7: 4 patriarch Abraham gave him a *t*

TENTMAKER* (TENT)
Ac 18: 3 and because he was a *t* as they were

TENTS (TENT)
Ge 13: 12 and pitched his *t* near Sodom.
Ps 84: 10 than dwell in the *t* of the wicked.

TERAH
Ge 11: 31 *T* took his son Abram, his

TERRIBLE (TERROR)
2Ti 3: 1 There will be *t* times

TERRIFIED (TERROR)
Dt 7: 21 Do not be *t* by them,
20: 3 do not be *t* or give way to panic
Ps 90: 7 and *t* by your indignation.
Mt 14: 26 walking on the lake, they were *t*.
17: 6 they fell facedown to the ground, *t*.
27: 54 they were *t*, and exclaimed,
Mk 4: 41 They were *t* and asked each other,

TERRIFYING (TERROR)
Heb 12: 21 The sight was so *t* that Moses said,

TERRITORY
2Co 10: 16 done in another man's *t*.

TERROR (TERRIBLE TERRIFIED TERRIFYING)
Dt 2: 25 very day I will begin to put the *t*
28: 67 of the *t* that will fill your hearts
Job 9: 34 so that his *t* would frighten me no
Ps 91: 5 You will not fear the *t* of night,
Pr 21: 15 but *t* to evildoers.
Isa 13: 8 *T* will seize them,
24: 17 *T* and pit and snare await you,
51: 13 live in constant *t* every day
54: 14 *T* will be far removed;
Lk 21: 26 Men will faint from *t*, apprehensive
Ro 13: 3 For rulers hold no *t*

TEST (TESTED TESTING TESTS)
Dt 6: 16 Do not *t* the LORD your God
Jdg 3: 1 to *t* all those Israelites who had not
1Ki 10: 1 came to *t* him with hard questions.
1Ch 29: 17 that you *t* the heart and are pleased
Ps 26: 2 *T* me, O LORD, and try me,
78: 18 They willfully put God to the *t*
106: 14 wasteland they put God to the *t*.
139: 23 *t* me and know my anxious
Jer 11: 20 and *t* the heart and mind,
Lk 4: 12 put the Lord your God to the *t*.'"
Ac 5: 9 How could you agree to *t* the Spirit
Ro 12: 2 Then you will be able to *t*
1Co 3: 13 and the fire will *t* the quality
10: 9 We should not *t* the Lord,
2Co 13: 5 unless, of course, you fail the *t*?
1Th 5: 21 *T* everything.
Jas 1: 12 because when he has stood the *t*,
1Jn 4: 1 *t* the spirits to see whether they are

TESTED (TEST)
Ge 22: 1 Some time later God *t* Abraham.
Job 23: 10 when he has *t* me, I will come forth
34: 36 that Job might be *t* to the utmost
Ps 66: 10 For you, O God, *t* us;
Pr 27: 21 man is *t* by the praise he receives.
Isa 28: 16 a *t* stone,
48: 10 I have *t* you in the furnace
1Ti 3: 10 They must first be *t*; and then
Heb 11: 17 By faith Abraham, when God *t* him

TESTIFIES (TESTIFY)
Jn 5: 32 There is another who *t* in my favor,
Ro 8: 16 The Spirit himself *t*

TESTIFY (TESTIFIES TESTIMONY)
Pr 24: 28 Do not *t* against your neighbor
Jn 1: 7 a witness to *t* concerning that light,
1: 34 and I *t* that this is the Son of God."
5: 39 are the Scriptures that *t* about me,
7: 7 because I *t* that what it does is evil.
15: 26 he will *t* about me. And you
Ac 4: 33 continued to *t* to the resurrection
10: 43 All the prophets *t* about him that
2Ti 1: 8 ashamed to *t* about our Lord,
1Jn 4: 14 *t* that the Father has sent his Son
5: 7 For there are three that *t*: the Spirit

TESTIMONY (TESTIFY)
Ex 20: 16 "You shall not give false *t*
31: 18 gave him the two tablets of the *T*,
Nu 35: 30 only on the *t* of witnesses.
Dt 19: 18 giving false *t* against his brother,
Pr 12: 17 A truthful witness gives honest *t*,
Isa 8: 20 and to the *t*! If they do not speak
Mt 15: 19 sexual immorality, theft, false *t*,

Mt 24: 14 preached in the whole world as a *t*
Lk 18: 20 not give false *t*, honor your father
Jn 2: 25 He did not need man's *t* about man
21: 24 We know that his *t* is true.
1Jn 5: 9 but God's *t* is greater because it is
Rev 12: 11 and by the word of their *t*;

TESTING (TEST)
Lk 8: 13 but in the time of *t* they fall away.
Heb 3: 8 during the time of *t* in the desert,
Jas 1: 3 because you know that the *t*

TESTS (TEST)
Pr 17: 3 but the LORD *t* the heart.
1Th 2: 4 but God, who *t* our hearts.

THADDAEUS
Apostle (Mt 10:3; Mk 3:18); probably also known as Judas son of James (Lk 6:16; Ac 1:13).

THANK (THANKFUL THANKFULNESS THANKS THANKSGIVING)
Php 1: 3 I *t* my God every time I remember
1Th 3: 9 How can we *t* God enough for you

THANKFUL (THANK)
Col 3: 15 And be *t*.
Heb 12: 28 let us be *t*, and so worship God

THANKFULNESS (THANK)
1Co 10: 30 If I take part in the meal with *t*,
Col 2: 7 taught, and overflowing with *t*.

THANKS (THANK)
1Ch 16: 8 Give *t* to the LORD, call
Ne 12: 31 assigned two large choirs to give *t*.
Ps 7: 17 I will give *t* to the LORD
28: 7 and I will give *t* to him in song.
30: 12 my God, I will give you *t* forever.
35: 18 I will give you *t* in the great
75: 1 we give *t*, for your Name is near;
100: 4 give *t* to him and praise his name.
107: 1 Give *t* to the LORD, for he is good;
118: 28 are my God, and I will give you *t*;
136: 1 Give *t* to the LORD, for he is good.
Ro 1: 21 as God nor gave *t* to him,
1Co 11: 24 when he had given *t*, he broke it
15: 57 *t* be to God! He gives us the victory
2Co 2: 14 *t* be to God, who always leads us
9: 15 *T* be to God for his indescribable
1Th 5: 18 give *t* in all circumstances,
Rev 4: 9 and *t* to him who sits on the throne

THANKSGIVING (THANK)
Ps 95: 2 Let us come before him with *t*
100: 4 Enter his gates with *t*
1Co 10: 16 cup of *t* for which we give thanks
Php 4: 6 by prayer and petition, with *t*,
1Ti 4: 3 created to be received with *t*

THEFT (THIEF)
Mt 15: 19 sexual immorality, *t*, false

THEFTS* (THIEF)
Rev 9: 21 their sexual immorality or their *t*.

THEME*
Ps 45: 1 My heart is stirred by a noble *t*
119: 54 Your decrees are the *t* of my song

THIEF (THEFT THEFTS THIEVES)
Ex 22: 3 A *t* must certainly make restitution
Pr 6: 30 Men do not despise a *t* if he steals
Lk 12: 39 at what hour the *t* was coming,
1Th 5: 2 day of the Lord will come like a *t*
1Pe 4: 15 or *t* or any other kind of criminal,
Rev 16: 15 I come like a *t*! Blessed is he who

THIEVES (THIEF)
Mt 6: 19 and where *t* break in and steal.
Jn 10: 8 who ever came before me were *t*
1Co 6: 10 nor homosexual offenders nor *t*

THINK (THINKING THOUGHT THOUGHTS)
Ps 63: 6 I *t* of you through the watches
Isa 44: 19 No one stops to *t*,
Mt 22: 42 "What do you *t* about the Christ?
Ro 12: 3 Do not *t* of yourself more highly
Php 4: 8 praiseworthy — *t* about such things

THINKING (THINK)
Pr 23: 7 who is always *t* about the cost.
1Co 14: 20 Brothers, stop *t* like children.
2Pe 3: 1 to stimulate you to wholesome *t*.

THIRST (THIRSTS THIRSTY)
Ps 69: 21 and gave me vinegar for my *t*.
Mt 5: 6 Blessed are those who hunger and *t*
Jn 4: 14 the water I give him will never *t*.
2Co 11: 27 I have known hunger and *t*
Rev 7: 16 never again will they *t*.

THIRSTS (THIRST)
Ps 42: 2 My soul *t* for God,

THIRSTY (THIRST)
Ps 107: 9 for he satisfies the *t*
Pr 25: 21 if he is *t*, give him water to drink.
Isa 55: 1 "Come, all you who are *t*,
Mt 25: 35 I was *t* and you gave me something
Jn 7: 37 "If anyone is *t*, let him come to me
Ro 12: 20 if he is *t*, give him something
Rev 21: 6 To him who is *t* I will give to drink
22: 17 Whoever is *t*, let him come;

THOMAS
Apostle (Mt 10:3; Mk 3:18; Lk 6:15; Jn 11:16; 14:5; 21:2; Ac 1:13). Doubted resurrection (Jn 20:24 – 28).

THONGS
Mk 1: 7 *t* of whose sandals I am not worthy

THORN (THORNBUSHES THORNS)
2Co 12: 7 there was given me a *t* in my flesh,

THORNBUSHES (THORN)
Lk 6: 44 People do not pick figs from *t*,

THORNS (THORN)
Ge 3: 18 It will produce *t* and thistles
Nu 33: 55 in your eyes and *t* in your sides.
Mt 13: 7 fell among *t*, which grew up
27: 29 and then twisted together a crown of *t*
Heb 6: 8 But land that produces *t*

THOUGHT (THINK)
Pr 14: 15 a prudent man gives *t* to his steps.
21: 29 an upright man gives *t* to his ways.
1Co 13: 11 I talked like a child, I *t* like a child,

THOUGHTS (THINK)
1Ch 28: 9 every motive behind the *t*.
Ps 94: 11 The LORD knows the *t* of man;
139: 23 test me and know my anxious *t*.
Isa 55: 8 "For my *t* are not your *t*,
Mt 15: 19 For out of the heart come evil *t*,
1Co 2: 11 among men knows the *t* of a man
Heb 4: 12 it judges the *t* and attitudes

THREE
Ge 6: 10 Noah had *t* sons: Shem, Ham
Ex 23: 14 "*T* times a year you are
Dt 19: 15 the testimony of two or *t* witnesses.
2Sa 23: 8 a Tahkemonite, was chief of the *T*;
Pr 30: 15 "There are *t* things that are never
30: 18 "There are *t* things that are too
30: 21 "Under *t* things the earth trembles,
30: 29 "There are *t* things that are stately
Ecc 4: 12 of *t* strands is not quickly broken.
Da 3: 24 "Weren't there *t* men that we tied up
Am 1: 3 "For *t* sins of Damascus,
Jnh 1: 17 inside the fish *t* days and *t* nights.
Mt 12: 40 so the Son of Man will be *t* days
12: 40 *t* nights in the belly of a huge fish,
12: 40 *t* nights in the heart of the earth.
17: 4 I will put up *t* shelters — one
18: 20 or *t* come together in my name,
26: 34 you will disown me *t* times."
26: 75 you will disown me *t* times."
27: 63 'After *t* days I will rise again.'
Mk 8: 31 and after *t* days rise again.
9: 5 Let us put up *t* shelters — one
14: 30 yourself will disown me *t* times."
Jn 2: 19 and I will raise it again in *t* days."
1Co 13: 13 And now these *t* remain: faith,
14: 27 or at the most *t* — should speak,
2Co 13: 1 testimony of two or *t* witnesses."
1Jn 5: 7 For there are *t* that testify:

THRESHER* (THRESHING)
1Co 9: 10 plowman plows and the *t* threshes,

THRESHING (THRESHER)
Ru 3: 6 So she went down to the *t* floor
2Sa 24: 18 an altar to the LORD on the *t* floor
Lk 3: 17 is in his hand to clear his *t* floor

THREW (THROW)
Da 6: 16 and *t* him into the lions' den.
Jnh 1: 15 took Jonah and *t* him overboard,

THRIVE
Pr 29: 2 When the righteous *t*, the people

THROAT (THROATS)
Ps 5: 9 Their *t* is an open grave;
Pr 23: 2 and put a knife to your *t*

THROATS (THROAT)
Ro 3: 13 "Their *t* are open graves;

THROB*
Isa 60: 5 your heart will *t* and swell with joy;

THRONE (ENTHRONED ENTHRONES THRONES)
2Sa 7: 16 your *t* will be established forever
1Ch 17: 12 and I will establish his *t* forever.
Ps 11: 4 the LORD is on his heavenly *t*.
45: 6 Your *t*, O God, will last for ever
47: 8 God is seated on his holy *t*.
89: 14 justice are the foundation of your *t*;
Isa 6: 1 I saw the Lord seated on a *t*,
66: 1 "Heaven is my *t*,
Eze 28: 2 I sit on the *t* of a god
Da 7: 9 His *t* was flaming with fire,
Mt 19: 28 Son of Man sits on his glorious *t*,
Ac 7: 49 prophet says: "'Heaven is my *t*,
Heb 1: 8 "Your *t*, O God, will last for ever
4: 16 Let us then approach the *t* of grace
12: 2 at the right hand of the *t* of God.
Rev 3: 21 sat down with my Father on his *t*.
3: 21 the right to sit with me on my *t*,
4: 2 there before me was a *t* in heaven
4: 10 They lay their crowns before the *t*
20: 11 Then I saw a great white *t*
22: 3 *t* of God and of the Lamb will be

THRONES (THRONE)
Mt 19: 28 me will also sit on twelve *t*,
Rev 4: 4 throne were twenty-four other *t*,

THROW (THREW)
Jn 8: 7 the first to *t* a stone at her."
Heb 10: 35 So do not *t* away your confidence;
12: 1 let us *t* off everything that hinders

THUNDER (THUNDERS)
Ps 93: 4 Mightier than the *t*
Mk 3: 17 which means Sons of *T*); Andrew,

THUNDERS (THUNDER)
Job 37: 5 God's voice *t* in marvelous ways;
Ps 29: 3 the God of glory *t*,
Rev 10: 3 the voices of the seven *t* spoke.

THWART* (THWARTED)
Isa 14: 27 has purposed, and who can *t* him?

THWARTED (THWART)
Job 42: 2 no plan of yours can be *t*.

THYATIRA
Rev 2: 18 the angel of the church in *T* write:

TIBNI
King of Israel (1Ki 16:21 – 22).

TIDINGS
Isa 40: 9 You who bring good *t* to Jerusalem
52: 7 who bring good *t*,

TIES
Hos 11: 4 with *t* of love;
Mt 12: 29 unless he first *t* up the strong man?

TIGHT*
Jas 1: 26 and yet does not keep a *t* rein

TIGHTFISTED*
Dt 15: 7 or *t* toward your poor brother.

TIME (TIMES)
Est 4: 14 come to royal position for such a *t*
Ecc 3: 1 There is a *t* for everything,
8: 5 wise heart will know the proper *t*
Da 7: 25 to him for a *t*, times and half a *t*.
12: 7 "It will be for a *t*, times and half a *t*.
Hos 10: 12 for it is *t* to seek the LORD,
Jn 2: 4 Jesus replied, "My *t* has not yet
17: 1 prayed: "Father, the *t* has come.
Ro 9: 9 "At the appointed *t* I will return,
13: 11 understanding the present *t*.
1Co 7: 29 brothers, is that the *t* is short.
2Co 6: 2 now is the *t* of God's favor,
2Ti 1: 9 Jesus before the beginning of *t*,
Tit 1: 2 promised before the beginning of *t*,
Heb 9: 28 and he will appear a second *t*,
10: 12 for all *t* one sacrifice for sins,
1Pe 4: 17 For it is *t* for judgment to begin

TIMES (TIME)
Ps 9: 9 a stronghold in *t* of trouble.
31: 15 My *t* are in your hands;
62: 8 Trust in him at all *t*, O people;
Pr 17: 17 A friend loves at all *t*,
Isa 46: 10 from ancient *t*, what is still to come
Am 5: 13 for the *t* are evil.
Mt 16: 3 cannot interpret the signs of the *t*.
18: 21 how many *t* shall I forgive my
Ac 1: 7 "It is not for you to know the *t*
Rev 12: 14 *t* and half a time, out

TIMID (TIMIDITY)
1Th 5: 14 encourage the *t*, help the weak,

TIMIDITY* (TIMID)
2Ti 1: 7 For God did not give us a spirit of *t*

TIMOTHY
Believer from Lystra (Ac 16:1). Joined Paul on second missionary journey (Ac 16 – 20). Sent to settle problems at Corinth (1Co 4:17; 16:10). Led church at Ephesus (1Ti 1:3). Co-writer with Paul (1Th 1:1; 2Th 1:1; Phm 1).

TIP
Job 33: 2 my words are on the *t* of my tongue

TIRE (TIRED)
2Th 3: 13 never *t* of doing what is right.

TIRED (TIRE)
Ex 17: 12 When Moses' hands grew *t*,
Isa 40: 28 He will not grow *t* or weary,

TITHE (TEN)
Lev 27: 30 "'A *t* of everything from the land,
Dt 12: 17 eat in your own towns the *t*
Mal 3: 10 the whole *t* into the storehouse,

TITHES (TEN)
Nu 18: 21 give to the Levites all the *t* in Israel
Mal 3: 8 'How do we rob you?' "In *t*

TITUS*
Gentile co-worker of Paul (Gal 2:1 – 3; 2Ti 4:10); sent to Corinth (2Co 2:13; 7 – 8; 12:18), Crete (Tit 1:4 – 5).

TODAY
Ps 2: 7 *t* I have become your Father.
95: 7 *T*, if you hear his voice,
Mt 6: 11 Give us *t* our daily bread.
Lk 2: 11 *T* in the town of David a Savior has
23: 43 *t* you will be with me in paradise."
Ac 13: 33 *t* I have become your Father.'
Heb 1: 5 *t* I have become your Father"?
3: 7 "*T*, if you hear his voice,
3: 13 daily, as long as it is called *T*,
5: 5 *t* I have become your Father."
13: 8 Christ is the same yesterday and *t*

TOIL (TOILED TOILING)
Ge 3: 17 through painful *t* you will eat of it

TOILED (TOIL)
2Co 11: 27 and *t* and have often gone

TOILING (TOIL)
2Th 3: 8 *t* so that we would not be a burden

TOLERANCE* (TOLERATE)
Ro 2: 4 for the riches of his kindness, *t*

TOLERATE (TOLERANCE)
Hab 1: 13 you cannot *t* wrong.
Rev 2: 2 that you cannot *t* wicked men,

TOMB
Mt 27: 65 make the *t* as secure as you know
Lk 24: 2 the stone rolled away from the *t*,

TOMORROW
Pr 27: 1 Do not boast about *t*,
Isa 22: 13 "for *t* we die!"
Mt 6: 34 Therefore do not worry about *t*,
1Co 15: 32 for *t* we die."
Jas 4: 13 "Today or *t* we will go to this

TONGUE (TONGUES)
Ex 4: 10 I am slow of speech and *t*."
Job 33: 2 my words are on the tip of my *t*.
Ps 5: 9 with their *t* they speak deceit.
34: 13 keep your *t* from evil
37: 30 and his *t* speaks what is just.
39: 1 and keep my *t* from sin;
51: 14 my *t* will sing of your righteousness
52: 4 O you deceitful *t*!
71: 24 My *t* will tell of your righteous acts
119: 172 May my *t* sing of your word,
137: 6 May my *t* cling to the roof
139: 4 Before a word is on my *t*
Pr 6: 17 a lying *t*,
10: 19 but he who holds his *t* is wise.
12: 18 but the *t* of the wise brings healing.
15: 4 The *t* that brings healing is a tree
17: 20 he whose *t* is deceitful falls
21: 23 He who guards his mouth and his *t*
25: 15 and a gentle *t* can break a bone.
26: 28 A lying *t* hates those it hurts,
28: 23 than he who has a flattering *t*.
31: 26 and faithful instruction is on her *t*.
SS 4: 11 milk and honey are under your *t*.
Isa 32: 4 and the stammering *t* will be fluent
45: 23 by me every *t* will swear.
50: 4 has given me an instructed *t*,
59: 3 and your *t* mutters wicked things.
Lk 16: 24 of his finger in water and cool my *t*,
Ro 14: 11 every *t* will confess to God.'"
1Co 14: 2 speaks in a *t* does not speak to men
14: 4 He who speaks in a *t* edifies himself
14: 9 intelligible words with your *t*,
14: 13 in a *t* should pray that he may
14: 19 than ten thousand words in a *t*.
14: 26 revelation, a *t* or an interpretation.
14: 27 If anyone speaks in a *t*, two —
Php 2: 11 every *t* confess that Jesus Christ is
Jas 1: 26 does not keep a tight rein on his *t*,
3: 5 Likewise the *t* is a small part
3: 8 but no man can tame the *t*.
1Jn 3: 18 or *t* but with actions and in truth.

TONGUES (TONGUE)
Ps 12: 4 "We will triumph with our *t*;
126: 2 our *t* with songs of joy.
Isa 28: 11 with foreign lips and strange *t*
66: 18 and gather all nations and *t*,
Jer 23: 31 the prophets who wag their own *t*
Mk 16: 17 in new *t*; they will pick up snakes
Ac 2: 3 to be *t* of fire that separated
2: 4 and began to speak in other *t*
10: 46 For they heard them speaking in *t*
19: 6 and they spoke in *t* and prophesied
Ro 3: 13 their *t* practice deceit."
1Co 12: 10 still another the interpretation of *t*.
12: 28 speaking in different kinds of *t*.
12: 30 Do all speak in *t*? Do all interpret?
13: 1 If I speak in the *t* of men
13: 8 where there are *t*, they will be
14: 5 greater than one who speaks in *t*,
14: 18 speak in *t* more than all of you.
14: 21 "Through men of strange *t*
14: 39 and do not forbid speaking in *t*.

TOOK (TAKE)
Isa 53: 4 Surely he *t* up our infirmities
Mt 8: 17 "He *t* up our infirmities
26: 26 they were eating, Jesus *t* bread,
26: 27 Then he *t* the cup, gave thanks
1Co 11: 23 the night he was betrayed, *t* bread,
11: 25 after supper he *t* the cup, saying,
Php 3: 12 for which Christ Jesus *t* hold of me.

TOOTH (TEETH)
Ex 21: 24 eye for eye, *t* for *t*, hand for hand,
Mt 5: 38 'Eye for eye, and *t* for *t*.'

TOP
Dt 28: 13 you will always be at the *t*,
Isa 1: 6 of your foot to the *t* of your head
Mt 27: 51 torn in two from *t* to bottom.

TORMENT (TORMENTED TORMENTORS)
Lk 16: 28 also come to this place of *t*.'
2Co 12: 7 a messenger of Satan, to *t* me.

TORMENTED (TORMENT)
Rev 20: 10 They will be *t* day and night

TORMENTORS (TORMENT)
Ps 137: 3 our *t* demanded songs of joy;

TORN
Gal 4: 15 you would have *t* out your eyes
Php 1: 23 I do not know! I am *t*

TORTURED*
Mt 18: 34 turned him over to the jailers to be *t*,
Heb 11: 35 Others were *t* and refused

TOSSED (TOSSING)
Eph 4: 14 *t* back and forth by the waves,
Jas 1: 6 of the sea, blown and *t* by the wind.

TOSSING (TOSSED)
Isa 57: 20 But the wicked are like the *t* sea,

TOUCH (TOUCHED TOUCHES)
Ge 3: 3 you must not *t* it, or you will die.'"
Ex 19: 12 go up the mountain or *t* the foot
Ps 105: 15 "Do not *t* my anointed ones;
Mt 9: 21 If I only *t* his cloak, I will be healed
Lk 18: 15 babies to Jesus to have him *t* them.
24: 39 It is I myself! *T* me and see;
2Co 6: 17 *T* no unclean thing,
Col 2: 21 Do not taste! Do not *t*!"?

TOUCHED (TOUCH)
1Sa 10: 26 men whose hearts God had *t*.
Isa 6: 7 With it he *t* my mouth and said,
Mt 14: 36 and all who *t* him were healed.
Lk 8: 45 "Who *t* me?" Jesus asked.
1Jn 1: 1 looked at and our hands have *t* —

TOUCHES (TOUCH)
Ex 19: 12 Whoever *t* the mountain shall
Zec 2: 8 for whoever *t* you *t* the apple

TOWER
Ge 11: 4 with a *t* that reaches to the heavens
Pr 18: 10 of the LORD is a strong *t*;

TOWN (TOWNS)
Mt 2: 23 and lived in a *t* called Nazareth.

TOWNS (TOWN)
Nu 35: 2 to give the Levites *t* to live
35: 15 These six *t* will be a place of refuge
Jer 11: 13 as many gods as you have *t*,
Mt 9: 35 Jesus went through all the *t*

TRACING*
Ro 11: 33 and his paths beyond *t* out!

TRACK
Job 14: 16 but not keep *t* of my sin.

TRADERS (TRADING)
1Ti 1: 10 for slave *t* and liars and perjurers —

TRADING (TRADERS)
1Ki 10: 22 The king had a fleet of *t* ships at sea
Pr 31: 18 She sees that her *t* is profitable,

TRADITION (TRADITIONS)
Mt 15: 2 "Why do your disciples break the *t*
15: 6 word of God for the sake of your *t*.
Mk 7: 13 by your *t* that you have handed
Col 2: 8 which depends on human *t*

TRADITIONS (TRADITION)
Mk 7: 8 are holding on to the *t* of men."
Gal 1: 14 zealous for the *t* of my fathers.

TRAIL
1Ti 5: 24 the sins of others *t* behind them.

TRAIN* (TRAINED TRAINING)
Ps 68: 18 you led captives in your *t*;
Pr 22: 6 *T* a child in the way he should go,
Isa 2: 4 nor will they *t* for war anymore.
6: 1 the *t* of his robe filled the temple.
Mic 4: 3 nor will they *t* for war anymore.
Eph 4: 8 he led captives in his *t*
1Ti 4: 7 rather, *t* yourself to be godly.
Tit 2: 4 they can *t* the younger women

TRAINED (TRAIN)
Lk 6: 40 everyone who is fully *t* will be like
Ac 22: 3 Under Gamaliel I was thoroughly *t*
2Co 11: 6 I may not be a *t* speaker,
Heb 5: 14 by constant use have *t* themselves
12: 11 for those who have been *t* by it.

TRAINING* (TRAIN)
1Co 9: 25 in the games goes into strict *t*.
Eph 6: 4 up in the *t* and instruction
1Ti 4: 8 For physical *t* is of some value,
2Ti 3: 16 correcting and *t* in righteousness,

TRAITOR (TRAITORS)
Lk 6: 16 and Judas Iscariot, who became a *t*.
Jn 18: 5 Judas the *t* was standing there

TRAITORS (TRAITOR)
Ps 59: 5 show no mercy to wicked *t*.

TRAMPLE (TRAMPLED)
Joel 3: 13 Come, *t* the grapes,
Am 2: 7 They *t* on the heads of the poor
5: 11 You *t* on the poor
8: 4 Hear this, you who *t* the needy
Mt 7: 6 they may *t* them under their feet,
Lk 10: 19 I have given you authority to *t*

TRAMPLED (TRAMPLE)
Isa 63: 6 I *t* the nations in my anger;
Lk 21: 24 Jerusalem will be *t*
Heb 10: 29 to be punished who has *t* the Son
Rev 14: 20 They were *t* in the winepress

TRANCE*
Ac 10: 10 was being prepared, he fell into a *t*.
11: 5 and in a *t* I saw a vision.
22: 17 into a *t* and saw the Lord speaking.

TRANQUILLITY*
Ecc 4: 6 Better one handful with *t*

TRANSACTIONS*
Ru 4: 7 method of legalizing *t* in Israel.)

TRANSCENDS*
Php 4: 7 which *t* all understanding,

TRANSFIGURED*
Mt 17: 2 There he was *t* before them.
Mk 9: 2 There he was *t* before them.

TRANSFORM* (TRANSFORMED)
Php 3: 21 will *t* our lowly bodies

TRANSFORMED (TRANSFORM)
Ro 12: 2 be *t* by the renewing of your mind.
2Co 3: 18 are being *t* into his likeness

TRANSGRESSED* (TRANSGRESSION)
Da 9: 11 All Israel has *t* your law

TRANSGRESSION* (TRANSGRESSED TRANSGRESSIONS TRANSGRESSORS)
Ps 19: 13 innocent of great *t*.
Isa 53: 8 for the *t* of my people he was
Da 9: 24 and your holy city to finish *t*,
Mic 1: 5 All this is because of Jacob's *t*,
1: 5 What is Jacob's *t*?
3: 8 to declare to Jacob his *t*,
6: 7 Shall I offer my firstborn for my *t*,
7: 18 who pardons sin and forgives the *t*
Ro 4: 15 where there is no law there is no *t*.
11: 11 Rather, because of their *t*,
11: 12 if their *t* means riches for the world

TRANSGRESSIONS* (TRANSGRESSION)
Ps 32: 1 whose *t* are forgiven,
32: 5 my *t* to the LORD"—
39: 8 Save me from all my *t*;
51: 1 blot out my *t*.
51: 3 For I know my *t*,
65: 3 you forgave our *t*.
103: 12 so far has he removed our *t* from us
Isa 43: 25 your *t*, for my own sake,
50: 1 of your *t* your mother was sent
53: 5 But he was pierced for our *t*,
Mic 1: 13 for the *t* of Israel
Ro 4: 7 whose *t* are forgiven,
Gal 3: 19 because of *t* until the Seed to whom
Eph 2: 1 you were dead in your *t* and sins,
2: 5 even when we were dead in *t*—

TRANSGRESSORS* (TRANSGRESSION)
Ps 51: 13 Then I will teach *t* your ways,
Isa 53: 12 and made intercession for the *t*.
53: 12 and was numbered with the *t*.
Lk 22: 37 'And he was numbered with the *t*';

TRAP (TRAPPED TRAPS)
Ps 69: 22 may it become retribution and a *t*.
Pr 20: 25 a *t* for a man to dedicate something
28: 10 will fall into his own *t*,
Isa 8: 14 a *t* and a snare.
Mt 22: 15 and laid plans to *t* him in his words.
Lk 21: 34 close on you unexpectedly like a *t*.
Ro 11: 9 their table become a snare and a *t*,
1Ti 3: 7 into disgrace and into the devil's *t*.
6: 9 and a *t* and into many foolish
2Ti 2: 26 and escape from the *t* of the devil,

TRAPPED (TRAP)
Pr 6: 2 if you have been *t* by what you said
12: 13 An evil man is *t* by his sinful talk,

TRAPS (TRAP)
Jos 23: 13 they will become snares and *t*
La 4: 20 was caught in their *t*.

TRAVEL (TRAVELER)
Pr 4: 15 Avoid it, do not *t* on it;
Mt 23: 15 You *t* over land and sea

TRAVELER (TRAVEL)
Job 31: 32 door was always open to the *t*—
Jer 14: 8 like a *t* who stays only a night?

TREACHEROUS (TREACHERY)
Ps 25: 3 who are *t* without excuse.
2Ti 3: 4 not lovers of the good, *t*, rash,

TREACHERY (TREACHEROUS)
Isa 59: 13 rebellion and *t* against the LORD,

TREAD (TREADING TREADS)
Ps 91: 13 You will *t* upon the lion

TREADING (TREAD)
Dt 25: 4 an ox while it is *t* out the grain.
1Co 9: 9 an ox while it is *t* out the grain."
1Ti 5: 18 the ox while it is *t* out the grain,"

TREADS (TREAD)
Rev 19: 15 He *t* the winepress of the fury

TREASURE (TREASURED TREASURES TREASURY)
Pr 2: 4 and search for it as for hidden *t*,
Isa 33: 6 of the LORD is the key to this *t*.
Mt 6: 21 For where your *t* is, there your
13: 44 of heaven is like *t* hidden in a field.
Lk 12: 33 a *t* in heaven that will not be
2Co 4: 7 But we have this *t* in jars of clay
1Ti 6: 19 In this way they will lay up *t*

TREASURED (TREASURE)
Ex 19: 5 you will be my *t* possession.
Dt 7: 6 to be his people, his *t* possession.
26: 18 his *t* possession as he promised,
Job 23: 12 I have *t* the words
Mal 3: 17 when I make up my *t* possession.
Lk 2: 19 But Mary *t* up all these things
2: 51 But his mother *t* all these things

TREASURES (TREASURE)
1Ch 29: 3 my God I now give my personal *t*
Pr 10: 2 Ill-gotten *t* are of no value,
Mt 6: 19 up for yourselves *t* on earth,
13: 52 out of his storeroom new *t*
Col 2: 3 in whom are hidden all the *t*
Heb 11: 26 of greater value than the *t* of Egypt,

TREASURY (TREASURE)
Mk 12: 43 more into the *t* than all the others.

TREAT (TREATED TREATING TREATMENT)
Lev 22: 2 sons to *t* with respect the sacred
Ps 103: 10 he does not *t* us as our sins deserve
Mt 18: 17 *t* him as you would a pagan
18: 35 my heavenly Father will *t* each
Eph 6: 9 *t* your slaves in the same way.
1Th 5: 20 do not *t* prophecies with contempt.
1Ti 5: 1 *T* younger men as brothers,
1Pe 3: 7 and *t* them with respect

TREATED (TREAT)
Lev 19: 34 The alien living with you must be *t*
25: 40 He is to be *t* as a hired worker
1Sa 24: 17 "You have *t* me well, but I have
Heb 10: 29 who has *t* as an unholy thing

TREATING (TREAT)
Ge 18: 25 *t* the righteous and the wicked
Heb 12: 7 as discipline; God is *t* you as sons.

TREATMENT (TREAT)
Col 2: 23 and their harsh *t* of the body,

TREATY
Ex 34: 12 not to make a *t* with those who live
Dt 7: 2 Make no *t* with them, and show
23: 6 Do not seek a *t* of friendship with them

TREE (TREES)
Ge 2: 9 and the *t* of the knowledge of good
2: 9 of the garden were the *t* of life
Dt 21: 23 hung on a *t* is under God's curse.
2Sa 18: 9 Absalom's head got caught in the *t*.
1Ki 14: 23 and under every spreading *t*.
Ps 1: 3 He is like a *t* planted by streams
52: 8 But I am like an olive *t*
92: 12 righteous will flourish like a palm *t*,
Pr 3: 18 She is a *t* of life to those who
11: 30 of the righteous is a *t* of life,
27: 18 He who tends a fig *t* will eat its fruit
Isa 65: 22 For as the days of a *t*,
Jer 17: 8 He will be like a *t* planted
Eze 17: 24 I the LORD bring down the tall *t*
Da 4: 10 before me stood a *t* in the middle
Mic 4: 4 and under his own fig *t*,
Zec 3: 10 to sit under his vine and fig *t*,'
Mt 3: 10 every *t* that does not produce good
12: 33 for a *t* is recognized by its fruit.
Lk 19: 4 climbed a sycamore-fig *t* to see him
Ac 5: 30 killed by hanging him on a *t*.
Ro 11: 24 be grafted into their own olive *t*!
Gal 3: 13 is everyone who is hung on a *t*."
Jas 3: 12 My brothers, can a fig *t* bear olives,
1Pe 2: 24 sins in his body on the *t*,
Rev 2: 7 the right to eat from the *t* of life,
22: 2 side of the river stood the *t* of life,
22: 14 they may have the right to the *t*
22: 19 from him his share in the *t* of life

TREES (TREE)
Jdg 9: 8 One day the *t* went out
Ps 96: 12 Then all the *t* of the forest will sing
Isa 55: 12 and all the *t* of the field
Mt 3: 10 The ax is already at the root of the *t*
Mk 8: 24 they look like *t* walking around."
Jude : 12 autumn *t*, without fruit

TREMBLE (TREMBLED TREMBLES TREMBLING)
Ex 15: 14 The nations will hear and *t*;
1Ch 16: 30 *T* before him, all the earth!
Ps 114: 7 *T*, O earth, at the presence
Jer 5: 22 "Should you not *t* in my presence?
Eze 38: 20 of the earth will *t* at my presence.
Joel 2: 1 Let all who live in the land *t*,
Hab 3: 6 he looked, and made the nations *t*.

TREMBLED (TREMBLE)
Ex 19: 16 Everyone in the camp *t*.
20: 18 in smoke, they *t* with fear.
2Sa 22: 8 "The earth *t* and quaked,
Ac 7: 32 Moses *t* with fear and did not dare

TREMBLES (TREMBLE)
Ps 97: 4 the earth sees and *t*.
104: 32 he who looks at the earth, and it *t*,
Isa 66: 2 and *t* at my word.
Jer 10: 10 When he is angry, the earth *t*;
Na 1: 5 The earth *t* at his presence,

TREMBLING (TREMBLE)
Ps 2: 11 and rejoice with *t*.
Da 10: 10 set me *t* on my hands and knees.
Php 2: 12 out your salvation with fear and *t*,
Heb 12: 21 terrifying that Moses said, "I am *t*

TRESPASS* (TRESPASSES)
Ro 5: 15 But the gift is not like the *t*.
5: 15 died by the *t* of the one man,
5: 17 For if, by the *t* of the one man,
5: 18 result of one *t* was condemnation
5: 20 added so that the *t* might increase.

TRESPASSES* (TRESPASS)
Ro 5: 16 but the gift followed many *t*

TRIAL (TRIALS)
Ps 37: 33 condemned when brought to *t*.
Mk 13: 11 you are arrested and brought to *t*,
2Co 8: 2 most severe *t*, their overflowing
Jas 1: 12 is the man who perseveres under *t*,
1Pe 4: 12 at the painful *t* you are suffering,
Rev 3: 10 you from the hour of *t* that is going

TRIALS* (TRIAL)
Dt 7: 19 saw with your own eyes the great *t*,
29: 3 own eyes you saw those great *t*,
Lk 22: 28 who have stood by me in my *t*.
1Th 3: 3 one would be unsettled by these *t*.
2Th 1: 4 the persecutions and *t* you are
Jas 1: 2 whenever you face *t* of many kinds,
1Pe 1: 6 had to suffer grief in all kinds of *t*.
2Pe 2: 9 how to rescue godly men from *t*

TRIBE (HALF-TRIBE TRIBES)
Heb 7: 13 no one from that *t* has ever served
Rev 5: 5 See, the Lion of the *t* of Judah,
5: 9 God from every *t* and language
11: 9 men from every people, *t*,
14: 6 to every nation, *t*, language

TRIBES (TRIBE)
Ge 49: 28 All these are the twelve *t* of Israel,
Mt 19: 28 judging the twelve *t* of Israel.

TRIBULATION*
Rev 7: 14 who have come out of the great *t*;

TRICKERY*
Ac 13: 10 full of all kinds of deceit and *t*.
2Co 12: 16 fellow that I am, I caught you by *t*!

TRIED (TRY)
Ps 73: 16 When I *t* to understand all this,
95: 9 where your fathers tested and *t* me,
Heb 3: 9 where your fathers tested and *t* me

TRIES (TRY)
Lk 17: 33 Whoever *t* to keep his life will lose

TRIMMED
Mt 25: 7 virgins woke up and *t* their lamps.

TRIUMPH (TRIUMPHAL TRIUMPHED TRIUMPHING TRIUMPHS)
Ps 25: 2 nor let my enemies *t* over me.
54: 7 my eyes have looked in *t*
112: 8 in the end he will look in *t*
118: 7 I will look in *t* on my enemies.
Pr 28: 12 When the righteous *t*, there is great
Isa 42: 13 and will *t* over his enemies.

TRIUMPHAL* (TRIUMPH)
Isa 60: 11 their kings led in *t* procession.
2Co 2: 14 us in *t* procession in Christ

TRIUMPHED (TRIUMPH)
Rev 5: 5 of Judah, the Root of David, has *t*.

TRIUMPHING* (TRIUMPH)
Col 2: 15 of them, *t* over them by the cross.

TRIUMPHS* (TRIUMPH)
Jas 2: 13 Mercy *t* over judgment! What

TROUBLE (TROUBLED TROUBLES)
Ge 41: 51 God has made me forget all my *t*
Jos 7: 25 Why have you brought this *t* on us?
Job 2: 10 good from God, and not *t*?"
5: 7 Yet man is born to *t*
14: 1 is of few days and full of *t*.
42: 11 him over all the *t* the LORD had
Ps 7: 14 conceives *t* gives birth
7: 16 The *t* he causes recoils on himself;
9: 9 a stronghold in times of *t*.

Ps 10:14 But you, O God, do see *t* and grief;
22:11 for *t* is near
27:5 For in the day of *t*
32:7 you will protect me from *t*
37:39 he is their stronghold in time of *t*.
41:1 LORD delivers him in times of *t*.
46:1 an ever-present help in *t*.
50:15 and call upon me in the day of *t*;
59:16 my refuge in times of *t*.
66:14 spoke when I was in *t*.
86:7 In the day of my *t* I will call to you,
91:15 I will be with him in *t*,
107:6 to the LORD in their *t*,
107:13 they cried to the LORD in their *t*,
116:3 I was overcome by *t* and sorrow.
119:143 *T* and distress have come upon me,
138:7 Though I walk in the midst of *t*,
143:11 righteousness, bring me out of *t*.
Pr 11:8 righteous man is rescued from *t*,
11:17 a cruel man brings *t* on himself
11:29 He who brings *t* on his family will
12:13 but a righteous man escapes *t*.
12:21 but the wicked have their fill of *t*.
15:27 A greedy man brings *t* to his family
19:23 one rests content, untouched by *t*.
22:8 He who sows wickedness reaps *t*,
24:10 If you falter in times of *t*,
25:19 on the unfaithful in times of *t*.
28:14 he who hardens his heart falls into *t*
Jer 30:7 It will be a time of *t* for Jacob,
Na 1:7 a refuge in times of *t*.
Zep 1:15 a day of *t* and ruin,
Mt 6:34 Each day has enough *t* of its own.
13:21 When *t* or persecution comes
Jn 16:33 In this world you will have *t*.
Ro 8:35 Shall *t* or hardship or persecution
2Co 1:4 those in any *t* with the comfort we
2Th 1:6 *t* to those who *t* you
Jas 5:13 one of you in *t*? He should pray.

TROUBLED (TROUBLE)
Ps 38:18 I am *t* by my sin.
Isa 38:14 I am *t*; O Lord, come to my aid!"
Mk 14:33 began to be deeply distressed and *t*.
Jn 14:1 "Do not let your hearts be *t*.
14:27 Do not let your hearts be *t*
2Th 1:7 and give relief to you who are *t*,

TROUBLES (TROUBLE)
Ps 34:6 he saved him out of all his *t*.
34:17 he delivers them from all their *t*.
34:19 A righteous man may have many *t*,
40:12 For *t* without number surround me
54:7 he has delivered me from all my *t*,
1Co 7:28 those who marry will face many *t*
2Co 1:4 who comforts us in all our *t*,
4:17 and momentary *t* are achieving
6:4 in *t*, hardships and distresses;
7:4 in all our *t* my joy knows no bounds
Php 4:14 good of you to share in my *t*.

TRUE (TRUTH)
Nu 11:23 not what I say will come *t* for you."
12:7 this is not *t* of my servant Moses;
Dt 18:22 does not take place or come *t*,
Jos 23:15 of the LORD your God has come *t*
1Sa 9:6 and everything he says comes *t*.
1Ki 10:6 and your wisdom is *t*.
2Ch 6:17 your servant David come *t*.
15:3 was without the *t* God,
Ps 33:4 of the LORD is right and *t*;
119:142 and your law is *t*.
119:151 and all your commands are *t*.
119:160 All your words are *t*;
Pr 8:7 My mouth speaks what is *t*,
22:21 teaching you *t* and reliable words,
Jer 10:10 But the LORD is the *t* God;
28:9 only if his prediction comes *t*."
Eze 33:33 "When all this comes *t*—
Lk 16:11 who will trust you with *t* riches?
Jn 1:9 The *t* light that gives light
4:23 when the *t* worshipers will worship
6:32 Father who gives you the *t* bread
7:28 on my own, but he who sent me is *t*
15:1 "I am the *t* vine, and my Father is
17:3 the only *t* God, and Jesus Christ,
19:35 testimony, and his testimony is *t*.
21:24 We know that his testimony is *t*.
Ac 10:34 "I now realize how *t* it is that God
11:23 all to remain *t* to the Lord
14:22 them to remain *t* to the faith.
17:11 day to see if what Paul said was *t*.
Ro 3:4 Let God be *t*, and every man a liar.
Php 4:8 whatever is *t*, whatever is noble,
1Jn 2:8 and the *t* light is already shining.
5:20 He is the *t* God and eternal life.
Rev 19:9 "These are the *t* words of God."
22:6 These words are trustworthy and *t*.

TRUMPET (TRUMPETS)
Isa 27:13 And in that day a great *t* will sound
Eze 33:5 Since he heard the sound of the *t*
Zec 9:14 Sovereign LORD will sound the *t*;
Mt 24:31 send his angels with a loud *t* call,
1Co 14:8 if the *t* does not sound a clear call,
15:52 For the *t* will sound, the dead will
1Th 4:16 and with the *t* call of God,
Rev 8:7 The first angel sounded his *t*,

TRUMPETS (TRUMPET)
Jdg 7:19 They blew their *t* and broke the jars
Rev 8:2 and to them were given seven *t*.

TRUST* (ENTRUST ENTRUSTED TRUSTED TRUSTFULLY TRUSTING TRUSTS TRUSTWORTHY)
Ex 14:31 put their *t* in him and in Moses his
19:9 and will always put their *t* in you."
Nu 20:12 "Because you did not *t*
Dt 1:32 you did not *t* in the LORD your
9:23 You did not *t* him or obey him.
28:52 walls in which you *t* fall down.
Jdg 11:20 did not *t* Israel to pass
2Ki 17:14 who did not *t* in the LORD their
18:30 to *t* in the LORD when he says,
1Ch 9:22 to their positions of *t* by David
Job 4:18 If God places no *t* in his servants,
15:15 If God places no *t* in his holy ones,
31:24 "If I have put my *t* in gold
39:12 Can you *t* him to bring
Ps 4:5 and *t* in the LORD.
9:10 Those who know your name will *t*
13:5 But I *t* in your unfailing love;
20:7 Some *t* in chariots and some
20:7 we *t* in the name of the LORD our
22:4 In you our fathers put their *t*;
22:9 you made me *t* in you
25:2 I lift up my soul; in you I *t*,
31:6 I *t* in the LORD.
31:14 But I *t* in you, O LORD;
33:21 for we *t* in his holy name.
37:3 *T* in the LORD and do good;
37:5 *t* in him and he will do this:
40:3 and put their *t* in the LORD.
40:4 who makes the LORD his *t*,
44:6 I do not *t* in my bow,
49:6 those who *t* in their wealth
49:13 of those who *t* in themselves,
52:8 I *t* in God's unfailing love
55:23 But as for me, I *t* in you.
56:3 I will *t* in you.
56:4 in God I *t*; I will not be afraid.
56:11 in God I *t*; I will not be afraid.
62:8 *T* in him at all times, O people;
62:10 Do not *t* in extortion
78:7 Then they would put their *t* in God
78:22 or *t* in his deliverance.
91:2 my God, in whom I *t*."
115:8 and so will all who *t* in them.
115:9 O house of Israel, *t* in the LORD—
115:10 O house of Aaron, *t* in the LORD
115:11 You who fear him, *t* in the LORD
118:8 than to *t* in man.
118:9 than to *t* in princes.
119:42 for I *t* in your word.
125:1 Those who *t* in the LORD are like
135:18 and so will all who *t* in them.
143:8 for I have put my *t* in you.
146:3 Do not put your *t* in princes,
Pr 3:5 *T* in the LORD with all your heart
21:22 the stronghold in which they *t*.
22:19 So that your *t* may be in the LORD
Isa 8:17 I will put my *t* in him.
12:2 I will *t* and not be afraid.
26:4 *T* in the LORD forever,
30:15 in quietness and *t* is your strength,
31:1 who *t* in the multitude
36:15 to *t* in the LORD when he says,
42:17 But those who *t* in idols,
50:10 *t* in the name of the LORD
Jer 2:37 LORD has rejected those you *t*;
5:17 the fortified cities in which you *t*.
7:4 Do not *t* in deceptive words
7:14 the temple you *t* in, the place I gave
9:4 do not *t* your brothers.
12:6 Do not *t* them,
28:15 you have persuaded this nation to *t*
39:18 you *t* in me, declares the LORD.'"
48:7 Since you *t* in your deeds
49:4 you *t* in your riches and say,
49:11 Your widows too can *t* in me."
Mic 7:5 Do not *t* a neighbor;
Na 1:7 He cares for those who *t* in him,
Zep 3:2 She does not *t* in the LORD,
3:12 who *t* in the name of the LORD.
Lk 16:11 who will *t* you with true riches?
Jn 12:36 Put your *t* in the light
14:1 *T* in God; *t* also in me.
Ac 14:23 Lord, in whom they had put their *t*.
Ro 15:13 you with all joy and peace as you *t*
1Co 4:2 been given a *t* must prove faithful.
9:17 discharging the *t* committed
2Co 13:6 I *t* that you will discover that we
Heb 2:13 "I will put my *t* in him."

TRUSTED* (TRUST)
1Sa 27:12 Achish *t* David and said to himself,
2Ki 18:5 Hezekiah *t* in the LORD, the God
1Ch 5:20 their prayers, because they *t*
Job 12:20 He silences the lips of *t* advisers
Ps 5:9 from their mouth can be *t*;
22:4 they *t* and you delivered them.
22:5 in you they *t* and were not
26:1 I have *t* in the LORD
41:9 Even my close friend, whom I *t*,
52:7 but *t* in his great wealth
Isa 20:5 Those who *t* in Cush and boasted
25:9 This is the LORD, we *t* in him;
25:9 we *t* in him, and he saved us.
47:10 You have *t* in your wickedness
Jer 13:25 and *t* in false gods.
38:22 those *t* friends of yours.
48:13 ashamed when they *t* in Bethel.
Eze 16:15 "'But you *t* in your beauty
Da 3:28 They *t* in him and defied the king's
6:23 because he had *t* in his God.
Lk 11:22 the armor in which the man *t*
16:10 *t* with very little can also be *t*
Ac 12:20 a *t* personal servant of the king,
Tit 2:10 but to show that they can be fully *t*,
3:8 so that those who have *t*

TRUSTFULLY* (TRUST)
Pr 3:29 who lives *t* near you.

TRUSTING* (TRUST)
Job 15:31 by *t* what is worthless,
Ps 112:7 his heart is steadfast, *t*
Isa 2:22 Stop *t* in man,
Jer 7:8 you are *t* in deceptive words that

TRUSTS* (TRUST)
Job 8:14 What he *t* in is fragile;
Ps 21:7 For the king *t* in the LORD;
22:8 "He *t* in the LORD;
28:7 my heart *t* in him, and I am helped.
32:10 surrounds the man who *t* in him.
84:12 blessed is the man who *t* in you.
86:2 who *t* in you.
Pr 11:28 Whoever *t* in his riches will fall,
16:20 blessed is he who *t* in the LORD.
28:25 he who *t* in the LORD will prosper.
28:26 He who *t* in himself is a fool,
29:25 whoever *t* in the LORD is kept safe
Isa 26:3 because he *t* in you.
28:16 one who *t* will never be dismayed.
Jer 17:5 "Cursed is the one who *t* in man,
17:7 blessed is the man who *t*
Eze 33:13 but then he *t* in his righteousness
Hab 2:18 For he who makes it *t*
Mt 27:43 He *t* in God.
Ro 4:5 but *t* God who justifies the wicked,
9:33 one who *t* in him will never be put
10:11 "Anyone who *t* in him will never
1Co 13:7 always protects, always *t*,
1Pe 2:6 and the one who *t* in him

TRUSTWORTHY* (TRUST)
Ex 18:21 *t* men who hate dishonest gain—
2Sa 7:28 you are God! Your words are *t*,
Ne 13:13 these men were considered *t*.
Ps 19:7 The statutes of the LORD are *t*,
111:7 all his precepts are *t*.
119:86 All your commands are *t*;
119:138 they are fully *t*.
Pr 11:13 but a *t* man keeps a secret.
13:17 but a *t* envoy brings healing.
25:13 is a *t* messenger to those who send
Da 2:45 and the interpretation is *t*."
6:4 he was *t* and neither corrupt
Lk 16:11 So if you have not been *t*
16:12 And if you have not been *t*
19:17 'Because you have been *t*
1Co 7:25 one who by the Lord's mercy is *t*.
1Ti 1:15 Here is a *t* saying that deserves full
3:1 Here is a *t* saying: If anyone sets his
3:11 but temperate and *t* in everything.
4:9 This is a *t* saying that deserves full
2Ti 2:11 Here is a *t* saying:
Tit 1:9 must hold firmly to the *t* message

Tit 3: 8 This is a *t* saying.
Rev 21: 5 for these words are *t* and true."
22: 6 "These words are *t* and true.

TRUTH* (TRUE TRUTHFUL TRUTHFULNESS TRUTHS)

Ge 42: 16 tested to see if you are telling the *t*.
1Ki 17: 24 LORD from your mouth is the *t*."
22: 16 the *t* in the name of the LORD?"
2Ch 18: 15 the *t* in the name of the LORD?"
Ps 15: 2 who speaks the *t* from his heart
25: 5 guide me in your *t* and teach me,
26: 3 and I walk continually in your *t*.
31: 5 redeem me, O LORD, the God of *t*
40: 10 do not conceal your love and your *t*
40: 11 your *t* always protect me.
43: 3 Send forth your light and your *t*,
45: 4 victoriously in behalf of *t*, humility
51: 6 Surely you desire *t*
52: 3 than speaking the *t*.
86: 11 and I will walk in your *t*;
96: 13 and the peoples in his *t*.
119: 30 I have chosen the way of *t*;
119: 43 of *t* from my mouth,
145: 18 to all who call on him in *t*.
Pr 16: 13 they value a man who speaks the *t*.
23: 23 Buy the *t* and do not sell it;
Isa 45: 19 I, the LORD, speak the *t*;
48: 1 but not in *t* or righteousness—
59: 14 *t* has stumbled in the streets,
59: 15 *T* is nowhere to be found,
65: 16 will do so by the God of *t*;
65: 16 will swear by the God of *t*.
Jer 5: 1 who deals honestly and seeks the *t*,
5: 3 do not your eyes look for *t*?
7: 28 *T* has perished; it has vanished
9: 3 it is not by *t*
9: 5 and no one speaks the *t*.
26: 15 for in *t* the LORD has sent me
Da 8: 12 and *t* was thrown to the ground.
9: 13 and giving attention to your *t*.
10: 21 what is written in the Book of *T*.
11: 2 "Now then, I tell you the *t*:
Am 5: 10 and despise him who tells the *t*.
Zec 8: 3 will be called the City of *T*,
8: 16 are to do: Speak the *t* to each other,
8: 19 Therefore love *t* and peace."
Mt 5: 18 I tell you the *t*, until heaven
5: 26 I tell you the *t*, you will not get out
6: 2 I tell you the *t*, they have received
6: 5 I tell you the *t*, they have received
6: 16 I tell you the *t*, they have received
8: 10 "I tell you the *t*, I have not found
10: 15 I tell you the *t*, it will be more
10: 23 I tell you the *t*, you will not finish
10: 42 I tell you the *t*, he will certainly not
11: 11 I tell you the *t*: Among those born
13: 17 For I tell you the *t*, many prophets
16: 28 I tell you the *t*, some who are
17: 20 I tell you the *t*, if you have faith
18: 3 And he said: "I tell you the *t*,
18: 13 And if he finds it, I tell you the *t*,
18: 18 "I tell you the *t*, whatever you bind
19: 23 to his disciples, "I tell you the *t*,
19: 28 "I tell you the *t*, at the renewal
21: 21 Jesus replied, "I tell you the *t*,
21: 31 Jesus said to them, "I tell you the *t*,
22: 16 of God in accordance with the *t*.
23: 36 I tell you the *t*, all this will come
24: 2 "I tell you the *t*, not one stone here
24: 34 I tell you the *t*, this generation will
24: 47 I tell you the *t*, he will put him
25: 12 'I tell you the *t*, I don't know you.'
25: 40 The King will reply, 'I tell you the *t*
25: 45 "He will reply, 'I tell you the *t*,
26: 13 tell you the *t*, wherever this gospel
26: 21 "I tell you the *t*, one
26: 34 "I tell you the *t*," Jesus answered,
Mk 3: 28 I tell you the *t*, all the sins
5: 33 with fear, told him the whole *t*.
8: 12 I tell you the *t*, no sign will be given
9: 1 he said to them, "I tell you the *t*,
9: 41 I tell you the *t*, anyone who gives
10: 15 I tell you the *t*, anyone who will not
10: 29 "I tell you the *t*," Jesus replied,
11: 23 "I tell you the *t*, if anyone says
12: 14 of God in accordance with the *t*.
12: 43 Jesus said, "I tell you the *t*,
13: 30 I tell you the *t*, this generation will
14: 9 I tell you the *t*, wherever the gospel
14: 18 "I tell you the *t*, one
14: 25 "I tell you the *t*, I will not drink
14: 30 "I tell you the *t*," Jesus answered,
Lk 4: 24 "I tell you the *t*," he continued,
9: 27 I tell you the *t*, some who are
Lk 12: 37 I tell you the *t*, he will dress himself
12: 44 I tell you the *t*, he will put him
18: 17 I tell you the *t*, anyone who will not
18: 29 I tell you the *t*," Jesus said to them,
20: 21 of God in accordance with the *t*.
21: 3 "I tell you the *t*," he said, "this
21: 32 tell you the *t*, this generation will
23: 43 answered him, "I tell you the *t*,
Jn 1: 14 from the Father, full of grace and *t*.
1: 17 and *t* came through Jesus Christ.
1: 51 "I tell you the *t*, you shall see
3: 3 "I tell you the *t*, no one can see
3: 5 Jesus answered, "I tell you the *t*,
3: 11 I tell you the *t*, we speak
3: 21 But whoever lives by the *t* comes
4: 23 worship the Father in spirit and *t*,
4: 24 must worship in spirit and in *t*."
5: 19 "I tell you the *t*, the Son can do
5: 24 "I tell you the *t*, whoever hears my
5: 25 I tell you the *t*, a time is coming
5: 33 and he has testified to the *t*.
6: 26 "I tell you the *t*, you are looking
6: 32 Jesus said to them, "I tell you the *t*,
6: 47 I tell you the *t*, he who believes has
6: 53 Jesus said to them, "I tell you the *t*,
7: 18 the one who sent him is a man of *t*;
8: 32 Then you will know the *t*,
8: 32 and the *t* will set you free."
8: 34 Jesus replied, "I tell you the *t*,
8: 40 who has told you the *t* that I heard
8: 44 to the *t*, for there is no *t* in him.
8: 45 I tell the *t*, you do not believe me!
8: 46 I am telling the *t*, why don't you
8: 51 I tell you the *t*, if anyone keeps my
8: 58 "I tell you the *t*," Jesus answered,
10: 1 "I tell you the *t*, the man who does
10: 7 "I tell you the *t*, I am the gate
12: 24 I tell you the *t*, unless a kernel
13: 16 I tell you the *t*, no servant is greater
13: 20 tell you the *t*, whoever accepts
13: 21 "I tell you the *t*, one of you is going
13: 38 I tell you the *t*, before the rooster
14: 6 I am the way and the *t* and the life.
14: 12 I tell you the *t*, anyone who has
14: 17 with you forever—the Spirit of *t*.
15: 26 the Spirit of *t* who goes out
16: 7 But I tell you the *t*: It is
16: 13 But when he, the Spirit of *t*, comes,
16: 13 comes, he will guide you into all *t*.
16: 20 I tell you the *t*, you will weep
16: 23 I tell you the *t*, my Father will give
17: 17 them by the *t*; your word is *t*.
18: 23 if I spoke the *t*, why did you strike
18: 37 into the world, to testify to the *t*.
18: 37 on the side of *t* listens to me."
18: 38 "What is *t*?" Pilate asked.
19: 35 He knows that he tells the *t*,
21: 18 I tell you the *t*, when you were
Ac 20: 30 and distort the *t* in order
21: 24 everybody will know there is no *t*
21: 34 commander could not get at the *t*
24: 8 able to learn the *t* about all these
28: 25 "The Holy Spirit spoke the *t*
Ro 1: 18 of men who suppress the *t*
1: 25 They exchanged the *t* of God
2: 2 who do such things is based on *t*.
2: 8 who reject the *t* and follow evil,
2: 20 embodiment of knowledge and *t*—
9: 1 I speak the *t* in Christ—I am not
15: 8 of the Jews on behalf of God's *t*,
1Co 5: 8 the bread of sincerity and *t*.
13: 6 in evil but rejoices with the *t*.
2Co 4: 2 setting forth the *t* plainly we
11: 10 As surely as the *t* of Christ is in me,
12: 6 because I would be speaking the *t*.
13: 8 against the *t*, but only for the *t*.
Gal 2: 5 so that the *t* of the gospel might
2: 14 in line with the *t* of the gospel,
4: 16 enemy by telling you the *t*?
5: 7 and kept you from obeying the *t*?
Eph 1: 13 when you heard the word of *t*,
4: 15 Instead, speaking the *t* in love,
4: 21 him in accordance with the *t* that is
5: 9 and *t*) and find out what pleases
6: 14 with the belt of *t* buckled
Col 1: 5 heard about in the word of *t*,
1: 6 understood God's grace in all its *t*.
2Th 2: 10 because they refused to love the *t*
2: 12 who have not believed the *t*
2: 13 and through belief in the *t*.
1Ti 2: 4 to come to a knowledge of the *t*.
2: 7 I am telling the *t*, I am not lying—
3: 15 the pillar and foundation of the *t*.
4: 3 who believe and who know the *t*.
6: 5 who have been robbed of the *t*
2Ti 2: 15 correctly handles the word of *t*.
2: 18 have wandered away from the *t*.
2: 25 them to a knowledge of the *t*,
3: 7 never able to acknowledge the *t*.
3: 8 so also these men oppose the *t*—
4: 4 will turn their ears away from the *t*
Tit 1: 1 the knowledge of the *t* that leads
1: 14 of those who reject the *t*.
Heb 10: 26 received the knowledge of the *t*,
Jas 1: 18 birth through the word of *t*,
3: 14 do not boast about it or deny the *t*.
5: 19 of you should wander from the *t*
1Pe 1: 22 by obeying the *t* so that you have
2Pe 1: 12 established in the *t* you now have.
2: 2 the way of *t* into disrepute.
1Jn 1: 6 we lie and do not live by the *t*.
1: 8 deceive ourselves and the *t* is not
2: 4 commands is a liar, and the *t* is not
2: 8 its *t* is seen in him and you,
2: 20 and all of you know the *t*.
2: 21 because no lie comes from the *t*.
2: 21 because you do not know the *t*,
3: 18 or tongue but with actions and in *t*.
3: 19 we know that we belong to the *t*,
4: 6 is how we recognize the Spirit of *t*
5: 6 testifies, because the Spirit is the *t*.
2Jn : 1 whom I love in the *t*—
: 2 who know the *t*—because of the *t*,
: 3 will be with us in *t* and love.
: 4 of your children walking in the *t*,
3Jn : 1 friend Gaius, whom I love in the *t*.
: 3 how you continue to walk in the *t*.
: 3 tell about your faithfulness to the *t*
: 4 my children are walking in the *t*.
: 8 we may work together for the *t*.
: 12 everyone—and even by the *t* itself.

TRUTHFUL* (TRUTH)

Pr 12: 17 A *t* witness gives honest testimony,
12: 19 *T* lips endure forever,
12: 22 but he delights in men who are *t*.
14: 5 A *t* witness does not deceive,
14: 25 A *t* witness saves lives,
Jer 4: 2 and if in a *t*, just and righteous way
Jn 3: 33 it has certified that God is *t*.
2Co 6: 7 in *t* speech and in the power

TRUTHFULNESS* (TRUTH)

Ro 3: 7 "If my falsehood enhances God's *t*

TRUTHS* (TRUTH)

1Co 2: 13 expressing spiritual *t*
1Ti 3: 9 hold of the deep *t* of the faith
4: 6 brought up in the *t* of the faith
Heb 5: 12 to teach you the elementary *t*

TRY (TRIED TRIES TRYING)

Ps 26: 2 Test me, O LORD, and *t* me,
Isa 7: 13 enough to *t* the patience of men?
Lk 12: 58 *t* hard to be reconciled to him
13: 24 will *t* to enter and will not be able
1Co 10: 33 even as I *t* to please everybody
14: 12 *t* to excel in gifts that build up
2Co 5: 11 is to fear the Lord, we *t*
1Th 5: 15 always *t* to be kind to each other
Tit 2: 9 to *t* to please them, not to talk back

TRYING (TRY)

2Co 5: 12 We are not *t* to commend ourselves
Gal 1: 10 If I were still *t* to please men,
1Th 2: 4 We are not *t* to please men but God
1Pe 1: 11 *t* to find out the time
1Jn 2: 26 things to you about those who are *t*

TUMORS

1Sa 5: 6 them and afflicted them with *t*.

TUNE

1Co 14: 7 anyone know what *t* is being

TUNIC (TUNICS)

Lk 6: 29 do not stop him from taking your *t*.

TUNICS (TUNIC)

Lk 3: 11 "The man with two *t* should share

TURMOIL

Ps 65: 7 and the *t* of the nations.
Pr 15: 16 than great wealth with *t*.

TURN (TURNED TURNING TURNS)

Ex 32: 12 *T* from your fierce anger; relent
Nu 32: 15 If you *t* away from following him,
Dt 5: 32 do not *t* aside to the right
28: 14 Do not *t* aside from any
30: 10 and *t* to the LORD your God
Jos 1: 7 do not *t* from it to the right
1Ki 8: 58 May he *t* our hearts to him,
2Ch 7: 14 and *t* from their wicked ways,

2Ch 30: 9 He will not *t* his face from you
Job 33: 30 to *t* back his soul from the pit,
Ps 28: 1 do not *t* a deaf ear to me.
34: 14 *T* from evil and do good;
51: 13 and sinners will *t* back to you.
78: 6 they in *t* would tell their children.
119: 36 *T* my heart toward your statutes
119: 132 *T* to me and have mercy on me,
Pr 22: 6 when he is old he will not *t* from it.
Isa 17: 7 *t* their eyes to the Holy One
28: 6 to those who *t* back the battle
29: 16 You *t* things upside down,
30: 21 Whether you *t* to the right
45: 22 "*T* to me and be saved,
55: 7 Let him *t* to the LORD,
Jer 31: 13 I will *t* their mourning
Eze 33: 9 if you do warn the wicked man to *t*
33: 11 *T*! *T* from your evil ways!
Jnh 3: 9 and with compassion *t*
Mal 4: 6 He will *t* the hearts of the fathers
Mt 5: 39 you on the right cheek, *t*
10: 35 For I have come to *t*
Lk 1: 17 to *t* the hearts of the fathers
Jn 12: 40 nor *t*— and I would heal them."
16: 20 but your grief will *t* to joy.
Ac 3: 19 Repent, then, and *t* to God,
26: 18 and *t* them from darkness to light,
1Co 14: 31 For you can all prophesy in *t*
15: 23 But each in his own *t*: Christ,
1Ti 6: 20 *T* away from godless chatter
1Pe 3: 11 He must *t* from evil and do good;

TURNED (TURN)
Dt 23: 5 *t* the curse into a blessing for you,
1Ki 11: 4 his wives *t* his heart
2Ch 15: 4 But in their distress they *t*
Est 9: 1 but now the tables were *t*
9: 22 when their sorrow was *t* into joy
Ps 14: 3 All have *t* aside,
30: 11 You *t* my wailing into dancing;
40: 1 he *t* to me and heard my cry.
Isa 9: 12 for all this, his anger is not *t* away,
53: 6 each of us has *t* to his own way;
Hos 7: 8 Ephraim is a flat cake not *t* over.
Joel 2: 31 The sun will be *t* to darkness
Lk 22: 32 And when you have *t* back,
Ro 3: 12 All have *t* away,

TURNING (TURN)
2Ki 21: 13 wiping it and *t* it upside down.
Pr 2: 2 *t* your ear to wisdom
14: 27 *t* a man from the snares of death.

TURNS (TURN)
2Sa 22: 29 the LORD *t* my darkness into light
Pr 15: 1 A gentle answer *t* away wrath,
Isa 44: 25 and *t* it into nonsense,
Jas 5: 20 Whoever *t* a sinner from the error

TWELVE
Ge 35: 22 Jacob had *t* sons: The sons of Leah:
49: 28 All these are the *t* tribes of Israel,
Mt 10: 1 He called his *t* disciples to him
Lk 9: 17 the disciples picked up *t* basketfuls
Rev 21: 12 the names of the *t* tribes of Israel.
21: 14 of the *t* apostles of the Lamb.

TWIN (TWINS)
Ge 25: 24 there were *t* boys in her womb.

TWINKLING*
1Co 15: 52 in a flash, in the *t* of an eye,

TWINS (TWIN)
Ro 9: 11 before the *t* were born

TWISTING* (TWISTS)
Pr 30: 33 and as *t* the nose produces blood,

TWISTS (TWISTING)
Ex 23: 8 and *t* the words of the righteous.

TYRANNICAL*
Pr 28: 16 A *t* ruler lacks judgment,

TYRE
Eze 28: 12 a lament concerning the king of *T*
Mt 11: 22 it will be more bearable for *T*

UNAPPROACHABLE*
1Ti 6: 16 immortal and who lives in *u* light,

UNASHAMED*
1Jn 2: 28 and *u* before him at his coming.

UNBELIEF* (UNBELIEVER UNBELIEVERS UNBELIEVING)
Mk 9: 24 help me overcome my *u*!"
Ro 4: 20 through *u* regarding the promise
11: 20 they were broken off because of *u*,
11: 23 And if they do not persist in *u*,
1Ti 1: 13 because I acted in ignorance and *u*.
Heb 3: 19 able to enter, because of their *u*.

UNBELIEVER* (UNBELIEF)
1Co 7: 15 But if the *u* leaves, let him do so.
10: 27 If some *u* invites you to a meal
14: 24 if an *u* or someone who does not
2Co 6: 15 have in common with an *u*?
1Ti 5: 8 the faith and is worse than an *u*.

UNBELIEVERS* (UNBELIEF)
Lk 12: 46 and assign him a place with the *u*.
Ro 15: 31 rescued from the *u* in Judea
1Co 6: 6 another— and this in front of *u*!
14: 22 however, is for believers, not for *u*.
14: 22 not for believers but for *u*;
14: 23 do not understand or some *u* come
2Co 4: 4 this age has blinded the minds of *u*,
6: 14 Do not be yoked together with *u*.

UNBELIEVING* (UNBELIEF)
Mt 17: 17 "O *u* and perverse generation,"
Mk 9: 19 "O *u* generation," Jesus replied,
Lk 9: 41 "O *u* and perverse generation,"
1Co 7: 14 For the *u* husband has been
7: 14 and the *u* wife has been sanctified
Heb 3: 12 *u* heart that turns away
Rev 21: 8 But the cowardly, the *u*, the vile,

UNBLEMISHED*
Heb 9: 14 the eternal Spirit offered himself *u*

UNCEASING
Ro 9: 2 and *u* anguish in my heart.

UNCERTAIN*
1Ti 6: 17 which is so *u*, but to put their hope

UNCHANGEABLE* (UNCHANGING)
Heb 6: 18 by two *u* things in which it is

UNCHANGING* (UNCHANGEABLE)
Heb 6: 17 wanted to make the *u* nature

UNCIRCUMCISED
Lev 26: 41 when their *u* hearts are humbled
1Sa 17: 26 Who is this *u* Philistine that he
Jer 9: 26 house of Israel is *u* in heart."
Ac 7: 51 stiff-necked people, with *u* hearts
Ro 4: 11 had by faith while he was still *u*.
1Co 7: 18 Was a man *u* when he was called?
Col 3: 11 circumcised or *u*, barbarian,

UNCIRCUMCISION
1Co 7: 19 is nothing and *u* is nothing.
Gal 5: 6 neither circumcision nor *u* has any

UNCLEAN
Ge 7: 2 and two of every kind of *u* animal,
Lev 10: 10 between the *u* and the clean,
11: 4 it is ceremonially *u* for you.
17: 15 he will be ceremonially *u* till evening.
Isa 6: 5 ruined! For I am a man of *u* lips,
52: 11 Touch no *u* thing!
Mt 15: 11 mouth does not make him '*u*,'
Ac 10: 14 never eaten anything impure or *u*."
Ro 14: 14 fully convinced that no food is *u*
2Co 6: 17 Touch no *u* thing,

UNCLOTHED*
2Co 5: 4 because we do not wish to be *u*

UNCONCERNED*
Eze 16: 49 were arrogant, overfed and *u*;

UNCOVERED
Ru 3: 7 Ruth approached quietly, *u* his feet
1Co 11: 5 with her head *u* dishonors her head
11: 13 to pray to God with her head *u*?
Heb 4: 13 Everything is *u* and laid bare

UNDERGOES* (UNDERGOING)
Heb 12: 8 (and everyone *u* discipline),

UNDERGOING* (UNDERGOES)
1Pe 5: 9 the world are *u* the same kind

UNDERSTAND (UNDERSTANDING UNDERSTANDS UNDERSTOOD)
Ne 8: 8 the people could *u* what was being
Job 38: 4 Tell me, if you *u*.
42: 3 Surely I spoke of things I did not *u*,
Ps 14: 2 men to see if there are any who *u*,
73: 16 When I tried to *u* all this,
119: 27 Let me *u* the teaching
119: 125 that I may *u* your statutes.
Pr 2: 5 then you will *u* the fear
2: 9 Then you will *u* what is right
30: 18 four that I do not *u*:
Ecc 7: 25 to *u* the stupidity of wickedness
11: 5 so you cannot *u* the work of God,
Isa 6: 10 *u* with their hearts,
Isa 44: 18 know nothing, they *u* nothing;
52: 15 they have not heard, they will *u*.
Jer 17: 9 Who can *u* it?
31: 19 after I came to *u*,
Da 9: 25 and *u* this: From the issuing
Hos 14: 9 Who is discerning? He will *u* them.
Mt 13: 15 *u* with their hearts
24: 15 Daniel— let the reader *u*—
Lk 24: 45 so they could *u* the Scriptures.
Ac 8: 30 "Do you *u* what you are reading?"
Ro 7: 15 I do not *u* what I do.
15: 21 those who have not heard will *u*."
1Co 2: 12 that we may *u* what God has freely
2: 14 and he cannot *u* them,
14: 16 those who do not *u* say "Amen"
Eph 5: 17 but *u* what the Lord's will is.
Heb 11: 3 By faith we *u* that the universe was
2Pe 1: 20 you must *u* that no prophecy
3: 3 you must *u* that in the last days
3: 16 some things that are hard to *u*,

UNDERSTANDING (UNDERSTAND)
1Ki 4: 29 and a breadth of *u* as measureless
Job 12: 12 Does not long life bring *u*?
28: 12 Where does *u* dwell?
28: 28 and to shun evil is *u*.'"
32: 8 of the Almighty, that gives him *u*.
36: 26 How great is God— beyond our *u*!
37: 5 he does great things beyond our *u*.
Ps 111: 10 follow his precepts have good *u*.
119: 34 Give me *u*, and I will keep your law
119: 100 I have more *u* than the elders,
119: 104 I gain *u* from your precepts;
119: 130 it gives *u* to the simple.
136: 5 who by his *u* made the heavens,
147: 5 his *u* has no limit.
Pr 2: 2 and applying your heart to *u*,
2: 6 his mouth come knowledge and *u*.
3: 5 and lean not on your own *u*;
3: 13 the man who gains *u*,
4: 5 Get wisdom, get *u*;
4: 7 Though it cost all you have, get *u*.
7: 4 and call *u* your kinsman;
9: 10 knowledge of the Holy One is *u*.
10: 23 but a man of *u* delights in wisdom.
11: 12 but a man of *u* holds his tongue.
14: 29 A patient man has great *u*,
15: 21 a man of *u* keeps a straight course.
15: 32 whoever heeds correction gains *u*.
16: 16 to choose *u* rather than silver!
16: 22 *U* is a fountain of life
17: 27 and a man of *u* is even-tempered.
18: 2 A fool finds no pleasure in *u*
19: 8 he who cherishes *u* prospers.
20: 5 but a man of *u* draws them out.
23: 23 get wisdom, discipline and *u*.
Isa 11: 2 the Spirit of wisdom and of *u*,
40: 28 and his *u* no one can fathom.
56: 11 They are shepherds who lack *u*;
Jer 3: 15 you with knowledge and *u*.
10: 12 stretched out the heavens by his *u*.
Da 5: 12 a keen mind and knowledge and *u*,
10: 12 that you set your mind to gain *u*
Hos 4: 11 which take away the *u*
Mk 4: 12 and ever hearing but never *u*;
12: 33 with all your *u* and with all your
Lk 2: 47 who heard him was amazed at his *u*
2Co 6: 6 in purity, *u*, patience and kindness;
Eph 1: 8 on us with all wisdom and *u*.
Php 4: 7 of God, which transcends all *u*,
Col 1: 9 through all spiritual wisdom and *u*.
2: 2 have the full riches of complete *u*,
1Jn 5: 20 God has come and has given us *u*,

UNDERSTANDS (UNDERSTAND)
1Ch 28: 9 and *u* every motive
Jer 9: 24 that he *u* and knows me,
Mt 13: 23 man who hears the word and *u* it.
Ro 3: 11 there is no one who *u*,
1Ti 6: 4 he is conceited and *u* nothing.

UNDERSTOOD (UNDERSTAND)
Ne 8: 12 they now *u* the words that had
Ps 73: 17 then I *u* their final destiny.
Isa 40: 13 Who has *u* the mind of the LORD,
40: 21 Have you not *u* since the earth was
Jn 1: 5 but the darkness has not *u* it.
Ro 1: 20 being *u* from what has been made,

UNDESIRABLE*
Jos 24: 15 But if serving the LORD seems *u*

UNDIVIDED*
1Ch 12: 33 to help David with *u* loyalty—
Ps 86: 11 give me an *u* heart,
Eze 11: 19 I will give them an *u* heart
1Co 7: 35 way in *u* devotion to the Lord.

UNDOING
Pr 18: 7 A fool's mouth is his *u*,

UNDYING*
Eph 6: 24 Lord Jesus Christ with an *u* love.

UNEQUALED*
Mt 24: 21 *u* from the beginning of the world
Mk 13: 19 of distress *u* from the beginning,

UNFADING*
1Pe 3: 4 the *u* beauty of a gentle

UNFAILING*
Ex 15: 13 "In your *u* love you will lead
1Sa 20: 14 But show me *u* kindness like that
2Sa 22: 51 he shows *u* kindness
Ps 6: 4 save me because of your *u* love.
13: 5 But I trust in your *u* love;
18: 50 he shows *u* kindness
21: 7 through the *u* love
31: 16 save me in your *u* love.
32: 10 but the LORD's *u* love
33: 5 the earth is full of his *u* love.
33: 18 those whose hope is in his *u* love,
33: 22 May your *u* love rest upon us,
36: 7 How priceless is your *u* love!
44: 26 redeem us because of your *u* love.
48: 9 we meditate on your *u* love.
51: 1 according to your *u* love;
52: 8 I trust in God's *u* love
77: 8 Has his *u* love vanished forever?
85: 7 Show us your *u* love, O LORD,
90: 14 in the morning with your *u* love,
107: 8 thanks to the LORD for his *u* love
107: 15 thanks to the LORD for his *u* love
107: 21 to the LORD for his *u* love
107: 31 to the LORD for his *u* love
119: 41 May your *u* love come to me,
119: 76 May your *u* love be my comfort,
130: 7 for with the LORD is *u* love
143: 8 bring me word of your *u* love,
143: 12 In your *u* love, silence my enemies;
147: 11 who put their hope in his *u* love.
Pr 19: 22 What a man desires is *u* love;
20: 6 Many a man claims to have *u* love,
Isa 54: 10 yet my *u* love for you will not be
La 3: 32 so great is his *u* love.
Hos 10: 12 reap the fruit of *u* love,

UNFAITHFUL (UNFAITHFULNESS)
Lev 6: 2 is *u* to the LORD by deceiving his
Nu 5: 6 and so is *u* to the LORD,
1Ch 10: 13 because he was *u* to the LORD;
Pr 11: 6 the *u* are trapped by evil desires.
13: 2 the *u* have a craving for violence.
13: 15 but the way of the *u* is hard.
22: 12 but he frustrates the words of the *u*.
23: 28 and multiplies the *u* among men.
25: 19 is reliance on the *u* in times
Jer 3: 20 But like a woman *u* to her husband,

UNFAITHFULNESS (UNFAITHFUL)
1Ch 9: 1 to Babylon because of their *u*.
Mt 5: 32 except for marital *u*, causes her
19: 9 for marital *u*, and marries another

UNFIT*
Tit 1: 16 and *u* for doing anything good.

UNFOLDING
Ps 119: 130 the *u* of your words gives light;

UNFORGIVING*
2Ti 3: 3 unholy, without love, *u*, slanderous

UNFRIENDLY*
Pr 18: 1 An *u* man pursues selfish ends;

UNFRUITFUL
1Co 14: 14 my spirit prays, but my mind is *u*.

UNGODLINESS (UNGODLY)
Tit 2: 12 It teaches us to say "No" to *u*

UNGODLY (UNGODLINESS)
Ro 5: 6 powerless, Christ died for the *u*.
1Ti 1: 9 the *u* and sinful, the unholy
2Ti 2: 16 in it will become more and more *u*.
2Pe 2: 6 of what is going to happen to the *u*;
Jude : 15 and to convict all the *u*

UNGRATEFUL*
Lk 6: 35 he is kind to the *u* and wicked.
2Ti 3: 2 disobedient to their parents, *u*,

UNHOLY*
1Ti 1: 9 and sinful, the *u* and irreligious;
2Ti 3: 2 ungrateful, *u*, without love,
Heb 10: 29 as an *u* thing the blood

UNINTENTIONALLY
Lev 4: 2 'When anyone sins *u* and does
Nu 15: 22 " 'Now if you *u* fail to keep any
Dt 4: 42 flee if he had *u* killed his neighbor

UNIT
1Co 12: 12 body is a *u*, though it is made up

UNITE (UNITED UNITY)
1Co 6: 15 and *u* them with a prostitute?

UNITED (UNITE)
Ge 2: 24 and mother and be *u* to his wife,
Mt 19: 5 and mother and be *u* to his wife,
Ro 6: 5 If we have been *u* with him like this
Eph 5: 31 and mother and be *u* to his wife,
Php 2: 1 from being *u* with Christ,
Col 2: 2 encouraged in heart and *u* in love,

UNITY* (UNITE)
2Ch 30: 12 the people to give them *u* of mind
Ps 133: 1 is when brothers live together in *u*!
Jn 17: 23 May they be brought to complete *u*
Ro 15: 5 a spirit of *u* among yourselves
Eph 4: 3 effort to keep the *u* of the Spirit
4: 13 up until we all reach *u* in the faith
Col 3: 14 them all together in perfect *u*.

UNIVERSE*
1Co 4: 9 made a spectacle to the whole *u*,
Eph 4: 10 in order to fill the whole *u*.)
Php 2: 15 which you shine like stars in the *u*
Heb 1: 2 and through whom he made the *u*.
11: 3 understand that the *u* was formed

UNJUST
Ro 3: 5 That God is *u* in bringing his wrath
9: 14 What then shall we say? Is God *u*?
1Pe 2: 19 up under the pain of *u* suffering

UNKNOWN
Ac 17: 23 TO AN *U* GOD.

UNLEAVENED
Ex 12: 17 "Celebrate the Feast of *U* Bread,
Dt 16: 16 at the Feast of *U* Bread, the Feast

UNLIMITED*
1Ti 1: 16 Jesus might display his *u* patience

UNLOVED
Pr 30: 23 an *u* woman who is married,

UNMARRIED
1Co 7: 8 It is good for them to stay *u*,
7: 27 Are you *u*? Do not look for a wife.
7: 32 An *u* man is concerned about

UNPLOWED
Ex 23: 11 the seventh year let the land lie *u*
Hos 10: 12 and break up your *u* ground;

UNPRODUCTIVE
Tit 3: 14 necessities and not live *u* lives.
2Pe 1: 8 and *u* in your knowledge

UNPROFITABLE
Tit 3: 9 because these are *u* and useless.

UNPUNISHED
Ex 34: 7 Yet he does not leave the guilty *u*;
Pr 6: 29 no one who touches her will go *u*.
11: 21 of this: The wicked will not go *u*,
19: 5 A false witness will not go *u*,

UNQUENCHABLE
Lk 3: 17 he will burn up the chaff with *u* fire

UNREPENTANT*
Ro 2: 5 stubbornness and your *u* heart,

UNRIGHTEOUS*
Zep 3: 5 yet the *u* know no shame.
Mt 5: 45 rain on the righteous and the *u*.
1Pe 3: 18 the righteous for the *u*, to bring you
2Pe 2: 9 and to hold the *u* for the day

UNSEARCHABLE
Ro 11: 33 How *u* his judgments,
Eph 3: 8 preach to the Gentiles the *u* riches

UNSEEN*
Mt 6: 6 and pray to your Father, who is *u*.
6: 18 who is *u*; and your Father,
2Co 4: 18 on what is seen, but on what is *u*.
4: 18 temporary, but what is *u* is eternal.

UNSETTLED*
1Th 3: 3 so that no one would be *u*
2Th 2: 2 not to become easily *u*

UNSHRUNK
Mt 9: 16 patch of *u* cloth on an old garment,

UNSPIRITUAL*
Ro 7: 14 but I am *u*, sold as a slave to sin.
Col 2: 18 and his *u* mind puffs him up
Jas 3: 15 down from heaven but is earthly, *u*,

UNSTABLE*
Jas 1: 8 he is a double-minded man, *u*
2Pe 2: 14 they seduce the *u*; they are experts
3: 16 ignorant and *u* people distort,

UNTHINKABLE*
Job 34: 12 It is *u* that God would do wrong,

UNTIE
Mk 1: 7 worthy to stoop down and *u*.
Lk 13: 15 each of you on the Sabbath *u* his ox

UNVEILED*
2Co 3: 18 with *u* faces all reflect the Lord's

UNWHOLESOME*
Eph 4: 29 Do not let any *u* talk come out

UNWISE
Eph 5: 15 how you live — not as *u* but as wise,

UNWORTHY*
Ge 32: 10 I am *u* of all the kindness
Job 40: 4 "I am *u* — how can I reply to you?
Lk 17: 10 should say, 'We are *u* servants;
1Co 11: 27 Lord in an *u* manner will be guilty

UPHOLD (UPHOLDS)
Isa 41: 10 I will *u* you with my righteous right
Ro 3: 31 Not at all! Rather, we *u* the law.

UPHOLDS* (UPHOLD)
Ps 37: 17 but the LORD *u* the righteous.
37: 24 for the LORD *u* him with his hand.
63: 8 your right hand *u* me.
140: 12 and *u* the cause of the needy.
145: 14 The LORD *u* all those who fall
146: 7 He *u* the cause of the oppressed

UPRIGHT
Dt 32: 4 *u* and just is he.
Job 1: 1 This man was blameless and *u*;
Ps 7: 10 who saves the *u* in heart.
11: 7 *u* men will see his face.
25: 8 Good and *u* is the LORD;
33: 1 it is fitting for the *u* to praise him.
64: 10 let all the *u* in heart praise him!
92: 15 proclaiming, "The LORD is *u*;
97: 11 and joy on the *u* in heart.
119: 7 I will praise you with an *u* heart
Pr 2: 7 He holds victory in store for the *u*,
3: 32 but takes the *u* into his confidence.
14: 2 whose walk is *u* fears the LORD,
15: 8 but the prayer of the *u* pleases him.
21: 29 an *u* man gives thought to his ways.
Isa 26: 7 O *u* One, you make the way
Tit 1: 8 who is self-controlled, *u*, holy
2: 12 *u* and godly lives in this present

UPROOTED
Dt 28: 63 You will be *u* from the land you are
Jer 31: 40 The city will never again be *u*
Jude : 12 without fruit and *u* — twice dead.

UPSET
Lk 10: 41 are worried and *u* about many

URIAH
Hittite husband of Bathsheba, killed by David's order (2Sa 11).

USEFUL
Eph 4: 28 doing something *u*
2Ti 2: 21 *u* to the Master and prepared
3: 16 Scripture is God-breathed and is *u*
Phm : 11 now he has become *u* both to you

USELESS
1Co 15: 14 our preaching is *u*
Tit 3: 9 these are unprofitable and *u*.
Phm : 11 Formerly he was *u* to you,
Heb 7: 18 *u* (for the law made nothing perfect
Jas 2: 20 faith without deeds is *u*?

USURY
Ne 5: 10 But let the exacting of *u* stop!
Ps 15: 5 who lends his money without *u*

UTMOST
Job 34: 36 that Job might be tested to the *u*

UTTER (UTTERS)
Ps 78: 2 I will *u* hidden things, things from of old —
Mt 13: 35 I will *u* things hidden

UTTERS (UTTER)
1Co 14: 2 he *u* mysteries with his spirit.

UZZIAH
Son of Amaziah; king of Judah also known as Azariah (2Ki 15:1–7; 1Ch 6:24; 2Ch 26). Struck with leprosy because of pride (2Ch 26:16–23).

VAIN
Ps 33: 17 A horse is a *v* hope for deliverance;
73: 13 in *v* have I kept my heart pure;
127: 1 its builders labor in *v.*
Isa 65: 23 They will not toil in *v*
1Co 15: 2 Otherwise, you have believed in *v.*
15: 58 labor in the Lord is not in *v.*
2Co 6: 1 not to receive God's grace in *v.*
Gal 2: 2 running or had run my race in *v.*

VALIANT
1Sa 10: 26 by *v* men whose hearts God had

VALID
Jn 8: 14 my own behalf, my testimony is *v,*

VALLEY (VALLEYS)
Ps 23: 4 walk through the *v* of the shadow
Isa 40: 4 Every *v* shall be raised up,
Joel 3: 14 multitudes in the *v* of decision!

VALLEYS (VALLEY)
SS 2: 1 a lily of the *v.*

VALUABLE (VALUE)
Lk 12: 24 And how much more *v* you are

VALUE (VALUABLE VALUED)
Lev 27: 3 set the *v* of a male between the ages
Pr 16: 13 they *v* a man who speaks the truth.
31: 11 and lacks nothing of *v.*
Mt 13: 46 When he found one of great *v,*
1Ti 4: 8 For physical training is of some *v,*
Heb 11: 26 as of greater *v* than the treasures

VALUED (VALUE)
Lk 16: 15 What is highly *v* among men is

VANISHES
Jas 4: 14 appears for a little while and then *v.*

VASHTI*
Queen of Persia replaced by Esther (Est 1–2).

VAST
Ge 2: 1 completed in all their *v* array.
Dt 1: 19 of the Amorites through all that *v*
8: 15 He led you through the *v*
Ps 139: 17 How *v* is the sum of them!

VEGETABLES
Pr 15: 17 of *v* where there is love
Ro 14: 2 whose faith is weak, eats only *v.*

VEIL
Ex 34: 33 to them, he put a *v* over his face.
2Co 3: 14 for to this day the same *v* remains

VENGEANCE (AVENGE AVENGER AVENGES AVENGING REVENGE)
Nu 31: 3 to carry out the LORD's *v* on them
Isa 34: 8 For the LORD has a day of *v,*
Na 1: 2 The LORD takes *v* on his foes

VERDICT
Jn 3: 19 This is the *v:* Light has come

VICTOR'S* (VICTORY)
2Ti 2: 5 he does not receive the *v* crown

VICTORIES* (VICTORY)
2Sa 22: 51 He gives his king great *v;*
Ps 18: 50 He gives his king great *v;*
21: 1 great is his joy in the *v* you give!
21: 5 Through the *v* you gave, his glory is
44: 4 who decrees *v* for Jacob.

VICTORIOUS (VICTORY)
Ps 20: 5 for joy when you are *v*

VICTORIOUSLY* (VICTORY)
Ps 45: 4 In your majesty ride forth *v*

VICTORY (VICTOR'S VICTORIES VICTORIOUS VICTORIOUSLY)
2Sa 8: 6 gave David *v* wherever he
Ps 44: 6 my sword does not bring me *v;*
60: 12 With God we will gain the *v,*
129: 2 they have not gained the *v* over me.
Pr 11: 14 but many advisers make *v* sure.
1Co 15: 54 "Death has been swallowed up in *v*
15: 57 He gives us the *v* through our Lord
1Jn 5: 4 This is the *v* that has overcome

VIEW
Pr 5: 21 are in full *v* of the LORD,
2Ti 4: 1 and in *v* of his appearing

VILLAGE
Mk 6: 6 went around teaching from *v* to *v.*

VINDICATED (VINDICATION)
Job 13: 18 I know I will be *v.*
1Ti 3: 16 was *v* by the Spirit,

VINDICATION (VINDICATED)
Ps 24: 5 and *v* from God his Savior.

VINE (VINEYARD)
Ps 128: 3 Your wife will be like a fruitful *v*
Isa 36: 16 one of you will eat from his own *v*
Jnh 4: 6 Jonah was very happy about the *v.*
Jn 15: 1 "I am the true *v,* and my Father is

VINEGAR
Pr 10: 26 As *v* to the teeth and smoke
Mk 15: 36 filled a sponge with wine *v,*

VINEYARD (VINE)
1Ki 21: 1 an incident involving a *v* belonging
Pr 31: 16 out of her earnings she plants a *v.*
SS 1: 6 my own *v* I have neglected.
Isa 5: 1 My loved one had a *v*
1Co 9: 7 Who plants a *v* and does not eat

VIOLATION
Heb 2: 2 every *v* and disobedience received

VIOLENCE (VIOLENT)
Ge 6: 11 in God's sight and was full of *v.*
Isa 53: 9 though he had done no *v,*
60: 18 No longer will *v* be heard
Eze 45: 9 Give up your *v* and oppression
Joel 3: 19 of *v* done to the people of Judah,
Jnh 3: 8 give up their evil ways and their *v.*

VIOLENT (VIOLENCE)
Eze 18: 10 "Suppose he has a *v* son, who sheds
1Ti 1: 13 and a persecutor and a *v* man,
3: 3 not *v* but gentle, not quarrelsome,
Tit 1: 7 not *v,* not pursuing dishonest gain.

VIPERS
Ps 140: 3 the poison of *v* is on their lips.
Lk 3: 7 "You brood of *v!* Who warned you
Ro 3: 13 "The poison of *v* is on their lips."

VIRGIN (VIRGINS)
Dt 22: 15 shall bring proof that she was a *v*
Isa 7: 14 The *v* will be with child
Mt 1: 23 "The *v* will be with child
Lk 1: 34 I am a *v?"* The angel answered,
2Co 11: 2 that I might present you as a pure *v*

VIRGINS (VIRGIN)
Mt 25: 1 will be like ten *v* who took their
1Co 7: 25 Now about *v:* I have no command

VIRTUES*
Col 3: 14 And over all these *v* put on love,

VISIBLE
Eph 5: 13 exposed by the light becomes *v,*
Col 1: 16 and on earth, *v* and invisible,

VISION (VISIONS)
Da 9: 24 to seal up *v* and prophecy
Ac 26: 19 disobedient to the *v* from heaven.

VISIONS (VISION)
Nu 12: 6 I reveal myself to him in *v,*
Joel 2: 28 your young men will see *v.*
Ac 2: 17 your young men will see *v,*

VOICE
Dt 30: 20 listen to his *v,* and hold fast to him.
1Sa 15: 22 as in obeying the *v* of the LORD?
Job 40: 9 and can your *v* thunder like his?
Ps 19: 4 Their *v* goes out into all the earth,
29: 3 The *v* of the LORD is
66: 19 and heard my *v* in prayer.
95: 7 Today, if you hear his *v,*
Pr 8: 1 Does not understanding raise her *v*
Isa 30: 21 your ears will hear a *v* behind you,
40: 3 A *v* of one calling:
Mk 1: 3 "a *v* of one calling in the desert,
Jn 5: 28 are in their graves will hear his *v*
10: 3 and the sheep listen to his *v.*
Ro 10: 18 "Their *v* has gone out
Heb 3: 7 "Today, if you hear his *v,*
Rev 3: 20 If anyone hears my *v* and opens

VOMIT
Lev 18: 28 it will *v* you out as it vomited out
Pr 26: 11 As a dog returns to its *v,*
2Pe 2: 22 "A dog returns to its *v,"* and,

VOW (VOWS)
Nu 6: 2 a *v* of separation to the LORD
30: 2 When a man makes a *v*
Jdg 11: 30 Jephthah made a *v* to the LORD:

VOWS (VOW)
Ps 116: 14 I will fulfill my *v* to the LORD
Pr 20: 25 and only later to consider his *v.*

VULTURES
Mt 24: 28 is a carcass, there the *v* will gather.

WAGE (WAGES WAGING)
2Co 10: 3 we do not *w* war as the world does.

WAGES (WAGE)
Mal 3: 5 who defraud laborers of their *w,*
Lk 10: 7 for the worker deserves his *w.*
Ro 4: 4 his *w* are not credited to him
6: 23 For the *w* of sin is death,
1Ti 5: 18 and "The worker deserves his *w."*

WAGING (WAGE)
Ro 7: 23 *w* war against the law of my mind

WAILING
Ps 30: 11 You turned my *w* into dancing;

WAIST
2Ki 1: 8 and with a leather belt around his *w."*
Mt 3: 4 he had a leather belt around his *w.*

WAIT (AWAITS WAITED WAITING WAITS)
Ps 27: 14 *W* for the LORD;
130: 5 I *w* for the LORD, my soul waits,
Isa 30: 18 Blessed are all who *w* for him!
Ac 1: 4 *w* for the gift my Father promised,
Ro 8: 23 as we *w* eagerly for our adoption
1Th 1: 10 and to *w* for his Son from heaven,
Tit 2: 13 while we *w* for the blessed hope—

WAITED (WAIT)
Ps 40: 1 I *w* patiently for the LORD;

WAITING (WAIT)
Heb 9: 28 to those who are *w* for him.

WAITS (WAIT)
Ro 8: 19 creation *w* in eager expectation

WAKE (AWAKE WAKENS)
Eph 5: 14 *"W* up, O sleeper,

WAKENS* (WAKE)
Isa 50: 4 He *w* me morning by morning,
50: 4 *w* my ear to listen like one being

WALK (WALKED WALKING WALKS)
Lev 26: 12 I will *w* among you and be your
Dt 5: 33 *W* in all the way that the LORD
6: 7 and when you *w* along the road,
10: 12 to *w* in all his ways, to love him,
11: 19 and when you *w* along the road,
11: 22 to *w* in all his ways and to hold fast
26: 17 and that you will *w* in his ways,
Jos 22: 5 to *w* in all his ways,
Ps 1: 1 who does not *w* in the counsel
15: 2 He whose *w* is blameless
23: 4 Even though I *w*
84: 11 from those whose *w* is blameless.
89: 15 who *w* in the light of your presence
119: 45 I will *w* about in freedom,
Pr 4: 12 When you *w,* your steps will not be
6: 22 When you *w,* they will guide you;
Isa 2: 3 so that we may *w* in his paths."
2: 5 let us *w* in the light of the LORD.
30: 21 saying, "This is the way; *w* in it."
40: 31 they will *w* and not be faint.
57: 2 Those who *w* uprightly
Jer 6: 16 ask where the good way is, and *w*
Da 4: 37 And those who *w* in pride he is able
Am 3: 3 Do two *w* together
Mic 4: 5 All the nations may *w*
6: 8 and to *w* humbly with your God.
Mk 2: 9 'Get up, take your mat and *w'?*
Jn 8: 12 Whoever follows me will never *w*
1Jn 1: 6 with him yet *w* in the darkness,
1: 7 But if we *w* in the light,
2Jn : 6 his command is that you *w* in love.

WALKED (WALK)
Ge 5: 24 Enoch *w* with God; then he was no
Jos 14: 9 which your feet have *w* will be your
Mt 14: 29 *w* on the water and came toward Jesus.

WALKING (WALK)
1Ki 3: 3 love for the LORD by *w* according
Da 3: 25 I see four men *w* around in the fire,
2Jn : 4 of your children *w* in the truth,

WALKS (WALK)
Pr 10: 9 The man of integrity *w* securely,
13: 20 He who *w* with the wise grows wise
Isa 33: 15 He who *w* righteously
Jn 11: 9 A man who *w* by day will not

WALL (WALLS)
Jos 6: 20 *w* collapsed; so every man charged
Ne 2: 17 let us rebuild the *w* of Jerusalem,
Eph 2: 14 the dividing *w* of hostility,
Rev 21: 12 It had a great, high *w*

WALLOWING
2Pe 2: 22 back to her *w* in the mud."

WALLS (WALL)
Isa 58: 12 be called Repairer of Broken *W*,
60: 18 but you will call your *w* Salvation
Heb 11: 30 By faith the *w* of Jericho fell,

WANDER (WANDERED)
Nu 32: 13 he made them *w* in the desert forty
Jas 5: 19 one of you should *w* from the truth

WANDERED (WANDER)
Eze 34: 6 My sheep *w* over all the mountains
Mt 18: 12 go to look for the one that *w* off?
1Ti 6: 10 have *w* from the faith and pierced
2Ti 2: 18 who have *w* away from the truth.

WANT (WANTED WANTING WANTS)
1Sa 8: 19 "We *w* a king over us.
Mt 19: 21 Jesus answered, "If you *w*
Lk 19: 14 'We don't *w* this man to be our king
Ro 7: 15 For what I *w* to do I do not do,
13: 3 Do you *w* to be free from fear
2Co 12: 14 what I *w* is not your possessions
Php 3: 10 I *w* to know Christ and the power

WANTED (WANT)
1Co 12: 18 of them, just as he *w* them to be.
Heb 6: 17 Because God *w* to make

WANTING (WANT)
Da 5: 27 weighed on the scales and found *w*.
2Pe 3: 9 with you, not *w* anyone to perish,

WANTS (WANT)
Mt 5: 42 from the one who *w* to borrow
20: 26 whoever *w* to become great
Mk 8: 35 For whoever *w* to save his life will
10: 43 whoever *w* to become great
Ro 9: 18 he hardens whom he *w* to harden.
1Ti 2: 4 who *w* all men to be saved
1Pe 5: 2 you are willing, as God *w* you to be;

WAR (WARRIOR WARS)
Jos 11: 23 Then the land had rest from *w*.
1Sa 15: 18 make *w* on them until you have
Ps 68: 30 the nations who delight in *w*.
120: 7 but when I speak, they are for *w*.
144: 1 who trains my hands for *w*,
Isa 2: 4 nor will they train for *w* anymore.
Da 9: 26 *W* will continue until the end,
Ro 7: 23 waging *w* against the law
2Co 10: 3 we do not wage *w* as the world does
1Pe 2: 11 which *w* against your soul.
Rev 12: 7 And there was *w* in heaven.
19: 11 With justice he judges and makes *w*

WARN* (WARNED WARNING WARNINGS)
Ex 19: 21 *w* the people so they do not force
Nu 24: 14 let me *w* you of what this people
1Sa 8: 9 but *w* them solemnly and let them
1Ki 2: 42 swear by the LORD and *w* you,
2Ch 19: 10 you are to *w* them not to sin
Ps 81: 8 O my people, and I will *w* you—
Jer 42: 19 I *w* you today that you made a fatal
Eze 3: 18 and you do not *w* him or speak out
3: 19 But if you do *w* the wicked man
3: 20 Since you did not *w* him, he will die
3: 21 if you do *w* the righteous man not
33: 3 blows the trumpet to *w* the people,
33: 6 blow the trumpet to *w* the people
33: 9 if you do *w* the wicked man to turn
Lk 16: 28 Let him *w* them, so that they will
Ac 4: 17 we must *w* these men
1Co 4: 14 but to *w* you, as my dear children.
Gal 5: 21 I *w* you, as I did before, that those
1Th 5: 14 brothers, *w* those who are idle,
2Th 3: 15 an enemy, but *w* him as a brother.
2Ti 2: 14 *W* them before God
Tit 3: 10 and then *w* him a second time.
3: 10 *W* a divisive person once,
Rev 22: 18 I *w* everyone who hears the words

WARNED (WARN)
2Ki 17: 13 The LORD *w* Israel and Judah
Ps 19: 11 By them is your servant *w*;
Jer 22: 21 I *w* you when you felt secure,
Mt 3: 7 Who *w* you to flee
1Th 4: 6 have already told you and *w* you.
Heb 11: 7 when *w* about things not yet seen,
12: 25 they refused him who *w* them

WARNING (WARN)
Jer 6: 8 Take *w*, O Jerusalem,
1Ti 5: 20 so that the others may take *w*.

WARNINGS (WARN)
1Co 10: 11 and were written down as *w* for us,

WARRIOR (WAR)
Ex 15: 3 The LORD is a *w*;
1Ch 28: 3 you are a *w* and have shed blood.'
Pr 16: 32 Better a patient man than a *w*,

WARS (WAR)
Ps 46: 9 He makes *w* cease to the ends
Mt 24: 6 You will hear of *w* and rumors of *w*,

WASH (WASHED WASHING)
Ps 51: 7 *w* me, and I will be whiter
Jer 4: 14 *w* the evil from your heart
Jn 13: 5 and began to *w* his disciples' feet,
Ac 22: 16 be baptized and *w* your sins away,
Jas 4: 8 *W* your hands, you sinners,
Rev 22: 14 Blessed are those who *w* their robes

WASHED (WASH)
Ps 73: 13 in vain have I *w* my hands
1Co 6: 11 you were *w*, you were sanctified,
Heb 10: 22 and having our bodies *w*
2Pe 2: 22 and, "A sow that is *w* goes back
Rev 7: 14 they have *w* their robes

WASHING (WASH)
Eph 5: 26 cleansing her by the *w* with water
1Ti 5: 10 showing hospitality, *w* the feet
Tit 3: 5 us through the *w* of rebirth

WASTED (WASTING)
Jn 6: 12 Let nothing be *w*."

WASTING (WASTED)
2Co 4: 16 Though outwardly we are *w* away,

WATCH (WATCHER WATCHES WATCHING WATCHMAN)
Ge 31: 49 "May the LORD keep *w*
Ps 90: 4 or like a *w* in the night.
141: 3 keep *w* over the door of my lips.
Pr 4: 6 love her, and she will *w* over you.
6: 22 when you sleep, they will *w*
Jer 31: 10 will *w* over his flock like a shepherd
Mic 7: 7 I *w* in hope for the LORD,
Mt 24: 42 "Therefore keep *w*, because you do
26: 41 *W* and pray so that you will not fall
Mk 13: 35 "Therefore keep *w* because you do
Lk 2: 8 keeping *w* over their flocks at night
1Ti 4: 16 *W* your life and doctrine closely.
Heb 13: 17 They keep *w* over you

WATCHER* (WATCH)
Job 7: 20 O *w* of men?

WATCHES* (WATCH)
Nu 19: 5 While he *w*, the heifer is
Job 24: 15 The eye of the adulterer *w* for dusk;
Ps 1: 6 For the LORD *w* over the way
33: 14 from his dwelling place he *w*
63: 6 of you through the *w* of the night.
119: 148 through the *w* of the night,
121: 3 he who *w* over you will not slumber
121: 4 indeed, he who *w* over Israel
121: 5 The LORD *w* over you—
127: 1 Unless the LORD *w* over the city,
145: 20 LORD *w* over all who love him,
146: 9 The LORD *w* over the alien
Pr 31: 27 She *w* over the affairs
Ecc 11: 4 Whoever *w* the wind will not plant;
La 2: 19 as the *w* of the night begin;
4: 16 he no longer *w* over them.

WATCHING (WATCH)
Lk 12: 37 whose master finds them *w*

WATCHMAN (WATCH)
Eze 3: 17 I have made you a *w* for the house
33: 6 but I will hold the *w* accountable

WATER (WATERED WATERING WATERS WELL-WATERED)
Ex 7: 20 all the *w* was changed into blood.
17: 1 but there was no *w* for the people
Nu 20: 2 there was no *w* for the community,
Ps 1: 3 like a tree planted by streams of *w*,
22: 14 I am poured out like *w*,
42: 1 As the deer pants for streams of *w*,
Pr 25: 21 if he is thirsty, give him *w* to drink.
Isa 12: 3 With joy you will draw *w*
30: 20 of adversity and the *w* of affliction,
32: 2 like streams of *w* in the desert
49: 10 and lead them beside springs of *w*.
Jer 2: 13 broken cisterns that cannot hold *w*.
17: 8 will be like a tree planted by the *w*
31: 9 I will lead them beside streams of *w*
Eze 36: 25 I will sprinkle clean *w* on you,
Zec 14: 8 On that day living *w* will flow out
Mt 14: 29 walked on the *w* and came toward Jesus.
Mk 9: 41 anyone who gives you a cup of *w*
Lk 5: 4 to Simon, "Put out into deep *w*,
Jn 3: 5 unless he is born of *w* and the Spirit.
4: 10 he would have given you living *w*."
7: 38 streams of living *w* will flow
Eph 5: 26 washing with *w* through the word,
Heb 10: 22 our bodies washed with pure *w*.
1Pe 3: 21 this *w* symbolizes baptism that now
2Pe 2: 17 These men are springs without *w*
1Jn 5: 6 This is the one who came by *w*
5: 6 come by *w* only, but by *w*
5: 8 the Spirit, the *w* and the blood;
Rev 7: 17 to springs of living *w*.
21: 6 cost from the spring of the *w* of life.

WATERED (WATER)
1Co 3: 6 I planted the seed, Apollos *w* it,

WATERING (WATER)
Isa 55: 10 it without *w* the earth

WATERS (WATER)
Ps 23: 2 he leads me beside quiet *w*,
Ecc 11: 1 Cast your bread upon the *w*,
SS 8: 7 Many *w* cannot quench love;
Isa 11: 9 as the *w* cover the sea.
43: 2 When you pass through the *w*,
55: 1 come to the *w*;
58: 11 like a spring whose *w* never fail.
Hab 2: 14 as the *w* cover the sea.
1Co 3: 7 plants nor he who *w* is anything,

WAVE (WAVES)
Lev 23: 11 He is to *w* the sheaf
Jas 1: 6 he who doubts is like a *w* of the sea,

WAVER*
1Ki 18: 21 "How long will you *w*
Ro 4: 20 Yet he did not *w* through unbelief

WAVES (WAVE)
Isa 57: 20 whose *w* cast up mire and mud.
Mt 8: 27 Even the winds and the *w* obey him
Eph 4: 14 tossed back and forth by the *w*,

WAY (WAYS)
Ex 13: 21 of cloud to guide them on their *w*
18: 20 and show them the *w* to live
Dt 1: 33 to show you the *w* you should go.
32: 6 Is this the *w* you repay the LORD,
1Sa 12: 23 I will teach you the *w* that is good
2Sa 22: 31 "As for God, his *w* is perfect;
1Ki 8: 23 wholeheartedly in your *w*.
8: 36 Teach them the right *w* to live,
Job 23: 10 But he knows the *w* that I take;
Ps 1: 1 or stand in the *w* of sinners
32: 8 teach you in the *w* you should go;
37: 5 Commit your *w* to the LORD;
86: 11 Teach me your *w*, O LORD,
119: 9 can a young man keep his *w* pure?
139: 24 See if there is any offensive *w* in me
Pr 4: 11 I guide you in the *w* of wisdom
12: 15 The *w* of a fool seems right to him,
14: 12 There is a *w* that seems right
16: 17 he who guards his *w* guards his life.
19: 2 nor to be hasty and miss the *w*.
22: 6 Train a child in the *w* he should go,
30: 19 and the *w* of a man with a maiden.
Isa 30: 21 saying, "This is the *w*; walk in it."
35: 8 it will be called the *W* of Holiness.
40: 3 the *w* for the LORD;
48: 17 you in the *w* you should go.
53: 6 each of us has turned to his own *w*;
55: 7 Let the wicked forsake his *w*
Jer 5: 31 and my people love it this *w*.
Mal 3: 1 who will prepare the *w* before me.
Mt 3: 3 'Prepare the *w* for the Lord,
Lk 7: 27 who will prepare your *w* before you
Jn 14: 6 "I am the *w* and the truth
Ac 1: 11 in the same *w* you have seen him go
9: 2 any there who belonged to the *W*,
24: 14 of the *W*, which they call a sect.
1Co 10: 13 also provide a *w* out so that you can
12: 31 will show you the most excellent *w*.
14: 1 Follow the *w* of love and eagerly
Col 1: 10 and may please him in every *w*:
Tit 2: 10 that in every *w* they will make
Heb 4: 15 who has been tempted in every *w*,
9: 8 was showing by this that the *w*
10: 20 and living *w* opened for us
13: 18 desire to live honorably in every *w*.

WAYS (WAY)
Ex 33: 13 teach me your *w* so I may know

Dt 10: 12 to walk in all his *w,* to love him,
26: 17 and that you will walk in his *w,*
30: 16 in his *w,* and to keep his commands
32: 4 and all his *w* are just.
Jos 22: 5 in all his *w,* to obey his commands,
2Ch 11: 17 walking in the *w* of David
Job 34: 21 "His eyes are on the *w* of men;
Ps 25: 4 Show me your *w,* O LORD,
25: 10 All the *w* of the LORD are loving
37: 7 fret when men succeed in their *w,*
51: 13 I will teach transgressors your *w,*
77: 13 Your *w,* O God, are holy.
119: 59 I have considered my *w*
139: 3 you are familiar with all my *w.*
145: 17 The LORD is righteous in all his *w*
Pr 3: 6 in all your *w* acknowledge him,
4: 26 and take only *w* that are firm.
5: 21 For a man's *w* are in full view
16: 2 All a man's *w* seem innocent
16: 7 When a man's *w* are pleasing
Isa 2: 3 He will teach us his *w,*
55: 8 neither are your *w* my *w,"*
Eze 28: 15 You were blameless in your *w*
33: 8 out to dissuade him from his *w,*
Hos 14: 9 The *w* of the LORD are right;
Ro 1: 30 they invent *w* of doing evil;
Jas 3: 2 We all stumble in many *w.*

WEAK (WEAKER WEAKNESS WEAKNESSES)
Ps 41: 1 is he who has regard for the *w;*
72: 13 He will take pity on the *w*
82: 3 Defend the cause of the *w*
Eze 34: 4 You have not strengthened the *w*
Mt 26: 41 spirit is willing, but the body is *w."*
Ac 20: 35 of hard work we must help the *w,*
Ro 14: 1 Accept him whose faith is *w,*
15: 1 to bear with the failings of the *w*
1Co 1: 27 God chose the *w* things
8: 9 become a stumbling block to the *w.*
9: 22 To the *w* I became *w,* to win the *w.*
11: 30 That is why many among you are *w*
2Co 12: 10 For when I am *w,* then I am strong.
1Th 5: 14 help the *w,* be patient
Heb 12: 12 your feeble arms and *w* knees.

WEAK-WILLED (WILL)
2Ti 3: 6 and gain control over *w* women,

WEAKER* (WEAK)
2Sa 3: 1 the house of Saul grew *w* and *w.*
1Co 12: 22 seem to be *w* are indispensable,
1Pe 3: 7 them with respect as the *w* partner

WEAKNESS* (WEAK)
La 1: 6 in *w* they have fled
Ro 8: 26 the Spirit helps us in our *w.*
1Co 1: 25 and the *w* of God is stronger
2: 3 I came to you in *w* and fear,
15: 43 it is sown in *w,* it is raised in power;
2Co 11: 30 boast of the things that show my *w.*
12: 9 for my power is made perfect in *w*
13: 4 he was crucified in *w,* yet he lives
Heb 5: 2 since he himself is subject to *w.*
11: 34 whose *w* was turned to strength;

WEAKNESSES* (WEAK)
2Co 12: 5 about myself, except about my *w.*
12: 9 all the more gladly about my *w*
12: 10 I delight in *w,* in insults,
Heb 4: 15 unable to sympathize with our *w,*

WEALTH
Dt 8: 18 gives you the ability to produce *w,*
2Ch 1: 11 and you have not asked for *w,*
Ps 39: 6 he heaps up *w,* not knowing who
Pr 3: 9 Honor the LORD with your *w,*
10: 4 but diligent hands bring *w.*
11: 4 *W* is worthless in the day of wrath,
13: 7 to be poor, yet has great *w.*
15: 16 than great *w* with turmoil.
22: 4 bring *w* and honor and life.
Ecc 5: 10 whoever loves *w* is never satisfied
5: 13 *w* hoarded to the harm of its owner,
SS 8: 7 all the *w* of his house for love,
Mt 13: 22 and the deceitfulness of *w* choke it,
Mk 10: 22 away sad, because he had great *w.*
12: 44 They all gave out of their *w;* but she
Lk 15: 13 and there squandered his *w*
1Ti 6: 17 nor to put their hope in *w,*
Jas 5: 2 Your *w* has rotted, and moths have
5: 3 You have hoarded *w*

WEAPON (WEAPONS)
Ne 4: 17 work with one hand and held a *w*

WEAPONS (WEAPON)
Ecc 9: 18 Wisdom is better than *w* of war,
2Co 6: 7 with *w* of righteousness
10: 4 The *w* we fight with are not

WEAR (WEARING)
Dt 8: 4 Your clothes did not *w* out
22: 5 nor a man *w* women's clothing,
Ps 102: 26 they will all *w* out like a garment.
Pr 23: 4 Do not *w* yourself out to get rich;
Isa 51: 6 the earth will *w* out like a garment
Heb 1: 11 they will all *w* out like a garment.
Rev 3: 18 and white clothes to *w,*

WEARIES (WEARY)
Ecc 12: 12 and much study *w* the body.

WEARING (WEAR)
Jn 19: 5 When Jesus came out *w* the crown
Jas 2: 3 attention to the man *w* fine clothes
1Pe 3: 3 as braided hair and the *w*
Rev 7: 9 They were *w* white robes

WEARY (WEARIES)
Isa 40: 28 He will not grow tired or *w,*
40: 31 they will run and not grow *w,*
50: 4 know the word that sustains the *w.*
Mt 11: 28 all you who are *w* and burdened,
Gal 6: 9 Let us not become *w* in doing good,
Heb 12: 3 so that you will not grow *w*
Rev 2: 3 my name, and have not grown *w.*

WEDDING
Mt 22: 11 who was not wearing *w* clothes.
Rev 19: 7 For the *w* of the Lamb has come,

WEEDS
Mt 13: 25 and sowed *w* among the wheat,

WEEK
Mt 28: 1 at dawn on the first day of the *w,*
1Co 16: 2 On the first day of every *w,*

WEEP (WEEPING WEPT)
Ecc 3: 4 a time to *w* and a time to laugh,
Lk 6: 21 Blessed are you who *w* now,
23: 28 *w* for yourselves and for your

WEEPING (WEEP)
Ps 30: 5 *w* may remain for a night,
126: 6 He who goes out *w,*
Jer 31: 15 Rachel *w* for her children
Mt 2: 18 Rachel *w* for her children
8: 12 where there will be *w* and gnashing

WEIGH (OUTWEIGHS WEIGHED WEIGHS WEIGHTIER WEIGHTS)
1Co 14: 29 others should *w* carefully what is

WEIGHED (WEIGH)
Job 28: 15 nor can its price be *w* in silver.
Da 5: 27 You have been *w* on the scales
Lk 21: 34 or your hearts will be *w*

WEIGHS (WEIGH)
Pr 12: 25 An anxious heart *w* a man down,
15: 28 of the righteous *w* its answers,
21: 2 but the LORD *w* the heart.
24: 12 not he who *w* the heart perceive

WEIGHTIER* (WEIGH)
Jn 5: 36 "I have testimony *w* than that

WEIGHTS (WEIGH)
Lev 19: 36 Use honest scales and honest *w,*
Dt 25: 13 Do not have two differing *w*
Pr 11: 1 but accurate *w* are his delight.

WELCOME (WELCOMES)
Mk 9: 37 welcomes me does not *w* me
2Pe 1: 11 and you will receive a rich *w*

WELCOMES (WELCOME)
Mt 18: 5 whoever *w* a little child like this
2Jn : 11 Anyone who *w* him shares

WELL (WELLED WELLING WELLS)
Mt 15: 31 crippled made *w,* the lame walking
Lk 14: 5 falls into a *w* on the Sabbath day,
17: 19 your faith has made you *w."*
Jas 5: 15 in faith will make the sick person *w*

WELL-WATERED (WATER)
Isa 58: 11 You will be like a *w* garden,

WELLED* (WELL)
2Co 8: 2 and their extreme poverty *w* up

WELLING* (WELL)
Jn 4: 14 of water *w* up to eternal life."

WELLS (WELL)
Isa 12: 3 from the *w* of salvation.

WELLSPRING* (SPRING)
Pr 4: 23 for it is the *w* of life.

WEPT (WEEP)
Ps 137: 1 of Babylon we sat and *w*
Lk 22: 62 And he went outside and *w* bitterly
Jn 11: 35 Jesus *w.*

WEST
Ps 103: 12 as far as the east is from the *w,*
107: 3 from east and *w,* from north

WHEAT
Mt 3: 12 gathering his *w* into the barn
13: 25 and sowed weeds among the *w,*
Lk 22: 31 Satan has asked to sift you as *w.*
Jn 12: 24 a kernel of *w* falls to the ground

WHEELS
Eze 1: 16 appearance and structure of the *w:*

WHIRLWIND (WIND)
2Ki 2: 1 to take Elijah up to heaven in a *w,*
Hos 8: 7 and reap the *w.*
Na 1: 3 His way is in the *w* and the storm,

WHISPER (WHISPERED)
1Ki 19: 12 And after the fire came a gentle *w.*
Job 26: 14 how faint the *w* we hear of him!
Ps 107: 29 He stilled the storm to a *w;*

WHISPERED (WHISPER)
Mt 10: 27 speak in the daylight; what is *w*

WHITE (WHITER)
Isa 1: 18 they shall be as *w* as snow;
Da 7: 9 His clothing was as *w* as snow;
7: 9 the hair of his head was *w* like wool
Mt 28: 3 and his clothes were *w* as snow.
Rev 1: 14 hair were *w* like wool, as *w* as snow,
3: 4 dressed in *w,* for they are worthy.
6: 2 and there before me was a *w* horse!
7: 13 "These in *w* robes — who are they,
19: 11 and there before me was a *w* horse,
20: 11 Then I saw a great *w* throne

WHITER (WHITE)
Ps 51: 7 and I will be *w* than snow.

WHOLE
Ge 1: 29 plant on the face of the *w* earth
2: 6 and watered the *w* surface
11: 1 Now the *w* world had one language
Ex 12: 47 The *w* community
19: 5 Although the *w* earth is mine,
Lev 16: 17 and the *w* community of Israel.
Nu 14: 21 of the LORD fills the *w* earth,
32: 13 until the *w* generation
Dt 13: 16 *w* burnt offering to the LORD your
19: 8 gives you the *w* land he promised
Jos 2: 3 come to spy out the *w* land."
1Sa 1: 28 For his *w* life he will be given
17: 46 the *w* world will know that there is
1Ki 10: 24 The *w* world sought audience
2Ki 21: 8 and will keep the *w* Law that my
Ps 72: 19 may the *w* earth be filled
Pr 4: 22 and health to a man's *w* body.
8: 31 rejoicing in his *w* world
Ecc 12: 13 for this is the *w* duty of man.
Isa 1: 5 Your *w* head is injured,
6: 3 the *w* earth is full of his glory."
14: 26 plan determined for the *w* world;
Eze 34: 6 were scattered over the *w* earth,
37: 11 these bones are the *w* house
Da 2: 35 mountain and filled the *w* earth.
Zep 1: 18 the *w* world will be consumed,
Zec 14: 9 will be king over the *w* earth.
Mal 3: 10 the *w* tithe into the storehouse,
Mt 5: 29 than for your *w* body to be thrown
6: 22 your *w* body will be full of light.
16: 26 for a man if he gains the *w* world,
24: 14 will be preached in the *w* world
Lk 21: 35 live on the face of the *w* earth.
Jn 12: 19 Look how the *w* world has gone
13: 10 to wash his feet; his *w* body is clean
21: 25 the *w* world would not have room
Ac 17: 26 they should inhabit the *w* earth;
20: 27 proclaim to you the *w* will of God.
Ro 1: 9 whom I serve with my *w* heart
3: 19 and the *w* world held accountable
8: 22 know that the *w* creation has been
1Co 4: 9 made a spectacle to the *w* universe,
12: 17 If the *w* body were an ear,
Gal 3: 22 declares that the *w* world is
5: 3 obligated to obey the *w* law.
Eph 4: 10 in order to fill the *w* universe.)
4: 13 attaining to the *w* measure
1Th 5: 23 May your *w* spirit, soul
Jas 2: 10 For whoever keeps the *w* law
1Jn 2: 2 but also for the sins of the *w* world.
Rev 3: 10 going to come upon the *w* world

WHOLEHEARTED* (HEART)
2Ki 20: 3 you faithfully and with *w* devotion

1Ch 28: 9 and serve him with *w* devotion
29: 19 my son Solomon the *w* devotion
Isa 38: 3 you faithfully and with *w* devotion

WHOLEHEARTEDLY* (HEART)
Nu 14: 24 a different spirit and follows me *w*,
32: 11 they have not followed me *w*,
32: 12 for they followed the LORD *w*.'
Dt 1: 36 because he followed the LORD *w*
Jos 14: 8 followed the LORD my God *w*.
14: 9 followed the LORD my God *w*.'
14: 14 the LORD, the God of Israel, *w*.
1Ki 8: 23 with your servants who continue *w*
1Ch 29: 9 for they had given freely and *w*
2Ch 6: 14 with your servants who continue *w*
15: 15 oath because they had sworn it *w*.
19: 9 and *w* in the fear of the LORD.
25: 2 in the eyes of the LORD, but not *w*
31: 21 he sought his God and worked *w*.
Ro 6: 17 you *w* obeyed the form of teaching
Eph 6: 7 Serve *w*, as if you were serving

WHOLESOME*
2Ki 2: 22 And the water has remained *w*
2Pe 3: 1 to stimulate you to *w* thinking.

WICK
Isa 42: 3 a smoldering *w* he will not snuff out
Mt 12: 20 a smoldering *w* he will not snuff out

WICKED (WICKEDNESS)
Ge 13: 13 Now the men of Sodom were *w*
39: 9 How then could I do such a *w* thing
Ex 23: 1 Do not help a *w* man
Nu 14: 35 things to this whole *w* community,
Dt 15: 9 not to harbor this *w* thought:
Jdg 19: 22 some of the *w* men
1Sa 2: 12 Eli's sons were *w* men; they had no
15: 18 completely destroy those *w* people,
25: 17 He is such a *w* man that no one can
2Sa 13: 12 in Israel! Don't do this *w* thing.
2Ki 17: 11 They did *w* things that provoked
2Ch 7: 14 and turn from their *w* ways,
19: 2 "Should you help the *w*
Ne 13: 17 "What is this *w* thing you are doing
Ps 1: 1 walk in the counsel of the *w*
1: 5 Therefore the *w* will not stand
7: 9 to an end the violence of the *w*
10: 13 Why does the *w* man revile God?
11: 5 the *w* and those who love violence
12: 8 The *w* freely strut about
26: 5 and refuse to sit with the *w*.
32: 10 Many are the woes of the *w*,
36: 1 concerning the sinfulness of the *w*:
37: 13 but the Lord laughs at the *w*,
49: 5 when *w* deceivers surround me —
50: 16 But to the *w*, God says:
58: 3 Even from birth the *w* go astray;
73: 3 when I saw the prosperity of the *w*.
82: 2 and show partiality to the *w*? *Selah*
112: 10 the longings of the *w* will come
119: 61 Though the *w* bind me with ropes,
119: 155 Salvation is far from the *w*,
140: 8 do not grant the *w* their desires,
141: 10 Let the *w* fall into their own nets,
146: 9 but he frustrates the ways of the *w*.
Pr 2: 12 you from the ways of *w* men,
4: 14 Do not set foot on the path of the *w*
6: 18 a heart that devises *w* schemes,
9: 7 whoever rebukes a *w* man incurs
10: 20 the heart of the *w* is of little value.
10: 28 the hopes of the *w* come to nothing
11: 5 *w* are brought down by their own
11: 10 when the *w* perish, there are shouts
11: 21 The *w* will not go unpunished,
12: 5 but the advice of the *w* is deceitful.
12: 10 the kindest acts of the *w* are cruel.
14: 19 the *w* at the gates of the righteous.
15: 3 keeping watch on the *w*
15: 26 detests the thoughts of the *w*,
21: 10 The *w* man craves evil;
21: 29 A *w* man puts up a bold front,
28: 1 *w* man flees though no one pursues,
28: 4 who forsake the law praise the *w*,
29: 7 but the *w* have no such concern.
29: 16 When the *w* thrive, so does sin,
29: 27 the *w* detest the upright.
Isa 11: 4 breath of his lips he will slay the *w*.
13: 11 the *w* for their sins.
26: 10 Though grace is shown to the *w*,
48: 22 says the LORD, "for the *w*."
53: 9 He was assigned a grave with the *w*
55: 7 Let the *w* forsake his way
57: 20 But the *w* are like the tossing sea,
Jer 35: 15 of you must turn from your *w* ways
Eze 3: 18 that *w* man will die for his sin,
13: 22 you encouraged the *w* not to turn
Eze 14: 7 and puts a *w* stumbling block
18: 21 "But if a *w* man turns away
18: 23 pleasure in the death of the *w*?
21: 25 "'O profane and *w* prince of Israel,
33: 8 When I say to the *w*, 'O *w* man,
33: 11 pleasure in the death of the *w*,
33: 14 to the *w* man, 'You will surely die,'
33: 19 And if a *w* man turns away
Da 12: 10 but the *w* will continue to be *w*.
Mt 12: 39 *w* and adulterous generation asks
12: 45 be with this *w* generation."
12: 45 with it seven other spirits more *w*
Lk 6: 35 he is kind to the ungrateful and *w*.
Ac 2: 23 and you, with the help of *w* men,
Ro 4: 5 but trusts God who justifies the *w*,
1Co 5: 13 "Expel the *w* man from among you
6: 9 not know that the *w* will not inherit
Rev 2: 2 that you cannot tolerate *w* men,

WICKEDNESS (WICKED)
Ge 6: 5 The LORD saw how great man's *w*
Ex 34: 7 and forgiving *w*, rebellion and sin.
Lev 16: 21 and confess over it all the *w*
19: 29 to prostitution and be filled with *w*.
Dt 9: 4 it is on account of the *w*
Ne 9: 2 and confessed their sins and the *w*
Ps 45: 7 You love righteousness and hate *w*;
92: 15 he is my Rock, and there is no *w*
Pr 13: 6 but *w* overthrows the sinner.
Jer 3: 2 land with your prostitution and *w*.
8: 6 No one repents of his *w*,
14: 20 O LORD, we acknowledge our *w*
Eze 18: 20 the *w* of the wicked will be charged
28: 15 created till *w* was found in you.
33: 19 wicked man turns away from his *w*
Da 4: 27 and your *w* by being kind
9: 24 to atone for *w*, to bring
Jnh 1: 2 its *w* has come up before me."
Mt 24: 12 Because of the increase of *w*,
Lk 11: 39 inside you are full of greed and *w*.
Ac 1: 18 (With the reward he got for his *w*,
Ro 1: 18 who suppress the truth by their *w*,
1Co 5: 8 the yeast of malice and *w*,
2Co 6: 14 what do righteousness and *w* have
2Ti 2: 19 of the Lord must turn away from *w*
Tit 2: 14 for us to redeem us from all *w*
Heb 1: 9 loved righteousness and hated *w*;
8: 12 For I will forgive their *w*
2Pe 2: 15 who loved the wages of *w*.

WIDE
Ps 81: 10 Open *w* your mouth and I will fill it
Isa 54: 2 stretch your tent curtains *w*,
Mt 7: 13 For *w* is the gate and broad is
2Co 6: 13 my children — open *w* your hearts
Eph 3: 18 to grasp how *w* and long and high

WIDOW (WIDOWS)
Ex 22: 22 "Do not take advantage of a *w*
Dt 10: 18 cause of the fatherless and the *w*,
Ps 146: 9 sustains the fatherless and the *w*,
Isa 1: 17 plead the case of the *w*.
Lk 21: 2 saw a poor *w* put in two very small
1Ti 5: 4 But if a *w* has children

WIDOWS (WIDOW)
Ps 68: 5 to the fatherless, a defender of *w*,
Ac 6: 1 their *w* were being overlooked
1Co 7: 8 to the unmarried and the *w* I say:
1Ti 5: 3 to those *w* who are really
Jas 1: 27 look after orphans and *w*

WIFE (WIVES WIVES')
Ge 2: 24 and mother and be united to his *w*,
19: 26 But Lot's *w* looked back,
24: 67 she became his *w*, and he loved her;
Ex 20: 17 shall not covet your neighbor's *w*,
Lev 20: 10 adultery with another man's *w* —
Dt 5: 21 shall not covet your neighbor's *w*.
24: 5 happiness to the *w* he has married.
Ru 4: 13 took Ruth and she became his *w*.
Pr 5: 18 in the *w* of your youth.
12: 4 *w* of noble character is her
18: 22 He who finds a *w* finds what is
19: 13 quarrelsome *w* is like a constant
31: 10 *w* of noble character who can find?
Hos 1: 2 take to yourself an adulterous *w*
Mal 2: 14 the witness between you and the *w*
Mt 1: 20 to take Mary home as your *w*,
19: 3 for a man to divorce his *w* for any
Lk 17: 32 Remember Lot's *w*! Whoever tries
18: 29 or *w* or brothers or parents
1Co 7: 2 each man should have his own *w*,
7: 33 how he can please his *w* —
Eph 5: 23 the husband is the head of the *w*
5: 33 must love his *w* as he loves himself,
1Ti 3: 2 husband of but one *w*, temperate,
Rev 21: 9 I will show you the bride, the *w*

WILD
Ge 1: 25 God made the *w* animals according
8: 1 Noah and all the *w* animals
Lk 15: 13 squandered his wealth in *w* living.
Ro 11: 17 and you, though a *w* olive shoot,

WILL (WEAK-WILLED WILLFUL WILLING WILLINGNESS)
Ps 40: 8 I desire to do your *w*, O my God;
143: 10 Teach me to do your *w*,
Isa 53: 10 Yet it was the LORD's *w*
Mt 6: 10 your *w* be done
7: 21 who does the *w* of my Father
10: 29 apart from the *w* of your Father.
12: 50 does the *w* of my Father
26: 39 Yet not as I *w*, but as you *w*."
26: 42 I drink it, may your *w* be done."
Jn 6: 38 but to do the *w* of him who sent me.
7: 17 If anyone chooses to do God's *w*,
Ac 20: 27 to you the whole *w* of God.
Ro 12: 2 and approve what God's *w* is —
1Co 7: 37 but has control over his own *w*,
Eph 5: 17 understand what the Lord's *w* is.
Php 2: 13 for it is God who works in you to *w*
1Th 4: 3 God's *w* that you should be sanctified:
5: 18 for this is God's *w* for you
2Ti 2: 26 has taken them captive to do his *w*.
Heb 2: 4 distributed according to his *w*.
9: 16 In the case of a *w*, it is necessary
10: 7 I have come to do your *w*, O God
13: 21 everything good for doing his *w*,
Jas 4: 15 "If it is the Lord's *w*,
1Pe 3: 17 It is better, if it is God's *w*,
4: 2 but rather for the *w* of God.
2Pe 1: 21 never had its origin in the *w*
1Jn 5: 14 we ask anything according to his *w*,
Rev 4: 11 and by your *w* they were created

WILLFUL (WILL)
Ps 19: 13 Keep your servant also from *w* sins;

WILLING (WILL)
1Ch 28: 9 devotion and with a *w* mind,
29: 5 who is *w* to consecrate himself
Ps 51: 12 grant me a *w* spirit, to sustain me.
Da 3: 28 were *w* to give up their lives rather
Mt 18: 14 Father in heaven is not *w* that any
23: 37 her wings, but you were not *w*.
26: 41 The spirit is *w*, but the body is weak
1Ti 6: 18 and to be generous and *w* to share.
1Pe 5: 2 but because you are *w*,

WILLINGNESS* (WILL)
2Co 8: 11 so that your eager *w*
8: 12 For if the *w* is there, the gift is

WIN (WINS WON)
1Co 9: 19 myself a slave to everyone, to *w*
Php 3: 14 on toward the goal to *w* the prize
1Th 4: 12 your daily life may *w* the respect

WIND (WHIRLWIND WINDS)
Ps 1: 4 that the *w* blows away.
Ecc 2: 11 meaningless, a chasing after the *w*;
Hos 8: 7 "They sow the *w*
Mk 4: 41 Even the *w* and the waves obey
Jn 3: 8 The *w* blows wherever it pleases.
Eph 4: 14 and there by every *w* of teaching
Jas 1: 6 blown and tossed by the *w*.

WINDOW
Jos 2: 21 she tied the scarlet cord in the *w*.
Ac 20: 9 in a *w* was a young man named
2Co 11: 33 in a basket from a *w* in the wall

WINDS (WIND)
Ps 104: 4 He makes *w* his messengers,
Mt 24: 31 gather his elect from the four *w*,
Heb 1: 7 "He makes his angels *w*,

WINE
Ps 104: 15 *w* that gladdens the heart of man,
Pr 20: 1 *W* is a mocker and beer a brawler;
23: 20 join those who drink too much *w*
23: 31 Do not gaze at *w* when it is red,
31: 6 *w* to those who are in anguish;
SS 1: 2 your love is more delightful than *w*.
Isa 28: 7 And these also stagger from *w*
55: 1 Come, buy *w* and milk
Mt 9: 17 Neither do men pour new *w*
Lk 23: 36 They offered him *w* vinegar
Jn 2: 3 When the *w* was gone, Jesus'
Ro 14: 21 not to eat meat or drink *w*
Eph 5: 18 on *w*, which leads to debauchery.
1Ti 5: 23 a little *w* because of your stomach
Rev 16: 19 with the *w* of the fury of his wrath.

WINEPRESS
Isa 63: 2 like those of one treading the *w*?
Rev 19: 15 He treads the *w* of the fury

WINESKINS
Mt 9: 17 do men pour new wine into old *w.*

WINGS
Ex 19: 4 and how I carried you on eagles' *w*
Ru 2: 12 under whose *w* you have come
Ps 17: 8 hide me in the shadow of your *w*
91: 4 under his *w* you will find refuge;
Isa 6: 2 him were seraphs, each with six *w:*
40: 31 They will soar on *w* like eagles;
Eze 1: 6 of them had four faces and four *w.*
Zec 5: 9 in their *w!* They had *w* like those
Mal 4: 2 rise with healing in its *w.*
Lk 13: 34 hen gathers her chicks under her *w,*
Rev 4: 8 the four living creatures had six *w*

WINS (WIN)
Pr 11: 30 and he who *w* souls is wise.

WINTER
Mk 13: 18 that this will not take place in *w,*

WIPE (WIPED)
Isa 25: 8 The Sovereign LORD will *w* away
Rev 7: 17 God will *w* away every tear
21: 4 He will *w* every tear

WIPED (WIPE)
Lk 7: 38 Then she *w* them with her hair,
Ac 3: 19 so that your sins may be *w* out,

WISDOM (WISE)
Ge 3: 6 and also desirable for gaining *w,*
1Ki 4: 29 God gave Solomon *w* and very
2Ch 1: 10 Give me *w* and knowledge,
Ps 51: 6 you teach me *w* in the inmost place
111: 10 of the LORD is the beginning of *w;*
Pr 2: 6 For the LORD gives *w,*
3: 13 Blessed is the man who finds *w,*
4: 7 *W* is supreme; therefore get
8: 11 for *w* is more precious than rubies,
11: 2 but with humility comes *w.*
13: 10 *w* is found in those who take advice
23: 23 get *w,* discipline and understanding
29: 3 A man who loves *w* brings joy
29: 15 The rod of correction imparts *w,*
31: 26 She speaks with *w,*
Isa 11: 2 Spirit of *w* and of understanding,
28: 29 in counsel and magnificent in *w.*
Jer 10: 12 he founded the world by his *w*
Mic 6: 9 and to fear your name is *w*—
Mt 11: 19 But *w* is proved right by her actions
Lk 2: 52 And Jesus grew in *w* and stature,
Ac 6: 3 known to be full of the Spirit and *w.*
Ro 11: 33 the depth of the riches of the *w*
1Co 1: 17 not with words of human *w,*
1: 30 who has become for us *w* from God
12: 8 through the Spirit the message of *w*
Eph 1: 17 may give you the Spirit of *w*
Col 2: 3 are hidden all the treasures of *w*
2: 23 indeed have an appearance of *w,*
Jas 1: 5 of you lacks *w,* he should ask God,
3: 13 in the humility that comes from *w.*
Rev 5: 12 and wealth and *w* and strength

WISE (WISDOM WISER)
1Ki 3: 12 give you a *w* and discerning heart,
Job 5: 13 He catches the *w* in their craftiness
Ps 19: 7 making *w* the simple.
Pr 3: 7 Do not be *w* in your own eyes;
9: 8 rebuke a *w* man and he will love
10: 1 A *w* son brings joy to his father,
11: 30 and he who wins souls is *w.*
13: 1 A *w* son heeds his father's
13: 20 He who walks with the *w* grows *w,*
16: 23 A *w* man's heart guides his mouth,
17: 28 Even a fool is thought *w*
Ecc 9: 17 The quiet words of the *w* are more
Jer 9: 23 "Let not the *w* man boast
Eze 28: 6 "'Because you think you are *w,*
Da 2: 21 He gives wisdom to the *w*
12: 3 Those who are *w* will shine like
Mt 11: 25 hidden these things from the *w*
25: 2 them were foolish and five were *w.*
1Co 1: 19 I will destroy the wisdom of the *w;*
1: 27 things of the world to shame the *w;*
3: 19 He catches the *w* in their craftiness
Eph 5: 15 but as *w,* making the most
2Ti 3: 15 able to make you *w* for salvation
Jas 3: 13 Who is *w* and understanding

WISER (WISE)
Pr 9: 9 a wise man and he will be *w* still;
1Co 1: 25 of God is *w* than man's wisdom,

WISH (WISHES)
Jn 15: 7 ask whatever you *w,* and it will be
Ro 9: 3 For I could *w* that I myself were
Rev 3: 15 I *w* you were either one

WISHES (WISH)
Rev 22: 17 let him come; and whoever *w,*

WITCHCRAFT
Dt 18: 10 engages in *w,* or casts spells,
Gal 5: 20 idolatry and *w;* hatred, discord,

WITHDREW
Lk 5: 16 But Jesus often *w* to lonely places

WITHER (WITHERS)
Ps 1: 3 and whose leaf does not *w.*
37: 19 In times of disaster they will not *w;*

WITHERS (WITHER)
Isa 40: 7 The grass *w* and the flowers fall,
1Pe 1: 24 the grass *w* and the flowers fall,

WITHHELD (WITHHOLD)
Ge 22: 12 you have not *w* from me your son,

WITHHOLD (WITHHELD WITHHOLDS)
Ps 84: 11 no good thing does he *w*
Pr 23: 13 Do not *w* discipline from a child;

WITHHOLDS (WITHHOLD)
Dt 27: 19 "Cursed is the man who *w* justice

WITNESS (EYEWITNESSES WITNESSES)
Pr 12: 17 truthful *w* gives honest testimony,
19: 9 A false *w* will not go unpunished,
Jn 1: 8 he came only as a *w* to the light.

WITNESSES (WITNESS)
Dt 19: 15 by the testimony of two or three *w.*
Mt 18: 16 by the testimony of two or three *w.'*
Ac 1: 8 and you will be my *w* in Jerusalem,

WIVES (WIFE)
Eph 5: 22 *W,* submit to your husbands
5: 25 love your *w,* just as Christ loved
1Pe 3: 1 words by the behavior of their *w,*

WIVES' (WIFE)
1Ti 4: 7 with godless myths and old *w* tales

WOE
Isa 6: 5 "*W* to me!" I cried.
Eze 34: 2 *W* to the shepherds
Mt 18: 7 "*W* to the world
23: 13 "*W* to you, teachers of the law
Jude : 11 *W* to them! They have taken

WOLF (WOLVES)
Isa 65: 25 *w* and the lamb will feed together,

WOLVES (WOLF)
Mt 10: 16 you out like sheep among *w.*

WOMAN (MAN)
Ge 2: 22 God made a *w* from
2: 23 she shall be called '*w,*'
3: 6 *w* saw that the fruit
3: 12 The *w* you put here with
3: 15 between you and the *w,*
3: 16 To the *w* he said,
12: 11 a beautiful *w* you are.
20: 3 because of the *w* you have
24: 5 if the *w* is unwilling
Ex 2: 1 married a Levite *w*
3: 22 Every *w* is to ask her
21: 10 If he marries another *w*
21: 22 hit a pregnant *w*
Lev 12: 2 *w* who becomes pregnant
15: 19 *w* has her regular flow
15: 25 a *w* has a discharge
18: 17 sexual relations with both a *w*
20: 13 as one lies with a *w,*
Nu 5: 29 when a *w* goes astray
30: 3 young *w* still living in
30: 9 by a widow or divorced *w*
30: 10 *w* living with her husband
Dt 20: 7 become pledged to a *w*
21: 11 the captives a beautiful *w*
22: 5 *w* must not wear men's
22: 13 married this *w* but when
Jdg 4: 9 hand Sisera over to a *w.*
13: 6 the *w* went to her husband
14: 2 have seen a Philistine *w*
16: 4 he fell in love with a *w*
20: 4 husband of the murdered *w*
Ru 3: 11 a *w* of noble character
1Sa 1: 15 a *w* who is deeply troubled
25: 3 intelligent and beautiful *w,*
28: 7 a *w* who is a medium,
2Sa 11: 2 he saw a *w* bathing
13: 17 "Get this *w* out of here
14: 2 had a wise *w* brought
20: 16 a wise *w* called from
1Ki 3: 18 this *w* also had a baby.
17: 24 the *w* said to Elijah,
2Ki 4: 8 a well-to-do *w* was there,
8: 1 Elisha had said to the *w*
9: 34 "Take care of that cursed *w,*"
Job 14: 1 Man born of *w* is of few
Pr 11: 16 A kindhearted *w* gains respect,
11: 22 a beautiful *w* who shows no
14: 1 a wise *w* builds her house,
30: 23 unloved *w* who is married,
31: 30 a *w* who fears the LORD
Isa 54: 1 O barren *w,* you who never
Mt 5: 28 looks at a *w* lustfully
9: 20 a *w* who had been subject
15: 28 *W* you have great faith!
26: 7 a *w* came to him with
Mk 5: 25 a *w* was there who had
7: 25 a *w* whose little daughter
Lk 7: 39 what kind of a *w* she is
10: 38 a *w* named Martha opened
13: 12 "*W,* you are set free
15: 8 suppose a *w* has ten silver
Jn 2: 4 *w,* why do you involve
4: 7 a Samaritan *w* came
8: 3 a *w* caught in adultery.
19: 26 *w,* here is your son,"
20: 15 *W,* 'he said, "Why are you crying?
Ac 9: 40 Turning toward the dead *w,*
16: 14 was a *w* named Lydia,
Ro 7: 2 a married *w* is bound to
1Co 7: 2 each *w* her own husband
7: 15 a believing man or *w* is
7: 34 an unmarried *w* or virgin
7: 39 *w* is bound to her husband
11: 3 the head of the *w* is man,
11: 7 the *w* is the glory of man
11: 13 a *w* to pray to God with
Gal 4: 4 his Son, born of a *w,*
4: 31 not children of the slave *w,*
1Ti 2: 11 A *w* should learn in
5: 16 any *w* who is a believer
Rev 2: 20 You tolerate that *w* Jezebel,
12: 1 a *w* clothed with the sun
12: 13 he pursued the *w* who had
17: 3 a *w* sitting on a scarlet

WOMEN (MAN)
Mt 11: 11 among those born of *w,*
28: 5 The angel said to the *w,*
Mk 15: 41 Many other *w* who had come
Lk 1: 42 Blessed are you among *w,*
8: 2 also some *w* who had been
23: 27 *w* who mourned and wailed
24: 11 they did not believe the *w,*
Ac 1: 14 along with the *w* and Mary
16: 13 speak to the *w* who had
17: 4 not a few prominent *w.*
Ro 1: 26 *w* exchanged natural relations
1Co 14: 34 *w* should remain silent in
Php 4: 3 help these *w* who have
1Ti 2: 9 want *w* to dress modestly
5: 2 older *w* as mothers,
Tit 2: 3 teach the older *w* to be
2: 4 train the younger *w* to love
Heb 11: 35 *W* received back their dead
1Pe 3: 5 the holy *w* of the past

WOMB
Job 1: 21 Naked I came from my mother's *w,*
Ps 139: 13 in my mother's *w.*
Pr 31: 2 "O my son, O son of my *w,*
Jer 1: 5 you in the *w* I knew you,
Lk 1: 44 the baby in my *w* leaped for joy.
Jn 3: 4 into his mother's *w* to be born!"

WON (WIN)
1Pe 3: 1 they may be *w* over without words

WONDER (WONDERFUL WONDERS)
Ps 17: 7 Show the *w* of your great love,
SS 1: 3 No *w* the maidens love you!

WONDERFUL* (WONDER)
2Sa 1: 26 Your love for me was *w,*
1: 26 more *w* than that of women.
1Ch 16: 9 tell of all his *w* acts.
Job 42: 3 things too *w* for me to know.
Ps 26: 7 and telling of all your *w* deeds.
31: 21 for he showed his *w* love to me
75: 1 men tell of your *w* deeds.
105: 2 tell of all his *w* acts.
107: 8 and his *w* deeds for men,
107: 15 and his *w* deeds for men,
107: 21 and his *w* deeds for men.
107: 24 his *w* deeds in the deep.
107: 31 and his *w* deeds for men.
119: 18 *w* things in your law.
119: 129 Your statutes are *w;*
131: 1 or things too *w* for me.

Ps 139: 6 Such knowledge is too *w* for me,
139: 14 your works are *w*,
145: 5 I will meditate on your *w* works.
Isa 9: 6 *W* Counselor, Mighty God,
28: 29 *w* in counsel and magnificent
Mt 21: 15 of the law saw the *w* things he did
Lk 13: 17 with all the *w* things he was doing.
1Pe 2: 9 out of darkness into his *w* light.

WONDERS (WONDER)
Ex 3: 20 with all the *w* that I will perform
Dt 10: 21 and awesome *w* you saw
2Sa 7: 23 awesome *w* by driving out nations
Job 37: 14 stop and consider God's *w*.
Ps 9: 1 I will tell of all your *w*.
89: 5 The heavens praise your *w*,
119: 27 then I will meditate on your *w*.
Joel 2: 30 I will show *w* in the heavens
Ac 2: 11 we hear them declaring the *w*
2: 19 I will show *w* in the heaven above
5: 12 many miraculous signs and *w*
2Co 12: 12 that mark an apostle — signs, *w*
2Th 2: 9 and *w*, and in every sort
Heb 2: 4 also testified to it by signs, *w*

WOOD
Isa 44: 19 Shall I bow down to a block of *w*?"
1Co 3: 12 costly stones, *w*, hay or straw,

WOOL
Pr 31: 13 She selects *w* and flax
Isa 1: 18 they shall be like *w*.
Da 7: 9 hair of his head was white like *w*.
Rev 1: 14 and hair were white like *w*,

WORD (BYWORD WORDS)
Nu 30: 2 he must not break his *w*
Dt 8: 3 but on every *w* that comes
2Sa 22: 31 the *w* of the LORD is flawless.
Ps 56: 4 In God, whose *w* I praise,
119: 9 By living according to your *w*.
119: 11 I have hidden your *w* in my heart
119: 105 Your *w* is a lamp to my feet
Pr 12: 25 but a kind *w* cheers him up.
15: 1 but a harsh *w* stirs up anger.
25: 11 A *w* aptly spoken
30: 5 "Every *w* of God is flawless;
Isa 55: 11 so is my *w* that goes out
Jer 23: 29 "Is not my *w* like fire," declares
Mt 4: 4 but on every *w* that comes
12: 36 for every careless *w* they have
15: 6 Thus you nullify the *w* of God
Mk 4: 14 parable? The farmer sows the *w*.
Jn 1: 1 was the *W*, and the *W* was
1: 14 The *W* became flesh and made his
17: 17 them by the truth; your *w* is truth.
Ac 6: 4 and the ministry of the *w*."
2Co 2: 17 we do not peddle the *w* of God
4: 2 nor do we distort the *w* of God.
Eph 6: 17 of the Spirit, which is the *w* of God.
Php 2: 16 as you hold out the *w* of life —
Col 3: 16 Let the *w* of Christ dwell
2Ti 2: 15 and who correctly handles the *w*
Heb 4: 12 For the *w* of God is living
Jas 1: 22 Do not merely listen to the *w*,
2Pe 1: 19 And we have the *w* of the prophets

WORDS (WORD)
Dt 11: 18 Fix these *w* of mine in your hearts
Ps 12: 6 the *w* of the LORD are flawless,
119: 103 How sweet are your *w* to my taste,
119: 130 The unfolding of your *w* gives light;
119: 160 All your *w* are true;
Pr 2: 1 My son, if you accept my *w*
10: 19 When *w* are many, sin is not absent
16: 24 Pleasant *w* are a honeycomb,
30: 6 Do not add to his *w*,
Ecc 12: 11 The *w* of the wise are like goads,
Jer 15: 16 When your *w* came, I ate them;
Mt 24: 35 but my *w* will never pass away.
Lk 6: 47 and hears my *w* and puts them
Jn 6: 68 You have the *w* of eternal life.
15: 7 in me and my *w* remain in you,
1Co 2: 13 but in *w* taught by the Spirit,
14: 19 rather speak five intelligible *w*
Rev 22: 19 And if anyone takes *w* away

WORK (WORKED WORKER WORKERS WORKING WORKMAN WORKMANSHIP WORKS)
Ge 2: 2 day he rested from all his *w*.
Ex 23: 12 "Six days do your *w*,
Nu 8: 11 ready to do the *w* of the LORD.
Dt 5: 14 On it you shall not do any *w*,
Ps 19: 1 the skies proclaim the *w*
Ecc 5: 19 his lot and be happy in his *w* —
Jer 48: 10 lax in doing the LORD's *w*!
Mt 20: 1 to hire men to *w* in his vineyard.
Jn 6: 27 Do not *w* for food that spoils,
9: 4 we must do the *w* of him who sent
Ac 13: 2 for the *w* to which I have called
1Co 3: 13 test the quality of each man's *w*.
4: 12 We *w* hard with our own hands.
Eph 4: 16 up in love, as each part does its *w*.
Php 1: 6 that he who began a good *w*
2: 12 continue to *w* out your salvation
Col 3: 23 Whatever you do, *w* at it
1Th 4: 11 and to *w* with your hands,
5: 12 to respect those who *w* hard
2Th 3: 10 If a man will not *w*, he shall not eat
2Ti 3: 17 equipped for every good *w*.
Heb 6: 10 he will not forget your *w*
2Jn : 11 him shares in his wicked *w*.
3Jn : 8 men so that we may *w* together

WORKED (WORK)
1Co 15: 10 No, I *w* harder than all of them —
2Th 3: 8 On the contrary, we *w* night

WORKER (WORK)
Lk 10: 7 for the *w* deserves his wages.
1Ti 5: 18 and "The *w* deserves his wages."

WORKERS (WORK)
Mt 9: 37 is plentiful but the *w* are few.
1Co 3: 9 For we are God's fellow *w*;

WORKING (WORK)
Col 3: 23 as *w* for the Lord, not for men,

WORKMAN (WORK)
2Ti 2: 15 a *w* who does not need

WORKMANSHIP* (WORK)
Eph 2: 10 For we are God's *w*, created

WORKS (WORK)
Ps 66: 5 how awesome his *w* in man's behalf
145: 6 of the power of your awesome *w*,
Pr 8: 22 As the first of his *w*,
31: 31 let her *w* bring her praise
Ro 4: 2 in fact, Abraham was justified by *w*
8: 28 in all things God *w* for the good
Eph 2: 9 not by *w*, so that no one can boast.
4: 12 to prepare God's people for *w*

WORLD (WORLDLY)
Ps 9: 8 He will judge the *w*
50: 12 for the *w* is mine, and all that is in it
96: 13 He will judge the *w*
Pr 8: 23 before the *w* began.
Isa 13: 11 I will punish the *w* for its evil,
Zep 1: 18 the whole *w* will be consumed,
Mt 5: 14 "You are the light of the *w*.
16: 26 for a man if he gains the whole *w*,
Mk 16: 15 into all the *w* and preach the good
Jn 1: 29 who takes away the sin of the *w*!
3: 16 so loved the *w* that he gave his one
8: 12 he said, "I am the light of the *w*.
15: 19 As it is, you do not belong to the *w*,
16: 33 In this *w* you will have trouble.
17: 5 had with you before the *w* began.
17: 14 not of the *w* any more than I am
18: 36 "My kingdom is not of this *w*.
Ac 17: 24 "The God who made the *w*
Ro 3: 19 and the whole *w* held accountable
10: 18 their words to the ends of the *w*."
1Co 1: 27 things of the *w* to shame the strong.
3: 19 the wisdom of this *w* is foolishness
6: 2 that the saints will judge the *w*?
2Co 5: 19 that God was reconciling the *w*
10: 3 For though we live in the *w*,
1Ti 6: 7 For we brought nothing into the *w*,
Heb 11: 38 the *w* was not worthy of them.
Jas 2: 5 poor in the eyes of the *w* to be rich
4: 4 with the *w* is hatred toward God?
1Pe 1: 20 before the creation of the *w*,
1Jn 2: 2 but also for the sins of the whole *w*.
2: 15 not love the *w* or anything in the *w*.
5: 4 born of God overcomes the *w*.
Rev 13: 8 slain from the creation of the *w*.

WORLDLY (WORLD)
1Co 3: 1 address you as spiritual but as *w* —
Tit 2: 12 to ungodliness and *w* passions,

WORM
Mk 9: 48 "'their *w* does not die,

WORRY (WORRYING)
Mt 6: 25 I tell you, do not *w* about your life,
10: 19 do not *w* about what to say

WORRYING (WORRY)
Mt 6: 27 of you by *w* can add a single hour

WORSHIP (WORSHIPED WORSHIPS)
Jos 22: 27 that we will *w* the LORD
2Ki 17: 36 arm, is the one you must *w*.
1Ch 16: 29 *w* the LORD in the splendor
Ps 95: 6 Come, let us bow down in *w*,
100: 2 *w* the LORD with gladness;
Zec 14: 17 up to Jerusalem to *w* the King,
Mt 2: 2 and have come to *w* him."
4: 9 "if you will bow down and *w* me."
Jn 4: 24 and his worshipers must *w* in spirit
Ro 12: 1 to God — this is your spiritual act of *w*.
Heb 10: 1 perfect those who draw near to *w*.

WORSHIPED (WORSHIP)
2Ch 29: 30 and bowed their heads and *w*.
Mt 28: 9 clasped his feet and *w* him.

WORSHIPS (WORSHIP)
Isa 44: 15 But he also fashions a god and *w* it;

WORTH (WORTHY)
Job 28: 13 Man does not comprehend its *w*;
Pr 31: 10 She is *w* far more than rubies.
Mt 10: 31 are *w* more than many sparrows.
Ro 8: 18 sufferings are not *w* comparing
1Pe 1: 7 of greater *w* than gold,
3: 4 which is of great *w* in God's sight.

WORTHLESS
Pr 11: 4 Wealth is *w* in the day of wrath,
Jas 1: 26 himself and his religion is *w*.

WORTHY (WORTH)
1Ch 16: 25 For great is the LORD and most *w*
Mt 10: 37 more than me is not *w* of me;
Lk 15: 19 I am no longer *w* to be called your
Eph 4: 1 to live a life *w* of the calling you
Php 1: 27 in a manner *w* of the gospel
Col 1: 10 in order that you may live a life *w*
1Ti 3: 8 are to be men *w* of respect, sincere,
Heb 3: 3 Jesus has been found *w*
3Jn : 6 on their way in a manner *w* of God.
Rev 5: 2 "Who is *w* to break the seals

WOUND (WOUNDS)
1Co 8: 12 and *w* their weak conscience,

WOUNDS (WOUND)
Pr 27: 6 *w* from a friend can be trusted
Isa 53: 5 and by his *w* we are healed.
Zec 13: 6 'What are these *w* on your body?'
1Pe 2: 24 by his *w* you have been healed.

WRAPS
Ps 104: 2 He *w* himself in light

WRATH
2Ch 36: 16 scoffed at his prophets until the *w*
Ps 2: 5 and terrifies them in his *w*, saying,
76: 10 Surely your *w* against men brings
Pr 15: 1 A gentle answer turns away *w*,
Isa 13: 13 at the *w* of the LORD Almighty,
51: 17 the cup of his *w*,
Jer 25: 15 filled with the wine of my *w*
Eze 5: 13 my *w* against them will subside,
20: 8 So I said I would pour out my *w*
Am 1: 3 I will not turn back ˹my *w*˺.
Na 1: 2 maintains his *w* against his enemies
Zep 1: 15 That day will be a day of *w*,
Jn 3: 36 for God's *w* remains on him."
Ro 1: 18 The *w* of God is being revealed
2: 5 you are storing up *w*
5: 9 saved from God's *w* through him!
9: 22 choosing to show his *w*
1Th 5: 9 God did not appoint us to suffer *w*
Rev 6: 16 and from the *w* of the Lamb!
19: 15 the fury of the *w* of God Almighty.

WRESTLED
Ge 32: 24 and a man *w* with him till daybreak

WRITE (WRITER WRITING WRITTEN WROTE)
Dt 6: 9 *W* them on the doorframes
10: 2 I will *w* on the tablets the words
Pr 7: 3 *w* them on the tablet of your heart.
Jer 31: 33 and *w* it on their hearts.
Heb 8: 10 and *w* them on their hearts.
Rev 3: 12 I will also *w* on him my new name.

WRITER* (WRITE)
Ps 45: 1 my tongue is the pen of a skillful *w*.

WRITING (WRITE)
1Co 14: 37 him acknowledge that what I am *w*

WRITTEN (WRITE)
Dt 28: 58 which are *w* in this book,
Jos 1: 8 careful to do everything *w* in it.
23: 6 to obey all that is *w* in the Book
Ps 40: 7 it is *w* about me in the scroll.
Da 12: 1 everyone whose name is found *w*
Mal 3: 16 A scroll of remembrance was *w*
Lk 10: 20 but rejoice that your names are *w*

Lk 24: 44 must be fulfilled that is *w* about me
Jn 20: 31 these are *w* that you may believe
21: 25 for the books that would be *w.*
Ro 2: 15 of the law are *w* on their hearts,
1Co 4: 6 "Do not go beyond what is *w.*"
10: 11 as examples and were *w* down
2Co 3: 3 *w* not with ink but with the Spirit
Col 2: 14 having canceled the *w* code,
Heb 10: 7 it is *w* about me in the scroll —
12: 23 whose names are *w* in heaven.
Rev 21: 27 but only those whose names are *w*

WRONG (WRONGDOING WRONGED WRONGS)
Ex 23: 2 Do not follow the crowd in doing *w*
Nu 5: 7 must make full restitution for his *w,*
Dt 32: 4 A faithful God who does no *w,*
Job 34: 12 unthinkable that God would do *w,*
Ps 5: 5 you hate all who do *w.*
Gal 2: 11 to his face, because he was clearly in the *w.*
1Th 5: 15 that nobody pays back *w* for *w,*

WRONGDOING (WRONG)
Job 1: 22 sin by charging God with *w.*
1Jn 5: 17 All *w* is sin, and there is sin that

WRONGED (WRONG)
1Co 6: 7 not rather be *w?* Why not rather

WRONGS (WRONG)
Pr 10: 12 but love covers over all *w.*
1Co 13: 5 angered, it keeps no record of *w.*

WROTE (WRITE)
Ex 34: 28 And he *w* on the tablets the words
Jn 5: 46 for he *w* about me.
8: 8 down and *w* on the ground.

XERXES
King of Persia, husband of Esther. Deposed Vashti; replaced her with Esther (Est 1 – 2). Sealed Haman's edict to annihilate the Jews (Est 3). Received Esther without having called her (Est 5:1 – 8). Honored Mordecai (Est 6). Hanged Haman (Est 7). Issued edict allowing Jews to defend themselves (Est 8). Exalted Mordecai (Est 8:1 – 2, 15; 9:4; 10).

YEAR (YEARS)
Ex 34: 23 Three times a *y* all your men are
Lev 16: 34 to be made once a *y* for all the sins
25: 4 But in the seventh *y* the land is
25: 11 The fiftieth *y* shall be a jubilee
Heb 10: 1 repeated endlessly *y* after *y,*

YEARS (YEAR)
Ge 1: 14 to mark seasons and days and *y,*
Ex 12: 40 lived in Egypt was 430 *y.*
16: 35 The Israelites ate manna forty *y,*
Job 36: 26 of his *y* is past finding out.
Ps 90: 4 For a thousand *y* in your sight
90: 10 The length of our days is seventy *y*
Pr 3: 2 they will prolong your life many *y*
Lk 3: 23 Jesus himself was about thirty *y* old
2Pe 3: 8 the Lord a day is like a thousand *y,*
Rev 20: 2 and bound him for a thousand *y.*

YEAST
Ex 12: 15 are to eat bread made without *y.*
Mt 16: 6 guard against the *y* of the Pharisees
1Co 5: 6 you know that a little *y* works

YESTERDAY
Heb 13: 8 Jesus Christ is the same *y*

YOKE (YOKED)
1Ki 12: 4 and the heavy *y* he put on us,
Mt 11: 29 Take my *y* upon you and learn
Gal 5: 1 be burdened again by a *y*

YOKED (YOKE)
2Co 6: 14 Do not be *y* together

YOUNG (YOUNGER YOUTH)
2Ch 10: 14 he followed the advice of the *y* men
Ps 37: 25 I was *y* and now I am old,
119: 9 How can a *y* man keep his way
Pr 20: 29 The glory of *y* men is their strength
Isa 40: 11 he gently leads those that have *y.*
Joel 2: 28 your *y* men will see visions.
Ac 2: 17 your *y* men will see visions,
7: 58 at the feet of a *y* man named Saul.
1Ti 4: 12 down on you because you are *y,*
Tit 2: 6 encourage the *y* men
1Pe 5: 5 *Y* men, in the same way be
1Jn 2: 13 I write to you, *y* men,

YOUNGER (YOUNG)
1Ti 5: 1 Treat *y* men as brothers, older
Tit 2: 4 Then they can train the *y* women

YOUTH (YOUNG)
Ps 103: 5 so that your *y* is renewed like
Ecc 12: 1 Creator in the days of your *y,*
2Ti 2: 22 Flee the evil desires of *y,*

ZACCHAEUS
Lk 19: 2 A man was there by the name of *Z;*

ZEAL (ZEALOUS)
Ps 69: 9 for *z* for your house consumes me,
Pr 19: 2 to have *z* without knowledge,
Isa 59: 17 and wrapped himself in *z*
Jn 2: 17 "*Z* for your house will consume me
Ro 10: 2 their *z* is not based on knowledge.
12: 11 Never be lacking in *z,*

ZEALOUS (ZEAL)
Nu 25: 13 he was *z* for the honor of his God
Pr 23: 17 always be *z* for the fear
Eze 39: 25 and I will be *z* for my holy name.
Gal 4: 18 fine to be *z,* provided the purpose is

ZEBULUN
Son of Jacob by Leah (Ge 30:20; 35:23; 1Ch 2:1). Tribe of blessed (Ge 49:13; Dt 33:18 – 19), numbered (Nu 1:31; 26:27), allotted land (Jos 19:10 – 16; Eze 48:26), failed to fully possess (Jdg 1:30), supported Deborah (Jdg 4:6 – 10; 5:14, 18), David (1Ch 12:33), 12,000 from (Rev 7:8).

ZECHARIAH
1. Son of Jeroboam II; king of Israel (2Ki 15:8 – 12).
2. Post-exilic prophet who encouraged rebuilding of temple (Ezr 5:1; 6:14; Zec 1:1).
3. Father of John the Baptist (Lk 1:13; 3:2).

ZEDEKIAH
1. False prophet (1Ki 22:11 – 24; 2Ch 18:10 – 23).
2. Mattaniah, son of Josiah (1Ch 3:15), made king of Judah by Nebuchadnezzar (2Ki 24:17 – 25:7; 2Ch 36:10 – 14; Jer 37 – 39; 52:1 – 11).

ZEPHANIAH
Prophet; descendant of Hezekiah (Zep 1:1).

ZERUBBABEL
Descendant of David (1Ch 3:19; Mt 1:3). Led return from exile (Ezr 2:2; Ne 7:7). Governor of Israel; helped rebuild altar and temple (Ezr 3; Hag 1 – 2; Zec 4).

ZILPAH
Servant of Leah, mother of Jacob's sons Gad and Asher (Ge 30:9 – 12; 35:26, 46:16 – 18).

ZIMRI
King of Israel (1Ki 16:9 – 20).

ZION
2Sa 5: 7 David captured the fortress of *Z,*
Ps 2: 6 King on *Z,* my holy hill."
9: 11 to the LORD, enthroned in *Z;*
74: 2 Mount *Z,* where you dwelt.
87: 2 the LORD loves the gates of *Z*
102: 13 and have compassion on *Z,*
137: 3 "Sing us one of the songs of *Z!*"
Isa 2: 3 The law will go out from *Z,*
28: 16 "See, I lay a stone in *Z,*
51: 11 They will enter *Z* with singing;
52: 8 When the LORD returns to *Z,*
Jer 50: 5 They will ask the way to *Z*
Joel 3: 21 The LORD dwells in *Z!*
Am 6: 1 to you who are complacent in *Z,*
Mic 4: 2 The law will go out from *Z,*
Zec 9: 9 Rejoice greatly, O Daughter of *Z!*
Ro 9: 33 I lay in *Z* a stone that causes men
11: 26 "The deliverer will come from *Z;*
Heb 12: 22 But you have come to Mount *Z,*
Rev 14: 1 standing on Mount *Z,*

ZIPPORAH*
Daughter of Reuel; wife of Moses (Ex 2:21 – 22; 4:20 – 26; 18:1 – 6).

ZOPHAR
One of Job's friends (Job 11; 20).

Index to Color Maps

The Index to Color Maps will lead you to place-names found on the color maps in the back of this Bible. References are to the map number and the margin markings.

Abana River **6** C/D1/2; **7** C/D1/2; **9** C/D1/2
Abarim Mts. **2** D4
Abel Meholah **7** B/C3
Abel Shittim **3** D2/3
Abila **9** C3
Abilene **9** D1; **13** D8
Acco *See* Akko
Achaia **13** C4/5; **14** C/D3
Adora **9** B5
Adriatic Sea **13** A/B3; **14** C2
Aegean Sea **1** A1; **13** C5; **14** C2
Africa **13** D1/2; **14** B/C3
Ai **1** C3; **3** C/D2/3
Aijalon **6** B3/4
Akko **2** D2; **4** B2; **5** B3/4; **6** B2; **9** B2/3
Aleppo **1** D2; **5** C1; **8a** B1/2; **8b** B4/5; **12** D1; **13** D8
Alexandria **14** D3/4
Alexandrium **9** B4
Altar **10** C3
Amathus **9** B/C4
Amman **2** D/E3
Ammon **3** D2/3; **4** D4; **5** B/C4/5; **6** D3; **7** C4
Amphipolis **13** B5
Anathoth **7** B4
Antinoe **14** D/E4
Antioch **12** C1/2; **13** D8; **14** E3
Antipatris **9** A/B4
Antonia Fortress **10** B2
Aphek **4** B3/4; **6** B3; **7** B3
Apollonia **13** B5
Arabah **2** D5
Arabia **1** D3; **13** E/F7/8
Arabians **8a** B/C2/3
Arad **7** B4; **9** B5
Aram **4** D1/2; **5** C3; **6** C/D2; **7** C/D2
Aramean Desert **5** D3
Ararat *See* Urartu
Ararat, Mt. **1** E1; **8a** C1
Araxes River **1** F1; **8a** D1
Arbela **8b** C4/5
Armenia **14** F2/3
Arnon River **2** D4; **3** D3; **4** C5; **6** C4; **7** C4; **9** C5
Aroer **4** C5
Arrapkha **8a** C2; **8b** C5
Arubu **8a** B/C2/3
Arvad **5** B2; **8a** B2; **8b** B5
Ashdod **4** A/B4; **5** A/B4/5; **6** B3/4; **9** A4
Asher **4** B/C2
Ashkelon **4** A4; **6** A/B4; **9** A4
Ashtaroth **4** C/D2/3; **5** B/C3/4; **6** C2/3
Asia **13** C6
Asshur **1** E2; **8a** C2; **8b** C4/5
Assos **13** C5/6
Athens **13** C5; **14** D3
Atlantic Ocean **14** A1
Attalia **13** C/D6/7
Auranitis **9** D3
Azekah **3** C3
Azotus **12** B5/6

Babylon **1** E3; **8a** C2; **8b** C5
Babylonians **1** E/F3
Bashan **3** D1/2
Batanea **9** C3
Beautiful, Gate **10** C/D3
Beersheba **1** C3; **2** C/D4; **3** C3; **4** B5; **5** B5; **6** B4; **7** B4; **9** A/B5
Beersheba, Desert of **7** A/B4/5
Behistun **8b** D5
Beirut **6** B/C1
Benjamin **4** B/C4
Berea **13** B/C4/5
Berothai **5** B/C2/3
Besor Brook **2** C4; **3** C3; **6** A/B4; **7** A/B4; **9** A5
Beth Horon **3** C2/3
Beth Shan **4** C3; **5** B4; **6** C3
Beth Shemesh **4** B4
Bethany **9** B4; **11** B5
Bethany beyond Jordan **9** B/C3; **11** C3, C5
Bethel **1** C/D3; **3** C/D2/3; **4** B4; **6** B3/4; **7** B3/4
Bethesda Pool **10** C2
Bethlehem **2** D3/4; **4** B4; **6** B4; **9** B4; **11** B5
Bethsaida **9** B/C2/3; **11** C2
Bethsura **12** B5/6
Betogabris **12** B5/6
Bezer **4** C4
Bithynia & Pontus **13** B7; **14** D/E2/3
Black Sea **1** B1; **8a** A/B1; **13** A/B7; **14** E2
Bozrah **6** C5
Britain **14** A/B1
Byblos **1** C/D2/3; **5** B2/3; **8a** B2; **8b** B5; **12** B/C3/4
Byzantium **14** D2/3

Cabul *See* Kabul
Caesarea **9** A/B3; **11** A3; **12** B5; **13** E7/8
Caesarea Philippi **9** B/C2; **11** C1; **12** C4
Calah **8a** C1/2
Cana **9** B3; **11** B2/3
Canaan **3** C/D2/3
Capernaum **9** B2/3; **11** B/C2; **12** B/C4/5
Caphtor **1** A2/3
Cappadocia **13** C8; **14** E2/3
Carchemish **1** D2; **8a** B1/2; **8b** B4/5
Carmel, Mt. **2** C/D2/3; **6** B2/3; **7** B2/3; **9** A/B3
Carthage **14** B/C3
Caspian Sea **1** F1; **8a** D1; **8b** D4; **14** F2
Caucasus Mts. **14** F2
Cenchrea **13** C/D5
Chorazin *See* Korazin
Cilicia **12** B1; **13** C/D7/8; **14** E3
Cnidus **13** C/D6
Cologna **14** B1
Colosse **13** C6

Commagene **13** C8
Corinth **13** C4/5; **14** C/D3
Corsica **13** A/B1/2; **14** B/C2
Cos **13** C/D6
Crete **1** A2/3; **13** D5; **14** D3
Cyprus (island) **1** C2/3; **5** A2; **12** A2/3; **13** D7; **14** D3
Cyprus (town) **9** B4
Cyrenaica **13** E/F4/5
Cyrene (region) **14** C/D4
Cyrene (town) **14** C/D3/4
Cyrus River **14** F2/3

Dacia **13** A5; **14** D2
Dalmatia **13** A3/4
Damascus **1** C/D3; **2** E1/2; **4** D1; **5** B/C3; **6** C/D2; **7** C/D2; **8a** B2; **8b** B5; **9** C/D2; **12** C4; **13** D/E8; **14** E3
Dan (town) **2** D2; **4** C1/2; **5** B3; **6** C2
Dan (tribe) **4** B4
Danube River **14** C1
Dead Sea **2** D4
Debir **3** C/D3
Decapolis **9** C/D3/4; **11** C/D3/4
Delphi **13** C4/5
Derbe **13** C7; **14** E3
Dibon **3** D3; **4** C4/5; **6** C4
Dion **9** C3
Dnieper River **14** D/E1
Dophkah **3** B/C4/5
Dor **4** B2/3; **9** A/B3
Dothan **1** C3; **7** B3
Dur Sharrukin **8a** C1/2; **8b** C4/5
Dura-Europos **14** E/F3

Eastern Desert **2** E/F4/5; **5** C/D4/5
Ebal, Mt. **2** D3; **4** B/C3; **6** B3; **9** B3/4
Ebla **1** C/D2
Ecbatana **8a** D2; **8b** D5
Edessa **14** E3
Edom **3** C/D3/4; **4** C6; **5** B5; **6** C5/6; **7** C5/6
Edom, Desert of **2** D/E5
Edrei **3** D2; **4** C/D3; **5** B/C4; **6** C3
Eglon **3** C3; **4** A/B4/5
Egypt **3** A3; **13** E/F6/7; **14** D4
Egyptians **1** C4
Egypt, Wadi of **2** B/C4; **5** A5
Ekron **4** B4
Elim **3** B4
Emmaus **9** B4; **11** A5; **12** B5
En Gedi **2** D4; **4** B/C5
Ephesus **13** C6; **14** D3
Ephraim **4** B4

Epirus **13** C4
Erech/Uruk **1** E/F3
Esbus *See* Heshbon
Essene Gate **10** A5
Essene Quarter **10** A/B5
Euphrates River **1**D2; **5** D1; **8a** C2; **8b** C5; **13** C8; **14** E3
Ezion Geber **2** C/D6; **3** C4; **5** B6

Fair Haven **13** D5
First Wall **10** B3/4
Fish Gate **10** A/B2
Foothills **2** C/D4
Forum of Appius **13** B2/3

Gad **4** C3/4
Gadara **9** B/C3; **11** C3
Galatia **13** C7; **14** D/E3
Galilean Mts. **2** D2
Galilee **7** B/C2; **9** B/C2/3; **11** B2; **12** B4/5
Galilee, Sea of **2** D2; **11** C2; **12** B/C4/5
Gallia **13** A1
Garden Tomb **10** B1
Gate Beautiful **10** C/D3
Gath **4** B4; **5** A/B4/5; **6** B4
Gath Hepher **7** B2/3
Gaul **14** B1/2
Gaulanitis **9** C2
Gaza **2** C4; **4** A4/5; **5** A4/5; **6** A/B4; **9** A5; **12** B6
Gebal **5** B2/3
Gennath Gate **10** A/B3/4
Gennesaret **9** B2/3
Gentiles, Court of the **10** C3
Gerar **1** C3; **4** A5; **6** A/B4
Gerasa **9** C3/4
Gergesa/Kursi **9** B/C3; **11** C2/3
Gerizim, Mt. **2** D3; **4** B/C3/4; **6** B3; **9** B4; **11** B4; **12** B5
Germania **13** A4
Germany **14** C1
Gethsemane **10** D2
Gezer **4** B4; **5** B4; **6** B3/4
Gibeah **5** B4
Gibeon **3** C2/3; **4** B4
Gihon Spring **10** D4/5
Gilboa, Mt. **2** D3; **3** C/D2; **5** B4; **6** B/C3
Gilead **7** C3/4
Gilgal **3** C/D2/3; **4** C4; **7** B/C3/4
Golan **4** C/D2/3
Golden Gate **10** D3
Golgotha **10** A/B3
Goshen **3** A/B3/4
Gozan **8a** C1/2; **8b** C4/5

Great Bitter Lake **2** A5; **3** A/B3/4
Great Sea, The **1** B3; **2** B2; **3** B2; **4** A2; **5** A3; **6** A2; **7** A2; **8a** A2; **8b** A5; **9** A2; **11** A2; **12** A3/4; **13** D3
Gulf of Aqaba **5** B6

Habor River **8a** B/C1/2; **8b** B/C4/5
Halak, Mt. **2** D4
Hamath (region) **5** C/D1/2
Hamath (town) **5** C2; **8a** B2; **8b** B5; **12** C/D2/3
Haran **1** D2; **8a** B/C1/2; **8b** B/C4/5
Hattusha **1** C1
Hazeroth **3** C4/5
Hazor **1** C/D3; **3** C/D2; **4** C2; **5** B3/4; **6** B/C2
Hebron **1** C3; **2** D4; **3** C/D3; **4** B4/5; **5** B4/5; **6** B4; **9** B5
Heliopolis **1** B/C3/4; **3** A4
Hermon, Mt. **2** D2; **4** C1/2; **5** B3; **6** C2; **9** C2; **11** C1
Herod Antipas's Palace **10** B4
Herod's Palace **10** A4
Herodium **9** B4/5
Heshbon **3** D2/3; **4** C4; **6** C3/4; **9** C4
Hezekiah's Tunnel **10** C/D5
High Priest's House **10** A/B5
Hinnom Valley **10** A/B6
Hippicus, Tower of **10** A3/4
Hippos **9** B/C3
Hittites **1** C1/2
Horeb, Mt. *See* Sinai, Mt.
Hormah **4** B5
Hula, Lake **9** B/C2
Huldah Gates **10** C/D4
Hyrcania **9** B4/5

Ibleam **6** B/C3
Iconium **13** C7
Idumea **9** A/B5
Ijon **4** C1/2
Illyricum **14** C1/2
Inner Court **10** C3
Ionian Sea **13** C4
Israel **6** B/C3/4
Israel, Court of **10** C3
Israel Pool **10** C/D2
Issachar **4** B/C3
Issus **13** C/D8
Italy **13** A/B2/3; **14** C2
Iturea **9** C1/2
Iye Abarim **3** D3

Jabbok River **2** D/E3; **4** C3/4; **6** C3; **7** C3; **9** C3/4; **11** C4

Jabesh Gilead **4** C3; **6** C3
Jahaz **3** D3
Jarmuk, Mt. **6** B/C2; **9** B2/3
Jamnia **9** A4
Jarmuth **3** C2/3
Jazer **4** C4
Jericho **2** D3; **3** C/D2/3; **4** C4; **6** B/C3/4; **7** B/C3/4; **9** B4; **11** B/C5
Jerusalem **2** D3/4; **3** C/D2/3; **4** B4; **5** B4/5; **6** B3/4; **7** B4; **8a** B2/3; **8b** B5/6; **9** B4; **11** B5; **12** B5/6; **13** E8; **14** E3/4
Jezreel **4** B/C3; **7** B3
Joppa **2** C/D3; **4** A/B3/4; **5** A/B4; **6** B3/4; **7** B3/4; **9** A/B4; **12** B5
Jordan River **2** D3; **3** C/D2; **4** C3; **5** B4; **6** C3; **7** B/C3; **8a** B2/3; **8b** B5/6; **9** B/C3/4; **11** B/C5; **12** B/C5; **13** E8
Judah **4** B4/5; **6** B4/5; **7** B4
Judea **9** B4/5; **11** B5; **12** B6; **13** E8; **14** E3
Judean Mts. **2** C/D4

Kabul **4** B/C2
Kadesh *See* Kedesh
Kadesh Barnea **1** C3/4; **3** C3/4; **5** A/B5/6; **6** A/B5
Kedesh **3** C/D1/2; **4** C2; **5** C2; **6** B/C2
Kerith Ravine **7** C3
Khersa *See* Gergesa/Kursi
Kidron Valley **10** D4/5
Kinnereth, Sea of **2** D2/3; **3** D2; **4** C2; **5** B3/4; **6** B/C2/3; **7** B/C2/3; **9** B/C2/3
Kios **13** C5/6
Kir Hareseth **5** B5; **6** C4/5; **7** C4/5
Kiriath Jearim **4** B4
Kishon River **2** D2/3; **4** B2/3; **6** B2/3; **7** B2/3; **9** B3
Kittim **1** C2/3; **5** A2
Knossos **1** A2
Korazin **9** B/C2/3; **11** B/C2

Lachish **3** C3; **4** B4/5
Laodicea **13** C6
Lasea **13** D5
Leontes River **9** B2
Libnah **3** C3
Litani River **2** D2; **4** C1; **5** B3; **6** C1/2; **12** C4
Little Bitter Lake **2** A/B5
Loire River **14** B1/2
London **14** B1
Lower City **10** B/C5

Lycaonia **13** C7
Lycia **13** C/D6/7
Lydda **12** B5
Lydia **13** C5/6
Lyon **14** B1/2
Lystra **13** C/D7

Macedonia, Former Yugoslav Republic of **13** B4/5; **14** D2
Machaerus **9** B/C4/5; **11** C5/6
Magdala **9** B3; **11** B/C2
Mahanaim **4** C3/4; **5** B4
Mainz **14** B/C1
Makkedah **3** C3
Malatha **9** B5
Malta **13** D2/3
Manasseh **4** B3
Manasseh, East **4** C/D2
Marah **3** B4
Mareshah **6** B4
Mari **1** D/E2/3
Mariamne, Tower of **10** A4
Masada **9** B5
Mauretania **14** A/B3
Medeba **5** B4/5; **6** C4
Media **8a** D2; **8b** D4/5
Mediterranean Sea **2** B/2; **14** C3
Megiddo **1** C3; **4** B/C3; **5** B4; **6** B3; **9** B3
Me Jarkon River *See* Yarkon River
Memphis **1** B/C4; **3** A4; **8a** A3; **8b** A6; **14** D/E4
Men, Court of *See* Israel, Court of
Menzaleh, Lake **3** A/B3
Merom **3** C/D2; **4** C2
Mesopotamia **14** E/F3
Midian **3** C5
Miletus **13** C/D6
Mitylene **13** C5/6
Mizpah **4** B/C4; **7** B3/4; **8b** B5/6
Moab **3** D3; **4** C5; **5** B5; **6** C4; **7** B/C4/5
Moesia **13** A6; **14** D2
Moreh, Mt. **2** D2/3; **4** B/C2/3; **6** B/C2/3
Moresheth Gath **7** B4
Mycenae **1** A2
Myra **13** D6/7
Mysia **13** B/C6; **14** D2/3

Nabatea **9** C5; **14** E3/4
Nain **9** B3; **11** B3
Naphtali **4** C2
Nazareth **2** D2/3; **9** B3; **11** B3
Neapolis **13** B5
Nebo, Mt. **2** D3/4; **3** D2/3; **4** C4; **6** C3/4

Negev **2** C/D4
Nile River **1** B/C4; **3** A4/5; **13** F7; **14** D/E4
Nineveh **1** E2; **8a** C1/2; **8b** C4/5
Nippur **1** E3; **8a** C/D2/3; **8b** C/D5
Noph *See* Memphis
Numidia **13** C/D1
Nuzi **1** E2

Oboth **3** C/D3/4
Olives, Mt. of **2** D3/4; **10** D3; **11** B5
Olympus, Mt. **13** B/C4/5
On *See* Heliopolis
Orontes River **5** B/C1; **8a** B1/2; **8b** B4/5; **12** C/D3

Paddan Aram **1** D2
Pamphylia **13** C/D6/7
Paphos **13** D7
Paran, Desert of **2** B/C5; **3** B/C4
Parthia **14** F3
Patara **13** C/D6
Patmos **13** C/D5/6
Pella **9** B/C3/4; **14** E3/4
Penuel **6** C3
Perea **9** B/C4; **11** C4
Perga **13** C/D6/7
Pergamum **13** C6; **14** D2/3
Persian Gulf **1** F4; **8a** D3; **8b** D6; **14** F4
Pharpar River **4** D1/2; **6** C2; **7** C2; **9** C2
Phasael, Tower of **10** A4
Philadelphia **9** C4; **13** C6
Philippi **13** B5; **14** D2
Philistia **3** C3; **5** A/B4; **6** A/B4/5; **7** A4/5
Phoenicia **5** B3; **6** B/C2; **7** C1/2; **9** B2; **11** B1; **13** D8
Phoenix **13** D5
Phrygia **14** D/E3
Pinnacle of the Temple **10** D4
Pisidia **13** C6/7
Pisidian Antioch **13** C7
Pithom **3** A/B3/4
Po River **14** B/C2
Ptolemais **11** A/B2; **12** B4/5; **13** D/E7/8
Punon **3** C/D3/4
Puteoli **13** B3; **14** C2/3

Qatna **5** C2

Rabbah **4** C/D4; **5** B/C4; **6** C3/4
Ramah **7** B4
Rameses **3** A/B3
Ramoth Gilead **4** C/D3; **5** B/C4; **6** C3; **7** C3

Raphana **9** C2/3
Raphia **6** A/B4; **9** A5
Red Sea **1** C4; **2** C/D8; **3** C6; **8a** B3; **8b** B6; **13** F7/8; **14** E4
Rephidim **3** B/C5
Reuben **4** C4/5
Rezeph **8a** B/C2; **8b** B/C5
Rhegium **13** C3
Rhine River **14** B/C1
Rhodes **13** D6
Rhone River **14** B2
Riblah **8b** B5
Rimmon **4** B/C2/3
Robinson's Arch **10** C4
Rome **13** B2; **14** C2
Royal Porch **10** C/D3/4

Salamis **13** D7/8
Salim **9** B/C3/4; **11** B/C3/4
Salmone **13** D5/6
Salt Sea **2** D4; **3** C/D3; **4** B/C5; **5** B5; **6** B/C4; **7** B/C4; **9** B5; **11** B/C6; **12** B/C6
Samaria (region) **7** B3; **9** B3/4; **11** B3/4; **12** B5
Samaria (town) **4** B3; **6** B3; **7** B3; **8a** B2/3; **12** B5
Samos **13** C5/6
Samothrace **13** B/C5/6
Sardinia **13** B/C1/2; **14** B/C2/3
Sardis **13** C6
Sarmatia **14** D1
Scythopolis **9** B/C3
Sebaste *See* Samaria (town)
Second Quarter **10** B3
Second Wall **10** B1/2
Seleucia **13** D8
Serpent's Pool **10** A5
Sharon, Plain of **2** C/D3
Shechem **1** C/D3; **2** D3; **3** C/D2/3; **4** B/C3/4; **5** B4; **6** B3
Sheep Gate **10** C/D2/3
Sheep Pool **10** C/D2
Shephelah **2** C/D4
Shiloh **3** C/D2/3; **4** B/C4; **6** B3; **7** B3/4
Shunem **7** B/C3
Shur, Desert of **2** B5; **3** B/C3/4
Sicily **13** C2/3; **14** C3
Sidon **5** B3; **6** B/C1/2; **7** B/C1/2; **9** B1/2; **12** B/C4; **13** D/E8; **14** E3
Siloam, Pool of **10** C5/6
Simeon **4** A/B5
Sin, Desert of **2** B6; **3** B/C4/5
Sinai **1** C4; **2** B/C5/6; **3** B/C4
Sinai, Desert of **2** B/C 7
Sinai, Mt. **2** C7; **3** C5
Smyrna **13** C6
Spain **14** A2
Sparta **13** C/D4/5
Succoth **1** B/C3/4; **3** A/B3/4; **4** C3/4; **6** C3
Susa **8a** D2/3; **8b** D5
Sychar **9** B3/4; **11** B4; **12** B5
Syracuse **13** C/D3; **14** C3
Syria **9** C/D2; **12** C/D2; **13** D8; **14** E3

Taanach **4** B/C3; **5** B4; **6** B3
Tabor, Mt. **2** D2/3; **3** C/D2; **4** C2/3; **6** B/C2/3; **9** B3; **11** B3
Tadmor **1** D2/3; **5** D2; **8a** B/C2; **8b** B/C5
Tagus River **14** A2
Tamar **5** B5
Tanis *See* Zoan
Tarsus **12** B1; **13** C/D7/8; **14** E3
Taurus Mts. **1** C2
Tekoa **7** B4
Tel Aviv **2** C/D3
Temple **10** C3
Tetrarchy of Philip **9** C2/3
Theater **10** B4/5
Thessalonica **13** B/C4/5; **14** C/D2/3
Thrace **13** B5; **14** D2/3
Three Taverns **13** B2/3
Thyatira **13** C6
Tiberias **2** D2/3; **9** B/C3; **11** B/C2/3
Tigris River **1** E2; **8a** C2; **8b** C5; **14** F3
Tiphsah **5** D1; **8a** B/C2
Tirzah **4** B/C3; **6** B/C3
Tishbe **7** C3
Tower Pool **10** A3
Trachonitis **9** C/D2/3
Tripolitania **13** E2/3
Troas **13** B/C5/6
Troy **1** A/B1
Tyre **2** D2; **4** B/C1/2; **5** B3; **6** B2; **7** B2; **9** B2; **11** B1; **12** B4; **13** D/E7/8; **14** E3/4
Tyropoeon Valley **10** B2/3
Tyrrhenian Sea **13** B/C2/3; **14** B/C2/3

Ugarit **1** C/D2/3
Upper City **10** B4
Upper Room **10** A/B5
Ur **1** E/F3; **8a** C/D2/3; **8b** C/D5/6
Urartu **8a** C1; **8b** C4
Urmia, Lake **1** E/F2; **8a** C/D1/2; **8b** C/D4
Uruk **1** E/F3

Valley Gate **10** C4
Van, Lake **8a** C1; **8b** C4
Vistula River **14** C/D1
Volga River **14** F1/2

Water Gate **10** C/D5/6
Wadi el-Arish **6** A4/5
Wilson's Arch **10** B/C3/4
Women, Court of **10** C3

Yarkon River **2** C/D3; **9** A/B4
Yarmuk River **2** D/E2/3; **4** C2/3; **6** C2/3; **7** C2/3; **9** C3; **11** C2/3

Zarephath **7** B/C2
Zebulun **4** B/C2/3
Zered Brook **2** D4; **3** C/D3; **4** C5/6; **6** C4/5; **7** B/C5; **9** B/C5/6
Ziklag **4** A/B5; **5** A/B5
Zin, Desert of **2** C/D5; **3** C3/4
Zoan **1** B/C3/4
Zoar **1** C/D3/4

NOTES

The NIV Study Bible

2008 Edition

General Editor: Kenneth Barker
Associate Editors: John Stek
Mark Strauss
Ronald Youngblood
Zondervan Editorial: Amy Ballor, Natalie Block, Pamela Fisher, Michael Vander Klipp
Production Management: Phil Herich
Art Direction and Cover Design: Ron Huizinga
Interior Design: Sharon VanLoozenoord, Belmont, MI
Ron Huizinga
Interior Proofreading: Peachtree Editorial and Proofreading Service, Peachtree City, GA
Interior Typesetting: Nancy Wilson

See Contributors page (xix) for a complete listing of individuals who contributed and/or reviewed material for the *NIV Study Bible*.

2002 Edition

General Editor: Kenneth Barker
Associate Editors: John Stek
Walter Wessel
Ronald Youngblood
Zondervan Editorial: Lois Brom, Ben Irwin, Michael Vander Klipp
Production Management: Phil Herich
Art Direction and Cover Design: Jamie DeBruyn
Interior Design: Sharon VanLoozenoord, Belmont, MI
Interior Proofreading: Peachtree Editorial and Proofreading Service, Peachtree City, GA
Interior Typesetting: Auto-Graphics, Pomona, CA

1985 Edition

General Editor: Kenneth Barker
Associate Editors: Donald Burdick
John Stek
Walter Wessel
Ronald Youngblood
Managing Editor: Doris Wynbeek Rikkers
Copy Editor/Stylist: June Gunden
Artist: Hugh O. Claycombe
Art Consultant: James E. Jennings

GUARANTEE

Thank you for choosing a Zondervan product. We want to make sure you're satisfied with the quality of your purchase. We stand behind every product we make; that's why we guarantee each one for a lifetime against manufacturing defects. For more information on our quality guarantee and product care instructions, visit us at www.zondervan.com/guarantee.

Map 1: **WORLD OF THE PATRIARCHS**

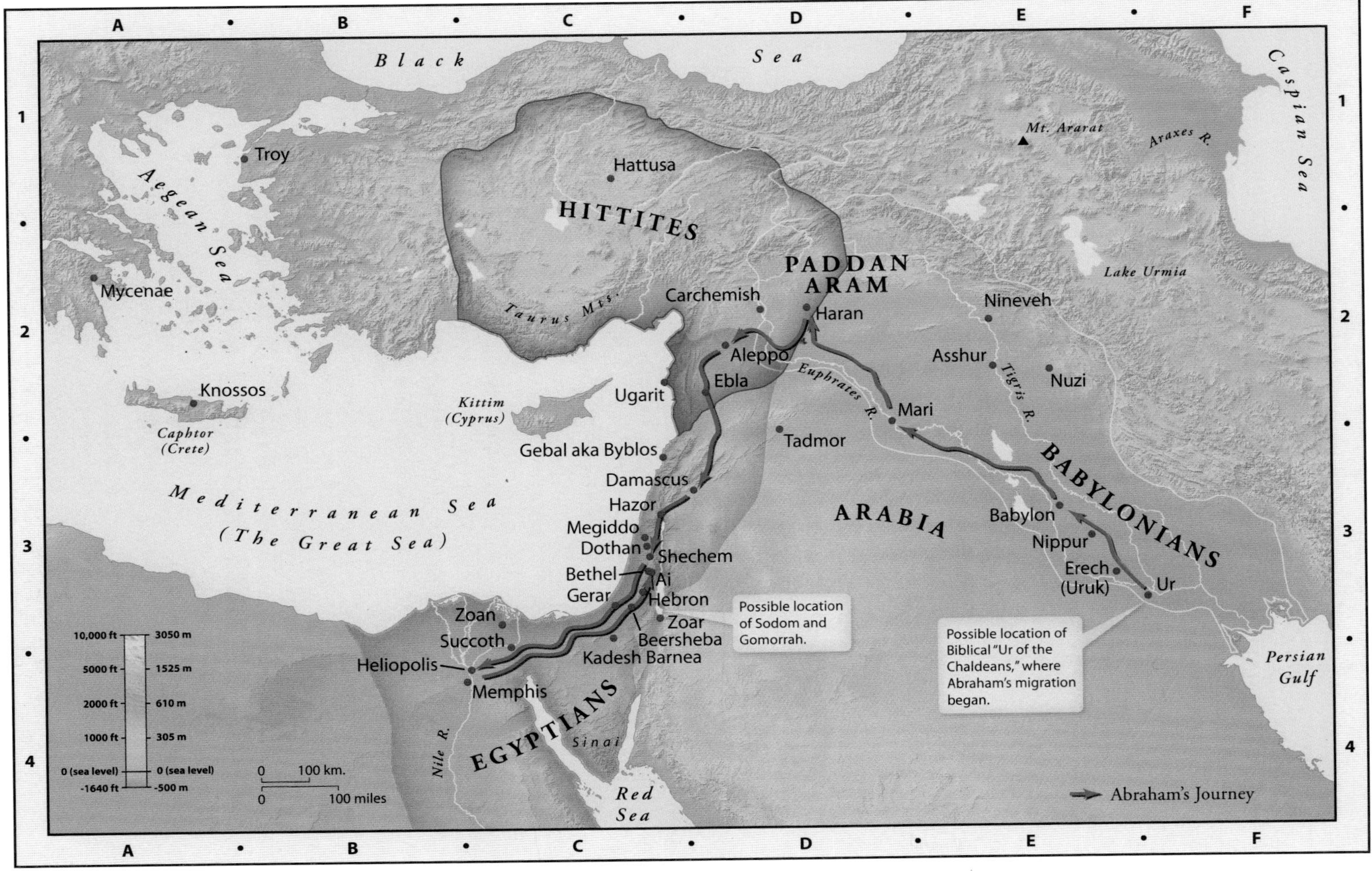

Black Sea
Caspian Sea
Aegean Sea
Mediterranean Sea
(The Great Sea)
Persian Gulf
Red Sea
Lake Urmia
Araxes R.
Mt. Ararat
Tigris R.
Euphrates R.
Nile R.
Taurus Mts.
Sinai
HITTITES
PADDAN ARAM
BABYLONIANS
ARABIA
EGYPTIANS
Troy
Mycenae
Knossos
Caphtor (Crete)
Kittim (Cyprus)
Hattusa
Carchemish
Haran
Aleppo
Ebla
Ugarit
Tadmor
Mari
Nineveh
Asshur
Nuzi
Babylon
Nippur
Erech (Uruk)
Ur
Gebal aka Byblos
Damascus
Hazor
Megiddo
Dothan
Shechem
Bethel
Ai
Gerar
Hebron
Zoar
Beersheba
Kadesh Barnea
Zoan
Succoth
Heliopolis
Memphis
Possible location of Sodom and Gomorrah.
Possible location of Biblical "Ur of the Chaldeans," where Abraham's migration began.
Abraham's Journey
0 100 km.
0 100 miles
10,000 ft 3050 m
5000 ft 1525 m
2000 ft 610 m
1000 ft 305 m
0 (sea level) 0 (sea level)
-1640 ft -500 m
A B C D E F
1 2 3 4

Map 2: **HOLY LAND AND SINAI**

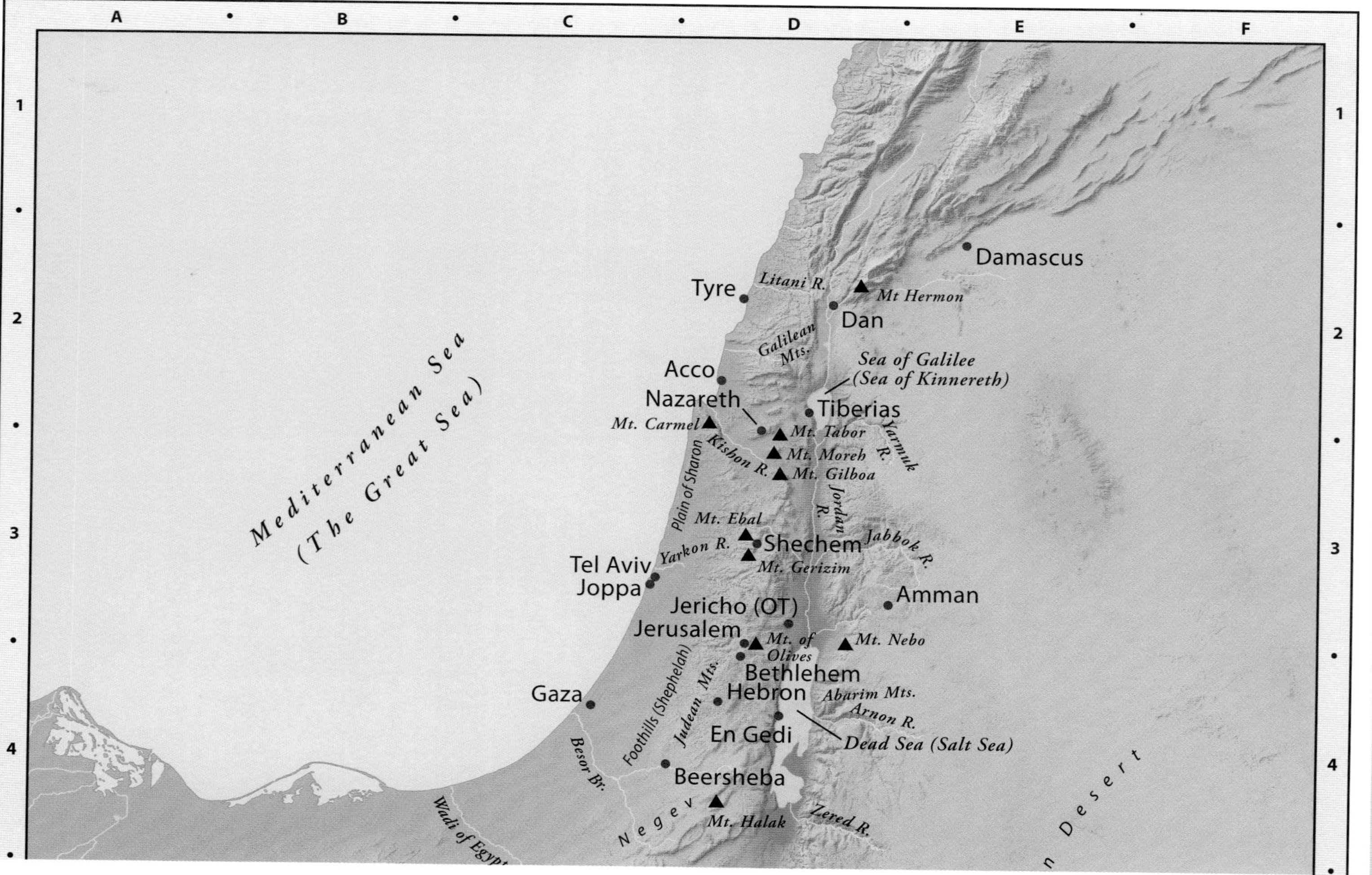

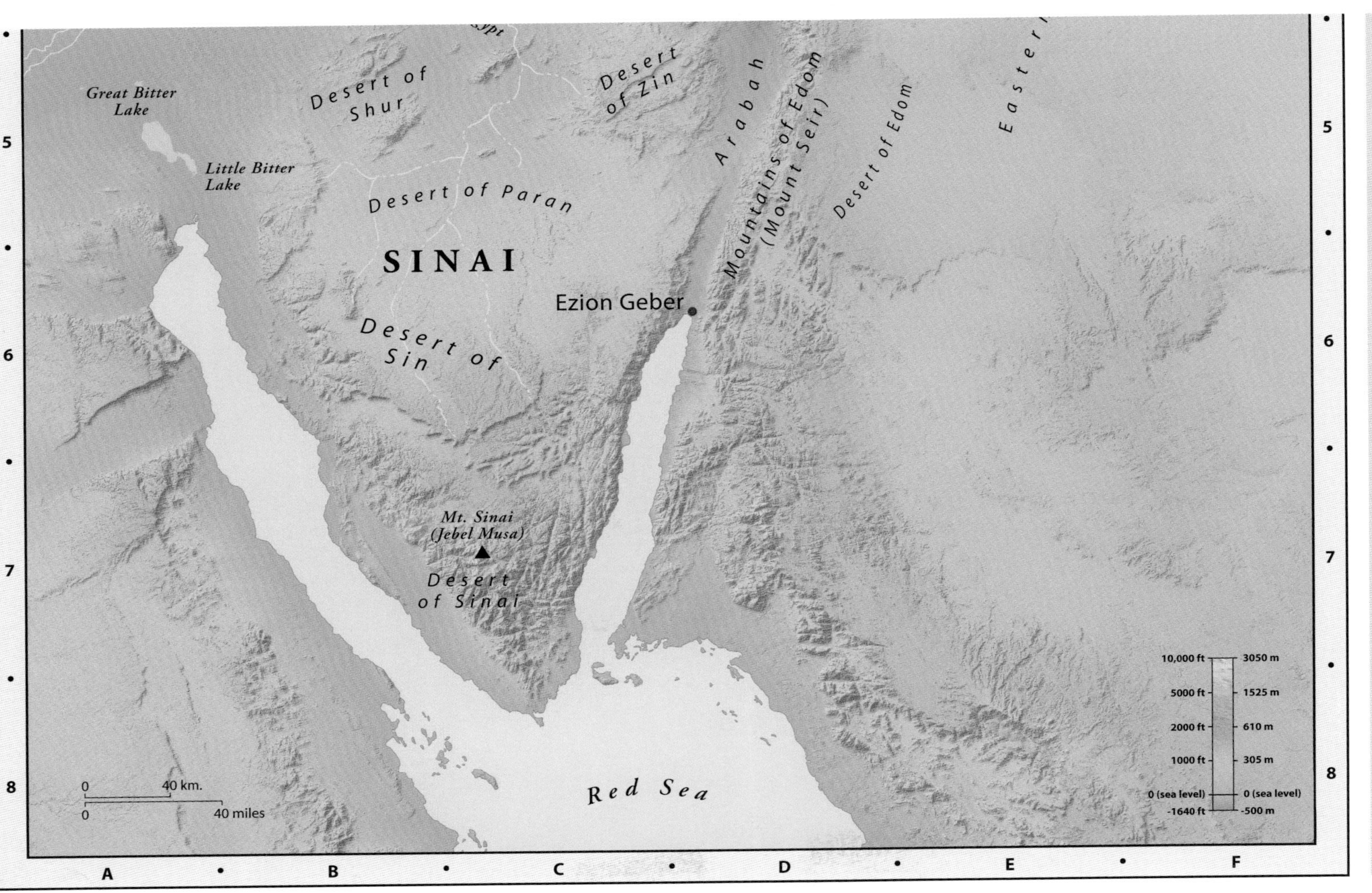
Great Bitter Lake
Little Bitter Lake
Desert of Shur
Desert of Zin
Desert of Paran
SINAI
Desert of Sin
Ezion Geber
Arabah
Mountains of Edom (Mount Seir)
Desert of Edom
Mt. Sinai (Jebel Musa)
Desert of Sinai
Red Sea
0 40 km.
0 40 miles
10,000 ft 3050 m
5000 ft 1525 m
2000 ft 610 m
1000 ft 305 m
0 (sea level) 0 (sea level)
-1640 ft -500 m
A B C D E F
5 6 7 8

Map 3: **EXODUS AND CONQUEST OF CANAAN**

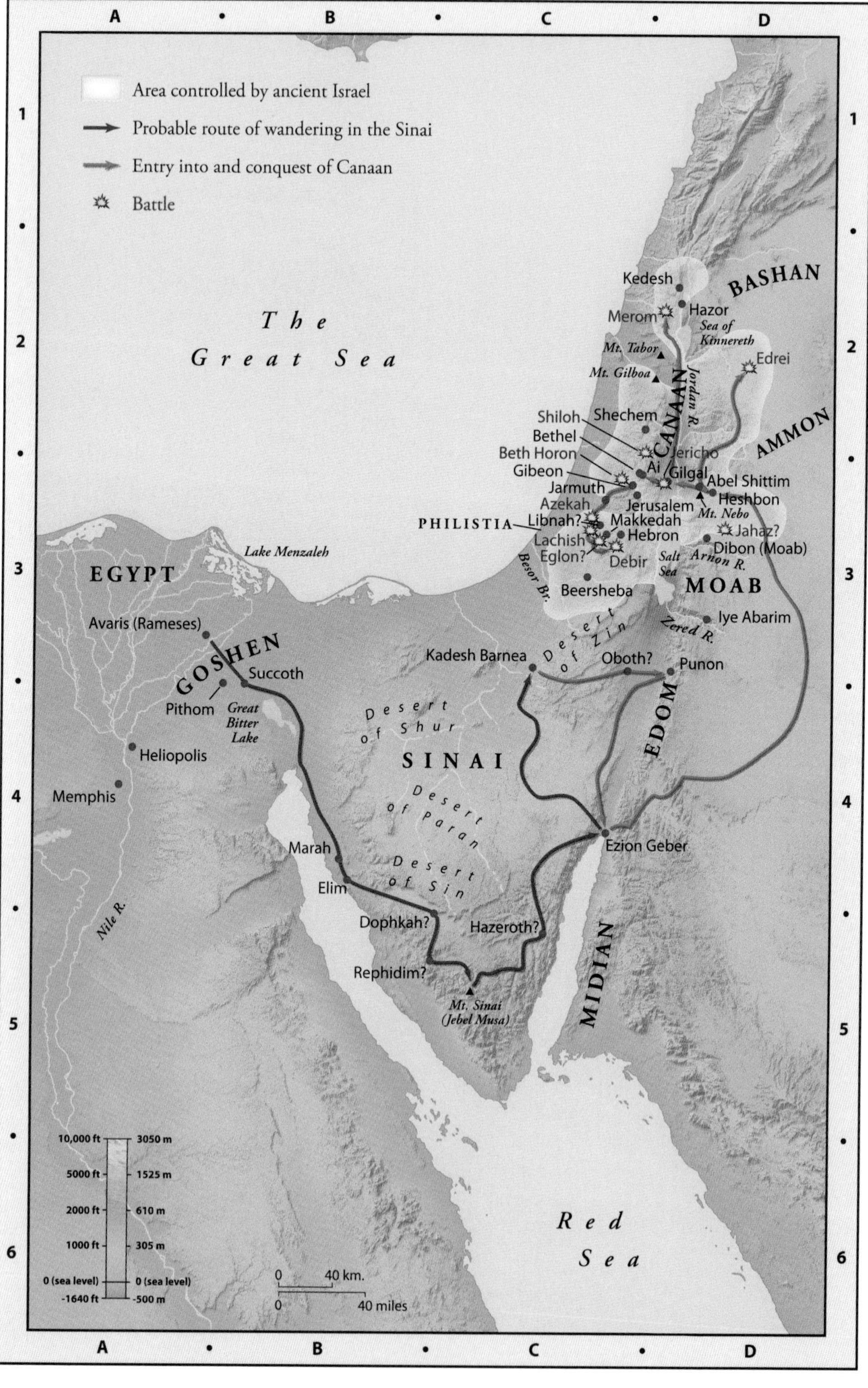

A
B
C
D
1
2
3
4
5
6
Area controlled by ancient Israel
Probable route of wandering in the Sinai
Entry into and conquest of Canaan
Battle
The Great Sea
Kedesh
BASHAN
Merom
Hazor
Sea of Kinnereth
Mt. Tabor
Mt. Gilboa
Edrei
Jordan R.
CANAAN
Shiloh
Shechem
Bethel
Beth Horon
Gibeon
Jericho
Ai
Gilgal
Abel Shittim
AMMON
Jarmuth
Azekah
Jerusalem
Heshbon
Mt. Nebo
PHILISTIA
Libnah?
Makkedah
Lachish
Hebron
Jahaz?
Eglon?
Debir
Dibon (Moab)
Salt Sea
Arnon R.
Besor Br.
Beersheba
MOAB
Lake Menzaleh
EGYPT
Avaris (Rameses)
GOSHEN
Succoth
Pithom
Great Bitter Lake
Heliopolis
Memphis
Iye Abarim
Zered R.
Desert of Zin
Kadesh Barnea
Oboth?
Punon
EDOM
Desert of Shur
SINAI
Desert of Paran
Desert of Sin
Ezion Geber
Marah
Elim
Dophkah?
Hazeroth?
Rephidim?
Mt. Sinai (Jebel Musa)
MIDIAN
Nile R.
Red Sea
10,000 ft
3050 m
5000 ft
1525 m
2000 ft
610 m
1000 ft
305 m
0 (sea level)
0 (sea level)
-1640 ft
-500 m
0
40 km.
0
40 miles

Map 4: **LAND OF THE TWELVE TRIBES**

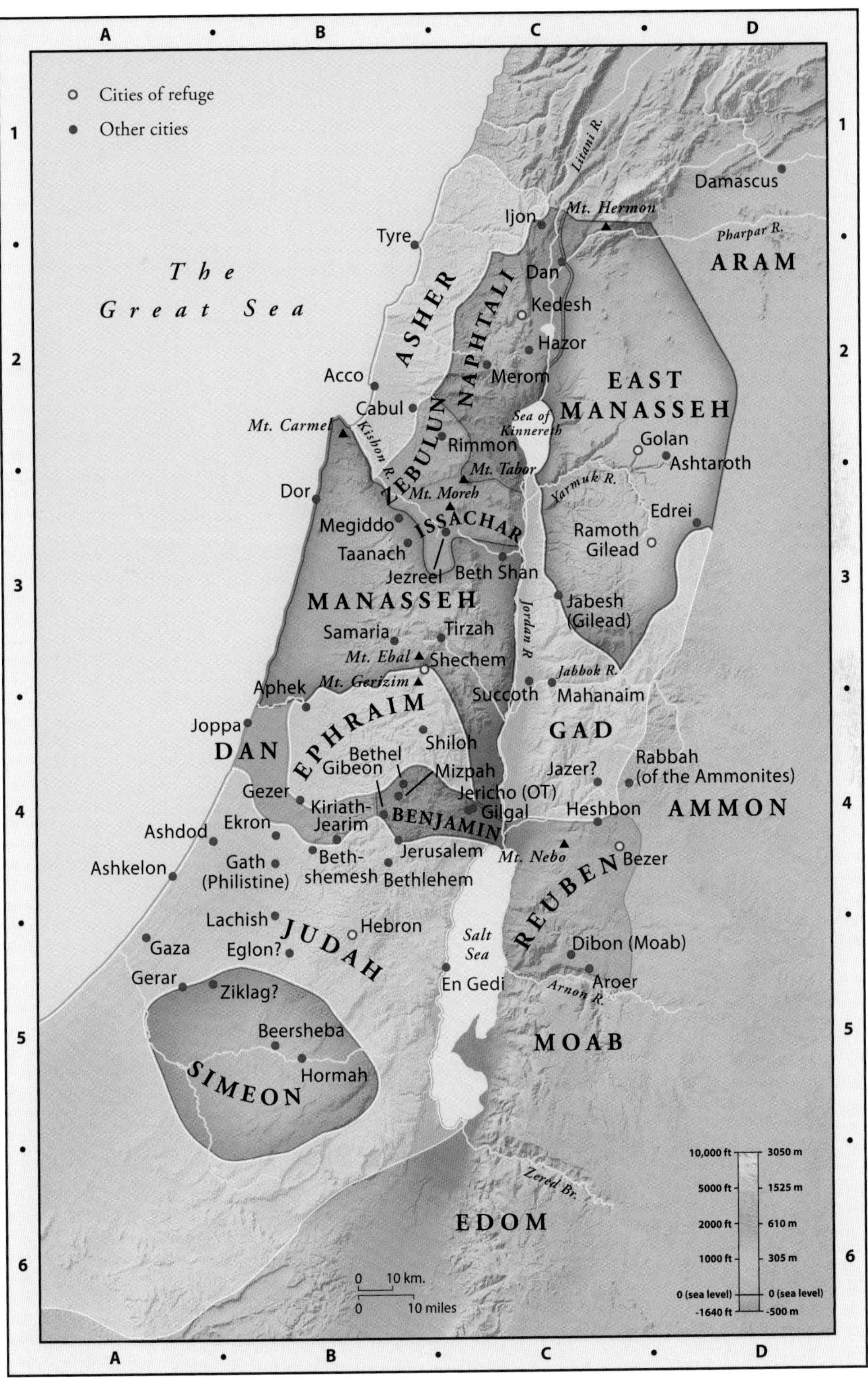

A
B
C
D
1
2
3
4
5
6
Cities of refuge
Other cities
The Great Sea
Litani R.
Damascus
Mt. Hermon
Ijon
Tyre
Pharpar R.
ARAM
Dan
ASHER
NAPHTALI
Kedesh
Hazor
Acco
Merom
EAST MANASSEH
Cabul
Sea of Kinnereth
Mt. Carmel
Kishon R.
Rimmon
ZEBULUN
Golan
Ashtaroth
Mt. Tabor
Yarmuk R.
Dor
Mt. Moreh
Edrei
Megiddo
ISSACHAR
Ramoth Gilead
Taanach
Beth Shan
Jezreel
MANASSEH
Jabesh (Gilead)
Jordan R.
Samaria
Tirzah
Mt. Ebal
Shechem
Jabbok R.
Aphek
Mt. Gerizim
Succoth
Mahanaim
EPHRAIM
Joppa
GAD
DAN
Shiloh
Bethel
Gibeon
Mizpah
Rabbah (of the Ammonites)
Jazer?
Gezer
Jericho (OT)
Kiriath-Jearim
Gilgal
Heshbon
AMMON
Ashdod
Ekron
BENJAMIN
Jerusalem
Mt. Nebo
Bezer
Ashkelon
Gath (Philistine)
Beth-shemesh
Bethlehem
REUBEN
Lachish
Hebron
JUDAH
Salt Sea
Gaza
Eglon?
Dibon (Moab)
Gerar
Ziklag?
En Gedi
Aroer
Arnon R.
Beersheba
MOAB
Hormah
SIMEON
Zered Br.
EDOM
0 10 km.
0 10 miles
10,000 ft
3050 m
5000 ft
1525 m
2000 ft
610 m
1000 ft
305 m
0 (sea level)
0 (sea level)
-1640 ft
-500 m

Map 5: **KINGDOM OF DAVID AND SOLOMON**

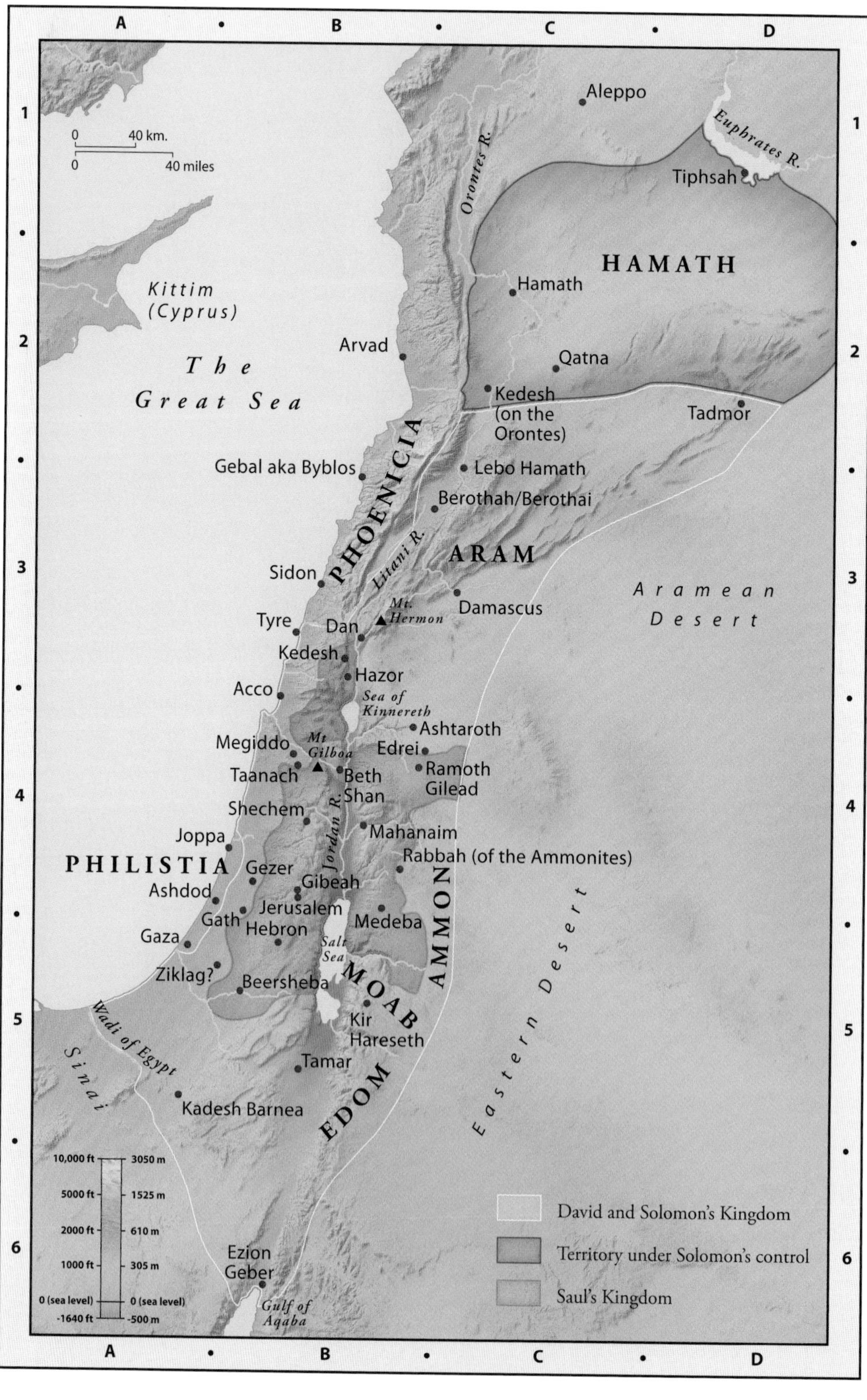

A
B
C
D
1
2
3
4
5
6
0 40 km.
0 40 miles
Aleppo
Euphrates R.
Tiphsah
Orontes R.
HAMATH
Hamath
Kittim (Cyprus)
Arvad
Qatna
The Great Sea
Kedesh (on the Orontes)
Tadmor
PHOENICIA
Gebal aka Byblos
Lebo Hamath
Berothah/Berothai
Litani R.
ARAM
Sidon
Damascus
Aramean Desert
Mt. Hermon
Tyre
Dan
Kedesh
Hazor
Acco
Sea of Kinnereth
Ashtaroth
Megiddo
Mt Gilboa
Edrei
Taanach
Beth Shan
Ramoth Gilead
Shechem
Jordan R.
Mahanaim
Joppa
Rabbah (of the Ammonites)
PHILISTIA
Gezer
Ashdod
Gibeah
Jerusalem
Gath
Hebron
Medeba
AMMON
Gaza
Salt Sea
Ziklag?
Beersheba
MOAB
Eastern Desert
Wadi of Egypt
Kir Hareseth
Sinai
Tamar
EDOM
Kadesh Barnea
10,000 ft
3050 m
5000 ft
1525 m
2000 ft
610 m
1000 ft
305 m
0 (sea level)
0 (sea level)
-1640 ft
-500 m
Ezion Geber
Gulf of Aqaba
David and Solomon's Kingdom
Territory under Solomon's control
Saul's Kingdom

Map 6: **KINGDOMS OF ISRAEL AND JUDAH**

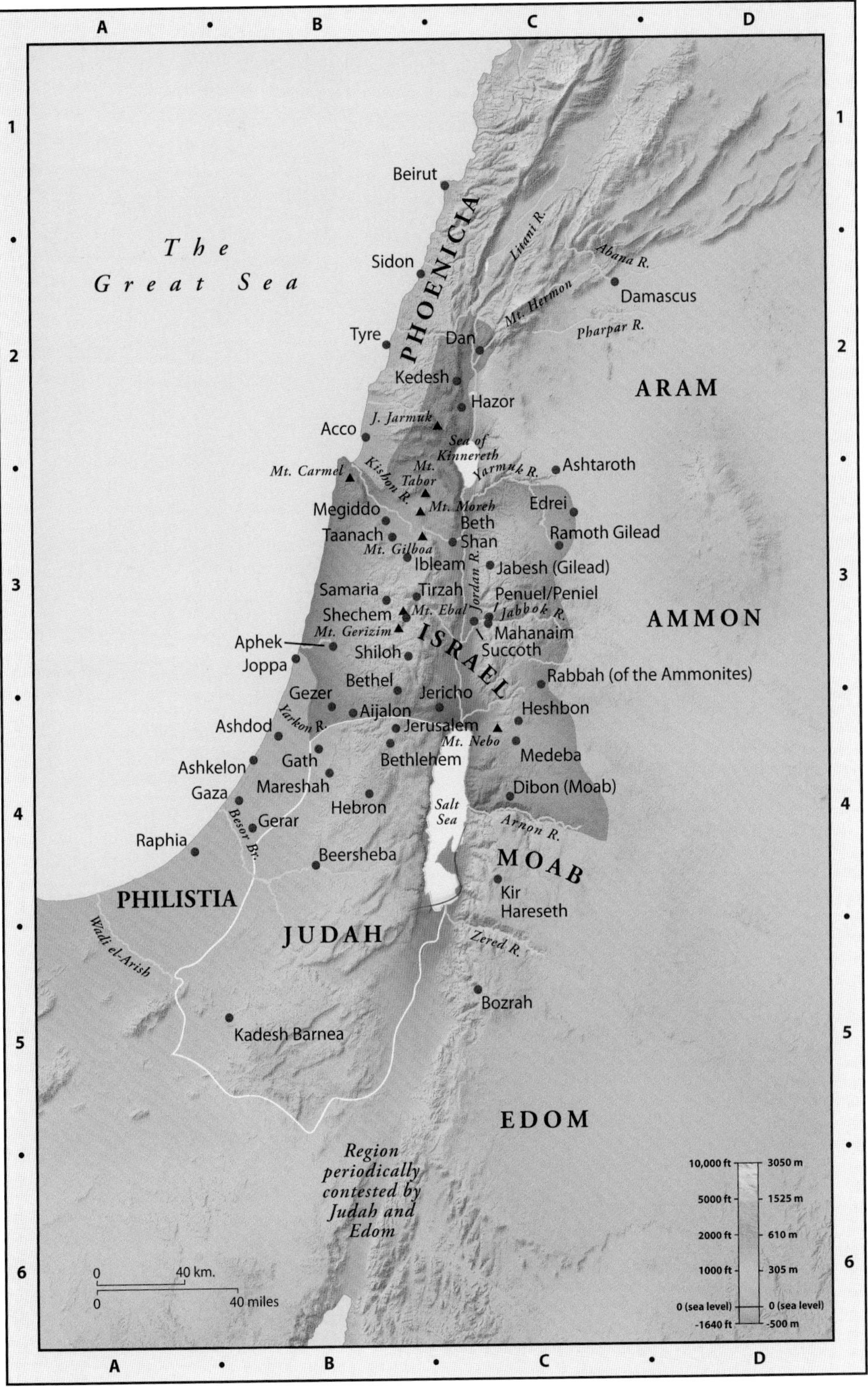

A
B
C
D
1
2
3
4
5
6
The Great Sea
PHOENICIA
Beirut
Sidon
Tyre
Dan
Kedesh
Hazor
Acco
J. Jarmuk
Sea of Kinnereth
Litani R.
Abana R.
Damascus
Mt. Hermon
Pharpar R.
ARAM
Mt. Carmel
Kishon R.
Mt. Tabor
Yarmuk R.
Ashtaroth
Megiddo
Mt. Moreh
Beth Shan
Edrei
Taanach
Mt. Gilboa
Ramoth Gilead
Ibleam
Jordan R.
Jabesh (Gilead)
Samaria
Tirzah
Penuel/Peniel
Shechem
Mt. Ebal
Jabbok R.
Mt. Gerizim
Mahanaim
AMMON
Aphek
ISRAEL
Succoth
Joppa
Shiloh
Bethel
Rabbah (of the Ammonites)
Gezer
Jericho
Yarkon R.
Aijalon
Heshbon
Ashdod
Jerusalem
Mt. Nebo
Gath
Bethlehem
Medeba
Ashkelon
Mareshah
Gaza
Dibon (Moab)
Hebron
Salt Sea
Besor Br.
Gerar
Arnon R.
Raphia
Beersheba
MOAB
Kir Hareseth
PHILISTIA
JUDAH
Wadi el-Arish
Zered R.
Bozrah
Kadesh Barnea
EDOM
Region periodically contested by Judah and Edom
0
40 km.
0
40 miles
10,000 ft
3050 m
5000 ft
1525 m
2000 ft
610 m
1000 ft
305 m
0 (sea level)
0 (sea level)
-1640 ft
-500 m

Map 7: **PROPHETS IN ISRAEL AND JUDAH**

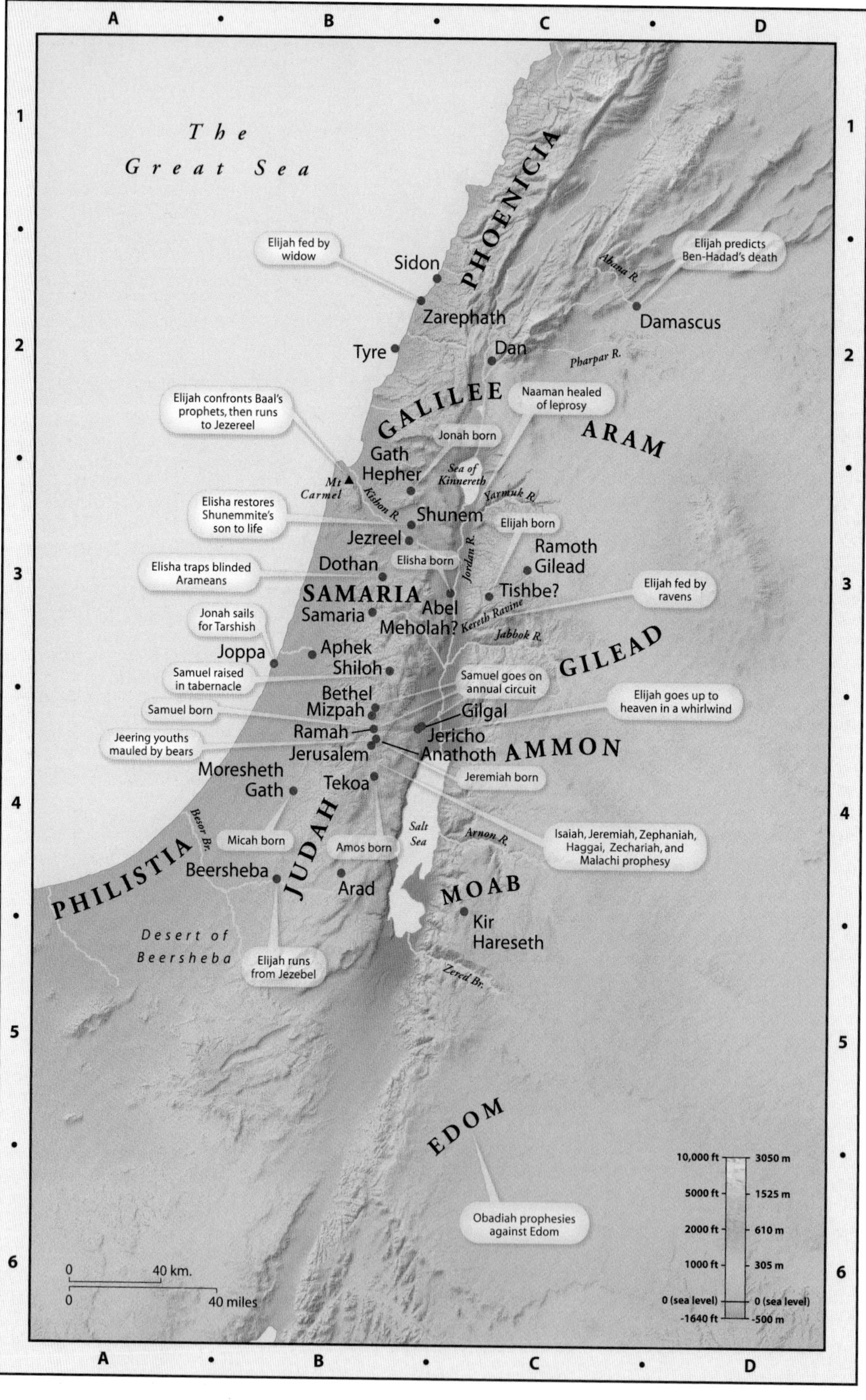

The Great Sea
PHOENICIA
Elijah fed by widow
Sidon
Zarephath
Tyre
Dan
Elijah predicts Ben-Hadad's death
Abana R.
Damascus
Pharpar R.
GALILEE
ARAM
Naaman healed of leprosy
Elijah confronts Baal's prophets, then runs to Jezereel
Jonah born
Gath Hepher
Mt Carmel
Sea of Kinnereth
Kishon R.
Yarmuk R.
Elisha restores Shunemmite's son to life
Shunem
Jezreel
Elijah born
Jordan R.
Elisha born
Ramoth Gilead
Elisha traps blinded Arameans
Dothan
SAMARIA
Tishbe?
Elijah fed by ravens
Samaria
Abel Meholah?
Kereth Ravine
Jonah sails for Tarshish
Jabbok R.
Joppa
Aphek
GILEAD
Samuel raised in tabernacle
Shiloh
Samuel goes on annual circuit
Bethel
Mizpah
Gilgal
Elijah goes up to heaven in a whirlwind
Samuel born
Ramah
Jericho
Jeering youths mauled by bears
Jerusalem
Anathoth
AMMON
Moresheth Gath
Tekoa
Jeremiah born
Besor Br.
JUDAH
Salt Sea
Arnon R.
Isaiah, Jeremiah, Zephaniah, Haggai, Zechariah, and Malachi prophesy
Micah born
Amos born
PHILISTIA
Beersheba
Arad
MOAB
Kir Hareseth
Desert of Beersheba
Elijah runs from Jezebel
Zered Br.
EDOM
Obadiah prophesies against Edom
0 40 km.
0 40 miles
10,000 ft 3050 m
5000 ft 1525 m
2000 ft 610 m
1000 ft 305 m
0 (sea level) 0 (sea level)
-1640 ft -500 m
A B C D
1 2 3 4 5 6

Map 8: ASSYRIAN AND BABYLONIAN EMPIRES

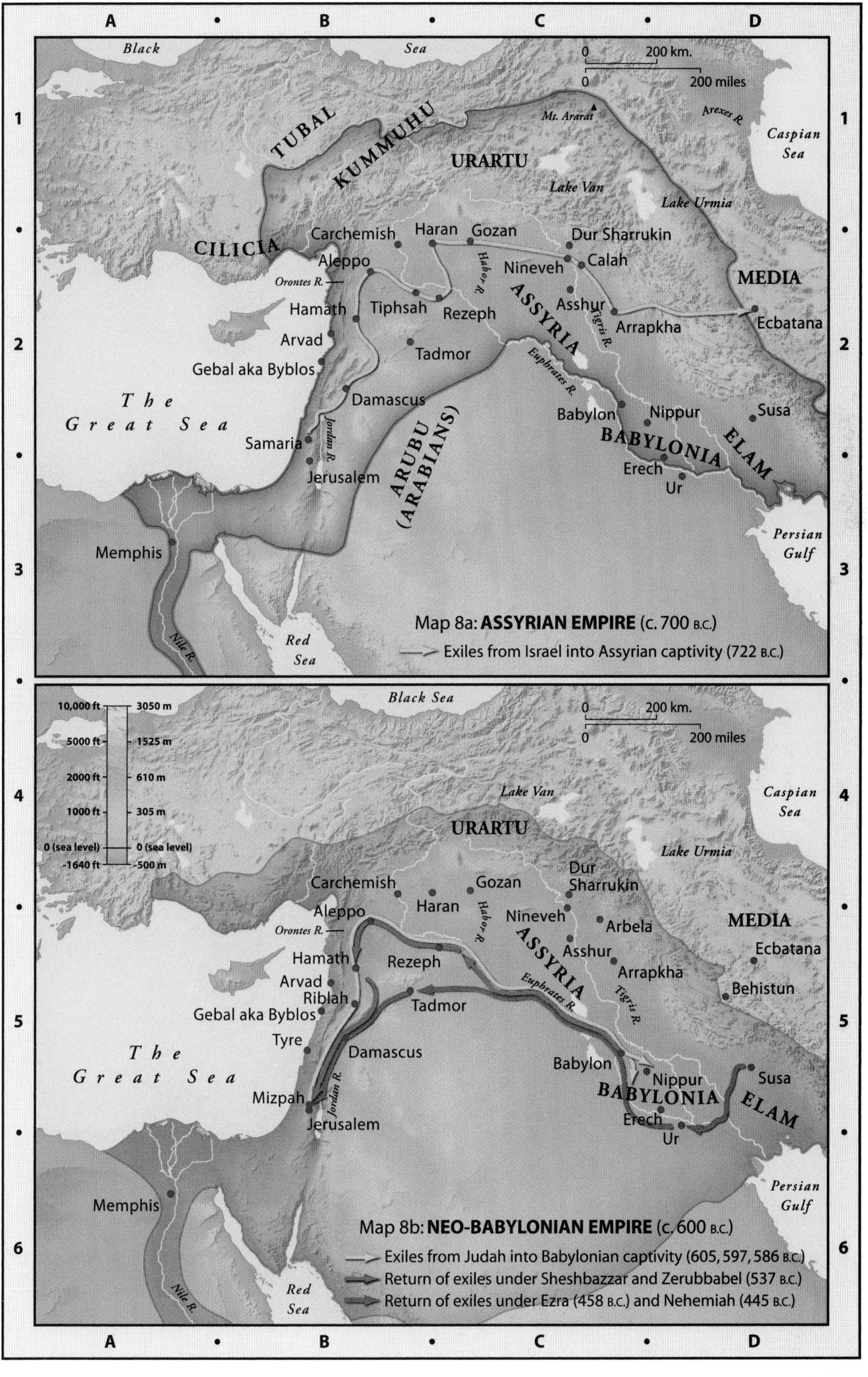

A
B
C
D
1
2
3
4
5
6
Black Sea
0 200 km.
0 200 miles
Mt. Ararat
Arexes R.
Caspian Sea
TUBAL
KUMMUHU
URARTU
Lake Van
Lake Urmia
CILICIA
Carchemish
Haran
Gozan
Dur Sharrukin
Aleppo
Calah
Nineveh
Orontes R.
Habor R.
MEDIA
Hamath
Tiphsah
Rezeph
ASSYRIA
Asshur
Arrapkha
Ecbatana
Tigris R.
Arvad
Tadmor
Gebal aka Byblos
Euphrates R.
The Great Sea
Damascus
Babylon
Nippur
Susa
Jordan R.
BABYLONIA
ELAM
Samaria
ARUBU (ARABIANS)
Erech
Ur
Jerusalem
Persian Gulf
Memphis
Red Sea
Nile R.
Map 8a: ASSYRIAN EMPIRE (c. 700 B.C.)
Exiles from Israel into Assyrian captivity (722 B.C.)
10,000 ft 3050 m
5000 ft 1525 m
2000 ft 610 m
1000 ft 305 m
0 (sea level) 0 (sea level)
-1640 ft -500 m
Arbela
Riblah
Behistun
Tyre
Mizpah
Map 8b: NEO-BABYLONIAN EMPIRE (c. 600 B.C.)
Exiles from Judah into Babylonian captivity (605, 597, 586 B.C.)
Return of exiles under Sheshbazzar and Zerubbabel (537 B.C.)
Return of exiles under Ezra (458 B.C.) and Nehemiah (445 B.C.)

Map 9: **HOLY LAND IN THE TIME OF JESUS**

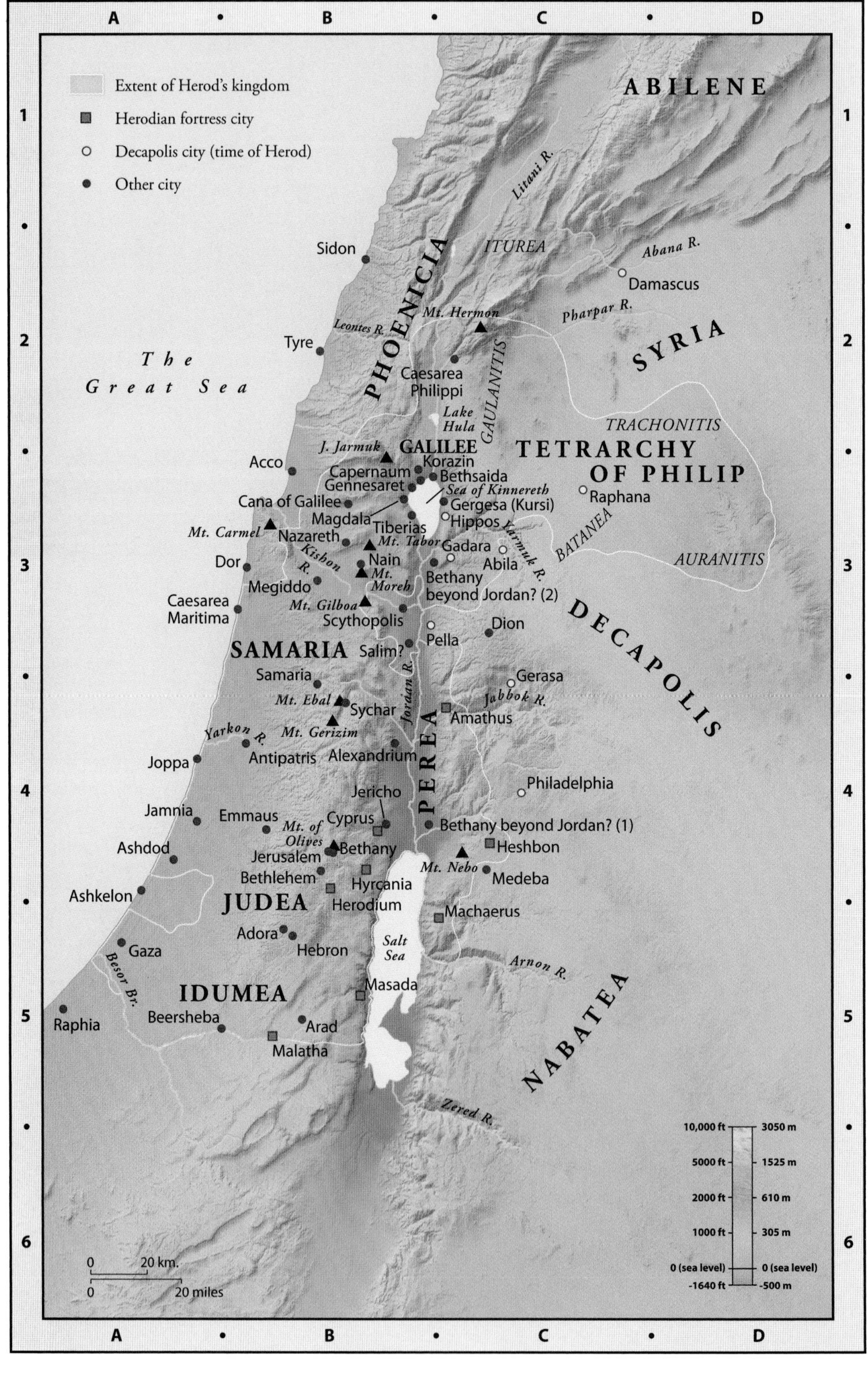

Extent of Herod's kingdom
Herodian fortress city
Decapolis city (time of Herod)
Other city
ABILENE
ITUREA
PHOENICIA
SYRIA
TRACHONITIS
TETRARCHY OF PHILIP
GAULANITIS
BATANEA
AURANITIS
GALILEE
DECAPOLIS
SAMARIA
PEREA
JUDEA
IDUMEA
NABATEA
The Great Sea
Litani R.
Abana R.
Pharpar R.
Leontes R.
Mt. Hermon
Sidon
Damascus
Tyre
Caesarea Philippi
Lake Hula
J. Jarmuk
Korazin
Acco
Capernaum
Bethsaida
Gennesaret
Sea of Kinnereth
Raphana
Cana of Galilee
Gergesa (Kursi)
Magdala
Tiberias
Hippos
Mt. Carmel
Nazareth
Mt. Tabor
Gadara
Yarmuk R.
Kishon R.
Dor
Nain
Abila
Mt. Moreh
Bethany beyond Jordan? (2)
Megiddo
Caesarea Maritima
Mt. Gilboa
Scythopolis
Dion
Pella
Salim?
Samaria
Gerasa
Mt. Ebal
Sychar
Jabbok R.
Jordan R.
Amathus
Yarkon R.
Mt. Gerizim
Joppa
Antipatris
Alexandrium
Philadelphia
Jericho
Jamnia
Emmaus
Cyprus
Bethany beyond Jordan? (1)
Mt. of Olives
Bethany
Heshbon
Ashdod
Jerusalem
Mt. Nebo
Bethlehem
Hyrcania
Medeba
Ashkelon
Herodium
Machaerus
Adora
Salt Sea
Gaza
Hebron
Arnon R.
Besor Br.
Masada
Raphia
Beersheba
Arad
Malatha
Zered R.
10,000 ft
3050 m
5000 ft
1525 m
2000 ft
610 m
1000 ft
305 m
0 (sea level)
0 (sea level)
-1640 ft
-500 m
0
20 km.
0
20 miles
A B C D
1 2 3 4 5 6

Map 10: **JERUSALEM IN THE TIME OF JESUS**

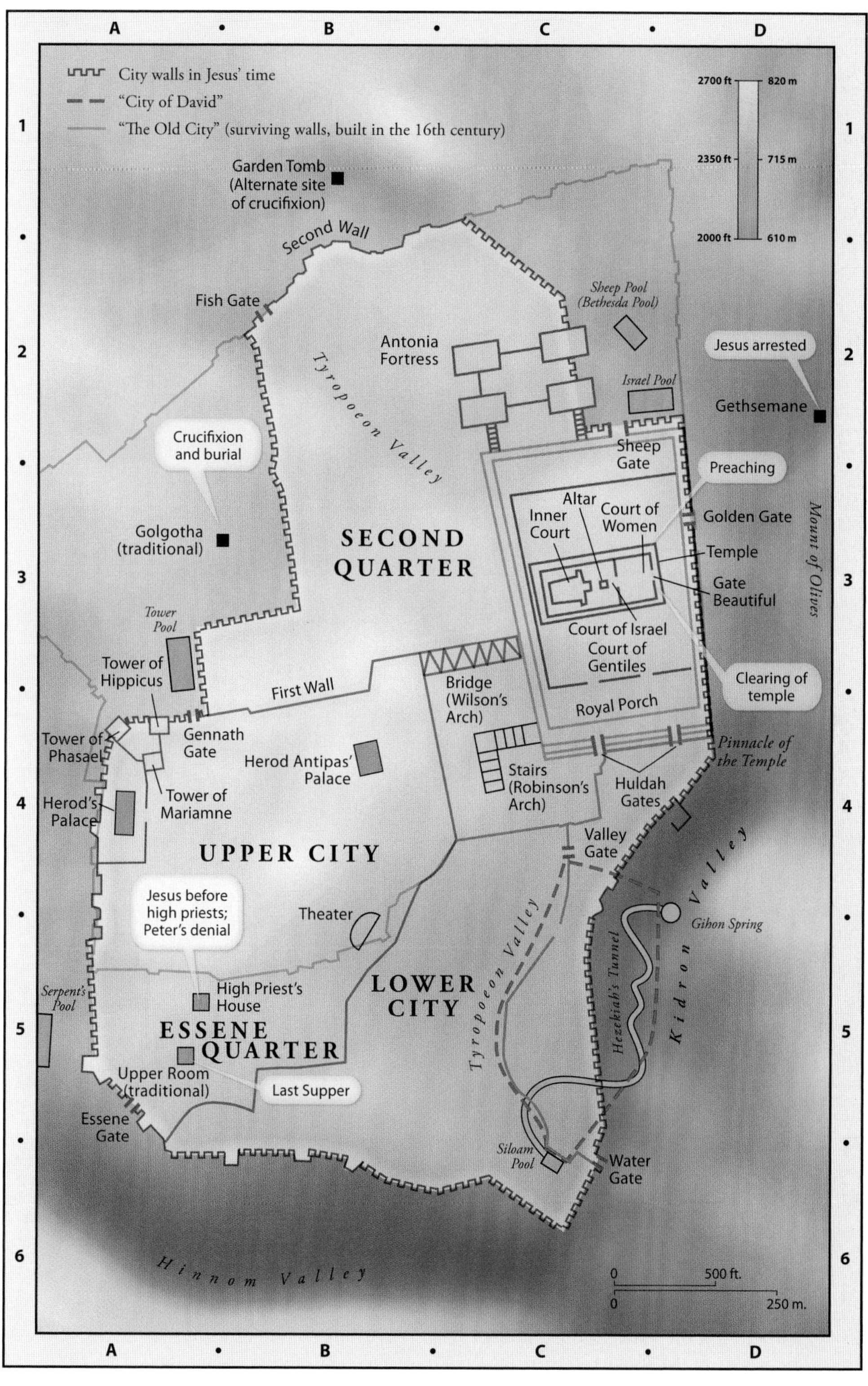

A
B
C
D
1
2
3
4
5
6
City walls in Jesus' time
"City of David"
"The Old City" (surviving walls, built in the 16th century)
2700 ft
820 m
2350 ft
715 m
2000 ft
610 m
Garden Tomb (Alternate site of crucifixion)
Second Wall
Fish Gate
Sheep Pool (Bethesda Pool)
Antonia Fortress
Jesus arrested
Israel Pool
Gethsemane
Tyropoeon Valley
Crucifixion and burial
Sheep Gate
Preaching
Altar
Inner Court
Court of Women
Golden Gate
Mount of Olives
Golgotha (traditional)
SECOND QUARTER
Temple
Gate Beautiful
Court of Israel
Court of Gentiles
Tower Pool
Tower of Hippicus
First Wall
Bridge (Wilson's Arch)
Royal Porch
Clearing of temple
Tower of Phasael
Gennath Gate
Herod Antipas' Palace
Pinnacle of the Temple
Stairs (Robinson's Arch)
Huldah Gates
Herod's Palace
Tower of Mariamne
Valley Gate
UPPER CITY
Kidron Valley
Jesus before high priests; Peter's denial
Theater
Gihon Spring
Serpent's Pool
High Priest's House
LOWER CITY
Tyropoeon Valley
Hezekiah's Tunnel
ESSENE QUARTER
Upper Room (traditional)
Last Supper
Essene Gate
Siloam Pool
Water Gate
Hinnom Valley
0
500 ft.
0
250 m.

Map 11: **JESUS' MINISTRY**

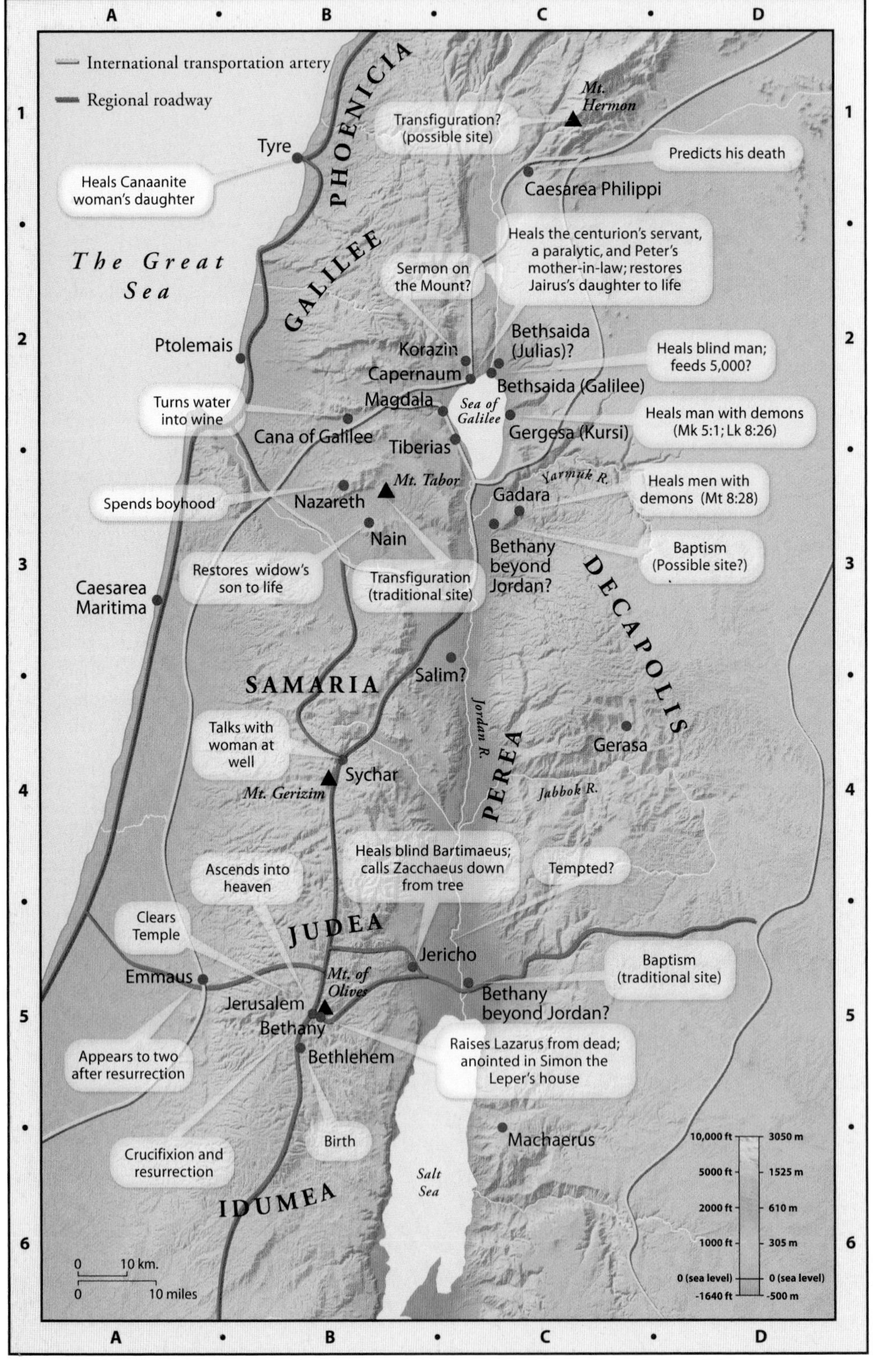

A
B
C
D
1
2
3
4
5
6
International transportation artery
Regional roadway
PHOENICIA
Tyre
Heals Canaanite woman's daughter
Transfiguration? (possible site)
Mt. Hermon
Predicts his death
Caesarea Philippi
The Great Sea
GALILEE
Sermon on the Mount?
Heals the centurion's servant, a paralytic, and Peter's mother-in-law; restores Jairus's daughter to life
Ptolemais
Korazin
Bethsaida (Julias)?
Heals blind man; feeds 5,000?
Capernaum
Bethsaida (Galilee)
Turns water into wine
Magdala
Sea of Galilee
Heals man with demons (Mk 5:1; Lk 8:26)
Cana of Galilee
Gergesa (Kursi)
Tiberias
Yarmuk R.
Mt. Tabor
Spends boyhood
Nazareth
Gadara
Heals men with demons (Mt 8:28)
Nain
Bethany beyond Jordan?
Baptism (Possible site?)
Restores widow's son to life
Transfiguration (traditional site)
Caesarea Maritima
DECAPOLIS
Salim?
SAMARIA
Jordan R.
Talks with woman at well
PEREA
Gerasa
Sychar
Mt. Gerizim
Jabbok R.
Heals blind Bartimaeus; calls Zacchaeus down from tree
Ascends into heaven
Tempted?
Clears Temple
JUDEA
Jericho
Baptism (traditional site)
Emmaus
Mt. of Olives
Jerusalem
Bethany beyond Jordan?
Bethany
Appears to two after resurrection
Bethlehem
Raises Lazarus from dead; anointed in Simon the Leper's house
Machaerus
Birth
Crucifixion and resurrection
Salt Sea
IDUMEA
0 10 km.
0 10 miles
10,000 ft 3050 m
5000 ft 1525 m
2000 ft 610 m
1000 ft 305 m
0 (sea level) 0 (sea level)
-1640 ft -500 m

Map 12: **APOSTLES' EARLY TRAVELS**

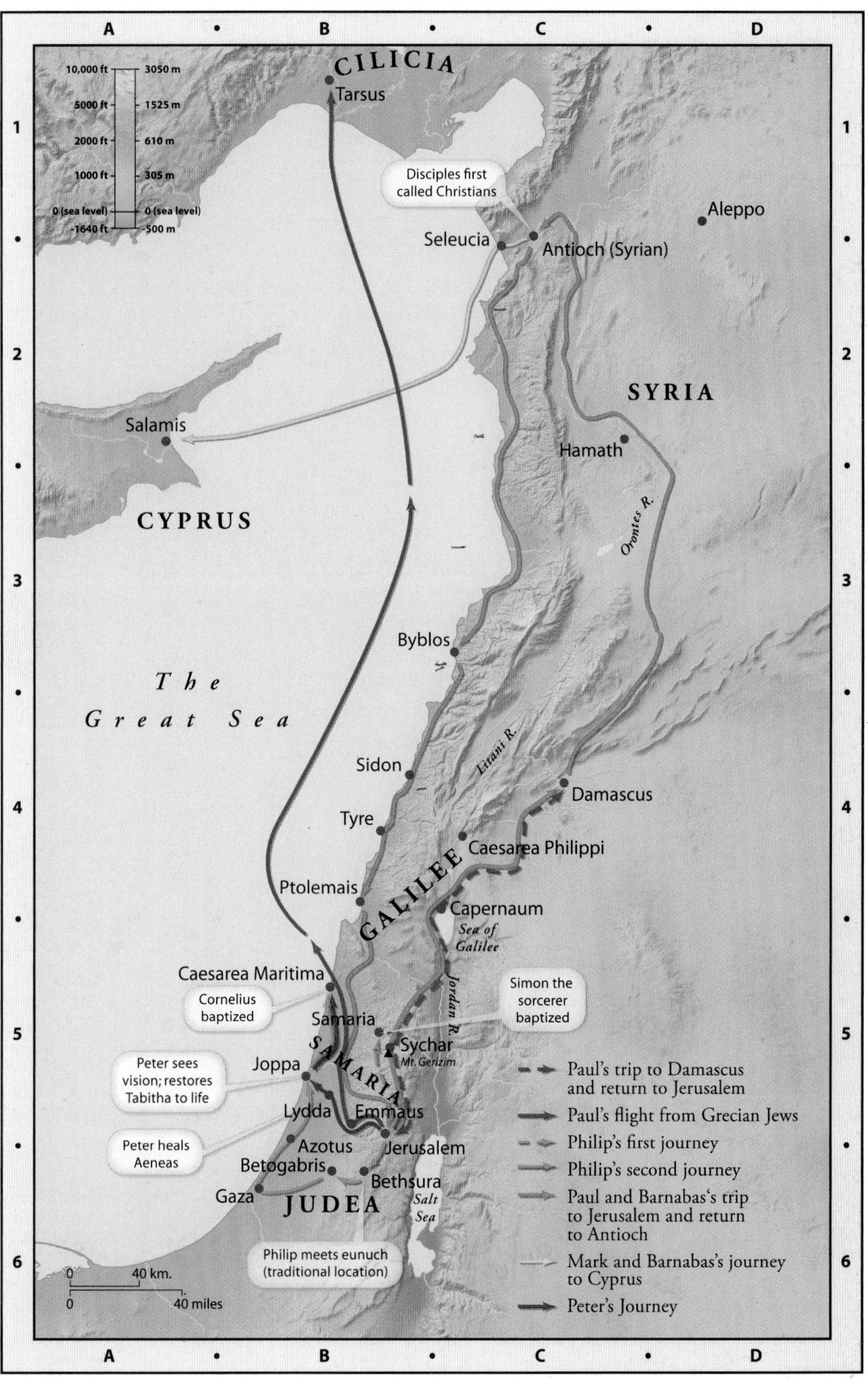

A
B
C
D
1
2
3
4
5
6
10,000 ft
3050 m
5000 ft
1525 m
2000 ft
610 m
1000 ft
305 m
0 (sea level)
0 (sea level)
-1640 ft
-500 m
CILICIA
Tarsus
Disciples first called Christians
Aleppo
Seleucia
Antioch (Syrian)
SYRIA
Salamis
Hamath
CYPRUS
Orontes R.
Byblos
The Great Sea
Litani R.
Sidon
Damascus
Tyre
Caesarea Philippi
GALILEE
Ptolemais
Capernaum
Sea of Galilee
Caesarea Maritima
Cornelius baptized
Jordan R.
Simon the sorcerer baptized
Samaria
SAMARIA
Sychar
Mt. Gerizim
Peter sees vision; restores Tabitha to life
Joppa
Lydda
Emmaus
Peter heals Aeneas
Azotus
Jerusalem
Betogabris
Bethsura
Gaza
JUDEA
Salt Sea
Philip meets eunuch (traditional location)
0
40 km.
0
40 miles
Paul's trip to Damascus and return to Jerusalem
Paul's flight from Grecian Jews
Philip's first journey
Philip's second journey
Paul and Barnabas's trip to Jerusalem and return to Antioch
Mark and Barnabas's journey to Cyprus
Peter's Journey

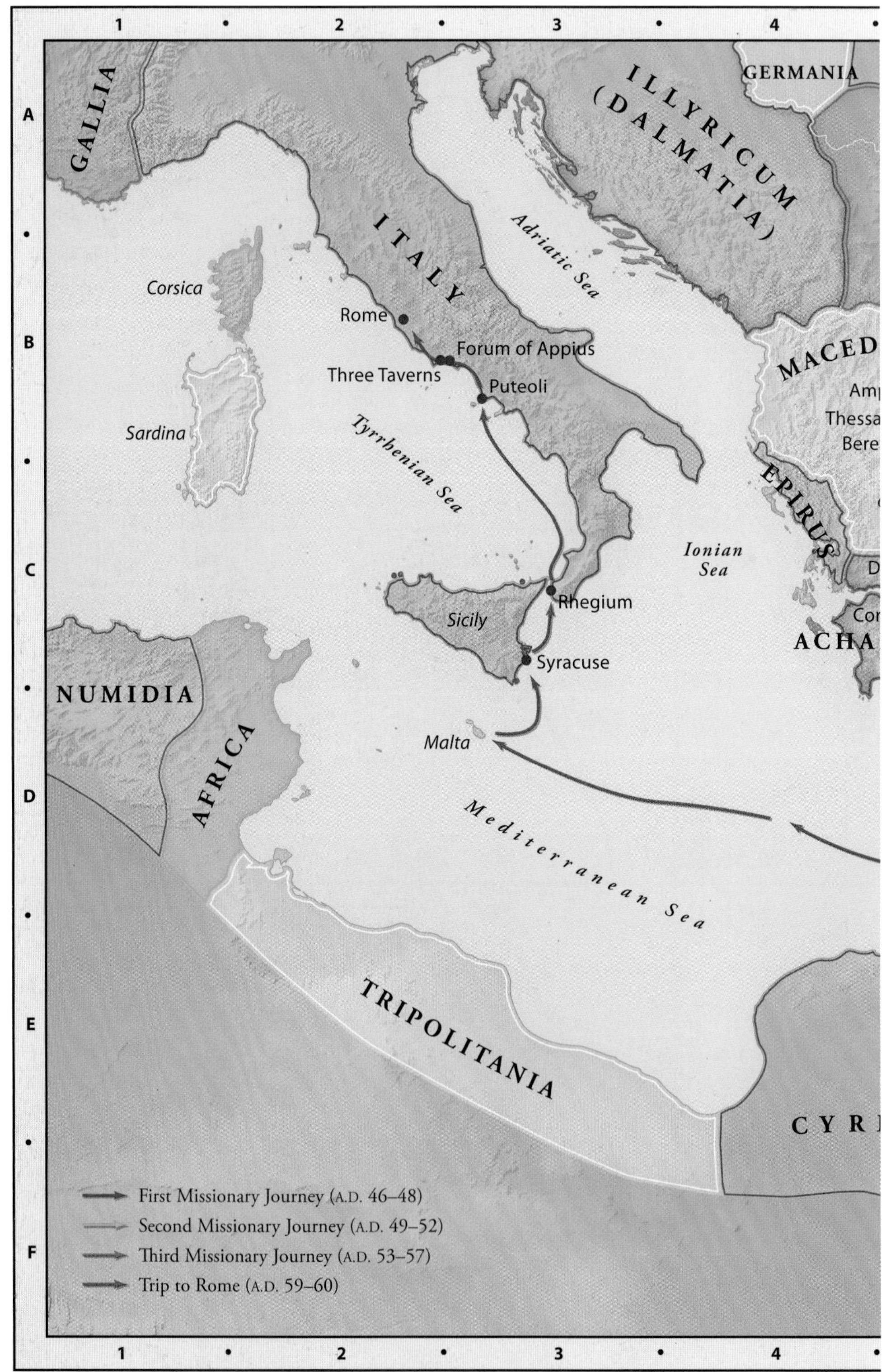
1
2
3
4
A
B
C
D
E
F
GALLIA
ITALY
ILLYRICUM (DALMATIA)
GERMANIA
Adriatic Sea
Corsica
Sardina
Rome
Forum of Appius
Three Taverns
Puteoli
Tyrrhenian Sea
MACED
Thessa
Bere
EPIRUS
Ionian Sea
Sicily
Rhegium
Syracuse
ACHA
NUMIDIA
AFRICA
Malta
Mediterranean Sea
TRIPOLITANIA
CYR
First Missionary Journey (A.D. 46–48)
Second Missionary Journey (A.D. 49–52)
Third Missionary Journey (A.D. 53–57)
Trip to Rome (A.D. 59–60)

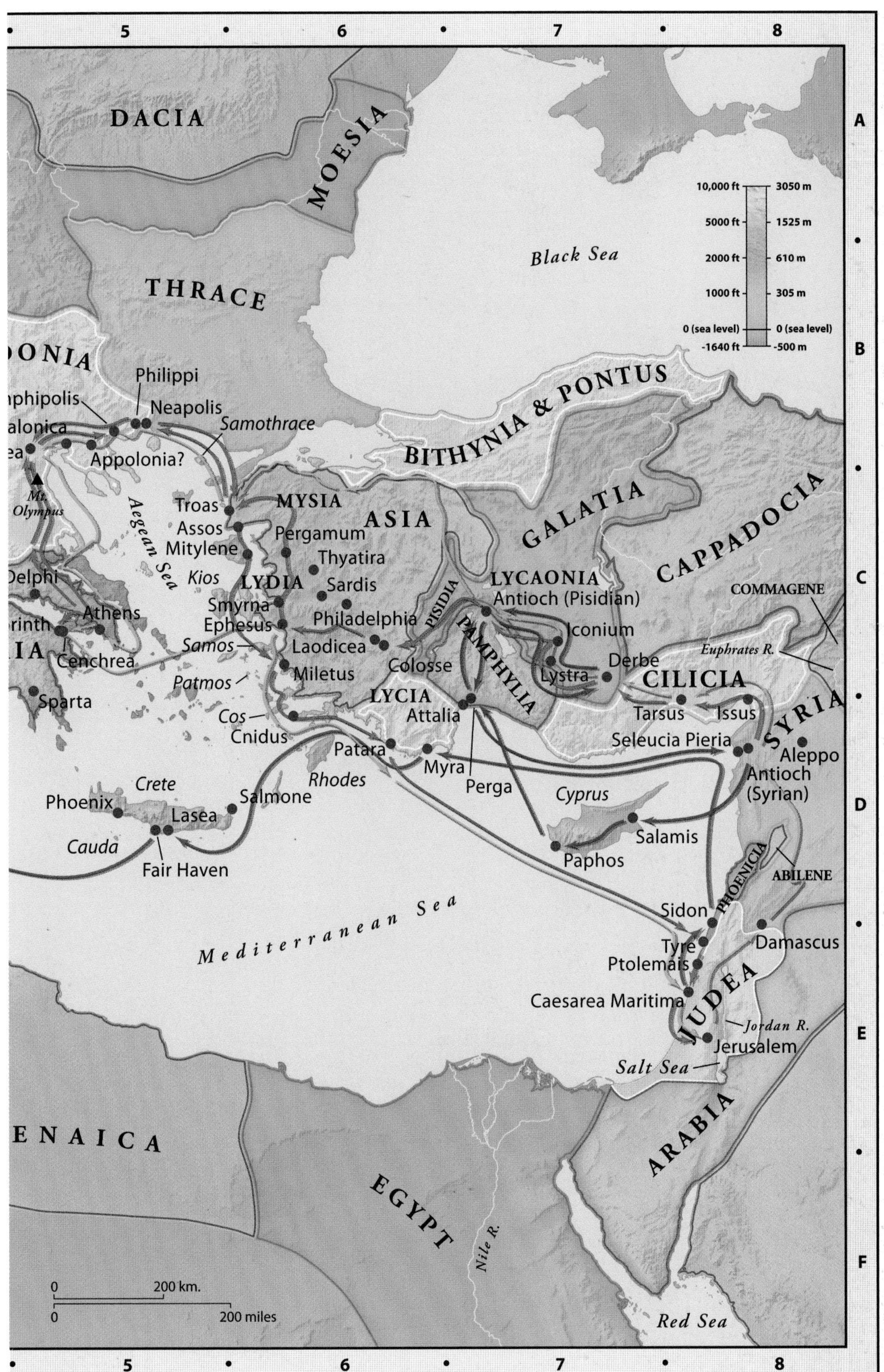

5
6
7
8
A
B
C
D
E
F
DACIA
MOESIA
THRACE
Black Sea
10,000 ft
3050 m
5000 ft
1525 m
2000 ft
610 m
1000 ft
305 m
0 (sea level)
0 (sea level)
-1640 ft
-500 m
BITHYNIA & PONTUS
Philippi
Neapolis
Samothrace
Appolonia?
Mt. Olympus
Aegean Sea
Troas
Assos
Mitylene
Kios
MYSIA
Pergamum
ASIA
Thyatira
LYDIA
Sardis
Smyrna
Ephesus
Philadelphia
Samos
Laodicea
Colosse
Miletus
Patmos
Cos
Cnidus
Delphi
Athens
Cenchrea
Sparta
GALATIA
CAPPADOCIA
LYCAONIA
Antioch (Pisidian)
PISIDIA
PAMPHYLIA
Iconium
Lystra
Derbe
COMMAGENE
Euphrates R.
CILICIA
Tarsus
Issus
SYRIA
Seleucia Pieria
Aleppo
Antioch (Syrian)
LYCIA
Attalia
Patara
Myra
Perga
Rhodes
Crete
Phoenix
Lasea
Salmone
Cauda
Fair Haven
Cyprus
Salamis
Paphos
PHOENICIA
ABILENE
Sidon
Tyre
Ptolemais
Damascus
Mediterranean Sea
Caesarea Maritima
JUDEA
Jordan R.
Jerusalem
Salt Sea
ARABIA
EGYPT
Nile R.
Red Sea
0
200 km.
0
200 miles

Map 14: **ROMAN EMPIRE**

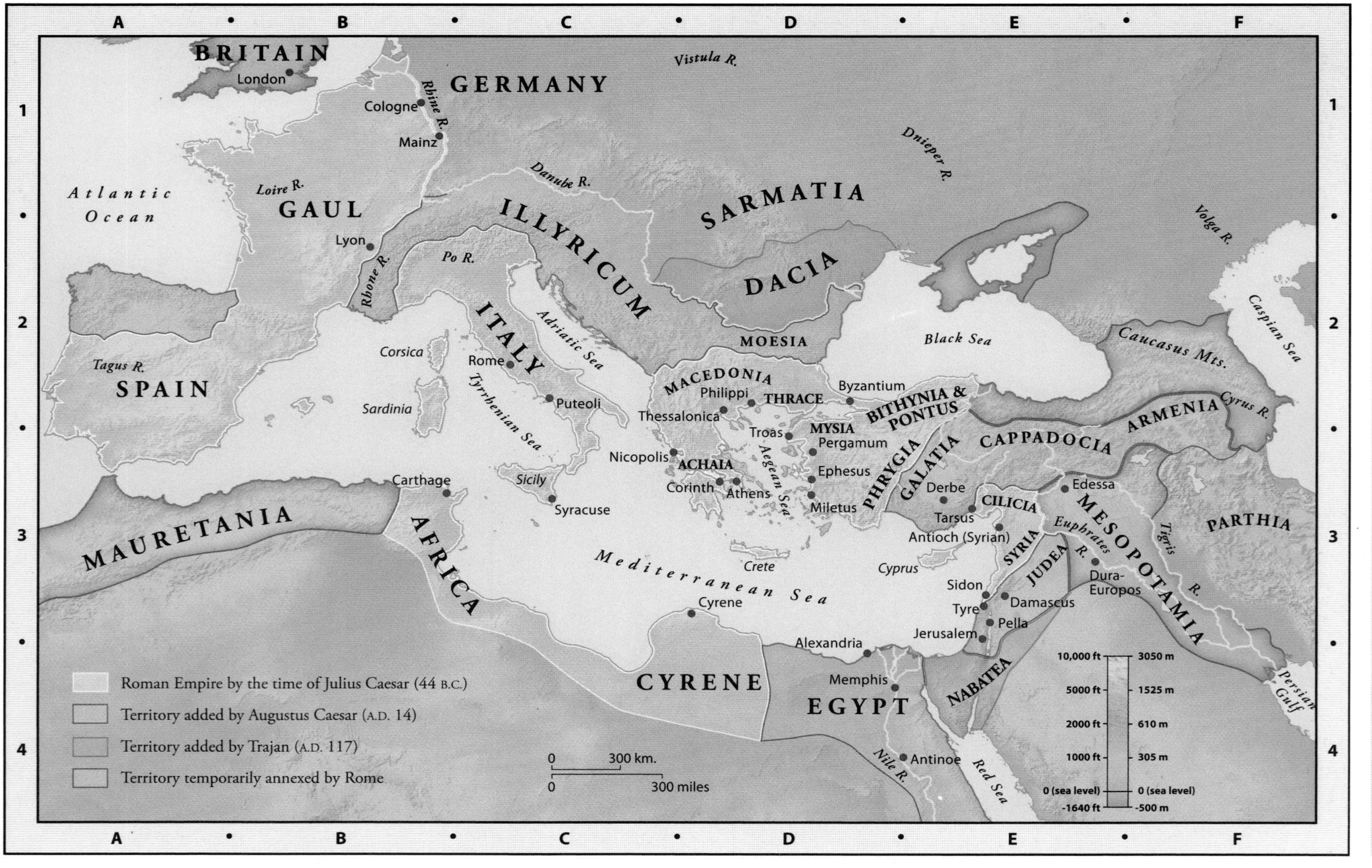

BRITAIN
London
GERMANY
Rhine R.
Cologne
Mainz
Vistula R.
Dnieper R.
Atlantic Ocean
Loire R.
GAUL
Lyon
Rhone R.
Po R.
Danube R.
ILLYRICUM
SARMATIA
DACIA
Volga R.
Caspian Sea
SPAIN
Tagus R.
Corsica
Sardinia
ITALY
Rome
Puteoli
Tyrrhenian Sea
Adriatic Sea
MOESIA
Black Sea
Caucasus Mts.
MACEDONIA
Philippi
THRACE
Thessalonica
Byzantium
BITHYNIA & PONTUS
Troas
MYSIA
Pergamum
Nicopolis
ACHAIA
Corinth
Athens
Aegean Sea
Ephesus
Miletus
PHRYGIA
GALATIA
CAPPADOCIA
ARMENIA
Cyrus R.
Derbe
CILICIA
Tarsus
Antioch (Syrian)
Edessa
MESOPOTAMIA
Euphrates R.
Tigris R.
PARTHIA
Carthage
Sicily
Syracuse
MAURETANIA
AFRICA
Mediterranean Sea
Crete
Cyprus
SYRIA
JUDEA
Dura-Europos
Sidon
Tyre
Damascus
Pella
Jerusalem
Cyrene
Alexandria
CYRENE
Memphis
EGYPT
NABATEA
Persian Gulf
Nile R.
Antinoe
Red Sea
Roman Empire by the time of Julius Caesar (44 B.C.)
Territory added by Augustus Caesar (A.D. 14)
Territory added by Trajan (A.D. 117)
Territory temporarily annexed by Rome
0 300 km.
0 300 miles
10,000 ft 3050 m
5000 ft 1525 m
2000 ft 610 m
1000 ft 305 m
0 (sea level) 0 (sea level)
-1640 ft -500 m
A B C D E F
1 2 3 4